DOMESDAY BOOK

A Complete Translation

Alecto Historical Editions

Editors: Dr Ann Williams, Professor G. H. Martin

PENGUIN BOOKS

PENGUIN BOOKS

Published by the Penguin Group
Penguin Books Ltd, 80 Strand, London, WC2R ORL, England
Penguin Putnam Inc., 375 Hudson Street, New York, New York 10014 U S A
Penguin Books Australia Ltd, 250 Camberwell Road, Camberwell, Victoria 3124, Australia
Penguin Books Canada Ltd, 10 Alcorn Avenue, Toronto, Ontario, Canada, M4V 3B2
Penguin Books India (P) Ltd, 11, Community Centre, Panchsheel Park, New Delhi – 110 017, India
Penguin Books (NZ) Ltd, Cnr Rosedale and Airborne Roads, Albany, Auckland, New Zealand
Penguin Books (South Africa) (Pty) Ltd, 24 Sturdee Avenue, Rosebank 2196, South Africa

Penguin Books Ltd, Registered Offices: 80 Strand, London, WC2R ORL, England

www.penguin.com

This translation first published by Alecto Historical Editions 1992
Published in this edition as a Penguin hardback 2002

1

Copyright © Editions Alecto (Domesday) Limited, 1992
All rights reserved

The moral right of the author has been asserted

Set in 8.25/10pt PostScript Monotype Octavian
Typeset by Tradespools, Frome, Somerset
Printed in England by Clays Ltd, St Ives plc

ISBN 0–141–00523–8

Contents

Introduction

Domesday Book is unique. A survey of England made in 1086–7, it is unmatched in its age, its scope and the consistent detail of its contents. It has been in official custody ever since it was made, and is celebrated now as the first of the public records and an endlessly rich source of historical material.

Its name, 'Domesday', the book of the day of judgment, attests the awe with which the work has always been regarded. The earliest names accorded to it, 'the King's book' and 'the great book of Winchester', where it was first kept, in the royal treasury, were displaced as early as the twelfth century by a title which recalled the wonder with which the subjugated English had seen their Norman lords called to deferential account.

The survey was commissioned at Christmas 1085, when William the Conqueror held court at Gloucester. Although the chroniclers of the time represented it as an act of the King's will, and royal authority manifestly enforced it, the finished text seems throughout to be the work not only of a single hand but also of a single mind. In a word, the man who devised it also compiled it, and must have secured the King's approval for the undertaking. No doubt William was gratified to be offered an account of his kingdom that recorded the disposition of wealth and power there over the twenty years since the Conquest, but it is highly unlikely that he thought of such a venture himself. The resolution to exploit in that way the apparatus of English government which the Normans had acquired, and which was probably the most valuable of all their acquisitions, was the mark of one thoroughly familiar with its workings. It produced an astonishing result: a complex return of the resources of the land, and their division between the King and the lords to whom he had granted them, based on local testimony.

The historic text of the book consists of two volumes, known as 'Great Domesday', now bound in two parts, and 'Little Domesday', now bound in three. Great Domesday describes thirty-one counties between the Channel and the Tees; Little Domesday covers Essex, Norfolk and Suffolk. Their names refer to the relative size of the parchment folios; Little Domesday is in fact the bulkier of the two, and its text, less tightly abbreviated than that of Great Domesday, contains a wider range of information. It is not a supplement to Great Domesday but an undigested remnant of an intermediate stage of the survey.

Contemporary references to the making of *Domesday* dwelt upon the searching nature of the inquiries made by the King's commissioners, some seven or eight panels of bishops and earls each taking a circuit of several counties. In particular, it was noted and deplored that the inquest extended even to details of livestock. There is no reference to animals in Great Domesday, but such returns duly appear in Little Domesday and in a closely analogous manuscript covering Cornwall, Devon, Dorset, Somerset and Wiltshire, known as 'Exon Domesday'. Those five counties figure in Great Domesday without their sheep, pigs and cows. The material presumably proved too dense to manage and was jettisoned by the masterly hand which had planned and executed the larger volume, and had also made some contributions to Exon Domesday while the earliest returns were being edited. By the time Little Domesday came to hand, with its detailed account of the prosperous eastern counties, it was put beside the larger volume but never assimilated to it.

In a sense *Domesday Book* was out of date as soon as it was completed; some estates changed hands even during the survey, and rents and values were as mortal as lords and tenants. Yet it has effortlessly retained the respect that it first commanded. It seems to have drawn attention at once to the wealth of the towns and so influenced taxation, and its word resolved many disputes over title. For centuries exemplifications of the text were made in a hand that carefully replicated the script of the original. *Doomsday*'s authority has long outlived the system of government that produced it, and over the last three hundred years historians have consulted it as assiduously as did its custodians in the past. Available for study today in facsimiles of archival quality and electronic texts it has as much as ever to impart to those who consult it.

Professor G. H. Martin, 2002

A Note on the Text

The text reproduced here is that of the Alecto Historical Editions translation of both *Great* and *Little Domesday* published with the facsimile in individual county volumes and also in complete sets for the whole of Domesday England. The Alecto translation of *Great Domesday*, while based on the *Victoria History of the Counties of England* translation, is a much overhauled and improved version – inconsistencies have been removed, the treatment of names standardized and out-of-date words replaced. New texts were commissioned for the Little Domesday counties.

The Alecto editions replicate exactly the page layout of the original *Domesday* manuscript. No attempt has been made here to do this as space did not permit it. However, we have retained some features of the original layout which might help readers of *Domesday* in this edition. We have included references to the original *Domesday* page numbers. These are marked on the text

[Folio number: COUNTY NAME]

There are generally two references for each number. The right-hand page is simply indicated

[Folio 275: DERBYSHIRE]

while the left-hand page is indicated with a 'V' (meaning 'verso')

[Folio 275V: DERBYSHIRE]

We have not included the Marginalia of Domesday.

We have retained a number of the editorial conventions used in the Alecto editions. […] indicates a gap in the manuscript text, either left blank by the scribe for an insertion to be added later, or as a result of erasure.

County abbreviations following a place name [Oxon] indicate that a locality recorded in the folios of this county lies within the boundaries of another in modern times.

Single inverted commas around a place name indicate the latest or most typical known form of a name which remained in use beyond the eleventh century, but which either has not survived into modern times at all, or appears on twentieth-century maps as the name of a feature, such as a river, hill, wood, etc., rather than a place of habitation.

Double inverted commas indicate a place name found only in *Domesday Book*, for which there is no known later equivalent, or of which the form may be corrupt.

Daggers enclose the tentative translation of a passage, phrase or numeral which is obscure in the manuscript.

[sic] indicates a scribal error in the manuscript.

The folios of the original text of *Great* and *Little Domesday* are self-contained: they both start at page 1. The page numbering within this edition is sequential: thus Little Domesday starts on page 967. The Index of Places shows the modern name, the contemporary name, the county and the page number in this edition.

There is a Glossary of Terms used in this translation at the end of the book. This explains terms which are either ambiguous to the modern reader or in need of further clarification after translation.

The Editorial Board

Great Domesday

KENT

[Blank in MS]

DOVER in the time of King EDWARD rendered £18, of which money King Edward had 2 parts and Earl Godwine the third. Besides this the canons of St Martin had the other half. The burgesses gave to the king once in the year 20 ships for 15 days, and in each ship were 21 men. They did this for him because he had remitted to them the sake and soke. Whenever the king's messengers came there they gave 3d for the passage of a horse in the winter and 2[d] in the summer. The burgesses found a steersman and one other helper; and if more help were needed it was hired out of his pay. From Michaelmas up to the feast of St Andrew there was a truce of the king, that is peace, in the vill. If anyone broke it the king's reeve took a common fine for it. Whoever dwelt permanently in the vill rendered a customary due to the king [and] was quit of toll throughout England. All these customs were there when King William came into England. On his very first arrival in England the vill itself was burned down, and therefore a valuation could not be made of what it was worth when the Bishop of Bayeux received it. It is now valued at £40, and yet the reeve pays from it £54: to the king £24 of pence at 20 to the ora, to the earl £30 by tale.

In Dover are 29 messuages from which the king has lost the customary due; of these Robert of Romney has 2, Ralph de Courbepine 3, William fitzTheobald 1, William fitzOgier 1, William fitzTheobald and Robert Black 6, William fitzGeoffrey 3, amongst which was the guildhall of the burgesses, Hugh de Montfort 1 house, Durand 1, Ranulph de Colombieres 1, Wadard 6, [and] the son of Modbert 1. And all these appeal for these houses to the Bishop of Bayeux as their warrantor and livery officer or giver [of seisin]. Of that messuage which Ranulph de Colombieres holds, which belonged to a certain exile, that is, outlaw, they agree that half the land belongs to the king, but Ranulph himself has both [halves]. Humphrey the Bandy-legged holds 1 messuage, half of which was forfeit to the king. Roger of Westerham has built a certain house on [the banks of] the king's stream, and hitherto he has kept back the king's customary due. Nor was there a house there TRE. At the entrance of the harbour of Dover is a mill which wrecks nearly all the ships through its great disturbance of the sea, and causes very great loss to the king and his men, and it was not there TRE. Concerning this, Herbert's nephew states that the

Bishop of Bayeux allowed it to be built by his uncle Herbert fitzIvo.

The men of 4 lathes agree as to these undermentioned laws of the king: this is, [the men of] the Borough Lathe and Eastry Lathe, and 'Limen' Lathe, and Wye Lathe. If anyone makes a fence or a ditch by which the king's public way is narrowed, or fells onto [the road] a tree standing outside the road and takes from it branch or foliage, for each offence of this sort he shall pay 100s to the king. And if he leaves for home not having been arrested nor having found security, a king's servant shall pursue him, and he shall pay the fine of 100s. Concerning breach of the peace, if anyone commits it and is charged [with it] on a road or has to find security [for it] he shall pay a fine of £8 to the king. Otherwise he shall be discharged as regards the king, but not as regards the lord whose man he is; with other forfeitures [it is] as with breach of the peace, but he shall pay a fine of 100s. The king has these forfeitures over all allodiaries in the whole shire of Kent and over their men. And when an allodiary dies the king has from him a relief from his land except from the land of HOLY TRINITY, and St Augustine, and St Martin, and except from these: Godric of Bourne, Godric son of Karli, Æthelnoth Cild, Esbiorn Bigga, Sigeræd of Chilham, Thorgisl, Northmann, and Azur. For these the king has only the personal amercements; and he has relief from the lands of those who have their sake and soke. And from these lands, namely: "Goslaches", and, [?] Buckland [in Luddenham], and another Buckland [?Buckland in Luddenham], and a third Buckland [?Buckland near Dover], and "Herste" [and] 1 yoke of Oare, and 1 yoke of 'Harty', [...] "Schildricheham", Macknade, "Ernulfitone", "Oslachintone", Perry, and another Perry, Throwley, Ospringe, [and] Horton, the king has these forfeitures: housebreaking, breach of the peace, and highway robbery. In the case of adultery, throughout Kent the king has [the fine from] the man and the archbishop [from] the woman, except on the land of HOLY TRINITY, and St Augustine, and St Martin, from which the king has nothing. The king has half the possessions of a thief who has been condemned to death. And from the man who takes in an exile without permission of the king, the king has the forfeiture.

From the above-named lands of Æthelnoth Cild and those like him the king has a bodyguard for 6 days at Canterbury or at Sandwich, and they have food and drink there from the king. If they do not have them, they leave without forfeiture. If they are summoned to attend at the shire [moot] they go as far as Penenden [in Maidstone], not further. And if they do not come, from the forfeiture for this and from all other [forfeitures] the king will have 100s except for breach of the peace, for which the fine is £8; and for [offences on] the [public] ways, as is written above.

In 'Limen' Lathe in "Briseuuei" the king has a customary due, namely, [service of] 2 carts, and 2 sticks of eels for 1 [term of] escort-service, and in the land of "Sophis" he has 12d for 1 [term of] escort-service; and from 1 yoke [of land] of "Northburg" 12d, or 1 [term of] escort-service; and from Dean 18d; and from "Gara" 1 [term of] escort-service. These lands belong to Wye, and the men of these lands used to guard the king at Canterbury or at Sandwich for 3 days, if the king came there.

[Folio 1V: KENT]

In Sutton Lathe and in Aylesford Lathe these men had sake and soke: Beorhtsige Cild, Æthelweald of Eltham, Eskil of Beckenham, Azur of Lessness, Alfwine Horne, Wulfweard White, Ording of Horton Kirby, Esbiorn of Chelsfield, Leofnoth of Sutton, Edward of Stone, Wulfstan and Leofric of Wateringbury, Osweard of Norton, Eadgyth of Aisiholte, Æthelræd of Yalding.

The land of the Canons of St Martin of Dover

IN THE LATHE of Eastry the canons of St Martin had TRE 21 sulungs, in the Hundred of 'Cornilo' and in the Hundred of Bewsbury. In the Lathe of 'Limen' they had 3 sulungs: one in Street Hundred, another in Bircholt Hundred, and the third in 'Blackbourne' Hundred. TRE the prebends were [held in] common and rendered £61 all together. They have now been divided among individuals by the Bishop of Bayeux.

IN BEWSBURY HUNDRED

Ralph de Saint-Samson holds 1 manor as a prebend. It is called 'Charlton' [in Dover], and it is assessed at 1 sulung. There he has 3 villans and 4 bordars with 1 plough. All together it is worth 70s; TRE 100s. Leofwine held it as a prebend.

In the same vill William fitzOgier holds 1 sulung, and there he has 1 villan and 7 bordars with half a plough, and 1 mill rendering 40s. There a certain Frenchman has 1 plough. The same William holds 1 minster in Dover of the bishop, and pays him 11s. The canons claim it. All this is worth £6; TRE £12. Sigeræd held it.

In Buckland [near Dover] Alwigc holds 1 sulung, and there he has 6 villans and 10 bordars with 1½ ploughs. All together it is worth £4; TRE 100s. The same man held it as a prebend.

In Guston Wulfric holds 1 yoke, and there he has 2 villans and 1 bordar with 1 plough. To this land belong 25 acres of land in 'Cornilo' Hundred, and there are 5 bordars with half a plough. All together it is worth 20s; TRE 10s. Alric held it as a prebend.

IN THIS SAME HUNDRED LIES ST MARGARET'S AT CLIFFE.

There Sigeræd has 1 sulung, and 1 plough in demesne, and 6 bordars with 4 slaves. It is worth 100s; TRE £4. The father of the same Sigeræd held it as a prebend.

In the same place Ralph holds 1 sulung, and has 1 plough in demesne, and 7 bordars. It is worth 69s2d; TRE £4. Ælfric held it in the same way as a prebend.

In the same place Æthelræd holds 1 sulung, and has in demesne 1 plough; and 2 villans and 2 bordars with half a plough. It is worth 60s; TRE 20s. This man's father held it as a prebend.

In the same place Robert Black holds 1 sulung, and has there 3 villans and 6 bordars with 1 plough. It is worth 30s; TRE 20s. Smelt, a chaplain of King Edward, held it.

In the same place Walter holds 1 sulung, and there he has 3 villans and 5 bordars with 1½ ploughs. It is worth 60s; TRE 70s. Sidgar held it as a prebend.

In the same place Turbat holds half a sulung, and there he has 2 villans and 1 bordar with half a plough; and the same Robert has half a sulung in 'CORNILO' Hundred, and there is half a plough in demesne, and 5 bordars. All together it is worth £3; TRE £4. Goldstan held it.

In the same place Edwin holds half a sulung and 25 acres of land besides. In demesne he has half a plough; and 1 villan with half a plough. In 'CORNILO' Hundred the same Edwin has 85 acres, and 1 villan with 1 plough there. It is worth £3; TRE £4. He himself held it TRE. From this prebend the Bishop of Bayeux took away 8 acres and gave them to Alan his clerk. Wulfric of Oxford has them now.

IN 'CORNILO' HUNDRED

In Deal Ansketil the archdeacon holds 1 sulung, and there he has in demesne 2 ploughs, with 6 bordars. Archbishop Stigand held this land. To this same Ansketil the Bishop of Bayeux gave 50 acres of land at Deal, and another 50 acres at St Margaret's at Cliffe, where he has 1 villan and half a plough. These 100 acres belonged to the prebends, as they testify. All together it is worth £8; TRE £7.

IN BEWSBURY HUNDRED

In Shepherdswell or Sibertswold William de Poitou holds half a sulung and 12 acres, and in Deal half a sulung less 12 acres; and there he has 2 villans and 3 bordars with 1½ ploughs. All this is worth 55s; TRE £4.

IN 'CORNILO' HUNDRED

In Deal Æthelweald holds 3 virgates, and there he has 3 villans and 8 bordars with 1 plough. It is and was always worth 60s. This man held it TRE.

IN BEWSBURY HUNDRED AND IN 'CORNILO' HUNDRED

In Deal the Abbot of St Augustine's holds 1 sulung, and there he has 3 villans and 7 bordars with $1\frac{1}{2}$ ploughs. It is worth 30s; TRE 40s. His predecessor held it as a prebend in the same way.

In Deal William fitzTheobald holds half a sulung and half a yoke, and he has there in demesne 1 plough, and 2 villans and 2 bordars. It is worth 60s; TRE 40s. Deoring son of Sigeræd held it.

In Shepherdswell or Sibertswold Sigar holds $1\frac{1}{2}$ yokes, and he has there in demesne half a plough, and 2 villans and 1 bordar. It is worth 25s; TRE 35s. His father held it as a prebend.

Nigel the physician holds $1\frac{1}{2}$ yokes at St Margaret's at Cliffe, and there he has 1 villan with 2 oxen. It is worth 20s; TRE 25s. Spirites held it as a prebend.

IN BEWSBURY HUNDRED

In Farthingloe William fitzGeoffrey holds 1 sulung, and there he has in demesne 1 plough; and 4 villans with 1 plough. It is worth £4; TRE £6. Sigeræd held it as a prebend.

In [Church or West] Hougham Baldwin holds 1 sulung, and there he has 4 villans and 5 bordars with 2 ploughs. It is worth £4; TRE 100s. Edwin held it.

In Buckland [near Dover] Godric holds 1 sulung, and there he has 2 ploughs in demesne; and 3 villans and 4 bordars with 1 plough, and [there is] 1 church. It is worth £6; TRE £8.

In Shepherdswell or Sibertswold Wulfstan son of Wulfwine holds 1 sulung, and there he has half a plough; and 3 villans and 9 bordars with 1 plough. TRE it was worth 100s; now 60s. His father held it. *Look what a sulung is on the following page at this note* [drawing of a hand]. *As it seems to me, it contains [...] because the English counted 120 for each 100 as appears under the city of Lincoln* [f.336]. *Written by me, Arthur Agarde, 1583.*

[Folio 2: KENT]

IN THE CITY OF CANTERBURY King EDWARD had 51 burgesses paying rent and 212 others over whom he had sake and soke, and 3 mills rendering 40s. Now there are 19 burgesses paying rent. Of [the houses of] the 32 others who were [there], 11 are waste in the city ditch, and the archbishop has 7 of them, and the Abbot of St Augustine's 14 others in exchange for the [site of the] castle; and there are still 212 burgesses over whom the king has sake and soke, and 3 mills render 108s, and a toll renders 68s. There are 8 acres of meadow which used to belong to the king's messengers: they now render 15s for rent; and 1,000 acres of unproductive woodland from which come 24s. All together it was worth £51 TRE; and as much when Hamo the sheriff received it; and now it is valued at £50. Yet he who holds it now pays £30 assayed and weighed and £24 by tale. Besides all this the sheriff has 110s.

A certain monk of the church of Canterbury took 2 houses of 2 burgesses, one outside, the other within the city. These were situated on the king's road.

The burgesses had 45 messuages outside the city for which they themselves had rent and customary dues; the king, however, had sake and soke. These burgesses also had from the king 33 acres of land for their gild. Ranulph de Colombieres holds these houses and this land. He has also 80 acres of land more than these which the burgesses used to hold in alod of the king. He holds also 5 acres of land which of right belong to a church. Concerning all these the same Ranulph appeals to the Bishop of Bayeux as his warrantor.

Ralph de Courbepine has 4 messuages in the city which a certain concubine of Harold held, the sake and soke of which are the king's; but hitherto he has not had it.

The same Ralph holds of the Bishop of Bayeux 11 other messuages in the city itself, which belonged to Esbiorn Bigga, and they render $11s2\frac{1}{2}d$.

Throughout the whole city of Canterbury the king has sake and soke except on the land of the church of HOLY TRINITY and of St Augustine, and of Queen Edith and of Æthelnoth Cild and of Esbiorn Bigga and of Sigeræd of Chilham.

It has been agreed as regards the main roads which have entrance to and exit from the city, that whoever incurs a fine on them shall pay it to the king, and likewise on the main roads outside the city for 1 league and 3 perches and 3 feet. If anyone digs or sets up a post on these roads inside or outside the city, the king's reeve pursues him wherever he goes and exacts a fine for the king's use.

The archbishop claims the forfeitures on the roads outside the city on each side where his land is. A certain reeve, Brunmann by name, TRE took customary dues from foreign merchants on the land of HOLY TRINITY and St Augustine. Afterwards, TRW, he acknowledged before Archbishop Lanfranc and the Bishop of Bayeux that he had taken them unjustly and he took his oath that these churches had their customary dues quit in the time of King Edward. And thenceforth both churches had their customary dues on their land by the judgement of the king's barons who tried the case.

The city of ROCHESTER TRE was worth 100s; when the bishop received it, the same. It is now worth £20, yet he who holds it pays £40.

Also the Possession of St Martin

Three canons of the community of ST MARTIN, that is Sigeræd, Godric and Seuen, have together 1 sulung and 16 acres. On this land are 4 villans and 9 bordars with 1 plough. They pay 22s. [They hold also] 1 sulung of the lathe of 'LIMEN' in 'Blackbourne' Hundred, and there are 9 villans with 2 ploughs. They pay 16s8d. In STREET Hundred lies 1 sulung of 'Stanstede' [in Aldington]. There 7 villans have $2\frac{1}{2}$ ploughs, and 7 bordars, and 1 meadow. They pay 16s8d. In BIRCHOLT Hundred [they have] 1 sulung of 'Stanstede' [in Aldington]: there are 7 villans and 7 bordars, and they have 4 ploughs and pay 20s less 2d. [Pertaining] to these 3 sulungs are 5 denes and 6 villans and 5 bordars and they pay 9s less 3d. They have 3½ ploughs. In Brenzett [they have] a very small piece of land: there are 2 villans and 3 bordars and they have half a plough. They pay 50d. The canons of the community of St Martin have those 4 sulungs mentioned above, in both woodland and field. TRE they were worth £10; now the same. The land of Norwood and the land of 'West Ripe' [in Lydd] and the land of Brenzett render 20s6d. to St Martin in alms.

On the inland of St Martin dwell 7 bordars with half a plough. They pay 60s for the footwear of the canons. St Margaret's at Cliffe renders £8. There is 1 peasant. The toll of Dover was worth TRE £8; now £22. 3 churches at Dover render 36s8d. From the pasture of 'Mederclive' [in Hougham] and from the gardens of Dover come 9s4d. A pasture in Shepherdswell or Sibertswold renders 16d. St Martin has 10½ mills: they render £7; TRE they rendered as much. They are now valued at £12, but [they yield] no profit to the canons. Subject to these mills dwell 8 men. At "Scortebroc" a pasture renders 2s.

From this community the archbishop has each year 55s. There are 6 men with 1½ ploughs.

In the common land of St Martin are 400½ acres which amount to 2½ sulungs. This land has never rendered any customary dues or tax because 24 sulungs discharge [the payment] for all these. At 'West Ripe' [in Lydd] are 100 acres which discharge [their payments] where they discharged them TRE. At Norwood are 50 acres, and 100 at Brenzett which discharge [their payments] where the aforesaid also [do]. On this land are 3 villans and 9 bordars; they have 1½ ploughs. If the canons had them as they ought, all these would be worth to them £60 each year; they have from them now only £47.6s4d.

Ranulph de Colombieres has taken from them a meadow; Robert of Romney has taken from them each year 20d, and 1 salt-pan and 1 fishery. Herbert fitzIvo gave to the Bishop of Bayeux a mark of gold for 1 of their mills against their will. Lambert [has] 1 mill, Wadard 1 mill, [and] Ralph de Courbepine 1.

Æthelnoth Cild, because of [Earl] Harold's violent action, took from St Martin "Merclesham" and [?] Hawkhurst, for which he gave the canons unfair compensation. Robert of Romney now holds [this] which the canons continue to claim from him.

Here Are Noted Those Holding Lands In Kent

I KING WILLIAM
II The Archbishop of Canterbury
III And his monks and men
IIII The Bishop of Rochester
V The Bishop of Bayeux
VI Battle Abbey
VII The Abbey of St Augustine
VIII The Abbey of Ghent
IX Hugh de Montfort
X Count Eustace
XI Richard of Tonbridge
XII Hamo the sheriff
XIII Albert the chaplain

I. The land of the King

IN THE HALF-LATHE OF SUTTON

IN 'AXTON' HUNDRED

King WILLIAM holds DARTFORD. It is assessed at 1½ sulungs. There is land for 40 ploughs. In demesne are 2 ploughs; and 142 villans with 10 bordars have 53 ploughs. There are 3 slaves, and 1 mill, 22 acres of meadow, 40 acres of pasture, [and] 8 small and 3 large woodland denes. There are 2 hithes, that is, 2 harbours. TRE it was worth £60; and as much when Hamo the sheriff received it. It is now valued by the English at £60; the French reeve, however, who holds it at farm, states that it is worth £80 and £10. He himself, however, pays from this manor £70 weighed and 111s of pence [at] 20 to the ora, and £7 and 26d by tale. Besides this he pays 100s to the sheriff.

The men of the hundred testify that from this manor of the king have been taken a meadow, and an alder-wood, and a mill, and 20 acres of land, and besides this as much meadow as pertains to 10 acres of land, all of which were in the farm of King Edward while he was living. This is worth 20s. They state also that Osweard, then sheriff, leased these to Alstan the reeve of London, and that now Helto the steward and his nephew hold them.

They also testify that HAWLEY, which is assessed at half a sulung, has been taken from this manor. The sheriff held this land, and when he lost the shrievalty it remained in the king's farm. It continued thus also after King Edward's death. Hugh de Port now holds it with 54 more acres of land. The whole of this is worth £15.

From the same manor of the king have also been taken 6 acres of land and a certain wood, which the same Osweard the sheriff put outside the manor by a certain pledge of 40s.

The Bishop of Rochester holds the church of this manor, and it is worth 60s. Apart from this there are also 3 small churches there.

IN THE LATHE OF AYLESFORD

IN LARKFIELD HUNDRED

King William holds AYLESFORD. It is assessed at 1 sulung. There is land for 15 ploughs. In demesne are 3 ploughs; and 40 villans with 5 bordars have 15 ploughs. There are 8 slaves, and 1 mill [rendering] 40d, and 43 acres of meadow, [and] woodland for 70 pigs. All together it was worth £15 TRE; and as much when Hamo the sheriff received it; now it is worth £20, yet it renders £31, and the sheriff has £3 from it. Ansgot holds close to Rochester as much land of this manor as is valued at £7. Also the Bishop of Rochester holds as much of this land as is worth 17s4d in exchange for the land on which the castle stands.

IN THE HALF-LATHE OF MILTON

IN MILTON HUNDRED

King William holds MILTON REGIS. It is assessed at 80 sulungs. Besides these there are in demesne 4 sulungs, and there are 3 ploughs in demesne. In this manor 309 villans with 74 bordars have 167 ploughs. There are 6 mills rendering 30s, and 18 acres of meadow. There are 27 salt-pans rendering 27s. There are 32 fisheries rendering 22s8d. From a toll, 40s; from pasture, 13s4d. [There is] woodland for 220 pigs, and the men of the Weald pay 50s for escort-service and cartage dues. In this manor are 10 slaves. All together it was worth TRE £200 by tale; and as much when Hamo the sheriff received it; and now the same.

Of this manor Hugh de Port holds 8 sulungs and 1 yoke which TRE were [rendering] customary dues with other sulungs. There he has 3 ploughs in demesne.

This land which Hugh de Port holds is worth £20, which are reckoned in the £200 of the whole manor of MILTON REGIS. He who holds it pays £140 assayed and weighed, besides £15.6s, less 2d, by tale. The reeve gives £12 to Hamo the sheriff.

Of the king's woodland Wadard has as much as renders 16d a year, and he holds half a dene which TRE a certain villan held, and Æthelnoth Cild took 2 parts away from a certain villan by force.

The Abbot of St Augustine's holds the churches and tithes of this manor; and 40s from 4 sulungs of the king go to him.

IN THE LATHE OF WYE

IN FAVERSHAM HUNDRED

King William holds FAVERSHAM. It is assessed at 7 sulungs. There is land for 17 ploughs. In demesne are 2 [ploughs]. There 30 villans with 40 bordars have 24 ploughs. There are 5 slaves, and 1 mill rendering 20s, and 2 acres of meadow, woodland for 100 pigs, and from woodland pasture, 31s2d. [There is] a market rendering £4, and 2 salt-pans rendering 3s2d, and in the city of Canterbury 3 closes rendering 20d pertain to this manor. In all it was worth TRE £60 less 5s; and afterwards £60; now it is worth £80.

[Folio 3: KENT]

II. The land of the Archbishop of Canterbury

IN THE CITY OF CANTERBURY the archbishop has 12 burgesses and 32 messuages which the clerks of the vill hold for their gild, and they pay 35s, and a mill rendering 5s.

SANDWICH lies in its own HUNDRED. The archbishop holds this borough, and it is for the clothing of the monks, and renders to the king the same sort of service as DOVER. And the men of this borough testify this, that before King Edward gave it to HOLY TRINITY it rendered to the king £15. At the time of King Edward's death it was not at farm. When the archbishop received it, it rendered £40 at farm and 40,000 herrings for the sustenance of the monks. In the year in which this record was drawn up Sandwich rendered £50 at farm and

herrings as before. TRE there were 307 messuages occupied; now there are 76 more - that is all together 383.

IN 'AXTON' HUNDRED

The Archbishop of Canterbury holds DARENTH in demesne. It is assessed at 2 sulungs. There is land [...]. In demesne is 1 plough; and 22 villans with 7 cottars have 7 ploughs. There are 6 slaves, and 2 mills rendering 50s. 5 burgesses in Rochester belonging to this manor pay 6s8d. There are 8 acres of meadow, [and] woodland for 20 pigs. In all it was worth £14 TRE; when received, £10; now £15.10s. Yet he who holds the manor pays £18.

The archbishop himself holds OTFORD in demesne. It is assessed at 8 sulungs. There is land for 42 ploughs. In demesne are 6 ploughs. There 101 villans with 18 bordars have 45 ploughs. There are 8 slaves, and 6 mills rendering 72s, and 50 acres of meadow, [and] woodland for 150 pigs.

Of this manor 3 thegns hold 1½ sulungs, and have there in demesne 3 ploughs; and 16 villans with 11 bordars having 4 ploughs. There are 5 slaves, and 2 mills rendering 24s, and 28 acres of meadow, [and] woodland for 30 pigs. In all, TRE and afterwards, it was worth [...]. The archbishop's demesne is now valued at £60, [the land] of the thegns at £12. What Richard of Tonbridge holds in his lowy is valued at £10.

The archbishop himself holds SUNDRIDGE. It is assessed at 1½ sulungs. There is land [...]. In demesne are 3 ploughs; and 27 villans with 9 bordars have 8 ploughs. There are 8 slaves, and 3½ mills rendering 13s and ½[s], that is 6d. There are 8 acres of meadow, [and] woodland for 60 pigs. There is a church. In all it was worth £12 TRE; when received, £16; and now £18. Yet it renders £23 and [provides] 1 knight in the service of the archbishop.

IN "HELMESTREI" HUNDRED

The archbishop himself holds OLD BEXLEY. It was assessed TRE at 3 sulungs, and now at 2. There is land [...]. In demesne are 2 ploughs; and 41 villans with 15 bordars have 10 ploughs. There is a church, and 3 mills rendering 48s, and 8 acres of meadow, [and] woodland for 100 pigs. In all, TRE and afterwards, it was worth £12; and now £20, and yet it renders £30.8s.

IN 'LITLELEE' HUNDRED

The archbishop himself holds CRAYFORD. It is assessed at 4 sulungs. There is land for 8 ploughs. In demesne are 2 [ploughs]; and 27 villans with 2 bordars have 8 ploughs. There is a church, and 3 mills rendering 50s6d. There are 5 slaves, and 10 acres of meadow, [and] woodland for 40 pigs. In all it was worth £12 TRE; and as much when received; now £16, and yet it renders £21.

IN THE LATHE OF AYLESFORD

IN LARKFIELD HUNDRED

The archbishop himself holds in demesne [East or West] Malling. It is assessed at 2 sulungs. There is land for 7 ploughs. In demesne are 3 ploughs; and 38 villans with 12 bordars have 5 ploughs. There is a church, and 5 slaves, and 2 mills rendering 10s, and 21 acres of meadow, [and] woodland for 60 pigs. In all it was worth £9 TRE; the same when received; and now as much, and yet it renders £15.

IN TOLLINGTROUGH HUNDRED

The archbishop himself holds NORTHFLEET in demesne. It was assessed at 6 sulungs TRE, and now at 5. There is land for 14 ploughs. In demesne are 2 [ploughs]; and 36 villans have 10 ploughs. There is a church, and 7 slaves, and 1 mill rendering 10s with 1 fishery, and 20 acres of meadow, [and] woodland for 20 pigs. In all it was worth £10 TRE; when received, £12; and now £27, and yet it renders £37.10s. What Richard of Tonbridge holds of this manor in his lowy is worth 30s.

IN WROTHAM HUNDRED

The archbishop himself holds WROTHAM. It is assessed at 8 sulungs. There is land for 20 ploughs. In demesne are 3 ploughs; and 76 villans with 18 bordars have 14 ploughs. There is a church, and 10 slaves, and 3 mills rendering 15s, and 9 acres of meadow. [There is] woodland for 500 pigs when it is productive.

Of this manor William the steward holds 1 sulung, and there he has 1 plough in demesne; and 2 villans with half a plough.

Of the same manor Geoffrey holds 1 sulung of the archbishop, and there he has 1 plough, and 6 villans with 1 bordar having 2 ploughs.

Of this manor Farman holds 1½ yokes of the archbishop, and there he has 3 ploughs, and 6 villans with 12 cottars having 2 ploughs. There are 10 slaves.

In all TRE this manor was worth £15; and afterwards £16. The archbishop's demesne is now valued at £24, and yet it renders £35; [the land] of the knights, £11. What Richard of Tonbridge holds in his lowy is valued at £15.

IN MAIDSTONE HUNDRED

The archbishop himself holds MAIDSTONE. It is assessed at 10 sulungs. There is land for 30 ploughs. In demesne are 3 ploughs; and 25 villans with 21 bordars have 25 ploughs. There is a church, and 10 slaves, and 5 mills rendering 36s8d. There are 2 fisheries rendering 270 eels. There are 10 acres of meadow, [and] woodland for 30 pigs.

Three knights hold of the archbishop 4 sulungs of this manor, and there they have 3½ ploughs in demesne; and 32 villans with 10 bordars having 6 ploughs, and 10 slaves; and they have 1 mill rendering 5s, and 13 acres of meadow, and 2½ fisheries rendering 180 eels, and 2 salt-pans. [There is] woodland for 23 pigs.

In all this manor TRE was worth £14; when received, £12; and now the archbishop's demesne is worth £20; [the land] of the knights, £15.10s. The monks of Canterbury have 20s every year from 2 men of this manor.

IN CHATHAM HUNDRED

The archbishop himself holds GILLINGHAM. It is assessed at 6 sulungs. There is land for 15 ploughs. In demesne are 2 ploughs; and 42 villans with 16 bordars have 15 ploughs. There is a church, and 3 slaves, and 3 fisheries rendering 42s8d, and 1 mill rendering 16s8d, and 14 acres of meadow, [and] woodland for 20 pigs. Of this manor a certain Frenchman holds land for 1 plough, and there he has 2 bordars. In all TRE this manor was worth £15; when received, £12; and now £23, and yet it renders £26 less 12d. What the Frenchman holds [is worth] 40s.

IN RECULVER HUNDRED

The archbishop himself holds RECULVER. It is assessed at 8 sulungs. There is land for 30 ploughs. In demesne are 3 ploughs; and 90 villans with 25 bordars have 27 ploughs. There is a church, and 1 mill rendering 25d, and 33 acres of meadow, woodland for 20 pigs, and 5 salt-pans rendering 64d, and 1 fishery. In all this manor was worth TRE £14; when received, the same; and now £35. Besides this the archbishop has £7.7s.

The archbishop himself holds 'NORTHWOOD' [in Whitstable] in demesne. It is assessed at 13 sulungs. There is land for 26 ploughs. In demesne are 2 ploughs; and 92 villans with 40 bordars have 59½ ploughs. There is a church, and 10 acres of meadow, [and] woodland for 50 pigs. In all this manor was worth TRE £24.5s; and afterwards as much; and now it renders to the archbishop £50.14s2d, and to the archdeacon 20s.

Vitalis holds of the archbishop 3 sulungs and 1 yoke and 12 acres of land of this manor, and there he has 5 ploughs, and 29 bordars and 5 slaves, and 7 salt-pans rendering 25s4d. There is a church, and 1 small woodland dene. All together it is worth £14.6s6d.

IN THE BOROUGH LATHE

IN PETHAM HUNDRED

The archbishop himself holds PETHAM. It is assessed at 7 sulungs. There is land for 20 ploughs. In demesne are 3 ploughs; and 32 villans with 21 bordars have 19 ploughs. There are 2 churches. There are 2 slaves, and 13 acres of meadow, [and] woodland for 20 pigs. In all this manor was worth TRE £17.6s3d; and afterwards as much; and now it is worth £20.

Godfrey and Nigel hold of the archbishop 1½ sulungs and [...] a yoke of this manor; and there they have 4 ploughs, and 4 villans with 8 bordars having 3 ploughs. All together it is worth £9. From these men the monks have 8s a year.

IN 'STURSETE' HUNDRED

The archbishop himself holds "ESTURSETE" [in Canterbury] in demesne. It is assessed at 7 sulungs. There is land for 20 ploughs. In demesne are 4 ploughs; and 17 villans with 83 bordars have 16 ploughs. There is a church, and 12 mills rendering £4.5s, and 100 acres of meadow, [and] woodland for 50 pigs. To this manor pertained, TRE, 52 messuages in the city, and now there are only 25 because the others have been destroyed for the new residence of the archbishop. In all, TRE and afterwards, it was worth £24.12s6d; now it is worth £40.

5 men of the archbishop have 1 sulung and 6 yokes of this manor; and there they have 5½ ploughs in demesne; and 8 villans with 26 bordars having 2 ploughs, and 3 mills, and 34 acres of meadow. [There is] woodland for 10 pigs. All together it is worth £9.

Hamo the sheriff holds of the archbishop half a sulung of this manor, and there he has 2 ploughs, with 5 bordars and 1 slave, and 2 mills rendering 15s. It is worth 100s.

IN BARHAM HUNDRED

The archbishop himself holds BISHOPSBOURNE in demesne. It is assessed at 6 sulungs. There is land for 50 ploughs. In demesne are 5 ploughs; and 64 villans with 53 bordars have 30½ ploughs. There is a church, and 2 mills rendering 8s6d, and 20 acres of meadow, [and] woodland for 15 pigs. From the herbage, 27d. In all, TRE and afterwards, it was worth £20; now £30.

IN BOUGHTON HUNDRED

The archbishop himself holds BOUGHTON STREET in demesne. It is assessed at 5½ sulungs. There is land [...]. In demesne are 2 ploughs; and 31 villans with 31 bordars having 15 ploughs. There are 4 acres of meadow, and a fishery rendering 10d, a salt-pan rendering 16d, [and] woodland for 45 pigs. In all, TRE and afterwards, it was worth £15.16s3½d; now it is worth £30.16s3½d.

IN CALEHILL HUNDRED

The archbishop himself holds CHARING in demesne. It is assessed at 8 sulungs. There is land for 40 ploughs. In demesne is 1 sulung, and there are 4½ ploughs. There 26 villans with 27 bordars have 27 ploughs. There are 12 slaves, and 1 mill rendering 40d. There are 25 acres of meadow, [and] woodland for 26 pigs. In all it was worth £24 TRE; when received as much; now it is valued at £34, and yet it renders £60.

The archbishop himself holds PLUCKLEY in demesne. It is assessed at 1 sulung. There is land for 12 ploughs. In demesne [are] 2½ ploughs; and 16 villans with 7 bordars have 11 ploughs. There are 8 slaves, and 12½ acres of meadow, [and] woodland for 140 pigs. All together it was worth TRE £12; when received, £8; and now £15, and yet it renders £20.

IN THE LATHE OF EASTRY

IN WINGHAM HUNDRED

The archbishop himself holds WINGHAM in demesne. It was assessed at 40 sulungs TRE, and now at 35. There is land [...]. In demesne are 8 ploughs; and 85 villans with 20 bordars having 57 ploughs. There are 8 slaves, and 2 mills rendering 34s, woodland for 5 pigs, and 2 small woods for fencing. In all TRE it was worth £77; when received the same; and now £100.

William d'Arques holds 1 sulung of this manor in Fleet, and there he has in demesne 1 plough; and 4 villans and 1 knight with 1 plough, and 1 fishery with a salt-pan rendering 30d. The whole is worth 40s.

Of this manor 5 men of the archbishop hold 5½ sulungs and 3 yokes, and there they have in demesne 8 ploughs, and 22 bordars and 8 slaves. All together it is worth £21.

IN LONGBRIDGE HUNDRED

The archbishop himself holds MERSHAM in demesne. It was assessed TRE at 6 sulungs, and now at 3. There is land for 12 ploughs. In demesne are 3 ploughs; and 39 villans with 9 bordars having 16 ploughs. There is a church, and 2 mills rendering 5s, and 2 salt-pans rendering 5s, and 13 acres of meadow, [and] woodland for 30 pigs.

[Folio 4: KENT]

In all, TRE and afterwards, it is worth £10; now £20.

IN 'LIMEN' LATHE

IN BIRCHOLT HUNDRED

The archbishop himself holds ALDINGTON [near Hythe] in demesne. It was assessed at 21 sulungs TRE, and now at 15 sulungs. [There is] land for 100 ploughs. In demesne are 13 ploughs; and 200 villans less 10 with 50 bordars have 70 ploughs. There is a church, and 13 slaves, and 3 mills rendering 16s, and 3 fisheries rendering 21d. There are 170 acres of meadow, [and] woodland for 60 pigs. In all it was worth TRE £62; and as much when received; now it renders £100 and 20s.

The archbishop himself holds a vill which is called St Martins [in Canterbury] and belongs to "Estursete" [in Canterbury] and it lies in this hundred and is assessed at 1½ sulungs. There is land [...]. In demesne are 2 ploughs, and 36 bordars. To this land belong 7 burgesses in Canterbury paying 8s4d. There are 5 mills rendering 20s, and a small wood.

In this vill Ralph holds half a sulung of the archbishop, and there he has 2 ploughs in demesne; and 5 villans with 3 bordars having 2½ ploughs. TRE the half-sulung of St Martins [in Canterbury] was worth £7, and the other half-sulung has always been worth £4.

In OLD ROMNEY are 85 burgesses who belong to ALDINGTON [near Hythe], the archbishop's manor, and they were and now are worth £6 to the lord.

Half a yoke and a half a virgate of this manor of Aldington [near Hythe] are in Lympne. The archbishop holds it in demesne, and there he has 1 plough; and 1 villan with 18 bordars having 1½ ploughs. There are 7 priests who pay £7.5s. There is land for 2 ploughs. It is and was worth £12, and yet it renders £15.

Of the same manor, the Count of EU holds Stowting as 1 manor. It was assessed at 1½ sulungs TRE, and now at 1 sulung only. There is land for 8 ploughs. In demesne are 2 [ploughs]; and 27 villans with 13 bordars having 7 ploughs, and 1 mill rendering 25d. There is a church, and 20 acres of meadow, woodland for 10 pigs, and 8 slaves. TRE, and afterwards, it was worth £8; now £10.

IN 'LONINGBOROUGH' HUNDRED

The archbishop himself holds LYMINGE in demesne. It is assessed at 7 sulungs. There is land for 60 ploughs. In demesne are 4 [ploughs]; and 101 villans with 16 bordars having 55 ploughs. There is a church, and 10 slaves, and 1 mill rendering 30d, and 1 fishery rendering 40 eels, and 30 acres of meadow, [and] woodland for 100 pigs. 6 burgesses in HYTHE belong there. TRE it was worth £24; and afterwards £40; and now the same, and yet it renders £60.

Three men of the archbishop hold 2½ sulungs and half a yoke of this manor, and there they have 5 ploughs in demesne; and 20 villans with 16 bordars having 5½ ploughs, and 1 slave, and 2 mills rendering 7s6d, and 40 acres of meadow. [There is] woodland for 11 pigs. There are 2 churches. All together it is worth £11.

IN SILVERDEN HUNDRED

The archbishop himself holds NEWENDEN. It is assessed at 1 sulung. There is land [...]. There are 25 villans with 4 bordars having 5 ploughs. There is a market rendering 40s. less 5d. [There is] woodland for 40 pigs. All together it was worth TRE 100s; when received, £12; and now £10; and yet the reeve pays £18.10s.

The land of His [The Archbishop's] Knights

IN 'AXTON' HUNDRED

Ansgot holds FARNINGHAM of the archbishop. It is assessed at 1 sulung. There is land [...]. In demesne are 2 ploughs; and 13 villans with 5 bordars having 3½ ploughs. There are 6 acres of meadow. [There is] woodland for 20 pigs, and Richard of Tonbridge has as much of the same woodland in his lowy. This manor TRE was worth £7; and now £11. Of these the monks of Canterbury have £4 for their clothing. And *[sic]*.

Ralph fitzOspak holds Eynsford of the archbishop. It is assessed at 6 sulungs. There is land [...]. In demesne are 5 ploughs; and 29 villans with 9 bordars have 15 ploughs. There are 2 churches, and 9 slaves, and 2 mills rendering 43s, and 29 acres of meadow, [and] woodland for 20 pigs. TRE it was worth £16; and now it is worth £20. Of this manor Richard of Tonbridge holds as much woodland as 20 pigs might come from, and 1 mill rendering 5s, and 1 fishery in his lowy.

Mauger holds of the archbishop 3 yokes in Orpington, and they were assessed at this much TRE outside Orpington. There are now 2 yokes inside Orpington, and a third outside. There is land [...]. In demesne [is] 1 plough; and 4 villans with 1 bordar and 4 slaves and half a plough, and 3 acres of meadow, and woodland for 11 pigs. TRE it was worth 40s; when received, 20s; and now 50s.

Hamo the sheriff holds BRASTED of the archbishop. It is assessed at 1½ sulungs. There is land for 10 ploughs. In

demesne are 2 [ploughs]; and 24 villans with 16 bordars have 12 ploughs. There is a church, and 15 slaves, and 2 mills rendering 24s, woodland for 80 pigs, and from the herbage 9s6d. All together TRE it was worth £10; and as much when received; and now £17. Abbot Æthelnoth held this manor of the Archbishop of Cantebury.

The Count of EU holds ULCOMBE of the archbishop. It was assessed at 2½ sulungs TRE, and now at 2 only. There is land for 9 ploughs. In demesne are 2 ploughs; and 23 villans with 8 bordars have 7 ploughs. There is a church, and 1 mill rendering 4s, and 8 acres of meadow, [and] woodland for 80 pigs. All together TRE it was worth £10; when received, £8; now £11. Ælfhere held this manor of the archbishop.

IN EYHORNE HUNDRED

Ralph fitzTurold holds BOUGHTON MALHERBE of the archbishop. It is assessed at half a sulung and it pertains to the 6 sulungs of Hollingbourne. There is land for 1½ ploughs. In demesne is 1 plough; and 3 villans with 2 bordars have 1 plough. There is a church, and 2 acres of meadow, and woodland for 16 pigs. All together it is and was always worth 40s.

IN FAVERSHAM HUNDRED

Richard, a man of the archbishop, holds of him LEAVELAND. It is assessed at 1 sulung. There is land [...]. In demesne [is] 1 plough; and 2 villans with 1 bordar have 1 plough. [There is] woodland for 5 pigs. TRE, and afterwards, it was worth 30s; now 20s.

IN BOUGHTON HUNDRED

The same Richard holds GRAVENEY of the archbishop. It is assessed at 1 sulung. There is land [...]. In demesne is 1 plough; and 8 villans with 10 bordars have 2 ploughs. There are 5 slaves, and 10 acres of meadow, and 4 salt-pans rendering 4s. TRE, and afterwards, it was worth 100s; now £6. Of these the monks of Canterbury have 20s.

[Folio 4V: KENT]

IN CALEHILL HUNDRED

Godfrey the steward holds LENHAM [? Heath] of the archbishop. It is assessed at 2 sulungs. There is land [...]. In demesne are 2 ploughs; and 15 villans with 2 bordars have 4 ploughs. There are 4 slaves, and 6 acres of meadow, and 1 mill rendering 7s, and woodland for 10 pigs. All together it is worth £8, and yet it renders £12.10s.

IN TEYNHAM HUNDRED

The same Godfrey holds half a sulung of the archbishop in SHEPPEY. There is land [...]. In demesne [is] 1 plough, with 2 bordars, and 4 slaves. TRE, and afterwards, it was worth 30s; now £4, and yet it renders 100s.

IN EASTRY HUNDRED

Osbern fitzLetard holds of the archbishop 1 yoke in BUCKLAND [in Woodnesborough], and there he has in demesne 1 plough, and it is worth 10s.

William Folet holds FINGLESHAM of the archbishop. It is assessed at half a sulung. There he has 6 villans with 1½ ploughs.

The same William holds Statenborough of the archbishop, and it is assessed at half a sulung, and there he has 12 villans with 1½ ploughs.

These lands were worth TRE 40s; when the archbishop received them, 10s; now 30s.

IN HEANE HUNDRED

Hugh de Montfort holds SALTWOOD of the archbishop. It was assessed at 7 sulungs TRE, and now at 3 sulungs. There is land for 15 ploughs. In demesne are 2 ploughs; and 33 villans with 12 bordars having 9½ ploughs. There is a church, and 2 slaves, and 9 mills rendering 20s, and 33 acres of meadow, [and] woodland for 80 pigs.

To this manor belong 225 burgesses in the borough of Hythe. Both borough and manor were worth TRE £16; when received, £8; now all together £29.6s4d.

IN STREET HUNDRED

William of Adisham holds BERWICK of the archbishop as 1 manor. It is assessed at half a sulung. There is land for 3 ploughs. In demesne are 2 [ploughs]; and 9 villans with 9 bordars have 1½ ploughs. There are 18 acres of meadow, and woodland for 20 pigs. TRE it was worth 60s; and afterwards 20s; now £7, and yet it renders £11.

IN 'LANGPORT' HUNDRED

Robert of Romney holds 'OLD LANGPORT' [in Lydd] of the archbishop. It is assessed at 1½ sulungs. There is land for 6 ploughs. In demesne are 2 [ploughs]; and 29 villans with 9 bordars have 9 ploughs. There are 7 salt-pans rendering 8s9d.

To this manor belong 21 burgesses who are in Old Romney, from whom the archbishop has 3 forfeitures: theft, breach of the peace, [and] highway robbery. But the king has all the service from them, and they themselves have all customary dues and the other forfeitures, in return for service on the sea, and they are in the king's hands. TRE, and afterwards, it was worth £10; and now £16.

William holds TILMANSTONE of the archbishop. It is assessed at 1 sulung. In demesne are 2 ploughs, and 5 bordars. Formerly [it was worth] 20s; now it is worth 30s.

III. The land of the Archbishop's Monks

IN "HELMESTREI" HUNDRED

The Archbishop of Canterbury holds ORPINGTON. It was assessed at 3 sulungs TRE, and now at 2½ sulungs. There is land [...]. In demesne are 2 ploughs; and 46 villans with 25 bordars having 23 ploughs. There are 3 mills rendering 16s4d, and 10 acres of meadow, and 5 woodland denes rendering 50 pigs. In all it was worth TRE £15; when received, £8; and now £25, and yet it renders £28. There are 2 churches.

IN AYLESFORD LATHE

IN 'LITTLEFELD' HUNDRED

The archbishop himself holds EAST PECKHAM. It was assessed at 6 sulungs TRE, and now at 5 sulungs and 1 yoke. There is land for 10 ploughs. In demesne are 2 [ploughs]; and 16 villans with 14 bordars have 4½ ploughs. There is a church, and 10 slaves, and 1 mill, and 6 acres of meadow, [and] woodland for 10 pigs.

Of the land of this manor a man of the archbishop holds half a sulung, and it paid geld TRE with these 6 sulungs although it did not belong to the manor except for [the payment of] tax because it was free land.

Of the same manor Richard of Tonbridge holds 2 sulungs and 1 yoke, and there he has 27 villans having 7 ploughs, and woodland for 10 pigs; and the whole is worth £4. The manor was worth £12 TRE; when the archbishop received it, £8; and now what he has is worth £8.

IN EYHORNE HUNDRED

The archbishop himself holds HOLLINGBOURNE. It is assessed at 6 sulungs. There is land for 24 ploughs. In demesne are 2 [ploughs]; and 61 villans with 16 bordars have 23 ploughs. There is a church, and 12 slaves, and 2 mills, and 8 acres of meadow, [and] woodland for 40 pigs. All together, TRE and afterwards, it was worth £20; and now it is worth £30.

To this manor belongs half a sulung which has never paid tax. The Bishop of Bayeux holds this of the archbishop at rent.

IN TOLLINGTROUGH HUNDRED

The archbishop himself holds MEOPHAM. It was assessed TRE at 10 sulungs; now at 7. There is land for 30 ploughs. In demesne are 4 [ploughs]; and 25 villans with 71 bordars have 25 ploughs. There is a church, and 17 slaves, and 16 acres of meadow, [and] woodland for 10 pigs. In all it was worth TRE £15.10s; when received, £15; now £26. Richard of Tonbridge has in his lowy what is worth 18s6d. [There is] woodland for 20 pigs.

IN MAIDSTONE HUNDRED

The archbishop himself holds EAST FARLEIGH. It is assessed at 6 sulungs. There is land for 26 ploughs. In demesne are 4 [ploughs]; and 35 villans with 56 bordars have 30 ploughs. There is a church, and 3 mills rendering 27s8d. There are 8 slaves, and 6 fisheries rendering 1,200 eels. There are 12 acres of meadow, [and] woodland for 115 pigs.

Of the land of this manor Godfrey holds in fee half a sulung, and there he has 2 ploughs; and 7 villans with 10 bordars having 3 ploughs, and 4 slaves, and 1 mill rendering 20d, and 4 acres of meadow, and woodland for 30 pigs.

The whole manor TRE was worth £16; and afterwards as much; and now £22; what Abel now holds, £6; what Godfrey [holds], £9; what Richard [has] in his lowy, £4.

IN 'SHAMWELL' HUNDRED

The archbishop himself holds CLIFFE. It is assessed at $3\frac{1}{2}$ sulungs. There is land for 6 ploughs. In demesne are $1\frac{1}{2}$ ploughs; and 20 villans with 18 bordars have $5\frac{1}{2}$ ploughs. There is a church, and 2 slaves, and 36 acres of meadow, [and] woodland rendering 12d. TRE the whole manor was worth £6; and afterwards £7; and now £16.

IN THE BOROUGH LATHE

IN THANET HUNDRED

The archbishop himself holds MONKTON. It was assessed TRE at 20 sulungs, and now at 18. There is land for 31 ploughs. In demesne are 4 [ploughs]; and 89 villans with 21 bordars have 27 ploughs. There are 2 churches, and 1 mill rendering 10s. There is a new fishery, and 1

[Folio 5: KENT]

salt-pan rendering 15d, [and] woodland for 10 pigs. In all it was worth, TRE and afterwards, £20; and now £40.

IN 'DOWNHAMFORD' HUNDRED

The archbishop himself holds ICKHAM. It is assessed at 4 sulungs. There is land for 12 ploughs. In demesne are 3 [ploughs]; and 29 villans with 60 cottars have $16\frac{1}{2}$ ploughs. There is a church, and 4 mills rendering 100s, and 35 acres of meadow, and woodland for 30 pigs. The whole manor was worth, TRE and afterwards, £22; now £32. Of the land of this manor William, his man, holds as much as is worth £7.

IN CANTERBURY HUNDRED

The archbishop himself holds 'NORTHGATE' in Canterbury. It is assessed at 1 sulung. There is land [...]. In demesne [are] $1\frac{1}{2}$ ploughs; and 7 villans with 26 bordars have 2 ploughs. To this manor belong in the city of Canterbury 100 burgesses less 3, paying £8.4s. There are 8 mills rendering 71s, and 24 acres of meadow, [and] woodland for 30 pigs. All together it is and was worth £17.

In the same BOROUGH LATHE lies a small borough named SEASALTER which properly belongs to the archbishop's kitchen. A certain person named Blize holds it of the monks. In demesne is 1 plough; and 48 bordars with 1 plough. There is a church, and 8 fisheries rendering, with the rent, 25s, [and] woodland for 10 pigs. TRE, and afterwards, it was worth 25s; and now 100s.

IN WYE LATHE

IN FAVERSHAM HUNDRED

The archbishop himself holds PRESTON [in Faversham]. It is assessed at 1 sulung. There is land for 6 ploughs. In demesne are 3 [ploughs]; and 13 villans with 14 bordars have 3 ploughs. There is a church, and 1 slave, and 1 mill without rent, and 1 fishery rendering 250 eels. There are 2 acres of meadow, [and] woodland for 5 pigs. TRE, and afterwards, it was worth £10; now £15.

IN FELBOROUGH HUNDRED

The archbishop himself holds CHARTHAM. It is assessed at 4 sulungs. There is land for 14 ploughs. In demesne are 2 [ploughs]; and 60 villans with 15 cottars have $15\frac{1}{2}$ ploughs. There is a church, and 1 slave, and $5\frac{1}{2}$ mills rendering 70s, and 30 acres of meadow, and woodland for 25 pigs. TRE, and when received, it was worth £12; now £25, and yet it renders £30.

The archbishop himself holds GODMERSHAM. It is assessed at 8 sulungs. There is land for 12 ploughs. In demesne are 2 [ploughs]; and 60 villans with 8 cottars have 17 ploughs. There is a church, and 2 slaves, and 1 mill rendering 25s, and 12 acres of meadow, [and] woodland for 40 pigs. TRE, and when received, it was worth £12; now £20, and yet it renders £30.

IN CHART HUNDRED

The archbishop himself holds GREAT CHART. It is assessed at 3 sulungs. There is land for 12 ploughs. In demesne are 2 [ploughs]; and 36 villans with 11 cottars have $22\frac{1}{2}$ ploughs. There are 5 slaves, and 2 mills rendering 6s, and a salt-pan rendering 6d, and 27 acres of meadow, and woodland for 100 pigs. TRE, and when received, it was worth £12; now £20, and yet it renders £27.

IN CALEHILL HUNDRED

The archbishop himself holds LITTLE CHART. TRE it was assessed at 3 sulungs, and now at $2\frac{1}{2}$ hides. There is land [...]. In demesne are 2 [ploughs]; and 19 villans with 5 bordars have 7 ploughs. There are 2 mills rendering 5s10d, and 11 acres of meadow, and woodland for 15 pigs.

Of the land of this manor William holds of the archbishop half a sulung, and there he has in demesne 1 plough, with 4 slaves, and 10 acres of meadow, and woodland for 20 pigs. The whole manor was worth, TRE and afterwards, 100s; now £8.8s4d. What William holds is valued at 40s.

The archbishop himself holds WESTWELL. TRE it was assessed at 7 sulungs, and now at 5. There is land for 18 ploughs. In demesne are 4 [ploughs]; and 81 villans with 5 bordars have $12\frac{1}{2}$ ploughs. There are 7 slaves, and 1 mill rendering 30d, and 20 acres of meadow, [and] woodland for 80 pigs. TRE it was worth £17.11s4d; when received as much; now £24.0s4d, and yet it renders £40.

IN THE LATHE OF EASTRY

IN EASTRY HUNDRED

The archbishop himself holds EASTRY. It is assessed at 7 sulungs. There is land [...]. In demesne are 3 ploughs; and 72 villans with 22 bordars have 24 ploughs. There are $1\frac{1}{2}$ mills rendering 30s, and 3 salt-pans rendering 4s, and 18 acres of meadow, [and] woodland for 10 pigs.

And in Geddinge the monks of Canterbury holds half a sulung and 1 yoke and 5 acres, and there they have 6 villans with $2\frac{1}{2}$ ploughs. All together, TRE and afterwards, it was worth £26.10s4$\frac{1}{4}$d; now £36.10s4$\frac{1}{4}$d.

The archbishop himself holds ADISHAM. It is assessed at 17 sulungs. There is land [...]. In demesne are $2\frac{1}{2}$ ploughs; and 100 villans with 14 bordars have 36 ploughs. There are 13 acres of meadow, and 3 slaves, [and] woodland for fencing.

Of the land of this manor 2 knights hold 3 sulungs of the archbishop, and there they have in demesne 4 ploughs; and 18 villans with 5 bordars have 1 plough. The whole manor TRE was worth £40; when received, the same; now it renders £46.16s4d and to the archbishop 100s of fine.

What the knights hold is worth £11, and yet it renders £13.

IN HAM HUNDRED

The archbishop himself holds WAREHORNE. It is assessed at 1 sulung. There is land for 2 ploughs. In demesne is 1 plough; and 6 villans with 3 bordars have 1 plough. There are 12 acres of meadow, and woodland for 6 pigs. TRE, and afterwards, it was worth 20s; and now 60s.

IN 'LIMEN' LATHE

IN 'BLACKBOURNE' HUNDRED

The archbishop himself holds APPLEDORE. TRE it was assessed at 2 sulungs, and now at 1. There is land for 8 ploughs. In demesne are 3 ploughs; and 37 villans with 41 bordars have 11 ploughs. There is a church, and 6 fisheries rendering 3s4d. There are 2 acres of meadow, and woodland for 6 pigs. TRE, and afterwards, it was worth £6; now £16.17s6d.

IN THE HUNDRED OF WYE

The archbishop himself holds 1 manor which was assessed at 1 sulung TRE, and now at a half. [There is] land for 2 ploughs. In demesne is 1 [plough]; and 3 villans with 4 bordars have $2\frac{1}{2}$ ploughs. There is a church, and 1 mill rendering 2s, and 2 slaves, and 7 acres of meadow, [and] woodland for 10 pigs. TRE, and afterwards, [it was worth] 50s; now £4.

IN ROMNEY MARSH

The archbishop himself holds "ASMESLANT". It is assessed at 1 sulung. There is land for 3 ploughs. There are 21 villans having 7 ploughs. It is and was always worth 53s.

Of this land William Folet has 1 yoke, and it is worth to him 10s a year.

SANDWICH is described above. It belongs to the demesne of the monks.

[Folio 5V: KENT]

IIII. The land of the Bishop of Rochester

The Bishop of Rochester holds SOUTHFLEET. It was assessed at 6 sulungs. There is land for 13 ploughs. In demesne is 1 plough; and 25 villans with 9 bordars having 12 ploughs. There are 7 slaves, and 20 acres of meadow, [and] woodland for 10 pigs. It is now assessed at 5 sulungs. There is a church. TRE, and afterwards, it was worth £11; now £21, and yet it renders £24 and 1 ounce of gold.

Of this manor there is in Tonbridge as much woodland and land as is valued at 20s.

The same bishop holds STONE. TRE it was assessed at 6 sulungs, and now at 4 sulungs. There is land for 11 ploughs. In demesne are 2 [ploughs]; and 20 villans with 12 bordars have 11 ploughs. There is a church, and 4 slaves, and 72 acres of meadow, and 1 mill rendering 6s8d, and 1 fishery rendering 3s4d, [and] woodland for 60 pigs. TRE, and afterwards, it was worth £13; and now £16, and yet it renders £20 and 1 ounce of gold and 1 porpoise. Richard of Tonbridge holds of this manor as much woodland as is worth 15s.

The same bishop holds FAWKHAM [Fawkham and Fawkham Green]. It is assessed at 2 sulungs. There is land [...]. In demesne is 1 plough; and 15 villans with 3 bordars have 4 ploughs. There is a church, and 3 slaves, and 2 mills rendering 15s, and 4 acres of meadow, [and] woodland for 30 pigs. TRE, and afterwards, it was worth £7; now £8.

The same bishop holds LONGFIELD, and Ansketil the priest [holds] of him. It is assessed at 1 sulung. There is land [...]. In demesne is 1 plough; and 9 villans with 7 bordars have 2 ploughs. It was worth 70s; and now 100s.

IN BROMLEY HUNDRED

The same bishop holds BROMLEY. It was assessed at 6 sulungs TRE, and now at 3. There is land for 13 ploughs. In demesne are 2 ploughs; and 30 villans with 26 bordars have 11 ploughs. There is 1 mill rendering 4s, and 2 acres of meadow, [and] woodland for 100 pigs. TRE, and afterwards, it was worth £12.10s; now £18, and yet it renders £21 less 2s.

The same bishop holds WOULDHAM. It was assessed at 6 sulungs TRE, and now at 3. There is land for 5 ploughs. In demesne are 2 [ploughs]; and 18 villans with 16 bordars have 6 ploughs. There are 6 slaves, and 1 fishery, and 60 acres of meadow, [and] woodland for 20 pigs. There is a church. TRE, and afterwards, it was worth £8; now £12.

The same bishop holds [East or West] MALLING. It was assessed at 3 sulungs TRE, and now at $1\frac{1}{2}$. There is land for 3 ploughs. In demesne is 1 [plough]; and 5 villans with 6 bordars have 2 ploughs. There is a church, and 1 mill rendering 2s, [and] woodland for 20 pigs. TRE, and afterwards, it was worth 40s; and now £4.

The same bishop holds TROTTISCLIFFE. It was assessed TRE at 3 sulungs, and now at 1 sulung. There is land for 3 ploughs. In demesne is 1 sulung, and there is 1 plough; and 10 villans with 2 ploughs. There is a church, and 1 slave, and 2 acres of meadow, and woodland for 10 pigs. TRE, and afterwards, it was worth 60s; and now £7.

The same bishop holds SNODLAND. It was assessed TRE at 6 sulungs, and now at 3. There is land for 6 ploughs. In demesne are 2 ploughs; and 10 villans with 6 bordars have 6 ploughs. There is a church, and 5 slaves, and 3 mills rendering 40s, and 30 acres of meadow, [and] woodland for 4 pigs. TRE, and afterwards, it was worth £6; and now £9.

IN 'SHAMWELL' HUNDRED

The same bishop holds CUXTON. It was assessed at $2\frac{1}{2}$ sulungs TRE, and now at only 2. There is land for 6 ploughs. In demesne are 2 [ploughs]; and 15 villans with 9 bordars have 5 ploughs. There is a church, and 2 slaves, and 1 mill rendering 30d, and 20 acres of meadow. TRE, and afterwards, it was worth £4.10s; and now £10.10s.

The same bishop holds DENTON [in Gravesend]. It was assessed at 2 sulungs TRE, and now at half a sulung. There is land for 2 ploughs. In demesne is 1 [plough]; and 6 villans have there 1 plough. There is a church, and 4 slaves, and 4 acres of meadow, [and] woodland for 15 pigs. TRE, and afterwards, it was worth 100s; and now £7.15s.

The same bishop holds HALLING [Halling, North Halling and Upper Halling]. It was assessed at 6 sulungs TRE, and now at $2\frac{1}{2}$. There is land for 7 ploughs. In demesne are 3 ploughs; and 15 villans with 9 bordars have 6 ploughs. There is a church, and 2 slaves, and 30 acres of meadow, and woodland for 5 pigs. TRE, and afterwards, it was worth £7; now £16. What Richard holds | in his lowy is worth 7s. |

The same bishop holds FRINDSBURY. It was assessed at 10 sulungs TRE, and now at 7. There is land for 15 ploughs. In demesne are 5 ploughs; and 40 villans with 28 bordars have 11 ploughs. There is a church, and 9 slaves, and 1 mill rendering 12s, and 40 acres of meadow, [and] woodland for 5 pigs. TRE, and afterwards, it was worth £8; and now £25. What Richard holds in his lowy is worth 10s.

IN THE HUNDRED OF ROCHESTER

The same bishop holds BORSTAL. It was assessed at 2 sulungs TRE, and now at $1\frac{1}{2}$ sulungs. There is land for 4 ploughs. In demesne are 2 ploughs; and 6 villans with 3 ploughs. There are 50 acres of meadow, and 2 mills rendering 20s. TRE, and afterwards, it was worth £6; and now £10.

In ROCHESTER the bishop had and still has 80 messuages which belong to Frindsbury and Borstal, his own manors. TRE, and afterwards, they were worth £3; now they are worth £8, and yet they render £11.13s4d a year.

IN HOO HUNDRED

The same bishop holds STOKE [Stoke, Lower Stoke and Middle Stoke]. TRE it was assessed at 5 sulungs, and now at 3. There is land for 5 ploughs. In demesne are 2 ploughs; and 10 villans with 5 bordars have 4 ploughs. There is a church, and 4 slaves, and 4 acres of meadow. TRE and afterwards, as now, worth £8 and 20d; and yet he who holds it pays £13 and 20d.

This manor was and is of the bishopric of Rochester; but Earl Godwine TRE bought it from 2 men who held it of the bishop, and this sale was made without his knowledge.

Afterwards, however, when King William was reigning, Archbishop Lanfranc proved his right to it against the Bishop of Bayeux; and the Church of Rochester is now seised of it.

V. The land of the Bishop of Bayeux

IN THE LATHE OF SUTTON

IN 'AXTON' HUNDRED

Hugh de Port holds HAWLEY of the Bishop of Bayeux. It is assessed at half a sulung. There is land [...]. In demesne are 2 ploughs; and 14 villans with 3 bordars have 4 ploughs. There are 3 slaves, and 12 acres of meadow, and 1 mill rendering 20s, and 1 woodland dene for 5 pigs. The whole manor is now worth £15 at 20[d] to the ora.

In this manor a man holds 20 acres of land worth 5s a year. He is called Wulfræd. He does not belong to this manor nor could he have [any] lord except the king.

Helto holds SWANSCOMBE of the bishop. It is assessed at 10 sulungs. There is land for 14 ploughs. In demesne are 3 [ploughs]; and 33 villans with 3 bordars have 13 ploughs. There is a knight, and 10 slaves, and 40 acres of meadow, [and] woodland for 3 pigs, and 5 fisheries rendering 30d, and a sixth which serves the hall, and 1 hithe rendering 5s4d. Of the woodland of this manor Richard holds in his lowy what is worth 4s. The whole manor was worth £20 [...]; and now it is worth £32.

Ralph fitzTurold holds HARTLEY of the bishop. It is assessed at 1 sulung. There is land [...]. In demesne are 2 ploughs; and 9 villans with 6 cottars have 3 ploughs. There are 3 slaves, and woodland for 10 pigs. The whole manor was worth £3 [...]; and now 100s. A certain woman held it.

Ralph holds of the bishop "EDDINTONE" for half a sulung. There is land for 1 plough, and there is [1 plough], with 4 bordars and 2 slaves, and there is 1 mill rendering 23s. The whole manor is valued at £4. TRE it was worth little. Leofstan held it of King Edward, and after his death he turned to Æthelnoth Cild; and now it is in dispute.

Ansgot of Rochester holds MAPLESCOMBE of the bishop for half a sulung. There is land [...]. In demesne is 1 plough, with 1 villan and 4 bordars and 4 slaves. There is 1 acre of meadow, and woodland for 8 pigs and 16d. besides. It was worth £4 [...]; and now 110s. Alstan held it of King Edward.

Adam fitzHubert holds RIDLEY of the bishop. It is assessed at 1 sulung. There is land [...]. In demesne are 2 ploughs; and 6 villans with 8 bordars have 2 ploughs. There are 5 slaves, and half an acre of meadow, and 1 woodland dene which Richard of Tonbridge holds. The manor was worth £3; and now £4.10s. Siward held it of King Edward.

Hugh de Port holds ASH of the bishop. It is assessed at 3 sulungs. There is land [...]. In demesne is 1 plough; and 12 villans with 8 bordars have 3 ploughs. There is a certain knight having 8 slaves and female slaves, and land for 1 plough. Besides this, Hugh has 2 men holding half a sulung who TRE could go where they pleased without leave. One estate is called Idleigh and the other, "Soninges". There is land for 1 plough, and it is valued at 20s. The whole manor was valued at £7; and now the same. What Richard of Tonbridge holds is valued at 40s. The king has there 2 denes which are valued at 7s. Godric held it of King Edward.

Geoffrey de Rots holds LULLINGSTONE. It is assessed at 1 sulung. There is land [...]. In demesne is 1 plough; and 4 villans with 1 cottar have 2 ploughs. There are 7 slaves, and 6 acres of pasture, [and] woodland for 20 pigs. When received, it was worth 60s; and now 100s. The king has in his own hand what is worth 10s. Beorhtsige Cild held it of King Edward.

Mauger holds LULLINGSTONE of the bishop. It is assessed at half a sulung. There is land [...]. In demesne is 1 plough; and 3 villans with 6 bordars have 1 plough. There are 5 acres of meadow. The whole manor was worth 60s; now 70s. Of this manor the king has what is worth 10s. Bruning held it of King Edward.

The same Mauger holds in FARNINGHAM half a yoke of land. There is land for 3 oxen. There are 2 oxen, with 1 bordar, and 2 acres of meadow. It was and is worth 15s. Brunsunu held it and could turn where he wished with his land. Of this manor the king holds what is worth 8s.

The same Mauger holds in Pinden half a sulung of the bishop. There is land for 7 oxen. There is 1 plough, with 6 villans, and 6 acres of meadow. It was and is worth 16s. Alfred held it TRE and could turn where he wished.

Osbern Paisforeire holds in Lullingstone half a sulung of the bishop. There is land [...]. In demesne is 1 plough; and 3 villans with 1 bordar and 1 slave have 1 plough. There are 5 acres of meadow, woodland for 5 pigs, and 1 mill rendering 15s and 150 eels. The king has woodland as a recent gift from the bishop, and it is worth 3s. The whole manor was worth 60s; now 77s. Sæweard Sot held it TRE and could turn where he wished with his land.

Wadard holds half a sulung in Farningham of the bishop. There is land for 3 ploughs. In demesne are 2 ploughs, with 1 villan and 2 cottars and 5 slaves. There is half a mill rendering 5 sulungs [sic], and 4 acres of meadow, [and] woodland for 5 pigs. Besides this half-sulung Wadard holds half a yoke in the same vill which has never discharged [its payments] to the king. All together it was worth £4; and now £6. Æstan held it TRE and could turn where he wished.

The same Wadard holds MAPLESCOMBE of the bishop. It is assessed at half a sulung. There is land for 2 ploughs. There are [2 ploughs], with 1 villan and 4 bordars and 5 slaves, and 1½ acres of meadow, [and] woodland for 8 pigs and 16d. [besides]. It was worth £3; and now £6. Wulfstan held it under Harold.

Ernulf de Hesdin holds FARNINGHAM. It is assessed at 3 yokes. There is land for 2 ploughs. There are now 6 oxen, with 2 villans and 3 bordars. There is a mill rendering 10s, and 8 acres of meadow, [and] pasture for 100 sheep. [There is] woodland for 10 pigs and 14d. [besides]. The king has of the woodland of this manor what is worth 8s. The whole manor was worth £3; and now 40s. Deoring held it and could turn where he wished.

Ansketil de Rots holds DARENTH of the bishop. It is assessed at half a sulung. There is land for 1½ ploughs. In demesne is 1 [plough]; and 4 villans with 4 bordars have 1 plough. There are 3 acres of meadow, and 2 mills rendering 18s, [and] woodland for 3 pigs. The king has of this manor as a recent gift from the bishop what is worth 10d. The whole manor was and is worth 100s. Ælfric held it of King Edward.

In the same vill the same Ansketil has 1 manor of the bishop. It is assessed at half a sulung. There is land for 1½ ploughs. There are 5 villans and 5 bordars, and 1 mill rendering 20s. There are 3 acres of meadow, and 1 slave. The whole manor was worth 60s; and now 70s. Osgeard held it of King Edward.

The same Ansketil holds HORTON KIRBY of the bishop. It is assessed at 1 sulung.

[Folio 6V: KENT]

There is land for 3 ploughs, and there are 4 bordars, and 1 mill rendering 5s, and 6 acres of meadow. There is a church, and woodland for 3 pigs. The king has as a recent gift from the bishop as much woodland of this manor as is worth 5s. The whole manor was worth £4; and now £6. Godel held it of Beorhtsige and could turn where he wished with this land.

The same Ansketil holds half a sulung of the bishop in the same manor. There is land for 1 plough, and there is [1 plough] in demesne; and 8 villans with 6 bordars have 1 plough. There is a mill rendering 15s, and 9 acres of meadow, [and] woodland for 5 pigs. The whole manor was worth 40s; and now 60s. Ording held it of the king.

The same Ansketil holds 1 sulung of the bishop in the same manor. There is land for 3 ploughs. In demesne is 1 plough; and 8 villans with 2 ploughs. There is 1 slave, and 8 acres of meadow, and half a mill rendering 5s, [and] woodland for 15 pigs. The whole manor was worth £4; and now 100s. Alweard held it of Harold. These 4 manors are now [held] as 1 manor.

IN 'LITLELEE' HUNDRED

Robert Latimer holds LESSNESS of the bishop. There is land for 17 ploughs. In demesne is 1 [plough]; and 60 villans with 3 bordars have 15 ploughs. There are 2 slaves and 3 cottars, and 3 fisheries rendering 4s, and 30 acres of meadow, [and] woodland for 20 pigs. TRE it was worth £20; when the bishop received it, £18; and now £22, and yet he who holds it pays £30. This manor TRE was assessed at 10 sulungs, and now at 4 sulungs. Azur held it.

Ansgot holds of the bishop HOWBURY which is assessed at 1 sulung. There is land [...]. In demesne is 1 plough; and 5 villans with 1½ ploughs, and 1 mill rendering 10s. There are 2 cottars and 1 slave, and 12 acres of meadow, [and] woodland for 3 pigs. TRE it was worth 60s; when received, as much; and now £4. Eskil held it of King Edward.

The Abbot of St Augustine's holds PLUMSTEAD of the Bishop of Bayeux. It is assessed at 2 sulungs and 1 yoke. [There is] land for 5 ploughs. In demesne is 1 plough; and 17 villans with 3 bordars have 4 ploughs. There is woodland for 5 pigs. TRE it was worth £10; when received, £8; and now as much, and yet he who holds it pays £12. Beorhtsige Cild held it of King Edward.

IN "HELMESTREI" HUNDRED

Mauger holds RUXLEY of the bishop. It is assessed at 1 sulung. There is land [...]. In demesne are 1½ ploughs; and 10 villans with 10 bordars have 2½ ploughs. There is a mill rendering 12s, [and] woodland for 3 pigs. TRE it was worth £4; when received, £3; and now 100s. Alweard held it of King Edward.

Ernulf de Hesdin holds CHELSFIELD of the bishop. It is assessed at 2 sulungs. There is land [...]. In demesne are 2 ploughs; and 20 villans with 4 bordars have 8 ploughs. There are 4 slaves, and 1 mill rendering 10s, and 10 acres of meadow, and woodland for 10 pigs. TRE it was worth £16; and afterwards £12; and now £25, and yet he who holds it pays £35. Toki held it of King Edward.

Adam fitzHubert holds ST MARY CRAY of the bishop. It is assessed at 1 sulung. There is land [...]. In demesne are 2 ploughs; and 14 villans with 1 bordar have 4 ploughs. There are 6 slaves, and 10 acres of meadow, [and] woodland for 10 pigs. TRE it was worth £6; and afterwards £4; and now £10. Toli held it of King Edward.

The same Adam holds WEST WICKHAM of the bishop. It is assessed at 1 sulung. There is land [...]. In demesne are 2 ploughs; and 24 villans have 4 ploughs. There are 13 slaves, and a church, and 1 mill rendering 20d, and a wood for 10 pigs. TRE it was worth £8; and afterwards £6; and now £13. Godric son of Karli held it of King Edward.

Geoffrey de Rots holds SEAL of the bishop. It is assessed at 7 sulungs. There is land [...]. In demesne are 3 ploughs; and 31 villans with 14 bordars have 16 ploughs. There are 10 slaves, and 1 fishery rendering 90 eels, [and] woodland for 75 pigs. The whole manor was worth £30 TRE; when received, £16; and now what Geoffrey holds, £24; what Richard of Tonbridge holds in his lowy is valued at £6; what the king holds of this manor, 22s. Beorhtsige Cild held it of King Edward.

Ansketil de Rots holds [? North] CARRY of the bishop. It is assessed at half a sulung. There is land [...]. In demesne is 1 plough; and 7 villans with 6 bordars have 1 plough. There is a church, and 1 acre of meadow and 3 acres of pasture. TRE, and afterwards, it was worth £4; and now £3. Leofric held it of King Edward.

The same Ansketil holds another CARY [?St Paul's Cray] of the bishop. It is assessed at half a sulung. There is land [...]. In demesne is 1 plough; and 7 villans with 5 bordars have 1 plough. There is 1 mill rendering 42d, and 5 slaves, [and] woodland for 7 pigs. TRE, and afterwards, it was worth £4; and now £3. These 2 estates were 2 manors TRE and are now 1 manor. Alwine held them of Æthelnoth Cild.

IN THE HALF-LATHE OF SUTTON

IN GREENWICH HUNDRED

The Bishop of Lisieux holds GREENWICH of the Bishop of Bayeux. It is assessed at 2 sulungs. There is land [...]. In demesne are 2 ploughs; and 24 villans have 4 ploughs, and [there are] 4 bordars and 1 cottar and 5 slaves. There are 4 mills rendering 70s, and 22 acres of meadow and 40 acres of pasture, and woodland for 10 pigs. These 2 sulungs TRE were 2 manors. Earl Harold held one and Beorhtsige the other, and now they are one. TRE, and afterwards, they were worth together £8; and are now valued at £12.

Hamo the sheriff holds ELTHAM of the bishop. It is assessed at 1½ sulungs. There is land for 12 ploughs. In demesne are 2 ploughs; and 42 villans with 12 bordars have 11 ploughs. There are 9 slaves, and 22 acres of meadow, [and] woodland for 50 pigs. TRE it was worth £16; when received, £12; and now £20. Æthelweald held it of the king.

The son of Turold of Rochester holds of the bishop 'WRICKLESMARSH' [in Charlton]. It is assessed at 1 sulung. There is land for 4 ploughs. In demesne are 2 ploughs; and 11 villans with 2 cottars have 2 ploughs. There are 4 acres of meadow, [and] woodland for 15 pigs. TRE it was worth 100s; when received, £4; and now 100s. Eskil held it of King Edward.

Walter de Douai holds LEE of the bishop. It is assessed at half a sulung. There is land for 4 ploughs. In demesne are 2 ploughs; and 11 villans with 2 cottars have 2 ploughs. There are 2 slaves, and 5 acres of meadow, [and] woodland for 10 pigs. TRE, and when the bishop received it, it was worth £3; now 100s. Alwine held it of the king.

William fitzOgier holds CHARLTON [near Greenwich] of the bishop. It is assessed at 1 sulung. There is land for 5 ploughs. In demesne is 1 plough; and 13 villans have 3 ploughs. There are 2 slaves, and 8 acres of meadow, [and] woodland for 5 pigs. TRE, and afterwards, as now, worth £7. 2 brothers, Godwine and Alweard, held this land of the king as 2 manors.

IN "HELMESTREI" HUNDRED

The same William holds FOOTS CRAY of the bishop. It is assessed at half a sulung. There is land [...]. In demesne is 1 plough; and 8 villans with 1½ ploughs, and 4 cottars, and 1 mill rendering 10s.

[Folio 7: KENT]

There is 1 slave, and woodland for 6 pigs. TRE it was worth £4; and afterwards £3; now £4. Godwine Fot held it of King Edward.

Ansketil holds CROFTON of the bishop. It is assessed at 1 sulung and 1 yoke. There is land [...]. In demesne is nothing, but there are 3 villans and 4 bordars.

TRE, and afterwards, it was worth 100s; and now £6. Alwine held this land of King Edward as 2 manors.

Gilbert Maminot holds CUDHAM of the bishop. It is

assessed at 4 sulungs. There is land for 10 ploughs. In demesne are 4 [ploughs]; and 15 villans with 6 bordars have 6 ploughs. There is a church, and 11 slaves, and 2 mills rendering 14s2d, [and] woodland for 40 pigs. TRE it was worth £20; and afterwards £16; now £24.

The same Gilbert holds KESTON of the bishop. It is assessed at half a sulung. There is land [...]. In demesne is 1 plough; and 4 villans with 1 plough. There is woodland for 5 pigs. TRE, and afterwards, it was worth 60s; now 40s. Esbiorn Bigga held it of King Edward.

Hugh nephew of Herbert holds 'SANDLINGS' [in St Mary Cary] of the bishop. It is assessed at 1½ sulungs. There is land [...]. In demesne are 2 ploughs; and 20 villans with 2 ploughs. There is a church, and 9 slaves, and 6 acres of meadow and 20 acres of pasture, [and] woodland for 8 pigs. TRE it was worth £8; and afterwards £6; now £8. Bondi held it of the archbishop.

IN BROMLEY HUNDRED

Ansgot of Rochester holds BECKENHAM of the bishop. It is assessed at 2 sulungs. There is land for 8 ploughs. In demesne are 2 [ploughs]; and 22 villans with 8 bordars have 8½ ploughs. There are 12 acres of meadow, and 4 slaves, and 1 mill, and woodland for 60 pigs. TRE, and afterwards, it was worth £9; now £13. Eskil held it of King Edward.

IN THE LATHE OF AYLESFORD

IN LARKFIELD HUNDRED

Adam holds LEYBOURNE of the bishop. It is assessed at 2 sulungs. There is land [...]. In demesne are 3 ploughs; and 16 villans with 2 bordars have 7 ploughs. There is a church, and 10 slaves, and 1 mill rendering 7s, and 12 acres of meadow, [and] woodland for 50 pigs. TRE it was worth £8; when received, £7; now £8. Richard of Tonbridge holds in his lowy what is worth 24s. The king holds as a recent gift from the bishop what is worth 24s2d. Thorgisl held this manor of Earl Godwine.

Ansketil holds ALLINGTON [near Maidstone] of the bishop. It is assessed at 1 sulung. There is land for 3 ploughs. In demesne are 2 [ploughs]; and 15 villans with 2 bordars have 1½ ploughs. There is a church, and 2 slaves, and half a mill, and 1 dene rendering 15s, woodland for 8 pigs, and 1 acre of meadow. TRE it was worth 100s; when received, 60s; now 100s. Wulfric held it of Æthelnoth Cild.

Hamo the sheriff holds DITTON of the bishop. It is assessed at 1 sulung. There is land for 4 ploughs. In demesne are 2 [ploughs]; and 20 villans with 5 bordars have 3 ploughs. There is a church, and 6 slaves, and 1 mill rendering 10s, and 8 acres of meadow and 35 acres of pasture, [and] woodland for 6 pigs. TRE it was worth £8; when received, 100s; now £8. Esbiorn held it of King Edward.

Vitalis holds 'SIFFLETON' [in Ditton] of the bishop. It is assessed at 3 yokes. There is land for 1 plough. In demesne [are] 1½ ploughs; and 6 villans with 1 bordar have half a plough. There are 6 slaves, and 1 mill rendering 10s. There are 10 acres of meadow and 30 acres of pasture. TRE it was worth

40s; when received, £4; now 100s. TRE 2 men, Leofwine and Wulfwine, held this land in parage, and they could turn where they wished with their land.

Ralph fitzTurold holds ECCLES of the bishop. It is assessed at 3 yokes. There is land [...]. In demesne is 1 plough; and 7 villans with 14 bordars have 1 plough. There is 1 slave, and 11 acres of meadow, [and] woodland for 10 pigs. TRE, and afterwards, it was worth £3; now £4; what Richard holds in his lowy, 15d. The king [has] as a recent gift from the bishop 8s5d, and in Rochester the bishop had 3 houses rendering 31d, which he took from this manor into his own hand. Æthelnoth Cild held this manor.

Hugh de Port holds PADDLESWORTH of the bishop. It is assessed at half a sulung. There is land [...]. In demesne is 1 plough; and 1 villan with 4 bordars have 3 oxen. There is a church, and 2 slaves, and 5 acres of meadow and 1 acre of pasture. TRE it was worth 20s; when received, 30s; now 40s. Godric held it of King Edward.

The same Hugh holds RYARSH of the bishop. It is assessed at 2½ sulungs. There is land for 5 ploughs. In demesne are 2 [ploughs]; and 10 villans with 2 bordars have 3 ploughs. There is a church, and 10 slaves, and 1 mill rendering 10s, and 9 acres of meadow, [and] woodland for 5 pigs. TRE it was worth £8; when received, 100s; now £6. Ælfric held it of King Edward.

The same Hugh holds OFFHAM of the bishop. It is assessed at 1 sulung. There is land for 3 ploughs. In demesne, nothing. There 6 villans with 1 bordar have 2 ploughs. There is a mill rendering 50d, and 3 slaves, and 4 acres of meadow, [and] woodland for 10 pigs. TRE it was worth 40s; when received, 20s; now 30s. Godric held it of King Edward.

Ranulph de Colombieres holds NASHENDEN of the bishop. It is assessed at 1 sulung. There is land [...]. In demesne is 1 plough; and 19 villans with 3 bordars have 3 ploughs. There are 3 slaves, and 8 acres of meadow. TRE it was worth £3; when received, £4; now £5. Earl Leofwine held it.

Robert Latimer holds TOTTINGTON of the king at farm by a recent gift from the Bishop of Bayeux. It is assessed at half a sulung. There is land for 1½ ploughs. In demesne is 1 [plough]; and 3 villans with 9 bordars have half a plough. There are 4 slaves, and 5 acres of meadow, [and] woodland for 2 pigs. TRE it was worth 30s; when received, 20s; now 40s. Wulfnoth held it of King Edward.

The same Robert holds in TOTTINGTON of the king at farm 1 yoke, and this is by a recent gift from the Bishop of Bayeux, and there is nothing there except 2 acres of meadow. It is and was always worth 10s. Godwine held it of King Edward.

Ralph fitzTurold holds ADDINGTON of the bishop. It is assessed at 2½ sulungs. There is land for 5 ploughs. In demesne are 2 [ploughs]; and 6 villans with 9 bordars have 1 plough. There is a church, and 10 slaves, and 2 mills rendering 11s2d, and 12 acres of meadow, [and] woodland for 10 pigs. TRE it was worth £8; when received, 100s; now £6. Æthelræd held it of King Edward.

IN TOLLINGTROUGH HUNDRED

Ralph fitzTurold holds MILTON [near Gravesend] of the bishop. It is assessed at 1 sulung and 3 yokes. There is land for 4 ploughs. In demesne is 1 [plough]; and 21 villans with 2 bordars have 2 ploughs. There is a church, and 1 mill rendering 49d, and a hithe rendering 20s, and 3 slaves. TRE it was worth £4; and afterwards £3; now £6; what Richard holds in a wood in his lowy, 5s. Earl Leofwine held it.

The same Ralph holds LUDDESDOWN of the bishop. It is assessed at 2½ sulungs and half a yoke. There is land for 6 ploughs. In demesne are 2 [ploughs]; and 17 villans with 4 bordars have 5 ploughs. There is a church, and 1 slave, and 3½ acres of meadow, [and] woodland for 20 pigs. TRE it was worth £6; and afterwards 100s; now £8; what Richard has in his lowy, 20d. The bishop holds in his own hand in the city of Rochester 4 houses belonging to this manor, from which he has 9s10d. Earl Leofwine held it.

Herbert fitzIvo holds GRAVESEND of the bishop. It is assessed at 2 sulungs and 1 yoke. There is land for 4 ploughs. In demesne is 1 [plough]; and 4 villans with 8 slaves have 2 oxen. There is a church, and 1 hithe. TRE it was worth £10; when received, as much; now £11. This manor was 3 manors TRE. Leofric and Wulfwine and Godwine held them. It is now one.

Wadard holds NURSTEAD of the bishop. It is assessed at 2 sulungs. There is land for 2 ploughs. In demesne is 1 [plough], and there are 4 bordars, and a church, and 4 slaves. [There is] woodland for 3 pigs. TRE it was worth £4; when received, £3; now £5. Wulfstan held it of King Edward.

IN LARKFIELD HUNDRED

Ansketil holds OFFHAM of the bishop. It is assessed at 1 sulung. There is land [...]. In demesne is 1 plough; and 6 villans with 2 bordars have 1 plough. There are 4 slaves, and 1 mill rendering 10s, and 7 acres of meadow, [and] woodland for 10 pigs; and in the city of Rochester 1 house rendering 30d. TRE the manor was worth 100s; when received, £4; now £4.9s; what Richard of Tonbridge holds is worth 11s. Wulfric held it of Æthelnoth Cild.

Ralph de Courbepine holds BIRLING of the bishop. It is assessed at 6 sulungs. There is land [...]. In demesne is 1 plough; and 10 villans with 14 bordars have 6 ploughs. There is a church, and 6 slaves, and 1 mill rendering 10s and 330 eels, and a fishery rendering 60 eels. There are 12 acres of meadow and pasture for 50 cattle, [and] woodland for 40 pigs. TRE it was worth £12; when received, £6; now £12. Esbiorn Bigga held it of King Edward.

The same Ralph holds BURHAM of the bishop. It is assessed at 6 sulungs. There is land for 8 ploughs. In demesne are 2 [ploughs]; and 15 villans with 20 bordars have 6 ploughs. There is a church, and 7 slaves, and 1 mill rendering 6s, and 10 acres of meadow, [and] woodland for 20 pigs. TRE

it was worth £10; and when received as much; now £12. The Bishop of Rochester has the houses of this manor and they are worth 7s. Earl Leofwine held this manor.

IN 'LITTLEFELD' HUNDRED

Corbin holds WEST PECKHAM of the bishop. It is assessed at 2 sulungs. There is land for 6 ploughs. In demesne is 1 [plough]; and 12 villans have 5 ploughs, and [there are] 8 bordars and 5 slaves, and 3 acres of meadow. [There is] woodland for 10 pigs. TRE, and afterwards, it was worth £12; now £8, | and yet it renders £12. | The king has in this manor | [in margin] | 3 denes where 4 villans live and they are worth 40s. Earl Leofwine held it.

Richard of Tonbridge holds HADLOW of the bishop. It is assessed at 6 sulungs. There is land for 12 ploughs. In demesne are 3 [ploughs]; and 47 villans with 15 bordars have 15 ploughs. There is a church, and 10 slaves, and 2 mills rendering 11s, and 12 fisheries rendering 7s6d, and 12 acres of meadow, [and] woodland for 60 pigs. TRE and afterwards, as now, worth £30. Eadgifu held it of King Edward.

Ralph fitzTurold holds half a sulung of the bishop in 'STOKENBURY' [in East Peckham]. TRE 2 free men held it and now likewise, and it is worth 20s.

IN THE LATHE OF AYLESFORD

IN WECHYLSTONE HUNDRED

Richard of Tonbridge holds TUDELEY of the bishop. It is assessed at 1 yoke. There is land for 1 plough, and there is [1 plough] in demesne, and a church, and woodland for 2 pigs. It is and was always worth 15s. Eadgifu held it of the king.

IN EYHORNE HUNDRED

Hugh nephew of Herbert holds HARRIETSHAM of the bishop. It is assessed at 2 sulungs. There is land for 6 ploughs. In demesne [...]; 18 villans with 10 bordars have 4 ploughs. There is a church, and 11 slaves, and 2 mills rendering 11s6d, and 7 acres of meadow, [and] woodland for 15 pigs. TRE it was worth £10; when received, £8; now £10. Osweard held it of King Edward.

The same Hugh holds FAIRBOURNE of the bishop. It is assessed at 1 sulung. There is land for 2 ploughs. In demesne [...]; 4 villans with 1½ ploughs, and 2 mills rendering 40d. TRE it was worth £4; afterwards, as now, £3. Alwine held it of Earl Godwine.

The same Hugh holds 1 yoke of free land in 'SHELBOROUGH' [in Harrietsham] of the bishop, and he has there half a plough, with 1 bordar and 5 slaves, and [there are] 1½ acres of meadow. It is and was always worth 20s. Alwine held it of Earl Godwine.

The same Hugh and Adelold the chamberlain hold FRINSTED of the bishop. It is assessed at 1 sulung. There is land for 3 ploughs. In demesne [...]; 3 villans have 7 oxen. There is a church, and 2½ acres of meadow, and woodland for 2 pigs. It is and was always worth 20s. Leofwine held it of King Edward.

Adelold holds LEEDS of the bishop. It is assessed at 3 sulungs. There is land for 12 ploughs. In demesne are 2 ploughs; and 28 villans with 8 bordars have 7 ploughs. There is a church, and 18 slaves. There are 2 arpents of vineyard and 8 acres of meadow, woodland for 20 pigs, and 5 mills of the villans. TRE it was worth £16; when received, the same; now £20, and yet it renders £25. Earl Leofwine held it.

The Abbot of St Augustine's has half a sulung of this manor, which is worth 10s, in exchange for the park of the Bishop of Bayeux. The Count of EU has 4 denes of this manor which are worth 20s.

Ansgot of Rochester holds ALDINGTON [in Thurnham] of the bishop. It is assessed at 2 sulungs. There is land for 3½ ploughs. In demesne are 2 [ploughs]; and 7 villans with 5 bordars have 1½ ploughs. There is a church, and 4 slaves, and 6 acres of meadow, and 1 mill rendering 4s2d, [and] woodland for 10 pigs. TRE, and afterwards, it was worth £4; now £7. Godwine and Alwine held it of King Edward as 2 manors.

The same Ansgot holds STOCKBURY of the bishop. It is assessed at 2 sulungs. There is land [...]. In demesne is 1 plough; and 5 villans with 9 bordars have 2 ploughs. There is a church, and 2 slaves, and 1 mill rendering 64d, [and] woodland for 15 pigs. TRE, and afterwards, it was worth £4; now £6. Ælfgifu held it of King Edward.

Hugh de Port holds ALLINGTON [in Hollingbourne]. It is assessed at 3 sulungs. There is land for 8 ploughs. In demesne are 2 ploughs; and 18 villans with 6 bordars have 6 ploughs. There is a church, and 8 slaves, and 2½ mills rendering 17s.

[Folio 8: KENT]

There are 5 acres of meadow, [and] woodland for 40 pigs. TRE it was worth £9; and when received, as much; and yet it renders £12. To this manor belong 3 messuages in Rochester and they render 5s a year. Osweard held it of King Edward.

Adam fitzHubert holds SUTTON [East Sutton or Sutton Valence] of the bishop. It is assessed at 4 sulungs. There is land for 7 ploughs. In demesne are 2 [ploughs]; and 18 villans with 5 bordars have 4 ploughs. There is a church, and 4 acres of meadow, and 1 mill [...], [and] woodland for 50 pigs. TRE it was worth £12; when received, £10; now £14, and yet it renders £18. Earl Leofwine held it.

The same Adam holds CHART SUTTON of the bishop. It is assessed at 3 sulungs. There is land for 8 ploughs. In demesne is 1 [plough]; and 20 villans with 5 bordars have 6 ploughs. There is a church, and 8 slaves, and 6 acres of meadow, [and] woodland for 50 pigs. There are 3 arpents of vineyard and a park for wild beasts. TRE and afterwards, as now, worth £12. Æthelnoth Cild held it.

The same Adam holds SUTTON [East Sutton or Sutton Valence] of the bishop. It is assessed at 1½ sulungs. There is land for 8 ploughs. In demesne are 2 [ploughs]; and 15 villans with 9 bordars have 4 ploughs. There is a church, and 10 slaves, and 8 acres of meadow, [and] woodland for 50 pigs.

TRE, and afterwards, it was worth £10; now £12, and yet it renders £18. Leofnoth held it of King Edward.

The same Adam holds BOWLEY of the bishop. It is assessed at 2 sulungs. There is land for 2½ ploughs. In demesne is 1 plough; and 2 villans with 2 bordars have half a plough. There is a church, and 4 slaves, and 1 mill rendering 5s, and 6 acres of meadow, [and] woodland for 20 pigs.

A man of Adam has 1 sulung of this manor, and it is called Marley, and there he has 1 plough, and 4 villans with 1 plough, and a church, and 2 slaves, and woodland for 4 pigs. The whole manor TRE was worth £6; and afterwards as much; now £7. Thorgisl held it of King Edward.

The same Adam holds LANGLEY of the bishop. It is assessed at 1½ sulungs. There is land for 4 ploughs. In demesne are 2 [ploughs]; and 7 villans with 5 bordars have 3 ploughs. There is a church, and 7 slaves, and 3 acres of meadow, [and] woodland for 25 pigs. TRE it was worth 60s; when received, 50s; now 60s. Thorgisl held it of King Edward.

The same Adam holds OTTERDEN of the bishop. It is assessed at half a sulung. There is land for 2 ploughs. In demesne is 1 [plough]; and 2 villans with 4 bordars have half a plough. There are 2 slaves, and 1 acre of meadow, [and] woodland for 5 pigs. TRE, and afterwards, it was worth 10s; now 30s. To this manor belong 2 messuages in Canterbury rendering 12d. Alweard held this manor of King Edward.

The same Adam holds OLD SHELVE of the bishop. It is assessed at half a sulung. There is land for 1 plough, and there is [1 plough] in demesne, with 1 villan and 1 bordar and 5 slaves. There are 4 acres of meadow, [and] woodland for 4 pigs. TRE and afterwards, as now, worth 20s. Godric held it of King Edward.

William fitzRobert holds NEW SHELVE of the bishop. It is assessed at 1 sulung. There is land for 3½ ploughs. In demesne are 2 [ploughs]; and a certain Frenchman with 10 villans and 1 bordar have 1½ ploughs. There are 5 slaves, and 1 acre of meadow, and 1 mill rendering 15d, [and] woodland for 15 pigs. TRE and afterwards, as now, worth £4. Edith held it of King Edward. To this manor belonged in Canterbury TRE 1 house rendering 25d.

Hugh nephew of Herbert holds BOUGHTON MALHERBE of the bishop. It is assessed at 1 sulung. There is land for 2 ploughs. In demesne, nothing, but 5 villans have 1 plough there, and [there are] 2 acres of meadow. [There is] woodland for 20 pigs. There is a church. TRE, and afterwards, it was worth £8; now £6. Alwine held it of Earl Godwine.

The same Hugh holds WORMSHILL of the bishop. It is assessed at 1 sulung. There is land for 2 ploughs. In demesne is 1 [plough]; and 5 villans have 1½ ploughs. There is a church, and 2 slaves, and 2 acres of meadow, and woodland for 10 pigs. TRE and afterwards, as now, worth £4. Edwin held it of King Edward and could go where he wished with his land.

The same Hugh holds WICHLING of the bishop. It is assessed at half a sulung. There is land for 1 plough, and there is [1 plough] in demesne, with 3 slaves, and a church, and woodland for 5 pigs; and TRE in Canterbury 3 houses rendering 40d belonged to this manor. The whole TRE was worth 100s; and afterwards, as now, 40s. Wulfgeat held it of King Edward and could go where he pleased.

The same Hugh holds OLD SHELVE of the bishop. It is assessed at half a sulung. There is land for 1 plough, and there is [1 plough] in demesne, with 1 villan and 1 bordar and 2 slaves. There are 4 acres of meadow, and woodland for 4 pigs. TRE and afterwards, as now, worth 40s. Wulfgeat held it of King Edward.

Geoffrey de Rots holds OTHAM of the bishop. It is assessed at 1 sulung and 1 yoke. There is land for 2½ ploughs. In demesne is 1 [plough]; and 9 villans with 3 bordars have 1 plough. There is a church, and 2 slaves, and 1 mill rendering 5s, and 3 acres of meadow, [and] woodland for 8 pigs. TRE it was worth £4; when received, £3; now £4. Alwine held it of King Edward.

Robert Latimer holds 'HARBILTON' [in Harrietsham] at farm. Adelold held it of the bishop. It is assessed at 1 sulung. There is land [...]. In demesne is 1 plough; and 2 villans with 1 bordar have 2 oxen, and there are 4 acres of meadow. TRE and afterwards, as now, worth 60s; and yet it is at farm for £4. Ælfirc held it of Earl Godwine.

The same Robert holds BROOMFIELD at farm. Adelold held it of the bishop. It is assessed at 1 sulung. There is land [...]. In demesne are 2 ploughs; and 5 villans with 10 bordars have 1½ ploughs. There is 1 mill rendering 6s8d, and pasture rendering 15s. There are 12 slaves, and 8 acres of meadow, [and] woodland for 20 pigs. TRE, and afterwards, it was worth £4; now 100s. Alwine held it of Earl Godwine. To this manor belongs a certain [piece of] free land for 3 oxen, and it is worth 5s.

Ralph de Courbepine holds THURNHAM of the bishop. It is assessed at 3 sulungs. There is land for 8 ploughs. In demesne is 1 [plough]; and 16 villans with 18 bordars have 4 ploughs. There is a church, and 6 slaves, and 1 mill rendering 6s, and 4 acres of meadow, [and] woodland for 40 pigs. TRE, and afterwards, it was worth £10; now £12, and yet it renders 14[l]. Esbiorn Bigga held it of King Edward.

The same Ralph holds FAIRBOURNE of the bishop. It is assessed at 1 sulung. There is land [...]. In demesne is 1 plough, and 2 villans with 1 bordar, and 2 slaves, and 1½ acres of meadow. [There is] woodland for 6 pigs. TRE and afterwards, as now, worth 30s. Esbiorn Bigga held it of King Edward.

Odo holds GILLINGHAM of the bishop. It is assessed at half a sulung. There is land for 1 plough. In demesne are 2 [ploughs]; and 6 bordars have half a plough. There is 1 mill rendering 16s7d, and 13 acres of meadow and 8 acres of pasture.

TRE it was worth 40s; when received, 30s; now 60s.

Robert Latimer holds CHATHAM of the bishop at farm. It is assessed at 6 sulungs. There is land for 16 ploughs. In demesne are 3 [ploughs]; and 33 villans with 4 bordars have 10 ploughs. There is a church, and 15 slaves, and 1 mill rendering 32d, and 20 acres of meadow, and 6 fisheries rendering 12d, [and] woodland for 1 pig. TRE, and afterwards, it was worth £12; now £15, and yet it renders £35. Earl Godwine held it.

IN THE LATHE OF AYLESFORD

IN ROCHESTER HUNDRED

The son of William de Thaon holds 'LITTLE DELCE' [in Rochester] of the bishop. It is assessed at 1 sulung and 1 yoke. There is land [...]. In demesne is 1 plough; and 5 villans have 2 ploughs. There are 12 acres of meadow, [and] woodland for 1 pig. TRE, and afterwards, it was worth £3; and now 70s. Godric held it of King Edward.

Ansgot of Rochester holds 'GREAT DELCE' [in Rochester] of the bishop. It is assessed at 1 sulung. There is land for 2 ploughs, and there are [2 ploughs] in demesne, with 1 villan and 5 bordars and 6 slaves. There are 12 acres of meadow and 60 acres of pasture. TRE and afterwards, as now, worth 100s. Osweard held it of King Edward.

IN HOO HUNDRED

The same Ansgot holds STOKE [Stoke, Lower Stoke and Middle Stoke] of the bishop. It is assessed at 2 sulungs. There is land for 2 ploughs, and there are [2 ploughs] in demesne, with 7 bordars. There is a fishery rendering 2s. TRE, and afterwards, it was worth 100s; now 110s. Eskil held it of King Edward.

The Bishop of Bayeux himself holds HOO [Allhallows, Hoo St Werburgh and St Mary Hoo] in demesne. [...] It was assessed at 50 sulungs TRE, and now at 33. There is land for 50 ploughs. In demesne are 4 [ploughs]; and 100 villans less 3 with 61 cottars have 43 ploughs. There are 6 churches, and 12 slaves, and 32 acres of meadow, [and] woodland for 30 pigs. The whole manor TRE was worth £60; when the bishop received it, the same; and now as much, and yet he who holds it pays £113. To this manor belonged 9 houses in the city of Rochester and they rendered 6s. They have now been taken away. Earl Godwine held this manor.

Of this manor Richard of Tonbridge holds half a sulung and woodland for 20 pigs. TRE and afterwards, as now, worth 40s. Adam fitzHubert holds of the bishop 1 sulung and 1 yoke of the same manor, and there a man of his has in demesne half a plough; and 4 villans with half a plough and 1 cottar. It is and was worth 30s.

Ansketil de Rots holds 3 sulungs of this manor and he has there in demesne 1 plough; and 5 villans with 12 cottars have 1½ ploughs. There are 5 slaves, and 1 mill rendering 10s, and 12 acres of meadow, and 2 fisheries rendering 5s. TRE, and afterwards, it was worth £6; now £6.5s.

IN TWYFORD HUNDRED

Adam holds of the bishop 1 yoke in PIMP. There is land [...]. There he has half a plough, with 2 slaves, and 4 acres of meadow, and half a fishery without rent. [There is] woodland for 6 pigs. TRE it was worth 6s; and afterwards 5s; now 10s, and yet it renders 15s. Godric held it of King Edward.

Ranulph de Colombieres holds WEST FARLEIGH of the bishop. It is assessed at 1 sulung. There is land for 4 ploughs. Ranulph holds only 3 yokes, and there he has in demesne 1 plough; and 10 villans with 4 cottars [who] have 3 ploughs. There is a church, and 7 slaves, and 1 mill rendering 5s, and 10 acres of meadow, [and] woodland for 15 pigs. TRE and afterwards, as now, worth £7. Æthelnoth held it of the king. Rayner holds of the bishop 1 yoke of this sulung in the manor of PIMP, and he has there 1 plough, with 9 slaves, and 3 acres of meadow. [There is] woodland for 4 pigs. TRE, and afterwards, it was worth 20s; now 40s. Æthelnoth Cild held it of King Edward.

Hamo holds NETTLESTEAD of the bishop. It is assessed at 3 sulungs. There is land for 6 ploughs. In demesne is 1 [plough]; and 14 villans have 5 ploughs. There is a church, and 14 slaves, and 2 mills rendering 14s, and a fishery rendering 2s, and 7 acres of meadow, [and] woodland for 35 pigs. TRE it was worth £8; and afterwards £6; now £8.5s. Northmann held it of King Edward. From this manor the bishop has 30s for 2 enclosures.

Ralph fitzTurold holds WATERINGBURY of the bishop. It is assessed at 2 sulungs. There is land for 5 ploughs. In demesne are 2 [ploughs]; and 6 villans with 8 bordars have 3 ploughs. There is a church, and 2 mills rendering 3s, and 2 acres of meadow, and a fishery rendering 30 eels, [and] woodland for 2 pigs. TRE, and afterwards, it was worth 40s; now £6. Leofgifu held it of King Edward. To this manor belong 4 closes in the city rendering 3s.

Hugh de Breboeuf holds WATERINGBURY of the bishop. It is assessed at 2 sulungs. There is land for 4 ploughs. In demesne is 1 [plough]; and 9 villans with 4 bordars have 2 ploughs. There are 3 slaves, and 1 mill rendering 16d, and 3 acres of meadow, [and] woodland for 2 pigs. TRE, and afterwards, it was worth £4; now 100s. Gothild held it of King Edward.

Adelold held TESTON of the bishop, and Robert now holds it at farm. It is assessed at 1 sulung. There is land [...]. In demesne are 2½ ploughs; and 7 villans with 3 bordars have 1 plough. There are 12 slaves, and 1 mill rendering 3s, and 8 acres of meadow, [and] woodland for 20 pigs. TRE it was worth 100s; and afterwards 60s; now 100s. Edward held it of King Edward. This land 3 brothers held TRE as 3 manors. It is now one.

The same Adelold held 'BENSTED' [in Hunton] of the bishop, and Robert holds it at farm. It is assessed at 1 yoke. There is land [...]. In demesne is 1 plough, with 5 slaves, and 1 acre of meadow. [There is] woodland for 6 pigs. TRE, and afterwards, it was worth 20s; now 40s. Godric held it of Æthelnoth Cild.

IN MAIDSTONE HUNDRED

Ranulph de Colombieres holds EAST BARMING of the bishop. It is assessed at 1 yoke. There is land [...]. In demesne is 1 plough, with 5 slaves, and 4 acres of meadow. [There is] woodland for 3 pigs. TRE it was worth 15s; when received, 20s; now 40s.

Robert Latimer holds BOXLEY at farm. It was assessed at 7 sulungs TRE; now at 5 sulungs. There is land for 20 ploughs. In demesne are 3 ploughs; and 47 villans with 11 bordars have 16 ploughs. There are 3 mills rendering 36s8d, and 16 slaves, and 20 acres of meadow, [and] woodland for 50 pigs. TRE, and afterwards, it was worth £25; now £30, and yet Robert pays £55. Æthelnoth Cild held it. Helto holds half a sulung of this manor, and there he has 1 plough, with 1 bordar and 1 Frenchman, and 2 acres of meadow, and woodland for 6 pigs, and it is worth 40s.

Ralph fitzTurold holds LITTLE WROTHAM of the bishop. It is assessed at 1½ sulungs. There is land [...]. In demesne is 1 plough; and 4 villans with 4 bordars have 2 ploughs. There are 2 slaves, and 2 mills rendering 4s, and 2 acres of meadow, [and] woodland for 5 pigs. TRE, and afterwards, it was worth 40s; now 60s and 54d. Richard of Tonbridge has in his lowy what is worth 13s, and woodland for 50 pigs, and the king has in the same manor what is worth 16d. TRE Godwine and Edwin held this land as 2 manors.

Adam holds CHALK of the bishop. It is assessed at 3 sulungs. There is land for 7 ploughs. In demesne are 2 [ploughs]; and 14 villans with 6 bordars have 5 ploughs. There is a church, and 4 slaves, and 1 mill rendering 5s, and 16 acres of meadow. TRE it was worth £7; and afterwards 100s;

[Folio 9: KENT]

now £10, and yet he who holds it pays £14. Of this manor there is in the king's hand what is worth 7s, by a recent gift from the bishop.

The bishop kept in his own hand 3 closes in the city of Rochester which are worth 50d.

In Essex is 1 hide which of right belongs to this manor. Godwine son of Dudemann held it. Now Ranulph Peverel holds it.

The same Adam holds HIGHAM [Higham and Lower Higham] of the bishop. It is assessed at 5 sulungs. There is land for 12 ploughs. In demesne are 3 ploughs; and 24 villans with 12 bordars have 6½ ploughs. There are 20 slaves, and 30 acres of meadow. There is a church, and 1 mill rendering 10s, and a fishery rendering 3s, and in Essex pasture for 200 sheep. TRE it was worth £12; and afterwards £6; now £15. Godwine son of Karli and Toli held this land TRE, as 2 manors.

The same Adam holds 1½ sulungs in COOLING of the bishop. There is land for 1½ ploughs. In demesne are 2 ploughs; and 5 villans have half a plough. There are 4 slaves, and 7 acres of meadow, [and] woodland for 10 pigs. TRE, and afterwards, it was worth 40s; now £4. What Richard of Tonbridge has in his lowy is worth 7s. Wulfwine held it of Earl Leofwine.

The same Adam holds 'BECKLEY' [in Higham] of the bishop. It is assessed at half a sulung. There is land for half a plough. In demesne is half a plough; and 1 villan with half a plough, and 2 bordars. There is 1 mill rendering 5s. TRE, and afterwards, it was worth 10s; now 15s. Wulfwine held it of Earl Leofwine.

IN 'SHAMWELL' HUNDRED

Ralph fitzTurold holds OAKLEIGH of the bishop. It is assessed at 1 sulung. There is land for half a plough, and there are besides 30 acres of land. In demesne is 1 plough; and 6 villans have half a plough. There are 12 acres of meadow. TRE, and afterwards, it was worth 40s; now £4. Hunæf held it of Earl Harold.

Ansgot of Rochester holds HENHURST. It is assessed at half a sulung. There is land for 1 plough. In demesne is 1 plough, and 2 villans with 4 slaves. TRE it was worth 20s; when received, 30s; now 40s. Godwine held it of Earl Godwine.

Ernulf de Hesdin holds CLIFFE of the bishop. It is assessed at half a sulung. There is land [...]. In demesne [is] half a plough, and 2 villans, and 10 acres of meadow and pasture for 100 sheep. TRE, and afterwards, it was worth 30s. 2 brothers, Ælfric and Ordric, held it of King Edward.

The same Ernulf holds 'HAVEN' [in Frindsbury] of the bishop. It is assessed at 3 yokes. There is land for 1 plough, and there is [1 plough] in demesne; and 6 villans with 1 bordar have 1 plough. There are 6 acres of meadow. TRE, and afterwards, it was worth 50s; now 60s. Osweard held it of King Edward.

Odo holds 1 yoke of the bishop in the same 'Haven' [in Frindsbury]. There is land for half a plough. In demesne is nothing. TRE and afterwards, as now, worth 20s.

The same Odo holds COOLING of the bishop. It is assessed at half a sulung. There is land for half a plough. There is [half a plough], with 1 bordar, and 4 acres of meadow. TRE, and afterwards, it was worth 20s; now 30s. God held it of King Edward.

Helto holds [?] 'MERSTON' [in Shorne] of the bishop. It is assessed at half a sulung. There is land for 1 plough, and there is [1 plough], with 5 villans, and 1 acre of meadow. TRE, and afterwards, it was worth 10s; now 30s. Wulfweard White held it of King Edward.

IN THE HALF-LATHE OF MILTON

IN MILTON HUNDRED

Hugh de Port holds TUNSTALL of the bishop. It is assessed at $3\frac{1}{2}$ sulungs [...]. There is land for 4 ploughs. In demesne are 2 ploughs; and 9 villans with 1 plough, and 9 slaves. [There is] woodland for 10 pigs, and a salt-pan rendering 12d. TRE, and afterwards, it was worth £7; now £8. Osweard held it of King Edward.

The same Hugh holds UPCHURCH of the bishop. It is assessed at 2 sulungs. There is land for 2 ploughs. In demesne

is 1 [plough], with 5 bordars and 1 slave, and 1 mill rendering 6s8d. It is worth £6. Osweard held it.

The same Hugh holds TONGE of the bishop. It is assessed at 2 sulungs. There is land for 3 ploughs. In demesne are 2 [ploughs]; and 5 villans with 1 plough. There is a church, and 4 slaves, and 1 mill rendering 8s, [and] woodland for 4 pigs. TRE, and afterwards, it was worth £7; now £10.10s. Osweard held it.

Of these sulungs which Hugh de Port has, Osweard held 5 at rent and 3 sulungs and $1\frac{1}{2}$ yokes which he took away from the king's villans.

IN THE BOROUGH LATHE

IN BRIDGE HUNDRED

Richard fitzWilliam holds PATRIXBOURNE of the bishop. It is assessed at 6 sulungs. There is land for 8 ploughs. In demesne are 3 ploughs; and 44 villans with 3 bordars have 10 ploughs. There is a church, and 1 slave, and 4 mills rendering 16s8d, a fishery rendering 6d, pasture, of which men from elsewhere have ploughed 6 acres of land, [and] woodland for 4 pigs. TRE it was worth £18; when received, £10; now £19.

The Bishop of Bayeux himself holds [Lower or Upper] HARDRES in demesne. It is assessed at 2 sulungs. There is land for 4 ploughs. In demesne is 1 [plough]; and 9 villans with 2 ploughs. There is a church, and 5 slaves, [and] woodland for 20 pigs. TRE it was worth £7; and afterwards 100s; now £7, and yet it renders £10. Edwin held it of King Edward.

The same bishop holds STELLING in demesne. It is assessed at 1 yoke. [There is] land for $1\frac{1}{2}$ ploughs. In demesne is nothing except 1 bordar. There is a church, [and] woodland for 2 pigs. TRE it was worth 60s; and afterwards, as now, 40s. Alræd held it of King Edward.

The same bishop holds BEKESBOURNE in demesne. It is assessed at 2 sulungs. There is land for 6 ploughs. In demesne are 2 [ploughs]; and 25 villans with 4 bordars have 7 ploughs. There is a church, and 6 slaves, and 1 mill rendering 38d, and 1 salt-pan rendering 30d, and half a fishery [rendering] 4d. From pasture, 40d [There is] woodland for $6\frac{1}{2}$ pigs. TRE it was worth £12; and afterwards £7; now £12, and yet it renders £18. What Hugh de Montfort holds is worth 5s. Lyfing held it of King Edward.

Ranulph holds these 3 manors of the Bishop of Bayeux at farm.

Ranulph de Colombieres holds [Lower or Upper] HARDRES of the bishop. It is assessed at 1 sulung. There is land for 4 ploughs. In demesne is half a plough; and 9 villans have 2 ploughs. There is a church, and 8 slaves, and 13 acres of meadow, [and] woodland for 4 pigs. TRE it was worth £6; and afterwards £4; now 100s. Azur held it of King Edward.

IN 'DOWNHAMFORD' HUNDRED

The bishop himself holds WICKHAMBREAUX in demesne. It is assessed at 4 sulungs. There is land for 11 ploughs. In demesne are 2 ploughs; and 36 villans with 32 cottars have 9 ploughs. There is a church, and a priest who gives 40s a year. There is a park, and 2 mills rendering 50s, and 2 salt-pans rendering 32d, and 3 fisheries rendering 4s, and 32 acres of meadow, pasture for 300 sheep and for 31 cattle, [and] woodland for 80 pigs. TRE it was worth £25; when received, £20; now £30. To this manor belong 3 messuages in Canterbury rendering 6s8d. Alfred Bigga held this manor of King Edward. In addition there belongs to this manor half a sulung of free land

[Folio 9V: KENT]

which Sigeræd held of Alfred Bigga and now Geoffrey fitzMalleterre holds of the Bishop of Bayeux; and it is and was always worth 60s.

IN THE HUNDRED and in the City of Canterbury Adam fitzHubert has of the bishop 4 houses and 2 outside the city which render 8s.

IN THE SAME HUNDRED

Hamo the sheriff holds NACKINGTON of the bishop. It is assessed at half a sulung. There is land for 1½ ploughs. In demesne is 1 [plough], with 2 bordars. There is a small wood containing 12 acres of pasture. TRE and afterwards, as now, worth £3.

The same Hamo holds of the bishop half a sulung, and there is land for 4 ploughs. In demesne are 2 ploughs; and 11 bordars with 3 ploughs, and 16 acres of scrubland. TRE it was worth 100s; and afterwards £6; and now £9.

The burgesses of Canterbury held these lands TRE and up to [the time of] the Bishop of Bayeux, who took them away from them.

IN 'LIMEN' LATHE

IN FOLKESTONE HUNDRED

William d'Arques holds FOLKESTONE. It was assessed TRE at 40 sulungs, and now at 39. There is land for 120 ploughs. In demesne are 14 ploughs; and 209 villans and 83 bordars. Among them all they have 45 ploughs. There are 5 churches from which the archbishop has 55s. There are 3 slaves, and 7 mills rendering £9.12s. There are 100 acres of meadow, [and] woodland for 40 pigs. Earl Godwine held this manor.

Of this manor Hugh fitzWilliam holds 9 sulungs of the land of the villans, and there he has in demesne 4½ ploughs; and 38 villans with 17 bordars who have 16 ploughs. There are 3 churches, and 1½ mills rendering 16s5d, and 1 salt-pan rendering 30d, [and] woodland for 6 pigs. It is worth £20.

Walter d'Appeville holds 3 yokes and 12 acres of land of this manor, and there he has 1 plough in demesne, and 3 villans with 1 bordar. It is worth 30s.

Alvred holds 1 sulung and 40 acres of land, and there he has in demesne 2 ploughs, with 6 bordars, and 12 acres of meadow. [...] It is worth £4.

Walter fitzEngelbert holds half a sulung and 40 acres, and

there he has in demesne 1 plough, with 7 bordars, and [there are] 5 acres of meadow. It is worth 30s.

Wesman holds 1 sulung, and there he has in demesne 1 plough; and 2 villans with 7 bordars having 1½ ploughs. [...] It is worth £4.

Alvred the steward holds 1 sulung and 1 yoke and 6 acres of land, and there he has in demesne 1 plough, with 11 bordars. [...] It is worth 50s.

Eudo holds half a sulung, and there he has in demesne 1 plough, with 4 bordars, and [there are] 3 acres of meadow. [...] It is worth 20s.

Bernard de Saint-Ouen [holds] 4 sulungs, and there he has in demesne 3 ploughs; and 6 villans with 11 bordars have 2 ploughs. There are 4 slaves, and 2 mills rendering 24s, and 20 acres of meadow, [and] woodland for 2 pigs.

From 1 dene and from land which has been given from these sulungs come £3 farm. All together it is worth £9.

Baldric holds half a sulung, and there he has 1 plough; and 2 villans with 6 bordars [who] have 1 plough, and 1 mill rendering 30d. It is worth 30s.

Richard holds 58 acres of land, and there he has 1 plough, with 5 bordars. It is worth 10s.

The whole of Folkestone TRE was worth £110; when received, £40; now what he has in demesne is worth £100; what the above-named knights hold together is worth £45.10s.

IN 'LONINGBOROUGH' HUNDRED

The Bishop of Bayeux holds ELHAM in demesne. It is assessed at 6 sulungs. There is land for 24 ploughs. In demesne are 5 ploughs; and 41 villans with 8 bordars have 18 ploughs. There is a church, and 8 slaves, and 2 mills rendering 6s, and 28 acres of meadow, [and] woodland for 100 pigs. TRE, and afterwards, it was worth £30; now 40[l], and yet it renders £50. Eadric held this manor of King Edward.

IN ROLVENDEN HUNDRED

Adam fitzHubert holds of the bishop 1 dene of half a yoke which remained outside the divisio of Hugh de Montfort, and it belonged to "Belice". He has there 2 villans with half a plough. This is and was always worth 10s.

IN STOWTING HUNDRED

Ansfrid holds half a sulung of the bishop in "Bochelande", and there he has in demesne 1 plough, with 1 villan. There is land for 2 ploughs. TRE it was worth 20s; when received, 30s; now 40s.

IN EASTRY LATHE

IN EASTRY HUNDRED

Ralph de Courbepine holds of the bishop 1 yoke in Barfrestone. There 1 very poor woman pays 3½d. This yoke is and was always worth 10s.

Ranulph de Colombieres holds there 1 yoke which paid its tax in [Lower or Upper] Hardres and now so far as the king's tax is concerned has not paid.

Adelold held EASOLE of the bishop. It is assessed at 3 sulungs. There is land [...]. In demesne is 1 plough; and 6 villans with 2 bordars have 3 ploughs. There are 2 slaves, and a small wood for fencing. TRE it was worth £9; now 15[l]. Æthelnoth Cild held it of King Edward.

Osbern fitzLetard holds of the bishop 1 sulung in 'SHELVING' [in Woodnesborough]. There he has 1 villan paying 2s. TRE it was worth 60s; and afterwards, as now, 30s. Alwine held it TRE.

The same Osbern holds 'NORTH PONSHALL' [in Waldershare] of the bishop. It is assessed at 1 sulung. There is land [...]. In demesne are 2 ploughs; and 1 villan with 4 bordars have half a plough. 2 free men held this land of King Edward. A certain knight of his holds half a yoke, and there he has 1 plough in demesne. The whole TRE was worth 60s; and afterwards 20s; now 100s.

IN BEWSBURY HUNDRED

Ralph de Courbepine holds half a yoke in 'South Ponshall' [in Coldred], and there he has 3 oxen. TRE, and afterwards, it was worth 4s; now 8s. Wulfric held it of King Edward.

IN BARHAM HUNDRED

Fulbert holds BARHAM of the bishop. It is assessed at 6 sulungs. There is land for 32 ploughs. In demesne are 3 ploughs; and 52 villans with 20 cottars have 18 ploughs. There is a church, and 1 mill rendering 20s4d. There are 25 fisheries rendering 35s less 4d. From cartage, that is, a service, 60s. From the herbage, 26s, and [there are] 20 acres of meadow. As pannage, 150 pigs.

The bishop gave to Herbert fitzIvo a Berewick of this manor, which is called [Church or West] HOUGHAM, and there he has 1 plough in demesne; and 12 villans with 9 ploughs, and 20 acres of meadow.

The bishop also gave from the same manor to Osbern Paisforiere 1 sulung, and 2 mills rendering 50s, and there is in demesne 1 plough; and 4 villans with 1 plough.

The whole of BARHAM TRE was worth £40; when the bishop received it, the same; and yet it rendered £100 to him.

Barham by itself is now worth £40 and [Church or West] Hougham £10; and that which Osbern has, £6, and the land of a certain Ranulph, a knight, is worth 40s. Archbishop Stigand held this manor, but it did not belong to the archbishopric but belonged to the demesne farm of King Edward.

[Folio 10: KENT]

IN WHITSTABLE HUNDRED

Vitalis holds SWALECLIFFE of the bishop. It is assessed at half a sulung. There is land for 1½ ploughs. In demesne is 1 plough, with 8 cottars who pay 4s6d, [and] woodland for 20 pigs. TRE it was worth 21s; when Vitalis received it, 12s; now 30s. Edward Snoch held it of King Edward.

The same Vitalis holds of the bishop 1 yoke in the same hundred, and there he has half a plough in demesne, with 4 bordars paying 6s. There is land for half a plough, [and]

woodland for 10 pigs. TRE, and afterwards, it was worth 10s; now 20s. Wulfsige held it of King Edward.

IN THE LATHE OF WYE

IN FAVERSHAM HUNDRED

Adam holds OARE of the bishop. It is assessed at 2 sulungs. There is land for 4 ploughs. In demesne is 1 [plough]; and 10 villans with 10 bordars have 2 ploughs. There is half a church, and 1 mill rendering 22s, and 2 fisheries without rent, and 1 salt-pan rendering 28d, [and] woodland for 6 pigs. TRE it was worth £4; and afterwards 60s; now 100s. Thorgisl held it of King Edward.

The same Adam holds STALISFIELD [Stalisfield and Stalisfield Green] of the bishop. It is assessed at 2 sulungs. There is land for [...]. In demesne is 1 plough; and 10 villans have 2 ploughs. There is a church, and †6† slaves, and 2 acres of meadow, [and] woodland for 60 pigs. TRE it was worth 60s; and afterwards 40s; now 100s. Thorgisl held it of Earl Godwine.

Hugh de Port holds NORTON of the bishop. It is assessed at 4 sulungs. There is land for 4 ploughs. In demesne are 3 ploughs; and 18 villans with 6 bordars have 5 ploughs. There are 3 churches, and 3 mills without rent, and 2 fisheries rendering 12d, and woodland for 40 pigs. TRE it was worth £8; and afterwards £6; now £12. Osweard held it of King Edward.

IN FELBOROUGH HUNDRED

Fulbert holds CHILHAM of the bishop. It is assessed at 5 sulungs. There is land for 20 ploughs. In demesne are 2 ploughs; and 38 villans with 12 cottars have 12 ploughs. There is a church, and 6½ mills rendering £6.8s, and 2 fisheries rendering 17d, and pasture rendering 18s7d. In the city of Canterbury 13 messuages belonging to this manor render 15s, and [there are] 9 acres of meadow, [and] woodland for 80 pigs. TRE it was worth £40; and afterwards £30; now £30 likewise, and yet it renders to the Bishop of Bayeux £80 and 40s. Sigeræd held it of King Edward.

IN FAVERSHAM HUNDRED

Hugh nephew of Herbert holds OSPRINGE of the bishop. It is assessed at 7½ sulungs. There is land for 20 ploughs. In demesne are no ploughs. [...] There 29 villans with 6 bordars have 11 ploughs. There is a church, and 1 mill rendering 11s8d, and a fishery rendering 10d, and a salt-pan rendering 4d, and 13 acres of meadow, [and] woodland for 80 pigs.

Of the land of this manor Herbert holds half a sulung and 3 virgates, and there he has in demesne 1 plough; and 1 villan with 10 bordars having 1 plough. Richard de le Marais holds half a sulung of this manor, and there he has 6 villans and 1 bordar with 1 plough; and a certain Turstin holds 1 yoke which renders 5s. The whole manor TRE was worth £20; when Herbert received it, £15; now £20. To this manor belongs in Canterbury 1 messuage rendering 30d. This manor [...] held.

Ansfrid holds "CILDRESHAM" of the bishop. It is

assessed at 1 sulung. There is land for 3 ploughs. In demesne is 1 [plough]; and 4 villans with 2 bordars have 1½ ploughs. There are 5 slaves, and 2 acres of meadow. There is woodland but it renders nothing. Of this manor a certain knight holds land for 1 plough. All together TRE it was worth 60s; and afterwards 40s; now £4.

The same Ansfrid holds "ERNOLTUN" of the bishop. It is assessed at 1 sulung. There is land for 3 ploughs. In demesne is 1 [plough]; and 8 villans with 2½ ploughs. There are 2 salt-pans […], and in the city of Canterbury 1 messuage rendering 21d. TRE it was worth £4; and afterwards 40s; now 100s. Burgnoth held this manor of King Edward. Of this manor Ranulph holds 10 acres which lie close to the city and rendered 42d. TRE.

The same Ansfrid holds MACKNADE of the bishop. It is assessed at 1 yoke. There is land for half a plough. There are 2 villans paying 50d. TRE it was worth 50d; now it is worth 60d. Sæweald held it TRE.

The same Ansfrid holds BADLESMERE of the bishop. It is assessed at 1 sulung. There is land for 2½ ploughs. In demesne is 1 [plough]; and 10 villans have 1½ ploughs. There is a church, and 2 slaves, and a fishery rendering 12d, [and] woodland for 4 pigs. TRE it was worth 60s; and afterwards 60s; now £4. The Abbot of St Augustine's claims this manor because he had it TRE, and the hundred testifies for him. But the son of the man states that his father could turn where he wished, but with this the monks do not agree.

The same Ansfrid holds PERRY of the bishop. It was assessed at 1 yoke. There is 1 bordar paying 5d. TRE and afterwards, as now, worth 16s. Wulfwig held it of King Edward.

The same Ansfrid holds PERRY of the bishop. It is assessed at half a sulung. There is land for 1 plough. There are 3 bordars, and 1 messuage in the city rendering 16d. TRE and afterwards, as now, worth 24s. Wulfgifu held it of King Edward.

Osbern holds BUCKLAND [in Luddenham] of the bishop. It is assessed at 3 yokes. There is land for 1 plough. In demesne is 1 [plough]; and 3 villans with 2 bordars have half a plough. There are 8 slaves. TRE it was worth £4; and afterwards £3; and now 70s. Sæweard held it of King Edward.

The same Osbern holds 1 yoke of the bishop in the same manor, and it is assessed at 1 yoke. TRE it was worth 20s; and afterwards, as now, worth 10s. Leofweard held it of King Edward.

Hugh de Port holds "HERSTE" of the bishop. It is assessed at 3 yokes. There is land for 1 plough. In demesne is [1 plough], with 2 bordars and 2 slaves. TRE, and afterwards, it was worth 10s; now 30s. Osweard held it of King Edward.

Adam holds of the bishop 1 yoke in OARE, and it is assessed at 1 yoke. There is land for 1 plough. 4 villans now holds this at farm and pay 20s, and it was always worth as much. There is a church. Leofweald held it of King Edward.

Herfrid holds THROWLEY. It is assessed at 3 sulungs.

There is land for 8 ploughs. In demesne is 1 [plough]; and 24 villans with 5 bordars have 6½ ploughs. There is a church, and 5 slaves, [and] woodland for 20 pigs, and in the city, 3 closes rendering 32d. TRE it was worth £7; and afterwards £6; now £8. Wulfnoth held it of King Edward.

Herbert held NORTH EASTLING of the bishop. There is land for 1 plough. It is assessed at half a sulung. There 2 bordars pay 2s. TRE, and afterwards, it was worth 20s; now 25s. Thorgot held it TRE.

Herbert fitzIvo held these 2 manors of the Bishop of Bayeux.

[Folio 10V: KENT]

Turstin de Gironde holds in Buckland [in Luddenham] 1 yoke of the bishop, and it is assessed at 1 yoke. There is 1 villan paying 6s. It is and was always worth 12s. Thorgot held it of King Edward.

Roger fitzAnsketil holds EASTLING of the bishop. It is assessed at 1 sulung. There is land for 1 plough. There is [1 plough] in demesne; and 1 bordar has half a plough. There is a church, and 1 mill rendering 10s, and 2 acres of meadow. TRE it was worth 60s; and afterwards 20s; now 40s. Wulfnoth held it of King Edward and could go where he wished with the land.

Fulbert holds EASTLING of the bishop. It was assessed at 5 sulungs TRE, and now at 2, and it was so after the bishop gave the manor to Hugh fitzFulbert. There is land for 6 ploughs. In demesne are 2 ploughs; and †30† villans have 3 ploughs. There is a church, and 28 slaves, and 1 mill rendering 10s, [and] woodland for 30 pigs. TRE it was worth £10; and when received, £6; now £4; and yet the bishop had £8. Sigeræd held it of King Edward.

The same Fulbert holds LUDDENHAM of the bishop. It is assessed at 1 sulung. There is land […]. In demesne is 1 plough; and 17 villans with 10 bordars have 2 ploughs. There is a church, and 6 slaves, and half a fishery rendering 300 herrings, and in the city of Canterbury, 5 closes rendering 7s10d. TRE it was worth £10; the bishop put it at farm for £10; when Fulbert received it, [it was worth] £6; and now the same. Sigeræd held it of King Edward.

Richard holds RINGLESTONE of the bishop. It is assessed at 1 sulung. There is land […]. There 2 villans have 1 plough, and pay 6s. TRE and afterwards, as now, worth 40s. Wulfgeat held it of King Edward.

IN FELBOROUGH HUNDRED

Ansfrid holds HORTON of the bishop. It is assessed at half a sulung. There is land for 1 plough. There is [1 plough] in demesne; and 13 villans have half a plough. There is 1 slave, and 2 mills rendering 1 mark of silver, and 8 acres of meadow, and 100 acres of scrubland. TRE it was worth †40s; afterwards † 30s; now 100s. Godric held it of King Edward.

IN WYE HUNDRED

Adam holds 'FANSCOMBE' [in Wye] of the bishop. It is assessed at half a sulung. There is land for 1½ ploughs. In demesne are 2 ploughs; and 3 villans and 3 slaves, and a church, and 13 acres of meadow. [There is] woodland for 10 pigs. TRE it was worth £4; and afterwards 20s; now £4. Hugh de Montfort holds of it what is worth 20s.

Wadard holds BUCKWELL of the bishop. It is assessed at half a sulung. There is land for 1 plough. There is [1 plough] in demesne; and 3 villans and 3 slaves, and 1 mill rendering 40d, and 10 acres of meadow and 1 alder-wood. TRE, and afterwards, it was worth 20s; now 40s. Wærhelm held it of the king.

The same Wadard holds COOMBE of the bishop. It is assessed at 1 sulung. There is land for 2 ploughs. In demesne is 1 [plough]; and 9 villans with 5 bordars have 1½ ploughs. There are 14 acres of meadow, [and] woodland for 5 pigs. TRE it was worth 60s; and afterwards 50s; now £4 and the service of 1 knight. Leofræd of Ruckinge held it of King Edward.

Ralph de Courbepine holds 'BEAMSTON' [in Westwell] of the bishop. It is assessed at 1 sulung. There is land for 6 ploughs. In demesne are 2 [ploughs]; and 13 villans with 1 bordar have 3 ploughs. There are 33 acres of meadow, and woodland for 40 pigs. Of this manor Hugh de Montfort holds, in both woodland and pasture, what was worth TRE £6; and afterwards, as now, as much. Æthelric held it of King Edward.

Adelold held DEAN of the bishop. It is assessed at 1 sulung. There is land for 2 ploughs. In demesne is 1 plough; and 4 bordars and 2 slaves, and 1 acre of meadow, and woodland for 7 pigs. Of this sulung Ralph de Courbepine holds 1½ yokes, which are and were always worth 10s. Adelold had half a sulung and half a yoke, and TRE they were worth 40s; and afterwards 20s; now 40s. This land is in the king's hand. Wulfnoth and Waua and Alweard and Wulfrun held this land of King Edward and it was divided amongst 3 places.

IN CALEHILL HUNDRED

Ralph de Courbepine holds PIVINGTON, of the bishop's fief, and Hugh [holds] of him. It is assessed at 1 sulung. There is land for 5 ploughs. In demesne are 1½ [ploughs]; and 7 villans with 7 bordars have 3½ ploughs. There is a church, and 9 slaves, and 1 mill rendering 55d, and 20 acres of meadow, [and] woodland for 60 pigs. TRE it was worth £8; and afterwards 100s; now £6. Esbiorn Bigga held it of King Edward.

The same Ralph holds 3 denes of Postling manor which remained outside the divisio of Hugh de Montfort, and there is 1 yoke of land and † 1 virgate †, and there are 2 villans. It is and was always worth 15s.

IN FELBOROUGH HUNDRED

Herfrid holds SHALMSFORD STREET of the bishop's fief. It is assessed at half a sulung. There is land for 1 plough. In demesne is 1 plough; and 3 villans with 1 bordar have 1

plough. There are 3 slaves, and 8 acres of meadow. TRE it was worth 60s; and afterwards 40s; now 60s. Alræd held it of King Edward.

IN BIRCHOLT HUNDRED

Osbert holds 'ALDGLOSE' [in Hastingleigh] of † the son of William † de Thaon. Half a sulung belongs there. There is land for 2 ploughs. In demesne is 1 plough; and 3 villans have half a plough. TRE it was worth 30s; and afterwards 20s; now 40s. This land belongs to the fief of the Bishop of Bayeux and remained outside his divisio. Godric held it of King Edward with the manor of BRABOURNE.

IN 'LIMEN' LATHE

IN OXNEY HUNDRED

Osbern Paisforeire holds PALSTRE of the bishop. It is assessed at 3 yokes. There is land for 2 ploughs. In demesne is 1 [plough]; and 9 bordars have half a plough. There is a church, and 2 slaves, and 10 acres of meadow, and 5 fisheries rendering 12d, [and] woodland for 10 pigs. TRE, and afterwards, it was worth 40s; now 60s. Eadwig the priest held it of King Edward.

IN THE LATHE OF EASTRY

IN BEWSBURY HUNDRED

The same Osbern holds of the bishop 12 acres of land which are worth 4s a year.

Hugh de Port holds 'POISON' [in East London] and PINEHAM of the bishop. They are assessed at 2 sulungs. There is land [...]. In demesne [are] 2½ ploughs; and 6 villans with 14 bordars have 1 plough. TRE they were worth 100s; and afterwards nothing; now £6. Leofstan and Leofwine and Alfred and Sigeræd and 2 others held them TRE and could go where they pleased with their lands.

IN 'LIMEN' LATHE

IN NEWCHURCH [HUNDRED]

The Bishop of Bayeux holds BILSINGTON in demesne. It is assessed at 4 sulungs. There is land for 15 ploughs. In demesne are 5 [ploughs]; and 47 villans with 27 bordars have 14 ploughs. There is a church, and 10 salt-pans rendering 100d, and 10 acres of meadow, woodland for 50 pigs, and 2 fisheries rendering 5d. TRE it was worth £10; and afterwards £30; now £50, and yet it renders at farm £70. Æthelnoth Cild held it. In this manor the bishop has put 3 denes which remained outside the divisio of the Count of Eu.

IN 'LANGPORT' HUNDRED

Robert of Romney holds "AFETTUNE" of the bishop. It is assessed at 1 sulung. There is land for 3 ploughs. In demesne is 1 [plough]; and 9 villans with 3 bordars have 3½ ploughs. There are 2 slaves. TRE it was worth 100s; and afterwards 50s; now £4.

The same Robert holds of the bishop in Denge Marsh half a sulung, and it is assessed at as much. There is land for 2 ploughs. There 11 villans with 2 bordars have 3 ploughs, and a fishery rendering 2s.

The same Robert has 50 burgesses in the borough of OLD ROMNEY; and from these the king has every service, and they are by reason of service at sea quit of every customary due except these 3: theft, breach of the peace, and highway robbery.

[Folio 11: KENT]

TRE, and afterwards, it was worth 40s; now 50s. Alsige held it of Earl Godwine.

The same Robert holds of the bishop half a sulung in Denge Marsh, and it is assessed at as much. There is land for 2 ploughs. In demesne is half a plough; and 15 villans with 2 bordars have 3½ ploughs. TRE, and afterwards, it was worth 30s; now 40s. 6 sokemen held it TRE.

IN ROLVENDEN HUNDRED

The same Robert holds BENENDEN of the bishop. It is assessed at half a sulung. There is land for 2 ploughs. In demesne is 1 plough; and 4 villans with 9 bordars have 2 ploughs. [There is] woodland for 5 pigs, and 1 church. TRE, and afterwards, it was worth 40s; now 50s. Osgeard held it of King Edward.

IN 'ALOESBRIDGE' HUNDRED

The same Robert holds half a yoke of the bishop, and it is assessed at as much. A widow paying 13d a year lives there. It is and was always worth 10s. 2 sokemen held it TRE without halls and demesnes.

The same Robert holds of the bishop half a dene of the manor of TINTON which Hugh de Montfort holds, and there he has land for half a plough, and 1 villan with 3 bordars, and half a plough, and 2 fisheries rendering 5s. The whole of this is and was worth 15s. This land is outside the divisio of Hugh.

IN THE LATHE OF EASTRY

IN EASTRY HUNDRED

Herbert holds RINGLETON of the king at farm. It is [part] of the fief of the bishop. There is land [...]. In demesne are 2 ploughs; and 4 villans with 7 bordars have 2½ ploughs. There is 1 mill rendering 40s. TRE it was worth £8; when received, 100s; now £8, and yet it renders £13. Edward held it of King Edward.

Adam holds half a yoke of the bishop's fief in HAMMIL. Riculf holds it of Adam, and Herbert holds another half-yoke of HAMMIL of Hugh nephew of Herbert. Each of these is worth 20s.

IN BEWSBURY HUNDRED

Hugh holds TEMPLE EWELL of the bishop. It is assessed at 3 sulungs. There is land [...]. In demesne is 1 plough; and 15 villans with 12 bordars have 2 ploughs. There are 2 mills rendering 46s, and 4 acres of meadow, [and] woodland for 4 pigs. TRE it was worth £12; and afterwards 100s; now £10, and yet it renders £12.12s. Eadric of Elham held it of King

Edward. Of this manor Hugh de Montfort holds 17 acres of land and 1½ denes, which are valued at 7s.

The same Hugh holds WEST CLIFFE of the bishop. It is assessed at 2 sulungs. There is land [...]. In demesne is 1 plough; and 17 villans have 2 ploughs. TRE it was worth £8; when received, £6; now £8. Hugh de Montfort holds 2 mills of this manor rendering 28s. Eadric held it of King Edward.

The same Hugh holds SOLTON of the bishop. It is assessed at 1 sulung. There is land [...]. In demesne is 1 plough, and 3 villans with 1 bordar pay 4s7d. TRE it was worth £15; and afterwards, as now, 30s. Godric lived in this manor and held 20 acres as his alod.

The same Hugh holds in DOVER 1 mill which renders 48 measures of wheat, and does not belong to any manor.

Ansfrid holds half a yoke of the bishop's fief in ''Leueberge'', and there he has 1 villan and 1 bordar. It is worth 5s. Leofwine held it of King Edward.

In the same place lived a certain Altet who held of King Edward 2 acres in alod and held these of Ansfrid, and it is valued at 6s.

Ralph de Courbepine holds COLDRED of the bishop. There is land [...]. In demesne [are] 1½ ploughs; and 6 villans with 7 bordars have 2 ploughs. There are 2 slaves, and 4 acres of meadow. It is assessed at 2 sulungs. TRE it was worth £8; and afterwards 20s; now £6. Molleve held it of King Edward.

The same Ralph holds TEMPLE EWELL. It is assessed at 3 sulungs. There is land [...]. In demesne is 1 plough; and 5 villans with 4 bordars have 2 ploughs. There is woodland for 10 pigs. A certain knight holds of Ralph 1 sulung of this manor, and there he has 1 plough, with 3 bordars. The whole manor TRE was worth £12; and afterwards 20s; now 40s, and yet what Ralph has renders £4. Hugh de Montfort has the capital manor, and there are 5½ mills rendering £6. Molleve held it of King Edward.

The same Ralph holds SWANTON [in Lydden] of the bishop. It is assessed at 2 sulungs. There is land [...]. In demesne [is] 1 plough; and 2 bordars with half a plough.

Robert de Barbes holds 1 sulung of this land, and there he has 3 villans with half a plough; and a certain Hugh holds 1 sulung, and has there 1 plough in demesne, and 1 bordar. TRE it was worth £10; when received, 30s; now 40s, and yet it renders £4. Kolsveinn held it of King Edward.

The same Ralph holds APPLETON of the bishop. It is assessed at 1 sulung. There is land [...]. In demesne are 2 ploughs, with 6 bordars. TRE it was worth 100s; and afterwards 10s; now 40s. Ascored held it of King Edward.

Herfrid holds 'BOSWELL' [in Ewell] of Hugh, and it is [part] of the bishop's fief. It was assessed at 1 sulung TRE. There is land [...]. In demesne is 1 plough, and 2 slaves. TRE it was worth 60s; and afterwards 60[s]; now 40[s]. When Herbert received it, [there were] 3 yokes; now 2 yokes. Wulfnoth held it of King Edward.

Turstin Tinel and his wife hold of King William at farm in

"Leueberge" 1 yoke and 5 acres, and there are 2 villans with 2 bordars. It is and was always worth 8s. Bucca held it of King Edward.

IN THE LATHE OF EASTRY

IN EASTRY HUNDRED

Ansfrid holds WOODNESBOROUGH of the bishop. It is assessed at 2 sulungs and 3 yokes. There is land [...]. In demesne are 2 ploughs, and 24 villans.

TRE it was worth £12; and afterwards 20s; now £9. In Sandwich the archbishop has 32 messuages belonging to this manor, and they render 42s8d, and Adelold has 1 yoke which is worth 10s.
    This manor [...] thegns held of King Edward and 3 lived there permanently [...] held 2 sulungs of it in parage, but not [...] there. When Ansfrid received it, he made it 1 manor.

Turstin holds KNOWLTON of the bishop. It is assessed at 1 sulung. There is land [...]. In demesne are 2 ploughs, with 2 bordars. TRE, and afterwards, [it was worth] £4; now £7, and yet it renders £8. Edward held it of King Edward.

Osbert fitzLetard holds BETTESHANGER of the bishop. It is assessed at 1½ yokes. There is land [...]. In demesne is 1 plough, with 1 villan and 4 bordars. TRE it was worth 60s; and afterwards 30s; now 50s. Godeza held it of King Edward.

In the same manor 10 thegns hold of Osbern himself 1 sulung and half a yoke, and there they themselves have 4½ ploughs. TRE it was worth 100s; and afterwards 30s; now 60s.

Ansfrid holds SOLE of the bishop. It is assessed at 1 sulung. There is land [...]. In demesne are 2 ploughs; and 8 villans with half a plough. TRE it was worth 100s; and afterwards 20s; now £6. Almær held it of King Edward.

Ralph fitzRobert holds 'HARTANGER' [in Barfreston] of the bishop. It is assessed at 1 sulung. There is land [...]. In demesne is 1 plough; and 5 villans with 2 bordars have 2 ploughs. TRE it was worth 40s; and afterwards 10s; now 60s. Edith held it of King Edward.

Osbern holds of the bishop 1½ yokes in the same hundred, and there he has 7 bordars. TRE it was worth £10; and afterwards 10s; now 30s. Ernald held it of King Edward.

[Folio 11V: KENT]

IN BEWSBURY HUNDRED

Hugh de Montfort holds of the bishop 1 sulung of vacant land outside his divisio and it belonged to NEWINGTON [near Folkestone], a manor which he has inside his divisio, and there he has 1 border. It is and was always worth 60s.

IN EASTRY HUNDRED

Wibert holds half a yoke which belonged to the gild of DOVER and now is assessed with the land of Osbert fitzLetard, and it is worth 4s a year.

Osbern fitzLetard holds HAM of the bishop. It is assessed at 1 sulung. There is land [...]. In demesne is 1 plough, with 1

villan and 2 bordars and 2 slaves. TRE it was worth 50s; and afterwards 20s; now 60s 3 thegns held it of King Edward.

The same Osbern holds CHILLENDEN of the bishop. It is assessed at 1 sulung and 1 yoke and 10 acres. There is land [...]. In demesne [there is] now nothing; but 9 villans have there 2½ ploughs. TRE it was worth 60s; and afterwards 30s; now 40s. Godwine held it of King Edward and [so did] 5 other thegns.[...] Osbern put their lands into 1 manor.

Alvred holds MIDLEY of the bishop. It is assessed at 3 yokes and 12 acres. There is land for 3 ploughs. In demesne are 1½ ploughs; and 5 villans with 9 bordars have 1 plough. There is a church, and 10 acres of meadow, [and] woodland for 10 pigs. TRE it was worth 60s; and afterwards 40s; now 60s. Godric held it of King Edward.

IN SOMERDEN HUNDRED

Robert Latimer holds 6 acres of land, and there he has half a plough. 1 sokeman held this land. And by a recent gift from the bishop he has in the king's hand from Richard son of Count Gilbert 10 villans with 3 ploughs, and woodland for 50 pigs, and from this Robert pays a farm of £6.

Turstin holds TICKENHURST of the bishop. It is assessed at 1½ sulungs. There is land [...]. In demesne is 1 plough, with 4 bordars, and a small wood. TRE it was worth £4; and afterwards 40s; now 100s. Eadric of Elham held it of King Edward.

The same Turstin holds of the bishop 1 yoke in WOODNESBOROUGH, and there are 2 bordars. [...] Toki held it of King Edward.

The same Turstin holds of the bishop 1 yoke in EACH, and there are 4 bordars.

These 2 yokes TRE were worth 15s; and afterwards 10s; now 20s.

Osbert holds of the bishop 1 yoke and 10 acres in MARSHBOROUGH, and there are 2 villans with half a plough. Godwine held them of King Edward.

The same Osbert holds of the bishop 15 acres in 'ELMTON' [in Eythorn], and there a priest dwells. Each of these TRE was worth 30s; and afterwards 20s; now 30s. Sigeræd held them of King Edward.

IN EASTRY HUNDRED

Ralph de Courbepine holds of the bishop 2 sulungs in WALDERSHARE. There is land [...]. In demesne [are] 1½ ploughs; and 14 villans with 2½ ploughs. Robert has half a sulung of this land, and there is 1 plough. TRE it was worth £7.10s; and afterwards 50s; now £7. Wulfweard held it of King King Edward.

Osbert fitzLetard holds of the bishop 1 yoke in EACH, and there are 3 villans. TRE it was worth 12s; and afterwards 6s; now 16s. Bernald held it of King Edward.

Ralph de Courbepine holds EASOLE of the bishop. It is assessed at 3 sulungs. There is land [...]. In demesne are 3 ploughs; and 1 villan with 7 bordars have half a plough. There is 1 slave. It is worth £6. Molleve held it of King Edward.

Osbern holds of the bishop 1 manor which 3 free men held of King Edward. It is assessed at 1½ sulungs. There is land [...]. In demesne is 1 plough; and 1 villan with 1 bordar has half a plough. TRE and afterwards, as now, worth £4.

Ralph de Colombieres holds 'SHELVING' [in Woodnesborough] of the bishop. It is assessed at 1½ sulungs. There is land [...]. In demesne is 1 plough; and 4 villans with 3 bordars have half a plough and 1½ ploughs. TRE it was worth £4; and afterwards 40s; now 100s. Wulfwig held it of King Edward.

Ralph de Courbepine holds DENTON [near Barham] of the bishop. It is assessed at half a sulung. There is land for 3 ploughs. In demesne is 1 [plough]; and 4 villans with 2 bordars have 1 plough. There is a church, and 4 messuages in Canterbury rendering 6s less 1d. TRE it was worth 60s; and afterwards 20s; now 60s. Molleve held it of King Edward.

The same Ralph holds of the bishop 1 yoke in 'Boswell' [in Ewell] which Molleve held of King Edward, and there is 1 villan paying 30d.

IN BEWSBURY HUNDRED

Ralph de Courbepine holds 40 acres of land which Molleve held of King Edward; and there is 1 villan paying 6s; and it is worth as much.

Ranulph de Vaubadon holds half a yoke in HEMSTED which 2 free men held of King Edward in Buckland [near Dover]; and now Ranulph states that the Bishop of Bayeux gave it to a certain brother of his. There is 1 villan paying 30d. It is worth 10s.

IN 'LONINGBROUGH' HUNDRED

Ansketil de Rots holds of the bishop's fief ACRISE, which 2 brothers held and each had a hall. It is now 1 manor and is assessed at 1 sulung. There is land for 2 ploughs. In demesne are 1½ ploughs; and 5 villans with 5 bordars have 1 plough. [There is] woodland for 10 pigs, and a church. TRE it was worth 40s; and afterwards 30s; now 60s.

IN BIRCHOLT HUNDRED

Roger fitzAnsketil holds of the bishop's fief HASTINGLEIGH, which Wulfnoth held of King Edward; and it was then assessed at 1 sulung, and now at 3 yokes, because Hugh de Montfort holds the other part in his divisio. There is land for 3 ploughs. In demesne are 2 [ploughs]; and 2 villans with 6 bordars have 1 plough. There are 4 slaves, and woodland for 1 pig. TRE it was worth 60s; and afterwards 30s; now 60s.

VI. The land of the Church of Battle

The ABBOT of St MARTIN of Battle holds the manor which is called WYE, which TRE, as now, was assessed at 7 sulungs. There is land for 52 ploughs. In demesne are 9 ploughs; and 114 villans with 22 bordars have 17 ploughs.

There is a church, and 7 slaves, and 4 mills rendering 23s8d, and 133 acres of meadow, and woodland for 300 pigs as pannage.

TRE it was worth £80 and 106s8d; when received, £125.10s at 20[d] to the ora; now £100 by tale; and if the abbot had had sake and soke it would be valued at £20 more.

Ralph de Courbepine holds 1 dene and 1 yoke of the land of the sokemen of this manor, paying 6d. as customary dues; and Adelulf 2 parts of 1 sulung, paying 12d; and Hugh de Montfort has 2 yokes, rendering 300 eels and 2s, and they rendered sake and soke TRE.

To this manor from 22 hundreds pertain sake and soke and all the forfeitures which of right belong to the king.

[Folio 12: KENT]

VII. The land of the Church of St Augustine

IN THE HALF-LATHE OF SUTTON

IN 'LITLELEE' HUNDRED

THE ABBOT OF ST AUGUSTINE'S has 1 manor, PLUMSTEAD by name, which is assessed at 2 sulungs and 1 yoke. There is land [...]. In demesne is 1 plough; and 17 villans with 6 cottars have 6 ploughs. There is woodland for 5 pigs as pannage. TRE, and afterwards, it was worth £10; now £12, and yet it renders £14.8s3d.

IN THE LATHE OF AYLESFORD

IN EYHORNE HUNDRED

The abbot himself holds LENHAM, which is assessed at 5½ sulungs. There is land for 18 ploughs. In demesne are 2 ploughs; and 40 villans with 7 bordars have 16 ploughs. There is 1 slave, and 2 mills rendering 6s8d, and 8 acres of meadow, and woodland for 40 pigs. TRE it was worth £28; and afterwards £16; now £28. Robert Latimer holds 1 yoke of this manor which is worth 5s.

IN THE BOROUGH LATHE

IN BRIDGE HUNDRED

The abbot himself holds BEKESBOURNE, which is assessed at 1 sulung. There is land for 2 ploughs. In demesne is 1 [plough]; and 9 villans with 1 bordar have 1 plough. There are 2 mills rendering 9s6d, and 3½ acres of meadow, [and] woodland for 5 pigs. TRE it was worth 100s; and afterwards 40s; now 100s.

The abbot himself holds the manor of 'LONGPORT' [in Canterbury], and there is 1 sulung and 1 yoke, and it has always been quit and without customary due; and 1 yoke which belongs to this manor lies in another hundred; and there were 70 burgesses in the city of Canterbury belonging to this manor. In this manor are 2½ ploughs in demesne; and 28 villans with 63 bordars have 6 ploughs. There are 17 acres of meadow. TRE it was worth £20; and afterwards £18; now £35.4s.

IN 'DOWNHAMFORD' HUNDRED

The abbot himself holds LITTLEBOURNE, which is assessed at 7 sulungs. There is land for 12 ploughs. In demesne are 3 ploughs; and 35 villans with 14 cottars have 6½ [ploughs]. There is a church, and 38 acres of meadow, [and] woodland for 4 pigs. TRE it was worth £25; and afterwards £20; now £32. Of this manor the Bishop of Bayeux has in his park as much as is worth 60s.

The abbot himself holds GARRINGTON, and the Bishop of Bayeux gave it to him in exchange for his park. It is assessed at half a sulung and 42 acres of land. There is land for 1 plough, and there is [1 plough] in demesne, with 3 cottars, and 16 acres of meadow. TRE it was worth £4; and afterwards 40s; now £4. Eadric held this manor of Esbiorn Bigga and now Ralph holds it of the abbot.

IN STURRY HUNDRED

The abbot himself holds STURRY, which is assessed at 5 sulungs quit. There is land for 12 ploughs. In demesne are 2 ploughs; and 39 [villans] with 32 bordars have 12 ploughs. There is a church, and 10 mills rendering £8, and 7 fisheries rendering 5s, and 28 acres of meadow. As pannage, 30 pigs. TRE it was worth 50s, when the abbot received it, £45; now £50, and yet it renders £54.

IN THANET, THE HUNDRED OF ST MILDRED

The abbot himself holds MINSTER, a manor which is assessed at 48 sulungs. There is land for 62 ploughs. In demesne are 2 [ploughs]; and 150 villans with 50 bordars have 63 ploughs. There is a church, and a priest who gives 20s a year. There is 1 salt-pan, and 2 fisheries rendering 3d, and 1 mill. TRE it was worth £80; when the abbot received it, £40; now £100. Of this manor, 3 knights hold as much of the villans' land as is worth £9 when there is peace in the land, and there they have 3 ploughs.

IN CHISLET HUNDRED

The abbot himself holds CHISLET, which is assessed at 12 sulungs. There is land for 30 ploughs. In demesne are 5 ploughs; and 72 villans with 68 bordars have 39 ploughs. There is a church rendering 12s, and 14 slaves. There are 50 acres of meadow, and 47 salt-pans rendering 50 summae of salt. As pannage, 130 pigs. TRE it was worth £53; and afterwards £40; now 78. There are 3 arpents of vineyard. Of this manor 4 French knights hold what is worth £12 a year.

IN FORDWICH HUNDRED

The abbot himself holds a small borough which is called FORDWICH. 2 parts of this borough King Edward gave to St Augustine; the third part, which had belonged to Earl Godwine, the Bishop of Bayeux granted to the same saint with the consent of King William. It is assessed at 1 yoke. There were 100 messuages less 4 rendering 13s. There are now 73 messuages; they render as much. TRE, and afterwards, it was worth 100s; now £11.2s.

In the same place are 24 acres of land which St Augustine always had, where there were and are 6 burgesses paying 22s.

In this borough Archbishop Lanfranc holds 7 messuages which TRE did service to St Augustine; now the archbishop has taken that service away from him.

Close by the city of Canterbury St Augustine has [...] half a sulung which has always been quit, and there is 1 plough in demesne, with 15 bordars, and 7 acres of meadow, and in the same place are 4 acres of land which 4 nuns hold of the abbot in alms and pay 2s and 1 summa of flour. The whole of this, TRE and afterwards, as now, worth £4.

IN THE LATHE OF WYE

IN FAVERSHAM HUNDRED

The abbot himself holds WILDERTON ['Wilderton' in Throwley, and South Wilderton], which is assessed at 1 sulung. There is land for 2 ploughs. In demesne is 1 [plough]; and 9 villans with 1 plough. There are 2 acres of meadow, and 5 pigs as pannage from the woodland. TRE it was worth 60s; when received, 40s; now £4.

IN WYE HUNDRED

The abbot himself holds ASHENFIELD, and Ansketil [holds] of him. It is assessed at 1 sulung. There is land for 1 plough; and there is [1 plough] in demesne, with 5 bordars, and 6 acres of meadow. [There is] woodland for 10 pigs. TRE [it was worth] 40s; and afterwards 20s; now 40s.

In 'DERNEDALE' [in Wye] Adam holds half a sulung of the abbot. There is land for half a plough. There are 2 slaves, and 7 acres of meadow. It is and was always worth 20s.

IN BOUGHTON HUNDRED

The abbot himself holds SELLING, a manor without a hall, which is assessed at 6 sulungs. There is land for 11 ploughs. [There is] nothing in demesne. There 30 villans have 10 ploughs. There is a church. TRE it was worth £15; when received, £8; now £13.5s.

IN CALEHILL HUNDRED

The abbot himself holds half a yoke in Rooting, which TRE was assessed at half a sulung. There was and is 1 plough in demesne. It is and was always worth 15s.

IN CHART HUNDRED

The abbot himself holds 1 yoke, 'REPTON' [in Ashford], and Ansered [holds] of him, and it is assessed at 1 yoke. There is land for 2 ploughs. In demesne is 1 [plough], with 4 bordars. There are 11 acres of meadow, and the fourth part of a mill rendering 15d, and woodland for 10 pigs, and besides he has 2 yokes which the abbot gave him out of his demesne, and 2 villans with 8 bordars there. TRE, and afterwards, it was worth £3; now £4.

[Folio 12V: KENT]

IN FELBOROUGH HUNDRED

Ansfrid holds 'SHILLINGHAM' [in Chilham] of the abbot. It is assessed at half a sulung. There is land for 1 plough. In demesne are 2 [ploughs]; and 8 villans have 1½ ploughs. TRE, and afterwards, it was worth 20s; now 30s.

IN THE LATHE OF EASTRY

IN 'CORNILO' HUNDRED

The abbot himself holds NORTHBOURNE. It is assessed at 30 sulungs. There is land for 54 ploughs. In demesne are 3 [ploughs]; and 79 villans with 42 bordars have 37 ploughs. There are 40 acres of meadow, and woodland for 10 pigs. TR [sic]

TRE it was worth £80; when received, £20; now 76.

Oidelard holds 1 sulung of the villans' land of this manor, and there he has 2 ploughs, with 11 bordars. It is worth £4.

Of the same land of the villans Gilbert holds 2 sulungs less half a yoke, and there he has 1 plough, and 4 villans with 1 plough. It is worth £6.

Wadard holds 3 sulungs less 60 acres of the villans' land of this manor, and there he has 1 plough, and 8 villans with 1 plough, and 2 slaves. It is worth £9. He himself renders no service to the abbot except 30s, which he pays each year.

Odelin holds 1 sulung of the same land of the villans, and there he has 1 plough, with 3 bordars. It is worth £3.

Marcher holds of the same land of the villans what is worth 8s.

Osbern fitzLetard holds half a sulung and 11 acres of meadow of the villans' land which is worth 25s. He himself pays to the abbot 15s.

Ranulph de Colombieres holds 1 yoke. It is worth 50d.
Ranulph de Vaubadon holds 1 yoke, and pays from it 50d. The above-named Oidelard also holds of this manor 1 sulung, and it is called 'BAWESFELD' [in Whitfield], and there he has 2 ploughs, with 10 bordars. It is worth £6.

The abbot himself holds [Great and Little] MONGEHAM. It is assessed at 2½ sulungs. There is land for 5 ploughs. In this manor the land which the monks hold has never paid geld; and Wadard holds there the land which TRE always paid geld; and at that time it was 1 manor. The monks have now in demesne 4 ploughs; and 20 bordars with 1 plough, and 1 mill rendering 16s, and woodland for 4 pigs. There is a church. It was worth £22 TRE; and afterwards £10; the abbot's part, £26.

Wadard has in demesne there 1 plough; and 8 villans, with 2 bordars having 4 ploughs. It is and was worth £10. He renders no service for it except 30s a year to the abbot.

IN BEWSBURY HUNDRED

The abbot himself holds SHEPHERDSWELL OR SIBERTSWOLD. It is assessed at 2 sulungs. There is land for 4 ploughs. In demesne are 1½ [ploughs]; and 11 villans with 6 bordars have 2½ ploughs. There is a church. TRE it was worth £8; when received, 40s; now £6, and yet it renders £8.

The abbot himself holds 'WADHOLT' [in Coldred]. It is assessed at 1 sulung. There is land [...]. In demesne, nothing; but 4 villans with 3 bordars have 1½ ploughs. There is

scrubland. Ralph de Courbepine has 25 acres of this land. TRE and afterwards, as now, worth 20s; yet it is valued at 40s because it is at farm.

IN PRESTON HUNDRED

The abbot himself holds PRESTON [near Forwich]. It is assessed at 5 sulungs. There is land for 8 ploughs. In demesne are 2 ploughs; and 25 villans with 17 bordars have 9 ploughs. There is a very small wood.

Of this manor Vitalts holds 1 sulung and half a yoke, and there he has in demesne 2 ploughs; and 17 bordars with half a plough. The whole manor TRE was worth £10; when received, £6; now what the abbot has is worth £14; what Vitalis holds is worth 100s.

Ansfrid holds ELMSTONE of the abbot. It is assessed at half a sulung and half a yoke. There is land [...]. In demesne is 1 plough; and 3 villans with 3 oxen in a plough.

In this manor Ansfrid holds half a sulung of the demesne of the monks, and pays from it to St Augustine 100d a year. Godeza held it in alod, and gave from it to St Augustine 25d in alms every year. TRE it was worth 40s; and afterwards 10s; now 60s.

IN THE LATHE and in the Hundred of EASTRY St Augustine has 3 virgates of land, and there is 1 plough in demesne, with 5 bordars. TRE it was worth 10s; and afterwards 5s; now 20s.

IN 'LIMEN' LATHE

IN STOWTING HUNDRED

Geoffrey holds BODSHAM of the abbot. It is assessed at 1 sulung. There is land for 2 ploughs, and there are [2 ploughs], with 8 bordars. [There is] woodland for 15 pigs. TRE it was worth £4; and afterwards 20s; now £4. A certain villan held it.

The abbot himself holds in 'LONGPORT' [in Canterbury] 2 sulungs and 1 yoke. There is land for 6 ploughs. There are 9 villans with 4 bordars having 6 ploughs. There are 10 acres of meadow, and woodland for 2 pigs. TRE it was worth £6; and afterwards £4; now £8.

IN THE LATHE OF WYE

IN LONGBRIDGE HUNDRED

The abbot himself holds KENNINGTON. It was assessed TRE at 4 sulungs, and belonged to BURMARSH. There is land for 10 ploughs. There are 30 villans having 10 ploughs. There is a church. [...] The villans held it | TRE |. With these 4 sulungs St Augustine has 1 yoke quit of all the king's taxes, and there is as much woodland as 40 pigs come from as pannage or 54½d. The whole of this TRE was worth £10; and afterwards £8; now £12.10s.

IN ROMNEY MARSH

The abbot himself holds BURMARSH. It is assessed at 2 sulungs and 3 yokes. There is land for 12 ploughs. In demesne are 4 [ploughs]; and 44 villans with 5 bordars have 10 ploughs. TRE it was worth £20; and afterwards £10; now £30.

The shire gives evidence that Badlesmere belonged to St Augustine TRE, and that from the man who held it the abbot had sake and soke.

VIII. The land of St Peter of Ghent

IN GREENWICH HUNDRED

The ABBOT of Ghent holds LEWISHAM of the king, and held it of King Edward, and then, as now, it was assessed at 2 sulungs. There is land for 14 ploughs. In demesne are 2 ploughs; and 50 villans with 9 bordars have 17 ploughs. There are 3 slaves, and 11 mills with the rent from the peasants render £8.12s. From the profits of the market, 40s. There are 30 acres of meadow. From the woodland, 50 pigs as pannage. The whole manor TRE was worth £16; and afterwards £12; now £30.

[Folio 13: KENT]

IX. The land of Hugh de Montfort

HUGH de Montfort holds 1 manor, EASTWELL, which Frederic held of King Edward, and it is assessed at 1 sulung. There are 3 yokes in Hugh's divisio, and a fourth yoke is outside, it and is [part] of the fief of the Bishop of Bayeux. There is land for 3 ploughs all together. In demesne are 2 ploughs; and 5 villans with 5 bordars have 1½ ploughs. There are 10 slaves, and 12 acres of meadow, and woodland [...]. TRE it was worth 70s; and afterwards 30s; now 70s.

Hugh himself holds of the king [?] HAMPTON, which Wulfsige the priest held of King Edward, and it is assessed at 1 sulung. There is land for 1 plough, and there is [1 plough], with 1 villan and 4 bordars, and 3 acres of meadow, TRE and afterwards, as now, worth 20s.

IN THE LATHE OF WYE

IN LONGBRIDGE HUNDRED

Mainou holds SEVINGTON of Hugh. Bresibalt held it of King Edward, and it is assessed at half a sulung. There is land for 1 plough, and there is [1 plough] in demesne, with 1 villan and 6 bordars. There is a church, and a priest, and 1 mill rendering 10d, and 8 acres of meadow. TRE it was worth 30s; and afterwards 20s; now 30s.

The same Mainou holds ASHFORD of Hugh. Thorgisl held it of Earl Godwine, and it is assessed at 1 sulung. There is land for half a plough. Yet in demesne is 1 plough; and 2 villans have 1 plough. There are 2 slaves, and 8 acres of meadow. TRE it was worth 25s; when received, 20s; now 30s.

Hugh himself holds "ESSELLA". 3 men held it of King Edward, and could go where they pleased with their lands. It is assessed at 3 yokes. There is land for 1½ ploughs. There 4 villans with 2 bordars now have 1 plough, and 6 acres of meadow. The whole TRE was worth 20s; and afterwards 15s; now 20s.

Mainou holds another ASHFORD of Hugh. William held it of King Edward. It is assessed at 1 sulung. There is land for 4 ploughs. In demesne are 2 [ploughs]; and 2 villans with 15 bordars have 3 ploughs. There is a church, and a priest, and 3 slaves, and 2 mills rendering 10s2d. TRE it was worth 70s; and afterwards 60s; now 100s.

IN 'LIMEN' LATHE

IN NEWCHURCH HUNDRED

The same Hugh holds 1 yoke in Romney Marsh. There is land [...]. 2 sokemen held half of this land, and 2 villans the other [half]. [...] There are now 4 villans having 1 plough. [...] This land was and is worth 12s.

The same Hugh holds half a yoke, which 1 sokeman held. There are now 2 bordars. This land is valued in Tinton, because it is ploughed with the demesne ploughs there.

The hundred and the burgesses of Dover and the men of the Abbot of St Augustine's and Eastry Lathe testify this concerning the land of 'ATTERTON' [in River], which the canons of St Martin of Dover claim against Hugh de Montfort: that Wulfwig Wild held it in alod TRE, and it is assessed at 1 yoke, and he has there 1 plough in demesne; and 5 bordars with 1 plough, and 1 mill rendering 20s. It is and was worth £10.

IN 'WORTH' HUNDRED

Hugh himself holds EASTBRIDGE in demesne. Alsige held it of Earl Godwine, and it is assessed at 1 sulung. There is land for 6 ploughs. In demesne are 3 ploughs; and 2 villans with 36 bordars have 4 ploughs. There are 8 salt-pans with the third part of a ninth salt-pan rendering 20s, half a fishery [rendering] 8d, [and] woodland for 3 pigs as pannage. There are 2 churches. TRE, and afterwards, it was worth £10; now £15.

Bertram holds of Hugh half a yoke and half a virgate. They are assessed at as much. Æthelhelm held them of King Edward. There is land for 1 plough. TRE it was worth 20s.

Hervey holds BLACKMANSTONE of Hugh. Blæcmannheld it TRE, and it is assessed at half a sulung. There is land for 2 ploughs. There are [2 ploughs] in demesne; and 3 villans with 10 bordars with 1 plough. There is a church, and 1 slave. TRE it was worth £4; and afterwards £3; now £6.

The same Hugh holds in Romney Marsh 1 sulung less half a virgate. It is assessed at as much. There is land for 3 ploughs. There 14 sokemen have 3 ploughs. TRE it was worth £4; and afterwards £3; now 100s.

Roger holds of Hugh 1 yoke in Romney Marsh. It is assessed at 1 yoke. 2 sokemen held it. There is land for 1 plough, and there is [1 plough], with 3 bordars. TRE it was worth 30s; and afterwards 15s; now 30s.

Robert holds of Hugh in the same Marsh the sixth part of 1 yoke. A sokeman held it. It is and was worth 5s.

IN HEANE HUNDRED

Roger holds POSTLING of Hugh. Esbiorn Bigga held it. It is assessed at $2\frac{1}{2}$ sulungs. There is land for 13 ploughs. In demesne are 3 [ploughs]; and 16 villans with 7 bordars have 7 ploughs. There are 2 small churches, and 2 mills rendering 6s, and 40 acres of meadow, [and] woodland for 40 pigs. TRE it was worth £10; and afterwards 100s; now £14.

Ralph de Courbepine holds 3 denes of this manor. They are outside the divisio, and are worth 15s.

The same Hugh holds half a sulung, which Ealdræd Bot held of King Edward without a hall. It is assessed at half a sulung. There is land for 3 ploughs. 1 villan dwells there with 4 bordars. There is no plough. [There is] a mill rendering 25d, and 5 acres of meadow.

The same Hugh holds "BELICE". Thorgisl held it to King Edward, and it is assessed at 1 sulung. There is land [...]. In demesne is 1 plough; and 2 villans with 1 bordar have 1 plough. There are 3 acres of meadow. These 2 estates TRE were worth 60s; and afterwards 20s; now 60s.

IN NEWCHURCH HUNDRED

Hugh himself holds 1 estate which Azur Rot held of King Edward without a hall. It is assessed at 1 sulung. There is land for 5 ploughs. There 8 villans with 3 bordars have 2 ploughs. TRE, and afterwards, it was worth £8; now £9.

Hugh himself holds half a sulung in Romney Marsh. It is assessed at as much. There is land for 4 ploughs. 12 sokemen having 4 ploughs held and hold it. It is and was worth 60s.

IN 'ALOESBRIDGE' HUNDRED

The same Hugh holds 1 yoke in this Marsh. It is assessed at as much. There is land for 2 ploughs. There are 12 sokemen with 8 bordars having 2 ploughs. These 2 estates TRE were worth 110s; and afterwards, as now, the same.

IN 'BLACKBOURNE' HUNDRED

Hugh himself holds TINTON. Wulfnoth held it of King Edward, and it was then assessed at 1 sulung; now at a half because it is outside the divisio. There is land for 5 ploughs. In demesne are 2 ploughs; and 21 villans with 6 bordars have 7 ploughs. There is a church, and 9 slaves, and 3 fisheries rendering 5s, and 38 acres of meadow, [and] woodland for 40 pigs. TRE it was worth £12; and afterwards £6; now £7.

The same Hugh holds half a yoke which 5 sokemen, having 1 plough there, with 4 bordars, held and hold now. It is and was always worth 5s.

[Folio 13V: KENT]

IN STREET HUNDRED

Hervey holds SELLINDGE of Hugh. Osweard held it of King Edward. It is assessed at 1 sulung. There is land for 7 ploughs. In demesne are 3 ploughs; and 8 villans with 25 bordars have 4 ploughs. There are 2 churches, and 1 mill rendering 30d, and 36 acres of meadow, and woodland for 6 pigs. TRE it was worth £8; and afterwards 100s; now £7.

IN STOWTING HUNDRED

Alnoth holds MONKS HORTON of Hugh. Leofwine held it of King Edward, and it is assessed at half a sulung. There is land for 3 ploughs. In demesne are 2 ploughs; and 5 villans with 6 bordars have $1\frac{1}{2}$ ploughs. There is a church, and 1 mill rendering 25d, and 24 acres of meadow, [and] woodland for 10 pigs. TRE it was worth 40s; and afterwards 20[s]; now 60s.

In the same place Alnoth holds 1 yoke of Hugh, but there is nothing there.

Hugh himself holds $3\frac{1}{2}$ virgates in the same LATHE, which 3 sokemen held of King Edward. [...] There 1 villan has now half a plough, with 3 bordars. It is and was always worth 10s.

IN HAM HUNDRED

William holds of Hugh 3 yokes and half a virgate in ORLESTONE. 11 sokemen held this land. There is land for 3 ploughs. There are now 2 ploughs in demesne; and 15 villans with 9 bordars have $3\frac{1}{2}$ ploughs. There are 2 churches, and 20 acres of meadow, [and] woodland for 6 pigs. TRE it was worth 60s; and afterwards 30s; now 100s.

Ralph fitzRichard holds of Hugh half a sulung in Ruckinge which Leofræd held of King Edward. It is assessed at half a sulung. There is land for 2 ploughs. There 12 villans now have $1\frac{1}{2}$ ploughs. From the woodland, 1 pig. TRE it was worth 50s; and afterwards 30s; now 50s.

IN STOWTING HUNDRED

Ralph holds MONKS HORTON of Hugh. 2 sokemen held it of King Edward, and it is assessed at $1\frac{1}{2}$ yokes. [There is] land for $1\frac{1}{2}$ ploughs. In demesne is 1 [plough], with 4 villans, and 1 mill rendering 30d, and 10 acres of meadow. From the woodland, 6 pigs. TRE it was worth 40s; and afterwards 20s; now 30s.

IN STREET HUNDRED

Hugh de Mandeville holds COURT-AT-STREET of Hugh. Wulfnoth held it of King Edward. It is assessed at 2 sulungs. There is land for 8 ploughs. In demesne are 2 [ploughs]; and 11 villans with 25 bordars have 5 ploughs. There is a church, and 7 slaves, and 30 acres of meadow. TRE it was worth 10s; and afterwards 4s; now £8.

Ansfrid holds of Hugh 1 yoke, which 1 sokeman held of King Edward in the same hundred, and it is assessed at 1 yoke. There is land for 1 plough. There is [1 plough], with 1 villan and 2 bordars, and 1 mill rendering 26d, and 8 acres of meadow. TRE, as now, worth 40s.

Robert the cook holds of Hugh 1 yoke which 1 sokeman held, and it is assessed at as much. There is 1 plough, with 1 bordar, and 4 acres of meadow. TRE, as now, worth 30s.

IN LONGBRIDGE HUNDRED

Gilbert holds of Hugh 1 yoke, which a certain sokeman held of King Edward. It is and was worth 4s. Nothing was nor is there.

Of Temple Ewell, which Herbert fitzIvo holds outside the divisio of Hugh, Hugh himself holds 14 acres of land within his divisio, and they are worth 2s.

IN EASTRY LATHE

IN BEWSBURY HUNDRED

Hugh de Montfort himself holds TEMPLE EWELL. Molleve held it. It was assessed at 3 sulungs, and now at 1 sulung.[...] There is land for 1 plough, and there is [1 plough] in demesne; and 19 bordars have 1 plough. There is a church, and 4½ mills rendering £4.17s4d, and 4 acres of meadow. TRE it was worth £11; and afterwards £4; now £8.

Hugh himself holds NEWINGTON [near Folkestone]. Eadric held it of King Edward, and it was assessed at 2 sulungs then, and now at 1, because the other is outside the divisio. There is land for 2 ploughs, and there are [2 ploughs] in demesne. There is a church, and 21 bordars and 3 slaves with 3 ploughs. There are 3½ mills rendering 105s. The whole TRE was worth £12; and afterwards £3; now what Hugh has in his divisio, £12.

Inside this divisio is 1 sokeman holding 16 acres of land, and the same man himself held them of King Edward.

In the same hundred the same Hugh holds 1 part of "Iaonei", which neither renders nor rendered anything, nor belonged to any manor, but it is inside his divisio and was [part] of the king's demesne. Alwine the priest held it.

In the same hundred Fulbert has 1 mill of Hugh, and it renders 24s.

Herfrid holds POULTON of Hugh. Wulfwine held it of King Edward, and it is assessed at 1 sulung. There is land for 2 ploughs. There are 3 villans, and a small church. TRE it was worth 40s; and afterwards 15s; now 30s.

IN WYE LATHE

IN BIRCHOLT HUNDRED

Hugh himself holds BRABOURNE. Godric of Bourne held it of King Edward, and it was assessed at 7 sulungs then, and now at 5½ sulungs and half a yoke, because the other part is outside the divisio of Hugh; and the Bishop of Bayeux holds it. There is land for 15 ploughs. In demesne are 2 [ploughs]; and 31 villans with 10 bordars have 10 ploughs. There is a church, and 8 slaves, and 2 mills rendering 7s, and 20 acres of meadow, [and] woodland for 25 pigs. TRE it was worth £20; and afterwards £8; now £16.

In the Hundred of Chart a certain woman holds of Hugh 1 virgate, which a sokeman held of King Edward. It is worth 3s.

IN 'BLACKBOURNE' HUNDRED

Hugh himself holds half a yoke in TIFFENDEN which Northmann held of King Edward, and it is assessed at half a yoke. There are 2 villans with half a plough. It always was and is worth 100d.

IN 'LIMEN' LATHE

IN STREET HUNDRED

Hugh himself holds "SIBORNE". Osgeard held it of King Edward, and it was assessed at 1 sulung, then as now. There is land for 2 ploughs. In demesne is 1 [plough]; and 1 villan with 4 bordars has 1 plough, and there is 1 slave. TRE it was worth 60s; and afterwards 20s; now £4.

The same Hugh has [...] half a sulung [in] SWANTON [in Bilsington]. There is land for 1 plough. Northmann held it of King Edward, and it is assessed at as much. There 4 villans have 1 plough. There is woodland for 5 pigs. TRE it was worth 25s; and afterwards 15s; now 30s.

Nigel holds of Hugh 1 yoke, and in "Aia" [are] 7 acres. 1 sokeman held them of King Edward. There is land for 1 plough. In demesne is half a plough, and 6 bordars and 2 slaves, and 5 acres of meadow. TRE it was worth 20s; and afterwards 10s; now 25s.

William fitzGrosse holds BONNINGTON of Hugh. Northmann held it of King Edward, and it is assessed at 1 sulung. There is land for 4 ploughs. In demesne is 1 [plough]; and 9 villans with 4 bordars have 2 ploughs.

[Folio 14: KENT]

There is a church, and 8 slaves, and woodland for 8 pigs. TRE it was worth £4; and afterwards £3; now 100s.

Hervey holds OTTERPOOL of Hugh. Ealdræd Bot held it of King Edward, and it is assessed at 1 sulung. There is land for 6 ploughs. In demesne is 1 [plough]; and 11 villans with 2 ploughs, and 1 slave, and 10 acres of meadow, and woodland rendering 5d as pannage. TR [sic].

TRE it was worth 50s; and afterwards 20s; now £4.

IN 'BLACKBOURNE' HUNDRED AND IN NEWCHURCH HUNDRED

Harold holds half a sulung less 1 virgate [...]. 6 sokemen held it of King Edward, and it is assessed at so much. There is land for 5 ploughs. In demesne are 2 [ploughs]; and 31 bordars have 3 ploughs. There is 1 slave. TRE it was worth 60s; and afterwards 30s; now £4.15s. And he has also 1 dene which belonged to 'FANSCOMBE' [in Wye], Adam's manor. There are 2 bordars paying 30d. It is and always was worth 5s.

IN BIRCHOLT HUNDRED

Hugh himself holds half a sulung in HASTINGLEIGH. Wulfnoth held it of King Edward, and it is assessed at as much. A certain man now holds it of Hugh, and has there 2 bordars paying 4s. It was always and is worth 10s.

IN LONGBRIDGE HUNDRED

Hugh himself holds 1½ yokes in demesne in EVEGATE. God held it of King Edward. There is now 1 villan with 1 plough, and there are 8 acres of meadow. TRE it was worth 20s; and afterwards 10s; now 20s.

In the same hundred is 1 virgate of land in [?] 'SWETTON'

[in Cheriton] which 1 sokeman held of King Edward. There is now 1 bordar paying 12d. TRE it was worth 30d; and afterwards 18[d.]; now 3s.

X. The land of Count Eustace

IN THE HALF-LATHE OF SUTTON

IN WESTERHAM HUNDRED

Count EUSTACE holds WESTERHAM of the king. Earl Godwine held it of King Edward, and it was assessed at 4 sulungs, then as now. There is land [...]. In demesne are 2 ploughs; and 42 villans with 7 bordars have 30 ploughs. There are 10 slaves, and 1 mill rendering 5s, and 16 acres of meadow, and from the woodland, 100 pigs. TRE it was worth £30; when received, £24; now £40.

IN THE LATHE OF WYE

IN WYE HUNDRED

The count himself holds BOUGHTON ALUPH. Earl Godwine held it, and it was assessed at 7 sulungs, then as now. There is land for 33 ploughs. In demesne are 3 [ploughs]; and 67 villans with 5 bordars have 30 ploughs. There is a church, and 17 slaves, and 2 mills rendering 7s2d, and 26 acres of meadow, [and] woodland for 200 pigs. TRE it was worth £20; and afterwards £30; now £40.

XI. The land of Richard fitzGilbert

IN TWYFORD HUNDRED

RICHARD of Tonbridge holds YALDING, and Æthelræd held it of King Edward, and then, as now, it was assessed at 2 sulungs. There is land for 16 ploughs. In demesne are 1½ [ploughs]; and 16 villans with 12 bordars have 6 ploughs. There are 2 churches, and 15 slaves, and 2 mills rendering 25s, and 4 fisheries rendering 1,700 eels less 20. There are 5 acres of meadow, and woodland for 150 pigs. TRE, and afterwards, it was worth £30; now £20 because the land has been stripped of livestock.

IN MAIDSTONE HUNDRED

The same Richard holds EAST BARMING. Æthelræd held it of King Edward, and then, as now, it was assessed at 1 sulung. There is land for 4 ploughs. In demesne [are] 2 ploughs; and 5 villans with 8 bordars have 5 ploughs. There are 13 slaves, and 1 mill rendering 5s, and 4 acres of meadow, [and] woodland for 10 pigs. TRE it was worth £4; and afterwards 100s; now £4.

XII. The land of Hamo the Sheriff

IN THE LATHE OF WYE

IN WYE HUNDRED

HAMO the sheriff holds of the king a manor which TRE was assessed at 2½ sulungs, and now at 1 sulung and 3 yokes. There is land for 8 ploughs. In demesne [are] 5 oxen ploughing; and 16 villans with 15 bordars have 10 ploughs. There is

a church, and 7 slaves, and 1 mill rendering 9s and 60 eels. There are 20 acres of meadow, and woodland for 30 pigs. TRE it was worth £10; and afterwards £7; now £14.6s6d. Of this manor Hugh de Montfort holds 3½ yokes. It is worth 60s.

IN THE HALF-LATHE OF SUTTON

IN GREENWICH HUNDRED

Hamo has there 63 acres of land which pertain to WOOLWICH. William the falconer held them of King Edward. There are 11 bordars paying 41d. [...] The whole is worth £3.

IN THE LATHE OF AYLESFORD

IN 'LITTLEFELD' HUNDRED

Hamo himself holds MEREWORTH. Northmann held it of King Edward, and then, as now, it was assessed at 2 sulungs. There is land for 9 ploughs. In demesne are 2 [ploughs]; and 28 villans with 15 bordars have 10 ploughs. There is a church, and 10 slaves, and 2 mills rendering 10s, and 2 fisheries rendering 2s. There are 20 acres of meadow, and as much woodland as 60 pigs come from as pannage. TRE it was worth £12; and afterwards £10; now £19.

IN THE LATHE OF THE BOROUGH

IN WHITSTABLE HUNDRED

Hamo himself holds BLEAN. Northmann held it of King Edward, and then, as now, it was assessed at 1 sulung. There is land for 4 ploughs, and 12 villans have there 2 ploughs. In demesne is 1 plough. There is a church, and 2 acres of meadow, and as pannage, 60 pigs. There is 1 fishery. TRE it was worth £8; and afterwards, as now, worth £6.

[Folio 14V: KENT]

XIII. The land of Albert the Chaplain

IN THE HALF-LATHE OF MILTON

IN MILTON HUNDRED

ALBERT the chaplain holds NEWINGTON [near Sittingbourne] of the king. Sidgar held it of Queen Edith, and then, as now, it was assessed at 7½ sulungs. There is land [...]. The land which was in demesne is at farm for 60s.

In the manor itself 10 villans with 48 bordars have 5 ploughs. There are 12 acres of meadow, and 4 woodland denes render 30 pigs as pannage. There is 1 fishery serving the hall, and 2 slaves, [and] a very small wood for fencing.

To this manor belong in the city of Canterbury 4 closes and in Rochester 2, which rendered 64d.

And from the manor of Milton Regis is rendered in Newington [near Sittingbourne] a customary due, that is, 28 weys of cheeses; and from 28 sulungs of Milton Regis pertaining to [this] Newington, £10.10s; and from the other part of 9 sulungs of Milton Regis pertaining to [this] Newington, 28½ weys of cheeses, and 58s of rent from these 9 sulungs; and from these 9 sulungs Sidgar used to render cartage at Milton Regis. Of this manor 3 denes are outside which were in it TRE as the hundred testifies.

The whole manor TRE was worth £40; and afterwards £36; now £34. The archbishop has from it £6; and the Bishop of Bayeux has 3 denes. It is worth 40s. Of the land of this manor Geoffrey de Rots holds 1 yoke, and it is worth 10s. Adam fitzHubert [has] as much woodland as 40d a year come from.

[Blank in MS]

[Blank in MS]

SUSSEX

Here Are Entered the Holders of Lands In Sussex

I KING WILLIAM
II The Archbishop of Canterbury
III The Bishop of Chichester
IIII The Abbot [...] of Westminster
V The Abbot [...] of Fecamp
VI Osbern, Bishop of Exeter
VII The Abbey of Winchester
VIII The Abbey of Battle
IX The Count of EU
X The Count of Mortain
XI Earl Roger
XII William de Warenne
XIII William de Braose
XIIII Oda of Winchester
XV Ealdræd

The land of the King

KING WILLIAM holds BOSHAM in demesne. Earl Godwine held it, and then there were 56½ [hides], and it paid geld for 38 hides, and now the same. There is land [...]. In demesne are 6 ploughs; and 39 villans with 50 bordars have 19 ploughs. There is a church, and 17 slaves, and 8 mills rendering £4 less 30d. There are 2 fisheries rendering 8s10d, [and] woodland for 6 pigs.

To this manor belonged 11 closes in Chichester TRE, which rendered 7s4d. Now the Bishop has 10 of those from the king, and there is now 1 in the manor. The whole manor TRE, and afterwards, was worth £40; now the same, £40; yet it renders £50 assayed and weighed, which are worth £65.

Of this manor Engeler has 2 hides of the king; and he has there 1 plough, and 1 bordar.

IN ROTHERFIELD HUNDRED

King William holds in demesne ROTHERFIELD of the fief of the Bishop of Bayeux. Earl Godwine held it, and then, as now, it was assessed at 3 hides. There is land for 26 ploughs. In demesne are 4 ploughs; and 14 villans with 6 bordars have 14 ploughs. There are 4 slaves, and woodland rendering 80 pigs as pannage. There is a park.

TRE it was worth £16; and afterwards £14; now 12, and yet it renders £30.

II. The land of the Archbishop

IN MALLING HUNDRED

ARCHBISHOP LANFRANC holds the manor of SOUTH MALLING, and it is in the rape of Pevensey; and TRE it was assessed at 80 hides, but now the archbishop has only 75 hides, because the Count of Mortain has 5 hides outside the hundred. The land of the whole manor [is] for 50 ploughs. In demesne are 5 ploughs; and 219 villans with 35 bordars have 73 ploughs and 43 crofts. [...] There are 5 mills rendering £4.10s and 2,000 eels. There are 200 acres less 5 of meadow, and woodland for 300 pigs as pannage. From the herbage, 38s6d and 355 pigs [for] herbage. TRE it was worth £40; when received, £30; now £70. Godfrey held this manor at farm for £90.

Of this manor Baynard holds 5 hides of the archbishop, and there he has in demesne 2 ploughs; and 14 villans with 2 bordars have 2 ploughs. There are 35 acres of meadow, and from the herbage 3 pigs. It is worth £8.

Of the same manor the son of Boselin holds 2 hides of the archbishop, and there he has in demesne 1 plough; and 11 villans with 2 bordars have 3 ploughs. There are 2 mills rendering 10s, and from the herbage 2 pigs, and from the woodland 20 pigs as pannage. It is worth 60s.

Of this manor Godfrey holds 1 hide of the archbishop, and there he has 2 ploughs in demesne, and 2 villans with 3 bordars, and a mill rendering 5s. [There is] woodland for 1 pig as pannage. It is worth 50s.

Of the same manor Walter holds of the archbishop 2 parts of half a hide, and there he has 2 ploughs in demesne; and 1 villan and 1 bordar with 1 plough, and [there are] 3 acres of meadow, and woodland for 3 pigs as pannage, and 1 pig from the herbage. It is worth 40s.

Of this manor, moreover, the canons of St Michael hold 4 hides, and there is in demesne 1 plough; and 4 villans with 16 bordars have 2 ploughs; and it is worth £3.

William de Keynes holds 1 virgate of this manor, and it is at 'Alchin' [in Buxted].

IN STREAT HUNDRED

The archbishop himself holds WOOTTON [in East Chiltington], for the clothing of the monks. TRE it was assessed at 6 hides, and now at 4½ hides, because the rest is in the rape of the Count of Mortain. There is land for 5 ploughs. In demesne are 2 ploughs; and 10 villans with 4 bordars have 3 ploughs. There is a mill rendering 39d, and 22 acres of meadow, and woodland for 2 pigs.

TRE it was worth £4; and afterwards 40s; now £4. Formerly it rendered £6, but it could not maintain it.

IN FALMER HUNDRED

The canons of South Malling hold STANMER of the archbishop. TRE, as now, it was assessed at 20 hides. There is land for 20 ploughs. In demesne are 4 ploughs; and 49 villans with 10 bordars have 26 ploughs. [There is] woodland for 6 pigs. TRE and afterwards, as now, worth £15. To this manor belong 7 closes in LEWES rendering 21d a year.

The archbishop himself has in LEWES 21 closes, rendering 8s8d a year, and they belong to South Malling manor.

IN PAGHAM HUNDRED

The archbishop himself holds PAGHAM in demesne. TRE it was assessed at 50 hides, and now at 34. There is land for 30 ploughs. In demesne are 7 ploughs; and 74 villans with 80 bordars less 2 have 23 ploughs. There is a mill rendering 10s, and 80 acres of meadow, and a small wood for fencing. From the herbage, 1 pig from every villan who has 7 pigs. TRE, and afterwards, it was worth £40; now £60, and yet it renders £80, but that is too heavy. There is a church, and a church in Chichester rendering 64d.

Of this manor Osmelin holds 1 hide of the archbishop. There he has 2 bordars.

The archbishop himself holds TANGMERE in demesne. [...] Clerks held it of the archbishop. TRE it was assessed at 10 hides, and now at 6 hides. There is land [...]. In demesne are 2 ploughs; and 15 villans with 15 bordars have 4 ploughs. There is a church.

TRE it was worth £6; and afterwards 100s; now £6, and the reeve of the manor has 20s of it.

To this manor belong 4 closes in Chichester rendering 22d.

IN SINGLETON HUNDRED

The archbishop himself holds EAST LAVANT in demesne. TRE it was assessed at 18 hides; now at 9½ hides. There is land [...]. In demesne are 3 ploughs; and 14 villans with 8 bordars have 4 ploughs. There is a mill rendering 6s, and 26 acres of meadow.

TRE, and afterwards, it was worth £12; now £15.

Of this manor Ralph holds 3 hides of the archbishop, and there 1 villan with 3 bordars have 1 plough. It is worth £3.

IN "RISBERG" HUNDRED

The archbishop himself holds PATCHING; it was always for the clothing of the monks. TRE it was assessed at 12 hides, and now at 3 hides and 3½ virgates. There is land for 9 ploughs. In demesne are 2 ploughs; and 22 villans with 21 bordars have 6 ploughs. There is a church, [and] woodland for 4 pigs. TRE it was worth £12; and afterwards £10; now £15. Lately it stood at £20, but it could not bear it.

IN 'BRIGHTFORD' HUNDRED

The archbishop himself holds WEST TARRING [in Worthing], which always belonged to the monastery. TRE it was assessed at 18 hides, and now at 7 hides and 1 virgate. There is land for 14½ ploughs. In demesne are 3 ploughs; and 27 villans with 14 bordars have 10 ploughs. There are 2 churches, and woodland for 6 pigs. TRE it was worth £14.4s; and afterwards £10; now £15.

Of this manor William de Braose holds 4 hides, [...] and there he has in demesne 1 plough; and 4 villans with 5 bordars have 1½ ploughs. There are 5 acres of meadow. From the woodland, 10d; as pannage 20s and 2 pigs. It is worth 70s.

II. The land of the Bishop of Chichester

IN 'FLEXBOROUGH' HUNDRED

THE BISHOP OF CHICHESTER holds BISHOPSTONE in demesne. TRE it was assessed at 25 hides, and now the same. There is land [...]. In demesne are 3 ploughs; and 30 villans with 9 bordars have 30 ploughs. There are 40 acres of meadow. [There is] woodland for 3 pigs as pannage, and from the herbage 1 pig of [every] 3 pigs.

TRE it was worth £26; and afterwards £11; now £20.

Of this manor Geoffrey holds 4 hides, and Harold 2 hides, and Richard 3 hides. There are 6 ploughs in demesne, and 13 bordars. The whole of this is worth 100s and 10s[sic].

IN HENFIELD HUNDRED

The bishop himself holds HENFIELD in demesne. TRE it was assessed at 15 hides, and now at 11 hides and 1 virgate. There is land for 20 ploughs. In demesne are 2 ploughs; and 23 villans with 15 bordars have 10 ploughs. There is a church, and 40 acres of meadow. A mill and a fishery are wanting because of an encroachment by William de Broase. Of these hides William holds of the bishop 3 hides; and there he has in demesne 1 hide; and 1 villan with 10 bordars have half a plough. [There is] woodland for 3 pigs. The whole manor TRE was worth £10; and afterwards £7; now what the bishop holds [is worth] £10, what the knight holds 40s; and yet it was at farm for £18.

In LEWES are 3 burgesses belonging to this manor, paying 21d.

IN BOXGROVE [...] HUNDRED

The bishop himself holds ALDINGBOURNE in demesne. TRE, as now, it was assessed at 36 hides. There is land for 20 ploughs. In demesne are 2 ploughs; and 16 villans with 13 bordars have 5 ploughs. There is a church, and 3 slaves, and 6 acres of meadow. [There is] woodland for 3 pigs as pannage, and from the herbage 1 pig of [every] 6 pigs. To this manor belong 16 enclosures which render 7s6d.

Of this manor a priest holds 1 hide, Robert 5 hides, Hugh 3 hides, Alweard 1 hide: these 3 are clerks; and these 4 [are] knights: Harold [who holds] 3 hides, Murdac 3 hides, Ansfrid 1 hide, Lovel 1 hide. Among them all they have 6 ploughs in demesne, and 12 villans and 25 bordars. The whole manor

TRE was worth £15; and afterwards £10; now what the bishop holds [is worth] £10, what the clerks [hold] £4, what the knights [hold] the same, £4.

IN "RISBERG" HUNDRED

The bishop himself holds FERRING in demesne. TRE it was assessed at 12 hides, and now at 8 hides. There is land [...]. In demesne are 2 ploughs; and 15 villans with 14 bordars have 5 ploughs. There is 1 slave, and 20 acres of meadow, and woodland for 4 pigs, and for the herbage 1 pig of [every] 7.

[Folio 17: SUSSEX]

Of this manor Ansfrid holds 2 hides, and he has in demesne half a plough, with 4 bordars. TRE it was worth £7; and afterwards 100s; now £7. What Ansfrid holds is worth 20s.

IN 'EASWRITHE' HUNDRED

The bishop himself holds AMBERLEY. TRE, as now, it was assessed at 24 hides. There is land [...]. In demesne are 2 ploughs; and 20 villans with 13 bordars have 12 ploughs, and [there are] 30 acres of meadow, and woodland for 7 pigs as pannage.

Of this manor William the clerk holds 2 hides, and Ealdæd the priest 3 hides, Baldwin 2½ hides, Ralph 2 hides less 1 virgate, Theodric 3 hides, Huscarl 2 hides. Among them all they have 5 ploughs in demesne; and 17 villans and 25 bordars having 5 ploughs.

The whole manor TRE was worth £20; and afterwards £15; now what the bishop holds [is worth] £14, what the others hold of the bishop is worth £7.

IN SOMERLEY HUNDRED

The bishop himself holds SIDLESHAM in demesne. TRE, as now, it was assessed at 12 hides. There is land for 12 ploughs. In demesne are 2 ploughs; and 16 villans with 14 bordars have 7 ploughs. There is 1 acre of meadow, and woodland for fencing.

Of this manor Gilbert holds 3 hides, Roscelin 1 hide, Ulf 1 hide, and in demesne they have 3 ploughs, with 12 bordars.

The whole manor TRE was worth £10; and afterwards £8; now what the bishop holds [is worth] £10, what the men [hold] 65s.

The bishop himself holds SELSEY in demesne. TRE, as now, it was assessed at 10 hides. There is land for 7 ploughs. In demesne are 2 ploughs; and 16 villans with 11 bordars have 5 ploughs. There are 2 slaves, and 6 closes in Chichester rendering 38d.

Of this manor Geoffrey holds 1 hide, and William half a hide and half a virgate, and they have 1½ ploughs, with 1 bordar.

The whole manor TRE was worth £12; and afterwards £10; now the demesne of the bishop [is worth] £12, [that] of his men 40s.

The bishop himself holds [? East] WITTERING in demesne. TRE, as now, it was assessed at 14 hides. There is land for 8 ploughs. In demesne are 2 [ploughs]; and 15 villans with 12 bordars have 5 ploughs. There is a mill rendering 30d, and 13 enclosures rendering 26d. [For] the herbage, 1 of [every] 7 pigs.

Of this manor Ralph holds 1 hide, Herbert 3 hides, and they have in demesne 2½ ploughs; and 2 villans with 12 bordars and half a plough.

The whole manor, TRE and afterwards, was worth £8; now what the bishop has is worth as much, what his men [have] 50s.

The bishop himself holds PRESTON [in Brighton], and it always belonged to the monastery. TRE, as now, it was assessed at 20 hides. There is land for 12 ploughs. In demesne are 1½ [ploughs]; and 30 villans with 20 bordars have 12 ploughs; and in LEWES, 3 closes rendering 18d. There is a church, and 15 acres of meadow, and woodland for 2 pigs as pannage.

Of this manor Lovel holds 2 hides, and there he has 2 ploughs, and 9 villans with 3 bordars having 2 ploughs, and a mill there. It is worth 40s.

The whole manor TRE was worth £18; and afterwards £10; now £18. Formerly it was at farm for £25, but it could not render [so much].

The canons of Chichester hold in common 16 hides which have never paid geld, as they say, and there they have 4 ploughs in demesne. This is worth £8.

IIII. The land of St Peter of Westminster

IN 'EASWRITHE' HUNDRED

THE ABBOT OF ST PETER of Westminster holds PARHAM, and held it of King Edward. Then it was assessed at 7 hides; now at 3. There is land for 4 ploughs. In demesne is 1 [plough]; and 8 villans with 5 cottars have 2 ploughs. There are 9 acres of meadow. It is and was worth £4.

V. The land of the Church of Fecamp

IN GUESTLING HUNDRED

THE ABBOT of Fecamp holds RYE of the king and held it of King Edward, and then it was assessed at 20 hides, now at 17½ hides. There is land for 35 ploughs. [...] In demesne is 1 plough; and 100 villans less 1 have 43 ploughs. There are 5 churches rendering 64s. There are 100 salt-pans rendering £8.15s, and 7 acres of meadow, and woodland for 2 pigs as pannage. In this manor is a new borough, and there are 64 burgesses paying £8 less 2s. In Hastings 4 burgesses and 14 bordars pay 63s.

Of this manor Robert of Hastings holds 2½ hides of the abbot, and Heoruwulf half a hide. They themselves have 4 villans and 4 cottars, and 2 ploughs. The whole manor TRE was worth £34; now the abbot's demesne [is worth] £50, but [that] of the men 44s.

IN STEYNING HUNDRED

The abbot himself holds STEYNING. Harold held it at the end [of the reign] of King Edward, and then it was assessed at 81 hides, and [there were] moreover in addition 18 hides and 7 acres outside the rape which have never paid geld. Now [there are] 67 hides. In the rape of Arundel are 33½ hides, and the others [are] in the rape of William de Braose, and yet the abbot holds them all now. The land of the whole manor [is] for 41 ploughs. In demesne are 7 ploughs; and 178 villans with 63 bordars have 48 ploughs. There are 2 churches, 9 slaves, and 4 mills rendering 47s and 68 pigs in addition. There are 113 acres of meadow, [and] woodland for 45 pigs as pannage.

In the borough were 118 messuages [which] rendered £4.2s. Now there are 123 messuages, and they render 100s and 100d, and [the burgesses] have 1½ ploughs. TRE they did villan service at the court. TRE it was worth £86; and afterwards £50; now £100, and yet it is at farm for £122 less 2s.

IN BURY HUNDRED

The abbot himself holds BURY of the king. Countess Gode held it of King Edward, and then it was assessed at 16 hides, now at 12 hides. There is land for 16 ploughs. In demesne are 2 ploughs; and 48 villans with 22 cottars have 18 ploughs. There is a church, and 30 acres of meadow, and woodland for 40 pigs, and 1 fishery.

TRE, and afterwards, it was worth £12; now £24.

VI. The land of Bishop Osbern

Bishop OSBERN holds of the king the church of BOSHAM, and held it of King Edward. To this church belonged 112 hides; now 47 are outside [the rape, and of these] Hugh fitzRanulph holds 30 hides, and Ralph de Quesnay 17 hides.

When Osbern received it, the church was assessed at 65 hides, and now the same. There is land [...]. In demesne are 2 ploughs; and 21 villans with 18 bordars have 8 ploughs. There are 3 mills rendering 14s, and 12 acres of meadow, and 1 salt-pan rendering 2s, and 1 enclosure rendering 8d.

Mauger holds of the land of this church 12 hides as 1 manor; it is called West Thorney and pays geld for 8 hides. There he has 32 villans with 8 ploughs.

Of the same land of the church Ralph has 1 hide, a certain clerk 1 hide, and 4 clerks 1 hide in common.

[Folio 17v: SUSSEX]

They themselves have 3 ploughs in demesne; and 3 villans and 10 bordars having 1½ ploughs; and there is a church and a priest, and 2 slaves, and 1 enclosure rendering 8d. The whole TRE was worth £300; and afterwards £50.

Now what the bishop holds [is worth] £16.10s, and yet he has 20s more from the farm; what Mauger holds is worth £6, and yet he has 50s more; what the others hold is worth £4.15s. The clerks hold the tithe of the church, and it is worth 40s.

TRE 1 hide in West Itchenor belonged to this manor. Now Warin, Earl Roger's man, holds it.

IN DUMPFORD HUNDRED

The bishop himself holds ELSTED, and held it of King Edward, and then it was assessed at 13 hides, now at 5½ hides. There is land [...]. In demesne are 2 ploughs; and 7 villans with 23 bordars have 2 ploughs. There are 2 slaves, and a mill rendering 4s, and there is a church. [There is] woodland for 10 pigs. [From] the herbage, 1 of [every] 7 pigs.

Of this manor Richard holds 1 hide, Osbern the clerk half a hide, Ralph the priest 1 hide which belongs to the church. The whole manor, TRE and afterwards, as now, was worth £15.

IN SINGLETON HUNDRED

Durand holds PRESTON [near Chichester] of the bishop. TRE, as now, it was assessed at 3 hides. There is land [...]. In demesne [are] 1½ ploughs; and 3 villans with 4 bordars have half a plough. There are 6 acres of meadow, and a small wood for fencing. TRE it was worth £4; and afterwards, as now, £3.

IN ROTHERBRIDGE HUNDRED

Richard holds EAST LAVINGTON of the bishop. Godwine the priest held it of King Edward in alms, and then, as now, it was assessed at 6 hides. There is land [...]. In demesne are 2 ploughs; and 11 villans with 7 bordars have 4 ploughs.

There is a church, and in Chichester 1 close rendering 3d, and 12 acres of meadow. [There is] woodland for 10 pigs, and 1 of [every] 7 pigs.

TRE it was worth £10; and afterwards £6; now £10.

All these lands belonged and belong to the church of Bosham in alms.

VII. The land of St Peter of Winchester

THE ABBOT OF ST PETER of Winchester holds SOUTHEASE. It always belonged to the monastery. TRE it was assessed at 28 hides, and now at 27 hides. There is land for 28 ploughs. [...]. In demesne is 1 plough; and 46 villans with 4 bordars have 21 ploughs. There is a church, and 130 acres of meadow.

In Lewes [are] 10 burgesses rendering 52d; and from villans [come] 38,500 herrings. For porpoises, £4. For the forfeiture of the villans, £9 and 3 summae of peas.

In all, TRE and afterwards, it was worth £20; now it is valued at as much, but yet it renders £28.

IN STOCKBRIDGE HUNDRED

The abbot himself holds DONNINGTON. TRE the abbey held it, and then, as now, it was assessed at 5 hides. There is land [...]. In demesne is 1 plough; and 15 villans with 4 bordars have 6½ ploughs. There are 2 slaves, and 25 acres of meadow, and woodland for fencing. In Chichester, 1 close rendering 4d. As pannage 1½ pigs.

TRE it was worth £4.10s7d; now £6.

VIII. The land of the Church of Battle

IN "WANDELMESTREI" HUNDRED

THE ABBOT OF ST MARTIN of Battle holds ALCISTON of the king. Æthelnoth Cild held it of King Edward, and then it was assessed at 50 hides, and now at 44½ hides. There is land for 28 ploughs.

Of these hides, 3½ hides belong to the rape of Hastings, and 2 hides to the rape of Lewes, as do 7 burgesses.

In demesne the abbot has 4 ploughs; and 65 villans with 7 bordars have 21½ ploughs. There are 12 slaves, and 50 acres of meadow. [There is] woodland for 4 pigs as pannage, and 6 pigs from the herbage.

Of the above-mentioned 5 hides, Robert holds 1 hide and 3 virgates of the abbot, Reinbert 5 virgates, Geoffrey half a hide, Alvred 3 virgates. They themselves have in demesne 4 ploughs; and 5 villans and 1 bordar with 1½ ploughs.

The whole manor TRE was worth £48; and afterwards £30; now what the abbot holds [is worth] £36, what his men [have] £4.5s.

IN 'TOTNORE' HUNDRED

The abbot himself holds 4 hides of the king. Æthelnoth Cild held them of King Edward, and then, as now, they were assessed at 4 hides. There the abbot has 6 villans with 3 ploughs. It is valued in another manor.

The abbot himself has 6½ hides in his rape. This land was assessed at 6 hides, and half [a hide] was exempt because [it was] outside the rape.

Among these hides the same abbot holds in demesne 'UCKHAM' [in Battle]. Wulfbeald held it of Earl Godwine. Then, as now, it was assessed at half a hide; now 1 virgate is in the rape of the Count of EU. In demesne the abbot has 1 plough; and 4 bordars with 1 plough. There are 3 acres of meadow, and woodland for 2 pigs. TRE, as now, worth 20s.

In [?]BEECH [in Whatlington], which Osbern holds of the Count of EU, the abbot has 3 virgates of land, and there are 3 villans with 1 plough. It is worth 6s.

In 'BATHURST' [in Battle], which Reinbert holds, the abbot has 1 virgate of land, with 1 villan, and half a plough. There is woodland for 2 pigs. It is worth 4s.

In WILMINGTON, which the Count of Mortain holds, the abbot has 6 virgates of land, and there are 6 villans with 4 ploughs, and woodland for 2 pigs. It is worth 15s.

In NETHERFIELD, which the Count of EU holds, the abbot has 6 virgates of land, and there are 5 villans and 1 bordar with 3 ploughs. It is worth 10s.

In PENHURST, which Osbern holds of the Count of EU, the abbot has half a hide, and there are 2 villans with 2 ploughs, and 1 acre of meadow, and woodland for 2 pigs. It is worth 15s.

In the manor of HOOE, which the Count of EU holds, the abbot has half a hide, and there are 2 villans with 1 plough. It is worth 5s.

In FILSHAM, which the Count of EU holds, the abbot has 1 virgate, and 1 villan with 1 plough, and [there is] 1 acre of meadow. It is worth 4s.

In CATSFIELD, which Warin holds of the Count of EU, the abbot has 3 virgates in demesne.

In 'BULLINGTON' [in Bexhill], which the Count of EU, holds, the abbot has 2 hides less 1 virgate, and there are 7 villans with 5 ploughs. It is worth 20s.

In CROWHURST, which Walter holds of the Count of EU, the abbot has 1 virgate of land, with 1 villan. It is worth 12d.

In [Lower and Upper] WILTING, which Ingelrann holds of the count, the abbot has 1 virgate of waste land.

In HOLLINGTON, which the Count of EU holds, the abbot has 1 virgate of waste land. There is also a wood for 5 pigs outside the rape.

Of all this land the abbot has 2½ hides in demesne, and there is 1 plough, with 21 bordars, and 2 mills without rent. It is worth 40s. These hides have not paid geld in the rape.

The land of St Edward [Of Shaftesbury]

IN BINSTED HUNDRED

The Abbey of ST EDWARD holds and held FELPHAM TRE. Then it was assessed at 21 hides; now at 15½ hides. There is land for 12 ploughs. In demesne is 1 plough; and 48 villans and 19 cottars with 15 ploughs. There is a church, and a fishery rendering 5s, and in Chichester, 6 burgesses paying 7s. There are 8 acres of meadow, [and] woodland for 30 pigs. TRE it was worth £10; now £20.

[Folio 18: SUSSEX]

IX. The land of the Count of Eu

THE COUNT OF EU holds in demesne a manor which is called HOOE. Earl Godwine held it, and TRE, as now, it was assessed at 12 hides. There is land for 44 ploughs. In demesne are 2 ploughs; and 44 villans with 12 bordars have 28 ploughs. There is a chapel, and 1 mill rendering 7s, and 71 acres of meadow, and 30 salt-pans rendering 33s. [There is] woodland for 10 pigs as pannage. From the herbage, 7 pigs.

Of the villans' land of this manor Reinbert holds half a hide, Robert 2½ virgates, Osbern 2 virgates, Alvred 2 virgates, Gerald 2 virgates, Ingelrann 2 virgates, Witbert 4½ virgates, Werelc 2 virgates, another Robert 2 virgates.

Among them all they have in demesne 3½ ploughs; and 12 villans and 3 bordars with 7 ploughs.

The whole manor TRE was worth £25; and afterwards £6; now the count's demesne [is worth] £14, [that] of his knights £7.7s.

Werenc holds CATSFIELD of the count. Ælfhelm held it of King Edward and could go with the land where he would.

Then it was assessed at 1½ hides; now at 1 hide and 1 virgate. There is land for 7 ploughs. In demesne is 1 plough; and 11 villans with 2 bordars have 8 ploughs. There is a chapel, and 1 mill serving the hall. There are 4 acres of meadow, and woodland for 3 pigs, and [from] the herbage 5 pigs. TRE it was worth 50s; and afterwards 20s; now 60s.

Wibert holds "MEDEHEI" of the count. Osweard held it of King Edward, and could go with the land where he would, and then, as now, it was assessed at 3 virgates. There is land for 4 ploughs. In demesne is 1 plough; and 4 villans with 4 ploughs, and 5 salt-pans rendering 64d, and 2½ acres of meadow, and woodland for 3 pigs as pannage.

TRE it was worth £4; and afterwards 20s; now 110s.

Robert holds NINFIELD of the count. Blæc held it of King Edward, and wished [sic] to go with the land where he would. Then it was assessed at 3 hides; now at 2½ hides. There is land for 12 ploughs. In demesne Robert has 1 plough, and a church, and 1 bordar. Of the land of this manor, the Count of EU himself holds 5 virgates in demesne, Osbern 3 virgates, Werenc 2 virgates, Reinbert 7 virgates. In demesne they have 2 ploughs; and 8 villans and 2 bordars have 6 ploughs. The aforesaid Robert the cook holds the capital manor, and he holds 2 virgates only, and a certain villan holds the others.

The whole manor TRE was worth £6; and afterwards 20s; now the whole [is worth] 105s.

IN 'FOXEARLE' HUNDRED

Wibert holds HERSTMONCEUX of the count. Eadmær the priest held it TRE, and could go with the land where he would; and then, as now, it was assessed at 5 hides. There is land for 12 ploughs. In demesne are 3 ploughs; and 30 villans with 12 cottars have 16 ploughs. There is a church, and 7 acres of meadow, and woodland for 2 pigs.

TRE it was worth £6; and afterwards 20s; now £10.

William holds WARTLING of the count. Alnoth held it of King Edward and could go with the land where he would; and then, as now, it was assessed at 5 hides. There is land for 16 ploughs. In demesne are 2 ploughs; and 30 villans with 10 cottars have 18 ploughs. There are 3 salt-pans rendering 7s, woodland for 30 pigs, and 30 acres of meadow. Of the land of this manor, Gerard holds 1 hide, Ralph 1 hide, Wenenc the priest 2 virgates. There are 12 villans with 4 cottars with 9 ploughs, and 8 acres of meadow. The whole manor, TRE and afterwards, was worth £10; now what William holds [is worth] £10, what the knights [hold] £4.

Robert de Criel holds ASHBURNHAM of the count. Siward held it of King Edward, and then, as now, it was assessed at 2½ hides. |There is land for 12 ploughs. In demesne is 1 [plough]|; and 21 villans with 3 cottars have 14 ploughs. There is a church, and 3 salt-pans rendering 58d.

TRE it was worth £6; and afterwards 20s; now £9.

The Count of EU holds 'FRANKWELL' [in Ashburnham], and 6 knights [hold] of him. One of them, Northmann, held it

TRE, and then, as now, it was assessed at 1½ hides. There is land for 2 ploughs.

Of this land the same Northmann has half a hide, Ralph 2 virgates, Hugh 2 virgates, Osbern 2 virgates, Wenenc 1 virgate, Gerard 1 virgate. In demesne [is] 1 plough; and 8 villans and 1 cottar with 4 ploughs.

In the manor [are] 12 acres of meadow, and woodland for 2 pigs.

The whole manor TRE was worth 40s; and afterwards 10s; now 46s.

Ingelrann holds of the count 1 hide in the same hundred. 2 free men held it TRE, and could go with the land where they would. Then, as now, it was assessed at 1 hide. There is land for 4 ploughs. In demesne is 1 [plough]; and 6 villans with 4 cottars have 4 ploughs.

TRE it was worth 30s; and afterwards 20s; now 30s.

Olaf holds of the count 1 virgate in this hundred. Hernetoc held it TRE, and could go where he pleased; and then, as now, it was assessed at 1 virgate. There is land for 1 plough, and there is [1 plough] in demesne, with 1 villan and 2 cottars. It is and | was worth | 10s.

IN BEXHILL HUNDRED

Osbern holds BEXHILL of the count. TRE Bishop Æthelric held it, because it belongs to the bishopric, and afterwards he held it until King William gave the jurisdiction of the castle of Hastings to the count. TRE, as now, it was assessed at 20 hides. There is land for 26 ploughs.

Of the land of this manor the count himself holds in demesne 3 hides, and there he has 1 plough; and 7 villans with 4 ploughs.

Of the same land Osbern has 10 hides, Wenenc 1 hide, William de Sept-Meules 2½ hides less half a virgate, Robert de Saint-Leger 1 hide and half a virgate, Reinbert half a hide, Ansketil half a hide, Robert de Criel half a hide, Geoffrey and Roger, clerks, 1 hide as a prebend. There are 2 churches. In demesne [are] 4 ploughs; and 46 villans and 27 cottars with 29 ploughs. In the whole manor [are] 6 acres of meadow.

The whole manor TRE was worth £20; and afterwards it was waste; now [it is worth] £18.10s. Of these the count's part accounts for 40s.

Osbern holds of the count 2 virgates of land in the same hundred, and they were always assessed at 2 virgates. There he has 5 oxen in a plough. It was worth 8s; now 16s.

Leofnoth held 'BULLINGTON' [in Bexhill] of King Edward, and it was assessed at 5 hides both then and now. There is land for 5 ploughs.

Of this land the count holds in demesne 3 virgates, and there he has 20 burgesses and 5 cottars with 2 ploughs.

The Abbey of Le Treport holds 3 hides less 2 virgates, and at so much it is assessed. In demesne [is] 1 plough; and 13 villans with 13 cottars have 5 ploughs ploughs [sic]. [There are] 20 acres of meadow.

TRE the whole manor was worth £6; and afterwards 50s; now the count has 43s, and the monks £4.

IN BALDSLOW HUNDRED

King Edward held FILSHAM in demesne. There are 15 hides which do not pay geld and have not paid geld. There is land for 30 ploughs.

Of this land the count himself holds 8 hides and 1 virgate, and there he has 2 ploughs,

[Folio 18V: SUSSEX]

and 48 villans with 7 cottars have 34 ploughs.

Of the land of the same manor, Geoffrey holds 2 hides, Robert 1 hide and 1 virgate, William half a hide, Hugh the crossbowman 5 virgates, Ingelrann 2 virgates, Robert the cook half a hide, Walter 5 virgates, Sasward 1 virgate, Wenenc the priest 1 virgate, Osweard 2 virgates, Roger Daniel half a hide. In demesne [are] $6\frac{1}{2}$ ploughs; and 13 villans and 17 cottars and 3 slaves with $7\frac{1}{2}$ ploughs. In the manor [are] 30 acres of meadow, and woodland for 8 pigs.

The whole manor TRE was worth £14; afterwards it was laid waste; now [it is worth] £22. Of these, £14 are accounted for in the count's part

Wulfweard the priest of this manor holds a church with 1 virgate, but it does not belong to the 15 hides. Wulfmær held it of King Edward, and it did not then pay geld, nor does it now. It is worth 5s.

Godwine and Alstan held HOLLINGTON TRE, and could go with the land where they would. Then it was assessed at $4\frac{1}{2}$ hides; now at 3 hides and 2 virgates. There is land for 8 ploughs.

Of this land the count holds in demesne $1\frac{1}{2}$ hides and 2 virgates, and there he has 1 plough, and 12 villans with 4 ploughs.

Of this land Reinbert has half a hide, William 1 hide, Hugh half a hide, Wulfweard 2 virgates.

In demesne [is] 1 plough; and 3 villans and 3 cottars with 3 ploughs. In the manor [are] 2 acres of meadow, and woodland for 2 pigs.

The whole manor TRE was worth 30s; and afterwards 20s; now 58s.

Goldwine held 'CORTESLEY' [in Hollington] TRE, and could go where he would; and then, as now, it was assessed at 6 hides. There is land for 8 ploughs.

Of this land he holds half a hide, and there is 1 villan with 1 plough. Of the same land William holds $4\frac{1}{2}$ hides and Godwine [holds] of him, Reinbert half a hide, Hugh half a hide. There they have 24 villans and 2 cottars with 8 ploughs.

In the manor [are] 27 acres of meadow.

The whole manor TRE, and afterwards, was worth 100s; now £6.7s.

Wynstan held WESTFIELD TRE, and could go where he would. Then, as now, it was assessed at 1 hide and 2 virgates. There is land for 3 ploughs. Wibert holds it of the count, and has in demesne $1\frac{1}{2}$ ploughs; and 7 villans and 1 cottar with 3 ploughs.

TRE it was worth 20s; and afterwards 70s; now 72s.

Earl Harold held CROWHURST. Then it was assessed at 6 hides; now at 3 hides. There is land for 22 ploughs. Walter fitzLambert holds it of the count, and has 2 ploughs in demesne; and 12 villans and 6 cottars have 12 ploughs. There are 15 acres of meadow, and woodland for 4 pigs. A certain Walo holds half a hide and 2 virgates. There are 3 villans with 1 plough. TRE it was worth £8; now 100s. It was laid waste.

Two free men held [Lower and Upper] WILTING TRE. Then, as now, it was assessed at 4 hides. There is land for 9 ploughs.

Of this land Ingelrann holds of the count 2 hides and 2 virgates, Reinbert half a hide and 2 virgates, Ralph half a hide, Robert 2 virgates. There are in demesne 3 ploughs; and 9 villans and 5 cottars with 6 ploughs. There are 16 acres of meadow. The whole manor TRE was worth 100s; now £4. It was laid waste. The count has 1 virgate of this manor in his park.

In the same hundred Ingelrann holds 3 virgates of the count, which 2 free men held TRE, but they have never paid geld. There are 3 villans with 2 ploughs. It is worth 10s.

IN "HAILESALTEDE" HUNDRED

Earl Harold held WHATLINGTON. Then, as now, it was assessed at half a hide. There is land for 6 ploughs. Reinbert holds it of the count, and there he has 2 ploughs, and 6 villans and 3 cottars with 3 ploughs. There are 10 acres of meadow, and woodland for 6 pigs. TRE, as now, worth 50s. It was laid waste.

The same Reinbert holds MOUNTFIELD of the count. Goda held it TRE, and could go where he would. Then, as now, it was assessed at 1 hide. There is land for 8 ploughs. In demesne are 2 [ploughs]; and 9 villans with 2 cottars have 6 ploughs. There are 8 acres of meadow, and woodland for 10 pigs. TRE it was worth £3; and afterwards 20s; now £4.

Herolf holds NETHERFIELD of the count. Goda held it of King Edward. Then it was assessed at $1\frac{1}{2}$ hides; now at 1 only. There is land for 4 ploughs. In demesne is 1 [plough]; and 7 villans have 3 ploughs. There are 8 salt-pans rendering 8s, and woodland for 10 pigs. TRE it was worth 100s; now 50s. It has been laid waste.

In this HUNDRED Hugh holds a manor of the count, which Alnoth held TRE, and he could go with it where he pleased; and then it was assessed at $1\frac{1}{2}$ hides; now at 1 only. There is land for 4 ploughs. In demesne is 1 plough; and 12 villans with 5 ploughs. There are 5 acres of meadow, and woodland for 4 pigs. TRE it was worth 100s; and afterwards 20s; now 50s.

The same Osbern holds 1 virgate of the count in [?] BEECH [in Whatlington]. Wulfbeald held it TRE. Then [it was assessed] at 1 virgate; now at nothing. Then it was worth 2s; now nothing.

Wenenc the priest holds BROOMHAM of the count. Edith held it TRE, and could go where she pleased; and it was assessed at half a hide then, as now. There is land for 3 ploughs. In demesne is 1 [plough]; and 4 villans and 2 cottars with 2 ploughs. [There is] 1 acre of meadow, [and] woodland for 2 pigs. TRE, as now, [worth] 20s. It was laid waste.

Hugh holds of the count 1 virgate in EYELIDS. Leofwine held it of Earl Leofwine. It has never paid geld. There is 1 plough, and woodland for 3 pigs. It was worth 5s; now 12s.

IN STAPLE HUNDRED

The same Hugh holds 2 virgates belonging to EYELIDS. Earl Leofwine held them, and they were assessed at 2 virgates then, as now. There is 1 villan with 1 plough.

The count himself holds 1 virgate belonging to EYELIDS. Earl Leofwine held it. It has never given geld. There is land for 1 plough, and there is [1 plough], with 1 villan. Then [worth] 4s; now 5s.

In the same hundred Hugh holds 1 virgate of the count. Cana held it TRE. Then, as now, it was assessed at 1 virgate. There is land for 1 plough. There is [1 plough], with 1 villan. It is and was worth 4s.

The Count of EU holds BRIGHTLING. TRE 2 brothers held it of the king. It was assessed at 1 hide then, as now. In demesne is 1 plough, and a church, and woodland rendering 5s. Of this hide Robert holds 4 virgates of the count, and there he has 10 villans with 2 cottars having 7 ploughs.

TRE it was worth 100s; and afterwards 10s; now 42s.

The Count of EU holds DALLINGTON. Northmann held it TRE, and could go where he pleased; and it was assessed at 1 hide, now at nothing. There is land [...]. Of this hide the count has a half in the forest, and it is worth 5s. William has the other half, and there he has 1 plough in demesne, with 2 cottars.

The same William has 1½ virgates in 'FOXEARLE' HUNDRED. King Edward held them, and they have never paid geld. There 1 villan and 2 cottars have 1 plough.

The whole TRE was worth 45s; now 35s.

IN 'HAWKESBOROUGH' HUNDRED

Wibert holds WARBLETON of the count. Countess Gode held it. Then, as now, it was assessed at 1 hide. There is land for 2 ploughs. In demesne is 1 [plough]; and 2 villans with 6 cottars have 1 plough. It was worth 40s; now 20s.

In BEDDINGHAM the count has 1 hide in demesne. Queen Edith held it. It has never paid geld. There is land for 3 ploughs. In demesne is 1 [plough]; and 3 villans have 2 ploughs.

[Folio 19: SUSSEX]

TRE it was worth 20s; and afterwards 10s; now 20s.

The count himself has half a hide in BEDDINGHAM. King Edward held it, and it has never paid geld. There are 2 villans with 3 ploughs. It was and is worth 10s.

Also in BEDDINGHAM, the count holds 4 hides less half a virgate. Countess Gode held it, and it has never paid geld.

There is land for 10 ploughs. There 18 villans have 13 ploughs. TRE it was worth £4; and afterwards 40s; now 70s.

The count himself holds in demesne 1½ hides and 1 virgate of the manor of WEST FIRLE. TRE the Abbey of Wilton held it. It has never paid geld. There is land for 6 ploughs. There 9 villans have 8 ploughs. TRE, as now, worth 30s.

The same count holds 1½ virgates of ARLINGTON. The Abbey of Wilton held it TRE. It has never paid geld. There is land for 1 plough. There 5 villans have 3 ploughs. TRE, as now, worth 7s.

The same count has 1½ virgates of the manor of LAUGHTON. Countess Gode held it. It has never paid geld. There 3 villans have 2 ploughs. TRE, as now, worth 8s.

The same count holds 1 virgate of land belonging to ECKINGTON. Aghmund held it TRE, and could go where he pleased, and it has not paid geld. There 2 villans have 2 ploughs. TRE, as now, worth 4s.

The same count holds half a hide and half a virgate of the manor of RIPE. Earl Harold held it, and it has never paid geld. There 2 villans have 1 plough. It is and was worth 5s.

The same count holds 1 virgate in the manor of TILTON. Earl Harold held it, and it has never paid geld. There 2 villans have 1 plough. It is and was worth 5s.

In the manor of EAST DEAN Countess Gode held 1½ virgates; it has never paid geld. There 2 villans have 1 plough. It is and was worth 3s.

In the manor of WILLINGDON Countess Gode held 1½ virgates, and it has never paid geld. There the count has 2 villans with 2 ploughs. It is and was worth 5s.

In the same place Wulfmær the priest held 1 virgate, and could go where he pleased, and it has never paid geld. There the count has 1 villan with 1 plough. It is and was worth 3s.

In the same place Alwine held 1 virgate and 1 furlong of the manor of SESSINGHAM, and could go where he pleased, and it has never paid geld. There the count has 2 villans with 2 ploughs. It is and was worth 10s.

Wibert holds half a hide of the count in RATTON. A certain free man, Cana, held it, and it has never paid geld. There 3 villans have 2 ploughs. It is and was worth 8s.

In EAST DEAN Countess Gode held 1 hide, and it has never paid geld. There Wibert has 2 villans with 2 ploughs. It is and was worth 14s.

In LAUGHTON Countess Gode held 1 hide, and it has never paid geld. There Wibert has 4 villans with 3 ploughs. It is and was worth 13s.

In 'BROUGHTON' [in Jevington] a certain free man, Wulfmær, held half a hide, and it has never paid geld. There Wibert has 1 villan and 1 cottar with 1 plough. Then, as now, [worth] 8s.

Osbern fitzGeoffrey holds 5 hides of the count in LAUGHTON. Countess Gode held it, and it has never paid geld. There is land for 10 ploughs. There 15 villans have 15 ploughs. TRE it was worth £4; and afterwards 40s; now £4.

In 'STOCKINGHAM' [in Laughton] Leofnoth held half a hide, and it has never paid geld. There Osbern has 1 cottar paying 12d. Then [worth] 3s; now 2s.

In ETCHINGWOOD Beorhtwine, a free man, held half a hide, and it has never paid geld. There Osbern has in demesne 1 plough; and 1 villan with 1 plough, and 2 acres of meadow. Then and afterwards, as now, worth 10s.

In ECKINGTON Aghmund held 1 hide of King Edward, and it has never paid geld. [There is] land for 2 ploughs. There Osbern has 3 villans with 3 ploughs. Then and afterwards, as now, [worth] 14s.

In WEST FIRLE the Abbey of Wilton held 1 virgate of King Edward, and it has never paid geld. There Osbern has 1 villan with 1 plough. Then, as now, [worth] 30d.

In PRESTON [in Beddingham] Botic, a free man, held half a hide, and it has never paid geld. There Osbern has 5 villans with 3 ploughs. Then, as now, [worth] 5s.

In WALDRON Ælfgifu, a free woman, held half a virgate, and it has never paid geld. There Osbern has 1 villan with 5 oxen. It is worth 2s.

In RIPE Earl Harold held 1 virgate. It has never paid geld. There Alwine, a man of the Count of EU, has 1 plough in demesne; and 1 villan and 1 cottar with 1 plough. There are 3 acres of meadow, and woodland for 3 pigs. Then, and afterwards, [worth] 4s; now 10s.

IN SHOYSWELL HUNDRED

THIS HUNDRED HAS NEVER PAID GELD

Walter fitzLambert holds HAZELHURST of the count. Bishop Æthelric held it in fief of King Edward. Then, as now, [there were] 4½ hides. There is land for 9 ploughs. There are in demesne 2 ploughs; and 6 villans and 1 cottar with 7 ploughs. There is a church, and woodland for 10 pigs. Of this land Walo holds 1 hide, and there he has 4 villans with 2 ploughs, and 1 cottar. The whole manor TRE was worth 114s; now £7. It was laid waste.

In CHALVINGTON 2 free men, Leofwine and Edward, held 1 virgate. There the count has 2 villans with 1 plough. Then and afterwards, as now, [worth] 40d.

In SHERRINGTON Leofwine, a free man, held 1 virgate. There the count has 2 villans with 1 plough. Then and afterwards, as now, [worth] 6s.

In ALCISTON the Abbey of Wilton held 1 virgate. There the count has 1 villan with 1 plough. Then and afterwards, as now, [worth] 5s.

Reinbert holds of the count 1 virgate in RATTON. Ulf, a free man, held it. There is 1 plough in demesne, and 15 acres of meadow, and 3 cottars pay 2s. Then and afterwards, as now, [worth] 5s.

In ALCISTON the Abbey of Wilton held 1 virgate. There Reinbert has 2 ploughs, and 3 cottars, and woodland for 2 pigs. Then and afterwards, as now, [worth] 5s.

In WINTON Countess Gode held 1 virgate. There Reinbert has in demesne 1 plough, with 1 cottar. Then [worth]5s; now 10s. It was laid waste.

In WILLINGDON Countess Gode held half a virgate. There Reinbert has 1 cottar paying 12d. Then, as now, [worth] 12d. It was laid waste.

In RATTON Countess Gode held 1 virgate. There Reinbert has 4 villans with 3 ploughs. Then and afterwards, as now, [worth] 10s.

In RIPE Godwine, a free man, held 1 virgate. There Reinbert has 1 villan with 1 plough. Then and afterwards, as now, [worth] 4s.

Osbern fitzGeoffrey holds of the count half a hide in WILLINGDON. Countess Gode held it. There are now 2 ploughs in demesne, with 1 cottar. Then and afterwards, as now, [worth] 40s.

In WEST FIRLE the Abbey of Wilton held 1 virgate. There Osbern has 1 villan with 1 plough. Then and afterwards, as now, [worth] 8s.

In RATTON Countess Gode held 1 virgate. There Eustace the clerk has in demesne 1 plough, with 1 villan. Then, and afterwards, [worth] 5s; now 6s.

In JEVINGTON Countess Gode held 1 virgate. There Hugh has of the count 1 villan with 1 plough. Then and afterwards, as now, [worth] 5s.

In RIPE Earl Harold held 1 hide. There Walter fitzLambert has in demesne 2 ploughs; and 3 villans with 2 ploughs, and 2 acres of meadow. Then, and afterwards, [worth] 20s; now 30s.

[Folio 19V: SUSSEX]

In WEST FIRLE the Abbey of Wilton held 1 hide and 1½ virgates. There Walter has 9 villans with 5 ploughs. There is land for 6 ploughs. TRE, and afterwards, worth £3; now £4.

In ECKINGTON Aghmund, a free man, held half a hide and 1 virgate. There Walter has 3 villans with 2 ploughs. Then and afterwards, as now, [worth] 20s.

In SHERRINGTON Alwine, a free man, held half a hide. There Walter has in demesne 1 plough; and 2 villans with 1 plough. Then, and afterwards, [worth] 10s; now 5[s].

In LAUGHTON Gode held 1 virgate. Walter has nothing there except 2s.

In "BURGELSTALTONE" Wulfsige held 1 virgate; he was a free man. There Walter has 2 villans with 1 plough. Then and afterwards, as now, [worth] 5s.

In EAST DEAN Gode held half a hide. There Walter has in demesne 2 ploughs, with 3 cottars. Then, and afterwards, [worth] 10s; now 20s.

In ALCISTON the Abbey of Wilton held 1 virgate. There Walter has 3 villans with 2 ploughs.

SHOYSWELL HUNDRED HAS NEVER PAID GELD

IN 'HENHURST' HUNDRED

Reinbert holds SALEHURST of the count. Countess Gode held it. Then, as now, it was assessed at half a hide. There is land for 4 ploughs. In demesne is 1 [plough]; and 7 villans and 8 cottars with 6 ploughs. There is a church, and 16 acres of meadow. TRE it was worth 20s; now 30s. It was laid waste.

Ælfric holds 'DRIGSELL' [in Salehurst] of the count. A certain free man, Cana, held it, and then, as now, it was assessed at 3½ hides #. There is land for 8 ploughs. In demesne are 2 [ploughs]; and 18 villans and 6 cottars have 12 ploughs. There are 10 acres of meadow, and woodland for 20 pigs. TRE it was worth £3; now £4. It was laid waste.

William holds of the count half a hide in this hundred. Leofgifu held it TRE, and then, as now, it was assessed at half a hide. There is land [...]. In demesne is 1 plough, and 6 acres of meadow, and woodland for 6 pigs. TRE, as now, worth 20s; when received, 10s.

Reinbert holds of the count 1 hide in this hundred. A certain free man, Cana, held it, but it has not paid geld. There are now 8 villans [and] 3 cottars with 6 ploughs. Then, as now, [worth] 30s. It was waste.

In this hundred Northmann held half a hide; he was a free man. It has never paid geld. There Reinbert has 1 plough, with 1 cottar, and 1 mill rendering 2s, and [there are] 3 acres of meadow, and woodland for 1 pig. Then, as now, [worth] 20s.

In this hundred Azur, a free man, held 1 virgate, but it has not paid geld. There Reinbert has 1 plough in demesne, with 1 villan. There are 10 acres of meadow. Then, as now, [worth] 10s; when received, 5s.

In EASTBOURNE King Edward held 1 hide. It has never paid geld. There Reinbert has 4 villans with 3 ploughs. Then and afterwards, as now, [worth] 20s.

In BERWICK King Edward held half a hide. It has never paid geld. There Reinbert has 1 villan and 4 cottars with 1 plough, and a mill rendering 10s, and 11 acres of meadow, and woodland for 6 pigs, and 2 fisheries rendering 6d. TRE it was worth 30s; and afterwards 10s; now 35s.

In EASTBOURNE King Edward held half a hide. It has never paid geld. There Reinbert has in demesne 3 ploughs, with 5 cottars, and [there is] 1 fishery. There is land for 2 ploughs. TRE it was worth 20s; and afterwards 10s; now 45s.

In the same hundred is half a hide and 1½ virgates. There is land for 3 ploughs. This land TRE belonged to 3 manors, Ratton, Willingdon [and] West Firle. It has never rendered geld. There Reinbert has 6 villans with 3 ploughs. TRE, as now, worth 22s.

In SELMESTON Ælfhere held half a hide of King Edward. It has never paid geld. There Reinbert has 1 plough, with 1 villan. There are 3 acres of meadow, and woodland for 1 pig. It is and was worth 10s.

In BURGHAM Wulfgar held half a hide of King Edward. It has never paid geld. There Reinbert has 2 villans with 2 ploughs. TRE, as now, worth 12s.

The same Reinbert holds of the count half a hide which belonged TRE to 2 manors, BERWICK and CLAVERHAM [Claverham and Lower Claverham]. The king held one, and Osweard held the other of King Edward. It has never paid geld. There is now 1 villan and 1 cottar. It was worth 5s; now 7s.

The same Reinbert holds 1 virgate which Cola held of King Edward. It has never paid geld. There is 1 villan with 1 plough. It was and is worth 5s.

In WILLINGDON Gode held of the count half a hide. It has never paid geld. There is land for 2 ploughs. There Reinbert has 2 ploughs in demesne; and 4 villans and 2 cottars with 2 ploughs. There are 5 acres of meadow, and woodland for 2 pigs, and 1 slave. TRE it was worth 20s; and afterwards 10s; now 30s.

In ECKINGTON Azur, a free man, held 1 virgate. It has never paid geld. There Reinbert has 3 villans with 1½ ploughs. Then, as now, [worth] 6s.

In "SEGNESCOME" Leofwine, a free man, held half a hide. It has never paid geld. There the count has 2 villans with 5 oxen, and 1 cottar. Then, as now, [worth] 5s.

In ALCISTON Countess Gode held 2½ virgates. They have never paid geld. There is land for 3 ploughs. There Robert has 4 villans and 5 oxen. It was worth 30s; now 20[s].

In ALCISTON Gode held half a virgate. It has never paid geld. There Hugh has 1 villan of the count. Then [worth] 5s; now 2s.

In WILLINGDON Gode held 1½ virgates. They have never paid geld. There Hugh has 2 villans with 1 plough. TRE, and afterwards, [worth] 10s; now 5s.

In WEST FIRLE the Abbey of Wilton held half a virgate. It has never paid geld. There the monks of Le Treport have 2 villans and 2 cottars with 1 plough. Then and afterwards, as now, [worth] 5s.

IN "BABINRERODE" HUNDRED

Rainer holds KITCHENHAM of the count. Eadric held it TRE; he was a free man. Then, as now, it was assessed at half a hide. There is land for 1 plough, and there is [1 plough] in demesne, with 3 cottars, and 2 acres of meadow. TRE, and afterwards, it was worth 10s; now 20[s].

Reinbert holds UDIMORE of the count. Algar held it of Earl Godwine. Then, as now, it was assessed at 6 hides. There is land for 10 ploughs. In demesne is 1 [plough]; and 22 villans have 15 ploughs. There is a church, and 2 acres of meadow. TRE, as now, [worth] £8; when received, 30s.

IN GUESTLING HUNDRED

Geoffrey de Flocques holds GUESTLING of the count. Wulfbeald held it of King Edward. Then, as now, it was assessed at 4½ hides. There is land for 7 ploughs. In demesne [are] 2 ploughs; and 12 villans with 5 cottars have 4 ploughs. There are 5 acres of meadow.

Of this land Robert of Ulcombe holds 1 hide, and there he has 2 ploughs in demesne; and 2 villans and 2 cottars with 1 plough. TRE, as now, [worth] 100s. It was laid waste.

William de Sept-Meules holds "IVET". Leofræd held it of Earl Godwine. It is 1 hide. It has never paid geld. There is land for 2 ploughs. In demesne is 1 [plough]; and [he has] 1 villan and 3 cottars with 2 ploughs. There are 3 acres of meadow. TRE, as now, [worth] 20s. It was laid waste.

In the same HUNDRED Robert holds 1 ferding of the count. Wulfmær held it of Earl Godwine. Then it was assessed at 6 hides; now at 2 hides. There is land for 12 ploughs. In demesne are 4 ploughs; and 14 villans and 5 cottars with 8 ploughs. There is a church. TRE it was worth 100s; and afterwards 40s; now £6.

IN 'GOLDSPUR' HUNDRED

In "EVEBENTONE" Earl Godwine held half a hide, and at so much it was assessed. There is land for 1 plough. There the count has 2 villans with 1½ ploughs. Then, as now, [worth] 12s.

The count himself holds PLAYDEN. Sigewulf held it of King Edward. Then, as now,

[Folio 20: SUSSEX]

it was assessed at 4 hides. There is land for 7 ploughs. These men hold this of the count: Eadnoth 1 hide, Walter 1 hide, Remir 1 hide, Geoffrey half a hide, Theobald the priest 3 virgates, and 1 church, and 1 plough in demesne.

Among them all they have 22 villans and 15 cottars with 10½ ploughs, and in demesne 1 plough. There are 5 acres of meadow. The whole manor TRE was worth £6; now 112s. The count has from it what is worth £7.3s.

Geoffrey, [who holds] 1 virgate, and Leofwine, 2 virgates, hold IDEN of the count. Eadnoth, a free man, held it TRE, and then, as now, it was assessed at 3 virgates. There is land for 2 ploughs, and there are [2 ploughs] in demesne, with 1 villan and 7 cottars. There are 6 acres of meadow. TRE, as now, [worth] 30s.

Three men hold 'GLOSSAMS' [in Beckley] of the count, and they held it TRE, and could go with this land where they pleased. Then, as now, it was assessed at 1½ hides. There is land for 2 ploughs. They themselves have in demesne 3 ploughs, and 1 villan and 2 cottars. There are 8 acres of meadow, and woodland for 10 pigs. TRE [worth] 40s; and afterwards 20s; now 30s.

In the same HUNDRED Alwine holds 1 virgate of the count. Edward, a free man, held it, and it was assessed at 1 virgate. There are 2 acres of meadow. Then and afterwards, as now, [worth] 5s.

IN BALDSLOW HUNDRED

In "IVET" Leofric held 1 virgate; he was a free man. It has never paid geld. Then it was worth 3s; now 12d. William holds it.

In CLAVERHAM [Claverham and Lower Claverham] Osweard, a free man, held 2 virgates. They have never paid geld. There William has 2 cottars. They were worth 5s; now 3s.

IN "HAILESALTEDE" HUNDRED

In CHALVINGTON Goda, a free man, held 2 virgates. They have never paid geld. There Reinbert has 1 villan and 1 cottar with 1 plough. Then [worth] 2s; now 4s.

In 'HEIGHTON' [in Beckley] Godwine, a free man, held 2 virgates. They have never paid geld. There Osbern has 2 villans with 1 plough. Then, as now, [worth] 4s.

In 'HEIGHTON' [in Beckley] Godwine, a free man, held 1 virgate. It has never paid geld. There Hugh has 1 cottar. Then [worth] 2s; now 12s.

In 'HEIGHTON' [in Beckley] Godwine held 1 virgate. It has never paid geld. There Hugh has 1 villan with 5 oxen. It is and was worth 20s.

In the same HUNDRED Saswalo holds 1 virgate of the count. 1 free man held this. It has never paid geld. Then [worth] 15d; now 12d.

IN STAPLE HUNDRED

The count himself holds EWHURST in demesne. Ælfhere held it of King Edward. Then it was assessed at 6 hides; now at 4 hides and 3 virgates; and there are 5 virgates in arrears because 1 hide is in the rape of the Count of Mortain. There is land for 20 ploughs. In demesne are 4 ploughs; and 12 villans and 10 bordars with 6 ploughs. There are 4 slaves, and 12 acres of meadow, and woodland for 10 pigs.

Of the land of this manor Osbern holds 1 hide and 3 virgates in BODIAM; and it always belonged to EWHURST, and there was a hall there. Rogar [holds] half a hide; Ralph 2 virgates. In demesne [are] 1½ ploughs; and 7 villans and 10 bordars with 4½ ploughs. The whole manor TRE was worth £10; and afterwards £6; now £9.

The count himself holds HIGHAM. Earl Godwine held it. TRE there were 2½ hides, but it was assessed at 2 hides, as they say, and now at 2 hides. There is land for 16 ploughs. In demesne is 1 [plough]; and 30 villans and 10 bordars with 19 ploughs. There are 6 acres of meadow, and woodland for 2 pigs. TRE it was worth 100s; now £6. It was waste.

Walter fitzLambert holds SEDLESCOMBE of the count. Leofsige held it of Countess Gode. It was assessed at 1 hide and 3 virgates outside the rape, and now at 1 hide. There is land for 4 ploughs. In demesne is 1 [plough]; and 6 villans with 2 bordars have 5 ploughs. There are 7 acres of meadow, and woodland for 6 pigs. There is a chapel. TRE [worth] 60s; and afterwards 20s; now 40s.

Wibert holds LORDINE of the count. Wynstan held it of

Osweard, and could not go where he pleased. Then, as now, it was assessed at half a hide. There is land for 3 ploughs. In demesne is 1 [plough]; and 4 villans and 3 bordars with 2 ploughs. There is 1 acre of meadow, and woodland for 1 pig. TRE, and afterwards, [worth] 14s; now 20[s].

In BELLHURST Ealdræd held 2 virgates in parage, and at so much it was assessed then, as now. There William has in demesne 1 plough; and 1 villan with 1 plough. It is and was worth 7s.

In SEDLESCOMBE Walter fitzLambert holds 1 virgate. It has never paid geld and has always been outside the rape. There is land for 1 plough. There is [1 plough] in demesne, and 3 acres of meadow, and woodland for 1 pig. Then, and afterwards, [worth] 10s; now 20s.

In the same place Geoffrey the canon holds half a hide. It belonged to Sedlescombe. It is assessed at half a hide. There are 2 bordars with 1 plough, and woodland for 3 pigs. It is worth 10s. It was waste.

The count himself holds in his demesne 1 villan, who belonged to Sedlescombe; and he holds 1 virgate outside the rape. It is worth 5s.

In the same HUNDRED Wynstan held half a hide at FOOTLAND, and could go where he pleased. It is assessed at 2 virgates. There Ansketil has 1 plough, with 1 villan, and woodland for 4 pigs. It is worth 10s.

In HURST Wulfwine held half a hide. TRE it was assessed at 2 virgates, and so it is now. There Eadnoth has in demesne 1 plough, and 1 acre of meadow. It is and was worth 10s.

Five men hold 'WELLHEAD' [in Ewhurst] of the count. There is 1 hide. 4 brothers held this, and could go where they would. There was only 1 hall. TRE, as now, it was assessed at 1 hide. Of this hide Alweald holds 2 virgates, Ansketil 3 virgates, Rogar 5 virgates, Hugh 1 virgate, Osbern 2 virgates. There is land [...]. In demesne [is] 1 plough; and 7 villans and 1 bordar have 4½ ploughs. There are 5 acres of meadow, and woodland for 20 pigs. TRE, as now, [worth] 66s.

Osbern holds "BASINGEHAM" of the count. Ælfgeat held it in parage; then, as now, it was assessed at 2 virgates. There is 1 villan. It is worth 8s.

[Folio 20V: SUSSEX]

X. The land of the Count of Mortain

IN THE BOROUGH OF PEVENSEY TRE there were 24 burgesses in the king's demesne, and they paid 14s6d as rent. From the toll, 20s; from the harbour, 35s; from the pasture, 7s3d.

The Bishop of Chichester had 5 burgesses, Eadmær the priest 15, Ordmær the priest 5, Dodda the priest 3.

When the count of Mortain received it, [there were] only 27 burgesses. Now he himself has in demesne 60 burgesses, paying 39s as rent. The toll [renders] £4; the mint, 20s.

The monks of Mortain [have] 8 burgesses paying 66d, Gilbert the sheriff 1 burgess paying 20d, William de Keynes 2 burgesses paying 2s, Boselin 5 paying 2s, William 4 paying 2s, Ansfrid 4 paying 2s, Gerald 2 paying 6s, Ansgot 3 paying 12d, Bernard 2 paying 7d, Ralph 2 paying 12d, Alan 6 paying 4s, Ralph 3 paying 56d, Azelin 3 paying 4s. He himself holds 1 house rendering 32d, and a little land rendering 3s. Walter [has] 2 burgesses paying 16d, Rogar 2 paying 12d, Hugh 1 paying 8d.

The count has a mill rendering 20s. Alvred has 15s4d from the herbage.

IN EASTBOURNE HUNDRED

The Count of Mortain holds EASTBOURNE in demesne. King Edward held it. There were and are 46 hides. There is land for 28 ploughs. In demesne are 4 ploughs; and 68 villans and 3 bordars with 28 ploughs. There is 1 mill rendering 5s, and 16 salt-pans rendering £4, and 40d, and 25 acres of meadow. From the pasture, £6.

Of the land of this manor 2 hides and 1 virgate are in the rape of Hastings.

Of the same land William holds 1 hide, Alvred 1 hide, the warders of the castle [of Pevensey] 2 hides, Roger the clerk 3 virgates.

In demesne [are] 1½ ploughs; and 2 villans and 6 bordars with half a plough. TRE it rendered one night's farm; when the count received it, £30; now his demesne [renders] £40, [that] of his men 67s.

IN 'TOTNORE' HUNDRED

The count himself holds BEDDINGHAM in demesne. King Edward held it. Then it was assessed at 52½ hides; now at 50 hides. 1½ hides and half a virgate are in the rape of Hastings. There is land for 33 ploughs. In demesne are 4 ploughs; and 68 villans and 6 bordars with 34 ploughs. There are 5 slaves, and 4 salt-pans rendering 40d, and 50 acres of meadow, and woodland for 30 pigs as pannage. From the herbage, 35s.

Of the land of this manor Geoffrey holds 4 hides, Gilbert 1½ hides. In demesne they have 3½ ploughs; and 15 bordars with half a plough, and a mill rendering 8s.

TRE it rendered 1 night's farm; when the count received it, £20; now what the count has [renders] £30, what the men [have] £6.

Walter holds 'EAST HALE' [in Eastbourne] of the count. 2 free men held it, and could go where they pleased. Then, as now, it was assessed at 3 hides. There is land for 3 ploughs. In demesne is 1 plough; with 1 villan and 8 bordars who have 1 plough. There are 2 acres of meadow. TRE it was worth 50s; and afterwards 30[s]; now 40s.

The same Walter holds 'BEVERINGTON' [in Eastbourne]. 2 men held it of King Edward, and could go where they would. It was assessed at 3 hides then, as now. [...] There is land for 3 ploughs. In demesne are 2 [ploughs]; and 2 bordars have half a plough. TRE it was worth 50s; and afterwards 30s; now 40s.

IN 'TOTNORE' HUNDRED

Hemming holds 'CHOLLINGTON' [in Eastbourne] of the count, and he himself held it of king Edward, and could go where he would. Then, as now, it was assessed at 2 hides. There is land for 2 ploughs. In demesne is 1 plough; and 1 villan and 5 bordars with 1 plough. TRE it was worth 40s; and afterwards 16s8d; now 30s.

William de Keynes holds 'BEVERINGTON' [in Eastbourne] and 'YEVERINGTON' [in Eastbourne]. 2 free men held them of King Edward. Then, as now, they were assessed at 2 hides. There is land for 3 ploughs. In demesne is half a plough, with 3 bordars, and 2 acres of meadow. TRE they were worth 30s; and afterwards 15s; now 24s.

In the same place Hugh and Mortin hold 2½ hides. Cana and Frani [held them] of King Edward, and could go where they pleased. There is land for 2 ploughs. There are [2 ploughs], with 6 villans and 1 bordar, and there is 1 acre of meadow. This land is valued in the manor of Willingdon.

Ralph fitzGunfrid holds in 1 hide 'EAST HALE' [in Eastbourne]. Edmund held it of king Edward, and could go where he pleased. It was assessed at 1 hide then, as now. TRE it was worth 15s; afterwards, as now, 10s.

In the same HUNDRED Ranulph holds 1 virgate of the count, and at so much it is assessed. Wulfhere held it of King Edward. There is land for half a plough. There is 1 villan. Then and afterwards, as now, worth 4s.

William holds ITFORD of the count. Beorhtsige held it of King Edward, and could go where he would. Then, as now, it was assessed at 4 hides. There is land for 4 ploughs. In demesne are 2 [ploughs]; and 4 villans and 2 slaves with 1 plough, and 50 acres of meadow. TRE, as now, worth £4; when received, 40s.

Ralph holds PRESTON [in Beddingham] of the count. Cola held it of King Edward. Then, as now, it was assessed at 4 hides. There is land for 3 ploughs. In demesne is 1 [plough]; and 5 villans with 2 oxen. TRE it was worth £4; and afterwards 30s; now 40s.

In the same HUNDRED the count himself holds 8 hides, but they are valued in another HUNDRED.

The Abbot of Grestain holds of the count 2 hides in BEDDINGHAM. Wulfnoth the priest held them of King Edward, and they were assessed at 2 hides then, as now. There is land for 2 ploughs. In demesne is 1 [plough]; and 2 villans and 2 bordars with 1 plough. TRE, as now, worth 40s; when received, 30[s].

Durand holds 6 hides of the count in CHARLESTON [in West Firle]. 3 free men held them of King Edward as 3 manors. Then, as now, they were assessed at 6 hides. There is land for 5 ploughs. In demesne [is] half a plough; and 1 villan and 1 bordar with 2 oxen.

Of this land Roger holds 2 hides, Gilbert 2 hides. These have in demesne 2 ploughs; and 2 villans and 2 bordars with 1 plough.

TRE it was worth 60s; and afterwards 40s; now 100s. for the whole.

In the same place Hubert holds 2 hides of the count. Alnoth held them of King Edward, and could go where he would. There is land for half a plough. In demesne is 1 plough; and 2 villans and 2 bordars with 1½ ploughs. TRE, and afterwards, it was worth 10s; now 20s.

In TILTON William de Keynes holds 2 hides of the count. Ælfhere held them as 1 manor of King Edward. There is land for 2 ploughs. Then, as now, it was assessed at 2 hides. In demesne is 1 plough; and 2 villans with half a plough. Then and afterwards, as now, [worth] 20s.

The same William holds SHERRINGTON of the count. Edward held it of King Edward, and could go where he would. There is land for 5 ploughs. Then it was assessed at 5 hides; now half a hide is in the rape of Hastings. In demesne is 1 plough, and 2 bordars. TRE it was worth 60s; and afterwards 25s; now 40s. For the half-hide which is not there they deduct 20s.

[Folio 21: SUSSEX]

In the same place Hemming holds 5 hides of the count, and he himself held them of King Edward. Then they were assessed at 5 hides; now half a hide is in the rape of Hastings. There is land for 4 ploughs. In demesne [are] 1½ ploughs; and 2 villans with half a plough, and 3 bordars. TRE it was worth 60s; and afterwards 25s; now 40s.

Osbern holds of the count 4 hides in TILTON. Godwine held them of King Edward as a manor. Then they were assessed at 4 hides; now at 2 hides and 1 virgate. There is land for 4 ploughs. There is nothing now except 2 villans, and 4 acres of meadow. TRE it was worth 70s; now 20s.

In the same place the count himself has 1 hide, William 1 hide, Ralph 1 hide. Godwine held this land. There is land for 4 ploughs. It was worth 18s; now 15s.

The count himself holds WEST FIRLE in demesne. The Abbey of Wilton held it TRE, and then it was assessed at 48 hides; now at nothing. Of this land 7 hides are in the rape of Hastings. There is land for 40 ploughs.[...] In demesne the count has 5 ploughs; and 80 villans with 34 ploughs. There are 2 mills rendering 30s, and 72 acres of meadow, and woodland for 40 pigs.

Of these hides the clerks of St Pancras have 2½ hides, Roger 1 mill, Joscelin 1 hide, William 1 hide, Gilbert 2 hides, the warders of the castle [of Pevensey] 3 hides and 20 acres. In demesne [are] 6 ploughs; and 3 villans and 11 bordars with 4 ploughs. There are 7 acres of meadow. Gilbert also holds 60 acres of waste land. The whole manor TRE was worth £60; and afterwards £30; now what the count has [is worth] £40, what the other men [have] £4.10s.

In 'COMPTON' [in West Firle] the count himself holds 4 hides. Harold held them of King Edward. Then, as now, they were assessed at 4 hides. This land is valued in LAUGHTON.

IN WILLINGDON HUNDRED

Walter holds 2½ hides of the count in EXCEAT. Dodda held them of King Edward, and could go where he would. Then, as now, they were assessed at 2½ hides. There is land for 2 ploughs. In demesne is 1 [plough]; and 7 bordars with 1 plough. TRE, as now, [worth] 40s.

In the same place William holds 3 hides of the count. Edward and Alwine held them of King Edward, and could go where they would. Then, as now, they were assessed at 3 hides. There is land for 3 ploughs. In demesne is 1 plough, with 7 bordars. TRE it was worth 50s; and afterwards 30s; now 40s.

Ralph holds of the count 7½ hides in JEVINGTON. Cola held them of King Edward as a manor. Then, as now, they were assessed at 7 hides. [There is] land for 14 ploughs. In demesne is 1 plough; and 16 villans with 5 bordars have 4 ploughs. There is 1 slave, and a mill rendering 8s. TRE it was worth £6; and afterwards £3; now £4.10s.

The count himself holds WILLINGDON in demesne. Earl Godwine held it. Then it was assessed at 50½ hides; now at nothing. Of this land there are 14½ hides in the rape of Hastings. There is land for 36 ploughs. In demesne are 6 ploughs; and 75 villans and 24 bordars with 26 ploughs. There are 60 acres of meadow, and 11 salt-pans rendering 35s. There is 1 slave, and woodland for 3 pigs.

Of this land Osbern holds of the count 4 hides, William 1 hide, Joscelin 2 hides, Gilbert 1 hide, Alwine 1 hide, Ansgot 2 hides, Godfrey the priest 1 hide and 1 virgate. In demesne [are] 3½ ploughs; and 2 villans and 4 bordars with 1 plough. The whole manor TRE was worth £60; and afterwards £30; now what the count holds [is worth] £40, what the men [hold] £7.

The count himself holds 'WEST BURTON' [in Friston] in demesne. Ælfric and Goldwine held it of King Edward, and could go where they would. Then [...] it was assessed at 2 hides; now at nothing. There is land for 2 ploughs. There are 3 villans with 1½ ploughs. It is worth 24s.

Hemming holds EXCEAT of the count, and he himself held it of King Edward. Then, as now, it was assessed at 4½ hides. There is land for 4 ploughs. In demesne [are] 1½ ploughs; and 3 villans and 6 bordars have half a plough, and there is 1 slave. TRE it was worth £4; now £3.

Ralph holds CHARLESTON [near Eastbourne] of the count. Wulfric held it of King Edward. Then it was assessed at 10 hides; now 2½ hides are in the rape of Hastings. There is land for 8 ploughs. In demesne is 1 [plough; and] 6 villans and 8 bordars with 4 ploughs. There are 3 slaves, and 3 salt-pans rendering 10s4d, and 20 acres of meadow. TRE it was worth £9; now £4.10s.

Joscelin holds RATTON of the count. Wulfhun held it of Earl Godwine. Then it was assessed at 6 hides, and now at 4 hides. In the rape of Hastings are 2 hides less 1 virgate. There is land for 7 ploughs. In demesne [is] 1 plough; and 8 villans and 5 bordars with 2½ ploughs. There is 1 mill rendering 4s, and 6 acres of meadow.

Of the land of this manor Azelin holds 1 hide in alms of the count, Ranulph half a hide, Ansfrid half a hide. The whole manor TRE was worth £6; now £4.10s.

Ralph holds of the count in the same HUNDRED 1 manor, which Wulfmær held of King Edward. Then it was assessed at 4½ hides; now half a hide is in the rape of Hastings. There is land for 6 ploughs. There is 1 villan and 2 bordars and 2 slaves. TRE it was worth £4; and afterwards, as now, 30s.

Osbern holds [?] WESTDEAN of the count. Edwin held it of King [Edward] as a manor. Then, as now, it was assessed at 2 hides. There is land for 1½ ploughs. There are 5 villans and 3 bordars with 2 ploughs. TRE it was worth 30s; and afterwards, as now, 20s.

In [?] WESTDEAN Ralph holds 8 hides of the count. Azur held them of King Edward as a manor. Then, as now, they were assessed at 8 hides. There is land for 8 ploughs. In demesne are 2 ploughs; and 11 villans and 4 bordars with 3 ploughs. There are 3 slaves, and 4 salt-pans rendering 8s. TRE it was worth £7; and afterwards 60s; now 100s.

IN WILLINGDON HUNDRED

Ralph holds RATTON of the count. Osweard held it of King Edward as a manor. Then it was assessed at 5 hides; now 1 is in the rape of Hastings. There is land for 5 ploughs. In demesne are 2 [ploughs]; and 4 villans and 4 bordars with half a plough. There are 4 acres of meadow, [and] pasture rendering 28s. TRE it was worth 100s; now £4.

In RATTON Morin holds 3 hides of the count. Cana held them of King Edward | as a manor | . Then they were assessed at 3 hides; now half a hide is in the rape of Hastings. There is land for 7 ploughs. In demesne is 1 [plough]; and 6 villans and 3 bordars with 1 plough. There are 2 acres of meadow, and the fourth part of a salt-pan rendering 10d. TRE it was worth 60s; and afterwards 20s; now 40s.

In RATTON Hugh holds 3 hides of the count. Frani held them of King Edward as a manor. Then they were assessed at 3 hides; now half a hide is in the rape of Hastings. There is land for 7 ploughs. In demesne is half a plough; and 5 villans and 3 bordars with 2 ploughs. There are 2 acres of meadow, and the fourth part of a salt-pan rendering 10d. TRE it was worth 60s; now 40s.

William holds WANNOCK of the count. Northmann held it of King Edward as a manor. Then, as now, it was assessed at 6 hides. There is land for 8 ploughs. In demesne are 3 ploughs; and 3 villans with 1 plough. There are 4 acres of meadow. TRE it was worth 110s; and afterwards 40s; now £4.10s.

IN "AVRONEHELLE" HUNDRED

[Folio 21V: SUSSEX]

The Abbot of Grestain holds WILMINGTON of the count. Alnoth held it of Earl Godwine. Then, as now, it was assessed at 8 hides. There is land for 9 ploughs. One of these hides lies in the rape of Hastings.

In the same place the same abbot holds 4 hides which Wulfnoth held of Earl Godwine. Then, as now, they were assessed at 4 hides.

In the same place the same abbot holds 2 hides of the count which Wulfstan held of Earl Godwine. Then, as now, they were assessed at 2 hides. [...] In demesne are 3 ploughs; and 16 villans and 10 bordars with 6 ploughs. There are 3 slaves. TRE, as now, worth £13.

William holds FOLKINGTON of the count. Goda held it of King Edward, and could go where he would. Then, as now, it was assessed at 6 hides. There is land for 5 ploughs. In demesne are 3 ploughs; and 4 villans and 6 bordars with 1½ ploughs. TRE it was worth 100s; and afterwards 40s; now 60s.

IN 'FLEXBOROUGH' HUNDRED

The count himself holds TARRING NEVILLE in demesne. Azur held it of Earl Godwine. Then, as now, it was assessed at 8 hides. There is land for 5 ploughs. In demesne are 2½ ploughs; and 11 villans and 9 bordars with 3 ploughs. There are 3 slaves, and 50 acres of meadow. From the pastures, 40d. TRE it was worth £8; and afterwards £6; now £10.

The Abbot of Grestain holds FROG FIRLE of the count. Queen Edith held it, and gave it to St John TRE. Then it was assessed at 8 hides; now at 5 hides.

In the same place the same abbot holds 1 hide which Earl Godwine held. There is land for 4 ploughs. In demesne are 2 [ploughs]; and 4 villans with 2 ploughs, and 3 bordars. TRE, and afterwards, worth £3; now £4.

In the same place Hemming holds 2 hides of the count. He himself held them of Earl Godwine. Then, as now, they were assessed at 2 hides. There is land for 1 plough. There is 1 villan and 1 bordar with 1 plough. TRE [worth] 30s; now 20s.

William holds SOUTH HEIGHTON of the count. Gundulf held it of King Edward as 1 manor. Then, as now, [it was assessed] at 2 hides. There is land for 2 ploughs. In demesne is 1 [plough]; and 2 villans and 3 bordars with 2 oxen. TRE, as now, [it was worth] 30s; when received, 20s.

In the same HUNDRED Durand holds 1 hide of the count. Alweard held it of King Edward as 1 manor. Then, as now, it was assessed at 1 hide. There is land for half a plough. There are 2 oxen, with 1 bordar. [There is] woodland for 1 pig. TRE it was worth 20s; now 10s.

In FROG FIRLE Alan holds 4 hides of the count. Almær and Godwine held them of King Edward as 2 manors. Then, as now, they were assessed at 4 hides. There is half a hide outside the rape which does not belong to these. There is land for 4 ploughs. In demesne are 2 ploughs, with 15 bordars. TRE, as now, worth 60s; and afterwards 30s.

IN 'DILL' HUNDRED

In "PENGEST" the count has in demesne 1 virgate of land. Wulfgeat held it of King Edward, and could go where he would. Then, as now, it was assessed at 1 virgate. There is land for 1 plough. There is 1 villan with half a plough. TRE, as now, worth 25d.

In 'HAWKRIDGE' [in Hellingly] the count has 1 hide, but half is in the rape of Hastings, and now it is assessed at half a

hide. Beorhtwig held it in alod. There is land for 2 ploughs. There is 1 villan with 2 ploughs, and woodland for 4 pigs as pannage. TRE it was worth 20s; and afterwards 10s; now 15s.

In 'HENDON' [in Hailsham] the count has half a hide, and at so much it is assessed. Almær held it in alod. There is land for 2 ploughs. There is 1 villan with 1 plough, and 2 bordars. TRE it was worth 9s; and afterwards 4s; now 5s.

IN "WANDELMESTREI" HUNDRED

William holds of the count SELMESTON and 'SIDNOR' [in Selmeston]. Ælfhere held them in alod. Then, as now, they were assessed at 4½ hides. There is land for 7 ploughs. In demesne are 3 ploughs; and 4 villans and 3 bordars with 4 ploughs. There is a church, and a priest, and 5 slaves. TRE, as now, worth 70s; when received, 40s.

Ralph holds of the count 1 hide in 'SIDNOR' [in Selmeston], and at so much it is assessed. Wulfmær Cild held it in alod. There is land for 1 plough, and there is [1 plough], with 1 villan. TRE it was worth 8s; and afterwards 6s; now 10s.

In the same place Walter holds half a hide of the count, and at so much it is assessed. Godwine held it. There is land for half a plough, and there is [half a plough], with 1 villan. It is and was worth 4s.

Gerald holds of the count 1 hide in SESSINGHAM. Half of it is in the rape of Hastings. Alwine held it in alod. There is land for 6 ploughs, and there are [6 ploughs], with 16 villans, and 1 mill rendering 10s and 500 eels. TRE, as now, [worth] 60s; when received, 20s.

Gilbert holds 1 hide at farm of the count in ALFRISTON. Ælfric held it in alod. There is land for 1 plough. There is now 1 bordar. TRE and afterwards, as now, [worth] 8s.

In ALFRISTON itself Ranulph holds of the count 1 hide, Ralph half a hide, William half a hide, Ralph 1 hide, Walter 2 hides. All together 5 hides, and at so much they are assessed. Leofwine, Alweald, Alnoth, and Godwine held this land in alod. There is land for 5 ploughs. In demesne now [are] 3½ ploughs; and 2 villans and 6 bordars do half the ploughing. TRE the whole was worth 20s; now 54s.

IN HARTFIELD HUNDRED

The count himself holds "WILDENE" in demesne. Earl Harold held it. Then, as now, it was assessed at 2 hides. There is land for 7 ploughs. In demesne are 2 [ploughs]; and 7 villans and 3 bordars have 5 ploughs. TRE, and afterwards, it was worth 60s; now 70s.

In HARTFIELD Walter holds 1 hide of the count, and at so much it is assessed. Karli held it in alod. There is land for 3 ploughs. In demesne are 1½ ploughs; and 6 villans and 2 slaves with 1½ ploughs. There is 1 mill rendering 4s and 350 eels, and 3 acres of meadow, and woodland for 5 pigs as pannage. TRE, as now, [worth] 40s; when received, 20s.

In the same HUNDRED the count has 1½ hides outside the rape, and they belong to the manor of Rodmell. Earl Godwine held them, and they have never paid geld. There is land for 6 ploughs. There are 7 villans and 1 bordar with 5 ploughs. There is woodland for 40 pigs. TRE, as now, [worth] 40s; when received, 30s.

In the same HUNDRED Ralph holds at farm of the count 1 hide outside the rape. Azur held it in alod, and it has never paid geld. There is land for 2 ploughs. There are 3 villans with 2 ploughs. TRE and afterwards, as now, [worth] 10s.

In [Little, Lower and Upper] PARROCK the count himself holds half a hide. It has never paid geld. It is outside the rape. Queen Edith held it. There is land for 2 ploughs. There are 2 villans with $1\frac{1}{2}$ ploughs. [There is] woodland for 40 pigs and 12s. There is 1 virgate where the count has his hall. In the same way Earl Harold had it, and he took it away from St John. TRE and afterwards, as now, [worth] 52s.

IN FRAMFIELD HUNDRED

There William holds of the count 1 virgate outside the rape. It has never paid geld. Leofwine held it in alod. There is land for half a plough, and there is [half a plough], with 3 bordars. [There is] woodland for 1 pig as pannage. TRE [worth] 10s; and afterwards, as now, 5s.

Ralph holds 1 hide and 1 virgate of the count in WORTH, and at so much

[Folio 22: SUSSEX]

they are assessed. Helghi held them of King Edward, and could go where he would. There is land for 6 ploughs. In demesne are $1\frac{1}{2}$ ploughs; and 8 villans and 1 bordar with 2 ploughs. There is 1 mill rendering 9s, and 2 acres of meadow, and woodland for 6 pigs. TRE, as now, [worth] 50s; when received, 30s.

Ranulph holds of the count in LITTLE HORSTED 5 hides and 3 virgates, and at so much they are assessed. Wulfhere held them of King Edward, and could go where he would. There is land for $7\frac{1}{2}$ ploughs. In demesne are 2 [ploughs]; and 9 villans and 6 bordars with $4\frac{1}{2}$ ploughs, and 1 mill rendering 8s.

Of this land, 1 hide lies in the rape of Lewes, and Azelin holds another hide in 'Bechington' [in Friston], and Grento holds $1\frac{1}{2}$ virgates. These men have $1\frac{1}{2}$ ploughs in demesne.

The whole TRE was worth 100s; and afterwards 50s; now 60s.

IN PEVENSEY HUNDRED

The count himself holds $4\frac{1}{2}$ hides at "LODINTONE", and at so much they are assessed. 6 thegns held this land in alod. There is land for 5 ploughs. In demesne are 2 ploughs; and 5 villans with 5 ploughs, and 1 mill rendering 20s, and pasture rendering 20s, and 5 salt-pans rendering 41s and 8s. [sic] TRE it was worth 30s; now £6.11s8d.

William holds $1\frac{1}{2}$ hides of the count at HAILSHAM, and at so much they are assessed. Alnoth held them in alod. There is land for 4 ploughs. There are 4 bordars with 1 ox, and 2 salt-pans rendering 7s. TRE it was worth 110s; now 20s.

In this manor the count has kept back 11 salt-pans, which are worth 24s6d.

Ansfrid holds 2 hides of the count at "CHENENOLLE". There is land for 2 ploughs. Toki held them in alod. In demesne is half a plough; and 1 villan with half a plough, and 5 acres of meadow. TRE it was worth 40s; now 15s.

The same Ansfrid holds half a hide of the count in WILLINGDON, and at so much it is assessed. Leofweard held it in alod. There is land for half a plough. Then, as now, it was worth 10s.

Godfrey the clerk holds 1 hide in alms in Peelings, and there he has 2 bordars; they pay 8d. It is and was worth 3s.

Roger the clerk holds 1 hide at 'CUDNOR' [in Westham] in alms. There is land for 1 plough, and there is [1 plough] in demesne with 1 bordar, and 1 ox. Beorhtwine held it.

The same Roger holds at Horse Eye 1 hide in alms of St Michael. Clerks held it in common. There is land for 1 plough. There is 1 villan with 1 plough. These 2 hides then, as now, were assessed at so much. Then [worth] 10s; now 22s.

Walter holds 1 hide of the count, and at so much it is assessed. Beorhtwine held it at 'CUDNOR' [in Westham]. There is land for half a plough, and there is [half a plough] in demesne. It is worth 5s.

Ansfrid holds 2 hides of the count at THE HORNS, and at so much they are assessed. 3 men held them in alod. There are 2 bordars, and 8 acres of meadow. TRE it was worth 25s; now 10s.

Ranulph holds 1 hide of the count at THE HORNS. [...] There is land for 2 ploughs. There is 1 bordar. Then it was worth 13s; now 63d.

In HOOE the count holds 4 salt-pans in demesne, which are worth 20s.

In 'RENCHING' [in Westham] William and Ralph and another Ralph hold 2 hides of the count, and at so much they are assessed. 2 free men held them in alod. There is land for 4 ploughs. There are 2 villans and 1 bordar, and 2 oxen ploughing. TRE it was worth 16s; now 15s.

In PEELINGS Alan and Godfrey and Ansfrid and Roger hold 4 hides of the count, and at so much they are assessed. There is land for 4 ploughs. Alweard and Algar held them of King [Edward] as 2 manors in alod. There is now 1 villan and 1 bordar.

In LANGNEY Ranulph holds 1 hide of the count, and at so much it is assessed. Leofmær and Beorhtstan held it in alod. There are 2 bordars.

In the same place William holds 1 hide, and at so much it is assessed. Ælfheah held it. There are 2 bordars. TRE it was worth 16s8d; now 10s.

William holds of the count at HANKHAM 2 hides, which were part of the manor of EASTBOURNE. There is land for 3 ploughs. There are 4 bordars. TRE it was worth 15s; now 8s.

In HANKHAM the count has 1 hide and half a virgate. King Edward held them. There is land for 1 plough. Of this [holding] no return [has been made].

In the same place Ansgot holds of the count half a hide which belonged to EASTBOURNE It is worth 9s.

In 'BOWLEY' [in Hailsham] William holds half a hide of the count. Earl Harold held it. There is land for 2 ploughs, and there are [2 ploughs], with 2 villans and 1 bordar, and 8 acres of meadow, and 4 salt-pans rendering 22s4d. TRE worth 15s; now 30s.

In "LODIUTONE" should be paid 13s from pasture which the count has given him.

IN "EDIVESTONE" HUNDRED

The count himself holds RIPE. Earl Harold held it. Then, as now, it was assessed at 22 hides. Of these, 8 lie in the rape of Hastings. There is land for 10 ploughs. In demesne are 2 ploughs; and 16 villans and 8 bordars with 8 ploughs. There are 12 acres of meadow, and 8 salt-pans rendering 20s. TRE it was worth £12; now £8.

The count himself holds CLAVERHAM [Claverham and Lower Claverham]. Osweard held it of King Edward. Then, as now, it was assessed at 4 hides. There is land for 4 ploughs. In demesne is 1 [plough]; and 2 villans and 2 bordars and 2 slaves with half a plough.

Of these 4 hides, half a hide is in the rape of Hastings, and Alvred holds 1 hide, and has there 1 villan. The whole TRE was worth 40s; now 36s.

In CLAVERHAM [Claverham and Lower Claverham] Morin holds of the count 1 hide and 1 virgate, Hugh 3 hides less 1 virgate. Cana and Frani held them as 2 manors of King Edward. Then, as now, they were assessed at 4 hides. There is land for 3½ ploughs. In demesne are 1½ ploughs, and 1 villan and 5 bordars. TRE it was worth 45s; now 40s.

William holds ECKINGTON of the count. Aghmund held it of King Edward. Then it was assessed at 5 hides; now at 3, because 2 lie in the rape of Hastings. There is land for 4 ploughs. In demesne are 2 ploughs; and 8 bordars with 1 plough. There is woodland for 10 pigs

Of this land a man of his holds half a hide, and there he has 1 plough in demesne. TRE it was worth 100s; now 60s.

In ECKINGTON and CHALVINGTON the count himself holds in demesne 5 hides, and at so much they are assessed. Queen Edith held them as 2 manors. There is land for 6 ploughs. There are 7 villans with 2 ploughs. TRE it was worth 40s; now 30s.

In CHALVINGTON Ansfrid holds 4 hides of the count, and at so much they are assessed. Osweard and Toti held them as 2 manors in alod. There is land for 1½ ploughs. In demesne is 1 plough, with 2 bordars and 2 slaves. Of this land, half a hide lies in the rape of Hastings, and Humphrey holds 1 hide, and there he has half a plough in demesne. TRE, as now, [worth] 40s.

In WALDRON Ansfrid holds 1 hide of the count, and at so much it is assessed. Ælfgifu held it of King Edward in alod. There is land for 3½ ploughs. In demesne is 1 plough, with 1 villan. Then, as now, [worth] 20s.

The count himself holds LAUGHTON in demesne. Earl Godwine held it. Then it was assessed at 10 hides; now at 6, because 4 lie in the rape of Hastings.

[Folio 22V: SUSSEX]

There is land for 16 ploughs. In demesne are 3 ploughs; and 14 villans and 3 bordars with 10½ ploughs. There are 16 salt-pans rendering 25s. TRE it was worth £15; now £10.5s.

The count himself holds 'STOCKINGHAM' [in Laughton]. Leofnoth held it of King Edward. Then, as now, it was assessed at 10 hides. There is land for 8 ploughs. In demesne is 1 plough; and 10 villans with 4½ ploughs. From the herbage, 12 pigs. TRE, as now, [worth] 60s.

In CHIDDINGLY Ralph and Godwine hold 1 virgate of the count. Almær held it of King [Edward] in alod. Then, as now, it was assessed at 1 virgate. There is land for 3 ploughs. In demesne is 1 plough; and 2 villans with 1 plough, and 1 mill with a miller rendering 4s. Another virgate lies in the rape of Hastings. TRE it was worth 20s; now the same.

IN EAST GRINSTEAD HUNDRED

In SHOVELSTRODE the count has 1 hide, which lay in the rape of Lewes. Now it is outside the rape. It does not pay geld. Alnoth held it of King Edward. There is land for 2 ploughs. There are [2 ploughs], with 1 villan and 3 bordars. From the herbage, 3 pigs; from the woodland, 5. TRE, as now, worth 20s.

In SHOVELSTRODE Ansfrid holds of the count 1 virgate outside the rape. It has never paid geld. Almær held it of King Edward. There is land for 1 plough. There is [1 plough], with 1 villan. [There is] woodland and herbage for 2 pigs. TRE it was worth 5s; now 7s.

In "FELESMERE" the count holds 1½ hides outside the rape. It has not paid geld. Villans held it, and it is valued in the manor.

In BURLEIGH William holds 1½ hides of the count. It is outside the rape. It has not paid geld. TRE Ælfhere held it of HOLY TRINITY in the manor of WOOTTON [in East Chiltington], as the hundred testifies. There is land for 4 ploughs. There are 3 villans with 1 plough. TRE it was worth 20s; now 10s.

The same William holds 'WARDLEIGH' [in East Grinstead] of the count. There are 2 hides. It has never paid geld. It is outside the rape. Wulfgifu held it of King Edward as 1 manor. There is land for 5 ploughs. There are 3 villans with 3 ploughs. From the herbage, 5 pigs, and woodland for 2 pigs. Then [worth] 20s; now 15s.

The same William holds of the count outside the rape 1 virgate, "Sperchedene". It belonged to "Wildetone", and has never paid geld. Cana held it of King Edward. There is land for half a plough. Then worth 3s; now 2s.

Ansfrid holds of the count outside the rape 2 hides less 1 virgate. King Edward held them. They belonged to the manor of Ditchling, and have not paid geld. There is land for 6 ploughs. From the woodland and the herbage, 6 pigs. There is 1 acre of meadow, and a forge. There are 6 villans with 2 ploughs. TRE it was worth 15s; now 20s.

The same Ansfrid holds half a hide outside the rape; it is called Hazelden. Wulfweard held it of King Edward. It belonged to Allington, and has never paid geld. There is land for 2 ploughs. It was worth 10s; now 5s.

The same Ansfrid holds of the count outside the rape half a hide, Brockhurst. Frani held it of King Edward. It belonged to Warningore. It has never paid geld. There is land for 1 plough, and there is [1 plough], with 1 villan. It was worth 15s; now 5s.

Ralph holds BRAMBLETYE of the count. Cola held it of King Edward. Then, as now, it was assessed at 1 hide. There is land for 1½ ploughs. There is a priest, with 1 villan, and 1½ ploughs, and 14 bordars. From the woodland and herbage, 12 pigs, and [there are] 5 acres of meadow, and 1 mill [rendering] 2s. TRE it was worth 30s; now 20s.

The same Ralph holds 'WHALESBEECH' [in Weir Wood Reservoir] of the count outside the rape. There is 1 hide. Folki held it of King Edward. It belonged to EAST LAVANT. It has never paid geld. There is land for 3 ploughs. There are 2 villans with half a plough. It was worth 30s; now 20s.

The count himself holds outside the rape 1½ virgates, Standen. Azur held it of King Edward. It belonged to Bevendean [Bevendean and Lower Bevendean]. It has never paid geld. It is accounted for and valued in the manor of Tarring Neville.

The count himself holds FAIRLIGHT as 1 virgate. It is outside the rape, in the rape of Lewes. It belonged to DITCHLING. It has never paid geld. There is land for half a plough. There is 1 villan with 1 plough. It was worth 10s; now 5s.

IN RUSTON HUNDRED

William holds HORSTED KEYNES of the count. It is outside the rape. Wulfgifu held it of King Edward. It belonged to HAMSEY. It has never paid geld. There are 4 hides. There is land for 8 ploughs. In demesne is 1 [plough]; and 9 villans with 3 ploughs. There is 1 mill rendering 2s, and 3 bordars. TRE it was worth 60s; now 40s.

The same William holds of the count outside the rape 1 virgate in Birchgrove. Goda held it of King Edward in alod. It belonged to Balmer. It has never paid geld. There is land for half a plough. It is and was worth 2s. There is 1 villan.

The count himself holds SHEFFIELD. Godwine held it of King Edward in alod. Then, as now, [it was assessed] at 6 hides. There is land for 11 ploughs. In demesne is 1 plough; and 9 villans and 5 bordars with 7 ploughs. There is 1 mill rendering 40d and 500 eels, and 10 acres of meadow. From the woodland and herbage, 32 pigs. TRE it was worth 100s; now £4.

Ansfrid holds 1 hide of the count in FLETCHING, and at so much it is assessed. Leofwine held it as a manor of King Edward. There is land for 3 ploughs. There are 4 villans and 3 bordars with 2 ploughs. From the woodland and herbage, 6 pigs, and there is 1 acre of meadow. TRE it was worth 40s; now 20s.

Morin and Hugh hold FLETCHING of the count. Cana held it of King Edward. Then, as now, it was assessed at 2 hides. There is land for 5 ploughs. In demesne [is] 1 plough; and 11 villans and 5 bordars with 4 ploughs. There are 6 acres of meadow, and from the woodland, 30 pigs. TRE it was worth £4; now 50s.

Gilbert holds of the count outside the rape half a hide at Barkham. Karli held it of King Edward. It has never paid geld. There is land for 1 plough, and there is [1 plough], with 3 villans. It was worth 7s; now 9s.

Warner holds 3 virgates of the count in BARKHAM, and at so much they are assessed. Earl Godwine held them of King Edward as a manor in alod. There is land for 3 ploughs. In demesne is 1 plough; and 4 villans and 5 bordars with 2 ploughs. There are 6 acres of meadow. From the woodland and herbage, 9 pigs. TRE and afterwards, as now, worth 20s.

Alan holds of the count 1 virgate, "Inode". It is outside the rape. It belonged to the New Minster, and has never paid geld. Almær held it as a manor of King Edward. There is land for 1½ ploughs. In demesne is 1 [plough]; and 2 villans and 2 bordars with half a plough. TRE it was worth 15s; now 10s.

IN ROTHERFIELD HUNDRED

The count himself holds 2 hides which Alweard and Wulfweard held of King Edward as 2 manors. There is land for 6 ploughs. Of this land Ansfrid holds 1 hide of the count, Humphrey 1 virgate, William 1 virgate and 1 ferding, and a certain Englishman 1 virgate. In demesne are 4½ ploughs; and 6 villans and 8 bordars with 6 ploughs. There is 1 slave, and 1 mill rendering 30d. TRE it was worth 30s; now 73s.

The count himself holds "MESEWELLE". Godwine held it. Then, as now, [it was assessed] at 4 hides. There is land for 2 ploughs, and there are [2 ploughs], with 4 villans and 5 bordars. In demesne is 1 plough. From the woodland, 30 pigs. TRE it was worth £4; now 40s.

Of this land William de Warenne holds 3 virgates of land and 1 mill.

[Folio 23: SUSSEX]

XI. The land of Earl Roger

IN CHICHESTER City TRE there were 100 closes less 2½, and 3 crofts, and they rendered 49s less 1d. Now the city itself is in the hand of Earl Roger, and there are on the same messuages 60 houses more than there were before, and there is 1 mill rendering 5s. It rendered £15: to the king £10, to the earl 100s; now it is worth £25, and yet it renders £35.

Humpery Flamme has there 1 close rendering 10s.

ARUNDEL CASTLE TRE rendered from a certain mill 40s, and for 3 entertainments 20s, and for 1 day's food-rent 20s. Now, between the borough and the port of the river and ship-dues it renders £12, and yet it is worth £13; of this St Nicholas has 24s. There is 1 fishery rendering 5s, and 1 mill rendering 10 modii of wheat, and 10 modii of rough corn, [and] in addition 4 modii. This is valued at £14.

Robert fitzTheobald has 2 closes rendering 2s, and he has his toll from outsiders.

Morin has there a customary due of 12d from 2 burgesses. Arnold [has] 1 burges paying 12d, Saint-Martin 1 burgess paying 12d, Ralph 1 close rendering 12d, William 5 closes rendering 5s, Nigel 5 closes [whose tenants] do service.

IN SINGLETON HUNDRED

Earl Roger holds SINGLETON in demesne. Earl Godwine held it. Then it was assessed at 100 hides less 2½ now at 47 hides. There is land for 40 ploughs. In demesne are 7 ploughs; and 86 villans and 52 bordars with 33 ploughs. There are 17 slaves, and 2 mills rendering 12s7d, and 60 acres of meadow, and from the woodland, 150 pigs. There is a church to which belong 3 hides and 1 virgate of this land. The clerks have 2 ploughs, and 5 bordars.

Of the land of this manor Pain holds of the earl 1 hide, William 1 hide, Geoffrey 2 hides. In demesne [is] 1 plough; and 3 villans and 1 bordar and 3 slaves with half a plough. To this manor belong 9 closes in Chichester; they render 7s4d, and [there is] 1 mill rendering 40d, and from the herbage, 15s. A monk of Saint-Evroul holds 1 hide of the land of this manor. It is worth 10s. The whole manor TRE was worth £89; and afterwards £57. Now it is valued at £93 and 1 mark of gold, yet what belongs to the earl renders £120 and 1 mark of gold. What the clerks hold [is worth] £8, and yet they have £10. What the knights [have is worth] £14.

The earl himself holds BINDERTON. Countess Gytha held it. Then it was assessed at 7 hides; now at 3 hides. There is land for 4 ploughs. In demesne are 2 ploughs; and 8 villans and 9 bordars with 2 ploughs. There are 4 acres of meadow. There is a church. TRE it was worth 100s; and afterwards 60s; now £7.

Ivo holds MID LAVANT of the earl. Godwine held it of Earl Godwine. Then, as now, it was assessed at 9 hides. There is land for 5 ploughs. In demesne are 2 [ploughs]; and 10 villans and 10 bordars with 3 ploughs. There is 1 mill rendering 7s, and in Chichester 1 close rendering 5d. TRE, as now, [worth] £8.

There Guy holds 1 hide, and at so much it is assessed. Alweard held it of Earl Godwine as a manor. There is nothing there; yet it is and was worth 20s.

IN DUMPFORD HUNDRED

The earl himself holds [East, South and West] HARTING in demesne. Countess Gytha held it of King Edward. Then it was assessed at 80 hides; now at 48 hides. There is land for 64 ploughs. In demesne are 10 ploughs; and 128 villans and 35 bordars with 51 ploughs. There are 20 slaves, and 9 mills rendering £4 and 18d. From the herbage 18s, and [there are] 30 acres of meadow, [and] woodland for 100 pigs. In Chichester, 11 closes rendering 15s.

Of the land of this manor the clerks of St Nicholas hold 6 hides, and there they have 6 villans and 7 bordars with 3 ploughs, and so it was TRE. The whole manor TRE was worth £80; and afterwards £60; now £100.

The earl himself holds TROTTON in demesne. Countess Gytha held it of King Edward. Then it was assessed at 9 hides; now at 3. There is land for 36 ploughs. In demesne are 2 [ploughs]; and 4 villans and 10 bordars with 3 ploughs. There is a church, and 1 mill rendering 12s6d, and 5 acres of meadow, and from the woodland 10 pigs. TRE it was worth 60s; and afterwards 30s; now 100s, and yet these 2 manors, [East, South and West] Harting and Trotton, render £120 and 1 mark of gold.

Robert fitzTheobald holds TREYFORD of the earl. Æthelheard held it of Earl Godwine. Then, as now, it was assessed at 11 hides. There is land for 6 ploughs. In demesne are 2 [ploughs]; and 8 villans and 8 bordars with 4 ploughs. There are 5 slaves, and 1 mill rendering 30d, and 6½ acres of meadow, and woodland for 10 pigs.

Of the land of this manor 2 hides belong to a prebend of the church of Chichester. Robert holds them of the bishop. Offa held them of the bishop in fief as a manor. They were assessed at 2 hides then, as now. It is valued at 8s, but yet it renders 15s. The whole manor TRE, as now, was worth 100s; when received, 60s. The Abbot of ST PETER of Winchester claims this manor. The HUNDRED testifies that TRE the man who held it of the abbot held it only for the term of his life.

Morin holds CHITHURST of the earl. Almær held it of Earl Godwine in alod. Then, as now, it was assessed at 4 hides. There is land for 2 ploughs. In demesne is 1 [plough]; and 6 villans and 5 bordars with 2 ploughs. There is a chapel, and 3 slaves, and 1 mill rendering 8s and 100 eels, and 5 acres of meadow, and from the woodland, 3 pigs. In Chichester, 1 close rendering 6d. TRE it was worth 40s; and afterwards 30s; now 60s.

Robert holds STEDHAM of the earl. Edith held it of Earl Godwine. Then, as now, it was assessed at 14 hides. There is land for 15 ploughs. In demesne are 4 ploughs; and 23 villans and 16 bordars with 10 ploughs. There is a church, and 10 slaves, and 3 mills rendering 30s, and 4 acres of meadow, and woodland for 40 pigs, a quarry rendering 6s8d, and in Chichester 1 close rendering 6d. Of this land a Frenchman holds 1 hide and 4 acres. The whole manor TRE was worth £15; and afterwards £8; now £12.

The same Robert holds COCKING of the earl. Azur held it of King Edward. Then, as now, it was assessed at 12 hides. There is land for 11½ ploughs. In demesne are 2 [ploughs]; and 18 villans and 8 bordars with 9 ploughs. There is a church, and 6 slaves, and 5 mills rendering 37s6d. Of this land Turold holds of Robert half a hide, and has half a plough there; and in Chichester [is] 1 close rendering 12d. TRE, as now, worth £15; when received, £10.

The same Robert holds LINCH of the earl. Wulfric held it of King Edward. Then, as now, it was assessed at 5 hides. There is land for 6 ploughs. In demesne is 1 [plough]; and 7 villans and 5 bordars with 2 ploughs. There is a church, and 2 slaves, and 3 acres of meadow, and woodland for 10 pigs. In Chichester, 1 close rendering 10d. TRE it was worth £8; and afterwards £4; now 100s.

[Folio 23V: SUSSEX]

The same Robert holds OLD BUDDINGTON of the earl, and Ralph [holds] of him. Edwin held it of Earl Godwine. Then, as now, it was assessed at 1 hide. There is land for 3 ploughs. In demesne is 1 [plough]; and 5 villans and 3 bordars with 2 ploughs. There are 2 slaves. TRE it was worth 30s; and afterwards, as now, 20s.

Robert holds SELHAM of the earl, and Fulk [holds] of him. Cuthwulf held it of Earl Godwine. Then, as now, it was assessed at 4 hides. There is land for 3 ploughs. In demesne is 1 [plough]; and 2 villans and 2 bordars with 1 plough. There are 2 slaves, and a mill rendering 10s and 100 eels, and 17 acres of meadow, and woodland for 10 pigs. In Chichester, 1 close rendering 7d. The whole manor TRE was worth £4; and afterwards 30s; now 64s.

Geoffrey holds BEPTON of the earl. Vigot held it of King Edward. Then, as now, it was assessed at 4 hides. There is land for 4 ploughs. In demesne is 1 [plough]; and 10 villans and 10 bordars with 3 ploughs. There is a church, and 3 slaves, and in Chichester 1 close rendering 10d. TRE it was worth £4; and afterwards 40s; now 100s.

William holds [Great and Little] TODHAM of the earl. Nigel holds it of him. Wulfnoth held it of Earl Godwine. Then, as now, it was assessed at 4 hides. There is land for 3 ploughs. In demesne is 1 [plough]; and 8 villans and 3 bordars with 1 plough, and the third part of a mill rendering 14d. There are 8 acres of meadow, and woodland for 3 pigs. TRE, as now, worth 40s; when received, 20s.

Four Frenchmen hold GRAFFHAM of the earl; Ralph Robert [sic] 4 hides, Roland 2½ hides, Arnold 2 hides. 6 thegns held it TRE as a manor, as alods of their own. Then, as now, it was assessed at 10 hides. There is land [...]. In demesne are 2½ ploughs; and 7 villans and 6 bordars with 2 ploughs. There is a church; and from the woodland, 8 pigs. TRE the whole manor was worth £8; and afterwards £7; now £8.

IN ROTHERBRIDGE HUNDRED

Robert holds PETWORTH of the earl. Edith held it of King Edward in alod. Then, as now, it was assessed at 9 hides. There is land for 12 ploughs. In demesne are 2 [ploughs]; and 22 villans and 10 bordars with 8 ploughs. There is a church, and 9 slaves, and 1 mill rendering 20s and 189 eels eels [sic], and 29 acres of meadow, and woodland rendering 80 pigs. In Chichester, 2 closes rendering 16d. Of this land 2 Frenchmen hold 2 hides, and there they have 3½ ploughs, and 2 villans and 1 bordar. The whole manor TRE was worth £18; and afterwards £10; now £18.

IN EASEBOURNE HUNDRED

Robert holds TILLINGTON of the earl. Edith held it of King Edward. Then, as now, it was assessed at 5 hides. There is land for 7 ploughs. In demesne are 2 [ploughs]; and 21 villans and 11 bordars with 5 ploughs. There are 8 slaves, and 1 mill rendering 20s and 120 eels, [...] and in Chichester 1 close rendering 8d, and 12 acres of meadow, and woodland for 20 pigs. Of this land 2 Frenchmen hold 1½ virgates, and there they have 5 bordars. TRE it was worth £8; and afterwards 100s; now £8.6s.

Robert holds GRITTENHAM of the earl. 2 thegns held it of King Edward in alod as 3 manors. Then, as now, it was assessed at 4 hides and 1 virgate. There is land for 7 ploughs. In demesne are 2 [ploughs]; and 14 villans and 9 bordars with 3 ploughs. There are 5 slaves, and 1 mill rendering 10s, and a quarry rendering 10s10d, and 20 acres of meadow, and woodland for 30 pigs. Of this manor Turstin holds half a hide and 1 virgate, and there he has 2 ploughs, with 3 villans and 3 bordars. TRE it was worth £6; and afterwards £4; and now £6.5s.

IN ROTHERBRIDGE HUNDRED

Robert holds DUNCTON of the earl. Leofwine held it of King Edward in alod. Then, as now, it was assessed at 5 hides. There is land for 5½ ploughs. In demesne are 2 ploughs; and 15 villans and 8 bordars with 3 ploughs. There is a church, and 2 slaves, and 4 mills rendering 38s, and 2 fisheries rendering 360 eels, and 25 acres of meadow, and woodland for 15 pigs, and in Chichester 1 close rendering 2s.

Of this manor 4 Frenchmen hold 1½ hides and 1½ virgates and 10 acres of land, and there they have 6 bordars with half a plough. The whole TRE was worth £6; and afterwards £3; now £7.3s.

The same Robert holds SUTTON of the earl, and 5 thegns held it as a manor in alod. Then, as now, it was assessed at 8½ hides. There is land for 8½ ploughs. In demesne are 2 [ploughs]; and 17 villans and 11 bordars with 4 ploughs. There are 5 slaves, and 3 mills rendering 13s9d, and 22 acres of meadow, and woodland for 30 pigs. Of this manor 3 Frenchmen hold 3 hides and 1 ferding, and there is 1 plough in demesne; and 8 villans and 7 bordars with 2 ploughs. TRE worth, as now, £10; and afterwards when received, £6.

Robert holds BARLAVINGTON of the earl, and Corbelin [holds] of him. Frawin held it of King Edward in alod. Then, as now, it was assessed at 5 hides. There is land for 6 ploughs. In demesne are 2 [ploughs]; and 8 villans and 8 bordars with 3 ploughs. There are 4 slaves, and 2 mills [...], and 7 acres of meadow, and woodland for 2 pigs. TRE it was worth 100s; and afterwards 60s; now £7.

Robert holds GLATTING of the earl, and Ralph [holds] of him. 4 free men held it in alod. Then, as now, it was assessed at 4 hides. There is land for 3 ploughs. In demesne are 2 [ploughs]; and 3 villans and 2 bordars with 1 plough. There are 6 slaves. TRE it was worth 60s; and afterwards 40s; now £4.

Robert holds STOPHAM of the earl; Ralph [holds] of him. 5 free men held it in alod. Then it was assessed at 5 hides; now at 3 hides. There is land for 5 ploughs. In demesne is 1 [plough]; and 4 villans and 4 bordars with 1 plough. There is 1 slave, and 8 acres of meadow, and 3 fisheries, and woodland for 10 pigs, and in Chichester 1 close rendering 3d.

In the same HUNDRED Thorkil holds 1 virgate of the earl, and he himself held it of Harold, and it is assessed at 1 virgate. There is land for 1 plough, and there is [1 plough] in demesne, with 1 bordar and 1 mill. Then, as now, it was worth 10s.

Robert holds ST MICHAELS BURTON of the earl, and Hamelin [holds] of him. Wulfmær held it of King Edward as 2 manors in alod. Then, as now, it was assessed at 5 hides. There is land for 5 ploughs. In demesne are 2 [ploughs]; and 8 villans and 3 bordars with 2 ploughs. There are 2 slaves, and 1 mill rendering 11s, a fishery rendering 280 [eels], and 4 acres of meadow, and woodland for 2 pigs. TRE, and afterwards, it was worth 40s; now 100s.

In the same HUNDRED Hamelin holds 1½ hides, and at so much they are assessed. Wulfwine held them of King Edward as a manor. There is land for 1 plough, and there is [1 plough] in demesne, with 1 villan and 3 bordars, and 6 acres of meadow. TRE, as now, worth 20s.

In the same HUNDRED Morin holds 1 manor of the earl. Eadric held it of King Edward in alod. Then, as now, it was assessed at 1 hide. There is land for 2 ploughs, and there are [2 ploughs], with 3 villans and 3 bordars and 2 slaves. TRE, as now, worth 20s; when received, 10s.

IN "GHIDENETROI" HUNDRED

The earl himself holds WESTBOURNE in demesne. Earl Godwine held it. There are 36 hides, but it was assessed then, as now, at 12 hides. There is land for 30 ploughs. In demesne are 2 ploughs; and 27 villans and 31 bordars with 15 ploughs. There are 7 slaves, and 4 mills rendering 40s, and a fishery rendering 16d, and woodland for 3 pigs. In Chichester, 6 closes rendering 30d.

To this manor belongs Warblington [Hants] in Hampshire. TRE it was assessed at 12 hides; now at 4 hides. There is land [...]. In demesne are 2 ploughs;

and 17 villans and 12 bordars with 5 ploughs. There are 2 churches, and 6 slaves, and 1 mill rendering 10s.

Of this land Pain holds 4 hides. Alric held them [as belonging] to the minster. In demesne is 1 plough; and 8 villans and 5 bordars with 2 ploughs, and a mill rendering 10s, and 2 acres of meadow. In Chichester, 1 close rendering 12d. The whole manor TRE was worth £30; and afterwards £10. Now what the earl holds [is worth] £40, and yet it renders £50; what Pain holds is and was worth 60s.

Robert holds [East, North, Up or West] MARDEN of the earl, and Corbelin [holds] of him. Alwine and Ælfric held it as 2 manors in alod. Then, as now, it was assessed at 5 hides. There is land for 6 ploughs. In demesne are 2 [ploughs]; and 13 villans and 2 bordars with 4 ploughs. There are 5 slaves, and in Chichester 1 close rendering 14d.

Fulk holds half a hide which belongs to this manor. Ælfric held it in alod. The whole TRE was worth £4.10s; and afterwards 45s; now 115s.

Ivo holds RACTON of the earl. Fulk held it of King Edward. Then, as now, it was assessed at 5 hides. There is land for 4 ploughs. In demesne is 1 plough; and 8 villans and 13 bordars with 2½ ploughs. There are 3 acres of meadow, and woodland for 4 pigs. In Chichester, 1 close rendering 20d. TRE it was worth 60s; and afterwards 40s; now £4.

Engeler holds [East, North, Up or West] MARDEN of the earl. Leofsige held it of Countess Gytha. Then, as now, it was assessed at 3 hides. There is land for 3 ploughs. In demesne is half a plough; and 2 villans and 3 bordars with 2 oxen. In Chichester, 1 close rendering 1d. TRE it was worth 50s; and afterwards 20s; now 30s.

Azo holds [East, North, Up or West] MARDEN of the earl. Alwine held it of King Edward in alod. Then, as now, it was assessed at 4 hides. There is land for 4 ploughs. In demesne are 2 [ploughs]; and 6 villans and 4 bordars with 1 plough. There are 3 slaves. In Chichester, 3 closes rendering 21d. TRE, as now, [worth] 60s; when received, 30s.

William holds LORDINGTON of the earl. Wulfstan held it of King Edward in alod. Then, as now, it was assessed at 4 hides. There is land for 4 ploughs. In demesne is 1 [plough]; and 8 villans and 7 bordars with 2 ploughs. There are 2 slaves, and a mill rendering 30d, and woodland for 3 pigs. TRE it was worth 50s; and afterwards 30s; now 70s.

Geoffrey holds COMPTON [near Chichester] of the earl. Esbiorn held it of Earl Godwine. Then, as now, it was assessed at 10 hides. There is land for 10 ploughs. In demesne is 1 plough; and 18 villans and 5 bordars with 5 ploughs. There is a church, and 4 slaves. In Chichester, 2 closes rendering 2s. A priest holds half a hide. TRE, as now, worth £8; when received, 100s.

The earl himself holds STOUGHTON in demesne. Earl Godwine held it. There are 36 hides, but then, as now, it was assessed at 15 hides. Of these, 16 hides were put in the manor of WESTBOURNE; now they are again in STOUGHTON. There is land for 26 ploughs. In demesne are 3 ploughs; and 54 villans and 35 bordars with 23 ploughs. There are 5 slaves, and 11 acres of meadow, and woodland for 100 pigs. In Chichester, 15 closes rendering 7s8d. In this manor is a church to which belong 1½ hides, and there the priest has half a plough. This is worth £4. The whole manor TRE was worth £40; and afterwards £30; now £40, and yet it renders £50. Of this manor there is 1 hide in the rape of William de Braose, and woodland for 1,500 pigs.

Alwine holds [East, North, Up or West] MARDEN of the earl. Godwine held it in alod. Then, as now, it was assessed at 2 hides. In demesne is 1 [plough], with 6 bordars. TRE, as now, [worth] 40s; when received, 20s.

Near [East, North, Up or West] Marden a certain falconer

holds half a hide of the earl. He himself held it as a manor in alod.

IN STOCKBRIDGE HUNDRED

The Church of Saint-Martin of Sees holds NEW FISH-BOURNE of the earl. Earl Tosti held it. Then, as now, it was assessed at 6 hides. There is land for 6 ploughs. In demesne are 2 [ploughs]; and 6 villans and 11 bordars with 2 ploughs. There is 1 slave, and 2 mills rendering 40s, and 27 acres of meadow. In Chichester, 2 closes rendering 21d. TRE it was worth £6; and afterwards 50s; now |£7|.

Hugh holds RUMBOLDSWHYKE of the earl, and Warin [holds] of him. 5 free men held it as 5 manors. Then it was assessed at 9 hides; now at 6 hides. There is land for 9 ploughs. In demesne is 1 plough; and 6 villans and 2 bordars with 2 ploughs. There is 1 slave. Then, as now, [worth] 100s; when received, 40s.

Ealhere holds NORTH MUNDHAM of the earl. Countess Gytha held it of Earl Godwine. Then it was assessed at 9 hides; now at 6 hides. There is land for 6 ploughs. In demesne are 2 [ploughs]; and 14 villans and 13 bordars with 2 ploughs. There are 2 slaves, and 1½ mills rendering 6s8d. There is a church to which belongs half a hide. A priest has half a plough. TRE, as now, worth £8; when received, 100s.

In the same HUNDRED Ketil holds land for 1 plough. It has never been assessed in hides. King William granted this to him. There he has 1 mill rendering 5s, and 1 bordar, and 5 acres of meadow. It is worth 25s.

William holds HUNSTON of the earl. 6 free men held it in alod. Then, as now, it was assessed at 4 hides. There is land for 4 ploughs. In demesne is 1 plough; and 5 villans and 19 bordars with 2 ploughs. There is 1 mill rendering 20s, and 2 salt-pans, and from 1 enclosure 6d. TRE it was worth 40s; and afterwards 30s; now £4.

IN WITTERING HUNDRED

The same William holds BIRDHAM of the earl, and Nigel [holds] of him. Alnoth held it in alod. Then, as now, it was assessed at 3½ hides. There is land for 5 ploughs. In demesne are 2 [ploughs]; and 5 villans and 8 bordars with 3 ploughs. There is 1 mill rendering 20s, and 2 fisheries, and 3 acres of meadow. From the woodland and herbage, 5 pigs.

Of this manor Ansketil holds 1½ hides, and he has there 1 plough, and 1 villan and 2 bordars. The whole TRE was worth 40s; and afterwards 30s; now 65s.

Warin holds WEST ITCHENOR of the earl. Leofwine held it of Earl Godwine. Then, as now, it was assessed at 1 hide. There is land for 1 plough. In demesne is 1 plough; and 3 villans and 3 bordars with 1 plough. There is 1 acre of meadow. TRE it was worth 20s; and afterwards 15s; now 22s.

Reginald holds SOMERLEY of the earl. Helghi held it of King Edward in alod. Then, as now, it was assessed at 1 hide. There is land for 1 plough. In demesne is 1 [plough]; and 2

villans and 3 bordars with 1 plough. There is 1 slave. TRE, as now, worth 20s; when received, 15s.

Ralph holds of Robert, and Robert of the earl, [?West] WITTERING. 2 free men held it as 2 manors. Then, as now, it was assessed at 1 hide. There is land for 1 plough. There are 4 villans with 2 ploughs, and 1 enclosure rendering 6d. TRE and afterwards, as now, worth 20s.

IN 'EASWRITHE' HUNDRED

Robert holds STORRINGTON of the earl, and Durand holds of him. Then it was assessed at 6 hides; now at 5½ hides. [There is] land for 3 ploughs. In demesne are 2 ploughs; and 6 villans and 7 cottars with 1 plough. There is a church, and 2 mills rendering 11s. TRE, as now, worth £4; and afterwards 40s.

Robert holds STORRINGTON of the earl, and Alwine [holds] of him, and this man held it TRE, and could go where he pleased. Then, as now, [it was assessed] at 3 hides.

[Folio 24V: SUSSEX]

There is land for 2 ploughs. In demesne is 1 plough, with 1 villan and 5 cottars and 2 slaves, and a mill rendering 5s. TRE and afterwards, as now, worth 30s.

Robert holds COOTHAM of the earl, and Aubrey [holds] of him. 2 free men held it TRE. Then, as now, it was assessed at 4 hides and 1 virgate. There is land for 3 ploughs. In demesne are 2 [ploughs]; and 4 villans and 5 cottars with half a plough. TRE and afterwards, as now, worth £3.

In the same manor Robert holds of the earl 2 hides and 1 virgate, and at so much they are assessed. 2 free men held them. There is land for 2 ploughs, and there are [2 ploughs] in demesne, with 1 villan and 1 cottar. TRE and afterwards, as now, worth 20s.

Robert holds PARHAM of the earl. A certain free man, Tovi, held it. Then, as now, it was assessed at 3 hides. There is land for 2 ploughs. In demesne are 1½ [ploughs]; and 2 villans and 1 cottar with half a plough, and 1 mill rendering 30d. TRE and afterwards, as now, worth £3.

The same Robert holds NUTBOURNE of the earl; Warin [holds] of him. 2 free men held it TRE. Then, as now, it was assessed at 6 hides. There is land for 6 ploughs. In demesne is 1 [plough]; and 20 villans and 4 cottars with 7 ploughs, and 2 mills rendering 25s. There are 7 acres of meadow, [and] woodland for 12 pigs. TRE, as now, worth £7; when received, £6.

Roger holds NYETIMBER of the earl, and Alweard [holds] of him. Leofwine held it TRE, and could go where he would. Then, as now, it was assessed at 4 hides. There is land for 5 ploughs, and [there are] 16 villans and 3 cottars with 4 ploughs, and 3 acres of meadow, and woodland for 10 pigs. TRE and afterwards, as now, worth £3.

Robert holds PULBOROUGH of the earl. Wulfric held it TRE. Then, as now, it was assessed at 16 hides. There is land for 18 ploughs. In demesne are 4 ploughs; and 35 villans and 15 cottars with 13 ploughs. There are 9 slaves, and 2 mills rendering 11s, and 30 acres of meadow, and woodland for 25 pigs, and 2 fisheries rendering 3s. There are 2 churches. Of the land of this manor Theobald and Ivo hold 2 hides and half a virgate, and there is in demesne 1 plough; and 3 villans and 4 cottars with 1 plough. The whole manor TRE was worth £16; and afterwards £16; now Robert's demesne [is worth] £22, [the holding] of the men, 35s.

Ernucion holds GREATHAM of the earl. Azur held it of King Edward. Then it was assessed at 5 hides. Now 1 hide is in the rape of William de Braose. There is land for 3 ploughs. In demesne are 2 [ploughs]; and 10 villans and 7 cottars with 2 ploughs, and 4 fisheries rendering 5s. TRE it was worth £6; and afterwards, as now, 100s.

Robert holds WEST CHILTINGTON of the earl, and Oswulf [holds] of him. Azur held it of King Edward. Then it was assessed at 6 hides; now 3 hides are in the rape of William de Braose. There is land for 3 ploughs. In demesne is 1 plough; and 4 villans and 2 cottars with 1 plough. There is a church. Then and afterwards, as now, [worth] 30s.

In SULLINGTON Robert holds 1 virgate. Wulfweard held it of King Edward. There is 1 villan with half a plough. It is and was worth 2s.

IN "RISBERG" HUNDRED

The earl himself holds LYMINSTER in demesne. King Edward held it in demesne. There are 20 hides. It has never paid geld. There is land for 44 ploughs. In demesne are 4 ploughs; and 68 villans and 43 cottars with 40 ploughs. There is a church, and a mill rendering 5s, and 2 salt-pans rendering 20d, and 8 acres of meadow, and woodland for 30 pigs. TRE and afterwards, as now, worth £50.

In the same place Robert holds 1 hide of the earl. Azur held it. It has never paid geld. There are 6 acres of meadow, and 60 acres of pasture. It is and was worth 10s.

Robert holds TODDINGTON of the earl. Azur held it of King Edward. Then, as now, it was assessed at 4 hides. There is land for 4 ploughs. In demesne are 2 ploughs; and 10 villans and 11 cottars with 2 ploughs, and 6 acres of meadow, and 1 slave. TRE, and afterwards, worth 60s; now 70s.

Nigel holds WARNINGCAMP. Thorgot held it of King Edward. Then, as now, it was assessed at 4 hides. There is land for 3 ploughs. In demesne is 1 plough; and 3 villans and 3 cottars with 1 plough, and 8 acres of meadow.

Of this land Rafin holds of Nigel 3 hides, and there is 1 plough in demesne; and 8 villans and 3 cottars with 2 ploughs. There are 24 acres of meadow, and 2 fisheries rendering 18d, [and] woodland for 3 pigs. The whole manor TRE was worth 60s; and afterwards 20s; now 50s.

The Abbey of Almeneches holds WEST PRESTON of the earl. Smelt the priest held it of King Edward. Then, as now, it was assessed at 13 hides. There is land for 12 ploughs. In demesne are 3 ploughs; and 59 villans and 12 cottars with 17 ploughs. There is a church, and 4 slaves, and 2 salt-pans rendering 30d, [and] woodland for 20 pigs. TRE it was worth £20; and afterwards £16; now £25.

In the same place Roger holds 1 hide of the abbey itself. Smelt the priest held it, and it has never paid geld. There is land for 1 plough. There is [1 plough] in demesne, with 9 cottars, and 25 acres of meadow, and 1 fishery rendering 2s, and 60 acres of pasture. And moreover Roger holds 1 hide of the abbey itself. Alwine held it of King Edward. There is land for 2 ploughs. It is assessed at 1 hide. There are 4 villans and 6 cottars with 2 ploughs, and a mill rendering 30d. These 2 hides TRE and afterwards, as now, were worth 60s.

Warin holds ANGMERING of the earl. Earl Godwine held it. Then it was assessed at 5 hides. Now 1 of these hides is in the rape of William de Braose. There is land for 2 ploughs. In demesne is 1 [plough]; and 6 villans and 4 cottars with 1 plough. TRE and afterwards, as now, worth 40s.

Geoffrey holds ANGMERING of the earl. 3 free men held it TRE. Then it was assessed at 5 hides. Now 1 of these hides is in the rape of William de Braose. There is land for 2 ploughs. In demesne is 1 [plough]; and 6 villans and 2 cottars with 2 ploughs. There are 3 acres of meadow, and woodland for 3 pigs. TRE, and afterwards, worth 50s; now 60s.

Reginald holds NORTH STOKE of the earl. Beorhtsige held it of King Edward. Then, as now, it was assessed at 8 hides. There is land for 7 ploughs. In demesne are 3 ploughs; and 16 villans and 16 cottars with 4 ploughs. There is a church, and 5 slaves, and 2 fisheries rendering 10d. TRE and afterwards, as now, worth £20.

Roger holds BURPHAM of the earl, and Alweard [holds] of him. Leofwine held it of King Edward. Then, as now, it was assessed at 5 hides. There is land for 4 ploughs. In demesne are 3 ploughs; and 8 villans and 12 cottars with 3 ploughs. There is a church, and 10 slaves, and 8 acres of meadow, and woodland for 3 pigs. TR [sic] TRE and afterwards, as now, worth £8; and yet it renders £10.

Robert holds EAST PRESTON of the earl. A certain free woman, Wulfgifu, held it TRE. Then, as now, it was assessed at 7 hides. There is land for 4 ploughs. There are 14 villans and 1 cottar with 4 ploughs, and 3 salt-pans rendering 30d. | It is worth £4. |

The same Robert holds GORING-BY-SEA of the earl. It was a Berewick of King Edward's. There are 6 hides. They have never paid geld. There is land for 7 ploughs. In demesne are 2 ploughs; and 20 villans and 12 cottars with 5 ploughs. It is and was always worth £4.

Robert holds GORING-BY-SEA of the earl. Godwine, a free man, held it TRE. Then it was assessed at 11 hides; now William de Braose has 2 hides in his rape. There is land for 4 ploughs. In demesne are 2 ploughs;

[Folio 25: SUSSEX]

and 13 villans and 8 cottars with 2 ploughs. TRE and afterwards, as now, worth 100s.

The same Robert holds GORING-BY-SEA of the earl. Gundrada held it of King Edward. Then it was assessed at 4 hides; now at $2\frac{1}{2}$ because $1\frac{1}{2}$ hides are in the rape of William de Braose. There is land for 1 plough, and there is [1 plough] in demesne, with 2 villans, and there are 3 acres of meadow. TRE and afterwards, as now, worth 20s.

The same Robert holds GORING-BY-SEA of the earl. 3 free men held it TRE. Then it was assessed at 8 hides; now at 5½ hides; the remainder is in the rape of William de Braose. There is land for 3 ploughs. In demesne are 2 ploughs; and 6 villans and 3 cottars with 1 plough, and 2 acres of meadow. It is and was always worth 40s.

Picot holds WEPHAM of the earl. 2 free men held it TRE. Then, as now, it was assessed at 8 hides. There is land for 6 ploughs. In demesne are 2 [ploughs], and a mill rendering 30d, and 10 acres of meadow, woodland for 3 pigs, and 2 fisheries rendering 3s, and 18 villans and 9 cottars with 4 ploughs. TRE it was worth £8; and afterwards £9; now £10.

The Abbey of Almeneches holds CLIMPING of the earl in alms. Earl Godwine held it. Then, as now, it was assessed at 11 hides. There is land for 9 ploughs; and [there are] 26 villans and 24 cottars with 7 ploughs. There is a church, and 12 acres of meadow, [and] woodland for 20 pigs. TRE it was worth £20; and afterwards, as now, £15.

In the same manor Saint-Martin of Sees holds 11 hides of the earl in alms, and at so much they were assessed TRE, as now. Earl Godwine held them. There is land for 9 ploughs. In demesne are 2 ploughs; and 26 villans and 24 cottars with 7 ploughs. There is a church, and 12 acres of meadow, and woodland for 20 pigs. TRE it was worth £20; and afterwards, as now, £15.

In Littlehampton William holds 1 hide of the earl. Countess Gode held it, and it is assessed at 1 hide. There is land for 1 plough, and there is [1 plough] in demesne, with 2 cottars, and 1 acre of meadow. It is and was always worth 10s.

IN BURY HUNDRED

Robert holds BIGNOR of the earl, and Ralph [holds] of him. 3 free men held it TRE. Then, as now, it was assessed at 4 hides. There is land for 3 ploughs. In demesne are 2 ploughs; and 9 villans and 5 cottars with 2 ploughs. There is a church, and 2 mills rendering 28s, and a quarry for mill-stones rendering 4s. There are 2 slaves, and 2 acres of meadow, and woodland for 3 pigs. TRE it was worth £3; and afterwards 40s; now £4.

Robert holds HARDHAM of the earl. Godwine, a free man, [held it] TRE. Then, as now, it was assessed at 5 hides. [There is] land for 4 ploughs. In demesne are 2 [ploughs]; and 10 villans and 4 cottars with 3 ploughs. There are 3 fisheries rendering 6s, and 15 acres of meadow, [and] woodland for 3 pigs. Of this land Ivo holds of Robert 3 virgates of land, and there he has 1 villan. TRE it was worth £4; and afterwards 40s; now 100s.

IN BINSTED HUNDRED

Osmelin holds BINSTED of the earl. 3 free men held it TRE. Then, as now, it was assessed at 4 hides. There is land for 2 ploughs. In demesne are 2 ploughs; and 2 villans with 6 cottars with half a plough. There are 8 acres of meadow,

and woodland for 6 pigs. TRE it was worth £3; and afterwards 40s; now £3.

William holds WALBERTON of the earl. 3 free men held it TRE. Then, as now, it was assessed at 11 hides and 2 virgates. There is land for 6 ploughs. In demesne [are] 3 ploughs; and 19 villans and 13 cottars with 5 ploughs. There is a church, and 6 slaves, and 14 acres of meadow, and woodland for 4 pigs. TRE it was worth £10; and afterwards £6; now £12.

Of this land Roland holds 1 hide less 1 virgate and this the earl himself has in his park, and there 2 villans with 4 cottars have 1 plough. And Acard the priest holds 2 virgates as a prebend, and there he has 1 villan. The whole of this is worth 20s.

William holds BARNHAM of the earl. Alnoth, a free man, held it TRE. Then, as now, it was assessed at 4 hides. There is land for 4 ploughs. In demesne is 1 [plough]; and 12 villans and 12 cottars with 4 ploughs. There is a church, and 20 acres of meadow, and woodland for 3 pigs, and 1 mill. TRE and afterwards, as now, worth £4.

William holds MIDDLETON-ON-SEA of the earl. 5 free men held it TRE. Then, as now, it was assessed at 5 hides and 2 virgates. There is land for 3 ploughs. There is a church, and 2 villans with half a plough.

Of the land of this manor 3 Frenchmen hold 4 hides and 5 virgates of William, and there is in demesne 1 plough; and 10 villans and 4 cottars with 1½ ploughs. The whole manor TRE was worth £4.

Arnold holds SOUTH STOKE of the earl. Wulfnoth, a free man, held it TRE. Then, as now, it was assessed at 4 hides. There is land for 2 ploughs. In demesne is 1 plough; and 10 villans and 4 cottars with 2 ploughs. There is a church, and 24 acres of meadow. TRE and afterwards, as now, [worth] £4.

Ernucion holds TORTINGTON of the earl. Leofwine, a free man, held it TRE. Then it was assessed at 4 hides; now at 3 hides, because the earl has 1 in his park. There is land for 2 ploughs, and there are [2 ploughs] in demesne, and 6 villans and 2 cottars. There are 30 acres of meadow, and woodland for 6 pigs. TRE it was worth 60s; and afterwards 30s; now 40s.

Hugh holds BILSHAM of the earl. Godwine, a free man, held it TRE. Then, as now, it was assessed at 4 hides. There is land for 3 ploughs. In demesne is 1 [plough]; and 14 villans with 2 ploughs, and 8 acres of meadow. TRE it was worth £4; and afterwards 40s; now 50s.

The same Hugh holds 3 hides of the earl, and Warin [holds] of him. 3 free men held them TRE. Then, as now, they were assessed at 3 hides. There is land for 2 ploughs. In demesne is 1 plough; and 5 villans and 5 cottars with 1 plough. There are 3 acres of meadow. TRE, as now, [worth] 30s; when received, 20s.

The same Hugh holds SLINDON of the earl. A certain free man, Azur, held it TRE. Then, as now, it was assessed at 8 hides. There is land for 8 ploughs. In demesne are 1½ ploughs;

and 23 villans and 12 cottars with 7 ploughs. There is a church [...]. TRE it was worth £20; and afterwards, as now, £16.

The same Hugh holds 8 hides of the earl. [...] 9 free men held them TRE. Then they were assessed at 8 hides; now [at] 1 virgate less, which the earl has and [which] does not pay geld. There is land for 4 ploughs; and 16 villans with 5 ploughs. There are 8 acres of meadow. TRE and afterwards, as now, worth £3.

Morin holds "BORHAM" of the earl. A free man held it TRE. Then, as now, it was assessed at 1 virgate. There are 2 virgates. There are 5 oxen ploughing, with 1 cottar. TRE, as now, worth 20s; when received, 10s.

In the same HUNDRED William holds 3 hides of the earl, and at so much they are assessed. 2 free men held them TRE. There is land for 3 ploughs. In demesne are 1½ [ploughs]; and 5 villans and 5 cottars and 2 slaves with 2 ploughs. TRE, as now, worth £4; when received, £3.

Azo holds OFFHAM of the earl. Alwine, a free man, held it TRE. Then, as now, it was assessed at 4 hides. There is land for 2 ploughs. In demesne is 1 [plough]; and 8 villans and 5 cottars with 2 ploughs. There are 5 slaves, and 48 acres of meadow, and a fishery rendering 2s, [and] woodland for 3 pigs. The whole TRE was worth £7; and afterwards £6; now £4.

There the earl has 2 mills, pasture, and the renders of the woodland. It is worth £4.10s.

[Folio 25v: SUSSEX]

Saint-Martin of Sees holds EASTER GATE in alms of the earl. Earl Harold held it. There are 3 hides, but then, as now, it was assessed at 2 hides. There is land for 4 ploughs. In demesne are 2 ploughs; and 18 villans and 10 cottars with 2 ploughs. There is a church, and 4 acres of meadow, [and] woodland for 5 pigs. TRE, as now, worth £4; when received, £3.

In this HUNDRED of BINSTED Warin holds half a hide of the earl. Azur, a free man, held it, and it has never paid geld. There is land for 1 plough, and there is [1 plough], with 2 villans. It is and was worth 30s.

Guntram holds of the earl in the same place 1 hide, and at so much it has always been assessed. Heoruwulf held it of Earl Godwine. There is land for 1 plough, and there is [1 plough] in demesne, with 1 villan and 4 cottars, and 2 acres of meadow, and woodland for 3 pigs. [It has] always [been worth] | 20s. |

In this HUNDRED Acard holds 2½ hides of the earl. They were assessed at 2 hides less half a virgate then, as now. There is land for 2 ploughs. In demesne is 1 plough; and 6 villans and 6 cottars with 1 plough. There is a church, and woodland for 6 pigs. Asgot held it of Earl Godwine. Then, as now, [worth] 40s; when received, | 20s. |

In the same place Pain holds 1 virgate of the earl, and at so much it has always been assessed. Asgot held it of Earl Godwine. There is 1 cottar. [It has] always [been worth] 30d.

In the same HUNDRED William holds of the earl half a hide and 2 virgates, and at so much they have always been assessed. 2 Englishmen held them of Earl Godwine. There is land for 1 plough. There are 4 villans and 1 cottar with half a plough. It is and was worth 10s.

In the same HUNDRED Hugh holds 5½ virgates of the earl, and at so much they have always been assessed. Azur, a free man, held them TRE. There is land for 2 ploughs. There is 1 villan and 1 cottar. Then and afterwards, as now, worth 8s.

In this HUNDRED Roland holds 1 hide of the earl, and at so much it has always been assessed. Godwine, a free man, held it. There is land for 2 ploughs. In demesne is 1 plough; and 2 villans and 4 cottars with 1 plough. It is and was worth 20s.

In the same HUNDRED Wineman holds 1 virgate of the earl, and at so much it has always been assessed. Thorkil held it; he was a free man. It is and was worth 5s.

IN BOXGROVE HUNDRED

William holds BOXGROVE of the earl. 2 free men held it TRE. Then, as now, it was assessed at 6 hides. There is land for 4 ploughs. Of this land Humphrey holds 3 hides and 1 virgate, Nigel 1 hide and 1 virgate, William half a hide, the clerks of the church 1 hide. In demesne are 2 ploughs; and 1 villan and 12 cottars with 1 plough. The whole TRE was worth 40s; and the same afterwards; and the same now.

The same William holds EAST HAMPNETT of the earl, and Nigel [holds] of him. Alweard, a free man, held it. Then, as now, it was assessed at 7 hides, and there are 8 villans and 11 cottars with 3 ploughs. There is land for 4 ploughs. In demesne are 2 ploughs, and 3 acres of meadow. TRE it was worth 60s; and afterwards 40s; now 50s.

The same William holds HALNAKER of the earl. Alweard held it TRE, and then, as now, it was assessed at 9 hides. There is land for 5 ploughs. In demesne are 2 ploughs; and 17 villans and 12 cottars with 2 ploughs. There are 8 acres of meadow, and woodland for 9 pigs. In Chichester, 3 burgesses paying 5s. TRE, and afterwards, it was worth £4; now 100s.

The same William holds WESTHAMPNETT of the earl. 2 free men held it of Earl Godwine. Then, as now, it was assessed at 9 hides. There is land [...]. There William has 1 mill rendering 5s, and 12 cottars, and [there is] woodland for 6 pigs, and in Chichester [he has] 1 close.

Of this land Williams holds 1 hide, Restold 1 hide, Richard 3 virgates, Godfrey 1 virgate. In demesne [is] 1 plough, and 4 cottars, and a church. The whole TRE was worth 60s; and afterwards 40s; now 60s.

The same William holds 3 hides of the earl, and at so much they are assessed in the same HUNDRED. 2 free men held them TRE. There is land for 1 plough. Of this land Richard holds 2 hides, Turgis 1 hide. In demesne [is] 1 plough, with 9 cottars, and 1 mill rendering 3s, and 2 enclosures rendering 9d. TRE it was worth 20s; and afterwards 15s; now 10s.

The same William holds STRETTINGTON of the earl. 4 free men held it TRE. Then, as now, it was assessed at 10 hides. There is land for 6 ploughs. There are 6 villans and 16 cottars with 2 ploughs. In Chichester, 3 closes rendering 2s. TRE it was worth £6; and afterwards, as now, 40s.

Augustine holds STRETTINGTON of the earl. Godwine, a free man, held it TRE. Then, as now, it was assessed at 3 hides. There is land for 1 plough, and there is [1 plough] in demesne, with 2 villans and 2 cottars, and 1 enclosure rendering 3d, and 2 slaves, and 1 acre of meadow. TRE it was worth 20s; and afterwards 10s; now 30s.

In the same manor Arnold holds 2 hides of the earl, and at so much they are assessed. Godwine, a free man, held them TRE. There is land for 1 plough, and there is [1 plough] in demesne, with 2 cottars and 2 slaves, and 1 enclosure rendering 8d. TRE it was worth £3; and afterwards, as now, 20s.

Osmelin holds MERSTON of the earl. Gyrth held it of King Edward. Then it was assessed at 8 hides; now at 6 hides. There is land for 3 ploughs. In demesne are 2 ploughs; and 10 villans with 6 cottars have 3 ploughs, and 3 mills rendering 7s, and 2 enclosures rendering 2s, and 10 acres of meadow. TRE it was worth £5; and afterwards £4; now £6.

The Abbey of Troarn holds RUNCTON in alms of the earl. 2 free men held it TRE. Then it was assessed at 8 hides; now at 2 hides. There is land for 3 ploughs. In demesne are 2 ploughs; and 6 villans and 15 cottars with 1 plough. There are 5 slaves, and 2 mills rendering 12s6d, and a fishery rendering 6d, and 2 enclosures rendering 18d. TRE it was worth £5; and afterwards £4; now £6.

Arnold holds UPWALTHAM of the earl. Godwine, a free man, held it. Then it was assessed at 6 hides; now at 4. Arnold has 2 hides, and there are 2 cottars and 1 slave; and the Abbey of Troarn has 2 hides, and there are 3 cottars, and 1 enclosure rendering 16d; and from the herbage, 2s; and the earl has 2 hides in his park. There is land for 1 plough. The whole TRE was worth 40s; and afterwards 20s; [now] what Arnold [has] is worth 10s, the abbey's part, 35s.

Geoffrey holds UPWALTHAM of the earl. 2 free men held it TRE. Then it was assessed at 4 hides; now at 3, because the earl has 1 in his park. There is land for 4 ploughs. In demesne is 1 [plough], with 5 cottars, and woodland for 10 pigs, and 1 enclosure rendering 7d. [From] the herbage, 2s. TRE [worth] 30s; and afterwards 10s; now 20s.

In this HUNDRED William holds 1 hide of the earl. Alweard, a free man, held it, and it was assessed at 1 hide in HALNAKER then, as now. Then [worth] 15s; and afterwards 5s; now 10s.

In this HUNDRED Siward holds 1 hide of the earl, and at so much it has always been assessed. Sigeræd held it; he was a free man. There is land for 1 plough. Then, as now, [worth] 20s.

In this HUNDRED Reginald holds half a hide of the earl, and at so much it is assessed. Helghi held it TRE. Then [worth] 3s; and afterwards 2s; now 12d.

XII. The land of William de Warenne

THE BOROUGH OF LEWES TRE rendered £6.4s1½d from rents and from tolls. There King Edward had 127 burgesses in demesne. Their custom was, if the king wished to send his men to patrol the sea without him, they collected from all the men, whosesoever land it was, 20s, and those who were in charge of the arms in the ships had those.

Whoever sells a horse in the borough gives to the reeve 1d and the buyer [gives] another; for an ox ½d; for a man, wherever he may buy him within the rape, 4d. A man who sheds blood pays a fine of 7s4d. A man who commits adultery or rape pays a fine of 8s4d, and a woman as much. The king has [the penalty from] the adulterous man, the archbishop [from] the woman.

From a fugitive, if he is retaken, 8s4d.

When the mint is renewed, each moneyer gives 20s.

Of all these, 2 parts were the king's and the third the earl's.

Now the borough renders in all [as much] as [it did] then and 38s in addition.

Of the rape of Pevensey, 39 inhabited messuages and 20 uninhabited, from which the king has 26s6d, and of these William de Warenne has half.

TRE the whole was worth [...] £26. The king had a half and the earl the other. Now it is worth £34, and from the new mint 100s. and 12 [sic]. Of all these William has a half and the king the other.

In the rape of Pevensey William de Warenne has 12 messuages, 7 inhabited and 5 not. [They belong] to Laughton, a manor of the Count of Mortain.

IN SWANBOROUGH HUNDRED

WILLIAM de Warenne holds IFORD in demesne. Queen Edith held it. TRE it was assessed at 77½ hides. When William received it, [there were] only 58 hides, because the others were within the rape of the Count of Mortain. These 58 hides are assessed now at 36 hides. There is land for 52 ploughs. In demesne are 5 ploughs; and 100 villans, less 3, and 32 bordars have 34 ploughs. There is a church, and 6 slaves, and 2 mills rendering 23s, and 208 acres of meadow, [and] woodland for 30 pigs. In the borough of Lewes, 26 burgesses paying 13s. From the pasture, 15s8d. and 16,000 herrings.

Of this land the monks of St Pancras hold 6½ hides, and there they have in demesne 2 ploughs; and 10 villans with 3 ploughs. These hides do not pay geld. Of the same land Hugh has 2 hides and Tosard 1½ hides. In demesne they have 2 ploughs, with 4 bordars. Villans held these lands.

The whole manor TRE was worth £50; and afterwards £20; now William's demesne [is worth] £35, [the holding] of the monks £3, [the holding] of the men 75s.

IN 'HOLMESTROW' HUNDRED

William himself holds RODMELL in demesne. Earl Harold held it. TRE it was assessed at 79 hides. William received 64 hides, because the others [are] in the rape of the count and [in that] of William de Braose. These 64 hides are now assessed at 33 hides. There is land for 36 ploughs. In demesne are 6 ploughs; and 107 villans and 25 bordars with 34 ploughs. There are 11 salt-pans rendering 26s, and 140 acres of meadow, and woodland for 23 pigs. In the manor is a church.

In LEWES, 44 closes rendering 22s. and 4,000 herrings.

Of this land Norman holds 2 hides of William, and there is 1 plough in demesne, with 2 bordars and a slave. The man who held this land could not withdraw with it.

The whole manor TRE was worth £60; and afterwards £20; now £37.

IN PRESTON HUNDRED

William himself holds PATCHAM in demesne. Earl Harold held it TRE. Then it was assessed at 60 hides, and now at 40. There is land for 80 ploughs. In demesne [are] 8 ploughs; and 163 villans and 45 bordars with 82 ploughs. There is a church, and 6 slaves, and 10 shepherds. There are 84 acres of meadow, and woodland for 100 pigs.

In Lewes [are] 26 closes rendering 13s.

Of this land, Richard holds 7 hides and a knight of his 1½ hides. In demesne they have 2 ploughs, with 2 bordars.

TRE the whole was worth £100; and afterwards £50; now £80.

IN SWANBOROUGH HUNDRED

William himself holds DITCHLING in demesne. King Edward held it. | It has never paid geld. | TRE it was assessed at 46 hides. When received, [there were] only 42 hides; the others were in the rape of the Count of Mortain, as were 6 woods, which used to belong to the capital manor. Now it is assessed at 33 hides. There is land for 60 ploughs. In demesne [are] 8 ploughs; and 108 villans and 40 bordars have 81 ploughs. There is a church, and 1 mill rendering 30d, and 130 acres of meadow, [and] woodland for 80 pigs. In Lewes [he has] 11 messuages rendering 12s. Of this land Gilbert holds 1½ hides, Hugh 2 hides, Alweard 3 hides, Warin 3 hides, Richard 1 hide. In demesne they have 7½ ploughs, with 29 bordars; and 3 villans and 10 slaves with 3 ploughs. In Lewes, 6 burgesses paying 43d.

The whole manor TRE was worth £80 and 66d; and afterwards £25; now William's demesne [is worth] £60, and [the holding] of the men £12.10s.

IN FALMER HUNDRED

St Pancras holds FALMER of William. The Abbey of Wilton held it TRE, and was seised [of it] on the day of his [King Edward's death]. TRE it was assessed at 21 hides, and now at 18 hides; the others are in the rape of the Count of Mortain and do not pay geld. [There is] land for 15 ploughs. In demesne [are] 2 ploughs; and 35 villans and 7 bordars with 13 ploughs. There is a church, and 1 slave. There are 4 acres of

meadow, and woodland for 20 pigs. TRE and afterwards, as now, [worth] £20.

IN 'HOLMESTROW' HUNDRED

Godfrey holds 'HARPINGDEN' [in Piddinghoe] of William. Alnoth held it TRE, and could go where he would. Then it was assessed at 10½ hides; now at 6 hides, but half a hide is in the rape of the Count of Mortain. There is land for 4 ploughs. In demesne are 2 ploughs; and 14 villans and 6 bordars with 2 ploughs. There are 17 acres of meadow, and woodland for 30 pigs. In Lewes, 4 closes rendering 20d. TRE it was worth 40s; and afterwards 50s; now 60s.

Nigel holds 'ORLESWICK' [in Piddinghoe] of the earl. [...] Earl Godwine held it, and 7 alodiaries [held] of him. TRE it was assessed at 6½ hides; now at 5 hides. There is land for 4 ploughs.

[Folio 26V: SUSSEX]

In demesne is 1 plough; and 11 villans and 6 bordars with 2 ploughs. There are 2 slaves, and 17 acres of meadow. In LEWES, 2 closes rendering 10s. TRE it was worth 30s; and afterwards 40s; now 60s.

IN "WELESMERE" HUNDRED

Hugh holds ROTTINGDEAN of William. Hemming held it of Earl Godwine. Then, as now, it was assessed at 2 hides, and it was part of FROG FIRLE which the count of Mortain holds in his rape. There is land for 2 ploughs. There are [2 ploughs] in demesne, with 10 bordars. TRE it was worth 40s; and afterwards 20s; now 60s.

Godfrey holds OVINGDEAN of William. Alnoth held it of King Edward, and could go where he would. Then it was assessed at 5 hides. In the same vill Edith held 3 hides of the king in parage. When Godfrey received it, he found it as 1 manor then. But of these 8 hides the Count of Mortain has 1½ hides in his rape. What Godfrey holds pays geld for 6 hides now. There is land for 4 ploughs. In demesne are 2 ploughs; and 5 villans and 5 bordars with 1 plough. There is a chapel, and 4 slaves. In Lewes, 10 closes rendering 5s.

With these hides Godfrey holds 2 hides of a certain manor of William, his lord, which have never paid geld, and there he has nothing. The whole TRE was worth £6; and afterwards £4; now £7.

In the same vill Beorhtmær holds 2 hides of William. He himself held them of Azur TRE, and then, as now, they were assessed at 2 hides. There he has 1 plough, with 2 bordars. It is and was always worth 20s.

Ralph holds BRIGHTON of William. Beorhtric held it by grant of Earl Godwine. TRE, as now, it was assessed at 5½ hides. There is land for 3 ploughs. In demesne is half a plough; and 18 villans and 9 bordars with 3 ploughs, and 1 slave. From rents, 4,000 herrings. TRE it was worth £8.12s; and afterwards 100s; now £12.

In the same vill Widard holds of William 6 hides and 1 virgate, and at so much they are assessed. 3 alodiaries held them of King Edward, and could go where they pleased. 1 of them had a hall, and villans held the shares of the other 2. There is land for 5 ploughs, and it is in 1 manor. In demesne [are] 1½ ploughs; and 14 villans and 21 bordars with 3½ ploughs. There are 7 acres of meadow, and woodland for 3 pigs. In Lewes, 4 closes. TRE it was worth £10; and afterwards £8; now £12.

In the same place William de Vatteville holds BRIGHTON of William. Wulfweard held it of King Edward. Then, as now, it was assessed at 5½ hides. There is land for 4 ploughs. In demesne is 1 plough; and 13 villans and 11 bordars with 1 plough. There is a church. TRE it was worth £10; and afterwards £8; now £12.

Goze holds BALMER of William. Villans who belonged to Falmer held it TRE. Then, as now, it was assessed at 4 hides. There is land for 2 ploughs. In demesne is 1 [plough], with 1 villan and 2 bordars and 2 slaves. There is a chapel, and woodland for 4 pigs. TRE it was worth 20s; and afterwards, as now, 30s.

IN FALMER HUNDRED

Eustace holds 1 hide of William. 1 villan of Falmer held it. It is assessed at 1 hide. It is worth 6s.

Walter holds BEVENDEAN [Bevendean and Lower Bevendean] of William. Azur held it of King [Edward]. Then, as now, it was assessed at 4 hides. There is 1 virgate in addition which does not pay geld, because it is outside the rape. There is land for 3 ploughs. In demesne are 2 ploughs; and 2 villans and 3 bordars with 1 plough. In Lewes, 2 closes rendering 18d. TRE it was worth 100s; and afterwards £4; now £6. Villans of [?] Keymer held this land.

IN SWANBOROUGH HUNDRED

Eldeid holds 'WINTERBOURNE' [in Lewes] of William; there is 1 hide, and at so much it is assessed. Edith held it of King Edward. There is land for half a plough, and there is [half a plough] in demesne, with 6 bordars, and 1½ acres of meadow. In Lewes, 3 closes and the third part of 1 close rendering 18d. TRE, and afterwards, it was worth 10s; now 20s.

IN THE HALF-HUNDRED OF ALDRINGTON

Godfrey holds ALDRINGTON of William. It belonged to Upper Beeding, a manor of King Edward, and now William de Braose holds it in his rape. Godfrey holds 7 hides and half a virgate. There is land for 7 ploughs. It has not paid geld. Villans held it TRE. There are 41 villans and 10 bordars with 7 ploughs. TRE, and afterwards, it was worth £4; now £6.

In the same vill the same Godfrey holds 9 hides of William, and at so much they are assessed. Vigot held them of King Edward and they belonged to Broadwater [in Worthing], which William de Braose holds in his rape. There is land for 4 ploughs. In demesne is 1 plough; and 10 villans and 12 bordars with 2 ploughs. TRE, and afterwards, it was worth £4; now 100s. In these 2 estates [there is] only 1 hall.

Nigel holds "ESMEREWIC" [? in Aldrington] of William. Azur held it of King Edward. Then, as now, it was assessed at 1½ hides. There is land for 4 ploughs. In demesne are 2 ploughs; and 4 villans and 6 bordars with 2 ploughs. TRE it was worth 40s; and afterwards 30s; now £4.

William de Vatteville holds HANGLETON of William. Azur held it of King Edward. Then it was assessed at 14 hides and 1 virgate; now at 8½ hides. There is land for 8 ploughs. In demesne are 2 ploughs; and 31 villans and 13 bordars with 5 ploughs.

This land belonged to Kingston by Sea, a manor of William de Braose. TRE, as now, worth £10; when received, £8.

Osweard holds of William PORTSLADE, half a hide. He himself held it TRE, and it has not paid geld. This man could go with the land where he would. There is 1 villan. It is worth 6s.

Albert holds half a hide in PORTSLADE. It has not paid geld. There is 1 villan with half a plough. It is and was worth 6s.

IN POYNINGS HUNDRED

Leofnoth holds PAYTHORNE of William. He himself held it of King Edward, and could go where he pleased. Then it was assessed at 4 hides; now at 1½ hides, because the others are in the rape of William de Braose. There is land for 1 plough, and there is [1 plough] in demesne, with 2 bordars. [...] In Lewes, 3 closes rendering 18d. It is and was worth 30s.

Osweard holds PERCHING of William. He himself held it TRE, and could go where he would. Then, as now, it was assessed at 3 hides. There is land for 2½ ploughs. In demesne is 1 [plough]; and 2 villans and 4 bordars with 1 plough, and half a mill rendering 40d, and 7 acres of meadow, [and] woodland for 2 pigs. In Lewes, 1½ closes rendering 9d. It is and was worth 40s.

In the same vill Tezelin holds 2 hides of William, and at so much they are assessed. They were part of Truleigh, which William de Braose holds. Bædling held them of Earl Godwine. In demesne is 1 plough; and 3 villans and 2 bordars with half a plough. [There is] half a mill rendering 13s4d, and 3 acres of meadow, [and] woodland for 2 pigs. In Lewes, half a close rendering 2d.

The same Tezelin holds FULKING of William. To Shipley

[Folio 27: SUSSEX]

it belonged, which William de Braose holds. Harold held it TRE. Then, as now, it was assessed at 3 hides and 1 virgate. There are 6 villans with 2 ploughs.

These 2 estates of Tezelin are together. They are and were always worth 50s.

William fitzReginald holds POYNINGS of William. Cola held it of Earl Godwine, because he gave it to him. TRE, as now, [it was assessed] at 8 hides, but it has never paid geld. There is land for 13 ploughs. In demesne are 2 ploughs; and 25 villans and 8 bordars with 15 ploughs. There is a church, and 2 slaves, and 2 mills rendering 12s, and 50 acres of meadow, [and] woodland for 40 pigs. TRE it was worth £12; and afterwards, as now, £10.

The same William holds PANGDEAN of William. Leofhelm held it of King Edward. Then, as now, it was assessed at 10 hides. There is land for 11 ploughs. In demesne is 1 plough; and 15 villans and 8 bordars with 8 ploughs. There is woodland for 2 pigs. In Lewes, 2 closes rendering 2s, and 1 acre of meadow. TRE, as now, worth 100s; when received, £6.

The same William holds PANGDEAN of William. Osweard held it of King Edward, and could go where he would. Then, as now, it was assessed at 9 hides. There is land for 10 ploughs. In demesne is 1 [plough]; and 15 villans and 6 bordars with 6 ploughs. In Lewes, 2 closes rendering 2s. TRE, and afterwards, it was worth £6; now 100s. Of the same land, Roger and Walter hold 2 carucates of William, with 4 bordars. It is worth 30s.

Ralph holds SADDLESCOMBE of William. Godwine the priest held it of Earl Godwine. It belonged to Bosham. Then, as now, it was assessed at 17 hides. There is land for 10 ploughs. In demesne are 2 ploughs; and 24 villans and 4 bordars with 7 ploughs. There are 13 acres of meadow. From salt, 15d. In Lewes, 1 close. There was woodland for 5 pigs, which is now in the rape of William de Braose. Of this land Ralph holds 4 hides, and there he has in demesne 1 plough; and 3 villans and 2 bordars with half a plough. The whole TRE was worth £15; and afterwards £10; now £11.

The same Ralph holds NEWTIMBER of William. Ælfheah held it of King Edward, and could go where he would. Then, as now, it was assessed at 10 hides. There is land for 7 ploughs. In demesne are 2 ploughs; and 14 villans and 7 bordars with 5 ploughs. There is 1 mill rendering 20d, and 2 acres of meadow, and woodland for 3 pigs. TRE, and afterwards, it was worth £7; now £8.

William de Vatteville holds PERCHING. Azur held it of King Edward, and 2 men [held] of Azur. It was assessed at 5½ hides then, as now. Then there were 2 halls. Now [it is] in 1 manor. There is land for 5½ ploughs. In demesne is 1 [plough]; and 4 villans and 3 bordars with 1 plough. There are 2 slaves, and 3 acres of meadow, [and] woodland for 3 pigs. From pasture, 6d. TRE it was worth 60s; and afterwards 40s; now 50s.

IN 'BUTTINGHILL' HUNDRED

Robert [...] holds HURSTPIERPOINT of William. Earl Godwine held it. Then it was assessed at 41 hides; now at nothing, because it has never paid geld. When received, [there were] only 18½ hides. In the rape of the Count of Mortain are 3½ hides. In the rape of William de Braose are 19 hides. There is land for 25 ploughs. [...] In demesne are 2 ploughs; and 35 villans and 8 bordars with 21½ ploughs. There is a church, and 8 slaves, and 3 mills rendering 9s, and 80 acres of meadow, [and] woodland for 50 pigs.

Of this land William holds 3 hides, Gilbert 3½ hides. Villans held them. The whole TRE was worth £36; and afterwards £9; now £12 all together.

The wife of William de Vatteville holds CLAYTON of William. Azur held it of King Edward. Then, as now, it was assessed at 7 hides. There is land for 12 ploughs. In demesne are 2 ploughs; and 26 villans and 5 bordars with 14 ploughs. There is a church, and 23 acres of meadow, [and] woodland for 15 pigs. In Lewes, 9 closes rendering 4s7d. TRE it was worth £10; and afterwards, as now, £8.

Alwine holds HURST WICKHAM of the woman herself. He himself held it of Azur. Then, as now, it was assessed at 3 hides. In demesne is 1 plough; and 3 villans with 1 plough; and in Lewes, 3 parts of a close rendering 15d.

William de Vatteville holds KEYMER of William. Azur held it of King Edward. Then, as now, it was assessed at 14 hides. There is land for 25 ploughs. In demesne are 2 ploughs; and 36 villans and 11 bordars with 17 ploughs. There is a church, and 3 slaves, and 40 acres of meadow, and 2 mills rendering 12s. In Lewes, 7 closes rendering 26d. TRE, and afterwards, it was worth £14; now £12.

IN STREAT HUNDRED

Ralph holds STREAT of William. Leofwine held it of King Edward. Then it was assessed at 9 hides; now at 8 hides. There is land for 16 ploughs. In demesne are 3 ploughs; and 20 villans and 12 bordars with 8 ploughs. There are 6 acres of meadow. From the woodland, 16 pigs. In Lewes, 3 closes rendering 18d.

Of this land a certain Ralph holds 1 hide, and there he has 1 plough, with 1 villan. There are 2 chapels. TRE and afterwards, as now, worth 100s.

Robert holds 12 hides of William in WESTMESTON. Countess Gytha held them, and villans held them under her. There was no hall there, and it did not pay geld, so they say. There is land for 9 ploughs. In demesne is 1 plough; and 4 villans and 12 bordars with 2 ploughs. There are 3 acres of meadow, and woodland for 10 pigs.

Of this land a knight holds 3 hides and 3 virgates, and there he has in demesne 1 plough, and [there are] 2 villans and 5 bordars. In Lewes 1 close renders nothing. TRE it was worth £7; and afterwards 100s; now £6.

Hugh fitzRanulph holds PLUMPTON of William. Godwine the priest held it of Earl Godwine. Then it was assessed at 32 hides; now at 30. There is land for 24 ploughs. In demesne are 3 ploughs; and 51 villans and 6 bordars with 22 ploughs. There is a church, and 8 slaves, and 2 mills rendering 20s, [and] woodland for 20 pigs. From rents, 17 pigs; meadow [...]. In Lewes, 9 closes rendering 4s5d. TRE, as now, worth £25; when received, l1s.

Robert holds EAST CHILTINGTON of William. Frederic held it of King Edward, and could go where he would. Then it was assessed at 7 hides; now at 5 hides and 1 virgate: the others are in the rape of the Count of Mortain. There is land for 6 ploughs. In demesne is 1 plough; and 3 villans with 1 plough. In Lewes, 1 close rendering 12d.

Of this land a certain knight holds 2½ hides, and there he has in demesne 1 plough; and [there are] 6 villans and 2 bordars with 1 plough, and half a mill rendering 15d, and 1½ closes rendering 8d. TRE, and afterwards, it was worth £4; now 100s.

Godfrey holds EAST CHILTINGTON of William. Godric held it of King Edward. Then it was assessed at 2 hides; now at 1½ hides, because half [a hide] is in the rape of the Count of Mortain. There is land for 2 ploughs. In demesne is 1 plough; and 5 villans and 3 bordars with 1 plough. There are 2 acres of meadow, [and] woodland for 12 pigs. In Lewes, 1 burgess paying 6d.

[Folio 27V: SUSSEX]

TRE, and afterwards, it was worth 16s; now 20s.

Nigel holds of William 1 hide in WOOTTON [in East Chiltington]. Godric held it of King Edward. It has not given geld. No one lives there. It is worth 12s.

Hugh holds WARNINGORE of William. 4 alodiaries held it of King Edward, and could go where they would with their lands. Then it was assessed at 3½ hides; now half [a hide] is in the rape of the Count of Mortain. There is land for 3 ploughs. In demesne are 3 ploughs; and 6 villans and 5 bordars with 3 ploughs. [...]. [There are] 3 closes rendering 21d. TRE it was worth 40s; and afterwards 30s; now 60s.

The same Hugh holds 3 virgates of William in Upper Beeding, which William de Braose holds. Villans held them TRE. They have never paid geld. In demesne is 1 plough; and 15 villans and 3 bordars with 5 ploughs. There is land for 5 ploughs. There are 3 acres of meadow, [and] woodland for 10 pigs. TRE, and afterwards, it was worth 15s; now 30s.

IN BARCOMBE HUNDRED

William de Vatteville holds BARCOMBE of William. Azur held it of Earl Godwine. Then it was assessed at 13 hides; now at 10½ hides; the others are in the rape of the Count of Mortain. They have never paid geld, so they say. There is land for 20 ploughs. In demesne are 2 ploughs; and 24 villans and 2 bordars with 9 ploughs. There is a church, and 3½ mills rendering 20s. In Lewes, 18 closes rendering 8s7d. TRE it was worth £12; and afterwards £6; now £8.

Ralph holds. HAMSEY of William. Wulfgifu held it of King Edward. Then it was assessed at 25 hides; now there are 14, because the others, namely 7 hides, are in the rape of the Count of Mortain, and 4 hides less half a virgate in the rape of Earl Roger. Now what Ralph has pays geld for 13 hides. There is land for 13 ploughs. In demesne are 2 hides; and 16 villans and 14 bordars with 10 ploughs. There is a church, and 200 acres of meadow, [and] woodland for 10 pigs. From the herbage, 13s.

Of the same land Hugh holds 1 hide, Ralph half a hide. The whole TRE was worth £20; and afterwards £10; now £10.

The same Ralph holds ALLINGTON of William. Wulfweard held it of King Edward. Then, as now, it was assessed at 6 hides. There is land for 6 ploughs. There are 8 villans and 3 bordars with 2½ ploughs. In Lewes, 1 close rendering 6d. Of this land Warner holds 1 hide, Osmund 1 hide. The whole TRE was worth £4.2s; and afterwards 62s; now 50s.

In the same vill Hugh holds 2 hides of William. Edith held

them TRE, and could go where she would. Then, as now, they were assessed at 2 hides. There is land for 1 plough. In demesne is half a plough; and 3 villans and 2 bordars with 1 plough. In Lewes, 4 closes rendering 4s. It is and was worth 20s.

In the same place Nigel holds half a virgate, and for so much it pays geld. There a certain villan has half a plough. It is and was worth 10s.

IN FALMER HUNDRED

Joscelin holds 1 hide of William in 'MOUSTONE' [in Falmer]. Azur held it of King Edward as of the manor of Ovingdean. It has not paid geld. In demesne is 1 plough. It is and was worth 20s.

IN WYNDHAM HUNDRED

Scolland holds 'BENEFELD' [in Twineham] of William. Thorgot held it of Cola, and Cola of King Edward. Then it was assessed at 2 hides; now at nothing. There is land for 3 ploughs. In demesne [are] 2 ploughs; and 5 villans with 8 bordars have 2 ploughs. TRE it was worth 60s; and afterwards the same; now £6.

Alfred holds 1 hide of William in 'Benefeld' [in Twineham] and 1 virgate, and at so much it was assessed TRE; now at nothing. Leofwine held it in parage. There is land for 1 plough, and there is [1 plough] in demesne; and 4 villans with half a plough. There are 4 acres of meadow, and woodland for 3 pigs. TRE, and afterwards, it was worth 10s; now 40s.

IN SWANBOROUGH HUNDRED

William fitzReginald holds ASHCOMBE of William. Cola held it TRE. Then, as now, it was assessed at 2 hides. In demesne is 1 plough; and 5 villans with 3 ploughs. The villans themselves are in the rape of the Count of Mortain, but they were always outside the rape. TRE and afterwards, as now, worth 26s.

[Folio 28: SUSSEX]

XIII. The land of William de Braose

IN 'BURGHBEACH' HUNDRED

WILLIAM DE BRAOSE holds UPPER BEEDING. King Edward held it in his farm. Then it was assessed at 32 hides. It has not paid geld. Of these hides William de Warenne has 10 hides in his rape. William de Braose holds the others. There is land for 28 ploughs. In demesne are 4 ploughs; and 62 villans and 48 bordars with 24 ploughs. There are 2 churches, and 6 acres of meadow, [and] woodland for 70 pigs, and 20 pigs from the rents, and 2 sesters of honey. TRE it rendered 1 day's farm and was worth £95.5s6d; and afterwards it was worth £50; now £40. All this land renders HERDIGELT.

William himself holds 8 hides which belonged to Rodmell, which William de Warenne holds in his rape, and they are assessed at 5½ hides. There are 10 villans having 5½ ploughs, and 4 acres of meadow. TRE and afterwards, as now, worth £8.

The same William holds 7 hides which belonged to 'BERTH' [in Wivelsfield], which William has in his rape. It was a Berewick. Now they are assessed at 1½ hides. In demesne are 2 ploughs; and 3 villans and 6 bordars with 2½ ploughs. TRE it was worth £6; and afterwards 55s; now £4.

William himself holds OLD ERRINGHAM. Frederic held it of King Edward, and could go where he would. Then it was assessed at 5 hides; now at half a hide. There are 2 villans and 5 bordars having nothing. TRE, as now, worth 40s; when received, 20s.

William himself holds OLD SHOREHAM. Azur held it of King Edward. Then it was assessed at 12 hides; now at 5 hides and half a virgate. There is land for 15 ploughs. In demesne are 3 ploughs; and 26 villans and 49 bordars with 12 ploughs. There is a church, and 6 acres of meadow, and woodland for 40 pigs. TRE it was worth £25; and afterwards £16; now £35, and yet it was at farm for £50, but it could not bear it.

William the knight holds TRULEIGH of William. Bædling [held it] of Earl Godwine TRE. Then it was assessed at 4 hides; now at nothing. There is land for 2½ ploughs. In demesne [is] 1 plough; and 3 villans and 6 bordars with half a plough, and 2 mills rendering 65d. Of this land Ansfrid holds half a hide, and there he has half a plough. The whole manor TRE was worth £4; and afterwards 60s; now 70s.

William himself holds TOTTINGTON in demesne. It belonged to Findon. [It is] a Berewick. Harold held it TRE. Then it was assessed at 6 hides; now at 1 hide. There is land for 5 ploughs. In demesne is 1 [plough]; and 3 villans and 7 bordars with 2 ploughs, and 4 acres of meadow. Of this land a certain William holds 2 hides, and there he has 3 villans with 1½ ploughs. The whole, TRE and afterwards, as now, was worth £6.

IN STEYNING HUNDRED

William himself holds ANNINGTON. Northmann held it of King Edward. Then it was assessed at 12 hides; now at 6 hides. There is land for 5 ploughs. In demesne is 1 [plough]; and 15 villans and 34 bordars with 4 ploughs. There is a church, [and] woodland for 10 pigs. TRE, and afterwards, it was worth £12; now £25.

William himself holds WASHINGTON. Earl Gyrth held it TRE. Then it was assessed at 59 hides. Now it does not give geld. In 1 of these hides is situated the castle of BRAMBER. There is land for 34 ploughs. In demesne are 5 ploughs; and 120 villans and 25 bordars with 34 ploughs. There are 5 salt-pans rendering 110 ambers of salt or 9s2d, and 4 acres of meadow. As pannage of the woodland, 60 pigs. There are 6 slaves.

Of this land Gilbert holds half a hide, Ralph 1 hide, William 3 virgates, Leofwine half a hide and he could withdraw with his land and gave geld to his lord and his lord gave nothing. These men have 4 villans and 2 bordars with 2½ ploughs, and 7 acres of meadow, and [there is] woodland for 10 pigs.

The whole manor TRE was worth £50; and afterwards £50; now William's demesne [is worth] £50.5s, [that] of the knights 50s and 12d; yet this manor was at farm for £100.

William himself holds STEYNING. King Edward held it as [part of] his farm. Then it was assessed at 18 hides and 3 virgates. It has never paid geld. Of these hides William has 12 hides; the others are in the rape of Earl Roger in Goring-by-Sea. In the hides which William has there is land for 21 ploughs. In demesne are 2 ploughs; and 45 villans and 33 bordars with 18 ploughs. There is 1 mill without rent, and 3 salt-pans rendering 30d, and 5 acres of meadow, [and] woodland for 20 pigs as pannage. TRE it was worth £28; and afterwards £20; now £25.

William himself holds FINDON. Harold held it TRE. Then it was assessed at 30½ hides. Of these, 10 hides are in the rape of Earl Roger. The others have not paid geld, except 3 hides. There is land for 17 ploughs. In demesne are 3 ploughs; and 27 villans and 17 bordars with 17 ploughs. There is a church, and 6 slaves, and woodland for 20 pigs.

Of this land a certain William holds 5 hides, and there are 2 ploughs in demesne; and 2 villans and 6 bordars with 1 plough.

The whole TRE was worth £28; and afterwards £20; now £28 | 10s | .

William himself holds SULLINGTON. Wulfweard held it of King Edward. Then it was assessed at 9 hides; now at 4 hides. Of this land 3 virgates are in the rape of Arundel. There is land for 7 ploughs. In demesne are 3 ploughs; and 20 villans and 14 bordars with 6 ploughs. There is 1 mill rendering 6s, and 6 acres of meadow, [and] woodland for 30 pigs. TRE it was worth £9; and afterwards, as now, £8.

Ralph holds WISTON of William. Azur held it of Earl Godwine. Then it was assessed at 12 hides; now at nothing. There is land for 8 ploughs. In demesne are 2 ploughs; and 10 villans and 24 bordars with 5 ploughs. There is a church, and 5 slaves, and 7 acres of meadow, [and] woodland for 30 pigs. TRE, as now, worth £12; when received, £4.

William fitzManni holds WAPPINGTHORN of William. Karli held it of King Edward. Then it was assessed at 6 hides; now at 2 hides. There is land for 6 ploughs. In demesne is 1 plough; and 7 villans and 15 bordars with 4 ploughs. There are 7 acres of meadow, [and] woodland rendering 5d. From salt, 20d; and 1 sester of honey. TRE it was worth 100s; and afterwards 20s; now £4.

Gilbert holds CLAPHAM of William. Alwine held it of King Edward, and it belonged to Lyminster, which Earl Roger holds in his rape. Then it was assessed at 8 hides, but 2 hides are in the rape of Earl Roger. What Gilbert holds has paid geld for 3 hides. There is land for 4 ploughs. In demesne are 2 ploughs; and 5 villans and 8 bordars with 2 ploughs. TRE it was worth £8; and afterwards £4; now £6.

The same Gilbert holds of William land for 3 ploughs. This belonged to Goring-by-Sea, which is in the rape of Earl Roger. It is outside the rape and not included in the number of hides. It has never paid geld. There are 6 villans and 5 bordars with 3 ploughs. TRE and afterwards, as now, worth 30s.

Richard holds [Lower and Upper] CHANCTON of William. Essocher held it of Earl Godwine. Then it was assessed at 4 hides; now at nothing. There is land for 2 ploughs. In demesne is 1 plough, with 5 bordars. TRE it was worth £4; and afterwards 40s; now 60s.

[Folio 28V: SUSSEX]

Tetbert holds 1 hide in [Lower and Upper] Chancton of William. Wulfrun held it of Earl Godwine. There is nothing there. It is worth 11s.

William fitzNorman holds COOMBES of William. Gyrth held it TRE. Then it was assessed at 10 hides; now at 5 hides. There is land for 8 ploughs. In demesne are 2 [ploughs]; and 27 villans and 4 bordars with 10 ploughs. There is a church, and 2 slaves, and from the salt-pans 50s5d, [and] woodland for 4 pigs. TRE it was worth £12; and afterwards £10; now £13.

The same William holds APPLESHAM of William. Leofwine held it of Earl Godwine. Then it was assessed at 7½ hides; now at nothing. There is land for 5 ploughs. In demesne are 3 ploughs; and 7 villans and 7 bordars with 2 ploughs. There is 1 slave, and 1 mill rendering 6s, and 5 acres of meadow, and woodland for 5 pigs. TRE and afterwards, as now, worth £6.

Two knights hold 1½ hides of this land, and there is 1 bordar, and 2 salt-pans rendering 5s. It is worth 23s4d.

The same William holds 2 hides of William in 'Offington' [in Worthing]. They have not paid geld. Godwine held them. There is 1 plough in demesne. Nothing more. It is and was worth 26s.

IN HENFIELD HUNDRED

William fitzRanulph holds WOODMANCOTE of William. Countess Gytha held it. Then it was assessed at 3½ hides; now at 2 hides. There is land for 9 ploughs. In demesne is 1 plough; and 16 villans and 4 bordars with 8 ploughs. There is a church, and 5 acres of meadow, [and] woodland for 13 pigs.

Of this land a certain knight holds 1 hide, and there he has 1 plough, with 1 villan. TRE and afterwards, as now, worth £3.10s.

Ralph holds WANTLEY of William. Beorhtmær held it of Azur, and Azur of Harold. Then it was assessed at 4½ hides; now at nothing. There is land for 2 ploughs. In demesne is 1 [plough]; and 2 villans and 2 bordars with half a plough. There are 2 slaves, and 1 mill rendering 20d, and 10 acres of meadow. TRE, and afterwards, it was worth 40s; now 22s.

[IN] WYNDHAM HUNDRED

The same Ralph holds half a hide of William in Woolfly. Alwine held it of Azur, and then it was assessed at half a hide, now at nothing. There is nothing except 10 acres of meadow. It is worth 5s.

The same Ralph holds SHERMANBURY of William. Azur held it of Harold. Then it was assessed at 2 hides; now at nothing. There is land for 2 ploughs. In demesne is 1 plough;

and 1 villan and 3 bordars with 1 plough. There is a chapel, and 4 slaves. TRE and afterwards, as now, worth 24s.

William fitzRanulph holds half a hide of William in Morley. Alweard held it of Azur, and it was assessed at half a hide then, as now. There is half a plough, with 2 bordars. TRE, and afterwards, it was worth 10s; | now 5s. |

The same William holds SAKEHAM of William. Beorhtwine held it of Azur. Then it was assessed at 2 hides; now at nothing. There is land for 2 ploughs. There are now only 2 oxen, and 1 villan and 2 bordars, [and] woodland rendering 10d TRE, and afterwards, it was worth 10s; now 5s.

IN ALDRINGTON HUNDRED

Ralph holds KINGSTON BY SEA of William. Azur held it of Harold. Then it was assessed at 21 hides. Of these, 6 hides are in the rape of William de Warenne. What Ralph holds has paid geld for 6 hides. There is land for 8 ploughs. In demesne are 2 ploughs; and 12 villans and 20 bordars with 10 ploughs. There is a church, and 6 salt-pans rendering 20s and 10 ambers of salt.

Of this land 3 knights hold 4½ hides, and there they have 2 ploughs, and 2 villans and 6 bordars.

The whole manor TRE was worth £15; now Ralph's part [is worth] £11.7s6d, what the knights hold is worth 100s.

In the same vill William fitzRanulph holds of William 7 hides less 1 virgate. Gunild held them of Harold, and at so much they are assessed. There is land for 3 ploughs. In demesne are 2 ploughs; and 4 villans and 8 bordars with 1 plough. There is a church, and 1 slave, and 3 salt-pans rendering 22d. From pasture, 16s, and [there are] 4 acres of meadow. TRE, as now, worth £7; when received, £3.

IN 'BRIGHTFORD' HUNDRED

Robert holds BROADWATER [in Worthing] of William. Vigot held it of King Edward. Then it was assessed at 29 hides. Of these, 9 hides are in the rape of William de Warenne, and William de Braose has 2 hides in demesne. What Robert holds has paid geld for 6 hides. There is land for 7 ploughs. In demesne are 2 ploughs; and 30 villans and 4 bordars with 10 ploughs. There is a church, and 3 slaves, and 1 mill rendering 7s, and 60 acres of meadow, [and] woodland for 20 pigs. Of this land 1 knight holds 1 hide. The whole, TRE and afterwards, was worth £15; now £14.

Ralph holds 'HEENE' [in Worthing] of William. Leofræd held it of Earl Godwine. Then, as now, it was assessed at 2½ hides. In demesne is 1 plough; and 3 villans and 2 bordars with 1 plough, and 1 slave, and 3 acres of meadow. It is and was worth 40s.

In the same vill Alweard holds 2½ hides of William. He himself held it of King Edward. Then, as now, it was assessed at 2½ hides. In demesne is 1 plough; and 3 villans and 5 bordars with 1 plough. It is and | was worth | 40s.

Robert holds DURRINGTON of William. Wulfweard held it of Earl Harold. Then it was assessed at 4 hides; now at 1 hide. There is land for 2 ploughs. There are 2 villans and 5 bordars with half a plough, and 4 acres of meadow, [and] woodland for 4 pigs. Of this land 1 Frenchman holds 1½ hides, and there are 2 bordars. TRE, and afterwards, it was worth 40s; now 60s.

The same Robert holds DURRINGTON in the same place of William. Edward held it of King Edward. Then it was assessed at 8 hides; now at 2 hides and 1 virgate. There is land for 6 ploughs. In demesne is 1 plough; and 9 villans and 9 bordars with 7 ploughs. There is a church, and 4 slaves, and 8 acres of meadow, [and] woodland for 10 pigs. TRE and afterwards, as now, worth 100s.

The same Robert holds WORTHING of William. 7 alodi-aries held it of Earl Godwine. Then it was assessed at 11 hides. Now Robert has 9 hides, and they have paid geld for 2 hides. There is land for 3 ploughs. In demesne are 2 ploughs; and 6 villans and 9 bordars with 1 plough. There is 1 slave, and 7 acres of meadow. TRE and afterwards, as now, worth 100s.

Robert holds WORTHING of William. There are 1½ hides. Leofwine held it of King [Edward], and it paid geld for half a hide.[...] There is 1 villan and 5 bordars, and half an acre of meadow. It is and was worth 12s.

In the same vill Ralph holds half a hide. It belonged to Sompting. Tosti held it of Leofwine, and it was assessed at so much, half a hide, then, as now. There are 4 oxen, and 1 bordar, and 1 acre of meadow. It is and was worth 5s.

Ralph holds SOMPTING of William. Leofwine held it of King Edward. Then it was assessed at 17 hides. Of these, 2 hides are in the rape of Earl Roger, in Goring-by-Sea; and elsewhere are 3½ hides

[Folio 29: SUSSEX]

which other men hold. Ralph has in his own hand 11½ hides. Now they pay geld for 2 hides and 3 virgates. There is land for 5 ploughs. In demesne are 2 ploughs; and 19 villans and 16 bordars with 9 ploughs. There is a church, and 5 slaves, and 1 mill rendering 3s, and 8 salt-pans rendering 13s, and 30 acres of meadow.

Of this land a knight holds 1 hide, and has in demesne 1 plough, and 2 villans and 4 bordars, and 1 salt-pan rendering 2s, and 2 acres of meadow. The whole, TRE and afterwards, was worth £8; now £7.8s.

Of the same manor another Ralph holds 2 hides of William, but they are additional to the above hides. Leofwine held them of King Edward, and then they were assessed at 2 hides; now at 1½. There are 4 villans and 1 bordar with half a plough, and 2 acres of meadow. There is land for 1 plough. TRE, and afterwards, it was worth 50s; now 70s.

Of this manor Robert holds 1 hide of William in addition to the above hides. Leofwine held it, and then it was assessed at 1 hide; now at half a virgate. There is 1 villan and 1 bordar, and 4 acres of meadow. It is and was worth 8s.

Ralph holds LOWER COKEHAM of William. Grene held it of Earl Harold. Then it was assessed at 2 hides and 1 virgate;

now at nothing. In demesne is 1 plough, with 5 bordars, and 8 acres of meadow. It is and always [was] worth 55s.

The same Ralph holds 'DANKTON' [in Sompting] of William. Auti held it of Earl Godwine. Then it was assessed at 5 hides; now at 1 hide and 3 virgates. There is land for 2 ploughs. Of this land William holds 2 hides and 1 virgate, Robert 1 hide and 1 virgate, and another knight 1½ hides. In demesne is nothing save only 2 villans and 3 bordars, and 10 acres of meadow. The whole, TRE and afterwards, as now, [worth] 72s.

Robert holds [North and South] LANCING of William. Leofwine held it of King Edward. Then it was assessed at 16 hides and 1 virgate. Of these, Robert himself has 12 hides and 1 virgate, and they have paid geld for 5 hides and 1½ virgates. There is land for 5 ploughs. In demesne are 2½ ploughs; and 13 villans and 7 bordars with 2 ploughs. There is 1 mill rendering 8s, and 7 salt-pans rendering 20s3d.

Of this land 2 knights hold 2½ hides and half a virgate, and there they have in demesne 2 ploughs, and [there are] 11 salt-pans rendering 12s6d. The whole TRE was worth £9; and afterwards £7; now £14.10s.

In the same vill Ralph holds 3½ virgates, and they are [part] of the above 16 hides, and have paid geld for 1 virgate. There is 1 villan and 2 bordars. It is worth 5s.

Of this manor another Ralph holds 3 hides and 1 virgate, and they are likewise [part] of the above 16 hides. This land of Ralph's paid geld for 3 virgates, and does now. In demesne is 1 plough; and 2 villans and 2 bordars with half a plough. There are 5 salt-pans rendering 12s6d. It is and was worth 50s.

And moreover Ralph holds 1 virgate which belonged to [North and South] Lancing and gave geld. 1 villan holds and held it. It is and was worth 5s.

Ralph fitzTheodric holds LOWER COKEHAM of William. Beorhtmær held it of Azur. Then, as now, it was assessed at 1½ hides. In demesne is half a plough; and 1 villan and 3 bordars with half a plough. [There is] a salt-pan rendering 40d, and 2 acres of meadow, [and] woodland for 1 pig. It is and was worth 20s.

William fitzBonard holds of William a Berewick which belonged to HURSTPIERPOINT, a manor which William de Warenne holds. It is called HOE. Earl Godwine held it. Then it was assessed at 6 hides; now at 2 hides less 1 virgate. There is land for 6 ploughs. In demesne are 2 ploughs; and 14 villans and 8 bordars with 4 ploughs. There are 6 salt-pans rendering 7s6d.

Of this land a knight holds 1 hide, and there he has half a plough. The whole, TRE and afterwards, was worth £4; now £6.

IN 'EASWRITHE' HUNDRED

Robert holds ASHINGTON of William. 2 alodiaries held it of Earl Godwine. Then it was assessed at 2½ hides; now at nothing. It belonged to Washington. There is land for 3 ploughs. In demesne is 1 [plough]; and 6 villans and 2 bordars with 1½ ploughs. It is and was always worth 30s.

Ralph holds 3 hides of William in West Chiltington, which is in the rape of Earl Roger. They have not paid geld. There is land for 6 ploughs. In demesne is half a plough; and 18 villans and 6 bordars with 3½ ploughs. There are 6 acres of meadow, and woodland for 30 pigs. TRE and afterwards, as now, worth 60s.

Morin holds THAKEHAM of William. Beorhtsige held it of King Edward. Then it was assessed at 20 hides and 3 virgates; now at 5 hides. There is land for 14 ploughs. In demesne are 2 ploughs; and 30 villans and 12 bordars with 8 ploughs. There is a church, and 1 mill rendering 3s, and 16 acres of meadow, [and] woodland for 60 pigs.

Of this land a knight holds 1 hide. There he has 5 oxen, with 1 bordar. The whole TRE, as now, was worth £14; when received, £10.

The same Morin holds MUNTHAM of William. Osweard held it of King Edward. Then it was assessed at 3 hides; now at nothing. There is land for 2 ploughs. There are 5 villans and 6 bordars with 2 ploughs. [There is] woodland for 5 pigs. TRE it was worth 50s; and afterwards 30s; now 70s.

The same Morin holds of William 1 hide which belonged to Washington. Edwin held it of Earl Godwine. Then it was assessed at 1 hide; now at nothing. There is 1 villan, and 1 mill rendering 15d. It is and always [was] worth 10s.

Ælfgeat holds of William land for 1 plough; [it is part] of William's demesne and is not included in the number of hides. There is 1 plough, and 1 mill rendering 3s. It belonged to Storrington as pasture. Now it has lately been settled. It is worth 10s.

IN WEST GRINSTEAD HUNDRED

William fitzBonard holds EATONS of William. Thorgot held it of Earl Godwine. Then it was assessed at 3½ hides; now at 1 hide. It belonged to Warningcamp, which is in the rape of Earl Roger. There is land for 2 ploughs. In demesne is 1 [plough]; and 5 villans and 3 bordars with 1 plough, and 6 acres of meadow. [There is] woodland rendering 5d. TRE it was worth 20s; and afterwards 15s; now 40s.

IN IFIELD HUNDRED

William fitzRanulph holds IFIELD of William. Alwig held it of King Edward. Then, as now, it was assessed at 1 hide. In demesne is nothing; and [there are] 5 villans and 4 bordars with 1 plough, and 6 acres of meadow, and woodland for 6 pigs. It is and was worth 20s.

The same William holds half a hide which belonged to OLD SHOREHAM, which William de Braose holds. This hide [sic] is quit of geld. There is 1 villan with half a plough. It is worth 6s.

IN STEYNING HUNDRED

Robert holds BUNCTON of William. Leofwine held it of King Edward. Then it was assessed at 4½ hides; now at nothing. There is land for 5 ploughs. In demesne is 1 plough; and 19 villans and 7 bordars with 5 ploughs. There are 2 acres of meadow, woodland for 10 pigs, and 1 mill rendering 2s. TRE, and afterwards, [worth] 30s; | now 40s. |

The same Robert has a small pasture, with 2 bordars who pay 5s. This is in Angmering, which Earl Roger holds in his rape.

[Folio 29v: SUSSEX]

XIIII. The land of Oda and Ealdræd

IN EASEBOURNE HUNDRED

Oda holds WOOLBEDING of the king. Fulcwig held it of King Edward [in] alod. Then, as now, it was assessed at 6 hides. There is land for 7 ploughs. In demesne is 1 plough; and 14 villans and 5 bordars with 6 ploughs. There are 5 slaves, and 1 mill rendering 10s, and 23 acres of meadow, [and] woodland for 30 pigs. There is a church. TRE, as now, worth £6; when received, £4.

Ealdræd holds IPING of the king.[...] Oualet held it of King Edward. Then, as now, it was assessed at 4 hides. There is land for 3 ploughs. In demesne is 1 plough; and 8 villans and 2 bordars with 2 ploughs. There are 5 slaves, and 1 mill rendering 3s4d, and 3 acres of meadow, woodland for 20 pigs, and a quarry rendering 9s4d, [and] 1 enclosure rendering 20d. From church-scot, 40d TRE, as now, [worth] £4; when received, £3.

SURREY

Here Are Noted the Landholders In Surrey

I KING WILLIAM
II The Archbishop of Canterbury
III The Bishop of Winchester
IIII Bishop Osbern
V The Bishop of Bayeux
VI The Abbot of Westminster
VII The Abbot of Winchester
VIII The Abbot of Chertsey
IX The Abbot of Saint-Wandrille
X The Abbot of La-Croix-Saint-Leufroy
XI The Abbot of Battle
XII The Abbess of Barking
XIII The canons of St Paul's of London
XIIII The Church of Lambeth
XV Count Eustace
XVI The Countess of Boulogne
XVII The Count of Mortain
XVIII Earl Roger
XIX Richard of Tonbridge
XX William de Braose
XXI William fitzAnsculf
XXII Walter fitzOther
XXIII Walter de Douai
XXIIII Gilbert fitzRicher
XXV Geoffrey de Mandeville
XXVI Geoffrey Orlateile
XXVII Edward of Salisbury
XXVIII Robert Malet
XXIX Miles Crispin
XXX Hamo the sheriff
XXXI Humphrey the chamberlain
XXXII Ralph de Feugeres
XXXIII Reginald fitzErchenbald
XXXIIII Albert the clerk
XXXV Odard the crossbowman
XXXVI Osweald, Theodric, and other servants of the king

The land of the King

IN WOKING HUNDRED

IN GUILDFORD KING WILLIAM HAS 75 closes in which dwell 175 men. TRE it rendered £18.0s3d; now it is valued at £30, and yet it renders £32.

Of the aforesaid closes, Ranulph the clerk has 3 closes in which 6 men dwell, and of these the same Ranulph has sake and soke unless the common geld from which no one may escape be laid upon the vill. If his man commits an offence in the vill, and, after being distrained, escapes, the king's reeve has nothing from him. But if he is accused and is distrained there, then the king has the fine. Archbishop Stigand held these [closes] thus.

Ranulph the sheriff holds 1 close, which he has up to this time held of the Bishop of Bayeux. The men, however, testify that it does not belong to any manor, but that he who held it TRE granted it to Tovi, the reeve of the vill, in compensation for a forfeiture of his.

There is another house which the reeve of the Bishop of Bayeux holds of the manor of Bramley. Concerning this the men of the shire say that he has no other right there, except that the reeve of the vill married a certain widow whose house it was, and therefore the bishop put that house into his own manor, and the king has hitherto lost the customary dues, but the bishop has them.

The jurors declare also concerning another house that it belongs to Bramley, only because the reeve of this vill was a friend of that man who had this house, and, on his [friend's] death, transferred it to the manor of Bramley.

Waleran also disseised a certain man of a house from which King Edward had the customary dues. Now Odbert holds it with the customary dues, as he says, by [grant from] King William.

Robert de Watteville holds 1 house, which rendered every customary due TRE; now it renders nothing.

King William holds in demesne WOKING. It was [part] of King Edward's farm. It was then assessed at 15½ hides. They have never paid geld. There is land for 6 ploughs. In demesne is 1 [plough]; and 33 villans and 9 bordars with 20 ploughs. There is a church. Osbern holds it. And there is 1 mill rendering 11s4d. There are 32 acres of meadow, [and] woodland for 133 pigs.

Of this land, Walter fitzOther holds 3 virgates. A certain forester held this TRE, and it was then put out of the manor by King Edward. Now there is nothing. TRE, and afterwards, it was worth £15 by tale; now £15 by weight, and 25s to the sheriff.

The king holds in demesne STOKE [in Guildford]. It was [part] of King Edward's farm. It was then assessed at 17 hides. They have paid no geld. There is land for 16 ploughs. In demesne are 2 ploughs; and 24 villans and 10 bordars with 20 ploughs. There is a church which William holds of the king, with half a hide in alms. There are 5 slaves, and 2 mills rendering 25s, and 16 acres of meadow. [There is] woodland for 40 pigs, and this is in the king's park. TRE, and afterwards, it was worth £12; now £15, yet he who holds it pays £15 by weight. The sheriff has 25s.

IN BRIXTON HUNDRED

The king holds BERMONDSEY. Earl Harold held it. It was then assessed at 13 hides; now at 12 hides. There is land for 8 ploughs. In demesne is 1 plough; and 25 villans and 33 bordars with 4 ploughs. There is a new and handsome church, and 20 acres of meadow. [There is] woodland for 5 pigs as pannage. In London, 13 burgesses paying 44d. TRE, as now, worth £15; and the sheriff has 20s. The Count of Mortain holds 1 hide, which, TRE and afterwards, was in this manor.

The king holds MERTON. Earl Harold held it. It was then assessed, as now, at 20 hides. There is land for 21 ploughs. In demesne are 2 ploughs; and 56 villans and 13 bordars with 18 ploughs. There is a church, and 2 mills rendering 60s, and 10 acres of meadow, [and] woodland for 80 pigs. TRE it was worth £25; and afterwards £16; now £35, yet he who holds it pays £43. In Southwark 16 messuages rendering 18s2d belong to this manor.

A certain Urk holds 2 hides, which always belonged in this manor, and are in another hundred. He himself held them TRE. It was then assessed at 2 hides; now at nothing. There is 1 plough in demesne, and 2 acres of meadow. It has always been worth 20s.

The Bishop of Lisieux holds in Kent 2 sulungs which belonged to this manor TRE and [in the time] of King William, as the men of the hundred testify. He himself calls to warranty the Bishop of Bayeux, and his reeve has not wanted to plead concerning it.

IN WALLINGTON HUNDRED

The king holds in demesne WALLINGTON. TRE, as now, it was assessed at 11 hides. There is land for 11 ploughs. In demesne is 1 plough; and 15 villans and 14 bordars with 10 ploughs. There are 3 slaves, and 2 mills rendering 30s, and 8 acres of meadow. [There is] woodland which is in Kent.

Richard of Tonbridge holds of this manor 1 virgate, with woodland, from which he evicted a peasant who dwelt there. Now it renders to the sheriff 10s a year. The whole manor TRE was worth £15; now £10.

IN REIGATE HUNDRED

The king holds in demesne REIGATE. Queen Edith held it. It was then assessed at 37½ hides; now for the king's use at 34 hides. There is land [...]. In demesne are 3 ploughs; and 67 villans and 11 bordars with 26 ploughs. There are 2 mills rendering 12s less 2d, and 12 acres of meadow. [There is] woodland for 140 pigs as pannage, and from the herbage, 43 pigs. It is now valued at £40, and renders as much.

IN KINGSTON HUNDRED

The king holds in demesne KINGSTON UPON THAMES. It was [part] of King Edward's farm. It was then assessed at 39 hides; now at nothing. There is land for 32 ploughs. In demesne are 2 ploughs; and 86 villans and 14 bordars with 25 ploughs. There is a church, and 2 slaves, and 5 mills rendering 20s, and 2 fisheries rendering 10s, and a third fishery very good but without rent. There are 40 acres of meadow, [and] woodland for 6 pigs. TRE and afterwards, as now, worth £30.

Of the villans of this vill, Humphrey the chamberlain had, and has, 1 villan in his charge for the purpose of collecting the queen's wool. He also received from this man 20s as a relief when his father was dead.

IN 'COPTHORNE' HUNDRED

The king holds in demesne EWELL. TRE it was assessed at 16 hides less 1 virgate; now at 13½ hides at farm. There is land [...]. In demesne is 1 plough; and 48 villans and 4 bordars with 15 ploughs. There are 2 mills rendering 10s, and 14 acres of meadow. [There is] woodland for 100 pigs. From the herbage, 11 pigs. TRE it was worth £20; and afterwards, as now, £16; and yet it renders £25. The men of the hundred testify that 2 hides and 1 virgate have been subtracted from this manor, which were there TRE; but the reeves let them out to their friends, and a woodland dene and a croft. The church of Leatherhead belongs to this manor, with 40 acres of land. It is worth 20s. Osbern de EU holds it.

The king holds in demesne FETCHAM. Queen Edith held it. It was then assessed at 7 hides; now at none. There is land [...]. In demesne is half a plough and 2 oxen; and 3 villans and 10 bordars with 2 ploughs. There are 4 mills rendering 4s, and 10 acres of meadow. From the pannage and herbage, 6 pigs. TRE, and afterwards, it was worth 60s; now 50s.

IN BLACKHEATH HUNDRED

The king holds in demesne GOMSHALL. Earl Harold held it. It was then assessed at 20 hides; now at nothing. There is land for 20 ploughs. In demesne are 2 [ploughs]; and 30 villans and 8 bordars with 18 ploughs. There are 6 slaves, and a mill rendering 40d, and 3 acres of meadow, [and] woodland for 30 pigs. TRE it was worth £15; and afterwards £10; now £20, and yet it renders £30. The villans of this vill are quit of every sheriff's matter. Of the land of this manor, the bishop put half a hide in the manor of Bramley wrongfully, and holds it, which had been in Gomshall TRE, and also [in the time] of [King] William.

In WOTTON Hundred the king has in demesne 1 hide, which belongs to Gomshall.

The king holds in demesne SHERE. Queen Edith held it. It was then assessed at 9 hides, and yet there were then 16 hides there. Recently it has not paid geld. There is land for 14 ploughs. In demesne are 2 ploughs; and 19 villans and 6 bordars with 12 ploughs. There is a church, and 6 slaves, and

2 mills rendering 10s, and 3 acres of meadow, [and] woodland for 50 pigs. TRE and afterwards, as now, worth £15.

In WOTTON Hundred the king has in demesne 3 virgates, which belong to Shere and are valued there.

IN WOTTON HUNDRED

The king holds in demesne DORKING. Queen Edith held it. It was then assessed at 10½ hides; now at nothing. There is land for 14 ploughs. In demesne are 2 ploughs; and 38 villans and 13 bordars with 14 ploughs. There is a church, and 4 slaves, and 3 mills rendering 15s4d. There are 3 acres of meadow. [There is] woodland for 50 pigs as pannage. From the herbage, 38 pigs. TRE and afterwards, as now, worth £18.

A certain Eadric, who held this manor, gave 2 hides to his daughters and they could go where they would with their lands. Of these hides, Richard of Tonbridge has 1, which does not belong to any manor, and he has there in demesne 1 plough, with 1 bordar, and a mill at the hall, and [there is] 1 acre of meadow. Herfrid holds the other hide of the Bishop of Bayeux. Richard's hide is worth 20s, Herfrid's 10s.

From the 3 manors which Queen Edith had in Surrey, the sheriff has £7, because he affords them aid when they have need.

IN GODALMING HUNDRED

The king holds in demesne GODALMING. King Edward held it. Then [there were] 24 hides. They have never paid geld. There is land for 30 ploughs. In demesne are 3 ploughs; and 50 villans and 29 bordars with 19 ploughs. There are 2 slaves, and 3 mills rendering 41s8d, and 25 acres of meadow, [and] woodland for 100 pigs. TRE it was worth £25; and afterwards £20; now £30 by tale, and yet it renders £30 weighed and assayed.

Ranulph Flambard holds of this manor a church, to which belong 3 hides. Wulfmær held it of King Edward. They have never paid geld. There is land for 2 ploughs. In demesne is 1 [plough]; and 5 villans and 12 cottars with 2 ploughs. There are 15 acres of meadow, and woodland for 3 pigs.

The same Ranulph holds another church in the same place, which renders 12s a year. These 3 hides TRE, as now, were worth £4; when received, £3.

The same Ranulph holds of the king TUESLEY. It belonged to Godalming. Leofwine held it of King Edward. Then, as now, [there was] 1 hide. It does not pay geld. There is land for 1 plough, and there is [1 plough], with 1 villan and 6 cottars and 1 slave. TRE it was worth 60s; and afterwards, as now, 40s.

In 'ELMBRIDGE' [Hundred] Ealdgyth, a certain woman, holds of the king 1 virgate. It is worth 3s.

II. The land of the Archbishop of Canterbury

IN WALLINGTON HUNDRED

ARCHBISHOP Lanfranc holds in demesne CROYDON. TRE it was assessed at 80 hides, and now at 16 hides and 1 virgate. There is land for 20 ploughs. In demesne are 4 ploughs; and 48 villans and 25 bordars with 34 ploughs. There is a church, and a mill rendering 5s, and 8 acres of meadow, [and] woodland for 200 pigs.

Of the land of this manor, Restold holds 7 hides of the archbishop; Ralph 1 hide; and they have £7.8s from them for rent. TRE, and afterwards, the whole was worth £12; now £27 to the archbishop, £10.10s to his men.

The archbishop himself holds CHEAM for the sustenance of the monks. TRE it was assessed at 20 hides, and now at 4 hides. There is land for 14 ploughs. In demesne are 2 ploughs; and 25 villans and 12 cottars with 15 ploughs. There is a church, and 5 slaves, and 1 acre of meadow, [and] woodland for 25 pigs. TRE, and afterwards, it was worth £8; now £14.

IN BRIXTON HUNDRED

The archbishop himself holds in demesne MORTLAKE. TRE it was assessed at 80 hides. The canons of St Paul's hold 8 of these hides, which with these [others] have paid, and do pay, geld. Now they pay geld for 25 hides all together. There is land for 35 ploughs. In demesne are 5 ploughs; and 80 villans and 14 bordars with 28 ploughs. There is a church, and 16 slaves, and 2 mills rendering 100s, and 20 acres of meadow. From the woodland, 55 pigs as pannage.

In London were 17 messuages rendering 52d. In Southwark, 4 messuages rendering 27d, and 20s from the toll of the vill of Putney, and a fishery without rent. This fishery belonged to

[Folio 31: SURREY]

Earl Harold in Mortlake TRE, and Archbishop Stigand had it a long while TRW; and yet they say that Harold set it up by force TRE in the land of Kingston upon Thames and in the land of St Paul's. The whole manor TRE was worth £32; and afterwards £10; now £38.

Baynard holds of the archbishop WALWORTH. TRE it was for the clothing of the monks. It was then [...] assessed at 5 hides; now at 3½ hides. There is land for 3 ploughs. In demesne is 1 plough; and 14 villans and 5 bordars with 3 ploughs. There is a church, and 8 acres of meadow. TRE it was worth 30s; and afterwards 20s; now 60s.

IN REIGATE HUNDRED

The archbishop himself holds MERSTHAM [Merstham and South Merstham] for the clothing of the monks. TRE it was assessed at 20 hides; now at 5 hides. There is land for 8 ploughs. In demesne are 2 ploughs; and 21 villans and 4 bordars with 8 ploughs. There is a church, and a mill rendering 30d, and 8 slaves, and 8 acres of meadow. [There is] woodland for 25 pigs. From the herbage, 16 pigs. TRE it was worth £8; and afterwards £4; now £12.

IN WOKING HUNDRED

The archbishop himself holds EAST HORSLEY for the sustenance of the monks. TRE it was assessed at 14 hides; now at 3 hides and 1½ virgates. There is land for 5 ploughs. In demesne is 1 [plough]; and 13 villans and 6 bordars with 7½ ploughs. There are 3 slaves. [There is] woodland for 50 pigs. TRE it was worth £4; and afterwards the same; now as much, and yet it renders 100s.

III. The land of the Bishop of Winchester

THE BISHOP OF WINCHESTER holds FARNHAM. ST PETER always held it. TRE it was assessed at 60 hides, and now at 40 hides. There is land [...]. In demesne are 5 ploughs; and 36 villans and 11 bordars with 29 ploughs. There are 11 slaves, and 6 mills rendering 46s4d, and 35 acres of meadow, [and] woodland for 150½ pigs as pannage. Of the land of this manor Ralph holds of the bishop 4 hides less 1 virgate; William 3 hides and 1 virgate; Wazo half a hide. In these lands [are] 3 ploughs in demesne; and 22 villans and 9 bordars with 6 ploughs. [There is] woodland for 25 pigs. TRE the manor, so far as it lies in Surrey, was worth £55; when received, £30; now the demesne of the bishop [is worth] £38, [the land] of this men £9. Osbern de EU holds the church of this manor of the bishop. It is worth £6, with 1 hide, which he has in Hampshire.

IIII. The land of Bishop Osbern

IN WOKING HUNDRED

Bishop OSBERN holds WOKING. He himself held it TRE, and it was then assessed at 8 hides; now at 3½ hides. There is land for 9½ ploughs. In demesne [are] 1½ ploughs; and 20 villans and 6 bordars with 8½ ploughs. There are 3 slaves, and a mill rendering 30d, and 14 acres of meadow, [and] woodland for 28 pigs.

This manor has, and had, a customary due in the king's woodland of Woking; it is this: that the lord of this vill can have in this woodland 120 pigs without [payment for] pannage. 2 men, Ansgot and Godfrey, hold this manor of the bishop; each [holds] 4 hides. The whole, TRE and afterwards, was worth £10; now £9.10s.

The bishop himself holds TYTING. Almær the huntsman held it TRE. It was then assessed at 1 hide; and the same now. There is land for 2 ploughs. In demesne is 1 plough; and 1 villan and 6 bordars with 1 plough. TRE, and afterwards, it was worth £3; now 40s. The men of the hundred testify that this manor was leased through the sheriff out of King Edward's farm, and that Bishop Osbern did not have this manor TRE.

V. The land of the Bishop of Bayeux

IN BLACKHEATH HUNDRED

The Bishop of BAYEUX holds in demesne BRAMLEY. Æthelnoth Cild held it of King Edward. It was then assessed at 34 hides. 4 of these hides belonged to free men who could withdraw from Æthelnoth. Over and above these is land for 2 ploughs in the manor itself which never have rendered geld. All these lands are now in the farm of Bramley. There is land for 35 ploughs. In demesne are 6 ploughs; and 84 villans and 40 cottars with 32 ploughs. There are 3 churches, and 18 slaves, and 5 mills rendering 26s, and 20 acres of meadow, [and] woodland for 100 pigs. TRE it was worth £40; and afterwards £30; now £60, and yet it renders £80 less 40d. Since the bishop was seised [of it] it has not paid geld.

The bishop himself holds CHILWORTH in Bramley. Alwine Boy held it, and could go where he would. It was then assessed at 3 hides; now at nothing. There is land [...]. In demesne is 1 plough; and 6 villans and 2 cottars with 2 ploughs. There is a mill rendering 7s. The whole is worth 70s.

In BRAMLEY there are 2 more hides. Eskil held them TRE, and could go where he would. It was then assessed at 2 hides; now at nothing. There are 3 villans and 1 cottar with 1 plough. There is land for 1 plough. It is worth 36s.

The bishop has 2½ more hides in the same place, which Ælfric held TRE, and could go with them where he would. There is land for 2 ploughs. It lies in Wotton Hundred. It is worth 32s.

The same bishop has 1 more hide there. A certain widow holds it, and held it TRE, and could go where she would. It was then assessed at 1 hide; now at nothing. It is worth 10s.

IN BLACKHEATH HUNDRED

The bishop himself has in demesne 3 hides. Alweard held these, and could go where he would with them. There are 5 villans and 8 cottars with 2 ploughs. There are 5 slaves, and a mill rendering 20d. The whole is worth 100s a year.

The bishop himself has in this hundred land for 1 plough. Alwine held it TRE. It is worth 30s. Then [...].

All the land that belongs to Bramley has not paid geld since the bishop received it.

IN GODALMING HUNDRED

The bishop himself holds in demesne RODSALL. Tovi held it TRE, and could go with it where he would. It was then assessed at 5 hides; now at nothing. There is land for 2 ploughs. There are 3 villans and 4 cottars with 1 plough, and 2 acres of meadow. [There is] woodland for 4 pigs. TRE and afterwards, as now, worth 40s.

The bishop himself holds in demesne FARNCOMBE. Asgot held it TRE, and could go with it where he would. It was then assessed at 3½ hides; now at nothing. There is land for 2 ploughs. There are 8 villans and 3 cottars with 2 ploughs, and 15 acres of meadow. [There is] woodland for 3 pigs. It is and was worth 24s. A certain reeve of the king, named Lufa, claims this manor, and the men of the hundred bear witness for him, that he was holding it of the king when the king was in Wales, and he afterwards held it until the Bishop of Bayeux arrived in Kent. The bishop himself has transferred Rodsall and Farncombe to the farm of Bramley.

IN TANDRIDGE HUNDRED

Ansketil de Rots holds of the bishop TATSFIELD. Ælfric held it of King Edward. Then, as now, it was assessed at half a hide. There is land [...]. In demesne is 1 plough; and 5 villans and 9 bordars with 1 plough. There are 12 slaves. TRE it was worth 30s; and afterwards 40s; now 60[s.].

Hugh holds of the bishop a manor which Cana held of King Edward. It was then assessed at 4 hides; now at half [a hide]. There is land for 4 ploughs. In demesne is 1 plough, and 5 villans and 2 bordars. TRE it was worth £4; and afterwards 20s; now 40s.

IN WALLINGTON HUNDRED

The canons of Bayeux hold of the bishop MITCHAM for 5 hides. Beorhtric held it of King Edward. He himself had 6½ hides, but Odbert holds 1, which his predecessor held in pledge of Beorhtric for half a mark of gold.

In the land of the canons are 4 villans and 1 cottar with 2 ploughs and 1 slave, and 40 acres of meadow. There is land for 2 ploughs. It is and was worth 40s.

In Odbert's land are 4 acres of meadow. They are worth 7s. [There is] nothing more. Ansgot holds half a hide of the bishop. It is worth 5s.

In this manor the canons themselves hold of the bishop 2½ hides, which 2 men held of King Edward. There is 1 plough in demesne; with 1 villan and 2 bordars and 1 slave, and half a plough, and 12 acres of meadow. [It has] always [been worth] 20s.

The canons themselves hold of the bishop 'WHITFORD' [in Mitcham]. Eadmær held it of King Edward. Then, as now, it was assessed at 3 hides. There is land for 2 ploughs. In demesne is 1 plough; and 2 villans and 6 cottars with 2 ploughs, and 4 acres of meadow. TRE, as now, worth 30s; when received, 10s.

Richard holds of the bishop BANSTEAD. Alnoth held it of King Edward. It was then assessed at 29 hides; now at 9½ hides. There is land for 16 ploughs. In demesne are 2 ploughs; and 28 villans and 15 cottars with 15 ploughs. There is a church, and 7 slaves, and a mill rendering 20s. [There is] woodland for 20 pigs, and in Southwark 1 house rendering 40d. belongs to this manor, and in London Alnoth had a demesne messuage belonging to this manor. Adam fitzHubert now holds it of the bishop. The whole manor TRE was worth £10; and afterwards 100s; now £8. Of the land of this manor, Geoffrey holds of Richard 5 hides, Ralph 2 hides, [and] Wulfsige 2 hides. The whole is worth £6.10s.

The same Ralph holds of the bishop CHALDON. Deoring

held it of King Edward. Then, as now, it was assessed at 2 hides. There is land for 2 ploughs, and there are [2 ploughs] in demesne, and a church. TRE it was worth 40s; and afterwards 20s; now £4.

IN BRIXTON HUNDRED

The Bishop of Lisieux holds of the bishop HATCHAM. Beorhtsige held it of King Edward. Then, as now, it was assessed at 3 hides. There is land for 3 ploughs. There are 9 villans and 2 bordars with 3 ploughs; and there are 6 acres of meadow, [and] woodland for 3 pigs. TRE and afterwards, as now, worth 40s.

IN REIGATE HUNDRED

Herfrid holds of the bishop GATTON. Earl Leofwine held it. It was then assessed at 10 hides; now at 2½ hides. There is land for 5 ploughs. In demesne are 2 ploughs; and 6 villans and 3 bordars with 2 ploughs. There is a church, and 6 acres of meadow, [and] woodland and herbage for 7 pigs. TRE, as now, worth £6; when received, £3.

Ansgot holds of the bishop half a hide in Wallington Hundred. Øpi held this TRE, and could go where he would. It is worth 5s.

IN BRIXTON HUNDRED

The Bishop of Lisieux holds of the bishop PECKHAM. Alflæd held it of Harold TRE, and it belonged to Battersea. Then, as now, it was assessed at 2 hides. There is land for 1 plough. There is 1 villan and 3 bordars, and 2 acres of meadow. TRE, as now, worth 30s; when received, 20s.

Ansgot holds of the bishop STREATHAM. Edwin held it TRE, and could go where he would. Then, as now, it was assessed at 1 hide. There is 1 plough, and 2 villans. It is and was worth 25s.

IN 'COPTHORNE' HUNDRED

Hugh holds of the bishop PACHESHAM. Almær held it of the king TRE. It was then assessed at 4 hides; and now at 3 virgates. There is land [...]. In demesne are 2 ploughs; and 11 villans and 8 bordars with 2 ploughs. There are 4 slaves, and 2 halves of a mill rendering 12s, and 5 acres of meadow, [and] woodland for 3 pigs. TRE it was worth 40s; and afterwards 20s; now 70s.

Ranulph holds of the bishop 1 hide and 1 virgate. Leofric held them of Harold, free, and could go where he would. This land is now assessed at 1 virgate. 2 villans have half a plough there. TRE [it was worth] 20s; and afterwards 12[s.]; now 10s.

Baynard holds of the bishop 1 hide, which Almær held of Earl Harold, and he could go where he pleased. It was then assessed at 1 hide; now at 1 virgate. In demesne is 1 plough, with 1 bordar, and half a mill rendering 6s. TRE it was worth 20s; and afterwards 10s; now 24s.

In Wallington Hundred Adam fitzHubert has 1 hide of the bishop, which has never paid geld.

The bishop himself holds CUDDINGTON. Earl Leofwine

held it. It was then assessed at 30 hides. Of these, the earl held 20 hides; and the allodial tenants of the vill, who could withdraw with their lands where they would, held 10 hides. The bishop now holds 6 of these 10 with the other 20 [hides]. These 26 hides are now assessed at 5 hides. The bishop holds this as 1 manor. Ilbert now holds of the bishop these 26 hides. He himself [has] 22 hides, and 1 of his men 4 hides. In demesne is 1 plough; and 7 villans and 9 bordars with 6 ploughs. There are 4 slaves, and a mill rendering 40d.

Of these hides, Ralph holds 4 hides. Wulfwine holds of the king 1 hide and 3 parts of 1 hide. In demesne is 1 plough; and 4 villans and 4 bordars with 1 plough. The whole manor TRE was worth £11; and afterwards 100s; now £9.12s. Of the land of this manor, Restald holds 2 hides, but he renders account in Wallington Hundred.

The canons hold ASHTEAD of the Bishop of Bayeux. Thorgisl held it of Earl Harold. It was then assessed at 9 hides; now at 3 hides and 1 virgate. There is land [...]. In demesne are 2 ploughs; and 33 villans and 11 bordars with 14 ploughs. There are 9 slaves, and 7 pigs from the herbage, and 4 acres of meadow. TRE it was worth £10; and afterwards £6; now £12.

Ralph holds of the bishop TADWORTH. 2 brothers held it of King Edward, and they could go where they would. It was then assessed at 5 hides; now at 1½ hides. There is land for 2 ploughs. In demesne [are] 1½ [ploughs]; and 3 villans and 4 bordars with 1½ ploughs. There is 1 slave, and 1 pig from the woodland. TRE it was worth 40s; and afterwards, as now, 30s.

Richard holds of the bishop FETCHAM. Bicga held it of King Edward. It was then assessed at 8½ hides; now at 4 hides. There is land for 5 ploughs. In demesne is 1 [plough];

[Folio 32: SURREY]

and 8 villans and 3 bordars with 1 plough. There are 2 slaves, and the sixth part of a mill, and the third part of another mill, and 10 acres of meadow; and from the pannage and herbage, 13 pigs. From the mills, 6½s. TRE, as now, worth 60s; when received, 50s.

Nigel holds of the bishop MICKLEHAM. Ansfrid held it of King Edward. Then, as now, it was assessed at 5 hides. There is land for 4 ploughs. In demesne are 2 ploughs, and 4 villans and 4 bordars and 2 slaves. There is a church, and 2 acres of meadow, [and] woodland for 3 pigs. TRE it was worth £3; and afterwards 50s; now £4.

Hugh de Port holds of the bishop GREAT BURGH. 3 free men held it, and they could go where they would. It was then assessed at 5 hides; now at 2½ hides. Hugh holds these 4 manors as 1 manor. It is valued in Wallington Hundred.

IN 'ELMBRIDGE' HUNDRED

The same Hugh holds of the bishop 1 free hide in Esher, and a certain woman [holds] of him. There is 1 villan. It is worth 5s. When Hugh was seised of this land, he did not have the livery officer or the king's writ for it, as the hundred testifies.

Herfrid holds of the bishop WEYBRIDGE. 2 sisters held it TRE, and they could turn with the land where they would. It was then assessed at 4 hides; now at 2 hides. There is 1 villan and 1 bordar, and 16 acres of meadow, [and] woodland for 5 pigs. It is and was worth 40s. When the bishop was seised of this land, they did not have the livery officer or the king's writ for it, as the hundred testifies.

IN KINGSTON HUNDRED

Wadard holds of the bishop THAMES DITTON. Leofgar held it of Harold, and served him, but could have gone with the land where he would. When he died, he divided this land between his 3 sons, TRE. It was then assessed at 6 hides; now at 2½ hides. There is land for 2 ploughs. There are 1½ ploughs, and 4 bordars and 4 slaves, and part of a mill rendering 15d, and 4 acres of meadow, [and] woodland for 20 pigs. TRE it was worth £4; and afterwards 40s; now £4. He who holds it of Wadard renders him 50s and the service of 1 knight.

The bishop himself has in SOUTHWARK 1 minster and 1 tideway. King Edward held them on the day on which he died. He who had the church held it of the king. From the dues of the waterway, where ships used to put in, the king had 2 parts, Earl Godwine the third. But the men of the hundred, both French and English, testify that the Bishop of Bayeux commenced a suit concerning these [tolls] with Ranulph the sheriff; but he, understanding that the suit was not being justly conducted to the king's advantage, withdrew the suit. The bishop at first gave the church and the tidal stream to Adelold, then to Ralph in exchange for a house. The sheriff also denies that he had ever received the king's precept or seal concerning this matter.

The men of Southwark testify that TRE no one took toll on the strand or on the water front except the king, and if anyone committing a trespass there had been charged, he paid a fine to the king. If, however, he had escaped uncharged to [the jurisdiction of] him who had sake and soke, that man was to have the fine from the accused.

The men of Southwark themselves have proved their right to an enclosure and its toll [belonging to] the farm of Kingston upon Thames. Count Eustace held this. What the king has in Southwark is valued at £16.

In Wotton Hundred and in the manor of Sutton [in Shere] the Bishop of Bayeux has 2½ hides. Heoruwulf held them TRE, and could go where he would. They were then assessed at 2½ hides; now at nothing. These are enumerated and valued in the bishop's manor of Bramley.

VI. The land of the Church of Westminster

IN BRIXTON HUNDRED

ST PETER of Westminster holds BATTERSEA. Earl Harold held it. It was then assessed at 72 hides, and now at 18 hides. There is land [...]. In demesne are 3 ploughs; and 45 villans and 16 bordars with 14 ploughs. There are 8 slaves, and 7 mills rendering £42.9s8d, or wheat of the same value, and 82 acres of meadow, and woodland for 50 pigs as pannage, and in Southwark 1 bordar paying 12d. From the toll of Wandsworth, £6. From a villan having 10 pigs, 1 pig; if less, he gives nothing.

A knight holds 4 hides of the land of this manor. His livestock is reckoned above with the other.

The whole was worth TRE £80; and afterwards £30; now £75.9s8d. King William gave this manor to St Peter's in exchange for Windsor [Berks.].

The Count of Mortain holds of the land of this manor 1½ hides, which belonged to it TRE, and for some time afterwards. Gilbert the priest holds 3 hides; they had been [held] in the same way. The Bishop of Lisieux [holds] 2 hides of which the church was seised in the time of King William; and afterwards the Bishop of Bayeux disseised it. The Abbot of Chertsey holds 1 hide, [...] which the reeve of this vill, on account of some enmity, took away from this manor, and put in Chertsey.

IN WALLINGTON HUNDRED

The Abbey of Westminster itself holds MORDEN. TRE it was assessed at 12 hides; now at 3 hides. There is land [...]. In demesne are 3 ploughs; and 8 villans and 5 cottars with 4 ploughs. There is 1 slave, and a mill rendering 40s. TRE it was worth £6; now £10, and yet it renders £15.

IN KINGSTON HUNDRED

The abbey itself holds CLAYGATE. TRE it was assessed at 2½ hides; now at half a hide. There is land for 2 ploughs. In demesne is 1 [plough]; and 3 villans and 2 bordars with 1 plough. There are 5 acres of meadow, [and] woodland for 1 pig. TRE it was worth 40s; now 50s.

IN BRIXTON HUNDRED

The abbey itself holds UPPER TOOTING. Swein held it of King Edward, and it was assessed at 4 hides. There is land for 1½ ploughs. There are 2 villans with half a plough, and 3 acres of meadow. TRE, as now, worth 40s; when received, 20s. Earl Waltheof received this land of Swein after the death of King Edward, and pledged it for 2 marks of gold to Alnoth of London, who granted it to St Peter's for his soul: namely, what he had there. Odbert holds it of St Peter's, and has paid nothing for geld.

IN 'GODLEY' HUNDRED

The abbey itself holds PYRFORD. Harold held it of King Edward. Before Harold had it, it was assessed at 27 hides; after he had it, at 16 hides at Harold's pleasure. The men of the hundred have never heard nor seen the writ on the king's behalf, which had fixed it at so much. [There is] land for 13 ploughs.

In demesne is 1 plough; and 37 villans and 14 bordars with 6 ploughs. There are 3 slaves, and 2 mills rendering 10s, and 15 acres of meadow. From the pannage and herbage, 80 pigs. TRE it was worth £12; and afterwards £10; now £18. The king has 3 hides of this land in his forest.

VII. The land of St Peter of Winchester

IN WALLINGTON HUNDRED

The ABBEY OF ST PETER of Winchester holds SANDERSTEAD. TRE it was assessed at 18 hides; now at 5 hides. There is land for 10 ploughs. In demesne is 1 [plough]; and 21 villans and 1 cottar with 8 ploughs.

[Folio 32V: SURREY]

There are 4 slaves, [and] woodland for 30 pigs. TRE it was worth 100s; and afterwards £7; now £12, yet it renders £15.

VIII. The land of the Church of Chertsey

IN WALLINGTON HUNDRED

THE ABBEY OF ST PETER of CHERTSEY holds 'WADDINGTON' [in Coulsdon]. TRE it was assessed at 20 hides; now at 5 hides. There is land for 8 ploughs. In demesne is 1 plough; and 17 villans and 2 cottars with 5 ploughs. There is a church, [and] woodland for 6 pigs as pannage. TRE it was worth £6; now £7.

The abbey itself holds COULSDON. TRE it was assessed at 20 hides; now at 3½ hides. There is land for 10 ploughs. In demesne is 1 plough; and 10 villans and 4 cottars with 6 ploughs. There is a church, [and] woodland for 3 pigs. TRE it was worth £6; now £7.

The abbey itself holds SUTTON [near Cheam]. TRE it was assessed at 30 hides; now at 8½ hides. There is land for 15 ploughs. In demesne are 2 ploughs; and 21 villans and 4 cottars with 13 ploughs. There are 2 churches, and 2 slaves, and 2 acres of meadow, [and] woodland for 10 pigs. TRE it was worth £20; now £15.

IN TANDRIDGE HUNDRED

The abbey itself holds 2 hides of land, and William holds of the abbot. But the men testify that it was the demesne land of Alwine TRE, and he could go where he would. [...] It was then assessed at 2 hides; now at nothing. There is 1 bordar and 1 slave. TRE it was worth 20s; and afterwards 5s; now 10s.

IN 'ELMBRIDGE' HUNDRED

The abbey itself holds COBHAM. TRE it was assessed at 30 hides; now at 12½ hides. There is land for 10 ploughs. In demesne is 1 plough; and 29 villans and 6 cottars with 9 ploughs. There are 3 mills rendering 13s4d, and 1 acre of meadow, [and] woodland for 40 pigs. TRE it was worth £20; now £14.

William de Watteville holds 2 hides of the abbey itself. An Englishman held them TRE, and in the lifetime of this king he gave this land to the same church in alms. This land belongs to the manor of Esher. There are 6 villans with 2 ploughs. TRE, as now, worth 14s6d.

In the same vill of Esher the same William has of the Abbey of Chertsey, as he says, 3½ hides. TRE 1 man and 2 women held them, and they could turn where they would; but for security they placed themselves with the land under the abbey. There are 2 villans with 1 plough. TRE it was worth 16s; and afterwards 5s; now 10s. These aforesaid 5½ hides are assessed at 5 virgates.

IN 'COPTHORNE' HUNDRED

The abbey itself holds EPSOM. TRE it was assessed at 34 hides; now at 11 hides. There is land for 17 ploughs. In demesne is 1 [plough]; and 34 villans and 4 bordars with 17 ploughs. There are 2 churches, and 6 slaves, and 2 mills rendering 10s, and 24 acres of meadow, [and] woodland for 20 pigs. TRE it was worth £20; now £17.

In WEYBRIDGE the abbey itself hitherto has held [...] 2 hides. Alfred held them TRE and after his [the king's] death, and could turn where he would. Then, as now, [there were] 2 hides. There are 3 villans, and 8 acres of meadow, [and] woodland for 2 pigs. [It has] always [been worth] 20s.

In the same vill an Englishman has 2 hides of the abbey itself. He himself held them TRE, and could turn with them where he would. There is 1 plough, and 2 villans with half a plough, and 8 acres of meadow, [and] woodland for 2 pigs. It is and was worth 20s.

IN KINGSTON HUNDRED

Eadric holds of the abbey itself half a hide which the abbey held for 2 years before the death of King Edward. 3 men held it of the king himself previously, but they could not withdraw without the king's precept, because they were beadles in Kingston upon Thames. Then, as now, it was assessed at half a hide. There is land for 3 oxen. There are 7 oxen, with 1 bordar, and 2 acres of meadow. TRE it was worth 7s; now 8s.

William de Watteville holds OLD MALDEN of the fief of the abbot. The abbot held it TRE. It was then assessed at 2 hides; now at 1 hide less 1 virgate. There is land for 1 plough. There are 4 villans with half a plough. It is and was worth 20s.

The abbey itself holds in demesne PETERSHAM. TRE it was assessed at 10 hides; now at 4 hides. There is land for 5 ploughs. In demesne is 1 plough; and 15 villans and 2 bordars with 4 ploughs. There is a church, and a fishery rendering 1,000 eels and 1,000 lampreys, and 3 acres of meadow. TRE it was worth 100s; now £6.10s.

Hamo the sheriff holds [?] STREATHAM of the abbey itself. Wulfweard held it of King Edward, and could go where he would. It was then assessed at 1 hide. There is land for 1 plough. There are 2 bordars. It is and was worth 20s.

IN 'ELMBRIDGE' HUNDRED

Reginald holds 1 hide in Esher of the abbey itself, and has paid geld for 15 acres. A certain woman held it TRE, and could go where she would, but for security she put herself under the abbey. There are 3 villans. It is worth 7s.

IN EFFINGHAM HUNDRED

The abbey itself holds GREAT BOOKHAM. TRE it was assessed at 26 hides; and now at 13 hides. There is land for 19 ploughs. In demesne is 1 plough; and 32 villans and 4 bordars

with 18 ploughs. There is a church, and 3 slaves, and a mill rendering 10s, and 6 acres of meadow. [There is] woodland for 80 pigs. From the herbage, 30 pigs. Of this land, Gunfrid holds 1 hide, and he has there 1 plough. The whole manor TRE was worth £16; now £15.

The abbey itself lies in 'GODLEY' HUNDRED, and the vill itself [Chertsey] TRE, as now, was assessed at 5 hides. There is land [...]. In demesne are 2 ploughs; and 39 villans and 20 bordars with 17 ploughs. There is a mill at the hall, and 200 acres of meadow. [There is] woodland for 50 pigs as pannage, and a forge which serves the hall. Of these 5 hides, Richard Sturmy holds 2½ hides under King William. But the hundred testifies that his predecessor held of the abbey, nor could he go elsewhere without leave of the abbot. He has in demesne there 1 plough; and 1 villan and 4 bordars with 1 plough. The whole manor TRE was worth £18; now £22; what Richard holds [is worth] 40s.

IN 'GODLEY' HUNDRED

The abbey itself holds THORPE. TRE it was assessed at 10 hides; now at 7 hides. There is land [...]. In demesne is 1 plough; and 24 villans and 12 bordars with 8 ploughs. There are 33 acres of meadow. From the herbage, 24 pigs. TRE, as now, worth £12.

IN EFFINGHAM HUNDRED

Osweald holds of the church itself EFFINGHAM. He himself held it TRE. It was then assessed at 6 hides; now at 2½ hides. There is land for 2 ploughs. There are 2 villans and 9 bordars with half a plough, and 1 acre of meadow, and from the woodland, 10 pigs as pannage. It is and was worth 40s.

IN 'GODLEY' HUNDRED

The abbey itself holds EGHAM. TRE it was assessed at 40 hides; now at 15 hides. There is land for 40 ploughs. In demesne are 2 ploughs; and 25 villans and 32 bordars with 10 ploughs. There are 120 acres of meadow. [There is] woodland for 50 pigs as pannage. From the herbage, 25 pigs. TRE it was worth £40; now £30.10s. Of this land Joscelin holds 3 hides, which were of the abbey's demesne TRE.

The abbey itself holds CHOBHAM. TRE, as now, it was assessed at 10 hides. There is land for 12 ploughs. In demesne is 1 [plough]; and 29 villans and 6 bordars with 11 ploughs. There are 3 slaves, and 10 acres of meadow, [and] woodland for 130 pigs. Of this land, Odin holds of the abbot 4 hides, [and] Corbelin 2 hides of the land of the villans. In demesne [is] 1 plough; and 7 villans and 4 bordars with 3 ploughs. There is a church and another chapel. [continued on f.34]

[Folio 33: [SURREY]]

IN WALLINGTON HUNDRED. Hamo the sheriff holds 1½ hides in fief of the Abbot of Chertsey. Alweard held them TRE, and could turn where he would. In demesne is 1 plough, with 6 cottars and 3 slaves, and 11 acres of meadow. TRE and afterwards, as now, worth 20s.

The same Hamo holds half a hide of the abbey itself. Wulfweard held it TRE, and could turn where he would.

There is 1 cottar, and 5 acres of meadow. It is and was worth 5s. These 2 hides which Hamo holds were assessed at 2 hides TRE; now at half [a hide].

In BRIXTON HUNDRED. The same Hamo holds TOOTING [?Graveney] of the Abbot of Chertsey. It was assessed at 6 hides less 1 virgate TRE; now at nothing. There is land for 3 ploughs. In demesne is 1 plough; and 3 villans and 2 bordars with 1 plough. There is a church, and 4 acres of meadow. TRE it was worth 40s; afterwards 20s; now 70s.

The same Hamo holds in Tooting [?Graveney] 1 hide of the Abbot of Chertsey. Osweard held it of King Edward, and could go where he would. There is 1 villan with half a plough, and 1 acre of meadow. TRE [it was worth] 15s; now 10s.

IN REIGATE HUNDRED. William de Watteville held CHIPSTEAD of the Abbot of Chertsey. Thorgisl and Ulf held it TRE. The land of Thorgisl belonged to the abbey. Ulf could go where he would. It was then assessed at 5 hides; now at 1 hide. There are 2 villans and 1 bordar. When William left, it was at farm for 40s.

[Folio 33V: [SURREY]]

[Blank in MS]

[Folio 34: SURREY]

[continued from f.32v] The whole manor TRE was worth £16; now the monk's part [is worth] £12.10s, but the men's [part] 60s.

Wulfwine holds of the abbey itself BYFLEET. The same man held it TRE. It was then assessed at 8 hides; now at 2½ hides. There is land for 2 ploughs. In demesne is 1 plough; and 7 villans and 2 bordars with 2 ploughs. There is a church, and 3 slaves, and a mill rendering 5s. [There are] 1½ fisheries rendering 325 eels, and 6 acres of meadow, [and] woodland for 10 pigs as pannage. TRE [it was worth] 100s; now £4.

IN WOKING HUNDRED

The abbey itself holds EAST CLANDON. TRE it was assessed at 10 hides; now at 4 hides. There is land for 5 ploughs. There are 6 villans and 12 bordars with 7 ploughs. [There is] woodland for 6 pigs. TRE it was worth £6; now £4, and yet the villans who hold it pay £6.

TRE the Abbot of Chertsey bought 2 hides in East Clandon, and put them in this manor. Eskil held them of the king. The Bishop of Bayeux put them in Bramley wrongfully, as the men of the hundred testify.

The abbey itself holds HENLEY. Azur held it until he died, and gave it to the church for his soul in the time of King William, as the monks say, and they have the king's writ for it. TRE it was assessed at 8 hides; now at 5½ hides. There is land for 5 ploughs. In demesne is 1 plough; and 10 villans and 6 bordars with 5 ploughs. There is a church, and 2 slaves, and 4 acres of meadow, [and] woodland for 50 pigs as pannage. TRE it was worth £6; now 100s.

IX. The land of Saint-Wandrille

IN BRIXTON HUNDRED

The Abbot of Saint-Wandrille holds WANDSWORTH, through Ingulf the monk. Swein held it of the king, and could go where he would. It was then assessed at 1 hide; now at nothing. There are 3 villans and 2 bordars with 1 plough. It was and is worth 20s.

X. The land of Saint-Leufroy

IN 'ELMBRIDGE' HUNDRED

The Abbot of La-Croix-Saint-Leufroy holds 7 hides and 3 virgates of land in ESHER by gift of King William. Tovi held them of King Edward.[...] There is land for 2 ploughs. In demesne is 1 [plough]; and 4 villans and 11 cottars with 2 ploughs. It is worth £3. Since the SAINT had it, it has never paid geld.

XI. The land of the Church of Battle

IN TANDRIDGE HUNDRED

THE ABBOT of Battle holds LIMPSFIELD. Harold held it TRE. It was then assessed at 25 hides. Now, since the abbot received it, it is not assessed. There is land for 12 ploughs. In demesne are 5 ploughs; and 25 villans and 6 bordars with 14 ploughs. There is a mill rendering 2s, and a fishery, and 1 church, and 4 acres of meadow. [There is] woodland for 150 pigs as pannage, 2 stone quarries rendering 2s, and 3 nests of hawks in the wood, and 10 slaves. TRE it was worth £20; and afterwards £15; now £24. "BRAMESELLE" belonged to this manor TRE, as the men of the hundred say.

XII. The land of the Church of Barking

IN 'ELMBRIDGE' HUNDRED

The Abbey of BARKING has 7 hides at WESTON GREEN. It is now assessed at 3 hides and 1 virgate. There is land for 3 ploughs. There are 9 villans with 3 ploughs. It is and was worth 40s.

IN WALLINGTON HUNDRED

The abbey itself has 2 hides of land. TRE it was assessed at 2 hides; now at 1. There are 2 villans with half a plough, and 6 acres of meadow. TRE it was worth 1 mark of silver; now 20s.

XIII. The land of St Paul's of London

IN BRIXTON HUNDRED

The canons of ST PAUL'S of London hold BARNES. TRE it was assessed at 8 hides. These hides have paid, and do pay, geld with Mortlake, the archbishop's manor, and are accounted for there. There is land for 6 ploughs. In demesne are 2 ploughs; and 9 villans and 4 bordars with 3 ploughs, and 20 acres of meadow. TRE it was worth £6; now £7.

XIIII. The land of the Church of Lambeth

IN BRIXTON HUNDRED

There is a manor [of] ST MARY'S which is called LAMBETH. Countess Gode, sister of King Edward, held it. It was then assessed at 10 hides; now at 2½ hides. There is land for 12 ploughs. In demesne are 2 ploughs; and 12 villans and 27 bordars with 4 ploughs. There is a church, and 19 burgesses in London who pay 36s, and there are 3 slaves, and 16 acres of meadow, [and] woodland for 3 pigs. TRE, and afterwards, it was worth £10; now £11. Of this manor the Bishop of Bayeux has a piece of arable land, which before and after the death of Gode belonged to this church.

XV. The land of Count Eustace

IN TANDRIDGE HUNDRED

Count EUSTACE holds OXTED. Gytha, the mother of Harold, held it TRE. It was then assessed at 20 hides; now at 5 hides. There is land for 20 ploughs. In demesne are 2 ploughs; and 34 villans with 18 ploughs. There are 2 mills rendering 12s6d, and 4 acres of meadow. [There is] woodland for 100 pigs as pannage, and in Southwark 1 messuage rendering 2d, and 6 slaves and 9 bordars. There is a church. TRE it was worth £16; when received, £10; now £14.

The count himself holds 'WALKINGSTEAD' [in Godstone]. Osweard held it of King Edward. It was then assessed at 40 hides; now at 6 hides. There is land for 30 ploughs. In demesne are 3 ploughs; and 39 villans and 2 bordars with 22 ploughs. There are 10 slaves, and a mill rendering 6s, and 3 acres of meadow, [and] woodland for 100 pigs. To this manor belong 15 messuages in Southwark and in London, rendering 6s and 2,000 herrings. TRE it was worth £20; and afterwards £16; now £20, yet it renders £28 by weight.

IN REIGATE HUNDRED

XVI. The Countess of Boulogne holds of the king NUTFIELD [Nutfield and South Nutfield]. Wulfwig held it of King Edward. It was then assessed at 13½ hides; now at 3 hides. There is land for 12 ploughs. In demesne are 3 ploughs; and 25 villans and 10 bordars with 12 ploughs. There is a church, and 10 slaves, and a mill rendering 2s, and 10 acres of meadow. From the herbage, 12 pigs. TRE it was worth £13; and afterwards £10; now £15 at 20[d], to the ora.

XVII. The land of the Count of Mortain

IN BRIXTON HUNDRED

The Count of MORTAIN holds LAMBETH. The canons of Waltham held it of Harold. It was then assessed at 6½ hides; now at nothing. There is land for 6 ploughs. In demesne is 1 plough; and 5 villans and 12 bordars with 3 ploughs. There is 1 slave, and 6 acres of meadow. TRE it was worth 100s; and afterwards, as now, £4.

The same count has in Bermondsey 1 hide of the king's land, where his house is situated. There is 1 bordar. It is worth 8s.

IN WALLINGTON HUNDRED

The same count has 2 hides of land and 1 virgate of the king. Æthelmær held them of King Edward. They are not now assessed. There are 4 villans and 9 cottars with 3 ploughs, and 9 acres of meadow. TRE, as now, worth 40s; when received, 20s. | It was assessed at 2 hides and 1 virgate. |

The count himself holds [?] STREATHAM. TRE it was assessed at 5 hides; now at nothing. Harold held 1½ hides; the canons of Waltham 1½ hides. 3 sokemen held 2 hides, and could go where they would with them. There is land for 2 ploughs. There are 3 villans and 3 bordars with 2½ ploughs. TRE it was worth 30s; and afterwards 15s; now 43s.

XVIII. The land of Earl Roger

IN WOTTON HUNDRED

Earl ROGER has of the king 1 hide, which belongs to Compton [near Chichester, Sussex], his manor in Sussex. TRE he who held [this] Compton held this hide of the king. It was then assessed at 1 hide; now at nothing. There is in demesne 1 plough. TRE it was worth 20s; and afterwards, as now 15s.

[Folio 34V: SURREY]

Turold holds of Earl Roger BURPHAM. Osmund held it of King Edward. It was then assessed at 4 hides; now at 3 hides. There is land for 5 ploughs. In demesne is 1 plough; and 7 villans and 2 bordars with 3½ ploughs, and a mill rendering 15s, and 25 acres of meadow. [There is] woodland for | 80 | pigs as pannage. There are 4 slaves. Of these hides, Godric has 1 hide which is called Wyke, in which was the hall belonging to this manor TRE; and there is in demesne 1 plough; and 4 villans and 3 bordars with 1 plough and 1 slave. [There is] woodland for 3 pigs. The whole manor, TRE and afterwards, was worth £8; now the lord [has] £7; his men 20s.

Turold holds of the earl WORPLESDON. Osmund held it of King Edward. It was then assessed at 8 hides; now at 6½ hides. There is land for 7 ploughs. In demesne is 1 plough; and 13 villans and 3 bordars with 6 ploughs. There is a church, and 1 slave, and 8 acres of meadow. [There is] woodland for 60 pigs as pannage. Of this land 2 knights hold 2 hides and 1 virgate; and they have there in demesne 2 ploughs, and 3 villans and 2 bordars, and a mill rendering 30d. The whole, TRE and afterwards, was worth 10s; now the same, £10 all together.

IN GODALMING HUNDRED

Turold holds of the earl LOSELEY. Osmund held it of King Edward. It was then assessed at 3 hides; now at 2 hides. There is land for 2 ploughs. In demesne is 1 plough; and 7 villans and 1 cottar with 3 ploughs. There are 2 slaves, and 5 acres of meadow. TRE it was worth 40s; and afterwards 20s; now 60s.

XIX. The land of Richard, son of Count Gilbert

IN TANDRIDGE HUNDRED

RICHARD of TONBRIDGE holds in demesne CHEV-INGTON. Alnoth held it of King Edward. It was then assessed at 20 hides; now at 6 hides. There is land for 12 ploughs. In demesne are $2\frac{1}{2}$ ploughs; and 23 villans and 1 bordar with 9 ploughs. There are 9 slaves, and a mill rendering 32d. From the herbage, 12 pigs. [There is] woodland for 50 pigs as pannage, and 16 acres of meadow. Of these hides, Roger holds half a hide, and he has there in demesne 1 plough, with 5 bordars. In Southwark [he has] 3 closes rendering 15d, and in London 2 messuages rendering 10d. TRE it was worth £11; and afterwards £6; now £10.

Richard himself holds BLETCHINGLEY. Ælfheah and Alwine and Alnoth held it of King Edward. It was then assessed at 10 hides; now at 3 hides. There is land for 16 ploughs. There were 3 manors; now it is in 1. In demesne are 3 ploughs; and 20 villans and 4 bordars with 9 ploughs. There are 7 slaves, and 14 acres of meadow. From the woodland, 40 pigs, and from the herbage, 18 pigs. In London and Southwark, 7 messuages rendering 5s4d. Of these 10 hides, Odin holds $2\frac{1}{2}$ hides, and Lemei 2 hides, and Peter $1\frac{1}{2}$ hides. In demesne [is] 1 plough; and 3 villans and 2 bordars with 1 plough, and 3 acres of meadow. The whole manor TRE was worth £13; and afterwards £8; now what Richard holds [is worth] £12, what his men [hold] 73s4d.

Robert de Watteville holds of Richard CHELSHAM. Wulfweard held it of King Edward. It was then assessed at 10 hides; now at 2 hides. There is land for 4 ploughs. In demesne are 2 ploughs; and 6 villans and 11 bordars with 3 ploughs. There are 4 slaves. 1 pig as a customary due. TRE it was worth £6; and afterwards £3; now £8.

The wife of Salie holds of Richard TANDRIDGE. Thorbiorn held it of King Edward. It was then assessed at 10 hides; now at 2 hides. There is land for 10 ploughs. In demesne are 3 ploughs; and 20 villans and 10 bordars. with 11 ploughs. There is 1 mill rendering 50d, and 5 acres of meadow. [There is] woodland for 40 pigs as pannage. From the herbage, 11 pigs. TRE it was worth £6; and afterwards 40s; now £11.

This same wife of Salie holds of Richard TILLINGDOWN. Alnoth held it of King Edward. It was then assessed at 10 hides; now at $1\frac{1}{2}$ hides. There is land for 4 ploughs. In demesne are 2 ploughs; and 5 villans and 8 slaves with $2\frac{1}{2}$ ploughs. There is a church. [There is] woodland for 30 pigs as pannage. TRE it was worth £7; and afterwards £3; now £6, and yet it renders £7.

Robert de Watteville holds of Richard a manor which Azur held of King Edward. It was then assessed at 14 hides; now at 2 hides. There is land for 4 ploughs. In demesne are 2 ploughs; and 11 villans and 7 bordars with 3 ploughs. [There is] woodland for 5 pigs as pannage. There is a church. TRE, as now, worth £8; when received, 100s.

The same Robert holds of Richard CHELSHAM. Toki held it of King Edward. It was then assessed at 10 hides; now at 2 hides. There is land for 4 ploughs. In demesne are 2 [ploughs]; and 11 villans and 7 bordars with 4 ploughs. There is a church, and 3 slaves. TRE, as now, worth 7; when received, £4.

The same Robert holds of Richard FARLEIGH. Tovi held it of King Edward. It was then assessed at 6 hides; now at half a hides. There is land for $2\frac{1}{2}$ ploughs. In demesne is 1 [plough]; and 4 villans and 1 bordar with 1 plough. There is 1 slave, and 1 ox. TRE, as now, worth 60s; when received, 20s.

John holds of Richard WOLDINGHAM. Wulfstan held it of King Edward. It was then assessed at 8 hides; now at 1. There is land [...]. In demesne are $1\frac{1}{2}$ ploughs; and 6 villans and 3 bordars with 3 ploughs. There are 3 slaves. TRE, as now, worth £4; when received, 20s.

IN BRIXTON HUNDRED

SAINTE-MARIE of Bec holds TOOTING BEC by gift of Richard. Starher held it of King Edward. It was then assessed at 11 hides; and now the same, at 1 hide [sic]. There is land for 4 ploughs. In demesne are 2 ploughs; and 5 villans and 4 bordars with 3 ploughs. There are 10 acres of meadow. TRE, as now, worth 100s; when received, 20s.

This same church holds of Richard STREATHAM. Hearding held it of King Edward. It was then assessed at 5 hides; and now the same, at 1 hide and 1 virgate of land [sic]. There is land for 3 ploughs. In demesne is 1 plough; and 4 villans and 5 bordars with 2 ploughs. There is a chapel rendering 8s. There are 4 acres of meadow. [There is] woodland for 10 pigs. From the herbage, 1 pig out of 10 pigs. TRE it was worth 50s; and afterwards, as now, 60s.

IN REIGATE HUNDRED

William, nephew of Bishop Walkelin, holds of Richard CHIPSTEAD. Wulfnoth held it of King Edward. It was then assessed at 15 hides; now at 2 hides. There is land for 7 ploughs. In demesne are 2 [ploughs]; and 8 villans and 5 bordars with 5 ploughs. There are 5 slaves, and a mill rendering 20s. [There is] woodland for 5 pigs; Richard has retained another wood for himself. TRE it was worth £7; and afterwards 100s; now £6.

Siward holds of Richard "ORDE". Osweald held it of King Edward. Then, as now, it was assessed at half a hide. There is 1 villan with half a plough. TRE it was worth 30s; and afterwards 2s; now 20s.

John holds of Richard BUCKLAND. Alnoth held it of King Edward. It was then assessed at 5 hides; now at 2 hides. There is land [...]. In demesne are $1\frac{1}{2}$ ploughs; and 17 villans and 8 bordars with 10 ploughs. There is a church, and 10 slaves, and a mill rendering 6s. TRE, and afterwards, it was worth 100s; now £8.

IN WALLINGTON HUNDRED

Robert de Watteville holds of Richard BEDDINGTON. Azur held it of King Edward. It was then assessed at 25 hides; now at 3 hides. There is land for 6 ploughs. In demesne is 1 plough;

[Folio 35: SURREY]

and 16 villans and 14 cottars with 5 ploughs. There is a church, and 5 slaves, and 2 mills rendering 40s, and 24 acres of meadow, [and] woodland for 5 pigs. 15 messuages in London, which belong to this manor, render 12s3d. TRE, as now, worth £10; when received, £6.

Richard himself holds in demesne WOODMANSTERNE. Azur held it of King Edward. Then, as now, it was assessed at 15 hides, but it has never paid geld. There is land for 3 ploughs. In demesne are 2 ploughs; and 1 villan and 12 cottars with 3 ploughs. There are 18 slaves, and a church, and a mill rendering 20s, and 4 acres of meadow, [and] woodland for 10 pigs. TRE it was worth £10; and afterwards 100s; now £8.

IN 'COPTHORNE' HUNDRED

John holds of Richard WALTON ON THE HILL. Alwine and Leofhelm and Coleman held it of King Edward as 3 manors, and could go where they would. It was then assessed at 15 hides; now at 2 hides and half a virgate. There is land for 5 ploughs. In demesne are 2½ ploughs; and 10 villans and 1 bordar with 2 ploughs, and 7 slaves. Of these hides, Roger holds 2 hides, and he has 1 plough there; and 1 messuage in Southwark. The whole TRE was worth £6; and afterwards £6; now £6.

IN 'ELMBRIDGE' HUNDRED

Richard himself holds of the king 1 hide, which Almær held of King Edward, and he could go with it where he would. It has never paid geld since Richard has had it. It is worth 6s9d.

IN 'COPTHORNE' HUNDRED

Osweald holds of Richard MICKLEHAM. The same man held it of King Edward. It was then assessed at 5 hides; now at 2 hides. There is land for 5 ploughs. In demesne is 1 plough; and 8 villans and 6 bordars with 4 ploughs. There are 2 slaves, and 1 acre of meadow, and 1 pig as pannage from the woodland. TRE it was worth 100s; now £6.

IN KINGSTON HUNDRED

Picot holds of Richard TOLWORTH. Alwine held it of King Edward, and he could go where he would. It was then assessed at 5 hides. [...] There is land for 3 ploughs. In demesne are 2 ploughs; and 7 villans and 8 bordars with 3 ploughs. There are 7 slaves, and a mill without rent, and 5½ acres of meadow, and half a virgate. TRE, as now, worth 60s; when received, 20s.

Picot holds of Richard LONG DITTON. Almær held it of King Edward. It was then assessed at 5 hides. This land, and that above, are now assessed at 4 hides. There is land for 4 ploughs. In demesne is 1 plough; and 2 villans and 9 bordars with 2½ ploughs. There is a church, and a mill rendering 9s,

[and] woodland for 15 pigs. There is 1 slave; and in Southwark 1 messuage rendering 500 herrings. TRE it was worth 60s; and afterwards 30s; now 50s, yet it is at farm for £4.

Picot holds of Richard a [piece of] land which is called 'EMBER' [in Thames Ditton]. Edwin and another man held it TRE, and they could go where they would. It was then assessed at half a hide; now at nothing. There are 6 oxen ploughing, with 2 bordars. It has always been worth 5s.

Robert de Watteville holds of Richard OLD MALDEN. Hearding held it of King Edward. It was then assessed at 8 hides; now at 4. There is land for 5 ploughs. In demesne is 1 plough; and 14 villans and 2 bordars with 4 ploughs. There is a chapel, and 3 slaves, and a mill rendering 12s, and 4 acres of meadow. From the herbage, 1 pig out of 7 pigs.

Of these hides, a knight holds 1 hide and 1 virgate, and there he has 1 plough, and 1 villan and 1 bordar, and 1 acre of meadow. The whole TRE was worth £7; and afterwards 100s; now £6.12s.

The same Robert holds of Richard CHESSINGTON. Hearding held it of King Edward. It was then assessed at 5 hides; now at half a hide. There is land for 2 ploughs. There are 3 villans and 1 bordar with 1 plough, and half a mill rendering 2s. [There is] woodland for 30 pigs. TRE it was worth £4; and afterwards 40s; now 70s.

A hide in OLD MALDEN which Robert de Watteville holds remains in dispute; and the men of the hundred say that Edward of Salisbury and Robert d'Oilly have proved their right to it against Richard of Tonbridge; and it has remained quit in the king's hands.

IN 'ELMBRIDGE' HUNDRED

Richard himself holds WALTON-ON-THAMES. Hearding held it of King Edward. It was then assessed at 6 hides; now at 3 hides. There is land for 8 ploughs. In demesne are 2 ploughs; and 8 villans and 3 cottars with 3 ploughs. There is a church, and a mill rendering 12s6d, and a fishery rendering 5s. TRE it was worth £8; and afterwards 100s; now £14.

The same Richard has in the manor of APPS 6 hides, which Abbot Wulfweald delivered to him in compensation for Walton-on-Thames, as Richard's men say. But the men of the hundred say that they have never seen the king's writ or livery officer who had given him seisin of it. 9 thegns held this land, and they could turn with it where they would. There are 10 villans and 6 cottars with 4 cottars [sic]. There are 2 slaves, and 46 acres of meadow, [and] woodland for 6 pigs. TRE it was worth £3; and afterwards 40s; now £4.

In Apps 1 villan holds half a hide, for which up till now he has given Richard's men 30d for rent. Now it remains quit in the king's hands. And Picot holds of Richard in Apps half a hide which Almær held without gift of the king now Picot holds it because his predecessor Almær held it. It is now worth 5s. Moreover, Picot holds of Richard in Apps half a hide which

Almær held TRE, and could go with it where he would. Now it is worth 12s.

John holds of Richard [East or West] MOLESEY. Ælfric held it of King Edward. It was then assessed at $3\frac{1}{2}$ hides; and now at 5 virgates. There is land for 3 ploughs. In demesne is 1 plough; and 7 villans and 8 bordars with $2\frac{1}{2}$ ploughs. There are 16 acres of meadow, [and] woodland for 4 pigs. TRE, as now, it was worth 60s; when received, 40s.

In that manor John holds of Richard 1 hide, which was given in compensation for Walton-on-Thames. Wulfweard held it of King Edward. There are 2 villans with 2 oxen. It is and was worth 5s.

Roger d'Abernon holds of Richard [East or West] MOLESEY. Toki held it of King Edward. It was then assessed at $6\frac{1}{2}$ hides; now at 6 virgates. There is land for 3 ploughs. In demesne is 1 plough; and 4 villans and 4 cottars with $2\frac{1}{2}$ ploughs. There are 6 slaves, and 16 acres of meadow, and woodland for 6 pigs. TRE it was worth £3; and afterwards 40s; now 70s.

Richard himself holds STOKE D'ABERNON. Beorhtsige Cild held it of King Edward. It was then assessed at 15 hides; now at 2 hides and 5 acres. There is land for 6 ploughs. In demesne are 2 ploughs; and 10 villans and 9 cottars with 2 ploughs. There is a church, and 7 slaves, and a mill rendering 7s, and 4 acres of meadow, [and] woodland for 40 pigs. TRE, as now, worth £4; when received, £3.

In the same manor the same Richard has 5 hides. Odo held them of King Edward. Now it is assessed at half a hide. There are 2 villans with 6 oxen, and a mill rendering 6s. There is land for 2 ploughs. It is and was worth 20s.

IN EFFINGHAM HUNDRED

In 'DIRTHAM' [in Effingham] Richard holds $1\frac{1}{2}$ hides. Almær held them of King Edward as a manor. The wife of Salie holds them of Richard, and she has there 1 villan and 2 bordars. It was worth 40s; now 30s.

[Folio 35V: SURREY]

In the same 'DIRTHAM' [in Effingham] are $1\frac{1}{2}$ hides which Ælfric held of King Edward as a manor, and he afterwards gave that land to his wife and daughter for the church of Chertsey, as the men of the hundred testify. Richard claims it. It does not belong to any manor, nor does he hold it as a manor, but it was delivered to him, and now 3 hides pay geld for $1\frac{1}{2}$ hides. There is land for 2 ploughs. In this land of Ælfric; there is in demesne 1 plough, and 2 bordars and 2 slaves. It is worth 40s.

IN BLACKHEATH HUNDRED

Roger holds of Richard ALBURY. Azur held it of King Edward. It was then assessed at 4 hides; now at $2\frac{1}{2}$ hides. There is land for 6 ploughs. In demesne is 1 [plough]; and 11 villans and 5 bordars with 6 ploughs. There is a church, and 4 slaves, and a mill rendering 5s, [and] woodland for 30 pigs.

Of these hides, a knight holds 1 hide; and [has] there in demesne $1\frac{1}{2}$ ploughs, and 1 villan and 1 slave; and an acre of meadow. The whole TRE was worth £10; and afterwards 100s; now £9.

Robert holds of Richard SHALFORD. 2 brothers held it TRE. Each one had his own house, and yet they resided in 1 court, and could go where they would. Then, as now, it was assessed at 4 hides. There is land for 6 ploughs. In demesne are 2 ploughs; and 29 villans and 11 bordars with 9 ploughs. There is a church, and 10 slaves, and 3 mills rendering 16s, and 4 acres of meadow, [and] woodland for 20 pigs. Of these hides, a knight holds a virgate, where he has half a plough, and 1 slave and 5 bordars [...]. The whole TRE was worth 16; and afterwards £9; now £20. To this manor belongs a close in Guildford rendering 3s.

IN KINGSTON HUNDRED

Ralph holds of Richard TOLWORTH. Eadmær held it, and could go where he would, TRE. It was then assessed at 5 hides; now at $2\frac{1}{2}$ hides. There is land for 4 ploughs. In demesne is 1 plough; and 6 villans and 1 bordar with 2 ploughs. There are 2 slaves, and 5 acres of meadow. TRE, and afterwards, it was worth 40s; now 60s.

IN 'COPTHORNE' HUNDRED

Richard himself holds in demesne THORNCROFT. Cola held it of King Edward. There are now in demesne 2 ploughs; and 5 villans and 4 bordars with 2 ploughs. There are 9 slaves, and a mill rendering 20s, and 5 acres of meadow, [and] woodland for 1 pig.

With that manor these lands were made over to Richard: 'West Betchworth' [in Dorking] at 6 hides; 1 hide and 1 virgate which Merewine held; and 1 hide which Alric and Almær held as a manor; and another hide which Coleman the huntsman held as a manor. These men were so free that they could go where they would; and these lands together with Thorncroft were assessed TRE at $25\frac{1}{2}$ hides less 1 virgate; now at 4 hides less 4 acres. In the hide which Alric and Almær held is half a plough and 2 oxen in demesne. In Merewine's hide is 1 plough in demesne, and 3 acres of meadow. In Coleman's hide are 2 bordars. All together there is land for 5 ploughs. TRE Thorncroft was worth 100s; when received, 60s; now 110s. 2 hides [have] always [been worth] 30s; Coleman's hide 10s.

In this hundred the Abbot of Westminster holds 2 hides, but they are valued in another hundred.

In MICKLEHAM there belongs 1 hide which Sæmann held of King Edward, and now holds of King William. He has there in demesne 1 plough, and 3 bordars; and half an acre of meadow. It is and was worth 20s.

In the same place Godwine holds 1 virgate of King William. The same man held it of King Edward. It is worth 30d a year.

In the same HUNDRED, William fitzAnsculf holds 2 hides, but they are valued in another hundred.

IN EFFINGHAM HUNDRED

Osweald holds of Richard EFFINGHAM. Azur held it of King Edward. It was then assessed at 6 hides; now at 2½ hides. With these 6 hides Osweald holds 1 hide and 1 virgate of land which a free man held under King Edward, but for a certain need of his he sold it to Azur in the time of King William. There is land for 5 ploughs all together. In demesne are 2 ploughs; and 6 villans and 5 bordars with 2 ploughs. There are 6 slaves, and 4 acres of meadow, and woodland for 5 pigs. From the herbage, 3 pigs. TRE it was worth 100s; and afterwards £4.10s; now £6.

IN WOKING HUNDRED

Richard himself holds OCKHAM in demesne. Almær held it of King Edward. It was then assessed at 9 hides; now at 1½ hides. There is land for 4 ploughs. In demesne is 1 plough; and 6 villans and 2 bordars with 2 ploughs. There is a church, and 3 slaves, and 2 fisheries rendering 10d, and 2 acres of meadow. [There is] woodland for 60 pigs. It is and always was worth 100s.

Ralph holds of Richard OCKLEY. Almær held it of King Edward. Then, as now, it was assessed at 1 hide. There is land for 4 ploughs. In demesne is 1 [plough]; and 9 villans and 3 bordars with 4 ploughs. [There is] woodland for 20 pigs, and 2 slaves. TRE it was worth 70s; and afterwards, as now, the same.

In this manor Richard himself holds half a hide. Alwine held it TRE, and could go with it where he would. The [it was assessed] at half a hide; now at nothing. It is valued in Ockley.

IN WOTTON HUNDRED

Richard himself holds in demesne 'WEST BETCHWORTH' [in Dorking]. Cola held it of King Edward. It was then assessed at 6 hides; and now at 2 hides. There is land for 7 ploughs. In demesne is 1 plough; and 6 villans and 10 bordars with 3 ploughs. There are 6 slaves, and a mill rendering 10s, and 3 acres of meadow. [There is] woodland for 80 pigs. From the herbage, 6 pigs. There is a church. TRE, and afterwards, [worth] £9; now £8.

Richard himself holds HARTSHURST. Almær held it of King Edward. Then, as now, it was assessed at 2 hides. There is land for 4 ploughs. There are 8 villans with 3 ploughs. [There is] woodland for 15 pigs. TRE and afterwards, as now, worth 45s. This land belonged to a certain free man, and he could go with it where he pleased; nor does it belong to any manor of Richard.

XX. The land of William de Braose

IN 'COPTHORNE' HUNDRED

William de Braose holds TADWORTH, and Halsart [holds] of him. Godtovi held it of Earl Harold, and could go where he would. It was then assessed at 5 hides; now at half a hide. There is land for 3 ploughs. In demesne is 1 plough; and 2 villans and 5 bordars with 1 plough. [There is] woodland for 3

pigs. TRE it was worth 100s; and afterwards 20[s.]; now 45[s.].

IN EFFINGHAM HUNDRED

Halsart holds of William LITTLE BOOKHAM. Godtovi held it of Earl Harold. It was then assessed at 5 hides; now at 2 hides. There is land for 3 ploughs. In demesne is 1 [plough]; and 3 villans and 4 bordars with 1 plough. There are 4 acres of meadow. From the pannage and herbage, 11 pigs. TRE, and afterwards, it was worth 50s; now 60s.

XXI. The land of William fitzAnsculf

IN WALLINGTON HUNDRED

WILLIAM fitzAnsculf holds 'WHITFORD' [in Mitcham], and William the chamberlain [holds] of him. Lang held held [sic] it of King Edward. It was then assessed at 2 hides; now at 1 hide. There is land [...]. In demesne is 1 plough; and 2 villans with 1 plough, and a mill rendering 20s, and 24 acres of meadow. TRE it was worth 50s; and afterwards 22s; now 60s.

The same William holds MITCHAM. Lemar held it of King Edward. Then, as now, it was assessed at 2 hides and 1 virgate. There are 2 villans and 6 cottars, and half a mill rendering 20s. TRE, as now, worth 40s; when received, 13s4d.

IN BRIXTON HUNDRED

William himself holds WANDSWORTH. 6 sokemen held it of King Edward, and they could go where they would. There were 2 halls.

[Folio 36: SURREY]

Then, as now, it was assessed at 12 hides. There is land for 4 ploughs. Ansculf had this land after he received the sheriffdom; but the men of the hundred say that they have not seen the [king's] seal nor livery officer.

Ansfrid['s land was assessed at] 5 hides; now at 1 hide. Ealdræd ['s at] 3 hides; now at nothing. Wulfweard ['s at] 3 hides. Walter the vineyard-keeper at 1 hide. They did not pay geld. In their land are 2½ ploughs in demesne; and 5 villans and 22 bordars with 2 ploughs, and 22 acres of meadow. The whole manor TRE was worth 110s; and afterwards 50s; now £8 all together.

IN WOTTON HUNDRED

Baldwin holds MILTON of William himself. Wulfric held it of King Edward. It was then assessed at 6 hides; now at 4½ hides. There is land for 5 ploughs. In demesne is 1 plough; and 10 villans and 9 bordars with 4 ploughs, and 4 slaves, and a mill rendering 2s, and 2 acres of meadow. [There is] woodland for 9 pigs. From the herbage, 10 pigs. TRE it was worth 70s; and afterwards, as now, 60s.

In the HUNDRED of 'Copthorne' are 2 hides which belong to this manor. They are worth 20s.

The same Baldwin holds of William 1 hide at Anstie. Ordwig held it; and Baldwin holds half a hide at "Litelfeld". Ælfthere held it. These 2 could go with their lands where they would. There is 1 plough in demesne, with 1 bordar. It is worth 11s3d.

William himself holds ABINGER. Huscarl held it of King Edward. It was then assessed at 6 hides; now at 4 hides. There is land for 9 ploughs. In demesne are 2 ploughs; and 10 villans and 7 bordars with 5 ploughs. There is a church, and 5 slaves, and a mill rendering 6s, and 3 acres of meadow. From the herbage and pannage, 40 pigs. TRE it was worth £8; and afterwards, as now, £7.

William himself holds PADDINGTON. Huscarl held it of King Edward. It was then assessed at 4 hides; now at 3 hides. There is land for 9 ploughs. In demesne is nothing; but there are 12 villans and 5 bordars with 6 ploughs, and a mill rendering 6s, and 4 acres of meadow. [There is] woodland for 40 pigs. From the herbage, 15 pigs. Of this manor, Hugh, a man of William, holds 3 hides, with a hall, and 1 plough in demesne. The whole manor TRE was worth £9; and afterwards £7; now the same £7.

XXII. The land of Walter fitzOther

IN GODALMING HUNDRED

WALTER fitzOther holds COMPTON. Beorhtsige held it of King Edward. It was then assessed at 14 hides; now at 11 hides. There is land for 10 ploughs. In demesne are 3 ploughs; and 21 villans and 8 cottars with 6 ploughs. There are 7 slaves, and 7 acres of meadow. There is a church. TRE it was worth £8; and afterwards £6; now £9.

Tezelin holds of Walter HURTMORE. Alwine held it of King Edward. It was then assessed at 15 hides; now at 3 hides. There is land for 3 ploughs. In demesne are 2 ploughs; and 3 villans and 2 cottars with 1½ ploughs. There is 1 mill rendering 11s, and 6 acres of meadow. TRE it was worth 50s; afterwards 30s; now 100s.

Walter himself holds PEPER HAROW, and Gerard [holds] of him. Alweard held it of King Edward. It was then assessed at 5 hides; now at 3 hides. There is land for 3 ploughs. In demesne are 2 ploughs, and a mill rendering 15s, and 7 acres of meadow. There are 4 villans and 3 cottars with 1 plough. TRE, and afterwards, it was worth 30s; now 100s.

IN KINGSTON HUNDRED

Walter himself holds 1 man of the soke of Kingston upon Thames, to whom he has committed the charge of the king's wild mares, but we know not on what terms. This man holds 2 hides, but he has no right in the land itself. It was assessed at 2 hides; now at nothing. There is 1 plough in demesne, with 3 slaves, and 1 fishery rendering 125 eels, and 1 acre of meadow. It is and was always worth 30s.

XXIII. The land of Walter de Douai

IN WALLINGTON HUNDRED

WALTER de Douai holds 2 hides of the king, as he says. But the men of the hundred say that they have never seen the writ or the king's commissioner who had given him seisin of it. But this they testify, that a certain free man holding this land, and able to go where he would, commended himself into Walter's hand for his own protection. This land is and was worth 20s.

XXIIII. The land of Gilbert fitzRicher

GILBERT fitzRicher de l'Aigle holds WITLEY. Earl Godwine held it. It was then assessed at 20 hides; now at 12 hides. There is land for 16 ploughs. In demesne are 2 ploughs; and 37 villans and 3 cottars with 13 ploughs. There is a church, and 3 acres of meadow, [and] woodland for 30 pigs. TRE, and afterwards, it was worth £15; now £16.

XXV. The land of Geoffrey de Mandeville

IN BRIXTON HUNDRED

GEOFFREY de Mandeville holds CLAPHAM. Thorbiorn held it of King Edward. It was then assessed at 10 hides; now at 3 hides. There is land for 7 ploughs. In demesne is 1 plough; and 8 villans and 3 bordars with 5 ploughs. There are 5 acres of meadow. TRE it was worth £10; afterwards the same; now £7.10s. The men say that Geoffrey has this manor wrongfully, because it does not belong to Esger's land. What Geoffrey gave in alms from this manor is worth 20s.

IN WALLINGTON HUNDRED

Geoffrey himself holds CARSHALTON. 5 free men [held it] of King Edward, and they could go where they would. Of these, 1 held 2 hides, and 4 [held] 6 hides apiece. There were 5 manors. Now it is in 1 manor. It was then assessed at 27 hides; now at 3½ hides. There is land for 10 ploughs. In demesne is 1 [plough]; and 9 villans and 9 cottars with 5 ploughs. There is a church, and 7 slaves, and 12 acres of meadow. The men of the shire and of the hundred say that they have never seen the writ or the livery officer who on the king's behalf had given Geoffrey seisin of this manor. TRE it was worth £20; when he was seised of it, 100s; now £10. Of these hides, Wesman holds 6 hides of Geoffrey son of Count Eustace. Geoffrey de Mandeville gave him [i. e. Geoffrey] this land with his daughter. In demesne is 1 plough; and 3 villans and 1 cottar with 3 ploughs, and a mill rendering 35s, and 3 slaves, and 10 acres of meadow. [There is] woodland for 2 pigs. There is land for 2 ploughs. TRE it was worth £4; and afterwards 40s; now 110s. Of the same hides, a certain smith of the king's has half a hide, which TRE he received with his wife, but he has never done service for it.

IN WOKING HUNDRED

Geoffrey himself holds WANBOROUGH. It is not [part] of Esger's land. Swein and Leofwine, brothers, held it of King Edward. It was then assessed at 7 hides; now at 3 hides. There is land for 7 ploughs. There were 2 manors; now there is 1. In demesne is 1 plough; and 12 villans and 17 bordars with 8 ploughs. There is a church, and 8 slaves, and 6 acres of meadow, [and] woodland for 30 pigs. The whole TRE was worth £7; afterwards 100s; now £7.

IN WOKING HUNDRED

Walter fitzOther holds WEST HORSLEY. Beorhtsige held it of King Edward. It was then assessed at 10 hides; now at 8 hides. There is land for 6 ploughs. In demesne are 2 ploughs; and 14 villans and 5 bordars with 5 ploughs. There is a church, and 8 slaves, [and] woodland for 20 pigs. TRE it was worth £8; afterwards 100s; now £6. Of this land, an Englishman holds 1 hide; and he has 1 plough there, with 1 bordar. It is worth 20s.

XXVII. The land of Edward of Salisbury

IN 'ELMBRIDGE' HUNDRED

EDWARD of Salisbury holds WALTON-ON-THAMES. Azur held it of King Edward. It was then assessed at 6 hides; now at 3 hides. There is land for 8 ploughs. In demesne are 2 ploughs; and 8 villans and 3 cottars with 7 ploughs. There are 8 slaves, and a mill rendering 12s6d, and 40 acres of meadow, [and] woodland for 50 pigs. There is a forester, paying 10s. TRE it was worth £8; afterwards 100s; now £12, yet it renders £14.

IN GODALMING HUNDRED

Ranulph holds of Edward HAMBLEDON. Azur held it of King Edward. It was then assessed at 5 hides; now at 3 hides. There is land for 4 ploughs. In demesne are 2 ploughs; and 8 villans and 1 cottar with 5 ploughs. There are 13 slaves, and a mill rendering 30d, and 3 acres of meadow, [and] woodland for 30 pigs. It is and always was worth 100s.

IN WOKING HUNDRED

Hugh holds of Edward WEST CLANDON. Fulcwig held it TRE. It was then assessed. at 5 hides; now at 2½ hides. There is land for 3 ploughs. In demesne is 1 [plough]; and 4 villans and 5 bordars with 1½ ploughs. [There is] a mill rendering 3s. There is a church, and woodland for 5 pigs. It was worth 50s; now 60s.

[Folio 36V: SURREY]

XXVIII. The land of Robert Malet

IN WOKING HUNDRED

ROBERT Malet holds SUTTON [in Woking]. Wynsige held it of King Edward. It was then assessed at 5 hides; now at 3 hides. There is land for 3 ploughs. In demesne is 1 [plough]; and 5 villans and 5 bordars with 2 ploughs. There are 6 slaves, and a mill rendering 5s, and 20 acres of meadow, [and] woodland for 25 pigs. TRE, and afterwards, it was worth £8; now 100s. Durand was seised of this land, and the men say that he has it wrongfully, for none of them has seen the king's writ or livery officer.

XXIX. The land of Miles Crispin

IN WALLINGTON HUNDRED

MILES Crispin holds BEDDINGTON, and William fitzTurold [holds] of him. Ulf held it of King Edward. It was then assessed at 25 hides; now at 3 hides. There is land for 6 ploughs. In demesne is 1 plough; and 13 villans and 13 cottars with 6 ploughs. There is 1 slave, and 2 mills rendering 35s, and 20 acres of meadow, [and] woodland for 5 pigs. TRE it was worth £10; afterwards £6; now £9.10s. From this manor [...] have been taken 21 messuages which Earl Roger holds, 13 in London, 8 in Southwark. They render 12s.

IN KINGSTON HUNDRED

Miles himself holds CHESSINGTON. Magni Svert held it TRE. It was then assessed at 5 hides; now at 1 hide. When King William came into England, Vigot did not have it. There is land for 3 ploughs. This land belonged to Beddington. Villans held it. In demesne is now 1 plough; and 6 villans with 2 ploughs. TRE it was worth £4; afterwards 40s; now 70s.

XXX. The land of Hamo the Sheriff

IN TANDRIDGE HUNDRED

HAMO the sheriff holds TITSEY. Godtovi held it of King Edward. It was then assessed at 20 hides; now at 2 hides. There is land for 8 ploughs. In demesne are 4 ploughs; and 14 villans and 31 bordars with 5 ploughs. There is a church, and 9 slaves. For the pasture, the seventh pig of the villans. TRE it was worth £10; afterwards £6; now £11.

IN BRIXTON HUNDRED

Hamo himself holds CAMBERWELL. Northmann held it of King Edward. It was then assessed at 12 hides; now at 6 hides and 1 virgate. There is land for 5 ploughs. In demesne are 2 [ploughs]; and 22 villans and 7 bordars with 6 ploughs. There is a church, and 63 acres of meadow, [and] woodland for 60 pigs. TRE it was worth £12; afterwards £6; now £14.

XXXI. The land of Humphrey the Chamberlain

IN KINGSTON HUNDRED

HUMPHREY the chamberlain holds of the queen's fief COOMBE. Alfred held it of the king, and could go where he would. It was then assessed at 3 hides; now at nothing. There is land for 2 ploughs. In demesne is 1 [plough]; and 3 villans and 4 bordars with 1 plough. There are 8 acres of meadow. TRE it was worth £4; afterwards 20s; now 100s. TRW the woman who held this land put herself with it in the queen's hand.

XXXII. The land of Ralph de Feugeres

IN 'COPTHORNE' HUNDRED

RALPH de Feugeres holds HEADLEY. Countess Gode held it of King Edward. It was then assessed at 7 hides; now at 2 hides and 1 virgate. There is land [...]. In demesne is 1 plough; and 9 villans and 5 bordars with 5 ploughs. There are 8 slaves, [and] woodland for 15 pigs. TRE it was worth £7; afterwards, as now, 100s.

IN WOTTON HUNDRED

Ralph himself holds WESTCOTT. Abbot Æthelsige held it of King Edward. It was then assessed at 10 hides; now at 3 hides. There is land for 7 ploughs. In demesne is 1 plough; and 14 villans and 5 bordars with 7 ploughs. There are 3 slaves, and a mill rendering 30d, and 2½ acres of meadow, [and] woodland for 30 pigs. TRE it was worth £9; afterwards, as now, £8.

XXXIII. The land of Alvred of Marlborough

IN WOKING HUNDRED

ALVRED holds of the king SEND, and Reginald [holds] of him. Karli held it TRE. Then, as now, it was assessed at 20 hides. There is land for 10 ploughs. In demesne are 2 ploughs and 8 slaves; and 14 villans and 10 bordars with 6 ploughs. There is a mill rendering 21s6d. There is a church, and 5 fisheries rendering 54d, and 100 acres of meadow, less 16, [and] woodland for 160 pigs.

Of this land, Walter holds 1½ hides, and Herbert 9 [hides] of the land of the villans. There are 2 ploughs in demesne, and 7 slaves, and 1 villan and 16 bordars. There is a mill rendering 2s. The whole TRE was worth £20; now the demesne [is worth] £10, and the rest 110s.

XXXIIII. The land of Albert

IN WALLINGTON HUNDRED

ALBERT the clerk holds of the king ADDINGTON. Osweard held it of King Edward. It was then assessed at 8 hides; now at 2. There is land for 4 ploughs. In demesne are 2 ploughs; and 5 villans and 4 cottars with 1½ ploughs. [There is] woodland for 20 pigs. TRE, as now, [worth] 100s.

XXXV. The land of Odard

IN 'ELMBRIDGE' HUNDRED

ODARD the crossbowman holds of the king 4 hides in Esher. Tovi held them of King Edward. It is now assessed at 1 hide. There are 10 villans with 2 ploughs, and 2 acres of meadow. It is worth 40s.

The same Odard holds [East or West] MOLESEY. Tovi held it of King Edward. It was then assessed at 6 hides and 1 virgate; now at 1 hide. There is land for 3 ploughs. In demesne is 1 [plough]; and 10 villans and 5 cottars with 4 ploughs.

There is a church, and 2 slaves. TRE it was worth 100s; afterwards 50s; now £4.

XXXVI. The Lands of Osweald and Other Thegns

IN EFFINGHAM HUNDRED

OSWEALD holds of the king "PECHINGEORDE". He himself held it of King Edward. Then, as now, it was assessed at 1 hide. There is land for 3 ploughs. In demesne is 1 plough; and 3 villans and 2 bordars with 2 ploughs. There are 2 slaves. TRE and afterwards, as now, worth 40s. The men of the Bishop of Bayeux claim from this land every year for the king's use 2 marks of gold or 2 hawks, and this by grant of the abbot, brother to Osweald, namely for the battle which he ought to have fought against Geoffrey the Little.

IN 'COPTHORNE' HUNDRED Sæmann holds 1 virgate of land which he held of King Edward. But from [the time] when King William came into England he has done service to Osweald, paying him 20d. This man could turn where he would TRE.

Osweald himself holds FETCHAM. He himself held it of King Edward. It was then assessed at 11 hides; now at 3 hides. There is land [...]. In demesne is 1 plough; and 6 bordars with 5 ploughs. From a mill, 6s6d. There are 10 acres of meadow, [and] woodland for 4 pigs. TRE it was worth £4; now 100s.

IN WOTTON HUNDRED

Osweald himself holds WOTTON. Harold held it TRE, but the men of the hundred say that they do not know how Harold had it. It was then assessed at 6 hides; now at 5 hides. There is land [...]. In demesne is 1 plough; and 20 villans and 7 bordars with 8½ ploughs. There is a mill rendering 20d, and 3 acres of meadow. [There is] woodland for 50 pigs. From the herbage, 23 pigs. TRE, and afterwards, it was worth £8; now £7.

Of these hides, [...] Richard of Tonbridge holds 1 hide, and Corbelin [holds] of him. Theodric held it of Harold as a manor. It was then assessed at 1 hide; now at half [a hide]. There is half a plough, and 2 villans and 1 slave. It was then worth 20s; now 10s.

IN WOKING HUNDRED

Osweald himself holds WISLEY. He himself held it of Earl Harold. It was then assessed at 3½ hides; now at 1½ hides. There is land for 2 ploughs. In demesne is 1 [plough]; and 4 villans and 4 bordars with 2 ploughs. There is a church, and 2 slaves, and a mill rendering 10s, and 6 acres of meadow, and a fishery rendering 5d, [and] woodland for 6 pigs. TRE it was worth 40s; now 60s.

IN BRIXTON HUNDRED

THEODRIC the goldsmith holds of the king KENN-INGTON. He himself held it of King Edward. It was then assessed at 5 hides; now at 1 hide and 3 virgates. There is land for 2½ ploughs. In demesne is 1 plough; and 4 villans and 3 bordars with 2 ploughs. There is 1 slave, and 4 acres of meadow. It was and is worth £3.

IN WALLINGTON HUNDRED

TEZELIN the cook holds of the king ADDINGTON. Godric held it of King Edward. It was then assessed at 8 hides; now at 1 hide. There is land for 4 ploughs. In demesne are 2 ploughs; and 8 villans and 9 cottars with 2½ ploughs. [There is] woodland for 20 pigs. It is and was worth 100s.

IN KINGSTON HUNDRED

ANSGOT the interpreter holds of the king COOMBE. Cola held it TRE. It was then assessed at 3 hides; now at 1½ hides. There is land for 3 ploughs. In demesne is 1 [plough]; and 6 villans and 1 bordar with 1 plough, and 4 acres of meadow. For the herbage, 4 pigs. It is worth 60s.

IN WOKING HUNDRED

KETIL the huntsman holds of the king [?] LOLLES-WORTH. His father held it of King Edward. It was then assessed at 1 hide; now at half [a hide]. There is land for 2 ploughs. In demesne is 1 [plough]; and 2 villans and 5 bordars with 1 plough. [There is] a mill rendering 2s, and 4 acres of meadow, [and] woodland for 20 pigs. It is and was worth 50s.

IN GODALMING HUNDRED

WULFWIG the huntsman holds of the king LITTLETON. He himself held it of King Edward. Then [it was assessed at] 2 hides, but they did not pay geld; now at 1 virgate. There is land for 1 plough. There is [1 plough] in demesne; with 1 villan and 1 cottar with 1 plough. There are 2 acres of meadow. It is and was worth 20s.

HAMPSHIRE

[Blank in MS]

Here Are Entered the Holders of Lands In Hampshire

I KING WILLIAM
II The Bishop of Winchester
III and his monks
IIII Archbishop Thomas
V Bishop Osbern
VI The Abbot of Winchester
VII The Abbot of Gloucester
VIII The Abbot of Westminster
IX The Abbot of Chertsey
X The Abbot of Jumieges
XI The Abbot of Glastonbury
XII The Abbot of Milton
XIII The Abbot of Grestain
XIIII The Abbess of Winchester
XV The Abbess of Romsey
XVI The Abbess of Wherwell
XVII The canons of Twynham
XVIII Count Alan
XIX The Count of Mortain
XX Earl Roger
XXI Earl Hugh
XXII Hugh de Port of the king
XXIII The same Hugh of the Bishop of Bayeux
XXIIII Hubert de Port
XXV William de Percy
XXVI Ernulf de Hesdin
XXVII Edward of Salisbury
XXVIII Robert fitzGerald
XXIX Ralph de Mortimer
XXX Eudo fitzHubert
XXXI William Bertram
XXXII William de Eu
XXXIII William de Braose
XXXIIII William de Warenne
XXXV William Mauduit
XXXVI Alvred of Marlborough
XXXVII Durand of Gloucester
XXXVIII Turstin fitzRolf
XXXIX Bernard Pauncevolt

XL Turstin the chamberlain
XLI Richard Sturmy
XLII Richard Puignant
XLIII Gilbert de Breteuil
XLIIII Hugh fitzBaldric
XLV Waleran the huntsman
XLVI Walter fitzOther
XLVII Walter fitzRoger de Pitres
XLVIII William fitzManni
XLIX William Alis
L William fitzBaderon
LI William fitzStur
LII William Bellet
LIII William the archer
LIIII Herbert fitzRemy
LV Herbert the chamberlain
LVI Henry the treasurer
LVII Humphrey the chamberlain
LVIII Herbrand de Pont Audemer
LIX Reginald fitzCroch
LX Croch the huntsman
LXI Joscelin de Cormeilles
LXII Geoffrey Marshal
LXIII Nigel the physician
LXIIII Alvred the priest
LXV Durand the barber
LXVI Ranulph Flambard
LXVII Geoffrey the chamberlain of the king's daughter
LXVIII Hugh a la Barbe and many more sergeants of the king
LXIX Oda of Winchester and many other thegns of the king

IN THE ISLE OF WIGHT

I KING WILLIAM II The Bishop of Winchester III The Church of St Nicholas IIII The Abbey of Lyre V The Abbey of Wilton VI William fitzStur VII William fitzAzor VIIII Joscelin fitzAzor IX Godric the priest and many more

ALSO IN THE SAME HAMPSHIRE AROUND THE NEW FOREST AND WITHIN IT

I KING WILLIAM II The Bishop of Winchester III Earl Roger IIII William de Eu V Ralph de Mortimer VI Hugh de Port VII Edward of Salisbury VIIII Ranulph Flambard IX Hugh and Oda and many more

I. The land of the King

IN ODIHAM HUNDRED

King WILLIAM holds ODIHAM in demesne. Earl Harold held it. There are 80 hides less 1½ hides. It was then assessed at 38 hides; now it does not pay geld. There is land for 56 ploughs. In demesne are 15 ploughs; and 137 villans and 60 bordars with 40 ploughs. There are 50 slaves, and 8 mills rendering 56s7d, and 21 acres of meadow, [and] woodland for 160 pigs.

TRE, and afterwards, it was worth £50 by tale; now £50 by weight.

Of this manor 2 hides belong to 2 churches of the same manor, and the priest has there 1 villan with 1 plough. It is worth £6.

Of the same manor another 2 priests hold 2 churches with 2 virgates of land; and they have there 1½ ploughs. It is worth 67s6d.

IN NEATHAM HUNDRED

The king himself holds NEATHAM in demesne. King Edward held it. They have not said how many hides are there. There is land for 52 ploughs. In demesne are 5 ploughs; and 54 villans and 26 bordars with 47 ploughs. There are 16 slaves, and 8½ mills rendering £4.14s less 3d. [There is] a market rendering £8, and 15 acres of meadow, [and] woodland for 150 pigs. TRE, and afterwards, it was worth £76.16s8d. It is now valued at the same sum, and yet it renders at farm £118.12s9d. From this manor has been taken 1 virgate of land which Leofwine the forester held, so the hundred says.

The king himself holds HOLYBOURNE. Wulfweard held it of King Edward. [It was assessed] then, as now, at 1 hide. [...] There is land for 4 ploughs. In demesne is half a plough; and 6 villans and 4 bordars with 1 plough. There is 1 slave, and 5 acres of meadow, [and] woodland for fencing and 1 pig as pannage. TRE, as now, [worth] 50s; when received, 40s.

The king himself holds ANSTEY. Queen Edith held it. It was then assessed at 5 hides; now it does not pay geld. There is land for 3 ploughs. There are 8 villans with 2½ ploughs. TRE and afterwards, as now, worth 50s.

The king himself holds GREATHAM. Queen Edith held it. It was then assessed at 1 hide; now it does not pay geld. There is land for 3 ploughs. There 7 villans have 3 ploughs. There is woodland for 30 pigs. TRE and afterwards, as now, worth 60s.

The king himself holds CHILTLEE. Lang held it of King Edward in alod. It was then assessed at 2 hides; now at half a hide. There is land for 2 ploughs. There 4 villans have 2 ploughs. There is woodland for 30 pigs. It is and was worth 53s.

The king himself holds SELBORNE. Queen Edith held it, and it never paid geld. Of this manor the king gave half a hide

with the church to Radfred the priest. TRE, and afterwards, it was worth 12s6d; now 8s4d.

IN CHALTON HUNDRED

The king himself holds MAPLEDURHAM in demesne. Wulfgifu held it, and Queen Matilda had it. TRE it was assessed at 20 hides; now at 13. There is land for 20 ploughs. In demesne are 4 ploughs; and 34 villans and 15 bordars with 15 ploughs. There is a church, and 8 slaves, and 3 mills rendering 20s, and 5 acres of meadow. [There is] woodland for 30 pigs as pannage. From the herbage, 6s3d.

Of this land Albold the cook holds 2½ hides. Theodger held them TRE, and could not go elsewhere. This land paid geld above at half a hide with the other hides. There is in demesne 1 plough; and 5 villans and 3 bordars with 1 plough, and 2 slaves, and 1 acre of meadow.

Of the same land of the said manor, Theobald holds 3½ hides. Richard of Tonbridge gave it to him when he had the land from the queen. Now they do not know through whom he holds it. 2 radknights held it and could not withdraw elsewhere. There are 2 ploughs in demesne; and 4 villans and 8 bordars with 1 plough, and 2 slaves, and 1 acre of meadow. [There is] woodland rendering 6d. The whole manor TRE was worth £25; and afterwards, as now, as much; and yet he who holds it pays £32. Albold's part [is worth] 40s; Theobald's part £4.

IN PORTSDOWN HUNDRED

The king himself holds WYMERING in demesne. King Edward held it. It was never assessed in hides. [...] In demesne are 2 ploughs; and 16 villans and 6 bordars with 4 ploughs. There are 2 slaves, [and] woodland for 5 pigs.

In COSHAM are 4 hides which belong to this manor, where there were, TRE, 8 boors, that is coliberts, with 4 ploughs paying 50s less 8d. There is in demesne 1 plough; and 8 villans and 8 bordars with 5 ploughs, and 2 slaves, and 1 salt-pan.

In PORTCHESTER is another part of this manor. It was never assessed in hides. There is in demesne 1 plough; and 1 villan and 6 bordars with 1 plough. There is 1 acre of meadow, [and] woodland for 10 pigs.

IN 'BOSBARROW' HUNDRED

The king himself holds in [North or South] HAYLING 2½ hides. Leofmann held it of King Edward in parage. Harold took it from him when he seized the kingdom and put it in his farm; and it is there still. It was then assessed at 2½ hides; now at nothing. There is land for 1½ ploughs. In demesne is 1 plough; and 1 villan and 8 bordars with half a plough, and 1½ acres of meadow. TRE it was worth 40s; and afterwards 20s; now 70s.

IN MEONSTOKE HUNDRED

The king himself holds SOBERTON. Leofmann held it of Earl Godwine. Harold, when he was reigning, took it from him and put it in his farm and it is still there. Leofmann himself could not withdraw where he would. They say that it was in parage in Chalton. It was then assessed at 4 hides; now at nothing. There is land for 2 ploughs. In demesne is half a plough; and 6 villans and 3 bordars with 2 ploughs, and 2 mills rendering 15s, and 1 acre of meadow. It is and always was worth £3.

The king himself holds SOBERTON. Godwine held it of King Edward in parage, and could not withdraw elsewhere. Harold took it from him and put it in his farm. It is still there. It was then assessed at 3 hides; now at nothing. There is land for 2 ploughs. In demesne is half a plough; and 3 villans and 2 bordars with 1 plough. There is 1 mill rendering 5s, and 3 acres of meadow. It is and always was worth 40s. These 2 estates render 40s more.

[The king] himself holds MEONSTOKE. It belonged to King Edward's farm. It was then assessed at 1½ hides; now at nothing. There is land for 4 ploughs. In demesne are 1½ ploughs; and 3 villans and 16 bordars with 1½ ploughs. There are 4 slaves and 4 coliberts, and 1 mill rendering 10s, and 3 acres of meadow. [There is] woodland for 10 pigs; for the herbage, 10s.

IN EAST MEON HUNDRED

The king himself holds EAST MEON. Archbishop Stigand held it TRE, for the use of the monks, and had it afterwards as long as he lived. There were then 72 hides, and it paid geld for 35 hides and 1 virgate. There is land for 64 ploughs. In demesne are 8 ploughs; and 70 villans and 32 bordars with 56 ploughs. There are 15 slaves, and 6 mills rendering 40s, and 8 acres of meadow. [There is] woodland for 200 pigs as pannage. For the herbage, 7s6d. TRE it was worth £60; and afterwards £40; now £60; and yet it renders at farm £100 by weight, but it cannot bear it.

Of this land of this manor, Bishop Walkelin holds 6 hides and 1 virgate with a church. These hides of the bishop have paid geld; now [...] 3 hides and 1 virgate; the others have not paid.

[Folio 38V: HAMPSHIRE]

IN BARTON HUNDRED

The king himself holds BARTON STACEY. It belonged to King Edward's farm; and it rendered half a day's farm in all things. To this [manor] belongs KING'S WORTHY, and it is a berewick. It was never assessed in hides, except 6 hides only, which coliberts held and hold. They have not stated the number of hides. [...] There is land for 25 ploughs. In demesne are 5 ploughs; and 28 villans and 47 bordars with 18 ploughs. There are 8 slaves, and 3 mills rendering 42s6d. There are 6 coliberts, and 37 acres of meadow, [and] woodland for 80 pigs as pannage. From the herbage, 46s.

TRE it was worth £38.8s4d; and afterwards as much; it is now worth £33; and yet it renders £52.6s1d.

IN ODIHAM HUNDRED

The king himself holds LASHAM. Hakun held it of King Edward in alod. It was then assessed at 5 hides; now at 2½ hides. There is land for 6 ploughs. In demesne is 1 [plough]; and 8 villans and 7 bordars with 4 ploughs. There are 5 slaves, and 1 acre of meadow. TRE, as now, worth 100s; when received, 60s.

IN BROUGHTON HUNDRED

The king himself holds [? Nether] WALLOP. Countess Gytha held it of Earl Godwine. It then paid geld for 22 hides; now for nothing. There is land for 15 ploughs. In demesne are 6 ploughs; and 30 villans and 39 bordars with 12 ploughs. There are 18 slaves, and 3 mills rendering 15s, and 9 acres of meadow, a salt-pan rendering 5d, woodland for 40 pigs, and 2 closes in Winchester rendering 65d.

There is a church to which belong 1 hide and half of the tithe of the manor, and the whole church-scot, and 46d from the villans' tithe, and half of the fields.

There is, besides, a chapel to which belong 8 acres of tithe.

To this manor belonged TRE the third penny of 6 hundreds; and in all the woods which belonged to the 6 hundreds, it had also free right of pasture and pannage. TRE it was worth £30; and afterwards £27; now £27; yet it renders at farm £31.5s. What belongs to the churches is worth 25s.

The king himself holds another [?Over] WALLOP. Earl Harold held it. It then paid geld for 17 hides; now for nothing. There is land for 10 ploughs. In demesne are 2 [ploughs]; and 22 villans and 16 bordars with 9 ploughs. There are 3 slaves, and 3 mills rendering 25s, and 4 acres of meadow, [and] woodland for 3 pigs. TRE, and afterwards, worth £20; now £23; and yet it renders £27.10s at 20[d.] to the ora.

The king himself holds BROUGHTON. King Edward held it in demesne. They have not given an account of the hides. There is land [...]. In demesne are 2 ploughs; and 8 villans and 11 bordars with 4½ ploughs. There are 4 coliberts, and 3 mills rendering 27s6d, and 50 acres of meadow, [and] woodland for 3 pigs.

What belongs to this manor TRE, and afterwards, was worth £76.16s8d; now £66; and yet it renders at farm £104.12s2d.

To this manor belongs a wood which is in the hand of Bishop Walkelin, but as yet [the right to it] has not been proved.

A certain [portion of] land was given TRE for a mill of this manor; but the reeve, TRW, received the mill, and has both.

In the same hundred is EAST DEAN, which belongs to this manor, and there is in demesne 1 plough; and 2 villans and 14 bordars with 1½ ploughs. There are 2 slaves, and 2 mills rendering 20s, and 4 acres of meadow, [and] woodland for 3 pigs.

Of this manor, he has in [? Nether] Wallop 5 villans and 1 slave, and a mill rendering 30d, and 2 ploughs in demesne; and the coliberts or boors, as above, render the customary dues of the others.

Formerly the reeve had the honey and pasture of these manors as his farm, and woodland for house-building. Now the foresters have this, the reeves nothing. 10s of the honey and 10s of the pasture are in the king's forest.

IN HURSTBOURNE HUNDRED

The king himself holds UPTON, [part] of Queen Edith's land. It was then assessed at 1 hide; now at nothing. There is land for 2 ploughs. In demesne is 1 plough; and 5 villans and 3 bordars with 2 ploughs. There is 1 slave, [and] woodland for fencing. TRE it was worth £4; and afterwards 40s; now 60s; yet it is at farm for £4.

IN ANDOVER HUNDRED

The king holds UPPER CLATFORD in demesne, of the fief of Earl Roger. Saxi held it of King Edward. It then paid geld for 11 hides; now for 4½ hides. There is land for 10 ploughs. In demesne are 3 ploughs; and 16 villans and 21 bordars with 7 ploughs. There are 8 slaves, and 3 mills rendering 57s6d, and 15 acres of meadow, woodland for 10 pigs, and 7 closes in Winchester rendering 10s. TRE it was worth £20; and afterwards, as now, £15.10s; yet it renders £20 at farm.

Of this manor, the Abbey of Lyre holds 3 virgates of land, and the tithe of the vill; and Adelina the jester 1 virgate, which Earl Roger gave her.

IN REDBRIDGE HUNDRED

The king himself holds STANSWOOD. Cypping held it of King Edward. It was then assessed at 2 hides, now at 1, because the other is in the forest. There is land for 7 ploughs. In demesne is 1 [plough]; and 13 villans and 20 bordars with 7 ploughs. There are 4 slaves, and a mill rendering 5s, and 4 acres of meadow, and 2 fisheries rendering 50d, [and] woodland for 10 pigs. TRE it was worth £10; and afterwards, as now, £7. This manor is included in the king's farm which he has from the Isle of Wight.

The king himself holds ELING in demesne. This manor, in the time of King Edward, rendered half a day's farm. They do not know the number of hides. There is land for 20 ploughs. In demesne are 5 ploughs; and 13 villans and 43 bordars with 7 ploughs. There are 13 slaves, and 2 mills rendering 25s. For the herbage, 45s. There is a fishery, and a salt-pan without rent, and 125 acres of meadow. [There is] woodland for 20 pigs, which has remained in the farm; other woodland is in the hand of the king. There is a church to which belongs half a carucate of land in alms. To this manor belonged 2 Berewicks in [the Isle of] Wight, and 3 outside it. When Hugh de Port received it, then those 2 which were in the island were wanting. Earl William held them. Into the forest were taken 16 villans' messuages and 3 of bordars, and woodland for 280 pigs as pannage, and 3 sesters of honey; all which are now lacking, and these things together are valued at £26. TRE it was worth £38.8s4d; and afterwards the same; now £20; and yet it renders £52.6s1d, with those things which fall within the forest.

IN 'EDGEGATE' HUNDRED

The king holds CHRISTCHURCH in demesne. It belonged to King Edward's farm. Then, as now, [it was assessed at] 1 virgate of land. There is land for 13 ploughs. In demesne are 2 ploughs; and 21 villans and 5 bordars with 12 ploughs. There is 1 slave, and 3 coliberts and 4 radknights with 2½ ploughs, and a mill rendering 5s, and 61 acres of meadow. The woodland is in the king's forest, where there were 5 villans with 3 ploughs. In the borough of Christchurch 31 messuages render 16d rent.

[Folio 39: HAMPSHIRE]

TRE, and afterwards, it was worth £19 by tale; now £10 at 20[d.] to the ora; and yet it renders £12.10s. What is in the forest is valued at £12.10s.

The king himself holds HOLDENHURST. Earl Tosti held it. It was then assessed at 29 hides and half a virgate. When Hugh de Port received it, there were then 22 hides and half a virgate, and they never paid geld. The other 7 hides are in the Isle [of Wight]. [There are] now 18½ hides and half a virgate. 3½ hides are in the New Forest. There is land for 20 ploughs. In demesne are 4½ ploughs; and 37 villans and 25 bordars with 19 ploughs. There is a chapel, and 14 slaves, and a mill rendering 15s, and 3 fisheries serving the hall, and 181 acres of meadow, [and] woodland for 6 pigs as pannage. On 7 hides, which are in the forest, dwelt 13 villans and 3 bordars with 8 ploughs; and with these hides there is, outside the manor, woodland for 129 pigs as pannage. TRE it was worth £44; and afterwards £34; now £24 by tale; and yet it renders £25 at 20[d] to the ora. What is in the forest is valued at £12.10s.

IN RINGWOOD HUNDRED

The king holds RINGWOOD in demesne. Earl Tosti held it. It was then assessed at 28 hides; now at nothing. When the sheriff received it, [there were] only 10 hides, the rest were in [the Isle of] Wight; [there are] now 6 hides, the remainder are in the forest. There is land for 16 ploughs. In demesne are 4 ploughs; and 56 villans and 21 bordars with 13 ploughs, and 1 radknight with half a plough. There is a church to which belongs half a hide in alms. There are 8 slaves, and a mill rendering 22s, and 105 acres of meadow. TRE it was worth £24; and afterwards £16; now £8.10s; yet it renders £12.10s at 20[d] to the ora. On 4 hides, which are in the forest, dwelt 14 villans and 6 bordars with 7 ploughs, and a mill rendering 30d, and woodland for 189 pigs as pannage. That which the king has is worth £7.10s by tale.

IN BOLDRE HUNDRED

The king himself holds LYNDHURST. It belonged to the king's farm of Amesbury [Wilts.]. It was then assessed at 2 hides. Of these 2 hides, Herbert the forester now [holds] 1 virgate, and it pays geld for as much; the others are in the forest. There are now only 2 bordars. It is worth 10s; TRE it was worth £6.

IN FORDINGBRIDGE HUNDRED

The king himself holds "SLACHAM" in his forest. Ælfstan held it of King Edward in alod. It then paid geld for half a hide; now for nothing. There is land for 1 plough. When Ralph de Limesy received it, there were 3 villans with 1 plough. It was worth 25s.

The king himself holds EYEWORTH in the forest. 2 free

men held it of King Edward in alod. It then paid geld for 1 virgate; now for nothing. It was worth 10s.

The king holds "BEDECOTE" in the forest. Dodda held it of King Edward in alod, and it then paid geld for half a hide. There is land for 1 plough. It is now in the forest except 11½ acres of meadow, which Picot holds. It was worth 20s; and afterwards 15s.

In the same HUNDRED the king holds 1 virgate of land which Eadric held of King Edward in alod, and it paid geld for 1 virgate; now for nothing. There is land for 1 plough. It is all in the forest except 1½ acres of meadow which the son of Alric holds. It was worth 7s6d.

The king holds ROCKBOURNE in demesne. King Edward held it. It never paid geld nor was it assessed in hides. In demesne are 2 ploughs; and 4 villans and 20 bordars with 3 ploughs. There are 3 acres of meadow.

BREAMORE belongs to this above manor, which the king holds and King Edward held. [...] In demesne is 1 plough; and 4 villans and 8 bordars with 4 ploughs, and 82 acres of meadow. Of this manor 2½ hides and woodland for 50 pigs are in the forest. This used to render 51s8d. To this manor belongs 1 hide in the Isle of Wight, which Gerwy holds. From it there used to come £9 to the king's farm, and the priest had 20s. Of this manor, half a hide which Wulfmær holds, lies in the king's forest. From Breamore, and Rockbourne, and Broughton, and Lower Burgate there falls within the forest £13.10s; and in the Isle [of Wight] £9 of farm; and from the priest 20s.

The king holds LOWER BURGATE, 1 virgate of land. King Edward held it. [...] In demesne is 1 plough; and 7 villans and 18 bordars and 8 coliberts with 7 ploughs. There is a mill rendering 10s and 1,000 eels, and 80 acres of meadow. The woodland of this manor is in the king's forest, and the pasture, which used to render 40 pigs and 10s.

IN ANDOVER HUNDRED

The king holds [?]MONXTON in demesne. Wulfgifu held it of King Edward in alod. It then paid geld for 10 hides; now for 2½ hides. There is land for 3 ploughs. In demesne are 2 ploughs; and 3 villans and 5 bordars with 2 ploughs. There are 3 slaves, and a mill rendering 7s6d, and 2 acres of meadow, and a small wood. TRE it was worth 100s; and afterwards, as now, £9.

The king himself holds [?]QUARLEY. Earl Harold held it. It then paid geld for 5 hides; now for nothing. There is land for 4 ploughs. In demesne is 1 plough; and 4 villans and 11 bordars with 3 ploughs. There is a church, and 12 slaves, [and] woodland without pannage. TRE it was worth £12; and afterwards, as now, £8.

The king holds ANDOVER in demesne. King Edward held it. They have not stated the number of hides. There is land [...]. In demesne are 2 ploughs; and 62 villans and 36 bordars and 3 coliberts and 6 slaves with 24 ploughs. There are 6 mills rendering 72s6d, and 18 acres of meadow, [and] woodland for 100 pigs as pannage.

IN BASINGSTOKE HUNDRED

The king holds BASINGSTOKE in demesne. It was always a royal manor. It never gave geld; nor was it ever hidated. There is land for 20 ploughs. In demesne are 3 ploughs; and 20 villans and 8 bordars with 12 ploughs. There are 6 slaves, and 3 mills rendering 30s, and 12 coliberts with 4 ploughs. There is a market rendering 30s, and 20 acres of meadow; and in Winchester 4 inhabitants of the suburbs paid 13s less 1d. Geoffrey the chamberlain holds the land of 1 of these; but neither the sheriff nor the hundred have ever seen the king's seal for it. There is woodland for 20 pigs.

The king holds KINGSCLERE in demesne. It belonged to King Edward's farm and belongs to the day's farm [rendered] from Basingstoke. They did not know the number of hides. There is land for 16 ploughs. In demesne are 3 ploughs; and 21 villans and 31 bordars with 13 ploughs. There are 2 mills rendering 100d, and 7 slaves. From the toll 15s, from the woodland 20s, and [there are] 6 acres of meadow. [There is] woodland for 15 pigs. There 2 coliberts pay 13s.

The king holds HURSTBOURNE TARRANT in demesne. It belonged to King Edward's farm. They have not the number of hides. There is land for 16 ploughs. In demesne are 2 ploughs; and 24 villans and 12 bordars with 15 ploughs. There are 10 acres of meadow, [and] woodland for 20 pigs; for the herbage, 20s.

Vitalis the priest holds the church of this manor, with half a hide, and there he has 1 plough with 2 bordars, and 1 acre of meadow, and the church-scot, which is valued at 14s. These 3 manors, Basingstoke, Kingsclere, [and] Hurstbourne Tarrant, render 1 day's farm.

IN TITCHFIELD HUNDRED

The king holds TITCHFIELD. It is a Berewick belonging to MEONSTOKE. King Edward held it. There are 2 hides; but they have not paid geld. There is land for 15 ploughs. In demesne, only 2 oxen; and 16 villans and 13 bordars with 9 ploughs. There are 4 slaves, and a mill rendering 20s. The market and toll [render] 40s.

[Folio 39V: HAMPSHIRE]

There is a mill rendering 20s, and 14 acres of meadow, and pasture [rendering] 51d.

IN SOMBORNE HUNDRED

The king holds KING'S SOMBORNE in demesne. It was a royal manor, but was not hidated. There is land for 10 ploughs. In demesne are 3 ploughs; and 25 villans and 8 bordars with 8 ploughs. There are 2 slaves, and 3 mills rendering 15s. There are 7 coliberts, and 20 acres of meadow, [and] pasture rendering 17s10d from the herbage. The soke of 2 hundreds belongs to this manor. There are 2 churches, to which half a hide belongs in alms. The reeve claims 1 virgate of land for the use of this manor, and pasture which they call [?]Furzedown, which render 15s. The Count of Mortain holds it; but the hundred asserts that it ought to belong to the king's demesne farm, and it was there TRE, and the meadow [was] in the same [manor].

THESE LANDS MENTIONED BELOW LIE IN THE ISLE OF WIGHT

The king holds KNIGHTON and "DONE" in demesne. 8 free men held them of King Edward in alod. They then paid geld for 2 hides; now for nothing. Oda, with 2 free men, had half a hide and the fourth part of a virgate, Alweald 1 virgate, Harold 1 virgate, Godwine 1 virgate, Alric 1 virgate, [and] Beorhtric half a hide. Each of these [had] part of a mill, each part [rendering] 22d. The land of these 5 [sic] thegns the king holds in his farm; and there he has 2 ploughs in demesne, and it is valued at 100s; and yet it renders £8 at farm. What Oda held [is worth] 11s; what Alweald [held] 5s; what Harold [held] 5s.

The king holds "LADONE" and BATHINGBOURNE in demesne. Oda held them of King Edward in alod. They then paid geld for 4 hides, and now for half a hide. There is land for 3 ploughs. The king holds them in his farm. Oda had £4 at farm.

The king holds SANDFORD WITH WEEK in demesne. King Edward held them. [There were] then 3 hides. When the sheriff received them, [there were] 2 hides and 1 virgate. There is land for 12 ploughs. In demesne are 3 ploughs; and 10 villans and 3 bordars with 6 ploughs. There are 10 slaves, and 2 mills rendering 70d, and 6 acres of meadow. From the herbage, 20s. [There is] woodland without pannage. TRE [it was worth] £25 weighed and assayed; when the king received it, £20 [measured] in the the same way; and now £20 by weight; and yet it renders at farm £26 by weight and 100d.

The king holds ARRETON in demesne. King Edward held it. There are 4 hides. There is land for 5 ploughs. In demesne are 3 ploughs; and 10 villans and 12 bordars with 10 ploughs. There are 7 slaves, and 1 mill rendering 15s. The Abbey of Lyre holds the church of this manor, with 1 virgate of land and 1 acre of meadow, and all the tithe of the manor; and it is valued at 20s. The whole manor was worth TRE £10; and afterwards, as now, £8; yet it renders £12 blanch at 20[d] to the ora.

The king holds YAVERLAND in demesne. King Edward held it. It was not assessed in hides. There is land for 5 ploughs. There are 12 villans with 5 ploughs. TRE it was worth 100s; and afterwards, as now, £4; yet it renders 100s.

The king holds "ABEDESTONE" [in Ryde] in demesne. 3 free men held it of King Edward in alod. It then, as now, paid geld for 1 hide. There is land for 3 ploughs. There are 11 villans with 4 ploughs. It is and was worth 40s; yet it renders 60s blanch.

The king has a plot of land in the island, from which come 6 ploughshares.

The king holds "SCALDEFORD" in demesne. Sæweard held it in alod of King Edward. It paid geld then, as now, for half a hide. There is land for 1 plough. There are 3 villans with 1½ ploughs. It is and was worth 13s; yet it renders 16s8d.

The king holds LESSLAND in demesne. 5 free men held it in alod as 5 manors of King Edward. It paid geld then for 1 hide

and half a virgate; now for half a hide and half a virgate. Almær had half a hide, Wulfnoth half a virgate, Swærting half a virgate, Wudumann half a virgate, [and] Godmann 1 virgate. There is land for 2 ploughs. There are 4 villans having 2½ ploughs in demesne, and 5 acres of meadow. It is and was worth 20s.

The king holds LUCCOMBE. Sæwine held it of King Edward in alod. It then paid geld for 1 hide; now for 2 parts of a virgate. There is land for 1 plough, and there is [1 plough] in demesne, with 6 bordars and 2 slaves. TRE it was worth £4; and afterwards, as now, £3; yet it renders £4 at farm.

The king holds NUNWELL. Wulfflæd held it of Earl Tosti, but it was not an alod. It then paid geld for 2 hides; now for 1 virgate. There is land for 1½ ploughs. In demesne is [1] plough; and 1 villan and 2 bordars with half a plough, and 3 slaves. TRE it was worth 60s; and afterwards, as now, 40s; and yet it renders a blanch farm.

The king holds KERN. Earl Harold held it. It then paid geld for 1 hide; now for nothing. There is land for 1 plough, and there is [1 plough] in demesne, with 2 bordars and 5 slaves. TRE it was worth 25s; and afterwards, as now, 20s.

The king holds 'WOOLVERTON' [in Bembridge]. Eadgifu held it of Earl Godwine. It then paid geld for half a hide; now for nothing. There is land for 1 plough, and there is [1 plough] in demesne, with 3 bordars and 1 slave. It is and was worth 10s.

The king holds SANDOWN. Wulfnoth held it of King Edward in alod. It then paid geld for 2 hides; now for half [a hide] and half a virgate. There is land for 3 ploughs. In demesne is 1 plough; and 7 villans and 1 bordar with 3 ploughs, and 4 acres of meadow. It was worth 40s; now 30[s].

The king holds WROXALL. Countess Gytha held it of Earl Godwine in alod. It then paid geld for 5 hides; now for 2½ hides. There is land for 10 ploughs. In demesne are 4 ploughs; and 10 villans and 24 bordars with 7 ploughs. There are 17 slaves, and 2 mills rendering 20s, and 3 acres of meadow, [and] woodland for 1 pig. TRE it was worth £27; and afterwards, as now, £20; yet it renders £22.

The king holds HEASLEY. Earl Harold held it. It then paid geld for 3 hides; now for 1½ virgates. There is land for 4 ploughs. In demesne are 2 [ploughs]; and 4 villans and 4 bordars with 2 ploughs. There are 15 slaves, and 10 acres of meadow, [and] woodland for 2 pigs. TRE it was worth £8; and afterwards, as now, 100s; yet it renders at farm £8 at 20[d] to the ora.

The king holds BARNSLEY. Godwine held it of King Edward in alod. It then paid geld for 1 hide; now for half a hide and half a virgate. There is land for 2 ploughs. There are 3 villans with 1 plough. [There is] woodland for 1 pig. It was worth 40s; now 20s.

The king holds PUCKPOOL and "ETHARIN". 2 free men held it of King Edward as 2 manors in alod. It then paid geld for 1 hide; now for 3 virgates. There is land for 1 plough, and there is [1 plough] in demesne, with 3 villans. It was worth 30s; now 20s; and yet it renders 30s.

The king holds NETTLESTONE. Alnoth held it of King Edward in alod. It then paid geld for the third part of a hide; now for half a virgate. There is land for half a plough, and there is [half a plough] in demesne, with 3 bordars. It was worth 10s; now 5s.

The king holds STENBURY and WHIPPINGHAM. Cypping held it of King Edward as 2 manors in alod. It then paid geld for 3 hides; now for 2 hides. There is land for 7 ploughs. In demesne are 2 [ploughs]; and 7 villans and 10 bordars with 6 ploughs. There are 12 slaves, and 5 acres of meadow. It is and was always worth £12.

The king holds "WENECHETONE". 2 free men held it of King Edward as 2 manors in alod. It then paid geld for 1 hide; now for nothing. There is land for 2 ploughs, and there are [2 ploughs] with 2 villans. It was and is worth £3.

Yet from these 2 manors comes at farm £18 at 20[d] to the ora.

[Folio 40: HAMPSHIRE]

1 virgate of this manor is in 'Shoofleet' [in Whippingham]. Bolla held this of King Edward in alod. The king has it now in his farm.

The king holds NITON and "ABLA". 2 free men held it as 2 manors of King Edward in alod. It then paid geld for 3 hides; now for 1 hide and 1 virgate. There is land for 8 ploughs. In demesne are 3 ploughs; and 7 villans and 18 bordars with 5 ploughs. There are 9 slaves. TRE it was worth £17; and afterwards, as now, £12; yet it renders £17.

The king holds WOOTTON. Queen Edith held it. It then, as now, paid geld for 1 hide. There are 4 villans with 3 ploughs. It is worth, and renders, £3.

The land of the Bishop of Winchester

IN FAWLEY HUNDRED

WALKELIN, Bishop of Winchester, holds OLD ALRESFORD in demesne. It belongs, and always did belong, to the bishopric. TRE it was assessed at 51 hides; now at 42 hides. There is land for 40 ploughs. In demesne are 10 ploughs; and 48 villans and 36 bordars with 13 ploughs. There are 31 slaves, and 9 mills rendering £9 and 30d. There are 8 acres of meadow. [There is] woodland for 10 pigs as pannage; for the herbage 50d. There are 3 churches rendering £4; these used to render £6 a year, but they could not support it.

Of this land of this manor, Robert holds 3½ hides, Walter 2 hides, Durand 4 hides in Soberton and 6 hides in Beauworth, and 1 Englishman 1½ hides. These men have 6 ploughs in demesne; and 17 villans and 6 bordars and 19 slaves with 6 ploughs, and a mill rendering 20s, and 6 acres of meadow. Wulfric Cepe, Robert's predecessor, could not go where he would; neither [could] Osbern, Walter's predecessor; nor Edward and Alric, the predecessors of Durand. The whole

manor TRE was worth £40; and afterwards £20; now the bishop's demesne [is worth] £40; Robert's [part] £4; Walter's 40s; [and] Durand's £11.

The bishop himself holds KILMESTON. Godwine held it of the bishop; he could not go elsewhere. Then, as now, it was assessed at 5 hides. There is land for 3 ploughs. In demesne is 1 [plough]; and 4 villans and 4 bordars with 1½ ploughs. There are 6 slaves, and 7 acres of meadow. TRE and afterwards, as now, worth 100s.

The bishop himself holds TWYFORD in demesne. He always held it. TRE it was assessed at 20 hides; now at 15 hides. There is land for 25 ploughs. In demesne are 4 [ploughs]; and 29 villans and 20 bordars with 21 ploughs. There is a church rendering 5s, and 4 mills rendering £4, and 10 acres of meadow, [and] woodland for 15 pigs as pannage. TRE, and afterwards, it was worth £20; now £32.

In the same place, in TWYFORD, the bishop has 1 manor. Ealdgyth, wife of Osweald, held it of the bishop. Wulfric held it TRE. It always belonged to the bishopric. It was then assessed at 10 hides; now at 5 hides. There is land for 8 ploughs. In demesne are 2 [ploughs]; and 17 villans and 20 bordars with 7 ploughs. There are 3 slaves, and 2 mills rendering £4.15s. There are 32 acres of meadow. For the herbage, 12s6d. TRE, and afterwards, it was worth £12; now £15.

The bishop himself holds EASTON in demesne. It always belonged to the bishopric. TRE, as now, it was assessed at 6 hides. There is land for 11 ploughs. In demesne are 6 ploughs; and 7 villans and 42 bordars with 4 ploughs. There are 12 slaves, and 2 chapels, and 2 mills rendering 30s, and 58 acres of meadow, [and] woodland for 15 pigs as pannage; for the pasture, 14d. Turstin holds 52 acres of the demesne, which Ælfheah held.

Of this land of this manor, Geoffrey holds 3 hides. Beorhtric held them of the bishop in parage, but he could not go elsewhere. There are 1½ ploughs, with 7 bordars, and 10 acres of meadow.

Of the same land Alwine holds 1 hide and 1 virgate. He held them himself TRE. There he has 1 plough, with 5 bordars, and 6 acres of meadow. The whole TRE was worth £24; and afterwards £12; now what the bishop holds, £30; what Geoffrey [holds], £3; what Alwine [holds], 25s.

The bishop himself holds BISHOPSTOKE in demesne, and it always belonged to the bishopric. It was assessed TRE, as now, at 5 hides. There is land for 5 ploughs. In demesne are 2 ploughs; and 6 villans and 5 bordars with 3 ploughs. There are 6 slaves, and a mill rendering 10s. There is a church, and 74 acres of meadow, [and] woodland for 10 pigs. TRE, and afterwards, it was worth £6; now £8.

Ealdræd holds KILMESTON of the bishop. His wife held it. TRE, as now, it was assessed at 5 hides. She could not go where she would. There is land for 3 ploughs. In demesne is 1 plough; and 6 villans and 3 bordars with 1½ ploughs. There is a chapel, and 7 acres of meadow. It is and was worth 100s.

IN 'BUDDLESGATE' HUNDRED

The bishop himself holds CRAWLEY in demesne. It always belonged to the bishopric. TRE, as now, it was assessed at 6½ hides. There is land for 14 ploughs. In demesne are 5 ploughs; and 6 villans and 25 bordars with 7 ploughs, and 20 slaves, and 26 acres of meadow. [There is] woodland for 15 pigs, and a church.

Of this land of this manor, Hugh holds 3 hides. Alwine Stilla held them of the bishop in parage; he could not go where he pleased. There is in demesne 1 plough; and 2 villans and 5 bordars with 1 plough. There are 9 slaves, [and] woodland rendering 6d. TRE the whole manor was worth £35; and afterwards £28; now the bishop's demesne [is worth] £35; what Hugh holds, £7.

IN WALTHAM HUNDRED

The bishop himself holds BISHOP'S WALTHAM in demesne. It always belonged to the bishopric. TRE, as now, it was assessed at 20 hides; although there are 30 hides in number. There is land for 26 ploughs. In demesne are 6 ploughs; and 70 villans and 15 bordars with 26 ploughs. There are 7 slaves, and 3 mills rendering 17s6d, and 2½ acres of meadow, [and] woodland for 10 pigs. There is a park for beasts. TRE it was worth £31; and afterwards £10.10s; now £30.

Of this land of this manor, Robert holds 3 virgates; villans held these TRE. There he has 1 plough, and 1 bordar and 1 slave. It is worth 30s. Ralph the priest holds 2 churches of this manor with 2½ hides; and there he has 2 ploughs; and 2 villans and 9 bordars and 6 slaves with 1 plough. It is worth 100s. Of the land of these churches, 1 man holds 1 hide of the villans' land. There he has 1 villan and 3 bordars with 9 oxen. It is worth 30s.

IN OVERTON HUNDRED

The bishop himself holds OVERTON in demesne. It always belonged to the bishopric. TRE, as now, it was assessed at 41 hides. There is land for 32 ploughs. In demesne are 5 ploughs; and 50 villans and 27 bordars with 27 ploughs. There are 2 churches, and 17 slaves, and 4 mills rendering 62s6d, and 4 acres of meadow, [and] woodland for 30 pigs as pannage. TRE it was worth £24; and afterwards the same; now £50; yet it is at farm for £61.

Of this land of this manor, Robert the clerk holds 2 hides of the bishop; [and] Gilbert his brother 2 hides. In BRADLEY, Geoffrey [holds] 5 hides. The predecessors of these men, Alnoth, Wulfstan, and Alric, held of the bishop; they could not go where they pleased. In demesne they have 3 ploughs; and 5 villans and 8 bordars and 7 slaves with 3 ploughs. TRE it was worth £10; and afterwards £6; now £7.10s.

[Folio 40V: HAMP[SHIRE]]

IN MEONSTOKE HUNDRED

The bishop himself holds WEST MEON in demesne. It always belonged to the bishopric. TRE it was assessed at 20 hides; now at 12 hides. There is land for 14 ploughs. In demesne are 3 ploughs; and 25 villans and 17 bordars with 11 ploughs. There is a church with 1 hide, and 8 slaves, and 2 mills rendering 10s. There are 10 acres of meadow, woodland for 40 pigs, and 8 closes in Winchester rendering 6s. TRE it was worth £20; and afterwards £16; now £30; yet it renders £40 at farm, but it cannot support it for long. The church renders 50s.

The bishop himself holds half a hide in the manor of Meonstoke. The bishop always held it in demesne. TRE, as now, it was assessed at half a hide. There he has half a plough, and 1 villan and 1 mill. It is and was worth 25s. The bishop has 20s from the church of Meonstoke.

IN EAST MEON HUNDRED

The bishop himself holds in EAST MEON 6 hides and 1 virgate with the church. There is land for 4 ploughs. In demesne are 1½ ploughs; and 11 villans and 8 bordars with 3 ploughs. There are 2 slaves, and 1 mill rendering 30d, and 4 acres of meadow. TRE, and afterwards, it was worth £4; now 100s.

The bishop himself holds [?]STOKE [in St Mary Bourne] in demesne. It always belonged to the bishopric. TRE it was assessed at 10 hides; now at 7 hides. There is land for 4 ploughs. In demesne are 2 ploughs; and 2 villans and 8 bordars with 1 plough. There are 6 slaves, and 4 acres of meadow.

Of this land of this manor, Geoffrey holds 4 hides of the bishop which formerly villans held. There he has 1 plough, and 2 bordars and 6 slaves, and 4 acres of meadow. Mauger holds the church of this manor. It is worth 15s. The whole manor was worth TRE £10; and afterwards £8; now what the bishop holds [is worth] £7; what Geoffrey [holds] £4.

IN FAREHAM HUNDRED

The bishop himself holds FAREHAM in demesne. It always belonged to the bishopric. TRE, as now, it was assessed at 20 hides; yet there are 30 hides in number. But King Edward granted it thus on account of the Vikings because it is on the sea. There is land for 20 ploughs. In demesne are 2 ploughs; and 30 villans and 16 bordars with 14 ploughs. There is a church, and 6 slaves, and 2 mills rendering 25s, and 25 acres of meadow. [There is] woodland for 10 pigs as pannage; for the herbage, 30d. TRE it was worth £18; and afterwards £10; now £16; and yet it is at farm for £20, but it cannot support it.

Of this land of this manor, Ralph holds of the bishop 7½ hides of villans' land, Geoffrey 4 hides. Herch held them. William [holds] 1 hide. Godwine held this. These hides paid geld with the others; those who held them could not withdraw from the bishop. There are now in demesne 4 ploughs; and 24 villans and 10 bordars with 5½ ploughs. There are 4 slaves, and 3 mills rendering 16s. There are 16 acres of meadow, [and] woodland for 3 pigs. The whole is worth £7.

IN BROUGHTON HUNDRED

Richer holds "CHINGESCAMP" of the bishop. The Abbot of Ely held it of Archbishop Stigand. TRE, as now, it paid geld for half a hide. There is land for 1 plough. There is 1 villan with half a plough. [There is] woodland for 3 pigs. TRE it was worth 15s; and afterwards, as now, 5s.

IN TITCHFIELD HUNDRED

In MEON the bishop himself holds 1 hide, and it was assessed at as much. There is land for 1 plough, and there is [1 plough] with 2 villans. There are 2 acres of woodland for fencing. It is and was worth 20s. Tovi had half of this hide by [gift of] Earl William, and the other part he had of the king for money, and, on account of the fact that Tovi held this land, the bishop now has it by the king's gift.

IN 'BOUNTISBOROUGH' HUNDRED

The bishop himself holds YAVINGTON. Archbishop Stigand held it. It was then assessed at 1½ hides; now at nothing. There is land for half a plough. There are 2 bordars, and half a mill rendering 7s, and 7 acres of meadow. TRE it was worth 25s; and afterwards 19s; now 20s.

IN 'MAINSBOROUGH' HUNDRED

Richer holds 1 manor, CHILTON CANDOVER, of the bishop. Godwine and Leofwine held it of the bishopric as 2 manors, 5 hides each. TRE, as now, it was assessed at 10 hides. There is land for 6 ploughs. In demesne are 3 ploughs; and 1 villan and 10 bordars [...]. The whole manor was worth TRE £8; and afterwards £6; now £7.

IN SOMBORNE HUNDRED

The bishop himself holds HOUGHTON in demesne. It always belonged to the bishopric. There are 24 hides. TRE, as now, it was assessed at 16 hides. There is land for 28 ploughs. In demesne are 4 ploughs; and 36 villans and 46 bordars with 23 ploughs. There are 14 slaves, and 4 mills rendering 70s, and a fishery rendering 3d, and 156 acres of meadow, woodland for 22 pigs as pannage, and 3 burgesses paying 30d.

There are 2 churches, to which 2 hides less 1 virgate belong. Wibert the clerk holds these; and there the priest has half a plough. It is worth 60s.

The whole manor, TRE and afterwards, was worth £24; now as much; yet it is at farm for £30.

William Peverel holds 1 hide of the same manor, but does not wish to give geld. There he has 1 plough with 2 bordars, and 4 acres of meadow. It is worth 20s.

Walter holds of the bishop 1 hide of the same manor, and there he has 1 plough with 1 bordar. It is worth 22s.

IN 'BOUNTISBOROUGH' HUNDRED

Durand holds [Lower and Upper] WIELD of the bishop. 2 free men held it of the bishop TRE, but they could not withdraw with the land. It was then, as now, assessed at 10 hides. There is land for 9 ploughs. In demesne are 5 ploughs; and 9 villans and 6 bordars with 4 ploughs. TRE it was worth, all together, £8; and afterwards £6; now £10. Of this manor, 2 free men hold 1 hide, and there they have 1 plough with 1 bordar. It is worth 20s.

IN 'ASHLEY' HUNDRED

Ranulph holds WEST TISTED of the bishop. It belongs to the bishopric. TRE, as now, it paid geld for 7 hides. There is land for 8 ploughs. In demesne are 3 ploughs; and 15 villans and 3 bordars with 3 ploughs. There is a church, and 2 slaves. TRE, and afterwards, it was worth £4; now £6.

IN 'BOUNTISBOROUGH' HUNDRED

Hugh de Port holds ABBOTSTONE of the bishop. It belongs and belonged to the bishopric. TRE, as now, it was assessed at 9 hides. There is land for 5 ploughs. In demesne are 2 [ploughs]; and 8 villans and 6 bordars with 3 ploughs. There are 5 slaves, and a mill rendering 15s, and 5 acres of meadow. It is and was always worth 100s.

Of this land Reginald holds 1½ hides, and there he has 1 plough and 1 acre of meadow. It is worth 20s.

IN TITCHFIELD HUNDRED

The bishop himself holds BROWNWICH of the king, as a fief. Ansgot holds it of the bishop. It does not belong to the bishopric. Eadric held it of King Edward. Then, as now, it was assessed at 1 hide. There is land for 3 ploughs. In demesne are 1½ ploughs; and 5 villans and 11 bordars with 3 ploughs. There is 1 slave. It is and was always worth £4.

The bishop himself holds BENTLEY [near Farnham] of the bishopric. [...] TRE it was assessed at 10 hides; now at 8 hides. There is land for 10 ploughs. In demesne are 2 ploughs; and 17 villans and 5 bordars with 8 ploughs. There are 4 slaves, and a mill rendering 10s, and 10 acres of meadow, [and] woodland for fencing.

Of this land, Osbern holds of the bishop 1 hide and 1 virgate, [and] William 1½ hides. There are 2 ploughs in demesne; and 3 villans with 1 plough, and 1 acre of meadow. [There is] woodland for 2 pigs.

The bishop's demesne is and was worth £12; Osbern's [part], 50s; William's, 20s.

[Folio 41: [HAMP]SHIRE]

III. These Lands Mentioned Below Are For the Sustenance of the Monks of Winchester

IN "FALEMERE" HUNDRED

Bishop WALKELIN holds CHILCOMB. TRE, as now, it was assessed at 1 hide. There is land for 68 ploughs. In demesne are 12 ploughs; and 30 villans and 115 bordars with 57 ploughs. There are 9 churches, and 20 slaves, and 4 mills rendering £4, and 40 acres of meadow; for the herbage, 23s5d. [There is] woodland for 30 pigs as pannage.

Of the same hide, William holds land for 3 ploughs. Manna held it. Cypping holds land for 1 plough. He held it himself. Walter holds land for 1 plough. Ælfhere held it. Hugh the mason holds land for 2 ploughs. Gerald held it. Turstin Rufus holds land for 1 plough. Æthelmær held it. Osbern holds land for 1 plough. Godwine held it. Turstin the Small holds 30 acres. Ælfheah held them. Those who held these lands TRE could not withdraw to another lord with the land. Those who hold now have 7 ploughs in demesne; and 7 villans and 30 bordars with 2 ploughs. There are 11 slaves, and 4 acres of meadow.

The whole manor was worth TRE £73.10s; and afterwards as much; now what the monks hold [is worth] £80; what the men hold, £24.

To this manor belonged TRE 6 hides, which Ralph de Mortimer now holds; but he performs no service to the church.

IN 'BUDDLESGATE' HUNDRED

The bishop himself holds NURSLING. It always belonged to the monastery. TRE, as now, it was assessed at 5 hides. There is land for 6 ploughs. In demesne is 1 plough; and 21 villans and 8 bordars with 10 ploughs. There is a church, and 1 slave, and a mill rendering 22s8d, and 140 acres of meadow, [and] woodland for 5 pigs as pannage. TRE it was worth £8; and afterwards 100s; now £9; yet it renders £10.

The bishop himself holds CHILBOLTON. It always belonged to the monastery. TRE it was assessed at 10 hides; now at 5 hides. There is land for 7 ploughs. In demesne are 2 ploughs; and 11 villans and 11 bordars with 7 ploughs. There is a church, and 4 slaves, and a mill rendering 15s, and 30 acres of meadow. TRE, and afterwards, it was worth £12; now £15.

Of the land of this manor, the bishop has only 5 hides and 3 virgates; and this is land for 7 ploughs. Richard Sturmy holds the remaining hides. A certain reeve held them, and could not go where he pleased; and of these hides, he had 2 by villan tenure.

IN FAWLEY HUNDRED

The bishop himself holds AVINGTON. It always belonged to the church. TRE, as now, it was assessed at 5 hides. There is land for 5 ploughs. In demesne are 2 ploughs; and 8 villans and 3 bordars with 4 ploughs. There is a church, and 3 slaves, and 16 acres of meadow. TRE it was worth £6; and afterwards 100s; now £10.

IN 'EVINGAR' HUNDRED

The bishop himself holds WHITCHURCH. It always belonged to the monastery. TRE there were 50 hides; and it was then assessed at 38 hides; now at 33 hides. There is land for 33 ploughs. In demesne are 5 ploughs; and 42 villans and 50 bordars with 28 ploughs. There are 10 slaves, and 3 mills rendering 40s, and 15 acres of meadow, [and] woodland for 40 pigs. TRE, and afterwards, it was worth £30; now £35.

Of this manor and of these hides Ralph fitzSeifrid holds 1 manor, which is called FREEFOLK, and it was for the sustenance of the monks. Eadnoth held it of the bishop, and could not go where he pleased. It was then assessed at 9 hides; now at 4 hides, with the others mentioned above. There is land for 5 ploughs. In demesne are 2 ploughs; and 2 villans and 17 bordars with 2 ploughs. There are 5 slaves, and a mill rendering 20s, and 4 acres of meadow. TRE, and afterwards, it was worth £16; now £10.

Of the same manor, William de Fecamp holds 7 hides in Whitnal and in 2 other places. 2 thegns held them of the bishop, and could not go where they pleased; and [these hides] paid geld with the above-mentioned hides. There is land for 7 ploughs. In demesne are 4½ ploughs; and 8 villans and 11 bordars with 3½ ploughs. There are 18 slaves, and a mill rendering 20s, and 4 acres of meadow. TRE, and afterwards, it was worth £10; now £7.

Of the same manor, Mauger holds 1 hide of the villans' land, and there he has 2 villans and 1 bordar with 1 plough. It is worth 20s. Ælfric the priest holds a church of this manor with 1 hide; and there he has in demesne 1 plough with 3 bordars, and 3 acres of meadow. It is worth 20s.

The bishop himself holds HURSTBOURNE PRIORS. It always belonged to the monastery. TRE, as now, it was assessed at 38 hides. There is land for 51 ploughs. In demesne are 4 ploughs; and 55 villans and 38 bordars with 45 ploughs. There are 14 slaves, and 5 mills rendering 25s, and 30 acres of meadow, [and] woodland for 20 pigs. TRE it was worth £36; and afterwards £26; now £40.

Of this manor, Geoffrey holds of the bishop 5 hides in the same vill. 3 thegns held them of the bishop, and could not go where they pleased. They had 3 halls, and in demesne there are 3 ploughs, and 19 bordars and 2 slaves, and a mill rendering 12s6d, and 20 acres of meadow. It was worth £8; now £6.

Of the same manor, Richer holds of the bishop 2 hides. Alnoth held them, and could not go where he pleased. In demesne is 1 plough, and 9 bordars and 3 slaves, and 5 acres of meadow. [There is] woodland for 3 pigs as pannage. It is worth 60s.

Of this manor, William holds of the bishop 2 hides less half a virgate. Sæwine held them of the bishop, and could not go where he pleased. There is 1 plough, with 1 villan and 12 bordars with 1 plough, and 4 acres of meadow. It was worth £6; now 40s. Leofwine holds of the bishop 1 hide, with a church; and there he has 7 oxen in a plough, and 2 acres of meadow. It is and was worth 50s.

The bishop himself holds HIGHCLERE [Burghclere and Highclere]. It always belonged to the church. TRE it was assessed at 10 hides; now at 7½ hides. There is land for 17 ploughs. In demesne is 1 [plough]; and 20 villans and 18 bordars with 16 ploughs, and 24 coliberts and 3 slaves, and a mill rendering 30d, and 6 acres of meadow. [There is] woodland for 10 pigs. TRE it was worth £12 and 38d; and afterwards £7; now £11.

Ælfric the priest holds of the bishop 1 hide, with a church; and there he has 1 plough with 1 bordar and 2 slaves and 1 acre of meadow. It is worth 40s.

IN CRONDALL HUNDRED

The bishop himself holds CRONDALL. It always belonged to the church. There were 50 hides TRE; and then, as now, they paid geld for 40 hides. There is land for 29 ploughs. In demesne are 4 ploughs; and 45 villans and 11 bordars with 25 ploughs. There is a church rendering 20s, and 12 slaves, [and] woodland for 80 pigs as pannage. TRE it was worth £15.10s; and afterwards £6; now £24.

Of the land of this manor, German holds of the bishop 8 hides in Itchel and in Cove. Leofwine and Wulfweard held them of the bishop in parage, and could not go where they pleased. Each of them had a hall. When German received it, there was only 1 hall. In demesne he has 3 ploughs; and 20 villans and 10 bordars with 6 ploughs, and 6 slaves, and a mill rendering 3s, and 2 acres of meadow. [There is] woodland for 15 pigs as pannage. It was worth £6; and afterwards 40s; now £8.

Of the same manor William holds of the bishop 3 virgates in 'Badley' [in Crondall]. Ælfric held them of the bishop by villan tenure. There is 1 plough, with 1 bordar and 4 slaves.

[Folio 41v: HAMP[SHIRE]]

Of the same manor, Turstin holds 7 hides in Long Sutton. Iusten and Leofsige held them of the bishop in parage, but could not go where they pleased, and they had 2 halls. There are in demesne 3 ploughs; and 3 villans and 4 bordars with half a plough. TRE it was worth £7; and now the same; when received, £4.

Of the same manor, Odin of Windsor holds of the bishop 3 hides in Farnborough. Alwine held them of the bishop in parage, and could not go where he pleased. There is now in demesne 1 plough; and 7 villans and 4 bordars with 3 ploughs. There are 5 slaves, and a mill rendering 10d, and 3 acres of meadow, [and] woodland for 6 pigs. TRE, as now, worth 60s; when received, 40s.

IN DROXFORD HUNDRED

The bishop himself holds DROXFORD. It always belonged to the church. TRE it was assessed at 16 hides; now at 14 hides. There is land for 16 ploughs. In demesne are 2 ploughs; and 32 villans and 13 bordars with 14 ploughs. There are 6 slaves, and a church rendering 20s, and 2 mills rendering 15s2d, for the money-rent of the land, 12s, and 10 acres of meadow, [and] woodland for 40 pigs as pannage. TRE, as now, worth £26; when received, £20.

Of the same manor, Hugh de Port holds of the bishop 2 hides in St Clair's. Aghmund held them of the bishop, and could not go where he pleased. There are in demesne 2 ploughs; and 3 villans and 3 bordars with 1 plough. There are 6 slaves, and a mill rendering 10s, and 7 acres of meadow, [and] woodland for 5 pigs. From the pasture, 10d. TRE, as now, worth 60s; when received, 40s.

Of this capital manor Ralph de Mortimer holds by force half a virgate which was there TRE, although the monks discharge its geld.

Ralph fitzSeifrid holds of the bishop POLHAMPTON. TRE it was for the sustenance of the monks. It was then assessed at 5 hides; now at 3½ hides. There is land for 4 ploughs. In demesne is 1 [plough]; and 2 villans and 16 bordars with 2 ploughs, and 2 mills rendering 33s, and 3 acres of meadow. [There is] woodland for 2 pigs. TRE it was worth £8; and afterwards, as now, £7.10s.

IN MEONSTOKE HUNDRED

The bishop himself holds EXTON. It always belonged to the church. TRE it was assessed at 12 hides; now at 8 hides. There is land for 6 ploughs. In demesne are 2 ploughs; and 13 villans and 24 bordars with 5 ploughs. There is a church, and 2 mills rendering 20s, and 4 acres of meadow. TRE it was worth £16; and afterwards £12; now £20, although it ought to render £30, but it cannot bear it.

Of the land of the same manor, Lyfing holds, and held, 2 hides, and they paid geld with the other hides. There he has in demesne 1 plough, and 3 villans and 3 bordars and 3 slaves, and a mill rendering 2s, and 1½ acres of meadow. It is worth 40s.

The bishop himself holds ALVERSTOKE. It always belonged to the monastery. TRE it was assessed at 16 hides; and King Edward allowed that it should be [assessed] at 10 hides, and it is so now. Villans held it and hold it. There are 48 villans with 15 ploughs. There is woodland for 2 pigs. There is land for 15 ploughs. It is and was always worth £6. Of the land of the same manor 1 knight holds half a hide, which paid geld with the other hides. Sæwine held it, but could not go where he pleased. There is 1 plough with 2 bordars. It is worth 25s.

The bishop himself holds MARTYR WORTHY. It always belonged to the monastery. TRE, as now, it was assessed at 3 hides. There is land for 4 ploughs. In demesne are 3 ploughs; and 7 villans and 9 bordars with 1 plough. There is a church, and 7 slaves, and a mill rendering 25s, and 6 acres of meadow. TRE, as now, worth £8; when received, £6.

IN BARTON HUNDRED

The bishop himself holds WONSTON. It always belonged to the monastery. TRE it was assessed at 10 hides; now at 7 hides. There is land for 7 ploughs. In demesne are 2 [ploughs]; and 10 villans and 6 bordars with 5 ploughs. There is a church, and 10 slaves, and a mill rendering 7s6d. TRE, and afterwards, it was worth £8; now £10.

Richer the clerk holds BRANSBURY, and claims it from the bishop. Abbot Æthelsige held it of Stigand and of the monks TRE, and it was for their sustenance. It was then, as now, assessed at 4 hides. There is land for 4 ploughs. In demesne is 1 [plough]; and 5 villans and 7 bordars with 2 ploughs, and a mill rendering 15s. TRE it was worth 100s; and afterwards £4; now £6.

IN MANSBRIDGE HUNDRED

The bishop himself holds SOUTH STONEHAM. It is for the clothing of the monks. TRE it was assessed at 5 hides; now at 3 hides. There is land for 9 ploughs. In demesne is 1 plough; and 11 villans and 9 bordars with 8 ploughs. There is 1 slave, and 23 acres of meadow, and 2 fisheries rendering 39d, [and] woodland for 20 pigs. TRE it was worth £7; and afterwards £4; now £8.

Richer the clerk holds the church of this manor, with 2 other churches near Southampton which belong to this mother church; and there belongs 1 hide of land, and all the tithes of the same vill and also of the king's land. What he holds of the bishop is worth 20s; what [he holds] of the king, 20s.

The bishop himself holds MILLBROOK. It always belonged to the monastery. TRE, as now, it was assessed at 5 hides. Villans held it and hold it. There is no hall. There is land for 5 ploughs. There are 28 villans with 5 ploughs, and 14 acres of meadow. [There is] woodland for 5 pigs. TRE and afterwards, as now, worth 100s.

The bishop himself holds HINTON AMPNER. It always belonged to the monastery. There are 8 hides. TRE, as now, it paid geld for 5 hides. There is land for 8 ploughs. In demesne are 3 ploughs; and 15 villans and 14 bordars with 5 ploughs. There are 6 slaves, and 8 acres of meadow, [and] woodland for 10 pigs. There is a church worth 40s, yet it renders 50s. TRE, as now, worth £8; when received, 100s.

IN REDBRIDGE HUNDRED

The bishop himself holds 2 hides in demesne in Fawley, which always belonged to the monastery, and were assessed at 2 hides, but now at 1 virgate only, because the 7 other [virgate] are in the forest. On this virgate are 3 villans and 5 bordars with 2 ploughs. There is a chapel, and 4 acres of meadow. There is land for 1 plough. TRE, and afterwards, it was worth 60s; now 15s.

IN KINGSCLERE HUNDRED

The bishop himself holds ECCHINSWELL. It always belonged to the monastery. TRE it was assessed at 10 hides; now at 7½ hides. There is land for 11 ploughs. In demesne are 2 ploughs; and 18 villans and 12 bordars with 9 ploughs. There are 2 slaves, and 2 mills rendering 100d, and 3 acres of meadow. TRE it was worth £7; and afterwards £6; now £8.

The bishop himself holds HANNINGTON. It always belonged to the monastery. TRE it was assessed at 7 hides; now at 6½ hides and 2 parts of a virgate. There is land for 8 ploughs. In demesne are 2 ploughs; and 17 villans and 7 bordars with 7 ploughs. There is a church and 4 slaves. TRE it was worth 100s; and afterwards £6; now £8; yet it is at farm for £15.

IN HODDINGTON HUNDRED

The bishop himself holds HODDINGTON. TRE it was assessed at 5 hides; now at 2 hides. There is land for 6 ploughs. In demesne are 2 ploughs; and 3 villans and 9 bordars with 2 ploughs. TRE and afterwards, as now, worth £4.

IN PORTSDOWN HUNDRED

In Boarhunt [Boarhunt or North Boarhunt] the Bishop of Winchester's monks have half a hide of the bishopric; and it is for the sustenance of the monks, and it is assessed at half a hide. There is nothing there except 1 villan. It is worth 6s6d.

IN 'CHUTELEY' HUNDRED

The monks hold WOOTTON ST LAWRENCE of the bishopric of Winchester. TRE, as now, it was assessed at 20 hides. There is land for 20 ploughs. In demesne are 2 ploughs; and 27 villans and 14 bordars with 15 ploughs. There are 10 slaves, and 4 acres of meadow. [continued on f.43]

IIII. What Archbishop Thomas Holds

IN BROUGHTON HUNDRED

Archbishop THOMAS holds in the manor of MOTTISFONT 1 church and 6 chapels, with all customary dues from the living and the dead. In Broughton, 1 chapel. In Pittleworth, 1. In [?West] Tytherley, 1, and [in] another [? East] Tytherley, 1. In East Dean, 1. In Lockerley, 1. There belong to this church 5 hides less 1 virgate. His predecessor held it in the same manner of King Edward. Then, as now, [it was assessed] at 4 hides less 1 virgate.

In demesne is 1 plough; and 5 villans and 5 bordars with 2 ploughs. 39½ acres of meadow belong there. [There is] woodland for fencing. 1 close in Winchester, rendering 30d. From these 5 hides, the king's reeves took 1 hide, and 12½ acres of meadow, and a grove, and a pasture, as the hundred declares. Cava the reeve did this without the knowledge of Hugh de Port.

The whole TRE was valued at £4; and afterwards at £3; now at £4 and 30d. The hide which is wanting was and is worth 10s.

[The land] of St Peter of Winchester

IN 'MAINSBOROUGH' HUNDRED

THE ABBEY OF ST PETER of Winchester holds BROWN CANDOVER. TRE it belonged to this monastery, and was assessed at 20 hides. 11 of these are in demesne. There is land for †18† ploughs. In demesne is 1 plough; and 13 villans and 4 bordars with 8 ploughs. There are 9 slaves, and 10 acres of meadow

Of the land of the same manor, Hugh de Port holds 2½ hides of the abbot. 1 hide is of the demesne land. TRE Elaf held this land. In demesne is 1 plough, and 3 slaves, and 1 acre of meadow.

Of this land of the same manor, Alsige the son of Beorhtsige holds a manor, WOODMANCOTT, of the abbey, and it is of the demesne land. TRE, as now, it was assessed at 6 hides and 2½ virgates of land. In demesne are 3 ploughs; and 3 villans with 2 ploughs, and 1 acre of meadow.

The whole manor TRE was worth £13; and afterwards as much; now the abbot's part [is worth] £8, yet it is at farm for £10; Hugh's [is worth] 20s; Alsige's, £7. These 20 hides of this manor are now assessed at 13 hides and 2½ virgates.

The abbey itself holds, in SOMBORNE Hundred, FULLERTON. It always belonged to the monastery. TRE it was assessed at 5 hides; now at 1 hide. There is land for 3 ploughs. In demesne are 2 ploughs; and 5 villans and 4 bordars with 1 plough. There are 4 slaves, and a mill rendering 10s, and 4 acres of meadow. It was worth 50s; now 60s.

The abbey itself holds LECKFORD in the same HUNDRED. TRE it was assessed at 5 hides; now at 2½ hides. There is land for 3 ploughs. In demesne is 1 plough; and 4 villans and 4 bordars with 1 plough. There are 2 slaves, and 1½ mills rendering 22s6d, and 20 acres of meadow. TRE, and afterwards, it was worth £3; now £4.

[Folio 42V: HAMPSHIRE]

IN MICHELDEVER HUNDRED

THE ABBEY OF ST PETER of Winchester holds MICHELDEVER in demesne. TRE it was assessed at 106 hides; now at 83 hides and half a virgate. There is land for 72 ploughs. In demesne are 9 ploughs; and 64 villans and 28 bordars have 25 ploughs. There are 22 slaves, and a mill rendering 30d, and 30 acres of meadow, [and] woodland for 4 pigs as pannage.

Of this land of this manor, Hugh de Port holds of the abbot 22½ hides and 1 virgate. 3 hides and 3 virgates are of the demesne land. 4 free men held them of the abbey TRE as 4 manors, Cranbourne [Cranbourne Grange and Upper Cranbourne], Drayton, [East and West] Stratton, [and] Popham, and could not withdraw with the land, as the men of the same hundred testify. There are in demesne 6½ ploughs; and 6 villans and 12 bordars with 1½ ploughs. There are 7 slaves, and 24 acres of meadow.

Of the same land of the same manor, Herbert the chamberlain holds 7 hides. Odo the steward [holds] 5 hides of the demesne land; Waleran the huntsman 4½ hides of the demesne land. 3 free men held them TRE. In demesne are 6 ploughs; and 9 villans and 9 bordars with 4 ploughs, and 2 slaves, and 5 acres of meadow.

Of this land of this manor, Alsige holds 6 hides. His father held it. And Ealdræd, Oda's brother, [holds] 1½ hides. His wife held it in dower TRE. Siward the huntsman [holds] 2 hides. He held it himself TRE. In demesne are 6½ ploughs; and 5 villans and 2 bordars with 1½ ploughs. There are 19 slaves, and 7 acres of meadow. The whole manor was worth, TRE, £60; when received, £40; now the demesne of the abbot [is worth] £57; what Hugh de Port holds, £19; what Herbert [holds], 100s; what Odo [holds], 50s; what Waleran [holds], 60s; what Alsige [holds], 100s; what Ealdræd [holds], 30s; what Siward [holds], 20s.

In another place, Alsige holds 1 hide of the demesne land of this manor; and there are 4 villans paying 7s.

The abbey itself holds ABBOTS WORTHY in demesne. It always belonged to the monastery. There are 7 hides, but it has never paid geld. There is land for 3 ploughs. In demesne are 2 ploughs; and 2 villans and 9 bordars without a plough. There are 4 slaves, and a mill rendering 20s, and 63 acres of meadow. The abbey itself has besides this 72 acres of meadow, which King Edward gave to the same church, and pasture which they call 'Hyde Moors' [in Winchester], [and] 80 acres of meadow.

All these were worth TRE £6; and afterwards 110s; now £6.10s.

[Folio 43: HAMPSHIRE]

[continued from f.41v] [There is] woodland for 5 pigs. TRE it was worth £15; and afterwards £16; now £20; yet it renders £28.12s6d.

IN 'BOSBARROW' HUNDRED

The monks hold [North or South] HAYLING of the bishopric of Winchester. They always held it. TRE it paid geld for 5 hides; and now for 4 hides. There is land for 2 ploughs. There are 11 villans with 3½ ploughs, and 1 acre of meadow. [There is] woodland for 1 pig. TRE it was worth 100s; and afterwards £4; and now £4.10s.

The monks hold BROCKHAMPTON of the bishopric of Winchester. They always held it. TRE it paid geld for 6 hides; now for 4 hides. There is land for 3 ploughs. There are 14 villans with 4 ploughs, and a mill rendering 15s, and 4 acres of meadow. [There is] woodland for 20 pigs.

The monks hold HAVANT of the bishopric of WINCHESTER. They always held it. TRE it paid geld for 10 hides; now for 7 hides. There is land for 4 ploughs. There are 20 villans with 6 ploughs, and 2 mills rendering 15s, and 3 salt-pans rendering 15d. [There is] woodland for 10 pigs. It is and was worth £8. BROCKHAMPTON is and was worth 100s.

V. The land of Bishop Osbern

IN NEATHAM HUNDRED

OSBERN, Bishop of EXETER, holds [Lower and Upper] FARRINGDON of the king. Godwine the priest held it of King Edward. It belongs to the church of BOSHAM. [It was] then [assessed] at 10 hides; now at 5 hides. There is land for 10 ploughs. In demesne is 1 plough; and 11 villans and 20 bordars with 8 ploughs. There are 2 slaves, and 12 acres of meadow. [There is] woodland for 30 pigs. TRE it was worth £15; and afterwards £12; now £21.

IN BASINGSTOKE HUNDRED

THE CHURCH OF MONT-SAINT-MICHEL holds 1 church of the king, with 1 hide and the tithe of the manor of Basingstoke. There is a priest and 2 villans and 4 bordars with 1 plough, and a mill rendering 20s, and 2 acres of meadow. The whole is worth £4.5s. Bishop Walter held it of King Edward, but it did not belong to his bishopric.

VI. The land of St Peter of Winchester

IN NEATHAM HUNDRED

THE ABBOT OF ST PETER of Winchester holds ALTON. Queen Edith held it TRE. There were then 10 hides, and the villans who dwelt there paid geld for 5 hides. The abbot now has 5 hides in demesne, but they have not paid geld. There is land for 4 ploughs. In demesne is 1 plough; and 11 bordars and 2 slaves with 2 ploughs, and half a mill rendering 4s7d, and 2 acres of meadow. [There is] woodland for fencing. TRE it was worth £6; and afterwards, as now, £7.

The shire testifies, concerning this manor, that [the abbot] received it unjustly, in exchange for the king's house, because the house [already] belonged to the king.

IN 'CHUTELEY' HUNDRED

The abbey itself holds WORTING. TRE, as now, it was assessed at 5 hides. There is land for 5 ploughs. In demesne are 2 ploughs; and 4 villans and 9 bordars with 2 ploughs. There are 2 slaves and a church. It is and was worth 100s.

The abbey itself holds BIGHTON. TRE it was assessed at 10 hides; now at 7 hides. There is land for 8 ploughs. In demesne are 1½ ploughs; and 8 villans and 3 bordars with 3 ploughs. There is a church, and 3 slaves, and 3 acres of meadow, [and] woodland for 10 pigs. Of this manor, Fulchred holds, 2 hides, [and] Borghill 2 hides. There are in demesne 2 ploughs; and 3 villans and 6 bordars with 1½ ploughs. There are 3 slaves. TRE the whole manor was worth 100s; and afterwards £6; now what the abbey holds [is worth] £8; what the men [hold], £4.

IN PORTSDOWN HUNDRED

Hugh de Port holds BEDHAMPTON of the abbey. Alsige held it of the abbot. TRE, as now, it was assessed at 10 hides. There is land for 8 ploughs. In demesne is 1 plough; and 12 villans and 7 bordars with 7 ploughs. There is a church, and 7 slaves, and 2 mills for the hall, and 2 salt-pans rendering 37s8d, and 3 acres of meadow, [and] woodland for 30 pigs. TRE, as now, worth £12; when received, £10.

IN MEONSTOKE HUNDRED

Ruald holds LOMER of the abbey. Alweard held it of the abbot. He bought it, TRE, to hold for his own life only, and rendered Of this manor of ALTON, the king holds 5 hides, as [part of] his farm, which Hearding holds; and they do not pay geld. to the abbot 10 sesters of wine a year. It was then, as now, assessed at 3 hides. There is land for 5 ploughs. In demesne is 1 [plough]; and 6 villans and 3 bordars with 3 ploughs. There is a church, and 3 acres of meadow, and 2 slaves.

Of this land, a man of the abbot holds 1 virgate.

The whole, TRE and afterwards, was worth £6; now 100s; what the man holds, 20s.

Hugh de Port holds WARNFORD of the Abbey of St Peter. Alweard and Ketil held it of the abbot, and could not go where they pleased. It was then, as now, assessed at 8 hides. There is land for 6 ploughs. In demesne are 3 ploughs; and 8 villans and 6 bordars with 3 ploughs. There are 6 slaves, and a mill rendering 10s, and 8 acres of meadow. TRE, as now, worth £8; when received, £6.

IN BASINGSTOKE HUNDRED

The same Hugh holds LYCHPIT of St Peter's Abbey. TRE, as now, it was assessed at 2 hides. There is land for 2 ploughs, and there are [2 ploughs] in demesne, with 8 bordars and 5 slaves, and 5 acres of meadow. It is and was worth 60s.

IN MANSBRIDGE HUNDRED

The abbey itself holds NORTH STONEHAM. It always belonged to the monastery. TRE, as now, it was assessed at 8 hides. There is land for 11 ploughs. In demesne are 2 ploughs; and 28 villans and 7 bordars with 9 ploughs. There is a church, and 13 slaves, and 2 mills rendering 30s, and 224 acres of meadow, [and] woodland for 20 pigs. From the pasture, 2s. TRE it was worth £12; and afterwards, as now, £10.

In KINGSCLERE, St Peter's Abbey has a church, and 4 hides and 1 virgate of land. These King William gave to the church, in exchange for the land on which is the king's house in the city. TRE it was assessed at 4 hides and 1 virgate; now at nothing. They vouch the king for [its exemption from] geld. Queen Edith held this; and there was a hall. There is land for 4 ploughs. In demesne is 1 [plough]; and 3 villans and 14 bordars with 3 ploughs. There are 2 slaves, and a mill rendering 5s, and 2 acres of meadow. For the herbage, 8d. TRE it was worth £7; and afterwards, as now, £6.

The abbey itself has half a hide in TATCHBURY. Eadsige the sheriff held it of King Edward in parage; and after the death of King Edward, he gave it to the same church for his soul before King William had come. It did not pay geld. It is waste; and yet it is and always was worth 10s.

IN ANDOVER HUNDRED

The abbey itself holds ABBOTTS ANN. It always belonged to the church. TRE it paid geld for 15 hides; now for 8 hides. There is land for 9 ploughs. In demesne are 2 [ploughs]; and 14 villans and 12 bordars with 7 ploughs. There are 4 slaves, and 3 mills rendering 37s6d. TRE, as now, worth £14; when received, £12.

IN OVERTON HUNDRED

The abbey itself holds LAVERSTOKE. Wulfgifu Beteslau held it of the abbey till her death. After her death, King William restored this manor to the same church for his own soul and [that] of his wife. TRE it was assessed at 10 hides; now at 6 hides and half a virgate. There is land for 6 ploughs. In demesne are 2 ploughs; and 7 villans and 19 bordars with 5 ploughs. There is a church, and 3 slaves, and 2 mills rendering 14s, and 3 acres of meadow. TRE it was worth £7; and afterwards, as now, £8.

VII. The land of the Church of Gloucester

IN HURSTBOURNE HUNDRED

THE ABBEY OF ST PETER of Gloucester holds LINKENHOLT; Ernulf de Hesdin gave it to the church, by permission of King William. Eadric held it of King Edward. It was then assessed at 5 hides; now at 1 hide; the others are in demesne. There is land for 5 ploughs. In demesne are 2 ploughs; and 4 villans and 8 bordars with 2 ploughs. There are 6 slaves, and 7 acres of meadow, [and] woodland for fencing. TRE it was worth 100s; and afterwards, as now, £4.

VIII. The land of St Peter of Westminster

IN HOLDSHOTT HUNDRED

THE ABBEY OF ST PETER of Westminster holds EVERSLEY. 4 free men held it as 4 manors of King Edward in alod. It then paid geld for 5 hides; now for 4 hides. There is land [...]. There are 10 villans and 4 bordars with 3 ploughs, and 2 mills rendering 105d. [There is] woodland rendering 30s, and 1 close in Winchester rendering 7d, and 12 acres of meadow. TRE it was worth 100s; and afterwards £4.10s; now £4.

IX. The land of the Church of Chertsey

IN ODIHAM HUNDRED

THE ABBEY of CHERTSEY holds WINCHFIELD, and Walter fitzOther [holds] of the abbey. Alwine held it of King Edward in alod, and it never belonged to the abbey. It was then, as now, assessed at 5 hides. There is land for 8 ploughs. There are 10 villans and 7 bordars with 1½ ploughs. TRE it was worth 100s; and afterwards 60s; now 30s.

Hugh de Port holds ELVETHAM of the Abbey of Chertsey. Eadric held it of King Edward in alod. It was then assessed at 3 [...] hides; now at 1 hide. [...] In demesne is 1 plough; and 4 villans and 4 bordars and 8 slaves with 2 ploughs, and 4 acres of meadow. [There is] woodland for 10 pigs. TRE, as now, worth 30s; when received, 25s.

X. The land of Saint-Pierre of Jumieges

IN 'BOSBARROW' HUNDRED

THE ABBEY of Jumieges holds [North or South] HAYLING. Wulfweard White held it of Queen Edith in alod. It then paid geld for 12 hides; now for 7 hides. There is land for 14 ploughs. In demesne are 2 ploughs; and 23 villans and 37 bordars with 17 ploughs. There are 3 slaves, and a salt-pan rendering 6s8d, and 2 fisheries rendering 20d, and 1 acre of meadow, [and] woodland for 20 pigs as pannage. TRE it was worth £15; and afterwards £10; now £12; and yet it renders £15 at farm.

The monks of the bishopric of Winchester claim this manor, because Queen Emma gave it to the Church of St Peter and St Swithun, and at that time gave the monks seisin of one half; the other half she demised to Wulfweard for his life only, on condition that, after his death, his body should return to the monastery for burial, and the manor [also]. And on these terms Wulfweard held part of the manor from the monks, till he died, TRW. Æthelsige, Abbot of Ramsey, attests to this and [so does] the whole hundred.

XI. The land of the Church of Glastonbury

IN REDBRIDGE HUNDRED

THE ABBEY of Glastonbury holds 1 hide in OWER, and Gilbert de Breteuil holds it of the abbey. Alsige held it of the abbot, and could not go where he would, but always paid rent to the abbot. There is land for 2 ploughs. In demesne is half a plough with 6 bordars. [There is] woodland for 5 pigs. It is and was worth 20s.

XII. The land of the Church of Milton

IN 'EDGEGATE' HUNDRED

THE ABBEY of Milton has 12 acres of land, and Edward the sheriff holds of the abbey. It has never paid geld. There is 1 villan with 2 oxen, and 1 acre of meadow. There was a fishery; now there is none. It is worth 40d.

XIII. The land of the Church of Grestain

IN ANDOVER HUNDRED

THE ABBEY of Grestain holds PENTON GRAFTON of the king. Queen Edith held it as a manor. It then paid geld for 3 hides; now for nothing. There is land for 6 ploughs. In demesne are 2 ploughs; and 5 villans and 27 bordars with 3 ploughs. There is a church, and 5 slaves. TRE, and afterwards, it was worth £10; now £8.

XIIII. The land of St Mary of Winchester

IN MEONSTOKE HUNDRED

THE ABBESS of Winchester holds LISS. It always belonged to the abbey. TRE it was assessed at 5 hides; now at 3 hides. There is land for 4 ploughs. There are 16 villans with 3½ ploughs, and a mill rendering 16d, and 1½ acres of meadow. [There is] woodland for 15 pigs. TRE and afterwards, as now, worth 50s; yet it renders £4 at farm.

IN NEATHAM HUNDRED

The abbey itself holds [Lower and Upper] FROYLE. It always belonged there. TRE it was assessed at 10 hides; now at 8 hides. There is land for 10 ploughs. In demesne are 3 ploughs; and 15 villans and 23 bordars with 8 ploughs. There is a church, and 10 slaves, and 2 mills rendering 22s6d, and 8 acres of meadow. TRE, and afterwards, it was worth £12; now £15; yet it renders £20 at farm.

IN SOMBORNE HUNDRED

The abbey itself holds LECKFORD. It always belonged to the church. TRE it was assessed at 5 hides; now at 1 hide. There is land for 3 ploughs. In demesne are 2 [ploughs]; and 5 villans and 2 bordars with 2 ploughs. There are 3 slaves, and 15 acres of meadow. TRE it was worth £3; and afterwards, as now, £4.

The abbey itself holds LONGSTOCK. It always held it. TRE it was assessed at 3 hides; now at half a hide. There is land for 2 ploughs. In demesne is 1 [plough], with 4 bordars and 1 slave, and a mill rendering 20s, and 5 acres of meadow. TRE it was worth 30s; and afterwards, as now, 40s.

The abbey itself holds TIMSBURY. It always held it. TRE, as now, it was assessed at 2 hides. There is land for 3 ploughs. In demesne is 1 [plough]; and 5 villans and 4 bordars with 3 ploughs. There is a mill rendering 12s6d, and 50 acres of meadow. TRE it was worth 50s; and afterwards, as now, 60s.

IN 'BOUNTISBOROUGH' HUNDRED

The abbey itself holds YAVINGTON. It belonged, and belongs, to the church. Archbishop Stigand held it. It was then assessed at 1½ hides; now at nothing, because it is for the sustenance of the nuns. There is land for half a plough. In demesne is 1 plough, and 3 slaves with 1 bordar, and half a mill rendering 7s, and 7 acres of meadow. TRE and afterwards, as now, worth 25s.

XV. The land of the Church of Romsey

THE ABBEY OF ROMSEY holds the whole vill [of Romsey] in which the church itself stands. TRE it was assessed at 14 hides; now at 10 hides. There is land for 18 ploughs. In demesne are 2 ploughs; and 39 villans and 53 bordars with 16 ploughs. There are 2 slaves, and 3 mills rendering 25s, and 536 acres of meadow, [and] woodland for 40 pigs. In Winchester, 14 burgesses paying 25s.

Of this land, Hunger holds 1 hide and 1 virgate; and 4 other free men hold 2 hides less half a virgate. There are in demesne 4 ploughs, and 13 bordars and 2 slaves. The whole TRE was worth £19; and afterwards the same; now what the abbess holds [is worth] £24; what the men [hold], 40s.

The abbey itself holds, and held, 1 hide, where are 4 villans with 1 plough, and a mill rendering 10s. It is and was worth 20s.

IN 'BOUNTISBOROUGH' HUNDRED

The abbey itself holds ITCHEN STOKE. It always held it.

[Folio 44: HAMPSHIRE]

TRE it was assessed at 8 hides; now at 6 hides. There is land for 6 ploughs. In demesne are 3 ploughs; and 8 villans and 8 bordars with 7 ploughs. There are 2 slaves, and 1½ mills rendering 22s6d, and 10 acres of meadow. TRE, and afterwards, it was worth £7; now £9.

IN KINGSCLERE HUNDRED

The abbey itself holds SYDMONTON. It always held it. TRE it was assessed at 10 hides; now at 7½ hides. There is land for 11 ploughs. In demesne are 2 ploughs; and 17 villans and 11 bordars with 9 ploughs. There is 1 slave, and 4 acres of meadow, [and] woodland for 5 pigs as pannage. TRE it was worth £7; and afterwards £8; now £10.

IN REDBRIDGE HUNDRED

The same abbey holds, and held, 1 hide in [?] TOTTON, and it is assessed at 1 hide. There is land for 3 ploughs. There are 8 villans and 7 bordars with 3 ploughs, and a mill rendering 10s, and a salt-pan rendering 10s, and 30 acres of meadow. It is and was worth 70s.

IN BOLDRE HUNDRED

The abbey itself holds, and always held, 1 hide in SWAY. TRE it was assessed at 1 hide; now at 3 virgates, and 1 virgate is in the forest. There is land for 1 plough. There are 2 villans with 2 ploughs, and 1 acre of meadow. It is and was worth 20s.

XVI. The land of the Church of Wherwell

IN "WELFORD" HUNDRED

THE ABBEY OF WHERWELL holds the whole vill [of Wherwell] in which the church itself stands. It always held it. TRE it was assessed at 22 hides; now at 13 hides. There is land for 14 ploughs. In demesne are 4 ploughs; and 5 villans and 12 bordars and 25 coliberts and 10 slaves with 10 ploughs. There are 3 mills rendering 27s6d, and 65 acres of meadow, [and] woodland for 25 pigs. TRE, and afterwards, it was worth £10; now £15.

The abbey itself holds TUFTON. It always held it. TRE it was assessed at 7 hides; now at 3½ hides. There is land [...]. In demesne are 2 ploughs; and 9 villans and 6 bordars with 1½ ploughs. There are 4 slaves, and 2 mills rendering 35s, and 8 acres of meadow, and woodland for fencing. It is and was worth £6.

The abbey itself holds GOODWORTH CLATFORD. It always held it. TRE it was assessed at 3 hides; now at half a hide. There is land for 3 ploughs. In demesne are 2 [ploughs]; with 6 bordars and 4 slaves, and 1 plough, and 10 acres of meadow. It is and was worth 40s.

The abbey itself holds LITTLE ANN. It always held it. TRE it was assessed at 5 hides; now at 3 virgates and the third part of a virgate. There is land for 3 ploughs. In demesne are 2 ploughs; and 10 bordars and 4 slaves with half a plough, and 2 mills rendering 30s, and 2 acres of meadow. [There is] woodland for fencing. It is and was worth 100s.

The abbey itself holds MIDDLETON. It always held it. TRE it was assessed at 20 hides; now at 10 hides. There is land for 9 ploughs. In demesne are 2 ploughs; and 14 villans and 10 bordars with 7 ploughs. There are 5 slaves, and 2 mills rendering 40s, and a fishery for the hall, and 9 acres of meadow. It is and was worth £12.

The abbey itself holds [Lower and Upper] BULLINGTON. It always held it as 10 hides. It has never paid geld. There is land for 6 ploughs. In demesne are 2 ploughs, and 8 villans and 4 bordars and 3 slaves, and a mill rendering 15s. It is and was worth £7.

The abbey itself holds in the city of Winchester 31 messuages, which it has quit of all customary dues, the king's geld excepted; of which geld, also, the abbess's own house is quit. TRE it was worth 50s; now 30s. There also, that is in Winchester, [the abbey] has 1 mill which renders 48s.

XVII. The land of the Canons of Twynham [Christchurch]

IN 'EDGEGATE' HUNDRED

THE CANONS OF HOLY TRINITY OF TWYNHAM hold, in the vill itself [Christchurch], 5 hides and 1 virgate, and 1 hide in the Isle of Wight. These hides always belonged to the church itself. They were then assessed at 6 hides and 1 virgate; and now [...]. In demesne are 5 ploughs; and 11 villans and 13 bordars with 1 plough. There are 2 slaves, and a mill rendering 30d, and 108 acres of meadow, [and] woodland for 2 pigs. In the borough, 6 messuages rendering 13s4d.

To this church belongs the whole tithe of Christchurch, and the third part of the tithes of Holdenhurst.

TRE it was worth £6; now £8.

Alnoth the priest holds of the king 'BOSLEY' [in Christchurch]; he held it in parage of King Edward. It was then assessed at 1½ virgates; now the same. There is land for half a plough, and there is half a plough with 2 slaves, and the third part of a mill rendering 25d, and 10½ acres of meadow, and 2 messuages in Christchurch. It was worth 5s; now 10s.

Alsige the priest holds BASHLEY of the king. He himself held it of King Edward. It was then assessed at 1 hide and 3 virgates; now at 3 virgates only. There is land for 1 plough. There is [1 plough] in demesne, with 2 slaves and 1 villan and 1 bordar, and half a mill rendering 3s, and 16 acres of meadow. It is and was worth 20s.

In Boldre Hundred the Church of HOLY TRINITY of Twynham had 8 acres of land in "Andret". This land is now in the forest.

XVIII. The land of Count Alan

IN TITCHFIELD HUNDRED

COUNT ALAN holds CROFTON. Wulfweard held it, and could go where he would with this land. TRE it was assessed at 7 hides; now at 3 hides less half a virgate. There is land for 5 ploughs. In demesne is 1 plough; and 11 villans and 2 bordars with 4½ ploughs. There is a church, and 4 slaves, and a mill rendering 12s6d, and a fishery with 2 salt-pans rendering 100d, and 24 acres of meadow, [and] woodland for 5 pigs. TRE it was worth £8; and afterwards 100s; now £4.

The count himself holds GREAT FUNTLEY. Wulfweard held it of Earl Godwine, and could not go where he would. It was then, as now, assessed at 1 hide. There is land for 3 ploughs. There are 7 villans and 2 slaves with 2½ ploughs, and a mill rendering 10s, and 3 acres of meadow. TRE, and afterwards, it was worth 40s; now 30s. Ealdræd and the men of the hundred testify that this manor does not belong to Crofton.

The count himself holds 1 manor, which Asgot and Almær his brother held of King Edward. It was then assessed at 5 hides; now at 1 hide. There is land for 3 ploughs. There are 2 villans and 4 bordars with 1 plough, and 3 slaves, and 2 acres of meadow. [There is] woodland for 5 pigs. TRE it was worth £4; and afterwards, as now, 40s. These [lands] the count received as 1 manor.

[Folio 44V: HAMPSHIRE]

XIX. The land of the Count of Mortain

IN SOMBORNE HUNDRED

THE COUNT of Mortain holds 1 manor of the king which 3 thegns, Leofwine, Godric, and Sæwulf, held of King Edward. It was then assessed at 4 hides; now at nothing. There is land for 4 ploughs. In demesne are 2 ploughs; and 20 bordars with 1 plough, and 4 slaves, and a mill rendering 15s, and 30 acres of meadow. TRE it was worth £10; and afterwards £11; it now renders £12. It is worth £8.

XX. The land of Count Eustace

IN 'ASHLEY' HUNDRED

COUNT EUSTACE holds BISHOP'S SUTTON of the king. Earl Harold held it. There are 25 hides. It is now assessed at 10 hides; and so it was TRE, as the hundred says. There is land for 50 ploughs. In demesne are 5 ploughs; and 60 villans and 60 bordars with 23 ploughs. There is a church with 1 hide, and 32 slaves, and 4 mills rendering 35s, and 6 acres of meadow, [and] woodland for 100 pigs as pannage. TRE it was worth £50; and afterwards, as now, £60; yet it renders £80 by tale.

IN NEATHAM HUNDRED

The count himself holds 5 hides in Headley, which were assessed TRE at 3 hides. Earl Godwine held them, and they are reckoned in Bishop's Sutton.

XXI. The land of Earl Roger

IN PORTSDOWN HUNDRED

EARL ROGER holds BOARHUNT [Boarhunt or North Boarhunt] of the king. 3 free men held it of King Edward in alod. It was then assessed at 11½ hides; now at 4 hides and 1½ virgates. There is land for 10 ploughs. In demesne are 2 ploughs; and 10 villans and 6 bordars with 3 ploughs. There are 6 slaves, and a church, and a mill rendering 42d, and another for the hall, and 2 salt-pans rendering 22s4d.

One knight holds of this manor 1 hide, and there he has 1 plough. It is worth 10s. The whole manor was worth TRE £11; and afterwards £11; now £14; and yet it renders £17 at farm.

Oda of Winchester claims half a hide of this manor, and he says it does not belong there.

IN BERMONDSPIT HUNDRED

Clerks hold PRESTON CANDOVER of the earl. Ælfric held it of Earl Harold. It then, as now, paid geld for 5½ hides. There is land for 5 ploughs. In demesne are 2 ploughs; and 9 villans and 1 bordar with 2½ ploughs. There are 3 slaves, and 5 acres of meadow, and a close in Winchester rendering 17d. TRE it was worth £10; and afterwards 60s; now 100s.

IN ANDOVER HUNDRED

Turold holds PENTON MEWSEY of the earl. Osmund held it in alod of King Edward as a manor. It then paid geld for 8 hides; now for 5 hides. There is land for 5 ploughs. In demesne is 1 [plough]; and 11 villans and 7 bordars with 4 ploughs. There is a church, and 3 slaves, and 5 acres of meadow, [and] woodland without pannage. TRE it was worth £7; and afterwards, as now, 100s.

IN SHIRLEY HUNDRED

William d'Anneville holds AVON of the earl. Ketil held it in alod of King Edward as a manor. It then, as now, paid geld for 1 hide. There is land for 1 plough, and there is [1 plough] in demesne, with 2 bordars, and 13 acres of meadow. All the woodland of this manor is in the king's forest. TRE it was worth 25s; and afterwards, as now, 15s.

IN SOMBORNE HUNDRED

Turold holds HOUGHTON of the earl. Osmund held it of King Edward. It was then, as now, assessed at 2½ hides. There is land for 1½ ploughs. In demesne is [1] plough, with 4 bordars and 4 slaves. It is and was worth 30s.

IN CHALTON HUNDRED

The earl himself holds CHALTON in demesne. Earl Godwine held it. It was then assessed at 60 hides; now at 27 hides. There is land for 35 ploughs. In demesne are 10 ploughs; and 55 villans and 27 bordars with 27 ploughs. There are churches, and 22 slaves, and 1 acre of meadow, [and] woodland for 50 pigs. From the pasture, 10s. TRE it was worth £56; and afterwards 35[l]; now £80; yet it renders £110 and 1 mark of gold.

Walter holds SUNWOOD of the earl. Tunbi held it of Earl Godwine. It was then, as now, assessed at 3 hides. There is land for 4 ploughs. In demesne are 2 ploughs; and 4 villans and 6 bordars with 2 ploughs. There is a chapel, and 1 slave, and 1 acre of meadow. [There is] woodland for 4 pigs: the greatest part of it has been blown down.

TRE, as now, worth £4; when received, £3; but it renders 100s.

IN 'BOSBARROW' HUNDRED

The Abbey of Troarn holds 5 hides of the earl. Alweard held them as a manor of King Edward in alod. It then paid geld for 5 hides; and now for 3 hides. There is land for 3 ploughs. There are 11 villans with 4 ploughs, and 1 acre of meadow. [There is] woodland for fencing. TRE, as now, worth £4; when received, £3; but it renders 100s.

Sigeræd holds 'NEWTIMBER' [in Warblington] of the earl.

He himself held it of Earl Harold. It was then, as now, assessed at 3 hides. There is land for 2 ploughs. In demesne [are] 2 oxen in a plough; and 2 [villans] and 4 bordars with half a plough, and a mill rendering 5s, and 3 acres of meadow, and a fishery. It is and was worth 30s.

The men of the hundred say that Sunwood was not in the earl's manor of Chalton, and that Earl William, who gave him Chalton, did not, however, grant him Sunwood.

IN MEONSTOKE HUNDRED

Edward holds 1 hide in HAMBLEDON. He himself held it of Earl Godwine, and could not go where he pleased without his leave. But it did not lie in Charlton, where it does now. It was then, as now, assessed at 1 hide. There is 1 plough in demesne with 2 bordars. [There is] woodland for 6 pigs. It is and was worth 20s.

XXII. The land of Earl Hugh

IN FORDINGBRIDGE HUNDRED

EARL HUGH holds BICKTON of the king, and Hugh Macy [holds] of him. Ketil held it of King Edward in alod. It then paid geld for 4 hides and half a virgate; now for 2 hides and half a virgate. There is land for 4 ploughs. In demesne is 1 plough; and 4 villans and 10 bordars with 3 ploughs. There are 4 slaves, and a mill rendering 7s6d, and 30 acres of meadow, [and] woodland for 4 pigs. The pasture of this manor, and some part of the woodland, is in the king's forest. TRE, and afterwards, it was worth 100s; now 60s.

XXIII. The land of Hugh de Port

IN FORDINGBRIDGE HUNDRED

HUGH de Port holds SOUTH CHARFORD, and William [holds] of him. 2 free men held it as 2 manors of King Edward in alod. It then, as now, paid geld for 5 hides. There is land for 4 ploughs. In demesne are 2 ploughs; and 20 bordars and 4 slaves with 1 plough, and 91 acres of meadow. TRE, as now, worth £4; when received, 100s.

The same William holds of Hugh in 'CLATTYNG' [in Charford] 1½ virgates. 2 free men held it of Alwine, but it was not an alod. There are 2 bordars, and 6 acres of meadow. It was worth 10s; now 8s.

In this hundred, and in this manor, Picot holds 2½ virgates of the king. Vitalis held it as a manor of King Edward in alod. Then, as now, it paid geld for 2½ virgates. There is land for half a plough, and there is [half a plough], with 1 villan and 2 bordars, and 10 acres of meadow.

William de Chernet claims this land, saying that it belongs to the manor of SOUTH CHARFORD, [in] Hugh de Port's fief, through inheritance from his predecessor; and he has brought as his testimony to this the better men and the old men of the whole shire and hundred; and Picot has brought against it as his testimony villans and common people and reeves, who are willing to maintain by oath, or by the judgement of God, that he who held the land was a free man, and could go with his land where he would. But the witnesses of William refuse to accept [any] law except that of King Edward until it be determined by the king. It was worth 15s; and afterwards 8s; now 10s.

[Folio 45: HAMPSHIRE]

IN BASINGSTOKE HUNDRED

XXIII. HUGH de Port holds SHERBORNE ST JOHN of the king. Wulfgifu held it of King Edward, and could go where she would. It was then assessed at 10 hides; now at 7 hides. There is land for 10 ploughs. In demesne are 3 ploughs; and 16 villans and 19 bordars with 5 ploughs. There is a church with half a hide rendering 20s, and 5 slaves, and 3 mills rendering 27s6d, and 20 acres of meadow. TRE, and afterwards, it was worth £10; now £15.

Hugh himself holds BRAMLEY. Ælfric held it of King Edward, and could go where he pleased. It was then assessed at 5 hides; now at 2½ hides. There is land for 8 ploughs. In demesne are 2 [ploughs]; and 14 villans and 14 bordars with 11 ploughs. There is a church, and 8 slaves, and 2 mills rendering 20s, and 2 acres of meadow, woodland for 80 pigs, and 3 burgesses [...] paying 22d. TRE it was worth 100s; and afterwards £7; now £9; yet it renders £12.

Hugh himself holds OLD BASING. Altei held it of King Edward, and could go where he would. It was then assessed at 11 hides; now at 6½ hides. There is land for 10 ploughs. In demesne are 3 ploughs; and 20 villans and 41 bordars with 11 ploughs. There are 7 slaves, and 3 mills rendering 50s, and 19 acres of meadow, [and] woodland for 25 pigs. TRE it was worth £12; and afterwards £8; now £16.

Hugh himself holds TUNWORTH. Alfred held it of Queen Edith, and could not go elsewhere. It was then assessed at 3 hides; now at 2 hides. There is land for 5 ploughs. In demesne are 2 ploughs; and 6 villans and 10 bordars with 2½ ploughs. There are 4 slaves, and 5 acres of meadow. TRE it was worth £3; and afterwards 50s; now £4.

Hugh himself holds NATELY [? Scures], and Ansketil [holds] of him. Edwin held it of King Edward, and could go where he would. It was then, as now, assessed at 2½ hides. There is land for 4 ploughs. In demesne are 1½ ploughs; and 5 villans and 4 bordars with 2 ploughs. There are 11 slaves, and a mill rendering 10s, and 5 acres of meadow. TRE it was worth 50s; and afterwards 30s; now 60s.

Hugh himself holds KEMPSHOTT, and Walter [holds] of him. Ealdræd held it TRE, and could go where he would. TRE, as now, it was assessed at 2 hides. There is land for 3 ploughs. In demesne are 2 ploughs; and 3 villans and 3 bordars with 1 plough. It has always been worth 30s.

Hugh himself holds CHINEHAM, and Aghmund [holds] of him. He himself held it of King Edward, and could go where he would. It was then, as now, assessed at 3 hides. There is land for 2 ploughs. In demesne is 1 plough; and 3 villans and 4 bordars with 2 ploughs. There are 7 slaves, and 2 acres of meadow. It has always been worth 50s.

Hugh himself holds WINSLADE, and Walter [holds] of him.

TRE, as now, it was assessed at 1 hide. There is land for 3 ploughs. In demesne is 1 [plough]; and 5 villans and 8 bordars with 4 ploughs. There are 4 slaves. It has always been worth 40s.

IN TITCHFIELD HUNDRED

Hugh himself holds WICKHAM. 4 brothers held it, as 2 manors, of King Edward. It was then, as now, assessed at 12 hides. Hugh received it as 1 manor. There is land for 7 ploughs. In demesne are 2 ploughs; and 15 villans and 6 bordars with 7 ploughs. There are 5 slaves, and 2 mills rendering 20s, and 8 acres of meadow, [and] woodland for 5 pigs. TRE it was worth £10; and afterwards £4; now £7.

Hugh himself holds 'SEGENSWORTH' [in Titchfield], and Herlebald [holds] of him. Wulfric held it of King Edward. It was then, as now, assessed at 1 hide. There is land for 3 ploughs. In demesne is 1 [plough]; and 5 villans and 2 bordars with 2 ploughs. There are 3 slaves, and a mill rendering 20s, and 5 acres of meadow, [and] woodland for 5 pigs. TRE, as now, worth 60s; when received, 30s.

Hugh himself holds HOOK, and German [holds] of him. Northmann held it of King Edward. It was then, as now, assessed at 1 hide. There is land for 1½ ploughs. In demesne is [1] plough; and 2 villans and 3 bordars with 1 plough. There are 3 slaves, and 1 acre of meadow, [and] woodland for 1 pig. It is worth 25s.

Hugh himself holds STUBBINGTON. Godwine held it of King Edward. It was then, as now, assessed at 3 hides. There is land for 3 ploughs. In demesne is 1 [plough]; and 5 villans and 4 bordars with 2 ploughs, and 2 acres of meadow. TRE it was worth 50s; and afterwards, as now, 60s; yet it renders 110s.

IN SOMBORNE HUNDRED

Hugh himself holds HOUGHTON, and Heldred [holds] of him. Godwine held it of King Edward. It was then, as now, assessed at 2½ hides. The same Godwine held AWBRIDGE as 1 manor. It was then, as now, assessed at 1½ hides. These 2 manors Hugh received as 1 manor. There is land for 4 ploughs. In demesne are 1½ ploughs; and 4 villans with 3 ploughs, and 23 slaves, and 18 acres of meadow. The whole TRE and afterwards, as now, was worth £4.

Hugh himself claims, for the use of this manor, 3 messuages and the corner of a meadow, and 1 virgate and 5 acres of land, against Turstin the chamberlain. Concerning this the whole hundred bears testimony that his predecessors were seised of it, and holding it on the day on which King Edward was alive and dead.

IN MEONSTOKE HUNDRED

Hugh himself holds WESTBURY, and Joscelin [holds] of him. Wulfnoth held it of King Edward. It was then, as now, assessed at 3 hides. There is land for 4 ploughs. In demesne are 2 ploughs; and 5 villans and 6 bordars with 2 ploughs. There are 2 slaves, and 3 acres of meadow, [and] woodland for 4 pigs. TRE, as now, worth £4; when received, 40s.

Hugh himself holds WARNFORD. Wulfric and Wulfweard held it in parage of King Edward, and had 2 halls. It was then assessed at 4 hides; now at 2 hides less 1 virgate.

In HOUND there are 3 hides and 4 acres of land, which belonged to Warnford and paid geld in Mansbridge Hundred. In all there are 7 hides. There is land for 9 ploughs. In demesne are 3 ploughs; and 31 villans and 9 bordars with 6 ploughs. There is a church, and 6 slaves, and 2 mills rendering 20s, and 20 acres of meadow. TRE, as now, worth £14; when received, £8.

Hugh himself holds [?] CORHAMPTON. Alwine held it of King Edward. It was then assessed at 3 hides; now at 1 hide. There is land for 3 ploughs. In demesne are 2 ploughs; and 2 villans and 6 bordars with 1 plough. There are 4 slaves, and a church, and 2 mills rendering 22s, and 1 acre of meadow, and a house in Winchester rendering 5s. TRE, as now, worth £8; when received, 5s.

Hugh himself holds EAST HOE. Wulfweard held it of King Edward. It was then assessed at 1½ hides; now at 1 hide. There is land for 2 ploughs. In demesne is 1 [plough]; and 3 villans and 2 bordars with 2 ploughs. There are 4 slaves, and 1 acre of meadow, [and] woodland for 4 pigs. TRE it was worth 40s; and afterwards 30s; now 60s; yet it is at farm for £14.

IN KINGSCLERE HUNDRED

Hugh himself holds EWHURST, and Walter [holds] of him. Godwine held it, and could go where he would. It was then, as now, assessed at 1 hide. There is land for 2 ploughs. In demesne is 1 [plough]; and 2 villans and 2 bordars with 1 plough. [There is] woodland for 5 pigs. It has always been worth 30s.

Hugh himself holds 1 hide in KINGSCLERE, and Faderlin [holds] of him. Sæwulf and Godwine held it in parage of King Edward, and there were 2 halls; now there is 1 hall. There is land for 1½ ploughs. In demesne is [1] plough, with 4 bordars and 3 slaves. There is a mill rendering 12s, and 2 acres of meadow. It is and was worth 20s.

Hugh himself holds KNOWL HILL, and Faderlin [holds] of him. Alnoth held it in parage of the king. It was then, as now, assessed at 3½ virgates. There is land for 1 plough, and there is [1 plough] in demesne; and 1 villan and 10 bordars with half a plough.

[Folio 45V: HAMPSHIRE]

There are 2 slaves, and 2 acres of meadow. It has always been worth 20s.

IN HURSTBOURNE HUNDRED

Hugh himself holds LITCHFIELD, and Faderlin [holds] of him. Eadsige held it of King Edward. It was then, as now, assessed at 3 hides. There is land for 4 ploughs. In demesne are 2 [ploughs]; and 5 villans and 10 bordars with 2 ploughs. [There is] woodland for fencing. TRE it was worth £4; and afterwards, as now, £3.

IN NEATHAM HUNDRED

Hugh himself holds CHAWTON. Oda held it of King Edward in alod. There were 10 hides, but King Edward assessed it for service and geld at 4 hides and 1 virgate. There is land for 8 ploughs. In demesne are 4 ploughs; and 19 villans and 8 bordars with 5 ploughs. There are 6 slaves, and 6 acres of meadow, [and] woodland for 50 pigs. #[1]

Hugh himself holds LUDSHOTT. Alwine held it of King Edward in alod. It was then assessed at 2 hides; now at 1 hide. There is land for 2 ploughs. In demesne is 1 [plough]; and 5 villans and 5 bordars with 5 ploughs, and a mill rendering 7s6d, and 4 acres of meadow. [There is] woodland for 50 pigs. TRE, and afterwards, it was worth 60s; now 100s.

CHAWTON TRE was worth £10; and afterwards £10; now £12.

IN 'CHUTELEY' HUNDRED

Hugh himself holds OAKLEY. Alwine held it of King Edward in alod. It was then assessed at 10 hides; now at 1½ hides and 1 virgate. There is land for 4 ploughs. In demesne are 2 ploughs; and 6 villans and 6 bordars with 2 ploughs. There are 4 slaves, and a church, [and] woodland for fencing. TRE, and afterwards, it was worth £6; now £8.

IN HODDINGTON HUNDRED

Hugh himself holds "AOLTONE". Azur held it of King Edward in alod. It was then assessed at 10 hides; now at 3½ hides. There is land for 6 ploughs. In demesne are 2 ploughs; and 7 villans and 9 bordars with 6 ploughs. There is a church, and 6 slaves, [and] woodland for fencing. TRE, as now, worth £10; when received, £8.

IN BERMONDSPIT HUNDRED

Hugh himself holds HERRIARD, and Walter [holds] of Hugh. Erlenc held it of King Edward in alod. It was then, as now, assessed at 5 hides. There is land for 6 ploughs. In demesne are 2 ploughs; and 8 villans and 2 bordars with 4 ploughs. There is 1 slave, [and] woodland for fencing. TRE it was worth £4; and afterwards £3; now 100s.

Hugh himself holds DUMMER, and 1 of his men [holds] of him. Alric held it of King Edward in alod. It was then, as now, assessed at 5 hides. There is land for 5 ploughs. In demesne are 2 ploughs; and 8 villans and 9 bordars with 2 ploughs. There is a church, and 3 slaves. TRE, as now, worth 100s; when received, 40s.

IN PORTSDOWN HUNDRED

Hugh himself holds BUCKLAND [in Portsmouth], and Heldred [holds] of him. Alweard held it of Earl Godwine in alod. It was then, as now, assessed at 3½ hides. There is land for 4 ploughs. In demesne are 2 ploughs; and 6 villans and 2 bordars with 2 ploughs. There are 2 slaves. TRE, as now, worth 60s; when received, 40s.

Hugh himself holds 1 hide in BOARHUNT [Boarhunt or North Boarhunt], and Tezelin [holds] of him. Leofsige and Mærwynn held it of King Edward in alod as 2 manors. It then, as now, paid geld for 1 hide. There is land for 1 plough. In demesne is this [plough]; and 2 villans and 2 bordars with half a plough, and a mill rendering 5s, and half an acre of meadow. It is worth 20s.

Hugh himself holds 'APPLESTEAD' [in Boarhunt], and Tezelin [holds] of him. Goding held it of King Edward in alod. It then, as now, paid geld for 1½ hides. There is land for 2 ploughs. In demesne is 1 [plough]; and 13 bordars with half a plough, and a mill rendering 15d, and half an acre of meadow. [There is] woodland for 3 pigs. 1 of his men holds half a hide of this land; and he has half a plough with 3 bordars. The whole was worth, TRE, and afterwards, 30s; now 40s.

IN 'BOSBARROW' HUNDRED

Hugh himself holds BROCKHAMPTON, and Herbert the chamberlain [holds] of him. Sigeræd held it of Earl Harold, and could not go elsewhere. It was then, as now, assessed at 2 hides. There is land for 1 plough, and in demesne is 1 [plough]; with 1 villan and 4 bordars and half a plough. It is worth 20s.

Hugh himself holds HECKFIELD. Stenesnoc held it of King Edward [...] in alod. It then, as now, paid geld for 2 hides. There is land for 5 ploughs. In demesne is 1 [plough]; and 14 villans and 8 bordars with 9 ploughs. There is a church, and 2 slaves, and a mill rendering 5s, and a fishery rendering 100 eels, and 3 acres of meadow, [and] woodland for 100 pigs. TRE, and afterwards, it was worth 100s; now £6; and yet it renders £8.

Hugh himself holds BRAMSHILL. 2 free men held it of King Edward in alod as 2 manors. It then paid geld for 1 hide; now for half a hide. There are 2 villans and 2 bordars with 1 plough, and the fourth part of a mill rendering 10d, and 3 acres of meadow. [There is] woodland for 2 pigs. TRE, and afterwards, it was worth 10s; now 20s.

IN HOLDSHOTT HUNDRED

Hugh himself holds STRATFIELD TURGIS, and Ælfric [holds] of him. Ælfric held it of King Edward in alod. It then, as now, paid geld for 1 hide. There is land for 4 ploughs. In demesne are 1½ ploughs; and 5 villans and 9 bordars with 3 ploughs. There are 4 slaves, and a forge rendering 2s2d, and a mill for the hall, and 15 acres of meadow, [and] woodland for 5 pigs. It has always been worth 30s.

IN BROUGHTON HUNDRED

Hugh himself holds SNODDINGTON. Tovi held it of King Edward in alod. It then, as now, paid geld for 5 hides. There is land for 3 ploughs. There is 1 plough in demesne, and 5 bordars and 2 slaves. TRE it was worth £3; and afterwards 40s; now £4.

Hugh himself holds LOCKERLEY. Sterre held it of King Edward in alod as a manor. Then, as now, it paid geld for 1 hide. There is land for 3 ploughs. In demesne is 1 plough; and 4 bordars and 4 slaves with half a plough, and a mill rendering 10s, and 6 acres of meadow. [There is] woodland for 3 pigs. The same Sterre held 1 hide, which has been put in the

king's forest. The whole was worth, TRE and afterwards, 15s; now 30s.

Hugh himself holds OVER WALLOP as half a manor. Godric held it of King Edward in alod. It then paid geld for 1½ hides; now for 1 virgate. In demesne [is] 1 plough with 4 bordars. TRE it was worth 20s; and afterwards, as now, 15s.

Hugh himself holds SHERFIELD ENGLISH. Eadric held it of King Edward in alod. It then paid geld for 6 hides; and now for 2½ hides. There is land for 8 ploughs. In demesne is 1 plough; and 11 villans and 6 bordars with 8 ploughs. There are 2 slaves, and a mill rendering 5s, and 2 acres of meadow, [and] woodland for 20 pigs. TRE, and afterwards, it was worth £3; now £4.

Hugh himself holds 1 hide in OVER WALLOP, and Boda [holds] of him. Eadric held it of King Edward. Then, as now, it paid geld for 1 hide. There is land for 1 plough. There are 2 villans and 2 bordars with 2 oxen. It has always been worth 10s.

IN ANDOVER HUNDRED

Hugh himself holds AMPORT. Eadric held it of King Edward in alod as 1 manor. It then paid geld for 10 hides; now for 6 hides. There is land for 5 ploughs. In demesne are 2 ploughs; and 7 villans and 12 bordars with 5 ploughs. There are 3 slaves, and a mill rendering 20s. Half a hide of this manor is in Over Wallop. TRE, and afterwards, it was worth £4; now £6.

To this manor belong 5 hides which Ralph de Mortimer holds. A brother of Eadric held them by the following agreement, that he should hold the land of him so long as he behaved well to him; and that, if he wished to sell, he should not sell nor give [the land] to anyone but him, of whom he held it. The hundred testifies to this.

Hugh himself holds LITTLETON. Azur held it of King Edward in alod. It then paid geld for 5 hides; now for 5 virgates. There is land for 4 ploughs. In demesne are 2 ploughs; and 5 villans and 6 bordars with 3 ploughs. The woodland [is] unproductive. TRE it was worth 100s; and afterwards, as now, £4.

Hugh himself holds 3 hides in EAST CHOLDERTON, and Ralph [holds] of him. Hugh himself holds PRESTON CANDOVER, and Ansketil [holds] of him. Godwine held it of King Edward. It then, as now, paid geld for 1 hide and 1 virgate of land. There is land for 1 plough, which [plough] is there in demesne, and 4 slaves; and 2 villans with half a plough. TRE and afterwards, as now, worth 30s.

[Folio 46: HAMPSHIRE]

Eadric held them of King Edward in alod as 1 manor. Then, as now, it paid geld for 3 hides. There is land for 1 plough, and this [plough] is in demesne, with 1 villan and 1 bordar. TRE it was worth 30s; and afterwards, as now, 20s.

Hugh himself holds KIMPTON, and Geoffrey [holds] of him. Wynsige held it of King Edward in alod. Then, as now, it paid geld for 2 hides. There is land for 3 ploughs. In demesne are 2 ploughs; and 2 villans and 8 bordars with 1 plough, and there is 1 slave, and unproductive woodland. TRE it was worth 60s; and afterwards 40s; now £4.

Hugh himself holds CLANVILLE, and Herbert [holds] of him. Azur held it of King Edward in alod. Then, as now, it paid geld for 1½ hides. There is land for 1 plough, and there is [1 plough] in demesne, with 4 bordars. TRE, and afterwards, it was worth 30s; now 20s.

IN SHIRLEY HUNDRED

Hugh himself holds AVON. 3 free men held it of King Edward in alod. It then paid geld for 8 hides; now for 3½ hides. There is land for 4 ploughs. William and Ralph, and a certain other man, hold this manor of Hugh, and they have in demesne 3 ploughs; and 9 villans and 6 bordars with 4 ploughs. There are 4 slaves, and 84 acres of meadow. There was woodland for 90 pigs; now the king has in [his] forest 1½ hides and half a virgate of this land, and half of the woodland, that is, for 45 pigs. The whole was worth TRE £10; and afterwards £8; now what the men have [is worth] 100s; and what the king has, 100s.

IN FORDINGBRIDGE HUNDRED

Hugh himself holds ROCKSTEAD. Ealdwine held it of King Edward in alod. Then, as now, it paid geld for 1 hide and half a virgate. There is land for 1 plough, and there is [1 plough] in demesne, with 7 bordars and 2 slaves, and a mill rendering 40d. TRE, and afterwards, it was worth 10s; now 25s.

Hugh himself holds ROCKFORD, and Hugh de St Quentin [holds] of him. Alsige the priest held it of King Edward in alod as a manor. It then paid geld for 2 hides; now for 1. There is land for 2 ploughs. In demesne is 1 [plough]; and 7 villans and 9 bordars with 1 plough. There are 6 slaves, and 50 acres of meadow. The woodland is in the king's forest. It was worth 30s. The whole, TRE and afterwards, was worth 60s; now 30s.

Hugh himself holds IBSLEY, and Ralph [holds] of him. Algar held it of King Edward in alod. It then paid geld for 4 hides; now for 2 hides. There is land for 5 ploughs. In demesne are 2 [ploughs]; and 6 villans and 10 bordars with 3 ploughs. There are 3 slaves, and a mill rendering 10s and 700 eels, and 75 acres of meadow, [and] woodland for 1 pig. 2 hides of this manor are in the forest. TRE it was worth £4; and afterwards 40s; what [is] in the forest [is worth] 20s.

Hugh himself holds SOUTH CHARFORD, and William [holds] of him. 2 free men held it of King Edward in alod. Then, as now, it paid geld for 5 hides. There is land for 4 ploughs. In demesne are 2 ploughs; and 20 bordars and 4 slaves with 1 plough, and 100 less 9 acres of meadow. [There is] woodland for 2 pigs. TRE it was worth 100s; and afterwards, as now, £4.

Hugh himself holds 1½ virgates of land in 'CLATTYNG' [in Charford], and William [holds] of him. 2 free men held them of Alwine, but it was not an alod. There are 2 bordars, and 6 acres of meadow, [and] unproductive woodland. It was worth 10s; now 8s.

IN NEATHAM HUNDRED

Hugh himself holds NORTON [in Selborne], and Robert [holds] of him. Godwine held it of King Edward in alod. It was then, as now, assessed at 2 hides. There is land for 1 plough, and there is [1 plough] in demesne, and 2 villans and 3 bordars, and 7½ acres of meadow. TRE it was worth 30s; and afterwards 20s; now 40s.

Hugh de Port Holds the Lands Mentioned Below of the Bishop of Bayeux

IN NEATHAM HUNDRED

Hugh holds 1 hide in BINSTED of the Bishop of Bayeux. Boda held it in alod of King Edward as a manor. Half this hide does not pay geld. There is land for 1 plough. There is [1 plough] in demesne, with 4 bordars, and half an acre of meadow. TRE, and afterwards, it was worth 10s; now 20s.

IN 'CHUTELEY' HUNDRED

Hugh himself holds MONK SHERBORNE. Æthelnoth Cild held it of King Edward in alod. It was then, as now, assessed at 10½ hides and half a virgate. There is land for 10 ploughs. In demesne are 3 ploughs; and 8 villans and 13 bordars with 4 ploughs. There are 5 slaves, and 16 acres of meadow, [and] woodland for 23 pigs. TRE, and afterwards, it was worth £8; now £10.

Hugh himself holds WOOTTON ST LAWRENCE. Almær and Ælfgeat held it of King Edward in alod. It was then, as now, assessed at 5 hides. There is land for 3 ploughs. In demesne is 1 [plough]; and 2 villans and 2 bordars with 1 plough, and 1 acre of meadow. TRE, and afterwards, it was worth 50s; now 100s.

IN BERMONDSPIT HUNDRED

Hugh himself holds ELLISFIELD. Auti held it of King Edward in alod. It was then, as now, assessed at 8 hides. There is land for 10 ploughs. In demesne is 1 [plough]; and 8 villans and 4 bordars with 5 ploughs. There is a church, and 4 slaves, and 5 acres of meadow, [and] woodland for fencing. TRE it was worth £10; and afterwards 60s; now 100s.

IN PORTSDOWN HUNDRED

Hugh himself holds COSHAM, and Geoffrey [holds] of him. Beorhtmær held it of King Edward in alod. It was then, as now, assessed at 2 hides. There is land for 2 ploughs. In demesne is 1 [plough]; and 2 villans and 4 bordars with half a plough, and there are 4 slaves. It was worth 40s; now 30[s].

IN 'EDGEGATE' HUNDRED

Hugh himself holds HURN, and Hugh [holds] of him. 2 alodiaries held it. It was then, as now, assessed at 1 hide. There is land for 1 plough, and there is [1 plough] with 3 bordars and 1 slave, and half a fishery rendering 2d. TRE, and afterwards, it was worth 20s; now 36s.

Hugh himself holds 1 hide in 'KNAPP' [in Christchurch], and Hugh [holds] of him. 3 alodiaries held it in parage of King Edward; and there were 3 halls. Then, as now, [it was assessed] at 1 hide. There is land for 1 plough, and there is [1 plough], with 1 slave, and a mill rendering 20s, and a fishery rendering 50d, and 16 acres of meadow. TRE it was worth 20s; now 30s.

Hugh himself holds 1 hide in demesne, and Wihtlac held this of King Edward, and he had a hall. Then, as now, [it was assessed] at 1 hide. It is called Stanpit. There is land for 1 plough. [...] It is and was worth 15s.

Hugh himself holds STANPIT. Godric the priest held it of King Edward. It was then, as now, assessed at 2 hides. There is land for 2 ploughs. In demesne is half a plough; and 2 villans and 2 bordars with half a plough. There are 8 acres of meadow. TRE, and afterwards, it was worth 20s; now 40s; and yet it renders 60s.

IN SHIRLEY HUNDRED

Hugh himself holds RIPLEY, and Hugh [holds] of him. Wihtlac held it of King Edward in alod. It then, as now, paid geld for half a hide. There is land [...]. In demesne is 1 plough, and 3 bordars, and 8 acres of meadow. The woodland is in the king's forest. TRE, and afterwards, it was worth 20s; now 15s.

IN MANSBRIDGE HUNDRED

Hugh himself holds 1 hide in REDBRIDGE. Tovi held it of the king. Then, as now, [it was assessed] at 1 hide. There are 4 villans and 1 bordar with 1 plough, and 2 mills rendering 50s, and 1 acre of meadow. TRE, and afterwards, it was worth 10s; now 60s.

IN REDBRIDGE HUNDRED

Hugh himself holds half a hide in "LESTRED", and Hugh [holds] of him. Alsige held it of King Edward. It was then, as now, assessed at half a hide. There is land for half a plough, and there is [half a plough], with 4 villans, and 2 acres of meadow. It is and was worth 10s.

[Folio 46V: [HAMPSHIRE]]

Hugh himself holds TIDGROVE, and Faderlin [holds] of him. Oswulf held it of King Edward. It was then, as now, assessed at 1 hide and 1 virgate. There is land for 2½ ploughs. In demesne is 1 plough, and 2 bordars, and a mill rendering 50d, and half an acre of meadow. It has always been worth 25s.

XXIIII. The land of Hubert de Port

IN BASINGSTOKE HUNDRED

HUBERT de Port holds MAPLEDURWELL of the king. Eskil held it of King Edward, and could go where he would. It was then assessed at 5 hides; now at 2½ hides. There is land for 6 ploughs. In demesne are 2 ploughs; and 12 villans and 8 bordars with 5 ploughs. There are 6 slaves, and 2 mills

rendering 32s6d. TRE and afterwards, as now, worth £10; and yet it renders £13.

XXV. The land of William de Percy

IN MEONSTOKE HUNDRED

WILLIAM de Percy holds HAMBLEDON; he received it with his wife. Alwine held it of King Edward. It was then, as now, assessed at 1 hide. There is land for 3 ploughs. In demesne is 1 [plough]; and 6 villans and 6 bordars with 2 ploughs. There are 2 slaves, and a mill rendering 12d, [and] woodland for 4 pigs. TRE, as now, worth £4; when received, £3.

XXVI. The land of Ernulf de Hesdin

IN HURSTBOURNE HUNDRED

ERNULF de Hesdin holds COMBE [Berks.] of the king. Eadric held it of King Edward. It was then assessed at 3 hides; now at 2. There is land for 9 ploughs. In demesne are 3 ploughs; and 10 villans and 12 bordars with 7 ploughs. There is a church, and 6 slaves, and woodland for fencing. TRE and afterwards, as now, worth £6.

XXVII. The land of Edward of Salisbury

IN NEATHAM HUNDRED

EDWARD of Salisbury holds BRAMSHOTT of the king. 2 free men held it of King Edward in alod. It was then, as now, assessed at 6 hides. There is land for 5 ploughs. In demesne is 1 [plough]; and 10 villans and 3 bordars with 4 ploughs. There are 2 mills rendering 100d, and 2 acres of meadow, [and] woodland for 4 pigs. TRE and afterwards, as now, worth 100s. William Mauduit claims 1 hide of this land, which was in Hartley Mauditt, and the hundred and the shire testify to this.

IN FORDINGBRIDGE HUNDRED

Edward himself holds NORTH CHARFORD, and Ranulph [holds] of him. Alnoth held it of King Edward in alod. It then, as now, paid geld for 5 hides. There is land for 4 ploughs. In demesne is 1 plough. There are 9 bordars and 4 slaves, and a mill rendering 15s and 1,250 eels. There are 50 acres of meadow, [and] woodland for 4 pigs. Ingulf holds 1 hide of this manor, and there he has 1 plough with 2 bordars. TRE, as now, worth 100s; when received, 60s.

XXVIII. The land of Robert fitzGerald

IN 'CHUTELEY' HUNDRED

ROBERT fitzGerald holds OAKLEY of the king. Tovi held it of King Edward. It was then, as now, assessed at 1½ hides. There is land for 1 plough. There are 2 villans and 2 bordars with 2 ploughs.

In MALSHANGER is half a virgate of land which Bolla held of King Edward in alod, but Robert added it to this manor.

The hundred, however, says that it never belonged there. The whole, TRE and afterwards, was worth 15s; now 20[s].

IN PORTSDOWN HUNDRED

Robert himself holds COPNOR, and Heldred [holds] of him. Tovi held it of Earl Godwine, nor could he go elsewhere. It was then, as now, assessed at 3 hides. There is land for 2 ploughs. In demesne is 1 [plough]; and 5 villans and 2 bordars and 2 slaves with 2 ploughs. There is a salt-pan rendering 8d. TRE, as now, [worth] 60s; when received, 30s.

IN BROUGHTON HUNDRED

Robert himself holds SOUTH TIDWORTH. [...] 2 free men held it of King Edward in alod as 2 manors. Then, as now, it paid geld for 4 hides. Robert made 1 manor [of it]. There is 1 villan with 5 bordars; they have 1 plough. TRE, and afterwards, it was worth 40s; now 30s.

Robert himself holds SHIPTON BELLINGER. Wulfstan held it of King Edward in alod. Then, as now, it paid geld for 1½ hides. There are 2 villans with half a plough. It [has] always [been worth] 20s.

The same Robert holds BOSSINGTON. Tovi held it of King Edward in alod as a manor. Then, as now, it paid geld for 2 hides and 1 virgate. There is land for 1 plough, and there is [1 plough] in demesne, with 3 bordars. TRE it was worth 50s; and afterwards 30s; now 40s.

IN ANDOVER HUNDRED

The same Robert holds SOUTH TIDWORTH, and Hugh [holds] of him. Cuthwulf held it of Earl Harold in alod. Then, as now, it paid geld for 7 hides. There is land for 4 ploughs. In demesne are 3 ploughs; and 3 villans and 9 slaves with 1 plough. There is a church, and 4 acres of meadow, and a small wood. TRE, as now, worth £10; when received, 100s.

IN BARTON HUNDRED

Robert himself holds SUTTON SCOTNEY. Tovi held it of Earl Godwine. It was then assessed at 5 hides; now at 2½ hides. There is land for 4 ploughs. In demesne is 1 [plough]; and 4 villans and 4 bordars with 2 ploughs. There is a church, and 8 slaves, and a mill rendering 6s3d, and 10 acres of meadow. TRE it was worth £6; and afterwards £4; now 100s.

IN TITCHFIELD HUNDRED

The same Robert holds half a hide in GREAT FUNTLEY. Tovi held it of King Edward. It was then, as now, assessed at half a hide. There is land for 1 plough. There are 3 bordars, and 6 acres of meadow, [and] woodland for 3 pigs. It is and was worth 20s.

IN FORDINGBRIDGE HUNDRED

The same Robert holds FORDINGBRIDGE, and Robert [holds] of him. Alwig held it of King Edward in alod. It then paid geld for 2 hides and 3 virgates; now for 2 hides. There is land for 2 ploughs. In demesne is 1 [plough]; and 13 bordars have 1 plough. There is a church, and 2 mills rendering 14s2d, and 30 acres of meadow. Of this manor, 3 virgate are in the king's forest, and the whole woodland, which is worth 20s.

XXIX. The land of Ralph de Mortimer

IN 'BUDDLESGATE' HUNDRED

RALPH de Mortimer holds OTTERBOURNE. Cypping held it of the bishopric of Winchester. He could not withdraw from the church. It was then, as now, assessed at 4 hides. There is land for 5 ploughs. In demesne is 1 plough; and 10 villans and 8 bordars with 2 ploughs. There is a church, and 6 slaves, and 50 acres of meadow, and a fishery rendering 2s; from the pasture, 10s. TRE it was worth £8; and afterwards, as now, 100s.

IN BARTON HUNDRED

The Church of SAINT-VICTOIRE [-en-Caux] holds BARTON STACEY of Ralph. Cypping held it of King Edward in parage. It was then assessed at 1 hide; now at 1 virgate. There is land for 2 ploughs. There are 9 oxen, and 1 villan and 5 bordars, and 6 acres of meadow, and 1 slave. TRE it was worth 60s; and afterwards, as now, 30s.

Ralph himself holds HEADBOURNE WORTHY. Cypping held it of King Edward. It was then, as now, assessed at 1 hide. There is land for 5 ploughs. In demesne are 3 ploughs; and 1 villan and 27 bordars with 2 ploughs. There is a church, and 24 slaves, and 3 mills rendering 60s, and 5 acres of meadow. For the herbage, 40s; and [there are] 8 closes in Winchester rendering 65s4d. TRE it was worth £25; and afterwards £10; now £15. This manor, TRE, was bought from the church on this term and condition, that the [episcopal] Church of St Peter should receive it back from the bishopric with all its stock after [the death of] the third heir. Ralph, who now holds it, is the third heir.

The same Ralph holds HEADBOURNE WORTHY. Eadsige held it TRE. It was then assessed at 1 hide and 1 virgate; now at nothing. There is land for 1 plough. It was a manor; it is now added to another manor. TRE, as now, worth 40s; when received, 30s.

IN MANSBRIDGE HUNDRED

The same Ralph holds SHIRLEY. Cypping held it of King Edward. It was then, as now, assessed at 1 hide. There is land for 8 ploughs. There are 4 villans and 3 bordars with 2 ploughs. There is a church, and 5 slaves, and a mill rendering 30d, and 12 acres of meadow, [and] woodland for 6 pigs. In Southampton, 4 messuages, rendering 40d. [There is] a fishery rendering 6s. TRE and afterwards, as now, worth 100s.

The same Ralph holds BOTLEY. Cypping held it of King Edward. Then, as now,

[Folio 47: HAMPSHIRE]

it was assessed at 2 hides. There is land for 6 ploughs. There are 8 villans and 4 bordars with 4 ploughs. There is a church, and 4 slaves, and 2 mills rendering 20s, and 12 acres of meadow. There is no woodland. TRE it was worth £10; and afterwards, as now, 100s.

The same Ralph holds NORTH BADDESLEY. Cypping held it of the king. Then, as now, it was assessed at 2 hides.

There is land for 4 ploughs. There are 4 villans and 7 bordars with 2 ploughs, and 7 slaves. There is a church, and woodland for 10 pigs, and, for the herbage, 10s. TRE it was worth £10; and afterwards 100s; now 60s.

IN KINGSCLERE HUNDRED

The same Ralph holds KNOWL HILL, and Oidelard [holds] of him. Cypping held it of King Edward. It was then, as now, assessed at 2 hides. There is land for 3 ploughs. In demesne are 2 [ploughs]; and 2 villans and 10 bordars with 1 plough. There are 4 slaves, and 2 mills rendering 11s3d, [and] woodland for 5 pigs. TRE, and afterwards, it was worth 60s; now 70s.

The same Ralph holds 1 hide in SWAMPTON. Cypping held it of the bishop and monks, and it always belonged to the monastery, but it was granted to this man to hold for his own life only, and after his death it was to revert to the church. This the monks say, but the hundred knowns nothing of the agreement; but they know this, that it belonged to the monastery, and that it did not give geld, nor does it now, and they know not why it has remained [in his hands]. There is land for 1 plough. This [plough] is in demesne, with 2 villans and 3 bordars, and a mill rendering 15s. TRE and afterwards, as now, worth 25s.

IN TITCHFIELD HUNDRED

The same Ralph holds 1 virgate of land. Cypping held this of King Edward. It paid geld then, as now, for 1 virgate. There is land for half a plough. 2 villans have this [half-plough] there, and half an acre of meadow. TRE it was worth 5s; and afterwards 3s; now 7s.

IN SOMBORNE HUNDRED

Ralph himself holds 1 manor, which Cypping held of King Edward. It was then assessed at 2 hides; now at 1½ hides. There is land for 3 ploughs. In demesne, however, are 2 ploughs; and 1 villan and 8 slaves with 1 plough, and a mill rendering 7s6d, and 15 acres of meadow. Of this land Waleran holds 1 hide of Ralph, and there he has 3 bordars. TRE [the whole] together was worth £7; and afterwards £4; now Ralph's part [is worth] £4; and Waleran's, 20s, and yet it renders 30s.

IN NEATHAM HUNDRED

The same Ralph holds 2 hides of the king, in Norton [in Selborne], which Alwine held in alod of King Edward as 1 manor. It was then, as now, assessed at 2 hides. There is land for 1 plough. This [plough] is in demesne, and 2 villans and 1 bordar and 1 slave, and 7½ acres of meadow. It is worth 40s.

IN BERMONDSPIT HUNDRED

Ralph himself holds PRESTON CANDOVER, and Oidelard [holds] of him. Cypping held it of King Edward in alod. It then paid geld for 5 hides; now for 4½ hides. There is land for 6 ploughs. In demesne is 1 plough, and 1 villan and 2 bordars and 3 slaves, and 5 acres of meadow. TRE it was worth £8; and afterwards 100s; now £4.

IN HOLDSHOTT HUNDRED

Ralph himself holds SILCHESTER. Cypping held it of Earl Harold in alod. It then paid geld for 5 hides; now for 3 hides. There is land for 5 ploughs. There are 9 villans and 13 bordars with 4 ploughs, and 3 slaves, and 6 acres of meadow. [There is] woodland for 20 pigs. TRE it was worth 100s; and afterwards, as now, 60s.

IN ANDOVER HUNDRED

The same Ralph holds SARSON, and Ingerlrann [holds] of him. Eadric held it TRE. It paid geld then, as now, for 5 hides. There is land for 3 ploughs. In demesne is 1 plough; and 7 villans and 6 bordars with 2 ploughs. There are 3 slaves, and a mill rendering 25s, and 2 acres of meadow, [and] woodland without pannage. TRE it was worth 100s; and afterwards 40s; now £4.

IN 'BOUNTISBOROUGH' HUNDRED

The same Ralph holds of the king a manor, Mortimer West End, which Cypping held TRE. It was then assessed at 5 hides; now at 1 hide. There is land for 5 ploughs. In demesne are 2 [ploughs]; and 4 villans and 9 bordars with 1 plough. There are 6 slaves, and 2 acres of meadow. TRE it was worth £12; and afterwards £10; now £6.

XXX. The land of Eudo fitzHubert

IN OVERTON HUNDRED

EUDO fitzHubert holds ASHE of the king. Ailwacre held it of Earl Harold. It was then assessed at 8 hides; now at 3 hides. There is land for 8 ploughs. In demesne are 2 [ploughs]; and 4 villans and 10 bordars with 3 ploughs. There is a church, and 10 slaves, and 3 acres of meadow. TRE it was worth £7; and afterwards, as now, £6.10s; and this [is] on account of half a hide which is missing because of Hugh the sheriff.

XXXI. The land of William Bertram

IN OVERTON HUNDRED

WILLIAM Bertram holds POLHAMPTON of the king. Tosti held it TRE. It was then assessed at 3½ hides. There is land for 6 ploughs. In demesne are 1½ ploughs; and 5 villans and 9 bordars with 3 ploughs. There is a church, and 10 slaves, and 3 acres of meadow, [and] woodland for 10 pigs as pannage. TRE it was worth £12; and afterwards, as now, £8; yet it was [farmed] at £9.

XXXII. The land of William de Eu

IN SOMBORNE HUNDRED

WILLIAM de EU holds KING'S SOMBORNE of the king. Tholf the Dane held it of King Edward. It was then assessed at 14 hides; now at 7½ hides. There is land for 12 ploughs. In demesne are 2 ploughs; and 19 villans and 5 bordars with 8 ploughs. There are 13 slaves, and a mill rendering 10s, and 68 acres of meadow, and 9 messuages of burgesses render 12s2d.

TRE and afterwards, as now, worth £14; yet it renders £16 at farm.

IN 'CHUTELEY' HUNDRED

The same William holds DEANE. Tholf held it of King Edward in alod. It was then assessed at 20 hides; now at 11 hides. There is land for 10 ploughs. In demesne are 3 ploughs; and 12 villans and 10 bordars with 7 ploughs. There are 11 slaves, and woodland for 1 pig. TRE it was worth £10; and afterwards £11; | now £12. |

The same William holds half a virgate of land and 4 acres in MALSHANGER. Edward held it of King Edward in alod. It is now placed with the above manor of DEANE, and belongs there, as the hundred says.

IN HOLDSHOTT HUNDRED

William himself holds SILCHESTER, and Ralph Bloiet [holds] of him. Ælfstan held it of King Edward in alod. Then, as now, it paid geld for 5 hides. There is land for 5 ploughs. In demesne is 1 plough; and 5 villans and 5 bordars with 3 ploughs. There are 4 slaves, and 2 acres of meadow, [and] woodland for 60 pigs. TRE, and afterwards, it was worth 100s; now £6.

XXXIII. The land of William de Braose

IN NEATHAM HUNDRED

WILLIAM de BRAOSE holds half a hide of the king. Wynsige held it of King Edward by customary service, as his predecessor, who was a goatherd, held it. He could not turn to another lord. It now pays geld for half a hide. There is 1 plough in demesne. Richard holds it of William. TRE it was worth 10s; and afterwards, as now, 5s.

XXXIIII. The land of William de Warenne

IN PORTSDOWN HUNDRED

WILLIAM de Warenne holds FRATTON, and Osmelin [holds] of him. Ketil held it of King Edward in alod. It was then, as now, assessed at 4 hides. There is land for 3 ploughs. In demesne is 1 [plough]; and 4 villans and 4 bordars with 2 ploughs. There are 4 slaves. TRE it was worth 60s; and afterwards 30s; now 40s.

[Folio 47V: HAMPSHIRE]

XXXV. The land of William Mauduit

IN TITCHFIELD HUNDRED

WILLIAM Mauduit holds ROWNER. Coleman held it of King Edward. It was then assessed at 5 hides; now at 2½ hides. There is land for 4 ploughs. In demesne are 1½ ploughs, and 2 slaves, and 1 acre of meadow, and woodland for 4 pigs; and 10 villans and 2 bordars with 2½ ploughs. TRE it was worth 70s; and afterwards 30s; now 70s.

IN NEATHAM HUNDRED

The same William holds HARTLEY MAUDITT. Gyrth held it of King Edward in alod. It was then assessed at 6 hides, and afterwards at 3 hides; but the shire has not seen the king's writ or seal for this. [It is] now [assessed] at 2 hides. There is land for 8 ploughs. In demesne are 2 ploughs; and 8 villans and 5 bordars with 5 ploughs, and 6 acres of meadow. [There is] woodland for 30 pigs. TRE it was worth £8; and afterwards £3; now £7.

William himself holds "BESSETE". Wulfweard and Ælfric [held it] as 2 manors of King Edward in alod. It was then, as now, assessed at 2½ hides. There is land for 4 ploughs. In demesne are 2 ploughs, and 14 villans and 4 bordars, and 2 slaves, and a mill rendering 40d, and 3 acres of meadow. [There is] woodland for 5 pigs. TRE it was worth £3; and afterwards, as now, £4.

IN PORTSDOWN HUNDRED

William himself holds PORTCHESTER. 3 free men held it as 3 manors of King Edward. It then paid geld for 5 hides; now for 2½ hides; and it is 1 manor. There is land for 5 ploughs. In demesne are 2 [ploughs]; and 5 villans and 4 bordars with 1½ ploughs. There are 4 slaves, and a fishery for the hall, [and] woodland for 5 pigs. Of this manor, Durand holds 1 hide of William, and he has in demesne 1 plough, and a mill rendering 30d. The whole was worth TRE £4.10s; and afterwards 100s; now £6.

The same William holds 1 hide, and Fulcold [holds] of him. Alweard held it of King Edward. It then, as now, paid geld for 1 hide. There is land for 1 plough. In demesne is half a plough; and 2 villans and 2 slaves with half a plough. It is worth 15s.

The same William holds 2 hides less 1 virgate. Ælfric held it as 1 manor in alod of the king. Then, as now, it paid geld for 2 hides less 1 virgate. There is land for 2 ploughs. In demesne is 1 [plough]; and 3 villans and 4 bordars with half a plough. There are 2 slaves, and 2 mills rendering 5s, and 2 acres of meadow. TRE, and afterwards, it was worth 25s; now 30s.

IN BERMONDSPIT HUNDRED

William himself holds PRESTON CANDOVER. 2 free men held it as 2 manors of King Edward. It then paid geld for 5 hides; now for 2½ hides; and it is 1 manor. There is land for 6 ploughs. In demesne are 1½ [ploughs]; and 7 villans and 2 bordars with 2 ploughs. There are 14 slaves, and 4 acres of meadow, [and] woodland for fencing. TRE, as now, worth 100s; when received, 60s.

IN ODIHAM HUNDRED

William himself holds SHALDEN. 4 free men held it of King Edward in alod. It then paid geld for 5 hides; now for 3 hides and 1 virgate. There is land for 6 ploughs. In demesne are 1½ ploughs; and 11 villans and 8 bordars with 7 ploughs. There are 8 slaves, TRE, as now, worth 100s; when received, 60s.

IN ANDOVER HUNDRED

The same William holds 5 hides of land. Wulfgifu held these as 1 manor in alod of King Edward. They then paid geld for 5 hides; now for 3 hides. There is land for 5 ploughs. In demesne is 1 [plough]; and 10 villans and 5 bordars with 3 ploughs. There is a church, and 2 slaves, and 2 acres of meadow. TRE, as now, worth 100s; when received, 50s.

XXXVI. The land of Alvred of Marlborough

IN BROUGHTON HUNDRED

ALVRED of Marlborough holds SHIPTON BELLINGER, and Reginald [holds] of him. Karli held it of King Edward in alod. Then, as now, it paid geld for 10½ hides. There is land for 5 ploughs. In demesne is 1 [plough]; and 5 villans and 3 bordars with 3 ploughs. [There is] woodland for fencing. There is a church, and 6 slaves. TRE and afterwards, as now, worth £6.

IN BASINGSTOKE HUNDRED

The same Alvred holds EASTROP, and Hugh [holds] of him. karli held it of King Edward, and could go where he would. It was then, as now, assessed at 3 hides. There is land for 3 ploughs. In demesne is 1 plough; and 2 villans and 15 bordars with 2 ploughs. There are 3 slaves, and a mill rendering 7s6d. TRE, as now, worth £4; when received, £3.

XXXVII. The land of Durand of Gloucester

IN BASINGSTOKE HUNDRED

DURAND of Gloucester holds CLIDDESDEN of the king, and Ralph [holds] of him. 2 brothers held it of King Edward, and could go where they would. It was then, as now, assessed at 2 hides. There is land for 5 ploughs. In demesne is 1 plough; and 6 villans and 10 bordars with 2 ploughs. There is a church, and 9 slaves. TRE it was worth £4; and afterwards, as now, £3.

IN HODDINGTON HUNDRED

The same Durand holds WESTON [? Corbett], and Geoffrey [holds] of him. Eadric held it of King Edward in alod. It was then, as now, assessed at 2 hides. There is land for 2 ploughs. In demesne is 1 [plough], with 3 bordars, and 1 slave. TRE, as now, worth 40s; when received, 20s.

The land of Turstin fitzRolf

IN NEATHAM HUNDRED

TURSTIN fitzRolf holds NEWTON VALENCE of the king. Beorhtric held it of King Edward in alod. [It was] then [assessed] at 10 hides; now at 5 hides. There is land for 12 ploughs. In demesne are 3 ploughs; and 9 villans and 5 bordars with 9 ploughs. There is a church, and 6 slaves, and 2 mills rendering 100d, and 6 acres of meadow, [and] woodland for 100 pigs. TRE, and afterwards, it was worth £15; now £12.

The land of Bernard Pauncevolt

IN SOMBORNE HUNDRED

BERNARD Pauncevolt holds AWBRIDGE of the king. Godwine held it of King Edward, and could go where he would. It was then assessed at 1 hide; now at 1 virgate. There is land for 2 [ploughs]. There are 2 villans with half a plough, and 7 acres of meadow. [There is] woodland for 2 pigs. TRE, and afterwards, it was worth 60s; now 30s.

The same Bernard holds LITTLE SOMBORNE. Godwine held it of King Edward. It was then assessed at 2 hides; now at 1 virgate. There is land for 2 ploughs. In demesne are 2 ploughs, and 1 villan and 7 slaves. TRE it was worth 60s; and afterwards, as now, 70s.

IN BARTON HUNDRED

The same Bernard holds HEADBOURNE WORTHY. Godwine held it of King Edward. It was then, as now, assessed at 1 hide. There is land for 2 ploughs. In demesne are [2 ploughs], and 3 slaves, and 2 acres of meadow, and 1 messuage in Winchester rendering nothing. TRE it was worth £12; and afterwards, as now, £6.

IN MANSBRIDGE HUNDRED

The same Bernald holds CHILWORTH. Godwine held it of King Edward. It was then, as now, assessed at 2 hides. There is land for 2 ploughs. In demesne is 1 [plough]; and 4 villans with 1 plough. There is a church, and 4 slaves, and 3 closes in Southampton rendering 18d. TRE it was worth £10; and afterwards £8; now £4, because he has no rights in his woodland.

IN BROUGHTON HUNDRED

The same Bernard holds EMBLEY. Godwine held it of King Edward in alod. It then paid geld for half a hide; now for nothing. There is land for half a plough. It was worth 10s. It is now waste.

[Folio 48: HAMPSHIRE]

XL. The land of Turstin the Chamberlain

IN SOMBORNE HUNDRED

TURSTIN the chamberlain holds HOUGHTON. Algar and Edward held it of King Edward. It was then assessed at 2½ hides; now at 1 hide and 1 virgate and 5 acres of land. In demesne are 1½ ploughs, with 5 bordars and 1 free man and 2 slaves. TRE, and afterwards, it was worth 40s; now 60s.

XLI. The land of Richard Sturmy

IN 'BUDDLESGATE' HUNDRED

RICHARD Sturmy holds CHILBOLTON. Ordweald held it of the Bishop of Winchester, and it belonged to the monastery TRE, and he could not go where he pleased. It was then assessed at 3 hides and 3 virgates; now at 1 hide. There is land for 3 ploughs. In demesne [are] 2 ploughs, and 1 villan and 11 bordars, and a mill rendering 7s6d. TRE, as now, worth £4; when received, 40s.

XLII. The land of Richard Puignant

IN MANSBRIDGE HUNDRED

RICHARD Puignant holds NETLEY. Alweard held it of King Edward, and could go where he would. It was then assessed at 3 hides; now at 1 hide. There is land for 5 ploughs. In demesne is 1 [plough]; and 9 villans and 2 bordars with 2 ploughs. There is a chapel, and 2 slaves, and 4 acres of meadow, [and] woodland for 40 pigs. TRE it was worth 60s; and afterwards 40s; now 100s.

XLIII. The land of Gilbert de Breteuil

IN ANDOVER HUNDRED

GILBERT de Breteuil holds 4 hides and 3 virgates in EAST CHOLDERTON of the king, and Ralph [holds] of him. 4 free men held them as 4 manors in alod of King Edward. It then, as now, paid geld for 4 hides and 3 virgates. There is land for 3 ploughs. In demesne is 1 [plough]; and 4 villans and 2 bordars with 1 plough. There are 2 slaves, and 3 acres of meadow. TRE it was worth 67s6d; and afterwards 40s; now 60s.

IN BROUGHTON HUNDRED

The same Gilbert holds DUNBRIDGE. Cyning held it in alod of King Edward as 1 manor. It then, as now, paid geld for 1 hide. There are 2 villans with 1 plough, and 3 acres of meadow, and woodland for 2 pigs. TRE and afterwards, as now, worth 25s2d.

The same Gilbert holds EAST TYTHERLEY, and Papald [holds] of him. Cyning held it in alod of King Edward as a manor. It then, as now, paid geld for 1 hide. There is land for 1 plough. In demesne is half a plough; and 2 villans and 1 bordar with 1 plough. It is worth 10s.

IN HOLDSHOTT HUNDRED

The same Gilbert holds BRAMSHILL, with the king's manor of SWALLOWFIELD, which is in Berkshire. Alwig and Alsige held it in alod of King Edward as 2 manors. Then, as now, it paid geld for 2 hides less 1 virgate. There is land for 2 ploughs. In demesne are 2 [ploughs]; and 4 villans with 1 plough, and a mill rendering 25d, and 6 acres of meadow. [There is] woodland for 2 pigs. TRE it was worth 40s; and afterwards 20s5d; now 25d. This manor, as the hundred says, never belonged to the king's manor.

The same Gilbert holds STRATFIELD SAYE with the king's manor of Swallowfield [Berks.]; but the hundred says that it never belonged there. Edward held it of King Edward in alod. It then paid geld for 1 hide; now it does not pay geld. There is land for 2 ploughs. There are 2 villans. Hugh holds it of Gilbert, and pays 15s.

IN SOMBORNE HUNDRED

The same Gilbert holds 1 hide of the king. Alnoth held this of King Edward. It was then, as now, assessed at 1 hide. There is land for 2 ploughs. There are 3 villans and 6 bordars with 4 ploughs, and a mill rendering 20s, and 12 acres of meadow. [There is] woodland for 10 pigs. TRE and afterwards, as now, worth 60s. Hugh de Port claims this hide, saying it belongs to his manors of South Charford and "Eschetune", and there his predecessors held it; and the whole hundred testifies to this.

XLIIII. The land of Hugh fitzBaldric

IN 'BOUNTISBOROUGH' HUNDRED

HUGH fitzBaldric holds ITCHEN ABBAS of the king. The abbey of nuns of ST MARY'S, Winchester, held this manor TRE. It was then assessed at 12 hides; now at 3½ hides. There is land for 3 ploughs. In demesne are 4 ploughs; and 9 villans and 9 bordars with 3 ploughs. There are 16 slaves, and a mill rendering 20s, and 24 acres of meadow. TRE it was worth £15; and afterwards £17; now £11. The Abbess of ST MARY'S claims this manor; and the whole hundred, and also the whole shire, bears witness that it was the abbey's TRE and [in the time] of King William, and ought of right to be.

IN 'CHUTELEY' HUNDRED

The same Hugh holds OAKLEY. Bondi held it of King Edward in alod. It was then, as now, assessed at 1½ hides. There is 1 villan and 1 bordar. TRE, and afterwards, it was worth 15s; now 20s.

IN HOLDSHOTT HUNDRED

The same Hugh holds STRATFIELD SAYE. Bondi held it of King Edward in alod. It then paid geld for 15 hides; now for 7½ hides. There is land for 17 ploughs. In demesne are 2 ploughs; and 30 villans and 10 bordars with 16 ploughs. There is a church, and 14 slaves, and 2 mills rendering 27s6d, and 40 acres of meadow, woodland for 100 pigs, and 1 close in Winchester. TRE it was worth £15; and afterwards £12; now £15.

IN HODDINGTON HUNDRED

The same Hugh holds South Warnborough, and Guy [holds] of him with his daughter. Bondi held it of King Edward. It was then assessed at 11 hides; now at 6 hides. There is land for 12 ploughs. In demesne are 2 ploughs; and 15 villans and 16 bordars with 6 ploughs. [There is] a church, | and 3 slaves, and a mill rendering 10s, and 12 acres of meadow. | TRE [it was worth] £12; and afterwards £6; now £10.

XLV. The land of Waleran the Huntsman

IN SHIRLEY HUNDRED

WALERAN holds WINKTON of the king, and Robert [holds] of him. Earl Tosti held it of King Edward in alod. It then paid geld for 7 hides; now for 3 hides and 1 virgate. There is land for 4 ploughs. In demesne are 1½ ploughs; and 14 villans and 7 bordars with 4 ploughs. There are 2 mills for the hall, and 450 eels from the mill, and 55 acres of meadow. TRE it was worth £10; and afterwards £7; now £4.10s.

Of this manor the king has 1 hide and half a virgate, and all the woodland, in his forest. This is valued at 110s; and of the remainder the king gave 1 virgate of land to a certain priest.

IN FORDINGBRIDGE HUNDRED

The same Waleran holds 1½ virgates in Outwick, and Joscelin holds of Waleran. Aghmund held it of King Edward in alod; and it belonged to East Wellow, as the hundred and the shire say. There is land for half a plough. There is [half a plough], with 1 villan and 1 bordar, and 3 acres of meadow, and a small wood. It was worth 10s; now 5s.

IN ANDOVER HUNDRED

The same Waleran holds FOXCOTTE, and Ralph [holds] of him. 2 free men held it in alod of King Edward as 2 manors. Then, as now, it paid geld for 3 hides. There is land for 4 ploughs. In demesne are 2 ploughs; and 10 villans and 13 bordars with 4 ploughs. There are 3 slaves. TRE it was worth 50s; and afterwards 40s; now 70s.

Waleran holds 1 virgate in [?] GREAT SHODDESDEN, and Ralph [holds] of him. Godric held it in alod of King Edward as a manor. Then, as now, it paid geld for 1 virgate. [There is] land for 3 ploughs. It is and was worth 5s.

IN BROUGHTON HUNDRED

The same Waleran holds EAST DEAN. Manna held it of King Edward. Then, as now, it paid geld for 1 virgate. There is land for half a plough, and there is [half a plough] with 1 villan and 1 bordar. There are 4 acres of meadow, and 2 slaves, [and] woodland for fencing. TRE it was worth 10s; and afterwards, as now, 5s. This land does not belong to any manor of his.

[Folio 48V: HAMPSHIRE]

The same Waleran holds WEST DEAN [Wilts.]. Boda held it of King Edward in alod. Then, as now, it paid geld for 2 hides and 1 virgate. There is land for 3 ploughs. In demesne is 1 plough; and 11 bordars with 2 ploughs, and a mill rendering 20s, and 4 acres of meadow. [There is] woodland for fencing. TRE it was worth £4; and afterwards 60s; now 40s.

The same Waleran holds EAST TYTHERLEY, and Roger [holds] of him. Ælfric held it in alod of King Edward as a manor. Then, as now, it paid geld for 1 hide. There is land for 1 plough, and there is [1 plough] in demesne, and 4 bordars. It is worth 10s.

IN SOMBORNE HUNDRED

The same Waleran holds KING'S SOMBORNE, and Roger [holds] of him. Eadnoth held it of King Edward. It was then, as now, assessed at 1½ hides. There is land for 1 plough. There are 2 villans with half a plough, and 18 acres of meadow. TRE, and afterwards, it was worth 30s; now 20s.

XLVI. The land of Walter fitzOther

IN NEATHAM HUNDRED

WALTER fitzOther holds WILL HALL. Ocsen held it of King Edward in alod. It was then, as now, assessed at 1 hide. There is land for 1½ ploughs. There is 1 plough; and 6 bordars with half a plough. There is a church, and 1½ acres of meadow. It is worth 40s.

IN 'CHUTELEY' HUNDRED

The same Walter holds MALSHANGER. Ocsen held it of King Edward in alod. It was then, as now, assessed at 3 hides. There is land for 3 ploughs. In demesne are 2 [ploughs]; and 5 villans and 6 bordars with 1 plough and 1 slave. There is woodland for fencing. TRE, and afterwards, it was worth 30s; now 40s.

XLVII. The land of Walter fitzRoger

IN BARTON HUNDRED

WALTER fitzRoger de Pitres holds half a hide in BARTON STACEY, and Hugh de Port [holds] of him. Eadsige the sheriff held it of King Edward. It was then, as now, assessed at half a hide. There is a church; and it is worth 15s.

IN BROUGHTON HUNDRED

The same Walter holds EAST DEAN, and Herbert [holds] of him. Wulfstan held it in alod of King Edward as 1 manor. Then, as now, it paid geld for half a hide. There is land for 1 plough. There are 2 bordars with half a plough. TRE and afterwards, as now, worth 7s; and yet it renders 15s at farm.

XLVIII. The land of William fitzManni

IN BARTON HUNDRED

WILLIAM fitzManni holds 1 hide in NEWTON STACEY. Ælfric held it of King Edward. [It was] then [assessed] at 1 hide; now at nothing. There is 1 plough in demesne; and it is farmed at 20s, and is worth as much. William received this land with his wife.

XLIX. [The land] of William Alis

IN MANSBRIDGE HUNDRED

WILLIAM Alis holds ALLINGTON. Godmann held it of King Edward. It was then, as now, assessed at 3 hides. There is land for 5 ploughs. In demesne is 1 plough; and 11 villans and 6 bordars with 7 ploughs. There is a church, and 10 slaves, and 2 mills rendering 20s, and 67 acres of meadow, and 30d for the herbage, [and] woodland for 20 pigs. TRE it was worth £15; and afterwards £7; now £6.10s.

L. The land of William fitzBaderon

IN KINGSCLERE HUNDRED

WILLIAM fitzBaderon holds BURGHCLERE. Saxi held it of King Edward. It was then assessed at 4 hides; now at 3 hides and 2½ virgates. There is land for 7 ploughs. In demesne are 2 ploughs; and 14 villans and 16 bordars with 5 ploughs. There is 1 slave, and 3 mills rendering 7s6d, and 7 acres of meadow. TRE and afterwards, as now, worth £7; and yet it renders £10.

IN ANDOVER HUNDRED

The same William holds EAST CHOLDERTON. 3 free men held it of King Edward in alod. It then paid geld for 3 hides and 2½ virgates; now for 1 hide and 2½ virgates. There is land [...]. In demesne is 1 plough, and 4 bordars and 2 slaves, and 5½ acres of meadow. TRE it was worth £4.10s; and afterwards, as now, 65s.

LI. The land of William fitzStur

IN SHIRLEY HUNDRED

WILLIAM fitzStur holds SOPLEY. Eadric held it of King Edward in alod. It then paid geld for 7 hides; now for 1 hide and half a virgate. There is land for 2 ploughs. In demesne is 1 [plough]; and 3 villans and 6 bordars with 2 ploughs. There is 1 slave, and a mill rendering 10s and 875 eels, and 60 less 1 acres of meadow. TRE it was worth £10; and afterwards 40s; now 50s; yet it renders 100s. The king has 4 hides of this manor in his forest and all the woodland. The whole of this is worth 110s.

IN SOMBORNE HUNDRED

The same William holds 1 hide, and Hugh [holds] of him. Oda held this of King Edward. It was then, as now, assessed at 1 hide. There is land for 1 plough, and there is [1 plough] in demesne, with 4 villans. There are 10 acres of meadow. TRE, and afterwards, it was worth 20s; now 25s.

LII. [The land] of William Bellet

WILLIAM Bellet holds WOODCOTT, and Faderlin [holds] of him with his daughter. Ansfrid held it of King Edward. It was then, as now, assessed at 1 hide. There is land for 1½ ploughs. In demesne is [1] plough, with 7 bordars, and 1 slave, and 2 acres of meadow. TRE it was worth 20s; and afterwards, as now, 30s.

LIII. The land of William the Archer

IN BROUGHTON HUNDRED

WILLIAM the archer holds BENTLEY [in Mottisfont]. Alwig held it as a manor in alod of King Edward. Then, as now, it paid geld for half a hide. There is land for 1 plough. There is [1 plough] in demesne; and 6 bordars with 1 plough. TRE it was worth 10s; and afterwards, as now, worth 12s6d.

IN SOMBORNE HUNDRED

The same William holds COMPTON. 5 thegns held it of King Edward, and could go where they would. It was then assessed at 4½ hides; now at 3 hides. There is land for 7 ploughs. In demesne is 1 [plough]; and 13 villans and 19 bordars with 7 ploughs. There is a mill rendering 20s, and 8 acres of meadow. TRE, and afterwards, it was worth £4; now £7.

Ealdræd, Oda's brother, claims 1 virgate of land of this manor, and says that he held it on the day on which King Edward was alive and dead and was disseised after King William had crossed the sea, and he proved his claim before the queen. Hugh de Port is his witness to this fact and [so are] the men of the whole hundred.

LIIII. [The land] of Herbert fitzRemy

IN SOMBORNE HUNDRED

HERBERT fitzRemy holds FARLEY. Alwine and Wulfwine held it of the king. It was then assessed at 5 hides; and now at 1 hide. There is land for 8 ploughs. In demesne are 3 ploughs; and 7 villans and 4 bordars with 4 ploughs. There are 6 slaves. TRE, and afterwards, it was worth 60s; now 100s.

The same Herbert holds FARLEY. Northmann held it of King Edward. It was then assessed at half a hide; now at nothing. There is land [...]. There are 3 bordars and 1 villan with half a plough. It is and was worth 20s. William de EU claims this hide, saying it belongs to his manor. But the men of the hundred do not bear witness that he ought to have it, but that it had been seized from the king.

LV. The land of H[erbert the Chamberlain]

IN NEATHAM HUNDRED

HERBERT the chamberlain holds RHODE of the king. Beorhtric held it of King Edward. There is 1 hide and 1 virgate of land, and it has not paid geld. There is land for 1 plough. In demesne is 1 plough, with 3 bordars, and 1 acre of meadow. [There is] woodland for fencing. TRE, as now, worth 20s; when received, 15s.

IN MEONSTOKE HUNDRED

The same Herbert holds SOBERTON of the king. Wulfnoth held it TRE. It was then assessed at 3 hides;

IN NEATHAM HUNDRED

Walter fitzRoger holds SELBORNE, and Herbert [holds] of him. Alweard held it of King Edward in alod. It was then, as now, assessed at 4 hides. There is land for 2 ploughs. In demesne is 1 plough; and 4 villans and 2 bordars with 2 ploughs, and 2 slaves, and 1 acre of meadow. [There is] woodland for 3 pigs. TRE it was worth 60s; and afterwards 40s; now 70s.

now at 2½ hides, because half a hide is in Earl Roger's park. There is land for 2 ploughs. In demesne is 1 plough; and 2 villans and 8 bordars with half a plough. There is a mill rendering 10s, and 2 acres of meadow. TRE it was worth 60s; and afterwards, as now, 40s, because it is diminished.

LVI. The land of Henry the Treasurer

IN MEONSTOKE HUNDRED

HENRY the treasurer holds SOBERTON of the king. Andrac held it of King Edward, and could go where he would. It was then assessed at 2 hides; now at 1, and Earl Roger has 1 virgate in his park. There is land for 2 ploughs. In demesne is 1 [plough]; and 4 villans and 5 bordars with 1 plough. There are 2 slaves, and 2 acres of meadow. TRE it was worth 30s; and afterwards 20s; now 60s.

IN MANSBRIDGE HUNDRED

The same Henry holds EASTLEIGH. Godwine held it of King Edward, and could go where he would. It was then assessed at 2 hides; now at 1. There is land for 2 ploughs. In demesne is 1 [plough]; and 4 villans and 7 bordars with 3 ploughs. There are 2 slaves, and 12 acres of meadow, [and] woodland for 5 pigs. TRE and afterwards, as now, worth 40s.

IN BERMONDSPIT HUNDRED

The same Henry holds NUTLEY. 4 free men held it of King Edward in alod. It was then assessed at 5 hides; now at 2½ hides. There is land for 5 ploughs. In demesne are 3 ploughs; and 4 villans and 7 bordars with 1½ ploughs. There are 8 slaves. TRE it was worth 100s; and afterwards 60s; now £4.10s. Of this manor Geoffrey Marshal holds half a hide, which, as the hundred says, belongs there.

The same Henry has in the same hundred 1 virgate which renders him 4s; but it does not belong to this manor.

LVII. The land of Humphrey the Chamberlain

IN BROUGHTON HUNDRED

HUMPHREY the chamberlain holds PITTLEWORTH. Wulfnoth held it of King Edward in alod. It then paid geld for 3½ hides; now for 1½ hides. There is land [...]. In demesne are 3 ploughs, and 2 bordars. TRE and afterwards, as now, worth 60s.

IN BARTON HUNDRED

The same Humphrey holds 1 hide in COLEMORE. Ælfric held it of Bondi, and could not go where he pleased. It was then assessed at 1 hide; now at half a hide. There is land for 2 ploughs. In demesne is 1 plough; and 2 villans and 4 bordars with 1 plough. There are 4 slaves. TRE it was worth 40s; and afterwards, as now, 30s; yet it renders 40s.

LVIII. [The land] of Herbrand

IN MANSBRIDGE HUNDRED

HERBRAND holds BOYATT of the king. Godric held it of King Edward. It was then assessed at 2 hides; now at half a hide. There is land for 2 ploughs. In demesne is 1 plough; and 1 villan and 8 bordars with half a plough. There are 2 slaves, and 2 mills rendering 16s, and 45 acres of meadow, [and] woodland for 1 pig. TRE it was worth £4; and afterwards, as now, 40s.

LIX. [The land] of Reginald [fitz]Croch

IN MANSBRIDGE HUNDRED

REGINALD fitzCroch holds 1 hide of the king in WOOLSTON. Tovi held it of King Edward. It was then assessed at 1 hide; now at half a virgate. There are 3 villans and 3 bordars with 1 plough. It was worth 10s; now 5s.

LX. The land of Croch the Huntsman

IN ANDOVER HUNDRED

CROCH holds 2 hides of the king in SOUTH TIDWORTH. Alwine held it as a manor of King Edward in alod. Then, as now, it paid geld for 2 hides. There is land for 1 plough, and there is [1 plough] in demesne, with 1 bordar and 1 slave. TRE it was worth 40s; and afterwards 20s; now 30s.

IN HURSTBOURNE HUNDRED

The same Croch holds CRUX EASTON. Linxi held it of King Edward in parage. It was then assessed at 6 hides; now at 3 hides and half a virgate. There is land for 5 ploughs. In demesne are 2 ploughs; and 7 villans and 10 bordars with 2 ploughs. There is a church, and 20 acres of meadow, [and] woodland for fencing. TRE it was worth £6; and afterwards £3; now £6.

LXI. The land of Joscelin de Cormeilles

IN ANDOVER HUNDRED

JOSCELIN de Cormeilles holds THRUXTON of the king. Saxi held it as a manor of King Edward in alod. It then paid geld for 10 hides; now for 4½ hides. There is land for 5 ploughs. In demesne are 2 [ploughs]; and 4 villans and 8 bordars with 3 ploughs. There are 4 slaves, and 4 acres of meadow, [and] woodland for 5 pigs. The Abbey of Cormeilles holds the church of this manor, with 1 virgate of land, and has there 1 villan. The whole manor TRE was worth £13; and afterwards, as now, £10.

LXII. The land of Geoffrey Marshal

IN NEATHAM HUNDRED

GEOFFREY Marshal holds EMPSHOTT of the king. Bondi and Saxi held it of King Edward in alod. It was then, as now, assessed at half a hide. There is land for 1 plough. There are 4 villans with 1½ ploughs. There is a mill rendering 50d, and half an acre of meadow, [and] woodland for 1 pig. TRE, and afterwards, it was worth 20s; now 25s.

The same Geoffrey holds EAST WORLDHAM. Alwine held it of King Edward in alod. It was then assessed at 5 virgates of land; now at 1 virgate. There is land for 1 plough. In demesne are 2 ploughs; and 2 villans and 12 bordars with 1½ ploughs, and a mill rendering 6s8d, and 10 acres of meadow. TRE, and afterwards, it was worth 20s; now 40s.

LXIII. The land of Nigel the Physician

IN NEATHAM HUNDRED

NIGEL the physician holds BROXHEAD of the king. Spirites held it of King Edward in alod. It was then, as now, assessed at 1 hide. There is land for 1 plough. This [plough] is in demesne; and 4 villans and 3 bordars with 2 ploughs. There are 3 slaves, and a mill rendering 5s, and 6 acres of meadow, [and] woodland for 50 pigs.

LXIIII. The land of Alvred the Priest

IN KINGSCLERE HUNDRED

ALVRED the priest holds WOLVERTON and 'Finley' [in Baughurst]. Ælfgifu held it of the king, and could go where she pleased. It was then, as now, assessed at 5 hides. There is land for 8 ploughs. In demesne is 1 [plough]; and 7 villans and 17 bordars with 5 ploughs. TRE, and afterwards, it was worth £6; now 100s.

IN TITCHFIELD HUNDRED

The same Alvred holds 1 hide. Wulfræd held this of the king, and it is a berewick of Wolverton. It was then, as now, assessed at 1 hide. There is land for 1 plough. There are 3 villans with half a plough, and woodland for 5 pigs. It is worth 20s.

LXV. The land of Durand the Barber

IN TITCHFIELD HUNDRED

DURAND the barber holds 1 hide of the king, which Blæcmann held of King Edward. It was then assessed at 1 hide; now at 1 virgate. There is land for 1 plough. This [plough] is in demesne; and 2 villans and 4 bordars with half a plough. TRE it was worth 20s; and afterwards 15s; now 25s.

LXVI.

IN TITCHFIELD HUNDRED

RANULPH Flambard holds GREAT FUNTLEY of the king. Thorir held it of Earl Godwine. It was then, as now, assessed at 1 hide; and yet there is 1 virgate of land more. There is land for 3 ploughs. In demesne is 1 [plough]; and 4 villans and 5 bordars with 2½ ploughs. There is 1 slave, and a mill rendering 12s6d, and 5 acres of meadow, [and] woodland for 10 pigs. TRE it was worth £4; and afterwards, as now, £3.

LXVII.

IN BASINGSTOKE HUNDRED

GEOFFREY, chamberlain to the king's daughter, holds HATCH WARREN of the king. Alsige held it TRE. It was then assessed at 1 hide; now at 3 virgates. There is land for 3 ploughs. In demesne are 2 [ploughs]; and 2 villans with 1 plough. There is a church, and 11 slaves. TRE it was worth 100s; and afterwards, as now, £4. Oda of Winchester claims this hide, saying he had it in pledge for £10 from Alsige with the permission of King William, and therefore he lost it unjustly. But Geoffrey holds it of the king, for the service he performed for his daughter Matilda.

[Folio 49V: HAMPSHIRE]

IN ODIHAM HUNDRED

LXVIII. HUGH a la Barbe holds DOGMERSFIELD of the king. Sven held it of King Edward in alod. It was then assessed at 5 hides; now at nothing. There is land for 6 ploughs. In demesne is 1 [plough]; and 10 villans and 8 bordars with 3 ploughs. There is a church, and 1 slave, and a mill rendering 6s6d, and 5 acres of meadow, [and] woodland for 100 pigs. It is worth 100s.

IN SOMBORNE HUNDRED

HUGH fitzOsmund holds [?]LONGSTOCK of the king. Edward held it of King Edward. It was then assessed at 1 hide; now at nothing. There is land for 1 plough, and there is [1 plough] in demesne, with 2 slaves. It is and was worth 20s.

IN SOMBORNE HUNDRED

ANSKETIL fitzOsmund holds HOUGHTON of the king. Godwine held it of King Edward. It was then assessed at 2½ hides; now at half a hide. There is land for 2 ploughs, and there are [2 ploughs] in demesne, with 4 bordars and 10 slaves. TRE it was worth 60s; and afterwards 20[s]; now 50s.

IN REDBRIDGE HUNDRED

The same Ansketil holds 1 virgate of the king in "NORTHAM". Eadsige held it of King Edward, and it belonged to the king's farm, and in his time it was alienated; but the hundred knows not how. It was then, as now, assessed at 1 virgate. It is worth 15s.

IN PORTSDOWN HUNDRED

Ansketil [...] holds COSHAM of the king. Beorhtmær held it of King Edward in alod. It then paid geld for 2 hides; now for half a hide. There is land for 3 ploughs. In demesne is 1 plough, and 6 bordars and 1 slave, and a salt-pan rendering 14d. Of this manor 1 of his men holds 1 virgate, and there he has 1 plough. TRE it was worth 40s; and afterwards 30s; now 50s.

The same Ansketil holds half a hide of the king. Northmann held this of King Edward in alod. It then, as now, paid geld for half a hide. There is land for 1 plough, and there is [1 plough] in demesne; and 2 villans and 3 bordars and 3 slaves with 1 plough, and half an acre of meadow. TRE, as now, [worth] 40s; when received, 30s.

IN 'ASHLEY' HUNDRED

MILES the porter holds BRAMDEAN of the king. 2 free men held it as 3 manors of King Edward. It then paid geld for 1 hide and 2½ virgates; now for nothing. There is land [...]. In demesne are 1½ ploughs; and 4 villans and 6 bordars with 1 plough, and 5 acres of meadow, and a close in Winchester rendering 3s. TRE it was worth 60s; and afterwards 40[s]; now 50s.

IN BERMONDSPIT HUNDRED

The same Miles holds 2½ virgates of the king. 2 free men held them as 2 manors of King Edward. There is land for half a plough. There is [half a plough] with 2 villans. It is and was worth 5s.

IN HOLDSHOTT HUNDRED

AUBREY the chamberlain holds HARTLEY WESPALL of the king. Ælfric held it of King Edward in alod. It then, as now, paid geld for 1½ hides. There is land [...]. There are 4 villans with 3 ploughs, and 1 slave, and a mill rendering 3s, and 6 acres of meadow. [There is] woodland for 5 pigs. TRE and afterwards, as now, worth 40s; and yet it renders 45s.

IN ANDOVER HUNDRED

ROBERT fitzMurdoch holds EAST CHOLDERTON of the king. 2 free men held it as 2 manors in alod of King Edward. It then paid geld for 3 hides and 1 virgate and 1½ acres; now for 2 hides and the fourth part of 1 virgate. There is land for 2 ploughs. In demesne is half a plough; and 2 villans and 2 bordars with half a plough. There are 2 slaves, and 1½ acres of meadow. TRE it was worth 60s; and afterwards 30s; now 40s.

IN FORDINGBRIDGE HUNDRED

OSBERN the falconer holds [North and South] GORLEY of the king. Wihtric held it of King Edward in alod. Then, as now, it paid geld for 1 hide. There is land [...]. There are 3 villans and 2 bordars with 1 plough, and 7 acres of meadow. It was worth 20s; now 10s. Half of this hide is in the forest, and is worth 7s.

LXIX. The land of the King's Thegns

IN BARTON HUNDRED

ODA holds SUTTON SCOTNEY of the king. Alweard held it of Earl Godwine. It was then assessed at 5 hides; now at 2 hides and 3 virgates. There is land for 4 ploughs. In demesne

is 1 [plough]; and 4 villans and 4 bordars with 2 ploughs. There is a church, and 8 slaves, and a mill rendering 6s3d, and 10 acres of meadow. TRE it was worth £6; and afterwards £4; now 100s.

The same Oda holds NORTON [in Wonston]. Folki held it of King Edward, and could go where he would. It was then assessed at 5 hides; now at 2 hides and 1 virgate. There is land for 3 ploughs. In demesne are 2 [ploughs]; and 3 villans and 5 bordars with 1 plough. There is a church, and 6 slaves, and a mill rendering 15s, and 10 acres of meadow. From the herbage, 12d, and in Winchester, 5 closes rendering 10s. TRE it was worth £6; and afterwards £3; now £6.10s.

IN 'ASHLEY' HUNDRED

The same Oda holds BRAMDEAN. Leofwine held it of King Edward in alod. It was then, as now, assessed at 1 hide and 1 virgate. There is land for 1 plough, and there is [1 plough] in demesne, with 3 bordars, and 3 acres of meadow. [There is] woodland for fencing. TRE, as now, it was worth 40s; when received, 5s.

IN NEATHAM HUNDRED

EDWIN holds OAKHANGER, and says that he bought it of King William, but the shire does not know this. Alwig held it of King Edward, and Richard now holds of Edwin. TRE it was assessed at 1 hide and 1 virgate. There is land for 4 ploughs. In demesne are 2 [ploughs]; and 8 villans and 6 bordars with 3 ploughs, and 2 slaves, and 2 acres of meadow. TRE, and afterwards, it was worth 40s; now 60s. Of this manor the king's reeve claims half a hide for pasture for the king's oxen. The shire, however, testifies that he cannot have pasture nor pannage in the king's woodland, as he claims, except through the sheriff.

IN ODIHAM HUNDRED

GODWINE holds 'BARTLEY' [in Odiham]. Edwin held it of King Edward in alod. It was then assessed at 1½ hides; now at 1 hide. There is land for 2 ploughs. In demesne is 1 [plough]; and 4 villans and 4 bordars with 2 ploughs. There are 2 slaves, and a mill rendering 20d, and 3 acres of meadow. It is and was worth 20s.

IN BERMONDSPIT HUNDRED

CYPPING holds PRESTON CANDOVER of the king. Esbiorn held it of Queen Edith. It then paid geld for 2½ hides; now for 2 hides. There is land [...]. In demesne is 1 plough; and 3 villans with 3 oxen in a plough and 1 slave. A certain Earnwulf holds 1 virgate of this land, and there he has half a plough. TRE it was worth £4; and afterwards 60s; now 50s. Half a hide has been taken from this manor and put in Odiham, so the hundred says.

ODA of Winchester holds DUMMER, and Hunger [holds] of him. Auti held it of King Edward. It then, as now, paid geld for 5 hides. There is land for 5 ploughs. In demesne are 3 ploughs; and 2 villans and 3 bordars with 1 plough. There is a church, and 3 closes in Winchester rendering 2s, and 1 acre of meadow. TRE, as now, worth 100s; when received, 60s.

EDWIN the priest holds 1 virgate in PRESTON CANDOVER of the king. The same man held it of King Edward in alod. Then, as now, it paid geld for 1 virgate. There is land for half a plough, and yet in demesne is 1 plough. It is worth 5s.

IN HOLDSHOTT HUNDRED

ALSIGE the son of Beorhtsige holds MATTINGLEY of the king. Alric held it of King Edward in alod. It then, as now, paid geld for 1½ hides. There is land for 3 ploughs. There are 8 villans and 3 bordars with 3 ploughs, and a mill rendering 5s, and 4 acres of meadow. It is and was worth 30s.

The same ALSIGE holds MINLEY. Alwig held it of King Edward in alod. Then, as now, it paid geld for 2 hides. There is land for 1 plough. There are 5 villans with 2 ploughs. It is and was worth 20s.

ÆLFRIC holds 2 hides in STRATFIELD SAYE. Godric and Siward held them as 2 manors of King Edward in alod, and this Ælfric has held them till now, without any warranty. There are 3 villans with 1 plough, and 2 acres of meadow. There is land for 3 ploughs. TRE, as now, it paid geld for 2 hides. TRE it was worth 15s; and afterwards, as now, 13s4d[10s].

[Folio 50: HAMPSHIRE]

The same ÆLFRIC holds HARTLEY WESTPALL. Alric held it of King Edward in alod. It then paid geld for 1 hide. There is land for 2 ploughs. There are 5 villans with 2 ploughs, and 6 acres of meadow. [There is] woodland for 4 pigs. It is and was worth 15s. He who holds this land says that he bought it of Earl William for 2 marks of gold, but he had never had it before.

IN BERMONDSPIT HUNDRED

Eadnoth and Eadwig held "SUDBERIE" in alod of King Edward, and after his death they also died. But Cola, a certain kinsman of theirs, redeemed this land of Earl William. Walter now holds it in pledge from the son of Cola of Basing. It was then, as now, assessed at 2½ hides. There is land for 3 ploughs. There is 1 villan and 1 bordar. TRE it was worth 40s; and afterwards 10s; now 20s.

SIGERIC the chamberlain holds FARLEIGH WALLOP of the king. Wulfgifu held it of King Edward. It then paid geld for 4 hides; now for 3 hides. There is land for 8 ploughs. In demesne is 1 plough; and 15 villans and 7 bordars with 6 ploughs. There are 3 slaves, and 16 acres of meadow, [and] woodland for fencing. TRE it was worth £8; and afterwards 60s; now £6.

IN BROUGHTON HUNDRED

OSMUND holds BENTLEY [in Mottisfont] of the king. The same man held it of King Edward in alod. It then, as now, paid geld for half a hide. There is land for 1 plough. There is 1 villan with half a plough. It is and was worth 5s.

ALWIG son of Thurbert holds [? West] TYTHERLEY of the king. 3 free men held it as 3 manors of King Edward in alod. It then paid geld for 4 hides and 1 virgate; now for 3 hides and 1 virgate. There is land for 6 ploughs. In demesne is 1 plough; and 2 villans and 22 bordars with 2 ploughs. There are 7½ acres of meadow, and woodland for fencing. The whole TRE was worth 50s; and afterwards, as now, 40s.

The men of the hundred say that they have never seen the king's seal, nor his officer who had given seisin of this manor to Alwine Ret, the predecessor of he who holds it now; and that, unless the king were to bear testimony, he has nothing there. 2 of those who held were killed in the Battle of Hastings.

ALWIG son of Sæwulf holds [? East] TYTHERLEY of the king. . His father held it of King Edward in alod. Then, as now, it paid geld for 3 hides. There is land for 4 ploughs. In demesne are 2 ploughs; and 2 villans and 9 bordars with 2 ploughs. There are 2 mills rendering 27s6d, and 26 acres of meadow, [and] woodland for 30 pigs. It was worth 60s; now 40[s].

WULFRIC holds LOCKERLEY of the king [...]. His father held it as a manor of King Edward in alod. Then, as now, it paid geld for half a virgate. There is land for 1 plough. In demesne [is] half [a plough]; and 2 bordars with half a plough. It is and was worth 5s.

Four Englishmen hold OVER WALLOP of the king. Their father held it of King Edward in alod. Then, as now, it paid geld for 1 hide. There is land for half a plough, and there is [half a plough] in demesne among these 4. It is and was worth 10s.

EDMUND holds 'MICHELTON' [in Broughton] of the king. His father held 1 virgate of King Edward, and another virgate was given him in exchange by Walter Giffard. Sceva held this of King Edward in alod. Then, as now, it paid geld for half a hide. There is land for 1 plough, and there is [1 plough] in demesne with 1 bordar. It is and was worth 5s.

ALSIGE son of Beorhtsige holds NETHER WALLOP of the king. Alric held it as a manor of King Edward in alod. Then, as now, it paid geld for 2 hides. There is land for 1 plough. There are 4 villans with 1 plough. TRE, as now, worth 20s; and afterwards 15s.

AGHMUND holds EAST WELLOW of the king. He himself held it in alod of King Edward. Then, as now, it paid geld for 5 hides. There is land for 3 ploughs. In demesne is 1 plough; and 10 bordars with 2 ploughs, and 2 mills rendering 100d, and 12 acres of meadow. [There is] woodland for 6 pigs. It was worth 60s; now 40s.

Waleran took away 1½ virgates from this manor, and put them out of the shire, and put them in Wiltshire, and 3 virgates of this land are in the king's forest.

Another AGHMUND holds "HOTLOP" of the king. He himself held it as a manor of King Edward in alod. It then paid geld for 3 hides; now for 1 hide. There is land for 2 ploughs. In demesne is 1 [plough]; and 1 villan and 2 bordars and 1 slave with half a plough. It was worth 40s; now 30s.

ALWIG holds LOCKERLEY of the king. The same man held it of King Edward in alod. It then, as now, paid geld for 1 virgate. There is land for half a plough. There is [half a plough] in demesne. It is and was worth 30d.

EADWULF holds 1 messuage of the king in MOTTISFONT in alod. His father held it. There is 1 bordar paying 7d; and it is worth as much.

IN ANDOVER HUNDRED

AGHMUND holds [? Little] SHODDESDEN of the king. He himself held it as a manor of Queen Edith in alod. It then, as now, paid geld for 1 hide. There is land for 1 plough. In demesne is half a plough; and 1 villan with half a plough. It was worth 15s; now 10s.

SÆRIC holds ENHAM ALAMEIN of the king. Alwine held it as a manor of King Edward in alod. Then, as now, it paid geld for 1½ hides. There is land for 2 ploughs. In demesne is 1 [plough]; and 2 villans and 7 bordars with half a plough, and half a mill rendering 5s, and 2 acres of meadow. [There is] woodland for 2 pigs. It was worth 60s; now 30s.

ALSIGE the †chamberlain† holds ENHAM ALAMEIN of the king. Wulfgifu held it of King Edward in alod. It then paid geld for 1½ hides. There is land for 1 plough. In demesne is 1 plough; and 2 villans and 9 bordars with 1 plough, and half a mill rendering 5s, and 2 acres of meadow. [There is] woodland for 2 pigs. It was worth 60s; now 30s. The monks of the bishopric of Winchester have on this manor a pledge of £12, which a certain man who is dead demised to them.

IN FORDINGBRIDGE HUNDRED

ALWIG son of Thurbert holds [? North] CHARFORD of the king. Wulfgeat held it of King Edward in alod. Then, as now, it paid geld for 1 hide. There is land for 2 ploughs. In demesne is 1 [plough]; and 14 bordars with 1 plough, and a mill rendering 30d, and 30 acres of meadow. [There is] woodland for 6 pigs. It was worth 30s; now 20s.

The same Alwig holds ROCKBOURNE. Wulfgeat held it as a manor of King Edward in alod. It then, as now, paid geld for 1 hide. There is land for 1 plough. There are 5 bordars. It was worth 40s; now 20s.

The hundred says that 1 virgate of this hide, which he claimed, was quit and geld-free TRE, and that Alwig has King Edward's seal for it.

The same Alwig holds MIDGHAM. Wulfgeat held it of King Edward in alod. It then paid geld for 1½ hides; now for nothing. There is land for 1½ ploughs. There are 8 bordars with half a plough. It is worth 13s.

COLA the huntsman holds ELLINGHAM of the king. Bolla held it of King Edward in alod. It then paid geld for 5½ hides; now for 1½ hides. There is land for 5 ploughs. In demesne are 2 ploughs; and 8 villans and 7 bordars and 5 slaves with 3½ ploughs, and a mill rendering 7s6d, and 103 acres of meadow. [There is] woodland for 40 pigs. TRE, and afterwards, it was worth £7; now 70s.

Of this manor, 1 hide is in the king's forest, and as much woodland as provides 20 pigs as pannage. All this is worth 70s.

SÆWINE holds half a hide of the king in ROCKBOURNE. He himself held it of King Edward in alod. It then paid geld for half a hide; now for nothing. There is land [...]. In demesne is half a plough with 2 bordars. It was worth 12s6d; now 7s6d. The sheriff's officers say that this half-hide belongs to the king's farm. But the hundred and the shire say that King Edward gave it to him [Sæwine], and he has his seal for it.

[Folio 50V: HAMPSHIRE]

EADGIFU holds MIDGHAM of the king. 2 free men held it of King Edward in alod. Then, as now, it paid geld for 1½ hides. There is land for 1 plough. There are 4 bordars. It was worth 20s; now 13s. Picot holds it of Eadgifu.

PICOT holds 1 virgate of the king in UPPER BURGATE. Wulfric and Goldgifu held it of King Edward in alod. It then, as now, paid geld for 1 virgate. There is land for half a plough; and there is [half a plough] with 2 bordars, and a mill rendering 8s8d, and 7 acres of meadow. [There is] woodland without pannage. TRE it was worth 10s; and afterwards 5s; now 12s.

IN SHIRLEY HUNDRED

WULFGEAT the huntsman holds RIPLEY of the king. He himself held it of King Edward in alod. It then paid geld for 5 hides; now for 2 hides. There is land for 2 ploughs. In demesne is 1 [plough]; and 8 bordars and 4 slaves with 2 ploughs, and 40 acres of meadow.

Of this manor, 3 hides and all the wood are in the king's forest. TRE it was worth £8; now 50s; what [is] in the forest, 100s.

IN REDBRIDGE HUNDRED

AGHMUND holds half a hide of the king in TOTTON. He himself held it TRE, and then, as now, it was assessed at half a hide. There is land for 1½ ploughs. There are 3 bordars and 2 villans with 1½ ploughs. There are 5 acres of meadow, and the fifth part of a mill rendering 5s. It was worth 12s; now worth 15s.

ALRIC holds [...] half a hide. His father held this of King Edward; but he did not apply to the king [for it] after the death of Godric, his uncle, who had the custody of it. There is land for 1½ ploughs. It was then, as now, assessed at half a hide. There are 2 villans and 5 bordars with 1½ ploughs, and 4 acres of meadow, and the fourth part of a mill rendering 5s. TRE, and afterwards, it was worth 12s; now 15s.

The sons of Godric Mal hold HANGER. Their father held it of King Edward. It was then, as now, assessed at 1 hide. There is land for 1 plough. There are 2 villans and 5 bordars with 1 plough, and 1 acre of meadow, and woodland for 1 pig. It was worth 20s; now 10s.

IN KINGSCLERE HUNDRED

ALWINE White holds 2 hides. He himself held them TRE. They were then assessed at 2 hides; now at half a hide. There is land for 1½ ploughs. There is 1 plough and 2 slaves; [and] 1 villan and 1 bordar with half a plough. It was worth 40s; now 30s. This Alwine held this land TRE under the protection of Vigot. He now holds the same [land] under Miles, and it was delivered by Humphrey Visdeloup to Vigot, in exchange for Broadwater [Sussex], as he himself says; but the hundred knows nothing of this.

EDWIN the huntsman holds 2 hides of the king's farm. King Edward gave them to him. They were then, as now, assessed at 1 virgate. There is land for 2 ploughs. In demesne is 1 plough; and 2 villans and 5 bordars with 1 plough. There are 2 slaves, and 3 acres of meadow. It is and was worth 18s.

RAVELIN holds KINGSCLERE of the king. He himself held it TRE, and it was then assessed at 3 hides and half a virgate; now at 2 hides. There is land for 5 ploughs. In demesne are 2 [ploughs]; and 3 villans and 18 bordars with 3 ploughs. There are 4 slaves, and a mill rendering 50d, and 3 acres of meadow. For the herbage, 6s2d. It is and was worth 65s.

LEOFWINE holds 1 virgate of the king in KINGSCLERE. He himself held it TRE; and it was then, as now, assessed at as much. There is land for half a plough, and there is [half a plough] with 1 slave, and 2 acres of meadow, and woodland for fencing. It is worth 5s.

The same Leofwine holds 1 hide in HANNINGTON. Æstan held it in parage of King Edward. It was then, as now, assessed at 1 hide. There is land for 1 plough. There is 1 villan, 2 bordars [and] 3 slaves with half a plough. It is and was worth 20s.

IN SOMBORNE HUNDRED

EALDRÆD, Oda's brother, holds half a hide of the king. He himself held it of King Edward; and it was then assessed at half a hide; now at 1 virgate. There is land for 1 plough. In demesne [is] half a plough; with 1 villan and 1 bordar and half a plough, and 2 acres of meadow. It is and was worth 6s.

ALMÆR holds half a hide of the king. Alwig held it of King Edward. It was then assessed at half a hide; now at 1 virgate. There is land for 1 plough. There are 3 bordars, and 1 acre of meadow. It is and was worth 5s.

WULFRIC the huntsman holds 1 manor of the king. His father held it of King Edward. It was then assessed at 1½ hides of land; now at 1 hide. There is land for 2 ploughs. In demesne is 1 [plough]; and 3 villans and 2 bordars with 1 plough. There are 12 acres of meadow. It is and was worth 20s.

IN BASINGSTOKE HUNDRED

ALSIGE the †chamberlain† holds STEVENTON of the king. Ælfhelm held it of King Edward. 5 hides were reckoned [to be there]; but it was then, and is now, assessed at 3 hides. There is land for 5 ploughs. In demesne are 2 [ploughs]; and 5 villans and 3 bordars with 2 ploughs, and 8 slaves. TRE it was worth 100s; and afterwards 70s; now £4.

GODWINE the falconer holds half a hide of the king. The same man held it of King Edward. It was then, as now, assessed at half a hide. It is and was worth 4s.

IN REDBRIDGE HUNDRED

ALWINE holds MARCHWOOD of the king. Wulfgeat his father held it. It was then, as now, assessed at half a hide. There is land for 1 plough. There 2 villans and 2 bordars have 1½ ploughs, and 2 acres of meadow. [There is] woodland rendering 8d. It was worth 10s; now 15s.

EDMUND son of Pain holds 1 virgate in DURLEY of the king, and Hugh [holds] of him. Sæwulf held it of King Edward in parage. There are 2 villans with 1 plough, and half an acre of meadow. [There was] woodland for 6 pigs; but it is not [there]. It was worth 10s; now 3s.

COLA the huntsman holds half a hide of his father Wulfgeat, in LANGLEY. He held this of the king in parage. It was then assessed at half a hide, now at the fourth part of a virgate. There is land for half a plough, and there is [half a plough] in demesne with 1 bordar, and half an acre of meadow. [There is] woodland for 5 pigs. It is and was worth 6s.

ÆLFRIC the Little holds 1 virgate in THE FOREST. A colibert held it at farm of the king; and now Ælfric claims this of the Bishop of Saintes. It was then, as now, assessed at 1 virgate. There is land for 1 plough. It was worth 6s; now 12s.

EDMUND holds STONE of the king. Sæwine and Almær held it in parage, and each had a hall. It was then, as now, assessed at half a hide. There is land for 2 ploughs. There is 1 bordar only. TRE it was worth 60s; and afterwards 10s; now 5s.

IN 'ROWDITCH' HUNDRED

Hugh de Port holds 1½ hides in OLD MILTON, and William Orenet [holds] of him. Alwine held them in parage. There is land for 3 ploughs. In demesne is 1 [plough]; and 5 villans have there 2 ploughs. There is 1 slave, and 3½ acres of meadow. TRE, and afterwards, it was worth 40s; now 20s. TRE it was assessed at 1½ hides; now at 1 hide. The woodland of this manor, for 20 pigs, the king has in his forest; it is worth 20s.

IN REDBRIDGE HUNDRED

HUGH de St Quentin holds LANGLEY, through the Bishop of Bayeux, as he says, in exchange for a mill, which he had of a man. 4 alodiaries held it in parage TRE. Then, as now, [it was assessed] at 1 hide. There is land for 2 ploughs. There are 6 villans and 7 bordars with 2 ploughs. TRE, and afterwards, it was worth 20s; now 30s.

IN 'ROWDITCH' HUNDRED

Hugh Latimer holds 1 hide and 1 virgate of the king in ARNEWOOD. Siward held it of Earl Tosti. It was then assessed at 1 hide and 1 virgate; now at nothing. There is land for 3 ploughs. There 1 villan and 9 bordars have 1 plough, and 5 acres of meadow. TRE and afterwards, as now, worth 30s; what is in the forest, 4s.

IN FORDINGBRIDGE HUNDRED

The king holds CANTERTON [Canterton and Upper Canterton] in his forest. Cynna held it of King Edward; and he is still there. It then paid geld for half a virgate; and now for 1 ferding. The other ferding is in the king's forest. In demesne is half a plough with 4 bordars. The woodland and meadow are in the forest. TRE it was worth 20s; now [what] Cynna [holds], 4s; [what] the king [holds], 16s.

In NEATHAM Hundred Godwine held [?West] Worldham TRE, and it paid geld for 1 hide and 1 virgate. The same Godwine held, in the same hundred, Holybourne, and it paid geld for 2 hides. There is land for 2 ploughs. The value of both lands [is] 40s.

[Folio 51: HAMPSHIRE]

In the New Forest and [...] Around It

IN REDBRIDGE HUNDRED

THE KING had, and has, 1 hide in "ACHELIE", and it belongs to the farm of the Isle of Wight. Cypping held it in parage. It was then assessed at 1 hide; now at nothing. There is land for 4 ploughs. TRE, and afterwards, it was worth 50s. It is now in the forest. The king put it there.

II. Bishop WALKELIN had 1 hide and 3 virgates of land in FAWLEY, and it paid geld for as much; now for nothing. There is land for 12 ploughs. TRE, and afterwards, it was worth 50s; it is now in the forest.

IN BOLDRE HUNDRED

The same bishop had 'THROUGHAM' [in Beaulieu] in demesne, and it belonged to the monastery. It was assessed at 2½ hides. There is land for 4 ploughs. TRE, and afterwards, it was worth 60s; it is now in the forest.

The same bishop had "SCLIVE" in demesne, and it always belonged to the monastery. It was assessed at 3 hides. There is land for 8 ploughs. TRE, and afterwards, it was worth £10. It is now in the forest, except the meadow, which the man who held the manor still holds. There are 8 acres of meadow.

III. Earl ROGER had "LESTEORDE". 2 alodiaries held it in parage, and this land was assessed at 1 hide. TRE, and afterwards, it was worth 40s. It is now in the forest, except the fourth part of a virgate, which a certain man holds of the earl, and there he has 3 bordars. It is worth 3s.

The earl himself holds 1 hide in SWAY, and Folcwine [holds] of him. Alfred held it in parage. It was then assessed at 1 hide; now at 3 virgates; and the fourth virgate is in the forest. There is land for 1 plough in the manor. There 4 bordars have half a plough, and 1 acre of meadow. TRE and afterwards, as now, worth 9s; what the king has, 2s.

The earl himself has 1 hide in SWAY, and Nigel [holds] of him. Durand held it in parage. It was then assessed at 1 hide; now at 1 virgate; the other [virgates] are in the forest. There 2 villans have 1 plough, and [there is] half an acre of meadow. It was worth 20s; now 5s; what the king has, 15s.

The earl himself has 1 hide in SOUTH BADDESLEY, and Durand [holds] of him. Swærting held it in parage. It was then assessed at 1 hide; now at 1 virgate; the other [virgates] are in the forest. There is land for 1 plough. There 1 villan and 3 bordars have 1 plough. It is worth 3s.

The earl himself has 1 hide in "OSELEI", and Nigel [holds] of him. Sælida held it in parage. It was then assessed at 1 hide. It is now in the forest, except 1 acre of meadow, which Nigel holds. It was worth 40s.

The earl himself holds 1 hide in "OSELEI", and Folcwine [holds] of him. Godwine held it in parage. It was then assessed at 1 hide; it is now in the forest, 2 acres of meadow excepted. There was land for 2 ploughs, and it was worth 20s.

The earl himself had 'THROUGHAM' [in Beaulieu] [as] 2 manors, and William [held] of him. Kolgrimr and Eadwig held it in parage; and it was assessed at 2½ hides. The whole [is] now in the forest. There was land for 4 ploughs. It was worth 60s.

The earl himself holds half a hide in WALHAMPTON, and Folcwine [holds] of him. Alnoth held it in parage. [It was] then [assessed] at half a hide; now at 1 virgate. There is land for 1 plough, and there is [1 plough] in demesne; with 1 bordar and 1 slave. TRE it was worth 15s; and afterwards, as now, 10s. The woodland in the forest and is worth 4s.

The earl himself holds 1 hide in LYMINGTON, and Folcwine [holds] of him. Lyfing held it in parage. [It was] then [assessed] at 1 hide; now at half [a hide], because the woodland is in the forest. There is land for 2 ploughs. There 1 villan, 2 slaves, [and] 3 bordars have 1 plough, and 4 acres of meadow. TRE it was worth 20s; and afterwards, as now, 15s.

The earl himself has half a hide in HINTON [Hinton and Hinton Admiral], and Folcwine [holds] of him. Wulfwig held it in parage. [It was] then [assessed] at half a hide; now at 1½ virgates, because the other [half-virgate] is in the forest. There is land for 1 plough, and there is [1 plough] with 3 villans, and 1½ acres of meadow. It is and was worth 15s; what the king has, 3s.

The earl himself has 5½ virgates in ASHLEY, and Nigel [holds] of him. Sæwulf held them in parage. It was then assessed at 5½ virgates; now at 4½ virgates, [bacause] 1 virgate is in the forest. There is land for 3 ploughs, and there is [1 plough] in demesne; and 2 villans and 10 bordars with 2 ploughs, and 5½ acres of meadow. It was worth 50s; now 20s; what the king has, 6s.

The earl himself has 7 virgates in BARTON ON SEA, and Durand [holds] of him. Ælfric held them of King Edward. [They were] then [assessed] at 7 virgates; now at 5 virgates, because the other [virgates] are in the forest. There is land for 3 ploughs. In demesne is 1 [plough]; and 3 villans and 3 bordars have 2 ploughs. There are 2 slaves. TRE it was worth 40s; and afterwards 30s; now 20s; what the king has, 6s.

The earl himself has 1 hide in BARTON ON SEA, and Durand [holds] of him. Wulfweard held it in parage. [It was] then [assessed] at 1 hide; now at half [a hide], [because] the other [half] is in the forest. There is land for 1 plough, and there is [1 plough] in demesne, with 1 bordar, and half an acre of meadow. It was worth 20s; now 10s; what the king has, 6s.

The earl himself has 1 hide in HINTON [Hinton and Hinton Admiral], and Nigel [holds] of him. Eadric held it in parage. [It was] then [assessed] at 1 hide; now at 3 virgates, [because] 1 [virgate] is in the forest. There is land for 3 ploughs. There 6 villans have 2 ploughs, and 6 acres of meadow. It is and was worth 15s; what the king has, 3s.

The earl himself has 1 hide in BECKLEY, and Nigel [holds] of him. Holmger held it in parage. [It was] then [assessed] at 1 hide; now at 3 virgates, [because] 1 virgate is in the forest. There is land for 4 ploughs. There 4 villans have 2 ploughs, and 4 acres of meadow. It was worth 20s; now 15s; what the king has, 5s.

The earl himself holds the third part of a hide in FERNHILL, and Nigel holds of the earl. Godric held it in parage. It was then assessed at 3 virgates; now at 1 virgate; [because] the other [virgates] are in the forest. There is land for 1 plough, and there is [1 plough] with 1 villan. It was worth 13s; now 10s; what the king holds, 3s.

IN 'ROWDITCH' HUNDRED

IIII. WILLIAM de EU holds 1 manor, and Bernard [holds] of him. Cuthwulf held it of King Edward. It was then assessed at 2 hides; now at 5 virgates. There is land for 3 ploughs. There 3 villans and 2 bordars have 2 ploughs, and 6 acres of meadow. TRE, and afterwards, it was worth 40s; now 30s. The king has 1 virgate, with the woodland; it is worth 5s.

V. RALPH de Mortimer holds HORDLE, and Oidelard [holds] of him. Iusten held it of King Edward. [It was] then [assessed] at 5 hides; now at 4 hides; the fifth is in the forest. There is land for 5 ploughs. There 6 villans and 9 bordars have 4 ploughs. There is a mill, and 6 salt-pans rendering 15d. TRE it was worth £8; and afterwards 100s; and now the same. The king holds the woodland, where 6 men dwelt, in [his] forest; it is worth 60s.

VI. HUGH de Port holds 1 [...]½ virgates in PILLEY, and Hugh de St Quentin [holds] of him. Algar held it in parage. It was then assessed at 1½ virgates; now at nothing, because it is all in the forest, 1½ acres of meadow excepted. There was land for 1 plough. It was worth 10s.

The same Hugh holds 1 hide in 'THROUGHAM' [in Beaulieu], and Hugh de St Quentin [holds] of him. Wihtlac held it in parage. [It was] then [assessed] at 1 hide; now at nothing, because it is all, 1 acre of meadow excepted, in the forest. There was land for 2 ploughs. It was worth 30s.

EDWARD of Salisbury holds 2 hides in ALLUM, and Robert [holds] of him. 2 alodiaries held these in parage. [They were] then [assessed] at 2 hides; now at nothing, because they are all, 12 acres of meadow excepted, in the forest. There was land for 4 ploughs. It was worth 100s.

RANULPH Flambard holds 1 hide of the king in "BILE". Alweald held it in parage. It was then assessed at 1 hide; now at nothing, because it is all, 4 acres of meadow excepted, in the forest.

The same Ranulph held 1 hide in the vill himself; and it was assessed TRE at as much. It is now all, except 4 acres of meadow, in the forest. There was land for 4 ploughs. These 2 estates were worth £4.

The same Ranulph holds 1 hide of the king in [?]BATCHLEY. 2 alodiaries held it. [It was] then [assessed] at 1 hide; now at 3 virgates. There is land for 2 ploughs. There 3 villans have 1 plough, and 2½ acres of meadow. It was worth 15s; now 4s, and [there is] a mill rendering 30d.

IN REDBRIDGE HUNDRED

Hugh fitzOsmund holds 1 hide of the king in HARFORD. Ælfric held it in parage. [It was] then [assessed] at 1 hide; now at nothing, because it is in the forest. There was land for 4 ploughs. It was worth 25s.

[Folio 51V: HAMPSHIRE]

IN REDBRIDGE HUNDRED

ODA holds DIBDEN of the king. Ketil held it of King Edward. It was then assessed at 5 hides; now at 2 hides, and it pays geld for 1 only, because 3 hides are in the forest. There is land for 4 ploughs. There are 4 villans and 15 bordars with 5 ploughs. There are 9 acres of meadow, woodland for 6 pigs, a salt-pan and a fishery. TRE it was worth £10; and afterwards £8; now 50s; and yet it renders 100s.

PAIN holds of the king 1 hide and 1 virgate in 'BUCK-HOLT'. Sæwine held it in parage. It was assessed at 5 virgates. It is now in the forest. There is land for 6 ploughs. It was worth 100s.

THURBERT the huntsman had 1 hide in OTTERWOOD, and it was assessed at as much. It is now in the forest. Land for 2 ploughs. It was worth 21s.

Two alodiaries had half a hide in 'NUTLEY' [in Fawley]. Land for 2 ploughs. It was worth 25s.

ÆLFRIC and 2 alodiaries had 1 hide and 1 virgate in OTTERWOOD; and they were assessed at as much. It is now in the forest. Land for 3 ploughs. It was worth 30s.

GODRIC and Alnoth had 2 hides in GATEWOOD; and they were assessed at as much. It is now in the forest. Land for 5 ploughs. It was worth 45s.

BOLLA and Wulfgeat had 2 hides in EXBURY; and they were assessed at as much. It is now in the forest. It was worth 40s.

GODRIC and Aghmund [held] 1 hide in ROLLSTONE in parage; and it was assessed at as much. It is now in the forest. Land for 2 ploughs. It was worth 15s.

BERNARD Pauncevolt [held] 3 virgates, and Sæwine 1 hide, in HARDLEY; and they were assessed at as much. It is now in the forest. Land for 2 ploughs. It was worth 30s.

IN 'EDGEGATE' HUNDRED

Sæwulf's wife holds HOBURNE of the king. Sæwulf held it of the king. It was then assessed at 1 hide; now at 1 virgate. There is land for 1 plough. There are 2 bordars, and 6 acres of meadow. It was worth 20s; now 15s. In the same HUNDRED Wihtlac has 4 acres of meadow, and Ælfric the physician 4 acres.

IN RINGWOOD HUNDRED

BERNARD the chamberlain holds HARBRIDGE of the king. Wulfgifu held it. It was then assessed at 5 hides; now at 3 hides and 1 virgate. There is land for 4 ploughs. In demesne is 1 [plough]; and 8 villans and 2 bordars with 4 ploughs, and 80 acres of meadow. [There is] woodland for 2 pigs. TRE it was worth £4.10s; and afterwards, as now, 70s.

IN BOLDRE HUNDRED

BOLLA had half a hide of the king in GRITNAM. Waleran the huntsman was holding it recently, and it was assessed at 1 hide. It is now in the forest. It was worth 40s.

CYPPING held 3 virgates of the king in "ACHELIE", and they were assessed at as much. It is now in the forest. It was worth 40s.

WIHTLAC held 1 hide of the king in BOLDERFORD. It is now in the forest, except 2 acres of meadow, which Hugh de St Quentin holds. It was worth £10.

EADRIC had 1 hide of the king in PILLEY; and it was assessed at as much. It is now in the forest, except 6 acres of meadow, which Hugh de St Quentin holds. It was worth 30s.

ÆLFRIC had 'WYGESTON' [in Beaulieu] of the king in parage. It was assessed at 1 hide. It is now in the forest, except 1 acre of meadow, which the same Ælfric holds. There was land for 2 ploughs. It was worth 5s.

PAIN held 2 manors called BOLDRE. 2 alodiaries held them in parage. They were then assessed at 2 hides. It is now in the forest, except 6 acres of meadow, which Hugh de St Quentin holds. There was land for 4 ploughs. It was worth £3.

BEORHTSIGE had [?] 'CHILDENHURST' [in Brockenhurst] of the king in parage. It was assessed at 5 hides. It is now in the forest, except 2 acres of meadow, which Ælfric the Little holds. There was land for 8 ploughs. It was worth £8.

ÆLFRIC the Little had 1 hide and 2 virgates in parage in 'THROUGHAM' [in Beaulieu] and they were assessed at as much. It is now in the forest. Land for 4 ploughs. It was worth £4.

HUNTA had 1 hide in 'THROUGHAM' [in Beaulieu], and it was assessed at as much. It is now in the forest. There is land for 3 ploughs. It was worth 30s.

SÆWINE had 1 virgate in the same HUNDRED, and it never paid geld. It is now in the forest, except 1 acre of meadow, which Hugh de St Quentin holds. It was worth 12d.

SÆWULF and ÆLFRIC had 2 hides in BATTRAMSLEY, and they were assessed at as much. It is now in the forest, except 4 acres of meadow, which Sæwulf holds. [There is] land for 5 ploughs. It was worth £3. There Peret the forester holds half a virgate of the king.

SÆWULF had half a hide in "SANHEST", and it was assessed at as much. It is now in the forest. Land for 2 ploughs. It was worth 20s.

HUNTA and Pain held 2½ virgates in parage, and they were assessed at as much. It is now in the forest, except 1 acre of meadow which Ælfric holds. Land for 2 ploughs. It was worth 20s.

ÆLFRIC had half a hide in PILLEY, and it was assessed at as much. It is now in the forest, except 3 acres of meadow, which the same Ælfric holds. Land for 2 ploughs. It was worth 15s.

ÆLFRIC and Aghmund held 3 virgates of land in FOXLEASE [High Coxlease and Foxlease]. It is now in the forest. Land for 2 ploughs. It was worth £3.

Two alodiaries held 1 virgate in "NUTLEI" in parage, and it was assessed at as much. It is now in the forest. There is land for 1 plough. It was worth 6s.

EADNOTH had 2 hides in parage in 'BROOKLEY' [in Brockenhurst] and "Mapleham", and they were assessed at 2 hides. It is now in the forest. Land for †6† ploughs. It was worth 20s.

WIHTLAC held half a hide in HINCHESLEA, and it was assessed at as much. It is now in the forest. Land for 2 ploughs. It was worth 20s.

IN 'ROWDITCH' HUNDRED

GODRIC held WOOTTON [in Milton] of the king. [It was] then [assessed] at 1 hide. It is now in the forest, except 15 acres of meadow, which Godric holds. Land for 2 ploughs. It was worth 40s.

WIHTLAC and Ælfric held in parage 2 hides in "OXELEI". Bolla held them. [They were] then [assessed] at 2 hides. It is now in the forest, except 4 acres of meadow, which they themselves hold. There was land for 4 ploughs. It was worth 40s.

WULFRIC has 1 virgate of land in "GODESMANESCAMP". Then, as now, it was assessed at 1 virgate. There is land for 1 plough, and there is [1 plough] in demesne. It is and was worth 4s.

WULFGAR has of the king 1 virgate of land in MILFORD ON SEA. He himself held it of King Edward, and it was then assessed at 1 virgate; now at 3 parts of a virgate. There is nothing there; and yet it is worth 3s. The king has the woodland in the forest; it is worth 12d.

The sons of Godric Malf hold 1 hide in ASHLEY. Their father held it of the king. [It was] then [assessed] at 1 hide; now at 1 virgate. There is land for 1 plough. There are 3 slaves, and 1 slave and 2 bordars with half a plough, and 4 acres of meadow. TRE, and afterwards, it was worth 20s; now 15s.

The king holds the woodland of this manor, for 8 pigs, in his forest; and it is worth 5s.

ÆLFRIC holds MILFORD ON SEA of the king, in exchange for [land in] the forest. Sæwulf held it of King Edward. It was then assessed at 1 hide; and now at half [a hide], because part [of] the church is in the forest. Land for 1 plough. In demesne is 1 plough; and 4 villans and 6 slaves with 1 plough, and a mill rendering 30d, and 2 acres of meadow. TRE it was worth 20s; and afterwards 10s; now 20s; the king's part, 10s.

The same Ælfric holds half a hide in EFFORD. His father held it in parage. It was then assessed at half a hide; and now the same. Land for 2 ploughs, and there are [2 ploughs] with 3 villans, and a mill which a certain keeper of the king's house holds. It was worth 5s; now 10s.

The same Ælfric holds 1½ virgates in "UTEFEL". Lyfing and Ketil held them. Ælfric bought them of them TRW. They were then, as now, assessed at 1½ virgates. There are 2 villans with half a plough. It is and was worth 5s.

The same Ælfric holds 3 virgates of land, and Alweald [holds] of him. He himself held them of King Edward. Then, as now, they were assessed at 3 virgates. There is land for 1 plough. There is [1 plough] with 1 villan and 3 bordars, and 1 acre of meadow. [There is] woodland for 4 pigs; but it is in the forest. It is and was worth 10s; what is in the forest [is worth] 4s.

The same Ælfric holds 1 hide in BROCKENHURST. His father and uncle held it in parage. [It was] then [assessed] at 1 hide; now at half [a hide]. There is land for 1 plough. In demesne is 1 plough; and 6 bordars and 4 slaves with 2½ ploughs. There is a church, [and] woodland for 20 pigs. TRE it was worth 40s; and afterwards, as now, £4.

EDMUND holds 1 hide in SWAY. Algar held it of King Edward. It was then, as now, assessed at 1 virgate. There is land for 2 ploughs, and there are [2 ploughs] with 5 bordars. There are 2 acres of meadow. TRE, and afterwards, it was worth 10s; now 15s.

The sons of Godric Malf have MINSTEAD of the king. Their father held it of King Edward. It was then assessed at 3½ hides. His sons have now only half a hide, which has paid geld for 1 virgate. The other land is in the forest. There is land for 1 plough, and there is [1 plough] in demesne, with 4 bordars and 3 slaves, and 16 acres of meadow. [There is] woodland for 10 pigs, and 1 close in Winchester rendering 12d. This land TRE was worth £8; and afterwards 15s; now 20s.

The same men themselves hold BISTERNE of the king. Their father held it in parage of King Edward. [It was] then [assessed] at 3 hides. There are now 2 hides, and they have paid geld for 1½ hides. The third hide is in the forest. There is land for 3 ploughs. In demesne is 1 [plough]; and 5 villans and 4 bordars have 2 ploughs. There are 32 acres of meadow, [and] woodland for 20 pigs. It is worth 60s; now 40[s].

The same men themselves hold 2 hides in CROW of the king. Their father held them of King Edward. [They were] then, as now, [assessed] at 2 hides. There is land for 2 ploughs, and there are [2 ploughs] with 4 villans and 5 bordars, and 36 acres of meadow. TRE it was worth 40s; and afterwards, as now, 25s.

[Folio 52: HAMPSHIRE]

IN THE BOROUGH OF SOUTHAMPTON the king has in demesne 80 less 4 men, who pay £7 for land-rent and they paid as much TRE. Of these, 27 pay 8d each, 2 [pay] 12d, and the others, 50 in number, pay 6d each.

These had quit land in the borough itself TRE from the king himself: Oda of Winchester; Eskil the priest; Ketil; Fugel; Tosti; the sons of Alric had 16 acres, Gerin 18 acres; Cypping had 3 houses quit, and now Ralph de Mortimer holds them; and Godwine 3 houses: Bernard Pauncevolt holds these. After King William came into England, there have been settled in Southampton 65 Frenchmen, and 31 Englishmen. These all pay between them £4.0s6d for all customary dues.

The following have the customary dues from their houses in Southampton by grant of King William: Bishop Geoffrey, from 1 house; the Abbot of Cormeilles 1; the Abbot of Lyre 1; the Count of Evreux 2; Ralph de Mortimer 2; Gilbert de Breteuil 2; William fitzStur 2; Ralph de Tosny 1; Durand of Gloucester 2; Hugh de Port 1; Hugh de Grandmesnil 2; the Count of Mortain 5; Aiulf the chamberlain 5; Humphrey his brother 1; Osbern Giffard 1; Nigel the physician 4; Richer de les Andelys 4; Richard Puignant 1; Stephen the steersman 2; Turstin the chamberlain 2; Turstin the engineer 2; Ansketil fitzOsmund 3; Reginald Croch 1. The Abbess of Wherwell has 1 fishery and a little land. It then rendered 100d; now 10s.

The land of the King In the Isle of Wight

IN BOWCOMBE HUNDRED

King WILLIAM holds BROOK in demesne. Earl Tosti held it. [It was] then [assessed] at 3 hides; now at 1 hide. There is land for 6 ploughs. In demesne are 2 ploughs; and 3 villans and 7 bordars with 2½ ploughs. There are 9 slaves, and a mill rendering 15d, and 6 acres of meadow. TRE it was worth £7; and afterwards £6; now £7; and yet it renders £7 more.

The king himself holds COMPTON in demesne. Earl Tosti held it. It was then assessed at 3 hides; now at 1 hide. There is land for 4 ploughs. In demesne is 1 [plough]; and 7 villans and 3 bordars with 2 ploughs. There is 1 slave, and 2 acres of meadow. TRE it was worth £6; and afterwards, as now, 100s; yet it renders 60s. more.

The king himself holds AFTON in demesne. Earl Tosti held it. [It was] then [assessed] at 4 hides; now at 3 hides less 1 virgate. There is land for 8 ploughs. In demesne are 2 [ploughs]; and 14 villans and 8 bordars with 6 ploughs. There are 12 slaves, and 6 acres of meadow. TRE it was worth £10; and afterwards, as now, £8; yet it renders £10.

The king himself holds WELLOW in demesne. Cuthwulf held it in parage of the king. [It was] then [assessed] at 2 hides; now at 3 virgates. There is land for 4 ploughs. In demesne are 2 [ploughs]; and 6 villans and 3 bordars with 1½ ploughs.

There are 4 slaves, and 6 acres of meadow. TRE and afterwards, as now, worth £10; yet it is at farm for £15.

The king himself holds FRESHWATER in demesne. Earl Tosti held it. It was then assessed at 15 hides; now at 6 hides. There is land for 15 ploughs. In demesne are 2 ploughs; and 18 villans and 10 bordars with 8 ploughs. There are 7 slaves, and 6 acres of meadow. TRE it was worth £16; and afterwards £20; yet it is at farm for £30.

Of these 15 hides the Abbey of Lyre holds 3 virgates, and William fitzAzor 1 hide.

The same king holds WILMINGHAM in demesne. Wulfgeat the huntsman held it in parage. Then, as now, [it was assessed] at 1 hide. There is land for 1 plough. There are 3 villans with 2 ploughs, and half an acre of meadow. It is and was worth 20s.

Of this manor of the king, Reginald fitzCroch holds 1 virgate, and says that Earl Roger gave it to his father. It was worth 5s; now it is waste.

The king himself holds BOWCOMBE in demesne. It belonged to King Edward's farm. It was then assessed at 4 hides; now at nothing. There is land for 15 ploughs. In demesne are 3 ploughs; and 25 villans and 15 bordars with 15 ploughs. There are 10 slaves, and 8 acres of meadow, and a mill rendering 40d. From a toll, 30s, and [there is] a salt-pan without rent, [and] woodland for 5 pigs.

Of the land of this manor William fitzStur holds half a virgate. There is 1 plough with 1 villan. It is worth 10s. Joscelin and William his brother hold 1 virgate, which before them rendered rent; but these men have not paid it.

The monks of Lyre hold the church of this manor, with 1 virgate of land.

Of this virgate of land Humphrey holds a portion where he has 8 men paying 5s, and William fitzAzor 2½ acres where he has 4 houses. They hold without the consent of the priest. There belong to this church 20 bordars' messuages, and they render 14s. There is a mill rendering 6s, and all the tithes of Bowcombe belong to this church. The whole, TRE and afterwards, as now, worth £20; what the abbot has, £4.

The same king holds 'HALDLEY' [in Carisbrooke] in demesne. Cypping held it of King Edward. It was then assessed at 6 virgates; now at 2 virgates less 1 ferding. There is land for 3 ploughs. In demesne is 1 [plough]; and 4 villans and 1 bordar have 2 ploughs. [There is] woodland for 2 pigs, and 5 slaves. It is worth £3.

[Folio 52V: HAMPSHIRE]

The king himself holds LUTON. Wulfgeat the huntsman held it in parage. [It was] then [assessed] at 1 hide; now at half [a hide]. There is land for 2 ploughs. There 4 villans and 2 bordars have 2 ploughs. There are 2 slaves, [and] woodland for fencing. It is and was worth 20s.

The same king holds SHIDE. Ketil held it in parage. [It was] then [assessed] at 1½ hides; now at 1 [hide] only. There is land for 4 ploughs. In demesne is 1 [plough]; and 5 villans and 8 bordars with 3 ploughs. There is 1 slave, and 4 mills rendering 12s6d, and 4 acres of meadow, [and] woodland for fencing. It is and was worth £4. William fitzStur pays for these aforesaid 4 manors £60, although they are worth less.

The same king holds SHORWELL. 3 thegns held it in parage, and they had 3 halls. [It was] then [assessed] at 1½ hides; now at 3 virgates. There is land for 3 ploughs. In demesne are 1½ ploughs; and 2 villans and 8 bordars with 1 plough. There are 6 slaves, [and] woodland for fencing. It is and was worth £4.

The same king holds 3 manors, ATHERFIELD [Atherfield and Atherfield Green], DUNGEWOOD, [and] WALPAN. 3 thegns held them. [They were] then [assessed] at 3 hides; now at 1 hide. There is land for 3 ploughs. In demesne are 2 [ploughs]; and 1 villan and 10 bordars with 2 ploughs. There are 4 slaves, and 6 acres of meadow. It is and was worth £3; yet it renders £7.

The same king holds KINGSTON. Wulfric held it in parage. [It was] then [assessed] at 1 hide; now at 1 virgate. There is land for 2 ploughs. There 6 bordars have 1 plough. There are 4 acres of meadow. It is and was worth 20s; yet it renders 30s.

The same king holds ALVINGTON. Dunna held it. [It was] then [assessed] at 2½ hides; now at 2 hides, because the castle stands on 1 virgate. There is land for 6 ploughs. There are 8 villans and 2 bordars with 4 ploughs. There are 2 mills rendering 5s, and 6 acres of meadow. It is and was worth £3; yet it renders £4.

IN CALBOURNE HUNDRED, WHICH LIES IN BOWCOMBE HUNDRED

II. WALKELIN, Bishop of Winchester, holds CALBOURNE in demesne. It always belonged to the monastery. There are 32 hides; but it only paid geld TRE, as now, for 17 hides. There is land for 25 ploughs. In demesne are 6 ploughs; and 27 villans and 15 bordars with 14 ploughs. There are 11 slaves, and 2 mills rendering 6s3d, and 8 acres of meadow, [and] woodland for 20 pigs.

Of this land Robert holds 6 hides, Herpul 2 hides, and Alsige 3½ hides. 7 alodiaries held these hides of the bishop, and could not withdraw elsewhere or from him. There are 3½ ploughs; and 3 villans and 22 bordars with 5 ploughs. There are 12 slaves, and 15 acres of meadow. Mauger holds the church of this manor, with half a hide, and there he has 1 plough with 1 bordar.

The whole manor, TRE and afterwards, was worth £16. Now what the bishop has [is worth] £30; and yet it is at farm for £40, but it cannot bear nor render it. What the men hold [is worth] £7; [what] the church [holds], 30s.

III. What St Nicholas Holds

ST NICHOLAS has of King William 1 hide in SHALCOMBE. Alwine Forst held it. It was then assessed at 1 hide; now at nothing. There is land for 2 ploughs, and there are [2 ploughs] in demesne, with 1 bordar. It was worth £4; now £3.

IIII. What Saint-Marie of Lyre Holds

The Abbey of SAINT-MARIE of Lyre has in the Isle of Wight 6 churches, to which belong 2 hides and $2\frac{1}{2}$ virgates of land; and in various manors they have 5 villans, who hold $1\frac{1}{2}$ hides less the fourth part of a virgate. They have the tithes of all the king's revenues. All that they have is valued at £20. It pays geld for 2 hides and half a virgate of land.

V. The land of St Mary of Wilton

THE ABBEY of Wilton holds [Lower and Upper] WATCHINGWELL. It always belonged to the monastery. TRE it was assessed at 3 hides; now at $2\frac{1}{2}$ hides, because half [a hide] is in the king's park. There is land for 8 ploughs. There 7 villans and 12 bordars have 5 ploughs. There is a salt-pan without rent, [and] woodland for 2 pigs. The meadow is in the park. It is and was worth £3; what the king has [is worth] 5s.

VI. The land of William fitzStur

IN BOWCOMBE HUNDRED

WILLIAM fitzStur holds CHALE in demesne of the king. Ketil was [sic] in parage. [It was] then [assessed] at 1 hide; now at 1 virgate. There is land for 1 plough, and there is [1 plough], with 4 bordars having 1 plough. There are 4 slaves, and 1 acre of meadow. TRE, as now, worth 40s; when received, 20s.

The same William holds GOTTEN. Bruning and his brother held it in parage. It was then, as now, assessed at 1 hide. There is land for 1 plough. There is [1 plough], with 2 bordars and 3 acres of meadow. It is and was worth 20s.

The same William holds [Great, North or Upper] APPLEFORD, and Robert [holds] of him. Ketil held it in parage. It was then, as now, assessed at 1 hide. There is land for 2 ploughs. In demesne is half a plough; and 3 bordars with 1 plough. There are 4 acres of meadow. It was worth 17s; now 18s.

The same William holds GATCOMBE. 3 brothers held it in parage of King Edward. It was then assessed at 2 hides; now at 1 hide. Each had a hall. There is land for 4 ploughs. In demesne are 3 ploughs; and 6 villans and 15 bordars with 5 ploughs. There are 6 slaves, and a mill rendering 40d. There are 26 acres of meadow, [and] woodland for fencing. TRE, as now, worth £6; when received, 100s.

The same William holds GREAT WHITCOMBE. Godric held it in parage. [It was] then [assessed] at 1 hide; now at nothing. There is land for 1 plough. There is [1 plough] in demesne, with 3 bordars, and $2\frac{1}{2}$ acres of meadow. It was worth 10s; now 15s.

The same William holds CALBOURNE. Bolla held it in parage. It was then assessed at 3 hides less half a virgate; now at $1\frac{1}{2}$ virgates. There is land for 2 ploughs. In demesne are 2 ploughs; and 1 villan and 3 bordars with 1 plough. There are 3

slaves, and a mill rendering 5s, and $2\frac{1}{2}$ acres of meadow, [and] woodland for fencing. TRE, and afterwards, it was worth 30s; now 40s.

The same William holds WOLVERTON, and Juran [holds] of him. He himself held it in parage of King Edward. It was then, as now, assessed at 1 hide. There is land for 1 plough, and there is [1 plough] with 1 villan and 2 bordars, and a mill rendering 35d, and half an acre of meadow. It is and was worth 10s.

The same William holds half a hide in [? Little] ATHERFIELD, and Travers holds of William. Wulfgeat held this in parage. It was then, as now, assessed at half a hide. There is land for 1 plough, and there is [1 plough] in demesne, with 1 bordar, and $1\frac{1}{2}$ acres of meadow. It is worth 10s.

The same William holds CHEVERTON, and Humphrey [holds] of him. Thorkil held it in parage. [It was] then, as now, [assessed] at 1 hide. There is land for $1\frac{1}{2}$ ploughs. In demesne is 1 [plough]; and 3 villans and 1 bordar with 1 plough. [There is] woodland for fencing. It was worth 20s; now 30s.

In the same place, the same William has of the king 1 villan with half a virgate of land, and $1\frac{1}{2}$ acres of land which Reginald the baker held of Earl William. The earl's bakehouse was there. It is worth 16d; the villan pays 10s a year.

William fitzSTUR himself holds 'HARDLEY' [in Brading]. Godric held it of King Edward in alod. It was then assessed at 1 hide; now at half a virgate. There is 1 plough; and 3 bordars with half a plough, and 8 slaves. [There is] a small wood without pannage. It is and was worth 40s.

[Folio 53: HAMPSHIRE]

The same William holds "ORHAM". Godric held it of King Edward in alod. It then paid geld for half a hide; now for 1 virgate. There is land for 1 plough. In demesne are $1\frac{1}{2}$ ploughs; and 5 bordars with half a plough. It was worth 40s; now 20s.

The same William holds WHIPPINGHAM. Bolla held it of King Edward in alod. Then, as now, it paid geld for 1 hide. There is land [...]. In demesne is half a plough; and 3 villans and 2 bordars with 1 plough. It is and was worth 10s.

The same William holds WHITEFIELD [Whitefield or Little Whitefield], and Reginald [holds] of him. Ketil held it of King Edward in alod. Then, as now, it paid geld for 1 hide. There is land [...]. In demesne is 1 plough; and 1 villan and 3 bordars and 1 slave with half a plough. There is salt-pan rendering 14s8d, and 1 acre of meadow. It is worth 20s.

The same William holds another WHITEFIELD [Whitefield or Little Whitefield]. Godric held it of King Edward in alod. It then paid geld for 3 hides; now for 1 hide. There is land for 6 ploughs. In demesne are 4 ploughs; and 4 villans have 2 ploughs. There are 3 mills rendering 11s, and 8 acres of meadow. TRE it was worth £4; and afterwards £3; now £7.

The same William holds HALE, and Nigel [holds] of him. Godric held it of King Edward in alod. It then, as now, paid geld for half a hide. There is land for 1 plough. In demesne is 1 [plough]; and 1 villan and 4 bordars with 1 plough, and 4 acres of meadow. It is worth 10s.

The same William holds BINSTEAD. Tovi held it as a manor of King Edward in alod. It then paid geld for 5 virgates; now for 2 virgates. There is land for 2 ploughs. There are [2 ploughs] with 2 villans. It is and was worth 10s.

The same William holds MERSTONE, and Humphrey [holds] of him. Beorhtwine held it of King Edward in alod. It then, as now, paid geld for half a hide. In demesne is 1 plough, with 1 villan. It is and was worth 10s.

The same William holds PRESTON. Tovi held it of King Edward in alod. It then, as now, paid geld for 2 hides and 1½ virgates. There is land for 1 plough. There are 8 villans with 1 plough, and 4 acres of meadow, and a fishery for the hall. [There is] woodland for 1 pig. It is and was worth 20s.

The same William holds [Great of Little] EAST STANDEN, and Humphrey [holds] of him. Bolla held it of King Edward. It then, as now, paid geld for 1½ hides. There is land [...]. In demesne is 1 plough; and 2 villans and 3 bordars with 1 plough. It is and was worth 20s.

The same William holds MERSTONE. King Edward held it in demesne; it belonged to his farm, and did not pay geld. There is land for 1 plough. In demesne is 1 plough; and 2 villans and 1 bordar and 2 slaves with 1 plough. It is and was worth 20s.

The same William holds ALVERSTONE, and Tovi [holds] of him. He himself held it of King Edward. It then, as now, paid geld for 1 hide. There is land for 2 ploughs. There is 1 bordar, and a mill rendering 40d. It was worth 20s; now 5s.

VII. The land of William fitzAzor

WILLIAM fitzAzor holds BONCHURCH [Bonchurch and Upper Bonchurch] of the king. Æstan held it of Earl Godwine in alod as a manor. It then paid geld for 1 virgate; now for nothing. There is land for half a plough. There are 3 bordars. TRE it was worth 30s; and afterwards, as now, 20s.

The same William holds LOVERSTON. 2 free men held it of King Edward in alod. It then paid geld for half a hide; now for 1 virgate. There is land for 1 plough, and there is [1 plough] with 9 bordars. It was worth 40s; now 30s.

The same William holds [Great or Little] EAST STANDEN. 2 free men held it of King Edward in alod. It then paid geld for 5 virgates; now for 1 virgate. There is land for 2 ploughs. In demesne is 1 plough with 1 bordar. Of this land, a certain Peveral holds half a virgate, and there he has 1 plough. TRE it was worth 30s; and afterwards 15s; now the demesne of William [is worth] 40s; of Peverel 10s.

The same William holds GREAT BRIDDLESFORD, and Nigel [holds] of him. Olaf held it of King Edward in alod. It then, as now, paid geld for 1 hide. There is land for 4 ploughs. In demesne is 1 [plough]; and 5 villans and 5 bordars with 4 ploughs. It was worth 20s; now 40s.

The same William holds YAVERLAND. Almær and Swærting held it of King Edward in alod. It then paid geld for 3 hides; now for 1 virgate. There is land for 3 ploughs. In demesne is 1 plough with 8 bordars, and a mill rendering 12s. There are 1½ acres of meadow. It was worth £3; and afterwards £4; now 100s.

The same William holds SHANKLIN. Algar held it of King Edward. It then paid geld for 1 hide; now for 3 virgates. There is land for 1 plough. In demesne is half a plough; and 3 villans and 2 bordars and 2 slaves with 1 plough. [There is] woodland for 2 pigs. TRE, as now, worth 40s; when received, 20s.

The same William holds BRADING, and his nephew holds of him. Alnoth held it as a manor of King Edward in alod. It then, as now, paid geld for 3 parts of virgate. There is land for half a plough. In demesne is 1 plough, with 4 bordars, and 1 acre of meadow. [There is] woodland for 2 pigs. It was worth 10s; now 20s.

The same William holds BORTHWOOD, and BRANSTONE, and LESSLAND. 2 free men [held them] as 2 manors of King Edward in alod. Then, as now, they paid geld for 1 hide and 1 virgate. There is land for 2 ploughs; and it is [now all] in one manor. In demesne [is] 1 villan and 2 bordars with half a plough, and 2 acres of meadow. Of this land, William's nephew holds 1 virgate, and Peverel [holds] half a hide and 1 virgate. The whole TRE was worth 30s; and afterwards 20s; now 16s.

The same William holds 10 acres in BLACK PAN, and there is 1 bordar. It is worth 3s.

The same William holds "SCALDEFORD". Asgot held it of King Edward in alod. Then, as now, it paid geld for 1 virgate. There is land for 1 plough, and there is [1 plough], with 3 villans. [There is] woodland for 2 pigs. It was worth 16s; now 10s.

The same William holds "WITESTONE", and William and Richard [hold] of him. Almær held it of King Edward in alod. It then, as now, paid geld for 1 hide. There is land for 2 ploughs. In demesne is 1 [plough], with 3 villans. It was worth 30s; now 20s.

The same William holds BARNSLEY, and Roger [holds] of him. Wulfnoth held it of King Edward. Then, as now, it paid geld for half a hide. There is land for 1 plough. There is 1 bordar. It was worth 10s; now 7s.

The same William holds ROWBOROUGH. The Abbot of Winchester held it of King Edward in alod. Then, as now, it paid geld for 1 virgate. There is land for 1 plough. There is [1 plough] in demesne, with 1 villan with 2 bordars and half a plough. It was worth 5s; now 20s.

The same William holds MOOR, and Ansketil [holds] of him. 3 free men held it of King Edward. It then, as now, paid geld for half a hide. There is land for 1 plough. In demesne is 1 plough; and 5 bordars with half a plough. It was worth 30s; now 20s.

The same William holds ADGESTONE. Godric held it of King Edward in alod. It then, as now, paid geld for 1 virgate and the third part of 1 virgate. There is land for 1 plough. A certain vavasour, having 2 cows, dwells there. It is and was worth 10s.

The same William has a certain plot of land in the island, from which come 3 ploughshares.

VIII. The land of Joscelin fitzAzor

JOSCELIN fitzAzor holds "SCALDEFORD" of the king. Asgot held it of King Edward in alod. Then, as now, it paid geld for 1 virgate. There is land for 1 plough, and there is [1 plough] in demesne. Azor holds it of Joscelin. TRE it was worth 40s; and afterwards 20s; now 30s.

The same Joscelin has a plot of land in the island, from which come 3 ploughshares.

The same Joscelin holds ROUD. Alnoth held it of King Edward in alod. It then paid geld for 3 hides; now for $5\frac{1}{2}$ virgates of land. There is land for 6 ploughs. In demesne are 2 ploughs; and 6 bordars and 4 slaves with 1 plough, and 4 acres of meadow.

Of this manor, Azor holds 1 virgate, and Sæwine half a hide and the fourth part of a virgate, and Nigel 3 parts of a virgate. In demesne is 1 plough; and 1 villan and 2 bordars with 1 plough. The whole TRE was worth £9; and afterwards £8; now £8.10s.

The same Joscelin holds SHANKLIN. 6 free men held it of King Edward in alod. It then paid geld for $3\frac{1}{2}$ hides; now for $5\frac{1}{2}$ virgates of land. There is land for 5 ploughs. In demesne are 2 ploughs; and 4 villans and 2 bordars and 2 slaves with 2 ploughs.

[Folio 53V: HAMPSHIRE]

Of this manor, Livol holds 1 hide, and there he has 2 bordars with half a plough. The whole TRE was worth £8; and afterwards £6; now £7.

The same Joscelin holds [?]BRIGHSTONE. 3 free men held it of King Edward in alod. Then, as now, it paid geld for 2 hides and 3 virgates and the third part of a virgate. There is land for 4 ploughs. 4 men, William, and another William, Geoffrey, and Douenold, hold this land of Joscelin. There is 1 plough in demesne. The whole TRE was worth 100s; and afterwards, as now, amongst them all, 50s.

Joscelin himself holds SHIDE of the king. Eadnoth [...] held it of King Edward. It was then assessed at 2 hides less 1 virgate; now at $1\frac{1}{2}$ hides. There is land for 4 ploughs. In demesne is 1 plough; and 3 villans and 2 bordars with $1\frac{1}{2}$ ploughs. There are 3 slaves, and 2 mills rendering 5s, and 2 acres of meadow. TRE, as now, worth 50s; when received, 40s.

The same Joscelin holds 1 virgate in CHILLERTON, and Geoffrey holds it of Joscelin. Blæcmann held it in parage. [It was] then, as now, [assessed] at 1 virgate. There is land for 1 plough, and there is [1 plough] in demesne. It is and was worth 10s.

The same Joscelin holds SHORWELL. Wulfnoth held it in parage. [It was] then [assessed] at 2 hides and 1 virgate; now at half a hide. There is land for $2\frac{1}{2}$ ploughs. In demesne is 1 [plough]; and 2 villans and 6 bordars with $1\frac{1}{2}$ ploughs. There are 3 slaves, and a mill rendering 40d, and 14 acres of meadow. TRE, and afterwards, it was worth 100s; now £4.

The same Joscelin holds SHALFLEET. Eadric held it TRE, and it was then assessed at 6 hides; now at 3 hides and half a virgate. There is land for 14 ploughs. In demesne are 2 [ploughs]; and 14 villans and 19 bordars with $9\frac{1}{2}$ ploughs. There is a mill rendering 11d, and 4 acres of meadow. There is a church, [and] woodland for 20 pigs.

Of this land, Geoffrey holds $2\frac{1}{2}$ virgates, and there is 1 plough with 2 villans and 1 bordar; and Turgis half a hide, Leof 1 hide. These have 2 ploughs in demesne; and 2 villans and 2 bordars with half a plough. The whole, TRE and afterwards, was worth £20; now £15 amongst them all.

The same Joscelin holds HAMSTEAD. Ælfric held it in parage. [It was] then, as now, [assessed] at half a hide. There is land for 1 plough. There are 2 slaves and 1 villan with half a plough. It is and was worth 20s.

The same Joscelin holds WOLVERTON. Ælfric held it in parage. [It was] then, as now, [assessed] at 1 hide. There is land for 2 ploughs. In demesne are $1\frac{1}{2}$ [ploughs]; and 1 villan and 3 bordars with 1 plough. There are 4 slaves, and 1 acre of meadow. It is and was worth 60s. Turold holds it of Joscelin.

The same Joscelin has half a hide in CHILTON. Ælfric held it, and it was then, as now, assessed at half a hide. There is land for 1 plough, and there is [1 plough], with 2 villans, and 4 acres of meadow. It is and was worth 10s.

ALSO WILLIAM fitzAzor holds MOTTISTONE of the king. 4 thegns held it in parage. [It was] then [assessed] at 2 hides; now at $2\frac{1}{2}$ virgates. There is land for 4 ploughs. In demesne is 1 plough and 7 slaves; and 7 bordars with 1 plough, and 16 acres of meadow. TRE it was worth £10; and afterwards, as now, £6.

The same William holds COOMBE. Lyfing held it in parage. [It was] then [assessed] at 1 hide; now at half a virgate. There is land for 1 plough. There are 2 bordars and 2 slaves, and a mill and 2 acres of meadow. It is worth 40s.

The same William holds half a hide in HAMSTEAD, and Nigel [holds] of him. Ælfric held it in parage. [It was] then, as now, [assessed] at half a hide. There is land for 1 plough, and there is [1 plough] with 2 villans and 2 bordars. It is and was worth 20s.

The same William holds half a hide in CHILTON, and William Forist [holds] of him. Ælfric held it in parage. It was then, as now, assessed at half a hide. There is land for 1 plough. It was worth 10s; now 5s.

The same William holds 1 hide and 1 virgate in SHIDE. Eadnoth held it in parage. [It was] then [assessed] at 5 virgates; now at 3 virgates. There is land for 3 ploughs. In demesne [is] nothing; but [there are] 15 bordars and 4 slaves with $1\frac{1}{2}$ ploughs. There is a mill rendering 10s, and 2 acres of meadow, [and] woodland for fencing. TRE, and afterwards, it was worth 40s; now 60s.

The same William holds in FRESHWATER 1 hide, and it pays geld for as much, and Roger [holds] of him. A certain reeve of Tosti held this in the manor of Freshwater. There is land for 1 plough, and there is [1 plough] in demesne, with 3 bordars. TRE, as now, worth 40s; when received, 20s.

The same William holds in CHILLERTON 1 virgate, and it is assessed at as much, and Geoffrey [holds] of him. Blæcmann held it in parage. There is land for 1 plough, and there is [1 plough] in demesne, with 2 bordars and 1 slave. It was worth 20s; now 30s.

IX. The Lands of the King's Thegns

GODRIC the priest holds "MELEUSFORD" of the king. He himself held it of King Edward in parage. [It was] then, as now, [assessed] at 1 hide and half a virgate. There is land for half a plough. In demesne, however, is 1 plough with 1 bordar, and a mill without rent, and $1\frac{1}{2}$ acres of meadow. It is and was worth 10s.

ALSIGE son of Beorhtsige holds THORLEY. Earl Tosti held it. It was then assessed at 3 hides; now at 2 hides. There is land for 7 ploughs. In demesne are 2 [ploughs]; and 10 villans and 11 bordars with 6 ploughs. There are 7 slaves, and 6 acres of meadow. TRE, and afterwards, it was worth £8; now £12.

ÆLFRIC holds and held 1 hide in SHEAT, and it is assessed at as much. There is land for half a plough. In demesne is 1 plough, and 2 slaves and 1 bordar, and a mill without rent. It was worth 10s; now 15s.

WULFNOTH holds and held [?]'LEA' [in Brading]. TRE, as now, it paid geld for 1 virgate. In demesne is half a plough. It is worth 5s; it was worth 7s.

HERBRAND holds [Great and Little] PAN of the king. Godric held it of King Edward. It then, as now, paid geld for 1 hide. There is land for 4 ploughs. In demesne is 1 plough; and 4 villans with 2 ploughs. There are 2 acres of meadow, [and] woodland without pannage. It was worth £4; now £3.

EADRIC holds ADGESTONE. He himself held it of King Edward. It then, as now, paid geld for half a virgate. There is land for half a plough. There is [half a plough] in demesne, with 2 bordars and 2 slaves. It is and was worth 5s.

OIRANT holds 'CHALCROFT' [in Brading]. His father held it of King Edward. It then, as now, paid geld for half a virgate. In demesne is half a plough, with 1 bordar. It is and was worth 5s.

ALSIGE holds [?]BAGWICH of the king. He himself held it of King Edward in alod. It then, as now, paid geld for 1 virgate. There is land for half a plough. There is half an acre of meadow. It was worth 5s; now 3s.

WULFWEARD holds WHIPPINGHAM of the king. He himself held it of King Edward in alod. It then, as now, paid geld for half a hide. In demesne is half a plough, with 3 bordars. It is and was worth 10s.

ALRIC and his nephew hold NETTLESTONE of the king. They themselves held it of King Edward in alod. It then, as now, paid geld for the third part of a hide. There is land for half a plough, and there is [half a plough] in demesne. It is and was worth 5s.

HUMPHREY holds the third part of a hide in NETTLESTONE of the king. Godeza held it of King Edward in alod. It then, as now, paid geld for the third part of a hide. There is land for 3 ploughs. In demesne is 1 plough, and 2 acres of meadow. It was worth 60s; now 20s.

EADWIG holds [Great, North or Upper] APPLEFORD. He himself held it of King Edward in alod. It then, as now, paid geld for half a hide. There is land for 1 plough. In demesne is half a plough, with 1 bordar, and $2\frac{1}{2}$ acres of meadow. It was worth 20s; now 10s.

[Folio 54: [HAMPSHIRE]]

SWÆRTING holds DURTON of the king. He himself and another free man held it of King Edward in alod. It then paid geld for $1\frac{1}{2}$ hides, less the third part of a virgate. [...] In demesne is half a plough; and 1 villan and 1 bordar with 1 plough. Of this manor, William holds at farm 2 parts of a hide, and there he has 1 plough. It was worth 32s; now 42s.

GODRIC holds 'HUFFINGFORD' of the king. He himself held it of King Edward. It then, as now, paid geld for 1 virgate. There 1 villan has half a plough. It is worth 40d.

TOVI holds, as a gift from the king, half a virgate in KNIGHTON. Bondi held it of King Edward in alod. It then, as now, paid geld for half a virgate. There is 1 villan. It is and was worth 3s.

IN "HEMRESWEL" HUNDRED

ÆLFRIC and Wihtlac have 1 hide and $2\frac{1}{2}$ virgates in YARMOUTH. They themselves held it in parage of King Edward. It was then, as now, assessed at 1 hide and $2\frac{1}{2}$ virgates. There is land for 2 ploughs. There are 7 villans and 2 bordars having 2 ploughs. It was worth 12s; now 25s.

WULFNOTH and Bruning have half a hide in [?]SHATE. They themselves held it in parage. [It was] then, as now, [assessed] at half a hide. There is land for 1 plough. There 3 villans have 1 plough, and a mill rendering 40d, and 2 acres of meadow. It is and was worth 10s.

GERIN has 1 hide in NINGWOOD. King Edward had it in his farm. [It was] then, as now, [assessed] at 1 hide. There is land for 4 ploughs. In demesne is 1 [plough]; and 6 villans and 10 bordars with 3 ploughs. There is half an acre of meadow, [and] woodland for fencing. It was worth £6; now £7.

IN BOWCOMBE HUNDRED

WULFSIGE holds half a hide in CHALE. He himself held it of King Edward in parage. [It was] then, as now, [assessed] at half a hide. There is land for 1 plough. In demesne is half a plough; and 2 bordars have half a plough, and [there is] 1 acre of meadow. It is worth 10s.

GODRIC has half a hide of the king in 'HUFFINGFORD'.

He himself held it TRE. It was then, as now, assessed at half a hide. There is land for 1 plough. In demesne is half [a plough], with 1 bordar, and a mill without rent, and 1 acre of meadow. It is and was worth 10s.

ALNOTH holds 1 hide of the king in LUTON. He himself held it in parage TRE. [It was] then, as now, [assessed] at 1 hide. There is land for 1 plough. In demesne is half a plough, with 2 bordars. It was worth 10s; now 12s.

WULFNOTH holds of the king half a virgate, and it was assessed at as much TRE, as now. There is land for half a plough. There is 1 bordar. It is worth 30d.

ÆLFRIC and Wihtlac hold half a hide in YAFFORD, and it was assessed at as much TRE, as now. 4 alodiaries held it in parage. There is land for 1 plough. In demesne is half a

plough; and 5 bordars have 1 plough, and [there is] half an acre of meadow. It is and was worth 10s.

BOLLA holds of the king 1 virgate in [Great, North or Upper] APPLEFORD, and it was assessed at as much TRE, as now. There is land for 1 plough, and there is [1 plough] in demesne with 3 slaves, and there are 5 acres of meadow. It is and was worth 10s.

[Folio 54V: [HAMPSHIRE]]

[Blank in MS]

[Folio 55: [HAMPSHIRE]]

[Blank in MS]

[Folio 55V: [HAMPSHIRE]]

[Blank in MS]

BERKSHIRE

HERE ARE NOTED DOWN THOSE WHO HOLD LANDS IN BERKSHIRE

I KING WILLIAM
II The Bishop of Winchester
III The Bishop of Salisbury
IIII The Bishop of Durham
V The Bishop of Exeter
VI The Bishop of Coutances
VII The Abbey of Abingdon
VIII The Abbey of Glastonbury
IX The Abbey of Westminster
X The Abbey of Winchester
XI The Abbey of Chertsey
XII The Abbey of St Albans
XIII The Abbey of Saint-PIERRE-sur-Dives
XIIII The Abbey of Battle
XV The Abbess of Winchester
XVI The Abbess of Amesbury
XVII The Count of Evreux
XVIII Earl Hugh
XIX The Count of Mortain
XX Walter Giffard
XXI Henry de Ferrers
XXII William fitzAnsculf
XXIII William de Eu
XXIIII William Peverel
XXV William de Braose
XXVI William Lovet
XXVII William fitzCorbucion
XXVIII William fitzRichard
XXIX William de Cailly
XXX Walter fitzPons
XXXI Walter fitzOther
XXXII Eudo fitzHubert
XXXIII Miles Crispin
XXXIIII Giles brother of Ansculf
XXXV Hascoit Musard
XXXVI Gilbert de Breteuil
XXXVII Gilbert de Ghent
XXXVIII Geoffrey de Mandeville
XXXIX Osbern Giffard
XL Robert fitzGerald
XLI Robert d'Oilly
XLII Robert of Stafford
XLIII Richard Puignant
XLIIII Roger d'Ivry
XLV Roger de Lacy
XLVI Ralph de Mortimer
XLVII Ralph de Tosny
XLVIII Ralph fitzCount
XLIX Ralph fitzSeifrid
L Ernulf de Hesdin
LI Hugh fitzBaldric
LII Hugh de Port
LIII Humphrey the chamberlain
LIIII Humphrey Visdeloup
LV Turstin fitzRolf
LVI Albert
LVII Aiulf the sheriff
LVIII Hugolin the steersman
LIX Matthew de Mortagne
LX Bernard the falconer
LXI Regenbald the priest
LXII Grimbald
LXIII Theodric the goldsmith, Odo, and several other thegns

IN THE BOROUGH OF WALLINGFORD KING EDWARD HAD 8 virgates of land, and in these were 276 closes rendering £11 from rent, and they who dwelt there did service for the king with horses or by water as far as Blewbury, Reading, Sutton Courtenay [and] Benson [Oxon.], and to those who did this the reeve gave cash or kind not from the rent of the king but from his own.

Now all the customs in this borough are as they were before; but of the closes there are 13 less: 8 were destroyed for the castle, and a moneyer has 1 quit so long as he does the coining; Sæwulf of Oxford has 1; the son of Alsige of Faringdon 1, which, he says, the king gave him; Humphrey Visdeloup has 1, for which he claims the king's warranty; Nigel [claims] 1 of Henry through inheritance from Swærting, but the burgesses give evidence that they never had it.

From these 13 the king does not have any customary due; and in addition William de Warenne has 1 close from which the king does not have any customary dues.

Over and above these are 22 messuages [held] by Frenchmen rendering 6s5d.

King Edward had 15 acres on which housecarls dwelt; Miles Crispin holds them, they do not know how; 1 of them belongs to Long Wittenham, a manor of Walter Giffard.

Bishop Walkelin has 27 closes rendering 25s, and they are appraised in his manor of Brightwell-cum-Sotwell.

The Abbot of Abingdon has 2 acres on which are 7 messuages rendering 4s, and belonging to Oxford.

Miles [has] 20 messuages rendering 12s10d, and they belong to Newnham Murren [Oxon.]; and also 1 acre on which are 6 closes rendering 18d. In [Great and Little] Haseley [Oxon.] 6 messuages rendering 44d. In North Stoke [Oxon.] 1 messuage rendering 12d. In Chalgrove [Oxon.] 1 messuage rendering 4d; and in Sutton Courtenay 1 acre on which are 6 messuages rendering 12d; and in Bray 1 acre, and there are 11 messuages rendering 3s. The whole of this land belongs to Oxfordshire, and yet it is in Wallingford.

Reginald has 1 acre on which are 11 messuages rendering 26d, and they belong to Albury [Oxon.], which is in Oxford[shire].

The archbishop has 6 messuages rendering 26d; Walter Giffard has 1 acre and 10 messuages rendering 6s1½d; Robert d'Oilly 4 messuages rendering 20d; Gilbert de Ghent 1 messuage rendering 2½d; Hugh the Great 1 messuage rendering 4d; R. fitzSeifrid 2 closes rendering 12d; Hugh de Bolbec 1 close rendering 4d; Ranulph Peverel 1 rendering 4d; Walter fitzOther 6 closes rendering 4d all but a halfpenny; William Lovet 1 plot of land rendering 4d; in [East and West] Ilsley 3 messuages rendering 3d. The Abbot of Battle [Abbey] has 5 messuages in Berkshire rendering 20d, [and there is] 1 close, which belonged to Bishop Peter, rendering 4d.

The king [has] 3 closes rendering 6d; Henry de Ferrers 6 closes which TRE and also TRW gave 62d customarily in the king's farm; now they give nothing.

Bishop Remigius [has] 1 close rendering 4d; Earl Hugh 1 close worth 16d;

[Folio 56V: BERKSHIRE]

Godric 1 close rendering 2d; Dodda 1 close rendering 2d; Algar 1 [close] rendering 2d; smiths [have] 5 closes rendering 10d.

The king [has] in Aldermaston 2 closes rendering 5d; the Count of Evreux 2 closes rendering 2½[d]; Hugh Bolbec 1 close rendering 2d; Roger de Lacy 1 close rendering 12d; Robert d'Oilly 1 close rendering 6d.

The king [has] 1 close rendering 6d; Bishop Osmund 7 closes rendering 28d; Robert d'Oilly 2 closes rendering 10d; Roger de Lacy 5 closes rendering 21d; Ralph Piercehedge 7 closes rendering 50d; Regenbald the priest 1 close rendering 4d; St Alban 1 close singa [sic], and it is in dispute; Beorhtric 1 close rendering 2d; Leofgifu 1 close rendering 2d; Godwine 1 close rendering 2d; Alwine 1 close rendering 2d; Almær the priest and another Almær the priest and Brunmann and Eadwig and Edmund and William son of Osmund and Leofflæd and Lambert the priest, Alweald and Godric have rent from their houses and [the fines due for] bloodshedding, if there is bloodshed there, [and] if the man [accused] is received in them before claim is made by the king's reeve, except on Saturday, on account of the market, because then the king has the fine; and they have the fines for adultery and theft in their houses; other fines, however, are the king's.

TRE it was worth £30; and afterwards £40; now £60, and yet it renders at farm £80 by tale. What belongs to Adbrei [is worth] 7s, and the land of Miles Molay 24[s]; what the Abbot of Abingdon has, 8s; what Roger de Lacy [has], 7s; what Reginald [has], 4s.

The following thegns of OXFORDSHIRE had land in WALLINGFORD:

Archbishop Lanfranc 4 houses belonging to NEWINGTON [Oxon.] rendering 6s; Bishop Remigius 1 house belonging to Dorchester [Oxon.] rendering 12d; the Abbot of St Alban's 1 house rendering 4s; Abbot R [...] 1 house [belonging] to Ewelme [Oxon.] rendering 3s.

Earl Hugh 1 house [belonging] to Pyrton [Oxon.] rendering 3s; Walter Giffard 3 houses [belonging] to Caversham rendering 2s; Robert d'Oilly 2 houses [belonging] to Watlington [Oxon.] rendering 2s, and [belonging] to Waterperry [Oxon.], 1 house rendering 2s.

Ilbert de Lacy, Roger fitzSeifrid, and Ordgar, 3 houses rendering 4s; Hugh de Bolbec 3 houses [belonging] to [?] Crowmarsh Gifford [Oxon.] rendering 3s; Hugh the Great of Scoca 1 house rendering 12d; Drogo [has, belonging] to Shirburn [Oxon.], and [belonging] to South Weston [Oxon.], 3 houses rendering 4s; Robert d'Armentieres, [belonging] to Ewelme [Oxon.], 1 house rendering 12d; Wazo 1 house [belonging] to Ewelme [Oxon.] rendering 3s.

When geld was commonly paid TRE, throughout the whole of Berkshire, a hide gave 3½d before [the Feast of] the Nativity of the Lord and as much at Pentecost. If the king sent out an army anywhere only 1 thegn went out from [each] 5 hides, and for his sustenance or pay 4s for 2 months was given him from each hide. This money, however, was not sent to the king but given to the thegns. If anyone summoned to military service did not go he forfeited all his land to the king. But if anyone having to stay behind promised to sent another in his stead, and yet he who should have been sent stayed behind, his lord was quit for 50s. When a thegn or a knight of the king's demesne was dying he left all his weapons to the king as heriot, and 1 horse with a saddle and 1 without a saddle. But if he possessed hounds or hawks these were presented to the king, to have if he wished. If any one slew a man having [the protection of] the king's peace, he forfeited both his person and all his possessions to the king. He who broke into the city at night paid a fine of 100s to the king, not to the sheriff. He who was summoned to [take part in] heading off [game] in the hunt [and] did not go, paid a fine of 50s to the king.

The land of the King

King WILLIAM holds WINDSOR in demesne. King Edward held it. There are 20 hides. There is land [...]. In demesne is 1 plough; and 22 villans and 2 bordars with 10 ploughs. There is 1 slave, and a fishery rendering 6s8d, and 40 acres of meadow. [There is] woodland for 50 pigs as pannage, and other woodland has been put in [the king's] preserve and there are, besides, 100 closes, less 5, in the vill. Of these, 26 are quit of rent and from the others come 30s.

Of the land of this manor Albert the clerk holds 1½ hides and the third part of a dene; Walter fitzOther 1½ hides and 1 virgate, and as much woodland as provides 5 pigs as pannage. Gilbert Maminot [holds] 3 virgates, William Belet 1 hide, Ælfric 1 hide, and another Ælfric half a hide, and a priest of the vill 1½ hides, and 2 sergeants of the king's court half a hide, Eudo Dapifer 2 hides. TRE it was worth £15; and afterwards £7; now £15.

IN THATCHAM HUNDRED

The king holds THATCHAM in demesne. King Edward held it. It was then assessed at 2 hides, and has never paid geld. There is land for 25 ploughs. There are 35 villans and 12 bordars with 25 ploughs, and there are 12 enclosures rendering at farm 55s, and 2 mills rendering 22s6d, and 147 acres of meadow. [There is] woodland for 60 pigs. The church of this manor 2 clerks hold with 3 hides which belong there; and these pay geld with the shire, and are worth £3. TRE it was worth £20; now £30; and yet it renders £34.

IN 'BEYNHURST' HUNDRED

The king holds COOKHAM in demesne. King Edward held it. Then [there were] 20 hides, but it never paid geld. There is land for 25 ploughs. There are 32 villans and 21 cottars with 20 ploughs, and there are 4 slaves, and 2 mills rendering 22s6d, and 2 fisheries rendering 13s4d, and 50 acres of meadow. [There is] woodland for 100 pigs and the other half is in the forest of Windsor. From the new market which is there now, 20s. The whole TRE was worth £50; and afterwards 50s. [sic]; now £36, and yet it renders £45.

Of these 20 hides, Regenbald the priest has of the king 1½ hides in alms, and the church of this manor with 8 cottars and 1 plough, and 15 acres of meadow. It is worth 50s. 2 other clerks have half a hide of this, and 2 cottars with 2 ploughs, and 8 acres of meadow. It is worth 5s.

The king holds WALTHAM ST LAWRENCE in demesne. Queen Edith held it. [It was] then [assessed] at 8 hides; now at nothing. There is land for 16 ploughs. In demesne are 2 [ploughs]; and 32 villans and 4 cottars with 15 ploughs. There are 4 slaves, [and] woodland for 150 pigs. TRE, and afterwards, it was worth £12; now £10, [and] yet it renders £15 by weight.

IN BLEWBURY HUNDRED

The king holds BLEWBURY in demesne. King Edward held it. Then, as now, [it was assessed at] 3 hides. There is land for 20 ploughs. In demesne are 4 ploughs; and 24 villans and 58 cottars with 15 ploughs, and there are 3 mills rendering 37s6d, and 16 acres of meadow. TRE and afterwards it was worth £50; now £60. Of this manor William Beaufour holds the church with 5 virgates of land. Ælfric held it of King Edward. There are 3 cottars, and 10 acres of meadow. It is and was worth 100s.

The king holds ASTON TIRROLD in demesne. The wife of Lang held it of King Edward. [It was] then [assessed] at 15 hides; now at 5 hides. There is land for 7 ploughs. In demesne is 1 [plough]; and 14 villans with 7 ploughs, and there are 3 slaves, and 60 acres of meadow. TRE it was worth £15; and afterwards £12; now £9.

IN 'SLOTISFORD' HUNDRED

The king holds CHOLSEY in demesne. King Edward held it. There were then 23 hides, but it was assessed at 22. There is land for 27 ploughs. Out of the whole of this land the king has 11 hides which pay no geld, and there are in demesne 4 ploughs; and 17 villans and 71 cottars with 16 ploughs. There are 6 slaves, and 3 mills rendering 62s, and 100 acres of meadow.

In this manor were 10 free men TRE and they held 12½ hides of the land of the same manor, but they could not withdraw from there. Richard Puignant now holds 8 hides of this land which are now assessed at 3 hides. William holds of Richard 3 hides, and Hugh 1 hide.

[Folio 57: BERKSHIRE]

There are 3 ploughs in demesne, and 4 villans and 11 cottars, and 26 acres of meadow, and 7 slaves. Of the land of the same manor Gilbert holds 5 virgates of the king, and they are assessed at 1 virgate; and Hervey holds of the king 3 hides and 1 virgate which pay no geld. In demesne are 2 ploughs; and 1 villan and 14 cottars with 1½ ploughs, and 2 slaves, and 3 acres of meadow. The whole, TRE and afterwards, was worth £64; the king's demesne now [renders] £47 by tale; the part held by Richard and the others £17.15s.

Of this manor the Abbey of Mont-Saint-Michel holds of the king 1 church with 1 hide, and there is 1 plough with 4 cottars, and 7 acres of meadow. It is worth £3. 2 priests also in the same vill hold of the king in tithe and church what is worth £4.

The king holds in demesne LOWER BASILDON of Earl Roger's fief. Æthelgifu, a free woman, held it TRE. [It was] then [assessed] at 20 hides; now at 6 hides. There is land for 20 ploughs. In demesne are 5 ploughs; and 28 villans and 15 cottars with 14 ploughs, and a mill rendering 15s, and 13 slaves; and in Wallingford, 3 closes rendering 9d, and 30 acres of meadow. [There is] woodland for 120 pigs. TRE, as now, worth £25; when received, £20. Of this manor 2 priests have 2 churches with 1 hide, and the same men themselves held them TRE. They have there 2 ploughs. It is and was worth 40s.

IN WANTAGE HUNDRED

The king holds WANTAGE in demesne. King Edward held it. Then, as now, [it was assessed at] 4 hides. It has never paid geld. There is land for 21 ploughs. In demesne are 5 ploughs; and 30 villans with 40 cottars have 17 ploughs. There are 5 slaves. It is worth £61; formerly £55. In this manor Bishop Peter held 2 parts of a church with 4 hides belonging there. These have never paid geld; they are now in the hand of the king because they did not belong to the bishopric. There is 1 plough, and 3 villans and 7 cottars with 1 plough, and a mill rendering 100d, and 12 acres of meadow. There is land for 2 ploughs. It was worth £3; now £4. The third part of the aforesaid church William the deacon holds of the king with 1 hide which does not pay geld. There are 4 villans with 1 plough. It was worth 25s; now 30s.

The king holds SPARSHOLT in demesne. 3 free men held it

TRE as 3 manors. Froger the sheriff had it afterwards and made it 1 manor. Then it was assessed at 16 hides; now at nothing. There is land for 10 ploughs. In demesne are 2 ploughs; and 28 villans and 17 cottars with 5 ploughs. There are 3 slaves, and 84 acres of meadow. The whole TRE was worth £9; and afterwards £15; now £19.5s, and yet it renders £23. The church of this manor with 1 hide Eadræd the priest holds, and he himself held it TRE. There he has 1 plough, and 1 cottar, and 4 acres of meadow. This hide does not pay geld. It is worth 20s.

The king holds CHARLTON in demesne. Almær, a free man, held it TRE. [It was] then [assessed] at 8 hides; now at 7 hides. There is land for 4 ploughs. Bishop Peter held it afterwards. There is 1 plough in demesne; and 1 villan and 7 cottars with 1 plough. There are 3 slaves, and 24 acres of meadow, and a mill rendering 7s6d which Walter Giffard holds unjustly, as the hundred says. TRE it was worth £8; and afterwards £4; now £8.

The king holds BETTERTON in demesne. Wulfric, a free man, held it TRE. [It was] then [assessed] at 10 hides; now at 2 hides less 1 virgate. There is land for 4 ploughs. In demesne are 1½ ploughs; and 4 villans and 5 cottars with 2 ploughs. TRE it was worth £6; and afterwards £3; now 100s.

The king has there half a virgate which Wulfflæd held TRE, and she could go where she wished. [It was assessed] then at half a virgate; now at nothing. Robert holds it in the farm of Wantage but it never belonged there. It is and was worth 16d.

In Sutton Courtenay the king holds half a virgate which Leofflæd held TRE, and she could go where she wished. [It was] then [assessed] at half a virgate; now at nothing. Robert holds it in the farm of Sutton Courtenay but it does not belong there. It is and was worth 16d.

IN 'RIPPLESMERE' HUNDRED

The king holds WARFIELD in demesne. Queen Edith held it. It was then, as now, assessed at 10 hides. There is land [...]. There are 13 villans with 8 ploughs. [There is] woodland for 100 pigs. TRE, and afterwards, it was worth £12; now £6. A priest of Geoffrey de Mandeville has 1 hide of this which always belonged to this manor; but he transferred it to a manor of his lord.

IN 'CHARLDON' HUNDRED

The king has WARGRAVE in demesne. Queen Edith held it. [It was] then [assessed] at 33 hides; now at nothing. There is land for 29 ploughs. In demesne are 2 ploughs; and 41 villans and 14 bordars with 25 ploughs. There are 6 slaves, and a mill rendering 9s2d, and 3 fisheries rendering 3,000 eels, and 16 acres of meadow, [and] woodland for 100 pigs. TRE it was worth £31; and afterwards, as now, £27.6s8d.

The king holds REMENHAM in demesne. Queen Edith held it. [It was] then [assessed] at 12 hides; now at 4 hides. There is land [...]. In demesne are 2 ploughs; and 20 villans and 4 bordars with 6 ploughs. There are 4 slaves, and a mill rendering 20s and 1,000 eels, and 52 acres of meadow, [and]

woodland for fencing. TRE it was worth £15; and afterwards, as now, £10.

The king holds SWALLOWFIELD in demesne. Saxi held it of King Edward in alod. [...] There is land for 7 ploughs. In demesne are 2 ploughs; and 8 villans and 8 bordars with 5 ploughs. There are 2 slaves, and a mill rendering 50d, and 5 fisheries rendering 40d, and 12 acres of meadow, [and] woodland for 20 pigs. TRE, and afterwards, it was worth £7; now £8.0s6d.

The king holds SHINFIELD in demesne. Saxi held it in alod of King Edward. [It was] then [assessed] at 5 hides; now at nothing. There is land for 6 ploughs. In demesne is 1 [plough]; and 8 villans and 5 bordars with 7 ploughs. There are 2 slaves, and a mill rendering 5s and 150 eels, and 5 fisheries rendering 550 eels, and 16 acres of meadow, [and] woodland for 90 pigs. It was worth £7; now £8.

The king holds FINCHAMPSTEAD in demesne. Earl Harold held it. [It was] then [assessed] at 5 hides. Now it does not pay geld but renders farm in Reading. There is land for 15 ploughs. In demesne is 1 [plough]; and 16 villans and 8 bordars with 14 ploughs. There are 6 slaves, and a mill rendering 7s6d, and 4 acres of meadow, [and] woodland for 200 pigs. It is and was worth £8.

The king holds BARKHAM in demesne. Almær held it of King Edward. Then, as now, [it was assessed] at 3 hides. There is land for 3 ploughs. In demesne is 1 [plough]; and 6 villans and 4 bordars with 3 ploughs. There are 5 acres of meadow, [and] woodland for 40 pigs. It was worth £4 TRE; and afterwards, as now, £3.

The king holds EARLEY in demesne. Almær held it in alod of King Edward. [It was] then [assessed] at 5 hides; now at 4 hides. There is land for 6 ploughs. In demesne is 1 plough; and 6 villans and 1 bordar with 3 ploughs. There are 2 slaves, and 1 close in Reading, and 2 fisheries rendering 7s6d, and 20 acres of meadow, [and] woodland for 70 pigs. TRE it was worth 100s; and afterwards, as now, 50s.

IN BRAY HUNDRED

The king holds BRAY in demesne. King Edward held it. There are 18 hides and they did not pay geld. There is land [...]. In demesne are 3 ploughs; and 56 villans and 7 bordars with 25 ploughs. There are 4 slaves, and a church, and 3 knights, and 50 acres of meadow, [and] woodland for 60 pigs. Rainbald holds 1 hide which belongs to the church, and there he has 1 plough. The whole TRE was worth £25; and afterwards £18; now £17.

IN BUCKLEBURY HUNDRED

The king holds BUCKLEBURY in demesne. King Edward held it. There are 2 hides but they do not pay geld. There is land [...]. In demesne is 1 plough; and 18 villans and 16 bordars with 20 ploughs. There is 1 slave, and a church to which belongs half a hide, and it is worth 15s. There are 11 acres of meadow, [and] woodland for 100 pigs. It is and was worth £11; and yet it renders £16.10s.

IN 'NAKEDTHORN' HUNDRED

The king holds 'NAKEDTHORN' [?in Compton] in demesne. Eadric held it in alod of King Edward. [It was] then [assessed] at 20 hides; now at 9 hides less 1 virgate. There is land for 12 ploughs. In demesne are 2 ploughs; and 8 villans and 4 bordars with 2 ploughs. Of this manor Ralph the priest holds the church, with 1 hide and half a virgate, and Reginald 2 hides and half a virgate. There is 1 plough and 1 villan. The whole, TRE, was worth £15; and afterwards £12; now what the king has, £10; what Ralph [has], 40s; what Reginald [has], 30s.

The king holds COMPTON in demesne. King Edward held it. There are 3 hides all but 1 virgate. There is land for 8 ploughs. In demesne are 2 ploughs; and 6 villans and 12 bordars with 6 ploughs. There are 3 slaves, and 4 acres of meadow. [There is] woodland for 3 pigs. This woodland Henry de Ferrers holds. TRE, and afterwards, it was worth £6; now £8.

IN KINTBURY HUNDRED

The king holds KINTBURY in demesne. King Edward held it. There are 2 hides. There is land for 10 ploughs. In demesne are 2 ploughs; and 15 villans and 16 bordars with 8 ploughs. There are 2 slaves, and 2 mills rendering 32s6d, and 40 acres of meadow, [and] woodland for 3 pigs. TRE and afterwards, as now, worth £10. Henry de Ferrers holds of this manor 43 acres of land which were in the king's farm TRE, as the shire says. They also say that Godric the sheriff made there pasture-land for his own horses; but they do not know how.

The king holds SHALBOURNE [Wilts.] in demesne. King Edward held it. There are 6½ hides. There is land for 10 ploughs. In demesne are 3 ploughs; and 14 villans and 13 bordars with 6 ploughs. There are 3 slaves, and a mill rendering 10s, and 8 acres of meadow, [and] woodland for fencing. TRE, and afterwards, it was worth £12; now £20. Of this manor 2½ hides have been put in the manor of Henry [de Ferrers]. 1 hide [belonged to] the reeve land, another [belonged] to the villans, and half a hide belonged to the king's farm, but it was alienated in the time of Godric the sheriff. The whole shire testifies to this.

The king holds EDDINGTON in demesne. Azur held it in alod of King Edward. [It was] then [assessed] at 10 hides; now at 2 [hides] all but half a virgate. There is land for 6 ploughs. In demesne is 1 plough; and 6 villans and 2 bordars with 2 ploughs. There is 1 slave, and a mill rendering 15s, and 34 acres of meadow, [and] woodland for 10 pigs. TRE it was worth £6; and afterwards 100s; now 70s.

IN LAMBOURN HUNDRED

The king holds LAMBOURN in demesne. King Edward held it. There are 20 hides. There is land for 42 ploughs. In demesne are 4 ploughs; and 44 villans and 60 bordars with 25 ploughs. There are 6 slaves, and a church with 1 hide belonging to it, and 2 mills rendering 20s, [and] woodland for 10 pigs. TRE it was worth £49; and afterwards £34; now £44.

IN 'EAGLE' HUNDRED

In SOUTH FAWLEY the king holds 1 hide. King Edward held it. There is land for 3 ploughs. In demesne are 2 ploughs, with 6 bordars, and 3 acres of meadow. It is and was worth 40s.

The king holds LETCOMBE REGIS in demesne. King Edward held it. There are 3 hides. There is land for 16 ploughs. In demesne are 3 ploughs; and 1 villan and 30 bordars and 18 boors and 2 slaves with 13 ploughs. There are 5 mills rendering £4, and 225 acres of meadow. The Abbey of Amesbury holds the church of this manor with 1 virgate. The whole, TRE and afterwards, as now, worth £55; yet it renders £60.

IN 'HILDSLOW' HUNDRED

The king holds KINGSTON LISLE in demesne. King Edward held it. There are 10 hides. There is land for 13 ploughs. In demesne are 3 ploughs; and 25 villans and 3 bordars with 10 ploughs. There are 3 slaves, and 200 acres of meadow. TRE it was worth £15; and afterwards £18; now £20, yet it renders £26. Of this manor Henry de Ferrers holds 1 virgate of land, and 12 acres of meadow, and 1 dairy rendering 6 weys of cheeses, which, as the shire testifies, remained in the king's farm when Godric lost the sheriffdom.

IN SHRIVENHAM HUNDRED

The king holds SHRIVENHAM in demesne. King Edward held it. There are 46 hides. There is land for 33 ploughs. In demesne are 4 ploughs; and 80 villans and 17 bordars with 30 ploughs. There is a church with 5 hides of the same land, and there is 1 plough, and 4 villans and 5 bordars with 2 ploughs. In the manor are 2 mills rendering 20s, and 240 acres of meadow. [There is] woodland for 20 pigs. TRE it was worth £35; and afterwards £20; now £45. What the priest has [is worth] £4.

IN 'WYFOLD' HUNDRED

The king holds FARINGDON in demesne. Harold held it. It was then assessed at 30 hides; now it does not pay geld. There is land for 15 ploughs. In demesne are 3 ploughs; and 17 villans and 10 bordars with 10 ploughs. There are 10 slaves, and a mill with a fishery rendering 35s, and 9 enclosures in the same vill rendering 40s, and 130 acres of meadow. [There is] woodland for fencing. Of this manor Bishop Osmund has 1 hide with the church; [...] and Alsige has 4 hides, and in demesne [are] 2 ploughs, and 2 bordars and 6 slaves. The whole TRE was worth £16; and afterwards £12; now £21.6s8d. What the church or priest [has is worth] 40s; what Alsige [has], 30s.

The king holds GREAT COXWELL in demesne. Harold held it. It was then assessed at 20 hides; now it does not pay geld. There is land for 8 ploughs. In demesne are 2 ploughs; and 9 villans and 4 bordars with 3 ploughs, and 7 slaves, and 80 acres of meadow less 3. There is a church with half a hide. TRE it was worth £8; and afterwards £6; now £10.

The king holds in demesne another [Little] COXWELL. Harold held it. [It was] then [assessed at] 10 hides; now it does not pay geld. There is land for 9 ploughs. In demesne are 2 [ploughs]; and 11 villans and 6 bordars with 6 ploughs, and 200 acres of meadow, [and] woodland for fencing. TRE it was worth £16; and afterwards £12; now £14.

IN SUTTON HUNDRED

The king holds SUTTON COURTENAY in demesne. It was assessed TRE at 23 hides and 1 virgate; now at nothing. There is land for 20 ploughs. In demesne are 3 ploughs; and 48 villans and 21 bordars with 17 ploughs. There are 2 slaves, and 3 mills rendering 50s, and 300 acres of meadow, [and] woodland for 40 pigs. In Wallingford, 1 close rendering 18d, but it is waste. TRE it was worth £30; and afterwards £20; now £50; yet it renders £60 by tale at farm.

Henry de Ferrers holds in this manor, of the demesne land of the king, 120 acres of land and 3 acres of meadow, for the reason that Godric his predecessor ploughed this land, when he was sheriff, with his own ploughs. But, as the hundred says, it belongs of right to the king's court, for Godric occupied it unjustly.

The king holds [East and West] HENDRED in demesne. King Edward held it. It was then assessed at 4½ hides; now at nothing. There is land for 5 ploughs. In demesne are 2 ploughs; and 8 villans and 13 bordars with 2 ploughs, and there are 2 slaves, and a mill rendering 42s, and 4 acres of meadow. TRE it was worth £10; and afterwards £8; now £15; and yet it renders £20.

Henry [de Ferrers] holds there 1 hide which had been in the king's farm. Godric held it. Ælfric of Thatcham says that he has seen the king's writ which gave it as a gift to Godric's wife because she was rearing his hounds. But there is no one in the hundred besides Ælfric who has seen the writ.

The king holds STEVENTON in demesne. Harold held it. It was then assessed at 20 hides; now at nothing. There is land for 20 ploughs. In demesne are 4 ploughs; and 38 villans and 28 bordars with 10 ploughs. There are 2 slaves, and 3 mills rendering 45s, and 268 acres of meadow. There is a church in the manor. TRE it was worth £25; and afterwards £20; now £32, yet it renders £40. To this manor belonged in Oxford 13 closes rendering 12s6d, and 1 meadow rendering 20s. The men of the hundred now say that they believe that Robert d'Oilly held this; they know no more about it because it is in another shire.

[Folio 58: BERKSHIRE]

IN GAINFIELD HUNDRED

The king holds LITTLEWORTH in demesne. Harold held it TRE. It was then assessed at 31 hides; now at nothing. There is land for 16 ploughs. In demesne are 3 ploughs; and 32 villans and 13 bordars with 12 ploughs. There are 14 slaves, and a mill rendering 12s6d, and a fishery rendering 10s, and 300 acres of meadow less 15.

Of this land Alsige holds 2 hides which belonged to the villans. He himself held them TRE; and Ælfgeat [holds] 2 hides, and another Ælfgeat held them. On this land [is] 1 plough in demesne, with 2 bordars and 1 slave, and 54 acres of meadow. The whole, TRE, was worth £30; and afterwards £20; now £25.10s.

IN READING HUNDRED

The king holds READING in demesne. King Edward held it. Then, as now, it was assessed at 43 hides. There is land for 40 ploughs. In demesne is 1 [plough]; and 55 villans and 30 bordars with 55 ploughs. There are 4 mills rendering 55s, and 3 fisheries rendering 17s6d, and 150 acres of meadow, [and] woodland for 100 pigs. From pasture, 16s6d. TRE, and afterwards, it was worth £40; now £48.

The king has in the borough of READING 28 closes, rendering £4.3s for all customary dues. Yet those who hold them pay 100s.

Henry de Ferrers has there 1 close, and half a virgate of land in which are 3 acres of meadow. It is worth 6s. Godric the sheriff held this land for the use of guests; therefore Henry holds it.

Reinbald son of Bishop Peter held 1 close there which he transferred to his manor of EARLEY. It is now in the king's hand and is worth 16d.

PANGBOURNE belonged to the farm TRE, and after that Alweald the chamberlain held it, but the hundred does not know how he had it. Froger afterwards attached it to the king's farm without pleading and judgement. Then it was assessed at 2 hides; now at nothing. There is land for 2 ploughs. There are 4 villans and 5 bordars, and a mill rendering 20s. It is and was worth 40s.

The king holds ALDERMASTON in demesne. Harold held it. It was then assessed at 15 hides; now at nothing. There is land for 30 ploughs. In demesne are 2 ploughs; and 36 villans and 12 bordars with 18 ploughs. There are 2 slaves, and a mill rendering 20s, and 2 fisheries rendering 5s. There is a church, and 124 acres of meadow, [and] woodland for 30 pigs. TRE and afterwards, as now, worth £20.10s. Yet for this, and for Wokefield, which is below, they who hold pay £26.

To Aldermaston belongs WOKEFIELD. Beorhtweard held it by a grant from Harold. It was then assessed at 1½ hides; now at nothing. There is land for 3 ploughs. There are 3 villans and 6 bordars with 2 ploughs. There are 2 slaves, and 6 acres of meadow, [and] woodland for 50 pigs. Its value [is included] above.

In the same HUNDRED the king has 1 hide, and it belongs to Swallowfield, which is in 'Charldon' Hundred. Saxi held it TRE. There are 4 villans and 2 bordars with 3 ploughs. It is appraised with Swallowfield, which is the capital manor.

IN ROWBURY HUNDRED

The king holds WINTERBOURNE. It was [part] of Queen Edith's land. Lang held it of her. Theodric holds it of the king at farm. It was then assessed at 5 hides; now at nothing. There is land for 5 ploughs. In demesne is 1 plough; and 4 villans and 11 bordars with 4 ploughs. There are 2 acres of meadow, [and] woodland for 3 pigs. TRE it was worth £6; and afterwards 50s; now £4.

II. The land of the Bishop of Winchester

IN 'HILDSLOW' HUNDRED

WALKELIN, Bishop of Winchester, has WOOLSTONE for the sustenance of the monks. TRE it was assessed at 20 hides; now at 10 hides. There is land for 11 ploughs. In demesne are 2½ ploughs; and 12 villans and 24 bordars with 2½ ploughs. There are 10 slaves, and 2 mills rendering 12s6d, and 150 acres of meadow. Of this manor Roger d'Ivry holds 3½ hides of the bishop, and there he has 1 plough. TRE it was worth £16; and afterwards £12; now £18, yet it renders at farm £22. What Roger holds [is worth] £3.

IN BLEWBURY HUNDRED

The bishop himself holds HARWELL in demesne as of his bishopric. Bishop Stigand held it TRE. [It was] then [assessed] at 15 hides; now at 10 hides. There is land for 8 ploughs. In demesne are 2 ploughs; and 18 villans and 5 cottars with 6 ploughs. There are 4 slaves, and a mill rendering 30d, and 45 acres of meadow; and in Wallingford 3 closes rendering 15d. TRE, and afterwards, it was worth £12; now £16.

IN 'SLOTISFORD' HUNDRED

The bishop himself holds BRIGHTWELL-CUM-SOTWELL as of his bishopric. Bishop Stigand held it TRE. [It was] then [assessed] at 20 hides; now at 10 hides. There is land for 16 ploughs. In demesne are 4 ploughs; and 17 villans and 16 cottars with 9 ploughs. There are 15 slaves, and a mill rendering 20s. There is a church, and from the pleas of the land which [is] in Wallingford belonging to this manor, 25s. TRE, and afterwards, it was worth £20; now £25.

III. The land of the Bishop of Salisbury

IN 'CHARLDON' HUNDRED

OSMUND, Bishop of Salisbury, holds SONNING in demesne as of his bishopric. TRE it was assessed at 60 hides; now at 24 hides. There is land for 46 ploughs. In demesne are 5 ploughs; and 40 villans and 16 bordars with 41 ploughs. There are 10 slaves, and 2 mills rendering 12s6d, and 5 fisheries rendering 30s, and 40 acres of meadow, [and] woodland for 300 pigs. TRE it was worth £50; and afterwards, as now, £40. Of the appurtenances of this manor Aubrey de Coucy held 20 hides in [East and West] ILSLEY which of right belong to the aforesaid manor of the bishop. Roger the priest holds 1 church in Wallingford which of right belongs to this manor.

IN WANTAGE HUNDRED

The same bishop holds of the king 1½ hides, and Thorir [holds] of him. Thorir's father held them TRE and could go where he wished; but for his protection he commended himself to Bishop Herman; and Thorir, in like manner, to Bishop Osmund. Then, as now, [it was assessed] at 1½ hides. There is land for 5 oxen. Yet in demesne is 1 plough with 1 cottar, and a

mill rendering 6s3d. TRE it was worth 15s; and afterwards 20s; now 30s.

IN ROWBURY HUNDRED

The same bishop holds WINTERBOURNE, and Ranulph Flambard [holds] of him. Bishop Herman held it. It was then assessed at 2 hides; now at nothing. There is land for 1 plough. In demesne [is] half a plough with 4 bordars. It is worth 20s.

IIII. The land of the Bishop of Durham

IN 'BEYNHURST' HUNDRED

The Bishop of DURHAM holds of the king WHITE WALTHAM in alms. Wulfwine the canon held it of Earl Harold and it belonged to the Church of Waltham. Then, as now, [it was assessed] at 3 hides. There is land for 6 ploughs. In demesne are 2 [ploughs]; and 8 villans and 3 cottars with 4 ploughs. There are 3 slaves, and 3 acres of meadow, [and] woodland for 6 pigs. TRE it was worth 60s; and afterwards 70s; now 100s.

[Folio 58V: BERKSHIRE]

V. The land of Bishop Osbern

IN GAINFIELD HUNDRED

Bishop OSBERN holds BUCKLAND in demesne as of his bishopric, he says. Wulfric Cemp dwelt there TRE. As a result, they did not judge the matter but sent it before the king to judge. It was then assessed at 15½ hides; now at 8 hides. There is land for 6 ploughs. There is nothing in demesne; but 9 villans and 7 cottars with 4 ploughs. There is a church, and 7 slaves, and a mill rendering 12s6d, and 4 fisheries rendering 20s6d, and 220 acres of meadow, and a dairy farm rendering 10 weys of cheeses worth 32s4d. TRE it was worth £16; and afterwards £12; now £8.

VI. The land of the Bishop of Coutances

IN 'NAKEDTHORN' HUNDRED

Bishop GEOFFREY holds COMPTON. Oda held it of King Edward. It was then assessed at 5 hides; now at 2½ hides. There is land [...]. In demesne are 2 ploughs; and 9 villans and 4 bordars with 5 ploughs. There are 5 slaves, [and] woodland for 10 pigs. TRE, and afterwards, it was worth £4; now 100s.

VII. The land of the Church of Abingdon

IN 'HORMER' HUNDRED

THE ABBEY of Abingdon holds CUMNOR. It has always belonged to the abbey. TRE it was assessed at 50 hides; now at 30 hides. There is land for 50 ploughs. In demesne are 9 ploughs; and 60 villans and 69 bordars with 26 ploughs. There are 4 slaves, and 2 mills rendering 50s, and from the fisheries 40s, and 200 acres of meadow. There is a church. TRE it was worth £30; and afterwards, as now, £50.

Of these 50 hides Ansketil holds 5 hides. Northmann held them TRE as 1 manor, called Seacourt, and he could not go where he wished. It paid geld for 5 hides with the others above. There is land for 7 ploughs. In demesne are 2 ploughs; and 12 villans and 15 bordars with 5 ploughs. TRE it was worth 100s; and afterwards 70s; now £8.

In Wytham Hubert holds of the abbot 5 hides. 4 [hides] were of the land of the villans and paid geld with the hides of the manor. The thegn's hide was quit, but he could not go where he wished. There is land for 2 ploughs. In demesne are 1½ ploughs; and 4 villans and 11 bordars. There are 64 acres of meadow. TRE, and afterwards, it was worth 50s; now £4.

Of the aforesaid hides Osbern holds in Cumnor 2½ hides and they paid geld for as much, with the other hides. 2 alodiaries held them of the abbot. There is land for 2 ploughs. In demesne is 1 plough, with 1 villan and 3 bordars. It was worth 60s; now 40s.

Reginald holds 1 hide in Cumnor; and it paid geld for 1 hide with the others. There is land for 1 plough. It was worth 20s; now 10s.

The abbey itself holds ABINGDON in demesne. TRE it was assessed at 60 hides; now at 40 hides. There is land for 40 ploughs. In demesne are 3 ploughs; and 64 villans and 36 bordars with 34 ploughs, and 10 merchants dwelling in front of the door of the church paying 40d, and in Abingdon 2 slaves and 24 coliberts, and 2 mills rendering 40s, and 5 fisheries rendering 18s4d, and 200 acres of meadow, and 15s. from pasture, and 2 mills in the court of the abbot without rent. TRE it was worth £20; and afterwards, as now, £40.

Of these 60 hides Reginald holds of the abbot in pledge 1 manor, SHIPPON. Eadnoth the staller held it TRE and it did not then belong to the abbey. Earl Hugh gave it to the abbot. It was then assessed at 5 hides; now at 1 hide. There are in demesne 2 ploughs; and 2 villans and 5 bordars with 1 plough, and 4 slaves, and 20 acres of meadow.

The same man holds in the same place 3 hides of the abbot. Alweard the priest and Leofwine the goldsmith held them of the abbot and could not withdraw. Then, as now, it was assessed at 3 hides. In demesne he has 1 plough with 1 bordar, and 18 acres of meadow, [and] a fishery rendering 5d. This land is for 4 ploughs. TRE it was worth £7; and afterwards 100s; now £6.

Hugh the cook holds of the abbot in Abingdon 1½ hides and in Sandford-on-Thames [Oxon.] 2 hides. Leofwine and Northmann held them but they could not withdraw. There are 1½ ploughs with 1 bordar, and 6 acres of meadow. There is land for 2 ploughs. It is worth 40s.

Of the aforesaid 60 hides Ansketil and Gilbert hold in BAYWORTH 10 hides of the abbot. Wulfric held them and could not withdraw. These 10 hides are assessed at 8. There are 3 ploughs; and 9 villans and 8 bordars with 4½ ploughs. There are 5 slaves, and 60 acres of meadow. There is land for 8 ploughs. It was worth £10; now £8.

Of the same manor and of the same land Warin holds 4 hides in Sugworth, and Berner 5 hides in Sunningwell and in

Kennington, and Alwine 1 hide in Kennington. 6 Englishmen held them and could not withdraw from the church. There is land for 6 ploughs and it paid geld with the other hides. There are 3 ploughs; and 7 villans and 18 bordars with 1 plough and 5 slaves, and 110 acres of meadow. It was worth £12; now £10.

IN ROWBURY HUNDRED

The abbey itself holds CHIEVELEY. It has always held it. TRE it was assessed at 27 hides; now at 7½ hides. There is land for 20 ploughs. In demesne are 3 ploughs; and 28 villans and 10 bordars with 18 ploughs. There are 3 slaves, and 4 acres of meadow, [and] woodland for 60 pigs. Of this land William holds of the abbot 5 hides, and Godfrey 1½ hides, and there is 1 plough, with 3 villans and 2 bordars having 1 plough, and 3 acres of meadow. The whole, TRE and afterwards, was worth £12; now the abbot's portion [is worth] £10; [that] of his men 50s.

The abbey itself holds WELFORD, and always held it. TRE it was assessed at 50 hides; and now at 37 hides. There is land for 24 ploughs. In demesne are 5 ploughs; and 33 villans and 34 bordars with 22 ploughs. There are 9 slaves, and 5 mills rendering 60s, and 2 churches, and 40 acres of meadow, [and] woodland for 20 pigs. TRE and afterwards, as now, worth £27.

Of this land of this manor Reinbald holds LECKHAMPSTEAD, 10 hides, and William 4 hides in WESTON and Berner 2 hides in BOXFORD. These Beorhtwine and Ælfric and a certain reeve held of the abbot, and they could not withdraw. There is land for 11 ploughs. There are 3 ploughs; and 12 villans and 24 bordars with 6 ploughs and 6 slaves, and 2 acres of meadow, and a church. It is and was worth £10.

Walter de Riviere holds of the abbot BEEDON. Northmann held it of the abbot and could not go where he wished. It was then assessed at 10 hides; now at 8 hides. However, it was [assessed] at 15 hides, but King Edward allowed it as 11 hides, so they say. There is land for 11 ploughs. In demesne are 2 [ploughs]; and 11 villans and 10 bordars with 6 ploughs, and there are 3 slaves. Of this land a certain knight holds 2 hides, and he has there 1 plough with 3 bordars. TRE it was worth £11; and afterwards £6; now £8.

The same Walter holds 2 hides in BENHAM. Edith held them TRE, and they were assessed at as much then, as now. Edith herself could go where she wished. There is land for 1 plough. There are 5 bordars, and 20 acres of meadow; nothing else. It is and was worth 30s. This land did not belong to the abbey TRE but it is quit to the king.

IN MARCHAM HUNDRED

The abbey itself holds MARCHAM. It has always held it. TRE it was assessed at 20 hides; now at 10 hides. There is land for 10 ploughs. In demesne are 3 ploughs; and 18 villans and 10 bordars with 10 ploughs. There is a church, and 6 slaves, and a mill rendering 15s, and 100 acres of meadow. Of this land Ansketil holds 1 hide. Alwine held it of the abbot, and there is in demesne 1 plough. The whole, TRE, was worth £12.10s; now as much.

The abbey itself holds FRILFORD. It has always held it. TRE it was assessed at 10 hides, as it is now. In demesne are 4 hides. There is land for 4 ploughs. There are 8 villans with 2 ploughs, and 40 acres of meadow. It is and was worth 40s. Of this land of this manor Reginald holds 4 hides and Renbald 1 hide and Salvi 1 hide. 5 thegns held them of the abbot and could not withdraw. There is land for 6 ploughs. There are 2½ ploughs; and 6 villans and 10 bordars with 2 ploughs and 2 slaves, and 60 acres of meadow. The whole, TRE, was worth 70s; and afterwards the same; now £6.

Rainbald holds of the abbot 1 hide in TUBNEY. Northmann and Ælfric held it. TRE, as now, it was assessed at 1 hide. There is land for 6 ploughs. In demesne, nothing. There are 2 villans and 16 bordars with 6 ploughs. There are 2 slaves, and 15 acres of meadow. TRE, and afterwards, it was worth 40s; now £4.

William holds BESSELS LEIGH of the abbot, and Northmann held it of the abbot TRE. Then, as now, it was assessed at 1 hide. There is land for 5 ploughs. In demesne are 2 ploughs; and 12 bordars with 3 ploughs. It was worth 40s; now £4.

[Folio 59: BERKSHIRE]

The abbey itself holds GARFORD, and always held it. TRE it was assessed at 10 hides; now at 6 hides. Of these the abbot has 8 hides, and Berner [holds] 2 of him. There is land for 7 ploughs. In demesne are 3 ploughs; and 10 villans and 10 bordars with 3 ploughs. There is a mill rendering 7s6d, and 30 acres of meadow, and Berner has 1 plough with 6 bordars, and 6 acres of meadow. The whole was worth TRE £12; and afterwards £10; now as much.

The abbey itself holds EAST HANNEY, and always held it. TRE, as now, it was assessed at 10 hides. There is land for 7 ploughs. There are 10 villans with 2 ploughs, and 100 acres of meadow. Of this land of this manor Wulfwig holds 3 hides which were [part] of the demesne for the sustenance of the monks TRE, and Nicholas holds 1 hide of the abbot which Edwin the priest held and could not withdraw from him. On these 4 hides are 2 ploughs, and 9 bordars with half a plough, and a mill rendering 12s, and 4 slaves, and 60 acres of meadow. The whole TRE was worth £8; and afterwards £7; now the same.

The abbey itself holds GOOSEY, and always held it. It was assessed TRE at 17 hides; now at 11 hides. There is land for 9 ploughs. In demesne are 2 ploughs; and 6 villans and 3 bordars with 2 ploughs, and 1 radknight with his own plough, and 100 acres of meadow, and from pasture, 16d. Of this land of this manor Hermer holds 7 hides, and it is [part] of the demesne for the sustenance of the monks. He has there 1 plough, and 7 villans with half a plough, and 35 acres of meadow. The whole TRE was worth £9; and afterwards £10; now the same.

Walter Giffard holds LYFORD of the abbot. TRE the sons of Algeard held it of the abbot and could not go elsewhere without leave, and yet they commended themselves to Walter without the abbot's licence. Then, as now, it was assessed at 7 hides. There is land for 3 ploughs. In demesne are 2 [ploughs]; and 8 villans and 7 bordars with 2 ploughs, and there are 4 acres of meadow. It was worth £4; now 100s.

Reginald holds of the abbot 3 hides in the same vill. Lindbald the monk held it of the abbey, and it was assessed at 3 hides then, as now. There is land for 1½ ploughs. In demesne is a plough; and 3 villans and 3 bordars with half a plough. There is 1 slave, and 36 acres of meadow. It was worth 20s; now 40s.

The abbey itself holds DRAYCOTT MOOR, and always held it. TRE, as now, it was assessed at 10 hides. There is land for 8 ploughs. There are 16 villans with 7 ploughs, and 40 acres of meadow. Of this land Gilbert holds 1 hide and a certain Englishman half a hide, and there is 1 plough, with 2 villans and 2 slaves, and 6 acres of meadow, and a fishery. The whole, TRE and afterwards, was worth 100s; now £6.

IN SUTTON HUNDRED

The abbey itself holds MILTON, and always held it. TRE it was assessed at 28 hides; now at 23 hides. There is land for 24 ploughs. In demesne are 4 ploughs; and 39 villans and 25 bordars with 15 ploughs. There are 4 slaves, and a mill rendering 10s, and 344 acres of meadow. Of the same land Azelin holds 2 hides and 1 virgate of the abbot, and Reginald 3 hides. There are 3 ploughs, and 5 villans and 11 bordars, and a mill rendering 12s6d, and 2 slaves, and 30 acres of meadow. The whole TRE was worth £25; now what the abbot has [is worth] as much; what his men [hold] £4.5s.

The abbey itself holds APPLEFORD in demesne. TRE, as now, it was assessed at 5 hides. There is land for 6½ ploughs. In demesne are 2 [ploughs]; and 14 villans and 20 bordars with 4 ploughs. There is 1 slave, and 2 mills rendering 25s, and a fishery rendering 10s, and 60 acres of meadow, and 21s of profits from the demesne land. Of this land Robert holds 1 hide and he has 2 bordars there. The whole TRE was worth £9; and afterwards, as now, the same.

In SUTTON COURTENAY Alwig the priest holds 1 hide of the abbot. His father held it, and it was assessed at as much then, as now. He has there half a plough with 3 bordars. It is worth 20s.

The abbey itself holds LITTLE WITTENHAM, and always held it. TRE it was assessed at 10 hides; now at 5 hides. There is land for 6 ploughs. In demesne are 2 ploughs; and 11 villans and 9 bordars with 3 ploughs. There is a church, and a mill rendering 10s, and 53 acres of meadow. TRE it was worth £15; and afterwards, as now, £12.

IN 'RIPPLESMERE' HUNDRED

The abbey itself holds WINKFIELD, and always held it. TRE it was assessed at 10 hides; now at 3½ hides. There is land for 20 ploughs. There are 20 villans with 9 ploughs, and 1 man holds half a hide against the will of the abbot, and he does so unjustly. Of this land 4 hides are in the king's forest. It is and was always worth £4.

IN 'CHARLDON' HUNDRED

The abbey itself holds WHISTLEY GREEN, and always held it. TRE it was assessed at 10 hides; now at 7 hides. There is land for 12 ploughs. There are 16 villans and 1 bordar with 9 ploughs, and a mill rendering 5s and 250 eels, and 10 acres of meadow, woodland for 50 pigs, and a fishery rendering 300 eels. It was worth £10; now £6.

IN 'NAKEDTHORN' HUNDRED

The abbey itself holds FARNBOROUGH. TRE it was assessed at 10 hides; now at $4\frac{1}{2}$ hides. There is land for 10 ploughs. In demesne are 2 ploughs; and 8 villans and 10 bordars with 6 ploughs. There is 1 slave, and 5 acres of meadow, [and] woodland for fencing. TRE it was worth £9; and afterwards £6; now £8.

Wynric holds CHILTON of the abbot. Blæcmann held it of Earl Harold in alod, and could go where he wished. Then, as now, [it was assessed] at 5 hides. There is land for 6 ploughs. In demesne are $1\frac{1}{2}$ ploughs; and 3 villans and 13 bordars with $2\frac{1}{2}$ ploughs. [There is] woodland for 10 pigs.

Hezelin holds LEVERTON of the abbot. Blæcmann held it in fief TRE. It was then assessed at $6\frac{1}{2}$ hides; now at $4\frac{1}{2}$ hides. There is land for 4 ploughs. In demesne is 1 [plough]; and 4 villans and 3 bordars with 2 ploughs. There are 2 slaves, and a mill rendering 10s, [and] woodland for 2 pigs. It was worth 60s; now 50s.

IN SHRIVENHAM HUNDRED

The abbey itself holds WATCHFIELD, and held it TRE. It was then assessed at 20 hides; now at 10 hides. There is land for 12 ploughs. In demesne are 3 ploughs; and 14 villans and 10 bordars with 6 ploughs. There are 8 slaves, and a mill rendering 25s, and 150 acres of meadow. Of this land Gilbert holds 3 hides and 1 virgate of the abbot, and Wimund 1 hide. There is in demesne 1 plough; and 2 villans and 7 bordars. The whole TRE was worth £15; and afterwards £10; now what the abbot has [is worth] £12; what the men [have] 50s.

IN 'HILDSLOW' HUNDRED

The abbey itself holds UFFINGTON, and always held it. TRE it was assessed at 40 hides; now at 14 hides. There is land for 14 ploughs. In demesne are 3 ploughs; and 17 villans and 16 bordars with 7 ploughs. There are 11 slaves, and a mill rendering 5s, and 85 acres of meadow. Of this land Gilbert holds 6 hides of the abbot, and there he has 1 plough, and 16 bordars with 1 plough. The whole, TRE, was worth £15; and afterwards £21; now £26.

Ansketil holds FAWLER of the abbot. Eadric held it in alod of King Edward and could go where he wished. Then, as now, it was assessed at 10 hides. There is land for 4 ploughs. In demesne are 2 ploughs; and 2 villans and 1 slave with 1 plough, and a mill rendering 5s, and 50 acres of meadow. TRE it was worth £7; and afterwards £4; now £6. About this manor the shire testifies that Eadric, who used to hold it, gave it over to his son, who was a monk in Abingdon, to hold it at farm and to provide him [Eadric] as long as he lived with the necessaries of life [and], after his death, to have the manor;

and therefore the men of the shire do not know that it belongs to the abbey, for they have seen neither king's writ nor seal concerning it. The abbot on the other hand testifies that TRE [Eadric's son] transferred the manor to the church to which he belonged, and concerning this he has the writ and seal of King Edward, according to the testimony of all his monks.

IN GAINFIELD HUNDRED

The abbey itself holds LONGWORTH in demesne, and held it TRE. [It was] then [assessed] at 30 hides; now at 8 hides. There is land for 8 ploughs.

[Folio 59V: BERKSHIRE]

In demesne are 3 ploughs; and 8 villans and 14 cottars with 6 ploughs. There is a church, and 8 slaves, and a fishery rendering 2s, and 100 acres of meadow. It is and always was worth £15.

The abbey itself holds CHARNEY BASSETT, and TRE, as now, it was assessed at 2 virgates. There is land for 5 ploughs. In demesne are 2 ploughs; and 13 cottars with 5 ploughs, and there are 4 slaves. It is and was worth £6.

Warin holds of the abbey half a hide [? in the same place]. Wulfwine held it of the abbot TRE. Then, as now, [it was assessed] at half a hide. There is 1 plough, with 2 cottars and 1 slave, and 16 acres of meadow. It is and was worth 12s.

The abbey itself holds SHELLINGFORD, and always held it. TRE [it was assessed] at 12 hides; now at 2 hides and 1 virgate. There is land for 9 ploughs. In demesne are 3 ploughs; and 13 villans and 1 cottar with 4 ploughs. There are 6 slaves, and a mill rendering 30d, and 104 acres of meadow, and from other meadows 12s6d, and from customary dues of cheeses £4.16s8d.

Of this manor Gilbert holds 2 hides of the abbot, and Wimund 1 hide. There are $1\frac{1}{2}$ ploughs with 1 slave. The whole, TRE and afterwards, was worth £12; now what the abbot holds [is worth] £9; what the men [hold], 60s.

Gilbert holds of the abbot PUSEY. Alfred held it of the abbot TRE. Then, as now, [it was assessed] at 2 hides. There is land for 3 ploughs. In demesne are 2 ploughs, and 1 cottar and 2 slaves. It was worth £4; now £3.

IN WANTAGE HUNDRED

The abbey itself holds [East and West] LOCKINGE, and held it TRE. [It was] then [assessed] at 10 hides; now at 6 hides and 1 virgate. There is land for 8 ploughs. In demesne is 1 plough; and 8 villans and 11 cottars with 4 ploughs. There are 3 slaves, and a mill rendering 30d, and 34 acres of meadow.

Of this land Gilbert holds 1 hide of the abbot, and 1 church with half a hide, and there he has 1 plough with 1 villan. The whole TRE was worth £9; now the abbey's demesne is worth £7; Gilbert's 36s.

The abbey itself holds WEST GINGE, and always held it. TRE it was assessed at 10 hides; now at 2 hides and 1 virgate. There is land for 5 ploughs. In demesne are 2 ploughs; and 4 villans and 18 cottars with 2 ploughs. There are 5 slaves, and a mill rendering 6s6d, and 3 acres of meadow. It was worth £8; now £7.

Reginald holds of the abbot 2 hides [? East and West Ginge]. Northmann held them of the abbot TRE. Then, as now, [they were assessed] at 2 hides. There is land for 1 plough. There are 2 cottars, and 2 acres of meadow. It was worth 40s; now 30s.

The abbey itself holds BUCKLAND. Almær held it TRE. Then, as now, [it was assessed] at 5 hides. There is land for 2 ploughs. In demesne is 1 plough; and 4 villans and 1 cottar and 1 slave with 1 plough, and half a fishery rendering 3s, and 15 acres of meadow. TRE it was worth 100s; and afterwards 40s; now 60s.

VIII. The land of the Church of Glastonbury

IN 'HILDSLOW' HUNDRED

The Abbey of GLASTONBURY holds ASHBURY, and always held it. TRE it was assessed at 40 hides; now at 16 hides and 2½ virgates. There is land for 20 ploughs. In demesne are 3 ploughs; and 13 villans and 26 bordars with 5 ploughs. There are 5 slaves, and a mill rendering 10s, and 200 acres of meadow, and a small wood.

Of this land of this manor Robert d'Oilly holds 4½ hides of the abbot, and Alwine 3 hides, and Edward 2 hides. There are in demesne 5 ploughs; and 2 villans and 7 bordars with 1 plough. There is a church, and a priest having 1 hide, and there are 4 slaves, and a mill rendering 12s6d.

The whole TRE was worth £35; and afterwards £20; now what the abbot holds [is worth] £20; what the men [hold] £12.

IX. The land of St Peter of Westminster

IN 'RIPPLESMERE' HUNDRED

THE ABBEY of WESTMINSTER holds EAST-HAMPSTEAD. It held it TRE, and then it was assessed at 10 hides; now at 5 hides. There is land for 8 ploughs. There are 14 villans with 5 ploughs, and woodland for 10 pigs. TRE it was worth 100s; and afterwards 50s; now 60s.

X. The land of the Abbey of St Peter of Winchester

IN 'EAGLE' HUNDRED

THE ABBEY of WINCHESTER holds CHADDLE-WORTH. 2 free men held it of Countess Gytha and of her son Gyrth as 2 manors. It was then assessed at 16 hides; now at 10 hides. There is land for 10 ploughs. In demesne is 1 plough; and 5 villans and 5 bordars with 4 ploughs. There are 6 slaves, and 2 acres of meadow, [and] woodland for 20 pigs. TRE it was worth £14; and afterwards £10; now £12.

This manor Odo of Winchester gave to Robert, steward to Hugh de Port. How the abbey has it the men of the shire do not know.

IN 'SLOTISFORD' HUNDRED

The abbey itself held BRIGHTWELL-CUM-SOTWELL in demesne for the sustenance of the monks TRE. Hugh de Port now holds it of the abbot in fief. Then, as now, it was assessed at 10 hides. There is land for 5 ploughs. In demesne are 2 ploughs; and 9 villans with 3 ploughs. There is a mill rendering 15s, and 30 acres of meadow, and 9 cottars; and in Wallingford 8 closes rendering 14s4d.

A man holds 1 hide of the same land and there he has 1 plough with 3 cottars. The whole, TRE, was worth £8; and afterwards as much; now £12.

XI. The land of the Church of Chertsey

IN 'BEYNHURST' HUNDRED

THE ABBEY OF CHERTSEY holds WHITE WALT-HAM as [part] of the demesne for the sustenance of the monks. It held it TRE. Then, as now, it was assessed at 10 hides. There is land for 12 ploughs. In demesne are 2 ploughs; and 18 villans with 10 ploughs. There is 1 slave, and a chapel, and 9 acres of meadow, [and] woodland for 5 pigs.

Of the same land Turold holds 1 hide and 1 virgate of the abbot, and there he has 2 ploughs with 2 cottars. The whole, TRE, was worth £8; now the abbot's part [is worth] £6; Turold's [part] 10s.

XII. The land of the Church of St Alban

IN WANTAGE HUNDRED

THE ABBEY of ST ALBAN holds [East and West] HENDRED. Nigel d'Aubigny gave it to the church. 3 thegns held it TRE and could go where they wished. It was then assessed at 10 hides; now at 4. There is land for 4 ploughs. In demesne are 2 ploughs; and 3 villans and 3 cottars with 1 plough, and there are 45 acres of meadow.

Of this land Ernucion holds 2 hides of the abbot, and there he has 1 plough with 4 cottars. There is a church and 5 acres of meadow. The whole, TRE and afterwards, was worth £10; now likewise the whole [is worth] £10.

XIII. The land of the Church of Saint-Pierre-Sur-Dives

IN GAINFIELD HUNDRED

THE ABBOT of Saint-Pierre-sur-Dives holds of the king PUSEY. 2 alodiaries held it and could go where they wished. It was then assessed at 2½ hides; now at nothing. There is 1 plough and 2 villans. It is and was worth 32s1d.

IN THATCHAM HUNDRED

The abbot himself holds 2 hides in CURRIDGE. Edward held them of King Edward as a manor. [It was] then [assessed] at 2 hides; now at nothing. There is 1 villan with 3 oxen. It is and was worth 10s.

XIIII. The land of St Mary of Winchester

IN 'WYFOLD' HUNDRED

THE ABBESS of WINCHESTER holds COLESHILL. Edmund held it of King Edward in alod. Walter de Lacy gave it to the church with his daughter; the shire does not know in what manner. TRE it was assessed at 8 hides; now at 2½ hides. There is land [...]. In demesne are 2 ploughs; and 6 villans and 3 bordars with 1 plough. There are 2 slaves, and the third part of a mill rendering 10s, and 69 acres of meadow. It was worth £7; and afterwards £6; now 100s.

XV. The land of the Church of Battle

IN 'NAKEDTHORN' HUNDRED

THE ABBOT of Battle holds BRIGHTWALTON of the king. Earl Harold held it. [It was] then [assessed] at 10 hides. A certain thegn who held it before him used to pay geld for 15 hides; now nothing. There is land [...]. In demesne are 2 ploughs; and 10 villans and 13 bordars with 7 ploughs. There are 3 slaves, and a church with a priest, [and] woodland for 20 pigs. In Wallingford, 5 closes. It was worth £10; now £9.

[Folio 60: BERKSHIRE]

The abbot himself holds a church in Reading with 8 hides belonging there. Leofgifu the abbess held it of King Edward. It was then assessed at 8 hides; now at 3 hides. There is land for 7 ploughs. In demesne is 1 [plough]; and 9 villans and 8 bordars with 5 ploughs. There are 2 mills rendering 40s, and 2½ fisheries rendering 5s. In Reading, 29 messuages rendering 28s8d, and 12 acres of meadow, [and] woodland for 5 pigs. From the church, £3. TRE it was worth £9; and afterwards £8; now £11.

XVI. The land of the Church of Amesbury

IN KINTBURY HUNDRED

THE ABBESS of AMESBURY holds KINTBURY. The church has always held it. TRE it was assessed at 11 hides; now at 8 hides. There is land for 10 ploughs. In demesne are 4 ploughs; and 12 villans and 18 bordars with 8 ploughs. There are 11 slaves, and a mill rendering 4s, and 60 acres of meadow, [and] woodland for 10 pigs. It was worth £12; now 11.

IN 'EAGLE' HUNDRED

The abbey itself holds WEST CHALLOW, and always held it. TRE it was assessed at 7 hides; now at 3½ hides. There is land for 5 ploughs. In demesne are 2 ploughs; and 10 villans and 8 bordars with 2 ploughs. There are 2 slaves, and 40 acres of meadow. It is and always was worth £7.

The abbey itself holds FAWLEY. TRE it was assessed at 10 hides; now at 5 hides. There is land for 5 ploughs. In demesne are 2 ploughs; and 8 villans and 4 slaves with 3 ploughs, and 20 acres of meadow. It is and always was worth £6.

XVII. The land of the Count of Evreux

IN READING HUNDRED

THE COUNT of Evreux holds SHEFFIELD BOTTOM of the king. Coleman and Beorhtweard held it of King Edward and could go where they wished. Then, as now, it was assessed at 2 hides. There is land for 3 ploughs. In demesne, nothing. There are 5 villans and 5 bordars with 2 ploughs, and 4 slaves, and a mill rendering 10s, and 20 acres of meadow, [and] woodland for 10 pigs. It is and was worth 40s.

The same count holds 1 hide in PEASEMORE. Alwine held it in parage, and it was assessed at 1 hide then; now at nothing. There is 1 bordar with half a plough. It is worth 10s.

IN BUCKLEBURY HUNDRED

The same count holds BUCKLEBURY. Leofwine held it of King Edward. [It was] then [assessed] at 4 hides; now at 1 hide and 1 virgate. There is land for 4 ploughs. In demesne are 2 [ploughs]; and 3 villans and 4 bordars with 2 ploughs. There are 7 slaves, and a mill rendering 4s. It is and was worth £4.

The same count holds [?] WESTROP GREEN. 4 free men held it of King Edward. Then, as now, [it was assessed] at 1 hide. There is nothing in demesne. There 3 villans have 1 plough and 4 acres of meadow. It is and was worth 10s.

IN KINTBURY HUNDRED

The same count holds 'CALCOT' [in Hungerford]. Beorhtweard held it of King Edward as a manor. [It was] then [assessed] at 3 hides; now at 1 hide. There is land for 2 ploughs. In demesne is 1 plough; and 3 villans and 4 bordars with 1 plough. There is a mill rendering 4s, and 5 acres of meadow, [and] woodland for fencing. It was worth 30s; now 20s.

The count himself holds BECKETT. 2 free men held it of King Edward in alod as 2 manors. It was then assessed at 5 hides; now at 2 hides and 4 acres. There is land for 4 ploughs. In demesne are 2 ploughs; and 2 villans and 13 bordars with 1½ ploughs, and 100 acres of meadow less 7. It was worth £4; and now the same.

IN BLEWBURY HUNDRED

The count himself holds BLEWBURY. Beorhtweard held it TRE. [It was] then [assessed] at 2 hides; now at 1 virgate. There is land for 1 plough. There are 4 cottars, and a mill rendering 4s, and 10 acres of meadow. It was worth 40s; now 20s.

IN WANTAGE HUNDRED

The same count holds EAST HANNEY. 2 free men held it TRE. It was then assessed at 6 hides; now at 2 hides. There is land for 5 ploughs. In demesne is 1 plough; and 20 cottars with 1 plough. There is 1 slave, and 2 mills rendering 27s6d, and 70 acres of meadow. It was worth 100s; now £6.

The same count holds [East and West] HENDRED. Alwine held it TRE. [It was] then [assessed] at 5 hides; now at 2 hides. There is land for 2 ploughs. There is 1 plough; and 6 cottars with 1 plough. There is a church, and a slave, and 5 acres of meadow. It was worth 60s; now 70s.

The same count holds 5 hides which 7 free men held TRE. It was then assessed at 5 hides; now at 30 acres of land. There is land for 2½ ploughs. There are 6 cottars with 1 plough, and 5 acres of meadow. It is and was worth 30s.

The same count has in the same HUNDRED 1 hide. A certain Wulfgar held it TRE. [It was] then [assessed] at 1 hide; now at 6 acres. There is land for 1 plough. There are 2 cottars and 12 acres of meadow. It is and was worth 10s.

IN GAINFIELD HUNDRED

The same count has 1 hide and 3 virgates and 2 acres. A certain Wulfwine held them TRE, and it was assessed at as much; now at nothing. There are 4 cottars. There are 7 acres of meadow. It was worth 30s; now 15s.

The same count holds 2 hides and 2 acres of land. 4 free men held these TRE, and it was assessed at as much; now at 5 virgates. There is 1 villan and 4 cottars, and 12 acres of meadow. TRE it was worth 37s6d; now 22s.

XVIII. The land of Earl Hugh

IN SUTTON HUNDRED

Earl HUGH holds DRAYTON, and William [holds] of him. Eadnoth held it of Harold and could not go where he pleased. It was then assessed at 2 hides; now at nothing. There is land for 1½ ploughs. In demesne is 1 plough; and 4 bordars and 2 slaves, and 13 acres of meadow. It is and was worth 50s.

IN 'WYFOLD' HUNDRED

The earl himself holds BUSCOT, and Robert [holds] of him. Earl Harold held it. It was then assessed at 40 hides; now at 6 hides. There is land for 20 ploughs. In demesne are 4 ploughs; and 25 villans and 25 bordars with 8 ploughs. There are 6 slaves, and a fishery rendering 18s8d, and 300 acres of meadow.

Of this land Drogo holds 8 hides and Ranulph 4 hides; and there are in demesne 2 ploughs; and 2 villans and 6 bordars.

The whole, TRE, was worth £20; and afterwards £17; now £26.

XIX. The land of the Count of Mortain

IN BLEWBURY HUNDRED

The Count of MORTAIN holds ASTON TIRROLD, and the Abbey of Preaux holds it of him. Eskil held it TRE. [It was] then [assessed] at 5 hides; now at 2 hides. There is land for 2 ploughs. In demesne is 1 plough; and 3 villans and 3 cottars and 6 slaves, and a church. It was and is worth £3.

XX. The land of Walter Giffard

IN WANTAGE HUNDRED

WALTER Giffard holds WEST HANNEY. Osbern and Theodric hold it of him. Edwin, a free man, held it of King Edward. Then, as now, [it was assessed] at 2 hides. There is land for 1 plough. There is 1 plough, and 11 cottars, and 24 acres of meadow. It is and was worth 40s.

Walter himself holds WEST HANNEY. Earl Tosti held it. [It was] then [assessed] at 14 hides; now at 7 hides. There is land for 8 ploughs. In demesne are 2 ploughs; and 14 villans and 8 cottars with 3 ploughs. There are 4 slaves, and a mill rendering 12s6d, and another mill rendering 7s6d, which belongs to the manor of Charlton, as the HUNDRED states. Turold the priest holds of Walter the church of this vill with 1 hide which always pays geld. It was worth £10; and afterwards £8; now £14.

XXI. The land of Henry de Ferrers

IN 'NAKEDTHORN' HUNDRED

HENRY de Ferrers holds CATMORE, and Henry [holds] of him. Eadsige held it of King Edward. [It was] then [assessed] at 5 hides; now at 3 hides. There is land for 6 ploughs. In demesne is 1 [plough]; and 5 villans and 12 bordars with 3 ploughs. It was worth £7; and afterwards 40s; now 70s.

The same Henry holds EAST ILSLEY, and Roger [holds] of him. Algar held it of King Edward. Then, as now, [it was assessed] at 3½ hides. There is land for 2 ploughs. In demesne is half a plough with 2 bordars and 1 slave. It was worth 60s; now 40s.

The same Henry holds 'ASHDEN' [? in Compton], and Ralph [holds] of him. Bondi held it of King Edward. [It was] then [assessed] at 10 hides and 1 virgate; now at 9 hides. There is land for 10 ploughs. In demesne are 4 ploughs; and 8 villans and 8 bordars. There are 9 slaves, and 6 acres of meadow, [and] woodland for 5 pigs. The whole was worth £12 TRE; and afterwards £6; now £10.

IN BUCKLEBURY HUNDRED

The same Henry holds FRILSHAM, and Roger [holds] of him. 2 free men held it of King Edward. Then, as now, it was assessed at 7½ hides. There is land [...]. In demesne are 1½ ploughs;

IN SUTTON HUNDRED

Walter himself holds LONG WITTENHAM. Queen Edith held it. It was then assessed at 20 hides; now at 13 hides and 1 virgate. There is land for 16 ploughs. In demesne are 3 ploughs; and 29 villans and 16 bordars with 9 ploughs. There are 6 slaves, and 163 acres of meadow; and in Wallingford 8 closes rendering 4s. For herbage, 5s. TRE it was worth £20; and afterwards £15; now £20.

and 5 villans and 11 bordars with $6\frac{1}{2}$ ploughs. There are 3 slaves, and a mill rendering 4s, and 10 acres of meadow, [and] woodland for 10 pigs. It is and always was worth £6.

IN THATCHAM HUNDRED

HENRY himself holds GREENHAM. Siward held it of King Edward in alod. [It was] then [assessed] at 5 hides; now at $2\frac{1}{2}$ hides. There is land for 10 ploughs. In demesne are 2 ploughs; and 11 villans and 19 bordars with 7 ploughs. There is a church, and 4 slaves, and $1\frac{1}{2}$ mills rendering 11s all but 2d, and 41 acres of meadow, and 80 acres of meadow [sic]. TRE, and afterwards, it was worth £8; now £6.

IN KINTBURY HUNDRED

The same Henry holds BAGSHOT [Wilts.]. Godric held it of King Edward as a manor. 2 hides did not pay geld because they belonged to the king's farm, and they have been claimed for the king's use. There is land for 4 ploughs. There are 9 villans and 10 bordars with 4 ploughs. There are 3 slaves, and a mill rendering 11s, and 8 acres of meadow. [There is] woodland for fencing. It was worth 30s; now 40s.

IN 'BEYNHURST' HUNDRED

The same Henry holds BISHAM. Bondi held it of King Edward. Then, as now, [it was assessed] at 8 hides. There is land for 10 ploughs. In demesne are 2 ploughs; and 17 villans and 2 cottars with 8 ploughs. There is a church, and 2 slaves, and 26 acres of meadow, and 12 arpents of vineyard. It was worth £8; now £12.

IN BLEWBURY HUNDRED

The same Henry holds WILLINGTON, and Nigel [holds] of him. Thorkil, a free man, held it of King Edward. There is land for 6 ploughs. [It was] then [assessed] at 8 hides; now at 4 hides and 1 virgate. There is a church, and 9 slaves, and 2 ploughs in demesne, and 10 villans and 2 cottars with 8 ploughs, and 40 acres of meadow. It was worth £6; now £9.

IN WANTAGE HUNDRED

The same Henry holds DENCHWORTH, and Reiner [holds] of him. Æthelric held it TRE. [It was] then [assessed] at 7 hides; now at $5\frac{1}{2}$ hides. There is land for 5 ploughs. In demesne is 1 plough; and 5 villans and 5 cottars with 1 plough, and 30 acres of meadow, and there is a church. TRE it was worth 70s; and afterwards 60s; now £4.

The same Henry holds CHARLTON, and Robert [holds] of him. Tovi, a free man, held it. Then, as now, [it was assessed] at $2\frac{1}{2}$ hides. There is land for 1 plough. In demesne is 1 plough, with 7 cottars, and half a mill rendering 5s, and 8 acres of meadow. It is and was worth 50s.

Henry himself holds [East and West] LOCKINGE, and Hubert [holds] of Henry. Siward held it of King Edward. Then, as now, [it was assessed] at 10 hides. There is land for 6 ploughs. In demesne are 2 ploughs; and 3 villans and 14 cottars with 2 ploughs. There is 1 slave, and 41 acres of meadow. It was worth £10; now £8.

The same Henry holds SPARSHOLT, and Fulchard [holds] of him. Godric, a free man, held it. Then, as now, [it was assessed] at $1\frac{1}{2}$ hides. There is land for 1 plough. There are 2 villans and 2 cottars and 4 slaves. It was worth 40s; now 30s.

The same Henry holds 3 hides and 1 virgate [?Kingston Lisle]. 4 free men held them TRE. It was then assessed at 3 hides and 1 virgate; now at 1 hide. There is land for 2 ploughs. There are 8 cottars with 1 plough, and 3 acres of meadow. TRE it was worth 60s; and afterwards, as now, 40s. This land Henry states to have been his predecessor Godric's; but according to the testimony of the hundred, Godric took possession of it at King William's expense after the Battle of Hastings, and he did not ever hold it in the time of King Edward.

IN MARCHAM HUNDRED

Henry himself holds KINGSTON BAGPUIZE, and Ralph [holds] of him. Stenkil held it TRE, and then, as now, it was assessed at 5 hides. There is land for 4 ploughs. In demesne are 2 ploughs; and 11 villans and 6 bordars with 2 ploughs. There are 3 slaves, and 30 acres of meadow. It was worth 60s; now 50s.

The same Henry holds FYFIELD, and another Henry [holds] of him. Godric the sheriff held it of the abbot, and could not go where he pleased with this land. Then, as now, it was assessed at 10 hides. There is land for 8 ploughs. In demesne are 2 ploughs; and 13 villans and 5 bordars with 3 ploughs. There is a church, and 7 slaves, and 100 acres of meadow. TRE, and afterwards, it was worth £10; and now £6.

The same Henry holds FYFIELD. Godric held it of King Edward, and then it was assessed at 10 hides; and now at 5 hides because King Edward so allowed, as the hundred testifies. There is land for 6 ploughs. In demesne are 2 ploughs; and 8 villans and 3 bordars with 2 ploughs, and half a fishery rendering 11s8d. There are 4 slaves, and 12 acres of meadow. It was worth £6; now 100s.

IN SUTTON HUNDRED

The same Henry holds [East and West] HENDRED, and another Henry [holds] of him. Godric the sheriff held it of King Edward. It was then assessed at 1 hide; now at nothing. This is that hide which belonged to the king's farm about which Ælfric gave evidence. There is land for 2 ploughs. There are [2 ploughs] in demesne with 8 bordars, and 6 acres of meadow. It was worth 100s; and now the same.

The same Henry holds STANFORD IN THE VALE. Siward held it of King Edward. It was then assessed at 40 hides, and, as they say, King Edward allowed it as 30 hides. It now pays geld for 6 hides. There is land for 20 ploughs. In demesne are 3 ploughs; and 21 villans and 22 bordars with 9 ploughs. There are 7 slaves, and 2 mills rendering 7s8d, and 318 acres of meadow. For pasture, 32d. Of this land Henry the steward holds half a plough [sic]; and there he has 1 bordar. The whole, TRE, was worth £30; and afterwards £24; now £20.10s.

The same Henry holds PUSEY, and another Henry [holds] of him. Dunnic held it of King Edward and could go where he wished. It was then assessed at 2½ hides and 2 acres of land; now at 2 hides. There is land for 1 plough, and there is [1 plough] in demesne with 4 bordars. TRE it was worth 40s; and afterwards 20s; now 30s.

IN READING HUNDRED

The same Henry holds 1½ hides in BURGHFIELD. 2 alodiaries held them TRE, and it was assessed at as much. One did service to the queen and the other to Bondi. They who then held it hold it still of Henry, but the hundred knows not why. There is land for 6 ploughs. In demesne are 2 ploughs; and 2 villans and 2 bordars with 1 plough, and a mill rendering 5s10d, and a fishery rendering 68d, and 40 acres of meadow, [and] woodland for 15 pigs. It was worth 40s; now 50s.

The same Henry holds 1 hide in "BURLEI". Leofwine held it of King Edward and could go where he wished. The same man holds it still, and it was assessed at 1 hide then, as now. There is 1 villan and 1 bordar with 1 plough, and a fishery rendering 8d, and 2 acres of meadow, [and] woodland for 5 pigs. It was worth 10s; now 20s.

The same Henry holds UPPER WOOLHAMPTON. Godric the sheriff held it of King Edward, and it was assessed at 3 hides then, as now. There is land for 5 ploughs. There are 12 villans and 4 bordars with 5 ploughs, and 4 slaves, and a mill rendering 15s, and 40 acres of meadow. It was worth £6; and afterwards, as now, £4. This land King Edward granted out of his farm to Godric; and the men of the shire have seen his seal concerning it. In addition to these hides Godric himself acquired from the king's farm 1 virgate of land, concerning which they have not seen the king's seal.

XXII. The land of William fitzAnsculf

IN READING HUNDRED

WILLIAM fitzAnsculf holds ENGLEFIELD, and Gilbert [holds] of him. Alwine held it of King Edward. Then, as now, it was assessed at 10 hides. There is land for 13 ploughs. In demesne are 2 ploughs; and 17 villans and 3 bordars with 11 ploughs. There are 4 slaves, and a mill rendering 10s, and 60 acres of meadow. TRE it was worth £10; and afterwards £7; now 7s. more.

The same William holds BRADFIELD. Horling held it of King Edward. It was then assessed at 9 hides; now at 6 hides. There is land for 30 ploughs. In demesne are 2 ploughs; and 20 villans and 31 bordars with 18 ploughs. There are 9 slaves, and 3 mills rendering 53s, and 20 acres of meadow, [and] woodland for 100 pigs. TRE, and afterwards, it was worth £24; now £16.

The same William holds HARTRIDGE. Alfred held it of King Edward, and now holds it of William. Then, as now, it was assessed at 1 hide. There is land for 5 ploughs. In demesne is 1 plough; and 2 villans and 2 bordars with 1 plough. There are 3 slaves, and woodland for 3 pigs. It was worth 60s; now 30s.

The same William holds ENGLEFIELD. Wulfmær held it of King Edward. Then, as now, it was assessed at 1 hide. There

is land for 1 plough. There are 2 bordars, and 4 acres of meadow.

[Folio 61: BERKSHIRE]

This land Stephen holds of William. It was worth 20s; now 7s.

The same William holds UFTON NERVET, and a certain knight [holds] of him. Horling held it of King Edward. It was then assessed at 5 hides; now at 4½ hides. There is land for 5 ploughs. In demesne is 1 [plough]; and 8 villans and 5 bordars with 5 ploughs. There is 1 slave, and 44 acres of meadow, and woodland for 1 pig. Of this land another knight holds 3 virgates and there he has 1 plough. The whole, TRE, was worth 100s; and afterwards, as now, 60s.

IN 'NAKEDTHORN' HUNDRED

The same William holds HODCOTT, and Stephen [holds] of him. Baldwin held it of King Edward. Then, as now, [it was assessed] at 5 hides. There is land for 3 ploughs. In demesne is 1 [plough] with 3 bordars. [...] It was worth £6; and afterwards 30s; now 60s.

The same William holds [East and West] ILSLEY, and Stephen [holds] of him. Baldwin held it of King Edward. Then, as now, it was assessed at 6½ hides. There is land for 3 ploughs. In demesne is 1 plough; and 4 villans and 2 bordars with 2 ploughs. There are 7 slaves. It was worth £7; and afterwards, as now, £4.

The same William holds YATTENDON, and Godebold [holds] of him. Baldwin held it of King Edward in alod. Then, as now, [it was assessed] at 8 hides; this the shire testifies. In demesne are 2 ploughs; and 4 villans and 6 bordars with 3 ploughs. There are 9 slaves, and a mill rendering 5s, and 5 acres of meadow. [There is] woodland for fencing. It was worth £7; now £8.

The same William holds STANFORD DINGLEY. Eadric held it of King Edward in alod. Then, as now, [it was assessed] at 5 hides. There is land for 4 ploughs. In demesne are 2 ploughs; and 8 villans and 2 bordars with 3 ploughs. There are 3 slaves, and a mill rendering 12s. It is and always was worth £4. Gilbert holds it of William.

IN KINTBURY HUNDRED

The same William holds INKPEN. 2 free men held it of King Edward as 2 manors in alod. Then [it was assessed] at 5 hides; now at 2½ hides. There is land [...]. In demesne are 4 ploughs; and 10 villans and 15 bordars with 7 ploughs. There are 20 slaves, and a mill rendering 12s6d, and 16 acres of meadow, [and] woodland for fencing. It was worth £14; and afterwards, as now, £12.

IN 'HILDSLOW' HUNDRED

The same William holds COMPTON BEAUCHAMP. Almær held it in alod of King Edward. Then, as now, it was assessed at 5 hides. There is land for 4 ploughs. In demesne are 2 ploughs; and 1 villan and 9 bordars with 1 plough. There is a church with half a hide of this land, and 60 acres of meadow. It was worth £8; and afterwards 100s; now £6.

IN MARCHAM HUNDRED

The same William holds KINGSTON BAGPUIZE, and Adelelm [holds] of him. Thorkil held it of King Edward and could go where he wished. It was then assessed at 5 hides; now at 4 hides. There is land for 4 ploughs. In demesne are 2 ploughs; and 6 villans and 9 bordars with 1 plough. There are 5 slaves, and a fishery rendering 5s, and 30 acres of meadow. It was worth 100s; now 60s.

XXIII. The land of William de Eu

IN READING HUNDRED

WILLIAM de Eu holds of the king PADWORTH, and Joscelin [holds] of him. Ælfstan held it of King Edward, and then, as now, it was assessed at 2½ hides. There is land for 2 ploughs. In demesne is 1 [plough]; and 3 villans and 4 bordars with 1 plough. There is half a mill rendering 7s6d, and 16 acres of meadow. It was worth 50s; now 40s.

IN KINTBURY HUNDRED

The same William holds DENFORD. Alweard held it in alod of King Edward. [It was] then [assessed] at 10 hides; now at 5 hides. There is land [...]. In demesne is 1 plough; and 4 villans and 4 bordars with 2½ ploughs. There are 3 slaves, and a church. It was worth 100s; now £4. With this manor William holds half a hide which belonged to 2 free men, and never belonged to this manor, as the shire says.

IN WANTAGE HUNDRED

The same William holds NORTH DENCHWORTH, and Joscelin [holds] of him. Alweard, a free man, held it of King Edward. Then, as now, [it was assessed] at 5 hides. There is land for 2 ploughs. In demesne is 1 [plough]; and 2 villans and 6 cottars with 1 plough. There are 2 slaves, and 27 acres of meadow. It was worth 50s; and afterwards 40s; now 60s.

XXIIII. The land of William Peverel

IN 'EAGLE' HUNDRED

WILLIAM Peverel holds of the king WOOLLEY. Earl Ralph held it of King Edward. It was then assessed at 10 hides; now at 3½ hides. There is land for 6 ploughs. In demesne are 2 ploughs; and 10 villans and 8 bordars with 4 ploughs. There are 4 slaves. It was worth £10; now £6.

XXV. The land of William de Braose

IN READING HUNDRED

WILLIAM de Braose holds SOUTHCOTE of the king. Beorhtweard held it of King Edward. It was then assessed at 2 hides; now at 1 hide. There is land for 3 ploughs. In demesne is 1 [plough]; and 5 villans and 8 bordars with 2 ploughs. There is a mill rendering 18s, and a fishery rendering 50d. It was worth £4; now 100s.

XXVI. The land of William Lovet

IN THATCHAM HUNDRED

WILLIAM LOVET Lovet holds DONNINGTON of the king. Toti held it of King Edward in alod. It was then assessed at 8 hides; now at 1 hide and 1 virgate. There is land for 5 ploughs. In demesne [is] half a plough; and 4 villans and 3 bordars with 2 ploughs. There are 2 slaves, and a mill rendering 15s, and 4 acres of meadow, [and] woodland for 5 pigs. It was worth £8; and afterwards 100s; now 70s.

IN KINTBURY HUNDRED

The same William holds ENBORNE. Toti held it of King Edward in alod as a manor. Then, as now, [it was assessed] at 3 hides and 1 virgate. There is land for 2 ploughs. There are 2 villans and 7 bordars with 2 ploughs, and 13 acres of meadow, [and] woodland for fencing. It was worth 40s; now 30s.

IN BLEWBURY HUNDRED

The same William holds [North and South] MORETON. Toti held it of King Edward. Then [it was assessed] at 5 hides; now at 2½ hides. There is land for 4 ploughs. In demesne is 1 [plough]; and 3 villans and 4 cottars with 1½ ploughs. There is a mill rendering 12s6d, and 40 acres of meadow. It was and is worth £6, although it renders £7.

XXVII. The land of William fitzCorbucion

IN KINTBURY HUNDRED

WILLIAM fitzCorbucion holds of the king 10 hides in ENBORNE. Tovi held them as a manor in alod of King Edward. [It was] then [assessed] at 10 hides; now at 8 hides. There is land for 3 ploughs. In demesne is 1 [plough]; and 4 villans and 7 bordars with 2 ploughs. There are 2 slaves, and a mill rendering 20s, and 20 acres of meadow, [and] woodland for 10 pigs. It was worth 100s; now £4.

IN BLEWBURY HUNDRED

The same William holds [North and South] MORETON, and Ralph [holds] of him. A certain free man held it TRE. Then, as now, [it was assessed] at 10 hides. There is land for 7 ploughs. In demesne are 2 ploughs; and 14 villans and 8 cottars with 6 ploughs, and a mill rendering 12s6d. There is a church, and 3 slaves, and in Wallingford 5 closes rendering 50d. It was worth £10; now £12.

IN WANTAGE HUNDRED

The same William holds CHARLTON, and Geoffrey [holds] of him. Tovi, a certain free man, held it TRE. Then, as now, [it was assessed] at 2½ hides. There is land for 1 plough. In demesne is 1 [plough]; and 1 villan and 5 cottars with half a plough. It was worth 40s; now 50s.

XXVIII. The land of William fitzRichard

IN 'WYFOLD' HUNDRED

WILLIAM fitzRichard holds COLESHILL. Asgot held it in alod of King Edward. It was then assessed at 8 hides; now at 5 hides. There is land for 3 ploughs. In demesne are 2 ploughs, and 2 villans and 5 bordars. There are 4 slaves, and the third part of a mill rendering 10s, and 69 acres of meadow. It was worth £7; and afterwards £6; now £4.

IN WANTAGE HUNDRED

The same William holds CHILDREY. A certain free man, Asgot, held it TRE. [It was] then [assessed] at 12 hides; now at 8 hides. There is land for 4 ploughs. In demesne William has 2 hides, and there he has 2 villans and 3 cottars with half a plough; and Godfrey holds of him 10 hides, and there are 6 villans and 8 cottars with half a plough, and a mill rendering 4s, and 36 acres of meadow. The whole, TRE and afterwards, was worth £9; now £6.12s.

XXIX. The land of William de Cailly

IN READING HUNDRED

WILLIAM de Cailly holds of the king SULHAM, and a certain knight [holds] of him. Godric held it of King Edward. Then, as now, it was assessed at 2 hides. There is land for 5 ploughs. In demesne are 2 ploughs; and 4 villans and 6 bordars with 2 ploughs. There is a church, and 2 slaves, and 4 acres of meadow. It was worth £4; and afterwards £3; now 100s.

XXX. The land of Walter fitzPons

WALTER fitzPons holds EATON HASTINGS of the king. Gyrth held it in alod of King Edward. It was then assessed at 20 hides; now at 6 hides. There is land [...]. In demesne are 3 ploughs; and 13 villans and 5 bordars with 4 ploughs. There 7 slaves did not pay geld [*sic*]. There are 2 fisheries rendering 16s, and 148 acres of meadow. TRE it was worth £10; and afterwards 100s; now £9.

Of this manor Pons gave 3 hides to St Peter of Westminster for his soul; and there is 1 plough with 4 bordars and 3 oxen. It is worth 20s.

IN 'HILDSLOW' HUNDRED

The same William holds ODSTONE. Asgot held it of King Edward in alod. It was then assessed at 10 hides; now at 5 hides. There is land for 7 ploughs. In demesne are 2 ploughs; and 18 bordars with 3 ploughs. There are 5 slaves, and 200 acres of meadow. TRE it was worth £12; and afterwards £8; now £10.

XXXI. The land of Walter fitzOther

IN 'RIPPLESMERE' HUNDRED

WALTER fitzOther holds "ORTONE". Godric held it of King Edward. It was assessed then, as now, at 1½ hides. There is land [...]. In demesne are 2 ploughs; and 3 bordars, and 1 acre of meadow. [There is] woodland for 2 pigs. It was worth 40s; now 30s.

IN 'NAKEDTHORN' HUNDRED

The same Walter holds CHILTON. Wynsige held it of King Edward. Then, as now, it was assessed at 5 hides. There is land [...]. In demesne are 2 ploughs; and 7 villans and 9 bordars with 1½ ploughs. There are 4 slaves, and 6 closes in Wallingford rendering 2s.

IN BUCKLEBURY HUNDRED

The same Walter holds BUCKLEBURY, 1 hide; and a certain man of his [holds] of him. It lies in the forest and has never paid geld, so the shire says. Ælfhild Dese held it of King Edward. There is 1 plough in demesne. It is and was worth 7s6d.

In KINTBURY the same Walter holds half a hide, which King Edward gave to his predecessor out of his farm, and freed from all customary dues in consideration of wardenship of the forest-except such forfeiture to the king as is [due from] theft, and manslaughter, and housebreaking, and breach of the peace. It is worth 5s.

IN BLEWBURY HUNDRED

The same Walter holds [East and West] HAGBOURNE. Alwine, a free man, held it. Then, as now, [there were] 10 hides, but it is assessed at 6½ hides. There is land for 6 ploughs. In demesne are 2 ploughs; and 14 villans and 10 cottars with 5 ploughs. There are 4 slaves, and a mill rendering 12s, and 24 acres of meadow. Of this land Robert holds 1 hide of Walter, and there he has 1 plough with 1 cottar, and 4 acres of meadow. The whole, TRE and afterwards, was worth £13; and now £13.

IN READING HUNDRED

The same Walter holds WOKEFIELD, and a certain knight [holds] of him. Wihtric held it of King Edward. Then, as now, it was assessed at 1½ hides. There is land for 2 ploughs. In demesne is 1 [plough]; and 6 bordars with 1 plough. There are 4 acres of meadow, [and] woodland for 15 pigs. It was worth 20s; now 30s.

XXXII. The land of Eudo fitzHubert

IN 'RIPPLESMERE' HUNDRED

EUDO the steward holds ST LEONARDS of the king. Ælfric held it of King Edward. [It was] then [assessed] at 2 hides; now at 1 hide. In demesne are 2 ploughs; and 7 villans with 2 ploughs, and 7 acres of meadow. [There is] woodland for 5 pigs. It was worth £4; now 30s.

XXXIII. The land of Miles Crispin

IN READING HUNDRED

MILES Crispin holds PANGBOURNE, and William [holds] of him. Baldwin held it of King Edward. There are 6 hides and 1 virgate, and they did not pay geld TRE; and now for only 5 hides. There is nothing in demesne; and 3 villans and 5 bordars with 2 ploughs, and a mill rendering 10s, and 12 acres of meadow. Of this land a knight holds 1 hide; and there he has 1 plough and 2 acres of meadow. The whole was worth £6; and afterwards £5; now £4.

The same William holds of Miles 1 hide in SULHAM. Baldwin held it of King Edward; and it was assessed at as much then, as now. There is 1 plough in demesne; and 3 bordars with half a plough. It was worth 20s; now 30[s].

IN 'SLOTISFORD' HUNDRED

Miles himself holds 'CLAPCOT' [in Wallingford]. Wulfnoth, a free man, held it TRE. [It was] then [assessed] at 7 hides; now at 1 hide and 1 virgate. There is land for 3 ploughs. In demesne are 1½ ploughs; and 7 villans and 2 cottars with 2 ploughs, and a mill rendering 26s, and 25 acres of meadow. It was worth £7; and afterwards £4; now 100s.

The same Miles holds 'CLAPCOT' [in Wallingford]. Seaxfrith, a free man, held it TRE, and [it was] then [assessed] at 7 hides; now at 1 hide and 1 virgate. There is land for 3 ploughs. In demesne are 1½ ploughs; and 2 villand and 6 cottars with 3 ploughs. There are 25 acres of meadow. Of this manor Harold holds 1½ virgates of Miles. The whole was worth £7; and afterwards £4; now 100s. These 2 manors Miles holds as 1 manor.

IN WANTAGE HUNDRED

The same Miles holds BETTERTON, and William [holds] of him. Leofric the monk held it TRE, and could go where he wished. Then [it was assessed] at 10 hides; now at 5 hides. There is land for 4 ploughs. There is 1 villan and 5 cottars with half a plough, and 2 slaves, and a mill rendering 5s, and 10 acres of meadow. It was worth £8; and afterwards £4; now £3.

IN MARCHAM HUNDRED

The same Miles holds APPLETON, and Richard [holds] of him. Healfdene held it TRE. It was then assessed at 5 hides; now at 2½ hides. There is land for 6 ploughs. In demesne is 1 [plough]; and 4 villans and 5 bordars with 1 plough. There are 3 slaves, and a fishery rendering 34s2d. It was worth 100s; and afterwards 70s; now 60s.

The same Miles holds EATON, and Richard [holds] of him. Healfdene held it of King Edward. Then, as now, it was assessed at 5 hides. There is land for 4 ploughs. In demesne are 2 ploughs; and 3 villans and 4 bordars with 3 ploughs, and a fishery rendering 5s, and 25 acres of meadow. It was worth 60s; now 50s.

The same Miles holds EATON, and Alvred [holds] of him. Bosi held it of King Edward. Then, as now, it was assessed at 5 hides. There is land for 4 ploughs. In demesne are 2 ploughs; and 3 villans and 6 bordars with 1 plough, and 2 fisheries rendering 18s, and 25 acres of meadow. It was worth 60s; now 70s.

In READING Hundred Leofweard holds in [?] 'LANGLEY' [in Tilehurst] 1 hide of Miles and could not go where he pleased without leave of Vigot. This land belongs to, and is appraised in "GRATENTUN" [Oxon.] which is in Oxfordshire, and nevertheless it pays tax in Berkshire.

XXXIIII. The land of Giles brother of Ansculf

IN THATCHAM HUNDRED

GILES holds MIDGHAM of the king. 5 free men [held it] of King Edward as a manor. It was then assessed at 5 hides; now at 2 hides. There is land for 10 ploughs. In demesne there is nothing; but 9 villans and 5 bordars with 5 ploughs, and a mill rendering 14s. Of this land Almær holds 3 virgates, Reiner 1 virgate, Gilbert 1 hide and 1½ virgates; and there are 2½ ploughs; and 5 villans and 8 bordars with 1½ ploughs, and 80 acres of meadow in the manor. The whole was worth, TRE, 100s; now, in all, £6.

IN 'BEYNHURST' HUNDRED

The same Giles holds MAIDENHEAD. Siward held it TRE. Then, as now, [it was assessed] at 3 hides. There is land for 4 ploughs. 2 men, Hugh and Landri, hold of Giles. They have there 2 ploughs; and 6 villans and 4 cottars with 1 plough. There are 16 acres of meadow, [and] woodland for 10 pigs. It was worth 60s; now 40s.

IN READING HUNDRED

The same Giles holds UFTON NERVET. Sæwulf held it of King Edward. It was then assessed at 5 hides; now at 3½ hides. There is land for 5 ploughs. There are 8 villans and 5 bordars with 3 ploughs, and 36 acres of meadow. It was worth 100s; now 60s.

XXXV. The land of Hascoit [Musard]

IN ROWBURY HUNDRED

HASCOIT holds of the king WINTERBOURNE, and Chemarhuec [holds] of him. Beorhtheah held it TRE and could go where he wished. It was then assessed at 2 hides; now at 1 hide and 3 virgates. In demesne is 1 plough; and 1 villan and 2 bordars with half a plough. It is and was worth 20s.

In the same vill Norman holds of Hascoit 5 hides. These Beorhtheah held of King Edward. It was then assessed at 5 hides; now at 2 hides and 1 virgate. There is land for 6 ploughs. In demesne are 2 ploughs; and 5 villans and 8 bordars with 4 ploughs. There are 2 slaves, and 2 acres of meadow, and woodland for 4 pigs. It was worth £8; now £4.

IN LAMBOURN HUNDRED

The same Hascoit holds LAMBOURN. Beorhtheah held it of King Edward in alod. It was then assessed at 8 hides; now at 2 hides and 1 virgate. There is land for 5 ploughs. In demesne are 2 [ploughs]; and 4 villans and 6 bordars with 2½ ploughs. There are 8 slaves. It was worth £12; now £6.

The same Hascoit holds DRAYTON. Godwine held it in alod of King Edward as a manor. [It was] then [assessed] at 3½ hides; now at 1 hide. There is land for 1 plough. There are 4 villans with 1 plough. It was worth 60s; now 20s.

IN WANTAGE HUNDRED

The same Hascoit holds SPARSHOLT. Beorhtric, a free man, held it TRE. Then, as now, [it was assessed] at 2 hides. There is land for 4 ploughs. In demesne is 1 plough; and 8 villans and 5 cottars with 2 ploughs. There are 2 slaves. It is and was worth £8.

XXXVI. The land of Gilbert de Breteuil

IN BUCKLEBURY HUNDRED

GILBBERT de Breteuil holds WYLD, and William [holds] of him. Alwine held it of King Edward. Then, as now, [it was assessed] at 1 hide There is land for 2 ploughs. In demesne are 2 ploughs; and 2 villans and 2 bordars with 1 plough. There are 2 slaves. It was worth 30s; now 40s.

The same Gilbert holds EAST HANNEY, and Joscelin [holds] of him. A certain free man, Godric, held it TRE. Then, as now, it was assessed at 6 hides. There is land for 3 ploughs. In demesne are 2 ploughs; and 12 cottars with half a plough. There are 2 mills rendering 30s,

IN KINTBURY HUNDRED

The same Giles holds ENBORNE. Sæwulf held it of King Edward as a manor in alod. It was then assessed at 3½ hides; now at 1 hide. There is land for 2 ploughs. In demesne is half a plough; and 2 villans and 2 bordars, and 13 acres of meadow. The villans [have] 2 ploughs. It was worth 40s; now 20s.

[Folio 62: BERKSHIRE]

and 38 acres of meadow. It was and is worth £6; and yet it renders £6 and an ounce of gold.

The same Gilbert holds half a hide. Ælfric, a free man, held it. Then, as now, [it was assessed] at half a hide. There is 1 villan and 1 slave, and 8 acres of meadow. It is worth 10s.

IN MARCHAM HUNDRED

The same Gilbert holds HATFORD, and Payne [holds] of him. 2 brothers held it in parage; each had a hall and they could go where they wished. Then, as now, it was assessed at 10 hides. There is land for 6 ploughs. In demesne are 2 ploughs; and 3 villans and 11 bordars with 2 ploughs. There is a church, and 3 slaves, and 100 acres of meadow. It was worth £8; and afterwards 100s; now £10.

The same Gilbert holds NEWTON, and Payne [holds] of him. Alric held it and could go where he wished. Then, as

now, it was assessed at 2 hides. There is land for 1 plough, and there is [1 plough] in demesne with 4 bordars and 2 slaves, and 13 acres of meadow. It is worth 30s.

IN MARCHAM HUNDRED

The same Gilbert holds PEASEMORE, and Richard [holds] of him Godwine and Herlewin held it TRE and could go where they wished. It was then assessed at 7 hides; now at 4 hides. There were 2 halls; now 1. There is land for 3 ploughs. In demesne are 1½ [ploughs]; and 2 villans and 5 bordars with half a plough. [There is] woodland for 2 pigs. It was and is worth £4.

XXXVII. The land of Gilbert de Ghent

IN ROWBURY HUNDRED

GILBERT de Ghent has of the king 1 manor, and Robert [holds] of him. Tunni held it TRE, and it was then assessed at 6 hides; now at 3 hides. There is land for 6 ploughs. In demesne is 1 [plough], and 2 villans and 4 bordars with 4 ploughs. There are 3 slaves, and woodland for 20 pigs. Of this land Algot holds 3 hides and he has there 1 plough, and 2 villans and 6 bordars with 2 ploughs. It was worth £6; and afterwards 60s; now the same.

XXXVIII. The land of Geoffrey de Mandeville

IN KINTBURY HUNDRED

GEOFFREY de Mandeville holds [East and West] ILSLEY, and Saswalo [holds] of him. Ordwulf held it as a manor in alod of King Edward. Then, as now, [it was assessed] at 1 hide. There is land for 2 ploughs. In demesne is 1 plough; and 1 villan and 7 bordars with 1 plough. There are 3 slaves, and 7 acres of meadow, [and] woodland for fencing. It is and was worth 20s.

The same Geoffrey holds [East and West] ILSLEY, and Saswalo [holds] of him. Ordwulf held it of King Edward in alod. Then, as now, [it was assessed] at 10 hides. There is land for 6 ploughs. In demesne are 2 ploughs; and 7 villans and 12 bordars with 3 ploughs. There are 4 slaves. It was worth £8; and afterwards £5; now £6.

IN LAMBOURN HUNDRED

The same Geoffrey holds EAST GARSTON. Esger held it of King Edward. [It was] then [assessed] at 30 hides; now at 10 hides. There is land for 20 ploughs. In demesne are 4 ploughs; and 23 villans and 12 bordars with 10 ploughs. There are 3 slaves, and 2 mills rendering 15s, and 5 acres of meadow, [and] woodland for 40 pigs. It was worth £20; and afterwards, as now, £12.

IN 'EAGLE' HUNDRED

The same Geoffrey holds WHATCOMBE. Sæweard held it in alod of King Edward. Then, as now, it was assessed at 2 hides. There is land for 3 ploughs. In demesne is 1 plough with 3 bordars, and half a plough. It was worth 30s; now 20s.

IN 'BEYNHURST' HUNDRED

The same Geoffrey holds HURLEY. Esger held it of King Edward. Then, as now, [it was assessed] at 14 hides less 1 virgate. There is land for 18 ploughs. In demesne are 4 ploughs; and 25 villans and 12 cottars with 15 ploughs. There are 10 slaves, and a mill rendering 20s. There is a church, and 2 fisheries rendering 12s, and 20 acres of meadow, [and] woodland for 5 pigs. It is and was worth £12.

IN 'SLOTISFORD' HUNDRED

The same Geoffrey holds STREATLEY. Esger held it of King Edward. [It was] then [assessed] at 25 hides; now at 10 hides. There is land for 15 ploughs. In demesne are 3 ploughs; and 18 villans and 10 cottars with 12 ploughs. There are 7 slaves, and a mill rendering 22s, and 2 fisheries rendering 11s, and 22 acres of meadow. In Oxford, 1 close rendering 10d. TRE, and afterwards, it was worth £20; now £24. Wibert the priest holds of Geoffrey the church of this manor with 1 hide, and he has there 1 plough with 1 cottar, and 4 acres of meadow. It is and was worth 50s.

XXXIX. The land of Osbern Giffard

IN 'CHARLDON' HUNDRED

OSBERN Giffard holds EARLEY of the king. Dunn held it in alod of King Edward. [It was] then [assessed] at 5 hides; now at 2 hides. There is land for 7 ploughs. In demesne are $1\frac{1}{2}$ ploughs; and 4 villans and 7 bordars with $2\frac{1}{2}$ ploughs. There is 1 slave, and 2 fisheries rendering 68d, and 20 acres of meadow, [and] woodland for 30 pigs. It was worth 100s; and afterwards 60s; now £4.

XL. The land of Robert fitzGerald

IN THATCHAM HUNDRED

ROBERT fitzGerald holds BRIMPTON. Beorhtric held it in alod of King Edward. [It was] then [assessed] at $4\frac{1}{2}$ hides; now at $3\frac{1}{2}$ hides. There is land for 4 ploughs. In demesne are $1\frac{1}{2}$ ploufgs; and 5 villans and 3 bordars and 1 English knight with 3 ploughs. There is 1 slave, and a church, and 2 mills rendering 26s 3d, and 35 acres of meadow. It is and was worth £4.10s.

IN KINTBURY HUNDRED

The same Robert holds INGLEWOOD. 2 free men held it of King Edward as 2 manors. Then, as now, [it was assessed] at 3 hides. There is land [...]. In demesne is 1 plough; and 7 bordars with 1 plough. There is 1 slave, and 4 acres of meadow, and a small wood. It was worth 30s; now 20s.

XLI. The land of Robert d'Oilly

IN 'EAGLE' HUNDRED

ROBERT d'Oilly holds CHADDLEWORTH. Edward held it in alod of king Edward as a manor. Then, as now, it was assessed at 4 hides. There is land for 2 ploughs. In demesne is 1 plough; and 2 villans and 2 bordars with half a plough, and 3 slaves, and 1 acre of meadow, [and] woodland for 10 pigs. It was worth 60s; and afterwards 30s; now 40s.

The same Robert holds LETCOMBE BASSETT. Vigot held it of King Edward. It was then assessed at 10 hides; now at 7 hides. There is land for 7 ploughs. In demesne are 2 ploughs; and 14 villans and 8 bordars with 5 ploughs. There are 4 slaves, and 2 mills rendering £3, and 36 acres of meadow. TRE, and afterwards, it was worth £15; now £16.

The same Robert holds in GREAT SHEFFORD $1\frac{1}{2}$ hides. of the Bishop of Bayeux's fief. Beorhtheah held it of King Edward and could go where he wished. Then, as now, it was assessed at $1\frac{1}{2}$ hides. In demesne is 1 plough; and 4 bordars and 2 slaves, and a mill rendering 8s, and 1 acre of meadow, [and] woodland for fencing. It was worth 30s; now 20s.

IN WANTAGE HUNDRED

The same Robert holds ARDINGTON. Edwin, a free man, held it TRE. [It was] then [assessed] at 5 hides; now at 2 hides and 1 virgate. There is land for 2 ploughs. In demesne is 1 [plough]; and 3 villans and 8 cottars with half a plough. There are 2 slaves, and a mill rendering 11s, and 26 acres of meadow. It is and was worth £4.

The same Robert holds ARDINGTON. Sæwine, a free man, held it TRE. [It was] then [assessed] at 9 hides; now at 4 hides and 3 virgates. There is land for 5 ploughs. In demesne is 1 [plough]; and 6 villans and 5 slaves, and 2 mills rendering 25s. Cola the Englishman claims 1 of these mills, but Alwine and Godwine and Ælfric give evidence that it always belonged to Ardington. It was worth £16; and afterwards £12; now £16.

The same Robert holds 1 hide which Azur, the steward of King Edward, held and could go with it where he wished. [It was] then [assessed] at 1 hide; now at nothing. There is land for 2 ploughs. In demesne is 1 [plough]; and 11 cottars with half a plough, and 10 acres of meadow. This land the same Azur holds of Robert, but the men of the hundred give evidence he ought to hold it of the king, since King William restored it to him at Windsor and gave him his writ concerning it. Robert holds it unjustly, for no one of them has seen the king's writ [granting it to him], nor the man who gave him seisin of it on his behalf. It is and was worth £3; although it renders £4.

XLII. The land of Robert of Stafford

IN WANTAGE HUNDRED

ROBERT of Stafford holds DENCHWORTH of the king, and Laurence [holds] of him. Leofgifu, a certain free woman, [held it] TRE. [It was] then [assessed] at 6 hides; now at $4\frac{1}{2}$ hides. There is land for 2 ploughs. In demesne is 1 [plough]; and 4 villans and 5 cottars with 1 plough, and 24 acres of meadow. It is and was worth £3.

XLIII. The land of Richard Puignant

IN 'SLOTISFORD' HUNDRED

RICHARD Puignant holds LOLLINGDON. Almær, a free man, held it TRE. [It was] then [assessed] at 3 hides; now at nothing.

[Folio 62v: BERKSHIRE]

There is land for 2 ploughs. In demesne is 1 [plough]; and 3 villans and 3 cottars with 1 plough, and 12 acres of meadow. It was worth 100s; and afterwards 40s; now 60s. When Richard received this manor he found it in the farm of Cholsey. It is now outside.

The same Richard holds AVINGTON. Gunnar held it of King Edward. It was then assessed at 10 hides; now at 2 hides. There is land [...]. In demesne are 3 ploughs; and 6 villans and 7 bordars with 3 ploughs. There are 4 slaves, and a mill rendering 10s, and 20 acres of meadow, [and] woodland for 10 pigs. It is and was worth 100s.

XLIIII. The land of Roger d'Ivry

IN BUCKLEBURY HUNDRED

ROGER d'Ivry holds of the king 1 virgate in [East and West] ELING. Sæwine held it of King Edward in his manor of [East and West] Hendred. This Roger transferred to his manor of Harwell, to which it never belonged, so the shire says, nor did it ever pay geld. There are 4 villans with 2 ploughs. [There is] woodland for 30 pigs. It is worth 20s.

IN 'EAGLE' HUNDRED

The same Roger holds in GREAT SHEFFORD 1½ hides of the Bishop of Bayeux's fief. Beorhtheah held it of King Edward as a manor in alod. Then, as now, it was assessed at 1½ hides. There is land for 1 plough, and there is [1 plough] in demesne; and 1 villan and 3 bordars, and half a mill rendering 7s6d, and 1 acre of meadow, and a small wood. It was worth 30s; now 20s.

IN BLEWBURY HUNDRED

The same Roger holds HARWELL. Wulfric, a free man, held it TRE. [It was] then [assessed] at 6 hides; now at 3 hides. There is land for 5 ploughs. In demesne are 2 ploughs; and 7 villans and 7 cottars with 2 ploughs. There are 2 slaves, and a chapel. It was worth £12; now £15.

The same Roger holds HARWELL of the fief of Earl William. Aki, a free man, held it TRE. [It was] then [assessed] at 5 hides; now at 2½ hides. There is land for 4 ploughs. In demesne is 1 [plough]; and 5 villans and 5 cottars with 1 plough, and there are 3 slaves. It was worth £5; now £6.

IN GAINFIELD HUNDRED

The same Roger holds PUSEY. Ælfric, a free man, held it TRE. Then, as now, [it was assessed] at 6 hides. There is land for 5 ploughs. In demesne are 2 [ploughs]; and 4 villans and 4 cottars with 1 plough. There is a church, and 4 slaves, and 5 acres of meadow. It is and was worth £4. It is [part] of the Bishop of Bayeux's fief.

XLV. The land of Roger de Lacy

IN KINTBURY HUNDRED

ROGER de Lacy holds ENBORNE of the king. Edmund held it of King Edward in alod. [It was] then [assessed] at 3 hides and 1 virgate; now at 1 hide. There is land for 2 ploughs. There are 6 villans and 8 bordars with 3 ploughs, and 13 acres of meadow, [and] woodland for 1 pig. It was worth 40s; now 50s.

IN WANTAGE HUNDRED

The same Roger holds CHILDREY. Edmund, a free man, held it TRE. [It was] then [assessed] at 13 hides; now at 8½ hides. There is land for 5 ploughs. In demesne are 2 ploughs; and 10 villans and 9 cottars with 3 ploughs. There are 2 slaves, and a mill rendering 50d. It is and always was worth £8.10s.

The same Roger holds 2 hides. Leofwine, a free man, held them TRE. [It was] then [assessed] at 2 hides; now at 1½ hides. There are 3 villans with half a plough. It is worth 30s.

XLVI. The land of Ralph de Mortimer

IN THATCHAM HUNDRED

RALPH de Mortimer holds BRIMPTON. Godwine held it of King Edward in alod. [It was] then [assessed] at 3½ hides; now at 2½ hides. There is land for 4 ploughs. In demesne are 1½ ploughs; and 6 villans and 3 bordars with 3 ploughs. There is a church, and 6 slaves, and a mill rendering 12s, and 30 acres of meadow. It is and was worth 70s.

The same Ralph holds CURRIDGE, and Baldwin [holds] of him. 2 free men held it of King Edward as 2 manors. It is now in 1 manor. [It was] then [assessed] at 7 hides; now at 3 hides less 1 virgate. There is land for 2 ploughs. In demesne is 1 plough; and 1 villan and 4 bordars with 1 plough. It was worth 60s; now 50s.

IN READING HUNDRED

The same Ralph holds STRATFIELD MORTIMER. 2 thegns, Cypping and Edwin, held it in parage TRE. [It was] then [assessed] at 6 hides; now at 3 hides. There is land for 21 ploughs. In demesne are 2 ploughs; and 14 villans and 13 bordars with 8 ploughs. There are 10 slaves, and a mill without rent, and 7 acres of meadow, [and] woodland for 40 pigs.

Of this land a knight holds half a hide, and there he has 1 plough, and a church with 4 bordars. It was worth £18; and afterwards £10; now £10.10s.

The same Ralph holds BURGHFIELD, and a certain knight [holds] of him. Abbot Æthelsige held it TRE of the Old Minster of the Church of Winchester, according to the testimony of the shire, and afterwards until he was an outlaw. Then, as now, [it was assessed] at 1½ hides. There is land for 6 ploughs. In demesne is 1 plough; and 6 villans and 8 bordars with 5 ploughs. There is a church, and half a mill rendering 5s10d, and a fishery rendering 68d, and 43 acres of meadow, [and] woodland for 15 pigs. It was worth 40s; now 50s.

The same Ralph holds HARTLEY. Regnild held it of King Edward. It was then assessed at 2 hides; now at 1 hide. There is land for 2 ploughs. In demesne is nothing; but 2 villans and 3 bordars have 2 ploughs. There is woodland for 15 pigs. It is worth 40s.

IN ROWBURY HUNDRED

The same Ralph holds PEASEMORE, and Oidelard [holds] of him. 2 thegns held it TRE and there were 2 halls; and they could go where they wished. It was then assessed at 8 hides; now at 3 hides. There is land for 6 ploughs. In demesne are 2 ploughs; and 4 villans and 11 bordars with 3 ploughs. [There is] woodland for 6 pigs. It was worth £6; and afterwards 60s; now 100s.

IN 'NAKEDTHORN' HUNDRED

The same Ralph holds Hodcott, and Oidelard [holds] of him. Alwine held it of King Edward. Then, as now, [it was assessed] at 5 hides. There is land [...]. In demesne are 2 ploughs; and 5 bordars with half a plough. It was worth £7; now £4.

XLVII. The land of Ralph de Tosny

IN WANTAGE HUNDRED

RALPH de Tosny holds CHARLTON of the king, and Drogo [holds] of him. 3 free men held it TRE. Then, as now, [it was assessed] at 7 hides. There is land for 7 ploughs. In demesne is 1 plough; and 4 villans and 13 cottars with 1 plough. There is half a mill rendering 5s, and 21 acres of meadow. It was worth 100s; now £6. This land is [part] of Earl Roger's fief.

XLVIII. The land of Ralph fitzCount

IN LAMBOURN HUNDRED

RALPH fitzCount holds [?] BOCKHAMPTON. 3 free men held it of King Edward as 3 manors in alod. [It was] then [assessed] at 8 hides; now at 3 hides less 1 virgate. There is land for 4 ploughs. In demesne are 2 ploughs; and 11 bordars with half a plough, and 1 slave, and a mill rendering 5s, and 5 acres of meadow, [and] woodland for 10 pigs. Of this manor Odo holds 1 hide, and there he has 1 plough with 1 bordar. It was worth £7; and afterwards £6; now £7.

XLIX. The land of Ralph fitzSeifrid

IN 'RIPPLESMERE' HUNDRED

RALPH fitzSeifrid holds CLEWER of the king. Earl Harold held it. It was then assessed at 5 hides; now at 4½ hides; and the castle of Windsor is on the half-hide. There is land [...]. In demesne are 1½ ploughs; and 9 villans and 6 bordars with 4 ploughs, and a mill rendering 10s, and 20 acres of meadow,

[and] woodland for 10 pigs. Of this land his son-in-law, Ralph, holds half a hide, and nothing is there. It was worth £7; now £4.10s.

IN BLEWBURY HUNDRED

Roger fitzSeifrid holds FULSCOT of the king. Ludric, a certain free man, held it TRE. Then at 3 hides it was assessed at 1 hide [sic]; now the same. There is land for 2 ploughs. In demesne is 1 [plough]; and 4 villans and 5 cottars with 1 plough, and 30 acres of meadow. It was worth 40s; now £4.

L. The land of Ernulf de Hesdin

IN THATCHAM HUNDRED

ERNULF de Hesdin holds NEWBURY of the king. Wulfweard held it of King Edward in alod. It was then assessed at 10 hides; now at 2½ hides. There is land for 12 ploughs. In demesne is 1 plough; and 11 villans and 11 bordars with 7 ploughs. There are 2 mills rendering 50s, and 27 acres of meadow, woodland for 25 pigs, and 51 enclosures rendering 20s7d. TRE it was worth £9; and afterwards £8; now £24.

LI. The land of Hugh fitzBaldric

IN THATCHAM HUNDRED

HUGH fitzBaldric holds SHAW of the king. Ælfric held it of King Edward in alod. [It was] then [assessed] at 5 hides; now at 2½ hides. There is land for 5 ploughs. In demesne is half a plough; and 4 villans and 12 bordars with 4 ploughs. There are 3 slaves, and a mill rendering 20s, and 5 acres of meadow, [and] woodland for 50 pigs. It is and was worth £6.

LII. The land of Hugh de Port

IN 'EAGLE' HUNDRED

HUGH de Port holds GREAT SHEFFORD of the king. Wulfgifu held it in alod of King Edward. [It was] then [assessed] at 20 hides; now at 7 hides and 2 acres.

IN READING HUNDRED

The same Roger holds PURLEY. Beorhtweard held it of King Edward. It was then assessed at 4½ hides; now at 4 hides. There is land for 4 ploughs. In demesne are 2 [ploughs]; and 9 villans and 3 bordars with 3 ploughs. and 16 acres of meadow. It was worth 100s; and afterwards £4; now 100s.

[Folio 63: BERKSHIRE]

There is land for 10 ploughs. In demesne are 3 ploughs; and 15 villans and 8 bordars with 6 ploughs. There are 6 slaves, and 6 acres of meadow, [and] woodland for 30 pigs. There is a mill rendering 10s. It was worth £6; now £12.

LIII. The land of Humphrey the Chamberlain

IN THATCHAM HUNDRED

HUMPHREY the champberlain holds BAGNOR of the king. Wulfgifu held it in alod of King Edward. It was then assessed at 3 hides; now at 1 hide. There is land for 3 ploughs. In demesne is 1 [plough]; and 3 villans and 3 bordars with 2 ploughs. There is 1 slave, and a mill rendering 20s, and 22 acres of meadow, [and] woodland for 4 pigs. It is and was worth £4.

LIIII. The land of Humphrey Visdeloup

IN THATCHAM HUNDRED

HUMPHREY Visdeloup holds SPEEN of the king. Karli held it of King Edward in alod. [It was] then [assessed] at 10 hides; now at 5 hides. There is land for 9 ploughs. In demesne are 3 ploughs; and 9 villans and 10 bordars with 6 ploughs. There is a church, and 7 slaves, and a mill rendering 22s, and 60 acres of meadow, [and] woodland for 3 pigs. It was worth £8; now £10. To the church belongs half a hide of this land.

IN KINTBURY HUNDRED

The same Humphrey holds BOXFORD. 3 brothers held it of King Edward in alod. It was then assessed at 9 hides; now at 4 hides. There is land for 2 ploughs. In demesne is 1 [plough]; and 1 villan and 6 bordars with 1 plough. There is a slave, and a mill rendering 27s6d, and 6 acres of meadow. Of this manor Æfric holds 1 hide and Almær 2 hides, and there is 1 plough in demesne. The whole, TRE and afterwards, was worth £8; now £6.10s.

The same Humphrey holds BENHAM. 3 thegns held it in alod of King Edward. [It was] then [assessed] at 5 hides; now at 4 hides. There is land for 3 ploughs. In demesne is 1 [plough]; and 6 villans and 8 bordars with 5 ploughs. There are 2 slaves, and 120 acres of meadow. Of this manor Ansketil holds 2 hides, and William 2 hides; and there are 2 ploughs. The whole, TRE and afterwards, as now, worth £6.

IN BLEWBURY HUNDRED

The same Humphrey holds [North and South] MORETON. Osmund, a free man, held it TRE. [It was] then [assessed] at 5 hides; now at 2½ hides. There is land for 3 ploughs. In demesne are 2 [ploughs]; and 4 villans and 4 cottars with 1 plough. There is a church, and 6 slaves, and 40 acres of meadow. It is and was worth £6.

LV. The land of Turstin fitzRolf

IN 'WYFOLD' HUNDRED

TURSTIN fitzRolf holds COLESHILL of the king. Beorhtric held it in alod of King Edward. It was then assessed at 8 hides; now at 5 hides. There is land for 3 ploughs. In demesne are 2 ploughs; and 7 bordars and 5 slaves with half a plough. There is a third part of a mill rendering 10s, and 69

acres of meadow. It was worth £7; and afterwards 40s; now 100s.

IN BLEWBURY HUNDRED

The same Turstin holds UPTON. Beorhtric, a free man, held it. [It was] then [assessed] at 10 hides; now at 5 hides. There is land for 9 ploughs. In demesne are 2 [ploughs]; and 16 villans and 7 cottars with 6 ploughs. There are 7 slaves, and 30 acres of meadow. It is and was worth £13.

IN 'SLOTISFORD' HUNDRED

The same Turstin holds CHILDREY, and Roger [holds] of him. Beorhtric, a free man, held it TRE. [It was] then [assessed] at 10 hides; now at 8 hides. There is land for 4 ploughs. In demesne is 1 [plough]; and 5 villans and 6 cottars with 1 plough. There are 3 slaves, and a mill rendering 2s, and a church. Of this manor another Roger holds 6 hides and 1 virgate, and there is 1 plough in demesne; and 6 villans and 2 cottars with 1 plough, and 2 slaves. TRE it was worth £10; and afterwards £8; now £9.5s.

The same Turstin holds SPARSHOLT, and Roger [holds] of him. Beorhtric, a free man, held it TRE. Then, as now, [it was assessed] at 2½ hides and a virgate. There is land for 1 plough, and there is [1 plough] in demesne, and 2 slaves, and 16 acres of meadow. It was worth 30s; and afterwards 20s; now 30s.

LVI. The land of Albert

IN 'RIPPLESMERE' HUNDRED

ALBERT holds of the king DEDWORTH. Hugh the chamberlain held it of King Edward. Then, as now, it was assessed at 1 hide. In demesne is 1 plough; and 4 villans and 1 bordar with 2 ploughs, and 20 acres of meadow, [and] woodland for 5 pigs. It was worth £4; and afterwards, as now, 30s.

LVII. The land of Aiulf the Sheriff

IN 'EAGLE' HUNDRED

AIULF holds EAST SHEFFORD of the king. Beorhtric held it in alod of King Edward. It was then assessed at 10 hides; now at 5 hides. There is land for 5 ploughs. In demesne are 2 ploughs; and 8 villans and 5 bordars with 3 ploughs. There are 5 slaves, and 2 mills rendering 22s6d, and 8 acres of meadow, [and] woodland for 10 pigs. It was worth £10; and afterwards £9; now £10.

LVIII. The land of Hugh the Steersman

IN KINTBURY HUNDRED

HUGOLIN the steersman holds HAMSTEAD MARSHALL of the king. Edward held it as a manor of King Edward in alod. It was then assessed at 4 hides; now at 1 hide. There is land for 5 ploughs. In demesne are 2 [ploughs]; and 4 villans and 8 bordars with 3 ploughs. There are 10 slaves, and a mill rendering 20s, and 6 acres of meadow, [and] woodland for 10 pigs. It is and was worth £4.

The same Hugolin has held up to the present IRISH HILL. Herling held it TRE as a manor. Then, as now, [it was assessed] at 1 hide. There is land for 2 ploughs. In demesne is nothing; but 4 villans and 4 bordars have 3 ploughs. There are 3 slaves, and a mill rendering 30s, and 3 acres of meadow, [and] woodland for fencing. It was worth £4; now £3. About this manor the shire testifies that it did not belong to the predecessor of Hugh through whom he claims it. His men, however, were unwilling to give an account of it. He has also transferred the hall and other buildings and the livestock to another manor.

The same Hugolin holds 1 virgate in BUCKLEBURY, and it has never paid geld; it belongs and belonged to Hamstead Marshall. It is worth 10s.

LIX. The land of Matthew de Mortagne

IN LAMBOURN HUNDRED

MATTHEW de Mortagne holds LAMBOURN of the king. Wulfweard held it of King Edward in alod as a manor. Then, as now, it was assessed at 4 hides. There is land for 2 ploughs. In demesne [is] half a plough; and 2 villans and 8 bordars with 1 plough. It was worth 60s; and afterwards 30s; now 50s.

LX. The land of Bernard the Falconer

IN THATCHAM HUNDRED

BERNARD the falconer holds WASHING of the king. Alwine held it of King Edward in alod. It was then assessed at 1 hide; now at half [a hide]. There is land for 4 ploughs. In demesne are 2 [ploughs]; and 5 villans and 1 bordar with 2 ploughs, and 1 slave, and a mill rendering 16s. It is and was worth £3.

LXI. The land of Regenbald of Cirencester

IN BLEWBURY HUNDRED

REGENBALD of Cirencester holds [East and West] HAGBOURNE of the king. He himself held it of King Edward. There are 15 hides; but then, as now, it was assessed at 12 hides less 1 virgate. There is land for 12 ploughs. In demesne are 2 ploughs; and 18 villans and 16 cottars with 10 ploughs. There are 6 slaves, and a mill rendering 12s6d, and 30 acres of meadow. It was worth £15; now £18.

The same Regenbald holds ASTON UPTHORPE. Æthelgifu, a certain free woman, held it TRE. Then there were 10 hides; but it was assessed at 6½ hides then, as now. There is land for 7 ploughs. In demesne are 2 ploughs; and 10 villans and 12 cottars with 5 ploughs. There are 3 slaves, and 41 acres of meadow. It was worth £10; now £12.

LXII. The land of Grimbald

IN WANTAGE HUNDRED

GRIMBALD holds [East and West] HENDRED of the king. Aki, a free man, held it TRE. [It was] then [assessed] at 5 hides; now at 1 hide. There is land for 2 ploughs. In demesne is 1 [plough]; and 2 villans and 5 cottars with 1 plough, and a mill rendering 10s, and 15 acres of meadow. It was worth £4; and afterwards 30s; now £4.

LXIII. The land of Theodric the Goldsmith

IN 'NAKEDTHORN' HUNDRED

THEODRIC the goldsmith holds ALDWORTH of the king. Edward held it in alod of King Edward. [It was] then [assessed] at 5 hides; now at 2 hides. There is land for 5 ploughs. In demesne are 2 ploughs; and 6 villans and 4 bordars with 3 ploughs. There are 4 slaves, [and] woodland for 10 pigs. It was and is worth 100s.

IN BUCKLEBURY HUNDRED

The same Theodric holds HAMPSTEAD NORREYS. Lang held it of King Edward. [It was] then [assessed] at 17 hides; now at 6 hides. There is land for 12 ploughs. In demesne are 2 ploughs; and 13 villans and 9 bordars with 8 ploughs. There are 8 slaves, and 4 acres of meadow, [and] woodland for 40 pigs. Of this land a priest of the church holds half a hide in alms and has nothing on it. It was worth £12; and afterwards £9; now £10.

IN READING HUNDRED

The same Theodric holds SULHAM. Edward held it of King Edward. [It was] then [assessed] at 1 hide; now at half [a hide]. There is land for 2 ploughs. In demesne is 1 plough, with 5 bordars, and 2 slaves and 2 acres of meadow. It is and was worth 30s.

The same Theodric holds in PURLEY half a hide. Edward held it; and it was assessed at as much then, as now. There is land for 2 ploughs. In demesne is 1 [plough]; and 1 villan and 3 bordars with 1 plough, and 5 acres of meadow. It was worth 40s; now 50[s].

The same Theodric holds WHITLEY. Edward held it of King Edward. It was then assessed at 3 hides; now at 1 hide. There is land for 3 ploughs. In demesne is 1 plough; and 2 villans and 2 bordars with 1 plough. There are 4 slaves, and 12 acres of meadow, and a fishery rendering 40d. It is and was worth 40s.

[Folio 63V: BERKSHIRE]

LXIIII. The land of Stephen fitzErhard

IN READING HUNDRED

STEPHEN fitzErhard holds of the king PADWORTH. 3 thegns held it in parage and could go with their lands where they wished. There are 7½ hides; but then, as now, it paid geld for 5½ hides. There is land for 5 ploughs. In demesne is 1 [plough]; and 3 villans and 2 bordars with 1 plough. There are 2½ mills rendering 37s6d, and 48 acres of meadow. Of these hides Nigel holds 1 hide, and a certain knight half a hide. There is in demesne 1 plough; and 4 villans and 3 bordars with 2½ ploughs. The whole, TRE, was worth 100s; and afterwards £4; now £4.10s.

The same Stephen holds 1 hide in SWALLOWFIELD, and Ælfric [holds] of him. 3 alodiaries held it TRE and could go where they pleased. Then, as now, it was assessed at 1 hide. There is land for 2 ploughs. There are 5 alodiaries with 2 ploughs and 1 bordar. It was and is worth 20s.

LXV. The land of Odo and Other Thegns

IN GAINFIELD HUNDRED

ODO of Winchester holds HINTON WALDRIST of the king. Wulfwynn held it TRE and could go where she wished. It was then assessed at 10 hides; now at 7½ hides. There is land for 8 ploughs. In demesne are 3 ploughs; and 13 villans and 8 bordars with 5 ploughs. There is a church, and 8 slaves, and 2 fisheries rendering 20s, and 40 acres of meadow. It was worth TRE £11; and afterwards 100s; now £9.

In the same vill Odo has 3 hides; these 2 thegns held, and they had 2 halls and could go where they wished; and it was assessed at 3 hides then, as now. There is land for 1½ ploughs. There are [1½ ploughs] with 3 villans, and 12 acres of meadow. This belongs to the manor above. It was worth 50s; now 30s.

The same Odo holds in the same place DUXFORD. Alwig held it and could go where he wished. Then, as now, [it was assessed] at 3 hides. There is land for 2 ploughs. In demesne is 1 plough; and 1 villan and 4 bordars with half a plough. There are 2 slaves, and a mill rendering 5s, and a fishery rendering 25s2d, and 16 acres of meadow. It is and was worth £4.

IN 'HILDSLOW' HUNDRED

The same Odo holds KNIGHTON. 5 free men [held it] in alod of King Edward. It was then assessed at 5 hides; now at 2 virgates and 2 parts of a virgate. There is land for 4 ploughs. In demesne [is] half a plough; and 3 villans and 6 bordars with 2½ ploughs. There are 3 slaves. It was worth 100s. TRE; and afterwards 60s; now £6.

IN 'BEYNHURST' HUNDRED

ALWEARD the goldsmith holds SHOTTESBROOKE of the king. His father held it of Queen Edith. Then, as now, [it was assessed] at 7 hides. There is land for 8 ploughs. In demesne are 2 ploughs; and 24 villans and 2 cottars with 10 ploughs. There is a church, and 2 slaves, [and] 7 acres of meadow. It was worth £7; now £6.

IN 'BEYNHURST' HUNDRED

ALWINE son of Cypping holds BRAY of the king. Tovi held it of King Edward. [It was] then [assessed] at 2 hides; now at 1 hide. There is land for 1 plough, and there is [1 plough], with 10 villans having 1 plough. There is a church. It was worth 60s; now 30[s].

IN GAINFIELD HUNDRED

ALSIGE of Faringdon holds [?] BARCOTE by gift of King William. Harold held it. It was then assessed at 5 hides; now at 2 hides. There is land for 4 ploughs. In demesne is 1 plough; and 5 villans and 5 bordars with 2 ploughs. There are 5 slaves. It was worth £4; now £5.

IN WANTAGE HUNDRED

The same Alsige holds of the king half a hide which Ælfric, a certain free man, held TRE. Then, as now, [it was assessed] at half a hide. There are 2 cottars and 6 acres of meadow. It is and was worth 10s.

IN THATCHAM HUNDRED

EDWARD holds of the king 1 hide in CURRIDGE. He himself held it in alod of King Edward, and it was assessed at 1 hide then, as now. There is land for 1 plough, and there is [1 plough] in demesne with 3 bordars. It is and was worth 5s.

IN THATCHAM HUNDRED

COLA holds of the king [East and West] GINGE. Beorhtric held it in alod of King Edward. [It was] then [assessed] at 3 hides; now at 2 hides. In demesne is 1 plough; and 5 villans and 3 bordars with 5 ploughs. There are 4 slaves, and a mill rendering 15s, and 25 acres of meadow, [and] woodland for 3 pigs. It is and was worth £3.

IN KINTBURY HUNDRED

WIGAR holds of the king 2 hides in BENHAM. Ordmær held them in alod, [...] as a manor, of King Edward. It was then assessed at 2 hides; now at half a hide. There is land for 1 plough, and there is [1 plough] in demesne, with 2 bordars, and 60 acres of meadow. It is and was worth 40s.

IN LAMBOURN HUNDRED

EDWARD holds [?] BOCKHAMPTON of the king. Eskil held it in alod of King Edward. [It was] then [assessed] at 3 hides; now at half a hide. There is land for 2 ploughs. In demesne is 1 plough with 5 bordars. It was worth 60s; now 40s.

IN WANTAGE HUNDRED

COLA holds of the king [East and West] HENDRED. Sæwine, a certain free man, held it TRE. [It was] then [assessed] at 7 hides; now at 1 hide and 3 virgates. There is land for 3 ploughs. There are 8 cottars, and a mill rendering 20s, and 8 acres of meadow. It was worth 100s; now £4.

There a certain free woman, Ealdgifu, has of the king 1 hide in alms which the same woman held TRE, and she could go where she wished. Then, as now, [it was assessed] at 1 hide. There are 2 cottars and 1 acre of meadow. It was worth 20s; now 5s.

In GAINFIELD Hundred a certain woman, Edith, has 1 virgate of the king in alms which she herself held TRE, and she could go where she wished. Then [it was assessed] at 1 virgate; now at nothing. It is worth 12d.

IN SUTTON HUNDRED

ALWEALD the chamberlain holds CARSWELL of the king. Queen Edith held it. It was then assessed at 5 hides; now at 1 hide. There is land for 2 ploughs. There are [2 ploughs] in demesne; and 4 villans and 6 bordars with 1 plough. There are 9 slaves, and a fishery rendering 40d, and 59 acres of meadow. It is and was worth £4.

IN READING HUNDRED

AUBREY, the queen's chamberlain, holds 1 hide of the queen in "BURLEI". Alweard held it of King Edward and could go where he wished. It was then assessed at 1 hide; now at nothing. There is land for 1½ ploughs. It was worth 30s; now 20s.

HEARDING holds 1 hide in "BURLEI". [...] This he himself held of Queen Edith. Ælfgifu held it TRE and could go where she wished. [It was] then [assessed] at 1 hide; now at nothing. There is land for 1½ ploughs. [There is] nothing in demesne; but there 3 villans have 1 plough. [There is] woodland for 5 pigs. It was worth 20s; now 12s.

IN KINTBURY Hundred is Inglewood, which Fulchard holds of William. [There is] 1 hide with 1 bordar. It is worth 3s.

And Alvred has 1 hide in the same manor and 1 plough in demesne. It is worth 15s.

And Godebold [has] 1½ hides with 3 bordars. They are worth 10s.

And Ralph de Feugeres [has] 2½ hides which belonged to Inkpen, so the shire says.

IN MARCHAM HUNDRED

BERNER, nephew of R. de Peronne, holds APPLETON, [part] of the Bishop of Bayeux's fief. Alwine held it of King Edward. It was then assessed at 5 hides; now at 2½ hides. There is land for 4 ploughs. In demesne is 1 [plough]; and 3 villans and 5 bordars with 1 plough. There are 3 slaves. It was worth £4; and afterwards 60s; now 50s.

ROBERT fitzRolf holds INGLEWOOD of the king. [...] 2 thegns held it of King Edward as 2 manors. Then, as now, [it was assessed] at 3 hides. [There is] land [...]. There is 1 plough in demesne. There is 1 villan and 7 bordars with 1 plough, and 1 slave, and 4 acres of meadow, and a small wood. It was worth 30s; and afterwards 20[s]; and now the same.

IN GAINFIELD HUNDRED

A certain woman, EALDGYTH, holds of the king 1 virgate of land in alms. She herself held it TRE. It then paid geld for 1 virgate of land; now for nothing. It was worth 30d; now 12d.

IN THATCHAM HUNDRED

Alwig Ceuresbert held Crookham TRE, and it was assessed at 1 hide. The same man holds it. [There is] land for 1 plough. There are 3 villans. It is worth 20s.

WILTSHIRE

[Folio 64: WILTSHIRE]

[Blank in MS]

[Folio 64V: WILTSHIRE]

In the borough of MALMESBURY the king has 26 inhabited messuages and 25 messuages in which are houses which pay no more geld than waste land. Each one of these messuages renders 10d as rent; this is all together 43s6d.

There is half a waste messuage, [part] of the fief of the Bishop of Bayeux, which renders no service.

The Abbot of Malmesbury has 4½ messuages and outside the borough 9 cotsets who pay geld with the burgesses. The Abbot of Glastonbury has 2 messuages; Edward the sheriff, 3 messuages; Ralph de Mortimer, 1½ Durand of Gloucester, 1½ William de Eu 1; Humphrey de l'Isle, 1; Osbern Giffard, 1; Alvred of Marlborough, half a waste messuage; Geoffrey Marshal, the same; Tovi, 1, and the fourth part of 1 messuage; Drogo fitzPons, half [a messuage]; the wife of Eadric, 1; Roger of Berkeley, 1 messuage belonging to the king's farm; and Ernulf de Hesdin, 1 [messuage] likewise belonging to the king's farm of which he incautiously took possession. These 2 render no service.

The king has 1 waste messuage of the land which Azur held.

Here Are Noted the Landholders In Wiltshire

I KING WILLIAM
II The Bishop of Winchester
III The Bishop of Salisbury
IIII The Bishop of Bayeux
V The Bishop of Coutances
VI The Bishop of Lisieux
VII The Abbey of Glastonbury
VIII The Abbey of Malmesbury
IX The Abbey of Westminster
X The Abbey of Winchester
XI The Abbey of Cranborne
XII The Abbess of Shaftesbury
XIII The Abbess of Wilton
XIIII The Abbess of Winchester
XV The Abbess of Romsey
XVI The Abbess of Amesbury
XVII The Church of Bec
XVIII Gerald the priest of Wilton
XIX The canons of Lisiecux
XX The Count of Mortain
XXI Earl Roger
XXII Earl Hugh
XXIII Earl Aubrey
XXIIII Edward of Salisbury
XXV Ernulf de Hesdin
XXVI Alvred of Marlborough
XXVII Humphrey de l'Isle
XXVIII Miles Crispin
XXIX Gilbert de Breteuil
XXX Durand of Gloucester
XXXI Walter Giffard
XXXII William de Eu
XXXIII William de Braose
XXXIIII William de Moyon
XXXV William de Falaise
XXXVI Walter de Douai
XXXVII Waleran the huntsman
XXXVIII William fitzGuy
XXXIX Henry de Ferrers
XL Richard son of Count Gilbert
XLI Ralph de Mortimer
XLII Robert fitzGerald
XLIII Robert fitzRolf
XLIIII Roger de Courseulles
XLV Roger of Berkeley
XLVI Bernard Pauncevolt
XLVII Berengar Giffard
XLVIII Osbern Giffard
XLIX Drogo fitzPons
L Hugh l'Asne
LI Hugh fitzBaldric
LII Humphrey the chamberlain
LIII Gunfrid Mauduit
LIIII Alvred d'Epaignes
LV Aiulf the sheriff
LVI Nigel the physician
LVII Osbern the priest
LVIII Richard Puignant
LIX Robert Marshal
LX Robert the Fair
LXI Richard Sturmy
LXII Reginald Canute
LXIII Matthew de Mortagne
LXIIII Joscelin [...] Riviere
LXV Godescal
LXVI Herman and other king's sergeants
LXVII Oda and other king's thegns
LXVIII Hervey and other king's servants

THE KING has from the borough of WILTON £50. When Hervey received it in custody, it rendered £22.

From WILTSHIRE the king has £10 for a hawk and 20s for a sumpter-horse, and 100s and 5 orae for fodder.

From half a mill at SALISBURY the king has 20s by weight.

From the third penny of SALISBURY the king has £6. From the third penny of MARLBOROUGH, £4. From the third penny of CRICKLADE, †£5†. From the third penny of BATH, [Som.], £11. From the third penny of MALMESBURY, £6.

As increment £60 by weight [is due]; EDWARD the sheriff pays this.

WALTER Hosed, from 2 parts of the borough of Malmesbury, pays £8 to the king; the borough itself rendered as much TRE, and in this farm were the pleas of the hundreds of "Cicementone" and Startley, which belonged to the king. From the mint the borough itself renders 100s. In the same borough Earl Harold had an acre of land, in which are 4 messuages, and 6 others [which are] waste, and 1 mill rendering 10s. All this rendered 100s. TRE. When the king was going on an expedition, whether by land or sea, he had from this borough either 20s for the support of his butsecarls or took with him 1 man for [each] honour of 5 hides.

The land of the King

THE KING holds CALNE. King Edward held it, and it has never paid geld; hence it is not known how many hides are there. There is land for 29 ploughs. In demesne are 8 ploughs, and 8 slaves. There are 37 villans and 78 bordars and 10 coliberts having 21 ploughs. There are 45 burgesses, and 7 mills rendering £4.12s6d, and 50 acres of meadow, and pasture 2 leagues long and 1 league broad. This vill renders a farm of 1 night with all customary dues.

Nigel holds the church of this manor of the king, with 6 hides of land. There is land for 5 ploughs. In demesne are 2 [ploughs], and 6 slaves. There are 7 villans and 2 bordars and 11 cotsets with 3 ploughs. There are 2 mills rendering 20s, and 25 burgesses paying 20s, woodland 2 furlongs long and 1 furlong and 24 acres broad, [and] pasture 4 furlongs long and 2 furlongs broad. The whole is worth £8.

Alvred d'Epaignes holds 5 hides of land which Nigel claims. This land, according to the testimony of the shire, belonged to the church TRE.

THE KING holds [Great and Little] BEDWYN. King Edward held it. It has never paid geld, nor has it been assessed in hides. There is land for 80 ploughs less 1. In demesne are 12 ploughs, and 18 slaves. There are 80 villans and 60 cotsets and 14 coliberts. There are 8 mills rendering 100s, [and] 2 woods having 2 leagues in length and 1 league in breadth. There are 200 acres of meadow, and pasture 12 furlongs long and 6 furlongs wide. To this manor belong 25 burgesses. This vill renders a farm of 1 night with all customary dues. In this manor there was TRE a grove, having half a league [in] length and 3 furlongs in breadth, and it was in the demesne of the king. Now Henry de Ferrers holds it.

THE KING holds AMESBURY. King Edward held it. It has never paid geld, nor has it been assessed in hides. There is land for 40 ploughs. In demesne are 16 ploughs, and 55 slaves and 2 coliberts. There are 85 villans and 56 bordars having 23 ploughs. There are 8 mills rendering £4.10s, and 70 acres of meadow, pasture 4 leagues long and 3 leagues broad, [and] woodland 6 leagues long and 4 leagues broad.

This manor, [...] with its appendages, renders a farm of 1 night with all customary dues.

In this manor are included the lands of 3 thegns, which they themselves held TRE. These [lands] in Amesbury Earl William gave in return for the loan of BOWCOMBE [I.o.W., Hants].

Of the land of this manor, King Edward, in his infirmity, gave 2 hides to the Abbess of Wilton, which she never had previously; afterwards, however, she held them. # Earl William gave "Quintone" and Swindon and [? Great] Cheverell, which were thegnlands, for land in the Isle of Wight, which belonged to the farm of Amesbury.

THE KING holds WARMINSTER. King Edward held it. It has paid no geld, nor has it been assessed in hides. There is land for 40 ploughs. In demesne are 6 ploughs, and 24 slaves and 13 swineherds. There are 15 villans and 8 cotsets and 14 coliberts with 36 ploughs. There are 7 mills rendering £4, and 80 acres of meadow, pasture 1 league long and half a league broad, [and] woodland 2 leagues long and 2 broad. There are 30 burgesses.

This manor renders a farm of 1 night with all its customary dues.

THE KING holds CHIPPENHAM. King Edward held it. It has paid no geld, nor has it been assessed in hides. There is land for 100 ploughs. In demesne are 16 ploughs, and 28 slaves. There are 48 villans and 45 bordars and 20 cottars and 23 swineherds. Among them all they have 66 ploughs. There are 12 mills rendering £6, and 100 acres of meadow, woodland 4 leagues in length and breadth, [and] pasture 2 leagues long and 1 league broad. This manor, with its appendages, renders a farm of 1 night with all customary dues, and it is worth £110 by tale.

Bishop Osbern holds the church of this manor, with 2 hides, from TRE. One of these hides is thegnland, the other belongs to the church. The whole is worth 55s.

To this manor belongs one [piece of] land which King Edward had given to Wulfgeat, his huntsman, and it was [part] of his demesne. This now belongs to the king's farm and it is reckoned as 1 hide. There is land for 2 ploughs, and these are there, and 3 slaves; and 4 villans and 4 cotsets with 1 plough. [There is] pasture 4 furlongs long and 1 furlong broad. It is worth £3. To the farm of this manor belongs half a virgate of land, which was thegnland. Eadric held it TRE.

[Folio 65: WILTSHIRE]

THE KING holds BRITFORD. King Edward held it, and it paid geld for 1 hide. There is land for 20 ploughs. In demesne are 2 ploughs, and 6 slaves and 10 coliberts. There are 12 villans and 6 bordars and 14 cotsets with 17 ploughs. There are 2 mills rendering 20s, and 100 acres of meadow, [and] pasture 1 league long and half a league broad. This manor renders £30 by weight. The woodland is in the hand of the king, and he has 40s from it in his farm. Osbern the priest holds the church of this manor, with 1 hide of land belonging to the church. It is worth 40s.

THE KING holds TILSHEAD. King Edward held it. It has paid no geld, nor has it been assessed in hides. There is land for 40 ploughs. In demesne are 9 ploughs, and 22 slaves and 10 coliberts. There are 34 villans and 32 cotsets with 18 ploughs. There are 9 mills rendering 100s and 30d, and 66 burgesses paying 50s. There is meadow 1 league in length and a half broad, pasture 1½ leagues long and 1 league broad, [and] woodland 2 leagues long and 1 league broad. This manor renders the farm of 1 night with its customary dues, and it is worth £100 by tale.

THE KING holds COMPTON CHAMBERLAYNE. Earl Harold held it, and it paid geld for 10 hides. There is land for 10 ploughs. In demesne are 2 ploughs, and 2 slaves; and 28 villans and 2 bordars with 8 ploughs. There is a mill rendering 12s6d, and 20 acres of meadow, and 8 acres of pasture and 15 acres of woodland. This manor renders £12 by weight.

THE KING holds RUSHALL. Gytha held it TRE, and it paid geld with its appendages for 37 hides. [...] There is land for 27½ ploughs. In demesne are 19 hides, and there are 12 ploughs, and 37 slaves. There are 28 villans and 40 bordars with 14 ploughs. There are 5 mills rendering 72s, and 112 acres of meadow, pasture 3½ leagues long and 1½ leagues in breadth, [and] woodland 1 league long and half a league broad. It was and is worth £32.10s. [The Abbey of] Saint-Wandrille has the church of this manor, with 2 hides of land, and there are 1½ ploughs. It is worth 40s.

THE KING holds ALDBOURNE. Gytha held it TRE, and it paid geld for 40 hides. There is land for 45 ploughs. In demesne are 18 hides, and there are 10 ploughs, and 25 slaves and 14 coliberts. There are 73 villans and 38 cotsets with 26 ploughs. There are 4 mills rendering 16s8d, meadow 1 league long and 5 furlongs broad, pasture 1 league long and half a league broad, [and] woodland 2 leagues long and half a league broad. To this manor belong 6 burgesses in Cricklade, paying 64d. This manor renders £70 by weight, but by the English it is only valued at £60 by tale. To the church of this manor belong 2 hides. There is land for 2 ploughs. These the priest of the same church has, and it is worth 40s.

THE KING holds CORSHAM. Earl Tosti held it TRE. There are 34 hides, but it renders geld for 18 hides. There is land for 50 ploughs. In demesne are 11 hides, and there are 7 ploughs, and 10 slaves. There are 65 villans and 48 cotsets and 9 cottars with 38 ploughs. There are 2 mills rendering 8s6d, and 32 acres of meadow, and 1 hide of pasture, and woodland 2 leagues in length and breadth. This manor with its appendages renders £30 by weight. The English, however, value it at £31 by tale. [The Abbey of] Saint-Etienne of Caen has the church of this manor with 3 hides of land. There is land for 5 ploughs. These 3 villans with 6 cotsets have there. It is

worth £7. Edgar holds the church of Poulshot, which belongs to this manor, and his father held it. It is worth 5s.

THE KING holds MELKSHAM. Earl Harold held it, and, with its appendages, it paid geld for 84 hides. There is land for 60 ploughs. In demesne are 34 hides, and there are 19 ploughs, and 35 slaves and 31 coliberts. There are 100 villans less 8 and 66 bordars having 39 ploughs. There are 8 mills rendering £7.6s, and 130 acres of meadow, and 8 leagues of pasture in length and breadth, [and] woodland 4 leagues in both length and breadth. This manor renders £111.11s by weight. The English, however, value it at as many pounds by tale. Rumold the priest has the church of this manor with 1 hide of land, and it is worth 40s.

THE KING holds COOMBE BISSETT. Gytha held it TRE, and it paid geld for 23½ hides. There is land for 20 ploughs. In demesne are 11 hides, and there are 3 ploughs, and 7 slaves. There are 28 villans and 7 bordars and 43 cotsets having 17 ploughs. There are 2 mills rendering 25s, and 60 acres of meadow, and pasture 1 league long and another wide, and 10 acres of scrubland. This manor renders £24 by weight; TRE as much by tale. Leofric the priest holds the church of this manor with half a hide of land, and it is worth 20s.

THE KING holds BROMHAM. Earl Harold held it, and it paid geld for 20 hides. There is land for 10 ploughs. In demesne are 10 hides, and there are 2 ploughs, and 4 slaves. There are 14 villans and 6 bordars and 30 cotsets with 8 ploughs. There are 2 mills rendering 5s, and 40 acres of meadow, and 12 acres of pasture, [and] woodland 5 furlongs long and 3 furlongs broad. It was worth £20; now £24. Of the land of the villans a priest holds of the king 1 hide and 1 virgate of land. It is worth 15s.

THE KING holds WOOTTON RIVERS. Queen Edith held it, and it paid geld for 30 hides less 1 virgate. There is land for 30 ploughs. In demesne are 13 hides and 1 virgate of land, and there are 2 ploughs, and 12 slaves. There are 40 villans and 17 cotsets with 14 ploughs. There are 6 acres of meadow, and pasture 6 furlongs long and 3 furlongs broad, [and] woodland 6 furlongs long and as much broad. It was worth £26; now £30. [The Abbey of] Mont-Saint-Michel holds 2 churches of this manor with 1 hide of land. It is worth 20s.

THE KING holds WESTBURY. Queen Edith held it, and it paid geld for 40 hides. There is land for 47 ploughs. In demesne are 17 hides, and there are 7 ploughs, and 28 slaves and 16 coliberts. There are 38 villans and 23 bordars and 9 bee-keepers. Among them all they have 40 ploughs. The potters there pay 20s a year, and 6 mills render 70s6d, and [there are] 80 acres of meadow, pasture 3 leagues long and 3 leagues broad, [and] woodland 3 leagues long and half a league broad. There are 29 swineherds. This manor renders £100 by tale. Of the same land of this manor the church has 1½ hides. William Scudet [holds] 4½ hides and has there 7 ploughs.

THE KING holds WINTERBOURNE STOKE. Queen Edith held it, and it paid geld for 2 hides and 1 virgate of land. There is land for 12 ploughs. In demesne is half a virgate of land, and there are 3 ploughs, and 11 slaves and 5 coliberts.

There are 15 villans and 15 bordars with 8 ploughs. There is a mill rendering 10s, and 8 acres of meadow, [and] pasture 2 leagues long and as much broad. It was and is worth £33. The church of the same manor has 1 hide of this land. The Abbot of Jumieges holds this church with the land, and it is worth 60s.

THE KING holds NETHERAVON. Earl Harold held it, and it paid geld for 20 hides. There is land for 22 ploughs. In demesne are 2 hides, and there are 6 ploughs, and 46 slaves and 8 coliberts. There are 30 villans and 40 bordars with 16 ploughs. To this manor belong 5 burgesses in Wilton; they pay 6s. There are 3 mills rendering 30s, and 70 acres of meadow, [and] pasture 3 leagues long and half a league broad. It was worth £40; now £57. Of this land of this manor Hervey holds 1½ hides, and there he has 1 plough. A thegn has 2½ hides, and he has there 1 plough. Nigel the physician holds the church of this manor with 1 hide. This with all its appendages is worth £32. [The church] itself, however, is waste, and the roof so damaged, that it is almost tumbling down.

THE KING holds COLLINGBOURNE DUCIS. Earl Harold held it, and it paid geld for 20 hides. There is land for 45 ploughs. In demesne are 5 hides, and there are 5 ploughs, and 12 slaves. There are 49 ploughs [sic] and 26 bordars with 15 ploughs, and 20 acres of meadow. [There is] pasture 2 leagues long and 1 league broad, [and] woodland 1 league long and as much broad, and a third part of the woodland which is called Chute. It was worth £40; now £60. To the church belongs half a hide. Gerald, the priest of Wilton [Church], holds the tithe of this church, and it is worth 10s. The church itself is waste and dismantled.

THE KING holds EAST KNOYLE. Æthelgifu held it TRE, and it paid geld for 30 hides. [There is] land for 15 ploughs. In demesne are 17½ hides, and there are 5 ploughs, and 10 slaves. There are 16 villans and 10 bordars and 18 cotsets with 10 ploughs. There are 15 acres of meadow, and pasture 1 league long and half a league wide, [and] woodland half a league long and as much wide. It was worth £28; now £30. Of this land Gilbert has 1 hide. There are 3 bordars. It is worth 7s6d.

THE KING holds LYDIARD MILLICENT. Godric held it TRE, and it paid geld for 10 hides. There is land for 8 ploughs. In demesne [are] 6 hides less 1 virgate, and there are 4 ploughs, and 9 slaves. There 10 villans and 6 bordars have 6 ploughs. There is a mill rendering 32d, and 20 acres of meadow, [and] woodland 1 league long and half a league broad. It was worth £10; now £12.

THESE 2 vills belonged to Earl William.

[Folio 65V: WILTSHIRE]

THE KING holds OGBOURNE ST GEORGE. [...] TRE it paid geld for 30 hides. There is land for 25 ploughs. In demesne are 18 hides, and there are 4 ploughs, and 6 slaves. There 24 villans and 14 bordars have 10 ploughs. There are 6 acres of meadow, and pasture half a league long and 4 furlongs broad, and as much woodland. It is worth £25.

Ralph the priest holds the church of HIGHWORTH, and to it belong 3 hides which did not pay geld TRE. There is land for 2 ploughs. These the priest has there, with 6 bordars, and 10 acres of meadow. It is worth 100s.

Vitalis the priest holds the church of BURBAGE with 1 virgate of land. It is worth 20s.

Regenbald the priest [...] holds the church of PEWSEY with 1 carucate of land. It is worth 20s.

Regenbald the priest holds the church of AVEBURY, to which belong 2 hides. It is worth 40s.

Alweard the priest holds the church of HEYTESBURY, to which belong 3 hides. There is land for 2 ploughs. These are there, with 2 villans and 6 cottars, and 6 acres of meadow. It is worth 60s.

Bishop Osbern has the church of HAZELBURY with half a virgate of land. It is worth 10s.

[The Abbey of] Saint-Wandrille holds the church of SHERSTON, to which belong 3 virgates of land. It is worth 28s. It also holds the church of UPAVON, to which belong 2½ hides. There is land for 2 ploughs. It is worth £10.15s.

Bishop Osmund holds of the king half a church in alms, to which belongs half a hide. There is 1 plough, with 5 bordars, and a mill rendering 6s. It is worth 25s.

William de Beaufour has 1 hide with a church in MARLBOROUGH. It is worth 30s.

Beorhtweard the priest holds the church of [Great and Little] BEDWYN. His father held it TRE. To it belong 1½ hides. There is land for 1 plough, which [plough] is there. It was and is worth 60s.

II. The land of the Bishop of Winchester

THE BISHOP OF WINCHESTER holds DOWNTON. [...] TRE it paid geld for 100 hides less 3. 2 of these [hides] are not the bishop's, because they were taken away, with 3 others, from the church and out of the hand of the bishop in the time of King Cnut. There is land for 46½ ploughs. Of this land 30 hides are in demesne, and there are 13 ploughs, and 40 slaves. There are 64 villans and 27 bordars having 17 ploughs. There are 7 mills rendering 60s, and 60 acres of meadow, pasture 2 leagues long and 1 league broad, [and] woodland 1½ leagues long and half a league broad.

Of the same land of this manor William de Braose holds 14 hides; Waleran 5 hides; Ralph 5 hides; Ansgot 3½ hides; and the king has, in his forest, 4 hides. The church of the same manor has 4 hides; and all these hold of the bishop. Those who held these lands TRE could not separate themselves from the church. When Bishop Walkelin received this manor, it was worth 60s; now what he has in demesne is worth £80; what the knights [hold] £23; what the church [holds] £3.

The same bishop holds FONTHILL BISHOP. TRE it paid geld for 10 hides. There is land for 7 ploughs. In demesne are 5 hides of this land, and there are 2 ploughs, and 5 slaves. There are 8 villans and 5 bordars with 3 ploughs. There is a mill rendering 5s, and 8 acres of meadow, pasture half a league long and 3 furlongs broad, and as much woodland. It was worth £10; now £14.

The same bishop holds FYFIELD, and Edward [holds] of him, and it paid geld for 5 hides TRE. This land belonged to the sacrist of the church; Alsige, a monk, held it of the bishop. There is land for 3 ploughs. Of this land 3 hides are in demesne, and there are 2 ploughs, with 1 slave. There are 3 villans and 9 bordars with 2 ploughs. There are 3 acres of meadow, and 30 acres of pasture, [and] woodland 3 furlongs long and 1 furlong broad. It was and is worth 100s.

THESE [LANDS] ARE FOR THE SUSTENANCE OF THE MONKS

The same bishop holds ALTON PRIORS, and it paid geld for 20 hides TRE. There is land for 14 ploughs. Of this land 6 hides and 1 virgate of land are in demesne, and there are 4 ploughs, and 8 slaves. There are 27 villans and 15 cotsets with 8 ploughs. There are 2 mills rendering $12\frac{1}{2}$s, and 100 acres of meadow, pasture 6 furlongs long and 4 furlongs broad, [and] woodland 7 furlongs long and 2 furlongs broad. Of the same land William Scudet holds 3 hides of the bishop, and he has there 2 ploughs. What the monks have is worth £24; what William [has] 100s.

The same bishop holds HAM. TRE it paid geld for $10\frac{1}{2}$ hides and half a virgate of land. There is land for 7 ploughs. Of this land $5\frac{1}{2}$ hides are in demesne, and there are 3 ploughs, with 1 slave. There are 9 villans and 10 cotsets with 3 ploughs. There are 8 acres of meadow, pasture 3 furlongs long and 1 furlong broad, [and] woodland 6 furlongs long and 3 furlongs broad. Of the same land William holds 2 hides of the bishop. He who held them before him could not withdraw from the church. This manor was worth £6 when the bishop received it; now the demesne is worth £9; what William holds [is worth] £3.

The same bishop holds WESTWOOD. TRE it paid geld for 3 hides. [There is] land for 5 ploughs. Of this land 2 hides [are] in demesne, and there are 3 ploughs, and 3 slaves. There are 6 villans and 4 bordars with 1 plough. There is a mill rendering 10s, and 6 acres of meadow, [and] woodland 2 furlongs long and 1 furlong broad. When the bishop received it, it was worth £6; now £4.

The same bishop holds 'ELINGDON' [in Wroughton]. TRE it paid geld for 30 hides. There is land for 12 ploughs. Of this land 15 hides are in demesne, and there are 4 ploughs, and 3 slaves. There are 25 villans and 14 bordars have 7 ploughs. There 6 mills render 42s6d, and [there are] 60 acres of meadow, pasture half a league long and 3 furlongs broad, and 20 acres of woodland.

Of this land 1 knight has $1\frac{1}{2}$ hides, and he has there 1 plough. Godric, who held it TRE, could not be separated from the church. When the bishop received it, it was worth £14; now it is worth £18.

The bishop himself holds BUSHTON. TRE it paid geld for 10 hides. There is land for 5 ploughs. Of the same land $6\frac{1}{2}$ hides are in demesne, and there are 2 ploughs, and 3 slaves. There are 7 villans and 3 cotsets with 2 ploughs. There are 30 acres of meadow, [and] woodland 2 furlongs long and 1 furlong broad. When the bishop received it, it was worth £3; now £6.

The same bishop holds WANBOROUGH. TRE it paid geld for 19 hides. There is land for 10 ploughs. Of the same land 9 hides are in demesne, and there are 3 ploughs, and 6 slaves. There are 19 villans and 13 bordars with 5 ploughs. There is a mill rendering 5s, and 40 acres of meadow, [and] pasture half a league long and 15 furlongs broad. Of this land Richer holds 1 hide. When the bishop received it, it was worth £15; now £18.

The same bishop holds ENFORD. TRE it paid geld for 30 hides. There is land for 24 ploughs. Of the same land 10 hides are in demesne, and there are 3 ploughs, and 6 slaves. There are 12 villans and 15 bordars with 10 ploughs. There are 2 mills rendering 25s, and 17 acres of meadow, [and] pasture $2\frac{1}{2}$ leagues long and $1\frac{1}{2}$ leagues broad. Of the same land William holds 5 hides and Harold 2 hides, an Englishman 3 hides. They have there 10 ploughs. A priest has 1 hide. Those who held [these lands] TRE could not be separated from the church. When the bishop received it, it was worth £34; now the demesne is worth £20; what the priest and the knights hold [is worth] £19.

The same bishop holds 'EAST OVERTON' [near Marlborough]. TRE it paid geld for 15 hides. There is land for 7 ploughs. Of this land $8\frac{1}{2}$ hides are in demesne, and there are 2 ploughs. There [...] villans have 5 ploughs. There are 15 acres of meadow, pasture 8 furlongs long and 4 furlongs broad, [and] woodland 5 furlongs long and 2 furlongs broad.

Of the same land Durand holds 2 hides less half a virgate. He who held them TRE could not be separated from the church. It was and is worth 20s. The demesne is worth £8; when the bishop received it, it was worth £6.

The same bishop holds STOCKTON. TRE it paid geld for 10 hides. There is land for 6 ploughs. Of this land $3\frac{1}{2}$ hides are in demesne, and there are 2 ploughs, and 3 slaves. There are 4 villans and 6 bordars with 2 ploughs. There is a mill rendering 10s, and 10 acres of meadow, pasture 5 furlongs long and 2 furlongs broad, and 40 acres of woodland.

Of the same land Richer holds 2 hides, and Ansketil $2\frac{1}{2}$ hides. They have there 2 ploughs. This manor when the bishop received it was worth £8; now the demesne is worth 100s and 10s; what the men hold is worth £4. The land which they hold could not be separated from the church TRE.

[Folio 66: WILTSHIRE]

III. The land of the Bishop of Salisbury

THE BISHOP OF SALISBURY holds POTTERNE. TRE it paid geld for 52 hides. There is land for 40 ploughs. Of this land 10 hides are in demesne, and there are 6 ploughs, and 4 slaves and 5 coliberts. There are 29 villans and 40 bordars with 30 ploughs. There 6 mills render 43s4d, and [there are] 40 acres of meadow, pasture $2\frac{1}{2}$ leagues long and 1 league and 3 furlongs broad, [and] woodland 1 league long and 10 furlongs broad. The demesne of the bishop is and was worth £60.

Of the same land of this manor 2 Englishmen hold 6 hides and

1 virgate of land. 1 of them is a knight by the command of the king, and was the nephew of Bishop Herman. And Alward holds 3 hides which Wulfweard White, TRE, bought from Bishop Herman, for his lifetime only, so that they should afterwards revert to the bishop's farm, because they were [part] of the demesne of the bishop. These thegns have there 4 ploughs, with 2 slaves and 9 bordars. It is worth £7; what the priest of this manor holds is worth 40s.

Of the land of the same manor Ernulf de Hesdin holds 3 hides and 1 virgate of the king. The bishop, however, claims them, since he who held them TRE could not be separated from the bishop.

The same bishop holds BISHOPS CANNINGS. TRE it paid geld for 70 hides. There is land for 45 ploughs. Of this, 10 hides are in demesne, and there are 5 ploughs, and 6 slaves. There are 48 villans and 40 bordars with 28 ploughs. There are 6 mills rendering 7s6d, and 30 acres of meadow, pasture 1 league long and 8 furlongs broad, [and] woodland 1 league long and 10 furlongs broad. In the borough of CALNE a house belonging to this manor renders 20d a year.

Of the same land of this manor a priest holds 2 hides; Everard 10 hides; Herman 4 hides; Quintin 3 hides; Walter 2 hides; Beorhtweard 5 hides; Alweard 1 hides; the wife of the reeve 1 hide. These have 8 ploughs, with 3 villans and 30 bordars having 4 ploughs. The demesne of the bishop is worth £60; what the others hold is worth £35.

The same bishop holds RAMSBURY. TRE it paid geld for 90 hides. There is land for 54 ploughs. Of this land 30 hides are in demesne, and there are 8 ploughs, and 9 slaves. There are 68 villans and 43 bordars having 29 ploughs. There are 80 acres of meadow, and 10 mills render £6 and 30d. [There is] pasture 14 furlongs long and 5 furlongs broad, [and] woodland 16 furlongs long and 4 furlongs broad.

Of the same land of this manor the priests hold 4 hides; Otbold 12 hides; Herbert 5 hides; Quintin 5 hides; the wife of the reeve 1 hide. These have in demesne 11 ploughs; and 31 bordars with 6 ploughs. In Cricklade 5 burgesses belonging to this manor pay 5s. The demesne of the bishop is worth £52.15s; what the others hold, £17.5s.

The same bishop holds SALISBURY. TRE it paid geld for 50 hides. There is land for 32 ploughs. Of this land 10 hides are in demesne, and there are 8 ploughs. There are 25 villans and 50 bordars with 17 ploughs. 7 burgesses in Wilton belonging to this manor pay 65d. In the manor [are] 4 mills rendering 47s7d, and half a mill rendering 30s, and 142 acres of meadow. [There is] pasture 20 furlongs long and 10 furlongs broad, and elsewhere pasture 5 furlongs long and 1 furlong broad. [There is] woodland 4 furlongs long and 2 furlongs broad.

Of the same land of this manor Edward holds 5 hides; Odo 5 hides; Hugh 3 hides less 1 virgate. Those who held them TRE could not be separated from the bishop. There are in demesne 5 ploughs; and 3 villans and 17 bordars with 2 ploughs.

The demesne of the bishop is worth £47; what the men hold is worth £17.10s.

The same bishop holds CHARNAGE. Algar held it TRE, and it paid geld for 5 hides. There is land for 3 ploughs. Of this land 4 hides are in demesne, and there are 2 ploughs; and 3 villans and 6 bordars and 2 cotsets with 1½ ploughs. There are 10½ acres of meadow, pasture 3 furlongs long and 2 furlongs broad, [and] woodland 2 furlongs long and 1 furlong broad. It was worth 40s; now £4. This is in exchange for "SCEPELEIA". Hugh holds it of the bishop.

IIII. The land of the Bishop of Bayeux

THE BISHOP OF BAYEUX holds NORTH TIDWORTH, and Odo [holds] of him. Eadwulf held it TRE, and it paid geld for 5 hides. There is land for 3 ploughs. Of this land 4 hides less 1 virgate are in demesne, and there are 2 ploughs, and 2 slaves. There is 1 villan and 6 bordars with 1 plough. [There is] pasture 3 furlongs long and 2 furlongs broad. It is worth £4.10s.

The same bishop holds WOODHILL, and Odo [holds] of him. Eadwulf held it TRE, and it paid geld for 6 hides. There is land for 3 ploughs. Of this land 5 hides are in demesne, and there are 2 ploughs, and 6 slaves. There is 1 villan and 4 bordars with 1 plough. There are 12 acres of meadow, and pasture 1 furlong long and as much broad, [and] woodland, 1 furlong long and 3 acres broad. It is worth £4.

The same bishop holds SWINDON, and Wadard [holds] of him. Leofgeat held it TRE, and it paid geld for 5 hides. Of these, 1 is in demesne, and there is 1 plough, and 4 slaves. There are 5 villans and 2 bordars with 2 ploughs. There is a mill rendering 4s, and 30 acres of meadow and as much pasture. | It was worth 40s; now £4. |

The same bishop holds DITCHAMPTON, and Robert [holds] of him. Azur held it TRE, and it paid geld for 2 hides. There is land for 2 ploughs. 18 cottars have these there; and there are 4 mills rendering 27s, and 4 acres of meadow and 10 acres of pasture. It was worth 100s; now £8.

V. The land of the Bishop of Coutances

THE BISHOP OF COUTANCES holds DRAYCOT FITZ PAYNE, and Roger [holds] of him. Alweard and Alnoth held it as 2 manors TRE, and it paid geld for 5 hides. There is land for 2½ ploughs. Of this land 4 hides less 1 virgate are in demesne, and there are 2 ploughs, and 3 slaves. There 4 bordars and 7 cotsets have half a plough. There are 60 acres of pasture. It was worth 30s; now 60s.

The same bishop holds 'WITTENHAM' [in Wingfield], and Roger [holds] of him. Ælfgeat held it TRE, and it paid geld for 5 hides. There is land for 5 ploughs. Of this land 3 hides are in demesne, and there is 1 plough, and 3 slaves. There are 5 villans and 5 bordars with 4 ploughs. There is a mill rendering 12s6d, and 10 acres of meadow, and 16 acres of woodland, [and] pasture 2 furlongs long and 1 furlong broad. It was and is worth £4.10s.

The same bishop holds WINGFIELD, and Roger [holds] of him. Azur held it TRE, and it paid geld for 3½ hides. There is land for 3 ploughs. Of this land 2 hides are in demesne, and there is 1 plough. There are 3 villans and 9 bordars with †1† plough. There is a mill rendering 20s, and 7 acres of meadow, and 20 acres of woodland, [and] pasture 3 furlongs long and 2 furlongs broad. It was and is worth 70s.

The same bishop holds MALMESBURY. Gilbert held it TRE, and it paid geld for 1 hide. There is land for half a plough. Of this land 3 virgates of land are in demesne, and there is half a plough, with 3 bordars. There are 4 acres of meadow, and pasture 2 furlongs long and 1 furlong broad. It is worth 13s.

The same bishop holds HIGHER PERTWOOD, and Osbert [holds] of him. Wulfweard held it TRE, and it paid geld for 2 hides. There is land for 2 ploughs. Of this land [...] $1\frac{1}{2}$ hides are in demesne, and there is 1 plough. There are 2 villans and 3 bordars with 1 plough. There are 20 acres of pasture and 4 acres of woodland. It was and is worth 40s.

The same bishop holds LITTLETON DREW, and Robert [holds] of him. Alweard held it TRE of the Abbot of Glastonbury, and he could not be separated from that church, and it paid geld for 5 hides. There is land for 8 ploughs. Of this land 2 hides are in demesne, and there are 2 ploughs, and 4 slaves. There are 6 villans and 6 bordars with 5 ploughs. There is a mill rendering 7s6d, and 15 acres of meadow. It was and is worth £7.

The same bishop holds WINTERBOURNE [? Dauntsey]. Leofsidu held it TRE, and it paid geld for $2\frac{1}{2}$ hides. There is land for 2 ploughs. Of this land $1\frac{1}{2}$ hides are in demesne, and there is 1 plough, and 2 slaves. There are 5 villans and 1 cottar and 4 bordars with 1 plough. There is a mill rendering 12s6d, and 20 acres of pasture. It was worth 30s when the bishop received it; now £4.

VI. The land of the Bishop of Lisieux

THE BISHOP OF LISIEUX holds [?] YATTON KEYNELL. Leofnoth held it TRE, and it paid geld for 2 hides and 3 virgates. There is land for 3 ploughs. Of this 2 hides are in demesne, and there is 1 plough; and 2 bordars and 6 cotsets with 1 plough. There is a mill rendering 10s, and 3 acres of meadow, [and] woodland 2 furlongs long and as much broad. It was and is worth 40s. Turstin holds it of the bishop.

The same bishop holds SOMERFORD KEYNES [Glos.]. Alweard held it TRE, and it paid geld for 10 hides. There is land for 7 ploughs. Of this 5 hides are in demesne, and there are 3 ploughs, and 5 slaves; and 14 villans and 8 bordars with 4 ploughs. There is a mill rendering 10s, and 100 acres of meadow, [and] woodland 3 furlongs long and 2 furlongs broad. It is worth £7.

[Folio 66V: WILTSHIRE]

VII. The land of the Church of Glastonbury

THE CHURCH OF ST MARY OF GLASTONBURY holds DAMERHAM [Hants], and TRE it paid geld for 52 hides. There is land for 30 ploughs. Of this land 16 hides are in demesne, and there are 4 ploughs, and 6 slaves and 38 coliberts. There are 14 villans and 17 bordars with 19 ploughs. There 4 mills render 20s, and [there are] 26 acres of meadow, pasture 3 leagues long and 1 league broad, [and] woodland 5 furlongs long and 4 furlongs broad.

Of the same land Serlo holds 5 hides; the wife of Hugh 3 hides; Roger 1 hide and 8 acres. Those who held [these lands] TRE could not be separated from the church. There are $3\frac{1}{2}$ ploughs.

The whole manor TRE was worth £36. It now renders £61, but by the men [the lands] are not valued at more than £45, on account of the confusion of the land, and on account of the farm, which is too high. The land of the thegns is worth £7.15s.

The same church holds HANNINGTON, and Robert [holds] of the abbot. There are 15 hides. There is land for 10 ploughs. In demesne are 3 ploughs, and 7 slaves; and 18 villans and 10 cotsets with 6 ploughs. There are 2 mills rendering 8s, and 1 house rendering 5d, meadow 3 furlongs long and 3 furlongs broad, [and] pasture 4 furlongs long and 3 furlongs broad. In all it is worth £15. Of this same land the abbot had sold 3 hides to a certain thegn TRE for the lives of 3 men, and the abbot himself had the service from them, and afterwards they were to return to the demesne, and so now they are with the other 12 hides.

The same church holds [? Monkton] DEVERILL. TRE it paid geld for 10 hides. There is land for 8 ploughs. Of this land 5 hides are in demesne, and there are 2 ploughs, and 2 slaves. There are 10 villans and 8 cotsets with 5 ploughs. There is a mill rendering 5s, and 1 acre of meadow, [and] pasture half a league long and as much broad.

Of the same land a thegn holds $1\frac{1}{2}$ hides and this land neither could nor can be separated from the church. The manor, when Abbot Turstin received it, was worth £8; now £10.

The same church holds CHRISTIAN MALFORD. TRE it paid geld for 20 hides. There is land for 10 ploughs. Of this land 14 hides are in demesne, and there are 3 ploughs, and 2 slaves. There are 11 villans and 12 bordars and 12 cotsets with 6 ploughs. There 2 mills render 40s, and [there are] 36 acres of meadow, [and] woodland 1 league long and half a league broad. Of the same land Robert holds half a hide, and Edward 1 virgate. This land [being] thegnland could not be separated from the church TRE. The whole manor is worth £10.10s.

The Abbot of Glastonbury leased 6 acres of meadow to Beorhtric TRE in Stanton [Stanton St Quintin and Lower Stanton St Quintin]. Osbern Giffard holds them now. In like manner he leased 4 acres of meadow in Littleton Drew to Alweard. Bishop Geoffrey holds them now. These 10 acres of meadow ought to belong to Christian Malford.

The church itself holds BADBURY. TRE it paid geld for 20 hides. There is land for 10 ploughs. Of this land $13\frac{1}{2}$ hides are in demesne, and there are 3 ploughs, and 4 slaves. There are 11 villans and 10 bordars with 3 ploughs. There is a mill rendering 40d, and 100 acres of meadow, [and] pasture 1 league long and 3 furlongs broad. In Cricklade 1 burgess pays 5d. It was worth £8; now £10.

The church itself holds MILDENHALL, and Edward [holds] of it. Hugolin had held it previously. It was in the hand of the abbot TRE, and it paid geld for 10 hides. There is land for 10 ploughs. Of this land 4 hides are in demesne, and there are 2 ploughs. There are 15 villans and 5 bordars with 4 ploughs. There is a mill rendering 30s, and 10 acres of meadow, and pasture half a league long and 3 furlongs broad, and as much woodland. It was worth £12; now £18.

The church itself holds WINTERBOURNE MONKTON. TRE it paid geld for 25 hides. There is land for 15 ploughs. Of this land 10 hides are in demesne, and there are 4 ploughs, and 7 slaves. There are 17 villans and 8 bordars with 7 ploughs. There are 6 acres of meadow and 100 acres of pasture. Of the same land Gilbert holds 3½ hides. Ordgar held them TRE, and he could not be separated from the church. The whole manor was worth £12; now £20.

The church itself holds NETTLETON. TRE it paid geld for 20 hides. There is land for 12 ploughs. Of this land 10 hides are in demesne, and there are 4 ploughs, and 2 slaves. There are 10 villans and 12 bordars with 6 ploughs. There are 3 mills rendering 22s6d, and 4 acres of meadow, [and] woodland half a league long and 2 furlongs broad. It was worth £8; now £13.

The church itself holds GRITTLETON. TRE it paid geld for 30 hides. There is land for 20 ploughs. Of this land 10 hides are in demesne, and there are 13 ploughs, and 2 slaves. There are 10 villans and 11 bordars with 7 ploughs. There are 10 acres of meadow and 8 acres of pasture.

Of the same land the Bishop of Coutances holds 5 hides, and Urse 4½ hides. Those who held them TRE could not be separated from the church. There are 10 ploughs.

The demesne of the abbot is worth £12; the bishop's [land] £7; Urse's [land] 40s.

The church itself holds KINGTON LANGLEY. TRE it paid geld for 29 hides. There is land for 16 ploughs. Of this land 11 hides are in demesne, and there are 4 ploughs, and 4 slaves. There are 15 villans and 5 bordars with 8 ploughs. There are 15 acres of meadow, and 10 acres of pasture, [and] woodland 1½ leagues long and half a league broad. In Malmesbury, 1 burgess, paying 15d, belongs to this manor.

Of the same land Urse holds 2½ hides; Roger 2 hides less 1 virgate; Ralph 1½ hides. They have there 3 ploughs. Those who held these lands TRE could not be separated from the church. The demesne of the abbot is worth £14.10s; the men's [land] 100s; when the abbot received it, it was worth £8.

In LITTLE LANGFORD the abbot of the same church holds 2 hides, and Edward [holds] of him. 2 thegns held them of the abbot TRE, and it paid geld for 2 hides. There is land for 1½ ploughs. Of this land 1 hide and 3 virgates are in demesne, and there is 1 plough, and 2 slaves, and 7 bordars, and 17 acres of meadow and 20 acres of pasture. It was and is worth 60s.

In the same vill Edward holds 1 hide of the king, which by right belongs to the thegnland of the abbey.

The church itself holds [?] IDMISTON. TRE it paid geld for 10 hides. 1 of these lies in Hampshire. There is land for 7 ploughs. Of this land 3 hides are in demesne, and there is 1 plough, and 2 slaves. There are 8 villans and 5 bordars with 2 ploughs. There are 6 acres of meadow, and 10 acres of woodland, [and] pasture 1 league long and 3 furlongs broad.

Of the same land Humphrey holds 2½ hides, and has there 1 plough, and 4 acres of meadow and 20 acres of pasture. He who held them TRE could not be separated from the church. It is worth 40s.

The demesne of the abbot is worth £6; when received, it was worth 100s.

The church itself holds [?] GOMELDON. TRE it paid geld for 5 hides. There is land for 3 ploughs. Of this land 2½ hides are in demesne, and there is 1 plough, and 2 slaves. There are 6 villans and 3 bordars with 1½ ploughs. There is a mill rendering 15s, and 6 acres of meadow and 60 acres of pasture. It was and is worth £4.

Of these 5 hides Waleran holds 1 virgate of land and the abbot claims it, which the thegns testify should belong to the church.

The church itself holds [? Longbridge] DEVERILL. TRE it paid geld for 10 hides. There is land for 9 ploughs. Of this land 5 hides are in demesne, and there are 3 ploughs, and 2 slaves. There are 14 villans and 24 bordars and 12 cottars with 6 ploughs. There are 3 mills rendering 14s10d, and 6 acres of meadow, pasture half a league long and 2 furlongs broad, [and] woodland 2 leagues long and half a league broad.

Of the same land a knight holds 1 hide and 1 virgate of land of the abbot. Æthelsige, who held it TRE, could not be separated from the church. The whole manor is worth £12.

VIII. The land of the Church of Malmesbury

THE CHURCH OF ST MARY OF MALMESBURY holds HIGHWAY. TRE it paid geld for 11 hides. There is land for 6 ploughs. In demesne are 3 ploughs. There 3 villans and 6 bordars and 4 cottars with 1 slave have 3 ploughs. There are 15 acres of meadow and as many acres of pasture. It was worth 100s; now £8.

The church itself holds DAUNTSEY. TRE it paid geld for 10 hides. There is land for 6 ploughs. Robert holds it of the abbot. Alweard, who held it of the abbot TRE, could not be separated from the church. In demesne are 2 ploughs and 2 slaves; and 10 villans and 11 cotsets and 3 cottars with 4 ploughs. There is a mill rendering 20s, and 12 acres of meadow, [and] woodland half a league long and as much broad. It was and is worth £6.

[Folio 67: WILTSHIRE]

The church itself holds LITTLE SOMERFORD, and Gunfrid [holds] of the abbot. TRE it paid geld for 5 hides. Alweard, who held it TRE, could not be separated from the church. There is land for 6 ploughs. Of this land 2 hides are in demesne, and there are 3 ploughs. There are 7 villans and 5 bordars and 12 cotsets and 3 slaves having 4 ploughs. There is a mill rendering 20s, and 40 acres of meadow, and 8 acres of woodland. At Malmesbury a burgess pays 12d. It was worth 60s; now 100s.

The church itself holds BRINKWORTH. TRE it paid geld for 5 hides. There is land for 8 ploughs. Of this land 1 hide is in demesne, and there are 2 ploughs, and 3 slaves. There are 9 villans and 13 cotsets and 18 cottars with 6 ploughs. There are 12 acres of meadow, [and] woodland 2 furlongs long and 1 furlong broad. Of the same land 1 knight holds 1 hide. It was and is worth £4; the land of the knight, 15s.

The church itself holds NORTON [near Malmesbury]. TRE it paid geld for 5 hides. There is land for 8 ploughs. Of this land 2½ hides are in demesne, and there are 2 ploughs, and 5 slaves. There are 7 villans and 3 cotsets with 3 ploughs. There is a mill rendering 15s, and 6 acres of meadow, [and] pasture 2 furlongs long and 1 furlong broad. It was worth £6; now £4.

The church itself holds BROKENBOROUGH. TRE it paid geld for 50 hides. There is land for 60 ploughs. Of this land 8 hides are in demesne, and there are 5 ploughs, and 16 slaves. There are 64 villans and 7 cottars and 15 cotsets having 59 ploughs. There are 8 mills rendering £6.12s6d, and 50 acres of meadow, and 30 acres of pasture, [and] woodland 3 leagues long and 2 leagues broad.

Of the same land Ranulph Flambard holds in CORSTON 6 hides. [There is] land for 5 ploughs. He has there 2 ploughs, and 2 villans and 2 cotsets and 2 slaves with 1 plough, and a mill rendering 12s6d, and 10 acres of meadow, and 15 acres of pasture, and woodland 3 furlongs long and 1 furlong broad.

Of the same land, also, Robert holds 3½ hides; William 2 hides; an Englishwoman 1 hide. Those who held these lands TRE could not be separated from the church.

Of the demesne of the monks, [and] of the land of the villans, 2 knights hold 3½ hides. The demesne of the abbot, when received, was worth £26; now £30; what Ranulph [...] and the others hold is worth £11.4s.

The church itself holds KEMBLE [Glos.]. TRE it paid geld for 30 hides. There is land for 30 ploughs. Of this land 12 hides are in demesne, and there are 2 ploughs, and 6 slaves. There are 30 villans and 15 cotsets with 18 ploughs. There are 2 mills rendering 15s, and 40 acres of meadow, [and] woodland 1 league long and 3 furlongs broad.

Of the same land Tovi holds 2 hides and 1 virgate of land, and William 4 hides, in CHELWORTH [in Crudwell]. Those who held them TRE could not be separated from the church. There are 2 ploughs, and 6 slaves, and 6 bordars, and a mill rendering 10s, and 8 acres of meadow. Of the land of the villans Ansketil holds 1 hide.

The demesne of the abbot is worth £13; when received, it was worth £10; what the men hold is worth £8.

The church itself holds LONG NEWNTON [Glos.]. TRE it paid geld for 30 hides. There is land for 23 ploughs. Of this land 15 hides are in demesne, and there are 4 ploughs, and 4 slaves. There are 19 villans and 5 cottars and 2 cotsets with 9 ploughs. There are 2 mills rendering 30s, and 18 acres of meadow and 80 acres of pasture.

Of the same land Osbern holds 3 hides, and William 2 hides. They have there 6 ploughs. Of the land of the villans the abbot gave 1 hide to a certain knight of his. When the abbot received it, it was worth £10; now his demesne is worth £12; what the men hold is worth £6.

The church itself holds CHARLTON [near Malmesbury]. TRE it paid geld for 20 hides. There is land for 13 ploughs. Of this land 12 hides are in demesne, and there are 2 ploughs, and 7 slaves. There are 23 villans and 13 cottars and 2 cotsets with 5 ploughs. There is a mill rendering 15s, and 12 acres of meadow, and 15 acres of pasture, [and] woodland 2 furlongs long and 1 furlong broad. Of the same land Ranulph Flambard holds 1½ hides, and has there 1½ ploughs. Of the land of the villans Ralph holds 1½ hides, and has there 1 plough. When the abbot received the manor, it was worth £8; now his demesne is worth as much; what the men hold is worth 40s.

The church itself holds GARSDON. Wulfgifu held it TRE, and it paid geld for 3 hides. There is land for 6 ploughs. Of this land 1½ hides are in demesne, and there are 2 ploughs, and 6 slaves. There are 5 villans and 5 cotsets with 3 ploughs. There are 2 mills rendering 25s, and 10 acres of meadow, and 10 acres of pasture, [and] woodland half a league long and 2 furlongs broad; and 1 burgess pays 3s. It was worth 60s; now 100s.

The church itself holds CRUDWELL. TRE it paid geld for 40 hides. There is land for 25 ploughs. Of this land 18 hides are in demesne, and there are 4 ploughs, and 5 slaves. There are 48 villans and 24 bordars and 10 cottars and 7 coliberts with 18 ploughs. There are 24 acres of meadow, [and] woodland 2 leagues long and as much broad. It was and is worth £16. Of the same land Everard holds 3 hides, and he has there 3 ploughs, and 7 villans with 1 bordar and 5 slaves and 1 plough. Werlin, who held it TRE, could not be separated from the church. It is worth £4. There are 9 acres of meadow.

The church itself holds BREMHILL. TRE it paid geld for 38 hides. There is land for 30 ploughs. Of this land 17 hides are in demesne, and there are 7 ploughs, and 12 slaves. There are 32 villans and 13 bordars with 20 ploughs. There are 2 mills rendering 30s, and 12 acres of meadow, [and] woodland 2 leagues long and 2 furlongs broad. It was worth £14 when the abbot received it; now £16.

Of the same land Edward holds 4 hides, and Theodric 4 hides. There is land for 7 ploughs, and there are as many ploughs, and 2 villans and 9 bordars and 7 cottars and 4 slaves. Among them there is a mill rendering 16s, and 10 acres of meadow, and 4 acres of spinney, and woodland 1 furlong long and as much broad. Each [of these holdings] is worth 100s. Those who held these 8 hides TRE could not be separated from the church. Of the land of the villans the same Theodric holds 1 hide which the abbot gave him.

Of the same [land] also, [...] Edward holds 2 hides of the king, and Gilbert [holds] of him. These a certain English abbot took away from the demesne of the church and gave to a certain reeve, and afterwards to a thegn, who could in no way be separated from the church. It is worth 40s. a year.

William de Eu also holds of the same land 1 hide which the abbot leased to Ælfstan TRE. It is worth 6s.

The church itself holds PURTON. TRE it paid geld for 35 hides. There is land for 24 ploughs. Of this land 21½ hides are in demesne, and there are 2 ploughs, and 5 slaves. There are 20 villans and 12 bordars and 13 cottars with 19 ploughs. There is a mill rendering 5s, and 60 acres of meadow, [and] woodland 2 leagues long and as much broad. In Cricklade a burgess belonging to this manor pays 6d. It was and is worth £16.

IX. What [The Church of] St Peter of Westminster Has

THE CHURCH OF ST PETER OF WESTMINSTER holds the church of CRICKLADE, and has there many burgesses, and the third penny of the same vill. The whole together renders £9.

X. The land of the Abbey of St Peter of Winchester

THE CHURCH OF ST PETER OF WINCHESTER holds MANNINGFORD ABBOTS. TRE it paid geld for 10 hides. There is land for 10 ploughs. Of this land 5 hides and half a virgate of land are in demesne, and there are 2 ploughs, and 5 slaves. There are 8 villans and 7 cotsets with 2½ ploughs. There is a mill rendering 12s6d, and 10 acres of meadow, [and] pasture 4 furlongs long and 1 furlong broad. It was worth £6; now £8.

The church itself holds COLLINGBOURNE KINGSTON. TRE it paid geld for 50 hides. There is land for 32 ploughs. Of this land 10 hides are in demesne, and there are 4 ploughs, and 13 slaves. There are 40 villans and 13 cotsets with 15 ploughs. There are 2 acres of meadow, woodland 1 league long and half a league broad, and as much pasture.

Of the same land Croch holds of the abbot 10 hides and half a virgate of land and half a hide, and Fulchred 2 hides. Those who held [these lands] TRE could not be separated from the church. There are 8 ploughs. Of the thegnland the abbot has in his demesne 1 hide.

The whole demesne of the abbot is now worth £28; what the men hold is worth £12; when received, it was worth 100s less.

[Folio 67v: WILTSHIRE]

The church itself holds PEWSEY. TRE it paid geld for 30 hides. There is land for 24 ploughs. Of this land 6 hides and 1 virgate of land are in demesne, and there are 3 ploughs, and 6 slaves. There are 46 villans and 24 cotsets and 1 bordar with 18 ploughs. There are 7 mills rendering £4.5s, and 15 acres of

meadow, pasture 1 league long and as much broad, [and] woodland 3 furlongs long and half a furlong broad. Of the same land a thegn holds 2 hides less 1 virgate, and he could not be separated from the church; and Ernulf de Hesdin holds 2 hides of the king, which the abbot gave TRE to a thegn who, however, could not be separated from the church. It is worth 30s. The demesne of the abbot was worth £26; now it is worth £28.

The church itself holds 2 hides in ADDESTONE. There is land for 2 ploughs. Of this land 1 hide is in demesne, and 1 plough, and 3 slaves. There is 1 villan and 4 bordars with 1 plough, and 4 acres of meadow and 60 acres of pasture. It was worth 10s; now 40s.

The church itself holds CHISELDON. TRE it paid geld for 40 hides. There is land for 22 ploughs. Of this land 17 hides are in demesne, and 5 ploughs, and 6 slaves. There are 45 villans and 13 bordars with 10 ploughs. There is a mill rendering 40d, and 40 acres of meadow, pasture half a league long and 4 furlongs broad, [and] woodland 3 furlongs long and 2 furlongs broad. It was worth £18; now £24. 6 burgesses in Cricklade belonging to this manor pay 4s1d.

XI. The land of the Church of Cranborne

THE CHURCH OF ST MARY OF CRANBORNE holds ASHTON KEYNES, and held it TRE, and it paid geld for 20 hides. There is land for 16 ploughs. Of this land 10 hides are in demesne, and there are 2 ploughs, and 5 slaves. There are 20 villans and 12 bordars and 4 cotsets with 13 ploughs. There is a mill rendering 5s, and 200 acres of meadow, [and] pasture 1 league long and half a league broad. The woodland is of like extent. It was and is worth £15.

The church itself holds 1 hide in DAMERHAM [Hants]. There is land for 1½ ploughs. The abbot has there 1 plough, and 5 bordars with half a plough. It is worth 20s.

XII. The land of the Church of Shaftesbury

THE CHURCH OF ST MARY OF SHAFTESBURY holds BEECHINGSTOKE, and Turstin holds it of the abbess. Hearding held it of the church TRE, and it paid geld for 5 hides. There is land for 5 ploughs. Of this land 3 hides are in demesne, and there are 2 ploughs, and 2 slaves. There are 6 villans and 6 cotsets with 3 ploughs. There is a mill rendering 12s, and 28 acres of meadow, and 40 acres of pasture. It was worth 60s; now 100s. Hearding, who by agreement was entitled to hold this land in his own lifetime, of his own accord restored it to the church.

The church itself holds TISBURY. TRE it paid geld for 20 hides. There is land for 40 ploughs. Of this land 5 hides are in demesne, and there are 3 ploughs. There are 40 villans and 50 bordars with 25 ploughs. There are 4 mills rendering 35s, and 40 acres of meadow, pasture 1 league long and half a league broad, [and] woodland 1 league long and as much broad.

Of the same land Turstin holds 3 hides of the abbess; Gunfrid 3 hides; Aubrey 2 hides. They have there 9 ploughs. Edward the sheriff has 3 ploughs in the land of the villans. The demesne of the abbess is worth £30; the knights' [land] £13.

The church itself holds DONHEAD [St Andrew and St Mary]. TRE it paid geld for 40 hides. There is land for 32 ploughs. Of this land 12 hides are in demesne, and there are 2 ploughs. There are 35 villans and 25 bordars with 25 ploughs. There are 8 mills rendering 66s8d, and 15 acres of meadow, pasture 1 league long and as much broad, [and] woodland 6 furlongs long and 2 furlongs broad. Of the same land Turstin holds 6 hides, and a certain thegn 1 hide, and there are 6 ploughs. Those who held them TRE could not be separated from the church. The demesne of the abbess is worth £22; the men's [land] £10; and it was worth as much previously.

The church itself holds BRADFORD ON AVON. TRE it paid geld for 42 hides. There is land for 40 ploughs. Of this land 13 hides are in demesne, and there are 8 ploughs, and 9 slaves | and 18 | coliberts. There are 36 villans and 40 bordars with 32 ploughs, and there are 22 swineherds, and 33 burgesses paying 35s9d, and 1 sergeant rendering 7 sesters of honey. There are 2 mills rendering £3. The market renders 45s. There is an arpent of vineyard, and 50 acres of meadow, pasture 11 furlongs long and 3 furlongs broad, [and] woodland half a league long and 2 furlongs broad.

To the same manor of Bradford on Avon belongs "ALVESTONE" [? in Bradford on Avon]. TRE it paid geld for 7 hides apart from the 42 hides above-mentioned. There is land for 6 ploughs. Of this land 4 hides are in demesne, and there are 3 ploughs. The whole of Bradford on Avon, with its appendages, was and is worth £60.

The church itself holds LIDDINGTON. TRE it paid geld for 38 hides. There is land for 16 ploughs. Of this land 24 hides are in demesne, and there are 4 ploughs, and 6 slaves. There are 23 villans and 17 bordars with 7 ploughs. There are 2 mills rendering 5s, meadow 4 furlongs long and 3 furlongs broad, [and] pasture half a league long and 4 furlongs broad. In Cricklade 1 burgess pays 6d. It was worth £18; now £22.

The church itself holds DINTON. TRE it paid geld for 20 hides. There is land for 15 ploughs. Of this land 7 hides and 3 virgates of land are in demesne, and there are 2 ploughs, and 4 slaves. There are 21 villans and 10 bordars with 11 ploughs. There are 2 mills rendering 12s6d, and 20 acres of meadow, and as many acres of woodland, [and] pasture 1 league long and half a league broad. 2 burgesses pay 10d.

Of the same land Gunfrid holds 2 hides, and has there 2 ploughs. He who held them TRE could not be separated from the church. The demesne of the abbess was and is worth £18; Gunfrid's [holding] 40s.

XIII. The land of the Church of Wilton

THE CHURCH OF ST MARY OF WILTON holds STANTON ST BERNARD. TRE it paid geld for 20 hides. There is land for 12 ploughs. Of this land 10 hides are in demesne, and there are 4 ploughs, and there are 8 slaves. There are 16 villans and 1 bordar and 21 cotsets with 8 ploughs. There are 2 mills rendering 12s6d, and 60 acres of meadow, and 3 acres of alder-wood, [and] pasture 1 league long and half a league broad. It was worth £16; now £24.

The church itself holds NORTH NEWNTON. TRE it paid geld for 13½ hides and half a virgate of land. Of this land 3 hides are in demesne, and there are 2 ploughs, and 4 slaves. There are 13 villans and 16 cotsets with 5 ploughs. 10 ploughs can plough the whole manor. There is a mill rendering 12s6d, and 30 acres of meadow, pasture 4 furlongs long and 2 furlongs broad, [and] woodland 1 league long and as much broad.

Of the land of the villans the abbess gave to a knight 3½ hides and half a virgate of land. He has there 2 ploughs, and his villans 1 plough.

Of the same land Ælfric the huntsman held of the abbess 1 hide and 1½ virgates of land, on the condition that after his death it should return to the church because it was [part] of the demesne farm. Richard Sturmy holds it now. The whole manor was worth £14 when received; now £18.

The church itself holds [Great and Little] DURNFORD. TRE it paid geld for 4 hides. There is land for 3 ploughs. Edward holds it of the abbess. 3 Englishmen held it TRE and they could not be separated from the church. 2 of them paid 5s, and the third rendered service as a thegn. There are 6 oxen in the demesne plough, with 4 bordars. 2 Englishmen there have 2 ploughs. There is a mill rendering 7½s, and there are 12 acres of meadow, [and] pasture 4 furlongs long and 1 furlong broad. It was worth 100s; now £9.

The church itself holds SWALLOWCLIFFE. TRE it paid geld for 4 hides and 1 virgate. There is land for 2 ploughs. There is 1 villan and 2 bordars, and 2 acres of meadow. It was and is worth 40s.

The church itself holds CHILMARK. TRE it paid geld for 20 hides. There is land for 14 ploughs. Of this land 8 hides are in demesne, and there are 2 ploughs. There are 15 villans and 12 bordars and 12 coliberts with 12 ploughs. There is a mill rendering 10s, and 5 acres of meadow, and 10 acres of thicket, [and] pasture 1 league long and half a league broad. It was worth £14; now £15.

[Folio 68: WILTSHIRE]

The church itself holds 1 hide of land in WARDOUR, and Beorhtmær holds it of the abbess. There is land for 1 plough. This [plough] is there with 4 bordars, and 3 acres of meadow. [There is] pasture 1 league long and half a league broad, [and] woodland 2 furlongs long and 1 furlong broad. It is worth 20s.

The church itself holds WEST KNOYLE. TRE [it paid geld] for 10 hides. There is land for 7 ploughs. Of this land 4½ hides are in demesne, and 3 slaves. There are 11 villans and 9 cotsets with 5 ploughs. There are 5 acres of meadow, and pasture half a league long and 3 furlongs broad, [and] woodland half a league long and as much broad. It was worth £6; now £8.

The church itself holds WEST OVERTON. TRE it paid geld for 10 hides. Of this land 7 hides and half a virgate of land are in demesne, and there are 2 ploughs, and 2 slaves. There are 3 villans and 8 bordars with 2 ploughs. There is a mill rendering 10s, and 5 acres of meadow, and 20 acres of pasture, and 20 acres of woodland. It is worth 100s.

The church itself holds CHALKE [Bowerchalke and Broad Chalke]. TRE it paid geld for 77 hides. There is land for 66 ploughs. Of this land 10 hides are in demesne, and there are 10 ploughs, and 20 slaves. There are 86 villans and 50 bordars and 10 coliberts having 50 ploughs. There are 5 mills rendering 65s, and 12 acres of meadow, pasture 3 leagues long and 1 league broad, and as much woodland.

Of the same land Gerard holds 3 hides. He who held them TRE could not be separated from the church. There are 2 ploughs. It is worth £3. The demesne of the abbess is worth £67.

Of the same land Richard Puignant holds 7½ hides of the king. Of these, Æthelgifu held 2 hides TRE, and the men of the church held the others, rendering service as villans. The abbess claims them. Richard has there 5 ploughs; and it is worth £7.

The church itself holds SOUTH NEWTON. TRE it paid geld for 19 hides and 3 virgates of land. There is land for 14 ploughs. Of this land 2 hides are in demesne, and there are 2 ploughs, and 6 coliberts. There are 20 villans and 16 bordars with 12 ploughs. There are 2 mills rendering 40s, and 20 acres of meadow, and 150 acres of pasture and 200 acres of woodland. To this manor belongs [the right] by custom to have in MELCHET WOOD [Hants] 80 cart-loads of wood |and fodder for 80 pigs, | and what may be necessary for the repair of the houses and fences.

The church itself holds WYLYE. TRE it paid geld for 10 hides. There is land for 5 ploughs. Of this land 5 hides are in demesne, and there are 2 ploughs, and 2 slaves. There are 9 villans and 10 bordars with 3 ploughs. There is a mill rendering 10s, and 12 acres of meadow, and 100 acres of pasture and 10 acres of scrubland. It was worth £6; now £8. #SOUTH NEWTON is worth £16.

The church itself holds LITTLE WISHFORD. TRE it paid geld for 4 hides. There is land for 3 ploughs. Of this land 2 hides are in demesne, and there are 2 ploughs. There is 1 villan and 16 bordars with 1 plough. There are 2 mills rendering 24s, and 8 acres of meadow, and 9 acres of pastures. It was worth £3; now £4.

The church itself holds LITTLE LANGFORD. TRE it paid geld for 3 hides. There is land for 2 ploughs. These [ploughs] 2 Englishmen have there with 2 bordars and 2 slaves. There is a mill rendering 5s, and 25 acres of meadow and 20 acres of pasture. It was worth 40s; now 50s. The father of those who now hold it, held it TRE, and could not be separated from the church.

The church itself holds UGFORD. TRE it paid geld for 4 hides. There is land for 3 ploughs. Of this land 3 hides are in demesne, and there is 1 plough. There are 2 villans and 4 bordars with 1 plough. There is a mill rendering 5s, and 6 acres of meadow. It was worth 40s; now 60s. The church itself has half a hide of land in DITCHAMPTON. It is worth 30d.

The church itself holds BURCOMBE. TRE it paid geld for 6 hides. There is land for 4 ploughs. Of this land 2 hides are in demesne, and there are 2 ploughs. There are 13 bordars, and a mill rendering 15s, and 18 acres of meadow, [and] pasture 8 furlongs long and 1 furlong broad. It is worth 100s. Of the same land Edward holds 1 hide which cannot be alienated from the church. It is worth 15s.

The church itself holds BAVERSTOCK. TRE it paid geld for 3 hides. There is land for 3 ploughs. Of these 2 hides are in demesne, and there is 1 plough, with 1 slave; and 4 bordars with 2 ploughs, and 6 acres of meadow and 4 acres of pasture. It is worth 60s.

The church itself holds WASHERN. TRE it paid geld for 8½ hides. There is land for 7 ploughs. Of this land 2 hides are in demesne, and there is 1 plough. There are 9 villans and 10 coliberts with 6 ploughs. There are 12 acres of meadow, [and] pasture 8 furlongs long and 6 furlongs broad. In MELCHET Wood [Hants] [there is] pasture for 80 pigs, and 80 cart-loads of wood, and what is necessary for [repairing] the houses and fences. It is worth £7.10s.

The church itself holds FOVANT. TRE it paid geld for 10 hides. There is land for 7 ploughs. Of this land 5 hides are in demesne, and there are 2 ploughs, and 7 coliberts. There are 8 villans and 7 bordars with 5 ploughs. There are 2 mills rendering 17s6d, and 8 acres of meadow, pasture 4 furlongs long and 1 furlong broad, [and] woodland 2 furlongs long and 1 furlong broad. It is worth £7.10s.

The church itself holds LAVERSTOCK. TRE it paid geld for 2 hides. There is land for 3 ploughs. Of this land 1 hide is in demesne, and there is 1 plough. There are 6 villans and 8 bordars with 2 ploughs. There is a mill rendering 7s6d, and 18 acres of pasture. It was worth 100s; now £6. Of this land a fourth part has been put in the king's forest.

The church itself held 2 hides TRE, which Thorth had given there with his 2 daughters, and from them they were always clothed, until the Bishop of Bayeux unjustly took them away from the church.

All the rents which the church has from this borough of Wilton are valued at £10.17s6d.

XIIII. The land of the Church of St Mary of Winchester

THE CHURCH OF ST MARY OF WINCHESTER holds URCHFONT. TRE it paid geld for 30 hides. There is land for 20 ploughs. Of this land 6 hides are in demesne, and there are 7 ploughs, and 17 slaves. There are 33 villans and 26 bordars and 6 cottars with 9 ploughs. There are 3 mills rendering 21s3d, and 64 acres of meadow, pasture 1 league long and half a league broad, and as much woodland. Of the same land Edward holds 1½ hides and the third part of half a hide; Walter 1 hide; Englishmen hold 2 hides and 2 parts of half a hide. Of the 6 hides which are in demesne, the abbess's reeve held 2 hides TRE. Afterwards, however, he restored them to the church with all his livestock and they are now in demesne. When the abbess received the manor, it was worth £15; now what she has in demesne [is worth] £27; what the knights [hold] £3.

The church itself holds ALL CANNINGS. TRE it paid geld for 18 hides and $1\frac{1}{2}$ virgates of land. There is land for 15 ploughs. Of this land 4 hides are in demesne, and there are 5 ploughs, and 8 slaves. There are 27 villans and 17 bordars and 6 cottars with 10 ploughs. There is a mill rendering 13s, and 108 acres of meadow, pasture 1 league long and 4 furlongs broad, [and] woodland 4 furlongs long and 2 furlongs broad. It was worth £20; now £30.

XV. The land of the Church of Romsey

THE CHURCH OF ST MARY OF ROMSEY holds EDINGTON. TRE it paid geld for 30 hides. There is land for $35\frac{1}{2}$ ploughs. Of this land $2\frac{1}{2}$ hides are in demesne, and there are 7 ploughs, and 10 slaves. There are 21 villans and 23 bordars and 10 coliberts with 15 ploughs. There are 2 mills rendering 19s, and 100 acres of meadow, pasture 1 league long and half a league broad, [and] woodland 10 furlongs long and 5 broad.

Of the same land William holds $4\frac{1}{2}$ hides; Osmund 4 hides; Hervey 2 hides; Englishmen 5 hides and 1 virgate of land. Those who held these 15 hides and 3 virgates TRE could not be separated from the church. There are $12\frac{1}{2}$ ploughs. The demesne of the church is worth £30; what the men hold £18.

The church itself holds [Steeple and West] ASHTON. TRE it paid geld for 40 hides. There is land for 37 ploughs. Of this land 10 hides are in demesne, and there are 9 ploughs, and 8 slaves. There are 40 villans and 30 bordars with 20 ploughs. There are 3 mills rendering 32s6d, and 100 acres of meadow, pasture 19 furlongs long and 1 furlong broad, [and] woodland 2 leagues long and half a league broad. Of the same land Edward holds 3 hides; William 1 hide; Englishmen 4 hides. Those who held them TRE could not be separated from the church. The demesne of the church is worth £30; [the holdings] of the men, £6.13s.

[Folio 68V: WILTSHIRE]

XVI. The land of the Church of Amesbury

THE CHURCH OF AMESBURY holds BULFORD. TRE it paid geld for 12 hides. There is land for 9 ploughs. Of this land 6 hides are in demesne, and there are 3 ploughs, and 13 slaves. There are 3 villans and 20 cotsets and 3 cottars with 5 ploughs. There are 2 mills rendering 65s, and 35 acres of meadow, [and] pasture 1 league long and half a league broad. Of the same land Alweard holds 3 hides. He who held them TRE could not be separated from the church. The demesne of the abbess is worth £13; what the thegn holds is worth 15s.

The church itself holds BOSCOMBE. TRE it paid geld for 4 hides. There is land for 2 ploughs. Of this land $2\frac{1}{2}$ hides are in demesne, and there is 1 plough, with 1 slave. There are 2 villans and 5 cotsets and 2 cottars with 1 plough. There are 4 acres of meadow, [and] pasture 1 furlong long and half a furlong broad. It was and is worth £3.

The church itself holds ALLINGTON [near Amesbury]. TRE it paid geld for 4 hides. There is land for 2 ploughs. Of this land 3 hides less 1 virgate are in demesne, and there is 1 plough, and 3 slaves. There are 3 villans and 5 cotsets and 1 cottar with 1 plough. There are 8 acres of meadow, [and] pasture 1 league long and 1 furlong broad. It was worth £3; now £4.

The church itself holds CHOULSTON, and Alweard holds it of the abbess. TRE it paid geld for $2\frac{1}{2}$ hides. There is land for $1\frac{1}{2}$ ploughs, and as many [ploughs] are there, with 2 slaves and 3 cotsets. There are 8 acres of meadow, [and] pasture 5 furlongs long and 1 furlong broad. It was worth 30s; now 40s.

The church itself used to hold 2 hides TRE, and held them afterwards in the time of King William, and they are for the sustenance of the nuns. These [hides] the Count of Mortain holds unjustly.

The church itself holds 6 hides in RABSON. There is land for 4 ploughs. Of this land 3 hides are in demesne, and there are 3 ploughs, and 2 slaves. There are 5 villans and 10 bordars with 1 plough. There are 3 acres of meadow, [and] pasture half a league long and as much broad. It was worth £4; now 100s.

The church itself holds MADDINGTON. TRE it paid geld for $4\frac{1}{2}$ hides. There is land for 2 ploughs. Of this land $2\frac{1}{2}$ hides are in demesne, and there is 1 plough. There are 4 villans and 4 bordars and 2 cottars with 1 plough. There are 8 acres of meadow and 10 acres of pasture. It was and is worth £4.

XVII. The land of Sainte-Marie of Bec

THE CHURCH OF SAINTE-MARIE OF BEC holds BRIXTON DEVERILL of the king. Beorhtric held it TRE, and it paid geld for 10 hides. There is land for 7 ploughs. Of this land $6\frac{1}{2}$ hides are in demesne, and there are 3 ploughs, and 8 slaves. There are 8 villans and 7 cotsets and 2 bordars with 4 ploughs. There is a mill rendering 30d, and 4 acres of meadow, pasture 1 league long and 5 furlongs broad, [and] woodland 3 furlongs long and 2 furlongs broad. The church of the same manor has 1 hide of the same land. The whole manor is worth £12. It was worth £15 during the lifetime of Queen Matilda, who gave it to the same church.

XVIII. The land of Gerald of Wilton

GERALD of Wilton holds UPTON LOVELL of the king in alms. The same man held it TRE, and it paid geld for 10 hides. There is land for 6 ploughs. Of this land 6 hides and $1\frac{1}{2}$ virgates are in demesne, and there are 3 ploughs, and 4 slaves. There are 9 villans and 6 bordars and 4 cotsets with 3 ploughs. There is a mill rendering 20s, and 15 acres of meadow, [and] pasture half a league long and 2 furlongs broad. It is worth £10.

[The land] of Regenbald

REGENBALD the priest holds LATTON and EYSEY. 2 thegns held them as 2 manors TRE. Earl Harold joined them into 1, and it paid geld for 9 hides. There is land for 8 ploughs. Of this land 3 hides are in demesne, and 8 slaves. There are 15 villans and 6 bordars and 4 cottars with 5 ploughs; and in demesne 3 ploughs. There are 2 mills, and 200 acres of meadow, [and] pasture 1 league long and half a league broad. It was and is worth £10.

XIX. [The land of] the Canons of Lisieux

THE CANONS OF LISIEUX hold KINGSTON DEVERILL. Eadgifu held it TRE, and it paid geld for 4 hides. There is land for 3 ploughs. Of this $3\frac{1}{2}$ hides less 3 acres are in demesne, and there is 1 plough, and 2 slaves; and 6 cotsets with 1 villan have 1 plough. There are 3 acres of meadow, [and] pasture 4 furlongs long and 3 furlongs broad. It was worth 40s; now 70s.

ALWEARD the priest has 5 hides which belong to the church of ALDERBURY of the alms of the king. There is land for 3 ploughs. In demesne is 1 plough; and 4 villans and 8 bordars with 2 ploughs. There are 10 acres of meadow, and 4 furlongs of woodland in length and 4 in breadth. To this same church belongs 1 hide which has never paid geld. The whole is worth 70s.

OSBERN the priest has 2 hides of the king in the church of ALDERBURY. It is worth 20s.

AGENULF holds HORNINGSHAM. His father held it of King Edward in alms. There is half a hide. [There is] land for 1 plough. There is 1 cotset, and 2 acres of meadow and 2 acres of woodland. It is worth 5s.

XX. The land of the Count of Mortain

THE COUNT OF MORTAIN holds CONOCK, and [the Church of] SAINTE-MARIE of Grestain [holds] of him. TRE it paid geld for 10 hides. There is land for 4 ploughs. Of this land $6\frac{1}{2}$ hides are in demesne, and there are 2 ploughs, and 3 slaves. There are 6 villans and 9 bordars with 2 ploughs. There are 20 acres of meadow, [and] pasture half a league long and 3 furlongs broad. It was worth £8; now £9.

The same count holds "NECHENDUNE", and Gilbert [holds] of him. Godwine held it TRE, and it paid geld for 3 hides. There is land for 2 ploughs. Of this land 2 hides are in demesne, and there is 1 plough, and 2 slaves. There is 1 villan and 8 bordars with 1 plough. There are 20 acres of meadow and 15 acres of pasture. It was worth 30[s]; it is now worth 40s.

The same count holds [?] CLYFFE PYPARD, and Gilbert [holds] of him. Godwine held it TRE, and it paid geld for 3 hides. There is land for $1\frac{1}{2}$ ploughs. In demesne is 1 plough, and 2 slaves, and 10 acres of meadow. It was worth 20s; now 40s.

The same count holds [?] CLYFFE PYPARD, and Gilbert [holds] of him. Godwine held it TRE, and it paid geld for 4 hides less 1 virgate. There is land for $1\frac{1}{2}$ ploughs. There is 1 villan and 3 bordars, and 16 acres of meadow and 14 acres of pasture. It is worth 40s.

The count himself holds HANGING LANGFORD. Ketil held it TRE, and it paid geld for 5 hides. There is land for $2\frac{1}{2}$ ploughs. Of this land 4 hides and 1 virgate of land are in demesne, and there are 2 ploughs. There are 2 villans and 4 bordars with half a plough. There is half a mill rendering 30d, and 20 acres of meadow and 30 acres of pasture. It was and is worth 100s.

The count himself holds [? West] WINTERSLOW. Hearding held it TRE, and it paid geld for $6\frac{1}{2}$ hides. There is land for 7 ploughs. Of this land 3 hides are in demesne, and there are 3 ploughs, and 6 slaves. There are 6 villans and 12 cotsets with 3 ploughs. There is a mill rendering 5s, and 3 acres of meadow, pasture 1 league long and as much broad, [and] woodland 1 league long and half a league broad. It is worth £10. Of this manor the Abbess of Amesbury held 2 hides TRE.

XXI. The land of Earl Roger

EARL ROGER holds CASTLE EATON. TRE it paid geld for 15 hides. There is land for 12 ploughs. Of this land half is in demesne, and there are $3\frac{1}{2}$ ploughs, and 6 slaves. There are 8 villans and 8 cotsets with 5 ploughs. There is a mill rendering 15s6d, and 100 acres of meadow, [and] pasture 6 furlongs long and 3 furlongs broad. It was worth £15 TRE; now £12.

The earl himself holds MILSTON. TRE it paid geld for $3\frac{1}{2}$ hides. There is land for 2 ploughs. Of this land 2 hides are in demesne, and there is 1 plough; and 3 villans and 5 cotsets with $1\frac{1}{2}$ ploughs. There are 8 acres of meadow, [and] pasture 1 league long and 3 furlongs broad. It was and is worth 70s. Turold holds these 2 manors of the earl. Osmund, a thegn, held them TRE.

The same earl holds POULTON [near Cirencester, Glos.]. Siward held it TRE, and it paid geld for 5 hides. There is land for 8 ploughs. Of this land $3\frac{1}{2}$ hides are in demesne, and there are 4 ploughs, and 8 slaves; and 8 villans and 7 cotsets with 4 ploughs. There are 15 acres of meadow, [and] pasture 3 furlongs long and 1 furlong broad. It was worth £12; now £16.

XXII. The land of Earl Hugh

EARL HUGH holds "RETMORE", and William [holds] of him. TRE it paid geld for half a hide. There is land for 3 ploughs. In demesne are 2 ploughs with 1 slave. There is 1 villan and 3 bordars and 11 cotsets with 1 plough. There is a mill rendering 14s, and 5 acres of meadow, pasture 3 furlongs long and 1 furlong broad, [and] woodland 3 furlongs long and 2 furlongs broad. It was worth 50s; now 60s.

The same earl holds [?] WILSFORD [near Amesbury], and Hamo [holds] of him. TRE it paid geld for 1 hide. There is land for 1 plough, and this [plough] is in demesne, and 2 slaves and 3 cotsets. There are 6 acres of meadow, [and] pasture 8 furlongs long and 1 furlong broad. It is worth 40s.

The same earl holds HARTHAM, and Edward [holds] of him. TRE it paid geld for 2 hides. There is land for 3 ploughs. Of this land 1 hide is in demesne, and there are 2 ploughs, and 2 slaves. There is 1 knight, and 3 cotsets, and 5 acres of meadow, and 3 acres of woodland and 12 acres of pasture. It is worth 40s.

The same earl holds BURCOMBE, and Hamo [holds] of him. TRE it paid geld for 4 hides. There is land for 2 ploughs. Of this land 3 hides are in demesne,

[Folio 69: WILTSHIRE]

and there is 1 plough, with 1 slave. There is 1 villan and 4 bordars, and a mill rendering 10s, and 6 acres of meadow, and 10 acres of woodland and 20 acres of pasture. It was worth £3; now £4.

The same earl holds CADENHAM, and William [holds] of him. TRE it paid geld for 2 hides. There is land for 2 ploughs. Of these [hides], 1 hide [is] in demesne, and 1 plough, and 2 slaves; and 8 bordars with 1 plough. There are 5 acres of meadow, [and] woodland 2 furlongs long and 1 furlong broad. It was worth 30s; now 40s.

Eadnoth the steward held these 5 manors TRE.

The same earl holds 'FISHERTON' [in Salisbury], and Hamo [holds] of him. Godric held it TRE, and it paid geld for 3 hides. There is land for 2 ploughs. In demesne are 2 hides of this land, and there is 1 plough, and 1 slave. There are 3 villans and 5 bordars, and a mill rendering 10s, and 40 acres of meadow and 40 acres of pasture. It was and is worth £3.

XXIII. The land Which Belonged To Earl Aubrey

EARL AUBREY held COMPTON [in Enford]. TRE it paid geld for 7 hides. There is land for 6 ploughs. Of this, 3 hides and 1 virgate of land are in demesne, and there is 1 plough, and 6 slaves. There are 5 villans and 5 cotsets with 3 ploughs. There is a mill rendering 10s, and 5 acres of meadow, [and] pasture 3 furlongs long and 1 furlong broad. It was and is worth £10.

DURRINGTON paid geld TRE for 1½ hides. There is land for 1 plough. In demesne is 1 hide, and 4 cotsets have the rest of the land there. There are 5 acres of meadow. In this vill is 1 hide. [There is] land for 1 plough. A thegn held this TRE. There is 1 bordar, and 5 acres of meadow. These 2½ hides are worth £4.

[? East] WINTERSLOW paid geld TRE for 2 hides. There is land for 2 ploughs. There is 1 villan and 3 bordars, and woodland 1 furlong long and half a furlong broad. It is worth £4.

ABLINGTON paid geld for 3 hides. There is land for 2 ploughs. Of this land 2½ hides are in demesne, and there is 1

plough, and 4 cotsets. There are 35 |acres| of meadow, and pasture 3 furlongs long and 1 furlong broad. It is worth £4.

CHITTERNE paid geld TRE for 6 hides. There is land for 5 ploughs. Of this land 3 hides are in demesne, and there is 1 plough, and 4 slaves. There are 4 villans and 2 bordars with 2 ploughs. [There is] pasture 4 furlongs long and 2 furlongs broad. It was worth £4; now £6.

TYTHERINGTON paid geld TRE for 2 hides. There is land for 2 ploughs. There is 1 villan, and half a mill rendering 30d, and 5 acres of meadow. It is worth 20s.

Hearding held these 6 estates TRE.

ALLINGTON [near Amesbury] paid geld TRE for 4 hides. There is land for 2 ploughs. Of this land 2½ hides are in demesne, and there is 1 plough, and 3 slaves. There is 1 villan and 4 cotsets with 1 plough. There is a mill rendering 20s, and 5 acres of meadow, [and] pasture 3 furlongs long and 1 furlong broad. Earl Harold held this land. In the same vill are 4 hides of land which Harold unjustly took away from the Church of Amesbury, by the testimony of the thegns of the shire. The church, however, now has it.

ELCOMBE paid geld TRE for 27 hides. There is land for 8 ploughs. Of this land 24 hides are in demesne, and there are 2 ploughs, and 6 slaves. There are 3 villans and 14 bordars with 3 ploughs. There are 60 acres of meadow, and as much pasture, and 20 acres of woodland. It was worth £27; now £20.

STRATFORD TONY paid geld TRE for 13 hides. There is land for 7 ploughs. Of this land 9 hides and 1 virgate of land are in demesne, and there are 2 ploughs, and 7 slaves. There are 6 villans and 4 bordars and 10 cotsets with 4 ploughs. There are 2 mills rendering 17s6d, and 15 acres of meadow, and 2 acres of pasture near the river, and other pasture 1 league long and 6 furlongs broad. In Wilton, 1 burgess paying 20d belongs to this manor. It is worth £20.

GUSSAGE ST MICHAEL [Dorset] paid geld TRE for 10 hides. There is land for 12 ploughs. Of this land 4½ hides are in demesne, and there are 2 ploughs, and 8 slaves. There are 5 villans and 8 bordars with 4 ploughs. There are 40 acres of meadow, [and] pasture 1 league long and half a league broad, and as much woodland. It was worth £40 when Aubrey received it; now £10. Azur held these 3 manors TRE.

The whole of this land belonged to Earl Aubrey. It is now in the hand of the king.

The Renders of Edward of Salisbury

EDWARD the sheriff has yearly from the pence which belong to the shrievalty, 130 pigs and 32 sides of bacon; of wheat, 2 modii and 8 sesters, and as much malt; of oats, 5 modii and 4 sesters; of honey, 16 sesters, or instead of honey 16s; 480 hens; 1,600 eggs; 100 cheeses; 52 lambs; 240 fleeces; of corn in the field, 162 acres. He has also £80 in value between the reeveland and what he has from it. When the reeves' farm falls short, Edward must make it up from his own resources.

XXIIII. The land of the Same Edward of Salisbury

EDWARD of Salisbury holds WILCOT of the king. TRE it paid geld for 15½ hides. There is land for 10 ploughs. Of this land 7 hides are in demesne, and there are 3 ploughs, and 6 slaves. There are 19 villans and 6 bordars and 12 cotsets. [...] There are 40 acres of meadow, and 20 acres of pasture, and 50 acres of scrubland, and a new church and an excellent house, and a good vineyard. It was worth £12; now £16.

The same Edward holds ALTON BARNES. TRE it paid geld for 5 hides. There is land for 4 ploughs. In demesne are 2 ploughs, and 4 slaves. There are 3 villans and 1 bordar and 6 cotsets with 1 plough. There is a mill rendering 10s, and 25 acres of meadow, [and] pasture 3 furlongs long and 2 furlongs broad. It was worth 100s; now £6.

The same Edward holds ETCHILHAMPTON. TRE it paid geld for 7 hides. There is land for 4 ploughs. Of this land 4 hides are in demesne, and there are 3 ploughs. There are 12 bordars and 6 cottars and 2 Frenchmen holding 2 hides and 1 virgate of land and they have 2 ploughs. There are 6 acres of meadow and 50 acres of pasture. It was worth £6; now the demesne of Edward [is worth] 6½l; the Frenchmen's [land] 40s.

The same Edward holds HEDDINGTON. TRE it paid geld for 10 hides. There is land for 6 ploughs. In demesne are 3 ploughs, and 4 slaves. There are 9 villans and 2 cottars and 24 cotsets with 3 ploughs. There are 10 acres of meadow, and 8 acres of pasture, and 8 acres of woodland. It was worth £8; now £12. Earl Harold held it.

The same Edward holds 6 hides in the HUNDRED OF HIGHWORTH [at] LUS HILL, and it paid geld for 6 hides TRE. There is land for 3 ploughs. In demesne are 2 ploughs; and 4 villans and 2 cotsets with 1 plough. There is a mill rendering 18d, and 24 acres of meadow and 1 furlong of pasture. It was worth 100s; now £6. Beorhtric held it. Huard holds it of Edward.

The same man holds 1 hide in RATFYN. Ælfric held it TRE, and it paid geld for 1 hide. Hervey holds it of Edward. There is land for half a plough. There are 3 bordars, and 4 acres of meadow, [and] pasture half a furlong long and as much broad. It is worth 15s.

The same Edward holds SHREWTON. Wulfgifu held it TRE, and it paid geld for 3 hides. There is land for 3 ploughs. Godfrey holds it of Edward. Of this land he holds 2 hides in demesne, and there are 2 ploughs, and 4 slaves. There are 4 villans and 4 bordars with 1 plough. There is a mill rendering 5s, and 6 acres of meadow, and 30 acres of woodland, [and] pasture 6 furlongs long and 4 furlongs broad. It was and is worth £3.

The same Edward holds in WINTERBOURNE STOKE 1½ hides, and Walter holds of him. There is land for 1 plough, which [plough] is there. It is worth 30s.

The same Edward holds in the same vill 1 hide. [There is] land for 1 plough. Walter holds of Edward. There he has 1 plough with 2 cottars, and 1 acre of meadow and 6 acres of pasture. It is worth 20s. Alwig, whose wife holds in the same place a hide [and] a half of the king, held it TRE.

The same Edward holds SHREWTON. Alric held it TRE, and it paid geld for 13 hides and 3 virgates. There is land for 7 ploughs. Of this land 7 hides are in demesne, and there are 4 ploughs, and 7 slaves. There are 12 villans and 5 bordars with 3 ploughs. There are 10 acres of meadow, [and] pasture 1 league long and half a league broad. It was worth £6; now £10.

The same Edward holds ORCHESTON; Hugh [holds] of him. Godric held it TRE, and it paid geld for 4½ hides. There is land for 2 ploughs. In demesne is 1 plough; and 4 bordars with 4 slaves have 1 plough. There is pasture 8 furlongs long and 2 furlongs broad. It was worth £3; now £4.

William holds of Edward in Orcheston 2 hides. Alwine held them TRE. There is land for 1 plough, which [plough] is there with 1 bordar and 3 slaves, and 80 acres of pasture. It was worth 20s; now 30[s].

Edward himself holds NORTH TIDWORTH. Alweard held it TRE, and it paid geld for 4 hides. There is land for 2 ploughs. In demesne are 3 hides of the same [land], and there are 2 ploughs, and 3 slaves. There is 1 villan and 2 cotsets with half a plough, [and] pasture 4 furlongs long and 3 furlongs broad. It was worth 50s; now 60s. In North Tidworth is 1 virgate of land which Croch proved ought to belong to him. This, however, Edward holds.

Edward himself holds LUDGERSHALL. Alweard held it TRE, and it paid geld for 1 hide. There is land for 3 ploughs. In demesne are 2 ploughs, and 3 slaves; and 8 cotsets with 1 plough. There is pasture 3 furlongs long and 1 furlong broad, [and] woodland half a league long and 2 furlongs broad. It was worth 100s; now £6.10s.

Osmund holds AMESBURY of Edward. Wulfær held it TRE, and it paid geld for 1 hide. There is land for 1 plough. There are 3 cotsets, and 6 acres of meadow, [and] pasture 2 furlongs long and half a furlong broad. It was worth 10s; now 20s.

[Folio 69V: WILTSHIRE]

The same Osmund holds of Edward 3 virgates of land which belong to Amesbury. There is land for 1 plough, which [plough] is there, with 2 cotsets and 3 slaves. 1 Englishman holds 1½ virgates of the same land, and has there half a plough, and 1 cotset and 3 slaves. The whole is worth 40s. Alric and Cola held it TRE.

Edward himself holds HILL DEVERILL, and Adelelm [holds] of him. Sæwulf held it TRE, and it paid geld for 4 hides. There is land for 2 ploughs. In demesne [are] 2½ hides of the same land, and there are 2 ploughs, with 1 slave. There is 1 villan and 9 cotsets with 1 plough. There are 2 acres of meadow, and 3 acres of woodland, [and] pasture 3 furlongs long and 2 furlongs broad. It was worth 40s; now 60s.

Edward himself holds BRADENSTOKE. Strami held it

TRE, and it paid geld for 16 hides and 1 virgate. There is land for 10 [...] ploughs. Of this 7½ hides are in demesne, and there are 4 ploughs, and 2 slaves. There are 8 villans and 16 bordars and 16 cottars with 6 ploughs. There is a mill rendering 30d, and 4 acres of meadow, and 12 acres of pasture, [and] woodland half a league long and 3 furlongs broad. It was worth £6; now £10. To this manor belong 1 hide and 1 virgate of land, as the Englishmen have proved. This land William de Picquigny holds.

Theodric holds of Edward 3½ virgates of land in [? Great] SOMERFORD, and it paid geld for as much. There is land for 1 plough, which [plough] is there, with 3 bordars and 3 cotsets. There is part of a mill rendering 15d, and 5 acres of meadow and 7 acres of pasture. In Malmesbury 1 house renders 15d. It was worth 15s; now 20s. Scirweald held it TRE.

Robert holds BROAD BLUNSDON of Edward. Aki held it TRE, and it paid geld for 5 hides. There is land for 3 ploughs. Of this 4½ hides are in demesne, and there are 2 ploughs; and 4 bordars with 1 plough. There is a mill rendering 25d, and 30 acres of meadow and as many of pasture. It was worth 40s; now 60s.

Edward himself holds CHITTERNE. Azur held it TRE, and it paid geld for 11 hides and 1 virgate of land. There is land for 14 ploughs. Of this 6 hides and 1 virgate of land are in demesne, and there is 1 plough, and 4 slaves and 11 coliberts; and 10 villans and 3 cotsets with 5 ploughs. There are 18 acres of meadow, and pasture 1 league long and half a league broad, and as much woodland. It was worth £20; now £30.

Edward himself holds CHITTERNE. Cynewine held it TRE, and it paid geld for 5 hides. There is land for 4 ploughs. Of this 3 hides are in demesne, and there are 2 ploughs, and 4 slaves; and 5 villans and 3 cotsets with 2 ploughs. There are 8 acres of meadow, and pasture 5 furlongs long and 1 furlong broad. It was worth £8; now £10.

Robert holds CHITTERNE of Edward. Wulfwynn held it TRE, and it paid geld for 5 hides. There is land for 4 ploughs. Of this 4½ hides are in demesne, and there are 2 ploughs, and 4 slaves; and 4 villans and 2 bordars with 2 ploughs. There is pasture 6 furlongs long and 2 furlongs broad. It was worth 60s; now 100s.

Edward himself holds BOYTON. Alwine held it TRE, and it paid geld for 11½ hides. There is land for 6 ploughs. Of this 8½ hides are in demesne, and there are 3 ploughs, and 5 slaves; and 7 villans and 5 cotsets with 2 ploughs. There is a mill rendering 15s, and 10 acres of meadow, and pasture 4 furlongs long and 3 furlongs broad, [and] woodland 3 furlongs long and as many broad. It was worth £8; now £11.10s.

Adelelm holds BAYCLIFFE of Edward. Winegot held it TRE, and it paid geld for 1 hide. There is land for 2 ploughs, which are there in demesne, with 10 bordars, [and] woodland 3 furlongs long and 1 furlong broad. It was worth 20s; now 40s.

Azelin holds POOLE KEYNES [Glos.] of Edward. Wulfwynn held it TRE, and it paid geld for 5 hides. There is land for 5 ploughs. Of this 3 hides are in demesne, and there are 3 ploughs, and 6 slaves; and 6 villans and 2 bordars with 2 ploughs. There is a mill rendering 10s, and 60 acres of meadow, pasture 3 furlongs long and 2 furlongs broad, [and] woodland 1 league in length and breadth. It was worth 100s; now £6.

Edward himself holds BISHOPSTROW. Eadræd held it TRE, and it paid geld for 7 hides. There is land for 6 ploughs. Of this 4 hides are in demesne, and there are 3 ploughs, and 4 slaves; and 9 villans and 6 bordars and 2 cottars with 3 ploughs. There is a mill rendering 15s, and 8 acres of meadow, and 8 acres of woodland, [and] pasture 5 furlongs long and 3 furlongs broad. It was worth £7; now £11.

Edward himself holds in MIDDLETON 3 virgates of land. Leofwine and Alric held them TRE, and it paid geld for as much. There is land for 1 plough, which [plough] is there, with 1 villan, and 4 acres of meadow, and 6 acres of pasture and 1 acre of woodland. It was and is worth 27s.

Gilbert holds THICKWOOD of Edward. Swein held it TRE, and it paid geld for 2 hides. There is land for 2½ ploughs. There are 2 ploughs in demesne, with 6 cotsets, and 3 acres of meadow and as many of pasture. It was worth 30s; now 40s.

Borel holds LANGLEY BURRELL of Edward. Wulfwig held it TRE, and it paid geld for 7 hides. There is land for 6 ploughs. Of this 2 hides are in demesne, and there are 2 ploughs, and 2 slaves; and 4 villans and 9 cottars and 7 cotsets with 3 ploughs. There are 8 acres of meadow and 6 acres of woodland. It was worth 40s; now £4. The same Wulfwig holds 1 hide of the same land. It is worth 10s.

Borel holds [East or West] TYTHERTON of Edward. Alric held it TRE, and it paid geld for 2 hides. There is land for 1 plough, which [plough] is there, and 2 slaves and 3 cotsets. There is the fourth part of a mill rendering 20d, and 6 acres of meadow. It was worth 10s; now 20s.

Edward himself holds LACOCK. Edwin held it TRE, and it paid geld for 7 hides. There is land for 9 ploughs. Of this 3½ hides are in demesne, and there are 3 ploughs, and 7 slaves, and 12 villans and 16 cotsets and 3 cottars. There are 2 mills rendering 17s6d, and 20 acres of meadow, and half an acre of vineyard, [and] 1 league of woodland in both length and breadth. It was and is worth £7.

Edward himself holds 1 hide in ROCKLEY. Azur held it TRE, [...]. There is land for 2 ploughs. In demesne is 1 plough; and 1 villan and 3 bordars with 1 plough, and 20 acres of pasture. It was and is worth 40s.

Theobald holds SHREWTON of Edward. Alweard held it TRE, and it paid geld for 3 hides and 1 virgate of land and 4 acres. There is land for 2 ploughs. In demesne is 1 plough; with 1 villan and 6 bordars, and 13 acres of pasture. It was worth 30s; now £4.

Azelin holds 2 hides of land of Edward in DEPTFORD. Osweard and Godwine held them TRE, and it paid geld for as much. There is land for 2 ploughs. Of this 1½ hides are in demesne, and there are 2 ploughs, with 1 villan and 3 bordars, and 2 cottars. There is a mill rendering 10s, and 8 acres of meadow and 16 acres of pasture. It was worth 20s; now 40s. Those who held [this land] could go where they wished.

Turchil holds of Edward 1 hide of land in HARTHAM. 2 thegns held it TRE, and it paid geld for as much. There is land for 6 oxen. There is 1 plough, with 1 slave and 4 cotsets, and 4 acres of meadow, and 12 acres of pasture, and 3 acres of scrubland. It was worth 10s; now 15s.

Godfrey holds NORTH WRAXALL of Edward. Baldwin held it TRE, and it paid geld for 7 hides. There is land for 9 ploughs. Of this 3 hides are in demesne, and there are 4 ploughs, and 3 slaves; and 16 villans and 5 bordars and 6 cotsets with 5 ploughs. There are 2 mills rendering 18s, and half an acre of meadow, [and] woodland 6 furlongs long and 4 furlongs broad; and 2 burgesses in Malmesbury pay 2s. It was worth 100s; now £6.

Aiulf holds TOLLARD ROYAL of Edward. Rozo held it TRE, and it paid geld for 2½ hides. There is land for as many ploughs. Of this 2 hides and half a virgate of land are in demesne, and there are 2 ploughs; and 3 villans and 7 cotsets with half a plough. There is pasture 2 furlongs long and 1 furlong broad, and as much woodland. It was worth 40s; now 50s.

Peter holds 1 hide of Edward in PORTON. God held it TRE. There is land for 1 plough, which [plough] is there, with 1 slave and 1 bordar. There is a mill rendering 32d, and 2 acres of meadow, [and] pasture for 50 sheep. It is worth 20s.

Edward himself holds WINTERBOURNE EARLS. Wulfwynn held it TRE, and it paid geld for 7 hides. There is land for 6 ploughs. Of this 3 hides are in demesne, and there are 2 ploughs, and 8 slaves; and 8 villans and 12 cotsets with 3 ploughs. There is a mill rendering 15s, and 13 acres of meadow, [and] pasture 5 furlongs long and 3 furlongs broad. It was worth £8; now £12.

Letard holds of Edward 1 hide of land in LITTLE LANGFORD. Azur held it TRE, and it paid geld for as much. There is land for half a plough. There are 9 acres of meadow and 10 acres of pasture. It was and is worth 20s. The thegns adjudge this land to the Church of Glastonbury.

XXV. The land of Ernulf de Hesdin

ERNULF de HESDIN holds KEEVIL of the king. Beorhtsige held it TRE, and it paid geld for 16 hides. Of this land 7 hides are in demesne, and there are 6 ploughs, and 10 slaves; and 18 villans and 14 bordars with 12 ploughs. There are 2 mills rendering 55s, and 16 acres of meadow, pasture 4 furlongs long and 4 broad, [and] woodland 1 league long and 2 furlongs broad. It is worth £26. When he received it, it was worth £20 apart from the farm of 2 thegns which was in the manor.

The same Ernulf holds in POTTERNE 3 hides and 1 virgate of land, which paid geld with the Bishop of Salisbury's manor of Potterne TRE. Bishop Osmund claims this land. Algar, who held it TRE, could not be separated from the church.

Robert holds it of Ernulf. There is land for 2 ploughs, and [2 ploughs] are in demesne;

[Folio 70: WILTSHIRE]

and 1 villan has there half a plough; and 6 slaves and 3 bordars. There is a mill rendering 7s6d, and 14 acres of meadow, [...] 3 furlongs long and 1 furlong broad. It was worth £4; now 100s.

Lethelin holds [? Little] CHEVERELL of Ernulf. Alweard held it TRE, and it paid geld for 3½ hides. There is land for 3 ploughs. In demesne are 2 ploughs; and 12 bordars with 1 plough. There is half a mill rendering 30d, and 3 acres of meadow, [and] pasture 10 furlongs long and 1 broad. It was worth 60s; now 100s.

In ETCHILHAMPTON are 2 hides. [There is] land for 1 plough. Eadric held it TRE, and his wife holds it now of Ernulf, and has there 1 plough, and 7 bordars with 1 cottar. There are 12 acres of meadow and 12 acres of pasture. It was and is worth 40s.

The same wife of Eadric holds CALSTONE WELLINGTON of Ernulf. Her husband held it TRE, and it paid geld for 2½ hides. There is land for 3 ploughs. Of this 1 hide and 1 virgate is in demesne, and there is 1 plough; and 1 villan and 10 bordars and 18 cotsets with 1 plough. There is a mill rendering 15s, and 12 acres of meadow, and 6 acres of woodland, [and] pasture 3 furlongs long and 1 furlong broad. In Calne 1 burgess pays 11d. It was and is worth £4.

In PEWSEY the same Ernulf holds 2 hides of the king. TRE a thegn held them of the Abbey of Winchester, and he could not be separated from it. It was and is worth 40s.

Benzelin holds NORTH STANDEN [Berks.] of Ernulf. Beorhtric held it TRE, and it paid geld for 2 hides. There is land for 2 ploughs. In demesne is 1 [plough]; and a mill rendering 6s, and 4 acres of meadow, pasture 3 furlongs long and 3 broad, [and] woodland 3 furlongs long and 1 furlong broad. It is worth 40s.

Ernulf himself holds [Great and Little] CHALFIELD. Waltheof held it TRE, and it paid geld for 2½ hides. There is land for 2 ploughs. Of this 1½ hides are in demesne, and there is 1 plough, with 1 slave and 4 bordars. There is half a mill rendering 18d, and 6 acres of meadow, and 6 acres of woodland and 8 acres of pasture. It was worth £4; now 50s.

Ernulf himself holds in the same vill as much land, as 1 manor. Godwine held it TRE. It is reckoned at as much as is contained in the above [manor], and it is valued at as much.

The same Ernulf holds 5 acres of land in BUTTERMERE.

Robert holds [?] CLYFFE PYPARD of Ernulf. Ketil held it TRE, and it paid geld for 3 hides. There is land for 2 ploughs. Of this 2½ hides are in demesne, and there are 2 ploughs, with 4 cotsets. There are 20 acres of meadow, and 15 acres of pasture and 4 acres of woodland. It was worth 30s; now 40s.

Robert holds "BICHENEHILDE" of Ernulf. Ketil held it TRE, and it paid geld for 1 hide. There is land for half a plough, which [half-plough] is there, with 1 cotset, and 6 acres of meadow, and 4 acres of woodland. It was worth 10s; now 15s.

Robert holds WITCOMB of Ernulf. Beorhtric held it TRE, and it paid geld for 2 hides. There is land for 2 ploughs. There are 7 cotsets with 1 plough, and 12 acres of meadow, and 6 acres of pasture and 12 acres of woodland. It was worth 20s; now 30s.

Robert holds HILMARTON of Ernulf. Eskil held it TRE, and it paid geld for 1 hide. There is land for 1 plough, which [plough] is there, with 3 cotsets. There is a mill rendering 7s6d, and 6 acres of meadow, and 1 acre of pasture and 8 acres of woodland. It was worth 15s; now 30s.

Wulfweard holds CHOLDERTON of Ernulf at farm. He himself held it TRE, and it paid geld for 1 hide and 4 acres. There is land for 1 plough, which [plough] is there in demesne, and pasture 2 furlongs long and 1 furlong broad. It was worth 25s; now 40s.

Ernulf himself holds CHOLDERTON. Sæwig held it TRE, and it paid geld for 1 hide. There is land for 1 plough, which [plough] is there, with 1 cotset, and pasture 2 furlongs long and 1 furlong broad. It was worth 25s; now 40s.

Godric holds 1 hide of Ernulf in CHOLDERTON. Alwine and Wulfric held it TRE as 2 manors, and it paid geld for 1 hide. There is land for $1\frac{1}{2}$ ploughs, and as many [ploughs] are there with 2 cotsets. There is pasture 2 furlongs long and 1 furlong broad. It was worth 20s; now 40s.

Robert holds "BECHENEHILDE" of Ernulf. Thorgot held it TRE, and it paid geld for 1 hide. There is land for half a plough. There is 1 cotset, and 6 acres of meadow and 6 acres of woodland. It was worth 10s; now 15s.

Urse holds "CHENEBUILD" of Ernulf. Wulfwith held it TRE, and it paid geld for $2\frac{1}{2}$ hides. There is land for 2 ploughs. In demesne is 1 [plough], and 2 slaves; and 6 acres of meadow and 2 acres of woodland. It was worth 20s; now 25s.

Ernulf himself holds CHEDGLOW. Wulfwig held it TRE, and it paid geld for 1 hide and $1\frac{1}{2}$ virgates. There is land for 1 plough, and $1\frac{1}{2}$ acres of meadow and 1 acre of woodland. It is worth 20s.

In the same vill a thegn holds of Ernulf $2\frac{1}{2}$ virgates of land. This man, TRE, could go to what lord he pleased, and TRW of his own accord he turned to Ernulf. This land was worth 15s; now 40d which he pays to Ernulf as farm.

Urse holds [? Hill] DEVERILL of Ernulf. Wulfær held it TRE, and it paid geld for $2\frac{1}{2}$ hides and half a virgate of land. There is land for 3 ploughs. Of this $1\frac{1}{2}$ hides are in demesne, and there are 2 ploughs, and 3 slaves; and 2 bordars and 6 cotsets with 1 plough. There is a mill rendering 5s, and 2 acres of meadow, pasture half a league long and 1 furlong broad, and as much woodland. It was worth 30s; now 50s.

Rainbald holds UPTON SCUDAMORE of Ernulf. Tous held it TRE, and it paid geld for $2\frac{1}{2}$ hides. There is land for 3 ploughs. Of this $1\frac{1}{2}$ hides are in demesne, and there are 2 ploughs, with 1 villan and 5 bordars. There are 4 acres of

meadow and 3 acres of woodland. It is worth 40s. In this land is included half a hide which paid geld TRE, but has paid no geld since King William came into England.

Within the same land Ernulf holds half a hide of the land of William de Eu; and also, of the demesne land of the king, as much as is worth 1 hide.

Nubold holds [?] BERWICK ST JAMES of Ernulf. Eadric held it TRE, and it paid geld for 1 hide and $2\frac{1}{4}$ virgates of land. There is land for 1 plough, which [plough] is there with 2 slaves, and 8 acres of pasture. It was worth 20s; now 40s.

Turchil holds HARDENHUISH of Ernulf. Alweard held it TRE, and it paid geld for 3 hides. There is land for 4 ploughs. There are 3 bordars, and 12 acres of meadow, [and] woodland 1 furlong long and 1 furlong broad. It was worth £4; now 40s.

Ernulf himself holds EASTON [Easton Piercy and Lower Easton Piercy]. God held it TRE, and it paid geld for 5 hides. There is land for 3 ploughs. In demesne are 2 ploughs, with 1 slave and 3 bordars. There are 10 acres of meadow and 12 acres of pasture. It was worth 60s; now 100s.

Iudichael holds YATTON KEYNELL of Ernulf. 2 thegns held it TRE, and it paid geld for 5 hides. There is land for 3 ploughs. Of this $3\frac{1}{2}$ hides are in demesne, and there are 2 ploughs, and 2 villans and 6 bordars, and 20 acres of meadow, and as many of pasture, and 10 acres of woodland. It was worth 30s; now 50s.

Hubold holds 1 manor of Ernulf. Ælfric held it TRE, and it paid geld for 1 hide. There is land for 1 plough, and 3 acres of meadow. It was worth 5s; now 10s.

XXVI. The land of Alvred of Marlborough

ALVRED of MARLBOROUGH holds ALLINGTON [in All Cannings]. TRE it paid geld for $11\frac{1}{2}$ hides and 5 acres of land. There is land for 7 ploughs. Of this $7\frac{1}{2}$ hides are in demesne, and there are 4 ploughs, and 7 slaves; and 6 villans and 7 bordars with 1 plough. There are 20 acres of meadow, [and] pasture 6 furlongs long and 3 furlongs broad. Of this land a knight has 2 hides, and there is 1 plough. The whole was worth £12; now £15.

William holds 18 hides, and Gilbert 1 hide, and Wulfgeat 1 hide, of Alvred [in] ROWDE. TRE it paid geld for 20 hides. There is land for 8 ploughs. In demesne are 4 ploughs, and 4 slaves; and 4 villans and 8 bordars and 11 cotsets and a priest with 4 ploughs. There are 2 mills of William's rendering 9s8d, and 20 acres of meadow, [and] woodland 6 furlongs long and $1\frac{1}{2}$ furlongs broad. The whole was worth £6; now £8.

Alvred himself holds TEFFONT EVIAS. TRE it paid geld for $6\frac{1}{2}$ hides. There is land for 5 ploughs. Of this 4 hides are in demesne, and there are 2 ploughs, and 9 slaves; and 4 villans and 3 bordars and 1 Frenchman with 2 ploughs. There is a mill rendering 10s, and 6 acres of meadow, and 6 of pasture and 6 of woodland. It was and is worth £6.

Hugh holds CROFTON of Alvred. TRE it paid geld for 8 hides. There is land for 5 ploughs. Of this 3 hides are in demesne, and there are 3 ploughs, and 3 slaves; and 2 villans and 5 cotsets with 2 ploughs. There is a mill rendering 30s, and 10 acres of meadow, and pasture 6 acres long and as many broad, [and] woodland 3 furlongs long and 1 furlong broad. It was and is worth £7.

Alvred himself holds NEWTON TONY. TRE it paid geld for 11 hides. There is land for 7 ploughs. Of this 6 hides are in demesne, and there are 2 ploughs, and 6 slaves; and 6 villans and 4 bordars with 3 ploughs. There is a mill rendering 10s, and 3 acres of meadow, and pasture 3 furlongs long and 3 furlongs broad.

Of the land Gerard has 3 hides, and there are 4 villans and 5 bordars with 2 ploughs. It was worth £10; now £18. By the English it is valued at £12.

Edward holds of Alvred 1 hide in "WINTREBURNE". [There is] land for 1 plough, which [plough] is there, with 1 slave and 1 bordar. It was worth 10s; now 20s.

Alvred himself holds LYDIARD TREGOZE. TRE it paid geld for 7 hides. There is land for 7 ploughs. Of this 3 hides are in demesne, and there is 1 plough, and 3 slaves; and 8 villans and 10 cotsets with 4 ploughs; and 40 acres of meadow, and 30 acres of pasture, [and] woodland 1 league long and a half broad. It was worth £10; now £6. In Cricklade 7 burgesses pay 5s.

[Folio 70V: WILTSHIRE]

Alvred himself holds in SWINDON 1½ hides. [There is] land for 6 oxen. It is worth 12s.

Albert holds MOREDON of Alvred. TRE it paid geld for 6 hides. There is land for 4 ploughs. Of this 3 hides are in demesne, and there are 2 ploughs, and 3 slaves; and 3 villans and 5 bordars with 2 ploughs. There are 30 acres of meadow, [and] pasture half a league long and 2 furlongs broad. It was worth 100s; now £4.

Gunfrid holds [Lower and Upper] WIDHILL of Alvred. TRE it paid geld for 5 hides. There is land for 3 ploughs. Of this 4 hides are in demesne, and there are 2 ploughs; and 2 villans and 4 bordars with 1 plough. There is a mill rendering 25d, and 30 acres of meadow and as many of pasture. It was worth 40s; now 60s.

Ralph holds UPTON SCUDAMORE of Alvred. TRE it paid geld for 9 hides. There is land for 6 ploughs. Of this 5 hides are in demesne, and there are 2 ploughs, and 5 slaves; and 9 villans and 22 bordars with 4 ploughs. There is a mill rendering 20s, and 5 acres of meadow, and 30 acres of pasture, [and] woodland 3 furlongs long and 1 furlong broad. It was worth £8; now £9.

Alvred himself holds NORTON BAVANT. TRE it paid geld for 11 hides. There is land for 8 ploughs. Of this 6 hides are in demesne, and there are 2 ploughs, and 2 slaves; and 12 villans and 8 bordars with 6 ploughs. There are 2 mills rendering 40s, and 10 acres of meadow, pasture 4 furlongs long and 2 furlongs broad, [and] woodland half a league long and 4 furlongs broad. It was worth £24; now £14. # It is worth £8.

Alvred himself holds ROCKLEY. TRE it paid geld for 10 hides. There is land for 6 ploughs. Of this 6 hides and 3 virgates of land are in demesne, and there is 1 plough, with 1 slave. There are 7 villans and 12 bordars with 3 ploughs. There are 3 acres of meadow, [and] pasture half a league long and 4 furlongs broad. #

Alvred himself holds FIFIELD BAVANT. Ralph [holds] of him. TRE it paid geld for 5 hides. There is land for 4 ploughs. Of this 3 hides are in demesne, and there is 1 plough, and 3 slaves. There are 9 villans and 6 bordars with 2 ploughs. There are 2 acres of meadow, pasture half a league long and 2 furlongs broad, [and] woodland half a league long and half a furlong broad. It was worth £4; now 100s. There 1 forge renders 12d a year. In Wilton 2 burgesses pay 18d.

Alvred himself holds 1 virgate of land in Lacock. There is land for 1 plough, which [plough] is there with 1 bordar, and 2 acres of meadow. It was worth 10s; now 5s.
Karli held all these above-mentioned lands TRE.

Roger holds CLEVANCY of Alvred. Godric and Theodger and Ælfric and Wulfric held it as 4 manors TRE, and it paid geld for 4 hides. There is land for 2 ploughs. In demesne is 1 plough, and 3 slaves and 2 cotsets. There are 24 acres of meadow, and 20 acres of pasture and 6 acres of woodland. It was worth 40s; now 50s.

Robert holds 2½ hides of Alvred in [?] CLYFFE PYPARD, and it paid geld for as much TRE. Sigar and Carlman held it. There is land for 1½ ploughs. There are 3 slaves with 1 bordar, and a mill rendering 5s, and 12 acres of meadow, and 20 acres of pasture and 50 acres of woodland. It was worth 20s; now 30s.

Siward holds GREAT SOMERFORD of Alvred. Alnoth held it TRE, and it paid geld for 3 hides and 24 acres of land. There is land for 3 ploughs. Of this 2 hides are in demesne, and there is 1 plough, and 2 slaves; and 3 villans and 2 bordars and 8 cotsets with 2 ploughs. There is a mill rendering 5s, and 6 acres of meadow, [and] woodland 2 furlongs long and 1 furlong broad. It was and is worth 40s.

Edward holds of Alvred in CHEDGLOW 1 hide and 1 virgate of land. There is land for 1 plough. In demesne is half a plough, with 1 slave and 1 cottar, and 1 acre of meadow, and 1 acre of woodland in length and breadth. In Malmesbury half a house renders 6d. It was worth 40s; now 10s. Besides this land Durand of Gloucester has half a virgate of land, which the same Edward held TRE. This Amalric de Dreux took from him unjustly, as all the thegns of the shire testify.

Osmund holds of Alvred in HORNINGSHAM half a hide, and it paid geld for as much TRE. Kolsveinn held it, and he could go where he wished. There is land for 1 plough, which [plough] is there, with 4 bordars. There are 8 acres of woodland, and 1 league of pasture, and a mill rendering 7s6d. It was worth 5s; now 10s.

Alvred holds in WEST KENNETT 13½ hides and 2 acres of land. Of these Nicholas has 2 hides; Turstin 3½ hides; Wulfgeat 2 hides; Leofric 3½ hides; Wulfmær 2½ hides and 2 acres of land. There is land for 6 ploughs. There are 4 ploughs, with 1 villan and 15 bordars. There is a mill rendering 12s, and 11 acres of meadow, and 106 acres of pasture and 7 acres of woodland. The whole was worth, when received, £4.10s; now £8.10s. Wulfgeat, Alnoth, Eadmær, Leofric and Wulfmeær held these hides in West Kennett TRE.

William Durus holds WEST TYTHERTON of Alvred. Wulfgifu and Ælfgifu held it as 2 manors TRE, and it paid geld for 4 hides. There is land for 4 ploughs. Of this 2 hides are in demesne, and there is 1 plough, and 2 villans and 4 bordars and 2 cottars. [...] There are 2 parts of a mill rendering 40d, and 10 acres of meadow. It was and is worth 60s.

Wulfmær holds 1 hide in FIFIELD BAVANT of Alvred. The same man held it TRE. It was and is worth 10s.

XXVII. The land of Humphrey de L'Isle

HUMPHREY de l'Isle holds BROUGHTON GIFFORD of the king. 3 thegns held it in parage TRE, and it paid geld for 12 hides. There is land for 8 ploughs. Of this 4½ hides are in demesne, and there are 3 ploughs, and 2 slaves; and 17 villans and 4 bordars with 7 ploughs. There are 2 mills rendering 9s, and 12 acres of meadow, and 8 acres of pasture, [and] woodland 1 league long and 2 furlongs broad. It was worth £13; now £10.

Pain holds COMPTON BASSETT of Humphrey. Leofnoth held it TRE, and it paid geld for 5½ hides. There is land for 4 ploughs. Of this 2 hides and 1 virgate of land are in demesne, and there are 2 ploughs, and 4 slaves; and 4 villans and 4 cotsets with 2 ploughs. There is the third part of 2 mills rendering 10s, and 20 acres of meadow, and 10 acres of pasture and as many of woodland. It was and is worth £4.10s.

Humphrey himself holds STERT. Ælfric held it TRE, and it paid geld with its appendages for 5 hides and 1½ virgates. There is land for 3 ploughs. Of this 4 hides are in demesne, and there are 3 ploughs, and 6 slaves; and 15 bordars, and 1 Frenchman having 1½ virgates. There are 2 mills rendering 8s, and 30 acres of meadow, and 10 acres of pasture and 2 acres of woodland. It was worth 100s; now £6.

Blæcmann holds BURBAGE of Humphrey. Eadric held it TRE, and it paid geld for 2½ hides. There is land for 2½ ploughs. Of this 1½ hides are in demesne, and there is 1 plough; and 2 villans and 3 cotsets with 1 plough. There is woodland 3 furlongs long and 2 furlongs broad. It was worth 50s; now 40s.

Pain holds [Great and Little] CUMBERWELL of Humphrey. Leofnoth held it TRE, and it paid geld for 4 hides. There is land for 5 ploughs. In demesne are 2 ploughs, with 1 slave; and 2 villans and 4 bordars with 3 ploughs. There are 4 acres of meadow and 5 acres of woodland. It is worth £3. Of the same land the king has 1 hide in his demesne, and there is nothing there, and 1 Englishman holds half of it of the king. It is worth 8s.

Gunter holds LUS HILL of Humphrey. Wulfric held it TRE, and it paid geld for 4 hides. There is land for 2 ploughs. In demesne is 1 [plough], with 2 bordars, and from a mill [are

rendered] 12d, and [there are] 8 acres of meadow and half a furlong of pasture. It is worth 40s.

Robert holds WROUGHTON of Humphrey. Alnoth held it TRE, and it paid geld for 10 hides. There is land for 4 ploughs. Of this 5½ hides are in demesne, and there are 2 ploughs; and 6 villans and 9 bordars with 2 ploughs; and there a Frenchman holds 2 hides of the same land. There is a mill rendering 15d, and 30 acres of pasture and 2 acres of woodland. It was and is worth 100s.

Robert holds SALTHROP of Humphrey. Wulfwine held it TRE, and it paid geld for 10 hides. There is land for 4 ploughs. Of this 8 hides are in demesne, and there are 2 ploughs, and 3 slaves; and 9 bordars with 1 plough. There are 20 acres of meadow and 30 acres of pasture. It was worth 100s; now £4.

Robert holds CLYFFE PYPARD of Humphrey. Edwin held it TRE, and it paid geld for 8 hides. There is land for 4 ploughs. Of this 6 hides are in demesne, and there are 2 ploughs, and 4 slaves; and 2 villans and 7 bordars with 2 ploughs. There are 20 acres of meadow and as much pasture; and 3 burgesses in Cricklade pay 3d. It was and is worth £4.

Robert holds GREAT SOMEFORD of Humphrey. Edwin held it TRE, and it paid geld for 3 hides and 24 acres. There is land for 3 ploughs. Of this 2 hides are in demesne. There 16 cotsets have 2 ploughs; and [there is] the third part of a mill rendering 8s, and 10 acres of meadow, [and] pasture 3 furlongs long and 1 furlong broad. In Malmesbury 1 burgess pays 12d. It was and is worth 60s.

Elbert holds [Great and Little] SMITHCOT of Humphrey. Sæwine held it TRE, and it paid geld for 5 hides. There is land for 4 ploughs. Of this 2½ hides are in demesne, and there are 3 ploughs, and 2 slaves; and 3 villans and 4 bordars with 1 cotset have 2 ploughs. There is a mill [rendering] 5s, and 20 acres of meadow, [and] woodland 4 furlongs long and 1 furlong broad; and 1 burgess pays 8d. It was worth 40s; now 60s.

Ilbert holds BLUNSDON ST ANDREW of Humphrey. Eadric held it TRE, and it paid geld for 5 hides. There is land for 2½ ploughs. Of this 2½ hides are in demesne, and there is 1 plough, with 1 slave; and 2 bordars with 1½ ploughs. It was worth 30s; now 50s.

Hugh and Gerald hold GROUNDWELL of Humphrey. Ordwulf held it TRE, and it paid geld for 5 hides. There is land for 3 ploughs. Of this 4 hides are in demesne, and there are 2 ploughs, with 1 slave; and 1 villan and 2 bordars with 1 plough. There are 12 acres of meadow. It was worth 40s; now 70s.

Robert holds ASHTON GIFFORD of Humphrey. Cynewig held it TRE, and it paid geld for 6 hides. There is land for 4 ploughs. Of this 3 hides are in demesne, and there are 2 ploughs, and 3 slaves; and 4 villans and 3 cotsets with 2 ploughs. There is half a mill rendering 6s3d, and 12 acres of meadow, [and] pasture 6 furlongs long and as much broad. It was worth £4; now £6.

Humphrey himself holds BATHAMPTON. Ælfric held it TRE, and it paid geld for 3 hides and 3 virgates. There is land for 4 ploughs. Of this 1 hide and 1 virgate of land is in demesne, and there are 3 ploughs, and 12 slaves; and 2 villans and 6 cotsets with 1½ ploughs. There is a mill [rendering] 15s, and 10 acres of meadow, [and] pasture half a league long and as much broad. It was worth £3; now £4.

Humphrey himself holds BATHAMPTON. Edwin held it TRE, and it paid geld for 3 hides. There is land for 2 ploughs. Of this 2 hides are in demesne, and there is 1 plough; and 2 villans and 1 cotset with 1 plough. There is a mill rendering 6s, and 5 acres of meadow and 8 acres of pasture. It was worth 40s; now 60s.

Humphrey himself holds COLERNE. Leofnoth held it TRE, and it paid geld for 10 hides. There is land for 12 ploughs. Of this 4½ hides are in demesne, and there are 3 ploughs, and 10 slaves; and 13 villans and 5 cotsets with 8 ploughs. There is a mill rendering 13s 6d, and 8 acres of meadow, [and] scrubland 1 league long and another broad. It was and is worth £10.

Humphrey himself holds WINTERBOURNE BASSETT. 2 thegns held it TRE, and it paid geld for 10 hides. There is land for 6 ploughs. Of this 4 hides and 10 acres of land are in demesne, and there are 3 ploughs, and 8 slaves; and 4 villans and 8 bordars with 3 ploughs. There are 14 acres of meadow and 20 acres of pasture. It was and is worth £10.

Humphrey himself holds POULTON [in Mildenhall]. Tovi held it TRE, and it paid geld for 10 hides. There is land for 4 ploughs. Of this 8 hides are in demesne, and there are 2 ploughs, and 2 slaves; and 2 villans and 7 bordars with 1 plough. There is a mill rendering 15s, and 4 acres of meadow, and 10 acres of pasture and 8 acres of woodland. It was and is worth £8.

Ranulph holds BROAD HINTON of Humphrey. Wulfgar held it TRE, and it paid geld for 10 hides. There is land for 4 ploughs. Of this 6 hides are in demesne, and there is 1 plough, with 1 slave; and 4 villans and 6 bordars with 2 ploughs. There are 12 acres of meadow and 14 acres of pasture. It was and is worth 100s.

Turchil holds BIDDESTONE of Humphrey. Ælfric held it TRE, and it paid geld for 1 hide and 1 virgate. There is land [...]. There are 4 cotsets, and 3 acres of meadow and 2 acres of woodland. It was worth 10s; now 20s.

Hugh holds HARTHAM of Humphrey. Godric held it TRE, and it paid geld for 1 hide. There is land for half a plough. There are 2 cotsets, and 2 acres of meadow, and 7 acres of pasture and 2 acres of woodland. It was worth 8s; now 12s.

Humphrey himself holds CASTLE COMBE. Swein held it TRE, and it paid geld for 10 hides. There is land for 10 ploughs. Of this 5 hides less 1 virgate are in demesne, and there are 4 ploughs, and 13 slaves; and 5 villans and 7 bordars and 5 cottars with 6 ploughs. There are 3 mills rendering 31s 6d, and 12 acres of meadow, [and] woodland 1 league long

and half a league broad. In Wilton 1 burgess pays 5s, and 2 burgesses in Malmesbury pay 18d. It was and is worth £10.

Robert holds SHERSTON of Humphrey. God held it TRE, and it paid geld for 6½ hides. There is land for 5 ploughs. Of this 3½ hides are in demesne, and there are 3 ploughs, and 2 slaves; and 3 villans and 9 bordars with 2 ploughs. There are 2 mills rendering 10s, and 6 acres of meadow and 10 acres of scrubland. It was worth £3; now £4.

Humphrey himself holds HURDCOTT [in Barford]. Ælfric held it TRE, and it paid geld for 3 hides. There is land for 4 ploughs. Of this 2 hides are in demesne, and there are 2 ploughs, with 1 slave; and 2 villans and 12 bordars with 2 ploughs. There is a mill rendering 6s, and 6 acres of meadow and 8 acres of pasture. It was worth 40s; now 60s.

Humphrey himself holds 'FRUSTFIELD' [in Whiteparish]. Eadric held it TRE, and it paid geld for 3 hides. There is land for 4 ploughs. Of this 2 hides are in demesne, and there is 1 plough, and 3 slaves; and 4 villans and 2 bordars and 2 coliberts with 3 ploughs. There are 12 acres of meadow, [and] woodland 2 furlongs long and 1 furlong broad. It was worth 40s; now 50s.

Joscelin holds half a hide of land of Humphrey in MILFORD, and it paid geld for as much TRE. Sæweald and Sæweard held it. There is land for 1 plough. There are 6 cottars, and 3 acres of meadow. It was worth 15d; now 7s. Half this land is in the king's forest.

XXVIII. The land of Miles Crispin

MILES CRISPIN holds WOOTTON BASSETT of the king. Leofnoth held it TRE, and it paid geld for 12 hides. There is land for 12 ploughs. Of this 6 hides are in demesne, and there are 3 ploughs, and 5 slaves; and 11 villans and 14 bordars with 6 ploughs. There is a mill rendering 30d, and 24 acres of meadow, and 33 acres of pasture, [and] woodland 2 leagues long and 1 league broad. In Malmesbury 1 house renders 13d. It was worth £10; now £9.

Reginald holds CHILTON FOLIAT of Miles. Earl Harold held it TRE, and it paid geld for 10 hides. There is land for 12 ploughs. Of this 6½ hides are in demesne, and there are 2 ploughs, and 2 slaves; and 7 villans and 10 cotsets with 5 ploughs. There are 2 mills rendering 40s, and meadow 2 furlongs long and 1 furlong broad, and as much pasture, [and] woodland 1 league long and 2 furlongs broad. It was worth £12; now £10.

Humphrey holds CLYFFE PYPARD of Miles. Harold held it TRE, and it paid geld for 5 hides. There is land for 2 ploughs. Of this 3½ hides are in demesne, and there is 1 plough, with 1 slave. There are 3 villans and 4 bordars and 1 cottar with half a plough. There are 20 acres of meadow and 12 acres of pasture. It was worth 30s; now 50s.

In the same CLYFFE PYPARD Miles holds 1 hide. [There is] land for half a plough. It is worth 6s. He who held it TRE could go to what lord he wished.

Turchil holds LITTLECOTT of Miles. Godric held it TRE,

and it paid geld for 1 hide and 1 virgate. There is land for half a plough, which [half-plough] is there, with 1 bordar. There are 4 acres of meadow, and as many of pasture and as many of spinney. It is worth 10s.

Reginald holds of Miles in WALCOT 2½ hides. Alnoth held them TRE; and in the same place [are] 3 virgates of land which Leofnoth held TRE. The whole is worth 23s.

Reginald holds DRAYCOT FOLIAT of Miles. Leofnoth held it TRE, and it paid geld for 10 hides. There is land for 6 ploughs. Of this 5 hides are in demesne, and there are 2 ploughs, with 1 slave; and 4 villans and 7 bordars with 3 ploughs. There are 18 acres of meadow and 40 acres of pasture. It was and is worth 100s.

Humphrey holds BRINKWORTH of Miles. Toki held it TRE, and it paid geld for 5 hides. There is land for 3 ploughs. Of this 4 hides are in demesne, and there is 1 plough. There are 8 bordars and 8 cotsets with 1 plough. There are 24 acres of meadow, and 3 acres of pasture, [and] woodland 4 furlongs long and as much broad. It was and is worth 50s. This Toki could go where he wished.

Reginald holds RODBOURNE of Miles. Vigot held it TRE, and it paid geld for 5 hides. There is land for 4 ploughs. Of this 2 hides are in demesne. [...] There are 3 villans and 5 bordars and 1 slave with 3 ploughs. [There is] meadow 6 furlongs long and 2 furlongs broad, [and] pasture 2 furlongs long and as many broad. It was worth 100s; now £4.

Siward, a thegn, holds CHEDGLOW of Miles. 2 thegns held it TRE, and it paid geld for 1 hide and 1½ virgates. There is land for 6 oxen, which are at plough there, and [there is] 1 cottar and 1 slave. There is 1 acre of meadow, and 1½ virgates and 1 acre of woodland. It was and is worth 10s. Those who held it TRE could go where they wished.

Besides this land Durand has half a virgate of land which Siward held TRE. Amalric de Dreux took this from him unjustly, as the thegns of the shire say.

Miles himself holds OGBOURNE [? St Andrew]. Earl Harold held it TRE, and it paid geld for 10 hides. There is land for 8 ploughs. Of this 6 hides are in demesne, and there are 3 ploughs, and 4 slaves; and 11 villans and 4 bordars with 3 ploughs. There is a mill rendering 30s, and 8 acres of meadow, [and] pasture half a league long and as much broad. It was and is worth £15.

Reginald holds MANTON of Miles. Vigot held it TRE, and it paid geld for 3 hides. There is land for 3 ploughs. Of this 1 hide is in demesne, and there is 1 plough, and 2 slaves; and 5 villans and 5 bordars with 2 ploughs. There are 4 acres of meadow, and 40 acres of pasture and as many of woodland. It was and is worth £3.

Reginald holds HAZELBURY of Miles. Leofnoth held it TRE, and it paid geld for 5 hides. There is land for 5 ploughs. Of this 1 hide is in demesne, and there are 2 ploughs, and 2 slaves; and 5 villans and 13 cotsets and 2 cottars with 3 ploughs. There are 2 mills rendering 35s, and 22 acres of

meadow, and woodland 2 furlongs long and 1 furlong broad. It was and is worth £6.

XXIX. The land of Gilbert de Breteuil

GILBERT de BRETEUIL holds CHISBURY of the king. Eadric held it TRE, and it paid geld for 5 hides. There is land for 9 ploughs. In demesne are 4 ploughs, and 7 slaves; and 12 villans and 3 bordars and 14 cotsets with 5 ploughs. There are 2 mills rendering 20s, and 15 acres of meadow, and 40 acres of woodland, [and] pasture 15 furlongs long and 3 furlongs broad. It was worth £8; now £12.

The same Gilbert holds 5 hides in [?] BINCKNOLL. Hakun held it TRE. There is land for 2 ploughs. Of this 4 hides are in demesne, and there is 1 plough, and 4 slaves; and 1 villan and 3 bordars with 1 plough. There are 10 acres of meadow, and 12 acres of pasture and 4 acres of woodland. It was worth 40s; now 50s.

In the same vill Toli held 2 hides less 1 virgate TRE. [There is] land for 6 oxen. Gilbert has there 1 villan. It is worth 18s.

In the same vill Sæwulf and Alwine held 3 hides and 1 virgate of land TRE. There is land for 10 oxen. Gilbert has there 2 villans, and 4 acres of meadow and 6 acres of pasture. It was worth 20s; now 27s.

Gilbert himself holds CLYFFE PYPARD. Ælfric and Burghelm and Godgifu held it TRE, and it paid geld for 16 hides less 1 virgate. There is land for 7 ploughs. Of the same land Ansfrid has 11 hides of Gilbert, and there are in demesne 3 ploughs, and [he has] 7 slaves; and 3 villans and 2 bordars and 10 cotsets with 2½ ploughs. There is a mill rendering 5s, and 50 acres of meadow, and 70 acres of pasture and 18 acres of woodland. One of these 11 hides, which lay in Clyffe Pypard TRE, is in THORNHILL.

[Folio 71V: WILTSHIRE]

There are in Clyffe Pypard 2 bordars and 2 slaves, and 16 acres of meadow and 17 acres of pasture, under Gilbert. This is worth 35s; what Ansfrid holds is worth £6.

Turstin holds MOREDON of Gilbert. Wulfgar held it TRE, and it paid geld for 3 hides less 1 virgate. There is land for 2 ploughs. Of this 1 hide and 1 virgate of land are in demesne, and there is 1 plough; and 2 villans and 4 bordars with 2 ploughs. There are 20 acres of meadow and 80 acres of pasture. It was and is worth 40s.

Gilbert himself holds BROAD HINTON. Wulfgar held it TRE, and it paid geld for 11 hides and 1 virgate. There is land for 5 ploughs. Of this 9 hides and 1 virgate of land are in demesne, and there are 2 ploughs; and 4 villans and 5 bordars with 2 ploughs. There are 16 acres of meadow and 30 acres of pasture. It was worth 100s; now £7.

Ansfrid holds BECKHAMPTON of Gilbert. Eadric held it TRE, and it paid geld for 2 hides. There is land for 3 ploughs. Of this 1 hide is in demesne, and there are 2 ploughs; and 4 villans and 7 bordars and 3 cottars with 2 ploughs. There are 8 acres of meadow and 40 acres of pasture. It was and is worth £6.

Ansfrid holds 'STANMORE' [in Preshute] of Gilbert. Bruning held it TRE, and it paid geld for 2½ hides. There is land for 2 ploughs. Of this 2 hides are in demesne, and there is 1 plough, and 2 slaves; and 1 villan and 3 bordars with half a plough. It was worth 20s; now 40s.

XXX. The land of Durand of Gloucester

DURAND of GLOUCESTER holds CHIRTON of the king. Almær held it TRE, and it paid geld for 10 hides. There is land for 5 ploughs. Of this 7 hides with 1½ ploughs are in demesne; and 7 villans and 10 bordars with 2 ploughs. There is a mill rendering 10s, and 30 acres of meadow, [and] pasture half a league long and 3 furlongs broad. It was worth £11; now £10.

Roger holds TOCKENHAM COURT of Durand. Dodda held it TRE of the Church of Malmesbury, and it could not be separated from it, and it paid geld for 5 hides. There is land [...]. In demesne is half a [...] and there are 2 ploughs, with 1 slave; and 7 villans and 3 bordars with 2 ploughs. There is a mill rendering 50d, and 12 acres of meadow, and 4 acres of pasture and 2 acres of woodland. It was worth 40s; now £4.

The same man holds 1½ hides in UFFCOTT. There is land for 1 plough. This [plough] is in demesne. It was and is worth 15s. Almær held it TRE.

Durand himself holds [Lower and Upper] SEAGRY. 2 thegns held it TRE, and it paid geld for 5 hides. There is land for 4 ploughs. Of this 2 hides are in demesne, and there is 1 plough; and 3 villans and 2 bordars with 3 ploughs. There are 40 acres of meadow. It was worth 40s; now 50s. 2 knights hold it of Durand. Those who held it TRE could go where they wished.

Durand himself holds ASHLEY [Glos]. Eadlræd held it TRE, and it paid geld for 5 hides less 1 virgate. There is land for 4 ploughs. Of these [hides], 3 hides are in demesne, and there are 2 ploughs, and 3 slaves; and 5 villans and 3 bordars with 2 ploughs and 2 cottars. There are 5 acres of meadow and 5 acres of woodland. It was and is worth £4. A knight of Miles Crispin claims 1 virgate of land in this vill.

Durand himself holds LOCKERIDGE. Almær held it TRE, and it paid geld for 2 hides. There is land for 1 plough. Of this 1 hide is in demesne. There is 1 villan and 2 bordars with 1 slave, and 1 acre of meadow, and 12 acres of pasture and 6 acres of woodland. It was worth 40s; now 30s.

Herman holds LUCKINGTON of Durand. Earl Harold held it TRE, and it paid geld for 4 hides. There is land for 5 ploughs. Of this 2 hides are in demesne, and there are 2 ploughs, with 1 slave; and 6 villans and 8 bordars with 2 ploughs. There is a mill rendering 5s, and 10 acres of meadow, and 8 acres of pasture and 4 acres of woodland. It was worth 100s; now £4.

XXXI. The land of Walter Giffard

WALTER GIFFARD holds MAIDEN BRADLEY of the king. Earl Tosti held it TRE, and it was assessed at 10 hides. There is land for 10 ploughs. Of this 4 hides are in demesne, and there are 2 ploughs, and 4 slaves; and 6 villans and 13 bordars with 6 ploughs. There are 2 mills rendering 12s6d, and 10 acres of meadow, pasture half a league long and 2 furlongs broad, [and] woodland 1 league long and 1 broad. It was worth £12; now £10.

XXXII. The land of William de Eu

WILLIAM de Eu holds [Great and Little] DURNFORD of the king. TRE it paid geld for 16 hides. There is land for 14 ploughs. Of this 4 hides are in demesne, and there are 2 ploughs, and 2 slaves; and 26 villans and 37 bordars with 12 ploughs. There are 3 mills rendering 24s6d, and 30 acres of meadow, pasture 10 furlongs long and 2 furlongs broad, [and] woodland 4 furlongs long and 2 furlongs broad. In Wilton 4 houses render 4s. It was and is worth £24.

William d'Audrieu holds LITTLETON PANNELL of William. TRE it paid geld for 6 hides and 1 virgate of land. There is land for 6 ploughs. In demesne are 2 ploughs, with 1 slave; and 3 villans and 21 bordars with 3 ploughs. There are 2 mills rendering 30s, and 12 acres of meadow, [and] pasture 10 furlongs long and 2 furlongs broad. It was worth £10; now £8.

TRE this land was thegnland of the Church of Salisbury. Ælfstan of Boscombe held it.

The same William holds COMPTON BASSETT of William. TRE it paid geld for 6 hides. There is land for 4 ploughs. In demesne are 2 ploughs, and 5 slaves; and 3 villans and 11 bordars with 2 ploughs. There is the third part of 2 mills rendering 10s, and 24 acres of meadow, and 10 acres of pasture and as many of woodland. It was and is worth 100s.

William Delamere holds BEVERSBROOK [Beversbrook or Lower Beversbrook] of William. TRE it paid geld for 2½ hides. There is land for 2 ploughs. Of this 1½ hides are in demesne, and there are 2 ploughs, and 2 slaves, and 1 villan and 8 bordars. It was and is worth 30s.

Hugh holds 'CHARLTON' [in Hungerford, Berks.] of William. TRE it paid geld for 5 hides. There is land for 7 ploughs. Of this 4½ hides are in demesne, and there is 1 plough; and 2 villans and 7 bordars with half a plough. There are 2 mills rendering 8s4d, and 15 acres of meadow, pasture 4 furlongs long and 1 furlong broad, [and] woodland 6 furlongs long and 3 furlongs broad. It was and is worth 100s.

The same Hugh holds [East or West] GRAFTON of William. TRE it paid geld for 1 hide. There is land for 1½ ploughs. There are 3 bordars, [and] pasture 2 furlongs long and 1 furlong broad. It was worth 60s; now 40s.

Edward holds BOSCOMBE of William. TRE it paid geld for 7 hides. There is land for 4 ploughs. Of this 4½ hides are in demesne, and there are 2 ploughs, and there are 2 slaves; and 3 villans and 4 cotsets with $1\frac{1}{2}$ ploughs. There are 6 acres of meadow, [and] pasture 12 furlongs long and as many broad. It is worth £10.

Bernard holds CHOLDERTON. TRE it paid geld for $3\frac{1}{2}$ hides, less 4 acres. There is land for 2 ploughs. Of this 3 hides are in demesne, and there are 2 ploughs, and 2 slaves; and 5 bordars and 2 cotsets. There is pasture 6 furlongs long and 5 furlongs broad. It was worth 100s; now £9.

Ralph holds HILMARTON of William. TRE it paid geld for 9 hides. There is land for 8 ploughs. Of this 3 hides are in demesne, and there are 2 ploughs; and 7 villans and 10 bordars with 6 ploughs. There is a mill rendering 7s, and 50 acres of meadow and 40 acres of pasture. It was and is worth £7.

Bernard holds CODFORD [? St Peter] of William. TRE it paid geld for $1\frac{1}{2}$ hides. There is land for 2 ploughs. Of this 1 hide [is] in demesne, and there is 1 plough, with 1 slave; and 2 cotsets with 1 plough. There are 10 acres of meadow, and the fourth part of a mill rendering 3s, [and] pasture 4 furlongs long and 2 furlongs broad. It was worth £4; now £3.

Warner holds DITTERIDGE of William. TRE it paid geld for 1 hide and 3 virgates of land. There is land for 1 plough, which [plough] is there in demesne, and 2 villans and 4 cotsets. There is half a mill rendering 5s, and 7 acres of meadow, and 15 acres of pasture and 17 acres of scrubland. It is worth 30s. A certain abbot of Malmesbury leased 1 hide of this land to Ælfstan.

Ralph holds LACKHAM of William. TRE it paid geld for $7\frac{1}{2}$ hides. There is land for 10 ploughs. Of this $1\frac{1}{2}$ hides are in demesne, and there are 2 ploughs, and 2 slaves; and 10 villans and 4 bordars and 24 cotsets with 8 ploughs. There are 2 mills rendering 30s, and 15 acres of meadow, [and] woodland 1 league long and as much broad. It was worth £6; now the same.

William holds SEVINGTON of William. TRE it paid geld for 10 hides. There is land for 7 ploughs. Of this 4 hides are in demesne, and there are 2 ploughs; and 10 villans and 5 bordars with 5 ploughs. There are 20 acres of meadow, [and] woodland 2 furlongs long and 1 furlong broad. It was worth £6; now £7.

An Englishman holds YATTON KEYNELL of William. TRE it paid geld for 1 virgate of land. There is land for half a plough, which [half-plough] is there. It renders 5s.

Ælfstan of Boscombe held all these above-mentioned lands of William de Eu.

Hugh holds SOPWORTH of William. Ælfric held it TRE, and it paid geld for 5 hides. There is land for 6 ploughs. Of this $3\frac{1}{2}$ hides are in demesne, and there are 2 ploughs, and 6 slaves; and 3 villans and 5 bordars with 3 ploughs. It was worth £6; now £4.

The same William holds TOLLARD ROYAL. Toli held it TRE as 1 manor, and it paid geld for 1 hide. There is land for 1

plough. There are [...] cotsets, and 5 acres of meadow and 1 furlong of woodland. It was and is worth 20s.

Ansfrid holds UPTON SCUDAMORE of William. Toli held it TRE, and it paid geld for 3 hides. There is land for $2\frac{1}{2}$ ploughs. Of this 2 hides are in demesne, and there is 1 plough; and 2 villans and 5 bordars with 1 plough. There is a mill rendering 5s, and 4 acres of meadow, [and] woodland 2 furlongs long and 1 furlong broad, and 20 acres of pasture. It was worth 15s; now 60s.

It has not paid geld for half a hide since King William came into England; and Ernulf de Hesdin holds unjustly half a hide in the vill itself. [...]

[Folio 72: WILTSHIRE]

XXXIII. The land of William de Braose

WILLIAM de BRAOSE holds SHAW [in Overton] of the king. Alwine held it TRE, and it paid geld for 2 hides and $1\frac{1}{2}$ virgates of land. There is land for $1\frac{1}{2}$ ploughs. Of this 2 hides are in demesne. There is 1 villan and 2 bordars with half a plough. There are 40 acres of pasture, and woodland 1 league long and 3 furlongs broad. It was worth 10s; now 20s. Robert holds it of William.

XXXIIII. The land of William de Moyon

WILLIAM de MOYON holds SUTTON VENY of the king, and Walter [holds] of him. Cola held it TRE, and it paid geld for 5 hides. There is land for 4 ploughs. Of this 3 hides and 1 virgate of land are in demesne, and there are 2 ploughs, and 3 slaves; and 3 villans and 6 bordars with 2 ploughs. There is a mill rendering 40s, and 4 acres of meadow, and 2 acres of woodland, [and] pasture half a league long and 1 broad. It was worth £4; now 100s.

XXXV. The land of William de Falaise

WILLIAM de Falaise holds of the king half a hide in STANDLYNCH, and Alweard [holds] of him. There is land for half a plough, which [half-plough] is there, and 4 acres of meadow. It was worth 20s; it now renders 10s. Lyfing held it TRE.

XXXVI. The land of Walter de Douai

WALTER de DOUAI holds "CELDEWELLE" of the king, and Godescal [holds] of him. Alsige held it TRE, and it paid geld for 5 hides. There is land for 3 ploughs. Of this 3 hides and 3 virgates of land are in demesne, and there is 1 plough, with 1 slave and 1 villan and 6 bordars with half a plough. There are 10 acres of meadow, and 7 acres of pasture and 8 acres of woodland. It was and is worth £3.

Ralph holds STOURTON of Walter. Ailwacre held it TRE, and it paid geld for 8 hides. There is land for 6 ploughs. Of this 5 hides are in demesne, and there are 2 ploughs, with 1 slave; and 6 villans and 13 cotsets and 8 cottars with 4 ploughs.

There are 2 mills rendering 20d, and 60 acres of pasture, [and] woodland 1 league long and 1 broad. It was worth £4; now £7.

XXXVII. The land of Waleran the Huntsman

WALERAN holds CODFORD [? St Mary] of the king. Herlebald held it TRE, and it paid geld for 6 hides. There is land for 6 ploughs. Of this 3 hides are in demesne, and there are 2 ploughs, and 3 slaves; and 7 villans and 6 bordars with 3 ploughs. There is a mill rendering 10s, and 10 acres of meadow, [and] pasture half a league long and 5 furlongs broad. It was worth £10; now £12.

Walter holds ANSTY of Waleran. Ælfric and Wulfweard held it TRE, and it paid geld for 7 hides. There is land for 4 ploughs. Of this 5 hides and 1 virgate of land are in demesne, and there are 2 ploughs, and 2 slaves; and 6 villans and 4 bordars with 2 ploughs. There is a mill rendering 5s, and 16 acres of meadow, and 15 acres of woodland, [and] pasture half a league long and 3 furlongs broad. It was and is worth 100s.

Azelin holds BUTTERMERE of Waleran. 8 thegns held it TRE, and it paid geld for 1 hide and 1 virgate of land. There is land for 2 ploughs. It is worth 20s.

Waleran himself holds 1 hide in STANDLYNCH. Cola held it TRE. There is land for half a plough. There are 6 acres of meadow. It was worth 5s; now 10s.

Richard holds EAST KENNETT of Waleran. Leofdæg held it TRE, and and [sic] it paid geld for 1½ hides and 1 virgate of land. There is land for 1 plough, which [plough] is there, with 1 slave and 2 bordars, and 1 acre of meadow and 4 acres of pasture. It was and is worth 20s.

Azelin holds STANLEY of Waleran. Selewine held it TRE, and it paid geld for 1 hide and 3 virgates of land. There is land for 1 plough. There are 3 villans and 3 bordars, and 10 acres of meadow. It was worth 15s; now 30s.

Waleran himself holds STEEPLE LANGFORD. Oswulf held it TRE, and it paid geld for 10 hides. There is land for 5 ploughs. Of this 5 hides are in demesne, and there are 2 ploughs, and 5 slaves; and 8 villans and 4 bordars with 3 ploughs. There is a mill rendering 15s, and 30 acres of meadow, [and] pasture half a league long and 2 furlongs broad. It was and is worth £10.

Erenburgis holds HANGING LANGFORD of Waleran. Northmann held it TRE, and it paid geld for 5 hides. There is land for 2 ploughs. Of this 4 hides are in demesne, and there is 1 plough, with 1 slave and 1 villan and 5 bordars with half a plough. There is half a mill rendering 30d, and 20 acres of meadow, [and] pasture 4 furlongs long and 1 furlong broad. It was and is worth 100s.

Engenold holds half a hide of Waleran in BARFORD ST MARTIN, and it paid geld for as much TRE. Bolla held it. There is land for half a plough. There are 2 bordars, and 3 acres of meadow. It was and is worth 7s.

Robert holds of Waleran 3 virgates of land in [? Great] WISHFORD, and it paid geld for as much TRE. Bolla held it. There is land for half a plough. There are 2 bordars, and 4 acres of meadow. It was and is worth 10s.

Herbert holds [East or West] GRIMSTEAD of Waleran. Aghmund held it TRE, and it paid geld for 3 hides. There is land for 3 ploughs. Of this 1½ hides are in demesne, and there is 1 plough, and 2 slaves; and 5 villans and 7 cotsets with 3 ploughs. There are 10 acres of meadow, [and] woodland 5 furlongs long and 2 furlongs broad. It was and is worth 60s.

Engenulf holds WHADDON [in Alderbury] of Waleran. Bolla held it TRE, and it paid geld for 2 hides. There is land for 1½ ploughs. Of this 1½ hides are in demesne, and there is 1 plough; and 4 cotsets with half a plough. There are 7 acres of meadow, [and] woodland 2 furlongs long and half a furlong broad. It was worth 15s; now 25s.

In WHADDON [in Alderbury] 2 knights hold 3½ virgates of land less 2 acres. TRE 4 thegns held them, who could go where they wished. There is land for half a plough, which [half-plough] is there, with 2 cotsets, and 4½ acres of meadow. It is worth 12s.

Engenulf holds 1 virgate of land of Waleran in ALDERBURY, and has there 1 cotset. It is worth 2s. Boda held it TRE.

Waleran himself holds WEST DEAN. Godric held it TRE, and it paid geld for 2 hides and 1 virgate of land. There is land for 3 ploughs. Of this 1 hide is in demesne, and there are 1½ ploughs, and 2 slaves; and 1 villan and 10 cotsets with 1½ ploughs. There are 1½ mills rendering 16s, and 5 acres of meadow, [and] woodland 1 furlong in both length and breadth. It was and is worth 60s.

In HURDCOTT [in Winterbourne Earl] [Waleran] holds half a hide. There is land for half a plough. He has there half a mill rendering 6s. The whole is worth 20s. Eadnoth held it TRE.

XXXVIII. The land of William fitzGuy

WILLIAM fitzGuy holds SUTTON VENY of the king. Alweald and his sister held it TRE, and it paid geld for 8 hides. There is land for 6 ploughs. Of this 4 hides are in demesne, and there are 2 ploughs, and 4 slaves; and 6 villans and 8 bordars with 4 ploughs. There are 2 parts of a mill rendering 13s4d, and 6 acres of meadow, [and] pasture 1 league long and 2 furlongs broad, and as much woodland. It was worth £8; now £10.

XXXIX. The land of Henry de Ferrers

HENRY de Ferrers holds STANDEN [Berks.] of the king. Godric held it TRE, and it paid geld for 1 hide. There is land for 5 ploughs. In demesne are 4 [ploughs], and 4 slaves, and 8 acres of meadow, and 10 acres of pasture and 6 acres of woodland. It is worth 100s. There is woodland belonging to [Great and Little] BEDWYN TRE.

The same man holds [?] CLYFFE PYPARD. Godric held it TRE, and it paid geld for 5 hides less 1 virgate. There is land for 3 ploughs. Of this 4 hides and 1 virgate are in demesne, and there are 3 ploughs, and 6 slaves and 5 bordars, and 30 acres of meadow and 12 acres of pasture. It was and is worth £4.

XL. The land of Richard fitzGilbert

RICHARD son of Count Gilbert holds SUTTON MANDEVILLE of the king, and Berengar [holds] of him. Wulfweard held it TRE, and it paid geld for 10 hides. There is land for 6 ploughs. Of this 7 hides are in demesne, and there are 3 ploughs, and 5 slaves; and 6 villans and 9 bordars with 3 ploughs. There is a mill rendering 10s, and 12 acres of meadow, and 3 acres of woodland, [and] pasture 6 furlongs long and 3 furlongs broad, and 5 burgesses pay 50d. It was and is worth £6.

XLI. The land of Ralph de Mortimer

RALPH de MORTIMER holds HULLAVINGTON of the king. Earl Harold held it, and it paid geld for 20 hides. There is land for 14 ploughs. Of this 14 hides are in demesne, and there are 4 ploughs, and 8 slaves; and 19 villans and 8 cotsets with 6 ploughs. There are 12 acres of meadow, and 10 acres of pasture and 8 acres of woodland. It was and is worth £12. In Malmesbury 1 house renders 12d.

Oidelard holds TOCKENHAM of Ralph. Alwine held it TRE, and it paid geld for 2½ hides. There is land for 3 ploughs. Of this 2 hides are in demesne, and there are 2 ploughs, with 1 slave; and 1 villan and 3 cotsets with half a plough. There are 12 acres of meadow, and as many of pasture and 2 acres of woodland. It was worth 30s; now 50s.

Edward holds BRADFIELD of Ralph. Beorhtwig and Alwig held it TRE, and it paid geld for 2½ hides. There is land for 2 ploughs. Of this 1½ hides are in demesne, and there are 2 ploughs, and 3 villans and 2 cotsets, and 12 acres of meadow. It was and is worth 30s.

In HIGHWAY Ralph holds 1 hide, and has there 1 bordar, and 4 acres of meadow. It is worth 15s. Toti purchased it TRE of the Church of Malmesbury, for the lives of 3 men, and within that term could go with it to what lord he wished.

Ralph himself holds CLATFORD. Alwine held it TRE, and it paid geld for 5 hides. There is land for 3 ploughs. Of this 3 hides are in demesne, and there are 2 ploughs, with 1 slave and 1 villan and 7 bordars with 1 plough. There is a mill rendering 20s, and 5 acres of meadow, pasture half a league long and 3 furlongs broad, [and] woodland half a league long and as much broad. It was and is worth 100s.

Ralph himself holds IMBER. Alwine held it TRE, and it paid geld for 2 hides. There is land for 2 ploughs. In demesne is 1 plough, and 2 slaves, and 1 villan and 4 bordars. There is

pasture 3 furlongs long and 2 furlongs broad. It was worth £3; now £4.

[Folio 72V: WILTSHIRE]

Richard holds [?] SURRENDELL of Ralph. Alwig held it TRE, and it paid geld for 5 hides. There is land for 6 ploughs. Of this 2½ hides are in demesne, and there are 2 ploughs, and 4 slaves; and 12 villans and 3 bordars with 4 ploughs. There are 7 acres of meadow. It was and is worth £7.

Roger holds KINGTON ST MICHAEL of Ralph. Alwine held it TRE, and it paid geld for 1½ hides. There is land for 1 plough, which [plough] is there in demesne, with 1 slave and 2 bordars. There is a mill rendering 2s, and 4 acres of meadow and 6 acres of woodland. It was worth 20s; now 30s. This Alwine held this land of the Church of Glastonbury and could not be separated from it, and rendered service to the abbot for it.

Richard holds 3 hides of Ralph in ALDERTON, and Walter holds 1 hide in the same place. Alric, Godwine, Algar and Godric held them in parage TRE, and it paid geld for 4 hides. There is land for 4 ploughs. There are 4 villans and 5 bordars and 2 slaves, and a mill rendering 37d, and 25 acres of meadow. A burgess in Malmesbury pays 7d. It was and is worth 60s.

Edward holds LUCKINGTON of Ralph. Alweard held it TRE, and it paid geld for 3 hides. There is land for 4 ploughs. Of this 2 hides less 1 virgate are in demesne, and there are 2 ploughs; and 2 villans and 4 bordars with 2 ploughs. There are 8 acres of meadow and 4 acres of woodland. It was and is worth £3.

XLII. The land of Robert fitzGerald

ROBERT fitzGERALD holds [?] WOODBOROUGH of the king. Sæwulf held it TRE, and it paid geld for 10 hides. There is land for 5 ploughs. Of this 7 hides are in demesne, and there are 4 ploughs, and 5 slaves; and 5 villans and 11 cotsets with 1 bordar have 1 plough. There is a mill rendering 12s6d, and 50 acres of meadow, and 50 acres of pasture and 10 acres of scrubland. It was worth £7; now £10. Joscelin holds it of Robert.

Rainer holds FOSBURY of Robert. Vitalis held it TRE, and it paid geld for 10 hides. There is land for 5 ploughs. Of this 6 hides are in demesne, and there are 2 ploughs, and 2 slaves; and 7 villans and 2 bordars with 1½ ploughs. There is pasture 5 furlongs long and 3 furlongs broad, [and] woodland half a league long and 3 furlongs broad. It was and is worth 100s.

Rainer holds FOSBURY of Robert. Alwine held it TRE, and it paid geld for 2 hides. There is land for 2 ploughs. There are 3 bordars with 1 plough, pasture 2 furlongs long and 1½ furlongs broad, [and] woodland 2 furlongs long and 2 furlongs broad. It was worth 15s; now 30s.

Robert holds BIDDESDEN. Cuthwulf held it TRE, and it paid geld for 1 virgate of land. There is land for 1 plough, which [plough] is there, with 1 villan and 2 bordars and 4 slaves, and pasture 2 furlongs long and 1 broad. It renders 30s.

Robert holds BRIGMERSTON of Robert. Beorhtmær held it TRE, and it paid geld for 4 hides. There is land for 2 ploughs, which are there in demesne, with 11 bordars. There is a mill rendering 12s, and 10 acres of meadow, [and] pasture 12 furlongs long and 4 furlongs broad. It was worth 10s; now £4.

The same Robert holds MILSTON of Robert. Beorhtmær held it TRE, and it paid geld for 1½ hides. There is land for 1 plough, which [plough] is there, with 2 slaves and 4 cotsets. There is a mill rendering 18s, and 4 acres of meadow, [and] pasture 12 furlongs long and 1 furlong broad. It was worth 20s; now 30s.

Hugh holds [?] WILSFORD [near Amesbury] of Robert. Tovi held it TRE, and it paid geld for 1 hide. There is land for 1 plough, which [plough] is there, with 1 villan and 3 cotsets. There is a mill rendering 10s, and 6 acres of meadow, [and] pasture 9 furlongs long and 2 furlongs broad. It was worth 30s; It is worth 60s.

Rainer holds FITTLETON of Robert. Vitalis held it TRE, and it paid geld for 10 hides. There is land for 12 ploughs. Of this 5 hides and 1 virgate of land are in demesne, and there are 3 ploughs and 6 slaves; and 6 villans and 12 bordars with 3 ploughs. There is a mill rendering 22s6d, and 3 acres of meadow, [and] pasture 1 league long and half a league broad. It was and is worth £12.

Hugh holds SHAW [in Overton] of Robert. Cuthwulf held it TRE, and it paid geld for 2 hides and 1½ virgates. There is land for 1 plough. There is 1 villan and 2 slaves, and 30 acres of pasture, [and] woodland 1 league long and 1 furlong broad. It was worth 20s; now 40s.

Robert holds EBBESBORNE WAKE of Robert. Alward and Vitalis held it TRE as 2 manors, and it paid geld for 14 hides. There is land for 10 ploughs. Of this 10 hides are in demesne, and there are 6 ploughs, and 4 slaves; and 18 villans and 7 bordars with 4 ploughs. There are 14 acres of meadow, pasture 14 furlongs long and 4 furlongs broad, [and] woodland 2 leagues in both length and breadth. It was worth £12; now £14.

XLIII. The land of Robert fitzRolf

ROBERT fitzRolf holds in MOREDON 1 hide and 1 virgate of land. Wulfgar held it TRE, and it paid geld for 5 virgates of land. There is land for 1 plough, which [plough] is there in demesne, with 1 slave and 1 villan, and 10 acres of meadow and 40 acres of pasture. It was and is worth 20s.

Robert fitzRolf holds BROAD HINTON. Wulfgar held it TRE, and it paid geld for 9 hides less 1 virgate. There is land for 5 ploughs. Of this 6 hides are in demesne, and there are 2 ploughs, with 1 slave, and 5 villans and 6 bordars. There are 12 acres of meadow, [and] pasture 1 furlong long and as much broad. It was and is worth £6.

XLIIII. [The land] of Roger de Courseulles

ROGER de COURSEULLES holds FISHERTON DE LA MERE of the king. Bondi held it TRE, and it paid geld for 10 hides. There is land for 10 ploughs. Of this 5½ hides are in demesne, and there are 3 ploughs; and 16 villans and 12 bordars and 14 cottars with 7 ploughs. There is a mill rendering 20s. and 12 acres of meadow, and 10 acres of woodland, [and] pasture half a league long and as much broad. It was and is worth £25.

XLV. [The land] of Roger Berkeley

ROGER of Berkeley holds FOXLEY of the king. Ealdræd held it TRE, and it paid geld for 2 hides. There is land for 4 ploughs. Of this 1 hide is in demesne, and there are 2 ploughs, and 3 slaves; and 4 villans and 3 cotsets with 3 ploughs. There is a mill [rendering] 7s6d, and 4 acres of meadow, and 8 acres of pasture, and 1 house in Malmesbury. It was and is worth 40s.

The same Roger holds 1 hide less half a virgate of the demesne farm of Chippenham. Celein held it TRE, on lease from Eadric the sheriff.

Roger himself holds EASTON GREY. Alwig held it TRE, and it paid geld for 3 hides less half a virgate. There is land for 3 ploughs. Of this 2 hides are in demesne, and there are 2 ploughs, and 4 slaves; and 2 villans and 3 bordars with 1 plough. There is a mill rendering 6s. It was worth 30s; now 40s.

XLVI.

BERNARD Pauncevolt holds 'FRUSTFIELD' [in Whiteparish]. Godwine held it TRE, and it paid geld for 1½ virgates of land. There is land for half a plough. It is worth 5s.

XLVII. The land of Berengar Giffard

BERENGAR Giffard holds FONTHILL GIFFORD of the king. Euing held it TRE, and it paid geld for 5 hides. There is land for 7 ploughs. Of this 1 hide is in demesne, and there are 3 ploughs, and 4 slaves; and 6 villans and 16 bordars with 4 ploughs. There is a mill rendering 5s, and 7 acres of meadow, pasture half a league long and 3 furlongs broad, [and] woodland 4 furlongs long and 2 furlongs broad. It was worth 100s; now £6.

The same man holds 1 hide in BARFORD ST MARTIN. Earl Harold held it TRE, and it paid geld for as much. There is land for 1 plough. There are 6 bordars, and 6 acres of meadow. It was worth 60s; now 20s.

XLVIII. The land of Osbern Giffard

OSBERN Giffard holds ELSTON of the king. Dunna held it TRE, and it paid geld for 11 hides. There is land for 6 ploughs. Of this 9 hides are in demesne, and there are 4 ploughs, and 5 slaves; and 4 villans and 5 bordars with 2 ploughs. There are 6 acres of meadow, and pasture 9 furlongs long and 6 furlongs broad. It was worth £7; now £9.

The same Osbern holds 2 hides in [?] ELSTON. There is land for 1 plough. There are 2 acres of meadow and 3 acres of pasture. It was worth 30s; now 40s.

The same Osbern holds 3½ hides in ORCHESTON. Wulfmær and Alwine held them TRE. There is land for 2 ploughs, which are there in demesne, and 3 slaves. [There is] pasture half a league and 40 acres long and broad. It was worth 40s; now 50s.

Osbern himself holds STANTON [Stanton St Quintin and Lower Stanton St Quintin]. Beorhtric held it TRE, and it paid geld for 18 hides. He has there 2 ploughs in demesne on 9 hides, and there are 7 slaves; and 9 villans and 3 cotsets with 6 ploughs. There are 6 acres of meadow, pasture 1 league long and 1 broad, [and] woodland 1 league long and 3 furlongs broad. It was worth £9; now £8.

The Church of Saint-Etienne of Fontenay holds of Osbern 2 hides and 1 virgate of land in MIDDLETON. Dunna held it TRE, and it paid geld for as much. There is land for 2 ploughs, which are there in demesne, with 1 slave and 2 bordars. There are 5 acres of meadow, and 20 acres of pasture and 1 acre of woodland. It was worth 20s; now 50s.

Osbern himself holds CODFORD [? St Peter]. Ælfric held it TRE, and it paid geld for 1½ hides. There is land for 2 ploughs. Of this 1 hide is in demesne, and there are 1½ ploughs, and 2 slaves; and 6 cotsets and 1 cottar with half a plough. There is the fourth part of a mill rendering 3s 1½d, and 10 acres of meadow, [and] pasture 4 furlongs long and 1 furlong broad. It was worth 50s; now 60s.

Osbern himself holds ORCHESTON. Trasmund held it TRE, and it paid geld for 5 hides. There is land for 3 ploughs. Of this 4 hides are in demesne, and there are 2 ploughs, and 3 slaves; and 4 villans and 3 cotsets and 5 cottars with 1½ ploughs. There is pasture 3 furlongs long and 1 furlong broad. It was worth £4; now 100s.

Osbern himself holds HILL DEVERILL. Smala held it TRE, and it paid geld for 3 hides and half a virgate of land. There is land for 3 ploughs. Of this 2 hides are in demesne, and there are 2 ploughs, with 1 slave and 9 cotsets and 3 bordars. There is a mill rendering 30d, and 2 acres of meadow, and pasture 2 furlongs long and 1 furlong broad, [and] woodland half a league long and as much broad. It was worth 40s; now 60s.

Osbern himself holds KELLAWAYS. Dunna held it TRE, and it paid geld for 10 hides. There is land for 6 ploughs. Of this 9 hides are in demesne, and there are 3 ploughs, and 4 slaves; and 2 villans and 4 cotsets and 3 bordars with 3 ploughs. There are 10 acres of meadow. It was worth £4; now 100s.

Osbern himself holds SHERRINGTON. Algar held it TRE, and it paid geld for 5 hides. There is land for 2½ ploughs. Of this 4½ hides are in demesne, and there are 2 ploughs, and 5 slaves; and 2 villans with half a plough. There is half a mill

rendering 7s 6d, and 6 acres of meadow, and 60 acres of pasture and 40 acres of woodland. It was worth £4; now 100s.

Osbern himself holds SHERRINGTON. Smala held it TRE, and it paid geld for 5 hides. There is land for 2½ ploughs. Of this 4½ hides are in demesne, and there are 2 ploughs, and 5 slaves; and 2 villans with half a plough. There is half a mill rendering 7s 6d, and 6 acres of meadow, and 60 acres of pasture, and 40 acres of woodland, and 1 burgess in Wilton paying 3s. It was worth £4; now 100s.

Gunduin holds UGFORD of Osbern. Eadnoth held it TRE, and it paid geld for 2½ hides. There is land for 1 plough, which [plough] is there, with 1 slave and 1 bordar. There is a mill rendering 4s, and 4 acres of meadow and 10 acres of pasture. It was worth 30s; now 40s. Earl Godwine took away this land from [the Church of] ST MARY of Wilton, and then Eadnoth recovered it.

XLIX. The land of Drogo fitzPons

DROGO fitsPons holds [Lower and Upper] SEAGRY of the king. Wigflæd held it TRE, and it paid geld for 5 hides. There is land for 4 ploughs. Of this 2 hides are in demesne. ROGER de Lacy, and Turstin fitzRolf, and William Leofric hold 1 hide in COLESHILL [Berks.]. 3 thegns held it TRE. The share of all is worth £4.

[Folio 73: WILTSHIRE]

and there is 1 plough; and 5 villans and 6 bordars and 5 cotsets with 1 plough. There are 2 mills rendering 22s 4d, and 30 acres of meadow. A house in Malmesbury renders 9d. It was worth 60s; now 70s.

Gilbert holds EASTON [Easton Piercy and Lower Easton Piercy] of Drogo. Osweard held it TRE, and it paid geld for 5 hides. There is land for 3 ploughs. Of this 4 hides are in demesne, and there are 2 ploughs, and 2 slaves, and 1 villan and 4 bordars and 2 cotsets. There are 10 acres of meadow, [and] woodland 2 furlongs long and 2 furlongs broad. It was worth 40s; now 50s.

Hugh holds ALDERTON of Drogo. Eadric held it TRE, and it paid geld for 3 hides. There is land for 3 ploughs. Of this 2 hides and 3 virgates of land are in demesne, and there is 1 plough, with 1 slave and 2 bordars. From part of a mill [comes] 22d; and [there are] 15 acres of meadow. It was and is worth 60s.

L. The land of Hugh L'Asne

HUGH L'Asne holds 1 hide of land and 3 virgates of the king in SHALBOURNE, and William holds of him. A thegn held it of King Edward, and it paid geld for as much. There is land for 2 ploughs. There is 1 villan and 4 cotsets with 1 plough. There is 1 arpent of meadow, and 2 acres of woodland. It is worth 30s.

Harold holds WESTLECOTT of Hugh. Leofric held it TRE, and it paid geld for 5 hides. There is land for 2 ploughs. Of this 4 hides are in demesne, and there are 1½ ploughs, with 1 slave;

and 3 villans and 6 bordars with half a plough. There is a mill rendering 5s, and 25 acres of meadow and 30 acres of pasture. It was and is worth 40s.

Hugh himself holds 2 hides in [?] CLYFFE PYPARD. Godgifu held it as 1 manor. There is land for 1 plough. There is 1 cotset, and 12 acres of meadow. It is worth 12s.

William holds CORTON of Hugh. Dene held it TRE, and it paid geld for 6 hides. There is land for 4 ploughs. Of this 4 hides are in demesne, and there are 1½ ploughs, and 2 slaves; and 4 bordars with half a plough. There is a mill rendering 20s, and 6 acres of meadow, pasture 3 furlongs long and 2 furlongs broad, and as much woodland. It was worth 100s; now £6.

The Church of ST MARY of Winchester holds [? East] KENNETT of Hugh for his daughter. Hunwine held it TRE, and it paid geld for 2 hides less 1 virgate. There is land for 1 plough, which [plough], is there in demesne, with 2 bordars, and 1 acre of meadow and 6 acres of pasture. It was worth 10s; now 20s.

LII. [The land] of Humphrey the Chamberlain

HUMPHREY the chamberlain holds SHORNCOTE [Glos.] of the king. Alweard held it TRE, and it paid geld for 5 hides. There is land for 4 ploughs. Of this, 2½ hides are in demesne, and there are 2 ploughs, and 3 slaves; and 8 villans with 2 ploughs. There are 50 acres of meadow, and pasture 2 furlongs long and 1 furlong broad. It was worth 40s; now 60s.

LIII. The land of Gunfrid Mauduit

GUNFRID Mauduit holds CALSTONE WELLINGTON of the king. Algar held it TRE, and it paid geld for 2 hides and 1 virgate of land. There is land for 2 ploughs. Of this 5 virgates of land are in demesne, and there are 2 ploughs, and 3 slaves; and 6 bordars with half a plough. There is a mill rendering 15s, and 8 acres of meadow, [and] pasture 2 furlongs long and 1 furlong broad. It was worth 40s; now 50s.

The same Gunfrid holds WHITLEY. Api held it TRE, and it paid geld for 1 hide. There is land for 2 ploughs, which are there in demesne, with 1 slave and 6 bordars. There are 8 acres of meadow, [and] woodland 3 furlongs long and 1 furlong broad. It was worth 40s; now 50s.

LIIII. The land of Alvred d'Epaignes

ALVRED d'Epaignes holds YATESBURY of the king. Alwig held it TRE, and it paid geld for 5 hides. There is land for 4 ploughs. Of this 3½ hides are in demesne, and there are 2 ploughs, and 2 slaves; and 7 bordars and 1 knight with 1 plough. There are 20 acres of pasture. It was worth £3; now £4.

LV. [The land] of Aiulf the Sheriff

AIULF the sheriff holds 5 hides and half a hide of the king in TOLLARD ROYAL. 5 thegns held it TRE, and it paid geld

for 5½ hides. There is land for 4 ploughs. Of this 4 hides are in demesne, and there are 2 ploughs, and 2 slaves, and 3 villans and 14 bordars. There are 2 arpents of vineyard, and 20 acres of pasture and 4 acres of woodland. It was worth £4; now £6.

The same Aiulf holds half a hide in BEMERTON. There is land for half a plough. It renders 12s. Radulf held it TRE.

LVI. The land of Nigel the Physician

NIGEL the physician holds STRATTON ST MARGARET of the king. TRE it paid geld for 30 hides. There is land for 14 ploughs. Of this 5 hides are in demesne, and there are 3 ploughs, and 2 slaves; and 24 villans and 18 bordars with 12 ploughs. There is a mill rendering 2s, and meadow 8 furlongs long and 5 furlongs broad, [and] pasture 1 league long and 5 furlongs broad. It was worth £18; now £16.

The same Nigel holds [East and West] CHISENBURY. TRE it paid geld for 8 hides. There is land for 5 ploughs. Of this 4½ hides are in demesne, and there are 2½ ploughs, and 2 slaves; and 8 villans and 12 bordars with 2 ploughs. There is a mill rendering 7½s, and 20 acres of meadow, and pasture 1 league long and 5 furlongs broad. It was and is worth £13.

The same Nigel holds 1 hide in NETHERAVON, and Durand [holds] of him. There is land for 1 plough. There are 3 bordars with half a plough, and 6 acres of meadow, [and] pasture 4 furlongs long and 2 furlongs broad. It was and is worth £3. These 3 manors belong to the Church of Netheravon.

The same Nigel holds 4 hides in SUTTON VENY, and it paid geld for as much TRE. There is land for 3 ploughs. [The Abbey of] SAINTE-MARIE of Montebourg holds it of Nigel. Of this land 2 hides are in demesne, and there is 1 plough, and 3 slaves; and 5 villans and 5 bordars with 2 ploughs. There is the third part of a mill rendering 6s8d, and 3 acres of meadow, pasture half a league long and 1 furlong broad, [and] woodland 1 league long and 1 furlong broad. It was worth £4; now 100s. Spirites the priest held these 4 manors TRE.

NIGEL holds half a hide in BEVERSBROOK [Beversbrook or Lower Beversbrook], and it paid geld for as much TRE. He has there 1 villan and 1 bordar; and woodland 1 furlong long and half a furlong broad. It is worth 7s.

The same Nigel holds HAZELBURY. TRE it paid geld for 1 virgate of land. There is land for 6 oxen. There are 3 bordars, and 3 acres of meadow, [and] pasture 4 furlongs long and 1 furlong broad. It is worth 10s. Alsige the priest held these 2 estates TRE.

LVII. The land of Osbern the Priest

OSBERN the priest holds HOMINGTON. Alsige held it TRE, and it paid geld for 2 hides. There is land for 1 plough. There are 2 cotsets, and 3 acres of meadow and 6 acres of pasture. It is worth 30s.

LVIII. The land of Richard Puignant

RICHARD Puignant holds CALSTONE WELL-INGTON of the king. Gunnar held it TRE, and it paid geld for 4 hides less 1 virgate. There is land for 4 ploughs. Of this 2 ploughs [sic] and 1 virgate are in demesne, and there are 3 ploughs, and 2 slaves; and 16 cotsets and 3 bordars with 1 plough. There are 2 mills rendering 33s6d, and 15 acres of meadow, and as many of pasture, [and] woodland 3 furlongs long and 2 furlongs broad, and in Calne 2 burgesses pay 20d. It was worth £4; now 100s.

The same Richard holds TROW. TRE it paid geld for 7½ hides. There is land for 4 ploughs. Of this 5 hides are in demesne, and there are 3 ploughs. There are 3 villans with 1 plough, and 2 acres of meadow, pasture 4 furlongs long and 3 furlongs broad, [and] woodland 6 furlongs long and 3 furlongs broad. It was worth 100s; now £7.

[The Church of] ST MARY of Wilton held this land TRE, and it could not be alienated from the church.

LIX. The land of Robert Marshal

ROBERT Marshal holds MARKET LAVINGTON of the king. Queen Edith held it, and it paid geld for 15 hides. There is land for 10 ploughs. Of this 7 hides are in demesne, and there are 4 ploughs, and 7 slaves; and 14 villans and 17 bordars with 5 ploughs. There are 2 mills rendering 16s4d, and 20 acres of meadow, and 12 acres of woodland, [and] pasture 1 league long and as much broad. It was and is worth £20.

The same Robert holds GORE. Osweard held it TRE, and it paid geld for 3 hides. There is land for 3 ploughs. Of this 2 hides are in demesne, and there are 2 ploughs, and 6 slaves; and 3 villans and 1 bordar with 1 plough, and 40 acres of pasture. It was worth 30s; now 50s.

LX.

ROBERT the Fair holds WEST LAVINGTON of the king. Aki held it TRE, and it paid geld for 10 hides. There is land for 7 ploughs. Of this 1 hide and 1 virgate are in demesne, and there is 1 plough. 2 sons-in-law of his hold 7 hides and 1 virgate of him, and they have there 5 ploughs with their men. There is a mill rendering 5s, and pasture 1½ leagues long and 4 furlongs broad. It was worth £15; now £12.

LXI. The land of Richard Sturmy

RICHARD Sturmy holds COWESFIELD of the king. Ælfric held it TRE, and it paid geld for 2 hides. There is land for 2 ploughs. Of this 1 hide is in demesne, and there is 1 plough; and 2 villans and 8 cotsets with 2 ploughs. There is pasture 2 furlongs long and 1 furlong broad, and as much woodland. It was worth 15s; now 30s.

LXII. [The land] of Reginald Canute

REGINALD Canute holds 1 hide in CHIPPENHAM of the king. Toki held it TRE. There is land for 1 plough. 2 bordars there have half a plough, and [there are] 20 acres of meadow, and half a mill rendering 15s. The whole was and is worth 20s.

LXIII. The land of Matthew de Mortagne

MATTHEW de Mortagne holds MADDINGTON of the king. Wulfweard held it TRE, and it paid geld for 4 hides. There is land for 2 ploughs. Of this 2 hides are in demesne, and there is 1 plough, with 1 slave; and 2 villans and 4 bordars with 1 plough. There is pasture 4 furlongs long and as much broad. It was worth 40s; now 60s.

LXIIII. [The land] of Joscelin Riviere

JOSCELIN Riviere holds ZEALS of the king. Almær held it TRE, and it paid geld for 2½ hides. There is land for 3 ploughs. In demesne is 1 plough, and 2 slaves; and 5 villans and 3 cotsets with 2 ploughs. There is a mill rendering 40d, and 3 acres of meadow, pasture 3 furlongs long and 3 broad, [and] woodland half a league long and as much broad. It was and is worth 30s.

LXV. [The land] of Godescal

GODESCAL holds WINTERBOURNE [? Gunner] of the king. Alwig held it TRE, and it paid geld for 2 hides. There is land for 2 ploughs. In demesne is 1 plough, and 3 slaves, and 4 bordars and 5 cotsets. There is half a mill rendering 3s9d, and half an acre of meadow, [and] woodland 2 furlongs long and as much broad. It was worth 30s; now 40s.

The same Godescal holds half a hide which Guthmund held TRE, and it paid geld for as much. There is 1 cotset. It is worth 12s.

LXVI.

HERMAN de Dreux holds "ETONE" of the king. Eadric held it TRE, and it paid geld for 2 hides. There is land for 2 ploughs. In demesne is 1 plough; and 2 bordars and 2 cotsets and 1 villan with 1 plough. There are 2 acres of meadow, [and] woodland 2 furlongs long and 1 furlong broad. It was and is worth 30s.

LI. The land of Hugh fitzBaldric

HUGH fitzBaldric holds MARDEN, and Walter, his son-in-law, [holds] of him. Wynsige held it TRE, and it paid geld for 10 hides. There is land for 8 ploughs. In demesne are 2 ploughs, and 4 slaves; and 9 villans and 14 cotsets and 2 bordars with 5 ploughs. There is a mill rendering 7½s, and 24 acres of meadow, [and] pasture 3 furlongs in length and 2 furlongs broad. A house in Wilton renders 10d. It was worth £7; now £10.

AMALRIC de Dreux holds MANNINGFORD BOHUNE of the king. Godric held it TRE, and it paid geld for 3½ hides. There is land for 1½ ploughs. There are 4 bordars, and the third part of a mill rendering 50d, and 12 acres of meadow, [and] pasture 4 furlongs long and 1½ furlongs broad. It was worth 30s; now 60s.

ANSGER the cook holds HILPERTON. 3 thegns held it in parage TRE, and it paid geld for 4 hides and 1 virgate and 6 acres. There is land for 3 ploughs, which are there in demesne, with 1 slave and 9 cotsels. There are 12 acres of meadow and 20 acres of pasture. It was worth £4; now 10s less.

WILLIAM Corniole holds HILPERTON of the king. 4 thegns held it in parage TRE, and it paid geld for 5 hides and 1 virgate of land. There is land for 5 ploughs. In demesne are 2 ploughs; and 1 villan with 1 plough, and 12 acres of meadow and 20 acres of pasture. It renders 40s.

FULCHRED holds 3 virgates of land in GILLINGHAM [Dorset]. Algar held them TRE. There is land for 2 ploughs, which are there, with 1 bordar. It was and is worth 15s.

STEPHEN the carpenter holds 1 hide and 1 virgate of land in EARLSCOURT. Oda held it TRE. There is land for 2 ploughs, which are there, with 1 slave and 3 villans and 2 bordars. There are 30 acres of meadow, and 8 acres of pasture, and in Cricklade a garden renders 2d. It was worth 30s; now 60s.

The same Stephen holds 3 hides. Aki held them TRE. There is land for 1 plough, which [plough] is there, with 1 villan and 4 bordars. There is pasture half a league long and 3 furlongs broad. It was worth 20s; now 40s.

OSMUND holds 1 hide in POMEROY. Alnoth held it TRE. There is land for 1 plough, which [plough] is there in demesne. It was worth 5s; now 10s.

LXVII. The land of Oda and Other King's Thegns

ODA of WINCHESTER holds CALCUTT of the king. There are 5 hides. TRE it paid geld for half a hide. There is land for 3 ploughs. Of this 4½ hides are in demesne. There 1 villan and 4 bordars with 1 slave have 1 plough; and [there are] 60 acres of meadow. In Cricklade 3 burgesses pay 21d. It is worth £4.

BEORHTRIC holds COULSTON of the king. TRE it paid geld for 5 hides. There is land for 4 ploughs. In demesne are 2 ploughs, and 6 slaves; and 5 villans and 3 bordars with 2 ploughs. There is a mill rendering 10s, and 30 acres of meadow and 5 furlongs of pasture. It is worth 100s.

BEORHTRIC holds in SWALLOWCLIFFE 1 hide and 1½ virgates of land. There is land for 1 plough, which [plough] is there, with 2 villans. It is worth 15s.

Beorhtric holds 1 hide in TROWLE. There is land for 1 plough, which [plough] is there, with 1 villan. It is worth 10s.

Beorhtric holds MONKTON FARLEIGH, and his brother [holds] of him. TRE it paid geld for 5 hides. There is land for 4 ploughs. In demesne is 1 plough, and 4 slaves; and 5 villans and 3 bordars with 3 ploughs. There are 20 acres of pasture and 3 acres of woodland. It is worth 70s.

BEORHTRIC holds OAKSEY. His father held it TRE, and it paid geld for 10 hides. There is land for 6 ploughs. In demesne are 2 ploughs, and 10 slaves; and 6 villans and 12 cotsets with 4 ploughs. There is a mill rendering 5s, and 40 acres of meadow, and 30 acres of pasture, [and] woodland 1 league long and half a league broad. It was worth £8; now £6.

BEORHTRIC holds TROWBRIDGE. His father held it TRE, and it paid geld for 10 hides. There is land for 9 ploughs. In demesne are 2 ploughs, and 7 slaves; and 11 villans and 6 cotsets with 7 ploughs. There is a mill rendering 10s, and 10 acres of meadow, and 12 acres of pasture, [and] woodland 5 furlongs long and 3 furlongs broad. It was worth £4; now £8.

BEORHTRIC holds STAVERTON. His father held it TRE, and it paid geld for 5 hides. There is land for 3 ploughs. In demesne are 2 ploughs, and 7 slaves; and 3 villans and 2 cotsets with 1 plough. There is a mill rendering 20s, and 20 acres of meadow and 20 acres of pasture. It is worth 70s.

BEORHTRIC holds ODSTOCK. His father held it TRE, and it paid geld for 12 hides. There is land for 6 ploughs. In demesne is 1 plough, and 3 slaves; and 9 villans and 16 cotsets with 2½ ploughs. There is a mill rendering 7s6d, and 40 acres of meadow, pasture 1 league long and 3 furlongs broad, and in another part 5 acres of pasture, [and] woodland 3 furlongs long and 3 furlongs broad. 1 burgess in Wilton pays 12d. It is worth £10.

BEORHTRIC and his brother Alwig hold COWESFIELD. TRE it paid geld for 1½ hides. There is land for 1 plough, which [plough] is there, with 3 cotsets. There are 2 furlongs of scrubland. It is worth 10s.

ALWEARD holds 3 hides in POTTERNE. TRE it paid geld with the bishop's manor. There is land for 3 ploughs. In demesne is 1 [plough]; and 3 villans and 4 bordars with 2 ploughs. There is [...] 4 furlongs long and 3 furlongs broad. It is worth 70s. Bishop Osmund claims it.

Alweard holds 1 hide in TILSHEAD. There is land for 1 plough, which [plough] is there, and 1 furlong of pasture. It is worth 20s.

Alweard holds SWALLOWCLIFFE. TRE it paid geld for 3 hides less half a virgate. There is land for 1½ ploughs. The villans hold it. It is worth 30s.

Alweard Colling holds KNOOK. TRE it paid geld for 4 hides. There is land for 3 ploughs. In demesne is 1 plough, and 3 slaves; and 4 villans and 3 bordars with 2 ploughs. There is a mill rendering 15s, and 5 acres of meadow, [and] pasture half a league long and 1 furlong broad. It is worth £4.

ÆLFRIC of Melksham holds WILSFORD [near Pewsey] of the king. Beorhtmær held it TRE, and it paid geld for 5 hides. There is land for 2½ ploughs, which are there, with 10 bordars. There are 8 acres of meadow, [and] pasture 5 furlongs long and 1 furlong broad. It was worth 100s; now 8s. Edward holds it in pledge.

ÆLFRIC holds MONKTON FARLEIGH. Beorhtmær held it TRE, and it paid geld for 5 hides. There is land for 4 ploughs. In demesne is 1 plough, and 4 slaves; and 5 villans and 3 bordars with 3 ploughs. There are 20 acres of pasture and 3 acres of woodland. It is worth 70s.

ÆLFRIC holds WHADDON [in Semington]. He himself held it TRE, and it paid geld for 3 hides. There is land for 2 ploughs. In demesne is 1 [plough], and 3 slaves and 3 cotsets. There is a mill rendering 5s, and 8 acres of meadow, [and] 1 furlong of pasture in length and breadth. It is worth 20s.

ÆLFRIC the Little holds 2½ virgates of land in TILSHEAD. There is land for half a plough. It is worth 7s6d.

The same man holds 1 hide in HILMARTON. There is land for 1 plough, and he has there 1 slave. It is worth 15s.

The same man holds 1 hide in TOCKENHAM, and it paid geld for as much. There is land for 1 plough. There are 6 acres of meadow and 6 acres of pasture. It is worth 13s.

The same man holds 2 hides less 1 virgate which 2 thegns held TRE. There is land for 6 oxen. It is worth 15s.

ALWINE the priest holds [? Great] SOMERFORD. TRE it paid geld for 2½ virgates of land. There is land for half a plough. There are 2 cotsets and 1 cottar, and part of a mill rendering 15d, and 4 acres of meadow and 4 acres of pasture. It is worth 11s.

In the same vill Alwig holds 2½ virgates of land, and it paid geld for as much TRE. There is land for half a plough. There are 2 cotsets, and part of a mill [rendering] 15d, and 4 acres of meadow and 4 acres of pasture. It was and is worth 8s.

In the same vill Edward holds half a hide. There is land for half a plough. It is worth 40d.

In the same vill Sægifu holds 2½ virgates of land. There is land for half a plough. There is 1 cotset and 1 cottar. Part of a mill renders 15d, and [there are] 4 acres of meadow and 4 acres of pasture. It is worth 11s.

ALWIG the son of Thorbiorn holds half a hide in STANDLYNCH. There is land for half a plough. There are 4 acres of meadow. It is worth 5s.

ALRIC holds half a hide paying geld in TOCKENHAM. There is land for half a plough. There are 3 acres of meadow and 3 acres of pasture. It is worth 7s.

AZUR holds 2 hides in 'BARLEY' [in South Wraxall]. Dunna held them TRE. There is land for 4 ploughs. In demesne are 2 ploughs, with 1 bordar and 2 villans. It was and is worth 40s.

ÆLFSTAN holds half a hide of land in TILSHEAD. It is worth 5s.

ALMÆR holds 2½ virgates of land in TILSHEAD. It is worth 5s.

ALGAR holds 1 hide paying geld in TOCKENHAM. There

is land for 1 plough. He has there half a plough, with 1 bordar; and 6 acres of meadow and as many of pasture. It is worth 13s.

ÆLFGEAT holds ZEALS. TRE it paid geld for 2½ hides. There is land for 3 ploughs. In demesne is 1 plough, and 4 slaves; and 8 villans and 9 bordars with 2 ploughs. There is a mill rendering 3s, and 4 acres of meadow, and 40 acres of pasture, [and] woodland half a league long and half a league broad. It is worth 30s.

AZUR holds 1 hide in CORSLEY. There is land for 1 plough, which [plough] is there in demesne, with 4 bordars. There is a mill rendering 40d, and woodland 1 furlong long and half a furlong broad. It is worth 20s.

EALDRÆD holds BEMERTON. He himself held it TRE, and it paid geld for 2 hides. There is land for 2 ploughs. There is 1 villan and 3 bordars, and 4 acres of meadow, and a mill rendering 12s6d. It is worth 40s.

EALDRÆD holds ALDERSTONE. He himself held it TRE, and it paid geld for 1 hide. There is land for 2 ploughs. There is 1 plough, with 1 villan and 3 cotsets. There is pasture 1 furlong long and 1 broad, [and] woodland 2 furlongs long and 1 furlong broad. It is worth 10s.

EALDRÆD holds WINTERBOURNE [? Gunner]. Godwine held it TRE, and it paid geld for 1½ hides. There is land for 1 plough. There is half a plough, with 1 villan and 1 bordar, and part of a mill rendering 22½d, [and] pasture 2 furlongs long and as much broad. It is worth 30s.

CUTHWULF holds [?] ROLLESTONE. He himself held it TRE. He has there 6 hides. There is land for 3 ploughs. In demesne are 2 ploughs; and 5 slaves with 1 villan and 2 bordars have 1 plough. There are 4 acres of meadow and half a league of pasture. It is worth £3.

KETIL holds 1 hide in MALMESBURY. Godwine held it TRE. There is land for 1 plough, which [plough] is there, with 2 bordars. There are 6 acres of meadow, [and] pasture 3 furlongs long and half a furlong broad. It is worth 20s.

CYPPING holds HAZELBURY. He himself held it TRE, and it paid geld for 1 virgate of land. There is land for 1 plough, which [plough] is there, and woodland 2 furlongs long and 1 furlong broad. It is worth 7s.

COLA holds [East or West] GRIMSTEAD. His father held it TRE, and it paid geld for 1½ hides. There is land for 1 plough. There are 4 villans. It is worth 15s.

Ealdræd holds 3 hides in ANSTY. There is land for 2 ploughs, which are there, with 1 slave and 1 villan and 3 bordars. There is a mill rendering 25d, and 5 acres of woodland, and 5 acres of meadow and 2 furlongs of pasture. It is worth 30s. Ealdræd holds 10 hides in WROUGHTON. There is land for 4 ploughs, which are there, with 5 slaves and 3 villans and 3 bordars. It was and is worth 100s. Beorhtnoth and Alwine held these 2 estates TRE.

[Folio 74: WILTSHIRE]

GRIMBALD the goldsmith holds MANNINGFORD BRUCE. Edward held it TRE, and it paid geld for 6½ hides. There is land for 4 ploughs. In demesne are 2 ploughs; and 1 villan and 10 cotsets and 2 bordars with 1 plough. There are 2 parts of a mill rendering 12s6d, and 20 acres of meadow, [and] pasture 12 furlongs in length and breadth. It was worth 100s; now £6.

The same Grimbald holds STANTON FITZWARREN. Langa held it TRE, and it paid geld for 10 hides. There is land for 6 ploughs. In demesne are 2 ploughs, and 2 slaves; and 4 villans and 10 cotsets with 3 ploughs. There are 3 acres of meadow, [and] pasture 6 furlongs long and 4 broad. It is worth £12.

GODRIC the huntsman holds 1 virgate of land paying geld in MERE. There is land for half a plough. He has there 1 cotset, and half an acre of meadow. It is worth 5s.

GODRIC holds HARTHAM. His father held it TRE, and it paid geld for 3½ virgates. There is land for half a plough. There are 2 acres of meadow and 3 acres of pasture. It is worth 10s.

GODWINE Clec holds 1 virgate of land in HILPERTON. It is worth 2s.

GODE holds 1 hide in STITCHCOMBE. She herself held it TRE. There is land for 3 ploughs. In demesne is 1 plough; and 2 villans and 5 bordars with 2 ploughs. There is a mill rendering 15s, and 50 acres of woodland. It is worth 50s.

ERLKING holds 1½ virgates of land in ETCHIL-HAMPTON. There is land for 2 oxen. It is worth 7s6d.

EADRIC holds 1 hide in PEWSEY. There is land for 1½ ploughs. It is worth 20s.

EDWIN holds CHEDGLOW. He himself held it TRE, and it paid geld for 1½ virgates of land. There is land for half a plough, which [half-plough] is there. It is worth 3s.

EDGAR the priest holds half a hide in [? Hill] DEVERILL. Algar held it TRE, and it paid geld for as much. There is land for half a plough. He has there 2 cotsets. [There is] pasture 3 furlongs long and 1 broad. It is worth 12s.

EADRIC the Blind holds HARTHAM. He himself held it TRE, and it paid geld for 1 virgate of land. There is land for 2 oxen, which are there. It is worth 30d.

EDWARD holds WITHERINGTON. His father held it TRE, and it paid geld for 3 hides. There is land for 3 ploughs. In demesne is 1 plough; and 4 villans and 5 cotsets and 3 bordars with 1 plough. There is a mill rendering 10s, and 20 acres of meadow and 3 furlongs of woodland. It was worth £3; now £4.

EDMUND holds half a virgate of land in BRAMSHAW [Hants]. It is worth 30d.

EDMUND holds PLAITFORD [Hants]. Algar held it TRE, and it paid geld for 1 virgate of land. There is land for half a plough, which [half-plough] is there, with 2 bordars and 2 cotsets. There is a mill rendering 10d, [and] woodland 3 furlongs long and 1 furlong broad.

The same Edmund holds 1 virgate of land, in which he has

half a plough, and 4 bordars and 2 cottars. These 2 estates together are worth 40s.

EDMUND son of Æthelwulf holds 1 hide in BRITFORD. It renders 12s6d.

The son of Æthelwulf holds [East or West] GRIMSTEAD. His father held it TRE, and it paid geld for 1½ hides. There is land for 2 ploughs. In demesne is 1 plough, with 1 villan and 2 cotsets and 2 cottars. There is a mill rendering 10s, and 14 acres of meadow, and 4 furlongs of pasture, [and] woodland 4 furlongs long and 4 furlongs broad. It is worth 40s.

HEARDING holds 'KNIGHTON' [in Durrington] of the king. He himself held it TRE, and it paid geld for 11 hides. There is land for 6 ploughs. In demesne are 2 ploughs, and 6 slaves; and 7 villans and 6 cotsets with 3 ploughs. There is a mill rendering 10s, and 20 acres of meadow, [and] pasture 12 furlongs long and 3 furlongs broad. It is worth £11.

HEARDING holds FIGHELDEAN. He himself held it TRE, and it paid geld for 11½ hides. There is land for 5 ploughs. In demesne is 1 plough, and 6 slaves; and 7 villans and 8 bordars with 4 ploughs. There is a mill rendering 15s, and 24 acres of meadow, [and] pasture 12 furlongs long and 3 furlongs broad. It is worth £9.

Of this land Earl Aubrey had 4½ hides. The king now holds them.

HEARDING holds OGBOURNE [? Maizey]. He himself held it TRE, and it paid geld for 5 hides. There is land for 3 ploughs. In demesne is 1 plough, with 1 slave; and 3 villans and 4 bordars with 1 ploughs. There are 2 acres of meadow, [and] pasture 2 furlongs long and 1 furlong broad. It is worth £4.

THORKIL holds [land] in COMPTON BASSETT. He himself held it TRE, and it paid geld for 6 hides. There is land for 4 ploughs. In demesne is 1 plough, and 4 slaves; and 5 villans and 10 cotsets and 3 bordars with 2 ploughs. There is the third part of 2 mills rendering 10s, and 24 acres of meadow, and 10 acres of pasture and 10 acres of woodland. It is worth 100s.

ULF holds 1 hide in BUDBURY. There is land for 1 plough. There are 4 bordars and 3 slaves, and 3 acres of woodland. It is worth 10s.

WULFRIC holds 1 hide and 1 virgate of land in SHALBOURNE. Ordweald held it TRE, and it paid geld for as much. There is land for 1½ ploughs, and there are 3 bordars. It is worth 20s.

WULFRIC holds 3 virgates of land in [?West] WIN-TERSLOW, and 1 virgate of land in WEST TYTHERLEY [Hants]. His father held it TRE, and it paid geld for 1 hide. There is land for 1 plough. This [plough] 4 peasants have there. [There is] woodland 4 furlongs long and 1 furlong broad. It is worth 20s.

WULFRIC holds 3½ hides in UFFCOTT. His father held it TRE. There is land for 1½ ploughs. It is worth 30s.

WULFRIC holds MERE. Ællic held it TRE, and it paid geld

for 1½ virgates of land. There is land for half a plough, which [half-plough] is there, with 4 bordars, and half an acre of meadow and 1 acre of pasture. It is worth 7s6d.

WULFRIC holds 1 hide and 1 virgate of land in SWINDON. There is land for half a plough. It is worth 7s.

WULFRIC holds 1 hide in BRITFORD. There is land for half a plough. It is worth 12s6d.

WULFRIC holds 1 hide in 'FRUSTFIELD' [in Whiteparish], and has there 6 bordars. It is worth 20s.

WULFRIC holds PORTON. His father held it TRE, and it paid geld for 2 hides. There is land for 2 ploughs. In demesne is 1 plough, with 1 slave; and 2 villans and 3 cotsets with 1 plough. There are 6 acres of meadow and 3 furlongs of pasture. It is worth 40s.

WULFWEARD holds 4 hides in [? West] WINTERSLOW. There is land for 3 ploughs. In demesne is 1 plough, and 2 slaves, and 1 villan and 3 bordars, [and] woodland 3 furlongs long and 1 furlong broad. It is worth 40s.

WULFWEARD the king's purveyor holds 2 hides in SWINDON. There is land for 6 oxen. It is worth 15s.

WULFRIC Waula holds half a hide in [?] CLYFFE PYPARD. There is land for half a plough. It is worth 4s.

WULFNOTH holds 1 hide in MERE, and it paid geld for as much TRE. There is land for 1 plough, which [plough] is there, with 6 cottars, and 4 acres of meadow and 1 acre of pasture. It is worth 20s.

WULFGEAT the huntsman holds LONGFORD. TRE it paid geld for 4 hides. There is land for 2 ploughs. In demesne is 1 plough, with 1 slave, and 2 villans and 6 bordars and 3 cottars. There is a mill rendering 5s, and 20 acres of meadow, [and] pasture 5 furlongs long and 2 furlongs broad. It is worth 60s.

WULFNOTH holds half a hide paying geld in BRAMSHAW [Hants]. His father held it. There is land for half a plough. It is worth 10s.

WULFGEAT holds half a hide in MILFORD. There is land for 2 oxen. It is worth 2s. Half this land is in the forest.

The wife of WYNSIGE holds TIDCOMBE. Her husband held it TRE, and it paid geld for 2 hides. There is land for 3 ploughs. In demesne is 1 plough, with 1 slave; and 2 villans and 6 bordars with 2 ploughs. There is a mill rendering 15s, and 4 acres of woodland, [and] pasture 5 furlongs long and 2 furlongs broad. It is worth 70s.

WADO holds 1 hide in BARFORD ST MARTIN. He himself held it TRE. There is land for 1 plough, which [plough] is there, with 1 bordar, and 6 acres of meadow. It is worth 15s.

ASGOT holds half a hide in SHALBOURNE. There is land for half a plough. It is worth 5s.

ODOLINA holds 1 hide in MARTEN. There is land for 1½

ploughs. There are 30 acres in both meadow and pasture. It is worth 40s.

SÆWULF holds 1 hide paying geld in "GATEGRAM". His father held it. There is land for half a plough. It is worth 10s.

THORKIL holds 2 hides in OGBOURNE [? Maizey]. His father held them. There is land for 1 plough. There are 30 acres of pasture. It is worth 10s.

LEOFGYTH holds KNOOK. Her husband held it TRE, and it paid geld for 3½ hides. There is land for 2½ ploughs, which are there, with 1 slave, and 4 villans and 4 bordars. There is a mill rendering 15s, and 5 acres of meadow, [and] pasture half a league long and 1 furlong broad. It is worth £3. This Leofgyth made and makes the gold fringe of the king and the queen.

ÆLFHILD holds HARTHAM. Her husband held it TRE, and it paid geld for 1 virgate. There is land for half a plough, which [half-plough] is there, and 1 acre of meadow. It is worth 3s.

SÆGIFU holds 1 virgate of land paying geld. Alwig held it TRE. There is land for 2 oxen. There is 1 acre of meadow. It is worth 3s.

LIDHSMAN holds 3 hides in MELKSHAM. He himself held it TRE, and it paid geld for as much. There is land for 2½ ploughs. In demesne is 1 plough; and 4 villans and 3 bordars and 3 cottars with 1 plough. There are 10 acres of meadow, and 5 acres of pasture and 5 acres of woodland. It is worth 30s.

EALDHILD holds 1 hide and 6 acres of land in HILPERTON. Her husband held them TRE. There is land for 1 plough. There is 1 bordar, and 4 acres of meadow. It is worth 8s.

OSWEARD holds 1 hide paying geld in BRITFORD. There is land for half a plough. His father held it. It is worth 12s6d.

ODA holds LANDFORD. His father held it TRE, and it paid geld for 2 hides. There is land for 2 ploughs. There are 6 bordars, and a mill rendering 20d. There is pasture 1 league long and half a league broad, [and] woodland 4 furlongs long and 4 furlongs broad. It is worth 15s.

ESBERN holds 1 virgate of land in 'FRUSTFIELD' [in Whiteparish]. It is worth 15d.

SWEIN holds STAPLEFORD. His father held it TRE, and it paid geld for 10½ hides. There is land for 10 ploughs. In demesne are 2 ploughs, with 1 slave; and 17 villans and 10 bordars with 8 ploughs. There are 2 mills rendering 30s, and 40 acres of meadow, pasture half a league long and as much broad, [and] woodland 1 league long and half a league broad. It is worth £12.

SÆRIC holds WINTERBOURNE [? Gunner]. Alwine held it TRE, and it paid geld for 1½ hides. There is land for 1 plough, which [plough] is there in demesne, with 1 villan and 4 cotsets. There is part of a mill rendering 22½d, [and] woodland 2 furlongs long and 1 furlong broad. It is worth 30s.

SÆRIC holds LAVERSTOCK. Gestr, his brother, held it TRE, and it paid geld for half a hide. There is land for half a plough, which [half-plough] is there. It is worth 10s.

SÆWEARD holds 3 hides in BROUGHTON GIFFORD. Alweald held them TRE. There is land for 2 ploughs, which are there. It is worth 40s.

RAGNBURH holds a manor which Godric held TRE, and it paid geld for 5 hides. There is land for 3 ploughs, which are there, and 5 slaves, and 6 villans and 1 bordar, and 4 acres of meadow, [and] pasture 5 furlongs long and 2 furlongs broad. It was worth £4; now 100s.

The king's FORESTERS hold 1½ hides in the forest of Grovely. It is worth 30s.

LANG held [?Broad] Blunsdon of King Edward, and it was assessed at 2 hides. Edward the sheriff now holds it in the hand of the king, and there are 3 bordars. It was worth 20s; now 7s.

[Folio 74V: WILTSHIRE]

LXVIII. The land of the King's Servants

HERVEY of WILTON holds 1 hide in EDINGTON of the king. Osweard held it TRE. There is land for 1 plough. There are 3 bordars, and as much meadow and pasture as is sufficient for 1 hide. It is worth 30s.

Hervey holds 1½ hides. Edwin held this TRE. There is land for 1 plough. There are 4 acres of pasture. It was and is worth 30s. This is in NETHERAVON.

RICHARD Sturmy holds 1 hide and 1½ virgates of land in HUISH. There is land for 3 ploughs. In demesne is 1 plough, and 4 slaves; and 3 villans and 4 cotsets with 2 ploughs. There are 4 acres of meadow, and woodland 1 league long and 4 furlongs broad. It was worth 30s; now 60s.

The same Richard holds BURBAGE, and William [holds] of him. Ælfric held it TRE, and it paid geld for 2½ hides. There is land for 2 ploughs, which are there, with 1 slave and 1 villan and 4 cotsets. There are 2 arpents of meadow, and woodland 4 furlongs long and 2 furlongs broad. It is worth 30s.

The same man holds 1 hide in [East or West] GRAFTON. It is worth 20s

The same man holds 1½ hides in HARDING, and Robert [holds] of him. Ælfric held them TRE. There is land for 1 plough, which [plough] is there in demesne. It is worth 10s.

The same man holds 1 hide and 3 virgates of land in SHALBOURNE. Ordweald held them TRE, and it paid geld for as much. There is land for 3 ploughs. In demesne are 2 ploughs, and 4 slaves; and 3 villans and 3 cotsets with 1 plough. There are 3 arpents of meadow, and woodland 4 furlongs long and 2 furlongs broad. It is worth 40s.

ROBERT fitzRalph holds 1 hide and 2½ virgates of land in [East or West] GRAFTON. Wulfmær held them TRE. There is land for 2 ploughs, which are there in demesne, with 1 slave and 5 cotsets, and 2 arpents of woodland. It is worth 30s.

RALPH de Hauville holds 3 hides and 1½ virgates of land in [East or West] GRAFTON. Alwine, and Alweald, and Leofwine and Ceolstan held of him TRE. There is land for 4½ ploughs. In demesne are 3 ploughs, and 3 slaves; and 4 cotsets with 1½ ploughs. There is pasture 2 furlongs long and half a furlong broad. It is worth £7.

The same Ralph holds 1 hide in MARTEN. 2 thegns held it TRE. There is land for 1 plough, which [plough] is there in demesne, with 2 slaves and 2 cotsets. There are 2 arpents of meadow and 2 acres of pasture. It is worth 40s.

The same Ralph holds in BURBAGE 2 hides and 1 virgate of land. Alric held it TRE. There is land for 2 ploughs, which are there with 1 slave, and 2 villans and 1 bordar. [There is] woodland 3 furlongs long and 2 furlongs broad. It is worth 30s.

In WOLFHALL he has 4 hides. Thorold and Alwine held them TRE, and it paid geld for as much. There is land for 3 ploughs, and [there is] no livestock. There is a mill rendering 16s, and 4 villans and 4 cotsets, [and] woodland 2 furlongs long and as much broad. It is worth 30s.

THORBERT holds 1 hide in MARTEN. Leofwine held it TRE, and it paid geld for as much. There is land for 1 plough. There are 2 cotsets, and 6 acres of meadow and 10 acres of pasture. It was and is worth 40s.

CROCH holds NORTH TIDWORTH. 3 thegns held it TRE, and it paid geld for 3 hides. There is land for 1½ ploughs. Of this, Croch holds 3 virgates of land, and a knight of his 2 hides. There is 1 plough, and 2 bordars and 1 villan, and pasture 2 furlongs long and 1 furlong broad. It was worth 20s; now 50s. Edward the sheriff holds 1 virgate of land which belongs to these 3 hides.

HERVEY holds RATFYN. Earl Harold held it TRE, and it paid geld for 2 hides. There is land for 1 plough, which [plough] is there in demesne, and 5 bordars. There are 8 acres of meadow, and pasture 2 furlongs long and 1 furlong broad. It was worth 30s; now 40s.

THEOBALD and Humphrey hold [Lower and Upper] WIDHILL. Robert fitzWimarc held it, and it paid geld for 5 hides. There is land for 5 ploughs. In demesne are 2 ploughs and 2 slaves, and 6 bordars. There are 50 acres of meadow and 60 acres of pasture. It was worth 20s; now 40s.

ANSKETIL holds BUTTERMERE. Godwine held it TRE, and it paid geld for half a virgate of land. There is land for 2 oxen. It is worth 40d.

JOHN the doorkeeper holds ALTON [in Figheldean]. Godric and Bolla held it TRE, and it paid geld for 5 hides. There is land for 4 ploughs. In demesne are 2 ploughs, and 3 slaves; and 4 villans and 2 cottars with half a plough. There are 8 acres of meadow, and pasture 3 furlongs long and 2 furlongs broad. Of this land Turstin holds 1 hide, and Frawine 1 hide. There is 1 bordar and 1 cottar with half a plough, and 2 acres of meadow. [There is] pasture 4 furlongs long and 2 furlongs broad. The whole is worth 100s.

The same man holds half a hide in BARFORD ST

MARTIN. Ælfric held it TRE. There is land for 1 plough. There is 1 bordar with 1 slave, and 8 acres of meadow. It was and is worth 10s.

WILLIAM Scudet holds WESTBURY. Wulfweard held it TRE, and it paid geld for 4½ hides. There is land for 7 ploughs. In demesne are 4 ploughs, and 4 slaves; and 20 bordars with 3 ploughs. There are 20 acres of meadow, and 4 acres of woodland, and 2 mills rendering 25s. It was and is worth £8.

GEOFFREY holds DRAYCOT CERNE. Eadric held it TRE, and it paid geld for 5 hides. There is land for 5 ploughs. In demesne are 2 ploughs, and 4 slaves; and 7 villans and 10 cotsets with 3 ploughs. There is a mill rendering 5s, and 40 acres of meadow, pasture 2 furlongs long and 1 furlong broad, [and] woodland 4 furlongs long and 2 furlongs broad, and 1 burgess pays 12d. It is worth 100s.

WILLIAM fitzAnsculf holds THORNHILL. Strami held it TRE, and it paid geld for 7½ hides. There is land for 5 ploughs. In demesne are 2 ploughs; and 5 villans and 5 bordars and 5 cotsets with 3 ploughs. There is a mill rendering 5s, and 11 acres of meadow, and 10 acres of woodland, and pasture 2 furlongs long and 2 broad. It was and is worth 100s.

WILLIAM holds 2 hides near those above-mentioned 7 hides. One belongs to Bradenstoke, the manor of Edward the sheriff, and the other to Clyffe Pypard, the manor of Gilbert de Breteuil, according to the testimony of the thegns. They are worth 20s.

WIBERT holds [?] CLYFFE PYPARD. This was of the land of Wulfgifu [of] Beslow, and it paid geld TRE for 5 hides and 1 virgate of land. There is land for 3 ploughs. In demesne are 2 ploughs; and 3 villans and 1 bordar and 1 cotset with 1 plough. A house in Cricklade renders 3d. There are 4½ acres of meadow, and 84 acres of pasture and 24 acres of woodland. It was worth 20s; now £3.10s.

ODIN the chamberlain holds SWINDON. Thorbert held it TRE, and it paid geld for 12 hides. There is land for 6 ploughs. In demesne are 2 ploughs, and 2 slaves; and 6 villans and 8 bordars with 3 ploughs. There is a mill rendering 4s, and 30 acres of meadow and 20 acres of pasture. It was worth 60s; now 100s. Of this land Miles Crispin holds 2 hides, and has there 1 plough. Odin claims them.

TURSTIN the chamberlain holds [?] CLYFFE PYPARD. Alwine held it TRE, and it paid geld for 4 hides. There is land for 1½ ploughs. In demesne is 1 plough, with 1 slave and 4 cotsets. There is a mill rendering 5s, and 12 acres of meadow and 8 acres of pasture. It is worth 50s.

AUBREY the chamberlain holds 'SMALLBROOK' [in Warminster]. Mainard held it TRE, and it paid geld for 2 hides. There is land for 3 ploughs. In demesne is 1 plough; and 1 villan and 12 bordars with 2 ploughs. There are 6 acres of meadow and 9 acres of woodland. It was worth 30s; now 40s.

AUBREY the chamberlain holds [? Hill] DEVERILL. 2 thegns held it TRE, and it paid geld for 1 hide. There is land for 1 plough. There are 8 cotsets with 1 plough, and a mill rendering 4s, and 1 acre of meadow. [There is] pasture 4 furlongs long and 2 furlongs broad, [and] woodland 5 furlongs long and 1 furlong broad. It was worth 40s; now 29s.

GUNDUIN the keeper of the granaries holds WHITE-CLIFF. Alwig held it TRE, and it paid geld for 2 hides. There is land for 1 plough, which [plough] is there in demesne, with 1 slave and 1 cotset. There are 2 acres of meadow, and pasture 4 furlongs long and 1 furlong broad, [and] woodland 1 furlong long and another broad. It was worth 20s; now 35s.

WARIN the crossbowman holds CHELWORTH [in Cricklade]. Eadric held it TRE, and it paid geld for 2 hides. There is land for 2 ploughs. In demesne is 1 plough, with 4 bordars. There are 8 acres of meadow and 10 acres of woodland. It was and is worth 40s.

CROCH holds half a hide in BRADENSTOKE. There is land for half a plough. It is worth 10s.

WILLIAM Corniole holds [? Great] WISHFORD. Æfic held it TRE, and it paid geld for 2 hides. There is land for 2 ploughs. There are 3 villans and 3 bordars with 1 plough, and a mill rendering 15s. There are 8 acres of meadow. It was and is worth 40s.

EDWARD holds 1 virgate of land in ALDERBURY. Boda held it TRE. It is worth 40d.

DORSET

IN DORCHESTER IN THE TIME OF KING EDWARD there were 172 houses. These were assessed for every service of the king and paid geld for 10 hides, that is, 1 silver mark for the use of the housecarls excepting the customs which belonged to the night's farm. There were 2 moneyers, each of them paying to the king 1 silver mark and 20s. when the coinage was changed.

Now there are 88 houses, and 100 have been completely destroyed from the time of Hugh the sheriff until now.

IN BRIDPORT IN THE TIME OF KING EDWARD there were 120 houses and they were assessed for every service of the king and paid geld for 5 hides, that is, half a silver mark for the use of the king's housecarls excepting the customs which belonged to the farm of 1 night. There was 1 moneyer paying to the king 1 silver mark and 20s when the coinage was changed.

Now there are 100 houses and 20 are so impoverished that those who dwell in them are not able to pay geld.

IN WAREHAM IN THE TIME OF KING EDWARD there were 143 houses in the king's demesne. This vill was assessed for every service of the king and paid geld for 10 hides, that is, 1 silver mark for the king's housecarls excepting the customs which belonged to the farm of 1 night. There were 2 moneyers each paying 1 silver mark to the king and 20s. when the coinage was changed.

Now there are 70 houses, and 73 have been completely destroyed from the time of Hugh the sheriff.

In the part belonging to Saint-Wandrille there are 45 houses standing and 17 are waste.

In the parts belonging to the other barons there are 20 houses standing and 60 have been destroyed.

IN THE BOROUGH OF SHAFTESBURY TRE there were 104 houses in the king's demesne. This vill was assessed for every service of the king and paid geld for 20 hides, that is, 2 silver marks for the king's housecarls. There were 3 moneyers; each paid 1 silver mark and 20s when the coinage was changed.

Now there are 66 houses, and 38 houses have been destroyed from the time of Hugh the sheriff until now.

In the part belonging to the abbess there were 153 houses TRE. Now there are 111 houses, and 42 have been utterly destroyed.

There the abbess has 151 burgesses and 20 vacant messuages and 1 garden. It is worth 65s.

Here Are Noted the Landholders In Dorset

I KING WILLIAM
II The Bishop of Salisbury
III And the monks of Sherborne
IIII The Bishop of Bayeux
V The Bishop of Coutances
VI The Bishop of Lisieux
VII The Bishop of London
VIII The Abbey of Glastonbury
IX The Abbey of Winchester
X The Abbey of Cranborne
XI The Abbey of Cerne
XII The Abbey of Milton
XIII The Abbey of Abbotsbury
XIIII The Abbey of Horton
XV The Abbey of Athelney
XVI The Abbey of Tavistock
XVII The Abbey of Caen
XVIII The Abbey of Saint-Wandrille
XIX The Abbess of Shaftesbury
XX The Abbess of Wilton
XXI The Abbess of Caen
XXII The Abbess of Montivilliers
XXIII The canons of Coutances
XXIIII Regenbald the priest and other clerks
XXV Count Alan
XXVI The Count of Mortain
XXVII Earl Hugh
XXVIII Roger de Beaumont
XXIX Roger de Courseulles
XXX Robert fitzGerald
XXXI Edward of Salisbury
XXXII Ernulf de Hesdin
XXXIII Turstin fitzRolf
XXXIIII William de Eu
XXXV William de Falaise
XXXVI William de Moyon
XXXVII William de Braose
XXXVIII William d'Ecouis
XXXIX Walter de Douai
XL Waleran the huntsman
XLI Walter de Claville
XLII Baldwin of Exeter

XLIII Berengar Giffard
XLIIII Osbern Giffard
XLV Matthew de Mortagne
XLVI Roger Arundel
XLVII Serlo de Burcy
XLVIII Aiulf the sheriff
XLIX Humphrey the chamberlain
L Hugh de Port
LI Hugh de St Quentin
LII Hugh de Boscherbert
LIII Hugh d'Ivry and other Frenchmen
LIIII The wife of Hugh fitzGrip
LV Isolde
LVI Guthmund and other thegns
LVII William Bellet and other king's sergeants
LVIII The Countess of Boulogne

The land of the King

THE KING holds the island which is called PORTLAND.
King Edward held it in his lifetime.

There the king has 3 ploughs in demesne, and 5 slaves. There
1 villan and 100 bordars, less 10, have 23 ploughs. There are 8
acres of meadow, [and] pasture 8 furlongs long and 8 wide.
This manor with what belongs to it renders £65 blanched.

THE KING holds BURTON BRADSTOCK and BERE
REGIS and Colber and Shipton Gorge and Bradpole and
Chideock [Chideock and North Chideock]. King Edward
held these in demesne. It is not known how many hides are
there, nor did they pay geld TRE. There is land for 55
ploughs. In demesne are 8 ploughs, and 20 slaves; and 41
villans and 30 bordars and 7 coliberts and 74 cottars. Among
them all they have 27 ploughs. There are 8 mills rendering £4
and 35d, and III acres of meadow, pasture 4 leagues long and
as much wide, [and] woodland 3 leagues long and 1 league
wide.

This manor with its appurtenances and customary dues
renders 1 night's farm. The wood of 'HAWCOMBE'
belongs to BURTON BRADSTOCK just as TRE
[when] two parts of it were in the king's farm; the third part
or the third oak belonged to Earl Edwin, which now belongs to
FRAMPTON, a manor of Saint-Etienne of Caen.

THE KING holds WIMBORNE MINSTER and
Shapwick and Moor Crichel and Wimborne St Giles. King
Edward held them in demesne. It is not known how many
hides are there because they did not pay geld TRE. There is
land for 45 ploughs. In demesne are 5 ploughs, and 15 slaves;
and 63 villans and 68 bordars and 7 cottars have 22 ploughs.
There are 8 mills rendering 110s, and 150 acres of meadow,
pasture 6 leagues long and 3 leagues wide, [and] woodland 5
leagues long and 1 league wide.

This manor with its appurtenances renders 1 night's farm.

THE KING holds DORCHESTER and Fordington and
Sutton Poyntz and Gillingham and "Frome". King Edward
held them. It is not known how many hides are there because
they did not pay geld TRE. There is land for 56 ploughs. In

demesne are 7 ploughs, and 20 slaves; and 12 coliberts and
114 villans and 89 bordars having 49 ploughs. There are 12
mills rendering £6.5s, and 160 acres of meadow, pasture 2
leagues long and 1 league wide, [and] woodland 4 leagues
long and 1 league wide.

This manor with its appurtenances renders 1 night's farm.

THE KING holds PIMPERNE and Charlton Marshall.
King Edward held them in demesne. It is not known how
many hides are there because they did not pay geld TRE.
There is land for 20 ploughs. In demesne are 4 ploughs, and 5
slaves; and 1 colibert and 18 villans and 68 bordars with 14
ploughs. There are 2 mills rendering 40s6d, and 94 acres of
meadow, pasture 2 leagues long and 2 leagues wide, [and]
woodland 1 league long and half a league wide. This manor
with its appurtenances renders half of 1 night's farm.

THE KING holds WINFRITH NEWBURGH and [East
or West] Lulworth and "Wintreborne" and Knowlton. King
Edward held them in demesne. It is not known how many
hides are there because they did not pay geld TRE. There is
land for 24 ploughs. In demesne are 4 ploughs, and 8 slaves;
and 30 villans and 30 bordars with 1 cottar having 16
ploughs. There are 4 mills rendering 50s, and 80 acres of
meadow, pasture 3 leagues long and as much wide, [and]
woodland as much in length and width. This manor with its
appurtenances and customary dues renders half of 1 night's
farm. EARL HAROLD HELD THESE FOLLOWING
MANORS TRE

THE KING holds CHILD OKEFORD. TRE it paid geld
for 5 hides. There is land for 6 ploughs. Of this 3 hides are in
demesne, and there are 2 ploughs, with 1 slave; and 6 villans
and 8 bordars with 2 ploughs. There are 2 mills rendering 20s,
and 40 acres of meadow and 2 furlongs of pasture, [and]
woodland 4 furlongs long and 1½ furlongs wide. It was and is
worth £10.

THE KING holds PUDDLETOWN. TRE it paid geld for
half a hide. There is land for 15 ploughs. In demesne are 4
ploughs, and 12 slaves; and 14 villans and 29 cotsets with 10
ploughs. There are 2 mills rendering 32s, and 126 acres of
meadow, pasture 1½ leagues long and 1 wide, [and] woodland
2 furlongs long and as much wide.

To this manor belong 1½ hides in PURBECK [?Hundred]
and half a hide in MAPPOWDER. There is land for 1½
ploughs.

To this manor of Puddletown also belongs the third penny
of the whole shire of DORSET. It renders with all its appurtenances £73.

THE KING holds CHARBOROUGH. TRE it paid geld
for 5 hides. There is land for 3½ ploughs. Of this 3½ hides are in
demesne, and there is 1 plough, and 4 slaves; and 5 villans and
4 bordars with 1½ ploughs. There is woodland 2 furlongs long
and 1 wide. It was and is worth £9.

[Folio 75v: DORSET]

THE KING holds IBBERTON. TRE it paid geld for 5
hides. There is land for 5 ploughs. Of this 2½ hides are in

demesne, and there are 2 ploughs, and 2 slaves; and 10 villans and 7 bordars with 3 ploughs. There are 11 acres of meadow, and pasture 7 furlongs long and 3 furlongs wide, [and] woodland 4 furlongs long and 2 furlongs wide. It was and is worth £10.

THE KING holds FLEET. TRE it paid geld for 5 hides. There is land for 5 ploughs. Of this 3½ hides are in demesne, and there are 2 ploughs, and 2 slaves; and 4 villans and 7 bordars with 3 ploughs. There are 6 furlongs of pasture. It was and is worth £7.

THE KING holds CHALDON HERRING OR EAST CHALDON. TRE it paid geld for 13 hides. There is land for 10 ploughs. Of this 6 hides are in demesne, and there is 1 plough, and 4 slaves; and 16 villans and 15 cottars with 6 ploughs. There is a mill rendering 10s, and 20 acres of meadow, [and] pasture 1 league long and half a league wide. It was and is worth £13.

THE KING holds LODERS. TRE it paid geld for 18 hides. There is land for as many ploughs. Of this 8 hides are in demesne, and there are 3 ploughs, and 9 slaves; and 28 villans and 24 bordars with 6 ploughs. There are 2 mills rendering 23s4d. There are 40 acres of meadow, [and] scrubland 3 furlongs long and 1 furlong wide. It was and is worth £33.

In this manor are 2 hides of thegnland which do not belong there. TRE 2 thegns held them. They are worth 30s.

THE KING holds LITTLE PUDDLE. Earl Harold's mother held it TRE, and it paid geld for 5 hides. There is land for 3 ploughs. Of this 2½ hides are in demesne, and there are 2 ploughs, and 8 slaves; and 2 villans and 3 bordars with half a plough. There are 8 acres of meadow and 10 furlongs of pasture. It was worth 100s; now £7. QUEEN MATILDA HELD THESE LANDS WRITTEN BELOW

THE KING holds FROME ST QUINTIN. TRE it paid geld for 13 hides. There is land for 8 ploughs. Of this 10½ hides are in demesne, and there are 3 ploughs, and 6 slaves; and 10 villans and 3 bordars with 3 ploughs. There is a mill rendering 4s, and 10 acres of meadow, pasture 20 furlongs long and 2 furlongs wide, [and] woodland 8 furlongs long and 6 furlongs wide. It was worth £12; now †£18†.

THE KING holds CRANBORNE. TRE it paid geld for 10 hides. There is land for 10 ploughs. Of this 3½ hides are in demesne, and there are 2 ploughs, and 10 slaves; and 8 villans and 12 bordars and 7 cottars with 8 ploughs. There are 4 mills rendering 18s, and 20 acres of meadow, pasture 2 leagues long and 1 furlong and 1 league wide, [and] woodland 2 leagues long and 2 wide. It was worth £24; now it renders £30.

Of this land 3 thegns hold 3 hides and pay £3 excepting service.

THE KING holds ASHMORE. TRE it paid geld for 8 hides. There is land for 7 ploughs. Of this 4 hides are in demesne, and there are 3 ploughs, and 8 slaves; and 10 villans and 6 bordars with 4 ploughs. There are 10 acres of meadow, pasture 10 furlongs long and 1 furlong wide, [and] woodland 2 leagues long and 1 league wide. It was and is worth £15.

Beorhtric held these 3 MANORS TRE.

THE KING holds EDMONDSHAM. Dodda held it TRE, and it paid geld for 2 hides. There is land for 3 ploughs. Of this 1 hide is in demesne, and there is 1 plough, with 1 slave and 8 bordars. There is a mill rendering 5s, and 2 acres of meadow, pasture 3 furlongs long and 1 furlong wide, [and] woodland 5 furlongs long and 1½ furlongs wide. It was and is worth £3.

THE KING holds HAMPRESTON. Sæwulf held it TRE, and it paid geld for 2 hides and 1 virgate of land. There is land for 2 ploughs. Of this 1 hide is in demesne, and there is 1 plough, and 2 slaves; and 5 villans and 4 bordars with 1 plough. There are 40 acres of meadow, and pasture 1 league long and 5 furlongs wide, and 2 acres of woodland. It renders 50s.

THE KING holds WITCHAMPTON. 2 thegns held it TRE, and it paid geld for 4 hides and 2 parts of 1 hide. There is land for 4 ploughs. Of this 2 hides and 1 virgate of land and 2 parts of 1 virgate are in demesne, and there are 2 ploughs, and 2 slaves; and 5 villans and 15 bordars with 2 ploughs. There is a mill rendering 10s, and 16 acres of meadow, pasture 5 furlongs long and 3 furlongs wide, [and] woodland 6 furlongs long and 2 furlongs wide. It was and is worth 100s.

THE KING holds WIMBORNE MINSTER. Oda held it TRE. There is half a hide, and it has never paid geld. There is land for 2 ploughs. In demesne is 1 virgate, and 1 plough, and 2 slaves; and 4 villans and 7 bordars with 2 ploughs. There are 14 acres of meadow, [and] woodland 1 furlong long and as much wide. It was and is worth £4. This land does not belong to the farm of WIMBORNE MINSTER. HUGH FITZGRIP HELD THESE EIGHT ESTATES OF THE QUEEN WRITTEN BELOW

Alwine held [?] UPWEY TRE, and it paid geld for 1½ hides. There is land for 1 plough. There are 2 bordars, and 5 furlongs of pasture. It is worth 30s.

THE KING holds LANGTON HERRING. Alweard held it TRE, and it paid geld for 1½ hides. There is land for 2 ploughs. There are 2 slaves and 8 bordars and 1 paying 30d. There are 8 acres of meadow, and pasture 5 furlongs long and 3 furlongs wide. It is worth 30s.

THE KING holds TARRANT [?Gunville]. Ælfric held it TRE, and it paid geld for 3½ hides. There is land for 4 ploughs. Of this 2 hides are in demesne, and there is half a plough, and 5 slaves; and 6 villans and 3 bordars with 2 ploughs. There is pasture 7 furlongs long and 2 furlongs wide, [and] woodland 5 furlongs long and 3 furlongs wide. It was worth £4; now 100s. To this manor belongs 1 virgate of land which Ælfric had in pledge for half a gold mark and it has not yet been redeemed.

THE KING holds TARRANT [?Gunville]. Alwine held it TRE, and it paid geld for half a hide. There is land for 1 plough. There are 2 bordars. It is worth 10s.

THE KING holds TARRANT [?Gunville]. 2 thegns held it TRE, and it paid geld for 3 hides and 1 virgate of land. There is land for 3 ploughs. Of this 2 hides and 3 virgates of land are in demesne, and there is 1 plough, and 4 slaves; and 2 villans and 4 bordars [...]. There is a mill rendering 4s, and 13 acres of meadow, [and] pasture 4 furlongs long and as much wide. It was worth £4; now £3.

THE KING holds "SCETRE". Wulfgeat held it TRE, and it paid geld for 5 hides. There is land for 4 ploughs. Of this 3½ hides are in demesne, and there is 1 plough, and 5 slaves; and 6 villans and 3 bordars with 1 plough. There are 4 acres of meadow, pasture 2 furlongs long and 2 wide, [and] woodland 3 furlongs long and 3 wide. It was worth £6; now 100s.

THE KING holds NUTFORD. Ælfric held it TRE, and it paid geld for 2½ hides. There is land for 2 ploughs. There are 2 slaves and 3 cotsets, and 8 acres of meadow, [and] pasture 1 furlong long and 1 wide. It was and is worth 25s.

THE KING holds WATERCOMBE. Ælfric held it TRE, and it paid geld for 1 hide. There is land for 1 plough. There is 1 cotset, and half a mill rendering 4s, [and] pasture 1 league long and 1 furlong [wide]. It renders 15s.

Those who held these lands TRE could go to any lord they wished.

THE KING holds MELCOMBE [Melcombe Bingham and Higher Melcombe]. Earl Harold unlawfully took it from ST MARY of Shaftesbury. TRE it paid geld for 10 hides. There is land for 10 ploughs. Of this 7½ hides and 1 virgate of land are in demesne, and there are 2 ploughs, and 4 slaves; and 9 villans and 20 bordars with 7 ploughs. There are 5 acres of meadow and 1 league of woodland. [There is] pasture 1 league long and 8 furlongs wide, and 12 acres of meadow were leased to Wulfgar White, belonging to the same manor. Now William Bellet holds them. To this manor Gode added 3½ virgates of land which 3 free thegns held TRE, and which paid geld for as much. There is land for 1 plough, which [plough] is there, with 3 villans, and 15 acres of meadow and 5 acres of woodland. These 3½ virgates are in BUCKLAND [Newton] HUNDRED. The whole was and is worth £16. Countess Gode held it.

II. The land of the Bishop of Salisbury

THE BISHOP OF SALISBURY holds CHARMINSTER. TRE it paid geld for 10 hides. There is land for 8 ploughs. In demesne are 2 ploughs, and 4 slaves; and 14 villans and 12 bordars with 6 ploughs. There is a mill rendering 6s, and 15 acres of meadow, pasture 1 league long and 3 furlongs wide, [and] woodland 2 furlongs long and 1 furlong wide.

In Wareham 2 burgesses with 12 acres of land, and in Dorchester 1 burgess with 10 acres of land, belong to this manor. It was and is worth £16. Of this land 1 king's reeve holds 1 hide, and there he has 1 plough, with 3 bordars.

In this manor the bishop has as much land as 2 ploughs can plough. This has never | paid geld. |

The same bishop holds ALTON PANCRAS. TRE it paid geld for 6 hides. Besides this he

has land for 2 ploughs in demesne which has never paid geld, and there he has 2 ploughs, and 4 slaves; and 6 villans and 10 bordars with 1 plough. There is a mill rendering 15s, and 7 acres of meadow, pasture 6 furlongs long and 2 furlongs wide, [and] woodland 2 furlongs long and 1 furlong wide.

Of the same land Edward has 2½ hides and Payne 2½ hides. There are 3 ploughs; and 1 villan and 5 bordars with 1 plough, and pasture 4 furlongs long and 2 wide.

The bishop's demesne is worth £13; [the land] of the men is worth £4.

The same bishop holds UP CERNE. TRE it paid geld for 2½ hides. There is land for 4 ploughs. Of this 1½ hides are in demesne, and there are 3 ploughs, and 6 slaves; and 4 villans and 8 bordars with 1 plough. There is a mill rendering 15s, and 7 acres of meadow, [and] pasture 1 league long and 3 furlongs wide. It is worth £10. Robert holds it of the bishop.

The same bishop holds YETMINSTER. TRE it paid geld for 15 hides. There is land for 20 ploughs. Besides this he has land for 6 ploughs which has never paid geld TRE. There are 4 ploughs in demesne, and 6 slaves; and 25 villans and 25 bordars with 8 ploughs. There is a mill rendering 5s, and 30 acres of meadow, pasture 2 furlongs long and 1 furlong wide, [and] woodland 1 league long and another wide. It was and is worth £22.

Of this same land William holds 6 hides of the bishop, and there he has 4 ploughs, and 4 slaves, and 6 villans and 10 bordars with 2 ploughs, and a mill, and 12 acres of meadow, and woodland 3 furlongs long and 1 furlong wide. It is worth £4. Those who held it TRE could not be separated from the church.

The same bishop holds LYME REGIS. There is land for 1 plough. It has never paid geld. Fishermen hold it and pay 15s. to the monks for the fish. There are 4 acres of meadow. There the bishop has 1 house rendering 6d.

[Folio 76: [DORSET]]

THE KING holds HINTON MARTELL. Countess Gode held it TRE, and it paid geld for 14 hides and 1 virgate of land. There is land for 12 ploughs. Of this 6 hides and 1 virgate of land are in demesne, and there is 1 plough; and 8 villans and 14 bordars have 3 ploughs. There is a mill rendering 10s, and 37 acres of meadow, pasture 5 furlongs long and as much wide, [and] woodland 1 league long and half a league wide. It is worth £13.5s.

Of this same land, a certain priest held 1 hide of thegnland and could go with it where he would. Now it is in the king's demesne.

Of the same land another priest held 2½ hides. The Bishop of Lisieux has 1 of these in demesne, and it is worth 20s. A priest of this manor has the other 1½ hides, and there he has 2 ploughs, with 4 villans and 2 bordars, and a mill rendering 5s, and 11 acres of meadow, and woodland 1 furlong in length and half a furlong in width, and 11 houses in Wimborne Minster. The whole is worth 30s. This priest could go where he would with his land TRE.

Of this same land another priest dwelling in

"TARENTE" holds 1 hide and the third part of 1 hide, and there he has 3 villans and 4 bordars with 1 plough, and [there is] 1 acre of meadow, and pasture 5 furlongs in length and 1 furlong in width. It is worth 30s. Of this same land Wulfric holds 1 virgate of land, and it is worth 2s.

Of this same land 1½ hides and half a virgate of land belong to the church of Wimborne Minster. Bishop Maurice holds them, and there he has 6 bordars and 8 burgesses, and a mill rendering 5s, and 15 acres of meadow, and pasture half a league in length and 4 furlongs in width. It is worth £6.7s6d.

[Folio 76v: [DORSET]]

[Folio 77: DORSET]

The bishop himself holds SHERBORNE. Queen Edith held it, and Bishop Ælfweald before her. TRE it paid geld for 43 hides. There is land for 46 ploughs.

Of this land the bishop holds 12 hides, and there he has 25 villans and 14 bordars with 12 ploughs. There are 130 acres of meadow, 3 acres of which are in Somerset near Milborne Port [Som.]. [There is] pasture 1 league long and 1 wide, [and] woodland 2 leagues long and as much wide.

Of the same land of this manor Otbold holds of the bishop 4 hides; Sinod 5½ hides; Engelbert 5 hides; Waleran 3 hides; Ralph 3 hides; the wife of Hugh fitzGrip 2 hides. In these 22½ hides are 21 ploughs, and 33 villans and 15 bordars and 10 cotsets and 4 slaves. There are 4 mills rendering 18½s.

Of the same land also 6 thegns hold 8½ hides, and there they have 8 ploughs, and 4 slaves and 17 villans and 19 bordars, and 3 mills rendering 30d.

In this manor of SHERBORNE besides the aforesaid land the bishop has in demesne 16 carucates of land. This land has never been hidated, nor has it paid geld. There are in demesne 5 ploughs; and 26 villans and 26 bordars and 8 slaves with 11 ploughs. There is a mill rendering 10s.

Of this quit land Sinod holds of the bishop 1 carucate of land, and Edward another. There are 2 ploughs, and 2 slaves and 8 bordars.

III. In this same SHERBORNE the monks of the same bishop hold 9½ carucates of land which have neither been hidated nor have they ever paid geld. There are in demesne 3½ ploughs, and 4 slaves; and 10 villans and 10 bordars with 5 ploughs, and 3 mills rendering 22s, and 20 acres of meadow, [and] woodland 1 league long and 4 furlongs wide.

Of this land of the monks Lambert holds of them 1 carucate of land, and there he has 1 plough, and a mill rendering 5s.

What the bishop has in demesne in this manor is worth £50; what the monks [have], £6.10s; what the knights of the bishop [have], £27; what the thegns [have], £6.

Moreover, besides these, Sinod holds of the bishop 1 hide in the same vill, and there he has 1 plough, and 2 slaves and 2 bordars. It is worth 12s.

Alweard held this hide of King Edward, but it had belonged to the bishopric previously.

The same bishop holds OBORNE. TRE it paid geld for 5 hides. There is land for 4 ploughs. Of this 2 hides are in demesne, and there is 1 plough, and 2 slaves; and 6 villans and 5 bordars with 3 ploughs. There are 8 acres of meadow and 4 acres of scrubland. It is worth £4.

The same bishop holds THORNFORD. TRE it paid geld for 7 hides. There is land for 6 ploughs. Of this 3 hides are in demesne, and there are 2 ploughs, with 1 slave; and 7 villans and 7 bordars with 4 ploughs. There is a mill rendering 12s6d, and 16 acres of meadow, [and] woodland 10 furlongs long and 1 furlong wide. It is worth 100s.

The same bishop holds BRADFORD ABBAS. TRE it paid geld for 10 hides. There is land for 10 ploughs. Of this 1½ hides are in demesne, and there are 3 ploughs, and 7 slaves; and 8 villans and 7 bordars with 7 ploughs. There is a mill rendering 15s, and 20 acres of meadow and 3 acres of scrubland. It is worth £10.

The same bishop [holds] [Nether and Over] COMPTON. TRE it paid geld for 6 hides and 3 virgates of land. There is land for 8 ploughs. Of this 1 hide and 3 virgates of land are in demesne, and there are 2 ploughs, and 6 slaves; and 13 villans and 10 bordars with 6 ploughs. There is a mill rendering 10s, and 16 acres of meadow, [and] woodland 2 furlongs long and wide. It is worth £6.

The same bishop holds STALBRIDGE. TRE it paid geld for 20 hides. There is land for 16 ploughs. Of this 6 hides are in demesne, and there are 2 ploughs, with 1 slave; and 19 villans and 2 bordars with 11 ploughs. There is a mill rendering 15s, and 25 acres of meadow, pasture 4 furlongs long and 2 furlongs wide, [and] woodland 1 league long and 3 furlongs wide. It is worth £12.

Of the same land Lambert holds 2 hides, and there he has 1 plough, with 6 bordars. It is worth 20s.

Of the same land also Manasses holds 3 virgates, which William the king's son took from the church without the consent of the bishop and the monks. There is 1 plough.

The bishop himself holds STALBRIDGE WESTON. TRE it paid geld for 8 hides. There is land for 6 ploughs. Of this 5 hides are in demesne, and there are 2 ploughs, with 1 slave; and 7 villans and 7 bordars with 3 ploughs. There are 12 acres of meadow, [and] scrubland 4 furlongs long and 1 furlong wide. It is worth £7.

The same bishop holds CORSCOMBE. TRE it paid geld for 10 hides less 1 virgate. There is land for 9 ploughs. Of this 4 hides and 3 virgates are in demesne, and there are 3 ploughs, with 1 slave; and 7 villans and 7 cotsets with 7 ploughs. There is a mill rendering 5s, and 10 acres of meadow, pasture 9 furlongs long and 4 furlongs wide, [and] woodland 1 league long and 4 furlongs wide. It is worth £7.

The same bishop holds STOKE ABBOTT. TRE it paid geld for 6½ hides. There is land for 7 ploughs. Besides this there are 2 carucates of land which have never been hidated, and there in demesne is 1 plough, with 1 slave and 6 cotsets. There 8 villans have 4 ploughs, and 2 thegns hold 2½ hides, and there they have 2 ploughs, and 12 cotsets and 5 slaves, and a mill rendering 5s. [...] [There is] pasture 5 furlongs long and 3 furlongs wide, [and] scrubland 3 furlongs long and 2 furlongs wide. The demesne is worth £6; what the thegns hold, 40s.

THESE NINE MANORS DESCRIBED ARE FOR THE SUSTENANCE OF THE MONKS OF SHERBORNE

The same bishop holds BEAMINSTER. TRE it paid geld for 16 hides and 1 virgate of land. There is land for 20 ploughs. Besides this land he has in demesne 2 carucates of land which have never paid geld, and there he has 2 ploughs, and a mill rendering 20d. Under the bishop are 19 villans and 20 bordars and 5 slaves, and 33 acres of meadow, pasture 1 league long and half a league wide, [and] woodland 1½ leagues long and half a league wide.

Of the same land Algar holds 2 hides of the bishop; Humphrey de Carteret 2 hides less 1 virgate; Sinod 5 hides; Beorhtwine 1½ hides. There are 9 ploughs, and 11 slaves and 19 bordars and 2 villans and 2 cotsets, and 2 mills rendering 28d, and 40 acres of meadow, pasture 4 furlongs long and 2 furlongs wide and a further 32 acres of pasture, [and] woodland 13 furlongs long and 9 furlongs wide.
   The bishop's demesne is worth £16; [the land] of the men, £7.

The same bishop holds NETHERBURY. TRE it paid geld for 20 hides. There is land for 20 ploughs. Besides this he has in demesne 2 carucates of land which have never paid geld, and there are 2 ploughs. There are 18 villans and 22 bordars and 6 slaves with 8 ploughs. There is a mill rendering 10s, and 16 acres of meadow, and 3 furlongs of pasture, [and] woodland 9 furlongs long and 1 furlong wide.

Of the same land Tezelin holds of the bishop 5 hides and 3 virgates of land; William 2 hides; Godfrey 2 hides; Serlo 1½ hides. There are 10 ploughs, and 12 villans and 24 bordars and 5 slaves. There is a mill rendering 5s, and 21 acres of meadow, and woodland †3† furlongs in length and width.
   The bishop's demesne is worth £16; [the land] of the men, £8.10s.
   In BRIDPORT the bishop has half an acre rendering 6d.

The same bishop holds CHARDSTOCK [Devon.], and 2 knights, Walter and William, [hold] of him. TRE it paid geld for 12 hides. There is land for 20 ploughs. Of this 4 hides are in demesne, and there are 4 ploughs, and 6 slaves; and 45 villans and 21 bordars with 17 ploughs. There are 2 mills rendering 20s, and 10 acres of meadow, pasture 3 leagues long and 1½ leagues wide, woodland 2 leagues in both length and width, and in another place scrubland 3 furlongs long and 2 furlongs wide. The whole is worth £16. THESE LANDS WHICH ARE LISTED BELOW THE BISHOP HAS IN EXCHANGE FOR "SCIPELEIA" [?Wilts.]

In "CERNEL" the bishop has 1½ hides and 10 acres of land. Almær held it TRE. There is land for 1 plough. 1 woman has this there, and she holds it of the bishop, with 4 bordars, and 3 acres of meadow. [There is] pasture 2 furlongs long and 1 furlong wide. It is worth 20s.

The same bishop holds 'BARDOLFESTON' [in Puddletown], and the wife of Hugh [holds] of him. Æthelric held it of King Edward, and it paid geld for 4 hides. There is land for 3 ploughs. In demesne is 1 [plough], and 3 bordars, and 34 acres of meadow and 6 furlongs of pasture. It was worth £4; now £3.

The same bishop holds ATHELHAMPTON, and Otbold [holds] of him. Æthelric held it TRE, and it paid geld for 4 hides. There is land for 2 ploughs, which are there, with 1 villan and 5 bordars and 5 slaves. There is a mill rendering 67d, and 20 acres of meadow, and 20 acres of pasture and 5 furlongs of woodland. It was and is worth £3.

The same bishop holds [North and South] BOWOOD, and 3 knights, Godfrey, Osmær and Ælfric, [hold] of him. 3 thegns held it TRE, and it paid geld for 6 hides. There is land for 6 ploughs. There are 5 ploughs, and 3 slaves and 14 villans and 18 bordars. There are 4½ acres of meadow, and 10 acres of pasture and 12 acres of scrubland. The whole is worth 70s.

The same bishop holds BUCKHAM, and Walter [holds] of him. 3 thegns held it TRE, and it paid geld for 3 hides. There is land for 3 ploughs. Of this 2 hides and 1 virgate of land are in demesne, and there is 1 plough, and 2 slaves; and 3 villans and 4 bordars with 2 ploughs. There are 4 acres of meadow and 30 acres of pasture, [and] woodland 4 furlongs long and 2 furlongs wide. It is worth 30s. To this manor belongs 1 hide in WELLWOOD. There is land for 1 plough. There is 1 bordar. It is worth | 40d. | Osmær holds it.

IIII. The land of the Bishop of Bayeux

THE BISHOP OF BAYEUX holds RAMPISHAM, and Wadard [holds] of him. Leofwine held it TRE, and it paid geld for 6 hides. There is land for 6 ploughs. Of this 3 hides are in demesne, and there are 2 ploughs, with 1 slave; and 10 villans and 6 bordars with 3 ploughs. There are 12 acres of meadow, pasture 1½ leagues and 2 furlongs long and 1 league and 1 furlong wide, [and] woodland 1 league and 2 furlongs long and 1 league and 1 furlong wide. It was worth £10; now £6.

With this manor Wadard has held till now 3 virgates of land which 5 thegns held TRE, and they could turn themselves where they would.

V. The land of the Bishop of Coutances

THE BISHOP OF COUTANCES holds "WINT-REBURNE", and Osbern [holds] of him. Thormund held it TRE, and it paid geld for 4½ hides. There is land for 4 ploughs. Of this 3 hides and 1 virgate of land are in demesne, and there are 2 ploughs, and 2 slaves; and 5 villans and 3 bordars with 1 plough. There is a mill rendering 16d, and 8 furlongs of pasture, [and] woodland 3½ furlongs long and 4 acres and 2 [sic] wide. It was worth 60s; now 100s.

The same bishop holds "WINTREBURNE". 2 brothers held it TRE, and it paid geld for 2 hides. There is land for 2 ploughs. In demesne is 1 plough, and 3 slaves, and 6 cottars. There is a mill rendering 15d, and pasture 8 furlongs long and 1 furlong wide. It was worth 30s; now 50s. Osbern holds it of the bishop.

VI. The land of the Bishop of Lisieux

THE BISHOP OF LISIEUX holds TARRANT CRAWFORD. Wulfweard held it TRE, and it paid geld for 5 hides. There is land for 3 ploughs. Of this 3 hides and 1 virgate of land are in demesne, and there are 2 ploughs, and 4 slaves; and 2 villans and 13 bordars with 1 plough. There is a mill rendering 5s, and 9 acres of meadow, pasture 5 furlongs long and 1 furlong wide, [and] woodland 2 furlongs long and 2 wide. It was worth £4; now 100s.

The same bishop holds PRESTON [in Tarrant Rushton]. Edward the clerk held it TRE, and it paid geld for 1 hide. There is land for 1 plough. There is half and acre of meadow, and pasture 4 furlongs long and as much wide. It was and is worth 20s.

The same bishop holds TARRANT KEYNESTON. Herling held it TRE, and it paid geld for 10 hides and the third part of half a hide. There is land for 8 ploughs. Of this 5½ hides are in demesne, and there are 3 ploughs, and 6 slaves; and 12 villans and 14 bordars with 4 ploughs. There are 2 mills rendering 30s and 1,000 eels, and 76 acres of meadow, and pasture 22 furlongs in length and width, [and] woodland 8 furlongs long and as many wide. It was and is worth £13.

The same bishop holds COOMBE KEYNES. Ælfric held it TRE, and it paid geld for 10 hides. There is land for 7 ploughs. Of this 6 hides and 1 virgate of land are in demesne, and there are 2 ploughs, and 4 slaves; and 6 villans and 9 bordars with 5 ploughs. There are 20 acres of meadow, and pasture 8 furlongs in length and as many wide, [and] woodland 6 furlongs long and as much wide. It is worth £7.

VII. [The land] of the Bishop of London

THE BISHOP OF LONDON, Maurice, holds half a hide in 'ODENHAM' [in Wimborne Minster]. Ælfric Dod held it TRE. There is land for half a plough and yet there is 1 plough, and 8 acres of meadow, and woodland 1 furlong long and half a furlong wide. It was and is worth 12s6d.

VIII. The land of St Mary of Glastonbury

THE CHURCH OF ST MARY OF GLASTONBURY holds STURMINSTER NEWTON. TRE it paid geld for 22 hides. There is land for 35 ploughs. Besides this there is land for 14 ploughs in demesne which has never paid geld. There are 21 villans and 18 bordars and 10 cottars and 13 coliberts and 15 slaves. [...] There are 3 mills rendering 40s, and 66 acres of meadow, [and] woodland 2½ leagues long and 1 league wide. It was worth £30; now £25.

Of that land of this manor Waleran holds 6 hides; Roger 1 hide; Ketil 1 hide. These 8 hides can be ploughed by 11 ploughs. They are worth £7.

Of the same land Goscelm the cook holds 4 hides of the king. There he has 2 ploughs, and 2 slaves; and 5 villans and 6 bordars with 4 ploughs, and a mill rendering 3s9d, and 16 acres of meadow. [There is] woodland half a league long and 1 furlong wide. It was and is worth £4.

The church itself holds OKEFORD FITZPAINE, and knights [hold] of it. 4 thegns held it TRE, and it paid geld for 8 hides. There is land for 16 ploughs. In demesne are 4 ploughs, and 10 slaves; and 15 villans and 15 bordars with 7 ploughs. There is a mill rendering 5s, and 21 acres of meadow, pasture 6 furlongs long and 3 furlongs wide, [and] woodland 9 furlongs long and 6 furlongs wide. It was and is worth £12. The wife of Hugh has 4 hides; Alvred 2 hides; Ketil 2 hides.

The church itself holds BUCKLAND NEWTON. TRE it paid geld for 15 hides. There is land for 24 ploughs. Besides this there is in demesne land for 8 ploughs which has never paid geld. There are in demesne 4 ploughs, and 4 slaves; and 22 villans and 22 bordars and 22 cottars with 8 ploughs. There are 20 acres of meadow, pasture 2 leagues long and half a league wide and as much woodland.

Of the same land of this manor the wife of Hugh holds of the abbot 7 hides and 1½ virgates of land, and Warmund 2 hides. There are in demesne 3 ploughs, and 4 slaves; and 3 villans and 7 bordars with 1 plough, and 3 acres of meadow, and woodland 2 furlongs long and 1 furlong wide.

The demesne of the church is worth £20; [the land] of the men, £6.10s.

The church itself holds WOODYATES, and the wife of Hugh [holds] of the abbot. TRE it paid geld for 4 hides. There is land for 4 ploughs. In demesne are 3 hides and 1 virgate of land, and there is 1 plough, and 3 slaves and 2 villans and 5 bordars [...]. There is pasture 16½ furlongs in both length and width, [and] woodland 7 furlongs long and 5½ furlongs wide. It was worth £4; now 40s.

The church itself held PENTRIDGE TRE, and it paid geld for 6 hides. There is land for 6 ploughs. Now the king holds it in demesne, and he has there 1 plough, and 4 slaves; and 6 villans and 6 bordars with 3 ploughs. There is pasture 8 furlongs long and 4 furlongs wide, [and] woodland 1 league long and 3 furlongs wide. It is worth £6. Wulfweard, who held it TRE, could not be separated from the church.

The church itself holds LYME REGIS. TRE it paid geld for 3 hides. There is land for 4 ploughs. Wulfgeat held and holds it of the abbot and there he has 2 ploughs, and 9 villans and 6 bordars, and 4 acres of meadow. [There is] pasture 4 furlongs long and 2 furlongs wide, and 10 acres of woodland. There are 13 salt-workers paying 13s. The whole is worth 60s.

IX. The land of the Abbey of St Peter of Winchester

THE CHURCH OF ST PETER OF WINCHESTER holds PIDDLETRENTHIDE. TRE it paid geld for 30 hides. There is land for 17 ploughs. Of this 15 hides and 2½ virgates of land are in demesne, and there are 5 ploughs, and 20 slaves; and 20 villans and 30 bordars with 8 ploughs. There are 3 mills rendering 60s, and 16 acres of meadow, [and] pasture 2 leagues long and half a league wide.

Of the same land 1 knight and a certain widow hold 3 hides, and there they have 2 ploughs.

The demesne of the church is worth £28; the rest is worth 40s. Almær and Æthelfrith held this manor TRE as 2 manors of King Edward and they could not go with this land to whichever lord they pleased. Afterwards Roger Arundel held it of King William.

X. The land of St Mary of Cranborne

THE CHURCH OF ST MARY OF CRANBORNE holds IN GILLINGHAM. There is land for 2 ploughs. There are 5 bordars, and 7 acres of meadow. It was worth 60s; now 20s. Hugh received this land from the king's farm and gave it to this church.

The church itself holds BOVERIDGE. Beorhtric held it TRE, and it paid geld for 5 hides. There is land for 7 ploughs. Of this 2½ hides are in demesne, and there are 2 ploughs, and 10 slaves; and 5 villans and 9 bordars with 3 ploughs. There is a mill rendering 6s, pasture 9½ furlongs in length and width, heathland 2 leagues long and wide, [and] woodland 1 league long and half a league wide. It was and is worth 100s. Of this land John holds 2½ virgates of land.

The church itself holds MONKTON UP WIMBORNE. TRE it paid geld for 5 hides. There is land for 6 ploughs. Of this 1 hide is in demesne, and there are 2 ploughs, and 7 slaves; and 7 villans and 7 bordars with 4 ploughs. There are 10 acres of meadow, pasture 1 league long and half a league wide, [and] woodland 4 furlongs long and 2 furlongs wide.

Of the same land Ralph holds 1 hide. The whole was and is worth 100s.

The church itself holds 'LEFTISFORD' [in Cranborne], and John [holds] of the abbot. There is half a hide, and 2 ploughs, with 4 villans and 1 bordar, and 4 acres of meadow. It is worth 15s.

The church itself holds half a hide in [?] 'LANGFORD' [in West Parley]. There is land for 1 plough. 2 villans have this [plough] there, and [there is] pasture 2 furlongs in length and width, [and] woodland 1 furlong in length and width. It is worth 5s.

The church itself holds TARRANT MONKTON. TRE it paid geld for 10 hides. There is land for 8 ploughs. Of this 4½ hides are in demesne, and there is 1 plough, and 4 slaves; and 12 villans and 12 bordars with 3 ploughs. There is a mill rendering 5s, and 35 acres of meadow, pasture 1½ leagues in length and width, [and] woodland 10 furlongs in length and width. It was worth £12; now £10.

XI. The land of St Peter of Cerne

THE CHURCH OF ST PETER OF CERNE holds CERNE ABBAS. TRE it paid geld for 22 hides. There is land for 20 ploughs. Of this 3 hides are in demesne, and there are 3 ploughs, and 5 slaves; and 26 villans and 32 bordars with 14 ploughs. There is a mill rendering 20s, and 20 acres of

meadow, pasture 2 leagues long and 8 furlongs wide, [and] woodland 1 league long and 8 furlongs wide.

Of the same land Beorhtwine holds 4 hides of the abbot and there he has 4 ploughs. He held them in the same way TRE and he could not withdraw from the church, nor can he.

The demesne of the church was and is worth £21; [the land] of Beorhtwine, 100s.

The church itself holds LITTLE PUDDLE. William [holds] of the abbot. TRE it paid geld for 3½ hides. There is land for 2 ploughs. In demesne is 1 plough, and 2 slaves; and 1 villan and 3 bordars with half a plough. There are 4 acres of meadow, [and] pasture 2 furlongs long and 1 furlong wide. It was and is worth 50s.

The church itself holds RADIPOLE. TRE it paid geld for 3 hides. There is land for 3 ploughs. Of this, half is in demesne, and there is 1 plough, with 1 slave and 1 villan and 5 bordars; they have 2 ploughs. There are 10 acres of meadow and 5 furlongs of pasture. It is worth 40s.

The church itself holds BLOXWORTH. TRE it paid geld for 5½ hides. There is land for 6 ploughs. Of this 2 hides are in demesne, and there are 2 ploughs, and 3 slaves; and 13 villans and 9 bordars and 7 cottars with 4½ ploughs. There are 8 acres of meadow, and 8 acres of woodland, and pasture 8 furlongs in length and as much wide. It is worth £7.10s.

The church itself holds AFFPUDDLE. TRE it paid geld for 9 hides. There is land for 6 ploughs. Of this 4 hides are in demesne, and there are 2 ploughs, and 3 slaves; and 6 villans and 4 bordars with 4 ploughs. There are 2 mills rendering 15s, and 55 acres of meadow, pasture 12 furlongs long and 6 furlongs wide, [and] woodland 7 furlongs long and as much [...].

[Folio 78: DORSET]

The church itself holds POXWELL. TRE it paid geld for 6 hides. There is land for 7 ploughs. Of this 1½ hides are in demesne, and there are 2 ploughs, with 1 slave; and 4 villans and 8 bordars with 3 ploughs. There are 15 acres of meadow, [and] pasture 8 furlongs and 26 virgates long and 3 furlongs and 14 perches wide.

Of the same land the wife of Hugh holds 3 hides, and there is 1 plough. This land belonged to the demesne farm of the monks, and it is worth 40s.

The church's demesne is worth £7.

The church itself holds WOODSFORD. TRE it paid geld for 2½ hides. There is land for 2 ploughs, which are there, with 4 villans and 3 bordars and 5 slaves. It is worth 30s.

The church itself holds 3 virgates of land in HETHFELTON. They were and are worth 5s.

The church itself holds 1 hide in WORGRET, and it paid geld for as much TRE. There are 2 slaves, and half a mill and 8 acres of meadow. The whole is worth 15s.

The church itself holds LITTLEBREDY. TRE it paid geld for 11 hides. There is land for 6 ploughs. Of this 5 hides are in demesne, and there are 2 ploughs, and 5 slaves; and 6 villans and 5 bordars with 6 ploughs. There are 12 acres of meadow, pasture 1 league long and another wide, [and] woodland 1 league long and 2 furlongs wide. It was and is worth £16.

The church itself holds WINTERBOURNE ABBAS. TRE it paid geld for 10 hides. There is land for 10 ploughs. Of this 5 hides are in demesne, and there are 4 ploughs, and 3 slaves; and 10 villans and 7 cotsets with 3 ploughs. There are 20 acres of meadow, pasture 11 furlongs long and 10 furlongs wide, [and] woodland 2 furlongs long and 1 furlong wide. It was and is worth £16.

The church itself holds LONG BREDY. TRE it paid geld for 9 hides. There is land for 9 ploughs. Of this 3 hides are in demesne, and there are 3 ploughs, and 3 slaves; and 7 villans and 9 cotsets with 5 ploughs; and 1 thegn has 1 hide, and there is 1 plough. There is a mill rendering 6s, and 11 acres of meadow, pasture 1 league long and as much wide, [and] woodland half a league long and 3 furlongs wide. The whole is worth £21.

The church itself holds NETTLECOMBE. TRE it paid geld for 5 hides. There is land [...]. Of this 1½ hides and half a virgate of land are in demesne, and there is 1 plough, and 2 slaves; and 5 villans and 7 cotsets with 2 ploughs. There are 10 acres of meadow, pasture 1 league long and 4 furlongs wide, [and] woodland 1 league long and 8 furlongs wide. It was worth £12; now £8 to the abbot, 55s to the knight.

The church itself holds WEST MILTON. TRE it paid geld for 4 hides. There is land for 4 ploughs. Of this 2 hides are in demesne, and there is 1 plough, and 2 slaves; and 5 villans and 13 bordars with 5 ploughs. There is a mill rendering 65d, and 16 acres of meadow, pasture 1 league long and 4 furlongs wide, [and] woodland 3 furlongs long and 2 furlongs wide. It was worth £10; now £9.

The church itself holds KIMMERIDGE. TRE it paid geld for 5 hides. There is land for 4 ploughs. Of this 3 hides less 1½ virgates are in demesne, and there are 2 ploughs, with 1 slave; and 2 villans and 8 bordars with 2 ploughs. There are 18 acres of meadow, [and] pasture 6 furlongs long and 2 furlongs wide. It was and is worth £8.

The church itself holds RENSCOMBE. TRE it paid geld for 5 hides and 1 virgate of land. There is land for 6 ploughs. Of this 2 hides and 3 virgates of land are in demesne, and there are 2 ploughs, and 3 slaves; and 7 villans and 7 bordars [...]. There are 12 acres of meadow, pasture 1 league long and 10 furlongs wide, [and] unproductive woodland 5 furlongs long and 1 furlong wide. It was and is worth £8.

The church itself holds SYMONDSBURY. TRE it paid geld for 19 hides. There is land for 20 ploughs. Of this 5 hides are in demesne, and there are 2 ploughs, with 1 slave; and 20 villans and 10 bordars with 14 ploughs. There are 14 acres of meadow, pasture 5 furlongs long and 1 furlong, less 10 virgates, wide, [and] woodland half a league long and 1 furlong wide. It was and is worth £21.

XII. The land of the Abbey of Milton

THE CHURCH OF MILTON holds SYDLING ST NICHOLAS. TRE it paid geld for 29 hides. There is land for 20 ploughs. Of these, 6 hides are in demesne, and there are 2 ploughs, and 6 slaves; and 25 villans and 10 bordars with 13 ploughs. There are 2 mills rendering 7s6d, and 12 acres of meadow, pasture 2½ leagues long and 6 furlongs wide, [and] woodland 1 league long and as much wide. It is worth £25.

The church itself holds MILTON ABBAS, and it is the chief [manor] of the abbey. TRE it paid geld for 24 hides. There is land for 18 ploughs. Of this 10 hides less 1 virgate are in demesne, and there are 2 ploughs, and 6 slaves; and 27 villans and 20 bordars with 13 ploughs. There is a mill rendering 15s, and 40 acres of meadow, [and] pasture 3 leagues long and 1 league wide. It is worth £20.

The church itself holds WEST COMPTON. TRE it paid geld for 5 hides. There is land for 3 ploughs. Of this 3 hides are in demesne, and there is 1 plough, and 3 slaves, and 6 villans and 5 bordars. There are 10 acres of meadow, and pasture 1 league long and 2 furlongs wide. It is worth £4.

The church itself holds CATTISTOCK. TRE it paid geld for 10 hides. There is land for 6 ploughs. Of this 3 hides are in demesne, and there is 1 plough, and 6 slaves; and 12 villans and 5 bordars with 5 ploughs. There is a mill rendering 15d, and 18 acres of meadow, pasture 1 league long and 2 furlongs wide, [and] woodland 6 furlongs long and 4 furlongs wide. It is worth £6.

The church itself holds [?] BURLESTON. TRE it paid geld for 3 hides. There is land for 2 ploughs. Of this 2½ hides are in demesne, and there are 2 ploughs, and 4 slaves and 5 bordars. There is a mill rendering 40d, and 16 acres of meadow. It is worth 40s.

The church itself holds CLYFFE. TRE it paid geld for 2 hides. There is land for 2 ploughs. There are 5 villans. It is worth 20s.

The church itself holds OSMINGTON. TRE it paid geld for 10 hides. There is land for 10 ploughs. Of this 4 hides are in demesne, and there are 2 ploughs, and 3 slaves; and 16 villans and 7 bordars with 6 ploughs. There is a mill rendering 5s, and 5 acres of meadow and 1 league of pasture. It is worth £8.

The church itself holds WHITCOMBE. TRE it paid geld for 6 hides. There is land for 6 ploughs. Of this 4 hides are in demesne, and there is 1 plough, and 2 slaves; and 7 villans and 5 bordars with 3 ploughs. There are 5 acres of meadow, and pasture 13 furlongs long and 2 furlongs wide. It is worth £4.10s.

The church itself holds LYSCOMBE. TRE it paid geld for 3 hides. There is land for 2 ploughs. Of this 2 hides are in demesne, and there is 1 plough, and 2 slaves; and 3 villans and 5 bordars with 1 plough. There is pasture 6 furlongs long and 3 furlongs wide. It is worth 40s.

The church itself holds WOOLLAND. TRE it paid geld for 5 hides. There is land for 4 ploughs. Of this 2 hides are in demesne, and there is 1 plough, and 3 slaves; and 5 villans and 5 bordars with 2 ploughs. There are 8 acres of meadow, [and] woodland 7 furlongs long and 4 furlongs wide. It is worth 60s.

The church itself holds WINTERBORNE WHITE-CHURCH. TRE it paid geld for 2 hides and 1 virgate of land. There is land for 1½ ploughs. Of this 1 hide is in demesne, and there is 1 plough, with 1 slave and 2 bordars. There are 6 acres of meadow and 10 acres of pasture. It is worth 25s.

The church itself holds HOLWORTH. TRE it paid geld for 5 hides. There is land for 5 ploughs. Of this 3 hides are in demesne, and there are 2 ploughs, and 4 slaves; and 4 villans and 5 cotsets with 2 ploughs. There are 3 acres of meadow, and pasture 5 furlongs long and as many wide. It is worth £3 and a sester of honey.

The church itself holds OWER. TRE it paid geld for 3 hides. No plough is [thought to be] there, but 13 salt-workers pay 20s.

The church itself holds STOCKLAND [Devon.], and Hervey [holds] of the abbot. TRE it paid geld for 10 hides. There is land for 16 ploughs. Of this 4 hides are in demesne, and there are 2 ploughs, and 4 slaves; and 40 villans have 20 ploughs. There are 3 mills rendering 37d, and 23 acres of meadow, [and] woodland 13 furlongs long and 12 wide. It is worth £9.

This manor always belonged to the monks' demesne for their sustenance and clothing.

The church itself holds [?] LITTLE PUDDLE. TRE it paid geld for 2 hides. There is land for 1 plough, which [plough] is there, and 12 acres of meadow and 2 acres of woodland, [and] pasture 1 league long and 3 furlongs wide. It is worth 10s.

The church itself holds [?] MINTERNE PARVA, and Aiulf [holds] of the abbot. TRE it paid geld for 1½ hides. There is land for 2 ploughs. Of this 1 hide and 1 virgate less 5 acres are in demesne, and there is 1 plough. There are 5 bordars, and a mill rendering 20d, and 13 acres of meadow and 19 acres of pasture. It was worth 10s; now 25s. He who held it TRE could not be separated from the church.

XIII. The land of the Abbey of Abbotsbury

THE CHURCH OF ABBOTSBURY holds ABBOTS-BURY. TRE it paid geld for 21 hides. There is land for 16 ploughs. Of this 8 hides are in demesne, and there are 5 ploughs, and 14 slaves; and 32 villans and 16 bordars with 16 ploughs. There are 2 mills rendering 16s3d, and 36 acres of meadow, pasture 27 furlongs long and 1 league and 3 furlongs wide, [and] 8 furlongs of woodland. It is worth £26.

To this manor belongs 1 hide. TRE it was for the sustenance of the monks. Hugh unlawfully took this and kept it and his wife still retains it by force.

[Folio 78v: DORSET]

The church itself holds TOLPUDDLE. TRE it paid geld for 18 hides. There is land for 12 ploughs, Of this 8 hides are in

demesne, and there are 3 ploughs, and 4 slaves; and 16 villans and 14 cotsets with 5 ploughs. There are 2 mills rendering 20s, and 6 furlongs of meadow and 18 furlongs of pasture. It is worth £12.

The church itself holds HILTON. TRE it paid geld for 18 hides. There is land for 10 ploughs. Of this 9 hides and 1 virgate of land are in demesne, and there are 3 ploughs, and 8 slaves; and 17 villans and 12 bordars with 7 ploughs. There is a mill rendering 20d, and 10 acres of meadow, pasture 1 league long and half a league wide, [and] 3 furlongs of woodland. It is worth £15.

The church itself holds PORTESHAM. TRE it paid geld for 12 hides. There is land for 9 ploughs. Of this 5 hides are in demesne, and there are 4 ploughs, and 12 slaves; and 12 villans and 10 bordars with 5 ploughs. There is a mill rendering 10s, and 24 acres of meadow, [and] pasture 1 league long and 2 furlongs wide. It is worth £12.

To this manor belongs 1 virgate of land which Hugh fitzGrip unlawfully took and his wife still holds by force. This was for the sustenance of the monks TRE.

The church itself holds SHILVINGHAMPTON. TRE it paid geld for 5 virgates of land. There is land for 1 plough, which [plough] is there, with 1 slave and 1 bordar. There are 6 acres of meadow and 3 furlongs of pasture. It is worth 15s6d.

The church itself holds ABBOTT'S WOOTTON. TRE it paid geld for 2½ hides. There is land for 4 ploughs. Of this 1 hide is in demesne, and there are 2 ploughs, and 4 slaves; and 4 villans with 2 ploughs. There are 5 acres of meadow, and 3 furlongs of pasture and 3 furlongs of woodland. It is worth 40s.

The church itself holds half a hide in NORTH POORTON. There is land for 1 plough. 2 villans have this [plough] there, and [there are] 3 furlongs of woodland. It is worth 10s.

The church itself holds ATRIM, and Bolla and a widow [hold] of the abbot. TRE it paid geld for 2 hides. There is land for 2 ploughs, which are there, and 2 slaves and 1 villan and 3 bordars. There are 5 acres of meadow and 3 furlongs of woodland. It is worth 20s.

XIIII. The land of the Abbey of Horton

THE CHURCH OF HORTON holds HORTON. TRE it paid geld for 7 hides. There is land for 7 ploughs. Of this 2 hides are in demesne, and there are 2 ploughs, and 3 slaves; and 4 villans and 10 bordars with 1 plough. There are 2 mills rendering 15s, and 6 acres of meadow, pasture 2 leagues long and wide, [and] woodland 1 league long and half a league wide. It is worth £4. The king holds the better 2 hides of these 7 in the forest of 'Wimborne'.

To this church belongs 1 chapel in WIMBORNE MINSTER and land for 2 houses, and in WAREHAM 1 church and 5 houses rendering 65d, and in Dorchester 1 house.

XV. The land of the Abbey of Athelney

THE CHURCH OF ATHELNEY holds PURSE CAUNDLE. TRE it paid geld for 4 hides and 1½ virgates of land. There is land for 4 ploughs. Of this 4 hides are in demesne, and there is 1 plough; and 2 villans and 14 bordars with 2 ploughs. There are 14 acres of meadow, [and] woodland 3 furlongs long and 2 furlongs wide. Of this land Alvred holds 1½ virgates of land. The whole is worth 67s6d.

XVI. The land of the Abbey of Tavistock

THE CHURCH OF TAVISTOCK holds ASKERSWELL. TRE it paid geld for 3 hides. There is land for 6 ploughs. Of this 1 hide is in demesne, and there are 2 ploughs, and 4 slaves; and 7 villans and 17 bordars with 4 ploughs. There are 2 mills rendering 7s, and 9 acres of meadow, pasture 15 furlongs long and 2 furlongs wide, and 2 rent-paying tenants paying 15s. It is worth £6.

The church itself holds NORTH POORTON. TRE it paid geld for 2 hides. There is land for 2 ploughs. Of this 1 hide is in demesne, and there is 1 plough, and 5 villans and 3 bordars, and 2 acres of meadow and 16 acres of woodland, [and] pasture 8 furlongs long and 2 furlongs wide. It was worth 25s; now 40s.

XVII. The land of Saint-Etienne of Caen

THE CHURCH OF SAINT-ETIENNE OF CAEN holds FRAMPTON. Gytha held it TRE, and it paid geld for 25½ hides. There is land for as many ploughs. Of this 9½ hides are in demesne, and there are 7 ploughs, and 27 slaves; and 24 bordars and 6 cottars with 14 ploughs. There are 2 mills rendering 20s, and 67 acres of meadow, pasture 1½ leagues long and half a league wide, [and] woodland 8 furlongs long and 3 furlongs wide.

To this manor are attached 2 hides which Queen Queen [sic] Matilda gave to Saint-Etienne. The whole was worth, and renders, £40.

The church itself holds BINCOMBE. Earl Harold held it TRE, and it paid geld for 8 hides. There is land for 6 ploughs. Of this 5 hides are in demesne, and there are 2 ploughs, and 3 slaves; and 2 villans and 10 bordars with 1 plough. There are 20 acres of meadow and 2 leagues of pasture. It was worth, and renders, £12.

XVIII. THE CHURCH OF SAINT-WANDRILLE holds the church of Burton Bradstock and of Bridport and of Whitchurch Canonicorum. 4 hides belong to them. They render £7.

The church itself holds 1 church in WAREHAM of the king, to which belongs 1 hide, and there is 1 plough, with 2 bordars. It is worth 70s. with its appurtenances.

XIX. The land of the Abbey of Shaftesbury

THE CHURCH OF ST MARY OF SHAFTESBURY holds SIXPENNY HANDLEY. TRE it paid geld for 20 hides. There is land for 20 ploughs. Of this 4 hides less 1 virgate are in demesne, and there are 4½ ploughs, and 4 slaves; and 30 villans and 15 bordars with 12 ploughs. There are 7 acres of meadow, and woodland 1 league long and half a league wide. It was and is worth £12. Of this land 2 free Englishmen hold 4 hides and they have there 3 ploughs.

The church itself holds HINTON ST MARY. TRE it paid geld for 8 hides. There is land for 9 ploughs. Of this 3 hides are in demesne, and there are 3 ploughs, and 3 slaves; and 16 villans and 9 bordars with 6 ploughs. There is a mill rendering 10s, and 30 acres of meadow, woodland 1 furlong long and as much wide, and the same amount of pasture. It was worth £8; now £10.

The church itself holds [East and West] STOUR. TRE it paid geld for 17 hides. There is land for 10 ploughs. Of this 10 hides less 1½ virgates are in demesne, and there are 2 ploughs; and 25 villans and 18 bordars with 5 ploughs. There are 3 mills rendering 30s, and 10 acres of meadow, [and] pasture 8 furlongs long and 6 furlongs wide. It was worth £8; now £10.

The church itself holds FONTMELL MAGNA. TRE it paid geld for 15 hides. There is land for 16 ploughs. Of this 3 hides and 1 virgate of land are in demesne, and there are 2 ploughs, and 3 slaves; and 45 villans and 20 bordars with 14 ploughs. There are 3 mills rendering 11s7d, and 8 acres of meadow, and 4 furlongs of pasture, and 8 furlongs and 2 acres of woodland. It was worth £10; now £15.

The church itself holds COMPTON ABBAS. TRE it paid geld for 10 hides. There is land for 10 ploughs. Of this 4 hides and 1 virgate of land are in demesne, and there are 2 ploughs. There are 18 villans and 14 bordars with 8 ploughs. There is a mill rendering 50d, and 3 acres of meadow, [and] pasture half a league long and 2 furlongs wide. It is worth £10.

The church itself holds MELBURY ABBAS. TRE it paid geld for 10 hides. There is land for 12 ploughs. Of this 3 hides are in demesne, and there are 6 ploughs; and 27 villans and 20 cotsets with 6 ploughs. There are 4 mills rendering 15s3d, pasture half a league long and 2 furlongs wide, [and] woodland 8 furlongs long and 2 furlongs wide. It was worth £9; now £13.

The church itself holds IWERNE MINSTER. TRE it paid geld for 18 hides. There is land for 16 ploughs. Of this 5½ hides are in demesne, and there are 2 ploughs; and 29 villans and 21 bordars with 14 ploughs. There are 3 mills rendering 17s, and 18 acres of meadow, #[1] [and] pasture 10 furlongs long and 2 furlongs wide. It was worth £10; now £14.

The church itself holds TARRANT HINTON. TRE it paid geld for 10 hides. There is land for 8 ploughs. Of this 2½ hides are in demesne, and there are 2 ploughs, and 3 slaves; and 18 villans and 14 bordars with 6 ploughs. There are 18 acres of meadow, pasture 1 league long and half a league wide, [and] woodland 50 perches long and 40 wide. It was worth £6; now

£10. In IWERNE MINSTER, woodland 1 league long and a half wide.

The church itself holds FIFEHEAD ST QUINTIN. TRE it paid geld for 5 hides. There is land for 4 ploughs. Of this 3½ hides are in demesne, and there are 2 ploughs, and 2 slaves; and 4 villans and 3 bordars with 2 ploughs. There is a mill rendering 5s, and 6 acres of meadow, [and] woodland 4 furlongs long and 3 furlongs wide. It is worth £3. Ketil holds it of the abbess.

The church itself holds KINGSTON [in Corfe Castle]. TRE it paid geld for 16 hides. There is land for 20 ploughs. Of this 3 hides and 3 virgates of land are in demesne, and there are 2 ploughs, and 2 slaves; and 22 villans and 16 bordars with 18 ploughs. There are 12 acres of meadow, [and] pasture 1 league long and as much wide. It was worth £16; now £23.

The church itself holds STOKE WAKE. TRE it paid geld for 5 hides. There is land for 4 ploughs. Of this 3 hides and 1 virgate of land are in demesne, and there are 2 ploughs, and 4 slaves; and 7 villans and 4 bordars with 2 ploughs. There is a mill rendering 12d, and 15 acres of meadow, pasture 6 furlongs long and 1 furlong wide, [and] woodland 12 furlongs long and 4 furlongs wide. It was and it worth £4.

The church itself holds MAPPERTON [in Almer]. TRE it paid geld for 11 hides. There is land for 4 ploughs. Of this 7 hides and 1 virgate of land are in demesne, and there are 2 ploughs, with 1 slave; and 6 villans and 4 bordars with 2 ploughs. There are 7 acres of meadow, [and] both pasture and woodland 11 furlongs long and as much wide. It was worth 30s; now 100s.

The church itself holds CHESELBOURNE. TRE it paid geld for 16 hides. There is land [...]. Of this 2 hides and 3 virgates are in demesne, and there are 3 ploughs and 5 slaves; and 21 villans and 10 bordars with 8 ploughs. There is a mill rendering 15s, and 10 acres of meadow, [and] pasture 1½ leagues long and 1 league wide. It was and is worth £16.

Earl Harold had taken this manor and [East and West] STOUR from ST MARY TRE, but King William caused her to be reseised of them because a writ with the seal of King Edward was found in the church itself ordering that they should be returned to the church with MELCOMBE [Melcombe Bingham and Higher Melcombe], which the king still holds. Earl Harold himself also took from the church [?] PIDDLEHINTON. The Count of Mortain holds it.

The king has 1 hide of the manor of KINGSTON [in Corfe Castle] on which he built 'WAREHAM' Castle and for this he gave to ST MARY the church of GILLINGHAM with its appurtenances, which is worth 40s. Of the same manor William de Braose has 1 virgate of land which the church held TRE.

The church itself holds 1 hide in FARNHAM which Aiulf and the wife of Hugh fitzGrip hold of it.

XX. The land of the Abbey of Wilton

THE CHURCH OF ST MARY OF WILTON holds DIDLINGTON. TRE it paid geld for 6 hides. There is land for 5 ploughs. Of this 2 hides and 3 virgates of land are in demesne, and there are 2 ploughs, and 4 slaves; and 7 villans and 12 bordars with 2 ploughs. There is a mill rendering 12s6d, and 36 acres of meadow, pasture half a league long and as much wide, [and] woodland 1 league long and half a league wide. It is worth £7.

The church itself holds 'PHILIPSTON' [in Wimborne St Giles]. TRE it paid geld for 3½ hides. There is land for 2 ploughs. It is all in demesne except for 1 virgate, and there is 1 plough, and 2 slaves with 1 villan and 6 bordars. There is a mill rendering 7s6d, and 7 acres of meadow, pasture 4 furlongs in both length and width, [and] woodland 3 furlongs long and 1 furlong wide. It was worth 40s; now 30s.

XXI. The land of La Trinite of Caen

THE CHURCH OF LA TRINITE OF CAEN holds TARRANT LAUNCESTON. Beorhtric held it TRE, and it paid geld for 10 hides. There is land for 8 ploughs. Of this 4 hides less 4 acres are in demesne, and there are 2 ploughs, and 14 slaves; and 9 villans and 1 bordar with 4 ploughs. There are 38 acres of meadow, pasture 33 furlongs in both length and width, [and] woodland 15 furlongs in both length and width. It was worth £11; now £14.

XXII. The land of the Canons of the Church of Coutances

THE CANONS of Coutances hold WINTERBORNE STICKLAND. TRE it paid geld for 8 hides. There is land for 9 ploughs. Of this 3 hides and 3 virgates of land are in demesne, and there are 4 ploughs, and 5 slaves; and 12 villans and 20 bordars with 4 ploughs. There is a mill rendering 12s6d, pasture 26 furlongs long and 4 furlongs wide, [and] woodland 5 furlongs long and 4 furlongs wide. It was worth £10; now £15.

XXIII. The land of Sainte-Marie of Montivilliers

THE CHURCH OF SAINTE-MARIE OF VILLIERS holds WADDON. 3 thegns held it TRE, and it paid geld for 6 hides. There is land for 5 ploughs. Of this 5½ hides are in demesne, and there are 3 ploughs, and 4 slaves; and 2 villans and 7 bordars with 2 ploughs. There are 20 acres of meadow and 15 furlongs of pasture. It was and is worth £10.

Hugh fitzGrip gave this land to the same church. Of this the Church of ABBOTSBURY. had 6 acres of crops and 3 church-scots as a customary due TRE, but Hugh never gave this.

XXIIII. The land of the King's Almsmen

BEORHTWEARD the priest holds the church of Dorchester and of BERE REGIS and the tithes. 1 hide and 20 acres of land belong there. They are worth £4.

Bolla the priest has the church of WINFRITH NEWBURGH with 1 virgate of land. There is half a plough. It is worth 10s.

Bolla the priest has the church of PUDDLETOWN and of Chaldon Herring or East Chaldon and of Fleet. To these belong 1½ hides. It renders 57s6d.

REGENBALD the priest holds [?West] PULHAM of the king. He himself held it TRE, and it paid geld for 10 hides. There is land for 10 ploughs. Of this 4 hides are in demesne [...] and 2 slaves; and 9 villans and 5 bordars with 4 ploughs. There is meadow 8 furlongs in both length and width, and woodland 2 leagues in both length and width. It is worth 110s.

WALTER the deacon holds [?] GODMANSTONE of the king, and Bernard [holds] of him. Godwine, a free man, held it TRE, and it paid geld for 3 hides. There is land for 5 ploughs. In demesne are 2 ploughs, and 3 slaves; and 8 villans and 6 bordars with 2 ploughs. There is a mill rendering 10s, and 3 acres of meadow, and pasture 7 furlongs in length and 6 furlongs wide. It was worth 100s; now £6.

XXV. The land of Count Alan

COUNT ALAN holds DEWLISH of the king. Beorhtric held it TRE, and it paid geld for 15 hides. There is land for 15 ploughs. Of this 5 hides are in demesne, and there are 3 ploughs, and 13 slaves; and 19 villans and 6 bordars with 6 ploughs. There are 15 acres of meadow, pasture 23 furlongs in both length and width, [and] woodland 6 furlongs in length and width. It was and is worth £23.

XXVI. The land of the Count of Mortain

THE COUNT OF MORTAIN holds BUCKHORN WESTON, and Hamo [holds] of him. Godric and Brune held it in parage TRE as 2 manors, and it paid geld for 7 hides. There is land for 6 ploughs. In demesne are 2 ploughs, and 5 slaves; and 14 villans and 7 bordars with 1½ ploughs. There are 40 acres of meadow, and woodland half a league long and as much wide. It was worth £4; now £7.

The same count holds 2 hides in [Higher and Lower] NYLAND, and Drogo [holds] of him. There is land for 1 plough. It is waste.

The count himself holds HANFORD. Alweard held it TRE, and it paid geld for 4 hides. There is land for 3 ploughs. In demesne are 2 ploughs, and 4 slaves; and 2 villans and 2 bordars with 1 plough. There are 2 mills rendering 16s, and 35 acres of meadow and 15 acres of woodland, [and] pasture 1 league long and 1 furlong wide. It was and is worth 100s.

The count himself holds CHILD OKEFORD. Alwine held it TRE, and it paid geld for 5 hides. There is land for 6 ploughs.

In demesne are 2 ploughs, with 1 slave; and 6 villans and 17 bordars with 5 ploughs. There is half of 2 mills rendering 10s, and 40 acres of meadow and as much pasture, [and] woodland 2 furlongs and half a league long and 1½ furlongs wide. It was and is worth £7.

The same count holds 1½ hides in FORSTON [Forston, Herrison or Pulston], and a certain woman [holds] of him. Brungar held it TRE. There is land for 1 plough, which [plough] is there, and 3 acres of meadow, [and] pasture 2 furlongs long and 1 furlong wide. It is worth 10s.

The same count holds BHOMPSTON, and William [holds] of him. Alweard held it TRE, and it paid geld for 4 hides. There is land for 3 ploughs. In demesne are 2 [ploughs], and 15 acres of meadow, [and] pasture 4 furlongs long and 2 furlongs wide. It was worth 40s; now 60s.

Robert holds [?] WEST STAFFORD of the count. Beorhtnoth held it TRE, and it paid geld for 3 hides. There is land for 2 ploughs. There is 1 villan and 3 bordars with half a plough. There is a mill [rendering] 4s, and 30 acres of meadow, [and] pasture 1 league long and 3 furlongs wide. It is worth 20s.

Ansgar holds FORSTON [Forston, Herrison or Pulston] of the count. 2 thegns held it freely TRE, and it paid geld for 3 hides. There is land for 2 ploughs, which are there in demesne, and 2 villans and 6 bordars. There is a mill rendering 5s, and 4 acres of meadow, [and] pasture 5 furlongs long and 3 furlongs wide. It was and is worth £3.

Ralph holds FORSTON [Forston, Herrison or Pulston] of the count. 10 thegns held it in parage TRE, and it paid geld for 3 hides. There is land for 2 ploughs. In demesne is 1 [plough]; and 2 villans and 2 bordars and 2 French sergeants with 1 plough. There are 3 acres of meadow, [and] pasture 5 furlongs long and 3 wide. It is worth 40s.

The count himself holds 2½ hides in FORSTON [Forston, Herrison or Pulston]. 6 thegns held it in parage TRE. There is land for 2 ploughs. There are 2 bordars with 1 plough, and a mill rendering 40d, and 3 acres of meadow, [and] pasture 3 furlongs long and 2 furlongs wide. It is worth 50s.

Ansgar holds FORSTON [Forston, Herrison or Pulston] of the count. Beorhtwine held it TRE, and it paid geld for 2 hides. There is land for 1 plough. It is worth 15s.

Bretel holds 1 hide in BHOMPSTON of the count. There is land for 1 plough. There are 5 acres of meadow and 30 acres of pasture. It is worth 12s.

Robert holds 1 hide in "WINTREBURNE" of the count. Alfred held it TRE. There is land for 1 plough, which [plough] is there, with 3 villans. It was and is worth 10s.

Dodman holds WEY [Broadwey or Upwey] of the count. Scirweald and Wulfweard held it in parage TRE, and it paid geld for 2 hides. There is land for 1½ ploughs. In demesne is 1 plough, with 1 slave, and 2 bordars. There are 2 mills rendering 20s, and 12 acres of meadow, [and] pasture 5 furlongs long and 2 wide. It was and is worth 40s.

Amund holds WEY [Broadwey or Upwey] of the count. 9 thegns held it freely TRE, and it paid geld for 4 hides. There is land for 4 ploughs. In demesne is 1 plough; and 3 cotsets with 1 villan have 1 plough. There are 2 mills rendering 32s, and 12 salt-pans, and 9 acres of meadow and 9 furlongs of pasture. It is worth £4.

Robert holds WEY [Broadwey or Upwey] of the count. 8 thegns held it freely TRE, and it paid geld for 4 hides less 1 virgate. There is land for 3 ploughs. There are 2 bordars, and 7 acres of meadow, [and] pasture 7 furlongs long and 4 furlongs wide. It is worth 40s.

Bretel holds HOLWELL of the count. Alwine held it TRE, and it paid geld for 2 hides. There is land for 1½ ploughs. There are 12 acres of meadow, and pasture 7 furlongs long and 1 furlong wide. It is worth 10s.

Robert holds "WINTREBURNE" of the count. Alfred held it TRE, and it paid geld for 3 hides. There is land for 2 ploughs. In demesne is 1 plough, and 2 slaves, and 1 villan and 3 bordars. There are 10 acres of meadow, and pasture 5 furlongs long and 3 furlongs wide. It was worth 40s; now 30s.

Robert holds "WINTREBURNE" of the count. 2 thegns held it in parage TRE, and it paid geld for 2½ hides. There is land for 1½ ploughs, which are there, with 2 villans and 2 slaves. There are 2 acres of meadow, [and] pasture 5 furlongs long and 1 furlong wide. It was and is worth 40s.

The Abbey of Marmoutier holds PIDDLEHINTON of the count. 2 thegns held it TRE as 2 manors, and it paid geld for 10 hides. There is land for 7 ploughs. Of this 5 hides are in demesne, and there are 2 ploughs, and 3 slaves; and 13 villans and 8 bordars with 3 ploughs. There are 33 acres of meadow and 15 furlongs of pasture. It is worth £10.

Humphrey holds "PIDELE" of the count. 1 thegn held it freely TRE, and it paid geld for 1½ hides. There is land for 1 plough. There are 4 bordars with half a plough. There is a mill rendering 40d, and 4 acres of meadow and 5 furlongs of pasture. It was worth 30s; now 40s.

[Folio 79v: DORSET]

Humphrey holds "PIDELE" of the count. 2 thegns held it freely TRE, and it paid geld for 2½ hides. There is land for 2 ploughs. There is 1 plough, with 1 slave and 7 bordars. There is a mill rendering 40d, and 1½ acres of meadow, [and] pasture 3 furlongs long and 1½ furlongs wide. It is worth 50s.

The count himself holds MAPPOWDER. Beorhtric held it TRE, and it paid geld for 3½ virgates and 7 acres of land. There is land for 1 plough. There is 1 slave, and 12 acres of meadow, [and] woodland 2 furlongs long and 1 furlong wide. It was worth 20s; now 12s.

Robert holds MORDEN [Morden and East Morden] of the count. 2 thegns held it TRE, and it paid geld for 1 hide. There is land for 1 plough. There are 2 villans, and a mill rendering 6s3d, and 5 acres of meadow and half a league of pasture. It was worth 20s; now 15s.

The count himself holds SPETISBURY. 3 thegns held it

TRE, and it paid geld for 1½ hides. There is land for half a plough. There is 1 bordar and 1 villan, and 16 acres of meadow and 34 acres of pasture. Of this land the count has 1 virgate of land and 3 acres, and Robert 3 virgates and 6 acres. The whole is worth 18s.

Ansgar holds UP SYDLING of the count. Eadmær held it TRE, and it paid geld for 5 hides. There is land for 4 ploughs. In demesne are 2 ploughs, and 5 slaves; and 4 villans and 4 bordars with 1 plough. There is a mill rendering 5s, and 12 acres of meadow, [and] pasture 1 league long and 4 furlongs wide. It was and is worth £4.

Amund holds SYDLING ST NICHOLAS of the count. Swein held it TRE, and it paid geld for 1 hide. There is land for 1 plough. There is pasture 4 furlongs in length and 2 furlongs wide. It is worth 10s.

Bretel holds LITTLETON of the count. Wulfgeat held it TRE, and it paid geld for 5 hides. There is land for 3 ploughs. In demesne is 1 plough, and 6 bordars and 2 slaves. There is a mill rendering 7s6d, and 20 acres of meadow and 30 acres of pasture. It was worth £4; now 40s.

Bretel holds BLANDFORD [Blandford St Mary and Lower Blandford St Mary] of the count. Alweard held it TRE, and it paid geld for 1½ hides. There is land for 1 plough. It renders 12s. It was worth 20s.

Robert holds "WINTREBURNE" of the count. Godwine held it TRE, and it paid geld for 2 hides. There is land for 1 plough, which [plough] is there, with 3 bordars, and 3 furlongs of pasture. It is worth 20s.

Robert holds "WINTREBURNE" of the count. Alweard held it TRE, and it paid geld for 3 hides. There is land for 2 ploughs. There are 7 cotsets with half a plough, and 2 furlongs of woodland, and pasture 3 furlongs long and 1 furlong wide. It is worth 30s.

Robert himself holds "WINBURNE" of the count. Eskil held it TRE, and it paid geld for 3 hides. There is land for 2 ploughs. In demesne is 1 plough, with 1 slave and 5 bordars. There is a mill rendering 2s, and 2½ acres of meadow, pasture 1 league long and 4 furlongs wide, [and] woodland 6 furlongs long and 2 furlongs wide. It was and is worth £3.

Hubert holds "WINTREBURNE" of the count. 2 thegns held it in parage TRE, and it paid geld for 5 hides. There is land for 3 ploughs. In demesne are 2 ploughs; and 2 villans and 4 bordars with half a plough. There are 20 acres of meadow, pasture 2 furlongs long and 1 wide, [and] woodland 3 furlongs long and 2 furlongs wide. It was worth £4; now 40s.

Mauger holds 2 hides in "WINTREBURNE" of the count. 3 thegns held them TRE. There is land for 1 plough, which [plough] is there, with 1 villan. There are 3 furlongs of pasture. It is worth 20s.

Dodman holds MELBURY OSMOND of the count. 3 thegns held it in parage TRE, and it paid geld for 2½ hides. There is land for 2 ploughs. There is 1 smith and 2 bordars and 2 slaves, and 9 acres of meadow, [and] woodland 8 furlongs long and 2 furlongs wide. It is worth 20s.

Dodman holds "WINTREBURNE" of the count. Alric held it TRE, and it paid geld for 1½ hides. There is land for 1 plough. There is 1 bordar with 1 slave, and 6 acres of meadow and 2½ furlongs of pasture. It is worth 15s.

In the same vill the count has 5½ virgates of land. There is land for 1 plough. There are 13 acres of meadow and 1½ furlongs of pasture. It was and is worth 14s.

Dodman holds [? Langton Long] BLANDFORD of the count. Særæd and his brother held it in parage TRE, and it paid geld for 1½ hides. There is land for half a plough. There are 3 bordars and 2 slaves, and 9 acres of meadow and 5 furlongs of pasture. It is worth 15s.

The count himself has 2 hides in MANNINGTON. There is land for 1 plough. Ælfric held them. There are 3 villans and 2 bordars with 1 plough, pasture 1 league long and half a league wide, [and] woodland half a league in length and width. It is worth 20s.

Hubert holds HEMSWORTH of the count. 1 thegn held it TRE, and it paid geld for 1 hide. There is land for 1½ ploughs, which are there, with 1 slave and 3 bordars. There is pasture 3 furlongs in length and width and as much woodland. It is worth 25s.

Hubert holds WITCHAMPTON of the count. 1 thegn held it TRE, and it paid geld for 2 hides. There is land for 1½ ploughs. There is 1 villan and 3 bordars with 1 plough, and a mill rendering 5s, and 8 acres of meadow, pasture 2 furlongs long and 1 furlong wide, [and] woodland 1 furlong long and 8 acres wide. It was and is worth 25s. Hubert has there 1 virgate of land and the third part of 1 virgate on which he has never paid geld.

Gerard holds 1 hide at MATRAVERS of the count. Wulfgeat held it TRE. There is land for 1 plough, which [plough] is there, with 5 bordars. There is a mill [rendering] 3s, and 4 acres of meadow and 26 acres of pasture. It is worth 25s.

The count himself holds 1 hide at MATRAVERS. Ælfric held it TRE. There is land for 1 plough. There are 6 bordars with 1 slave, and 2 acres of meadow and 30 acres of pasture. It is worth 25s. Alvred holds half this hide of the count.

Ansgar holds 2 hides in KNOWLTON of the count. Æthelmær held it TRE, and it paid geld. There is land for 1 plough, which [plough] is there, with 1 slave and 1 bordar. There is a mill rendering 12s6d. It was and is worth 25s.

The count himself holds GUSSAGE ALL SAINTS. Eadmær held it TRE, and it paid geld for 15 hides. There is land for 12 ploughs. In demesne are 3 ploughs, and 9 slaves; and 8 villans and 18 bordars with 5 ploughs. There is a mill rendering 25s, and 60 acres of meadow, pasture 2 leagues long and 1 league wide and as much woodland. It was and is worth £15.

William holds KNIGHTON [in Durweston] of the count. 5 thegns held it TRE, and it paid geld for 2½ hides. There is land for 2 ploughs, which are there in demesne, and 2 slaves; and 2 villans and 5 bordars with 1 plough. There are 8 acres of meadow, and 7 furlongs of pasture and scrubland 1 furlong in length and width. It is worth 50s.

The count himself holds BRYANSTON. Eadmær held it TRE, and it paid geld for 10 hides. There is land for 6 ploughs. In demesne are 3 ploughs. and 8 slaves; and 7 villans and 9 bordars with 2 ploughs. There is a mill rendering 20s, and 20 acres of meadow, pasture 9 furlongs long and 3 furlongs wide, [and] 5½ furlongs of woodland. It was worth £10; now £11.

The count himself holds BROCKINGTON. Godric held it, and it paid geld for 1½ hides. There is land for 1 plough, which [plough] is there, and 10 acres of meadow and pasture 2 furlongs long and 1 furlong wide. It is worth 20s.

The count himself holds WINTERBORNE [?Muston]. Alfred and 2 others held it TRE, and it paid geld for 1 hide and 1 virgate of land. There is land for 1 plough. There are 3 bordars, and pasture 4 furlongs long and 2 furlongs wide, [and] woodland 2 furlongs long and 2 wide. It is worth 20s. Dodman holds 2 virgates | of this land. |

The count himself holds BESTWALL. Eadmær held it TRE, and it paid geld for 3 hides. There is land for 1½ ploughs. In demesne is 1 plough, and 4 slaves; and 4 cottars and 1 villan with half a plough. There are 20 acres of meadow, and 20 acres of pasture, [and] woodland 2 furlongs long and 1 furlong wide. It was worth 30s; now 60s.

The count himself holds [East or West] LULWORTH. Alsige held it TRE, and it paid geld for 3½ hides. There is land for 2 ploughs. In demesne is 1 plough, with 1 slave and 4 bordars [...]. There are 2 acres of meadow, [and] pasture 3 furlongs long and 1 furlong wide. It was worth 60s; now 30s.

The count himself holds [East or West] LULWORTH. Trawin held it TRE, and it paid geld for 2 hides. There is land for 1½ ploughs. In demesne is 1 plough, and 2 bordars, and 2 acres of meadow, [and] pasture 2 furlongs long and 2 wide. It was worth 40s; now 20s.

The count himself holds EAST STOKE. Eadmær held it TRE, and it paid geld for 2 hides. There is land for 2 ploughs, which are there in demesne, and 2 slaves; and 2 villans and 3 bordars with 1 plough. There is a mill rendering 15s, and 20 acres of meadow, [and] pasture 5 furlongs long and as much wide. It was and is worth 50s.

The count himself has 1 mill in STOBOROUGH with half a hide and 3 bordars. The whole is worth 40s.

Bretel holds CREECH [Creech, East Creech and West Creech] of the count. Scirweald held it TRE, and it paid geld for 2 hides. There is land for 1 plough, which [plough] is there, with 1 villan and 1 bordar, and 4 acres of meadow, [and] pasture 6 furlongs long and as much wide, and 1 house in Wareham. It was worth 20s; now 40s.

Bretel holds TYNEHAM of the count. 6 thegns held it TRE, and it paid geld for 3½ hides. There is land for 3 ploughs. There are 3 villans and 4 bordars, and 2 acres of meadow, [and] pasture 5 furlongs long and 2 furlongs wide. It was and is worth 47s.

Robert holds MORETON of the count. 6 thegns held it TRE, and it paid geld for 3 hides. There is land for 3 ploughs. 6 villans with 3 cotsets have these [ploughs] there. There is a mill rendering 3s, and 30 acres of meadow, [and] pasture 1 league long and as much wide. It was and is worth £4.

Robert holds WARMWELL of the count. Leofwine held it TRE, and it paid geld for 1 hide. There is land for 1 plough. There are 3 bordars, and pasture 9 furlongs in length and 1 in width. It is worth 16s.

The count himself holds UPLODERS. Beorhtric held it TRE, and it paid geld for 1½ hides. There is land for 2 ploughs, which are there, with 1 cotset and 3 slaves, and 15 acres of meadow, and pasture 6 furlongs in length and 1 furlong wide. It was and is worth 47s6d.

William holds HOOKE of the count. Ælfric held it TRE, and it paid geld for 2 hides. There is land for 3 ploughs. In demesne are 2 ploughs, with 1 slave; and 4 villans and 3 bordars with 1 ploughs. There is a mill rendering 6s, and 6 acres of meadow, and 5 furlongs of pasture and 4 furlongs of woodland. It was and is worth 40s.

Bretel and Mauger hold WOOL of the count. 3 thegns held it TRE as 2 manors, and it paid geld for 1 hide and 3 virgates of land. There is land for 1½ ploughs. There are 2 villans and 6 cotsets. There are 4 acres of meadow, [and] pasture 5 furlongs long and 2 furlongs wide. It was and is worth 23s.

Hamo holds STUDLAND of the count. Almær held it TRE, and it paid geld for 3½ hides. There is land for 4 ploughs. In demesne are 2 ploughs, and 6 slaves, and 5 villans and 13 bordars.

[Folio 80: DORSET]

[There is] pasture 1 league long and as much wide, [and] woodland 2 furlongs long and 1 furlong wide. There are 32 salt-pans rendering 40s. The whole is worth £8.

Alvred holds half a hide in ST GABRIEL'S of the count. Eadwig held it TRE. There is land for 6 ploughs. In demesne are 2½ ploughs, and 5 slaves; and 3 villans and 8 bordars with 3½ ploughs. There are 24 acres of meadow, and 2½ leagues of pasture and 2 furlongs of woodland. It was and is worth 60s.

Bretel holds WOOTTON FITZPAINE of the count. Eadmær held it TRE, and it paid geld for 2 hides. There is land for 7 ploughs. In demesne are 2 ploughs, and 2 slaves; and 12 villans and 9 bordars with 5 ploughs. There is a mill rendering 15d, and 6 acres of meadow, and 7 furlongs and 4 acres of pasture, and 1 league and 5 furlongs of woodland. It is worth 100s.

William holds [?] CATHERSTON LEWESTON of the count. Ealdbeorht held it TRE, and it paid geld for 3 hides. There is land for 4 ploughs. In demesne are 2 ploughs, and 5 slaves; and 6 villans and 2 bordars with 2 ploughs. There is a mill rendering 3d, and 8 acres of meadow, pasture 10 furlongs long and 1 furlong wide, [and] woodland 2 furlongs long and 2 wide. It was and is worth 60s.

In the same vill William holds half a hide which belonged to the demesne farm of Cerne [?Abbas] TRE.

The same William holds CORSCOMBE of the count. Leofwine held it TRE, and it paid geld for 1 hide. There is

land for 1½ ploughs, which are there, with 1 villan and 7 bordars and 2 slaves. There is pasture 1 furlong long and half a furlong wide and as much woodland. It was and is worth 15s.

Drogo holds TOLLER WHELME of the count. Almær held it TRE, and it paid geld for 3 hides. There is land for 3 ploughs. In demesne is 1 plough, with 6 bordars. There is half an acre of meadow, [and] pasture 5 furlongs long and 2 furlongs wide. It was worth 20s; now 40s.

Robert holds CHARMOUTH of the count. Algar held it TRE, and it paid geld for 3 hides. There is land for 3 ploughs. In demesne are 2 ploughs, and 3 slaves; and 3 villans with 2 ploughs. There are 16 salt-workers, and 16 acres of meadow, pasture 3 furlongs long and 1 furlong wide, [and] woodland 7 furlongs long and 1 furlong wide. It is worth 60s.

The count himself holds SHILVINGHAMPTON. 3 thegns held it in parage TRE, and it paid geld for 1 hide and 1 virgate. There is land for 1 plough, which [plough] is there, with 1 cotset. There is pasture 2 furlongs long and 2 wide. It was and is worth 15s.

Bretel holds WOOTTON FITZPAINE of the count. Wulfræd held it TRE, and it paid geld for half a hide. There is land for 1 plough. There are 2 villans with half a plough, and 5 acres of meadow and 4 acres of woodland. It is worth 5s.

The count himself holds STOURTON CAUNDLE. Alstan held it TRE, and it paid geld for 1 hide. There is land for 1 plough. There are 3 bordars and 2 slaves, and 6 acres of meadow and 8 acres of scrubland. It was worth 20s; now 10s.

Alwine holds STOURTON CAUNDLE of the count. Ælfgifu held it TRE, and it paid geld for 3 hides. There is land for 3 ploughs, which are there, with 1 slave and 2 villans and 5 bordars. There are 3 acres of meadow and woodland 4 furlongs long and as much wide. It was and is worth 40s. All who had these lands TRE held them freely.

XXVII. The land of Earl Hugh

EARL HUGH holds FIFEHEAD MAGDALEN, and Gilbert [holds] of him. Alnoth held it TRE, and it paid geld for 5 hides. There is land for 5 ploughs. In demesne are 3 ploughs, and 6 slaves; and 4 villans and 4 bordars with 2 ploughs. There are 2 mills rendering 22s6d, and 30 acres of meadow, [and] woodland 4 furlongs long and 2 furlongs wide. It was and is worth £7.

William holds ILSINGTON of the earl. Alnoth held it TRE through Earl Harold, who took it from a certain clerk. Then it paid geld for 2 hides. There is land for 1½ ploughs, which are there, and a mill, and 8 acres of meadow, and 5 furlongs of pasture and 3 furlongs of woodland. It was and is worth 20s.

William holds TINCLETON of the earl. Eadnoth held it TRE, and it paid geld for 2 hides. There is land for 2 ploughs. In demesne is 1 plough, with 1 slave and 1 villan and 4 bordars. There are 5 acres of meadow, and 5 furlongs of pasture and 2 furlongs of woodland. It is worth 20s.

William holds [?] LITTLEMAYNE of the earl. Eadnoth held it TRE, and it paid geld for 3 hides. There is land for 2 ploughs. In demesne is 1 plough, and 3 slaves; and 6 villans and 2 bordars with 1 plough. There are 3 acres of meadow and 140 acres of pasture. In Wareham, 1 house rendering 5d. It was and is worth 40s.

William holds [?] LITTLEMAYNE of the earl. Eadric held it TRE, and it paid geld for 2 hides. There is land for 1½ ploughs. In demesne is 1 plough, with 1 slave, and 4 bordars. There are 3 acres of meadow, [and] pasture 8 furlongs long and 1 furlong wide. It is worth 40s.

William holds CLIFTON MAYBANK of the earl. Eadnoth held it TRE, and it paid geld for 6 hides. There is land for 4 ploughs. In demesne are 3 ploughs; and 3 villans and 14 bordars with 2 ploughs. There is a mill rendering 10s, and 12 acres of meadow, [and] woodland 8 furlongs long and 4 furlongs wide. It was and is worth £6.

To this manor of Clifton Maybank are attached 3 hides in TRILL which 3 thegns held |in parage| TRE, and it paid geld for 3 hides. There is land for 2 ploughs. There are 3 villans and 4 bordars with 1 plough, and a mill rendering 50d, and 8 acres of meadow, [and] woodland 6 furlongs long and 2 furlongs wide. It was and is worth £3.

William holds WARMWELL of the earl. 2 thegns held it TRE, and it paid geld for 2 hides and 1 virgate of land. Besides this there is 1 virgate of land which has never paid geld. There is land for 2 ploughs. In demesne is 1 plough, with 1 slave; and 2 villans and 7 bordars with half a plough. There is a mill rendering 5s, [and] pasture 9 furlongs long and 2 furlongs wide. It is worth 50s.

The same William holds 1 hide and 1 virgate of land in TYNEHAM of the earl. Alnoth held it TRE. There is land for 1 plough. There are 3 villans, and 1 acre of meadow, and 6 acres of woodland and 4 furlongs of pasture. It was and is worth 20s.

The same William holds SOUTH PERROTT of the earl. Alnoth held it TRE, and it paid geld for 5 hides. There is land for 5 ploughs. In demesne are 2 ploughs, and 3 slaves; and 6 villans and 14 bordars with 3 ploughs. There is a mill rendering 2s, and 12 acres of meadow, pasture 14 furlongs long and 3 furlongs wide, [and] woodland 7 furlongs long and 5 furlongs wide. It was worth 100s; now £6. Alnoth bought this manor from Bishop Ælfweald for his lifetime only on the condition that after his death it should be restored to the church.

The same man holds CATSLEY of the earl. Alnoth held it TRE, and it paid geld for 1 hide. There is land for 1½ ploughs. There is 1 villan and 3 bordars with 1 slave, and 12 acres of meadow, pasture 4 furlongs long and as much wide, [and] woodland 1 furlong long and 1 furlong wide. It was worth 5s; now 10s; and this land Alnoth bought in the same way from Bishop Ælfweald on that condition that after his death it should return to the church.

The same William holds BURSTOCK. 1 thegn held it TRE, and Alnoth took it from him TRW, and it paid geld for 3

hides. There is land for 3 ploughs. In demesne are 1½ ploughs, and 3 slaves; and 4 villans and 5 bordars with 1½ ploughs. There are 8 acres of meadow and pasture 2 furlongs long and 2 furlongs wide. It was worth 20s; now 40s.

XXVIII. The land of Roger de Beaumont

ROGER DE BEAUMONT holds STOUR PROVOST of the king. Alfred held it TRE, and it paid geld for 7 hides. There is land for 9 ploughs. Of this 4½ hides are in demesne, and there are 2 ploughs, and 6 slaves; and 12 villans and 12 bordars with 3 ploughs. There is a mill rendering 100d, and 20 acres of meadow, [and] woodland 1½ leagues long and half a league wide. It was worth £9; now £8.

The same Roger holds STURMINSTER MARSHALL. Archbishop Stigand held it TRE, and it paid geld for 30 hides. There is land for 25 ploughs. Of this 12½ hides are in demesne, and there are 3 ploughs, and 8 slaves; and 64 villans and 26 bordars with 15 ploughs. There are 2 mills rendering 28s, and 124 acres of meadow, pasture 3 leagues long and 1½ leagues wide, [and] woodland 1 league long and half a league wide. It was worth £66 when he received it; now £55.

The same Roger holds CREECH [Creech, East Creech and West Creech]. Kolbrand held it TRE, and it paid geld for 2 hides. There is land for 2 ploughs, which are there, with 2 villans and 4 slaves. There are 4 acres of meadow, pasture 6 furlongs long and as much wide, [and] woodland 6 furlongs long and 3 furlongs wide. It was and is worth 40s.

The same Roger holds STEEPLE. Leofwine held it TRE, and it paid geld for 2½ hides. There is land for 3 ploughs. In demesne is 1 plough, and 2 slaves; and 1 villan and 3 bordars with 1 plough. There are 4 acres of meadow, and 3 acres of woodland, [and] pasture 3 furlongs long and 1 furlong wide. It was and is worth 50s.

The same Roger holds CHURCH KNOWLE. 3 thegns held it in parage TRE, and it paid geld for 3½ hides. There is land for 3 ploughs. There is a priest and 1 villan and 1 bordar with 1 plough. There are 3 acres of meadow, and pasture 3 furlongs long and 1 furlong wide. It was and is worth 40s.

The same Roger holds AFFLINGTON. Ælfrun held it TRE, and it paid geld for 2 hides. There is land for 2 ploughs, which are there, with 2 villans and 2 bordars. There are 2½ acres of meadow, and 2 acres of woodland, [and] pasture 4 furlongs long and 1 furlong wide. It was and is worth 50s.

The same Roger holds AFFLINGTON. Leodmær held it TRE, and it paid geld for half a hide and 4 acres of land. There is land for 1 plough. There are 2 villans. It is worth 7s6d.

XXIX. The land of Roger de Courseulles

ROGER de COURSEULLES holds CORTON of the king. 2 thegns held it |in parage| TRE, and it paid geld for 5 hides. There is land for 4 ploughs. In demesne are 2 ploughs, and 12 bordars, and 15 acres of meadow, [and] pasture 1 league long and half a league wide. It was worth £9; now £7. Vitalis holds it of Roger.

XXX. The land of Robert fitzGerald

ROBERT fitzGerald holds CORFE MULLEN of the king. Wada and Æthelric held it TRE, and it paid geld for 10 hides. There is land for 10 ploughs. Of this $7\frac{1}{2}$ hides are in demesne, and there is 1 plough, and 4 slaves; and 12 villans and 12 bordars with 5 ploughs. There is a mill rendering 20s, and 102 acres of meadow, pasture 2 leagues in length and width, [and] woodland 2 leagues long and 1 league wide. It was and is worth £15.

The same Robert holds [?] LEIGH [in Wimborne Minster]. 2 thegns held it TRE, and it paid geld for 1 hide. There is land for 1 plough. 3 villans have this [plough] there. There are 2 acres of meadow, [and] woodland 1 furlong long and 5 virgates wide. It was worth 13s; now 20s.

Robert holds of Robert holds [sic] RANSTON. 2 brothers held it in parage TRE, and it paid geld for 3 hides. There is land for $2\frac{1}{2}$ ploughs. In demesne is 1 plough; and 6 villans and 3 bordars with 1 plough. There is a mill rendering 3s, and 10 acres of meadow, pasture 3 furlongs long and 1 furlong wide, [and] woodland 5 furlongs long and 3 furlongs wide. It was and is worth £3.

Robert himself holds POVINGTON. Almær held it TRE, and it paid geld for $8\frac{1}{2}$ hides. There is land for 6 ploughs. In demesne are 3 ploughs, and 8 slaves; and 4 villans and 5 bordars with 3 ploughs. There is a mill rendering 25s, and 8 acres of meadow and 6 acres of woodland, [and] pasture 6 furlongs long and as much wide. It was and is worth £11. The mill of this manor is claimed for the king's use.

XXXI. The land of Edward of Salisbury

EDWARD OF SALISBURY holds CANFORD MAGNA of the king. Wulfwynn held it TRE, and it paid geld for 25 hides. There is land for 18 ploughs. Of this $11\frac{1}{2}$ hides are in demesne, and there are 3 ploughs, and 9 slaves; and 35 villans and 40 bordars with 15 ploughs. There are 2 mills rendering 15s, and 118 acres of meadow, pasture 2 leagues in both length and width, [and] woodland 1 league long and half a league wide. At Wimborne Minster [are] 3 bordars and 1 house belonging to this manor, and there is 1 league of water-meadow.

The same EDWARD holds KINSON [Hants]. Wulfwynn held it TRE, and it paid geld for 13 hides. There is land for 9 ploughs. Of this 5 hides and 1 virgate of land are in demesne, and there are 2 ploughs, and 7 slaves; and 18 villans and 14 cotsets and 4 cottars with 7 ploughs. There is a mill rendering 5s, and 1 acre of woodland, and 100 acres of meadow less 5, [and] pasture 3 leagues long and 2 leagues less 3 furlongs wide. These 2 manors were worth £50 when he received them; now £70.

XXXII. The land of Ernulf de Hesdin

ERNULF holds KINGTON MAGNA of the king. Eadric held it TRE, and it paid geld for 6 hides #[1]. There is land for 5 ploughs. Of this 4 hides and 3 virgates of land are in demesne, and there are 2 ploughs, and 6 slaves; and 6 villans and 1 bordar with 2 ploughs. There are 20 acres of meadow and 1 furlong of woodland. It was and is worth £4. Urse holds of Ernulf.

Urse holds MELBURY [?Osmond] of Ernulf. 3 thegns held it in parage TRE, and it paid geld for $4\frac{1}{2}$ hides. There is land for 4 ploughs. In demesne are 3 ploughs; with 1 villan and 7 bordars with half a plough. There are 12 acres of meadow, [and] woodland 8 furlongs long and 4 furlongs wide. It was worth 40s; now £4.

Ernulf himself holds [Higher and Lower] KINGCOMBE. 5 thegns held it TRE, and it paid geld for 3 virgates of land and the fourth part of 1 virgate. There is land for 1 plough. 5 villans have this [plough] there, and there are 3 acres of meadow and pasture 8 furlongs long and 2 furlongs wide. It is worth 10s.

Ernulf himself holds MAPPERTON [near Beaminster]. 7 thegns held it TRE, and it paid geld for 3 hides and 3 virgates of land. There is land for $3\frac{1}{2}$ ploughs. In demesne are 2 ploughs; and 3 villans and 10 bordars with $1\frac{1}{2}$ ploughs. There are 8 acres of meadow, pasture 1 league long and 4 furlongs wide, [and] woodland 5 furlongs long and 4 furlongs wide. It was worth 40s; now 60s.

XXXIII. The land of Turstin fitzRolf

TURSTIN fitzRolf holds GILLINGHAM of the king, and Bernard [holds] of him. Alweald held it TRE, and it paid geld for $3\frac{1}{2}$ hides. There is land for 4 ploughs. In demesne are 2 ploughs, and 8 slaves; and 1 villan with 2 ploughs. There are 12 acres of meadow. It was and is worth 60s.

Ranulph holds [Higher and Lower] NYLAND of Turstin. Eadric and Dachelin and Alweard held it in parage TRE, and it paid geld for 2 hides. There is land for 2 ploughs. In demesne is 1 plough, with 1 slave; and 2 villans and 2 bordars with half a plough. There are 8 acres of meadow. It was and is worth 20s.

Bernard holds 1 hide of Turstin in the same vill. Dodda held it TRE. There is 1 plough, and it is worth 10s. It was worth 5s.

Turstin himself holds ALLINGTON. Beorhtwig held it TRE, and it paid geld for 3 hides. There is land for 3 ploughs. In demesne are 2 ploughs; and 12 bordars with half a plough, and 9 rent-paying tenants paying 11s. There is a mill rendering 15s.

The same Ernulf holds NORTH POORTON. 7 thegns held it TRE, and it paid geld for half a hide. There is land for 1 plough. 7 villans have this [plough] there, and [there is] pasture 2 furlongs in length and width. It is worth 12s6d. and 10 acres of meadow and 6 acres of woodland, [and] pasture 7½ furlongs long and 1 furlong wide. It was worth £3; now £4.

Ranulph holds 'STOKE WALLIS' [in Whitchurch Canonicorum] of Turstin. Wulfgeat held it TRE, and it paid geld for 1 hide. There is land for 1 plough, which [plough] is there, with 1 slave and 5 bordars. There are 10 acres of meadow and 16 acres of woodland. It is worth 20s.

Ranulph holds 'STOKE WALLIS' [in Whitchurch Canonicorum] of Turstin. Beorhtwine held it TRE, and it paid geld for 3 virgates of land. There is land for 1 plough, which [plough] is there, and 4 acres of meadow and 16 acres of woodland. It is worth 10s.

XXXIIII. The land of William de Eu

WILLIAM de Eu holds THORNTON of the king, and William [holds] of him. Ælfstan held it TRE, and it paid geld for 2 hides. There is land for 3 ploughs. In demesne are 2 ploughs, and 4 slaves; and 3 villans and 6 bordars with 1 plough. There are 10 acres of meadow, [and] woodland 3 furlongs long and 2 furlongs wide. It was and is worth 40s.

The same William holds BRADFORD PEVERELL of William. Tholf held it TRE, and it paid geld for 17 hides. There is land for 8 ploughs. In demesne are 2 ploughs, and 4 slaves; and 10 villans and 13 bordars with 5 ploughs. There are 2 mills rendering 20s, and 30 acres of meadow, [and] pasture 10 furlongs long and 4 furlongs wide. It was and is worth £12.

William holds 1 hide in "HIWES" of William. There is land for half a plough. It is worth 20s.

Hugh holds MAPPOWDER of William. Wulfweard and Almær held it TRE, and it paid geld for 3 virgates of land. There is land for 1 plough. There are 4 acres of meadow and 5 acres of woodland. It was worth 15s; now 7s.

The same Hugh holds LYTCHETT MATRAVERS of William. Toli held it TRE, and it paid geld for 12 hides. There is land for 8 ploughs. In demesne are 2 ploughs, and 3 slaves; and 16 villans and 11 cotsets with 5 ploughs. There are 40 acres of meadow, 11 furlongs of pasture, woodland half a league in both length and width, [and] water-meadow 1 league in length and width. In Wareham, 2 gardens and 1 bordar. It was worth £9; now £10.

William holds BLANDFORD [Blandford St Mary and Lower Blandford St Mary] of William. Tholf held it TRE, and it paid geld for 3½ hides. There is land for 2 ploughs. In demesne is 1 plough, and 3 slaves and 3 bordars. There are 12 acres of meadow and 56 acres of pasture. It was and is worth 40s.

In the vill itself William holds half a hide which Tholf had in pledge and it was redeemed, [but] which Ralph de Limesy took with that other land. Afterwards the king did not have geld from it. It is worth 3s.

Hugh holds WOOLCOMBE [in Melbury Bubb] of William. Beorhtmær held it TRE, and it paid geld for 5 hides. There is land for 4 ploughs. In demesne is 1 plough, and 2 slaves; and 2 villans and 8 bordars with 1 plough, and 3 cottars. There are 8 acres of meadow, pasture 8 furlongs long and 2 furlongs wide, [and] woodland 2 furlongs long and 1 furlong wide. It was and is worth 50s.

William holds SWYRE of William. Tholf held it TRE, and it paid geld for 9 hides. There is land for 7 ploughs. In demesne are 3 ploughs, and 5 slaves; and 5 villans and 11 bordars with 3 ploughs. There is a mill rendering 16s, and 30 acres of meadow, [and] pasture 7 furlongs long and 1 furlong wide. It was and is worth £9.

In that vill William holds a certain piece of land which never paid geld TRE but was in the demesne, and in the farm, of the king. A certain king's reeve had let this [land] to Toxus the priest; later he took it back into the king's hand. Toxus was given seizin of it again by King Edward, as he says, and thus he held it in the life and at the death of King Edward and in the time of Harold. Formerly it was for grazing, now it is for sowing.

William himself holds WYNFORD EAGLE in demesne. Ælfstan held it TRE, and it paid geld for 14 hides. There is land for 11 ploughs. In demesne are 6 hides of this land, and there are 3 ploughs, and 2 slaves; and 13 villans and 18 bordars with 8 ploughs. There is a mill rendering 10s, and 8 acres of meadow, pasture 2 leagues long and 1 league and 4 furlongs wide, [and] woodland 5 furlongs long and 3 furlongs wide. It was worth £12; now £19.

Ansfrid holds FROME VAUCHURCH of William. Ælfstan held it TRE, and it paid geld for 6 hides. There is land for 3 ploughs. In demesne is 1 plough, and 2 slaves; and 4 villans and 8 bordars with 2 ploughs. There is a mill rendering 10s, and 10 acres of meadow, pasture 6 furlongs long and 2 furlongs wide, [and] woodland 2 furlongs long and 1 furlong wide. It was worth £3; now £4.

William himself holds LONG CRICHEL. Ælfstan held it TRE, and it paid geld for 12 hides. There is land for 9 ploughs. Of this 7½ hides are in demesne, and there are 2 ploughs, and 8 slaves and 3 female slaves; and 13 villans and 7 bordars with 4 ploughs. There are 2 acres of meadow, pasture 20 furlongs long and 3 furlongs wide, [and] woodland 3 furlongs long and 2 furlongs wide. It was worth £10; now £15.

William holds "TERENTE" of William. Tholf held it TRE, and it paid geld for 3½ hides. There is land for 3 ploughs. In demesne is 1 plough, and 2 slaves; and 4 villans and 2 bordars with 1½ ploughs. There is pasture 5 furlongs long and 3 furlongs wide, [and] woodland 8 furlongs long and 4 furlongs wide. It was worth 20s; now £4.

Ansfrid holds ELWORTH of William. Ælfstan held it TRE, and it paid geld for 2 hides. There is land for 2 ploughs. In demesne is 1 plough, with 1 slave; and 3 villans

[Folio 81: [DORSET]]

XLII. The land of Baldwin

BALDWIN the sheriff holds IWERNE COURTNEY COUNTRY OR SHROTON of the king. Sæweard held it TRE, and it paid geld for 8 hides. There is land for 8 ploughs. In demesne are 3 ploughs, and 4 slaves; and 4 villans and 9 bordars with 4 ploughs. There are 2 mills rendering 12s, and 30 acres of meadow, [and] pasture 9 furlongs long and 6 furlongs wide. It was worth £15; now £10.

[Folio 81v: [DORSET]]

The same William de MOYON holds [?East] PULHAM. 21 thegns held it TRE, and it paid geld for 10 hides. There is land for 8 ploughs. In demesne are 3 ploughs, and 6 slaves; and 14 villans and 25 bordars with 7 ploughs. There is a mill rendering 40d, and 32 acres of meadow, [and] woodland 2 leagues long and 8 furlong wide. It was worth £10; now £8.

The same William holds HAMMOON. Godric held it TRE, and it paid geld for 5 hides. There is land for 4 ploughs. In demesne are 2 ploughs, and 4 slaves; and 6 villans and 5 bordars with 2 ploughs. There is a mill rendering 7s6d, and 50 acres of meadow, and pasture 3 furlongs in length and 1 furlong in width. It was worth 60s; now 100s.

The same William holds CHILFROME. 3 thegns held it in parage TRE, and it paid geld for 10 hides. There is land for 6 ploughs. In demesne are 4 ploughs, and 4 slaves, and 4 villans and 7 bordars. There is a mill rendering 3s, and 20 acres of meadow and 9 acres of woodland, [and] pasture 17 furlongs long and as much wide. It was and is worth £6. 2 men hold it of William.

Robert holds CRUXTON of William. Æthelweard held it TRE, and it paid geld for 4 hides. There is land for 2 ploughs, which are there in demesne, with 1 slave and 9 bordars. There is a mill rendering 10s, and 7 acres of meadow, and pasture 7 furlongs in length and 5 furlongs in width. It was worth £4; now £3.

Ranulph holds WEST CHELBOROUGH of William. Godric held it TRE, and it paid geld for 3 hides. There is land for 3 ploughs. In demesne is 1 plough; and 1 villan and 5 bordars with 1 plough. There are 10 acres of meadow, and pasture 7 furlongs in length and 3 furlongs in width. It was and is worth £3. The son of Odo the chamberlain claims these 3 hides.

Geoffrey holds STEPLETON of William. Godwine held it TRE, and it paid geld for 3 hides. There is land for 3 ploughs. In demesne are 2 ploughs, and 2 slaves; and 6 villans and 6 bordars with 1 plough. There are 8 furlongs of woodland, and pasture 10 furlongs in length and 3 furlongs in width. It was and is worth £4.

The same William holds LITTLEWINDSOR, and Alweard held it TRE, and it paid geld for 4 hides. There is land for 3 ploughs. In demesne are 2 ploughs, and 2 slaves; and 9 villans and 2 bordars with 1 plough. There are 30 acres of meadow, and pasture 7 furlongs in length and 6 furlongs in width, and

woodland 6 furlongs in length and 3 furlongs in width. It is worth 60s.

The same William holds MAPPERTON [near Beaminster]. Almær held it TRE, and it paid geld for 5 hides and 1 virgate of land. There is land for 4 ploughs. In demesne are 3 ploughs, and 6 slaves; and 6 villans and 7 bordars with 1 plough. There is a mill rendering 5s, and 8 acres of meadow and 12 acres of pasture, [and] woodland 6 furlongs in length and 4 furlongs wide. It is worth 70s.

[Folio 82: DORSET]

and 4 bordars with 1 plough. There are 8 acres of meadow and pasture 3 furlongs long and 2 furlongs wide. It was and is worth 60s.

Hugh holds STOCK GAYLARD of William. Tholf held it TRE, and it paid geld for 1 hide. There is land for 3 ploughs. 8 villans and 3 bordars have these [ploughs] there. There are 8 acres of meadow, [and] woodland 10 furlongs long and 4 furlongs wide. It was and is worth 50s. Tholf held this land in pledge of the land of Sherborne TRE.

The same Hugh holds STOURTON CAUNDLE of William. Tholf held it TRE, and it paid geld for 3½ hides. There is land for 3 ploughs. In demesne is 1 plough, and 2 slaves; and 4 villans and 2 bordars with 1 plough. There are 7 acres of meadow, and pasture 4 furlongs long and 1 furlong wide. It was and is worth 60s.

XXXV. The land of William de Falaise

WILLIAM de FALAISE holds SILTON of the king. Wulfweard White held it TRE, and it paid geld for 8 hides. There is land for 8 ploughs. In demesne are 2 ploughs, and 6 slaves; and 8 villans and 10 bordars with 4 ploughs. There are 3 mills rendering 5s, and 20 acres of meadow, [and] woodland 1 league long and half a league wide. It was worth £11; now £6.

With this land the same William holds 1 hide and half a virgate of land. There is land for 1 plough. 3 villans have this [plough] there, and it is worth 10s. Wulfweard held this land in pledge TRE from a certain reeve of his.

With the land itself the same William also holds 1 hide. There is land for 1 plough, which [plough] is there in demesne, and it is worth 20s. Wulfweard bought this hide [...] from the Bishop of Exeter TRE but it did not belong to the manor itself.

With the same aforesaid land the same William holds 3 hides in MILTON ON STOUR, and Roger [holds] of him. Wihtnoth held them TRE. There is land for 1½ ploughs. There are 5 bordars with 1 plough, and a mill rendering 15d, and 8 acres of meadow and woodland 8 furlongs long and 2 furlongs wide. It was and is worth 20s.

XXXVI. The land of William de Moyon

WILLIAM de MOYON holds TODBER of the king, and Geoffrey [holds] of him. Godric held it TRE, and it paid geld for 2 hides. There is land for 2 ploughs, which are there in demesne, and a mill rendering 10s, and 12 acres of meadow, [and] woodland half a league long and 1 furlong wide. It was worth £3; now |£4.|

William himself holds SPETISBURY. Æthelweard and Godric held it as 2 manors TRE, and it paid geld for 7 hides and 1 virgate of land and 6 acres. There is land for 6 ploughs. In demesne are 4 ploughs, and 6 slaves; and 10 villans and 12 bordars with 3 ploughs. There is a mill rendering 12s6d, and 50 acres of meadow, and pasture 5½ furlongs long and 2 furlongs wide, and in another place, above the water, pasture 2½ furlongs long and 1½ furlongs wide. It was worth 100s; now £7.10s.

Ogis holds WINTERBORNE HOUGHTON of William. Alweard held it TRE, and it paid geld for 2½ hides. There is land for 2 ploughs. There are 4 bordars with 1 slave, and 2 acres of meadow, and 6 furlongs of pasture and 13 acres of scrubland. It was worth 50s; now 40s.

XXXVII. The land of William de Braose

WILLIAM de BRAOSE holds GLANVILLES WOOTTON of the king, and Ralph [holds] of him. The Abbot of Milton held it TRE, and it paid geld for 3 hides. There is land for 3 ploughs. In demesne is 1 plough, with 1 slave; and 3 villans and 4 bordars with 1 plough. There are 16 acres of meadow and 4 acres of pasture, [and] woodland 5 furlongs long and 4 furlongs wide. It was and is worth £3.

Ralph holds 2 hides in the same vill of William. There is land for 1 plough. There are 2 slaves and 1 bordar, and 6 acres of meadow and 2 acres of pasture, [and] woodland 5 furlongs long and 2 furlongs wide. It was worth 30s; now 40s.

William himself holds half a hide in EAST HOLTON. There is land for half a plough. It is worth 10s.

David holds ASH of William. 2 thegns held it TRE, and it paid geld for 2½ hides. There is land for 2 ploughs. There is 1 plough, and 3 slaves and 3 cotsets, and 10 acres of meadow and pasture 10 furlongs long and 2 furlongs wide. It was and is worth 40s.

Richard holds KIMMERIDGE of William. Beorhtweald held it TRE, and it paid geld for 1½ hides. There is land for 1½ ploughs. In demesne is 1 plough, and 4 acres of meadow, and pasture 2 furlongs long and 1 furlong wide. It was and is worth 30s.

The same William holds half a hide in CREECH [Creech, East Creech and West Creech], and Walter [holds] of him. Eadnoth held it TRE. There are 2 bordars, and 3 acres of meadow and 3 acres of woodland, and pasture 7 furlongs long and 4 furlongs wide. It was and is worth 10s.

The same Walter holds 3½ virgates of land in AFFLINGTON of William. There is land for 1 plough, which [plough] is there, with 2 bordars, and 1 acre of meadow and 1 furlong of pasture. It was and is worth 16s.

The same Walter holds 1 hide in CHURCH KNOWLE of William. There is land for 1 plough. There is 1 acre of

meadow, [and] pasture 4 furlongs long and 2 furlongs wide. It is worth 20s. Sæwine held it TRE.

The same Walter holds 1½ hides in RUSHTON. There is land for 1 plough, which [plough] is there, and a mill, and 20 acres of meadow and 1 league of pasture. It renders 30s and 4 sesters of honey.

The same Walter holds 1 hide and 3 virgates of land in WORGRET of William. Beorhtwine held them TRE. There is land for 1½ ploughs. There is 1 villan and 1 bordar, and half a mill rendering 10s. The whole renders 28s.

Robert holds 2 hides of land in HETHFELTON of William. Æthelflæd held them TRE. There is land for 1 plough. There are 2 villans with 1 slave, and 10 acres of meadow, [and] pasture 1 league long and half a league wide. It was and is worth 10s.

Richard holds half a hide in SMEDMORE of William. There is land for half a plough. There is 1 villan and 1 slave, and 3 acres of meadow. It is worth 10s.

Richard holds of William 7 hides less half a virgate in PURBECK HUNDRED. 12 thegns held them TRE and could go where they would. There is land for 7 ploughs. In demesne are 2 ploughs, and 4 villans and 2 bordars. It is worth 70s.

The wife of Hugh fitzGrip holds part of this land, and there she has 2 ploughs, and 4 villans and 5 bordars, and pasture 1 league long and 6 furlongs wide. It is worth £4.

Humphrey holds WOOLGARSTON [Woolgarston and Little Woolgarston] of William. 5 thegns held it TRE, and it paid geld for 2 hides less 4 acres. There is land for 2 ploughs. There are 6 villans, and 8 acres of meadow, [and] pasture half a league long and 1 furlong wide. It is worth 40s.

XXXVIII. The land of William d'Ecouis

WILLIAM d'ECOUIS holds WEST KNIGHTON [near Dorchester] of the king. 2 thegns held it |in parage| TRE, and it paid geld for 6 hides. There is land for 4 ploughs. In demesne are 2 ploughs, and 6 slaves; and 5 villans and 5 bordars [...] with 1 plough. There are 2 mills rendering 12s, and 20 acres of meadow, and 20 acres of woodland and 250 acres of pasture. It was worth £7; now £6.

The same William holds the land of 5 thegns in STOURTON CAUNDLE as 1 manor. There are 5 hides. Of this 3½ hides are in demesne, and there are 2 ploughs, and 3 slaves; and 7 villans and 3 bordars with 3 ploughs. There is a mill rendering 9s, and 10 acres of meadow and 12 acres of woodland, [and] pasture 6 furlongs long and 3 furlongs wide. It was and is worth £7.

XXXIX. The land of Walter de Douai

WALTER de DOUAI holds "WINTREBURNE" of the king, and Walcher [holds] of him. Alweard and Alwine held it TRE as 2 manors, and it paid geld for 6 hides. There is land for 4 ploughs. In demesne are 2 ploughs, and 3 slaves; and 5 villans and 3 bordars with half a plough. There are 12 acres of meadow and 8 acres of woodland, [and] pasture 4 furlongs long and 3 furlongs wide. It was worth £6; now £4.

Wimer holds STOURTON CAUNDLE of Walter. Alsige held it TRE, and it paid geld for 3 hides. There is land for 3 ploughs. In demesne are 2 ploughs, and 2 slaves; and 2 villans and 2 bordars with 1 plough. There is a mill rendering 3s, and 10 acres of meadow and 3 acres of scrubland. It was and is worth 40s.

XL. The land of Waleran

WALERAN holds MANSTON of the king, and Warenger [holds] of him. Trasmund held it TRE, and it paid geld for 5 hides. There is land for 8 ploughs. In demesne are 2 ploughs, and 3 slaves; and 10 villans and 6 bordars with 2 ploughs. There are 2 mills rendering 12s, and 25 acres of meadow, [and] woodland 4 furlongs long and 1 furlong wide. It was worth £6; now 100s.

Ranulph holds KINGTON [Little Kington and Kington Magna] of Waleran. Leofgeat held it TRE, and it paid geld for 3 hides. There is land for 2 ploughs. In demesne are 1½ ploughs, and 2 slaves; and 7 bordars with half a plough. There are 8 acres of meadow and 4 acres of pasture. It was worth 30s; now 50s.

Waleran himself holds SUTTON WALDRON. Guthmund held it TRE, and it paid geld for 8 hides. There is land for 6 ploughs. In demesne is 1 plough, with 1 slave; and 11 villans and 12 bordars with 3 ploughs. There is a mill rendering 7s6d, and 6 acres of meadow and 40 acres of woodland. It was and is worth £8.

Urse holds WINTERBORNE [Muston or Tomson] of Waleran. Alfred held it TRE, and it paid geld for 4 hides. There is land for 2 ploughs, which are there, and 3 slaves and 6 villans, and 80 acres of pasture and 35 acres of meadow, [and] woodland 9 furlongs long and 1 furlong wide. It was and is worth 40s.

Azelin holds DUDSBURY of Waleran. Godwine held it TRE, and it paid geld for 1 hide. There is land for 1 plough, which [plough] is there, with 4 bordars, and 7 acres of meadow and 6 acres of woodland, [and] pasture half a league long and 5 furlongs wide. It was and is worth 20s.

Ingelrann holds FIFEHEAD NEVILLE of Waleran. 1 thegn held it TRE, and it paid geld for 5 hides. There is land for 3 ploughs, which are there, with 4 bordars and 4 slaves. There is a mill rendering 40d, and 15 acres of meadow, [and] woodland 8 furlongs long and 4 furlongs wide. It is worth £4.

Beulf holds CHURCH KNOWLE of Waleran. 1 thegn held it TRE and he was free with this land, and it paid geld for 1 hide. There is land for 1 plough, which [plough] is there, with 3 slaves. There is pasture 2 furlongs long and as much wide, [and] woodland 1 furlong long and as much wide. It is worth 25s. Waleran held this of Earl William. Now, as he says, he holds of the king.

Waleran himself holds MAIDEN NEWTON. Alward held it TRE, and it paid geld for 6 hides. There is land for 7 ploughs. Of this half a hide is in demesne, and there are 2 ploughs, and 5 slaves; and 7 villans and 14 bordars with 5 ploughs. There are 2 mills rendering 20s, and 18 acres of meadow, pasture 14 furlongs long and 7 furlongs wide, [and] woodland 5 furlongs long and 3 furlongs wide. It is worth £10.

Ogier holds TOLLER [Fratrum and Porcorum] of Waleran. Alweard held it TRE, and it paid geld for 5 hides. There is land for 4 ploughs. In demesne are 2 ploughs, and 3 slaves; and 4 villans and 5 bordars with 1 plough. There is a mill rendering 30d, and 15 acres of meadow, pasture 12 furlongs long and 10 furlongs wide, [and] woodland 5 furlongs long and 3 furlongs wide. It was worth £3; now £4.

XLI. The land of Walter de Claville

WALTER de CLAVILLE holds AFFLINGTON of the king. Beorhtric held it TRE, and it paid geld for 2 hides and 1½ virgates of land. There is land for 2½ ploughs. In demesne are 2 ploughs, with 1 slave, and 1 bordar. There are 3 acres of meadow and 4 acres of scrubland, [and] pasture 4 furlongs in length and width. It was and is worth 50s.

The same man holds CHURCH KNOWLE. Beorn held it TRE, and it paid geld for 2 hides. There is land for 2 ploughs. In demesne is 1 plough, with 1 slave, and 2 villans, and 3 acres of meadow and pasture 3 furlongs long and as much in width. It was and is worth 40s.

The same man holds EAST HOLME. Ealdræd held it TRE, and it paid geld for 2 hides and 1 virgate of land. There is land for 2 ploughs. In demesne is 1 plough, and 4 villans, and 10 acres of meadow and 3 acres of woodland, [and] pasture 6 furlongs long and as much wide. It was and is worth 20s.

The same man holds COOMBE KEYNES. 2 thegns held it TRE, and it paid geld for 3 hides. There is land for 3 ploughs. In demesne is 1 plough, and 2 slaves; and 2 villans and 1 bordar with 1½ ploughs. There are 2 acres of meadow, and pasture 2 furlongs in both length and width. It was and is worth 60s.

The same man holds MORDEN [Morden and East Morden]. 4 thegns held it TRE, and it paid geld for 3 hides and 2½ virgates of land. There is land for 3 ploughs. In demesne is 1 plough; and 8 villans and 10 bordars with 2 ploughs. There is a mill rendering 45d, and 14 acres of meadow, and pasture 3 leagues in both length and width, [and] woodland 2 furlongs long and 1 furlong wide. It was and is worth 60s.

XLIII. The land of Berengar Giffard

BERENGAR Giffard holds BREDY of the king. Hearding held it TRE, and it paid geld for 4 hides. There is land for 3 ploughs. In demesne is 1 plough, and 2 slaves; and 5 villans and 7 bordars with 2 ploughs. There is a mill rendering 10s, and 15 acres of meadow and pasture 3 furlongs long and 1 wide. It is [sic] worth £3; now £4.

XLIIII. The land of Osbern Giffard

OSBERN Giffard holds [?] GOLD HILL of the king. Trasmund held it TRE, and it paid geld for 2 hides. There is land for 1 plough, which [plough] is there in demesne, and 20 acres of meadow and 20 acres of pasture. It was and is worth 20s.

XLV. The land of Alvred d'Epaignes

ALVRED d'Epaignes holds TURNWORTH of the king. Alwig held it TRE, and it paid geld for 5 hides. There is land for 6 ploughs. In demesne are 4 ploughs, and 4 slaves; and 7 villans and 8 bordars with 1 plough. There are 10 acres of meadow, and pasture 10 furlongs in length and 4 in width, [and] woodland 10 furlongs in length and 5 furlongs in width. It was worth £6; now £10.

XLVI. The land of Matthew de Mortagne

MATTHEW de Mortagne holds MILBORNE ST ANDREW of the king. John held it TRE, and it paid geld for 5 hides. There is land for 4 ploughs. In demesne are 2 ploughs, with 1 villan and 9 bordars. There is a mill rendering 32d, and 5 acres of meadow and 6 furlongs of scrubland. It was and is worth 100s.

The same man holds OWERMOIGNE. John held it TRE, and it paid geld for 10 hides less 1 virgate. There is land for 8 ploughs. In demesne are 2 ploughs, and 6 slaves; and 7 villans and 6 cotsets with 5 ploughs. There is a mill rendering 6s, and 20 acres of meadow, and pasture 1 league in length and half a league in width. It was and is worth £10.

XLVII. The land of Roger Arundel

ROGER Arundel holds WYNDHAM of the king. Alnoth held it TRE, and it paid geld for 2 hides. There is land for 1½ ploughs. In demesne is 1 plough, with 1 slave. There are 3 acres of meadow and 4 furlongs of woodland. It was worth 30s; now 20s. Roger holds it of Roger.

Roger himself holds MELBURY BUBB. Beorhtnoth held it TRE, and it paid geld for 6 hides. There is land for 4 ploughs. There are 4 villans and 7 bordars and 4 slaves with 2 ploughs. There is a mill rendering 5s, and 12 acres of meadow and 3 furlongs of pasture, [and] woodland 10 furlongs long and 4 furlongs wide. It was and is worth £4.

He himself holds [?East] CHELBOROUGH. Æthelfrith held it TRE, and it paid geld for 5 hides. There is land for 2 ploughs. In demesne is 1 plough, with 1 slave; and 4 villans and 7 bordars with 1 plough. There are 2 acres of meadow, and pasture 1 furlong in length and 1 wide, [and] woodland 4 furlongs long and 2 furlongs wide. It was and is worth 50s.

Robert holds LANGTON LONG BLANDFORD of Roger. Æthelfrith held it TRE, and it paid geld for 5 hides. There is land for 4 ploughs. In demesne are 3 ploughs, and 4 slaves, and 1 villan and 2 bordars. There are 4 acres of

meadow, and pasture 6 furlongs in length and 4 furlongs in width. It was and is worth £4.

Roger himself holds [East and West] BEXINGTON. Æthelmær held it TRE, and it paid geld for 9½ hides. There is land for 7 ploughs. In demesne are 2 ploughs, and 8 slaves; and 4 villans and 8 bordars with 4 ploughs. There are 4 acres of meadow and pasture 8 furlongs in length and 1 furlong in width. It was worth £4; now £6.

Hugh holds POWERSTOCK of Roger. Æthelmær held it TRE, and it paid geld for 6 hides. There is land for 6 ploughs. In demesne are 2½ ploughs, and 5 slaves; and 5 villans and 9 bordars with 2½ ploughs. There are 2 mills rendering 3s, and 13 acres of meadow, and pasture 15 furlongs in length and 2 furlongs wide, [and] woodland 11 furlongs long and 2½ furlongs wide. It was worth £4; now £6.

Ralph holds WRAXALL of Roger. Æthelmær held it TRE, and it paid geld for 10 hides. There is land for 8 ploughs. In demesne are 2 ploughs, and 4 slaves; and 4 villans and 14 bordars with 2 ploughs. There is a mill rendering 5s, and 5 acres of meadow and pasture 8 furlongs in length and 2½ furlongs wide, [and] woodland 8 furlongs long and 3 furlongs wide. It is worth 100s.

In the same vill William holds 3 hides of Roger. There are 4 villans. They are worth £3; and 1 knight holds 1 hide of Roger and it is worth 20s. All together the manor is worth £9; when he received it, £4.

Guy holds NORTH POORTON of Roger. Alwine and Ulf held it for 2 hides. There is land for 2 ploughs. In demesne is 1 plough, and there are 9 cotsets, and 6 acres of meadow and pasture 15 furlongs in length and width. It is worth 30s.

Roger himself holds WORTH MATRAVERS. Æthelfrith held it of the king TRE, and it paid geld for 16½ hides and half a virgate. There is land for 12 ploughs. In demesne are 4 ploughs, and 8 slaves; and 9 villans and 8 bordars with 9 ploughs. There is a mill rendering 7s6d, and 15 acres of meadow, and pasture 15 furlongs in length and in width, and woodland 7 furlongs in both length and width. It was and is worth £16.7s6d.

Robert holds ROLLINGTON of Roger. 9 thegns held it |freely| TRE, and it paid geld for 2½ hides |less| the fourth part of a virgate. There is land for 2 ploughs. There are 4 acres of meadow, and pasture 14 furlongs in length and width. It is worth 40s.

Roger himself holds WORTH MATRAVERS. Alweard held it TRE, and it paid geld for half a hide. There is land for half a plough, which [plough] is there, with 3 bordars. It is worth 10s.

Roger himself holds HERSTON. Her held it TRE, and it paid geld for 2 parts of 1 hide. There is land for half a plough. There are 2½ acres of meadow. It is worth 10s.

XLVIII. The land of Serlo de Burcy

SERLO de BURCY holds WATERSTON [Waterston and Lower Waterston] of the king. Earl Harold held it TRE, and it paid geld for 10 hides. There is land for 6 ploughs. In demesne are 3 ploughs, and 2 slaves; and 12 villans and 12 bordars with 3 ploughs. There is a mill rendering 3s, and 40 acres of meadow and 20 acres of woodland, [and] pasture 16 furlongs long and 4 furlongs wide. It is worth £10.

The same man holds WHITECLIFF. Alweard held it TRE, and it paid geld for 3 hides. There is land for 3 ploughs. In demesne are 2 ploughs, and 2 slaves, and 1 villan and 4 bordars. There is pasture 6 furlongs in length and 1 furlong wide. It was and is worth 60s.

XLIX. The land of Aiulf the Chamberlain

AIULF holds BLANDFORD [Blandford St Mary and Lower Blandford St Mary] of the king. Leofgifu held it TRE, and it paid geld for 1½ hides. There is land for 1 plough, which [plough] is there, and 5 acres of meadow and 2 furlongs of pasture. It was worth 20s; now 30s.

Aiulf himself holds MORDEN [Morden and East Morden]. Æthelgifu held it TRE, and it paid geld for 3 virgates of land. There is land for half a plough. It is worth 25s.

Aiulf himself holds HAMPRESTON. 5 thegns held it TRE, and it paid geld for 6 hides. There is land for 5 ploughs. In demesne are 2 ploughs, and 4 slaves; and 6 bordars with 2 ploughs. There are 20 acres of meadow, and pasture 8 furlongs in length and as many in width, and woodland 4 furlongs in length and as many wide. It is worth £4.10s.

Aiulf himself holds "SELAVESTUNE". 2 thegns held it TRE, and it paid geld for 4 hides and 1½ virgates of land. There is land for 3 ploughs. In demesne are 2 ploughs, and 2 slaves; and 5 villans and 1 bordar with 1 plough. There are 30 acres of meadow and pasture 4 furlongs in length and 2 furlongs wide. It is worth 60s.

The same Aiulf holds TARRANT [?Gunville]. 1 free man held it TRE, and it paid geld for 2 hides. There is land for 1 plough, which [plough] is there in demesne, and 3 villans and 2 bordars and 2 slaves. There are 15 acres of pasture and as much woodland. It is worth 40s.

The same Aiulf holds STUBHAMPTON. 1 thegn held it TRE, and it paid geld for 1 hide. There is land for 1 plough, which [plough] is there in demesne, and 4 slaves. There are 3 acres of pasture and 25 acres of woodland. It is worth 20s.

[Folio 83: DORSET]

The same Aiulf holds CHETTLE, and Airard [holds] of him. 1 thegn held it TRE, and it paid geld for 1 hide. There is land for 1 plough. There are 12 acres of pasture. It is worth 20s.

Aiulf himself holds FARNHAM. 1 thegn held it TRE, and it paid geld for 2 hides, which are there, with 1 slave and 4 bordars. There are 10 acres of pasture, and woodland 3 furlongs in length and 2 furlongs in width. It is worth 30s.

The same Aiulf holds BRADLE. 1 thegn held it TRE, and it paid geld for 4 hides. There is land for 2 ploughs. In demesne is 1 plough, and 2 slaves; and 1 villan and 2 bordars with half a plough. There is 1 acre of meadow, and 2 furlongs of pasture and woodland 1 furlong in length and a half in width. It was worth 40s; now 60s.

Aiulf himself holds TATTON. 1 thegn held it TRE of the Church of Cerne and could not be separated from it, and it paid geld for 3 hides. There is land for 2 ploughs. In demesne is 1 plough, and 2 slaves, and 1 villan and 4 bordars. There are 4 acres of meadow and pasture 2 furlongs in length and width. It is worth 75s.

Aiulf himself holds DURWESTON. 3 thegns held it TRE, and it paid geld for 4½ hides. There is land for 3 ploughs. In demesne are 2 ploughs, and 4 slaves; and 8 bordars with 1 plough. There are 2 acres of vineyard, and 15 acres of meadow, and pasture 3 furlongs in length and 1 furlong wide, [and] woodland 3 furlongs long and 2 furlongs wide. It was worth 60s; now £4.10s.

Aiulf himself holds WOOTTON FITZPAINE. Beorhtsige, a thegn of King Edward, held it, and it paid geld for 12 hides. There is land for 16 ploughs. Of this 4 carucates are in demesne, and there are 3 ploughs, and 6 slaves; and 12 villans and 11 bordars with 9 ploughs. There are 2 mills rendering 15s, and 2 arpents of vineyard, and 50 acres of meadow and 40 acres of woodland, and pasture 1 league in length and as much wide. It was worth £10; now £20.

The same Aiulf holds 1 virgate of land at BRIDGE. Sæweard held it TRE. There is land for 2 oxen. There are 2 fishermen, and it renders 5s.

The same Aiulf holds 1½ hides in HETHFELTON. Azur held them TRE. There is land for 1 plough, which [plough] is there in demesne, and 5 acres of meadow and 6 furlongs of pasture. It was worth 5s; now 40s.

Aiulf himself holds [East or West] LULWORTH. Alfred the sheriff held it TRE, and it paid geld for 8 hides and 3 virgates of land. There is land for 5 ploughs. In demesne are 3 ploughs, and 3 slaves; and 3 villans and 8 bordars with 1 plough. There are 12 acres of meadow and pasture 6 furlongs in length and as much in width. It was worth £6; now £7.

Aiulf himself holds LONG CRICHEL. Ælfric held it TRE, and it paid geld for 4 hides. There is land for 3 ploughs. In demesne are 2 ploughs, and 2 slaves; and 4 villans and 7 bordars with half a plough. There is a mill rendering 20s, and 18 acres of meadow, and pasture 4 furlongs in length and 1 furlong wide, and woodland 6 furlongs long and 1 furlong wide. It was worth 40s; now 65s8d. Aiulf holds this of the king as long as he shall be sheriff.

The same Aiulf holds FARNHAM, which 1 thegn held TRE of the Church of Shaftesbury and he could not be separated from it, and it paid geld for half a hide. There is land for half a plough. There is pasture 1 furlong in length and a half in width, and woodland 2 furlongs in length and 1 furlong wide. It is worth 30s.

L. The land of Humphrey the Chamberlain

HUMPHREY holds EDMONDSHAM of the king. Dodda held it TRE, and it paid geld for $1\frac{1}{2}$ hides. There is land for $1\frac{1}{2}$ ploughs, which are there, with 1 villan and 2 bordars and 1 slave. There is a mill rendering 30d, and $1\frac{1}{2}$ acres of meadow, and pasture 8 furlongs in length and 3 furlongs in width, and woodland 5 furlongs in length and $1\frac{1}{2}$ furlongs in width. It is worth 60s.

The same man holds EDMONDSHAM. TRE it paid geld for $1\frac{1}{2}$ hides. There is land for 1 plough, which [plough] is there. It is worth 30s. Eadgifu holds it of Humphrey.

The same man holds HEMSWORTH. 1 free thegn held it TRE, and it paid geld for 1 hide. There is land for 1 plough, which [plough] is there, with 1 slave and 3 bordars. There are 2 acres of meadow and pasture 2 furlongs in length and 1 furlong in width. It was and is worth 60s.

The same man holds STOURPAINE. Alweard held it TRE, and it paid geld for 6 hides and $1\frac{1}{2}$ virgates of land. There is land for 4 ploughs. In demesne are 2 ploughs, with 1 slave; and 6 villans and 7 bordars with $1\frac{1}{2}$ ploughs. There is a mill rendering 3s, and 40 acres of meadow and pasture 8 furlongs in length and 5 furlongs in width. It was worth £4.10s; now £6.

LII. The land of Hugh de St Quentin

HUGH de St Quentin holds STINSFORD of the king. 6 thegns held it | in parage | TRE, and it paid geld for 2 hides and $2\frac{1}{2}$ virgates of land. There is land for 2 ploughs, which are there in demesne, and 3 villans and 2 bordars with 1 plough. There are 23 acres of meadow and pasture 2 furlongs in length and 1 furlong wide. It was and is worth 15s.

The same man holds RINGSTEAD. 4 thegns held it in parage TRE, and it paid geld for 2 hides. There is land for 2 ploughs, which are there in demesne, with 6 bordars. There is half a mill rendering 4s, and 8 acres of meadow and pasture 12 furlongs in length and 1 furlong in width. It was worth 30s; now 40s.

LIII.

HUGH de Boscherbert holds "CERNEL" of the king. Godwine held it TRE, and it paid geld for $1\frac{1}{2}$ hides. There is land for 1 plough, which [plough] is there in demesne, with 1 slave and 2 villans and 1 bordar. There are $1\frac{1}{2}$ acres of meadow and pasture 3 furlongs in length and 1 in width. It was worth 25s; now 20s.

The same man holds 1 manor which 2 brothers held TRE, and it paid geld for 10 hides. There is land for 8 ploughs. In demesne are 2 ploughs, and 6 slaves; and 9 villans and 5 bordars with 4 ploughs. There is a mill rendering 30d, and 12 acres of meadow, [and] pasture 1 league and 4 furlongs long and 1 league in width. It was worth £6; now £9.

LIIII.

HUGH d'IVRY holds of the king land in 3 places which 11 thegns held, and it paid geld for 5 hides. There is land for 4 ploughs. Ralph holds it of Hugh. In demesne is half a plough; and 12 villans with $3\frac{1}{2}$ ploughs. There are 10 acres of meadow and pasture 5 furlongs in length and 2 furlongs in width. It was and is worth £4.

HUGH Sylvester holds half a hide of land in STOURTON CAUNDLE. Leofrun held it TRE. There is land for half a plough. There are 2 bordars, and 2 acres of meadow. Nothing more.

FULCHRED holds "WAIA" of the king. Hwætmann held it TRE, and it paid geld for $2\frac{1}{2}$ hides. [There is] land for 2 ploughs. In demesne is 1 plough, and 3 slaves, and 1 villan and 2 bordars. There are 4 acres of meadow and 7 furlongs of pasture. It is worth 30s.

FULCHRED holds MOORBATH. Alric held it TRE, and it paid geld for 2 hides. There is land for 2 ploughs, which are there in demesne, and 3 villans and 4 bordars. There are 11 acres of meadow, and 50 acres of pasture and 30 acres of woodland. It is worth 30s.

RICHARD de Reviers holds MOSTERTON. Almær held it TRE, and it paid geld for 6 hides. There is land for 5 ploughs. In demesne are 2 ploughs, and 5 slaves; and 8 villans and 5 bordars with 3 ploughs. There is a mill rendering 7s6d, and 30 acres of meadow, [and] woodland 1 league long and half a league wide. It was and is worth £12.

SCHELIN holds SHILLINGSTONE. Earl Harold held it TRE, and it paid geld for 16 hides. There is land for 16 ploughs. In demesne are 3 ploughs, and 5 slaves; and 15 villans and 26 bordars with 8 ploughs. There is a mill rendering 23s6d, and 200 acres of meadow less 17, pasture 42 furlongs long and 8 furlongs wide, [and] woodland 23 furlongs long and 9 furlongs wide. It was worth £16; now £19.

DAVID the interpreter holds NORTH POORTON. 8 thegns held it TRE, and it paid geld for 1 hide and $2\frac{1}{2}$ virgates of land. There is land for 2 ploughs, which are there, with 8 villans. There is a mill, and 4 acres of woodland and pasture 2 furlongs in length and half a furlong in width. It was and is worth 30s. Godescal holds it of David.

ANSKETIL fitzAmelina holds TYNEHAM. Beorhtric held it TRE, and it paid geld for 3 hides. There is land for 3 ploughs. In demesne are 2 ploughs, and 9 slaves; and 4 villans with 1 plough. There are 4 acres of meadow and pasture 8 furlongs in length and 4 furlongs in width. It was worth £3; now £4. Ansketil held this land of the queen, as he says, but after her death he did not seek it of the king.

RALPH holds TARRANT [?Rawston]. Beorhtric held it TRE, and it paid geld for 2 hides. There is land for $1\frac{1}{2}$ ploughs. In demesne is 1 plough, and 2 slaves; and 2 villans and 2 cotsets with half a plough. There are 3 acres of meadow, and pasture 7 furlongs in length and $1\frac{1}{2}$ furlongs in width, [and] woodland 1 furlong long and 4 acres wide. It was and is worth 40s.

RALPH of Cranborne holds WEST PARLEY. Beorhtnoth held it TRE, and it paid geld for 2 hides. There is land for 2 ploughs, which are there, and 5 villans and 4 bordars and 2 slaves, and 15 acres of meadow, pasture 1 league long and 7 furlongs wide, [and] woodland 4 furlongs long and 1 furlong wide. It was and is worth 30s.

Odo fitzEurebold holds FARNHAM. Wulfgeat held it TRE, and it paid geld for 2 hides. There is land for 2 ploughs, which are there in demesne, and 4 slaves and 3 bordars. [There is] pasture 10 acres in both length and width, [and] woodland 3 furlongs long and 2 furlongs wide. It is worth 40s.

The same man holds 'MILBORNE STILEHAM'. Dodda held it TRE, and it paid geld for 2 hides. There is land for 1 plough, which [plough] is there in demesne, and 4 acres of meadow and 2 furlongs of pasture. It was worth 44s; now 30s.

The son of Eurebold holds 3 virgates of land in RUSHTON. There is land for 1 plough, which [plough] is there, with 4 villans, and 1 acre of meadow and 4 acres of woodland, and pasture 1 league in length and width. It is worth 10s.

The same man holds PETERSHAM. Sæweard held it TRE, and it paid geld for 3 virgates of land. There is land for 1 plough, which [plough] is there, and 6 acres of meadow.

LI. The land of Hugh de Port

HUGH de Port holds COMPTON VALENCE of the king. Bondi held it TRE, and it paid geld for 10 hides. There is land for 8 ploughs. In demesne are 2 ploughs, and 3 slaves; and 10 villans and 12 bordars with 3 ploughs. There are 32 acres of meadow, [and] pasture 18 furlongs long and 1 league wide. It was and is worth £20.

[Folio 83v: DORSET]

LV. The land of the wife of Hugh fitzGrip

THE WIFE OF HUGH fitzGrip holds MARTINSTOWN of the king. 9 thegns held it | in parage | TRE, and it paid geld for 6 hides. There is land for 6 ploughs. In demesne are 3 hides of this land, and there are 2 ploughs, and 5 slaves; and 17 bordars with 2 ploughs. There is a mill rendering 16d, and 13 acres of meadow, [and] pasture 9 furlongs long and 8 furlongs wide. It was worth £10; now £6.

William holds FROME WHITFIELD of her. Godric held it TRE, and it paid geld for 4 hides. There is land for 3 ploughs. In demesne are 2 ploughs, with 1 slave, and 8 bordars and 4 cottars. There is a mill rendering 5s, and 30 acres of meadow, [and] pasture 4 furlongs long and 2 furlongs wide. It was worth 40s; now £4.

Roger holds 'LITTLE CHESELBOURNE' [in Puddletown] of the same woman. Ælfgar and Alstan held it TRE, and it paid geld for 2 hides. There is land for 2 ploughs. In demesne is 1 plough, with 6 bordars. There is a mill rendering 30d, and 5 acres of meadow and 1 furlong of pasture. It was worth 50s;

now 25s. Hugh held this land of the Abbot of Abbotsbury, as his men say, but the abbot denies it.

The woman herself holds BUCKLAND RIPERS. 4 thegns held it in parage TRE, and it paid geld for 4 hides. There is land for 3 ploughs. In demesne are 2 ploughs, with 1 slave; and 2 villans and 5 bordars with 1 plough. There is a mill rendering 20s, and 10 acres of meadow, [and] pasture 15 furlongs long and 1 furlong wide. It was and is worth 100s.

She herself holds WEY [Broadwey or Upwey]. 9 thegns held it in parage TRE, and it paid geld for 4 hides and 1 virgate of land. There is land for 4 ploughs. In demesne are 2 ploughs, and 3 slaves, and 6 bordars. There are 3 mills rendering 35s, and meadow 9 furlongs long and 1 furlong wide, [and] pasture 3 furlongs long and 1 furlong wide. It was worth £6; now 100s.

She herself holds WEY [Broadwey or Upwey]. 5 thegns held it freely TRE, and it paid geld for 6 hides. There is land for 5 ploughs. In demesne are 2 ploughs, with 1 slave; and 1 villan and 10 bordars with 1 plough. There are 3 mills rendering 37s6d, and 25 acres of meadow, [and] pasture 20 furlongs long and 3 furlongs wide. It was worth £7; now £10.

AZO holds "WINTREBURNE" of her. Almær held it TRE, and it paid geld for 1 hide. There is land for half a plough. There are 2 bordars, and 1 acre of meadow and pasture 2 furlongs in length and 1 furlong wide. It is worth 10s.

Hugh and William hold [?] WEST STAFFORD of her. 3 thegns held it in parage TRE as 2 manors, and it paid geld for 6 hides. There is land for 3 ploughs. In demesne are 2 ploughs, with 1 slave, and 8 bordars. There are 24 acres of meadow and 16 furlongs of pasture and 8 acres. It was worth £4; now 70s.

The woman herself holds "WINTREBURNE". Alric held it TRE, and it paid geld for 8 hides. There is land for 4 ploughs. In demesne are 2 ploughs, and 3 slaves; and 3 villans and 5 bordars with half a plough. There are 9 acres of meadow and 200 acres of pasture. It was and is worth £6.

William holds MORDEN [Morden and East Morden] of her. Alnoth held it TRE, and it paid geld for 5 virgates of land. There is land for 1 plough. [...] It was worth 25s; now 20s.

She herself holds "WINTREBURNE". 3 thegns held it TRE, and it paid geld for 5 hides. There is land for 3 ploughs. In demesne is 1 plough, and 2 slaves, and 5 villans and 4 bordars. There are 4 acres of meadow and pasture 5 furlongs in length and as much wide. It was worth 100s; now 40s.

Ralph holds 1½ virgates of land in WINTERBORNE [?Muston] of her. There is land for 3 oxen. Godwine held it TRE, and it was and is worth 3s.

William holds WIMBORNE [?St Giles] of her. Ealdwine held it TRE, and it paid geld for 1 hide. There is land for 1 plough. There are 2 bordars, and a third of a mill rendering 15d. There is pasture 4 furlongs in length and width, [and] woodland 1 furlong long and half a furlong wide. It was worth 20s; now 5s.

The same William holds HAMPRESTON of her. Æthelweard held it TRE, and it paid geld for 1 hide. There is land for 1 plough. There is 1 villan and 2 bordars, and 2 acres of meadow and woodland 1 furlong in length and another in width. It was and is worth 12s.

William holds BERE REGIS of her. Leomer held it TRE, and it paid geld for half a hide. There is land for half a plough, which [half-plough] is there, and a mill rendering 20s, and 1 bordar, and 6 acres of meadow and 6 acres of pasture. It is worth 30s.

William holds 1½ virgates of land of her. It renders 20s.

Walter holds TURNERS PUDDLE of her. Gerling held it TRE, and it paid geld for 6 hides. There is land for 3 ploughs. In demesne are 2 ploughs, and 4 slaves; and 2 villans and 4 bordars with half a plough. There are 10 acres of meadow and 20 acres of woodland, [and] pasture 12 furlongs long and 6 wide. It was worth £3; now £4.

Hugh holds WINTERBORNE HOUGHTON of her. Wulfgar held it TRE, and it paid geld for 2 hides and 1 virgate of land. There is land for 1½ ploughs. In demesne is 1 plough, with 1 slave; and 2 villans and 2 bordars with half a plough. There are 14 acres of scrubland and pasture 6 furlongs in length and 6 in width. It was worth 20s; now 30s.

With this manor the same Hugh holds 1 virgate of land unlawfully which belongs to William de Moyon.

Hugh holds 1 virgate of land at BRIDGE of the same woman. There is land for 2 oxen, and there is 1 villan. It was and is worth 10s.

William holds [Higher and Lower] STURTHILL of the same woman. Ælfric held it TRE, and it paid geld for 5 hides. There is land for 4 ploughs. In demesne are 2 ploughs, and 4 slaves; and 2 villans and 4 bordars with 1½ ploughs. There is a mill rendering 6s3d, and 27 acres of meadow, [and] pasture 4 furlongs long and 1 furlong wide. It was worth £4; now 100s.

William holds GRASTON of the same woman. Alweard held it TRE, and it paid geld for 2½ hides. There is land for 2 ploughs. In demesne is 1 plough, and 2 slaves; and 1 villan and 8 bordars with half a plough. There is a mill rendering 7s6d, and 16 acres of meadow. It was worth 40s; now 60s.

Ilbert holds half a hide in FARNHAM of the same woman. There is land for half a plough, and yet there is 1 plough, and pasture 1½ furlongs in length and 1 furlong wide. It is worth 10s. Alwine held this land of the Church of Shaftesbury and he could not be separated from it.

William holds PUNCKNOWLE of the same woman. Alweard held it TRE, and it paid geld for 5 hides. There is land for 4 ploughs. In demesne are 2 ploughs, and 4 slaves; and 4 villans and 5 bordars with 2 ploughs. There is a mill rendering 12s6d, and 35 acres of meadow, and 30 acres of woodland and 3 furlongs of pasture. It was worth 60s; now 100s.

The woman herself holds 2 hides in TATTON which were in the demesne of Cerne Abbey. TRE 2 thegns held them on lease. Hugh took these despite the abbot. It is worth 20s.

Walter holds 1 hide at MATRAVERS of the same woman. 2 thegns held it TRE. There is land for 1 plough, which [plough] is there in demesne, with 1 slave and 1 villan and 4 bordars. There are 2 acres of meadow and 30 acres of pasture. It was worth 20s; now 30s.

She herself holds half a hide in "TARENTE". There is land for 1 plough. There is 1 villan and 1 bordar, and 2 acres of meadow and pasture 3 furlongs in length and 1 furlong wide. It is worth 10s.

Robert holds DURWESTON of the same woman. Ælfric held it TRE, and it paid geld for 2 hides. There is land for 2 ploughs. In demesne is 1 plough, with 3 bordars. There are 8 acres of meadow, and pasture 4 furlongs in length and 2 furlongs in length [sic]. It was and is worth 40s.

Robert holds QUARLESTON of the same woman. Godwine held it TRE, and it paid geld for 1½ hides. There is land for 1½ ploughs. In demesne is 1 plough, with 1 slave, and 4 bordars. There is a mill rendering 5s, 1½ furlongs of woodland and pasture 3 furlongs in length and 1 furlong in width. It is worth 30s.

In Quarleston Robert holds 1 hide and 1 virgate of land. In demesne is half a plough, with 1 bordar. It was worth 25s; now 20s.

Ralph holds TARRANT [?Rawston] of the same woman. 1 thegn held it TRE, and it paid geld for 5 hides. There is land for 3 ploughs. In demesne is 1 plough, and 4 slaves; and 2 villans and 4 bordars with 1 plough. There is a mill rendering 30d, and 16 acres of meadow, [and] pasture 3 furlongs long and 2 furlongs wide and in another place 8 furlongs of pasture. It was worth 100s; now £4.

Berold holds TARRANT [?Gunville] of the same woman. 1 thegn held it TRE, and it paid geld for 1 hide and 3 virgates of land. There is land for 1½ ploughs. There are 3 bordars with 1 slave, and 7 acres of meadow, and pasture 2 furlongs in length and 2 wide. It was worth 40s; now 15s.

She herself holds LANGTON HERRING. 1 thegn held it TRE, and it paid geld for 1½ hides. There is land for 3 ploughs. In demesne are 2 ploughs, with 1 slave; and 1 villan and 7 bordars with 1 plough. There are 4 acres of meadow and 40 acres of pasture. It was worth 30s; now 40s.

Two knights hold half a hide in RUSHTON of the same woman. 3 thegns held it freely TRE, and it paid geld for as much. There is land for half a plough. There are 20 acres of meadow and 200 acres of pasture. It is worth 10s.

Hugh holds WEST CHALDON of the same woman. 9 thegns held it in parage TRE, and it paid geld for 5 hides. There is land for 4 ploughs. In demesne are 2 ploughs, and 2 slaves; and 5 villans and 8 bordars with 2 ploughs. There are 3 acres of meadow, and pasture 7 furlongs in length and 5 furlongs in width. It was worth £10; now £8.

Hugh holds RINGSTEAD of the same woman. Wulfnoth held it freely TRE, and it paid geld for 1 hide. There is land for 1 plough. There are 2 villans and 2 bordars, and 8 acres of meadow, and pasture 2 furlongs in length and 1 furlong in width. It was worth 30s; now 25s.

Turold holds WARMWELL of the same woman. Almær held it TRE, and it paid geld for 1½ hides. There is land for 2 ploughs, which are there in demesne, and 5 bordars. There is a mill rendering 5s, [and] pasture half a league and 3 furlongs long and 3 furlongs wide. It was worth 30s; now 40s.

Ralph holds RINGSTEAD of the same woman. Hunwine held it TRE, and it paid geld for 1½ hides. There is land for 2 ploughs. In demesne is 1 plough; and 1 villan and 3 bordars with half a plough, and 4 furlongs of pasture. It is worth 40s.

[Folio 84: DORSET]

Robert holds CREECH [Creech, East Creech and West Creech] of the same woman. Boln held it TRE, and it paid geld for half a hide. There is land for half a plough, which [half-plough] is there, with 4 bordars, and 3 acres of meadow, and pasture 7 furlongs in length and 3 furlongs in width. It is worth 10s.

Robert holds HURPSTON of the same woman. Alweard held it TRE, and it paid geld for 3 hides. There is land for 3 ploughs. In demesne are 1½ ploughs, and 3 slaves and 2 cotsets. There is a mill rendering 20d, and 9 acres of meadow and 4 furlongs of pasture and 1 furlong of woodland, and 1 burgess paying 8d. It was worth 100s; now £4.

In the same vill Robert holds half a hide of the woman herself. Sæwine held it as a manor TRE. There is land for half a plough. It is worth 12s6d.

She herself holds WILKSWOOD. Æthelweard held it TRE, and it paid geld for 3½ hides and 2 parts of 1 virgate. There is land for 3½ ploughs. In demesne is 1 plough, and 2 slaves; and 2 villans and 4 bordars with 1 plough, and 2 acres of meadow and 4 furlongs of woodland. It was and is worth £4.

She herself holds ACTON. Æthelweard held it TRE, and it paid geld for 2½ hides. There is land for 2 ploughs. In demesne is 1 plough, and 3 slaves; and 2 villans and 1 bordar with 1 plough. There is a mill rendering 12s6d, [and] woodland 2 furlongs long and 1½ furlongs wide. It was worth 60s; now 40s.

Walter holds SWANAGE of the same woman. Æthelweard held it in parage TRE, and it paid geld for 1½ hides. There is land for 1 plough, which [plough] is there, with 1 slave and 1 bordar. There are 7 acres of meadow. It was worth 20s; now 25s.

Ralph holds 3 virgates of land in WORTH MATRAVERS of the same woman. 2 thegns held it in parage TRE, and it paid geld for as much. There is land for half a plough, which [half-plough] is there, with 2 bordars. It is worth 15s.

Walter holds 'THORNE' [in Langton Matravers] of the same woman. Ælfric held it in parage TRE, and it paid geld for 1 hide. There is land for 1 plough [...]. It is worth 18s.

Robert holds 'THORNE' [in Langton Matravers] of the same woman. Sæwine held it in parage TRE, and it paid geld for 1 hide. There is land for 1 plough, which [plough] is there in demesne. It was worth 10s; now 20s.

Hugh holds BRENSCOMBE of the same woman. Algar held it in parage TRE, and it paid geld for 1 virgate of land. There is land for 1 plough. There are 3 bordars, and pasture half a league long and 4 furlongs wide, [and] woodland 4 furlongs long and 1 furlong wide. It is worth 10s.

She herself holds [East and West] ORCHARD. 4 thegns held it TRE, and it paid geld for 1½ hides. There is land for 1½ ploughs. There are 2 bordars, and an orchard. Hugh gave this hide to the Church of Cranborne for the sake of his soul, and it is worth 20s. The wife of Hugh holds half a hide. It is worth 20s.

Durand holds half a hide in WILKSWOOD of the same woman. There is land for half a plough. It is worth 10s. 2 thegns held it TRE.

All the thegns who held these lands TRE could go to whichever lord they wished.

ISOLDE holds PETERSHAM of the king. Wada held it TRE, and it paid geld for 1 hide. There is land for 1 plough. There are 11 bordars, and a mill rendering 5s10d, and 7 acres of meadow, pasture 1 furlong long and half a furlong wide, [and] woodland 1 furlong long and another wide. It is worth 15s.

LVI. The Lands of the King's Thegns

GUTHMUND holds MILTON ON STOUR. The same man held it TRE, and it paid geld for 4½ hides. There is land for 3 ploughs. In demesne is 1 plough, and 2 slaves; and 2 villans and 8 bordars with 1 plough. There is a mill [rendering] 12d, and 10 acres of meadow, [and] woodland 8 furlongs long and half a furlong wide. It was worth 60s; now 30s.

KETIL holds KINGTON [?Magna]. Dodda held it TRE, and it paid geld for 3 hides and 3 virgates of land. There is land for 3 ploughs. In demesne are 2 ploughs, with 1 slave, and 1 villan and 3 bordars. There are 15 acres of meadow and 5 acres of woodland. It was and is worth 40s.

EDWIN holds 1 virgate of land in GILLINGHAM. There is land for half a plough. It is worth 5s.

GODRIC holds 1 virgate of land in GILLINGHAM. There is land for half a plough. There are 4 bordars, and 3 acres of meadow. It is worth 5s.

WULFWINE holds 1½ virgates of land in GILLINGHAM. There is land for half a plough. It is worth 6s.

ÆLFRIC holds 1 hide in WINTERBORNE [?Kingston]. There is land for 1 plough. It is worth 10s.

Bolla the priest holds MAPPOWDER. He himself held it with 7 other free thegns TRE, and it paid geld for 5 hides and 3 virgates of land. There is land for 5 ploughs. In demesne are 2 ploughs, and 2 slaves; and 8 villans and 4 bordars with 3 ploughs. There is a certain amount 16 [sic] of meadow, and woodland 4 furlongs long and 3 furlongs wide. It is worth £4.

BOLLA holds of CHICKERELL. Sæwulf held it TRE, and it paid geld for 3 hides and half a virgate of land. There is land for 3 ploughs, which are there in demesne, and 4 slaves and 1 villan and 6 bordars. There are 6 acres of meadow and 7 furlongs of pasture. It is worth 60s.

BEORHTWINE holds WEY [Broadwey or Upwey]. He himself held it TRE, and it paid geld for 2 hides. There is land for 2 ploughs, which are there in demesne, and 3 slaves and 2 villans and 4 bordars. There is a mill rendering 15s, and 3 acres of meadow and 2 acres of pasture. It is worth 40s.

BEORHTWINE holds 1½ hides in "WINTREBURNE". He himself held them TRE. There is land for 1 plough, which [plough] is there. It is worth 15s.

BEORHTWINE holds 1 virgate of land in LEWELL. He himself held it TRE. It is worth 10d.

ÆLFRIC holds 'GREAT CRAWFORD' [in Spetisbury], and Edward [holds] of him. TRE it paid geld for 2 hides. There is land for 1½ ploughs. However, there are 2 ploughs, with 1 cotset, and 3 slaves, and the fourth part of a mill rendering 30d, and 12 acres of meadow and woodland 6 furlongs in length and 2 furlongs wide. It was worth 30d; it is worth 40s.

WULFRIC holds MORDEN [Morden and East Morden]. His father held it TRE, and it paid geld for 2½ hides. There is land for 2 ploughs, which are there, with 2 villans and 6 bordars, and 11d from part of a mill, and 5 acres of meadow and pasture 1 league in length and width. It is worth 30s. The wife of Wulfric's brother has there 1 hide and half a virgate of land. There is land for 1 plough. It is worth 20s.

EDWIN holds BLANDFORD [Blandford St Mary and Lower Blandford St Mary]. Alwine held it TRE, and it paid geld for 5 hides and 1½ virgates. There is land for 3 ploughs. In demesne is 1 plough, and 3 slaves; and 2 villans and 1 bordar and 3 cottars with 1 plough. There are 18 acres of meadow, [and] pasture 8 furlongs long and 2 furlongs wide. It was worth £4; it is worth 40s.

ÆTHELWEARD holds THORNICOMBE. He himself held it TRE, and it paid geld for 2 hides. There is land for 1 plough, which [plough] is there, with 1 slave and 4 bordars. It is worth 20s.

WULFGEAT holds WIMBORNE ST GILES. He himself held it TRE, and it paid geld for 1 hide. There is 1 plough, with 1 slave, pasture 4 furlongs long and 1 wide, [and] woodland 1 furlong long and half a furlong wide. It was worth 20s; now 10s.

BEORHTWINE holds MELBURY [Bubb or Osmond]. TRE it paid geld for 5 hides. There is land for 4 ploughs. In demesne are 2 ploughs, and 5 slaves; and 4 villans and 9 bordars with 2 ploughs. There are 3 acres of meadow and woodland 3 furlongs in length and 3 in width. It is worth 60s.

WULFRIC holds THORNHILL. His father held it TRE,

and it paid geld for half a hide. There is land for 1 plough, which [plough] is there, with 5 bordars and 5 cottars, and 5 acres of meadow. It is worth 10s.

THORKIL holds HAMPRESTON. TRE it paid geld for 3 virgates of land and the third part of 1 virgate. There is land for 1 plough. There is half a plough, with 1 bordar, and 6 acres of meadow and 2 furlongs of woodland, and pasture 2 furlongs long and 1 furlong wide. It is worth 8s. The queen gave this land to Schelin. Now the king has it in demesne.

Dodda holds half a hide, and it paid geld for as much TRE. There is land for half a plough. However, there is 1 plough, and a mill rendering 10s, and 14 acres of meadow, and half an acre of woodland, [and] pasture half a league long and 3 furlongs wide. It is worth 17s6d. The queen gave this land to Dodda in alms.

The same man holds 1 hide in WILKSWORTH, and it paid geld for as much TRE. There is land for 1 plough, which [plough] is there, with 2 slaves and 2 villans; and 2 bordars having half a plough. There are 14 acres of meadow, and woodland 2 furlongs in length and 1 furlong wide. It is worth 10s.

ALWEARD holds the third part of 1 virgate of land, and it renders 30d.

ÆTHELRUN holds WILKSWORTH. There is 1 hide. There is land for 1 plough, which [plough] is there, with 2 bordars and 2 slaves, and pasture 4 furlongs long and 1 furlong wide and as much woodland. It is worth 10s.

GODWINE the huntsman holds 'WALFORD' [in Wimborne Minster]. Almær held it TRE, and it paid geld for 1 hide. There is land for 1 plough, which [plough] is there, with 3 bordars, and 7 acres of meadow, and pasture 5 furlongs long and 2 furlongs wide and 1 furlong of woodland. It is worth 15s.

ÆTHELWEARD holds 1 virgate of land in RUSHTON. There is land for 2 oxen. It is worth 30d.

GODWINE the reeve holds 1 hide in "WINTREBURNE". He himself held it TRE. There is land for 1 plough. There is 1 bordar. It is worth 12s6d.

GODWINE the huntsman holds 1 virgate of land and 4 acres, and there he has half a plough, with 5 bordars, and 9 acres of meadow. It is worth 10s. Godric held it TRE.

SWEIN holds WINTERBORNE HOUGHTON. His father held it TRE, and it paid geld for 10 hides. There is land for 6 ploughs. In demesne are 2 ploughs, and 5 slaves; and 7 villans and 17 bordars with 3 ploughs. There are 10 acres of meadow, pasture 1½ leagues long and a half wide, [and] woodland 1½ leagues long and 4 furlongs wide. It was worth 100s; now £8. Robert holds it of Swein.

The same Swein holds PLUMBER, and Ralph [holds] of him. His father held it TRE, and it paid geld for 5 hides. There is land for 3 ploughs. In demesne is 1 plough, and 4 slaves; and 3 villans and 6 bordars with 1 plough. There are 15 acres of meadow, [and] woodland 5 furlongs long and 3 furlongs wide. It was worth 30s; now 60s.

WULFRIC the huntsman holds 1 hide of the king. His father held it TRE, and it paid geld for as much. There is land for 1 plough. There are 3 bordars, and 3 acres of meadow. It is worth 10s.

EDWIN holds LANGTON LONG BLANDFORD. Alwig held it TRE, and it paid geld for 5 hides. There is land for 4 ploughs. In demesne are 1½ ploughs, and 3 slaves; and 3 villans with a priest and 6 bordars and 3 cottars with 1 plough. There is a mill rendering 18s4d, and 18 acres of meadow, [and] pasture 5 furlongs long and 2 furlongs wide. It is worth £4.

EDWIN holds LAZERTON. Alweard held it TRE, and it paid geld for 3 hides. There is land for 2 ploughs, which are there, with 1 villan and 3 cotsets and 3 slaves. There is a mill rendering 2s, and pasture 4½ furlongs in length and 2 furlongs in width, [and] woodland

Folio 84v: DORSET]

6 furlongs long and 2 furlongs wide. It was worth 60s; now 30s.

The same Edwin holds SHILVINGHAMPTON. Alwig held it TRE, and it paid geld for 2½ hides. There is land for 2 ploughs. There is 1 villan and 5 slaves with half a plough, and 15 acres of meadow and pasture 3 furlongs in length and width. It is worth 40s.

WULFGEAT holds [?] BRYANSTON. He himself held it TRE, and it paid geld for 1 hide. There is land for 1 plough. There are 4 cotsets, and 3 acres of meadow and 5 acres of pasture. It was and is worth 10s.

BEORHTWINE holds CHILCOMBE. He himself held it TRE, and it paid geld for 3 hides. There is land for 3 ploughs. In demesne are 2 ploughs, and 5 slaves; and 1 villan and 8 bordars with half a plough. There is a mill rendering 5s, and 25 acres of meadow and 20 acres of pasture. It is worth 60s.

The same man holds WADDON. Alweard held it TRE, and it paid geld for 2 hides. There is land for 2 ploughs, which are there in demesne, and 4 slaves and 1 villan and 3 bordars. There are 16 acres of meadow and 14 acres of pasture. It is worth 40s.

Hugh fitzGrip exchanged this land with Beorhtwine [for a manor] which the Count of Mortain now holds and the exchange itself is worth twice as much.

The same Beorhtwine holds 1 hide and 8 acres of land in MORETON. He himself held them TRE. There is land for 1 plough. 3 villans and 4 bordars have this [plough] there. There are 11 acres of meadow and pasture 6 furlongs in length and 4 furlongs in width. It is worth 21s3d.

The same Beorhtwine holds GALTON. He himself held it TRE, and it paid geld for 2 hides and 1½ virgates of land. There is land for 2 ploughs. In demesne is 1 plough, and 3 slaves, and 2 villans and 6 cottars. There is a mill rendering

12s6d, and 2 acres of meadow and pasture 8 furlongs in length and 3 furlongs in width. It is worth 40s.

The same Beorhtwine holds 1 hide in RINGSTEAD. He himself held it TRE. There is land for 1 plough. 6 men hold it at farm. It is worth 25s.

The same Beorhtwine holds 2½ virgates of land in STINSFORD, and Aiulf [holds] of him. There is land for half a plough. There are 3 bordars. It is worth 7s.

The same man holds 1 virgate of land in BRIDGE. There is land for 2 oxen. There are 2 fishermen. It is worth 5s. The same Beorhtwine held these lands TRE.

EADRIC holds 1 hide in RUSHTON less the fourth part of 1 virgate. Sæwine held it TRE. There is land for 1 plough. There are 5½ acres of meadow. It is worth 9s2d.

The same man holds 1 hide at EAST HOLME. There is land for 1 plough. It is worth 20s.

The same man holds 1 hide at 'STOKE WALLIS' [in Whitchurch Canonicorum]. There is land for 2 ploughs. In demesne is 1 plough, and 2 slaves; and 1 villan and 8 bordars with half a plough. There is a mill rendering 40d, and 14 acres of meadow, and 16 acres of woodland and 12 acres of pasture. It is worth 30s.

The same man holds 2 hides at 'STUDLEY' [in Whitchurch Canonicorum]. There is land for 2 ploughs. In demesne is 1 plough, and 2 slaves; and 2 villans and 3 bordars with 1½ ploughs. There are 5 acres of meadow and 3 acres of woodland, and pasture 1 furlong in length and another in width. It is worth 25s.

The same man holds PILSDON. TRE it paid geld for 3 hides. There is land for 4 ploughs. There are 7 villans and 8 bordars with 3 ploughs, and 12 acres of meadow and 100 acres of pasture. It was worth 20s; now 40s.

The same man holds 1 virgate of land at 'STUDLEY' [in Whitchurch Canonicorum]. There is land for half a plough. It is worth 5s. Sæwine held these lands of Eadric TRE.

GODRIC holds BRIANTSPUDDLE. Azur held it TRE, and it paid geld for 5 hides. There is land for 3 ploughs. In demesne is 1 plough, and 7 slaves; and 2 villans and 4 bordars with 2 ploughs. There is a mill rendering 7s6d, and 38 acres of meadow, and 12 acres of woodland and pasture 11 furlongs in length and 4 wide. It is worth £4.

EADRIC holds 1 virgate of land in TYNEHAM. There is land for 2 oxen. It is worth 65d.

DODDA holds 1 virgate of land in WOOLCOMBE [in Toller Porcorum]. There is land for 2 oxen. There are 2 acres of meadow and pasture 3 furlongs in length and width. It was and is worth 20d.

ÆLFRIC and Beorhtric hold half a hide in UPLODERS. There is land for 1 plough. There are 5 acres of meadow and 20 acres of pasture. It was and is worth 10s.

ÆLFRIC holds BLACKMANSTON. He himself held it TRE, and it paid geld for 1 hide. There is land for 1 plough.

SWEIN holds 'MILBORNE STILEHAM', and Osmund [holds] of him. Swein's father held it TRE. There is land for 2 ploughs. There are 7 bordars with 1 slave, and a mill rendering 25d, and 10 acres of meadow and 30 acres of pasture. It was and is worth 20s.

GODRIC holds 1 hide in STOURTON CAUNDLE. Leofrun held it TRE. There is land for 1 plough. There are 2 slaves with 1 bordar, and 6 acres of meadow and 10 acres of pasture and 2 furlongs of scrubland. It is worth 10s.

SÆWEARD holds 2½ virgates of land in [? Purse] CAUNDLE. He himself held them TRE. There is land for half a plough. There is 1 acre of pasture. It is worth 5s.

Two bordars hold the fourth part of 1 virgate of land. It is worth 15d. They themselves held it freely TRE.

ÆLFRIC holds COOMBE [in Langton Matravers]. He himself held it TRE, and it paid geld for 5 hides and 1 virgate of land. There is land for 3 ploughs. In demesne are 2 ploughs, and 4 slaves; and 1 villan and 4 bordars [...]. There are 6 acres of meadow and woodland 4 furlongs in length and 2 furlongs wide. It is worth £6.

SWEIN holds AILWOOD. Azur held it TRE, and it paid geld for 5 hides less 1 virgate. There is land for 6 ploughs. In demesne are 3 ploughs, with 1 slave and 1 villan and 1 cotset. There are 10 acres of meadow, and pasture 8 furlongs in length and 1 furlong wide, [and] woodland 1 league long and as much wide. It was and is worth 40s. The wife of Hugh holds of Swein.

ÆLFRIC holds BOVINGTON. He himself held it TRE, and it paid geld for 4 hides. There is land for 3 ploughs. In demesne is 1 plough, with 1 slave; and 3 villans with 2 ploughs. There are 40 acres of meadow, [and] pasture 1 league long and half a league wide. It is worth 40s.

ÆLFRIC holds WINTERBORNE [?Kingston]. He himself held it TRE, and it paid geld for 1 hide. There is land for 1 plough. There are 5 bordars with 1 slave, and 5 acres of meadow and pasture 8 furlongs in length and 4 furlongs in width. It is worth 20s.

Ten thegns hold [Higher and Lower] KINGCOMBE. They themselves held it TRE as 1 manor, and it paid geld for 1 hide and 3 parts of 1 virgate. There is land for 1 plough, which [plough] is there [...].

ALWEARD holds WOOL. He himself held it TRE, and it paid geld for 1½ hides. There is land for 1 plough, which [plough] is there in demesne, with 1 villan and 2 bordars. There are 7½ acres of meadow and 2 acres of pasture. It is worth 15s.

ALMÆR holds WOOL. Alweard held it TRE, and it paid geld for 1 virgate of land. There is land for 2 oxen. It is worth 2s.

GODWINE holds CORSCOMBE. Ealdwine held it TRE, and it paid geld for 1 hide. There is land for 1½ ploughs. There is 1 villan with 1 plough and 4 bordars and 1 slave, and half a furlong of pasture and 2 furlongs of woodland. It was worth 30s; now 20s.

ÆLFRIC holds 1 hide in BLACKMANSTON. He himself held it TRE. There is land for 1 plough. It is worth 20s.

EDWARD the huntsman holds half a virgate of land in GILLINGHAM. Eskil held it TRE. There is land for 3 oxen. It is worth 30d.

All who held these lands TRE could go to any lord they wished.

LVII. The Lands of the King's Sergeants

WILLIAM Bellet holds 'FROME BILLET' [in West Stafford] of the king. Wulfweard and Beorhtfrith held it TRE as 2 manors, and it paid geld for 3 hides. There is land for 2 ploughs. However, there are 3 ploughs, and 6 slaves, and 2 villans with 1 bordar. There is a mill rendering 5s, and 23 acres of meadow, [and] pasture 3 furlongs long and 2 furlongs wide. It is worth £6.

HUGH holds 3 virgates of land in LEWELL. Alweard held them TRE. There is land for 2 oxen. There are 2 bordars paying 20d.

WILLIAM holds 'WINTERBORNE BELET'. 2 thegns held it in parage TRE, and it paid geld for 2½ hides. There is land for 1½ ploughs. However, there are 2 ploughs, and 5 slaves, and 18 acres of meadows, [and] pasture 6 furlongs long and 3 furlongs wide. It was worth 40s; now £4.15s.

WILLIAM [...] de DAUMERAY holds the lands of 3 thegns, which paid geld TRE for 3 hides and 2½ virgates of land. There is land for 2 ploughs, which are there, and 5 slaves and 5 bordars. There are 3 parts of a mill rendering 9s, and 4 acres of meadow, [and] woodland 6 furlongs long and 3 furlong wide. It is worth 60s.

HUGH holds 1 virgate of land. Sæwulf held it TRE. It is worth 30d.

The same Hugh holds "WINTREBURNE". 2 thegns held it TRE, and it paid geld for half a hide. There is land for half a plough. There are 2 villans. It is worth 40d.

The same Hugh holds 1 virgate of land in WORGRET. Almær held it TRE. There is land for 2 oxen. It was and is worth 12d.

The same Hugh holds 3 virgates of land in WOOLCOMBE [in Toller Porcorum]. Dodda the monk held it TRE, and it paid geld for as much. There is land for 1 plough, which [plough] is there, with 2 bordars, and 4 acres of meadow and 6 furlongs of pasture and 8 acres of scrubland. It was worth 5s; now 15s.

[Folio 85: DORSE]

HERVEY the chamberlain holds WIMBORNE ST GILES. Beorhtric held it TRE, and it paid geld for 2½ hides. There is land for 3 ploughs. In demesne is 1 plough; and 5 villans and 5 bordars with 2 ploughs. In the mill of the vill 22½ [...]. There are 2 acres of meadow, and pasture 1 league long and 3 furlongs wide, [and] woodland 6 furlongs long and 2 furlongs wide. It was worth 30s; now 50s.

JOHN holds WINTERBORNE [?Muston]. Alweard held it TRE, and it paid geld for 2 hides and 1½ virgates. There is land for 2 ploughs. In demesne are 1½ ploughs, and 3 slaves; and 2 villans and 3 bordars with half a plough. There is pasture 5 furlongs long and as much wide. It was and is worth 40s.

WILLIAM de DAUMERAY holds WALDITCH. Alwig held it TRE, and it paid geld for 2 hides. There is land for 1 plough, which [plough] is there in demesne, with 1 slave; and 1 villan and 8 bordars with half a plough. There is a mill rendering 45d, and 4 acres of meadow, [and] woodland 4 furlongs long and 1 furlong wide. It was and is worth 40s.

WILLIAM Bellet holds NUTFORD. Alnoth held it TRE, and it paid geld for 1 hide and 2½ virgates of land. There is land for 1 plough. However, there are 2 ploughs, and 3 slaves, and 8 acres of meadow, [and] pasture 3 furlongs long and 1 furlong wide. It was worth 15s; now 30s.

The same William holds WOODSFORD. Leofgar held it TRE, and it paid geld for 2½ hides. There is land for 2 ploughs, which are there in demesne, and 4 slaves and 2 villans and 2 bordars. There is a mill rendering 6s, and 28 acres of meadow and pasture 12 furlongs in length and width. It was worth 100s; now 60s.

The same William holds LYME REGIS. Ælfgifu held it TRE, and it paid geld for 1 hide. There is land for 1 plough. There is 1 villan with half a plough, and 14 salt-workers. There is a mill rendering 39d, and 3 acres of meadow, pasture 4 furlongs long and 1 furlong wide, and 1 furlong of woodland in length and width. It is worth 60s.

HUNGER fitzOdin holds BROADWINDSOR. Bondi held it TRE, and it paid geld for 20 hides. There is land for 20 ploughs. In demesne are 2 ploughs, and 7 slaves; and 38 villans and 12 bordars with 16 ploughs. There are 12 acres of meadow, and woodland 30 furlongs in length and 8 furlongs wide and 8 furlongs of pasture. It was and is worth £20.

In the same vill Hunger has 1 hide of land which 1 free man held TRE.

OSMUND the baker holds 1 hide and half a virgate of land in GALTON. 4 free men held them TRE. There is land for 1 plough. There are 4 men paying 12s4d. It was worth 15s.

The same Osmund holds 3 virgates of land in WOODSTREET. 3 free men held them TRE. There is land for 6 oxen. There are 2 bordars. It was and is worth 7s6d. Those who held these lands TRE could go where they would.

WILLIAM Bellet holds 1 hide and 2½ virgates of land in STOURPAINE of the king. Alnoth held them of Edward Lipe, and he could not be separated from his lord.

LVIII. The land of the Countess of Boulogne

THE COUNTESS OF BOULOGNE holds [Higher and Lower] BOCKHAMPTON of King William. TRE it paid geld for 4 hides. There is land for 3 ploughs. In demesne is 1 plough, with 1 slave; and 4 villans with 1 bordar have 2 ploughs. There is a mill rendering 5s, and 20 acres of meadow and woodland 4 furlongs in length and 1 furlong wide. It is worth £3.

The same woman holds WINTERBORNE MONKTON. TRE it paid geld for 6 hides. There is land for 5 ploughs. In demesne are 2 ploughs, and 4 slaves; and 4 villans and 2 bordars with 2 ploughs. There are 9 acres of meadow and pasture 9 furlongs in length and 3 furlongs wide. It is worth £6.

The same woman holds SWANAGE. TRE it paid geld for 1 hide and the third part of 1 virgate. There is land for 1 plough. 1 villan has this [plough] there, and there are 4 acres of meadow. It is worth 15s. Wulfgifu held these 3 manors TRE, and she could go with the land where she would.

DURAND the carpenter holds AFFLINGTON. Leofwine held it TRE, and it paid geld for 1 virgate of land. There is land for half a plough. It is worth 6s.

The same man holds 'MOULHAM' [in Swanage]. 3 thegns held it TRE, and it paid geld for 1 hide. There is land for 1 plough, which [plough] is there, with 1 cottar. There is a mill rendering 6d, and 1 acre of meadow. It was worth 5s; now 30s.

GODFREY the scullion holds 1 virgate of land in HERSTON. His father held it TRE, and it paid geld for 1 virgate of land and 4 acres. These [...].

[Folio 85v: [DORSET]]

[Blank in MS]

SOMERSET

[Folio 86: SOMERSET]

Here Are Entered the Holders of Lands In Somerset

I KING WILLIAM
II The Bishop of Winchester
III The Bishop of Salisbury
IIII The Bishop of Bayeux
V The Bishop of Coutances
VI The Bishop of Wells
VII The Church of Bath
VIII The Church of Glastonbury
IX The Church of Muchelney
X The Church of Athelney
XI The Church of St PETER at Rome
XII The Church of Caen
XIII The Abbey of Montebourg
XIIII The Church of Shaftesbury
XV Bishop Maurice
XVI Clerks holding of the king
XVII Count Eustace
XVIII Earl Hugh
XIX The Count of Mortain
XX Baldwin of Exeter
XXI Roger de Courseulles
XXII Roger Arundel
XXIII Walter Giffard
XXIIII Walter or Walscin de Douai
XXV William de Moyon
XXVI William de Eu
XXVII William de Falaise
XXVIII William fitzGuy
XXIX Ralph de Mortimer
XXX Ralph de la Pommeraye
XXXI Ralph Paynel
XXXII Ralph de Limesy
XXXIII Robert fitzGerald
XXXIIII Alvred of Marlborough
XXXV Alvred d'Epaignes
XXXVI Turstin fitzRolf
XXXVII Serlo de Burcy
XXXVIII Odo fitzGamelin
XXXIX Osbern Giffard
XL Edward of Salisbury
XLI Ernulf de Hesdin
XLII Gilbert fitzTurold

XLIII Godebold
XLIIII Matthew de Mortagne
XLV Humphrey the chamberlain
XLVI Robert d'Auberville and other sergeants of the king
XLVII The king's thegns

The land of the King

The KING holds SOMERTON. King Edward held it. It has never paid geld, nor is it known how many hides are there. There is land for 50 ploughs. In demesne are 5 ploughs and 4 slaves; and 80 villans and 28 bordars with 40 ploughs. There are 100 acres of meadow, and pasture 1 league in length and half a league in breadth, [and] woodland 1 league long and 1 furlong broad.

There is a borough which is called LANGPORT, in which dwell 34 burgesses paying 15s, and [there are] 2 fisheries rendering 10s. It renders yearly £79.10s7d at 20[d] to the ora.

To this manor have been added 3 estates which 3 thegns, Beorhtnoth, Ælfric, and Sæwine, held TRE; and they paid geld for 5½ hides. There are 7 villans and 5 bordars with 4 ploughs. They render £7.15s. From this manor has been taken away half a hide at 'DEADMAN'S WELL' [in Broomfield], which was [part] of the demesne farm of King Edward. Alvred d'Epaignes holds it, and it is worth 10s.

The KING holds CHEDDAR. King Edward held it. It has never paid geld, nor is it known how many hides are there. There is land for 20 ploughs. In demesne are 3 ploughs and 2 slaves and 1 colibert; and 17 villans and 20 bordars with 17 ploughs; and 7 rent-payers pay 17s.

In AXBRIDGE 32 burgesses pay 20s. There are 2 mills rendering 12s6d, and 3 fisheries rendering 10s, and 15 acres of meadow, [and] pasture 1 league long and as much broad. It renders yearly £21.0s2½d at 20[d] to the ora. [There is] woodland 2 leagues long and half a league broad.

Of this manor Bishop Giso holds a member, WEDMORE, which he held of King Edward. For it William the sheriff reckons in the king's farm £12 every year. From this same manor has been taken away half a virgate of land which was of the demesne farm of King Edward. Robert d'Auberville holds it, and it is worth 15d.

These 2 manors, SOMERTON and CHEDDAR, with their attached members rendered the farm of 1 night TRE.

The KING holds NORTH PETHERTON. King Edward held it. It has never paid geld, nor is it known how many hides are there. There is land for 30 ploughs. In demesne are 3 ploughs; and 20 villans and 19 bordars and 6 slaves and 20 swineherds with 23 ploughs. There is a mill rendering 15d, and 100 acres of meadow, and 2 leagues of pasture rendering 20s a year. This manor renders £42.8s4d at 20[d] to the ora.

The KING holds SOUTH PETHERTON. King Edward held it. It has never paid geld, nor is it known how many hides are there. There is land for 28 ploughs. In demesne are 2 ploughs and 5 slaves and 22 coliberts; and 63 villans and 15 bordars with 26 ploughs. There is a mill rendering 20s, and 50 acres of meadow, [and] woodland 11 furlongs long and 10 furlongs broad. It renders £42 and 100d at 20[d] to the ora.

Of this manor Mærle;-Sveinn held 2 hides in [Lower and Over] STRATTON TRE; and it was thegnland. It now renders 60s in the king's farm. From the same manor has been taken half a hide. Norman holds it of Roger de Courseulles, and it is worth 16s.

To this manor TRE there was yearly rendered from Cricket St Thomas a customary due, that is, 6 sheep with as many lambs, and [from] each free man 1 bloom of iron. Turstin holds it of the Count of Mortain, but he has not rendered the customary due since the count has had the land.

The KING holds CURRY RIVEL. King Edward held it. It has never paid geld, nor is it known how many hides are there. There is land for 13 ploughs. In demesne are 3 ploughs and 5 slaves; and 20 villans and 2 bordars with 10 ploughs. There are 40 acres of meadow, and woodland 2 leagues long and 1 league broad. It renders £21 and 50d at 20[d] to the ora.

From this manor has been taken away 1 virgate of land. Bretel holds it of the Count of Mortain, and it is worth 10s8d.

These 3 manors, North Petherton and South Petherton and Curry Rivel, TRE rendered the farm of 1 night with their customary dues.

[Folio 86V: SOMERSET]

The KING holds WILLITON and CANNINGTON and CARHAMPTON. King Edward held them. They have never paid geld, nor is it known how many hides are there. There is land for 100 ploughs. In demesne are 11½ ploughs and 11 slaves and 30 coliberts; and 38 villans and 50 bordars with 37½ ploughs. There are 2 mills rendering 5s, and 104 acres of meadow, pasture 5 leagues in length and 3 leagues [...] in breadth, [and] woodland 4 leagues in length and 2½ leagues in breadth. It rendered [sic] £100 and 116s6½d at 20[d] to the ora. TRE it rendered the farm of 1 night.

To this manor of Williton has been added half a hide. Særic held it TRE as 2 manors and it paid geld for half a hide. There is land for 5 ploughs. There 6 villans and 4 bordars have 3 ploughs, and there are 4 acres of meadow, and woodland 4 furlongs in length and 1 furlong in breadth. It renders 31s8d.

To the same manor has been added another half a hide at WESTOWE which Alwine held TRE, and it paid geld for half a hide. There is land for 1 plough. It renders 40d. To this manor has been added a further half a hide, and it renders 7s to the king's farm. From Alvred's manor of MONKSILVER

has been added to this manor a customary due, that is, 18 sheep a year. TRE this did not belong to Williton.

The KING holds BEDMINSTER [in Bristol]. King Edward held it. It has never paid geld, nor is it known how many hides are there. There is land for 26 ploughs. In demesne are 3 ploughs and 3 slaves; and 25 villans and 22 bordars with 10 ploughs. There is a mill rendering 5s, and 34 acres of meadow, [and] woodland 2 leagues long and 1 league broad. It renders £21.0s2½d at 20[d] to the ora. The priest of this manor holds land for 1 plough, and it is worth 20s. Of this manor the Bishop of Coutances holds 112 acres of meadow and woodland.

The KING holds FROME. King Edward held it. It has never paid geld, nor is it known how many hides are there. There is land for 50 ploughs. In demesne are 3 ploughs and 6 coliberts; and 31 villans and 36 bordars with 40 ploughs. There are 3 mills rendering 25s, and a market rendering 46s8d. There are 30 acres of meadow, and 50 acres of pasture, [and] woodland 1 league long and as much broad. It renders £53.0s5d at 20[d] to the ora.

Of this manor the Church of St John of Frome holds 8 carucates of land and it held the same TRE. Regenbald is priest there.

The KING holds BRUTON. King Edward held it. It has never paid geld, nor is it known how many hides are there. There is land for 50 ploughs. In demesne are 3 ploughs and 5 slaves and 4 coliberts; and 28 villans and 26 bordars with 18 ploughs. There are 5 burgesses and 1 swineherd. There are 6 mills rendering 20s, and 38 acres of meadow, and 150 acres of pasture, [and] woodland 5 leagues in length and 1 league in breadth. It renders £53.0s5d at 20[d] to the ora.

This manor with the above FROME TRE rendered the farm of 1 night.

From this manor have been taken away 9 acres which Bretel holds of the Count of Mortain, and they are worth 18d.

From this manor has been taken away half a hide in KILMINGTON [Wilts.]. Serlo de Burcy holds it, and it is worth 10s. They were [part] of the demesne farm.

From the same manor has been taken away 1 hide. Joscelin holds it of Robert fitzGerald. There is land for 3 ploughs. It was worth 40s; now 20s.

The KING holds MILBORNE PORT. King Edward held it. It has never paid geld, nor is it known how many hides are there. There is land for 50 ploughs. In demesne are 4 ploughs and 5 slaves; and 70 villans and 18 bordars with 65 ploughs. There are 6 mills rendering 77s6d, and 170 acres of meadow, woodland 2 leagues in length and 9 furlongs broad, pasture 4 furlongs long and 2 furlongs broad, and 1 league of moor.

In this manor are 56 burgesses, with a market also, paying 60s.

In ILCHESTER are 107 burgesses paying 20s. A market with its appurtenances renders £11.

The whole of MILBORNE PORT with the aforesaid appurtenances renders £80 of blanch silver less 9s5d. TRE it rendered a half and a quarter of the farm of 1 night.

Regenbald holds the church with I hide. There he has I plough. It is worth 30s.

The KING holds BROMPTON REGIS. Gytha held it TRE and it paid geld for 10 hides. There is land for 60 ploughs. Of this 3 hides are in demesne, and there are 3 ploughs and 7 slaves; and 50 villans and 17 bordars with 20 ploughs. There are 2 mills rendering 3s, and 60 acres of meadow, pasture 3 leagues long and I league broad, and as much woodland in length and breadth. It renders £27.12s1d of blanch silver.

Of these 10 hides a priest holds I in alms of the king. There he has I plough, and 4 villans with I plough, and 3 acres of meadow. It is worth 20s.

Of this manor the Count of Mortain holds I hide in 'TORREL'S PRESTON' [in Milverton], which was [part] of the demesne farm TRE. There is land for 4 ploughs. There are 2 ploughs. It is and was worth 40s.

From this manor has been taken away the third penny from Milverton which was rendered there TRE.

The KING holds DULVERTON. Earl Harold held it TRE and it paid geld for 2½ hides. There is land for 11 ploughs. Of this I hide is in demesne, and there are 2 ploughs and 6 slaves; and 17 villans and 6 bordars with 3½ ploughs. There are 3 acres of meadow, and pasture I league long and half a league broad, and as much woodland. It renders £11.10s of blanch silver.

To this manor have been added 2 hides of land less half a ferding. 13 thegns held them TRE. There is land for 10 ploughs. There are 8 villans with 4½ ploughs, and 3 acres of meadow, and pasture half a league long and 4 furlongs broad, [and] woodland I league long and half a league broad. It is worth 64s2d.

From this manor has been taken away a customary due from BRUSHFORD, a manor of the Count of Mortain, that is, 24 sheep a year which were rendered there TRE. Mauger keeps it back [...] through the count.

The KING holds OLD CLEEVE. Earl Harold held it TRE and it paid geld for 4 hides and I virgate of land. There is land for 33 ploughs. Of this I hide is in demesne, and there are 3 ploughs and 4 slaves; and 19 villans and 9 bordars with 18 ploughs. There are 2 mills rendering 54d, and 24 acres of meadow, [and] woodland I league long and half a league broad. It renders £23 of blanch silver.

To this manor belonged the third penny of the borough-right and [sic] Carhampton and Williton and Cannington and North Petherton.

The KING holds NETTLECOMBE. Godwine son of Harold held it TRE and it paid geld for 2 hides and 3 virgates of land. There is land for 12 ploughs. Of this 1½ virgates are in demesne, and there are 2 ploughs and 3 slaves; and 15 villans and 4 bordars with 7 ploughs. There are 6 acres of meadow, and 100 acres of pasture and 50 acres of woodland. It renders l[...].12s of blanch silver.

The KING holds CAPTON. Earl Harold held it and it paid geld for I hide. There is land for 5 ploughs. Of this half a hide is in demesne, and there is I plough; and 5 villans with I plough.

There are 8 acres of meadow, and 20 acres of pasture and 10 acres of woodland. It renders 46s of blanch silver.

The KING holds LANGFORD BUDVILLE. Godwine son of Harold held it TRE and it paid geld for 5 hides. There is land for 10 ploughs. Of this 1½ hides are in demesne, and there is I plough and 4 slaves; and 21 villans and 4 bordars with 8 ploughs. There is a mill rendering 7s6d, and 8 acres of meadow, and 100 acres of pasture and 30 acres of woodland. It renders £4.12s.

The KING holds WINSFORD. Earl Tosti held it TRE and paid geld for 3½ hides. There is land for 60 ploughs. Of this half a hide is in demesne, and there are 2 ploughs and 9 slaves; and 38 villans and 11 bordars with 13 ploughs. There is a mill rendering 6d, and 8 acres of meadow, and 40 acres of woodland, [and] pasture 4 leagues long and 2 leagues broad. It renders £10.10s of blanch silver.

To this manor has been added half a hide. 3 thegns held it TRE and did customary service to the reeve of the manor without paying any farm. There is land for 4 ploughs. There are 3 villans and 23 bordars. It renders 20s.

The KING holds CREECH ST MICHAEL. Gunild held it TRE and it paid geld for 10½ hides. There is land for 8 ploughs. Of this 6 hides are in demesne, and there are 2 ploughs and 6 slaves; and 20 villans and 10 bordars with 6 ploughs. There is a mill rendering 8d, and 8 acres of meadow, pasture I league long and as much broad, [and] woodland I furlong long and as much broad. It renders £9.4s of blanch silver. There is a fishery, but it does not belong to the farm.

The KING holds NORTH CURRY. Earl Harold held it TRE and it paid geld for 20 hides. There is land for 40 ploughs. Of this 5 hides are in demesne, and there are 5 ploughs and 18 slaves and 23 coliberts; and 100 villans less 5 and 15 bordars with 30 ploughs. There are 60 acres of meadow, and 50 acres [...] of woodland, [and] pasture 2 leagues long and I league broad. To this manor belong 5 burgesses in Langport, paying 38d, and 18 slaves and 4 swineherds and 2 cottars. The whole renders £23 of blanch silver. There is a fishery but it does not belong to the farm, and 7 acres of vineyard.

Bishop Maurice holds the church of this manor with 3 hides of the same land. He has there 7 villans and 11 bordars and 2 slaves with 4 ploughs, and 18 acres of meadow, and 5 acres of pasture and 12 acres of woodland. It renders 60s.

Of the same land of this manor Ansgar holds I hide of the Count of Mortain. It is worth 20s.

The KING holds CREWKERNE. Eadgifu held it TRE, and it did not pay geld, nor is it known how many hides are assessed there. There is land for 40 ploughs. In demesne are 5 ploughs and 12 slaves and 26 coliberts; and 42 villans and 45 bordars with 20 ploughs. There are 4 mills rendering 40s, and a market rendering £4. There are 60 acres of meadow, pasture half a league long

[and] 4 furlongs broad, [and] woodland 4 furlongs long and 2 furlongs broad. It renders £46 of blanch silver.

From this manor has been taken away [? Lower] EASTHAMS. TRE it belonged to the farm of the manor and could not be separated from it. Turstin holds it of the Count of Mortain. It is worth 50s.

The KING holds CONGRESBURY. Earl Harold held it TRE and it paid geld for 20 hides. There is land for 50 ploughs. Of this 5 hides are in demesne, and there are 6 ploughs and 12 slaves; and 34 villans and 34 bordars with 34 ploughs. There are 2 mills rendering 17s6d, and 250 acres of meadow, pasture 2 leagues long and half a league broad, [and] woodland 2½ leagues long and half a league broad. It renders £28.15s of blanch silver.

Of this land of this manor 3 thegns, Alweard, Ordric, and Ordwulf, hold 3 hides and 3 virgates of land. They themselves held them TRE, nor could they be separated from the lord of the manor. There are in demesne 3 ploughs and 4 slaves; and 6 villans and 17 bordars with 3½ ploughs. There are 20 acres of meadow and 30 acres of woodland. The whole is worth 60s.

Bishop Maurice holds the church of this manor with half a hide. It is worth 20s.

From this land of this manor have been taken away 2 hides which belonged there TRE. Bishop Giso holds 1, and it is worth £4. Serlo de Burcy and Gilbert fitz Turold hold the other hide, and it is worth 40s.

The KING holds QUEEN CAMEL. Gytha held it TRE and it paid geld for 8½ hides. But there are 15 hides. There is land for 15 ploughs. Of this 5 hides are in demesne, and there are 4 ploughs and 6 slaves; and 28 villans and 10 bordars with 11 ploughs. There are 2 mills rendering 20s, and 100 acres of meadow, and 100 acres of pasture and 100 acres of woodland. It renders £23 of blanch silver.

The KING holds [East, North and West] COKER. Gytha held it TRE. There are 15 hides, and it paid geld for 7 hides. There is land for 15 ploughs. Of this 5½ hides are in demesne, and there are 3 ploughs and 7 slaves and 4 coliberts; and 35 villans and 42 bordars with 12 ploughs. There is a mill rendering 5s, and 100 acres of meadow, pasture 1 league long and half a league broad, [and] woodland 8 furlongs long and 6 furlongs broad. It renders £19 and 12d of blanch silver.

The KING holds HARDINGTON MANDEVILLE. Gunild held it TRE, and there are 10 hides, and it paid geld for 5 hides. There is land for 10 ploughs. Of this 5½ hides are in demesne, and there are 2 ploughs and 7 slaves; and 16 villans and 16 bordars with 8 ploughs. There are 40 acres of meadow, [and] woodland 5 furlongs long and 4 furlongs broad. It renders £12.14s of blanch silver.

The KING holds HENSTRIDGE. Earl Harold held it TRE and it paid geld for 10 hides. There is land for 16 ploughs. Besides these 10 hides there is land for 8 ploughs, which has never paid geld. There are in demesne 5 ploughs and 8 slaves; and 37 villans and 15 bordars with 16 ploughs. There is a mill

rendering 30d, and 160 acres of meadow, pasture 1 league long and half a league broad, and as much woodland. It renders £23 of blanch silver.

In this manor 1 free man held 9 acres of land and 2 acres of woodland. They are worth 30d. He could not separate himself from the lord of the manor.

Queen Edith Held These Lands Entered Below

The KING holds MILVERTON. TRE it paid geld for half a virgate of land. There is land for 16 ploughs. In demesne is 1 plough and 3 slaves and 3 cottars; and 16 villans and 7 bordars with 9 ploughs. There is a mill rendering 7s6d, and 6 acres of meadow, and 100 acres of pasture and 100 acres of scrubland. There is a market rendering 10s. The whole renders £25 by tale; in Queen Edith's time it rendered £12.

The KING holds MARTOCK. There are 38 hides. TRE it paid geld for 13 hides. There is land for 40 ploughs. Of this 8 hides are in demesne, and there are 3 ploughs and 6 slaves and 14 coliberts; and 65 villans and 24 bordars with 28 ploughs. There are 2 mills rendering 35s, and 50 acres of meadow, pasture 1 league long and as much broad, [and] woodland 1 league long and 2 furlongs broad. A fishery renders 5s. It renders £70 by tale, and [would render] 100s more if Bishop Walkelin bears witness.

To this manor have been added 3 hides. TRE 3 thegns held them. They render £4.10s in Martock.

From this manor have been taken away 1 hide and 1 virgate of land in COMPTON[? Nether or Over Compton, Dorset]. Ansgar the cook holds it. There is land for 2 ploughs. There 4 men have 1 plough. It was worth 50s; now 30s.

From this same manor have been taken away 1½ hides. Ælfric the Little holds them, and they are worth 40s.

The KING holds KEYNSHAM. TRE it paid geld for 50 hides. There is land for 100 ploughs. Of this 15½ hides are in demesne, and there are 10 ploughs and 20 slaves and 25 coliberts; and 70 villans and 40 bordars with 63 ploughs. There are 6 mills rendering 60s, and 100 acres of meadow, and 100 acres of pasture, [and] woodland 1 league long and as much broad.

It renders £108 by tale; it used to render £80.

To this manor belong 8 burgesses in Bath paying 5s a year.

Of these 50 hides Count Eustace holds in BELLUTON 4 hides, and Alvred [holds] of him. Tovi held it as 1 manor TRE. There are in demesne 1½ ploughs with 1 slave; and 5 villans and 2 bordars with 2 ploughs. There is a mill rendering 15s, and 22 acres of meadow, and 20 acres of pasture, [and] woodland 3 furlongs long and 2 furlongs wide. It was worth £3; now £4.

Of the same land of this manor Roger holds 10 hides in STANTON DREW. He has there in demesne 1 plough; and 15 villans and 13 bordars have 7 ploughs. There is a mill rendering 10s, and 15 acres of meadow, pasture 4 furlongs long and 1½ furlongs broad, and as much woodland. It is worth 100s.

Of this land the Bishop of Coutances holds half a hide, and has there half a plough. It is worth 5s. Wulfweard held it, and could not be separated from the manor.

The wife of this Wulfweard holds 1 hide of the above-mentioned 50 hides and has there 4 ploughs with 3 slaves and 3 villans and 4 bordars. There are 12 acres of meadow and 4 acres of scrubland. It was and is worth £4.

Ælfric holds of the same land 1 hide which Wulfmær held TRE, and it could not be alienated from the manor. There is 1 plough, and 17 acres of meadow and 2 acres of pasture. It is worth 20s.

The KING holds CHEWTON MENDIP. There are 29 hides. TRE it paid geld for 14 hides. There is land for 40 ploughs. Of this 18 hides are in demesne, and there are 9 ploughs and 20 slaves and 2 coliberts; and 18 villans and 25 bordars with 19 ploughs. There are 5 mills rendering 30s less 5d, and 100 acres of meadow, pasture 2 leagues long and 1 league broad, [and] woodland 1 league in length and breadth. In Bath 4 burgesses pay 40d. It renders £50 by tale; in the time of Queen Edith it rendered 30.

The Abbot of Jumièges holds the church of this manor with half a hide of land. There are 2½ ploughs, and 2 slaves, and 2 villans and 8 bordars and 8 cottars. It was and is worth 40s.

The KING holds BATHEASTON. There are 2 hides, and it paid geld for 1 hide. There is land for 10 ploughs. In demesne is 1 plough, and 2 slaves and 7 coliberts; and 13 villans and 3 bordars and 3 cottars with 5 ploughs. There are 2 mills rendering 100d, and 50 acres of meadow, and scrubland 2 leagues in length and breadth. These 2 hides were and are [part] of the demesne farm of the borough of Bath.

The KING holds BATH. TRE it paid geld for 20 hides when the shire paid geld. There the king has 64 burgesses paying £4, and 90 burgesses of other men pay there 60s. There the king has 6 waste houses.

That borough with the aforesaid BATHEASTON renders £60 by tale and 1 mark of gold. Besides this the mint renders 100s. Edward pays £11 of the third penny of this borough. From this borough 1 house has been taken away. Hugh the interpreter holds it, and it is worth 2s.

William de Moyon pays of the third penny of ILCHESTER £6 at 20[d] to the ora. From MILBORNE PORT 20s. From BRUTON 20s. From LANGPORT 10s. From AXBRIDGE 10s. From FROME 5s.

Wulfweard White Held These Lands Entered Below

The KING holds CORTON DENHAM. TRE it paid geld for 7 hides. There is land for 7 ploughs. Of this 3½ hides and 1 ferding are in demesne, and there is 1 plough and 3 slaves; and 10 villans and 8 bordars with 3 ploughs. There are 6 acres of meadow, [and] woodland 2 furlongs long and 1 furlong broad. It was and is worth £7.

The KING holds WHITCOMBE. TRE it paid geld for 5 hides. There is land for 4 ploughs. Of this 3 hides and

3 virgates of land are in demesne, and there is 1 plough and 2 slaves; and 3 villans and 3 bordars having 2 ploughs. There are 6 acres of meadow, [and] woodland 4 furlongs long and 1 furlong broad. It renders £4.

The KING holds PITNEY. TRE it paid geld for 1 hide. There is land for 1½ ploughs. Humphrey holds there half a hide, and he has there 1 plough, and 6 acres of meadow and 3 acres of woodland. It was and is worth 20s. What the king has there is worth 10s.

Warmund holds MUDFORD [Mudford, Up Mudford and West Mudford] in pledge from Wulfweard on the evidence of the king's writ. TRE it paid geld for 5 hides. There is land for 5 ploughs. Of this 2 hides are in demesne, and there are 2 ploughs. There are 12 acres of meadow and as much of pasture. It was and is worth £3.

[Folio 87V: SOMERSET]

The land of the Bishop of Winchester

The BISHOP OF WINCHESTER holds TAUNTON. Archbishop Stigand held it TRE and it paid geld for 54 hides and 2½ virgates of land. There is land for 100 ploughs. Besides this the bishop has in demesne land for 20 ploughs which has never paid geld, and there he has 13 ploughs. There are 80 villans and 82 bordars and 70 slaves and 16 coliberts and 17 swineherds paying £7.10s. Among them all they have 60 ploughs. There are 64 burgesses paying 32s. There are 3 mills rendering 100s less 60d. The market renders 50s, and from the mint 50s. There are 40 acres of meadow, pasture 2 leagues long and 1 league broad, [and] woodland 1 league long and as much broad.

When Bishop Walkelin received it, it rendered £50; now it renders £154 and 13d with all its appurtenances and customary dues.

These customs belong to TAUNTON: borough-right; thieves; breach of the peace; house-breaking; hundred pence and St Peter's pence; church-scot; thrice in the year the bishop's pleas to be held without summons; setting out on military service with the bishop's men.

These lands render the said customs at TAUNTON: Tolland, Oake, [Rich's or Treble's] Holford, and Upper Cheddon and Cheddon Fitzpaine, Maidenbrook, Ford, Hillfarrance and Hele, Nynehead [Nynehead and East Nynehead], Norton Fitzwarren, Bradford-on-Tone, Halse and Heathfield, Shopnoller, and Stoke St Mary. These 2 estates do not owe military service. Those of West Bagborough owe the same customs except military service and burial.

From all these lands those who have to make oath or undergo the ordeal come to Taunton. When the lords of these lands die, they are buried at Taunton.

Hillfarrance and Hele TRE could not be separated from Taunton.

Of the aforesaid 54½ hides and half a virgate of land, Geoffrey now holds of the bishop 4 hides and 1 virgate of land; Robert

4½ hides; Hugh 2½ hides. There are in demesne 10 ploughs and 12 slaves; and 20 villans and 37 bordars with 10 ploughs. There are 37 acres of meadow, and 43 acres of woodland, and a mill rendering 3s: this is Hugh's. In all it is worth £27.

Also of the aforesaid hides Godwine holds of the bishop 2 hides less half a virgate of land; Leofgifu 2 hides; Alweard 1 hide and 1½ virgates of land; Ælfric and Eadær 3 hides; Leofwig half a virgate of land. There are in demesne 7 ploughs and 13 slaves; and 13 villans and 20 bordars with 3½ ploughs. There are 2 mills rendering 6s8d, and 45 acres of meadow and 61 acres of woodland. In all it is worth £8.3s. Those who held these lands TRE could not be separated from the church.

Of the aforesaid hides the Count of Mortain holds 1 hide; Alvred 1 hide; John 2 hides and half a virgate of land. In demesne are 2 ploughs and 6 slaves; and 12 villans and 17 bordars with 3½ ploughs. There are 2 mills rendering 14s2d, and 19 acres of meadow and 100 acres of pasture and 20 acres of woodland. These 3 estates belonged to TAUNTON TRE and were worth 70s; now they render £6.10s.

To this manor of Taunton have been added 2½ hides in Lydeard St Lawrence and Leigh [Chapel Leigh, Pyleigh and West Leigh, in Lydeard St Lawrence] which 1 thegn held in parage TRE, and he could go to any lord he wished. Now Wulfweard and Alweard hold them of the bishop by grant of King William. There is land for 5 ploughs. There are 6 villans and 3 bordars and 4 slaves, and 11 acres of meadow, and 100 acres of pasture and 49 acres of woodland. It was and is worth 45s.

The customary dues and service from these estates always belonged to TAUNTON; and King William granted these lands for St Peter and Bishop Walkelin to have, as he himself recognized at Salisbury [Wilts.] in the hearing of the Bishop of Durham, whom he commanded to write this his grant in the returns.

The same bishop holds PITMINSTER. Archbishop Stigand held it and it paid geld for 15 hides. There is land for 20 ploughs. Of this 5 hides are in demesne, and there are 2 ploughs; and 17 villans and 8 bordars with 14 ploughs. There are 6 acres of meadow, and 400 acres of pasture and as many acres of woodland. It was worth £13; now £16.

The same bishop holds BLEADON. It was and is for the monks' sustenance. TRE it paid geld for 15 hides. There is land for 17 ploughs. Of this 10 hides are in demesne, and there are 3 ploughs and 8 slaves; and 16 villans and 10 bordars with 11 ploughs. There are 50 acres of meadow, and pasture 1 league long and half a league broad. It was and is worth £15. Of these 10 hides Sæwulf holds of the bishop 1 hide, and there he has 1 plough with 1 slave, and 1 bordar, and 16 acres of meadow and 1 acre of scrubland. It is worth 20s.

The same bishop holds RIMPTON. Stigand held it TRE and it paid geld for 5 hides. There is land for 5 ploughs. Of this 2 hides and 1½ virgates of land are in demesne, and there are 3 ploughs and 2 slaves; and 8 villans and 7 bordars with 3 ploughs. There are 10 acres of meadow, [and] woodland 4 furlongs long and 1 furlong broad. It was and is worth £7.

The land of the Bishop of Salisbury

The Bishop of SALISBURY holds SEABOROUGH [Dorset]. Alweard held it TRE and it paid geld for 1½ hides. There is land for 1½ ploughs. Yet there are 2 ploughs, and 2 villans and 4 bordars and 2 slaves. There is half a mill rendering 10d, and 9 acres of meadow, and 10 acres of woodland, [and] pasture half a league long and half a furlong broad. To this manor has been added another SEABOROUGH [Dorset]. Alfred held it TRE and it paid geld for 1½ hides. There are 2 ploughs with 1 villan and 5 bordars, and half a mill rendering 10d, and 9 acres of meadow and 10 acres of woodland, [and] pasture half a league long and half a furlong broad. These 2 estates do not belong to the bishopric of Salisbury. Bishop Osmund holds them as 1 manor, and Walter [holds] of him. It was and is worth 60s. TRE they belonged to CREWKERNE, the king's manor, and those who held them could not be separated from it, and they paid as a customary due in CREWKERNE 12 sheep with lambs, and a bloom of iron from every free man.

The same bishop holds CHILCOMPTON, and Walter [holds] of him. Alweard held it TRE and it paid geld for 5 hides. There is land for 3 ploughs. In demesne are 2 ploughs and 2 slaves; and 5 villans and 4 bordars and 7 cottars with 2 ploughs. There is a mill rendering 30d, and 14 acres of meadow, and 80 acres of woodland and 1 league of pasture. It was and is worth 60s.

The land of the Bishop of Bayeux

The Bishop of BAYEUX holds TEMPLECOMBE, and Samson [holds] of him. Earl Leofwine held it TRE and it paid geld for 8 hides. There is land for 8 ploughs. Of this 5 hides are in demesne, and there are 3 ploughs and 7 slaves; and 10 villans and 6 bordars with 2 ploughs. There are 40 acres of meadow, and 40 acres of pasture and 60 acres of scrubland. It was and is worth £10. To this manor have been added 3 virgates of land in 'THORENT' [in Milborne Port]. Alweard held them TRE as 1 manor and it paid geld for as much. There is land for half a plough. It was and is worth 13s.

The land of the Bishop of Coutances

The Bishop of COUTANCES holds DOWLISH [Dowlish Wake and West Dowlish]. Alweard held it TRE and it paid geld for 2 hides and 1 virgate of land. There is land for 1½ ploughs, which are there with 3 villans and 3 bordars and 1 slave. It was and is worth 24s.

To this manor have been added 7 hides, which 3 thegns held as 3 manors TRE. There are in demesne 2 ploughs and 2 slaves; and 11 villans and 11 bordars with 5 ploughs. There are 44 acres of meadow, and pasture 4 furlongs in length and as much in breadth and 20 acres more, [and] woodland 8 furlongs long and 3 furlongs broad and 20 acres in addition. It is worth £6.10s. William holds this land of the bishop.

The same bishop holds CHAFFCOMBE, and Ralph [holds] of him. 2 thegns held it TRE and it paid geld for 3½ hides.

There is land for 3 ploughs. In demesne is 1 [plough]; and 2 villans and 6 bordars have 1 plough. There is woodland 8 furlongs long and as much broad. It is worth 40s. To this manor has been added 1 hide and 3 virgates of land. 2 thegns held it TRE as 2 manors. There is land for 2 ploughs. 3 villans there have these [ploughs]. It is worth 20s.

The same bishop holds 'HISCOMBE' [in West Coker], and William [holds] of him. 4 thegns held it TRE and it paid geld for 2 hides and 3 virgates of land. There is land for 3 ploughs. In demesne are 2 ploughs with 1 slave; and 4 villans and 8 bordars with 2 ploughs. There are 31 acres of meadow and 10 acres of scrubland. It was worth 40s; now 50s.

The same bishop holds RODNEY STOKE. Ælfgeat held it TRE. There are 5 hides and 1 virgate of land, and it paid geld for 4 hides. There is land for 5 ploughs. Of this 2½ hides are in demesne, and there are 2 ploughs and 3 slaves; and 9 villans and 3 bordars with 4½ ploughs. There is a mill rendering 3s, and 15 acres of meadow, pasture 2 leagues long and 1 league broad, and 2s more in addition, [and] woodland 1 league long and 1 furlong broad. It was worth £6; now £4.

The same bishop holds EXTON, and Drogo [holds] of him. Edwin held it TRE and it paid geld for 3 hides and a ferding. There is land for 12 ploughs. In demesne are 2 ploughs and 6 slaves; and 20 villans and 13 bordars with 7 ploughs. There are 8 acres of meadow, and 60 acres of woodland, [and] pasture 1 league long and as much broad. It is worth £6. Of this same land TRE 3 virgates of land belonged to NETTLECOMBE, a manor of the king.

[Folio 88: SOMERSET]

The same bishop holds WILMERSHAM, and Drogo [holds] of him. TRE it paid geld for 1 hide and 1 virgate of land. There is land for 5 ploughs. Of this 3 virgates are in demesne, and there is 1 plough and 3 slaves; and 5 villans and 3 bordars with 1 plough. There are 200 acres of pasture and as much woodland. It is worth 30s.

The same Drogo holds of the bishop CULBONE. TRE it paid geld for 1 hide and 1 virgate. There is land for 2 ploughs. There are 2 villans and 1 bordar and 1 slave with 1 plough, and 50 acres of pasture and 100 acres of woodland. It is worth 15s. These 2 manors Osmund held TRE.

Eadmær holds of the bishop WITHYCOMBE. Alnoth held it and it paid geld for 3 hides TRE. There is land for 10 ploughs. In demesne are 2 ploughs and 6 slaves; and 14 villans and 7 bordars with 8 ploughs. There are 10 acres of meadow, and 550 acres of pasture, and 100 less 4 acres of woodland. It was worth £4; now £6.

Azelin holds of the bishop EAST HARPTREE. Alric and Wulfwig held it TRE as 2 manors and it paid geld for 5 hides. There is land for 5 ploughs. Of this 3 hides are in demesne, and there are 2 ploughs and 2 slaves; and 9 villans and 1 bordar and 4 cottars with 3 ploughs. There is a mill rendering 5s, and 40 acres of meadow, pasture 8 furlongs long and 5 furlongs broad, [and] woodland 4 furlongs long and 2½ furlongs broad. It was and is worth 40s.

Azelin holds of the bishop HUTTON. 2 thegns held it TRE as 2 manors and it paid geld for 5 hides. There is land for 5 ploughs. There is 1 plough in demesne; and 5 villans and 6 bordars have 2 ploughs. There are 30 acres of meadow, and 200 acres of pasture and 15 acres of scrubland. It was worth £4; now 60s.

Azelin holds of the bishop ELBOROUGH. Alweard held it TRE and it paid geld for 3 hides. There is land for 4 ploughs. In demesne are 2 ploughs with 1 slave; and 1 villan and 5 bordars with 1 plough. There are 20 acres of meadow and 40 acres of pasture. It was worth 60s; now 40s.

Herlwin holds of the bishop WINTERHEAD. Beorhtric held it TRE and it paid geld for 1 hide. There is land for 2 ploughs. There are [2 ploughs] with 2 villans and 2 bordars and 2 slaves. There are 8 acres of meadow and 3 acres of scrubland. It was and is worth 20s. These 3 manors belonged to the Church of Glastonbury TRE. Those who held them could not be separated from the church.

Herlwin holds of the bishop ASHCOMBE. Beorhtric held it TRE and it paid geld for 3½ hides. There is land for 5 ploughs. In demesne are 2 ploughs and 7 slaves; and 6 villans and 5 bordars with 3 ploughs. There are 40 acres of meadow, and 3 acres of scrubland and 100 acres of pasture. It was and is worth 100s.

William holds of the bishop CLUTTON. Thorkil held it TRE and it paid geld for 10 hides. There is land for 8 ploughs. In demesne are 3 ploughs with 1 slave; and 10 villans and 12 bordars with 6 ploughs. There is a mill rendering 30d, and 107 acres of meadow, pasture 10 furlongs long and 4 furlongs broad, [and] woodland half a league long and as much broad. It was worth £3; now £6.

William holds of the bishop TIMSBURY. Api held it TRE and it paid geld for 3 hides. There is land for 3 ploughs. In demesne is 1 plough and 2 slaves; and 2 villans and 1 bordar with 1 plough. There are 2 parts of a mill rendering 3s, and 26 acres of meadow and as much pasture. It was worth 26s; now 50s.

To this manor have been added 2 hides which Sibbi held as 1 manor TRE, and it paid geld for as much. There is land for 2 ploughs, which are there with 1 slave, and 1 villan and 3 bordars. There is the third part of a mill rendering 2s, and 16 acres of meadow and as much pasture. It was worth 14s; now 30s.

Wulfgifu holds of the bishop NORTON MALREWARD. Alweald held it TRE and it paid geld for 5 hides. There is land for 8 ploughs. In demesne is 1 plough and 3 slaves; and 5 villans and 11 bordars with 3 ploughs. There is a mill rendering 40d, and 34 acres of meadow, and 6 acres of scrubland, and woodland 1 league in length and as much in breadth. It was worth 100s; now 60s.

Fulcran holds of the bishop CLAVERHAM. Gunild held it TRE and it paid geld for 2 hides. There is land for 3 ploughs. In demesne is 1 plough with 1 slave; and 3 villans and 12 bordars with 2 ploughs. There are 7 acres of meadow, woodland 1 furlong long and as much broad, [and] scrubland half a league long and as much broad. It was worth 20s; now 30s.

William holds of the bishop FARMBOROUGH. Eadric held it TRE and it paid geld for 5 hides. There is land for 5 ploughs. In demesne are 2 ploughs and 5 slaves; and 4 villans and 3 bordars with 2 ploughs. There are 77 acres of meadow and 74 acres of pasture. It was and is worth £4.

To this manor have been added 5 hides. Ælfric held them TRE as 1 manor, and it paid geld for 5 hides. There is land for 5 ploughs. Nigel holds them of the bishop. In demesne are 2 ploughs with 1 slave, and 1 villan and 5 bordars. There are 77 acres of meadow and 74 acres of pasture. It was and is worth £4.

Fulcran and Nigel hold of the bishop CLEWER. Thorkil held it TRE and it paid geld for 3 virgates of land less a ferding. There is land for 2 ploughs, which are there with 6 villans, and 10 acres of meadow. It is worth 15s.

Herlwin holds of the bishop BISHOPSWORTH [in Bristol]. Algar held it TRE and it paid geld for 2 hides. There is land for 2 ploughs. In demesne is 1 plough and 3 slaves, and 2 bordars. There are 12 acres of meadow, [and] woodland 6 furlongs long and 1 furlong broad. In Bristol, 10 houses. In Bath, 2 houses render 10d. It was worth 20s; now 40s.

Azelin holds of the bishop BISHOPSWORTH [in Bristol]. Eadric held it TRE and it paid geld for 1½ hides. There is land for 2 ploughs, which are there with 4 villans and 4 bordars and 4 cottars. There are 10 acres of meadow and 45 acres of pasture. It was worth 20s; now 30s.

Azelin holds of the bishop WESTON IN GORDANO. Beorhtnoth held it TRE and it paid geld for 7 hides. There is land for 6 ploughs. In demesne are 3 ploughs and 2 slaves; and 6 villans and 7 bordars with 3 ploughs. There are 33 acres of meadow, pasture 12 furlongs long and 8 furlongs broad, [and] woodland 7 furlongs long and 3 furlongs broad. It was and is worth £4. 10s.

Roger holds of the bishop SALTFORD. 4 thegns held it TRE and it paid geld for 4 hides. There is land for 6 ploughs. In demesne are 3 ploughs and 6 slaves; and 7 villans and 10 bordars with 4 ploughs. There is a mill rendering 12s6d, and 32 acres of meadow. It was and is worth £6.

Roger holds of the bishop EASTON-IN-GORDANO. Æthelric held it TRE and it paid geld for 12 hides. There is land for 9 ploughs. In demesne are 2 ploughs and 3 slaves; and 14 villans and 7 bordars with 7 ploughs. There is a mill rendering 50d, and 36 acres of meadow, and 30 acres of woodland and 100 acres of pasture. It was worth £10; now £7.

William holds of the bishop PORTISHEAD. Ælfric held it TRE and it paid geld for 8 hides. There is land for 8 ploughs. In demesne are 2 ploughs with 1 slave; and 9 villans and 4 bordars with 5 ploughs. There is a mill rendering 8s, and 20 acres of meadow, and 100 acres of pasture, [and] scrubland 12 furlongs long and 3 furlongs broad. It was and is worth 70s.

William holds of the bishop WESTON IN GORDANO.

Algar held it TRE and it paid geld for 3 hides and 1 virgate of land. There is land for 3 ploughs. In demesne are 2 ploughs and 2 slaves; and 4 villans and 4 bordars with 2 ploughs. There are 17 acres of meadow, and 12 acres of scrubland, pasture 12 furlongs long and 2 furlongs broad, and 6 furlongs of moor. It was and is worth 60s.

Herlwin holds of the bishop CLAPTON IN GORDANO. Algar held it TRE and it paid geld for 5½ hides. There is land for 5 ploughs. In demesne are 2 ploughs and 2 slaves; and 10 villans and 10 bordars with 3 ploughs. There are 50 acres of meadow, pasture 18 furlongs long and 3 furlongs broad, [and] woodland 7 furlongs long and 1 furlong broad. It was worth 40s; now 70s.

Brungar holds of the bishop HAVYATT. Tidwulf held it TRE and it paid geld for 1½ hides. There is land for 1 plough, which [plough] is there in demesne with 3 bordars. There are 10 acres of meadow and 20 acres of woodland. It was and is worth 20s.

The bishop himself holds an estate, which is called KENN. There is half a hide, and there he has 1 slave. It is worth 5s.

Fulcran and Nigel hold of the bishop BACKWELL. Thorkil held it TRE and it paid geld for 10 hides. There is land for 14 ploughs. 32 villans and 21 bordars and 2 slaves have these [ploughs] there. There is a mill rendering 4s, and 24 acres of meadow, pasture 1 league long and half a league broad, [and] scrubland 1 league long and 2 furlongs broad. It was and is worth £8.

Fulcran holds of the bishop BUTCOMBE. Alweard held it TRE and it paid geld for 3 hides. There is land for 3 ploughs. In demesne is 1 plough and 2 slaves; and 11 villans and 4 bordars with 5 ploughs. There is a mill rendering 20d, and 10 acres of meadow and 30 acres of woodland. It was and is worth £4.

Nigel holds of the bishop BARROW GURNEY. Eadric held it TRE and it paid geld for 10 hides. There is land for 14 ploughs. In demesne are 2 ploughs and 3 slaves, and 15 villans and 7 bordars. There is a mill rendering 5s, and 35 acres of meadow, and 30 acres of pasture, [and] woodland 1 league long and 1 furlong broad. It was and is worth £10.

[Folio 88V: SOMERSET]

The bishop himself holds PORTBURY. Godwine held it TRE and it paid geld for 8 hides. There is land for 18 ploughs. In demesne are 2 ploughs and 13 slaves; and 20 villans and 17 bordars with 16 ploughs. There are 2 mills rendering 6s, and 150 acres of meadow, pasture 17 furlongs long and 2 furlongs broad, [and] woodland 1 league long and 5 furlongs broad. It was and is worth I5.

The bishop himself holds LONG ASHTON. 3 thegns held it TRE and it paid geld for 20 hides. There is land for 30 ploughs. In demesne are 2 ploughs and 5 slaves; and 12 villans and 6 bordars with 7 ploughs. There is a mill rendering 40d, and 25 acres of meadow, pasture 1 league long and half a league broad, and 100 acres of woodland. It was worth £12; now £10.

Of the land of this manor Roger holds 7 hides of the bishop, and has there in demesne 2 ploughs and 4 slaves; and 8 villans and 10 bordars with 5 ploughs. There are 18 acres of meadow and 30 acres of woodland. It is worth £7. Of the same land of this manor Guy the priest holds 3 hides, and there he has 2 ploughs and 2 slaves, and 3 villans and 2 bordars with 2 ploughs. It is worth 100s. To the church of this manor belongs 1 virgate of the same land.

Roger holds of the bishop FRESHFORD. Tovi held it TRE and it paid geld for 2½ hides. There is land for 3 ploughs. In demesne are 2 ploughs; and 8 bordars with 1 plough. There is half a mill rendering 5s, and 12 acres of meadow, and 30 acres of pasture and 12 acres of scrubland. It was worth 40s; now 60s.

Azelin holds of the bishop LANGRIDGE. Æthelsige held it TRE and it paid geld for 2½ hides. There is land for 5 ploughs. In demesne are 3 ploughs and 3 slaves; and 5 villans and 7 bordars with 2 ploughs. There is a mill rendering 40d, and 4½ acres of meadow and 130 acres of pasture. It was worth 40s; now 60s.

The bishop himself holds BATHWICK [in Bath]. Ælfric; held it TRE and it paid geld for 4 hides. There is land for 4 ploughs. In demesne are 3 ploughs and 4 slaves, and 1 villan and 10 bordars. There is a mill rendering 35s, and 50 acres of meadow and 120 acres of pasture. It is worth £7.

To this manor has been added 1 hide in WOOLLEY, which Ælfric held TRE as 1 manor and it paid geld for 1 hide. There are 2 ploughs and 6 slaves, and 9 bordars with 1 plough. There are 2 mills rendering 2s, and 20 acres of scrubland. It was and is worth 60s.

Nigel holds of the bishop [Lower and Upper] SWAINSWICK. Alfred held it TRE and it paid geld for 1 hide. There is land for 1 plough. It was and is worth 20s.

The bishop himself holds COMPTON DANDO. Eadric held it TRE and it paid geld for 10 hides. There is land for 14 ploughs. In demesne is 1 plough and 4 slaves; and 16 villans and 6 bordars with 6 ploughs. There are 2 mills rendering 25s, and 15 acres of meadow, and 100 acres of pasture and 15 acres of woodland. It was and is worth 10.

The bishop himself holds WRAXALL. Ælfric held it TRE and it paid geld for 20 hides. There is land for 26 ploughs. In demesne is 1 plough and 2 slaves; and 34 villans and 30 bordars with 25 ploughs. There are 2 mills rendering 12s6d, and 150 acres of meadow and as much woodland, [and] pasture 2 leagues long and 7 furlongs broad. It was and is worth £15. Of the same land of this manor 1 knight holds 4½ hides of the bishop, and there he has 2 ploughs with 3 villans and 4 bordars. It was and is worth 50s. To this manor has been added 1 hide which 1 thegn held TRE. There is land for 1 plough. It is worth 10s.

The bishop holds WINFORD. Alweald held it TRE and it paid geld for 10 hides. There is land for 22 ploughs. Of this Roger holds 4 hides, Fulcran 5 hides, Kolsveinn 1 hide. In demesne they have 5 ploughs and there are 7 slaves; and 19 villans and 12 bordars with 14 ploughs. There is a mill

rendering 40d, and 20 acres of meadow, pasture 2 furlongs long and 1 furlong broad, [and] woodland 1 league long and 2 furlongs broad. The whole was worth £9.5s; now 20s more.

To this manor has been added 1 hide which Ælfric held TRE. Now Kolsveinn holds it of the bishop, and has there 2 ploughs and 2 bordars. It was and is worth 25s.

William holds FOXCOTE. Ealdgyth held it TRE and it paid geld for 5 hides. There is land for 4 ploughs. In demesne are 2 ploughs and 3 slaves and 2 cottars; and 6 villans and 6 bordars with 2 ploughs. There is a mill rendering 10s, and 19 acres of meadow, and 6 acres of pasture and 20 acres of scrubland. It was and is worth £4.

The same William holds of the bishop STRATTON-ON-THE-FOSSE. Alweald held it TRE of the Church of Glastonbury, nor could he be separated from it, and it paid geld for 3 hides. There is land for 3 ploughs. In demesne are 2 ploughs and 3 slaves; and 5 villans and 6 bordars with 1½ ploughs. There is a mill rendering 5s, and 20 acres of meadow, pasture 4 furlongs in both length and breadth, [and] woodland 3 furlongs long and 2 furlongs broad. It was worth 50s; now £4.

To this manor have been added 1½ hides in PITCOTE. Wulfmær held them TRE and could go where he would. There is land for 1 plough. There are 2 villans and 2 bordars with 1 slave. There is a mill rendering 40d, and 7 acres of meadow, and 2 furlongs of pasture and 1 furlong of woodland. It was and is worth 20s. William holds it of the bishop.

Nigel holds of the bishop ENGLISHCOMBE. 1 thegn held it TRE and it paid geld for 10 hides. There is land for 10 ploughs. In demesne are 3 ploughs and 6 slaves; and 3 villans and 17 bordars with 6 ploughs. There are 2 mills rendering 11s7d. There are 12 acres of meadow and 100 acres of scrubland. It was and is worth £10.

The same Nigel holds of the bishop TWERTON [in Bath]. 3 thegns held it TRE and it paid geld for 7½ hides. There is land for 10 ploughs. In demesne are 3 ploughs and 6 slaves; and 7 villans and 13 bordars with 6 ploughs. There are 2 mills rendering 30s, and 15 acres of meadow. It was and is worth £10.

Geoffrey holds of the bishop TWERTON [in Bath]. 1 thegn held it TRE and it paid geld for 2½ hides. There is land for 2½ ploughs, which are there in demesne with 4 bordars and 2 slaves. There are 2 mills rendering 30s, and 7 acres of meadow and 3 acres of scrubland. It was and is worth 60s. Alfred held this land of Queen Edith. Now the bishop holds it of the king, as he says.

Roger holds of the bishop RADSTOCK. Ælfgeat, Alwine, and Algar held it TRE and it paid geld for 7 hides and 3 virgates. There is land for 9 ploughs. In demesne are 3 ploughs and 2 slaves; and 9 villans and 12 bordars and 3 cottars with 4 ploughs. There is a mill rendering 13s, and 12 acres of meadow. It was and is worth £7.

Ralph holds of the bishop HARDINGTON. 3 thegns held it TRE and it paid geld for 4 hides. There is land for 4 ploughs.

In demesne are 2 ploughs and 4 slaves; and 1 villan and 7 bordars with 3 ploughs. There are 36 acres of meadow and 12 acres of scrubland. It was and is worth £4. In this manor is 1 hide belonging to HEMINGTON. Baldwin holds it and has common pasture in this manor.

Azelin holds of the bishop BABINGTON. 2 thegns held it TRE and it paid geld for 5 hides. There is land for 4 ploughs. In demesne are 2 ploughs and 7 slaves; and 2 villans and 2 bordars with 3 ploughs. There is a mill rendering 40d, and 12 acres of meadow, and 15 acres of pasture, [and] woodland 6 furlongs long and 2 furlongs broad. It was worth 40s; now 60s.

Azelin holds of the bishop 'MIDDLECOTE' [in Mells]. 2 thegns held it of the Church of Glastonbury, nor could they be separated from it, and it paid geld for 5½ hides. There is land for 5 ploughs. In demesne are 1½ ploughs and 3 slaves; and 9 villans and 6 bordars and 5 cottars with 5 ploughs. There is a mill rendering 6s6d, and 3 acres of meadow, pasture 4 furlongs long and 2 furlongs broad, and as much woodland. It was worth 40s; now £4.

The bishop himself holds LULLINGTON. Earl Harold held it TRE and it paid geld for 7 hides. There is land for 5 ploughs. In demesne are 2 ploughs and 2 slaves; and 7 villans and 10 bordars with 4 ploughs. There is a mill rendering 20s, and 20 acres of meadow, [and] woodland 6 furlongs long and 2 furlongs broad. It was worth £4; now 100s.

The bishop himself holds ORCHARDLEIGH. 3 thegns held it TRE and it paid geld for 5 hides. There is land for 4 ploughs. In demesne are 3 ploughs and 2 slaves; and 3 villans and 9 bordars with 2 ploughs. There is a mill rendering 12s6d, and 24 acres of meadow, [and] woodland 6 furlongs long and 2 furlongs broad. It was and is worth £4.

Moses holds of the bishop TELLISFORD. Edward held it TRE and it paid geld for 2 hides. There is land for 3 ploughs. In demesne are 2 ploughs and 5 cottars; and 4 bordars with 1½ ploughs. There is half a mill rendering 7s6d, and 7 acres of meadow, and 10 acres of pasture and 1½ acres of woodland. It is worth 30s. To this manor have been added 3 hides. Ælfgeat held them TRE and they paid geld for as much. There is land for 4 ploughs. In demesne is 1 plough and 3 slaves; and 3 villans and 8 bordars with 2 ploughs. There is half a mill rendering 9s, and 11½ acres of meadow, and 30 acres of pasture and 4½ acres of woodland. It was worth 60s; now 40s.

The bishop holds RODE as 3 manors. 7 thegns held it TRE and it paid geld for 9 hides. There is land for 9 ploughs. Of this land Robert holds of the bishop 1 hide; Moses half a hide; Robert 1½ hides; Roger 2½ hides; Scirweald 2½ hides; Richard 1 hide. In demesne are 7 ploughs and 6 slaves; and 3 villans and 29 bordars with 4½ ploughs. From the mills come 27s, and [there are] 33 acres of meadow, and 33 acres of woodland and 25 acres of pasture. The whole was worth £7.10s; now among them all it is worth £8.5s.

Nigel holds of the bishop KEYFORD. Leofdæg held it TRE and it paid geld for 1 hide and 1 virgate of land. There is land for 1 plough, which [plough] is there in demesne with 12 cottars. There is a mill rendering 30d, and 6 acres of meadow and 5 acres of pasture. It was worth 10s; now 15s.

[Folio 89: SOMERSET]

Osmund holds of the bishop STONY LITTLETON. Godwine held it TRE and it paid geld for 2 hides. There is land for 2 ploughs, which are there in demesne with 1 bordar and 6 slaves. There is a mill rendering 10s, and 2 acres of meadow and 6 acres of pasture. It is worth 40s.

The bishop himself holds NEWTON ST LOE. Ælfric held it TRE and it paid geld for 3 hides. There is land for 4 ploughs. In demesne are 2 ploughs and 4 slaves; and 4 villans and 3 bordars with 2 ploughs. There is a mill rendering 7s6d, and 9 acres of meadow and 40 acres of scrubland. It was worth 60s; now 100s.

To this manor have been added 7 hides which 2 thegns held TRE. There is land for 8 ploughs. There are 14 villans and 8 bordars and 7 slaves with 6 ploughs, and 23 acres of meadow. It was worth 100s; now £10.

Azelin holds of the bishop FARRINGTON GURNEY. Beorhtmær held it TRE and it paid geld for 5 hides. There is land for 7 ploughs. In demesne are 3 ploughs and 4 slaves; and 7 villans and 7 bordars with 4 ploughs. There are 100 acres of meadow. It was worth 50s; now £4.

Azelin holds of the bishop STON EASTON. 3 thegns held it TRE and it paid geld for 4½ hides. There is land for 6 ploughs. In demesne are 3 ploughs and 4 slaves; and 5 villans and 4 bordars and 2 cottars with 4 ploughs. There is a mill rendering 30d, and 40 acres of meadow and 40 acres of pasture. It was and is worth 70s.

Azelin holds of the bishop WEST HARPTREE. Eadric held it TRE and it paid geld for 5 hides. There is land for 4 ploughs. In demesne is half a plough; and 7 villans and 4 bordars and 5 cottars with 3 ploughs. There is a mill rendering 5s, and 58 acres of meadow, and 42 acres of woodland, [and] pasture 1 league long and half a league broad. It was and is worth 40s.

Robert holds of the bishop EMBOROUGH. 2 thegns held it TRE and it paid geld for 3 hides. There is land for 4 ploughs. In demesne are 2 ploughs and 2 slaves; and 6 villans and 4 bordars with 5 ploughs. There are 29 acres of meadow. It was worth 20s; now 70s.

The bishop himself holds CAMELEY. 2 thegns held it TRE and it paid geld for 9 hides and half a virgate of land. There is land for 9 ploughs. In demesne are 3 ploughs and 13 slaves; and 9 villans and 1 bordar and 7 cottars with 4 ploughs. There is a mill rendering 5s, and 120 acres of meadow, and 30 acres of pasture and 50 acres of scrubland. It was worth £7; now £10.

Of this land of this manor Humphrey holds 1 hide, and there he has 1 plough, and 3 villans and 1 cottar with 1 plough. There are 40 acres of meadow. It is worth 20s.

William holds of the bishop KINGSTON SEYMOUR. Ealdræd held it TRE and it paid geld for 1 hide. There is land for 17 ploughs. In demesne are 3 ploughs with 1 slave;

and 18 villans and 4 bordars with 11 ploughs. There are 40 acres of pasture. It was and is worth £6.

Of this land of this manor Fulcran holds of the bishop land for 1 plough, and there he has 2 bordars. It is worth 3s.

The same William holds KINGSTON SEYMOUR of the bishop. 4 thegns held it TRE and it paid geld for 4½ hides. There is land for 7 ploughs. There are 9 villans and 8 bordars with 1 slave having 6½ ploughs. It was and is worth 60s. TRE this manor paid geld for 1 hide only.

Roger holds of the bishop HALLATROW. 4 thegns held it TRE and it paid geld for 5 hides less half a virgate of land. There is land for 6 ploughs. In demesne are 1½ ploughs; and 4 villans and 3 bordars and 3 cottars with 2 ploughs. There are 27 acres of meadow and 33 acres of pasture. It was and is worth 60s.

Ralph holds of the bishop HIGH LITTLETON. Alweald held it TRE and it paid geld for 5 hides. There is land for 5 ploughs. In demesne are 2 ploughs with 1 slave; and 4 villans and 6 bordars with 3 ploughs. There is a mill rendering 50d, and 32 acres of meadow and 66 acres of pasture. In Bath 1 burgess pays 15d. It was and is worth 60s.

The same Ralph holds of the bishop UPTON NOBLE. Leofmær held it TRE and it paid geld for 3 hides. There is land for 3 ploughs. In demesne is 1 plough and 2 slaves; and 5 villans and 4 bordars and 2 cottars with 3 ploughs. There are 5 acres of meadow, [and] woodland half a league long and 4 furlongs broad. It was and is worth 60s.

Leofwine holds of the bishop MIDGELL. Almær held it TRE and it paid geld for 1 hide. There is land for 2 ploughs, which are there with 2 villans and 3 bordars and 1 slave, and 6 acres of meadow. It was worth 4s; now 20s.

Ralph holds of the bishop WEATHER GROVE [Dorset]. 3 thegns held it TRE and it paid geld for 2 hides. There is land for 1 plough, which [plough] is there in demesne, and 2 slaves; and 1 villan and 5 bordars and 2 cottars with half a plough. There is a mill rendering 3s, and 3 acres of meadow and 5 acres of woodland. It was worth 20s; now 30s.

Azelin holds of the bishop STOWELL. Thormund held it TRE and it paid geld for 3 hides. There is land for 4 ploughs. In demesne are 2 ploughs and 2 slaves; and 5 villans and 7 bordars and 2 cottars with 2 ploughs. There are 16 acres of meadow, and 5 acres of pasture and 6 acres of scrubland. It was worth 40s; now 60s.

VI. The land of the Bishop of Wells

The Bishop of WELLS holds WELLS. He himself held it TRE and it paid geld for 50 hides. There is land for 60 ploughs. Of this 8 hides are in demesne, and there are 6 ploughs and 6 slaves; and 20 villans and 14 bordars with 15 ploughs. There are 4 mills rendering 30s, and 300 acres of meadow, pasture 3 leagues long and 1 league broad, woodland 2 leagues long and 2 furlongs broad, and 3 leagues of moor. It is worth £30 for the use of the bishop.

Of this land of the same manor the canons hold 14 hides. They have there in demesne 6 ploughs and 8 slaves; and †16† villans and 12 bordars with 8 ploughs. There are 2 mills rendering 50d. It is worth £12.

Of the same land of the same manor Fastrad holds of the bishop 6 hides, Richard 5 hides, [and] Erneis 5 hides. There are in demesne 6 ploughs and 10 slaves; and 17 villans and 16 bordars with 11 ploughs, and 2 mills rendering 10s. Among them all it is worth £13.

Of this land of this manor Fastrad holds of the bishop 2 hides [and] Ralph 2 hides. These 4 hides are [part] of the bishop's demesne. There are in demesne 2 ploughs and 3 slaves; and 5 villans and 5 bordars with 1 plough. There is a mill rendering 7s6d. The whole is worth 70s.

Of the same 50 hides the wife of Manasses holds 2 hides, but not of the bishop. It is worth 20s.

Besides these 50 hides the bishop has 2 hides which never paid geld TRE. Alweard and Eadric hold them of the bishop. They are worth 30s.

The same bishop holds COMBE ST NICHOLAS. Azur held it TRE and it paid geld for 20 hides. There is land for 16 ploughs. Of this 8 hides are in demesne, and there are 3 ploughs and 12 slaves; and 15 villans and 13 bordars with 12 ploughs. There are 12 acres of meadow, and half a league of pasture in both length and breadth, and woodland 1 league in both length and breadth. It was worth £10; now £18.

The same bishop holds KINGSBURY EPISCOPI. He himself held it TRE and it paid geld for 20 hides. There is land for 24 ploughs. Of this 6 hides are in demesne, and there are 2 ploughs and 4 slaves; and 16 villans and 4 bordars with 11 ploughs. There are 2 mills rendering 30s, and 100 acres of meadow, [and] pasture 1 league long and 3 furlongs broad. Of the same land of this manor 3 knights and 1 clerk hold 8 hides. It is worth for the use of the bishop £12; for the use of the knights £8.

The same bishop holds CHARD. He himself held it TRE and it paid geld for 8 hides. There is land for 20 ploughs. Of this 2 hides are in demesne and there are 2 ploughs and 11 slaves; and 20 villans with 14 ploughs. There is a mill rendering 30d, and 20 acres of meadow, woodland 2 leagues long and 4 furlongs broad, and as much pasture. Of the same land 1 thegn, who cannot be separated from the church, holds 2 hides. The whole is worth £16.

The same bishop holds 'LITNES' [in Huish Episcopi]. He himself held it TRE and it paid geld for 2 hides. There is land for 8 ploughs. Of this 1 hide is in demesne and there are 2 ploughs and 2 slaves; and 3 villans and 6 bordars with 2 ploughs. There are 12 acres of meadow, and 100 acres of pasture and 20 acres of woodland. It was and is worth 40s.

The same bishop holds WIVELISCOMBE. He himself held it TRE and it paid geld for 15 hides. There is land for 36 ploughs. Of this 3 hides are in demesne, and there are 4 ploughs and 8 slaves; and 16 villans and 3 bordars with 7 ploughs. There is a mill rendering 50d, and 34 acres of meadow, and 200 acres of pasture and 80 acres of woodland.

Of this land of this manor 3 knights hold of the bishop 9

hides, and there they have 16 ploughs. This land belongs to the demesne of the bishopric, nor can it be alienated from the bishop. It is worth £10 to the bishop; to the knights £15.

The same bishop holds WELLINGTON. He himself held it TRE and it paid geld for 14 hides. There is land for 30 ploughs. Of this 3 hides are in demesne, and there are 4 ploughs and 31 slaves; and 53 villans and 61 bordars with 25 ploughs. There are 2 mills rendering 15s, and 105 acres of meadow, pasture 1 league long and half a league broad, [and] woodland 3 furlongs long and as much broad.

Of this land of this manor John holds of the bishop 2 hides of the villans' land. The whole is worth £25.

To this manor has been added 1 hide which Ælfgifu held TRE as a manor. There is land for 3 ploughs, which are there with 8 villans and 4 bordars and 1 slave. There are 5 acres of meadow, [and] woodland 3 furlongs long and as much broad. It is worth 30s.

The same bishop holds BISHOPS LYDEARD. He himself held it TRE and it paid geld for 10 hides less 1 virgate. There is land for 16 ploughs. Of this 3 hides are in demesne, and there are 2 ploughs and 5 slaves; and 20 villans and 12 bordars with 6 ploughs. There is a mill rendering 31d, and 30 acres of meadow, pasture 1 league long and 3 furlongs broad, and as much woodland. Of this land of this manor 2 knights hold 3 hides of the villans' land, and have 3 ploughs there. The whole is worth £13.

[Folio 89V: SOMERSET]

The same bishop holds BANWELL. Earl Harold held it TRE and it paid geld for 30 hides. There is land for 40 ploughs. Of this 6 hides are in demesne, and there are 3 ploughs and 5 slaves; and 24 villans and 12 bordars with 18 ploughs. There are 100 acres of meadow, pasture 1 league long and broad, [and] woodland 2½ leagues in length and breadth.

Of this land of this manor Serlo holds of the bishop 3 hides; Ralph 5½ hides; Rohard 5½ hides; Fastrad 1 hide; Bono 1 hide; [and] Alwig 1 hide. There are in demesne 9 ploughs and 5 slaves; and 25 villans and 15 bordars having 13½ ploughs. There are 2 mills belonging to Rohard rendering 10s. Ordwulf [has] 1 mill rendering 40d. The whole manor is worth £15 for the use of the bishop; for the use of the men £15 as well.

The same bishop holds EVERCREECH. He himself held it TRE and it paid geld for 20 hides. There is land for 20 ploughs. Of this 3 hides are in demesne, and there are 3 ploughs and 6 slaves; and 3 villans and 10 bordars with 2 ploughs. There is a mill rendering 7s6d, and 60 acres of meadow, and 200 acres of pasture, [and] woodland 1 league long and 1 furlong broad. It is worth £10.

Of the same land of the same manor Erneis holds of the bishop 7 hides; Macharius 1½ hides; [and] Ildebert 1 hide. In demesne are 4 ploughs and 4 slaves; and 5 villans and 4 bordars with 2 ploughs. Among them all it is worth 110s. Of the same land a priest and 2 other Englishmen hold 5 hides and 1 virgate of land. It is worth £4.

The same bishop holds WESTBURY-SUB-MENDIP. He himself held it TRE and it paid geld for 6 hides. There is land for 8 ploughs. Of this 3 hides are in demesne, and there are 2 ploughs and 2 slaves; and 6 villans and 10 bordars with 5 ploughs. There are 30 acres of meadow, and woodland 1 league long and 2 furlongs broad. It is worth £8.

Osmund holds of the bishop WINSHAM. Alsige held it TRE and it paid geld for 10 hides. There is land for 16 ploughs. Of this 4 hides are in demesne, and there are 3 ploughs and 12 slaves; and 50 villans with 9 ploughs. There are 2 mills rendering 20s, and 6 acres of meadow, [and] woodland half a league long and 1½ furlongs broad. It was worth £6; now £10.

The bishop himself holds CHEW MAGNA. He himself held it TRE and it paid geld for 30 hides. There is land for 50 ploughs. Of this 4 hides are in demesne, and there are 6 ploughs and 14 slaves; and 30 villans and 9 bordars with 24 ploughs. There are 3 mills rendering 20s, and 100 acres of meadow, and 50 acres of pasture, [and] woodland 2 leagues long and half a league broad. It is worth £30 to the bishop.

Of this land of this manor Richard holds of the bishop 5 hides; Rohard 6 hides; Stephen 5 hides; Ælfric 7 virgates; [and] Wulfric 2 hides. There are in demesne 7 ploughs and 8 slaves; and 18 villans and 27 bordars with 10 ploughs. There are 2 mills rendering 10s. Among them all it is worth £13.

The same bishop holds YATTON. John the Dane held it TRE and it paid geld for 20 hides. There is land for 22 ploughs. Of this 6 hides are in demesne, and there are 2 ploughs and 3 slaves; and 10 villans and 14 bordars with 6 ploughs. There are 32 acres of meadow, woodland 1 league long and 2 furlongs broad, [and] moorland 1 league in length and breadth. It is worth £6 to the bishop.

Of this land of this manor Fastrad holds of the bishop 5 hides, [and] Ildebert 4 hides. In demesne are 3 ploughs and 4 slaves; and 18 villans and 23 bordars with 11 ploughs. Among them it is worth £9.

A pasture called Wemberham is there which TRE belonged to Congresbury, the king's manor.

Benthelin holds of the bishop the church of this manor with 1 hide. It is worth 20s.

The same bishop holds WEDMORE. He himself held it TRE and it paid geld for 10 hides. Yet there are 11 hides. There is land for 36 ploughs. Of this 5 hides less 1 virgate are in demesne, and there are 4 ploughs and 4 slaves; and 13 villans and 14 bordars with 9 ploughs and 18 cottars. There are 70 acres of meadow, and 2 fisheries rendering 10s, and 50 acres of woodland, and pasture 1 league in both length and breadth. It was worth £20; now £17.

The canons of St Andrew [of Wells] hold of the bishop WANSTROW. They themselves held it TRE and it paid geld for 4 hides. There is land for 4 ploughs. Of this 2 hides are in demesne, and there are 2 ploughs and 4 slaves; and 5 villans and 2 bordars with 3 ploughs. There are 12 acres of meadow, [and] woodland 3 furlongs long and 2 furlongs broad. It is worth £3.

[The canons] themselves hold LITTON. They themselves

held it TRE and it paid geld for 8½ hides. There is land for 7 ploughs. Of this 6½ hides are in demesne, and there are 2 ploughs and 6 slaves; and 8 villans and 7 bordars with 4 ploughs. There are 3 mills rendering 10s, and 60 acres of meadow, and 1,000 acres of pasture, and woodland 3 furlongs in length and breadth. It is worth 100s.

The king holds a manor, MILVERTON. Bishop Giso held it TRE and it paid geld for 1 virgate of land.

Roger Arundel holds a manor, ASH PRIORS, and TRE it belonged to BISHOPS LYDEARD, the bishop's manor. Bishop Giso held it and it paid geld for 3 hides and 1 virgate. Roger holds it of the king unjustly. It is worth £3.

VII. The land of the Church of Bath

The CHURCH of ST PETER of Bath has in the borough itself 24 burgesses paying 20s, There is a mill rendering 20s, and 12 acres of meadow. The whole is worth 40s.

The church itself holds PRISTON. TRE it paid geld for 6 hides. There is land for 8 ploughs. Of this 2 hides are in demesne, and there is 1 plough and 3 slaves; and 7 villans and 8 bordars with 6 ploughs. There is a mill rendering 7s6d, and 20 acres of meadow and 80 acres of pasture. It was and is worth £6.

The church itself holds STANTON PRIOR. TRE it paid geld for 3 hides. There is land for 3 ploughs. Of this half a hide is in demesne, and there is 1 plough and 5 slaves; and 4 villans and 3 bordars with 2 ploughs. There are 12 acres of meadow, and 30 acres of pasture and 30 acres of scrubland. It was and is worth £3.

Walter holds of the church WILMINGTON. 1 thegn held it of the church TRE and it paid geld for 3 hides. There is land for 4 ploughs. In demesne are 2 ploughs and 2 slaves; and 7 bordars with 1 plough. There is a mill rendering 5s, and 10 acres of meadow and 10 acres of pasture. It was and is worth 60s.

The church itself holds WESTON [near Bath]. TRE it paid geld for 15 hides. There is land for 10 ploughs. Of this 8½ hides are in demesne, and there are 2 ploughs and 7 slaves; and 7 villans and 10 bordars with 6 ploughs. There is a mill rendering 10s, and 20 acres of meadow, [and] scrubland 1 league in both length and breadth. It was worth £8; now £10.

The church itself holds BATHFORD. TRE it paid geld for 10 hides. There is land for 9 ploughs. Of this 5 hides are in demesne, and there are 2 ploughs and 6 slaves; and 5 villans and 7 bordars with 6 ploughs. There is a mill rendering 10s, and 12 acres of meadow, and scrubland 1 league in both length and breadth. It was and is worth £10.

The church itself holds MONKTON COMBE. TRE it paid geld for 9 hides. There is land for 8 ploughs. Of this 6 hides are in demesne, and there are 3 ploughs and 6 slaves; and 6 villans and 8 bordars with 5 ploughs. There are 2 mills rendering 13s6d, and 32 acres of meadow, and scrubland 1 league in length and breadth. It was worth £7; now £8.

William holds of the church CHARLCOMBE. 1 thegn held it of the church TRE and it paid geld for 4 hides. There is land for 4 ploughs. In demesne are 2 ploughs and 3 slaves; and 5 villans and 4 bordars with 2 ploughs. There are 5 acres of meadow and 10 acres of scrubland. It was worth 50s; now £6.

The church itself holds LYNCOMBE [in Bath]. TRE it paid geld for 10 hides. There is land for 8 ploughs. Of this 7 hides are in demesne, and there are 3 ploughs and 8 slaves; and 4 villans and 10 bordars with 3 ploughs. There are 2 mills rendering 10s, and 30 acres of meadow and 200 acres of pasture. It was worth £6; now £8.

Walter holds of this church BATHEASTON. Abbot Wulfweald held it TRE and it paid geld for 1½ hides. There is land for 2 ploughs. In demesne is 1 plough, with 1 villan and 8 bordars with 1 plough. There are 2 mills rendering 6s8d. There are 2 acres of meadow. It was worth 30s; now 40s.

Hugh, 3 hides, and Kolgrimr, 2 hides, hold of this church BATHAMPTON. 2 thegns held it TRE nor could they be separated from the church, and it paid geld for 5 hides. There is land for 6 ploughs. In demesne are 3 ploughs and 3 slaves; and 3 villans and 6 bordars with 3 ploughs. There are 28 acres of meadow, and pasture 6 furlongs in both length and breadth, and scrubland 10 furlongs in length and breadth. It is worth 110s.

Ranulph Flambard holds of this church 'WOODWICK' [in Freshford]. 1 monk of the same monastery held it TRE and it paid geld for 2½ hides. There is land for 3 ploughs. There are 5 bordars, and half a mill rendering 5s, and 12 acres of meadow and 30 acres of pasture. It was and is worth 20s.

The church itself holds CORSTON. TRE it paid geld for 10 hides. There is land for 9 ploughs. Of this 5 hides are in demesne, and there are 2 ploughs and 4 slaves; and 5 villans and 8 bordars with 3 ploughs. There is a mill rendering 30d, and 6 acres of meadow. It is worth £8.

The church itself holds 'EVERSY' [in Dunkerton]. TRE it paid geld for 1 hide. There is land for 1 plough, which [plough] is there in demesne, and 3 slaves, and 4 acres of meadow. It is worth 20s.

The church itself holds ASHWICK. TRE it paid geld for half a hide. There is land for half a plough. There is 1 slave, and 2 villans paying 42d, and 12 acres of meadow and 3 acres of scrubland. It is and was worth 42d. All this land belonged to this church TRE, and could not be alienated from it.

[Folio 90: SOMERSET]

VIII. The land of St Mary of Glastonbury

The CHURCH of GLASTONBURY has in the vill itself 12 hides which have never paid geld. There is land for 30 ploughs. Of this 10 hides less half a virgate are in demesne, and there are 5 ploughs and 17 slaves; and 21 villans and 33 bordars with 5 ploughs. There are 8 smiths, and 3 arpents of vineyard, and 60 acres of meadow, and 200 acres of pasture, and 20 acres of woodland and 300 acres of scrubland. It is worth £20.

To this manor belongs an island which is called MEARE. There are 60 acres of land. [There is] land for I plough which [plough] is there, and 10 fishermen and 3 fisheries rendering 20d, and 6 acres of meadow, and 6 acres of woodland and 2 arpents of vineyard. It is worth 20s.

Another island belongs there which is called PANBOROUGH. There are 6 acres of land, and 3 arpents of vineyard, and 1 bordar. It is worth 4s.

A third island belongs there, and it is called 'ANDERSEY' [in Cheddar], in which are 2 hides which have never paid geld. There is I plough with I bordar, and 2 acres of meadow and I acre of scrubland. It is worth 15s. Godwine holds it of the abbot.

The church itself holds WINSCOMBE. TRE it paid geld for 15 hides. There is land for 30 ploughs. Of this 5 hides less 1 virgate are in demesne, and there are 2 ploughs and 3 slaves; and 28 villans and 6 bordars with 9 ploughs. There is a mill rendering 5s, and 60 acres of meadow, and pasture 1 league in length and breadth, [and] woodland 2 leagues long and 1 league broad.

Of this land of this manor Roger holds of the abbot 2½ hides; Ralph 1 hide and 1 virgate; [and] Pipe half a hide. There are 5 ploughs.

This manor is worth £8 to the abbot; to his men 55s.

Of the land of this manor the Bishop of Coutances holds of the king 1 hide, and it is worth 20s. Beorhtric held it freely TRE, but he could not be separated from the church.

The church itself holds PODIMORE. TRE it paid geld for 6 hides. There is land for 6 ploughs. Of this 4 hides and 7 acres are in demesne, and there are 2 ploughs; and 8 villans and 6 bordars with 4 ploughs. There are 50 acres of meadow and 100 acres of pasture. It was and is worth £6.

Roger holds of the church EAST LYDFORD. Alweard held it TRE, nor could he be separated from the church, and it paid geld for 4 hides. There is land for 5 ploughs. Of this 3 hides and half a virgate of land are in demesne, and there are 2 ploughs and 6 slaves; and 6 villans and 3 bordars with 1½ ploughs. There is a mill rendering 10s, and 40 acres of meadow. It was and is worth £4.

The church itself holds SHAPWICK. TRE it paid geld for 30 hides. There is land for 40 ploughs. Besides this the abbot has land for 20 ploughs, which has never paid geld. There are 12 villans' ploughs, and elsewhere 4 ploughs in demesne and 6 slaves, and 5 coliberts and 15 villans and 16 bordars. There are 60 acres of meadow, and 60 acres of pasture and 57 acres of scrubland.

Of these 30 hides Roger holds of the abbot 5 hides in Sutton Mallet, and 5 hides in Edington, and 5 hides in Chilton Polden, and 5 hides in Catcott, 14 thegns held these TRE, and they could not be separated from the church. There are in demesne 9 ploughs and 11 slaves; and 19 villans and 23 bordars with 8½ ploughs. There are 100 acres of meadow less 1, and 31 acres of scrubland.

Of the same 30 hides Alvred holds 5 hides in Woolavington, and has 2 ploughs there. There are 5 slaves, and 12 villans and 8 bordars with 6 ploughs.

Of the same land Warmund holds half a hide of the abbot, and has there 1 plough and 4 bordars. It is worth 10s.

This manor is worth to the abbot £12, to Roger £19, to Alvred £7.

The church itself holds MIDDLEZOY [Middlezoy and Westonzoyland]. TRE it paid geld for 12 hides. There is land for 20 ploughs. Of this 5 hides are in demesne, and there are 2 ploughs and 2 slaves and 12 coliberts; and 27 villans and 13 bordars with 14 ploughs. There are 30 acres of meadow and 12 acres of scrubland. It was worth £10; now £24.

Walter holds of the abbot COSSINGTON. Alwine Pic held it of the abbot TRE and it paid geld for 3 hides. There is land for 6 ploughs. Of this 1 hide is in demesne, and there is I plough and 4 slaves; and 9 villans and 9 bordars with 5 ploughs. There are 10 acres of meadow and 2 acres of scrubland. It was and is worth £6.

Roger holds of the abbot DURBOROUGH. Osweald held it of the abbot TRE and it paid geld for 2 hides. There is land for 3 ploughs. There are 3 villans and 3 bordars with 2 ploughs, and in demesne half a plough, and 11 acres of meadow, and 20 acres of pasture and 10 acres of woodland. It is worth 30s; when received, it was worth 40s.

Ailwacre holds of the abbot BLACKFORD [near Wincanton]. Alnoth held it of the abbot TRE and it paid geld for 4 hides. There is land for 6 ploughs. In demesne are 3 ploughs and 5 slaves; and 7 villans and 10 bordars with 4 ploughs. There are 115 acres of meadow and 43 acres of pasture and 47 acres of woodland. It is worth 100s; when received £4.

Godescal holds of the abbot STAWELL. Alweard held it TRE and it paid geld for 2½ hides. There is land for 2½ ploughs. In demesne is 1 plough, and 3 slaves, and 3 bordars with I plough, and 20 acres of meadow. It is worth 40s; when received 5s.

The church itself holds WALTON [near Glastonbury]. TRE it paid geld for 30 hides. There is land for 40 ploughs. Of this 10 hides are in demesne, and there are 4 ploughs and 4 slaves; and 27 villans and 12 bordars with 18 ploughs. There are 50 acres of meadow, pasture 7 furlongs long and I furlong broad, [and] woodland 7 furlongs long and 3 furlongs broad. It is worth £15 to the abbot.

Of these 30 hides Roger holds of the abbot 5 hides in COMPTON DUNDON, Walter 3 hides in ASHCOTT and 3 hides in PEDWELL. Those who held them TRE could not be separated from the church. In demesne are 3 ploughs and 6 slaves; and 15 villans and 12 bordars with 8 ploughs. Roger has 20 acres of meadow and woodland 6 furlongs in length and I furlong in breadth. Walter [has] 12 acres of meadow and 40 acres of scrubland. Between them it is worth £8.

Roger holds of the abbot [?] BUTLEIGH. Winegot held it TRE and it paid geld for 3 virgates of land. There is land for

1½ ploughs which are there with 7 bordars. There are 6 acres of meadow and 2 acres of woodland. It is worth 10s.

The same Roger holds of the abbot DUNDON. Algar held it TRE and it paid geld for 5 hides. There is land for 4 ploughs. Of this 3 hides and half a virgate of land are in demesne, and there are 2 ploughs and 4 slaves, and 5 villans and 10 bordars with 3 ploughs. There are 40 acres of meadow and 10 acres of woodland. It is worth 100s.

The same Roger holds of the abbot ASHCOTT, and it belongs to WALTON [near Glastonbury], a manor of the abbot. TRE it paid geld for 2 hides. There is land for 3 ploughs. There are 2 villans and 3 bordars and 2 slaves with 1 plough, and 4 acres of meadow. It was and is worth 40s.

Gerard holds of the abbot GREINTON. Wulfmær held it TRE and it paid geld for 2½ hides. There is land for 2½ ploughs. In demesne is 1 plough and 5 slaves; and 2 bordars and 2 coliberts with 1 plough. There are 20 acres of meadow and 3 acres of woodland. It is and was worth 50s.

The church itself holds LEIGH [Lower Leigh, Mid Leigh and Overleigh, in Street]. TRE it paid geld for 4 hides. There is land for 10 ploughs. Of this 2 hides are in demesne. 1 of these was thegnland, yet it could not be alienated from the church. In demesne are 4 ploughs with 1 slave; and 7 villans and 10 bordars with 5 ploughs. There are 35 acres of meadow, and 30 acres of pasture and 6 acres of woodland. It is worth £8.

The church itself holds [High and Low] HAM [near Street]. TRE it paid geld for 17 hides. There is land for 20 ploughs. Of this 5 hides and 2½ virgates are in demesne, and there are 3 ploughs and 5 slaves; and 22 villans and 21 bordars with 8 ploughs. There are 30 acres of meadow and 16 acres of woodland. It is worth £10.

Of this land of this manor Robert holds of the abbot 1 hide and 1 virgate, and Serlo 5 hides, [and] Gerard 3 virgates of land. Leofric and Alweald and Almær held TRE, nor could they be separated from the church. In demesne are 2 ploughs and 4 slaves; and 2 villans and 14 bordars with 2 ploughs. There are 30 acres of meadow and 20 acres of pasture. All together it is worth 110s.

The church itself holds BUTLEIGH. TRE it paid geld for 20 hides. There is land for 20 ploughs. Of this 5 hides are in demesne, and there are 5 ploughs and 7 slaves; and 11 villans and 7 bordars with 6 ploughs. There are 50 acres of meadow and 100 acres of woodland. It is worth £10 to the abbot.

Of this land of this manor Turstin holds 8 hides, Roger 2 hides. 2 thegns held them of the church TRE, and could not be separated from it. In demesne are 4 ploughs and 6 slaves; and 11 villans and 6 bordars with 3 ploughs. There are 14 acres of meadow and 12 acres of scrubland. Between them it was and is worth £7.

Of the same land Alstan holds of the abbot half a hide and there he has 1 plough. It is worth 10s.

Humphrey holds of the king 2 hides in LATTIFORD, and it belongs to this manor. Ælfric held it TRE, nor could he be separated from the church. There is land for 2 ploughs. It is worth 20s.

The same church holds PILTON. TRE it paid geld for 20 hides. There is land for 30 ploughs. Besides this the abbot has there land for 20 ploughs which has never paid geld. In demesne are 10 ploughs and 15 slaves; and 21 villans and 42 bordars with 10 ploughs upon the land which does not pay geld. There are 2 mills rendering 10s, and 46 acres of meadow, and 40 acres of pasture, [and] woodland 1 league long and half a league broad. Of the land which does not pay geld Alnoth the monk holds 1 hide of the abbot freely by the king's grant. This was thegnland, nor can it be alienated from the church. The whole is worth £24; it was worth £16.

Of this land of this manor Roger holds 6½ hides in SHEPTON MALLET, and 3 hides in CROSCOMBE. Wulffrith and Almær held them TRE, and they could not be separated from the church.

In demesne are 3 ploughs and 8 slaves; and 13 villans and 19 bordars with 6 ploughs. There are 2 mills rendering 6s3d, and 50 acres of meadow, and 42 acres of scrubland, [and] pasture 3 furlongs long and 1 furlong broad. The whole is worth £9.

Of the same land of the same manor Eadræd holds of the abbot 5 hides in NORTH WOOTTON, and Serlo 5 hides in PYLLE, and Ralph 2 hides in PILTON itself. Those who held them TRE could not be separated from the church. In demesne are 4½ ploughs and 8 slaves; and 8 villans and 18 bordars with 3 ploughs. There are 2 mills rendering 4s6d, and 36½ acres of meadow, and 20 acres of pasture and 4 acres of woodland. Among them the whole is worth £7.10s.

The church itself holds EAST PENNARD. TRE it paid geld for 10 hides. Yet there are 20 hides. There is land for 12 ploughs. Of this 12 hides are in demesne, and there are 5 ploughs and 4 slaves; and 17 villans and 9 bordars and 10 cottars with 6 ploughs. There are 30 acres of meadow, and 40 acres of pasture, [and] woodland 1½ leagues long and 4 furlongs broad. It is worth £12 to the abbot.

Of this land of this manor Serlo holds of the abbot 1 hide. Æthelmær held it TRE. There are 4 villans having 2 ploughs, and 8 acres of meadow and 30 acres of woodland. It was and is worth 30s.

The church itself holds BALTONSBOROUGH. TRE it paid geld for 5 hides. There is land for 6 ploughs. Of this 4 hides and 1 virgate are in demesne, and there are 2 ploughs and 4 slaves; and 5 villans and 9 bordars and 3 cottars with 2 ploughs. There is a mill rendering 5s, and 30 acres of meadow, [and] woodland 1½ leagues long and half a league wide. It was and is worth £6.

The church itself holds DOULTING. TRE it paid geld for 20 hides. There is land for 20 ploughs. Of this 12 hides are in demesne, and there are 2 ploughs and 5 slaves; and 10 villans and 6 bordars and 4 cottars with 6 ploughs. There are 30 acres of meadow, and 60 acres of pasture and 60 acres of scrubland. It is worth £14 to the abbot.

Of this land Roger holds 3 hides and 1 virgate of land in CHARLTON [in Shepton Mallet], and elsewhere 2 hides and 3 virgates of land. In demesne is 1 plough with 1 slave; and 8 villans and 6 bordars with 2 ploughs. There is a mill rendering 9d, and 23 acres of meadow, and 10 acres of pasture and 30 acres of scrubland. It is worth 100s.

The church itself holds BATCOMBE. TRE it paid geld for 20 hides. There is land for 16 ploughs. Of this 9 hides and 3 virgates of land are in demesne, and there are 2 ploughs and 6 slaves; and 4 villans and 14 bordars with 3 ploughs. There is a mill rendering 5s. and 20 acres of meadow, and 6 acres of pasture and 40 acres of woodland. It is worth £7 to the abbot.

Of this land of this manor Roger holds 2 hides. Wulfwig held them TRE and could not be separated from the church. He has there 1 plough with 1 slave and 3 bordars. There are 12 acres of meadow and 10 acres of pasture. It is worth 20s.

Of this land of the same manor Azelin holds in WEST-COMBE 7 hides and 3 virgates of land. Ælfhild held them TRE and could not be separated from the church. In demesne are 2 ploughs; and 6 villans and 7 bordars and 6 cottars with 1 slave have 2½ ploughs. There are 2 mills rendering 5s, and 12 acres of meadow, and 12 acres of pasture and 16 acres of woodland. It is worth £4.10s 2 hides of this land were villans' land and the other 5 were thegnland.

The church itself holds MELLS. TRE it paid geld for 20 hides. There is land for 20 ploughs. Of this 10 hides are in demesne, and there are 2 ploughs and 2 slaves; and 8 villans and 7 bordars and 5 cottars with 3 ploughs. There is a mill rendering 5s, and 15 acres of meadow, and 12 acres of pasture, [and] woodland 1 league long and 2 furlongs broad. It is worth £10 to the abbot.

Of this land of this manor Godgifu holds of the abbot 1 hide. Her husband held it TRE, nor could he be separated from the church. It is worth 78d.

The Bishop of Coutances holds of the king 5½ hides belonging to this manor. 2 thegns held them TRE, but they could not be separated from the church. Azelin holds them of the bishop.

Walter holds of the abbot in WHATLEY [near Frome] 4 hides. Wulfgar, a monk, held them TRE and could not be separated from the church. There is land for 4 ploughs. Of this 2½ hides are in demesne, and there are 2 ploughs and 4 slaves; and 8 villans and 5 bordars with 2 ploughs. There is a mill rendering 5s, and 6 acres of meadow, and 50 acres of pasture and 14 acres of woodland. It is worth 70s.

In the same manor John holds of the abbot 1 hide of villans' land. There is land for 1 plough, which [plough] is there with 2 villans. It is worth 15s.

The church itself holds WRINGTON. TRE it paid geld for 20 hides. There is land for 32 ploughs. Of this 11 hides are in demesne, and there are 6 ploughs and 7 slaves; and 41 villans and 12 bordars with 20 ploughs. There are 3 mills rendering 14s2d, and 44 acres of meadow, and 200 acres of pasture, [and] woodland 2 leagues long and as much broad. It is worth £30 to the abbot.

Of this land of this manor Roger holds 1½ hides of the abbot. A thegn held them TRE, and could not be separated from the church. There are 3 ploughs, and 2 villans and 6 bordars. It is worth 30s.

Of this land Sæwulf holds 1½ hides. He himself held them TRE. There he has 1½ ploughs, and 1 villan with 4 cottars have 1 plough. It is worth 30s.

The church itself holds WEST MONKTON. TRE it paid geld for 15 hides. There is land for 20 ploughs. Of this Bishop Walkelin holds of the abbot 5 hides and 1 virgate of land in demesne, and there are 3 ploughs and 7 slaves; and 20 villans and 7 bordars with 7 ploughs. There are 20 acres of meadow, and 100 acres of pasture and 24 acres of woodland. It is worth £7.

In this vill Roger holds of the abbot 4 hides and 3 virgates of land, and Serlo 2½ hides. Those who held them TRE could not be separated from the church. There are 4 ploughs in demesne and 3 slaves; and 8 villans and 11 bordars with 2½ ploughs, and 19 acres of meadow and 40 acres of pasture. Between them it is worth £4.10s.

The church itself holds MARKSBURY. TRE it paid geld for 10 hides. There is land for 8 ploughs. Of this 4½ hides are in demesne, and there are 2 ploughs and 5 slaves; and 6 villans and 5 bordars with 3 ploughs. There are 19 acres of meadow and 40 acres of woodland. It is worth £10. A thegn holds 2½ hides of this land. It is worth 20s. Osweald held it TRE, and could not be separated from the church.

The church itself holds DITCHEAT. TRE it paid geld for 30 hides. There is land for 30 ploughs. Of this 3 hides are in demesne, and there are 3½ ploughs and 2 slaves; and 13 villans and 18 bordars and 3 cotsets with 7 ploughs. There is a mill rendering 7s5d, and 40 acres of meadow, and pasture 6 furlongs long and 2 furlongs broad, [and] woodland 1½ leagues long and 2 furlongs broad. To the abbot it is worth £12.

Of this land of this manor Serlo holds 5½ hides in HORNBLOTTON; Ralph 6½ hides in ALHAMPTON; Nigel 5½ hides in LAMYATT. Those who held TRE could not be separated from the church. IN demesne are 4 ploughs and 4 slaves; and 29 villans and 12 bordars and 3 cotsets with 15 ploughs. There are 3 mills rendering 13s4d, and 55 acres of meadow, and 20 acres of pasture, [and] woodland 9 furlongs long and 1½ furlongs broad. Among them the whole is worth £14.10s; it was worth £11.

Of the same 30 hides, Ælfric and Everard hold of the king 1 hide. A thegn held it TRE, and could not be separated from the church. It is worth 20s.

Of the same 30 hides, the Count of Mortain holds of the king 7 hides. A thegn held them of the abbot TRE, and could not be separated from the church. It is worth 100s.

The church itself holds CAMERTON. Eadmær [...] held it TRE and it paid geld for 10 hides. There is land for 10 ploughs. Of this 7 hides are in demesne, and there are 2 ploughs and 8 slaves; and 6 villans and 6 bordars with 2 ploughs. There are 2 mills rendering 5s, and 80 acres of meadow, and 20 acres of pasture and 40 acres of woodland. It is worth £7.

Of this land of this manor Roger holds of the abbot 1 hide, and there he has 1 plough with 1 slave and 1 bordar. There are 10 acres of meadow and 6 acres of woodland. It is worth 10s. The Count of Mortain gave this manor to the abbot in exchange for TINTINHULL.

Hearding holds of the abbot CRANMORE. He held it likewise TRE, and it paid geld for 12 hides. There is land for 10 ploughs. Of this 6 hides are in demesne, and there is 1 plough and 6 slaves; and 8 villans and 2 bordars and 7 cottars with 3 ploughs. There is a mill rendering 30d, and 50 acres of meadow, and 60 acres of pasture and 100 acres of woodland. It is worth £4. This land cannot be alienated from the church.

The church itself holds BRENT [East Brent and Brent Knoll]. TRE it paid geld for 20 hides. There is land for 30 ploughs. Of this 4 hides are in demesne, and there are 8 ploughs and 5 slaves; and 50 villans and 47 bordars with 16 ploughs, and 20 acres of meadow. To the abbot it is worth £50.

Of these 20 hides Roger holds of the abbot 1 hide; Ralph 5 virgates; Ælfric 5 virgates; Godwine 1½ hides. Those who held them of the abbot TRE could not be separated from the church. In demesne are 4 ploughs with 1 slave; and 3 villans and 5 bordars and 10 cottars with 3 ploughs. Among them it is worth £4.10s.

Walscin holds of the abbot EDINGWORTH. A thegn held it TRE, and could not be separated from the church, and it paid geld for 2 hides. There is land for 5 ploughs. In demesne are 2 ploughs and 4 slaves; and 4 villans and 5 bordars and 5 cottars with 4 ploughs. It is worth 40s.

Erneis holds of the abbot DOWNHEAD. Wulfgar the monk held it TRE and it paid geld for 3 hides. There is land for 5 ploughs. Of this 2 hides are in demesne, and there are 3 ploughs with 5 villans and 4 bordars. There are 5 acres of meadow, pasture 5 furlongs long and 2 furlongs broad, [and] woodland half a league long and as much broad. It was and is worth 40s.

Siward holds 3 virgates of land of the Church of Glastonbury in a manor which is called DINNINGTON. It is worth 13s2d.

[Folio 91: SOMERSET]

Bishop Maurice holds the Church of St Andrew in [Northover in] Ilchester with 3 hides of land of the king. Beorhtric held this TRE of the Church of Glastonbury, nor could he be separated from it.

The Bishop of Coutances holds of the king Hutton, Elborough, Elborough, 'Hiscombe' [in West Coker], and Stratton-on-the-Fosse. These lands were thegnland TRE, nor could they be alienated from the church. They are worth 100s, and more. From them the church has no service.

The Count of Mortain holds these manors of the king: Kingstone, Stoke Sub Hamdon and [another] Stoke Sub Hamdon, and Draycott [in Limington]. These lands were thegnland in Glastonbury TRE, nor could they be alienated from it. They are worth £13.

The same count holds in the manor of Butleigh woodland 2 furlongs in length and 1 furlong in breadth, which [manor] TRE was in Glastonbury.

Roger de Courseulles has 1 manor, Limington, for which his father gave in exchange 5 hides which he held of the Church of Glastonbury, nor could they be alienated from it. From these the church loses service.

IX. The land of the Church of Muchelney

The CHURCH of ST PETER OF MUCHELNEY has 4 carucates of land which have never paid geld in these 3 islands, Muchelney, Midelney, and Thorney. There are in demesne 2 ploughs and 1 arpent of vineyard. There are 4 slaves, and 3 villans and 18 bordars with 2 ploughs. There are 2 fisheries rendering 6,000 eels, and 25 acres of meadow, and 12 acres of woodland and 100 acres of pasture. It was and is worth £3.

The church itself holds CHIPSTABLE. Ceolric held it TRE and it paid geld for 2½ hides. There is land for 6 ploughs. Of this half a hide is in demesne, and there is 1 plough and 2 slaves; and 16 villans and 2 bordars with 5 ploughs. There is half an acre of meadow, and 100 acres of pasture, [and] woodland half a league long and 2 furlongs broad. It is worth 50s.

The church itself holds ILMINSTER. Abbot Leofweard held it TRE and it paid geld for 20 hides. There is land for 20 ploughs. Of this 9 hides and 1½ virgates are in demesne, and there are 3 ploughs and 10 slaves; and 25 villans and 22 bordars with 20 ploughs. There are 3 mills rendering 22s6d, and 80 acres of meadow, [and] woodland 3 leagues long and 1½ leagues broad. There is a market rendering 20s.

Of this land 2 thegns, who could not be separated from the church, hold 1½ hides. It is worth in all £20. When the abbot died it was worth £26.

The church itself holds ISLE ABBOTTS. Godric[A] held it TRE and it paid geld for 5 hides. There is land for 5 ploughs. Of this 3 hides are in demesne, and there are 2 ploughs and 6 slaves; and 12 villans and 5 bordars with 2 ploughs. There is a mill rendering 15s, and 40 acres of meadow, and 7 acres of pasture, [and] woodland 3 leagues long and 1½ leagues broad. It was and is worth £4.

The church itself holds ISLE ABBOTTS. Edwin[B] held it TRE and it paid geld for 1½ hides. There is land for 1½ ploughs. There are 3 bordars holding 15 acres. The rest is in demesne, and [there are] 10 acres of meadow and 7 acres of pasture, [and] woodland 3 furlongs long and 1 furlong broad. It is worth 16s.

The church itself holds DRAYTON. TRE it paid geld for 20 hides. There is land for 15 ploughs. Of this 11 hides and 2½ virgates of land are in demesne, and there are 6 ploughs and 10 slaves; and 16 villans and 14 bordars with 9 ploughs. There are 50 acres of meadow, and pasture 2 leagues long and 1 league broad, [and] woodland 2 leagues long and 1½ leagues broad.

Of these 20 hides Ceolric and Wulfweard hold 2 hides. Beorhtwine and Lyfing held them of the abbey TRE nor could they be separated from it. There are 4 bordars, and 3 acres of meadow, and 35 acres of pasture and 7 acres of woodland. The whole is worth £10.

The church itself holds WEST CAMEL. TRE it paid geld for 10 hides. There is land for 16 ploughs. Of this 4½ hides are in demesne, and there are 4 ploughs and 5 slaves; and 7 villans and 8 bordars with 6 ploughs. There is a mill rendering 10s, and 60 acres of meadow and 60 acres of pasture. Of these 10 hides Dodman holds of the abbot 1 hide, and there he has 1 plough, and 3 villans with 1 plough, and 2 acres of meadow. The whole is worth £10.10s.

The church itself holds CATHANGER. Wadel^C held it TRE and it paid geld for 1½ hides. There is land for 1½ ploughs. There is 1 villan with 1 bordar holding 15 acres. Of this land Ingulf holds 1 hide and there he has 1 plough with 3 bordars. There are 6 acres of meadow and 15 acres of woodland. It is worth 20s; the monks' share, 7s. Godric^A, and Edwin^B and Wadel^C did not belong to the abbey TRE.

X. The land of the Church of Athelney

The CHURCH of ST PETER of ATHELNEY holds ILTON. TRE it paid geld for 8 hides. There is land for 12 ploughs. In demesne are 4 hides, and there are 3 ploughs and 4 slaves; and 10 villans and 6 bordars with 4 ploughs. There is a mill rendering 7s6d, and 40 acres of meadow, and 30 acres of pasture, [and] woodland 1 league long and another in breadth. It is worth 100s. Of the land of this manor the Count of Mortain holds 2 hides which belonged to the church itself TRE. There is land for 4 ploughs, and it is worth 30s.

The church itself holds LONG SUTTON. TRE it paid geld for 10 hides. There is land for 16 ploughs. Of this 4 hides are in demesne, and there are 2 ploughs and 4 slaves; and 8 villans and 6 bordars with 6 ploughs. There are 40 acres of meadow and 100 acres of pasture. To the abbot it is worth £8. Of this land Roger the Breton holds half a hide and has 1 plough.

Of the same land of this manor Roger de Courseulles holds 2 hides against the will of the abbot. 2 thegns held them of the church TRE, and they could not be separated from it. There is land for 2 ploughs, which are there in demesne, and 6 acres of meadow. It is worth 50s. 2 men hold it of Roger.

The church itself holds SEAVINGTON ABBOTS. TRE it paid geld for 2 hides. There is land for 2 ploughs, which are there with 7 villans and 3 bordars and 2 slaves. There are 6 acres of meadow. It is worth 30s.

The church itself holds HAMP. TRE it paid geld for 1 hide. There is land for 4 ploughs. In demesne is 1 plough and 4 slaves; and 1 villan and 7 bordars with 1 plough. There are 15 acres of meadow and 3 acres of scrubland. It is worth 30s.

The church itself holds LYNG. There is 1 hide but it did not pay geld TRE. In demesne are 2 ploughs and 6 slaves; and 3 villans and 4 bordars with 2 ploughs. There are 12 acres of meadow and 50 acres of woodland. It is worth 40s.

The Count of Mortain holds 2 hides of the abbot's manor which is called in ASHILL, and Roger de Courseulles holds 2 hides of the manor of LONG SUTTON, and Ralph de Limesy holds 1 hide of the manor in BOSSINGTON. These lands belonged to Athelney [Abbey] TRE and could not be alienated from it.

XI. The land of the Church of Rome

The CHURCH of the blessed Apostle PETER at Rome holds of the king PURITON. Queen Edith held it TRE. There are 6 hides, but it did not pay geld except for 5 hides. There is land for 12 ploughs. Of this 3 hides are in demesne, and there are 2 ploughs and 4 slaves; and 11 villans and 4 bordars with 6 ploughs. There are 150 acres of meadow and 150 acres of pasture. It renders £12 a year.

XII. The land of Saint-Etienne of Caen

The CHURCH OF SAINT-ETIENNE of Caen holds of the king the church of CREWKERNE. There are 10 hides. There is land for 13 ploughs. Of this 2 hides are in demesne, and there is 1 plough with 1 slave; and 11 villans and 2 coliberts and 17 bordars with 6 ploughs. There are 10 acres of meadow, and pasture half a league in length and in breadth.

Of these 10 hides a knight holds of the abbot 3 hides, and there he has 2 ploughs with 1 slave, and 6 villans and 2 bordars with 4 ploughs. He has a mill rendering 5s, and 10 acres of meadow, and pasture half a league in length and in breadth. To the abbot it is worth £7; to the knight £4.

XIII. The land of Saint-Marie of Montebourg

The CHURCH OF SAINT-MARIE of Montebourg holds of the king a manor by the gift of Nigel the physician. Spirites the priest held it TRE and it paid geld for 5 hides. There is land for 3 ploughs. Of this 2½ hides are in demesne, and there are 2 ploughs and 2 slaves; and 5 villans and 12 bordars with 2 ploughs. There is a mill rendering 30d, and 20 acres of pasture, [and] woodland half a league long and as much broad. Formerly, as now, worth £4.

XIIII. The land of St Edward

The CHURCH of St EDWARD [Shaftesbury] holds ABBAS COMBE. TRE it paid geld for 5 hides. There is land for 5 ploughs. Of this 2½ hides are in demesne, and there are 2 ploughs; and 4 villans and 7 bordars with 2 ploughs. In Milborne Port 6 burgesses pay 50d. [There is] meadow 4 furlongs long and 2 furlongs broad, woodland 3 furlongs long and 2 furlongs broad, [and] pasture 2 furlongs long and 1 furlong broad. It was and is worth £6.

XV. What Bishop Maurice Holds

Bishop Maurice holds of the king the Church of ST ANDREW [Northover in Ilchester]. Beorhtric held it TRE and it paid geld for 3 hides. There is land for 3 ploughs. In demesne are 2 ploughs and 3 slaves; and 1 villan and 6 bordars with 1 plough. There is a mill rendering 20s, and 30 acres of meadow. It was and is worth 100s.

XVI. What the King's Clerks [Hold]

REGENBALD holds the church of FROME with 8 carucates of land. In demesne are 2½ ploughs and 4 slaves; and 8 villans and 12 bordars with 6 ploughs. There is a mill rendering 5s, and 35 acres of meadow, [and] woodland 6 furlongs long and 2 furlongs broad. It is worth £6.

RICHER holds the church of STOGUMBER of the king. TRE it paid geld for 2 hides. There is land for 4 ploughs. There are 5 villans and 4 bordars and 2 slaves with 2 ploughs. There are 3 acres of meadow, and 20 acres of pasture and 4 acres of woodland. It is worth £3 and 4 cows.

[Folio 91V: SOMERSET]

Erchenger holds of the king in the church of CANNINGTON 2½ virgates of land. There is land for 2 ploughs. In demesne is half a plough, with I villan and 6 bordars. There are 7 acres of pasture, and 30 acres of meadow and 4 acres of scrubland. It is worth 30s.

Stephen the chaplain holds the church of MILVERTON with I virgate of land and a ferding. There is land for I plough. There are 10 acres of woodland. It is worth 40s.

Ælfgeat the priest holds of the king I hide in SOUTH PETHERTON. There is land for I plough, which [plough] is there with I bordar and I slave. There are 8 acres of meadow. It is worth 20s.

To the church of CARHAMPTON belong 1½ hides. There are in demesne 1½ ploughs, with a priest and I villan and 8 bordars. There are 40 acres of pasture and 15 acres of woodland. It is worth 30s.

To the church of NORTH PETHERTON belong 3 virgates of land. There is land for I plough, which [plough] is there. It is worth 20s.

Bishop Peter held these 2 churches. Now they are in the king's hand.

Leofa holds BEERE, which he also held of King Edward and it paid geld for I virgate of land. There is land for I plough, which [plough] is there with I slave and 2 bordars. There is a mill rendering 6d, and 6 acres of meadow. It is worth 10s.

Thorsten holds ABBOTS LEIGH. His father held it TRE and it paid geld for I hide. There is land for I plough. There are 2 bordars. It is worth 10s.

Godwine holds half a hide, in a manor which is called Ridgehill, of the king in alms. It is worth 3s.

In the church of CURRY RIVEL is half a hide. There a priest has I plough. It is worth 12s.

Edith the nun has in alms of the king 12 acres of land. There she has 80 acres of woodland and pasture. It is worth 5s.

Two nuns hold of the king in alms 2½ virgates of land in HOLNICOTE. There is land for 2 ploughs. There is I plough and 5 acres of meadow. It is worth 5s.

In KILMERSDON there is half a hide of land. It is worth 10s. Bishop Peter held it. Now it is in the king's hand.

XVII. The land of Count Eustace

COUNT EUSTACE held [sic] of the king [North or West] NEWTON. Leofwine held it TRE and it paid geld for I hide and I virgate of land. There is land for 4 ploughs. Of this 2½ virgates of land are in demesne, and there is I plough and 2 slaves; and 7 villans and 6 bordars with 3 ploughs. There is a mill rendering 15d, and 7 acres of meadow, and 33 acres of pasture and 17 acres of woodland. It was and is worth £4. Alvred of Marlborough holds it of the count.

The same Alvred holds of the count COMBWICH. Leofwine held it TRE and it paid geld for 1½ hides. There is land for 6 ploughs. In demesne is I plough and 2 slaves; and 2 villans and I bordar with 2 ploughs. There are 26 acres of meadow, and 10 acres of pasture and 2 acres of woodland. It was worth 50s; now 40s.

Everard holds of the count LEXWORTHY. Alweard held it TRE and it paid geld for I virgate of land. There is land for 2 ploughs. In demesne is half a plough and 4 slaves; and 4 villans and 3 bordars with 1½ ploughs. There are 2 mills rendering 2 blooms of iron, and 3 acres of meadow and 20 acres of woodland. It was and is worth 30s.

The count himself holds LOXTON. Wulfgifu held it TRE and it paid geld for 5 hides. There is land for 7 ploughs. Of this 4 hides are in demesne, and there are 2 ploughs and 2 slaves; and 5 villans and 6 bordars with 3 ploughs. There is a mill rendering 6d, and 50 acres of meadow, and 60 acres of pasture and 6 acres of scrubland. It was and is worth 100s.

Alvred holds of the count CHELWOOD. Thorir held it TRE and it paid geld for 3 hides. There is land for 3 ploughs. Of this 2½ hides are in demesne; and [there are] 3 villans and 2 bordars with 1 plough, and the other [plough is] in demesne. There are 5 acres of meadow, [and] woodland 5 furlongs long and I furlong broad. It is worth 60s.

Alvred holds of the count BELLUTON. Tovi held it freely TRE and it paid geld for 4 hides. There is land for 4 ploughs. In demesne are 1½ ploughs with I slave; and 5 villans and 2 bordars with 2 ploughs. There is a mill rendering 15s, and 22 acres of meadow, and 20 acres of pasture, [and] woodland 4 furlongs long and 2 furlongs broad. It was worth £3; now £4.

Countess Ida of Boulogne holds of the king KINGWESTON. Wulfgifu held it TRE and it paid geld for 5 hides. There is land for 8 ploughs. Of this 2 hides and 3 virgates are in demesne, and there are 2 ploughs and 6 slaves;

and 8 villans and 8 bordars with 5 ploughs. There are 25 acres of meadow, and 22 acres of pasture, [and] woodland 3 furlongs long and 1 acre broad. It was and is worth £6.

Matilda holds of the count COMPTON DURVILLE. Wulfnoth held it TRE and it paid geld for 5 hides. There is land for 5 ploughs. Of this 3 hides are in demesne, and there are 2 ploughs and 4 slaves; and 5 villans and 10 bordars with 3 ploughs. There is a mill rendering 64d, and 5 acres of meadow, [and] pasture 4 furlongs long and 2 furlongs broad. It is worth 100s.

XVIII. The land of Earl Hugh

Earl Hugh holds of the king TETTON, and William [holds] of him. Eadnoth held it TRE and it paid geld for 1 hide. There is land for 4 ploughs. In demesne is 1 plough and 4 slaves; and 5 villans and 8 bordars with 2 ploughs. There are 5 acres of meadow, and 100 acres of pasture and 40 acres of woodland. It was and is worth 40s.

William holds of the earl SAMPFORD BRETT. TRE it paid geld for 2 hides. There is land for 5 ploughs. In demesne is 1 plough with 1 slave; and 8 villans with 1 plough. There are 9 acres of meadow, and 50 acres of woodland and a mill. It was and is worth £3.

William holds of the earl ALLER [in Sampford Brett]. Eadnoth held it TRE and it paid geld for half a hide. There is land for 2 ploughs, with 1 slave and 1 bordar and 1 villan, and 1 acre of meadow, and 36 acres of pasture and 6 acres of woodland. It was worth 20s; now 15s.

The Church of SAINT-SEVER holds of the earl HENSTRIDGE. Eadnoth held it TRE and it paid geld for 4 hides. There is land for 3 ploughs. Of this 3½ hides are in demesne, and there are 2 ploughs and 4 slaves; and 6 bordars with 1 plough. There are 30 acres of meadow, and 30 acres of pasture and woodland 4 furlongs long and 1 furlong broad. It is worth £4.9s.

XIX. The land of the Count of Mortain

The COUNT OF MORTAIN holds of the king CRICKET ST THOMAS, and Turstin [holds] of him. Scirweald held it TRE and it paid geld for 6 hides. There is land for 5 ploughs. Of this 4 hides are in demesne, and there are 3 ploughs and 2 slaves; and 6 villans and 5 bordars with 3 ploughs. There is a mill rendering 12s, and 1½ acres of meadow, [and] woodland 7 furlongs long and 2 furlongs broad. It was worth £4; now 100s.

Mauger holds of the count SEAVINGTON ST MARY. Alweard held it TRE and it paid geld for 7 hides. There is land for 7 ploughs. Of this 5½ hides are in demesne, and there are 3 ploughs and 6 slaves; and 8 villans and 7 bordars with 3 ploughs. There is a mill rendering 5s, and 40 acres of meadow. It was worth £8; now 100s.

From this manor have been taken away 10 acres of woodland and 25 acres of moor and meadow, and they are in South Petherton, the king's manor.

Mauger holds of the count COMPTON DURVILLE. Godric held it TRE and it paid geld for 3 hides. There is land for 3 ploughs. In demesne is 1 plough; and 6 villans with 6 bordars have 1 plough. It is worth 60s.

Ansgar holds WHITESTAUNTON of the count. Alweard held it TRE and it paid geld for 3 hides. There is land for 8 ploughs. In demesne are 1½ ploughs and 6 slaves; and 18 villans and 4 bordars with 3½ ploughs. There is a mill without rent, and 260 acres of woodland, and 50 acres of pasture rendering 4 blooms of iron. It is worth 60s.

The count himself holds SHEPTON BEAUCHAMP. Algar held it TRE and it paid geld for 6 hides. There is land for 4 ploughs. Of this 4 hides less half a virgate are in demesne, and there are 1½ ploughs and 3 slaves; and 9 villans and 3 bordars [...], and 15 acres of meadow. It was worth 100s; now £4.

Gerard holds of the count LOPEN. Alweard held it TRE and it paid geld for 1 hide. There is land for 1 plough. There is 1 bordar with 1 slave, and 10 acres of meadow. It is worth 20s.

Robert holds of the count CROWCOMBE. The Church of St Swithun of Winchester held it TRE. There are 10 hides, but it paid geld for 4 hides only. There is land for 12 ploughs. Of this 1 hide is in demesne, and there are 3 ploughs and 6 slaves; and 31 villans and 10 bordars with 10 ploughs. There are 11 acres of meadow, and 20 acres of woodland, [and] pasture 1 league long and half a league broad. It was and is worth £8.

Ansgar holds of the count ISLE BREWERS. Wulfnoth held it TRE and it paid geld for 6 hides. There is land for 6 ploughs. In demesne are 2 ploughs and 5 slaves; and 5 villans and 4 bordars with 2 ploughs. There is a mill rendering 14s, and 17 acres of meadow, [and] woodland 3½ furlongs long and 2 furlongs broad. It is worth 100s.

The count himself holds TINTINHULL. The Church of Glastonbury held it TRE. There are 7 hides and 1 virgate of land, but it paid geld for 5 hides. There is land for 10 ploughs. Of this 4 hides are in demesne, and there are 2 ploughs and 5 slaves; and 19 villans and 9 bordars with 8 ploughs. There is a mill rendering 30d, and 60 acres of meadow, and 200 acres of pasture and 57 acres of woodland. It is worth £16. Drogo holds of the count 1 virgate of this land, and it is worth 1 mark of silver.

Hubert holds of the count KINGSTONE. The Church of Glastonbury held it TRE and it paid geld for 8 hides. There is land for 8 ploughs. Of this 4 hides are in demesne, and there are 2 ploughs and 3 slaves; and 11 villans and 13 bordars with 5 ploughs. There are 41 acres of meadow, [and] woodland 6 furlongs long and 3 furlongs broad. It was and is worth £9. The church does not have the service.

Mauger holds of the count STOKE SUB HAMDON. Alwine held it TRE and it paid geld for 2 hides and 1½ virgates of land. There is land for 3 ploughs. In demesne are 2 ploughs and 7 slaves, with 1 villan and 1 bordar. There is a mill rendering 40d, and 10 acres of meadow. It is worth 40s.

William holds of the count DRAYCOTT [in Limington]. Wulfwig held it TRE and it paid geld for 2 hides. There is land for 3 ploughs. In demesne are $1\frac{1}{2}$ ploughs; and 9 bordars with $1\frac{1}{2}$ ploughs. There is a mill rendering 15s, and $26\frac{1}{2}$ acres of meadow, and 31 acres of pasture and as much scrubland. It is worth 40s.

Robert holds of the count STOKE SUB HAMDON. 5 thegns held it TRE and it paid geld for $5\frac{1}{2}$ hides. There is also 1 virgate of land which did not pay geld TRE. There is land for 8 ploughs. In demesne are 2 ploughs and 5 slaves; and 2 villans and 14 bordars with 3 ploughs. There are 2 mills rendering 9s, and 25 acres of meadow, and 2 furlongs of pasture and 3 acres of woodland. It was and is worth £7.

Robert holds of the count STOKE SUB HAMDON. 3 thegns held it TRE and it paid geld for 2 hides less half a virgate of land. There is land for 2 ploughs. There are 4 bordars, and 10 acres of meadow, and 15 acres of pasture and 4 acres of woodland. It was and is worth 40s.

Bretel holds of the count SWELL. Alweald held it TRE and it paid geld for 3 hides. There is land for 4 ploughs. In demesne is 1 plough with 1 slave; and 6 villans and 12 bordars with 2 ploughs. There are 34 acres of meadow, [and] woodland 5 furlongs and 10 perches long and 2 furlongs broad. It is worth 60s.

Mauger holds of the count BRUSHFORD. Ordwulf held it TRE and it paid geld for 2 hides. There is land for 12 ploughs. In demesne is 1 plough and 2 slaves; and 10 villans and 5 bordars with 2 ploughs. There is a mill rendering 12s6d, and 6 acres of meadow, and 17 acres of woodland, [and] pasture half a league long and 3 furlongs broad. It is worth £4.

Mauger holds of the count NORTH BRADON. Ælfric held it TRE and it paid geld for 1 hide. There is land for 1 plough. There is 1 bordar. It is worth 10s. This manor owes as a customary due 1 sheep with a lamb to CURRY RIVEL, the king's manor.

Mauger holds of the count ASHILL. 2 thegns held it TRE and it paid geld for 5 hides. There is land for 5 ploughs. In demesne are 2 ploughs; and 4 villans and 17 bordars with 2 ploughs. There are 40 acres of meadow, [and] woodland 40 furlongs long and 20 furlongs broad. It is worth 60s. This manor ought to render 30d to CURRY RIVEL, the king's manor.

Mauger holds of the count BROADWAY. Alnoth held it TRE and it paid geld for 1 hide. There is land for 1 plough. There are 3 villans and 3 bordars with 1 slave. There are 12 acres of meadow and 4 acres of woodland. It was and is worth 10s.

Bretel holds of the count [?] ASHBRITTLE. Wada held it TRE and it paid geld for 4 hides. There has been added 1 hide which 2 thegns held. In all there is land for 10 ploughs. In demesne are 2 ploughs and 8 slaves; and 16 villans and 22 bordars with 4 ploughs. There are 2 mills rendering 15s, and 4 acres of meadow, and 40 acres of pasture and 38 acres of woodland. It is worth 100s.

Bretel holds of the count GREENHAM. Alric held it TRE and it paid geld for 1 hide. There is land for 2 ploughs. In demesne is 1 plough and 2 slaves; and 3 villans and 2 bordars with half a plough. There is a mill rendering 5s, and 3 acres of meadow, and 3 acres of pasture and 10 acres of woodland. It is worth 15s.

Bretel holds of the count APPLEY. Beorhtmær held it TRE and it paid geld for 1 hide. There is land for 2 ploughs. There are 2 villans with 1 plough, and 2 acres of meadow, and 3 acres of pasture and 3 acres of woodland. It is worth 10s.

Drogo holds of the count NORTH BRADON. Ceolræd held it TRE and it paid geld for 1 hide. There is land for 1 plough, which [plough] is there with 1 slave. There are 7 acres of meadow and 3 acres of scrubland. It is worth 15s. This manor owes as a customary due 1 sheep with a lamb to CURRY RIVEL, the king's manor.

Drogo holds of the count DONYATT. Adulf, Sæwine, and Dunstan held it as 3 manors TRE and it paid geld for 5 hides. There is land for 5 ploughs. In demesne is 1 plough and 3 slaves; and 6 villans and 9 bordars with 2 ploughs. There is a mill without rent, and 20 acres of meadow, and 50 acres of meadow [sic], and a park. It was and is worth 100s. This manor owes as a customary due to CURRY RIVEL, the king's manor, 5 sheep with lambs.

The count himself holds STAPLE FITZPAINE. 2 thegns held it TRE and it paid geld for 10 hides. There is land for 9 ploughs. Of this 7 hides are in demesne, and there are 3 ploughs and 6 slaves; and 20 villans with 6 ploughs. There is a mill rendering 30d, and 24 acres of meadow, pasture half a league long and 1 furlong broad, [and] woodland 1 league long and 2 furlongs broad. It was worth £10; now £12. To this manor belongs a garden in Langport rendering 50 eels.

William holds of the count BICKENHALL. Ælfric held it TRE and it paid geld for 5 hides. There is land for 5 ploughs. In demesne are 2 ploughs and 3 slaves; and 9 villans and 7 bordars with 3 ploughs. There are 14 acres of meadow, [and] woodland 1 league long and 1 furlong broad. It was worth 20s; now 70s. This manor owes as a customary due to CURRY RIVEL, the king's manor, 5 sheep with as many lambs, and each free man [owes] 1 bloom of iron.

Reginald holds of the count BEER CROCOMBE. Algar held it TRE and it paid geld for 5 hides. There is land for 4 ploughs. In demesne are 3 ploughs and 4 slaves, and 6 villans and 7 bordars. There are 20 acres of meadow, and 12 acres of pasture and 5 acres of woodland. It was worth 100s; now 60s.

Robert holds of the count HATCH BEAUCHAMP. Godric and Godwine and Bolla held it TRE as 3 manors, and it paid geld for 5 hides. There is land for 6 ploughs. In demesne are 2 ploughs and 3 slaves; and 11 villans and 4 bordars with 3 ploughs. There are 8 acres of meadow and 60 acres of woodland. It was worth £8; now £4. From 1 of these hides which Bolla held is owed as a customary due to CURRY RIVEL manor 1 sheep with a lamb.

Drogo holds of the count THURLBEAR. Wulfgeat held it TRE and it paid geld for 3 hides. There is land for 9 ploughs. In demesne are 2 ploughs and 5 slaves; and 21 villans with 7 ploughs. There are 15 acres of meadow and 20 acres of woodland. It was and is worth £6.

Ansgar holds of the count THORNFALCON. Algar held it TRE and it paid geld for 6 hides. There is land for 6 ploughs. In demesne are 2 ploughs and 3 slaves; and 5 villans and 4 bordars with 2 ploughs. There are 8 acres of meadow and 2 acres of scrubland. It was and is worth £3.

Dodman holds of the count MERRIOTT. Leofwine and Beorhtweard held it TRE and it paid geld for 7 hides. There is land for 7 ploughs. In demesne are 2 ploughs and 6 slaves; and 10 villans and 6 bordars with 4 ploughs. There are 3 mills rendering 30s, and 25 acres of meadow, and pasture half a league in length and breadth. It was worth £4; now £7.

Turstin holds of the count [? Lower] EASTHAMS. Godwine, the king's reeve, held it with CREWKERNE, the king's manor, and TRE it could not be alienated from the farm and it paid geld for 2 hides. There is land for 2 ploughs, which are there in demesne with 10 bordars and 1 slave. There is a mill rendering 12s, and 12 acres of meadow and 20 acres of woodland. It was and is worth 50s.

Drogo holds of the count CRICKET MALHERBIE. 2 thegns held it TRE and it paid geld for 3 hides. There is land for 4 ploughs. In demesne is 1 plough with 1 slave; and 5 villans and 4 bordars with half a plough. There are 8 acres of meadow and 80 acres of woodland. It was worth 10s; now 30s.

Robert holds of the count 1 hide in 'TORREL'S PRESTON' [in Milverton]. Earl Harold held this. There is land for 4 ploughs. In demesne is half a plough with 1 slave; and 6 villans and 2 bordars with 2 ploughs. There is a mill rendering 12d, and 5 acres of meadow, and 3 acres of pasture and 11 acres of woodland. It was and is worth 30s. This land belonged to BROMPTON REGIS, the king's manor, with the farm.

Ansgar holds of the count in ASHBRITTLE 1 hide. Beorhtwine held it TRE. There is land for 1 plough, which [plough] 2 villans have there. There is 1 acre of meadow and 2 acres of scrubland. It was and is worth 10s.

Robert holds of the count EAST HARPTREE. Ealdwine held it TRE and it paid geld for 5 hides. There is land for 5 ploughs. In demesne are 2 ploughs; and 6 villans and 6 bordars with 2 ploughs. There is a mill rendering 5s, and 40 acres of meadow, and 60 acres of woodland, [and] pasture 8 furlongs long and 5 furlongs broad. It was and is worth 40s.

Two porters of Montacute hold of the count STEART. Beorhtnoth held it TRE and it paid geld for 2 hides. There is land for 3 ploughs. In demesne are 3 ploughs and 4 slaves; with 1 bordar and 1 villan [who] have 1 plough. There are 16 acres of meadow. It was worth 30s; now 50s.

Alvred holds of the count BRADFORD-ON-TONE. Edwin held it TRE and it paid geld

Drogo holds of the count SOUTH BRADON. Orda held it TRE and it paid geld for 2 hides. There is land for 2 ploughs, which are there in demesne with 1 slave and 3 bordars. There is a mill rendering 12s6d, and 18 acres of meadow, and 20

acres of pasture and 20 acres of woodland. It is and was worth 40s. This manor ought to render as a customary due 2 sheep with lambs to CURRY RIVEL, the king's manor.

[Folio 92V: SOMERSET]

for 5 hides. There is land for 8 ploughs. In demesne are 2 ploughs and 5 slaves; and 19 villans and 7 bordars with 6 ploughs. There is a mill rendering 10s, and 30 acres of meadow, and 10 acres of pasture and 72 acres of woodland. It was worth £8; now £11.

Alvred holds of the count HELE. Ealdræd held it TRE and it paid geld for 1 hide. There is land for 3 ploughs. In demesne is 1 plough and 4 slaves; and 2 villans and 7 bordars with 1 plough. There is a mill rendering 10s, and 10 acres of meadow and 15 acres of woodland. It was worth 40s; now £4.

This land TRE could not be alienated from Taunton, the manor of Walkelin, Bishop of Winchester.

Alvred holds of the count NORTON FITZWARREN. Osmund held it TRE and it paid geld for 5 hides. There is land for 10 ploughs. In demesne are 3 ploughs and 6 slaves; and 13 villans and 8 bordars with 8 ploughs. There are 2 mills rendering 11s3d, and 25 acres of meadow and 40 acres of woodland. It was worth £8; now £15.

Alvred holds of the count FORD. Theodric held it TRE and it paid geld for half a hide. There is land for 1 plough, which [plough] is there with 2 bordars, and there are 2 acres of meadow. It was worth 20s; now 30s.

Reginald holds of the count CHARLTON ADAM. 3 thegns with 1 clerk held it TRE and it paid geld for 5 hides. There is land for 6 ploughs. In demesne are 3 ploughs and 6 slaves; and 5 villans and 6 bordars with 1½ ploughs. There are 50 acres of meadow, and 40 acres of pasture and 20 acres of scrubland.

The count himself holds EAST CHINNOCK. Eadmær held it TRE and it paid geld for 7 hides. There is land for 7 ploughs. In demesne are 3 ploughs and 4 slaves; and 10 villans and 12 bordars with 4 ploughs. There is a mill rendering 15d, and 60 acres of meadow and 20 acres of pasture. It was worth 100s; now £12.

Bretel holds of the count NORTH PERROTT. Algar held it TRE and it paid geld for 10 hides. There is land for 8 ploughs. In demesne is 1 plough and 2 slaves; and 8 villans and 12 bordars with 3 ploughs. There are 2 mills rendering 14s, and 18 acres of meadow, [and] woodland 6 furlongs long and 3 furlongs broad. It was and is worth £7.

Ansgar holds of the count ODCOMBE. Eadmær held it TRE and it paid geld for 5 hides. There is land for 5 ploughs. In demesne are 2 ploughs and 4 slaves; and 10 villans and 16 bordars with 3 ploughs. There is a mill rendering 7s6d. There are 20 acres of meadow, and 12 acres of pasture and 1 furlong of scrubland. It was and is worth 100s.

Alvred holds CHISELBOROUGH. 2 thegns held it TRE and it paid geld for 5 hides. There is land for 5 ploughs. In demesne is 1 plough and 2 slaves; and 10 villans and 12 bordars with 4 ploughs. There is a mill rendering 15s, and 38 acres of meadow and 3 acres of scrubland. It was worth 60s; now 100s.

Mauger holds of the count MIDDLE CHINNOCK. 1 thegn held it TRE and it paid geld for 3 hides. There is land for 3 ploughs. In demesne is 1 plough and 3 slaves; and 2 villans and 9 bordars with 1 plough. There are 36 acres of meadow. It was worth £4; now £3.

Alvred holds of the count WEST CHINNOCK. 1 thegn held it TRE and it paid geld for 4 hides. There is land for 4 ploughs. In demesne are 2 ploughs and 5 slaves; and 5 villans and 10 bordars with 2 ploughs. There is a mill rendering 10s, and 40 acres of meadow and 2 acres of pasture. It is worth £4.

The Church of SAINTE-MARIE of Grestain holds of the count NORTON SUB HAMDON. 1 thegn held it TRE and it paid geld for 5 hides. There is land for 5 ploughs. Of this 2 hides are in demesne, and there is 1 plough and 5 slaves; and 8 villans and 6 bordars with 3 ploughs. There are 2 mills rendering 20s, and 25 acres of meadow, [and] woodland 2 furlongs long and 1 furlong broad. It was and is worth 100s.

Alvred holds of the count PENDOMER. Alweard held it TRE and it paid geld for 5 hides. There is land for 5 ploughs. In demesne are 3 ploughs and 2 slaves; and 5 villans and 10 bordars with 4 ploughs. There are 10 acres of meadow, and pasture 4 furlongs in length and breadth, [and] woodland 7 furlongs long and 3 furlongs broad. It was worth 40s; now 60s.

The count himself holds CLOSWORTH. 1 thegn held it TRE and it paid geld for 7 hides. There is land for 6 ploughs. In demesne are 3 ploughs and 3 slaves; and 10 villans and 7 bordars with 3 ploughs. There is a mill rendering 15s, and 12 acres of meadow, [and] woodland 4 furlongs long and 2 furlongs broad. It was and is worth £7.

Alvred holds of the count CLOFORD. 5 thegns held it TRE and it paid geld for 10 hides. There is land for 9 ploughs. In demesne are 3 ploughs and 2 slaves and 3 cottars; and 12 villans and 17 bordars with 7 ploughs. There is a mill rendering 3s, and 20 acres of meadow, and 300 acres of pasture and 160 acres of woodland. It was worth £7; now £10.

The count himself holds YARLINGTON. Alnoth held it TRE and it paid geld for 7 hides. There is land for 7 ploughs. In demesne is 1 plough and 6 slaves; and 8 villans and 6 bordars with 2 ploughs. There is a mill rendering 7s, [and] woodland 6 furlongs long and 3 furlongs broad. It was worth £7; it is worth 100s.

Drogo holds of the count WOOLSTON [in North Cadbury]. 3 thegns held it TRE and it paid geld for 3 hides and 1½ virgates of land. There is land for 2½ ploughs. In demesne is 1 plough and 8 cottars; with 1 villan and 5 bordars with 1 plough. There is a mill rendering 30d, and 10 acres of meadow. It was worth 50s; now 40s.

Drogo holds of the count SUTTON MONTIS. Bondi held it TRE and it paid geld for 5 hides. There is land for 5 ploughs. In demesne are 2 ploughs and 2 slaves; and 3 villans and 9 bordars with 2 ploughs. There is a mill without rent, and 16

acres of meadow and 8 acres of woodland. It was and is worth 100s.

Drogo holds of the count SHEPTON MONTAGUE. Toli held it TRE and it paid geld for 5 hides. There is land for 5 ploughs. In demesne are 2 ploughs and 8 slaves; and 8 villans and 5 bordars with 3 ploughs. There are 2 mills, 1 without rent, the other renders 7s6d. There are 30 acres of meadow, [and] woodland 10 furlongs long and 4 furlongs broad. It was worth £7; now 100s.

To this manor has been added STONEY STOKE. Drogo holds it of the count. Robert fitzWimarc held it TRE and it paid geld for 3 hides. There is land for 4 ploughs. In demesne is 1 plough and 2 slaves; and 5 villans and 8 bordars with 2 ploughs. There are 5 acres of meadow and 2 acres of woodland. It is worth £3.

Bretel holds of the count REDLYNCH. Ælfric held it TRE and it paid geld for 4 hides. There is land for 6 ploughs. In demesne is 1 plough; and 4 villans and 3 bordars and 7 cottars with 1 plough. There are 15 acres of meadow, [and] woodland 2 furlongs long and half a furlong broad. It is worth 40s.

Mauger holds of the count KEINTON MANDEVILLE. 2 thegns held it TRE and it paid geld for 5 hides. There is land for 5 ploughs. In demesne are 3 ploughs and 5 slaves; and 2 villans and 4 bordars with 1 cottar have 1½ ploughs. There are 30 acres of meadow. It is worth £4.

Richard holds of the count CARLINGCOTT. Godmann held it TRE and it paid geld for 3½ hides. There is land for 3 ploughs. In demesne are 2 ploughs with 1 slave, and 1 villan and 3 bordars. There is a mill rendering 5s, and 10 acres of meadow. It is worth 50s.

Alvred holds of the count ECKWEEK. Ælfstan held it TRE and it paid geld for 1 virgate of land. There is 1 villan and 1 slave. It was and is worth 10s.

Bretel holds of the count [North and South] BARROW. Almær held it TRE and it paid geld for 5 hides. There is land for 5 ploughs. In demesne is 1 plough and 2 slaves; and 10 villans and 1 bordar and 4 cottars with 4 ploughs. There are 8 acres of meadow, and 20 acres of pasture and 40 acres of woodland. It was and is worth £4.

Bretel holds of the count STOKE TRISTER. 2 thegns held it TRE and it paid geld for 3 hides. There is land for 5 ploughs. In demesne is 1 plough and 7 slaves; and 3 villans and 8 bordars and 5 cotsets with 2 ploughs. There is a mill rendering 10d, and 15 acres of meadow, [and] woodland 1 league long and 1 furlong broad. It was and is worth 60s.

Bretel holds of the count CUCKLINGTON. Lyfing and Sven held it TRE and it paid geld for 7 hides. There is land for 6 ploughs. In demesne is 1 plough with 1 slave; and 12 villans and 8 bordars with 2 ploughs. There are 22 acres of meadow, [and] woodland 18 furlongs long and 4 furlongs broad. It was worth £7; now 100s.

Ansgar holds of the count ALFORD. Godric held it TRE and it paid geld for 5 hides. There is land for 5 ploughs. In demesne is 1 plough and 3 slaves; and 7 villans and 4 bordars and 4 cottars with 2 ploughs. There is a mill rendering 7s, and 50 acres of meadow, and from the villans 8 blooms of iron. It was worth 100s; now £4.

Robert holds of the count BABCARY. Godric held it TRE and it paid geld for 2½ hides. There is land for 3 ploughs. In demesne are 2 ploughs and 3 slaves; and 6 villans and 4 bordars with 1 plough. There are 14 acres of meadow and 8 acres of pasture. It was worth 50s; now 60s.

Hugh holds of the count FODDINGTON. Ceolræd held it TRE and it paid geld for 1 hide and 1½ virgates of land. There is land for 2 ploughs. In demesne is 1 plough; with 1 villan and 1 bordar with 1 plough, and 4 acres of meadow. It was worth 30s; now 20[s].

Mauger holds of the count CLAPTON [in Cucklington]. 2 thegns held it TRE and it paid geld for 3 hides. There is land for 3 ploughs. In demesne is 1 [plough] and 2 slaves, and 2 villans and 3 bordars. It is worth 30s.

Alvred holds of the count WESTON BAMPFYLDE. Beorhtwig held it TRE and it paid geld for 1 hide and 2½ virgates. There is land for 1 plough, which [plough] is there with 5 bordars. There is half a mill rendering 30d. It was worth 20s; now 30s.

Humphrey holds of the count 1 hide in GOATHILL [Dorset]. Godric held it TRE. There is land for 2 ploughs, which are there with 2 villans and 3 bordars. There is a mill rendering 10s, and 15 acres of meadow and 15 acres of woodland. It is worth 30s.

[Folio 93: SOMERSET]

Warmund holds of the count in MILBORNE PORT 1 hide. There is land for 1 plough, which [plough] is there in demesne with 2 bordars and 2 slaves, and there are 11 acres of meadow, and a mill rendering 16d, and 5 burgesses paying 3s. The whole is worth 20s.

The count himself holds MARSTON MAGNA. 4 thegns held it TRE and it paid geld for 5 hides. There is land for 5 ploughs. In demesne is 1 plough with 1 slave; and 5 villans and 10 bordars with 3 ploughs. There are 40 acres of meadow and 30 acres of woodland. It was and is worth £10.

Robert holds of the count MARSTON MAGNA. 5 thegns held it TRE and it paid geld for 2 hides. There is land for 2 ploughs. 5 villans and 2 bordars have these [ploughs] there, and 24 acres of meadow. It was worth 40s; now 60s.

Drogo holds of the count in ADBER [Dorset] 3 virgates of land. Alwig held it TRE. There is land for half a plough, which [half-plough] is there with 3 bordars. There are 6 acres of meadow and 10 acres of woodland. It was and is worth 10s.

Ansgar holds of the count TRENT [Dorset]. Beorhtnoth held it TRE and it paid geld for 7 hides. There is land for 5 ploughs. In demesne is 1 plough and 6 slaves; and 7 villans and 10 bordars with 4 ploughs. There are 30 acres of meadow, and 60 acres of pasture and 30 acres of woodland. It was and is worth £8.

William holds of the count POYNTINGTON [Dorset].

Adulf held it TRE and it paid geld for 2½ hides. There is land for 3 ploughs. In demesne is 1 plough; and 4 villans and 6 bordars with 2 ploughs. There is a mill rendering 32d, and half an acre of meadow and 20 acres of pasture. It is worth 40s.

Drogo holds of the count THORNE COFFIN. Cynegifu held it TRE and it paid geld for 1 hide and 1 virgate. There is land for 2 ploughs. In demesne is 1 plough and 3 slaves, and 3 bordars, and 10 acres of meadow. It was worth 10s; now 20s.

Ralph the priest holds of the count THORNE COFFIN. 2 thegns held it TRE and it paid geld for 2 hides. There is land for 3 ploughs. In demesne is 1 plough; and 5 villans and 2 bordars with 1 plough, and 14 acres of meadow. It was worth 40s; now 32s.

Alvred holds of the count CHILTHORNE [Chilthorne Domer or Vagg]. Beorhtwine held it TRE and it paid geld for †3† hides. There is land for 3 ploughs. In demesne are 2 ploughs and 2 slaves; and 3 villans and 5 bordars with 2 ploughs. There are 15 acres of meadow and 20 acres of woodland. It was and is worth 60s.

Alvred holds of the count CHILTHORNE [Chilthorne Domer or Vagg]. Alwig held it TRE and it paid geld for 2 hides. There is land for 3 ploughs. In demesne are 2 ploughs and 5 slaves; and 2 villans and 4 bordars with 2 ploughs, and 30 acres of meadow. It was worth 30s; now 40s.

Ansgar holds of the count HOUNDSTONE. 3 thegns held it TRE and it paid geld for 1 hide. There is land for 1 plough, which [plough] is there in demesne and 2 slaves, and 2 villans and 3 bordars, and 3½ acres of meadow. It was worth 10s; now 20s.

Ansgar holds of the count in LUFTON 1 hide. Alwine held it TRE. There is land for 1 plough, which [plough] is there in demesne and 2 slaves, and 3 bordars, and 10 acres of meadow. It is worth 20s.

The count himself holds in YEOVIL 1 hide. There is land for 2 ploughs. There are 2 bordars. It is worth 3s.

In the same vill Amund holds of the count 1 hide. There is land for 1 plough, which [plough] is there with 2 bordars. There is a mill rendering 5s. The whole is worth 20s 4 thegns held these 2 hides TRE and it paid geld for as much.

Robert holds of the count SOCK DENNIS. 7 thegns held it TRE and it paid geld for 3½ hides. There is land for 5 ploughs. In demesne are 2 ploughs with 1 slave; and 8 villans and 2 bordars with 2 ploughs. There are 70 acres of meadow. It was and is worth 65s.

The count himself holds in demesne 'BISHOPSTONE' [in Montacute] and there is his castle which is called MONTACUTE. TRE this manor paid geld for 9 hides; and it belonged to the abbey of Athelney and for it the count gave to that church a manor which is called PURSE CAUNDLE [Dorset]. In this manor, 'Bishopstone', there is land for 7 ploughs. Of this 2½ hides are in demesne, and there are 2 ploughs and 4 slaves; and 4 villans and 3 bordars with 2 ploughs. There is a mill rendering 50d, and 15 acres of meadow.

Of these 9 hides Alvred holds of the count 1½ hides; Drogo 1 hide; Bretel 1 hide; Donecan 1 hide. There are 5 ploughs with 1 slave and 19 bordars. This manor is worth to the count £6; to the knights £3.3s.

XX. The land of Baldwin of Exeter

BALDWIN the sheriff holds HEMINGTON of the king. Siward held it TRE and it paid geld for 21 hides. There is land for 20 ploughs. Of this 8 hides are in demesne, and there are 4 ploughs and 11 slaves; and 26 villans and 8 bordars with 12 ploughs. There are 12 acres of meadow, and 50 acres of scrubland, [and] pasture half a league long and half a league broad. It was and is worth £19. Of this land 1 hide is in the common pasture in 6 villans and Hardington, a manor of the Bishop of Coutances.

Drogo holds of Baldwin APPLEY. Northmann held it TRE and it paid geld for 3 virgates of land. There is land for 2 ploughs. There are 4 villans and 3 bordars, and 5 acres of meadow and 10 acres of pasture. It is worth 15s.

The same man holds of Baldwin PORLOCK. Algar held it TRE and it paid geld for 3 hides. There is land for 12 ploughs. There are 6 villans and 3 bordars and 6 slaves, and 300 acres of woodland and 500 acres of pasture. It was worth £4 when received; now 25s.

Dodman holds of the count MUDFORD [Mudford, Up Mudford and West Mudford]. Winulf held it TRE and it paid geld for 4½ hides. There is land for 4 ploughs. In demesne are 2 ploughs and 7 slaves; and 1 villan and 7 bordars with 1 plough. There is a mill rendering 20s, and 15 acres of meadow and 40 acres of pasture. It was and is worth £4.

XXI. The land of Roger de Courseulles

ROGER de COURSEULLES holds of the king CURRY MALLET. Beorhtric held it TRE and it paid geld for 3½ hides. There is land for 4 ploughs. Of this 1 hide is in demesne, and there are 2 ploughs and 2 slaves; and 11 villans and 7 bordars with 3½ ploughs. There are 12 acres of meadow, and 5 acres of pasture, and half a league of woodland in both length and breadth. It was worth £4; now 100s.

Roger himself holds CURRY MALLET. Ceolric held it TRE and it paid geld for 3½ hides. There is land for 4 ploughs. Of this 1 hide is in demesne, and there is 1 plough with 1 slave; and 10 villans and 7 bordars with 3½ ploughs. There are 10 acres of meadow, and 5 acres of pasture, and woodland half a league in length and breadth. It was worth £4; now 100s.

These 2 estates Roger holds as 1 manor.

Robert holds of Roger [North or West] NEWTON. Elaf held it TRE and it paid geld for 3 virgates of land. There is land for 1 plough, which [plough] is there with 1 villan and 5 bordars and 2 slaves. There are 6 acres of woodland. It is worth 20s.

Robert holds of Roger HADWORTHY. Algar held it TRE and it paid geld for 1 hide. There is land for 1½ ploughs. There are 2 slaves and 1 villan and 9 bordars, and 4 acres of meadow, and 7 acres of woodland and 36 acres of pasture. It was worth 15s; now 20s.

Of this hide Walter de Douai has 1 virgate of land.

Geoffrey holds of Roger PERRY. 4 thegns held it TRE and it paid geld for 1 hide and 1 ferding. There is land for 2 ploughs. In demesne is 1 plough; and 2 villans and 5 bordars with 1 plough. There are 33 acres of meadow, and 43 acres of pasture and 37 acres of woodland. It is worth 30s.

William holds of Roger WALDRON. Alwig held it TRE and it paid geld for 1 hide and 1 ferding. There is land for 2 ploughs. In demesne is 1 plough with 1 slave; and 3 villans and 3 bordars with 1 plough. There are 11 acres of meadow, and 7 acres of pasture and 13 acres of woodland. It was and is worth 22s.

To this manor has been added 1 hide in PERRY. Alweard held it TRE and it paid geld for 1 hide. There is land for 2 ploughs. In demesne is 1 plough; and 2 villans and 3 bordars with 1 plough. There are 10 acres of meadow, and 7 acres of pasture and 13 acres of woodland. It was and is worth 20s.

Ansketil holds of Roger CLAYHILL. Ordgar held it TRE and it paid geld for 1 hide. There is land for 3 ploughs. In demesne is 1 plough; and 2 villans and 7 bordars with 2 ploughs. There are 3 acres of meadow, and 8 acres of pasture and 12 acres of woodland. It was and is worth 20s.

Robert holds of Roger SHEARSTON. Sigeræd held it TRE and it paid geld for half a hide. There is land for 1 plough, which [plough] is there in demesne with 1 slave; and 2 villans and 5 bordars with 1 plough. It was worth 10s; now 15s.

Ansketil holds of Roger "RIME". Alwig held it TRE and it paid geld for half a virgate of land. There is land for 2 oxen. There is 1 bordar, and 2 acres of meadow. It is worth 30d.

Ansketil holds of Roger CHILTON TRINITY. Godric held it TRE and it paid geld for 1 virgate of land. There is land for 1 plough. There is 1 bordar. It was and is worth 20s.

Robert holds of Roger REXWORTHY. Godric held it TRE and it paid geld for 1 virgate of land. There is land for half a plough. There are 2 bordars, and 6 acres of woodland. It was and is worth 4s.

Roger himself holds CHARLYNCH. Alwig held it TRE and it paid geld for 1½ hides. There is land for 3 ploughs. In demesne are 2 ploughs and 4 slaves; and 3 villans and 3 bordars with 2 ploughs. There is a mill rendering 6d, and 3 acres of meadow, and 14 acres of pasture and 2 acres of woodland. It was and is worth 40s.

Roger himself holds CURRYPOOL. Alwig held it TRE and it paid geld for 1 hide. There is land for 4 ploughs. In demesne is half a plough; and 6 villans and 5 bordars have 3 ploughs. There are 7 acres of meadow, and 100 acres of pasture and 6 acres of woodland. It was and is worth 40s.

Geoffrey holds of Roger PIGHTLEY. Almær held it TRE and it paid geld for 1 hide. There is land for 4 ploughs. In demesne are 2 ploughs and 5 slaves; and 2 villans and 4 bordars with 2 ploughs. There are 6 acres of meadow and 6 acres of pasture. It was and is worth 40s.

Geoffrey holds of Roger GOTHELNEY. Alweard held it TRE and it paid geld for half a hide. There is land for 2 ploughs. In demesne is 1 plough; and 5 villans and 5 cotsets with 1 plough and 1 slave. There is half a mill rendering 10d, and 20 acres of pasture. It is worth 20s; it was worth 30s.

Geoffrey holds of Roger "KOLGRIMR'S LAND". Kolgrimr held it TRE and it paid geld for half a virgate of land. There is land for 2 oxen. There are 3 bordars. It is worth 4s.

Robert holds of Roger OTTERHAMPTON. Edwin held it TRE and it paid geld for half a hide. There is land for 1½ ploughs. There are 4 villans and 1 bordar and 1 slave. There are 2½ acres of meadow, and 12 acres of pasture and 7 acres of scrubland. It was and is worth 18s.

[Folio 93V: SOMERSET]

Robert holds of Roger WOOLSTONE [in Stogursey]. Ulf held it TRE and it paid geld for half a hide. There is land for half a plough. There is 1 villan, and 17 acres of meadow and 42 acres of pasture. It was worth 10s; now 15s.

Alweard holds of Roger 'HOLCOMBE' [in Aisholt]. He himself held it TRE and it paid geld for 1 virgate of land. There is land for 2 ploughs. In demesne is 1 plough and 2 slaves; and 1 villan and 5 bordars with half a plough. There is a mill rendering 6d, and 75 acres of pasture and 15 acres of woodland. It was and is worth 10s.

Ansketil holds of Roger 'DODISHAM' [in Cannington]. 3 thegns held it TRE and it paid geld for 3½ virgates and 5 acres of land. There is land for 2 ploughs, which are there with 6 bordars. There are 5 acres of meadow and 12 acres of pasture. It was and is worth 20s.

Ansketil holds of Roger 'PETHERHAM' [in Otterhampton]. Godwine held it TRE and it paid geld for half a virgate of land. There is land for 1 plough. 4 bordars there have this [plough]. There is 1 acre of meadow. It was and is worth 10s.

Ansketil holds of Roger "Alwine's Land". Alwine held it TRE and it paid geld for 1 virgate of land and a ferding. There is land for 1 plough, which [plough] is there in demesne with 1 bordar. There is a mill rendering 12d, and 2 acres of meadow and 2 acres of pasture. It was and is worth 10s.

Ansketil holds of Roger CHILTON TRIVETT. Leofgar held it TRE and it paid geld for half a hide. There is land for 2 ploughs. In demesne is 1 plough with 1 slave; and 2 villans and 5 bordars with 2 ploughs. There are 6 acres of meadow, and 8 acres of pasture and 16 acres of woodland. It was worth 20s; now 40s.

Ansketil holds of Roger CHILTON TRIVETT. Mereswet held it TRE and it paid geld for half a hide. There is land for 2 ploughs. 4 villans and 6 bordars have these [ploughs] there, and in demesne is half a plough, and [there is] half a mill rendering 20s. There are 6 acres of meadow, and 8 acres of pasture and 16 acres of woodland. It was and is worth 40s.

Ansketil holds of Roger 'PILLOCK' [in Cannington]. Godric held it TRE and it paid geld for half a ferding. There is land for half a plough. Yet in demesne is 1 plough, and 2 bordars, and 3 acres of meadow and 7 acres of pasture. It was and is worth 6s.

Ansketil holds of Roger STOCKLAND BRISTOL. 2 thegns held it TRE and it paid geld for 1½ hides. There is land for 2 ploughs, which are there in demesne and 2 slaves; and 3 villans and 2 bordars with 1 plough. There are 24 acres of meadow and 12 acres of woodland. It was worth 30s. when received; now 65s.

Ansketil holds of Roger IDSON. Alwine held it TRE and it paid geld for 2½ hides. There is land for 4 ploughs. In demesne are 2 ploughs and 7 slaves; and 7 villans with 1 bordar have 3 ploughs. There are 40 acres of meadow and 5 acres of woodland. It was and is worth 100s.

Robert holds of Roger RADLET. Godric held it TRE and it paid geld for half a hide. There is land for 2 ploughs. There is 1 villan and 2 bordars, and a mill rendering 6d. and 5 acres of meadow, and 24 acres of pasture and 1 acre of woodland. It was worth 20s; now 15s.

Ranulph holds of Roger [?] SWANG. Alweard held it TRE and it paid geld for 1 virgate of land. There is land for 1 plough, which [plough] is there in demesne and 2 slaves, and 5 bordars, and a mill rendering 3d, and 1 acre of meadow, and 3 acres of pasture and 7 acres of woodland. It was worth 15s; now 20s.

Herbert holds of Roger "Theodric's Land". Theodric held it TRE and it paid geld for 1 virgate of land. There is land for 1 plough. There are 1½ acres of meadow. It is worth 10s.

Robert holds of Roger [?] Aisholt. Alweard held it TRE and it paid geld for 1 virgate of land. There is land for 1 plough. There are 2 bordars, and 1½ acres of meadow. It was and is worth 10s.

John holds of Roger 'EDSTOCK' [in Cannington]. Ulf held it TRE and it paid geld for 1 virgate of land. There is land for half a plough, which [half-plough] is there in demesne with 7 bordars, and 20 acres of meadow and 7 acres of scrubland. It is worth 12s.

William holds of Roger WITHIEL. Eadric held it TRE and it paid geld for 3 virgates of land. There is land for 1½ ploughs. There are 2 villans and 5 bordars with a plough [...], and a mill rendering 6d. It was and is worth 15s.

William holds of Roger STRINGSTON. Siward held it TRE and it paid geld for 1½ virgates of land. There is land for half a plough, which [half-plough] is there in demesne with 1 bordar, and 1 acre of meadow and 6 acres of pasture. It was and is worth 8s.

Ansketil holds of Roger BLACKMORE. Ælfric held it TRE and it paid geld for 1 virgate of land. There is land for half a plough. To this manor has been added 1 acre of land which

rendering 20s. There are 6 acres of meadow, and 8 acres of pasture and 16 acres of woodland. It was and is worth 40s.

TRE 1 thegn held. There are 2 bordars. The whole was and is worth 8s.

William holds of Roger 'WORTH' [in Cudworth]. 2 thegns held it TRE and it paid geld for 1½ hides. There is land for 3 ploughs. There are 10 villans with 2½ ploughs, and 4 acres of meadow, and woodland 4 furlongs in length and 2 furlongs in breadth. It was and is worth 60s.

The same man holds of Roger KNOWLE ST GILES. Godric and Ælfric held it TRE and it paid geld for 1 hide and 1 virgate of land. There is land for 2 ploughs. In demesne is 1 plough; and 5 villans and 4 bordars with half a plough. There is woodland 4 furlongs in length and 2 furlongs in breadth. It is worth 25s.

To this manor has been added ELEIGH. Bruning held it TRE as a manor and it paid geld for 3 virgates of land. There is land for 2 ploughs. There is 1 plough with 1 villan and 1 bordar and 1 slave. It was and is worth 15s.

Gerard holds of Roger LOPEN. Leofwine held it TRE and it paid geld for 1 hide. There is land for 1 plough, which [plough] is there in demesne with 1 bordar, and 10 acres of meadow. It is worth 20s.

Ealdræd holds of Roger MONKSILVER. He himself held it TRE and it paid geld for half a hide. There is land for 1½ ploughs. There 1 villan and 2 bordars with 1 slave have 1 plough. There are 3 acres of meadow and 62 acres of pasture. It was and is worth 20s.

Alric holds of Roger MONKSILVER. Beorhtmær held it TRE and it paid geld for half a hide. There is land for 1½ ploughs. There 4 villans with 1 bordar have 1 plough. There are 6 acres of meadow, and 16 acres of pasture and 16 acres of scrubland. It was and is worth 20s.

Alric holds of Roger HALSWAY. He himself held it TRE and it paid geld for 3 virgates of land. There is land for 3 ploughs. In demesne are 1½ ploughs and 3 slaves; and 4 villans with 1 bordar have 1½ ploughs. There are 3 acres of meadow and 400 acres of pasture. It is worth 20s.

Alric holds of Roger COLEFORD. He himself held it TRE and it paid geld for 3 ferdings of land. There is land for half a plough. Yet in demesne is 1 plough. It is worth 4s.

Bertram holds of Roger HUISH [in Nettlecombe]. Wulfgar held it TRE and it paid geld for 3 virgates of land. There is land for 2 ploughs. In demesne is 1 [plough] with 1 slave; and 3 villans and 2 bordars have 1 plough. There are 3 acres of meadow and 30 acres of pasture. It is worth 20s.

Alric holds of Roger [Higher and Lower] VEXFORD. Dunna held it TRE and it paid geld for half a hide. There is land for 1 plough. 2 villans with 1 bordar have this [plough] there, and in demesne is half a plough. There are 4 acres of meadow, and 3 acres of pasture and 11 acres of woodland. It is worth 10s.

Robert holds of Roger [Higher and Lower] VEXFORD. Beorhtmær held it TRE and it paid geld for half a hide. There is land for 2 ploughs. In demesne is 1 plough; and 1

villan and 3 bordars have 1 plough. There are 2 acres of meadow, and 20 acres of pasture and 40 acres of woodland. It was and is worth 17s.

Alric holds of Roger EMBLE. Wulfgar held it TRE and it paid geld for half a hide. There is land for 2 ploughs. In demesne is half a plough, and 1½ acres of meadow and 4 acres of pasture. It is worth 5s.

Roger himself holds KILVE. Beorhtric held it TRE and it paid geld for 2½ hides. There is land for 4 ploughs. In demesne are 2 ploughs with 1 slave; and 5 villans and 5 bordars with 2 ploughs. There is a mill rendering 6s, and 13 acres of meadow, and 12 acres of woodland, [and] pasture 1½ leagues long and half a league broad. It was and is worth £4.

To this manor has been added [Higher and Low] HILL. Eadweald held it as a manor TRE and it paid geld for 2 hides. There is land for 2 ploughs. There 1 villan and 5 bordars and 2 slaves have half a plough. There is a mill rendering 12d, and 7 acres of meadow and 20 acres of woodland. It was and is worth 30s.

To the same manor has been added PARDLESTONE. Perlo held it TRE and it paid geld for half a hide. There is land for 1 plough, which [plough] is there in demesne; and 2 villans and 4 bordars with half a plough. There are 3 acres of meadow, and 12 acres of pasture and 6 acres of woodland. It was and is worth 10s. Norman holds it.

Geoffrey and William hold of Roger WEACOMBE. 3 thegns held it TRE and it paid geld for 1 hide. There is land for 1½ ploughs. There is 1 bordar. The whole is worth 32s.

William holds of Roger WESTOWE. Æthelweald held it TRE and it paid geld for 1 hide. There is land for 2 ploughs. In demesne is 1 plough and 3 slaves; and 2 villans and 3 bordars with half a plough. There are 4 acres of meadow, and 8 acres of pasture and 15 acres of woodland. It was and is worth 40s.

Hugh holds of Roger ASHWAY. Ælfric held it TRE and it paid geld for half a hide and a ferding. There is land for 6 ploughs. In demesne is 1 plough and 2 slaves; and 11 villans and 3 bordars with 2 ploughs. There is 1 acre of meadow, and 60 acres of woodland, [and] pasture 1 league long and half a league broad. It is worth 25s.

William holds of Roger BROFORD. Wulfwine held it TRE and it paid geld for 1 virgate of land. There is land for 2 ploughs. In demesne is 1 [plough]; and 4 villans have the other [plough]. There are 5 acres of woodland. It is worth 7s.

William holds of Roger BROFORD. Almær held it TRE and it paid geld for a ferding. There is land for half a plough. There are 2 bordars, and 4 acres of woodland. It is worth 26d.

Roger himself holds PIXTON. Beorhtric held it TRE and it paid geld for 1 virgate of land. There is land for 2 ploughs. There are 20 acres of pasture and 3 acres of woodland. It was and is worth 30d.

William holds of Roger PUCKINGTON. Lyfing held it TRE and it paid geld for 1½ hides. There is land for 1½ ploughs. There are 3 villans and 3 bordars and 2 slaves with 1 plough, and 11½ acres of meadow, and 6 acres of pasture and 66 acres of woodland.

To this manor has been added PUCKINGTON. Alweard held it TRE as a manor and it paid geld for 1½ hides. There is land for 1½ ploughs. There are 4 bordars with 1 villan and 1 slave, and 2 acres of meadow, and 6 acres of pasture and 66 acres of woodland.

[Folio 94: SOMERSET]

These 2 estates Lyfing and Alweard held of the Church of St Peter nor could they be separated from it TRE. They were worth 50s; now 60s.

Ogis holds of Roger MOORTOWN. Swet held it TRE of the Church of Muchelney nor could he be separated from this [church]; and it paid geld for 1 hide and half a virgate of land, and it is [part] of the 20 hides of DRAYTON and is thegnland. There is land for 1 plough, which [plough] is there in demesne and 6 slaves, and 10 acres of meadow and 7 acres of woodland. It was and is worth 20s.

Roger himself holds 'ALMSWORTHY' [in Exford]. Eadric held it TRE and it paid geld for 1 virgate of land. There is land for 6 ploughs. In demesne is 1 plough and 2 slaves; and 6 villans and 9 bordars with 3 ploughs. There are 8 acres of meadow, and 30 acres of scubland, [and] pasture 2 leagues long and 2 broad. It is worth 25s.

Æthelgifu holds of Roger DOWNSCOMBE. Leofmær held it TRE and it paid geld for a ferding. There is land for 1 plough. There is 1 bordar with half a plough, and 6 acres of meadow, and 3 acres of woodland and 6 acres of pasture. It is worth 2s.

Roger himself holds EXFORD. Æthelwulf held it TRE and it paid geld for half a virgate. There is land for 2 ploughs. There is 1 bordar and 1 slave with half a plough, and 10 acres of meadow, and 10 acres of pasture and 12 acres of scrubland. It is worth 3s.

Eadnoth holds of Roger EXFORD. Eadric held it TRE and it paid geld for a ferding. There is land for 1 plough. There is 1 bordar with half a plough, and 2 acres of woodland, and 3 acres of meadow and 10 acres of pasture. It is worth 30d.

Roger himself holds STOKE PERO. Ailhalle held it TRE and it paid geld for half a virgate of land. There is land for 2 ploughs. There is 1 plough with 1 slave, and 2 bordars, and 50 acres of pasture and 60 acres of woodland. It was and is worth 5s.

Kafle holds of Roger 'BAGLEY' [in Stoke Pero]. He himself held it TRE and it paid geld for half a virgate of land. In demesne is 1 plough; and 2 bordars have half a plough. There are 50 acres of pasture and 12 acres of woodland. It was worth 12d; now 40d.

Roger himself holds COMBE [in Withycombe]. Alric held it TRE and it paid geld for 1 virgate of land. There is land for 1 plough. There is half a plough with 1 bordar, and 16 acres of pasture and 18 acres of woodland. It is worth 5s.

Ogis holds of Roger ALLER [in Carhampton]. Beorhtmær

and Eadmær held it TRE and it paid geld for half a hide. There is land for 1½ ploughs. In demesne is 1 plough with 1 slave; and 1 villan and 1 bordar who have half a plough. There are 60 acres of pasture. It is worth 8s.

Alric holds of Roger 'GILCOTT' [in Withycombe]. Edwin held it TRE and it paid geld for half a hide. There is land for 1½ ploughs. There is 1 plough with 3 bordars, and 6 acres of meadow, and 50 acres of pasture and 15 acres of woodland. It is worth 10s.

William holds of Roger HOLNICOTE. Ælfric and Beorhtwine held it TRE and it paid geld for half a hide and for half a virgate of land. There is land for 2½ ploughs. There are 4 villans with 1 bordar and they have 2 ploughs. There are 16 acres of pasture. It is worth 22s.

Alric holds of Roger DOVERHAY. Eadgifu held it TRE and it paid geld for 1 virgate of land. There is land for 1 plough. There are 2 villans with 1 bordar. It is worth 8s.

William holds of Roger 'HOLNE' [? in Holnicote]. Godric held it TRE and it paid geld for 1 virgate of land. There is land for 2½ ploughs. There are 3 villans and 4 bordars with 1½ ploughs, and half and acre of meadow, and 30 acres of pasture and 14 acres of scrubland. It is worth 6s.

William holds of Roger EXFORD. Wulfwine held it TRE and it paid geld for a ferding. There is land for 1 plough. There are 2 bordars with half a plough, and 3 acres of meadow and 10 acres of pasture. It was and is worth 30d.

Roger himself holds STONE [in Exford]. Beorhtric held it TRE. There is half a virgate of land. There is land for 2 ploughs, but it is waste.

Bertram holds of Roger FIVEHEAD. Ealdræd held it TRE and it paid geld for 1½ hides. There is land for 2 ploughs. In demesne is 1 plough and 2 slaves, and 4 bordars. There are 15 acres of meadow and 20 acres of woodland. It was worth 30s; now 40s.

Wulfweard holds of Roger EARNSHILL. Lyfing held it TRE and it paid geld for half a hide. There is land for 1½ ploughs. In demesne is 1 plough with 1 slave, and 3 bordars. There are 8 acres of meadow and 8 acres of pasture. It is worth 12s.

Ogis holds of Roger SAMPFORD ARUNDEL. Alwine held it TRE and it paid geld for 2 hides. There is land for 7 ploughs. In demesne are 2 ploughs and 5 slaves; and 11 villans and 6 bordars with 3 ploughs. There is a mill rendering 8d, and 5 acres of meadow, and 200 acres of pasture and 47 acres of woodland. It was worth 20s; now 50s.

Alric holds of Roger THORNE ST MARGARET. 3 thegns held it TRE and it paid geld for 1 hide and 3 virgates of land. There is land for 5 ploughs. In demesne is 1 plough and 3 slaves; and 9 villans and 5 bordars with 3 ploughs. There is a mill rendering 10s, and 4 acres of meadow, and 30 acres of pasture and 8 acres of woodland. It was worth 20s; now 40s.

Geoffrey holds of Roger ENMORE. Algar held it TRE and it paid geld for 1 hide. There is land for 4 ploughs. In demesne is

1 plough and 2 slaves; and 3 villans and 3 bordars with 3 ploughs. There are 68 acres of woodland. It was and is worth 40s.

Geoffrey holds of Roger LEXWORTHY. Ordgar held it TRE and it paid geld for 1 virgate of land. There is land for 1 plough. This [plough] 2 villans and 2 bordars have there. There is a mill rendering 2 blooms of iron, and 4 acres of woodland there. It was and is worth 15s.

Geoffrey holds of Roger LEXWORTHY. Æthelstan held it TRE and it paid geld for 1 virgate of land. There is land for 3 ploughs. There 4 villans and 4 bordars and 2 slaves have 2 ploughs. There is a mill rendering 2 blooms of iron, and 5 acres of meadow and 20 acres of woodland. It was and is worth 40s.

Geoffrey holds of Roger BLAXHOLD. Leofric held it TRE and it paid geld for 1 virgate of land. There is land for 3 ploughs. There 3 villans and 3 bordars with 1 slave have 2 ploughs. There are 60 acres of woodland. It was worth 20s; now 30s.

Robert holds of Roger CHEDDAR. Adulf held it TRE and it paid geld for 2 hides and 1 virgate of land. There is land for 4 ploughs. In demesne are 2 ploughs, with 5 villans and 5 bordars. There are 15 acres of meadow. It was worth 40s; now 30s.

Robert holds of Roger SHIPHAM. Ealdwine held it TRE and it paid geld for 4 hides. There is land for 6 ploughs. In demesne are 2 ploughs; and 2 villans and 7 bordars with 1 plough. There are 3 acres of meadow, and 200 acres of pasture and 10 acres of scrubland. It was worth 40s; now 30s.

Roger himself holds half a hide in 'PONTESIDE' and there he has half a plough with 1 slave. There is half an acre of meadow. It was and is worth 10s.

Geoffrey holds of Roger OAKE. Dunna held it TRE and it paid geld for 3½ hides. There is land for 6 ploughs. In demesne are 2 ploughs and 4 slaves; and 14 villans and 14 bordars have 3½ ploughs. There is a mill rendering 4s, and 17 acres of meadow, and 15 acres of pasture and 10 acres of woodland. In Milverton 1 house renders 11d. The whole is worth £4; when received, it was worth 50s.

William holds of Roger TOLLAND. Wulfwine held it TRE and it paid geld for 2 hides. There is land for 6 ploughs. In demesne are 2 ploughs with 1 slave; and 11 villans and 4 bordars have 4 ploughs. There are 10 acres of meadow, and 15 acres of woodland and 60 acres of pasture. It was and is worth 50s.

William holds of Roger [Rich's or Treble's] HOLFORD. Æthelweald held it TRE and it paid geld for half a hide. There is land for 1 plough. There are 2 bordars and 2 slaves, and 1 acre of meadow, and 10 acres of pasture and 1 acre of woodland. It is worth 18s.

Alric holds of Roger [Rich's or Treble's] HOLFORD. Alweard held it TRE and it paid geld for half a virgate of land. There is land for half a plough, which [half-plough] is there with 1 villan, and it renders 3s.

Norman holds of Roger LITTLETON [in Compton Dundon]. Almær and Osbern and Godric held it as 3 manors TRE and it paid geld for 3 hides. There is land for 4 ploughs. In demesne are 2 ploughs and 3 slaves; and 4 villans and 3 bordars with 1 plough. There are 40 acres of meadow and as many acres of scrubland. It was and is worth 40s.

Robert holds of Roger STANDERWICK. Smeawine held it TRE and it paid geld for 1½ hides. There is land for 3 ploughs. In demesne is 1 plough, and 2 villans and 7 bordars. There are 6 acres of meadow and 4 acres of woodland. It was worth 50s; now 20s.

Almær holds of Roger FAIROAK. Ælfric held it TRE and it paid geld for 1 hide. There is land for 4 ploughs. There are 6 villans and 3 bordars with 3 ploughs, and 13 cotsets. There are 6 acres of meadow and 60 acres of woodland. It was worth 60s; now 40s.

Almær holds of Roger FARLEIGH HUNGERFORD. Smeawine held it TRE and it paid geld for half a hide. There 1 villan and 3 bordars and 2 cottars have 1 plough. There are 3 acres of meadow and 6 acres of woodland. It was worth 20s; now 10s.

Robert holds of Roger WHITE OX MEAD. 2 thegns held it TRE and it paid geld for 1 hide. There is land for 2 ploughs, which are there in demesne with 1 slave, and 6 bordars. There are 3 acres of meadow and 30 acres of woodland. It was and is worth £3.

William holds of Roger WITHAM FRIARY. Erlebald held it TRE and it paid geld for 2 hides. There is land for 3 ploughs. In demesne is 1 plough and 2 slaves; and 4 villans and 3 bordars and 4 cotsets with 2 ploughs. There are 20 acres of meadow and 30 acres of pasture, [and] woodland 1 furlong long and half a furlong broad. It was worth 20s; now 30s. This land TRE belonged to [North and South] Brewham, a manor of William de Moyon, nor could it be alienated from it.

Erneis holds of Roger BRUTON. Godwine held it TRE and it paid geld for 1 hide and 1 virgate of land. There is land for 2 ploughs. There is 1 plough with 3 bordars, and a mill rendering 30d. It was and is worth 30s.

Norman holds of Roger BARTON ST DAVID. Alstan held it TRE and it paid geld for 1½ hides. There is land for 2 ploughs. In demesne is 1 plough; and 2 villans and 4 bordars with 1 plough. There is a mill rendering 5s, and 24 acres of meadow and as many acres of pasture. It was worth 40s; now 30s. To this manor belonged KEINTON MANDEVILLE TRE. There is 1 hide. The Count of Mortain holds it.

Roger himself holds LIMINGTON. Sæwulf held it TRE and it paid geld for 7 hides. There is land for 8 ploughs. In demesne are 3 ploughs and 3 slaves; and 1 villan and 13 bordars with 1 plough. There is a mill rendering 20s, and 60 acres of meadow, [and] pasture 12 furlongs long and 2 furlongs broad. It was and is worth £7.

Vitalis holds of Roger ASHINGTON. Godwine held it TRE and it paid geld for 3 hides. There is land for 3 ploughs. In demesne is 1 plough with 1 slave; and 2 villans and 4 bordars with 1 plough. There are 43 acres of meadow and 20 acres of pasture. It was and is worth 40s.

[Folio 94V: SOMERSET]

Vitalis holds of Roger MUDFORD SOCK. Toki held it TRE and it paid geld for 1½ hides. There is land for 2 ploughs. In demesne is 1 plough, and 3 bordars, and 10 acres of meadow and 15 acres of pasture. It was and is worth 15s.

Herbert holds of Roger BRYMPTON D'EVERCY. Sæwulf held it TRE and it paid geld for 3 hides. There is land for 4 ploughs. In demesne are 2 ploughs and 2 slaves; and 2 villans and 8 bordars with 2 ploughs. There are 13 acres of meadow and 4 acres of scrubland. It was worth 40s; now 60s.

Roger himself holds half a hide which is worth 10s. TRE this belonged to Barrington, the king's manor.

Dodman and Warmund hold of Roger LONG SUTTON. 2 thegns held it TRE of the Church of Athelney and could not be separated from this [church], and it paid geld for 2 hides. There is land for 3 ploughs. In demesne are 3 ploughs with 1 slave; and 4 villans and 3 bordars have 1 plough. There are 8 acres of meadow. It is worth 50s.

XXII. The land of Roger Arundel

ROGER Arundel holds of the king HALSE. Æthelmær held it TRE and it paid geld for 4 hides. There is land for 7 ploughs. In demesne are 2 ploughs and 3 slaves; and 16 villans and 7 bordars with 3½ ploughs. There is a mill rendering 10s, and 8 acres of meadow, and 12 acres of woodland and 20 acres of pasture. When received, it was worth 100s; now £6.

Roger himself holds HUISH CHAMPFLOWER. Æthelric held it TRE and it paid geld for 2 hides and 3 virgates of land. There is land for 12 ploughs. In demesne are 2 ploughs and 5 slaves; and 20 villans and 6 bordars with 6 ploughs. There is a mill rendering 12d, and 20 acres of meadow, and 60 acres of woodland, [and] pasture 1 league long and half a league broad. It was worth when received £6; now £7.

Roger himself holds WHITELACKINGTON. Almær held it TRE and it paid geld for 10 hides. There is land for 10 ploughs. In demesne is 1 plough and 7 slaves; and 9 villans and 30 bordars with 7 ploughs, and 7 swineherds rendering 40 pigs. There is a mill rendering 15s, and 50 acres of meadow, and 61 acres of pasture and 240 acres of woodland. It was worth when received £12; now £9.

Richard holds of Roger DURSTON. Alwig held it TRE and it paid geld for 2 hides and 3 virgates of land. There is land for 4 ploughs. In demesne is 1 plough and 4 slaves; and 4 villans and 5 bordars and 4 cottars with 3 ploughs. There are 15 acres of meadow, and 20 acres of pasture and 20 acres of woodland. It was and is worth 40s.

Ralph holds of Roger SANDFORD [in Wembdon]. Æthelweard held it TRE and it paid geld for 1 hide and half a virgate of land and a ferding. There is land for 3 ploughs. In demesne is 1 plough and 3 slaves; and 2 villans and 4 bordars with 1 plough, and 12 acres of meadow. It was and is worth 30s.

Ralph holds of Roger PERRY. Wulfric held it TRE and it paid geld for half a hide. There is land for 1 plough, which [plough] is there in demesne, and 8 acres of meadow. It was and is worth 10s.

Ralph holds of Roger 1 virgate of land in [North or West] NEWTON. Beorhtweald held it TRE. There is land for half a plough. There is 1 acre of meadow and 2 acres of woodland. It is worth 5s.

Hugh holds of Roger FIDDINGTON. Æthelweard held it TRE and it paid geld for 4 hides. There is land for 6 ploughs. In demesne are 2 ploughs and 2 slaves; and 6 villans and 5 bordars with 3 ploughs. There are 2 mills rendering 2s, and 21 acres of meadow, and 80 acres of pasture, and 43 acres of moor and 42 acres of woodland. It was and is worth £4.

Hugh holds of Roger TUXWELL. Æstan held it TRE and it paid geld for 1 virgate of land. There is land for half a plough. There 2 villans and 3 bordars have 1 plough. There are 140 acres of woodland, and 41 acres of moor and 40 acres of pasture. It was worth when received 20s, now 12s6d.

Odo holds of Roger CUDWORTH. 3 thegns held it TRE and it paid geld for 3½ hides. There is land for 4 ploughs. In demesne is 1 plough and 2 slaves; and 4 villans and 2 bordars with half a plough. There are 4 acres of meadow, [and] pasture 8 furlongs long and 2 furlongs broad. It was worth 40s; now 30s.

Robert holds of Roger SKILGATE. Goda held it TRE and it paid geld for 1 hide and 1 virgate of land. There is land for 4 ploughs. In demesne are 2 ploughs and 5 slaves; and 5 villans and 2 bordars with half a plough. There is a mill rendering 10d, and 2 acres of meadow, and 60 acres of woodland, [and] pasture 4 furlongs long and 1 furlong broad. It is worth 30s.

The same man holds of Roger 'MILTON' [in Skilgate]. Dunna held it TRE and it paid geld for 1 hide less a ferding. There is land for 3 ploughs. In demesne is 1 plough and 2 slaves; and 3 villans and 1 bordar with 1 plough. There are 2 acres of meadow, and 5 acres of woodland, [and] pasture 3 furlongs long and 1 furlong broad. It was worth 30s; now 20s.

Robert holds of Roger RADDINGTON. 2 thegns held it TRE and it paid geld for 2 hides. There is land for 8 ploughs. In demesne are 2 ploughs and 3 slaves; and 5 villans and 5 bordars with 4 ploughs. There is a mill grinding for the hall, and 3 acres of meadow, and 6 acres of woodland, [and] pasture 4 furlongs long and 3 furlongs broad. It was and is worth 30s.

Drogo holds of Roger TIMBERSCOMBE. Æthelfrith held it TRE and it paid geld for 1½ hides. There is land for 8 ploughs. In demesne is 1 plough and 2 slaves; and 3 villans and 8 bordars with 1 ploughs. There are 11 acres of meadow, and 150 acres of pasture and 61 acres of woodland. It was worth when received 100s; now 40s.

To this manor has been added a ferding. Algar held it TRE. There is land for 1 plough. There is half a plough, with 2 bordars, and 8 acres of pasture and 4 acres of woodland. It is worth 5s.

William holds of Roger KITTISFORD. Osmund Stramun held it TRE and it paid geld for 2 hides. There is land for 7 ploughs. In demesne are 2 ploughs and 3 slaves; and 5 villans and 6 bordars with 3½ ploughs. There is a mill rendering 7s, and 3 acres of meadow, and 10 acres of pasture and 12 acres of woodland. It was worth 40s; now 60s.

William holds of Roger 1 virgate of land in SYDENHAM. Cypping held it TRE. There is land for 1 plough. There are 15 acres of pasture. It is worth 15d.

Guy holds of Roger HALSWELL. Alweard held it TRE and it paid geld for 1 hide. There is land for 2 ploughs. In demesne is 1 plough and 2 slaves; and 2 villans and 3 bordars with 1 plough. There are 14 acres of woodland. It is worth 25s.

Robert holds of Roger CARY FITZPAINE. 2 thegns held it TRE and it paid geld for 1 hide less a ferding. There is land for 1 plough, which [plough] is there in demesne with 4 cottars. There are 20 acres of meadow. It was and is worth 20s.

Roger himself holds CHARLTON MACKRELL. Æthelfrith held it TRE and it paid geld for 3 hides. There is land for 6 ploughs. In demesne is 1 plough and 4 slaves; and 3 villans and 9 bordars with 3 ploughs. There are 30 acres of meadow and 2 acres of woodland. It was worth £6; now 100s.

Roger himself holds ASH PRIORS. Æthelric held it TRE and it paid geld for 2 hides. There is land for 4 ploughs. In demesne is 1 plough and 3 slaves; and 5 villans and 5 bordars with 2 ploughs. There are 8 acres of meadow, and 10 acres of woodland, [and] pasture 2 furlongs long and 1 furlong broad. It is worth 20s.

To this manor has been added ASH PRIORS. Sæwine held it of the Bishop of Wells and could not be separated from him TRE, and it paid geld for 1 hide and 1 virgate of land. There is land for 3 ploughs. In demesne is 1 plough; and the villans have 2½ ploughs. It was and is worth 30s. Roger holds it of the king, and Givold [holds] of him.

Roger himself holds UPPER CHEDDON. Dunna held it TRE and it paid geld for 3½ hides. There is land for 5 ploughs. In demesne is 1 plough and 2 slaves; and 6 villans and 6 bordars have 3 ploughs. There are 23 acres of meadow, and 15 acres of pasture and 2 acres of woodland. It was worth 50s; now 60s.

Of this land of this manor Robert holds 1 hide and there he has 1 plough with 1 slave, and 5 bordars, and a mill rendering 3s. There are 3 acres of meadow, and 5 acres of pasture and 4 acres of woodland. It was worth 15s; now 20s.

Roger himself holds CHEDDON FITZPAINE. Wulfwine held it TRE and it paid geld for 2½ hides. There is land for 4 ploughs. In demesne is 1 plough and 3 slaves; and 6 villans and 6 bordars with 3 ploughs. There are 24 acres of meadow and 15 acres of pasture. It is worth 60s.

Roger Buissel holds of Roger SUTTON BINGHAM. Wulfweard held it TRE and it paid geld for 5 hides. There

is land for 5 ploughs. There are 6 bordars and 4 cottars, and a mill rendering 16s. There are 12 acres of meadow, [and] pasture 3 furlongs long and 2 furlongs broad. It was worth 100s; now 30s.

Roger himself holds BECKINGTON. Æthelfrith held it TRE and it paid geld for 10 hides. There is land for 10 ploughs. In demesne are 2 ploughs; and 9 villans and 7 bordars have 6 ploughs. There is a mill rendering 20s, and 12 acres of meadow, and 8 acres of pasture and 100 acres of woodland. It was worth when received £10; now £6.

Robert holds of Roger BERKLEY. Tovi held it TRE and it paid geld for 2½ hides. There is land for 3 ploughs. In demesne are 2 ploughs with 1 slave; and 3 villans and 4 bordars with 1 plough. There is a mill rendering 12s6d, and 6 acres of meadow and 70 acres of woodland. It was and is worth 40s.

Roger himself holds MARSTON BIGOT. Æthelfrith held it TRE and it paid geld for 3½ hides. There is land for 5 ploughs. In demesne is 1 plough and 2 slaves; and 5 villans and 14 bordars have 5 ploughs. There is a mill rendering 6s, and 16 acres of meadow, and 100 acres of pasture, [and] woodland 1 league long and as much broad. It is worth £7.

William holds of Roger PENSELWOOD. Beorhtnoth held it TRE and it paid geld for 3 hides. There is land for 3 ploughs. In demesne is 1 plough; and 4 villans and 8 bordars and 4 cottars with 1½ ploughs. There is a mill rendering 40d, and 12 acres of meadow, and 20 acres of pasture, [and] woodland 12 furlongs long and 4 furlongs and 12 perches broad. It was worth when received £7; now £3.

Azelin holds of Roger LYDE [in Yeovil]. Godwine and Særic held it TRE and it paid geld for 2 hides. There is land for 2 ploughs, which are there in demesne and 4 slaves with 1 bordar. There are 4 acres of meadow and 2 acres of woodland. It was and is worth 40s.

[Folio 95: SOMERSET]

XXIII. The land of Walter Giffard

WALTER Giffard holds of the king YARNFIELD [Wilts.] and William [holds] of him. Ernebald held it TRE and it paid geld for 2 hides. There is land for 3 ploughs. In demesne are 2 ploughs with 1 slave; and 5 bordars with 1 plough. There are 20 acres of pasture and 60 acres of woodland. It was worth 40s, now 30s.

XXIIII. The land of Walter de Douai

WALTER DE DOUAI holds of the king WORLE. Esger held it TRE and it paid geld for 6½ hides. There is land for 15 ploughs. In demesne are 4 ploughs and 5 slaves; and 22 villans and 3 bordars with 9 ploughs. There are 50 acres of meadow, [and] pasture 13 furlongs long and 2 furlongs broad. It was worth £10; now £7.

WALSCIN holds STRETCHOLT, and Renewald [holds] of him. Leofgar held it TRE and it paid geld for half a hide. There is land for 2 ploughs. In demesne is 1 plough with 1 slave, and 3 bordars, and 10 acres of meadow. It was and is worth 50s.

Renewald holds of Walter STRETCHOLT. Eadweald held it TRE and it paid geld for half a hide. There is land for 1 plough. In demesne are 2 ploughs and 2 slaves; and 1 villan and 2 bordars with 1½ ploughs. There are 10 acres of meadow. It is worth 50s.

Rademer holds of Walter WALPOLE. Edward held it TRE and it paid geld for 3 virgates of land. There is land for 1 plough, which [plough] is there in demesne; and 1 villan and 3 bordars with half a plough. It was and is worth 20s.

Walter holds 1 virgate of land which is called [?] Dunwear. Algar held it TRE. This is [part] of that land which the king gave to him between the two waters. It is worth 12d.

Rademer holds of Walter [?] 'CROOK' [in Bawdrip]. Edward held it TRE and it paid geld for 1 virgate. There is land for 1 plough, which [plough] is there in demesne with 4 bordars. It is worth 10s.

Rademer holds of Walter [East and West] BOWER. Særic held it TRE and it paid geld for half a hide. There is land for 3 ploughs. In demesne is 1 plough with 1 slave; and 3 villans and 2 bordars have 2 ploughs. It was and is worth 40s. TRE this land belonged to Melcombe which Robert d'Auberville now holds.

Walscin holds WEARE [Weare and Lower Weare]. Ailwacre held it TRE and it paid geld for 5 hides. Yet there are 6 hides. There is land for 8 ploughs. Of this 3½ hides are in demesne, and there are 2 ploughs and 2 slaves; and 5 villans and 8 bordars with 2 ploughs. There are 2 mills rendering 42s, and 32 acres of meadow. When received it was worth £10; now 100s.

Folcwine holds of Walter BADGWORTH. 2 thegns held it as 2 manors TRE and it paid geld for 2 hides. There is land for 2 ploughs. In demesne is 1 plough; and 2 villans and 8 bordars with 1 plough. There are 9 acres of meadow. It was worth 15s; now 20s.

Ralph holds of Walter [Chapel and Stone] ALLERTON. Wulfnoth held it TRE and it paid geld for 5 hides. There have been added 6 hides which 2 thegns held TRE as 2 manors. In all there is land for 8 ploughs. Of this 9 hides less half a virgate are in demesne, and there are 3 ploughs and 4 slaves; and 9 villans and 9 bordars with 4 ploughs. There are 40 acres of meadow and 300 acres of pasture. It was worth £8 when received; now 100s.

Ludo holds of Walter TARNOCK. Alweard held it TRE and it paid geld for 1 hide. There is land for 2½ ploughs, which are there in demesne and 2 slaves, and 4 bordars. There are 20 acres of meadow, and pasture 5 furlongs in length and as much in breadth. It is worth 20s.

Richard holds of Walter TARNOCK. Leofwine held it TRE and it paid geld for 1 hide. There is land for 2½ ploughs. Yet there are 3 ploughs in demesne and 2 slaves, and 1 villan and 2 bordars. There are 30 acres of meadow, and pasture 6 fur-

longs in length and as much in breadth. It was worth 15s; now 25s.

Hubert holds of Walter ALSTON SUTTON. 2 thegns held it TRE and it paid geld for 4½ hides. There is land for 6 ploughs. In demesne are 3 ploughs with 1 slave; and 6 villans and 3 bordars with 2 ploughs. There are 15 acres of meadow and 20 acres of woodland. It was and is worth 60s.

Gerard holds of Walter BRATTON SEYMOUR. Alsige held it TRE and it paid geld for 4 hides. There is land for 8 ploughs. In demesne are 2 ploughs and 6 slaves; and 7 villans with 4 ploughs. There are 4 acres of meadow, and woodland 6 furlongs in length and breadth. It was worth £7 when received; now £4. Richard holds of Walter MILTON [in Weston-super-Mare]. Ailwacre held it TRE and it paid geld for 1½ hides. There is land for 2 ploughs. There 3 villans have 1 plough. It is and was worth 25s.

Reneward holds of Walter WINCANTON. Alsige held it TRE and it paid geld for 3½ hides. There is land for 7 ploughs. In demesne is 1 plough and 2 slaves; and 16 villans and 6 bordars and 5 cottars with 7 ploughs. There are 50 acres of meadow and as many of woodland. It was and is worth 70s.

To this manor has been added half a hide which Beorhtmær held as a manor TRE and | it paid geld for half a hide |. There is land for 5 ploughs. There Reneward has 1 plough and 2 slaves; and 7 villans and 9 bordars | and 2 cottars | with 3 ploughs. There is a mill rendering 30d, and 60 acres of meadow, and 30 acres of pasture and 100 acres of woodland. It was and is worth 40s.

Walter holds CASTLE CARY. Alsige held it TRE and it paid geld for 15 hides. There is land for 20 ploughs. Of this 8 hides are in demesne, and there are 6 ploughs and 6 slaves; and 23 villans and 20 bordars with 17 ploughs. There are 3 mills rendering 34s, and 100 acres of meadow, woodland 1 league long and half a league broad, and 1 burgess in Ilchester and another in Bruton pay 16½d. When received it was worth £16; now £15.

Folcwine holds of Walter SPARKFORD. Ailwacre held it TRE and it paid geld for 5 hides and 1 virgate of land. There is land for 5 ploughs. In demesne are 2½ ploughs and 6 slaves; and 9 villans and 7 bordars with 4 ploughs. There is a mill rendering 7½s, and 40 acres of meadow, and 100 acres of pasture, and woodland 1 furlong in length and breadth. It was worth £4; now 100s.

Wulfric holds of Walter ANSFORD. Ketil held it TRE and it paid geld for 5 hides. There is land for 6 ploughs. In demesne are 2 ploughs and 3 slaves; and 5 villans and 4 bordars with 5 ploughs. There is a mill rendering 7½s, and 20 acres of meadow, and 20 acres of pasture, [and] woodland 4 furlongs long and 1½ broad. When received it was worth £4; now £3.

Ralph holds of Walter [North and South] BARROW. Alsige held it TRE and it paid geld for 5 hides. There is land for 5 ploughs. In demesne are 2 ploughs and 3 slaves; and 7 villans and 5 bordars with 3 ploughs. There are 25 acres of meadow, and woodland 3 furlongs in length and 1 furlong in breadth. When received it was worth 100s; now 60s.

Walscin holds BRIDGWATER. Mærle-Sveinn held it TRE and it paid geld for 5 hides. There is land for 10 ploughs. In demesne are 3 ploughs and 5 slaves; and 13 villans and 9 bordars and 5 cottars with 8 ploughs. There is a mill rendering 5s, and 10 acres of meadow, and 100 acres of scrubland and 30 acres of pasture. When received it was worth 100s; now £7.

Ludo holds of Walter WEMBDON. Mærle-Sveinn held it TRE and it paid geld for 2 hides. There is land for 6 ploughs. In demesne are 2 ploughs with 1 slave; and 5 villans and 6 bordars with 4 ploughs. There are 10 acres of meadow, and 13 acres of pasture and 5 acres of woodland. When received it was worth £3; now £4.

Renewald holds of Walter BAWDRIP. Mærle-Sveinn held it TRE and it paid geld for 2 hides. There is land for 8 ploughs. In demesne is 1 plough and 6 slaves; and 11 villans and 7 bordars and 3 cottars with 5 ploughs. There is a mill rendering 4s, and 100 acres of meadow and 40 acres of pasture. It was worth 50s; now 60s..

Renewald holds of Walter BRADNEY. Alnoth held it TRE and it paid geld for 1 hide. There is land for 1½ ploughs. There is 1 villan and 5 bordars and 1 cottar and 1 slave with 1½ ploughs. There are 25 acres of meadow. It is worth 20s.

Rademer holds of Walter HORSEY. Alweard held it TRE and it paid geld for 2 hides. There is land for 7 ploughs. In demesne are 2 ploughs and 2 slaves; and 8 villans and 6 bordars and 3 cottars with 5 ploughs, and 24 acres of pasture. It is worth £4.

Rademer holds of Walter PAWLETT. Sæmær held it TRE and it paid geld for 1 virgate of land. There is land for 1 plough, which [plough] is there in demesne with 1 slave, and 2 bordars and 3 cottars, and 5 acres of meadow. It was and is worth 10s.

Walter himself holds BURNHAM-ON-SEA. Beorhtsige held it TRE and it paid geld for 4 hides. There is land for 12 ploughs. In demesne is 1 plough and 3 slaves; and 7 villans and 8 bordars with 5 ploughs. There are 150 acres of meadow, and 20 acres of pasture. It is worth £4.

Of this land Rademer holds of Walter 2 hides and there he has 1 plough and 3 slaves, and 7 villans and 8 bordars and 3 cottars with 5 ploughs, and 150 acres of meadow, and 20 acres of pasture. It is worth £4.

Walter himself holds [East and West] HUNTSPILL. Ailwacre held it TRE and it paid geld for 1 hide. There is land for 13 ploughs. In demesne are 2 ploughs and 5 slaves; and 21 villans and 5 bordars and 7 cottars with 11 ploughs. There are 100 acres of meadow and 200 acres of pasture. It was and is worth £8.

Walter himself holds BREAN. Mærle-Sveinn held it TRE and it paid geld for 2 hides. There is land for 8 ploughs. In demesne are 3 ploughs with 1 slave; and 9 villans and 7 bordars

and 8 cottars with 3½ ploughs. There are 30 acres of pasture. It is worth 100s.

Ralph holds of Walter CHILCOMPTON. Ailwacre held it TRE and it paid geld for 4 hides. There is land for 3 ploughs. In demesne are 2 ploughs; and 4 bordars and 7 cottars and 1 villan with half a plough. There is a mill rendering 6d, and 12 acres of meadow, and pasture 10 furlongs in length and 2 furlongs broad, and woodland 3 furlongs in length and 2 furlongs in breadth. It was and is worth 50s.

To this manor has been added 1 hide called CHILCOMPTON. Alric held it as a manor TRE and it paid geld for as much. There is land for 1 plough. There is half a plough, with 1 villan and 2 bordars, and 2 acres of meadow, and 4 acres of pasture and 4 acres of scrubland. It was and is worth 10s.

Ralph holds of Walter WEST HARPTREE. Ailwacre held it TRE and it paid geld for 5 hides. There is land for 4 ploughs. In demesne is 1 plough and 2 slaves; and 5 villans and 2 bordars with 2 ploughs. There is a mill rendering 5s, and 58 acres of meadow, and 62 acres of woodland, [and] pasture 1 league in length and breadth. It was and is worth 40s.

Ralph holds of Walter ECKWEEK. Ailwacre held it TRE and it paid geld for 1½ virgates of land and 8 acres. There is land for 1 plough. There is 1 bordar. It is worth 10s.

Rademer holds of Walter ALSTONE. Alweald held it TRE and it paid geld for 1 hide. There is land for 3 ploughs. In demesne is 1 plough with 1 slave; and 1 villan and 4 bordars and 3 cottars having 1 plough, and 40 acres of pasture. It was and is worth 20s.

Walter himself holds [East and West] HUNTSPILL. Alwine held it TRE and it paid geld for 3 virgates of land. There is land for 2 ploughs. In demesne is 1 plough and 4 slaves; and 2 villans and 5 bordars and 4 cottars with 1 plough. There are 20 acres of meadow. It was and is worth 20s.

Raimar the clerk holds of Walter 'HUISH' [in Burnham-on-Sea]. Cynesige held it TRE and it paid geld for 1 virgate of land. There is land for 1 plough, which [plough] is there with 1 slave and 1 cottar and 3 bordars. It was and is worth 10s.

Ralph holds of Walter 'HUISH' [in Burnham-on-Sea]. Alwig held it TRE and it paid geld for 1 virgate of land. There is land for 1 plough, which [plough] is there with 5 bordars. It was and is worth 10s.

The same Ralph holds of Walter ADBER [Dorset]. Alsige held it TRE and it paid geld for 1 hide and 1 virgate of land. There is land for 1 plough, which [plough] is there with 1 villan and 1 bordar. There are 10 acres of meadow and 20 acres of woodland. It was and is worth 15s.

XXI. The land of William de Moyon

WILLIAM de MOYON holds of the king SHURTON. Algar held it TRE and it paid geld for 4 hides and 1 virgate of land. There is land for 5 ploughs. In demesne are 3 ploughs and 6 slaves; and 5 villans and 4 bordars with half a plough. There is a mill rendering 10d, and 48 acres of meadow and 12 acres of woodland. When received it was worth 60s; now £4.10s.

To this manor has been added 'SEABERTON' [in Stogursey]. Ælfric held it TRE as 1 manor and it paid geld for 3 virgates of land. There is land for 1 plough. There are 13 acres of meadow and 6 acres of woodland. It was and is worth 10s.

He himself holds DUNSTER and his castle is there. Ælfric held it TRE and it paid geld for half a hide. There is land for 1 plough. There are 2 mills rendering 10s, and 15 bordars, and 5 acres of meadow and 30 acres of pasture. It was formerly worth 5s; now 15s.

Hugh holds of William ADSBOROUGH. 6 thegns held it TRE and it paid geld for 2 hides. There is land for 4 ploughs. In demesne is 1 plough and 3 slaves; and 6 villans and 12 bordars with 3½ ploughs. There are 6 acres of meadow, and 100 acres of pasture, and 10 acres of moor and 2 acres of woodland. It was and is worth 40s.

Garmund holds of William ALEY. Algar held it TRE and it paid geld for half a hide. There is land for 2 ploughs. In demesne is 1 [plough] with 1 slave; and 6 bordars with 1 plough. There are 10 acres of woodland. It was and is worth 20s.

Robert holds of William LEIGH [in Winsham]. Scirweald held it TRE and it paid geld for 3 hides. There is land for 4 ploughs. In demesne is 1 plough with 1 slave; and 5 villans and 2 bordars, and 8 acres of meadow, and woodland 2 furlongs long and 1 furlong broad. It was formerly worth 30s; now 20s.

Roger holds of William STREET. Huscarl and Almær held it TRR [sic] and it paid geld for 1½ hides. There is land for 2 ploughs. There are 3 villans and 1 bordar with 1 plough, and 1½ acres of meadow, and pasture 5 furlongs long and 2 furlongs broad. It was and is worth 15s.

Turgis holds of William BROMPTON RALPH. Beorhtric held it TRE and it paid geld for 3½ hides. There is land for 12 ploughs. In demesne are 2 ploughs and 7 slaves; and 16 villans and 2 bordars with 8 ploughs.

There is a mill rendering 30d, and 6 acres of meadow, and 20 acres of woodland and 1 league of pasture. When received it was worth 40s; now £4.

This land belonged to the Church of Glastonbury, and could not be alienated from it TRE.

Ogis holds of William CLATWORTHY. Ælfgyth held it TRE and it paid geld for 1½ hides. There is land for 7 ploughs. In demesne are 2 ploughs and 2 slaves; and 16 villans and 5 bordars with 5 ploughs. There is a mill rendering 6d, and 5 acres of meadow, and 25 acres of woodland, [and] pasture half a league long and 4 furlongs broad. It was formerly worth 20s; now 40s.

This land could not be alienated from the Church of Glastonbury, but was thegnland there TRE.

William himself holds CUTCOMBE. Almær held it TRE and it paid geld for 3 hides. There is land for 15 ploughs. In demesne are 4 ploughs and 6 slaves; and 18 villans and 5 bordars with 5 ploughs. There are 6 swineherds rendering 31 pigs, and a mill rendering 5s, and 6 acres of meadow, pasture 2 leagues long and 1 league broad, [and] woodland 1 league long and half a league broad. It was formerly worth £3; now £6. Of this land of this manor 3 knights hold of William 1 hide and half a virgate of land, and there they have 2 ploughs, and 4 villans and 6 bordars with 1 plough. There are 2 acres of meadow, and 14 acres of woodland, [and] pasture half a league long and 5 furlongs broad. It was and is worth 35s6d.

William himself holds MINEHEAD. Algar held it TRE and it paid geld for 5 hides. There is land for 12 ploughs. In demesne are 3 ploughs and 12 slaves; and 27 villans and 22 bordars with 10 ploughs. There is a mill rendering 3s, and 12 acres of meadow, and 24 acres of woodland, [and] pasture 4 leagues long and 2 leagues broad. When received it was worth 100s; now £6.

William himself holds ALCOMBE. Algar held it TRE and it paid geld for 1 hide. There is land for 3 ploughs. In demesne is 1 plough and 4 slaves; and 3 villans and 4 bordars with 2 ploughs. There are 8 acres of meadow and 3 furlongs of pasture. It was and is worth 20s.

Durand holds of William 'BROWN' [in Treborough]. Eadweald held it TRE and it paid geld for 1 hide. There is land for 6 ploughs. In demesne are 2½ ploughs and 2 slaves; and 13 villans and 3 bordars with 4 ploughs. There is 1 acre of meadow, and 80 acres of pasture and 12 acres of woodland. It was formerly worth 20s; now 40s.

Three knights hold of William LANGHAM. 3 thegns held it TRE and it paid geld for 1 hide. There is land for 6 ploughs. In demesne are 3 ploughs with 1 slave; and 5 villans and 8 bordars with 3½ ploughs. There is a mill rendering 3s, and 4 acres of meadow, and 60 acres of pasture and 36 acres of woodland. It was and is worth 30s.

Mainfrid holds of William NORTH QUARME. Æthelweard held it TRE and it paid geld for half a hide. There is land for 4 ploughs. In demesne is 1 plough with 1 slave; and 5 villans and 4 bordars with 1 plough. There is 1 acre of meadow, and 10 acres of woodland, [and] pasture 5 furlongs long and 5 broad. It was formerly worth 7s; now 15s.

Richard holds of William BICKHAM. 2 thegns held it TRE and it paid geld for 1 virgate of land. There is land for 2 ploughs. In demesne is 1 plough; and 3 villans and 6 bordars with half a plough. There are 3 acres of meadow and 40 acres of pasture. It was formerly worth 6s; now 15s.

William himself holds BROADWOOD. Alric held it TRE and it paid geld for half a hide. There is land for 1 plough, which [plough] is there in demesne and 2 slaves; and 3 villans and 2 bordars with 1 plough. There are 5 acres of meadow, pasture 1 league long and half a league broad, [and] woodland 1 league long and 4 furlongs broad. It was formerly worth 10s; now 15s.

Ralph holds of William AVILLE. Ælfric held it TRE and it

paid geld for half a hide. There is land for 2 ploughs. In demesne is 1 plough; and 1 villan and 5 bordars with half a plough. There is a mill rendering 20d, and 4 acres of meadow, and 2 acres of woodland and 50 acres of pasture. It was and is worth 10s.

William himself holds STAUNTON. Walo held it TRE and it paid geld for 3 virgates of land. There is land for 2 ploughs. There are 2 villans and 2 slaves and 2 bordars with 1 plough, and 5 acres of meadow and 40 acres of pasture. It is worth 15s.

To this manor has been added 1 virgate of land which 1 thegn held TRE as 1 manor. There is land for 1 plough. There is 1 bordar, and 3 acres of meadow and 50 acres of pasture. It is worth 3s.

William himself holds EXFORD. Dunna held it TRE and it paid geld for a ferding. There is land for 2 oxen. There is 1 villan, and 15 acres of pasture. It was and is worth 15d.

William himself holds EXFORD. Sarpo held it TRE and it paid geld for 1½ ferdings. There is land for half a plough. But it lies as pasture, and it renders 12d.

[Folio 96: SOMERSET]

Durand holds of William OLD STOWEY. Lyfing held it TRE and it paid geld for 1 virgate of land. There is land for 1 plough, which [plough] is there in demesne, with 1 villan and 1 bordar. There are 14 acres of woodland. It was worth 3s; now 10s.

Durand holds of William OAKTROW. Manni held it TRE and it paid geld for half a virgate of land. There is land for 1 plough. There are 2 villans with half a plough, and 4 acres of woodland. It was worth 4s; now 6s.

Durand holds of William ALLERCOTT. Leofwine held it TRE and it paid geld for half a virgate. There is land for 2 ploughs. There is 1 plough, with 2 villans and 2 bordars, and 8 acres of pasture and 2 acres of woodland. It was and is worth 6s.

Geoffrey holds of William [East and West] MYNE. Leofwine held it TRE and it paid geld for half a hide. There is land for 2 ploughs, which are there in demesne and 4 slaves with 1 bordar. There is 1 acre of meadow, and 4 acres of woodland and 50 acres of pasture. It was worth 15s.

Roger holds of William BRATTON. Ælfric held it TRE and it paid geld for 3 virgates of land. There is land for 4 ploughs. In demesne are 2 ploughs with 1 slave; and 2 villans and 4 bordars with 2 ploughs. There are 2 acres of meadow and 100 acres of pasture. It was formerly worth 5s; now 30s.

Roger holds of William KNOWLE [in Timberscombe]. Paulinus held it TRE and it paid geld for 1 hide. There is land for 3 ploughs. In demesne are 1½ ploughs and 1 slave; and 1 bordar and 4 villans with 1 plough. There is scrubland 1 league in length and half a league broad. It was formerly worth 5s; now 25s.

Ranulph holds LUXBOROUGH. 2 thegns held it TRE and it paid geld for 1 hide. There is land for 4 ploughs. In demesne is 1 plough and 3 slaves; and 6 villans and 3 bordars with 3 ploughs. There are 100 acres of pasture and 30 acres of woodland. It is worth 20s.

Nigel holds of William LUXBOROUGH. Beorhtmær held it TRE and it paid geld for 1 hide. There is land for 3 ploughs. There are 2 acres of meadow, and 100 acres of pasture and 30 acres of woodland. It was and is worth 15s.

William himself holds WEST QUANTOXHEAD. Alnoth held it TRE and it paid geld for 3½ hides. There is land for 8 ploughs. In demesne are 3 ploughs and 7 slaves; and 10 villans and 4 bordars with 6 ploughs. There are 16 acres of meadow, and 50 acres of woodland, [and] pasture 1 league long and 1 league broad. It was worth £3; now £4.

William himself holds KILTON. Alweard and Leofric held it as 2 manors TRE and it paid geld for 10½ hides. There is land for 10 ploughs. In demesne are 4 ploughs and 7 slaves; and 16 villans and 6 bordars with 5 ploughs. There are 60 acres of meadow, and 60 acres of pasture and 100 acres of woodland. It was formerly worth 100s; now £7.

Of the same land Ralph holds of William 1 hide, and has there 1 plough, and 2 villans with 1 plough. There are 5 acres of meadow and 1 virgate of pasture. It is worth 20s.

William himself holds NEWTON [in Bicknoller]. Ælfgeat held it TRE and it paid geld for 4½ hides. There is land for 7 ploughs. In demesne are 2 ploughs and 4 slaves; and 13 villans and 4 bordars with 5 ploughs. There is a mill rendering 40d, and 18 acres of meadow, and 50 acres of woodland, and pasture 1 league in length and breadth. It was worth 60s; now 100s.

William himself holds WOOLSTON [in Bicknoller]. Beorhtmær held it TRE and it paid geld for half a hide. There is land for 1 plough. There 2 villans and 2 bordars have 2 ploughs. There are 7 acres of meadow, and 10 acres of pasture and 7 acres of woodland. It was formerly worth 10s; now 20s.

Dodman holds ELWORTHY of William. Dunna held it TRE and it paid geld for 4 virgates, a hide. There is land for 5 ploughs. In demesne are 2 ploughs and 2 slaves; and 9 villans and 8 bordars with 3 ploughs. There is a mill rendering 4s, and 1½ acres of meadow, and 120 acres of pasture and 50 acres of woodland. It was formerly worth 20s; now 40s. Of this hide the king holds 1 virgate of land [as belonging] to the manor of Williton.

Dodman holds of William WILLETT. Dunna held it TRE and it paid geld for half a hide. There is land for 4 ploughs. In demesne is 1 plough with 1 slave; and 9 villans and 6 bordars with 3 ploughs. There is a mill without rent, and 3 acres of meadow, and 50 acres of pasture and 40 acres of woodland. It was formerly worth 10s; now 20s.

The same man holds of William COLEFORD. Beorhtwine held it TRE and it paid geld for half a hide less a ferding. There is land for 2 ploughs. There 2 villans have 1 plough. It is worth 6s.

The same Dodman holds of William WATCHET. Alweald held it TRE and it paid geld for 1 virgate of land. There is land for half a plough. Yet there is 1 plough with 1 slave and 1 bordar. There is a mill rendering 10s. It is worth 15s.

Hugh holds of William TORWESTON. Leofsige held it TRE and it paid geld for 1½ hides. There is land for 3 ploughs. In demesne are 2 ploughs; and 5 villans and 6 bordars with 2 ploughs. There is a mill without rent, and 15½ acres of meadow, and 11 acres of pasture and 46 acres of woodland. It was formerly worth 30s; now 50s.

Hugh holds of William HOLFORD [near Nether Stowey]. Alweald held it TRE and it paid geld for 1 hide. There is land for 2 ploughs, which are there in demesne with 1 slave; and 1 villan and 5 bordars with 1 plough. There is a mill rendering 10d, and 3 acres of meadow, and 60 acres of pasture and 4 acres of woodland. It was formerly worth 10s; now 20s..

Roger holds of William HARTROW. Wulfweald held it TRE and it paid geld for 1 hide. There is land for 4 ploughs. In demesne is 1 plough with 1 slave; and 2 villans and 6 bordars with 1 plough. There is a mill rendering 6d, and 5 acres of meadow, and 100 acres of pasture and 6 acres of woodland. It was formerly worth 10s; now 20s.

Mainfrid and Robert hold of William CHUBWORTHY. 2 thegns held it TRE and it paid geld for 1 hide. There is land for 3 ploughs. In demesne is 1 plough; and 1 villan and 4 bordars with half a plough. There are 4 acres of meadow, and 50 acres of pasture and 5 acres of woodland. It was formerly worth 10s; now 12s.

Turgis holds of William COMBE SYDENHAM. Æthelmær held it TRE and it paid geld for 1 hide. There is land for 3 ploughs. In demesne is 1 plough with 1 slave; and 6 bordars with half a plough. There is a mill without rent, and 4 acres of meadow, and 50 acres of pasture, and woodland 4 furlongs in length and 2 furlongs in breadth. It was formerly worth 15s; now 20s.

Beorhtric holds of William 'SHORTMANSFORD'. The same Beorhtric held it TRE and it paid geld for 1 virgate of land. There is land for half a plough. 1 bordar has this [half-plough] there and 7 acres of woodland. It was and is worth 6s.

Nigel holds of William BATHEALTON. 2 thegns held it TRE and it paid geld for 2 hides. There is land for 5 ploughs. In demesne is 1 plough and 3 slaves; and 12 villans and 1 bordar and 5 cottars with 4 ploughs. There is a mill rendering 7s6d, and 6 acres of meadow, and 40 acres of pasture and 12 acres of woodland. It was formerly worth 20s; now 50s.

Ranulph holds of William 'MANWORTHY' [in Milverton]. Ulf held it TRE for 1 hide. There is land for 3 ploughs. In demesne is 1 plough with 1 slave; and 3 villans and 2 bordars with half a plough. There are 7 acres of meadow, and 12 acres of woodland and 12 acres of pasture. It was formerly worth 10s; now 20s.

Dodman holds of William RUNNINGTON. 2 thegns held it TRE and it paid geld for 2 hides. There is land for 2 ploughs. In demesne is 1 plough and 4 slaves; and 1 villan and 8 bordars with 1 plough. There is a mill rendering 5s, and 8 acres of meadow and 10 acres of woodland. It was formerly worth 20s; now 50s.

Dodman holds of William POLESHILL. Wulfric held it TRE and it paid geld for half a hide. There is land for 2 ploughs. There is 1 slave, and 3 acres of meadow and 20 acres of woodland. It is worth 10s. To this manor has been added 1 hide which 1 thegn held freely TRE. There is land for 1 plough. It was and is worth 30d.

Mainfrid holds of William LEIGH [in Milverton]. Cypping held it TRE and it paid geld for half a hide. Yet there is 1 hide. [There is] land for 2 ploughs. In demesne is 1 plough and 2 slaves; and 2 villans and 3 bordars with half a plough. There is 1 acre of meadow, and 12 acres of pasture and 20 acres of woodland. It was formerly worth 5s; now 12s.

Roger holds of William STOCKLINCH ST MAGDALEN. Edith held it TRE and it paid geld for 2 hides. There is land for 2 ploughs, which are there in demesne with 8 bordars. There are 8 acres of meadow and 4 acres of scrubland. It was and is worth 30s.

William himself holds BROOMFIELD. Alnoth held it TRE and it paid geld for 3 hides. In demesne is 1 plough and 8 slaves; and 12 villans and 2 bordars with 4 ploughs. There are 10 acres of meadow, and 1 league of pasture, and woodland 1 league in length and breadth. When received it was worth 40s; now 60s.

William himself holds EAST LYDEARD. Alric held it TRE and it paid geld for 2 hides. There is land for 6 ploughs. In demesne is 1 plough and 4 slaves; and 10 villans and 6 bordars with 1 plough. There is a mill rendering 8s, and 15 acres of meadow, and 10 acres of pasture and 20 acres of woodland. It was and is worth £7.

William himself holds WEST BAGBOROUGH. Leofric held it TRE and it paid geld for 3 hides. There is land for 10 ploughs. In demesne are 3 ploughs and 7 slaves; and 21 villans and 2 bordars with 4 ploughs. There are 11 acres of meadow, and 200 acres of pasture and 10 acres of woodland. It was and is worth 100s.

William himself holds STOKE ST MARY. Alweard held it TRE and it paid geld for 2 hides. There is land for 6 ploughs. There 6 villans and 2 bordars with 1 slave have 2 ploughs. There is 1 acre of meadow, and 200 acres of pasture and 6 acres of woodland. It was and is worth 30s.

Ralph holds of William HEATHFIELD. Æthelwine held it TRE and it paid geld for 3½ hides. There is land for 6 ploughs. In demesne is 1 plough and 5 slaves; and 7 villans and 5 bordars with 1 plough. There is a mill rendering 30d, and 18 acres of meadow, and 50 acres of pasture and 30 acres of woodland. It was worth 30s; now £4.

[Folio 96V: SOMERSET]

Turgis holds of William NUNNEY. Cola held it TRE and it paid geld for 5 hides. There is land for 3 ploughs. In demesne is 1 plough and 4 slaves; and 3 villans and 8 bordars with 1 plough. There is half a mill rendering 30d, and 20 acres of meadow and as many of pasture, and 100 acres of woodland. It was formerly worth 40s; now 60s.

William himself holds [North and South] BREWHAM. Robert fitzWimarc held it TRE and it paid geld for 12 hides. There is land for 15 ploughs. In demesne are 4 ploughs and 2 slaves; and 22 villans and 28 bordars with 13 ploughs. There are 2 mills rendering 9s2d, and 60 acres of meadow and 200 acres of woodland. When received it was worth £12; now £14.12s.

To this manor have been added 3 virgates of land. Æthelmær held them TRE. [...] There is land for half a plough. There are 3 cottars. It was and is worth 5s.

From this manor have been taken away 3 hides which Erlebald held TRE of Robert, nor could he be separated from the manor. Roger de Courseulles now holds them.

Warmund holds of William NORTH CHERITON. Earnwig held it TRE and it paid geld for 3 hides. There is land for 3 ploughs. In demesne are 1½ ploughs; and 1 villan and 4 bordars with half a plough. There are 10 acres of meadow and as many of pasture, and 12 acres of woodland. It was and is worth 40s.

XXII. The land of William de Eu

WILLIAM de EU holds of the king WHATLEY [in Winsham]. TRE it paid geld for 1 hide. There is land for 1 plough. There are 2 villans, and woodland 6 furlongs in length and 4 in breadth. It is worth 10s.

William himself holds HINTON ST GEORGE. TRE it paid geld for 13 hides. There is land for 12 ploughs. Of this 5 hides are in demesne, and there are 4 ploughs and 5 slaves; and 16 villans and 24 bordars with 10 ploughs. There are 2 mills rendering 7s6d, and 60 acres of meadow, [and] woodland 1 league in length and half a league broad. When received it was worth £12; now £15.

Ralph holds of William YEOVILTON. TRE it paid geld for 8 hides. There is land for 8 ploughs. In demesne are 3 ploughs and 4 slaves; and 6 villans and 4 bordars with 5 ploughs. There are 2 mills rendering 30s, and 90 acres of meadow and 40 acres of pasture. When received it was worth £9; now as much. To this manor have been added 2 hides which 5 thegns held in parage TRE. There is land for 2 ploughs. It is worth 30s.

Herbert holds of William LAVERTON. TRE it paid geld for 10 hides. There is land for 10 ploughs. In demesne are 3 ploughs and 2 slaves; and 6 villans and 8 bordars with 4 ploughs. There are 12 acres of meadow, and 60 acres of pasture and 60 acres of woodland. When received it was worth £7; now £8.

Ralph holds of William HINTON BLEWETT. TRE it paid geld for 8 hides. There is land for 6½ ploughs. In demesne are 2½ ploughs and 4 slaves; and 7 villans and 3 bordars and 4 cottars with 3 ploughs. There is a mill rendering 4s, and 60 acres of meadow, [and] woodland 1 league long and 1 furlong broad. It was worth £6; now 100s. Of this land Hugh holds of William half a hide. It has always been worth 3s.

Hugh holds of William YEOVIL. TRE it paid geld for 6 hides. There is land for 6 ploughs. In demesne is 1 plough and 3 slaves; and 11 villans and 14 bordars with 6 ploughs. There is 1 mill rendering 10s, and 33 acres of meadow and 30 acres of pasture. It has always been worth £8. To this manor have been added 22 messuages which 22 men held in parage TRE. They pay 12s.

Warner holds of William CHILTON CANTELO. TRE it paid geld for 1 hide. There is land for 1 plough. It is worth 10s. These above-mentioned lands Ælfstan of Boscombe held TRE.

William himself holds TICKENHAM. Sæwulf and Teolf held it TRE as 2 manors and it paid geld for 8½ hides. There is land for 9 ploughs. In demesne are 3 ploughs and 4 slaves; and 12 villans and 5 bordars with 6 ploughs. There are 30 acres of meadow, and 60 acres of pasture and 110 acres of woodland. It was worth 100s. when received; now £6.

XXIII. The land of William de Falaise

WILLIAM de FALAISE holds of the king STOGURSEY. Beorhtsige held it TRE and it paid geld for 4½ hides. There is land for 14 ploughs. In demesne are 4 ploughs and 5 slaves; and 38 villans and 3 bordars and 3 coliberts with 10 ploughs. There is a mill rendering 16d, and 150 acres of meadow, and 19 acres of pasture and 100 acres of woodland. When received, it was worth £25; now £20.

To this manor has been added half a hide which TRE 1 thegn held in parage and he could go where he would. There is land for 1 plough, which [plough] is there with 1 bordar and 2 slaves. It has always been worth 10s.

William himself holds WOOTTON COURTENAY. Algar held it TRE and it paid geld for 3 hides. There is land for 10 ploughs. In demesne are 3 ploughs and 6 slaves; and 10 villans and 8 bordars with 3 ploughs. There is 1 mill rendering 10d, and 4 acres of meadow, pasture 1 league long and a half broad and as much woodland. It was and is worth 100s.

William himself holds WOODSPRING by permission of King William. Serlo de Burcy gave it to him with his daughter. Everwacer held it TRE and it paid geld for 6 hides and 1 virgate of land. There is land for 12 ploughs. In demesne [...]. There 13 villans and 6 bordars have 6 ploughs. There are 10 acres of pasture and 10 acres of scrubland. It has always been worth 100s.

To this manor have been added 3 hides which TRE Alweard and Cola held as 2 manors and it paid geld for 3 hides. There is land for 8 ploughs. In demesne are 3 ploughs and 4 slaves; and 7 villans and 4 bordars with 3 ploughs, and 8 acres of pasture. It has always been worth £4.

XXXIIII [sic]. the land of William fitzGuy

WILLIAM fitzGUY holds of the king HORSINGTON. Sæweard and Ealdgifu held it TRE as 2 manors and they could go where they would, and it paid geld for 11 hides. There is land for 10 ploughs. In demesne is 1 plough and 4 slaves; and 12 villans and 10 bordars and 12 cottars with $7\frac{1}{2}$ ploughs. There is a mill rendering 42d, and 100 acres of meadow, pasture 6 furlongs long and 5 furlongs broad, [and] woodland 7 furlongs long and 6 furlongs broad. When received it was worth £8.15s; now as much.

Of this land Ralph holds of William $1\frac{1}{2}$ hides and there he has $1\frac{1}{2}$ ploughs. It has always been worth 25s.

Bernard holds of William [?South] CHERITON. Alweald held it TRE and it paid geld for 6 hides. There is land for 6 ploughs. In demesne are 2 ploughs and 6 slaves; and 5 villans and 4 bordars and 2 cottars with 3 ploughs. There are 125 acres of meadow, pasture 5 furlongs long and 3 furlongs broad, [and] woodland 7 furlongs long and as much broad. When received it was worth 100s; now £6.

Of this same land Alweald purchased 5 hides of the Abbey of Cerne [in Dorset] for the term of his life only, and after his death the land ought to return to the church.

XXV. The land of Ralph de Mortimer

RALPH de Mortimer holds of the king WALTON IN GORDANO, and Richard [holds] of him. Gunni held it TRE and it paid geld for $3\frac{1}{2}$ hides. There is land for 4 ploughs. In demesne is 1 plough; and 7 villans and 5 bordars with 3 ploughs. There are 20 acres of meadow, and 100 acres of pasture and 50 acres of woodland. When received it was worth 50s; now 20s more, that is 70[s].

XXVI. The land of Ralph de La Pommeraye

RALPH de la Pommeraye holds 'STOWEY' [in Oare], and Beatrice [holds] of him. Almær held it TRE and it paid geld for 1 virgate of land. There is land for 3 ploughs. In demesne are 2 ploughs and 3 slaves, and 1 villan and 4 bordars. There are 2 acres of meadow, and 6 acres of woodland, and pasture half a league long and 4 furlongs broad. It was and is worth 20s.

Ralph himself holds OARE. Eadric held it TRE and it paid geld for 1 hide. There is land for 6 ploughs. In demesne are 2 ploughs and 4 slaves; and 7 villans and 5 bordars with 4 ploughs. There are 2 acres of meadow, and 15 acres of woodland, [and] pasture 2 leagues long and 1 broad. | It is worth 30s. | This manor rendered to the king's manor of Carhampton as a customary due 12 sheep a year. Ralph keeps back this customary due.

XXVII. The land of Ralph Paynel

RALPH Paynel holds of the king STOCKLAND BRISTOL, and Ralph [holds] of him. TRE it paid geld for 3 hides. There is land for 5 ploughs. In demesne are 2 ploughs

and 4 slaves; and 7 villans and 4 bordars with 3 ploughs. There are 50 acres of meadow and 80 acres of pasture. It has always been worth 100s.

The same Ralph holds of Ralph EAST QUANTOXHEAD. TRE it paid geld for 7 hides. There is land for 20 ploughs. In demesne are 2 ploughs and 5 slaves; and 13 villans and 7 bordars with 7 ploughs. There is a mill rendering 7s6d, and 20 acres of meadow, and 50 acres of woodland, [and] pasture 2 leagues long and 1 league broad. It was worth £11 when received; now £8.

The same Ralph holds of Ralph BEGGEARN HUISH. TRE it paid geld for $1\frac{1}{2}$ hides. There is land for 6 ploughs. In demesne are 2 ploughs and 5 slaves; and 9 villans and 6 bordars with 3 ploughs. There is a mill rendering 3s, and 12 acres of meadow and 100 acres of pasture. It has always been worth £3.

The same Ralph holds of Ralph WEST BAGBOROUGH. TRE it paid geld for 1 hide. There is land for 4 ploughs. In demesne is half a plough and 3 slaves; and 5 villans and 5 bordars with $2\frac{1}{2}$ ploughs. There are 3 acres of meadow and 60 acres of pasture. It has always been worth 50s.

Robert holds of Ralph NEWHALL. TRE it paid geld for 1 virgate of land. There is land for 2 ploughs. There are 2 bordars, and half a league of woodland. It has always been worth 10s. These above-mentioned lands Mærle-Sveinn held TRE.

[Folio 97: SOMERSET]

XXVIII. The land of Ralph de Limesy

RALPH de LIMESY holds of the king COMBWICH, and Walter [holds] of him. Leofwaru held it TRE and it paid geld for $1\frac{1}{2}$ hides. There is land for 6 ploughs. In demesne is 1 plough with 1 slave; and 4 villans and 5 bordars with 2 ploughs. There are 28 acres of meadow, and 5 acres of pasture and 2 acres of woodland. It has always been worth 40s.

Ralph himself holds LUCCOMBE. Queen Edith held it TRE and it paid geld for 2 hides. There is land for 8 ploughs. In demesne are 3 ploughs and 2 slaves; and 18 villans and 6 bordars with 4 ploughs. There are 5 acres of meadow, and 50 acres of woodland, [and] pasture 1 league long and half a league broad. It was worth £3; now £4.

Ralph himself holds SELWORTHY. Queen Edith held it TRE and it paid geld for 1 hide. There is land for 5 ploughs. In demesne are 2 ploughs and 2 slaves; and 7 villans and 5 bordars with 3 ploughs. There is a mill rendering 20d, and 5 acres of meadow, and 60 acres of pasture and 40 acres of woodland. It was worth 20s; now 25s.

Ralph himself holds ALLERFORD. Eadric held it TRE and it paid geld for 1 hide. There is land for 5 ploughs. In demesne are 2 ploughs and 2 slave; and 6 villans and 2 bordars with 1 plough. There is a mill rendering 15d, and 6 acres of meadow, and 20 acres of pasture and 1 acre of woodland. It was worth 15s; now 20s.

This manor rendered as a customary due 12 sheep a year to Carhampton, the king's manor. Ralph has kept back this customary due to the present time.

Ralph himself holds BOSSINGTON. The Church of Athelney held it TRE, and it was for the sustenance of the monks, and it paid geld for 1 hide. There is land for 5 ploughs. In demesne is 1 plough with 1 slave; and 5 villans and 2 bordars with 1 plough. [There is] pasture 1 league in length and half a league broad. It was and is worth 20s. The church was seised of this manor when the king gave his land to Ralph.

Ralph himself holds TREBOROUGH. Eadric held it TRE and it paid geld for half a hide. There is land for 5 ploughs. In demesne is 1 plough. There is 1 villan, and 30 acres of woodland, [and] pasture 1 league long and as much broad. It is worth 7s for it has been laid waste.

Ralph himself holds [?] RAPPS. Wulfweard held it TRE and it paid geld for half a hide. There is land for 1 plough. There is 1 villan, and 16 acres of meadow. It is worth 3s.

Ralph himself holds ALLER [near Langport]. Wulfweard held it TRE and it paid geld for 2 hides. There is land for 4 ploughs. In demesne are 2 ploughs and 2 slaves; and 5 villans and 12 bordars with 2 ploughs. There are 15 acres of meadow, and 200 acres of pasture and 10 acres of woodland. When received it was worth 100s; now £6.

XXIX. The land of Robert fitzGerald

ROBERT fitzGerald holds of the king CHARLTON MUSGROVE, and Jocelyn [holds] of him. Godmann held it TRE and it paid geld for 5 hides. There is land for 12 ploughs. In demesne are 3 ploughs and 7 slaves; and 4 villans and 15 bordars and 3 cotsets with 8 ploughs. There is a mill rendering 5s, and 50 acres of meadow, pasture 4 furlongs long and 3 furlongs broad, [and] woodland half a league long and as much broad. It was worth £10; now £6.

Robert himself holds [...]. Vitalis held it TRE and it paid geld for 10 hides. There is land for 10 ploughs. In demesne are 3 ploughs and 8 slaves and 4 coliberts; and 11 villans and 17 bordars with 5 ploughs. There are 30 acres of meadow, and 100 acres of pasture, [and] woodland 3 furlongs long and 2 furlongs broad. When received it was worth £18; now it renders 100 cheeses and 10 bacons.

XXX. The land of Alvred of Marlborough

ALVRED of Marlborough holds of the king CHELWOOD, and Nicholas [holds] of him. Karli held it TRE and it paid geld for 5 hides. There is land for 5 ploughs. In demesne is 1 plough and 4 slaves; and 3 villans and 4 cotsets with 1 plough. There are 7 acres of meadow and 30 acres of woodland. It was and is worth 100s.

XXXI. The land of Alvred d'Epaignes

ALVRED d'Epaignes holds of the king WOOL-MERSDON, and Walter [holds] of him. Alwig held it TRE and it paid geld for half a hide. There is land for 3 ploughs. In demesne is 1 plough with 1 slave; and 4 villans and 13 bordars with 1 plough. There are 10 acres of meadow and 20 acres of woodland. It was and is worth 30s.

To this manor have been added 1½ virgates of land. This land belonged to North Petherton, the king's manor. Alwig the reeve leased it TRE. It was and is worth 10s.

Alvred himself holds [East and West] BOWER. Alwig held it TRE and it paid geld for half a hide. There is land for 5 ploughs. There are 8 villans and 6 bordars and 3 slaves. It has always been worth 100s. To this manor has been added 1 virgate of land which belonged to the king's farm in North Petherton. There is land for 1 plough. It is worth 10s.

Richard holds of Alvred HUNTWORTH. Alwig held it TRE and it paid geld for 1 hide. There is land for 2 ploughs, which are there with 2 slaves and 7 bordars. There are 4 acres of meadow and 10 acres of moor. When received it was worth 5s; now 20s.

Ranulph holds of Alvred STRINGSTON. Alwig held it TRE and it paid geld for 1 hide. There is land for 3 ploughs. In demesne are 2 ploughs and 4 slaves; and 3 villans with 1 plough. There are 4 acres of meadow and 50 acres of pasture. It is worth 50s.

To this manor has been added half a virgate of land which Beorhtgifu held freely TRE. There is land for half a plough. 1 villan has this [half-plough] there. It has always been worth 5s.

Alvred himself holds SPAXTON. Alwig held it TRE and it paid geld for 2½ hides. There is land for 8 ploughs. In demesne is 1 plough and 2 slaves; and 3 villans and 2 bordars with 1 plough. There are 26 acres of meadow and 9 acres of woodland. When received it was worth 50s; now the same.

Of this same land 1 knight holds of Alvred 1½ hides, and there he has 2 ploughs and 3 slaves, and 3 cottars and 6 villans and 5 bordars. There are 4 acres of meadow and 120 acres of woodland. It was worth £3; now as much.

Herbert holds of Alvred OTTERHAMPTON. Æstan held it TRE and it paid geld for 1 hide and 2½ virgates of land. There is land for 3 ploughs. In demesne are 2 ploughs with 1 slave; and 5 villans and 3 bordars and 3 cottars with 2½ ploughs. There are 5 acres of meadow, and 3 acres of pasture and 3 acres of woodland. It has always been worth 40s.

Herbert holds of Alvred RADLET. Æstan held it TRE and it paid geld for half a hide less a ferding. There is land for 1½ ploughs. There are 2 villans with 1 bordar, and 5 acres of meadow, and 21 acres of pasture and 3 acres of woodland. It was and is worth 15s.

Hugh holds of Alvred PLAINSFIELD. Eadræd held it TRE

and it paid geld for 1 hide. There is land for 2 ploughs. There are 3 bordars and 1 slave, and 2 acres of meadow and 15 acres of woodland. When received it was worth 20s; now 10s.

Hugh holds of Alvred MARSH MILLS. Alwine held it TRE and it paid geld for 1 hide. There is land for 1 plough. There is 1 bordar with 1 slave, and 15 acres of meadow. It has always been worth 15s.

Richard holds of Alvred MONKSILVER. Alwig held it TRE and it paid geld for $1\frac{1}{2}$ hides. There is land for 9 ploughs. In demesne are 2 ploughs and 4 slaves; and 11 villans and 5 bordars with 7 ploughs. There is a mill rendering 3s, and 2 acres of meadow, and 160 acres of pasture, [and] woodland 3 furlongs long and 2 furlongs broad. It was worth £3; now £4.

Alvred himself holds NETHER STOWEY. Earl Harold held it TRE and it paid geld for 3 hides. There is land for 5 ploughs. In demesne is 1 plough and 5 slaves; and 8 villans and 4 bordars with 2 ploughs. There is a mill rendering 4d, and 7 acres of meadow, and 100 acres of pasture, [and] woodland $1\frac{1}{2}$ leagues in both length and breadth.

Osweard and Æthelweard hold of Alvred NETHER STOWEY. They themselves held it TRE and it paid geld for 2 hides. There is land for 4 ploughs. In demesne are $1\frac{1}{2}$ ploughs with 1 slave; and 4 villans and 3 bordars with 1 plough. There are 3 acres of meadow. It has always been worth 20s. This land has been added to the land of Alwig which Alvred holds.

Ranulph holds of Alvred ALFOXTON and DYCHE. Alwig held them TRE and they paid geld for 2 hides. There is land for 3 ploughs. In demesne is 1 plough with 1 slave; and 4 villans and 2 bordars with 2 ploughs. There are 8 acres of meadow, and 30 acres of pasture | and 35 acres of woodland. | It was and is worth 20s.

Hugh holds of Alvred [?] LEIGH [in Old Cleeve]. Dunna held it TRE and it paid geld for half a hide. There is land for $1\frac{1}{2}$ ploughs. There are 2 bordars, and 2 acres of meadow, [and] woodland 3 furlongs long and half a furlong broad. It was and is worth 17s. This land has been added to the lands of Alwig which Alvred holds.

Hugh holds of Alvred RODHUISH. Alwig held it TRE and it paid geld for 1 virgate of land. There is land for 1 plough, which [plough] is there in demesne, with 1 bordar, and 1 acre of meadow and 12 acres of pasture. When received it was worth 2s; now 6s.

Robert and Herbert hold of Alvred STAWLEY. Alwig held it TRE and it paid geld for 3 hides. There is land [...]. In demesne are 2 ploughs with 1 slave; and 2 villans and 4 bordars [...]. There are 4 acres of meadow and 20 acres of woodland. When received it was worth 100s; now 60s.

Richard holds of Alvred ISLE BREWERS. Alwig held it TRE and it paid geld for 2 hides. There is land for 2 ploughs. In demesne is 1 plough with 1 slave; and 8 villans and 2 bordars with 1 plough. There is a mill rendering 20d, and 10 acres of meadow, and 10 acres of pasture and 30 acres of woodland. When received it was worth 20s; now 40s.

Hugh holds of Alvred PRESTON BOWYER. Alwig held it TRE and it paid geld for 3 hides less 1 virgate. There is land for 5 ploughs. In demesne is 1 plough and 2 slaves; and 14 villans with 1 plough. There is a mill rendering 20d, and 8 acres of meadow and 15 acres of woodland. When received it was worth 30s; now 60s.

[Folio 97V: SOMERSET]

Walter, 5 virgates, and Ansgar, 2 virgates of land, hold of Alvred GOATHURST. Alwig held it TRE and it paid geld for 1 hide and 3 virgates of land. There is land for 6 ploughs. In demesne are 2 ploughs and 4 slaves; and 13 villans and 5 bordars with 4 ploughs. There are 62 acres of woodland. When received it was worth 70s; now the same.

Ranulph holds of Alvred MERRIDGE. Alwig held it TRE and it paid geld for half a hide. There is land for $2\frac{1}{2}$ ploughs. In demesne is 1 plough and 2 slaves; and 4 villans and 1 bordar with $1\frac{1}{2}$ ploughs. There is a mill rendering 6d, and 30 acres of pasture and 20 acres of woodland. It was and is worth 20s.

Robert holds of Alvred QUANTOCK. Alwig held it TRE and it paid geld for 1 virgate of land. There is land for $1\frac{1}{2}$ ploughs. 3 villans have these [ploughs] there, and [there are] 8 acres of scrubland. When received it was worth 20s; now 25s.

Walter holds of Alvred HILLFARRANCE. Alwig held it TRE and it paid geld for 3 hides. There is land for 6 ploughs. In demesne is 1 plough and 4 slaves; and 11 villans and 4 bordars and 1 cottar with 1 plough. There is a mill rendering 30d, and 17 acres of meadow, and 10 acres of pasture and 17 acres of woodland. It was worth £3; now £4.

Alvred himself holds LUCKINGTON. Alwig held it TRE and it paid geld for 5 hides. There is land for 5 ploughs. In demesne are 2 ploughs and 3 slaves; and 8 bordars with 1 plough. There is a mill rendering 10s, and 12 acres of meadow, [and] woodland half a league long and 3 furlongs broad. When received it was worth £6; now £3.

Alvred himself had OAKLEY. Alwig held it TRE. This has been added to Martock, the king's manor, and is worth 50s a year.

XXXII. The land of Turstin fitzRolf

TURSTIN fitzRolf holds of the king PITCOMBE. Alweald held it TRE and it paid geld for 5 hides. There is land for 5 ploughs. In demesne are 2 ploughs; and 5 villans and 19 bordars with 3 ploughs. There are 2 mills rendering 15s, and 22 acres of meadow and 5 acres of woodland. In Bruton 11 burgesses pay 23s. The whole is worth £7; when received it was worth £8.

Butolf holds of Turstin WITHAM FRIARY. Ketil held it TRE and it paid geld for 1 hide. There is land for 2 ploughs. In demesne is 1 plough; and 6 cottars with 1 plough. When received it was worth 15s; now 20s.

To this manor has been added 1 hide in "Wltune", which Ketil held as a manor TRE. There is land for 1 plough, which [plough] is there with 1 slave and 6 cottars. There are 2 acres of meadow. It is worth 10s; when received it was worth 30s.

This land has been added to the lands of Alweald which Turstin holds.

Rippe holds of Turstin 'EASTRIP' [in Bruton]. Æthelwine held it TRE and it paid geld for 1 hide. There is land for 1 plough, which [plough] is there with 3 cottars. [There is] woodland 1 furlong long and broad. It has always been worth 20s. Hugh holds of Turstin 'SYNDERCOMBE' [in Clatworthy Reservoir]. Ceolric held it TRE and it paid geld for 1 plough hide. There is land for 5 ploughs. In demesne is 1 plough; and 7 villans and 7 bordars with 3 ploughs. There are 17 acres of meadow, and pasture 1 league in length and breadth, and 50 acres of woodland. It was and is worth 20s.

Turstin himself holds NORTH CADBURY. Alweald held it TRE and it paid geld for 12 hides. There is land for 12 ploughs. In demesne are 3 ploughs and 6 slaves; and 16 villans and 20 bordars with 8 ploughs, and 1 swineherd renders 12 pigs a year. There are 2 mills rendering 22s, and 50 acres of meadow, and 70 acres of pasture, [and] woodland 4 furlongs long and 1 furlong broad. It was worth £20; now £12.

To this manor has been added WESTON BAMPFYLDE. Alwig held it TRE as a manor, and could go where he would, and it paid geld for 2 hides and 2½ virgates of land. In demesne are 1½ ploughs and 2 slaves; and 6 bordars with 1 plough. There is half a mill rendering 45d, and 24 acres of meadow, [and] woodland 2 furlongs long and 1 furlong broad. It was and is worth 40s. Richard holds it of Turstin.

Alwine holds of Turstin WESTON BAMPFYLDE. He himself held it TRE and it paid geld for half a hide. There is land for half a plough. Yet there is 1 plough with 1 villan. It is worth 10s.

Bernard holds of Turstin SOUTH CADBURY. Alweald held it TRE and it paid geld for 3 virgates of land. There have been added 2 hides and 1 virgate of land which 4 thegns held freely TRE. In all there is land for 3 ploughs. Bernard has 2 hides, a clerk half a hide, an Englishman half a hide. It was and is worth £3. All these lands have been added to the lands of Alweald which Turstin holds.

1 hide in WOOLSTON [in North Cadbury] which Alnoth held freely TRE has also been added. There is land for 1 plough. Leofgeat holds it of Turstin, and has there 1 slave and 3 cotsets, and 4 acres of meadow and 3 acres of scrubland. It is worth 10s.

CLAPTON [Clapton and Higher Clapton, in Maperton] has also been added. Alnoth held it freely TRE and it paid geld for 2 hides. There is land for 3 ploughs. Ralph holds it of Turstin, and has there 1 plough, with 1 villan and 4 bordars and 2 slaves. There are 10 acres of meadow, and woodland 4 furlongs in length and 2 furlongs broad. When received it was worth 40s; now 20s.

Alweard holds of Turstin BLACKFORD [near Wincanton]. The same man held it TRE and it paid geld for 1 hide. There is land for 1 plough, which [plough] is there with 3 bordars. It is worth 15s.

Geoffrey holds of Turstin COMPTON PAUNCEFOOT. Alweard held it TRE and it paid geld for 6 hides. There is land for 6 ploughs. In demesne is half a plough and 4 slaves; and 9 villans and 11 bordars with 5 ploughs. There is a mill rendering 8s, and 15 acres of meadow, [and] woodland 4 furlongs long and 1 furlong broad. It is worth 100s; formerly £6.

Geoffrey holds of Turstin MAPERTON. Alweald held it TRE and it paid geld for 5 hides. There is land for 6 ploughs. In demesne are 2 ploughs and 10 slaves; and 3 villans and 9 cotsets with 3 ploughs. There are 2 mills rendering 5s5d, and 5 acres of meadow, and 10 acres of pasture, [and] woodland 5 furlongs long and 3 furlongs broad. It was formerly worth £8; now £6.

Norman holds of Turstin WANSTROW. Alweald held it TRE and it paid geld for 5 hides. There is land for 5 ploughs. In demesne are 2 ploughs and 4 slaves; and 4 villans and 4 bordars with 1 plough. There are 36 acres of meadow, and 30 acres of pasture, [and] woodland 1 league long and half a league broad. It is worth £3; formerly £6.

Norman holds of Turstin LITTLE KEYFORD. Leofdæg held it TRE and it paid geld for half a hide. There is land for half a plough, which [half-plough] is there in demesne with 4 cottars. There are 4 acres of meadow and 4 acres of pasture. It is worth 7s.

Bernard holds of Turstin DUNKERTON. Alweald held it TRE and it paid geld for 3 hides. There is land for 8 ploughs. In demesne are 4 ploughs and 8 slaves; and 10 villans and 6 bordars with 4 ploughs. There is a mill rendering 7s6d, and 6 acres of meadow, [and] pasture 4 furlongs long and 2 furlongs broad. It is worth £6; it was formerly worth 100s.

To this manor has been added 1 virgate of land, and it is worth 5s. Eadwig held it freely TRE.

Robert holds of Turstin [?North] CHERITON. Alweald held it TRE and it paid geld for 2 hides. There is land for 2 ploughs. In demesne is 1 plough, with 1 villan and 4 bordars. There are 6 acres of meadow, and woodland 1 furlong in length and in breadth. It is worth 30s; formerly it was worth 40s.

XXXIII. The land of Serlo de Burcy

SERLO de BURCY holds of the king BLAGDON. Almær held it TRE and it paid geld for 10 hides. There is land for 10 ploughs. In demesne are 2 ploughs with 1 slave; and 5 villans and 8 bordars with 5 ploughs. There are 2 mills rendering 5s, and 10 acres of meadow, and 200 acres of woodland, [and] pasture 1 league in length and breadth. When received it was worth £10; now £7.

Of this land Lambert holds 1 hide of Serlo and there he has 2 ploughs with 2 villan [sic]. It is worth 20s.

Four knights hold of Serlo UPHILL. Everwacer held it TRE and it paid geld for 6½ hides. There is land for 10 ploughs. In demesne are 4 ploughs with 1 slave; and 7 villans and 4 bordars with 3 ploughs. There are 70 acres of meadow and 100 acres of pasture. It was and is worth £6.

Serlo himself holds CHEW STOKE. Everwacer held it TRE and it paid geld for half a hide. There is land for 1 plough, and with 1 slave [the plough] is there in demesne, and 1½ acres of meadow, and woodland 4 furlongs long and 1 furlong broad. It is worth 10s.

Serlo himself holds CHILLYHILL. Everwacer held it TRE and it paid geld for 3 virgates of land. There is land for 2 ploughs, which are there with 1 villan and 1 bordar and 1 slave. There are 1½ acres of meadow. It is worth 15s.

To this has been added CHEW STOKE. Ælfric held it TRE as a manor and it paid geld for half a hide. There is land for 1 plough, which [plough] is there with 2 bordars, and 1½ acres of meadow. It is worth 10s.

Walter holds of Serlo ALDWICK. Almær held it TRE and it paid geld for 2 hides. There is land for 5 ploughs. In demesne is 1 plough and 2 slaves; and 4 villans and 1 bordar [...] There is a mill rendering 3s, and 15 acres of meadow and 49 acres of woodland. Formerly, as now, worth 40s.

[Folio 98: SOMERSET]

Guntard holds of Serlo RIDGEHILL. 4 thegns held it TRE and it paid geld for 2 hides. There is land for 2 ploughs. In demesne is 1 plough with 1 slave, and 1 villan. There are 5 acres of meadow and 5 acres of scrubland. It is worth 30s.

To this has been added 1 hide and 1 virgate of land. A thegn held it freely TRE. There is land for 3 ploughs. Walter holds it of Serlo and has there 1 plough and 4 slaves, with 1 villan and 1 bordar. There are 3 acres of meadow, and woodland 3 furlongs in length and breadth. Formerly [worth] 10s; now 30s. This land did not belong to Everwacer.

The Church of St Edward [of Shaftesbury] holds of Serlo KILMINGTON [Wilts.] for his daughter who is there. Alsige held it TRE. There are 5 hides but it pays geld for 1 hide. There is land for 5 ploughs. In demesne is 1 plough; and 4 villans and 3 bordars with 4 ploughs. There is woodland 1 league in length and 3 furlongs broad. Formerly [worth] 30s; now 40s.

Serlo himself holds LOVINGTON. 3 thegns held it TRE as 3 manors and it paid geld for 6 hides. There is land for 8 ploughs. In demesne are 2 ploughs and 2 slaves; and 8 villans and 9 bordars with 6 ploughs. There is a mill rendering 10s, and 40 acres of meadow, [and] woodland 4 furlongs long and 2 furlongs broad. Formerly [worth] £6; now 100s.

Of this land Lambert holds 1 hide and has there 1 plough with 3 villans. There are 12 acres of meadow. It is worth 20s.

Serlo himself holds WHEATHILL. Æthelmær held it TRE of the Church of Glastonbury, nor could he be separated from it, and it paid geld for 3 hides. There is land for 4 ploughs. In demesne is 1 plough with 1 slave and 1 bordar. Formerly [worth] 40s; now 40s. Of this land Geoffrey holds of Serlo 1 hide and it is worth 10s.

Serlo himself holds COMPTON MARTIN. Everwacer held it TRE and it paid geld for 5 hides. There is land for 5 ploughs. In demesne are 2 ploughs and 2 slaves; and 5 villans and 6 cottars | and 5 | bordars with 4 ploughs. There are 15 acres of meadow, and pasture 1 league in length and 2 furlongs broad, [and] woodland 11 furlongs long and 9 furlongs broad. Formerly [worth] 100s; now £4.

Of this land Richard holds of Serlo 1 virgate of land and 1 ferding, and has there 1 plough with 2 bordars, and 5 acres of meadow. Formerly [worth] 5s; now 15s.

Serlo himself holds 'MORETON' [in Chew Valley Lake]. 3 thegns held it as 3 manors TRE and it paid geld for 5 hides. There is land for 5 ploughs. Godric holds 2 hides of this land and Alric 2 hides. In demesne are 2 ploughs; and 9 villans and 11 bordars with 2 ploughs. There is a mill rendering 5s, and 40 acres of meadow and 15 acres of woodland. Formerly, as now, worth £3.

Of this land Richard holds 3 virgates of land and Humphrey 1 virgate of land. There is 1 plough, and 2 villans and 3 bordars, and 18 acres of meadow, and 4 acres of woodland and 2 acres of pasture. Formerly, as now, worth 15s.

Reginald holds of Serlo MUDFORD [Mudford, Up Mudford and West Mudford]. Æthelmær held it TRE and it paid geld for 3 hides. There is land for 3 ploughs. In demesne are 1½ ploughs; and 3 villans and 4 bordars with 2 ploughs. Formerly, as now, worth £3.

To this manor has been added STONE [in Mudford]. Særæd held it freely as a manor TRE and it paid geld for 2 hides. There is land for 1½ ploughs. Formerly, as now, worth 10s.

XXXIIII. The land of Odo fitzGamelin

Odo fitzGamelin holds of the king LUCCOMBE, and Vitalis [holds] of him. Vitalis held it TRE and it paid geld for 1 hide. There is land for 6 ploughs. In demesne is 1 plough and 2 slaves; and 8 villans and 1 bordar with 2½ ploughs. There are 2 acres of meadow, and 12 acres of woodland and 50 acres of pasture. Formerly, as now, worth 40s.

XXXV. The land of Osbern Giffard

OSBERN Giffard holds of the king KNOWLE [in Bristol]. Alnoth held it TRE and it paid geld for 2 hides. There is land for 3 ploughs. In demesne is 1 plough; and 5 villans and 6 bordars with 2 ploughs. There are 16 acres of meadow, and 20 acres of pasture, [and] woodland 2½ furlongs long and 1½ furlongs broad. Formerly 30s; now it is worth 40s.

Osbern himself holds GREAT ELM. Dunna held it TRE and it paid geld for 5 hides. There is land for 4 ploughs. In demesne is 1 plough and 2 slaves; and 3 villans and 4 bordars with 3 ploughs. There are 2 mills rendering 100d, and 14 acres of meadow, and 16 acres of scrubland and 14 acres of pasture. Formerly [worth] £3; now £4.

Osbern himself holds WOODBOROUGH. Dunna held it

TRE and it paid geld for 1 hide. There is land for 2 ploughs. In demesne is 1 plough, and 6 bordars with 1 slave, and 8 acres of meadow. Formerly [worth] 30s; now 40s.

XXXVI. The land of Edward of Salisbury

EDWARD OF SALISBURY holds of the king HINTON CHARTERHOUSE. Wulfwynn held it TRE and it paid geld for 10 hides. There is land for 10 ploughs. In demesne are 3 ploughs and 9 slaves; and 12 villans and 15 bordars with 6 ploughs. There are 2 mills rendering 34s, and 12 acres of meadow, [and] woodland 1 league long and half a league broad. In BATH, 2 houses, 1 rendering 7½d. Formerly £10; now it is worth £12.

Edward himself holds NORTON ST PHILIP. Iving held it TRE and it paid geld for 10 hides. There is land for 10 ploughs. In demesne are 3 ploughs and 3 slaves; and 3 villans and 13 bordars with 3 ploughs. There is a mill rendering 5s, and 20 acres of meadow and as many of pasture, [and] woodland 1 league long and as much broad. Formerly [worth] £6; now £7. Of these 10 hides King Edward gave to the aforesaid Iving 2 carucates of land.

XXXVII. The land of Ernulf de Hesdin

ERNULF de Hesdin holds of the king WESTON [near Bath]. Eadric held it TRE and it paid geld for 5 hides. There is land for 7 ploughs. In demesne are 2 ploughs and 10 slaves; and 6 villans and 1 bordar with 3 ploughs. There is a mill rendering 20s, and 13 acres of meadow, and 60 acres of pasture and 30 acres of woodland. In BATH 3 houses render 27d. The whole formerly, as now, worth £8.

Engeler holds of Ernulf TICKENHAM. Eadric held it TRE and it paid geld for 1 hide and 3 virgates of land. There is land for 3 ploughs. There are 3 villans and 1 bordar and 1 slave, and 6 acres of meadow, [and] woodland 3 furlongs long and 1 furlong broad. It is worth 40s.

Ingelrann holds of Ernulf RODDEN. Eadric held it TRE and it paid geld for 1 hide. There is land for 3 ploughs, which are there in demesne and 3 slaves, and 28 bordars. There are 2 mills rendering 15s, and 20 acres of meadow, and 30 acres of pasture, [and] woodland 1 league long and as much broad. Formerly, as now, worth £4.

XXXVIII. The land of Gilbert fitzTurold

GILBERT fitzTurold holds of the king KEWSTOKE, and Osbern [holds] of him. Eadric held it TRE and it paid geld for 1½ hides. There is land for 2 ploughs, which are there in demesne and 2 slaves, and 2 bordars, and 20 acres of meadow and 10 acres of scrubland. Formerly 20s; now it is worth 30s.

Walter holds of Gilbert UBLEY. Eadric held it TRE and it paid geld for 5 hides. There is land for 5 ploughs. In demesne is 1 plough and 2 slaves; and 5 villans and 4 bordars and 4 cotsets with 3 ploughs. There is a mill rendering 30d, and 35 acres of meadow, pasture 1 league long and half a league

broad, and as much woodland. When received it was worth 100s; now as much.

The same man holds STON EASTON. Eadric held it TRE and it paid geld for 1 hide. There is land for 1 plough, which [plough] is there with 3 bordars. It renders 30s.

XXXIX. The land of Godebold

GODEBOLD holds of the king SOUTH QUARME. Æthelbeorht held it TRE and it paid geld for 3 virgates of land. There is land for 3 ploughs. In demesne is 1 plough with 1 slave, and 3 villans with 1 bordar. There are 3 acres of meadow and 50 acres of pasture. Formerly 20s; now it is worth 10s.

XL. The land of Matthew de Mortagne

MATTHEW holds of the king CLEVEDON, and Ildebert [holds] of him. John held it TRE and it paid geld for 5½ hides and 2 ferdings. There is land for 6 ploughs. In demesne are 2 ploughs with 1 slave; and 8 villans and 10 bordars with 4 ploughs. There are 46 acres of meadow, pasture 1½ leagues long and as much broad, [and] woodland 2 furlongs long and half a furlong broad. Formerly 40s; now it is worth £4.

Rumald holds of Matthew CHELVEY. Thorkil held it TRE and it paid geld for 1 hide. There is land for 3 ploughs. In demesne is 1 plough and 2 slaves; and 3 villans and 4 bordars with 2 ploughs. There are 6 acres of scrubland. Formerly, as now, [worth] 40s.

From this manor has been taken away 1 virgate of land which Thorkil held with the aforesaid land. The Bishop of Coutances holds it.

Ildebert holds of Matthew MILTON CLEVEDON. Wulfweard held it TRE and it paid geld for 10 hides. There is land for 6 ploughs. In demesne are 2 ploughs and 4 slaves; and 9 villans and 9 bordars with 3 ploughs. There is a mill rendering 5s, and 24 acres of meadow, [and] woodland 10 furlongs in length and breadth. When received it was worth 100s; now £6.

[Folio 98V: SOMERSET]

XLV. The land of Humphrey

HUMPHREY the chamberlain holds of the king LYTE'S CARY. Ordric and Lyfing held it TRE and it paid geld for 1 hide and a ferding. There is land for 1 plough, which [plough] is there in demesne with 1 bordar and 2 cottars. There are 20 acres of meadow. Formerly 20s; now it is worth 40s. This land has been added to the lands of Beorhtric but those who held it TRE could go where they would.

The same Humphrey holds LYTE'S CARY. Lyfing held it TRE and it paid geld for 2 hides. There is land for 3 ploughs. In demesne are 2 ploughs; and 3 villans and 3 bordars with 1 plough. There are 24 acres of meadow. Formerly 30s; now it is worth 40s; and this has been joined to the lands of Beorhtric, but he who held it TRE could go where he would.

XLVI.

ROBERT d'Auberville holds of the king in WEARNE $2\frac{1}{2}$ virgates of land which have never paid geld. There is land for half a plough. There is 1 bordar with 1 slave. It is worth 15s. [It was] waste [when] received.

The same Robert holds half a hide in WITHYPOOL. 3 foresters held it TRE. There is land for 4 ploughs. From this Robert used to pay 20s to the king's farm at WINSFORD. Now it has been adjudged as thegnland.

The same Robert holds WELLISFORD. 2 thegns held it TRE and it paid geld for 1 hide. There is land for 2 ploughs. In demesne is 1 plough and 2 slaves; and 8 bordars have 1 plough. There are 4 acres of meadow, and 10 acres of pasture and 3 acres of scrubland. Formerly 10s; now it is worth 15s. Of this hide the Count of Mortain holds 1 virgate, and Bretel [holds] of him.

The same Robert holds MELCOMBE. Særic held it TRE and it paid geld for $1\frac{1}{2}$ virgates of land. There is land for $1\frac{1}{2}$ ploughs, and there are [$1\frac{1}{2}$ ploughs] with 10 bordars. There is a mill rendering 12d, and 10 acres of scrubland. Formerly, as now, worth 15s. From this manor has been taken away half a hide which TRE belonged there. Walter de Douai holds it with his manor of [East and West] BOWER.

JOHN the usher holds of the king 'PIGNES' [in Bridgwater]. Beorhtric held it TRE and it paid geld for 1 hide and 1 virgate of land. There is land for 2 ploughs. In demesne is 1 plough, and 2 villans with 1 bordar. There is a priest with 1 plough, and 2 bordars. There are 5 acres of meadow. Formerly 40s; now it is worth 30s.

The same John holds PERRY. Ordgar held it TRE and it paid geld for half a hide and half a virgate of land and half a ferding. There is land for 1 plough, which [plough] is there with 2 villans and 2 bordars. There are 5 acres of meadow. Formerly 10s; now it is worth 15s.

Stable holds of John [North or West] NEWTON. Sæmær held it TRE and it paid geld for half a hide. There is land for 1 plough, which [plough] is there with 2 villans and 2 bordars and 3 slaves. There are 5 acres of meadow and 5 acres of woodland. Formerly 10s; now it is worth 15s.

Robert holds of John CANNINGTON. Sæmær held it TRE and it paid geld for half a hide. There is land for 1 plough, which [plough] is there in demesne, with 1 villan and 4 bordars. There is a mill rendering 5s, and 23 acres of meadow and 6 acres of pasture. Formerly 15s; now it is worth 20s.

John himself holds WIGBOROUGH. Alweard held it TRE and it paid geld for 2 hides. There is land for $1\frac{1}{2}$ ploughs, and there are [$1\frac{1}{2}$ ploughs] with 2 villans and 3 bordars. There are 8 acres of meadow. Formerly [worth] 20s; now 30s.

John himself holds HUNTSTILE. Alweard held it TRE and it paid geld for 1 virgate of land. There is land for 2 ploughs, which are there with 3 villans and 4 bordars. There are 10 acres of pasture. Formerly 10s; now it is worth 20s. Of this

land half a virgate and a ferding TRE belonged to SOMERTON. It is worth 5s.

ANSGAR Fower holds of the king CHILTON TRINITY. Alwine held it TRE and it paid geld for 1 virgate of land. There is land for 1 plough, which [plough] is there with 1 villan and 1 slave. There are 14 acres of meadow and 5 acres of pasture. Formerly 5s; now it is worth 15s.

The same Ansgar holds ST MICHAEL CHURCH. Alwig held it TRE and it paid geld for half a hide. There is land for 1 plough. Formerly, as now, worth 5s.

The same Ansgar holds "SIWOLDESTONE". 2 thegns held it freely TRE and it paid geld for 1 virgate of land. There is land for half a plough. Formerly, as now, worth 4s.

The same man holds DURLEIGH. Alsige held it TRE and it paid geld for $2\frac{1}{2}$ virgates of land and a ferding. There is land for 3 ploughs, which are there with 4 villans and 2 bordars and 3 slaves. There are 20 acres of woodland. Formerly, as now, worth 20s.

ANSGAR the cook holds of the king LILSTOCK. Beorhtsige held it TRE and it paid geld for 5 hides. There is land [...]. In demesne are 3 ploughs and 2 slaves, and 11 villans and 7 bordars, and 20 acres of woodland in one place and, in another, woodland 1 league long and half a league broad. Formerly, as now, worth 100s.

ANSKETIL Parcher holds of the king [North or West] NEWTON. Osweard held it TRE and it paid geld for 1 hide and 1 virgate of land. There is land for 3 ploughs, which are there with 8 bordars. There are 15 acres of meadow, and 20 acres of moor and 10 acres of woodland. Formerly, 40s; now it is worth 30[s].

The same Ansketil holds HONIBERE. Ælfric held it TRE and it paid geld for 1 hide. There is land for 2 ploughs. There are 3 bordars with 1 slave, and 60 acres of pasture. Formerly 20s; now it is worth 5s.

The same Ansketil holds MILTON [in Weston-super-Mare]. Osweard held it TRE and it paid geld for 1 hide. There is land for 1 plough, which [plough] is there with 1 villan and 2 slaves. There are 6 acres of meadow, and 2 acres of scrubland and 20 acres of pasture. Formerly, as now, worth 15s.

Gerard holds EARNSHILL. Lyfing held it TRE and it paid geld for 1 hide of land. There is land for 1 plough. There is 1 bordar and 2 slaves, and 6 acres of meadow and 10 acres of woodland. Formerly, as now, worth 30s.

EDMUND son of Pain holds BARTON ST DAVID of the king. Eadwulf held it TRE and it paid geld for $3\frac{1}{2}$ hides. There is land for 6 ploughs. In demesne is 1 plough with 1 slave, and 2 villans and 4 bordars and 6 cottars. There is a mill rendering 10s, and 50 acres of meadow and 60 acres of pasture. Formerly [worth] £6; now £3. From this manor has been taken away 1 hide which Mauger de Carteret holds.

The same Edmund holds PITCOTE. Eadwulf held it TRE and it paid geld for $3\frac{1}{2}$ hides. There is land for 4 ploughs. In demesne are 2 ploughs and 2 slaves; and 3 villans and 8 bordars with 2 ploughs. There is a mill rendering 50d. There are 8 acres of meadow, and 12 acres of pasture and 50 acres of woodland. Formerly, as now, worth £4.

The same Edmund holds WALTON [in Kilmersdon]. Æthelmær held it TRE and it paid geld for 3 hides. There is land for 4 ploughs. There is 1 plough in demesne; and 1 villan and 6 bordars with $1\frac{1}{2}$ ploughs. There are 6 acres of meadow, and 40 acres of pasture, [and] scrubland 1 furlong in length and breadth. Formerly [worth] £4; now 40s.

The wife of Manasses the cook holds HAY STREET. Eadric held it TRE and it paid geld for 2 hides. There is land for 2 ploughs. There are 2 bordars with 1 cottar, and 6 acres of meadow and 12 acres of pasture. Formerly 20s; now it is worth 15s.

The same woman holds STON EASTON. Ealdwine held it TRE and it paid geld for 1 hide and 1 virgate of land. There is land for 2 ploughs, which are there in demesne, with 1 villan and 3 bordars and 1 cottar. There are 8 acres of meadow and 6 acres of pasture. Formerly, as now, worth 20s.

XLVII. The land of the King's Thegns

BEORHTRIC and Wulfweard hold of the king BUCKLAND ST MARY. The same men themselves held it TRE and it paid geld for $1\frac{1}{2}$ hides. There is land for 3 ploughs. In demesne are 2 ploughs, and 2 villans and 4 bordars. It is worth 20s.

These men held this land of Bishop Peter while he lived, and paid him 10s. Now they hold it of the king, but since the bishop's death the king has had nothing from it.

Of this land the wife of Bolla held 3 virgates TRE.

SIWARD holds SEAVINGTON ST MICHAEL. TRE it paid geld for 3 hides. There is land for 3 ploughs. In demesne is 1 plough, and 2 villans and 3 bordars and 2 slaves, and 8 acres of meadow. It is worth £3.

HEARDING son of Eadnoth holds LOPEN. Tovi held it TRE and it paid geld for 2 hides. There is land for 2 ploughs. In demesne is 1 plough and 2 slaves, and 2 villans and 5 bordars, and 20 acres of meadow. Formerly 20s; now it is worth 40s.

Hearding holds GOOSEBRADON. Tovi held it TRE and it paid geld for 1 hide. There is land for 2 ploughs. In demesne is 1 plough, with 1 villan. Formerly [worth] 20s; now 10s.

The same man holds CAPLAND. Tovi held it TRE and it paid geld for 1 hide. There is land for 2 ploughs. In demesne is 1 plough, with 1 bordar and 1 slave, and 6 acres of meadow and 30 acres of woodland. Formerly 5s; now it is worth 20s.

To this manor has been added half a hide which belonged to CURRY RIVEL, the king's manor. It is worth 5s.

The same man holds MERRIOTT. Godwine held it TRE and it paid geld for 5 hides. There is land for 6 ploughs. In demesne are 2 ploughs and 2 slaves; and 9 villans and 6 bordars with 2 ploughs. There is a mill rendering 5s, and 10

acres of meadow and 3 furlongs of pasture. Formerly 100s; now it is worth £4.

Hearding holds BUCKLAND ST MARY. Tovi held it TRE and it paid geld for 1 hide. There is land for 4 ploughs. There are 3 acres of meadow, and pasture 10 furlongs in length and 4 broad,

[Folio 99: SOMERSET]

[and] woodland 2 furlongs long and 1 broad. Formerly [worth] 40s; now 10s.

Hearding holds DISCOVE. Tovi held it TRE and it paid geld for 1 hide. There is land for 3 ploughs. In demesne are 2 ploughs, with 3 villans. There are 8 acres of meadow, and pasture 3 furlongs in length and breadth. Formerly, as now, worth 40s.

Beorhtric holds TUXWELL. Godwine held it TRE. There is half a virgate of land and it did not pay geld TRE. There is land for 1 plough. There are 4 bordars with 1 slave. Formerly, as now, worth 12s6d.

Siward holds DINNINGTON. Eadmær [...] held it TRE and it paid geld for 3 hides. There is land for 3 ploughs which are there with 6 villans and 3 bordars. There is a mill rendering 8d, and 8 acres of meadow, pasture 3 furlongs long and 2 furlongs broad, [and] woodland 3 furlongs long and 2 furlongs broad. Formerly 20s; now it is worth 40[s].

Siward holds ADBER [Dorset]. The same man himself held it TRE and it paid geld for 1 hide. There is land for $1\frac{1}{2}$ ploughs, and there are [$1\frac{1}{2}$ ploughs] with 2 villans and 3 bordars. There are 6 acres of meadow, and woodland 1 furlong in length and breadth. Formerly, as now, worth 20s.

Dodda holds DODINGTON. Sigeweald held it TRE and it paid geld for 3 virgates of land. There is land for 3 ploughs. In demesne is 1 plough and 3 slaves, and 6 villans and 2 bordars, and a mill without rent, and 5 acres of meadow, and 30 acres of pasture and 3 acres of woodland. Formerly, as now, worth 20s.

ULF holds HAWKWELL. The same man himself held it TRE and it paid geld for 1 virgate of land and a ferding and the fourth part of a ferding. There is land for 3 ploughs. There are 3 ploughs with 1 slave, and 3 villans and 4 bordars. It is worth 25s.

ALWEARD and his brothers hold STOCKLINCH OTTERSEY. Their father held it TRE and it paid geld for 3 hides. There is land for 2 ploughs, which are there with 1 villan and 1 slave and 13 bordars. There are 15 acres of meadow and 8 acres of pasture. Formerly 60s; now it is worth 50s.

GODWINE holds DRAYCOTT [in Rodney Stoke]. He himself and his mother held it TRE and it was assessed at 1 virgate of land. There is land for half a plough. It renders 2s a year.

EALDWIG holds CHEW STOKE. The same man himself held it TRE and it paid geld for 1 hide and 3 virgates of land. There is land for 2 ploughs. There are 3 bordars and 2 slaves with 1 plough. There is a mill rendering 6s8d, and 6 acres of meadow, pasture 5 furlongs long and 2 furlongs broad, [and] woodland 3 furlongs long and 2 furlongs broad.

BEORHTMÆR holds HASELBURY PLUCKNETT. The same man himself held it TRE and it paid geld for 10 hides. There is land for 8 ploughs. In demesne is 1 plough and 2 slaves; and 8 villans and 16 bordars with 5 ploughs. There is a mill rendering 5s, and 13½ acres of meadow, and pasture half a league in length and breadth, and as much woodland. It is worth £8.

ALFRED holds [Lower and Upper] SWAINSWICK. The same man himself held it TRE and it paid geld for 2 hides. There is land for 3 ploughs, which are there with 2 villans and 6 bordars and 3 slaves. There is a mill rendering 5s, and 5 acres of meadow and 10 acres of spinney. It is worth 40s.

DUNNA holds BUCKLAND DINHAM. The same man himself held it TRE and it paid geld for 12 hides. There is land for 7 ploughs. There are 5 ploughs, and 11 villans and 5 bordars and 7 slaves, and 40 acres of meadow, and 30 acres of scrubland, and pasture half a league in length and 1½ furlongs in breadth, and a mill rendering 7s. Formerly £8; now it is worth 100s.

ÆTHELRIC holds COMBE [?Hay]. Queen Edith held it TRE and it paid geld for 2 hides. There is land for 5 ploughs, which are there, and 6 villans and 5 bordars and 3 slaves. There is a mill rendering 50d, and 8 acres of meadow and 20 acres of woodland. Formerly [worth] 20s; now £4.

ÆLFRIC holds WEST LYDFORD. Beorhtric held it TRE and it paid geld for 9 hides. There is land for 8 ploughs. There are 7 ploughs, and 6 villans and 9 bordars and 2 cottars and 8 slaves. There is a mill rendering 15s, and 60 acres of meadow, and 30 acres of pasture, and woodland 1 league in length and breadth, and a swineherd rendering 10 pigs. Formerly, as now, worth £8.

ÆLFRIC holds "SCEPEWORDE" [? in West Lydford]. Beorhtric held it TRE and it paid geld for half a hide. There is land for half a plough. It is worth 5s.

BEORHTWEARD holds WRITHLINGTON. Beorhtweald held it TRE and it paid geld for 6 hides. There is land for 5 ploughs, and as many are there with 8 villans and 3 cottars. There are 12 acres of meadow, and 24 acres of pasture and 12 acres of scrubland. Formerly 100s; now it is worth £4.

Huscarl holds 1 virgate of land which he himself held TRE in 'EASTRIP' [in Bruton]. There he has half a plough. It is worth 40d.

OSMÆR holds 1 virgate of land in OTTERHAMPTON. His father held it TRE. Of this 2 parts have been taken away and placed in CANNINGTON, the king's manor.

The land of Humphrey and of Certain Others

HUMPHREY holds BABCARY. Brune held it freely TRE and it paid geld for 2½ hides. There is land for 3 ploughs. Yet in demesne are 2 ploughs and 2 slaves; and 6 villans and 3 bordars with 3 ploughs. There are 14 acres of meadow and 8 acres of pasture. Formerly 40s; now it is worth 50s. This has been added to the lands of Beorhtric.

Humphrey holds HOLTON. Alnoth held it TRE and it paid geld for 2 hides. There is land for 2 ploughs. In demesne is 1 plough; and 1 villan and 4 bordars with half a plough and 1 slave. There are 6 acres of meadow and 6 acres of woodland. Formerly 20s; now it is worth 30s.

Humphrey holds SANDFORD ORCAS [Dorset]. 3 thegns held it freely TRE and it paid geld for 6 hides. There is land for 6 ploughs, and as many are there, and 4 villans and 15 bordars and 4 slaves, and 8 acres of meadow. [There is] pasture 2 furlongs long and 1 furlong broad, [and] woodland 4 furlongs long and 1 furlong broad. Formerly £8; now it is worth £9.

Odo the Fleming holds TIMSBURY. Gunnfrothr held it TRE and it paid geld for 5 hides. There is land for 4 ploughs. There are 2 ploughs, and 5 villans and 3 bordars, and a mill rendering 40d, and 40 acres of meadow less 1, and 39 acres of pasture. It is worth £3.

William Hosed holds TADWICK. 3 thegns held it TRE and it paid geld for 1½ hides. There is land for 1 plough, which [plough] is there in demesne and 3 slaves, and 2 bordars, and half an acre of meadow and 10 acres of scrubland. Formerly 10s; now it is worth 30s.

RALPH of Berkeley holds TADWICK. Godric held it TRE and it paid geld for half a hide. There is land for 1 plough, which [plough] is there with 3 slaves. There is 1 acre of woodland. Formerly 10s; now it is worth 15s.

HUGOLIN the interpreter holds of the king WARLEIGH. Azur held it TRE and it paid geld for 1 hide. There is land for 3 ploughs, and as many are there with 1 villan and 5 bordars and 2 slaves. There is half an acre of meadow, and scrubland 3 furlongs in both length and breadth. Formerly, as now, worth 50s.

The same man holds BATHEASTON. Ingulf held it TRE and it paid geld for 3 hides. There is land for 5 ploughs. There are 3 ploughs, and 3 villans and 6 bordars and 2 slaves, and a mill rendering 5s. Formerly 40s; now it is worth 60s.

The same man holds CLAVERTON. Sven held it TRE and it paid geld for 5 hides. There is land for 6 ploughs, and as many are there, and 4 villans and 7 bordars and 4 slaves, and a mill rendering 7s6d, and 20 acres of meadow, and pasture 12 furlongs in length and breadth. Formerly, as now, worth £7.

DROGO of Montacute holds KNOWLE [in Shepton Montague]. Alnoth held it TRE and it paid geld for 1½ hides. There is land for 3 ploughs, and as many are there, and 6 villans and 4 slaves with 1 cottar. There are 15 acres of meadow, [and] woodland 4 furlongs in length and 3 furlongs in breadth. Formerly 40s; now it is worth £4. From this land has been taken away 1 hide of land which was there TRE. Turstin fitzRolf holds it. It is worth 20s.

HUGH holds FODDINGTON. Alweard held it TRE and it

paid geld for 2 hides and 1 virgate of land. There is land for 3 ploughs, and as many are there, and 2 villans and 1 cottar and 6 slaves, and 14 acres of meadow. Formerly 30s; now it is worth 40s.

Richard holds in RODE 1 hide which he himself held of Regenbald the priest by leave of the king, as he says. Regenbald indeed held it TRE. There is land for half a plough. There is 1 bordar. Formerly, as now, worth 10s.

SCHELIN holds FODDINGTON. Beorhtweard held it TRE and it paid geld for 1 hide and 1½ virgates of land. There is land for 2 ploughs, which are there with 1 slave and 1 bordar. There are 6 acres of meadow. Formerly, as now, worth 20s.

EALDRÆD holds BROCKLEY. The same man himself held it TRE and it paid geld for 4 hides. There is land for 4 ploughs, and as many are there, and 6 villans and 7 bordars, and 16 acres of meadow. It is worth 30s.

EALDRÆD holds CRANDON. The same man himself held it TRE and it paid geld for half a hide. There is land for half a plough. There are 4 bordars with 1 slave, and a mill rendering 30d, and 3 acres of meadow and 2 acres of scrubland. It is worth 5s.

ANSGAR of Montacute holds of the king PRESTON PLUCKNETT. Alweard held it TRE and it paid geld for 2 hides. There is land for 1 plough, which [plough] is there in demesne with 1 slave and 8 bordars. There are 10 acres of meadow. Formerly 15s; now it is worth 40s.

DEVONSHIRE

[Folio 100: DEVONSHIRE]

IN THE CITY OF EXETER THE KING HAS 300 houses, less 15, rendering customary dues. This [city] renders £18 a year. Of these Baldwin the sheriff has £6 weighed and assayed and Colwin £12 by tale from the administration of [the property of] Queen Edith.

In this city 48 houses have been destroyed since the king came to England.

TRE this city did not pay geld except when London, and York and Winchester paid geld and that was half a mark of silver for the use of the thegns.

Whenever an expedition went out by land or by sea, this city gave [as much] service as 5 hides of land [did].

Barnstaple, and Lydford and Totnes gave [as much] service as this city [did]. The burgesses of the city of Exeter have outside the city land for 12 ploughs which renders no customary dues except to the city itself.

Those Holding Lands In Devonshire Are Listed Here

I KING WILLIAM
II The Bishop of Exeter
III The Bishop of Coutances
IIII The Church of Glastonbury
V The Church of Tavistock
VI The Church of Buckfast
VII The Church of Horton
VIII The Church of Cranborne
IX The Church of Battle
X The Church of SAINTE-MARIE of Rouen
XI The Church of Mont-Saint-Michel
XII The Church of Saint-Etienne of Caen
XIII The Church of LA TRINITE of Caen
XIIII Earl Hugh
XV The Count of Mortain
XVI Baldwin the sheriff
XVII Iudichael of Totnes
XVIII William de Moyon
XIX William Chevre
XX William de Falaise
XXI William de Poilley
XXII William de Eu
XXIII Walter de Douai
XXIIII Walter de Claville
XXV Walter

XXVI Goscelm
XXVII Richard son of Count Gilbert
XXVIII Roger de Bully
XXIX Robert d'Aumale
XXX Robert the Bastard
XXXI Richard fitz Turolf [sic]
XXXII Ralph de Limesy
XXXIII Ralph Paynel
XXXIIII Ralph de Feugeres
XXXV Ralph de la Pommeraye
XXXVI Roald Dubbed
XXXVII Theobald fitzBerner
XXXVIII Turstin fitzRolf
XXXIX Alvred d'Epaignes
XL Alvred the Breton
XLI Ansgar
XLII Aiulf
XLIII Odo fitzGamelin
XLIIII Osbern de Sacey
XLV The wife of Hervey de Hellean
XLVI Gerald the chaplain
XLVII Gerard
XLVIII Godebold
XLIX Nicholas
L Fulcher
LI Haimeric
LII William and others of the king's sergeants
LIII Colwin and others of the king's thegns

The land of the King

THE KING has the borough of BARNSTAPLE. King Edward had it in demesne. There are 40 burgesses within the borough and 9 are outside the borough. Among them all they pay 40s by weight to the king and 20s by tale to the Bishop of Coutances. 23 houses have been destroyed there since the king came to England.

THE KING has the borough of LYDFORD. King Edward held it in demesne. There are 28 burgesses within the borough and 41 outside. Among them all they pay 60s by weight to the king, and have 2 carucates of land outside the borough. 40 houses have been destroyed there since the king came to England. But if an expedition goes out by land or by sea it [Lydford] renders as much service as Barnstaple or Totnes.

THE KING holds NORTH TAWTON. TRE it paid geld for half a virgate of land. There is land for 30 ploughs. In demesne are 3 ploughs, and 3 slaves; and 31 villans and 28 bordars with 27 ploughs. There are 40 acres of meadow, and 5 acres of pasture, and 40 acres of woodland and 30 acres of scrubland. It renders £15 by weight.

THE KING holds EXMINSTER. TRE it was assessed at 1 hide. There is land for 20 ploughs. In demesne are 2 ploughs, and 6 slaves; and 18 villans and 7 bordars with 16 ploughs. There is a fishery rendering 20s, and 18 acres of meadow, pasture 3½ leagues in length and breadth, [and] scrubland 12 furlongs long and 6 furlongs broad. It renders £8.

Of this manor's land William de Eu holds half a virgate of land which belonged there TRE; and Ecca the reeve leased 1 ferding of land to a certain priest TRE: now the monks of Battle hold it.

THE KING holds BRAUNTON. TRE it was assessed at 1 hide. There is land for 40 ploughs. In demesne is 1 plough, and 4 slaves; and 40 villans and 30 bordars with 30 ploughs. There are 2 acres of meadow, and 40 acres of pasture and 40 acres of scrubland. It renders £16 by weight.

From this manor has been taken away 1 virgate of land which rendered 20s in the king's farm. Robert de Pontchardon holds it.

To this manor has been added 1 virgate of land which TRE belonged to Filleigh, Baldwin the sheriff's manor, and it is worth 20s.

THE KING holds SOUTH MOLTON. There are 1½ virgates of land. There is land for 40 ploughs. In demesne is 1 plough, and 2 slaves; and 12 villans and 4 bordars with 20 ploughs. There are 10 acres of meadow, and 30 acres of pasture, [and] woodland 1 league long and 3 furlongs broad. It renders £10 by weight.

Half a virgate of land has been added to this manor; and it is called "RINGEDONE". It is worth 5s.

THE KING holds SILVERTON. It is not known how many hides are there because it never pays geld. There is land for 41 ploughs with all that belongs there. In demesne are 3 ploughs, and 15 slaves; and 45 villans and 31 bordars with 33 ploughs. There are 3 mills rendering 20s, and 50 acres of meadow, and 200 acres of pasture and 4 acres of woodland. It renders £40 weighed and assayed.

THE KING holds HEMYOCK. TRE it paid geld for 1 virgate of land. There is land for 12 ploughs. In demesne is 1 plough, and 7 slaves; and 12 villans and 12 bordars with 9 ploughs. There are 16 acres of meadow, pasture 2 leagues long and 1½ leagues broad, and 8 furlongs of woodland. It renders £6 by weight.

THE KING holds EAST BUDLEIGH. TRE it paid geld for half a hide. There is land for 13 ploughs. There are 16 villans and 20 bordars and 10 swineherds and 4 slaves with 12 ploughs. There are 5 acres of meadow, and 100 acres of pasture and 20 acres of woodland. It renders £10 by weight.

The king holds KINGSTEIGNTON. TRE it paid geld for 1 hide and 1 virgate of land. There is land for 16 ploughs. In demesne is 1 plough, and 3 slaves; and 14 villans and 30 bordars with 12 ploughs. There are 4 acres of meadow, and 15 acres of woodland. It renders £14 by weight and 10s by tale.

THE KING holds AXMINSTER. It is not known how many hides are there because it has never paid geld. There is land for 40 ploughs. In demesne are 2 ploughs, and 4 slaves; and 30 villans and 20 bordars with 18 ploughs. There are 2 mills rendering 10s, and 30 acres of meadow, and 100 acres of pasture and 100 acres of scrubland. It renders £26 weighed and assayed.

To this manor are owed 15d from 'Charlton' [?in Upottery], a manor of the Bishop of Coutances; and from HONITON [near Axminster], a manor of the Count of Mortain, 30d; and from Smallridge, a manor of Ralph de la Pommeraye, 30d; and from Membury, a manor of William Chevre, 30d; and from Rawridge, a manor of SAINTE-MARIE of Rouen, 30d. For many years now the king has not had these pence.

[Folio 100V: DEVONSHIRE]

'DENEWORTHY' [in Membury] has been added to this manor of AXMINSTER. Æthelric held it TRE, and it paid geld for 2 virgates. There is land for 1½ ploughs. There are 2 villans and 1 bordar, and it renders 10s.

UNDERCLEAVE is attached to the same manor. Eadric the Cripple held it in alms from King Edward. Now Edward the son of Eadric holds it, and it paid geld for 1 virgate of land. There is land for 1 plough, which [plough] 2 villans with 1 bordar have there. It is worth 5s.

Half a hide of the same land belongs to the church of the same manor, and there are 2 ploughs, with 12 bordars. It is worth 20s.

THE KING holds KINGSKERSWELL. TRE it paid geld for 1½ hides. There is land for 17 ploughs. In demesne is 1 plough, and 3 slaves; and 16 villans and 33 bordars with 16 ploughs. There are 9 acres of meadow and 20 acres of woodland. It renders £14 by weight. There is half a virgate of land in [the lands of] this manor's church.

THE KING holds COLYTON. TRE it paid geld for 1 hide. There is land for 16 ploughs. In demesne is 1 plough, and 3 slaves; and 21 villans and 10 bordars with 14 ploughs. There is a mill rendering 40d, and 36 acres of meadow, and 200 acres of pasture and 10 acres of scrubland. It renders £11.10s weighed and assayed. Half a virgate of land lies in [the lands of] this manor's church; and it is worth 5s.

THE KING holds AXMOUTH. It is not known how many hides are there because it has never paid geld. There is land for 12 ploughs. In demesne is half a plough, and 4 slaves; and 8 villans and 12 bordars with 6 ploughs. There are 16 acres of meadow, and 8 acres of scrubland, [and] pasture 1 league long and 4 furlongs broad. It renders £8 by weight and 1 mark of silver.

THE KING holds DIPTFORD. TRE it paid geld for 3 virgates of land. There is land for 10 ploughs. In demesne is 1 plough, and 4 slaves; and 8 villans and 7 bordars with 8 ploughs. There are 2 acres of meadow and 12 acres of pasture. It renders £7.5s by weight.

FARLEIGH was added to this manor in the time of William de Vauville. A thegn held it freely TRE, and it paid geld for 1 virgate of land. There are 2 villans and 5 bordars and they have 1 plough. It renders 10s by weight in the king's farm.

THE KING holds WEST ALVINGTON. TRE it paid geld for 1 hide. There is land for 10 ploughs. In demesne is 1 plough, and 4 slaves; and 10 villans and 5 bordars with 5 ploughs. There are 2 furlongs of woodland. It renders £7.5s by weight.

THE KING holds PLYMPTON. TRE it paid geld for $2\frac{1}{2}$ hides. There is land for 20 ploughs. In demesne are 2 ploughs, and 6 slaves; and 15 villans and 12 bordars with 12 ploughs. There are 6 acres of meadow, and 20 acres of pasture, [and] woodland 1 league long and a half broad. It renders £13.10s by weight.

Besides this land the canons of the same manor hold 2 hides. There is land for 6 ploughs. There 12 villans have 4 ploughs. It is worth 35s.

THE KING holds YEALMPTON. TRE it paid geld for $2\frac{1}{2}$ hides. There is land for 20 ploughs. In demesne is 1 plough, and 10 slaves; and 16 villans and 9 bordars with 12 ploughs. There are 6 acres of meadow, and 10 acres of pasture, [and] woodland 3 furlongs long and half a furlong broad. It renders £12.10s by weight.

The clerks of the same vill hold 1 hide. There is in demesne 1 plough, and 2 slaves; and 3 villans and 4 bordars with 1 plough. There are 2 acres of meadow and 10 acres of pasture. It is worth 10s. The king grants it to them in alms.

THE KING holds WALKHAMPTON. TRE it paid geld for half a virgate of land. There is land for 4 ploughs. There are 6 villans and 4 bordars and 2 slaves with 4 ploughs. There is 1 acre of meadow, and 100 acres of pasture, [and] woodland 1 league long and half a league broad. It renders £3 by weight.

THE KING holds 'SUTTON' [in Plymouth]. TRE it paid geld for 1 virgate of land. There is land for 6 ploughs. In demesne is half a plough with 1 slave; and 4 villans and 2 bordars with 5 ploughs. There are 2 acres of meadow and 20 acres of pasture. It renders 20s by weight.

THE KING holds KINGS TAMERTON [in Plymouth]. TRE it paid geld for geld for 1 virgate of land. There is land for 6 ploughs. There 6 villans and 2 bordars with 1 slave have $4\frac{1}{2}$ ploughs. [There is] woodland 3 furlongs long and 1 furlong broad. It renders 20s by weight.

From Walkhampton has been taken away Maker [Corn.], which paid geld TRE for 1 virgate of land. There is land for 10 ploughs, and it rendered £6, less 30d, in the king's farm.

These 3 manors belongs to Walkhampton.

THESE 19 MANORS WERE IN KING EDWARD'S DEMESNE AND BELONG TO THE KING

THE KING holds ERMINGTON. Esger held it TRE, and it paid geld for 3 hides. There is land for 20 ploughs. In demesne are 3 ploughs, and 10 slaves; and 16 villans and 36 bordars with 17 ploughs. There are 8 acres of meadow, [and]

woodland 2 leagues long and half a league broad. There is 1 salt-pan. It renders £13.10s. weighed and assayed.

To this manor belong these customary dues; from Fardel 30d and the customary dues of the hundred; likewise from Dinnaton and from the other Dinnaton; likewise from Broadaford and from Ludbrook [Ludbrook or Higher Ludbrook].

The Count of Mortain's men hold these lands and withhold the king's customary dues, that is, 30d from each vill and the customary dues of the hundred.

THE KING holds BLACKAWTON. Esger held it TRE, and it paid geld for 6 hides. There is land for 24 ploughs. In demesne are 2 ploughs, and 9 slaves; and 25 villans and 22 bordars with 24 ploughs. There is 1 salt-pan, and 5 acres of meadow, and 30 acres of pasture and 30 acres of woodland. It renders £14.10s.

These 2 manors are in exchange for BAMPTON.

QUEEN EDITH HELD THESE UNDER-MENTIONED LANDS. NOW THE KING HOLDS THEM

LIFTON. TRE it paid geld for $3\frac{1}{2}$ virgates of land. [There is] land for 25 ploughs. In demesne are 5 ploughs, and 12 slaves; and 26 villans and 24 bordars with 14 ploughs. There are 40 acres of meadow, and 42 acres of pasture and 40 acres of woodland. It renders £15.

To this manor 2 estates, Landinner [Corn.] and Trebeigh [Corn.], belonged TRE. The Count of Mortain holds them.

KENTON. TRE it paid geld for 3 hides and 1 ferding. There is land for 20 ploughs. In demesne are 4 ploughs, and 6 slaves; and 30 villans and 10 bordars with 15 ploughs. There are 4 swineherds rendering 20s, and 8 salt-workers rendering 20s. There is a mill rendering 50d, and 10 acres of meadow, and 150 acres of pasture, [and] woodland half a league long and 4 furlongs broad. It renders £30.

NORTH MOLTON. TRE it paid geld for $1\frac{1}{2}$ hides. There is land for 100 ploughs. In demesne are 7 ploughs, and 11 slaves; and 44 villans and 50 bordars and 4 iron-workers with 40 ploughs, and 15 swineherds. There are 2 leagues of meadow and as much pasture, and 1 league of woodland in length and breadth. It renders £45.

WONFORD [in Exeter]. TRE it was assessed at half a hide. There is land for 20 ploughs. In demesne are 2 ploughs, and 10 slaves; and 18 villans and 10 bordars with 8 ploughs. There are 30 acres of meadow, and 60 acres of woodland, and pasture half a league in length and breadth. It renders £18 of pence at 20[d] to the ora.

GYTHA, MOTHER OF EARL HAROLD, HELD THESE FOLLOWING MANORS

SOUTH TAWTON. TRE it paid geld for 3 hides and 1 virgate of land. There is land for 50 ploughs. In demesne are 8 ploughs, and 12 slaves; and 50 villans and 30 bordars with 36 ploughs. There are 60 acres of meadow, pasture 4 leagues long and 4 leagues broad, [and] woodland 2 leagues long and 2 broad. It renders £48 by weight.

[?East] ASH [in South Tawton] is attached to this manor. Wulfric held it TRE as a manor, and it paid geld for 1½ virgates of land. There is land for 3 ploughs. 6 villans with 1 slave have these [ploughs] there. There are 10 acres of meadow and 8 acres of pasture. It is worth 30s. It was appropriated into the above-mentioned manor in the time of King William.

HARTLAND. TRE it paid geld for 9 hides. There is land for 110 ploughs. In demesne are 15 ploughs, and 30 slaves; and 60 villans and 45 bordars with 30 ploughs. There are 10 acres of meadow, and 12 acres of woodland, [and] pasture 1 league long and another broad. It renders £48 by weight. Before Baldwin it rendered £23.

LITTLE TORRINGTON. TRE it paid geld for 1 virgate of land and 1 ferding. There is land for 7 ploughs. In demesne is 1 plough, and 3 slaves; and 6 villans and 4 bordars with 5 ploughs. There is 1 acre of meadow, and 8 acres of pasture and 2 acres of woodland. It renders 40s by weight.

WITHERIDGE. TRE it paid geld for 1 virgate of land. There is land for 3 ploughs. In demesne is 1 plough, and 2 slaves; and 3 villans and 3 bordars with 3 ploughs. There are 6 acres of meadow and 40 acres of pasture, and 12 acres of woodland. It is worth £6. To this manor has been added the land of 2 thegns which they held freely TRE, and it paid geld for 3 ferdings. There is land for 1 plough. There are 3 villans, and it renders 5s.

WOODBURY. TRE it paid geld for 10 hides. There is land for 35 ploughs. In demesne are 2 ploughs, and 6 slaves; and 30 villans and 22 bordars with 20 ploughs. There is a mill rendering 7s6d. There are 30 acres of meadow, and 300 acres of pasture, [and] woodland 1 league long and half a league broad. It renders £23 by weight. Before Baldwin [it rendered] £18.

| The Church of [Mont-]Saint-Michell holds this manor's church with 1 hide and 1 virgate and half a ferding. It is worth 20s.

CHILLINGTON. TRE it paid geld for 7 hides. There is land for 53 ploughs. In demesne are 2 ploughs, and 10 slaves, and 43 villans and 48 bordars. There are 12 acres of meadow, and 150 acres of pasture, [and] woodland 20 furlongs long and half a league broad. It renders £24 weighed and assayed.

SHERFORD [near Kingsbridge] belonged to this manor TRE, and it paid geld for half a hide. There is land for 8 ploughs. Now the Abbot of Battle holds it, and he has there 4 villans and 11 bordars and 2 slaves with 6 ploughs. There are 4 acres of meadow, and 6 acres of scrubland. It was and is worth £3.

TIVERTON. TRE it paid geld for 3½ hides. There is land for 36 ploughs. There are 35 villans and 24 bordars and 19 slaves with 30 ploughs. There are 3 swineherds rendering 10 pigs. There are 2 mills rendering 66d.

[Folio 101: DEVONSHIRE]

There are 14 acres of meadow, and 40 acres of common pasture, and 4 furlongs of woodland and 1 league in length

and 6½ furlongs in breadth. It is worth £18 weighed and assayed.

EARL HAROLD HELD THESE FOLLOWING 14 ESTATES

BRADSTONE. TRE it paid geld for half a hide. There is land for 8 ploughs. In demesne is 1 plough, and 3 slaves; and 17 villans and 4 bordars with 6 ploughs. There is 1 acre of meadow, and 15 acres of woodland. It renders £3 by weight.

BLACK TORRINGTON paid geld TRE for 2 hides, less 1 virgate of land. There is land for 31 ploughs. In demesne are 6 ploughs, and 15 slaves; and 20 villans and 22 bordars with 25 ploughs. There are 10 swineherds, and 20 acres of meadow, pasture 1 league long and 1 league broad, [and] woodland 1 league long and half a league broad. It renders £18 by weight. WEST PUTFORD renders 30d to this manor.

HOLSWORTHY. TRE it paid geld for 1 hide and 2½ virgates of land. There is land for 30 ploughs. In demesne are 8 ploughs, and 15 slaves; and 40 villans and with 20 bordars with 20 ploughs. There are 80 acres of meadow, and 1 acre of woodland, [and] pasture 1 league long and another broad. It renders £12 by weight.

SHEBBEAR. TRE it paid geld for 5 hides. There is land for 37 ploughs. In demesne are 10 ploughs, and 20 slaves; and 36 villans and 14 bordars with 23 ploughs. There are 30 acres of meadow, and pasture 1 league long and another broad, and as much woodland. It renders £18 by weight.

TAWSTOCK. TRE it paid geld for 5 hides. There is land for 80 ploughs. In demesne are 10 ploughs, and 18 slaves; and 60 villans having 21 ploughs, and 7 swineherds rendering 35 pigs. There are 12 acres of meadow, and 20 acres of woodland, [and] pasture 1 league long and another broad. In Exeter [are] 5 houses. It renders £24 by weight.

From this manor has been taken away LANGLEY, which was attached to it TRE and paid geld for 1½ virgates of land. There is land for 10 ploughs. There are 12 villans, and 20 acres of meadow and 100 acres of pasture. It renders £4. This land wrongfully lies in HIGH BICKINGTON.

MOLLAND [near West Anstey]. TRE it paid geld for 4 hides and 1 ferding. There is land for 40 ploughs. In demesne are 3 ploughs, and 10 slaves; and 30 villans and 20 bordars with 16 ploughs. There are 12 acres of meadow, and 15 acres of woodland, [and] pasture 3 leagues in length and breadth. It renders £24 by weight.

[Higher, Lower and Middle] BLACKPOOL has been joined to this manor. Æthelweard held it as a manor TRE, and it paid geld for half a hide. There is land for 2 ploughs. There are 5 villans with 1 slave. It is worth 20s weighed and assayed.

'NIMETE' has been wrongfully joined to the same manor and it is worth 15s.

To the manor itself belongs the third penny of North Molton, Bampton and Braunton HUNDREDS and the third animal on moorland pasture.

MOREBATH. TRE it paid geld for 3 hides. There is land for

20 ploughs. In demesne is 1 plough, and 12 slaves; and 20 villans and 13 bordars with 15 ploughs. There are 10 acres of meadow, and 20 acres of pasture and 40 acres of woodland. It renders £7.

ALPHINGTON [in Exeter]. TRE it paid geld for 2½ hides. There is land for 16 ploughs. In demesne are 2 ploughs, and 6 slaves; and 32 villans and 5 bordars with 14 ploughs. There are 3 acres of meadow, and 20 acres of woodland, [and] scrubland 1 league long and half a league broad. It renders £6 by weight.

TOPSHAM. TRE it paid geld for 1 hide. There is land for 12 ploughs. In demesne is 1 plough, and 5 slaves; and 16 villans and 12 bordars with 12 ploughs. There are 10 acres of meadow and 60 acres of pasture. It renders £6 by weight.

MORETONHAMPSTEAD. TRE it paid geld for 3 hides. There is land for 20 ploughs. In demesne are 3 ploughs, and 6 slaves; and 16 villans and 6 bordars with 8 ploughs. There are 20 acres of meadow, and 60 acres of pasture, [and] woodland 1 league long and 1 furlong broad. It renders £12 weighed and assayed. #²

COLATON RALEIGH. TRE it paid geld for 3 hides. There is land for 16 ploughs. In demesne are 2 ploughs, and 6 slaves; and 20 villans and 8 bordars with 12 ploughs. There is a mill rendering 7s6d, and 16 acres of meadow, and 400 acres of pasture and 40 acres of woodland. It renders £8 by weight.

To this manor has been added half a virgate of land which a thegn held freely TRE. It is worth 4s.

LITTLEHEMPSTON. TRE it paid geld for 2 hides. There is land for 6 ploughs. In demesne is 1 plough, and 4 slaves; and 8 villans and 7 bordars with 5 ploughs. There are 4 acres of meadow, and 24 acres of pasture and as many of woodland. It renders 40s by weight.

To the manor of MORETONHAMPSTEAD belongs the third penny of TEIGNBRIDGE HUNDRED.

SPITCHWICK. TRE it paid geld for 1 hide. There is land for 8 ploughs. There are 8 villans and 4 bordars and 5 slaves with 4 ploughs. There are 100 acres of pasture, [and] woodland 1 league long and 1 furlong broad. It renders 60s by weight.

KING'S NYMPTON. TRE it paid geld for 3 hides. There is land for 50 ploughs. In demesne are 3 ploughs, and 7 slaves; and 40 villans and 4 bordars with 16 ploughs. There are 6 swineherds, and 8 acres of meadow, and 1 league of pasture in length and breadth. It renders £18 by weight.

To this manor has been added half a virgate of land which a thegn held freely TRE, and it renders 7s in the king's farm.

WERRINGTON [Corn.]. TRE it paid geld for 6½ hides. Gytha held it TRE. There is land for 86 ploughs. In demesne are 6 ploughs, and 20 slaves and 25 coliberts; and 16 villans and 25 bordars with 27 ploughs. There are 100 acres of meadow, and 20 acres of woodland, and 500 acres of pasture. It renders £20 by tale; formerly it rendered £24.

EARL LEOFWINE HELD THESE 5 ESTATES MENTIONED BELOW

BEAFORD. TRE it paid geld for 1 hide and 1½ virgates of land. There is land for 18 ploughs. In demesne are 2 ploughs, and 5 slaves; and 16 villans and 5 bordars with 9 ploughs. There are 5 acres of meadow, and 50 acres of pasture and as much woodland. It renders £8 by weight.

PINHOE. TRE it paid geld for 1 hide and 3 virgates of land. There is land for 10 ploughs. In demesne is 1 plough, with 1 slave; and 8 villans and 6 bordars with 7 ploughs. There are 20 acres of meadow, and 100 acres of pasture and as much woodland. It renders £6 by weight.

The Abbey of Battle holds this manor's church with 1 virgate of the aforesaid land. It is worth 5s.

KILMINGTON. TRE it paid geld for 2 hides. There is land for 10 ploughs. In demesne is 1 plough, and 2 slaves; and 12 villans and 8 bordars with 6 ploughs. There is a mill rendering 5s, and 30 acres of meadow, and 6 acres of woodland, and 12 furlongs | and 12 acres | of pasture. It renders £7 weighed and assayed.

WHITFORD. TRE it paid geld for 5 hides. There is land for 16 ploughs. In demesne is 1 plough, and 2 slaves; and 14 villans and 13 bordars with 12 ploughs. There is a mill rendering 5s, and 27 acres of meadow, and 3 furlongs of pasture and 5 furlongs of woodland. It renders £11 weighed and assayed.

LANGFORD [in Ugborough]. TRE it paid geld for 3 hides. There is land for 20 ploughs. In demesne is 1 plough, and 6 slaves; and 16 villans and 10 bordars with 13 ploughs. There are 4 acres of meadow, and 200 acres of pasture and 7 acres of woodland. It renders £11 by weight.

To this manor the borough of Totnes rendered 20s to the king's farm. The king granted these [shillings] to Iudichael.

THE KING holds BROADCLYST. Ordwulf held it TRE, and it paid geld for 9½ hides. There is land for 35 ploughs. In demesne is 1 plough, and 11 slaves and 7 coliberts; and 35 villans and 30 bordars with 26 ploughs. There is a mill rendering 20s, and 40 acres of meadow, and 150 acres of woodland and half a league of pasture. It is worth £24 by weight.

BEORHTRIC HELD THE UNDERMENTIONED LANDS, AND LATER QUEEN MATILDA [HELD THEM]

THE KING holds NORTHLEW. TRE it paid geld for 1 hide and 1 virgate of land. There is land for 12 ploughs. In demesne [are] 4 ploughs, and 7 slaves; and 20 villans and 7 bordars with 10 ploughs. There are 30 acres of meadow, and 20 acres of woodland, [and] pasture 8 furlongs long and 4 furlongs broad. It renders £9 by tale.

HALWILL paid geld TRE for 1 virgate of land. There is land for 5 ploughs. In demesne are 2 ploughs, and 6 slaves; and 10 villans and 1 bordar with 5 ploughs. There are 40 acres of meadow, and 2 acres of woodland, [and] pasture 1 league long and 2 furlongs broad. It renders 70s by tale.

CLOVELLY. TRE it paid geld for 3 hides. There is land for 12 ploughs. In demesne are 5 ploughs, and 10 slaves; and 16 villans and 11 bordars with 7 ploughs. There are 30 acres of meadow, and 40 acres of woodland, [and] pasture 1 league long and half a league broad. It renders £12 by tale; formerly it rendered £6.

BIDEFORD. TRE it paid geld for 3 hides. There is land for 26 ploughs. In demesne are 4 ploughs, and 14 slaves; and 30 villans and 8 bordars with 20 ploughs. There are 10 acres of meadow, and 20 acres of pasture and 150 acres of woodland. It renders £16. A fishery was attached to this manor TRE; it renders 25s.

LITTLEHAM [near Bideford]. TRE; it paid geld for 1 hide. There is land for 8 ploughs. In demesne are [sic] is 1 plough, and 7 slaves; and 12 villans and 3 bordars with 4 ploughs. There are 10 acres of meadow, and 20 acres of pasture and 60 acres of woodland. It renders £3.

LANGTREE. TRE it paid geld for 2 hides, less half a virgate. There is land for 20 ploughs. In demesne are 2 ploughs, and 8 slaves; and 24 villans and 2 bordars with 16 ploughs.

[Folio 101V: DEVONSHIRE]

There are 15 acres of meadow, [and] woodland 1 league long and as much broad. It renders £7.5s.

IDDESLEIGH. TRE it paid geld for 3 hides. There is land for 22 ploughs. In demesne are 4 ploughs, and 15 slaves; and 24 villans with 16 ploughs. There are 15 acres of meadow, [and] woodland 2 leagues long and 1 league broad. It renders £14.

Of this land Walter holds 1 virgate of land from the king. There is land for 3 ploughs. Alware held it from Beorhtric TRE and she could not be separated from him. 2½ virgates of land in [North] TAWTON HUNDRED belong to this manor. They are worth 20s.

WINKLEIGH. TRE it paid geld for 5½ hides. There is land for 40 ploughs. In demesne are 8 ploughs, and 16 slaves; and 60 villans with 40 ploughs, and 10 swineherds. There are 80 acres of meadow, and 500 acres of woodland, pasture 1 league long and another broad, and a park for beasts. It renders £30 by tale. Of this land Norman holds 1½ virgates of land. They are worth 12s6d.

ASHREIGNEY. TRE it paid geld for 2 hides, less half a virgate. There is land for 15 ploughs. In demesne are 2 ploughs, and 10 slaves; and 14 villans and 6 bordars with 10 ploughs, and 2 swineherds rendering 10 pigs. There are 20 acres of meadow, and 200 acres of woodland, [and] pasture half a league long and as much broad. It renders £7 by tale.

LAPFORD. TRE it paid geld for 2½ hides. There is land for 11 ploughs. In demesne are 3 ploughs, and 6 slaves; and 7 swineherds and 18 villans and 12 bordars with 8 ploughs. There are 20 acres of meadow, and 10 acres of pasture and 130 acres of woodland. It is worth £12.12s.

IRISHCOMBE is attached to this manor and there is half a virgate of land.

HIGH BICKINGTON. TRE it paid geld for 1 hide and 2½ virgates of land. There is land for 16 ploughs. In demesne are 2 ploughs, and 3 slaves; and 14 villans and 2 bordars with 7 ploughs. There are 8 acres of meadow, and 100 acres of pasture and 100 acres of woodland. It renders £12.

To this manor has been added LANGLEY which belonged in Tawstock TRE. It renders £4 in High Bickington.

MORCHARD BISHOP. TRE it paid geld for half a hide. There is land for 8 ploughs. In demesne are 2 ploughs, and 2 slaves; and 8 villans with 3 ploughs. There are 2 acres of meadow and 40 acres of woodland. It renders £4 by tale.

HOLCOMBE BURNELL. TRE it paid geld for 1 hide. There is land for 7 ploughs. In demesne are 2 ploughs, and 4 slaves; and 10 villans and 8 bordars with 5 ploughs. There are 110 acres of woodland. It renders £8.15s.

HALBERTON. TRE it paid geld for 5 hides. There is land for 28 ploughs. In demesne are 4 ploughs, and 8 slaves; and 43 villans and 10 bordars with 22 ploughs. There are 2 mills rendering 10s, and 36 acres of meadow, pasture 5 furlongs long and 3 furlongs broad, [and] woodland 16 furlongs long and 13 furlongs broad. It renders £27.

Of this land of this manor Goscelm holds 1 virgate of land, and he has there 1 plough with 1 slave, and 1 bordar. It renders 10s in Halberton.

ASHPRINGTON. TRE it paid geld for 3 hides. There is land for 10 ploughs. In demesne are 2 ploughs, and 4 slaves; and 7 villans and 8 bordars with 3 ploughs. There are 2 fisheries, and 1 salt-pan, and 3 acres of meadow, and 40 acres of pasture, [and] woodland 1 league long and half a league broad. It renders £4. Iudichael held it from the queen.

THE KING holds [?] DOWN ST MARY. Boia held it TRE, and it paid geld for 1½ virgates of land. There is land for 2 ploughs, which are there, with 3 villans and 2 slaves. There are 3 acres of meadow, and 2 furlongs of pasture, [and] woodland 2 furlongs long and 1 furlong broad. It renders 10s. Adulf holds it from the king.

II. The land of the Bishop of Exeter

The BISHOP of EXETER has in the city [Exeter] 1 church which renders 1 mark of silver, and 47 houses rendering 10s10d, and 2 houses have been destroyed by fire. There are 2½ acres of land, and they lie with the land of the burgesses, who belong to the church.

The bishop himself holds CREDITON. TRE it paid geld for 15 hides. There is land for 185 ploughs. 6 hides of this [land] are in demesne, and there are 13 ploughs, and 40 slaves; and 264 villans and 73 bordars with 172 ploughs. There are 30 swineherds rendering 150 pigs, and a mill rendering 30d. There are 80 acres of meadow, and 200 acres of pasture, [and] woodland 5 leagues long and half a league broad. Formerly it was worth £21; now £75.

The same bishop holds NEWTON ST CYRES with this manor, and it pays geld for 3 hides. Bishop Osbern has produced his charters for this manor, which testify that the Church of ST PETER had been in possession of it before the reign of King Edward. In addition, in the time of King William he has proved before the king's barons that it is his. It is worth £3. Dunna holds it.

The bishop himself holds BURY. TRE it paid geld for 1 virgate of land. There is land for 3 ploughs. There are 4 villans and 3 bordars have 2 ploughs. There are 5 acres of meadow. It is worth 7s6d.

The bishop himself holds BISHOPSTEIGNTON. TRE it paid geld for 18 hides. There is land for 55 ploughs. In demesne are 4 ploughs, and 14 slaves; and 57 villans and 36 bordars with 51 ploughs. There are 10 swineherds rendering 35 pigs. There are 24 salt-pans rendering 10s, and 10 acres of meadow, pasture 4 leagues long and half a league broad, [and] woodland 1 league long and as much broad. In Exeter 9 houses render 3s. The whole of this manor was formerly worth £14; now £24.

The bishop himself holds DAWLISH. TRE it paid geld for 7 hides. There is land for 30 ploughs. In demesne are 2 ploughs, and 3 slaves; and 30 villans and 8 bordars with 24 ploughs. There are 6 acres of meadow, and 12 acres of pasture, [and] scrubland 3 furlongs long and 1 furlong broad. Formerly [it was worth] £7; now £8.

The bishop himself holds IDE. TRE it paid geld for 2 hides. There is land for 6 ploughs. In demesne is 1 plough, and 2 slaves; and 11 villans and 11 bordars with 5 ploughs. There are 3 acres of scrubland. Formerly, as now, worth 40s.

The bishop himself holds STAVERTON. TRE it paid geld for 2½ hides. There is land for 20 ploughs. In demesne is 1 plough, and 9 slaves; and 20 villans and 12 bordars with 16 ploughs. There are 12 acres of meadow, and 41 acres of scrubland and 30 furlongs of pasture. It is worth £7.

The bishop himself holds ST MARYCHURCH. TRE it paid geld for 2 virgates of land. There is land for 3 ploughs, which are there, with 4 villans and 4 bordars. It is worth 15s.

THESE 4 VILLS, MARKED ABOVE, ARE FOR THE CANONS' SUSTENANCE

The bishop himself holds HAXTON. Ordwulf held it TRE, and it paid geld for 2 virgates of land. There is land for 5 ploughs. There 6 villans have 3 ploughs, and there are 2 acres of meadow, and common pasture with Bratton Fleming. It was and is worth 25s.

The bishop himself holds BENTON. Eadnoth held it freely TRE, and it paid geld for 1 virgate of land. There is land for 2 ploughs. This has been added to the above vill. There is 1 villan, and common pasture with Bratton Fleming. It is worth 5s.

The Count of Mortain gave these 2 manors to the bishop in exchange for a castle in Cornwall.

The bishop himself holds BISHOP'S TAWTON. There are 12 hides. 3 of these have never paid geld, but only 9 [have]. There is land for 150 ploughs. In demesne are 6 ploughs, and 18 slaves; and 80 villans and 11 bordars having 100 ploughs. There are 22 swineherds rendering 100 pigs, and 24 acres of meadow, and 100 acres of pasture and 12 acres of scrubland. When received, it was worth £50; now £40.

The bishop himself holds CULMSTOCK. TRE it paid geld for 5 hides. There is land for 15 ploughs. In demesne are 2 ploughs, and 5 slaves; and 24 villans and 8 bordars with 11 ploughs. There is a mill rendering 5s, and 50 acres of meadow, and 7 furlongs of woodland in length and 1 furlong in breadth, [and] pasture 1 league long and as much broad. Formerly £4; now it is worth £6.

The bishop himself holds STOKE CANON. TRE it paid geld for 1 hide. There is land for 6 ploughs. In demesne is 1 plough, and 2 slaves; and 4 villans and 8 bordars with 6 ploughs. There are 2 mills rendering 30s, and 8 acres of meadow, and 50 acres of pasture and 4 acres of scrubland. It is worth 50s.

[Folio 102: DEVONSHIRE]

Robert holds TALATON from the bishop. TRE it paid geld for 7 hides. There is land for 16 ploughs. In demesne is 1 plough, and 6 slaves; and 20 villans and 12 bordars with 9 ploughs. There is a mill rendering 50d, and 20 acres of meadow, and 150 acres of pasture and 6 acres of scrubland. Formerly [it was worth] 100s; now £6.

The bishop himself holds SIDBURY. Alwine and Godwine held it TRE; it paid geld for 5 hides. There is land for 30 ploughs. In demesne are 2 ploughs, and 2 slaves; and 32 villans and 5 bordars with 25 ploughs. There are 12 acres of meadow, and 100 acres of pasture and 300 acres of woodland. Formerly, as now, worth £6.

The bishop himself holds SALCOMBE REGIS. TRE it paid geld for 3 hides. There is land for 6 ploughs. In demesne is 1 plough, and 2 slaves; and 16 villans and 7 bordars with 7 ploughs. There are 6 acres of meadow, and 14 acres of woodland, [and] pasture 1 league long and 4 furlongs broad. Formerly, as now, worth 60s.

The bishop himself holds 'BRIGHTSTON' [in Clyst Honiton]. TRE it paid geld for 1 hide. There is land for 5 ploughs. In demesne is 1 plough; and 3 villans and 6 bordars with 3 ploughs. There are 40 acres of meadow and 50 acres of pasture. Formerly, as now, worth 20s.

The bishop himself holds PAIGNTON. TRE it paid geld for 20 hides. There is land for 60 ploughs. In demesne are 8 ploughs, and 36 slaves; and 52 villans and 40 bordars with 42 ploughs. There are 5 swineherds rendering 50 swineherds [sic]. There is a salt-pan rendering 10d, and 18 acres of meadow, and 40 acres of pasture and 41 acres of woodland. When received, it was worth £13; now £50.

The bishop himself holds ASHBURTON. TRE it paid geld for 6 hides. There is land for 20 ploughs. In demesne are 2 ploughs. There are 10 slaves and 34 villans and 16 bordars with 16 ploughs. There are 3 acres of meadow, and 1 league of pasture and as much woodland. When received, it was worth £8; now £20.

Roger holds CHUDLEIGH KNIGHTON from the bishop. TRE it paid geld for half a hide. There is land for 3 ploughs, which are there, with 4 villans and 3 slaves. There are 3 acres of meadow and 6 acres of pasture. Formerly, as now, worth 10s.

The bishop himself holds BISHOP'S NYMPTON. TRE it paid geld for 3 hides. There is land for 52 ploughs. In demesne are 4 ploughs; and 56 villans and 25 bordars with 44 ploughs. There are 17 swineherds rendering 90 pigs, and there are 14 slaves. There is a mill rendering 40d, and 150 acres of meadow, and 140 acres of pasture and 200 acres of woodland. Formerly, £7; now it is worth £16.

The bishop himself holds BRANSCOMBE. TRE it paid geld for 5 hides. There is land for 16 ploughs. In demesne is 1 plough, with 1 slave; and 22 villans and 5 bordars with 15 ploughs. There are 2 acres of meadow and 12 acres of scrubland. It is worth £6. This is for the canons' sustenance.

Baldwin holds DITTISHAM from the bishop. TRE it paid geld for 3 hides. There is land for 16 ploughs. In demesne are 2 ploughs, and 2 slaves; and 22 villans and 10 bordars with 10 ploughs. There are 60 acres of pasture and 40 acres of scrubland. Formerly 60s; now it is worth 100s.

Baldwin holds SLAPTON from the bishop. TRE it paid geld for 6 hides. There is land for 26 ploughs. In demesne are 2 ploughs, and 6 slaves; and 26 villans and 21 cotsets with 21 ploughs. There are 10 acres of meadow, and 50 acres of pasture and 31 acres of woodland. Formerly £10; now it is worth £12.

III. The land of the Bishop of Coutances

THE BISHOP OF COUTANCES has in Exeter 3 houses and 1 waste [house], which were in king Edward's demesne and rendered customary dues.

Drogo holds 6 houses there from him. Of these, 4 were quit TRE, but 2 rendered 16d in customary dues. Drogo withholds these [dues].

The bishop himself has 10 burgesses in BARNSTAPLE paying 45d, and 7 waste houses and half a virgate of land, and a mill rendering 20s, and 20s from the customary dues of the king's burgesses.

The bishop himself holds ASHWATER. Alwine held it TRE, and it paid geld for 1 hide. There is land for 20 ploughs. In demesne are 2 ploughs, and 6 slaves; and 40 villans and 12 bordars with 17 ploughs. There are 100 acres of meadow, and 200 acres of pasture and 15 acres of scrubland. Formerly, as now, worth £7.10s.

The bishop himself holds MERTON. TRE it paid geld for 2½ virgates of land and half a ferding. There is land for 10 ploughs. In demesne 3 ploughs; and 12 villans and 8 bordars with 6 ploughs, and 9 swineherds rendering 25 pigs,

and 3 slaves. There are 15 acres of meadow, and 30 acres of pasture and 60 acres of woodland. Formerly £6; now it is worth £8. Thorkil held it TRE.

The bishop himself holds FREMINGTON. Earl Harold held it TRE, and it paid geld for 3 hides. There is land for 30 ploughs. In demesne are 3 ploughs, and 6 slaves; and 40 villans and 30 bordars with 27 ploughs. There are 13 swineherds rendering 21 pigs. There are 20 acres of meadow, and 100 acres of pasture and 10 acres of woodland. Formerly £12; now it is worth £22.

The bishop himself holds CLYST ST MARY. Vigot held it TRE, and it paid geld for 3 virgates of land. There is land for 6 ploughs. In demesne are 2 ploughs, and 5 slaves; and 9 villans and 5 bordars with 5 ploughs. There are 20 acres of meadow and 12 acres of pasture. Formerly 20s; now it is worth 60s.

The bishop himself holds BOVEY TRACEY. Eadric held it TRE, and it paid geld for 2 hides. There is land for 10 ploughs. In demesne are 3 ploughs, and 8 slaves; and 16 villans and 8 bordars with 10 ploughs. There is a mill rendering 10s, and 5 acres of meadow, and 50 acres of pasture and 60 acres of woodland. It renders £10, less 30d.

To this manor has been added the land of 15 thegns in Little Bovey, and Warmhill, and Scobitor, and "Brungarstone", and Elsford, and Woolleigh [in Bovey Tracey], and Hawkmoor, and Hatherleigh [in Bovey Tracey] and Pullabrook.

On these lands the 15 thegns have 2 hides and half a virgate of land. There is land for 8 ploughs, and there are 7 ploughs. These [thegns] pay to Bovey Tracey £4 and 30d. in rent; [this is] apart from the above-mentioned £10.

DROGO HOLDS THE UNDERMENTIONED LANDS FROM THE BISHOP

CORYTON. Alwine held it TRE, and it paid geld for half a hide. There is land for 8 ploughs. In demesne is 1 plough, and 6 slaves; and 8 villans and 7 cotsets with 1 plough. There are 12 acres of meadow, and 30 acres of woodland, [and] pasture half a league long and 2 furlongs broad. Formerly £4; now it is worth £3.

HAMSWORTHY. Alweard held it TRE, and it paid geld for half a virgate of land. There is land for 2 ploughs. There is 1 plough, with 2 slaves, and 20 acres of meadow. [There is] pasture 5 furlongs in length and 2 furlongs in breadth. Formerly 2s; now it is worth 5s.

HORTON. Oswulf held it TRE, and it paid geld for 1 virgate of land. There is land for 2 ploughs. There is 1 plough, with 2 slaves, and 20 acres of meadow and 100 acres of pasture. It is worth 5s. It has been joined to HORWOOD, the bishop's manor, but it did not belong there TRE.

HENSCOTT. 3 thegns held it as [...] a manor TRE, and it paid geld for half a virgate of land. There is land for 3 ploughs. There are 2 villans and 4 slaves, and 10 acres of meadow, and 60 acres of woodland and 2 furlongs of pasture. Formerly 20s; now it is worth 15s.

BUCKLAND FILLEIGH. Wulfgifu held it TRE, and it

paid geld for 1 hide and 1 virgate of land and 1 ferding. There is land for 8 ploughs. In demesne are 2 ploughs, and 5 slaves; and 10 villans and 4 bordars with 5 ploughs. There are 8 acres of meadow, and 1 league of pasture in length and breadth, [and] woodland half a league long and 3 furlongs broad. Formerly, as now, worth 40s.

HARTLEIGH. Wulfgifu held it TRE, and it paid geld for half a virgate of land. There is land for 5 ploughs. In demesne is 1 plough, and 3 slaves; and 2 villans and 1 bordar with 3 ploughs. There are 3 acres of meadow, and 15 acres of pasture, [and] woodland 4 furlongs long and 2 furlongs broad. Formerly, as now, worth 20s.

[Great or Middle] BARLINGTON. Alweard held it TRE, and it paid geld for 1½ virgates of land. There is land for 3 ploughs. There are 3 villans and 2 bordars, and 5 acres of woodland. It is worth 10s.

HUISH [in Instow]. Wulfgifu held it TRE, and it paid geld for 1 hide. There is land for 6 ploughs. In demesne is 1 plough, and 2 slaves; and 4 villans with 2 ploughs. There are 4 acres of meadow, and 30 acres of pasture and 8 acres of woodland. Formerly, as now, [worth] 30s.

HORWOOD. Oswulf held it TRE, and it paid geld for 3 virgates of land. There is land for 5 ploughs. There are 1½ ploughs, and 6 villans and 4 slaves, and 3 acres of meadow. Formerly, as now, [worth] 30s.

WORLINGTON [in Instow]. Dodda held it TRE, and it paid geld for half a hide. There is land for 5 ploughs. In demesne is 1 plough, with 1 slave; and 4 villans and 3 bordars with 2½ ploughs. There are 2 acres of meadow, and 10 acres of woodland and 12 acres of pasture. Formerly 30s; now it is worth 20s.

ROBOROUGH. Wulfgifu held it TRE, and it paid geld for 1½ hides. There is land for 14 ploughs. In demesne is 1 plough, and 5 slaves; and 15 villans and 3 bordars with 8 ploughs. There are 16 acres of meadow, and 20 acres of pasture and 20 acres of woodland. Formerly £4; now it is worth £3.

BONLEIGH. Alwine held it TRE, and it paid geld for 1 hide, less half a virgate. There is land for 12 ploughs. In demesne are 2 ploughs, and 8 slaves; and 6 villans with 2 ploughs. There are 3 swineherds rendering 15 pigs, and 12 acres of meadow and 30 acres of pasture and as much woodland. Formerly 30s; now it is worth 40s.

[Great or Middle] BARLINGTON has been added to this manor. Alfred held it freely as a manor TRE, and it paid geld for 1 virgate of land. There is land for 3 ploughs. It was and is worth 10s.

[Folio 102V: DEVONSHIRE]

NYMET TRACEY. Alwine held it TRE, and it paid geld for 1½ hides. There is land for 12 ploughs. In demesne is 1 plough, and 6 slaves; and 11 villans and 8 bordars with 6 ploughs. There are 6 acres of meadow, and pasture 1 league long and 3

furlongs broad, [and] woodland half a league long and 6 furlongs broad. Formerly, as now, worth £4.

COLDRIDGE. 2 thegns held it freely TRE, and it paid geld for 1 hide. There is land for 8 ploughs. In demesne are 2 ploughs, and 2 slaves; and 11 villans and 1 bordar with 6 ploughs. There are 3 swineherds rendering 50 pigs. There are 6 acres of meadow, and 30 acres of pasture, [and] woodland 1 league in length and half a league broad. Formerly 100s; now it is worth £4.

Of this hide Engelbald holds 1 virgate of land from Drogo. Algar held it freely TRE. Formerly 5s; now it is worth 10s.

MARTINHOE. Dodda held it TRE, and it paid geld for 1 hide. There is land for 8 ploughs. In demesne is 1 plough, with 1 slave; and 8 villans and 4 bordars with 3 ploughs. There are 50 acres of woodland and 1 league of pasture. It is worth 30s.

PILLAND. Eadmær held it TRE, and it paid geld for half a hide. There is land for 5 ploughs. In demesne are 2 ploughs, and 5 slaves; and 3 villans and 5 bordars with 3 ploughs. There are 4 acres of meadow, and 40 acres of pasture and 8 acres of woodland. Formerly 50s; now it is worth 40s.

PILTON. Dodda held it TRE, and it paid geld for half a hide. There is land for 5 ploughs. In demesne is 1 plough, and 4 slaves; and 6 villans and 7 bordars with 3 ploughs. There are 8 acres of meadow, and 40 acres of pasture and 60 acres of woodland. Formerly 40s; now it is worth 30s.

WEST DOWN. Algar held it TRE, and it paid geld for half a hide. There is land for 5 ploughs. In demesne is 1 plough, and 4 slaves; and 15 villans and 3 bordars with 7 ploughs. There are 3 acres of meadow, and woodland 1 league long and half a league broad. Formerly, as now, [worth] 40s.

To this manor have been added 3 estates of 3 thegns, which they held freely TRE, and they paid geld for half a hide. There is land for 4 ploughs. There are 3 villans with 2 ploughs. Formerly, as now, worth 20s.

[?East] HAGGINTON. Wulffrith held it TRE, and it paid geld for 1 virgate of land. There is land for 2 ploughs. 2 villans and 1 bordar have these [ploughs] there. There are 20 acres of pasture. Formerly 10s; now it is worth 6s.

RALEIGH. Beorhtric held it TRE, and it paid geld for half a hide. There is land for 4 ploughs. In demesne is 1 plough, and 4 slaves; and 4 villans and 4 bordars with 1 plough. There are 2 acres of meadow, and 5 acres of pasture and 30 acres of woodland. Formerly, as now, worth 30s.

METCOMBE. Beorhtric held it TRE, and it paid geld for half a virgate of land. There is land for 1 plough. 2 villans with 1 slave have this [plough] there. There are 4 acres of meadow and 20 acres of pasture. Formerly, as now, worth 10s.

[High and Little] BRAY [near Stoke Rivers]. Alwine held it TRE, and it paid geld for 1½ virgates of land. There is land for 6 ploughs. In demesne is 1 plough, with 1 slave; and 6 villans and 2 bordars with 3 ploughs. There are 30 acres of meadow, and 20 acres of woodland, [and] pasture 2 leagues long and half a league broad. Formerly, as now, worth 20s.

WHITEFIELD [in High Bray] has been added to this manor. Sæwine held it as a manor TRE, and it paid geld for 1 virgate of land. There is land for 2 ploughs. There is 1 plough, and 2 villans with 1 bordar, and 10 acres of woodland. Formerly, as now, worth 10s.

BEARA CHARTER. Beorhtric held it TRE, and it paid geld for half a hide. There is land for 5 ploughs. In demesne is 1 plough, with 1 slave; and 4 villans and 1 bordar with 2 ploughs. There are 2 acres of meadow and 6 acres of woodland. Formerly, as now, worth 20s.

Beorhtric held 1 virgate of land TRE [Boode] which before had been in Braunton, the king's manor, and William de Vauville put it back there TRW. The Bishop of Coutances claims this, but the thegns do not know how Beorhtric came to have it.

CHALLACOMBE. Wulfmær held it TRE, and it paid geld for 1 virgate of land. There is land for 3 ploughs. In demesne is 1 plough, with 1 slave; and 3 villans and 2 bordars with half a plough. There are 7 acres of meadow and 10 acres of pasture. Formerly, as now, worth 20s.

WHITEFIELD [in Challacombe]. Beorhtric held it TRE, and it paid geld for half a virgate of land. There is land for 2 ploughs. It was waste; now it is worth 6s.

BUSCOMBE. Ælfric held it TRE, and it paid geld for half a virgate of land. There is land for 2 ploughs. There 1 villan has half a plough, and [there are] 7 acres of meadow and 40 acres of pasture. It is worth 2s.

PATCHOLE. Eadnoth held it TRE, and it paid geld for half a hide. There is land for 5 ploughs. In demesne is 1 plough, and 2 slaves; and 9 villans and 2 bordars with 3½ ploughs. There are 3 acres of woodland. Formerly, as now, worth 40s.

KILLINGTON. Algar held it TRE, and it paid geld for half a virgate of land. There is land for 2 ploughs. In demesne is 1 plough, and 2 slaves; and 1 villan and 1 bordar have 6 oxen in a plough. There is 1 acre of meadow, and 30 acres of pasture and 6 acres of woodland. Formerly, as now, worth 15s.

PILLAND. Ælfric held it TRE, and it paid geld for half a hide. There is land for 4 ploughs. In demesne are 1½ ploughs, and 4 slaves; and 6 villans with 1½ ploughs. There is 1 acre of meadow, and 30 acres of pasture and 3 acres of woodland. Formerly [it was worth] 10s; now 20s.

PICKWELL. Ulf held it TRE, and it paid geld for half a hide. There is land for 5 ploughs. In demesne is 1 plough, with 1 slave; and 4 villans and 5 bordars with 1½ ploughs. There are 12 acres of meadow and 100 acres of pasture. Formerly [it was worth] 10s; now 20s.

[Higher and Lower] AYLESCOTT. 2 brothers held it freely TRE, and it paid geld for half a hide. There is land for 5 ploughs. In demesne is 1 plough, with 1 slave; and 5 villans and 3 bordars with 1½ ploughs. There are 20 acres of meadow and 100 acres of pasture. Formerly 10s; now it is worth 20s.

WEST STOWFORD [in West Down]. Eadric held it TRE, and it paid geld for half a virgate of land. There is land for 2

ploughs. There are 2 villans, and 6 acres of meadow and 50 acres of pasture. Formerly, as now, [worth 5s.

GRATTON. Ealdceorl held it TRE, and it paid geld for 1½ virgates of land. There is land for 8 ploughs. There 6 villans and 3 bordars with 1 slave have 2 ploughs. There are 12 acres of meadow, and 200 acres of pasture and 30 acres of woodland. Formerly 20s; now it is worth 15s.

WINSHAM. Dodda held it TRE, and it paid geld for 1½ hides and 1½ ferdings. There is land for 8 ploughs. In demesne is 1 plough, and 2 slaves; and 7 villans with 1 plough. There are 2 acres of meadow, and 100 acres of pasture and 20 acres of woodland. Formerly, as now, worth 20s.

HELE [in Ilfracombe]. Eadwig held it TRE, and it paid geld for half a virgate of land. There is land for 3 ploughs. In demesne is 1 plough, with 1 slave and 1 villan and 1 bordar. There are 30 acres of pasture and 20 acres of woodland. Formerly 5s; now it is worth 10s.

'BRAY' [in South Molton]. Æthelweard held it TRE, and it paid geld for half a virgate of land. There is land for 4 ploughs. In demesne is 1 plough; and 8 villans with 1 plough. There are 5 acres of meadow, and 30 acres of pasture and as much woodland. In Barnstaple a garden renders 4d. Formerly 10s; now it is worth 20s.

NORTHCOTE. Ulf held it TRE, and it paid geld for 2½ ferdings. There is land for 4 ploughs. In demesne is 1 plough, with 1 slave and 2 villans. There are 3 acres of meadow, and 100 acres of pasture and 12 acres of woodland. Formerly [it was worth] 5s; now 15s.

BRIDWICK. Æthelmær held it TRE, and it paid geld for 1 virgate of land. There is land for 3 ploughs. In demesne is 1 plough; and 5 villans and 5 bordars have 1 plough. There are 3 acres of meadow and 60 acres of pasture. Formerly 10s; now it is worth 20s.

TRENTISHOE. Beorhtsige held it TRE, and it paid geld for half a hide. There is land for 5 ploughs. There is 1 plough, with 1 slave and 4 villans and 3 bordars. There are 60 acres of pasture and 50 acres of woodland. Formerly, as now, worth 10s.

NORTHCOTE. Æthelmær held it TRE, and it paid geld for half a hide. There is land for 6 ploughs. In demesne is 1 plough, and 3 slaves; and 5 villans and 9 bordars with 2½ ploughs. There are 4 acres of meadow, and 40 acres of pasture and 4 acres of woodland. Formerly 10s; now it is worth 25s.

WALLOVER. Leofgar held it TRE, and it paid geld for 1 virgate of land. There is land for 3 ploughs. There are 2 villans and 2 bordars have 1 plough. There are 60 acres of pasture. Formerly, as now, worth 6s.

WARCOMBE [Warcombe and Higher Warcombe]. Beorhtric held it TRE, and it paid geld for 1 virgate of land. There is land for 2 ploughs, which are there, with 1 slave, and 4 villans and 1 bordar. There are 4 acres of meadow and 50 acres of pasture. Formerly 5s; now it is worth 10s.

[East and West] MIDDLETON. Eadmær held it TRE, and it

paid geld for half a virgate of land. There is land for 4 ploughs. In demesne is 1 plough; and 2 villans have another. There are 6 acres of meadow, and 30 acres of pasture and 3 acres of woodland. Formerly 8s; now it is worth 12s.

STOODLEIGH [in West Buckland]. Beorhtweald held it TRE, and it paid geld for half a virgate of land. There is land for 3 ploughs. In demesne is 1 plough; with 1 slave and 1 villan and 1 plough. There is 1 acre of meadow, and 20 acres of pasture and 30 acres of woodland. Formerly 5s; now it is worth 10s.

EAST BUCKLAND [near South Molton]. Wulfmær held it TRE, and it paid geld for half a virgate of land. There is land for 2 ploughs. There is 1 plough, with 1 villan and 2 slaves. There are 6 acres of meadow, and |6 acres of woodland| and 12 acres of pasture. Formerly 3s; now it is worth 5s.

BREMRIDGE. Eadmær held it TRE, and it paid geld for half a hide. There is land for 6 ploughs. In demesne are 2 ploughs, with 1 slave; and 3 villans and 3 bordars with 1 plough. There are 15 acres of woodland and 30 acres of pasture. Formerly [it was worth] 10s; now 20s.

SOUTH ALLER [in South Molton]. Eadmær held it TRE, and it paid geld for half a virgate of land. There is land for 2 ploughs. In demesne is 1 plough, with 1 slave and 1 villan. There are 6 acres of meadow and 12 acres of pasture. Formerly 5s; now it is worth 10s.

PLAISTOW. Beorhtweald held it TRE, and it paid geld for 1 virgate of land. There is land for 4 ploughs. In demesne is 1 plough, and 2 slaves; and 5 villans and 3 bordars with 2 ploughs. There are 6 acres of meadow and 30 acres of pasture. Formerly [it was worth] 10s; now 20s.

VARLEY [in Marwood]. Beorhtweald held it TRE, and it paid geld for 1 ferding of land.

EAST BUCKLAND [near South Molton]. Ulf held it TRE, and it paid geld for 1 ferding of land. There is land for 2 ploughs. There is 1 plough, with 1 villan and 2 slaves, and 3 acres of meadow and 3 acres of pasture. It is worth 5s.

[Folio 103: DEVONSHIRE]

There is land for 2 ploughs. In demesne is 1 plough, with 1 slave; and 1 villan and 2 bordars with half a plough. There are 6 acres of meadow and 4 acres of woodland. Formerly, as now, worth 5s.

BITTADON. Æthelmær held it TRE, and it paid geld for half a hide. There is land for 6 ploughs. In demesne are 1½ ploughs, and 3 slaves; and 4 villans and 3 bordars with 2 ploughs. There are 5 acres of meadow, and 60 acres of pasture and 1 acre of woodland. Formerly 15s; now it is worth 25s.

MOLLAND [near West Anstey]. Wulfwynn held it TRE, and it paid geld for half a hide. There is land for 4 ploughs. In demesne is 1 plough, and 2 slaves; and 3 villans and 4 bordars with 1 plough. There are 1½ acres of meadow and 30 acres of woodland. Formerly, as now, [worth] 25s.

WEST ANSTEY. Algar held it TRE, and it paid geld for half a hide, less 1 ferding. There is land for 3 ploughs. In demesne

are 2 ploughs, and 6 slaves; and 3 villans with 1 plough. There is 1 acre of meadow, and 20 acres of woodland, [and] pasture 1 league long and half a league broad. Formerly 15s; now it is worth 20s.

EAST BUCKLAND [near South Molton]. Ealdceorl held it TRE, and it paid geld for 1 virgate of land. There is land for 3 ploughs. In demesne is 1 plough, and 2 slaves; and 2 bordars with 1 plough. There are 12 acres of meadow, and 20 acres of pasture and 20 acres of woodland. Formerly 20s; now it is worth 10s.

ROWLEY. Alweard held it TRE, and it paid geld for half a virgate of land. There is land for 2 ploughs. There are 3 villans and 2 bordars with 1 plough. There is 1 acre of meadow, and 20 acres of pasture and 10 acres of woodland. Formerly [it was worth] 10s; now 7s6d.

CHAGFORD. Dodda held it TRE, and it paid geld for 1 hide. There is land for 6 ploughs. In demesne is 1 plough, and 4 slaves; and 8 villans and 5 bordars with 1½ ploughs. There are 18 acres of meadow, and 60 acres of pasture and 15 acres of woodland. Formerly 20s; now it is worth 30s.

TEIGNCOMBE. Alric held it TRE, and it paid geld for half a hide. There is land for 4 ploughs. In demesne is 1 plough, and 2 slaves; and 6 villans and 2 bordars with 1½ ploughs. There are 4 acres of meadow, and 4 acres of woodland, [and] pasture 3 leagues long and 1 league broad. Formerly 15s; now it is worth 20s.

BRAMPFORD SPEKE. Wulfnoth held it TRE, and it paid geld for 1 hide. There is land for 8 ploughs. In demesne is 1 plough; and 10 villans and 8 bordars and 6 slaves with 5 ploughs. There are 60 acres of pasture and 8 acres of woodland. Formerly, as now, worth 60s.

REWE. Wulfnoth held it TRE, and it paid geld for 1 hide. There is land for 5 ploughs. There are 5 villans and 3 bordars and 2 slaves, and 7 acres of meadow and 10 acres of woodland. Formerly 60s; now it is worth 20s.

NETHER EXE. Wulfnoth held it TRE, and it paid geld for 1 hide and 1 virgate of land. There is land for 8 ploughs. In demesne is 1 plough, and 6 slaves; and 10 villans and 8 bordars with 6 ploughs. There are 4 acres of meadow and 12 acres of pasture. Formerly 70s; now it is worth 60s.

UP EXE. Wulfnoth held it TRE, and it paid geld for 1 virgate of land. There is land for 3 ploughs. In demesne is 1 plough, and 3 slaves; and 7 villans and 7 bordars |with 1 plough.| There is a mill rendering 12s, and 10 acres of meadow, and 12 acres of pasture and 6 acres of woodland. Formerly 60s; now it is worth 40s.

Wulfnoth held 1 hide of land TRE. There the bishop has 1 villan, and a mill rendering 20s. The whole is worth 30s.

LOWER CREEDY. Gode held it TRE, and it paid geld for 1 virgate of land. There is land for 2 ploughs. There 4 villans have half a plough. It is worth 5s. This land belongs to Cruwys Morchard.

CRUWYS MORCHARD. Algar held it TRE, and it paid

geld for 1 virgate of land and 1 ferding. There is land for 4 ploughs. In demesne is 1 plough, with 1 slave; and 4 villans and 4 bordars with 1 plough. There are 6 acres of meadow, and 100 acres of pasture and 10 acres of woodland. Formerly [it was worth] 5s; now 12s6d.

SPURWAY. Algar held it TRE, and it paid geld for 1 virgate of land. There is land for 3 ploughs. There are 2 ploughs in demesne, and 2 slaves, and 2 villans and 2 bordars. There are 3 acres of meadow, and 20 acres of pasture and 10 acres of woodland. Formerly [it was worth] 5s; now 10s.

"CELVERTESBERIE". Alwine held it TRE, and it paid geld for 1 hide, less 1 ferding. There is land for 6 ploughs. In demesne is 1 plough. and 2 slaves, and 3 villans and 2 bordars. There are 15 acres of meadow, and 100 acres of pasture and 6 acres of scrubland. Formerly 5s; now it is worth 15s.

[North or South] COOMBE [in Templeton] has been added to this manor. Weland held it TRE, and it paid geld for 1 virgate of land and 1 ferding.

[North or South] COOMBE [in Templeton]. Æthelweard held it TRE, and it paid geld for half a hide. There is land for 3 ploughs. There are 2 ploughs, and 3 villans with 1 slave, and 3 acres of meadow, and 20 acres of pasture and 6 acres of woodland. It is worth 10s.

STOODLEIGH [near Oakford]. Alwine held it TRE, and it paid geld for 1 hide. There is land for 10 ploughs. In demesne are 2 ploughs, and 4 slaves; and 5 villans and 9 bordars with 2 ploughs. There are 2 acres of meadow, and 16 acres of pasture and 40 acres of woodland. Formerly 20s; now it is worth 40s.

[North or South] COOMBE [in Templeton]. Brungar held it TRE, and it paid geld for 1 virgate of land. There is land for 1 plough, which [plough] is there, with 1 slave. There are 3 acres of meadow and 2 acres of scrubland. Formerly 3s; now it is worth 5s.

[?West] BRADLEY. Heardwulf held it TRE, and it paid geld for half a hide. There is land for 4 ploughs. There is 1 plough, with 1 villan and 1 slave, and 5 acres of woodland. Formerly 10s; now it is worth 5s.

THELBRIDGE. Wulfgifu held it TRE, and it paid geld for half a hide and half a virgate of land. There is land for 10 ploughs. In demesne is 1 plough, and 6 slaves; and 15 villans with 2½ ploughs. There are 12 acres of meadow, and 12 acres of pasture and 16 acres of woodland. Formerly 50s; now it is worth 40s.

MIDDLEWICK has been added to this manor. Beorhtmær held it TRE as 1 manor. There is land for 2 ploughs. There are 3 villans, and 6 acres of meadow. It is worth 5s.

EAST WORLINGTON [near Witheridge]. Wulfgifu held it TRE, and it paid geld for 1 virgate of land. There is land for 3 ploughs. In demesne is 1 plough, with 1 slave; and 7 villans with 1½ ploughs. There are 4 acres of meadow, and 10 acres of pasture and 3 acres of scrubland. Formerly 20s; now it is worth 7s6d.

[?West] BRADLEY. Algar held it TRE, and it paid geld for 1 ferding. There is land for 1 plough. There is 1 bordar. It renders 30d.

LOXBEARE. Algar held it TRE, and it paid geld for 3 virgates of land. There is land for 4 ploughs. In demesne is 1 plough, and 2 villans and 4 bordars. There are 3 acres of meadow. Formerly 10s; now it is worth 15s.

PEADHILL. Algar held it TRE, and it paid geld for 3 virgates of land. There is land for 4 ploughs. In demesne is 1 plough, and 3 men, and 3 acres of meadow and 5 acres of woodland. Formerly, as now, worth 15s.

FARWAY. Æthelmær held it TRE, and it paid geld for half a hide. There is land for 4 ploughs. In demesne is 1 plough, and 2 slaves; and 5 villans and 4 bordars with 3 ploughs. There are 5 acres of meadow and 40 acres of pasture. Formerly 10s; now it is worth 20s.

DROGO HOLDS THESE 73 ESTATES FROM THE BISHOP

Engelbald's wife holds SOURTON from the bishop. Alwine held it TRE, and it paid geld for 3 virgates of land. There is land for 12 ploughs. In demesne are 3 ploughs, and 7 slaves; and 14 villans and 7 cotsets with 4 ploughs, and 2 swineherds. There are 60 acres of meadow, and 12 acres of scrubland, [and] pasture 1 league long and half a league broad. Formerly £11; now it is worth £7.

The same woman holds MILFORD [in Stowford] from the bishop. Alwine held it TRE, and it paid geld for 1 virgate of land. There is land for 5 ploughs. In demesne is 1 plough, and 3 slaves, and 3 villans and 1 cotset. There are 6 acres of meadow, and 6 acres of pasture and 15 acres of woodland. Formerly 40s; now it is worth 20s.

The same woman holds THORNE from the bishop. Sæwine held it TRE, and it paid geld for half a virgate of land. There is land for 3 ploughs. In demesne is 1 plough, and 4 villans and 4 bordars. There are 12 acres of meadow, [and] pasture half a league long and 2 furlongs broad. Formerly 15s; now it is worth 10s.

The bishop's niece holds KIMWORTHY from him. Edwin held it TRE, and it paid geld for 1 virgate of land. There is land for 3 ploughs. There are 2 ploughs, with 2 villans and 2 slaves, and 20 acres of meadow and 30 acres of pasture. It is worth 20s.

Wulfrun holds WELCOMBE from the bishop. Asgot held it TRE, and it paid geld for 1 hide and half a virgate of land. There is land for 15 ploughs. In demesne are 2 ploughs, and 3 slaves; and 15 villans and 7 bordars with 7 ploughs. There are 10 acres of meadow, and 20 acres of pasture and 1 league of woodland. Formerly 100s; now it is worth 60s.

Eadric holds SUTCOMBE from the bishop. He himself held it TRE, and it paid geld for half a hide. There is land for 7 ploughs. In demesne is 1 plough. and 4 slaves; and 9 villans and 6 cotsets with 6 ploughs. There are 14 acres of meadow, and 12 acres of pasture and 6 acres of woodland. Formerly 50s; now it is worth 40s.

Osbern holds TAPELEY from the bishop. Wulfgifu held it TRE, and it paid geld for 1 hide. There is land for 8 ploughs. In demesne are 2 ploughs, and 2 slaves; and 3 villans and 2 bordars with 1 plough. There are 3 acres of meadow, and 10 acres of pasture and 3 acres of woodland. It is worth 30s from this hide has been taken away 1 virgate of land which was there TRE. Roger holds it from the bishop.

Geoffrey holds SOWTON from the bishop. Eadric held it TRE, and it paid geld for 1 hide. There is land for 5 ploughs. In demesne are 2 ploughs, and 7 slaves; and 9 villans with $3\frac{1}{2}$ ploughs. There are 20 acres of meadow and 12 acres of pasture. Formerly 50s; now it is worth £4.

Eadmær holds CREALY from the bishop. Alwine held it TRE, and it paid geld for 1 virgate of land. There is land for 2 ploughs, which are there, with 1 slave and 2 villans and 1 bordar. There are 8 acres of meadow. Formerly 5s; now it is worth 10s.

[Folio 103V: DEVONSHIRE]

Eadhild holds RUSTON from the bishop. Abbud held it TRE, and it paid geld for 1 ferding. There is land for 1 plough, which [plough] is there, with 1 villan and 1 bordar and 1 slave. There are 6 acres of meadow. It was and is worth 5s.

Robert holds 'CHARLTON' [? in Upottery] from the bishop. Eadric held it TRE, and it paid geld for 3 virgates of land. There is land for 3 ploughs. In demesne is 1 plough; and 1 villan and 2 bordars with half a plough. There are 6 acres of meadow, and 12 acres of pasture and 6 acres of woodland. It renders 10s at farm.

Geoffrey holds CANONTEIGN from the bishop. Eadric held it TRE, and it paid geld for 1 hide. There is land for 7 ploughs. In demesne is 1 plough, and 5 slaves; and 16 villans with 6 ploughs. There is 1 acre of meadow, and 60 acres of pasture and 12 acres of woodland. Formerly, as now, worth 100s.

Leofric holds LANGAGE from the bishop. Sæwine held it TRE, and it paid geld for half a hide, less 1 ferding. There is land for $1\frac{1}{2}$ ploughs. There is 1 plough, and 2 bordars, and 2 acres of meadow and 10 acres of scrubland. Formerly 5s; now it is worth 10s.

Ansgar holds from the bishop 1 ferding of land in POLSLOE [in Exeter]. Alwine held it TRE. There is land for 1 plough, which [plough] is there, with 2 slaves. There are 2 acres of meadow and 16 acres of pasture. Formerly 4s; now it is worth 10s.

IIII. The land of Glastonbury Church

GLASTONBURY CHURCH holds UPLYME. TRE it paid geld for 6 hides. There is land for 7 ploughs. In demesne are 2 ploughs, and 4 slaves; and 16 villans and 4 bordars with 5 ploughs. There are 8 acres of meadow, pasture 2 leagues long and 1 league broad, [and] woodland 20 furlongs long and 1 furlong broad. Formerly, as now, worth £4.

V. The land of the Church of Tavistock

TAVISTOCK CHURCH holds TAVISTOCK Manor. TRE it paid geld for $3\frac{1}{2}$ hides. There is land for 40 ploughs. In demesne are 5 ploughs, and 12 slaves; and 17 villans and 20 bordars with 14 ploughs. There is a mill serving the court, and 16 acres of meadow, pasture 10 furlongs long and as much broad, [and] woodland 2 leagues long and 1 league broad.

Of this land of this manor Ermenald holds half a virgate of land; Ralph, as much; another Ralph, 3 parts of 1 virgate of land; Robert, 1 virgate and 2 ferdings; Geoffrey, 1 ferding; Hugh, half a hide and the third part of 1 virgate of land and 1 ferding. 4 thegns held these lands from the abbot TRE and they could not be separated from the church. There are in demesne $6\frac{1}{2}$ ploughs, and 4 slaves; and 6 villans and 17 bordars and 3 cotsets with 4 ploughs. The whole is worth £12 to the abbot, 100s to the knights. Formerly it was worth £22 in total.

The church itself holds MILTON ABBOT. TRE it paid geld for half a hide. There is land for 15 ploughs. In demesne are 5 ploughs, and 12 slaves; and 14 villans and 12 bordars with 10 ploughs. There are 20 acres of meadow, and 400 acres of pasture and 10 acres of woodland. Formerly £4; now it is worth £8.

With this manor the abbot holds 2 estates, Leigh [in Milton Abbot] and Liddaton. 2 thegns held them as 2 manors TRE, and they paid geld for half a hide. There is land for 15 ploughs. In demesne is 1 plough, and 3 slaves; and 4 villans and 5 bordars with 4 ploughs. Formerly 30s; now it is worth 60s.

Geoffrey holds LIDDATON from the abbot. TRE it paid geld for half a hide. There is land for 3 ploughs. There are [3 ploughs], with 5 villans and 2 bordars and 3 slaves. There are 10 acres of meadow, and 80 acres of pasture and 12 acres of woodland. Formerly 20s; now it is worth 30[s].

The church itself holds HATHERLEIGH [near Okehampton]. TRE it paid geld for 3 hides. There is land for 30 ploughs. In demesne are 3 ploughs, and 6 slaves; and 26 villans and 6 cotsets with 10 ploughs. There are 100 acres of meadow, pasture 3 leagues long and half a league broad, [and] woodland $2\frac{1}{2}$ leagues long and half a league broad.

Of this land of this manor Nigel holds half a virgate of land, less half a ferding; Walter, 3 virgates of land; Geoffrey, half a virgate of land and half a ferding; Ralph, half a virgate of land. There are in demesne 4 ploughs, and 3 slaves; and 12 villans and 4 bordars and 5 cotsets with 6 ploughs, and a mill rendering 6d on Geoffrey's land. This manor is worth £10 to the abbot, £3 to the knights. Formerly it was worth £9 in total.

Ralph holds THORNBURY [near Holsworthy] from the abbot. TRE it paid geld for 1 hide. There is land for 10 ploughs. In demesne are 2 ploughs, and 3 slaves; and 10 villans and 6 bordars with 4 ploughs. There are 100 acres of meadow, and 120 acres of pasture and 20 acres of woodland. It is worth £3.

The church itself holds ABBOTSHAM. TRE it paid geld for

2 hides. There is land for 20 ploughs. In demesne are 2 ploughs, and 4 slaves; and 21 villans and 6 bordars with 15 ploughs. There are 6 acres of meadow, and 60 acres of pasture and 2 acres of woodland. Formerly 60s; now it is worth 100s.

The church itself holds [Higher and Lower] WORTHYGATE. TRE it paid geld for half a hide. There is land for 5 ploughs. In demesne is 1 plough, with 1 slave; and 6 villans and 5 bordars with 1 plough. There are 8 acres of meadow and 12 acres of woodland. Formerly 10s; now it is worth 20s.

The church itself holds BURRINGTON [near Chulmleigh]. TRE it paid geld for 3 hides. There is land for 24 ploughs. In demesne are 3 ploughs, and 4 slaves; and 15 villans and 11 bordars with $8\frac{1}{2}$ ploughs. There are 4 boors, and 4 swineherds rendering 40 pigs. There are 8 acres of meadow, and 60 acres of woodland and 1 league of pasture. Formerly 100s; now it is worth £7.

To this manor have been added 2 estates which 2 thegns held as 2 manors TRE, and they paid geld for half a hide. There is land for 11 ploughs. In demesne are $4\frac{1}{2}$ ploughs, and 6 villans and 4 bordars. There are 3 acres of meadow, and 6 acres of scrubland and common pasture. Formerly 60s; now it is worth 35s. William Chevre and Geoffrey hold them now from the abbot.

William holds RADDON [in Thorverton] from the abbot. Wulfmær held it TRE, and it paid geld for 1 virgate of land. There is land for 2 ploughs. There is 1 villan with half a plough and 1 slave, and 13 acres of meadow and 50 acres of pasture. It is worth 5s.

Nigel and Robert hold ROMANSLEIGH from the abbot. TRE it paid geld for 1 hide. There is land for 1 plough. In demesne are 3 ploughs, and 7 slaves; and 10 villans and 10 bordars with 5 ploughs. There are 30 acres of meadow, and 60 acres of pasture and 38 acres of woodland. The whole is worth 40s.

Reginald holds GREAT HOUNDTOR from the abbot. Abbot Sigtrygg held it TRE, and it paid geld for half a hide. There is land for 4 ploughs. In demesne is 1 plough, and 2 slaves; and 2 villans and 4 bordars with 1 plough. There are 9 acres of meadow, and 2 acres of woodland and 1 league of pasture. It is worth 20s.

The church itself holds DENBURY. Archbishop Ealdræd held it TRE, and it paid geld for half a hide. There is land for 5 ploughs. In demesne is 1 plough, and 2 slaves; and 4 villans and 5 bordars with 4 ploughs. There are 2 acres of meadow, and 15 acres of pasture and 25 acres of woodland. Formerly 10s; now it is worth 40s.

Grento holds COFFINSWELL from the abbot. Archbishop Ealdræd held it TRE, and it paid geld for 2 hides. There is land for 8 ploughs. In demesne are 2 ploughs, and 4 slaves; and 10 villans and 12 bordars with 5 ploughs. There are 4 acres of meadow and 20 acres of pasture. Formerly 40s; now it is worth £4.

The church itself holds PLYMSTOCK. Sigtrygg held it

TRE, and it paid geld for half a hide. There is land for 4 ploughs. In demesne is 1 plough, and 5 slaves; and 4 villans and 9 bordars with 3 ploughs. There is half an acre of meadow and 30 acres of pasture. Formerly 20s; now it is worth 40s.

In the city of Exeter the abbot has 1 house which he had in pledge from a burgess, and it used to pay the king 8d in customary dues.

VI. The land of the Church of Buckfast

BUCKFAST CHURCH holds PETROCKSTOWE. TRE it paid geld for $1\frac{1}{2}$ virgates of land. There is land for 5 ploughs. In demesne is 1 plough, and 2 slaves; and 6 villans and 1 bordar with 2 ploughs. There are 6 acres of meadow, pasture 8 furlongs long and 5 furlongs broad, [and] woodland 3 furlongs long and $1\frac{1}{2}$ furlongs broad. Formerly, as now, worth 15s.

The church itself holds ASH [in Petrockstow]. TRE it paid geld for $1\frac{1}{2}$ virgates of land. There is land for 3 ploughs. In demesne is 1 plough, and 3 slaves; and 5 villans and 3 bordars with 2 ploughs. There are 6 acres of meadow, and 6 acres of woodland, [and] pasture 3 furlongs in length and breadth. Formerly 10s; now it is worth 20s.

The church itself holds ZEAL MONACHORUM. TRE it paid geld for 1 hide. There is land for 8 ploughs. In demesne is 1 plough, and 4 slaves; and 10 villans and 14 bordars with 6 ploughs. There are 3 acres of meadow and 4 acres of scrubland. It is worth 50s.

The church itself holds DOWN ST MARY. TRE it paid geld for 2 hides. There is land for 10 ploughs.

[Folio 104: DEVONSHIRE]

In demesne is 1 plough, and 7 slaves; and 12 villans and 9 bordars with 5 ploughs. There are 8 acres of meadow, and 12 acres of pasture and 7 furlongs of scrubland. It is worth £3.

The church itself holds TRUSHAM. TRE it paid geld for 1 hide. There is land for 4 ploughs. In demesne is 1 plough, and 10 slaves; and 4 villans and 9 bordars with 3 ploughs. There are 3 acres of meadow, and 10 acres of pasture and 16 acres of woodland. Formerly 25s; now it is worth 30s.

The church itself holds [?Lower] ASHTON. TRE it paid geld for $1\frac{1}{2}$ ferdings and 3 acres of land. 1 villan pays 40d there.

The church itself holds 'ABBOTS ASH'. TRE it paid geld for $1\frac{1}{2}$ hides. There is land for 10 ploughs. In demesne is 1 plough, and 6 slaves; and 8 villans and 9 bordars with 5 ploughs. There are 4 acres of meadow, pasture 1 league long and half a league broad, [and] woodland 3 furlongs long and 1 furlong broad. Formerly, as now, worth 30s.

The church itself holds HEATHFIELD. TRE it paid geld for 2 hides. There is land for 12 ploughs. In demesne is 1 plough, and 6 slaves; and 10 villans and 9 bordars with 5 ploughs. There are 40 acres of pasture and 2 acres of scrubland.

The church itself holds NORTON [in Churchstow]. TRE it paid geld for 2 hides. There is land for 10 ploughs. In demesne is 1 plough, and 6 slaves; and 9 villans and 12 bordars with 5 ploughs. There are 2 acres of meadow, and 20 acres of pasture, [and] woodland 2 furlongs long and 1 broad. Formerly 30s; now it is worth 40s.

The church itself holds CHARFORD. TRE it paid geld for 1 hide. There is land for 8 ploughs. In demesne is 1 plough, and 4 slaves; and 7 villans and 6 bordars with 3 ploughs. There are 2 acres of meadow and 20 acres of pasture. Formerly [it was worth] 20s; now 30s.

The church itself holds SOUTH BRENT. TRE it paid geld for 2 hides. There is land for 10 ploughs. In demesne is 1 plough, and 5 slaves; and 10 villans and 8 bordars with 5 ploughs. There are 4 acres of meadow, and 4 acres of woodland and 30 acres of pasture. Formerly 30s; now it is worth 40s.

The church itself holds SOUTH BRENT. TRE it paid geld for 2 hides. There is land for 6 ploughs. In demesne is half a plough, and 4 slaves; and 8 villans and 6 bordars with 3 ploughs. There are 2 acres of meadow, pasture 1 league long and half a league broad, [and] woodland 1 league long and 1 furlong broad. Formerly [it was worth] 20s; now 30s.

BUCKFAST is the capital manor of the abbey. It has never paid geld. There is 1 smith and 10 slaves with 2 ploughs. [There is] woodland 1 league long and half a league broad.

VII. The land of the Church of Horton

HORTON CHURCH holds LITTLEHAM [near Exmouth]. TRE it paid geld for half a hide. There is land for 8 ploughs. In demesne is 1 virgate of land; and 15 villans and 20 bordars with 8 ploughs. There are 6 acres of meadow, and 5 acres of scrubland, [and] pasture 6 furlongs in length and breadth. It is worth 40s.

The church itself holds ABBOTSKERSWELL. TRE it paid geld for 1½ hides. There is land for 8 ploughs. In demesne are 2 ploughs, and 2 slaves; and 10 villans and 9 bordars with 4 ploughs. There are 12 acres of meadow, pasture 5 furlongs in length and 30 acres in breadth, [and] woodland 12 furlongs in both length and breadth. It is worth 40s.

The church itself holds SEATON. TRE it paid geld for half a hide. There is land for 6 ploughs. In demesne is 1 plough, and 2 slaves; and 6 villans and 19 bordars with 3 ploughs. There are 8 acres of meadow, and pasture 5 furlongs in length and as much in breadth, and 11 salt-pans rendering 11d a year. It is worth 40s.

The church itself holds BEER [near Seaton]. TRE it paid geld for half a hide. There is land for 7 ploughs. In demesne is 1 plough, and 2 slaves; and 6 villans and 20 bordars with 5 ploughs. There are 7 acres of meadow, [and] pasture 1 league long and half a league broad. It is worth 60s.

From this manor have been taken away 1 ferding of land and 4 salt-pans. Drogo holds them from the Count of Mortain.

VIII. The land of Cranborne Church

CRANBORNE CHURCH holds LOOSEBEARE. TRE it paid geld for half a hide. There is land for 6 ploughs. In demesne are 2 ploughs, and 4 slaves; and 8 villans and 7 bordars with 4 ploughs. There are 3 acres of meadow, and 30 acres of pasture and 6 acres of woodland. It is worth 60s.

IX. What the Church of Battle Holds

THE CHURCH of Battle holds the Church of CULLOMPTON with 1 hide, and there is 1 plough in demesne; and 6 villans and 4 bordars with 3 ploughs, and 8 acres of meadow and 2 acres of woodland. It is worth 30s. Thorbert held it TRE.

The church itself has in Exeter the Church of St Olaf, and 7 houses rendering 4s8d in customary dues and 1 house which did not render customary dues.

X. The land of Sainte-Marie of Rouen

THE CHURCH OF SAINTE-MARIE of Rouen holds OTTERY ST MARY from the king. The church itself held it TRE, and it paid geld for 25 hides. There is land for 46 ploughs. In demesne are 3 ploughs, and 17 slaves; and 55 villans and 24 bordars with 40 ploughs. There are 5 swineherds paying 30s and 15d. There are 3 mills rendering 30s, and 200 acres of meadow, and 8 hides of pasture, and 20 acres of woodland, and 1 garden, and 1 salt-pan rendering 30d in Sidmouth, Mont-Saint-Michel's land.

The church itself holds RAWRIDGE. Wulfgifu held it TRE, and it paid geld for 3 hides. There is land for 12 ploughs. King William gave it to SAINTE-MARIE. In demesne are 2 ploughs, and 4 slaves; and 20 villans and 8 bordars with 10 ploughs. There are 20 acres of meadow and half a hide of woodland.

These 2 manors render £70 of Rouen pence a year.

XI. The land of Mont-Saint-Michel

THE CHURCH OF MONT-SAINT-MICHEL holds OTTERTON from the king. Countess Gytha held it TRE, and it paid geld for 14 hides. There is land for 25 ploughs. In demesne are 6 ploughs; and 50 villans and 20 bordars with 40 ploughs. There are 33 salt-workers, and 3 mills rendering 40s. There are 45 acres of meadow, and 150 acres of woodland and 1½ leagues of pasture. When the abbot received it, it was worth £10; now £18.

The church itself holds DENNINGTON. Earl Harold held it TRE, and it paid geld for 3 hides. There is land for 10 ploughs. In demesne is 1 plough, and 3 slaves; and 9 villans and 4 bordars with 2 ploughs. There are 200 acres of pasture and 100 acres of woodland. Formerly, as now, worth 40s.

The church itself holds YARCOMBE. Earl Harold held it

TRE, and it paid geld for 3 hides. There is land for 12 ploughs. In demesne is 1 plough, and 4 slaves; and 16 villans and 8 bordars with 11 ploughs. There is 1 swineherd rendering 10 pigs, and a mill rendering 6s. There are 4 acres of meadow, and 50 acres of pasture and 40 acres of woodland. Formerly, as now, worth 60s.

XII. The land of Saint-Etienne of Caen

THE CHURCH OF SAINT-ETIENNE, Caen, holds NORTHAM from the king. Beorhtric held it TRE, and it paid geld for 2 hides and half a virgate of land. There is land for 20 ploughs. In demesne are 3 ploughs, and 8 slaves; and 23 villans and 5 bordars with 14 ploughs. There are 2 salt-pans rendering 10s, and a fishery rendering 30d, and 15 acres of meadow, and 24 acres of woodland, and 30 acres of scrubland and 15 acres of pasture. Formerly, as now, worth £12.

XIII. The land of La Trinite of Caen

THE CHURCH OF LA TRINITE, Caen, holds UMBERLEIGH from the king. Beorhtric held it TRE, and it paid geld for 1 hide and 1 virgate of land. There is land for 12 ploughs. In demesne are 2 ploughs; and 12 villans and 2 bordars with 8 ploughs. There are 6 slaves, and 3 swineherds rendering 30 pigs. There are 100 acres of pasture, [and] woodland 6 furlongs long and 2 furlongs broad. Formerly £10; now it is worth £11.

What the Clergy Hold From the King

In SOUTH MOLTON 4 priests hold from the king 1 virgate of land in alms. It is worth 20s.

Sæwine the priest holds SWIMBRIDGE from the king. Beorhtfrith held it TRE, and it paid geld for 3 virgates of land. There is land for 4 ploughs. In demesne is half a plough, with 1 slave; and 3 villans with 1 plough. There are 2 acres of meadow. Formerly 5s; now it is worth 10s.

Algar the priest holds 1 hide in BRAUNTON from the king in alms. There is land for 8 ploughs. In demesne he has 3 ploughs; and 3 villans and 23 bordars have 5 ploughs. There are 20 acres of pasture. It is worth 50s.

[Folio 104V: DEVONSHIRE]

XIIII. The land of Earl Hugh

EARL HUGH holds EAST ANSTEY from the king. Eadnoth held it TRE, and it paid geld for half a hide. There is land for 6 ploughs. There 7 villans and 4 slaves with 1 bordar have 3 ploughs. There are 12 acres of meadow, and 48 acres of woodland, [and] pasture 1 league long and half a league broad. Formerly, as now, worth 20s.

The earl himself holds EAST ANSTEY. Northmann held it TRE, and it paid geld for half a hide. There is land for 6 ploughs. There 8 villans and 2 slaves with 1 bordar have 2 ploughs. There are 40 acres of woodland, [and] pasture half a

league long and 3 furlongs broad. Formerly, as now, worth 20s.

The earl himself holds STOWFORD [in Colaton Raleigh]. Eadnoth held it TRE, and it paid geld for 1 hide. There is land for 3 ploughs. Formerly, as now, [worth] 10s.

The earl himself holds "LANDESHERS". Eadnoth held it TRE, and it paid geld for half a virgate of land. There is land for 2 ploughs. Formerly 3s; now it is worth 10s.

XV. The land of the Count of Mortain

THE COUNT OF MORTAIN has in Exeter 1 church and 1 house and 1 orchard, which were in King Edward's demesne.

The count himself holds "STOCHELIE". Hademar held it TRE, and it paid geld for 1 virgate of land. There is land for 2 ploughs. There is 1 plough, with 2 villans and 3 bordars. It is worth 10s.

The count himself holds WYKE [near Crediton]. Ordwulf held it TRE, and it paid geld for 1 hide. There is land for 4 ploughs, which are there, with 5 villans and 3 bordars and 6 slaves. There are 2 acres of meadow and 4 acres of woodland. Formerly 10s; now it is worth 60s.

The count himself holds SHOBROOKE [near Crediton]. Ordwulf held it TRE, and it paid geld for 2 hides. There is land for 4 ploughs. In demesne are 2 ploughs, and 6 slaves; and 7 villans and 4 bordars with 8 ploughs. There are 4 acres of meadow and 30 acres of pasture. Formerly 20s; now it is worth £4.10s.

The count himself holds WEST RADDON [in Shobrooke]. Ordwulf held it TRE, and it paid geld for 1 hide and 3 virgates of land. There is land for 7 ploughs. In demesne are 2 ploughs, and 6 slaves; and 8 villans and 4 bordars with 4 ploughs. There are 4 acres of meadow, and as many of woodland and 10 acres of pasture. Formerly 20s; now it is worth £4.10s.

Alweard holds STOCKLEIGH [in Highampton] from the count. He himself held it TRE, and it paid geld for 1 ferding. There is land for 1 plough, which [plough] is there, with 3 bordars and 2 slaves. It is worth 10s.

Godwine holds GIDLEIGH from the count. He himself held it TRE, and it paid geld for 3 ferdings. There is land for 1 plough. [...] It is worth 5s.

Hamelin holds ALWINGTON from the count. Ordwulf held it TRE, and it paid geld for 1 hide and 3 virgates of land. There is land for 20 ploughs. In demesne are 2 ploughs, and 10 slaves; and 15 villans and 15 bordars with 9 ploughs. There are 3 acres of meadow, and 60 acres of pasture and 30 acres of woodland. Formerly 30s; now it is worth £4.

Alvred holds MONKLEIGH from the count. Ordwulf held it TRE, and it paid geld for 1 hide. There is land for 10 ploughs. In demesne are 2 ploughs, and 4 slaves; and 15 villans and 6 bordars with 6 ploughs. There are 10 acres of meadow, and 60 acres of pasture and 4 acres of woodland. Formerly, as now, worth £4.

Robert holds FRITHELSTOCK from the count. Ordwulf held it TRE, and it paid geld for 3 hides. There is land for 20 ploughs. In demesne are 4 ploughs, and 10 slaves; and 30 villans and 12 bordars with 11 ploughs. There are 20 acres of meadow, and 60 acres of pasture and 60 acres of woodland. Formerly, as now, worth £8.

Erchenbald holds CULLEIGH from the count. Cypping held it TRE, and it paid geld for 1 virgate of land. There is land for 2 ploughs. In demesne is 1 plough, with 1 slave; and 2 villans and 4 bordars with half a plough. There are 2 acres of meadow and 4 acres of woodland. Formerly 4s; now it is worth 12[s].

Ansgar holds BUCKLAND BREWER from the count. Eadmær [...] held it TRE, and it paid geld for 3 hides, less half a virgate of land. There is land for 20 ploughs. In demesne are 3 ploughs, and 7 slaves; and 42 villans and 5 bordars with 8½ ploughs. There are 40 acres of meadow, and 100 acres of woodland, [and] pasture 1 league long and half a league broad. Formerly, as now, worth £7.10s.

GALSWORTHY has been added to this manor. Eadwig held it as 1 manor TRE, and it paid geld for half a virgate of land. There is land for 1 plough, which [plough] is there, with 3 villans, and 20 acres of pasture. Formerly, as now, worth 10s.

The same Ansgar holds EAST PUTFORD from the count. Eadmær Atule held it TRE, and it paid geld for 1 hide. There is land for 6 ploughs. In demesne are 1½ ploughs, and 7 slaves; and 9 villans with 1 bordar have 1 plough. There are 30 acres of meadow, and pasture 1 league long and half a league broad. Formerly, as now, worth 30s.

The same Ansgar holds BULKWORTHY from the count. Iric held it TRE, and it paid geld for 1 virgate of land. There is land for 4 ploughs. In demesne is 1 plough, with 1 slave; and 6 villans and 3 bordars with 1 plough. There are 5 acres of meadow and 30 acres of pasture. Formerly, as now, worth 20s.

The same Ansgar holds SMYTHAM from the count. Ælfric held it TRE, and it paid geld for the third part of 1 ferding. There is land for 1 plough, which [plough] is there, with 1 villan and 1 bordar and 1 slave. There are 2 acres of meadow and 4 acres of pasture. Formerly, as now, worth 5s.

Alvred holds LITTLE TORRINGTON from the count. Alweard held it TRE, and it paid geld for the third part of 1 ferding, and he could go where he would. There 1 villan and 1 bordar and 2 slaves have 1 plough. There are 4 acres of pasture. Formerly, as now, worth 5s.

The same Alvred holds "STOCHELIE" from the count. Ordgar held it TRE, and it paid geld for 1 hide. There is land for 10 ploughs. In demesne are 2 ploughs, and 5 slaves; and 8 villans and 4 bordars with 7 ploughs. There are 7 acres of meadow, and 40 acres of pasture and 6 acres of woodland. Formerly 60s; now it is worth 50s.

The same Alvred holds "STOCHELIE" from the count. Hademar held it TRE, and it paid geld for 1 hide. There is land for 7 ploughs. In demesne are 2 ploughs, and 5 slaves; and 4 villans and 4 bordars with 5 ploughs. There are 6 acres of meadow, and 4 acres of pasture and 12 acres of woodland. Formerly 40s; now it is worth 30s.

The same Alvred holds POUGHILL from the count. 2 thegns held it freely TRE, and it paid geld for half a hide and 2 parts of 1 virgate of land. There is land for 4 ploughs. In demesne are 2 ploughs, and 3 slaves; and 3 villans and 4 bordars with 2 ploughs. There are 2 acres of meadow. Formerly 10s; now it is worth 25s.

Bretel holds HOLBROOK from the count. Sæmær held it TRE, and it paid geld for 3 virgates of land. There is land for 3 ploughs. In demesne is 1 plough, with 1 slave; and 2 villans and 1 bordar with 1 plough. There are 4 acres of meadow and 8 acres of woodland. Formerly, as now, worth 15s.

The same Bretel holds FARRINGDON from the count. 2 brothers held it TRE, and it paid geld for 1 virgate of land. There is land for 2 ploughs. There is 1 plough, and 2 cottars, and 8 acres of meadow, and 12 acres of pasture and 3 acres of woodland. Formerly, as now, worth 7s.

Alweard holds ROCKBEARE. Sæ;wine held it TRE, and it paid geld for 1 virgate of land. There is land for 2 ploughs. There is 1 plough, and 2 villans and 2 bordars and 2 slaves, and 8 acres of meadow, and 25 acres of pasture and 3 acres of woodland. Formerly 12s; now it is worth 7s6d.

Drogo holds HONITON [near Axminster] from the count. Almær held it TRE, and it paid geld for 5 hides. There is land for 18 ploughs. There are 24 villans and 6 bordars and 3 slaves with 16 ploughs. There are 18 acres of meadow, and 50 acres of woodland. There is a mill rendering 6s6d, and 2 salt-workers paying 5s. There is pasture 1 league long and 5 furlongs broad. Formerly, as now, worth £6.

Drogo holds 'WOMBERFORD' [in Cotleigh] from the count. Wulfweard held it TRE, and it paid geld for 1 virgate of land. There is land for 3 ploughs, which are there, with 1 slave and 6 villans. There are 3 acres of meadow, and 40 acres of woodland and 40 acres of pasture. Formerly [it was worth] 3s; now 5s.

Alweard holds NORTHLEIGH from the count. Sæwine held it TRE, and it paid geld for half a hide. There is land for 5 ploughs, which are there, and 2 slaves and 7 villans and 4 bordars with 3 ploughs, and 8 acres of meadow, and 40 acres of pasture and 30 acres of woodland. Formerly 5s; now it is worth 30s.

Reginald holds LUDBROOK [Ludbrook or Higher Ludbrook] from the count. Colbert held it freely TRE, and it paid geld for half a hide. There is land for 3 ploughs. In demesne is 1 plough, and 2 slaves; and 5 villans and 3 bordars with 1½ ploughs. There is a mill rendering 2s, and 2 acres of meadow. Formerly [it was worth] 25s; now 20s.

The same Reginald holds LUPRIDGE from the count. Eadric held it freely TRE, and it paid geld for 1 virgate of land. There is land for 3 ploughs. In demesne is 1 plough, and 2 slaves; and 3 villans and 2 bordars with 1½ ploughs. Formerly 19s; now it is worth 15s.

The same Reginald holds "HEWIS" from the count. Eadric held it TRE, and it paid geld for 1 virgate of land. There is land for 2 ploughs. There 2 villans have 1 plough. Formerly, as now, worth 10s.

The same Reginald holds HARESTON from the count. Eadric held it TRE, and it paid geld for half a hide. There is land for 2 ploughs. There is 1 plough. and 2 villans and 1 bordar, and 2 acres of meadow. Formerly 15s; now it is worth 10s.

The same Reginald holds WINSTON. Eadwine held it TRE, and it paid geld for half a hide. There is land for 1½ ploughs. There is 1 plough, and 3 villans and 2 bordars with 1 slave, and 1 acre of meadow. Formerly 20s; now it is worth 8s.

Alvred holds [East, Higher or Lower] DENSHAM from the count. Æthelmær held it TRE, and it paid geld for 1 virgate and 1 ferding. There is land for 3 ploughs, which are there, with 1 slave and 6 bordars. There are 4 acres of meadow and 5 acres of woodland. Formerly 5s; now it is worth 10s.

The Count of Mortain holds these aforesaid 17 estates with the land of Eadmær Atule which was handed over to him. But the above- mentioned thegns held them freely TRE.

[Folio 105: DEVONSHIRE]

Alvred holds FRIZENHAM from the count. Eadmær held it TRE, and it paid geld for 1 virgate of land. There is land for 3 ploughs. In demesne is 1 plough, and 2 slaves; and 5 villans and 3 bordars with 3 ploughs. There are 1½ acres of meadow and 20 acres of pasture. Formerly, as now, worth 20s.

The same Alvred holds WEDFIELD from the count. Æthelmær held it TRE, and it paid geld for 1 virgate of land. There is land for 2 ploughs, which are there, with 1 slave and 3 villans and 2 bordars. There are 10 acres of meadow and 30 acres of pasture. Formerly, as now, worth 10s.

Drogo holds FENITON from the count. Eadmær held it TRE, and it paid geld for 3 hides. There is land for 6 ploughs. There are 8 villans and 4 bordars and 2 slaves, and 15 acres of meadow, and 100 acres of pasture and 6 acres of woodland. Formerly £4; now it is worth 40s.

Richard holds COTLEIGH from the count. Eadmær held it TRE, and it paid geld for 2 hides. There is land for 8 ploughs. In demesne are 2 ploughs, with 1 slave; and 17 villans and 4 bordars with 6 ploughs. Formerly, 20s; now it is worth 40s.

Reginald holds CORNWOOD from the count. Eadmær held it TRE, and it paid geld for 1 hide. There is land for 5 ploughs. In demesne are 1½ ploughs, and 8 slaves; and 8 villans and 8 bordars with 2 ploughs. There is pasture 1 league long and half a league broad, [and] woodland 2 leagues long and half a league broad. Formerly, as now, worth 40s.

The same Reginald holds NEWTON FERRERS from the count. Eadmær held it TRE, and it paid geld for 2 hides. There is land for 10 ploughs. In demesne is half a plough, and 12 slaves; and 16 villans and 5 bordars with 3 ploughs. There are 2 acres of meadow, and 60 acres of pasture, [and] woodland 1 league long and 1 furlong broad. Formerly £6; now it is worth 70s.

Hugh holds BOLBERRY from the count. Eadmær held it TRE, and it paid geld for 1 hide. There is land for 4 ploughs. In demesne is 1 plough; with 1 slave and 1 villan and 3 bordars with 1 plough. Formerly 30s; now it is worth 10s.

BUCKLAND [in Thurlestone] has been added to this manor. Eadgifu held it freely TRE, and it paid geld for 1 virgate of land. There is land for 1½ ploughs, which are there, with 2 villans and 2 bordars. Formerly, as now, worth 4s.

Erchenbald holds ALVERDISCOTT from the count. Ordwulf held it TRE, and it paid geld for 1½ hides. There is land for 10 ploughs. In demesne are 3 ploughs, and 6 slaves; and 8 villans and 7 bordars with 6 ploughs. There are 5 acres of meadow and 20 acres of pasture. Formerly £6; now it is worth £3.

The same man holds BRATTON FLEMING from the count. Ordwulf held it TRE, and it paid geld for 1 hide. There is land for 12 ploughs. In demesne are 4 ploughs, and 8 slaves; and 14 villans and 4 bordars with 10 ploughs. There are 4 acres of meadow, and 100 acres of pasture and 60 acres of woodland. Formerly, as now, worth £8.

To this manor have been joined 3 estates which 3 thegns held freely as 3 manors TRE. 2 of them were Ordwulf's men, the third [was] not; and they paid geld for 3 virgates of land. There is land for 7 ploughs. There 5 villans and 3 slaves have 5 ploughs. There are 8 acres of meadow, and 50 acres of pasture and 10 acres of woodland. They are worth 22s.

Erchenbald holds CROYDE from the count. Ordwulf held it TRE, and it paid geld for 1 hide. There is land for 10 ploughs. In demesne are 3 ploughs, and 2 slaves; and 10 villans and 9 bordars with 6 ploughs. There are 5 acres of meadow. Formerly, as now, worth £4.

Ordwulf's sister held 1 virgate of this land and could not separate herself from him.

Richard holds ST MARYCHURCH from the count. Ordwulf held it TRE, and it paid geld for 1 hide. There is land for 4 ploughs. In demesne are 2 ploughs, and 3 slaves; and 5 villans and 8 bordars with 1½ ploughs, and 1 acre of meadow. Formerly 20s; now it is worth 40s.

Hamelin holds BROADHEMPSTON from the count. Ordwulf held it TRE, and it paid geld for 2 hides. There is land for 10 ploughs. In demesne are 2 ploughs, and 3 slaves; and 10 villans and 9 bordars with 6 ploughs. There are 4 acres of meadow, and 10 acres of pasture and 12 acres of woodland. Formerly 40s; now it is worth 60s.

Reginald holds BIGBURY from the count. Ordwulf held it TRE, and it paid geld for 2 hides. There is land for 12 ploughs. In demesne are 2 ploughs; and 12 villans and 12 bordars with 3½ ploughs. There is a salt-pan rendering 30d. There are 5 acres of meadow, and 30 acres of pasture, [and] woodland 1 league long and 1 furlong broad. Formerly £7; now it is worth £3.

Reginald holds HARFORD from the count. Ordwulf held it TRE, and it paid geld for 1 hide. There is land for 5 ploughs. In demesne is 1 plough, and 2 slaves; and 6 villans and 6 bordars with 2 ploughs. [There is] pasture 1 league long and half a league broad. Formerly £3; now it is worth 30s.

Reginald holds BERE FERRERS from the count. Ordwulf held it TRE, and it paid geld for 4 hides. There is land for 15 ploughs. There are 16 villans and 5 bordars and 5 slaves having 6 ploughs. There are 3 swineherds rendering 15 pigs, and 7 salt-pans rendering 10s. There is pasture 5 furlongs long and 1 furlong broad, [and] woodland 1½ leagues long and 1 furlong broad. Formerly 60s; now it is worth 100s.

THE COUNT HOLDS THESE UNDER-MENTIONED 7 ESTATES WITH THE LAND OF ORDWULF

Erchenbald holds [Crockers and Friars] HELE from the count 2 thegns held it freely TRE, and it paid geld for 1 virgate of land. There is land for 4 ploughs. In demesne is 1 plough; with 1 slave and 6 villans and 1 bordar and 1 plough. There are 10 acres of meadow, and 20 acres of pasture and 3 acres of woodland. Formerly 20s; now it is worth 10s.

Reginald holds STOCKLEIGH ENGLISH from the count. Sæwulf held it TRE, and it paid geld for 1 hide. There is land for 5 ploughs. In demesne is 1 plough, and 3 slaves; and 6 villans and 4 bordars with 4 ploughs. There are 2 acres of meadow, and 32 acres of pasture and 20 acres of woodland. Formerly 15s; now it is worth 25s.

Richard holds MODBURY from the count. Wada held it freely TRE, and it paid geld for 1 hide. There is land for 5 ploughs. In demesne is 1 plough, with 1 slave; and 4 villans and 2 bordars with 3 ploughs. There are 2 acres of woodland. Formerly, as now, worth 30s. The count holds this land wrongfully.

In the same place he holds 1 virgate of land which could not be alienated from Ordwulf TRE. It is worth 2s.

Reginald holds 'TORRIDGE' [in Plympton St Mary] from the count. Wada held it freely TRE, and it paid geld for 1 hide. There is land for 4 ploughs. In demesne is 1 plough, and 2 slaves; and 3 villans and 5 bordars with half a plough. There are 3 acres of meadow, and 5 acres of pasture and 5 acres of woodland. Formerly 20s; now it is worth 15s.

The same man holds HARESTON from the count. Swet held it TRE, and it paid geld for 3 virgates of land. There is land for 2 ploughs. There is 1 plough, and 3 slaves and 3 villans. [There is] woodland half a league long and 1 furlong broad. Formerly 15s; now it is worth 10s.

The same Reginald holds SPRIDDLESTONE from the count. 4 thegns held it freely TRE, and it paid geld for 1 virgate of land. There is land for 2 ploughs. There is 1 plough, and 4 villans and 3 bordars, and 1 acre of meadow and 10 acres of pasture. Formerly 20s; now it is worth 10s.

The same Reginald holds "WEDERIGE" from the count. Ottar held it TRE, and it paid geld for 1 ferding. There is land

for half a plough. There is 1 slave, and 6 acres of pasture and 2 acres of woodland. It renders 3s.

UP TO THIS POINT THESE ARE ADDED LANDS

Erchenbald holds STOCKLEIGH [in Meeth] from the count. Alsige held it TRE, and it paid geld for 3 ferdings. There is land for 3 ploughs. There are 2 ploughs, and 2 slaves and 3 villans, and 8 acres of meadow and 30 acres of pasture. Formerly 20s; now it is worth 10s.

Alvred holds MATFORD from the count. Alwig held it TRE, and it paid geld for 1 virgate of land. There is land for 2 ploughs. There are 1½ ploughs, with 1 villan and 4 slaves, and 4 acres of meadow. Formerly, as now, worth 10s.

William holds TATTISCOMBE from the count. Eadric held it TRE, and it paid geld for half a hide. There is land for 6 ploughs. In demesne is 1 plough, and 2 slaves; and 5 villans and 3 bordars with 2 ploughs. There are 7 acres of meadow, and 8 acres of woodland, [and] pasture half a league long and 2 furlongs broad. Formerly 40s; now it is worth 20s.

Mauger holds DENSCOMBE from the count. Dunning held it TRE, and it paid geld for 3 virgates of land and half a [...] ferding. There is land for 5 ploughs. In demesne is 1 plough; and 12 villans and 6 bordars with 4 ploughs. There is a mill rendering 7s6d. There are 13 acres of meadow, and 20 acres of pasture and 12 acres of woodland. Formerly, as now, worth 40s.

"ALWINESTONE" has been added to this manor. Alwine held it TRE, and it paid geld for 3 virgates of land. There is land for 5 ploughs. In demesne is 1 plough, and 2 slaves, and 4 villans and 2 bordars. There is a mill rendering 8d. There are 6 acres of meadow, and 30 acres of pasture and 7 acres of woodland. Formerly 40s; now it is worth 15s.

Alweard holds CLYST ST LAWRENCE from the count. He held it himself TRE, and it paid geld for 4 hides. There is land for 7 ploughs. In demesne are 2 ploughs, and 4 slaves; and 17 villans and 9 bordars with 3 ploughs. There are 50 acres of meadow, and 130 acres of pasture and 150 acres of woodland. Formerly 30s; now it is worth 60s.

[Folio 105V: DEVONSHIRE]

Alvred holds THORNBURY [in Drewsteignton] from the count. Ealdceorl held it TRE, and it paid geld for 1 virgate of land. There is land for 3 ploughs. There 3 villans with 1 slave have 1 plough. There are 2 acres of meadow and 40 acres of pasture. It was worth 7s; now 10s.

The same Alvred holds CHITTERLEY from the count. Hademar held it TRE, and it paid geld for 3 virgates of land. There is land for 4 ploughs, which are there, with 1 slave, and 4 villans and 2 bordars, and 9 acres of meadow and 16 acres of pasture. Formerly 30s; now it is worth 40s.

Alweard holds BICKLEIGH [near Silverton] from the count. He held it himself TRE, and it paid geld for 1 hide. There is land for 8 ploughs. In demesne are 2 ploughs, and 6 slaves; and 11 villans and 13 bordars with 6 ploughs. There is a mill rendering 5s, and 13 acres of meadow, and 20 acres of pasture and 59 acres of woodland. Formerly 40s; now it is worth 60s.

Drogo holds CURSCOMBE from the count. Ingvar held it TRE, and it paid geld for 1 hide. There is land for 4 ploughs, and 1 slave; and 4 villans and 4 bordars with 1½ ploughs. There are 2 acres of meadow [...] and 2 acres of woodland. Formerly 40s; now it is worth 20s.

Bretel holds [Higher and Lower] CHERITON [in Payhembury] from the count. Sæmær held it TRE, and it paid geld for 1 hide. There is land for 2 ploughs. There is 1 plough, and 3 villans and 1 bordar, and 4 acres of meadow, and 15 acres of pasture and 8 acres of woodland. Formerly, as now, worth 15s.

Reginald holds MODBURY from the count. Ordric held it TRE, and it paid geld for 4 hides. There is land for 23 ploughs. In demesne are 3 ploughs, and 7 slaves; and 22 villans and 16 bordars with 11 ploughs. There is 1 swineherd, and 1 acre of meadow, [and] woodland 5 furlongs long and 1 furlong broad. Formerly £12; now it is worth £6.

The same Reginald holds [Great and Little] ORCHETON from the count. Northmann held it TRE, and it paid geld for 1 hide. There is land for 4 ploughs. There are 2 ploughs, and 3 villans and 5 bordars, and 1 acre of meadow, and 6 acres of woodland, and 1 salt-pan rendering 5s. Formerly 40s; now it is worth 20s.

Ralph holds HOLLOWCOMBE [in Ermington] from the count. Leofgar held it TRE, and it paid geld for half a hide. There is land for 4 ploughs. In demesne are 2 ploughs, with 1 slave; and 5 villans and 3 bordars with 2 ploughs. There are 10 acres of meadow and 4 acres of woodland. There are 4 salt-pans rendering 40d and 2 summae of salt. Formerly 30s; now it is worth 40s.

Reginald holds FARDEL from the count. Dunna held it TRE, and it paid geld for 1 hide. There is land for 4 ploughs. In demesne is 1 plough, and 4 slaves; and 5 villans and 4 bordars with 1½ ploughs. There are 10 acres of meadow, and 300 acres of pasture, [and] woodland 4 furlongs long and 1furlong broad. Formerly 40s; now it is worth 30s.

From this manor 30d are owed in customary dues to Ermington, the king's manor, and the customary dues of the pleas, as the reeves and the king's men state.

Reginald holds VENN from the count. Northmann held it TRE, and it paid geld for 1 virgate of land. There is land for 3 ploughs. There are 4 villans and 2 bordars, and 7 acres of pasture. Formerly 20s; now it is worth 10s.

The same Reginald holds BROADAFORD from the count. Eadric held it TRE, and it paid geld for 1 virgate of land. There is land for 2 ploughs. Formerly 10s; now it is worth 5s.

The same Reginald holds DINNATON. Dunna held it TRE, and it paid geld for 1 hide. There is land for 4 ploughs. In demesne is 1 plough, and 4 slaves; and 4 villans and 4 bordars with 1 plough. There is 1 acre of meadow, and half a league of pasture, [and] woodland 4 furlongs long and 2 furlongs broad. Formerly 30s; now it is worth 20s.

The same Reginald holds TORPEEK. Ealdceorl held it TRE, and it paid geld for 1 virgate of land. There is land for 2 ploughs. There is 1 plough, with 1 slave, and 3 villans and 2 bordars, and 2 acres of scrubland and 1 league of pasture. Formerly 15s; now it is worth 10s.

The same Reginald holds LUDBROOK [Ludbrook or Higher Ludbrook] from the count. Alwine held it TRE, and it paid geld for 3 virgates of land. There is land for 3 ploughs. In demesne is 1 plough, and 6 slaves; and 3 villans and 5 bordars with 1½ ploughs. There is 1 acre of meadow and 1 furlong of woodland. Formerly 30s; now it is worth 20s.

Richard holds BOLBERRY from the count. Wada held it TRE, and it paid geld for half a hide. There is land for 4 ploughs. In demesne is 1 plough, with 1 slave; and 3 villans and 1 bordar with half a plough. Formerly 27s; now it is worth 7s6d.

Hugh holds BATSON from the count. Wulfric held it TRE, and it paid geld for 1½ hides. There is land for 4 ploughs. In demesne is 1 plough, with 1 slave; and 3 villans and 3 bordars with 1 plough. There are 3 acres of meadow, and 50 acres of pasture and 10 acres of woodland. Formerly 35s; now it is worth [...] 15s.

Reginald holds BOWCOMBE from the count. Ælfric held it TRE, and it paid geld for half a hide. There is land for 4 ploughs. In demesne is 1 plough, with 1 slave; and 3 villans and 3 bordars with 1 plough, and 1 acre of meadow. Formerly 20s; now it is worth 10s.

Richard holds SHILSTON from the count. Wada held it TRE, and it paid geld for half a hide. There is land for 3 ploughs. In demesne is 1 plough, and 2 slaves; and 4 villans and 3 bordars with 1 plough, and half an acre of meadow. Formerly 20s; now it is worth 10s.

Dunn holds SPRIDDLESCOMBE [Spriddlescombe and Higher Spriddlescombe] from the count. Asgot held it TRE, and it paid geld for 1 virgate of land. There is land for 2 ploughs. There is 1 plough, with 1 villan and 2 bordars, and 1 acre of meadow and half an acre of woodland. Formerly, as now, worth 7s.

Reginald holds, HONICKNOWLE [in Plymouth] from the count. Wada held it TRE, and it paid geld for half a hide. There is land for 2 ploughs. There are 2 villans and 2 slaves, and 1 acre of meadow, and 3 acres of woodland, [and] pasture 3 furlongs long and 1 furlong broad. Formerly, as now, worth 10s.

The same Reginald holds LIPSON [in Plymouth] from the count. Godwine held it freely TRE, and it paid geld for half a hide. There is land for 3 ploughs. There is 1 plough, and 4 villans and 3 bordars with 1 slave, and 1 acre of meadow, and 1 virgate of pasture and 6 acres of scrubland. Formerly 20s; now it is worth 10s. This has been added to Algar's lands.

XVI. The land of Baldwin the Sheriff

BALDWIN the sheriff holds from the king in Exeter 7 houses which were in King EDWARD'S demesne. Besides these he has 12 other houses in the city itself which belonged to his manor of Kenn.

The same Baldwin has in Barnstaple 7 burgesses and 6 waste houses; these renders 7s6d a year.

Baldwin himself holds OKEHAMPTON from the king, and the castle is sited there. OSFRITH held this manor TRE, and it paid geld for 3 virgates of land and 1 ferding. There is land for 30 ploughs. In demesne are 4 ploughs, and 18 slaves; and 21 villans and 11 bordars with 20 ploughs. There is a mill rendering 6s8d, and 5 acres of meadow, pasture 1 league long and half a league broad, [and] woodland 3 leagues long and 1 league broad. There are 4 burgesses, and a market rendering 4s. The whole is worth £10; when received £8.

Roger holds CHICHACOTT from Baldwin. Beorhtmær held it TRE, and it paid geld for half a virgate of land. There is land for 3 ploughs. In demesne is 1 plough, with 1 slave, and 4 villans with 1 bordar. There are 3 acres of meadow, and 3 acres of pasture and 30 acres of woodland. Formerly, as now, worth 15s.

Baldwin himself holds BRATTON CLOVELLY. Beorhtric held it TRE, and it paid geld for 1 virgate of land. There is land for 15 ploughs. In demesne are 3 ploughs, and 12 slaves; and 12 villans with 6 ploughs. There are 20 acres of meadow, and 200 acres of pasture and 5 acres of woodland. Formerly £9; now it is worth £7.

There were 2 thegns in this manor TRE holding half a virgate of land freely and they could go to whichever lord they would. Formerly 60s; now it is worth 30s.

Rolf holds BOASLEY from Baldwin. Beorhtric held it TRE, and it paid geld for 1 virgate of land. There is land for 8 ploughs. In demesne are 1½ ploughs; and 7 slaves with 1 plough. There are 60 acres of meadow, and 60 acres of pasture and 2 acres of scrubland. Formerly 30s; now it is worth 40s.

Ralph de la Pommeraye holds BRIDESTOWE from Baldwin. Eadmær held it TRE, and it paid geld for half a hide and half a ferding. There is land for 6 ploughs. In demesne are 2 ploughs, and 8 slaves; and 9 villans and 4 bordars with 4 ploughs. There are 12 acres of meadow, and 30 acres of pasture and 40 acres of woodland. Formerly £3; now it is worth £4.

With this manor Baldwin holds the land of 6 thegns which did not belong there TRE, and it paid geld for half a hide and 1½ ferdings. There is land for 6 ploughs. Formerly 30s; now it is worth 60s; less 20d. These 6 held it: Sæwine, Dodda, Dodda, Godwine, Godwine, Abbot Sigtrygg.

[Folio 106: DEVONSHIRE]

Rainer holds GERMANSWEEK from Baldwin. Eadnoth held it TRE, and it paid geld for half a virgate of land. There is land for 5 ploughs. In demesne are 2 ploughs, and 4 slaves; and 5 villans and 8 bordars with 1 plough. There are 10 acres of meadow, and 20 acres of woodland, and pasture half a league long and 3 furlongs broad. Formerly 40s; now it is worth 30s.

Roger de MEULLES holds LEWTRENCHARD from Baldwin. Beorhtric held it TRE, and it paid geld for half a hide. There is land for 7 ploughs. In demesne is 1 plough, and 6 slaves; and 12 villans and 8 bordars with 6 ploughs. There are 20 acres of meadow, and 60 acres of pasture and 30 acres of woodland. Formerly £3; now it is worth £4.

Roger holds WARSON from Baldwin. Wadel held it TRE, and it paid geld for 1 virgate of land. There is land for 2 ploughs. There are 3 villans with 1 bordar and 2 swineherds with 1 plough. There is 1 acre of woodland, and 5 acres of meadow and 40 acres of pasture. Formerly 15s; now it is worth 20s.

Modbert holds KELLY from Baldwin. Osfrith held it TRE, and it paid geld for half a hide. There is land for 8 ploughs. In demesne are 2 ploughs, and 10 slaves; and 7 villans and 15 bordars with 5 ploughs. There are 5 acres of meadow, and 8 acres of pasture, [and] woodland 2 furlongs long and 1 furlong broad. Formerly £3; now it is worth £4.

Ralph holds DUNTERTON from Baldwin. Beorhtmær held it TRE, and it paid geld for half a hide. There is land for 6 ploughs. In demesne are 2 ploughs, and 6 slaves; and 4 villans and 8 bordars with 3½ ploughs. There is 1 acre of meadow, and 40 acres of pasture and 60 acres of woodland. Formerly 20s; now it is worth 40s.

Colwin holds 'GUSCOTT' [in Bratton Clovelly] from Baldwin. Beorhtric held it TRE, and it paid geld for 1 virgate of land. There is land for 4 ploughs. In demesne is 1 plough, and 3 slaves; and 6 villans and 4 bordars with 2 ploughs. [There is] woodland 3 furlongs long and 1 furlong broad. Formerly 20s; now it is worth 25s.

Baldwin himself holds SAMPFORD COURTENAY. Northmann held it TRE, and it paid geld for 2½ hides. There is land for 40 ploughs. In demesne are 4 ploughs, and 8 slaves; and 40 villans and 30 bordars with 20 ploughs. There are 60 acres of meadow, and 40 acres of woodland, [and] pasture 2 leagues long and 1 league broad. Formerly £9; now it is worth £12.

Richard holds BELSTONE from Baldwin. Osfrith held it TRE, and it paid geld for half a hide. There is land for 6 ploughs. In demesne are 2 ploughs, and 4 slaves; and 8 villans and 5 bordars with 3 ploughs. There are 8 acres of meadow, and half a league of woodland and 1 league of pasture. Formerly, as now, worth 30s.

Cadio holds DUNSLAND from Baldwin. Wulfric held it TRE, and it paid geld for half a virgate of land. There is land for 4 ploughs, which are there, with 1 slave and 6 villans and 4 bordars. There are 20 acres of meadow, and as many of pasture and 4 acres of woodland. Formerly 30s; now it is worth 25s.

Baldwin himself holds MONKOKEHAMPTON. Wulfnoth held it TRE, and it paid geld for half a hide. There is land for 6 ploughs. In demesne are 2 ploughs, and 5 slaves; and 12 villans and 6 bordars with 8 ploughs. There are 12 acres of meadow, and 10 acres of pasture and 20 acres of woodland. Formerly 20s; now it is worth 60s.

Roger holds EXBOURNE from Baldwin. Almær held it TRE, and it paid geld for half a hide. There is land for 9 ploughs. In demesne are 2 ploughs, and 13 slaves; and 10 villans and 5 bordars with 5 ploughs. There are 20 acres of meadow, [and] woodland 3 furlongs long and 2 furlongs broad. Formerly £3; now it is worth £4.

Roger holds HIGHAMPTON from Baldwin. Beorhtmær held it TRE, and it paid geld for 3 virgates of land. There is land for 10 ploughs. In demesne are 2 ploughs, and 9 slaves; and 19 villans and 3 bordars with 7 ploughs. There are 60 acres of meadow, and 4 furlongs of pasture, [and] woodland half a league long and as much broad. Formerly, as now, worth £3.

Roger holds LASHBROOK from Baldwin. Algar held it TRE, and it paid geld for 1 virgate of land. There is land for 8 ploughs. In demesne are 2 ploughs, and 10 slaves; and 10 villans and 6 bordars with 3 ploughs. There are 50 acres of meadow, and 50 acres of pasture and 15 acres of woodland. Formerly, as now, worth 50s.

Baldwin himself holds BRADFORD [near Cookbury]. Algar held it TRE, and it paid geld for half a hide. There is land for 6 ploughs. In demesne is 1 plough, and 6 slaves; and 5 villans and 2 bordars with 2 ploughs. There are 12 acres of meadow, and 30 acres of pasture and 60 acres of woodland. Formerly 20s; now it is worth 40s.

Rainer holds KIGBEARE from Baldwin. Sæwine held it TRE, and it paid geld for 1 virgate of land. There is land for 5 ploughs. In demesne is 1 plough, with 1 slave; and 6 villans and 5 bordars with 3 ploughs. There are 12 acres of meadow, and 20 acres of pasture and 2 acres of woodland. Formerly 20s; now it is worth 30s.

Otelin holds INWARDLEIGH from Baldwin. Ingvar held it TRE, and it paid geld for 1 hide. There is land for 10 ploughs. In demesne is 1 plough, and 6 slaves; and 12 villans and 8 bordars with 9 ploughs. There are 30 acres of meadow, and 50 acres of pasture and 60 acres of woodland. Formerly, as now, worth 70s.

Richard holds [Higher and Lower] OAK from Baldwin. Asgot held it TRE, and it paid geld for 3 ferdings. There is land for 5 ploughs. In demesne is 1 plough, with 1 slave; and 6 villans and 3 bordars with 2 ploughs. There are 20 acres of meadow, and 60 acres of pasture and 8 acres of woodland. Formerly 30s; now it is worth 40s.

Bernard holds [Higher and Lower] GORHUISH from Baldwin. Alnoth held it TRE, and it paid geld for 1 ferding. There is land for 1 plough. There 2 villans with 1 bordar have half a plough. There are 6 acres of meadow, and 2 acres of scrubland and 40 acres of pasture. It is worth 5s.

Modbert holds BROADWOOD KELLY from Baldwin. Leofric held it TRE, and it paid geld for 1 virgate of land. There is land for 4 ploughs. In demesne is 1 plough, and 2 slaves; and 3 villans and 5 bordars with 1½ ploughs. There are 8 acres of meadow, and half a league of pasture, [and] woodland half a league long and 2 furlongs broad. Formerly, as now, worth 20s.

Walter holds HONEYCHURCH from Baldwin. Alwine held it TRE, and it paid geld for half a hide. There is land for 5 ploughs. In demesne are 2 ploughs, and 4 slaves; and 4 villans with 1 plough. There are 4 acres of meadow, and 10 acres of pasture and 2 acres of scrubland.

Ranulph holds MIDDLECOTT [in Broadwood Kelly] from Baldwin. Alweald held it TRE, and it paid geld for 1 virgate of land. There is land for 2 ploughs, which are there, with 1 slave and 2 villans and 4 bordars. Formerly 10s; now it is worth 20s.

Richard holds BRIXTON [in Broadwood Kelly] from Baldwin. Wulfnoth held it TRE, and it paid geld for 1 virgate of land. There is land for 4 ploughs. In demesne is 1 plough, and 2 slaves; and 4 villans and 3 bordars with 1 plough. There are 15 acres of meadow, and 10 acres of pasture, [and] woodland 6 furlongs long and 1 furlong broad. Formerly 12s6d; now it is worth 20s.

Richard holds MIDDLECOTT [in Broadwood Kelly] from Baldwin. Alweald held it TRE, and it paid geld for half a virgate of land. There is land for 2 ploughs. There are 2 villans with 1 bordar and 1 slave, having 1½ ploughs. There are 10 acres of meadow, and 15 acres of pasture, [and] woodland 4 furlongs long and 1 furlong broad. Formerly 10s; now it is worth 20s.

Gilbert holds ASHMANSWORTHY from Baldwin. Beorhtmær held it TRE, and it paid geld for half a hide. There is land for 5 ploughs. In demesne is 1 plough, and 4 slaves; and 6 villans and 4 bordars with 3 ploughs. There are 60 acres of meadow, [and] pasture 1 league long and half a league broad. Formerly [it was worth] 10s; now 30s.

Robert holds YARNSCOMBE from Baldwin. Godwine held it TRE, and it paid geld for half a hide. There is land for 10 ploughs. In demesne is 1 plough, with 1 slave and 3 villans. There are 10 acres of meadow, and 100 acres of woodland and 1 league of pasture. Formerly 40s; now it is worth 20s.

Richard holds PARKHAM from Baldwin. Algar held it TRE, and it paid geld for 2 hides. There is land for 10 ploughs. In demesne are 2 ploughs, and 4 slaves; and 9 villans and 3 bordars with 5 ploughs. There are 10 acres of meadow, [and] pasture 3 furlongs long and 1 furlong broad, and half a league of woodland. Formerly 30s; now it is worth 40s.

Sedborough was attached to this manor TRE. Beorhtmær held it, and it paid geld for 1 virgate of land.

Richard holds LITTLE TORRINGTON from Baldwin. Eadmær held it TRE, and it paid geld for 1 hide and 1 virgate of land. There is land for 8 ploughs. In demesne are 2 ploughs, and 5 slaves; and 6 villans and 5 bordars with 5 ploughs. There are 8 acres of meadow, and 1 league of pasture and half a league of woodland. Formerly 20s; now it is worth 40s.

Ralph holds HEANTON SATCHVILLE from Baldwin. Edwin held it TRE, and it paid geld for half a hide and half a virgate of land and 1 ferding. There is land for 5 ploughs. In demesne is 1 plough, with 1 slave; and 5 villans and 4 bordars with 3 ploughs. There are 10 acres of meadow, and 30 acres of pasture and 2 acres of scrubland. Formerly 10s; now it is worth 20s.

Aubrey holds [Great and Little] POTHERIDGE from Baldwin. Ulf held it TRE, and it paid geld for 2 virgates of land, less half a ferding. There is land for 7 ploughs. In demesne are 2 ploughs, and 3 slaves; and 6 villans and 5 bordars with 2 bordars [sic]. There are 3 acres of meadow, and 4 furlongs of pasture, [and] woodland 5 furlongs long and 2 furlongs broad. Formerly, as now, worth 40s.

Aubrey holds STOCKLEIGH [in Meeth] from Baldwin. Colwin held it TRE, and it paid geld for 1 virgate of land. There is land for 3 ploughs. In demesne is 1 plough, with 1 slave; and 3 villans and 3 bordars with half a plough. There are 9 acres of meadow, and 2 acres of scrubland, and sufficient common pasture. It is worth 15s.

Aubrey holds WOOLLADON from Baldwin. Sæwine held it TRE, and it paid geld for 1 virgate of land. There is land for 1½ ploughs. There is 1 villan and 2 bordars with 1 slave, and 9 acres of meadow. It is worth 5s.

[Folio 106V: DEVONSHIRE]

Bernard holds MEETH from Baldwin. Alnoth held it TRE, and it paid geld for half a hide. There is land for 4 ploughs. In demesne is 1 plough; and 2 villans and 3 bordars with 1 plough. There are 4 acres of meadow, and 2 furlongs of scrubland, and common pasture. Formerly 10s; now it is worth 20s.

Robert holds LANDCROSS from Baldwin. Ælfgifu held it TRE, and it paid geld for 1 virgate of land. There is land for 3 ploughs. In demesne is 1 plough, and 2 slaves; and 3 villans with half a plough. There are 3 acres of meadow, and 20 acres of pasture and 20 acres of woodland. Formerly 30s; now it is worth 20s.

Colwin holds WOOLLEIGH [in Beaford] from Baldwin. Alsige held it TRE, and it paid geld for 1 virgate of land. There is land for 4 ploughs, which are there, with 1 slave and 3 villans and 3 bordars. There is 1 acre of meadow and 5 acres of scrubland. Formerly 10s; now it is worth 20s

William holds "HELESCANE" from Baldwin. Eadric held it TRE, and it paid geld for 1 virgate of land. There is land for 8 ploughs. In demesne is 1 plough; and 4 villans and 4 bordars with 3 ploughs. There are 2 acres of meadow and 5 acres of scrubland. Formerly 30s; now it is worth 40s.

Baldwin himself holds CHAWLEIGH. Siward held it TRE, and it paid geld for 3 hides. There is land for 30 ploughs. In demesne are 6 ploughs, and 12 slaves; and 30 villans and 6 bordars with 10 ploughs. There are 10 acres of meadow, and 20 acres of woodland, [and] pasture 1 league long and half a league broad. Formerly £10; now it is worth £12.

William holds DOLTON from Baldwin. Ulf held it TRE, and it paid geld for 1 hide. There is land for 18 ploughs. In demesne are 2 ploughs; and 19 villans and 9 bordars and 2 swineherds with 12 ploughs. There are 10 acres of meadow, and 50 acres of pasture and 150 acres of woodland. Formerly, as now, worth £8.

Walter holds NYMET ROWLAND from Baldwin. Æthelric held it TRE, and it paid geld for half a hide. There is land for 6 ploughs. In demesne is 1 plough, and 2 slaves; and 4 villans and 5 bordars with 3 ploughs. There are 4 acres of meadow, and 3 acres of pasture and 5 acres of woodland. Formerly 20s; now it is worth 30s.

Walter holds [East and West] LEIGH [in Coldridge] from Baldwin. Æthelric held it TRE, and it paid geld for 3 virgates of land. There is land for 6 ploughs, which are there, and 3 slaves and 5 villans and 5 bordars, and 5 acres of meadow, and 5 acres of pasture and 3 acres of woodland. Formerly 30s; now it is worth 40s.

Walter holds [East, Great and Little] BEERE [in North Tawton] from Baldwin. Alnoth held it TRE, and it paid geld for 1 virgate of land and half a ferding. There is land for 4 ploughs. In demesne is 1 plough, with 1 slave; and 3 villans and 3 bordars with 2 ploughs. There are 4 acres of meadow, and 10 acres of pasture and 4 acres of woodland. Formerly 10s; now it is worth 20s.

Ralph holds BROADNYMETT from Baldwin. Wado held it TRE, and it paid geld for 3 virgates of land. There is land for 6 ploughs. In demesne is 1 plough, and 5 slaves; and 5 villans and 7 bordars with 3½ ploughs. There are 10 acres of meadow and 50 acres of pasture. Formerly 20s; now it is worth 25s.

The same Ralph holds APPLEDORE [in Clannaborough] from Baldwin. Leofnoth held it TRE, and it paid geld for 1 virgate of land. There is land for 1½ ploughs, and as many [ploughs] are there, with 1 slave and 2 villans and 1 bordar, and 2 acres of meadow. Formerly 5s; now it is worth 10s.

Modbert holds HALSE from Baldwin. Æthelmær held it TRE, and it paid geld for 1 virgate of land. There is land for 2 ploughs. There is 1 plough, and 2 bordars and 2 slaves, and 1 acre of meadow and 40 acres of pasture. Formerly 10s; now it is worth 13s.

Ralph holds CLANNABOROUGH from Baldwin. Godmann held it TRE, and it paid geld for 3 virgates of land. There is land for 6 ploughs. In demesne are 2 ploughs, and 3 slaves; and 2 villans and 5 bordars with half a plough. There are 5 acres of meadow, and 4 acres of pasture and 15 acres of woodland. Formerly, as now, worth 25s.

The same Ralph holds WALSON from Baldwin. Wado held it TRE, and and it paid geld for 1 virgate of land. There is land for 4 ploughs. There are 3 ploughs, and 2 slaves and 4 villans and 1 bordar, and 4 acres of meadow, and 12 acres of pasture and as much woodland. Formerly 15s; now it is worth 25s.

Godfrey holds BRUSHFORD from Baldwin. Leofric held it TRE, and it paid geld for half a hide. There is land for 3 ploughs. There is 1 plough, and 4 slaves and 4 villans, and 4 acres of meadow, and 12 acres of pasture and 8 acres of woodland. Formerly 7s6d; now it is worth 20s.

The same Godfrey holds BRUSHFORD from Baldwin. Leofric held it TRE, and it paid geld for half a hide. There is land for 3 ploughs. There is 1 plough, with 1 villan and 4 bordars, and 3 acres of meadow, and 6 acres of pasture and 8 acres of woodland. Formerly 7s6d; now it is worth 10s.

Otelin holds BURSTON from Baldwin. Osfrith held it TRE, and it paid geld for 1 hide. There is land for 4 ploughs. In demesne are 2 ploughs, and 3 slaves; and 6 villans and 5 bordars with 4 ploughs. There are 8 acres of meadow and 6 acres of woodland. Formerly, as now, worth 40s.

Rainer holds GREENSLADE from Baldwin. Wado held it TRE, and it paid geld for half a virgate of land. There is land for 3 ploughs. In demesne is 1 plough; and 2 villans and 2 bordars with half a plough. There is 1 acre of meadow and 10 acres of pasture. Formerly 7s6d; now it is worth 10s. Half of this land has been joined to the king's manor which is called North Tawton.

Richard holds WEMBWORTHY from Baldwin. Leofric held it TRE, and it paid geld for 1 hide. There is land for 12 ploughs. In demesne are 2 ploughs, and 3 slaves; and 5 villans and 5 bordars with $1\frac{1}{2}$ ploughs. There are 10 acres of meadow, and woodland half a league in length and as much broad. Formerly 20s; now it is worth 40s.

Baldwin himself holds KENN. Beorhtmær held it TRE, and it paid geld for 6 hides. There is land for 25 ploughs, and as many [ploughs] are there, and 20 slaves and 42 villans and bordars, and 5 swineherds rendering 44 pigs. There is a mill rendering 30d, and 30 acres of meadow, and 10 acres of woodland and 100 acres of pasture. Formerly £12; now it is worth £10.

11 burgesses in Exeter are attached to this manor; they pay 53d.

Roger holds GEORGE TEIGN from Baldwin. Uhtræd held it TRE, and it paid geld for 3 virgates of land. There is land for 4 ploughs, which are there, and 3 slaves and 4 villans and 8 bordars. There are 3 acres of meadow, pasture 5 furlongs long and 2 furlongs broad, [and] woodland $4\frac{1}{2}$ furlongs long and $2\frac{1}{2}$ furlongs broad. Formerly, as now, worth 20s.

Ansgar holds BEETOR from Baldwin. Eadwulf held it TRE, and it paid geld for 1 virgate of land. There is land for 4 ploughs. There are 3 ploughs with 1 slave, and 4 villans and 1 bordar, and 8 acres of meadow. Formerly 20s; now it is worth 25s.

Robert holds SHAPLEY [in Chagford] from Baldwin. Ætherlæd held it TRE, and it paid geld for 1 virgate of land. There is land for 2 ploughs, which are there, with 1 plough [sic], and 4 villans, and 5 acres of meadow and 2 acres of woodland. Formerly, as now, worth 12s6d.

Robert holds SHAPLEY [in Chagford] from Baldwin. Eadwig held it TRE, and it paid geld for half a hide. There is land for 3 ploughs. There are 5 acres of meadow. Formerly, as now, worth 7s6d.

Ralph holds MAMHEAD from Baldwin. Algar held it TRE, and it paid geld for 3 virgates of land. There is land for 5 ploughs. In demesne are 2 ploughs, and 3 slaves; and 6 villans and 4 bordars with 5 ploughs. There are 6 acres of meadow,

and 50 acres of pasture and 2 acres of woodland. Formerly 20s; now it is worth 30s.

Godwine holds SHAPLEY [in Chagford] from Baldwin. Wulfric held it TRE, and it paid geld for 1 virgate of land. There is land for 3 ploughs. There are $1\frac{1}{2}$ ploughs, with 1 slave, and 4 villans, and 5 acres of meadow. Formerly 10s; now it is worth 15s.

Robert holds SHIRWELL from Baldwin. Beorhtmær held it TRE, and it paid geld for 1 hide. There is land for 12 ploughs. In demesne are 2 ploughs, and 2 slaves; and 9 villans and 6 bordars with $4\frac{1}{2}$ ploughs. There are 3 acres of meadow, and 300 acres of scrubland, [and] pasture 1 league long and half a league broad. Formerly, as now, worth 60s.

The same Robert holds ASHFORD from Baldwin. Æthelmær held it TRE, and it paid geld for half a hide. There is land for 5 ploughs. There are 2 ploughs, with 1 slave, and 9 villans and 2 bordars. There are 4 acres of meadow, and 4 acres of scrubland and 30 acres of pasture. Formerly 30s; now it is worth 20s.

The same Robert holds LOXHORE [Loxhore and Lower Loxhore] from Baldwin. Doleswif held it TRE, and it paid geld for half a hide. There is land for 3 ploughs. There are 2 ploughs, with 1 slave, and 3 villans and 2 bordars, and 100 acres of woodland and 200 acres of pasture. Formerly, as now, worth 20s.

The same Robert holds LOXHORE [Loxhore and Lower Loxhore] from Baldwin. Wulfweard held it TRE, and it paid geld for half a hide. There is land for 5 ploughs. There are 3 ploughs, and 2 slaves and 7 villans and 2 bordars, and 4 acres of alder-wood and 100 acres of pasture. Formerly, as now, worth 20s.

Robert holds HEANTON PUNCHARDON from Baldwin. Beorhtmær held it TRE, and it paid geld for 2 hides. There is land for 12 ploughs. In demesne are 3 ploughs, and 11 slaves; and 24 villans with 5 ploughs. There is a mill rendering 4s, and a fishery rendering 2s, and 10 acres of meadow, and 100 acres of pasture and 100 acres of woodland. Formerly, as now, worth £4.

Robert holds WEST HAGGINTON from Baldwin. Ulf held it TRE, and it paid geld for 1 hide. There is land for 10 ploughs. In demesne are 2 ploughs, and 2 slaves; and 12 villans and 4 bordars with 5 ploughs, and 50 acres of pasture. Formerly, as now, worth 60s.

Robert holds CHARLES from Baldwin. Beorhtmær held it TRE, and it paid geld for 1 virgate of land. There is land for 12 ploughs. In demesne are 2 ploughs, and 3 slaves; and 6 villans and 6 bordars with 5 ploughs. There are 100 acres of woodland and 53 acres of pasture. Formerly, as now, worth 40s.

The same Robert holds MOCKHAM from Baldwin. Ealdceorl held it TRE. This acquitted its geld with the aforesaid manor for 1 virgate of land. Now they are accounted for as 2 virgates of land. There is land here for 3 ploughs, which are there, with 1 slave and 2 villans. There are 20 acres of pasture. Formerly 15s; now it is worth 20s.

Ansgar holds WEST BUCKLAND [near South Molton] from Baldwin. Alnoth held it TRE, and it paid geld for 1 virgate of land. There is land for 6 ploughs. In demesne are 2 ploughs, and 2 slaves; and 6 villans and 4 bordars with 4 ploughs. There are 4 acres of meadow and 24 acres of woodland. Formerly, as now, worth 40s.

[Folio 107: DEVONSHIRE]

Robert holds BLAKEWELL from Baldwin. This paid geld for 1 virgate of land TRE. There is land for 4 ploughs. There are 2 ploughs, with 1 slave, and 3 villans, and 60 acres of scrubland and as much pasture. Formerly, as now, worth 20s. This land is [part] of Braunton, the king's manor, so the men of the hundred state.

Baldwin himself holds KENTISBURY. Almær held it TRE, and it paid geld for 2 hides. There is land for 20 ploughs. In demesne is 1 plough, and 5 slaves; and 11 villans with 5 ploughs. There are 100 acres of pasture and 20 acres of woodland. It is worth 40s.

Roggo holds HOLCOMBE ROGUS from Baldwin. Sæweard held it TRE, and it paid geld for 9 hides. There is land for 22 ploughs. In demesne are 2 ploughs, and 8 slaves; and 30 villans and 5 bordars with 7 ploughs. There are 2 mills rendering 10s, and 24 acres of meadow, and 200 acres of pasture and 50 acres of scrubland. Formerly £10; now it is worth £6.

Roggo holds HOCKWORTHY from Baldwin. Kolbrand held it TRE, and it paid geld for 2 virgates of land and 2½ ferdings. There is land for 3 ploughs. [...] There are 4 villans and 2 bordars and 2 slaves with half a plough. There are 2 acres of meadow, and 40 acres of pasture and 30 acres of woodland. Formerly 20s; now it is worth 12s6d.

Ansgar holds WEST ANSTEY from Baldwin. Godwine held it TRE, and it paid geld for 1 hide. There is land for 9 ploughs. In demesne are 2 ploughs, and 7 slaves; and 7 villans and 5 bordars with 4 ploughs. There are 6 acres of meadow, and 120 acres of woodland and 1 league of pasture in length and breadth. Formerly 30s; now it is worth 40s.

Ansgar holds RINGCOMBE from Baldwin. Cypping held it TRE, and it paid geld for 1 virgate of land. There is land for 2 ploughs. There 2 villans have half a plough. Formerly 12d; now it is worth 3s.

Baldwin himself holds FILLEIGH. Osfrith held it TRE, and it paid geld for 1 hide. There is land for 8 ploughs. In demesne are 3 ploughs, and 3 slaves; and 9 villans and 6 bordars with 6 ploughs. There are 7 acres of meadow, and 30 acres of pasture and 10 acres of woodland. Formerly 40s; now it is worth 60s.

A certain estate which is called Lobb [Lobb and North Lobb] has been taken away from this manor and has been added to Braunton, the king's manor. This paid geld for 1 virgate of land. There is land for 3 ploughs. It is worth 20s.

Ansgar holds [North and South] NEWTON [in Chittlehampton] from Baldwin. Alweald held it TRE, and it paid geld for 1 virgate of land. There is land for 2 ploughs. There 2 villans with 1 bordar have 1 plough, and [there is] half

an acre of meadow and 5 acres of pasture. Formerly, as now, worth 10s.

Ansgar holds WHITSTONE from Baldwin. Eadmær held it TRE, and it paid geld for half a virgate of land. There is land for 2 ploughs. There is 1 plough, and 2 villans with 1 bordar, and 3 acres of meadow and 5 acres of pasture. Formerly, as now, worth 10s.

Robert holds LINCOMBE from Baldwin. Beorhtmær held it TRE, and it paid geld for 2 hides. There is land for 8 ploughs. In demesne are 2 ploughs, and 3 slaves; and 8 villans and 9 bordars with 5 ploughs. There are 1½ acres of meadow and 100 acres of pasture. Formerly, as now, worth 60s.

An estate which is called Yarde [in Ilfracombe] has been added to this manor. Godric held it TRE, and it paid geld for 1 virgate of land. There is land for 2 ploughs. Formerly 20s; now it is worth 10s.

Robert holds ILFRACOMBE from Baldwin. Almær held it TRE, TRE, and it paid geld for 1 hide. There is land for 9 ploughs. In demesne are 2 ploughs; and 12 villans and 12 bordars with 9 ploughs, and 5 slaves, and 5 acres of meadow and 100 acres of pasture. Formerly, as now, worth £4.

Robert holds ASHFORD from Baldwin. Beorhtmær held it. TRE, and it paid geld for half a hide and 1 ferding of land. There is land for 4 ploughs. In demesne are 2 ploughs, and 2 slaves; and 3 villans and 3 bordars with 1 plough. There are 15 acres of pasture. Formerly, as now, worth 20s.

Otelin holds CLYST HYDON from Baldwin. Burgræd held it TRE, and it paid geld for 3 hides. There is land for 8 ploughs. In demesne are 2 ploughs, and 8 slaves; and 9 villans and 5 bordars with 5 ploughs. There are 44 acres of meadow, and 20 acres of pasture and 80 acres of woodland. Formerly, as now, worth 60s.

Robert holds MIDDLE MARWOOD from Baldwin. Alwine held it TRE, and it paid geld for 1 virgate of land. There is land for 2 ploughs. There are 2 villans and 1 bordar and 2 slaves with 1½ ploughs. There are 2 acres of meadow, and 20 acres of pasture and 16 acres of woodland. Formerly, as now, worth 15s.

Gilbert holds SNYDLES from Baldwin. Eadric held it TRE, and it paid geld for 1 virgate of land. There is land for 3 ploughs. There are 2 ploughs, and 3 villans and 2 bordars and 2 slaves. There are 4 acres of meadow and 40 acres of pasture. Formerly 10s; now it is worth 15s.

The canons of ST MARY'S hold ASHCLYST from Baldwin. 4 thegns held it TRE, and it paid geld for 1 hide and half a virgate of land. There is land for 9 ploughs. In demesne are 2 ploughs, with 1 slave; and 10 villans and 4 bordars with 1 plough. There are 17 acres of meadow, and 50 acres of pasture and 5 acres of woodland. Formerly, as now, worth 40s.

The canons themselves hold POLTIMORE from Baldwin. Wulfmær held it TRE, and it paid geld for half a hide. There is land for 2 ploughs. There is 1 plough, and 2 bordars and 5 slaves, and 6 acres of meadow and 80 acres of pasture. Formerly, as now, worth 10s.

The canons themselves hold POLSLOE [in Exeter] from Baldwin. Ælfric held it TRE, and it paid geld for half a virgate of land. There is land for 2 ploughs, which are there, with 1 bordar and 4 slaves. There are 2 acres of meadow. Formerly 5s; now it is worth 10s.

The canons themselves holds WEST CLYST from Baldwin. Wulfgifu held it TRE, and it paid geld for 2½ virgates of land. There is land for 3 ploughs. There are 3½ ploughs, and 3 villans and 3 bordars and 3 slaves, and 3 acres of pasture and 10 acres of meadow. Formerly 20s; now it is worth 15s.

From this manor 1 ferding of land has been taken away, which belonged there TRE, and it has been added to Poltimore, Odo's manor. It is worth 12d.

The monks of Mont-Saint-Michel hold FURSHAM from Baldwin. Eadwulf held it TRE, and it paid geld for 1 virgate of land. There is land for 6 ploughs. In demesne is 1 plough, with 1 slave; and 5 villans and 2 bordars with 2 ploughs. There are 3 acres of meadow, and 20 acres of pasture and 10 acres of woodland. Formerly 20s; now it is worth 30s.

Baldwin's wife holds WHIMPLE from Baldwin. Almær held it TRE, and it paid geld for 2 hides and 1 virgate of land. There is land for 10 ploughs. In demesne are 2 ploughs, and 9 slaves; and 13 villans and 8 bordars with 6 ploughs. There are 50 acres of meadow, and 100 acres of pasture and 50 acres of scrubland. Formerly £6; now it is worth £10.

Rainer holds PAYHEMBURY from Baldwin. Alnoth held it TRE, and it paid geld for 2 hides. There is land for 8 ploughs. In demesne is 1 plough, with 1 slave; and 12 villans and 8 bordars with 5 ploughs. There is a mill rendering 40d, and 14 acres of meadow and 40 acres of pasture. Formerly 40s; now it is worth 60s.

Half a hide belonged TRE to the aforesaid manor of Whimple and it is called Larkbeare. There is land for 2 ploughs. There is half a plough, with 1 slave, and 8 acres of meadow, and 13 acres of pasture and 12 acres of woodland. It is worth 5s. Almær held it formerly. Now Alvred the Breton holds it.

Rainer holds LANGFORD [in Cullompton] from Baldwin. Beorhtmær held it TRE, and it paid geld for 1 hide and 3 virgates of land. There is land for 6 ploughs. In demesne are 2 ploughs, and 2 slaves; and 10 villans and 7 bordars with 3 ploughs. There are 12 acres of meadow and 2 acres of scrubland. Formerly, as now, worth 40s.

William holds PONSFORD from Baldwin. Edwin held it TRE, and it paid geld for half a hide. There is land for 2 ploughs, which are there, with 1 slave, and 3 villans and 4 bordars, and 8 acres of meadow and 60 acres of pasture. Formerly 30s; now it is worth 15s.

William holds PONSFORD from Baldwin. Siduwine held it TRE, and it paid geld for half a hide. There is land for 2 ploughs. There are 4 bordars, and 4 acres of meadow and 60 acres of pasture. Formerly, as now, worth 10s.

William holds KINGSFORD from Baldwin. Eadsige held it TRE, and it paid geld for half a virgate of land. There is half a plough, and 2 bordars with 1 slave, and 6 acres of meadow and 4 acres of woodland. Formerly, as now, worth 5s.

William holds KENTISBEARE from Baldwin. Eadwig held it TRE, and it paid geld for 1 virgate of land. There is land for 2 ploughs. There is 1 plough, with 1 slave and 4 bordars. There are 10 acres of meadow and 10 acres of woodland. Formerly 5s; now it is worth 10s.

William holds BLACKBOROUGH from Baldwin. Godric held it TRE, and it paid geld for half a hide. There is land for 1 plough, which [plough] is there, with 1 slave and 1 villan and 4 bordars. There are 5 acres of meadow and 20 acres of pasture. Formerly 5s; now it is worth 10s.

William holds KENTISBEARE from Baldwin. Northmann held it TRE, and it paid geld for half a hide. There is land for 4 ploughs, which are there, with 2 slaves and 3 villans and 5 bordars. There is a mill rendering 5s, and 10 acres of meadow and 10 acres of woodland. Formerly 40s; now it is worth 30s.

William holds ALLER [in Kentisbeare] from Baldwin. Æthelweard held it TRE, and it paid geld for 1 virgate of land. There is land for 2 ploughs. There is 1 plough, with 1 slave and 1 villan and 5 bordars. There are 10 acres of meadow and 10 acres of woodland. Formerly, as now, worth 10s.

Roggo holds 'MONK CULM' [? in Silverton] from Baldwin. Beorhtmær held it TRE, and it paid geld for 1 hide. There is land for 4 ploughs. There are 2 ploughs, and 2 slaves and 3 villans with 1 bordar, and 8 acres of meadow, and 16 acres of pasture and 12 acres of woodland. Formerly 20s; now it is worth 30s.

[Folio 107V: DEVONSHIRE]

Roggo holds 'BERNARDSMOOR' [? in Silverton] from Baldwin. Almær held it TRE, and it paid geld for half a hide. There is land for 3 ploughs, which are there, with 1 slave and 6 villans and 2 bordars. There is a mill rendering 5s, and 6 acres of meadow and 6 acres of pasture. Formerly 15s; now it is worth 20s.

Baldwin himself holds COWICK [In Exeter]. Æthelmær held it TRE, and it paid geld for 1 hide. There is land for 8 ploughs. In demesne are 2 ploughs, and 2 slaves; and 8 villans and 3 bordars with 6 ploughs. There is a mill rendering 10s, and 3 acres of meadow and 3 acres of woodland. Formerly 20s; now it is worth 30s.

Baldwin himself holds DREWSTEIGNTON. Osfrith held it TRE, and it paid geld for 2 hides. There is land for 12 ploughs. In demesne are 2 ploughs, and 4 slaves; and 12 villans and 8 bordars with 6 ploughs. There are 6 acres of meadow, and 60 acres of pasture, [and] woodland 1 league long and 3 furlongs broad. Formerly 40s; now it is worth 50s.

Baldwin himself holds SPREYTON. Osfrith held it TRE, and it paid geld for 2 hides. There is land for 12 ploughs. In demesne are 2 ploughs, and 3 slaves; and 14 villans and 10 bordars with 6 ploughs. There are 3 acres of meadow, and 10 acres of pasture, [and] woodland 1 league long and 2 furlongs broad. Formerly 50s; now it is worth 60s.

Baldwin himself holds EXWICK [in Exeter]. Everwacer held it TRE, and it paid geld for 1 hide. There is land for 8 ploughs. In demesne is 1 plough, and 5 slaves; and 9 villans with 6 ploughs. There is a mill rendering 10s, and 3 acres of meadow, and 50 acres of pasture and 3 acres of scrubland. Formerly 20s; now it is worth 30s.

Stephen holds CLIFFORD from Baldwin. Beorhtmær held it TRE, and it paid geld for 1 hide. There is land for 8 ploughs. In demesne are 3 ploughs, and 4 slaves; and 10 villans and 6 bordars with 4½ ploughs. There are 3 acres of meadow, and 4 acres of woodland and 6 furlongs of pasture. Formerly 20s; now it is worth 40s.

Otelin holds CLAYHIDON from Baldwin. Godwine held it TRE, and it paid geld for 3 hides. There is land for 12 ploughs. In demesne are 3 ploughs, and 6 slaves; and 14 villans and 6 bordars with 5 ploughs. There is a mill rendering 30d, and 26 acres of meadow, pasture 3 furlongs long and 1 furlong broad, [and] woodland 1 league long and half a league broad. Formerly, as now, worth £4.

Stephen holds RINGMORE [in Shaldon St Nicholas] from Baldwin. Beorhtric held it TRE, and it paid geld for 1 hide and 1 virgate of land. There is land for 8 ploughs. In demesne are 2 ploughs, and 4 slaves; and 8 villans and 6 bordars with 4 ploughs. There are 3 acres of meadow and 15 acres of pasture. Formerly 20s; now it is worth 30s.

Eadwig holds RUSHFORD from Baldwin. He himself held it TRE, and it paid geld for 1 hide. There is land for 5 ploughs. In demesne is 1 plough, with 1 slave; and 8 villans and 5 bordars with 3 ploughs. There are 5 acres of meadow, and 4 acres of pasture and 4 acres of scrubland. Formerly, as now, worth 30s.

Ralph holds HITTISLEIGH from Baldwin. Dodda held it TRE, and it paid geld for half a hide. There is land for 7 ploughs. In demesne are 2 ploughs, and 2 slaves; and 7 villans with 3 ploughs. There are 6 acres of meadow, [and] woodland 1 league long and half a league broad. Formerly 20s; now it is worth 30s.

Richard holds MARTIN from Baldwin. Eadwulf held it TRE, and it paid geld for 1 virgate of land. There is land for 3 ploughs. There are 1½ ploughs, with 1 slave and 2 villans, and 2 acres of meadow and 5 acres of woodland. Formerly, as now, worth 10s.

Hugh holds MELHUISH from Baldwin. Beorhtmær held it TRE, and it paid geld for half a hide. There is land for 7 ploughs, and there are as many [ploughs], with 4 slaves and 8 villans and 4 bordars. There are 3 acres of meadow, and 15 acres of pasture and 24 acres of woodland. Formerly 20s; now it is worth 30s.

Hugh holds TEIGNHARVEY from Baldwin. Ælfric held it TRE, and it paid geld for 2 virgates of land. There is land for 4 ploughs. There are 3 ploughs, and 2 slaves and 4 villans with

1 bordar, and 2 acres of meadow and 20 acres of pasture. Formerly 10s; now it is worth 15s.

Joscelin holds OLDRIDGE from Baldwin. Dodda held it TRE, and it paid geld for half a virgate of land. There is land for 6 ploughs. In demesne is 1 plough, and 3 slaves; and 6 villans and 3 bordars with 4 ploughs. There are 6 acres of meadow, and 100 acres of pasture and 60 acres of woodland. Formerly, as now, worth 20s.

Rainer holds TEDBURN ST MARY from Baldwin. Almær held it TRE, and it paid geld for 1 virgate of land. There is land for 4 ploughs. In demesne is 1 plough, with 1 slave; and 2 villans and 3 bordars with 1 plough. There are 3 acres of meadow, and 40 acres of pasture and 45 acres of woodland. Formerly 15s; now it is worth 10s.

Ralph holds TEDBURN ST MARY from Baldwin. Dodda held it TRE, and it paid geld for 1 virgate of land. There is land for 4 ploughs. There are 3 ploughs, and 2 slaves and 4 villans and 2 bordars, and 3 acres of meadow, and 45 acres of pasture and as much woodland. Formerly, as now, worth 10s.

Otelin holds BOLHAM WATER from Baldwin. Almær held it TRE, and it paid geld for 2 hides. There is land for 6 ploughs. In demesne are 2 ploughs, and 2 slaves; and 8 villans and 6 bordars with 2 ploughs. There are 24 acres of meadow, pasture 1 league long and half a league broad, [and] woodland half a league long and 1 furlong broad. Formerly 20s; now it is worth 35s.

Otelin holds CULM PYNE from Baldwin. Godwine held it TRE, and it paid geld for half a hide and 1 ferding. There is land for 4 ploughs. In demesne are 2 ploughs, and 2 slaves; and 4 villans and 4 bordars with 1 plough. There is a mill rendering 30d, and 4 acres of meadow, and 6 acres of woodland, [and] pasture 2 furlongs long and 1 furlong broad. Formerly 10s; now it is worth 20s.

Walter holds BRAMPFORD SPEKE from Baldwin. Brungar held it TRE, and it paid geld for half a hide. There is land for 2 ploughs. There are 1½ ploughs, with 1 slave and 2 villans and 2 bordars. There are 3 acres of meadow and 6 acres of pasture. Formerly 10s; now it is worth 15s.

Otelin holds HOLE [in Clayhidon] from Baldwin. Eadwulf held it TRE, and it paid geld for half a hide. There is land for 2 ploughs, which are there, with 2 villans, and 5 acres of pasture. Formerly waste; now it is worth 5s.

Bernard holds WHITESTONE from Baldwin. Cniht held it TRE, and it paid geld for half a hide. There is land for 4 ploughs. There are 1½ ploughs, with 1 slave and 4 villans and 2 bordars. There are 2 acres of meadow and 3 acres of woodland. Formerly 5s; now it is worth 10s.

Bernard holds MAIDENCOMBE from Baldwin. Cniht held it TRE, and it paid geld for half a hide and half a ferding. There is land for 3 ploughs. There is 1 plough, with 1 slave and 1 villan and 2 bordars. Formerly 30d; now it is worth 5s.

Bernard holds [Higher, Lower and Middle] ROCOMBE. Osmær held it TRE, and it paid geld for half a hide. There is land for 3 ploughs. There is 1 plough, with 1 villan and 2 bordars and 2 slaves. Formerly 30d; now it is worth 5s.

Baldwin's wife holds BRIDFORD from him. Beorhtric held it TRE, and it paid geld for 2 hides. There is land for 14 ploughs. In demesne are 3 ploughs, and 6 slaves; and 13 villans and 8 bordars with 7 ploughs. There are 12 acres of meadow, and 30 acres of pasture and 24 acres of woodland. Formerly 30s; now it is worth 40s.

Vitalis holds BRAMPFORD SPEKE from Baldwin. Godmann held it TRE, and it paid geld for 1 hide. There is land for 9 ploughs. In demesne are 2 ploughs, and 4 slaves; and 16 villans and 8 bordars with 6 ploughs. There is a mill rendering 8s, and 5 acres of meadow, and 20 acres of pasture and 40 acres of woodland. Formerly 20s; now it is worth 45s.

Modbert holds [Higher and Lower] EGGBEER from Baldwin. Leofgar held it TRE, and it paid geld for 2½ virgates of land. There is land for 6 ploughs. In demesne are 2 ploughs, and 2 slaves; and 4 villans and 4 bordars with 2½ ploughs. There are 10 acres of meadow, and 30 acres of pasture and 6 acres of woodland. Formerly 15s; now it is worth 20s.

Modbert holds UPPACOTT from Baldwin. Almær held it TRE, and it paid geld for 1 virgate of land. There is land for 5 ploughs. In demesne is 1 plough, with 1 slave; and 2 villans and 3 bordars with 1 plough. There are 6 acres of meadow, and 5 acres of pasture and 1 acre of woodland. Formerly, as now, worth 10s.

Modbert holds GREAT FULFORD from Baldwin. Æthelric held it TRE, and it paid geld for 1 virgate of land. There is land for 3 ploughs, which are there, with 1 slave and 3 villans and 4 bordars. There are 4 acres of meadow and 20 acres of pasture. Formerly 7s; now it is worth 15s.

Rainer holds ROCKBEARE from Baldwin. Eadmær held it TRE, and it paid geld for half a hide. There is land for 4 ploughs. In demesne are 2 ploughs, and 4 slaves; and 6 villans with 1 plough. There are 10 acres of meadow, and 40 acres of pasture and 6 acres of woodland. Formerly 10s; now it is worth 15s.

Rainer holds ROCKBEARE from Baldwin. Sæwine held it TRE, and it paid geld for 3 ferdings. There is land for 1 plough. 1 villan has this [plough] there. Formerly, as now, worth 5s.

Rainer holds DOTTON from Baldwin. Dodda held it TRE, and it paid geld for 1 virgate of land and 3 ferdings. There is land for 2 ploughs. There are 1½ ploughs, with 1 slave and 2 bordars, and a mill rendering 5s, and 2 acres of meadow and 10 acres of pasture. Formerly, as now, worth 7s.

[Folio 108: DEVONSHIRE]

Baldwin himself holds AYLESBEARE. Æthelmær held it TRE, and it paid geld for 2½ hides. There is land for 8 ploughs. In demesne are 2 ploughs, and 4 slaves; and 8 villans and 3 bordars with 5 ploughs. There are 6 acres of meadow and 50 acres of scrubland. Formerly, as now, worth 40s.

Robert holds WHITESTONE from Baldwin. Eadric held it

TRE, and it paid geld for 1 virgate of land. There is land for 2 ploughs, which are there, with 1 slave and 2 villans and 1 bordar. There are 4 acres of meadow and 8 acres of woodland. Formerly, as now, worth 10s.

Goscelm holds ROCKBEARE from Baldwin. Wulfmær held it TRE, and it paid geld for 3 hides, less 1 virgate of land. There is land for 6 ploughs. In demesne are 2 ploughs, and 4 slaves; and 9 villans and 5 bordars with 3½ ploughs. There are 55 acres of meadow, and 50 acres of pasture and 50 acres of woodland. Formerly 15s; now it is worth 40s.

Roger holds "PETECOTE" from Baldwin. Alweald held it TRE, and it paid geld for half a hide. There is land for 3 ploughs. In demesne is 1 plough, and 2 slaves; and 3 villans and 3 bordars with 1 plough. There are 5 acres of meadow and 5 acres of pasture. Formerly, as now, worth 20s.

Baldwin himself holds CHULMLEIGH. Beorhtmær held it TRE, and it paid geld for 5 hides. There is land for 40 ploughs. In demesne are 10 ploughs, and 20 slaves; and 30 villans and 20 bordars with 20 ploughs. There are 30 acres of meadow, and 40 acres of woodland and 1 league of pasture in length and breadth. Formerly £12; now it is worth £13.

Gilbert holds MESHAW from Baldwin. Alfred held it TRE, and it paid geld for 3 virgates of land. There is land for 10 ploughs. In demesne is half a plough, and 5 slaves; and 12 villans and 9 bordars with 6 ploughs, and 2 swineherds rendering 15 pigs. There are 40 acres of meadow, and 40 acres of woodland, [and] pasture 1 league long and half a league broad. Formerly 20s; now it is worth 30s.

Ansgar holds YARD [in Rose Ash] from Baldwin. Almær held it TRE, and it paid geld for 3 virgates of land. There is land for 6 ploughs. In demesne are 2 ploughs, and 5 slaves; and 8 villans and 4 bordars with 3 ploughs. There are 25 acres of meadow, and 80 acres of woodland and 100 acres of pasture. Formerly 10s; now it is worth 30s.

Ansgar holds ROSE ASH from Baldwin. Siward held it TRE, and it paid geld for 1 hide and 1 virgate of land. There is land for 18 ploughs. In demesne are 4 ploughs, and 8 slaves; and 20 villans and 12 bordars with 10 ploughs. There are 60 acres of meadow, and 150 acres of woodland, [and] pasture half a league long and half a league broad. Formerly 60s; now it is worth 100s.

Ansgar holds CREACOMBE [near Witheridge] from Baldwin. Siward held it TRE, and it paid geld for 3 ferdings, less the fourth part of 1 ferding. There is land for 2 ploughs. There are 2 ploughs, and 3 villans and 2 slaves, and 6 acres of meadow, and 7 acres of pasture and 2 acres of woodland. Formerly, as now, worth 10s.

To this manor has been added CREACOMBE [near Witheridge], which Leofgar held freely TRE, and it paid geld for 1 ferding and the fourth part of 1 ferding. There is land for 1½ ploughs. There is 1 villan and 1 bordar and 1 slave, and 6 acres of meadow, and 7 acres of pasture and 1 acre of scrubland. Formerly [it was worth] 2s; now 5s.

Ansketil holds WORTHY from Baldwin. Almær held it

TRE, and it paid geld for 1 virgate of land. There is land for 1 plough, which [plough] is there, with 1 villan and 1 slave. There are 6 acres of meadow and 8 acres of pasture. Formerly 2s; now it is worth 5s.

William holds WILSON from Baldwin. Topi held it TRE, and it paid geld for 1 virgate of land. There is land for 1 plough, which [plough] is there, with 1 villan and 1 slave. There are 12 acres of meadow and 10 acres of pasture. Formerly 3s; now it is worth 5s.

Walter holds CHELDON from Baldwin. Almær held it TRE, and it paid geld for 3 ferdings. There is land for 1 ploughs, which [plough] is there, with 1 slave. There are 6 acres of meadow, and 60 acres of pasture and 2 acres of woodland. Formerly [it was worth] 2s; now 3s.

Joscelin holds RACKENFORD from Baldwin. Siward held it TRE, and it paid geld for 2½ virgates of land. There is land for 6 ploughs. In demesne is 1 plough, and 2 slaves; and 4 villans and 4 bordars with 2 ploughs. There are 3 acres of woodland, and 20 acres of meadow and 200 acres of pasture. Formerly 10s; now it is worth 15s.

Reginald holds "ELTEMETONE" from Baldwin. Almær held it TRE, and it paid geld for half a virgate of land. There is land for 2 ploughs. There are 3 villans and 3 bordars with half a plough, and 6 acres of meadow, and 100 acres of pasture and 40 acres of scrubland. Formerly, as now, it was worth 5s.

Roggo holds [East and West] TAPPS from Baldwin. Ælfric held it TRE, and it paid geld for 1 virgate of land. There is land for 3 ploughs. In demesne is 1 plough, and 2 slaves; and 2 villans and 2 bordars with 1 plough. There are 30 acres of pasture and 10 acres of scrubland. Formerly 2s; now it is worth 10s.

Oswig holds WOODBURN from Baldwin. Ealdræd held it TRE, and it paid geld for 3 ferdings. There is land for 2 ploughs. 1 villan and 4 bordars have 1 plough there. There are 15 acres of meadow and 10 acres of pasture. Formerly, as now, worth 5s.

Stephen holds HACCOMBE from Baldwin. Ulf held it TRE, and it paid geld for half a hide. There is land for 5 ploughs. In demesne is 1 plough, and 3 slaves; and 8 villans and 4 bordars with 3 ploughs. There are 2 acres of meadow and 4 furlongs of scrubland. Formerly, as now, worth 20s.

Ralph holds TEIGNGRACE from Baldwin. Ulf held it TRE, and it paid geld for 2 hides. There is land for 5 ploughs. In demesne is 1 plough, and 4 slaves; and 4 villans and 7 bordars with 3 ploughs. There are 20 acres of meadow, and 35 acres of woodland, [and] pasture 1 league long and 4 furlongs broad. Formerly 10s; now it is worth 20s.

Hugh holds LANGSTONE from Baldwin. Eadwig held it TRE, and it paid geld for 1 virgate of land. There is land for 2 ploughs, which are there, with 1 slave and 4 villans and 4 bordars. There are 11 acres of meadow and 12 acres of pasture. Formerly 5s; now it is worth 10s.

Roger holds HENNOCK from Baldwin. Alnoth held it

TRE, and it paid geld for 1 hide. There is land for 13 ploughs. In demesne are 2 ploughs, and 5 slaves; and 9 villans and 6 bordars with 6 ploughs. Formerly 10s; now it is worth 30s.

Hervey's wife holds 'NEADON' [in Manaton] from Baldwin. Æthelræd held it TRE, and it paid geld for 1 virgate of land. There is land for 1 plough, which [plough] is there, with 1 slave and 2 bordars. There are 4 acres of meadow and 5 acres of pasture. Formerly 12d; now it is worth 5s.

Ranulph holds WHITEWAY from Baldwin. Osfrith held it TRE, and it paid geld for half a hide. There is land for 2 ploughs, which are there, with 1 slave and 1 villan and 4 bordars. There is a salt-pan rendering 12d, and 1 acre of woodland. Formerly 10s; now it is worth 15s.

Roggo holds CHEVITHORNE from Baldwin. Almær held it TRE, and it paid geld for 1 virgate of land. There is land for 5 ploughs. There are 1½ ploughs, and 3 slaves and 3 villans and 3 bordars, and 11 acres of meadow, and 12 acres of pasture and 100 acres of woodland. Formerly, as now, worth 20s.

Ansgar holds CHETTISCOMBE from Baldwin. Wulfmær held it TRE, and it paid geld for 1 hide. There is land for 6 ploughs. In demesne are 2 ploughs, and 4 slaves; and 6 villans and 5 bordars with 3 ploughs. There is a mill rendering 2s, and 10 acres of meadow, and 40 acres of pasture and 60 acres of woodland. Formerly 10s; now it is worth 40s.

Eadwig holds MANATON from Baldwin. The same man held it TRE, and it paid geld for 1 virgate of land. There is land for 1 plough, which [plough] is there, with 1 slave and 3 villans and 3 bordars. There are 5 acres of meadow, and 10 acres of pasture, [and] woodland half a league long and half a furlong broad. It is worth 10s.

Goscelm holds SELLAKE from Baldwin. Beorhtmær held it TRE, and it paid geld for half a hide. There is land for 2 ploughs. There are 1½ ploughs, and 2 villans and 2 bordars, and 2 acres of meadow and 6 acres of woodland. Formerly 5s; now it is worth 10s.

Richard holds SPARKWELL from Baldwin. Beorhtric held it TRE, and it paid geld for half a hide. There is land for 4 ploughs. In demesne is 1 plough, and 2 slaves; and 4 villans and 2 bordars, and 4 acres of meadow, and 20 acres of pasture and 8 acres of woodland. Formerly 10s; now it is worth 15s.

Ralph holds WOLBOROUGH from Baldwin. Siward held it TRE, and it paid geld for 1 hide. There is land for 8 ploughs. In demesne are 2 ploughs, and 4 slaves; and 6 villans and 7 bordars with 4 ploughs. There is a mill rendering 5s, and 15 acres of meadow, and 30 acres of pasture and as much woodland. Formerly 20s; now it is worth 40s.

Baldwin himself holds MUSBURY. Almær held it TRE, and it paid geld for 7 hides. There is land for 16 ploughs. In demesne are 3 ploughs, and 8 slaves; and 16 villans and 4 bordars with 6 ploughs. There is a mill rendering 5s, and 50 acres of pasture and 43 acres of meadow. Formerly £3; now it is worth £4.

Baldwin himself holds THORNCOMBE [Dorset]. Edward

held it TRE, and it paid geld for 2 hides. There is land for 12 ploughs. In demesne are 2 ploughs, and 2 slaves; and 16 villans and 8 bordars with 10 ploughs. There are 18 acres of meadow, and 30 acres of pasture and 15 acres of woodland. Formerly £4; now it is worth 100s.

Ranulph holds 'FORD' [in Musbury] from Baldwin. Ælfgifu held it TRE, and it paid geld for half a hide. There is land for 4 ploughs. In demesne are 2 ploughs, with 1 slave; and 2 villans and 5 bordars with 2 ploughs. There is a mill rendering 30d, and 12 acres of meadow, and 50 acres of pasture and 15 acres of woodland. It is worth 25s.

[Folio 108V: DEVONSHIRE]

Ranulph holds "ALREFORD" from Baldwin. Iuing held it TRE, and it paid geld for 1 virgate of land. There is land for 1½ ploughs. There are 3 bordars, and 3 acres of meadow and 20 acres of pasture. Formerly, as now, worth 5s.

Roger holds SMALLICOMBE from Baldwin. Godwine held it TRE, and it paid geld for half a hide. There is land for 1 plough, which [plough] is there, with 1 slave, and 3 acres of meadow and 6 acres of pasture. Formerly, as now, worth 4s.

Morin holds STEDCOMBE from Baldwin. Ulf held it TRE, and it paid geld for 1 hide. There is land for 4 ploughs. There are 3 slaves, and 6 acres of meadow, and 10 acres of pasture and 6 acres of scrubland. It is worth 12s.

Roggo holds COLWELL from Baldwin. Almær held it TRE, and it paid geld for 1½ hides. There is land for 8 ploughs. In demesne is 1 plough, and 2 slaves; and 6 villans and 2 bordars with 1½ ploughs. There are 300 acres of pasture and 80 acres of woodland. Formerly 10s; now it is worth 20s.

Odo holds COMBPYNE from Baldwin. Godmann held it TRE, and it paid geld for 1 hide. There is land for 4 ploughs. In demesne is 1 plough, and 3 slaves; and 4 villans and 2 bordars with half a plough. There are 9 acres of meadow and 30 acres of pasture. Formerly, as now, worth 20s.

Reginald holds OFFWELL from Baldwin. Burgræd held it TRE, and it paid geld for 1 virgate of land. There is land for 2 ploughs. In demesne is 1 plough; and 6 villans and 2 bordars with 2 ploughs. There are 80 acres of pasture, [and] woodland 5 furlongs long and 20 perches broad. Formerly 12d; now it is worth 13s.

Morin holds WILMINGTON from Baldwin. Eadmær held it TRE, and it paid geld for 1 virgate of land. There is land for 2 ploughs. In demesne is 1 plough, with 1 slave; and 2 villans and 2 bordars with half a plough. There are 7 acres of meadow and 15 acres of woodland. Formerly 5s; now it is worth 7s6d.

Morin holds 'BEER' [in Offwell] from Baldwin. Æthelweald held it TRE, and it paid geld for 3 virgates of land. There is land for 2 ploughs. It is worth 3s.

W[...] holds [Great or Key's] ENGLEBOURNE from Baldwin. Beorhtmær held it TRE, and it paid geld for half a hide. There is land for 5 ploughs. There is 1 plough, with 1 slave, and 3 villans and 1 bordar, and 13 acres of meadow and 40 acres of pasture. Formerly, as now, worth 15s.

Otelin holds WEST PRAWLE from Baldwin. Osfrith held it TRE, and it paid geld for 1 hide. There is land for 6 ploughs. In demesne are 2 ploughs, and 4 slaves; and 10 villans and 8 bordars with 4 ploughs. There are 4 acres of meadow, and 64 acres of pasture and 60 acres of woodland. Formerly 10s; now it is worth 20s.

XVII. The land of Iudichael of Totnes

IUDICHAEL holds from the king TOTNES, a borough which King Edward held in demesne. Within the borough there are 100 burgesses, less 5, and 15 outside the borough working the land. Among them all they pay £8 by tale. Formerly they paid £3 weighed and assayed.

This borough only pays geld when Exeter pays geld and then it renders 40d as geld. If an expedition travels by land or by sea, Totnes and Barnstaple and Lydford between them render as much service as Exeter renders.

Iudichael himself has in Exeter 1 house which TRE rendered 8d in customary dues.

Iudichael himself holds THRUSHELTON from the king. Grim held it TRE, and it paid geld for 1 hide. There is land for 14 ploughs. In demesne are 3 ploughs, and 11 slaves; and 20 villans and 20 bordars with 11 ploughs. There are 100 acres of meadow, and 100 acres of pasture and 20 acres of woodland. Formerly, as now, worth £10.

Nigel holds RADDON [in Marystow] from Iudichael. Oswulf held it TRE, and it paid geld for 1 hide. There is land for 15 ploughs. In demesne are 3 ploughs, and 5 slaves; and 8 villans and 15 bordars with 2 ploughs. There are 10 acres of meadow, pasture half a league long and 1 furlong broad, and as much woodland. Formerly £7.10s; now it is worth 100s.

Nigel holds BROADWOODWIDGER from Iudichael. Cynestan held it TRE, and it paid geld for half a hide, less 1½ ferdings. There is land for 6 ploughs. In demesne are 1½ ploughs, and 8 slaves; and 10 villans and 11 bordars with 2½ ploughs. There are 50 acres of meadow, pasture 1 league long and 1 furlong broad, and as much woodland. Formerly £6; now it is worth £4.

William holds NORTON [in Broadwoodwidger] from Iudichael. Beorhtric held it TRE, and it paid geld for 1 virgate of land. There is land for 6 ploughs. In demesne is 1 plough, and 3 slaves; and 7 villans and 4 bordars with 5 ploughs. There are 70 acres of meadow, pasture half a league long and 3 furlongs broad, [and] woodland 3 furlongs long and 1 furlong broad. Formerly, as now, worth £3.

Waldin holds DOWNICARY from Iudichael. Cynestan held it TRE, and it paid geld for 1½ virgates of land. There is land for 6 ploughs. In demesne is 1 plough, and 3 slaves; and 8 villans and 6 cotsets with 3½ ploughs. There are 40 acres of meadow, and 20 acres of woodland, [and] pasture 2 furlongs long and 1 furlong broad. Formerly 50s; now it is worth 40s.

William holds SYDENHAM [in Marystow] from Iudichael. Beorhtric held it TRE, and it paid geld for 1 virgate of land.

There is land for 5 ploughs. In demesne is 1 plough, and 5 slaves; and 5 villans and 7 cotsets with 4 ploughs. There are 10 acres of meadow, and woodland 3 furlongs long and 1 furlong broad. Formerly 30s; now it is worth 40s.

Ralph holds ASHLEIGH from Iudichael. Grim held it TRE, and it paid geld for 1 virgate of land. # There is land for 5 ploughs. In demesne is 1 plough; and 7 villans and 3 bordars with 3 ploughs. There are 8 acres of meadow and 2 acres of alder-wood. Formerly 30s; now it is worth 25s.

Nigel holds MOOR from Iudichael. Ealdræd held it TRE, and it paid geld for 1 virgate of land. There is land for 5 ploughs. In demesne is 1 plough, and 6 slaves; and 8 villans and 1 cotset with 2 ploughs. There are 40 acres of meadow, pasture 1 league long and 4 furlongs broad, [and] woodland 2 furlongs long and 12 perches broad. Formerly 40s; now it is worth 30s.

Nigel holds BRADAFORD from Iudichael. Sæwine held it TRE, and it paid geld for half a virgate of land. There is land for 2 ploughs. There is 1 villan, and 8 acres of meadow, and 1 acre of pasture and 10 acres of woodland. Formerly, as now, worth 30d.

Nigel holds TILLISLOW from Iudichael. Sæwine held it TRE, and it paid geld for half a virgate of land. There is land for 2 ploughs. There are 1½ ploughs, with 1 slave and 1 villan and 2 bordars. There are 7 acres of meadow, and 2 acres of pasture and 10 acres of woodland. Formerly, as now, worth 10s.

Sæwine, who held these lands TRE, could go where he would.

Nigel holds MARY TAVY from Iudichael. Beorhtwig held it TRE, and it paid geld for 1 virgate of land. There is land for 4 ploughs. In demesne are 1½ ploughs, and 6 slaves; and 6 villans and 2 bordars with 1 plough. There are 12 acres of meadow, and pasture half a league long and 6 furlongs broad. Formerly 30s; now it is worth 40s.

To this manor have been added the lands of 3 thegns, Ælfric and Alwine and Ealdwulf; they held them │as 3│ manors and could go where they would TRE; and they paid geld for 1 virgate of land. There is land for 3 ploughs. There is half a plough, with 1 slave and 2 villans and 5 bordars. There are 12 acres of meadow, [and] pasture 1 league long and half a league broad. Formerly, as now, these 3 estates were worth 25s.

Nigel holds SYDENHAM DAMEREL from Iudichael. 4 thegns held it freely TRE, and it paid geld for half a hide. There is land for 8 ploughs. In demesne are 2 ploughs, and 2 slaves; and 5 villans and 8 bordars with 1 plough. There are 5 acres of meadow, and 20 acres of pasture and 20 acres of woodland. Formerly 40s; now it is worth 30s.

Iudichael himself holds CLAWTON. Alfred held it TRE, and it paid geld for 1 hide, less 1 ferding. There is land for 20 ploughs. In demesne are 4 ploughs, and 16 slaves; and 28 villans and 6 bordars with 11 ploughs. There is meadow 1

league long and half a league broad, and 1 league of pasture and 1 league of woodland. Formerly £10; now it is worth £8.

Iudichael himself holds PYWORTHY. Alfred held it TRE, and it paid geld for 3 virgates of land. There is land for 16 ploughs. In demesne are 5 ploughs, and 8 slaves; and 30 villans and 5 bordars with 5 ploughs. There is 1 league of meadow, and 1 league of pasture, [and] woodland 4 furlongs long and 20 perches broad. Formerly £11; now it is worth £8.

Iudichael himself holds TETCOTT. Ealdræd held it TRE, and it paid geld for half a hide. There is land for 7 ploughs. In demesne is 1 plough, and 6 slaves; and 12 villans and 4 bordars with 2½ ploughs. There are 30 acres of meadow, and 40 acres of woodland, [and] pasture half a league long and 4 furlongs broad. Formerly 100s; now it is worth £4.

To this manor has been added 1 ferding of land which Alwine held freely TRE. There is land for 1 plough. 2 villans have this [plough] there. Formerly, as now, worth 10s.

[Folio 109: DEVONSHIRE]

Æthelwulf holds "LIDEMORE" from Iudichael. The same man held it TRE, and it paid geld for 1 ferding. There is land for 2 ploughs, which are there. Formerly, 25s; now it is worth 20s.

William holds BRADFORD [in Pyworthy] from Iudichael. Æthelgifu held it TRE, and it paid geld for 1 ferding. There is land for 2 ploughs. There is 1 plough, and 2 slaves. [There is] meadow 3 furlongs long and 1 furlong broad, [and] pasture 2 furlongs long and 1 furlong broad. Formerly, as now, worth 10s.

Ralph holds HENFORD from Iudichael. Brothir held it TRE, and it paid geld for 1 virgate of land. There is land for 3 ploughs. There are 2 ploughs, with 1 slave and 1 villan and 3 bordars. There are 15 acres of meadow, and 15 acres of woodland and half a league of pasture. Formerly 12s; now it is worth 15s.

Iudichael himself holds BRIDFORD. Alwine held it TRE, and it paid geld for 2 hides. There is land for 12 ploughs. In demesne are 2 ploughs, and 4 slaves; and 20 villans and 7 bordars with 9 ploughs. There are 14 acres of meadow, and 70 acres of pasture, [and] woodland 1 league long and 1 furlong broad. Formerly, as now, worth £3.

Turgis holds NORTH BOVEY from Iudichael. John held it TRE, and it paid geld for 1 hide and 3 virgates of land. There is land for 8 ploughs. In demesne is 1 plough, and 5 slaves; and 11 villans and 6 bordars with 5 ploughs. There are 20 acres of meadow, and 10 acres of woodland and 1 league of pasture. Formerly, as now, worth 40s.

Ralph holds COMBE FISHACRE from Iudichael. Alweald held it TRE, and it paid geld for half a hide. There is land for 3 ploughs. There are 1½ ploughs, and 3 villans and 2 bordars, and 3 acres of meadow and 1 acre of pasture. Formerly, as now, worth 15s.

Ralph holds COMBE FISHACRE from Iudichael. Ælfric

held it TRE, and it paid geld for 1 virgate of land. There is land for 1 plough, which [plough] is there, with 2 villans and 1 bordar. There are 1½ acres of meadow. Formerly, as now, worth 10s.

The same Ralph holds LITTLEHEMPSTON from Iudichael. Algar held it TRE, and it paid geld for 1 virgate of land. There is land for 1 plough, which [plough] is there, with 4 bordars. Formerly [it was worth] 30d; now 5s.

The same Ralph holds LOVENTOR from Iudichael. Ottar held it TRE, and it paid geld for half a hide. There is land for 3 ploughs. In demesne is 1 plough, with 1 slave and 3 bordars, and 2 acres of meadow, and 5 acres of pasture and 2 acres of woodland. Formerly 5s; now it is worth 10s.

The same Ralph holds SHIPHAY from Iudichael. Ælfric held it. TRE, and it paid geld for 1 virgate of land. There is land for 2 ploughs, which are there, with 1 slave and 1 villan and 5 bordars. There are 5 acres of meadow and 2 acres of pasture. Formerly 5s; now it is worth 10s.

The same Ralph holds LUPTON from Iudichael. Ottar held it TRE, and it paid geld for 1 virgate of land. There is land for 3 ploughs. There are 2 ploughs, with 1 slave, and 2 villans and 2 bordars, and 4 acres of woodland. Formerly 5s; now it is worth 10s.

Iudichael himself holds BRIXHAM. Ulf held it TRE, and it paid geld for 2½ hides. There is land for 10 ploughs. In demesne are 2 ploughs, and 12 slaves; and 15 villans and 12 bordars with 8 ploughs. There are 4 acres of meadow, and 12 acres of pasture and 12 acres of woodland. Formerly £3; now it is worth £4.

Iudichael himself holds CHURSTON FERRERS. Ulf held it TRE, and it paid geld for 1½ hides. There is land for 6 ploughs. In demesne are 2 ploughs, and 7 slaves; and 3 cottars and 8 villans and 7 bordars with 4 ploughs. There are 15 acres of woodland and 12 acres of pasture. Formerly, as now, worth 60s.

Warin holds COLETON from Iudichael. Alweard held it TRE, and it paid geld for half a hide. There is land for 2 ploughs, which are there, with 1 slave and 5 villans and 2 bordars, and 4 acres of pasture. Formerly 5s; now it is worth 15s.

Iudichael himself holds LODDISWELL. Heca held it TRE, and it paid geld for 2 hides. There is land for 12 ploughs. In demesne are 2 ploughs, and 8 slaves; and 20 villans and 10 bordars and 6 cottars with 8 ploughs. There is a fishery rendering 30 salmon, and 13 acres of meadow, and 1 league of woodland and half a league of pasture. Formerly, as now, worth 100s.

Iudichael himself holds THURLESTONE. John held it TRE, and it paid geld for 2 hides. There is land for 6 ploughs. In demesne are 2 ploughs, and 5 slaves; and 15 villans and 6 bordars and 4 cottars with 6 ploughs. There are 2 acres of meadow and 2 acres of pasture. Formerly £4; now it is worth £3.

A knight holds from Iudichael 1 virgate of land of this manor and he has 1 plough there, and 2 villans and 3 bordars with half a plough. Formerly 5s; now it is worth 10s.

Osbern holds BAGTON from Iudichael. Algar held it TRE, and it paid geld for half a hide. There is land for 2 ploughs, which are there, and 3 villans and 3 bordars and 2 slaves, and 2 acres of meadow and 2 acres of pasture. Formerly, as now, worth 15s.

Turgis holds COLLATON from Iudichael. Cola held it TRE, and it paid geld for half a hide. There is land for 3 ploughs. There is 1 plough, with 3 villans and 1 bordar. There is half an acre of meadow, and 2 acres of pasture and 6 acres of woodland. Formerly 20s; now it is worth 5s.

Ralph holds SOUTH HUISH [near Thurlestone] from Iudichael. Algar held it TRE, and it paid geld for 1 hide. There is land for 4 ploughs. In demesne is 1 plough, and 2 slaves; and 6 villans and 4 bordars with 3 ploughs. There are 6 acres of meadow and 20 acres of pasture. Formerly, as now, worth 25s.

Ralph holds GALMPTON [near Thurlestone] from Iudichael. Alweard held it TRE, and it paid geld for 1 hide. There is land for 5 ploughs. In demesne is 1 plough, with 1 slave; and 8 villans and 6 bordars with 4 ploughs. Formerly 40s; now it is worth 50s.

Fulk holds WEST PORTLEMOUTH from Iudichael. Heca held it TRE, and it paid geld for 1 hide. There is land for 4 ploughs. In demesne is 1 plough, with 1 slave and 3 bordars, and 2 acres of meadow and 60 acres of pasture. Formerly, 40s; now it is worth 10s.

Fulk holds ILTON from Iudichael. Algar held it TRE, and it paid geld for half a hide. There is land for 3 ploughs. There is 1 plough, with 1 slave and 1 villan and 4 bordars, and 2 acres of meadow. Formerly 20s; now it is worth 5s.

Fulk holds ALSTON from Iudichael. Alwine held it TRE, and it paid geld for half a hide. There is land for 2 ploughs. There are 1½ ploughs, and 3 bordars, and 2 acres of meadow and 3 acres of pasture. Formerly 20s; now it is worth 10s.

Odo holds SOAR from Iudichael. Algar held it TRE, and it paid geld for 1 hide. There is land for 4 ploughs. In demesne is 1 plough, and 2 slaves; and 1 villan and 3 bordars with 1½ ploughs. There is 1 acre of meadow, and 100 acres of pasture and 4 acres of scrubland. Formerly 40s; now it is worth 20s.

Fulk holds SORLEY from Iudichael. Algar held it TRE, and it paid geld for half a hide. There is land for 3 ploughs. In demesne is 1 plough, with 1 slave; and 3 villans and 4 bordars with 2 ploughs, and 1 acre of meadow. Formerly 10s; now it is worth 15s.

Robert holds POULSTON from Iudichael. Beorhtweald held it TRE, and it paid geld for 1 virgate of land. There is land for 1 plough. There are 1½ ploughs, and 3 slaves and 2 villans and 2 bordars, and half an acre of meadow. Formerly 5s; now it is worth 10s.

Ralph holds CURTISKNOWLE from Iudichael. Alwine held it TRE, and it paid geld for half a hide. There is land for 3 ploughs. There are 1½ ploughs, and 2 villans and 5 bordars, and 5 acres of pasture, and 5 acres of woodland and half an acre of meadow. Formerly 10s; now it is worth 15s.

Ralph holds BROADLEY from Iudichael. Alwine held it TRE, and it paid geld for 1 virgate of land. There is land for 2 ploughs. In demesne is 1 plough, with 1 slave; and 3 villans and 4 bordars with 1½ ploughs, and 1 acre of scrubland. Formerly 10s; now it is worth 15s.

Ralph holds NORTH HUISH [near Diptford] from Iudichael. Alwine held it TRE, and it paid geld for 3 virgates of land. There is land for 6 ploughs. In demesne is 1 plough, and 3 slaves; and 5 villans and 7 bordars with 4 ploughs. There are 2 acres of meadow. Formerly, as now, worth 30s.

Colbert holds WOOLSTON from Iudichael. Uhtræd held it TRE, and it paid geld for half a hide. There is land for 3 ploughs, which are there, and 3 slaves and 3 villans and 3 bordars, and 2 acres of meadow. Formerly 10s; now it is worth 15s.

Iudichael himself holds CORNWORTHY. Ulf held it TRE, and it paid geld for 3 hides. There is land for 13 ploughs. In demesne are 2 ploughs, and 8 slaves; and 20 villans and 15 bordars with 8 ploughs. There is a mill rendering 15s, and a fishery rendering 30 salmon, and 100 acres of pasture, and 30 acres of woodland and 70 acres of scrubland. Formerly, as now, worth 60s.

Iudichael himself holds [East and West] CHARLETON. Heca held it TRE, and it paid geld for 5 hides. There is land for 15 ploughs. In demesne are 2 ploughs, and 11 slaves; and 20 villans and 15 bordars with 8 ploughs. There are 5 acres of meadow and 2 acres of pasture. Formerly, as now, worth 100s.

William holds [East and West] LEIGH [in Harberton] from Iudichael. Osmær held it TRE, and it paid geld for half a hide. There is land for 2 ploughs. In demesne is 1 plough, and 2 slaves; and 3 villans and 3 bordars with 1 plough. There are 10 acres of pasture and 10 acres of pasture. Formerly, as now, worth 15s.

William holds SOUTH POOL from Iudichael. Algar held it TRE, and it paid geld for 2 hides. There is land for 4 ploughs. In demesne is 1 plough, and 3 slaves; and 6 villans and 7 bordars with 3 ploughs. There are 4 acres of meadow and 10 acres of scrubland. Formerly, as now, worth 20s.

William holds COMBE [in South Pool] from Iudichael. Alric held it TRE, and it paid geld for half a hide. There is land for 2 ploughs, which are there, with 1 slave, and 6 villans and 4 bordars, and half an acre of meadow and 2 acres of scrubland. Formerly, as now, worth 10s.

Turgis holds SOUTH ALLINGTON from Iudichael. Goda held it TRE, and it paid geld for 1 hide.

[Folio 109V: DEVONSHIRE]

There is land for 2 ploughs, which are there, and 4 villans and 4 bordars and 2 slaves. There are 1½ acres of meadow and 15 acres of pasture. Formerly, as now, worth 15s.

Turgis holds STANCOMBE from Iudichael. Snot held it TRE, and it paid geld for half a hide. There is land for 2 ploughs, which are there, and 2 villans and 3 bordars, and 1 acre of meadow. Formerly, as now, worth 10s.

Ralph holds MALSTON from Iudichael. Beorhtric held it TRE, and it paid geld for 1 hide. There is land for 4 ploughs, which are there, with 1 slave, and 6 villans and 4 bordars, and 2 acres of meadow and 5 acres of scrubland. Formerly, as now, worth 40s.

Ralph holds FORD [in Chivelstone] from Iudichael. Ottar held it TRE, and it paid geld for 1 hide. There is land for 2 ploughs. In demesne is 1 plough, with 1 bordar; and 2 villans with 2 ploughs. There are 4 acres of meadow, and 6 acres of pasture and 15 acres of scrubland. Formerly, as now, worth 10s.

Ralph holds CHIVELSTONE from Iudichael. Ælfric held it TRE, and it paid geld for 1 hide. There is land for 3 ploughs, which are there, and 3 villans and 3 bordars, and 3 acres of meadow and 6 acres of pasture. Formerly, as now, worth 15s.

The clerks of ST MARY'S hold FOLLATON from Iudichael. Ælfric held it TRE, and it paid geld for 1 virgate of land. There is land for 2 ploughs. There is 1 plough, with 1 slave and 1 villan, and 1 acre of meadow and 1 acre of scrubland. Formerly 8s; now it is worth 10s.

Iudichael himself holds [East and West] WORTHELE. Alwine held it TRE, and it paid geld for 1 hide. There is land for 5 ploughs. In demesne are 2 ploughs, and 5 slaves; and 7 villans and 7 bordars with 4 ploughs. There are 10 acres of meadow, and 100 acres of pasture and 8 acres of scrubland. Formerly, as now, worth £6.

Iudichael himself holds [East and West] LEIGH [in Modbury]. Alwine held it TRE, and it paid geld for 1 hide. There is land for 5 ploughs. In demesne are 2 ploughs, and 5 slaves; and 7 villans and 2 bordars with 3 ploughs. There are 3 acres of meadow, and 12 acres of pasture and 12 acres of scrubland. Formerly, as now, worth £6.

Turgis holds BUTTERFORD from Iudichael. Alric held it TRE, and it paid geld for half a hide. There is land for 3 ploughs. There are 2 ploughs, and 2 slaves and 4 villans and 2 bordars, and 1 acre of meadow and 2 acres of scrubland. Formerly 20s; now it is worth 15s.

Turgis holds BUTTERFORD from Iudichael. Tovi held it TRE, and it paid geld for half a hide. There is land for 2 ploughs. There 2 villans have half a plough, and [there is] half an acre of meadow. Formerly 10s; now it is worth 5s.

Ralph holds STADBURY from Iudichael. Tovi held it TRE, and it paid geld for 1 virgate of land. There is land for 3 ploughs, which are there, and 2 slaves and 5 villans and 4 bordars, and 20 acres of woodland. Formerly, as now, worth 15s.

Ralph holds RINGMORE [near Bigbury] from Iudichael. Heca held it TRE, and it paid geld for 1½ hides. There is land for 6 ploughs. In demesne are 2 ploughs, and 2 slaves; and 6 villans and 6 bordars with 3 ploughs, and 6 acres of meadow and 2 acres of pasture. Formerly, as now, worth 30s.

Ralph holds OKENBURY from Iudichael. Tovi held it TRE, and it paid geld for half a hide. There is land for 3 ploughs, which are there, with 1 slave, and 5 villans and 2 bordars, and 2 acres of meadow. Formerly, as now, worth 40s.

Ralph holds BLACHFORD from Iudichael. Alwine held it TRE, and it paid geld for 1 virgate of land. There is land for 3 ploughs, which are there, and 3 slaves and 4 villans, and 2 acres of meadow, and 20 acres of woodland and 1½ leagues of pasture. Formerly, as now, worth 10s.

Ralph holds LAMBSIDE from Iudichael. Tovi held it TRE, and it paid geld for 1½ hides. There is land for 6 ploughs. In demesne is 1 plough, and 3 slaves; and 6 villans and 12 bordars with 3 ploughs. There are 3 acres of meadow. Formerly, as now, worth 30s.

Waldin holds MEMBLAND from Iudichael. Ælfric held it TRE, and it paid geld for 1 hide. There is land for 5 ploughs. There are 2½ ploughs, with 1 slave and 5 villans and 3 bordars. There are 4 acres of meadow and 1 acre of scrubland. Formerly, as now, worth 20s.

Iudichael himself holds EGGBUCKLAND [in Plymouth]. Heca held it TRE, and it paid geld for 1 hide. There is land for 6 ploughs. In demesne are 2 ploughs, and 10 slaves; and 10 villans and 8 bordars with 6 ploughs. There is a salt-pan rendering 2s, and 1 acre of meadow, and 200 acres of woodland, [and] pasture half a league long and 2 furlongs broad. Formerly, as now, worth 50s.

Odo holds MUTLEY [in Plymouth] from Iudichael. Godwine held it TRE, and it paid geld for 1 virgate of land. There is land for 1 plough. 2 villans have this [plough] there. There are 3 acres of pasture and 2 acres of woodland. Formerly, as now, worth 5s.

Odo holds MUTLEY [in Plymouth] from Iudichael. Alwine held it TRE, and it paid geld for 1 virgate of land. There is land for 1 plough. There 1 villan and 2 bordars have half a plough. There is 1 acre of meadow and 3 acres of scrubland. Formerly, as now, worth 5s.

The same Odo holds "LEURICESTONE" from Iudichael. Sæwulf held it TRE, and it paid geld for 1 virgate of land. There is land for 2 ploughs, which are there, with 1 slave and 2 villans. There are 3 acres of meadow and 8 acres of woodland. Formerly, as now, worth 10s.

The same Odo holds WESTON [in Plymouth]. Wulfnoth held it TRE, and it paid geld for 3 virgates of land. There is land for 4 ploughs. In demesne are 2 ploughs, and 3 slaves; and 1 villan and 1 bordar with half a plough. There are 3 acres of meadow, and 4 acres of pasture and 4 acres of woodland. Formerly 10s; now it is worth 30s.

The same Odo holds 'BURRINGTON' [in Plymouth]. Alwine held it TRE, and it paid geld for 1 ferding. There is land for 1½ ploughs. However, there are 2 ploughs, and 2 slaves and 3 villans, and 3 acres of meadow. Formerly, as now, worth 10s.

The same Odo holds MANADON [in Plymouth] from Iudichael. Colbert held it TRE, and it paid geld for half a hide. There is land for 3 ploughs. There are 2 ploughs, with 1 slave, and 3 villans with 1 bordar, and 2 acres of meadow and 30 acres of woodland. Formerly 20s; now it is worth 12s6d.

The same Odo holds WHITLEIGH [in Plymouth] from Iudichael. Godwine held it TRE, and it paid geld for half a hide. There is land for 2 ploughs. There is 1 plough, with 1 slave, and 2 villans with 1 bordar, and 15 acres of scrubland. Formerly 2s; now it is worth 7s6d.

The same Odo holds COLERIDGE [in Plymouth] from Iudichael. Eadmær held it TRE, and it paid geld for half a virgate of land. There is land for 2 ploughs. There are 2 bordars, and 30 acres of scrubland. It is worth 15d; formerly it was waste.

Stephen holds COMPTON [in Plymouth] from Iudichael. Oswulf held it TRE, and it paid geld for 1 hide and 1 virgate of land. There is land for 4 ploughs, which are there, and 2 slaves and 6 villans and 4 bordars, and 1 acre of meadow and 20 acres of scrubland. Formerly, as now, worth 30s.

William holds MEAVY [Goodameavy, Hoo Meavy or Meavy] from Iudichael. Alweard held it TRE, and it paid geld for half a hide. There is land for 2 ploughs. There is 1 plough, with 1 slave and 2 bordars, and 2 acres of meadow and half an acre of scrubland. [There is] pasture half a league long and 2 furlongs broad. Formerly 5s; now it is worth 7s6d.

Turgis holds MEAVY [Goodameavy, Hoo Meavy or Meavy] from Iudichael. Alwine held it TRE, and it paid geld for 1 virgate of land. There is land for 2 ploughs. There is 1 plough, with 1 slave, and 3 villans and 2 bordars, and 5 furlongs of pasture and 4 furlongs of woodland. Formerly [it was worth] 5s; now 10s.

Turgis holds MEAVY [Goodameavy, Hoo Meavy or Meavy] from Iudichael. Edward held it TRE, and it paid geld for 1½ virgates of land. There is land for 4 ploughs. There are 4 villans and 2 bordars and 2 slaves with 1½ ploughs. There are 3 acres of meadow, and half a league of pasture, [and] woodland 5 furlongs long and 2 furlongs broad. Formerly 15s; now it is worth 30s.

Nigel holds MEAVY [Goodameavy, Hoo Meavy or Meavy] from Iudichael. Oswulf held it TRE, and it paid geld for 1 virgate of land. There is land for 1 plough. There is half a plough, with 1 villan and 1 bordar, and 3 acres of meadow. Formerly 5s; now it is worth 10s.

William holds [East and West] SHERFORD [near Plymouth] from Iudichael. Ælfric held it TRE, and it paid geld for half a hide. There is land for 3 ploughs. There are 2 ploughs, and 2 slaves and 4 villans and 6 bordars, and 2 acres of meadow and 1 acre of moor. Formerly, as now, worth 20s.

The same William holds CHITTLEBURN from Iudichael [...]. Æthelric held it TRE, and it paid geld for half a hide. There is land for 2 ploughs. There is scrubland 2 furlongs long and half a furlong broad. Formerly 5s; now it is worth 12d.

The same William holds WOLLATON from Iudichael.

Ælfric; held it TRE, and it paid geld for half a hide. There is land for 2 ploughs. There 4 villans and 4 bordars have half a plough, and there is half an acre of meadow and 2 furlongs of pasture. Formerly 4s; now it is worth 5s.

The same William holds BRIXTON [near Yealmpton] from Iudichael. Siduwine held it TRE, and it paid geld for half a hide. There is land for 2 ploughs. There is land for 2 ploughs, which are there, and 4 villans and 5 bordars, and 1 acre of meadow. Formerly, as now, worth 15s.

The same William holds BRIXTON [near Yealmpton] from Iudichael. Ælfric; held it TRE, and it paid geld for half a hide. There is land for 2 ploughs. There 4 villans and 5 bordars have 1 plough, and [there is] 1 acre of meadow. Formerly, as now, worth 5s.

The same William holds DOWN THOMAS from Iudichael. Ælfric held it TRE, and it paid geld for 3 ferdings of land. There is land for 3 ploughs. There are 2 ploughs, with 1 slave and 4 villans, and 12 acres of pasture. Formerly, as now, worth 15s.

The same William holds STADDISCOMBE from Iudichael. Ælfric held it TRE,

[Folio 110: DEVONSHIRE]

[and] it paid geld for 1 virgate of land. There is land for 2 ploughs. There is 1 plough, with 1 villan and 1 bordar, and half an acre of meadow and 20 acres of pasture. [There is] woodland 2 furlongs long and 1 furlong broad. Formerly 5s; now it is worth 7s6d.

William holds STADDON from Iudichael. Alwine held it TRE, and it paid geld for 1 virgate of land. There is land for 2 ploughs. There is 1 bordar, and 20 acres of pasture, [and] woodland 1 furlong long and half a furlong broad. Formerly, as now, worth 5s.

Ralph holds BRIXTON [in Shaugh Prior] from Iudichael. Almær held it TRE, and it paid geld for 1 virgate of land. There is land for 3 ploughs. There are 2 ploughs, and 4 villans and 2 bordars, and 2 acres of meadow and 10 acres of pasture. Formerly, as now, worth 10s.

The same Ralph holds BACCAMORE from Iudichael. Elous held it TRE, and it paid geld for half a hide. There is land for 4 ploughs. In demesne is 1 plough; and 4 villans and 3 bordars with 1 plough. There are 4 acres of meadow, and 20 acres of scrubland, and pasture 1 league long and half a league broad.

Another BACCAMORE has been added to this manor. Sigeric held it TRE. These 2 estates together pay geld for half a hide. They are worth 20s.

William holds 'WALFORD' [in Plympton St Mary] from Iudichael. Ælfric held it TRE, and it paid geld for half a virgate of land. There is land for 1 plough. There is half a plough, with 1 villan and 1 bordar. [There is] woodland 2 furlongs long and 1 furlong broad. Formerly, as now, worth 5s.

Ralph holds HOLLAND from Iudichael. Ælfric and Algar held it TRE, and it paid geld for 1 virgate of land. There is land for 2 ploughs. There is 1 villan and 1 bordar, and 2 acres of meadow and 8 acres of woodland. Formerly 10s; now it is worth 5s.

Waldin holds LANGDON from Iudichael. Heca held it TRE, and it paid geld for half a hide. There is land for 2 ploughs, which are there, with 1 slave, and 4 villans and 3 bordars, and 2 acres of meadow and 4 acres of pasture. Formerly, as now, worth 10s.

Waldin holds LANGDON from Iudichael. Goda held it TRE, and it paid geld for half a hide. There is land for 2 ploughs. There 4 villans and 3 bordars have 1 plough. There are 2 acres of meadow and 6 acres of pasture. Formerly, as now, worth 10s.

Turgis holds COLDSTONE from Iudichael. Ælfric held it TRE, and it paid geld for half a hide. There is land for 3 ploughs. There are 2 ploughs, with 1 slave, and 3 villans and 2 bordars, and 4½ acres of meadow and 14 acres of woodland. [There is] pasture half a league long and 2 furlongs broad. Formerly, as now, worth 10s.

The same Turgis holds 'FERNHILL' [in Shaugh Prior] from Iudichael. Alwine held it TRE, and it paid geld for 1 ferding. There is land for 1 plough. There is 1 villan, and 1 acre of meadow, and 10 acres of woodland, [and] pasture half a league long and 2 furlongs broad. Formerly, as now, worth 3s.

The same Turgis holds PITHILL from Iudichael. Ælfric held it TRE, and it paid geld for 1 ferding. There is land for 1 plough. There 2 villans have half a plough, and [there is] half an acre of meadow, [and] woodland 2 furlongs long and half a furlong broad. Formerly 2s; now it is worth 4s.

The same Turgis holds SHAUGH PRIOR from Iudichael. Ælfric held it TRE, and it paid geld for 1 virgate of land. There is land for 1½ ploughs. There 3 villans with 1 bordar and 1 slave have 1 plough. There is half an acre of meadow, and pasture half a league long and 4 furlongs broad. Formerly, as now, worth 10s.

The same Turgis holds SHAUGH PRIOR from Iudichael. Ælfric held it TRE, and it paid geld for 1 virgate of land. There is land for 1½ ploughs. There 4 villans with 1 bordar have 1 plough. There are 5 acres of woodland, and pasture 4 furlongs broad and half a league long. Formerly, as now, worth 10s.

Ralph holds 'TORRIDGE' [in Plympton St Mary] from Iudichael. Ælfric held it TRE, and it paid geld for 1 virgate of land. There is land for 1 plough. However, there are 1½ ploughs, with 1 slave and 2 villans and 1 bordar, and 1 acre of meadow, and 12 acres of pasture and 8 acres of scrubland. Formerly 5s; now it is worth 10s.

The same Ralph holds LOUGHTOR from Iudichael. Ælfric held it TRE, and it paid geld for 1 virgate of land. There is land for 2 ploughs. There are 1½ ploughs, with 1 slave and 5 villans and 3 bordars, and 30 acres of pasture and 5 acres of woodland. Formerly, as now, [worth] 12s.

The same Ralph holds ELFORDLEIGH from Iudichael.

Ælfric held it TRE, and it paid geld for 1 ferding. There is land for 1½ ploughs. There 3 villans have half a plough, and [there are] 1½ acres of meadow, and 30 acres of pasture and 10 acres of scrubland. Formerly, as now, worth 3s.

Ralph holds WOODFORD from Iudichael. Almær held it TRE, and it paid geld for half a hide. There is land for 2 ploughs. There is 1 plough, with 1 slave, and 2 villans and 2 bordars, and 1 acre of meadow, and 1 salt-pan and 1 fishery. [There is] woodland 3 furlongs long and 1 furlong broad.

Another WOODFORD has been added to this [manor]. Ælfric held it TRE, and it paid geld for half a hide. There is land for 2 ploughs. There 3 villans and 2 bordars with 1 slave have 1 plough. [There is] pasture 1 league long and half a league broad. These 2 estates are worth 40s.

Stephen holds HOOE from Iudichael. Ælfric held it TRE, and it paid geld for 1 virgate of land. There is land for 2 ploughs, which are there, with 1 slave, and 6 villans and 2 bordars, and 5 acres of pasture. Formerly, as now, worth 20s.

William holds HALWELL from Iudichael. Ælfric held it TRE, and it paid geld for half a hide. There is land for 2 ploughs. There is half a plough, with 1 slave and 1 villan and 3 bordars, and 2 acres of meadow and 2 acres of woodland. Formerly 12s; now it is worth 10s.

XVIII. The land of William de Moyon

WILLIAM de Moyon holds CLAYHANGER from the king, and Robert [holds] of him. Uhtraelig;d held it TRE, and it paid geld for 3 virgates of land and 3½ ferdings. There is land for 5 ploughs. In demesne are 2 ploughs, and 2 slaves; and 5 villans and 3 bordars with 2 ploughs. There are 12 acres of meadow, and 12 acres of pasture and 3 acres of scrubland. Formerly 30s; now it is worth 20s.

XIX. The land of William Chevre

WILLIAM Chevre has in Exeter 2 houses which TRE rendered 16d a year in customary dues.

William himself holds VIRWORTHY from the king. Godric held it TRE, and it paid geld for half a virgate of land. There is land for 1 plough, which [plough] is there, and 2 slaves, and 10 acres of meadow and 20 acres of pasture. Formerly 10s; now it is worth 20s.

Ansketil holds INSTAPLE from William. Godric held it TRE, and it paid geld for half a virgate of land. There is land for 1 plough. Formerly 7s; now it is worth 5s.

Ansketil holds WEST PUTFORD from William. 2 thegns [...] held it TRE, and it paid geld for 1 virgate of land. There is land for 4 ploughs. In demesne is 1 plough, with 1 slave and 1 villan, and 10 acres of meadow and 10 acres of pasture. Formerly 20s; now it is worth 7s6d.

William himself holds HUNTSHAW. Alweard held it TRE, and it paid geld for 1 hide. There is land for 10 ploughs. In demesne are 3 ploughs, and 5 slaves; and 12 villans with 4 ploughs, and 2 swineherds rendering 20 pigs, and 10 acres of meadow and 30 acres of woodland. [There is] pasture 1 league long and half a league broad. Formerly, as now, worth £4.

Ansketil holds EASTLEIGH from William. Alweard held it TRE, and it paid geld for half a hide. There is land for 5 ploughs. In demesne are 2 ploughs, and 2 slaves; and 6 villans with 1½ ploughs, and 2 acres of meadow, and 1 acre of woodland and 40 acres of pasture. Formerly, as now, worth 25s.

To this manor has been added half a virgate of land; and it has been concealed, so the king has no geld from it.

William himself holds SHILLINGFORD ABBOT. Eadmær held it TRE, and it paid geld for 2 hides, less 1 virgate of land. There is land for 8 ploughs. In demesne are 2 ploughs, and 4 slaves; and 6 villans and 9 bordars with 3 ploughs. There are 4 acres of meadow and 6 acres of scrubland. Formerly £3; now it is worth £4.

William himself holds EXMINSTER. Viking held it TRE, and it paid geld for 1 hide. There is land for 5 ploughs. In demesne are 2 ploughs, and 4 slaves; and 6 villans and 2 bordars with 2 ploughs. There are 6 acres of meadow and 6 acres of pasture. Formerly 20s; now it is worth 30s.

Ralph holds MATFORD from William. Viking held it TRE, and it paid geld for half a virgate of land. There is land for 1 plough, which [plough] is there, with 1 slave and 1 bordar. There are 3 acres of meadow and 4 acres of pasture. Formerly, as now, worth 5s.

Robert holds HACCOMBE from William. Ottar held it TRE, and it paid geld for half a hide. There is land for 4 ploughs. In demesne are 2 ploughs, and 2 slaves; and 4 villans and 3 bordars with 1 plough. There are 2 acres of meadow, and 20 acres of pasture, and 1 salt-pan and 1 fishery. Formerly 20s; now it is worth 30s.

William himself holds WOOLACOMBE. Edwin held it TRE, and it paid geld for 2 hides. There is land for 10 ploughs. In demesne are 4 ploughs, and 7 slaves; and 12 villans with 6 ploughs. There are 9 acres of meadow, and 30 acres of pasture and 20 acres of scrubland. Formerly, as now, worth £13.15s.

William himself holds NORTH BUCKLAND [in Braunton]. Beorhtric held it TRE, and it paid geld for 1 hide. There is land for 6 ploughs. In demesne are 3 ploughs, and 5 slaves; and 10 villans and 2 bordars with 3 ploughs. There is 1 acre of meadow, and 60 acres of pasture and 15 acres of woodland. Formerly 30s; now it is worth 60s.

[Folio 110V: DEVONSHIRE]

Godfrey holds BUCKLAND [in Braunton] from William. Ulf held it TRE, and it paid geld for 1 virgate of land. There is land for 3 ploughs, which are there, with 1 slave and 4 villans. There is 1 acre of meadow, and 5 acres of woodland and 50 acres of pasture. Formerly, as now, worth 20s.

Ralph holds ASH [in Braunton] from William. Alweard held it TRE, and it paid geld for 1 virgate of land. There is land for 3 ploughs, which are there, and 2 slaves and 3 villans with 1 bordar. There are 3 acres of meadow, and 40 acres of pasture and 40 acres of scrubland. Formerly, as now, worth 20s.

William himself holds COUNTISBURY. Æthelmær held it TRE, and it paid geld for half a hide. There is land for 10 ploughs. In demesne are 4 ploughs, and 15 slaves; and 12 villans and 6 bordars with 6 ploughs, and 1 swineherd rendering 10 pigs. There are 2 acres of meadow, and 50 acres of woodland, [and] pasture 1 league long and 1 furlong broad. Formerly 20s; now it is worth £4.

William himself holds LYNTON and [East and West] ILKERTON as 1 manor. Æthelweard and Algar held them TRE as 2 manors, and they paid geld for 1 hide. There is land for 12 ploughs. In demesne are 5 ploughs, and 12 slaves; and 13 villans with 1 bordar have 7 ploughs. There are 7 furlongs of woodland, and pasture 2 furlongs long and half a league broad. Formerly 35s; now it is worth £7.

William himself holds [East and West] LYN. Algar held it TRE, and it paid geld for 3 virgates of land. There is land for 7 ploughs. In demesne are 2 ploughs, and 5 slaves; and 9 villans and 5 bordars with 5 ploughs. There is a new mill, and pasture 2 leagues long and half a league broad, [and] woodland half a league long and 2 furlongs broad. Formerly 40s; now it is worth £4.

Fulcold holds 'BADGWORTHY' [in Brendon] from William, which has been added to the aforesaid manor of [East and West] Lyn. TRE it paid geld for 1 virgate of land. There is land for 2 ploughs, which are there, with 1 slave and 1 villan. There are 5 acres of meadow and 30 acres of pasture. It is worth 10s.

William himself holds [North and South] RADWORTHY [in North Molton]. Æthelweard held it TRE, and it paid geld for 1 virgate of land. There is land for 3 ploughs, which are there, and 8 villans and 4 slaves, and 1 acre of meadow and 40 acres of pasture. [There is] woodland 1 league long and 1 furlong broad. Formerly 15s; now it is worth 60s.

Ralph holds WHIMPLE from William. Uhtræd held it TRE, and it paid geld for 1 hide and half a virgate of land. There is land for 4 ploughs. In demesne are 1½ ploughs, with 1 slave; and 2 villans with 1 plough. There are 19 acres of meadow, and 40 acres of pasture and 9 acres of scrubland. Formerly 15s; now it is worth 30s.

Hamo holds PIRZWELL from William. Ælfric held it TRE, and it paid geld for 1 hide and 1 virgate of land. There is land for 4 ploughs. In demesne are 2 ploughs, and 5 slaves; and 8 villans and 4 bordars with 2 ploughs. There are 8 acres of meadow, and 14 acres of scrubland and 30 acres of pasture. Formerly 30s; now it is worth 40s.

The same Hamo holds "HEWISE" from William. Viking held it TRE, and it paid geld for half a hide. There is land for 1 plough. There are 7 acres of meadow. Formerly, as now, worth 5s.

Manfred holds COLEBROOK from William. Almær held it TRE, and it paid geld for half a hide. There is land for 2 ploughs. There are 1½ ploughs, and 2 slaves and 2 villans and

2 bordars, and 4 acres of meadow. Formerly, as now, worth 10s.

William himself holds CADELEIGH. Alweard held it TRE, and it paid geld for 3 virgates of land. There is land for 3 ploughs, which are there, and 3 slaves and 2 villans and 2 bordars, and 2 acres of meadow, and 8 acres of pasture and 4 acres of woodland. Formerly 20s; now it is worth 30s.

Ralph holds AWLISCOMBE from William. Æthelweard held it TRE, and it paid geld for half a hide. There is land for 2 ploughs. In demesne is 1 plough, with 1 slave; and 2 villans with 1 bordar and half a plough. There are 10 acres of meadow, and 10 acres of woodland and 12 acres of pasture. Formerly, as now, worth 15s.

Hamo holds AWLISCOMBE from William. Viking held it TRE, and it paid geld for 1 hide. There is land for 5 ploughs. In demesne are 2 ploughs, and 2 slaves; and 5 villans and 4 bordars with 1½ ploughs. There are 7 acres of meadow and 15 acres of pasture. Formerly, as now, worth 25s.

Warin holds WESTON [in Awliscombe] from William. Beorhtric held it TRE, and it paid geld for half a hide and 1 virgate of land and 1½ ferdings. There is land for 2 ploughs. There are 1½ ploughs, and 2 slaves and 1 villan and 3 bordars, and 5 acres of meadow and 2 furlongs of pasture.

William himself holds COMBEINTEIGNHEAD. Ælfric held it TRE, and it paid geld for half a hide. There is land for 4 ploughs. In demesne is 1 plough, and 2 slaves; and 1 villan and 6 bordars with 1 plough, and 5 acres of meadow. Formerly 10s; now it is worth 20s.

William himself holds [Higher, Lower and Middle] ROCOMBE. Eadric held it TRE, and it paid geld for half a hide. There is land for 3 ploughs. In demesne are 2 ploughs, and 2 slaves; and 2 villans and 3 bordars with 1 plough, and 1 acre of meadow and 10 acres of scrubland. Formerly 10s; now it is worth 30s.

William himself holds TEDBURN ST MARY. Burgræd held it TRE, and it paid geld for 1 hide. There is land for 5 ploughs. In demesne is 1 plough, and 2 slaves; and 8 villans and 7 bordars with 3 ploughs. There are 6 acres of meadow, and 40 acres of pasture and 40 acres of woodland. Formerly 20s; now it is worth 40s.

William himself holds BRADNINCH. Beorhtweald held it TRE, and it paid geld for 2½ hides. There is land for 20 ploughs. In demesne are 6 ploughs, and 7 slaves; and 42 villans and 16 bordars with 15 ploughs. There are 33 acres of meadow, and 200 acres of pasture, and 30 acres of woodland and 30 acres of scrubland. There is a mill rendering 5s. Formerly 100s; now it is worth £14.

William himself holds half a virgate of land in AWLISCOMBE. There 2 villans have 1 plough. It is worth 4s.

Ralph holds YOWLESTONE from William. Eadsige held it TRE, and it paid geld for 1 hide. There is land for 2 ploughs. Ralph holds half of this land | from William | and he has there 1 plough, and 2 slaves. There are 4 acres of meadow, and 12 acres of pasture and 6 acres of woodland. Formerly 12d; now it is worth 7s6d.

Warin holds half a hide of land in RAPSHAYES from William. There 3 villans have 3 oxen in a plough. There are 5 acres of meadow, and 1 acre of woodland, [and] pasture 1 furlong long and half a furlong broad. Formerly, as now, worth 30d.

William himself holds CRUWYSMORCHARD. Almær held it TRE, and it paid geld for 1 hide. He took this away from Æthelweard son of Toki after King William came to England. There is land for 20 ploughs. In demesne are 4 ploughs, and 7 slaves; and 20 villans and 4 bordars with 7 ploughs. There is 1 smith, and 40 acres of meadow, and 200 acres of pasture and 30 acres of woodland. Formerly 40s; now it is worth £6. William holds this [land] with Æthelweard's land.

Hamo holds MACKHAM from William. Almær held it TRE, and it paid geld for half a virgate of land. There is land for 1 plough. There is 1 villan. It is worth 30d. This land has been joined to Awliscombe.

William himself holds OAKFORD. Beorhtmær held it TRE, and it paid geld for 1 hide. There is land for 14 ploughs. In demesne are 4 ploughs, and 2 slaves; and 20 villans and 7 bordars with 9 ploughs. There is a mill rendering 30d, and 100 acres of woodland, and 12 acres of meadow and 8 acres of pasture. Formerly £3; now it is worth £6.

MILDON has been added to this manor. Edith held it TRE, and it paid geld for 1 virgate of land. There is land for 3 ploughs. There 8 villans have 2 ploughs, and [there are] 3 acres of meadow. Formerly 3s; now it is worth 10s.

William himself holds WHIPTON [in Exeter]. Viking held it TRE, and it paid geld for 1 hide. There is land for 8 ploughs. In demesne are 2 ploughs, and 7 slaves; and 5 villans and 3 bordars with 4 ploughs. There are 12 acres of meadow, and 100 acres of pasture and 2 acres of scrubland. Formerly 20s; now it is worth £6.

Ralph holds PUDDINGTON from William. Æthelweard held it TRE, and it paid geld for 1 hide. There is land for 8 ploughs. In demesne are 2 ploughs, and 3 slaves; and 8 villans and 6 bordars with 4 ploughs. There are 9 acres of meadow, and 30 acres of pasture and 6 acres of woodland. Formerly 20s; now it is worth 40s.

Beatrice holds BRADFORD TRACY [in Witheridge] from William. Almær held it TRE, and it paid geld for 1 virgate of land. There is land for 4 ploughs. In demesne is 1 plough, and 2 slaves; and 5 villans and 6 bordars with 2 ploughs. There are 6 acres of meadow and 6 acres of pasture. Formerly, as now, worth 20s.

"TOREDONE" has been added to this manor. Ælfric held it freely TRE, and it paid geld for half a virgate of land. There is land for 1 plough. It is worth 40d.

Robert holds BUCKLAND [in Combeinteignhead] from William. Alric held it TRE, and it paid geld for 1 virgate of land. There is land for 2 ploughs, which are there, and 3

villans and 3 bordars and 2 slaves. There is 1 acre of meadow and 25 acres of pasture. Formerly 6s; now it is worth 10s.

Warin holds IVEDON from William. Wulfnoth held it TRE, and it paid geld for 2 hides. There is land for 4 ploughs. There is 1 plough, with 1 villan and 1 bordar and with [sic] 1 slave. There are 12 acres of meadow and 2 furlongs of pasture. Formerly, as now, worth 10s.

Ralph holds IVEDON from William. Sæmær held it TRE, and it paid geld for 1 virgate of land. There is land for half a plough. Half a villan has this [half-plough] there. It is worth 30d. This land has been added to Awliscombe.

Warin holds MEMBURY from William. Ealdhild held it TRE, and it paid geld

[Folio 111: DEVONSHIRE]

for 1 hide. There is land for 3 ploughs. In demesne is 1 plough, with 1 slave; and 4 villans and 2 bordars with 1 plough. There are 6 acres of meadow, pasture 7 furlongs long and 2 broad, [and] woodland 6 furlongs long and 3 furlongs broad. Formerly, as now, worth 10s.

Eadwulf holds AXMINSTER from William. Viking held it TRE, and it paid geld for 1 virgate of land. There is land for 2 ploughs. There are 1½ ploughs, and 4 slaves and 12 bordars, and 8 acres of meadow, and common pasture. Formerly, as now, worth 20s.

Beatrice holds SOUTHLEIGH from William. Almær held it TRE, and it paid geld for 2 hides. There is land for 10 ploughs. In demesne are 2 ploughs, and 3 slaves; and 7 villans and 6 bordars with 3 ploughs. There are 15 acres of meadow, and 200 acres of pasture and 40 acres of woodland. Formerly 50s; now it is worth 40s.

XX. The land of William de Falaise

WILLIAM DE FALAISE holds COMBE MARTIN from the king. Beorhtric and Eadwig held it freely TRE, and it paid geld for 2 hides and 1 virgate of land. There is land for 20 ploughs. In demesne are 3 ploughs, and 9 slaves; and 18 villans and 10 bordars with 14 ploughs. There is pasture 1 league long and as much broad, and 5 acres of woodland. Formerly, as now, worth 100s.

William himself holds FURZE. Ealdceorl held it TRE, and it paid geld for half a virgate of land. There is land for 3 ploughs, and it is waste.

William himself holds PARRACOMBE. Beorhtweald held it TRE, and it paid geld for half a hide. There is land for 8 ploughs. In demesne are 2 ploughs, and 5 slaves; and 5 villans and 8 bordars with 4 ploughs. There are 8 acres of meadow, and 30 acres of woodland and 1 league of pasture. Formerly, as now, worth 40s.

Norman holds CHURCHILL from William. Beorhtweald held it TRE, and it paid geld for 1 virgate of land. There is land for 8 ploughs. In demesne is 1 plough, and 5 slaves; and 8 villans and 4 bordars with 4 ploughs. There is 1 league of pasture and 40 acres of woodland. Formerly, as now, worth 40s.

Roger holds 'BEARE' [?in East Worlington] from William. Beorhtweald held it TRE, and it paid geld for 1 virgate of land. There is land for 2 ploughs. There is 1 plough, with 1 slave and 2 bordars, and 3 acres of meadow and 1 league of pasture. Formerly, as now, worth 15s.

Peter holds WASHFORD PYNE from William. Cynegar held it TRE, and it paid geld for 1 virgate of land. There is land for 2 ploughs. There is 1 plough, and 3 bordars, and 4 acres of meadow and 15 acres of pasture. Formerly, as now, worth 5s.

Hugh holds [East or West] WORLINGTON [near Witheridge] from William. 2 thegns held it freely TRE, and it paid geld for 1 ferding. There is land for 1 plough. 2 villans have this [plough] there. There are 2 acres of meadow and half an acre of woodland. Formerly, as now, worth 10s.

William himself holds BRADFORD [in Witheridge]. Brungar held it TRE, and it paid geld for $1\frac{1}{2}$ ferdings. There is land for 1 plough. 1 villan has this [plough] there. There are 2 acres of meadow. Formerly, as now, worth 5s.

An Englishman holds [East, Higher or Lower] DENSHAM from William. Algar held it TRE, and it paid geld for half a virgate of land. There is land for 1 plough. Formerly, as now, worth 5s.

William himself holds COCKINGTON. Alric held it TRE, and it paid geld for 3 hides. There is land for 13 ploughs. In demesne are 5 ploughs, and 14 slaves; and 18 villans and 6 bordars with 7 ploughs. There are 15 acres of meadow, and 50 acres of pasture and 50 acres of woodland. Formerly, as now, worth 50s.

Of the same land Alric holds 1 virgate of land in 'DEWDON' [in Widecombe in the Moor], and it paid geld for as much. Formerly, as now, worth 10s. This land has been added to the above, and William holds them as 1 manor.

William himself holds HOLNE. Alwine held it TRE, and it paid geld for $1\frac{1}{2}$ hides. There is land for 12 ploughs. In demesne is 1 plough, and 8 slaves; and 13 villans and 7 bordars with 5 ploughs. There is 1 league of pasture and 1 league of woodland. Formerly, as now, worth £3.

Winemar holds STOKE [in Holne] from William. Wulfgifu held it TRE, and it paid geld for half a hide. There is land for 2 ploughs. There is 1 plough, with 1 slave, and 4 villans and 2 bordars, and half a league of pasture. [There is] woodland 1 league long and 1 furlong broad. Formerly, as now, worth 10s.

Four knights holds DEAN PRIOR from William. Alwine held it TRE, and it paid geld for 3 hides. There is land for 12 ploughs. In demesne are 3 ploughs, and 2 slaves; and 19 villans and 15 bordars with 6 ploughs. There are 10 acres of meadow, and 1 league of pasture and 6 acres of woodland. Formerly, as now, worth £4.

Of this land an Englishman holds from William as much land as renders 10s.

William himself holds RATTERY. Alwine held it TRE, and it paid geld for 3 hides. There is land for 12 ploughs. In demesne are 2 ploughs, and 6 slaves; and 13 villans and 4 bordars with 5 ploughs, and 2 swineherds rendering 8 pigs. There is half an acre of meadow and 5 acres of pasture. Of this land 2 knights hold 1 virgate of land and a half, and an Englishman 1 virgate of land. In demesne are 2 ploughs, and 2 slaves, and 8 villans and 7 bordars [...]. Formerly, as now, worth £3.10s.

William himself holds DARTINGTON. Alwine held it TRE, and it paid geld for 1 virgate of land. There is land for 15 ploughs. In demesne are 2 ploughs, and 9 slaves; and 13 villans and 7 bordars with 8 ploughs, and 2 swineherds rendering 21 pigs. There are 100 acres of pasture, woodland half a league long and $2\frac{1}{2}$ furlongs broad, and 30 acres of scrubland. Formerly, as now, worth £4.5s.

Ansketil holds 1 ferding of this land from William, and it paid geld for as much. TRE a thegn held it; and it is called Luscombe. There are $2\frac{1}{2}$ ploughs, and 4 villans with 1 slave, and half an acre of meadow. Formerly 10s; now it is worth 5s.

Reginald holds HARBOURNEFORD from William. Alric held it TRE, and it paid geld for half a hide. There is land for 4 ploughs. There are 3 villans and 2 bordars with 1 slave have 1 plough. There are 2 acres of meadow and 4 acres of woodland. Formerly 8s; now it is worth 10s.

Reginald holds [Great or Key's] ENGLEBOURNE from William. Alric held it TRE, and it paid geld for half a hide. There is land for 3 ploughs. There are $2\frac{1}{2}$ ploughs, and 4 bordars with 1 slave, and 10 acres of meadow. Formerly, as now, worth 20s.

XXI. The land of William de Poilley

WILLIAM DE POILLEY holds 'RADWORTHY' [in Challacombe] from the king. Alric held it TRE, and it paid geld for 1 virgate of land. There is land for 6 ploughs. In demesne is 1 plough, with 1 slave; and 3 villans with 2 oxen in a plough. There are 3 acres of meadow, and 20 acres of woodland and 2 leagues of pasture. Formerly 6s; now it is worth 10s.

William himself holds SHIRWELL. Wulfweard held it TRE, and it paid geld for 3 virgates of land. There is land for 8 ploughs. In demesne are 2 ploughs, and 4 slaves; and 8 villans with 3 ploughs. There is 1 acre of meadow, and 100 acres of woodland and 2 leagues of pasture. Formerly 20s; now it is worth 40s.

Of the same land 2 knights hold 1 virgate of land from William and they have 2 ploughs there.

William himself holds STOKE RIVERS. Alric held it TRE, and it paid geld for 3 virgates of land. There is land for 12 ploughs. In demesne are 2 ploughs, and 7 slaves; and 6 villans and 2 bordars with 3 ploughs. There is 1 acre of meadow, and

40 acres of pasture and 30 acres of woodland. Formerly 20s; now it is worth 40s.

William himself holds BEAWORTHY. Leofric held it TRE, and it paid geld for 1½ virgates of land. There is land for 8 ploughs. In demesne is 1 plough, and 3 slaves; and 3 villans with 1 plough. There are 20 acres of meadow, and pasture 1 league long and half a league broad. Formerly, as now, worth 20s.

William himself holds MELBURY. Wulfnoth held it TRE, and it paid geld for 1 virgate of land. The whole of it is waste.

Ralph holds DART [in Cadeleigh] from William. Alric held it TRE, and it paid geld for 1 hide. There is land for 6 ploughs. In demesne is 1 plough, and 2 slaves; and 5 villans and 7 bordars with 2 ploughs. There is a mill, and 20 acres of meadow, and as many acres of pasture and as many of woodland. Formerly, as now, worth 30s.

William himself holds CADBURY. Ingvar held it TRE, and it paid geld for 3 virgates of land. There is land for 5 ploughs. In demesne are 2 ploughs, and 3 slaves; and 7 villans and 1 bordar with 3 ploughs. There are 4 acres of meadow and 3 virgates of pasture. Formerly 20s; now it is worth 30s.

William himself holds BOWLEY. Wulfmær held it TRE, and it paid geld for half a hide. There is land for 2 ploughs, which are there, and 4 villans and 3 slaves, and 4 acres of meadow. Formerly 15s; now it is worth 20s.

William himself holds BLAGROVE. Hache held it TRE, and it paid geld for 1 virgate of land. There is land for 6 ploughs. In demesne is 1 plough; and 4 bordars and 8 villans with 1 plough. There are 12 acres of meadow and 60 acres of pasture. Formerly 5s; now it is worth 20s.

Ralph holds PEDLEY from William. Hache held it TRE, and it paid geld for 2½ ferdings. There is land for 2 ploughs. There is 1 plough, with 1 villan and 1 bordar, and 6 acres of meadow and 4 acres of woodland. Formerly 5s; now it is worth 10s.

Hildwine holds "ASSECOTE" from William. Almær held it TRE, and it paid geld for half a ferding. There is land for half a plough. There is 1 villan and he pays 30s.

These 2 estates, PEDLEY and "ASSECOTE", have been joined to BLAGROVE and render 12s6d.

[Folio 111v: DEVONSHIRE]

William himself holds WOOLFARDISWORTHY [near Witheridge]. Wulfnoth held it TRE, and it paid geld for half a hide, less half a ferding. There is land for 4 ploughs. In demesne is 1 plough, with 1 slave; and 6 villans and 1 bordar with 3 ploughs. There are 4 acres of meadow and 20 acres of woodland. Formerly 5s; now it is worth 15s.

Ralph holds DART RAFFE from William. Leofgar held it TRE, and it paid geld for 1 virgate of land. There is land for 2 ploughs. There 3 villans with 1 slave have 1 plough. There are 2 acres of meadow, and 3 acres of woodland and 20 acres of pasture. Formerly 10s; now it is worth 13s.

Ralph holds WORTH from William. Sæweard held it TRE, and it paid geld for half a hide. There is land for 5 ploughs. In demesne is 1 plough, and 2 slaves; and 5 villans with 1 plough, and 2 acres of meadow. Formerly, as now, worth 10s.

Herbert holds FARWOOD from William. Leofmær held it TRE, and it paid geld for half a hide. There is land for 5 ploughs. In demesne is 1 plough; and 4 villans and 2 bordars with 2 ploughs. There are 4 acres of meadow, and 30 acres of pasture and 16 acres of woodland. Formerly 10s; now it is worth 20s.

William himself holds CHALLONSLEIGH. Osfrith held it TRE, and it paid geld for 2 hides. There is land for 8 ploughs. In demesne are 2 ploughs, and 7 slaves; and 9 villans with 2 ploughs. There are 2 acres of meadow, and pasture 4 furlongs long and 2 furlongs broad and as much woodland. Formerly 20s; now it is worth 40s.

William himself holds BATTISFORD. Alwine held it TRE, and it paid geld for half a hide. There is land for 3 ploughs. In demesne is 1 plough; and 3 villans and 1 bordar with 1 plough, and 3 acres of meadow. Formerly 5s; now it is worth 10s.

Robert holds GOOSEWELL from William. Heca held it TRE, and it paid geld for half a hide. There is land for 2 ploughs. There is 1 plough, with 1 villan and 3 bordars, and 2 acres of woodland. It is worth 5s.

William himself holds BICKLEIGH [near Plymouth]. Beorhtmær held it TRE, and it paid geld for 1 hide. There is land for 8 ploughs. In demesne are 2 ploughs, and 7 slaves; and 7 villans and 4 bordars with 3 ploughs. There is a fishery rendering 5s; and 4 acres of meadow, pasture 1 league long and 4 furlongs broad, [and] woodland 1 league long and 1 league broad. Formerly 20s; now it is worth 40s.

William himself holds BUCKLAND MONACHORUM. Beorhtmær held it TRE, and it paid geld for 3 hides and 1½ virgates of land. There is land for 15 ploughs. In demesne are 3 ploughs, and 12 slaves; and 24 villans and 10 bordars with 7 ploughs. There is a salt-pan, and a fishery rendering 10s, and 8 acres of meadow, pasture 1 league long and as much broad, [and] woodland 4 leagues long and 2 furlongs broad. Formerly 50s; now it is worth 100s.

Robert holds SAMPFORD SPINEY from William. Beorhtær held it TRE, and it paid geld for half a hide. There is land for 8 ploughs. In demesne is 1 plough, with 1 slave; and 12 villans and 1 bordar with 2 ploughs. There is pasture half a league long and 1 furlong broad, [and] woodland 1 league long and 4 furlongs broad. Formerly 10s; now it is worth 20s.

XXII. The land of William de Eu

WILLIAM DE EU holds POWDERHAM from the king, and Ranulph [holds] from him. Thurs held it TRE, and it paid geld for half a hide. There is land for 12 ploughs. In demesne are 3 ploughs, and 8 slaves; and 12 villans and 12 bordars with 8 ploughs. There is a mill rendering 50d, and 20 acres of meadow, and 50 acres of pasture and 4 acres of scrubland. Formerly, as now, worth £6.

In this manor there is half a virgate of land which lay in Exminster TRE, and there is 1 plough. It is worth 5s.

The same Ranulph holds WHITESTONE from William. Toli held it TRE, and it paid geld for 1 virgate of land. There is land for 2 ploughs. 6 villans and 2 slaves have this [sic] [ploughs] there. There are 2 acres of meadow and 4 acres of woodland. Formerly 6s; now it is worth 10s.

XXIII. The land of Walter de Douai

WALTER de DOUAI holds HOLLACOMBE [in Kentisbury] from the king. Alwine held it TRE, and it paid geld for half a virgate of land. There is land for 1 plough, which [plough] is there, with 1 villan and 1 slave. There are 6 acres of meadow, and 10 acres of pasture and 1 furlong of woodland. It is worth 5s.

Walter himself holds BERRYNARBOR. Edith held it TRE, and it paid geld for 2 hides. There is land for 17 ploughs. In demesne are 4 ploughs, and 6 slaves; and 20 villans and 10 bordars with 7 ploughs. There is 1 acre of meadow, and 200 acres of pasture and 100 acres of woodland. Formerly, as now, worth £6.

Wulfric holds EAST HAGGINTON from Walter. Wulfmær and Godric held it in parage TRE, and it paid geld for 3 virgates of land. There is land for 5 ploughs. In demesne are 2 ploughs, and 3 slaves; and 10 villans and 2 bordars with 1 plough. There are 100 acres of pasture and 20 acres of woodland. Formerly 15s; now it is worth 30s.

Ernald holds [?] STOODLEIGH [in West Buckland] from Walter. Algar held it TRE, and it paid geld for half a virgate of land. There is land for 2 ploughs. There are 1½ ploughs, with 2 bordars and 3 slaves, and 20 acres of pasture and 6 acres of woodland. Formerly 5s; now it is worth 10s.

Walter himself holds BAMPTON. King Edward held it. This land has never paid geld. There is land for 25 ploughs. In demesne are 2 ploughs, and 2 slaves; and 31 villans and 20 bordars with 18 ploughs, and 15 swineherds rendering 106½ pigs. There is a mill rendering 10s, and 320 acres of woodland.

To this manor is attached 1 hide which 5 thegns held in parage as 5 manors TRE. There is land for 4 ploughs. Rademer, and Rademer and Gerald hold from Walter. There are 4 ploughs, and 3 villans and 3 bordars and 2 slaves, and 4½ acres of meadow and 10 acres of pasture. William de Moyon wrongfully acquired half a ferding of this hide to Walscin's loss.

The whole of BAMPTON with its dependencies is worth £18; formerly it was worth £21 by weight.

Wulfric holds DIPFORD from Walter. There is land for 6 ploughs. In demesne are 2 ploughs, and 3 slaves; and 6 villans and 4 bordars with 6 ploughs. There is a mill rendering 8d, and 2½ acres of meadow, and 10 acres of pasture and 10 acres of woodland. Formerly 20s; now it is worth 30s. 2 thegns held it in parage as 2 manors.

Walscin holds this manor from the queen and calls upon the king [to warrant it].

Walter himself holds HOCKWORTHY. Eadnoth held it TRE, and it paid geld for 3 virgates of land. There is land for 5 ploughs. In demesne is 1 plough, and 2 slaves; and 7 villans and 6 bordars with 3 ploughs. There are 2 acres of meadow, and 50 acres of pasture and 3 furlongs of woodland. Formerly 30s; now it is worth 35s.

Gerard holds KERSWELL [in Hockworthy] from Walter. Ordric held it TRE, and it paid geld for half a hide. There is land for 1 plough. There is 1 slave, and 2 acres of meadow. It is worth 5s.

Walter himself holds UFFCULME. Eadgifu held it TRE, and it paid geld for 14 hides. There is land for 30 ploughs. In demesne are 2 ploughs, and 6 slaves; and 45 villans and 6 bordars with 15 ploughs. There are 2 mills rendering 10s, and 25 acres of meadow, and 25 acres of scrubland, and 60 acres of pasture, and there are 2 swineherds rendering 15 pigs. Formerly £10; now it is worth £12.

Rolf holds KNOWSTONE from Walter. Algar held it TRE, and it paid geld for half a hide. There is land for 7 ploughs. In demesne is 1 plough, with 1 slave; and 6 villans with 1 bordar and 1 plough. There are 12 acres of meadow and 60 acres of pasture. Formerly 30s; now it is worth 20s.

The same Rolf holds KNOWSTONE from Walter. Leofwine held it TRE, and it paid geld for 3 ferdings. There is land for 4 ploughs. In demesne is 1 plough, with 1 slave; and 3 villans with 1 bordar and 1 plough. There are 16 acres of meadow, and 30 acres of pasture, [and] woodland 4 furlongs long and 1 furlong broad. It is worth 10s.

Gerard holds DUNSFORD from Walter. Alsige held it TRE, and it paid geld for 1½ hides. There is land for 10 ploughs. In demesne is 1 plough, and 7 slaves; and 12 villans and 8 bordars with 5 ploughs. There are 20 acres of meadow, and 10 acres of woodland, [and] pasture 5 furlongs long and 2 furlongs broad. Formerly 40s; now it is worth 50s.

Ludo holds LITTLE RACKENFORD from Walter. Godric held it TRE, and it paid geld for half a virgate of land. There is land for 1 plough, which [plough] is there, with 2 slaves, and 2 acres of meadow and 20 acres of pasture. Formerly 30d; now it is worth 5s.

Hermer holds WEST SPURWAY from Walter. Wulfric held it TRE, and it paid geld for 1 hide. There is land for 6 ploughs. In demesne are 2 ploughs, with 1 slave; and 9 villans with 3 ploughs. There are 5 acres of meadow, and 5 acres of woodland and 40 acres of pasture. Formerly 15s; now it is worth 20s.

Ansgar holds "SUTREWORDE" from Walter. Esger held it TRE, and it paid geld for 1 virgate of land. There is land for 12 ploughs. In demesne are 2 ploughs, and 5 slaves; and 11 villans and 14 bordars with 8 ploughs, and 5 swineherds rendering 61 pigs, and 5 bee-keepers rendering 7 sesters of honey. There are 23 acres of meadow, and 10 furlongs of pasture, [and] woodland 1 league long and a half broad. Formerly, as now, worth £7.

Ralph holds GOODRINGTON from Walter. Esger held it TRE, and it paid geld for 2 hides. There is land for 8 ploughs. In demesne are 2 ploughs, and 4 slaves; and 9 villans and 6 bordars with 6 ploughs. There are 20 acres of woodland. Formerly 25s; now it is worth 50s.

Ludo holds "HETFELLE" from Walter. Æthelsige held it TRE, and it paid geld for 3 hides. There is land for 8 ploughs. In demesne is 1 plough, and 2 slaves; and 8 villans and 6 bordars with 4 ploughs. There are 20 acres of meadow, and 100 acres of pasture and 10 acres of woodland. Formerly, as now, worth 40s.

Ludo holds MOHUN'S OTTERY from Walter. Æthelsige held it TRE, and it paid geld for 5 hides. There is land for 12 ploughs. In demesne are 3 ploughs, and 7 slaves; and 9 villans and 9 bordars with 7 ploughs. There is a mill which renders 10s, and 150 acres of pasture, and 100 acres of woodland and 20 acres of meadow. Formerly £4; now it is worth 100s.

Ludo holds LUPPITT from Walter. Æthelsige held it TRE, and it paid geld for 2 hides. There is land for 6 ploughs. In demesne are 2 ploughs, and 3 slaves; and 3 villans and 1 bordar with 2 ploughs. There are 10 acres of meadow, and 10 acres of scrubland and 15 acres of pasture. Formerly, as now, worth 20s.

Ludo holds GREENWAY from Walter. Æthelsige held it TRE, and it paid geld for 1 hide. There is land for 5 ploughs. In demesne are 3 ploughs, and 4 slaves; and 3 villans and 4 bordars with 1 plough. There are 10 acres of meadow, and 10 acres of pasture and 10 acres of scrubland. Formerly 30s; now it is worth 40s.

To this manor has been added SHAPCOMBE, which TRE lay in Broadhembury, Beorhtric's land, and paid geld for 1 hide. There is land for 4 ploughs. In demesne is 1 plough, with 1 slave; and 3 villans with 1 bordar and 1 plough. There are 12 acres of meadow, and 15 acres of pasture and 20 acres of woodland. Formerly, as now, worth 20s.

Hubert holds COMBE RALEIGH from Walter. Æthelsige held it TRE, and it paid geld for 4 hides. There is land for 8 ploughs. In demesne are 3 ploughs, and 4 slaves; and 5 villans and 6 bordars with 2 ploughs. There are 24 acres of meadow, and 50 acres of woodland and 1 hide of pasture. Formerly £4; now it is worth 40s.

Ludo holds STOKE FLEMING from Walter. Esger held it TRE, and it paid geld for 5 hides. There is land for 24 ploughs. In demesne are 4 ploughs, and 12 slaves; and 27 villans and 16 bordars with 12 ploughs. There is a mill in demesne rendering service, and 4 acres of meadow and 30 acres of scrubland. Formerly, as now, worth 100s.

Ralph holds half a hide of this land, and he has there 1 plough, with 1 slave; and [there are] 2 villans and 3 bordars with 1 plough. There are 4 acres of woodland. It is worth 15s.

A woman holds half a hide of the same land from Walter, and she has there 1 plough, with 1 slave, and [there are] 6 villans and 1 bordar with 1 plough. It is worth 10s.

Alric holds COLERIDGE [in Stokenham] from Walter. Bicca held it TRE, and it paid geld for 1 virgate of land. There is land for 2 ploughs. There is 1 plough, and 3 bordars, and 6 acres of scrubland. Formerly, as now, worth 5s.

This manor has been added to Esger's lands. He who held it TRE could go with the land where he would.

Alric holds [?]WOODCOMBE from Walter. Eadric held it TRE, and it paid geld for half a hide. There is land for 2 ploughs. There are 1½ ploughs, and 4 villans, and 1 acre of meadow. It is worth 15s. This land has been added to Esger's lands. He who held it TRE could go where he would.

Ælfgifu holds COLERIDGE [in Stokenham] from Walter. She herself held it TRE, and it paid geld for 1 virgate of land. There is land for 1 plough, which [plough] is there, and 7 acres of scrubland. Formerly, as now, worth 40d.

Ralph holds TOWNSTALL from Walter. Esger held it TRE, and it paid geld for half a hide. There is land for 2 ploughs, which are there, and 2 slaves and 5 villans and 4 bordars, and 6 acres of woodland. Formerly, as now, worth 10s.

Walter himself has in Exeter 10 houses which Esger held TRE. He also has there 1 house in pledge from a burgess, from which the customary due has been withheld.

XXIIII. The land of Walter de Claville

WALTER de CLAVILLE holds BYWOOD from the king. Mahthild held it TRE, and it paid geld for 3½ virgates of land. There is land for 3 ploughs. In demesne is 1 plough; and 4 villans have half a plough, and [there are] 150 acres of pasture. Formerly, as now, worth 10s.

Walter himself holds BRAMPFORD SPEKE. Ælfgifu held it TRE, and it paid geld for half a hide. There is land for 2 ploughs, which are there, and 2 villans and 2 bordars, and 5 acres of meadow, and 50 acres of pasture and 20 acres of woodland. Formerly 5s; now it is worth 15s.

Walter himself holds WITHYCOMBE RALEIGH. Ælfgifu held it TRE, and it paid geld for 1 hide. There is land for 5 ploughs. In demesne is 1 plough, and 2 slaves; and 3 villans and 6 bordars with 3 ploughs. There are 5 acres of meadow, and 30 acres of pasture and 4 acres of woodland. Formerly, as now, worth 20s.

Walter holds WEST RADDON [in Shobrooke] from Walter. Ælfgifu held it TRE, and it paid geld for 2 parts of 1 virgate of land. There is land for 1 plough, which [plough] is there, with 1 villan and 1 bordar and 1 slave. There are 2 acres of meadow. Formerly, as now, worth 6s.

Walter holds WASHFORD PYNE from Walter. 2 thegns held it TRE, and it paid geld for 1 hide, less 1 ferding. There is land for 6 ploughs. In demesne are 2 ploughs, and 4 slaves; and 7 villans and 4 bordars with 2½ ploughs. There are 5 acres of meadow, pasture half a league long and 1 furlong broad, [and] woodland 4 furlongs long and 1 furlong broad. Formerly 25s; now it is worth 40s. 1 ferding of land has been added to this manor. It is worth 3s.

Walter himself holds DRAYFORD. Ælfrun held it TRE, and it paid geld for 3 virgates of land, less half a ferding. There is land for 3 ploughs. In demesne is 1 plough; and 2 villans and 3 bordars with 2 ploughs. There are 4 acres of meadow, and 12 acres of pasture, [and] woodland 2 furlongs long and 1 furlong broad. Formerly 10s; now it is worth 15s.

Osbern holds SYDEHAM from Walter. Ælfrun held it TRE, and it paid geld for 1 virgate of land. There is land for 2 ploughs, which are there, with 1 slave and 1 villan and 3 bordars. There are 8 acres of meadow, and 10 acres of pasture, [and] woodland 3 furlongs long and 1 furlong broad. Formerly, as now, worth 10s.

Walter himself holds CRAZE LOWMAN. Ælfrun held it TRE, and it paid geld for 3 virgates of land. There is land for 3 ploughs. In demesne are 2 ploughs, and 5 slaves; and 3 villans and 2 bordars with 2 ploughs. There are 6 acres of meadow, and 6 acres of pasture and 30 acres of woodland. Formerly, as now, worth 30s.

'KIDWELL' [in Uplowman] has been added to this manor. Ælfrun held it freely TRE, and it paid geld for 1 virgate of land. There is land for 1 plough. There 3 villans and 2 bordars have 1 plough. There are 2 acres of meadow and 8 acres of scrubland. It is worth 10s.

Walter holds MURLEY from Walter. Alnoth held it TRE, and it paid geld for half a hide. There is land for 2 ploughs, which are there, and 2 slaves and 2 villans with 1 bordar. There is 1 acre of meadow and 1 perch and 30 acres of pasture and 8 acres of woodland. Formerly 5s; now it is worth 15s.

The same Walter holds COOMBE [in Uplowman] from Walter. Gundhard held it TRE, and it paid geld for half a hide. There is land for 3 ploughs, which are there, and 3 villans and 2 bordars and 4 slaves, and 6 acres of meadow and 30 acres of pasture. Formerly, as now, worth 15s.

Walter himself holds BOEHILL. Wulfrun held it TRE, and it paid geld for half a hide. There is land for 1 plough. 4 bordars have this [plough] there. There are 5 acres of meadow, and 20 acres of pasture and 10 acres of scrubland. It is worth 10s.

Walter himself holds BOEHILL. Leofræd held it TRE, and it paid geld for 3 virgates of land and 1½ ferdings. There is land for 2 ploughs. There are 2 villans and 4 bordars with 1 slave, and 2 acres of meadow, and 35 acres of pasture and 12 acres of scrubland.

Walter holds AYSHFORD from Walter. Wulfweard held it TRE, and it paid geld for 1 hide. There is land for 3 ploughs, which are there, and 4 villans and 7 bordars and 3 slaves, and 12 acres of meadow, and 60 acres of pasture and 12 acres of woodland. Formerly 10s; now it is worth 20s.

Walter himself holds APPLEDORE [in Burlescombe]. Wulfwig held it TRE, and it paid geld for 2 hides. There is land for 6 ploughs. In demesne are 2 ploughs, and 3 slaves; and 14 villans and 5 bordars with 4 ploughs. There are 8 acres of meadow, and 50 acres of pasture and 40 acres of woodland. Formerly 20s; now it is worth 40s. This thegn could go where he would.

Walter himself holds CANONSLEIGH. Ælfrun held it TRE, and it paid geld for 1½ virgates of land. There is land for 1 plough. There is 1 villan, and 2 acres of meadow, and 20 acres of pasture and 40 acres of woodland. Formerly, as now, worth 7s 6d.

Walter himself holds LEONARD. Sæmær held it TRE, and it paid geld for 3 virgates of land. There is land for 2 ploughs. There 3 villans and 3 bordars have 1 plough, and there are 5 acres of meadow and 12 acres of pasture. It is worth 10s.

Walter himself holds "BERE". Wordrou held it TRE, and it paid geld for half a hide. There is land for 4 ploughs. In demesne is 1 plough, with 1 slave; and 4 villans and 2 bordars with 4 ploughs. There are 4 acres of meadow and 20 acres of scrubland. Formerly, as now, worth 20s.

Walter himself holds BUCKLAND-TOUT-SAINTS. Wudumann held it TRE, and it paid geld for half a virgate of land. There is land for 1½ ploughs. There are 5 bordars, and 2 acres of meadow. It renders 10s. This land, which was free TRE, has been added to Beorhtric's lands.

[Folio 112V: DEVONSHIRE]

Ansfrid holds NORTH POOL from Walter. Beorhtric held it TRE, and it paid geld for 1 hide. There is land for 4 ploughs. In demesne is 1 plough, with 1 slave; and 4 villans and 4 bordars with 1½ ploughs. There are 4 acres of meadow, and 10 acres of pasture and 5 acres of scrubland. Formerly 10s; now it is worth 25s.

Walter himself holds LUPRIDGE. Cola held it TRE, and it paid geld for 1½ virgates of land. There is land for 2 ploughs. There 1 villan with 1 burgess has 1 plough, and [there is] 1 acre of meadow and 1 furlong of pasture. [There is] woodland 1 furlong long and half a furlong broad. It is worth 5s.

Walter himself holds LEIGH [in Churchstow]. 2 thegns held it from Beorhtric TRE, and it paid geld for 1 hide, less half a virgate of land. There is land for 4 ploughs. In demesne are 2 ploughs, and 4 slaves; and 7 villans and 6 bordars with 3 ploughs. There are 4 acres of meadow and 4 acres of woodland. Formerly, as now, worth 30s.

WALTER holds 1 virgate of land which belongs to IDDESLEIGH, the king's manor. Ælfgifu thief held it TRE, and she could not be separated from the king's manor. There is land for 3 ploughs, which are there, and 4 villans and 2 bordars, and 15 acres of meadow and 8 acres of woodland. Formerly 15s; now it is worth 20s.

Walter holds DOWLAND. Alweard held it TRE, and it paid geld for half a hide; and he could go where he would. There is land for 4 ploughs. In demesne is 1 plough, and 4 slaves; and 3 villans and 7 bordars with 2 ploughs. There are 3 acres of meadow, and 4 furlongs of pasture and 2 furlongs of woodland. Formerly 20s; now it is worth 30s.

Walter holds LOOSEDON. Beorhtric held it TRE, and it paid geld for half a hide. There is land for 3 ploughs. There 5 villans and 2 bordars have 2½ ploughs. There are 6 acres of meadow, and 2 furlongs of pasture, [and] woodland 5 furlongs long and half a furlong broad. Formerly 20s; now it is worth 15s.

Walter has in DOWLAND 1 virgate of land, which 2 thegns held TRE, and it paid geld for as much. There is land for 3 ploughs. There are 2 ploughs, with 1 villan and 2 bordars and 2 slaves. There are 2 acres of meadow and 1 furlong of scrubland. Formerly, as now, worth 12s6d.

Walter holds INSTOW. Alweard held it TRE, and it paid geld for 1 virgate of land. There is land for 2 ploughs. There is a priest and 7 bordars and 3 slaves. There are 2 acres of meadow, and 60 acres of pasture and 4 acres of woodland. Formerly, as now, worth 15s.

Riculf holds "CHETELESCOTE" from Walter. Ketil held it TRE, and it paid geld for 1 virgate of land. There is land for 1 plough. However, there are $1\frac{1}{2}$ ploughs, with 1 slave, and 2 villans and 5 bordars, and 10 acres of meadow, and common pasture. Formerly, as now, worth 10s.

Walter holds WOLFIN. Alweard, a free man, held it TRE, and it paid geld for 1 virgate of land. There is land for 1 plough. However, there are 2 ploughs, with 1 villan and 3 bordars and 2 slaves. There are 3 acres of meadow and 20 acres of pasture. Formerly 5s; now it is worth 15s.

Walter holds SHOBROOKE [in Morchard Bishop]. Beorhtric, a free man, held it TRE, and it paid geld for 1 virgate of land. There is land for 2 ploughs. 4 villans and 5 bordars have these [ploughs] there. There is 1 acre of meadow and 6 acres of pasture. Formerly, as now, worth 10s.

Walter holds BURLESCOMBE. Wulfgeat held it TRE, and it paid geld for 1 hide and $1\frac{1}{2}$ virgates of land. There is land for 4 ploughs. In demesne are 2 ploughs, and 2 slaves; and 2 villans and 4 bordars with 3 ploughs. There are 2 acres of meadow, and 50 acres of pasture and 70 acres of woodland. Formerly 20s; now it is worth 25s.

Walter holds "CICLET". Gunnar held it TRE, and it paid geld for half a hide. There is land for 4 ploughs. There 4 villans and 3 bordars have 2 ploughs. There are 2 acres of meadow, and 24 acres of woodland and 85 acres of pasture. Formerly 10s; now it is worth 20s.

Walter and Goscelm hold VIRWORTHY from the king, and Riculf [holds] of them. Edwin held it TRE, and it paid geld for 1 virgate of land. There is land for 3 ploughs, which are there, and 4 villans and 3 bordars and 2 slaves, and 20 acres of meadow. [There is] pasture half a league long and 3 furlongs broad. Formerly 15s; now it is worth 20s.

XXV. The land of Goscelm

Goscelm holds VILLAVIN from the king. Eadlufu thief and Eadgifu held it TRE, and it paid geld for half a hide. There is land for 4 ploughs. In demesne is 1 plough, and 3 slaves; and 5 villans and 3 bordars with 4 ploughs. There are 8 acres of meadow, and 3 acres of scrubland and half a league of pasture. Formerly 100s; now it is worth 20s.

Goscelm himself holds HUISH [near Dolton]. Alwig held it

TRE, and it paid geld for half a virgate of land. There is land for 1 plough, which [plough] is there, with 1 bordar and 1 slave. There are 2 acres of meadow, [and] woodland 2 furlongs long and half a furlong broad. Formerly, as now, worth 5s.

Walter holds NEWTON TRACEY from Goscelm. Alweard held it TRE, and it paid geld for half a hide. There is land for 4 ploughs. In demesne are $1\frac{1}{2}$ ploughs, and 2 slaves; and 4 villans and 3 bordars with $2\frac{1}{2}$ ploughs. There are 6 acres of meadow, and 2 acres of woodland and 5 acres of pasture. Formerly 10s; now it is worth 20s.

Kolsveinn, a man of the Bishop of Coutances, has taken away from this manor the common pasture which was attached to it TRE, and also for 5 years TRW.

Walter holds DODSCOTT from Goscelm. Dodda held it TRE, and it paid geld for 1 virgate of land. There is land for $1\frac{1}{2}$ ploughs. There are 3 villans and 1 bordar and 2 slaves, and 6 acres of meadow and 20 acres of pasture. Formerly it was worth 7s6d; now 15s.

Goscelm himself holds RIDDLECOMBE. Algar held it TRE, and it paid geld for 1 hide. There is land for 5 ploughs. In demesne are 2 ploughs, and 3 slaves; and 7 villans and 4 bordars with 3 ploughs. There are 10 acres of meadow, and 150 acres of pasture and 140 acres of woodland. Formerly 30s; now it is worth 40s.

Goscelm himself holds LOOSEDON. Ælfric held it TRE, and it paid geld for half a hide. There is land for 4 ploughs. In demesne are 2 ploughs, and 2 slaves; and 5 villans and 3 bordars with 2 ploughs. There are 8 acres of meadow, and 50 acres of pasture and 10 acres of woodland. Formerly 10s; now it is worth 20s.

Godfrey holds BRUSHFORD from Goscelm. Alous held it TRE, and it paid geld for 1 virgate of land. There is land for 2 ploughs, which are there, with 1 slave, and 3 villans and 2 bordars, and 1 acre of meadow and 2 acres of scrubland. Formerly 5s; now it is worth 10s.

Hermer holds HAMPSON from Goscelm. Alweald held it TRE, and it paid geld for 1 virgate of land and half a ferding. There is land for 2 ploughs, which are there, and 3 villans and 5 bordars, and 6 acres of meadow. Formerly 9s; now it is worth 12s.

Osmund holds NICHOLS NYMET from Goscelm. Alweard held it TRE, and it paid geld for 1 hide. There is land for 6 ploughs. In demesne is 1 plough, and 2 slaves; and 6 villans and 3 bordars with 4 ploughs. There are 5 acres of meadow, and 3 acres of pasture and 6 acres of woodland. Formerly 10s; now it is worth 30s.

Osmund holds [Lower or Man's] NEWTON [in Zeal Monachorum] from Goscelm. Beorhtwine held it TRE, and it paid geld for half a ferding. There is land for 1 plough. There 2 villans have half a plough. There are 2 acres of meadow, and 4 acres of pasture and 3 acres of scrubland. Formerly 30d; now it is worth 7s.

Goscelm himself holds GOODCOTT. Godgifu held it TRE,

and it paid geld for 1 virgate of land. There is land for 2 ploughs, which are there, with 1 slave and 2 villans. There are 2 acres of meadow. Formerly 5s; now it is worth 10s.

Osmund holds FENACRE from Goscelm. Wulfgeat held it TRE, and it paid geld for $2\frac{1}{2}$ virgates of land. There is land for $1\frac{1}{2}$ ploughs. There are 2 ploughs, however, with 1 slave and 2 villans. There are 2 acres of meadow and 5 acres of pasture. Formerly 15s; now it is worth 20s.

Godfrey holds WOODBEARE from Goscelm. Winemar held it TRE, and it paid geld for 1 hide. There is land for 4 ploughs. In demesne are 2 ploughs, and 3 slaves; and 6 villans and 3 bordars with $1\frac{1}{2}$ ploughs. There are 2 acres of meadow, and 50 acres of pasture and 10 acres of woodland. Formerly 10s; now it is worth 25s.

Goscelm himself holds AWLISCOMBE. Chenias held it TRE, and it paid geld for 1 hide. There is land for 3 ploughs. In demesne is 1 plough, and 5 slaves; and 5 villans with 1 bordar and 2 ploughs. There are 18 acres of meadow and 14 acres of woodland. Formerly 15s; now it is worth 20s.

Goscelm himself holds GITTISHAM. Chenias held it TRE, and it paid geld for $4\frac{1}{2}$ hides. There is land for 10 ploughs. In demesne are 3 ploughs, and 5 slaves; and 28 villans with 1 bordar have 5 ploughs. There is a mill rendering 10s, and 40 acres of meadow, and pasture 9 furlongs in length and 8 furlongs in breadth, and 2 acres of woodland. Formerly, as now, worth 60s.

Goscelm himself holds UPLOWMAN. Alnoth held it TRE, and it paid geld for half a hide. There is land for 6 ploughs. In demesne are 2 ploughs, and 2 slaves; and 8 villans and 5 bordars with 4 ploughs. There are 8 acres of meadow, and 10 acres of pasture and 30 acres of woodland. Formerly 20s; now it is worth 30s.

Goscelm himself holds COOMBE [in Uplowman]. Alnoth held it TRE, and it paid geld for half a hide. There is land for 2 ploughs. There is 1 plough, with 1 slave and 4 bordars. There is a mill rendering 4s, and 4 acres of meadow. Formerly 5s; now it is worth 10s.

Goscelm himself holds "LOTELAND". Sotmann held it TRE, and it paid geld for 1 virgate of land. There is land for 1 plough. There 1 villan has half a plough. Formerly, as now, [worth] 5s.

Almær holds UPLOWMAN from Goscelm. He himself held it TRE, and it paid geld for 3 ferdings. There is land for half a plough. It is worth 4s.

Godfrey holds ASH THOMAS from Goscelm. Ælfgifu, a free woman, held it TRE, and it paid geld for half a hide. There is land for $1\frac{1}{2}$ ploughs. There are 2 villans and 2 bordars and 2 slaves. There are 4 acres of meadow, and 8 acres of woodland and 25 acres of pasture. Formerly, as now, worth 10s. This land has been added to Beorhtric's lands.

[Folio 113: DEVONSHIRE]

Goscelm himself holds EAST MANLEY. Alweard held it TRE, and it paid geld for half a hide and half a virgate of land.

There is land for 3 ploughs, which are there, with 1 slave and 5 villans and 2 bordars. There are 5 acres of meadow and 60 acres of pasture. Formerly, as now, worth 15s.

Goscelm himself holds WHITNAGE. Wulfmær held it TRE, and it paid geld for 1 hide. There is land for 3 ploughs. There are 4 villans and 3 bordars and 2 slaves, and 2 acres of meadow, and 5 acres of woodland and 40 acres of pasture. Formerly, as now, worth 15s.

Ludo holds FARWAY from Goscelm. Chenias held it TRE, and it paid geld for 1 virgate of land. There is land for 4 ploughs. In demesne is 1 plough, with 1 slave; and 5 villans and 3 bordars with 2 ploughs. There are 5 acres of meadow and 20 acres of woodland. Formerly, as now, worth 20s.

Hermer holds WASHBOURNE from Goscelm. Algar held it TRE, and it paid geld for 1 hide. There is land for 3 ploughs. In demesne are 2 ploughs, with 1 slave; and 2 villans with 5 bordars with $1\frac{1}{2}$ ploughs. There is 1 acre of meadow, and 2 acres of scrubland and 1 virgate of pasture. Formerly 10s; now it is worth 20s.

Baldwin holds BUCKLAND-TOUT-SAINTS from Goscelm. Ælfric held it TRE, and it paid geld for half a virgate of land. There is land for $1\frac{1}{2}$ ploughs. However, there are 2 ploughs, and 4 villans and 2 bordars, and 2 acres of meadow and half an acre of scrubland. It is worth 10s. This land has been added to Beorhtric's lands. He who held it TRE was a free man.

Baldwin holds LUPRIDGE from Goscelm. Snotta held it TRE, and it paid geld for half a hide. There is land for 4 ploughs. There is 1 plough, and 2 bordars. [There is] pasture 2 furlongs long and 1 furlong broad, and as much woodland. It is worth 7s.

Goscelm himself holds "ULESTANECOTE". Wulfstan held it TRE, and it paid geld for 1 virgate of land. There is land for 1 plough. There is 1 bordar with 1 slave, and 3 acres of meadow. Formerly, as now, worth 10s. He who held it TRE held it freely from Beorhtric.

Goscelm of Exeter holds "HERSTANHAIA" from the king. Cniht held it TRE, and it paid geld for $1\frac{1}{2}$ hides; and he could go where he would. There is land for 3 ploughs. 6 villans have these [ploughs] there. There is a mill rendering 15d, and 5 acres of meadow, [and] pasture 2 furlongs long and 1 furlong broad. It renders 20s.

XXVI. The land of Richard son of Count Gilbert

RICHARD son of Count Gilbert holds LYMPSTONE from the king, and William [holds] of him. Sæweard held it TRE, and it paid geld for 1 hide and 1 virgate of land. There is land for 8 ploughs. There are 10 villans and 6 bordars and 2 slaves. Formerly £10; now it renders [and] is worth £8.

XXVII. The land of Roger de Bully

ROGER de Bully holds SAMPFORD PEVERELL from the king. Beorhtric held it TRE, and it paid geld for $3\frac{1}{2}$ hides. There is land for 12 ploughs. In demesne is 1 plough, and 6 slaves; and 20 villans and 8 bordars with 9 ploughs. There are 30 acres of meadow, and 150 acres of pasture and 80 acres of woodland. Formerly 100s; now it is worth £10. The queen gave it to Roger with his wife.

XXVIII. The land of Robert D'Aumale

ROBERT d'Aumale holds MILTON DAMEREL from the king. Wulfgifu held it TRE, and it paid geld for half a hide. There is land for 10 ploughs. In demesne is 1 plough, and 7 slaves; and 10 villans and 11 bordars with 5 ploughs. There are 15 acres of meadow, and 50 acres of woodland, [and] pasture 1 league long and half a league broad. Formerly 100s; now [it is worth] 50s.

Robert himself holds OTTERY [in Lamerton], and COLLACOMBE and WILLESTREW as 1 manor. 3 thegns held them as 4 manors, and they paid geld for 3 virgates of land. There is land for 8 ploughs. In demesne is 1 plough, and 8 slaves; and 12 villans and 8 bordars with 5 ploughs. There are 10 acres of meadow, and woodland 20 acres in length and 2 in breadth, [and] pasture half a league long and as much broad. It is worth 60s.

Robert himself holds COOKBURY WICK. Wulfrun, a free woman, held it TRE, and it paid geld for $1\frac{1}{2}$ virgates of land. There is land for 10 ploughs. In demesne are 2 ploughs, and 5 slaves; and 9 villans and 7 bordars with 4 ploughs. There are 50 acres of meadow, and 12 acres of scrubland, [and] pasture 1 league long and as much broad. Formerly £4; now it is worth £3.

Frank holds THUBOROUGH from Robert. Beorhtweald held it TRE, and it paid geld for 1 virgate of land. There is land for 5 ploughs. In demesne are 2 ploughs, with 1 slave; and 4 villans and 6 bordars with 1 plough. There are 30 acres of meadow, and 40 acres of pasture and 2 acres of woodland. Formerly, as now, worth 35s.

Gilbert holds GIDCOTT from Robert. Wulfweard held it TRE, and it paid geld for 1 virgate of land. There is land for 4 ploughs. In demesne is 1 plough, and 2 slaves; and 2 villans with 1 plough. There are 4 acres of meadow, and 50 acres of pasture and 20 acres of scrubland. Formerly, as now, worth 10s.

Robert himself holds WESTLEIGH [near Bideford]. Wulfweard held it TRE, and it paid geld for half a hide. There is land for 5 ploughs. In demesne are 2 ploughs, and 3 slaves; and 4 villans and 5 bordars with 2 ploughs. There are 2 acres of meadow, and 2 acres of woodland and 3 acres of pasture. Formerly 40s; now it is worth 30s.

Robert himself holds GOODLEIGH. Wulfweard held it TRE, and it paid geld for 1 hide. There is land for 10 ploughs. In demesne are 3 ploughs, and 8 slaves; and 13 villans and 5 bordars with 7 ploughs. There is 1 acre of meadow, and 20 acres of woodland and as many of pasture. Formerly, as now, worth 60s.

Two knights hold MARWOOD from Robert. Wulfweard held it TRE, and it paid geld for 1 virgate of land. There is land for 4 ploughs. In demesne is 1 plough, and 2 slaves; and 3 villans and 2 bordars with $1\frac{1}{2}$ ploughs. There are 4 acres of meadow, and woodland half a league long and 2 furlongs broad. Formerly, as now, worth 15s.

Two knights hold WHITEFIELD [in Marwood] from Robert. Alwine held it TRE, and it paid geld for 1 virgate of land. There is land for 5 ploughs. In demesne is 1 plough, and 3 slaves; and 4 villans and 7 bordars with 4 ploughs. There are 5 acres of meadow, pasture half a league long and 2 furlongs broad, and as much woodland. Formerly, as now, worth 30s.

Robert holds BICKHAM from Robert. Æthelmær held it TRE, and it paid geld for 4 virgates of land. There is land for 4 ploughs. In demesne is 1 plough, with 1 slave; and 2 villans with 1 bordar and half a plough. There are 10 acres of meadow, and 20 acres of woodland and 40 acres of pasture. Formerly 5s; now it is worth 15s.

Robert himself holds FLETE. Beorhtweald held it TRE, and it paid geld for 1 hide. There is land for 6 ploughs. In demesne is 1 plough, and 2 slaves; and 8 villans and 2 bordars with 3 ploughs. There are 4 acres of meadow, and 10 acres of pasture and 10 acres of woodland. Formerly, as now, worth 20s.

Gilbert holds BEENLEIGH from Robert. Æthelweard held it TRE, and it paid geld | for half a hide. | There is land for 4 ploughs. There are 2 ploughs, and 3 villans and 3 bordars, and 10 acres of pasture. Formerly 8s; now it is worth 12s.

Robert himself holds WOODLEIGH. Ælfric Pike held it TRE, and it paid geld for 1 hide and 1 virgate of land. There is land for 12 ploughs. In demesne are 3 ploughs, and 7 slaves; and 15 villans and 8 bordars with 9 ploughs, and 2 swineherds rendering 16 pigs. There are 2 acres of meadow, and 30 acres of pasture, and 10 acres of scrubland and 100 acres of woodland. Formerly 40s; now it is worth 60s.

Robert himself holds 'HALSTOW' [in Woodleigh]. Beorhtric and Alweard held it TRE, and it paid geld for half a virgate of land. There is 1 villan paying 30d. Formerly it was worth 5s.

Robert himself holds STOKE [in Plymouth]. Beorhtmær held it TRE, and it paid geld for 2 hides. There is land for 12 ploughs. In demesne are 2 ploughs, and 5 slaves; and 16 villans and 4 bordars with 8 ploughs. There are 2 acres of woodland and 12 acres of pasture. Formerly 40s; now it is worth 70s.

Oswulf holds 'WIDEY' [in Plymouth] from Robert. Wadilo held it TRE, and it paid geld for half a hide. There is land for 4 ploughs. In demesne is 1 plough; and 3 slaves with 1 villan have half a plough. There are 40 acres of pasture. There is woodland half a league long and 4 furlongs broad. It is worth 10s.

WHITLEIGH [in Plymouth] has been added to this manor. Wadilo held it freely TRE, and it paid geld for half a hide. There is land for 3 ploughs. In demesne is 1 plough; and 3 bordars with 1 plough. There are 30 acres of pasture and 9 acres of woodland. Formerly 5s; now it is worth 10s.

Robert himself has in BARNSTAPLE 2 waste houses rendering 4d.

XXIX. The land of Robert the Bastard

ROBERT the Bastard holds [East, North and West] BACKSTONE from the king. Ælfric held it TRE, and it paid geld for 3 ferdings of land. There is land for 1 plough, which [plough] is there, and 2 slaves; and 2 bordars with half a plough. There are 10 acres of meadow and 80 acres of pasture. Formerly 5s; now it is worth 10s.

Robert himself holds HAZARD. Ælfric held it TRE, and it paid geld

[Folio 113V: DEVONSHIRE]

for 1 virgate of land. There is land for 5 ploughs. In demesne are 2 ploughs, with 1 slave; and 6 villans and 3 bordars with 3 ploughs. There are 2 acres of meadow and 40 acres of pasture. Formerly 10s; now it is worth 20s.

Osbern holds COMBE ROYAL from Robert. Ælfric held it TRE, and it paid geld for 1 virgate of land. There is land for 3 ploughs. In demesne is 1 plough, with 1 slave; and 2 villans and 2 bordars with 1 plough. There are 2 acres of meadow and 6 acres of woodland. Formerly 3s; now it is worth 10s.

Ranulph holds DUNSTONE [in Yealmpton] from Robert. Alwig held it TRE, and it paid geld for half a hide. There is land for 3 ploughs. In demesne is 1 plough; and 2 villans and 3 slaves with 2 ploughs, and 4 acres of woodland. Formerly 5s; now it is worth 20s.

Robert himself holds BLACHFORD. Alwine held it TRE, and it paid geld for 1 virgate of land. There is land for 3 ploughs. In demesne is 1 plough, with 1 slave; and 3 villans and 3 bordars with 1 plough. There are 3 acres of meadow and 20 acres of woodland. Formerly 5s; now it is worth 10s.

Robert himself holds EFFORD [in Plymouth]. Alwine held it TRE, and it paid geld for half a hide. There is land for 4 ploughs. In demesne are 2 ploughs, and 2 slaves; and 3 villans with 1 bordar and 1 plough. There is a fishery rendering 12d, and 2 acres of meadow and 20 acres of woodland. Formerly 10s; now it is worth 20s.

Robert himself holds STONEHOUSE [in Plymouth]. Alwine held it TRE, and it paid geld for 1 ferding. There is land for 1 plough. There is 1 villan paying 5s.

Robert himself holds BICKFORDTOWN. Alwine held it TRE, and it paid geld for 1 virgate of land. There is land for 2 ploughs. There is 1 plough, with 1 slave and 1 villan and 1 bordar, and 4 acres of meadow and 60 acres of pasture. Formerly 5s; now it is worth 10s.

Robert himself holds LOVATON. Alwine held it TRE, and it

paid geld for 1 virgate of land. There is land for 2 ploughs, which are there, with 1 slave and 5 villans. There are 3 acres of meadow, and 100 acres of pasture, [and] woodland 3 furlongs long and 1 furlong broad. Formerly 10s; now it is worth 20s.

Robert himself has on the land of ST PETER'S of Plympton 2 villans whom Alwine held TRE. They pay 5s.

XXX. The land of Richard fitzTurold

RICHARD fitz Turolf [sic] holds WOODHUISH from the king. Ordwulf held it TRE, and it paid geld for 1 hide. There is land for 5 ploughs. In demesne are 2 ploughs, and 5 slaves; and 6 villans and 6 bordars with 2½ ploughs. There are 2 acres of meadow and 6 acres of woodland. Formerly 20s; now it is worth 40s.

Richard himself holds NATSWORTHY. Edward held it TRE, and it paid geld for 1 ferding. There is land for 2 ploughs, which are there, with 1 slave and 2 villans and 2 bordars. There are 5 acres of meadow and 6 acres of scrubland. Formerly 5s; now it is worth 15s.

Richard himself holds EAST ALLINGTON. Wulfnoth held it TRE, and it paid geld for 3 hides. There is land for 16 ploughs. In demesne are 2 ploughs, and 10 slaves; and 17 villans and 15 bordars with 10 ploughs, and 5 acres of meadow and 8 acres of scrubland. Formerly, as now, worth 100s.

Richard himself has in Exeter 1 house from which he withholds the king's customary dues, that is, 8d.

XXXI. The land of Ralph de Limesy

RALPH de Limesy holds EAST DOWN from the king. Eadric held it TRE, and it paid geld for 5 virgates of land. There is land for 12 ploughs. In demesne is 1 plough, and 10 slaves; and 14 villans and 6 bordars with 10 ploughs. There are 20 acres of pasture and 20 acres of scrubland. Formerly, as now, worth £4.

The same Ralph holds BRADWELL. Eadric held it TRE, and it paid geld for 1 hide. There is land for 10 ploughs. In demesne are 2 ploughs, and 8 slaves; and 11 villans and 5 bordars with 4 ploughs. There are 23 acres of meadow and 50 acres of pasture. Formerly £4; now it is worth £3.

Ralph himself holds ROADWAY. Eadric held it TRE, and it paid geld for 1 virgate of land. There is land for 2 ploughs. There are 2 villans, and 10 acres of scrubland. It is worth 30d.

Ælfric holds MORTEHOE from Ralph. Eadric held it TRE, and it paid geld for half a hide. There is land for 3 ploughs. There are 2 ploughs, with 1 slave and 2 villans. Formerly, as now, worth 10s.

XXXII. The land of Ralph Paynel

RALPH Paynel holds DUNCHIDEOCK from the king. Mærle-Sveinn held it TRE, and it paid geld for 1 hide. There is land for 5 ploughs. In demesne is 1 plough, and 2 slaves; and 8 villans and 4 bordars with 4 ploughs. There are 2 acres of meadow and 20 acres of woodland. Formerly 60s; now it is worth 100s.

Gunter holds KERSWELL [in Broadhembury] from Ralph. TRE it paid geld for 2 hides. There is land for 8 ploughs. In demesne is 1 plough, and 4 slaves; and 8 villans and 5 bordars with 2½ ploughs. There is a mill rendering 5s, and 10 acres of meadow, and 30 acres of woodland and 100 acres of pasture. Formerly 40s; now it is worth 60s.

Ralph himself holds ALLER [in Kentisbeare]. TRE it paid geld for 1 hide. There is land for 10 ploughs. In demesne is 1 plough, and 5 slaves; and 14 villans and 9 bordars with 7 ploughs. There are 20 acres of meadow, and 20 acres of woodland and 50 acres of pasture. Formerly 60s; now it is worth 100s.

Ralph himself holds THROWLEIGH. TRE it paid geld for 1 hide. There is land for 8 ploughs. In demesne are 2 ploughs, and 3 slaves; and 10 villans with 1 bordar have 6 ploughs. There are 8 acres of meadow, and 12 acres of woodland, [and] pasture half a league long and 4 acres broad. It is worth £4.

Ralph himself holds CHAGFORD. TRE it paid geld for half a hide. There is land for 4 ploughs. In demesne is 1 plough, and 3 slaves; and 6 villans with 3 ploughs. Formerly, as now, worth £3.

Ralph himself holds ILSINGTON. TRE it paid geld for 2 hides. There is land for 12 ploughs. In demesne is 1 plough, and 7 slaves; and 22 villans and 6 bordars with 7 ploughs. There is 1 acre of meadow, and 210 acres of woodland, [and] pasture 2 leagues and 8 furlongs in both length and breadth. It is worth £9. In Exeter 1 house renders 10s.

Ralph himself holds INGSDON. TRE it paid geld for 2 hides. There is land for 9 ploughs. In demesne are 2 ploughs, and 5 slaves; and 20 villans and 8 bordars with 5 ploughs. There is 1 acre of meadow, and 70 acres of woodland and 4 acres of pasture. Formerly, as now, worth £9.

Gerard holds TIVERTON from Ralph. TRE it paid geld for 1 virgate of land. There is land for 2 ploughs. There are 4 villans with 1 slave, and 2 acres of meadow. Formerly 40s; now it is worth 30s.

Gerard holds 'LITTLE WASHFIELD' from Ralph. TRE it paid geld for 1 virgate of land. There is land for 2 ploughs. There 1 villan and 3 bordars have 1 plough, and [there is] 1 acre of meadow and 1 acre of woodland. Formerly 10s; now it is worth 20s.

Ralph himself holds EDGINSWELL. TRE it paid geld for 2 hides. There is land for 5 ploughs. In demesne are 2 ploughs, and 7 slaves; and 16 villans and 2 bordars with 4 ploughs. There are 12 acres of meadow, and 32 acres of pasture and 56 acres of woodland. Formerly £6; now it is worth 105s.

Mærle-Sveinn held all these lands TRE.

XXXIII. The land of Ralph de Feugeres

RALPH de Feugeres holds IPPLEPEN from the king. Goda held it TRE, and it paid geld for 4 hides, less half a virgate of land. There is land for 20 ploughs. In demesne are 3 ploughs, and 3 slaves; and 37 villans and 16 bordars with 12 ploughs. There are 30 acres of meadow, and half a league of scrubland and 10 acres of pasture.

Ralph himself holds GALMPTON [in Churston Ferrers]. Goda held it TRE, and it paid geld for 2 hides. There is land for 6 ploughs. In demesne are 2 ploughs, and 2 slaves; and 14 villans and 2 bordars with 5½ ploughs. There is 1 acre of meadow, and 4 acres of pasture, [and] scrubland 1 league long and 12 perches broad.

These 2 manors are worth £30.

XXXIIII. The land of Ralph de La Pommeraye

RALPH de LA POMMERAYE holds SOUTHWEEK from the king. Æthelweard held it TRE, and it paid geld for half a virgate of land. There is land for 5 ploughs. In demesne is 1 plough, and 2 slaves; and 4 villans and 3 bordars with 2 ploughs. There are 30 acres of meadow, and 12 acres of pasture and 2 acres of woodland. Formerly 40s; now it is worth 50s.

Roald himself holds BRIDGERULE. Frawin held it TRE, and it paid geld for 1½ virgates of land. There is land for 8 ploughs. In demesne are 2 ploughs, and 3 slaves; and 14 villans and 8 bordars with 6 ploughs. There is a mill rendering 4s, and meadow 7 furlongs long and 2 furlongs broad, [and] pasture 1 league long and half a league broad. Formerly, as now, worth 50s.

Walter holds WONFORD [Wonford and South Wonford, in Thornbury] from Roald. Eadmær held it TRE, and it paid geld for half a virgate of land. There is land for 2 ploughs, which are there, and 2 slaves and 2 villans, and 50 acres of meadow and 2 furlongs of pasture. [There is] scrubland 1 furlong long and half a furlong broad. Formerly 5s; now it is worth 15s.

Alvred holds [East or West] PANSON from Roald. Leofgar held it TRE, and it paid geld for 1 virgate of land. There is land for 4 ploughs. In demesne is 1 plough, and 2 slaves; and 5 villans with 2 ploughs. There are 12 acres of meadow, and 4 acres of woodland, [and] pasture 4 furlongs long and 1 furlong broad. Formerly 30s; now it is worth 20s. Roald holds this land in exchange for BRUCKLAND and 'RADISH' [in Southleigh].

Walter holds "TAMERLANDE" from Roald. Siduwine held it TRE.

[Folio 114: DEVONSHIRE]

Ralph himself holds DUNSDON. Tovi held it TRE, and it paid geld for 3 virgates of land. There is land for 12 ploughs. In demesne are 2 ploughs, and 9 slaves; and 6 villans and 7 bordars with 3 ploughs. There are 40 acres of meadow and 60 acres of pasture. It is worth 100s; formerly it was worth £4.

1 virgate has been taken away from these 3 virgates of land. The Count of Mortain holds this. There is land for 2 ploughs.

Roger holds LYDFORD from Ralph. Wadel held it TRE, and it paid geld for half a ferding. There is land for 1 plough. It is worth 3s.

Ralph himself holds "ALWINECLANCAVELE". Leodwine held it TRE, and it paid geld for half a virgate and half a ferding. There is land for 2 ploughs, which are there, with 1 slave and 2 villans and 4 bordars. There are 20 acres of meadow and 30 acres of pasture. Formerly 15s; now it is worth 10s.

Ralph himself holds [East and West] ASH [in Bradworthy]. Leodmær held it TRE, and it paid geld for 1 virgate of land. There is land for 3 ploughs. There 4 villans and 2 bordars have 2 ploughs. There are 10 acres of meadow and as much pasture. Formerly 20s; now it is worth 10s. Ralph seized this, as the French and English testify. Leodmær was a free man.

Ralph himself holds BRADWORTHY. Tovi held it TRE, and it paid geld for 3 hides and 1 virgate of land. There is land for 12 ploughs. In demesne are 3 ploughs, and 9 slaves; and 20 villans and 10 bordars with 7 ploughs. There are 40 acres of meadow, and pasture 3 leagues long and 1 league broad. Formerly 100s; now it is worth £8.

Roger holds WEST PUTFORD from Ralph. Leodmær held it TRE, and it paid geld for half a virgate of land. There is land for 2 ploughs, which are there, with 1 slave and 2 villans and 4 bordars. There are 12 acres of meadow, and 2 acres of woodland, [and] pasture half a league long and 2 furlongs broad. Formerly 15s; now it is worth 10s.

Ralph himself holds HORWOOD. Æthelweard held it TRE, and it paid geld for 3 virgates of land. There is land for 5 ploughs. In demesne are 3 ploughs, and 4 slaves; and 2 villans and 4 bordars with 2 ploughs. There are 8 acres of meadow and 1 acre of woodland. Formerly 40s; now it is worth 60s.

Roger holds [?Great] TORRINGTON from Ralph. Almær held it TRE, and it paid geld for the third part of 1 ferding. There is land for 1 plough, which [plough] is there, with 1 slave and 3 bordars. Formerly, as now, worth 5s.

Ralph himself holds ASHCOMBE. Ælfric held it TRE. 3 estates have been added to this, which 3 thegns held freely in parage as 3 manors TRE. These 4 estates paid geld for 2 hides TRE. There is land for 9 ploughs. In demesne are 4 ploughs, and 4 slaves; and 8 villans and 4 bordars with 7 ploughs. There are 5 acres of meadow, and 4 acres of woodland and 150 acres of pasture. Formerly £9; now it is worth £10.

Ralph himself holds HOLCOMBE [in Dawlish]. Æthelmær held it TRE, and it paid geld for 1 virgate of land. There is land for 1 plough. There are 4 salt-workers paying 6s5d.

Roger holds PEAMORE from Ralph. Viking held it TRE, and it paid geld for 1 virgate of land. There is land for 3

ploughs. In demesne is 1 plough, with 2 slaves; and 4 villans and 3 bordars with 2 ploughs. There are 3 acres of meadow. Formerly 10s; now it is worth 15s.

Richard holds MOWLISH from Ralph. Leofgar held it TRE, and it paid geld for 1 virgate of land. There is land for 1 plough. There are 2 villans and 2 bordars. Formerly, as now, worth 5s.

Ralph himself holds BRENDON. Æthelweard held it TRE, and it paid geld for 1 hide. There is land for 8 ploughs. In demesne are 2 ploughs, and 5 slaves; and 7 villans and 6 bordars with 6 ploughs. There are 30 acres of woodland and 2 leagues of pasture. Formerly 30s; now it is worth 100s.

'LANK COMBE' [in Brendon] has been added to this manor. Edwin held it TRE, and it paid geld for 1 ferding. There is land for 1 plough. There is 1 villan paying 3s.

Ralph himself holds CHERITON [in Brendon]. Ketil held it TRE, and it paid geld for half a virgate of land. There is land for 2 ploughs, which are there, and 2 slaves and 4 villans and 2 bordars. There are 20 acres of woodland and 2 leagues of pasture. Formerly 10s; now it is worth 40s.

Ralph himself holds CAFFYNS HEANTON. Ulf held it TRE, and it paid geld for 1 virgate of land. There is land for 3 ploughs. In demesne is 1 plough, and 2 slaves; and 3 villans with 1 plough. There are 30 acres of pasture and 12 acres of woodland. Formerly 20s; now it is worth 37s.

Ralph himself holds "STANDONE". Algar held it TRE, and it paid geld for 1 virgate of land. There is 1 villan, and 30 acres of pasture. It is worth 3s.

Ralph himself holds AUNK. Burgræd held it TRE, and it paid geld for 3 hides. There is land for 7 ploughs. In demesne are 3 ploughs, and 6 slaves; and 12 villans and 6 bordars with 3 ploughs. There are 20 acres of meadow and 23 acres of pasture. Formerly, as now, worth £3.

Ralph himself holds SHELDON. Alric held it TRE, and it paid geld for 1 hide. There is land for 6 ploughs. In demesne is 1 plough, and 2 slaves; and 9 villans and 2 bordars with 6 ploughs. There are 30 acres of scrubland and 300 acres of pasture. Formerly 40s; now it is worth 70s.

Ralph himself holds BLACKBOROUGH. Alnoth held it TRE, and it paid geld for half a hide. There is land for 2 ploughs, which are there, and 2 villans and 3 bordars. There are 3 acres of meadow and 100 acres of pasture. Formerly 10s; now it is worth 20s.

Ralph himself holds [Higher and Lower] TALE. Alnoth held it TRE, and it paid geld for 1½ hides, less 1 ferding. There is land for 3 ploughs. In demesne is 1 plough; and 4 villans and 3 bordars with half a plough. There are 2 acres of meadow, and 50 acres of pasture and 15 acres of scrubland. It is worth 20s.

Ralph himself holds [Higher and Lower] TALE. Burgræd held it TRE, and it paid geld for 1 hide. There is land for 4 ploughs. In demesne are 2 ploughs, and 3 slaves; and 5 villans with 1 bordar have 1 plough. There is a mill rendering 5s, and

20 acres of meadow, and 50 acres of pasture and 20 acres of scrubland. Formerly 20s; now it is worth 40s.

Ralph himself holds AWLISCOMBE. Eadmær held it TRE, and it paid geld for half a hide. There is land for 4½ ploughs. In demesne are 2 ploughs, and 3 slaves; and 5 villans and 5 bordars with 2½ ploughs. There is half a mill rendering 5s, and 5 acres of meadow and 2 furlongs of woodland. Formerly, as now, worth 40s.

Roscelin holds WESTON [in Awliscombe] from Ralph. Godric held it TRE, and it paid geld for half a hide. There is land for 2 ploughs. There is 1 plough, with 1 slave and 1 villan and 3 bordars, and 5 acres of meadow and 2 furlongs of pasture. Formerly, as now, worth 10s.

Ralph himself holds DUNKESWELL. Almær held it TRE, and it paid geld for 1½ hides. There is land for 10 ploughs. In demesne is 1 plough, and 3 slaves; and 11 villans with 5 ploughs. There are 4 acres of meadow, and 8 acres of scrubland and 10 furlongs of pasture. Formerly, as now, worth 50s.

Helgot holds AWLISCOMBE from Ralph. Alwine held it TRE, and it paid geld for half a hide and half a virgate of land. There is land for 3 ploughs, which are there, with 1 slave and 4 villans and 2 bordars. There are 8 acres of meadow, and 6 acres of woodland, and 11 acres of scrubland and 4 furlongs of pasture. Formerly, as now, worth 20s.

William holds [East and West] OGWELL from Ralph. Ælfric held it TRE, and it paid geld for 3 virgates of land. There is land for 4 ploughs. In demesne is 1 plough, with 1 slave; and 3 villans and 3 bordars with 1 plough. There is 1 acre of meadow [...] and 12 acres of pasture. Formerly 10s; now it is worth 30s.

The same William holds [East and West] OGWELL from Ralph. Eadric held it TRE, and it paid geld for half a hide. There is land for 3 ploughs. In demesne is 1 plough, with 1 slave; and 2 villans and 3 bordars with 1 plough. There is 1 acre of meadow, and 6 acres of woodland and 10 acres of pasture. Formerly 5s; now it is worth 10s.

Roger holds HUXHAM from Ralph. Viking held it TRE, and it paid geld for 3½ virgates. There is land for 6 ploughs. In demesne is 1 plough, with 1 slave; and 10 villans and 3 bordars with 5 ploughs. There is a mill rendering 6s, and 8 acres of meadow and 20 acres of pasture. Formerly 10s; now it is worth 25s.

Roger holds CLYST ST GEORGE from Ralph. Viking held it TRE, and it paid geld for 1 virgate of land. There is land for 6 ploughs. In demesne is 1 plough, with 1 slave; and 3 villans and 13 bordars with 5 ploughs. There are 8 acres of meadow. Formerly 10s; now it is worth 40s.

Ralph himself holds STOCKLEIGH POMEROY. Ælfgifu held it TRE, and it paid geld for 1 hide. There is land for 6 ploughs. In demesne are 3 ploughs, and 3 slaves; and 7 villans and 18 bordars with 3 ploughs. There are 3 acres of meadow, and 10 acres of pasture and 8 acres of woodland. Formerly, as now, worth 40s.

Roscelin holds half a hide in RAPSHAYES from Ralph.

Godric held it TRE. [...] There is land for 1 plough. There are 3 villans with half a plough, and 5 acres of meadow and 1 acre of woodland. [There is] pasture 1 furlong long and half a furlong broad. Formerly 12d; now it is worth 30d.

[Folio 114V: DEVONSHIRE]

William holds DUNSCOMBE from Ralph. Sægar held it TRE, and it paid geld for half a hide. There is land for 3 ploughs, which are there, with 2 slaves and 3 bordars. There are 3 acres of meadow and 30 acres of pasture. Formerly, as now, worth 30s.

Ralph himself holds "HEPPASTEBE". Wulfweard held it TRE, and it paid geld for 1 virgate of land. There is land for 1 plough. There is 1 slave, and 5 acres of meadow. It is worth 5s. Ralph took possession of this with another manor, AUNK.

William holds LOWER CREEDY from Ralph. Goda held it TRE. There is land for 2 ploughs, and it paid geld for 1 virgate of land. There are 2 ploughs, and 4 slaves and 4 bordars. There are 5 acres of meadow and 30 acres of pasture. Formerly 5s; now it is worth 10s.

The same William holds YEADBURY from Ralph. Særic held it TRE, and it paid geld for half a virgate of land. There is land for 1 plough. There are 2 slaves, and 30 acres of pasture. Formerly, as now, worth 3s.

The same William holds 1 ferding of land in LOWER CREEDY from Ralph. Edwin held it TRE. [...] There is land for 1 plough. There is 1 acre of meadow. It is worth 2s.

Turstin holds STRETE RALEGH from Ralph. Æthelmær held it TRE, and it paid geld for half a hide. There is land for 2 ploughs, which are there, and 3 slaves and 2 villans and 6 bordars, and 8 acres of meadow, and 12 acres of woodland and 60 acres of pasture. Formerly, as now, worth 10s.

Ralph himself holds WASHFIELD. Goda held it TRE, and it paid geld for 3 virgates of land. There is land for 4 ploughs. In demesne are 2 ploughs, and 2 slaves; and 7 villans and 4 bordars with 2 ploughs. There are 4 acres of meadow, and 15 acres of pasture and 40 acres of woodland. Formerly 6s; now it is worth 30s.

Robert holds STOODLEIGH [near Oakford] from Ralph. Almær held it TRE, and it paid geld for 3 virgates of land. There is land for 10 ploughs. In demesne are 3 ploughs, and 6 slaves; and 12 villans with 1 bordar have 3 ploughs. There are 2 acres of meadow, [and] woodland 1 league long and half a league broad. Formerly 30s; now it is worth 40s.

Ralph himself holds HIGHLEIGH. Beorhtmær held it TRE, and it paid geld for 1 virgate of land. There is land for 3 ploughs. In demesne is 1 plough; and 1 villan and 2 bordars with 1 plough. Formerly, as now, worth 10s.

William holds ADWORTHY from Ralph. Særic held it TRE, and it paid geld for 1 ferding. There is land for half a plough, which [half-plough] is there, with 1 slave, and 2 acres of meadow. It is worth 30d.

Beatrice [holds] CHEVITHORNE from Ralph. Almær held it TRE, and it paid geld for 1 virgate of land. There is land for

4 ploughs. In demesne are 2 ploughs, and 8 slaves; and 4 villans and 2 bordars with 2 ploughs. There are 8 acres of meadow, and 15 acres of pasture and 3 acres of woodland. Formerly, as now, worth 40s.

UPLOWMAN has been added to this manor. Alwine held it TRE, and it paid geld for 1 virgate of land and 1 ferding. There is land for 1 plough. It is worth 5s. The same Alwine holds it from Ralph.

Roger holds GAPPAH from Ralph. 5 thegns held it TRE, and it paid geld for 3 virgates of land. There is land for 4 ploughs. In demesne are 3 ploughs, and 2 slaves; and 10 bordars with 1 plough. There are 6 acres of meadow, and 14 acres of woodland and 4 furlongs of pasture. Formerly 5s; now it is worth 30s.

Ralph himself holds IVEDON. Sæmær held it TRE, and it paid geld for 1 virgate of land. There is land for 1 plough, which [plough] is there, with half a villan. It is worth 30d. Ralph has added this land to AWLISCOMBE.

Roger holds DUNSTONE [in Widecombe in the Moor] from Ralph. Edwin held it TRE, and it paid geld for half a virgate of land. There is land for 1 plough. There are 3 villans and 4 bordars have half a plough. There are 3 acres of meadow and 30 acres of pasture. It is worth 7s6d.

BLACKSLADE has been added to this manor. Edwin held it TRE, and it paid geld for 1 virgate of land. There is land for 1 plough. There are 2 villans and 3 bordars, and 2 acres of meadow. It is worth 3s.

Ralph himself holds IVEDON. Leofric held it TRE, and it paid geld for 1½ virgates of land and 1 ferding. There is land for 1 plough, which [plough] is there, with 1 slave. It is worth 3s.

Ralph himself holds BERRY POMEROY. Alric held it TRE, and it paid geld for 2 hides. There is land for 25 ploughs, and 16 slaves, and 45 villans and 17 bordars with 17 ploughs. There are 10 acres of meadow, and 100 acres of woodland and 40 acres of pasture. Formerly 16s; now it is worth £12.

Ralph himself holds AFTON. Æthelsige held it TRE, and it paid geld for 3 virgates of land. There is land for 5 ploughs. In demesne is 1 plough, and 3 slaves; and 6 villans and 3 bordars with 3 ploughs. There is 1 acre of meadow, and 8 acres of pasture and 10 acres of woodland. Formerly 15s; now it is worth 25s.

1 virgate of land has been added to this manor. A certain woman held it freely TRE in parage. There is land for 1 plough. There 1 villan has half a plough. It is worth 5s.

Ralph himself holds UPOTTERY. Æthelric held it TRE, and it paid geld for 4 hides. There is land for 15 ploughs. In demesne are 3 ploughs, and 8 slaves; and 18 villans and 4 bordars with 8 ploughs. There is a mill rendering 20d, and 20 acres of meadow, and 60 acres of woodland and 500 acres of pasture. Formerly, as now, worth 100s.

Ralph himself holds SMALLRIDGE. Wulfnoth held it TRE, and it paid geld for 1 hide. There is land for 4 ploughs. In

demesne are 2 ploughs, and 5 slaves; and 8 villans and 5 bordars with 2½ ploughs. There is a mill rendering 5s, and 15 acres of meadow, and 31 acres of pasture and half a hide of woodland. Formerly, as now, worth 40s.

Roger holds WEYCROFT from Ralph. Viking held it TRE, and it paid geld for 1 hide. There is land for 4 ploughs. In demesne is 1 plough, and 2 slaves; and 3 villans and 6 bordars with 1½ ploughs. There are 2 mills rendering 7s6d, and 3 acres of meadow and 25 acres of woodland. Formerly 10s; now it is worth 20s.

Geoffrey holds BRUCKLAND from Ralph. Æthelheard held it TRE, and it paid geld for 1 hide. There is land for 4 ploughs. There are 3 bordars, and 4 acres of meadow and 4 acres of pasture. It is worth 12d.

Geoffrey holds 'RADISH' [in Southleigh] from Ralph. 2 thegns held it TRE, and it paid geld for half a hide. There is land for 2 ploughs. There are 15 acres of scrubland. Formerly, as now, worth 3s.

These 3 manors had been given to Ralph in exchange for 1 manor of 1 virgate.

Roger holds KEYNEDON from Ralph. Eadwig held it TRE, and it paid geld for half a hide. There is land for 3 ploughs. In demesne is 1 plough, and 2 slaves; and 4 villans and 10 bordars, and 2 acres of meadow, and 8 acres of pasture and 2 furlongs of woodland. Formerly 7s; now it is worth 10s.

[?North] POOL has been added to this manor. Eadwig held it freely in parage TRE, and it paid geld for half a hide. There is land for 2 ploughs. It is worth 10s.

Roger holds HEAVITREE [in Exeter] from Ralph. Viking held it TRE. There are 2 carucates of land, and there are 2 ploughs. There is 1 villan and 2 slaves. | It is worth 20s. |

Roger has half a virgate of land. There is land for 1 plough. There is 1 villan, and a mill rendering 30d. Ælfric held it TRE, and it has been added to WEYCROFT.

Ralph himself holds in Exeter 6 houses from which he has withheld the king's customary dues, that is, 3s4d.

XXXV. The land of Roald Dubbed

ROALD Dubbed holds LAMERTON from the king. Ordwulf held it TRE, and it paid geld for 1½ hides. There is land for 17 ploughs. In demesne are 5 ploughs, and 16 slaves; and 34 villans with 12 ploughs. There are 2 mills rendering 9s, and 40 acres of meadow, pasture 1½ leagues long and 1 league broad, [and] woodland 7 furlongs long and 3 furlongs broad. Formerly £9; now it is worth £12.

[Folio 115: DEVONSHIRE]

and it paid geld for 1 virgate of land. There is land for 3 ploughs. In demesne is 1 plough; with 1 slave and 1 villan and 1 plough. There are 12 acres of meadow, and 3 acres of scrubland, [and] pasture 2 furlongs long and 1 furlong broad. Formerly 40s; now it is worth 10s.

The same Walter holds [East and West] PEEKE from Roald.

Edwin held it in parage TRE, and it paid geld for half a virgate of land. [...] There are 2 villans, and 6 acres of meadow, [and] pasture 4 furlongs long and 2 furlongs broad. Formerly 10s; now it is worth 5s.

Roger holds [East and West] KIMBER from Roald. Æthelwulf held it TRE, and it paid geld for 1 virgate of land. There is land for 3 ploughs. There is 1 plough, and 3 villans and 2 bordars with 1 slave. There are 20 acres of meadow, and 2 acres of scrubland, [and] pasture 3 furlongs long and 2 furlongs broad. Formerly 5s; now it is worth 10s.

The same Roger holds GREAT RUTLEIGH from Roald. Alric held it freely in parage TRE, and it paid geld for 1 ferding. There is land for 2 ploughs. There is half a plough, with 3 bordars, and 15 acres of meadow and as many of pasture, and 10 acres of woodland. Formerly, as now, [worth] 5s.

Reginald holds WEST PUTFORD from Roald. 2 thegns held it in parage TRE, and it paid geld for 2½ virgates of land. There is land for 6 ploughs. In demesne are 2 ploughs, and 2 slaves; and 3 villans and 3 bordars with 1 plough. There are 30 acres of meadow, [and] pasture 1 furlong long and as much broad. Formerly 10s; now it is worth 20s.

Roald himself holds WEARE GIFFARD. Ordwulf held it TRE, and it paid geld for 1 hide. There is land for 7 ploughs. In demesne are 2 ploughs, and 9 slaves; and 16 villans with 5½ ploughs. There is half a fishery rendering 40d, and 10 acres of meadow, and 15 acres of woodland and 20 acres of pasture. Formerly, as now, worth 40s.

The Count of Mortain holds half a virgate of land of the same manor. There is land for 1 plough. There are 2 slaves. It is worth 5s.

Roald himself holds HUXHILL. Alweard held it TRE, and it paid geld for 1 virgate of land. There is land for 2 ploughs. There 3 villans have 1 plough. There is 1 acre of meadow, and 4 acres of pasture and 3 acres of scrubland. Formerly 30d; now it is worth 5s.

Gilbert holds HOLLAM from Roald. Eadmær held it TRE, and it paid geld for 1 ferding. There is land for 3 ploughs. There are 1½ ploughs, and 4 villans and 2 bordars with 1 slave, and 2 acres of meadow, and 4 acres of pasture and 2 acres of scrubland. Formerly 5s; now it is worth 10s.

Reginald holds PETERS MARLAND from Roald. Alric held it TRE, and it paid geld for 3 virgates of land. There is land for 9 ploughs. There are 6 ploughs, and 4 slaves and 7 villans, and 10 acres of meadow and 6 acres of scrubland. [There is] pasture 2 furlongs long and 1 furlong broad. Formerly 20s; now it is worth 30s.

Roald himself holds TWIGBEARE. Æthelsige held it TRE, and it paid geld for 1 virgate of land. There is land for 3 ploughs, which are there, and 5 villans and 4 slaves, and 5 acres of meadow, and 6 acres of pasture and 4 acres of woodland. Formerly 10s; now it is worth 15s.

Roald himself holds WINSCOTT. Ælfhere held it TRE, and it paid geld for 1 virgate of land. There is land for 3 ploughs.

There are 2 ploughs, with 1 slave and 5 villans. There are 4 acres of meadow and as many of pasture, and as many of woodland. Formerly 10s; now it is worth 15s.

Roald himself holds WINSWELL. Alwine held it TRE, and it paid geld and it paid geld [sic] for 1 virgate of land. There is land for 2 ploughs; which are there, with 3 villans. There are 4 acres of meadow, and 6 acres of pasture and 2 acres of scrubland. Formerly 5s; now it is worth 10s.

Roald himself holds LOVACOTT. Lufa held it TRE, and it paid geld for half a virgate of land. There is land for 2 ploughs. There are 2 villans, and 4 acres of meadow and 12 acres of pasture. Formerly 30d; now it is worth 50d.

Roald himself holds TWIGBEARE. Alweard held it TRE, and it paid geld for half a virgate of land. There is land for 2 ploughs. There are 3 villans with 1 slave, and 2 acres of meadow, and 5 acres of pasture and 6 acres of woodland. Formerly 30d; now it is worth 4s.

Reginald holds HANKFORD from Roald. Eadmær held it TRE, and it paid geld for 1 ferding. There is land for 1 plough. 1 villan has this [plough] there, with 1 bordar. There are 4 acres of meadow and 6 acres of pasture. Formerly, as now, worth 40d.

Reginald holds LOBB [Lobb and North Lobb] from Roald. Ulf held it TRE, and it paid geld for half a hide. There is land for 4 ploughs. There is 1 plough, and 4 villans and 2 bordars and 2 slaves, and 7 acres of meadow and 30 acres of pasture. Formerly 30s; now it is worth 20s.

The same Reginald holds CROCKERNWELL from Roald. it TRE, and it paid geld for 1 virgate of land. There is land for 4 ploughs. There are 2 ploughs, with 1 slave, and 2 villans and 2 bordars, and 4 acres of meadow and 30 acres of pasture. Formerly, as now, worth 15s.

The same Reginald holds PULHAM from Roald. 2 thegns held it freely in parage TRE, and it paid geld for 1½ virgates of land. There is land for 3 ploughs. There is 1 plough, with 1 villan and 2 bordars, and 6 acres of woodland and 5 acres of meadow. It is worth 13s. This [land], which could go to whichever lord, is called Praunsley, and there is half a virgate of land in it, and it is worth 3s.

Salomon holds SIGFORD from Roald. Beorhtric held it TRE, and it paid geld for 1 virgate of land. There is land for 1½ ploughs. There is half a plough, and 8 acres of pasture and 6 acres of woodland. Formerly 3s; now it is worth 5s.

Roald himself holds POUGHILL. Eadmær held it TRE, and it paid geld for 1 virgate and 1 ferding. There is land for 2 ploughs, which are there. Formerly 3s; now it is worth 5s.

Walter holds WEST DOCKWORTHY. Alflæd held it TRE, and it paid geld for 1 virgate of land. There is land for 2 ploughs. There is 1 plough, with 1 slave and 2 bordars. There are 3 acres of meadow, and 4 acres of woodland, and pasture 1 furlong long and a half broad. Formerly 3s; now it is worth 5s.

Roald himself holds AVETON GIFFORD. Sæwine held it

TRE, and it paid geld for 3 hides. There is land for 12 ploughs. In demesne are 3 ploughs, and 8 slaves; and 16 villans and 17 bordars with 4 ploughs. There are 20 acres of meadow, and 30 acres of pasture and 44 acres of scrubland. Formerly 20s; now it is worth £3.

Reginald holds TRAIN from Roald. Osfrith held it TRE, and it paid geld for half a hide. There is land for 4 ploughs. There are 1½ ploughs, and 5 villans and 3 bordars, and 1 salt-pan, and 4 acres of meadow and 20 acres of scrubland. Formerly 10s; now it is worth 15s.

Walter holds HEMERDON from Roald. Goda held it TRE, and it paid geld for 1 hide. There is land for 4 ploughs. There 2 villans and 2 bordars have half a plough. There are 60 acres of pasture. Formerly, as now, worth 10s.

Roald himself holds WHITCHURCH. Sæwine held it TRE, and it paid geld for 1 hide. There is land for 12 ploughs. In demesne are 3 ploughs, and 8 slaves; and 20 villans and 15 bordars with 5 ploughs. There are 20 acres of meadow, pasture 1 league long and 4 furlongs broad, [and] woodland 2 leagues long and 4 furlongs broad. Formerly 30s; now it is worth 70s.

Reginald holds MONKSWELL from Roald. Sæwine held it TRE, and it paid geld for 1 ferding. There is land for 1 plough. There is half a plough, with 1 bordar and 1 slave. Formerly 2s; now it is worth 3s.

Roald himself has in Exeter 1 house which renders the king's customary dues.

XXXVI. The land of Theobald fitzBerner

THEOBALD fitzBerner holds YARNSCOMBE from the king. 2 thegns held it TRE, and it paid geld for 1 virgate of land. There is land for 8 ploughs. In demesne is 1 plough, and 2 slaves; and 8 villans and 5 bordars with 3 ploughs. There are 5 acres of meadow, and 60 acres of pasture and 12 acres of woodland. Formerly 100s; now it is worth 20s.

Theobald himself holds BUCK'S CROSS. 3 thegns held it TRE, and it paid geld for half a hide. There is land for 4 ploughs. There are 4 villans, and 5 acres of meadow, and 10 acres of pasture and 20 acres of scrubland. Formerly 5s; now it is worth 12s6d.

Gosbert holds SOUTH HOLE [in Hartland] from Theobald. Sæwine held it TRE, and it paid geld for 5 virgates of land. There is land for 4 ploughs. There are 1½ ploughs, with 1 slave and 7 bordars, and 5 acres of meadow and 10 acres of pasture. Formerly 10s; now it is worth 25s.

The same Gosbert holds MILFORD [in Hartland] from Theobald. Sæwine held it TRE, and it paid geld for half a hide. There is land for 3 ploughs. There are 2½ ploughs, and 2 slaves and 5 villans, and 2 acres of meadow and 10 acres of pasture. Formerly 15s; now it is worth 25s.

The same Gosbert holds SPECCOTT from Theobald. Elaf held it TRE, and it paid geld for 1 virgate of land. There is

land for 3 ploughs. There is 1 villan, and 15 acres of meadow and 40 acres of pasture. Formerly, as now, worth 7s6d.

[Folio 115V: DEVONSHIRE]

The same Gosbert holds LITTLE MARLAND from Theobald. Leofgar held it TRE, and it paid geld for 1 virgate of land and 1 ferding. There is land for 3 ploughs. There are 3 villans with 1 slave, and 10 acres of meadow, and 20 acres of pasture, [and] scrubland 3 furlongs long and 1 furlong broad. Formerly 5s; now it is worth 10s.

Goscelm holds OWLACOMBE from Theobald. Ælfgifu held it TRE, and it paid geld for half a hide. There is land for 4 ploughs. There are 3 ploughs, with 1 bordar and 2 villans. There is 1 acre of meadow, and 60 acres of pasture and 20 acres of scrubland. Formerly 25s; now it is worth 20s.

Bernard holds BICKLETON from Theobald. Godwine held it TRE, and it paid geld for half a hide. There is land for 4 ploughs. There is 1 plough, with 1 slave, and 3 acres of meadow and half an acre of woodland. Formerly 20d; now it is worth 7s6d.

Theobald himself holds HOLLOWCOMBE [in Fremington]. Æthelmaelig;r held it TRE, and it paid geld for 1 virgate of land. There is land for 1 plough. There are 3 salt-workers; they render 4s9d and 5 summae of salt and 1 summa of fish.

Theobald himself holds SAUNTON. Dodda held it TRE, and it paid geld for 2 hides. There is land for 10 ploughs. In demesne is 1 plough, and 2 slaves; and 12 villans and 10 bordars with 6 ploughs. There is a salt-pan rendering 30d, and 16 acres of meadow and 60 acres of pasture. Formerly, as now, worth 60s.

Theobald himself holds [North and South] HOLE [in Georgeham]. Eadmær held it TRE, and it paid geld for half a virgate of land. There is land for 2 ploughs. There 2 villans have 1 plough, and they pay 5s.

Theobald himself holds GEORGEHAM. Eadmær held it TRE, and it paid geld for 3 virgates of land. There is land for 6 ploughs. There are 3 ploughs, and 5 villans and 2 slaves. Formerly, as now, worth 20s.

Theobald himself holds SPREACOMBE [Spreacombe and Higher Spreacombe]. Vitalis held it TRE, and it paid geld for 1 virgate of land. There is land for 3 ploughs. There are 2½ ploughs, with 1 slave, and 2 villans and 2 bordars, and 1 acre of meadow, and 40 acres of pasture and 7 acres of scrubland. Formerly 60s; now it is worth 20s.

Theobald himself holds OSSABOROUGH. Wadel held it TRE, and it paid geld for 1 virgate of land. There is land for 3 ploughs. There is 1 plough, with 1 slave and 1 villan and 2 bordars, and 1 acre of meadow, and 2 acres of woodland and 30 acres of pasture. Formerly 20s; now it is worth 5s.

Joscelin holds WOOLACOMBE from Theobald. Beorhtgyth held it TRE, and it paid geld for 1 virgate of land. There is land for 2 ploughs. There are 1½ ploughs, with 1 villan, and 1 acre of meadow and 20 acres of pasture. Formerly, as now, worth 20s.

Oliver holds MIDDLE MARWOOD from Theobald. Beorhtric held it TRE, and it paid geld for 1 virgate of land. There is land for 2 ploughs, which are there, with 1 slave and 1 villan and 2 bordars. There are 6 acres of meadow, and 60 acres of pasture and 20 acres of woodland. Formerly, as now, worth 15s.

Bernard holds [Higher and Lower] MOLLAND [in North Molton] from Theobald. Northmann held it TRE, and it paid geld for 1 virgate of land. There is land for 2 ploughs. There are 3 oxen, with 1 slave, and 3 acres of meadow and 12 acres of woodland. Formerly 3s; now it is worth 7s6d.

Oliver holds CULM DAVY from Theobald. Kolbrand held it TRE, and it paid geld for 1 hide. There is land for 4 ploughs. There are 3 ploughs, and 2 slaves and 6 villans and 6 bordars. There is a mill rendering 5s, and 12 acres of meadow, and 48 acres of woodland and 4 furlongs of pasture. Formerly 70s; now it is worth 50s.

With this manor Oliver holds GORWELL from Theobald. Kolbrand held it as a manor TRE, and it paid geld for half a virgate of land. It is worth 10s.

Theobald himself holds CHERITON FITZPAINE. Almær held it TRE, and it paid geld for 1 hide, less half a virgate of land. There is land for 5 ploughs. In demesne is 1 plough, and 2 slaves; and 5 villans and 10 bordars with 3 ploughs. There are 3 acres of meadow and 6 acres of woodland. Formerly 40s; now it is worth 20s.

Jagelin holds COOMBE [in Cheriton Fitzpaine] from Theobald. Æthelmær held it TRE, and it paid geld for half a hide. There is land for 3 ploughs. In demesne are 2 ploughs, and 11 slaves; and 2 villans and 2 bordars with 1½ ploughs. There are 28 acres of woodland, and 6 acres of meadow and 60 acres of pasture. Formerly, as now, worth 15s.

Theobald himself holds WASHFORD PYNE. Colbert held it TRE, and it paid geld for 1 virgate of land. There is land for 1 plough. There 2 villans and 2 bordars have half a plough. There are 2 acres of meadow. Formerly, as now, worth 10s.

Theobald himself holds WASHFORD PYNE. 4 thegns held it in parage TRE, and it paid geld for 1 virgate of land. There is land for 1½ ploughs. There is 1 plough, with 2 bordars, and 1 acre of meadow. Formerly, as now, worth 5s.

Alweald holds WASHFORD PYNE from Theobald. Wulfmær held it TRE, and it paid geld for half a hide. There is land for 3 ploughs. There are 2 ploughs, and 3 villans and 2 bordars, and 5 acres of meadow and 2 acres of woodland. It is worth 12s6d. Theobald holds these 3 manors as 1 manor. 6 thegns held them freely.

The same Alweald holds "DERTRE" from Theobald. The same Alweald held it TRE, and it paid geld for 1 virgate of land. There is land for 3 ploughs. There are 1½ ploughs, and 2 slaves and 3 villans, and 7 acres of meadow and 12 acres of pasture. Formerly 20s; now it is worth 12s6d.

Aubrey holds RIFTON from Theobald. Æthelmær held it TRE, and it paid geld for half a hide. There is land for 3 ploughs. There are 1½ ploughs, and 3 villans and 2 bordars, and 5 acres of meadow and 10 acres of pasture. It is worth 10s.

To this manor has been added 1 virgate of land which a thegn held freely TRE. It is worth 4s.

Oliver holds WIDWORTHY from Theobald. Æthelmær held it TRE, and it paid geld for 1 hide. There is land for 5 ploughs. There are 2 ploughs, and 3 slaves and 7 villans and 4 bordars. There is a mill rendering 5s, and 1 acre of meadow, and 30 acres of pasture and 160 acres of woodland. Formerly, as now, worth 30s.

WILMINGTON has been added to this manor. Alweard held it TRE, and it paid geld for half a hide. There is land for 2 ploughs. It is worth 5s.

Theobald himself has in Exeter 1 house which renders 8d to the king in customary dues.

XXXVII. The land of Turstin fitzRolf

TURSTIN fitzRolf holds CHURCHSTANTON [Som.] from the king, and Geron from him. Ælfgifu held it TRE, and it paid geld for 3 hides. There is land for 20 ploughs. In demesne is 1 plough, and 4 slaves; and 24 villans and 8 bordars with 9½ ploughs. There are 7 acres of meadow, pasture 1½ leagues long and 1 league broad, [and] woodland 5 furlongs long and 4 furlongs broad. Formerly £10; now it is worth 100s.

XXXVIII. The land of Alvred D'Epaignes

ALVRED d'Epaignes holds ARLINGTON from the king. Alwig held it TRE, and it paid geld for 1 hide. There is land for 15 ploughs. In demesne are 2 ploughs, and 3 slaves; and 11 villans with 5 ploughs. There are 3 acres of meadow, and 4 acres of woodland and half a league of pasture. Formerly £8; now it is worth £3.

TWITCHEN has been added to this manor. Beorhtweald held it freely TRE, and it paid geld for 1 virgate of land. There is land for 3 ploughs. There 4 villans have 1 plough, and there are 30 acres of woodland. Formerly 20s; now it is worth 5s.

Alvred himself holds ORWAY. Alwig held it TRE, and it paid geld for half a hide. There is land for 3 ploughs. In demesne is 1 plough, with 1 slave, and 8 villans and 6 bordars, and 5 acres of meadow, and 100 acres of pasture and 4 acres of woodland. Formerly, as now, worth 30s.

XXXIX. The land of Alvred the Breton

ALVRED the Breton holds WILLSWORTHY from the king. Siward held it TRE, and it paid geld for 1 virgate of land. There is land for 4 ploughs. In demesne is 1 plough, and 4 slaves, and 12 acres of woodland. [There is] pasture 2 leagues long and 1 league broad. Formerly, as now, worth 30s.

Wihanoc holds SPRYTOWN from Alvred. Ealhhere held it TRE, and it paid geld for 1 virgate of land. There is land for 2 ploughs. There are $1\frac{1}{2}$ ploughs, with 1 slave and 4 bordars. There are 3 acres of meadow and 5 acres of woodland. Formerly, as now, worth 10s.

Fulk holds "FERDING" from Alvred. Sæwine held it TRE, and it paid geld for 1 ferding of land. There is land for $1\frac{1}{2}$ ploughs. There 5 bordars with 1 slave have half a plough. There are 10 acres of meadow. Formerly, as now, worth 10s.

[Folio 116: DEVONSHIRE]

Alvred himself holds INGLEIGH [Ingleigh Green and Lower Ingley]. Godric held it TRE, and it paid geld for 1 virgate of land. There is land for 6 ploughs. In demesne is 1 plough, with 1 slave; and 4 villans and 4 bordars with 1 plough. There are 8 acres of meadow and as many of woodland, and 10 acres of pasture. Formerly 30s; now it is worth 20s.

Alvred himself holds EXBOURNE. Wulfnoth held it TRE, and it paid geld for 1 virgate of land. There is land for 6 ploughs. In demesne is 1 plough, with 1 slave; and 2 villans and 2 bordars with 1 plough. There are 6 acres of meadow, and 8 acres of pasture and 10 acres of woodland. Formerly 30s; now it is worth 20s.

Three thegns holds CURWORTHY from Alvred. They themselves held it TRE, and it paid geld for 1 virgate of land. There is land for 3 ploughs. There is 1 villan and 1 slave, and 12 acres of meadow and as many of woodland, and 300 acres of pasture. Formerly, as now, worth 10s6d. They were 3 manors.

Wihanoc holds ASHBURY from Alvred. Leofric held it TRE, and it paid geld for 1 virgate of land. There is land for 5 ploughs. There are 2 ploughs, and 2 slaves and 5 villans and 4 bordars, and 10 acres of meadow, and 6 acres of woodland and 200 acres of pasture. Formerly 5s; now it is worth 20s.

The same Wihanoc holds GIFFORDS HELE from Alvred. Æthelwulf held it TRE, and it paid geld for half a hide. There is land for 5 ploughs. There are 4 ploughs, and 3 slaves and 5 villans and 2 bordars, and 6 acres of meadow, and 30 acres of pasture and 20 acres of woodland. Formerly 20s; now it is worth 25s.

William holds [?] ROADWAY from Alvred. Godric held it TRE, and it paid geld for half a virgate of land. There is land for 2 ploughs. There is 1 plough, with 1 slave and 1 villan, and 2 acres of meadow and 20 acres of pasture. Formerly, as now, worth 10s.

Alvred himself holds LARKBEARE. Ulf held it TRE, and it paid geld for half a hide. There is land for 2 ploughs. There is 1 plough, and 2 slaves and 5 villans with 1 bordar. There are 20 acres of meadow and as many of woodland, and 200 acres, less 7, of pasture. Formerly, as now, worth 20s.

To this manor has been added half a hide which belongs to Whimple, Baldwin's manor. Formerly, as now, worth 5s.

William holds BATTLEFORD from Alvred. Sæwulf held it TRE, and it paid geld for 1 hide. There is land for 3 ploughs.

There are $1\frac{1}{2}$ ploughs, with 1 slave, and 3 villans with 1 bordar. There are 7 acres of meadow, and 20 acres of pasture and half an acre of scrubland. Formerly 20s; now it is worth 15s.

The same William holds GRIMPSTONE from Alvred. Alnoth held it TRE, and it paid geld for half a hide. There is land for 2 ploughs. However, in demesne is 1 plough, with 1 slave; and 2 villans and 2 bordars with 2 ploughs, and 15 acres of pasture. Formerly 10s; now it is worth 15s.

The same William holds GRIMPSTONLEIGH from Alvred. Alnoth held it TRE, and it paid geld for 1 virgate of land. There is land for 3 ploughs, which are there, with 1 slave and 3 villans, and 10 acres of pasture. Formerly 10s; now it is worth 20s.

Alvred himself holds [North and South] BATTISBOROUGH. Almær held it TRE, and it paid geld for 1 hide. There is land for 8 ploughs. In demesne is 1 plough, with 1 slave; and 6 villans and 5 bordars with 2 ploughs. There are 15 acres of pasture and 4 acres of scrubland. Formerly, as now, worth 30s.

CREACOMBE [in Newton Ferrers] has been added to this manor. Almær held it as a manor TRE, and it paid geld for half a hide. There is land for 2 ploughs. There is half a plough. It is worth 10s.

Tovi holds SOUTH MILTON from Alvred. 2 thegns held it freely TRE, and it paid geld for 2 hides. There is land for 12 ploughs. In demesne are 2 ploughs, with 1 slave; and 8 villans and 6 bordars with 3 ploughs. There are 6 acres of meadow. Formerly, as now, worth 60s.

William holds MORELEIGH from Alvred. Ælfric held it TRE, and it paid geld for half a hide. There is land for 4 ploughs. There are 3 ploughs, and 4 slaves and 5 villans, and 4 acres of meadow, and 40 acres of pasture and 7 acres of woodland. Formerly, as now, worth 20s. This land has been added to the manor of GRIMPSTONLEIGH.

Alvred himself holds UGBOROUGH. Alwine held it TRE, and it paid geld for 3 hides and 1 virgate of land. There is land for 15 ploughs. In demesne are 2 ploughs, and 5 slaves; and 9 villans and 9 bordars with 6 ploughs. There are 12 acres of meadow, and 50 acres of pasture and 15 acres of scrubland. It is worth 60s.

Alvred himself holds BUDSHEAD [in Plymouth]. Alwine held it TRE, and it paid geld for half a hide. There is land for 5 ploughs. In demesne are 2 ploughs, and 4 slaves; and 5 villans with 1 plough. There are 4 acres of meadow, [and] scrubland half a league long and 2 furlongs broad. Formerly, as now, worth 30s.

Alvred himself holds TAMERTON FOLIOT [in Plymouth]. Ingvar held it TRE, and it paid geld for 2 hides. There is land for 10 ploughs. In demesne are 3 ploughs, and 7 slaves; and 16 villans and 6 bordars with 5 ploughs. There is a salt-pan rendering 5s, and 3 acres of meadow, pasture 3 furlongs long and 1 furlong broad, [and] woodland half a league long and 3 furlongs broad. Formerly 60s; now it is worth 100s.

Alvred himself holds BLAXTON. Ingvar held it TRE, and it paid geld for 1 hide. There is land for 4 ploughs. In demesne are 2 ploughs, and 5 slaves; and 4 villans with 1 plough, and 1 swineherd rendering 5 pigs, and a salt-pan rendering 30d. [There is] woodland 1 league long and 3 furlongs broad, [and] pasture 3 furlongs long and 1 furlong broad. Formerly 20s; now it is worth 50s.

Alvred himself holds PETER TAVY. Siward held it TRE, and it paid geld for 1 hide. There is land for 7 ploughs. In demesne are 2 ploughs, and 9 slaves; and 5 villans and 6 bordars with 2 ploughs. There are 4 acres of meadow, pasture 16 furlongs long and 9 furlongs broad, woodland 3 furlongs long and 1 furlong broad, and 16 acres of scrubland. Formerly 20s; now it is worth 60s.

Alvred himself has in Exeter 1 house which renders 8d in customary dues.

XLI. The land of Ansgar

ANSGAR of Montacute holds STAFFORD from the king. Ælfric held it TRE, and it paid geld for half a virgate of land. There is land for 1 plough, which [plough] is there, with 1 slave and 5 bordars. There are 4 acres of meadow, and 2 acres of woodland, [and] pasture 2 furlongs long and 1 furlong broad. Formerly 7s6d; now it is worth 12s6d.

Ansgar himself holds 1 virgate of land in GREAT TORRINGTON. Ælfric held it TRE. There is land for 2 ploughs, which are there, with 1 villan and 3 bordars. There are 4 acres of meadow. Formerly, as now, worth 15s.

Ansgar himself holds BRIMBLECOMBE. Ealhhere held it TRE, and it paid geld for half a virgate of land. There is land for 1½ ploughs. There is 1 plough, with 3 bordars. Formerly 5s; now it is worth 7s6d.

Ansgar himself holds CHELDON. Mahthild held it TRE, and it paid geld for 1½ virgates of land. There is land for 2 ploughs. In demesne, however, is 1 plough, with 1 slave, and 4 villans and 4 bordars. There are 2 acres of meadow, and 7 acres of woodland and 10 acres of pasture.

Half a virgate of land and half a ferding have been added to this manor. Beorhtmær held them TRE as a manor. There is land for 1½ ploughs. These 2 estates render 50s.

Ansgar himself holds MUXBERE. 5 thegns held it freely in parage from Beorhtric TRE, and it paid geld for 1 hide. There is land for 5 ploughs. In demesne is 1 plough; and 9 villans with 1 bordar and half a plough. There is a mill rendering 60d, and 26 acres of meadow, and 6 acres of woodland, [and] pasture 4 furlongs long and 2 furlongs broad. Formerly 40s; now it is worth 30s. Ansgar holds it as 1 manor.

Ansgar himself holds SUTTON [in Halberton]. Godric held it TRE, and it paid geld for half a hide. There is land for 1½ ploughs. There are, however, 2 ploughs, with 1 slave, and 3 villans with 1 bordar, and 8 acres of meadow, and 10 acres of

pasture and as many of scrubland. Formerly, as now, worth 10s.

This land has been wrongfully added to Beorhtric's lands.

Ansgar himself holds DOLTON. Eadric held it TRE, and it paid geld for 2 virgates of land. There is land for 6 ploughs. In demesne is 1 plough, with 1 slave; and 4 villans and 4 bordars with 2 ploughs. There are 4 acres of meadow, and 10 acres of pasture and 5 acres of scrubland. It is worth 50s.

This land has been wrongfully added to Beorhtric's lands. The man who held it TRE could go where he would.

XLII. The land of Aiulf

AIULF holds SUTTON [in Halberton] from the king. Eadric held it TRE, and it paid geld for half a hide. There is land for 1½ ploughs. There are 4 villans with 1 bordar, and 3 acres of meadow and 10 acres of pasture. Formerly, as now, worth 10s.

William holds WESTLEIGH [in Burlescombe] from Aiulf. Eadmær held it TRE, and it paid geld for 2½ virgates of land. There is land for 1½ ploughs. There are, however, 2 ploughs, and 2 slaves and 2 villans and 5 bordars. There is a mill rendering 36d, and 6 acres of meadow, and 38 acres of pasture and 25 acres of woodland. Formerly 10s; now it is worth 20s.

[Folio 116V: DEVONSHIRE]

XLIII. The land of Odo fitzGamelin

ODO fitzGamelin holds DELLEY from the king. Beorhtric held it |T| [sic] TRE, and it paid geld for 1 virgate of land. There is land for 4 ploughs. In demesne is 1 plough, with 1 slave; and 4 villans with 1 plough. There are 2 acres of meadow, and 10 acres of pasture and 4 acres of woodland. Formerly 10s; now it is worth 20s.

Ralph holds STOWFORD [near Lifton] from Odo. Sæwine held it TRE, and it paid geld for half a hide, less half a ferding. There is land for 6 ploughs. There are 4 ploughs, and 2 slaves and 10 villans and 3 bordars, and 10 acres of meadow, and 15 acres of pasture and 12 acres of woodland. Formerly 50s; now it is worth 40s.

Colwin holds ALMISTON from Odo. Leofgar held it TRE, and it paid geld for 1 virgate of land. There is land for 3 ploughs, which are there, with 1 slave and 6 villans. There are 10 acres of meadow and 40 acres of pasture. Formerly 3s; now it is worth 20s.

Ralph holds HUISH [near Dolton] from Odo. Sæwine held it TRE, and it paid geld for 3 virgates and 1 ferding. There is land for 7 ploughs. There are 5 ploughs, with 1 slave, and 7 villans and 3 bordars. There are 12 acres of meadow, and 50 acres of pasture and 30 acres of woodland. Formerly 60s; now it is worth 40s.

A thegn held 1 ferding of this land freely TRE and he could go where he would.

Odo himself holds LITTLE WEARE and it is attached to his

manor of GREAT TORRINGTON. Beorhtric held it TRE, and it paid geld for 1 virgate of land. There is land for 4 ploughs. There 4 villans and 3 bordars have 1 plough. There are 4 acres of pasture. Formerly, as now, worth 10s.

Odo himself holds GREAT TORRINGTON. Beorhtric held it TRE, and it paid geld for 3½ hides. There is land for 40 ploughs. In demesne are 4 ploughs, and 7 slaves; and 45 villans and 10 bordars with 26 ploughs. There are 20 acres of meadow, and 300 acres of woodland, [and] pasture 2 leagues long and 1 league broad. There are 25 swineherds rendering 110 pigs. Formerly £24; now it is worth £20.

Of this same land 3 Frenchmen hold 3 virgates. They are worth 45s.

Almær holds BUCKLAND [in Dolton] from Odo. Goda held it TRE, and it paid geld for 1½ virgates of land. There is land for 4 ploughs. There are 3½ ploughs, and 2 slaves and 6 villans and 3 bordars, and 2 acres of meadow, and 30 acres of pasture and 12 acres of woodland. Formerly 15s; now it is worth 20s.

Ralph holds WHIDDON from Odo. Northmann held it TRE, and it paid geld for 1 virgate of land. There is land for 2 ploughs. There are 1½ ploughs, with 1 slave and 2 villans and 1 bordar. There is half an acre of meadow, and 40 acres of pasture and 5 acres of scrubland. Formerly, as now, worth 10s.

Gilbert holds SHIRWELL from Odo. Vitalis held it TRE, and it paid geld for 1 virgate of land. There is land for 2 ploughs. There is 1 plough, with 1 slave and 1 villan, and 1 acre of meadow. It is worth 5s.

Odo himself holds GEORGE NYMPTON. 4 thegns held it freely in parage TRE, and it paid geld for 1 hide. There is land for 10 ploughs. In demesne are 4 ploughs, and 5 slaves; and 10 villans and 5 bordars with 4 ploughs. There are 10 acres of meadow and as many of woodland. Formerly 10s; now it is worth 40s.

Odo himself holds HONITON [in South Molton]. Alweald held it TRE, and it paid geld for half a virgate of land. There is land for 2 ploughs, which are there, with 3 villans and 2 bordars. There are 7 acres of meadow. Formerly 2s; now it is worth 5s.

Odo himself holds NORTH ALLER [in South Molton]. Godgifu held it TRE, and it paid geld for half a virgate of land. There is land for 2 ploughs. There are, however, 3 ploughs, with 1 slave and 4 villans and 1 bordar. There are 4 acres of meadow and 30 acres of pasture. It is worth 10s. Edda held 1 ferding of this land TRE and she could go where she would. There is land for 1 plough.

Alwig holds HACCHE from Odo. Vitalis held it TRE, and it paid geld for half a hide. There is land for 4 ploughs. There are 3 ploughs, and 3 slaves and 4 villans and 4 bordars, and 4 acres of meadow, and 10 acres of woodland and 20 acres of pasture. Formerly, as now, worth 20s.

Odo himself holds STALLENGE THORNE. Æthelric held it TRE, and it paid geld for 1 hide. There is land for 2 ploughs,

which are there, with 1 villan and 4 bordars. There are 2 acres of meadow and 2 acres of scrubland. It is worth 10s.

This land is [part] of his manor of HUNTSHAM.

Reginald holds BRAYLEY from Odo. Wulfwynn held it TRE, and it paid geld for 1 virgate of land. There is land for 6 ploughs. There are 1½ ploughs, and 4 slaves and 2 villans and 1 bordar, and 2 acres of meadow, and 10 acres of scrubland and half a league of pasture. It is worth 20s.

Odo himself holds BROADHEMBURY. Beorhtric held it TRE, and it paid geld for 4 hides. There is land for 14 ploughs. In demesne are 2 ploughs; and 11 bordars and 29 villans with 10 ploughs, and 2 swineherds rendering 10 pigs. There is a mill rendering 10s, and 10 acres of meadow, and 50 acres of pasture and 80 acres of woodland. Formerly £11; now it is worth £8.

1 hide in SHAPCOMBE was attached to this manor TRE. There is land for 3 ploughs. Ludo holds it wrongfully with Walter's land, and he has there 2 ploughs, and 6 villans. It is worth 30s.

Odo himself holds PLYMTREE. Beorhtric held it TRE, and it paid geld for 2 hides and 1 virgate of land. There is land for 5 ploughs. In demesne are 2 ploughs, and 4 slaves; and 15 villans and 4 bordars with 3 ploughs. There are 20 acres of meadow and 20 acres of woodland. Formerly, as now, worth 100s.

Reginald holds HILLERSDON from Odo. Scirweald held it TRE, and it paid geld for half a hide. There is land for 3 ploughs. There is 1 plough, with 1 slave, and 5 villans and 7 bordars, and 3 acres of meadow and 7 furlongs of pasture. Formerly, as now, worth 10s.

Hubert holds ESSEBEARE from Odo. Eadmær held it TRE, and it paid geld for 1 virgate of land. There is land for half a plough, which [half-plough] is there, and 4 acres of meadow. Formerly, as now, worth 3s.

Odo himself holds "DERTE". Beorhtric held it TRE, and it paid geld for 1½ virgates of land. There is land for 4 ploughs. In demesne is 1 plough, and 3 slaves; and 4 villans and 3 bordars with 1 plough. There are 5 acres of meadow and 40 acres of pasture. Formerly 20s; now it is worth 30s.

Alwig holds WEST WORLINGTON [near Witheridge] from Odo. Ælfric held it TRE, and it paid geld for 1 ferding of land. There is land for half a plough. It is worth 30d.

To this manor has been added the land of 9 thegns which they held freely in parage TRE, and it paid geld for 3 virgates of land. There is land for 6 ploughs. Alwig has 3½ ploughs there, with 1 slave and 12 villans and 3 bordars. There are 12 acres of meadow, and 5 acres of scrubland and 30 acres of common pasture. Formerly, as now, worth 30s.

2 virgates of land have also been joined to the same manor. 2 thegns held them in parage TRE as 2 manors. There is land for 3 ploughs. They are worth 10s.

Odo himself holds CHILTON. Æthelmær held it TRE, and it paid geld for half a virgate of land. There is land for 2 ploughs, which are there, and 3 slaves and 2 villans and 2 bordars, and 1 acre of meadow, and 5 acres of pasture and as many of woodland. Formerly 5s; now it is worth 10s.

Odo himself holds HUNTSHAM. Æthelric held it TRE, and it paid geld for 1 hide. There is land for 8 ploughs. In demesne are 2 ploughs, and 2 slaves; and 20 villans and 4 bordars with 5 ploughs. There are 6 acres of meadow, and 15 acres of pasture and 50 acres of woodland. Formerly 20s; now it is worth 40s.

Vitalis holds WILLAND from Odo. Eadmær held it TRE, and it paid geld for 1 hide. There is land for 6 ploughs. There are 2 ploughs, with 1 slave, and 8 villans and 3 bordars, and a mill rendering 40d. [There is] meadow 3 furlongs long and 1$\frac{1}{2}$ furlongs broad, pasture 8 furlongs long and 3 furlongs broad, [and] woodland 4 furlongs long and 1 furlong broad. Formerly, as now, worth 40s.

XLIIII. The land of Osbern de Sacey

OSBERN de Sacey holds PARFORD from the king. Godric held it TRE, and it paid geld for 1 virgate of land. There is land for 5 ploughs. There 6 villans with 1 slave have 1 plough. There are 12 acres of meadow and 20 acres of pasture. Formerly, as now, worth 20s.

This land owes either 1 ox or 30d a year in customary dues to South Tawton, the king's manor.

Osbern himself holds CLYST GERRED. Uhtræd held it TRE, and it paid geld for 3 hides and 1 virgate of land. There is land for 8 ploughs. In demesne is 1 plough, and 2 slaves; and 3 villans and 6 bordars with 6 ploughs. There are 40 acres of meadow, and 60 acres of pasture and 26 acres of woodland. Formerly 15s; now it is worth 40s.

Osbern himself holds SHILSTONE. Eadric held it TRE, and it paid geld [...]

[Folio 117: DEVONSHIRE]

for 1 virgate of land. There is land for 3 ploughs. In demesne are 2 ploughs, and 2 slaves; and 2 villans and 2 bordars with 1 plough. There are 8 acres of meadow and 40 acres of pasture. Formerly 10s; now it is worth 20s.

1 virgate of land was attached to this manor TRE. No one holds it. There are 2 villans. It is worth 3s.

Osbern himself holds LAMBERT. Leofgar held it TRE, and it paid geld for 1 virgate of land. There is land for 2 ploughs. There is 1 plough, and 2 villans with 1 bordar, and 5 acres of meadow and as many of woodland, and 20 acres of pasture. Formerly 5s; now it is worth 10s.

Osbern himself holds INGSDON. Frawin held it TRE, and it paid geld for 1$\frac{1}{2}$ hides. There is land for 6 ploughs. In demesne is 2 slaves; and 15 villans and 3 bordars with 5 ploughs. There are 8 acres of meadow, and 12 acres of woodland and 40 acres of pasture. Formerly 20s; now it is worth 40s.

Osbern himself has in Exeter 1 house from which he withholds the king's customary dues, that is, 8d.

XLV. The land of Hervey de Hellean

The wife of HERVEY de Hellean holds [?Higher] ASHTON from the king. Almær held it TRE, and it paid geld for 1 hide and 2 ferdings. There is land for 3 ploughs. There 4 villans and 4 bordars with 1 slave have 2 ploughs. There are 2 acres of meadow, and 40 acres of pasture and as many of woodland. Formerly, as now, worth 20s.

2 virgates of land and half a ferding have been added to this manor. 2 thegns held them in parage TRE as 2 manors. There is land for 3 ploughs. There 3 villans and 2 bordars have 1 plough. There is 1 swineherd rendering 4 pigs. There are 2 acres of meadow, and 10 acres of woodland and 40 acres of pasture. Formerly, as now, worth 10s.

Hervey's wife has these 3 estates as 1 manor.

She herself holds HACKWORTHY. Eadric held it TRE, and it paid geld for 1 virgate of land. There is land for 2 ploughs, which are there, with 3 villans and 2 bordars and 2 slaves. There are 4 acres of meadow and 24 acres of pasture. Formerly, as now, worth 10s.

Hervey's wife holds these lands in exchange for CHILTON.

XLVI. The land of Gerald the Chaplain

GERALD the chaplain holds [?] SHAPLEY [in Chagford] from the king. A thegn held it TRE, and it paid geld for 1 virgate of land and 1 ferding. This land owes 10s in customary dues to South Tawton, the king's manor.

Gerald himself holds ABBOTS BICKINGTON. Goda held it TRE, and it paid geld for 2 parts of 1 virgate. There is land for 3 ploughs, which are there, with 2 slaves and 8 bordars. There are 5 acres of meadow, and pasture 2 furlongs long and 1 furlong broad and as much woodland.

Gerald himself holds STOKE [in Hartland], and the canons of the same place [hold] from him. They themselves held it TRE, and it paid geld for 2 hides. There is land for 12 ploughs and as many [ploughs] are there. It is worth 40s a year to Gerald.

XLVII. The land of Gerard

GERARD holds WEST MANLEY from the king. Alstan held it TRE, and it paid geld for 1 virgate of land. There is land for 2 ploughs, which are there, with 4 villans and 3 bordars. There are 5 acres of meadow and 4 acres of woodland. Formerly 5s; now it is worth 10s.

Gerard himself holds NUTCOTT. Alstan held it TRE, and it paid geld for 1 virgate of land. There is land for 2 ploughs. There is 1 plough, with 1 slave and 1 villan and 4 bordars. There are 5 acres of meadow and 5 acres of scrubland. Formerly 5s; now it is worth 10s.

XLVIII. The land of Godebold

GODEBOLD holds HELE [in Petrockstow] from the king. Ulf held it TRE, and it paid geld for $1\frac{1}{2}$ virgates of land. There is land for 5 ploughs. In demesne is 1 plough; and 4 villans and 4 bordars with 2 ploughs. There is 1 acre of meadow and 2 acres of pasture. It is worth 10s.

Godebold himself holds HOOK. Ulf held it TRE, and it paid geld for 1 virgate of land. There is land for 2 ploughs. There are 6 acres of meadow and 80 acres of pasture. Formerly 10s; now it is worth 4s.

Godebold himself holds BRUSHFORD. Ælfric held it TRE, and it paid geld for 1 virgate of land. There is land for 3 ploughs. There are 2 bordars with 1 slave. Formerly 10s; now it is worth 20s.

Godebold himself holds [Lower or Man's] NEWTON [in Zeal Monachorum]. Ælfric held it TRE, and it paid geld for 1 virgate of land. There is land for 3 ploughs. There 2 villans have 1 plough, and [there is] 1 acre of meadow and 10 acres of pasture. Formerly 5s; now it is worth 6s6d.

Godebold himself holds DODDISCOMBSLEIGH. Alsige held it TRE, and it paid geld for 3 virgates of land. There is land for 8 ploughs. In demesne are 2 ploughs, and 2 slaves; and 10 villans and 5 bordars and 2 cottars with 4 ploughs. There are 10 acres of meadow, and 30 acres of pasture and 1 virgate of woodland. Formerly 40s; now it is worth 60s.

Godebold himself holds LOWLEY. Alsige held it TRE, and it paid geld for 1 virgate of land. There is land for 4 ploughs. There are $2\frac{1}{2}$ ploughs, and 2 slaves and 2 villans and 4 bordars, and 2 acres of meadow, and 20 acres of pasture and 1 ferding of scrubland. Formerly 10s; now it is worth 20s.

Godebold himself holds MULLACOTT. Ealhhere held it TRE, and it paid geld for half a hide. There is land for 4 ploughs. There are 2 ploughs, and 2 slaves and 5 villans and 2 bordars, and 1 acre of meadow and 10 acres of pasture. Formerly 10s; now it is worth 20s. A thegn held 1 ferding of this land TRE. There is 1 bordar.

Godebold himself holds SATTERLEIGH. Wulfnoth held it TRE, and it paid geld for 1 virgate of land. There is land for 5 ploughs. There are 3 ploughs, and 2 slaves and 6 villans and 2 bordars. There are 4 acres of meadow, and 10 acres of pasture and as many of woodland. Formerly 20s; now it is worth 25s.

Godebold himself holds BURN. Cypping held it TRE, and it paid geld for 1 virgate of land. There is land for half a plough. There are 4 slaves. It is worth 6s.

Godebold himself holds YARDE [in Silverton]. Cypping held it TRE, and it paid geld for 1 virgate of land. There is land for half a plough. 2 villans have this [half-plough] there. It is worth 5s.

Godebold himself holds CLIFFORD. Æthelræd held it TRE, and it paid geld for half a hide. There is land for 6 ploughs. In demesne are 2 ploughs, and 3 slaves; and 5 villans and 3 bordars with 2 ploughs. There are 3 acres of meadow, and 20 acres of pasture and 20 acres of woodland. Formerly, as now, worth 20s.

Godebold himself holds HALSTOW [in Dunsford]. Ealdræd held it TRE, and it paid geld for half a hide. There is land for 6 ploughs. There are 2 ploughs, and 2 slaves and 5 villans and 5 bordars, and 4 acres of meadow, and 3 acres of woodland and 20 acres of pasture. Formerly, as now, worth 15s.

Jagelin holds WEST WHITNOLE from Godebold. Cypping held it TRE, and it paid geld for $1\frac{1}{2}$ virgates of land. There is land for 2 ploughs. There are, however, 3 ploughs, with 1 slave, and 2 villans and 4 bordars, and 5 acres of meadow and 3 acres of pasture. Formerly 30d; now it is worth 10s.

Rainer holds LOWTON from Godebold. 2 thegns held it in parage TRE, and it paid geld for half a hide. There is land for 4 ploughs. There 4 villans and 2 bordars with 1 slave have 1 plough. There are 4 acres of meadow and 20 acres of pasture. Formerly, as now, worth 10s.

Godebold himself has in Exeter 2 houses which rendered 16d in customary dues TRE.

XLIX. The land of Nicholas the Crossbowman

NICHOLAS holds WEBBERY from the king. Ordric held it TRE, and it paid geld for half a hide. There is land for 3 ploughs. There 4 bordars have 1 plough, and [there are] 4 acres of woodland and 20 acres of pasture. Formerly 12d; now it is worth 15s.

Nicholas himself holds GREENSLINCH. 4 thegns held it in parage TRE, and it paid geld for 3 virgates of land. There is land for 3 ploughs, which are there, with 1 slave, and 4 villans and 3 bordars, and 2 acres of meadow. Formerly 10s; now it is worth 20s.

Nicholas himself holds STOKEINTEIGNHEAD. Ordric held it TRE, and it paid geld for $2\frac{1}{2}$ virgates. There is land for 5 ploughs. There are 4 ploughs, and 6 villans and 7 bordars and 5 slaves, and 3 acres of meadow and 20 acres of pasture. Formerly, as now, worth 30s.

Ralph holds [Higher, Lower and Middle] ROCOMBE from Nicholas. Ordric held it TRE, and it paid geld for 1 hide. There is land for 5 ploughs. There are 3 ploughs, and 3 bordars with 1 slave. There are 2 acres of meadow and 15 acres of pasture. Formerly 10s; now it is worth 20s.

Nicholas himself holds EAST OGWELL. Ordric held it TRE, and it paid geld for $2\frac{1}{2}$ virgates of land. There is land for 5 ploughs. There are 4 villans and 7 bordars and 3 slaves, and a mill rendering 30d, and 3 acres of meadow, and 10 acres of pasture and 6 acres of scrubland. Formerly 20s; now it is worth 30s.

Roger holds HOLBEAM from Nicholas. Ordric held it TRE, and it paid geld for 1 virgate of land. There is land for 3 ploughs. There are 2 ploughs, and 2 slaves and 2 villans with 1 bordar, and 1 acre of meadow and 10 acres of woodland. Formerly 10s; now it is worth 20s.

Roger holds BAGTOR from Nicholas. Ordric held it TRE, and it paid geld for 1 virgate of land. There is land for 5 ploughs. In demesne is 1 plough, with 1 slave; and 6 villans and 2 bordars with 4 ploughs. There are 3 acres of woodland, [and] pasture 1 league long and half a league broad. Formerly 15s; now it is worth 20s.

Nicholas himself holds IDEFORD. Ordric held it TRE, and it paid geld for $3\frac{1}{2}$ hides. There is land for 10 ploughs. In demesne are 2 ploughs, and 4 slaves; and 8 villans

[Folio 117V: DEVONSHIRE]

and 7 bordars with 4 ploughs. There are 8 acres of meadow, and 3 of woodland and 1 league of pasture. Formerly, as now, worth 40s.

Nicholas himself holds STAPLEHILL. Beorhtweald held it TRE, and it paid geld for half a hide. There is land for 2 ploughs. There are 3 villans and 4 bordars with half a plough, and 6 acres of meadow and 12 acres of pasture. Formerly, as now, worth 5s.

Nicholas himself holds BUCKLAND IN THE MOOR. Æthelsige held it TRE, and it paid geld for 3 virgates of land. There is land for 4 ploughs. There are $3\frac{1}{2}$ ploughs, and 3 slaves and 8 villans and 2 bordars, and 4 acres of meadow and 4 furlongs of pasture. [There is] woodland half a league long and 1 furlong broad. Formerly, as now, worth 10s.

Of this land Roger holds 1 virgate of land from Nicholas. It is worth 7s.

Nicholas himself holds ALLER [in Abbotskerswell]. Eadmær held it TRE, and it paid geld for half a virgate of land. There is land for 2 ploughs. There is 1 plough, and 2 villans and 5 bordars with 2 oxen. There are 10 acres of meadow, and 3 acres of woodland and 30 acres of pasture. Formerly [it was worth] 5s; now 10s.

L. The land of Fulcher

FULCHER holds SHILLINGFORD ST GEORGE from the king. Beorhtmær held it TRE, and it paid geld for 1 hide. There is land for 3 ploughs. There are, however, 2 ploughs in demesne, and 3 slaves; and 3 villans and 6 bordars with $3\frac{1}{2}$ ploughs. There are 3 acres of meadow. Formerly 20s; now it is worth 30s.

Fulcher himself holds COLUMBJOHN. Beorhtmær held it TRE, and it paid geld for 3 virgates of land. There is land for 3 ploughs. In demesne is 1 plough, and 3 slaves, and 4 villans and 4 bordars. There is a mill rendering 25s, and 7 acres of meadow, and 6 acres of scrubland and 36 acres of pasture. Formerly 60s; now it is worth 45s.

Fulcher himself holds 'EVELEIGH' [? in Broad Clyst]. Beorhtmær held it TRE, and it paid geld for 1 virgate of land. There is land for 1 plough, which [plough] is there, with 3 bordars. There are 2 acres of meadow, and 40 acres of pasture and 100 acres of woodland. Formerly, as now, worth 15s.

Fulcher himself has 1 virgate of land in [?] CULM VALE, and there is 1 villan paying 10s.

Fulcher himself holds FARRINGDON. Alric held it TRE, and it paid geld for 1 virgate of land. There is land for 3 ploughs, which are there, and 3 slaves and 3 villans and 1 bordar. There are 4 acres of meadow, and 8 acres of pasture and as many of woodland. Formerly 10s; now it is worth 20s.

Fulcher himself holds LEIGH [in Loxbear], and Roger [holds] from him. Godwine held it TRE, and it paid geld for 3 virgates of land. There is land for 5 ploughs. There are 3 ploughs, and 4 slaves and 4 villans and 2 bordars, and 8 acres of meadow and 30 acres of pasture. Formerly 40s; now it is worth 30s.

LI. The land of Haimeric

HAIMERIC holds POLTIMORE from the king. Beorhtric and Scirweald held it in parage TRE, and it paid geld for 3 hides and 1 virgate and 3 ferdings. There is land for 9 ploughs. In demesne are 2 ploughs, and 4 slaves; and 22 villans and 3 bordars with 4 ploughs. There are 47 acres of meadow, and 100 acres of woodland and 53 acres of pasture. Formerly 20s; now it is worth 50s.

Haimeric himself holds [East and West] RUCKHAM. Almær held it TRE, and it paid geld for half a virgate of land. There is land for 1 plough, which [plough] is there, with 1 [...] slave, and 1 acre of meadow, and 4 acres of woodland, and common pasture. It is worth 5s.

Haimeric himself holds HILL. Eadmær held it TRE, and it paid geld for half a ferding. There is half a plough, with 1 slave, and 20 acres of meadow and 100 acres of pasture. It is worth 40d.

Haimeric himself holds COOMBE [in Cruwys Morchard]. Eadmær held it TRE, and it paid geld for half a ferding. There is land for half a plough, which [half-plough] is there, with 1 villan, and 1 acre of meadow. It is worth 30d.

Haimeric himself holds [?Great] BRADLEY. Eadmær held it TRE, and it paid geld for 1 virgate of land. There is land for 1 plough. There are, however, 2 ploughs, and 2 slaves and 3 bordars, and 3 acres of pasture and 12 acres of woodland. Formerly 5s; now it is worth 18s.

LII. The land of the King's Seargents

William the porter holds BICTON from the king. Æthelsige held it TRE, and it paid geld for 1 hide. There is land for 4 ploughs. There are, however, 5 ploughs, with 1 slave, and 4 villans and 8 bordars, and 16 acres of meadow and 8 acres of woodland. Formerly 50s; now it is worth 100s.

WILLIAM the usher holds TAW GREEN from the king. Godric held it TRE, and it paid geld for 1 virgate of land. There is land for 3 ploughs. In demesne is 1 plough,

Fulcher himself holds [East and Great] HUISH [in Tedburn St Mary]. 2 thegns held it in parage TRE, and it paid geld for $2\frac{1}{2}$ virgates of land. There is land for 5 ploughs, which are there, with 1 slave and 4 villans and 3 bordars. There are 4 acres of meadow, and 3 acres of woodland and 20 acres of pasture. Formerly [it was worth] 15s; now 30s. and 2 slaves; and 3 villans with 1½ ploughs. There are 8 acres of meadow, and 50 acres of pasture and 10 acres of woodland. Formerly 10s; now it is worth 20s. This manor owes either 1 ox or 30d in customary dues to SOUTH TAWTON, the king's manor.

William himself holds CROOKE BURNELL. Æthelweard held it TRE, and it paid geld for 3 virgates of land. There is land for 6 ploughs. In demesne are 2 ploughs, and 6 slaves; and 10 villans and 3 bordars with 4 ploughs. There are 23½ acres of meadow and 200 acres of pasture. Formerly 10s; now it is worth 30s. These 2 manors are in exchange for [some of] William's lands.

Ralph holds 1 virgate of land from William. There is land for 2 ploughs. There is 1 slave with 1 female slave. It renders 5s.

William himself holds CADELEIGH. 2 thegns held it freely in parage TRE, and it paid geld for 1 hide. There is land for 7 ploughs. In demesne are 3 ploughs, and 3 slaves; and 14 villans and 5 bordars with 6 ploughs. There are 11 acres of meadow, and 20 acres of pasture and 44 acres of woodland. There is a mill rendering 4s. Formerly 15s; now it is worth 50s.

William himself holds RADDON [in Thorverton]. Edward held it TRE, and it paid geld for 2½ virgates of land. There is land for 3 ploughs, which are there, with 3 villans and 2 bordars. There are 6 acres of meadow and 11 acres of pasture. Formerly 10s; now it is worth 25s.

Ralph holds BLACKBOROUGH from William. Leofwine held it TRE, and it paid geld for 1 hide and 1 virgate of land. There is land for 3 ploughs. There are 9 villans and 2 slaves, and 4 acres of meadow, and 100 acres of pasture and 2 acres of scrubland. Formerly 10s; now it is worth 20s.

William himself holds BOLHAM [in Tiverton]. Beorhtric held it TRE, and it paid geld for 3 virgates of land. There is land for 5 ploughs. In demesne is 1 plough, and 3 slaves; and 11 villans and 6 bordars with 4 ploughs. There is a mill rendering 7s, and 6 acres of meadow, and 20 acres of pasture and 4 acres of woodland. Formerly 50s; now it is worth 40s.

William himself holds ILSHAM. Bera held it TRE, and it paid geld for 1 hide. There is land for 3 ploughs. There are 1½ ploughs, and 2 slaves and 2 villans and 2 bordars, and 20 acres of pasture. Formerly, as now, worth 10s. Roger holds it from William.

Richard holds SUTTON [in Widworthy] from William. Wulfwine held it TRE, and it paid geld for 1 hide. There is land for 7 ploughs. In demesne is 1 plough, and 2 slaves; and 7 villans and 4 bordars with 4 ploughs. Formerly 10s; now it is worth 20s.

The above-mentioned manors are [part] of William's [lands acquired by] exchange.

William himself holds MARIANSLEIGH. Ealdræd held it TRE, and it paid geld for 1 virgate of land. There is land for 9 ploughs. In demesne are 2 ploughs, and 4 slaves; and 12 villans and 5 bordars with 5 ploughs. There are 24 acres of

meadow, and 25 acres of pasture and 100 acres of woodland. Formerly 20s; now it is worth 40s.

William himself holds TORRE. Æthelric held it TRE, and it paid geld for 2 hides. There is land for 7 ploughs. In demesne are 2 ploughs, and 4 slaves; and 16 villans and 12 bordars with 4 ploughs. There are 24 acres of meadow, and 12 acres of woodland and 200 acres of pasture. Formerly, as now, worth 60s.

ANSGAR holds GATCOMBE. Burgræd held it TRE, and it paid geld for 1 hide. There is land for 4 ploughs. In demesne is 1 plough, and 3 slaves; and 6 villans and 3 bordars with 3 ploughs. There are 2 acres of meadow, and 3 acres of scrubland and 27 acres of pasture. Formerly 10s; now it is worth 20s.

MORIN holds LEONARD from the king. Frawin held it TRE, and it paid geld for 3 virgates of land. There is land for 2 ploughs. There is 1 plough, with 1 villan and 3 bordars and 2 slaves. There are 8 acres of meadow, and 16 acres of woodland and 60 acres of pasture. Formerly [it was worth] 40s; now 15s.

THE PRIESTS OF BODMIN holds HOLLACOMBE [near Holsworthy]. They themselves held it TRE, and it paid geld for 1 virgate of land. There is land for 3 ploughs, which are there, and 2 slaves and 6 villans, and 30 acres of meadow. [There is] pasture 4 furlongs long and 2 furlongs broad. It is worth 20s.

The priests themselves hold NEWTON ST PETROCK, which pays geld for 1 hide. There is land for 7 ploughs. In demesne are 2 ploughs, and 2 slaves; and 8 villans and 4 bordars with 5 ploughs. There are 8 acres of meadow, and 20 acres of pasture, [and] woodland half a league long and 3 furlongs broad. It is worth 20s.

[Folio 118: DEVONSHIRE]

LIII. The Lands of the King's Thegns

COLWIN holds CHILSWORTHY from the king. Odeua held it TRE, and it paid geld for half a virgate of land. There is land for 3 ploughs, which are there, with 1 slave and 6 bordars. There are 20 acres of meadow and as many of pasture. It is worth 20s.

The same Colwin holds BREXWORTHY. He himself held it TRE, and it paid geld for 1½ ferdings. There is land for 1 plough. There are 3 slaves with 1 villan, and 15 acres of meadow and 30 acres of pasture. It is worth 5s.

The same Colwin holds CULSWORTHY. He himself held it TRE, and it paid geld for 1 ferding and the third part of 1 ferding. There is land for 2 ploughs. There are 3 bordars with 1 villan, and 5 acres of meadow and 20 acres of pasture. It is worth 7s6d.

The same Colwin holds WOOLFARDISWORTHY [near Hartland]. Godric held it TRE, and it paid geld for half a hide. There is land for 4 ploughs, which are there, and 2 slaves and

2 villans and 4 bordars, and 5 acres of meadow and 10 acres of pasture. Formerly 20s; now it is worth 40s.

The same Colwin holds DUNSBEARE. Godric held it TRE, and it paid geld for 1 virgate of land. There is land for 4 ploughs, which are there, and 2 slaves and 4 bordars. There are 5 acres of meadow and 10 acres of pasture. Formerly, as now, worth 20s.

The same Colwin holds ALLISLAND. Godric held it TRE, and it paid geld for 1½ virgates of land. There is land for 6 ploughs. There are 4 ploughs, and 4 villans and 3 bordars and 2 slaves, and 5 acres of meadow and 12 acres of pasture. Formerly, as now, worth 30s.

The same Colwin holds "HAME". Godric held it TRE, and it paid geld for half a virgate of land. There is land for 1 plough. There is 1 villan. It is worth 5s.

The same Colwin holds WEST HEANTON. Beorhtgifu held it TRE, and it paid geld for 1 virgate of land. There is land for 2 ploughs. There is 1 villan and 2 bordars, and 5 acres of meadow, and 10 acres of pasture and 5 acres of woodland. It is worth 5s.

GODWINE holds NATSON. Alstan held it TRE, and it paid geld for 1 virgate of land. There is land for 2 ploughs, which are there, with 2 villans and 1 bordar. There are 5 acres of meadow and 30 acres of pasture. Formerly 15s; now it is worth 10s.

GODWINE holds CHITTLEHAMPTON. He himself held it TRE, and it paid geld for 1 virgate of land. There is land for 30 ploughs. In demesne are 5 ploughs, and 8 slaves; and 7 villans with 10 ploughs, and 22 swineherds rendering 64 pigs. There are 12 acres of meadows, pasture 9 furlongs long and 3 furlongs broad, [and] woodland 1½ leagues long and half a league broad. It is worth £7.

GODWINE holds CHERITON BISHOP. Alstan held it TRE, and it paid geld for 1 virgate of land. There is land for 3 ploughs. There are 2 ploughs, and 3 villans and 2 slaves, and 1 furlong of woodland. Formerly 20s; now it is worth 10s.

GODWINE holds LAMBERT. Alstan held it TRE, and it paid geld for 1 virgate of land. There is land for 12 ploughs. There are 6 ploughs, and 15 villans and 5 slaves, and 3 acres of meadow, and 4 acres of pasture and 15 acres of woodland. Formerly 40s; now it is worth 20s.

The same Godwine holds MEDLAND. Alstan held it TRE, and it paid geld for 1 hide. There is land for 8 ploughs. In demesne is 1 plough, with 1 slave; and 13 villans with 3 ploughs. There are 10 acres of pasture and 3 acres of woodland. Formerly 40s; now it is worth 20s.

The same Godwine holds WEST OGWELL. Alstan held it TRE, and it paid geld for half a hide. There is land for 3 ploughs. There are 2 ploughs, and 2 slaves and 3 villans and 3 bordars, and 6 acres of pasture. Formerly 20s; now it is worth 10s.

The same Godwine holds COOMBE [in Drewsteignton]. Alstan held it TRE, and it paid geld for 1 virgate of land.

There is land for 2 ploughs. There is 1 plough, and 6 bordars. Formerly, as now, it is worth 5s.

The same Godwine holds WRAY. Alstan held it TRE, and it paid geld for 1 hide. There is land for 6 ploughs, which are there, and 4 slaves and 11 villans and 3 bordars, and 8 acres of meadow and 5 acres of pasture. Formerly 60s; now it is worth 30s.

The same Godwine holds COMBESATCHFIELD. Alstan held it TRE, and it paid geld for 1 hide. There is land for 3 ploughs, which are there, and 3 slaves and 6 villans and 3 bordars, and 6 acres of meadow. Formerly 40s; now it is worth 20s.

The same Godwine holds HOLBROOK. He himself held it TRE, and it paid geld for half a hide of land. There is land for 3 ploughs. There is 1 plough, with 1 slave, and 2 villans and 4 bordars, and 6 acres of meadow. It is worth 10s.

Godwine holds 'DOWN UMFRAVILLE' [in Rousdon]. He himself held it TRE, and it paid geld for 1 hide. There is land for 6 ploughs. There are 3 ploughs, and 2 slaves and 7 villans and 4 bordars, and 3 acres of meadow, and 6 acres of pasture and 10 acres of woodland. It is worth 20s.

Godric holds BULWORTHY. Almær held it TRE, and it paid geld for 1 virgate of land and 1 ferding. There is land for 3 ploughs. There are 2 ploughs, and 3 slaves and 3 villans with 1 bordar. There are 20 acres of meadow, and 20 acres of pasture and 1 acre of woodland. Formerly 5s; now it is worth 10s.

The same Godric holds CALVERLEIGH. Almær held it TRE, and it paid geld for half a hide. There is land for 4 ploughs. There are 2½ ploughs, and 5 slaves and 3 villans and 5 bordars, and 7 acres of meadow and 40 acres of woodland. Formerly 10s; now it is worth 30s.

Oda holds PAYHEMBURY. Eadric held it TRE, and it paid geld for 1 hide. There is land for 2 ploughs, which are there, and 3 slaves and 2 villans and 2 bordars. There are 7 acres of meadow and 40 acres of pasture. Formerly, as now, worth 15s.

The same Oda holds CODDIFORD. Eadric held it TRE, and it paid geld for 1 virgate of land. There is land for 2 ploughs. There is 1 plough, with 1 slave and 1 villan and 2 bordars. There are 3 acres of meadow and 2 acres of pasture. Formerly, as now, worth 6s.

Oda holds WYKE GREEN. Beorhtric held it TRE, and it paid geld for 1 virgate of land. There is land for 1 plough, which [plough] is there, with 1 villan and 3 bordars and 2 slaves. There are 6 acres of meadow, and 5 acres of pasture and 6 acres of woodland. Formerly 10s; now it is worth 8s.

Oda holds ROUSDON. Mahthild held it TRE, and it paid geld for 1 virgate of land. There is land for 2 ploughs, which are there, with 1 villan and 6 bordars and 2 slaves. There are 2 acres of meadow, and 3 acres of pasture and 3 acres of scrubland. Formerly, now, worth 20s.

Ealdæd holds [?] WEEK [in Thornbury]. [...] TRE, and it paid geld for 1 virgate of land. There is land for 3 ploughs. There are 2 ploughs, and 3 slaves and 3 villans, and 10 acres of meadow, and 15 acres of pasture and 5 acres of woodland. It is worth 20s.

Ealdæd holds MANATON. He himself held it TRE, and it paid geld for 1 virgate of land. There is land for 2 ploughs, which are there, with 1 slave and 3 villans and 2 bordars. There are 5 acres of woodland and as many of meadow, and 2 acres of pasture. It is worth 20s.

Æthelræd holds 1 ferding of land in BICKFORDTOWN. He himself held it TRE. There is land for 1 plough, which [plough] is there, with 1 slave and 2 villans. There is 1 acre of meadow, and 1 furlong of woodland and 12 acres of pasture. It is worth 5s.

Alweard holds COLSCOTT. He himself held it TRE, and it paid geld for half a virgate of land. There is land for 2 ploughs, which are there, with 1 villan and 3 bordars and 1 slave. There are 30 acres of pasture. It is worth 5s.

Alweard Mert holds half a virgate of land [...]. He has 1 plough there. It is worth 5s. There is land for 2 ploughs. The queen gave it to him in alms.

Asgot holds MEDDON. He himself held it TRE, and it paid geld for half a hide. There is land for $2\frac{1}{2}$ ploughs, which are there, with 1 slave, and 3 villans and 3 bordars, and 60 acres of meadow and 8 acres of pasture. [There is] woodland 2 furlongs long and 1 furlong broad. It is worth 20s.

Asgot holds VARLEYS [in Petrockstow]. Dunna held it TRE, and it paid geld for half a virgate of land. There is land for 1 plough. There is 1 bordar and 2 slaves, and 12 acres of meadow and as many of woodland, and 15 acres of pasture. It is worth 5s.

Asgot holds SEDBOROUGH. Beorhtmær held it TRE, and it paid geld for 1 virgate of land. There is land for 1 plough. There are 3 slaves with 1 bordar, and 6 acres of meadow and 12 acres of pasture. It is worth 5s.

TRE this Sedborough belonged to PARKHAM, Baldwin the sheriff's manor.

DUNNA holds NEWTON ST CYRES. He himself held it TRE, and it paid geld for 3 hides. There is land for 30 ploughs. In demesne is 1 plough, and 6 slaves; and 21 villans and 8 bordars with 20 ploughs. There is a mill rendering 32d, and 20 acres of meadow, and 28 acres of pasture, [and] scrubland 1 league long and half a league broad. It is worth £6.

He held it from King Edward and now he states he holds it from King William.

Dunna holds NUTWELL. He himself held it TRE, and it paid geld for $1\frac{1}{2}$ hides. There is land for 6 ploughs. There are 3 ploughs, and 2 slaves and 7 villans and 4 bordars, and 4 acres of meadow and 5 acres of pasture. It is worth 20s.

Alnoth holds 'BRAY' [in South Molton]. Wulfwine held it TRE, and it paid geld for half a hide. There is land for 6 ploughs. There are 4 ploughs, and 4 slaves and 4 villans and 4 bordars, and 4 acres of meadow. [There is] pasture half a

league long and 1 furlong broad, [and] woodland 3 furlongs long and 1 furlong broad. It is worth 30s.

[Folio 118V: DEVONSHIRE]

Alwine holds MIDDLECOTT [in Chagford]. He himself held it TRE, and it paid geld for half a ferding of land. There is land for 1 plough, which is there, with 1 slave. There are 2 acres of scrubland. It is worth 5s.

Edwin holds BUTTERLEIGH. He himself held it TRE, and it paid geld for 1 virgate of land. There is land for 2 ploughs. There are, however, 3 ploughs, with 1 bordar and 1 slave and 4 villans. There are 8 acres of woodland. It is worth 15s.

Edwin holds CLYST WILLIAM. Alwine held it TRE, and it paid geld for half a hide. There is land for half a plough. There is 1 villan and 2 slaves, and 2 acres of scrubland, and 3 acres of meadow and 2 acres of pasture. It is worth 6s.

Ulf holds WADHAM. He himself held it TRE, and it paid geld for 1 virgate of land. There is land for 3 ploughs, which are there, and 3 slaves and 4 villans, and 6 acres of meadow and 50 acres of pasture. [There is] woodland 4 furlongs long and 3 furlongs broad. It is worth 20s.

Algar holds KNOWSTONE. He himself held it TRE, and it paid geld for 1 virgate of land. There is land for 3 ploughs. There are 2 ploughs, and 2 slaves and 2 villans and 3 bordars, and 5 acres of meadow, and 30 acres of pasture and 1 acre of scrubland. It is worth $7\frac{1}{2}$s.

Algar holds DUNSTONE [in Yealmpton]. He himself held it TRE, and it paid geld for half a hide. There is land for 3 ploughs. There are 2 ploughs, and 2 slaves with 1 villan and 1 bordar. There are 4 acres of woodland. It is worth 10s.

Alric holds WASPLEY. He himself held it TRE, and it paid geld for half a hide. There is land for 4 ploughs. There are 3 ploughs, with 1 slave, and 4 villans and 3 bordars. There are 5 acres of meadow, and 30 acres of pasture and 6 acres of woodland. Formerly, as now, worth 20s.

Ælfric holds SHAPLEY [in North Bovey]. He himself held it TRE, and it paid geld for half a virgate of land. There is land for 2 ploughs, which are there, with 1 slave and 3 villans and 1 bordar. There are 10 acres of pasture. It is worth 8s.

Ælfric holds SKERRATON. He himself held it TRE, and it paid geld for 1 virgate of land. There is land for 2 ploughs, which are there, with 1 slave and 3 villans and 3 bordars. There are 20 acres of woodland and 60 acres of pasture. It is worth 7s6d.

Leofric holds TWINYEO. He himself held it TRE, and it paid geld for 1 virgate of land. There is land for 1 plough. There 2 villans with 1 bordar have half a plough, and there are 2 acres of meadow. It is worth 20d.

Sæwulf holds DUNSFORD. He himself held it TRE, and it paid geld for 1 virgate of land. There is land for 1 plough. There are 3 bordars, and 20 acres of pasture. It is worth 40d.

The same man holds MAMHEAD. He himself held it TRE,

and it paid geld for 1 virgate of land. There is land for 1 plough. There is 1 villan and he pays 45d.

The same man holds MOWLISH. He himself held it TRE, and it paid geld for 1 virgate of land. There is land for 1 plough. There are 2 villans with 1 bordar. It is worth 50d.

ÆLFGIFU holds 'ST JAMES CHURCH' [in Exeter]. She herself held it TRE, and it paid geld for 1½ virgates of land. There is land for 1 plough, which [plough] is there, with 1 slave and 2 cottars. It is worth 40d.

Ælfhild holds KNOWSTONE. She herself held it TRE, and it paid geld for half a virgate of land. There is land for 1 plough. There is half a plough, and 2 slaves. There are 2 acres of meadow, and 15 acres of pasture and 1 acre of scrubland. It is worth 30d.

Godgifu holds TORBRYAN. Beorhtric held it TRE, and it paid geld for 3 hides. There is land for 12 ploughs. In demesne are 4 ploughs, and 4 slaves; and 16 villans and 12 bordars with 8 ploughs. There are 100 acres of woodland, and 6 acres of meadow and 20 acres of pasture. It is worth 100s.

Godgifu holds DODBROOKE. Beorhtric held it TRE, and it paid geld for 2 hides. There is land for 12 ploughs. In demesne are 4 ploughs, and 8 slaves; and 16 villans and 18 bordars with 12 ploughs. There are 4 acres of meadow, [and] scrubland 8 furlongs long and 1 furlong broad. It is worth 100s.

[Folio 119: [DEVONSHIRE]]

[Blank in MS]

[Folio 119V: [DEVONSHIRE]]

[Blank in MS]

CORNWALL

Here Are Noted Those Holding Lands In Cornwall

I KING WILLIAM
II The Bishop of Exeter
III The Church of Tavistock
IIII Churches of various saints
V The Count of Mortain
VI Iudichael of Totnes
VII Goscelm

The land of the King

THE KING holds WINNIANTON. There were TRE 15 hides. There is land for 60 ploughs. Of this, 1 hide is in demesne, and there are 2 ploughs; and the villans have 3 hides and 24 ploughs. There are 24 villans and 41 coliberts and 33 bordars and 14 slaves. There are 6 acres of meadow, pasture 4 leagues long and 2 leagues broad, [and] woodland 1 league long and half a league broad. It renders £12 weighed and assayed.

Of these 15 hides, the Count of Mortain holds 11 hides. TRE 17 thegns who could not be separated from the manor held these.

Of this land the count himself has in demesne 1 manor and it is called Rinsey. There is 1 virgate of land. [There is] land for 2 ploughs. It is worth 15s.

Wulfweard holds 1 manor, RINSEY, of the count. There is 1 hide. There is land for 12 ploughs. There Wulfweard has 1 plough, and 8 coliberts and 4 slaves. [There is] pasture half a league long and as much broad. It is worth 10s.

Cenræd holds SKEWES of the count. There is 1 virgate of land.

Blechu holds TRENANCE [in Mullion]. There is half a hide.

Godwine holds [?] GARAH. There is the third part of 1 virgate of land.

Beorhtsige holds TREMBRAZE. There is the third part of 1 virgate of land.

Wihumar holds TREGOOSE. There is 1 hide.

Hamelin holds 'CRAWLE' [in Breage]. There is half a hide.

Richard holds LIZARD. There is 1 hide.

Beorhtric holds MAWGAN. There is 1 hide.

Andrew holds BODEN [Higher Boden and Boden Vean]. There is 1 virgate of land.

Turstin holds TRELOWARREN. There is 1 hide.

Turstin holds HALLIGGYE. There is 1 virgate of land and the third part of a virgate.

Beorhtric holds BOJORROW. There is 1 virgate of land.

Turstin holds TRUTHALL. There is half a hide.

Alwine holds TREWARNEVAS. There is 1 acre of land.

Dodda holds TRELAN. There are 4 acres of land.

Leofnoth holds TREDOWER. There is 1 hide.

Alweard holds [?] TREWORDER. There is 1 hide.

Griffin holds ROSCARNON. There is 1 virgate of land.

Turstin holds TREAL. There are 2 acres of land.

Wulfweard holds [?] TREVEADOR. There is 1 virgate of land.

Among them all is land for 68 ploughs. Formerly £20.10s; now they are worth £6.14s.

THE KING holds HELSTON. There are 6½ hides, of which only 2 hides paid geld TRE. There is land for 40 ploughs. Of this, 1 hide is in demesne, and there are 3 ploughs and 23 slaves; and 30 tenants paying ale-rent and 20 bordars with 17 ploughs. There are 4 acres of meadow, pasture 5 leagues long and 3 leagues broad, [and] woodland 1 league long and half a league broad. It renders £8 weighed and assayed.

THE KING holds TOWAN. There are 3 hides, but it paid geld for 1 hide TRE. There is land for 20 ploughs. Of this, half a hide is in demesne, and there are 2 ploughs and 9 slaves; and 16 villans and 40 bordars with 16 ploughs. There are 2 acres of meadow, pasture 3 leagues long and 1 league broad, [and] woodland half a league long and 3 furlongs broad. It renders 100s weighed and assayed.

THE KING holds LANOW. There are 5 hides, but it paid geld for 2 hides. There is land for 22 ploughs. Of this, 1 hide is in demesne, and there are 2 ploughs and 8 slaves; and 59 villans and 26 bordars with 20 ploughs. There is 1 acre of meadow, and 40 acres of pasture, [and] woodland 1 league long and 3 furlongs broad. It renders £6 weighed and assayed.

From this manor have been taken 2 manors, Poundstock and St Gennys. There are 1½ hides. There is land for 12 ploughs. Jovin holds them of the Count of Mortain. Formerly 60s; now it is worth 40s.

THE KING holds KILKHAMPTON. TRE it paid geld for 7 hides. There is land for 40 ploughs. Of this, 1 hide is in demesne, and there are 9 ploughs and 20 slaves; and 26 villans and 23 bordars with 26 ploughs. There are 30 acres of meadow, pasture 5 furlongs long and 4 furlongs broad, [and] woodland 1 league long and 1 furlong broad. It renders £18 by weight.

THE KING holds BLISLAND. There are 4 hides, but it paid geld for 2 hides. There is land for 30 ploughs. Of this, 1 hide is in demesne, and there are 2 ploughs and 12 slaves; and 40 villans and 20 bordars with 17 ploughs. There is 1 acre of meadow, pasture 3 leagues long and 1½ leagues broad, [and] woodland 1 league long and half a league broad. It renders £6 by weight.

From this manor has been taken 1 hide in PENDAVEY. There is land for 6 ploughs. Boia the priest holds it of the Count of Mortain. Formerly 20s; now it is worth 10s.

THE KING holds PENDRIM. There is 1 hide, but it paid geld for half a hide. There is land for 6 ploughs. Of this, 1 virgate of land is in demesne, and there is 1 plough and 3 slaves; and 13 bordars with 1 plough. There are 200 acres of pasture, [and] woodland 1 league long and half a league broad. It renders £3 by weight.

From this manor have been taken 3 estates, Bonyalva, and Bucklawren, and Bodigga. There are 2½ hides. There is land for 10 ploughs.

The canons of St Stephen of St Stephens [Launceston] hold them of the Count of Mortain. Formerly 40s; now it is worth 20s.

THE KING holds [?] CARNANTON. There are 5 hides, but it paid geld for 3 hides. There is land for 30 ploughs. Of this, half a hide is in demesne, and there are 3 ploughs and 20 slaves; and 43 villans and 17 bordars with 17 ploughs. There are 2 acres of meadow, [and] pasture 1 league long and as much broad. It renders £7 by weight.

THE KING holds CLIMSOM. There are 5 hides, but TRE it paid geld for 2½ hides. There is land for 24 ploughs. Of this, 1 hide is in demesne, and there are 3 ploughs and 9 slaves; and 30 villans and 24 bordars with 17 ploughs. There are 3 acres of meadow, pasture 4 leagues long and as much broad, [and] woodland 3 leagues long and 1 league broad. It renders £6 by weight.

THE KING holds CALLINGTON. There are 4 hides, but it paid geld for 2 hides. There is land for 30 ploughs. Of this, 1 hide is in demesne, and there are 3 ploughs and 11 slaves; and 24 villans and 14 bordars with 15 ploughs. There is pasture 3 leagues long and half a league broad, [and] woodland half a league long and 2 furlongs broad. It renders £6 by weight.

THE KING holds ROSEWORTHY. TRE it paid geld for 1 hide. There is land for 30 ploughs. Of this, 1 virgate of land is in demesne, and there are 3 ploughs and 8 slaves; and 13 villans and 15 bordars with 10 ploughs. There are 2 acres of meadow, pasture 1 league long and half a league broad, [and] woodland half a league long and 2 furlongs broad. It renders £4 by weight.

THE KING holds PENHEALE. There are 2½ hides, but it paid geld for 1 hide. There is land for 30 ploughs. Of this, half a hide is in demesne, and there are 2 ploughs and 10 slaves; and 24 villans and 16 bordars with 20 ploughs. There are 11 acres of meadow, and 30 acres of pasture and 13 acres of woodland. It renders 100s by weight. EARL HAROLD HELD THESE 12 ABOVE-WRITTEN ESTATES TRE. BUT THE BELOW-WRITTEN Beorhtric held, and afterwards Queen Matilda.

THE KING holds 'CONNERTON' [in Gwithian]. There are 7 hides, but it paid geld for 3 hides. There is land for 40 ploughs. Of this, 1 hide is in demesne, and there are 6 ploughs

[Folio 120v: CORNWALL]

and 30 slaves; and 30 villans and 20 bordars with 25 ploughs. There is a mill rendering 30d, and 1 acre of meadow, [and] pasture 2 leagues long and 1 league broad. It renders £12 by tale.

THE KING holds COSWARTH. There is 1 hide and 3 virgates of land, and it paid geld for 1 virgate TRE. There is land for 16 ploughs. Of this, 1 virgate of land is in demesne, and there is 1 plough with 1 slave; and 7 villans and 6 bordars with 9 ploughs. It renders £3.

From this manor St Petroc had TRE, as a customary due, 30d or 10x.

THE KING holds BINNERTON. There are 8 hides, but it paid geld for 4 hides TRE. There is land for 60 ploughs. Of this, half a hide is in demesne, and there are 3 ploughs and 10 slaves; and 32 villans and 25 bordars with 15 ploughs. There are 2 acres of meadow, pasture 2 leagues long and as much broad, [and] woodland 1 league long and half a league broad. It renders £10.

THE KING holds TREVALGA. There is 1 hide, and it paid geld for half a hide. There is land for 8 ploughs. Of this, half a hide is in demesne, and there are 2 ploughs and 3 slaves; and 4 villans and 7 bordars with 3 ploughs. There is pasture 1 league long and half a league broad. It renders £4.

Of the lands of Beorhtric, Aiulf holds 1 manor, CARWORGIE. TRE it, paid geld for 1 virgate of land. There is land for 2 ploughs. There is 1 plough with 3 bordars. Formerly, as now, worth 7s6d. It renders to St Petroc 8d. as a customary due.

Of the lands of Beorhtric, Walter de Claville holds 1 virgate of land. There is land for 2 ploughs. Formerly 10s; now it is worth 5s.

II. The land of the Bishop of Exeter

THE BISHOP OF EXETER holds TRELIEVER. TRE it paid geld for 1½ hides. There is land for 20 ploughs. In demesne are 2 ploughs and 4 slaves; and 30 villans and 4 bordars with 12 ploughs. There is pasture 2 leagues long and 2 leagues broad, and 60 acres of woodland. Formerly, as now, worth £4.

The same bishop holds METHLEIGH. TRE it paid geld for 1 hide, but yet there are 1½ hides. There is land for 15 ploughs.

In demesne is 1 plough and 3 slaves; and 15 villans and 4 bordars with 8 ploughs. There are 40 acres of pasture and 60 acres of scrubland. Formerly, as now, worth 40s.

The Count of Mortain has the market of this manor, which the bishop had TRE.

The same bishop holds TREGEAR. TRE it paid geld for 2 hides, but yet there are 12 hides. There is land for 60 ploughs. In demesne are 2 ploughs and 6 slaves; and 18 villans and 12 bordars with 16 ploughs. There is pasture half a league long and as much broad, [and] woodland 1 league long and a half broad. Formerly 100s; now it is worth £8.

The same bishop holds PAWTON. TRE it paid geld for 8 hides, but yet there are 44 hides. There is land for 60 ploughs. In demesne are 3 ploughs and 6 slaves; and 40 villans and 40 bordars with 40 ploughs. There is pasture 6 leagues long and 2 leagues broad, [and] woodland 2 leagues long and 1 broad. Formerly £10; now it is worth £24.

The same bishop holds BURNIERE. TRE and [sic] it paid geld for 1 hide. There is land for 12 ploughs. In demesne are 2 ploughs and 6 slaves; and 8 villans and 12 bordars with 6 ploughs. There are 60 acres of pasture and 10 acres of woodland. Formerly, as now, worth 40s.

The same bishop holds a manor which is called the Church of St Germans. There are 24 hides. Of these, 12 hides are the canons', which have never paid geld, and the other 12 hides are the bishop's and paid geld for 2 hides TRE. In this bishop's part there is land for 20 ploughs. In demesne are 2 ploughs and 4 slaves; and 30 villans and 12 bordars with 16 ploughs. There is pasture 4 leagues long and 2 leagues broad, [and] woodland 2 leagues long and 1 league broad. Formerly 100s; now it is worth £8.

In the canon's part there is land for 40 ploughs. In demesne are 2 ploughs and 2 slaves; and 24 villans and 20 bordars with 24 ploughs. There is pasture 2 leagues long and 1 league broad, [and] woodland 4 leagues long and 2 leagues broad. It is worth 100s to the canons.

In this manor there is a market on Sunday, but it is reduced to nothing, on account of the Count of Mortain's market, which is very near to it.

The same bishop holds [?Lower] LANHERNE. TRE it paid geld for 1 hide, but yet there are 3 hides. There is land for 10 ploughs. In demesne is 1 plough and 4 slaves; and 8 villans and 6 bordars with 3 ploughs. There is pasture 2 leagues long and 1 league broad. Formerly 100s; now it is worth 50s. Fulcard holds of the bishop.

Richard holds TINTEN of the bishop. TRE it paid geld for half a hide. Yet there is 1 hide. There is land for 6 ploughs. In demesne are 1½ ploughs with 1 slave; and 5 villans and 2 bordars with 3 ploughs, and 1 acre of woodland. Formerly, as now, worth 25s.

The bishop himself holds LAWHITTON. TRE it paid geld for 4 hides. Yet there are 11 hides. There is land for 40 ploughs. In demesne are 2 ploughs and 7 slaves; and 27 villans and 20 bordars with 29 ploughs. There are 8 acres of meadow, and 100 acres of pasture and 10 acres of scrubland. Formerly £8; now it is worth £17.

Roland holds GULVAL of the bishop. TRE it paid geld for 1 hide. Yet there are 1½ hides. There is land for 12 ploughs. In demesne is 1 plough and 3 slaves; and 13 villans and 4 bordars with 3 ploughs. There are 2 acres of meadow, and pasture 2 leagues long and 1 league broad. Formerly, as now, worth £3.

Godfrey holds ST WINNOW of the bishop. TRE it paid geld for 1 hide. There is land for 6 ploughs. In demesne is 1 plough and 2 slaves; and 5 villans and 6 bordars with 2 ploughs. There is pasture half a league long and as much broad, [and] woodland half a league long and 1 furlong broad. Formerly 40s; now it is worth 20s.

From the Church of St Germans there has been taken 1 hide of land which rendered as a customary due a cask of ale and 30d. to the same church TRE.

From the same church has been taken 1 acre of land, and there is land for 1 plough.

From the same church has been taken 1 virgate of land.

These were in the demesne of the same church TRE. Reginald and Hamelin now hold them of the Count of Mortain.

ALL THESE LANDS Bishop Leofric held TRE.

IIII. The land of St Michael

THE CHURCH OF ST MICHAEL holds TRUTHWALL. Beorhtmær held it TRE. There are 2 hides which have never paid geld. There is land for 8 ploughs. There is 1 plough, with 1 villan and 2 bordars, and 10 acres of pasture. It is worth 20s.

Of these 2 hides, the Count of Mortain has taken away 1 hide. It is worth 20s.

THE CANONS OF ST STEPHEN hold ST STEPHENS. There are 4 hides of land which have never paid geld. There is land for 20 ploughs. There are 3 ploughs, and 3 leagues of pasture and 60 acres of woodland. Formerly £8; now it is worth £4.

From this manor the Count of Mortain has taken away a market which was situated there TRE, and it is worth 20s.

THE CHURCH OF ST PETROC holds BODMIN. There is 1 hide of land which has never paid geld. There is land for 4 ploughs. There 5 villans have 2 ploughs with 6 bordars. There are 30 acres of pasture and 6 acres of scrubland. There St Petroc has 68 houses and 1 market. The whole is worth 25s.

The church itself holds PADSTOW, which has never paid geld. There is 1 hide. [There is] land for 4 ploughs. There 8 villans with 4 bordars have 2 ploughs. There are 24 acres of pasture. The whole is worth 10s.

The church itself holds RIALTON, which was quit from all service TRE. There are 7 hides. [There is] land for 30 ploughs. In demesne is 1 plough and 2 slaves; and 30 villans and 15 bordars with 11 ploughs. There are 60 acres of woodland and 300 acres of pasture. It is worth £4.

Berner holds NANCEKUKE of St Petroc. Cadwalant held it of the saint TRE, nor could he be separated from him. There is 1 hide. [There is] land for 4 ploughs. There is 1 plough, and 2 slaves and 6 bordars, and pasture 1 league long and as much broad. It is worth 10s.

[Folio 121: CORNWALL]

The Count of Mortain holds 'TYWARNHAYLE' [in Perranzabuloe] of St Petroc. Algar held it TRE, and he could not be separated from the saint. There are 7 hides. [There is] land for †20† ploughs. In demesne are 4 ploughs and 10 slaves; and 15 villans and 16 bordars with 10 ploughs. There are 12 acres of woodland, and pasture 5 leagues long and 1 league broad. It renders £14, less 20d.

The same count holds 'HALWYN' [in Perranzabuloe] of St Petroc. A thegn held it TRE and could not be separated from the saint. There is 1 hide. [There is] land for 3 ploughs, which [ploughs] are there with 1 slave and 2 villans and 6 bordars. There is 1 acre of meadow and 20 acres of pasture. Formerly 40s; now it is worth 20s.

The same count holds CALLESTICK [Callestick, Higher Callestick and Callestick Vean] of St Petroc. A thegn held it TRE and could not be separated from the saint. There is 1 hide. [There is] land for 4 ploughs. There are 12 slaves, and 10 acres of woodland. Formerly 20s; now it is worth 3s.

The same count holds CARGOLL of St Petroc. A thegn held it TRE, nor could he be separated from the saint. There are 2 hides. [There is] land for 15 ploughs. In demesne are 3 ploughs and 16 slaves; and 12 villans and 22 bordars with 6 ploughs. There is a mill rendering 30d, and 4 acres of woodland, [and] pasture 2 leagues long and 1 league broad. Formerly £10; now it is worth £3.

The same count holds TRELOY of St Petroc. Godric held it TRE, nor could he be separated from the saint. There is 1 hide. [There is] land for 4 ploughs. There are 2 ploughs, and 5 slaves and 8 bordars, and 15 acres of pasture. Formerly 40s; now it is worth 20s.

The same count holds ST ENODER of St Petroc. Godric held it TRE. There is 1 hide which has never paid geld. [There is] land for 6 ploughs. There are 2 ploughs, and 3 slaves and 2 villans and 8 bordars, and 20 acres of pasture. Formerly, as now, worth 20s.

The same count holds BOSSINEY of St Petroc. Alwig held it TRE and could not be separated from the saint. There is 1 hide. [There is] land for 6 ploughs. There is 1 plough, with 1 slave and 3 villans and 3 bordars, and 30 acres of pasture. Formerly 20s; now it is worth 15s.

The same count holds TREMAIL of St Petroc. Æthelwulf held it TRE and could not be separated from the saint. There are 3 virgates of land. There is land for 5 ploughs. There are 3 ploughs, and 2 slaves and 2 villans and 6 bordars, and 100 acres of pasture. Formerly 30s; now it is worth 20s.

The same count holds POLROAD. A thegn held it TRE and could not be separated from the saint. There is half a hide. [There is] land for 3 ploughs. There are 2 ploughs with 1 slave, and 4 villans and 3 bordars, and 3 acres of woodland and 17 acres of pasture. Formerly 20s; now it is worth 15s.

Richard holds [?] TRENGALE of St Petroc. Godric held it of the saint TRE, nor could he be separated from him. There is 1 hide. [There is] land for 6 ploughs. There are 4 ploughs, and 3 slaves and 4 villans and 4 bordars, and 60 acres of pasture and 3 acres of scrubland. Formerly, as now, worth 20s.

Macco holds FURSNEWTH of St Petroc. He himself held it TRE, nor could he be separated from the saint. There is 1 hide. [There is] land for 8 ploughs. There are 4 ploughs with 1 slave, and 8 villans and 8 bordars, and 30 acres of pasture. It renders 10s.

St Petroc himself holds ELLENGLAZE. There are 2 hides. [There is] land for 8 ploughs. There are 4 ploughs, and 4 slaves and 8 villans and 8 bordars. [There is] pasture 1 league long and half a league broad. It is worth 20s.

St Petroc himself holds WITHIEL. There is 1 hide. There is land for 8 ploughs. There are 4 ploughs, and 2 slaves and 8 villans and 15 bordars, and 12 acres of woodland. [There is] pasture 1 league long and as much broad. Formerly 25s. When the count received it; now it is worth 15s.

St Petroc himself holds TREKNOW. There are 2 hides. [There is] land for 8 ploughs. There are 3½ ploughs, and 2 slaves and 7 villans and 8 bordars, and 100 acres of pasture. When the count received it, [worth] 25s; now it is worth 15s.

Earl Harold unjustly took away 1 hide of land from St Petroc, for which King William ordered a judicial enquiry to be held and the saint to be reseised by justice.

From the Church of St Petroc has been taken away COSWARTH, which TRE rendered as a customary due to the church itself 1 ox and 7 sheep. The king holds it.

THESE BELOW-WRITTEN LANDS HAVE BEEN TAKEN AWAY FROM ST PETROC. The Count of Mortain holds them and his men [hold] of him.

In [?] TREGENNA is 1 virgate of land which rendered 15d. as a customary due.

In TREVORNICK half a hide of land rendered 12 sheep and 15d.

In TRENHAILE 1 virgate of land rendered 6 sheep and 8d.

In [?Higher] TOLCARNE [in St Mawgan] half a hide of land rendered 1 ox.

In TREMORE half a hide of land rendered 1 ox and 15d. and 12 sheep.

In LANCARFFE 1 virgate of land rendered 15d.

In TRENINNICK 1 virgate of land rendered 15d. and 5 sheep.

St Petroc held all the lands described above TRE. The lands of this saint have never paid geld except to the church itself.

THE CANONS OF ST ACHEBRAN hold ST KEVERNE

and held it TRE. There are 11 acres of land. There is land for 7 ploughs. There is 1 plough, and 20 acres of pasture. When the count received it, it was worth 40s; now it is worth 5s.

THE CANONS OF ST PROBUS hold PROBUS. King Edward held it in his lifetime. There is 1 hide and 1 virgate of land, and it has never paid geld. There is land for 8 ploughs. There are $4\frac{1}{2}$ ploughs, and 5 slaves and 3 villans and 8 bordars, and 20 acres of pasture. It is worth 40s.

THE CANONS OF ST CARANTOC hold CRANTOCK and held it TRE. There are 3 hides, less 2 acres, and it has never paid geld. [There is] land for 10 ploughs. There are $1\frac{1}{2}$ ploughs, and 3 villans. It is worth 5s; when the count received possession of the land, it was worth 40s.

THE CANONS OF ST PIRAN hold 'PERRAN' [in Perranzabuloe], which was always free TRE. There are 3 hides. There is land for 8 ploughs. There are 2 ploughs, and 2 slaves and 4 villans and 8 bordars, and 10 acres of pasture. It is worth 12s; when the count received it, it was worth 40s.

From this manor have been taken away 2 estates, which rendered to the canons TRE a farm of 4 weeks, and 20, to the dean as a customary due.

Berner holds one of these of the Count of Mortain, and from the other hide which Odo holds of St Piran, the count has taken all the livestock.

THE CANONS OF ST BURYAN hold ST BURYAN, which was free TRE. There is 1 hide. [There is] land for 8 ploughs. There is half a plough, and 6 villans and 6 bordars, and 20 acres of pasture. It is worth 10s; when the count received the land, it was worth 40s.

THE CLERKS OF ST NEOT hold ST NEOT and held it TRE. There are 2 hides which have never paid geld. There are 4 bordars. It is worth 5s.

All this land, except 1 acre of land which the priests have, the count has taken from the church. Odo holds it of him, and it is worth 5s; before it was worth 20s.

ST CONSTANTINE has half a hide of land which was quit from all service TRE, but after the count received the land, it rendered geld unjustly as villans' land. There is land for 4 ploughs. It is worth 10s; when the count received the land, it was worth 40s.

III. The land of the Church of Tavistock

THE CHURCH OF TAVISTOCK holds SHEVIOCK, and Ermenald [holds] of it. TRE it paid geld for 1 hide. There is land for 9 ploughs. In demesne are 2 ploughs and 4 slaves; and 6 villans and 17 bordars with 3 ploughs. There are 30 acres of pasture and 60 acres of woodland. Formerly, as now, worth 60s.

The same Ermenald holds ANTONY of this church. TRE it paid geld for half a hide. There is land for 6 ploughs. In demesne are 2 ploughs and 4 slaves; and 12 villans and 15 bordars with 5 ploughs. There are 10 acres of pasture and 30

acres of scrubland. Formerly, as now, worth 100s. The Abbot of Horton claims this land.

The same Ermenald holds RAME of this church. There is 1 hide, and it pays geld for half a hide. There is land for 7 ploughs. In demesne is 1 plough and 4 slaves; and 4 villans and 15 bordars with 3 ploughs. There are 30 acres of pasture and 10 acres of scrubland. Formerly, as now, worth 40s.

[Folio 121V: CORNWALL]

The same Ermenald holds TREWORNAN of this church. TRE it paid geld for half a hide. There is land for 4 ploughs. There are 3 ploughs, and 2 slaves and 9 villans, and 1 acre of meadow and 2 acres of pasture. Formerly, as now, worth 20s.

The same Ermenald holds PENHARGET of this church. There is 1 virgate of land, and it paid geld for half a virgate. There is land for 2 ploughs. There is 1 plough, and 6 villans, and 10 acres of woodland and 10 acres of pasture. Formerly, as now, worth 10s.

The same man holds TOLCARNE [in North Hill] of this church. TRE it paid geld for half a virgate of land. There is land for 1 plough. There are 2 bordars, and 1 acre of pasture. Formerly, as now, worth 5s.

From the church itself the Count of Mortain unjustly holds 4 manors, BOYTON, [?] ILLAND, TREBEIGH, and TREWANTA. The abbot claims them [...] because they have been taken from the church.

The land of the Count of Mortain

THE COUNT OF MORTAIN holds FAWTON of the king. Mærle-Sveinn held it TRE and it paid geld for 1 hide. Yet there are 2 hides. [There is] land for 30 ploughs. In demesne are 6 ploughs and 20 slaves; and 30 villans and 20 bordars with 15 ploughs. There are 200 acres of woodland, and pasture 7 leagues long and 4 leagues broad. Formerly £8; now it is worth £16.18s4d.

The count himself holds LISKEARD. Mærle-Sveinn held it TRE and it paid geld for 2 hides. Yet there are 12 hides. There is land for 60 ploughs. In demesne are 3 ploughs and 20 slaves; and 35 villans and 37 bordars with 13 ploughs. There is a market rendering 4s, and a mill rendering 12s, and 400 acres of woodland, [and] pasture 4 leagues long and 2 leagues broad. Formerly £8; now it is worth £26, less 20d.

The count himself holds STRATTON. Bishop Osbern and Alvred the marshal held it TRE and it paid geld for 1 hide. Yet there are 2 hides. There is land for 30 ploughs. In demesne are 4 ploughs and 20 slaves; and 30 villans and 20 bordars with 15 ploughs. There are 10 salt-pans rendering 10s, and 20 acres of woodland and 200 acres of pasture. Formerly £30; now it is worth £36, less 20d.

The count himself holds HELSTONE. Algar held it TRE and it paid geld for 1 hide. Yet there are 2 hides. There is land for 15 ploughs. In demesne are 4 ploughs and 18 slaves; and 20 villans and 15 bordars with 8 ploughs. There are 10 acres of woodland, and pasture 3 leagues long and 2 leagues broad. Formerly, as now, it rendered £16, less 20d.

The count himself holds TREGLASTA. Earl Harold held it TRE and it paid geld for 2 hides. Yet there are 6 hides. There is land for 20 ploughs. In demesne are 2 ploughs and 15 slaves; and 24 villans and 20 bordars with 12 ploughs. There are 300 acres of pasture. Formerly 12 marks of silver; now it is worth £16, less 20d.

The count himself holds 'TYBESTA' [in Creed]. Radulf the staller held it TRE and it paid geld for 1 hide. Yet there are 3 hides. [There is] land for 30 ploughs. In demesne are 3 ploughs and 14 slaves; and 27 villans and 20 bordars with 10 ploughs. There are 40 acres of woodland, [and] pasture 3 leagues long and 1 league broad. Formerly £12; now it is worth £15.18s4d.

The count himself holds TRENOWTH. Abbot Sigtrygg held it TRE and it paid geld for 2 hides. Yet there are 6 hides. [There is] land for 40 ploughs. In demesne are 5 ploughs and 16 slaves; and 30 villans and 30 bordars with 12 ploughs. There are 40 acres of woodland and 1,000 acres of pasture. Formerly 12 marks of silver; now it renders £25.18s4d.

The count himself holds BRANNEL. Beorhtmær held it TRE and it paid geld for 1 hide. Yet there are 1½ hides. There is land for 20 ploughs. In demesne are 3 ploughs and 10 slaves; and 12 villans and 18 bordars with 20 ploughs. There are 40 acres of woodland, [and] pasture 4 leagues long and 2 leagues broad. Formerly 12 marks of silver; now it is worth £12.18s4d.

The count himself holds 'MORESK' [in St Clement]. Ordwulf held it TRE and it paid geld for 1 hide. Yet there are 2 hides. There is land for 10 ploughs. In demesne are 2 ploughs and 3 slaves; and 5 villans and 10 bordars with 5 ploughs. There are 100 acres of pasture and 200 acres of woodland. Formerly 100s; now it is worth £9.18s4d.

The count himself holds TREWIRGIE. Mærle-Sveinn held it TRE and it paid geld for 1 hide. Yet there are 2 hides. There is land for 16 ploughs. In demesne are 5 ploughs and 7 slaves; and 15 villans and 17 bordars with 8 ploughs. There are 60 acres of woodland and 300 acres of pasture. Formerly 100s; now it is worth £8.

The count himself holds ALVERTON [in Penzance]. Alweard held it TRE and it paid geld for 2 hides. Yet there are 3 hides. [There is] land for 60 ploughs. In demesne are 3 ploughs and 11 slaves; and 35 villans and 25 bordars with 12 ploughs. There are 3 acres of meadow, [and] pasture 2 leagues long and 1 league broad. Formerly £8; now it renders £20.

The count himself holds TEHIDY. Ordwulf held it TRE and it paid geld for 2 hides. Yet there are 3 hides. There is land for 50 ploughs. In demesne are 5 ploughs and 13 slaves; and 25 villans and 30 bordars with 12 ploughs. There are 2 acres of meadow, pasture 3 leagues long and 1 league broad, [and] woodland 1 league long and as much broad. Formerly £8; now it is worth £20.

The count himself holds RILLATON. Beorhtmær held it

TRE and it paid geld for 1 hide. There is land for 15 ploughs. In demesne are 2 ploughs and 12 slaves; and 15 villans and 24 bordars with 8 ploughs. There are 60 acres of woodland and 300 acres of pasture. Formerly £30; now it is worth £15 and 1 mark of silver and 5s.

The count himself holds LANDINNER. Edith held it TRE and it paid geld for 1 ferding of land. Yet there is 1 virgate of land. [There is] land for 2 ploughs. There are 6 bordars, and 5 acres of meadow and 40 acres of pasture. Formerly 10s; now it is worth 30d.

The count himself holds [? South] HILL. Æthelhelm held it TRE and it paid geld for half a ferding. Yet there is 1 ferding of land. [There is] land for 1 plough. There are 2 bordars, and 1 acre of meadow and 30 acres of pasture. Formerly 30d; now it is worth 12d.

The count himself holds TREWANTA. Sigtrygg held it TRE and it paid geld for 1 ferding. Yet there is 1 virgate of land. There is land for 2 ploughs. There are 5 bordars, and 30 acres of pasture. Formerly 10s; now it is worth 30d.

The count himself holds [?] ILLAND. Sigtrygg held it TRE and it paid geld for 1 ferding of land. Yet there is half a hide of land. [There is] land for 2 ploughs. There are 2 villans and 2 bordars, and 30 acres of pasture. Formerly 15s; now it is worth 5s.

The count himself holds PATRIEDA. Wadel held it TRE and it paid geld for 1 ferding of land. Yet there is 1 virgate of land. There is land for 2 ploughs. There are 2 villans and 2 bordars, and 5 acres of pasture. Formerly 7s; now it is worth 2s.

The count himself holds TREVILLA. Alstan held it TRE and it paid geld for 1 ferding of land. Yet there is half a hide, and 1 bordar, and 5 acres of woodland and 60 acres of pasture. Formerly 10s; now it is worth 3s.

The count himself holds TREBEIGH. Oswulf held it TRE and it paid geld for 1 ferding. Yet there is half a hide. There is land for 2 ploughs. There are 3 bordars, and 200 acres of pasture. Formerly 20s; now it is worth 5s.

The count himself holds [?] HENNETT. Alstan held it TRE and it paid geld for 2 ferdings of land. There is land for 2 ploughs. There are 3 bordars, and 30 acres of pasture. Formerly 20s; now it is worth 2s.

The count himself holds LAUNCESTON. TRE it paid geld for 1 virgate of land. Yet there is 1 hide. There is land for 10 ploughs. In demesne is 1 plough and 3 slaves; and 1 villan and 13 bordars with 4 ploughs. There are 2 mills rendering 40s, and 40 acres of pasture. Formerly £20; now it is worth £4. The count's castle is there.

[Folio 122: CORNWALL]

Reginald holds [?] TORWELL of the count. Beorhtmær held it TRE with the manor which is called [?] TREGARLAND and it paid geld for 1 virgate of land. There is land for 5 ploughs. In demesne is 1 plough and 4 slaves; and 6 villans and 6 bordars with 3 ploughs. There is woodland 3 leagues long and 1 league broad. Formerly 60s; now it is worth 25s.

The same man holds TRELAWNE of the count. Alwine held it TRE and it paid geld for 3 ferdings of land. Yet there is half a hide. There is land for 6 ploughs. In demesne is 1 plough and 8 slaves; and 4 villans and 4 bordars with 2 ploughs. There are 40 acres of pasture and 60 acres of woodland. Formerly, as now, worth 60s.

The same man holds LARNICK [Little Larnick and Muchlarnick] of the count. Eadmær held it TRE and it paid geld for 1 ferding. Yet there is 1 virgate of land. [There is] land for 1 plough, which [plough] is there with 2 bordars and 6 slaves. There are 10 acres of pasture and 30 acres of woodland. Formerly, as now, worth 8s.

The same man holds LEWARNE. Grim held it TRE and it paid geld for 1 ferding. Yet there is 1 virgate of land. [There is] land for 1 plough. There are 2 bordars, and 10 acres of woodland. Formerly 4s; now it is worth 2s.

The same man holds BRADDOCK. Ælfric held it TRE and it paid geld for 1 virgate of land. Yet there is half a hide. [There is] land for 4 ploughs. There are 2 ploughs, and 2 slaves and 3 villans and 4 bordars, and 100 acres of pasture and 20 acres of woodland. Formerly 12s; now it is worth 10s.

The same man holds RAPHAEL. Ælfgifu held it TRE and it paid geld for 1 virgate of land. Yet there is half a hide. [There is] land for 3 ploughs. There are 2 ploughs, and 3 slaves and 2 villans and 2 bordars, and 30 acres of pasture. Formerly 10s; now it is worth 7s.

The same man holds KILLIGORRICK. Uhtræd held it TRE and it paid geld for half a ferding. There is 1 acre of land. [There is] land for 1 plough. There is 1 slave, and 10 acres of woodland. Formerly, as now, worth 3s.

The same man holds ELLBRIDGE. Ælfric held it TRE and it paid geld for half a ferding. There is 1 acre of land. [There is] land for 1 plough. There is 1 bordar, and 30 acres of pasture. Formerly it was worth 15d.

The same man holds LANTYAN. Alric held it TRE and it paid geld for 1 ferding. There is land for 2 ploughs. Yet there is 1 virgate of land. There are 3 bordars, and 3 acres of woodland. Formerly 10s; now it is worth 2s.

The same man holds LANHADRON. Esbiorn held it TRE and it paid geld for 1 ferding. Yet there is 1 virgate of land. There is land for 3 ploughs. There is 1 plough, and 2 slaves and 4 bordars, and 60 acres of pasture and 5 acres of woodland. Formerly 10s; now it is worth 5s.

The same man holds TREMATON of the count. Beorhtmær held it TRE and it paid geld for 2½ hides. Yet there are 5 hides. There is land for 24 ploughs. In demesne are 3 ploughs and 50 slaves; and 20 villans and 30 bordars with 7 ploughs. There are 40 acres of pasture and 20 acres of woodland. Formerly £10; now it is worth £8.

There the count has a castle, and a market rendering 3s.

The same man holds CALSTOCK of the count. Esger held it

TRE and it paid geld for 1 hide. Yet there are 2½ hides. There is land for 12 ploughs. In demesne are 2 ploughs and 12 slaves; and 30 villans and 30 bordars with 6 ploughs. There are 100 acres of woodland, [and] pasture 3 leagues long and 1 league broad. Formerly £6; now it is worth £3.

The same man holds PENHAWGER. Almær held it TRE and it paid geld for 1 virgate of land. Yet there is 1 hide. There is land for 16 ploughs. In demesne is 1 plough and 4 slaves; and 11 villans and 30 bordars with 7 ploughs. There are 30 acres of pasture and 4 acres of woodland. Formerly 60s; now it is worth 30s.

The same man holds MAKER of the count. Edward held it TRE and it paid geld for 1 virgate of land. Yet there is 1 hide. There is land for 8 ploughs. There are 3 ploughs, and 4 slaves and 6 villans and 8 bordars, and 60 acres of pasture. Formerly 30s; now it is worth 20s.

The same man holds [?] TREDINNICK. Algar held it TRE and it paid geld for 1 acre of land. Yet there is 1 virgate of land. There is land for 1 plough, which [plough] is there with 1 slave, and 2 villans and 2 bordars. Formerly, as now, worth 10s.

The same Reginald holds [Higher and Lower] TREGANTLE. Beorhtmær held it TRE and it paid geld for 1 virgate of land. There is land for 3 ploughs. There are 2 ploughs, and 3 villans and 6 bordars. Formerly 20s; now it is worth 15s.

The same man holds HALTON of the count. Earl Harold held it TRE and it paid geld for 1 virgate of land. Yet there is 1 hide. There is land for 10 ploughs. There are 4 ploughs, and 7 slaves and 10 villans and 10 bordars, and 40 acres of pasture and 12 acres of woodland. Formerly 40s; now it is worth 30s.

The same man holds PILLATON. Mærle-Sveinn held it TRE and it paid geld for 1 virgate of land. Yet there is half a hide. There is land for 6 ploughs. There are 3 ploughs, and 3 slaves and 7 villans and 7 bordars, and 100 acres of pasture and 40 acres of woodland. Formerly 30s; now it is worth 20s.

The same Reginald holds [?] TREMEER. Beorhtmær held it TRE and it paid geld for 1 ferding. Yet there is 1 virgate of land. There is land for 2 ploughs. There is 1 plough with 1 villan and 3 bordars, and 10 acres of woodland and 10 acres of pasture. Formerly, as now, worth 5s.

The same man holds LEWARNE. Grim held it TRE and it paid geld for 1 ferding. Yet there is 1 virgate of land. [There is] land for 1 plough. There are 2 bordars with 1 slave, and 10 acres of woodland. It is worth 2s.

The same man holds TREHAWKE. Beorhtmær held it TRE and it paid geld for 1 ferding. Yet there is 1 virgate of land. [There is] land for 2 ploughs. There is 1 plough, and 2 bordars, and 5 acres of pasture. Formerly, as now, worth 5s.

The same man holds PENPOLL. Ælfric held it TRE and it paid geld for 1 acre of land. There is land for 3 ploughs, which [ploughs] are there, and 4 slaves and 6 villans and 6 bordars, and 3 acres of meadow, and 6 acres of woodland and 30 acres of pasture. Formerly, as now, worth 30s.

The same man holds [?] TREFRIZE. Leofrun held it TRE and it paid geld for 1 ferding. Yet there is 1 virgate of land. [There is] land for 3 ploughs. There are $2\frac{1}{2}$ ploughs with 1 slave, and 5 villans and 5 bordars, and 10 acres of woodland and 60 acres of pasture. It is worth 10s.

The same man holds NEWTON FERRERS. Ælfric held it TRE and it paid geld for 1 virgate of land. Yet there is half a hide. [There is] land for 6 ploughs. There are 2 ploughs, and 3 slaves and 3 villans and 12 bordars, and 12 acres of pasture. Formerly 30s; now it is worth 20s.

The same man holds APPLEDORE. Cynestan held it TRE and it paid geld for 1 virgate of land. There is land for 6 ploughs. There are 2 ploughs with 1 slave, and 3 villans and 3 bordars, and 100 acres of pasture and 5 acres of woodland. Formerly 20s; now it is worth 15s.

The same man holds BICTON. Cynestan held it TRE and it paid geld for 1 ferding. Yet there is 1 virgate of land. [There is] land for 2 ploughs. There are 2 slaves and 4 bordars, and 10 acres of pasture and 15 acres of woodland. Formerly 5s; now it is worth 3s.

The same man holds ASHTON. Ælfric held it TRE and it paid geld for 1 virgate of land. Yet there is half a hide. There is land for 2 ploughs. There are 4 bordars with half a plough, and 1 acre of pasture. [There is] woodland 6 furlongs long and 3 furlongs broad. It is worth 10s.

The same man holds NEWTON FERRERS. Ælfric held it TRE and it paid geld for 1 virgate of land. Yet there is 1 hide. [There is] land for 8 ploughs. There are 10 villans and 20 bordars with 1 plough, and 3 slaves, and half a league of pasture. [There is] woodland 2 leagues long and 1 furlong broad. Formerly 40s; now it is worth 30s.

The same man holds [?] LANDREYNE. Sæwulf held it TRE and it paid geld for 1 ferding. Yet there is 1 virgate of land. [There is] land for 1 plough, which [plough] is there with 1 slave and 1 villan and 3 bordars. There are 8 acres of meadow and 30 acres of pasture. Formerly, as now, worth 5s.

The same man holds TRECAN. Walo held it TRE and it paid geld for 1 ferding. Yet there is 1 virgate of land. There is land for 2 ploughs. There are 2 slaves and 2 bordars, and 10 acres of pasture. Formerly 10s; now it is worth 3s.

The same man holds LANGUNNETT. Beorhtric held it TRE and it paid geld for 1 ferding. Yet there is 1 virgate of land. There is land for 2 ploughs. There are 8 bordars and 3 slaves, and 10 acres of woodland and 5 acres of pasture. Formerly 10s; now it is worth 5s.

The same man holds [?] TREVELYAN. Alric held it TRE and it paid geld for half a ferding. Yet there is 1 ferding of land. There is land for 1 plough. There are 2 slaves. Formerly, as now, worth 2s.

The same man holds GEAR. Beorhtmær held it TRE and it paid geld for 1 ferding. Yet there is 1 virgate of land. [There is] land for 2 ploughs. There are 3 slaves, and 5 acres of pasture and 12 acres of woodland. Formerly 25s; now it is worth 5s.

RICHARD holds COSAWES of the count. Alwine held it TRE and it paid geld for 1 hide. There is land for 12 ploughs. In demesne are 4 ploughs and 12 slaves; and 15 villans and 20 bordars with 5 ploughs. There are 60 acres of woodland, [and] pasture 5 leagues long and 2 leagues broad. Formerly 100s; now it is worth 40s.

Richard holds POLSCOE. Alnoth held it TRE and it paid geld for 1 ferding. Yet there are 2 ferdings of land. There is land for 1 plough. There are 3 bordars, and 40 acres of pasture. Formerly, as now, worth 30d.

The same man holds TREZANCE. Alwine held it TRE and it paid geld for 1 hide. Yet there are 2 hides. There is land for 12 ploughs. In demesne are 2 ploughs and 6 slaves; and 5 villans and 11 bordars with 5 ploughs. There is pasture 3 leagues long and 2 leagues broad, [and] woodland 1 league long and half a league broad. Formerly 30s; now it is worth 20s.

The same man holds BOSENT. Beorhtweald held it TRE and it paid geld for 1 ferding. Yet there is 1 virgate of land. There is land for 2 ploughs. There is half a plough, and 4 bordars, and 20 acres of pasture and 20 acres of woodland. Formerly, as now, worth 3s.

[Folio 122V: CORNWALL]

The same Richard holds CARTUTHER of the count. Cola held it TRE and it paid geld for half a hide. Yet there are 17 frac12; hides. There is land for 10 ploughs. There are 4 ploughs, and 2 slaves and 6 villans and 7 bordars, and 20 acres of pasture and 12 acres of woodland. Formerly 40s; now it is worth 25s.

The same man holds LANREATH. Ælfric held it TRE and it paid geld for 3 virgates of land. Yet there is 1 hide. [There is] land for 8 ploughs. There are 3 ploughs, and 4 slaves and 4 villans and 10 bordars, and 30 acres of pasture and 40 acres of woodland. Formerly 30s; now it is worth 25s.

The same man holds LANSALLOS. Ærlfric held it TRE and it paid geld for 1 virgate of land. Yet there is 1 hide. [There is] land for 5 ploughs. There are 2 ploughs, and 3 slaves and 2 villans and 2 bordars, and 30 acres of pasture. Formerly, as now, worth 10s.

Richard holds TYWARDREATH of the count. Cola held it TRE and it paid geld for 1 hide. Yet there are 2 hides. [There is] land for 12 ploughs. In demesne are 4 ploughs and 7 slaves; and 8 villans and 18 bordars with 3 ploughs. There are 6 acres of woodland and 100 acres of pasture. Formerly 4d; now it is worth 40s.

The same man holds BODIGGO. Ælfric held it TRE and it paid geld for half a hide. Yet there is 1 hide. [There is] land for 7 ploughs, and as many [ploughs] are there, and 9 slaves and 10 villans and 22 bordars, and 1 league of pasture. Formerly 40s; now it is worth 30s.

The same man holds BODRUGAN. Alwine held it TRE and it paid geld for 3 virgates of land. Yet there is 1 hide. [There is] land for 10 ploughs. There are 3 ploughs, and 4 slaves and 4 villans and 12 bordars, and 4 acres of woodland and 200 acres of pasture. Formerly 60s; now it is worth 30s.

The same man holds TUCOYSE [in St Ewe]. Godric held it TRE and it paid geld for 1 virgate of land. There is land for 5 ploughs. There are 3 ploughs, and 5 slaves and 4 villans and 8 bordars, and 8 acres of woodland and 40 acres of pasture. Formerly 30s; now it is worth 20s.

The same man holds GOVILEY [Major and Vean]. Godric held it TRE and it paid geld for half a hide. Yet there is 1 hide. [There is] land for 6 ploughs. There are 5 ploughs, and 8 slaves and 5 villans and 13 bordars, and 5 acres of woodland and 100 acres of pasture. Formerly 40s; now it is worth 30s.

The same man holds POLSUE. Alwine held it TRE and it paid geld for 1 hide. There is land for 10 ploughs. There are 5 ploughs, and 8 slaves and 8 villans and 14 bordars, and 15 acres of woodland. [There is] pasture 3 leagues long and 1 league broad. Formerly 40s; now it is worth 30s.

The same man holds GOODERN. Alwine held it TRE and it paid geld for 1 virgate of land. Yet there is half a hide. [There is] land for 3 ploughs. There are 1½ ploughs, and 2 slaves and 2 villans and 4 bordars, and 60 acres of woodland. [There is] pasture 5 leagues long and 1 league broad. Formerly 20s; now it is worth 10s.

The same man holds TREVERBYN. Alwine held it TRE and it paid geld for half a virgate of land. Yet there is 1 virgate of land. [There is] land for 3 ploughs. There are 1½ ploughs, and 2 slaves and 2 villans and 3 bordars, and 2 acres of woodland and 20 acres of pasture. Formerly 10s; now it is worth 5s.

The same man holds BURTHY. Æthelbeorht held it TRE and it paid geld for 2 ferdings. There is land for 4 ploughs. There are 1½ ploughs, and 5 slaves and 5 bordars, and 20 acres of pasture. Formerly 20s; now it is worth 10s.

The same man holds LANESCOT. Æthelbeorht held it TRE and it paid geld for 1 ferding. [There is] land for 5 ploughs. There are 2 ploughs, and 2 slaves and 4 bordars, and 1 acre of woodland and 20 acres of pasture. Formerly 15s; now it is worth 10s.

The same Richard holds WEEK ST MARY. Cola held it TRE and it paid geld for half a hide. Yet there is 1 hide. [There is] land for 8 ploughs. There are 3 ploughs, and 4 slaves and 6 villans and 10 bordars, and 2 acres of woodland, and pasture 1 league long and as much broad. Formerly 20s; now it is worth 30s.

The same man holds PENHALLYM. Erneis held it TRE and it paid geld for half a hide. Yet there are 1½ hides. [There is] land for 10 ploughs. There are 6 ploughs, and 6 slaves and 8 villans and 22 bordars, and 6 acres of woodland. [There is] pasture 1 league long and as much broad. Formerly 40s; now it is worth 30s.

The same man holds DOWNINNEY. Mærle;-Sveinn held it TRE and it paid geld for 1 hide. Yet there are 2 hides. There is land for 12 ploughs. There are 10 ploughs, and 10 slaves and

10 villans and 20 bordars. [There is] pasture 1 league long and as much broad. Formerly 60s; now it is worth 40s.

The same man holds OTTERHAM. Eadwig held it TRE and it paid geld for half a hide. Yet there is 1 hide. [There is] land for 6 ploughs. There are 4 ploughs, and 6 slaves and 6 villans and 8 bordars. [There is] pasture 1 league long and broad. Formerly 30s; now it is worth 20s.

The same Richard holds HAMATETHY. Alric held it TRE and it paid geld for half a hide. Yet there is 1 hide. [There is] land for 6 ploughs. There are 4 ploughs, and 3 slaves and 4 villans and 8 bordars, and 2 acres of woodland, and pasture 5 leagues long and 2 leagues broad. Formerly 40s; now it is worth 30s.

The same man holds COLQUITE. Cola held it TRE and it paid geld for 1½ hides. There is land for 10 ploughs. There are 3 ploughs, and 3 slaves and 6 villans and 8 bordars, and 20 acres of woodland and 40 acres of pasture. Formerly 40s; now it is worth 20s.

The same man holds TREVISQUITE. Mærle;-Sveinn held it TRE and it paid geld for 1 hide. Yet there are 2 hides. [There is] land for 12 ploughs. There are 6 ploughs, and 8 slaves and 8 villans and 9 bordars, and a mill rendering 2s, and 20 acres of woodland and 50 acres of pasture. Formerly 30s; now it is worth 25s.

The same man holds TRETHEVY. Beorhtnoth held it TRE and it paid geld for half a ferding of land. Yet there is 1 virgate of land. [There is] land for 1 plough. There is 1 villan and 2 bordars, and 30 acres of pasture. Formerly 5s; now it is worth 2s.

The same man holds LANDULPH. Alnoth held it TRE and it paid geld for 1 virgate of land. Yet there is half a hide. There is land for 5 ploughs. There is 1 plough, and 2 slaves and 2 villans and 5 bordars, and 10 acres of pasture. Formerly 15s; now it is worth 10s.

The same man holds LUDGVAN. Alwine held it TRE and it paid geld for 1 hide. Yet there are 3 hides. [There is] land for 15 ploughs or 30 ploughs. There are 3 hides. There are 12 ploughs, and 9 slaves and 14 villans and 40 bordars, and 300 acres of pasture. Formerly 100s; now it is worth 60s.

The same man holds KELYNACK. Godric held it TRE and it paid geld for half a hide. Yet there is 1 hide. [There is] land for 8 ploughs. There are 5 ploughs, and 5 slaves and 10 bordars and 6 villans, and 100 acres of pasture. Formerly 30s; now it is worth 20s.

TURSTIN holds TRELAN of the count. Torhtweald held it TRE and it paid geld for 1 virgate of land. Yet there is 1 hide. There is land for 5 ploughs. There are 3 ploughs, and 4 slaves and 2 villans and 6 bordars, and pasture 3 leagues long and 2 leagues broad. Formerly 30s; now it is worth 25s.

Turstin holds PENCARROW of the count. Beorhtmær held it TRE and it paid geld for half a ferding. There is 1 acre. [There is] land for 1 plough. There are 2 bordars and 2 slaves, and 10 acres of woodland and 7 acres of pasture. Formerly 10s; now it is worth 3s.

Turstin holds [?] TRENEWAN of the count. Wulfnoth held it TRE and it paid geld for 1 ferding. Yet there is 1 virgate of land. [There is] land for 2 ploughs. There is half a plough with 1 slave and 2 bordars, and 12 acres of woodland and 20 acres of pasture. Formerly, as now, worth 5s.

The same man holds 'LANTIVET' [in Lanteglos-by-Fowey] of the count. Beorhtmær held it TRE and it paid geld for half a ferding. Yet there is 1 virgate of land. [There is] land for 2 ploughs. There are 2 slaves with 1 bordar, and 6 acres of pasture. Formerly 25s; now it is worth 12d.

The same man holds TRENODE of the count. Mærle-Sveinn held it TRE and it paid geld for 1 ferding. Yet there is 1 virgate of land. There is land for 2 ploughs. There is 1 plough, and 2 slaves with 1 villan and 2 bordars, and 15 acres of woodland. Formerly 5s; now it is worth 3s.

Turstin holds ST JULIOT of the count. Eadwig held it TRE and it paid geld for 1 ferding. Yet there is 1 virgate of land. [There is] land for 3 ploughs. There is half a plough, and 2 slaves and 2 villans, and 30 acres of pasture. Formerly 7s; now it is worth 5s.

The same man holds WILLSWORTHY. Cynesige held it TRE and it paid geld for half a ferding. Yet there is 1 virgate of land. There is land for 2 ploughs. There is 1 plough with 1 slave, and 2 villans and 6 bordars, and 4 acres of woodland and 100 acres of pasture. Formerly 7s; now it is worth 5s.

The same man holds TREBARWITH. Edwin held it TRE and it paid geld for 3 ferdings. Yet there is 1 hide. [There is] land for 3 ploughs. There are 2 ploughs, and 7 slaves and 6 bordars, and 40 acres of pasture. Formerly, as now, worth 20s.

The same man holds MINSTER. Edwin held it TRE and it paid geld for 1 ferding. Yet there is half a hide. [There is] land for 3 ploughs. There 2 villans and 6 bordars have 1 plough and [there are] 20 acres of pasture. Formerly, as now, worth 5s.

The same man holds [Chapel and Lower] AMBLE. Grim held it TRE and it paid geld for 2 ferdings. Yet there is half a hide. [There is] land for 3 ploughs. There is 1 plough, and 4 bordars and 5 slaves, and 20 acres of pasture. Formerly 10s; now it is worth 6s.

[Folio 123: CORNWALL]

The same Turstin holds CARADON of the count. Beorhtfrith held it TRE and it paid geld for 1 ferding. Yet there is 1 virgate of land. There is land for 2 ploughs. There are 6 bordars and 4 slaves, and 10 acres of woodland and 100 acres of pasture. Formerly 10s; now it is worth 10s.

The same man holds ARRALLAS. Beorhtmær held it TRE and it paid geld for 1 ferding. Yet there is half a hide. There is land for 3 ploughs. There is half a plough, and 7 bordars with 1 slave, and 10 acres of woodland and 1 league of pasture. Formerly 20s; now it is worth 2s.

The same man holds BODARDLE. Grim held it TRE and it paid geld for 1 virgate of land. Yet there is 1 hide. There is land

for 8 ploughs. There are 4 ploughs, and 7 slaves and 10 villans and 24 bordars, and 20 acres of woodland and 30 acres of pasture. Formerly 35s; now it is worth 20s.

The same man holds TRELOWTH. Alweard held it TRE and it paid geld for 1 virgate of land. Yet there is half a hide. There is land for 4 ploughs. There are 2 ploughs, and 3 slaves and 3 villans and 6 bordars, and 20 acres of woodland and 300 acres of pasture. Formerly 25s; now it is worth 15s.

The same man holds TRETHEAKE. Æthelric held it TRE and it paid geld for 1 virgate of land. Yet there is 1 hide. [There is] land for 7 ploughs. There are 2 ploughs, and 6 slaves and 4 villans and 8 bordars, and 40 acres of pasture. Formerly 20s; now it is worth 15s.

The same man holds TREWORRICK. Alric held it TRE and it paid geld for half a virgate of land. Yet there is 1 hide. There is land for 5 ploughs. There is 1 plough, and 2 slaves and 2 villans and 8 bordars, and 20 acres of woodland and 60 acres of pasture. Formerly 10s; now it is worth 5s.

The same man holds EGLOSROOSE. Earl Harold held it TRE and it paid geld for 1 ferding. Yet there is 1 virgate of land. [There is] land for 2 ploughs. There is half a plough, and 3 slaves and 3 bordars, and 20 acres of pasture. Formerly, as now, worth 10s.

Turstin holds GURLYN of the count. Dodda held it TRE and it paid geld for 1 virgate of land. Yet there is 1 hide. There is land for 5 ploughs. There is 1 plough, and 7 slaves and 16 bordars, and 2 acres of scrubland and 100 acres of pasture. Formerly 25s; now it is worth 15s. HAMELIN holds 'CRAWLE' [in Breage] of the count. Eadwig held it TRE and it paid geld for 1 ferding. There is land for 3 ploughs. There are 2 ploughs, and 4 bordars, and 6 acres of woodland and 100 acres of pasture. Formerly 15s; now it is worth 10s.

Hamelin holds MILTON of the count. Alwine held it TRE and it paid geld for 2½ hides. Yet there are 5 hides. [There is] land for 20 ploughs. There are 8 ploughs, and 7 slaves and 14 villans and 20 bordars, and 6 acres of woodland and 100 acres of pasture. Formerly 60s; now it is worth 50s.

The same Hamelin holds LEE. Alwine held it TRE and it paid geld for 1½ hides. Yet there are 3 hides. [There is] land for 15 ploughs. There are 6 ploughs, and 6 slaves and 8 villans and 12 bordars, and 10 acres of woodland and 30 acres of pasture. Formerly 40s; now it is worth 30s.

The same man holds BOYTON. Alnoth held it TRE and it paid geld for 1 virgate of land. Yet there is half a hide. There is land for 4 ploughs. There are 2 ploughs, and 3 slaves and 2 villans and 3 bordars, and 5 acres of woodland and 60 acres of pasture. Formerly 20s; now it is worth 15s.

The same man holds MARHAMCHURCH. Brothir held it TRE and it paid geld for 1½ ferdings. Yet there is 1 virgate of land. There is land for 2 ploughs. There is 1 plough with 1 slave and 1 villan and 2 bordars, and 20 acres of pasture. Formerly 10s; now it is worth 6s.

The same man holds WEEK ORCHARD. Sæwine held it TRE and it paid geld for 2½ ferdings. Yet there is half a hide.

[There is] land for 3 ploughs. There are 2 ploughs with 1 slave and 1 villan and 5 bordars, and 2 acres of woodland and 20 acres of pasture. Formerly 20s; now it is worth 15s.

The same man holds WADFAST. Siward held it TRE and it paid geld for 1½ virgates of land. Yet there is 1 hide. [There is] land for 6 ploughs. There are 3 ploughs, and 3 slaves with 1 villan and 5 bordars, and 15 acres of woodland and 100 acres of pasture. Formerly, as now, worth 20s.

The same man holds THORNE. Wulfric held it TRE and it paid geld for half a virgate of land.

Yet there is 1 virgate of land. [There is] land for 1 plough. There are 3 bordars with 1 slave, and 20 acres of pasture. Formerly, as now, worth 2s.

Hamelin holds ROSECRADDOC of the count. Godwine held it TRE and it paid geld for 1 hide. Yet there are 2 hides. [There is] land for 15 ploughs. There are 4½ ploughs, and 6 slaves and 7 villans and 16 bordars, and 6 acres of woodland. [There is] pasture 3 leagues long and 2 leagues broad. Formerly 60s; now it is worth 40s.

The same man holds [?] TREWALL. Beorhtric held it TRE and it paid geld for 1 acre. [There is] land for 2 ploughs. There is 1 plough, and 2 slaves with 1 villan and 2 bordars, and 10 acres of pasture. Formerly 5s; now it is worth 3s.

The same man holds TRELOWIA. Eadwig held it TRE and it paid geld for 1 acre. There is land for 2 ploughs. There is half a plough, and 2 slaves, and 10 acres of woodland and 10 acres of pasture. Formerly 5s; now it is worth 3s.

The same man holds TREGAMELLYN. Eadwig held it TRE and it paid geld for 1 acre. There is land for 2 ploughs. There is 1 plough, and 2 bordars with 1 slave, and 10 acres of pasture. Formerly, as now, worth 5s.

The same man holds TRETHAKE. Alwine held it TRE and it paid geld for 1 virgate of land. There is land for 2 ploughs. There are 1½ ploughs with 1 slave and 1 villan and 7 bordars, and 20 acres of pasture. Formerly 15s; now it is worth 10s.

The same man holds DAWNA. Beorhtric held it TRE and it paid geld for 1 ferding. Yet there is 1 virgate of land. [There is] land for 1 plough. There is half a plough with 1 slave and 2 bordars, and 5 acres of woodland and 40 acres of pasture. Formerly 10s; now it is worth 5s.

Hamelin holds PENPELL of the count. Beorhtric held it TRE and it paid geld for 1 virgate of land. Yet there is half a hide. There is land for 3 ploughs. There is 1 plough, and 2 slaves and 4 bordars, and 2 acres of woodland and 60 acres of pasture. Formerly 10s; now it is worth 5s.

The same man holds TREMODDRETT. Godwine held it TRE and it paid geld for 1 hide. Yet there are 1½ hides. [There is] land for 15 ploughs. There are 5 ploughs, and 7 slaves and 8 villans and 17 bordars, and 1 acre of woodland. [There is] pasture 4 leagues long and 2 leagues broad. Formerly 60s; now it is worth 40s.

The same man holds TREWOON. Beorhtmær held it TRE and it paid geld for 1 virgate of land. Yet there is half a hide.

[There is] land for 4 ploughs. There are 1½ ploughs, and 2 slaves and 5 bordars. [There is] pasture 1 league long and half a league broad. Formerly 10s; now it is worth 7s.

Turstin holds [?] KILMINORTH of the count. Wine held it TRE and it paid geld for half a ferding. There are 2 acres of land. [There is] land for 2 ploughs. There are 2 bordars with 1 slave, and 4 acres of woodland and 15 acres of pasture. Formerly 5s; now it is worth 3s.

Hamelin holds TREGAVETHAN of the count. Beorhtric held it TRE and it paid geld for 2 ferdings. Yet there is half a hide. [There is] land for 2 ploughs. There is 1 plough with 1 slave, and 4 bordars. [There is] pasture 1 league long and half a league broad. Formerly 10s; now it is worth 7s6d.

The same man holds PENVENTINUE. Alsige held it TRE and it paid geld for 1 virgate of land. Yet there is 1 hide. [There is] land for 4 ploughs. There are 2 ploughs, and 2 slaves and 6 bordars, and 5 acres of woodland and 10 acres of pasture. Formerly 20s; now it is worth 10s.

The same man holds TRENANCE [in St Austell]. Beorhtmær held it TRE and it paid geld for 1 virgate of land. Yet there is 1 hide. [There is] land for 5 ploughs. There are 3 ploughs, and 3 slaves and 6 bordars, and 10 acres of pasture. Formerly 20s; now it is worth 15s.

The same man holds TREHAVERNE [in Truro]. Leofric held it TRE and it paid geld for 1 acre of land. [There is] land for 1 plough. There is 1 bordar with 1 slave, and 40 acres of pasture. Formerly, as now, worth 12d.

The same man holds [?] BENNACOTT. Almær held it TRE and it paid geld for half a ferding. There is land for 1 plough. There is 1 villan with 1 bordar, and 40 acres of pasture. Formerly 5s; now it is worth 3s.

Turstin holds TREBARTHA of the count. Wulfnoth held it TRE and it paid geld for 1 ferding. Yet there is half a hide. [There is] land for 4 ploughs. There are 3½ ploughs, and 2 villans and 6 bordars. Formerly, as now, worth 15s.

NIGEL holds WOOLSTONE of the count. Alric held it TRE and it paid geld for half a hide. Yet there is 1 hide. [There is] land for 6 ploughs. There are 4½ ploughs, and 5 slaves and 4 villans and 12 bordars, and 1 acre of woodland and 10 acres of pasture. Formerly, as now, worth 20s.

The same Nigel holds WORTHYVALE. Beorhtmær held it TRE

[Folio 123V: CORNWALL]

and it paid geld for half a hide. There is land for 8 ploughs. There are 6 ploughs, and 12 slaves and 10 villans and 21 bordars, and 1 acre of scrubland, and 1 acre of meadow and 20 acres of pasture. Formerly £4; now it is worth 40s.

The same Nigel holds [?] TRENUTH of the count. Alric held it TRE and it paid geld for half a hide. Yet there is 1 hide. There is land for 4 ploughs. There are 2½ ploughs, and 5 slaves and 4 villans and 6 bordars, and 1 acre of meadow and 30 acres of pasture. Formerly 40s; now it is worth 25s.

The same Nigel holds ROSEBENAULT. Eadnoth held it TRE and it paid geld for 1 virgate of land. Yet there is half a hide. There is land for 3 ploughs. There are 1½ ploughs, and 3 slaves and 6 bordars, and 20 acres of pasture.

The same Nigel holds [?] ROSCARROCK. Alwine held it TRE and it paid geld for 1 virgate of land. Yet there are 3 virgates of land. There is land for 4 ploughs. There are 2 ploughs, and 4 slaves and 2 villans and 5 bordars, and 1 acre of meadow and 10 acres of pasture. Formerly, as now, worth 15s.

The same man holds LANCARFFE. Alweald held it TRE. There is 1 virgate of land which has never paid geld. There is land for 2 ploughs, which [ploughs] are there, and 2 slaves and 10 bordars, and 30 acres of woodland and 10 acres of pasture. Formerly 20s; now it is worth 10s. This land is of the honour of St Petroc.

The same Nigel holds TREVAGUE. Alwine held it TRE and it paid geld for 1 virgate of land. Yet there is half a hide. There is land for 6 ploughs. There are 4½ ploughs, and 6 slaves and 8 villans and 18 bordars, and 1 acre of scrubland. [There is] pasture 2 leagues long and 1 league broad. Formerly 40s; now it is worth 30s.

The same Nigel holds POLYPHANT. Wulfric held it TRE and it paid geld for 1 virgate of land. Yet there is half a hide. There is land for 3 ploughs. There are 2 ploughs, and 3 slaves and 3 villans and 6 bordars, and 2 acres of meadow, and 1 acre of woodland and 10 acres of pasture. Formerly, as now, worth 15s.

The same Nigel holds GALOWRAS. Sæwulf held it TRE and it paid geld for 1 ferding. Yet there is 1 virgate of land. There is land for 2 ploughs. There is 1 plough, and 2 slaves and 2 bordars, and 4 acres of woodland and 10 acres of pasture. Formerly, as now, worth 7s.

JOVIN holds ROSCARNON of the count. Griffin held it TRE and it paid geld for 1 ferding of land. There is land for 2 ploughs. There is half a plough, and 2 slaves, and 60 acres of pasture. Formerly 10s; now it is worth 5s.

The same Jovin held LAMETTON. Ælfheah held it TRE and it paid geld for half a ferding. There is 1 acre of land. [There is] land for 1 plough, which [plough] is there with 1 slave, and 3 bordars, and 3 acres of woodland. Formerly 3s; now it is worth 4s.

The same man holds NORTON. Almær held it TRE and it paid geld for 1 virgate of land. Yet there is half a hide. There is land for 5 ploughs. There are 3½ ploughs, and 3 slaves and 3 villans and 5 bordars, and 7 acres of woodland and 60 acres of pasture. Formerly 20s; now it is worth 25s.

The same man holds GREAT MORETON. Beorthmær held it TRE and it paid geld for 1 ferding. Yet there is 1 virgate of land. [There is] land for 3 ploughs. There are 2 ploughs, and 2 slaves and 5 bordars, and 20 acres of pasture. Formerly, as now, worth 10s.

The same man holds [East and West] BALSDON. Ketil held it TRE and it paid geld for half a ferding. Yet there is 1 ferding of land. There is land for 1 plough. There is half a plough with 1 villan and 2 bordars, and 20 acres of pasture. Formerly, as now, worth 5s.

The same man holds POUNDSTOCK. Gytha held it TRE and it paid geld for 1 virgate of land. Yet there is 1 hide. [There is] land for 6 ploughs. There are 2 ploughs with 1 slave and 1 villan and 5 bordars, and 10 acres of woodland and 40 acres of pasture. Formerly, as now, worth 20s. This land belongs to Lanow.

The same man holds TRESPARRETT. Beorhtsige held it TRE and it paid geld for 2 ferdings. Yet there is half a hide. [There is] land for 6 ploughs. There are 1½ ploughs with 1 slave and 1 villan and 4 bordars, and 300 acres of pasture. Formerly, as now, worth 12s.

The same man holds TREBLARY. Beorhtsige held it TRE and it paid geld for 1 ferding. Yet there is 1 virgate of land. [There is] land for 2 ploughs. There is 1 plough with 1 slave and 1 villan and 4 bordars, and 40 acres of pasture. Formerly 5s. now it is worth 10s.

The same Jovin holds ST GENNYS of the count. Gytha held it TRE and it paid geld for 1 virgate of land. Yet there is half a hide. [There is] land for 10 ploughs. There are 3 ploughs, and 3 slaves and 2 villans and 8 bordars, and 40 acres of pasture. Formerly, as now, worth 20s.

The same man holds DIZZARD. Beorhtsige held it TRE and it paid geld for 1 ferding. Yet there is 1 virgate of land. [There is] land for 2 ploughs. There is 1 plough, and 3 bordars, and 60 acres of pasture. Formerly 10s; now it is worth 5s.

JOVIN holds TRERICE of the count. He himself held it TRE and it paid geld for 1 ferding. Yet there is 1 virgate of land. [There is] land for 2 ploughs. There are 1½ ploughs, and 4 slaves with 1 villan and 2 bordars, and 20 acres of pasture. Formerly, as now, worth 20s.

The same man holds [?] TREWORGIE. Æthelwulf held it TRE and it paid geld for 1 ferding of land. [There is] land for 2 ploughs. There is 1 plough with 1 slave and 2 bordars, and 40 acres of pasture. Formerly 4s; now it is worth 8s.

The same man holds [East and West] CURRY. Godwine held it TRE and it paid geld for half a ferding. of land. There is land for half a plough. There is 1 slave, and 100 acres of pasture. Formerly 4s; now it is worth 2s.

Nigel holds TREDAULE of the count. Alweald held it TRE and it paid geld for half a hide. Yet there is 1 hide. [There is] land for 8 ploughs. There are 6 ploughs, and 8 slaves and 7 villans and 20 bordars, and 1 acre of meadow and 1 acre of woodland. [There is] pasture 2 leagues long and as much broad. Formerly 60s; now it is worth 40s.

BERNER holds HORNACOTT of the count. Eadsige held it TRE and it paid geld for half a virgate. Yet there is 1 virgate of land. There is land for 4 ploughs. There are 1½ ploughs with 1 slave, and 2 villans and 3 bordars, and 10 acres of scrubland and 30 acres of pasture. Formerly 20s; now it is worth 12s.

The same man holds ALVACOTT. Ælfgeat held it TRE and

it paid geld for half a virgate of land. Yet there is a virgate. There is land for 3 ploughs. There † are † 1½ ploughs with 1 slave and 1 villan and 3 bordars, and 3 acres of woodland and 30 acres of pasture. Formerly 20s; now it is worth 12s.

The same man holds WESTCOTT. Wulfnoth held it TRE and it paid geld for half a ferding. Yet there is 1 ferding. There is land for half a plough. There are 2 villans with 1 bordar, and 30 acres of pasture. Formerly 10s; now it is worth 5s.

The same man holds ROSECARE. Eadwig held it TRE and it paid geld for 1 ferding. Yet there is 1 virgate of land. [There is] land for 2 ploughs. There is 1 plough with 1 slave, and 2 bordars, and 5 acres of pasture. Formerly, as now, worth 7s6d.

The same man holds 'TREFREOCK' [in St Gennys]. Waso held it TRE and it paid geld for 1 ferding. Yet there is 1 virgate of land. [There is] land for 1 plough. There are 3 bordars, and 100 acres of pasture. Formerly 5s; now it is worth 3s.

The same man holds CRACKINGTON [Crackington Haven, Higher Crackington and Middle Crackington]. Eadwig held it TRE and it paid geld for 1 virgate of land. Yet there is half a hide. There is land for 3 ploughs. There is 1 plough, and 2 slaves and 6 bordars, and 4 acres of scrubland and 20 acres of pasture. Formerly 20s; now it is worth 10s.

The same man holds TRESLAY. Eadwig held it TRE and it paid geld for half and acre of land. Yet there is 1 acre of land. There is land for 1 plough. There are 3 bordars with half a plough, and 30 acres of pasture. Formerly, as now, worth 5s.

The same man holds [?] TREWEN. Eadwig held it TRE and it paid geld for 1 acre of land. There is 1 virgate of land. [There is] land for 1 plough. There are 2 bordars, and 30 acres of pasture. Formerly 5s; now it is worth 40s.

The same man holds LAMELLEN. Eadwig held it TRE and it paid geld for 1 virgate of land. Yet there is half a hide. [There is] land for 4 ploughs. There are 1½ ploughs, and 2 slaves and 5 bordars, and 20 acres of pasture. Formerly, as now, worth 15s.

The same man holds "TREGREBRI". Eadwig held it TRE. There is 1 hide which has never paid geld. There is land for 3 ploughs. There are 1½ ploughs with 1 slave, and 4 bordars, and 30 acres of pasture. Formerly 20s; now it is worth 10s. This land is [part] of the possessions of ST PIRAN.

[Folio 124: CORNWALL]

BRAIN holds WIDEMOUTH of the count. Wulfgeat held it TRE and it paid geld for 1 virgate of land. Yet there is half a hide. [There is] land for 4 ploughs. There are 2½ ploughs, and 2 slaves and 3 villans and 3 bordars, and 1 acre of meadow and 10 acres of pasture. Formerly 20s; now it is worth 15s.

The same man holds WHALESBOROUGH. Sæwine held it TRE and it paid geld for half a virgate of land. Yet there is 1 virgate. [There is] land for 3 ploughs. There are 2 ploughs with 1 slave, and 2 villans and 3 bordars, and 2 acres of meadow and 10 acres of pasture. Formerly, as now, worth 15s.

The same man holds PENFOUND. Eadgifu held it TRE and it paid geld for half a virgate of land. Yet there is 1 virgate. [There is] land for 2 ploughs. There is 1 plough with 1 slave, and 2 bordars, and 2 acres of meadow and 10 acres of pasture. Formerly, as now, worth 20s.

BRAIN holds TRENANT [in Fowey] of the count. Æthelmær held it TRE, and it paid geld for 1 ferding of land. Yet there is half a hide. [There is] land for 3 ploughs. There is 1 plough, and 2 slaves and 7 bordars, and 300 acres of pasture. Formerly, as now, worth 25s.

WILLIAM holds POUGHILL of the count. Alweard held it TRE and it paid geld for half a hide. Yet there is 1 hide. [There is] land for 16 ploughs. There are 5 ploughs, and 2 slaves and 8 villans and 13 bordars, and 40 acres of scrubland and 100 acres of pasture. Formerly 100s; now it is worth 40s.

ALVRED holds HILTON of the count. Esbiorn held it TRE and it paid geld for 3 virgates of land. Yet there are 2 hides. There is land for 10 ploughs. There are 5 ploughs, and 3 slaves and 7 villans and 11 bordars, and 10 acres of woodland and 50 acres of pasture. Formerly 100s; now it is worth 50s.

The same man holds THURLIBEER. Sæwine held it TRE and it paid geld for 1 virgate of land. Yet there are 3 virgates of land. There is land for 7 ploughs. There are 2 ploughs, and 3 slaves and 3 villans and 7 bordars, and 8 acres of scrubland and 30 acres of pasture. Formerly 40s; now it is worth 30s.

The same man holds BUTTSBEAR. Alwig held it TRE and it paid geld for half a ferding. Yet there is half a virgate of land. There is land for 1 plough, which [plough] is there with 1 slave, and 4 acres of woodland and 10 acres of pasture. Formerly 10s; now it is worth 7s6d.

The same man holds LAUNCELLS. Ælfric held it TRE and it paid geld for 1½ virgates of land. Yet there are 2 hides. [There is] land for 9 ploughs. There are 3½ ploughs, and 2 slaves and 3 villans and 11 bordars, and 30 acres of scrubland and 50 acres of pasture. Formerly 20s; now it is worth 40s.

The same man holds CANN ORCHARD. Ælfric held it TRE and it paid geld for 1 ferding. Yet there is 1 virgate of land. [There is] land for 2 ploughs, which [ploughs] are there with 1 villan, and 4 bordars and 2 slaves, and 2 acres of woodland and 10 acres of pasture. Formerly 15s; now it is worth 12s.

The same man holds BOROUGH [Devon.]. Algar held it TRE and it paid geld for half a ferding. Yet there is 1 virgate of land. [There is] land for 3 ploughs. There are 2 ploughs with 1 slave, and 2 villans and 2 bordars, and 5 acres of scrubland and 15 acres of pasture. Formerly 10s; now it is worth 15s.

The same man holds [?] ROSCARROCK. Alwine held it TRE and it paid geld for half a ferding. Yet there is 1 virgate of land. [There is] land for 1 plough. There are 2 bordars. Formerly 10s; now it is worth 2s.

ERCHENBALD holds BODBRANE. Alnoth held it TRE and it paid geld for 1 ferding. Yet there is 1 virgate of land. [There is] land for 2 ploughs. There is half a plough, and 2 slaves and 2 villans, and 12 acres of woodland and 10 acres of pasture. Formerly 10s; now it is worth 7s6d.

The same man holds "AVALDE". Dodda held it TRE and it paid geld for 1 ferding. Yet there is 1 virgate of land. [There is] land for 3 ploughs. There is 1 plough, and 3 slaves and 2 villans and 1 bordar, and 60 acres of pasture. [There is] woodland 3 furlongs long and 1 furlong broad. Formerly 20s; now it is worth 10s.

The same man holds BERA. Dodda held it TRE and it paid geld for 1 ferding. Yet there is half a hide. [There is] land for 3 ploughs. There are 1½ ploughs, and 3 slaves with 1 villan and 5 bordars, and 40 acres of pasture. Formerly 20s; now it is worth 12s6d.

OSFRITH holds MANELY of the count. Alric held it TRE and it paid geld for half a hide. Yet there are 2 hides. [There is] land for 12 ploughs. There are 3 ploughs, and 4 slaves and 5 villans and 16 bordars, and 8 acres of woodland. [There is] pasture 1 league long and half a league broad. Formerly £4; now it is worth 30s.

The same man holds BOCONNOC. The same man held it TRE and it paid geld for 1 virgate of land. Yet there is half a hide. [There is] land for 8 ploughs. There is 1 plough with 1 slave, and 2 villans and 6 bordars, and 100 acres of woodland and 40 acres of pasture. Formerly 40s; now it is worth 10s.

The same man holds TREMADART. Eadwig held it TRE and it paid geld for 1 virgate of land. Yet there is half a hide. [There is] land for 6 ploughs. There †are† 2½ ploughs, and 2 slaves and 3 villans and 9 bordars, and 10 acres of woodland and 40 acres of pasture. Formerly 60s; now it is worth 15d.

The same man holds TRENANT [Trenant and Little Trenant, in Duloe]. Osfrith himself held it TRE and it paid geld for 1 virgate of land. Yet there is half a hide. [There is] land for 8 ploughs. There are 2 ploughs, and 2 slaves and 4 villans and 12 bordars, and 6 acres of woodland and 40 acres of pasture. Formerly 60s; now it is worth 15s.

The same man holds GLYNN. He himself held it TRE and it paid geld for 1 virgate of land. There is land for 2 ploughs. There is 1 plough with 1 slave, and 2 villans and 6 bordars, and 100 acres of woodland and 40 acres of pasture. Formerly 40s; now it is worth 10s.

The same man holds BOWITHICK. Osfrith himself held it TRE and it paid geld for 1 ferding. There is land for 2 ploughs. There is 1 villan and 2 bordars. Formerly 5s; now it is worth 2s.

The same man holds PENHALT. He himself held it TRE and it paid geld for half a virgate of land. Yet there is 1 virgate of land. [There is] land for 4 ploughs. There are 6 bordars, and 10 acres of pasture. Formerly 20s; now it is worth 3s.

The same man holds PENPONT. He himself held it TRE and it paid geld for half a hide. Yet there is 1 hide. [There is] land for 16 ploughs. There are 2½ ploughs, and 5 slaves and 4 villans and 18 bordars, and 60 acres of pasture. Formerly 100s; now it is worth 25s.

The same man holds LANTYAN. He himself held it TRE and it paid geld for 1 virgate of land. Yet there is 1 hide. [There is] land for 8 ploughs. There are 1½ ploughs, and 4 slaves and 2 villans and 6 bordars, and 8 acres of woodland and 20 acres of pasture. Formerly 60s; now it is worth 20s.

The same man holds TREVILLYN. Bretel held it TRE and it paid geld for 1 ferding. Yet there are 2 ferdings. There is land for 2 ploughs. There is 1 villan and 3 bordars, and 5 acres of pasture. Formerly 10s. now it is worth 2s.

Osfrith holds TRELASKE of the count. He himself held it TRE and it paid geld for 1 virgate of land. Yet there is half a hide. [There is] land for 8 ploughs. There are 2½ ploughs, and 2 slaves and 3 villans and 12 bordars, and 10 acres of woodland and 50 acres of pasture. Formerly 60s; now it is worth 20s.

The same man holds TREGRILL. Alric held it TRE and it paid geld for 1 virgate of land. Yet there is 1 hide. There is land for 7 ploughs. There are 2 ploughs, and 2 slaves and 4 villans and 16 bordars, and 1 acre of woodland and 60 acres of pasture. Formerly 60s; now it is worth 20s.

Odo holds BOTELET of the count. Oswulf held it TRE and it paid geld for 1 virgate of land. Yet there are 2 hides. [There is] land for 8 ploughs. There are 2½ ploughs, and 4 slaves and 4 villans and 12 bordars, and 60 acres of woodland and 50 acres of pasture. Formerly 40s; now it is worth 50s.

The same man holds ST NEOT. Godric the priest held it TRE. There is 1 hide which has never paid geld. [There is] land for 5 ploughs. There is 1 plough, and 3 slaves and 3 villans and 6 bordars, and 60 acres of pasture. Formerly 20s; now it is worth 5s.

Odo holds TRELIGGA of the count. Beorhtmær held it TRE and it paid geld for 1 ferding. Yet there is 1 hide. [There is] land for 2 ploughs. There is 1 plough, and 2 slaves with 1 villan and 2 bordars, and 6 acres of pasture. Formerly 10s; now it is worth 5s.

The same man holds TREVENIEL. Beorhtmær held it TRE and it paid geld for 1 ferding. Yet there is half a hide. [There is] land for †2† ploughs. There is 1 plough, and 2 slaves and 2 villans and 4 bordars, and 2 acres of scrubland and 20 acres of pasture. Formerly 20s; now it is worth 10s.

The same Odo holds [?] TREVELL. Oswulf held it TRE and it paid geld for 1 ferding. Yet there is half a hide. [There is] land for 2 ploughs. There are 2 villans and 4 bordars with 1 slave, and 10 acres of pasture. Formerly 15s; now it is worth 5s.

Odo holds PORTHALLOW of the count. Leofrun held it TRE and it paid geld for 1 ferding. There is land for 2 ploughs. There are 2 bordars with 1 slave, and 4 acres of pasture. Formerly 7s; now it is worth 2s.

ALGAR holds TRENANCE [in St Keverne] of the count. Oswulf held it TRE and it paid geld for 1 ferding. Yet there is 1 hide. [There is] land for 6 ploughs. There are 2 ploughs, and

3 slaves and 2 villans and 9 bordars, and 100 acres of pasture. Formerly 40s; now it is worth 15s.

The same man holds TREWINCE. Oswulf held it TRE and it paid geld for 2 ferdings. Yet there is 1 hide. [There is] land for 6 ploughs. There are 2 ploughs, and 3 slaves and 3 villans and 7 bordars, and 500 acres of pasture. Formerly 30s; now it is worth 15s.

Algar holds PELYNT. Oswulf held it TRE and it paid geld for 1 virgate of land. Yet there is half a hide. [There is] land for 8 ploughs. There are 3½ ploughs, and 6 slaves and 4 villans and 12 bordars, and 30 acres of woodland and 40 acres of pasture. Formerly 50s; now it is worth 20s.

Algar holds PENTEWAN. Oswulf held it TRE and it paid geld for 2 ferdings. Yet there is half a hide. There is land for 3 ploughs. There are 2 ploughs, and 2 slaves and 3 villans and 7 bordars, and 4 acres of woodland and 10 acres of pasture. Formerly 20s; now it is worth 10s.

The same man holds [?] TREVESSON. Oswulf held it TRE and it paid geld for 2 ferdings. Yet there is half a hide. [There is] land for 4 ploughs. There are 2 ploughs, and 3 slaves and 3 villans and 4 bordars, and 20 acres of woodland and as many of pasture. Formerly 20s; now it is worth 10s.

The same man holds IDLESS. Oswulf held it TRE and it paid geld for 1 virgate of land. Yet there is 1 hide. [There is] land for 6 ploughs. In demesne are 3 ploughs, and 4 slaves, and 4 villans and 7 bordars, and 40 acres of woodland. [There is] pasture 2 leagues long and 1 league broad. Formerly 40s; now it is worth 15s.

ALWEARD holds TREGARDOCK of the count. He himself held it TRE and it paid geld for 3 ferdings. Yet there is half a hide. [There is] land for 3 ploughs. There are 2½ ploughs, and 2 slaves and 4 villans and 6 bordars, and 10 acres of pasture. Formerly 20s; now it is worth 10s.

The same man holds 'CARMAR' [in St Kew]. He himself held it TRE and it paid geld for half a virgate of land. Yet there is 1 virgate. [There is] land for 1 plough, which [plough] is there with 1 slave, and 3 bordars. There are 10 acres of pasture. Formerly 10s; now it is worth 7s.

ALNOTH holds TOLGULLOW of the count. The same man held it TRE and it paid geld for 2 ferdings. There is land for 3 ploughs. There are 1½ ploughs, and 3 slaves and 4 bordars and 2 acres of woodland and 60 acres of pasture. Formerly 20s; now it is worth 4s.

The same man holds TRESCOWE, and he himself held it TRE and it paid geld for 1 ferding. [There is] land for 3 ploughs. There is 1 plough with 1 slave, and 3 bordars, and 3 acres of woodland and 100 acres of pasture. Formerly 25s; now it is worth 5s.

Alnoth holds DIZZARD. Ælfric held it TRE and it paid geld for 1 acre. Yet there is 1 virgate of land. [There is] land for 1 plough. There is half a plough, and 2 villans with 1 slave, and 1 acre of meadow and 10 acres of pasture. Formerly 10s; now it is worth 5s.

Alnoth holds TREHUDRETH. Mærle-Sveinn held it TRE and it paid geld for 1 ferding. Yet there is 1 virgate of land. [There is] land for 2 ploughs. There is 1 plough, and 2 villans and 4 bordars, and 100 acres of pasture. Formerly 15s; now it is worth 10s.

Eadnoth holds PENGELLY. The same man held it TRE and it paid geld for half a ferding. There is 1 acre. [There is] land for 1 plough. There are 2 bordars, and 20 acres of pasture. Formerly 5s; now it is worth 2s.

Alnoth holds WOOLSTON. Sæwulf held it TRE and it paid geld for 1 ferding. Yet there is 1 virgate of land. [There is] land for 1 plough, which [plough] is there with 1 villan and 3 bordars. There are 100 acres of pasture. Formerly, as now, worth 5s.

ALRIC holds LANWARNICK of the count. The same man held it TRE and it paid geld for 1 ferding. Yet there is 1 virgate of land. [There is] land for 2 ploughs. There is half a plough with 1 slave and 2 villans and 3 bordars, and 10 acres of woodland and 60 acres of pasture. Formerly 20s; now it is worth 8s.

Alric holds DRAYNES. The same man held it TRE and it paid geld for half a ferding. Yet there is 1 ferding of land. [There is] land for 1 plough. There is half a plough, and 2 villans and 2 bordars, and 3 acres of scrubland and 30 acres of pasture. Formerly 20s; now it is worth 3s.

ALSIGE holds "TRELAMAR" of the count. The same man held it TRE and it paid geld for half a ferding of land. There is 1 acre of land. [There is] land for 1 plough. There is 1 slave, and pasture half a league long and as much broad. It is worth 12d.

ALMÆR holds HIGHER CABILLA of the count. The same man held it TRE and it paid geld for half a virgate. Yet there are 3 virgates of land. There is land for 6 ploughs. There is 1 plough, and 3 slaves and 3 villans and 7 bordars, and 40 acres of woodland and 50 acres of pasture. Formerly 40s; now it is worth 10s.

BEORHTRIC holds LESNEWTH of the count. He himself held it TRE and it paid geld for half an acre. Yet there is 1 virgate of land. [There is] land for 2 ploughs. There is 1 plough with 1 slave, and 3 bordars, and 2 acres of meadow and 15 acres of pasture. Formerly 15s; it is worth 10s.

The same man holds [?] TREGOLE. Burgræd held it TRE and it paid geld for 1 acre of land. There is land for 2 ploughs. There is half a plough, and 2 bordars, and 1 acre of woodland and 2 acres of meadow and 10 acres of pasture. Formerly 20s; now it is worth 8s.

Beorhtric holds [?] TREGEAGLE. He himself held it TRE and it paid geld for 1 ferding. Yet there is half a hide. There is land for 3 ploughs. There is 1 villan and 1 bordar with 1 slave, and 8 acres of woodland and 20 acres of pasture. Formerly 15s; now it is worth 5s.

Beorhtric holds TRETHURFFE. Leofric held it TRE and it paid geld for 1 ferding. Yet there is 1 virgate of land. [There is] land for 2 ploughs. There is 1 bordar with 1 slave, and 4 acres of woodland and 40 acres of pasture. Formerly 20s; now it is worth 5s.

Beorhtric holds PERRANUTHNOE. Hademar held it TRE and it paid geld for 1 virgate of land. Yet there is 1 hide. [There is] land for 2 ploughs. There are $1\frac{1}{2}$ ploughs, and 3 slaves and 7 villans and 8 bordars, and 30 acres of pasture. Formerly 30s; now it is worth 10s.

WULFSIGE holds DRAYNES of the count. The same man held it TRE and it paid geld for half a ferding. Yet there are 2 ferdings of land. [There is] land for 2 ploughs. There is 1 plough with 1 slave, and 2 villans and 3 bordars, and 3 acres of woodland and 30 acres of pasture. Formerly 10s; now it is worth 5s.

The same man holds "TREVILIUD". He himself held it TRE and it paid geld for 1 ferding. Yet there are 2 ferdings. [There is] land for 3 ploughs. There is 1 plough with 1 slave, and 2 villans and 2 bordars, and 20 acres of woodland and 5 acres of pasture. Formerly 20s; now it is worth 5s.

COLA holds HELE of the count. He himself held it TRE and it paid geld for 1 acre. There is 1 virgate of land. There is land for 2 ploughs. There is half a plough, and 4 bordars, and 1 acre of meadow, and 2 acres of woodland and 5 acres of pasture. Formerly 10s; now it is worth 5s.

LEOFNOTH holds ELERKEY of the count. Mærle-Sveinn held it TRE and it paid geld for 1 hide. Yet there are 4 hides. There is land for 20 ploughs. There are 5 ploughs, and 10 slaves and 17 villans and 18 bordars, and 30 acres of woodland and 100 acres of pasture. Formerly 100s; now it is worth 50s.

Leofnoth holds HALVANA. The same man held it TRE and it paid geld for half a virgate of land. Yet there is 1 virgate of land. There is land for 6 ploughs. There is half a plough, and 2 slaves and 5 bordars, and 15 acres of woodland and 20 acres of pasture. Formerly 15s; now it is worth 5s.

Wulfweard holds 1 ferding of land in RINSEY of the count. Alwine held it TRE. There is 1 villan, and 10 acres of pasture. It is worth 5s.

WULFSIGE holds PENHOLE. Wulfwine held it TRE and it paid geld for 1 ferding of land. Yet there is 1 virgate. [There is] land for 2 ploughs. There is 1 bordar, and 3 acres of meadow and 60 acres of pasture. Formerly 10s; now it is worth 15d.

Wulfric holds [?] 'BOSVISACK' [in Kenwyn] of the count. Leofric held it TRE and it paid geld for 1 ferding. Yet there is 1 virgate of land. [There is] land for 2 ploughs. There are 2 bordars with 1 slave, and 12 acres of woodland. [There is] pasture half a league long and half a league broad. Formerly 20s; now it is worth 5s.

Dodda holds CARSELLA of the count. He himself held it TRE and it paid geld for half a ferding. There is 1 acre of land. [There is] land for 1 plough. There are 3 slaves, and 30 acres of pasture. Formerly 10s; now it is worth 12d.

Scirweald holds GOTHERS. He himself held it TRE and it paid geld for 1 ferding. There are 2 acres of land. [There is] land for 1 plough. There is 1 villan with 1 slave. [There is]

pasture half a league long and as much broad. Formerly 10s; now it is worth 3s.

GUNNAR holds DOMELLICK. Æthelmær held it TRE and it paid geld for half a ferding. There is 1 acre of land. [There is] land for 1 plough. There are 2 bordars, and pasture half a league long and as much broad. Formerly 10s; now it is worth 12d.

GODWINE holds LANDEGEA. Alsige held it TRE and it paid geld for 1 virgate of land. Yet there is 1 hide. [There is] land for 5 ploughs. There are $1\frac{1}{2}$ ploughs, and 3 slaves and 2 villans and 4 bordars, and 2 acres of meadow and 3 acres of woodland. [There is] pasture 1 league long and as much broad. Formerly 30s; now it is worth 10s.

[Folio 125: CORNWALL]

WIHUMARC holds TUCOYSE [in Constantine] of the count. Eadmær held it TRE and it paid geld for 1 ferding of land. [There is] land for 4 ploughs. There are 2 villans and 3 bordars, and 2 acres of woodland and 1 league of pasture. Formerly 60s; now it is worth 5s.

Wihumar holds TRERSOOSEL. Eadmær held it TRE †and it paid geld†. There are 2 acres of land. There is land for 1 plough. There are 2 slaves with 1 bordar, and 1 acre of meadow and 1 acre of woodland. Formerly 10s; now it is worth 30d. The land belongs to the honour of St Kew.

HUECHE holds BODUEL of the count. The same man held it TRE and it paid geld for half a ferding. Yet there is 1 ferding of land. [There is] land for 1 plough. There is half a plough with 1 slave, and 2 villans and 3 bordars, and 10 acres of woodland and 60 acres of pasture. Formerly 20s; now it is worth 8s.

RABEL holds TREGUNNICK of the count. Ælfheah held it TRE and it paid geld for half a virgate of land. Yet there is 1 virgate. [There is] land for 3 ploughs. There is 1 bordar, and 20 acres of woodland and 10 acres of pasture. Formerly 5s; now it is worth 12d.

Rabel holds PENGOLD of the count. Alsige held it TRE and it paid geld for 1 ferding. Yet there is 1 virgate of land. [There is] land for 2 ploughs. There 4 bordars have 1 plough. There are 3 acres of scrubland and 20 acres of pasture. Formerly, as now, worth 5s.

Bernard the priest holds TACKBEAR [Devon.] of the count. Ælfric held it TRE and it paid geld for half a ferding of land. Yet there are 2 ferdings. [There is] land for 1 plough, which [plough] is there with 3 bordars, and 5 acres of scrubland and 40 acres of pasture. Formerly 4s; now it is worth 7s.

Humphrey holds TREVILLIS of the count. Ælfstan held it TRE and it paid geld for 1 virgate of land. Yet there is half a hide. [There is] land for 4 ploughs. There is 1 villan, and 20 acres of woodland and 30 acres of pasture. Formerly 10s; now it is worth 2s.

Seibert holds HELLAND of the count. Æthelmær held it TRE and it paid geld for 1 ferding. Yet there is 1 virgate of land. [There is] land for 4 ploughs. There is 1 plough, and 2 villans and 3 bordars, and 4 acres of woodland and 20 acres of pasture. Formerly, as now, worth 10s.

Frawin holds TREGONY of the count. Ælfric held it TRE and it paid geld for half a virgate of land. Yet there is 1 hide. [There is] land for 5 ploughs. There are 2 ploughs, and 5 slaves and 3 villans and 6 bordars, and 12 acres of woodland and 100 acres of pasture. Formerly 25s; now it is worth 15s.

ANDREW holds POLSCOE of the count. Ælfric held it TRE and it paid geld for 1 ferding. Yet there is 1 virgate of land. [There is] land for 1 plough. There is half a plough, and 2 villans and 5 bordars, and 3 acres of woodland and 5 acres of pasture. Formerly, as now, worth 3s.

Andrew holds "CARBIHAN" of the count. Merken held it TRE and it paid geld for 1 ferding. There are 4 acres of land. [There is] land for 4 ploughs. There are 2 ploughs, and 4 slaves and 2 villans and 3 bordars, and 5 acres of woodland and 20 acres of pasture. Formerly, as now, worth 10s.

RALPH holds WHITSTONE of the count. Alweald held it TRE and it paid geld for half a ferding of land. Yet there is 1 ferding. There is half a plough with 1 slave, and 12 acres of woodland. Formerly 20s; now it is worth 15s.

HELDRIC holds TREDWEN of the count. Beorhtmær held it TRE and it paid geld for 1 ferding of land. Yet there is 1 virgate. [There is] land for 3 ploughs. There are 2 ploughs, and 2 slaves and 6 bordars, and 40 acres of pasture. Formerly 15s; now it is worth 10s.

BLOHIN holds DELAMERE of the count. Iolfr held it TRE and it paid geld for 1 virgate of land. Yet there is half a hide. There is land for 2 ploughs, which [ploughs] are there with 1 slave, and 2 villans and 4 bordars, and 1 acre of meadow and 20 acres of pasture. Formerly 30s; now it is worth 20s.

The same man holds TREFREOCK [in St Endellion]. Iolfr held it TRE and it paid geld for 1 virgate of land. Yet there is half a hide. [There is] land for 2 ploughs. There is 1 plough with 1 slave, and 2 villans and 3 bordars, and 20 acres of pasture. Formerly 20s; now it is worth 10s.

The same man holds DANNONCHAPEL. Alweard held it TRE and it paid geld for 1 virgate of land. Yet there is half a hide. There is land for 3 ploughs. There are 1½ ploughs, and 4 slaves with 1 villan, and 40 acres of pasture. Formerly 25s; now it is worth 15s.

The same man holds TREWETHART. Ælfric held it TRE and it paid geld for half a ferding of land. Yet there is 1 ferding. [There is] land for 2 ploughs. There is 1 villan. Formerly, as now, worth 2s.

The same man holds TRUTHWALL. Beorhtmær held it TRE. There is 1 hide of land.

[There is] land for 8 ploughs. There are 4 ploughs, and 7 villans and 7 bordars, and 2 acres of meadow and 60 acres of pasture. Formerly 40s; now it is worth 20s.

This land the count took from the Church of ST MICHAEL.

ROGER holds TREWINT of the count. Burgræd held it TRE and it paid geld for 2 ferdings. Yet there is 1 virgate of land. [There is] land for 1 plough, which [plough] is there with 1 slave, and 4 bordars, and 2 acres of pasture. Formerly 10s; now it is worth 5s.

The same man holds DELABOLE. Leofwine held it TRE and it paid geld for 2 ferdings. Yet there is 1 hide. [There is] land for 4 ploughs. There is 1 plough with 1 slave and 1 villan and 3 bordars, and 1 acre of meadow and 40 acres of pasture. Formerly 30s; now it is worth 10s.

The same man holds LEIGH. Alnoth held it TRE and it paid geld for 2 ferdings of land. Yet there is half a hide. [There is] land for 4 ploughs. There are 2 ploughs, and 2 slaves and 10 bordars, and 2 acres of meadow, and 1 acre of woodland and 5 acres of pasture. Formerly 20s; now it is worth 10s.

The same man holds HAMMETT. Alnoth held it TRE and it paid geld for 1 ferding. There are 3 acres of land. [There is] land for 2 ploughs. There is 1 plough, and 3 slaves and 4 bordars, and 1 acre of woodland and 30 acres of pasture. Formerly 10s; now it is worth 5s.

VI. The land of Iudichael of Totnes

IUDICHAEL of Totnes holds FROXTON of the king and Turstin [holds] of him. There are 3 ferdings of land, but it pays geld for 1 ferding. There is land for 3 ploughs. There is half a plough, and 4 slaves and 2 bordars, and 50 acres of pasture and 40 acres of scrubland. Formerly 15s; now it is worth 11s.

VII. The land of Goscelm

GOSCELM holds [Higher and Lower] PIGSDON. Wadel held it TRE and it paid geld for 1 virgate of land. There is land for 1 plough, which [plough] is there with 1 bordar. There are 10 acres of meadow. Formerly, as now, worth 5s.

MIDDLESEX

[Folio 126: MIDDLESEX]

[Blank in MS]

[Folio 126V: MIDDLESEX]

Here Are Noted the Landholders In Middlesex

I KING WILLIAM
II The Archbishop of Canterbury
III The Bishop of London and his canons
IIII The Abbey of Westminster
V The Abbey of LA TRINITE, Rouen
VI The Abbey of Barking
VII Earl Roger
VIII The Count of Mortain
IX Geoffrey de Mandeville
X Ernulf de Hesdin
XI Walter fitzOther
XII Walter de Saint-Valery
XIII Richard son of Count Gilbert
XIIII Robert Gernon
XV Robert Fafiton
XVI Robert fitzRoscelin
XVII Robert Blund
XVIII Roger de Raismes
XIX William fitzAnsculf
XX Edward of Salisbury
XXI Aubrey de Vere
XXII Ranulph brother of Ilger
XXIII Deormann
XXIIII Countess Judith And the King's Almsmen

[Folio 127: MIDDLESEX]

IN 'OSSULSTONE' Hundred King WILLIAM holds 12½ acres of land of "Nanesmaneslande". This land was and is worth 5s. King EDWARD had this in the same way.

In the same hundred the king has 30 cottars [...] who pay 14s10½d a year.

At Holborn the king has 2 cottars who pay 20d a year to the king's sheriff.

TRE the Sheriff of Middlesex always had custody of these cottars [...].

William the chamberlain pays 6s a year to the king's sheriff for the land on which his vineyard is situated.

II. The land of the Archbishop of Canterbury

[...]

Archbishop Lanfranc holds HAYES for 59 hides. There is land for 40 ploughs. To the demesne belong 12 hides, and there are 2 ploughs. Among the Frenchmen and the villans are 26 ploughs, and there could be 12 more. There a priest has 1 hide; and 3 knights 6½ hides; and 2 villans 2 hides; and 12 villans each half a hide; and 20 villans each 1 virgate of land; and 40 villans each half a virgate; and [there are] 16 bordars on 2 hides. There are 12 cottars and 2 slaves. There is 1 mill [rendering] 4s, and meadow for 1 plough, [...] pasture for the livestock of the vill, [and] woodland for 400 pigs and [rendering] 3s.

In all it is worth £30; and when received, £12; TRE £40. Archbishop Stigand held this manor.

In THE HUNDRED of GORE Archbishop Lanfranc holds HARROW ON THE HILL. It was assessed at 100 hides TRE, and is so now. There is land for 70 ploughs. To the demesne belong 30 hides, and there are 4 ploughs and there could be a fifth. Among the Frenchmen and the villans, 45 ploughs, and there could be 16 more. A priest there [has] 1 hide, and 3 knights 6 hides, and under them well 7 men. There are 13 villans each [on] half a hide, and 28 villans each on 1 virgate, and 48 villans each [on] half a virgate, and 13 villans on 4 hides, and 2 cottars on 13 acres, and 2 slaves. [There is] pasture for the livestock of the vill, [and] woodland for 2,000 pigs. In all it is worth £56; and when received, £20; TRE £60. Earl Leofwine held this manor on the day on which King Edward was alive and dead.

In THE HUNDRED of 'Elthorne' Geoffrey de Mandeville holds 2 hides of Archbishop Lanfranc. [There is] land for 1 plough, and there is 1 villan with 1 plough who holds the land, and 4 cottars. [There is] woodland for 20 pigs. This land is worth 12s; and when received, the same; TRE 14s. Thurbert, the man of Earl Leofwine, held this. He could not place or sell it outside Harrow on the Hill, the archbishop's manor.

III. The land of the Bishop of London

In 'Ossulstone' HUNDRED the Bishop of London holds STEPNEY [for] 32 hides. There is land for 25 ploughs. To the demesne belong 14 hides, and there are 3 ploughs; and 22 ploughs among the villans. There are 44 villans each on 1 virgate, and 7 villans each on half a hide, and 9 villans each on half a virgate, and 46 cottars on 1 hide; they pay 30s a year. There are 4 mills rendering £4.16s less 4d, meadow for 25 ploughs, pasture for the livestock of the vill and [rendering] 15s, [and] woodland for 500 pigs and [rendering] 40s. In all it is worth £48; and when received, the same; TRE £50. This manor belonged and belongs to the bishopric.

In the same vill Hugh de Bernieres holds under the bishop 5 hides and 1 virgate of land. There is land for 4 ploughs. In demesne [is] 1 plough; and the villans [have] 3 ploughs. There is 1 villan on half a hide, and 6 villans on 3 virgate, and 2 bordars on half a virgate, and 3 cottars on 2½ acres, and 1 mill rendering 66s8d. [There is] meadow for 4 ploughs, [and] woodland for 150 pigs and [rendering] 3s6d. All together it is worth £6; when received, the same; TRE £7. Sigeræd held 2½ hides of this manor. He was a canon of St Paul's. He could give and sell them to whom he would without the bishop's permission. TRE the canon of St Paul's held 2½ hides for their demesne sustenance and Doding held 1 virgate and 1 mill from the bishop's own manor. He could not give or sell it except with his permission.

In the same vill the wife of Brian holds 5 hides of the bishop. There is land for 2½ ploughs. In demesne is 1 plough; and there could be 1 plough among the villans. There 1 villan on half a hide pays 4s a year for his house, and another villan on half a hide pays 8s. Roger the sheriff holds half a hide, and 15 bordars on 10 acres pay 9s. [There is] woodland for 60 pigs, [and] pasture for the livestock of the vill and [rendering] 5s. All together it is worth 60s; when received, the same; TRE 100s. Bishop William held this land in demesne, in the manor of Stepney, on the day on which King Edward was alive and dead.

In the same vill Ranulph Flambard holds 3½ hides of the bishop.

[Folio 127V: MIDDLESEX]

There is land for 5 ploughs. There are in demesne 2 ploughs; and 3 ploughs among the villans. There are 14 bordars on 1½ hides. [There is] meadow for 2 ploughs and [rendering] 2s. There is no pasture. [There is] a wood for making fences. All together it is worth £4; when received, the same; TRE 100s. Godwine held this land under Bishop William. He could not give or sell it without the bishop's permission TRE.

In the same vill William de Vere holds 1 hide of the bishop. There is land for 1 plough, and there is [1 plough] in demesne. This land is worth 16s; when received, the same; TRE 20s. Bishop William held this land in demesne with his manor of Stepney TRE.

In the same vill Engelbert the canon holds of the bishop 1 hide and 1 virgate. There is land for 1 plough, and there is [1 plough] in demesne. There is 1 villan on 1 virgate, and 4 bordars each on 7 acres, and 1 cottar. All together it is worth 40s; when received, the same; TRE 50s. The same canon held of Bishop William TRE. He could not sell it.

In the same vill the Bishop of Lisieux holds 1½ hides of the Bishop of London. There is land for 1 plough, and there is half a plough and there could be half [a plough more]. There are 2 bordars each on 5 acres, and 2 cottars on 4 acres, and 1 cottar. All together it is worth 40s; when received, the same; TRE 50s. Bishop William held this land in demesne on the day on which King Edward was alive and dead.

In the same vill William the chamberlain holds of the bishop 1½ hides and 1 virgate. There is land for 1½ ploughs. There is in demesne 1 plough, and there could be half [a plough more]. There is 1 villan on 1 virgate, and 6 bordars on 5 acres. All together it is worth 30s; when received, the same; TRE 40s. Bishop William held this land in demesne on the day on which King Edward died.

In the same [vill] Ælfric Chacepul holds 1 hide of the bishop. There is land for 1 plough, but the plough is wanting. This land is worth 10s; when received, the same; TRE 13s4d. Bishop William held this land in demesne TRE.

In the same vill Edmund son of Algot holds of the bishop 1 mill which is worth 32s6d; when received, the same, but it was not there TRE.

In the same vill Æthelwine, Beorhtmær's son, holds 1 mill which is worth 20s; when received, the same; TRE the same. He himself held it of Bishop William.

In FULHAM the Bishop of London holds 40 hides. There is land for 40 ploughs. To the demesne belong 13 hides, and there are 4 ploughs. Among the Frenchmen and the villans [are] 26 ploughs and there could be 10 more. There are 5 villans each [on] 1 hide, and 13 villans each on 1 virgate, and 34 villans each [on] half a virgate, and 22 cottars on half a hide, and 8 cottars with their gardens. Among the Frenchmen and certain burgesses of London [are] 23 hides of the land of the villans. Under them dwell 31 villans and bordars. [There is] meadow for 40 ploughs, [and] pasture for the livestock of the vill. From half a weir, 10s. [There is] woodland for 1,000 pigs and [rendering] 17d. In all it is worth £40; when received, the same; TRE £50. This manor belonged and belongs to the bishopric.

In the same vill Fulchred holds 5 hides of the Bishop of London. There is land for 3 ploughs. In demesne [is] 1 plough; and 1 plough among the villans, and there could be a third. There are 6 villans on half a hide, and 4 cottars on 8 acres, and 3 cottars. [There is] meadow for 1 ox, pasture for the livestock of the vill, [and] woodland for 300 pigs. In all it is worth 60s; when received, the same; TRE 100s. 2 sokemen held this land; they were the men of the Bishop of London. They could not give or sell it without the bishop's permission TRE.

In the same vill the canons of St Paul's hold 5 hides of the king as 1 manor. There is land for 5 ploughs. To the demesne belong 3 hides, and there are 2 ploughs. The villans [have] 2 ploughs, and there could be a third. There are 8 villans each on 1 virgate, and 7 villans each on half a virgate, and 7 bordars each on 5 acres, and 16 cottars and 2 slaves. [There is] meadow for 5 ploughs, pasture for the livestock of the vill, [and] woodland for 150 pigs. All together it is worth £8; when received, the same; TRE £10. The same canons of St Paul's held this manor in demesne TRE, and it is for their sustenance.

IN 'OSSULSTONE' HUNDRED

Durand, a canon of St Paul's, holds of the king 2 hides of land in TWYFORD. There is land for $1\frac{1}{2}$ ploughs. There are 3 villans on half a hide and half a virgate. [There is] pasture for the livestock of the vill, [and] woodland for 100 pigs. This land is worth 30s; when received, the same; TRE 20s.

In the same vill Gueri, a canon of St Paul's, holds 2 hides of land. There is land for $1\frac{1}{2}$ ploughs. In demesne is a plough, and there could be half [a plough more]. There are 2 villans on 1 virgate, and 1 bordar on 6 acres, and 3 cottars. [There is] woodland for 50 pigs. This land is worth 30s; when received, the same; TRE 20s. This manor belonged and belongs to St Paul's Church in the demesne of the canons.

The canons of St Paul's hold WILLESDEN. It was always assessed at 15 hides. There is land for 15 ploughs. There the villans [have] 8 ploughs, and there could be 7 [more]. There are 25 villans and 5 bordars. [There is] woodland for 500 pigs. In all it is worth £6.6s6d; when received, the same; TRE £12. The villans hold this manor at farm † of the canons†. There is nothing reckoned in demesne. This manor belonged to their demesne sustenance TRE.

The canons holds HARLESDEN as 1 manor. | It is assessed at 5 hides. | There is land for 4 ploughs. In demesne [are] 2 ploughs; and the villans [have] half a plough. There could be $1\frac{1}{2}$ ploughs. There are 12 villans each on 1 virgate, and 10 villans each on half a virgate. [There is] woodland for 100 pigs. All together it is worth 35s; when received, the same; TRE £4. TRE this manor belonged, as now, to the demesne of the canons of St Paul's.

Ralph the canon holds 'Rug Moor' [in St Pancras]. | It is assessed | at 2 hides. There is land for $1\frac{1}{2}$ ploughs. There is in demesne 1 plough, and there could be half a plough [more. There is] a wood for fences and [rendering] 4s. This land is worth 35s; when received, the same; TRE 40s. TRE it belonged, and it belongs now, | to the demesne of the canons. |

[Folio 128: MIDDLESEX]

The canons of St Paul's hold 'TOTTENHAM COURT' [in St Pancras]. It was always assessed at 5 hides. There is land for 4 ploughs. There are $3\frac{1}{2}$ ploughs, and there could be half [a plough] more. There are 4 villans and 4 bordars. [There is] woodland for 150 pigs, and 20s from the herbage. In all it is worth £4; when received, the same; TRE 100s. This manor belonged and belongs to the demesne of St Paul's.

Near St Pancras the canons of St Paul's hold 4 hides. There is land for 2 ploughs. The villans have 1 plough, and there could be another plough. [There is] a wood for fences, [and] pasture for the livestock and [rendering] 20d. There are 4 villans who hold this land under the canons, and 7 cottars. In all it is worth 40s; when received, the same; TRE 60s. This manor belonged and belongs to the demesne of St Paul's.

In Islington the canons of St Paul's have 2 hides. [There is] land for $1\frac{1}{2}$ ploughs. There is 1 plough, and there could be half [a plough more]. There are 3 villans on 1 virgate. [There is]

pasture for the livestock of the vill. This land is and was worth 40s. This belonged and belongs to the demesne of St Paul's Church.

In the same vill the canons themselves have 2 hides of land. There is land for $2\frac{1}{2}$ ploughs, and there are [$2\frac{1}{2}$ ploughs] now. There are 4 villans who hold this land under the canons, and 4 bordars and 13 cottars. This land is worth 30s; when received, the same; TRE 40s. This belonged and belongs to the demesne of St Paul's Church.

In Stoke Newington the canons of St Paul's have 2 hides. There is land for $2\frac{1}{2}$ ploughs, and there are [$2\frac{1}{2}$ ploughs] now. There are 4 villans, and 37 cottars on 10 acres. This land is worth 41s; when received, the same; TRE 40s. This belonged and belongs to the demesne of St Paul's.

In Hoxton the canons of St Paul's have 1 hide. [There is] land for 1 plough, and there is [1 plough] now, and 3 villans holding this land under the canons. [There is] pasture for the livestock. This land was and is worth 20s. This belonged and belongs to the demesne of St Paul's Church.

The canons hold HOXTON for 3 hides. There is land for 3 ploughs, and there are [3 ploughs]; and 7 villans who hold this land, and 16 cottars. All together it is worth 55s; when received, the same; TRE 60s. This manor belonged and belongs to St Paul's Church.

The canons of St Paul's have near the bishop's gate 10 cottars on 9 acres who pay 18s6d a year. TRE they held it in the same way and had as much.

In "Stanestaple" the canons have 4 hides. There is land for 2 ploughs, and there are [2 ploughs] now; and 7 villans who hold this land under the canons, and 2 cottars. [There is] pasture for the livestock of the vill, [and] woodland for 150 pigs and [rendering] 10s. In all it is worth 50s; when received, the same; TRE 60s. This land belonged and belongs to St Paul's Church.

Near St Pancras Walter, a canon of St Paul's, holds 1 hide. [There is] land for 1 plough. There is a plough, and 24 men who pay 30s a year. This land belonged and belongs to the demesne of St Paul's Church.

The canons of St Paul's hold WEST DRAYTON. It has always been assessed at 10 hides. [There is] land for 6 ploughs. To the demesne belong 5 hides, and there is 1 plough. The villans have 5 ploughs. There are 8 villans on 2 hides, and 6 bordars on 30 acres, and 2 cottars on 4 acres, and 1 bordar on 5 acres. There is 1 mill rendering 13s5d, meadow for 1 plough, [and] pasture for the livestock of the vill. From 1 weir, 32d. In all it is worth £6; when received, the same; TRE £8. This manor belonged and belongs to the demesne of St Paul's Church.

IIII. The land of St Peter of Westminster

IN 'OSSULSTONE' HUNDRED

In the vill in which ST PETER's Church is situated [Westminster] the abbot of the same place holds $13\frac{1}{2}$ hides. There is land for 11 ploughs. To the demesne belong 9 hides and 1 virgate, and there are 4 ploughs. The villans have 6 ploughs, and there could be 1 plough more. There are 9 villans each on 1 virgate, and 1 villan on 1 hide, and 9 villans each on half a virgate, and 1 cottar on 5 acres, and 41 cottars who pay 40s a year for their gardens. [There is] meadow for 11 ploughs, pasture for the livestock of the vill, woodland for 100 pigs, and 25 houses of the abbot's knights and other men who pay 8s a year. In all it is worth £10; when received, the same; TRE £12. This manor belonged and belongs to the demesne of ST PETER'S Church, Westminster.

In the same vill Baynard holds 3 hides of the abbot. There is land for 2 ploughs, and there are [2 ploughs] in demesne, and 1 cottar. [There is] woodland for 100 pigs, [and] pasture for the livestock. There are 4 arpents of newly-planted vineyard. In all it is worth 60s; when received, 20s; TRE £6. This land belonged and belongs to ST PETER'S Church.

The Abbot of ST PETER'S holds HAMPSTEAD [for] 4 hides. [There is] land for 3 ploughs. To the demesne belong $3\frac{1}{2}$ hides, and there is 1 plough. The villans have 1 plough, and there could be another. There is 1 villan on 1 virgate, and 5 bordars on 1 virgate, and 1 slave. [There is] woodland for 100 pigs. All together it is worth 50s; when received, the same; TRE 100s.

In the same vill Ranulph Peverel holds under the abbot 1 hide of the land of the villans. [There is] land for half a plough, and there is [half a plough]. This land was and is worth 5s. The whole of this manor belonged and belongs to the demesne of ST PETER'S Church.

IN SPELTHORNE HUNDRED

The Abbot of ST PETER'S holds STAINES [Surrey] for 19 hides. There is land for 24 ploughs. To the demesne belong 11 hides, and there are 13 ploughs. The villans have 11 ploughs. There are 3 villans each [on] half a hide, and 4 villans on 1 hide, and 8 villans each on half a virgate, and 36 bordars on 3 hides, and 1 villan on 1 virgate, and 4 bordars on 40 acres, and 10 bordars each [on] 5 acres, and 5 cottars each on 4 acres,

and 8 bordars on 1 virgate, and †3† cottars on 9 acres, and 12 slaves, and 46 burgesses who pay 40s a year. There are 6 mills rendering 64s, and 1 weir rendering 6s8d, and 1 weir [...] which renders nothing. [There is] pasture for the livestock of the vill, meadow for 24 ploughs and 20s in addition, woodland for 30 pigs, and 2 arpents of vineyard. To this manor belong 4 Berewicks, and they were there TRE. In all it is worth £35; when received, the same; TRE 40s. This manor belonged and belongs to the demesne of ST PETER'S Church.

The Abbot of St Peter's holds SUNBURY [Surrey] for 7 hides. There is land for 6 ploughs. To the demesne belong 4 hides, and there is 1 plough. The villans have 4 ploughs. There a priest has half a virgate, and [there are] 8 villans each [on] 1 virgate, and 2 villans on 1 virgate, and 5 bordars on 1 virgate, and 5 cottars and 1 slave. [There is] meadow for 6 ploughs, [and] pasture for the livestock of the vill. In all it is worth £6; when received, the same; TRE £7. This manor belonged and belongs to the demesne of ST PETER'S Church.

The Abbot of ST PETER'S holds SHEPPERTON [Surrey] for 8 hides. There is land for 7 ploughs. To the demesne belong $3\frac{1}{2}$ hides, and there is 1 plough. The villans have 6 ploughs. There are 17 villans each on 1 virgate, a priest [on] 15 acres, and 3 cottars on 9 acres, and 2 cottars and 2 slaves. [There is] meadow for 7 ploughs, pasture for the livestock of the vill, and 1 weir rendering 6s8d. All together it is worth £6#; when received, the same; TRE £7. This manor belonged and belongs to the demesne of ST PETER'S Church.

IN 'ELTHORNE' HUNDRED

The Abbot of ST PETER'S holds GREENFORD for $11\frac{1}{2}$ hides. There is land for 7 ploughs. To the demesne belong 5 hides, and there is 1 plough, and there could be another. The villans have 5 ploughs. There 1 villan has 1 hide and 1 virgate, and [there are] 4 villans each on half a hide, and 4 villans on 1 hide, and 7 bordars on 1 hide. A certain Frenchman [has] 1 hide and 1 virgate, and [there are] 3 cottars and 6 slaves. [There is] woodland for 300 pigs, [and] pasture for the livestock of the vill. In all it is worth £7; when received, the same; TRE £10. This manor belonged and belongs to the demesne of ST PETER'S Church.

The Abbot of ST PETER'S holds HANWELL. It is assessed at 8 hides. [There is] land for 5 ploughs. To the demesne belong 4 hides and 1 virgate, and there is 1 plough. The villans have 4 ploughs. There is 1 villan on 2 hides, and 4 villans on 1 hide, and 6 bordars on 3 virgates, and 4 cottars and 2 slaves. There is 1 mill rendering 2s2d, meadow for 1 plough, [and] woodland for 50 pigs. In all it is worth 110s; when received, the same; TRE £7. This manor belonged and belongs to the demesne of ST PETER'S.

The Abbot of ST PETER'S holds COWLEY. It is assessed at 2 hides. There is land for 1 plough. To the demesne belong $1\frac{1}{2}$ hides, and there is 1 plough. There are 2 villans on half a hide, and 1 cottar. [There is] meadow for half a plough, pasture for the livestock of the vill, woodland for 40 pigs, and a mill rendering 5s. This land is worth 30s; when received, the same; TRE 40s. St Peter's of Westminster held and holds this land in demesne.

In the HUNDRED of Gore William the chamberlain holds under the Abbot of ST PETER'S $2\frac{1}{2}$ hides in Kingsbury. [There is] land for 2 ploughs. In demesne [is] 1 plough; and the villans [have] 1 plough. There are 5 villans each on 1 virgate, and 1 cottar. [There is] woodland for 200 pigs. This land is worth 30s; when received, the same; TRE 60s. Alwine Horne, a thegn of King Edward, held this land in pledge from a certain man of ST PETER'S.

The Abbot of ST PETER'S holds HENDON. It is assessed

at 20 hides. [There is] land for 16 ploughs. To the demesne belong 10 hides, and there are 3 ploughs. The villans have 8 ploughs, and there could be 5 more. There a priest has 1 virgate, and 3 villans each [have] half a hide, and 7 villans 1 virgate each, and 16 villans half a virgate each, and [there are] 12 bordars who hold half a hide, and 6 cottars and 1 slave. [There is] meadow for 2 oxen, [and] woodland for 1,000 pigs and [rendering] 10s. In all it is worth £8; when received, the same; TRE £12. This manor belonged and belongs to the demesne of ST PETER'S Church.

V. The land of La Trinite of the Mount, Rouen

The Abbot of LA TRINITE, Rouen, holds HAR-MONDSWORTH of the king. It is assessed at 30 hides. There is land for 20 ploughs. To the demesne belong 8 hides, and there are 3 ploughs. Among the Frenchmen and the villans are 10 ploughs, and there could be 7 more. There a certain knight has 2 hides, and [there are] 2 villans each [on] 1 hide, and 2 villans on 1 hide, and 14 villans each on 1 virgate, and 6 villans each on half a virgate, and 6 bordars each [on] 5 acres, and 7 cottars and 6 slaves. There are 3 mills rendering 60s and 500 eels, and from the fishponds, 1,000 eels. [There is] meadow for 20 ploughs, pasture for the livestock of the vill, woodland for 500 pigs, and 1 arpent of vineyard. In all it is worth £20; when received, £12; TRE £25. Earl Harold held this manor, and in this manor was a certain sokeman holding 2 hides of these 30 hides. He could not give or sell them outside Harmondsworth TRE.

In SPELTHORNE HUNDRED Hertald of La Trinite now holds 1 hide of the king. [There is] land for half a plough. There is 1 villan who holds it. [There is] meadow for half a plough. This land is worth 10s; when received, the same; TRE the same. Golding, the man of Earl Harold, held this land. He could not sell or give it without his permission.

VI. The land of the Church of Barking

IN 'OSSULSTONE' HUNDRED

The Abbess of Barking holds MARYLEBONE of the king. It is assessed at 5 hides. [There is] land for 3 ploughs. In demesne [are] 2 hides, and there is 1 plough. The villans have 2 ploughs. There are 2 villans on half a hide, and 1 villan on half a virgate, and 2 bordars on 10 acres, and 3 cottars. [There is] pasture for the livestock of the vill, [and] woodland for 50 pigs. From the herbage, 40d. All together it is worth 52s; when received, the same; TRE 100s. This manor always belonged and belongs to the Church of Barking.

[Folio 129: MIDDLESEX]

VII. The land of Earl Roger

SPELTHORNE HUNDRED

Earl Roger holds 1½ hides in Hatton. [There is] land for 1 plough, and there is [1 plough]. 2 villans hold this land. [There is] meadow for 1 plough. This land is worth 15s; when received, the same; TRE 20s. 2 sokemen held it; they were the men of Albert of Lorraine. They could sell and give it. Now it is placed in Colham Green, to which it did not belong TRE.

HANWORTH is assessed at 5 hides. Robert holds it of Earl Roger. [There is] land for 3 ploughs. In demesne [are] 1½ ploughs. The villans [have] 2½ ploughs. There is 1 villan on 1 hide, and 5 villans each on 1 virgate, and 2 villans on 1 virgate, and 2 cottars. [There is] meadow for 1 plough, [and] pasture for the livestock of the vill. All together it is worth 40s; when received, the same; TRE 60s. Ulf, a house-carl of King Edward, held this manor.

'ELTHORNE' HUNDRED

Earl Roger holds 1 hide in Harmondsworth. [There is] land for 1 plough. There is half a plough; and there could be half [a plough more]. 2 villans hold this land. It was and is worth 10s. Alwine, the man of Vigot, held this and he could do with it what he would. Now it belongs to Colham Green, to which it did not belong TRE.

HARLINGTON is assessed at 10 hides. Alvred and Olaf hold it of Earl Roger. There is land for 6 ploughs. In demesne [are] now 2 ploughs; and the villans have 3 ploughs, and there could be a fourth. There a priest [has] half a hide, and [there are] 12 villans each [on] 1 virgate, and 4 villans each [on] half a virgate, and 2 bordars on 11 acres, and 8 cottars and 1 slave. [There is] meadow for 2 ploughs. In all it is worth 100s; when received, the same; TRE £8. Vigot held this manor, and 1 sokeman held 2 hides of this land. He could not sell it without his permission.

COLHAM GREEN is assessed at 8 hides. Earl Roger holds it. [There is] land for 7 ploughs. In demesne [are] 6 hides, and there are 3 ploughs; and the villans have 3 ploughs. There are 6 villans each on 1 virgate, and 4 others on 2 virgates, a priest [on] 1 hide, and 10 bordars each on 5 acres, and 4 cottars and 8 slaves. There are 2 mills rendering 41s, and half a mill rendering 5s, meadow for 3 ploughs, pasture for the livestock of the vill, woodland for 400 pigs, and 1 arpent of vineyard. In all it is worth £8; when received, £6; TRE £10. Vigot held this manor of King Edward.

HILLINGDON is assessed at 4 hides. Earl Roger holds it. There is land for 2 ploughs. In demesne [are] 2 hides, and there could be 1 plough. The villans have 1 plough. There are 2 villans on half a hide, and 2 bordars on 10 acres, and 1 cottar. 2 Frenchmen [have] 1½ hides; under them dwell 3 men. [There is] meadow for 4 oxen, [and] woodland for 1,000 pigs. From 1 weir, 5s. In all it is worth £3; when received, the same; TRE £4. Ulf, a thegn of King Edward, held this manor and he could do with it what he would.

Alnoth holds 'DAWLEY' [in Harlington] of Earl Roger. It is assessed at 3 hides. There is land for 2 ploughs. In demesne [is] 1 plough; and the villans have 1 plough. There are 4 villans each on 1 virgate, and 4 bordars on 5 acres. [There is] meadow for 6 oxen, pasture for the livestock of the vill, [and] woodland for 15 pigs. All together it is worth 30s; when received the same; TRE 60s. This manor belongs to Colham Green, to which it did not belong TRE. Godwine

Ælfgyth, the man of Vigot, held it and he could do with it what he would.

ICKENHAM is assessed at 9½ hides. 3 knights and 1 Englishman hold it of Earl Roger. There is land for 6 ploughs. There are 4 ploughs, and there could be 2 more. There are 6 villans on 1 hide, and 2 others on 1 hide and 1 virgate, and 2 others on 2 virgates, and 4 bordars on 20 acres, and 3 cottars. [There is] meadow for 4 ploughs, pasture for the livestock of the vill, [and] woodland for 200 pigs. In all it is worth £4; when received, the same; TRE £6. Toki held │2 hides│ of this manor: he was a housecarl of King Edward; and 2 sokemen [held] 2 hides and 1 virgate: they were the men of Wulfweard; and Alwine [held] 1 hide and 3 virgates: he was the man of Wulfsige son of Manni. They could sell to whom they would TRE. The whole of this land now belongs to Colham Green, to which it did not belong TRE.

VIII. The land of the Count of Mortain

IN SPELTHORNE HUNDRED

The Count of Mortain holds 2 hides in Laleham [Surrey], and the Abbot of Fecamp [holds] of him. [There is] land for 1½ ploughs, and there are [1½ ploughs. There are] 6 villans on half a hide, and 7 cottars. [There is] meadow for 1½ ploughs, [and] pasture for the livestock of the vill. This land is worth 40s; when received and TRE, 50s. The reeve of Staines [Surrey] held this land under the Abbot of Westminster. He could not give or sell it outside of Staines except with the permission of the abbot.

In Ashford [Surrey] the same count holds 1 hide. There is land for 1 plough, and there is [1 plough. There is] meadow for 1 plough. This land is worth 14s; when received, the same; TRE 20s. Ælfric, the man of the Abbot of Chertsey, held this, and he could do with it what he would. Now it is placed in the count's manor of Kempton [Surrey], to which it did not belong TRE. The soke, however, belonged to Staines [Surrey].

In East Bedfont the same count holds 2 hides. There is land for 1 plough. Now there is half a plough, and there could be half [a plough more]. There is 1 villan [on] 8 acres, and a certain knight [has] half a hide. [There is] meadow for 1 ox, [and] pasture for the livestock. This land is worth 5s; when received, the same; TRE 20s. Gøti, a housecarl of Earl Harold, held this land, and he could do with it what he would. This land belonged and belongs to Feltham.

The same count holds FELTHAM. It is assessed at 12 hides. There is land for 10 ploughs. In demesne [are] 6 hides, and there is 1 plough, and there could be 3 more. The villans have 8 ploughs. There are 14 villans each on 1 virgate, and 5 others each on half a virgate, and 2 slaves. [There is] meadow for 10 ploughs, [and] pasture for the livestock of the vill. All together it is worth £6; when received, £4; TRE £8. 2 thegns held this manor. One of these, the man of King Edward, had 5 hides │as 1 manor,│ and the other, the man of Earl Harold, 7 hides as 1 manor, and they could do with them what they would.

The same count holds KEMPTON [Surrey]. It is assessed at 5 hides. There is land for 5 ploughs. In demesne [are] 2 hides

and half a virgate, and there is 1 plough, and there could be another. The villans have 3 ploughs. There are 6 villans each on 1 virgate, and 8 others each on half a virgate, and 3 bordars on 1 virgate, and 2 slaves. [There is] meadow for 5 ploughs, pasture for the livestock of the vill, and 8 arpents of newly-planted vineyard. All together it is worth £4; when received, £3; TRE £6. Wulfweard White, a thegn of King Edward, held this manor, and he could do [with it] what he would.

IN GORE HUNDRED

[Folio 129V: MIDDLESEX]

The same count holds STANMORE. It is assessed at 9½ hides. There is land for 7 ploughs. In demesne [are] 6½ hides, and there are 2 ploughs, and there could be another. The villans have 1½ ploughs, and there could be 2½ ploughs [more]. There a priest has half a hide, and [there are] 4 villans each on 1 virgate, and 2 others on 1 virgate, and 3 cottars on 10 acres, and 3 others on 1 acre. [There is] pasture for the livestock of the vill, woodland for 800 pigs, and from the herbage, 12d. In all it is worth 60s; when received, 10s; Eadmær Atule, a thegn of King Edward, held this manor.

IX. The land of Geoffrey de Mandeville

'OSSULSTONE' HUNDRED

GEOFFREY de Mandeville holds 'EBURY' [in Westminster]. It is assessed at 10 hides. There is land for 8 ploughs. In demesne [are] 5 hides, and there are 2 ploughs. The villans have 5 ploughs, and there could be a sixth. There is 1 villan [on] half a hide, and 4 villans each on 1 virgate, and 14 others each on half a virgate, and 4 bordars on 1 virgate, and 1 cottar. [There is] meadow for 8 ploughs, and from the hay, 60s. From the pasture, 7s. In all it is worth £8; when received, £6; TRE £12. Harold, the son of Earl Ralph, of whom Queen Edith had the custody together with the manor on the day on which King Edward was alive and dead, held this manor. Afterwards William the chamberlain held it of the queen in fee at a farm of £3 a year, and after the queen's death he held it in the same way of the king. It is now 4 years since William lost the manor, and from that time the king's farm, namely £12, has not been paid.

In the same hundred Ralph holds 1½ hides of Geoffrey. [There is] land for 1 plough, and there is [1 plough], and 4 bordars on 14 acres, and 1 slave. [There is] meadow for 1 plough, pasture for the livestock and [rendering] 13d, [and] a wood for fences. This land is worth 30s; when received and TRE, 30s. 2 sokemen of King Edward held this land; they could sell it to whom they would.

In ISLINGTON Gilbert holds half a hide of Geoffrey. There is land for half a plough, and there is [half a plough], and 1 villan and 1 bordar. This land is worth 12s; when received, the same; TRE 20s. Grim, the man of King Edward, held this and he could sell it.

IN 'ELTHORNE' HUNDRED

In Greenford Ernulf holds 3 hides of Geoffrey. [There is] land for 1½ ploughs. There is 1 plough, and there could be half a plough [more]. There are 2 villans on half a hide, and 2 cottars and 1 slave. [There is] woodland for 40 pigs. This land is worth 20s; when received, 10s; TRE 40s. 2 sokemen held this land. One of these was a canon of St Paul's. He had 2 hides. He could do what he would with them. The other was the man of Esger the staller. He could not give it except with his permission.

In the same vill Ansgot holds half a hide of Geoffrey. [There is] land for 2 oxen. This land is worth 3s; and when received and TRE, the same. Azur held this land. He was the man of Esger the staller. He could not sell it without his permission.

In Ickenham 2 Englishmen hold 3½ hides of Geoffrey. There is land for 2 ploughs, and there are [2 ploughs]. [There are] 3 villans each on half a virgate, and 5 bordars. [There is] meadow for 2 ploughs, pasture for the livestock of the vill, [and] woodland for 40 pigs. This land is worth 30s; when received, the same; TRE 60s. 2 sokemen held this land. One of these was the man of Esger the staller and he had 1 hide; he could not sell it except with his permission, and the other was the man of Earl Leofwine. He had 2½ hides and he could sell them TRE.

Geoffrey de Mandeville holds NORTHOLT. It is assessed at 15 hides. There is land for 10 ploughs. In demesne [are] 8 hides, and there are 2 ploughs. The villans have 6 ploughs, and there could be 2 ploughs [more]. There is a priest [on] half a hide, and 1 villan [on] 1 hide, and 5 others each [on] half a hide, and 8 others each [on] 1 virgate, and 8 others each [on] half a virgate, and 3 cottars and 6 slaves. [There is] pasture for the livestock, [and] woodland for 200 pigs. In all it is worth £10; when received, £5; TRE £12. Esger the staller held this manor.

EDMONTON HUNDRED

Geoffrey de Mandeville holds EDMONTON. It is assessed at 35 hides. There is land for 26 ploughs. In demesne [are] 16 hides, and 4 ploughs. The villans have 22 ploughs. There is 1 villan on 1 hide, and 3 others each [on] half a hide, and 20 villans each on 1 virgate, and 24 others each [on] half a virgate, and 9 bordars on 3 virgates, and 4 bordars each on 5 acres, and 4 bordars each [on] 4 acres, and 4 cottars on 4 acres, 10 cottars, and 4 villans on 1 hide and 1 virgate, and 4 slaves. There is 1 mill [rendering] 10s, meadow for 26 ploughs and 25s in addition, pasture for the livestock, woodland for 2,000 pigs, and 12s from the renders of the woodland and of the pasture. In all it is worth £40; when received, £20; TRE £40. Esger, the staller of King Edward, held this manor. To this manor belonged and belongs a Berewick which is called South Mimms [Herts.] and it is assessed with the manor.

Geoffrey de Mandeville holds ENFIELD. It is assessed at 30 hides. [There is] land for 24 ploughs. In demesne [are] 14 hides, and there are 4 ploughs. The villans have 16 ploughs. There is 1 villan on 1 hide, and 3 villans each on half a hide, a priest [on] 1 virgate, and 17 villans each [on] 1 virgate, and 36 villans each [on] half a virgate, and 20 bordars on 1 hide and 1 virgate, and 7 cottars on 23 acres, and 5 cottars on 7 acres, and 18 cottars and 6 slaves. There is 1 mill [rendering] 10s. From the fishponds, 8s. [There is] meadow for 24 ploughs and [rendering] 25s. In addition, pasture for the livestock of the vill, [and] woodland for 2,000 pigs. From the woodland and pasture, 43s; and there is a park. In all it is worth £50; when received, £20; TRE £50. Esger, the staller of King Edward, held this manor. There were on this land 5 sokemen on 6 hides which they could give or sell without their lords' permission.

X. The land of Ernulf de Hesdin

'ELTHORNE' HUNDRED

ERNULF de Hesdin holds RUISLIP. It is assessed at 30 hides. There is land for 20 ploughs. In demesne [are] 11 hides, and there are 3 ploughs. Among the Frenchmen and the villans are 12 ploughs, and there could be 5 more. There a priest [has] half a hide, and [there are] 2 villans on 1 hide, and 17 villans each [on] 1 virgate, and 10 villans each [on] half a virgate, and 7 bordars each [on] 4 acres, and 8 cottars and 4 slaves, and 4 Frenchmen on 3 hides and 1 virgate. [There is] pasture for the livestock of the vill. There is a park for wild beasts, [and] woodland for 1,500 pigs and [rendering] 20d. In all it is worth £20; when received, £12; TRE £30. Wulfweard White, a thegn of King Edward, held this manor. He could sell it to whom he would.

In Kingsbury Albold holds 7½ hides of Ernulf.

[Folio 130: MIDDLESEX]

There is land for 7 ploughs. In demesne [are] 2 ploughs; and the villans [have] 5 ploughs. There are 8 villans each on 1 virgate, and 3 villans each [on] half a virgate. A priest [has] 1 virgate, and [there are] 5 bordars each on 5 acres. There is 1 mill [rendering] 3s, meadow for half a plough, [and] woodland for 1,000 pigs and [rendering] 20s. In all it is worth £4; when received, 20s; TRE £6. Wulfweard White, a thegn of King Edward, held this manor.

XI. The land of Walter fitzOther

SPELTHORNE HUNDRED

WALTER fitzOther holds STANWELL [Surrey] of the king. It is assessed at 15 hides. There is land for 10 ploughs. In demesne [are] 3 hides, and 3 ploughs. Among the Frenchmen and the villans [are] 10 ploughs. There is 1 villan on 1 hide, and 8 villans each [on] half a hide, and 10 villans each [on] 1 virgate, and 8 villans each [on] half a virgate, and 4 bordars on 28 acres, and 2 cottars and 8 slaves, and 2 knights [have] 2½ hides and under them dwell 6 bordars. There are 4 mills rendering 70s. and 400 eels less 25. From 3 weirs, 1,000 eels. [There is] meadow for 12 ploughs, pasture for the livestock of the vill, [and] woodland for 100 pigs. In all it is worth £14; when received, £6; TRE £14. Azur, a housecarl of King Edward, held this manor and he could do with it what he would.

In East Bedfont Richard holds of Walter fitzOther 10 hides as

1 manor. There is land for 5 ploughs. In demesne [is] 1 plough; and 4 ploughs among the Frenchmen and the villans. There are 4 villans on 1 hide, and 4 others each [on] half a virgate, and 3 bordars on 13 acres. A certain knight [has] 2 hides. [There is] meadow for 2 oxen, [and] pasture for the livestock of the vill. All together it is worth £4; when received, 20s; TRE £6. Azur held 8½ hides of this manor and it was a Berwick of Stanwell [Surrey], and 3 sokemen had 1½ hides. One of these was the man of King Edward, another the man of Leofwine, the third the man of Azur. Each had half a hide and they could sell or give them; and they did not belong to the manor TRE.

In West Bedfont [Surrey] Walter de Muchedent holds of Walter fitzOther 8 hides as 1 manor. There is land for 4 ploughs. In demesne [is] 1 plough; and the villans have 3 ploughs. There are 2 villans on 4 hides, and 2 villans on 2 virgates, and 2 villans on 1 virgate, and 1 bordar on 5 acres, a priest [on] 1 virgate, and 1 cottar on 5 acres, and 2 slaves. [There is] meadow for 2 oxen, [and] pasture for the livestock of the vill. All together it is worth £3; when received, the same; TRE £6. Beorhtmær held 4 hides of this manor. He was the man of Earl Harold. He could sell to whom he would; and 2 sokemen held 4 hides: they were the men of Azur. They could not sell or give them without his permission.

In Hatton Walter de Muchedent holds of Walter fitzOther 1 hide and 3 virgates and the third part of 1 virgate. There is land for 1 plough. There is half a plough, and there could be half a plough [more]. There is 1 villan on 1 virgate, and 2 virgates *[sic]* on 1 virgate, and 1 bordar on 5 acres. [There is] meadow for 1 plough, [and] pasture for the livestock. This land is worth 20s; when received, the same; TRE 30s. 2 sokemen held this land. They were the men of Azur. They could not sell it except with his permission.

XII. The land of Walter de Saint-Valery

HOUNSLOW HUNDRED

WALTER de Saint-Valery holds ISLEWORTH. It has always been assessed at 70 hides. There is land for 55 ploughs. In demesne [are] 6½ hides, and there are 6 ploughs. Among the Frenchmen and the villans [are] 28 ploughs and there could be 11 more. There a priest has 3 virgates, and [there are] 51 villans each on 1 virgate, and 24 villans each on half a virgate, and 18 villans each [on] half a virgate, and 6 cottars. The Frenchmen and a certain Englishman [have] 4 hides, and they are proven knights. Under them dwell 12 villans and bordars and 6 of the lord's villans who hold 2 hides and half a virgate. There are 2 mills rendering 10s, meadow for 20 ploughs, pasture for the livestock of the vill, 1½ weirs rendering 12s8d, [and] woodland for 500 pigs. From the herbage, 12d. In all it is worth £72; when received, the same; TRE £80. Earl Ælfgar held this manor.

The same Walter holds HAMPTON. It is assessed at 35 hides. There is land for 25 ploughs. In demesne [are] †18† hides, and 3 ploughs. The villans have 17 ploughs, and there could be 5 ploughs more. There are 30 villans each on 1 virgate, and 11 villans on 2½ hides, and 4 bordars each on half a virgate. [There is] meadow for 3 ploughs and [render-

ing] 10s, [and] pasture for the livestock of the vill. From the seines and drag-nets in the river Thames, 3s. In all it is worth £39; when received, £20; TRE £40. Earl Ælfgar held this manor.

XIII. The land of Richard fitzGilbert

'ELTHORNE' HUNDRED

RICHARD son of Count Gilbert holds HAREFIELD [Harefield and South Harefield]. It is assessed at 5 hides. There is land for 5 ploughs. In demesne [are] 2 hides, and there are 2 ploughs. The villans have 3 ploughs. There a priest has 1 virgate, and [there are] 5 villans each on 1 virgate, and 5 others each [on] half a virgate, and 7 bordars each on 5 acres, and 1 bordar on 3 acres, and 3 cottars and 3 slaves. There are 2 mills rendering 15s. From 4 fishponds, 1,000 eels. [There is] meadow for 1 plough, pasture for the livestock of the vill, [and] woodland for 1,200 pigs. In all it is worth £12; when received, £8; TRE £14. Countess Gode held this manor TRE.

XIIII. The land of Robert Gernon

'OSSULSTONE' HUNDRED

ROBERT Gernon holds of the king 2 hides in HAGGERSTON. There is land for 2 ploughs, and there are 3 ploughs. There are 3 villans and 7 bordars who hold this land; and it is worth 45s; when received, 40s; TRE 50s. Alwine, the man of King Edward, held this manor. He could sell it to whom he would.

In 'Elthorne' Hundred Nigel holds 2 hides of Robert Gernon. There is land for 1 plough. There is half a plough now, and there could be half a [plough more]. There is 1 cottar, [and] woodland for 30 pigs. This land is worth 14s; when received, the same; TRE 20s. Thurbert, the man of Earl Leofwine, held this land and he could sell it to whom he would.

XV. The land of Robert Fafiton

'OSSULSTONE' HUNDRED

ROBERT Fafiton holds of the king 4 hides in Stepney. There is land for 3 ploughs, and there are [3 ploughs] now. There is 1 villan on 14 acres, and another on 12 acres, and Roger the sheriff [has] 1 hide, and [there are] bordars on half a hide and half a virgate. [There is] woodland for 60 pigs and [rendering] 4s. All together it is worth 70s; when received, the same; TRE £8. Sigeræd, a canon of St Paul's, held this manor. He could sell it to whom he would TRE. The Bishop of London claims that he ought to have it. With these 4 hides there are now 53 acres of land which were not there TRE, which Hugh de Bernieres usurped to the loss of the canons of St Paul's and placed in this manor, according to the testimony of the hundred.

In 'Elthorne' Hundred Robert Fafiton holds of the king 2 hides in Ickenham. There is land for 1 plough, but there is no [plough] now.

[There is] meadow for 1 plough, pasture for the livestock of the vill, [and] woodland for 30 pigs. This land is worth 5s; when received, 40s; TRE 40s. Almær, the man of Wulfweard White, held this land, and he could sell it.

XVI. The land of Robert fitzRoscelin

'OSSULSTONE' HUNDRED

ROBERT fitzRoscelin holds of the king 3½ hides in Stepney. [There is] land for 2 ploughs. In demesne [are] 2 hides, and there is 1 plough. The villans [have] 1 plough. There is 1 villan on 1 virgate, and 8 bordars each on half a virgate, and 4 cottars on 19 acres. [There is] meadow for 2 ploughs, and a wood for fences. All together it is worth 53s; when received, 10s; TRE £4. Æthelwine Stichehare, the man of King Edward, held this land as 1 manor. He could sell it to whom he would. The Bishop of London claims it.

XVII. The land of Robert Blund

SPELTHORNE HUNDRED

ROBERT Blund holds in LALEHAM [Surrey] 8 hides of the king. Estrild, a certain nun, holds of him. There is land for 5 ploughs. In demesne [are] 4 hides, and there is 1 plough. The villans have 4 ploughs. There is 1 villan on 1 virgate, and 7 villans each [on] half a hide, and 3 bordars on 1 virgate, and 3 cottars. [There is] meadow for 5 ploughs, [and] pasture for the livestock of the vill. In all it is worth 60s; when received, 40s; TRE £6. Aki, a housecarl of King Edward, held this manor. He could sell it to whom he would, and the soke belonged to Staines [Surrey].

XVIII. The land of Roger de Raismes

SPELTHORNE HUNDRED

ROGER de Raismes holds CHARLTON [Surrey] of the king. It is assessed at †5† hides. There is land for 4 ploughs. In demesne [are] 4½ hides, and there is 1 plough. The villans [have] half a plough, and there could be 2½ ploughs. There is 1 villan on half a hide, and 1 bordar on 8 acres, and 6 slaves. [There is] meadow for 4 ploughs, [and] pasture for the livestock of the vill. This land is worth 30s; when received 60s; TRE 100s. 2 brothers held this manor. One was the man of Archbishop Stigand, the other the man of Earl Leofwine. They could sell it to whom they would, but the soke belonged to Staines [Surrey].

In the hundred of GORE the same Roger holds 9½ hides in Little Stanmore. There is land for 7 ploughs. In demesne [are] 4 hides, and there is 1 plough, and there could be 2 more. The villans have 3 ploughs, and there could be 1 more. There is 1 villan on 1 virgate, and 8 villans each [on] half a virgate, and 3 bordars each on 5 acres, and 2 slaves. [There is] woodland for 800 pigs, [and] pasture for the livestock of the vill and [rendering] 2s. In all it is worth 60s; when received, 20s; TRE £10.

Algar, the man of Earl Harold, held this manor and he could sell it.

XIX. The land of William fitzAnsculf

'ELTHORNE' HUNDRED

WILLIAM fitzAnsculf holds CRANFORD of the king, and Hugh [holds] of him. It is assessed at 5 hides. There is land for 3 ploughs. There is 1 plough in demesne; and the villans [have] 2 ploughs. There a priest has 1 virgate, and [there are] 8 villans each on 1 virgate, and 2 cottars on 2 acres, and 3 slaves. [There is] a wood for fences. All together it is worth 60s; when received, 40s; TRE 100s. Thorsten, a thegn of King Edward, held this manor, and he could sell it to whom he would.

XX. The land of Edward of Salisbury

'OSSULSTONE' HUNDRED

EDWARD of Salisbury holds CHELSEA for 2 hides. There is land for 5 ploughs. In demesne [is] 1 hide, and there are 2 ploughs now. The villans [have] 1 plough, and there could be 2 ploughs more. There are 2 villans on 2 virgates, and 4 villans each on half a virgate, and 3 bordars each on 5 acres, and 3 slaves. [There is] meadow for 2 ploughs, pasture for the livestock of the vill, [and] woodland for 60 pigs and [rendering] 52d. In all it is worth £9; when received and always, the same. Wulfwynn, the man of King Edward, held this manor. She could sell it to whom she would.

XXI. The land of Aubrey de Vere

'OSSULSTONE' HUNDRED

AUBREY de Vere holds KENSINGTON of the Bishop of Coutances. It is assessed at 10 hides. There is land for 10 ploughs. There are in demesne 4 ploughs; and the villans have 5 ploughs, and there could be a sixth. There are 12 villans each [on] 1 virgate, and 6 villans on 3 virgates. A priest [has] half a virgate, and [there are] 7 slaves. [There is] meadow for 2 ploughs, pasture for the livestock of the vill, woodland for 200 pigs, and 3 arpents of vineyard. In all it is worth £10; when received, £6; TRE £10. Edwin, a thegn of King Edward, held this manor and he could sell it.

XXII. The land of Ranulph brother of Ilger

'OSSULSTONE' HUNDRED

RANULPH brother of Ilger holds 'TOLLINGTON' [in Islington] of the king, for 2 hides. There is land for 2 ploughs. In demesne [is] 1 hide, and there is 1 plough. The villans have 2 ploughs. There are 5 villans each on half a virgate, and 2 bordars on 9 acres, and 1 cottar and 1 slave. [There is] pasture for the livestock of the vill, [and] woodland for 60 pigs and [rendering] 5s. This land is worth 40s; when received, 60s; TRE 40s. Edwin, the man of King Edward, held this and he could sell it.

XXIII. The land of Deormann of London

'OSSULSTONE' HUNDRED

DEORMANN holds of the king half a hide in ISLINGTON. There is land for half a plough. There is 1 villan. This land is and was worth 10s. Algar, the man of King Edward, held this land and he could sell and give it.

XXIIII. The land of Countess Judith

EDMONTON HUNDRED

Countess JUDITH holds TOTTENHAM of the king. It is assessed at 5 hides. There is land for 10 ploughs. In demesne are 2 carucates of land besides these 5 hides, and there are 2 ploughs. The villans have 12 ploughs. A priest has half a hide, and [there are] 6 villans on 6 virgates, and 24 villans each on half a virgate, and 12 bordars each on 5 acres, and 17 cottars. There are 2 Frenchmen on 1 hide and 3 virgates, and 4 slaves. [There is] meadow for 10 ploughs and [rendering] 20s in addition, pasture for the livestock of the vill, [and] woodland for 500 pigs. From 1 weir, 3s. In all it is worth £25.15s and 3 ounces of gold; when received, £10; TRE £26. Earl Waltheof held this manor.

XXV. The land Given In Alms

'OSSULSTONE' HUNDRED

LISSON GROVE is assessed at 5 hides. Eadgifu holds it of the king. There is land for 3 ploughs. In demesne [are] $4\frac{1}{2}$ hides, and there are 2 ploughs. The villans have 1 plough.

There are 4 villans each on half a virgate, and 3 cottars on 2 acres, and 1 slave. [There is] meadow for 1 plough, pasture for the livestock of the vill, [and] woodland for 100 pigs. From the herbage, 3d. In all it is worth 60s; when received, the same; TRE 40s. Edward the son of Swein, the man of King Edward, held this manor and he could sell it.

In the hundred of Spelthorne Ælfgifu, the wife of Hwætmann of London, holds of the king half a hide and the third part of half a hide. [There is] land for 4 oxen, but there are no [oxen. There is] meadow for 4 oxen, [and] pasture for the livestock of the vill. All together it is and was worth 4s. Alwine White, the man of Earl Leofwine, held this land, and he could sell it. Geoffrey de Mandeville was seised of this land when he crossed the sea in the king's service, as his men and the whole hundred say.

In the hundred of 'Elthorne' Ælfgifu holds of the king half a hide in Greenford. There is land for half a plough, but there is no [plough] now. This land is worth 10s; when received, the same; TRE 20s. Leofric, the man of Earl Leofwine, held this land and he could sell it to whom he would.

[Folio 131: [MIDDLESEX]]

[Blank in MS]

[Folio 131V: [MIDDLESEX]]

[Blank in MS]

HERTFORDSHIRE

THE BOROUGH OF HERTFORD was assessed at 10 hides TRE and now it is not. There were 146 burgesses in the soke of King Edward.

Of these, Count Alan now has 3 houses which rendered customary dues then, as now.

Eudo the steward has 2 houses which belonged to Algar of Cokenach and then, as now, rendering customary dues; and the same Eudo has a third house which belonged to Wulfmær of Eaton Socon: it renders no customary dues.

Geoffrey de Bec [has] 3 houses rendering customary dues.

Humphrey d'Anneville holds under Eudo 2 houses with 1 garden. Of these, one was leased to a certain king's reeve; and the other, together with the garden, belonged to a certain burgess, and now the burgesses themselves claim them back as having been taken from them unjustly.

King William has 18 other burgesses who were the men of Earl Harold and Earl Leofwine. All of them render customary dues.

Peter de Valognes has 2 churches with a house, which he bought of Wulfwig of Hatfield, rendering all customary dues. Wulfwig himself could both give and sell them.

Geoffrey de Mandeville has a certain holding which belonged to Esger the staller and 7 houses which rendered no customary due except the king's geld when it was collected.

Ralph Baynard has 2 houses and then, as now, they rendered customary dues.

Hardwin de Scales has 14 houses which Aki had TRE. They gave no customary dues except the king's geld. For these Hardwin claims the king as warrantor. Hardwin has 1 more house by the king's gift which belonged to a certain burgess, rendering every customary due.

This township renders £20 assayed and weighed, and 3 mills render £10 by tale. When Peter the sheriff received it, it rendered £15 by tale; TRE £7.10s by tale.

I KING WILLIAM
II The Archbishop of Canterbury
III The Bishop of Winchester
IIII The Bishop of London
V The Bishop of Bayeux
VI The Bishop of Lisieux
VII The Bishop of Chester
VIII The Abbot of Ely
IX The Abbot of Westminster
X The Abbot of St Albans

XI The Abbess of Chatteris
XII The canons of London
XIII The canons of Waltham
XIIII The Count of Mortain
XV Count Alan
XVI Count Eustace
XVII Earl Roger
XVIII Robert d'Oilly
XIX Robert Gernon
XX Robert de Tosny
XXI Ralph de Tosny
XXII Ralph de Limesy
XXIII Ralph Baynard
XXIIII Ranulph brother of Ilger
XXV Hugh de Grandmesnil
XXVI Hugh de Beauchamp
XXVII William de Eu
XXVIII William d'Auberville
XXIX Walter the Fleming
XXX Eudo the steward
XXXI Edward of Salisbury
XXXII Geoffrey de Mandeville
XXXIII Geoffrey de Bec
XXXIIII Gosbert de Beauvais
XXXV Peter de Valognes
XXXVI Hardwin de Scales
XXXVII Edgar
XXXVIII Mainou the Breton
XXXIX Gilbert fitzSalomon
XL Sigar de Chocques
XLI Deormann and other Englishmen of the King
XLII Rohais wife of Richard
XLIII Adeliza wife of Hugh
XLIIII The daughter of Ralph Taillebois

The land of the King

IN BROADWATER HUNDRED

KING WILLIAM holds [?Great] WYMONDLEY. | It is assessed at 8 hides. | There is land for 18 ploughs. In demesne [are] 2½ hides, and there are 3 ploughs; and 24 villans and 1 sokeman and 5 bordars and 5 cottars have 15 ploughs. There are 6 slaves, and 1 mill rendering 20s. [There is] meadow for 1 plough and 2 oxen, pasture for the livestock of the vill, [and] wood for fences. This manor belonged to the demesne of the Church of ST MARY of Chatteris, but Earl Harold took it away from it, as the whole shire testifies, and attached it to his manor of Hitchin 3 years before King Edward's death.

King William holds MINSDEN. It is assessed at 4 hides. There is land for 8 ploughs. In demesne [are] 2 hides and 2½ virgates, and there are 3 ploughs. A priest with 8 villans and 2 cottars have 3 ploughs, and there can be 2 more. There are 6 slaves, meadow for 1 plough, pasture for the livestock of the vill, and woodland for 30 pigs. This manor belonged and belongs to Hitchin. Earl Harold held it.

[Folio 132V: HERTFORDSHIRE]

IN THE HALF-HUNDRED OF HITCHIN

King WILLIAM holds HITCHIN. It is assessed at 5 hides. There is land for 34 ploughs. In demesne [is] 1 hide, and there are 6 ploughs; and 41 villans with 17 bordars have 20 ploughs, and there can be 8 more. There are 22 cottars and 12 slaves, and 4 mills rendering 53s4d, meadow for 4 ploughs, pasture for the livestock of the vill, [and] woodland for 600 pigs. Earl Harold held this manor. Of these 5 hides, 2 belong to the minster of this vill. There is land for 4 ploughs. In demesne [are] 1½ hides, and there is 1 ploughs, and there can be another; and 4 villans have 2 ploughs there, and there are 7 cottars. [There is] meadow for 2 oxen, [and] pasture for the livestock. These 2 hides are worth £6; when received, 40s; TRE £4. Earl Harold held this manor.

King William holds 'WEYLEYE' [in Ippollitts]. It is assessed at 2 hides. There is land for 7 ploughs. In demesne [is] 1 hide, and there are 2 ploughs; and 8 villans with 5 bordars have 4 ploughs, and there can be a fifth. There are 2 cottars and 4 slaves, pasture for the livestock of the vill, [and] woodland for 300 pigs. Earl Harold held this manor, and it belongs to Hitchin, to which it belonged TRE.

King William holds WESTONING [Beds.]. It is assessed at 5 hides. There is land for 14 ploughs. In demesne [are] 2 hides, and there are 2 ploughs; and 16 villans with 3 bordars have 5 ploughs, and there can be 5 more. There are 4 slaves, meadow for 7 ploughs, pasture for the livestock of the vill, [and] woodland for 400 pigs and [rendering] 3s. Earl Harold held this manor, and it belonged, and belongs, to Hitchin. But the wara of this manor was in Bedfordshire TRE, in the Hundred of 'Manshead', and there the manor is and always was; and since King Edward's death it has not discharged the king's geld.

King William holds KING'S WALDEN. It is assessed at 2 hides. There is land for 20 ploughs. In demesne [are] 2 virgates, and there are 2 ploughs. A priest with 13 villans and 4 bordars have 6 ploughs, and there can be 2 more. There are 2 cottars and 4 slaves, meadow for half a plough, pasture for the livestock of the vill, [and] woodland for 400 pigs. In all it is and was worth £8; TRE £10. Leofgifu held this manor of Earl Harold and could sell without his leave. For the king's service she found 1 cartage-due and 1 escort-service, but unjustly and by force, as the shire testifies. Of these 2 hides a certain widow, Esger's wife, holds 1 hide of the king as 1 manor; and she has there 1 plough, and 17 villans with 7 bordars; they have 6 ploughs, and there can be 3 [more].

There are 5 cottars, meadow for half a plough, woodland for 400 pigs, [and] pasture for the livestock of the vill. In all it is and was worth £4; TRE £8. The same woman held this manor TRE of Earl Harold and could sell without his leave, and she found, [but] unjustly and by force, 1 cartage-due and escort-duty for the king's service, as the shire testifies. Ilbert added these 2 manors to Hitchin when he was sheriff, as the hundred attests.

King William holds WANDON [End and Green]. It is assessed at 3 virgates. There is land for 2 ploughs and 6 oxen, and there are [2 ploughs and 6 oxen], with 6 villans. [There is] woodland for 40 pigs. Earl Harold held this land in his manor of Hitchin, and it now belongs there.

King William holds CHARLTON. It is assessed at 1 virgate. There is land for 1 plough, and there is [1 plough], with 2 cottars, and 1 mill rendering 20d. It is and was always worth 10s 2 sokemen held this land of Earl Harold and could sell without his leave. The soke was always in Hitchin. Ilbert added it to Hitchin when he was sheriff.

King William holds TEMPLE DINSLEY. It is assessed at 7 hides. There is land for 20 ploughs. In demesne [are] 3½ hides, and there are 3 ploughs; and 19 villans have 8 ploughs, and there can be 9 more. There are 7 bordars and 7 cottars and 6 slaves and 1 Frenchman, a king's almsman. There are 2 mills rendering 16s, meadow for 1 plough, pasture for the livestock of the vill, [and] woodland for 300 pigs. In all it renders £14 a year assayed and weighed, and £5 by tale; the same TRE and when Peter the sheriff received it. 2 sokemen held this manor as 2 manors of Earl Harold TRE and could sell. Yet they each found 2 cartage-dues and 2 escort-services in Hitchin, but by force and unjustly, as the hundred testifies. These 2 manors Ilbert held as 1 manor and he was seised of it by the king's writ for as long as he was sheriff, as the shire testifies. But after he lost the shrievalty, Peter de Valognes and Ralph Taillebois took the manor from him and put it in Hitchin because he refused to find the cartage-due for the sheriff. Geoffrey de Bec, Ilbert's successor, claims the king's mercy in regard to this manor.

King William holds GREAT OFFLEY. It is assessed at 2 hides. There is land for 9 ploughs. 5 sokemen held it TRE and they hold it now of King William. There are 8 ploughs, and there can be a ninth. There are 2 villans and 17 bordars and 3 cottars and 3 slaves, meadow for 1 plough, pasture for the livestock, woodland for 120 pigs, [and] wood for fences. All together it is and was always worth £4.4s. These men held it of Earl Harold and could give and sell. The soke, however, always belonged to Hitchin, and they found 2 cartage-dues and 2 escort-services.

In the same vill Edward of Pirton holds 3 virgates. There is land for 2 ploughs. There is half [a plough], and there can be 1½. There is 1 villan, and wood for fences. It is worth 5s; when received, 6s8d; TRE 10s. Of this land Alwine, a man of Archbishop Stigand, held half a hide, and a man of Earl Harold, Abba by name, had 1 virgate. These could give and sell their land; the soke remained in Hitchin.

In the other Offley [Little Offley] 1 sokeman holds 1 hide.

There is land for 2 ploughs. There is 1 [plough], and there can be another. There is 1 villan and 1 bordar and 1 cottar, [and] wood for fences. It is and was always worth 26s8d.

[Folio 133: HERTFORDSHIRE]

The same man who now holds it held it TRE of Earl Harold and could sell it. The soke remained in Hitchin. He renders 1 cartage-due and 1 escort-service. This sokeman and the 5 above from Great Offley, Ilbert of Hertford placed in Hitchin.

In Wellbury 1 sokeman holds 1 hide. There is land for 5 ploughs. In demesne is 1 [plough], and there can be 2. There 4 bordars have 1 plough, and there can be another. [There is] pasture for the livestock of the vill, [and] wood for fences. All together it is worth 26s8d; when Peter received it, 40s; TRE 60s. Leofgifu held this land of Earl Harold and could sell. Ilbert put it in his manor of Lilley while he was sheriff. After he lost the shrievalty, Peter de Valognes and Ralph Taillebois took it from him and put it in Hitchin, as the whole shire testifies. It did not belong there TRE nor did it render any customary dues.

In 'Weyleye' [in Ippollitts] 1 sokeman holds 1 hide. There is land for 2 ploughs, and there are [2 ploughs]. There are 2 villans with 1 bordar and 9 cottars, meadow for half a plough, pasture for the livestock of the vill, [and] wood for fences. To this land belongs woodland for 50 pigs which Osmund de Vaubadon seized to King William's loss, and it was in the soke of Hitchin TRE, as the shire testifies. This land is and was worth 20s; TRE 30s. Godwine, Earl Harold's man, held this land and could sell. Peter the sheriff put it at farm in Hitchin, to which it did not belong TRE nor did it render customary dues there. Ilbert had given this land to a certain knight of his while he was sheriff; for which land Geoffrey de Bec claims the king's mercy.

In 'Weyleye' [in Ippollitts] 1 sokeman holds half a hide. There is land for 1 plough, and there is [1 plough], with 1 cottar. [There is] wood for fences. It is worth 10s; when received, 5s; TRE 16s. Edmund, a man of Earl Harold, held this land and could sell, [but] the soke remained in Hitchin. He found 1 cartage-due.

In 'Flexmore' [in Kings Walden] 1 sokeman holds half a virgate. There is land for half a plough, and there is [half a plough], with 4 cottars. [There is] pasture for the livestock, [and] woodland for 5 pigs. It is and was worth 40d; TRE 60d. This man, a man of Earl Harold, held it TRE and he could sell. It rendered a cartage-due in Hitchin.

In [?] Ley Green 3 sokemen hold 1 virgate. There is land for 1½ ploughs, and there are [1½ ploughs], with 4 bordars. [There is] woodland for 40 pigs. It is and was always worth 26s8d. 3 men of Earl Ælfgar held this land; they could not sell outside Hitchin.

In Hextone 1 sokeman of the king holds 1 virgate. There is land for half a plough, and there is [half a plough], with 1 villan. It is and was worth 20d; TRE 40d. This man who holds it, a man of the Abbot of St Albans, held it TRE and could sell. This land Earl Harold put in Hitchin by force and unjustly, as the shire testifies.

IN HERTFORD HUNDRED

King William holds BAYFORD. It is assessed at 10 hides. There is land for 20 ploughs. In demesne [are] 2 hides and 3 virgates, and there are 3 ploughs. A priest and the reeve of this vill with 22 villans have 15 ploughs, and 2 more can be there. There are 9 cottars and 1 slave, and 2 mills rendering 26s, meadow for 20 ploughs, pasture for the livestock and [rendering] 2s, [and] woodland for 500 pigs. In all it renders £16 by tale; when the sheriff received it, £8; TRE £20. Earl Tosti held this manor, but King Edward had it in demesne on the day on which he died.

All together, HITCHIN with its appurtenances renders £106 a year assayed and weighed, and £10 by tale; when Peter the sheriff received it, £86; TRE £60 from Hitchin, and from the sokemen belonging there, £40 by tale.

II. The land of the Archbishop of Canterbury

IN BROADWATER HUNDRED

ARCHBISHOP LANFRANC holds 1 hide in Datchworth, and Ansketil [holds] of him. There is land for 2 ploughs. In demesne [is] 1 plough; and 3 villans with 2 bordars have 1 plough. [There is] meadow for half an ox, [and] woodland for 50 pigs. It is worth 30s; when received, 20s; TRE 60s. Ælfric Black held this land of the Abbot of Westminster TRE; he could not alienate it from the church, as the hundred testifies, but in respect of other lands he was Archbishop Stigand's man.

In Watton at Stone Ansketil holds 2½ hides of the archbishop. There is land for 6 ploughs. In demesne is 1 [plough], and there can be another. There 3 villans with a priest and 2 bordars have 2 ploughs, and there can be another 2. [There is] meadow for half a plough, woodland for 100 pigs, pasture for the livestock, and 2 mills rendering 17s. It is and was worth 50s; TRE £4. †Oft [sic] Of this land Ælfric Black held 2 hides of the Abbot of Westminster; he could not alienate them from the church; and Almær, a man of the same Ælfric, held half a hide and could sell.

In Shephall Ansketil holds 2 hides of the archbishop. There is land for 5 ploughs. In demesne is 1 [plough], and there can be another; and 3 villans have 2 ploughs, and there can be a third. [There is] meadow for half a plough, [and] woodland for 20 pigs. It is worth £3; when received, 40s; TRE £4. Ælfric, a man of Archbishop Stigand, held this land. It belonged to the demesne of the Church of St Alban TRE, and he could neither sell nor alienate it from the church.

In Libury 1 Englishman holds 2 acres of land of the archbishop. It is and was always worth 2s. The same man held it TRE in pledge. He could sell.

In Sacombe Ansketil holds half a virgate of the archbishop. There is land for 2 oxen. It is and was always worth 15d. Ælfric Black, a man of Archbishop Stigand, held this land and could sell.

III. The land of the Bishop of Winchester

IN ODSEY HUNDRED

BISHOP WALKELIN of Winchester holds COTTERED. It is assessed at 5 hides. There is land for 6 ploughs. In demesne [are] 1½ hides, and there is 1 plough; and 13 villans with 6 bordars have 5 ploughs. There is 1 slave, pasture for the livestock, [and] woodland for 100 pigs and [rendering] 12d. All together it is worth 60s; when received, 40s; TRE £6. This manor belonged and belongs to the demesne of the Church of St Peter of Winchester.

[Folio 133V: HERTFORDSHIRE]

IIII. The land of the Bishop of London

THE BISHOP OF LONDON holds 1½ hides in Throcking, and Humphrey [holds] of him. There is land for 1½ ploughs, and there [1½ ploughs], with 2 villans and 1 bordar and 1 cottar. [There is] meadow for 1 plough, pasture for the livestock, [and] wood for fences. It is worth 52s; when received, 30s, TRE 40s, 2 brothers, Bishop William's men, held this land. It belonged to the king's soke and they could sell it. As customary dues they paid 6d. to the sheriff or [rendered] 1½ cartage-dues. Of this land 1 virgate was and is in pledge. Humphrey discharges the king's geld on it, and yet he does not have it. This land is [part] of the purchase of Bishop William, as the bishop's men say, but the men of the shire do not bear witness on their [behalf].

The bishop himself holds MUCH HADHAM. It is assessed at 7½ hides. There is land for 22½ ploughs. In demesne [are] 2 hides, and there are 6 ploughs. A priest with 35 villans and 1 knight have 15 ploughs. There are 6 bordars and 2 cottars and 12 slaves, and 1 mill rendering 4s, meadow for 4 ploughs, pasture for the livestock, [and] woodland for 200 pigs. In all it is and was worth £20; TRE £24. This manor belonged and belongs to the bishopric of London.

The bishop himself holds WIDFORD. It is assessed at 3 hides. There is land for 5 ploughs. In demesne [are] 2 hides, and there are 2 ploughs; and 5 villans with 8 bordars have 3 ploughs. There is 1 cottar and 3 slaves, and 1 mill rendering 5s, meadow for 2 ploughs, [and] woodland for 50 pigs. It is and was worth 100s; TRE £8. Ealdræd, a thegn of King Edward, held this manor and could sell.

In Widford Theodbert holds 1 hide of the bishop. There is land for 2 ploughs. There is 1 [plough], and there can be another. There are 8 bordars, meadow for half a plough, [and] woodland for 30 pigs. It is and was worth 40s; TRE 60s. Alweard, a man of Archbishop Stigand's, held this land; he could sell.

In Chaldean Rodhere holds half a hide of the bishop. There is land for 2 ploughs. There is 1 [plough], and there can be another. There is 1 bordar and 4 slaves. [There is] woodland for 50 pigs, [and] meadow for 1 plough. It is and was worth 30s; TRE 40s. Ealdræd, a thegn of King Edward, held this land and could sell.

William holds Little Hadham of the bishop. It is assessed at 2 hides. There is land for 3 ploughs. In demesne are 2 [ploughs]; and 4 bordars with 1 plough. There are 4 cottars and 3 slaves, meadow for 2 oxen, pasture for the livestock, [and] woodland for 30 pigs. It is and was always worth £4. 3 sokemen held this manor. One of these, a man of Archbishop Stigand, had 1 hide less half a virgate; and another, a man of Robert fitz Wimarc, had 3½ virgates; and the third, a sokeman of King Edward, 1 virgate. This man paid 1d to the sheriff; and they could sell.

In Much Hadham William holds half a hide of the bishop. There is land for 1 plough. There is half a plough, and there can be another half [a plough]. There is 1 cottar. It is and was worth 15s. Eadric, a man of Esger the staller, held it and could sell.

In 'Levenage' [in Widford] William holds 1½ hides of the bishop. There is land for 4 ploughs. In demesne are 2 ploughs, and there can be a third. 3 villans there have 1 plough. There are 2 cottars and 4 slaves, meadow for 2 oxen, pasture for the livestock of the vill, [and] wood for fences. This land is and was worth 50s; TRE 60s. Leofwaru held this manor of Bishop William. Half a hide she could sell, but 1 hide she could not [sell] without his leave.

In Much Hadham Osbern holds 1 hide of the bishop. There is land for 2 ploughs. In demesne [are] 1½ ploughs; and 1 villan has half a plough. There are 6 cottars and 1 slave. It is and always was worth 40s. 2 sokemen held this land. One of these, a man of Earl Ælfgar, had half a hide; and the other half a hide belonging to the king's soke, [and] he paid 2d to the sheriff. Both, however, could sell.

In Patmore Baldwin holds of the bishop 1 hide and 3 virgates. There is land for 4 ploughs. In demesne are 2 [ploughs]; and 2 villans have 1 plough, and there can be another. There are 2 bordars and 6 cottars and 3 slaves, meadow for 2 oxen, [and] woodland for 60 pigs. It is and always was worth £4. Alweard, a man of Earl Ælfgar, held this land and could sell.

Ralph holds Albury of the bishop. It is assessed at 2½ hides. There is land for 9 ploughs. In demesne are 2 [ploughs]; and 6 villans and 9 bordars have 6 ploughs, and there can be a seventh. There are 3 cottars and 3 slaves, meadow for 2 oxen, pasture for the livestock, [and] woodland for 30 pigs. It is and was worth £7; TRE £8. Siward, a man of Archbishop Stigand, held this manor and could sell.

In [Brent, Furneaux and Stocking] Pelham Ralph holds of the bishop 1 hide and 1 virgate. There is land for 5 ploughs. In demesne are 2 [ploughs], and there can be a third. There 2 villans and 3 bordars have 2 ploughs. There are 5 slaves and 1 cottar, pasture for the livestock, [and] woodland for 20 pigs. It is and was worth £4; TRE £5. 2 brothers, Esger the staller's men, held it, and could sell.

In [Brent, Furneaux and Stocking] Pelham Payne holds 1 hide of the bishop. There is land for 3 ploughs. In demesne are 2 [ploughs]; and 1 villan has half a plough, and there can be [another] half [a plough]. There are 3 bordars and 3 cottars, [and] woodland for 6 pigs. It is and was worth 40s; TRE 50s. Alfred, a man of Esger the staller, held this manor and could sell.

In [Brent, Furneaux and Stocking] Pelham Ranulph holds $2\frac{1}{2}$ hides of the bishop. There is land for 8 ploughs. In demesne are 2 [ploughs]; and 7 villans with 5 bordars have 6 ploughs. There are 6 cottars and 6 slaves, meadow for 1 plough, pasture for the livestock, [and] woodland for 30 pigs. It is and was worth £10; TRE £15. 2 thegns held this manor. One of them [was] a man of Eskil of Ware, and the other a man of Godwine of Bentfield. They could sell.

In [Brent, Furneaux and Stocking] Pelham Gilbert and Ranulph hold of the bishop 1 hide and 1 virgate. There is land for 3 ploughs. In demesne is 1 [plough]; and 1 villan with 3 bordars has 1 plough, and there can be another. There are 7 cottars, meadow for half a plough, pasture for the livestock, [and] woodland for 100 pigs. It is and was worth 40s; TRE 60s. 2 brothers held it and could sell. One [was] a man of Esger the staller; and the other of the Abbot of Ely.

In [Brent, Furneaux and Stocking] Pelham 2 knights hold 3 hides and 1 virgate of the bishop. There is land for 7 ploughs. In demesne are 3 [ploughs]; and a priest with 7 villans have 4 ploughs. There are 7 bordars and 6 cottars and 1 slave, meadow for $2\frac{1}{2}$ ploughs, pasture for the livestock, [and] woodland for 100 pigs. It is and was worth £5; TRE £6. 2 thegns held this manor, one a man of Eskil of Ware, and the other a man of Almær of Benington; and, together with these, 5 sokemen of King Edward's soke had 2 virgates and could sell.

In Meesden Payne holds 1 hide of the bishop. There is land for 5 ploughs. In

[Folio 134: HERTFORDSHIRE]

demesne there can be 2 ploughs; and 3 villans with a priest have 3 ploughs. There is 1 [sic] and 1 slave, meadow for 3 ploughs, pasture for the livestock, [and] woodland for 400 pigs. It is and was worth 20s; TRE £6. Alweard, a man of Archbishop Stigand, held this manor and could sell.

In [Brent, Furneaux and Stocking] Pelham Ealdræd holds 1 hide of the bishop. There is land for 2 ploughs. There are $1\frac{1}{2}$ [ploughs], and there can be [another] half [-plough]. There are 8 bordars and 2 slaves, meadow for 1 plough, pasture for the livestock, [and] woodland for 20 pigs. It is and was worth 20s; TRE 40s. Alwine, a man of Godwine of Bentfield, held this land and could sell.

In [Brent, Furneaux and Stocking] Pelham Riculf holds 2 hides of the bishop. There is land for 4 ploughs. In demesne [are] 2 ploughs; and 4 villans with 3 bordars have 2 ploughs. There are 10 cottars and 3 slaves, meadow for 1 plough, pasture for the livestock, [and] woodland for 40 pigs. It is and was worth 100s; TRE £5.10s. Wulfwig, a man of Godwine of Bentfield, held this manor and he could sell.

In Hixham William and Ranulph hold $1\frac{1}{2}$ hides of the bishop. There is land for 3 ploughs. In demesne are 2 [ploughs]; and 2 villans with 3 bordars have 1 plough. There is 1 cottar and 1 slave, woodland for 60 pigs, [and] pasture for the livestock. It is and was worth 40s; TRE 60s. Wulfwig, a man of Esger the staller, [held] this land and could sell.

These 36 hides the Bishop of London and his knights hold; and with these he claims 4 hides which the Abbot of Ely holds in [?Little] Hadham.

IN BRAUGHING HUNDRED

The same bishop holds BISHOP'S STORTFORD. It is assessed at 6 hides. There is land for 10 ploughs. In demesne [are] $4\frac{1}{2}$ hides, and there are 2 ploughs, and there can be a third. There 6 villans with 8 bordars have 4 ploughs, and there can be 3 [more]. There is a priest, with 2 knights and 12 cottars, and 2 mills rendering 30s, meadow for 1 plough, [and] woodland for 300 pigs. In all it is and was worth £8; TRE £10. Eadgifu the Fair held this manor, and it is [part] of the fief which Bishop William bought.

In Thorley Rodhere holds half a hide of the bishop. There is land for 1 plough, and there is [1 plough], with 2 slaves. [There is] meadow for half a plough, [and] woodland for 2 pigs. It is and was worth 20s; TRE 30s. Eadsige, a man of Godgyth, held this land and could sell; and he paid 2d to the sheriff.

In Wickham Humphrey holds 2 hides and 20 acres as 1 manor of the bishop. There is land for 3 ploughs. In demesne are 2 [ploughs]; and 4 villans with 2 bordars have 1 plough. There are 8 cottars and 1 slave, meadow for half a plough, [and] woodland for 30 pigs. It is and was worth 40s; TRE 60s. 4 sokemen held this land and could sell.

In Wickham 2 knights hold $1\frac{1}{2}$ virgates of the bishop. There is land for half a plough, but [the half-plough] is not there. [There is] woodland for 20 pigs, and 1 villan. It is and was worth 8s; TRE 10s. 3 sokemen held this land and could sell. One of these [was] a man of Bishop William, another a man of Esger the staller, and the third a man of Eadgifu the Fair. This land belongs to the fief of Bishop William.

V. The land of the Bishop of Bayeux

IN TRING HUNDRED

THE BISHOP OF BAYEUX holds PUTTENHAM. It [is assessed] at 4 hides. Roger holds it of the bishop. There is land for 4 ploughs. In demesne is 1 [plough], and there can be another. There 4 villans with 2 bordars have 2 ploughs. There are 4 cottars and 2 slaves, and 2 mills rendering 10s8d, meadow for 4 ploughs and [rendering] 4s, [and] pasture for the livestock. It is worth 60s; when received, 40s; TRE £4. Earl Leofwine held this manor.

IN 'DANISH' HUNDRED

In 'Theobald' [in Aldenham] Adam holds half a hide of the bishop. There is land for 2 oxen. There is 1 bordar, [and] woodland for 20 pigs. It is worth 10s; when received, 5s; and as much TRE. Alweard held this land of the Abbot of St Albans [and] could not sell without his leave.

IN ST ALBANS HUNDRED

The same Adam holds of the bishop "Lampeth" for half a hide. There is land for 1 plough, but there is no [plough] there. [There is] woodland for 50 pigs. It is worth 10s; when received, 5s; TRE 20s. Alnoth Grutt held this land and could sell.

IN BROADWATER HUNDRED

In Graveley Adam holds of the bishop 1½ hides and 10 acres. There is land for 3 ploughs. In demesne is 1 [plough], and there can be another. There 4 villans with 3 bordars have 1 plough. There are 2 slaves, wood for fences, [and] pasture for the livestock. It is worth 20s; when received, 50s; and as much TRE. Alnoth held 1½ hides of this land, and Bruning 10 acres. Both could sell. Yet this [Bruning] paid ½d as customary dues to the sheriff.

In Almshoe [Almshoe Bury and Little Almshoe] Adam holds 1 hide of the bishop. There is land for 1 plough, and there is [1 plough], with 3 bordars. [There is] woodland for 60 pigs. It is worth 20s; when received, 10s; TRE 30s. Edmund, a man of Earl Harold, held this land and could sell.

In [?Little] Wymondley Adam holds of the bishop 1 hide and 1 virgate. There is land for 1 plough, and there is [1 plough], with 3 bordars. [There is] meadow for half a plough. It is and was worth 10s; TRE 20s. Alflæd held this land of Robert fitzWimarc; she could not sell without his leave, as the shire testifies.

In Boxbury Osbern holds half a hide of the bishop. There is land for 1 plough, and there is 1 bordar. It is and was always worth 10s. Sæmær, a man of Alnoth, held it and could sell.

The bishop himself holds ASTON. It is assessed at 10 hides. There is land for 15 ploughs. In demesne [are] 4 hides, and there are 4 ploughs, and there can be a fifth. There is a priest, and 11 villans with 5 bordars have 5 ploughs, and there can be another 5. There are 6 cottars and 4 slaves, meadow for 2 ploughs, pasture for the livestock, [and] woodland for 200 pigs. In all it is worth £18; when received, £14; TRE £20. 3 of Archbishop Stigand's men held this manor and could sell.

In Libury Peter holds of the bishop 1 hide and 1 virgate and 10 acres. There is land for 1 plough, and there is [1 plough], with 2 villans and a certain Frenchman. [There is] woodland for 30 pigs. It is worth 10s; when received, 7s; TRE 20s. 2 sokemen, Earl Leofwine's men, held this land of King Edward's soke, and they could sell, and they found for the king's sheriff 1 cartage-due or 5 ¼d a year.

In the same vill the bishop holds 2 hides and 1 virgate and 9 acres. There is land for 2 ploughs,

[Folio 134V: HERTFORDSHIRE]

but no [plough] is there. In demesne [are] 2 hides and 9 acres, and 3 bordars, and 1 mill rendering 16d. [There is] meadow for 2 oxen, [and] woodland for 55 pigs. It is and was worth 20s; TRE 40s. 3 of Archbishop Stigand' men held this land and could sell; and 1 man of Leofwine Scova had half a hide and could sell. He found half a cartage-due or 2d for the sheriff.

In the same vill Turstin holds 2 hides of the bishop. There is land for 2 ploughs, but there are no [ploughs] there, only 2 cottars, and 1 mill rendering 4s. [There is] meadow for 2 oxen,

[and] woodland for 100 pigs. It is and was worth 30s; TRE 60s. Almær, a man of Esger the staller, held this land of the king's soke, and could sell. He rendered to the sheriff 2 cartage-dues or 8d.

In the same vill the bishop himself holds 11 acres. They are and were always worth 11d. Alweard held them of Archbishop Stigand.

IN ODSEY HUNDRED

In Luffenhall Osbern holds of the bishop 2½ hides [...]. There is land for 5 ploughs. In demesne [are] 3 ploughs; and 3 bordars with 3 villans have 2 ploughs. There are 4 cottars and 4 slaves, [and] wood for fences. It is and was worth 40s; TRE 60s. 3 sokemen held this land 2 of these, Archbishop Stigand's men, had 1½ hides and could sell them; and the third, a man of Almær of Benington, had 1 hide and could sell. He rendered 1 cartage-due or 4d.

In Clothall Osbern holds of the bishop 7 hides and 3½ virgates. There is land for 10 ploughs. In demesne are 2 [ploughs], and there can be a third. There 8 villans with 12 bordars have 7 ploughs. There are 3 cottars and 4 slaves, wood for fences, [and] pasture for the livestock. In all it is worth £7; when received, £5; TRE £10. Alnoth Grud, a man of Archbishop Stigand, held this manor and could sell; and of this land 3 sokemen, Archbishop Stigand's men, had 2 hides and 3 virgates; they were not there TRE, but after his death they were put in this manor and could sell their land; and they paid as a customary due to the sheriff 11d a year, and 2 other sokemen, Archbishop Stigand's men, hold and held half a virgate and could give and sell.

In Orwell Bury Osbern holds half a hide of the bishop. There is land for 1 plough, and there is [1 plough], with 2 villans. It is and was always worth 15s 3 of Archbishop Stigand's men held this land and could sell.

In Reed Osbern holds 1 hide of the bishop. There is land for 3 ploughs. In demesne is 1 [plough], and there can be another. There 6 bordars have 1 plough. It is worth 40s; when received, 60s; and as much TRE. Eadgifu the girl held this land, so the hundred testifies. She was Archbishop Stigand's man and could sell.

In Radwell Adam holds 4 hides under the bishop. There is land for 7 ploughs. In demesne are 2 [ploughs], and there can be another 2. There 8 villans with 4 bordars have 3 ploughs. There are 4 slaves, and 1 mill rendering 8s, meadow for half a plough, [and] pasture for the livestock. It is worth 100s; when received, 40s; TRE £10. Alnoth, a man of Archbishop Stigand, held this manor and could sell.

IN 'EDWINSTREE'

In Barley Adam holds 1½ hides of the bishop. There is land for 2 ploughs. There is 1 [plough], and there can be another. There are 3 villans and 2 slaves. It is worth 20s; when received, 12s; TRE 40s. He held this land of Archbishop Stigand and could sell.

In "Haslehangra" Adam holds of the bishop the third part of 1 hide. There is land for half a plough. It is worth 4s; when received, 2s; TRE 10s. Leofflæd held this land of Archbishop Stigand and could sell.

Osbern holds Buckland of the bishop. It is assessed at 3 hides and 3 virgates. There is land for 6 ploughs. In demesne [are] 2 ploughs, and there can be a third. There a priest and 8 villans and 6 bordars have 3 ploughs. There are 8 cottars and 4 slaves, meadow for 1 plough, pasture for the livestock, [and] woodland for 40 pigs; from pasture and woodland, 10s. In all it is worth £6; when received, £8; TRE £10. Sæhild, a man of Earl Leofwine, held this manor and could sell.

In Hodenhoe Osbern holds of the bishop 1 hide and half a virgate. There is land for $2\frac{1}{2}$ ploughs, and there are [$2\frac{1}{2}$ ploughs], with 3 villans and 6 bordars and 1 Frenchman. It is worth 40s; when received, 30s; TRE 60s. 4 sokemen held this land. 3 of these were Archbishop Stigand's men and the fourth a man of Earl Ælfgar, and they could sell it.

In Throcking Osbern holds 12 acres of the bishop. There is land for 1 ox. It is and was always worth 2s. Ælfric Scova held it and could sell.

In 'Echington' [in Layston] Osbern holds 1 hide of the bishop. There is land for $2\frac{1}{2}$ ploughs. In demesne is 1 [plough]; and 2 villans with 2 bordars have 1 plough, and there can be half [a plough more]. There is 1 cottar and 4 slaves, meadow for 1 plough, pasture for the livestock, [and] woodland for 10 pigs. It is worth 40s; when received, 30s; TRE 60s. 4 sokemen held this land. 1 of these was a man of Archbishop Stigand, and 2, men of King Edward, paid as a customary due 2d, and the fourth was a man of Earl Harold. All these could sell their land.

IN THE HALF-HUNDRED OF HITCHIN

Ralph holds Kimpton of the bishop. It is assessed at 4 hides. There is land for 10 ploughs. In demesne are 2 [ploughs], and there can be a third. There 2 Frenchmen and 12 villans with 2 bordars have 7 ploughs. There are 3 cottars and 5 slaves, meadow for 6 oxen, woodland for 800 pigs, and 1 mill rendering 8s. In all it is and was worth £12; TRE £15. Ælfgifu mother of Earl Morcar held this manor.

IN BRAUGHING HUNDRED

In RYE Peter holds half a hide of the bishop. There is land for half a plough, but [the half-plough] is not there. [There is] a mill rendering 3s. [and] 200 eels from the weirs, meadow for half a plough, and from hay 10s. This land is worth 20s; when received, 10s; TRE 30s. Swein, a man of Earl Harold, held it and could sell.

In Thundridge Hugh de Grandmesnil holds 1 hide of the bishop. There is land for 4 ploughs. In demesne is 1 [plough], and there can be another. There 4 villans with 3 bordars have 2 ploughs. There are 2 slaves, and 1 mill rendering 5s, meadow for 4 [...], [and] woodland for 16 pigs. This land is worth 30s; when received, 40s; TRE 100s. Alnoth, a man of Archbishop Stigand, held this manor and could sell.

VI. The land of the Bishop of Lisieux

IN 'DANISH' HUNDRED

THE BISHOP OF LISIEUX has in Redbourn 1 virgate of land. Vigot holds it of him. There is land for half a plough, and there is [half a plough], with 1 bordar. It is worth 8s; when received, 2s; TRE 10s. Alwine the huntsman, a man of Earl Leofwine, held it and could sell.

[Folio 135: HERTFORDSHIRE]

VII. The land of Robert, Bishop of Chester

IN 'DANISH' HUNDRED

The Bishop of CHESTER holds NORTH MYMMS. It was assessed TRE at 8 hides and 1 virgate; and now at 8 hides. There is land for 13 ploughs. In demesne [are] 4 hides, and there are 2 ploughs, and there can be a third. There 17 villans with 8 bordars have 10 ploughs. There are 3 cottars and 1 slave, pasture for the livestock, [and] woodland for 400 pigs. In all it is and was worth £8; TRE £10. 3 thegns, Queen Edith's men, held this manor and could sell. This manor does not belong to the bishopric, but belonged to Rayner, the father of Bishop Robert.

IN ODSEY HUNDRED

The bishop himself holds BYGRAVE. It is assessed at 5 hides. There is land for 12 ploughs. In demesne [are] 2 hides, and there are 3 ploughs. A priest and 2 sokemen with 10 villans and 9 bordars have 9 ploughs. There are 6 cottars and 7 slaves, and 1 mill rendering 10s. In all it is worth £10; when received, £8; TRE £12. Leodmær, a man of Archbishop Stigand, held this manor and could sell; and 2 sokemen who are in the same place held 3 virgates, but could not sell without the leave of the archbishop.

In Broadfield the same bishop holds 1 virgate of land. There is land for 3 oxen. There is 1 slave. It is and was worth 3s; TRE 5s. Leodmær, a man of Archbishop Stigand, held it and could sell.

IN BROADWATER HUNDRED

In Welwyn the same bishop holds half a hide. There is land for half a plough. It is and was always worth 3s. This land belongs to Bygrave, a manor of the same bishop. Archbishop Stigand held it.

VIII. The land of the Abbot of Ely

IN BROADWATER HUNDRED

THE ABBOT of ELY holds HATFIELD. It is assessed at 40 hides. There is land for 30 ploughs. In demesne [are] 20 hides, and there are 2 ploughs, and there can be 3 more. There a priest with 18 villans and 18 bordars have 20 ploughs, and there can be 5 ploughs more. There are 12 cottars and 6 slaves, and 4 mills rendering 47s4d, meadow for 10 ploughs, pasture for the livestock, [and] woodland for 2,000 pigs; and from the customary dues of woodland and pasture, 10s. In all it is and was worth £25; TRE £30. This manor belonged and belongs to the demesne of the Church of Ely.

IN ODSEY HUNDRED

The abbot himself holds KELSHALL. It is assessed at 5 hides. There is land for 10 ploughs. In demesne [are] 2 hides, and there are 3 ploughs, and there can be a fourth. There 12 villans with 9 bordars have 6 ploughs. There are 7 slaves, meadow for 1 plough, [and] pasture for the livestock. All together it is and was always worth £10. This manor belonged and belongs to the demesne of the Church of Ely.

IN 'EDWINSTREE' HUNDRED

The abbot himself holds [?Little] HADHAM. It is assessed at 4 hides. There is land for 13 ploughs. In demesne [are] 2 hides, and there are 3 ploughs, and there can be a fourth. There 15 villans have 8 ploughs, and there can be a ninth. There are 15 bordars and 7 slaves, meadow for 2 ploughs, pasture for the livestock, [and] woodland for 100 pigs. In all it is and was worth £15; TRE £12. This manor belonged and belongs to the demesne of the Church of Ely, and it belonged to it on the day when King Edward was alive and dead, as the whole shire testifies.

IX. The land of the Abbey of Westminster

IN 'DANISH' HUNDRED

THE ABBOT of ST PETER OF WESTMINSTER holds WHEATHAMPSTEAD. It is assessed at 10 hides. There is land for 10 ploughs. In demesne [are] 5 hides, and there are 3 ploughs, and there can be 2 more. There a priest with 15 villans have 5 ploughs. There are 12 bordars and 9 cottars, and 4 mills rendering 40s, meadow for 4 ploughs, pasture for the livestock, [and] woodland for 400 pigs. In all it is and was worth £16; TRE £30. This manor belonged and belongs to the demesne of the Church of ST PETER.

In 'Theobald' [in Aldenham] the same abbot holds 1 hide. There is land for half a plough, [and] woodland for 40 pigs. It is and was worth 10s; TRE 13s4d.

In the same vill Geoffrey de Mandeville holds 3 virgates of the abbot. There is land for half a plough, [and] woodland for 12 pigs. It is and was worth 6s8d; TRE 10s.

In ALDENHAM the same abbot holds 9 hides. There is land for 6 ploughs. In demesne [are] 4 hides, and there is 1 plough, and there can be another. A reeve with 8 villans have 3 ploughs, and there can be a fourth. There are 5 cottars and 2 slaves, and 1 mill rendering 5s, meadow for 1 plough, pasture for the livestock, [and] woodland for 800 pigs. It is and was worth £3; TRE £8. This manor belonged and belongs to the demesne of the Church of ST PETER of Westminster.

IN BROADWATER HUNDRED

The abbot himself holds STEVENAGE. It is assessed at 8 hides. There is land for 10 ploughs. In demesne [are] 4 hides, and there are 2 ploughs. There 16 villans with 8 bordars have 7 ploughs, and there can be an eighth. There are 4 slaves, pasture for the livestock, [and] woodland for 50 pigs. In all it

is and was worth £12; TRE £13. This manor belonged and belongs to the demesne of the Church of ST PETER.

The abbot himself holds Tewin. It is assessed at 2½ hides. There is land for 1 plough, and there is [1 plough] in demesne, with 2 cottars. [There is] meadow for 1 plough, pasture for the livestock, [and] woodland for 50 pigs. This land is a herdwick of Stevenage, and it is valued with it.

In Datchworth the same abbot holds 3 hides and 1 virgate. There is land for 3 ploughs. In demesne [are] 2 hides, and there is 1 plough; and 6 villans have 2 ploughs. There are 2 cottars, meadow for half a plough, pasture for the livestock, [and] woodland for 50 pigs. It is and was worth 40s; TRE 60s. This manor belonged and belongs to the demesne of the Church of St Peter.

In Watton at Stone the same abbot holds 1 hide. There is land for 2 ploughs. In demesne is 1 [plough]; and 4 bordars have 1 plough. There are 2 cottars, and 1 mill rendering 2s, pasture for the livestock, [and] woodland for 100 pigs. It is and and was worth 10s; TRE 20s. This land belonged to the Church of St Peter.

In Ayot St Lawrence Geoffrey holds 2½ hides of the abbot. There is land for 7 ploughs. In demesne is 1 [plough], and there can be another. There 13 villans with 4 bordars have 5 ploughs. There are 5 cottars, and 1 mill rendering 6s8d, meadow for 1 plough, [and] woodland for 24 pigs. It is worth all together 60s; when received, 20s; TRE 100s. Ælfwine, a thegn of King Edward, held this manor and could sell. In regard to this manor the abbot claims that King William granted it to him.

IN ODSEY HUNDRED

The abbot himself holds ASHWELL. It is assessed at 6 hides.

[Folio 135V: HERTFORDSHIRE]

There is land for 12 ploughs. In demesne [are] 2½ hides, and there are 2 ploughs. A priest with 16 villans and 9 bordars have 5 ploughs; and there can be another 5 ploughs. There are 14 burgesses and 9 cottars. From toll and from other customary dues of the borough, 49s4d. There are 4 slaves, and 2 mills rendering 14s, meadow for 6 ploughs, pasture for the livestock, [and] woodland for 100 pigs. In all it is and was worth £20; TRE £22. Of this land Peter the sheriff holds of the abbot half a hide; and Geoffrey de Mandeville 1 virgate, and 1 mill rendering 10s. This manor belonged and belongs to the demesne of the Church of ST PETER of Westminster.

X. The land of the Church of St Alban

IN ST ALBANS HUNDRED

THE ABBOT OF ST ALBANS holds HANSTEAD. It is assessed at 20 hides. There is land for 20 ploughs. In demesne [are] 6 hides, and there are 3 ploughs, and there can be a fourth. There 26 villans with 4 Frenchmen have 13 ploughs, and there can be 3 more. There are 3 bordars and 1 slave, and 2 mills rendering 20s, meadow for 3 ploughs and [rendering] 13s, pasture for the livestock, [and] woodland for 1,000 pigs.

In all it is and was worth £22.10s; TRE £25. This manor belonged and belongs to the demesne of the Church of St Alban.

The abbot himself holds SHENLEY. It is assessed at 6 hides. There is land for 8 ploughs. In demesne [are] 2 hides, and there are 2 ploughs. There 11 villans with 1 Frenchman have 5 ploughs, and there can be a sixth. There are 3 cottars, meadow for half a plough, pasture for the livestock, [and] woodland for 400 pigs. In all it is worth £12; when received, £6; and as much TRE. This manor belonged and belongs to the demesne of the Church of St Alban.

The abbot himself holds SANDRIDGE. It is assessed at 10 hides. There is land for 13 ploughs. In demesne [are] 3 hides, and there are 2 ploughs, and there can be a third. There 26 villans have 10 ploughs. There are 2 cottars and 1 slave, and 1 mill rendering 10s, meadow for 2 ploughs, pasture for the livestock, [and] woodland for 300 pigs. In all it is worth £18; when received, £12; and as much TRE. This manor belonged and belongs to the demesne of the Church of St Alban.

The abbot himself holds ST PAUL'S WALDEN. It is assessed at 10 hides. There is land for 14 ploughs. In demesne [are] 3 hides, and there are 2 ploughs, and there can be a third. There 17 villans with 1 Frenchman have 10 ploughs, and there can be 1 more. There are 9 bordars and 3 slaves, and 2 mills rendering 15s, meadow for 1 plough, pasture for the livestock, [and] wood for fences and houses. In all it is and was worth 18[l]10s; TRE £20.10s. This manor belonged and belongs to the demesne of the Church of St Alban.

The vill of ST ALBANS is assessed at 10 hides. There is land for 16 ploughs. There is land for 16 ploughs [sic]. In demesne [are] 3 hides, and there are 2 ploughs, and there can be a third. There 4 Frenchmen and 16 villans with 13 bordars have 13 ploughs. There are 46 burgesses. From toll and from other renders of the vill, £11.14s a year, and [there are] 3 mills rendering 40s, meadow for 2 ploughs, [and] woodland for 1,000 pigs and [rendering] 7s. In all it is worth £20; when received, £12; TRE £24. In the same vill there are also 12 cottars, and there is a park for wild beasts and a fishpond. The above-mentioned burgesses have half a hide.

IN BROADWATER HUNDRED

CODICOTE and 'OXWYCE' were 2 manors TRE, and now they are 1. It is assessed at 8 hides. There is land for 12 ploughs. In demesne [are] 3 hides and 1 virgate, and there are 4 ploughs. There 16 villans have 7 ploughs, and there can be an eighth. There is 1 Frenchman, and 3 cottars and 4 slaves, and 2 mills rendering 12s, meadow for 2 ploughs, pasture for the livestock, [and] woodland for 200 pigs. In all it is worth £6; when received, £5; TRE £12. These 2 manors belonged to the Church of St Alban TRE. Ælfwine of Gotton held there 3 hides under the abbot; he could not alienate them from the church. The Count of Mortain's men seized 15 acres of this land to the abbot's loss, so the men of the hundred testify.

The abbot himself holds NORTON. It is assessed at 4 hides. There is land for 10 ploughs. In demesne [are] 2 hides, and there are 3 ploughs. A priest and a certain Frenchman with 14 villans have 7 ploughs. There are 5 cottars and 1 slave, and 2 mills rendering 16s, meadow for 2 ploughs, [and] pasture for the livestock. In all it is and was worth £16; TRE £17. St Alban held and holds this manor in demesne.

The abbot himself holds SHEPHALL [as] 3 hides. There is land for 5 ploughs. In demesne [are] 1½ hides, and there is 1 plough, and there can be another. There 8 villans have 3 ploughs. There are 2 cottars and 1 slave, meadow for 1 plough, pasture for the livestock, [and] woodland for 10 pigs. All together it is worth £4; when received, £3; TRE £4. This manor belonged and belongs to the demesne of the Church of St Alban.

IN 'DANISH' HUNDRED

The abbot himself holds ABBOTS LANGLEY. It was assessed at 5½ hides TRE; and now at 3 hides. There is land for 15 ploughs. In demesne [are] 2½ hides, and there are 4 ploughs, and there can be a fifth. There a priest and a Frenchman with 10 villans have 10 ploughs. There are 5 bordars and 2 slaves, and 2 mills rendering 20s, meadow for 5 ploughs, pasture for the livestock, [and] woodland for 300 pigs. Of this land a knight has half a hide. In all it is worth £10; when received, £12; TRE £15. This manor belonged and belongs to the Church of St Alban. From this manor Herbert fitzIvo took and seized 1 hide, both wood and field, in the Bishop of Bayeux's time. This hide belonged to the Church of St Alban on the day when King Edward was alive and dead. The Count of Mortain now holds it.

In REDBOURN the same abbot holds 7 hides and 1 virgate. There is land for 16 ploughs. In demesne [are] 3 hides and 1 virgate, and there are 4 ploughs. There 16 villans have 12 ploughs. There is 1 slave, and 2 mills rendering 26s, meadow for 1½ ploughs, pasture for the livestock, [and] woodland for 300 pigs. In all it is worth £30; when received, £15; TRE £16. This manor belonged and belongs to the Church of St Alban. Archbishop Stigand held it on the day of King Edward's death, but he could not alienate it from the church.

The abbot himself holds NAPSBURY. It was assessed at 3 hides TRE; and now at half a hide. There is land for 4 ploughs. In demesne [are] 2½ hides, and there are 2 ploughs; and 2 villans with 4 bordars have 2 ploughs. There are 2 slaves, and 1 mill rendering 10s, meadow for 1 plough, pasture for the livestock, [and] woodland for 300 pigs. This manor is worth 60s; when received, 20s; TRE £4. Godric, a man of Archbishop Stigand, held this manor. He could not put it outside St Alban's Church.

In Windridge Geoffrey de Bec holds 1½ hides of the abbot. There is land for 2 ploughs. In demesne is 1 [plough]; and 5 villans with 2 bordars have 1 plough. [There is] pasture for the livestock, [and] woodland for 300 pigs. It is worth 40s; when received [sic]; TRE 50s. This land Osbern, a monk, held, and Goding his man. They could not alienate it from the church, as the hundred testifies.

In 'Theobald' [in Aldenham] Geoffrey holds half a hide of the abbot. It is and was always worth 6s. A certain sokeman, a man of the Abbot of St Albans, held it TRE. He could not sell outside the church.

[Folio 136: HERTFORDSHIRE]

In Redbourn Amelger holds 3½ virgates of the abbot. There is land for 2 ploughs, and there are [2 ploughs], with 2 villans and 2 cottars. [There is] woodland for 200 pigs. It is worth 30s; when received, 20s; TRE 40s. St Alban held and holds this land.

IN ST ALBANS HUNDRED

The abbot himself holds RICKMANSWORTH. It is assessed at 15 hides. There is land for 20 ploughs. In demesne [are] 5 hides, and there are 3 ploughs, and there can be 2 more. There 4 Frenchmen and 22 villans with 9 bordars have 14 ploughs, and there can be 1 more. There are 5 cottars and 5 slaves, and 1 mill rendering 5s4d, meadow for 4 ploughs, from fish, 4s, pasture for the livestock, [and] woodland for 1,200 pigs. In all it is worth £20.10s; when received, £12; TRE £20. St Alban held and holds this manor in demesne.

The abbot himself holds 'CASSIO' [in Watford]. It is assessed at 20 hides. Of these the abbot holds 19. There is land for 22 ploughs. In demesne [are] 6 hides, and there are 5 ploughs, and there can be a sixth. There 3 Frenchmen and 36 villans with 8 bordars have 15 ploughs, and there can be 1 more. There are 3 bordars besides and 2 slaves, and 4 mills rendering 26s8d, meadow for 22 ploughs, pasture for the livestock, [and] woodland for 1,000 pigs. In all it is worth £28; when received, £24; TRE £30. St Alban held and holds this manor in demesne.

In Aldenham Geoffrey de Bec holds 1 hide under the abbot. There is land for 1 plough, but the plough is not there. There are 2 cottars, [and] woodland for 100 pigs. It is and was worth 12s; TRE 20s. Blaca, a man of St Alban, held this land. He could not sell.

IN ODSEY HUNDRED

The abbot himself holds NEWNHAM. It is assessed at 3 hides and 3 virgates. There is land for 8 ploughs. In demesne [is] 1 hide and 3 virgates, and there are 2 ploughs. There 10 villans with 8 bordars have 4 ploughs, and there can be 2 more. There are 3 cottars, meadow for 1 plough, [and] pasture for the livestock. In all it is and was worth £9; TRE £10. This manor belonged and belongs to the demesne of the Church of St Alban.

IN THE HALF-HUNDRED OF HITCHIN

In Hexton the same abbot holds 8 hides and 3 virgates. There is land for 12 ploughs. In demesne [are] 4 hides, and there are 4 ploughs, and there can be a fifth. There 13 villans with 3 bordars have 3 ploughs, and there can be 4 more. There are 3 cottars and 4 slaves, and Geoffrey de Bec holds there half a hide under the abbot. There are 2 mills rendering 3s4d, meadow for 2 ploughs, [and] pasture for the livestock. In all it is worth £17.10s; when received, £12; TRE £16. This manor belonged and belongs to the demesne of the Church of St Alban. Of this land 1 Englishman holds 3 hides under the abbot.

The abbot himself holds BENDISH. It is assessed at 1 hide. There is land for 2 ploughs, and there are [2 ploughs], with 4 villans who hold this land. There are 2 cottars, wood for fences, meadow for half a plough, [and] pasture for the livestock of the vill. It is and was worth 50s; TRE 40s. This land belonged and belongs to the demesne of the Church of St Alban.

XI. The land of St Benedict of Ramsey

IN ODSEY HUNDRED

THE ABBOT of RAMSEY holds in Therfield 10 hides and 1 virgate. There is land for 20 ploughs. In demesne [are] 3½ hides, and there are 2½ ploughs, and there can be another half [-plough]. There 27 villans with a priest and 1 Frenchman have 11 ploughs, and there can be 6 more. There are 14 cottars and 4 slaves, pasture for the livestock, [and] woodland for 20 pigs. In all it is worth £11; when received, £10; TRE £12. This manor belonged and belongs to the demesne of the Church of St Benedict.

XII. The land of the Church of Chatteris

IN 'EDWINSTREE' HUNDRED

THE ABBESS of CHATTERIS holds in BARLEY 3½ hides as 1 manor. There is land for 4 ploughs. In demesne [are] 1½ hides, and there can be half [a plough]. There 8 v [sic] free men have 2½ ploughs. There are 6 bordars and 2 slaves, [and] woodland for 20 pigs. All together it is and was worth 70s; TRE £4. This manor belonged and belongs to the demesne of the Church of St MARY of Chatteris.

XIII. The land of St Paul of London

IN 'DANISH' HUNDRED

THE CANNONS of London hold KENSWORTH [Beds.]. It is assessed at 10 hides. There is land for 10 ploughs. In demesne [are] 5 hides, and there are 2 ploughs, and there can be 3 more. There 8 villans with 3 bordars have 2 ploughs, and there can be 3 more. There are 3 slaves, pasture for the livestock, [and] woodland for 100 pigs and from the render of the woodland, 2s. In all it is worth 70s; when received, 100s; and as much TRE. Leofwine Cild held this manor of King Edward.

The canons themselves hold CADDINGTON [Beds.]. It is assessed at 10 hides. There is land for 10 ploughs. In demesne [are] 4 hides, and there is 1 plough, and there can be 3 more. There 22 villans have 6 ploughs. There are 5 bordars and 2 slaves, pasture for the livestock, [and] woodland for 100 pigs and [rendering] 2s. In all it is worth 110s; when received, £6; and as much TRE. Leofwine held this manor of King Edward.

IN ODSEY HUNDRED

The canons themselves hold ARDELEY. It is assessed at 6 hides. There is land for 10 ploughs. In demesne [are] 3 hides, and there are 2 ploughs, and there can be a third. There 12 villans have 7 ploughs. There are 6 bordars and 2 cottars and

4 slaves, meadow for 2 oxen, pasture for the livestock, [and] woodland for 200 pigs. In all it is and was worth £7; TRE £10. This manor belonged and belongs to the Church of ST PAUL.

In Luffenhall the canons hold 2 hides. There is land for 2 ploughs. In demesne [are] 1½ hides, and there is 1 plough; and 1 villan with 2 bordars has half a plough, and there can be another half [a plough]. There is 1 slave, pasture for the livestock, [and] wood for fences. It is and was worth 20s; TRE 40s. St Paul held this manor TRE.

The canons themselves hold SANDON. It is assessed at 10 hides. There is land for 20 ploughs. In demesne [are] 5 hides, and there are 6 ploughs. A priest with 24 villans have 13 ploughs, and there can be another. There are 12 bordars and 16 cottars and 11 slaves, meadow for 2 ploughs, pasture for the livestock, [and] woodland for 150 pigs. In all it is and was worth £16; TRE £20. This manor belonged and belongs to the Church of ST PAUL.

[Folio 136V: HERTFORDSHIRE]

XIIII. The land of the Canons of Waltham

IN HERTFORD HUNDRED

THE CANONS OF HOLY CROSS OF WALTHAM hold WORMLEY. It is assessed at 5 hides. There is land for 4 ploughs. In demesne [are] 3 hides and 2½ virgates, and there is 1 plough, and there can be another. There 5 villans have 2 ploughs. There are 4 bordars and 3 cottars and 2 slaves, meadow for 4 ploughs, meadow for 4 ploughs *[sic]*, pasture for the livestock, [and] woodland for 300 pigs. In all it is and was worth £4; TRE 100s. This manor belonged and belongs to the Church of HOLY CROSS of Waltham.

The canons themselves hold BRICKENDON. It is assessed at 5 hides. There is land for 8 ploughs. In demesne [are] 3½ hides, and there are 2 ploughs, and there can be a third. There 9 villans have 4 ploughs, and there can be a fifth. There are 9 bordars and 24 cottars and 2 slaves, and 1 mill rendering 8s, meadow for 2 ploughs, pasture for the livestock of the vill and [rendering] 2s, [and] woodland for 200 pigs. In all it is and was worth 100s; TRE £8. This manor belonged and belongs to the Church of HOLY CROSS of Waltham.

XV. The land of the Count of Mortain

IN TRING HUNDRED

THE COUNT OF MORTAIN holds BERKHAMSTED. It is assessed at 13 hides. There is land for 26 ploughs. In demesne [are] 6 hides, and there are 3 ploughs, and there can be another 3. There a priest with 14 villans and 15 bordars have 12 ploughs, and there can be 8 more. There 6 slaves and a certain ditcher have half a hide, and Ranulph, a sergeant of the count, 1 virgate.

In the borough of this vill [are] 52 burgesses who pay £4 in toll and have half a hide, and 2 mills rendering 20s. There are 2 arpents of vineyard, meadow for 8 ploughs, pasture for the

livestock of the vill, [and] woodland for 1,000 pigs and [rendering] 5s. In all it is worth £16; when received, £20; TRE £24. Eadmær, a thegn of Earl Harold, held this manor.

Ranulph holds "SCENLIE" of the count. It is assessed at 1 hide. There is land for 2 ploughs. There is 1 [plough], and there can be another. There are 2 bordars, pasture for the livestock, [and] woodland [rendering] 100s. All together it is worth 5s; when received, £3; TRE £4. 2 sokemen held this land. One [was] a housecarl of King Edward, and the other a man of Earl Leofwine; they could sell.

The count himself holds ALDBURY. It is assessed at 10 hides. There is land for 7 ploughs. In demesne [are] 6 hides, and there are 3 ploughs; and 8 villans with 1 sokeman and 1 Frenchman have 4 ploughs. There is 1 bordar and 4 slaves, half a hide [of] meadow, [and] woodland for 500 pigs. In all it is worth 110s; when received, £8; and as much TRE. Alwine, a thegn of King Edward, held this manor.

In Pendley the count himself holds 2 hides. There is land for 2 ploughs. There 1 villan with 6 bordars have 1 plough, and there can be another. [There is] meadow for 1½ ploughs. It is worth 30s; when received, 20s; TRE 40s. Eadgifu the nun held this land of Ingelric; she could not give it. These 2 hides are [part] of the 7 hides which the Count of Mortain took from Tring.

Humphrey holds WIGGINTON of the count. It is assessed at 7½ hides and the third part of half a hide. There is land for 5 ploughs. In demesne is 1 [plough], and there can be another. There 5 villans have 2 ploughs, and there can be a third. There are 6 cottars and 1 slave, and 1 mill rendering 5s, meadow for 1 plough, [and] woodland for 100 pigs. In all it is worth £4; when received, 40s; TRE £6. Of this manor Beorhtric, Queen Edith's man, held 3½ hides; and Godwine, Ingelric's man, had 3 hides and the third part of half a hide. He could not give nor sell [the land] outside Tring, and these are [part] of the 7 hides which the Count of Mortain took out of Tring; and Leofric, Oswulf's man, held half a hide and could sell; and the other half-hide belonged to Berkhamsted.

Fulcold holds Gubblecote of the count. It is assessed at 1½ hides. There is land for 1½ ploughs. In demesne is [1] plough; and 3 villans have half [a plough]. There are 2 bordars, and 1 mill rendering 12s4d, [and] meadow for 2 ploughs. It is and was worth 30s; TRE 40s. Eadgifu held this land of Ingelric. She could not put it outside Tring. This land is [part] of the 7 hides which the Count of Mortain took out of Tring.

In Miswell Ralph holds half a hide of the count. There is land for half a plough, [and] meadow for half a plough. It is and was worth 4s; TRE 10s. Wicga, a man of Oswulf son of Frani, held this land; he could sell.

Leofwine holds BOARSCROFT of the count. It is assessed at 1½ hides. There is land for 1 plough, and there is [1 plough] in demesne, and 4 cottars. [There is] meadow for half a plough. It is worth 20s9d; when received, 10s; TRE 20s9d. The same Leofwine held this land of King Edward and he could sell. He holds it now of the count at farm.

In Dunsley [Dunsley and Upper Dunsley] a certain widow

holds of the count the third part of half a hide. There is land for 1 ox. It is and was always worth 12d. Ingelric held this land, [part] of the 7 hides of land in Tring which the count took.

The count himself holds HEMEL HEMPSTEAD. It is assessed at 10 hides. There is land for 30 ploughs. In demesne [are] 3 hides, and there are 4 ploughs, and there can be 2 more ploughs. There 2 Frenchmen with 13 bordars have 20 ploughs, and there can be 4 more. There are 8 slaves, and 4 mills rendering 37s4d and 300 eels less 25, meadow for 4 ploughs, pasture for the livestock and [rendering] 2s, [and] woodland for 1,200 pigs. In all it is worth £22; when received, £25; and as much TRE. 2 brothers held this manor; they were Earl Leofwine's men.

Ralph holds KINGS LANGLEY of the count. It is assessed at 1½ hides. There is land for 16 ploughs. In demesne is no [plough], but there can be 2. There 1 Frenchman with 4 villans and 5 bordars have 2 ploughs, and there can be 12 ploughs. There are 2 mills rendering 16s, and 2 slaves, meadow for 3 ploughs, pasture for the livestock, [and] woodland for 240 pigs. In all it is worth 40s; when received, £4; TRE £8. 2 of Earl Leofwine's men, Thorir and Særic, held this manor.

Humphrey holds LITTLE GADDESDEN of the count. It is assessed at 5 hides. There is land for 3 ploughs. In demesne is 1 [plough]; and 5 villans with 2 bordars have 2 ploughs. There is 1 slave, pasture for the livestock, [and] woodland for 50 pigs. In all it is worth 40s; when received, 60s; TRE £4. Eadmær Atule held this manor, and it was a Berewick of Berkhamsted.

In Redbourn Ranulph holds half a hide of the count. There is land for 1 plough, but there is no [plough] there, only 2 bordars. [There is] meadow for 1 plough, [and] pasture for the livestock. It is worth 17s4d; when received, 20s; TRE 40s. Siward, a sokeman of King Edward, held it and could sell.

XVI. The land of Count Alan

IN BROADWATER HUNDRED

COUNT ALAN holds 1½ hides in Watton at Stone. Godwine holds of him. There is land for 4 ploughs. In demesne there can be 2 [ploughs]. There 3 bordars and 2 cottars have 2 ploughs. [There is] meadow for 2 oxen, [and] pasture for the livestock. It is and was worth 20s; TRE 30s. Godwine held this land of the Church of St Peter; he could not sell, but after his death it ought to have reverted to the church, as

[Folio 137: HERTFORDSHIRE]

the hundred testifies. But his wife turned with this land by force to Eadgifu the Fair, and held it on the day when King Edward was alive and dead. From this land 16 acres were taken after the coming of King William, which now Ansketil de Rots holds under the archbishop, and yet Count Alan discharges the king's geld on them.

The count himself holds [?Great] MUNDEN. It was assessed at 7 hides and half a virgate TRE. There is land for 14 ploughs. In demesne [are] 4 hides and 1 virgate, and there are 4 ploughs. There 16 villans with 6 bordars have 10

ploughs. There is 1 cottar and 2 slaves, and 1 mill rendering 10s. [There is] woodland for 150 pigs; and other woodland, on which 200 pigs might feed, Roger de Mussegros took away from this manor after Earl Ralph's forfeiture, as the whole shire testifies. In all it is worth £16; when received, £12; TRE £16. Eadgifu the Fair held this manor.

IN ODSEY HUNDRED

In Clothall Leofgeat holds 1 virgate of the count. There is land for 1 plough, and there is [1 plough]. It is and was always worth 20s. Asgot, a man of Eadgifu, held this and he could sell it. It now beongs to [?Great] Munden, to which it did not belong TRE.

In Wallington Wimund holds of the count 2 hides less 10 acres. There is land for 2 ploughs. There is 1 [plough], and there can be another. There is 1 villan and 2 cottars and 2 slaves, [and] pasture for the livestock. It is worth 30s; when received, 10s; TRE 60s. 2 sokemen, Eadgifu's men, held this land and could sell.

In Reed Hardwin holds 1 hide of the count. There is land for 3 ploughs. There is 1 [plough], and there can be 2. There is 1 villan, and wood for fences. It is worth 20s; when received, 10s; TRE 60s. Lyfing the priest, a man of Eadgifu, held this land and could sell.

In Reed Alweard holds 1 hide of the count. There is land for 3 ploughs. There is 1 [plough], and there can be 2. There are 6 cottars. It is and was worth 20s; TRE 60s. Thorbiorn, a man of Eadgifu, held this land and could sell.

IN 'EDWINSTREE' HUNDRED

In Wakeley Ralph holds of the count 40 acres of land. There is land for 1 plough. There is 1 sokeman and 1 slave, [and] meadow for 2 oxen. It is and was worth 10s; TRE 20s. Eadgifu the Fair held this manor.

In 'Langport' [in Great Hormead] Roger holds half a hide of the count. There is land for half a plough, and there is [half a plough], with 1 cottar and 2 slaves. It is worth 10s; when received, 5s; TRE 13s. Alric, a man of Archbishop Stigand, held this land and could sell.

IN HERTFORD HUNDRED

The count himself holds CHESHUNT. It is assessed at 20 hides. There is land for 33 ploughs. In demesne [are] 10 hides, and there are 4 ploughs, and there can be 2 more. There 41 villans with a priest and 12 bordars have 17 ploughs. There 10 merchants pay 10s of customary dues. There are 8 cottars and 6 slaves, and 1 mill rendering 10s, from the weir 16d, meadow for 23 ploughs and for the horses of the demesne, pasture for the livestock, [and] woodland for 1,200 pigs and [rendering] 40d.

The count himself holds Hoddesdon. It is assessed at 2 hides and 3 virgates. It is a Berewick of Cheshunt. There is land for 4 ploughs. In demesne [are] 2 hides, and there are 2 ploughs; and 2 villans with 8 bordars have 2 ploughs. There is 1 slave, meadow for 4 ploughs, pasture for the livestock, [and] woodland for 260 pigs. From the weir, 100 eels. In all, the manor with the Berewick is worth £24; when received, £22; TRE £30. Eadgifu the Fair held this manor, and there was and is 1 sokeman having half a hide; he could sell TRR [sic].

Wimund holds WORMLEY of the count. It is assessed at †1½† hides. There is land for 2 ploughs. In demesne is 1 [plough]; and 6 bordars with 1 cottar have 1 plough. [There is] meadow for 2 ploughs, pasture for the livestock, [and] woodland for 150 pigs. From half a weir, 50 eels. It is and was worth 40s; TRE 60s. Alsige, a man of Eadgifu, held this manor and could sell. This land belongs to Cheshunt.

In Bengeo the count holds 1 virgate. There is land for half a plough, [and] meadow for 2 oxen. It is and was always worth 5s. Snerrir, a man of Eadgifu the Fair, held this land and could sell.

XVII. The land of Count Eustace

COUNT EUSTACE holds TRING. It was assessed at 39 hides TRE, and now at 5 hides and 1 virgate. There is land for 20 ploughs. In demesne [are] 12 hides, and there are 3 ploughs, and there can be 2 more. There 21 villans with 6 bordars and 16 cottars and 3 sokemen have 9 ploughs, and there can be 6 more. There are 8 slaves, and 2 mills rendering 9s, meadow for 10 ploughs, pasture for the livestock of the vill and [rendering] 3s, [and] woodland for 1,000 pigs. In this vill is a Berewick where 8 villans having 2 ploughs are settled, and there can be a third. In all it is worth £22 of blanched pennies by this count's measure; when received, £20; TRE £25. Ingelric held this manor TRE, and there were 2 sokemen, men of Oswulf son of Frani; they held 2 hides and could sell them; the same Ingelric attached these sokemen to this manor after King William came, as the men of the hundred testify; and a man of the Abbot of Ramsey had 5 hides of this manor on the same terms. This man could not give or sell his land outside the Church of St Benedict. Ingelric attached him to this manor after the arrival of King William; he did not belong to it TRE, as the hundred attests. These aforesaid 3 sokemen who are still there, having 1 hide, were Ingelric's men and could sell their land.

IN ODSEY HUNDRED

In Reed Robert fitzRoscelin holds of the count 4 hides and 1½ virgates. There is land for 5 ploughs. In demesne are 2 [ploughs]; and 7 villans with 2 bordars have 3 ploughs. There are 4 slaves, meadow for half a plough, [and] pasture for the livestock. It is worth £4; when received, 50s; TRE £4. Alweard, a man of Earl Harold, held this manor and could sell.

The count himself holds ANSTEY. It is assessed at 5 hides. There is land for 10 ploughs. In demesne [are] 3 hides, and there are 2 ploughs, and there can be a third. There 8 villans with a priest and 6 bordars have 5 ploughs, and there can be 2 more. There are 5 cottars and 6 slaves, meadow for half a plough, pasture for the livestock, [and] woodland for 50 pigs. In all it is and was worth £14; TRE £15. Alweard, a thegn of Earl Harold, held this manor; he could sell.

IN 'EDWINSTREE' HUNDRED

In Carney Bury Robert holds 1 hide of the count. There is land for 1 plough, and there is [1 plough], with 4 bordars and 4 cottars and 2 slaves. [There is] meadow for half a plough, pasture for the livestock, [and] woodland for 10 pigs. All together it is worth 13s4d; when received, 10s; TRE 20s. Of this land Alweard, Harold's man, held 1 virgate and could sell it, and Goda, King Edward's man, had 3 virgates [and] could sell; as a customary due they rendered to the sheriff 3d or 3 parts of 1 cartage-due.

In Throcking Rumold holds 18 acres of the count. There is land for 2 oxen. It is and was always worth 2s. Alric, a man of Archbishop Stigand, held this land.

In 'Echington' [in Layston] Rumold holds of the count half a hide. There is land for 1 plough. There is 1 bordar. It is worth 20s; when received, 40s; and as much TRE. Godgyth, a man of Esger the staller, held this land; she could sell.

In the same vill 2 knights hold 20 acres of the count. There is land for 2 oxen, and there are [2 oxen]. It is and was always worth 3s. Godgyth, a man of Esger the staller, held this land and could sell.

In 'Berkesdon' [in Aspenden] Robert holds of the count 1 hide as 1 manor. There is land for 4 ploughs. In demesne are 2 [ploughs]; and 2 villans with a priest and 5 bordars have 2 ploughs. There are 6 slaves, meadow for half a plough, wood for fences and for 30 pigs, and 1 mill rendering 2s8d. All together is worth £3;

[Folio 137v: HERTFORDSHIRE]

when received, 40s; TRE 100s. Alweard, Earl Harold's man, held this manor and could sell.

In Wakeley Robert holds 40 acres of the count. There is land for 1 plough. [There is] meadow for 2 oxen, [and] wood for fences. It is and was always worth 5s. Alweard, Earl Harold's man, held this land and could sell.

In Beauchamps Rumold holds 2 hides of the count. There is land for 2 ploughs, and there are [2 ploughs], with 7 bordars and 2 slaves. There is 1 mill rendering 2s, meadow for 2 oxen, pasture for the livestock, [and] woodland for 20 pigs. It is worth 30s; when received, 40s; and as much TRE. Godgyth, a man of Esger, held this land and could sell.

In Little Hormead 2 Englishmen hold of the count 3 hides and 1 virgate. There is land for 3½ ploughs. In demesne are 2 [ploughs]; and a priest with 2 cottars has 1½ ploughs. [There is] meadow for 1 plough, [and] woodland for 12 pigs. All together it is worth £3; when received, £4; TRE 100s. Wulfweard, Esger the staller's man, held this manor and could sell.

In Bozen Green the count holds 1 hide and 1 virgate and 4 acres. There is land for 3 ploughs. In demesne [are] 3 virgates, and there is 1 plough; and 11 villans with a priest have 2 ploughs. There are 2 slaves, meadow for half a plough, pasture for the livestock, [and] woodland for 20 pigs. All together it is and was worth £3; TRE £4. 9 sokemen of Esger the staller held this land and could sell.

The count himself holds COCKHAMPSTEAD. It is assessed at 2 hides. There is land for 6 ploughs. In demesne [are] 3 virgates, and there is 1 plough. There 5 villans with 3 bordars have 5 ploughs. There is 1 cottar and 4 slaves, meadow for 1 plough, pasture for the livestock, [and] woodland for 10 pigs. In all it is and was always worth £7. Gøti, a thegn of Earl Harold, held this manor and could sell.

In Hoddesdon the canons of St Martin, London, hold 1 hide of the count. There is land for 1 plough, and there is [1 plough], with 3 bordars. [There is] meadow for 1 plough, pasture for the livestock, [and] woodland for 50 pigs. From the weir, 21 eels. It is worth 15s; when received, 5s; TRE 40s. Godgyth, a man of Esger the staller, held this land and could sell.

IN BRAUGHING HUNDRED

The count himself holds BRAUGHING. It is assessed at 5 hides. There is land for 11 ploughs. In demesne [are] 3 hides, and there are 3 ploughs. There 10 villans with a priest and 9 bordars have 8 ploughs. There are 3 cottars and 6 slaves, and 1 mill rendering 12d, meadow for 3 ploughs, pasture for the livestock of the vill, [and] woodland for 6 pigs. In all it is and was worth £16; TRE £20. 2 thegns held this manor. Of these, one, King Edward's man, had 4 hides; and the other, Esger the staller's man, had 1 hide. They could not sell them because [the holdings] were always in alms in the time of King Edward and of all his predecessors, as the shire attests.

XVIII. The land of Earl Roger

IN ODSEY HUNDRED

EARL Roger holds half a hide in Broadfield. There is land for half a plough, but [the half-plough] is not there. [There is] woodland for 40 pigs. It is and was worth 5s; TRE 10s. Goda held this land of Queen Edith and could sell.

XIX. The land of Robert d'Oilly

ROBERT d'Oilly holds 'TISCOTT' [in Tring], and Ralph Basset [holds] of him. It was assessed at 4 hides TRE; and now at 2. There is land for 4 ploughs. In demesne are 2 [ploughs]; and 3½ villans with 2 sokemen on 1 hide and 5 bordars have 2 ploughs. There is 1 cottar and 1 slave, and 1 mill rendering 10s, [and] meadow for 3 ploughs. All together it is worth 70s; when received, £4; TRE 100s. 5 sokemen held this manor. 2 of these, Beorhtric's men, had 1½ hides; and 2 others, men of Oswulf son of Frani, 1½ hides; and the fifth, Eadmær Atule's man, held 1 hide. None of these belonged to Vigot, [Robert's] predecessor, but each of them could sell his land. One of these bought his land from King William for 9 ounces of gold, as the men of the hundred attest, and afterwards turned to Vigot for protection.

In Polehanger [Beds.] Martell holds half a hide of Robert d'Oilly. There is land for 1 plough, and there is [1 plough], with 2 cottars and 2 slaves. [There is] meadow for 1 plough,

[and] woodland for 2 pigs. It is and was worth 10s; TRE 20s. Ælfric, a man of Earl Waltheof, held this land and could sell.

XX. The land of Robert Gernon

ROBERT Gernon holds 1 hide in Mardleybury, and Alweard [holds] of him. There is land for 3 ploughs. In demesne is 1 [plough]; and 4 villans with 2 bordars have 2 ploughs. There are 3 cottars, pasture for the livestock, [and] woodland for 200 pigs. It is worth 30s; when received, 40s; TRE 50s. The same man who holds it held it TRE and could sell.

In Ayot St Peter William holds 2½ hides of Robert. There is land for 6 ploughs. In demesne is 1 [plough], and there can be another. There 6 villans with 3 bordars have 3 ploughs, and there can be a fourth. There is 1 slave, meadow for 1 plough, pasture for the livestock, [and] woodland for 150 pigs. All together it is worth 40s; when received, 60s; TRE £6. 2 thegns, King Edward's men, held this land and could sell. William, Robert's man, seized this to the king's loss, but he claims his lord as his warrantor.

In Graveley William holds half a hide of Robert. There is land for 1 plough, but no [plough] is there. It is worth 4s; when received, 5s; and as much TRE. 2 men of Godwine of Bentfield held this land and could sell.

In Chells William holds half a hide of Robert. There is land for 1 plough, but no [plough] is there. There is 1 cottar. It is and was worth 10s; TRE 20s. Ælfric, a man of Ælfric of Benington, held this land and could sell.

In 'Woolwicks' [in Stevenage] William holds of Robert half a hide and half a virgate. There is land for 1 plough, and there is [1 plough], with 2 bordars and 2 cottars. [There is] meadow for half a plough, [and] woodland for 20 pigs. It is worth 6s; when received, 10s; TRE 20s. Godwine, a man of Almær of Benington, held this land; he could sell.

In [?Little] Wymondley William holds 1 hide of Robert. There is land for 1 plough, but no [plough] is there. There is 1 cottar, [and] meadow for half a plough. It is worth 6s; when received, 10s; TRE 15s. Alflæd held this land under Robert fitzWimarc on the day when King Edward was alive and dead; she could not sell without his leave.

The same William holds LETCHWORTH of Robert. It is assessed at 10 hides. There is land for 7 ploughs. In demesne are 2 [ploughs]; and 9 villans with a priest have 5 ploughs. There are 2 sokemen on 1½ hides, and 4 cottars and 1 slave, meadow for half a plough, pasture for the livestock, [and] woodland for 100 pigs. In all it is worth £6; when received, £7; TRE £8.

[Folio 138: HERTFORDSHIRE]

Godwine of Soulbury, a thegn of King Edward, held this manor and could sell; and there 3 sokemen, his men, had 2 hides and 3 virgates and could sell them.

In Welwyn Robert de Pontchardon holds 1½ hides of Robert, and 20 acres. There is land for 3 ploughs. In demesne is 1 [plough], and there can be another. There 3 villans with 6 bordars have 1 plough. There is 1 cottar and 2 slaves, meadow for 2 oxen, [and] pasture for the livestock. It is and was worth 30s; TRE 40s. Godric, a man of Almær of Benington, held this land and could sell.

IN ODSEY HUNDRED

In Wallington William holds of Robert 3 hides less 20 acres. There is land for 4 ploughs. There are 2 [ploughs], and there can be another 2. There are 3 villans and 6 cottars, pasture for the livestock, [and] wood for fences. It is worth 35s less 4d; when received, 60s; TRE 100s. Ælfric, a man of Godwine son of Wulfstan, held this land and could sell.

In Hyde William holds half a hide of Robert. There is land for 1 plough, and there is [1 plough], with 1 cottar. [There is] meadow for half a plough, [and] wood for fences. It is worth 6s8d; when received, 10s; TRE 20s. Alfred, a man of Esger the staller, held this land and could sell.

In "Sapeham" William holds 2 hides of Robert. There is land for 4 ploughs. In demesne are 1½ [ploughs], and there can be another half [-plough]. There 4 bordars have 1 plough, and there can be another. There are 3 cottars and 2 slaves, meadow for half a plough, pasture for the livestock, [and] wood for fences. This land is worth 40s; when received, 60s; TRE £4. 2 sokemen, men of Godwine of Bentfield, held this manor and could sell.

In Bozen Green William holds half a virgate of Robert. There is land for half a plough, and there is [half a plough], with 4 bordars. [There is] meadow for 2 oxen, [and] wood for fences. It is and was always worth 12s8d. Leofwine, a man of Godwine of Bentfield, held this land. The soke belonged to Esger the staller. He could sell.

IN BRAUGHING HUNDRED

Ansketil holds WESTMILL of Robert. It is assessed at 7 hides and 1 virgate. There is land for 14 ploughs. In demesne are 4 [ploughs]; and 18 villans and 5 Frenchmen with 12 bordars have 10 ploughs. There are 15 cottars and 2 slaves, and 3 mills rendering 21s8d, meadow for 4 ploughs, pasture for the livestock, [and] woodland for 100 pigs. In all it is worth £17; when received, £10; TRE £20. Aki, a thegn of Earl Harold, held this manor and could sell.

XXI. The land of Robert de Tosny

IN TRING HUNDRED

ROBERT de Tosny holds MISWELL and Ralph [holds] of him. It was assessed at 14 hides TRE; and now at 3 hides and 2½ virgates. Yet there are still 14 hides. There is land for 7 ploughs. In demesne are 2 [ploughs]; and 15 villans with 4 bordars have 5 ploughs. [There is] meadow for 7 ploughs, pasture for the livestock and [rendering] 2s, [and] woodland for 500 pigs. In all it is worth 100s and 1 ounce of gold; when received, £7; TRE £8. Oswulf son of Frani, a thegn of King Edward, predecessor of Robert de Tosny, held this manor.

IN 'DANISH' HUNDRED

In Barwythe [Beds.] Baldric holds 5 hides of Robert. There is land for 3 ploughs. In demesne are 2 [ploughs], and there can be a third. There are 3 villans with a priest, and a certain Frenchman with 4 bordars, meadow for 1 plough, pasture for the livestock of the vill, [and] woodland for 100 pigs. All together it is worth 40s; when received, 30s; TRE 60s. Oswulf son of Frani held this land and could sell to whom he wished.

XXII. The land of Ralph de Tosny

IN 'DANISH' HUNDRED

RALPH de Tosny holds FLAMSTEAD. It was assessed at 4 hides TRE; and now at 2. There is land for 12 ploughs. In demesne [are] 2 hides, and there are 2 ploughs; and 22 villans have 8 ploughs, and there can be 2 more. There are 7 cottars and 4 slaves, [and] woodland for 1,000 pigs. In all it is worth £11; when received, £9; TRE £12. Aki, a thegn of King Edward, held this manor.

IN BRAUGHING HUNDRED

Roger holds WESTMILL of Ralph. It is assessed at 4 hides and 3 virgates. There is land for 10 ploughs. In demesne are 2 [ploughs], and there can be a third. There 14 villans with 9 bordars have 7 ploughs. There are 3 cottars and 2 slaves, and a mill rendering 10s, meadow for 2 ploughs, pasture for the livestock, [and] woodland for 60 pigs. In all it is worth £12; when received, £10; TRE £14. Saxi, a housecarl of King Edward, held this manor; and a sokeman, a man of Eskil of Ware, had there 1 virgate and could sell. And after the arrival of King William it was sold and attached to this manor, where it did not belong TRE.

XXIII. The land of Ralph de Limesy

IN ODSEY HUNDRED

RALPH de Limesy holds in "Hainstone" half a hide and the fourth part of a virgate. There is land for half a plough. There is 1 cottar, and meadow for 2 oxen. It is and was worth 10s; TRE 20s. Leodmær, a man of Archbishop Stigand, held this land and could sell.

Ralph himself holds Caldecote as 1 hide and 1 virgate. There is land for 5 ploughs. In demesne [are] 3 virgates and the fourth part of a virgate. There 9 villans with a priest have 2½ ploughs, and there can be [another] 1½ ploughs. There are 4 cottars, [and] meadow for 2 oxen. This land is and was worth 40s; TRE 100s. Leodmær, a man of Archbishop Stigand, held this manor and could sell.

Ralph himself holds PIRTON. It is assessed at 10 hides. There is land for 20 ploughs. In demesne [are] 2 hides, and there are 6 ploughs. There 24 villans with a priest and 29 bordars have 12 ploughs, and there can be 2 more. There is an English knight and 1 sokeman with 4 cottars. There are 4 mills rendering 73s4d. On the land of the Englishman and the sokeman, that is, on 2 hides, dwell 1 villan and 8 cottars. [There is] meadow for 10 ploughs. There are 10 slaves, pasture for the livestock of the vill, [and] woodland for 500 pigs. From pasture and woodland, 10s. In all it is worth £20; when received, £22; TRE £25. Archbishop Stigand held this manor, and there were 2 sokemen, and they are there still; they could not sell. This above is [in] the half-HUNDRED of HITCHIN.

IN HERTFORD HUNDRED

Ralph himself holds [Great and Little] AMWELL. It is assessed at 14½ hides. There is land for 16 ploughs. In demesne [are] 7 hides, and there are 2 ploughs, and there can be another 2. There 24 villans with a priest and 4 Frenchmen and 7 bordars have 8 ploughs, and there can be 4 [more]. There are 19 cottars and 2 slaves, and 1 mill rendering 6s, meadow for 16 ploughs, pasture for the livestock of the vill, woodland for 200 pigs, and from pasture and hay, 10s. In all it is worth £14.10s; when received, £12; TRE £18. Earl Harold held this manor.

XXIIII. The land of Ralph Baynard

RALPH Baynard holds ALSWICK, and William [holds] of him. It is assessed at 6 hides. There is land for 7 ploughs. In demesne are 2 [ploughs], and there can be a third. There 4 villans have 3 ploughs, and there can be a fourth. There are 11 cottars and 7 slaves, meadow for 1 plough, pasture for the livestock of the vill, [and] woodland for 10 pigs. In all it is worth £7; when received, 100s; TRE £8. Almær, a man of Earl Gyrth, held this manor and could sell.

[Folio 138V: HERTFORDSHIRE]

In Little Hormead William holds 1 virgate of Ralph. There is land for half a plough, but no [plough] is there. [There is] wood only for fences. It is and was always worth 5s. Wulfweard, a man of Esger the staller, held this land. The men of Count Eustace claim this [land], of which they had been seised for 2 years after the count himself came into [possession of] this honour, as the men of the hundred testify.

IN HERTFORD HUNDRED

Ralph himself holds HERTINGFORDBURY. It is assessed at 5 hides. There is land for 10 ploughs. In demesne [are] 3 hides and 1 virgate, and there are 2 ploughs, and there can be a third. There 5 villans with 1 Frenchman and 6 bordars have 5 ploughs, and there can be 2 more. There are 11 cottars and 4 slaves, and 2 mills rendering 6s, meadow for 3 ploughs, pasture for the livestock of the vill, [and] woodland for 200 pigs. From woodland and pasture, 7s. In all it is worth £8; when received, £6; TRE £10. Alwine, a thegn of Earl Harold, held this manor and could sell.

XXV. The land of Ranulph, Ilger's Brother

RANULPH brother of Ilger holds 1 hide in Stagenhoe, and William [holds] of him. There is land for 3 ploughs. In demesne is 1 [plough]; and 6 villans have another, and there can be a third. There are 2 cottars, [and] woodland for 20 pigs. This land is worth 50s; when received, 20s; TRE £4.

Thorbiorn, a man of King Edward, held this manor and could sell.

IN BRAUGHING HUNDRED

Ranulph himself holds in STANSTEAD ABBOTTS 17 hides and half a virgate. There is land for 16 ploughs. In demesne [are] 13 hides, and there are 2 ploughs, and there can be a third. There 4 villans with a priest and the reeve of the vill and 4 Frenchmen have 8 ploughs, and there can be 5 more. There are 6 cottars and 2 slaves, and 1 mill rendering 10s, meadow for 16 ploughs, pasture for the livestock of the vill, [and] woodland for 100 pigs. There are also 7 burgesses, who pay 23s. with other customary dues of meadow and woodland. In all it is worth £17; when received, £10; TRE £20. Ælfwine of Gotton held 11 hides and half a virgate of this manor, and of these Ralph Taillebois gave [...] with his niece as a marriage portion to Ranulph, and the eleventh hide he put in Hunsdon. 4 [sic] sokemen held the other 7 hides. 4 of these, Eskil's men, had 4 hides; the other 10, men of Ælfwine of Gotton, had 3 hides and paid as a customary due to the king's sheriff 12d a year. But all the 14 could sell their land.

XXVI. The land of Hugh de Grandmesnil

IN BRAUGHING HUNDRED

HUGH de Grandmesnil holds 24 hides in WARE. There is land for 38 ploughs. In demesne [are] 13 hides, and there are 3 ploughs, and there can be another 3. There 38 villans with a priest and the reeve of the vill and with 3 Frenchmen and 2 Englishmen have 26½ ploughs, and there are 27 bordars and 12 cottars and 9 slaves. Under the Frenchmen and the Englishmen are 32 men, both villans and bordars. There are 2 mills rendering 24s and 400 eels less 25; and other men have 3 mills rendering 10s a year. [There is] meadow for 20 ploughs, [and] woodland for 400 pigs. There is a park for wild beasts and 4 arpents of vineyard just planted. In all it is worth £45; when received, £50; and as much TRE. Eskil of Ware held this manor, and 1 sokeman, his man, had there 2 hides, and another sokeman, Earl Gyrth's man, held half a hide. Both could sell. After the arrival of King William, these 2 were attached to this manor, where they did not belong TRE, as the shire testifies.

XXVII. The land of Hugh de Beauchamp

IN HERTFORD HUNDRED

HUGH de Beauchamp holds in Bengeo as 1 manor |6 hides|, and 2 knights [hold] of him. There is land for 8 ploughs. In demesne [are] 2 ploughs; and 7 villans with 6 bordars have 2 ploughs, and there can be 4 more. There are 2 slaves, and 1 mill rendering 6s8d, meadow for 3 ploughs, pasture for the livestock of the vill, [and] woodland for 20 pigs. In all it is and was worth £3; TRE £6. Brand, a housecarl of King Edward, held this manor.

XXVIII. The land of William de Eu

WILLIAM de EU holds 1½ virgates in Graveley, and Peter [holds] of him. There is land for half a plough, but no [plough] is there. There are 2 villans. This land is worth 3s; when received, 4s; and as much TRE. Ælfstan of Boscombe held 1 virgate of this land, and it belonged to Weston, and Leofsige, a sokeman of King Edward, [held] half a virgate [which] he could sell, and as a customary due he paid ½d to the sheriff; and of this half-hide [sic] 8 acres and 1 toft belonged to Stevenage, which King Edward gave to St Peter of Westminster; and Roger, officer of Peter de Valognes, now holds them.

In Welwyn William de EU holds half a hide. There is land for half a plough, but no [plough] is there. This land is and was always worth 3s. Ælfstan of Boscombe held this, and it belonged to Weston.

In the same vill William de la Mare holds 2 hides of William de EU. There is land for 3 ploughs. In demesne is 1 [plough]; and 5 villans have another, and there can be a third. There are 2 cottars, [and] pasture for the livestock. This land is and was worth 32s; TRE £4. Ælfstan of Boscombe held 1 hide of this land, and it belonged to Weston, and Ælfgeat, his man, held 1 hide. Both could sell.

William de EU himself holds WESTON. It is assessed at 10 hides. There is land for 23 ploughs. In demesne [are] 5 hides, and there are 5 ploughs, and there can be a sixth. There 33 villans with 2 priests and 1 knight and 2 Frenchmen have 16 ploughs, and there can be 1 more. There are 15 bordars and 12 cottars and 10 slaves, and 1 mill rendering 10s, meadow for 3 ploughs, pasture for the livestock, [and] woodland for 500 pigs. From wood and pasture, 13s4d. In all it is worth £20; when received, £25; TRE £30. Ælfstan, a thegn of King Edward, held this manor.

In Boxbury Peter holds of William de EU 2 hides and 3 virgates. There is land for 5 ploughs. In demesne are 2 [ploughs], and there can be a third. There 2 villans with 4 bordars have 2 ploughs. There are 3 cottars and 3 slaves, [and] wood for fences. In all it is worth 50s; when received, 30s; TRE 60s. Alweard, a man of Ælfstan of Boscombe, held this land. He could sell only 3 virgates of it.

IN ODSEY HUNDRED

In Clothall William holds half a virgate and 3 acres. There is land for half a plough, and there is [half a plough]. This land is and was worth 29d; TRE 3s. Ælfstan held this land, and it belonged to Weston.

In Hinxworth 2 knights hold of William 2 hides and half a virgate. There is land for 2 ploughs, and there are [2 ploughs], with 4 villans. There are 3 cottars and 2 slaves, meadow for 1 plough, [and] pasture for the livestock. This land is worth 42s6d; when received, 20s; TRE 60s. 3 sokemen held this land 2 of these, King Edward's men, held 2 hides and half a virgate; and the third, a man of Ælfstan of Boscombe, had 1 virgate. All of them could sell their land. As a customary due they paid the king's sheriff 8½d a year.

In Great Offley William de la Mare holds 8 hides and 8 acres of William de EU. There is land for 16 ploughs. In demesne are 4 [ploughs]; and 16 villans with a priest and 3 knights have 9 ploughs, and there can be 3 more. There are 8 bordars and 4 cottars and 8 slaves, pasture for the livestock of the vill, [and] woodland for 12 pigs. In all it is worth £11; when received, £8; TRE £15. Ælfstan of Boscombe, a thegn of King Edward, held this manor.

XXIX. The land of William d'Auberville

IN 'EDWINSTREE' HUNDRED

WILLIAM d'Auberville holds in Barley 4½ hides and 10 acres. There is land for 5 ploughs. In demesne [are] 2½ hides and 10 acres, and there are 2 ploughs; and 9 villans with 3 bordars have 3 ploughs. There is 1 cottar and 2 slaves, [and] wood for fences. All together it is worth £4; when received, 50s; TRE 100s. Leofwine, a thegn of King Edward, held this manor, and there 1 of his men had 1 virgate, and they could sell.

XXX. The land of Walter the Fleming

WALTER the Fleming holds [?Little] MUNDEN. It is assessed at 5 hides and 1 virgate. There is land for 8 ploughs. In demesne [are] 3½ hides, and there is 1 plough, and there can be 2 more. There 12 villans with a priest and 2 bordars have 5 ploughs. There are 2 slaves, pasture for the livestock of the vill, [and] woodland for 200 pigs. In all it is worth £6; when received, £7; TRE £8. Leofwine, Earl Harold's man, held this manor and could sell.

In Libury Walter holds 1 hide and half a virgate. There is land for 2 ploughs. There is 1 [plough], and there can be another. In demesne [is] 1 hide, and 1 villan. [There is] woodland for 15 pigs. It is and was worth 20s; TRE 30s. This land is a Berewick of [?Little] Munden. Thorkil held it of Leofwine; he could not sell without his leave.

In the same [vill] the same Walter holds 11 acres. They are and always were worth 12d. Leofwine held them and could sell.

XXXI. The land of Eudo fitzHubert

IN BROADWATER HUNDRED

EUDO the steward holds OLD KNEBWORTH, and Humphrey [holds] of him. It is assessed at 8 hides and 1 virgate. There is land for 12 ploughs. In demesne [are] 2 ploughs, and there can be another 2. There 20 villans with 2 knights and 2 bordars have 8 ploughs. There are 3 cottars and 4 slaves and 2 peasants, and 1 mill rendering 12s, meadow for half a plough, pasture for the livestock of the vill, [and] woodland for 1,000 pigs. In all it is worth £10; when received, 100s; TRE £12. Eskil, a thegn of King Edward, held this manor and there 1 of his men had 1 hide and 1 virgate and could sell. As a customary due he found 1 cartage-due when the king came into the shire; if not, he paid 5d.

IN ODSEY HUNDRED

In Reed Eudo holds 1 virgate. There is land for 2 oxen. It is and was always worth 2s. Sigenoth, a man of St Mary of Chatteris, held this land and could sell.

IN 'EDWINSTREE' HUNDRED

In Barley Eudo holds 2 hides and 20 acres. There is land for 2 ploughs. In demesne [are] 1½ hides and 20 acres, and he works it with his own ploughs from Newsells. There 4 villans have 1 plough. There are 2 slaves. This land is worth 30s; when received, 10s; TRE 40s. 2 brothers held this land. One of them, a sokeman, was a man of King Edward; he had 1 hide and 10 acres. The other, a man of Toki, had 1 hide and 10 acres. Both could sell.

In Barkway Eudo holds NEWSELLS. It is assessed at 4 hides and half a virgate.

In 'Echington' [in Layston] Walter holds 6 acres of Eudo. There is land for 1 ox. It is and was always worth 12d. Ealdræd, a thegn of King Edward, held this land and could sell.

Richard Sackville holds ASPENDEN of Eudo. It is assessed at 1½ hides. There is land for 3 ploughs. In demesne are 2 ploughs. A priest with 6 bordars has 1 plough. There are 3 slaves, meadow for 1 plough, [and] woodland for 20 pigs. All together it is worth £4; when received, 30s; TRE 60s. Ealdræd, a thegn of King Edward, held this manor.

Eudo himself holds NEWSELLS. It is assessed at 5 hides and half a virgate. There is land for 14 ploughs. In demesne [are] 3 hides and half a virgate, and there are 5 ploughs. There 10 villans with 6 bordars have 9 ploughs. There are 7 cottars and 21 slaves, meadow for 1 plough, woodland for 100 pigs, [and] pasture for the livestock of the vill. In all it is worth £18; when received, £6; TRE £12. Of this manor Ealdræd, a thegn of King Edward, held 4 hides and half a virgate; and there 1 sokeman, Earl Ælfgar's man, held 3 virgates, and another sokeman, a man of the aforesaid Ealdræd, had 1 virgate. This last paid 1d a year to the sheriff. All of them could sell their land.

IN HERTFORD HUNDRED

Humphrey holds of Eudo half a hide [...]. There is land for 2 ploughs. In demesne is 1 [plough]; and 4 bordars have 1 plough. There are 7 cottars, and 1 mill rendering 6s8d, [and] woodland for 50 pigs. All together it is and was always worth 60s. Leofsige, King Edward's reeve, held this land and could sell. The Bishop of Bayeux took this land from the same Leofsige and gave it to Eudo, and it was seized to the king's loss. With this [land] when Humphrey took it from Eudo he got 68 oxen and 350 sheep and 150 pigs and 50 goats and 1 mare, and 13s4d of the king's rent, and, between cloths and vessels, 20s.

XXXII. The land of Edward the Sheriff

IN 'DANISH' HUNDRED

EDWARD of Salisbury holds GREAT GADDESDEN. It was assessed at 6 hides TRE; and now at 3 hides, but 1 of these is assessed in Tring Hundred and [yet] it should be valued here. There is land for 12 ploughs. In demesne [are] 2 hides, and there are 4 ploughs; and 15 villans with a priest have 6 ploughs, and there can be 2 more. There are 2 bordars and 1 cottar and 8 slaves, and 1 mill rendering 5s, meadow for 1½ ploughs, pasture for the livestock of the vill, [and] woodland for 500 pigs. In all it is worth £22; when received, £20; TRE £25. Wulfwynn held this manor of the Abbot of St Albans on the day when King Edward was alive and dead. She could not put it outside the church, but it ought to have returned to the church after her death, as the hundred testifies.

IN HERTFORD HUNDRED

In Hoddesdon Edward holds 4 hides less 30 acres. There is land for 3 ploughs. In demesne [are] 3 hides, and there is 1 plough; and 4 villans with 2 bordars have 1 plough, and there can be another. There are 5 cottars and 2 slaves, meadow for 4 ploughs, [and] woodland for 20 pigs. From the fishery, 150 eels. It is worth 60s; when received, 30s; TRE 60s. Goda held this manor of Queen Edith and could sell.

XXXIII. The land of Geoffrey de Mandeville

IN 'DANISH' HUNDRED

GEOFFREY de Mandeville holds 3 virgates in 'Theobald' [in Aldenham], and Ralph [holds] of him. There is land for half a plough.

[Folio 139V: HERTFORDSHIRE]

There is 1 villan and 1 bordar, [and] woodland for 12 pigs. It is and was worth 5s; TRE 10s. 3 sokemen held held [sic] this land. 2 of these [were] Esger the staller's men, and the third a man of St Alban; he could not sell, but the other 2 could.

Geoffrey himself holds BUSHEY. It is assessed at 15 hides. There is land for 10 ploughs. In demesne [are] 5 hides, and there are 2 ploughs, and there can be a third. There 10 villans with 1 Frenchman and 8 bordars have 5 ploughs, and there can be a sixth. There are 2 mills rendering 8s, pasture for the livestock, [and] woodland for 1,000 pigs. In all it is and was worth £10; TRE £15. Leofwine, a thegn of King Edward, held this manor. There is a sokeman who was not there TRE; he has 1 hide. He was a man of Queen Edith TRE and could sell.

Geoffrey himself holds SHENLEY. It is assessed at 8 hides and 3 virgates. There is land for 9 ploughs. In demesne [are] 3 hides, and there are 2 ploughs. There 12 villans have 4 ploughs, and there can be 3 more. [There is] meadow for 1 plough, pasture for the livestock, [and] woodland for 600 pigs. In all it is worth £4; when received, £5; TRE £8. Esger held this manor, and there 2 sokemen, his men, had 1 hide and 3 virgates and could sell.

IN ST ALBANS HUNDRED

In 'Cassio' [in Watford] Turold holds 1 hide of Geoffrey. There is land for 1 plough, but no [plough] is there. [There is] meadow for 1 plough, [and] woodland for 30 pigs. It is and was worth 5s; TRE 20s. Alwine the huntsman, a man of Queen Edith, held this land and could sell. Geoffrey put this in Bushey, where it did not belong TRE.

IN BROADWATER HUNDRED

In Digswell Thorkil holds 2 hides of Geoffrey. There is land for 8½ ploughs. In demesne are 2 ploughs; and 12 villans with 3 bordars have 6½ ploughs. There are 4 cottars and 2 slaves, and 1½ mills rendering 8s8d, pasture for the livestock, [and] woodland for 100 pigs. All together it is worth £4; when received, 50s; TRE £4. The same man who holds it now held it TRE. He was a man of Esger the staller and could sell.

IN ODSEY HUNDRED

In Wallington Siward holds 1 virgate of Geoffrey. There is land for half a plough, but there is only 1 cottar there. It is worth 5s; when received, 3s; TRE 10s. Eadræd, a man of Esger, held this land and could sell.

In Ashwell Germund holds 1 virgate of Geoffrey. There is land for half a plough, and there is [half a plough], with 2 bordars. [There is] meadow for half a plough. It is and was always worth 10s. Godgifu held this land of Esger. She could not sell without his leave.

In "Hainstone" Germund holds of Geoffrey 2 hides and the fourth part of a virgate as 1 manor. There is land for 2 ploughs. There is 1 [plough] in demesne, and there can be another. There are 5 villans with 4 bordars, pasture for the livestock, [and] meadow for 1 plough. This land is worth 3s; when received, 30s; TRE £4. Wulfric, a man of Esger the staller, held this land; he could sell.

IN 'EDWINSTREE' HUNDRED

In Barkway Hugh holds of Geoffrey 3 hides as 1 manor. There is land for 7 ploughs. In demesne are 3 [ploughs]; and 12 villans with a priest and 15 bordars have 4 ploughs. There are 4 cottars and 6 slaves, meadow for half a plough, pasture for the livestock, [and] woodland for 50 pigs. From pasture and woodland, 2s and 3 ploughshares. In all it is worth £6; when received, £3; TRE £6. 2 men of Esger the staller held this manor and could sell.

In 'Longport' [in Great Hormead] Sæweard holds 1 virgate of Geoffrey. There is land for half a plough, and there is [half a plough], with 1 cottar and 2 slaves. It is and was always worth 5s. Alfred, a man of Esger, held it; he could sell.

In Bozen Green Turold holds of Geoffrey half a hide and 9 acres. There is land for 2½ ploughs. In demesne is 1 [plough]; and 2 villans with 2 bordars have 1½ ploughs. [There is] pasture for the livestock, meadow for 1 plough, [and] wood for fences. This land is worth 20s; when received, 10s; TRE 40 sokemen [sic]. 4 sokemen of Esger the staller's soke held this land and could sell.

IN HERTFORD HUNDRED

In "Stivicesuuorde" Germund holds 1 hide of Geoffrey. There is land for 1½ ploughs. There is 1 [plough], and there can be a half [-plough more]. There are 3 cottars and 2 slaves, meadow for 1½ ploughs and for the use of the demesne, woodland for 100 pigs, [and] pasture for the livestock. It is and was worth 20s; TRE 40s. Burghi, a man of Esger, held this manor and could sell.

In Hoddesdon Ralph holds 1 hide of Geoffrey. There is land for 1 plough, and there is [1 plough], with 3 bordars and 2 cottars. There is 1 slave, meadow for 1 plough, pasture for the livestock, [and] woodland for 50 pigs. From the weir, 22 eels. This land is worth 20s; when received, 5s; TRE 40s. Godgyth, a man of Esger the staller, held this land and could sell.

In Brickendon Walter holds 1 virgate of land of Geoffrey. There is land for half a plough, and there is [half a plough], with 1 cottar. [There is] woodland for 40 pigs. It is and was worth 5s; TRE 10s. Oswig, a man of Esger the staller, held this land and could sell.

In Bengeo Huard holds of Geoffrey 3 hides and 1 virgate. There is land for 4 ploughs. In demesne is 1 [plough]; and there can be another plough. There 3 villans with 2 bordars have 2 ploughs. There are 6 cottars, and 1 mill rendering 10s, meadow for 1 plough, pasture for the livestock, [and] woodland for 4 pigs. All together it is worth 45s; when received, 40s; TRE £4. Thorkil, a man of Esger the staller, held this manor and could sell.

IN BRAUGHING HUNDRED

In Stanstead Abbotts a certain sokeman holds half a virgate of Geoffrey. There is land for 2 oxen, and there are [2 oxen]. [There is] meadow for 6 oxen, [and] woodland for 1 pig. It is and was always worth 2s. This man held it TRE. He was Esger's man and could sell.

Geoffrey himself holds SAWBRIDGEWORTH at 24½ hides. There is land for 40 ploughs. In demesne [are] 15 hides, and there are 10 ploughs, and there can be 2 more. There 50 villans and 4 sokemen with a priest have 28 ploughs. The reeve has half a hide, a priest 1 hide. Of the villans 14 [have] 1 virgate each, and 35 villans half a virgate each; and these aforesaid villans hold 1½ virgates and 9 acres, from which they pay 17s4d a year. There are 46 bordars [and] each has 8 acres; and [there are] 2 bordars on 10 acres and 20 cottars on 26 acres, and there are 30 cottars and 30 slaves. Under the sokemen are 7 cottars. Esger has 2 hides. Under him are 2 villans and 7 bordars and 3 cottars and 4 slaves. Kip has half a hide, and 1 mill rendering 20s; and [there is] another sokeman paying 5s4d. [There is] meadow for 20 ploughs, pasture for the livestock, [and] woodland for 300 pigs and from their render, 4s. In all it is worth £50; when received, £60; and as much TRE.

[Folio 140: HERTFORDSHIRE]

Esger the staller held this manor, and there were 4 sokemen. 2 of these, men of the same Esger, had half a hide and could sell, except the soke. The third, a man of Earl Harold, had 1 virgate; and the fourth, a man of Ælfwine of Gotton, had 1 virgate. These could sell and give [their land]. The soke was Esger the staller's; and besides, 1 sokeman, a man of Esger, had 2 hides, but he could not sell.

Geoffrey himself holds THORLEY. It is assessed at 4 hides. There is land for 8 ploughs. In demesne [are] 2 hides, and there are 4 ploughs. There are 5 villans and with a certain knight and with a priest and 9 bordars they have 3½ ploughs, and there can be half [a plough] more. There are 11 slaves, and 1 mill rendering 10s, meadow for 2 ploughs, woodland for 40 pigs, [and] pasture for the livestock. In all it is worth £8; when received, 100s; TRE £10. Godgyth, a man of Esger the staller, held this manor and could sell. William, Bishop of London, bought this manor from King William by the grant of the same Godgyth, and now the Bishop of London claims it.

In Wickham 1 sokeman holds 8 acres of Geoffrey. There is land for 2 oxen, [and] woodland for 2 pigs. It is and was always worth 16d. This man held it TRE. He was Godgyth's man and could sell. He was of the king's soke. It belonged to Wickham TRE. This sokeman Geoffrey put in Thorley, where he did not belong TRE.

In Wickham 2 knights hold of Geoffrey 1 hide and 3 acres. There is land for 2 ploughs. In demesne is 1 [plough], and there can be another. [There is] meadow for 1 plough, [and] woodland for 14 pigs. All together it is worth 10s; when received, 20s; TRE 40s. 2 sokemen, men of Esger, held this land and could sell.

XXXIIII. The land of Geoffrey de Bec

IN 'DANISH' HUNDRED

GEOFFREY de Bec holds 1½ hides in Windridge, and Ralph [holds] of him. There is land for 2 ploughs. There is 1 [plough], and there can be another. There are 3 bordars, woodland for 300 pigs, [and] pasture for the livestock. This land is and was worth 20s; TRE 50s. Æthelmær, a man of Earl Leofwine, held this land and could sell.

In 'Theobald' [in Aldenham] Lovet holds half a hide of Geoffrey. There is land for 6 oxen, and there is 1 villan. [There is] woodland for 24 pigs. It is and was always worth 5s. A certain sokeman, a man of the Abbot of St Albans, held this land and could sell.

IN BROADWATER HUNDRED

In Datchworth 2 knights hold 2½ virgates of Geoffrey. There is land for 1 plough, and there is [1 plough], with 3 villans. It is and was worth 12s8d; TRE 20s. 3 sokemen, men of King Edward, held this land and could sell.

In Welwyn Roger holds 2 hides of Geoffrey. There is land for 7 ploughs. In demesne is 1 [plough], and there can be another. There 6 villans with 4 bordars have 4 ploughs, and there can be a fifth. There are 4 cottars and 1 slave, and 1 mill rendering 8s, meadow for 2 ploughs, pasture for the livestock, [and] woodland for 20 pigs. All together it is worth 50s; when received, 20s; TRE £6. Goda and his son held this land of Queen Edith and could sell.

In Langley Otbert holds 1½ hides of Geoffrey. There is land for 3 ploughs. There is 1 [plough], and there can be 2. There are 2 villans and 4 cottars. There is 1 slave, meadow for 1 ox, [and] woodland for 150 pigs. It is worth 30s; when received, 25s; TRE 30s. Swein, a man of Earl Harold, held this manor and could sell.

In Chells Ælfric Bush holds half a virgate of Geoffrey. There is land for 2 oxen, and there are [2 oxen]. This land is and was always worth 5s. This man held it TRE; a man of Swein, he was of King Edward's soke. As a customary due he paid the sheriff ½d a year.

In William Geoffrey de Bec himself holds 5 hides and 1 virgate. There is land for 9 ploughs. In demesne [are] 2 hides, and there are 2 ploughs, and there can be another 2. There 10 villans with 1 knight and 4 bordars have 5 ploughs. [There is] meadow for half a plough, pasture for the livestock, [and] wood for fences. All together it is worth £10.14s; when received, £4; TRE £12. Leofric, a housecarl of Earl Leofwine, held this manor and could sell; and there 1 sokeman, a man of Almær of Benington, had half a hide and could sell; and a widow had half a hide less 10 acres. She could not sell without the leave of Godwine of Letchworth.

In "Rodehangre" [in Letchworth] Lovet holds 1 virgate of Geoffrey. There is land for 2 oxen. It is and was always worth 44d. Alwine, a sokeman of King Edward, held this land and could sell, and he paid 1d as a customary due to the sheriff.

IN 'EDWINSTREE' HUNDRED

In Barley Ansfrid holds 20 acres of Geoffrey. There is land for 2 oxen. It is and was always worth 3s. Algar, a man of Wigar, held this land and could sell.

In Cokenach Ansfrid holds of Geoffrey 1 hide and 12 acres. There is land for 4 ploughs. In demesne are 2 [ploughs]; and there 1 villan with 8 bordars have 2 ploughs. There are 6 cottars and 1 slave, meadow for 1 plough, [and] woodland for 50 pigs. This manor is worth 60s; when received, 40s; TRE 100s. Algar, Wigar's man, held this manor and could sell.

IN THE HALF-HUNDRED OF HITCHIN

In Hexton Ralph holds 1 hide of Geoffrey. There is land for 1½ ploughs. There is half a plough, and there can be another plough. There are 2 bordars, meadow for half a plough, [and] pasture for the livestock. There are 2 cottars, and 1 mill rendering 40d. This land is worth 30s; when received, 10s; TRE 40s. Alric, a man of Esger the staller, held this land; he could sell. The soke remained in Hitchin, and there he found 1 cartage-due.

Geoffrey himself holds LILLEY. It is assessed at 5 hides. There is land for 9 ploughs. In demesne [are] 2 hides, and there are 3 ploughs. There 19 villans with a priest have 5 ploughs, and there can be a sixth. There are 6 bordars and 4 cottars and 6 slaves, pasture for the livestock, [and] woodland for 6 pigs. In all it is and was worth 100s; TRE £7. Leofgifu held this manor of Earl Harold; and there 1 sokeman, a man of Harold, had 3½ virgates of the same land and could sell, and he rendered 1 cartage-due in Hitchin or 3½d.

IN HERTFORD HUNDRED

Geoffrey himself holds HAILEY. It is assessed at 2 hides. There is land for 2 ploughs. In demesne [is] 1 hide and 3 virgates, and there is 1 plough, and there can be a half [-plough] more. There 2 villans with 2 bordars have half a plough. There are 3 cottars and 1 slave, meadow for 1 plough, pasture for the livestock, [and] woodland for 50 pigs. From the weir, 50 eels. It is worth 30s; when received, 10s; TRE £4. Wulfwine, a man of Earl Harold, held this land. Ralph de Limesy claims as much of a certain wood as belongs to the 3 hides of [Great and Little] Amwell, and 2 villans

[Folio 140v: HERTFORDSHIRE]

on 1 virgate and 1 bordar on 10 acres, and also 24 acres of land which Ilbert of Hertford took away and attached to this manor, as the men of the shire attest; and the canons of Waltham claim as much woodland as belongs to 1 hide.

In Brickendon Isembard holds of Geoffrey 5 virgates as 1 manor. There is land for 1 plough, and there is [1 plough]. [There is] meadow for 1 plough, [and] woodland for 40 pigs. It is and was worth 10s; TRE 40s. Leofrun, a man of Archbishop Stigand, held this land and could sell.

In Bengeo the same Geoffrey holds 5 hides and 1 virgate as 1 manor. There is land for 5 ploughs. In demesne [are] 3½ hides, and there is 1 plough, and there can be another. There 2 Frenchmen and 2 villans with 6 bordars have 3 ploughs. There are 34 cottars, meadow for 2 ploughs, pasture for the livestock and [rendering] 8d, [and] wood for fences. In all it is and was worth 100s; TRE £8. Anund, a housecarl of King Edward, held this manor, and there 1 sokeman had half a virgate and could sell.

In the same vill the same Geoffrey holds 6½ hides as 1 manor. There is land for 8 ploughs. In demesne [are] 2½ hides. There 4 knights, having 4 hides, with 2 villans have 3½ ploughs, and there can be 4½ ploughs more. There are 10 bordars and 5 slaves, meadow for 3 ploughs, pasture for the livestock, [and] woodland for 30 pigs. In all it is worth 100s; when received, 60s; TRE £8. Elaf, a thegn of King Edward, held this manor.

In the same vill 3 knights hold of Geoffrey 1 hide and 1½ virgates. There is land for 3 ploughs. There are no ploughs except demesne ploughs. There are 4 bordars, meadow for 4 oxen, [and] wood for fences. It is and was worth 20s; TRE 40s. 3 sokemen held this land. 2 of these, Walcra and Leofsige, had 1 hide of the king's soke and paid 4d. as a customary due; and the third, Alstan, held 1½ virgates of the king's soke and paid 1½d. All, however, could sell their lands.

In the same vill Roger holds 5½ virgates of Geoffrey. There is land for 2 ploughs. There is 1[plough], and there can be another. There are 4 villans. It is and was worth 20s; TRE 40s. 4 sokemen of King Edward held this land and could sell, and they paid the sheriff 6d. a year.

In the same vill a certain priest and a certain Frenchman hold 3½ virgates of Geoffrey. There is land for 1 plough. There is half [a plough], and there can be [another] half [a plough]. It is

and was worth 5s; TRE 10s. 2 sokemen of King Edward held this land and could sell; and they paid 2d. a year to the sheriff.

In 'Sele' [in Hertford] Godwine holds half a hide of Geoffrey. There is land for 1 plough, and there is [1 plough], with 2 slaves, and 1 mill rendering 2s, meadow for 1 plough, wood for fences, [and] pasture for the livestock. It is and was always worth 10s. This man held it TRE and could sell.

In Roxford Guy the priest holds half a hide of Geoffrey. There is land for 1½ ploughs. In demesne is 1 [plough], and there can be a half [-plough more]. There are 3 bordars, and 1 mill rendering 5s, meadow for 1 plough, pasture for the livestock, [and] woodland for 50 pigs. All together it is and was worth 15s; TRE 20s. Godwine, a thegn of King Edward, held this land and could sell.

In 'Blakemore' [in Hertford] Geoffrey Runevile holds 1 hide of Geoffrey. There is land for 2 ploughs. In demesne is 1 [plough], and there can be another. There is 1 villan and 2 bordars, meadow for 2 ploughs, pasture for the livestock, [and] woodland for 40 pigs. This land is and was worth 15s; TRE 40s. 2 thegns of King Edward held this land and could sell.

IN BRAUGHING HUNDRED

In Stanstead Abbotts Geoffrey holds half a hide of Geoffrey de Bec. There is land for half a plough, and there is [half a plough], with 1 cottar. [There is] meadow for half a plough. This land is worth 10s; when received, 5s; TRE 10s. Bettica, a man of Wulfwine of Eastwick, held this land and could sell, and he paid 2d.

In Eastwick Reginald holds 2 hides of Geoffrey. There is land for 4 ploughs. In demesne are 3 [ploughs]; and 4 villans with a priest and 2 bordars have 2 ploughs. There are 5 slaves, and 1 mill rendering 5s, meadow for 5 ploughs, [and] woodland for 20 pigs. In all it is worth 60s; when received, 40s; TRE £4. Wulfwine, a thegn of Earl Harold, held this manor and could sell.

In Wickham Roger and Osbert hold of Geoffrey 3 virgates and 5 acres. There is land for 1½ ploughs, and there are [1½ ploughs], with 8 bordars. [There is] meadow for half a plough, [and] woodland for 8 pigs. It is and was worth 30s; TRE 40s. 3 sokemen of King Edward held this land and could sell, and they paid the sheriff 3d a year.

XXXV. The land of Gosbert de Beauvais

GOSBERT de Beauvais holds [?Great] WYMONDLEY. It is assessed at 3 hides and 1 virgate. There is land for 4 ploughs. In demesne [are] 2 hides and 2½ virgates, and there are 2 ploughs, and there can be a third. There 4 villans with 3 bordars have 1 plough. There are 4 cottars and 2 slaves, meadow for 1 plough, pasture for the livestock, [and] woodland for 10 pigs. In all it is worth 60s; when received, 20s; TRE 60s. Swein, a man of Earl Harold, held this manor and could sell.

In Graveley the same Gosbert holds 2 hides. There is land for 3 ploughs. In demesne [are] 5½ virgates, and there is 1 plough, and there can be another. There 3 villans have 1 plough. There is 1 cottar and 1 slave, pasture for the livestock, [and] paling for fences. It is worth 40s; when received, 20s; TRE 40s. Swein, a man of Earl Harold, held this manor and could sell.

IN ODSEY HUNDRED

In Wallington Fulk holds of Gosbert 3 hides and 40 acres of land. There is land for 5 ploughs. In demesne are 2 [ploughs]; and 4 villans with 3 bordars have 2 ploughs, and there can be a third. There is 1 cottar and 2 slaves, pasture for the livestock, [and] wood for fences. All together it is worth 50s; when received, 30s; TRE 100s. Eadric, a man of Earl Ælfgar, held this manor and could sell, and a certain sokeman, a man of Eadgifu the Fair, held 24 acres of the same land and could sell. Of these Earl Ralph had been seised, but he was not seised of them on the day of his forfeiture, as the hundred testifies.

XXXVI. The land of Peter de Valognes

IN BROADWATER HUNDRED

PETER de Valogenes holds half a virgate in Datchworth, and Robert [holds] of him. There is land for 2 oxen, but there are no [oxen]. This land is and always was worth 6s. Ælfstan, a man of Almær of Benington, held this land and could sell.

[Folio 141: HERTFORDSHIRE]

In Digswell Roger holds 1 hide of Peter. There is land for 3 ploughs. In demesne is 1 [plough]; and 5 villans with 3 bordars have 2 ploughs. There are 8 cottars, and half a mill rendering 40d, meadow for 2 oxen, pasture for the livestock, [and] woodland for 50 pigs. All together it is worth 35s; when received, 20s; TRE 50s. Topi, a man of Almær, held this land and could sell.

In Graveley Godfrey holds of Peter 2 hides and 1½ virgates. There is land for 3 ploughs. In demesne are 2 [ploughs]; and 3 villans with 4 bordars have 1 plough. There are 2 cottars and 2 slaves, pasture for the livestock, [and] wood for fences and houses. It is worth 40s; when received, 10s; TRE £4. Lemar held this manor of Almær of Benington and could sell.

In Chells Godfrey holds 1½ hides of Peter. There is land for 1 plough, and there is [1 plough], with 2 bordars and 1 slave. It is worth 30s; when received, 20s; TRE 40s. Of this land Alwine held 1½ hides, less 10 acres, and 1 toft, which Alwine Dodda, a man of Ælfric the Little, held, and they belonged to Welwyn. He could not sell outside [the manor].

In 'Woolwicks' [in Stevenage] Roger holds 1½ virgates of Peter. There is land for half a plough, but there is no [plough] there. There are 5 cottars, meadow for 2 oxen, [and] woodland for 10 pigs. It is and was worth 3s; TRE 10s. Alwine, a man of Almær of Benington, held this land and could sell.

In Boxbury Peter holds 1 hide and 3 virgates. There is land for 2 ploughs. There is 1 bordar. This land belongs to Benington and is valued [there], and is worked by its own ploughs.

Peter himself holds BENINGTON. It is assessed at 10 hides. There is land for 11 ploughs. In demesne [are] 6½ hides, and there are 3 ploughs, and there can be 2 more. There 16 villans with a priest and 17 bordars have 8 ploughs. There is 1 cottar and 5 slaves, woodland for 100 pigs, [and] a park for wild beasts. In all it is worth £12; when received, £6; TRE £14. Almær of Benington held this manor.

In Libury 2 sokemen hold of Peter 1 hide and 3 virgates. There is land for 2 ploughs, and there are [2 ploughs], with 1 bordar. [There is] meadow for half a plough, [and] pasture for the livestock. All together it is and was worth 20s; TRE 40s. Of this land, Leofrun, a man of Almær of Benington, held 1 hide. She could not sell without his leave; and Alwine, the same Almær's man, had 3 virgates; he belonged to King Edward's soke and could sell, and he found 3 parts of a cartage-due or 3d for the sheriff.

In Libury Peter holds half a virgate and 10 acres. There is land for 3 oxen. There is 1 bordar, [and] woodland for 4 pigs. This land was worth 2s TRE. A certain sokeman of King Edward held and could sell this, and as a customary due he found the fourth part of a cartage-due or 1d a year for the king's sheriff. Peter the sheriff took this land from this sokeman of King William into the same king's hand as a fine for his not having rendered the king's geld, as his men say. But the men of the shire do not bear witness for the sheriff because it was always quit of geld and other [dues] to the king, as long as [the sokeman] held it, as the hundred testifies.

In the same vill Alweard holds half a virgate of Peter. There is land for 1 ox. It is and was always worth 16d. A certain woman held this land of Almær.

In Sacombe Peter holds 9 hides less 1 virgate. There is land for 7 ploughs. In demesne [are] 6 hides, and there are 3 ploughs, and there can be a fourth. There 5 villans with 6 bordars and 1 clerk have 3 ploughs. There are 6 cottars and 4 slaves, and 1 mill rendering 20s, [and] woodland for 60 pigs. In all it is and was worth £6; TRE £8. Of this manor Almær held 4 hides as 1 manor, as the hundred testifies, and Leofwine held 2 hides less 1 virgate as 1 manor. He was a man of Earl Harold and could sell. In the manor which Almær held were 4 sokemen. One of these held half a hide and could sell; and another held 1 virgate but could not sell without the leave of Almær, his lord. The third and fourth had half a hide less 6 acres and could sell. Over these 2 King Edward had sake and soke, and each found for the sheriff the fourth part of a cartage-due or 1d a year. These 4 were men of Almær of Benington. In this same manor a certain woman held 5 virgates under Eskil of Ware, and could sell, except for 1 virgate, which she pledged with Almær of Benington for 10s; and she found 1 cartage-due and the fourth part of another cartage-due, or 5d.

IN 'EDWINSTREE' HUNDRED

In 'Echington' [in Layston] Humphrey holds half a hide of Peter. There is land for 1 plough, and there is [1 plough], with 2 bordars. [There is] meadow for 2 oxen. This land is worth 15s; when received, 10s; TRE 20s. Almær of Benington held this land and could sell.

Peter himself holds STONEBURY. It is assessed at 1½ hides. There is land for 1½ ploughs. There is 1 [plough], and there can be half [a plough more]. There is 1 villan with 4 bordars. It is worth 15s; when received, 10s; TRE 40s. 4 sokemen held this land; 1 of these, the king's reeve, had half a hide and seized the lands of the other 3 sokemen to King William's loss, as the whole shire testifies. He paid as a customary due 4½d a year. Peter the sheriff now holds it.

IN ODSEY HUNDRED

In Ashwell Peter holds 2 hides as 1 manor. There is land for 6 ploughs. In demesne [are] 3 virgates, and there are 2 ploughs; and 8 villans with 8 bordars have 4 ploughs. There are 2 cottars and 4 slaves, and 1 mill rendering 10s, meadow for 1 plough, [and] pasture for the livestock. All together it is worth 100s; when received, 60s; TRE £7. Almær of Benington, a thegn of King Edward, held this manor.

In Hinxworth the same Peter holds 1 hide and 1 virgate. There is land for 2 ploughs, and there are [2 ploughs]. In demesne [is] half a hide, and there is 1 plough; and 1 villan with 4 bordars have 1 plough. There are 2 cottars, [and] meadow for half a plough. It is worth 20s; when received, 10s; TRE 30s. This land was a Berewick of Ashwell. Almær held it.

In Radwell Roger holds of Peter 2 hides as 1 manor. There is land for 3 ploughs. In demesne are 2 [ploughs]; and 5 bordars have half a plough, and there can be half [a plough] more. There are 2 slaves, and 1 mill rendering 6s8d, meadow for half a plough, [and] pasture for the livestock. Almær of Benington held this manor, and his brother held half a hide of the same land; he was his man and could sell.

IN THE HALF-HUNDRED OF HITCHIN

In 'Flexmore' [in Kings Walden] Peter holds half a virgate. There is land for half a plough. There is 1 bordar, [and] woodland for 5 pigs. It is and was worth 3s; TRE 40d. Ælfric, a man of Almær of Benington, held this land and could sell. He rendered 1 cartage-due in Hitchin.

IN HERTFORD HUNDRED

In Bengeo Peter holds half a virgate. There is land for half a plough, and there is [half a plough], with 1 villan. It is and was always worth 5s. Almær of Benington, a thegn of King Edward, held this land.

In Tewin Healfdene holds 5½ hides of Peter. There is land for 5½ ploughs. In demesne is 1 [plough], and there can be another;

[Folio 141V: HERTFORDSHIRE]

and 4 villans with 5 bordars have 3½ ploughs. There are 5 cottars and 1 slave, and 1 mill rendering 8s, meadow for 2 ploughs, pasture for the livestock, [and] woodland for 50 pigs, and from a render from the woodland, 2s. In all it is worth 60s; when received, 30s; TRE £4. The same Healfdene, a thegn of King Edward, held this manor and could sell. But King William gave this manor to this Healfdene and his mother for the soul of Richard his son, as he himself says, and shows by his writ. Peter now says that he has this manor by gift of the king.

XXXVII. The land of Hardwin de Scales

IN BROADWATER HUNDRED

HARDWIN de Scales holds 1 hide in Sacombe. There is land for 1 plough, and there is [1 plough], with 4 villans. It is and was worth 8s; TRE 20s. 3 sokemen held this land. 2 of these, men of Eskil of Ware, held 3 virgates and could sell, and the third, a man of Ælfric Black, had 1 virgate and could sell. These 3 rendered 1 cartage-due or 4d a year to the sheriff.

IN ODSEY HUNDRED

In Luffenhall Theobald holds half a hide of Hardwin. There is land for 1 plough. There is no [plough], only 2 bordars. It is and was worth 5s; TRE 10s. Alweard, a man of Earl Ælfgar, held this land and could sell.

In Clothall Theobald holds of Hardwin 1 virgate less 3 acres. It is and was worth 5s; TRE 10s. Thorbert, a priest of Archbishop Stigand, held this land and could sell. He found 1d.

In Wallington Siward holds of Hardwin 1½ hides and 26 acres. There is land for 2 ploughs. There is 1 [plough], and there can be another. There are 3 bordars. It is worth 25s; when received, 20s; TRE 30s. Wulfweard, a man of Eskil of Ware, held this land and could sell.

In Broadfield Theobald holds of Hardwin 1 hide and the fourth part of 1 virgate. There is land for 1 plough, and there is [1 plough], with 3 bordars and 2 slaves and 1 cottar. [There is] meadow for half a plough, [and] pasture for the livestock. It is worth 20s; when received, 10s; TRE 40s. 2 brothers, Archbishop Stigand's men, held this land and could sell.

In Orwell Bury Wisgar holds of Hardwin 1½ hides less 5 acres. There is land for 1½ ploughs, and there are [1½ ploughs], with 1 villan and 3 cottars. There are 2 slaves, no meadow, [but] pasture for the livestock. This land is worth 28s; when received, 15s; TRE 25s. 2 sokemen, Archbishop Stigand's men, held this land and could sell.

In Therfield Wigar holds 3 virgates of Hardwin. There is land for 1 plough. There are 2 villans and 2 cottars with 1 slave. [There is] pasture for the livestock. It is and was worth 10s; TRE 20s. Alric, a priest, held this land under the Abbot of Ramsey; he could not sell without the abbot's leave.

In Reed Hardwin holds 5 hides and 1½ virgates. There is land for 6 ploughs. In demesne [are] 3½ hides and 8 acres, and there are 2 ploughs. There 10 villans with a priest and 5 bordars have 4 ploughs. There are 2 cottars and 6 slaves, meadow for half a plough, pasture for the livestock, [and] woodland for 10 pigs. In all it is worth 100s; when received, £4; TRE £6.

Of this manor Sigeræd, Earl Harold's man, held 4 hides and 1½ virgates, and Sigenoth, a man of St Mary of Chatteris, held 1 hide. Both could sell.

In Ashwell Theobald holds half a hide of Hardwin. There is land for 1 plough, but there is no [plough]. There are 6 cottars, [and] meadow for half a plough. This land is worth 20s; when received, 10s; TRE 30s. Uhtræd held this land under Robert fitzWimarc; he could not sell without his leave, as the men of the hundred testify.

In Hinxworth Theobald holds 2 hides of Hardwin. There is land for 2 ploughs, and there are [2 ploughs], with 5 villans and a certain Frenchman and 3 cottars. [There is] meadow for 1 plough, [and] pasture for the livestock. This land is worth 40s; when received, 20s; TRE 60s. 6 sokemen held this land. 4 of these, men of Almær of Benington, had 1 hide and 1 virgate and paid 5d a year; and the fifth, a man of Archbishop Stigand, had half [a hide]; and the sixth, a man of King Edward, had 1 virgate and paid 1d. All could sell.

IN 'EDWINSTREE' HUNDRED

In Barley Theobald holds of Hardwin 4 hides and 10 acres. There is land for $3\frac{1}{2}$ ploughs. In demesne are 2 [ploughs]; and 3 villans with a priest and 8 bordars have $1\frac{1}{2}$ ploughs. There are 4 cottars and 2 slaves. All together it is worth 45s; when received, 15s; TRE 60s. 5 sokemen held this manor. 3 of these, Earl Ælfgar's men, had 1 hide and 10 acres; and the fourth, a man of Earl Gyrth, had 2 hides, and the fifth, a man of Earl Harold, had 1 hide. All these could sell.

In Barkway 2 men hold $1\frac{1}{2}$ virgates of Hardwin. There is land for 1 plough, but there is no [plough], only 1 cottar. This land is and was worth 7s; TRE 10s 2 sokemen held this land. 1 of these, Earl Ælfgar's man, had 1 virgate; and the other, Ealdræd's man, held half a virgate; he paid $\frac{1}{2}$d a year; he could sell.

In "Helsangre" 3 men hold of Hardwin 2 parts of 1 hide. There is land for 1 plough, and there is [1 plough]. This land is worth 10s; when received, 5s; TRE 20s. Ordmær, a man of the Abbot of Ramsey, held this land and could sell.

Hardwin himself holds WYDDIAL. It is assessed at $5\frac{1}{2}$ hides. There is land for 8 ploughs. In demesne [are] 2 hides less 20 acres, and there are 3 ploughs. There 11 villans with a priest with 5 bordars have 5 ploughs. There are 4 cottars and 6 slaves, meadow for half a plough, pasture for the livestock, [and] wood for fences. In all it is worth £9; when received, £6; TRE £10. 9 sokemen held this manor. 1 of these, Sigeræd, a man of Earl Harold, had 1 hide and 3 virgates as 1 manor, and Alweard, a man of Earl Ælfgar, $1\frac{1}{2}$ hides as 1 manor, and the other 7, King Edward's sokemen, had 2 hides and 1 virgate. These found for the sheriff 9d or 2 cartage-dues and the fourth part of a cartage-due a year.

In Hodenhoe Theobald holds of Hardwin 1 hide and 1 virgate. There is land for 1 plough, and there is [1 plough], with 1 bordar. [There is] wood for fences. This land is worth 20s; when received, 10s; TRE 25s. 2 sokemen, men of Earl Ælfgar, held this land; they could sell.

In Throcking Theobald holds 1 hide and 1 virgate of Hardwin. There is land for $1\frac{1}{2}$ ploughs, and there are [$1\frac{1}{2}$ ploughs], with 2 bordars and 1 sokeman on 3 virgates. There are 6 cottars and 2 slaves, meadow for 6 oxen, pasture for the livestock, [and] wood for fences. All together it is worth 25s; when received, 10s; TRE 25s. 2 sokemen, Archbishop Stigand's men, held this land and could sell.

In 'Echington' [in Layston] Theobald holds of Hardwin 3 virgates and 6 acres. There is land for 1 plough, and there is [1 plough], with 1 villan and 6 bordars and 1 cottar. [There is] meadow for 5 oxen, [and] pasture for the livestock. It is worth 15s; when received, 10s; TRE 20s. 2 sokemen of King Edward held this land; they could sell, and they paid to the sheriff 3d a year.

In Wakeley Theobald holds 40 acres of Hardwin. There is land for 1 plough, and there is [1 plough], with 7 cottars. [There is] meadow for 2 oxen, [and] wood for fences. This land is worth 15s; when received, 7s; TRE 15s. Eadric, a man of Earl Ælfgar, held this land and could sell.

In 'Berkesdon' [in Aspenden] Peter and Theobald hold 1 virgate of Hardwin. There is land for 1 plough, and there is [1 plough], with 2 bordars. [There is] meadow for 2 oxen. It is and was always worth 10s. 3 sokemen held this land. 1 of these, a man of Eadgifu the Fair, had the fourth part of 1 virgate; and another, a man of Ælfgar, had the fourth part [of a virgate] in like manner; and the third, a man of Gyrth, had half a virgate; and they could sell. Count Alan claims that he ought rightly to have 3 parts of this virgate, for he was seised of it when he crossed the sea very recently, as the men of the hundred testify for him. But Hardwin claims Peter the sheriff

[Folio 142: HERTFORDSHIRE]

as warrantor and livery officer by order of the Bishop of Bayeux, that he delivered it to him in exchange for Libury.

In Anstey Payne holds half a hide of Hardwin. There is land for $1\frac{1}{2}$ ploughs, and there are [$1\frac{1}{2}$ ploughs], with 4 bordars and 4 cottars and 1 slave. [There is] meadow for half a plough, pasture for the livestock, [and] woodland for 12 pigs. This land is worth 20s; when received, 10s; TRE 20s. Alweard, a man of Earl Ælfgar, held this and could sell.

IN HERTFORD HUNDRED

Hardwin himself holds LITTLE BERKHAMSTED. It is assessed at 5 hides. There is land for 8 ploughs. In demesne [are] 3 hides, and there are 2 ploughs, and there can be a third. There 6 villans with 5 bordars have 4 ploughs, and there can be a fifth. There are 6 cottars and 1 slave, meadow for 3 ploughs, [and] woodland for 50 pigs. In all it is worth 100s; when received, 50s; TRE 100s. Of this manor Sæmær the priest held 2 hides, and a certain widow, Leofgifu, [held] 2 hides, and Wulfric Werden 1 hide. These lands belonged to the alms of King Edward and all the kings his predecessors, as the shire testifies.

Hardwin himself holds BRAMFIELD. It is assessed at 5 hides. There is land for 6 ploughs. In demesne [are] 4 hides, and there are $1\frac{1}{2}$ ploughs, and there can be [another] half [-plough]. There 10 villans have $2\frac{1}{2}$ ploughs, and there can be $1\frac{1}{2}$ ploughs more. There is 1 slave, meadow for 1 plough, pasture for the livestock, [and] woodland for 100 pigs and 12d from it. In all it is worth £4; when received, 40s; TRE 100s. Aki, a thegn of Earl Harold, held this manor and could sell.

In "Briceuuold" Baldwin holds 3 virgates of Hardwin. There is land for 2 ploughs. There is 1 [plough], and there can be another. There are 2 villans and 3 bordars, meadow for 4 oxen, [and] woodland for 15 pigs. This land is worth 5s; when received, 10s; and as much TRE.

XXXVIII. The land of Edgar Ætheling

IN 'EDWINSTREE' HUNDRED

EDGAR Ætheling holds 1½ hides in Barkway, and Godwine [holds] of him. There is land for 2 ploughs. In demesne is 1 [plough]; and 4 bordars with 4 cottars have 1 plough. There is 1 slave, pasture for the livestock, [and] woodland for 15 pigs. This land is worth 40s; when received, 10s; TRE 40s. 2 sokemen, Esger the staller's men, held this and could sell.

The same Godwine holds GREAT HORMEAD of Edgar. It is assessed at 6 hides and 3 virgates. There is land for 10 ploughs. In demesne are 4 [ploughs], and there can be a fifth. There 6 villans with 15 bordars have 5 ploughs. There are 2 cottars and 6 slaves, meadow for 1 plough, pasture for the livestock, [and] woodland for 24 pigs. In all it is worth £8; when received, £6; TRE £12. Of this manor Alnoth, a thegn of Archbishop Stigand, held 1½ hides as 1 manor, and Wulfwine, a man of Esger the staller, 1 hide, and Alweard, a man of Almær of Benington, 1 hide, and 7 sokemen of King Edward held 3 hides and 1 virgate and paid the sheriff 13d a year. All these could sell their land. Ilbert the sheriff attached these 2 sokemen and Wulfwine and Alweard to this manor in the time of King William; they did not belong to it TRE, as the hundred testifies.

XXXIX. The land of Mainou the Breton

IN TRING HUNDRED

MAINOU the Breton holds in Dunsley [Dunsley and Upper Dunsley] the third part of half a hide. There is land for 1 ox. It is and was always worth 12d. Ingelric held this land TRE, and it belonged to Tring, and is [part] of the 7 hides which the Count of Mortain took.

XL. The land of Gilbert fitzSalomon

GILBERT fitzSalomon holds MEPPERSHALL [Beds.]. It is assessed at 3 hides and 1 virgate. There are 3 villans and 4 cottars. This land is valued in Bedfordshire with [his] other land. Leofwine, a thegn of King Edward, held this land.

XLI. The land of Sigar de Chocques

IN ODSEY HUNDRED

SIGAR de Chocques holds RUSHDEN. It is assessed at 5 hides. There is land for 8 ploughs. In demesne [are] 3 hides, and there are 2 ploughs, and there can be a third. There 8 villans with 3 bordars have 5 ploughs. There is 1 sokeman and 3 cottars and 4 slaves, meadow for half a plough, pasture for the livestock, [and] woodland for 50 pigs. In all it is and was worth 110s; TRE 10s. 2 sokemen, Archbishop Stigand's men, held this manor and could sell.

In Broadfield Sigar holds 1 hide and 3 parts of 1 virgate. There is land for 2 ploughs. There is 1 [plough] and there can be another. There are 4 villans with 2 bordars, meadow for half a plough, pasture for the livestock, [and] woodland for 50 pigs. All together it is and was worth 30s; TRE 60s. Asgot, a man of Archbishop Stigand, held this land and could sell.

XLII. The land of the King's Thegns

IN BROADWATER HUNDRED

DEORMANN and ALWEARD hold WATTON AT STONE of the king. It is assessed at 5 hides. There is land for 7 ploughs. In demesne [are] 3½ hides, and there are 2 ploughs, and there can be half [a plough] more. There 10 villans with 4 bordars have 4½ ploughs. There are 4 slaves, and 1 mill rendering 13s4d, meadow for 1 plough, pasture for the livestock, [and] woodland for 100 pigs. All together it is and was worth 100s; TRE £7. Alwine Horne, a thegn of King Edward, held this land and could sell.

Deormann himself holds WALKERN. It is assessed at 10 hides. There is land for 12 ploughs. In demesne [are] 5 hides, and there are 2 ploughs, and there can be another 2. There 14 villans with a priest and 6 bordars have 8 ploughs. There are 8 cottars and 4 slaves, pasture for the livestock, [and] woodland for 200 pigs. In all it is worth £10; when received, £8; TRE £16. Alwine Horne, a thegn of King Edward, held this manor and could sell.

In Libury Deormann holds 3 virgates. There is land for 1 plough, but there is no plough. This land is valued in Watton at Stone, Deormann's manor.

In the same vill Deormann holds 3 acres. They are and were always worth 3d.

In Sacombe Deormann holds half a virgate. There is land for 2 oxen. It is and was always worth 12d. Alwine Horne, a thegn of King Edward, held this land and the others above and could sell.

IN HERTFORD HUNDRED

In Wormley Alwine son of Dodda holds 2½ hides of the king. There is land for 2 ploughs, and there are [2 ploughs], with 6 villans and 1 slave. [There is] meadow for 2 ploughs, pasture for the livestock, [and] woodland for 150 pigs. All together it is worth 40s; when received, 50s; TRE 60s. Wulfweard, a man of Esger the staller, held this manor and could sell. This manor was sold for 3 marks of gold after the arrival of King William.

Peter, a certain burgess, holds 2 hides of the king in Hoddesdon. There is land for 1½ ploughs, and there are [1½ ploughs], with 1 villan and 3 cottars and 2 slaves. [There is] meadow for 2 ploughs, pasture for the livestock, [and] woodland for 10 pigs. All together it is worth 20s; when received, 10s; TRE 30s. Goda, a man of Queen Edith, held this manor and could sell.

Baldwin, a certain sergeant of the king, holds 3 virgates in Brickendon. There is land for 1 plough, and there is [1 plough]. [There is] woodland for 40 pigs. This land is and was worth 10s; TRE 15s. 3 brothers held this land and could sell.

In "Briceuuolde" a certain priest and his sister hold 3 virgates of the king. There is land for 2 ploughs. There is 1 [plough], and there can be another. There is 1 villan and 1 cottar, meadow for 4 oxen, [and] woodland for 15 pigs. This land is worth 5s; when received, 10s; and as much TRE. These men held it TRE of his soke and could sell.

In Epcombs a certain priest holds of the king's alms half a hide. There is land for 1 plough, and there is [1 plough], with 2 slaves. [There is] meadow for 1 plough, and 1 mill rendering 12d. This land is and was worth 15s; TRE 20s. This man held it TRE and still holds it in alms.

IN BROADWATER HUNDRED

In WELWYN a certain priest holds 1 hide in alms of the king. There is land for 3 ploughs. In demesne is 1 [plough], and there can be another. There 6 bordars have 1 plough. There are 2 cottars, meadow for 1 plough, pasture for the livestock, [and] woodland for 50 pigs. All together it is and was always worth 25s. This man held it of King Edward

[Folio 142V: HERTFORDSHIRE]

in alms and it belongs to the church of the same vill. William Black, a man of the Bishop of Bayeux, seized 12 acres of this almsland to the king's loss, as the hundred attests.

In Ayot St Lawrence the reeve of this hundred holds 9 acres of the king. There is land for 1 ox. It is and was always worth 9d. Siward, a man of Ælfwine of Gotton, held this land and could sell.

In "Rodenehangre" [in Letchworth] Alweard of Mardleybury holds 3 virgates of the king. There is land for 1 plough, but there is no [plough], only 1 cottar. [There is] woodland for 24 pigs. This land is and was always worth 5s. This man held it TRE and could give it to whom he wished, and paid 3d a year to the sheriff.

In Sacombe 1 king's sokeman holds half a virgate. There is land for 2 oxen. It is and was always worth 15d. This man held it TRE. [He was] a man of Earl Leofwine, and paid ½d a year as a customary due.

IN BRAUGHING HUNDRED

In Stanstead Abbotts Guthmund holds 3 virgates of the king. There is land for 6 oxen, and there are [6 oxen], with 4 bordars. [There is] meadow for 1 plough, [and] woodland for 8 pigs. This land is and was always worth 10s. This man held it of King Edward and could sell.

XLII. The land of Richard fitzGilbert's Wife

IN BRAUGHING HUNDRED

ROHAIS wife of Richard son of Count Gilbert holds STANDON. It is assessed at 11 hides. There is land for 24 ploughs. In demesne [are] 6 hides, and there are 5 ploughs. There 29 villans with a priest and 15 bordars and 2 sokemen and a certain Frenchman have 12 ploughs, and there can be 7 more. There are 9 cottars and 8 slaves, and 5 mills rendering 45s, meadow for 24 ploughs, pasture for the livestock, [and] woodland for 600 pigs. There are 2 arpents of vineyard. In all it is worth £33; when received, £16; TRE £34. Archbishop Stigand held this manor. In this manor were 6 sokemen, men of the same archbishop, and each had 1 hide and could sell but not the soke. 1 of them, however, could also sell his soke with the land.

XLIII. The land of Hugh de Grandmesnil's Wife

IN HERTFORD HUNDRED

ADELIZA wife of Hugh de Grandmesnil holds BROX-BOURNE. It is assessed at 5½ hides. There is land for 6 ploughs. In demesne [are] 3 hides and 3 virgates, and there is 1 plough. There 4 villans with a priest and 1 sokeman and 2 bordars have 5 ploughs. There are 2 slaves, and 1 mill rendering 8s, meadow [rendering] 6s. and 4s from the hay, pasture for the livestock, [and] woodland for 200 pigs. In all it is worth £4; when received, 60s; TRE £7. Archbishop Stigand held this manor, and there was 1 sokeman, the man and reeve of the same archbishop; he had half a hide and could sell.

XLIIII. The land of the Daughter of Ralph Taillebois

IN BRAUGHING HUNDRED

The daughter of Ralph Taillebois holds in Hunsdon 4 hides of the fief of Hugh de Beauchamp. There is land for 5 ploughs. In demesne [are] 2 hides, and there is 1 plough, and there can be another. There 4 villans with a priest and a certain Frenchman and 8 bordars have 2 ploughs, and there can be a third. There are 2 cottars and 3 slaves, and 1 mill rendering 10s, meadow for 5 ploughs, pasture for the livestock, [and] woodland for 40 pigs, and 10d from the pasture. In all it is and was worth 70s; TRE £6. Leofwine, a man of Earl Harold, held this manor and could sell, and of this land Ælfwine of Gotton, a man of King Edward, held 1 hide and could sell. Ralph Taillebois took it from Stanstead Abbotts and attached it to this manor.

BUCKINGHAMSHIRE

BUCKINGHAM with Bourton was assessed at 1 hide TRE, and is so now. There is land for 8 ploughs. In demesne are 2 [ploughs]; and the villans have $3\frac{1}{2}$ ploughs, and there could be $2\frac{1}{2}$ more. There are 26 burgesses and 11 bordars and 2 slaves. There is 1 mill rendering 14s, meadow for 8 ploughs, [and] pasture for the livestock of the vill. In all it rendered TRE £10 by tale; now it renders £16 of blanch silver.

Bishop Remigius holds the church of this borough, and land for 4 ploughs which belongs to it. There are 4 ploughs, and 3 villans and 3 bordars and 10 cottars, and 1 mill [rendering] 10s. [There is] meadow for 2 ploughs, [and] wood for fences. It is and was worth £6; TRE £7. This church Bishop Wulfwig held of King Edward.

In this borough the Bishop of Coutances has 3 burgesses whom Wulfweard son of Eadgifu held. These pay 6s6d. yearly, and to the king they pay 11d.

Earl Hugh has 1 burgess who was a man of Burgheard of Shenley. This man pays 26d yearly, and to the king 5d.

Robert d'Oilly has 1 burgess who was a man of Azur son of Toti. This man pays 16d, and to the king 5d.

Roger d'Ivry has 4 burgesses who were men of the same Azur. These pay 7s6d, and to the king 13d.

Hugh de Bolbec has 4 burgesses who were men of Ælfric. These pay 28d, and to the king 12d.

Mainou the Breton has 4 burgesses who were men of Eadgifu wife of Sigeræd. These pay 29d. They owe nothing to the king.

Hascoit Musard has 1 burgess who was a man of Azur son of Toti. This man pays 16d, and to the king 2d.

Ernulf de Hesdin has 1 burgess who was Wiglaf's [man]. This man pays 2s yearly, and to the king 3d.

William de Castellion has of the Bishop of Bayeux's fief 2 burgesses who were men of Earl Leofwine. These pay 16d, and to the king now nothing, but TRE they paid 3d.

1 burgess of Earl Aubrey's fief pays to the king 2d.

Leofwine of Nuneham Courtenay has 5 burgesses, and he had them TRE. These pay him 4s yearly, and to the king 12d.

I King WILLIAM
II The Archbishop of Canterbury
III The Bishop of Winchester
IIII The Bishop of Lincoln
V The Bishop of Bayeux
VI The Bishop of Coutances
VII The Bishop of Lisieux
VIII The Abbot of Westminster
IX The Abbot of St Albans
X The Abbess of Barking
XI The Canons of Oxford
XII Regenbald the priest
XIII The Count of Mortain
XIIII Earl Hugh of Chester
XV Walter Giffard
XVI William de Warenne
XVII William Peverel
XVIII William fitzAnsculf
XIX Robert de Tosny
XX Robert d'Oilly
XXI Robert Gernon
XXII Geoffrey de Mandeville
XXIII Gilbert de Ghent
XXIIII Miles Crispin
XXV Edward of Salisbury
XXVI Hugh de Beauchamp
XXVII Hugh de Bolbec
XXVIII Henry de Ferrers
XXIX Walter de Vernon
XXX Walter fitzOther
XXXI Walter the Fleming
XXXII William de Feugeres
XXXIII William the chamberlain
XXXIIII William fitzConstantine
XXXV William fitzManni
XXXVI Turstin fitzRolf
XXXVII Turstin Mantel
XXXVIII Ralph de Feugeres
XL Bertram de Verdum
XLI Nigel d'Aubigny
XLII Nigel de Berville
XLIII Roger d'Ivry
XLIIII Richard Engaine
XLV Mainou the Breton
XLVI Joscelin the Breton
XLVII Urse de Bercheres
XLVIII Winemar [the Fleming]
XLIX Martin
L Hervey the legate
LI Hascoit Musard
LII Gunfrid de Chocques
LIII Giles brother of Ansculf
LIIII Queen Matilda
LV Countess Judith
LVI Azelina wife of [Ralph] Taillebois

LVII Thegns of the king and almsmen

The land of the King

AYLESBURY, a demesne manor of the king, has always been assessed at 16 hides. There is land for 16 ploughs. In demesne are 2 [ploughs]. There 20 villans with 14 bordars have 10 ploughs, and there could be 4 more. There are 2 slaves, and 2 mills rendering 23s, meadow for 8 ploughs, and from the remainder, 20s. In all it renders £56 assayed and weighed, and from the toll £10 by tale; TRE it rendered £25 by tale.

In this manor was and is 1 sokeman having 1 virgate of land, which he could give or sell to whom he wished, and yet he always does service to the king's sheriff. The church of this manor the Bishop of Lincoln holds.

[Folio 143V: BUCKINGHAMSHIRE]

WENDOVER has always been assessed at 24 hides. There is land for 26 ploughs. In demesne are 3 ploughs. There 26 villans with 6 bordars have 17 ploughs, and there could be 6 more. There are 2 mills rendering 10s, meadow for 3 ploughs, and from the remainder, 20s, [and] woodland for 2,000 pigs. In all it renders yearly £38 assayed and weighed; TRE it rendered £25 by tale. In this manor are 2 sokemen holding 1½ hides. They did not belong there TRE.

PRINCES RISBOROUGH was Earl Harold's vill. It has always been assessed at 30 hides. There is land for 24 ploughs. In demesne [are] 20 hides, and there are 4 ploughs. There 30 villans with 12 bordars have 20 ploughs. There are 3 slaves, and 2 mills rendering 14s8d, meadow for 7 ploughs, [and] woodland for 1,000 pigs. All together it renders yearly £47 of blanch silver, less 16d; TRE it rendered £10 by tale. To this manor belongs and belonged a certain burgess of Oxford paying 2s. In addition a salt-worker of Droitwich [Worcs.] renders summae [sic] of salt, and in the same manor was and is a certain sokeman holding 3 virgates. He could indeed sell [his land], but yet he has done service to the sheriff.

SWANBOURNE was Earl Harold's vill. It is assessed at 4½ hides. There is land for 4 ploughs. In demesne [are] 3 hides and 3 virgates, and there is 1 plough and there could be another. There 3 villans have 1½ ploughs, and there could be as many more. There is 1 slave, and meadow for 5 ploughs. All together it renders yearly 30s of blanch silver; TRE 30s by tale.

UPTON [in Slough] was Earl Harold's vill. It is assessed at 18 hides. There is land for 10 ploughs. In demesne [are] 2½ hides, and there are 2 ploughs. There 19 villans with 5 bordars have 15 ploughs. There are 2 slaves, and 1 mill rendering 4s. From a fishery, 1,000 eels. [There is] meadow for 2 ploughs, [and] woodland for 200 pigs. All together it renders yearly £21 assayed and weighed; TRE it rendered £15 by tale.

BRILL was King Edward's manor. It has always been assessed at 20 hides. There is land for 25 ploughs. In demesne are 3 [ploughs]. There 19 villans with 13 bordars have 17

ploughs, and there could be 5 more. There are 2 slaves, and 1 mill rendering 10s, meadow for 20 ploughs, [and] woodland for 200 pigs. All together it renders yearly £38 of blanch silver, and for the forest £12 assayed and weighed; TRE it rendered £18 by tale.

IN 'STOTFOLD' HUNDRED

King William holds BIDDLESDEN. Earl Aubrey had it of him. There are 4 hides and 1 virgate. There is land for 8 ploughs. In demesne [are] 2 hides, and there is 1 plough, and there could be 2 more. There 4 villans and 5 bordars have 2 ploughs, and there could be 3 more. There are 4 slaves, and 2 mills rendering 28d, meadow for 1 plough, [and] woodland for 200 pigs. It is worth 30s; when received £4; TRE 40s. Azur son of Thorth, a thegn of King Edward, held this manor.

II. The land of Archbishop Lanfranc

IN STONE HUNDRED

ARCHBISHOP LANFRANC holds HADDENHAM. It is assessed at 40 hides. There is land for 30 ploughs. In demesne [are] 18 hides, and there are 6 ploughs. There 40 villans with 16 bordars have 14 ploughs, and there could be 10 more. There are 15 slaves, and 2 mills rendering 20s, meadow for 6 ploughs, pasture for the livestock, and for the farm of the archbishop 8 days' hay. In all it is worth £40; when received £20; TRE £40. Of this land Gilbert the priest holds of the archbishop 3 hides and 1 church with the tithes. There is land for 1 plough, and there is [1 plough] with 1 villan and 3 bordars. It is and always was worth 60s. This manor Earl Tosti held.

The archbishop himself holds HALTON. It is assessed at 5 hides. There is land for 7 ploughs. In demesne [are] 2½ hides, and there are 2 ploughs. There 10 villans with 15 bordars have 5 ploughs. There is 1 mill rendering 15s, meadow for 2 ploughs, woodland for 100 pigs and 2s [besides]. In all it is and always was worth £8. This manor Earl Leofwine held.

IN RISBOROUGH HUNDRED

The archbishop himself holds MONKS RISBOROUGH. It is assessed at 30 hides. There is land for 14 ploughs. In demesne [are] 16 hides, and there are 2 ploughs. There 32 villans with 8 bordars have 12 ploughs. There are 4 slaves, meadow for 6 ploughs, [and] woodland for 300 pigs. In all it is worth £16; when received 100s; TRE £16. This manor Esger the staller held of Christ Church, Canterbury, but with the condition that it could not be separated from that church TRE.

III. The land of the Bishop of Winchester

WALKELIN, Bishop of Winchester, holds WEST WYCOMBE. It is assessed at 19 hides. There is land for 23 ploughs. In demesne [are] 5 hides, and there are 3 ploughs. There 27 villans with 8 bordars have 19 ploughs. There are 7 slaves, and 3 mills rendering 20s, and 1 fishery rendering 1,000 eels, meadow for 7 ploughs, [and] woodland for 1,000 pigs. In all it is worth £15; when received £10; TRE £12. This manor was and is for the sustenance of the monks of the Church of Winchester. Stigand held it TRE.

IN YARDLEY HUNDRED

The Bishop of Winchester himself holds IVINGHOE. It is assessed at 20 hides. There is land for 25 ploughs. In demesne [are] 5 hides, and there are 3 ploughs, and there could be a fourth. There 28 villans with 4 bordars have 20 ploughs, and there could be 1 more. There are 6 slaves, meadow for 5 ploughs, woodland for 600 pigs and 10s [besides]. In all it is worth £18; when received £10; TRE £15. This manor belonged and belongs to the demesne of the Church of ST PETER of Winchester.

The land of Bishop of Lincoln

IN AYLESBURY HUNDRED

REMIGIUS, Bishop of Lincoln, holds STOKE MANDEVILLE. It is assessed at 8 hides. There is land for 21 ploughs. In demesne [are] 3 hides, and there are 6 ploughs. There 20 villans with 4 bordars have 15 ploughs. There are 3 slaves, and 1 mill rendering 10s, woodland for 30 pigs, [and] meadow for 3 ploughs. This manor belongs to the Church of Aylesbury. There are 18 bordars who pay 20s yearly. In all it is worth £20; when received £12; TRE £18. This manor with the church Bishop Wulfwig held TRE. From the 8 hundreds which lie round Aylesbury each sokeman who has 1 hide or more renders 1 summa of corn to this church. Besides this also 1 acre of corn or 4d was paid by each sokeman to this church TRE, but after the coming of King William it was not paid.

[Folio 144: BUCKINGHAMSHIRE]

Walter holds BUCKLAND of Bishop Remigius. It is assessed at 10 hides. There is land for 8 ploughs. In demesne are 2 [ploughs]; and and [sic] 14 villans with 6 bordars have 6 ploughs. [There is] meadow for 2 ploughs, [and] woodland for 300 pigs. In all it is worth £8; when received £3; TRE £10. This manor Godric, brother of Bishop Wulfwig, held; he could not give or sell it without his leave.

IN BURNHAM HUNDRED

The same Walter holds of the same bishop half a hide. There is land for half a plough. It is and always was worth 5s. This land Leofric, a man of Earl Harold, held and could sell.

IN DESBOROUGH HUNDRED

Walter himself holds of the same bishop WOOBURN. It is assessed at 8½ hides. There is land for 9 ploughs. In demesne are 2 [ploughs]; and 12 villans with 13 bordars have 10 ploughs. There is 1 slave, and 8 mills rendering 104s, [and] meadow for 6 ploughs and for the horses. From a fishery, 300 eels. [There is] woodland for 200 pigs and 7s4d [besides]. In all it is worth £15; when received 100s; TRE £12. This manor Earl Harold held.

In Lude Walter holds of the same bishop 1½ hides. There is land for 2 ploughs. There are 1½ [ploughs], and there could be half [a plough more]. There are 2 villans with 1 bordar. There is 1 slave, and 3 mills rendering 14s. It is and always was

worth 30s. Leofric, a man of Earl Harold, held this manor and could sell it.

IN 'ROWLEY' HUNDRED

The bishop himself holds Gawcott, which belongs to the Church of Buckingham. There is 1 hide. There is land for 1½ ploughs, and there are [1½ ploughs] with 2 bordars and 1 slave. [There is] meadow for half a plough. It is and was worth 30s; TRE 40s. This land Bishop Wulfwig held.

IIII. The land of the Bishop of Bayeux

IN STONE HUNDRED

The BISHOP of Bayeux holds in Stone 7 hides. Helto holds of him. There is land for 7 ploughs. In demesne are 3 [ploughs]; and 1 villan with 15 bordars have 1 plough, and there could be 2 more. There are 7 slaves. [There is] meadow for plough [sic]. In all it is and was worth 100s; TRE £6. This manor 2 brothers held: one a man of Ulf, and the other a man of Eadgifu. They could give or sell it to whom they wished.

The same Helto holds of the same bishop DINTON. It is assessed at 15 hides. There is land for 13 ploughs. In demesne are 3 [ploughs]; and 35 villans with 7 bordars have 10 ploughs. There are 8 slaves, meadow for 13 ploughs, and 1 mill rendering 4s. In all it is and always was worth £15. This manor Avelin, a thegn of King Edward, held.

In Lower Hartwell Helto holds of the bishop 3 hides. There is land for 3 ploughs, and there are [3 ploughs] with 1 villan and 7 bordars, and 1 mill rendering 8s. In all it is and always was worth 50s. This land 3 sokemen held. One, a man of Archbishop Stigand, [held] half a hide; another, a man of Earl Leofwine, 2 hides; the third, a man of Avelin, half a hide; and they could sell and give [their land].

In the same vill Robert holds of the bishop 1 hide. There is land for 2 ploughs. There is 1 [plough], and there could be another. There is 1 villan and 4 slaves. It is and was worth 20s; TRE 40s. This land Avelin, a thegn of King Edward, held and could sell.

Roger holds WESTON TURVILLE of the bishop. It is assessed at 20 hides. There is land for 17 ploughs. In demesne are 3 [ploughs], and there could be a fourth. There 12 villans have 12 ploughs, and there could be 1 more. There are 12 slaves, and 4 mills rendering 33s4d, meadow for 10 ploughs and 6s. [besides], [and] woodland for 100 pigs. In all it is worth £15; when received £8; TRE £15. Of the land of this manor Earl Leofwine held 9½ hides, and Godric the sheriff 3½ hides as 1 manor, and 2 men of the same Godric 3½ hides, and 1 man of Earl Tosti 2 hides, and 2 men of Earl Leofwine 1½ hides. All could sell [their land]. Of these hides, the Bishop of Lisieux has 1 of the Bishop of Bayeux. There is land for 1 plough, but the plough is not there. It is and always was worth 5s. Those men whom Roger holds in Weston Turville [...] did not belong to Earl Leofwine TRE.

Roger himself holds Bedgrove. It is assessed at 2 hides. There is land for 3 ploughs. In demesne is 1 [plough]; and 5 villans with 5 bordars have 2 ploughs. [There is] meadow for 1 plough. It is worth 30s; when received 10s; TRE 40s. This manor Swein, a man of Alwine Varus, held and could sell.

In Bierton the same Roger holds of the bishop 1 hide and 3 virgates. There is land for 1½ ploughs, and there are [1½ ploughs] with 3 bordars. It is and was worth 20s; TRE 50s. This land 2 sokemen held: one a man of Alwine Varus, and the other a man of Earl Leofwine, and they could sell.

IN RISBOROUGH HUNDRED

In HORSENDEN Roger holds of the bishop half a hide. There is land for half a plough, and there is [half a plough] with 1 bordar. It is and was worth 3s; TRE 5s. This land a man of Earl Leofwine held and could sell.

In the same vill Robert holds of the bishop half a hide. There is land for half a plough, but the plough is not there. It is and was worth 2s; TRE 5s. This land Godwine, a man of Earl Leofwine, held and could sell.

IN BURNHAM HUNDRED

In Chalfont St Peter Roger holds of the bishop 4 hides and 3 virgates. There is land for 15 ploughs. In demesne is 1 [plough]; and 14 villans with 4 bordars have 14 ploughs. There are 2 slaves, and 1 mill rendering 6s, meadow for 2 ploughs, woodland for 600 pigs, and a hawk's eyrie. In all it is worth 110s; when received 60s; TRE 110s. This manor Earl Leofwine held.

In Amersham Roger holds of the bishop half a hide. There is land for 1 plough, and there is [1 plough] with 3 bordars, and 1 mill rendering 4s, [and] meadow for 1 plough. This land is and always was worth 20s. This land Alwine, a man of Queen Edith, held and could sell.

In Chesham Roger holds half a hide. There is land for 2 ploughs. In demesne [is] 1 plough; and 1 villan with 2 bordars have 1 plough. [There is] woodland for 50 pigs. It is and always was worth 20s.

In Chesham the Bishop of Bayeux himself holds 1½ hides. There is land for 3 ploughs. In demesne is 1 hide, and there is 1 plough; and 2 villans with 3 bordars have 2 ploughs. There are 2 slaves, and 2 mills rendering 3s, [and] meadow for 3 ploughs. It is and always was worth 60s. This manor 2 sokemen held: one a man of Earl Leofwine, the other a man of Earl Harold, and they could sell.

GILBERT, Bishop of Lisieux, holds of the Bishop of Bayeux 'DILEHURST' [in Taplow]. It is assessed at 10 hides. There is land for 10 ploughs. In demesne are 2 [ploughs], and there could be a third. There 14 villans with 1 bordar have 6 ploughs, and there could be a seventh. There is 1 slave, and 1 mill rendering 3s, meadow for 2 ploughs, [and] woodland for 300 pigs. In all it is worth £6; when received 40s; TRE £6. This manor Earl Leofwine held in demesne.

Roger holds of the bishop TAPLOW. It is assessed at 8 hides and 1 virgate. There is land for 16 ploughs. In demesne is 1 [plough]; and 18 villans with 4 bordars have 15 ploughs. There are 2 slaves. From a fishery, 1,000 eels. [There is] meadow for 1 plough, [and] woodland for 700 pigs. In all it

is worth £8; when received 60s; TRE £9. This manor Asgot, a man of Earl Harold, held, and in the same place 1 man of Archbishop Stigand had 1 hide and could sell it.

[Folio 144V: BUCKINGHAMSHIRE]

IN DESBOROUGH HUNDRED

WILLIAM fitzOgier holds of the bishop HUGHENDEN. It is assessed at 10 hides. There is land for 10 ploughs. In demesne are 2 [ploughs]; and 15 villans with 3 bordars have 8 ploughs. There are 5 slaves, meadow for 2 ploughs, [and] woodland for 600 pigs. In all it is worth £10; when received £6; TRE £7. This manor Queen Edith held.

In West Wycombe Roger holds of the bishop half a hide. There is land for 1 plough, and there is [1 plough] with 1 bordar. It is and was worth 7s; TRE 10s. This land a man of Archbishop Stigand held; he could not sell or give it away from West Wycombe, his manor, as the hundred testifies.

In MARLOW [Marlow or Little Marlow] Tedald holds of the bishop 5 hides. There is land for 4 ploughs. In demesne [are] 1½ hides, and there are 1½ ploughs. There 6 villans with 4 bordars have 2½ ploughs. There is 1 slave, and 1 mill [rendering] 20s. From a fishery, 500 eels. [There is] meadow for 2 ploughs, [and] woodland for 50 pigs. In all it is worth £7; when received £4; TRE as much. This manor Queen Edith held.

In Saunderton Roger holds of the bishop 5 hides. There is land for 5 ploughs. In demesne are 2 [ploughs]; and 13 villans with 3 bordars have 3 ploughs. There are 2 slaves, and 1 mill, meadow for 1 plough, [and] woodland for 50 pigs. It is and was worth 100s; TRE £6. This manor a man of Earl Leofwine held and could sell.

In "Hanechedene" Tedald held of the bishop 3 hides. Now it is of the king's farm. There is land for 7 ploughs. In demesne [is] half a hide, and there are 2 ploughs. There 6 villans, with 3 bordars, and 5 slaves have 5 ploughs. In all it is and was worth 100s; TRE £4. Of this manor Fridebert, a man of Earl Leofwine, held 2½ hides, and Alric Gangemere and his sister held half a hide which TRE was unjustly taken from them.

IN IXHILL HUNDRED

In Waldridge Helto holds of the bishop 2 hides and 1 virgate. There is land for 2 ploughs. In demesne is 1 [plough]; and 2 villans have 1 plough. There is 1 slave, and meadow for 2 ploughs. It is and was worth 20s; TRE 40s. This land 2 sokemen held: one a man of Avelin, and the other a man of Ælfgifu, sister of Earl Harold; they could sell.

In Ilmer Robert holds of the bishop 4 hides. There is land for 5 ploughs. In demesne are 2 [ploughs]; and 8 villans with 1 bordar have 3 ploughs. There are 4 slaves, and 1 mill rendering 10s, [and] meadow for 5 ploughs. It is worth £4; when received 100s; and as much TRE. This manor Godwine, a man of Earl Leofwine, held and could sell.

The same Robert holds of the bishop Aston Sandford as 2 hides. There is land for 5 ploughs. In demesne are 2 [ploughs]; and 7 villans have 3 ploughs. There are 4 slaves, [and] meadow for 5 ploughs. It is worth £4; when received 100s; and as much TRE. This manor Avelin, a thegn of King Edward, held.

IN ASHENDON HUNDRED

In Beachendon 2 Englishmen hold of the bishop 1 virgate. There is land [...]. It is and always was worth 5s. They themselves held it TRE: one a man of Beorhtric, and the other a man of Azur; they could sell.

IN WADDESDON HUNDRED

In [?North] Marston Robert holds 1 hide of the bishop. There is land for 1 plough, and there is [1 plough], [and] meadow for 1 plough. It is and was always worth 20s. This land a man of Azur son of Toti held and could sell.

IN YARDLEY HUNDRED

In Whaddon [in Slapton] Roger holds 3 virgates of the bishop. There is land for half a plough, and there is [half a plough] with 1 villan, [and] meadow for half a plough. It is and was worth 5s; TRE 10s. This land a man held; he could sell it.

IN MURSLEY HUNDRED

TURSTIN de Gironde holds of the bishop DUNTON. It is assessed at 10 hides. There is land for 8 ploughs. In demesne are 2 [ploughs], and there could be a third. There 6 bordars have 3 ploughs, and there could be 2 more. There are 4 slaves, [and] meadow for 8 ploughs. All together it is and was always worth 100s. This manor Earl Leofwine held.

In Drayton Parslow Roger holds of the bishop 3 virgates. There is land for 3 ploughs, and there are [3 ploughs] with 2 villans and 3 bordars. [There is] meadow for plough [sic]. It is and was worth 25s; TRE 30s. This land 2 brothers, men of Alweard Cild, held, and they could sell it.

IN 'STOTFOLD' HUNDRED

In Westbury [near Brackley] Roger holds of the bishop 2½ hides as 1 manor. There is land for 7 ploughs. In demesne are 2 [ploughs]; and 8 villans with 3 bordars have 5 ploughs. There is 1 slave, meadow for 5 ploughs, [and] woodland for 250 pigs. It is worth £3; when received 50s; TRE 60s. This manor Æthelnoth Cild, a thegn of King Edward, held.

The bishop himself holds SHALSTONE, 5 hides, as 1 manor. There is land for 5 ploughs. In demesne are 2 [ploughs]; and 4 villans with 1 bordar have 2 ploughs, and there could be a third. There are 3 slaves, [and] woodland for 50 pigs. It is worth 30s; when received 20s; TRE £4. This manor 2 thegns held as 2 manors, Godric 3 hides and Wiglaf 2 hides, and they could sell to whom they wished.

Robert d'Oilly and Roger d'Ivry hold of the bishop STOWE. It is assessed at 5 hides. There is land for 5 ploughs. In demesne is 1 [plough], and there could be 2 more. There 3 bordars have half a plough, and there could be 1½ [ploughs more]. [There is] meadow for 6 ploughs, [and] woodland for 50 pigs. It is worth 40s; [it was] waste when received; TRE [it was worth] 60s. This manor Thorgisl, a man of Baldwin son of Herluin, held and could sell.

Turstin holds of the bishop Foscote. It is assessed at 6 hides. There is land for 4 ploughs. In demesne are 2 [ploughs]; and 1 villan with 2 bordars have 2 ploughs. There is 1 slave, and meadow for 4 ploughs, [and] woodland for 30 pigs. It is and always was worth £3. This manor Leithr, a thegn of King Edward, held and could sell.

Gilbert Maminot holds of the bishop LECKHAMPSTEAD. It is assessed at 18 [hides]. There is land for 12 ploughs. In demesne are 3 [ploughs], and there could be a fourth. There 18 villans with 6 bordars have 4 ploughs, and there could be another 4. There are 2 slaves, meadow for 12 ploughs, [and] woodland for 400 pigs. In all it is and was worth £6; TRE £8. This manor Earl Leofwine held.

IN 'ROWLEY' HUNDRED

Ernulf de Hesdin holds of the bishop in Lenborough 7 hides as 1 manor. There is land for 5 ploughs. In demesne are 2 [ploughs]; and 1 villan with 6 bordars have 1 plough, and there could be 2 more. There are 3 slaves, [and] meadow for 5 ploughs. From woodland, 4s yearly. It is and was worth 60s; TRE £4. This manor Wiglaf, a man of Earl Leofwine, held and could sell.

Ansgot de Rots holds of the bishop Preston Bissett. It is assessed at 15 hides. There is land for 8 ploughs. In demesne are 3 [ploughs]; and 11 villans with 7 bordars have 5 ploughs. There are 6 slaves, and 1 mill rendering 32d, meadow for 8 ploughs, [and] woodland for 200 pigs. It is worth 100s; when received £4; TRE as much. This manor Wiglaf, a man of Earl Leofwine, held and could sell.

[Folio 145: BUCKINGHAMSHIRE]

Robert of Thame holds of the bishop CHETWODE. It is assessed at 10 hides. There is land for 5 ploughs. In demesne are 2 [ploughs]; and 7 villans with 2 bordars have 2½ ploughs, and there could be half [a plough more]. There are 6 slaves, and 1 mill rendering 30d, meadow for 5 ploughs, [and] woodland for 100 pigs. It is worth 60s; when received 40s; TRE 60s. This manor Æthelnoth the Kentishman, a thegn of King Edward, held and could sell.

Ernulf de Hesdin holds of the bishop Barton Hartshorn. It is assessed at 10 hides. There is land for 5 ploughs. In demesne [are] 2 ploughs. There 3 bordars have 1 plough, and there could be 2 ploughs [more]. There are 4 slaves, [and] meadow for 3 ploughs. From pasture, 30s. [There is] woodland for 100 pigs. In all it is worth £14; when received 40s; TRE 60s. This manor Wiglaf, a thegn of Earl Leofwine, held and could sell.

Ilbert de Lacy holds of the bishop TINGEWICK. It is assessed at 10 hides. There is land for 8 ploughs. In demesne are 3 [ploughs]; and 3 villans with 2 bordars have 4 ploughs, and there could be a fifth. There are 10 slaves, and 1 mill rendering 4s, and from other renders of the vill, 20s. [There is] meadow for 8 ploughs, [and] woodland for 800 pigs. All together it is worth £10; when received £6; TRE £10. This manor Æthelnoth, a thegn of King Edward, held and could sell.

IN 'MOW' HUNDRED

The Bishop of Bayeux himself holds 3 hides and 3 virgates. There is land for 3 ploughs. In demesne [are] 2 hides, and there is half a plough, and there could be 1½ ploughs [more]. There 2 villans with 1 bordar have half a plough. There are 2 slaves, [and] meadow for 2 ploughs. It is worth 20s; when received 13s4d; TRE 40s.

Robert of Romney holds of the bishop in Addington 6 hides. There is land for 6 ploughs. In demesne are 2 [ploughs]; and 8 villans with 2 bordars have 3 ploughs, and there could be a fourth. There are 4 slaves, [and] meadow for 6 ploughs. It is and was worth 60s; TRE 100s. This manor Godwine, a man of Earl Leofwine, held and could sell.

IN BUNSTY HUNDRED

In Lathbury the Bishop of Lisieux holds of the Bishop of Bayeux 1 hide, less 5 feet. There is land for 1 plough, and there is [1 plough] with 3 villans, [and] meadow for 1 plough. It is and was worth 10s; TRE 20s. This land Sigeric, a man of Earl Leofwine, held and could sell.

GAYHURST the Bishop of Lisieux holds of the Bishop of Bayeux, and Robert de Noyers [holds] of him. It is assessed at 5 hides. There is land for 4 ploughs. In demesne are 2 ploughs; and 10 villans have 2 ploughs. There are 2 slaves, and 1 mill rendering 13s4d, meadow for 4 ploughs, [and] woodland for 80 pigs. All together it is and was worth 100s; TRE £8. This manor Sigeric, a man of Earl Leofwine, held and could sell.

In [Great or Little] Brickhill Turstin holds of the bishop 1 hide. There is land for 1 plough, but there is no plough, only 3 villans with 2 bordars. It is and was worth 14s; TRE 20s. This manor Alwine, a man of Æstan, held. He could not give nor sell it away from [Great or Little] Brickhill, Æstan's manor.

V. The land of the Bishop of Coutances

IN IXHILL HUNDRED

The Bishop of Coutances holds WORMINGHALL, and Robert holds of him. It has always been assessed at 5 hides. There is land for 5 ploughs. In demesne are 2 [ploughs]; and 16 villans with 6 bordars have 3 ploughs. There are 4 slaves, meadow for 2 ploughs, [and] woodland for 200 pigs. It is and was worth £6; TRE £7. This manor Eadgifu, wife of Wulfweard, held under Queen Edith and could sell.

IN ASHENDON HUNDRED

The bishop himself holds LUDGERSHALL. It is assessed at 9 hides. There is land for 8 ploughs. In demesne [are] 4 hides, and there are 2 ploughs, and there could be a third. There 13 villans with 4 bordars have 5 ploughs. There are 5 slaves, meadow for 8 ploughs, [and] woodland for 40 pigs. In all it is and was worth 100s; TRE £6. This manor Eadgifu held of Queen Edith and could sell.

Two knights hold OVING of the bishop. It is assessed at 10 hides. There is land for 9 ploughs. In demesne are 4 [ploughs], and there could be a fifth. There 18 villans have 3 ploughs, and there could be a fourth. There are 8 bordars, meadow for 4

ploughs, [and] woodland for 200 pigs. In all it is worth £10; when received 100s; TRE £7. This manor Edwin, a thegn of King Edward, held and could sell.

IN WADDESDON HUNDRED

In [? North] Marston Ranulph holds under the bishop 1 virgate. There is land for half a plough, and there are 2 oxen. It is and always was worth 40d. This land Leofric, a man of Edwin, held and could sell.

IN MURSLEY HUNDRED

In Stewkley William holds 3½ hides as 1 manor. There is land for 9 ploughs. In demesne are 2 ploughs. There 10 villans with 10 bordars have 6½ ploughs, and there could be half [a plough] more. There are 5 slaves, [and] meadow for 8 ploughs. It is and was always worth £4. This manor Wulfweard Cild, a thegn of King Edward, held.

IN 'SECKLEY' HUNDRED

The bishop himself holds SIMPSON as 8 hides and 3 virgates, as 1 manor, of William Bonvalet in pledge. There is land for 8 ploughs. In demesne are 3 hides, and there are 3 ploughs. There 13 villans with 2 bordars have 5 ploughs. There are 6 slaves, and 1 mill rendering 10s, [and] meadow for 8 ploughs. In all it is worth £6; when received 20s; TRE £8. This manor Queen Edith held and could sell.

The bishop himself holds EATON LEYS. It is assessed at 10 hides. There is land for 18 ploughs. In demesne [are] 4 ploughs. There 35 villans with 6 bordars have 14 ploughs. There are 12 slaves, and 1 mill rendering 20s, [and] meadow for 12 ploughs. In all it is worth £12; when received £8; TRE £10. Eadgifu held this manor and could sell it to whom she wished.

IN BUNSTY HUNDRED

LITTLE LINFORD Eadgifu holds of the bishop. It is assessed at 4 hides. There is land for 4 ploughs. In demesne are 2 [ploughs]; and 6 villans have 2 ploughs, and [there is] 1 mill rendering 8s8d, meadow for 4 ploughs, [and] woodland for 40 pigs. It is and was worth 40s; TRE 60s. This manor the same Eadgifu held TRE.

In Lathbury William holds of the bishop 5 hides as 1 manor. There is land for 4 ploughs. In demesne are 2 [ploughs]; and 6 villans with 6 bordars have 2 ploughs. There are 3 slaves, and meadow for 4 ploughs, [and] woodland for 100 pigs. It is worth £4; when received 40s; TRE 60s. This manor Edwin son of Burgræd, a thegn of King Edward, held.

In Tyringham Ansketil holds of the bishop 2½ hides and 3 parts of 1 virgate as 1 manor. There is land for 4 ploughs. In demesne are 3 [ploughs]; and 3 villans with 6 bordars have 1 plough. There are 4 slaves.

[Folio 145V: BUCKINGHAMSHIRE]

All together it is worth 50s; when received 20s; TRE 60s. This land is in exchange for [?] Bleadon [Som.]. This manor 2 thegns held. One, a man of Earl Waltheof, had 2 hides and half a virgate as 1 manor, and the other held 3 parts of 1 virgate, and they could sell.

In Stoke Goldington a certain Englishman holds of the bishop 1 hide and 1 virgate. There is land for 1 plough, and there is [1 plough] with 4 bordars. [There is] meadow for 1 plough, [and] woodland for 50 pigs. It is worth 20s; when received 10s. TRE 20s. This land 2 thegns held as 2 manors. Each held 2½ virgates and they could sell.

In WESTON UNDERWOOD the bishop holds 7½ hides. There is land for 7 ploughs. In demesne is 1 hide, and 1 plough; and 4 villans with 3 bordars have 6 ploughs, and with them are 7 sokemen and a certain Frenchman. There are 3 slaves, meadow for 7 ploughs, [and] woodland for 200 pigs. It is and was worth 100s; TRE £6. This manor 10 thegns held, men of Burgræd, held and could sell, and in the same place was 1 man of Alric [who] had 3 virgates and could sell them.

The bishop himself holds OLNEY. It is assessed at 10 hides. There is land for 10 ploughs. In demesne [are] 3 hides, and there are 3 ploughs. There 24 villans with 5 bordars have 7 ploughs. There are 5 slaves, and 1 mill rendering 40s and 200 eels, meadow for 10 ploughs, [and] woodland for 400 pigs. All together it is worth £12; when received £7; TRE £12. This manor Burgræd held, and there 1 sokeman, his man, had 1½ virgates and could sell them.

In Lavendon the bishop holds 2 hides as 1 manor. There is land for 4 ploughs. In demesne [is] 1 hide, and there are 2 ploughs; and 4 villans with 3 bordars have 2 ploughs. There are 3 slaves, meadow for 1 plough, [and] woodland for 100 pigs. It is worth 40s; when received 20s. TRE 60s. This manor a man of Burgræd held and could sell.

In the same vill William holds of the bishop 4 hides and 2 parts of 1 virgate as 1 manor. There is land for 4 ploughs. In demesne [are] 2 ploughs; and 7 villans with 6 bordars have 2 ploughs. There are 3 slaves, and 1½ mills rendering 27s and 250 eels, meadow for 4 ploughs, [and] woodland for 60 pigs. It is worth 60s; when received 20s; TRE £4. This manor 8 thegns held, and 1 of these, Alli, a man of King Edward, was lord of the others. All could sell their land.

In the same vill Ansketil holds 1½ hides and 2 parts of 1 virgate of the bishop. There is land for 1½ ploughs, and there are [1½ ploughs]. [There is] meadow for the like number, [and] woodland for 12 pigs. It is worth 20s; when received 5s; TRE 20s. This land Burgræd and Wulfric, his man, held and could sell.

In the same vill 3 sokemen hold 1 hide of the bishop, and 1 virgate. There is land for 1 plough. There is half [a plough], and there could be half [a plough more]. There is 1 villan with 2 bordars, meadow for 4 oxen, [and] woodland for 8 pigs. It is and was worth 10s; TRE 20s. This land 2 thegns, Burgræd and Wulfric God's man held and could sell.

IN MOULSOE HUNDRED

In Clifton Reynes Morcar holds 1½ hides of the bishop. There is land for 2 ploughs, and there are [2 ploughs], with 6 villans and 4 bordars. There is 1 slave, meadow for 2 ploughs, and 1

mill. All together it is and was worth 20s; TRE 40s. This manor Alli, a thegn of King Edward, held and could sell. This land is in exchange for [?] Bleadon [Som.], as the bishop's men say.

In the same vill Thorbert holds of the bishop 1 hide. There is land for 1 plough, and there is [1 plough], with 1 villan and 3 bordars. There is 1 slave, meadow for 1 plough, [and] woodland for 20 pigs. It is and was worth 10s; TRE 20s. This land Wulfwine God's man held and could sell.

The bishop himself holds SHERINGTON. It is assessed at 10 hides. There is land for 11 ploughs. In demesne [are] 3 hides, and there are 4 ploughs. There 22 villans with 6 bordars have 6 ploughs, and there could be a seventh. There are 8 slaves, and 1 mill rendering 26s, meadow for 4 ploughs, [and] woodland for 100 pigs. All together it is worth £10; when received £7; TRE £10. Of this manor Edwin son of Burgræd held 6 hides as 1 manor, and Alwine, his man, 1 hide as 1 manor, and Oswulf, a man of King Edward, had 3 hides as 1 manor. These 2 could give and sell their land.

In Emberton 2 thegns hold of the bishop 3 hides. There is land for 2 ploughs, and there are [2 ploughs]. [There is] meadow for 2 ploughs, [and] woodland for 50 pigs. There are 2 villans and 2 bordars. It is and was worth 40s; TRE £4. These men held it who now hold it. One of them, Godric, had 1 hide, and the other, Wulfric, 2 hides as 1 manor; and they could sell.

VI. The land of the Bishop of Lisieux

IN COTTESLOE HUNDRED

The Bishop of Lisieux holds in Crafton 2½ hides. Robert de Noyers holds them of him as 1 manor. There is land for 5 ploughs. In demesne are 2 [ploughs], and there could be a third; and 4 villans with 4 bordars have 2 ploughs. It is and was worth 60s; TRE £4. This manor Blæcmann, a man of Earl Tosti, held. He could not sell without his leave.

IN MOULSOE HUNDRED

In BOW BRICKHILL Robert holds of the bishop 5 hides. [...] There is land for 4 ploughs. In demesne is 1 [plough]; and 7 villans with 3 bordars have 3 ploughs. There is 1 slave, meadow for 4 ploughs, [and] woodland for 150 pigs. It is and was always worth £4. This manor Blæcmann, a man of Earl Tosti, held and could sell.

VII. The land of St Peter of Westminster

IN STOKE HUNDRED

THE ABBOT OF ST PETER of Westminster holds DENHAM. It is assessed at 10 hides. There is land for 12 ploughs. In demesne [are] 3 hides, and there are 2 ploughs. There 15 villans with 3 bordars have 7 ploughs, and there could be 3 more. [There is] meadow for 12 ploughs, and 2 mills rendering 7s, and 3 fisheries render 3s yearly [There is] woodland for 300 pigs. In all it is and was worth £7; TRE £10. This manor Wulfstan the thegn gave to ST PETER of

Westminster and there it belonged in demesne on the day on which King Edward was alive and dead.

IN BURNHAM HUNDRED

The abbot himself holds in EAST BURNHAM 8 hides. There is land for 6 ploughs. In demesne [are] 4 hides, and there is 1 plough; and 6 villans with 1 bordar have 5 ploughs. [There is] meadow for 6 ploughs, [and] woodland for 100 pigs. In all it is worth 100s and 28d; when received the same; TRE £6. This manor 3 thegns held TRE and could sell, and yet these 3 paid yearly 5 orae as a customary due to the minster of Staines. One of these, Wulfric, had 3 hides and 3 virgates, and another, a man of Eadric of Marlow, had 3 hides and 1 virgate, and the third had 1 hide: he was a man of Sæwulf.

VIII. The land of St Alban

IN WADDESDON HUNDRED

THE ABBOT OF ST ALBAN'S holds GRAN-BOROUGH. It is assessed at 5 hides. There is land for 9 ploughs. In demesne [are] 2 hides, and there are 2 ploughs; and 7 villans with 4 bordars have 7 ploughs. There is 1 slave, [and] meadow for 2 ploughs. All together it is worth it is worth [sic] 100s; when received £4; TRE 100s. This manor belonged and belongs to the demesne of the Church of St Alban.

IN COTTESLOE HUNDRED

The abbot himself holds ASTON ABBOTS. It is assessed at 10 hides. There is land for 12 ploughs. In demesne [are] 6 hides, and there are 3 ploughs, and there could be 2 more. There 7 villans with 12 bordars have 6 ploughs. There is 1 slave, [and] meadow for 3 ploughs. It is worth £10; when received £6; TRE £10. This manor belonged and belongs to the demesne of the Church of St Alban.

[Folio 146: BUCKINGHAMSHIRE]

IN MURSLEY HUNDRED

The abbot himself holds WINSLOW. It is assessed at 15 hides. There is land for 19 ploughs. In demesne [are] 5 hides, and there are 3 ploughs, and there could be a fourth. There 17 villans with 5 bordars have 15 ploughs. There are 3 slaves, [and] meadow for 19 ploughs. From woodland, 10s yearly. In all it is and always was worth £11.13s4d. This manor belonged and belongs to the demesne of the Church of St Alban.

IX. The land of the Church of Barking

IN YARDLEY HUNDRED

THE ABBESS of Barking holds SLAPTON. It is assessed at 6 hides. There is land for 6 ploughs. In demesne [is] 1 hide, and there are 2 ploughs; and 18 villans with 4 bordars have 4 ploughs. There are 4 slaves, [and] meadow for 6 ploughs. In all it is and always was worth £6. This manor belonged and belongs to the Church of Barking.

X. The land of the Canons of Oxford

IN ASHENDON HUNDRED

THE CANONS of Oxford hold of the king UPPER WINCHENDON. It is assessed at 10 hides. There is land for 9 ploughs. In demesne [are] 1½ hides, and there are 2 ploughs; and 18 villans with 1 bordar have 7 ploughs. There is 1 slave, [and] meadow for 2 ploughs. In all it is and was worth £6; TRE £8. This manor belonged and belongs to the demesne of the Church of the canons of Oxford.

XI. The land of Regenbald the Priest

IN BURNHAM HUNDRED

REGENBALD the priest holds of the king 1 hide in Boveney which belongs to the Church of Cookham. There is land for 1 plough, and there is [1 plough] with 1 villan. [There is] meadow for 1 plough. It is and always was worth 10s. This man held it in alms of King Edward.

XII. The land of the Count of Mortain

IN STONE HUNDRED

THE COUNT OF MORTAIN holds in Little Missenden 1 hide, and Vigot holds of him. There is land for 1½ ploughs. There is 1 plough, and there could be half [a plough more]. There are 4 bordars, meadow for 1 plough, [and] woodland for 100 pigs. It is and was worth 100s; TRE 40s. This land Alwine, a man of Sigeræd son of Sibbi, held and could sell.

IN RISBOROUGH HUNDRED

In Horsenden Ralph holds of the count 6 hides and 3 virgates. There is land for 4 ploughs. In demesne is 1 [plough]; and 7 villans with 1 bordar have 3 ploughs. There are 2 slaves, and 1 mill rendering nothing, [and] meadow for 1 plough. It is and was worth 50s; TRE 100s. This manor 3 sokemen held; 2 of these, men of Earl Harold, had 2 hides, and the third, a man of Ingeld, had 4 hides and 3 virgates. All, however, could sell.

The count HIMSELF holds BLEDLOW. It is assessed at 30 hides. There is land for 18 ploughs. In demesne [are] 16 hides, and there are 4 ploughs; and 32 villans with 3 bordars have 14 ploughs. There are 8 slaves, and 1 mill rendering 24 summae of malt, woodland for 1,000 pigs and from the rents of the woodland enough iron for the ploughs, [and] meadow for 18 ploughs. In all it is worth £22; when received £12; TRE £20. This manor Eadmær Atule, a thegn of King Edward, held and could sell.

IN BURNHAM HUNDRED

In Amersham Almær holds of the count half a hide. There is land for 2 ploughs, and there are [2 ploughs] with 1 villan and 1 bordar. [There is] meadow for 2 ploughs, [and] woodland for 20 pigs. It is and always was worth 20s. This land Siward, a man of Ealdgifu, held and could sell.

IN DESBOROUGH HUNDRED

In West Wycombe William holds of the count half a hide. There is land for half a plough, and there is [half a plough] with 1 bordar. It is and always was worth 10s. This land 1 sokeman, a man of Archbishop Stigand, held. He could not give nor sell it away from the manor of West Wycombe on the day on which King Edward was alive and dead, as the hundred testifies.

IN IXHILL HUNDRED

In Ickford the monks of Grestain hold 6 hides of the count. There is land for 6 ploughs. In demesne [are] 3 hides, and there are 2 ploughs, and there could be 2 others. There 3 villans with 10 bordars have 2 ploughs. [There is] meadow for 6 ploughs. It is and was worth £6; TRE £7. This manor Ulf, a man of Earl Harold, held and could sell.

IN COTTESLOE HUNDRED

The count himself holds WING. It is assessed at 5 hides. There is land for 40 ploughs. In demesne is 1 hide, and there are 4 ploughs. There 51 villans with 20 bordars have 21 ploughs, and there could be 15 more ploughs. [There is] meadow for 25 ploughs. From the pasture, iron for 5 ploughs. In all it is worth £31; when received the same; TRE £32. This manor Edward Cild, a man of Earl Harold, held and could sell.

In Crafton the monks of Saint-Nicolas hold 2½ hides of the count. There is land for 5 ploughs. In demesne are 3 [ploughs]; and 8 villans have 2 ploughs. [There is] meadow for 5 ploughs. It is and was worth £4; TRE £6. This manor Edward Cild held and could sell.

In Wingrave Alan holds 1½ hides of the count. There is land for 1 plough. There is 1 [plough], and there could be half [a plough more]. There is 1 villan and 1 bordar, [and] meadow for 1 plough. It is and always was worth 20s. This land Ordmær, a man of Beorhtric, held and could sell.

In Helsthorpe Ranulph holds of the count 3 virgates. There is land for 1 plough, and there is [1 plough] with 2 bordars. There is 1 slave, and meadow for 1 plough. It is and always was worth 20s. This land Leofwine, a man of Godric, held and could sell.

In Hardwick Almær holds of the count 2 hides. There is land for 2 ploughs, and there are [2 ploughs], with 2 villans and 1 bordar. There is 1 slave, [and] meadow for 2 ploughs. It is and always was worth 40s. This land Sæweard, a man of Earl Harold, held and could sell.

In [Lower or Upper] Burston Alan holds of the count 2 hides. There is land for 2 ploughs. In demesne is 1 [plough]; and 3 villans with 1 bordar have 1 plough. [There is] meadow for 2 ploughs. It is worth 30s; when received 10s; TRE 40s. This land 3 thegns held. V [sic] Of these one [was] a man of Earl Leofwine, another a man of Godwine Cild, Abbot of Westminster, the third a man of Alfred of Wing; and all could sell their land.

In the same vill Almær holds 1 virgate of the count, and there are 2 villans. It is and was worth 5s. This land Siward, a man of Earl Harold, held and could sell.

IN YARDLEY HUNDRED

In Drayton Beauchamp William fitzNigel holds 1½ hides. There is land for 1 plough. [There is] meadow for 1 plough, [and] woodland for 25 pigs. It is and always was worth 20s. This land a widow held of Beorhtric and could sell.

In the same vill Leofsige holds of the count 1½ hides and 2 parts of 1 virgate. There is land for 1 plough. There are 2 villans and 2 slaves, meadow for 1 plough, [and] woodland for 25 pigs. It is and always was worth 20s. This land Wicga, a man of King Edward, held and could sell.

In Pitstone Ralph holds of the count 3 hides and 1 virgate as 1 manor. There is land for 1 plough, and there is [1 plough] with 1 bordar. [There is] woodland for 30 pigs. It is worth 20s; when received 5s; TRE 25s. This land Ælfgeat of Aylesbury held and could sell.

In the same vill Bernard holds of the count 3 hides and 1 virgate as 1 manor. There is land for 1 plough. There is half [a plough], and there could be half [a plough more]. There are 2 bordars, [and] woodland for 30 pigs. It is and always was worth 20s. This land 2 men of the Abbot of St Alban's held and could sell.

In the same vill Fulcold holds of the count 1 hide and 1 virgate. There is land for 4 oxen, and there are [4 oxen]. [There is] woodland for 10 pigs. It is and always was worth 10s. This land Glædwine, a man of the Abbot of St Alban's, held and could sell.

[Folio 146V: BUCKINGHAMSHIRE]

From the manor of Pitstone, Turgis the count's man, took away 6 hides which the count himself holds unjustly in his demesne.

In Ivinghoe Aston Ralph holds of the count 3 virgates. There is land for half a plough, and there is [half a plough] with 1 villan. It is and was worth 5s; TRE 10s. This land Godwine, a priest of Archbishop Stigand, held and could sell.

In Cheddington Ralph holds of the count 1 hide and 1 virgate. There is land for 1 plough, and there is [1 plough] with 1 bordar. It is and always was worth 10s. This land 3 men of Archbishop Stigand held and could sell.

In the same vill Ranulph holds of the count half a hide. There is land for half a plough, and there is [half a plough] with 1 villan. It is and always was worth 10s. This land Lyfing, a man of the Abbot of St Alban's, held and could sell.

In Horton [in Ivinghoe] Æfstan holds of the count 1 virgate. There is land for 2 oxen. It is and was worth 2s. This land Brunmann, a man of Archbishop Stigand, held and could sell.

IN MURSLEY HUNDRED

In Swanbourne Ralph and Almær hold 5 hides. There is land for 5 ploughs. There is 1 [plough], and there could be 4 [more]. There are 2 villans, [and] meadow for 5 ploughs. This land is worth 40s; when received £6; TRE 100s. Of this manor

Beorhtwine, a thegn of King Edward, held 4½ hides, and Almær, a man of Earl Harold, 1½ hides, and they could sell.

In Salden Ralph holds of the count 3 hides and half a virgate as 1 manor. There is land for 3 ploughs, and there are [3 ploughs], with 3 villans and 2 bordars. [There is] meadow for 3 ploughs. It is and was worth 30s; TRE 40s. This manor 4 thegns held. Of these one [was] a man of Alwine, and another a man of Alwine of Newham, and the third a man of Alweard, and the fourth a man of Azur. All these could sell.

In Mursley Alvred holds of the count 1 hide. There is land for half a plough. It is and was worth 7s; TRE 10s. This land Edwin, a man of Azur, held and could sell.

IN 'STOTFOLD' HUNDRED

In Biddlesden the same count holds 3 virgates. There is land for 1 plough, but it has been laid waste. This land Alric, a man of Alwine son of Goding, held and could sell.

IN 'ROWLEY' HUNDRED

In Hillesden Ranulph holds of the count 1 hide. There is land for 1 plough, and there is [1 plough] with 3 bordars. [There is] meadow for 1 plough, [and] woodland for 10 pigs. It is worth 30s; when received 12s; TRE 30s. This land Leofwine, a man of Ælfric son of Goding, held and could sell.

IN 'MOW' HUNDRED

In MARSH GIBBON the monks of Grestain hold 11 hides of the count. There is land for 13 ploughs. In demesne [are] 4 hides, and there are 3 ploughs. There 17 villans with 3 bordars have 10 ploughs. There are 8 slaves. All together it is and always was worth £8. This manor Ulfson of Burgræd held and could sell, and a man of Bondi the staller had there half a hide and could sell it.

IN 'SECKLEY' HUNDRED

In Caldecote Alvred holds 4 hides and 1 virgate of the count as 1 manor. There is land for 4 ploughs. In demesne are 1½ [ploughs], and there could be half [a plough] more. There are 2 vavasours paying 32s6d, and 1 villan and 5 bordars with 2 ploughs. There is 1 slave, and a mill rendering 5 orae and 4d, meadow for 2 ploughs, [and] woodland for 24 pigs and 28d as a customary due. In all it is and always was worth £4. This manor 4 thegns held TRE and they could sell and give it to whom they wished.

In Woughton on the Green Ralph holds of the count 4 hides as 1 manor. There is land for 4 ploughs. In demesne is 1 [plough], and there could be another. There 3 villans with 6 bordars have 1 plough, and there could be another. There are 2 slaves, [and] meadow for 4 ploughs. All together it is worth £3; when received £4; TRE £3. This manor 8 thegns held. Of these, 4, the men of Ælfric Varus, had half a hide, and 1, a man of Ælfric; son of Goding, 1 hide and half a virgate, and 1, a man of Wulfweard son of Eadgifu, 1 hide and 1 virgate, and 1, a man of Leofwine son of Æstan, half a hide, and 1, a man of Baldwin, half a hide, and 1, a man of Morcar, half a hide, and 1, a man of Sæweald, had 1 virgate. All these could sell.

In Loughton Walter holds of the count half a hide. There is

land for half a plough, and there is [half a plough] with 1 villan. This land is worth 20s; when received 5s; TRE 20s. This land Almær, a man of Ælfric son of Goding, held and could sell.

In Great Linford Ranulph holds of the count 2 hides. There is land for 2 ploughs, and there are [2 ploughs], with 4 villans and 3 bordars and 1 slave. [There is] meadow for 2 ploughs. It is and was always worth 40s. This land 2 men of Ælfric son of Goding held and could sell.

IN BUNSTY HUNDRED

In Weston Underwood Ivo holds of the count 1 hide and 2 parts of 1 virgate. There is land for 1 plough. There are 2 oxen with 2 bordars, meadow for 1 plough, [and] woodland for 20 pigs. It is and always was worth 20s. This land 3 thegns held. Of these, 2, men of Burgræd had 3 virgates and 2 parts of 1 virgate, the third, a man of Ælfric son of Goding, 1 virgate, and they could sell.

In Lavendon Humphrey holds of the count 2½ hides as 1 manor. There is land for 2½ ploughs. In demesne [are] 1½ hides, and there is 1 plough; and 3 villans with 5 bordars have 1½ ploughs. There are 2 slaves, and 1 mill rendering 10s and 50 eels, meadow for 2 ploughs, [and] woodland for 40 pigs. It is worth 40s; when received 20s; TRE £4. This manor a man of Ælfric son of Goding held and could sell.

IN MOULSOE HUNDRED

In Wavendon Ralph holds of the count 2 hides as 1 manor. There is land for 2½ ploughs. In demesne is 1 [plough]; and 2 villans with 3 bordars have 1 plough, and there could be half [a plough more]. There is 1 slave, and meadow for 2 ploughs, [and] woodland for 15 pigs. It is worth 20s when received 10s; TRE 40s. This manor Goldnir, a housecarl of King Edward, held and could sell.

In the same [vill], Walter holds of the count 2 hides as 1 manor. There is land for 2½ ploughs. In demesne is 1 [plough]; and 2 villans with 3 bordars have 1 plough, and there could be half [a plough] more. There are 2 slaves, meadow for 2 ploughs, [and] woodland for 15 pigs. It is worth 20s; when received 10s; TRE 40s. This manor Beorhtwine, a man of Earl Harold, held and could sell.

In the same vill Humphrey holds of the count 3 virgates. There is land for 1 plough. There is 1 bordar, [and] meadow for 1 plough. It is and was worth 5s; TRE 10s. This land Centisc, a man of Leofnoth son of Osmund, held and could sell.

XIII. The land of Earl Hugh

IN COTTESLOE HUNDRED

Earl HUGH holds MENTMORE. Robert holds it of him. It is assessed at 18 hides. There is land for 10 ploughs. In demesne [are] 4 ploughs; and 18 villans have 6 ploughs. There are 3 slaves, [and] meadow for 4 ploughs. In all it is worth £12; when received £10; TRE £14. This manor Eadgifu the Fair held.

IN 'SECKLEY' HUNDRED

Hugh holds of the earl SHENLEY CHURCH END. It is assessed at 2 hides. There is land for 10 ploughs. In demesne are 3 ploughs; and 5 villans with 6 slaves have 5 ploughs, and there could be 2 more. [There is] meadow for 5 ploughs, [and] woodland for 50 pigs. It is and was worth 100s; TRE £6. This manor Burgheard, a housecarl of King Edward, held and could sell.

[Folio 147: BUCKINGHAMSHIRE]

In Shenley Church End Hugh holds of Earl Hugh 5 hides as 1 manor. There is land for 5 ploughs, and there are 4 ploughs, and there could be a fifth. There are 8 villans, meadow for 5 ploughs, [and] woodland for 50 pigs. In all it is and was worth £3; TRE £4. This manor Burgheard, a thegn of King Edward, held.

IN MOULSOE HUNDRED

William holds [Great or Little] BRICKHILL. It is assessed at 9 hides. There is land for 9 ploughs. In demesne [are] 4 ploughs; and 16 villans with 6 bordars have 6 s [sic] ploughs. There are 6 slaves, and 2 mills rendering 30s, meadow for 10 ploughs, [and] woodland for 100 pigs. All together it is worth £9; when received £7; TRE £10. This manor Earl Tosti held.

XIIII. The land of Walter Giffard

IN STONE HUNDRED

WALTER Giffard holds in Lower Hartwell 2 hides, and Hugh de Bolbec [holds] of him. There is land for 2 ploughs, and there are [2 ploughs], with 4 villans and 3 bordars. There are 4 slaves. It is and always was worth 30s. This land 2 men of Sigeræd held and could sell, and they now hold it.

Hugh himself holds of Walter GREAT KIMBLE. It is assessed at 20 hides. There is land for $11\frac{1}{2}$ ploughs. In demesne are 2 [ploughs], and there could be a third. There 22 villans with 8 bordars have $8\frac{1}{2}$ ploughs. There are 6 slaves, meadow for 11 ploughs, [and] wood for fences. In all it is and always was worth £10. This manor Sigeræd, a thegn of King Edward, held and could sell.

Turstin fitzRolf holds of Walter GREAT MISSENDEN. It is assessed at 10 hides. There is land for 8 ploughs. In demesne are 2 [ploughs]; and 9 villans with 1 bordar have 6 ploughs. There are 2 slaves, meadow for 2 ploughs, woodland for 500 pigs, and from the rents of the woodland, 4 orae yearly. In all it is and was worth £4; TRE £7. This manor Sigeræd son of Ælfgifu, a thegn of King Edward, held and could sell.

IN DESBOROUGH HUNDRED

Herbrand holds of Walter FAWLEY. It is assessed at 10 hides. There is land for 14 ploughs. In demesne are 2 ploughs; and 13 villans with 1 bordar have 12 ploughs. There are 5 slaves, meadow for 2 ploughs, [and] woodland for 100 pigs. All together it is worth £6; when received 100s; TRE £6. This manor Earl Tosti held.

IN IXHILL HUNDRED

Walter himself holds LONG CRENDON. It is assessed at 20 hides. There is land for 25 ploughs. In demesne [are] 10 hides, and there are 5 ploughs; and 52 villans with 10 bordars have 20 ploughs. There are 10 slaves, and 1 mill rendering 18s, meadow for 10 ploughs, woodland for 100 pigs, and there is a park for wild beasts. In all it is worth £20; when received and TRE £15. This manor Særic son of Ælfgifu, held.

Hugh holds of Walter ADDINGROVE. It is assessed at $3\frac{1}{2}$ hides. There is land for 4 ploughs. In demesne are 2 [ploughs]; and 2 villans with 7 bordars have 3 ploughs. There is 1 slave, [and] meadow for 1 plough. All together it is worth 60s; when received 40s; TRE £4. This manor Wulfweard, a man of Queen Edith, held and could sell.

Walter himself holds CHILTON. It is assessed at 10 hides. There is land for 10 ploughs. In demesne [are] 4 hides, and there are 4 ploughs; and 10 villans with 4 bordars have 6 ploughs. There are 3 slaves, meadow for 3 ploughs, [and] woodland for 100 pigs. All together it is worth £7; when received £8; and as much TRE. This manor, Ælfric son of Goding, a thegn of King Edward, held.

Roger holds of Walter EASINGTON. It is assessed at 5 hides. There is land for 4 ploughs. In demesne are 2 [ploughs]; and 5 villans have 2 [ploughs]. There are 2 slaves, and meadow for 2 ploughs. It is and always was worth 60s. This manor Ælfric son of Goding held and could sell.

Walter himself holds DORTON. It is assessed at 5 hides. There is land for 7 ploughs. In demesne [are] $2\frac{1}{2}$ hides, and there are 3 ploughs. There 12 villans with 6 bordars have 4 ploughs. There are 3 slaves, meadow for 3 ploughs, [and] woodland for 100 pigs. In all it is and always was worth 100s. This manor Ælfric, a thegn of King Edward, held and could sell.

IN ASHENDON HUNDRED

Walter himself holds [Lower or Upper] POLLICOTT. It is assessed at 10 hides. There is land for 8 ploughs. 2 knights hold it of Walter. In demesne [are] 4 ploughs; and 13 villans with 1 bordars have 4 ploughs. There are 4 slaves, [and] meadow for 8 ploughs. In all it is and was worth £6; TRE £7. Ælfric son of Goding held 5 hides of this manor, and 3 brothers held 5 hides, and they could sell to whom they wished.

In ASHENDON Richard holds of Walter 8 hides. There is land for 6 ploughs. In demesne are 2 [ploughs]; and 4 villans with 4 bordars have 4 ploughs. There are 2 slaves, and meadow for 6 ploughs. In all it is worth £3; when received £4; TRE 100s. This manor 3 brothers held and could sell to whom they wished.

In CHEARSLEY Earnwulf and Geoffrey hold of Walter $8\frac{1}{2}$ hides. There is land for 6 ploughs. In demesne [are] 4 ploughs; and 6 villans with 2 bordars have 2 ploughs. There are 4 slaves, [and] meadow for 6 ploughs. It is and was worth £6; TRE £7. This manor 6 thegns held and could sell to whom they wished.

Walter himself holds LOWER WINCHENDON. It is assessed at 10 hides. There is land for 11 ploughs. In demesne [are] 3 hides, and there are 3 ploughs; and 23 villans with 8 bordars have 8 ploughs. There is 1 slave, and meadow for 7 ploughs, and 1 mill rendering 20s and 80 eels. In all it is and always was worth £12. This manor Edith held of Queen Edith.

Ralph holds of Walter WOTTON UNDERWOOD. It is assessed at 10 hides. There is land for 10 ploughs. In demesne are 3 [ploughs]; and 10 villans with 13 bordars have 7 ploughs. There are 5 slaves, and meadow for 5 ploughs, [and] woodland for 200 pigs. All together it is and was worth £7; TRE £8. This manor Eadgifu, wife of Wulfweard, held and could sell.

IN COTTESLOE HUNDRED

Two Englishmen hold of Walter in this hundred 1 virgate. There is land for half a plough, [and] meadow for half a plough. It is and always was worth 3½s. These men who hold it held it TRE and could sell.

Hugh de Bolbec holds of Walter WHITCHURCH. It is assessed at 8 hides. There is land for 12 ploughs. In demesne [are] 3 ploughs, and there could be 2 [more]. There 14 villans with 2 bordars have 7 ploughs. There are 8 slaves, [and] meadow for 6 ploughs. All together it is and was worth £8; TRE £10. This manor 2 brothers, thegns of King Edward, held as 2 manors and could sell.

In Littlecote Robert holds of Walter 2½ hides as 1 manor. There is land for 3 ploughs. In demesne [are] 2 ploughs; and 2 villans with 3 bordars have 1 plough. There are 3 slaves, and meadow for 1 plough. This land is and was worth 40s; TRE 60s. This manor Wicga, a thegn of King Edward, held and could sell.

In [Lower or Upper] Burston Turstin holds of Walter 1 hide. There is land for 1 plough, and there is [1 plough], with 2 bordars and 1 slave. [There is] meadows for 1 plough. It is worth 20s; when received 10s; TRE 20s. This land Alwynn, a certain woman, held under Siward, and she could sell it.

IN YARDLEY HUNDRED

Ralph holds of Walter in Pitstone 5½ hides as 1 manor. There is land for 2 ploughs, and there are [2 ploughs], with 3 villans and 3 bordars and 1 slave. [There is] woodland for 40 pigs. It is worth 40s; when received 20s; TRE 40s. This manor Thorulf, a man of Earl Leofwine, held and could sell.

IN MURSLEY HUNDRED

William holds of Walter in SWANBOURNE 7 hides and 3 virgates as 1 manor. There is land for 7 ploughs. In demesne are 2 [ploughs]; and 7 villans with 5 bordars have 4 ploughs. There are 2 slaves, [and] meadow for 6 ploughs. All together it is and was worth £4; TRE 100s.

[Folio 147V: BUCKINGHAMSHIRE]

This manor 2 thegns held-Alweard 5 hides all but 1 virgate, and Alwig his man, 2 hides and 3 virgates. They had them as 2 manors and could sell them.

Walter himself holds [Great and Little] HORWOOD. It is assessed at 10 hides. There is land for 9 ploughs. In demesne [are] 5 hides, and there are 4 ploughs; and 8 villans with 10 bordars have 5 ploughs. There are 2 slaves, and meadow for 9 ploughs, [and] woodland for 100 pigs. In all it is and always was worth £7. This manor Alweard Cild, a thegon of King Edward, held.

Walter de Bec holds of Walter Singleborough. It is assessed at 6 hides. There is land for 6 ploughs. In demesne are 3 ploughs; and 4 villans with 4 bordars have 3 ploughs. There are 4 slaves, and meadow for 3 ploughs, [and] woodland for 40 pigs. In all it is and always was worth £4. This manor Edward Cild, a thegn of King Edward, held.

Walter himself holds WHADDON [near Bletchley]. It is assessed at 10 hides. There is land for 10 ploughs. In demesne [are] 5 hides, and there are 5 ploughs; and 14 villans with 9 bordars have 5 ploughs. There are 10 slaves, meadow for 10 ploughs, [and] woodland for 100 pigs. In all it is and always was worth £8. This manor Edward Cild, a thegn of King Edward, held.

In MURSLEY William holds of Walter 5 hides as 1 manor. There is land for 4 ploughs. In demesne are 2 [ploughs]; and 2 villans with 5 bordars have 2 ploughs. There are 2 slaves, [and] meadow for 2 ploughs. It is and always was worth £3.

In LAMPORT Berner holds of Walter 3½ hides as 1 manor. There is land for 4 ploughs. In demesne is 1 [plough], and there could be another. There 2 villans with 2 bordars have 2 ploughs. There are 2 slaves, meadow for 2 ploughs, [and] woodland for 50 pigs. It is and always was worth 40s. This manor Swein Swart, a man of Earl Edwin, held and could sell.

Robert holds of Walter AKELEY. It is assessed at 3 hides. There is land for 4 ploughs. In demesne are 4 oxen, and there could be 2 ploughs [more]. There 2 villans with 4 bordars have 2½ ploughs. There are 2 slaves, meadow for 1 plough, [and] woodland for 806 pigs. In all it is and was worth 40s; TRE 60s. This manor Ælfric son of Goding held and could sell.

Hugh holds of Walter LILLINGSTONE DAYRELL. It is assessed at 5 hides. There is land for 5 ploughs. In demesne are 1½ [ploughs], and there could be half [a plough more]. There 6 villans with 5 bordars have 2 ploughs, and there could be a third. [There is] meadow for 5 ploughs, [and] woodland for 1,200 pigs. It is worth 60s; when received 40s; TRE 50s. This manor Sigeric, a man of Queen Edith, held and could sell.

In MAIDS MORETON Turstin holds of Walter 2 hides. There is land for 2 ploughs, and there are 1½ [ploughs], and there could be half [a plough more]. There are 2 villans and 4 bordars, [and] meadow for 2 ploughs. It is worth 30s; when received 10s; TRE 20s. This manor Wulfric, a man of Ælfric son of Goding, held and could sell.

In the same vill the same Turstin holds of Walter 4 hides as 1 manor. There is land for 4 ploughs. In demesne are 2 [ploughs], and there could be another 2. There is 1 villan with 3 bordars, [and] meadow for 4 ploughs. It is worth £4; when received 20s; TRE 60s. Of this manor Ælfric son of Goding held 2 hides as 1 manor, and Eadric, a man of Esger the staller, 1½ hides as 1 manor, and Sæweard, a man of Azur son of Toti, held half a hide, and they could give and sell [their land].

In Leckhampstead Hugh holds of Walter 2 hides. There is land for 1 plough, and there is [1 plough], with 1 villan and 2 bordars and 1 slave. There is 1 mill rendering 20d, meadow for 1 plough, [and] woodland for 50 pigs. In all it is worth 30s; when received 20s; TRE 30s. This manor Swærting, a man of Esger the staller, held. He could neither sell nor give it but by his leave.

IN 'ROWLEY' HUNDRED

In Beachampton Hugh holds of Walter 5 hides as 1 manor. There is land for 5 ploughs. In demesne are 2 [ploughs]; and 5 villans with 9 bordars have 3 ploughs. There is 1 slave, and 1 mill rendering 10s, [and] meadow for 2 ploughs. In all it is worth £4; when received 30s; TRE £4.10s. This manor Ælfric, a man and thegn of King Edward, held and could sell.

The same Hugh holds Bourton of Walter. It is assessed at 1 hide. There is land for 2 ploughs. In demesne is 1 [plough]; and 2 villans with 2 bordars have 1 plough. [There is] meadow for 2 ploughs. It is and was worth 30s; TRE 20s. This manor Ælfric, a thegn of King Edward, held and could sell.

In Lenborough Ralph holds of Walter 3 hides as 1 manor. There is land for 2 ploughs. There is 1 [plough], and there could be another. There are 2 bordars, and meadow for 2 ploughs. It is worth 30s; when received 60s; TRE 40s. This manor Tovi, a man of Ælfric son of Goding, held and could sell.

In Hillesden Hugh holds of Walter 18 hides as 1 manor. There is land for 14 ploughs. In demesne are 4 [ploughs]; and 17 villans with 9 bordars have 10 ploughs. There are 7 slaves, and 1 mill rendering 4s, meadow for 14 ploughs, [and] woodland for 100 pigs. In all it is worth £6; when received £8; and as much TRE. This manor Ælfric, a thegn of King Edward, held and could sell.

Ralph holds of Walter EDGCOTT. It is assessed at 5 hides. There is land for 8 ploughs. In demesne are 2 [ploughs]; and 10 villans with 9 bordars have 6 ploughs. There are 2 slaves, meadow for 2 ploughs, [and] woodland for 100 pigs. In all it is and was worth 100s. This manor 4 thegns held. One of these, Alwine, had 2½ hides as 1 manor, and another, Edwin, 1 hide and 1 virgate as 1 manor, and Almær half a hide, and Thorir, a housecarl of King Edward, 3 virgates. All could sell [their land].

In Woolstone Ralph [...] holds of Walter 3½ hides as 1 manor. There is land for 3 ploughs. In demesne are 2 [ploughs]; and 4 villans have 1 plough. [There is] meadow for 2 ploughs, and 1 mill rendering 10s. It is worth 40s; when received 20s; TRE 60s. This manor Edward, a thegn of King Edward, held and could sell.

In Woolstone the monks of Saint-Pierre-de-la-Couture hold of Walter 5 hides as 1 manor. There is land for 5 ploughs. In demesne are 2 [ploughs]; and 8 villans with 1 bordar have 3

ploughs. There is 1 mill rendering 6s4d, meadow for 4 ploughs, [and] woodland for 100 pigs. It is and was worth £3; TRE £4. This manor Ælfric son of Goding held and could sell.

Walter himself holds NEWTON LONGVILLE. It is assessed at 10 hides. There is land for 12 ploughs. In demesne [are] 4 hides, and there are 4 ploughs; and 20 villans with 8 bordars have 8 ploughs. There are 11 slaves, and meadow for 6 ploughs. In all it is worth £12; when received £10; and as much TRE. This manor Edward Cild held.

In Loughton Ivo holds of Walter 4½ hides. There is land for 4½ ploughs. In demesne are 2 [ploughs]; and 5 villans with 2 bordars have 1 plough, and there could be another 1½ [ploughs]. [There is] meadow for 4 ploughs. It is worth 60s; when received 30s; TRE £4. This manor 5 thegns held and could sell.

[Folio 148: BUCKINGHAMSHIRE]

In Bradwell Walter Hackett holds of Walter Giffard 1½ hides. There is land for 2 ploughs. In demesne is 1 [plough], and there could be another. There is 1 bordar and 1 slave, [and] meadow for 1 plough. It is worth 20s; when received 10s; TRE 30s. This land Ælfgeat, a man of Queen Edith, held and could sell.

In Great Linford Hugh holds of Walter 2 hides and 1½ virgates as 1 manor. There is land for 5 ploughs. In demesne is 1 [plough]; and 16 villans with 2 bordars have 4 ploughs. There are 4 slaves, and meadow for 4 ploughs. It is worth £3; when received 40s; TRE £4. This manor Ælfric son of Goding held and could sell.

IN BUNSTY HUNDRED

The same Hugh holds of Walter RAVENSTONE. It is assessed at 5 hides. There is land for 6 ploughs. In demesne are 2 [ploughs]; and 10 villans with 6 bordars have 4 ploughs. There are 4 slaves, and 1 mill rendering 25s, meadow for 6 ploughs, [and] woodland for 300 pigs. It is and was worth 100s; TRE £6. This manor Leofwine, a thegn of King Edward, held and could sell.

In Lavendon Ralph holds of Walter 2 hides and 1 virgate and the fourth part of 1 virgate. There is land for 2 ploughs. In demesne is 1 [plough]; and 5 villans with 8 bordars have 1 plough. [There is] meadow for 1 plough, [and] woodland for 30 pigs. It is worth 25s; when received 10s; TRE 40s. This land a man of Bishop Wulfwig held and could sell.

IN MOULSOE HUNDRED

In Hardmead Hugh holds of Walter 2½ hides as 1 manor. There is land for 2½ ploughs, and there are [2½ ploughs], with 4 villans and 2 bordars. [There is] meadow for 1 plough, [and] woodland for 50 pigs. It is and always was worth 40s. This manor a man of Ælfric son of Goding held and could sell.

Richard holds of Walter MOULSOE. It is assessed at 10 hides. There is land for 7 ploughs. In demesne is 1 [plough]; and 7 villans with 9 bordars have 6 ploughs. There is 1 slave, and meadow for 5 ploughs, [and] woodland for 100 pigs. All together it is worth £6; when received 100s; TRE 8d. This manor 8 thegns held and could sell. One of these, Alwine, held 2 hides as 1 manor; and another, Ulf, a man of Esger the staller, 2 hides as 1 manor; and Algar, a man of Edward Cild, 1½ hides as 1 manor; Alsige 1 hide; Thorkil 1 hide; Lodi 1 hide; Oswulf 1 hide; Alric half a hide.

In Broughton [near Moulsoe] Hugh holds of Walter 4 hides as 1 manor. There is land for 5 ploughs. In demesne [is] 1 plough; and 8 villans with 5 bordars have 4 ploughs. There are 2 slaves, and 1 mill in demesne, [and] meadow for 3 ploughs. It is and was worth 60s; TRE 4d. This manor Oswig, a man of Ælfric son of Goding, held and could sell.

In Milton Keynes Hugh holds of Walter half a hide. There is land for 1 plough, but no [plough] is there. [There is] meadow for 1 plough. It is worth 4s; TRE 10s. This land Oswig, a man of Ælfric, held and could sell.

In Bow Brickhill Ralph holds of Walter 5 hides as 1 manor. There is land for 5 ploughs. In demesne are 2 [ploughs]; and 8 villans with 2 bordars have 3 ploughs. There are 2 slaves, [and] meadow for 5 ploughs. It is worth 60s; when received 40s; TRE 100s. Of this land Godwine, a man of Bishop Wulfwig, held 2 hides as 1 manor; Godbald 1 hide; Ælfric 1 hide; Ordric 1 hide; and they all could sell their land.

In the same vill Robert holds of Walter 4 hides as 1 manor. There is land for 5 ploughs. In demesne are 3 [ploughs]; and 9 villans with 5 bordars have 2 ploughs. There are 3 slaves, and 1 mill rendering 10s, meadow for 5 ploughs, [and] woodland for 100 pigs. It is and always was worth 100s. Of this land Godwine, a man of Bishop Wulfwig, held 2 hides as 1 manor, and 5 other thegns held the other land, that is, 2 hides, and they could sell.

XV. The land of William de Warenne

IN AYLESBURY HUNDRED

WILLIAM de Warenne holds BROUGHTON [in Aylesbury]. It is assessed at 10 hides. There is land for 8 ploughs. In demesne [are] 2 hides, and there are 2 ploughs; and 13 villans with 5 bordars have 6 ploughs. There are 4 slaves, and 1 mill rendering 10s, meadow for 5 ploughs, [and] woodland for 100 pigs. In all it is and was worth £8; TRE £10. This manor Edward, a thegn of King Edward, held and could sell.

IN 'ROWLEY' HUNDRED

Brian holds of William CAVERSFIELD [Oxon.]. It is assessed at 5 hides. There is land for 8 ploughs. In demesne are 3 [ploughs]; and 12 villans with 9 bordars have 5 ploughs. There is a fishpond. In all it is and always was worth 100s. This manor Edward, a man of Earl Tosti, held and could sell.

XVI. The land of William Peverel

IN STONE HUNDRED

WILLIAM Peverel holds LOWER HARTWELL, 6 hides and 3 virgates. Tehel holds of him. There is land for 8 ploughs. In demesne are 3 [ploughs]; and 16 villans with 4 bordars have 5 ploughs. There are 4 slaves, and meadow for 8 ploughs. In all it is and was worth 100s; TRE £7. This manor Alwine, a thegn of King Edward, held and could sell.

In Upton [in Dinton] Robert holds of William 3½ hides. There is land for 5 ploughs. In demesne are 2 [ploughs]; and 8 villans with 3 bordars have 3 ploughs. There are 3 slaves, and meadow for 5 ploughs. It is and always was worth 60s. This manor Alwine, a man of Queen Edith, held and could sell.

IN ASHENDON HUNDRED

Payne holds of William Tetchwick as 2 hides. There is land for 2 ploughs. In demesne is 1 [plough]; and 3 villans have 2 ploughs. There is 1 slave, meadow for 2 ploughs, [and] woodland for 50 pigs. This land is worth 30s; when received 20s; TRE 30s. This manor Alwine, a thegn of King Edward, held and could sell.

In Shipton Lee William holds 1 hide. There is land for half a plough, and there is [half a plough] with 1 villan. It is and was worth 5s. This land Alwine, a thegn of King Edward, held.

IN WADDESDON HUNDRED

William himself holds MIDDLE CLAYDON. It is assessed at 10 hides. There is land for 10 ploughs. In demesne [are] 3 hides, and there are 3 ploughs; and 16 villans with 2 bordars have 5 ploughs, and there could be 2 more. There are 3 slaves, meadow for 4 ploughs, [and] woodland for 150 pigs. In all it is worth £10; when received £12; TRE £10. This manor Alwine, a thegn of King Edward, held.

William himself holds HOGSHAW. It is assessed at 5 hides. There is land for 3½ ploughs. In demesne [are] 3 hides, and there are 2 ploughs; and 6 villans with 2 bordars have 1½ ploughs. [There is] meadow for 3 ploughs, [and] woodland for 40 pigs. It is and always was worth 60s. This manor Alwine, a thegn of King Edward, held.

Ralph holds in [Botolph or East] Claydon of William 3 hides and 1 virgate as 1 manor. There is land for 3 ploughs. In demesne is 1 [plough]; and 4 villans have another, and there could be a third. [There is] meadow for 1 plough, [and] wood for fences. It is and always was worth 40s. This manor Alwine, a thegn of King Edward, held and could sell. Of this land a certain man of his held 1 virgate and could sell it without his leave.

Ambrose holds of William ADSTOCK. It is assessed at 10 hides. There is land for 7 ploughs. In demesne are 3 [ploughs]; and 5 villans with 2 bordars have 3 ploughs, and there could be a fourth. [There is] meadow for 7 ploughs. In all it is and was worth 100s; TRE £8. This manor Gytha, wife of Earl Ralph, held and could sell.

William himself holds HAVERSHAM. It is assessed at 10

hides. There is land for 10 ploughs. In demesne are hides [sic], and there are 1½ ploughs, and there could be another 1½. There 16 villans with 8 bordars have 7 ploughs. There are 5 slaves, and 1 mill rendering 8s. and 75 eels, meadow for 9 ploughs, [and] woodland for 300 pigs. It is and was worth £6; TRE £7. This manor Countess Gytha held.

Drogo holds of William Stoke Goldington, 3 hides and 3 virgates, as 1 manor. There is land for 4 ploughs. In demesne are 2 [ploughs]; and 5 villans with 4 bordars have 2 ploughs. There are 2 slaves, meadow for 4 ploughs, [and] woodland for 200 pigs. It is and always was worth £4. This manor Countess Gytha held.

[Folio 148V: BUCKINGHAMSHIRE]

XVII. The land of William fitzAnsculf

IN STONE HUNDRED

WILLIAM fitzAnsculf holds in this hundred half a hide, and a certain Englishman [holds] of him. There is land for half a plough, and there is [half a plough], with 1 bordar. It is and always was worth 10s. This land Leofwine brother of Alsige held and could sell.

IN AYLESBURY HUNDRED

Ralph holds of William in ELLESBOROUGH 13½ hides. There is land for 11 ploughs. In demesne are 2 [ploughs]; and 17 villans with 3 bordars have 9 ploughs. There are 2 slaves, and meadow for 2 ploughs, [and] woodland for 105 pigs. In all it is and was worth £8; TRE £9. This manor Earl Harold held, and this same manor Ansculf de Picquigny exchanged for half of Princes Risborough with Ralph Taillebois, by order of King William.

In the same vill Otbert holds of William 1½ hides. There is land for 2 ploughs, and there are 2 oxen with 1 villan. It is and was worth 5s; TRE 20s. This land Baldwin, a man of Archbishop Stigand, held and could sell.

The same Otbert holds of William [Great and Little] HAMPDEN. It is assessed at 3 hides. There is land for 5 ploughs. In demesne are 2 [ploughs]; and 4 villans have 3 ploughs. There are 2 slaves, woodland for 500 pigs, and from the rents of the woodland, iron for 2 ploughs. It is and was worth £4; TRE 100s. This manor Baldwin, a man of Archbishop Stigand, held and could sell.

IN STOKE HUNDRED

Walter holds of William DITTON. It is assessed at 5 hides. There is land for 3 ploughs. In demesne is 1 [plough]; and 4 villans have 2 ploughs. There is 1 slave, and meadow for 3 ploughs, [and] woodland for 16 pigs. It is and was worth 30s; TRE 40s. This manor Sigeræd, a man of Earl Harold, held and could sell.

The same Walter holds of William STOKE POGES. It is assessed at 10 hides. There is land for 10 ploughs. In demesne are 2 [ploughs]; and 10 villans with 3 bordars have 6 ploughs, and there could be 2 more. There are 4 slaves, and 1 mill rendering 4s, [and] woodland for 500 pigs. In all it is worth £5;

when received £3; TRE £6. This manor sigeræd, a man of Earl Harold, held and could sell, and 1 hide of this land a certain sokeman, a man of Tubbi, held and could sell.

IN WADDESDON HUNDRED

In NORTH MARSTON Ranulph holds of William 6½ hides as 1 manor. There is land for 6 ploughs. In demesne are 2 [ploughs]; and 8 villans with 3 bordars have 3 ploughs, and there could be a fourth. [There is] meadow for 2 ploughs. All together it is worth 100s; when received 60s; TRE £4. Of this manor Leofric, a man of Earl Edwin, held 5 hides as 1 manor; and another man had 1 hide and 1 virgate of King Edward's soke; and Beorhtwine, a man of Earl Tosti, had 1 virgate. All these could sell.

In the same vill Bernard holds of William 1 hide. There is land for 1 plough, and there is [1 plough], with 1 bordar. It is and was worth 10s; TRE 20s. This land Alwig, a man of Beorhtric, held, and it was of the king's soke, and he could sell it.

In Hoggeston Payne holds of William 8 hides and 2½ virgates. There is land for 10 ploughs. In demesne are 2 [ploughs]; and 12 villans with 7 bordars have 8 ploughs. There are 5 slaves, [and] meadow for 10 ploughs. All together it is and was worth £7; TRE 100s. Of this manor Almær, a man of Bondi the staller, held 7 hides as 1 manor; and a man of the Abbess of Barking 1 hide, and a man of Eadgifu the Fair held 2½ virgates; and all these could sell [their land].

IN COTTESLOE HUNDRED

In Soulbury Payne holds of William 5½ hides and the third part of 1 virgate. There is land for 17 ploughs. In demesne are 3 [ploughs]; and 14 villans with 5 bordars have 9 ploughs, and there could be 5 ploughs more. There are 3 slaves, and 1 mill rendering 16s, [and] meadow for 3 ploughs. All together it is and was worth £7; TRE £8. This manor 11 sokemen held and could sell.

In Hollingdon Payne holds of William 3½ virgates. There is land for 1 plough, and there is [1 plough] with 3 villans. It is and always was worth 10s. This land 4 sokemen held: of these, 3 men of Beorhtric had 2½ virgates, and the fourth, a man of Wicga, had 1 virgate; and all these could sell their land.

In Littlecote Payne holds of William 1½ hides. There is land for 1½ ploughs. There is 1 [plough] with 1 bordar, and there could be half [a plough more]. [There is] meadow for 1 plough. It is worth 20s; when received 40s; TRE 30s. This land 2 men of Beorhtric held and could sell.

IN YARDLEY HUNDRED

In CHEDDINGTON Swæting holds of William half a hide. There is land for 2 oxen. It is and was worth 5s; TRE 10s. This land Lyfing, a man of King Edward, held and could sell.

IN MURSLEY HUNDRED

In Swanbourne Payne holds of William 1 virgate. There is land for 2 oxen. It is and always was worth 2s. This land Oswig, a man of Beorhtric, held and could sell.

IN 'MOW' HUNDRED

Baldwin holds of William at farm 2 hides. There is land for $1\frac{1}{2}$ ploughs, and there are [$1\frac{1}{2}$ ploughs], with 1 villan and 1 bordar. [There is] meadow for 1 plough. All together it is and was worth 26s. This man held it TRE and could sell it.

In MARSH GIBBON Æthelric holds of William 4 hides as 1 manor. There is land for 5 ploughs. In demesne [are] 2 [ploughs]; and 5 villans with 3 bordars have 3 ploughs. There are 3 slaves, meadow for 5 ploughs, [and] woodland for 30 pigs. It is and always was worth 70s. This man held it TRE, but he now holds it at farm of William in heaviness and misery.

IN 'SECKLEY' HUNDRED

William himself holds NEWPORT PAGNELL. It is assessed at 5 hides. There is land for 9 ploughs. In demesne [are] 4 carucates of land, and there are 4 ploughs; and 5 villans have 5 ploughs. The burgesses have $6\frac{1}{2}$ ploughs, and † [the ploughs] of other men working outside the 5 hides †. There are 9 slaves, and 2 mills rendering 40s, meadow for all the ploughs and 10s [besides], woodland for 300 pigs and 2s [besides], and, in addition, 4s from men who dwell in the woodland; and in all other rents it renders yearly 100s and 16s4d. In all it is and was worth £20; TRE £24. This manor Ulf, a thegn of King Edward, held.

In Caldecote William holds 3 hides and 1 virgate. There is land for 2 ploughs. In demesne is 1 [plough], and there could be another. There is 1 villan, and 1 mill rendering 8s; and a certain knight has there half a hide with half a plough. [There is] meadow for 1 plough, [and] woodland for 100 pigs. It is and always was worth 40s. This manor 2 men of Ulf held and could sell.

In Woolstone William holds $1\frac{1}{2}$ hides. There is land for $1\frac{1}{2}$ ploughs. In demesne is 1 [plough]; and 1 villan has half a plough. There are 2 slaves. It is and was worth 20s; TRE 30s. This land Ulf, a thegn of King Edward, held and could sell.

In Bradwell William holds 3 virgates. There is land for 1 plough, and there is [1 plough], with 1 villan and 2 bordars and 1 slave. [There is] meadow for 1 plough. It is and always was worth 10s. This land Alweard, a man of Goding, held and could sell. Of this land Ansculf, when he was sheriff, dispossessed William of Cholsey, unjustly, as the men of the hundred say, and without the livery officer of the king or of anyone.

In Great Linford Robert holds of William 1 virgate. There is land for 2 oxen, and there is 1 villan. It is and always was worth 2s. This land Grimbold, a man of Bisi, held and could sell.

In TYRINGHAM Acard holds of William 7 hides and 1 virgate and the fourth part of 1 virgate as 1 manor. There is land for 8 ploughs. In demesne are 3 [ploughs]; and 9 villans with 6 bordars have 5 ploughs. There are 6 slaves, meadow for 8 ploughs, [and] woodland for 200 pigs and 26d from minor customary dues. All together it is worth £6;

when received £8; and as much TRE. This manor 5 thegns held; one of them, Harold, had 3 hides as 1 manor, and Godwine the priest half a hide, Æstan 2 hides as 1 manor, Godric, a man of Harold, 1 virgate, and Ælfgifu; wife of Harold, $1\frac{1}{2}$ hides as 1 manor. All these could sell to whom they wished.

IN MOULSOE HUNDRED

Wilbert holds of William 4 hides as 1 manor. There is land for 4 ploughs. In demesne is 1 [plough]; and 7 villans with 6 bordars have 3 ploughs. There is 1 slave, and 1 mill rendering 20s, meadow for 3 ploughs, [and] woodland for 150 pigs and 16d [besides]. It is and was worth 40s; TRE £4. This manor 2 thegns, Harold and Alwig, held and could sell.

In CHICHELEY Baldwin holds of William 3 hides as 1 manor. There is land for 3 ploughs. In demesne is 1 [plough]; and 5 villans with 4 bordars have 2 ploughs. [There is] meadow for 1 plough, [and] woodland for 100 pigs. It is and always was worth 40s. This man held it TRE and could sell it.

In the same [vill], Andrew holds of William 3 hides as 1 manor. There is land for 3 ploughs. In demesne is 1 [plough]; and 7 villans with 4 bordars have 2 ploughs. There are 2 slaves, meadow for 2 ploughs, [and] woodland for 100 pigs. It is and always was worth 40s. This manor Eadstan, a man of Æthelnoth the Kentishman, held and could sell.

In the same [vill], Payne holds of William 3 hides and 3 virgates as 1 manor. There is land for 4 ploughs. In demesne is 1 [plough]; and 5 villans with 6 bordars have 3 ploughs. [There is] meadow for the ploughs. It is worth 60s; when received 100s; TRE £4. This manor 9 thegns held and could sell without leave of their lords.

William himself holds TICKFORD END. It is assessed at 5 hides. There is land for 8 ploughs. Besides the 5 hides, [there are] in demesne 2 carucates of land, and there are 2 ploughs. There 6 villans with 4 slaves have 6 ploughs. [There is] meadow for 5 ploughs, [and] woodland for 50 pigs. There 5 sokemen pay 27s. It is worth 100s; when received £6; and as much TRE. This manor Ulf, a thegn of King Edward, held, and there were 5 thegns who held $3\frac{1}{2}$ virgates of this land and could sell to whom they wished.

In Hardmead Hervey holds 1 hide all but half a virgate, as 1 manor, of William. There is land for 1 plough, and there is [1 plough], with 2 villans and 2 bordars and 1 slave. [There is] woodland for 24 pigs. It is and was worth 12s; TRE 20s. This land Godwine, a man of Ulf, held and could sell.

In the same [vill], Payne holds of William half a virgate. There is land for 2 oxen, and there are [2 oxen]. [There is] meadow for 2 oxen, [and] woodland for 5 pigs. It is and was worth 2s; TRE †£2† [...]. This land Godric, a man of Oswig, held and could sell.

In the same [vill], Baldwin holds 1 hide of William as 1 manor. There is land for 1 plough, and there is [1 plough] with 3 villans. It is and always was worth 1 mark of silver. This manor 3 brothers held. One of them [was] a man of Toki, and 2 were men of Baldwin, and they could sell. Of this land half a virgate belongs to the minster of St Firmin of [North] Crawley and it belonged to it TRE.

In Milton Keynes Otbert holds of William 1 hide. There is land for 1 plough. There is 1 villan and 5 bordars and 1 slave, [and] meadow for 1 plough. It is worth 5s; when received 20s; and as much TRE. This land Sæweald, a man of Wulfweard Cild, held and could sell.

XVIII. The land of Robert de Tosny

IN STONE HUNDRED

ROBERT de Tosny holds 7 hides in Stone, and Gilbert [holds] of him. There is land for 6 ploughs. In demesne are 2 [ploughs]; and 7 villans with 11 bordars have 4 ploughs. There are 4 slaves; and 1 sokeman pays 15s yearly. In all it is and always was worth 100s. This manor Ulf, a housecarl of King Edward, held

IN YARDLEY HUNDRED

In Cheddington Gilbert holds of Robert 5½ hides as 1 manor. There is land for 3½ ploughs. In demesne is 1 [plough], and there could be another. There 6 villans have 1½ ploughs. There are 4 slaves, [and] meadow for 2 ploughs. It is and was worth 60s; TRE 100s. This manor Oswulf son of Frani, a thegn of King Edward, held and could sell.

IN MOULSOE HUNDRED

In CLIFTON REYNES William de Boisrohard and his brother hold of Robert 4 hides as 1 manor. There is land for 4 ploughs. In demesne are 2 [ploughs]; and 6 villans with 7 bordars have 2 ploughs. There are 3 slaves, meadow for 4 ploughs, [and] woodland for 400 pigs. All together it is and was worth 100s; TRE £6. This manor Oswulf, a thegn of King Edward, held and could sell. In this vill of Clifton Reynes, Sigefrith and Thorbert held 3 virgates which William and Roger have taken possession of and concealed, to the king's hurt, as the men of the hundred say. Of the 4 above-mentioned hides Alric, a man of Oswulf, held 1 virgate and could sell to whom he wished.

XX. The land of Robert d'Oilly

IN STOKE HUNDRED

ROBERT d'Oilly holds IVER. It is assessed at 17 hides. There is land for 30 ploughs. In demesne [are] 2 hides, and there are 4 ploughs; and 32 villans have 26 ploughs. Of these villans, 5 have 6 hides. There are 6 bordars and 4 slaves, and 3 mills rendering 44s, [and] meadow for 30 ploughs. From 4 fisheries, 1,500 eels and fish on Fridays for the use of the reeve of the vill. [There is] woodland for 800 pigs, and 2 arpents of vineyard. In all it is worth £22; when received 100s; TRE £12. This manor Toki, a thegn of King Edward, held, and there were 3 sokemen. Of these, one, a man of Toki, held 3 virgates, but he could not sell except by his leave, and another, a man of Queen Edith, [held] 2½ hides, and the third, a man of Sæwulf, had 2½ hides: these 2 could give or sell [their land] to whom

they wished, and they did not belong to this manor. This manor Robert exchanged with Clarenbold de Le Marais for Padbury, and it is [part] of his wife's fief.

IN DESBOROUGH HUNDRED

Robert himself holds HIGH WYCOMBE from his wife's fief. It is assessed at 10 hides. There is land for 30 ploughs. In demesne [are] 4 hides, and there are 3 ploughs. There 40 villans with 8 bordars have 27 ploughs. There are 8 slaves and 4 boors, and 6 mills rendering 75s yearly, meadow for 3 ploughs and for the horses of the court and the villans' ploughs, [and] woodland for 500 pigs. In all it is worth £26; when received £10. This manor Beorhtric held of Queen Edith.

IN IXHILL HUNDRED

Robert fitzWalter holds of Robert OAKLEY. It is assessed at 5 hides and 3 virgates. There is land for 7 ploughs. In demesne are 3 [ploughs]; and 9 villans with 7 bordars have 4 ploughs. There are 3 slaves. There is woodland for 200 pigs, if it were not for the king's park in which it lies. In all it is and was worth £6; TRE £7. There 5 hides and 3 virgates are 8 hides. Of these, Ælfgyth the maid held 2 hides which she could give or sell to whom she wished, and of the demesne farm of King Edward she herself had half a hide which Godric the sheriff granted her as long as he was sheriff, on condition of her teaching his daughter gold embroidery work. This land Robert fitzWalter holds now, as the hundred testifies.

[Folio 149V: BUCKINGHAMSHIRE]

IN YARDLEY HUNDRED

Ralph Basset holds of Robert MARSWORTH. It is assessed at 20 hides. There is land for 9 ploughs. In demesne are 4 [ploughs]; and 22 villans have 5 ploughs. There are 8 slaves, and 3 mills rendering 15s, meadow for 6 ploughs, [and] woodland for 800 pigs. In all it is and always was worth £20. This manor Beorhtric, a thegn of King Edward, held and could sell.

In Cheddington Ralph holds of Robert 1½ hides. There is land for 1 plough, and there is [1 plough] with 2 bordars. [There is] meadow for 1 plough. It is and always was worth 20s. This land Fin the Dane held and could sell.

IN 'STOTFOLD' HUNDRED

In SHALSTONE Robert holds of Robert 4 hides as 1 manor. There is land for 5 ploughs. In demesne [are] 2 ploughs; and 4 villans with 3 bordars have 3 ploughs. There are 4 slaves, [and] woodland for 50 pigs. This land is worth 40s; when received 30s; TRE 60s. This manor Azur son of Toti held and could sell.

Turstin holds of Robert WATER STRATFORD. It is assessed at 8 hides. There is land for 8 ploughs. In demesne are 3 [ploughs]; and 10 villans with 5 bordars have 5 ploughs. There are 3 slaves, and 1 mill rendering 8s, [and] meadow for 6 ploughs. It is worth £7; when received 100s; TRE £7. This manor Azur son of Toti held and could sell.

XX. The land of Robert Gernon

IN STOKE HUNDRED

ROBERT Gernon holds WRAYSBURY. It is assessed at 20 hides. There is land for 25 ploughs. In demesne [are] 5 hides, and there are 2 ploughs; and 32 villans with 18 bordars have 15 ploughs, and there could be 8 ploughs more. There are 7 slaves, and 2 mills rendering 40 yearly [sic], meadow for 5 ploughs and hay for the beasts of the court, woodland for 500 pigs, and 4 fisheries in the Thames rendering 27s, less 4d. In all it is and was worth £20; TRE £22. This manor Edmund, a thegn of King Edward, held.

XXI. The land of Geoffrey de Mandeville

IN BURNHAM HUNDRED

GEOFFREY de Mandeville holds AMERSHAM. It is assessed at 7½ hides. There is land for 16 ploughs. In demesne [are] 2 hides, and there are 3 ploughs; and 14 villans with 4 bordars have 9 ploughs. There could be 4 more. There are 7 slaves, meadow for 16 ploughs, [and] woodland for 400 pigs. In all it is and was worth £9; TRE £16. This manor Queen Edith held.

IN IXHILL HUNDRED

In Waldridge Swærting holds of Geoffrey half a hide. There is land for 1 plough, and there is [1 plough, and] meadow for 1 plough. It is and was worth 10s; TRE 15s. This land Doding, a man of Esger the staller, held and could sell.

IN WADDESDON HUNDRED

In [Botolph or East] Claydon Geoffrey holds 7 hides as 1 manor. There is land for 5 ploughs. In demesne [are] 3 hides, and there are 2 ploughs; and 4 villans with 3 bordars have 3 ploughs. [There is] meadow for 2 ploughs, [and] woodland for 40 pigs. All together it is worth £4; when received £3; TRE £5. This manor Swein, a man of Esger the staller, held. He could not give nor sell it without his leave.

Geoffrey himself holds QUARRENDON. It is assessed at 10 hides. There is land for 10 ploughs. In demesne [are] 4 hides, and there are 4 ploughs; and 20 villans with 8 bordars have 8 ploughs. [There is] meadow for 10 ploughs, [and] woodland for 300 pigs. In all it is worth £8; when received 100s; TRE £6. This manor Swein, a man of Esger the staller, held. He could not sell it without his leave.

IN YARDLEY HUNDRED

In IVINGHOE ASTON Germund holds of Geoffrey 4 hides and 1 virgate as 1 manor. There is land for 3½ ploughs. In demesne are 2 ploughs; and 1 villan with 4 slaves has 1½ ploughs. [There is] meadow for 3 ploughs. It is and was worth 50s; TRE 60s. This manor Esger the staller held in demesne.

IN MURSLEY HUNDRED

Geoffrey himself holds in Swanbourne 2 hides. There is land for 2 ploughs. In demesne [is] 1 hide, and there is 1 plough; and 3 villans with 2 bordars have 1 plough. [There is]

meadow for 2 ploughs. It is and always was worth 30s. This manor Swein, a man of Esger the staller, held. He could not sell it without his leave.

IN 'STOTFOLD' HUNDRED

In Leckhampstead Osbert holds of Geoffrey 3½ hides. There is land for 3 ploughs. In demesne is 1 [plough]; and [...] villans have 1½ ploughs, and there could be half [a plough] more. [There is] woodland for 150 pigs. It is worth 30s; when received 20s; TRE 30s. This manor Swærting, a man of Esger, held. He could not sell it.

IN 'MOW' HUNDRED

William de Keynes holds of Geoffrey 3½ hides as 1 manor. There is land for 3½ ploughs. In demesne is 1 [plough]; and 3 villans with 1 bordar have 2 ploughs, and there could be half [a plough more]. There is 1 slave, [and] meadow for 3 ploughs. In all it is and always was worth 40s. This manor Ulf, a man of Esger the staller, held and could sell, and of the same land Alwig held half a hide; he was a man of Alwine Varus and could sell it.

XXII. The land of Gilbert de Ghent

IN YARDLEY HUNDRED

GILBERT de Ghent holds EDLESBOROUGH. It is assessed at 20 hides. There is land for 14 ploughs. In demesne [are] 10 hides, and there are 4 ploughs; and 26 villans with 4 bordars have 10 ploughs. There are 10 slaves, and 2 mills rendering 15s4d, meadow for 4 ploughs, [and] woodland for 400 pigs. In all it is and was worth £13; TRE £14. This manor Ulf, a thegn of King Edward, held and could sell.

In Horton [in Ivinghoe] Swærting holds of Gilbert 3 virgates. There is land for half a plough, and there is a plough. This land is and always was worth 6s8d. This land a certain man of Ulf held. He could not give nor sell it without his leave.

XXIII. The land of Miles Crispin

IN STONE HUNDRED

MILES Crispin holds in Upton [in Dinton] 1½ hides, and Alric holds of him. There is land for 1 plough, and there is [1 plough], with 1 villan and 2 bordars. There are 2 slaves. It is and always was worth 20s. This thegn held it TRE.

IN BURNHAM HUNDRED

Ralph holds of Miles DORNEY. It is assessed at 3 hides. There is land for 3 ploughs. In demesne is 1 [plough]; and 5 villans with 4 bordars have 2 ploughs. There are 2 slaves, meadow for 3 ploughs and for the horses, and 1 fishery rendering 500 eels, [and] woodland for 150 pigs. It is worth 30s; when received 10s; TRE 60s. This manor Ealdræd, a man of Earl Morcar, held and could sell.

Ralph and Roger hold of Miles HITCHAM. It is assessed at 6 hides. There is land for 6 ploughs. In demesne are 2 [ploughs]; and 8 villans have 4 ploughs. There are 3 slaves, meadow for the ploughs, [and] woodland for 100 pigs.

From a fishery, 500 eels. In all it is worth £4; when received 20s; TRE 100s. This manor Hemming, a thegn of King Edward, held and could sell.

IN DESBOROUGH HUNDRED

In Marlow [Marlow or Little Marlow] Ralph and Roger hold of Miles 8½ hides and half a virgate. There is land for 6 ploughs. In demesne are 2 [ploughs]; and 14 villans with 6 bordars have 4 ploughs. There are 2 slaves, meadow for 6 ploughs, [and] woodland for 200 pigs and 12d [besides]. It is and was worth 60s; TRE £4. This land Hemming, a thegn of King Edward, held and could sell.

In Saunderton Osbert holds of Miles 5 hides. There is land for 5 ploughs. In demesne are 2 [ploughs]; and 13 villans with 5 bordars have 3 ploughs. There are 2 slaves, and 2 mills rendering 8s, meadow for 1 plough, [and] woodland for 50 pigs. It is and was worth 100s; TRE £6. This manor Alric, a man of Earl Harold, held and could sell.

In Aston Sandford 2 men hold of Miles half a hide. There is land for half a plough, and there is [half a plough] with 2 villans. [There is] meadow for half a plough. It is and was worth 10s; TRE 15s. This land Wulfric and Coleman, men of Beorhtric, held and could sell.

IN IXHILL HUNDRED

Miles himself holds SHABBINGTON. It is assessed at 10 hides. There is land for 10 ploughs. In demesne are 3 hides, and there are 3 ploughs; and 12 villans with 7 bordars have 7 ploughs. There are 6 slaves, and 1 mill rendering 10s, [and] meadow for 6 ploughs. From a fishery, 100 eels. [There is] woodland for 100 pigs. This manor is and always was worth £10. Vigot of Wallingford held it.

In Ickford Richard holds of Miles 4 hides. There is land for 4 ploughs. In demesne is 1 [plough]; and 6 villans have 3 ploughs. There are 2 slaves, [and] meadow for 4 ploughs. In all it is worth £3; when received £4; TRE as much.

IN ASHENDON HUNDRED

In Ashendon Viking holds of Miles 2 hides. There is land for 2 ploughs, and there are [2 ploughs] with 3 bordars. [There is] meadow for 2 ploughs. It is and always was worth 30s. This man held it TRE and could sell.

In Chearsley Richard holds of Miles 1½ hides. There is land for 1 plough, and there is [1 plough], with 1 villan and 1 bordar. There are 2 slaves, [and] meadow for 1 plough. It is and always was worth 22s. This land Healfdene, a man of Earl Harold, held and could sell.

In 'Shortley' [in Quainton] 2 men hold of Miles 1 hide. There is land for 1 plough, and there is [1 plough], with 1 villan and 1 bordar. [There is] meadow for 1 plough, [and] woodland for 30 pigs. It is and always was worth 10s. This land 2 thegns, men of Beorhtric, held and could sell.

In QUAINTON Miles holds 7½ hides. There is land for 9 ploughs. In demesne [are] 3 hides, and there are 3 ploughs;

and 21 villans with 6 bordars have 6 ploughs. There are 6 slaves, meadow for 2 ploughs, [and] woodland for 100 pigs, meadow for 2 ploughs, [and] woodland for 100 pigs [sic]. In all it is and was worth £7; TRE £8. This manor Vigot of Wallingford held.

Two men hold of Miles Beachendon as 2 hides. There is land for 3 ploughs, and there are [3 ploughs], with 2 villans and 3 bordars. [There is] meadow for 2 ploughs. It is and always was worth 25s. These men held it TRE-one a man of Beorhtric, and the other a man of Azur-and could sell it.

IN WADDESDON HUNDRED

Miles himself holds WADDESDON. It is assessed at 27 hides. There is land for 28 ploughs. In demesne [are] 10 hides, and there are 8 ploughs; and 50 villans with 10 bordars have 20 ploughs. There are 17 slaves, and 1 mill rendering 12s, meadow for 28 ploughs, [and] woodland for 150 pigs. In all it is worth £30; when received £16; TRE £30. This manor Beorhtric, a man of Queen Edith, held.

In [Botolph or East] Claydon 2 Englishmen hold of Miles 2 hides. There is land for 1 plough, and there is [1 plough] with 3 bordars. [There is] meadow for 1 plough. It is and always was worth 20s. These men held it TRE. They were men of Hemming, and they could sell.

In [Botolph or East] Claydon Geoffrey holds of Miles 7 hides and 3 virgates as 1 manor. There is land for 5 ploughs. In demesne are 2 [ploughs]; and 4 villans with 3 bordars have 3 ploughs. There are 3 slaves, meadow for 2 ploughs, [and] woodland for 100 pigs. All together it is worth £4; when received 20s; TRE £4.

In [? North] Marston Særic holds of Miles 1 hide. There is land for 1 plough, and there is [1 plough] with 1 bordar. [There is] meadow for 1 plough. It is and always was worth 20s. This man held it TRE; he was a man of Beorhtric and could sell it.

IN COTTESLOE HUNDRED

In Soulbury Roger holds of Miles 1 hide and 1½ virgates. There is land for 3 ploughs. In demesne is 1 [plough]; and 2 villans have another, and there could be a third. [There is] meadow for 2 ploughs. It is and always was worth 20s. This land Almær, a man of Beorhtric, held. He could not sell it without his leave.

In Hollingdon Nigel holds of Miles 1 virgate. There is land for half a plough, and there is [half a plough] with 1 villan. It is and was worth 3s; TRE 4s. He who held this land could not give nor sell it TRE.

In Wingrave Nigel holds of Miles 5 hides as 1 manor. There is land for 5 ploughs. There 7 villans with 2 bordars have 2½ ploughs and there could be as many [more]. There is 1 slave, [and] meadow for 5 ploughs. It is worth 40s; when received 100s; and as much TRE. This manor Beorhtric, a man of Queen Edith, held and could sell.

In the same vill Turstin the priest holds of Miles half a hide. There is land for half a plough. There is 1 villan, [and] meadow for half a plough. It is and always was worth 10s. This land Leofmær, a man of Beorhtric, held and could sell.

In the same vill Almær holds of Miles 2 hides as 1 manor. There is land for 3 ploughs. In demesne is 1 [plough]; and 7 villans have 2 ploughs. [There is] meadow for 3 ploughs. It is and always was worth 40s. This manor Almær, a man of Beorhtric, held and could sell.

In Littlecote Robert holds of Miles 1 hide. There is land for 1 plough, and there is [1 plough] with 1 villan, [and] meadow for 1 plough. It is worth 15s; when received 5s; TRE 25s. This land Herch, a man of Beorhtric, held and could sell.

In Hardwick William holds of Miles 1 hide. There is land for 1 plough, and there is [1 plough] with 2 bordars. [There is] meadow for 1 plough. It is worth 20s; when received 10s; TRE 20s. This land Oswulf held and could sell.

In [Lower or Upper] Burston William holds of Miles 3 virgates. There is land for 1 plough. There are 3 villans, [and] meadow for 1 plough. It is and was worth 15s; TRE 20s. This land Oswulf, a man of Beorhtric, held and could sell.

IN YARDLEY HUNDRED

In Pitstone Roger holds of Miles 5 hides as 1 manor. There is land for 2 ploughs. In demesne is 1 [plough]; and 3 villans with 1 bordar have half a plough, and there could be half [a plough more. There is] woodland for 40 pigs. It is worth 30s; when received 20s; TRE 40s. This manor Leofsige, a man of Beorhtric, held and could sell.

In the same vill Swærting holds of Miles 2 hides. There is land for 1 plough, and there is [1 plough], with 1 bordar and 2 slaves. [There is] woodland for 25 pigs. It is and was worth 10s; TRE 20s. This land Leofsige, a man of Beorhtric, held and could sell.

In Horton [in Ivinghoe] Swærting holds of Miles 1 hide. There is land for half a plough.

[Folio 150V: BUCKINGHAMSHIRE]

There is a plough, with 1 villan and 2 slaves, [and] meadow for half a plough. It is and always was worth 13s4d. Leofsige, a man of Beorhtric, held and could sell it.

IN MURSLEY HUNDRED

In Stewkley Nigel holds of Miles 3½ hides as 1 manor. There is land for 9 ploughs. In demesne is 1 [plough], and there could be 2 [more]. There 9 villans with 2 bordars have 3½ ploughs, and there could be 2½ [ploughs] more. [There is] meadow for 9 ploughs. It is and was worth £4. This manor Beorhtric, a thegn of King Edward, held and could sell.

IN 'MOW' HUNDRED

In Addington Eadwulf holds half a hide. There is land for half a plough, and there is [half a plough]. It is worth 10s; when received 5s; TRE 10s. This land Leofwig, a man of Eadwig, held and could sell.

IN 'SECKLEY' HUNDRED

In Bradwell William holds of Miles 2 hides and 3 virgates. There is land for 3 ploughs. In demesne [are] 2 ploughs; and 5 villans there could have 1 plough. There are 2 slaves, [and] meadow for 2 ploughs. It is worth 40s; when received 20s; TRE 60s. This manor 2 thegns, Sibbi and Godwine, a men of Ælfric son of Goding, held and could sell.

Ralph holds Stanton Bury of Miles. It is assessed at 5 hides. There is land for 5½ ploughs. In demesne are 2 [ploughs]; and 7 villans with 3 bordars have 3 ploughs, and there could be half [a plough] more. There are 4 slaves, and 1 mill rendering 10s8d and 50 eels, [and] meadow for 4 ploughs. In all it is worth £6; when received 100s; TRE £6. This manor Bisi, a thegn of King Edward, held and could sell.

IN MOULSOE HUNDRED

Almær of Wotton holds 1 hide of Miles. There is land for 1 plough, and there is [1 plough], with 3 villans and 2 bordars. [There is] meadow for 1 plough. It is and always was worth 10s. This land Ordwig, a man of Vigot of Wallingford, held and could sell.

XXIIII. The land of Edward of Salisbury

IN AYLESBURY HUNDRED

EDWARD of Salisbury holds ASTON CLINTON. It is assessed at 20 hides. There is land for 17 ploughs. In demesne [are] 9 hides and 1 virgate, and there are 6 ploughs; and 28 villans with 4 bordars have 11 ploughs, and there could be a twelfth besides. There are 13 slaves, and 1 mill rendering orae of silver, meadow for 17 ploughs, [and] woodland for 300 pigs and iron for the demesne ploughs. In all it is worth £18; when received £10; TRE £20. This manor Wulfwynn, a man of King Edward, held and could sell.

IN WADDESDON HUNDRED

Ranulph holds of Edward 1 hide and 1½ virgates. There is land for 1 plough, and there is [1 plough], with 1 villan and 1 bordar and 4 slaves. [There is] meadow for 1 plough. It is and was worth 10s; TRE 20s. This land Almær held of Wulfwynn of Creslow and could sell.

The same Ranulph holds CRESLOW. It is assessed at 5 hides. There is land for 6 ploughs. In demesne are 4 [ploughs]; and 6 villans with 1 bordar have 2 ploughs. There are 5 slaves, [and] meadow for 5 ploughs. In all it is worth 100s; when received £4; TRE £6. This manor Wulfwynn, a certain woman, held TRE and could sell.

XXV. The land of Hugh de Beauchamp

IN COTTESLOE HUNDRED

HUGH de Beauchamp holds LINSLADE [Beds.]. It is assessed at 15 hides. There is land for 16 ploughs. In demesne [are] 5 hides, and there are 2 ploughs, and there could be 3 more. There 22 villans with 6 bordars have 11 ploughs. There are 5 slaves, and 1 mill rendering 20s, [and] meadow for 2 ploughs. All together it is worth £10; when received 100s; TRE £10, This manor Alwine, a man of Queen Edith, held and could sell.

In Soulbury Hugh holds 2 parts of 1 virgate. There is land for 4 oxen. It is and was worth 3s; TRE 4s. This land Dot God's man held; he could sell to whom he wished.

IN BUNSTY HUNDRED

In Lathbury William d'Orange holds 4 hides of Hugh as 1 manor. There is land for 3 ploughs. In demesne are 2 [ploughs]; and 4 villans with 4 bordars have 1 plough. There are 3 slaves, meadow for 3 ploughs, [and] woodland for 100 pigs. It is worth £4; when received 20s; TRE 60s. This manor 2 thegns, Leofric and Wulfgeat, held as 2 manors and could sell.

XXVI. The land of Hugh de Bolbec

IN STONE HUNDRED

HUGH de Bolbec holds in Little Missenden half a hide, and Wulfgeat [holds] of him. There is land for 1 plough, and there is [1 plough] with 1 bordar. [There is] meadow for 1 plough, [and] woodland for 30 pigs. It is and always was worth 10s. This man held it TRE. He was a man of Bishop Wulfwig and could sell.

IN BURNHAM HUNDRED

In Amersham Wulfgeat holds of Hugh half a hide. There is land for 2 ploughs, and there are [2 ploughs], with 2 villans and 3 bordars. There is 1 mill rendering 5s, [and] woodland for 20 pigs. It is and always was worth 20s. This man held it TRE and could sell.

Hugh himself holds in CHESHAM 8½ hides. There is land for 16 ploughs. In demesne [are] 1½ hides, and there are 2 ploughs; and 16 villans with 6 bordars have 12 ploughs, and there could be 2 more. There are 6 slaves, and 1 mill rendering 10s, meadow for 16 ploughs, [and] woodland for 800 pigs and iron for the ploughs. In all it is worth £10, less 3s; TRE £12. This manor Beorhtric, a man of Queen Edith, held, and there 2 sokemen held 4 hides: they were men of Beorhtric and they could sell.

IN DESBOROUGH HUNDRED

Hugh himself holds MEDMENHAM. It is assessed at 10 hides. There is land for 10 ploughs. In demesne [are] 4 hides, and there are 2 ploughs; and 10 villans with 8 bordars have 8 ploughs. There are 4 slaves. From a fishery, 1,000 eels. [There is] meadow for all the ploughs, [and] woodland for 50 pigs. All together it is and was worth 100s; TRE £8. This manor Wulfstan, a thegn of King Edward, held and could sell to whom he wished.

Hugh himself holds "BROCH" [? in Medmenham] as 1 hide. There is land for 1 plough, and there is [1 plough], with 1 villan and 2 bordars. It is and always was worth 10s. This land Oda held; he was a man of Beorhtric and could sell it.

IN YARDLEY HUNDRED

In Cheddington Hugh holds half a hide, but it has been laid waste. This land Wulfwine of Whaddon held and could sell.

In Whaddon [in Slapton] Hugh holds holds [sic] 1 hide. There is land for 1 plough, and there is [1 plough] with 1 villan. [There is] meadow for 1 plough. It is and was worth 10s; TRE 20s. This land 2 men of Beorhtric held and could sell.

IN 'SECKLEY' HUNDRED

Hugh himself holds CALVERTON. It is assessed at 10 hides. There is land for 10 ploughs. In demesne [are] 3 hides, and there are 3 ploughs; and 18 villans with 8 bordars have 7 ploughs and there could be a ninth [sic]. There are 9 slaves, and 1 mill rendering 13s4d, [and] meadow for 5 ploughs. In all it is and was worth £10; TRE £12. This manor Bisi, a thegn of King Edward, held; and there 1 man of Queen Edith had 2 hides as 1 manor and could sell them.

In Great Linford Hugh holds 2 hides and 1½ virgates as 1 manor. There is land for 2 ploughs. In demesne is 1 [plough]; and 5 villans with 2 bordars have 1 plough. There is meadow for 1 plough. It is and was worth 20s; TRE 40s. This manor 3 thegns held and could give and sell.

In Hardmead Hugh holds half a virgate. There is land for 2 oxen, meadow for 2 oxen, [and] woodland for 5 pigs. It is and was worth 2s. This land Wulfgrim, a man of Earl Leofwine, held and could sell.

In Wavendon Ansel holds of Hugh 3 hides, less 1 virgate, as 1 manor. There is land for 3 ploughs. There are 4 oxen,

[Folio 151: BUCKINGHAMSHIRE]

with 2 villans and 3 bordars, [and] meadow for 3 ploughs. It is and was worth 40s; TRE 60s. This land Swein, a man of Earl Harold, held and could sell.

XXVII. The land of Henry de Ferrers

IN ASHENDON HUNDRED

HENRY de Ferrers holds Grendon Underwood. It is assessed at 2 hides. There is land for 8 ploughs. In demesne [is] 1 hide, and there are 3 ploughs; and 12 villans with 2 bordars have 5 ploughs. There are †4† slaves, meadow for 2 ploughs, [and] woodland for 500 pigs. In all it is and was worth £6; TRE £7. This manor Bondi the staller held TRE and could sell.

In Shipton Lee Henry holds 7 hides. There is land for 7 ploughs. In demesne [are] 3 hides, and there are 2 ploughs, and there could be 2 others. There 4 villans with 1 bordar have 2 ploughs, and there could be a third. There is 1 slave, [and] meadow for 1 plough. It is and was worth 60s; TRE 100s. This manor Bondi the staller held TRE.

XXVIII. The land of Walter de Vernon

IN STONE HUNDRED

WALTER de Vernon holds in in [sic] Lower Hartwell half a hide. There is land for half a plough, but there is no plough. It is and always was worth 10s. This land Thorgot, a thegn of King Edward, held and could sell.

In Marlow [Marlow or Little Marlow] Walter holds 6 hides and 1½ virgates. There is land for 6 ploughs. In demesne [are] 3½ hides, and there are 2 ploughs; and 8 villans with 6 bordars have 2½ ploughs, and there could be 1½ ploughs more. There is 1 slave, and meadow for 2 ploughs. It is and was worth 100s; TRE £4. This land Godric, a man of Esger the staller, held and could sell.

IN WADDESDON HUNDRED

Walter himself holds [? Fleet] MARSTON. It is assessed at 3 hides. There is land for 6 ploughs. In demesne is 1 hide, and there is 1 plough, and there could be another. There 6 villans with 5 bordars have 3 ploughs, and there could be a fourth. There is 1 slave, [and] meadow for 2 ploughs. It is worth 40s; when received 100s; and as much TRE. This manor Thorgot, a man of Earl Leofwine, held and could sell.

XX. The land of Walter fitzOther

IN STOKE HUNDRED

WALTER fitzOther holds HORTON [near Slough]. It is assessed at 10 hides. There is land for 9 ploughs. In demesne [are] 2 hides, and there are 2 ploughs; and 15 villans with 5 bordars have 6 ploughs, and there could be a seventh. There are 4 slaves, and 1 mill rendering 20s, [and] meadow for 3 ploughs. In all it is worth £6; when received 50s; TRE £6. This manor Ealdræd, a man of Archbishop Stigand, held and could sell.

IN BURNHAM HUNDRED

Walter himself holds ETON. It is assessed at 12 hides. There is land for 8 ploughs. In demesne [are] 3 hides, and there are 2 ploughs; and 15 villans with 4 bordars have 6 ploughs. There are 4 slaves, and 2 mills rendering 20s, meadow for 2 ploughs, [and] woodland for 200 pigs. From a fishery, 1,000 eels. In all it is worth £6; when received 100s; TRE £6. This manor Queen Edith held.

Walter himself holds BURNHAM. It is assessed at 18 hides. There is land for 15 ploughs. In demesne [are] 3 hides, and there are 3 ploughs; and 28 villans with 7 bordars have 12 ploughs. There are 2 slaves, meadow for 3 ploughs, [and] woodland for 600 pigs and iron for the ploughs. In all it is worth £10; when received £6; TRE £10. This manor Almær, a thegn of King Edward, held.

IN MOULSOE HUNDRED

Ralph holds of Walter 4 hides as 1 manor. There is land for 6 ploughs. In demesne are 2 [ploughs]; and 9 villans with 7 bordars have 4 ploughs. There are 2 slaves, meadow for 2 ploughs, [and] woodland for 100 pigs. All together it is worth 60s; when received 100s; TRE £4. This manor Oswig, a man of Alric, held and could sell.

XXX. The land of Walter the Fleming

IN MOULSOE HUNDRED

WALTER the Fleming holds 1 hide and 1 virgate as 1 manor, and Fulkwin [holds] of him. There is land for 1 plough. There is 1 villan, [and] meadow for 1 plough. It is worth 10s; when received 20s; and as much TRE. This land Swening, a man of Earl Harold, held and could sell.

XXXI. The land of William de Feugeres

IN 'STOTFOLD' HUNDRED

WILLIAM de Feugeres holds TURWESTON. It is assessed at 5 hides. There is land for 8 ploughs. Besides these 5 hides there are 3 carucates of land in demesne, and there is 1 plough, and there could be 2 more; and 6 villans with 4 bordars have 5 ploughs. There are 4 slaves, and 1 mill rendering 7s6d, [and] meadow for 8 ploughs. In all it is and was worth £4; TRE 100s. This manor Wynsige, the chamberlain of King Edward, held and could sell.

XXXII. The land of William the Chamberlain

IN STONE HUNDRED

WILLIAM the chamberlain holds 2 hides in Lower Hartwell, and Robert [holds] of him. There is land for 2 ploughs. In demesne is 1 [plough]; and 2 villans with 4 bordars have 1 plough. It is and always was worth 30s. This land Wulfmær, a priest of King Edward, held and could sell.

XXXIII. The land of William fitzConstantine

IN STONE HUNDRED

WILLIAM fitzConstantine holds in 'Southcote' [in Stone] 1 virgate of land and 6 acres, and Sweeting [holds] of him. There is land for half a plough. It is and always was worth 6s. This land Wulfric, a man of Archbishop Stigand, held and could sell.

XXXIIII. The land of William fitzManni

IN ASHENDON HUNDRED

WILLIAM fitzManni holds in Ludgershall 2 hides. There is land for 2 ploughs. In demesne [are] 1 hide and 1 virgate, and there is 1 plough; and 3 villans have 1 plough. [There is] meadow for 1 plough. It is and always was worth 20s. This manor Ælfric, the chamberlain of King Edward, held and could sell.

XXXV. The land of Turstin fitzRolf

IN STONE HUNDRED

TURSTIN fitzRolf holds Little KIMBLE, and Albert [holds] of him. It is assessed at 10 hides. There is land for 10 ploughs. In demesne are 2 [ploughs], and there could be another 2. There 10 villans with 1 bordar have 3 ploughs, and there could be 3 others. There are 2 slaves, and 1 mill rendering 16s, [and] meadow for 10 ploughs. In all it is and was worth 100s; TRE £6. This manor Beorhtric, a thegn of King Edward, held.

IN COTTESLOE HUNDRED

In HARDWICK Turstin holds 19 hides. There is land for 19 ploughs. In demesne [are] 9½ hides, and there are 3 ploughs, and there could be a fourth. There 24 villans with 4 bordars have 14½ ploughs, and there could be half [a plough] more. There are 8 slaves, [and] meadow for 10 ploughs. In all it is worth £15; when received £10; TRE £16. This manor Saxi, a thegn of King Edward, held.

In [Lower or Upper] Burston Reginald holds 1 hide of Turstin. There is land for 1 plough, and there is [1 plough], with 2 bordars and 1 slave. [There is] meadow for 1 plough. It is worth 20s; when received 10s; TRE 20s. Alwynn, a certain woman of Siward, held this land, and she could give it to whom she wished.

[Folio 151V: BUCKINGHAMSHIRE]

XXXVI. The land of Turstin Mantel

IN STONE HUNDRED

TURSTIN Mantel holds half a hide in Little Missenden. There is land for 2 ploughs. In demesne is 1 [plough]; and 2 villans with 1 bordar have 1 plough. [There is] meadow for 2 ploughs, [and] woodland for 30 pigs. It is and was worth 20s; TRE 30s. This land Særic, a man of Sigeræd, held and could sell.

IN BURNHAM HUNDRED

In Amersham Turstin holds half a hide. There is land for 2 ploughs. There is 1 [plough], and there could be another. There are 2 villans with 1 bordar, meadow for 2 ploughs, [and] woodland for 30 pigs. It is and was worth 13s4d; TRE 20s. This land Thorkil, a man of King Edward, held and could sell.

In Chesham Turstin holds half a hide. There is land for 1 plough, but it has been laid waste. It is and always was worth 5s. This is land Øpi, a man of Beorhtric, held and could sell.

XXXVII. The land of Ralph de Feugeres

IN 'MOW' HUNDRED

RALPH de Feugeres holds TWYFORD. It is assessed at 17 hides. There is land for 18 ploughs. In demesne [are] 6 hides, and there are 3 ploughs, and there could be 2 more. There 15 villans with 10 bordars have 11 ploughs, and there could be 2 more. There are 9 slaves, meadow for 3 ploughs, [and] woodland for 100 pigs. In all it is worth £10; when received £8; TRE £12. This manor Countess Goda held, and there a certain man of Earl Harold had 3 hides as 1 manor and could sell it.

Ralph himself holds CHARNDON. It is assessed at 10 hides. There is land for 10 ploughs. In demesne [are] 2 hides, and there are 2 ploughs; and 18 villans with 11 bordars have 8 ploughs. There are 4 slaves, [and] meadow for 2 ploughs. All together it is and was worth £8; TRE £9. This manor Einger, a man of Earl Harold, held and could sell.

XXXVIII. The land of Bertram de Verdun

IN STOKE HUNDRED

BERTRAM de Verdun holds FARNHAM ROYAL. It is assessed at 10 hides. There is land for 8 ploughs. In demesne [are] 5 hides, and there are 2 ploughs; and 5 villans with 3 bordars have 4 ploughs, and there could be 2 more. There are 2 slaves, meadow for 2 ploughs, [and] woodland for 600 pigs. All together it is worth 100s; when received £4; and as much TRE. This manor Countess Goda held. Of this manor, Geoffrey de Mandeville holds in Amersham half a hide, of which he dispossessed the aforesaid Bertram whilst he was overseas in the service of the king; the HUNDRED testifies to this; and Ralph Taillebois set up on Bertram's land a mill which was not there TRE, as the hundred testifies.

XXXIX. The land of Nigel d'Aubigny

IN DESBOROUGH HUNDRED

NIGEL d'Aubigny holds TURVILLE, and Roger [holds] of him. It is assessed at 5 hides. There is land for 11 ploughs. In demesne are 3 [ploughs]; and 13 villans with 1 bordar have 7 ploughs, and there could be an eighth. [There is] woodland for 20 pigs. All together it is worth £7; when received 100s; TRE £7. This manor Thorbert, a man of Earl Ælfgar, held and could sell.

IN IXHILL HUNDRED

In TOWERSEY [Oxon.] Nigel de Le Vast holds of Nigel 9 hides and 1 virgate. There is land for 7 ploughs. In demesne are 3 [ploughs]; and 10 villans have 4 ploughs. There are 4 slaves, [and] meadow for 7 ploughs. In all it is worth £7; when received 100s; TRE £8. This manor 7 thegns, men of King Edward, held and could sell.

XL. The land of Nigel de Berville

IN MURSLEY HUNDRED

NIGEL de Berville holds in Drayton Parslow 2 hides and 1 virgate as 1 manor. There is land for 8 ploughs. In demesne is 1 [plough], and there could be 2 more. There 8 villans with 2 bordars have 4½ ploughs, and there could be half [a plough] more. There are 3 slaves, [and] meadow for 8 ploughs. It is worth 40s; when received 100s; and as much TRR [sic]. This manor Leofwine of Nuneham Courtenay held of the king, and afterwards, TRW, Ralph Passaquam held it of the same Leofwine, and found 2 men with hauberks for the guard of Windsor [Berks.]. The Bishop of Coutances dispossessed this Ralph and delivered [the manor] to the aforesaid Nigel.

XLI. The land of Roger d'Ivry

IN IXHILL HUNDRED

ROGER d'Ivry holds NASHWAY, and Picot [holds] of him. It is assessed at 2 hides. There is land for 4 ploughs. In demesne are 2 [ploughs]; and 4 villans with 2 bordars have 2 ploughs. There are 2 slaves, meadow for 1 plough, [and] woodland for 200 pigs. In all it is worth 40s; when received 30s; TRE 50s. This manor Azur son of Toti, a man of Queen Edith, held and could sell.

IN MURSLEY HUNDRED

In Westbury [in Shenley] Payne holds of Roger 2½ hides as 1 manor. There is land for 7 ploughs. In demesne are 2½ ploughs; and 8 villans with 2 bordars have 4½ ploughs. There is 1 slave, and 2 mills rendering 18s, meadow for 5 ploughs, [and] woodland for 250 pigs. In all it is worth 60s; when received 50s; TRE 60s. This manor Alwine, brother of Bishop Wulfwig, held and could sell.

In Dadford Haimard holds of Roger 2 hides as 1 manor. There is land for 4 ploughs. There is 1 [plough], and there could be 3 more. There are 4 bordars and 1 slave, meadow for 4 ploughs, [and] woodland for 200 pigs. All together it is and was worth 20s; TRE 30s. This manor Leofwine, a man of Burgræd, held and could give and sell.

Fulk holds of Roger RADCLIVE. It is assessed at 5 hides. There is land for 8 ploughs. In demesne are 3 [ploughs]; and 6 villans with 4 bordars have 3 ploughs, and there could be 2 more. There are 3 slaves, and 1 mill rendering 5s, [and] meadow for 8 ploughs. All together it is worth 100s; when received £4; TRE £6. This manor Azur son of Toti held and could sell.

IN 'ROWLEY' HUNDRED

In Beachampton Leofwine holds of Roger 1 hide. There is land for 1 plough, and there is [1 plough] with 2 villans. [There is] meadow for 1 plough. It is and always was worth 10s. This land Leofric, a man of Azur, held and could sell.

Godfrey holds of Roger THORNTON. It is assessed at 8 hides. There is land for 10 ploughs. In demesne are 3 [ploughs], and there could be a fourth. There 12 villans with 5 bordars have 5 ploughs, and there could be a sixth. There are 3 slaves, and 1 mill rendering 10 orae, [and] meadow for 6 ploughs. In all it is and was worth £6; TRE £8. This manor Azur son of Toti held and could sell.

Fulk holds of Roger 'Haseley' [in Thornton] as 1 hide. There is land for 1½ ploughs. There is 1 plough, and there could be half [a plough more]. There is 1 bordar and 1 slave, [and] meadow for 1½ ploughs. It is and was worth 30s; TRE 40s. This manor Thorir, a man of King Edward, held and could sell.

XLII. The land of Richard Engaine

IN MURSLEY HUNDRED

RICHARD Engaine holds in SHENLEY BROOK END 2½ hides as 1 manor. There is land for 2 ploughs, and there are [2 ploughs] with 8 villans and 2 slaves. [There is] meadow for 2 ploughs, [and] woodland for 50 pigs. It is and always was worth 40s. This manor Wulfweard, a thegn of King Edward, held.

XLIII. The land of Mainou the Breton

IN AYLESBURY HUNDRED

MAINOU the Breton holds in ELLESBOROUGH 14½ hides. There is land for 11 ploughs. In demesne [are] 5 hides, and there are 3 ploughs; and 8 villans with 10 bordars have 8 ploughs. There are 4 slaves, meadow for 3 ploughs, [and] woodland for 100 pigs. In all it is worth £6; when received £4; TRE £10. This manor Leofnoth, a man of King Edward, held.

IN BURNHAM HUNDRED

In Chalfont St Giles Mainou holds 4 hides and 3 virgates. There is land for 15 ploughs.

[Folio 152: BUCKINGHAMSHIRE]

In demesne [is] 1 hide, and there are 3 ploughs; and 13 villans and 8 bordars have 12 ploughs. There are 4 slaves, and 3 mills: 1 renders 5 orae and the other 2 render nothing. [There is] meadow for 1 plough, woodland for 600 pigs, and in the same woodland a hawk's eyrie. In all it is worth £6.10s; when received 100s; TRE £6.10s. This manor Tovi, a thegn of King Edward, held, and there Alweard, his man, had half a hide and could sell it.

In Aston Sandford Odo holds of Mainou 4½ hides. There is land for 4½ ploughs. In demesne are 3 [ploughs]; and 3 villans with 4 bordars have 1½ ploughs. There are 6 slaves, [and] meadow for 2 ploughs. All together it is worth 100s; when received £4; TRE 100s. This manor Soting, a man of Earl Tosti, held and could sell.

IN COTTESLOE HUNDRED

In Helsthorpe Helgot holds of Mainou 4 hides and 1 virgate as 1 manor. There is land for 3 ploughs. In demesne [are] 2 ploughs; and 2 villans with 1 plough. There are 2 slaves, [and] meadow for 3 ploughs. It is worth 40s; when received 20s; TRE £4. This manor 4 thegns held, one a man of Earl Leofwine, another a man of Wulfwynn, and the third a man of Earl Leofwine, of Mentmore, and the fourth a man of Beorhtric. All could sell.

IN YARDLEY HUNDRED

In Drayton Beauchamp Helgot holds of Mainou 6 hides and 3 virgates as 1 manor, and 3 acres. There is land for 4 ploughs. In demesne is 1 [plough]; and 13 villans have 3 ploughs. There are 2 slaves, meadow for 3 ploughs, [and] woodland for 200 pigs. All together it is and was worth £4; TRE 100s. This manor Ælfric, a thegn of King Edward, held and could sell.

IN 'STOTFOLD' HUNDRED

In Lamport Gerard holds of Mainou 2½ hides. There is land for 3 ploughs. In demesne is 1 [plough]; and 1 villan with 3 bordars have 1 plough, and there could be another. There is 1 slave, meadow for 1 plough, [and] woodland for 40 pigs. All together it is worth 30s; when received 16s; TRE 30s. This land Rawn, a man of Bishop Wulfwig, held and could sell.

IN 'MOW' HUNDRED

In Thornborough Berner holds of Mainou 14 hides and 1 virgate as 1 manor. There is land for 11 ploughs. In demesne are 3 [ploughs]; and 14 villans with 8 bordars have 8 ploughs. There are 3 slaves, and 1 mill rendering 20s, [and] meadow for 4 ploughs. In all it is worth £8; when received £6; TRE £8. This manor Thorir, a thegn of King Edward, held.

Mainou himself holds PADBURY. It is assessed at 20 hides. There is land for 14 ploughs. In demesne are 3 [ploughs], and there could be a fourth. There 15 villans with 6 bordars have 8 ploughs, and there could be 3 more. There are 8 slaves, and 1 mill rendering 15s, [and] woodland for 30 pigs. In all it is worth £12; when received £7; TRE £12.

IN 'SECKLEY' HUNDRED

Mainou himself holds STOKE HAMMOND. It is assessed at 10 hides. There is land for 10 ploughs. In demesne [are] 3 hides, and there are 3 ploughs; and 12 villans with 4 bordars have 6 ploughs, and there could be a seventh. There are 6 slaves, and 1 mill rendering 8s, [and] meadow for 6 ploughs. In all it is and always was worth £10. This manor 8 thegns held. 1 of them held 6 hides, less half a virgate, as 1 manor, and he and all the other 7 could sell their land to whom they wished.

In Loughton 2 knights hold of Mainou 5 hides as 1 manor. There is land for 5 ploughs. In demesne are 2 [ploughs]; and 6 villans with 2 bordars have 1½ ploughs, and there could be half [a plough more]. There is 1 slave, [and] meadow for 5 ploughs. In all it is and was worth £3; TRE £4. This manor Ælfric, a thegn of King Edward, held and could sell.

Mainou himself holds Wolverton. It is assessed at 20 hides. There is land for 20 ploughs. In demesne [are] 9 hides, and there are 5 ploughs; and 32 villans with 8 bordars have 10 ploughs, and there could be 5 more. There are 10 slaves, and 2 mills rendering 32s8d, [and] meadow for 9 ploughs. In all it is worth £20; when received £15; TRE £20. This manor 3 thegns held. One of these, Godwine, a man of Earl Harold, had 10 hides, and another, Thorir, a housecarl of King Edward, had 7½ hides, and the third, Ælfric, a man of Queen Edith, had 2½ hides. All these could sell to whom they wished.

XLIIII. The land of Joscelin the Breton

IN BURNHAM HUNDRED

JOSCELIN the Breton holds in Amersham half a hide. There is land for 1 plough, and there is [1 plough] with 5 bordars, and 1 mill rendering 4s. [There is] meadow for 1 plough. It is and always was worth 20s. This land Ælfric, a man of Godric the sheriff, held and could sell.

IN COTTESLOE HUNDRED

In Soulbury Joscelin holds 1½ hides and the third part of a virgate as 1 manor. There is land for 4 ploughs. In demesne [is] half a hide, and there is 1 plough; and 4 villans with 2 bordars have 3 ploughs. There are 3 slaves, and 1 mill rendering 16s, [and] meadow for 1 plough. It is and always was worth 40s. This manor Alwine, a man of Eadgifu the Fair, held and could sell.

Joscelin himself holds CUBLINGTON. It is assessed at 10 hides. There is land for 9 ploughs. In demesne [are] 6 hides, and there are 4 ploughs; and 8 villans with 8 bordars have 5 ploughs. There are 5 slaves, [and] meadow for 4 ploughs. All together it is worth £6; when received £3; TRE £6. This manor 2 men of King Edward held as 2 manors-Godwine 2 hides and Thorkil 8 hides-and they could sell.

In Grove Robert holds of Joscelin 2½ hides. There is land for 2 ploughs. In demesne is 1 [plough]; and 2 villans have another plough. It is and was worth 20s; TRE 27s. This manor 2 brothers held and could sell.

IN YARDLEY HUNDRED

Ralph holds of Joscelin 1½ hides. There is land for 1 plough, and there is [1 plough] with 1 villan and 2 bordars, [and] meadow for 1 plough. It is and was worth 15s; TRE 20s. This land Alwine, a man of Eadgifu the Fair, held and could sell.

XLV. The land of Urse de Bercheres

IN MURSLEY HUNDRED

URSE de Bercheres holds in SHENLEY BROOK END 2½ hides as 1 manor. There is land for 2 ploughs. In demesne [are] 1½ hides, and there is 1 plough; and the villans have 1 plough. [There is] woodland for 50 pigs. It is and was worth 30s; TRE 40s. This manor Morcar, a man of Earl Harold, held and could sell.

XLVI. The land of Winemar the Fleming

IN BUNSTY HUNDRED

WINEMAR holds HANSLOPE. It is assessed at 10 hides. There is land for 26 ploughs. In demesne are 5 hides, and, besides these, 5 carucates of land, and there are 2 ploughs, and there could be 4 more. There 36 villans with 11 bordars have 18 ploughs, and there could be 2 more ploughs. There are 8 slaves, and 1 mill rendering 12s, meadow for 11 ploughs, [and] woodland for 1,000 pigs. In all it is worth £24; when received £20; TRE £24. This manor Healfdene, a housecarl of King Edward, held and could sell.

XLVII. The land of Martin

IN 'SECKLEY' HUNDRED

MARTIN holds in Woughton on the Green 5½ hides as 1 manor. There is land for 5 ploughs. In demesne are 1½ [ploughs].

[Folio 152V: BUCKINGHAMSHIRE]

and there could be half [a plough more]. There 6 villans with 3 bordars have 3 ploughs. [There is] meadow for 2 ploughs. There are 4 slaves. All together it is and was worth 100s; TRE £6. This manor Azur son of Toti, a thegn of King Edward, held, and another thegn, his man, held 1 hide and could sell it.

XLVIII. The land of Hervey

IN DESBOROUGH HUNDRED

HERVEY the legate holds in Ibstone [Ibstone and Ibstone Common] 2 hides of the king. There is land for 5 ploughs. In demesne [is] half a hide, and there are 2 ploughs; and 7 villans have 2 ploughs, and there could be a third. There is 1 smith, and 4 slaves, [and] woodland for 100 pigs. In all it is and was worth £4; TRE 100s. This manor Tovi, a thegn of King Edward, held and could sell.

XLIX. The land of Hascoit Musard

HASCOIT Musard holds in Quainton 2½ hides as 1 manor, and Eudo [holds] of him. There is land for 4 ploughs. In demesne [are] 2 ploughs; and 4 villans with 3 bordars have 1 plough, and there could be another. There are 2 slaves, meadow for 2 ploughs, [and] woodland for 100 pigs. All together it is and always was worth 50s. This manor Azur son of Toti, a housecarl of King Edward, held and could sell.

L. The land of Gunfrid de Chocques

IN COTTESLOE HUNDRED

GUNFRID de Chocques holds in Wingrave 6 hides as 1 manor, and Wibald [holds] of him. There is land for 5 ploughs. In demesne are 3 [ploughs]; and 8 villans with 3 bordars have 2 ploughs. There is 1 slave, [and] meadow for 5 ploughs. In all it is and was worth 100s; TRE £6. This manor Swein, a thegn of King Edward, held and could sell.

LI. The land of Giles brother of Ansculf

IN STOKE HUNDRED

GILES brother of Ansculf holds DATCHET as 13½ hides. There is land for 12 ploughs. In demesne [are] 5 hides, and there is 1 plough, and there could be 4 [more] ploughs. There 16 villans with 6 bordars have 7 ploughs. There are 3 slaves, meadow for 5 ploughs, woodland for 300 pigs, and 2 fisheries [rendering] 2,000 eels. In all it is and was worth £6; TRE £12.

Of this manor, Sæwulf, a man of Earl Leofwine, held 6 hides and 3 virgates as 1 manor, and Siward his brother, a man of Earl Harold, 6 hides and 3 virgates; and these men could sell.

IN BURNHAM HUNDRED

In Boveney Gerard holds of Giles 3 hides. There is land for 2½ ploughs. There is half [a plough], and there could be 2 ploughs [more]. [There is] meadow for 2 ploughs, [and] woodland for 60 pigs. It is and was worth 20s; TRE 60s. This manor Siward, a man of Earl Harold, held and could sell.

IN IXHILL HUNDRED

Alvred of Thame holds of Giles 1 hide and 3 virgates. There is land for 2 ploughs, and there are [2 ploughs], with 2 villans and 1 slave. [There is] meadow for 2 ploughs. It is worth 30s; when received 10s; TRE 40s. This manor Sæwulf, a man of Earl Ralph, held and could sell.

LII. The land of Queen Matilda

IN DESBOROUGH HUNDRED

Queen MATILDA holds [sic] MARLOW [Marlow or Little Marlow]. It is assessed at 15 hides. There is land for 26 ploughs. In demesne [are] 5 hides, and there are 2 ploughs; and 35 villans with 23 bordars have 24 ploughs. There is 1 slave, and 1 mill rendering 20s, meadow for 26 ploughs, woodland for 1,000 pigs, and from 1 fishery, 1,000 eels, In all it is worth £25; when received £10; and as much TRE. This manor Earl Ælfgar held.

The queen herself holds [sic] HAMBLEDEN. It is assessed at 20 hides. There is land for 30 ploughs. In demesne are 5 [hides], and there are 3 ploughs; and 50 villans with 9 bordars have 27 ploughs. There are 9 slaves, and 1 mill rendering 20s, and from 1 fishery, 1,000 eels, meadow for 8 ploughs, [and] woodland for 700 pigs. From all rents, it renders yearly £35 and by tale; when the queen was living £15; TRE £16. This manor Earl Ælfgar held.

LIII. The land of Countess Judith

IN COTTESLOE HUNDRED

Countess JUDITH holds in Hollingdon 1 hide and 3½ virgates. Thorkil holds of her. There is land for 2 ploughs. In demesne is 1 [plough]; and 1 villan with 3 bordars has 1 plough. It is and was worth 20s; TRE 30s. This man held it TRE and could sell it.

IN BUNSTY HUNDRED

In Weston Underwood Ansketil holds of Countess Judith 3 virgates. There is land for half a plough, and there is [half a plough]. [There is] meadow for 4 oxen, [and] woodland for 20 pigs. It is and was worth 10s; TRE 20s. This land Wulfric, a man of Earl Waltheof, held and could sell.

In Lavendon Roger holds of the countess 2 hides and 1 virgate and the fourth part of 1 virgate. There is land for 2 ploughs. In demesne is 1 [plough]; and 3 villans with 2 bordars have 1 plough. [There is] meadow for 2 ploughs, [and] woodland for

30 pigs. It is worth 30s; when received 10s; TRE 40s. This manor Hunmann, a man of Alli, held and could sell.

In the same vill Gilbert de Blosseville holds holds [sic] of the countess 2 hides and 1 virgate. There is land for 3 ploughs, but there are no ploughs, only 4 bordars. [There is] meadow for 3 ploughs, [and] woodland for 20 pigs. It is and always was worth 20s. This manor Alli, a housecarl of King Edward, held and could sell.

In the same vill Ralph holds of the countess 1 hide. There is land for 1½ ploughs. There is 1 villan and 3 bordars, meadow for 1½ ploughs, [and] woodland for 15 pigs. It is and was worth 10s; TRE 20s. This manor Thorbert, a man of Countess Goda, held and could sell.

In Clifton Reynes Roger of Olney holds 1 hide and half a virgate. There is land for 1 plough, but there is no [plough]. There are 2 bordars, meadow for 1 plough, [and] woodland for 10 pigs. It is and always was worth 10s. This land 2 thegns, men of Ælfric son of Goding, held and could sell.

In the same [vill] Nigel holds of the countess 1½ hides. There is land for 2 ploughs, and there are [2 ploughs], with 2 villans and 4 bordars. There is 1 slave, and half a mill rendering 11s, meadow for 2 ploughs, [and] woodland for 20 pigs. From a fishery, 125 eels. It is and was worth 30s; TRE 40s. This manor Ælfric, a man of Bishop Wulfwig, held and could sell.

In Emberton Roger holds of the countess 3 hides as 1 manor. There is land for 3 ploughs. In demesne are 2 [ploughs]; and 6 villans with 3 bordars have 1 plough. [There is] meadow for 2 ploughs, [and] woodland for 60 pigs. It is worth 60s; when received 40s; TRE 60s. This manor Alric, a man of Bishop Wulfwig, held.

In Hardmead Morcar holds 1 hide and 1 virgate of the countess. There is land for 1 plough, and there is [1 plough], with 3 villans and 1 bordar. [There is] meadow for 1 plough, [and] woodland for 50 pigs. It is and was worth 10s; TRE 20s. This man held it TRE and could sell it without the leave of his lord.

In Broughton [near Moulsoe] Morcar holds of the countess 1 hide as 1 manor. There is land for 1 plough, and there is [1 plough], with 1 villan and 1 bordar. [There is] meadow for 1 plough. It is and was worth 10s; TRE 20s. This man held it TRE and could sell it.

[Folio 153: BUCKINGHAMSHIRE]

LIIII. [The land of Azelina, wife of Ralph Taillebois]

IN COTTESLOE HUNDRED

AZELINA, wife of Ralph Taillebois, holds of the king half a hide in Soulbury. There is land for 1 plough, and there is [1 plough]. [There is] meadow for 1 plough. It is and always was worth 10s. 2 Englishmen hold it, and they themselves held it TRE.

LV. [The land of Alric the Cook]

IN 'MOW' HUNDRED

ALRIC the cook holds of the king STEEPLE CLAYDON. It is assessed at 20 hides. There is land for 24 ploughs. In demesne [are] 5 hides, and there are 5 ploughs; and 50 villans with 3 bordars have 19 ploughs. There are 7 slaves, meadow for 4 ploughs, [and] woodland for 100 pigs. In all it is worth £16; when received £11; and as much TRE. This manor Queen Edith held.

LVI. The land of Alsige

IN BURNHAM HUNDRED

ALSIGE holds of the king in CHESHAM 4 hides. There is land for 9 ploughs. In demesne [are] 1½ hides, and there are 2 ploughs; and 10 villans with 5 bordars have 7 ploughs. There are 6 slaves, and meadow for 2 ploughs, woodland for 800 pigs, and 1 mill rendering 6s8d. It is and was worth £4; TRE 100s. This manor Queen Edith held and she herself gave it to the same Alsige after the coming of King William.

IN ASHENDON HUNDRED

In 'shortley' [in Quainton] Alsige holds 4 hides as 1 manor. There is land for 6 ploughs. In demesne [are] 2 hides, and there are 2 ploughs; and 5 villans with 4 bordars have 3 ploughs. There are 2 slaves, meadow for 2 ploughs, [and] woodland for 400 pigs. In all it is and always was worth £3. This manor Wulfweard, a man of Queen Edith, held TRE, and she herself gave it to this Alsige with Wulfweard's daughter.

In Shipton Lee Alsige holds 2 hides of the king. There is land for 1 plough. There is half a plough, and there could be [another] half. [There is] meadow for 1 plough. It is and was worth 10s; TRE 20s; and this land he received with his wife.

LVII. The land of Leofwine of Nuneham Courtenay

IN MURSLEY HUNDRED

LEOFWINE of Nunehaam Courtenay holds of the king in salden 2 hides and 3½ virgates as 1 manor. There is land for 3 ploughs. In demesne [is] 1 plough; and 6 villans with 3 bordars have 2 ploughs. There are 2 slaves, [and] meadow for 3 ploughs. It is and was worth 30s; when received 40s. This manor this man held TRE and could sell.

In Mursley Leofwine holds 4 hides. There is land for 3 ploughs. There are 2 [ploughs], and there could be a third. There are 4 villans with 2 bordars, [and] meadow for 1 plough. It is and was worth 20s; TRE 30s. This manor this man held TRE and could sell.

IN 'STOTFOLD' HUNDRED

In Maids Moreton Leofwine holds 5 hides as 1 manor. There is land for 5 ploughs. In demesne [are] 2 hides, and there is half a plough, and there could be another 1½ [ploughs]. There 3 villans with 2 bordars have 1½ ploughs, and there could be half [a plough] more. There are 5 slaves, and 1 mill rendering 10s, [and] meadow for 2 ploughs. In all it is and always was worth 40s. This manor this man held TRE and could sell.

IN 'ROWLEY' HUNDRED

In Beachampton Leofwine holds 4 hides as 1 manor. There is land for 4 ploughs. In demesne [is] 1 hide, and there are 2 ploughs; and 5 villans with 6 bordars have 2 ploughs. There are 2 slaves, [and] meadow for 3 ploughs. It is and was worth 40s; TRE 50s. This manor the same Leofwine held TRE and could sell.

IN MOULSOE HUNDRED

In Wavendon Godwine the priest holds of Leofwine 1 virgate. There is land for 4 oxen. There are 3 bordars, and meadow for 4 oxen. It is and was worth 2s; TRE 5s. This man held it TRE and could sell.

IN 'STOTFOLD' HUNDRED

A certain bandy-legged man holds in alms of the king Evershaw as 1 hide. There is land for 2 ploughs, and there are [2 ploughs] with 2 villans. It is and always was worth 20s. This man held it TRE.

IN 'STOTFOLD' HUNDRED

HUGH fitzGozhere holds in Dadford of the king 2 hides in alms. There is land for 4 ploughs. There is 1 [plough], and there could be 3 [more]. There are 3 bordars, meadow for 4 ploughs, [and] woodland for 200 pigs. It is and was worth 20s; TRE 40s. This land 2 thegns, Rawn and Wulfweard, held and could sell.

IN MOULSOE HUNDRED

Leofwine Chava holds of the king 1 hide in Wavendon. There is land for 1 plough, and there is [1 plough], with 3 villans and 5 bordars. There is 1 slave, and meadow for 1 plough, [and] woodland for 50 pigs. It is and always was worth 10s. This land Leofwine himself, reeve of the king, held and could sell.

IN 'SECKLEY' HUNDRED

Leofwine Oaura holds of the king 1 hide and 1 virgate in Simpson. There is land for 1 plough, and there is [1 plough], with 2 villans and 2 bordars. [There is] meadow for 1 plough. It is and always was worth 10s. This man held it TRE and could sell it.

IN AYLESBURY HUNDRED

Leofwine holds of the king half a hide in "Wandene". There is land for 1 plough. There is half [a plough], and there could be [another] half. There is 1 bordar, [and] woodland for 30 pigs and rendering 10s. It is and always was worth 10s. This man

held it TRE and could sell it. This land Ralph attached to Wendover but it did not belong to it TRE.

In Wendover 3 men hold 1 hide of the king. There is land for 1 plough, and there is [1 plough] with 1 bordar. It is and was worth 20s; TRE 40s. The same men held it TRE and could sell it. Now they are in the farm of the king in Wendover, in which they were not TRE.

IN BUNSTY HUNDRED

Ketil holds of the king half a hide in Lavendon. There is land for half a plough, and there is [half a plough] with 1 bordar. [There is] meadow for 1 plough, [and] woodland for 10 pigs. It is and was worth 7s; TRE 10s. This man held it TRE and could sell it.

IN MOULSOE HUNDRED

Godric Cratel holds of the king 8½ hides as 1 manor in Milton Keynes. There is land for 10 ploughs. In demesne [are] 2½ ploughs, and there could be half [a plough more]. There 18 villans with 6 bordars have 8 ploughs. There are 6 slaves, and 1 mill rendering 6s8d, [and] meadow for 8 ploughs. All together it is and was worth 100s; TRE £8. This manor Queen Edith held.

IN RISBOROUGH HUNDRED

Hearding holds of the king 1½ hides in Horsenden. There is land for 1 plough, and there is [1 plough] with 2 bordars. It is and was worth 10s; TRE 20s. This land Wulfræd held and could sell.

IN DESBOROUGH HUNDRED

Swærting and Hearding hold of the king Bradenham as 2 hides. There is land for 2 ploughs, and there are [2 ploughs] with 2 villans. It is and always was worth 20s. 2 brothers, men of King Edward, held it and could sell it.

IN YARDLEY HUNDRED

In Cheddington Swærting holds of the king 2 hides and 1 virgate. There is land for 1 plough, and there is [1 plough], with 1 villan and 2 slaves. [There is] meadow for 1 plough. It is and always was worth 20s. Fin the Dane held it and could sell it.

IN 'SECKLEY' HUNDRED

In Caldecote Swærting holds 2½ hides. There is land for 1 plough. There is 1 [plough], and there could be another. In demesne [are] 1½ hides. There are 2 bordars, and meadow for 1 plough. It is and always was worth 20s. This land Gunni, a man of Ælfric son of Goding, held and could sell.

IN COTTESLOE HUNDRED

In Soulbury Godwine the beadle holds of the king half a hide. There is land for 1 plough, and there is [1 plough] with 1 bordar. [There is] meadow for 1 plough. It is and always was worth 7½s. Alric Bolest held it TRE, and he who now holds it says this, that after the coming of King William it was forfeit.

OXFORDSHIRE

IN THE TIME OF KING EDWARD OXFORD in fact rendered yearly to the king for toll and rent and all other customary dues £20 and 6 sesters of honey. Also to Earl Ælfgar £10 with the addition of the mill which he had within the city.

When the king went on an expedition 20 burgesses went with him for all the others or else they gave £20 to the king that all might be free.

Now OXFORD renders £60 by tale at 20[d.] to the ora.

In this vill, within the wall as without, there are 243 houses paying geld, and besides these there are 500 houses, less 22, so waste and destroyed that they cannot pay geld.

The king has 20 wall-houses which belonged to Earl Ælfgar TRE, rendering then, as now, 14s less 2d, [...] and he has 1 messuage rendering 6d pertaining to Shipton-under-Wychwood, and another rendering 4d pertaining to Bloxham, and a third rendering 30d pertaining to Princes Risborough [Bucks.], and 2 others rendering 4d pertaining to Twyford [Bucks.] in Buckinghamshire; 1 of these is waste.

They are called wall-houses for this reason, because if there is need and the king commands it they will repair the wall.

To the lands which Earl Aubrey held there pertain 1 church and 3 messuages; 2 of these belong to the Church of ST MARY, rendering 28d, and the third belongs to Burford, rendering 5s.

To the lands which Earl William held there pertain 9 messuages rendering 7s; 3 of these are waste.

The Archbishop of Canterbury has 7 messuages: they render 38d; 4 of these are waste. The Bishop of Winchester, 9 messuages: they render 62d; 3 of these are waste. The Bishop of Bayeux, 18 messuages: they render 13s4d; 4 of these are waste. The Bishop of Lincoln has 30 messuages rendering 18s6d; 16 of these are waste. The Bishop of Coutances has 2 messuages rendering 14d. The Bishop of Hereford has 3 messuages rendering 13d; 1 of these is waste.

The Abbot of St Edmundsbury has 1 messuage rendering 6d, pertaining to Taynton.

The Abbot of Abingdon has 14 messuages rendering 7s3d; 8 of these are waste. The Abbot of Eynsham has 1 church and 13 messuages, rendering 9s; 7 of these are waste.

The Count of Mortain has 10 messuages: they render 3s. All are waste except 1. Earl Hugh has 7 messuages; they render 5s8d; 4 of these are waste. The Count of Evreux has 1 waste messuage and it renders nothing.

Henry de Ferrers has 2 messuages rendering 5s.

William Peverel, 4 messuages rendering 17d; 2 of these are waste.

Edward the sheriff, 2 messuages rendering 5s.

Ernulf de Hesdin, 3 messuages rendering 18d; 1 of these is waste.

Berengar de Tosny, 1 messuage rendering 6d.

Miles Crispin, 2 messuages rendering 12d.

Richard de Courcy, 2 messuages rendering 19d.

Robert d'Oilly, 12 messuages rendering 64d; 4 of these are waste.

Roger d'Ivry, 15 messuages rendering 20s4d; 6 of these are waste.

Ranulph Flambard, 1 messuage rendering nothing.

Guy de Raimbeaucourt, 2 messuages rendering 20d.

Walter Giffard, 17 messuages rendering 22s; 7 of these are waste. Walter's predecessor had 1 of these by the gift of King Edward out of the 8 virgates which were subject to custom TRE.

Gernio has 1 messuage rendering 6d pertaining to Hampton Poyle. The son of Manasses has 1 messuage rendering 4d. [pertaining] to Bletchingdon.

All the above-written hold these aforesaid messuages free on account of the repair of the wall.

All the messuages which are called wall[-houses] were free TRE from every customary due except military service and the repair of the wall.

The priests of St Michael have 2 messuages rendering 52d.

The canons of St Frideswide have 15 messuages rendering 11s; 8 of these are waste.

Coleman had while he lived 3 messuages rendering 3s8d.

William has 1 [messuage] rendering 20d. Spracheling, 1 messuage which renders nothing.

Wulfwig the fisherman, 1 messuage rendering 32d.

Alwine has 5 messuages rendering 37d; 3 of these are waste.

Eadric, 1 messuage which renders nothing. Hearding and Leofgifu, 9 messuages: they render 12s; 4 of these are waste.

Æthelric, 1 messuage which renders nothing. Deormann, 1 messuage rendering 12d.

Segrim, 1 messuage rendering 16d. Another Segrim, 1 messuage rendering 2s.

Smeawine, 1 messuage which renders nothing. Goldwine, 1 messuage rendering nothing.

Edith, 1 messuage rendering nothing. Swetmann, 1 messuage rendering 8d.

Sæwig, 1 messuage rendering nothing. Leofgifu, 1 waste messuage rendering 10d. TRE.

Ælfgifu, 1 messuage rendering 10d. Alweard, 1 messuage rendering 10d.

Alwine, 1 waste messuage. Beorhtræd and Deormann, 1 messuage rendering 16d.

Alwig, 1 messuage from which he has nothing. Deorwynn, 1 messuage rendering 6d.

Alwine the priest, 1 waste house which renders nothing. Leofric, 1 [house] likewise rendering nothing.

Wulfric, 1 waste messuage; and yet if there is need he will repair the wall.

Swetmann the moneyer, 1 free house rendering 40d.

Godwine 1, Wulfmær 1, Guthrun 1, Godric 1, Alwig 1; these 5 [houses] render nothing. Swetmann has 2 messuages responsible for the wall; they render 3s.

Another Swetmann, 1 messuage, free on account of the same service, and he has 9d.

Sæweald, 9 messuages; they render 13s; 6 of these are waste.

Lodowin, 1 house in which he dwells, free on account of the wall.

Segrim, 3 free houses rendering 64d; 1 of these is waste.

Alwine, 1 house, free on account of repairing the wall; from this he has 32d a year. And if the wall is not repaired when there is need by him who should, either he will pay a fine of 40s to the king or he loses his house.

All the burgesses of Oxford have pasture in common outside the wall rendering 6s8d.

Here Are Entered the Landholders In Oxfordshire

I KING WILLIAM
II The Archbishop of Canterbury
III The Bishop of Winchester
IIII The Bishop of Salisbury
V The Bishop of Exeter
VI The Bishop of Lincoln
VII The Bishop of Bayeux
VIII The Bishop of Lisieux
IX The Abbey of Abingdon
X The Abbey of Battle
XI The Abbey of Winchcombe
XII The Abbey of Preaux
XIII The Church of Saint-Denis of Paris
XIIII The Canons of Oxford and other clerks
XV Earl Hugh

XVI The Count of Mortain
XVII The Count of Evreux
XVIII Earl Aubrey
XIX Count Eustace
XX Walter Giffard
XXI William fitz Ansculf
XXII William de Warenne
XXIII William Peverel
XXIIII Henry de Ferrers
XXV Hugh de Bolbec
XXVI Hugh d'Ivry
XXVII Robert of Stafford
XXVIII Robert d'Oilly
XXIX Roger d'Ivry
XXX Ralph de Mortimer
XXXI Ranulph Peverel
XXXII Richard de Courcy
XXXIII Richard Puignant
XXXIIII Berengar de Tosny
XXXV Miles Crispin
XXXVI Guy de Raimbeaucourt
XXXVII Giles brother of Ansculf
XXXVIII Gilbert de Ghent
XXXIX Geoffrey de Mandeville
XL Ernulf de Hesdin
XLI Edward of Salisbury
XLII Swein the sheriff
XLIII Alfred nephew of Vigot
XLIIII Guy d'Oilly
XLV Walter Pons
XLVI William Leofric
XLVII William fitzManni
XLVIII Ilbod brother of Ernulf de Hesdin
XLIX Reinbald
L Robert fitzMurdoch
LI Osbern Giffard
LII Benzelin
LIII Countess Judith
LIIII Christina
LV The wife of Roger d'Ivry
LVI Hascoit Musard
LVII Thorkil
LVIII Richard Engaine and other servants of the king
LIX The land of Earl William

[Folio 154V: OXFORDSHIRE]

The land of the King

THE KING holds BENSON. There are 12 hides, less 1 virgate of land. TRE there were 50 ploughs. Now in demesne [are] 8 ploughs, and 5 slaves; and 32 villans with 29 bordars have 24 ploughs. There are 2 mills rendering 40s. From the meadows and the pastures and the fisheries and the woods together there come £18.15s5d a year. From the church-scot 11s. From the corn-rent for 1 year £30. The soke of 4½ HUNDREDS belongs to this manor.

All together it renders £80 and 100s a year.

THE KING holds HEADINGTON. There are 10 hides. [...] In demesne [are] now 6 ploughs; and 20 villans with 24 bordars have 14 ploughs. There are 2 mills rendering 50s, and 5 fisheries rendering 20s.

From the meadows and pastures £4. From the corn-rent for a year £8.

From helvewecha [meaning unknown] 30s. From the church-scot 10s6d.

From other customary dues 100s and 25d.

The soke of 2 HUNDREDS belongs to this manor. Richard de Courcy retains for himself [the soke] of 16 hides.

All together it renders £60 by tale.

THE KING holds KIRTLINGTON. There are 11½ hides. In demesne are 10 ploughs; and 42 villans with 24 bordars and 2 slaves have 21 ploughs. There are 2 mills rendering 35s. From the meadows and the pastures and the pannage and other customary dues £8. From the corn-rent for a year £20. The soke of 2½ HUNDREDS belongs to this manor, except for 2½ hides in LAUNTON which used to belong there. King Edward gave these to St Peter of Westminister and to Baldwin his godson.

All together it renders £52 by tale a year.

THE KING holds WOOTTON. There are 5 hides. [...] In demesne are 4 ploughs; and 10 villans with 11 bordars have 6 ploughs. There are 2 mills rendering 10s4d. From other customary dues 50s. From the corn-rent for a year 40s. The woodland is in the king's preserve. TRE it rendered 10s. The soke of 3 HUNDREDS belongs to this manor.

All together it renders £18 by tale.

THE KING holds SHIPTON-UNDER-WYCHWOOD. There are 33 hides and 3 virgates of land. In demesne are 10 ploughs; and 54 villans with 64 bordars and 6 slaves have 43 ploughs. There are 6 mills rendering 55s. From the meadows and the pannage and rent and other customary dues £12.17s. From the corn-rent for a year £15. The woodland, which rendered 50s. TRE, is in the king's preserve. The soke of 3 HUNDREDS belongs to this manor.

All together it renders £72 by tale.

THE KING holds BAMPTON. There are 27½ hides. In demesne are 6 ploughs, and 6 slaves; and 40 villans and 17 boors and 13 bordars have 16 ploughs. TRE they had 26 ploughs. There are 4 mills [rendering] 25s. From the fisheries 20s. From the meadows 65s. From the market 50s. From the pannage and from the salt-pans at Droitwich [Worcs.], and other customary dues of the men, £9.13s. From the corn-rent for a year £15. The soke of 2 HUNDREDS belongs to this manor.

All together it renders £80 and 40s by tale a year.

Ilbert de Lacy holds half a hide by the gift of the Bishop of Bayeux, and Walter fitzPons holds a certain parcel of land, and Henry de Ferrers holds a certain wood which Bondi the forester held. The shire bears witness that all this belongs to the king's demesne.

Joseph, TRE, had 60 acres of land in STOCKLEY belonging to the king's demesne. But afterwards Earl Harold put it into his demesne, and it was in the king's demesne when the king crossed the sea.

THE KING holds BLOXHAM and ADDERBURY. There are 34½ hides. TRE there were 48 ploughs. In demesne there are now 13 [ploughs], and 27 slaves; and 72 villans with 16 bordars having [...] ploughs. There are 6 mills rendering 56s4d, meadow 2 leagues and 5 furlongs long and 4 furlongs broad, pasture 2 leagues in length and breadth, [and] woodland 13½ furlongs in length and 9 furlongs broad. From wool and cheeses 40s. From the pannage 24s7d and 40 pigs when it is stocked, and formerly 66 pigs. From the corn-rent for a year £28.10s. The soke of 2 HUNDREDS belongs to this manor. Earl Edwin held this manor. TRE it rendered £56; now £67.

To this manor belong 1 hide and 1 virgate of land in LEDWELL. There is land for 1 plough. It was and is worth 20s.

From the time of Earl Tosti, Sægeat, a thegn, dwelt in Bloxham and served as a free man. Earl Edwin gave this man to Ralph d'Oilly. Ralph d'Oilly drew this same man back into the king's demesne.

The king holds LANGFORD. There are 15 hides. [There is] land for 15 ploughs. Now in demesne [are] 5 ploughs, and 12 slaves; and 21 villans with 4 bordars have 5 ploughs. There are 2 mills rendering 20s, and 40 acres of meadow and 5 acres of pasture. TRE and afterwards, as now, worth £18.

THE KING holds SHIPTON-UNDER-WYCHWOOD. There are 8 hides. [There is] land for 12 ploughs. Now in demesne [are] 2 ploughs, and 8 slaves; and 18 villans with 5 bordars have 7 ploughs. There are 36 acres of meadow. It was worth £10; now £9. Earl Harold held these 2 manors; now Ælfsige of Faringdon holds them at farm.

In Shotover, Stowford, Woodstock, Cornbury and Wychwood are the king's demesne forests; they are 9 leagues long and as many broad. To these forests belong 4½ hides, and there 6 villans with 8 bordars have 3½ ploughs. From them and everything belonging to the forest Reginald pays £10 a year to the king.

IN BENSON HALF-HUNDRED

In "VERNEVELD" the king has half a hide waste. Hervey had the profit of this land unjustly.

The shire of OXFORD renders a farm of 3 nights, that is £150.

As increment £25 by weight. From the borough £20 by weight.

From the mint £20 [...] in pennies at 20 to the ora. For weapons 4s.

From the queen's exactions 100s by tale. For a hawk £10.

For a sumpter-horse 20s. For hounds £23 in pennies at 20 to the ora; and 6 sesters of honey and 15d as a customary due.

From the land of Earl Edwin in OXFORD [shire] and in WARWICKshire the king has £100 and 100s.

If anyone breaks the king's peace given under his hand or seal so that he kills a man to whom this peace has been given, both his members and life will be subject to the king's judgement, if he is taken. And if he cannot be taken he will be considered an outlaw by everybody, and if anyone succeeds in killing him he will lawfully have his spoils.

If any stranger choosing to dwell in Oxford and having a house ends his life there without kinsmen, the king will have whatsoever he has left.

If anyone violently breaks into or enters anyone's court or house so that he kills or wounds or assails a man, he pays a fine of 100s to the king.

Likewise the man who, when summoned to go on an expedition does not go, will give 100s to the king.

If anyone kills any man within his own court or house, his body and all his substance are in the king's power, except his wife's dower if he received her with a dowry.

[Folio 155: OXFORDSHIRE]

II. The land of the Archbishop of Canterbury

THE ARCHBISHOP OF CANTERBURY holds NEWINGTON. It belonged and belongs to the church. There are 15 hides. There is land for 18 ploughs. [...] Now in demesne [are] 6 ploughs, and 5 slaves; and 22 villans with 10 bordars have 13 ploughs. There are 15 acres of meadow and 2 furlongs of pasture, [and] woodland 1 league long and 1 broad; when it is stocked it is worth 25s. Of this land Robert d'Oilly holds 1 hide and Roger 1 hide. TRE it was worth £11; now £15.

III. The land of the Bishop of Winchester

THE BISHOP OF WINCHESTER holds WITNEY. Archbishop Stigand held it. There are 30 hides. There is land for 24 ploughs. Now in demesne [are] 5 ploughs, and 9 slaves; and 36 villans with 11 bordars have 20 ploughs. There are 2 mills rendering 32s6d, and 100 acres of meadow, [and] woodland 3 leagues long and 2 leagues broad: when it is stocked it is worth 50s. TRE it was worth £22; now £25.

The same bishop holds ADDERBURY. It belonged and belongs to the church. There are 14½ hides. There is land for 20 ploughs. [...] Now in demesne [are] 4 ploughs, and 9 slaves; and 27 villans with 9 bordars have 19 ploughs. There are 2 mills rendering 30s, and 36 acres of meadow rendering 10s. The whole [is] 3 leagues and 3 furlongs long and 1½ leagues broad. TRE it was worth £12; now £20.

IIII. The land of the Bishop of Salisbury

THE BISHOP OF SALISBURY holds DUNSDEN. It belonged and belongs to the church. There are 20 hides. There is land for 20 ploughs. Now in demesne [are] 2 ploughs; and 40 villans with 18 bordars have 20 ploughs; and there is 1 slave, and 50 acres of meadow. [There is] woodland 1 league and 4 furlongs long and half a league broad. It was and is worth £15.

V. The land of the Bishop of Exeter

THE BISHOP OF EXETER holds of the king 6 hides in BAMPTON, and Bishop Robert [holds] of him. Bishop Leofric held them. There is land for 6 ploughs. Now in demesne [are] 2 ploughs, and 2 slaves; and 10 villans with 7 bordars have 3 ploughs. There are 2 fisheries rendering 33s, and 48 acres of meadow. TRE it was worth £4; now £6.

VI. The land of the Bishop of Lincoln

IN DORCHESTER HUNDRED

THE BISHOP OF LINCOLN holds DORCHESTER. There are 100 hides, less 10. Of these the bishop has in his farm 60 hides, less 1 virgate, and the knights 30 hides and 1 virgate of land.

Now in demesne [is] land for 4 ploughs, but there are only 3 ploughs; and 34 villans with 22 bordars have 15 ploughs. There is a mill rendering 20s. A fisherman renders 30 sticks of eels, and 1 man [pays] 12s for half a hide. From the meadow 40s. [There is] scrubland 6 furlongs long and 3 broad. In addition to these this manor renders £30 a year. TRE it was worth £18.

Of the same land of this manor Beorhtgifu holds 20½ hides at farm. There is land for 16 ploughs. Now in demesne [are] 4 ploughs; and 46 villans with 15 bordars have 20 ploughs. There are 4 mills rendering 38s. From the meadows and fisheries, 22s8d. and 9 sticks of eels. In addition to these this land renders £20; TRE £10; when received, £8.

In this same [land] the bishop has in SOUTH STOKE [...] 17 hides and 1 virgate of land. Of these hides 8 are in demesne, and there are 2 ploughs; and 19 villans with 5 bordars and 1 slave have 8 ploughs. There are 24 acres of meadow. It was worth £6 TRE; now it renders £12 and 12 sticks of eels.

The bishop himself holds THAME. There are 60 hides. Of these he has 37 hides in his farm and his knights have the others [...]. There is land for 34 ploughs. Now in demesne [are] 5 ploughs, and 5 slaves; and 27 villans with 26 bordars have 19 ploughs. There is a mill rendering 20s. From the meadows 60s. TRE it was worth £20; when received, £16; now £30.

The same bishop holds GREAT MILTON. There are 40 hides. Of these he has 31 hides in his farm and [his] knights [have] the others. [...] There is land for 26 ploughs. Now in demesne [are] 5 ploughs; and 24 villans with 31 bordars and a priest have 19 ploughs. There is a mill rendering 15s, and meadow rendering 10s. TRE, and afterwards, it was worth £18; now £30.

The bishop himself holds BANBURY. There are 50 hides. Of these the bishop has in demesne land for 10 ploughs, and 3 hides in addition to the inland. The men of the vill [have] 33½ hides. TRE there were 33½ ploughs and Bishop Remigius found as many. Now in demesne [are] 7 ploughs, and 14 slaves; and 76 villans with 17 bordars have 33 ploughs. There are 3 mills rendering 45s. The pasture is 3 furlongs long and 2 furlongs broad. TRE it was worth £35; when received, £30; now it is worth as much.

The bishop himself holds CROPREDY. It belonged and belongs to the Church of ST MARY of Lincoln. There are 50 hides. Of these the bishop has in his farm 25 hides and [his] knights as much. In addition to these 50 hides there is land in demesne for 10 ploughs. All together there is land for 30 ploughs. The bishop found 35. Now in demesne [are] 6 ploughs, and 12 slaves; and 55 villans with 22 bordars have 34 ploughs. There are 2 mills rendering 28s, and 120 acres of meadow and 132 acres of pasture. TRE it was worth £28; when received, £30; now it is worth as much.

The bishop himself holds EYNSHAM, and Columban the monk [holds] of him. There are 15½ hides belonging to the same church. [...] There is land for 18 ploughs, and he found as many. In demesne is land for 2 ploughs [which is] inland. Now in demesne [are] 3 ploughs; and 3 knights with 34 villans and 33 bordars have 15 ploughs. There is a mill rendering 12s and 450 eels, and 255 acres of meadow and 100 acres of pasture, [and] woodland, 1½ leagues long and 1 league and 2 furlongs broad: when stocked it is worth 25s. It was and is worth £20.

The same Columban holds SHIFFORD of the bishop. There are 3 hides. There is land for 5 ploughs. Now in demesne [is] 1 plough; and 8 villans with 5 bordars have 5 ploughs. There are 50 acres of meadow, and pasture 2 furlongs long and 1 furlong broad, [...] and 250 eels, and 4s4d. It was worth £4; now 100s.

The same Columban holds of the bishop 5 hides in LITTLE ROLLRIGHT, and it belongs to the church. There is land for 6 ploughs. In demesne are 2 ploughs, and 2 slaves; and 12 villans with 3 bordars have 6 ploughs. There are 25 acres of meadow. It was and is worth 100s.

Of the land of DORCHESTER English free men hold 3½ hides; and Conan [holds] 8 hides, less 1 virgate; Walcher, 6½ hides; Iseward, 5½ hides; Jacob, 2 hides; Reginald and Vitalis, 5 hides. There is land all together for 20 ploughs. There are 10 ploughs in demesne; and 26 villans with 5 bordars and 3 slaves have 17 ploughs. They have there among themselves 50 acres of meadow. The whole TRE was worth £16; when received, £13; now £27.

[Folio 155V: OXFORDSHIRE]

Of the land of the manor of THAME Robert holds of the bishop 10 hides; Sæweald, 4 hides; William, 3 hides; Alvred and his companion 6 hides. There are 10 ploughs in demesne; and 16 villans with 21 bordars and 8 slaves have 10 ploughs. The whole is worth £20.

In GREAT MILTON Ælfric holds of the bishop 6 hides; William, 3 hides and 3 virgates of land. There are 2 ploughs in demesne; and 10 villans with 4 bordars and 4 slaves have 4 ploughs. There is a mill rendering 8s. The whole is worth £6.

Of the land of the manor of BANBURY Robert holds of the bishop 4 hides; Goislen, 5 hides; another Robert, 2½ hides; William, 5 hides; Humphrey half a hide. There is land for 12½ ploughs. There are 8 ploughs in demesne; and 13 villans with 3 bordars and 12 slaves have 4 ploughs. There is a mill [belonging to] one of them, Robert fitzWalkelin, rendering 5s4d, and 4 acres of meadow. The whole TRE was worth £11.10s; when received, £9.10s; now £14.

Of the land of the manor of CROPREDY, Ansgered holds of the bishop 10 hides; Gilbert, 5 hides; Theodric, 2 hides; Richard, 3 hides; Edward, 6 hides; Roger, 1 hide and 1 virgate of land; Robert and another Robert, 3 hides, less 1 virgate. There is land for 34 ploughs. There are 13 ploughs; and 28 villans with 27 bordars and 4 Frenchmen and 10 slaves have 18 ploughs. There are 3 mills rendering 35s4d, and 22 acres of meadow and 5 acres of a grove. The whole TRE was worth £27; when received, £29; now £30.10s.

Roger d'Ivry holds YARNTON of the bishop. This belongs to the Church of Eynsham. There are 9½ hides. There is land for 9 ploughs. Now in demesne [are] 2 ploughs; and 20 villans with 3 bordars have 7 ploughs. There are 200 acres of meadow, less 20, and 80 acres of pasture. There a certain Maino had 1 hide and he could go where he wished. The whole TRE was worth £10; now with the fishery and with the meadows it is worth £14.

Robert holds of the bishop's inland 2 hides in WYKHAM. There is land for 3 ploughs. Now in demesne [are] 2 ploughs, and 4 slaves; and 5 villans have 1½ ploughs. There is a mill rendering 30s. It was worth 60s; now 100s.

Sæweald holds WATERSTOCK of the bishop. This belongs to the fief of ST MARY of Lincoln. There are 5 hides. There is land for 5 ploughs. Now in demesne [are] 3 hides of this land, and there are 2 ploughs, and a mill [rendering] 9s5d, and 5 slaves, and 36 acres of meadow. It was worth 20s; now 50s. Alwig held it freely.

In MARSH BALDON Iseward holds of the bishop 5 hides and Beorhtgifu 2½ hides. There is land for 7 ploughs. There 10 villans with 3 slaves have 6 ploughs, and there is 1 acre of meadow. TRE it was worth £4; now £7.

VII. The land of the Bishop of Bayeux

THE LAND OF THE BISHOP OF BAYEUX holds COMBE of the king. There is 1 hide. There is land for 4 ploughs. Now in demesne [are] 2 ploughs, and 2 slaves; and 6 villans with 6 bordars have 3 ploughs. There is a mill rendering 3s, and 15 acres of meadow, [and] woodland 1½ leagues long and as much broad. It was worth £6; now £10. Alwine and Algar held it freely.

The same bishop holds DEDDINGTON. There are 36 hides. There is land for 30 ploughs. In demesne there were 11½ hides in addition to the inland. Now there are 18½ hides in demesne, and there are 10 ploughs, and 25 slaves; and 64 villans with 10 bordars have 20 ploughs. There are 3 mills rendering 41s and 100 eels, and there are 140 acres of meadow and 30 acres of pasture. From the meadows 10s. TRE, and afterwards, it was worth £40; now £60. 5 thegns [...].

The same bishop holds STANTON HARCOURT. There

are 26 hides which paid geld TRE. There is land for 23 ploughs. Now in demesne [is] 1 hide and 1 virgate of this land in addition to the inland, and there are 5 ploughs, and 12 slaves; and 55 villans with 28 bordars have 17 ploughs. There are 3 mills rendering 40s, and 2 fisheries rendering 30s, and 200 acres of meadow and as many of pasture, [and] woodland 1 league long and half a league broad: when stocked it is worth 25s. TRE, and afterwards, it was worth £30; now £50. Alnoth held it freely.

The same bishop holds [Great and Little] TEW. There are 16 hides. There is land for 26 ploughs. Now in demesne [are] 6 ploughs, and 14 slaves; and 31 villans with 8 bordars have 16 ploughs. There are 300 acres of meadow, less 12, and 101 acres of pasture. TRE, and afterwards, it was worth £20; now £40. Æthelnoth of Kent held it.

IN LEWKNOR HUNDRED

ILBERT de Lacy holds of the Bishop of Bayeux 2½ hides in TYTHORP [Bucks.]. There is land for 3 ploughs. Now in demesne [is] 1 plough; and 4 villans have another. There are 10 acres of meadow. It was worth 60s; now 40s.

Wadard holds 2½ hides and 12 acres of land in the same vill. There is land for 3 ploughs. Now in demesne [is] 1 plough, and 2 slaves; and 2 villans have another. There are 10 acres of meadow. It was worth 60s; now 40s.

Hervey holds [Great and Little] HASELEY. There are 9 hides. There is land for 9 ploughs. Now in demesne [are] 2 ploughs, with 1 slave; and 8 villans with 3 bordars have 6 ploughs. There are 30 acres of meadow. It was worth £7; now £6.

The same Hervey holds 2 hides in BRIGHTWELL BALDWIN. There is land for 6 ploughs. Now in demesne [are] 2 ploughs; and 5 villans with 5 bordars have 2 ploughs. There is a mill rendering 20d, and 6 acres of meadow and 20 acres of woodland. It was worth 50s; now 70s.

Roger holds 2 hides and the third part of 1 virgate in COWLEY. There is land for 2 ploughs. These are there in demesne, with 4 bordars and 2 slaves. There are 4 acres of meadow and 2 acres of pasture. It was worth 60s; now 40s.

Reginald Wadard holds SOMERTON of the bishop. There are 9 hides. There is land for 9 ploughs. Now in demesne [are] 2 ploughs, with 1 slave; and 17 villans with 9 bordars have 7 ploughs. There is a mill rendering 20s and 400 eels, and 40 acres of meadow and 156 acres of pasture. It was worth £9; now £12.

The same man holds 6 hides in FRITWELL. There is land for 4 ploughs. Now in demesne [is] 1 plough, with 1 slave; and 4 villans with 1 bordar have 1½ ploughs. There are 12 acres of meadow. It was and is worth £3.

Adam holds of the bishop 2 hides in 'SAXINTON' [in Bucknell]. There is land for 3 ploughs. 6 villans have these there. It was worth 40s; now 60s.

Alvred holds of the bishop 1½ hides in 'SAXINTON' [in Bucknell]. There is land for 1½ ploughs. Now in demesne he has 1½ ploughs; and 3 villans with 4 bordars have 2 ploughs. It was and is worth 30s.

Wadard holds FRINGFORD of the bishop. There are 8 hides. There is land for 8 ploughs. Now in demesne [are] 2 ploughs, and 4 slaves; and 18 villans with 8 bordars have 6 ploughs. There are 2 mills [rendering] 10s. It was and is worth £8.

In the same vill the same man holds 2½ hides. There is land for 1 plough, and this [plough] is in demesne, with 4 bordars. It was worth 20s; now 40s.

Robert holds of the bishop 2 hides in FINMERE. There is land for 2 ploughs. There his men have 1 plough. It was worth 30s; now 40s.

Roger holds FOREST HILL of the bishop. There are 3 hides. [There is] land for 3 ploughs.

[Folio 156: OXFORDSHIRE]

Now in demesne [is] 1 plough, with 1 slave; and 3 villans with 2 bordars have 1 plough. [There is] a grove 2 furlongs long and 1 broad. It was worth 40s; now 20s.

The same man holds WOODPERRY of the bishop. There are 4 hides. [There is] land for 4 ploughs. Now in demesne [is] 1 plough, and 4 slaves; and 5 villans with 2 bordars have 2 ploughs. There are 30 acres of meadow and 15 acres of pasture, [and] woodland 5 furlongs long and 2 furlongs broad. It was and is worth 40s.

Robert d'Oilly holds of the bishop 1½ hides in TOOT BALDON. [There is] land for 1 plough. It was worth 20s; now 10s.

Ilbert holds STANTON ST JOHN of the bishop. There are 10 hides. There is land for 11 ploughs. Now in demesne [are] 3 ploughs, and 8 slaves; and 16 villans with 8 bordars have 5 ploughs. There are 60 acres of meadow and 60 acres of pasture, [and] woodland 1 league long and 4 furlongs broad. It was worth £12; now £10.

Wadard holds of the bishop 1 hide in WILCOTE. [There is] land for 1½ ploughs. Now in demesne [is] 1 plough, with 2 bordars, and 12 acres of meadow. [There is] woodland 4 furlongs long and 1 furlong broad. It was worth 30s; now 40s.

Adam holds of the bishop 5 hides in BLADON. [There is] land for 7 ploughs. Now in demesne [are] 2 ploughs, and 2 slaves; and 8 villans with 18 bordars have 3 ploughs. There are 2 mills rendering 14s and 125 eels, and from a pottery [come] 10s. There are 14 acres of meadow, [and] woodland 1 league long and half a league broad. It was and is worth £6.

Ansgar holds 5 virgates of land in HENSINGTON. [There is] land for 1 plough. There are 3 acres of meadow and 6 acres of scrubland. It was worth 10s; now 12[s].

Wadard holds 1½ hides in "PEREIO". [There is] land for 1 plough. This [plough] is there in demesne, with 1 bordar and 1 slave, and 12 acres of meadow. It was and is worth 30s.

Roger holds 3 virgates of land in [Lower or Old] WHITEHILL. [There is] land for 1 plough. This [plough] he has in demesne, with 1 slave, and 3 acres of meadow. It was worth 20s; now 25s.

Ilbert holds SHIPTON-ON-CHERWELL. There are $2\frac{1}{2}$ hides. [There is] land for 3 ploughs. Now in demesne [are] 2 [ploughs], and 4 slaves, and 3 villans with 3 bordars, and 2 acres of meadow and 3 acres of pasture. It was worth 40s; now £4.

Wadard hold COGGES. There are 5 hides. [There is] land for 8 ploughs. Now in demesne are 2 [ploughs], and 3 slaves. From a mill 10s. From a hay 10s. [There is] meadow 11 furlongs long and 2 furlongs broad, pasture 3 furlongs long and 1 furlong broad, [and] woodland 18 furlongs long and 6 furlongs broad. It was and is worth £10.

Roger holds $1\frac{1}{2}$ hides in TOOT BALDON. [There is] land for $1\frac{1}{2}$ ploughs. It was worth 20s; now 12s.

Wadard hold $1\frac{1}{2}$ hides in BRIGHTHAMPTON. [There is] land for 1 plough. He has this [plough] in demesne, with 1 slave and 1 villan and 5 bordars. There are 16 acres of meadow. It was and is worth 40s.

Ilbert holds 1 hide in STANTON ST JOHN. [There is] and for $1\frac{1}{2}$ ploughs. Now in demesne [is] 1 plough, with 1 villan. It was worth 20s; now 10s.

Hervey holds THOMLEY. There are $4\frac{1}{2}$ hides. [There is] and for 4 ploughs. Now in demense [are] 2 ploughs; and 5 villand with 6 bordars have 2 ploughs. There are 20 acres of meadow, [and] woodland 7 furlongs long and 3 furlongs broad. It was worth 60s; now 40s.

Wadard holds $2\frac{1}{2}$ hides in CASSINGTON. [There is] land for 3 ploughs. Now in demesne [are] 2 [ploughs], with 1 slave; and 4 villans with 1 bordar have 1 plough. From a mill and a fishery 15s6d and 175 eels. There are 12 acres of meadow, pasture 2 furlongs long and 1 furlongs broad, and 7 acres of spinney. It was worth 60s; now 100s.

Ilbert holds 3 hides in BAMPTON. [There is] land for 3 ploughs. Now in demesne [is] 1 plough; and 6 villans with 10 bordars have half a plough. There are 20 acres of meadow. It was worth 40s; now 60s.

Roger holds half a hide in YARNTON. [There is] land for 1 plough. This [plough] is there, with 2 villans and 1 bordar. It was worth 10s; now 20s.

Hugh hods of the bishop 1 hide and half a virgate of land in NETHER COTT. [There is] land for 1 plough. He has this [plough] in demesne, with 4 bordars, and [there are] 4 acres of meadow and $2\frac{1}{2}$ acres of pasture. It was and is worth 20s.

Earl aubrey held BURFORD of the bishop's land. There ae 8 hides. [There is] land for 20 ploughs. Now in demesne [are] 4 ploughs, and 3 slaves; and 22 villans and 18 bordars have 12 ploughs. There are 2 mills rendering 25s and 25 acres of meadow, [and] pasture 1 league in length and in breadth. It was worth £16; now £13.

Wadard holds $2\frac{1}{2}$ hides in CASSINGTON. [There is] land for 3 ploughs. Now in demesne [are] 2 ploughs, with 1 slave; and 4 villans with 1 bordar have 1 plough. From a mill and a fishery 15s6d and 175 eels, and [there are] 12 acres of meadow, pasture 2 furlongs long and 1 furlong broad, and 7 acres of spinney. It was worth 60s; now 100s.

Wadard holds 1 hide in [Great Little] TEW. [There is] land for 1 plough. There is 1 villan, and 5 acres of meadow. it was worth 20s; now 12s.

Adam holds $2\frac{1}{2}$ hides in SOUTH NEWINGTON. [There is] land for 2 ploughs. Now in demesne [is] plough, and 5 salves, and 1 villans and 2 bordars, and half a mill [rendering] 16d. and 11 acres of meadow. It was and is worth 30s.

In the same vill he holds 4 hides. [There is] land for 3 ploughs. Now in demesne [are] 2 ploughs, and 2 slaves; and 3 villans with 2 bordars have 1 plough. From half a mill 25d. and [ther are] 22 acres of meadow, [and] pasture 1 furlong long and half a furlong broad. it was worth 40s now 50s.

Wadard holds $3\frac{1}{2}$ hides in the same place. [There is] land for 4 ploughs. Now in demesne [is[1 plough; and the men [have] half a plough. From half a mill 16d and [there are] 17 acres of meadow. it was worth 50s; now 60s.

In the same vill he holds 1 waste hide. There is land for 1 plough. It was worth 20s.

Wadard hold DUNS TEW. There are $3\frac{1}{2}$ hides. There is land for as many ploughs. Now in demesne [is] 1 plough; and 1 villan with 6 bordars have 2 ploughs. There are 39 acres of meadow. It was and is worth £3.

Humphery holds $3\frac{1}{2}$ hides in [Great and Little] TEW. There is land for 4 ploughs. Now in demesne [is] 1 plough; and 2 bordars have another. There are $39\frac{1}{2}$ acres of meadow. It was and is worth 50s.

Humphery hold of Adam fitzHubert 5 hides in STEEPLE ASTON. There is land for 9 ploughs. Now iN demesne [are] 4 ploughs, and 6 slaves; and 12 villans with 2 bordars have 6 ploughs. There are 29 acres of meadow. It was worth £10; now £14.

Wadard holds $1\frac{1}{2}$ hides and 6 acres of land in SESSWELL'S BARTON. [There is] land for 3 ploughs. Now in demesne [are] 2 ploughs, with 1 slave; and 4 villans with 1 Frenchman and 1 bordar have 2 ploughs. There is a mill [rendering] 2s, and 5 acres of meadow. It was worth 40s; now 60s.

Adam holds 10 hides in the same vill. [There is] and for 16 ploughs. now in demesne [are] 4 ploughs, and 9 slaves; and 18 villans with 5 bordars have 14 ploughs. There are 2 mills rendering 10s and 9 acres of meadow. It was worth 12s; now 20s.

Wadard holds $1\frac{1}{2}$ hides in LUDWELL. [There is] land for 1 plough. he has this [plough] in demesne, with 2 bordars. it was and is worth 23s.

Robert d'Oilly hods $2\frac{1}{2}$ hides in BARFORD ST JOHN. [There is] land for $1\frac{1}{2}$ ploughs. Now in demesne [are] 2 ploughs, with 1 slave; and 2 villans with 3 bordars have half a plough. It was worth 30s; now 50s.

Ralph holds 3½ hides in ALKERTON. [There is] land for 5 ploughs. Now in demesne [are] 2 ploughs, with 6 bordars and 1 villan. It was and is worth 60s.

Wimund, 3 [hides], and Godric, 1 [hide], and the Count of Evreux, 1 hide, holds 5 hides in SHOWELL of the fief of the Bishop of Bayeux. [There is] land for 4 ploughs. Now in demesne [are] 2 ploughs, and 6 slaves; and 4 villans with 1 bordar have 2 ploughs. There are 18 acres of meadow and 26 acres of pasture. It was worth 50s; now 100s.

Adam holds 3 hides and half a virgate of land in [? Over] WORTON. [There is] land for 5 ploughs. Now in demesne [are] 2 ploughs; and 3 villans with 7 bordars have 2½ ploughs. There are 2 mills rendering 6s8d, and 38 acres of meadow. It was worth 40s; now 60s.

Adam holds 14 hides, less 1 virgate, in SANDFORD ST MARTIN. [There is] land for 16 ploughs. Now in demesne [are] 3 ploughs, and 2 slaves; and 24 villans with 13 bordars have 13 ploughs. There is a mill rendering 30d, and 100 acres of meadow, pasture 4 furlongs long and 3 furlongs broad, and 1 furlong of spinney. It was worth £10; now £20.

Urse holds 1 hide in CHASTLETON. [There is] land for 1 plough. There is 1 villan. It was and is worth 6s.

Ilbert holds 1 hide and 1 virgate of land in the same vill. These 2 hides are and were waste, with the 1 virgate of land, neithere do they pay geld nor [render] any customary due to the king.

Ralph holds 1 hide and the third part of half a hide in the same vill of the bishop's fief, which Robert d'Oilly has. There is land for 2 ploughs. Now in demesne [is] 1 plough, with 1 slave and 2 bordars. There are 10 acres of meadow. It was and is worth 20s.

Ilbert holds in the same vill 3 virgates of land and the third part of half a hide. [There is] land for half a plough. Now in demesne [is] 1 plough, with 1 villan and 1 bordar, and 7 acres of meadow. It was and is worth 10s.

Ansketil holds in the same vill 3 virgates of land which belong to SALFORD, | in which there are 5 hides and 1 virgate of land. | [He holds it] of Archbishop Thomas, and it belongs to the fief of the Bishop of Bayeux. There is land for 7 ploughs. Now in demesne [are] 3 ploughs, and 3 slaves; and 7 villans with 4 bordars have 3½ ploughs. There is a mill rendering 50d, and 38 acres of meadow, [and] pasture 2 furlongs long and 1 furlong broad. It was and is worth £6.

Ilbert holds LYNEHAM of the bishop. There are 10 hides. [There is] land for 14 ploughs. Now in demesne [are] 4 ploughs, and 6 slaves; and 30 villans and 7 bordars have 11 ploughs. There is a mill rendering 7s6d, and 120 acres of meadow and 200 acres of pasture. It was worth £12; now £10.

Hervey holds 3 hides in WARPSGROVE. [There is] land for 2 ploughs. Now in demesne [are] 2 ploughs, with 1 slave and 1 villan and 4 bordars. It was and is worth £4.

Ilbert holds 4½ hides in ASCOTT EARL. [There is] land for 7 ploughs. Now in demesne [are] 2 ploughs, and 4 slaves; and 3 villans with 6 bordars have 2 ploughs. There are 16 acres of meadow. It was worth £6; now £4.

The same man holds 2 hides in [Great and Little] TEW. [There is] land for 2 ploughs. Now in demesne [is] 1 plough; and 3 villans with 2 bordars have 1 plough. There are 22 acres of meadow. It was and is worth 40s.

The same man holds 1 hide in STANTON ST JOHN. [There is] land for 1 plough, which [plough] is there, with 1 villan. It was worth 20s; now 10s.

The same man holds 6 hides in CASSINGTON. [There is] land for 6 ploughs. Now in demesne [are] 2 ploughs; and 14 villans with 6 bordars have 4 ploughs. There are 29 acres of meadow, [and] pasture 1 furlong long and a half broad. It was worth £4; now 110s.

Wadard holds 5 hides in BALSCOTE. [There is] land for 5 ploughs. Now in demesne [is] 1 plough; and 3 villans with 6 bordars have 2 ploughs. There are 20 acres of meadow. It was worth £4; now £6.

VIII. The land of the Bishop of Lisieux

THE BISHOP OF LISIEUX holds of the king 1 hide in [Great and Little] TEW. [There is] land for 1 plough. 2 villans have this [plough] there. There are 11 acres of meadow. It was and is worth 30s. Leofwine, a free man, held it TRE. Routrou holds it now of the bishop.

The same bishop holds DUNS TEW. There are 3 hides. [There is] land for 4 ploughs. Now in demesne [is] 1 plough, and 2 slaves; and 5 villans have 1 plough. There are 5 acres of meadow and 6 acres of pasture. It was worth 40s; now 60s.

The same bishop holds 5 hides in DUNTHROP. [There is] land for 8 ploughs. Now in demesne [is] 1 plough, and 3 slaves; and 3 villans have 1 plough. There are 15 acres of meadow. It was and is worth £3.

The same bishop holds WESTCOTT BARTON, and Routrou [holds] of him. There are 5 hides. [There is] land for 8 ploughs. Now in demesne [are] 3 ploughs, and 5 slaves; and 10 villans with 4 bordars have 5 ploughs. There are 3 acres of meadow, [and] pasture 1 furlong long and a half broad. It was and is worth £7. Leofwine held these lands as he wished.

IX. The land of St Mary of Abingdon

THE ABBEY of Abingdon holds LEWKNOR. There are 17 hides. There is land for 26 ploughs. Of these, 4½ hides are in demesne, and there are 3 ploughs, with 6 slaves; and 30 villans with 26 bordars have 23 ploughs. There is a mill rendering 20d, meadow 4 furlongs long and 2 furlongs broad, [and] woodland 1 league long and 4 furlongs and 1 league broad: when stocked it is worth 25s. TRE it was worth £10; and afterwards £20; now £20 likewise.

The same abbey holds CUDDESDON. There are 18 hides. There is land for 18 ploughs. Of these, 4 hides are in demesne, and there are 4 ploughs, and 8 slaves; and 24 villans with 12 bordars have 18 ploughs. There is a mill and 2 fisheries [rendering] 12s. There are 60 acres of meadow, [and] woodland 8 furlongs long and half a league broad. It was worth £9; now £12.

Wynric holds SANDFORD-ON-THAMES of the abbey. There are 10 hides. [There is] land for 8 ploughs. Of this land 4 hides are in demesne, and there are 2 ploughs; and 7 villans with 4 bordars have 3½ ploughs. [There is] woodland 28 perches long and 30 perches broad. From 2 fisheries, 10s. TRE it was worth £8; and afterwards 100s; now 60s. Blæcmann the priest held it from the Church.

In the same vill Robert and Roger hold 1 hide of the abbot. [There is] land for 1 plough. They have this [plough] there. It was worth 15s; now 20s. Siward held it and could not withdraw from the Church.

Wynric holds SANDFORD-ON-THAMES of the abbot. There are 4 hides. [There is] land for 5 ploughs. There 3 villans with 4 bordars have 1 plough. There are 10 acres of meadow. It was and is worth 40s.

The son of Wadard holds of Roger, and he himself of the abbot, 5 hides in BARFORD ST MICHAEL. [There is] land for 5 ploughs. Now in demesne [are] 2 ploughs, and 2 slaves; and 6 villans with 1 Frenchman and 2 bordars have 3 ploughs. There is a mill rendering 9s, and 40 acres of meadow and 20 acres of pasture. It was and is worth £6.

Gilbert holds of the abbot 7½hides in GARSINGTON. [There is] land for 6 ploughs. Now in demesne [are] 2 ploughs, and 2 slaves; and 6 villans with 9 bordars have 3 ploughs. There are 12 acres of meadow, [and] woodland 2 furlongs long and 1 broad. It was worth £4; now 100s. There is 1 hide of inland which has never paid geld lying dispersed among the king's land.

In the same vill Sweting holds 1½ hides of the abbot. [There is] land for 1 plough. He has this [plough] there in demesne, with 1 villan and 2 bordars. It was and is worth 40s.

The same abbey holds 20 hides in TADMARTON. [There is] land for 16 ploughs. Of this land 6 hides are in demesne, and there are 3 ploughs, and 2 slaves; and 15 villans with 7 bordars have 5 ploughs. There is a mill rendering 4s, and 32 acres of meadow and 60 acres of pasture. It was worth £16; now £12.

Of this land 1 knight holds 5 hides of the abbot, and has there 2 ploughs, with 1 slave; and 8 villans with 5 bordars have 2 ploughs, and [there is] a mill rendering 5s. It was worth 40s; now £6.

All this land belonged and belongs to the demesne of ST MARY of Abingdon.

Robert d'Oilly and Roger d'Ivry hold of the abbot another ARNCOTT [Lower or Upper Arncott] of the fief of the church. There are 2 hides. [There is] land for 3½ ploughs. In demesne is 1 plough. [There is] woodland 1 league long and 3 furlongs broad. It was and is worth 30s.

X. The land of the Church of Battle

Battle ABBEY holds PRESTON CROWMARSH of the king. There are 5 hides. There is land for 6 ploughs. Of this land 2½ hides are in demesne, and there are 2 ploughs, and 2 slaves; and 4 villans with 7 bordars have 2 ploughs. It was worth £6; now £8. Earl Harold held it.

XI. The land of the Church of Winchcombe

THE ABBEY of WINCHCOMBE holds 24 hides in ENSTONE. There is land for 26 ploughs. In demesne are 3 ploughs, and 6 slaves; and 25 villans and 4 free men with 7 bordars have 18 ploughs. There are 4 mills rendering 19s, and 50 acres of meadow, pasture 4 furlongs long and 2 furlongs broad, [and] woodland 1 league long and and [sic] half a league and 4 furlongs broad.

Of this land Urse has 2 hides of the abbot, and there is 1 plough; and 3 villans with 2 bordars have 1 plough.

In CHASTLETON the abbot has 1 waste hide. The whole, TRE and afterwards, was worth £20; now £18.

XII. The land of the Abbey of Preaux

IN PYRTON HUNDRED

THE ABBEY OF PREAUX holds of the king 5 hides in WATLINGTON. [There is] land for 4½ ploughs. There 7 villans with 2 bordars and 2 slaves have 3 ploughs. There are 6 acres of meadow, [and] woodland 7 furlongs long and 3 furlongs broad. It was worth £4; now 100s. Ælfhelm, a free man, held it TRE.

XIII. The land of Saint-Denis of Paris

THE CHURCH OF SAINT-DENIS of Paris holds TAYNTON of the king. King Edward gave it to it. There are 10 hides. [There is] land for 15 ploughs. Now in demesne are 4 [ploughs], and 4 slaves; and 17 villans with 30 bordars have 17 ploughs. There are 2 mills rendering 32s6d, and 62s6d for eels. There are 170 acres of meadow, pasture 1 league long and half a league broad, [and] woodland 1 league long and 4 furlongs broad. Including the quarry and the meadows and the pastures it renders 24s7d TRE, and afterwards, it was worth £10; now £15 all together.

XIIII. The land of the Canons of Oxford and Other Clerks

THE CANONS OF ST FRIDESWIDE holds 4 hides of the king close to OXFORD. They themselves held them TRE. [There is] land for 5 ploughs. There 18 villans have 5 ploughs, and 105 acres of meadow, and 8 acres of spinney. It was and is worth 40s. This land has never paid geld and it neither belongs nor belonged to any HUNDRED.

Siward holds of the canons themselves 2 hides in CUTTESLOWE. [There is] land for 2 ploughs which are now there. It was and is worth 40s. It belonged and belongs to the Church.

Osmund the priest holds of the king 1 hide in KIRTLINGTON. [There is] land for 1 plough. He has this [plough] there in demesne. It was and is worth 20s.

Brun the priest holds of the king 3 virgates of land in CADWELL. [There is] land for 1 plough. This [plough] is there in demesne. It was worth 20s; now 30s. The same man held it TRE.

Edward holds half a hide of the king. There was 1 plough. It was worth 20s; now 6s.

Ranulph Flambard holds 4 hides of the king in MILTON-UNDER-WYCHWOOD. [There is] land for 4 ploughs. Now in demesne [is] 1 plough, and 2 slaves; and 4 villans with 2 bordars have 1 plough. There are 6 acres of meadow, [and] pasture 2 furlongs long and half a furlong broad. It was and is worth £3.

XV. The land of Earl Hugh

EARL HUGH holds of the king 9 hides in SOUTH WESTON, and Robert [holds] of him. There is land for 8 ploughs. Now in demesne [are] 2 ploughs; and 15 villans with 9 bordars have 6½ ploughs. There is a mill rendering 4s, and 12 acres of meadow and 4 acres of scrubland. It was worth £6; now £7.

IN PYRTON HUNDRED

William holds of Earl Hugh 40 hides in PYRTON. [There is] land for 26 ploughs. Now in demesne [are] 6 ploughs, and 8 slaves; and 42 villans and 4 free men with 2 bordars have 20 ploughs. There is a mill [rendering] 5s, and 200 acres of meadow, pasture 2 furlongs long and 1 furlong broad, [and] woodland 18 furlongs long and half a league broad. TRE it was worth £16; when received, £25; now £30. Archbishop Stigand held it.

Robert holds TACKLEY of the earl. There are 8 hides. [There is] land for 10 ploughs. Now in demesne [are] 4 ploughs, and 2 slaves; and 20 villans with 9 bordars have 6 ploughs. There is a mill [rendering] 10s, and 30 acres of meadow, pasture 9 furlongs long and 2 furlongs broad, [and] a grove 5 furlongs broad and 9 furlongs long. TRE, and afterwards, it was worth £8; now £17. Hugh the chamberlain held it.

Walter holds CHURCHILL of the earl. There are 20 hides. [There is] land for 20 ploughs. Now in demesne [are] 3 ploughs; and 24 villans with 14 bordars have 9 ploughs. There are 2 mills [rendering] 20s, and 170 acres of meadow and 120 acres of pasture. It was and is worth £10. Earl Harold held it.

Robert holds ARDLEY of the earl. There are 5 hides. [There is] land for 11 ploughs. In demesne are 4 [ploughs]; and 8 villans and 15 bordars with 6 ploughs. It is worth £6. Drogo holds it of Robert.

XVI. The land of the Count of Mortain

THE COUNT OF MORTAIN holds of the king 10 hides in HORLEY. [There is] land for 8 ploughs. Now in demesne [are] 3 ploughs, and †6† slaves; and 5 villans have 2 ploughs. There are 20 acres of meadow, and from part of the mill [come] 16d. It was and is worth 100s. Ralph holds it of the count. Toki held it freely TRE.

Of the same count the monks of SAINT-PIERRE hold 1 hide. [There is] land for 1 plough. This [plough] is there in demesne, and [There are] 6 acres of meadow and pasture. It was worth 10s; now 20s.

XVII. The land of the Count of Evreux

THE COUNT OF EVREUX holds of the king 3 hides in CHIPPINGHURST. [There is] land for 3 ploughs. Of this land 2 hides are in demesne, and there are 2 ploughs, with 1 slave; and 4 villans have 2 ploughs. There are 24 acres of meadow. It was and is worth 40s.

The same count holds 3½ hides in TOOT BALDON. [There is] land for 3 ploughs. Now in demesne [is] 1 plough, and 3 slaves; and 5 villans with 1 bordar have 2 ploughs. It was and is worth 30s.

The same count holds GRAFTON. There are 2 hides. [There is] land for 3 ploughs. Now in demesne [is] 1 plough, with 1 slave; and 1 villan with 10 bordars have 2 ploughs. There are 63 acres of meadow and they render 10s, [and there is] pasture 1 league in length and in breadth. It was and is worth 40s.

The same count holds DUNTHROP. There are 5 hides. [There is] land for 5 ploughs. Now in demesne [are] 2 ploughs, with 1 slave; and 4 villans with 2 bordars have 2 ploughs. There are 10 acres of meadow and 30 acres of pasture. It was worth 60s; now 100s.

The same count holds 4½ hides in MILCOMBE. [There is] land for 3 ploughs. Now in demesne [is] 1 plough, with 1 slave and 3 bordars. From part of a mill [come] 2s, and [there are] 15 acres of meadow, [and] pasture 2 furlongs long and 1½ furlongs and 5 perches broad. It was worth 40s; now 30s.

The same count holds 1 hide and 2½ virgates of land in BODICOTE. [There is] land for 1 plough. This [plough] is there in demesne, with 2 slaves and 5 bordars. It was worth 20s; now 30s.

The same count holds 1 hide in MOLLINGTON. [There is] land for 1 plough, which [plough] is there in demesne, with 1 slave and 2 bordars. There are 4 acres of meadow. It was worth 10s; now 20s.

The same count holds 1 hide in SHOWELL. [There is] land for 1 plough, which [plough] he has in demesne; and 2 villans with 1 bordar have half a plough. It was worth 10s; now 20s. Those who held these lands TRE could go where they wished.

[Folio 157V: OXFORDSHIRE]

XVIII. The land of Earl Aubrey

EARL AUBREY held IFFLEY of the king. There are 4 hides. There is land for 6 ploughs. In demesne is 1 plough, and 5 slaves; and 14 villans with 6 bordars have 4 ploughs. There is a fishery [rendering] 4s, and 24 acres of meadow, and 1 furlong of pasture, [and] a grove 2 acres in length and in breadth. It was worth 100s; now £4. Azur held it freely TRE.

The same [earl] held 7 hides in MINSTER [Little Minster and Minster Lovell]. [There is] land for 10 ploughs. Now in demesne [are] 6 ploughs, and 2 slaves; and 17 villans with 10 bordars have 7 ploughs. There are 2 mills rendering 20s, and 78 acres of meadow, [and] woodland 1 league long and 4 furlongs broad. It was worth £10; now £7.

XIX. The land of Count Eustace

COUNT EUSTACE holds of the king 3 hides in COWLEY, and Roger [holds] of him. [There is] land for 5 ploughs. Now in demesne [are] 2 ploughs, and 3 slaves; and 6 villans have 3 ploughs. There are 5 acres of meadow, [and] a grove 2 acres in length and breadth. From a mill and 1 virgate of land [come] 35s. The whole was and is worth 40s.

XX. The land of Walter Giffard

WALTER GIFFARD holds of the king 20 hides in CAVERSHAM [Berks.]. [There is] land for 21 ploughs. Now in demesne [are] 4 ploughs, and 2 slaves; and 28 villans with 13 bordars have 13 ploughs. There is a mill rendering 20s, and 13 acres of meadow, [and] woodland 1 league and 2 furlongs long and 1 league broad. TRE and afterwards, as now, worth £20. Swein held it freely TRE.

Hugh holds 'LYSBROOK' [in Shiplake] of Walter. There are 12 hides. [There is] land for 9 ploughs. There 6 villans with 5 bordars and 2 slaves have 3 ploughs. There is the site of a mill rendering 10s, and 22 acres of meadow. TRE it was worth £12; and afterwards £8; now 30s.

The same man holds CROWMARSH GIFFORD of Walter. There are 10 hides. [There is] land for 12 ploughs. Now in demesne [are] 2 ploughs, and 4 slaves; and 12 villans with 11 bordars have 5 ploughs. There are 2 mills rendering 40s, and 6 acres of meadow, [and] woodland 1 league long and 2 furlongs broad. TRE, and afterwards, it was worth £10; now £20.

Ralph holds HEMPTON of Walter. There are 10 hides. [There is] land for 10 ploughs. Now in demesne [are] 2 ploughs; and 13 villans with 4 bordars have 7½ ploughs. There is a mill [rendering] 12s, and meadow 2 furlongs broad and 1½ leagues long, and 3 acres of pasture, [and] woodland 1½ leagues long and 3½ furlongs broad. TRE and afterwards, as now, worth £6. Queen Edith held it.

Hugh holds STOKE LYNE of Walter. There are 10½ hides. [There is] land for 14 ploughs. Now in demesne [are] 4

ploughs, and 2 slaves; and 34 villans with 9 bordars have 13 ploughs. There are 12 acres of meadow and 10 acres of pasture, [and] woodland 3 furlongs long and 2 furlongs broad. It was and is worth £12. Earl Tosti held it.

The same man holds 1½ hides in LEW. [There is] land for 1 plough. This [plough] is there in demesne, with 1 bordar. [There is] pasture 1½ furlongs in length and breadth. It was worth 10s; now 20s.

The same man holds 2 hides, less half a virgate of land [...]. [There is] land for 2 ploughs. Now in demesne [is] 1 plough, with 2 villans. It was and is worth 40s.

The same man holds 2½ hides in BIX. [There is] land for 7 ploughs. Now in demesne are 2 [ploughs]; and 6 villans have 2 ploughs. There are 3 acres of meadow and 12 acres of woodland. It was and is worth £3.

The same man holds 5½ hides in EWELME. [There is] land for 6 ploughs. Now in demesne are 2 [ploughs]; and 7 villans with 3 bordars have 2½ ploughs. [There is] woodland 5 furlongs long and 1 furlong broad. It was and is worth 100s.

Turold holds of Walter 3 virgates of land in STOKE LYNE and 3 virgates of land in TUSMORE. [There is] land for 2 ploughs. There he has 1 plough. It was and is worth 20s.

XXI. The land of William fitzAnsculf

IN DORCHESTER HUNDRED

WILLIAM fitz ANSCULF holds of the king 5 hides in "HUNESWORDE", and Walter [holds] of him. [There is] land for 5 ploughs. Now in demesne [are] 2 ploughs; and 8 villans have 1½ ploughs. There is a mill rendering 8s, and 20 acres of meadow. It was and is worth £4.

XXII. The land of William de Warenne

WILLIAM DE WARENNE holds MAPLEDURHAM of the king. There are | 7 hides. | [There is] land for 12 ploughs. Now in demesne [are] 2 ploughs, and 2 slaves; and 16 villans with 8 bordars have 10 ploughs. There is a mill rendering 20s, and 10 acres of meadow. TRE, and afterwards, it was worth £8; now £12.

Brian holds of William 1½ hides in GATEHAMPTON. [There is] land for 1½ ploughs. In demesne is 1 plough; and 4 villans with 2 bordars have half a plough. There are 6 acres of meadow. It was worth 20s; now 40s.

XXIII. The land of William Peverel

WILLIAM PEVEREL holds 10 hides in CROWELL of the king. [There is] land for 5 ploughs. Now in demesne [are] 2 ploughs, and 4 slaves; and 15 villans with 5 bordars have 7 ploughs. There are 12 acres of meadow and 2 furlongs of woodland. It was worth £6; now £7.

The same Williams holds 10 hides in EMMINGTON. [There is] land for 5 ploughs. Now in demesne [are] 2 ploughs, and 6 slaves; and 10 villans with 4 bordars have 5 ploughs.

There are 12 acres of meadow. It was worth £6; now £7. Alwine held these 2 estates freely.

14 ploughs. There are 65 acres of meadow. It was worth £8; now £10. Ælfgifu held it freely TRE.

[Folio 158: OXFORDSHIRE]

XXIIII. The land of Henry de Ferrers

HENRY de Ferrers holds BADGEMORE of the king, and Ralph [holds] of him. There are 5 hides. [There is] land for 8 ploughs. Now in demesne [are] 2 ploughs, with 1 slave; and 7 villans with 3 bordars with have [sic] 3 ploughs. There are 12 acres of meadow, [and] woodland 2 furlongs long and 1 broad. TRE and afterwards, as now, worth £4.

The same man holds 3 hides in OLD CHALFORD. [There is] land for 3 ploughs. Now in demesne [are] 3 ploughs, and a mill rendering 3s4d, and 4 acres of meadow. It was worth 60s; now 30s. Robert holds it of him. Alric and Alnoth held it freely.

The same Henry holds of the king 10 hides in SIBFORD FERRIS, and Rolf [holds] of him, and there is land for 10 ploughs. Now in demesne [are] 3 ploughs, and 3 slaves; and 7 villans with 3 ploughs. There are 40 acres of meadow, [and] pasture 2 furlongs long and 1 furlong broad. TRE it was worth £10; and afterwards 100s; now £7.

The same Henry holds FIFIELD. There are 5 hides. [There is] land for 7 ploughs. Now in demesne [are] 2 ploughs, and 4 slaves; and 9 villans with 4 bordars have 5 ploughs. There are 24 acres of meadow, [and] pasture 1 league in length and in breadth. It was and is worth 100s.

The same Henry holds 8 hides in DEAN and in OLD CHALFORD. Robert holds of him. [There is] land for 8 ploughs. Now in demesne [are] 5 ploughs, and 4 slaves; and 13 villans with 3 bordars have 8 ploughs. There are 2 mills [rendering] 5s. and 13 acres of meadow, [and] a grove 1 league long and 2 furlongs broad. TRE, and afterwards, it was worth £7; now £9. Henry holds 5 hides of this land of the king and he bought 3 hides from Edwin the sheriff. Bondi held these lands freely TRE.

The same Henry holds 2 hides in "ASCE". [There is] land for 2 ploughs. There 1 villan dwells, with 3 bordars. It was worth 40s; now £4. Cynewig held it. From these 2 hides he has rendered neither geld nor any due to the king's servants. He has joined them to his land in Gloucestershire.

The same man holds 1 hide in CHASTLETON of the fief of the abbey. It is waste.

XXV. The land of Hugh de Bolbec

HUGH de BOLBEC holds of the king 4 hides in RYCOTE. [There is] land for 4 ploughs. There are 3 villans. It was worth £4; now it renders nothing.

XXVI. The land of Hugh d'Ivry

HUGH d'Ivry holds AMBROSDEN of the king. There are 10 hides. [There is] land for 16 ploughs. Now in demesne [are] 2 ploughs, and 3 slaves; and 24 villans with 11 bordars have

XXVII. The land of Robert of Stafford

ROBERT of STAFFORD holds of the king 1 hide in HORLEY, and Richard [holds] of him. [There is] land for 3 ploughs. Now in demesne [are] 2 ploughs, and 3 slaves; and 3 villans with 2 bordars have 1 plough. There is a mill rendering 5s, meadow 1 furlong long and 30 perches broad, [and] a grove 3 furlongs long and as many broad. It was worth 30s; now 40s.

The same man holds 5 hides and 1 virgate of land in GREAT ROLLRIGHT. [There is] land for 6 ploughs. Now in demesne [are] 2 ploughs, and 5 slaves; and 9 villans with 1 bordar have 4 ploughs. There are 50 acres of meadow and 50 acres of pasture. TRE and afterwards, as now, worth 100s. Ælfric held it freely.

Gosbert holds 2 hides and 1 virgate of land in BROMSCOTT and PEMSCOTT. [There is] land for 3 ploughs. Now in demesne [are] 2 ploughs, and 5 slaves; and 3 villans with 1 bordar have half a plough. There are 47 acres of meadow rendering 10s, and pasture 3 furlongs in length and breadth. It was worth 40s; now 50s. Ælfric and Alwine held it freely.

Ælfric holds of Robert 1 hide in STONESFIELD. [There is] land for 1 plough. Now in demesne [is] 1 plough, and 2 slaves; and 4 villans with 2 bordars have 1 plough. [There is] woodland 5 furlongs long and 2 furlongs broad. It was worth 20s; now 30s.

Evruin holds of Robert 3½ hides in DUNS TEW. [There is] land for 2 ploughs. There 1 villan with 2 bordars have half a plough, and 10 acres of meadow. It was worth 60s; and afterwards 10s; now 50s.

Robert holds of Robert 1 hide in ADDERBURY. [There is] land for 1 plough. He has this [plough] in demesne, with 1 slave and 1 villan and 3 bordars. There are 4 acres of meadow. It was worth 20s; now 30s.

Gadio holds of Robert 1 hide and 1 virgate of land in ILBURY. [There is] land for 2 ploughs. Now in demesne [are] 1½ ploughs, and 2 slaves; and 3 villans have half a plough. There are 6 acres of meadow. It was worth 20s; now 40s.

Reginald holds of Robert 2 hides in NORTHBROOK. [There is] land for 2 ploughs. Now in demesne [is] 1 plough with 1 slave; and 2 villans have 1 plough. There are 4 acres of meadow. It was and is worth 25s.

Gosbert holds of Robert in MIDDLE ASTON 1 hide. [There is] land for 1 plough. There are 3 villans, and 6 acres of meadow. It was worth 15s; now 20s.

Gilbert holds of Robert in MIDDLE ASTON 2 hides and 2½ virgates of land. [There is] land for 4 ploughs. Now in demesne [are] 2 ploughs, and 3 slaves; and 2 villans with 4 bordars have 2 ploughs. There are 11 acres of meadow and $6\frac{1}{2}$ acres of pasture. TRE and afterwards, as now, worth £3. 3 thegns held it freely.

XXVIII. The land of Robert d'Oilly

PYRTON HUNDRED

ROBERT D'OILLY holds of the king WATLINGTON. There are 8 hides. [There is] land for 11 ploughs. Of this land 3 hides are inland, and there are 2 ploughs, and 4 slaves; and 22 villans with 5 bordars have 11 ploughs. There are 2 mills rendering 10s8d. There are 4 acres of meadow and 11 acres of pasture, [and] woodland $1\frac{1}{2}$ leagues long and half a league broad. TRE, and afterwards, it was worth £6; now £10.

The same Robert holds GORING. There are 20 hides. [There is] land for 10 ploughs. Now in demesne [are] 3 ploughs, and 7 slaves; and 21 villans with 2 bordars have 10 ploughs, and there are 3 free men, and there is a mill rendering 20s. [There is] woodland 5 furlongs long and as many broad. TRE, and afterwards, it was worth £10; now £15. Vigot held it.

The same Robert [...] holds BICESTER as 2 manors. There are $15\frac{1}{2}$ hides. [There is] land for 22 ploughs. Of this land 3 hides are in demesne, and there are 6 ploughs, and 5 slaves; and 28 villans with 14 bordars have 16 ploughs. There are 2 mills rendering 40s, and 12 acres of meadow, [and] woodland 1 furlong long and 1 broad. It was worth £15; now 16[l].

The same Robert holds KIDLINGTON. There are 14 hides. [There is] land for 12 ploughs. Of this land 3 hides are in demesne, and there are 3 ploughs, with 2 slaves and 32 villans with 8 bordars [who] have 4 ploughs. There is meadow 3 furlongs long and 2 furlongs broad, pasture 4 furlongs long and 3 furlongs broad, [and] woodland 3 furlongs long and as many broad. There is a mill rendering 30s. It was worth £8; now £14.

The same Robert holds WATER EATON. There are 5 hides. [There is] land for 5 ploughs. In addition to these hides he has $3\frac{1}{2}$ hides of inland which have never paid geld. There 26 villans with 7 bordars have 9 ploughs, and there is a mill rendering 15s, and 3 fisheries rendering 12s. There is meadow 10 furlongs long and as many broad. The pasture has the same [dimensions]. It was worth £6; now 100s.

The same Robert holds HOOK NORTON as 3 manors. There are 30 hides. [There is] land for 30 ploughs. Of this land 5 hides are in demesne, and there are 5 ploughs, and 5 slaves; and 76 villans with 3 bordars have 30 ploughs. There are 2 mills rendering 20s, and 140 acres of meadow, pasture 5 furlongs long and 2 furlongs broad, [and] spinney 2 furlongs long and half a furlong broad. TRE and afterwards, as now, worth £30. 3 brothers held it freely.

The same Robert holds DRAYTON. There are 10 hides. [There is] land for 9 ploughs. Now in demesne [are] 3 ploughs, and 5 slaves; and 13 villans with 5 bordars have 7 ploughs. There is a mill rendering 10s, and 30 acres of meadow, [and] pasture 7 furlongs long and 5 furlongs broad. It was and is worth £7.

The same Robert has 42 inhabited houses in OXFORD, both within and without the wall. 16 of these pay geld and rent. The others pay neither because they cannot on account of their poverty; and he has 8 waste messuages, and 30 acres of meadow close to the wall, and a mill [rendering] 10s. The whole is worth £3, and he holds it as 1 manor with the benefice of ST PETER.

Drogo holds of Robert 10 hides in SHIRBURN. [There is] land for 6 ploughs. Now in demesne [are] 2 ploughs; and 12 villans with 7 bordars have $4\frac{1}{2}$ ploughs. There are 20 acres of meadow and 30 acres of pasture. The woodland is 3 furlongs long and 1 broad. TRE, and afterwards, it was worth £4; now £6.

Peter holds 2 hides in WHEATFIELD of Robert. [There is] land for 1 plough. Now in demesne is a plough, with 1 slave; and 2 villans with 2 bordars have half a plough. There are 12 acres of meadow and 5 acres of pasture. It was and is worth 20s.

The same Peter holds of Robert 1 hide in LEWKNOR. [There is] land for 1 plough, which [plough] is there, with 2 slaves; and 2 villans have half a plough. There are 6 acres of meadow. It was and is worth 20s.

Roger holds UPPER HEYFORD of Robert. There are 10 hides. [There is] land for 10 ploughs. Now in demesne [are] 3 ploughs, and 3 slaves; and 10 villans with 1 bordar have 6 ploughs. There is a mill rendering 12s, and 18 acres of meadow, and 2 fisheries rendering 900 eels, and $6\frac{1}{2}$ acres of pasture. TRE it was worth £8; when received, £10; now £12.

Gilbert holds BUCKNELL of Robert. There are 7 hides. [There is] land for 10 ploughs. Now in demesne [are] 2 ploughs, and 3 slaves; and 6 villans with 3 bordars have 5 ploughs. [There is] woodland 1 furlong long and half a furlong broad. It was worth £10; now £7.

The same Gilbert holds of Robert $3\frac{1}{2}$ hides in FULWELL. [There is] land for 3 ploughs. Now in demesne [is] 1 plough, with 1 slave; and 3 villans with 2 bordars have 1 plough. There is a mill [rendering] 10s, and 20 acres of pasture. It was worth £6; now £3.

Turstin holds ELSFIELD of Robert. There are 5 hides. [There is] land for 8 ploughs. Now in demesne [are] 3 ploughs, and 2 slaves; and 11 villans with 7 bordars and 6 others have 5 ploughs. There are 18 acres of meadow and 24 acres of pasture, [and] woodland 3 furlongs long and 3 broad. It was worth £4; now 100s.

Drogo holds HARDWICK of Robert. There are $7\frac{1}{2}$ hides. [There is] land for 6 ploughs. Now in demesne [is] 1 plough; and 5 villans with 2 bordars have $2\frac{1}{2}$ ploughs. It was and is worth 100s. Robert exchanged this land with Walter Giffard.

Alweard holds STRATTON AUDLEY of Robert. There are 5 hides. [There is] land for 6 ploughs. Now in demesne [is] 1 plough, with 1 slave; and 8 villans with 2 bordars have 2 ploughs. There are 25 acres of meadow. It was worth 40s; and afterwards, as now, 60s.

Gilbert holds WESTON-ON-THE-GREEN of Robert. There are 10 hides. [There is] land for 12 ploughs. Now in demesne [are] 4 ploughs, and 5 slaves; and 17 villans with 11 bordars have 8 ploughs. There are 2 mills [rendering] 4s, and 30 acres of meadow. It was worth £8; now £12.

The same Gilbert holds BLETCHINGDON of Robert. There are 8 hides. [There is] land for 6 ploughs. Now in demesne [are] 2 ploughs, and 5 slaves; and 9 villans with 7 bordars have 4 ploughs. There are 11 acres of meadow, [and] pasture 6 furlongs long and 3 furlongs broad. TRE, and afterwards, it was worth £4; now 100s. Robert bought this back from the king.

Roger holds DUCKLINGTON of Robert. There are 4 hides. [There is] land for 4 ploughs. Now in demesne [are] 3 ploughs, and 6 slaves; and 6 villans with 9 bordars have 2 ploughs. There is a mill [rendering] 12s, and 30 acres of meadow, pasture 1 furlong long and 1 broad, [and] woodland 3 furlongs long and 2 furlongs broad. It was worth £4; now £6.

Roger holds BAMPTON of Robert. There are 4 hides. [There is] land for 3 ploughs. Now in demesne [are] 2 ploughs, and 3 slaves; and 7 villans with 6 bordars have 3½ ploughs. There are 24 acres of meadow. It was worth 40s; now £4.

Robert holds of Robert holds [sic] WATERPERRY. There are 10 hides. [There is] land for 10 ploughs. Now in demesne [are] 3 ploughs, and 2 slaves; and 18 villans with 4 bordars have 8 ploughs. There are 40 acres of meadow, [and] woodland 5 furlongs long and 3 furlongs broad. TRE it was worth 100s; and afterwards £7; now £8.

Reginald holds of Robert in ROUSHAM 3 hides and 1 virgate of land, less 3 acres. [There is] land for 9 ploughs. Now in demesne [are] 3 ploughs, with 1 slave; and 8 villans with 6 bordars have 3 ploughs. From part of 2 mills, 11s6d. There are 8 acres of meadow, [and] a grove 2 furlongs long and 2 broad. It was and is worth £4. Robert bought this back from the king.

The same Reginald holds of Robert 1½ hides in LUDWELL. [There is] land for 1 plough. There is half an acre of meadow. It was worth 20s; now 5s. King William gave this to Robert at the siege of Sainte-Suzanne [Mayenne, France].

Roger holds of Robert 6 hides in ASCOTT D'OYLEY. [There is] land for 5 ploughs. Now in demesne [are] 3 ploughs, and 6 slaves; and 7 villans with 1 bordar have 4 ploughs. [There is] a mill [rendering] 5s, and 15 acres of meadow, and 4 acres of pasture, [and] woodland 3 furlongs long and 2 furlongs broad. It was worth 100s; now £8.

The same Roger holds of Robert 4 hides in KENCOT. [There is] land for 6 ploughs. Now in demesne [are] 5 ploughs, and 4 slaves; and 11 villans with 3 bordars have 5 ploughs. There are 12 acres of meadow. It was and is worth £6.

Herbert holds of Robert 2 hides in KIRTLINGTON. [There is] land for 2 ploughs. This he has in demesne. It was worth 20s; now 30s.

The Church of ST PETER of Oxford holds of Robert 2 hides in 'HOLYWELL' [in Oxford]. [There is] land for 1 plough. There are 1½ ploughs, and 23 men having little gardens. There are 40 acres of meadow. It was worth 20s; now 40s. This land has not paid geld nor rendered any due.

Evruin holds of Robert 7 hides in DUNS TEW. [There is] land for 7 ploughs. Now in demesne [are] 3 ploughs, and 3 slaves; and 8 villans with 3 bordars have 4 ploughs. There are 34 acres of meadow. It was worth £7; now £9.

XXIX. The land of Roger d'Ivry

ROGER d'IVRY holds MIXBURY of the king. There are 17 hides. [There is] land for 15 ploughs. Now in demesne [is] 1 plough, with 1 slave; and 18 villans with 11 bordars have 6 ploughs. There are 2 mills rendering 9s4d, and 50 acres of pasture. It was and is worth £15.

The same man holds BECKLEY. There are 6 hides. [There is] land for 7 ploughs. Now in demesne [are] 2 ploughs, and 6 slaves; and 11 villans with 6 bordars have 5 ploughs. There are 20 acres of meadow, and pasture 1 league long and 2 furlongs broad, [and] woodland 1 league long and a half broad. It was worth 100s; now £8.

The same Roger holds ASTHALL of the king. There are 11 hides. [There is] land for 15 ploughs. Of this land 4 hides are in demesne, and there are 4 ploughs, and 5 slaves; and 24 villans with 11 bordars have 9 ploughs. There are 2 mills rendering 22s, and 137 acres of meadow, [and] woodland 13 furlongs long and 10 furlongs broad. It was worth £11; now £12. He has this land with 2 hides and 1 virgate of land as 3 manors.

Fulk holds of Roger 14 hides and 1½ virgates of land in BRIZE NORTON. [There is] land for 12 ploughs. Now he has in demesne 5 hides of the villans' land, and there are 5 ploughs, with 1 knight of his. There are 8 slaves and 13 villans with 17 bordars, and 24 acres of meadow. [There is] a grove 1 furlong long and half a furlong broad. It was worth £9; now £13. 14 thegns held this land.

Roger himself holds FULBROOK as 4 manors. There are 12 hides. [There is] land for 15 ploughs. Now in demesne [are] 5 ploughs, and 12 slaves; and 22 villans with 7 bordars have 12 ploughs. [There is] a mill rendering 10s, and 63 acres of meadow, pasture 10 furlongs long and 3 furlongs broad, [and] woodland 6 furlongs long and 2 furlongs broad. It was and is worth £16.

Ralph holds of Roger 10 hides in SHIRBURN. [There is] land for 6 ploughs. Now in demesne are 2 [ploughs], and 4 slaves; and 13 villans with 3 bordars have 5 ploughs. There are 20 acres of meadow and 30 acres of pasture, [and] woodland 3 furlongs long and 1½ broad. It was worth £4; now £7.

Fulk holds of Roger 3 hides in WOODEATON. [There is] land for 4 ploughs. Now in demesne are 2 [ploughs], and 2 slaves; and 13 bordars with 2 ploughs. There are 18 acres of meadow, and 26 acres of moor, [and] woodland 6 furlongs long and 4 furlongs broad. It was and is worth 60s.

Godfrey holds HOLTON of Roger. There are 5 hides. [There

is] land for 7 ploughs. Now in demesne [are] 2 ploughs, and 4 slaves; and 10 villans with 3 bordars have 4 ploughs. There are 15 acres of meadow and 12 acres of pasture, [and] woodland 2 furlongs long and 1½ furlongs broad. It was and is worth £4.

Reginald holds of Roger 1 hide in NORTHBROOK. [There is] land for 1½ ploughs. In demesne is 1 plough; and 3 villans with 2 bordars have half a plough. It was and is worth 20s.

Godfrey holds NORTH LEIGH of Roger. There are 10 hides. [There is] land for 10 ploughs. Now in demesne [are] 2 ploughs, with 1 slave; and 33 villans with 8 bordars have 12 ploughs. There is a mill rendering 12s8d, and 100 acres of meadow, less 10, [and] woodland 1½ leagues long and 1 league broad. It was and is worth £10.

Hugh holds of Roger 7½ hides in [...]. [There is] land for 5 ploughs. Now in demesne [are] 2 ploughs, and 4 slaves; and 6 villans and 3 bordars with 3 ploughs. There are 24 acres of meadow. It was and is worth £3.

Gilbert holds of Roger 5½ hides in HORSPATH. [There is] land for 5 ploughs. Now in demesne [are] 2½ ploughs, and 2 slaves; and 7 villans with 6 bordars have 3 ploughs. There are 13 acres of meadow, [and] a grove 3 furlongs long and 2 furlongs broad. It was worth £4; now 100s.

Reginald holds of Roger 3 hides in BROOKHAMPTON. [There is] land for 3 ploughs. These are in demesne, with 1 villan. [There is] meadow 3 furlongs long and 1½ broad. It was worth 50s; now 60s. Besides these 3 hides there are in addition 2 hides which have been proved [to belong] to the king's demesne. Nevertheless Reginald keeps them despite the king's seisin.

William holds of Roger 2½ hides in HENSINGTON. [There is] land for 2½ ploughs. Now in demesne [are] 2 ploughs, and 2 slaves; and 4 villans have half a plough. [There is] meadow 1 furlong long and a half broad, and 5 acres of scrubland. It was and is worth 40s.

Godfrey holds of Roger [Lower of Old] WHITEHILL. There are 1½ hides. [There is] land for 2 ploughs, which are there in demesne. There is a mill [rendering] 8s, and 1 burgess paying 10s. There are 2 bordars, and 6 acres of meadow. It was worth 40s; now 60s.

The son of Wadard holds THRUPP of Roger. There are 3 hides. There is land for 6 ploughs. Now in demesne [are] 2 ploughs, with 1 slave, and a mill rendering 6s and 125 eels. There are 30 acres of meadow and as many acres of pasture. It was and is worth £6. Leofwig, a man of Archbishop Stigand, held it.

Alvred the clerk holds CUTTESLOWE of Roger. There are 3 hides. [There is] land for 3 ploughs. Now in demesne are 2 ploughs. [...] It was worth £3; now £4.

Pain holds CLANFIELD of Roger. There are 7 hides, less 1 virgate of land. There is land for 11 ploughs. Now in demesne [are] 4 ploughs, and 4 hides of the same land [are] in demesne.

There are 4 slaves, and 14 villans with 13 bordars have 7 ploughs. There are 100 acres of meadow, and 6 furlongs of pasture in length and in breadth. It was and is worth £7. This land belongs to the king's first fief.

William holds of Roger in ROUSHAM and in STEEPLE BARTON 3 hides and half a virgate of land and 3 acres. There is land for 6 ploughs. Now in demesne [are] 3 ploughs, and 3 slaves; and 7 villans with 8 bordars have 3 ploughs. There are 8 acres of meadow. It was worth £4; now 100s.

IN THE FIRST "GADRE" HUNDRED

Reginald holds of Roger half a hide in NORTHBROOK. [There is] land for half a plough. Nevertheless there is 1 [plough] in demesne; and 6 villans with 3 bordars have another. It was worth 10s; now 30s.

IN THE SECOND "GADRE" HUNDRED

Hugh holds of Roger 10 hides in STOKE TALMAGE. [There is] land for 6½ ploughs. Now in demesne [are] 3 ploughs, and 3 slaves; and 10 villans with 9 bordars have 3½ ploughs. There are 100 acres of meadow, less 3, [and] pasture 13 furlongs long and 1 furlong and 12 perches broad. It was worth £7; now £10.

Roger himself holds of the king 4 hides in WALTON. [There is] land for 2 ploughs. Now in demesne [is] 1 plough, with 1 slave and 13 bordars. There is a fishery [rendering] 16d, and 6 acres of meadow. It was worth 40s; now 60s.

Godfrey holds of Roger 5 hides in WOLVERCOTE. [There is] land for 6 ploughs. Now in demesne [is] 1 plough; and 13 villans with 7 bordars have 4 ploughs. There are 120 acres of meadow, [and] pasture 6 furlongs long and 3½ furlongs broad. It was and is worth 100s.

XXX. The land of Ralph de Mortimer

RALPH DE MORTIMER holds IDBURY of the king, and Oidelard [holds] of him. There are 14 hides. [There is] land for 12 ploughs. Now in demesne [are] 5 ploughs, and 5 slaves; and 13 villans with 5 bordars have 6 ploughs. There are 60 acres of meadow, [and] pasture 7 furlongs long and 4 furlongs broad. It was and is worth £12. 3 thegns held it freely.

XXXI. The land of Ranulph Peverel

RANULPH PEVEREL holds 2½ hides in EWELME. [There is] land for 3 ploughs. Now in demesne [are] 2 ploughs, with 1 villan and 4 bordars and 1 slave. [There is] woodland 3 furlongs long and 1½ furlongs broad. It was worth 40s; now 80s.

XXXII. The land of Richard de Courcy

RICHARD de COURCY holds NUNEHAM COURTENAY of the king. There are 16 hides. [There is] land for 10 ploughs. Besides the inland he has 2 hides and 1 virgate of the villans' land. Now in demesne [are] 3 ploughs; and 35 villans with 3 fishermen have 14 ploughs and pay 30s. There are 7 slaves, and a mill rendering 20s. There are 40 acres of meadow and 10 acres of pasture, [and] a grove 2 furlongs long and 1 furlong broad. TRE and afterwards, as now, worth £13. Hakun held it.

The same Richard holds 20 hides in SARSDEN. [There is] land for 28 ploughs. Now in demesne [are] 9 ploughs, and 34 slaves; and 37 villans with 26 bordars have 19 ploughs. There are 3 mills rendering 12s, and 155 acres of meadow, pasture 4 furlongs long and as many broad, [and] woodland 1 league long and 7 furlongs broad. TRE it was worth £18; and afterwards, as now, £27.

The same Richard holds 1 hide in FOSCOT. [There is] land for 1 plough. There are 4 acres of meadow. It was and is worth 10s.

XXXIII. The land of Richard Puignant

RICHARD Puignant holds of the king 10 hides in MIDDLETON STONEY. [There is] land for 16 ploughs. Now in demesne [are] 3 ploughs, and 5 slaves; and 25 villans with 7 bordars have 13 ploughs. [There is] woodland 8 furlongs long and as many broad. TRE and afterwards, as now, worth £10. Thorir held it freely.

William holds GODINGTON of Richard. There are 7 hides. [There is] land for 7 ploughs. Now in demesne [are] 2 ploughs, with 1 slave; and 16 villans with 2 bordars have 6½ ploughs. There is a mill rendering 3s. It was and is worth 100s. Siward and Sighwat held it freely.

XXXIIII. The land of Berengar de Tosny

BERENGAR de Tosny holds of the king 20 hides in BROUGHTON, and Robert and Reginald and Gilbert [hold] of him. [There is] land for 16 ploughs. Now in demesne [are] 8 ploughs, and 4 slaves; and 4 villans with 10 bordars have 2 ploughs. There are 2 mills rendering 16s, and 37 acres of meadow. TRE it was worth £16; now £20. Thorgot held it freely.

The same Berengar holds 10 hides in HORLEY, and Ralph [holds] of him. [There is] land for 8 ploughs. Now in demesne [are] 3 ploughs, and 5 slaves; and 4 villans with 3 bordars have 4 ploughs. There are 20 acres of meadow, and from part of a mill [come] 16d. TRE, and afterwards, it was worth 100s; now £7. Queen Edith, 5 hides, and Thorgot, 5 hides, held it.

The same Berengar holds of Robert his father 1½ hides in BODICOTE. [There is] land for 1½ ploughs. In demesne is 1 plough, with 3 bordars. It was and is worth 30s. 2 men held it but could not withdraw.

XXXV. The land of Miles Crispin

MILES CRISPIN holds GATEHAMPTON of the king. There are 5 hides. [There is] land for 4 ploughs. Now in demesne [are] 2 ploughs, and 4 slaves; and 4 villans with 2 bordars have 2 ploughs. There is a mill rendering 11s, and 10 acres of meadow. TRE and afterwards, as now, worth £4. Vigot held it.

The same man holds [Great and Little] HASELEY. There are 16 hides. [There is] land for 18 ploughs. Now in demesne [are] 3 ploughs, and 5 slaves; and 15 villans with 13 bordars have 15 ploughs. There are 60 acres of meadow, [and] woodland 2 furlongs long and 2 furlongs broad. TRE and afterwards, as now, worth £15. Queen Edith held it.

IN LEWKNOR HUNDRED

The same man holds ASTON ROWANT. There are 20 hides. [There is] land for 33 ploughs. Now in demesne [are] 3 ploughs, and 6 slaves; and 26 villans with 3 bordars, and 15 free men have 30 ploughs. There are 20 acres of meadow, [and] woodland 1 league long and half a league broad. TRE, and afterwards, it was worth £15; now £20. Wulfstan held it freely. In this vill Ælfric held 1 virgate of land and could go where he wished.

The same man holds KINGSTON BLOUNT. There are 7 hides. [There is] land for 6 ploughs. Now in demesne [are] 2 ploughs, and 6 slaves; and 4 villans with 1 bordar have 2 ploughs. There are 16 acres of meadow. It was worth £6; now £7.

The same man holds the other NETHERCOTE. There are 2 hides. [There is] land for 2 ploughs. Now in demesne [is] 1 plough; and 5 villans have another. There is a mill [rendering] 2s. It was worth 30s; now 40s.

IN BENSON HALF-HUNDRED

The same man holds CHALGROVE. There are 10 hides. [There is] land for 12 ploughs. Now in demesne [are] 4 ploughs, and 9 slaves; and 23 villans with 10 bordars have 9 ploughs. There are 5 mills rendering 60s, and meadow 3 furlongs long and 3 furlongs broad, and 60 acres of pasture. It was worth £10; now £12. Thorkil held it freely.

The same man holds 5 hides in ROTHERFIELD PEPPARD. There is land for 7 ploughs. Of this land 2 hides are in demesne, and there are 2 ploughs, and 2 slaves; and 10 villans with 5 bordars have 3 ploughs. There is a mill rendering 20s, and 9 acres of meadow, [and] woodland half a league long and 3 furlongs broad. It was worth £7; now £10. Wulfric held it freely.

The same man holds MAPLEDURHAM. There are 3 hides. [There is] land for 5 ploughs. Now in demesne [are] 2 ploughs, with 1 slave; and 7 villans with 5 bordars have 3 ploughs. There are 4 acres of meadow. It was worth 100s; now £7.

The same man holds WHITCHURCH. There are 10 hides. [...] [There is] land for 15 ploughs. Now in demesne [are] 3 ploughs, and 5 slaves; and 20 villans with 7 bordars have 12 ploughs. There is a mill rendering 20s, and 12 acres of meadow, [and] woodland 2 furlongs long and 1 furlong broad. It was worth £15; now £20. Leofric and Alwine held it freely TRE.

The same man holds NORTH STOKE. There are 10 hides. [There is] land for 15 ploughs. Now in demesne [are] 4 ploughs, and 8 slaves; and 26 villans with 9 bordars have 14 ploughs.

[Folio 159V: OXFORDSHIRE]

There are 2 mills rendering 20s, and 9 acres of meadow, [and] woodland 4 furlongs long and 3 furlongs broad. It was worth £13; now £15. Edwin held it.

The same Miles holds NEWHAM MURREN. There are 10 hides. [...] [There is] land for 16 ploughs. Now in demesne [are] 4 ploughs, and 9 slaves; and 13 villans with 10 bordars have 5 ploughs. There are 8 acres of meadow, [and] woodland 6 furlongs long and 3 furlongs broad. It was worth £10; now £12. Engelric held it.

Reginald holds of Miles 1 hide in [Hempton and Lower] WAINHILL. [There is] land for 1 plough. He has this [plough] there. It was and is worth 10s. Beorhtric held it.

Toli holds of Miles 1½ hides and the third part of 1 virgate of land in COWLEY. [There is] land for 1 plough. He has this [plough] there, with 1 slave and 2 villans and 2 bordars. There are 1½ acres of meadow, [and] a grove 3 acres in length and in breadth. It was and is worth 20s. The same Toli held it freely.

Reginald holds of Miles 1 hide in SOMERTON. [There is] land for 1 plough. It was and is worth 20s. Beorhtric held it.

Roger holds of Miles half a hide in THOMLEY. It is worth 5s.

Richard holds DRAYCOT of Miles. There are 2 hides and 1 virgate of land. [There is] land for 2 ploughs. Now in demesne [is] 1 plough, and 2 slaves; and 5 villans have 1 plough. There are 10 acres of meadow. It was worth 20s; now 30s.

Geoffrey holds of Miles 10 hides in MARSH BALDON. [...] [There is] land for 5 ploughs. Now in demesne [are] 2 ploughs; and 10 villans with 6 bordars have 5 ploughs. It was and is worth 100s. Azur held it.

William holds CHESTERTON of Miles. There are 12 hides. [There is] land for 16 ploughs. Now in demesne [are] 2 ploughs, and 2 slaves; and 22 villans with 10 bordars have 10 ploughs. There is a mill rendering 10s, and 39 acres of meadow, [and] woodland 3 furlongs long and as many broad. It was and is worth £10. Vigot held it.

Ralph holds of Miles 5 hides in UPPER HEYFORD. [There is] land for 6 ploughs. Now in demesne [are] 2 ploughs; and 6 villans with 5 bordars have 3 ploughs. There is a mill rendering 10s, and 30 acres of meadow. It was and is worth £6. Besi held it freely.

William holds HENTON of Miles. There are 8 hides and 1 virgate of land. [There is] land for 6 ploughs. Now in demesne [are] 2 ploughs, and 5 slaves; and 8 villans with 2 bordars have 2 ploughs. There are 46 acres of meadow, [and] a grove 1 furlong long and 1 broad. TRE it was worth £8; and afterwards 40s; now 100s. Leofnoth held it.

The same William holds ADWELL of Miles. There are 3 hides. [There is] land for 3 ploughs. Now in demesne [are] 2 ploughs, and 3 slaves; and 1 villan with 6 bordars have 2

ploughs. There is a mill rendering 6s, [and] meadow 1 furlong long and 1 furlong broad. It was and is worth £6. Wulfstan held it freely.

Amalric holds of Miles 5 hides in BRITWELL SALOME. [There is] land for 3 ploughs. Now in demesne [is] 1 plough, and 2 slaves; and 7 villans with 1 bordar have 1 plough. There are 7 acres of meadow, [and] scrubland 3 furlongs long and 1 furlong broad. It was and is worth £3. Wulfstan held it freely. From † the 5 hides † of this land Amalric has rendered neither geld nor anything else.

In the same vill William holds 1 hide of Miles. [There is] land for 1 plough. There are 2 villans, and 6 acres of a grove. It was and is worth 10s.

Ordgar holds of Miles 4 hides in BERRICK SALOME. [There is] land for 4 ploughs. Now in demesne [are] 2 ploughs, and 4 slaves; and 10 villans with 6 bordars have 3 ploughs. There are 4 acres of meadow and 2 acres of pasture, [and] woodland 2 furlongs long and 1 furlong broad. It was worth £3; now £4.

The same man holds of Miles 1 hide in GANGSDOWN. [There is] land for 2 ploughs. Now in demesne [is] 1 plough, and 3 slaves; and 4 bordars with 1 plough. There are 24 acres of pasture. It was and is worth 20s.

These 2 estates which Ordgar holds of Miles he ought to hold of the king. For he himself and his father and uncle held them freely TRE.

Alvred holds HARPSDEN of Miles. There are 5 hides. [There is] land for 6 ploughs. Now in demesne [are] 2 ploughs, and 4 slaves; and 12 villans with 2 bordars have 4 ploughs. There are 20 acres of meadow. It was worth £6; now 100s.

Humphrey holds KINGSTON BLOUNT of Miles. There are 5 hides. Now in demesne [is] 1 plough; and 7 villans with 1 bordar have 4 ploughs. There are 10 acres of meadow, [and] woodland 1 furlong long and 1 broad. It was and is worth 100s.

Tovi holds of Miles 2 hides in the other NETHERCOTE. [There is] land for 3 ploughs. Now in demesne [is] 1 plough; and 5 villans with 2 bordars have 2 ploughs. There are 12 acres of meadow and as many acres of pasture. It was and is worth £3.

Toli holds of Miles 1 hide in GARSINGTON. [There is] land for 1 plough. He has this [plough] in demesne, with 2 slaves and 3 bordars. It was and is worth 20s.

Geoffrey holds of Miles 2 hides in WATCOMBE. [There is] land for 2 ploughs. There 1 villan with 1 bordar has 1 plough. It was and is worth 20s.

Alvred holds 5 hides of Miles in CUXHAM. [There is] land for 4 ploughs. Now in demesne [are] 2 ploughs, and 4 slaves; and 7 villans with 4 bordars have 3 ploughs. There are 3 mills rendering 18s, and 18 acres of meadow. It was worth £3; now £6. Vigot held it.

Richard holds 6 hides of Miles in ALKERTON. [There is] land for 6 ploughs. Now in demesne [are] 3 ploughs; and 3 villans with 8 bordars have 1 plough. There are 10 acres of meadow. It was and is worth £4.

The monks of Bec hold 2½ hides of Miles in SWYNCOMBE. [There is] land for 2½ ploughs. Now there is no [plough]. There are 10 acres of meadow. It was worth 40s; now 60s. This land has never paid geld.

Reginald holds SOMERTON of Miles. [...] There is 1 hide. [There is] land for 1 plough. He has this [plough] in demesne, with 1 slave. There are 8 acres of meadow. It was and is worth 20s. Ketil held it.

XXXVI. The land of Guy de Raimbeaucourt

GUY de Raimbeaucourt holds WROXTON of the king, and Ingelrann his son holds of him. There are 17 hides. There is land for 14 ploughs. Now in demesne [are] 3 ploughs, and 2 slaves; and 12 villans with 10 bordars have 8 ploughs. There is a mill rendering 8s, and 60 acres of meadow. It was worth £12; now £16.

XXXVII. The land of Giles

GILES the brother of Ansculf holds of the king 2½ hides in BAINTON, and Erchenbald [holds] of him. [There is] land for 3 ploughs. Now in demesne [is] 1 plough; and 1 villan with 2 bordars has 1 plough. There are 4 acres of meadow. It was and is worth 40s.

XXXVIII. The land of Gilbert de Ghent

GILBERT DE GHENT holds CHURCH HAN-BOROUGH of the king, and Robert [holds] of him. There are 9 hides. [There is] land for 12 ploughs. Now in demesne [are] 2 ploughs, and 5 slaves; and 20 villans with 6 bordars have 10 ploughs. There is a mill rendering 10s, and 100 acres of meadow, [and] woodland 7 furlongs long and 6 furlongs broad. It was and is worth £10. Tonni held it.

The same Robert [holds] EWELME of Gilbert. There are 8 hides. [There is] land for 10 ploughs. Now in demesne [are] 2 ploughs, and 4 slaves; and 10 villans and 3 bordars have 6 ploughs. There are 20 acres of meadow, [and] woodland 3 furlongs long and 1 furlong broad. It was and is worth £6. Ulf held it.

XXXIX. The land of Geoffrey de Mandeville

GEOFFREY de Mandeville holds 10 hides in KINGHAM of the king. [There is] land for 16 ploughs. Now in demesne [are] 4 ploughs, and 4 slaves; and 19 villans with 10 bordars have 12 ploughs. There is a mill rendering 44d, and 109 acres of meadow and 33 acres of pasture. It was worth £12; now £15.

Saswalo holds of Geoffrey in RYCOTE 1 hide and 1 virgate of land. [There is] land for 1 plough. He has this [plough] in demesne, with 1 villan. There are 5 acres of meadow. It is worth 5s.

The same Saswalo holds WENDLEBURY of Geoffrey. There are 8 hides. [There is] land for 8 ploughs. Now in demesne [are] 2 ploughs, and 3 slaves; and 4 villans with 5 bordars

LVI. HASCOIT Musard holds of the king 2½ hides in CHILWORTH. [There is] land for 5 ploughs. Now in demesne [is] 1 plough, with 1 slave; and 2 villans with 8 bordars have 1 plough. There are 23 acres of meadow. It was worth 60s; now 20s. Leofwig held it freely. The same man holds of the king 2½ hides waste. [There is] land for 3 ploughs. It was worth 40s.

The same man holds 5 hides in HEYTHROP. [There is] land for 8 ploughs. In demesne are 2 ploughs,

[Folio 160: OXFORDSHIRE]

have 3 ploughs. [There is] meadow 8 furlongs long and 2 furlongs broad, [and] pasture 15 furlongs long and 2 furlongs broad. It was and is worth 100s. Esger held it.

XL. The land of Ernulf de Hesdin

ERNULF de Hesdin holds of the king 5 hides in BLACK BOURTON, and Wimund [holds] of him. [There is] land for 6 ploughs. Now in demesne [are] 3 ploughs, and 2 slaves; and 9 villans with 3 bordars have 3 ploughs. There is a mill [rendering] 4s, and 20 acres of meadow, [and] pasture 4 furlongs long and as many broad. It was and is worth £4. Thorgot held it freely.

The same Ernulf holds 1 hide in LUDWELL, and Osmund [holds] of him. [There is] land for 1 plough. It was worth 15s; now 40s.

The same Ernulf holds CHIPPING NORTON. There are 15 hides and 1 virgate of land. [There is] land for 21 ploughs. Now in demesne [are] 10 ploughs, and 15 slaves; and 22 villans with 16 bordars have 11 ploughs. There are 3 mills rendering 62d, and 60 acres of meadow, [and] pasture 1 league long and broad. It was worth £16; now £22. Wulfweard White and Ælfric Whelp held it.

XLI. The land of Edward of Salisbury

EDWARD of Salisbury holds NORTH ASTON of the king, and Ansketil [holds] of him. There are 9 hides. [There is] land for 20 ploughs. Now in demesne [are] 3 ploughs, and 7 slaves; and 6 villans with 2 Frenchmen and 10 bordars have 5 ploughs. There is a mill with a fishery rendering 30s, and 30 acres of meadow. It was worth £10; now £12.

The same Edward holds 1 hide in HEMPTON. [There is] land for 1 plough. He has this [plough] in demesne, with 1 slave. There are 4 acres of meadow. It was and is worth 20s.

XLII. The land of Swein the Sheriff

SWEIN the sheriff holds of the king 6 hides in TOOT BALDON, and Hugh [holds] of him. [There is] land for 5 ploughs. Now in demesne [is] 1 plough, and 2 slaves; and 7 villans with 2 bordars have 1 plough. It was and is worth 60s.

XLIII. The land of Alfred the Nephew of Vigot

ALFRED the nephew of Vigot holds LITTLESTOKE of the king. There are 3 hides. [There is] land for 4 ploughs. Now in demesne [is] 1 plough, and 2 slaves; and 6 villans with 2 bordars have 2 ploughs. There is a mill [rendering] 20s, [and] woodland 1½ furlongs long and as much broad. It was worth £4; now £3. Wulfræd held it freely.

The same man holds CHECKENDON. There are 5 hides. [There is] land for 7 ploughs. Now in demesne [is] 1 plough, and 4 slaves; and 8 villans with 3 bordars have 2 ploughs. There are 6 acres of meadow, [and] woodland 1 furlong long and 1 broad. It was worth £4; now £3. Wulfræd held it freely.

XLIIII. The land of Guy d'Oilly

GUY d'Oilly holds of the king 10 hides in WIGGINTON. [There is] land for 6 ploughs. Now in demesne [are] 3 ploughs, and 6 slaves; and 9 villans with 1 knight and 5 bordars have 5 ploughs. There is a mill [rendering] 8s, and 16 acres of meadow. It was and is worth 100s. Leofric held it freely TRE.

XLV. The land of Walter fitzPons

WALTER [fitz] Pons holds YELFORD of the king, as he says. There are 3 hides. [There is] land for 3 ploughs. Now in demesne [are] 2 ploughs, and 4 slaves; and 3 villans with 3 bordars have half a plough. There are 36 acres of meadow, and 15 acres of pasture. It was worth 60s; now 50s.

Walter fitzPons holds 5 hides of the king in WESTWELL. [There is] land for 10 ploughs. Now in demesne [are] 5 ploughs, and 8 slaves; and 8 villans with 3 bordars have 2 ploughs. [There is] pasture 8 furlongs long and as many broad. It was and is worth £7.

The same Walter holds 4 hides in "ALWOLDESBERIE". [There is] land for 6 ploughs. Now in demesne [is] 1 plough, and 2 slaves; and 5 villans with 6 bordars have 3 ploughs. There are 6 acres of meadow, and pasture 6 furlongs long and broad. It was worth £3; now £4. Ealdwine and Sæweald and Edwin held these lands freely.

XLVI. The land of William Leofric

WILLIAM Leofric holds of the king 3 hides and 1 virgate of land and 2 parts of 1 virgate, and Godfrey [holds] of him. [There is] land for 5 ploughs. Now in demesne [are] 2 slaves and 4 bordars. From part of a mill [come] 40d, and [there are] 4 acres of meadow, [and] woodland 10 furlongs long and 1½ furlongs broad. It was worth 40s; now 30s.

XLVII. The land of William fitzManni

WILLIAM fitzManni holds of the king, 3 hides in [Lower or Upper] ARNCOTT. [There is] land for 5 ploughs. Now in demesne [are] 2 ploughs, with 1 slave; and 4 villans with 2 bordars have 3 ploughs. There is woodland 8 furlongs long and 4 furlongs broad. It was and is worth 40s. 3 free men held it freely.

XLVIII. The land of Ilbod

ILBOD holds of the king 4 hides in BARFORD ST MICHAEL. [There is] land for 4 ploughs. Now in demesne [are] 2 ploughs, and 3 slaves; and 6 villans with 1 bordar have 2 ploughs. There are 18 acres of meadow. It was worth £3; now £4. Alwine held it freely.

XLIX. The land of Reinbald

REINBALD holds of the king 1 hide in BOYCOTT [Bucks.]. [There is] land for 3 ploughs. Now in demesne [is] 1 plough, with 1 villan. [There is] woodland 4 furlongs long and 2 broad. It was worth 40s; now 20s. Blæcmann held it freely.

L. The land of Robert fitzMurdoch

ROBERT fitzMurdoch holds of the king in BROUGHTON POGGS 7 hides, less 1 virgate. [There is] land for 10 ploughs. Now in demesne [are] 2 ploughs, and 9 slaves; and 11 villans with 11 bordars have 7 ploughs. There are 2 mills rendering 12s6d, and 36 acres of meadow and 40 acres of pasture. It was worth £6; now £7. 3 free men held it freely.

LI. The land of Osbern Giffard

OSBERN Giffard holds of the king 2½ hides in "BISPESDONE". [There is] land for 4 ploughs. Now in demesne [is] 1 hide of this land, and there is 1 plough; and 7 villans with 3 bordars have 3 ploughs. There are 7 acres of meadow, [and] woodland 1½ furlongs long and 1 furlong broad. It was and is worth 50s. Ledric held it.

LII. The land of Benzelin

BENZELIN holds LILLINGSTONE LOVELL [Bucks.] of the king. There are 2½ hides. [There is] land for 2 ploughs. Now in demesne [is] 1 plough; and 3 villans with 1 bordar have 1 plough. [There is] woodland 10 furlongs long and 5 furlongs broad. It was and is worth 40s. Azur held it freely TRE.

LIII. The land of Countess Judith

Countess JUDITH holds MERTON of the king. There are 10 hides. [There is] land for 12 ploughs. Now in demesne [are] 2 ploughs, and 2 slaves; and 19 villans with 6 bordars have 5 ploughs. There are 100 acres of meadow, [and] a grove 4 furlongs long and $1\frac{1}{2}$ furlongs broad. It was and is worth £8.

The same countess holds PIDDINGTON. There are 4 hides. [There is] land for 9 ploughs. Now in demesne [are] 3 ploughs, with 1 slave; and 12 villans with 6 bordars have 5 ploughs. There are 30 acres of meadow, [and] woodland 2 leagues long and 5 furlongs broad. It was worth £6; now £4. Hakun held these 2 estates freely.

LIIII. The land of Christina

CHRISTINA holds BROADWELL of the king. There are 24 hides and 1 virgate of land. [There is] land for 30 ploughs. Now in demesne [are] 6 ploughs, and 14 slaves; and 52 villans with 8 bordars have 24 ploughs. There 2 mills with a fishery and meadows render 20s, and [there are] 200 acres of meadow, less 15, and 100 acres of pasture. TRE it was worth £25; and afterwards £30; now £31. Algar held it freely TRE.

LV. The land of the wife of Roger d'Ivry

THE WIFE OF ROGER d'IVRY holds of the king 5 hides in ISLIP. 3 hides of these have never paid geld. [There is] land for 15 ploughs. Now in demesne [are] 3 ploughs, and 2 slaves; and 10 villans with 5 bordars have 3 ploughs. There is a mill rendering 20s, and 30 acres of meadow, pasture 3 furlongs long and 2 broad, and 5 slaves; and 4 villans with 1 bordar have 2 ploughs. There is a mill [rendering] 5s, and 40 acres of meadow. It was worth 100s; now £4.

The same man holds 5 hides in KIDDINGTON, and Mainou [holds] of him. [There is] land for 6 ploughs. Now in demesne [are] 2 ploughs, and 4 slaves; and 7 villans with 10 bordars have $2\frac{1}{2}$ ploughs. There is a mill [rendering] 5s, and 12 acres of meadow, [and] woodland 1 league long and 3 furlongs broad. It was worth £3; now £4. Godric held these 2 estates freely.

[Folio 160V: OXFORDSHIRE]

[and] woodland 1 league long and half a league broad. It was worth £7 TRE; when received, £8; now £10. Godric and Alwine held it freely.

The same woman holds of the king 3 hides and half a virgate of land in ODDINGTON. [There is] land for 3 ploughs. Now in demesne [are] 2 ploughs, and 2 slaves; and 10 villans with 4 bordars have 2 ploughs. There are 40 acres of meadow, [and] pasture 3 furlongs long and 2 furlongs broad. It was worth 40s; now 60s. Alwig held it freely TRE.

The wife of Roger has these 2 estates of the king in commendation.

LVII. The land of Thorkil

THORKIL holds of the king 5 hides in DRAYTON. [There is] land for 5 ploughs. Now in demesne [are] 3 ploughs, and 2 slaves; and 12 villans with 4 bordars have 3 ploughs. There is a mill rendering 4s. It was worth 100s; now £8.

LVIII. The land of Richard and Other Servants of the King

RICHARD Engaine holds of the king $2\frac{1}{2}$ hides in LILLINGSTONE LOVELL [Bucks.]. [There is] land for 2 ploughs. Of this land 1 hide and 1 virgate are in demesne. There 5 villans with 1 bordar and 1 slave have 2 ploughs. [There is] woodland 10 furlongs long and 5 furlongs broad. It was worth 40s; now 60s.

REGINALD the archer holds of the king $2\frac{1}{2}$ hides in IPSDEN. [There is] land for 4 ploughs. Now in demesne [is] 1 plough; and 6 villans with 5 bordars have 3 ploughs. There are 7 acres of meadow, [and] woodland $1\frac{1}{2}$ furlongs long and 1 furlong broad. It was and is worth 50s.

The same Reginald holds $2\frac{1}{2}$ hides in CHADLINGTON. [There is] land for 2 ploughs, and there are [2 ploughs] in demesne, with 4 slaves and 2 bordars. It was and is worth 40s.

Robert fitz Turstin holds 5 hides and 1 virgate of land of the king in GREAT ROLLRIGHT. [There is] land for 6 ploughs. Now in demesne [is] 1 plough, and 2 slaves; and 7 villans with 5 bordars have $3\frac{1}{2}$ ploughs. There are 50 acres of meadow, and 50 acres of pasture and 3 summae of salt at Droitwich [Worcs.]. It was and is worth 100s.

Turstin's son [holds], and Osmund [holds] of him, 2 hides of the king in LUDWELL. [There is] land for $1\frac{1}{2}$ ploughs. Now in demesne [is] 1 plough, with 2 slaves and 2 bordars. It was worth 20s; now 40s.

RANULPH holds of the king 1 hide in LUDWELL. [There is] land for 1 plough. It was worth 15s; now 10s.

ROGER holds of the king 2 hides in BRIGHTWELL BALDWIN. [There is] land for 6 ploughs. Now in demesne [are] 2 ploughs, and 2 slaves; and 8 villans with 2 bordars have 3 ploughs. There are 6 acres of meadow and 20 acres of woodland. It was worth 50s; now 100s.

ROBERT fitzRalph holds of the king 5 hides, less 1 virgate, in EWELME. [There is] land for 5 ploughs. Now in demesne [is] 1 plough, and 2 slaves; and 5 villans with 6 bordars have 2 ploughs. There are 8 acres of meadow, [and] 80 acres of pasture. It was and is worth 100s.

The same Robert holds 2 hides in EASINGTON. [There is] land for 2 ploughs. In demesne is 1 [plough]; and 4 villans with 3 bordars have 1 plough. There are $1\frac{1}{2}$ acres of meadow. It was worth 25s; now 40s.

WILLIAM holds of the king $4\frac{1}{2}$ hides in Great ROLLRIGHT. [There is] land for 5 ploughs. Now in demesne [are] 2 ploughs; and 5 villans with 3 bordars have 2 ploughs. There are 20 acres of meadow. It was and is worth £3.

HERVEY holds of the king 1 hide in IBSTOEN [Ibstone and Ibstone Common, Bucks.]. [There is] land for 1 plough. There is 1 villan, and 3 acres of meadow. It was and is worth 20s. This land does not pay geld.

The same man holds $2\frac{1}{2}$ hides in BIX. [There is] land for 7 ploughs. Now in demesne [is] 1 plough, with 1 slave; and 8 villans with 2 bordars have 5 ploughs. There are 3 acres of meadow, [and] 12 acres of woodland. It was and is worth £3.

These 2 estates have neither paid geld nor [rendered] other service to the king.

WILLIAM holds of the king 1 hide in BENSON and it belongs to the king's soke. [There is] land for 1 plough. There are 4 acres of meadow. It was worth 20s; now 12s6d. The same Hervey holds IBSTONE [Ibstone and Ibstone Common, Bucks.]. There is 1 hide. [There is] land for 1 plough. It is worth 10s. Ulf held it.

GEOFFREY holds of the king SWINBROOK and SHIPTON-UNDER- WYCHWOOD. There are $4\frac{1}{2}$ hides. [There is] land for 3 ploughs. Now in demesne [is] 1 plough, with 1 slave; and 2 villans with 4 bordars have 1 plough. There are 3 acres of meadow, [and] woodland 3 furlongs long and 1 broad. It was worth 60s; now 40s.

GERNIO holds of the king 10 hides in HAMPTON POYLE. 5 thegns held it as 5 manors. [There is] land for 6 ploughs. In demesne are 3 ploughs, and 2 slaves; and 7 villans with 2 bordars have 3 ploughs. There is a mill rendering 15s, and 60 acres of meadow, [and] woodland half a league long and 16 furlongs broad. It was worth £6; now £10.

THEODRIC the goldsmith holds of the king 1 hide in BRIZE NORTON. [There is] land for 1 plough. He has this [plough] in demesne. It was worth 10s; now 20s.

The same man holds $2\frac{1}{2}$ hides in CLAYWELL. [There is] land for 2 ploughs. He has these and 2 slaves in demesne; and 3 villans with 5 bordars have 1 plough. There are 24 acres of meadow. It was and is worth 40s. His wife held these 2 estates freely TRE.

The same man holds 2 hides in BENSON. [There is] land for 2 ploughs. There are 3 bordars, and 4 acres of meadow. It was and is worth 20s. Sæweald held it freely TRE.

ARETIUS holds of the king 2 hides, less 1 virgate, in LEW. [There is] land for 1 plough. In demesne he has 1 plough; and 3 villans with 2 bordars have 1 plough. There is pasture 1 furlong long and half a furlong broad. It was worth 20s; now 35s. Alwine held it.

SÆRIC holds ALVESCOT of the king. There are 2 hides. [There is] land for 2 ploughs. In demesne are 2 ploughs, and 2 slaves; and 4 bordars with $1\frac{1}{2}$ ploughs, and 3 acres of pasture. It was worth 20s; now 50s. Goda held it freely.

The same man holds 1 hide and 1 virgate of land in MIDDLE ASTON. [There is] land for 10 oxen. In demesne are 2 ploughs, and 2 slaves, with 1 villan and 4 bordars. There are 5 acres of meadow and 3 acres of pasture. It was worth 20s; now 40s.

SIWARD the huntsman holds of the king $2\frac{1}{2}$ hides in CHADLINGTON. [There is] land for 2 ploughs. He has these in demesne, with 1 slave, and 3 bordars. There are 3 acres of meadow. It was and is worth 40s. Siward himself held it freely TRE.

IN LEWKNOR HUNDRED

LEOFWINE holds CHINNOR, 13 hides, of the king. [There is] land for 11 ploughs. In demesne are 2 [ploughs], and 4 slaves; and 26 villans with 2 bordars have 8 ploughs. There are 20 acres of meadow, [and] woodland 5 furlongs long and 3 furlongs broad. It was worth £6; now £10.

The same man holds COWLEY of the king. There are $4\frac{1}{2}$ hides. [There is] land for 10 ploughs. There is 1 hide of warland in demesne, and 1 plough, and 2 slaves; and 20 villans with 5 bordars have 8 ploughs. There is a mill rendering 40s, and 2 fisheries [rendering] 8s, and 10 acres of meadow, [and] a grove 4 furlongs long and 2 furlongs broad. It was and is worth 100s. The same Leofwine held these lands freely TRE.

GODWINE holds of the king $2\frac{1}{2}$ virgates of land in BRIZE NORTON. [There is] land for half a plough. Nevertheless, he has 1 plough there. It was and is worth 10s.

ALWIG the sheriff holds of the king $2\frac{1}{2}$ hides in BLETCHINGDON. [There is] land for $1\frac{1}{2}$ ploughs, and he has as many in demesne, and there are 2 slaves. There is a mill rendering 7s6d, and 3 acres of meadow. It was and is worth 40s. Manasses bought this land from him without the king's leave.

ALSIGE holds RYCOTE of the king. There are 2 hides. [There is] land for 2 ploughs. He has these in demesne, and 24 acres of meadow. It was worth 40s; now £4.

The same man holds 2 hides in SHIPTON-UNDER-WYCHWOOD. [There is] land for 2 ploughs. He has these in demesne. It was and is worth 40s. Earl Harold held it.

LEOFWINE holds of the king 5 hides in HANWELL. [There is] land for 8 ploughs. Now in demesne [are] 3 ploughs, and 6 slaves; and 20 villans with 2 bordars have 7 ploughs. There are 14 acres of meadow. It was worth 100s; now £7. The same man held it.

SÆWEALD holds ROFFORD of the king. There are 3 hides [...]. [There is] land for 5 ploughs. Now in demesne [are] 2 ploughs; and 7 villans with 3 bordars have 3 ploughs. There are 5 acres of meadow and 16 acres of pasture. It was worth 40s; now 60s. Robert d'Oilly has this land in pledge.

The same man holds TIDDINGTON. There are 2 hides and 3 virgates of land. There is land for 2 ploughs. He has these in demesne, with 1 bordar. There are 15 acres of meadow. It was worth 30s; now 40s. Alwig held it freely TRE.

SÆWEALD holds of the king 3 hides in MINSTER [Little Minster and Minster Lovell], and Robert [holds] of him in pledge. [There is] land for 3 ploughs. In demesne is 1 [plough], and 2 slaves, with 2 bordars. There is a mill [rendering] 10s. It was and is worth £3. The same man held it TRE.

The same man holds of the king 2 mills which the king granted to him with his wife; they are close to the wall and are worth 40s.

Ælfric holds of the king 3½ hides in MILCOMBE. [There is] land for 2 ploughs. In demesne he has 1½ ploughs, with 2 slaves, and 2s. from part of a mill, and 15 acres of meadow. [There is] pasture 2 furlongs long and 1 furlong broad. There 3 villans with 1 bordar have half a plough. It was and is worth 30s.

The same man holds 6 hides, less 1 virgate, in CHASTLETON. [There is] land for 6 ploughs. In demesne are 2 ploughs, and 4 slaves; and 6 villans with 1 bordar have 4 ploughs. There are 26 acres of meadow. It was worth £4; when received, 40s; now 60s. Coleman and Azur held these lands.

ALWIG holds of the king 2 hides, less half a virgate of land, in [? Over] WORTON. [There is] land for 3 ploughs. In demesne he has 1 [plough]; and 2 villans with 3 bordars have another plough. There are 25 acres of meadow. It was and is worth 40s. Leofgeat held it freely.

ORDGAR holds of the king "ADLACH", 2 hides. [There is] land for 2 ploughs. He has these in demesne, with 2 slaves; and 2 villans have half a plough. There are 2 acres of meadow. It was and is worth 40s. Godwine held it freely.

LIX. These Lands Written Below Belong To the Fief of Earl William

IN LEWKNOR HUNDRED

GILBERT de Breteuil holds BOLNEY at farm. There are 8 hides. [There is] land for 7 ploughs. Now in demesne [are] 2 ploughs, and 3 slaves; and 11 villans with 2 bordars have 4 ploughs. There are 8 acres of meadow. It was and is worth £8. 3 thegns held it freely.

The same man holds SYDENHAM at farm. There are 15 hides. [There is] land for 14 ploughs. Now in demesne [are] 3 ploughs, and 5 slaves; and 16 villans with 5 bordars have 6 ploughs. There are 60 acres of meadow, [and] woodland half a league long and 3 furlongs broad. It was worth £10; now £16. Almær held it freely.

Robert holds 3½ hides in WATLINGTON. [There is] land for 3 ploughs. 8 villans with 2 bordars and 2 slaves have these [ploughs] there. It was worth 40s; now 100s.

The same man holds 1 hide in WATCOMBE. [There is] land for 1 plough. A widow has this [plough] there. It was and is worth 10s.

Ansketil holds ROTHERFIELD GREYS. There are 5 hides. [There is] land for 7 ploughs. Now in demesne [are] 2 ploughs; and 12 villans with 8 bordars have 5 ploughs, and [there are] 12 acres of meadow. [There is] woodland 4 furlongs long and as many broad. It was and is worth 100s.

Robert holds 7 hides in DUCKLINGTON. [There is] land for 6 ploughs. In demesne are 2 ploughs, and 3 slaves; and 7 villans with 2 bordars have 5 ploughs. There are 30 acres of meadow, pasture 1 furlong long and 1 broad, [and] woodland

3 furlongs long and 2 furlongs broad. It was worth £6; now £7.

The same Robert and Roger hold half a hide waste in NOKE.

The same Robert holds 1 hide in KIRTLINGTON. [There is] land for 1 plough. He has this [plough] in demesne, with 1 bordar and 2 slaves. There are 3 acres of meadow. It was and is worth 15s.

The same man holds 5 virgates of land in HENSINGTON, and Peter [holds] of him. [There is] land for 1 plough. He has this [plough] in demesne, with 1 slave and 1 villan and 2 bordars. There is a mill [rendering] 5s, and 3 acres of meadow and 6 acres of woodland. It was worth 20s; now 25s.

Roger holds 1 hide in ASTROP. [There is] land for 2 ploughs. He has these there, with 4 slaves and 1 villan and 4 bordars. There is pasture 3 furlongs in length and 2 furlongs in breadth. It was worth 20s; now 30s.

Roger de Lacy holds BEGBROKE, and Ralph [holds] of him. There are 4 hides and 1 virgate of land. [There is] land for 6 ploughs. Now in demesne [are] 2 ploughs; and 6 villans with 3 bordars have 2 ploughs. There are 50 acres of meadow and 40 acres of pasture. It was worth 100s; and afterwards £6; now £4.

Roger d'Ivry holds 3 hides in BLACK BOURTON, and Pain [holds] of him. [There is] land for 8 ploughs. Now in demesne [are] 2 ploughs, with 1 slave; and 10 villans with 6 bordars have 10 ploughs. There are 50 acres of meadow and 8 acres of pasture. It was and is worth £4.

Ansketil holds 2 hides in BLACK BOURTON. [There is] land for 2½ ploughs. There are 2 ploughs, and 2 slaves. There is a mill [rendering] 3s, and 6 acres of meadow and as many of pasture. It was worth 20s; now 40s.

The same Ansketil de Graye holds 3 hides in RADFORD. [There is] land for 4 ploughs. Now in demesne [are] 2 ploughs, and 2 slaves; and 4 villans with 8 bordars have 3 ploughs. There is a mill rendering 20d, and 6 acres of meadow and 3 acres of spinney. It was worth 50s; now £4.

Roger de Lacy holds 1 hide and 2½ virgates of land in KIDDINGTON, and Ralph holds of him. [There is] land for 2½ ploughs. Now in demesne [is] 1 plough; and 3 villans with 3 bordars have 1 plough. From part of a mill, 20d, and [there are] 2 acres of meadow, [and] woodland 5 furlongs long and 1 furlong broad. It was worth 30s; now 40s.

Reginald holds 2½ hides in [Hempton and Lower] WAINHILL. [There is] land for 1½ ploughs. In demesne is 1 plough, with 2 bordars, and 7 acres of meadow. It was worth 40s; now 40s.

The same man holds FRITWELL. There are 10 hides. [There is] land for 8 ploughs. Now in demesne [are] 2 ploughs, and 2 slaves; and 8 villans with 6 bordars have 4 ploughs. There are 20 acres of meadow. 6 hides of this land are in demesne. It was worth £7; now £6.

The same man holds NOKE. There are 2½ hides. [There is] land for 1 plough. 5 virgates of this land are in demesne, and there is 1 plough, and 2 slaves; and 3 villans with 6 bordars have 1 plough. [There is] pasture 3 furlongs long and 2 furlongs broad, [and] woodland 4 furlongs long and 3 furlongs broad. It was worth 30s; now 40s.

Ansketil holds 4 hides in SOUTH NEWINGTON, and Robert [holds] of him. [There is] land for 3 ploughs. Now in demesne [is] 1 plough; and 1 villan with 4 bordars have 1 plough. There is a mill rendering 25d, and 22 acres of meadow. It was worth 40s; now 50s.

Robert holds 5 hides in SWERFORD. [There is] land for 8 ploughs. Now in demesne [are] 3 ploughs, and 3 slaves; and 7 villans with 6 bordars have 6 ploughs. There is a mill rendering 6s, and 12 acres of meadow and 12 acres of pasture. It was and is worth 100s.

Roger holds 1 hide in MILTON-UNDER-WYCHWOOD, and Alwig [holds] of him. [There is] land for 1 plough. He has this [plough] in demesne. There are 2 acres of meadow, [and] woodland 1 league long and 4 furlongs broad. It was worth 20s; afterwards 15s; now £7.

Reginald holds 3 hides in ALBURY. [There is] land for 3 ploughs. Now in demesne [is] 1 plough, with 1 slave; and 5 villans with 3 bordars have 2 ploughs. There are 2 acres of meadow. It was and is worth £3.

Roger de Lacy holds MONGEWELL. There are 10 hides. [There is] land for 10 ploughs. Of this land 7 hides are in demesne, and there are 3 ploughs, and 5 slaves; and 6 villans and 1 knight with 11 bordars have 6 ploughs. There are 2 mills rendering 45s, and 5 acres of meadow, [and] woodland 1½ leagues in length and 4 furlongs broad. It was worth £10; now £14.

Ansketil de Graye holds WOODLEYS. There are 2 hides,

and they are in demesne except 1 virgate of land. [There is] land for 2 ploughs. He has these in demesne, and [there are] 3 slaves with 2 bordars. There are 12 acres of meadow. It was worth 40s; now 50s.

The same Ansketil holds 6 hides in BRIGHTHAMPTON. [There is] land for 7 ploughs. Now in demesne [are] 2 ploughs, and 4 slaves; and 15 villans with 16 bordars have 7 ploughs. There is a mill rendering 11s, and 90 acres of meadow, [and] pasture 10 furlongs long and 4 furlongs broad. It was worth 100s; now £6.

The same Ansketil holds in CORNWELL 2 hides and the third part of half a hide. [There is] land for 2 ploughs. Now in demesne [is] 1 plough, with 1 slave and 6 bordars. There is a mill rendering 2s, and 20 acres of meadow, and pasture 2 furlongs long and 2 furlongs broad. It was and is worth 30s.

Roger de Lacy holds 3 hides and 1 virgate of land in SALFORD. [There is] land for 5 ploughs. Now in demesne [are] 2 ploughs, and 3 slaves; and 2 villans with 1 bordar have half a plough. From part of a mill, 12d, and there are 23 acres of meadow, [and] pasture 1 furlong long and half a furlong broad. It was and is worth £3.

Robert holds 2½ hides in INGHAM. [There is] land for 3 ploughs. In demesne is 1 plough. It was and is worth 50s.

Roger holds WORTON, and Robert [holds] of him. There are 5 hides. [There is] land for 5 ploughs. Now in demesne [are] 2 ploughs; and 8 villans with 5 bordars have 3 ploughs. There are 48 acres of meadow, [and] pasture 3 furlongs long and as many broad. It was worth £4; now £6.

[Folio 161V: [OXFORDSHIRE]]

[Blank in MS]

GLOUCESTERSHIRE

In THE TIME of King EDWARD the city of Gloucester rendered £36 by tale, and 12 sesters of honey according to the measure of the same borough, and 36 dickers of iron, and 100 rods of iron, drawn out, for nails for the king's ships, and certain other small customary dues in the hall and in the king's chamber.

This city now render the king £60 at 20[d] to the ora, and the king has £20 from the mint.

In the king's demesne land Roger of Berkeley holds 1 house and 1 fishery in this vill, and it is out of the king's hand. Baldwin held this TRE.

Bishop Osbern holds the land and messuages which Eadmær held; he pays 10s with other customary dues.

Geoffrey de Mandeville holds 6 messuages. TRE these rendered 6s8d with other customary dues. William [fitz] Baderon [holds] 2 messuages rendering 30d. William the scribe, 1 messuage rendering 51d. Roger de Lacy, 1 messuage rendering 26d. Bishop Osbern, 1 messuage rendering 41d. Berner, 1 messuage rendering 14d. William the Bald, 1 messuage rendering 12d. Durand the sheriff, 2 messuages rendering 14d.

The same Durand holds 1 messuage rendering 26d, and in addition 1 messuage which renders no customary dues.

Hadewin holds 1 messuage which pays rent but withholds other customary dues.

Gosbert [holds] 1 messuage, Dunning 1 messuage, Widard 1 messuage. Arnulf the priest [holds] 1 messuage which pays rent and withholds other customary dues.

All these messuages rendered the royal customary dues TRE. Now King William has nothing from these, nor does Robert, his minister.

These messuages were in King Edward's farm on the day on which he was alive and dead. Now they have been removed from the king's farm and customary dues. TRE the whole of the king's demesne in the city was for lodging or clothing. When Earl William received it at farm, it was for clothing in the same way.

Where the castle stands were 16 houses which are not there now, and in the fortified area of the city 14 houses have been destroyed.

Earl William built the CASTLE of CHEPSTOW [Mon.], and in his time it rendered only 40s from ships going into the woodland. In the time of his son, Earl Roger, however, the vill

itself rendered £16, and Ralph de Limesy had half. Now the king has £12 from it.

All together from the renders of Caerleon [Mon.] and 1 plough [sic] which is there, and from 7 fisheries in the Wye and the Usk, come £7.10s.

In WALES are 3 hardwicks, Llanvair Discoed [Mon.], and Portskewett [Mon.] and Dinham [Mon.]. In these are 8 ploughs, and 11 half-villans and 15 bordars with 6 ploughs. For these 3 hardwicks Roger d'Ivry wished to have 100s.

Under Waswic the reeve are 13 vills; under Elmui 14 vills; under Bleio are 13 vills; under Iudichael are 14 vills.

These render 47 sesters of honey and 40 pigs and 41 cows and 28s. for hawks. The whole of this is worth £9.10s4d.

For a piece of waste land Walter the crossbowman renders 1 sester of honey and 1 pig.

Berdic the king's jester has 3 vills, and there are 5 ploughs. He pays nothing.

Morin [has] 1 vill; Cynesige 1; the son of Waswic 1; Sessisbert 1; Abraham the priest 2 vills; these men have 6 ploughs, and they pay nothing. Earl William placed these within the customary dues of King Gruffydd, with the leave of King William. Under the same reeves are 4 vills made waste by King Caradoc.

In the king's alms is 1 vill which renders to the church for his soul on the feast of St Martin 2 pigs and 100 loaves with beer.

I carucate of land belongs to St Michael, and 1 carucate to St David. These render no service except to the saints.

One Beluard of Caerwent has half a carucate of land and pays nothing.

From the pannage come 66 pigs, and they are valued at 44s. All these render £40.12s8d. Durand the sheriff gave these same things to William de EU for £55 at farm.

Walter the crossbowman holds 2 carucates of land of the king, and has there 3 ploughs, and 3 slaves and 3 female slaves. This is worth 20s.

Gerard has 2 carucates of land, and there are 2 ploughs. It is worth 20s.

Ows the king's reeve [has] 2 carucates of land, and there are 4 ploughs. It is worth 20s. There is in the king's demesne 1 carucate of land which Dagobert held.

Joscelin the Breton holds 5 carucates of land in Caerwent [Mon.], and there are 2 ploughs, with 2 Welshmen. It is worth 20s.

The Bishop of Coutances holds 5 carucates of land of the

king, and one of his men [holds] of him. There are 2 ploughs in demesne; and 3 [ploughs] of the villans. It is worth 40s.

Roger of Berkeley holds 2 carucates of land at Rogerstone [Mon.], and has there 6 bordars with 1 plough. It is worth 20s.

Durand the sheriff holds of the king in Caerwent [Mon.] 1 estate called Caldicot [Mon.]. There he has in demesne 3 ploughs; and 15 half-villans and 4 slaves and 1 knight. All these have 12 ploughs. There is a mill rendering 10s. The whole of this is worth £6.

William de EU has, as he says, £9 as customary dues from Chepstow [Mon.]. But Gerard and other men say that he has no more by right from the £10 of customary dues of Chepstow, even if it should be valued at £100.

In Wales the same William has in fief 3 fisheries in the Wye [which] render 70s, and in the same fief Earl William gave Ralph de Limesy 50 carucates of land as it is done in Normandy. Hugh and other livery-officers attest that he granted it to Ralph thus. Now William de EU says that he has only 32 carucates of this land. There are in demesne 8 ploughs; and the men have 16 ploughs. There are 2 mills rendering 10s. The whole is worth £12.10s.

Roger de Lacy holds in the fief of Chepstow [Mon.] as much inhabited land with 1 mill as is worth 36s.

Turstin fitzRolf has 17 ploughs [sic] between the Usk and the Wye. 4½ of these are in demesne; the others are the men's. There are 11 bordars, and a mill rendering 7s. The whole is worth £9. The king's reeves claim 5½ carucates of this land, saying that Turstin took them without any grant.

The same Turstin has 6 carucates of land beyond the Usk, and there his men have 4 ploughs, and a mill rendering 15s, and [there is] half a fishery rendering 10s. The whole is worth 54s6d.

Alvred d'Epaignes has in fief 2 carucates of land, and there are 2 ploughs in demesne. The same Alvred has in Wales 7 vills which belonged to Earl William, and to Roger, his son, in demesne. These render 6 sesters of honey and 6 pigs and 10s.

[Folio 162V: GLOUCESTERSHIRE]

The BOROUGH of WINCHCOMBE rendered £6 as farm TRE. Earl Harold had the third penny of this [6l], that is, 40s. Afterwards, it rendered £20 with the whole hundred of the same vill. Durand the sheriff added 100s, and Roger d'Ivry 60s. Now with the 3 hundreds associated with it, it renders £28 at 20[d] to the ora.

Here Are Noted the Landholders of Gloucestershire

I KING WILLIAM
II The Archbishop of York
III The Bishop of Worcester
IIII The Bishop of Hereford
V The Bishop of Exeter
VI The Bishop of Saint-Lo
VII The Church of Bath
VIII The Abbey of Glastonbury
IX The Abbey of Malmesbury
X The Abbey of Gloucester
XI The Abbey of Winchcombe
XII The Abbey of Evesham
XIII The Abbey of Abingdon
XIIII The Abbey of Pershore
XV The Abbey of Coventry
XVI The Abbey of Cormeilles
XVII The Abbey of Lyre
XVIII The Abbey of Eynsham
XIX The Abbey of Westminster
XX The Church of Saint-Denis of Paris
XXI The Church of Lambeth
XXII The Church of Saint-Evroul
XXIII The Church of LA TRINITE, Caen
XXIIII The Church of Troarn
XXV The Church of Cirencester
XXVI Regenbald the priest
XXVII Earl Roger
XXVIII Earl Hugh
XXIX The Count of Mortain
XXX Gilbert Maminot, Bishop of Lisieux
XXXI William de EU
XXXII William fitzBaderon
XXXIII William the chamberlain
XXXIIII William Goizenboded
XXXV William fitzGuy
XXXVI William Froisseloup
XXXVII William fitzNorman
XXXVIII William Leofric
XXXIX Roger de Lacy
XL Roger de Beaumont
XLI Roger d'Ivry
XLII Roger of Berkeley
XLIII Ralph, his brother
XLIIII Ralph Paynel
XLV Ralph de Tosny
XLVI Robert de Tosny
XLVII Robert Despenser
XLVIII Robert d'Oilly
XLIX Richard the legate
L Osbern Giffard
LI Geoffrey Orlateile
LII Gilbert fitzTurold
LIII Durand the sheriff
LIIII Drogo fitzPons
LV Walter fitzPons
LVI Walter fitzRoger
LVII Walter the deacon
LVIII Walter the crossbowman
LIX Henry de Ferrers
LX Ernulf de Hesdin
LXI Harold son of Ralph
LXII Hugh de Grandmesnil
LXIII Hugh l'Asne
LXIIII Miles Crispin
LXV Urse d'Abetot
LXVI Hascoit Musard
LXVII Turstin fitzRolf
LXVIII Ansfrid de Cormeilles

LXIX Humphrey the chamberlin
LXX Humphrey of Maidenhill
LXXI Humphrey the cook
LXXII Sigar de Chocques
LXXIII Matthew de Mortagne
LXXIIII Joscelin the Breton
LXXV Roger fitzRalph
LXXVI The wife of Gerwy
LXXVII Baldwin
LXXVIII Ælfsige and other thegns of the king

The land of the King

King EDWARD held CHELTENHAM.. There were 8½ hides. 1½ hides belong to the church. Regenbald holds them. In demesne were 3 ploughs; and 20 villans and 10 bordars and 7 slaves with 18 ploughs. The priests, 2 ploughs. There, 2 mills rendering 11s8d. To this manor King William's reeve added 2 bordars and 4 villans, and 3 mills-2 of these are the king's, the third the reeve's - and there is 1 plough more. TRE it rendered £9.5s and 3,000 loaves for the hounds. Now it renders £20 and 20 cows and 20 pigs and 16s. for loaves.

In 'BARTON' [in Gloucester] King Edward had 9 hides. 7 of these were in demesne, and there are 3 ploughs; and 14 villans and 10 bordars with 9 ploughs. There are 7 slaves. Of this manor 2 free men hold 2 hides, and they have there 9 ploughs. These men cannot separate themselves nor the land from the manor. There is a mill rendering 4s. King William's reeve added 8 bordars and 2 mills and 1 plough. TRE it rendered £9.5s and 3,000 loaves for the hounds. Now it renders £20, 20 cows, 20 pigs and 16s for loaves.

Archbishop Ealdræd leased 1 member of this manor, BRAWN. There are 3 virgates of land and 3 men. Miles Crispin holds it.

Alwig the sheriff leased another member, called UPTON ST LEONARDS. There is 1 hide of land, and there are 4 men. Humphrey holds it.

The same Alwig leased a third member, called 'MORWENT' [in Hartpury]. There are 3 virgates of land. Nigel the physician holds it.

IN "DUDSTONE" HUNDRED a certain thegn, Eadmær, had 3 manors, Haresfield and Down Hatherley and Sandhurst. This man could give and sell his land to whom he wished. This land was assessed at 2 hides. In demesne were 8 ploughs; and 4 villans and 4 bordars and 30 slaves with 5 ploughs. There is sufficient meadow for the ploughs.

In HARESCOMBE Wigflæd held 3 free virgates of land, like Eadmær. She had 2 ploughs there, and 2 bordars and 5 slaves, and meadow for the ploughs.

In BROOKTHORPE Ælfric held 3 virgates of land. [...] He had 2 ploughs, and 1 villan, 3 bordars [and] 4 slaves. Earl Harold took these 5 lands after the death of King Edward. Roger d'Ivry put these same [lands] to farm for £46.13s4d.

In the same HUNDRED, adjoining the city, Wulfweard had half a hide of King Edward quit, and there are 2 ploughs, and 4

slaves. Earl William gave this to one of his cooks, for Wulfweard was outlawed.

IN CIRENCESTER HUNDRED King Edward had 5 hides of land. There are in demesne 5 ploughs; and [he has] 31 villans with 10 ploughs. There are 13 slaves and 10 bordars, and 3 mills rendering 30s, meadows, and 2 woods rendering 50s, and there are 2 free men having 2 ploughs. The queen had the wool from the sheep. TRE this manor rendered 3½ modi of wheat and 3 modii of malt, and 6½ sesters of honey, and £9.5s, and 3,000 loaves for the hounds. Now it renders £20.5s, 20 cows, 20 pigs, and 16s for loaves, and from the new market 20s, of which ST MARY'S has the third penny.

In Cirencester 1 free man held 2 hides of land and paid 20s in farm, and did service for the sheriff throughout the whole of England. Earl William put this land outside the farm and gave it to one of his men.

IN 'SWINESHEAD' HUNDRED there were TRE 36 hides at farm in BITTON, with 2 members, Wapley and Winterbourne. In demesne were 5 ploughs; and 41 villans and 29 bordars with 45 ploughs. There are 18 slaves, with 1 mill. TRE this manor rendered the farm of 1 night, and now it does the same.

IN SALMONSBURY HUNDRED King Edward held LOWER SLAUGHTER. There were 7 hides, and in demesne 3 ploughs; and 9 villans and 11 bordars with 8 ploughs. 7 slaves there, and 2 mills rendering 1 mark of silver, meadows rendering 10s, and from 1 of these hides 10s, and 5s for the hounds.

[Folio 163: GLOUCESTERSHIRE]

From this manor the sheriff paid what he wished TRE. Therefore they do not know [how] to value it. Now the sheriff has added there 1 plough, and 5 bordars with 1 plough. Now he pays from this manor and from the hundred £27 by tale.

In WESTBURY-ON-SEVERN [were] 30 hides. There King Edward had 5 ploughs in demesne; and 32 villans and 15 bordars with 28 ploughs. There is 1 slave.

This manor rendered the farm of 1 night TRE; the same for 4 years TRW. Afterwards 6 hides were taken away from this manor in Kyre ['Little Kyre' and Kyre Magna, Worcs.], and 10 hides in Clifton upon Teme [Worcs.], 8 hides in Newent and Kingstone [in Weston under Penyard, Herefs.], [and] 1 hide in Edvin Loach [Herefs.].

Now the Abbot of Cormeilles and Osbern and William fitzRichard hold these lands, and yet from what remains the sheriff finds the whole farm. The men of the shire, however, say that "Sapina" lay in Westbury-on-Severn in the farm of King Edward.

In KIFTSGATE Hundred King Edward held "LANGEBERGE" [?War.], with 1 member called MEON [Meon and Lower Meon, War.]. In each were 8 hides. In demesne, 3 ploughs; and 10 villans and 4 bordars with 6 ploughs, and a mill rendering 5s, and 6 slaves. Meadow rendering 10s. TRE the sheriff paid from this manor whatever it produced at farm. Now it renders £15 with the 2 hundreds which the sheriff placed there.

In BLEDISLOE Hundred King Edward held AWRE. There are 5 hides, and in demesne 1 plough; and 12 villans and 8 bordars with 14 ploughs. There is 1 slave, and a mill rendering 30d, and a salt-pan rendering 30 summae of salt, and a church with 1 virgate of land.

This manor rendered half of the farm of a night TRE, and now it does the same. In the same manor there lies waste half a hide and accordingly it only renders £12. Yet the sheriff pays the whole farm.

Outside the manor are 3 members which were always within it, and ought to be, as the men of the shire bear witness, that is, Purton, Etloe [and] Bledisloe. In these are 7 hides, and in demesne 1 plough; and 20 villans and 3 bordars with 13 ploughs, and 2 slaves, and a fishery.

Purton is in the fief of Earl William. Roger of Berkeley holds Etloe. William fitzBaderon holds Bledisloe. Alwig the sheriff put these outside the farm.

In 'LANGLEY' HUNDRED Earl Harold held ALVESTON. There were 10 hides. In demesne [is] 1 plough; and 23 villans and 5 bordars with 22 ploughs, and 2 slaves. There reeve has added there 2 ploughs, and 5 slaves. It renders £12 by weight.

IN BERKELEY King Edward had 5 hides, and in demesne [are] 5 ploughs; and 20 villans and 5 bordars with 11 ploughs, and 9 slaves, and 2 mills rendering 12s. There are 10 radknights having 7 hides and 7 ploughs. There is 1 market in which 17 men dwell, and they pay rent in the farm.

These BEREWICKS pertain to BERKELEY:

In Hill 4 hides; in [?] Alkington 4 hides; in Hinton 4 hides; in Cam 6 hides, and another 11 hides; in Gossington 4 hides; in Dursley 3 hides; in Coaley 4 hides; in Uley 2 hides; in Nympsfield 3 hides; in Wotton-under-Edge 15 hides and half a virgate; in Symonds' Hall half a hide; in Kingscote 4½ hides; in Beverston 10 hides; in Ozleworth half a hide; in Almondsbury 2 hides; in Horfield [in Bristol] 8 hides; in Kingsweston [in Bristol] 7 hides and 1 virgate; in Elberton 5 hides; in Cromhall 2 hides; in Arlingham 9 hides; in Ashleworth 3 hides.

All these members, written above, pertain to Berkeley. All together [...].

In these [lands] TRE [were] in demesne 49½ ploughs; and 242 villans and 142 bordars with 126 ploughs. There are 127 slaves. There are 19 free men, radknights, having 48 ploughs with their men. There are 22 coliberts and 15 female slaves. There are 8 mills rendering 57s6d.

In this manor TRE 2 brothers held 5 hides in CROMHALL, having in demesne 2 ploughs; and 6 villans and 5 bordars having 6 ploughs. These 2 brothers could turn where they would with their land. Then it was worth £4; now £3. These men Earl William commended to the reeve of Berkeley so that he might have their service; so says Roger. From this manor with all its appurtenances Roger pays at farm £170 assayed and weighed.

Roger himself has of the land of this manor 2 hides in Slimbridge, 1 hide in Clingre, 1 hide in Hurst [Hurst and Old Hurst], [and] 7 hides in Newington Bagpath. There are in demesne 10 ploughs; and 13 villans and 21 bordars with 22 ploughs. There are 16 slaves, and a mill rendering 5s. The whole was worth £9 TRE; now £11.10s.

The same Roger holds 5 hides, the land of Bernard the priest. There he has 3 ploughs, and 2 villans and 6 bordars with 5 ploughs. It is and was worth 60s.

In SHARPNESS are 5 hides pertaining to Berkeley which Earl William put outside [the farm] to build a little castle. Roger claims these.

In "EDREDESTANE" Hundred Queen Edith held MARSHFIELD. There are 14 hides. In demesne [are] 5 ploughs; and 36 villans and 13 bordars with 30 ploughs. There are 18 slaves. A priest has 1 of these hides. TRE it rendered £35; now £47.

In BARTON in BRISTOL were 6 hides. In demesne [are] 3 ploughs; and 22 villans and 25 bordars with 25 ploughs. There are 9 slaves and 18 coliberts having 14 ploughs. There are 2 mills rendering †27s†. When Roger received this manor from the king he found there 2 hides, and 2 ploughs in demesne; and 17 villans and 24 bordars with 21 ploughs. 4 slaves and 13 coliberts with 3 ploughs. In 1 member of the same manor, Mangotsfield, 6 oxen in demesne. Of the same land, the Church of Bristol holds 3 hides, and 1 plough is reckoned there. 1 radknight holds 1 hide, and has 1 plough, and 4 bordars with 1 plough. This manor and BRISTOL render to the king 110 marks of silver. The burgesses say that, besides the king's farm, Bishop Geoffrey has 33 marks of silver and 1 mark of gold.

In 'BRADLEY'HUNDRED Baldwin son of Herluin had 1 manor in which were 10 hides. The Bishop of Bayeux held this manor. Now it is in the king's hand and pays geld. In demesne are 2 ploughs; and 7 villans and 5 bordars with 6 ploughs. There are 5 slaves, and 2 mills rendering 20s. There is a priest. TRE it was worth £12; now £6.

In CIRENCESTER HUNDRED Almær had HULLASEY, in which were 3½ hides. The Bishop of Bayeux held it. Now it is in the king's hand. In demesne is 1 plough; and 4 villans and 4 bordars with 3 ploughs. It was worth £4; now 50s.

In TEWKESBURY were 95 hides TRE. Of these, 45 are in demesne, and were quit of all royal service and geld except the service of the lord himself whose manor it was. In the capital manor were in demesne 12 ploughs, and all together 50 slaves and female slaves, and 16 bordars lived around the hall, and [there were] 2 mills rendering 20s, and 1 fishery, and 1 salt-pan at Droitwich [Worcs.] pertaining to the manor.

At Southwick 3 hides; in Tredington 6 hides; in Fiddington 6 hides; in Pamington 8 hides; in Natton |3½ hides;| in Walton Cardiff 3 hides; [...] in Aston on Carrant 6 hides.

There were 21 villans and 9 radknights having 26 ploughs, and 5 coliberts and 1 bordar with 5 ploughs. These radknights ploughed and harrowed at the lord's court.

In Gloucester were 8 burgesses paying 5s4d and serving at court.

In the whole of Tewkesbury are 120 acres of meadow, and woodland 1½ leagues long and as much broad.

[Folio 163V: GLOUCESTERSHIRE]

At Tewkesbury are now 13 burgesses paying 20s a year. The market which the queen established there renders 11s8d. There is 1 plough more, and 22 slaves and female slaves all together. [There is] 1 fishery, and 1 salt-pan at Droitwich [Worcs.].

Three radknights belonged there TRE. One of them held 6 hides in Aston on Carrant. Now Gerard holds them. Another held 3 hides in Walton Cardiff. Now Ralph holds them. The third held 2 hides in Fiddington. Now Bernard holds them.

In these 11 hides are 10 ploughs in demesne; and 4 villans and 1 bordar and 9 slaves with 1 plough. There are 18 acres of meadow. The whole was worth £10 TRE; now as much.

At OXENTON TRE was a hall and 5 hides pertaining to Tewkesbury. There are 5 ploughs in demesne; and 5 villans and 2 radknights having 7 ploughs, and 12 slaves and female slaves all together. There are 24 acres of meadow. At Winchcombe 3 burgesses pay 40d. All this is and was worth £8. This land listed below belongs to the Church of Tewkesbury.

IN STANWAY [Stanway and Wood Stanway] are 7 hides belonging to the church. There are 2 ploughs in demesne; and 8 villans and 2 bordars with 8 ploughs. There is a minster, and 5 slaves and female slaves all together, and a salt-pan at Droitwich [Worcs.], and 8 acres of meadow, [and] woodland 3 furlongs long and 1 broad. TRE it was worth £8; now £7.

In TADDINGTON, 4 hides. There are 2 ploughs, and 11 villans and 1 radknight with 2 ploughs, and 3 bordars and 9 slaves. It was worth £6; now 100s.

In LOWER LEMINGTON, 3 hides. There are 2 ploughs, and 8 villans with 4 ploughs, and 6 slaves and 1 bordar. It was worth 60s; now 40s.

In GREAT WASHBOURNE, 3 hides. There are 2 ploughs, and 6 villans with 3 ploughs, and 1 bordar and 9 slaves with a female slave. It was and is worth 60s.

In FIDDINGTON, 2 hides. There is 1 villan and 2 coliberts with 2 ploughs. It is and was worth 10s. 1 of these hides was quit land.

In NATTON, 1 hide of quit land, and there is 1 plough. It is worth 10s.

In STANLEY PONTLARGE, 4½ hides. There is 1 plough, and 4 villans with 2 ploughs, and 3 bordars and 5 slaves. This land was quit. It was worth £4; now 40s.

All the land belonging to the church paid geld for 20 hides TRE.

To the same manor of Tewkesbury belonged, besides the demesne, 4 hides which are in Hanley Castle [Worcs.]. TRE there were in demesne 2 ploughs, and 40 villans and bordars all together, and 8 slaves and female slaves all together, and a mill rendering 16d. Woodland in which there was an enclosure. This land belonged to Earl William. Now it is in the king's farm in Hereford. TRE it was worth £15; now £10.

In Forthampton 9 hides belonged to this manor. There are 2 ploughs in demesne, and 20 villans and bordars all together, and 6 slaves and female slaves all together. There is woodland. It was worth £10 TRE; now £8. Earl William held these 2 estates, and they paid geld with Tewkesbury.

In Shenington [Oxon.] 10 hides belonged to the same manor. There are 4 ploughs, and 8 villans and 4 bordars and 5 radknights with 8 ploughs. There are 12 slaves, and a mill rendering 3s. This land paid geld for 7 hides. TRE it was worth £20; now £8. It is in the king's hand. Robert d'Oilly holds it at farm.

In CLIFFORD CHAMBERS [War.], 7 hides belonging to the same manor. 3 ploughs in demesne there; and 14 villans with 5 ploughs, and a mill rendering 12s, and 2 acres of meadow. All together there were 13 slaves and female slaves, and a church and a priest with 1 plough. It was worth £8; now £6. The queen gave this land to Roger de Bully, and it paid geld for 4 hides in Tewkesbury.

The 50 hides described above have made quit and freed from all geld and royal service the 95 hides which belonged to Tewkesbury. This manor of Tewkesbury, when it was complete TRE, was worth £100; when Ralph received it, £12, since it had been dismembered and broken up; now it is valued at £40, but Ralph pays £50.

Beorhtric son of Ælfgar held this manor TRE and at that time he had these lands of other thegns, listed below, in his power.

In ASHTON UNDER HILL [Worcs.] 1 thegn held 4 hides, and it was a manor. Now Gerard holds it and has 1 plough there, and 2 villans with 1 plough. It is and was worth 40s.

In KEMERTON [Worcs.] Liut held 8 hides, and it was a manor. Now Gerard holds it and has 3 ploughs there, and 14 villans with 6 ploughs. There are 8 slaves, and 3 mills rendering 15s. It was worth £8; now £6. 3 hides in Boddington belong to this manor. The same Gerard holds them, and has there 2 ploughs, and 4 villans with 3 ploughs, and there are 3 slaves, and a mill rendering 8s, and 8 acres of meadow. It is and was worth 40s.

In WINCOT [War.] 1 thegn held 3 hides. The queen gave this land to Regenbald the chaplain. There are 3 villans with half a plough. It was worth 40s.

In ALDERTON Dunning held 6½ hides, and in Dixton 4½ hides, and in [?] 'Hentage' [in Alderton] 1 thegn held 1 hide. Humphrey holds these lands of the king, and has 4 ploughs in demesne there; and [there are] 5 villans and 8 bordars with 3 ploughs, and 1 radknight with 1 plough, and in Winchcombe 1 burgess; and 12 acres of meadow are reckoned there. TRE the whole was worth £11; now £6.

In THE MYTHE 4 villans held 2 hides, and 1 thegn half a hide. There are 4 ploughs, and 3 acres of meadow. The queen gave this land to John the chamberlain. It is and was worth 35s.

In STOKE ORCHARD Hermar and Alwine held 3 hides, less 1 virgate. Now Bernard holds them of the king, and has 1 plough in demesne there, and 4 acres of meadow. It was worth 60s; now 40s.

Those who held these lands TRE submitted themselves and their lands under the power of Beorhtric.

IN 'LANGLEY' HUNDRED

BEORHTRIC son of Ælfgar held Thornbury. TRE there were 11 hides, and 4 ploughs in demesne; and 42 villans and 18 radknights with 21 ploughs, and 24 bordars and 15 slaves and 4 coliberts. 2 mills rendering 6s4d there, [and] woodland 1 league long and 1 broad. A market rendering 20s there. Now the reeve has added a mill there rendering 8d. This manor belonged to Queen Matilda. Humphrey pays from it £50 by tale. In this manor is 1 meadow rendering 40s, and at Droitwich [Worcs.] 40 sesters of salt or 20d, and a fishery at Gloucester rendering 58d.

IN "EDREDESTANE" HUNDRED

The same Beorhtric held OLD SODBURY. TRE there were 10 hides, and 4 ploughs in demesne; and 12 villans with 5 ploughs, and 4 bordars and 18 slaves, and a park, and a mill rendering 5s. Now the reeve has added 1 mill rendering 40d. There is woodland 1 league long and 1 broad.

From this manor Humphrey pays £16.10s. To this manor belongs 1 virgate in Droitwich [Worcs.] which rendered 25 sesters of salt. Urse the sheriff oppressed the men to such an extent that now they cannot render the salt.

IN LONGTREE HUNDRED

The same Beorhtric held AVENING. TRE there were 10 hides, and 8 ploughs in demesne; and 24 villans and 5 bordars and 30 slaves with 16 ploughs. There were 4 mills rendering 19s2d. Now the reeve has added 1 mill rendering 40d. There is woodland 2 leagues long and half a league broad. There is a hawk's eyrie.

IN 'BRIGHTWELLS BARROW' HUNDRED

The same Beorhtric held FAIRFORD. TRE there were 21 hides, and [he had] 56 villans and 9 bordars with 30 ploughs. There was a priest, who held 1 virgate of the demesne, and 3 mills rendering 32s6d. In demesne are only 13 hides and 1 virgate. Queen Matilda held this manor. Humphrey pays £38.10s by tale. From the land of this manor the queen gave 4 hides to John the chamberlain. There are 2 ploughs, and 9 villans and 4 bordars with 4 ploughs. There are 14 slaves. It renders £9 at farm.

[Folio 164: GLOUCESTERSHIRE]

The queen herself gave Baldwin 3 hides and 3 virgates of the same land, and he has 2 ploughs there, and 5 slaves, and 1 free man having 1 plough, and 2 bordars. It is worth £4.

Those who held these 2 estates TRE were not able to withdraw from the capital manor.

IN BOTLOE HUNDRED

King Edward held DYMOCK. There were 20 hides, and 2 ploughs in demesne; and 42 villans and 10 bordars and 11 coliberts having 41 ploughs. A priest there holding 12 acres, and 4 radknights with 4 ploughs. Woodland there 3 leagues long and 1 broad. From this manor the sheriff paid what he wished TRE. King William held it in his demesne for 4 years. Afterwards Earl William had it and [then] Roger, his son. The men of the shire do not know by what means. Now it renders £21.

IN BLEDISLOE HUNDRED

Earl Harold held NAAS. There were 5 hides, and in demesne 1 plough; and 10 villans and 2 bordars with 9 ploughs. TRE it was not at farm. Earl William joined it to 2 other manors, namely Poulton [in Awre] and Purton. In these there were 9 hides, and 2 ploughs in demesne; and 15 villans and 2 bordars and 2 slaves with 9 ploughs. 1 fishery there. Now the reeve has added in Poulton [in Awre] 1 plough. Purton is claimed for the king's farm. All together they render £11.

In LYDNEY Earl William made 1 manor out of 4 estates which he received from their lords. From the demesne of the Bishop of Hereford, 3 hides. From the demesne for the sustenance of the monks of Pershore, 6 hides where there were 6 villans with 4 ploughs. From 2 thegns he received 3½ hides. There are in demesne 3 ploughs, and 8 bordars, and a mill rendering 40d. [There is] woodland 1league long and a half broad. All together it renders £7.

In TIDENHAM HUNDRED the Abbot of BATH had 1 manor called TIDENHAM. 30 hides were reckoned there. 10 of these were in demesne. There were 38 villans having 38 ploughs, and 10 bordars. In the Severn, 11 fisheries in demesne, and 42 fisheries of the villans. In the Wye, 1 fishery, and 2½ fisheries of the villans. Earl Roger added 2 fisheries in the Wye. There is woodland 2 leagues long and half a league broad, and there are 12 bordars more.

From this land Earl William gave 1 virgate of land to his brother, Bishop Osbern, with 1 villan, and to Walter de Lacy he gave 2 fisheries in the Severn and half [a fishery] in the Wye with 1 villan. To Ralph de Limesy he gave 2 fisheries in the Wye with 1 villan. To the Abbey of Lyre he gave half a hide of land and the church of the manor, with tithe.

This manor did not pay rent TRE, except for the sustenance of the monks. Archbishop Stigand was holding it when Earl William received it. Now it renders £25 at 20[d] to the ora, and in blanch money. There is now a mill rendering 40d.

IN RAPSGATE HUNDRED

WULFWEARD held CHEDWORTH. There were 15 hides in woodland and field and meadow, and 7 ploughs in demesne TRE; and 16 villans and 3 bordars with 6 ploughs, and 3 mills rendering 14s2d, and a toll of salt which came to the hall. There the sheriff has added 8 villans and 3 bordars having 4 ploughs.

IN BIBURY HUNDRED

CYNEWIG CHELLE, a thegn of King Edward, held ARLINGTON. There were 5 hides, and 4 ploughs in demesne; and 12 villans and 1 bordar with 6 ploughs; and 16 slaves and female slaves all together, and 2 mills rendering 20s. Woodland 1 league long and a half broad. The reeves of these 2 manors paid what they wished TRE. Now they pay £40 of blanch money at 20[d] to the ora. Earl Roger held them.

IN TIBBLESTONE HUNDRED

ROTLESC, a housecarl of King Edward, held BECKFORD [Worcs.]. There were 11 hides, and 3 ploughs in demesne; and 34 villans and 17 bordars having 30 ploughs. There are 12 slaves and 4 female slaves. From this manor Earl William gave 3 hides to Ansfrid de Cormeilles in which there were 12 villans with 5 ploughs.

THORBERT, a thegn of Earl Harold, held ASHTON UNDER HILL [Worcs.]. There are 8 hides, and 4 ploughs in demesne; and 10 villans and 4 bordars with 6 ploughs. There are 8 slaves and 3 female slaves. Earl William made 1 manor of these 2 vills and they were not [held] at farm until Roger d'Ivry put them at farm for £30. The earl himself gave to the Abbey of Cormeilles the tithes and the churches with 2 villans and 3 virgates of land.

The men of the shire, when questioned, said that they had never seen the king's writ which said this land had been given to Earl William.

IN 'LANGLEY' HUNDRED

WULFGAR, a thegn of King Edward, held TOCK-INGTON. There were 8 hides, and 5 ploughs in demesne; and 20 villans and 12 bordars and 10 slaves with 20 ploughs. This manor did not render farm TRE but the person who owned it lived off it. Earl William held it in demesne and there the reeve added 1 plough, and a mill rendering 8d. Now it renders £24 of blanch money at 20[d] to the ora.

IN 'DUDSTONE' HUNDRED

EADRIC Lang, a thegn of Earl Harold, held HEMP-STED[in Gloucester]. There were 5 hides, and in demesne 3 ploughs; and 6 villans and 8 bordars with 6 ploughs. 6 slaves there, and half a fishery. Earl William took this manor in demesne and it was not at farm. But now the sheriff has put it [at farm] for 60s by tale.

IN LONGTREE HUNDRED

GYTHA, the mother of Earl Harold, held WOOD-CHESTER. Earl Godwine bought it from Azur and gave it to his wife so that she could live off it while she stayed at Berkeley. She was unwilling to use up anything from that manor because of the destruction of the abbey. Edward holds this land in the farm of Wiltshire, unjustly as the shire says, since it does not pertain to any farm. No one gave any account of this manor to the king's commissioners, nor did any of them come to this registration. This land renders £7.

IN WYVERN HUNDRED

BEORHTRIC held 3 hides in MADGETTS, and they paid geld. In demesne there the king has 2 fisheries. Roger de Lacy has 1 fishery with half a hide. The Abbot of Malmesbury has 1 fishery with half a hide and this by the king's gift, as they say. William de EU has 2 hides, and he claims these 4 fisheries. These fisheries are in the Wye, and they rendered £4.

IN "GERSDONES" HUNDRED

EADNOTH held DOWN AMPNEY TRE. There are 15 hides paying geld. Of these King Edward pardoned Eadnoth 5 hides, as the shire says, and afterwards this manor paid for 10 hides. In demesne [are] 4 ploughs; and a priest and 19 villans and 3 bordars with 10 ploughs. There are 12 slaves. This manor belonged to the Bishop of Bayeux and was worth £20. Now it renders £26 to the king's farm.

IN BARRINGTON HUNDRED

TOVI the Wend, a housecarl of Earl Harold, held GREAT BARRINGTON. There are 4 hides. In demesne are 2 ploughs; and 10 villans and 5 bordars with 5 ploughs. There are 4 slaves, and a mill rendering 5s. It is and was worth £7. Ælfsige of Faringdon holds it in the king's farm.

ÆTHELMÆR held 4 hides in GREAT BARRINGTON as a manor TRE. In demesne is 1 plough; and 7 villans and 3 bordars with 4 ploughs. There are 6 slaves, and a mill rendering 5s. It was worth 100s; now 60s. Godwine of Stanton holds it in the king's farm.

[Folio 164V: GLOUCESTERSHIRE]

II. The land of Archbishop Thomas

Archbishop STIGAND held CHURCHDOWN. There were 15½ hides, and 2 ploughs in demesne; and 18 villans and 5 bordars and 7 radknights with 30 ploughs. There is woodland half a league long and 3 furlongs broad. Then it was worth £13; now £12.

The same Stigand held HUCCLECOTE [in Gloucester]. There were 4 hides, and in demesne 2 ploughs; and 11 villans and 5 bordars with 11 ploughs. There is a mill rendering 32d, and woodland 1 league long and a half broad. Then, as now, worth £4.

The same Stigand held BISHOP'S NORTON. There were 5½ hides, and in demesne 2 ploughs; and 15 villans with 15 ploughs, and 4 slaves, and a mill rendering 32d. Then, as now, worth £4.

Archbishop Thomas now holds these 3 manors. Walkelin, a nephew of the Bishop of Winchester, holds Bishop's Norton of him.

IN SALMONSBURY HUNDRED

Archbishop EALDRÆD held [Lower and Upper] ODDINGTON, with the BEREWICK of Condicote. There were 10 hides, and 2 ploughs in demesne; and 16 villans and 2 radknights and 4 bordars with 14 ploughs. This land never paid geld TRE. It was worth £6; now £10. Archbishop

Thomas holds it. St Peter of Gloucester had it in demesne until King William came to England.

IN CHELTENHAM HUNDRED

Archbishop Stigand held SWINDON. There were 3 hides, and 2 ploughs in demesne; and 7 villans and 2 bordars and they have 7 ploughs. There are 4 slaves. Then it was worth £3; now £4.10s. Archbishop Thomas holds this manor from the land of St Oswald and it pays geld.

IN "WACRESCUMBE" HUNDRED

Gundulf held and holds in SHIPTON SOLERS 1 manor of 1 hide, and it pays geld, and there is 1 plough in demesne, and it is worth 8s. He holds it of Archbishop Thomas.

PINN held 1 manor of 1 hide in HAMPEN, and it paid geld. Ansgar holds it of Archbishop Thomas, and he has 1 plough in demesne. It was worth 20s; now 10s.

IN 'BRADLEY' HUNDRED

St Peter of Gloucester held NORTHLEACH, and Archbishop Ealdræd held it with the abbey. There were 24 hides. In demesne are 4 ploughs; and 33 villans and 16 bordars with 30 ploughs. There are 4 slaves, and 2 mills rendering 7s4d.

Stowell belongs to this manor. There are 2 ploughs in demesne; and 5 villans with 5 ploughs, and a mill rendering 40d, and 4 slaves and 2 female slaves; and in Upper Coberley is 1 hide belonging to this manor.

Of this land of this manor Walter fitzPons holds 1 manor of 12 hides which belonged to the same manor TRE. There are 2 ploughs in demesne at Farmington; and 25 villans with 12 ploughs, and 4 slaves.

The whole manor was worth £18 TRE. Archbishop Thomas put it at farm for £27. The hide of Upper Coberley is valued at 20s; what Walter holds is worth £14. Archbishop Thomas claims it.

Archbishop Stigand held COMPTON ABDALE. There were 9 hides. There are 2 ploughs, and 5 acres of meadow, and 22 villans and 5 bordars with 11 ploughs. There are 5 slaves, and a mill rendering 5s. TRE it was worth £9; now £7. Archbishop Thomas holds it. A man of Roger d'Ivry holds 1 manor of 3 hides belonging to this manor. The archbishop himself claims this.

IN 'WHITSTONE' HUNDRED

Archbishop EALDRÆD held STANDISH. It belonged to the demesne of St Peter of Gloucester. There were 15 hides TRE. In demesne are 3 ploughs; and 9 villans and 14 bordars with 16 ploughs, and 7 radknights having 17 ploughs. There are 8 slaves, and half a fishery, [and] woodland half a league long and 1 furlong broad. TRE the whole manor was worth £16; now £12. Archbishop Thomas holds it and it pays geld in the same way.

Of this land of this manor the Abbot of Gloucester holds 1 hide and ought by right to hold it. Earl Hugh holds 1 hide unjustly. Durand the sheriff holds 3 hides which Earl William gave to his brother Roger. Archbishop Thomas claims these.

IN BARRINGTON HUNDRED

St OSWALD of Gloucester held WIDFORD [Oxon.]. There were 2 hides TRE, and 2 ploughs in demesne; and 4 villans and †3† bordars with 2 ploughs. There are 4 slaves, and 8 acres of meadow, and a mill rendering 10s. TRE it was worth 40s; now 60s. Ranulph holds it of the same saint. As it was then, so it is now.

IN RAPSGATE HUNDRED

St OSWALD held NORTH CERNEY, a manor of 4 hides, TRE. The same saint still holds it and has 2 ploughs in demesne; and 6 villans and 2 bordars with 5 ploughs. There is 1 slave, and a mill rendering 7s, and 2 acres of meadow. Then it was worth 100s; now £4.

IN "LANGEBRIGE" HUNDRED

Ulfkil held LASSINGTON, a manor of 2 hides. Now Roger holds it of Archbishop Thomas. This land pays geld. In demesne is 1 plough; and 5 villans and 2 bordars with 3 ploughs. There are 3 slaves, and 20 acres of meadow. It was worth 40s; now |30s|.

III. The land of the Church of Worcester

IN BRENTRY HUNDRED

St MARY of Worcester held and holds WESTBURY ON TRYM [in Bristol]. There were and are 50 hides. In demesne are 2 ploughs; and 8 villans and 6 bordars with 8 ploughs. There are 4 slaves and 1 female slave.

These members belong to this manor: Henbury [in Bristol], Redwick, Stoke Bishop [in Bristol], Yate. In these are 9 ploughs in demesne; and 27 villans and 22 bordars with 26 ploughs. There are 20 slaves and 2 female slaves and 20 coliberts with 10 ploughs, and a mill rendering 20d.

To this manor belong 6 radknights having 8 hides and 8 ploughs. They could not be separated from the manor. And in Bristol 2 houses rendered 16d.

Of this land of this manor Turstin fitzRolf holds 5 hides in Aust, and Gilbert fitzTurold 3½ hides in Compton Greenfield, and Constantine 5 hides in Itchington. In these lands are 5 ploughs in demesne; and 16 villans and 12 bordars with 12 ploughs. There are 11 slaves. Of the same land of this manor Osbern Giffard holds 5 hides and he does no service. The whole manor with its members was worth £24 TRE.

Now the demesne of ST MARY is worth £29.14s6d; what the men hold, £9.

IN RAPSGATE HUNDRED

The church itself held COLESBOURNE, and Swein [held] of it. He could not withdraw. There are 8 hides paying geld. Walter fitzRoger holds it of the church. In demesne is 1 plough; and 18 villans and 2 bordars with 5 ploughs. There are 2 slaves, and 3 acres of meadow, and 2 mills rendering 7s6d. Then it was worth £8; now £4.

The church itself held AYCOTE, and Æthelric [held] of it. It belongs to Bibury. There is 1 hide. In demesne are 2 ploughs;

and 2 villans and 4 bordars with 2 ploughs. There are 2 slaves, and 8 acres of meadow, and a mill rendering 64d. It was worth 20s; now 30s. Ordric holds it of the bishop.

IN BIBURY HUNDRED

The church itself held BIBURY. There are 21 hides. In demesne are 4 ploughs; and 19 villans and 2 bordars with 11 ploughs. There are 3 radknights having 4 hides and 4 ploughs, and a priest having 3 hides and, with his men, 4 ploughs. There are all together 11 slaves and female slaves, and 2 mills rendering 17s, and 10 acres of meadow.

Of the same land of this manor Durand holds of the bishop 1 manor of 3 hides and 1 virgate in Barnsley, and Eudo [holds] 7 virgates as a manor in the same place. In these are 5 ploughs in demesne; and 12 villans with 6 ploughs. There are 12 slaves. The whole manor was worth £18 TRE; and now the same. Bishop Wulfstan holds it, and it pays geld.

IN "WACRESCUMBE" HUNDRED

The church itself holds WITHINGTON. There are 30 hides. 3 of these have never paid geld. In demesne are 2 ploughs; and 16 villans and 8

[Folio 165: GLOUCESTERSHIRE]

IN 'WITLEY' HUNDRED

The church itself holds 2 hides in CONDICOTE, and Osbern [holds] of the bishop. It is and was worth 40s. bordars with 7 ploughs. There are 6 slaves, and 10 acres of meadow, [and] woodland 1 league long and a half broad, and in Cassey Compton is 1 plough, and 2 villans and 2 bordars with 1 plough, and 2 slaves, and a mill rendering 5s.

In the same manor are 4 radknights having 2 hides and 3 virgates, and they have 2 ploughs, and [there is] a priest having half a hide and 1 plough. In Gloucester 4 burgesses pay 7½d.

Of this land of this manor Morin holds of the bishop 3 hides in Foxcote, Ansketil [holds] 2 hides in Little Colesbourne and Hilcot, Robert 4½ hides in Dowdeswell and Pegglesworth, Schelin 5 hides in Notgrove, [and] Drogo 10 hides in Cold Aston.

In these lands are 16 ploughs in demesne; and 51 villans and 7 bordars with 28 ploughs. There are 41 slaves, and 3 mills rendering 13s4d. In Winchcombe 1 burgess pays 3s. In certain places [are] meadow and woodland but not much.

The whole manor was worth £38 TRE; now £33 among them all. Bishop Wulfstan holds this manor.

IN TIBBLESTONE HUNDRED

The church itself held BISHOP'S CLEEVE. There are 30 hides. In demesne are 3 ploughs; and 16 villans and 19 bordars with 16 ploughs. There are 8 slaves, and 1 pack-horse. There a priest has 1 hide and 2 ploughs, and [there is] 1 radknight having 1 hide and 2 ploughs. There is a very little wood.

Of this land of the same manor Durand the sheriff holds of the church 6 hides in Southam, Ralph [holds] 4 hides in

'Sapperton' [in Bishops Cleeve], [and] Turstin fitzRolf 6 hides in Gotherington. In these lands are 8 ploughs in demesne; and 22 villans and 7 bordars with 13 ploughs. There are 20 slaves, and 3 pack-horses, and a mill rendering 12d, and a certain amount of meadow. Of the same land Bernard and Reginald hold 7 hides in Stoke Orchard, and they are not willing to do service to ST MARY. The whole of this manor was worth †£36† TRE; now £26 among them all. Bishop Wulfstan holds this manor.

IIII. The land of the Church of Hereford

IN CHELTENHAM HUNDRED

THE BISHOP OF HEREFORD held PRESTBURY. There are 30 hides. In demesne are 3 ploughs; and 18 villans and 5 bordars with 9 ploughs. There is a priest and 1 radknight with 2 ploughs, and in Winchcombe 1 burgess paying 18d, and 11 slaves and female slaves all together. There are 20 acres of meadow, and woodland 1 league long and a half broad.

To this manor belongs 1 vill outside this HUNDRED, SEVENHAMPTON. There are 20 hides of the above-mentioned 30 hides; [...] and there are 2 ploughs, and 21 villans with 11 ploughs. There are 3 free men having 7 ploughs with their men.

Of these 20 hides Durand holds 3 hides of the bishop. The whole manor was worth £12 TRE; now £16. Robert, the bishop of the same city, holds this manor.

V. The land of Bishop Osbern

IN 'SWINESHEAD' HUNDRED

The BISHOP of EXETER holds OLDLAND. Alwig, a man of Earl Harold, held it and he could go where he would. There are 2 hides; one pays geld, the other does not. In demesne are 2 ploughs; and 1 villan and 6 bordars with 1 plough. There are 2 slaves, and 10 acres of meadow. Then it was worth £4; now 20s.

IN BAGSTONE HUNDRED

The same bishop holds TYTHERINGTON. Alwig held it TRE. There are 5 hides, and 2 ploughs are in demesne, and 1 villan and 5 bordars and 2 slaves, and 20 acres of meadow. [There is] woodland half a league in length and breadth. It was worth 100s; now 40s.

VI. The land of the Bishop of Coutances

IN BAGSTONE HUNDRED

The BISHOP of SAINT-LO holds IRON ACTON, and Ilger [holds] of him. There are 2½ hides. In demesne is 1 plough; and 4 villans and 5 bordars and 1 slave and 2 female slaves with 1½ ploughs. There is half a mill rendering 16d, and 10 acres of meadow and 1 furlong of woodland. It is and was worth 40s. Ebbi, a man of Beorhtric son of Ælfgar, held this manor.

IN 'SWINESHEAD' HUNDRED

The same bishop holds HAMBROOK, and Oswulf [holds] of him. Algar held it of King Edward, | [in margin] | and he could go where he would. There are 2 hides. | There is land for 5 ploughs. | In demesne are 2 ploughs; and 2 villans with 2 ploughs, and 2 slaves, and 6 acres of meadow. It was worth 100s; now 60s.

The same bishop holds 1 manor of 1 hide, and Goismer [holds] of him. In this hide when it is ploughed there are only 64 acres of land. There is 1 plough in demesne. It was worth 20s; now 16s.

The same bishop holds HARRY STOKE, and Theobald [holds] of him. Ealdræd held it of Earl Harold, and could go where he would. There are 2 hides; one pays geld, the other does not. In demesne is 1 plough; and 2 villans and 1 bordar with 1 plough. There are 6 slaves, and 5 acres of meadow. It was worth 40s; now 20s.

IN PUCKLECHURCH HUNDRED

The same bishop holds DOYNTON, and Robert [holds] of him. Alweard, a thegn of King Edward, held it. There are 5 hides paying geld. In demesne are 3 ploughs; and 14 villans and 8 bordars with 8 ploughs. There are 10 slaves, and 2 mills rendering 10s10d, and 2 men paying 5s, and 12 acres of meadow, [and] woodland half a league long and a half broad. It is and was worth £8.

The same bishop holds WAPLEY, and Ealdræd [holds] of him. The same man held it TRE. There is 1 hide, and in demesne 1 plough, and 2 slaves. It is and was worth 20s.

IN "LETBERGE" HUNDRED

The same bishop holds 'LEE' [in Almondsbury], and Robert [holds] of him. Algar held it TRE. There is 1 hide paying geld, and 2 ploughs in demesne; and 3 bordars and 2 slaves with 1 plough. It is and was worth 20s.

IN 'LANGLEY' HUNDRED

The same bishop holds GAUNT'S EARTHCOTT, and Robert [holds] of him. Cuthwulf held it TRE. There are 2 hides paying geld, and 2 ploughs are in demesne and 2 bordars and 4 slaves and | 4 villans |, and 10 acres of meadow, and woodland [...]. It is and was worth 40s.

IN "EDREDESTANE" HUNDRED

The bishop himself holds DODINGTON, and Roger [holds] of him. Wulfnoth held it TRE. There are 1½ hides and the third part of half a hide. In demesne is 1 plough; and 4 villans and 1 bordar with 1 plough. There are 3 slaves. It is and was worth 30s.

VII. The land of the Church of Bath

IN 'LANGLEY' HUNDRED

ST PETER of BATH held OLVESTON. There are 5 hides. Of thses, and 2 [hides] do not pay geld by gift of King Edward and King William. In demesne are 2 ploughs; and 9 villans and 6 bordars and a priest and 1 radknight with 10 ploughs. There are 7 slaves, and meadows and woodland to maintain the manor. It was worth 100s; now £4. The church itself still holds it.

IN PUCKLECHURCH HUNDRED

The church itself holds COLD ASHTON. There are 5 hides. Of these, 2 are quit of geld by gift of King Edward and King William. But 3 pay geld. In demesne is 1 plough; and 3 villans and 3 bordars and 1 radknight. Among them all [they have] 3 ploughs. There is 1 colibert, and a mill rendering 50d, and 6 acres of meadow. It is and was worth £4.

VIII. The land of the Church of Glastonbury

IN PUCKLECHURCH HUNDRED

ST MARY of GLASTONBURY holds PUCKLE-CHURCH. There are 20 hides. In demesne are 6 ploughs; and 23 villans and 8 bordars with 18 ploughs. There are 10 slaves, and 6 men render 100 ingots of iron, less 10, and in Gloucester 1 burgess pays 5d, and 2 coliberts pay 34d, and there are 3 Frenchmen, and 2 mills rendering 100d. There are 60 acres of meadow, and woodland half a league long and a half broad. It was worth £20; now £30.

IX. The land of the Church of Malmesbury

IN 'LANGLEY' HUNDRED

ST MARY of MALMESBURY holds LITTLETON-ON-SEVERN. There are 5 hides. Of these, 2½ pay geld, the others are quit. in demesne are 2 ploughs; and 13 villans and 2 bordars with 8 ploughs. There is a church and a priest, and 20 acres of meadow. It was worth 60s; now 100s.

[Folio 165V: GLOUCESTERSHIRE]

X. The land of St Peter of Gloucester

IN 'DUDSTONE' HUNDRED

ST PETER OF GLOUCESTER held TRE the manor of 'BARTON' [in Gloucester] with the members belonging to it: Barnwood [in Gloucester], Tuffley [Tuffley and Lower Tuffley, in Gloucester], 'Morwent' [in Hartpury]. There are 22 hides, less 1 virgate. There are 9 ploughs in demesne; and 42 villans and 21 bordars with 45 ploughs. There are 12 slaves, and a mill rendering 5s, and 120 acres of meadow, and woodland 5 furlongs long and 3 broad. It was worth £8; now £24.

This manor was always quit of geld and from all royal service.

IN "BLACHELAUE" HUNDRED

The same church itself held FROCESTER. There are 5 hides. In demesne are 4 ploughs; and 8 villans and 7 bordars with 7 ploughs. There are 3 slaves, and 10 acres of meadow, and woodland 3 furlongs long and 2 furlongs broad. It was worth £3; now £8.

IN "GRIMBOLDESTOU" HUNDRED

The church itself holds BOXWELL. There are 5 hides. In demesne are 2 ploughs; and 12 villans and 1 radknight having 12 ploughs. There are 8 slaves, and a mill rendering 5s. It was worth 70s; now 100s.

IN 'BRIGHTWELLS BARROW' HUNDRED

The church itself holds COLN ST ALDWYNS. There are 4 hides. In demesne are 3 ploughs; and 11 villans and 7 bordars with 12 ploughs. There are 4 slaves. It was worth £6; now £8. 2 mills rendered 25s.

IN BIBURY HUNDRED

The church itself holds ALDSWORTH. There are 11 hides. In demesne are 3 ploughs; and 21 villans and 5 bordars and 2 Frenchmen with 15 ploughs. There are 6 slaves. It was worth 100s; now £8.

IN 'WITLEY' HUNDRED

The church itself holds BUCKLAND. There are 10 hides. In demesne are 3 ploughs; and 22 villans and 6 bordars with 12 ploughs. There are 8 slaves, and 10 acres of meadow. It was worth £3; now £9.

IN TIBBLESTONE HUNDRED

The church itself holds HINTON ON THE GREEN [Worcs.]. There are 15 hides. In demesne are 2 ploughs; and 30 villans and 7 bordars with 16 ploughs. There are 11 slaves and 1 Frenchman.

It was worth £3; now £10. This manor is quit of geld and of all public service except to the church.

IN "LANGEBRIGE" HUNDRED

The church itself holds HIGHNAM. There are 7 hides. In demesne are 3 ploughs; and 22 villans and 4 bordars with 7 ploughs. There are 8 slaves, and 30 acres of meadow, [and] sufficient woodland for the manor. It was worth 40s; now £4.

The church itself holds PRESTON [in Dymock]. There are 2 hides. In demesne are 2 ploughs; and 8 villans and 4 bordars with 8 ploughs. There are 4 slaves. It was worth 30s; now £4.

IN BOTLOE HUNDRED

The church itself holds UPLEADON. There are 4 hides. In demesne are 2 ploughs; and 8 villans and 1 bordar with 8 ploughs. There are 4 slaves, and a mill rendering 4s, and 10 acres of meadow, [and] woodland 2 leagues long and 2 furlongs broad. It is worth scarcely 30s.

IN WESTBURY HUNDRED

The church itself holds CHURCHAM and 'MORTON' [in Churcham]. In both woodland and field [are] 5 hides. In demesne are 2 ploughs; and 7 villans and 2 bordars with 6 ploughs. [There is] woodland 1 league long and 1 broad. There the church had its hunting in 3 enclosures TRE and in the time of [King] William. It was worth 20s; now 40s.

IN "GERSDONES" HUNDRED

In AMPNEY ST PETER the brother of Regenbald holds 2 hides. There are 2 ploughs, and 5 villans with 3 ploughs, and 4 slaves, and 24 acres of meadow, and a mill rendering 5s. It was worth 40s; now scarcely 20s.

IN CIRENCESTER HUNDRED

With King William's consent the wife of Walter de Lacy gave to St Peter for the soul of her husband DUNTISBOURNE ABBOTS, a manor of 5 hides. In demesne [are] 3 ploughs; and 8 villans with 5 ploughs. There are 16 slaves, and a mill rendering 2s. It is worth £4.

TRE St Peter of Gloucester had from its burgesses 19s5d and 16 salmon. Now it has as many salmon and 50s. There is a mill rendering 12s, and 4 fisheries for the sustenance of the monks.

XI. The land of the Church of Winchcombe

IN SALMONSBURY HUNDRED

THE CHURCH OF ST MARY of WINCHCOMBE holds SHERBORNE. There are 30 hides. 10 of these are free [and] pertain to the court. There are 5 ploughs in demesne; and 40 villans and 7 bordars with 22 ploughs. There are 12 slaves, and 4 mills rendering 40s, and 30 acres of meadow. TRE it was worth £20; now £14.

The church itself holds BLEDINGTON. There are 7 hides. In demesne are 2 ploughs; and 8 villans and 4 bordars with 5 ploughs, and 8 slaves and 2 female slaves. There is a mill rendering 5s, and 30 acres of meadow. It was worth £4; now £3.

IN 'GRESTON' HUNDRED

The church itself holds TWYNING. There are 3 hides paying geld. In demesne are 2 ploughs; and 24 villans and 8 bordars with 27 ploughs. There are 8 slaves and 2 female slaves, and 40 acres of meadow, [and] woodland 2 furlongs long and 1 broad. It was worth £8; now £7.

The church itself holds FRAMPTON COURT. There is 1 hide, and in demesne 4 ploughs, and 6 slaves and 2 female slaves. This land was free and quit of all geld and royal service. It was worth 40s; now 50s.

The church itself holds FRAMPTON, and a certain knight [holds] of the abbot. There are 2½ hides. In demesne are 2 ploughs; and 1 villan with 1 plough, and there can be 3 [ploughs] more. There are 4 slaves. It is and was worth 30s.

The church itself holds NAUNTON [in Toddington], and 2 knights [hold] of the abbot. There are 3½ hides. In demesne are 3 ploughs and 3 slaves; and 2 villans with 1 plough, and 6 more [ploughs] could be there. It is and was worth 40s.

The church itself holds STANTON. There are 3 hides. In demesne are 2 ploughs; and 14 villans with 7 ploughs. There are 3 bordars and 6 slaves, and 6 acres of meadow, [and] woodland 1 league long and a half broad. It is and was worth £3.

The church itself holds CHARLTON ABBOTS. There are 2 hides free and quit. In demesne is 1 plough; and 4 villans and 2 bordars with 4 ploughs. There are 6 slaves, and a mill rendering 20d, and 2 acres of meadow. It is and was worth 20s.

IN 'HOLFORD' HUNDRED

The church itself holds SNOWSHILL. There are 7 hides paying geld. In demesne are 3 ploughs; and 12 villans and 2 bordars with 6 ploughs. There are 6 slaves. It is and was worth 100s.

IN "CELFLEDETORN" HUNDRED

The church itself holds COW HONEYBOURNE [Worcs.]. There are 10 hides. Of these, 2 [are] in demesne, and 8 [liable] for service. In demesne are 5 ploughs; and 15 villans with 5 ploughs. There are 9 slaves and 3 female slaves. It was worth £6; now £8.

The church itself holds ADMINGTON [War]. There are $3\frac{1}{2}$ hides. In demesne are 2 ploughs; and 13 villans with 6 ploughs. There are 4 slaves and 2 female slaves. It was worth £4; now £3.

The church itself holds HIDCOTE BOYCE. There are 2 free hides. In demesne is 1 plough, with 1 slave. It is and was worth 40s.

TRE this church was assessed in GLOUCESTER shire at 60 hides.

ÆLFSIGE of Faringdon holds of the abbey itself $3\frac{1}{2}$ hides in WINDRUSH. Bolla held it and gave it to the abbey. He could go with this land where he would. In demesne are 5 ploughs; and 1 villan and 7 bordars with 1 plough, and 10 slaves, and $1\frac{1}{2}$ mills

XII. The land of St Mary of Evesham

IN SALMONSBURY HUNDRED

THE CHURCH OF ST MARY OF EVESHAM holds MAUGERSBURY near Stow-on-the-Wold. There were 8 hides TRE, and a ninth hide belongs to the Church of St Edward. King Æthelræd gave it there quit. In demesne are 3 ploughs; and 12 villans and 1 free man and a priest having among them 7 ploughs. There are 6 slaves, and a mill rendering 8s, [and] a certain amount of meadow. TRE it was worth 100s; now £7.

The church itself holds ADLESTROP. There are 7 hides. In demesne are 2 ploughs; and 10 villans and 2 bordars with 3 ploughs. There are 4 slaves, and 1 knight with 2 ploughs. There is little meadow. It was worth £4; now 100s.

The church itself holds BOURTON-ON-THE-WATER. There are 10 hides. In demesne are 6 ploughs; and 16 villans and 8 bordars and 2 free men with 7 ploughs.

rendering 12s6d. All together it is worth £8. Wulfric held 2 hides of this land as a manor, and Tovi 5 virgates as a manor, and Leofwine 1 virgate as a manor. This manor which Ælfsige holds of the abbot unjustly lay in Salmonsbury Hundred after

Bolla died. Now it lies in Barrington Hundred by the judgement of the men of the same hundred.

[Folio 166: GLOUCESTERSHIRE]

There is a priest with half a plough. It was worth £8; now £12.

The church itself holds BROADWELL. There are 10 hides. There are 6 ploughs in demesne; and 25 villans and 8 bordars and 1 free man and a priest. Among them all they have 12 ploughs. in Gloucester 4 burgesses, and in Winchcombe 1 [burgess], pay 27d. The whole was worth £8; now £12.

IN 'WITLEY' HUNDRED

The church itself holds UPPER SWELL. There are 3 hides, and 9 villans and 2 bordars and a priest. Among them all [they have] 4 ploughs. There are 6 slaves. It was worth £4; now £5. In demesne are 3 ploughs. There are 3 mills [rendering] 20s.

The church itself holds WILLERSEY. There are 8 hides, 1 at Wickhamford [Worcs.]. There are 3 ploughs in demesne; and 16 villans and 4 bordars and a priest with 6 ploughs. There are 2 slaves, and little meadow. It was worth £4; now 100s.

The church itself holds WESTON-ON-AVON [War.]. There are 3 hides and 1 free [hide]. In demesne are 2 ploughs; and 5 villans and a priest with 2 ploughs. It was worth 20s; now 40s.

The church itself holds STOKE [Lark Stoke and Lower Lark Stoke, War.]. There are 2 hides. In demesne is 1 plough; and 7 villans and 2 bordars with 2 ploughs. There is 1 slave. It is and was worth 40s.

The church itself holds HIDCOTE BARTRIM. There are 3 hides. In demesne is 1 plough and 2 slaves; and the wives of 4 villans who have recently died have 1 plough. It is and was worth 20s.

The abbot has these 2 vills commended to 2 of his knights.

In the ferding of WINCHCOMBE, ST MARY of EVESHAM had 56 hides TRE.

XIII. The land of St Mary of Abingdon

IN 'GRESTON' HUNDRED

THE CHURCH OF ST MARY of ABINGDON holds DUMBLETON. There are $7\frac{1}{2}$ hides. In demesne are 4 ploughs; and 13 villans and 8 bordars with 8 ploughs. There are 6 slaves, and a mill rendering 6s. TRE it was worth £12; now £9. This manor paid geld TRE.

XIIII. The land of St Mary of Pershore

IN RAPSGATE HUNDRED

THE CHURCH OF ST MARY of PERSHORE holds COWLEY. There are 5 hides paying geld. In demesne are 2 ploughs; and 14 villans and 1 bordar with 7 ploughs. There are 5 slaves, and a mill rendering 50d, and 6 acres of meadow, and woodland 3 furlongs long and 1 broad. It is worth 100s.

IN "GRIMBOLDESTOU" [HUNDRED]

The church itself holds HAWKESBURY. There are 17 hides. In demesne [are] 5 ploughs; and 18 villans and 25 bordars with 15 ploughs. There are 2 slaves and 7 coliberts. There are 3 mills rendering 19s2d, and 10 acres of meadow, [and] woodland 2 leagues long and 1 broad. It was worth £16; now £10.

XV. The land of St Mary of Coventry

IN "CELFLEDETORN" HUNDRED

THE CHURCH OF ST MARY of COVENTRY holds LONG MARSTON [War.]. There are 10 hides. In demesne are 3 ploughs; and 15 villans and 3 bordars with 12 ploughs. There are 6 slaves, and meadow rendering 10s. It was worth £8; now 100s.

XVI. The land of Sainte-Marie of Cormeilles

IN BOTLOE HUNDRED

THE CHURCH OF SAINTE-MARIE of CORMEILLES holds NEWENT. King Edward held it. 6 hides there did not pay geld. Earl Roger gave it to this church for the soul of his father with the consent of King William. In demesne are 3 ploughs; and 9 villans and 9 bordars with 12 ploughs. There is a reeve having 1½ villans and 5 bordars. Among them all they have 5 ploughs, and a mill rendering 20d. There are 2 slaves, and 2 mills rendering 6s8d. From the woodland, 30d.

Of this land Durand holds 1 hide of the abbot, and has there 1 plough, and 5 bordars and 2 slaves with 2 ploughs. There are 2 enclosures of which the king has seisin. The whole manor was worth £4 TRE; now 100s. Durand's hide [is worth] 12s. Of the land of this manor William fitzBaderon holds 1 virgate by force.

XVII. The land of Sainte-Marie of Lyre

IN RAPSGATE HUNDRED

THE CHURCH OF SAINTE-MARIE of LYRE holds DUNTISBOURNE LEER. There is 1 hide and 1 virgate. In demesne is 1 plough, and 2 bordars. It is and was worth 20s. Roger de Lacy gave this land to the church itself. Eadmær held it TRE.

XVIII. The land of the Church of Eynsham

IN "CELFLEDETORN" HUNDRED

The CHURCH of EYNSHAM holds MICKLETON. There are 14 hides. In demesne are 5 ploughs; and 20 villans and 7 bordars with 10 ploughs. There are 8 slaves and 2 female slaves, and 24 measures of salt from Droitwich [Worcs.]. It is and was worth £10. The same church held it TRE.

XIX. The land of St Peter of Westminster

IN DEERHURST HUNDRED

THE CHURCH OF ST PETER OF WESTMINSTER holds DEERHURST. There are 59 hides.

In the capital manor were 5 hides TRE. There are 3 ploughs, and 20 villans and 8 bordars with 10 ploughs. There are 6 slaves, and 60 acres of meadow, [and] woodland 2 leagues long and half a league broad. It is and was worth £10. To this manor belong these BEREWICKS: Hardwicke 5 hides; Bourton-on-the-Hill 8 hides; Todenham 7 hides; Sutton-under-Brailes [War.] 5 hides; all together 25 hides. There are 13 ploughs in demesne; and 45 villans and 27 bordars with 21 ploughs. There are 37 slaves, and 4 mills rendering 20s, and 20 acres of meadow, woodland 1 league long and a half broad, and water-meadow 3 furlongs long and 1 broad.

Of the land of this manor, radknights, that is free men, held TRE, who, however, all ploughed and harrowed, mowed |and reaped| for the lord's work.

At Elmstone Hardwicke Beorhtric [...] 1 hide. Reinbald holds it.

At 'Ellings' [in Tirley] Godric [held] 2 hides. At Wightfield Eadwig [held] 1 hide. At Todenham Eadwig [held] 1 hide. Walter Ponther holds these.

At Boddington 2 hides. At Bourton-on-the-Hill 2 hides. Wulfwig held these. At Kemerton [Worcs.] half a hide. Leofwine held it. Gerard holds these lands. Abbot Baldwin holds half a hide in the same place.

At Evington Alwig [held] 1 hide and 1 virgate. At Oridge Street Leofwine [held] half a hide. At Tirley Eadric [held] 2½ virgates. William fitzBaderon holds these.

At Tirley Eadric [held] 2½ virgates. At Kemerton [Worcs.] Alwine [held] half a hide. Abbot Baldwin holds these.

At Hasfield Beorhtric [held] 1½ hides. Turstin fitzRolf holds them.

At Lemington Auti [held] 3 hides. Gilbert fitzTurold holds them.

At Moreton-in-Marsh Alfrith [held] half a hide. The same man holds it himself.

In these lands 11½ ploughs are in demesne; and 14 villans and 27 bordars with 7 ploughs. There are 14 slaves, and 20 acres of meadow.

Besides these, Gerard the chamberlain holds 8 hides in Kemerton [Worcs.] and 3 hides in Boddington, which always paid geld and did other services in Deerhurst Hundred. But after Gerard had them he neither rendered geld nor service.

TRE the whole manor gave as farm £41, and 8 sesters of honey according to the king's measure; now it is worth £40. Of these, £26, belong to the demesne manor and £14 to the men.

XX. The land of Saint-Denis of Paris

IN DEERHURST HUNDRED

THE CHURCH OF SAINT-DENIS holds these vills in DEERHURST HUNDRED: Uckington 5 hides; Staverton 3 hides; Coln St Dennis and Calcot 5 hides; Little Compton [War.] 12 hides; Preston on Stour [War.] 10 hides; Welford-on-Avon [War.] 15 hides. In these lands 15 ploughs are in demesne; and 75 villans and 12 bordars with 39 ploughs. There are 38 slaves, and 4 mills rendering 40s, and 36 acres of meadow, [and] woodland 2½ leagues long and 1 league and 2 furlongs broad.

Of this above-mentioned land, 5 free men hold 4½ hides. To the same manor belong 2½ hides beyond the Severn. In Woolstone 5 hides; in The Leigh 1 hide; in Deerhurst Walton 1 hide; in Kemerton [Worcs.] half a hide. In these lands are 5 ploughs in demesne; and 5 villans and 18 bordars with 9 ploughs. 1 free man lives there. There are 38 acres of meadow, [and] woodland half a league long and 2 furlongs broad. To this manor belong 30 burgesses in Gloucester paying 15s8d, and 2 burgesses in Winchcombe paying 10d. TRE the whole manor was worth £26.10s; now £30.

[Folio 166V: GLOUCESTERSHIRE]

XXI. The land of the Church of Lambeth

IN "CELFLEDETORN" HUNDRED

THE CHURCH OF ST MARY of LAMBETH holds ASTON SUBEDGE. Countess Gode held it TRE. There are 4 hides. In demesne are 3 ploughs; and 6 villans and 1 knight with 3½ ploughs. There are 6 slaves and 3 female slaves. It was worth 100s; now £4.

XXII. The land of Saint-Evroul

IN 'HOLFORD' HUNDRED

THE CHURCH OF SAINT-EVROUL holds ROEL of the king. Wulfweard held it TRE. There are 10 hides. In demesne are 4 ploughs; and 16 villans and 2 bordars with 6 ploughs. There are 3 slaves. It is and was worth £10. This manor has never paid geld.

XXIII. The land of the Church of the Nuns of Caen

IN CIRENCESTER HUNDRED

THE CHURCH of the nuns of LA TRINITE of CAEN holds PINBURY of the king. There are 3 hides. In demesne are 3 ploughs; and 8 villans and a smith with 3 ploughs. There are 9 slaves, and a mill rendering 40d. It is and was worth £4.

IN LONGTREE HUNDRED

The church itself holds MINCHINHAMPTON. Countess Gode held it TRE. There are 8 hides. In demesne are 5 ploughs; and 32 villans and 10 bordars with 24 ploughs.

There is a priest and 10 slaves, and 8 mills rendering 45s, and 20 acres of meadow, [and] woodland 2 leagues long and half a league broad. It is worth £28.

XXIIII. The land of the Church of Troarn

IN LONGTREE HUNDRED

THE CHURCH OF SAINT-MARTIN of TROARN holds HORSLEY by gift of King William. Gode, the sister of King Edward, held it. There are 10 hides. In demesne are 4 ploughs; and 6 villans and 5 bordars with 6 ploughs, and 1 radknight, and in Gloucester 1 house rendering 6d. There is a mill rendering 50d. It was worth £12; now £14.

XXVII. The land of Earl Roger

IN "GERSDONES" HUNDRED

EARL ROGER holds MEYSEY HAMPTON, and Thorvald, the nephew of Vigot, [holds] of him.

XXVIII. The land of Earl Hugh

IN BISLEY HUNDRED

EARL HUGH holds BISLEY, and Robert [holds] of him. There are 8 hides. In demesne are 4 ploughs; and 20 villans and 28 bordars with 20 ploughs. There are 6 slaves and 4 female slaves. There are 2 priests and 8 radknights having 10 ploughs, and 23 other men paying 44s and 2 sesters of honey. There are 5 mills rendering 16s, and woodland rendering 20s, and in Gloucester 11 burgesses paying 66d. It was worth £24; now £20.

In the same place the earl himself holds 1 hide at THROUGHAM. Leofnoth held it of King Edward and could go where he would. This land pays geld. There are 4 bordars with 1 plough, and 4 acres of meadow. It is worth 20s.

In the same place the earl himself holds half a hide which Roger de Lacy claims in Edgeworth by witness of the shire. It is worth 10s, and it pays geld.

IN 'WITLEY' HUNDRED

The earl himself holds CHIPPING CAMPDEN. Earl Harold held it. There are 15 hides paying geld. In demesne [are] 6 ploughs; and 50 villans and 8 bordars with 21 ploughs. There are 12 slaves, and 2 mills rendering 6s2d. There are 3 female slaves. It was worth £30; now £20.

IN LONGTREE HUNDRED

The earl himself holds 2 manors of 4 hides paying geld, and 2 of his men [hold] of him. Alnoth and Leofwine held them TRE. There has been no one to answer for these lands, but they are valued by the men of the shire at £8.

XXIX. The land of the Count of Mortain

IN 'WITLEY' HUNDRED

THE COUNT OF MORTAIN holds LONG-BOROUGH. Tovi held it TRE. There are 2 hides. In demesne are 2 ploughs; and 3 villans and 1 bordar with 1 plough, and 4 slaves. It was worth £4; now 40s, and it pays geld.

XXV. The land of the Church of Cirencester

IN CIRENCESTER HUNDRED

THE CHURCH of CIRENCESTER holds of the king 2 hides in alms, and held them of King Edward quit of all customary dues. There are 6 acres of meadow. This is and was worth 40s.

XXVI. The land of Regenbald the Priest

IN "GERSDONES" HUNDRED

XXVI

REGENBALD holds AMPNEY ST MARY of the king. Godric held it TRE. There are 4 hides and 1 virgate. In demesne [are] 2 ploughs; and 8 villans and 1 bordar with 6 ploughs, and a priest. There are 8 slaves, and 2 mills rendering 10s, and 20 acres of meadow. It is and was worth 100s.

The same Regenbald holds DRIFFIELD. Elaf held it of Earl Tosti. There are 7 hides. In demesne [are] 4 ploughs; and 8 villans and 2 bordars and a priest with 5 ploughs. There are 15 slaves, and a mill rendering 5s, and 20 acres of meadow. It is and was worth £8.

IN CIRENCESTER HUNDRED

The same Regenbald holds 1 hide in NORCOTE. Godric held it TRE. In demesne is 1 plough; and 2 villans and 2 bordars with 2 ploughs. There are 6 slaves. It is worth 40s. This thegn could go where he would.

The same Regenbald holds PRESTON [near Cirencester]. Elaf held it TRE. There are 8 hides paying geld besides the demesne. In demesne are 4 ploughs; and 7 villans and 6 bordars with 6 ploughs. There are 9 slaves, and 12 acres of meadow. It is and was worth £8. Elaf himself could go where he would.

XXX. The land of Gilbert, Bishop of Lisieux

IN LONGTREE HUNDRED

HUGH Maminot holds RODMARTON of Gilbert, Bishop of Lisieux, and he himself [holds] of the king. There are 2 hides. In demesne are 2 ploughs; and 1 villan and 2 bordars and a priest with 1 plough. There are 2 slaves. It was worth £4; now £3. Leofwine held it of King Edward.

The same Hugh holds LASBOROUGH of the bishop himself. Leofwine held it. There are 5 hides. In demesne is 1 plough; and 5 villans and a priest with 2 ploughs. There are 7 slaves. It was worth £10; now 50s.

IN "GRIMBOLDESTOU" HUNDRED

The same Hugh holds LITTLE SODBURY of the same bishop. Alweard held it TRE. There are 5 hides paying geld. In demesne are 2 ploughs; and 4 villans and 2 bordars with 2 ploughs. There are 4 slaves, and 20 acres of meadow, [and] a small amount of woodland. It was worth £8; now £4.

XXXI. The land of William de Eu

IN "BLACHELAUE" HUNDRED

WILLIAM de EU holds STONEHOUSE. Tovi held it TRE. There were 7 hides. There are 2 ploughs in demesne; and 21 villans and 9 bordars with 20 ploughs. There are 4 slaves, and 2 mills rendering 17s6d. There are 2 arpents of vineyard. It is and was worth £8. This manor pays geld.

IN LYDNEY HUNDRED

The same William holds 'ALVERSTON' [in Woolaston]. Bondi held it TRE. There are 3 hides paying geld. There is nothing in demesne; but 5 villans and 3 bordars have 3 ploughs. There is a fishery rendering 12d, and 10 acres of meadow, [and] woodland half a league long and a half broad. It was worth 20s; now 30s. Henry de Ferrers claims it because Bondi held it. Ralph de Limesy, the predecessor of William, held it.

The same William holds 2 hides in the same place paying geld, and there are 2 villans with 2 ploughs. Wulfnoth held it. It is and was worth 10s.

The same William held WYEGATE, and Ralph de Limesy [held it] before him. Ælfstan held it TRE. Now, by the king's order, it is in his forest. There were 6 hides, and they paid geld and were worth 60s. Now there is only a fishery rendering 10s.

IN WYVERN HUNDRED

The same William holds WOOLASTON. Beorhtric son of Ælfgar held it. There are 2 hides. There is nothing in demesne, except 5 villans with 5 ploughs. There is 1 fishery in the Severn rendering 5s, and a mill rendering 40d. It is and was worth 20s. This land pays geld.

The same William holds in TIDENHAM 1½ virgates paying geld. Archbishop Stigand held them. There is 1 villan with 1 plough, and 2 fisheries. It is and was worth 10s.

IN CIRENCESTER HUNDRED

The same William holds DAGLINGWORTH. Ælfstan held it TRE. There are 5½ hides paying geld. In demesne are 2 ploughs; and 6 villans and 4 bordars with 5½ ploughs. There are 7 slaves, and a mill rendering 8s. Ralph holds this manor of William and it pays geld, but he himself retains the geld on 3 hides. 1 Frenchman holds half a hide of this land and has 1 plough there with his men. The whole was worth £10 TRE; now £8.

The same William holds 1 hide in TARLTON, and Herbert [holds] of him. Leofric held it TRE and could go where he would. In demesne is 1 plough and 4 slaves. It was worth 40s; now 20s.

IN LONGTREE HUNDRED

Leofnoth held it. There are 5 hides. In demesne is 1 plough, and 4 villans and 2 bordars and a priest and 2 other men. Among them all they have 2½ ploughs. There are 6 slaves. It was worth £8; now £3.

[Folio 167: GLOUCESTERSHIRE]

The same William holds SHIPTON MOYNE as Ralph de Limesy held it. Wulfwig held it TRE. There are 2 hides. In demesne are 2 ploughs, and 2 bordars and 8 slaves. It is and was worth 40s. Wulfwig himself could go where he would. Hugh holds it of William.

The same William holds CULKERTON, and Herbert [holds] of him. Scirweald held it TRE. There are 3 virgates and 5 acres. In demesne is 1 plough, and 3 slaves. It is and was worth 35s. Ralph de Limesy held this land but it did not belong to Ælfstan.

IN 'DUDSTONE' HUNDRED

The same William holds BADGEWORTH. Ælfstan held it. There are 8 hides. In demesne are 6 ploughs; and 20 villans and 14 bordars with 24 ploughs. There are 17 slaves, and a mill rendering 12d, [and] woodland 2 leagues long and 1 broad. It was worth £15; now £13.

IN SALMONSBURY HUNDRED

The same William holds LOWER SWELL. Earnsige held it TRE. There are 3 hides paying geld. It was worth 40s; now 10s.

XXXII. The land of William fitzBaderon

IN CIRENCESTER HUNDRED

WILLIAM fitzBADERON holds 2 hides in CIRENCESTER, and Hugh holds of him. In demesne is 1 plough; and 1½ villans and 4 bordars with 1 plough. There are 2 slaves. It was worth 100s; now 70s. Alwig held this land.

The same William holds DAGLINGWORTH. Ketil and Ælfric held it and could go where they would. There are 3½ hides. In demesne are 1½ ploughs; and 1 villan and 2 bordars with 1 plough. There is 1 slave. It was worth £10; now 70s.

The same William holds 1 hide in SIDDINGTON. Aswith held it TRE and could go where he would. In demesne is 1 plough, and 4 slaves. It is and was worth 24s.

IN LONGTREE HUNDRED

The same William holds WESTONBIRT. Beorhtsige held it TRE. There are 3 hides. In demesne are 2 ploughs; and 2 villans and 3 bordars with 2 ploughs. There are 4 slaves, and 6 acres of meadow. It was worth £6; now £3.

IN BOTLOE HUNDRED

The same William holds TIBBERTON. There are 5 hides. Wulfhelm held it of King Edward and he could go where he would. In demesne are 3 ploughs; and 10 villans and 8 bordars with 8 ploughs. There are 4 slaves, and woodland 3 leagues long and 1 broad. It was worth £6.10s; now 100s.

The same William holds HUNTLEY. Alwine held it of Archbishop Ealdræd and could go where he would. There are 2 hides. In demesne is 1 plough; and 4 villans and 6 bordars with 3 ploughs. There is 1 slave, [and] woodland 2 leagues long and 1 broad. It was worth 40s; now 30s.

IN WESTBURY HUNDRED

The same William holds LONGHOPE. Forne and Wulfheah held it of King Edward, and these thegns could go where they would. There are 5 hides paying geld. In demesne are 2 ploughs; and 12 villans and 1 bordar with 12 ploughs. There are 3 slaves, and a mill rendering 17d. It was worth £8; now 100s.

The same William holds STEARS. Wulfheah held it TRE. It was worth 10s; now 5s. There is 1 hide and it does not pay geld.

The same William holds 2½ virgates, and he has there 1 villan and 1 bordar. His predecessor Winhanoc held them, but the shire affirms that this land belonged to the king's demesne farm in Westbury-on-Severn. It is worth 3s.

The same William holds NEWNHAM. There is 1 hide, and 3 villans and 3 bordars paying 20s. This land does not pay geld. There is woodland 2 furlongs long and 1 broad.

IN LYDNEY HUNDRED

The same William holds ST BRIAVELS. Ælfhere held it TRE. There are 6 hides paying geld. In demesne are 2 ploughs; and 3 villans and 5 bordars with 2 ploughs. There are 3 slaves, and a mill rendering 5s, and 20 acres of meadow, and half a fishery in the Wye, [and] woodland 1 league long and a half broad. It was worth £4; now 40s.

The same William held HEWELSFIELD. Wulfheah held it TRE. There are 3 hides. By the king's order this land is in the forest. It was worth 30s.

XXXIII. The land of William the Chamberlain

IN 'WITLEY' HUNDRED

WILLIAM the Chamberlain holds WINCOT [War.]. Wynric held it TRE. There are 3 hides. In demesne are 3 ploughs; and 2 villans and 2 bordars with 1 plough. There are 4 slaves. It is and was worth £4. This manor pays geld.

IN "WACRESCUMBE" HUNDRED

The same William [fitzBaderon] holds HAMPEN, and Geoffrey [holds] of him. Eadwig held it. There are 5 hides. In demesne are 2 ploughs; and 6 villans with 3 ploughs. There are 4 slaves. This land pays geld. It was worth 100s; now 60s.

XXXIIII. The land of William Goizenboded

IN "CELFLEDETORN" HUNDRED

WILLIAM Goizenboded holds PEBWORTH [Worcs.] of the king. Wulfgeat and Wulfweard held it TRE as 2 manors. There are 6 hides and 1 virgate. In demesne is 1 plough, and 1 bordar and 1 slave. It was worth £7; now £4.10s.

The same William holds ULLINGTON [Worcs.]. A thegn held it TRE. There are 5 hides. In demesne are 2 ploughs; and 2 villans and a Frenchman holding 1½ hides with 1 plough. Earl Ælfgar placed this manor in Pebworth [Worcs.]. It was worth 100s; now 40s.

The same William holds LOWER CLOPTON [War.]. Huscarl held it TRE. There are 10 hides. In demesne [are] 3 ploughs; and 12 villans and 4 bordars and 1 radknight with 9 ploughs. In Winchcombe [is] 1 burgess. It was worth £8; now 100s.

IN 'WITLEY' HUNDRED

The same William holds EBRINGTON. Beorhtmær held it. There are 10 hides. In demesne [are] 4 ploughs; and 18 villans and 4 bordars with 14 ploughs. There are 8 slaves and 3 female slaves, and 2 mills rendering 15s. It was worth £12; now £7.

IN SALMONSBURY HUNDRED

The same William holds 'CALDICOTT' [in Hawling], and Ranulph [holds] of him. Alwine held it TRE. There are 3 hides paying geld. In demesne [are] 3 ploughs, and 8 slaves and female slaves all together. It was worth 60s; now 40s.

The same William holds AYLWORTH. Alwine held it TRE. There is 1 hide paying geld. In demesne [is] 1 plough, and 2 slaves. It was worth 6s; now 3s.

IN 'HOLFORD' HUNDRED

The same William holds FARMCOTE. Alwine held it. There are 3 hides paying geld. In demesne [are] 2 ploughs; and 4 villans with 4 ploughs, and 13 slaves and female slaves all together. Geoffrey holds it of William. It was worth £10; now £3.

The same William holds GUITING POWER. King Edward held it and he leased it to Alwine his sheriff, so that he should have it for his lifetime. But it was not a gift, as the shire bears witness. On the death of Alwine, King William gave his wife and land to a certain young man, Richard. Now William, the successor of Richard, holds this land thus. There are 10 hides. Of these, 9 pay geld. In demesne are 4 ploughs; and 4 villans and 3 Frenchmen and 2 radknights and a priest with 2 bordars. Among them all they have 5 ploughs. All together [there are] 11 slaves and female slaves, and 2 mills rendering 14s. There 5 salt-pans render 20 summæ of salt. In Winchcombe 2 burgesses pay 11s4d. It was worth £16; now £6.

The same William holds CASTLETT. Alwine held it. There are 2 hides paying geld. In demesne [are] 2 ploughs, and 4 slaves, and a mill rendering 5s. It was worth 40s; now 10s.

IN BOTLOE HUNDRED

The same William holds TAYNTON. Alwine held it. There are 6 hides. In demesne is 1 plough; and 9 villans and 7 bordars with 9 ploughs. It was worth £6; now £3.

IN BARRINGTON HUNDRED

The same William holds 2 hides in LITTLE BARRINGTON, and Ralph [holds] of him. Alwine held them TRE. In demesne is 1 plough, and 1 slave, and a mill rendering 40d, and 6 acres of meadow. It is and was worth 40s.

IN WESTBURY HUNDRED

The same William holds half a hide of land and half a fishery. Alwine the sheriff held it and gave it to his wife. These were, however, [part] of the king's farm in Westbury-on-Severn.

IN 'GRESTON' HUNDRED

The same William holds 1 hide in DUMBLETON. Sæwine held it TRE and could go where he would. It was worth 20s; now 12s.

XXXV. The land of William fitzGuy

IN "GRIMBOLDESTOU" HUNDRED

WILLIAM fitzGuy holds DYRHAM of the king. Ælfric held it TRE. There are 7 hides paying geld. In demesne is 1 plough; and 13 villans and 13 bordars with 2 ploughs. There are all together 8 slaves and female slaves, and 3 mills rendering 15s, and 6 acres of meadow. It was worth £12; now £8.

The same William held 3 hides of this manor of which Durand the sheriff had given seisin to ST MARY of Pershore, by order of the king; these Earl William had given to Turstin fitzRolf with this manor.

[Folio 167V: GLOUCESTERSHIRE]

XXXVI. The land of William Froisseloup

IN 'DUDSTONE' HUNDRED

WILLIAM Froisseloup holds [?] WOTTON [in Gloucester] of the king. Godric held it. There are 2 hides. In demesne are 2 ploughs, and 4 bordars and 4 slaves. It was worth 30s; now 60s.

The same William holds in CONDICOTE half a hide paying geld. There was 1 plough, and 4 slaves. It was worth 20s; now 3s. Beorhtric held it TRE.

IN 'GRESTON' HUNDRED

The same William holds 1 hide in 'LITTLETON' [in Dumbleton]. Godric held it. In demesne are 2 ploughs, and 2 bordars and 3 slaves, and a mill rendering 4s. It was worth 40s; now 30s, and it pays geld.

XXXVII. The land of William fitzNorman

IN "LANGEBRIGE" HUNDRED

WILLIAM fitzNorman holds MOORCROFT [Moorcroft and Upper Moorcroft]. Wulfheah held it TRE. There is 1 hide. In demesne is 1 plough, with 2 bordars. It was worth 8s; now 10s. This land does not pay geld.

IN WESTBURY HUNDRED

The same William holds ENGLISH BICKNOR. Morganau held it TRE. There is half a hide. In demesne is half a plough, with 6 bordars. It was worth 5s; now 10s.

The same William holds in MITCHELDEAN 2 hides and 2½ virgates of land. 3 thegns, Godric, Alric and Earnwig, held these TRE. In demesne are 3 ploughs. There are 38 bordars having 7½ ploughs, and 3 of them pay 8s. It was worth 33s; now 44s. King Edward granted these lands quit of geld in return for guarding the forest.

IN BOTLOE HUNDRED

The same William holds TAYNTON. Wulfgar held it of King Edward. This land is free. [...] There are 6 bordars with 1 plough. It is and was worth 20s.

1 virgate of land in the same place belongs to the forest and renders 12d.

IN BLEDISLOE HUNDRED

The same William holds 1 hide and half a virgate of land. Siward and Wynstan held them. In demesne are 2 ploughs; and 17 bordars with 5 ploughs. It was worth 15s; now 30s.

XXXVIII. The land of William Leofric

IN CHELTENHAM HUNDRED

WILLIAM Leofric holds LECKHAMPTON of the king. Asgot held it TRE. There are 3 hides paying geld. In demesne are 2 ploughs; and 2 villans and 8 bordars with 1 plough. There are 4 slaves, [and] woodland 1 furlong long and 1 broad. It is and was worth 40s.

IN 'GRESTON' HUNDRED

The same William holds HAILES. Asgot held it TRE. There are 11 hides. In demesne are 3 ploughs; and 9 villans and 11 bordars with 8 ploughs. There were 12 slaves whom William made free. There is a mill rendering 10s, [and] woodland 1 league long and a half broad. It was worth £12; now £8. This manor pays geld.

IN "WACRESCUMBE" HUNDRED

The same William holds WHITTINGTON. Asgot held it. There are 3 hides and they pay geld. In demesne are 2 ploughs; and 6 villans and 1 radknight and 4 bordars with 4 ploughs. There is a mill rendering 10s, [and] woodland 1 league long and a half broad. It was worth 100s; now 60s.

The same William holds in SHIPTON OLIFFE 3 hides less 1 virgate, and they pay geld. Geoffrey holds them of him. Asgot

held them. In demesne are 2 ploughs; and a priest and 1 villan and 4 slaves without a plough. It was worth 40s; now 20s.

IN 'BRADLEY' HUNDRED

The same William holds TURKDEAN, and Geoffrey [holds] of him. Asgot held it. There are 5 hides and 1½ virgates. [There is] nothing in demesne. There are 2 villans and 3 bordars with 1 plough. This land pays geld. It was worth £4; now 10s.

XXXIX. The land of Roger de Lacy

IN BOTLOE HUNDRED

ROGER de Lacy holds KEMPLEY [Kempley and Kempley Green] of the king. Eadric and Leofric held it TRE as 2 manors and they could go where they would. There are 3 hides. In demesne are 3 ploughs; and 10 villans and 7 bordars with 12 ploughs. There are 7 slaves. It was worth £4; now 100s.

The same Roger holds OXENHALL. Thorkil held it of Earl Harold and he could go where he would. There are 3 hides. In demesne are 2 ploughs; and 5 villans and 3 bordars with 5 ploughs. There are 2 slaves, and in Gloucester 3 burgesses paying 15d. It is and was worth 40s.

The same Roger holds CARSWALLS, and Odo [holds] of him. Wulfhelm held it TRE and he could go where he would. There is 1 hide and 1 virgate. In demesne is 1 plough; and 3 villans and 1 bordar with 3 ploughs. It is and was worth 20s.

IN SALMONSBURY HUNDRED

The same Roger holds ICOMB PLACE, and Ralph [holds] of him. Healfdene held it. There are 2 hides. In demesne are 2 ploughs; and 2 villans and 2 bordars with 1 plough. There are 4 slaves and 3 female slaves. It is and was worth 40s. This land pays geld.

The same Roger holds WYCK RISSINGTON, and Hugh [holds] of him. There are 8 hides paying geld. Alweard and Eskil and Alweard and Wulfwig held them as 4 manors. In demesne are 7 ploughs; and 4 villans with 2 ploughs. There are 12 slaves and 2 female slaves. There is a mill rendering 10s. It is and was worth £7; and £10 [sic].

IN 'HOLFORD' HUNDRED

The same Roger holds TEMPLE GUITING. There are 10 hides paying geld besides the demesne which does not pay geld. Beorhtric, a thegn of King Edward, held it. In demesne are 5 ploughs; and 25 villans and a priest and 7 radknights with 18 ploughs. There are 18 slaves and female slaves all together, and 3 mills rendering 24s, and a salt-pan rendering 20s and 12 summae of salt; and in Winchcombe 3 burgesses paying 32d, and in Gloucester 2 burgesses paying 10d. From the woodland and pasture, 40 hens. It is and was worth £10.

IN RAPSGATE HUNDRED

The same Roger holds DUNTISBOURNE ABBOTS, and Gilbert [holds] of him. Cyneweard, a thegn of King Edward, held it and he could go where he would. There are 2 hides. In demesne is 1 plough; and 2 villans and 2 bordars with 1½ ploughs. There are 2 slaves. It is and was worth 40s.

IN BISLEY HUNDRED

The same Roger holds PAINSWICK. There is 1 hide paying geld. Earnsige held it. In demesne is 1 plough; and 35 villans and 16 bordars and a priest and 3 radknights. Among them all they have 52 ploughs. There are 11 slaves, and 4 mills rendering 24s, [and] woodland 5 leagues long and 2 broad. It was worth £20; now £24. The thegn himself could go where he would. In this land ST MARY of Cirencester holds 1 villan and part of the woodland. King William granted it this. It is worth 10s.

The same Roger holds EDGEWORTH. There are 1½ hides paying geld. Alwine held them. In demesne are 4 ploughs; and 4 villans and 3 bordars with 2 ploughs. There are 2 free men with 2 ploughs. There are 15 slaves, and a mill rendering 30d, and 2 acres of meadow, [and] woodland 1 league long and a half broad. It is and was worth £6.

The same Roger holds half a hide with 1 fishery in the Wye, and there is 1 villan with 1 plough. This land is called MADGETTS. It is and was worth 20s. Beorhtric held it.

The same Roger holds half a hide in TIDENHAM. Archbishop Stigand held it. There is 1 villan with 1 plough, and 4½ fisheries. It is and was worth 20s.

IN 'BRIGHTWELLS BARROW' HUNDRED

The same Roger holds QUENINGTON. There are 8 hides. 3 free men, Dodda, and another Dodda, and Alweald, held them as 3 manors and they could go where they would, and they paid geld. In demesne are 3 ploughs, and 20 villans and 7 bordars and a priest and a reeve. Among them all they have 12 ploughs, and [there are] 2 radknights with 1 plough. There are 12 slaves, and 2 mills rendering 20s, and 10 acres of meadow. In Gloucester 1 burgess renders 4 iron tips for ploughshares, and 1 smith pay 2s. It was worth £8; now £10.

The same Roger holds EASTLEACH TURVILLE, and William [holds] of him. There are 5 hides. Ealdwine held it TRE. In demesne are 2 ploughs; and 12 villans and 1 bordar with 5 ploughs. There are 5 slaves, and 8 acres of meadow. It is and was worth £6.

The same Roger holds WILLIAMSTRIP, and William [holds] of him. There are 2 hides. Dunning held it TRE. In demesne are 2 ploughs; and 3 villans and 3 bordars with 1 plough. There are 6 slaves. It is and was worth 100s.

IN BARRINGTON HUNDRED

The same Roger holds WINDRUSH, and Ralph [holds] of him. There are 2 hides. Wulfric held it TRE. In demesne is 1 plough; and 3 villans and 2 bordars with 1 plough. There are 5 slaves, and a mill rendering 5s, and 10 acres of meadow. It was worth 100s; now £4.

[Folio 168: GLOUCESTERSHIRE]

In the same place the same Roger holds 1 hide and 1 virgate, and Hugh [holds] of him. Godric, a thegn of King Edward,

held them. In demesne is 1 plough, and 2 bordars and 1 slave, and a mill rendering 3s, and 8 acres of meadow. It is and was worth 24s.

IN CIRENCESTER HUNDRED

The same Roger holds STRATTON. There are 5 hides paying geld besides the demesne. Edmund held it TRE. In demesne are 3 ploughs; and 16 villans and 7 bordars with a priest having 9 ploughs. There are 5 slaves, and 2 mills rendering 20s. It was worth £8; now £6.

The same Roger holds SIDDINGTON, and his mother holds it as her dower-land. There are 6 hides. Godric and Leofwine held it as 2 manors. In demesne are 3 ploughs; and 9 villans and 6 bordars and a priest with 7 ploughs. There are 2 slaves, and a mill rendering 10s. It was worth £8; now £9.

The same Roger holds COATES. There are 1½ hides. Leofwine held it. Now Gerard holds it of Roger. In demesne are 2 ploughs; and 2 villans with a priest having 2½ ploughs. There are 9 slaves. It was worth £4; now £3.

IN SALMONSBURY HUNDRED

The same Roger and his mother hold UPPER SLAUGHTER. There are 3 hides. Offa and Leofwine held it as 2 manors and could go where they would. In demesne are 4 ploughs, and 4 bordars and 8 slaves, and a mill rendering 12s. It is and was worth £6. Of these 3 hides, 1 hide paid geld each year at 10s for the king's use.

IN 'GRESTON' HUNDRED

The same Roger holds WORMINGTON; Walter fitzErcold [holds] of him. There are 5 hides paying geld. Eadwig held it. In demesne are 2 ploughs; and 6 villans with 2 ploughs. There are 2 slaves, and a mill rendering 8s, and 10 acres of meadow. It was worth 100s; now £4.

XL. The land of Roger de Beaumont

IN "CELFLEDETORN" HUNDRED

ROGER de Beaumont holds DORSINGTON [War.], and Robert [holds] of him. There are 10 hides. Saxi held it. In demesne [are] 3 ploughs; and 8 villans with 5 ploughs, and 6 slaves. It was worth £8; now 100s.

XLI. The land of Roger D'Ivry

IN 'BRADLEY' HUNDRED

ROGER d'IVRY holds HAMPNETT. There are 10 hides. Archbishop Ealdræd held it. Out of these 10, King Edward gave him 2 hides quit [of geld], as they say. In demesne are 3 ploughs; and 10 villans with a priest and 1 bordar with 5 ploughs. There are 11 slaves, and in Winchcombe 10 burgesses pay 65d. It was worth £8; now £6.

IN LONGTREE HUNDRED

The same Roger holds TETBURY. There are 23 hides paying geld. Siward held it TRE. In demesne are 8 ploughs; and 32 villans and 2 bordars and 2 radknights with a priest having among them all 14 ploughs. There are 19 slaves, and a mill rendering 15d, and pasture rendering 10s, and 10 acres of meadow.

The same Roger holds TETBURY UPTON. There are 2 hides and 1 virgate paying geld. Ælfric held it of King Edward. In demesne are 2 ploughs; and 5 villans and 3 bordars with 3 ploughs. There are 8 slaves.

These 2 manors were worth £33 TRE; now they are at farm for £50.

The same Roger holds CULKERTON, and Ansketil [holds] of him. Ælfric held it. There are 1½ hides. In demesne [are] 2 ploughs, and 4 slaves. It was worth 20s; now 30s.

The same Roger holds HAZELTON [in Rodmarton]. There are 3 hides and 3 virgates paying geld. Alnoth held it TRE. In demesne are 4 ploughs; and 7 half-villans and 1 bordar with 3 ploughs, and 17 slaves, and half a mill rendering 30d, and 15 acres of meadow. A certain man, Roger, held this manor of the Bishop of Bayeux for £16. Afterwards the bishop gave it to the same Roger with the farm.

XLII. The land of Roger of Berkeley

IN RAPSGATE HUNDRED

ROGER of Berkeley holds COBERLEY. There are 10 hides. Dene, a thegn of King Edward, held it. In demesne are 2 ploughs; and 19 villans and 4 bordars with 5 ploughs. There are 4 slaves, and 5 acres of meadow, [and] woodland 3 furlongs long and 2 broad. It was worth £7; now £8.

IN "EDREDESTANE" HUNDRED

The same Roger holds DODINGTON. There are 3 hides and 2 parts of half a hide. Alwine held it TRE. In demesne is 1 plough; and 7 villans and 4 bordars with 4 ploughs. There are 4 slaves, and 10 acres of meadow. It is and was worth £3.

IN PUCKLECHURCH HUNDRED

The same Roger holds SISTON. Anna held it. There are 5 hides paying geld. In demesne are 2 ploughs; and 8 villans and 10 bordars with 4 ploughs. There are 4 slaves, and 8 acres of meadow. It is and was worth 100s.

XLIII. The land of Ralph of Berkeley

IN PUCKLECHURCH HUNDRED

RALPH, the brother of this Roger, holds WAPLEY of the king. There is 1 hide. Godric held it. In demesne is 1 plough, and 4 slaves. It is and was worth 20s.

IN "BLACHELAUE" HUNDRED

The same Ralph holds LEONARD STANLEY. There are 4½ hides. Godric and Wihtnoth held it as 2 manors. In demesne are 2 ploughs; and 6 villans and 14 bordars with 12 ploughs. There are 5 slaves, and 10 acres of meadow. It was and is worth 100s.

XLIIII. The land of Ralph Paynel

IN CIRENCESTER HUNDRED

RALPH Paynel holds TARLTON, and Ralph [holds] of him. There are 4½ hides paying geld. Mærle-Sveinn held it. In demesne are 3 ploughs; and 10 villans and 1 bordar with 3 ploughs. There are 10 slaves. It was worth £10; now 100s.

IN LONGTREE HUNDRED

XLV. The land of Ralph de Tosny

IN 'WITLEY' HUNDRED

RALPH de Tosny holds CHARINGWORTH, and Roger [holds] of him. There are 10 hides. Beorhtmær held it. In demesne [are] 3 ploughs; and 13 villans and 1 radknight with 6 ploughs, and 9 slaves and female slaves all together. It was worth £8; now £6.

IN SALMONSBURY HUNDRED

The same Ralph holds ICOMB [Place or Proper], and Roger [holds] of him. There are 10 hides paying geld. In demesne [are] 3 ploughs; and 12 villans and 2 bordars with 7 ploughs. There are 8 slaves. It is and was worth £6.

IN BOTLOE HUNDRED

The same Ralph holds BROMSBERROW. There are 5 hides. Earl Harold held it. In demesne is 1 plough; and 11 villans and 8 bordars with 14 ploughs. There is 1 slave, [and] woodland 2 leagues long and 1 broad. It was worth £8; now 100s.

IN "GERSDONES" HUNDRED

The same Ralph holds HARNHILL, and Roger [holds] of him. There are 5 hides. Alric and Alwine and Wulfric held them as 3 manors.

The same Ralph holds 'AMPNEY' [in Driffield] and CERNEY WICK, and Roger [holds] of him. There are 4 hides. 4 thegns held them as 4 manors and could go where they would. In demesne [are] 10 ploughs, and 1 villan and 1 bordar. There are 21 slaves, and a mill rendering 5s, and 30 acres of meadow. It was worth £10; now £6.

IN SALMONSBURY HUNDRED

The same Ralph holds LOWER SWELL, and Drogo [holds] of him. Earnsige held it. There are 7 hides paying geld. In demesne are 4 ploughs; and 10 villans with 6 ploughs, and a mill rendering 7s6d. It was worth £8; now £7.

XLVI. The land of Robert de Tosny

IN SALMONSBURY HUNDRED

ROBERT de Tosny holds GREAT RISSINGTON. Ulf held it. There are 13 hides paying geld. In demesne are 3 ploughs; and 23 villans and 6 bordars with 10 ploughs. There are 8 slaves and female slaves all together, and a mill rendering 10s, and 1 burgess in Gloucester paying 3d. It was worth £12; now £10.

IN "GRIMBOLDESTOU" HUNDRED

The same Robert holds HORTON. There are 10 hides paying geld. Ulf held it. In demesne are 3 ploughs; and 11 villans and 8 bordars with 8 ploughs. There are 7 slaves, and a mill rendering 6s, and 20 acres of meadow, [and] woodland 2 leagues long and 1 broad. It was worth £12; now £7.

IN BISLEY HUNDRED

The same Robert holds SAPPERTON [near Cirencester] and FRAMPTON MANSELL. In the one [are] 5 hides, and in the other 5 hides. Ulf held them. In demesne are 7 ploughs; and 17 villans and 9 bordars with 10 ploughs. There are 13 slaves, and 2 mills rendering 6s, [and] woodland half a league long and 2 furlongs broad. These 2 manors together were worth £14 TRE; now £16.

XLVII. The land of Robert Despenser

IN 'GRESTON' HUNDRED

ROBERT Despenser holds CHILDSWICKHAM [Worcs.]. There are 10 hides paying geld. Baldwin held it. In demesne are 3 ploughs; and 32 villans and 10 bordars with 12 ploughs. There is 1 slave, and 2 mills rendering 10s, and 10 acres of meadow. In Winchcombe [is] 1 burgess paying 16d. It was worth £12; now £16.

[Folio 168V: GLOUCESTERSHIRE]

XLVIII. The land of Robert d'Oilly

IN SALMONSBURY HUNDRED

ROBERT d'Oilly holds LITTLE RISSINGTON. There are 10 hides paying geld. Siward held it. In demesne [are] 4 ploughs; and 12 villans and 2 bordars with 5 ploughs. There are 8 slaves, and 2 mills rendering 20s. It was worth £10; now £8.

IN 'BRADLEY' HUNDRED

The same Robert holds TURKDEAN. There are 5 hides and $2\frac{1}{2}$ virgates paying geld. Siward held it. In demesne are 4 ploughs; and 12 villans with 6 ploughs. All together there are 8 slaves and female slaves. It was worth £6; now 100s.

IN SALMONSBURY HUNDRED

Roger d'Oilly holds NAUNTON [near Bourton-on-the-Water] of Osbern fitzRichard. There are 5 hides paying geld. Thorsten held it. In demesne [are] 2 ploughs; and 8 villans with $4\frac{1}{2}$ ploughs. It is worth £3.

XLIX. The land of Richard the Legate

IN "EDREDESTANE" HUNDRED

RICHARD the legate holds TORMARTON of the king. There are 8 hides. [...] Alric held it of King Edward. In demesne are 6 ploughs; and 20 villans and 4 bordars and a priest and 1 radknight. Among them all they have 12 ploughs. There are 12 slaves. It was worth £12; now £15.

L. The land of Osbern Giffard

IN 'LANGLEY' HUNDRED

OSBERN Giffard holds ROCKHAMPTON of the king. There are 3 hides paying geld. Dunna held it TRE. In demesne are 2 ploughs; and 6 villans and 7 bordars with 3 ploughs. There are 5 slaves, and 20 acres of meadow, and a salt-pan at Droitwich [Worcs.] rendering 4 summae of salt, [and] woodland 1 league long and a half broad.

IN "LETBERGE" HUNDRED

The same Osbern holds STOKE GIFFORD. There are 5 hides paying geld. Dunna held it. In demesne are 4 ploughs; and 8 villans and 3 bordars and a priest with 8 ploughs. There are 4 slaves. It was worth £6; now £8.

IN RAPSGATE HUNDRED

The same Osbern holds BRIMPSFIELD. There are 9 hides paying geld. Duns held it of Earl Harold. In demesne are 3 ploughs; and 16 villans and 6 bordars and a priest with 12 ploughs. There are 8 slaves and 4 female slaves, and 2 mills rendering 64d. In Gloucester [are] 5 burgesses paying 2s. It is and was worth £12.

The same Osbern holds 'OLDBURY' [in Elkstone], but it did not pertain to the land of the man Duns which Osbern holds, as the shire says. [...] Æthelric held it and could go where he would. There is 1 hide and 1 plough. It is and was worth 10s.

LI. The land of Geoffrey Orlateile

GEOFFREY Orlateile holds of the king in BAUNTON 2 hides and 1 virgate paying geld. Bolli held them. There is nothing in demesne. There are 2 villans and 8 bordars with 3 ploughs. It is and was worth 40s. There are 8 acres of meadow.

LII. The land of Gilbert fitzTurold

IN CIRENCESTER HUNDRED

GILBERT fitzTurold holds 1 hide of the king in COATES, and Oswulf [holds] of him. Cyneweard held it TRE. In demesne are 2 ploughs, and 3 bordars and 6 slaves. It was worth 40s; now 30s.

The same Gilbert holds half a hide in TREWSBURY, and Osweard [holds] of him. Alweard held it. In demesne is 1 plough. It was worth 10s; now 15s.

IN RAPSGATE HUNDRED

The same Gilbert holds NORTH CERNEY. There are 7 hides. 2 thegns, Elaf and his brother, held it as 2 manors and could go where they would. In demesne are 4 ploughs; and 7 villans and 6 bordars with 5 ploughs. There are 6 slaves, and a mill rendering 8s, and 6 acres of meadow, [and] woodland 2 furlongs long and 1 broad. There 4 knights of Gilbert with their men have 7 ploughs, and a mill rendering 8s. The whole was worth £14 TRE; now £12.

The same Gilbert holds RENDCOMB. There are 5 hides paying geld. Ælfric held it. In demesne is 1 plough; and 3 villans and 7 bordars with 3 ploughs. There are 7 slaves, and 1 Frenchman holds the land of 2 villans, and [there is] a mill rendering 8s, and 4 acres of meadow. It was worth £7; now 100s.

The same Gilbert holds RENDCOMB, and Walter [holds] of him. There are 3 hides paying geld. In demesne are 2 ploughs; and 4 villans and 3 bordars with 2 ploughs. There are 6 slaves, and a mill rendering 5s, and 3 acres of meadow. It is and was worth £6.

The same Gilbert holds AYLWORTH, and Walter [holds] of him. Alwine held it. There are 4 hides paying geld. In demesne [are] 2 ploughs; and 3 villans with 2 ploughs, and 6 slaves and female slaves all together. It is and was worth 40s.

The same Gilbert holds [Lower and Upper] HARFORD. Ælfhere held it. There is 1 hide paying geld. In demesne [are] 2 ploughs; and 4 villans and 1 bordar with 2 ploughs, and 2 slaves, and a mill rendering 5s. It is and was worth 40s.

LIII. The land of Durand of Gloucester

IN WESTBURY HUNDRED

DURAND the sheriff holds 1 manor of 3 hides. Alweald held it, and it paid geld. In demesne is 1 plough; and 4 villans and 3 bordars with 4 ploughs. There are 2 slaves. It was worth 60s; now 40s.

IN "GERSDONES" HUNDRED

The same Durand holds 1 hide in ASHBROOK, and a certain knight of his [holds] of him. In demesne [is] 1 plough, and 1 bordar and 1 slave. It is and was worth 10s.

IN CIRENCESTER HUNDRED

The same Durand holds 2 hides in DUNTISBOURNE ROUSE, and Ralph [holds] of him. Wulfweard held it of King Edward as a manor. In demesne are 2 ploughs; and 3 villans and 1 bordar with 1 plough. There are 4 slaves, and 2 acres of meadow. It is and was worth 40s.

IN LONGTREE HUNDRED

The same Durand holds CULKERTON, and Roger d'Ivry [holds] of him. There are 2 hides and 2½ virgates. Grim held it. In demesne are 2 ploughs; and 6 villans with 3 ploughs. It is and was worth £4.

IN "GRIMBOLDESTOU" HUNDRED

The same Durand holds DIDMARTON, and Ansketil [holds] of him. There are 3 hides paying geld. Leofwine held it of Earl Harold. In demesne are 3 ploughs; and 8 bordars with 1 plough, and 4 slaves, and 6 acres of meadow. It was worth 30s; now 40s.

IN 'DUDSTONE' HUNDRED

The same Durand holds WHADDON. There are 5 hides. 5 brothers held them as 5 manors, and they could go where they would and were equals. In demesne are 5 ploughs; and 1 villan and 7 bordars with 5 ploughs. TRE it was worth £8; now 100s.

IN "CELFLEDETORN" HUNDRED

The same Durand holds SEZINCOTE, and Walter [holds] of him. There are 2½ hides. Leofwine and Leofwig held it as 2 manors. In demesne are 2 ploughs, and 4 bordars. It was worth 40s; now 60s.

IN SALMONSBURY HUNDRED

The same Durand holds ICOMB PROPER, and Walter [holds] of him. There are 2 hides paying geld. Thorsten held it. In demesne [are] 2 ploughs; and 2 villans and 2 bordars with 1 plough, and 6 slaves and female slaves all together. It was worth 30s; now 40s.

IN "WACRESCUMBE" HUNDRED

The same Durand holds SHIPTON SOLERS, and Ralph [holds] of him. Eadwig held it. There are 3½ hides paying geld. In demesne are 2 ploughs; and 3 villans with 2 ploughs, and 4 slaves, and 10 acres of meadow. It was worth £4; now 40s.

IN 'WHITSTONE' HUNDRED

The same Durand holds in HARESFIELD COURT 7 hides paying geld. 2 brothers, Godric and Eadric, held them as 2 manors and could go where they would. In demesne are 3 ploughs; and 9 villans and 11 bordars with 9 ploughs. There are 4 slaves, and 5 potters pay 44d. [There is] woodland half a league long and 3 furlongs broad. It is and was worth £6.

The same Durand holds MORETON VALENCE. There are 3 hides paying geld. Auti held it. In demesne is 1 plough; and 4 villans and 6 bordars with 3½ ploughs. There are 4 slaves, and 20 acres of meadow. It was worth £4; now 40s.

IN 'GRESTON' HUNDRED

The same Durand holds 'LITTLETON' [in Dumbleton], and Ralph [holds] of him. There is half a hide paying geld. Leofnoth held it as 1 manor. There is 1 plough. It is and was worth 10s.

IN 'WITLEY' HUNDRED

In CONDICOTE Osbern holds of Durand 1½ hides. It is and was worth 20s.

LIIII. The land of Drogo fitzPons

IN "BLACHELAUE" HUNDRED

DROGO fitzPons holds FRAMPTON ON SEVERN of the king. There are 10 hides paying geld. Earnsige held it. In demesne are 3 ploughs; and 10 villans and 8 bordars with 6 ploughs. There are 9 slaves, and a mill rendering 10s, and 10 acres of meadow, [and] woodland 1 league long and 3 furlongs broad. In Gloucester, 1 burgess paying 6d. It is and was worth 100s. Of this manor Roger de Lacy holds 1 hide unjustly.

IN 'BRIGHTWELLS BARROW' HUNDRED

The same Drogo holds EASTLEACH MARTIN. There are 10 hides paying geld. Cola held it. In demesne are 4 ploughs; and 15 villans and 4 bordars with 9 ploughs. There are 9 slaves, and a mill rendering 10s, and 10 acres of meadow. It was worth £8; now £10.

LV. The land of Walter fitzPons

IN 'BRIGHTWELLS BARROW' HUNDRED

WALTER fitzPons holds SOUTHROP of the king. There are 10 hides paying geld. Earl Tosti held it. In demesne are 4 ploughs; and 16 villans and 6 bordars and a priest with 8 ploughs. There are 12 slaves, and a mill rendering 10s, and 20 acres of meadow. It was worth £12; now £15.

[Folio 169: GLOUCESTERSHIRE]

LVI. The land of Walter fitzRoger

IN BARRINGTON HUNDRED

WALTER fitzRoger holds GREAT BARRINGTON of the king. There are 8 hides. [...] Thorsten and Eadwig held it as 2 manors. In demesne are 4 ploughs; and 14 villans and a priest and 2 bordars with 9 ploughs. There are 14 slaves, and a mill rendering 10s, and 20 acres of meadow. It is and was worth £8.

IN "GERSDONES" HUNDRED

The same Walter holds SOUTH CERNEY. There are 14 hides and 1 virgate. Archbishop Stigand held it. In demesne are 2 ploughs; and 25 villans and a priest and 9 bordars with 10 ploughs. There are 4 slaves, and 100 acres of meadow, and there were 3 mills rendering 30s. It was worth £16; now £12.

This manor is claimed for the Church of ST MARY of Abingdon, but the whole shire bore witness that Archbishop Stigand had held it for 10 years while King Edward was alive. Earl William gave this manor to Roger the sheriff, the father of Walter.

LVII. The land of Walter the Deacon

IN 'WITLEY' HUNDRED

WALTER the deacon holds SEZINCOTE of the king. There are 4½ hides. Godwine held it and could go where he would. In demesne [are] 2 ploughs; and 8 villans with 6 ploughs, and 10 slaves. It is and was worth £3.

LVIII. The land of Walter the Crossbowman

IN WESTBURY HUNDRED

WALTER the crossbowman holds BULLEY of the king. There are 4 hides paying geld. Tovi held it of King Edward. In demesne are 2 ploughs; and 4 villans and 6 bordars with 4 ploughs. There are 4 slaves, and 10 acres of meadow. In Gloucester 1 burgess pays 18d. It was worth 60s; now 40s.

The same Walter holds RUDDLE. There is 1 hide paying geld. Tovi held it. In demesne is 1 plough; and 2 villans and 4 bordars with 2 ploughs. It was worth 40s; now 10s.

IN BLEDISLOE HUNDRED

The same Walter holds half a hide which does not pay geld. Palli held it. There is a mill. It is worth 19s.

IN 'LANGLEY' HUNDRED

The same Walter holds FRAMPTON COTTERELL. There are 5 hides paying geld. Ælfstan of Boscombe held it. In demesne is 1 plough; and 10 villans and 11 bordars with 5 ploughs. There are 5 slaves, and 2 mills rendering 5s. And there is a church which was not [there before]. It was worth £8; now £3.

LIX. The land of Henry de Ferrers

IN 'BRIGHTWELLS BARROW' HUNDRED

HENRY de Ferrers holds LECHLADE. Siward Barn held it. There were 15 hides TRE paying geld. But the king himself granted 6 hides quit of geld. The whole shire bears witness to this, and the man himself who bore the king's seal. In demesne are 4 ploughs; and 29 villans and 10 bordars and 1 Frenchman holding the land of 1 villan. Among them all they have 16 ploughs. There are 13 slaves, and 3 mills rendering 30s, and a fishery rendering 200 eels, less 25. From the meadows, £7.7s, besides the hay for the oxen. In Winchcombe 2 burgesses pay 16d, and 1 in Gloucester pays nothing. The whole manor was worth £20 TRE; and now the same.

LX. The land of Ernulf de Hesdin

IN 'BRIGHTWELLS BARROW' HUNDRED

ERNULF de Hesdin holds KEMPSFORD. There are 21 hides paying geld. Asgot held it of Earl Harold. In demesne are 6 ploughs; and 38 villans and 9 bordars and 1 radknight with 18 ploughs. There are 14 slaves, and 4 mills rendering 40s. and 40d, and from the meadows £9 besides pasture for the oxen, and from the sheep-fold 120 weys of cheese. In

Gloucester 7 burgesses pay 2s. The whole was worth £30 TRE; now £66.6s8d.

The same Ernulf holds in HATHEROP. There are 7 hides. Wulfweard White held it. In demesne are 6 ploughs; and 23 villans with 10 ploughs. There are 12 slaves, and a mill rendering 15s. It was worth £8; now £12.

IN "GERSDONES" HUNDRED

The same Ernulf holds in 'AMPNEY ST NICHOLAS' 4 hides and 2½ virgates. Alric and Godric held them as 2 manors. [...] In demesne are 3 ploughs; and 7 villans and 2 bordars with 2 ploughs. There are 4 slaves. The whole was and is worth £6.

IN "GRIMBOLDESTOU" HUNDRED

The same Ernulf holds OLDBURY ON THE HILL. There are 5 hides paying geld. Eadric held it. In demesne are 3 ploughs; and 4 villans with 4 ploughs, and there are 9 slaves, and 1 Frenchman having 1 plough. There are 6 acres of meadow. It is and was worth £10.

The same Ernulf holds BADMINTON. There are 4 hides paying geld. Eadric held it. In demesne are 2 ploughs; and 6 villans and 8 bordars with a priest have 13 ploughs. There are 9 slaves, and 8 acres of meadow. It is and was worth £10.

The same Ernulf holds ACTON TURVILLE. There are 5 hides paying geld. Eadric held it. In demesne are 3 ploughs; and 4 villans and 3 bordars with 4 ploughs. There are 15 acres of meadow. It is and was worth 100s.

IN 'SWINESHEAD' HUNDRED

The same Ernulf holds HANHAM, and Humbald [holds] of him. Eadric held it. There is half a hide [...]. In demesne are 2 ploughs, with 8 bordars and 4 slaves. It is and was worth 40s.

LXI. The land of Harold son of Earl Ralph

HAROLD son of Earl Ralph holds SUDELEY of the king. Ralph his father held it. There are 10 hides paying geld. In demesne are 4 ploughs; and 18 villans and 8 bordars with 13 ploughs. There are 14 slaves and female slaves all together, and 6 mills rendering 52s, [and] woodland 3 leagues long and 2 broad.

The same Harold holds TODDINGTON. His father held it. There are 10 hides paying geld. In demesne are 3 ploughs; and 17 villans and 7 bordars and 2 free men have among them all 8 ploughs. There are 10 slaves and female slaves all together, and 2 mills rendering 20s. From 1 salt-pan, 50 mittae of salt. These 2 manors are and were worth £40.

LXII. The land of Hugh de Grandmesnil

IN "CELFLEDETORN" HUNDRED

HUGH de Grandmesnil holds PEBWORTH [Worcs.]. There are 2 hides and 1 virgate. 2 thegns held it as 2 manors. There are 3 ploughs, and 1 villan and 1 bordar and 7 slaves.

The same Hugh holds BROAD MARSTON [Worcs.]. There are 2 hides [...].

The same Hugh holds UPPER QUINTON [War.]. There are 2 hides. 1 thegn held it. In demesne [are] 2 ploughs; and 5 villans and 1 bordar with 3 ploughs. There are 4 slaves and 1 female slave. They were worth £7; now £4.

The same Hugh holds LOWER QUINTON [War.], and Roger [holds] of him. There are 12 hides. Baldwin held it TRE. In demesne [are] 3 ploughs; and 17 villans and 2 bordars with 9 ploughs. There are 6 slaves. It was worth £7; now £6.

The same Hugh holds WESTON-ON-AVON [War.], and Roger [holds] of him. There are 4 hides. Baldwin held it. In demesne [are] 2 ploughs; and 6 villans with 3 ploughs. There are 4 slaves and 5 female slaves, and a mill rendering 10s. It was worth £7; now £6.

The same Hugh holds WILLICOTE [Willicote and Little Willicote, War.], and his clerk [holds] of him. There are 2½ hides. In demesne [are] 2 ploughs; and 2 villans and 1 bordar with 1 plough. There are 4 slaves and 1 female slave. It was worth 40s; now 30[s]. Leofric held it.

LXIII. The land of Hugh l'Asne

IN 'DUDSTONE' HUNDRED

HUGH l'Asne holds of the king BROCKWORTH. There are 5 hides. Thorkil held it of King Edward. In demesne are 2 ploughs; and 8 villans and 6 bordars and a priest and 2 free men and a reeve. Among them all they have 15 ploughs. There are 4 slaves, and a mill rendering 2s, [and] woodland 1 league long and a half broad. It was worth £6; now 100s.

The same Hugh holds SHIPTON SOLERS. There are 5 hides paying geld. Wulfweard held it. In demesne are 2 ploughs; and 4 villans and 1 bordar with 2 ploughs. There are 5 slaves, and a mill rendering 10s. It was worth £4; now £3.

IN 'BRADLEY' HUNDRED

The same Hugh holds SALPERTON. There are 10 hides paying geld. Wulfweard held it. In demesne are 3 ploughs; and 10 villans and a priest with 7 ploughs, and 11 slaves and female slaves all together, and 5 acres of meadow. It was worth £9; now £7.

| IN CIRENCESTER HUNDRED |

The same Hugh holds BAGENDON, and Gilbert [holds] of him. There are 3 hides paying geld. Wulfweard held it. In demesne are 3 ploughs; and 5 villans with 3 ploughs, and 6 slaves, and a mill rendering 10s, and 8 acres of meadow. It is and was worth £4.

LXI. The land of Miles Crispin

IN 'DUDSTONE' HUNDRED

MILES Crispin holds in BRAWN 3 virgates of land. Vigot held them. [...] In demesne [is] 1 plough; and 7 bordars with 2 ploughs, and half a fishery. It was worth 40s; now 30s.

IN LONGTREE HUNDRED

The same Miles holds CHERINGTON, and Geoffrey [holds] of him. Hemming held it of King Edward. There are 2 hides paying geld. In demesne are 3 ploughs; and 3 villans and 8 bordars with 3½ ploughs. There are 12 slaves, and a mill rendering 30d, and 4 acres of meadow. It is and was worth £4.

IN "GRIMBOLDESTOU" HUNDRED

The same Miles holds ALDERLEY. Vigot held it. There is 1 hide. In demesne are 2 ploughs; and 7 villans and 5 bordars with 7 ploughs. There are 4 slaves, and a mill rendering 10s, and 12 acres of meadow. It is and was worth 100s.

LXII. The land of Urse d'Abetot

IN 'WITLEY' HUNDRED

URSE of Worcester holds in SEZINCOTE 1 hide. Alwine held it as a manor, and it paid geld. In demesne [is] 1 plough, and 4 slaves. It was worth 40s; now 10s.

LXIII. The land of Hascoit Musard

IN 'WITLEY' HUNDRED

HASCOIT Musard holds of the king SAINTBURY. Cynewig Chelle held it. There are 10 hides. In demesne [are] 3 ploughs; and 18 villans and 3 bordars with 9 ploughs, and 10 slaves and female slaves all together, and a mill rendering 6d. It was worth £12; now £10.

The same Hascoit holds 1 hide in SEZINCOTE, and it pays geld. Wulfwine held it as a manor. There is 1 plough, and 1 bordar. It is and was worth 10s.

IN SALMONSBURY HUNDRED

The same Hascoit holds EYFORD. There are 5 hides paying geld. Earnsige held it. In demesne are 2 ploughs; and 12 villans and 1 bordar with 5 ploughs. All together there are 8 slaves and female slaves. It is worth £4.

IN 'GRESTON' HUNDRED

The same Hascoit holds ASTON SOMERVILLE [Worcs.]. There are 6 hides paying geld. Earnsige held it. In demesne are 3 ploughs; and 12 villans with 4 ploughs, and 9 slaves and female slaves all together. There is a mill rendering 8s, and 20 acres of meadow. It is and was worth £6.

IN CIRENCESTER HUNDRED

The same Hascoit holds UPPER SIDDINGTON. There are 10 hides paying geld, besides the demesne. Earnsige held it. In demesne are 3 ploughs; and 8 villans and 10 bordars with a priest having 5½ ploughs. There are 7 slaves, and 20 acres of meadow. It was worth £10; now £8.

IN BISLEY HUNDRED

The same Hascoit holds MISERDEN. There is 1 hide paying geld. Earnsige held it. In demesne are 3 ploughs; and 8 villans and 5 bordars and a priest and 1 radknight. Among them all they have 9 ploughs. There are 10 slaves, and 8 acres of meadow, [and] woodland 1 league long and a half broad. It was worth 100s; now £7.

LXIIII. The land of Turstin fitzRolf

IN "GERSDONES" HUNDRED

TURSTIN fitzRolf holds of the king AMPNEY CRUCIS. There are 7 hides. Tovi held it of King Edward. In demesne are 3 ploughs; and 8 villans and a priest with 8 ploughs. There are 8 slaves. Of this land Tovi holds the land of 2 villans, and a certain knight the land of 4 villans. Half a hide and 4 acres of meadow belong to the church. It was worth £8; now £6.

In the same place Turstin himself holds 1 hide. Wulfwig held it as a manor and could go where he would. In demesne [are] 2 ploughs, with 1 bordar. It was worth 40s.

IN CIRENCESTER HUNDRED

The same Turstin holds in COATES 1 hide. Beorhtric held it as a manor of King Edward. In demesne is 1 plough; and 3 villans with 3 ploughs. There are 6 slaves, and 4 acres of meadow. It is and was worth 50s. Gerwy holds it of Turstin.

IN "GRIMBOLDESTOU" HUNDRED

The same Turstin holds HILLESLEY, and Bernard [holds] of him. There is 1 hide. Ælfric held it. In demesne are 2 ploughs; and 5 half-villans and 7 bordars with 2 ploughs. There are 8 slaves, and 3 mills rendering 18s, and 8 acres of meadow. It was worth 40s; now 60s.

IN BAGSTONE HUNDRED

The same Turstin holds TORTWORTH. There is 1 hide. Alweald held it. In demesne are 2 ploughs; and 6 villans and 7 bordars with 7 ploughs. There are 6 slaves, and 3 mills rendering 15s, and 10 acres of meadow. Woodland 1 league long and a half broad renders 5s. It was worth £7; now 100s.

IN "BLACHELAUE" HUNDRED

The same Turstin holds KING'S STANLEY. There are 5 hides. Tovi held it of King Edward. In demesne are 2 ploughs; and 8 villans and 6 bordars with 10 ploughs. There are 4 slaves, and 2 mills rendering 35s, and 10 acres of meadow, [and] woodland 1 league long and a half broad. It is and was worth 100s. Tovi holds 2 hides of this land in alms of King William.

The same Turstin holds FRETHERNE. Auti held it. There are 3 hides paying geld. In demesne is 1 plough; and 3 villans and 3 bordars with 2 ploughs, and 1 slave. It was worth 60s; now 30s.

LXV. The land of Ansfrid de Cormeilles

IN BISLEY HUNDRED

ANSFRID de Cormeilles holds WINSTONE. There are 5 hides. Wulfweard held it. In demesne are 3 ploughs; and 10 villans and 4 bordars and 1 Frenchman with 8 ploughs. There are 8 slaves, and a mill rendering 20d. It is and was worth £7.

IN "CELFLEDETORN" HUNDRED

The same Ansfrid holds WESTON-SUB-EDGE. 2 thegns held it, one the man of Earl Harold, the other of Leofric. There are 10 hides [held] as 2 manors, and [the men] could go where they would. In demesne [are] 4 ploughs; and 18 villans and 1 bordar with 9 ploughs, and 12 slaves. They were worth 100s; now £7.

The same Ansfrid holds 5 hides in BURNT NORTON. 2 thegns held them as 2 manors and they could go where they would. In demesne [are] 4 ploughs; and 9 villans and 2 bordars with 4 ploughs, and 10 slaves. They were worth £4; now £6.

IN 'WITLEY' HUNDRED

The same Ansfrid holds BATSFORD. Beorhtmær held it. There are 3 hides. In demesne [are] 3 ploughs; and 10 villans with 6 ploughs, and 16 slaves, and 1 man rendering 6 plough-shares. It was worth £8; now £6.

IN 'GRESTON' HUNDRED

The same Ansfrid holds POSTLIP. Godric held it. There are 3 hides paying geld. In demesne are 2 ploughs; and 3 villans and 5 bordars with 2 ploughs. There are 11 slaves, and 2 mills rendering 15s, [and] woodland 1 league long and 1 broad. It was worth 100s; now £4.

IN "WACRESCUMBE" HUNDRED

The same Ansfrid holds in SHIPTON SOLERS 3 virgates of land. Bil held it as a manor, and it paid geld. In demesne is 1 plough. It is and was worth 10s. This Bil could go where he would.

IN 'BRADLEY' HUNDRED

The same Ansfrid holds WINSON. Eadric and Leofric and Alric held it as 3 manors and could go where they would. There are 5 hides paying geld. In demesne are 4 ploughs; and 9 villans and 4 bordars with 5 ploughs. There are 10 slaves and female slaves all together, and a mill rendering 7s6d, and 15 acres of meadow. It was worth £8; now £7.

IN CIRENCESTER HUNDRED

The same Ansfrid holds 1 hide in DUNTISBOURNE ABBOTS. Almær held it as a manor and could go where he would. In demesne is 1 plough, and 1 villan and 2 bordars and 5 female slaves. It was worth 40s; now 20s.

IN RAPSGATE HUNDRED

The same Ansfrid holds ELKSTONE. 2 Leofwines held it as 2 manors. There are 4½ hides, and in COLESBOURNE 1½ hides. Alwine held them as a manor, and these 3 thegns could go where they would. [...] In demesne are 2 ploughs; and 5 villans and 2 bordars with 3½ ploughs. There are 4 slaves, and 10 acres of meadow, [and] woodland half a league long and 2 furlongs broad.

1 knight holds half of this manor of Ansfrid, and has 2 ploughs there, and 5 villans and 2 bordars with 3 ploughs.

And another knight holds Colesbourne of him, and has half a plough there, and [there are] 2 villans and 2 bordars with 1 plough, and a mill rendering 50d. This was worth £8; now £7.10s.

The same Ansfrid holds SYDE, and Turstin [holds] of him. Leofwine held it of King Edward. There are 3 hides paying geld. In demesne are 2 ploughs; and 1 villan with a priest and 3 bordars with 1 plough, and 6 slaves, and 4 acres of meadow. It was worth £4; now 40s.

The same Ansfrid holds 2½ virgates in DUNTISBOURNE ABBOTS, and Bernard [holds] of him. Almær held them as a manor and could go where he would. There is 1 bordar. It is and was worth 4s.

[Folio 170: GLOUCESTERSHIRE]

The same Ansfrid holds PAUNTLEY, 1½ hides, and KILCOT, 1 hide, and KETFORD, 1 hide, and HAYES, 1 hide. All together [there are] 4½ hides. Wulfhelm and Alweard and Wicga held them as 4 manors. 1½ hides [are] free from geld. [...] In demesne are 2 ploughs; and 7 villans and 3 bordars with 7 ploughs. There are 2 slaves, and a mill rendering 7s6d. It was worth £3.10s; now £4. Those who held these lands could go where they would.

These lands, and WINSTONE and DUNTISBOURNE ABBOTS, entered above, Ansfrid had of Walter de Lacy when he married his niece. But the other lands he holds of the king.

LXIX. The land of Humphrey the Chamberlain

IN 'WITLEY' HUNDRED

HUMPHREY the chamberlain holds of the king LONGBOROUGH. There are 4 hides paying geld. Alstan and Blæcmann and Eadric and Alric held it as 4 manors and could go there they would. In demesne were 4 ploughs; and 3 villans and 5 bordars with 3 ploughs. There are 9 slaves. It was worth £16; now 100s.

IN "GERSDONES" HUNDRED

The same Humphrey holds in AMPNEY CRUCIS 1 hide. Alwig held it of King Edward as a manor. In demesne [are] 2 ploughs, and 4 slaves and 1 bordar, and a mill rendering 5s. It is and was worth 25s.

IN CIRENCESTER HUNDRED

The same Humphrey holds 1 hide in PRESTON [near Cirencester]. Alwine held it as a manor. In demesne is 1 plough and 2 slaves; and 3 bordars with 1 plough. It is and was worth 30s. The man who held it could go where he would.

The same Humphrey holds 1 hide in NORCOTE. Alweard held it as a manor. In demesne are 2 ploughs; and 2 bordars with half a plough. It is and was worth 40s. William holds these 2 estates of Humphrey. Those who held them could go where they would.

The same Humphrey holds 2 hides in SIDDINGTON, and Ansketil [holds] of him. Alweard held them as a manor. In demesne is 1 plough; and 2 bordars with half a plough, and a mill rendering 5s. It is and was worth 40s. The man who held them could go where he would.

IN BAGSTONE HUNDRED

The same Humphrey holds IRON ACTON. Harold held it, the man of Alwig Hiles, who could go where he would. There are $2\frac{1}{2}$ hides. In demesne is 1 plough; and 3 villans and 3 bordars with half a plough. There are 2 slaves, and $1\frac{1}{2}$ mills rendering 64d, and 5 acres of meadow. It is and was worth 40s.

The same Humphrey holds WICKWAR. There are 4 hides. 3 men of Beorhtric son of Ælfgar held it TRE and could go where they would. In demesne were 3 ploughs; and 9 villans and 14 bordars with 9 ploughs. There are 5 slaves, and 20 acres of meadow and 6 furlongs of woodland. It was and is worth £12.

The queen gave Humphrey these 2 vills, Iron Acton and Wickwar.

IN "GERSDONES" HUNDRED

The same Humphrey holds 1 virgate of land in ASHBROOK, and William [holds] of him. Alwine held it as a manor. There is 1 villan. It is and was worth 2s.

LXX. The land of Humphrey of Maidenhill

IN 'DUDSTONE' HUNDRED

HUMPHREY of Maidenhill holds UPTON ST LEONARDS. Paganus held it. There is 1 hide. In demesne [is] 1 plough and 3 slaves; and 4 bordars with 2 ploughs. It was worth 30s; now 20s.

IN 'WITLEY' HUNDRED

The same Humphrey holds 1 hide in SEZINCOTE. Alwig held it as a manor, and it paid geld. In demesne were 2 ploughs and 6 slaves, and 1 bordar, and it was worth 50s; now only 12d because of the meadows.

LXXI. [The land] of Humphrey the Cook

IN SALMONSBURY HUNDRED

HUMPHREY the cook holds in LATTON [Wilts]. 1 hide, and has 1 plough there, with 4 bordars, and it is worth 15s, and it pays geld. Osbern of Cherbourg held it. Ordric held it as a manor TRE.

LXXII. The land of Sigar de Chocques

IN 'HOLFORD' HUNDRED

SIGAR de Chocques holds of the king HAWLING. Countess Gode held it. There are 10 hides paying geld. In demesne are 3 ploughs, and 20 villans and 5 bordars with 9 bordars [sic]. There are 6 slaves and 3 female slaves. There is woodland. It was worth £7; now £8.

IN 'BRADLEY' HUNDRED

The same Sigar holds HAZLETON [near Andoversford]. Gode held it. There are 10 hides. King William granted 3 of these hides quit of geld, as the shire attests. In demesne are 3 ploughs; and 14 villans and a priest with 10 ploughs. There are 6 slaves. It was worth £8; now £7.

The same Sigar holds YANWORTH. Gode held it. There are 5 hides. 3 of these are quit of geld by [grant of] King William, as Sigar's man says. In demesne are 3 ploughs; and 14 villans and 2 bordars with 7 ploughs. There are 7 slaves, and a mill rendering 40d, [and] woodland 3 furlongs long and 2 broad. It was worth £7; now £6.

LXXIII. The land of Matthew de Mortagne

IN LONGTREE HUNDRED

MATTHEW de Mortagne holds of the king SHIPTON MOYNE. Strang the Dane held it. There are 10 hides paying geld. In demesne are 2 ploughs; and 4 villans and 2 bordars with 4 ploughs. There are 4 slaves, and a mill rendering 10s. From the pasture, 2s. It was worth £15; now £8.

The same Matthew holds SHIPTON MOYNE, and Rumbald [holds] of him. There are 10 hides paying geld. John held it TRE. In demesne are 3 ploughs; and 4 villans and 8 bordars with 4 ploughs. There are 4 slaves, and a mill rendering 12s. From the pasture, 2s. It was worth £15; now £8.

The same Matthew holds 1 hide there, and Rumbald [holds] of him. Alwine held it and could go where he would, and afterwards Reinbert the Fleming had it. In demesne is 1 plough; and 1 villan and 1 bordar with half a plough. It was worth 20s; now 14s.

LXIIII. The land of Joscelin the Breton

IN BAGSTONE HUNDRED

JOSCELIN the Breton holds of the king CHARFIELD. Ælfhild held it of King Edward. There are 3 hides. In demesne are 2 ploughs; and 4 villans and 7 bordars with 4 ploughs. There are 4 slaves, and a mill rendering 10s, and 8 acres of meadow, [and] woodland half a league long and wide. It was worth £4; now 40s.

LXXV. The land of Roger fitzRalph

IN 'SWINESHEAD' HUNDRED

ROGER fitzRalph holds 1 manor, called CLIFTON [in Bristol], which Sæwine, reeve of Bristol, held of King Edward, and he could go where he would with this land, nor did he give any farm for it. There are 3 hides. In demesne are 3 ploughs; and 6 villans and 6 bordars with 2 ploughs. There are 3 slaves, and 8 acres of meadow. It was worth 100s; now 60s.

IN 'SWINESHEAD' HUNDRED

Roger has 1 manor of 1 hide of land and he has 2 slaves there. This is valued at 10s. There has been no one to answer for this land.

Walter has 1 manor of 1 virgate of land. It was worth 20d; now 2s.

LXXVI. The land of the wife of Gerwy

IN 'HOLFORD' HUNDRED

THE WIFE OF GERWY de Loges holds of the king 4 hides in TEMPLE GUITING. 3 thegns, Wulffrith, Tovi and Thorbiorn, held it as 3 manors, and it paid geld. In demesne is 1 plough; and 1 villan with half a plough. It was worth 40s; now 20s.

LXXVII.

IN "GERSDONES" HUNDRED

BALDWIN holds of the king 3 virgates of land in AMPNEY CRUCIS. Alwine held them TRE. There is 1 plough, with 2 bordars. It is and was worth 10s.

[Folio 170V: GLOUCESTERSHIRE]

LXVIII. The Lands of the King's Thegns

IN BARRINGTON HUNDRED

ÆLFSIGE of Faringdon holds of the king 3½ hides in WINDRUSH. Wulfric and Tovi and Leofwine held them as 3 manors and could go where they would. In demesne are 5 ploughs; and 1 villan and 7 bordars with 1 plough. There are 10 slaves, and 1½ mills rendering 12s6d. It was worth £3; now £8.

IN "GERSDONES" HUNDRED

KETIL holds of the king 1 hide and 1 virgate in WINDRUSH. He himself held them TRE. There is 1 plough, and 4 slaves. It is and was worth 20s.

IN RAPSGATE HUNDRED

The same Ketil holds 3½ virgates in DUNTISBOURNE ABBOTS. He himself held them TRE. There is 1 plough, and 2 bordars and 2 slaves. It was worth 10s; now 15[s].

IN LONGTREE HUNDRED

OSWEARD holds of the king RODMARTON. There are 3 virgates paying geld. He himself held it TRE. There is 1 plough. It was worth 20s; now 10s.

IN CIRENCESTER HUNDRED

EADRIC son of Ketil holds BAUNTON of the king. His father held it TRE. There are 3 hides and 3 virgates paying geld. In demesne are 2 ploughs; and 3 villans with 1 plough, and 4 slaves, and 15 acres of meadow. It is and was worth 60s.

IN 'DUDSTONE' HUNDRED

EDWARD holds of the king half a hide as a manor, and has there in demesne 1 plough; and 6 bordars with 2 ploughs. It is worth 30s.

IN "CELFLEDETORN" HUNDRED

EDITH holds of the king BICKMARSH [Worcs.]. She herself held it TRE. There is 1 hide, and in demesne 2 ploughs, and 1 villan and 1 bordar and 4 slaves. It is and was worth 20s.

IN SALMONSBURY HUNDRED

CWENHILD the nun holds of the king 9 hides in NAUNTON [near Bourton-on-the- Water]. Of these, 4 hides paid geld. Æthelmær held them as a manor. In demesne are 4 ploughs; and 7 villans with 5 ploughs, and now 1 plough is reckoned [there], and [there is] a mill rendering 5s, and 13 slaves and female slaves all together. It was worth £8; now £5.

IN CHELTENHAM HUNDRED

BEORHTRIC holds of the king 4 hides in LECKHAMPTON, and it pays geld. He himself [held] 2 hides TRE and Ordric held the other 2. King William, when he was setting out for Normandy, gave them both to the same Beorhtric. In demesne he has 1 plough; and 9 bordars with 3 ploughs, and 2 slaves and 1 female slave. [There is] woodland 2 furlongs long and 2 broad. It is worth 30s.

IN 'HOLFORD' HUNDRED

ALWEALD holds of the king PINNOCK. He himself held it TRE. There are 4 hides. One of these did not pay geld. In demesne are 4 ploughs; and 11 villans and 5 bordars with 4 ploughs. There are 8 slaves, and a mill rendering 30d. In Winchcombe 1 burgess pays 8d. [There is] woodland half a league long and 1 furlong broad. It is and was worth £4.

IN BIBURY HUNDRED

ALWEARD son of Regenbald holds ALDSWORTH. Balki held it. There are 2 hides paying geld. In demesne is 1 plough; and 4 villans and 2 bordars with 2 ploughs, and 1 slave. It was worth 40s; now 30s.

IN 'WHITSTONE' HUNDRED

ÆLFSIGE holds of the king LONGNEY. There are 5 hides paying geld. He himself held it TRE. In demesne are 2 ploughs; and 6 villans and 12 bordars with 9 ploughs. There are 4 slaves, and 10 acres of meadow and a fishery. It was worth 100s; now 60s.

IN 'SWINESHEAD' HUNDRED

DUNS holds of the king BITTON. He himself held it TRE. There are 2 hides. One of these paid geld, the other belonged to the church. In demesne are 2 ploughs; and 5 villans and 2 bordars with 5 ploughs. There are 4 slaves, and 10 acres of meadow. It was worth £6; now £3.

IN "BLACHELAUE" HUNDRED

BEORHTRIC holds of the king WOODCHESTER. He himself held it TRE. There is 1 hide paying geld. There are 16 villans and 12 bordars with 16 ploughs. [There is] nothing in demesne. In Gloucester 1 burgess renders 20 [pieces of] iron. There is a mill rendering 10s. It is and was worth 100s.

HEARDING holds in pledge from Beorhtric WHEATENHURST. Beorhtric himself held it TRE. There are 5 hides paying geld. In demesne is 1 plough; and a priest and 2 villans and 6 bordars with 5 ploughs. There are 3 slaves, and a mill rendering 10s, and 10 acres of meadow. It was worth 100s; now 30s.

EADRIC son of Ketil holds ALKERTON. His father held it TRE. There are 4½ hides paying geld. In demesne is 1 plough; and 6 villans and 4 bordars with 8 ploughs. There are 3 slaves, and a mill rendering 10s, and 10 acres of meadow. [There is] woodland 1 league long and a half broad. It is and was worth £3.

IN BOTLOE HUNDRED

MATOC holds of the king RUDFORD. He himself held it TRE. There are 2 hides. [...] In demesne [are] 2 ploughs; and 3 villans and 4 bordars with 3 ploughs, and a mill rendering as much grain as it is possible to make a profit from. It is and was worth 40s.

WORCESTERSHIRE

IN THE CITY OF WORCESTER, KING EDWARD HAD this customary due: when the coinage was changed, each moneyer gave 20s at London for receiving the dies for the coinage. When the shire paid geld, the city was reckoned at 15 hides. From the same city the king himself had £10 and Earl Edwin £8. The king took no other customary due there except the rent on the houses according to the liability of each.

Now King William has in demesne both the king's part and the earl's part. Thence the sheriff pays £23.5s by weight, for the city; and for the demesne manors of the king he pays £123.4s by weight. For the shire he pays £17 by weight; and he further pays £10 of pennies, at 20 to the ora, or a Norway hawk; [...] and to the queen also 100s by tale; and 20s, at 20[d] to the ora, for a sumpter horse. These £17 by weight and £16 by tale are for the pleas of the shire and for the hundreds, and if he does not receive [so much] thence, he pays it out of his own [means].

In this shire are 12 hundreds; 7 of these are so quit, the shire says, that the sheriff has no [rights] in them, and therefore, as he says, he loses much on the farm.

In this shire, if anyone has wittingly broken the peace which the king has given with his own hand, he is adjudged an outlaw; but if anyone has wittingly broken the king's peace which the sheriff gives, he shall pay a fine of 100s. He who has committed highway robbery shall pay a fine of 100s; he who has committed house-breaking 100s; [for him] who has committed rape, there should be no other emendation but corporal punishment. These forfeitures the king has in this shire except in the land of [the Abbey of] St Peter of Westminster, to which King Edward gave all his [rights] there, as the shire says.

When the king marches against the enemy, if anyone summoned by his edict says behind, if he is a man so free that he has his soke and sake, and can go where he will with his land, he is at the king's mercy with all his land; but if the free man of another lord stays away from the enemy, and his lord takes another man in his place, he who was summoned shall pay a fine of 40s to his lord. If, however, no one at all goes in his place, he himself shall give 40s to his lord, and his lord shall pay a fine of as many shillings to the king.

Here Are Entered the Holders of land In Worcestershire

I KING WILLIAM
II The Church of Worcester
III The Bishop of Hereford
IIII The Church of Saint-Denis
V The Church of Coventry
VI The Church of Cormeilles
VII The Church of Gloucester
VIII The Church of Westminster
IX The Church of Pershore
X The Church of Evesham
XI The Bishop of Bayeux
XII The Church of St Guthlac
XIII The clerks of Wolverhampton
XIIII Earl Roger
XV Ralph de Tosny
XVI Ralph de Mortimer
XVII Robert of Stafford
XVIII Roger de Lacy
XIX Osbern fitzRichard
XX Gilbert fitzTurold
XXI Drogo fitzPons
XXII Harold son of Ralph
XXIII William fitzAnsculf
XXIIII William fitzCorbucion
XXV William Goizenboded
XXVI Urse d'Abetot
XXVII Hugh l'Asne
XXVIII Ealdgifu

The land of the King

King William holds in demesne BROMSGROVE with 18 berewicks: Moseley [War.], King's Norton [War.], 'Lindsworth' [in Birmingham, War.], Wythall, Wythwood, Houndsfield, 'Tessall' [in Birmingham, War.], Rednal [War.], Lea Green, 'Comble' [in Bromsgrove], Burcot, Ashborough, Tutnall, 'Tynsall' [in Tutnall and Cobley], Fockbury, 'Shurvenhill', Woodcote [Woodcote and Woodcote Green], Timberhonger. Among them all, together with the manor, are 30 hides. Earl Edwin held this manor TRE.

In demesne are now 2 ploughs; and 20 villans and a reeve and a beadle with a priest and 92 bordars; among them all they have 77 ploughs. There are 9 slaves and 1 female slave, and 3 mills rendering 13s4d. [There is] woodland 7 leagues long and 4 leagues wide, and there are 4 eyries of hawks. To this manor belong 13 salt-pans in Droitwich and 3 salt-workers rendering from these salt-pans 300 mittae of salt, for which they were given 300 cart-loads of wood by the keepers of the woodland TRE. There are 6 leaden vats.

To this manor belonged, TRE, SUCKELY, a manor of 5 hides, but Earl William took it thence and put it in the farm of Hereford.

In all it rendered TRE a farm of £18. Urse the sheriff paid £24 by weight so long as he had the woodland.

To this manor belonged and belongs GRAFTON [near Bromsgrove], [where] there are 3½ hides, and COOKSEY [?Corner], [where] there are 2½ hides, and 'WILLINGWICK' [in Bromsgrove], [where] there are 2 hides and 3 virgates, and CHADWICH [in Bromsgrove], [where] there are 3 hides; in all 12 hides less 1 virgate.

These lands 5 thegns of Earl Edwin, Earngeat, Alwine, Beorhtræd, Frani, [and] Alweald, held; and they could not withdraw from the lord of the manor. Now 4 knights hold these lands of Urse the sheriff. Roger [holds] the 3½ hides, William the 2½ hides, Walter the 2 hides and 3 virgates, [and] Alvred the 3 hides.

In these lands are in demesne 5½ ploughs; and 1 radknight and 29 bordars having 11½ ploughs. There are 2 slaves and 6 oxmen, and 1 plough more can be there. In 'Willingwick' [in Bromsgrove] and Chadwich [in Bromsgrove] are 3 leagues of woodland, but the king has put them in his forest. In Droitwich, 1 salt-pan rendering 10s. In all it was worth TRE £6.13s; now 100s in all.

Of the land of the same manor William fitzAnsculf holds 3 virgates in 'Willingwick' [in Bromsgrove], and Baldwin [holds] of him. Wulfwine, a thegn of Earl Edwin, held it. There is 1 villan with half a plough, and 1½ ploughs more could be there. It was worth 5s; now 2s.

King William holds in demesne KIDDERMINSTER with 16 Berewicks: Wannerton, Trimpley, Hurcott, Franche, and another Franche, "Bristitune", [High and Low] Habberley, "Fastochesfelde", Wribbenhall, Ribbesford, and another Ribbesford, Sutton, Oldington, Lower Mitton, "Teulesberge", "Suduuale". In these lands, together with the manor, there are 20 hides. The whole of this manor was waste. In demesne is 1 plough; and 20 villans and 30 bordars with 18 ploughs, and 20 ploughs more can be there. There are 2 slaves and 4 female slaves; and 2 mills rendering 16s, and 2 salt-pans rendering 30s, and a fishery rendering 100d. [There are] 4 leagues of woodland. In this manor the reeve holds the land of 1 radknight, and has there 1 plough, and 1 mill rendering 5 orae. To this manor belong a house in Droitwich and another in Worcester rendering 10d.

The whole manor rendered TRE a farm of £14; it now renders £10.4s by weight. The king has put the woodland of this manor in his forest.

Of the land of this manor William holds 1 hide and the land of 1 radknight, and has there 1 villan and 8 bordars having 4½ ploughs. It is worth 11s.

Of the same land Aiulf holds 1 virgate. There is 1 plough, and 2 slaves. It is worth 2s.

In DROITWICH King Edward had 11 houses, and in 5 brine-pits King Edward had his share. In 1 brine-pit, 'Upwich' [in Droitwich], 54 salt-pans and 2 hocci render 6s8d. In another brine-pit, Helpridge, 17 salt-pans. In a third brine-pit, 'Middlewich' [in Droitwich], 12 salt-pans and 2 parts of a hoccus render 6s8d. In 5 other brine-pits, 15 salt-pans.

From all these King Edward had a farm of £52.

[Folio 172V: WORCESTERSHIRE]

In these brine-pits Earl Edwin had 51½ salt-pans, and from the hocci he had 6s8d. All this rendered as farm £24. Now King William has in demesne both what King Edward and what Earl Edwin had. The sheriff paid thence £65 by weight and 2 mittae of salt while he had the woodland. For if he does not have the woodland, he says, he cannot possibly pay that [amount].

For KINVER [Staffs.] he pays 100s at 20[d] to the ora. This land is in Staffordshire, so also is KINGSWINFORD [Staffs.]. For this manor and 2 others which are in Worcestershire-that is, Tardebigge of 9 hides and Clent of 9 hides-for these 3 manors the sheriff pays £15 of pennies at 20 to the ora.

IN 'CAME' HUNDRED

King William holds TARDEBIGGE. King Edward held it. There are 9 hides. In demesne is 1 plough and another can be [there]. There are 2 villans and 28 bordars with 12 ploughs. In Droitwich are 7 salt-pans and 2 lead vats, and they render 20s and 100 mittae of salt.

The sheriff of Staffordshire receives, and pays in KINGSWINFORD [Staffs.], the farm of this manor, that is £11 of pennies at 20 to the ora.

IN CLENT HUNDRED

King William holds CLENT. King Edward held it. There are 9 hides. In demesne are 1½ ploughs; and 12 villans and 3 bordars with 9½ ploughs. There are 3 oxmen, and 2 leagues of woodland.

The farm of this manor, £4, is paid in KINGSWINFORD in Staffordshire.

In Droitwich is half a hide which belongs to the [King's] hall at Gloucester.

II. The land of the Church of Worcester

THE CHURCH OF ST MARY OF WORCESTER has a HUNDRED, called 'OSWALDSLOW', in which belong 300 hides. From these the bishop of that church has, by an arrangement of ancient times, all render from jurisdiction and all customary dues there belonging to his demesne sustenance, both the king's service and his own, so that no sheriff can have any claim there, either in any plea or in any other matter. The whole shire testifies to this. These said 300 hides were of the demesne itself of the church, and if any portion of them was allotted or leased to any man in whatever manner, for service to be done for it to the bishop, he who held that land on lease to him could not retain for himself any customary due from it whatsoever except by permission of the bishop, nor retain the land beyond the completion of the term agreed upon between them, nor could he betake himself anywhere with that land.

In this hundred the bishop of the same church holds KEMPSEY. There are 24 hides paying geld. Of these hides 5 hides are waste. In demesne are 2 ploughs; and 15 villans and 27 bordars with 16 ploughs. There is a priest, and 4 slaves and 2 female slaves, and 40 acres of meadow, [and] woodland 1 league long and half a league wide. In demesne are 13 hides. TRE it was worth £16; now £8.

Of this manor Urse the sheriff holds 3 BEREWICKS of 7 hides, Mucknell, Stoulton, Upper Wolverton. There are 7 ploughs, and 7 villans and 7 bordars and 7 slaves, and 16 acres of meadow. For these 3 estates farm was rendered TRE, for they were always for the sustenance [of the bishop]. They are worth 100s.

Of this manor Roger de Lacy holds 2 hides at Lower Wolverton, and Aiulf [holds] of him. They were in demesne TRE, and Æthelric was still holding them TRW and was rendering thence all the customary dues of the farm that his predecessors rendered except the peasant's labour on such terms as he could obtain from the reeve. There are 2 ploughs with 1 villan, and 2 slaves, and a mill rendering 40d. TRE it was worth 50s; now 40s.

Of the same manor Walter Ponther holds 2 hides at WHITTINGTON. They were in demesne TRE; Æthelric held them in the same manner as the above hides. In demesne are 2 ploughs and 4 slaves; and 3 villans and 7 bordars with 4 ploughs, and a fishery rendering 4s, and 12 acres of meadow. [There is] woodland 1 league long and a half wide. TRE it was worth 30s; now 40s.

In the same hundred the same bishop holds WICK EPISCOPI. There are 15 hides paying geld. In demesne are 4 hides less 1 virgate, and there are 4 ploughs; and 12 villans and 12 bordars with 12 ploughs, and 2 mills rendering 12s, and 2 fisheries rendering 6s8d, and 60 acres of meadow. [There is] woodland 2 leagues long and 1 league wide. TRE as now, worth £8.

Of this manor Urse the sheriff holds 5 hides at Holt. Æthelric held them in the above manner. In demesne are 2 ploughs; and 12 villans and 24 bordars with 10 ploughs, and a fishery rendering 5s, and in Droitwich 1 salt-pan rendering 13d, and 12 acres of meadow. [There is] woodland half a league long and as much wide. There is an enclosure.

The same Urse holds 1 hide at Little Witley, and Walter [holds] of him. In demesne is 1 plough; and a priest and 2 bordars with 1 plough. [There is] woodland 3 furlongs long

and 2 wide. Earnwine the priest held it [and] rendered to the church all the customary dues of the farm and 1 sester of honey. It is and was worth 10s.

The same Urse holds 1 hide at KENSWICK, and Walter [holds] of him. In demesne are 2 ploughs, and 6 bordars and 4 slaves. Wulfwine held it, rendering all the customary dues to the reeve of the farm. [There is] woodland half a league long and a half wide. TRE it was worth 20s; now 15s.

The same Urse holds 1 hide at 'CLOPTON' [in St John in Bedwardine]. In demesne is 1 plough, and 1 bordar, and 6 acres of meadow. Beorhtmær held it, rendering all [that] the above [tenants did]. TRE it was worth 20s; now 15s.

The same Urse holds 3 virgates at LAUGHERN [Temple Laughern and Lower Temple Laughern]. He has there in demesne 1 plough, and 2 bordars. Sæwine held it of the bishop's demesne. There are 6 acres of meadow. It was and is worth 7s. In the same place Urse has 1 virgate of the bishop's demesne. It is worth 6s.

The same Urse holds 1 hide at GREENHILL, and Godfrey [holds] of him. There 2 bordars have 1 plough. Edith held it, rendering what the above [tenants rendered]. It was and is worth 6s.

Of the same manor Robert Despenser holds half a hide at LAUGHERN [Temple Laughern and Lower Temple Laughern], and there he has 1 plough with 1 bordar, and a mill rendering 5s, and 6 acres of meadow and 12 oaks. Cyneweard held it and performed such service as the bishop willed. It was and is worth 20s.

Of this manor Osbern fitzRichard holds 1 hide at COTHERIDGE, and there he has 1 plough in demesne; and 6 villans and 4 bordars with 4 ploughs, and a mill rendering 5s. There are 12 acres of meadow and 3 furlongs of woodland. Richard held it by such service as the bishop willed. It was and is worth 40s.

In the same HUNDRED the same bishop holds FLADBURY. There are 40 hides paying geld. In demesne are 7 hides, and there are 9 ploughs; and a priest having half a hide, and 23 villans and 17 bordars with 19 ploughs. There are 16 slaves and 3 female slaves, and a mill rendering 10s and 20 sticks of eels, and 50 acres of meadow. [There is] woodland 2 leagues long and a half wide, from which the bishop has all its proceeds

[Folio 173: WORCESTERSHIRE]

in hunting and honey and wood for the salt-pans of Droitwich, and 4s. It was worth £10; now £9.

Of this manor the Bishop of Hereford holds 5 hides at INKBERROW, and there he has a priest and 7 villans with 4 ploughs, and meadow for the oxen. Bishop Walter held it TRE, [performing] all the service [due] to the Bishop of Worcester. It was and is worth 30s.

Of the manor itself Urse holds 5 hides at ABBOTS LENCH, and there he has 2 ploughs in demesne; and 7 villans and 1 bordar and 1 Frenchman with 6 ploughs. There are 4 slaves and 2 female slaves, and meadow [...], [and] woodland 2 furlongs long and 2 furlongs wide. It was and is worth £4. Godric held it doing service for it to the bishop [on such terms] as he could obtain.

The same Urse holds 7 hides at ROUS LENCH, and Alvred [holds] of him. He has there in demesne 3½ ploughs; and a priest and 5 villans and 7 bordars with 5½ ploughs. There are 2 slaves and 2 female slaves, and a mill rendering 4s, and 6 acres of meadow. It was worth £6; now £7. Frani held 5 hides performing all the service [due], and the bishop had 2 hides in demesne.

Of the same manor Robert Despenser holds 5 hides at WYRE PIDDLE and [Lower and Upper] MOOR and HILL. In demesne are 4 ploughs; and 4 villans and 1 bordar with 1 plough. There are 3 slaves, and 24 acres of meadow. It was and is worth 60s. Cyneweard held it in the same manner as the other above.

Of the manor itself Æthelric the archdeacon holds 1 hide at BRADLEY GREEN, and there he has 1 plough in demesne; and 3 villans and 3 bordars with 1½ ploughs, and 1 slave. It was and is worth 20s. Archbishop Ealdræd leased it to his reeve TRE and took it from him justly when he would.

Of the same manor Roger de Lacy holds 10 hides at BISHAMPTON, and 2 Frenchmen [hold] of him. In demesne are 2 ploughs; and a priest having half a hide, and 8 villans and 2 bordars with 5 ploughs. There are 4 slaves and 4 female slaves, and a mill rendering 12d, and 20 acres of meadow. It was worth £12; now £10. 4 free men held it of the bishop TRE, rendering all soke and sake, and church-scot and fees for burial, and military service by land and sea, and [attendance at] pleas at the aforesaid hundred, and now those who hold it do likewise.

In the same HUNDRED the same bishop holds BREDON. There are 35 hides paying geld. In demesne are 10 hides, and there are 3 ploughs; and 33 villans and 13 bordars with 20 ploughs. There are 6 slaves, and a mill rendering 6s8d, and 80 acres of meadow. [There is] woodland 2 leagues long and 1½ leagues wide. The bishop has from it 10s and all its proceeds in honey and hunting and other things. TRE it was worth £10; now 10s less.

To this manor belong 3 hides in TEDDINGTON [Glos.] and 1 hide at MITTON [Glos.], and they are for the sustenance of the monks. There are in demesne 5 ploughs; and 12 villans and 6 bordars with 9 ploughs. There are 10 slaves and 3 female slaves, and 40 acres of meadow and 2 furlongs of woodland. It was and is worth £4.

Of this manor Æthelric the archdeacon holds 2 hides at CUTSDEAN [Glos.], and he has there 2 ploughs, and a priest and 4 villans and 7 bordars with 3 ploughs. It was and is worth 30s. Bishop Beorhtheah had leased this land to Dodda, but Archbishop Ealdræd proved his right to it against his son |TRW|.

Of this manor Urse holds 7 hides at REDMARLEY D'ABITOT [Glos.], and William [holds] of him 2 hides out of those. In demesne are 4 ploughs; and 23 villans and 9 bordars with 10 ploughs. There are 6 slaves and 2 female slaves, and a mill rendering 5s8d, [and] woodland 1 league long and a half wide. It was worth £8; now 10s. less. Azur and Godwine held it of the bishop and performed their service.

The same Urse holds 2 hides at PENDOCK, and there he has 2 ploughs, and 3 bordars and 3 slaves and 1 female slave. [There is] woodland half a league long and a half wide. It was worth 30s; now 4s less. Godwine held it on the same terms as above.

The same Urse holds 3 hides at LITTLE WASHBOURNE [Glos.], and there he has 2 ploughs; and 5 villans and 4 bordars with 2 ploughs. There are 5 acres of meadow. It was and is worth 40s. Almær held it and afterwards became a monk. The bishop received his land.

The same Urse holds 4 hides at WESTMANCOTE [Westmancote and Lower Westmancote], and there he has 3 ploughs, and 1 villan and 2 bordars with 1 plough. There are 14 slaves, and 12 acres of meadow. It was worth 50s; now 60s. Beorhtwine held it, and did service for it to the bishop [on such terms] as he could obtain.

Of the same manor Durand holds 2 hides at BREDON'S NORTON, and there he has 1 plough, and 2 bordars with 1 plough, and 6 acres of meadow. It was and is worth 20s. Leofwine held it and was the bishop's radman for it.

Of this manor Beorhtric son of Ælfgar held of the bishop 1 hide at BUSHLEY and paid farm for it to the bishop himself every year; and yet he rendered to the soke of the bishop whatever he owed to the king's service. It is now in the hand of King William. It is and was worth 40s. There are 20 acres of meadow, and woodland half a league long and 3 furlongs wide.

In the aforesaid HUNDRED the same bishop holds RIPPLE with 1 member, UPTON UPON SEVERN. There are 25 hides paying geld. Of these, 13 are in demesne, and there are 4 ploughs; and 2 priests having 1½ hides with 2 ploughs; and 40 villans and 16 bordars with 36 ploughs. There are 8 slaves and 1 female slave, and a mill, and 30 acres of meadow. [There is] woodland half a league long and 3 furlongs wide in [?Little] Malvern; from it [the bishop] had the honey and the hunting and all proceeds, and 10s over and above; it is now in the [king's] forest; but the bishop receives from it pannage, and [wood for] fuel and the repair of houses. It was and is worth £10.

Of this manor Ordric holds 1 hide at EARL'S CROOME and there he has 3 ploughs, and 3 villans and 5 bordars with 3 ploughs. There are 24 acres of meadow and 3 furlongs of woodland. It was worth 20s; now 40[s]. Godric held it and performed service to the bishop. Archbishop Ealdræd received it legally from him.

In the same place at CROOME Siward holds 5 hides, and there he has 1 plough, and 6 villans and 4 bordars with 4 ploughs. There are 12 acres of meadow, [and] woodland 4 furlongs long and 2 wide. This land Sigrefr held of the bishop TRE; on his death the bishop gave his daughter, with this land, to a certain knight of his, who was to support her mother and to render the bishop service for it. It was and is worth 40s.

Of this manor Roger de Lacy holds 3 hides at HILL CROOME, and there he has 1 plough, and 8 villans and 4 bordars with 4 ploughs. There are 30 acres of meadow, [and] woodland half a league long and 2 furlongs wide. It was worth £3; now £4.

Of the same manor Urse holds 1 hide at HOLDFAST, and there he has 1 plough, and 7 bordars with 1 plough. There are 5 acres of meadow and 2 furlongs of woodland. It was and is worth 20s. 2 priests held it of the bishop.

Of this manor Ralph de Bernay had 1 hide at QUEENHILL. Æthelric held it TRE, and did service for it to the bishop. It is now in the king's hand; and there are 8 acres of meadow and 2 furlongs of woodland. It was worth 40s.

Of the same manor Beorhtric son of Ælfgar held 1 hide at BARLEY in the same way as above, and it was worth 15s. It is now in the king's hand.

In the same hundred the same bishop holds BLOCKLEY [Glos.]. There are 38 hides paying geld. Of these, 25½ hides are in demesne, and there are 7 ploughs; and a priest having 1 hide, and 4 radmen having 6 hides, and 63 villans and 25 bordars; among them all they have 51 ploughs. There are 14 slaves, and 12 mills rendering 52s less 3d, and 24 acres of meadow, [and] woodland half a league long and wide. It was worth £16; now £20.

Of this manor Richard holds 2 hides at DITCHFORD [Glos.], and there he has 1 plough, and 2 villans and 1 bordar and 2 slaves with 1 plough. There are 4 acres of meadow. It was and is worth 30s. Alweard held it and rendered service [for it].

Ansgot holds 1½ hides of the villans' own land, and has 1 plough with 1 bordar. There are 3 acres of meadow. It is and was worth 15s.

To the above manor belongs 1 hide at ICOMB [Glos.] for the sustenance of the monks. There are 2 ploughs, and 4 villans and 2 bordars and 4 slaves with 2 ploughs. This is valued in the capital manor. There are 12 acres of meadow.

Stephen fitzFulchred holds 3 hides at DAYLESFORD [Glos.], and there he has 2 ploughs, and a priest and 6 villans with 5 ploughs, and 4 slaves and 1 female slave. There are 20 acres of meadow. It is and was worth £3.

Hereweard held 5 hides at EVENLODE [Glos.]. There are 2 ploughs, and 9 villans with 3 ploughs, and 1 slave, and there was a mill rendering 32d. It is and was worth £3.

These 2 estates, Daylesford [Glos.] and Evenlode [Glos.], the Abbot of EVESHAM held of the Bishop of Worcester until the Bishop of Bayeux received them from the abbey, and these lands were for the sustenance of the monks.

In the same HUNDRED the same bishop holds TREDINGTON [War.] with 1 member, TIDMINGTON [War.]. There are 23 hides paying geld. 1 of these is waste.

In demesne are 5 ploughs; and 42 villans and 30 bordars, and a priest having 1 hide, and 1 radman. Among them all they have 29 ploughs. There are 10 slaves, and 3 mills rendering 32s6d. There are 36 acres of meadow. It was worth £10; now £12.10s.

At BLACKWELL [War.] are 2 hides assigned to the sustenance of the monks. In demesne are 3 ploughs; and 10 villans and 6 bordars with 4 ploughs. There are 6 slaves and 1 female slave, and 10 acres of meadow. It was and is worth 50s.

Of the same manor Gilbert fitzTurold holds 4 hides at LONGDON [War.]. There he has 2 ploughs, and 8 villans and 2 bordars with 4 ploughs. There are 4 slaves and 4 female slaves, and 8 acres of meadow. It was worth £4; now £3. Leofric the reeve held it at the will of the bishop.

In the same HUNDRED the same bishop holds NORTHWICK with 1 member, TIBBERTON. There are 25 hides paying geld. Of these, 3½ hides are in demesne, and there are 4 ploughs; and a reeve having 3 virgates, and 1 radman having 3 virgates, and 13 villans and 18 bordars. Among them all they have 18 ploughs. There are 8 slaves, and 3 mills rendering 50s, and in Droitwich 1 salt-pan renders 100 mittae of salt for 100 cart-loads of wood. From the fishery, 4s; from the pastures, 2s. There are 40 acres of meadow, [and] woodland 1 league long and 1 wide. To this manor belong 90 houses in Worcester. Of these, the bishop has in demesne 45; they render nothing but labour at the bishop's court. Urse holds 24 houses of these, Osbern fitzRichard 8, Walter Ponther 11, Robert Despenser 1.

The bishop had the third penny of the borough of Worcester TRE, and now he has it with the king and the earl. [It was] then [worth] £6; now £8. To the same manor belong in Droitwich 3 houses [which] render 3 mittae of salt and 2s from the lead-works. It was worth £13; now £16.10s. In the market-place of Worcester Urse holds of the bishop 25 houses and they pay 100s a year.

Of the same manor Urse holds 5 hides at HINDLIP and OFFERTON, and Godfrey [holds] of him. In demesne are 2 ploughs; and a priest and 3 villans and 4 bordars with 2 ploughs. There are 24 acres of meadow, [and] woodland half a league long and a half wide. It was worth 30s; now 20s. The woodland is in the [king's] forest. Eadric the steersman held it and performed service with the other services belonging to the king and bishop.

The same Urse holds 1 hide and 3 virgates at WARNDON and WHITE LADIES ASTON, and Robert [holds] of him. He has there 2 ploughs with 2 slaves, and there are 16 acres of meadow. [There is] woodland 2 furlongs long and as much wide, and it is in the [king's] forest. It is and was worth 16s. This land was and is [part] of the villans' land.

The same Urse holds 1 hide at CUDLEIGH and there he has 2 ploughs and 3 bordars and 2 slaves. There is 1 furlong of woodland and it is in the [king's] forest. It was and was worth 10s. Ælfgifu the nun held it [on such terms] as she could obtain.

Of this manor Ordric holds 3 hides and 1 virgate at WHITE LADIES ASTON and there he has 3 ploughs, and 5 villans and 4 bordars with 4 ploughs. It was worth 20s; now 40s. This land was and is [part] of the demesne capital manor.

Ordric holds 1 hide at ODDINGLEY, and there he has 1 plough, and 1 villan and 3 bordars with 1 plough, and a salt-pan rendering 4s, and 12 acres of meadow. [There is] woodland 2 furlongs long and as much wide, and it is in the [king's] forest. Thorkil held it and did service for it to the bishop.

Æthelric the archdeacon holds 1 hide at HUDDINGTON, and there he has 2 ploughs, and 4 villans and 4 bordars with 2 ploughs. There is a mill rendering 3 summae of corn. [There is] woodland rendering 3s, and it is in the king's forest. It is and was worth 30s. Wulfric held it serving as a peasant.

Of the same manor Walter Ponther holds 1½ hides at WHITTINGTON and 'RADLEY' [in St Peter the Great], and there he has 1 plough, and 7 bordars with 2 ploughs, and 2 slaves. There are 16 acres of meadow, [and] woodland [sufficient] only for firewood. It was worth 20s; now 25s. Æthelric held it like those above.

The same Walter holds 3 hides at CHURCHILL [near Worcester], and there he has 2 ploughs, and a priest and 3 villans and 3 bordars with 3 ploughs. There are 3 slaves, and a mill rendering 4s, and 3 acres of meadow, and 2 furlongs of woodland, and it is in the [king's] forest. It was worth 50s; now 40s. Azur held it like the above.

The same Walter holds 3 hides at BREDICOT, and there he has 1 plough with 2 bordars and 2 slaves. There are 16 acres of meadow, [and] 2 furlongs of woodland. It was worth 25s; now 20s. Beorhtweald the priest held it and performed service as the bishop willed. The woodland is in the king's forest.

Herlebald holds 1 hide at 'PERRY' [in Worcester], and there he has 2 ploughs, and 3 villans and 1 bordar and 3 slaves with 1 plough. There are 10 acres of meadow. [There is] woodland 2 furlongs long and 1 wide and it is in the [king's] forest. It was worth 30s; now 20s. Godric held it at the will of the bishop.

In the same HUNDRED the church itself holds OVERBURY with PENDOCK. There are 6 hides paying geld. In demesne are 3 ploughs; and 15 villans and 7 bordars with 11 ploughs. There is a priest having half a hide and 1 plough. There are 6 slaves and 2 female slaves, and 10 acres of meadow, and woodland 1 league long and 1 wide. TRE it was worth £6; and now the same.

The church itself holds SEDGEBERROW. There are 4 hides paying geld. In demesne are 2 ploughs; and 11 villans and 4 bordars with 7 ploughs. There is a priest having half a hide and half a plough, and 4 slaves and 1 female slave, and 2 mills rendering 10s, and 8 acres of meadow. It was and is worth £3. Dodda holds it [sic], and it is for the sustenance of the monks. Archbishop Ealdræd proved [their] right [to it] against Beorhtric, his [Dodda's] son.

The church itself holds SHIPSTON ON STOUR [War.]. There are 2 hides paying geld. In demesne are 2 ploughs; and

15 villans and 5 bordars with 6 ploughs. There are 4 slaves and 1 female slave, and a mill rendering 10s, and 16 acres of meadow. It was and is worth 50s.

The church itself holds HARVINGTON with "WIBURGESTOKE" [in Harvington]. There are 3 hides paying geld. In demesne are 2 ploughs; and 12 villans and 3 bordars with 6 ploughs. There are 4 slaves and 1 female slave, and a mill rendering 10s, and 24 acres of meadow. It was and is worth 50s.

The church itself holds GRIMLEY. There are 3 hides paying geld. In demesne are 3 ploughs; and 12 villans and 15 bordars with 15 ploughs. There are 6 slaves and 1 female slave, and a mill without rent, and half a fishery rendering [...] sticks of eels, and 6 acres of meadow, [and] woodland half a league long and wide. It was and is worth £3.

Robert Despenser holds 1 of these 3 hides and it is called KNIGHTWICK, and there he has 1 plough, and 7 bordars with 2 ploughs, and 6 acres of meadow, and woodland 2 furlongs long and 1 wide. It was and is worth 20s.

This hide rendered TRE in the aforesaid manor sake and soke and all service due to the king; and it is of the demesne for the sustenance of the monks, but it was leased to a certain Edith the nun, so that she might have it and perform the service so long as the brethren were willing and could dispense with it. With the growth of the community TRW, she returned it [to them], and she herself, still living, is witness to this.

The church itself holds HALLOW with BROADWAS. There are 7 hides paying geld. In demesne there is but 1 hide and there are 2 ploughs; and 10 villans and 16 bordars with 10 ploughs. There are 4 slaves and 2 female slaves, and 2 mills rendering 10s, and a fishery rendering 20 sticks of eels, and 20 acres of meadow, and woodland 1 league long and 1 wide.

To this manor belong in Droitwich 10 houses rendering 5s, and a salt-pan rendering 50 mittae of salt.

Of this land 2 radmen hold 2 hides, and there they have 2 ploughs. TRE it was worth 100s; and now the same.

Of this manor Walter of Burgh holds half a hide in EASTBURY, and there he has 1 plough. Alric held it, and it is [part] of the villans' land. It is worth 5s.

Of this manor Roger de Lacy holds 3½ hides at HIMBLETON and SPETCHLEY. Himbleton was waste. There are now 2 villans and 2 bordars with 1½ ploughs, and 8 acres of meadow. [There is] woodland half a league long and a half wide. At Spetchley 2 Frenchmen have 4 ploughs, and 6 bordars with 2 ploughs. There are 16 acres of meadow, [and] 2 furlongs of woodland. It was and is worth 50s. Æthelric held this land, of the demesne for the sustenance of the monks, and did service for it at their pleasure.

[Folio 174: WORCESTERSHIRE]

Of the same manor Hugh de Grandmesnil holds half a hide at LEOPARD, and Baldwin [holds] of him; and it did and does belong to the bishop's soke. There are 3 villans and 2 bordars. There is a priest and a huntsman. These have 1 plough and 6 oxen. [There is] woodland 1 league long and a half wide. It was and is worth 20s. From this land is rendered every year 8d to the Church of Worcester for church-scot and acknowledgement of the land.

The church itself holds CROPTHORNE with NETHERTON. There are 50 hides. Of these, 14 hides are in demesne, and there are 5 ploughs; and a priest having half a hide with 1 plough, and 18 villans and 12 bordars with 11 ploughs. There are 10 slaves and 4 female slaves, and a mill rendering 10s and 20 sticks of eels, and 20 acres of meadow, and 3 furlongs of woodland in all. There are 5 hides waste. It was worth £7; now £6.

Of this manor Robert Despenser holds 11 hides, and there he has 9 ploughs, and 10 villans and 12 bordars with 7 ploughs. There were 8 slaves and 2 female slaves. It was worth £6; now £7. Cyneweard and Godric held it, and performed service [on such terms] as they could obtain from the bishop.

Of this manor the Abbot of Evesham holds 5 hides at HAMPTON [Hampton and Little Hampton]. From these the Bishop of Worcester, TRE, only had the geld of his hundred. From all else it was quit [as belonging] to the Church of Evesham, as the shire says.

Of the same manor the Abbot of EVESHAM holds 4 hides at BENGEWORTH, and in the same place Urse the sheriff holds 6 hides, and there he has 2 ploughs, and 12 villans and 2 bordars with 3½ ploughs. There are 6 slaves and 1 female slave, and 6 acres of meadow. It was worth 60s; now £4.10s. Azur held it and did service [for it] at the bishop's pleasure.

IN 'ASH' HUNDRED

The church itself holds CLEEVE PRIOR with ATCH LENCH. There are 10½ hides. In demesne are 2 ploughs; and a priest having 1 hide and 2 ploughs, and 9 villans and 5 bordars with 4 ploughs, and a mill rendering 1 sester of honey. There are 4 slaves and 4 female slaves, and 20 acres of meadow. It was worth £7; now £6. Of this land 2 hides, less 1 virgate, are waste.

The church itself holds PHEPSON. There are 6 hides. 1 of these does not pay geld. Walter Ponther holds it. The other 5 pay geld, and there are 2 ploughs, and 4 villans with 2 ploughs, and 4 slaves, and 6 acres of meadow. [There is] woodland half a league long and 1 furlong wide; and in Droitwich, from the salt-pans, 10s. It was and is worth 10s.

To this manor belongs 1 Berewick, CROWLE. There are 5 hides paying geld. Roger de Lacy holds it, and Odo [holds] of him. In demesne are 2 ploughs; and 7 villans and 3 bordars with 4 ploughs. There are 4 slaves and 1 female slave, and a mill rendering 2s, and a salt-pan in Droitwich rendering 3s. There are 16 acres of meadow. [There is] woodland half a league long and 1 furlong wide. This is in the [king's] forest. Sigmund held it-it was [part] of the demesne-and rendered for it to the bishop all service and geld, and could not betake himself anywhere with this land. It was worth £4; now 70s.

The church itself holds HANBURY. There are 14 hides

paying geld. In demesne are 2 ploughs; and 16 villans and 18 bordars and a priest and a reeve. Among them all they have 24 ploughs. There are 4 slaves and 1 female slave, and 20 acres of meadow. [There is] woodland 1 league long and a half wide, but it is in the king's forest. In Droitwich, from the salt-pans, 105 mittae of salt. It was worth £7; now £6. Of this land 2 hides are waste.

Urse holds half a hide of this land, and Ralph [holds] of him. He has there 1 plough. It was and is worth 5s.

In all of these manors there cannot be more ploughs than is stated. The shire says that from every hide of land, free or villan, which belongs to the Church of Worcester the bishop ought to have at Martinmas 1 summa of the better corn that grows there. But if that day passes without the corn being rendered, he who has kept it back shall render the corn, and shall pay elevenfold; and the bishop moreover shall receive such fine as he ought to have from his land.

IN 'CAME' HUNDRED

The church itself holds STOKE PRIOR with 2 Berewicks, ASTON FIELDS and 'BADDINGTON' [in Stoke Prior]. There are 10 hides. In demesne are 2 ploughs; and 13 villans and 7 bordars and a priest; among them all they have 14 ploughs. There are 4 slaves and 1 female slave, and 2 mills which render 7 orae. [There is] woodland 1½ leagues long. This woodland is in the [king's] forest. It was worth 40s; now 100s.

IN 'CRESSLOW' HUNDRED

The church itself holds HARTLEBURY [...] with 6 Berewicks. There are 20 hides, and in demesne 4 ploughs; and 24 villans and 3 bordars and a priest; among them all they have 21 ploughs. There are 12 slaves and 3 female slaves, and 2 mills rendering 4s and 10 summae of corn, [and] woodland 1 league long and a half wide; and in Droitwich 5 houses render 5 mittae of salt. TRE it was worth £16; now £13.10s.

The church itself holds WOLVERLEY. There are 5 hides. [...] In demesne are 2 ploughs; and 4 villans and 5 bordars with 4 ploughs. There is a priest having half a plough, and 1 free man having 1 hide and rendering 2 sesters of honey. There are 6 slaves and female slaves all together, and a mill rendering 6s. TRE it was worth £4; now 30s.

IN 'CAME' HUNDRED

The church itself holds ALVECHURCH with 4 Berewicks, COFTON HACKETT, WAST HILLS, 'TONGE' [in Alvechurch], "OVRETONE". In these, with the manor, are 13 hides. In demesne are 2 ploughs; and a priest and a reeve and a radknight and 12 villans and 7 bordars; among them all they have 14 ploughs. There are 7 slaves and female slaves all together, and 4 leagues of woodland, of which the king has taken half into his woodland. In Droitwich, 8 salt-pans; 1 of these renders 50 mittae of salt; the other 7 render 70 mittae of salt. TRE it was worth 100s; and now the same.

IN 'DODDINGTREE' HUNDRED

ST MARY holds EARDISTON and KNIGHTON ON TEME, for the sustenance of the monks. The 2 manors are of 15 hides. [...] In demesne are 8 ploughs; and a priest and 15 villans and 10 bordars with 15 ploughs, and 3 more ploughs could be there. There are 17 slaves, and a mill rendering 10s, and a fishery, and 6 acres of meadow, [and] woodland half a league long and 3 furlongs wide. It is worth £8.

III. The land of the Bishop of Hereford

IN 'DODDINGTREE' HUNDRED

THE BISHOP of Hereford holds BOCKLETON of the king. Thorkil held it and could go where he would. There are 8 hides paying geld. In demesne are 2 ploughs; and 2 radmen and 4 villans and 8 bordars with 10 ploughs. There are 12 slaves, [and] woodland 1½ leagues long and half a league wide. It was worth £6; now £4; and 4 ploughs more can be there.

The same bishop holds KYRE ['Little Kyre' and Kyre Magna]. Bishop Walter held it. There are 2 hides paying geld. In demesne is 1 plough, and 3 bordars and 3 slaves. It was worth 12s; now 10s. Urse holds it of the bishop, and 2 ploughs more can be there.

IN 'ASH' HUNDRED

The same bishop holds INKBERROW. Earl Harold held it wrongfully, but King William restored it to Bishop Walter because it belonged to the bishopric. There are 15½ hides. Of these, 10 hides pay geld, the others do not. In demesne are 4 ploughs; and 15 villans and 12 bordars with 13 ploughs, and 4 ploughs more could be there. There are 3 slaves, and a salt-pan rendering 15 mittae of salt. [There is] woodland 2 leagues long and 1 league wide, rendering 100 pigs as pannage. TRE it was worth £12; and afterwards £10; now £12.

IIII. The land of Saint-Denis

IN CLENT HUNDRED

The Church of SAINT-DENIS holds 1 hide in Droitwich, and there are 18 burgesses paying 4s6d, and a salt-pan rendering 20d.

V. The land of the Church of Coventry

IN CLENT HUNDRED

The Church of ST MARY of Coventry holds SALWARPE. There is 1 hide in Droitwich. Urse holds it of the abbot, and this land is in his park, and he has 4 burgesses and 6 salt-pans in Droitwich. It was worth 45s; now 35s.

VI. The land of the Church of Cormeilles

IN 'DODDINGTREE' HUNDRED

The Church of SAINTE-MARIE of Cormeilles holds half a hide in TENBURY WELLS and it pays geld. There is a priest with 1 plough, and it is worth 5s. Earl William gave it to the church.

VII. The land of the Church of Gloucester

IN CLENT HUNDRED

The Church of ST PETER of Gloucester holds half a hide in Droitwich with the same customary dues as the king's half hide in Droitwich that belongs to Gloucester.

[Folio 174V: WORCESTERSHIRE]

VIII. The land of St Peter of Westminster

The Church of ST PETER OF WESTMINSTER holds PERSHORE. King Edward held this manor and gave it to that church as quit and free of every claim as he was holding it in his demesne, the whole shire being witness. There are 200 hides; of these, there are in Pershore 2 hides which never paid geld TRE. There are 5 ploughs in demesne; and 10 villans with 7 ploughs, and 11 slaves and 1 female slave. There 28 burgesses pay 30s, and the toll renders 12s. There are 3 mills rendering 50s, and 100 acres of meadow, [and] woodland 2 leagues long and 3 furlongs wide. 1 church renders 16s. It is worth £14. In this manor a certain Frenchman holds the land of Thorkil, King Edward's steersman, and has 1 plough, and 2 slaves and 2 villans with 2 ploughs.

In WICK are 6 hides. There is in demesne 1 plough; and 9 villans and 25 bordars with 12 ploughs, and 1 slave, and a fishery. It is worth £3. Of these 6 hides, Urse holds 1 hide and Gilbert half a hide. Thor and Osweard held them. There is 1 plough, and 2 bordars and 2 slaves and 1 female slave. It is worth 25s.

In PENSHAM [are] 2 hides, and they are in demesne. There are 2 ploughs, and 3 villans and 9 bordars with 4 ploughs. There are 4 slaves, and 12 acres of meadow. It is worth £3.

In BIRLINGHAM are 3 hides and 1 virgate. There are in demesne 2 ploughs; and 3 villans and 4 bordars with 4 ploughs, and a fishery, and 20 acres of meadow. It is worth 50s.

Of this land Urse holds 2 hides and 1 virgate. Ælfric and Dunning held them. There are 2 ploughs, and 2 bordars and 4 slaves, and 10 acres of meadow. It was worth 60s; now 40s.

In BRICKLEHAMPTON are 10 hides. There are 10 villans and 10 bordars with 6 ploughs, and they plough and sow 6 acres with their own seed. There are 20 acres of meadow. It is worth 20s.

In DEFFORD are 10 hides between woodland and field. There are 8 villans and 10 bordars with 6 ploughs, and they plough and sow 4 acres with their seed. Of this land 2

Frenchmen have 2 hides, and they have 2 ploughs and 4 oxmen. There are 10 acres of meadow. It is worth 50s. Of this land Algot the monk held 1 hide TRE, and did the service that he was bidden.

In ECKINGTON are 16 hides. Of these, 9 hides less 1 virgate are in demesne. There are in demesne 2 ploughs; and 6 villans and 2 cottars with 2 ploughs. There are 6 coliberts paying 11s2d a year and they plough and sow 12 acres with their own seed. There are 4 slaves and 1 female slave. It is worth 100s. Of this land Urse holds 4 hides less 1 virgate. Dunning held them. There are in demesne 2 ploughs; and 5 villans and 8 bordars with 3 ploughs. There are 4 slaves and 3 female slaves, and a mill rendering 10s, and 16 acres of meadow. It is worth 40s.

Of this land Turstin fitzRalph holds 3 hides. Beorhtric held them. In demesne are 2 ploughs; and 7 villans and 4 bordars with 1 plough. There are 4 slaves and 3 female slaves, and 16 acres of meadow, [and] woodland 2 furlongs long and as much wide. It is worth 60s. These 2, Dunning and Beorhtric, mowed in the meadows of their lord for 1 day as a customary due.

In BESFORD are 10 hides. Of these, 4 hides are in demesne. William the priest holds them of the abbot. There, with his men, he has 1½ ploughs and 10 acres of meadow. [There is] woodland half a league long and 3 furlongs wide. It is worth 20s. Of this land Urse holds 5 hides. Edward and Leofric held them. He has there 2 ploughs, and 2 villans and 2 bordars with 1 plough. There are 4 slaves and 2 female slaves, and 10 acres of meadow, [and] woodland half a league long and 3 furlongs wide. It is worth 30s. Of the same land Walter Ponther holds 1 hide which never paid geld. It is and was waste; and yet it was and is worth 16d.

In LONGDON are 30 hides. Of these, 11 hides are in demesne. There are 3 ploughs; and 10 villans and 17 bordars with a priest having 6 ploughs. There are 6 slaves and 2 female slaves, and 40 acres of meadow, [and] woodland 3 leagues long and 2 leagues wide. It is worth £9.

Of this land, TRE, 9 free men held 18 hides, and they mowed in the meadows of their lord for 1 day, and did service as was commanded of them. [They were] Alric, Reinbald, Ælfweard, Beorhtric, Ælfric, Godric Cloch, Godric, Alwig and Alwig Black. What they held was worth in all £11.11s.

Of this land King William holds 5 hides and 3 virgates. Reinbald and Ælfric held them. In demesne are 3 ploughs; and 12 villans and 12 bordars with 14 ploughs. There are 7 slaves and 3 female slaves, and a mill rendering 2s.

Of the same land Drogo fitzPons holds 1 hide. Godric held it. There is 1 plough, and 2 oxmen, and 6 acres of meadow. It is worth 15s.

Of the same land Urse holds 5 hides. 4 of the above men, Ælfweard, Beorhtric, Alwig, and Godric, held them. There are in demesne 5 ploughs; and 3 villans and 9 bordars with 3 ploughs. There are 8 slaves and 3 female slaves, and 28 acres of meadow, [and] woodland 3 furlongs long and 2 furlongs wide. It is worth 70s.

Of this land William fitzBaderon holds 2½ hides. Alwig held them. He has there 2 ploughs; and 4 villans and 5 bordars with 3 ploughs. It is worth 40s. There are 12 acres of meadow.

Of the same land Roger de Lacy holds 5 hides. Alric held them. He has nothing in demesne. There is woodland is 1 league long and a half wide. Of him 1 radman, Leofric, holds 1 hide and 1 virgate, and there he has 1 plough, and 3 villans and 8 bordars with 4 ploughs. There is 1 slave and 3 female slaves, and a mill rendering 8s, and 12 acres of meadow. It is worth 20s.

In POWICK are 3 hides. There are in demesne 2 ploughs; and 16 villans and 5 bordars with 10 ploughs. There are 4 slaves and 1 female slave, and 3 boors, [that is] coliberts, render 3 sesters of honey and 45d, and [there is] 1 mill serving the hall. There are 20 acres of meadow, and from a certain render, 30s. It is worth £20. There is a priest having 1 plough, and 2 oxmen and 5 bordars with 2 ploughs.

There were 8 radmen, Æthelweard, Edward, Beorhtmær, Sæwulf, Alwine, Godric, Alwig, Ketilbert, having among them 10 ploughs, and many bordars and slaves with 7 ploughs. What they held was worth 100s. These radmen mowed for 1 day a year in the meadows of their lord, and did every service that they were bidden.

Urse holds the lands which Æthelweard and Sæwulf and Beorhtmær and Alwine held, and has there 7 ploughs, and 22 bordars and 14 slaves. The whole is worth £9.5s.

Gilbert fitzTurold holds what Alwig and Ketilbiorn held [sic], and there are in demesne 2 ploughs; and 7 bordars and 3 slaves with 1 plough, and a mill rendering 16d. It is worth 43s.

Walter Ponther holds what Godric held, and there he has half a plough, and 1 villan and 6 bordars and 2 slaves with 2 ploughs. It is worth 25s.

A certain Arthur the Frenchman holds what Edward held, and has there 1 plough and 2 oxen.

In UPTON SNODSBURY are 11 hides. Of these, 7 hides and 1 virgate are in demesne; 1 of these hides has never paid geld. There are in demesne 2 ploughs; and 6 villans and 16 cottars and 2 French sergeants; among them all they have 11 ploughs. There are 4 slaves, and 20 acres of meadow, [and] woodland 1 league long and as much wide. It is worth £7.10s.

Of this land Urse holds 4 hides, less 1 virgate. Alweard held them, and, as a customary due, mowed for 1 day the meadows of his lord and did the services he was bidden. There are 1½ ploughs, and 5 cottars and 4 oxmen with 1½ ploughs, and 6 acres of meadow. [There is] woodland 3 furlongs long and 2 furlongs wide. It is worth 50s.

In MARTIN HUSSINGTREE are 6 hides. There 11 villans have 4 ploughs and render annually 100 cart-loads of wood for the salt-pans of Droitwich. He who has the custody of this land has 1 hide of it, and 1 plough there, and 1 villan and 6 bordars with 2 ploughs. The whole is worth 30s.

In DROITWICH, there were and are 4 furnaces, and they rendered annually TRE 60s and 100 mittae of salt; and 31 burgesses pay 15s8d. There 2 priests hold 1 hide which has never paid geld and is in the abbot's demesne; and Leofnoth the priest 1 salt-pan rendering 10s. The whole of this is worth 112s8d.

From the king's tithes of Droitwich St Peter [of Westminster] has £8.

William fitzCorbucion holds DORMSTON. Waland held it TRE. There are 5 hides, and in demesne 2 ploughs; and 2 villans and 14 bordars with 3 ploughs. There are 6 slaves and 1 female slave, and 3 acres of meadow, [and] woodland half a league long and 3 furlongs wide. Albert holds of William 2 hides, and has there 1 plough, and 1 villan with half a plough. There are 2 slaves. The aforesaid Waland mowed the meadows of his lord and did every service he was bidden. It is worth £4.10s.

[Folio 175: WORCESTERSHIRE]

Urse the sheriff holds NORTH PIDDLE. Toli, a free man, held it. There are 5 hides, and in demesne 2 ploughs; and 4 villans and 4 bordars with 3 ploughs. There are 2 slaves, and 8 acres of meadow. It was worth 30s; now 60s. The above-mentioned Toli did service for this land like other free men.

The same Urse holds NAUNTON BEAUCHAMP. 3 free men held it TRE, Alweard, Sæwulf, and Alweard. In demesne are 4 ploughs; and 4 villans with 2 ploughs. There are 8 slaves, and 12 acres of meadow, [and] woodland 2 furlongs long and 1 furlong wide. It was worth 100s; now £4.

Of these 10 hides, Herbrand holds of Urse 3 hides and 1 virgate, and has there 2 ploughs, and 4 slaves and 2 female slaves, and 6 acres of meadow, and 2 cottars. It was worth 60s; now 40s. Those who held these lands did service like other free men.

The same Urse holds GRAFTON FLYFORD. Alwine, a free man, held it. There are 2 hides less 1 virgate. In demesne is 1 plough, and 3 bordars and 2 cottars and 2 slaves, and 6 acres of meadow. It was worth 40s; now 30s. He who held this land mowed in the meadow for 1 day and performed other services.

The same Urse holds NORTH PIDDLE. Alwine held it. There are 4 hides; of these, 1 never paid geld. In demesne are 2 ploughs; and 1 villan and 4 bordars and 4 oxmen and 1 female slave; among them all they have 1 plough. It was worth 50s; now 60s.

WALTER Ponther holds PIRTON. Godric held it. There are 6 hides, and in demesne 1 plough; and 3 villans and 10 bordars with 3½ ploughs. There are 4 slaves, and 8 acres of meadow, [and] woodland 1 league long and half a league wide. It was worth £4; now 50s.

The same Walter holds GRAFTON FLYFORD. Algar and Thorkil held it. There are 7 hides and in demesne 3 ploughs; and a priest and 1 Frenchman and 6 villans with 5 ploughs. There are 5 slaves, and 12 acres of meadow, [and] woodland half a league long and 4 furlongs wide. It was worth £4; now 70s.

In PEOPLETON are 4½ hides in demesne, and there 1 rad-man holds 3 virgates, and 1 Frenchman holds the land of 1 villan, and [there is] 1 villan and 4 bordars; among them all they have 4 ploughs, and there 2 cottars pay 3s.

In the same Berewick Godric held 3½ hides: this half-hide never paid geld; and Alwig held 1 hide, and 1 virgate: this virgate never paid geld; and another Alwig [...] held 1 hide; and Wulfric held 3 virgates: 1 of them did not pay geld TRE. They did service like other free men.

Now Walter Ponther holds the land of Godric and of Alwig and has there 1 plough, and 3 villans and 6 bordars with 3 ploughs. There are 4 slaves, and 10 acres of meadow.#

Urse the sheriff holds the hide which the other Alwig held. There is nothing there but 2 acres of meadow, and yet it renders 100d. #What Walter holds is worth 50s.

GILBERT fitzTurold holds [Great and Little] COMBERTON. Eadric, a free man, held it. There are 9 hides, and in demesne 1 plough; and a priest and 7 villans and 2 bordars with 4 ploughs. There are 2 slaves and 2 female slaves, and 30 acres of meadow. There a Frenchman holds 1 hide, and has there 1 plough and 2 slaves and 1 female slave. The same Eadric did the same service as other free men. It was worth £6; now 70s.

To this belongs a Berewick of 10 hides. Ulf and Asgot held it, and mowed 1 day a year in the lord's meadow, and did service like the others. Now the aforesaid Gilbert holds these 10 hides and he has there 3 ploughs in demesne; and 14 villans and 6 bordars with 11 ploughs. There are 4 slaves and 1 female slave, and a mill rendering 30 summae of corn, and 30 acres of meadow, [and] woodland 1 league long and as much wide. The whole was worth £10; now 100s.

The sheriff [Urse] holds BROUGHTON HACKETT, and Aiulf [holds] of him. Beorhtmær held it. There are 3 hides, and in demesne are 1½ ploughs; and 2 villans and 2 cottars with 1½ ploughs. There are 2 slaves, and 6 acres of meadow. It was worth 40s; now 30s. Beorhtmær who held it did service like the others.

In WORCESTERSHIRE Robert Parler holds of Gilbert fitzTurold a piece of land and it is called Nafford. This land neither pays geld nor owes service at the hundred. There is a priest without a plough [and] without livestock. It is worth 5s.

ALVRED of MARLBOROUGH holds SEVERN STOKE. There are 15 hides. The same man himself held 12 hides and 1 virgate TRE. 2 radmen, Alweard and Wulfric, held 3 hides less 1 virgate. Now Alvred has the whole. He has there in demesne 3 ploughs; and 10 villans and 10 bordars with 5 ploughs, and 4 slaves. A priest has 1 plough. There are 20 acres of meadow, [and] woodland 2 leagues long and 1 league wide.

Of this land 2 radmen hold 1 hide, and there they have 2 ploughs, and they pay 10s.

Of the same land, 2 men, William and Boselin, hold 2 hides and 3 virgates, and there they have 2 ploughs, and 11 bordars with 3 ploughs. TRE it was worth in all £13; now £10.

URSE holds [Great and Little] COMBERTON. There are 2

hides. Azur held it. There are 4 villans with 2 ploughs. It was worth 10s; now 20s.

ALL THESE ABOVE-MENTIONED LANDS BELONGED AND BELONG to PERSHORE. THIS MANOR, TRE, rendered £83 and 50 sesters of honey with all [the profits of] the pleas of the free men.

IX. The land of St Mary of Pershore

The Church of ST MARY OF PERSHORE held and holds the manor itself [of] PERSHORE. There are 26 hides paying geld. These Berewicks belong there: Chivington, Abberton, Wadborough, Drake's Broughton, Abberton, Wick, [Great and Little] Comberton. Of the above-mentioned 26 hides the church itself now holds 21 hides. In demesne are 5 ploughs; and 24 villans and 8 bordars with 22 ploughs. There are 7 slaves, and a mill rendering 4s, and at Wyre Piddle half a mill rendering 10s and 20 sticks of eels. There are 60 acres of meadow, [and] woodland 1 league long and half a league wide. In Droitwich 1 salt-pan renders 30 mittae of salt. TRE it was worth £13; now £12.

Of this land Urse holds 1½ hides, and there he has 2 ploughs, and 2 villans and 3 bordars with 1 plough. There are 4 slaves, and a mill rendering 10s. | It is worth 50s. | Azur held this land, and he did service for it to the church, and gave annually to the monks, in acknowledgement, 1 farm or 20s; and the agreement was that, after his death and that of his wife, the land was to revert to the church's demesne. He was living on the day of King Edward's death and was holding the land on these terms. After that, his wife being now dead, he was made an outlaw.

Of the same land the same Urse holds 1 hide at Drake's Broughton, and says that King William gave it him; and he ought to render service for it to the church. | It was and is worth 10s. |

Of this land Robert Despenser holds 3½ hides at Wadborough, and there he has 2 ploughs, and 9 bordars and 4 slaves, and a park. It is worth 40s. This was land of the demesne villans with half a hide which a man of the abbot holds.

In the same Wadborough is 1 hide of land in which was the monks' dairy farm. A certain Godric, a thegn of King Edward, bought this for 3 lives, and he gave annually to the monks, in acknowledgement, 1 farm. The third heir, namely Urse who holds it, now has this land. After his death it ought to revert to the Church of ST MARY.

The church itself holds BEOLEY with 1 member, YARDLEY [War.]. There are 21 hides between field and woodland. In demesne is 1 plough; and 8 villans and 10 bordars and 1 radman with 9 ploughs. There is woodland 6 leagues long and 3 leagues wide, and it renders 40d. It was worth £8; now 100s.

The church itself holds ALDERMINSTER [War.]. There are 20 hides, and in demesne 4 ploughs; and 24 villans and 8 bordars with 11 ploughs. There are 5 slaves, and 2 mills

rendering 17s6d There 1 knight holds 2 hides and 2 radmen. There are 20 acres of meadow. It was worth £12; now £9.

The church itself holds BROADWAY. There are 30 hides paying geld. In demesne are 3 ploughs; and a priest and 42 villans with 20 ploughs. There are 8 slaves. The whole TRE was worth £12.10s; now £14.10s.

Of this land 1 free man held TRE 2½ hides, and he bought them of Abbot Edmund. This land belonged to the demesne. Now there are 2 ploughs in the abbot's demesne for his sustenance. It was and is worth 30s. Urse claims this land by gift of the king, and says that he himself exchanged it with the abbot for a manor which belonged to the demesne.

The church itself held at LEIGH 3 hides paying geld. Of these hides the abbot has 1 hide in demesne, and has there 2 ploughs; and 12 villans and 32 bordars with 29 ploughs. There are 2 slaves, and 2 mills rendering 10s9d, and 30 acres of meadow, [and] woodland 3 leagues long and 2 leagues wide. TRE it was worth £20; now £16.

Of this aforesaid land 2 radmen held 1½ hides. Urse the sheriff holds them now, and has there 2 ploughs, and 2 villans and 11 bordars and 1 Frenchman; among them all they have 4 ploughs. There are 2 slaves, and a mill rendering 4s. It is worth 50s.

Of this land the same Urse holds the third hide at Bransford, and there he has in demesne 1 plough; and 9 bordars with 4 ploughs, and a mill rendering 20s. It is worth £4. The shire says of this hide that it belonged to the Church of Pershore TRE, and yet the Abbot of Evesham held it on the day of King Edward's death, but they know not how.

IN 'DODDINGTREE' HUNDRED

The church itself held MATHON [Herefs.]. There are 5 hides, but only 3 pay geld. 1 of these 5 hides lies in Herefordshire in RADLOW HUNDRED; 2 radmen hold this. The shire of Worcester has adjudged it to the use of ST MARY of Pershore, and it belongs to the above-mentioned manor. In this same manor are 2 ploughs in demesne; and 6 villans and 20 bordars and 1 smith with 12 ploughs. There is a mill rendering 30d. It was worth £9; now 100s.

Of this manor Urse holds 3 virgates, and has there 1 plough, and [there is] a priest and 1 villan and 3 bordars and a reeve. Among them they have 3 ploughs. It is worth 20s.

Of the same land Walter Ponther holds 1 virgate, but the whole is waste. | It is worth 5s. |

The shire says that the Church of Pershore ought to have church-scot from all 300 hides; that is, from each hide where a free man dwells, 1 summa of corn at Martinmas, and if he has more hides, they should be free, and if that day is missed, he who has kept back the corn shall dischrage [the obligation] elevenfold, but shall first pay what he owes; and the Abbot of Pershore himself has the forfeiture from his 100 hides, as he ought to have from his land. From the other 200 hides the abbot himself has the summa and payment in full, and the Abbot of Westminster has the forfeiture, because it is his land;

and the Abbot of Evesham has the same from his own land, and all the others similarly from their lands.

X. The land of the Church of Evesham

IN EVESHAM, the vill where the abbey is situated, are, and always were, 3 hides free [from geld]. [...] There in demesne are 3 ploughs; and 27 bordars serving the court and they have 4 ploughs. There is a mill rendering 30s, and 20 acres of meadow. From the rent of the men dwelling there, 20s a year. TRE it was worth 60s; and afterwards £4; now 110s.

In 'FISHBOROUGH' Hundred the Church of Evesham has 65 hides; of these, 12 hides are free. In that HUNDRED lie 20 hides of 'Doddingtree' [Hundred]; and the 15 hides of Worcester make up the hundred.

The church itself holds LENCHWICK. There is, and always was, 1 hide free [from geld]; and in NORTON are 7 hides. [...] In demesne are 5 ploughs; and 13 villans and 11 bordars and 1 Frenchman; among them all they have 11 ploughs. There are 10 slaves, and 2 mills rendering 22s6d and 2,000 eels. There are 12 acres of meadow. TRE it was worth £7; and afterwards 110s; now £7.

In Oldberrow [War.] are 12 acres of land, and there are 2 peasants-swineherds-and 1 league of woodland. It is worth 5s.

The church itself holds OFFENHAM. There is 1 hide free [from geld]; and at [Middle, North and South] LITTLETON are 6 hides, and at BRETFORTON 6 hides. In demesne are 3 ploughs; and 25 villans with 7 ploughs; and 2 radmen and 2 Frenchmen: each of them has 1 plough. There are 20 bordars, and 20 acres of meadow, and a mill rendering 12s6d [...] There are oxen for 1 plough, but they draw stone to the church. TRE, and afterwards, it was worth £8; now £6.10s.

To this manor belongs 1 Berewick, ALDINGTON. There is 1 hide free [from geld, belonging] to the church; and in demesne are 2 ploughs; and 5 bordars with 1 plough. There are 4 slaves, and a mill rendering 5s. It was and is worth 40s.

The church itself holds WICKHAMFORD. There are 3 hides free [from geld], and at BRETFORTON 6 hides. In demesne are 4 ploughs; and 16 villans and 7 bordars with 10 ploughs. There is a mill rendering 40d, and 10 acres of meadow. It was and is worth £6.

The church itself holds BADSEY. There were 6½ hides TRE. In demesne are 2 ploughs [...]; and 12 villans with 8 ploughs. There are 4 slaves and 1 widow. It was worth £6; now £3.10s.

The church itself holds [Middle, North and South] LITTLETON. There were 7 hides TRE. In demesne are 2 ploughs; and 15 villans, and 1 Frenchman with 2 villans; among them all they have 7 ploughs. There are 3 slaves, and 8 acres of meadow. It was worth £4.10s; now 70s.

The church itself holds CHURCH HONEYBOURNE. There were 2½ hides TRE. In demesne are 4 ploughs; and a priest and 10 villans and 4 bordars with 4 ploughs. There are 4

slaves. It was worth £3; now £4. There are 11 acres of meadow.

The church itself holds OMBERSLEY. This [land] was of old free for 3 hides, as the charters of the church say, but it was reckoned at 15 hides TRE, between woodland and field, and of these, 3 hides are free [from geld]. There are in demesne 5 ploughs; and 30 villans and 12 bordars and 2 priests and 2 radmen and 10 oxmen. Among them all they have 20 ploughs. There are 1½ fisheries rendering 2,000 eels, and 2 mills rendering 8s, and 4 acres of meadow, [and] 2 leagues of woodland, and in Droitwich 1 salt-pan. TRE, and afterwards, it was worth £18; now £16.

IN 'OSWALDSLOW' HUNDRED

The church itself holds HAMPTON [Hampton and Little Hampton]. There were 5 hides TRE. In demesne are 3 ploughs; and 15 villans and 5 bordars, and 1 Frenchman with 4 bordars; among them all they have 7 ploughs. There are 8 slaves, and 10 acres of meadow, and there is a newly-planted vineyard, and 2 mills rendering 20s. It was worth 100s; now £6.

The church itself holds 4 hides at BENGEWORTH, and Urse holds a fifth hide. Abbot Walter proved his right to these 5 hides at "Ildeberga" [in Evenlode, Glos.] in [the court of] 4 shires before the Bishop of Bayeux and other barons of the king. There are 2 ploughs; and 5 villans and 2 bordars with 2 ploughs. There are 6 slaves. TRE it was worth 60s; and afterwards 50s; now 60s.

IN 'ASH' HUNDRED

The church itself holds ABBOTS MORTON. There were 5 hides TRE, but a large part of them had been leased out. In demesne is 1 plough; and 7 villans and 2 oxmen with 4 ploughs. There are 15 acres of meadow, [and] woodland 3 furlongs long and 1 furlong wide. It was and is worth 30s. Ranulph holds it of the abbot.

The church itself holds ATCH LENCH. There are 4½ hides. In demesne is 1 plough; and 3 villans and 4 bordars with 1 plough. There are 2 slaves, and 6 acres of woodland. TRE it was worth 25s; and afterwards 20s; now 15s.

The church itself holds 'BEVINGTON' [in Abbots Morton]. There is 1 hide, and 1 plough, and 3 bordars, and 3 acres of woodland. It was worth 20s; and afterwards 15s; now 10s.

The church itself holds CHURCH LENCH. There were 4 hides TRE. In demesne are 2 ploughs; and a priest and 3 villans and 2 bordars and 4 oxmen and 1 Frenchman; among them all they have 3 ploughs. It was and is worth 30s.

In the city of WORCESTER the Church of Evesham has 28 messuages. Of these, 5 are waste, and the others render 20s.

XI. The land of the Bishop of Bayeux

IN 'DODDINGTREE' HUNDRED

The Bishop of Bayeux held ACTON BEAUCHAMP [Herefs.], and Urse [held] of him. It belonged to the Church of ST MARY of Evesham TRE, and Urse received it afterwards from the abbot in exchange [...] for other land. He holds it now of the Bishop of Bayeux's fief. There are 6 hides. of these, 3 pay geld, the other 3 do not pay gled. In demesne [are] 6 ploughs; and 1 villan and 9 bordars with 4 ploughs. There are 12 slaves. TRE it was worth 70s; now £4.

IN 'ASH' HUNDRED

The same bishop holds SHERIFF'S LENCH, and Urse [holds] of him. There are 4 hides paying geld. 2 thegns held 2 of these, and a certain woman, Ælfgifu, the other 2. They could go where they would, and held [the lands] as 3 manors. [...] In demesne are 2 ploughs; and 6 villans and 2 bordars and 4 slaves with 2 ploughs; and 8 ploughs more can be there. There is woodland rendering 2s. TRE it was worth 110s; and afterwards 30s; now 42s. Of this land, Gilbert fitzTurold gave 2 hides to the Church of Evesham for the soul of Earl William by permission of King William, and accordingly 1 monk was placed in the church. For the other 2 hides Abbot Æthelwig gave 1 mark of gold to King William, and [the king] himself granted the same land to the church for his soul, Gilbert fitzTurold, who received the gold for the king's use, being witness. The church itself was seised of these 4 hides for many years, until the Bishop of Bayeux took them away from the church and gave them to Urse.

XII. The land of St Guthlac

IN CLENT HUNDRED

Of ST GUTHLAC Nigel the physician holds 1 hide in DROITWICH. There are 9 burgesses paying 30s from the salt-pans and for everything.

XIII.THE PRIESTS of Wolverhampton hold LUTLEY. There are 2 hides. They themselves held it TRE. They have there 2 villans and 2 slaves and 1 bordar with 4 ploughs. It is worth 15s.

XIIII. The land of Earl Roger

IN CLENT HUNDRED

EARL ROGER holds of the king 1 manor, HALESOWEN. There are 10 hides. [...] In demesne are 4 ploughs; and 36 villans and 18 bordars, 4 radmen, and a church with 2 priests; among them all they have 41½ ploughs. There are 8 slaves and 2 female slaves. Of this land Roger the huntsman holds of the earl 1½ hides, and has there 1 plough, and 6 villans and 5 bordars with 5 ploughs. It is worth 25s. TRE this manor was worth £24; now £15. Wulfwine held it and had in Droitwich a

salt-pan rendering 4s, and in Worcester 1 house rendering 12d.

The same earl holds SALWARPE, and Urse [holds] of him. Æthelwine Cild held it. There are 5 hides. [...] In demesne is 1 plough; and 6 villans and 5 bordars with 7 ploughs. There are 3 slaves and 3 female slaves, and a mill rendering 10s, and 5 salt- pans rendering 60s. There is half a league of woodland and a park. TRE it was worth 100s; now £6. 2 ploughs more can be there.

XV. The land of Ralph de Tosny

IN 'DODDINGTREE' HUNDRED

RALPH de Tosny holds WORSLEY. Eadwig and Alnoth held it as 2 manors. There are 2 hides paying geld. In demesne are 3 ploughs; and 2 radmen and 8 bordars with 7 ploughs. There are 6 slaves. TRE it was worth 40s; and afterwards 20s; now £4.

The same Ralph holds 'LINDON' [in Rock]. Alweard, a thegn of Earl Ælfgar, held it. There are 2 hides paying geld. In demesne are 4 ploughs; and 16 bordars and 6 oxmen with 4 ploughs. There are 2 slaves. TRE it was worth 40s; and afterwards 20s; now 16s.

The same Ralph holds "HALAC". Wulfmær, a thegn of King Edward, held it. There is 1 hide paying geld. There are 5 bordars; they pay 5s. It was worth 4s. 2 ploughs can be there.

IN 'CRESSLOW' HUNDRED

The same Nigel holds DUNCLENT, and Urse [holds] of him. There are 3 hides. In demesne is 1 plough; and 2 bordars and 2 oxmen; and 5 ploughs can be there. It was worth 25s; now 10s. Oda held it of St Guthlac.

The same Ralph holds ALTON. Godric, a thegn of Earl Ælfgar, held it, and could go where he would. There are 2 hides paying geld. In demesne are 4 ploughs; and a priest and 2 bordars and 2 radmen with 4 ploughs. There are 6 slaves, and woodland 3 leagues long and 2 leagues wide. TRE it was worth 40s; and afterwards 20s; now 52s.

The same Ralph holds ROCK MOOR. Grim held it, and could go where he would. There is 1 hide paying geld. There are 2 bordars with 1 plough, and 1 free man with 1 plough. It was and is worth 20s. There is a little wood.

The same Ralph holds BAYTON. Eadric and Leofwig held it as 2 manors, and could go where they would. There are 3½ hides paying geld. In demesne are 3 ploughs; and 4 villans and 14 bordars and 1 radman with 12 ploughs. There is a mill rendering 5s. TRE it was worth 60s; and afterwards 30s; now £4. Reiner holds it of Ralph.

The same Ralph holds ROCK MOOR. Leofnoth held it, and could go where he would. There is 1 virgate paying geld. There is 1 villan with 1 plough. [...] [There is] woodland half a league long and 3 furlongs wide. It was and is worth 2s.

The same Ralph holds ABBERLEY. Wulfmær, held it, and

could go where he would. There are 2½ hides paying geld. [...] In demesne are 2 ploughs; and 18 villans and 8 bordars and 1 Frenchman and 3 cottars with 17 ploughs. There is a priest and 1 slave. TRE it was worth £7; and afterwards £4; now £10.10s.

The same Ralph holds ASTLEY, and the Church of Saint-Taurin [holds] of him. Earnsige held it, and could go where he would. There are 6 hides paying geld. Of these, Saint-Taurin holds 4 hides quit and free from all customary dues belonging to the king, as King William himself granted, when Ralph gave it to the saint. There in demesne are 2 ploughs; [and] a church and a priest and 11 villans and 3 bordars and 1 radman; among them all they have 11½ ploughs. There are 3 slaves, and 2 mills rendering 10s. At Worcester, 2 burgesses paying 2s; at Droitwich, 1 salt-pan rendering 18 mittae of salt and 64d. There is woodland rendering nothing. TRE this manor was worth £10; and afterwards, as now, 100s.

There Urse holds of Ralph 1 hide, and has 3 ploughs in demesne; and 3 villans and 15 bordars and 2 free men with 7 ploughs. There are 4 slaves, and 2 mills rendering 20s. It is worth £3.10s.

Ralph himself holds REDMARLEY. There are 1½ hides paying geld. Wulfmær and Ulfkil held it as 2 manors, and could go where they would. In demesne is 1 plough; and 14 bordars and 1 smith with 8 ploughs. There are 4 slaves. TRE it was worth 30s; and afterwards as much; now 40s. Ralph the knight holds it of Ralph.

The same Ralph holds SHELSLEY BEAUCHAMP, and Walter [holds] of him. Wulfmær held it, and could go where he would. There is 1 hide. In demesne are 2 ploughs; and 2 villans and 13 bordars with 8 ploughs. There are 2 slaves, and a fishery rendering 2s, and 30 acres of meadow, [and] woodland half a league long and 3 furlongs wide. TRE it was worth 50s; and afterwards 30s; now 50s.

The same Ralph holds EASTHAM and 'BASTWOOD' [in Eastham], and Herbert [holds] of him. Eadric held them as 2 manors. There are 3 hides [...]. In demesne are 2 ploughs; and a priest and 5 villans and 8 bordars with 5 ploughs. There are 6 slaves, and 1 man paying 32d, and a mill rendering 6s8d, and 60 acres of meadow, [and] woodland 2 leagues long and 1 league wide. TRE it was worth £4.5s; and afterwards 45s; now £4.

IN 'CRESSLOW' HUNDRED

The same Ralph holds ELMLEY LOVETT, and Walter [holds] of him. Alweald held it of Queen Edith. There are 11 hides. In demesne are 2 ploughs; and a priest and 14 villans and 15 bordars with 8 ploughs. There 3 mills render 109s4d, and 4 salt-pans render 70s; and at Droitwich 5 houses rendering 20d; and there 7 villans pay 3s. [There is] woodland 1 league long and half a league wide. TRE it was worth £10; now £16.

The same Ralph holds in DROITWICH 1 hide | or land | of the 10 geld-paying hides and Walter [holds] of him.

XVI. The land of Ralph de Mortimer

IN 'DODDINGTREE' HUNDRED

RALPH de Mortimer holds of the king SODINGTON, and a knight of his [holds] of him. Alsige held it, and could not withdraw from his lord. There is 1 hide [...] and in demesne 1 plough; and 1 smith and 2 bordars with half a plough. There are 3 slaves, and 3 furlongs of woodland; and 1 plough more can be there. It was worth 20s; now 10s.

The same Ralph holds MAMBLE. Sæweald held it, and could go where he would. There is half a hide paying geld. In demesne are 1 ploughs; and 3 villans and 6 bordars with 4 ploughs. There are 3 slaves, [and] woodland half a league long and 3 furlongs wide. It was worth 30s; now 40s.

The same Ralph holds [?] BROOK. Feche held it, and could go where he would. There is half a hide paying geld. In demesne are 1½ ploughs; and 1 villan and 11 bordars with 2½ ploughs. There are 4 slaves, and half a fishery, [and] 3 furlongs of woodland. It was worth 10s; now 20s.

The same Ralph holds CONNINGSWICK. Sæweald held it, and could go where he would. There is 1 hide paying geld. The son of this Sæweald has there 1 plough, and there is 1 bordar and 2 slaves. It was and is worth 10s.

XVII. The land of Robert of Stafford

IN 'ASH' HUNDRED

ROBERT of Stafford holds MORTON [?Underhill]. Alwig held it. There are 4 hides paying geld. This Alwig could go where he would. Arnold holds it of Robert, and has 2 ploughs in demesne, and 7 villans and 6 bordars with 4 ploughs. There are 6 slaves, and 1 burgess pays 10s, and a salt-pan renders 2s and 8 mittae of salt. [There is] woodland 1 league long and a half wide. TRE it was worth £4; and afterwards 30s; now £4.

XVIII. The land of Roger de Lacy

IN 'DODDINGTREE' HUNDRED

ROGER de Lacy holds STOCKTON ON TEME. Godric held it, and could go where he would. There are 3 hides paying geld. In demesne [is] 1 plough; and 3 villans and 6 bordars with 3 ploughs; and in addition 2 more can be [there]. There are 3 slaves, and a mill rendering 20s, and 3 furlongs of woodland. TRE it was worth 50s; now 70s.

The same Roger holds STANFORD ON TEME. Queen Edith held it, and Godric [held] of her as 2 manors. There are 2½ hides paying geld. Hugh holds it of Roger, and has there 1 ploughs, and 7 villans and 2 bordars, and 4 ploughs more can be there. [There is] woodland half a league long and 2 furlongs wide. TRE it was worth 50s; now 30s.

IN 'ASH' HUNDRED

The same Roger holds SHELL, and Herman [holds] of him. Alwig held it as 2 manors, and could go where he would. There is 1 hide paying geld. In demesne is 1 plough, and 2 bordars and 3 slaves, and 4 salt-pans with woodland half a league long and 2 furlongs wide, rendering 60 mittae of salt. TRE it was worth 60s; and afterwards 30s; now 15s. The woodland has been put in the king's preserve.

The same Roger holds KINGTON. Alwig and Elaf and Thorir held it as 3 manors. There are 5 hides paying geld. They could go where they would, and had 1 enclosure in which wild animals were captured. There are in demesne 2 ploughs; and 5 villans and 7 bordars with 2 ploughs. There are 2 slaves, and woodland 1 league long and 2 furlongs wide. TRE it was worth £4; and afterwards, as now, 50s. 2 knights hold it of Roger.

In MARTLEY Roger has 1 radman and he pays him 4s.

XIX. The land of Osbern fitzRichard

IN 'DODDINGTREE' HUNDRED

OSBERN fitzRichard Scrob holds BERRINGTON of the king. Richard his father held it. There are 2 hides paying geld. In demesne are 2 ploughs; and 8 villans and 4 bordars and a smith and a miller with 9 ploughs; and 1 plough more can be there. There are 4 slaves and 4 female slaves, and a mill rendering 22 summae of corn, and 10 acres of meadow, [and] woodland 1½ leagues long and 1 league wide. It was and is worth 20s.

The same Osbern holds TENBURY WELLS. His father held it. There are 3 hides paying geld. In demesne is 1 plough; and 14 villans and bordars altogether with 12 ploughs; and in addition 2 ploughs more can be there. There are 2 slaves.

The same Roger holds half a hide in Droitwich. Ælfric Mappesone held it. There are 11 burgesses, and 1½ salt-pans render 32½ mittae. This manor belongs to his manor of Hereford. There is woodland 2 leagues long and 1 league wide. It was worth 60s; now 40s.

The same Osbern holds CLIFTON UPON TEME. King Edward held it. There are 3 hides paying geld. Robert d'Oilly holds it of Osbern, and has there 3 ploughs in demesne; and 6 villans and 4 bordars and 4 oxmen; among them all, with a priest, they have 6 ploughs; and in addition 5 more ploughs could be there. There is woodland 3 fulongs long and 2 furlongs wide. TRE, and afterwards, it was worth 20s; now 40s.

The same Osbern holds KYRE ['Little Kyre' and Kyre Magna]. King Edward held it. There are 3 hides paying geld. In demesne is 1 plough; and 5 villans and 4 bordars with 8 ploughs. There are 3 slaves. TRE and afterwards, as now, worth 40s. There is a mill rendering 10 summae of wheat.

The same Osbern holds STANFORD ON TEME. Beorhtric, a thegn of Queen Edith, held it. There are 1½

hides paying geld. In demesne is 1 plough; and 1 villan and 1 bordar with 1 plough; and 1 plough more could be there. There is 1 slave. It was and is worth 20s.

The same Osbern holds SHELSLEY WALSH. Sigmund, a thegn of Earl Edwin, held it, and could not withdraw from him without his leave. There is 1 hide paying geld. In demesne is 1 plough; and a reeve with 3 villans and 2 bordars have 2 ploughs. There are 3 slaves, and a fishery rendering 16 sticks of eels. There could be 2 more ploughs. TRE it was worth 40s; and now 30s.

The same Osbern holds KYRE ['Little Kyre' and Kyre Magna]. His father held it. There is 1 hide paying geld. In demesne is 1 plough, and another could be [there]. There are 2 bordars and 1 radman with 1 plough. It was worth 15s; now 10s. Herbert holds it of Osbern.

The same Osbern holds HAMCASTLE. He himself held it. There is 1 hide paying geld. In demesne [is] 1 plough; and 7 bordars with 5 ploughs; and 1 plough more could be [there]. There are 4 slaves, and a fishery rendering 2s, and a mill rendering 16 summae of corn. It was worth 20s; now 30s.

The same Osbern holds LOWER SAPEY. He himself held it. There are 3 hides paying geld. In demesne [is nothing] but 9 oxen; and a priest and 9 villans and 4 bordars with 11 ploughs; and 3 ploughs more could be there. There is a mill rendering 6 summae of corn. It was worth 45s; now 30s.

The same Osbern holds CARTON, and Odo [holds] of him. His father held it. There is 1 hide and 1 virgate paying geld. In demesne are 2 ploughs; and 2 villans and 2 bordars with 1½ ploughs; and 3 ploughs more can be there. There are 7 slaves. [There is] woodland half a league long and 3 furlongs wide. It was worth 10s; now 5s.

The same Osbern holds EDVIN LOACH [Herefs.]. Wulfheah held it, and could go where he would. Herbert holds it of Osbern. There is 1 hide paying geld, and in demesne [is] 1 plough; and 1 villan and 5 bordars with 3 ploughs. There are 2 slaves. It was worth 20s; now 28s.

The same Osbern holds WYCHBOLD. Earl Godwine held it. There are 11 hides. Of these, 4 hides were quit from geld. In demesne is 1 plough, and 2 ploughs more could be [there]; and 19 villans and 27 bordars with 18 ploughs. There are 2 slaves, and 5 mills rendering £4.8s, and 26 salt-pans render £4.12s, and 13 burgesses in Droitwich reaping for 2 days in August and March and doing service at the court. [There is] 1 league of woodland. TRE, and afterwards, it was worth £14; now £15.

The same Osbern holds ELMBRIDGE. Ealdgyth held it. There are 8 hides. Of these, 3 hides are quit from geld by the testimony of the shire. There are 8 villans and 26 bordars with 10 ploughs, and another 10 ploughs could be [there]. There is 1 slave, and a salt-pan rendering 4s, and 50 acres of meadow, [and] woodland 1 league long and a half wide. TRE it was worth 100s; now 50s.

IN 'ASH' HUNDRED

The same Osbern holds CROWLE, and Urse [holds] of him. Ketilbert held it, and could go where he would. There are 5 hides paying geld. In demesne are 1½ ploughs; and 3 bordars and 3 cottars.

XX. The land of Gilbert fitzTurold

IN 'DODDINGTREE' HUNDRED

GILBERT fitzTurold holds DODDENHAM of the king. Ceolmær held it, and could go where he would. There is 1 hide paying geld. In demesne is 1 plough; and 3 villans and 8 bordars and 4 cottars and 1 miller; among them all they have 7 ploughs. There are 2 oxmen, and a mill rendering 12s. It was worth 20s; now 42s.

The same Gilbert holds REDMARLEY. Sæweard held it, and could go where he would. There are 1½ hides. [...] Ralph holds it of Gilbert, and has in demesne 1 plough; and 11 bordars and 1 Frenchman with 3 ploughs, and 1 plough more could be [there]. There are 2 slaves. It was worth 30s; and afterwards 15[s]; now 30s.

The same Gilbert holds HANLEY [Child and William], and Roger [holds] of him. Eadwig held it, and could go where he would. There are 1½ hides paying geld. In demesne are 2 ploughs;

[Folio 177: WORCESTERSHIRE]

and 11 bordars and 1 Frenchman with 3 ploughs, and 3 more could be [there]. There are 2 slaves. TRE it was worth 60s; and afterwards 20s; now 40s.

The same Gilbert holds HANLEY [Child and William], and Hugh [holds] of him. [...] Cyneweard and Ulfkil held it as 2 manors, and could go where they would. There are 3 hides paying geld. In demesne are 2 ploughs; and 10 bordars and 1 smith and 1 Frenchman with 3 ploughs, and in addition 5 ploughs more could be [there]. TRE it was worth 70s; now 50s

The same Gilbert holds ORLETON, and Hugh [holds] of him. Eadwig and Edwin held it as 2 manors, and could go where they would. There are 1½ hides paying geld. In demesne are 3 ploughs; and 2 villans and 2 bordars with 1 plough. There are 2 slaves, and 2 fisheries render 40 sticks of eels. [There are] 2 furlongs of woodland. TRE it was worth 40s; and afterwards, as now, 30s

IN CLENT HUNDRED

The same Gilbert holds HADZOR, and Walter, his son-in-law, [holds] of him. Beorhtmær, a thegn of King Edward, held it. There are 2 hides. In demesne are 2 ploughs; and 2 villans and 8 bordars and 4 cottars with 2 ploughs, and a third could be there. There are 4 oxmen, and 7 salt-pans render 1 1 1 mittae of salt. TRE it was worth 60s; now 45s.

XXI. The land of Drogo fitzPons

IN 'DODDINGTREE' HUNDRED

DROGO fitzPons holds HOLLIN of the king. Wulfmær held it, and could go where he would. There is 1 hide paying geld, and 1 plough could be there. It is waste and was waste. TRE it was worth 5s.

The same Drogo holds STILDON. Ulfkil held it, and could not withdraw from his lord Wulfmær. There is half a hide paying geld. There is land for 2 ploughs. It was worth 5s. It is now waste.

The same Drogo holds GLASSHAMPTON. Wulfmær held it, and could go where he would. There is 1 hide paying geld. In demesne [is] half a plough; and 1 villan and 3 bordars with 1 plough, and another could be there. There is a mill rendering 4s8d. It was worth 20s; now 10s

The same Drogo holds 1 virgate in MARTLEY, the king's manor, and it pays geld. He has there 1 radman paying 6s a year. Earnwine held it.

XXII. The land of Harold son of Earl Ralph

HAROLD son of Earl Ralph holds of the king 1 hide in DROITWICH, and has there 20 burgesses with 7 salt-pans; they render 50 mittae of salt. It was and is worth 40s.

XXIII. The land of William fitzAnsculf

IN 'CAME' HUNDRED

William fitzAnsculf holds SELLY OAK [War.] of the king, and Wibert [holds] of him. Wulfwine held it. To it belongs 1 Berewick, BARTLEY ['Bartley' in Bartley Reservoir, War., and Bartley Green, War.]. In all [there are] 4 hides. [. . .] In demesne is half a plough; and 2 villans and 9 bordars with 4 ploughs. [There is] woodland 1 league long. TRE it was worth 100s; now 60s.

The same Wulfwine bought this manor from the Bishop of Chester for 3 lives TRE. When he was ill and had come to the end of his life, he called his son, Bishop Li[. . .], and his wife and several of his friends, and said: 'Hear ye, my friends. I will that my wife hold this land which I bought from the church so long as she lives; and after her death, let the church from which I had it receive it; and let him who takes it thence be excommunicated.'

The better men of the whole shire testify that this was so.

The same William holds NORRTHFIELD [War.]. Alweald held it. There are 6 hides. [. . .] In demesne is 1 plough; and a priest and 7 villans and 16 bordars and 6 cottars with 13 ploughs, and 5 more ploughs could be [there]. There are 2 slaves and 1 female slave, [and] woodland half a league long and 3 furlongs wide. TRE it was worth £8; now 100s

The same William holds FRANKLEY, and Baldwin [holds] of him. Wulfwine held it. There is 1 hide. [...] In demesne is 1 plough. There are 9 bordars with 5 ploughs, and 2 slaves. [There is] woodland 1 league long and a half wide. TRE it was worth 40s; now 30s.

The same William holds 'WILLINGWICK' [in Bromsgrove], and Baldwin [holds] of him. There are 3 virgates of land. [...] There is 1 villan and 1 bordar with half a plough. There could be 2½ ploughs more. It was worth 5s; now 3s.

The same William holds SELLY OAK [War.]. Tumi and Algifu held it as 2 manors. Robert holds it of William. There is 1 hide. In demesne is 1 plough; and 3 villans and 2 bordars and 2 oxmen with 2 ploughs. [There is] 1 league of woodland. TRE it was worth 20s; now 15s.

The same William holds 'WARLEY WIGORN' [in Birmingham, War.], and Alelm [holds] of him. IEthelweard held it. There is half a hide. [...] In demesne is 1 plough; and 2 villans and 8 bordars with 4½ ploughs. There are 2 slaves. TRE it was worth 17s; now 10s.

The same William holds CHURCHILL [near Kidderminster], and Walter [holds] of him. Wigar held it. There are 2 hides. [...] In demesne is 1 plough, and 5 ploughs more can be there. It was worth 60s; now 8s.

The same William holds BELL. Leofnoth, a thegn of King Edward, held it. There are 3 hides. [...] Robert holds it of William. In demesne is 1 plough; and 7 villans and 4 bordars with 4 ploughs. There are 2 slaves, and a salt-pan rendering 2 orae. There could be 3 ploughs more. It was worth 25s; now 15s Ralph fitzHubert held this manor for more than years, but William fitzOsbern took it from him wrongfully.

The same William holds HAGLEY, and Roger [holds] of him. Godric, a thegn of King Edward, held it. There are 5½ hides. In demesne is 1 plough; and a priest and villans and 10 bordars with 5 ploughs; and in addition 8 ploughs more can be [there]. There are 2 slaves, [and] woodland half a league long and 3 furlongs wide. TRE it was worth 60s; now 50s.

The same William holds DUDLEY, and his castle is there. Earl Edwin held this manor. There is 1 hide. [...] In demesne is 1 plough; and 3 villans and 10 bordars and 1 smith with 10 ploughs. There are 2 slaves, and 2 leagues of woodland. TRE it was worth £4; now £3.

The same William holds OLD SWINFORD, and Acard [holds] of him. Wulfwine held it. There are 3 hides. [...] In demesne is 1 plough; and a priest and 5 villans and 11 bordars with 7 ploughs. There are 2 slaves, and a mill rendering 5s, [and] 1 league of woodland. TRE it was worth £6; now £3.

The same William holds PEDMORE, and Acard [holds] of him. Thorger held it. There are 3 hides. [...] In demesne is 1 plough; and 3 villans and a priest and 10 bordars and 3 cottars with 5½ ploughs, and 3 more ploughs can be there. In Worcester, 2 messuages rendering 2s, and 1 league of scrubland. TRE it was worth £4; now 50s.

The same William holds CRADLEY, and Pain [holds] of him. Wigar held it. There is 1 hide [...]. In demesne, nothing.

There are 4 villans and 11 bordars with 7 ploughs. It was worth 40s; now 24s.

The same William holds BELLINGTON in the jurisdiction of his castle. Alric and Holand held it as 2 manors. There are 5 hides. There is land for 5 ploughs. It was and is waste. There are 4 furlongs of woodland, but it is in the king's forest. The meadows of this manor are worth 4d.

[Folio 177V: WORCESTERSHIRE]

XXIIII. The land of William fitzCorbucion

IN CLENT HUNDRED

WILLIAM fitzCorbucion holds of the king WITTON IN DROITWICH. Tumi, a thegn of King Edward, held it. There are 2 hides. In demesne are 2 ploughs; and 18 bordars and a priest with 1 plough. There are 4 slaves and 1 female slave, and in Worcester 1 burgess paying 2s, and 3 salt-pans rendering 60 mittae of salt; and part of a salt-pan rendering 10 mittae of salt. [There is] half a league of woodland. It was and is worth £3.

XXV. The land of William Goizenboded

IN CLENT HUNDRED

WILLIAM Goizenboded holds CHAWSON, and William [holds] of him. Richard the Young held it TRE. There is 1 hide, and there are 4 bordars with 1 plough. TRE it was worth 10s; now 4s.

XXVI. The land of Urse d'Abetot

IN 'DODDINGTREE' HUNDRED

URSE holds COOKHILL, and Herlebald [holds] of him. Godric, a free man, held it. There are 2½ hides paying geld. In demesne is 1 plough, and 2 bordars, and 2 ploughs more can be there. There are 2 slaves, and 1 burgess paying 16d and 4 mittae of salt, and [there is] woodland 3 furlongs long and 2 furlongs wide. TRE it was worth 70s; and afterwards 40s; now 50s.

IN 'CAME' HUNDRED

The same Urse holds 'OSMERLEY' [in Alvechurch], and Herlebald [holds] of him. Alweald held it. There is 1 hide. In demesne is 1 plough; and 10 bordars with 3 ploughs. There are 2 slaves and 2 female slaves. In Worcester, 1 house rendering 16d, and in Droitwich 1 salt-pan rendering 12 mittae of salt. [There is] half a league of woodland. It was worth 20s; it is worth 13s.

The same Urse holds COFTON HACKETT. Leofgeat and Ælfric and Æthelric held it as 3 manors. There are 3 hides. Turold holds 2, and Walter 1 hide, of Urse. In demesne are 2 ploughs; and 11 bordars and 3 cottars with 4 ploughs, and in addition 1 plough more can be [there]. There is a mill serving the hall of 1 of them. [There is] woodland 3 furlongs long and 1 wide, but it is in the king's forest. TRE it was worth 35s; now 27s.

The same Urse holds [Lower and Upper] BENTLEY, and William [holds] of him. Leofric held it of Earl Edwin. There is 1 hide. In demesne is 1 plough; and 4 bordars with 3 ploughs. [There is] woodland 1 league long and a half wide. TRE it was worth 30s; now 16s.

The same Urse holds WOODCOTE [Woodcote and Woodcote Green], and Herlebald [holds] of him. Wulfsige, a thegn of King Edward, held it. There are 1½ hides. There is 1 villan and 2 bordars with 1 plough. [There is] half a league [of] woodland, but the king has put it in the forest. TRE it was worth 10s; now it is worth 5s.

IN 'CRESSLOW' HUNDRED

The same Urse holds RUSHOCK, and Hunulf [holds] of him. Aki held it. There are 5 hides. In demesne are 1½ ploughs; and 13 villans and 1 bordar and 3 cottars with 6½ ploughs. [There are] 4 slaves and female slaves all together. [There is] a salt-pan rendering 5 orae, [and] 1½ leagues of woodland. TRE it was worth 50s; now 30s.

The same Urse holds STONE. Tumi and Alfkil held it as 2 manors. There are 6 hides. Herlebald holds it of Urse. In demesne are 2 ploughs; and 7 villans and 15 bordars with 6 ploughs. There are 4 slaves, and a mill rendering 3 orae. TRE it was worth 40s; now 30s.

The same Urse holds DOVERDALE, and William [holds] of him. Thorbiorn, a thegn of King Edward, held it. There are 2 hides. In demesne are 2 ploughs; and a church and a priest and a smith and 4 villans and 4 bordars with 4 ploughs. There is a mill rendering 4s, and a salt-pan at Droitwich rendering 4s. TRE it was worth 30s; now 40s.

The same Urse holds "HATETE", and Gunfrid [holds] of him. Earngeat and Algeat held it as 2 manors, and could go where they would. There is 1 hide. [...] In demesne is 1 plough, and another can be [there]. There is a mill rendering 2s, and 1 bordar having nothing. TRE it was worth 30s; now 10s.

IN CLENT HUNDRED

The same Urse holds HAMPTON LOVETT, and Robert [holds] of him. Alweald held it. There are 4 hides. In demesne is 1 plough; and a priest and 5 villans and 2 bordars with 4 ploughs, and 4 ploughs more can be [there]. There 7 salt-pans render 14 orae. There are 2 oxmen. It was worth £4; now £3.

The same Urse holds HORTON, and Robert [holds] of him. Ælfric held it, and could go where he would. There are 2 hides. In demesne are 2 ploughs, and 4 oxmen and 2 bordars. There is a little wood. There is a salt-pan rendering 40d. TRE it was worth 50s; now 18s.

The same Urse holds COOKSEY [?Green], and Herbrand and William [hold] of him. Alwine and Atilic held it as 2 manors. There are 2 hides. In demesne is 1 plough; and 3 bordars and 2 Frenchmen having between them 4 ploughs, and 1 plough more can be [there]. This land is largely waste. [There is] woodland half a league long and 3 furlongs wide. TRE it was worth 45s; now 27s.

The same Urse holds BELBROUGHTON. Countess Godgifu held it. There are 2 hides. In demesne are 2 ploughs; and 5 villans and 10 bordars and a church and a priest; between them all they have 6 ploughs. There are 4 slaves. In Droitwich 5 salt-pans render 100 mittae of salt and 5 orae. [There are] 3 leagues of woodland. TRE it was worth £4; now £4.10s.

IN THE SAME HUNDRED

The same Urse holds 1 hide quit from geld and from every customary due, and Robert holds of him. There are 3 bordars having nothing. It was and is worth 3s. Ælfric held it TRE.

The same Urse holds UPTON WARREN, and Herlebald [holds] of him. Æthelwig, Abbot of Evesham, held it, and it ought, rightfully, to be in the abbey ['s possession], by the witness of the shire. There are 3 hides. [...] In demesne are 2 ploughs; and 7 villans and 13 bordars and a priest with 5 ploughs. There are 4 slaves, and a mill rendering 4s. In Worcester, 1 burgess paying 2s. In Droitwich 3 salt-pans render 40 mittae of salt. [There is] woodland 3 furlongs long and 2 furlongs wide. It was worth 60s; now 50s.

The same Urse holds WITTON in Droitwich, and Gunfrid [holds] of him. The Church of Evesham held it TRE. There is half a hide. In demesne is 1 plough, and 2 slaves and 2 bordars, and 7 burgesses in Droitwich, and 1½ salt-pans rendering 30d. It was worth 20s; now 15s. This land a certain Wulfgeat gave to the same Church of Evesham, and he placed his gift upon the altar when his son Ælfgeat was made a monk there. This was done in the fifth year of the reign of King Edward. Afterwards, Abbot Æthelwig leased this land to his uncle for so long as that man lived. The latter died, subsequently, in Harold's battle against the Northmen, and the church received its land back before King William had come into England, and the same abbot held it so long as he lived, and his successor also, Abbot Walter, held it similarly for more than 7 years.

The same Urse holds HAMPTON LOVETT. The Abbot of Evesham held it TRE. There are 4 hides. Robert holds it of Urse. In demesne is 1 plough; and 4 villans and 6 bordars with 2 ploughs, and 2 ploughs more can be [there]. There are 2 slaves, and a mill rendering 30s, and a salt-pan rendering 3 orae. TRE it was worth £4; now 50s.

The abbot of the same church bought this manor from a certain thegn who could rightfully sell his land to whom he would, TRE, and gave it, when bought, to the church by placing a copy [of the gospels] on the altar, by the witness of the shire.

XXVII. The land of Hugh l'Asne

IN 'CAME' HUNDRED

HUGH l'Asne holds 'THICKENAPPLETREE' [in Hampton Lovett] of the king, and William [holds] of him. Alweald held it. There are 3 hides. [...] In demesne are 2 ploughs; and 8 bordars and 1 Frenchman with 3 ploughs. There are 4 oxmen, and 1 female slave, and 12 acres of meadow. In Droitwich, a salt-pan rendering 30 mittae of salt. TRE it was worth 40s; now 30s.

[Folio 178: WORCESTERSHIRE]

IN 'CRESSLOW' HUNDRED

XXVII.

A certain woman, EADGIFU, holds CHADDESLEY CORBETT of the king. She herself held it TRE. There, with 8 Berewicks, are 25 hides. Of these, 10 hides were quit from geld, by witness of the shire. In demesne are 3 ploughs; and 33 villans and 20 bordars, and 2 priests with 4 bordars; among them all they have 25 ploughs. There are 8 slaves and female slaves all together, and 3 mills rendering 12 summae of corn. In Worcester, 2 burgesses pay 12d, and in Droitwich 5 salt-pans render 215⁄4d. There is woodland of 2 leagues and other woodland of 1 league. TRE, as now, worth £12.

Wulfmær held HILLHAMPTON. There is 1 virgate of land, and it is waste. TRE it was worth 12d.

In 'ASH' HUNDRED lie 10 hides in FECKENHAM and 3 hides in HOLLOW, and they are entered in the Hereford return.

In 'DODDINGTREE' HUNDRED lie 13 hides of MARTLEY and 5 hides of SUCKLEY, which plead and pay geld here, and render their farm at Hereford, and are entered in the king's return.

HEREFORDSHIRE

IN THE CITY OF HEREFORD IN THE TIME OF KING EDWARD there were 103 men dwelling within and without the wall, and they had the following customs.

If any of them wished to withdraw from the city he could with the consent of the reeve sell his house to another man who was willing to do the service due from it, and the reeve had the third penny of this sale. But if anyone through his poverty could not perform his service, he surrendered his house, without payment, to the reeve, who saw that the house did not remain empty and that the king did not lack [his] service.

Within the wall of the city each whole messuage rendered 7½d, and 4d for the hire of horses, and 3 days reaping in August at Marden, and 1 day gathering the hay where the sheriff pleased. He who had a horse went 3 times a year with the sheriff to the pleas and to the hundred [courts] at Wormelow. When the king was engaged in the hunt, 1 man from each house by custom went to head off [game] in the wood.

Other men not having whole messuages provided guards for the hall when the king was in the city.

When a burgess serving with a horse died, the king had his horse and weapons. From him who had no horse, if he died, the king had either 10s or his land with the houses [on it]. If anyone, overtaken by death, had not bequeathed his possessions the king had all his goods. Those living in the city, and others likewise dwelling without the wall, had these customs except only that a whole messuage outside the wall only gave 3½d. The other customs were common [to both]. Whosoever wife brewed within or without the city gave 10d according to custom.

There were 6 smiths in the city; each of them paid 1d from his forge, and each of them made 120 shoes of the king's iron, and to each one of them was given 3d on that account according to custom, and those smiths were quit from every other service.

There were 7 moneyers there. One of these was the bishop's moneyer.

When the coinage was renewed each of them gave 18s for receiving the dies, and within 1 month of the day on which they returned, each of them gave the king 20s, and likewise the bishop had from his moneyer 20s.

When the king came into the city the moneyers coined pennies for him, as many as he willed, that is of the king's silver. And these 7 had their sake and soke.

Upon the death of any of the king's moneyers, the king had 20s. for relief. But if he died intestate, the king had all his money.

If the sheriff went into Wales with the army these men went with him. But if anyone commanded to go did not go, he paid 40s fine to the king.

In the city itself Earl Harold had 27 burgesses having the same customs as the other burgesses.

From this city the reeve paid £12 to King Edward and £6 to Earl Harold, and he had in his farm all the aforesaid customs.

The king, however, had in his demesne the 3 forfeiture, namely breaking his peace, housebreaking, and highway robbery.

Whosoever committed one of these, paid 100s fine to the king, no matter whose man he was.

Now the king has the city of Hereford in demesne, and the English burgesses dwelling there have their former customs; but the French burgesses are quit for 12d from all their forfeitures, except the 3 aforesaid.

This city renders to the king £60 by tale of blanched pennies. Between them the city and 18 manors which render their farms in Hereford account for £335.18s, besides the pleas in the hundred and shire [courts].

IN ARCHENFIELD THE KING HAS 3 churches. The priests of these churches bear the king's embassies into Wales, and each of them sings 2 masses every week for the king. If one of them dies the king has 20s from him as a customary due.

If one of the Welshmen steals a man or woman, horse, ox, or cow, upon conviction for it, he first restores the stolen [goods], and [then] gives 20s as a forfeiture.

For a stolen sheep, however, or a bundle of sheaves, he pays 2s. fine.

If anyone kills one of the king's men, and commits housebreaking, he gives the king 20s in payment for the man, and as a forfeiture 100s. If he kills a thegn's man he gives 10s to the dead man's lord.

But if a Welshman kills a Welshman, the relatives of the slain meet together, and plunder the slayer and his kin, and burn their houses until on the morrow at about noon the corpse of the dead man is buried.

Of this plunder the king has the third part, but they have all the rest quit.

Otherwise, however, he who sets a house on fire, and is accused of it, defends himself by 40 men. But if he is unable to do so, he pays 20s fine to the king.

If anyone conceals a sester of honey due by custom, upon proof of it he renders for 1 sester 5, if he holds as much land as should give it.

If the sheriff calls them out to the shiremoot, 6 or 7 of the better of them go with him. He who does not go when called upon gives 2s or an ox to the king, and he who stays away from the hundred [court] pays as much.

He who does not go forth when ordered by the sheriff to go with him into Wales pays a like fine. But if the sheriff does not go, none of them goes.

When the army goes forth against the enemy these men, according to custom, make up the vanguard, and on the return the rearguard.

These were the customs of the Welsh TRE in ARCHENFIELD.

RHYS of Wales renders to King William £40.

From the land of "Calcebuef" the king has 10s over and above the farm.

Here Are Noted Those Holding Lands In Herefordshire and In Archenfield and In Wales

I KING WILLIAM
II The Bishop of Hereford
III The Church of Cormeilles
IIII The Church of Lyre
V The Church of Gloucester
VI The Church of St Guthlac
VII Nigel the physician
VIII Ralph de Tosny
IX Ralph de Mortimer
X Roger de Lacy
XI Roger de Mussegros
XII Robert Gernon
XIII Henry de Ferrers
XIIII William d'Ecouis
XV William fitzBaderon
XVI William fitzNorman
XVII Turstin fitzRolf
XVIII Albert of Lorraine
XIX Alvred of Marlborough
XX Alvred d'Epaignes
XXI Ansfrid de Cormeilles
XXII Durand of Gloucester
XXIII Drogo fitzPons
XXIIII Osbern fitzRichard
XXV Gilbert fitzTurold
XXVI Ilbert fitzTurold

XXVII Herman de Dreux
XXVIII Humphrey de Bouville
XXIX Hugh l'Asne
XXX Urse d'Abetot
XXXI Gruffydd
XXXII Rainier
XXXIII Carbonell
XXXIIII The wife of Ralph the chaplain
XXXV Stephen
XXXVI Madoc. Eadric. Almær

[Folio 179V: HEREFORDSHIRE]

The land of the King

IN BROMSASH HUNDRED

King William holds LINTON. King Edward held it. There were 5 hides and they rendered the fourth part of 1 night's farm. Now it is greatly decreased. There are in demesne 3 ploughs; and 10 villans and 5 bordars with 12 ploughs. There are 6 slaves, and a mill rendering 8d. There 1 Frenchman holds half a hide which rendered 4s. TRE.

This manor as it is now renders £10 of blanched pennies.

Of this manor SAINTE-MARIE of Cormeilles holds the church and [its] priest with its land, and all the tithes, and 1 villan with 1 virgate of land.

Of this manor Ansfrid de Cormeilles holds 2 hides, and 9 villans and 9 ploughs, and William fitzBaderon holds 1 virgate of land which belonged there TRE.

Ilbert the sheriff has as his farm from Archenfield all the customary dues of honey and sheep, which belonged to this manor TRE.

William fitzNorman has from this 6 sesters of honey and 6 sheep with lambs and 12d.

IN 'GREYTREE' HUNDRED

The king holds LUGWARDINE. King Edward held it. There are 4 hides. In demesne are 3 ploughs; and 9 villans and 3 bordars and 1 sergeant of the king. Among them all they have 10 ploughs. There are 3 slaves, and a mill rendering 10s.

This manor renders now £10 of blanched pennies #. TRE it was not put out to farm and therefore it is not known how much it was then worth.

SAINTE-MARIE of Cormeilles has the tithes of this manor and 1 villan with 1 virgate of land. 1 of these 4 hides was and is in the reeveland. There are 4 bordars and 1 female slave with 2 ploughs, and there are 2 mills rendering 15s.

Of the other 3 hides Ralph de Bernay added 50 acres to his reeveland, and 1 bordar, and a mill rendering 7s.

What the sheriff has for his use is worth 60s.

The king holds KINGSTONE [near Hereford]. King Edward held it. There are 4 hides. In demesne are 2 hides less 1 virgate, and there is 1 plough, and there could be another; and 6 villans with a reeve and 3 bordars, and 1 smith. Among them all they have 6 ploughs. There is a wood called Treville rendering no customary dues except venison. The villans living there TRE carried venison to Hereford, and they did no other service, as the shire says. SAINTE-MARIE of Cormeilles holds all the tithes of this manor and 1 villan with 1 virgate of land. Ilbert fitzTurold holds of this manor 2 hides as 1 manor.

To this manor belonged TRE a piece of land, CUSOP, and the customary dues from it went into Kingstone [near Hereford]. Roger de Lacy holds it of the king.

To this manor the sheriff added "WAPLEFORD" in the time of Earl William. Alwine held this manor and he could go to what lord he pleased. There is 1 hide. [There is] land for 2 ploughs. There are 2 villans with 1 plough.

All this thus added together renders to the king 50s of blanched pennies and 1 hawk.

The king holds MARDEN. King Edward held it. There were several hides there, but of these only 2 pay geld. This land is divided among many men. The king has in demesne 3 ploughs; and 25 villans and 5 bordars and 2 oxmen and 4 slaves and 4 coliberts. Among them all they have 21 ploughs. There is a mill rendering 20s and 25 sticks of eels. The woodland renders 20s. There is a fishery which pays no rent. From the salt-pans in Droitwich [Worcs.], 9 loads of salt, or 9d; and also 8 sergeants of the king have 7 ploughs.

Of this manor William fitzNorman holds 3 hides less 1 virgate, and Norman the swineherd holds half a hide of this manor, and Earl William alienated from this manor 1 virgate and gave it to a certain burgess of Hereford, and Ansketil holds 40 acres of open land and meadow, which the reeve of King Edward leased to his kinsman.

Three radknights held the land of William fitzNorman and they could not be separated from this manor. From the profits of the land of this manor come 9s. TRE it rendered £9 of blanched pennies; now it is valued at £16.

The king holds KINGSLAND. King Edward held it. There are 15 hides. [...] In demesne are 5 ploughs, and there can be 3 more ploughs; and 21 villans and 9 bordars with 17 ploughs. There are 10 oxmen and 2 slaves and 6 coliberts. There are 2 mills rendering 26s4d and 500 eels.

From the woodland and pasture, 8s; from customary dues and from the mills and villans and coliberts come 100s less 5s, besides the eels.

Of this manor Ralph de Mortimer holds 1 member, "MERESTONE" [in Wigmore], of 2 hides, and Roger de Lacy a manor of 2 hides called 'HOPE' [in Lyonshall], and another manor of 1 hide called STREET, and a third manor of 1 hide called LAWTON.

The same Roger holds half a hide which a swineherd held TRE. This land Earl William gave to Walter de Lacy.

Of the same manor Ilbert fitzTurold holds half a virgate which 1 swineherd held. This land is called "Alac".

TRE it was worth £6; now it is at farm for £13.3s.

IN "LENE" HUNDRED

The king holds EARDISLAND. Earl Morcar held it. There are 15 hides. In demesne are 3 ploughs; and 19 villans and 9 bordars and 2 radknights with 16 ploughs. There are 6 slaves

and 2 female slaves and 6 coliberts. There are 2 mills rendering 25s. The woodland renders 40d. The villans give as a customary due 13s4d, and the coliberts render 3 sesters of wheat and barley and 2½ sheep with their lambs and 2½d.

Of these 2 manors SAINTE-MARIE of Cormeilles holds the churches and priests and tithes and 2 villans in alms of the king.

TRE it was worth £6; now £12 of blanched pennies.

The reeve of this manor had the custom TRE that on the arrival of his lady at the manor he would present to her 18 orae of pence so that she should be well disposed, and the steward and the other servants had 10s from him.

IN "WIMUNDESTREU" HUNDRED

The king holds MUCH MARCLE. Earl Harold held it. There are 17 hides paying geld. In demesne are 4 ploughs; and 36 villans and 10 bordars with 40 ploughs. These villans plough and sow with their own seed 80 acres of wheat and as many of oats, save 9 acres. Of these, 6 belong to William fitzBaderon and 3 to SAINTE-MARIE of Cormeilles.

In this manor is a reeve and a Frenchman and a radknight. These have 3 ploughs. There are 8 slaves and an oxman and 6 female slaves. The mill there renders nothing beyond the sustenance of him who keeps it. The woodland there renders 5s. which are given to Droitwich [Worcs.] for 60 mittae of salt. At Hereford are 4 burgesses rendering to this manor 18 ploughshares.

Of this manor there is 1 hide at "Turlestane" which TRE rendered 50 masses of iron and 6 salmon. Now this land is in the forest.

Of this manor the sheriff holds 1 hide, and has there 2 ploughs.

In the same manor are 58 acres of land taken [or] assarted from the woodland, and the reeve and 2 other men hold several acres of this land. SAINTE-MARIE of Cormeilles has the tithes of this manor and a priest and the church with 1 villan holding 1 virgate of land. TRE it was worth £30; and now it is worth as much.

IN BROMSASH HUNDRED

The king holds CLEEVE [Cleeve and Lower Cleeve]. Earl Harold held it. There are 14½ hides with a Berewick called WILTON. In demesne are 4 ploughs; and 20 villans and a reeve and 11 bordars with 16 ploughs. There are 9 slaves and 5 female slaves and 1 oxman. There are 2 mills rendering 6s, and a fishery rendering nothing.

To this manor belong as many Welshmen as have 8 ploughs and render 10½ sesters of honey and 6s5d.

Of this manor SAINTE-MARIE of Cormeilles holds the church, a priest and the tithes, with 1 villan.

Of this manor there is in the forest of King William as much land as rendered TRE 6 sesters of honey and 6 sheep with their lambs.

Of that manor William fitzBaderon holds 1 hide and 3 virgates, and Godfrey holds 1 virgate. Roger de Lacy holds half a fishery which belonged to this manor in the time of King Edward; and then 25 mittae of salt from DROITWICH [Worcs.] belonged there, and at that time there were in this manor 2 hides less 1 virgate which are in ASHE INGEN. Alvred of Marlborough holds them now. Harold was holding them when he died, and the shire says that they are [part] of this manor.

This manor renders £9.10s of blanched pennies.

IN "PLEGELGETE" HUNDRED

The king holds 'STANFORD REGIS' [in Bishops Frome]. Queen Edith held it. There are 4 hides. [...] In demesne are 3 ploughs; and 4 villans and 4 bordars [...] with 3 ploughs. There are 6 oxmen and 4 female slaves. There is a mill rendering 6s, and 1 swineherd and 1 cowherd. SAINTE-MARIE of Cormeilles has the tithes of this manor with 1 villan. TRE it was worth 100s; now it renders 100s of blanched pennies.

The king holds LEOMINSTER. Queen Edith held it, with 16 members: Luston, Yarpole, Aymestrey, Brimfield, Ashton, Stockton, Stoke Prior, [?] Marston Stannett, Nun Upton, Hope under Dinmore, Brierley, Ivington, Cholstrey, Leinthall [?Earls], Edwyn Ralph, Farlow [Shrops.].

In this manor with these members were 80 hides, and in demesne 30 ploughs. There were 8 reeves and 8 beadles, and 8 radknights, and 238 villans and 75 bordars, and 82 slaves and female slaves.

All these together had 230 ploughs. The villans ploughed 140 acres of the lord's land and sowed them with their own wheat-seed and gave as a customary due £11 and 52d. The rad-knights gave 14s4d and 3 sesters of honey, and there were 8 mills rendering 73s and 30 sticks of eels. The woodland rendered 24s and pannage.

Now the king has in this manor in demesne 60 hides and 29 ploughs; and 6 priests, and 6 radmen, and 7 reeves and 7 beadles, and 224 villans and 81 bordars, and 25 slaves and female slaves. Among them all they have 201 ploughs.

These plough and sow with their own wheat 125 acres and give as a customary due £7.14s8½d, and 17s for fish, and 8s. for salt and 65s [worth] of honey. There are 8 mills rendering 108s and 100 sticks of eels less 10.

Woodland 6 leagues long and 3 leagues wide renders 22s. Out of these, 5s are given towards buying wood in Droitwich [Worcs.] and 30 mittae of salt come from there. Each villan having 10 pigs gives 1 pig as pannage.

From [the land] assarted from the woodland come 17s4d. There is a hawk's eyrie.

To this manor Hugh l'Asne pays 5s, Roger de Lacy 6s8d, Ralph de Mortimer 15s, Bernard a la Barbe 5s, Ilbert 5s, Osbern 6s8d, Godmund 5s, Godwine 40d, Alweard 40d, Sæmær 40d, Vitard 3s, Alweard 30d, Beorhtmær 20d, Alweard 20d.

In all this render, besides the eels, £23.2s are accounted for.

This manor is at farm for £60, besides the sustenance of the nuns.

The shire says that if it were freed this manor could be valued at six-score pounds, that is 120[l].

Of the 80 hides of this manor Urse d'Abetot holds 3 hides in Edwyn Ralph; and Roger de Lacy 3½ hides in HUMBER, and 1½ hides in Brockmanton; and Ralph de Mortimer 1 hide in Aymestrey, and 8 hides paying geld in Leinthall [?Earls]; and William fitzNorman half a hide in [?] LYE [in Birley] and 1 hide in [?] Eyton.

In these [hides] are 3 ploughs in demesne; and 11 villans and 22 bordars and 2 priests. Among them all they have 10 ploughs and [there are] 16 slaves, and 2 mills rendering 24s. At Leinthall [?Earls] is woodland 1 league long and 1 league broad.

In all these lands are worth £12.11s.

Leofwine Latimer holds as much of the land of Leominster as is worth 25s.

Of the land of Ralph de Mortimer in Aymestrey, St Peter has 15s.

To this manor belonged TRE 2 manors, 'Stanford Regis' [in Bishops Frome] and Much Marcle, which now render to the king £30, as is said above.

The Following Lands Belonged To Leominster TRE

HUGH l'Asne holds HATFIELD. Leodfæd held it. There are 5 hides. | Of these, 2 hides and 1 virgate paid geld. | In demesne are 3 ploughs. There is a reeve and 2 radknights and 2 Frenchmen and 8 bordars with 6½ ploughs, and also 2 men holding nothing. TRE it was worth £4; now 100s.

OSBERN fitzRichard holds [?] 'WAPLEY' [in Staunton on Arrow], by the king's gift, as he says. He himself held it TRE. There are 2 hides paying geld. There is 1 radknight, and 1 villan and 22 bordars. Among them all they have 6 ploughs. It is worth 20s.

URSE d'Abetot holds BUTTERLEY. Ketil held it. There is 1 hide. In demesne are 2 ploughs; and 4 bordars with 1 plough, and 4 oxmen. It is worth 40s.

The ABBESS holds FENCOTE, and she herself held it TRE. There is 1 hide [geld-] free, and 4 villans with 2 ploughs.

Roger de Lacy holds HAMPTON WAFER. Bruning held it. There is half a hide. In demesne is 1 plough. TRE it was worth 40s; now 30s.

The same Roger holds HAMPTON [in Hope under Dinmore], and Gilbert [holds] of him. Eadwig held it. There are 2 hides. In demesne are 2 ploughs; and a reeve and 2 radknights and 2 bordars with 4 ploughs. It was worth 20s; now 40s.

The same Roger holds SARNESFIELD, and Gothmund [holds] of him. Særic held it. There are 1½ hides. In demesne is 1 plough; and 10 bordars with 3 ploughs. There is 1 slave and 1 female slave. This land was waste; now it is worth 20s.

The same Roger holds GATTERTOP, and Walter [holds] of him. Alwine held it. There is 1 hide, and in demesne 1 plough. There is 1 villan and 7 bordars with 2 ploughs. There are 2 slaves and 2 female slaves, and in addition there can be 1 plough. It is worth 30s.

RALPH de Mortimer holds WIGMORE. Alweard held it. There is half a hide. WIGMORE Castle lies there.

The same Ralph holds BRIMFIELD. Earnsige held it. There are 3 virgates of land. In demesne [is] 1 plough and 2 slaves. It is worth 7s6d.

RALPH de Tosny holds FORD for 1 hide and 1 virgate, and BROADFIELD [Broadfield and Lower Broadfield] for 1 hide, and LITTLE SARNESFIELD for half a hide. Drogo holds them of Ralph. In demesne are 3 ploughs, and 2 villans and 5 bordars, and 3 slaves and 2 female slaves, and 3 oxmen, and a fishery rendering 600 eels. It was worth 55s; now 75s. Alweard held it.

The same Ralph holds EATON, and Herbert [holds] of him. Leofnoth held it. There are 1½ hides. In demesne are 2 ploughs; and 3 villans and 4 bordars with 4½ ploughs. It was worth 40s; now 60s.

WILLIAM d'Ecouis holds RISBURY, and Robert [holds] of him. Edwin held it. There are 2 hides, and in demesne 2 ploughs, and 1 villan and 3 bordars and 4 slaves, and a mill rendering 4s. The villan pays 10d. It was worth 20s; now 60s.

The same William holds WHARTON, and Bernard [holds] of him. There is 1 hide. In demesne are 2 ploughs; and 1 villan with half a plough, and 4 oxmen. It was and is worth 20s. Wulfweard held it.

The same William holds NEWTON [in Hope under Dinmore], and Bernard [holds] of him. Bruning held it. There is half a hide. This land is waste.

The same William holds [?Little] DILWYN, and Richard [holds] of him. Almær held it. There is 1 hide, and in demesne 1 plough; and a radknight with 1 plough. There is 1 Frenchman and 4 bordars paying 25d. There are 2 slaves and 1 female slave. It was worth 5s; now 20s.

The same William holds HATFIELD, and Ralph [holds] of him. Almær held it. There is half a hide, and in demesne 1 plough and 2 slaves. It was worth 65d; now 8s.

WILLIAM fitzNorman holds BROADWARD. Leofnoth held it. There is half a hide, and in demesne 1 plough; and 2 villans and a smith and 5 bordars with 2 ploughs. There are 2 slaves, and a mill rendering 10s, and a fishery rendering 500 eels. It was worth 20s; now 30[s.].

DROGO fitzPons holds HAMPTON [in Hope under Dinmore], and Stephen [holds] of him. There is 1 hide, and in demesne 1 plough; and 1 bordar with 1 plough, and a mill rendering 40d. Eadric held it. It has always been worth 20s.

The same Drogo holds HAMNISH [Hamnish Clifford and Upper Hamnish], and Walter [holds] of him. Earnsige held it. There is 1 hide, and in demesne 2 ploughs, and 2 bordars and 4 slaves. It was worth 20s; now 40d more.

DURAND the sheriff holds MIDDLETON ON THE HILL, and Bernard [holds] of him. Ælfric held it. There are 1½ hides, and in demesne 1 plough, and 2 bordars and 2 slaves. It was worth 20s; now 10s.

ILBERT holds [?Sollers] DILWYN. Ramkel held it. There are 2 hides, and in demesne 2 ploughs; and 8 bordars with 4 ploughs. There are 4 oxmen. It was worth 20s; now 40s.

[Folio 180V: HEREFORDSHIRE]

The same Ilbert holds LUNTLEY. Ramkel held it. There are 2 hides, and in demesne 1 plough. There is a reeve and 4 bordars and 2 oxmen with 2 ploughs. It was worth 40s; now 30s.

GRUFFYDD the boy holds "ALAC", and Godwine [holds] of him. Alweard held it. There is 1 hide, and in demesne 1 plough and 2 slaves. It was and is worth 10s.

The same Gruffydd holds half a hide, and Alweard [holds] of him. There he has 1 plough with his men. It was waste; now it is worth 15s.

LEOFWINE Latimer holds YARPOLE. Ælfric held it. There is 1 virgate. It was waste. Now there are 2 bordars with 1 plough, and it is worth 3s.

In all there are 32 hides and they all paid geld TRE and rendered customary dues at LEOMINSTER.

What Hugh l'Asne holds rendered 5s What Osbern [holds] rendered 5 orae.

What Urse holds rendered 40d. What the abbess [holds] 40d.

What Roger de Lacy [holds] 13s4d and 25d as rent.

What Ralph de Mortimer [holds] rendered 50d; now it renders nothing.

What Ralph de Tosny [holds] 11s10d.

What William d'Ecouis [holds] 11s10d and 2 sesters of honey.

What William fitzNorman [holds] 20d.

What Drogo fitzPons [holds] 8s8d.

What Durand the sheriff [holds] 5s. What Ilbert [holds] 5s.

What Gruffydd holds 5s. What Leofwine [holds] 10d, and they work 2 days in the week.

IN 'DODDINGTREE' HUNDRED

The king holds MARTLEY [Worcs]. Queen Edith held it. There are 10 hides and 1 virgate of land. In demesne are 8 ploughs; and 47 villans and 16 bordars and 2 radmen with 43 ploughs. There is a mill rendering 8s, and 2 weirs render 2,500 eels and 5 sticks [of eels].

There a reeve and a beadle have 2 virgates of land and 2 ploughs. In Worcester are 3 houses rendering 12d. The villans and bordars pay 12s for fish and for firewood.

This manor renders to Hereford £24 of pence at 20 to the ora, and 12s as a fine.

Earl William gave to SAINTE-MARIE of Cormeilles the church of this manor with the land belonging to it and with its tithe, and 2 villans with 2 virgates of land.

The earl himself gave to Ralph de Bernay 2 radmen and put them outside this manor with the land which they held. These men have 2 ploughs.

The same earl gave to Druward 1 virgate of land which he still holds.

IN 'ASH' HUNDRED

The king holds FECKENHAM [Worcs.]. 5 thegns held it of Earl Edwin, and could go with the land where they would, and had under them 4 knights as free as they themselves were. Among them all were 13 ploughs. There are 10 hides, and in demesne 6 ploughs; and 30 villans and 11 bordars, and a reeve and a beadle, and a miller and a smith. Among them all they have 18 ploughs. There are 12 slaves and 5 female slaves, and a radman holds half a hide and 2 parts of half a hide and a croft, and he has 1 plough. There is a mill rendering 2s.

In Droitwich [Worcs.], 4 salt-pans. The woodland of this manor has been put outside in the king's wood, and 1 hide of land which Earl William gave to Joscelin the huntsman.

The tithes and church of this manor with a priest, and 2 virgates of land with 1 villan, Earl William gave to the Church of SAINTE- MARIE.

Walter de Lacy gave to a certain Hubert 1 hide of demesne land. This man has half a plough.

The king holds HOLLOW [Worcs.]. Siward, thegn and kinsman of King Edward, held it. There are 3 hides, and in demesne 3 ploughs; and 4 villans and 1 bordar and a reeve and a beadle with 3 ploughs, and 6 slaves and female slaves. There is a park for wild beasts, but it has been put outside the manor with all the woodland. In Droitwich [Worcs.], 4 salt-pans and a hoccus.

In Worcester 1 house renders 2 ploughshares, and 2 other houses belonging to Feckenham [Worcs.] rendered nothing and have been put outside.

These 2 manors render to Hereford £18 of pence at 20 to the ora.

IN GLOUCESTERSHIRE

The king holds HANLEY CASTLE [Worcs.]. Beorhtric held it There are 4 hides. In demesne [are] 2 ploughs; and 20 villans and 17 bordars and a reeve. Among them all they have 17½ ploughs. There are 9 slaves and female slaves, and 6 swine-herds render 60 pigs and have 4 ploughs. There is a mill rendering 2s [There is] woodland 5 league in both length and breadth. This has been put outside the manor. There is a hawk's eyrie. A forester holds half a virgate of land, and a villan from Baldenhall [in Guarlford, Worcs.] pays 2 orae of pence to this manor.

The king holds FORTHAMPTON [Glos.]. Beorhtric held it. [...]There are 9 hides which paid geld for 4 hides. In demesne are 3 ploughs; and 7 villans with 5 ploughs. 4 swineherds there with 1 plough render 35 pigs. The woodland is 3 leagues in both length and breadth. It is within the preserve of the king's wood, and there is a hawk's eyrie and 2½ hides, and Ansgot holds 3 virgates of land. SAINTE-MARIE holds the tithe of this manor with 1 villan and 1 virgate of land.

IN WORCESTERSHIRE

The king holds BUSHLEY [Worcs.]. Beorhtric held it, who also bought it from Lyfing, Bishop of Worcester, for 3 marks of gold, together with a house in the city of Worcester, which renders yearly a mark of silver, and together with a wood 1 league long and as much broad. All this he bought thus and held quit so that he did not serve any man for it.

In this manor [is] 1 hide, and in demesne are 2 ploughs; and 4 villans and 8 bordars and a reeve and a beadle. Among them all they have 4 ploughs. There are 8 slaves and female slaves, and a cowherd and a diarymaid. A forester there holds half a virgate of land.

In PULL [Worcs.] are 3 virgates of land which belonged to Longdon [Worcs.], the manor of Earl Oda. This land Earl William added to Bushley [Worcs.]. There is 1 plough, and a man of the monks of Lyre holds 1 virgate of land.

Earl William put outside his manors 2 foresters, one from Hanley Castle [Worcs.] and the other from Bushley [Worcs.], in order to guard the woods.

The king holds QUEENHILL [Worcs.]. Æthelric, brother of Bishop Beorhtric, held it. There is 1 hide, and in demesne 1 plough; and 7 villans and 3 bordars with 4½ ploughs. There is 1 swineherd and 2 oxmen and a diarymaid. The woodland has been put outside the manor.

Earl William gave the tithes of this manor to SAINTE-MARIE of Lyre with 1 villan who holds half a virgate of land.

Herman holds of this manor 1 villan who has half a virgate of land.

The king holds ELDERSFIELD [Worcs.]. Regenbald the chancellor held it TRE. Earl William had it in exchange from him. There are 5 hides. In demesne are 3 ploughs; and 12 villans and 13 bordars with 11 ploughs. There are 5 slaves and female slaves, and 6 oxmen, and a mill rendering 2s. [There is] woodland 2 leagues long and as much broad. It has been put outside the manor. Ansgot, a man of Earl William, holds half a virgate of land, and Wulfgeat 1 hide of free land.

Sainte-MARIE has there 1 villan who holds 1 virgate of land.

The king holds SUCKLEY [Worcs.]. Earl Edwin held it. There are 5 hides. In demesne are 2 ploughs; and 22 villans and 24 bordars with 27 ploughs. There are 10 other bordars, poor men, and a mill rendering 6s, and a bee-keeper with 12 hives. The woodland is 5 leagues in both length and breadth, and there is a fishery. In Worcester [is] 1 burgess, but he pays nothing. There is a mill rendering 6s.

Sainte-MARIE holds the tithes of this vill with 1 villan and half a virgate of land. Earl Roger gave to a certain Richard half a virgate of land in complete freedom.

These 6 manors render to Hereford £50 as farm and 25s as a fine.

In MONMOUTH CASTLE the king has in demesne 4 ploughs. William fitzBaderon has the custody of them. What the king has in this castle is worth 100s. There

William has 8 ploughs in demesne, and there can be more. There are Welshmen having 24 ploughs; they render 33 sesters of honey and 2s. There are 15 slaves and female slaves, and 3 mills rendering 20s. The knights of this William have 7 ploughs. What William holds is worth £30.

The church of this castle and all the tithes with 2 carucates of land Saint-Florent of Saumur holds.

[Folio 181: HEREFORDSHIRE]

In ARCHENFIELD the king has 100 men less 4, who have 73 ploughs with their men, and give as a customary due 41 sesters of honey, and 20s for the sheep which they used to give, and 10s for smoke-sliver, nor do they pay geld or any other customary due except that they go forth in the king's army if they are ordered to.

If a free man dies there, the king has his horse with his weapons.
From a villan when he dies, the king has 1 ox.
King Gruffydd and Bleddyn laid waste this land TRE and so it is not known what it was like at that time.

GARWAY belonged to Archenfield TRE and there were 4 carucates of land. Herman holds this land, and 3 bordars there have 3 oxen.

Gilbert fitz Turold holds a manor [Ballingham] there in which are 4 free men with 4 ploughs. and they render 4 sesters of honey and 16d as a customary due. Of the same Archenfield Wærstan holds 1 vill [Harewood, near Llanwarne], and there he has with his men 6 ploughs, and the forest renders half a sester of honey and 6d.

These Vills Or Lands Which Follow Are Situated Within the Boundary of Archenfield

WILLIAM fitzNorman holds KILPECK. Cadiand held it TRE. In demesne are 3 ploughs and 2 slaves and 4 oxmen; and 57 men with 19 ploughs, and they render 15 sesters of honey and 10s, nor do they give any other geld nor do service save with the army. It is worth £4.

The same William holds BAYSHAM, and Walter [holds] of him. Merewine held it of King Edward. In demesne are 2 ploughs; and 14 men with 7 ploughs, and they pay 5s as a customary due. It is worth 30s.

The same William holds KINGS CAPLE, and Walter [holds] of him. him. King Edward held it in demesne. There are 5 Welshmen having 5 ploughs, and they render 5 sesters of honey and 5 sheep with their lambs and 10d. It is worth 30s. There is 1 Frenchman with 1 plough.

ALVRED of Marlborough holds PONTRILAS. Earl Harold held it. In demesne are 1½ ploughs; and a priest and 3 villans and 4 bordars and 4 slaves with 5 ploughs, and they give 3 sheep. It is worth 30s.

The same Alvred holds ASHE INGEN. It was waste TRE. There is 1 man having 1½ ploughs, and he pays 10s as farm.

ROGER de Lacy holds [Little and Much] BIRCH. Costelin

held it TRE. Now his son holds it of Roger, and there are 4 ploughs, and it renders 6 sesters of honey and 10s.

There Roger has 1 Welshman paying 5s and a sester of honey.

The same Roger holds "PENEBECDOC", and Novi [holds] of him. The same man held it TRE. There are 4 ploughs. This land renders 6 sesters of honey and 10s.

GODRIC Mappesone holds GODRICH. Taldus held it TRE. In demesne are 2 ploughs, and 4 oxmen and 1 female slave. There are 12 villans and 12 bordars with 11 ploughs, and they render 18 sesters of honey. There is a smith, and a fishery. It is worth 40s.

IN WORMELOW HUNDRED

ST PETER of Gloucester holds 'WESTWOOD' [in Llanwarne], the head of this manor. King Edward held it. There are 6 hides. 1 of these has Welsh customs and the others English. In demesne is 1 ploughs, and 2 bordars and 2 oxmen. This land of ST PETER gives as farm 30s. Durand gave it to the church for the soul of his brother Roger.

Of this manor Roger de Lacy holds a part, and Odo [holds] of him. Earl William gave it to him. In demesne are 2 ploughs; and 9 bordars with 2 ploughs, and 2 slaves and 2 oxmen. There is 1 Frenchman with 2 bordars having 2 ploughs. It is worth £3.

Ralph de Sacey holds part of the same manor and has land for 2 ploughs. There is 1 plough with 2 oxmen; and 1 Welshman having half a plough and rendering 1 sester of honey. It is worth 20s.

RALPH de Tosny holds DEWSALL, and William and Ilbert [hold] of him. Wulfheah held it. There is 1 hide, and in demesne 2 ploughs and a slave; and 4 bordars with 2 ploughs. It is worth 30s. SAINTE-MARIE of Lyre holds the church of this manor and a priest and land for 1 plough.

The king has in Herefordshire 9 waste manors [assessed] at 19 hides. For the forests which he holds William fitz Norman pays £15 to the king.

IN "HEZETRE" HUNDRED

The king holds BURLINGJOBB [Wales]. Sol held it TRE. There are 2 hides. They were and are waste. There is land for 4 ploughs.

The king holds OLD RADNOR [Wales]. Earl Harold held it. There are 15 hides. They are and were waste. There is land for 30 ploughs.

Hugh l'Asne says that Earl William gave this land to him, when he gave him the land of Thorkil his predecessor.

IN ELSDON HUNDRED

The king holds WHITNEY. Alweard held it TRE, and could go where he would. There is half a hide paying geld. It was and is waste.

Earl Harold held "MATEURDIN", a manor of 2 hides paying geld. Part of this land the king has, and it is and was waste.

The same Harold held EARDISLEY. There are 2½ hides, waste.

The same Harold held CHICKWARD. There is 1 hide and 3 virgates of land, waste. In [?][Lower and Upper] Welson 2 hides. In Chickward 1 hide. In Huntington [near Kington] 3 hides. In Bollingham 1 hide. In [Lower and Upper] Hergest 1 hide. In Breadward 2 hides. In Kington 4 hides. In Rushock 4 hides. These lands Earl Harold held. Now the king has them. | They are waste |. In [Lower and Upper] Hergest 3 hides. In Barton [in Kington] 2 hides. In Rushock 1 hide.

These 3 manors King Edward held and they paid geld. Now the king has them and they are waste.

IN ELSDON HUNDRED

In WOONTON [in Almeley] are 1½ hides paying geld. Algar and Alwine held them as 2 manors and could go where they would. Ralph de Bernay, when he was sheriff, added these 2 estates unjustly to the farm of Leominster. There are 1½ ploughs; nothing else. TRE it was waste; now it renders 62d to the king's farm.

IN "PLEGELGETE" HUNDRED

In ROWDEN is 1 hide paying geld. Grim held it as a manor and could go where he would. There Grimkel has 1 plough, and 1 bordar and 1 oxman. It was worth 12s; now 10s at farm.

IN BROMSASH HUNDRED

In 'NEWARNE' [in East Dean, Glos.] are 2½ hides, which used to convene and do service, but Roger de Pitres in the time of Earl William transferred them to Gloucestershire.

In [?] REDBROOK [Glos.] are 2½ hides. Ælfric and Alweard and Beorhtsige held them as 2 manors. They were waste and are still in the king's woodland.

In the same place Beorhtric held 1 manor as 1 hide, and Earl Godwine held STAUNTON [Glos.], 1 manor, as 1 hide. They were waste, and are still in the king's woodland.

In YATTON Hwætmann held 1 hide paying geld, and could go where he would. Hugh held it at farm of Humphrey the chamberlain, and paid 30s and still pays as much.

This land was thegnland TRE, but was afterwards changed into reeveland and therefore the king's commissioners say that this land and the revenue issuing from it is being stealthily taken away from the king.

[Folio 181V: HEREFORDSHIRE]

II. The land of the Church of Hereford

In THE TOWN OF HEREFORD TRE Bishop Walter had 100 messuages less 2. They who dwelt in them paid 100s less 6s. The same bishop also had a moneyers.

When Robert succeeded to the bishopric he found 60 messuages. They who dwelt in them paid 43s4d. Now it is valued at 50s.

Bishop Robert found 40 hides waste when he succeeded to the bishopric, and they are so still.

Bishop Walter had 1 manor, DIDLEY, which is valued at 40s, and next to it lies another manor, "STANE", which by rights belongs to the bishopric. In these 2 manors are 10 hides. All these hides are waste, and were waste, save 1 hide in DIDLEY.

Of these 9 hides one part is in the jurisdiction of Alvred's castle at EWYAS HAROLD and the other part in the preserve of the king['s woodland].

These hides paid geld with Bishop Walter TRE. In Tedstone Delamere 2½ hides. In Sawbury Hill half a hide. In Yarsop 3 virgates of land. In Noakes 1 hide and 1 virgate.

These Lands Which Follow Belong To the Canons of Hereford

IN STRETFORD HUNDRED

In LULHAM are 8 hides paying geld. In demesne is 1 plough; and 11 villans and 5 bordars with 13 ploughs. There is 1 female slave, and 3 acres of meadow, and there could be 1 more plough in demesne. Of this land 2 clerks hold 2 hides and 3 virgates, and 1 knight 1 hide. These have in demesne 2 ploughs; and 13 villans and 2 bordars with 8 ploughs. TRE it was waste; now it is worth £10.

In PRESTON ON WYE are 6 hides paying geld. In demesne is 1 plough; and 9 villans and 8 bordars with 8½ ploughs. There is a mill rendering 2s, [and] woodland 1 league long and a half broad, and there could be 1 more plough in demesne. Of this land 2 clerks hold 2½ hides, and 1 hide is waste. | These have | 7 villans with 3 ploughs. The villans have more ploughs than arable land. TRE it was waste; now [worth] 100s.

In TYBERTON are 6 hides paying geld. There is 1 plough in demesne; and 16 villans and 6 bordars with 9 ploughs, and there could be 1 more plough in demesne. There are 3 acres of meadow, [and] woodland 1 league long and half a league wide. TRE it was waste; now it is worth £3.

In this hundred 1 radman holds 1 hide which belongs to "Canons' Barton", and pays geld, and there is 1 plough in demesne. It is worth 5s.

In EATON BISHOP are 5 hides [...]. In demesne are 2 ploughs; and 12 villans and 6 bordars with 7 ploughs. There are 2 slaves, and a mill rendering 5s, and 12 acres of meadow, [and] woodland 1 league long and 2 furlongs wide. It is worth £4.

This manor Earl Harold held, and Earl William gave it to Bishop Walter for land in which the market is now, and for 3 hides of LYDNEY [Glos.].

In MADLEY are 3 hides, and it belongs to "Bishop's Barton". In demesne is 1 plough; and 16 villans with 4 ploughs. There is woodland half a league long and 1 furlong broad. This woodland is within the king's preserve.

In the same HUNDRED 2 free men hold 4 hides, and they belong to "Bishop's Barton". In demesne they have 1½ ploughs; and 6 bordars with 2 ploughs. The whole manor is worth 100s; the knight's land, 15s8d.

IN DINEDOR HUNDRED

In 'BARTON' [in Hereford] are 10 hides paying geld. In demesne is 1 plough; and 1 villans and 2 bordars with 1 plough. There is 1 female slave, and 4 acres of meadow. The woodland of this manor the king has in his demesne.

Of this land 4 clerks hold 4½ hides, and 4 knights hold 5 hides. These have in demesne 7½ ploughs; and 22 villans and 12 bordars with 10½ ploughs. Half a hide is waste. In demesne could be 2 more ploughs than there are. TRE it was waste; now it is worth £7.

In HOLME LACY are 6 hides paying geld. In demesne are 2 ploughs; and 16 villans, and a priest and a reeve, and a Frenchman and 4 boors. Among them all they have 20½ ploughs. There is 1 slave and 2 female slaves, and 10 acres of meadow, [and] woodland half a league long and as much wide.

To this manor belongs a church, and it is called LLANWARNE, and there are 3 ploughs, but the land of this church does not pay geld. A priest pays 2s from this. This land Roger de Lacy holds under the bishop.

This manor Earl Harold held unjustly, because it is for the sustenance of the canons. King William restored it to Bishop Walter. TRE it was worth £9; now £8.

IN 'GREYTREE' HUNDRED

In WOOLHOPE are 16 hides paying geld. In demesne is 1 plough, and there could be another; and 35 villans and 7 bordars with 35 ploughs. There are 8 acres of meadow, [and] woodland 3 furlongs long and 1 furlong wide.

Of this land 2 clerks hold 1 hide and 1 virgate, and 1 knight 1½ hides. In demesne is 1 plough; and 5 villans and 4 bordars with 4 ploughs. The knight pays 5s to the canons of St Æthelbert. TRE it was worth £16; and now the same.

In HOW CAPLE are 5 hides paying geld. In demesne are 3 ploughs; and 9 villans and 1 bordar with 8 ploughs. There is 1 slave and 2 female slaves, and a mill rendering 3s, and 8 acres of meadow. TRE it was worth 40s; and afterwards, as now, 60s.

In BROCKHAMPTON are 5 English hides paying geld, and 3 Welsh hides rendering 6s a year to the canons. In the 5 hides is 1 plough in demesne; and 8 villans with 7 ploughs, and 3 acres of meadow. TRE it was worth 70s; and afterwards, as now, as much.

IN "TORNELAUS" HUNDRED

In PRESTON WYNNE are 4 hides paying geld. 1½ virgates are waste. 2 canons held them TRE, and afterwards a clerk and a knight. In demesne [are] 4 ploughs; and 5 villans with 4½ ploughs. There is 1 female slave, and 20 acres of meadow. TRE it was worth 65s; now 5s less.

In WITHINGTON are 8 hides paying geld. In demesne is 1 plough; and 4 villans and 2 bordars with 3 ploughs. There are

2 acres of meadow, and a mill rendering 2s. Of this manor 3 clerks hold 4 hides, and have in demesne 3 ploughs; and 6 villans and 4 bordars with 6 ploughs, and 1 slave and 2 female slaves, and 7 acres of meadow.

Of the same manor the nuns of Hereford hold 2 hides, and have there 1 plough, and 3 villans with 2½ ploughs, and 14 acres of meadow. In all it is and was always worth £6.5s.

In ULLINGSWICK are 6 hides. Of these, 3 hides pay geld, and 3 are waste. In demesne are 3 ploughs; and 8 villans and 4 bordars with 6½ ploughs. There are 2 slaves, and part of a salt-pan in Droitwich [Worcs.]. TRE and afterwards, as now, worth 100s. One of the bishop's knights holds it of him.

IN "WIMUNDESTREU" HUNDRED

In DONNINGTON is 1 hide paying geld. In demesne is 1 plough; and 6 villans and 6 bordars with 7 ploughs. There is 1 female slave, and 8 acres of meadow. TRE and afterwards, as now, worth 25s. One of the bishop's clerks holds it of him.

IN RADLOW HUNDRED

In MORETON JEFFRIES are 4 hides paying geld. In demesne are 3 ploughs; and 2 villans and 1 bordar with 2 ploughs. There are 4 slaves and 6 female slaves, and 7 acres of meadow, and 1 salt-pans in Droitwich [Worcs.]. TRE and afterwards, as now, worth 100s.

In BISHOP'S FROME are 10 hides paying geld. Of these, 4 hides lie in "PLEGELGETE" HUNDRED. In demesne is 1 plough; and 22 villans and 4 bordars with 21 ploughs. There is 1 slave, and a mill rendering 8s, and 6 acres of meadow. The woodland renders nothing.

Of this manor 2 knights hold 3 hides, and the bishop's chaplain 1 hide, and the priest of the vill 1 virgate of land. These men have 6 ploughs; and 5 villans and 1 bordar

[Folio 182: HEREFORDSHIRE]

with 4 ploughs, and 3 slaves. The reeve of the vill has 1 mill rendering 32d. TRE and afterwards, as now, worth £10.15s

IN BROMSASH HUNDRED

In 'WHIPPINGTON' [in Staunton, [Glos.] are 3 hides which by rights belong to the bishopric. They are waste and were waste. There is a fishery.

In WALFORD are 7 hides paying geld. In demesne is 1 plough, and there could be 2 more. There are 6 villans and 4 bordars with 5 ploughs. There are 14 acres of meadow and 3 enclosures. The villans pay 10s for the waste land.

In ROSS-ON-WYE are 7 hides paying geld. In demesne is 1 plough, and there could be another. There are 18 villans and 6 bordars and a priest with 23 ploughs. There are 3 slaves, and a mill rendering 6s8d, and 16 acres of meadow. The woodland is in the king's preserve. The villans pay 18s as revenue.

In UPTON BISHOP are 7 hides paying geld. In demesne are 2 ploughs; and 18 villans and 11 bordars and 2 boors and a priest. Among them all they have 28½ ploughs. There are 5 slaves, and 4 acres of meadow and an enclosure, and woodland rendering nothing. The villans pay 20s as a customary due. These 3 manors, Walford, and Ross-on-Wye, and Upton Bishop, are valued at £14.

IN "WIMUNDESTREU" HUNDRED

In LEDBURY are 5 hides. In demesne are 2 ploughs; and 10 villans and 1 boor with 11 ploughs. There is a mill rendering 32d, and 7 acres of meadow. [There is] woodland half a league long and a half broad, and it renders nothing. Of this manor a priest holds 2½ hides, and 2 knights 1 hide, and a radman 3 virgates. These have in demesne 10 ploughs; and 7 bordars with other men having 8 ploughs, and [there is] part of a salt-pan in Droitwich [Worcs.]. TRE it was worth £10; and afterwards, as now, £8. What the priest holds is worth 50s.

Of this manor Earl Harold held 1 hide, HAZLE unjustly, and Godric [held] of him. King William restored it to Bishop Walter. In demesne are 3 ploughs; and 4 villans with 3 ploughs, and a mill rendering 2s, and 7 acres of meadow. TRE and afterwards, as now, worth 25s.

In EASTNOR are 4 hides paying geld. In demesne are 3 ploughs; and 8 villans and 7 bordars with 11 ploughs. There are 6 acres of meadow, and 2 enclosures, and woodland which renders nothing, and part of a salt-pan in Droitwich [Worcs.]. [There is] woodland 4 furlongs long, and 2 broad.

Of this, 1 knight holds half a hide, and a mason half a hide and half a virgate. In demesne [is] 1 plough; and 2 bordars with some others [have] 3 ploughs. TRE and afterwards, as now, worth £4.

In 'BAGBURROW' [in Mathon] are 5 hides paying geld. In demesne are 2 ploughs; and 16 villans and 13 bordars with 20 ploughs. There is a mill rendering 32d, and 8 acres of meadow, and woodland rendering nothing, and part of a salt-pan in Droitwich [Worcs.].

Of this manor 2 knights hold 1 hide and 3 virgates, and 2 radmen 3½ virgates. These have in demesne 4 ploughs; and their men 6 ploughs, and a mill rendering 16d. TRE and afterwards, as now, worth £8 less 5s.

In BOSBURY are 6 hides paying geld. In demesne [are] 2 ploughs; and 17 villans and 16 bordars and a boor with 22 ploughs. There are 2 slaves, and a mill rendering 30d, and 8 acres of meadow, and woodland rendering nothing. A priest holds 1 hide and has 1 plough. TRE and afterwards, as now, worth £6.

In CRADLEY are 12 hides. 1 of these is waste. The other pay geld. In demesne are 3 ploughs; and 23 villans and 3 bordars and 6 boors with 28 ploughs. There are 5 slaves, and a mill rendering 32d, and 7 acres of meadow. [There is] woodland 1 league long and half a league broad, and it renders nothing. There is 1 enclosure.

Of this manor a priest holds 1½ virgates, and a reeve half a hide, and 2 knights 1 hide and 1½ virgates, and 1 radman half a hide. These have in demesne 5 ploughs; and their bordars [have] 6 ploughs. TRE and afterwards, as now, worth £10.

In COLWALL are 3 hides paying geld, and they belong to

Cradley. In demesne are 2 ploughs; and 8 villans and 8 bordars with 10 ploughs. There are 6 slaves, and a mill rendering 16d, and 8 acres of meadow, and an enclosure.

Of this manor 1 radman holds half a hide, and he has 1 plough there. TRE and afterwards, as now, worth 60s.

This manor Earl Harold held unjustly, and Thormoth [held] of him. King William restored it to Bishop Walter.

In CODDINGTON are 3 hides. Half a hide is waste. The other hides pay geld. In demesne are 2 ploughs; and 6 villans and a bordar with 6 ploughs. 1 radman there holds 1 hide and has 1 plough. There are 3 acres of meadow, and woodland rendering nothing. To this manor belong 3 messuages in Worcester; they render 30d. TRE and afterwards, as now, worth 45s.

This manor Earl Harold held unjustly. King William restored it to Bishop Walter.

IN "CUTESTORNES" HUNDRED

In HAMPTON BISHOP are 4 hides paying geld. In demesne are 2 ploughs; and 6 villans and 5 bordars with 7 ploughs. There are 2 female slaves, and 2½ mills rendering 35s, and 28 acres of meadow. Of this manor 1 knight holds 3 virgates, and 1 radman 1 virgate, and they have in demesne 3 ploughs. TRE and afterwards, as now, worth 100s.

This manor Earl Harold held unjustly. King William restored it to Bishop Walter.

In TUPSLEY is 1 hide paying geld. In demesne are 2 ploughs; and 4 villans and 6 bordars with 2 ploughs. There is a mill rendering 20s, and 20 acres of meadow, and a salt-pan at Droitwich [Worcs.] rendering 16 mittae of salt. 1 Frenchman holds half this hide, and has 1 plough. TRE, and afterwards, it was worth 40s; now 5s more.

In SHELWICK are 2 hide paying geld. In demesne is 1 plough; and 6 villans and 6 bordars with 4 ploughs. There is 1 female slave, and a mill rendering 30s, and 18 acres of meadow. TRE, and afterwards, it was worth 60s; now 100s.

In SHELWICK are 3 hides paying geld. In demesne is 1 plough; and 5 villans with 3 ploughs, and 1 Frenchman there holds half a hide and has 1 plough with 2 bordars. There are 8 acres of meadow. TRE, and afterwards, it was worth 30s; now 5s more.

In SUGWAS are 2 hides paying geld. In demesne is 1 plough. 1 knight holds at farm 1 of these hides for 8s. TRE and afterwards, as now, worth 23s.

This manor Earl Harold held unjustly. King William restored it to Bishop Walter.

In WARHAM are 2½ hides paying geld. There are 8 villans with 4 ploughs. It is and was worth 30s.

In CANON PYON are 12 hides paying geld. In demesne is 1 plough; and 15 villans and 10 bordars with 16 ploughs. There is 1 beadle and 2 female slaves, and 2 acres of meadow.

Of the land of this manor 3 clerks of the bishop hold 4½ hides, and 3 knights holds 3½ hides. These have in demesne 6 ploughs; and 14 villans and 9 bordars with 6 ploughs. They have there 4 slaves, and a mill rendering 32d. TRE and afterwards, as now, worth £12.10s.

In HUNTINGTON [near Hereford] are 10 hides. Of these, 4 are waste, and the others pay geld. In demesne is 1 plough; and 5 villans and 4 bordars with 7 ploughs. There are 5 acres of meadow, and in addition there could be 1 plough more in demesne. Of this manor a clerk holds 2 hides, and a knight 3 hides. In demesne they have 2 ploughs; and 3 bordars and a smith with 1 plough. TRE and afterwards, as now, worth £4.

In HOLMER is 1 hide paying geld. There are 4 villans with 4 ploughs. It is and was worth 10s.

In MORETON ON LUGG are 4 hides paying geld. 3 clerk hold them of the bishop, and have 3 ploughs in demesne; and 8 villans and 4 bordars with 2½ ploughs. There are 3 slaves and 2 female slaves, and a mill rendering 4s, and 20 acres of meadow. TRE it was worth £4; and afterwards, as now, £3.

[Folio 182V: HEREFORDSHIRE]

In PIPE is 1 hide paying geld. There is 1 plough, and 16 acres of meadow. It is worth 5s.

In [Lower or Upper] LYDE are 2 hides paying geld. There are 1½ ploughs in demesne; and 3 villans with 3½ ploughs. There is 1 female slave; and in addition there could be in demesne half a plough. There are 8 acres of meadow. It is and was worth 40s. A knight holds it of the bishop.

IN "STEPLESET" HUNDRED

In NORTON CANON are 6 hides paying geld. In demesne is 1 plough; and 8 villans and 3 bordars with 8½ ploughs. There is 1 female slave, and 1 acre of meadow, and woodland rendering 2s. TRE, and afterwards, it was worth 60s; now 100s.

In BISHOPSTONE are 5 hides paying geld. In demesne is 1 plough and another [which is] idle; and 9 villans and a reeve and 4 bordars with 6½ ploughs. There is 1 female slave, and 6 acres of meadow. TRE it was worth £3; and afterwards, as now, £4.

In WORMSLEY is half a hide paying geld. A knight holds it of the bishop, and has 2 villans with 1 plough. TRE and afterwards, as now, worth 4s.

In BRIDGE SOLLERS are 5 hides paying geld. A knight holds them of the bishop. In demesne are 2 ploughs; and 4 villans with 2 ploughs, and another knight holds 1 hide there, and has 1 plough, and 4 bordars with 1 plough. There is 1 slave and a female slave. TRE it was worth 50s; now 60s.

IN "PLEGELGETE" HUNDRED

In BROMYARD are 30 hides. Of these, 3 hides are and were waste; the others pay geld. In demesne are 5 ploughs; and 42 villans and 9 bordars with 39 ploughs. There are 6 slaves, and a mill rendering 10s, and 12 acres of meadow. There is woodland rendering nothing. Of this manor 3 knights of the bishop hold 9 hides and 1 virgate, and 2 priests 1 hide, and a chaplain 1 hide and 3 virgates, and a reeve 1 hide, and a

radman 1 hide. In demesne they have 11½ ploughs; and their men have 20 ploughs. One of them has 2 slaves, and 3 acres of meadow. TRE and afterwards, as now, the whole manor was worth £45.10s.

In COLLINGTON are 3 hides paying geld. In demesne are 3 ploughs; and 2 villans and 4 bordars with 2½ ploughs. There are 2 acres of meadow. TRE and afterwards, as now, worth 30s. This manor and the above-mentioned BRIDGE SOLLERS Earl Harold held unjustly. King William restored them to Bishop Walter.

IN 'WOLFHAY' HUNDRED

In LITTLE HEREFORD are 7 hides. 3 of these are waste; the others pay geld. In demesne are 3 ploughs; and 17 villans and 3 bordars with 11 ploughs. There are 2 female slaves, and a mill rendering 6s8d. There are 4 mills, half of which belong by rights to the said manor. There are 5 acres of meadow, and woodland 2 furlongs long and half a furlong broad and rendering nothing. Of this manor a priest holds half a hide, and a radman half a hide. They have 3 ploughs. TRE it was worth 100s; and afterwards, as now, £4.

In "WINETUNE" is half a hide [...]. This radman holds, and has there 1 plough and 2 villans. It is and was worth 5s.

IN "CUTESTORNES" HUNDRED

In CREDENHILL are 2 hides [...]. 2 villans there with 1 plough pay 5s rent. It is worth 20s.

IN STRADEL HUNDRED

In 'MOOR' [in Hereford] is 1 hide which is worth 5s.

The canons themselves have 4 hides. There 3 clerks have 3 villans with 4 ploughs. It is worth 15s.

Bishop Walter himself had 1 Welsh hide TRE, waste. There are 2 ploughs in demesne; and 3 villans and 6 bordars and 2 other men with 6 ploughs. It is worth 40s. Of this land the greatest part is within the preserve of the king ['s woodland].

About the market town of HEREFORD Bishop Walter had lands TRE which did not pay geld. There Bishop Robert has 4 ploughs in demesne; and 2 villans and 5 boors with 5½ ploughs. It was worth 40s; now £4. Of this land 2 chaplains of the bishop hold a certain part, and a knight [holds] 1 hide. These have in demesne 6 ploughs, and a villan and 6 bordars and 2 slaves and 3 female slaves. In all it is worth 67s.

IN ALL THERE ARE IN THE BISHOPRIC 300 HIDES, although of 33 hides the bishop's men have given no account.

IN 'GREYTREE' HUNDRED

ST PETER of Hereford holds PRIORS FROME. Walter de Lacy gave it to the church with the consent of King William. There is 1 hide and 1 virgate and they pay geld. Eadwig Cild held it and could go where he would. In demesne is 1 plough; and 3 villans and 3 bordars with 2 ploughs. There are 7 slaves. It was worth 15s; now 30s.

III. The land of the Church of Cormeilles

IN BROMSASH HUNDRED

THE CHURCH OF SAINTE-MARIE of Cormeilles holds 2 hides in KINGSTONE [in Weston under Penyard], and they pay geld and do service in Gloucestershire, but those who dwell here come to this hundred for pleas to do and to receive justice.

IIII. [The land] of the Church of Lyre

THE CHURCH OF SAINTE-MARIE of LYRE has half a hide in MUCH MARCLE.

V. The land of St Peter of Gloucester

IN BROMSASH HUNDRED

THE CHURCH OF ST PETER of Gloucester holds BRAMPTON ABBOTTS. There are 2 hides. One pays geld, the other is free from geld and from every customary due.

In this free hide are 3 ploughs in demesne; and 5 villans and 5 bordars with 5 ploughs. There are 16 slaves. It is worth £4.

In the other hide is 1 villan and 1 bordar with 1 plough, and a mill rendering 8s. It is worth 10s.

The church itself holds LEA by the gift of Walter de Lacy. Asgot held it TRE. There is 1 hide paying geld. This man could go where he would. In demesne is 1 plough, and 2 slaves and 1 bordar. It is and was worth 10s. There can be 1 more plough.

VI. The land of St Guthlac

IN BROMSASH HUNDRED

THE CHURCH OF ST GUTHLAC holds GATSFORD. There is 1 hide paying geld. There is land for 2 ploughs. It was and is waste; yet it renders 5s.

IN 'GREYTREE' HUNDRED

The church itself held DORMINGTON, and Æstan the canon held of it. There is 1 hide paying geld. Walter holds it now and has there 1 plough, and 1 bordar and 1 slave. It is and was worth 10s.

The church itself holds HINTON. There is 1 hide paying geld [...]. In demesne is 1 plough; and 4 villans with 2½ ploughs. There are 3 slaves and 4 cottars, and a mill rendering 4s. It is worth 25s.

IN "TORNELAUS" HUNDRED

The church itself holds THINGHILL. There is 1 hide paying geld. In demesne are 2 ploughs; and 4 villans and 1 bordar with 2 ploughs. There are 5 slaves. It is and was worth 30s.

The church itself holds FELTON. There are 3 hides paying geld except half a hide. In demesne are 3 ploughs, and 5 slaves

and 1 bordar. There is 1 Frenchman with 1 plough paying 6s. It was worth 60s; now 40s.

IN STRETFORD HUNDRED

The church itself holds MOCCAS. There are 2 hides paying geld. There are 6 villans and 3 bordars with 4 ploughs. There is 1 Frenchman. It is worth 30s.

IN ELSDON HUNDRED

The church itself holds ALMELEY, and Roger de Lacy [holds] of it. There are 4 hides paying geld. There is land for 8 ploughs. The men of another vill labour in this vill and pay 37s8d.

The church itself holds 'MIDDLEWOOD' [in Winforton], and Drogo [holds] of it. There is 1 hide paying geld. In demesne is 1 plough; and 2 oxmen and 3 bordars with 1 plough.

It is worth 10s.

The church itself holds WHITNEY, and Harold [holds] of it. There are 4 hides paying geld. They are and were waste; yet they render 6s.

The church itself holds DUDALE'S HOPE. There are 2 hides. One pays geld, the other does not. In demesne are 2 ploughs; and 1 villan and 2 bordars with 1½ ploughs. There are 3 slaves. It is worth 30s.

IN 'WOLFHAY' HUNDRED

St Guthlac had 1 hide, "WESTELET". It was and is waste.

[Folio 183: HEREFORDSHIRE]

VII. The land of Nigel the Physician

IN 'GREYTREE' HUNDRED

Of the land of ST GUTHLAC, NIGEL the physician holds BARTESTREE. Leofflæd held it. There are 2 hides; 1 of them pays geld, as the shire witnesses. In demesne are 3 ploughs and 3 slaves; and a reeve with 1 plough. There is meadow.[...] There is land for 3 ploughs. It was worth 60s; now 50s.

To this manor belongs a Berewick. Leofflæd held it. There are 2 hides. 1 of them pays geld, as the shire witnesses. There Nigel has in demesne 2 ploughs and 2 slaves; and 1 bordar and a radman with land without a plough. It is and was worth 40s.

IN "TORNELAUS" HUNDRED

The same Nigel holds BOWLEY, and Ralph [holds] of him. Leofflæd held it. There is 1 hide free from geld and from the king's service. In demesne are 2 ploughs and 2 oxmen. There is land for 4 ploughs. It was worth 25s; now 20s.

The same Nigel holds SUTTON [St Michael and St Nicholas]. Leofflæd held it. [...] There are 2 hides paying geld. In demesne is 1 plough and 2 oxmen; and 4 bordars and 2 cottars with 1 plough, and a Frenchman with 1 plough. There is meadow for the oxen, and a mill which Hugh l'Asne holds of Nigel renders 8s. and 8 sticks of eels. TRE it was worth 60s; and afterwards 30s; now 50s. This manor Hugh held in the time of William [...].

The same Nigel holds SUTTON [St Michael and St Nicholas]. Spirites the priest held it. There is 1 hide paying geld. There is land for 2 ploughs. There are [2 ploughs] in demesne and 4 slaves, and 1 bordar, and a mill rendering 10s, and 7 sticks of eels, and meadow for the oxen only. It is and was worth 30s.

The same Nigel holds MAUND [Maund Bryan or Rosemaund]. Leofflæd held it of St Guthlac. There are 2 hides paying geld. [...] There are 7 villans with 5 ploughs. It was worth 40s; now 30[s].

The same Nigel holds THINGHILL, and Geoffrey [holds] of him. Spirites held it. There is 1 hide not paying geld. In demesne are 2 ploughs and 4 slaves. It is and was worth 20s.

IN DINEDOR HUNDRED

The same Nigel holds MOCCAS, and Ansfrid [holds] of him. Earnwine held it of St Guthlac. There is 1 hide, and in demesne 1 plough. It is worth 15s.

IN "PLEGELGETE" HUNDRED

The same Nigel holds LITTLE COWARNE. Spirites held it. There are 3 hides paying geld. In demesne are 3 ploughs and 7 slaves; and 2 bordars and 1 free man with 1 plough, and 2 bordars. It was worth 50s; now 40s.

The same Nigel holds AVENBURY. Spirites held it. There are 6 hides paying geld. [...] In demesne are 3 ploughs and 4 slaves; and 22 villans and 2 priests and 1 bordar with 12 ploughs. There is a mill rendering nothing. It is and was worth 100s.

VIII. The land of Ralph de Tosny

RALPH de Tosny holds the castle of CLIFFORD. Earl William erected it on waste land which Bruning held TRE. There Ralph has land for 3 ploughs, but there is only 1 plough. This castle is part of the kingdom of England; it is not subject to any hundred nor any customary due.

Gilbert the sheriff holds it at farm, and the borough and a plough [sic]. For the whole he pays 60s.

In the jurisdiction of this castle Roger holds land for 4 ploughs, and Gilbert for 12 ploughs, and Drogo for 5 ploughs, and Herbert for 2 ploughs. These have in demesne 9 ploughs, and 16 burgesses and 13 bordars, and 5 Welshmen, and 6 slaves and 4 female slaves, and a mill rendering 3 modii of corn, and 4 oxmen are there. The men have 3 ploughs. In all, what they have is worth £8.5s. And these, and whatever other men have anything there, hold of Ralph.

IN "HEZETRE" HUNDRED

The same Ralph holds MONKLAND, and Saint-Pierre of Castellion [holds] of him. Almær and Ulfkil held it as 2 manors and could go where they would. There are 5 hides paying geld. 1 of these did not pay geld because it was in demesne. There are 2 ploughs; and 10 villans and 8 bordars with 7 ploughs. There are 3 slaves and a free oxman, and a mill rendering 11s, and 25 sticks of eels. From the meadow 5s, besides pasture for the oxen. TRE [sic] it was worth £6; now £7.

IN ELSDON HUNDRED

The same Ralph holds WILLERSLEY and WINFORTON. Earl Harold held them. There are 4 hides paying geld. In demesne are 4 ploughs; and 17 bordars with 3 ploughs, and 3 free men with 3 ploughs. There are 8 slaves. TRE it was waste, and was worth 10s; now £7.

The same Ralph holds in the same place 1 hide paying geld. Alweard held it and could go where he would. 1 Welshman holds it of Ralph, and has there 8 men having 1½ ploughs. It is worth 12s.

IN STRETFORD HUNDRED

The same Ralph holds CHADNOR [Chadnor and Lower Chadnor]. There are 3 hides paying geld. Earnwig and Hadwin and Alweard held them as 3 manors. In demesne are 2 ploughs; and 4 villans and 6 bordars and 1 smith with 3 ploughs. There are 6 slaves, and meadow for the oxen only. The woodland renders nothing; and, in addition, there could be 3 more ploughs.

In the same vill lies a third part of a hide, and there is 1 plough. The whole TRE was worth £4.10s; now 110s.

IN "STEPLESET" HUNDRED

The same Ralph holds MONNINGTON ON WYE, and Roger [holds] of him. Earl Harold held it. There are 5 hides paying geld. Of these, Almær held 2 as a manor, and could go where he would. In demesne are 3 ploughs; and 5 villans and 6 bordars with 3 ploughs. TRE it was worth 60s; now £4.

IN DINEDOR HUNDRED

The same Ralph holds DINEDOR, and William and Ilbert his brother [hold] of him. Godric and Wulfheah held it as 2 manors. There are 6 hides paying geld. [...] In demesne are 2 ploughs; and 13 villans with a reeve and 5 bordars with 12 ploughs. There are 4 oxmen and 3 female slaves, and a mill rendering 28d. The woodland of this [place] the king has in demesne. No one, moreover, fishes in the river without leave. TRE these 2 manors were worth £7.5s; now the same.

IN RADLOW HUNDRED

The same Ralph holds WESTHIDE. Edith held it and could go where she would. There are 2 hides and 1 virgate paying geld. In demesne are 3 ploughs; and 6 villans and 5 bordars and 4 cottars with 4 ploughs. There are 7 slaves; and in addition there could be 1 more plough. TRE it was worth £6; now 105s. Of this land Ralph gave half a hide to a certain knight of his, and therefore the manor renders less.

[Folio 183V: HEREFORDSHIRE]

The same Ralph holds 1 virgate of land in RADLOW Hundred, and Beorhtweald the priest [holds] of him. Wulfwig held it as a manor, and could go where he would.

This land pays geld. It is called ASHPERTON. There is half a plough, and 1 villan and 1 bordar. It is worth 4s.

The same Ralph holds STOKE EDITH. Edith held it and could go where she would. There are 2½ hides paying geld. In demesne are 2 ploughs; and 6 villans and 6 bordars and 2 priests with 7 ploughs. There are 7 slaves, and a mill rendering 10s. TRE it was worth £7; now £6 less 5s.

IX. The land of Ralph de Mortimer

IN "HEZETRE" HUNDRED

RALPH de Mortimer holds WIGMORE Castle. Earl William erected it on the waste land which is called "MERESTUN" [in Wigmore], which Gunnfrothr held TRE. There are 2 hides paying geld. In demesne Ralph has 2 ploughs and 4 slaves. The borough which is there renders £7.

IN "HEZETRE" HUNDRED

The same Ralph holds DOWNTON ON THE ROCK, and Oidelard [holds] of him. Almær and Ulfkil held it as 2 manors and could go where they would. There are 4 hides. 2 of them do not pay geld. In demesne are 2 ploughs; and 3 villans and 3 bordars with half a plough. There are 6 slaves, and a fishery, [and] woodland half a league long and 5 furlongs broad. There are 2 enclosures. It was worth 30s; now as much. This land Earl William gave to Turstin the Fleming.

The same Ralph holds BURRINGTON. Eadric the Wild held it. There are 3 hides and 1 virgate. In demesne are 3 ploughs; and 7 villans and 4 bordars with 3 ploughs. There are 9 slaves, and very little woodland. It is and was worth 40s.

The same Ralph holds ASTON. 5 men held it as 3 manors. There are 3 hides paying geld. In demesne are 2 ploughs; and 5 villans and 2 bordars with 3 ploughs. This land was waste; now it is worth 30s.

The same Ralph holds ELTON. Eadric held it. There are 2 hides. [...] In demesne are 2 ploughs; and 6 villans and 3 bordars and 2 radknights. Among them all they have 3 ploughs. There are 4 slaves, and 2 furlongs of woodland. It was worth 12s; now 20s.

The same Ralph holds LEINTHALL [? Starkes]. Azur held it. There are 2 hides paying geld. In demesne are 2 ploughs; and 7 villans and 10 bordars and 2 radmen and a smith with 5 ploughs among them all. There is 1 slave and 3 free oxmen. TRE it was worth 20s; now 40s.

The same Ralph holds LEINTHALL [? Strakes]. Queen Edith held it. There are 4 hides paying geld. In demesne are 3 ploughs; and 10 villans and 7 bordars and 3 radknights with 7 ploughs. There are 6 free oxmen, and a mill rendering 30s. TRE it was worth 50s; now 100s.

The same Ralph holds [? Lower] LYE. Alsige held it, and could go where he would. There is half a hide paying geld. There he has 1 plough with 3 bordars, and there could be another plough. It is and was worth 5s.

The same Ralph holds COVENHOPE. Almær held it, and could go where he would. There is 1 hide paying geld. In demesne is 1 plough; and 6 bordars and a smith with 2 ploughs. There is 1 slave and a free oxman, and a very small wood. It is worth 10s.

The same Ralph holds SHOBDON. Edith held it.[...] There are 4 hides paying geld. In demesne are 3 ploughs; and 20 villans and 20 bordars. and a radknight and a smith with 9 ploughs. There are 6 slaves, [and] woodland 1 league in both length and breadth. It was worth £6; now £7.

The same Ralph holds STAUNTON ON ARROW. Eadric held it. There are 2 hides paying geld. In demesne are 2 ploughs; and 6 villans and 3 bordars with 4 ploughs. It was waste; now it is worth 40s.

The same Ralph holds LEDICOT. Beorhtmær held it and could go where he would. There is 1 hide paying geld. There dwell 3[men] having 1 plough, and there could be another plough. It is worth 10s6d.

The same Ralph holds in PILLETH [Wales] 2 hides; in HARPTON [Wales] 2 hides; in MIDDLETON [in Lower Harpton] 3 hides; in [Lower and Upper] WESTON [Wales] 2 hides. In all, there are 9 hides, waste, on the marches of Wales. There is land for 18 ploughs. There were 7 manors, and 5 thegns held them.

The same Ralph has 57 acres of land and all the woodland in [? Lower] LYE, Gruffydd's manor.

IN ELSDON HUNDRED

The same Ralph holds KINNERSLEY, and Richard [holds] of him. Eadric held it, and could go where he would. There is 1 hide paying geld. In demesne are 2 ploughs; and 3 villans and 6 bordars with 4 ploughs. It was waste; now it is worth 30s.

IN STRETFORD HUNDRED

The same Ralph holds BIRLEY, and Richard [holds] of him. Eadric and Ruillic and Leofgeat held it as 3 manors and could go where they would. There are 2 hides and 3 virgates of land paying geld. In demesne are 2 ploughs; and 3 villans and 1 radknight and 1 bordar with 3 ploughs. The woodland renders 2s. These 3 manors TRE were worth £4; now 50s.

The same Ralph holds BIRLEY, and Richard [holds] of him. Grimkel held it, and could go where he would. There is half a hide paying geld. In demesne is half a plough and 2 slaves. It is and was worth 3s.

IN "PLEGELGETE" HUNDRED

The same Ralph holds 2 hides in [Lower and Upper] UNDERLEY. Alwine held them. This land pays geld. In demesne he has 1 plough; and 1 villan with half a plough, and in addition there can be 3 more ploughs. It is worth 10s.

IN 'WOLFHAY' HUNDRED

The same Ralph holds ORLETON. Edith held it. There are 4 hides paying geld. In demesne are 4 ploughs; and 11 villans and 15 bordars and a reeve and a radman. Among them all

[are] 7 ploughs. There are 6 slaves and 5 oxmen and a smith. TRE it was worth £7; now 100s.

[Folio 184: HEREFORDSHIRE]

X. The land of Roger de Lacy

IN "CUTESTORNES" HUNDRED

In the jurisdiction of EWYAS HAROLD Castle, Earl William gave to WALTER de Lacy 4 carucates of waste land.

ROGER de Lacy his son holds them, and William and Osbern [hold] of him. In demesne they have 2 ploughs; and 4 Welshmen rendering 2 sesters of honey, and they have 1 plough. There they have 3 slaves and 2 bordars. This land is worth 20s.

The same Roger has an estate called LONGTOWN within the boundary of EWIAS. This land does not belong to the jurisdiction of the castle nor to a HUNDRED. From this land Roger has 15 sesters of honey and 15 pigs, when the men are there, and pleas over them.

Within the jurisdiction of CLIFFORD Castle the same Roger holds 4 carucates of land. His father held them. They were and are waste.

IN 'GREYTREE' HUNDRED

The same Roger holds PUTLEY, and William [holds] of him. Tosti held it. There is 1 hide paying geld. In demesne are 2 ploughs; and 2 villans and 1 bordar with 2 ploughs. There are 2 slaves. It is and was worth 20s.

IN "TORNELAUS" HUNDRED

The same Roger holds OCLE PYCHARD. 6 free men held it as 6 manors and could go where they would. There are 7 hides paying geld. In demesne are 2 ploughs; and 7 villans and 10 bordars and a reeve and a smith with 9 ploughs among them all. There are 12 slaves.

Of this land Walter de Lacy gave to St Peter of Hereford 2 carucates of land with the consent of King William, and 1 villan and 1 bordar with their lands. There are in demesne 2 ploughs; and 1 villan and 1 bordar with 1 plough, and there is 1 slave. It is worth 25s.

What Roger holds [is worth] 75s. The whole TRE was worth £7.15s.

The same Roger has in the WYE a fishery [Hadnock] which is valued at £6, and the burgesses whom he has in Hereford pay him 20s.

The same Roger holds [?] ROSEMAUND, and Hugh [holds] of him. Wonni held it. There is 1 hide paying geld, and 1 plough is in demesne, and there are 3 slaves. It was worth 20s; and afterwards 10s; now 15s.

The same Roger holds BODENHAM, and Herbert [holds] of him. Eadwig held it. There are 1½ hides paying geld. In demesne are 2 ploughs; and 6 villans and 3 bordars and a smith and a beadle and 6 cottars with 6 ploughs. There are 6

slaves, and a mill rendering 16s and 30 sticks of eels. There is meadow for the oxen only. TRE it was worth 50s; now 60s.

The same Roger holds in the same HUNDRED, and Herbert [holds] of him, a manor of 1 virgate. It does not pay geld. This Eadwig Cild held with 1 plough. It is and was worth |26d|.

The same Roger holds 1 hide [Burghope] of the farm of MARDEN, the king's manor. Ingelran holds it of him. In demesne are 2 ploughs; and 4 villans and 1 bordar with 2 ploughs. There are 3 slaves. TRE, and afterwards, it was worth 40s; now 60s. Eadwig Cild held it.

IN 'WOLFHAY' HUNDRED

The same Roger holds WOONTON [in Laysters], and Gerald [holds] of him. Earnwig held it. There are 3 virgates paying geld, and there is 1 plough. It was worth 6s; now 4s.

The same Roger holds [Great and Little] HEATH, and Gerald [holds] of him. Leofwine held it. There are 3 virgates paying geld. It is worth 6s.

The same Roger holds PUDLESTONE, and Hugh [holds] of him. Wulfweard held it. There are 3 hides paying geld. In demesne are 2 ploughs; and 3 bordars with 1 plough, and a Frenchman with 1 plough, and 2 bordars. There are 8 slaves. TRE it was worth 30s; now 40s.

The same Roger holds 1 manor of 1½ hides paying geld. Alwine holds of him. His father Eadwig held it. There he has 1 plough; and 2 villans with half a plough. There are 3 slaves. It is and was worth 10s.

The same Roger holds ROSEMAUND, and William [holds] of him. Æthelric held it. There are 2 hides paying geld. In demesne are 2 ploughs and 5 slaves, and there can be 2 more ploughs. It was worth 30s; now 25s.

In the STRADEL Valley the same Roger holds Bacton as 5 hides, and [?] Howton as 1 hide. These 2 manors Gilbert holds of Roger. Eadwig and Alweard held these 6 hides, and they were waste. In demesne is 1 plough and a slave; and 3 Welshmen render 3 sesters of honey. It is worth 9s.

In the same valley the same Roger holds [?] CHANSTONE as 3 hides, and William holds of Roger, and has 2 ploughs in demesne, and 6 bordars. It is worth 10s.

In the same place the same Roger holds "EDWARDESTUNE", and Walter [holds] of him, as 1 hide. It was waste; now it is worth 8s.

IN DINEDOR HUNDRED

The same Roger holds BULLINGHOPE [Lower Bullingham or Bullinghope]. Alnoth held it of John the sheriff. There are 2 hides paying geld. In demesne is 1 plough; and 4 villans and 4 bordars with 2½ ploughs. There are 5 slaves, and a third part of 2 mills which is worth 14s8d. The woodland is in the king's forest. TRE it was worth 50s; now as much.

The same Roger holds COBHALL. Alweard held it and could go where he would. There is 1 hide paying geld. Gerald holds of Roger. In demesne he has 2 ploughs; and 4 bordars with 1 hide [sic], and 9 slaves and female slaves. TRE it was worth 50s; now as much.

The same Roger holds MAWFIELD, and Ingelran [holds] of him. Eadwig Cild held it. There are 2 hides paying geld. In demesne are 2 ploughs, and 5 bordars and a smith and 2 slaves and a female slave. Of this land Leofwine holds 1 virgate of Roger himself. TRE it was worth 20s; now 46s.

The same Roger holds WEBTON, and Berner [holds] of him. Alweard held it. There is half a hide [...]. There is 1 plough. It is and was worth 15s.

The same Roger holds WEBTON, and Gerald and Berner [hold] of him. Eadwig held it. There are 2½ hides. [...] There are 7 bordars with 3 ploughs. It was waste; now it is worth 10s.

IN "CUTESTORNES" HUNDRED

The same Roger holds STRETTON SUGWAS, and Robert [holds] of him. Eadwig Cild held it. There are 2½ hides paying geld. In demesne are 2 ploughs; and 1 villan and 9 bordars and 4 oxmen and 2 radknights. Among them all they have 3 ploughs. TRE it was worth 40s; now 50s. There is a mill rendering 32d.

The same Roger holds [Lower or Upper] LYDE, and Ralph [holds] of him. Thorkil held it of Earl Harold. There are 2 hides paying geld. In demesne is 1 plough, and there can be another. There are 3 bordars and 1 free man with 2½ ploughs. TRE it was worth 20s; now 25s.

The same Roger holds [Lower or Upper] LYDE, and Ralph [holds] of him. Bruning held it. There is 1 hide. In demesne are 2 ploughs. It was worth 40s; now 60s.

IN RADLOW HUNDRED

The same Roger holds WESTON BEGGARD. Gunnfrothr held it and could go where he would. There are 6 hides paying geld. In demesne are 2 ploughs; and 9 villans and a priest and 2 bordars with 9 ploughs. There are 6 slaves, and a mill rendering 10s, and meadow for the oxen. TRE it was worth 100s; and now as much.

The same Roger holds YARKHILL. Arnketil, a thegn of Earl Harold, held it. There are 2 hides paying geld. In demesne are 2 ploughs; and 7 villans and 4 bordars with 7 ploughs. There are 7 slaves, and a mill rendering 100d. TRE it was worth 50s; now as much.

The same Roger holds HALMOND'S FROME. Tosti held it of Queen Edith. There are 4 hides paying geld. In demesne are 2 ploughs; and 7 villans and 4 bordars and a reeve with 8 ploughs. There are 10 slaves, and a mill rendering 7s6d and 5 sticks of eels. TRE it was worth 60s; now as much.

The same Roger holds CASTLE FROME. Beorhtmær held it of Earl Harold. There are 5 hides paying geld. In demesne are 3 ploughs; and 7 villans and a reeve and a free man with 7 ploughs. There are 10 slaves, and a mill rendering 10s. TRE it was worth 70s; now 60s.

The same Roger holds MUNSLEY, and Ralph [holds] of him. Beorhtmaelig;r held it, and could go where he would. There are 3 hides and 1 virgate paying geld. In demesne are 2 ploughs; and 11 villans and 7 bordars with 9 ploughs. TRE it was worth 70s; now 60s.

The same Roger holds LITTLE MARCLE, and Odo [holds] of him. Thorkil held it of Earl Harold. There are 5 hides paying geld. In demesne is 1 plough; and 10 villans and 4 bordars with 10 ploughs. There is 1 free man and 1 radknight with 1½ ploughs. There are 5 slaves, and a mill rendering corn. The woodland renders 17d. TRE it was worth 100s; now as much.

Of these 5 hides Alric held half as a manor and could go where he would. Now Odo holds it with the other land. It is and was worth 6s.

The same Roger holds CANON FROME, and Gerard [holds] of him. Thorkil held it. There are 4 hides paying geld. In demesne are 2 ploughs; and 8 villans and 2 bordars and a reeve with 7 ploughs. There are 6 slaves, and a mill rendering 10s10d. TRE it was worth 70s; now 3s more.

The same Roger holds EVESBATCH, and Odo [holds] of him. Almaelig;r and AElig;lfric and Thorkil held it as 3 manors of Earl Harold, and could go where they would. There is 1 hide only and it pays geld. In demesne are 4 ploughs; and 1 villan and 1 radknight with 2 ploughs, and 3 female slaves. TRE it was worth 28s; now as much.

The same Roger holds MONKHIDE, and Tezelin [holds] of him. Asgot held it and could go where he would. There is 1 hide paying geld. In demesne is 1 plough, and 1 bordar and 4 slaves. It is and was worth 5s.

The same Roger holds LITTLE TARRINGTON, and Ansfrid [holds] of him. Alric held it and could go where he would. There is half a hide paying geld. In demesne is 1 plough, and 1 bordar and 3 slaves. It was worth 5s; now 6s.

The same Roger holds LEADON, and St Peter [holds] of him by the gift of his father and the grant of King William. Thorkil held it. and could go where he would. There is half a hide paying geld. In demesne is 1 plough; and 8 bordars have 1 plough there. TRE it was worth 20s; now as much.

The same Roger holds LEADON. Thorkil held it and could go where he would. There is half a hide paying geld. There is land for 1 plough. It is waste. It is worth 4s.

IN "HEZETRE" HUNDRED

The same Roger holds LAWTON, and an Englishman [holds] of him. Wulfric held it. There is 1 hide paying geld. In demesne is 1 plough; and 3 bordars having 1½ ploughs. There are 4 slaves. TRE it was worth 20s; now as much.

The same Roger holds STREET. King Edward held it. There is 1 hide, of which one half was in the king's demesne and does not pay geld, [and] the other half pays geld. This land in the king's farm Earl William gave to Ewen the Breton. Now William holds it of Roger de Lacy, and there he has 3 villans. TRE it was worth 20s; now 15s.

The same Roger holds LEDICOT, and Gilbert [holds] of him. There is 1 hide paying geld. Alflæd held it and could go where she would. In demesne is 1 plough; and 1 man with 1 plough. It was waste; now it is worth 10s.

IN ELSDON HUNDRED

The same Roger holds 'HOPE' [in Lyonshall], and Walter [holds] of him. Wulfric held it. There are 2 hides paying geld. There is land for 4 ploughs. There are men paying 10s8d for their [right of] settlement. There is nothing else there.

The same Roger holds LYONSHALL, and Walter [holds] of him. Thorkil held it of Earl Harold. There are 5 hides paying geld. In demesne are 2 ploughs; and 3 villans and 11 bordars and 3 radknight with 5 ploughs. There are 5 slaves and female slaves; and from certain men settled there 100d are had so long as they themselves wish [to remain]. TRE it was worth 60s; now 50s.

The same Roger holds MATHON, and Odo [holds] of him. Merewine, a thegn of Earl Oda, held it, and could not go without the leave of the lord. There is half a hide paying geld. There is 1 plough. It is and was worth 10s.

The same Roger holds WOONTON [in Almeley]. Algar held it and could go where he would. There is 1 hide paying geld. There is nothing in demesne, but 5 villans have 1½ ploughs there. It was worth 3s8d; now 64d.

The same Roger holds EARDISLEY, and Robert [holds] of him. Eadwig held it. This land pays no geld, neither does it give any customary dues, nor does it lie in any hundred. It is situated in the midst of a certain wood, and there is 1 fortified house. In demesne is 1 plough and 2 slaves, and a Welshman paying 3s.

The same Roger holds LETTON, and Tezelin [holds] of him. Eadwig Cild held it, and could go where he would. There are 3 hides paying geld. In demesne is 1 plough; and a priest and 7 settlers with 1 plough pay 5s. There is 1 mill rendering nothing, and 2 slaves. It was worth 2s; now 30s.

IN STRETFORD HUNDRED

The same Roger holds WEOBLEY. Eadwig Cild held it. There are 3½ hides paying geld. In demesne are 3 ploughs; and 10 villans and a priest and a reeve and a smith and 5 bordars with 9½ ploughs. There are 11 slaves, and woodland half a league long and 4 furlongs broad. There is a park, and land for 1 plough from the assarts renders 11s9d. St Peter has 1 of these villans by the gift of Walter de Lacy. TRE it was worth 100s; and afterwards 60s; now 100s.

The same Roger holds FERNHILL. Eadwig Cild held it. There are 2 hides paying geld. In demesne is 1 plough; and 9 villans and 3 bordars and 1 radknight holding half a virgate. Among them all they have 10 ploughs. There are 3 slaves. There is woodland half a league long and 4 furlongs broad, and land for 1 plough from the assarts renders 54d. TRE it was worth 60s; now as much.

The same Roger holds KING'S PYON. King Edward held it. There are 5 hides paying geld. In demesne are 2 ploughs;

and 8 villans and 3 bordars and a priest and a reeve and 1 radknight. Among them all they have 9 ploughs, and in addition there could be 4 more there. There are 4 slaves.

Of this land Gruffydd holds half a hide [...], and Sainte-MARIE of Cormeilles 1 virgate and the tithes of the vill. It is worth 12s. The whole manor TRE was worth £4; and now as much. This land Ewen the Breton held of Earl William, but King William gave it to Walter de Lacy.

The same Roger holds BIRLEY, and Gothmund [holds] of him. Særic, a thegn of Earl Harold, held it. There is half a hide not paying geld. In demesne are 2 ploughs; and 8 bordars with 1 plough. There are 4 slaves, and woodland rendering nothing. TRE it was worth 30s; now 40s.

The same Roger holds ALTON, and Osbern [holds] of him. Alnoth held it and could go where he would. There are 2 parts of 1 hide, and they pay geld. There is land for 2 ploughs. There are 2 slaves and nothing more. It is and was worth 10s.

The same Roger holds SWANSTONE, and Gothmund [holds] of him. Særic held it, and could go where he would. There is 1 hide paying geld. In demesne, nothing. 3 villans and 3 bordars have 2 ploughs. It was worth 10s; now 15s.

IN "STEPLESET" HUNDRED

The same Roger holds BROBURY, and Robert [holds] of him. Earnwig held it of Eadwig Cild and could not withdraw from him. There are 2 hides paying geld. In demesne are 2 ploughs; and 2 villans and 6 bordars and 1 free man with 3 ploughs. There are 2 slaves. TRE it was worth 10s; now 20s.

The same Roger holds STAUNTON ON WYE, and Leofric [holds] of him. Earwig held it of Eadwig Cild. There are 2 hides paying geld. There is half a plough, and in addition there could be 1 plough. There 2 villans have 1 plough. It is worth 5s.

The same Roger holds MANSELL GAMAGE. Alflæd held it of Earl Harold. There are 8 hides paying geld. In demesne are 3 ploughs, and there could be a fourth. There are 10 villans and a reeve and 2 Frenchmen and 1 bordar with 10 ploughs. TRE it was worth £7; and afterwards 100s; now £8.

The same Roger holds STAUNTON ON WYE, and William [holds] of him. Alric held it and could go where he would. There are 4 hides paying geld. In demesne are 2 ploughs;

[Folio 185: HEREFORDSHIRE]

and 3 villans and 4 bordars with 1 plough, and in addition there could be 3 ploughs. There are 7 slaves, and woodland 1 league long and half a league broad. It was worth 25s; now 30s.

The same Roger holds YAZOR, and Robert [holds] of him. Luderic, a thegn of Earl Ælfgar, held it, and could go where he would. There are 5 hides paying geld. In demesne are 2 ploughs; and 6 villans and a smith with 3 ploughs, and 1 radman pays 2s. There are 4 oxmen and 1 female slave. TRE it was worth 15s; and afterwards 30s; now 60s.

The same Roger holds YAZOR, and Robert [holds] of him. Eadwig and Leofwine and Sæmær held it as 3 manors, and could go where they would. There are $1\frac{1}{2}$ hides paying geld. In demesne is 1 plough; and 1 Frenchman with half a plough, and 1 slave, and there could be 2 more ploughs. TRE it was worth 4s; and afterwards 30s; now 15s.

The same Roger holds BYFORD, and Walter [holds] of him. Æthelweard held it and could go where he would. There are 5 hides paying geld. In demesne is 1 plough; and 6 villans and 3 bordars with 2 ploughs. There are 2 slaves, and a mill rendering 20s, and there could be 4 more ploughs. TRE it was worth 40s; and afterwards 60s; now 100s.

The same Roger holds WORMSLEY, and Leofric [holds] of him. Alwig and Wulfnoth held it of him as 2 manors and could go where they would. There is 1 hide and 1 virgate paying geld. In demesne are $1\frac{1}{2}$ ploughs; and 2 bordars and a priest with $1\frac{1}{2}$ ploughs, and in addition there can be 1 plough. TRE it was worth 10s; now 15s.

The same Roger holds WORMSLEY. Haduic held it and could go where he would. There is 1 virgate of land not paying geld. There is land for 1 plough. It was worth 2s; now 3s.

IN "PLEGELGETE" HUNDRED

The same Roger holds STOKE LACY. Almær Cild held it, and could go where he would. There are 10 hides paying geld. In demesne are 3 ploughs; and 22 villans with 6 ploughs, and in addition there could be 6 others. There are 11 slaves, and a mill rendering 5s. TRE it was worth £10; now the same.

The same Roger holds COLLINGTON, and Hugh [holds] of him. Wulfweard the priest held it and could go where he would. There are 2 hides paying geld. In demesne is 1 plough; and 1 villan with half a plough. There are 2 slaves. It is and was worth 20s.

The same Roger holds SAWBURY HILL, and Hugh [holds] of him. Wynric held it. There are $2\frac{1}{2}$ virgates. There is land for 1 plough. It was and is waste.

The same Roger holds in WOLFERLOW 6 hides paying geld, and Hugh and Walter [hold] of him. Earl William gave to Walter his father $4\frac{1}{2}$ hides, and King William gave to Roger $1\frac{1}{2}$ hides. This land Alwine the sheriff held TRE and he could go where he would. In demesne are 2 ploughs; and 6 villans with 3 ploughs, and in addition there could be 3 others. There are 3 slaves. TRE it was worth 40s; now 65s.

The same Roger holds BISHOP'S FROME, and Hugh [holds] of him. Leofsige held it and could go where he would. There is 1 hide paying geld. In demesne is 1 plough; and 3 villans with 1 plough. There are 2 slaves, and a mill rendering 32d. TRE it was worth 20s; now 15s.

The same Roger holds TEDSTONE WAFRE. Earnsige held it and could go where he would. There is 1 hide paying geld. In demesne are 2 ploughs; and 4 villans and 1 bordar with 2 ploughs. There are 7 slaves. TRE it was worth 30s; and afterwards 15s; now 20s.

The same Roger holds BREDENBURY. Leofsige held it

and could go where he would. There is 1 hide paying geld. In demesne is 1 plough; and 4 villans with 4 ploughs, and in addition there could be 3 ploughs in demesne. There are 5 slaves. TRE it was worth 30s; now 10s. Herman holds it of Roger.

The same Roger holds BUTTERLEY, and Alwine [holds] of him. Eadwig Cild, his father, held it. There are $3\frac{1}{2}$ hides paying geld. In demesne is 1 plough; and 4 villans and 8 bordars with 3 ploughs. There are 5 slaves, and a mill rendering 16d. TRE it was worth 20s; now 30s; and in addition there could be 1 plough.

The same Roger holds MARSTON STANNETT, and Gothmund [holds] of him. Særic his father held it and could go where he would. There is half a hide paying geld. There is 1 plough and 2 slaves. It was worth 4s; now 5s.

The same Roger holds GRENDON, and William [holds] of him. Eadwig held it, and Ordric, as 2 manors. There are 4 hides paying geld. There is land for 8 ploughs. Nothing is reckoned to be there.

The same Roger holds STANFORD BISHOP, and Turstin [holds] of him. Eadwig Cild held it. There is 1 hide paying geld. In demesne is 1 plough, and 2 oxmen and 1 bordar. It was worth 5s; now 10s; and in addition there could be 1 plough.

The same Roger holds 'CUPLE', and Eadric [holds] of him. Leofsige held it and could go where he would. There is 1 hide paying geld. In demesne is 1 plough; and 1 villan and 1 oxman with 1 plough. There are 3 slaves. It was worth 5s; now 12s.

The same Roger holds HANLEY [Child and William, Worcs.], and St Peter [holds it] in alms of the gift by Walter de Lacy. Alnoth held it and could go where he would. There is half a hide paying geld. There is 1 villan who has 1 plough. It was worth 6s; now 8s.

XI. The land of Roger de Mussegros

IN 'WOLFHAY' HUNDRED

ROGER de Mussegros holds of the king LOWER UPTON. Arnketil and Arngrim held it as 2 manors. There are 2 hides paying geld. In demesne are 2 ploughs; and 1 Frenchman with 1 plough. There are 4 slaves and 2 bordars. It was and is worth 22s.

The same Roger holds LAYSTERS. Arnketil and Arngrim held it as 2 manors. There is 1 hide paying geld. It was worth 4s; now it is waste.

XII. The land of Robert Gernon

IN 'WOLFHAY' HUNDRED

ROBERT Gernon holds of the king YARPOLE. Richard Scrob held it. There are 3 hides paying geld. There are 4 villans and 8 bordars with 3 ploughs. TRE it was worth 25s; now 20s.

IN "CUTESTORNES" HUNDRED

The same Robert holds 5½ hides in the jurisdiction of the castle at RICHARDS CASTLE. Richard held them. This land does not pay geld. In demesne are 5 ploughs; and 34 villans and 6 bordars and a smith with 15 ploughs among them all, and they pay 20s. There are 10 slaves, and a mill rendering 4 modii of corn and 15 sticks of eels. TRE and afterwards, as now, worth £7.

XIII. The land of Henry de Ferrers

IN 'GREYTREE' HUNDRED

HENRY de Ferrers holds PRIORS FROME. Ælfgeat held it of Bishop Æthelstan and could go where he would. There are 2 hides and 1 virgate paying geld. In demesne are 2 ploughs; and 4 villans and 10 bordars with 2 ploughs, and 1 burgess in Hereford pays 12d. TRE and afterwards, as now, worth £3.

IN "CUTESTORNES" HUNDRED

In the jurisdiction of the castle of EWYAS HAROLD Roger holds of Henry 3 churches and a priest and 32 acres of land, and they render 2 sesters of honey. In the castle he has 2 messuages.

[Folio 185V: HEREFORDSHIRE]

XIIII. The land of William d'Ecouis

WILLIAM d'Ecouis holds 8 carucates of land in the jurisdiction of CARELEON Castle [Mon.], and Turstin holds of him. There he has in demesne 1 plough; and 3 Welshmen, living under the Welsh law, with 3 ploughs, and 2 bordars with half a plough, and they render 4 sesters of honey. There are 2 slaves and 1 female slave.

This land was waste TRE and when William received it; now it is worth 40s.

IN "TORNELAUS" HUNDRED

The same William holds MAUND BRYAN. Edwin held it. There is 1 hide paying geld and half [a hide] not paying geld. In demesne are 2 ploughs; and 2 villans and 3 bordars with 2 ploughs, and 4 slaves and 3 cottars, and meadow for the oxen. TRE, and afterwards, it was worth 40s; now 5s more. The clerks of St Guthlac claim this manor.

The same William holds BROADWARD. Edwin held it. There are 2 hides paying geld. In demesne is 1 plough; and 3 bordars with half a plough, and 2 slaves and a smith, and meadow for the oxen. Stephen holds it of William. TRE it was worth 40s; and afterwards 20s; now 25s.

The same William holds in NEWTON [in Hope under Dinmore] half a hide paying geld [...] Bruns held it. Bernard holds it of William. In demesne is 1 plough; and 2 villans with 1 plough, and 4 slaves. It was worth 10s; now 12s.

IN 'WOLFHAY' HUNDRED

The same William holds CROFT, and Bernard [holds] of him. Edwin held it. There is 1 hide paying geld. In demesne is 1 plough; and 2 oxmen and 1 Frenchman and 3 bordars with 2 ploughs. It was worth 20s; now 25[s].

The same William holds POSTON in the Stradel Valley, and Ralph [holds] of him. Edwin held it. There are 2 hides. In demesne is 1 plough; and 2 villans with 1 plough. It was waste; now [it is worth] 5s.

IN ELSDON HUNDRED

The same William holds RUSHOCK. Earl Harold held it. There is 1 hide paying geld. It was and is waste. There is 1 enclosure in a great wood.

The same William holds DILWYN. Edwin held it and could go where he would. There are 3 hides paying geld. In demesne is 1 plough; and 8 villans and 5 bordars with 7 ploughs, and in addition there could be 2 more ploughs. There is 1 female slave. TRE it was worth £4; and afterwards, as now, 75s.

The same William holds in this vill 1 hide paying geld. Earnwig held it, and could go where he would. There is land for 3 ploughs. There is 1 villan and 3 bordars. TRE it was worth 25s; and afterwards 10s; now 15s.

IN "STEPLESET" HUNDRED

The same William holds YARSOP. Almær held it and could go where he would. There is 1 hide paying geld. In demesne are 2 ploughs; and 2 bordars with half a plough, and 2 slaves. TRE it was worth 20s; and afterwards 15[s]; now 20s.

The same William holds in this vill 1 virgate of land paying geld. Ælfric held it and could go where he would. There is nothing there. Yet it was and is worth 3s.

The same William holds MARSTON STANNETT. Edwin held it and could go where he would. There is half a hide paying geld. In demesne is 1 plough, and 2 slaves. TRE, and afterwards, it was worth 4s; now 6s.

XV. The land of William fitzBaderon

IN BROMSASH HUNDRED

WILLIAM fitzBaderon holds HOPE MANSELL. Leofric and Eadwulf held it as 2 manors. There are 4 hides paying geld. Salomon holds it of William. In demesne are 2 ploughs; and 1 villan and 1 bordar with 1½ ploughs. TRE it was worth 40s; and now the same.

A third part of this manor belonged to the Church of St Peter of Gloucester TRE, as the shire witnesses.

The same William holds RUARDEAN [Glos.], and Salomon [holds] of him. Haduic held it. There are 4 hides paying geld. In demesne could be 3 ploughs. There is 1 bordar and 2 villans and 1 Welshman with 3 ploughs. It was and is worth 30s.

The same William holds 1 virgate of land of LINTON, the king's manor. Leofstan held it and could not withdraw from this manor. There is 1 plough and nothing more. It is and was worth 3s.

IN "WIMUNDESTREU" HUNDRED

The same William holds half a hide in MUCH MARCLE, the king's manor.

The same William holds BICKERTON, and Geoffrey [holds] of him. Adulf held it, and could go where he would. There is 1 hide paying geld. In demesne are 2 ploughs; and 2 villans with 1 plough, and 2 bordars and 3 slaves. It is and was worth 30s.

IN RADLOW HUNDRED

The same William holds STRETTON GRANDISON. Thorkil held it of Earl Harold. There are 3½ hides paying geld. In demesne are 2 ploughs; and 7 villans and 1 bordar with 7 ploughs, and 3 slaves, and 30 acres of meadow, and 2 mills rendering 6s8d. TRE it was worth £9; now £7.

The same William holds WHITWICK. Thorkil held it of Earl Harold. There are 2 hides paying geld. In demesne are 2 ploughs; and 1 villan and 2 bordars with 1 plough, and 3 slaves, and 2 acres of meadow. It was and is worth 20s.

The same William holds ASHPERTON. Wulfwig held it of Earl Harold, and could go where he would. There are 5½ hides paying geld. In demesne are 4 ploughs; and 6 villans and 2 bordars with 3 ploughs, and 13 slaves, and 20 acres of meadow. [There is] woodland 1 league in both length and breadth. TRE it was worth 110s; now as much.

The same William holds WALSOPTHORNE, and Gerald [holds] of him. Wulfmær, Thorkil's man, held it and could go where he would. There is 1 hide and 1 virgate paying geld. In demesne is 1 plough; and 2 bordars and 1 free man with 1 plough, and 2 acres of meadow. TRE it was worth 25s; now as much.

The same William holds MUNSLEY. Ælfric held it and could go where he would. There are 1½ hides paying geld. In demesne is 1 plough, and 3 bordars and 1 slave, and there can be 1 plough more. TRE it was worth 30s; and afterwards, as now, 15s.

XVI. The land of William fitzNorman

IN RADLOW HUNDRED

WILLIAM fitzNorman holds MUNSLEY. Wada held it and could go where he would. There is 1 hide paying geld. In demesne is 1 plough, and 6 bordars and 1 slave, and there could be half a plough more. It is and was worth 10s.

IN "PLEGELGETE" HUNDRED

The same William holds HOPTON SOLLERS, and Richer [holds] of him. Beorhtmær held it and could go where he would. There is 1 hide and 1 virgate paying geld. In demesne is 1 plough; and 3 villans and 2 bordars with 3 ploughs, and 4 slaves. TRE it was worth 30s; and now as much.

IN "TORNELAUS" HUNDRED

The same William holds VENN'S GREEN. Stenulf held it. There are 1½ hides paying geld. In demesne is 1 plough; and 2 villans and 7 bordars with 3 ploughs, and 2 slaves. TRE it was worth 20s; now 30s.

The same William holds THE VERN. 2 radmen held it TRE. There is half a hide [...] In demesne are 2 ploughs; and 1 villan and 2 bordars with 1 plough, and 4 slaves and 1 female slave. It was worth 10s; now 16s. These 2 manors belonged to the farm of Marden, the king's manor.

XVII. The land of Turstin fitzRolf

IN BROMSASH HUNDRED

TURSTIN fitzRolf holds ALVINGTON [Glos.]. Beorhtric held it TRE. There are 6 hides [...]. In demesne are 2 ploughs; and 12 villans with 9 ploughs, and they render 20 blooms of iron and 8 sesters of honey. There are 5 slaves, and a mill rendering 40d. TRE it was worth 20s; now £4.

IN RADLOW HUNDRED

The same Turstin holds AYLTON, and another Turstin [holds] of him. Beorhtric held it of Earl Harold and could go where he would. There are 3 hides paying geld. In demesne are 2 ploughs; and 7 villans and 4 bordars with 8 ploughs, and 4 slaves. TRE and afterwards, as now, worth 60s.

[Folio 186: HEREFORDSHIRE]

XVIII. The land of Albert of Lorraine

IN RADLOW HUNDRED

ALBERT of Lorraine holds UPLEADON. Edith sister of Earl Oda held it. There are 9 hides paying geld. In demesne are 2 ploughs, and there could be a third. There are 32 villans and 13 bordars with 32 ploughs. There are 6 slaves, and a mill rendering 32d. TRE it was worth £14; now £15.

IX. The land of Alvred of Marlborough

ALVRED of Marlborough holds the castle of EWYAS HAROLD of King William. For the king himself granted to him the lands which Earl William, who had refortified this castle, had given him; that is, 5 carucates of land there and another 5 carucates at Monnington. The king also granted him the land of Ralph de Bernay which used to belong to the castle. There he has in demesne 2 ploughs; and 9 Welshmen with 6 ploughs rendering 7 sesters of honey, and 12 bordars working 1 day a week. There are 4 oxmen and 1 man paying 6d.

His 5 knights, Richard, Gilbert, William, and William and Hernold, have 5 ploughs in demesne, and 12 bordars, and 3 fisheries and 22 acres of meadow.

Two others, William and Ralph, hold land for 2 ploughs. Turstin holds land rendering 19d, and Warner land rendering 5s. These men have 5 bordars.

This castle of Ewyas Harold is worth £10.

IN "CUTESTORNES" HUNDRED

The same Alvred holds BURGHILL. Earl Harold held it. There are 8 hides paying geld. In demesne are 2 ploughs; and 16 villans and 19 bordars and a priest with 24 ploughs. There are 4 slaves, and a mill rendering 20s, and 25 sticks of eels. The woodland renders 4s. In Hereford 5 burgesses pay to this manor 52d.

In this manor 2 knights have 2 ploughs and 2 oxmen, and Godric, a certain thegn, has 1 plough, and a certain other man has 1 villan. TRE there belonged to this manor the third penny of 2 hundreds, Stretford and "Cutestornes". Then it was worth £20; now £15.

The same Alvred holds BRINSOP, and Richard [holds] of him. Earl Harold held it. There are 5 hides paying geld. In demesne are 2½ ploughs; and 7 villans and a priest and †15† bordars with 5½ ploughs. There are 5 oxmen. TRE it was worth £8; now £6.

These 2 manors Osbern uncle of Alvred held TRE when Godwine and Harold had been exiled.

IN THE STRADEL VALLEY

The same Alvred holds MONNINGTON. Earl Harold held it. There are 5 hides [...] Ralph de Bernay unjustly withdrew thence 1 hide. There are 3 Frenchmen with 3 ploughs, and 9 bordars and 1 radman with half a plough. It was waste; now it renders 30s.

The same Alvred holds BREDWARDINE. Earl Harold held it. There are 5 hides. [...] In demesne is 1 plough; and 6 villans and 6 bordars and 1 man and 1 Welshman. Among them all they have 3 ploughs, and 3 slaves. It was waste; now it is worth £3.

IN "TORNELAUS" HUNDRED

The same Alvred holds 1 manor of 15 hides paying geld [Pencombe], and his daughter [holds] of him. Alvred himself held it TRE. In demesne are 3 ploughs; and 21 villans and 4 bordars, and a priest with a church, and a smith. Among them all they have 20 ploughs. There are 6 slaves and 6 oxmen, and a mill rendering 5s. TRE it was worth £14; now £10.

IN "BROMSASH" HUNDRED

The same Alvred holds HILL OF EATON. Earl Harold held it. There are 2½ hides paying geld. In demesne is 1 plough; and 9 villans and 6 bordars with 7 ploughs. TRE it was worth 50s; and afterwards, as now, 40s.

The same Alvred holds PEMBRIDGE. Earl Harold held it. There are 11 hides less 1 virgate, and it pays geld. In demesne are 3 ploughs; and 20 villans and 7 bordars and 1 radknight with 12 ploughs. There are 3 slaves, and a mill rendering 10s. There was woodland for 160 pigs if it had borne mast.

This manor of Pembridge the canons of St Guthlac claim, and they say that Earl Godwine and Harold his son unjustly took it away from St Guthlac. TRE it was worth £16; and afterwards it was waste; now it is worth £10.10s.

IN STRETFORD HUNDRED

The same Alvred holds STRETFORD. Earl Harold held it. There are 2 hides paying geld. Gilbert holds of Turstin, and Turstin of Alvred. In demesne is 1 plough; and 1 villan and 4 bordars with half a plough, and there could be 3 ploughs. There are 3 slaves, and meadow rendering 3s. There is woodland. TRE it was worth 30s; now 20s.

IN RADLOW HUNDRED

The same Alvred holds MUCH COWARNE. Earl Harold held it. There are 15 hides paying geld, but King William allowed 6 hides quit from geld. This manor Alvred's daughter Agnes, wife of Turstin of Wigmore, holds. In demesne are 2 ploughs; and a priest and a reeve and 26 villans and 8 bordars. Among them all they have 32 ploughs. There are 4 slaves and a smith, and the meadow and woodland render nothing, and 1 hide of this land lies in the king's woodland. To this manor belonged the third penny of 3 hundreds TRE; now it has been withdrawn. Then it was worth £25; now 100s less.

XX. The land of Alvred d'Epaignes

IN "PLEGELGETE" HUNDRED

ALVRED d'Epaignes holds THORNBURY. Siward held it and could go where he would. There are 6 hides paying geld. In demesne are 3 ploughs; and 4 villans and 4 bordars with 3 ploughs. There are 6 slaves, and there could be 2 more ploughs. TRE it was worth £6; and afterwards, 100s; now £4.10s.

The same Alvred holds in the same vill 1 hide. Leofric and Lyfing and Earnwig held it as 3 manors. This land was waste. There is half a plough, and 2 villans with half a plough, and there could be another plough. This land pays geld. They who held it could go where they would. It was worth 13s4d; now 2s.

XXI. The land of Ansfrid de Cormeilles

IN RADLOW HUNDRED

ANSFRID de Cormeilles holds TARRINGTON. Alweald and Earnwig held it as 2 manors and could go where they would There are 3 hides paying geld. In demesne are 2 ploughs; and 5 villans and 12 bordars with 9 ploughs, and there are 8 other men paying nothing, and in addition there could be 1 plough. There are 4 slaves and 3 female slaves. TRE it was worth 110s; and afterwards £4; now £6.

The same Ansfrid holds PIXLEY. Thorger held it and could go where he would. There is half a hide paying geld. In demesne is 1 plough, and 2 free men and 2 bordars. TRE it was worth 8s; now 10s.

IN BROMSASH HUNDRED

The same Ansfrid holds ASTON INGHAM, and Godfrey [holds] of him. King Edward held it. There are 2 hides paying geld. In demesne is 1 plough; and 4 villans and 9 bordars with 8 ploughs, and 8 other men paying nothing. There are 2 oxmen, and a mill rendering nothing. TRE it was worth 50s; now 100s.

IN 'GREYTREE' HUNDRED

The same Ansfrid holds SOLLERS HOPE. Haghni held it and could go where he would. There are 5 hides paying geld. Richard holds of Ansfrid, and has 2 ploughs in demesne and 11 slaves. 1 knight holds 1½ hides, and has 1 plough and 1 bordar, and a mill rendering 5s. There could be 3 more ploughs. TRE it was worth £4; and afterwards £3; now £4.

IN "TORNELAUS" HUNDRED

The same Ansfrid holds AMBERLEY, and Richard [holds] of him. There is 1 hide paying geld. In demesne is 1 plough and 3 slaves, and 1 bordar. It was and is worth 20s.

IN DINEDOR HUNDRED

The same Ansfrid holds BULLINGHOPE [Lower Bullingham or Bullinghope]. Reuer held it. There are 2 hides. [...] In demesne is 1 plough; and 3 villans and 5 bordars with 2 ploughs, and a third part of 2 mills rendering 14s8d. There is woodland, but placed in the king's forest. It was worth 50s; now the same.

[Folio 186V: HEREFORDSHIRE]

IN STRETFORD HUNDRED

The same Ansfrid holds CLEHONGER. Earl Harold held it. There are 5 hides paying geld, and in demesne 2 ploughs; and 3 villans and 4 bordars with 3 ploughs. There are 4 oxmen, and a mill rendering 5s, [and] woodland rendering nothing, and there is 1 hide waste.

Of this land Gerard holds 3 virgates, and has half a plough with 1 man of his own. It was waste; now it is worth 70s.

XXII. The land of Durand of Gloucester

IN RADLOW HUNDRED

DURAND of Gloucester holds ASHPERTON, and Ralph [holds] of him. Earnwig, a thegn of Earl Harold, held it and could go where he would. There are 3 virgates paying geld. In demesne are 2 ploughs, and 2 bordars and 4 slaves and 2 female slaves. It was and is worth 20s.

IN BROMSASH HUNDRED

The same Durand holds PONTSHILL, and Bernard [holds] of him. Gunnar held it and could go where he would. There is 1 hide paying geld. There 6 bordars have 3 ploughs. It was and is worth 6s.

The same Durand holds WESTON UNDER PENYARD, and Bernard [holds] of him. The aforesaid Gunnar held it. There are 2 hides paying geld. There 2 bordars have 1 plough, and in addition there can be 3 ploughs. It is and was worth 4s.

The same Durand holds COLDBOROUGH, and Bernard [holds] of him. The same Gunnar held it. There is 1 hide paying geld. In demesne is 1 plough, and 1 slave. It is and was worth 64d.

IN 'WOLFHAY' HUNDRED

The same Durand and Walter his nephew hold ROCH-FORD [Rochford and Upper Rochford, Worcs.], and Widard [holds] of them. Leofnoth held it. There are 1½ hides paying geld. In demesne are 2 ploughs; and 4 bordars with 2 ploughs, and 5 slaves, and woodland rendering nothing. TRE it was worth 40s; and afterwards, as now, 30s.

The same Durand and Walter his nephew hold LAYSTERS, and Bernard [holds] of him [sic]. Godric held it. There are 2 hides paying geld. It is and was waste.

IN STRETFORD HUNDRED

The same Durand holds THRUXTON, and Bernard [holds] of him. Robert fitzWimarc held it. There are 3 hides paying geld. In demesne is 1 plough; and 3 villans with 2 ploughs. There are 2 slaves and 1 bordar. It was waste; it is worth 40s.

IN "CUTESTORNES" HUNDRED

The same Durand holds LITLEY, and Widard [holds] of him. Reuer held it, and Alwine, as 2 manors. There is 1 hide [...]. In demesne is 1 plough, and 2 oxmen. This land King William gave to Roger de Pitres. It was worth 15s; now 10s.

XXIII. The land of Drogo fitzPons

IN 'WOLFHAY' HUNDRED

DROGO fitzPons holds ROCHFORD [Rochford and Upper Rochford, Worcs.]. Wulfmær held it. There is 1 hide and 1 virgate paying geld. In demesne are 2 ploughs; and 4 bordars with 1 plough, and 6 slaves. TRE it was worth 30s; now 28s.

The same Drogo holds DORSTONE. Earl Harold held it. There are 7 hides.

The same Drogo holds "BURCSTANESTUNE". Edwin and Ælfhild and Alweard held it as 3 manors. There are 3 hides.

The same Drogo holds MYNYDD-BRITH. [...]

There is 1 hide. There Drogo has 4 ploughs in demesne; and 7 villans and 2 bordars with 3 ploughs. There are 4 slaves, and a mill rendering 2s. There is a priest and a smith. It is worth 100s.

The same Drogo holds 'HANLEY'S END' [in Cradley]. Lyfing and Godwine and Alweard held it as 3 manors, and could go where they would. There is 1 hide and 1½ virgates and they pay geld. In demesne is 1 plough; and 4 bordars with 2 ploughs, and there could be a third plough. There is 1 slave, and a burgess paying 4d. It was worth 13s; now 12s. Adelelm holds it.

IN RADLOW HUNDRED

The same Drogo holds MATHON. Alweard, a thegn of Earl Oda, held it, and could not withdraw without the lord's leave. There is half a hide paying geld. Adelelm holds it and has there 1 plough. It was worth 5s; and afterwards 4s; now 10s.

XXIIII. The land of Osbern fitzRichard

IN "HEZETRE" HUNDRED

OSBERN fitzRichard holds MILTON. He himself held it TRE. There are 2 hides paying geld. In demesne is 1 plough; and 6 villans with 3 ploughs. There are 3 slaves and 1 bordar, [and] woodland 4 furlongs in both length and breadth. It was waste; now it is worth 20s.

The same Osbern holds BYTON. He himself held it TRE. There are 2 hides [...]. In demesne is half a plough; and 4 villans and 2 bordars with 2 ploughs, and there could be 2 others. There is 1 watermeadow. It was worth 12s; now 20s.

The same Osbern holds and held 'BRADLEY' [in Presteigne] as 1 hide, and TITLEY as 3 hides, and LITTLE BRAMPTON as 1 hide, and KNILL as 2 hides, and LOWER HARPTON as half a hide, and HARPTON [Wales] as 3 hides, and [?] BROAD HEATH as 1 hide, and CLATTERBRUNE [Wales] as 2 hides, and "QUERENTUNE" as 1 hide, and DISCOED [Wales] as 3 hides, and CASCOB [Wales] as half a hide.

In these 11 manors is land for 36 ploughs, but it was and is waste. It has never paid geld. It lies on the marches of Wales.

The same Osbern holds [? LOWER]LYE, and held it. There is half a hide, and there could be 1 plough. There is only 1 villan. It is worth 5s.

On these waste lands have grown up woods in which the same Osbern hunts, and thence he has whatever he can take. [There is] nothing else.

IN ELSDON HUNDRED

The same Osbern holds TITLEY. Earl Harold held it. There are 3 hides paying geld. There is land for †6† ploughs. It was and is waste. However, there is 1 enclosure in a little wood.

IN STRETFORD HUNDRED

In NEWTON [in Dilwyn] is half a hide which pays geld, and 1 virgate which does not pay geld. Særic held them as a manor and could go where he would. Herbert had them of Richard Scrob. In demesne are 3 oxen; and 3 villans and 1 bordar with 1 plough. It was worth 40s; now 24s. There could be 1 [more] plough.

IN "STEPLESET" HUNDRED

The same Osbern holds STAUNTON ON ARROW, and Drogo [holds] of him. Saissil held it, and could go where he would. There are 4 hides paying geld. In demesne are 2 ploughs; and 6 villans and 4 bordars with 4 ploughs. There are 4 slaves. It was waste; now it is worth 60s.

IN "TORNELAUS" HUNDRED

The same Osbern holds, and held, BODENHAM. There are 1½ hides paying geld. In demesne are 3 ploughs; and 6 villans and a smith and 2 bordars and a priest and 1 radman with 8 ploughs among them all. TRE it was worth 60s; now 48s.

IN 'WOLFHAY' HUNDRED

The same Osbern holds, and held, WHYLE. There is 1 hide paying geld. In demesne are 1½ ploughs, and 3 bordars and 2 slaves. It was worth 12s; now 8s.

IN "CUTESTORNES" HUNDRED

The same Osbern holds [Lower or Upper] LYDE, and Roger de Lacy [holds] of him. Saissil held it. There are 2 hides paying geld. In demesne are 2 ploughs; and 1 villan and a reeve and a smith with 2 ploughs. It was worth 25s; now 30s.

The same Osbern holds LUDFORD [Shrops.]. There is 1 hide, and in demesne 2 ploughs; and 5 bordars with 1 plough, and a mill rendering 6s. It is worth 20s.

The same Osbern has 23 men in RICHARDS CASTLE, and they pay 10s. This castle is worth 20s to him.

XXV. The land of Gilbert fitzTurold

IN DINEDOR HUNDRED

GILBERT fitzTurold holds ROTHERWAS. Sigeric held it TRE. There are 3 hides paying geld. In demesne are 2 ploughs; and 2 villans and 3 bordars with 2 ploughs. TRE it was worth £6; now £3. There were 10 villans with 13 ploughs.

The same Gilbert holds BULLINGHOPE [Lower Bullingham or Bullinghope]. Edwin held it. There are 2 hides. In demesne are 2 ploughs; and 4 villans and 3 bordars with 2 ploughs, and there are 4 slaves, and a third part of a mill rendering 14s8d. It was worth 50s; now as much.

[Folio 187: HEREFORDSHIRE]

IN STRETFORD HUNDRED

The same Gilbert holds WINNALL. Robert fitzWimarc held it. There are 3 hides. In demesne is 1 plough, and there could be another. There are 3 villans and 3 bordars and 2 oxmen with 1 plough. Picot holds of Gilbert. It was waste; now it is worth 30s.

IN THE STRADEL VALLEY

The same Gilbert holds BACH. Edwin held it. There are 3 hides. [...] There are 8 Welshmen with 2 ploughs; they render 1 hawk and 2 dogs.

The same Gilbert holds MIDDLEWOOD [in Clifford]. Earl Harold held it. There are 2 hides.

The same Gilbert holds HAREWOOD [in Clifford]. Eadwig held it. There are 4 hides. This land has all been converted into woodland. It was waste and renders nothing.

IN THE STRADEL VALLEY [are] 56 hides [which] 112 PLOUGHS COULD PLOUGH, and they pay geld.

IN "PLEGELGETE" HUNDRED

The same Gilbert holds "CHETESTOR". Earnwig and Godwine held it as 2 manors, and could go where they would. There are 2 hides paying geld. In demesne are 3 ploughs; and 7 villans with 7 ploughs; and there could be in addition 1 plough in demesne. There are 6 slaves, and a mill rendering 4½s. TRE it was worth 50s; and afterwards 45s; now 70s.

IN ELSDON HUNDRED

The same Gilbert holds [?] AILEY. Earl Harold held it. There are 2 hides paying geld. These Earl William gave to Gilbert as 4 hides. There is land for 12 ploughs. There is a fortified house, and a large wood for hunting. It was waste; now it is worth 5s.

XXVI. The land of Ilbert fitzTurold

IN 'GREYTREE' HUNDRED

ILBERT fitzTurold holds PRIORS FROME. Wulfweard held it. There are 1½ hides [...] In demesne is 1 plough; and 2 villans and 6 bordars with 1 plough, and 2 slaves. It was and is worth 30s.

IN DINEDOR HUNDRED

The same Ilbert holds CLEHONGER. Leofnoth held it and could go where he would. There is 1 hide paying geld. In demesne is 1 plough; and 1 villan and 4 bordars with 2 ploughs. There are 2 oxmen. It was waste; now it is worth 25s.

XXVII. The land of Herman de Dreux

HERMAN de Dreux holds of the king MARSTON [in Pembridge]. Sæmær and Wulfwine and Grim held it as 3 manors, and could go where they would. There are 3 hides paying geld. In demesne is 1 plough; and 3 radknights and 7 bordars with 1 plough, and in addition there could be 4 more ploughs. There are 2 slaves, and woodland 5 furlongs in both length and breadth. TRE it was worth 34s; and afterwards 10s; now 20s.

XXVIII. The land of Humphrey de Bouville

IN RADLOW HUNDRED

HUMPHREY de Bouville holds of the king PIXLEY. Eskil, a man of the Bishop of Hereford, held it and could go where he would. There is half a hide paying geld. In demesne is 1 plough; and 2 bordars with 1 plough. It was and is worth 8s.

The same Humphrey holds MUNSLEY. Sæmær held it, and could go where he would. There is 1 hide paying geld. It was worth 16s; now these 2 manors are at farm for 30s.

XXIX. The land of Hugh l'Asne

IN "STEPLESET" HUNDRED

HUGH l'Asne holds KENCHESTER. Wulfwig Cild held it and could go where he would. There are 4 hides paying geld. Of this land a certain Godric bought half a hide from the said Wulfwine [sic], and held it as a manor.

In demesne Hugh has 2 ploughs, and 3 slaves, and a mill

rendering 2s, and the said Godric has there 1 plough under Hugh, and half a hide.

Of this land the same Hugh leased to Earl William 1 hide, which the same earl gave to King Maredudd. There his son Gruffydd has 2 bordars. TRE it was worth 60s; now 70s; what Gruffydd holds, 5s.

IN 'GREYTREE' HUNDRED

The same Hugh holds FOWNHOPE. Thorkil White held it. There are 15 hides. 10 of them pay geld. In demesne are 3 ploughs; and 14 villans and 10 bordars and 2 priests with a church having half a hide of land. There is a reeve and a smith and a carpenter. Among them all they have 25 ploughs. There are 18 slaves and 8 female slaves, and a mill rendering 5s, and 3 fisheries rendering 300 eels. From the waste lands the lord has 12s4d. 1 member of this manor Hugh gave to a certain knight of his with 1 plough. TRE it was worth £12; and afterwards £15; now £16.

IN "TORNELAUS" HUNDRED

The same Hugh holds 1 manor of 1 hide not paying geld [Livers Ocle]. Leofflæd held it. In demesne are 2 ploughs, and 3 bordars and 4 slaves. TRE it was worth 30s; now 20s.

The same Hugh holds 1 manor of 3 virgates paying geld [Westhide]. Leofflæd held it. There were and are 3 radknights with 3 ploughs, and they serve the lord. TRE it was worth 13s; now 10s.

The same Hugh holds SUTTON [St Michael or St Nicholas]. Leofflæd held it. There are 2 hides not paying geld. There is 1 villan and 6 bordars with 3 ploughs, and 1 Frenchman with 1 plough. It is and was worth 30s.

IN THE STRADEL VALLEY

The same Hugh holds "BELTROU". Leofflæd held it. There is half a hide.

The same Hugh holds "WLVETONE" [In Lyonshall]. Leofflæd held it. There are 2 hides [...]. These 2 estates were and are waste.

The same Hugh holds WILMASTONE. Leofflæd held it. There are 5 hides. In demesne are 2 ploughs; and 7 villans and 2 bordars and a smith and 1 radman with 2 bordars. Among them all they have 2½ ploughs. There are 4 slaves, and a mill rendering 3s. It was waste; now it is worth 30s.

The same Hugh holds [?] PETERCHURCH. Alweard held it. There are 3 hides. There are 2 Frenchmen with 2 ploughs, and a priest with a church having half a plough, and 3 slaves and 1 bordar and 2 men pay 8s. It was waste; now it is worth 20s.

The same Hugh holds "ALCAMESTUNE". Leofflæd held it. There is 1 hide. It was and is waste, but nevertheless it renders 3s.

IN "CUTESTORNES" HUNDRED

The same Hugh holds WELLINGTON. Thorkil White held it. There are 5 hides paying geld. In demesne are 2 ploughs; formerly there were 5 ploughs; and [there are] 9 villans and 8 bordars and a priest and a reeve and a smith and 4 radknights. Among them all they have 8 ploughs. There are 11 slaves and 9 female slaves, and 2 mills rendering 13s. At Droitwich [Worcs.] he has 17 mittae of salt for 30d. TRE it was worth £8; now £7. There were more ploughs there than there are now.

The same Hugh holds CREDENHILL. Thorkil held it. There are 2 hides not paying geld. In demesne are 2 ploughs. It was and is worth 30s.

The same Hugh holds STRETTON SUGWAS. Alweard held it. Vitalis holds it of Hugh. There is half a hide. [...] In demesne is 1 plough, and 2 slaves. It is and was worth 10s.

The same Hugh [holds] half a hide in WELLINGTON, and Ralph [holds] of him. Wulfwine held it. There is 1 plough. It is and was worth 10s.

IN RADLOW HUNDRED

The same Hugh holds "LINCUMBE" [in Westhide]. Leofflæd held it. There are 3 virgates [...]. There is land for 1 plough. It was worth 9s; now 7s.

IN "HEZETRE" HUNDRED

The same Hugh holds [?] BARLAND [Wales]. Thorkil held it. There are 2 hides. There is a large wood, but its extent has not been told. There is 1 enclosure in which he keeps what he can catch. The other land is waste.

IN ELSDON HUNDRED

The same Hugh holds in EARDISLEY half a hide paying geld. Earl Harold held it, and it was and is waste.

The same Hugh holds 1 hide and 1 virgate of land in CHICKWARD, and it pays geld. Earl Harold held it. Earl William gave it to Hugh himself. It was and is waste.

The same Hugh holds "LEGE". Leofgeat held it and could not withdraw without the leave of his lord. There is half a hide [...] paying geld. The same man holds it who held it and has there 1 plough. It was waste; now it is worth 10s.

IN SELLACK HUNDRED

The same Hugh holds STRANGFORD. Alric held it of Thorkil White. There is half a hide, and 2 men having 2 ploughs, and rendering 2 sesters of honey. This land does not pay geld.

[Folio 187V: HEREFORDSHIRE]

XXX. The land of Urse d'Abetot

IN "PLEGELGETE" HUNDRED

URSE d'Abetot holds WICTON. Alwine held it and could go where he would. There is 1 hide and 1 virgate paying geld. There is land for 4 ploughs. It was worth 6s; now 3s.

This manor Roger de Lacy holds by exchange from Urse.

XXXI. The land of Gruffydd Ap Maredudd

IN ELSDON HUNDRED

GRUFFYDD ap Maredudd holds of the king in "MATEURDIN" a third part of 2 hides paying geld. Earl Harold held it. Earl William gave it to King Maredudd. It was and is waste, but yet Robert holds there of Gruffydd 1 enclosure.

The same Gruffydd holds "CURDESLEGE". Earl Harold held it. There is 1 hide paying geld. There is land for 2 ploughs. It was and is waste, except for 3 acres of land lately ploughed there.

IN "STEPLESET" HUNDRED

The same Gruffydd holds BUNSHILL. Godric held it, and could go where he would. There is 1 hide paying geld. There are 3 villans and 1 bordar with 1 plough, and there could be 3 ploughs. It was and is worth 10s.

The same Gruffydd holds MANSELL LACY. Godric held it, and could go where he would. There are 4 hides paying geld. In demesne is 1 plough; and 6 villans and 3 radmen with 9 ploughs, and in addition there could be 3 ploughs. There are 2 slaves. It was worth 100s; now 10s. less.

The same Gruffydd holds MANSELL LACY. Godwine and Ulfkil held it as 2 manors, and could go where they would. There is 1 hide paying geld. [...] In demesne is 1 plough, and there could be another. TRE it was worth 30s; now 10s.

IN "PLEGELGETE" HUNDRED

The same Gruffydd holds STOKE BLISS [Worcs.]. Godric held it, and could go where he would. There is 1 hide paying geld, and 1 plough, and 6 villans with 3 ploughs, and 3 slaves. It was and is worth 25s.

IN "HEZETRE" HUNDRED

The same Gruffydd holds [?Lower] LYE. Owen and Almær held it as 2 manors, and they were waste. There are 3 hides not paying geld. Earl William gave them to King Maredudd. There are 4 villans and 3 bordars with 2 ploughs. It is worth 15s. The woodland of this manor together with 57 acres of land Ralph de Mortimer holds King William remitted the geld to King Maredudd and afterwards to his son.

XXXII. [The land] of Rainier

IN "PLEGELGETE" HUNDRED

RAINIER the carpenter holds of the king MARSTON STANNETT. Ludi held it and could go where he would. There is half a hide paying geld. In demesne is 1 plough with 1 bordar. It was and is worth 4s.

XXXIII.

CARBONELL holds of the king NOAKES. Kolgrimr held it and could go where he would. There is 1 hide paying geld, and half a plough, and 2 villans with 1 plough. It was worth 30s; and afterwards 20s; now 24s.

XXXIIII.

IN "STEPLESET" HUNDRED

The wife of Ralph the chaplain holds YARSOP of the king. Wulfnoth held it, and could not leave his lord. There are 3 virgates of land paying geld. There are 2 slaves and 4 oxen. It was worth 8s; now 12s.

In ROWDEN the same woman with her son Walter holds half a hide paying geld. It is waste and yet it renders 2s. Ælfgifu held it, and it was worth 3s.

XXXV.

IN "TORNELAUS" HUNDRED

STEPHEN holds of the king in MARDEN 1 virgate of land. Alweard held it of King Edward as a manor. In demesne he has 1 plough, and 3 bordars and 4 slaves. It was and is worth 10s.

XXXVI.

IN RADLOW HUNDRED

MADOC holds of the king ASHPERTON. Godric held it. There is 1 hide paying geld, and 1 plough in demesne and 2 slaves; and 1 villan and 1 bordar with 1 plough. It was and is worth 15s.

IN 'WOLFHAY' HUNDRED

EADRIC holds of the king LAYSTERS, and he himself held it of King Edward. There are 1½ hides paying geld. Then it was worth 15s; now it is waste.

IN THIS HUNDRED

ALMÆR holds of the king half a hide. He himself held it of King Edward, and it paid geld. It is worth 10d.

CAMBRIDGESHIRE

[Folio 189: CAMBRIDGESHIRE]

THE BOROUGH of CAMBRIDGE was assessed as a single HUNDRED TRE. In this borough were and are 10 wards. In the first ward [were] 54 messuages; 2 of these are waste. In this first ward Count Alan has 5 burgesses paying nothing. The Count of Mortain has 3 messuages of the land of Iudichael, and there are 3 burgesses who paid 5s8½d. TRE; now they pay nothing. Ralph de Baons-le-Comte has 3 burgesses paying nothing. Roger, the man of Bishop Remigius, [has] 3 burgesses paying nothing. Erchenger has 1 burgess [who] pays nothing. This same 1 ward was reckoned as 2 TRE, but 27 houses have been destroyed for the castle.

In the second ward were 48 messuages TRE; 2 of these are waste. Of these, 13 messuages render nothing; the remaining 32 render all the customs. Of these, Count Alan has 5 burgesses paying nothing, and 9 dwell on the lands of the English.

In the third ward were 41 messuages TRE. Of these, 11 are waste; the remaining 30 render all the customs.

In the fourth ward were 45 messuages TRE. Of these, 24 are waste; the remaining 21 render all the customs.

In the fifth ward were 50 messuages TRE. 1 of these is waste; all the others render their customs.

In the seventh ward were 37 messuages TRE. 3 Frenchmen have [...] 3 of these messuages but they pay nothing.

In the eighth ward were 37 messuages TRE. A certain priest holds 1 of these and pays nothing.

In the ninth ward were 32 messuages TRE. Of these, 3 are waste.

In the tenth ward were 29 messuages TRE. Of these, 6 are waste, yet they pay their dues.

From the customs of this vill, £7 a year, and from land-rent £7 and 2 orae and 2d.

TRE the burgesses lent the sheriff their plough-teams 3 times a year; now they are demanded 9 times.

They provided neither cartage-dues nor carts TRE, which they now do because a custom has been imposed. They claim back from Picot the sheriff, however, the common pasture taken from them through and by him.

Picot himself has built 3 mills there, which have taken up the pasture and destroyed many houses and 1 mill of the Abbot of Ely and another of Count Alan. The mills themselves render £9 a year.

The same Picot had £8 and a riding-horse and the arms of 1 knight from the heriot of the lawmen.

Ælfric son of Godric, when he was sheriff, had 20s. heriot of 1 of these men.

I KING WILLIAM
II The Bishop of Winchester
III The Bishop of Lincoln
IIII The Bishop of Rochester
V The Abbot of Ely
VI The Abbot of St Edmundsbury
VII The Abbot of Ramsey
VIII The Abbot of Thorney
VIIII The Abbot of Crowland
X The Abbot of Saint-Wandrille
XI The Abbess of Chatteris
XII The Count of Mortain
XIII Earl Roger
XIIII Count Alan
XV Count Eustace
XVI The canons of Bayeux
XVII Walter Giffard
XVIII William de Warenne
XIX Richard son of Count Gilbert
XX Robert de Tosny
XXI Robert Gernon
XXII Geoffrey de Mandeville
XXIII Gilbert de Ghent
XXIIII Gilbert fitzTurold
XXV Eudo the steward
XXVI Hardwin de Scales
XXVII Hugh de Bernieres
XXVIII Hugh de Port
XXVIIII Aubrey de Vere
XXX Eustace of Huntingdon
XXXI Guy de Raimbeaucourt
XXXII Peter de Valognes, b
XXXIII Picot of Cambridge, a
XXXIIII Ranulph brother of Ilger, c
XXXV John fitzWaleran
XXXVI William fitzAnsculf
XXXVII William de Keynes
XXXVIII Robert Fafiton
XXXVIIII David d'Argentan
XL Two of the king's carpenters
XLI Countess Judith
XLII Azelina wife of Ralph Taillebois
XLIII The wife of Boselin de Dives
XLIIII Erchenger the baker

The land of the King

IN 'STAPLOE' HUNDRED

SOHAM, the king's manor, is assessed at $9\frac{1}{2}$ hides. There is land for 14 ploughs. There are 16 villans and 16 bordars with 12 ploughs. In demesne [are] 2 ploughs, and 4 slaves, and 2 mills [rendering] 24s. From the fisheries, 3,500 eels. [There is] meadow for 14 ploughs, [and] pasture for the livestock of the vill. There are 7 fishermen rendering to the king a gift of fish 3 times a year according to their ability. In all it renders £25 a year, assayed and weighed, and 138s4d by tale in blanch pennies for wheat, malt, honey and other minor customary dues. TRE it rendered £25 by tale

[Folio 189V: CAMBRIDGESHIRE]

and 3 days' farm in wheat, honey and malt and in everything else. King Edward always had this manor in demesne.

FORDHAM, a demesne vill of the king, is assessed at $5\frac{1}{2}$ hides. There is land for 10 ploughs. In demesne [are] 2 ploughs, and there can be 4 more. There are 6 villans and 15 bordars with 15 acres with 4 ploughs. There is 1 slave, and 2 mills [render] 16s and feed 2 pigs a year. [There is] meadow for 6 ploughs, [and] pasture for the livestock of the vill. It renders £10 assayed and weighed and £13.8s4d in blanch money for honey, wheat and malt; TRE it rendered £10 by tale, and 3 days' farm in honey, wheat and malt. King Edward always had this manor in demesne. In this vill a certain sokeman, Brunmann, holds 1 hide of the king's soke. TRE this man could give his land to whom he would, but yet he always provided cartage-due or 8d in the king's service, and he paid amercements to the sheriff.

ISLEHAM, a demesne vill of the king, is assessed at 6 hides and 40 acres of land. There is land for 10 ploughs. In demesne are 2 [ploughs]; and 16 villans and 10 bordars with 8 ploughs. There are $3\frac{1}{2}$ mills rendering 22s8d and 1,250 eels, meadow for 10 ploughs, [and] pasture for the livestock of the vill. It renders £10 assayed and weighed and £13.8s4d in blanch money for honey, wheat and malt and other minor customary dues. King Edward always had this manor in demesne. In this manor were 4 sokemen of King Edward, and of this land they had 1 hide and 40 acres [and] could give and sell to whom they would, but they always provided cartage-due or 8d in the king's service, and they paid their amercements to the sheriff.

IN CHEVELEY HUNDRED

CHEVELEY, a demesne vill of the king, is assessed at 8 hides and 40 acres. There is land for 12 ploughs. In demesne are 2 [ploughs], and there can be a third. There are 12 villans and 7 bordars with 8 ploughs, and there can be a ninth. [There is] meadow for 1 plough, woodland for 20 pigs, [and] pasture for the livestock of the vill. It renders £10 assayed and weighed and £13.8s. 4d in blanch money, for honey, wheat and malt. TRE it rendered £15 by tale. King Edward always had this manor in demesne.

IN 'STAINE' HUNDRED

GREAT WILBRAHAM is a demesne vill of the king. There are 2 hides, and land for 8 ploughs. In demesne is 1 [plough], and there can be 3 more. There are 5 villans and 5 bordars with 5 ploughs. There are 2 slaves, and 1 mill [rendering] 10s, and 2 orae from a toll. [There is] meadow for 8 ploughs. It renders £10 assayed and weighed and £13.8s4d in blanch money for honey, wheat and malt. The farm of King Edward was £14 by tale for all things pertaining to the farm. This manor was always in the king's demesne.

IN 'WETHERLEY' HUNDRED

COMBERTON is a demesne vill of the king. There are $2\frac{1}{2}$ hides. There is land for 5 ploughs. In demesne are 2 [ploughs], and there can be a third. There are 7 villans and 5 bordars with 2 ploughs. [There is] meadow for 2 ploughs. It renders 100s by tale and rendered as much TRE. This land always belonged to the king's farm. With these 2 hides is half a virgate which a sokeman holds who was not there TRE; and it was then worth 2s; now 12d. This man was under Earl Waltheof.

In HASLINGFIELD the king holds 7 hides and 1 virgate. There is land for 8 ploughs. In demesne are 2 [ploughs], and there can be a third. There are 11 villans and 9 bordars with 4 ploughs, and there can be a fifth. [There is] meadow for 3 ploughs. [There is] a wood to repair fences, and 2 slaves. It renders £10 assayed and weighed and £13.8s4d in blanch money by tale for honey, wheat and malt, and other customary dues. TRE it rendered £10 by tale and, as distinct from this, as much as was necessary in wheat, malt and honey. This land always belonged to the king's farm.

IN LONGSTOWE HUNDRED

In KINGSTON the king holds 1 hide and 3 virgates. There is land for 2 ploughs. In demesne is 1 [plough]; and 1 villan and 3 bordars with 1 plough. There is 1 slave. It renders 40s by tale; TRE it rendered 60s. This land always belonged to the king's farm.

IN CHESTERTON HUNDRED

CHESTERTON, a demesne vill of the king, is assessed at 30 hides. There is land for 16 ploughs. In demesne are 3 [ploughs], and there can be 9 more. There are 2 villans and 16 bordars and 6 cottars with 4 ploughs. The priest has 1 virgate of land. [There is] meadow for 8 ploughs. From the fen, 1,000 eels. It renders £15 assayed and weighed and £13.8s4d in blanch money for honey, wheat and malt and other customary dues. TRE it rendered £15 by tale and, as distinct from this, as much as was necessary in customary dues.

In Whittlesford Hundred. In Hinxton lies the wara of $1\frac{1}{2}$ hides of the manor of Great Chesterford [Essex] and it is valued in Essex. Earl Ælfgar held this land.

IN CHEVELEY HUNDRED

WOODDITTON was assessed at 10 hides TRE, and now at 1 hide. There is land for 16 ploughs. In demesne [are] 2 ploughs; and 7 villans and 3 bordars with 3 ploughs, and there can be 13 more. There are 3 slaves, pasture for the livestock of the vill, [and] woodland for 300 pigs. From the herbage of the vill, 6s8d. In all it is worth £12; when received, £15; and as much TRE. William de Noyers holds this manor at farm from the king. This manor belonged to the Church of St Æthelthryth of Ely TRE, but Archbishop Stigand took it away, the men of the hundred do not know how.

IN 'STAPLOE' HUNDRED

In EXNING [Suffolk] King William has 13½ hides. There is land for 34 ploughs. In demesne are 7 ploughs, and there can be 3 more. There are 35 villans and 34 bordars with 24 ploughs. There are 7 slaves, and 3 mills [rendering] 20s and 7,000 eels, [and] meadow for 4 ploughs. In all it is worth £53; when Godric received it, £12; TRE £56. Eadgifu the Fair held this manor, and in this manor were 7 sokemen, men of the same Eadgifu, and they could depart without her leave but she herself had their soke, and each of them provided cartage-due or 8d in the king's service or [gave] a pledge.

In Soham King William has 6 hides and 40 acres in his return.

[Folio 190: CAMBRIDGESHIRE]

In Fleamdyke Hundred. In Fulbourn Picot holds 26 sokemen who have 4 hides under the king's hand. There is land for 6 ploughs, and there are [6 ploughs], [and] meadow for the ploughs. They pay £8 a year assayed and weighed, and every year [provide] 12 horses and 12 watchmen if the king should come into the shire. If he should not come [they pay] 12s8d. TRE they rendered nothing to the sheriff but cartage-dues and escort-service, or 12s8d, and the rest Picot has usurped in defiance of the king.

IN CHILFORD HUNDRED

In Babraham Picot holds half a hide and half a virgate from the king. This land pertains to Great Chesterford [Essex] and is valued there at 30s. in Essex. Wulfwine held this land under Earl Ælfgar, [and] could not depart nor sell it.

In Great Abington Picot holds under the king's hand half a virgate, and a sokeman, Sagar, [holds] of him. It is worth 12d. Almær held this land TRE and could give and sell it. Aubrey de Vere usurped this in defiance of the king, and Picot proved his right to it against him. Of the livestock which Aubrey took from there he still retains 400 sheep, less 20, and a plough, as the men of the hundred bear witness.

IN THRIPLOW HUNDRED

In [?Great] Shelford Peter de Valognes holds 3 hides of the king's farm in Newport [Essex]. There is land for 4 ploughs. In demesne is 1 [plough], and there can be another; and 5 villans and 6 bordars have 2 ploughs. [There is] meadow for 4 ploughs. It renders £4 assayed and weighed and 20s by tale. This land is a Berewick of Newport, but its wara pertains to Cambridge. Earl Harold held this land.

IN 'ARRINGFORD' HUNDRED

In Litlington William the chamberlain and Otto the goldsmith hold 4½ hides and half a virgate from the king at farm. There is land for 10 ploughs. In demesne [are] 2 hides and 3 ploughs.

There are 26 villans and 10 bordars with 7 ploughs. There are 6 slaves, meadow for 2 ploughs, [and] woodland for 30 pigs. In all it is and always was worth £22. Earl Ælfgar held this manor. The men of this manor paid wardpenny to the king's sheriff or did ward.

In Abington Pigotts the king holds half a hide which pertains to Litlington. There is land for 1 plough, and there is [1 plough], and it is valued with the same manor.

In Abington Pigotts Alwine Coc the beadle holds half a virgate from the king. There is land for half a plough, and there is [half a plough]. It is worth 5s; TRE 10s. The same man held it TRE and could neither give nor sell it. It pertained to Ickleton.

IN PAPWORTH HUNDRED

In Fen Drayton 2 sokemen hold half a hide from the king. There is land for 4 oxen, and meadow. It is and always was worth 2s. The same men themselves held and could give and sell it.

In Whittlesford Hundred. In Hinxton lies the wara of 1½ hides of Great Chesterford [Essex] manor and it is valued in Essex. Earl Ælfgar held it.

Picot has under the king's hand 1 hide. 7 sokemen held this TRE and they could sell it.

II. The land of the Bishop of Winchester

IN 'ARRINGFORD' HUNDRED

WALKELIN, Bishop of Winchester, holds Steeple Morden. It is assessed at 8 hides. There is land for 16 ploughs. In demesne [are] 4 hides, and there are 5 ploughs; and 15 villans and 15 bordars with 11 ploughs. There are 11 slaves, and 1 mill rendering 16d and 2 other mills rendering 32d, meadow for 16 ploughs, [and] pasture for the livestock of the vill. In all it is worth £20; when received, £10; TRE £16. This manor pertains and pertained to the Church of St PETER of Winchester.

In 'Clopton' [in Croydon] the same bishop holds 3½ hides. There is land for 5 ploughs. In demesne [is] 1 hide and 3 virgates, and there is 1 plough. There are 6 villans and 5 bordars with 3 ploughs, and there can be a fourth. [There is] meadow for 5 ploughs, [and] pasture for the livestock of the vill. It is worth 60s; when received, 40s; TRE £4. This land pertained to the demesne of the Church of St PETER of Winchester.

In Abington Pigotts Hugh holds 2½ hides and half a virgate from Bishop Walkelin. There is land for 5 ploughs. In demesne [are] 3 ploughs; and 9 bordars, each with 5 acres, with 2 ploughs. [There is] meadow for 5 ploughs, and [rendering] 2s. It is worth £7; when received, £3; TRE £8. This manor pertained and pertains to the Church of St Peter of Winchester, and there a sokeman held half a virgate under Archbishop Stigand, and could depart without his leave.

In Bassingbourne the same bishop holds 1 hide and 2½ virgates. There is land for 3 ploughs. In demesne [is] 1 hide, and there is 1 plough. There is 1 villan and 4 bordars with 1 plough, and there can be another. There are 2 mills rendering 20s, [and] meadow for 1 plough. It is worth 60s; when received, 40s; TRE 60s. This land pertained and pertains to the Church of St PETER of Winchester, and there was 1 sokeman, the man of Archbishop Stigand; he held half a virgate and could give and sell it.

III. The land of the Bishop of Lincoln

IN WHITTLESFORD HUNDRED

The Bishop of Lincoln holds 2 hides in Hinxton, and Robert [holds], of him. There is land for 2 ploughs. There is 1 [plough], and there can be another. There are 2 villans and 2 bordars. [There is] meadow for 2 ploughs, and 1 mill rendering 8s. It is worth 40s; when received, 20s; TRE £4. Siward held this land from Earl Harold and could give it to whom he would.

IN 'NORTHSTOWE' HUNDRED

In Madingley Picot holds 1½ virgates of land from Bishop Remigius. It is and was worth 5s; TRE 10s. Blæcwine, the man of King Edward, held this land and could depart; but the soke remained with Bishop Wulfwig.

IN CHESTERTON HUNDRED

HISTON is assessed at 26½ hides. This manor is 1 of the 12 demesne manors of the bishopric of Lincoln. Bishop Remigius holds there 17 hides, less 1 virgate. There is land for 13 ploughs. In demesne [are] 8 hides, and there are 2 ploughs, and there can be a third. There are 18 villans and 18 bordars with 9 ploughs,

[Folio 190V: CAMBRIDGESHIRE]

and there can be a tenth plough. There are 4 cottars and 4 slaves, meadow for 13 ploughs, [and] pasture for the livestock of the vill. In all it is worth £10; when received, £12; TRE £14.

Of the 26½ hides, Picot holds 9 hides and 3 virgates from the bishop. There is land for 6 ploughs. In demesne [is] 1 plough, and there can be another. There are 10 villans and 19 cottars with 2 ploughs, and there can be another 2. [There is] meadow for 6 ploughs, [and] pasture for the livestock of the vill. It is worth £4; when received, £6; TRE £7. 9 sokemen held this land and could sell, but the soke remained with the bishop.

In the same vill Bishop Remigius holds 1 hide and 1 virgate and 2 parts of a virgate. There is land for 1 plough, but there is no plough. There is 1 villan and 1 cottar, [and] meadow for 1 plough. It is worth 5s; when received, 10s; TRE 20S. Wulfwine, the man of the Abbot of Ely, held this land and rendered yearly a sester of honey. Bishop Remigius usurped this land in defiance of the abbot, as the hundred bears witness. Picot the sheriff holds it from the bishop.

In Childerley Roger holds 3 hides from Bishop Remigius. There is land for 2½ ploughs. In demesne is 1 [plough]; and 1 villan and 5 bordars with 1 plough, and there can be half a plough [more]. There is 1 cottar and 3 slaves, [and] a wood for

fences. It is worth 50s; when received, 40s; TRE 100s. Siward, the man of Earl Harold, held this manor and could sell it.

IIII. The land of the Bishop of Rochester

IN 'STAPOLE' HUNDRED

THE BISHOP of Rochester holds 1½ hides and 20 acres in Isleham under Archbishop Lanfranc. There is land for 3 ploughs. In demesne [is] 1 plough; and 11 villans with 2 ploughs. There is half a mill [rendering] 2s8d and 300 eels, meadow for 3 ploughs, and 2,000 eels, [and] pasture for the livestock of the vill. It is and was worth 40s TRE 60s. Wulfwine, King Edward's huntsman, held half a hide and 20 acres of this land, and 12 sokemen, who could all give and sell, had 1 hide under Thurbert.

V. The land of the Abbey of Ely

IN 'RADFIELD' HUNDRED

THE ABBOT of Ely holds STETCHWORTH. He has there 8½ hides and half a virgate. There is land for 12 ploughs. In demesne [are] 3½ hides, and there are 3 ploughs, and there can be 2 more. There are 16 villans and 5 bordars with 6 ploughs, and there can be a seventh. There are 4 slaves, woodland for 260 pigs, [and] pasture for the livestock of the vill. All together it is worth £10; and as much when received; TRE £12. This land pertained and pertains to the demesne of the Church of Ely.

In the same vill Hardwin de Scales holds 1 virgate of the abbot. There is land for 2 oxen. It was always worth 5s. Godwine held this land, but could not sell it. The Abbot of Ely has half a hide of meadow in demesne in the vill itself. Særic d'Auberville took 1½ virgates of the demesne farm of the Abbot of Ely from this manor, and put them in the manor of Saint-Wandrille, as the hundred bears witness.

In WESTLEY WATERLESS the abbot holds 3 hides. There is land for 5 ploughs. There are 2 [ploughs], and there can be 3 more. There are 4 villans and 5 bordars and 2 slaves, [and] meadow for 2 oxen. It is and was worth 10s; TRE 100s. This land pertains and always pertained to the demesne of the Church of Ely, the hundred bearing witness.

The abbot himself holds WEST WRATTING. There are 4½ hides. There is land for 7 ploughs. In demesne [are] 3 hides, and there are 2 ploughs, and there can be 2 more. There are 6 villans and 3 bordars with 3 ploughs. There are 3 slaves, meadow for 1 plough, woodland for 20 pigs, [and] pasture for the livestock of the vill. All together it is worth £4; when received, 40s; TRE 100s. This manor pertains and always pertained to the demesne of the Church of Ely.

In the same vill Hardwin holds 3 hides from the abbot. There is land for 4 ploughs. In demesne [are] 2 ploughs; and 5 villans and 4 bordars with 2 ploughs. There are 4 slaves, and 4 acres of meadow, [and] woodland for 12 pigs. It is worth £4; when received, 20s; TRE 40s. 10 sokemen held this land: they were the men of the abbot, and without his leave they could not sell their land. 6 of them provided cartage-dues and 4 provided escort-service if the king came to the shire. If not, they paid 8d. for cartage-due, and 4[d] for escort-service.

The abbot himself holds BALSHAM. There are 9 hides. [There is] land for 19 ploughs. In demesne [are] 5 hides, and there are 5 ploughs, and there can be 2 more. There are 12 villans and 12 bordars with 12 ploughs. There are 2 slaves, and 1 mill [rendering] 4s, woodland for 200 pigs, and 12 acres of meadow, [and] 32d from pasture. In all it is worth £17; when received, £10; TRE £12. This manor pertains and always pertained to the demesne of the Church of Ely.

In the same vill Hardwin holds 80 acres from the abbot. There is land for 1 plough, and there is [1 plough]. It is and always was worth 13s4d. 3 sokemen, the men of the Abbot of Ely, held this land: they could neither give nor sell their land without his leave, yet they provided cartage-due, and escort-service.

IN 'STAPLOE' HUNDRED

In Soham the same abbot holds half a hide. There is land for 2 ploughs. In demesne is 1 [plough]; and 3 villans and 10 bordars with 1 plough. [There is] meadow for 2 ploughs, pasture for the livestock of the vill, and a boat which fishes in the mere by custom. It is worth 30s; when received, 20s; TRE 30s. This land always pertained to the church.

IN 'STAINE' HUNDRED

In SWAFFHAM PRIOR the same abbot holds 3 hides. There is land for 5 ploughs. In demesne [is] 1 hide and 3 virgates, and there are 2 ploughs; and 5 villans and 2 bordars with 3 ploughs. There are 2 slaves, and 6s. from a fishing-net toll, [and] 6d. from the fen. It is and always was worth 100s. This land pertains and always pertained to the church.

In the same vill Hardwin holds 2 hides and 3 virgates under the abbot. There is land for 3 ploughs. In demesne [is] 1 plough; and 2 villans with 2 ploughs. [There is] meadow for 2 oxen. It is and always was worth 70s. 4 sokemen held this land, and could not depart without the leave of the abbot.

In Stow cum Quy Picot holds 3 hides and 3 virgates under the abbot. There is land for 4 ploughs. In demesne [are] 2 ploughs; and 5 villans with 2 ploughs. There is 1 slave,

[Folio 191: CAMBRIDGESHIRE]

| and half a mill [rendering] 40d |, [and] meadow for 4 ploughs. It is worth £6; when received and TRE, £4. 2 sokemen held this land under the abbot; they could not depart without his leave.

IN FLEAMDYKE HUNDRED

In Fulbourn the same abbot holds 4½ hides. There is land for 6 ploughs. In demesne [are] 3 hides, where there can be 3 ploughs, but none is reckoned there. There are 8 villans and 6 bordars with 3 ploughs. [There is] meadow for the ploughs. It is and was worth 20s; TRE £6. This land pertains and always pertained to the demesne of the Church of Ely at farm.

In Teversham the same abbot holds 1 hide. There is land for 1½ ploughs. In demesne is 1 plough, and 2 villans and 2

bordars. It is and was worth 20s; TRE 40s. This land always pertained to the church.

HORNINGSEA is assessed at 7 hides. There is land for 17 ploughs. In demesne [are] 3½ hides, and there are 8½ ploughs. There are 22 villans and 14 bordars with 9 ploughs. There are 15 slaves, and 1 mill rendering 10s. and 1,000 eels, [and] meadow for the ploughs. In all it is worth £18; when received, £14; and as much TRE. This land always pertained and pertains to the demesne of the Church of Ely.

IN CHILFORD HUNDRED

In West Wickham the same abbot holds 1½ hides. There is land for 4 ploughs. In demesne [is] half a hide, and there are 2½ ploughs. There are 6 villans and 2 bordars with 2 ploughs. There are 2 slaves, and 4 acres of meadow, [and] woodland for 50 pigs. It is worth 65s; when received, 60s; TRE 40s. This land pertains and always pertained to the demesne of the Church of Ely.

In Barham a sokeman holds half a virgate under the abbot. It is and was worth 40d. This man provided escort-service for the sheriff TRE.

In Babraham Hardwin holds half a virgate of land under the abbot. It is and was worth 40d. 2 sokemen held it; they could not depart.

In Pampisford the same abbot holds 2 hides and 3½ virgates. There is land for 6 ploughs. In demesne [is] 1 hide and 1½ virgates, and there are 2 ploughs. There are 12 villans and 5 bordars with 4 ploughs. There are 3 slaves, and 1 mill rendering 20s, [and] meadow for 1 plough. It is and always was worth £7. This land always pertained and pertains to the demesne of the Church of Ely.

In the same vill Hardwin holds 10 acres from the abbot. [There is] land for 1 ox. It is worth 12d. Snelling held this land from the abbot, but he could not depart.

IN THRIPLOW HUNDRED

The abbot himself holds 6½ hides in Thriplow. There is land for 8 ploughs. In demesne [are] 3 hides, and there are 3 ploughs. There are 12 villans and 5 bordars with 5 ploughs. There are 5 slaves, and meadow for 1 plough [and] pasture for the livestock of the vill. In all it is and was worth £11; TRE £12. This land pertains and always pertained to the demesne of the church.

In the same vill Hardwin holds under the abbot as it were by the grace of the abbot himself 1 hide of the demesne for the sustenance of the monks till he confers with the king about it. There is land for 1 plough. It is and always was worth 20s. TRE this land always pertained to the demesne of the Church of Ely.

In the same vill Hardwin held 2 acres of the abbot's land, for which he does not have a warrantor nor a livery officer, but seized them in defiance of the abbot, as the men of the hundred bear witness.

HAUXTON is assessed at 8½ hides. There is land for 12 ploughs. In demesne [are] 5 hides, and there are 4 ploughs;

and 16 villans and 4 bordars with 8 ploughs. There are 3 slaves, and 2 mills rendering 50s, meadow for 4 ploughs, [and] pasture for the livestock of the vill. In all it is and was worth £13; TRE £14. This manor pertains and always pertained to the demesne of the Church of Ely.

In Harston Picot holds 1½ hides from the abbot by the king's command, and they are valued in Harston. A certain sokeman held this land under the Abbot of Ely TRE. He could depart without his leave, but the soke remained with the abbot.

GREAT SHELFORD is assessed at 9 hides and 24 acres. There is land for 11 ploughs. In demesne [are] 5 hides, and there are 3 ploughs. there are 20 villans and 8 bordars with 8 ploughs. There are 7 slaves, and 2 mills at 45s and rendering 2 pigs, [and] meadow for 4 ploughs. In all it is and was worth £12; TRE £14.

In the same vill Hardwin holds 2½ hides and 9 acres and a minster of the demesne farm of the monks of Ely, and they were there TRE, as the hundred bears witness. Now the abbot does not have them.

In the same vill 7 sokemen hold 1½ hides and 6 acres of the soke of the abbot. They could not depart with the land, but the soke remained with the Church of Ely. This manor always pertained and pertains to the demesne of the Church of Ely. |

STAPLEFORD is assessed at 10 hides. There is land for 11 ploughs. In demesne [are] 6½ hides, and there are 4 ploughs. There are 16 villans and 4 bordars with 7 ploughs. There are 7 slaves, and meadow for 5 ploughs, pasture for the livestock of the vill, [and] woodland to repair fences. In all it is and was worth £12; TRE £13. This manor pertains and always pertained to the demesne of the Church of Ely.

In Whaddon Hardwin holds 2½ hides. There is land for 3 ploughs. In demesne [is] 1 hide, and 1 plough. There are 6 villans and 15 cottars with 1½ ploughs, and there can be another half [-plough]. [There is] meadow for 2 ploughs, [and] pasture for the livestock of the vill. This land is valued with the land of Hardwin. Thorbiorn held 1 hide of this land from the abbot; he could not alienate it from the church [or put it] outside the farm of the monks TRE nor on the day of his [King Edward's] death; and 12 sokemen had 1½ hides; they could sell them, but the soke remained with the abbot.

In Meldreth Hardwin holds 1 virgate of the abbot's soke.

In the same vill the abbot holds 2 hides and 3 virgates. There is land for 7 ploughs. In demesne [are] 1½ hides, and 1½ ploughs, and there can be [another] half [-plough]. There are [...] 10 bordars with 3 ploughs. There are 3 slaves, and 1 mill [rendering] 3s, [and] meadow for 5 ploughs. It is and was worth 100s; TRE £6. This land pertains and always pertained to the demesne of the church.

In the same vill Hardwin holds 1½ hides and 1 minster

[Folio 191V: CAMBRIDGESHIRE]

In the same vill Guy de Raimbeaucourt holds 10 sokeman. One of them could not sell [his land] in the time of King Edward; the others could; the hundred bears witness to this.

of the demesne farm of the monks, which they held both during the life and at the death of King Edward, as the men of the hundred bear witness.

In Melbourn the Abbot of Ely holds 2 hides and 1 virgate of land. There is land for 5 ploughs. In demesne [is] 1 hide and 1 virgate, and there are 1½ ploughs, and there can be [another] half [-plough]. There are 6 villans and 9 bordars with 3 ploughs. There are 3 cottars, and 1 mill rendering 2s8d, meadow for 5 ploughs, [and] pasture for the livestock of the vill. It is and was worth 100s; TRE £6. This land pertains and always pertained to the demesne of the Church of Ely.

In Shepreth Hardwin holds half a virgate, which belonged to the Church of Ely on the day of King Edward's death.

IN LONGSTOWE HUNDRED

In Hardwick the Abbot of Ely holds 3 hides and 1 virgate and 12 acres. There is land for 6 ploughs. In demesne [are] 1¼ hides and 12 acres, and there are 2 ploughs. There are 7 villans with 4 ploughs. There are 4 slaves, meadow for 4 ploughs, [and] a wood for fences. It is and was worth 100s; TRE £6. This land pertains and always pertained to the demesne of the Church of Ely.

In the same vill Ralph holds 10 acres from the abbot. [There is] land for 1 ox. It is and was worth 12d. Cabe held this land under the abbot; he could not depart from him.

LITTLE GRANSDEN is assessed at 5 hides. There is land for 9 ploughs. In demesne [are] 2½ hides, and there is 1 plough, and there can be 2 [ploughs]. There are 8 villans and 3 bordars with 6 ploughs. There are 4 slaves, meadow for 3 ploughs, [and] pasture for the livestock of the vill. [There is] woodland for 60 pigs, and from the customary dues of the woodland, 2s. In all it is worth £8; when received, £9; TRE 15L. This manor pertains and always pertained to the demesne of the Church of Ely.

IN PAPWORTH HUNDRED

WILLINGHAM is assessed at 7 hides. There is land for 7 ploughs. In demesne [are] 4 hides, and there are 2 ploughs. There are 12 villans with 5 ploughs. There are 8 cottars and 1 slave. [There is] meadow for 7 ploughs, [and] pasture for the livestock of the vill. From the fen, 6s. In all it is and was worth 100s; TRE £8. This manor pertains and always pertained to the demesne of the Church of Ely.

IN 'NORTHSTOWE' HUNDRED

In Oakington Ælfgeat the priest holds 15 acres from the abbot. There is land for 1 ox. It is and always was worth 3s. The same man held it TRE and could give it, but the soke remained with the abbot.

IMPINGTON is assessed at 6½ hides. There is land for 6 ploughs. In demesne [are] 3½ hides, and there is half a plough, and there can be 1½ ploughs. There is 1 villan and 8 bordars with 2 ploughs, and there can be 2 [...]. There are 7 cottars and 1 slave, [and] meadow for 2 ploughs. It is and was worth 40s; TRE £8. This manor pertains and always pertained to the demesne of the Church of Ely.

IN CHESTERTON HUNDRED

COTTENHAM is assessed at 10 hides. There is land for 8 ploughs. In demesne [are] 6 hides, and 1 plough. There are 16 villans and 10 cottars with 6 ploughs. There are 2 slaves, meadow for 8 ploughs, [and] pasture for the livestock of the vill. In all it is and was worth 100s; TRE £8. This manor pertains and pertained to the demesne of the Church of Ely.

In Histon the abbot holds 1 hide and 3 virgates. This land is valued with Impington.

IN THE TWO HUNDREDS OF ELY WHICH MEET AT WITCHFORD

The Church of Ely holds WHITTLESEY for 2 hides. There is land for 4½ ploughs. In demesne [is] 1 hide, and there are 1½ ploughs. There are 8 villans and 4 cottars with 3 ploughs. There are 3 slaves, meadow for 1 plough, [and] pasture for the livestock of the vill. From the weir, 2s. It is worth £4; when received, £3; TRE 100s. This manor pertains and always pertained to the Church of Ely in demesne farm.

The Abbot of Ely holds DODDINGTON for 5 hides. There is land for 8 ploughs. In demesne [are] 2½ hides, and there are 3 ploughs. There are 24 villans with 5 ploughs. There are 8 sokemen with 1 hide, and 8 cottars and 1 slave. [There is] meadow for 8 ploughs, pasture for the livestock of the vill, [and] woodland for 250 pigs. From the fisheries, 27,150 eels, [and] from gifts [of fish], 24s. In all it is worth £16; when received, £10; TRE £12. This manor pertains and pertained to the demesne of the Church of Ely. To this manor pertains 1 Berewick, March, where there are 12 villans, each with 12 acres. This is valued with the manor.

In Chatteris the same abbot holds 2 hides and half a virgate. There is land for 3 ploughs. In demesne [is] half a hide, and there are 6 oxen. There are 6 villans and 2 bordars and 2 cottars with 2 ploughs and 2 oxen. [There is] meadow for 3 ploughs, [and] woodland for 20 pigs. From the fisheries, 1,500 eels. It is worth 40s; when received, 30s; TRE 50s. This land pertained and pertains to the demesne of the Church of Ely.

The Abbot of Ely holds LITTLEPORT for 2½ hides. There is land for 6 ploughs. In demesne [is] 1 hide, and there are 2 ploughs. There are 15 villans and 8 cottars with 4 ploughs. There are 8 slaves, and meadow for 6 ploughs, [and] pasture for the livestock of the vill. From the fisheries, 17,000 eels, [and] 12s9d from gifts of fish. In all it is worth £10; when received, £7; TRE £6. This manor pertains and always pertained to the Church of Ely in demesne.

In Stuntney the abbot holds 1½ hides. There is land for 3 ploughs. In demesne [is] 1 hide, and 1 plough. There are 6 villans and 5 cottars and 3 slaves with 2 ploughs. [There is] meadow for 3 ploughs, [and] pasture for the livestock of the vill. From the fisheries, 24,000 eels, and from gifts [of fish], 18s. All together it is and was worth £10.14s; TRE £12. This land is a BEREWICK of the manor of Ely.

The same abbot holds Little Thetford [for] 1 hide. There is land for 1 plough, and there is [1 plough] in demesne. There is 1 villan with 6 acres, and 4 cottars, meadow for 1 plough,

[and] pasture for the livestock of the vill. From the fishery, 500 eels, [and] 4½d from gifts [of fish]. It is worth 40s; when received, 20s; TRE 30s. This land is a Berewick of Ely.

STRETHAM is assessed at 5 hides. There is land for 9 ploughs. In demesne [are] 3 hides, and there are 4 ploughs. There are 12 villans, each [having] 10 acres, and 11 villans with 1 hide; these have 5 ploughs. There are 10 cottars and 2 slaves. [There is] meadow for 9 ploughs, [and] pasture for the livestock of the vill. From the fisheries, 3,250 eels, [and] 7s7d from gifts [of fish]. In all it is worth £9;

[Folio 192: CAMBRIDGESHIRE]

when received, £6; TRE £12. This manor pertains and always pertained to the demesne of the Church of Ely.

The Abbot of Ely holds WILBURTON. There are 5 hides. There is land for 7 ploughs. In demesne [are] 3 hides and 1 virgate, and there are 3 ploughs. There are 4 sokemen who neither could nor can depart, and 9 villans with 4 ploughs. There are 9 cottars and 8 slaves, meadow for 7 ploughs, [and] pasture for the livestock of the vill. From reeds, 16d. All together it is worth £7; when received, £4; TRE £10. This manor pertains and always pertained to the demesne of the Church of Ely.

The Abbot of Ely holds 'LINDEN' [in Haddenham]. There are 4 hides. There is land for 6 ploughs. In demesne [are] 2½ hides, and there are 4 ploughs. There are 2 sokemen who neither could nor can depart, and 14 villans with 2 ploughs. There are 9 cottars and 1 bordar and 10 slaves. From the fisheries, 3,333 eels, [and] 4s. from gifts [of fish]. [There is] meadow for 6 ploughs, [and] pasture for the livestock of the vill. All together it is worth £8; when received, £4; TRE £9. This manor pertains and pertained to the demesne of the church.

The Abbot of Ely holds HILL ROW. There are 2 hides. There is land for 5 ploughs. In demesne [is] 1 hide and 1 virgate and 10 acres, and there are 3 ploughs. There are 10 villans with 2 ploughs. There are 4 cottars and 5 slaves, meadow for 5 ploughs, pasture for the livestock of the vill, and from the port, 3 ploughshares. It is worth 100s; when received, 40s; TRE £6. This land is a Berewick of 'Linden' [in Haddenham].

Under the abbot 7 sokemen, who neither could nor can depart, hold Haddenham. There are 3 hides. There is land for 5 ploughs, and there are [5 ploughs]. There are 8 villans, each [having] half a virgate, and 4 bordars, each [having] 5 acres. There are 6 cottars, meadow for 5 ploughs, [and] pasture for the livestock of the vill. It is and was worth £8; TRE £12.

SO FAR ONE HUNDRED. NOW THE OTHER

The Abbot of Ely holds WISBECH. There are 10 hides. There is land for 10 ploughs. In demesne [is] 1 hide and 1 virgate, and there are 2 ploughs. There are 15 villans, each [with] 10 acres, and 13 sokemen with 2½ hides who neither could nor can depart. All these men [have] 8 ploughs. There are 17 cottars and 2 slaves. From the fisheries, 1,500 eels. [There is] meadow for 10 ploughs, [and] pasture for the livestock of the vill. All together it is and was worth 100s; TRE £6. This manor pertains and pertained to the demesne of the church.

In the same vill 2 fishermen render to the abbot 14,000 eels, and 13s4d from gifts [of fish]. The abbot has soke over all the men of this vill.

ELY is assessed at 10 hides. There is land for 20 ploughs. In demesne [are] 5 hides, and there are 5 ploughs, and there can be a sixth. There are 40 villans, each [with] 15 acres, with 14 ploughs. There are 28 cottars and 20 slaves. From the fisheries, 3,750 eels, [and] from gifts [of fish], 2s3d. [There is] meadow for 20 ploughs, [and] pasture for the livestock of the vill. There are 3 arpents of vineyard. In all it is worth £30; when received, £20; TRE £33. All this manor always was and is demesne.

Hainey is an is land on which is half a hide of land. This does not pay geld nor did it ever pay it TRE.

The Abbot of Ely holds LITTLE DOWNHAM. There are 4 hides. There is land for 8 ploughs. In demesne [are] 2½ hides, and there are 4 ploughs. There are 15 villans, each with 12 acres, with 4 ploughs. There are 8 cottars and 8 slaves. [There is] meadow for 8 ploughs, pasture for the livestock of the vill, 300 eels and 2s. from a fishery, [and] woodland for 100 pigs. In all it is worth £10; when received, 100s; TRE £12. This manor pertains and always pertained to the demesne of the Church of Ely.

The Abbot of Ely holds WITCHFORD. There are 3 hides. There is land for 7 ploughs. In demesne [are] 1½ hides, and there are 2 ploughs, and there can be a third. There are 5 sokemen with half a hide, who neither could nor can depart, and 17 villans, each with 7 acres. All these together [have] 4 ploughs. There are 7 cottars and 8 slaves, meadow for 7 ploughs, [and] pasture for the livestock of the vill. In all it is worth £10; when received, £8; TRE £12. This manor belonged and belongs to the demesne of the church.

The Abbot of Ely holds WENTWORTH. There are 3½ hides. There is land for 7 ploughs. In demesne [is] 1 hide, and there is 1 plough, and there can be another. There are 9 villans, each with 10 acres, and 2 sokemen with 1 hide, who neither could nor can sell [their land] without the abbot's leave, and 1 sokeman with 1 virgate, [holding] in the same manner, and under these sokemen 9 villans, each with 10 acres. There are 17 cottars, and meadow for 7 ploughs, pasture for the livestock of the vill, [and] woodland for 20 pigs. In all it is worth £10.10s; and as much when received; TRE £12. This manor pertains and always pertained to the demesne of the church.

The Abbot of Ely holds WITCHAM. There are 4 hides and 1 virgate. There is land for 7 ploughs. In demesne [are] 2 hides, and there are 2 ploughs, and there can be a third. There are 12 sokemen with 2 hides less half a virgate, who neither could nor can give [their land] without the abbot's leave. There are 2 villans with 10 acres, and 2 bordars, each with 5 acres. All these men [have] 4 ploughs. There are 4 cottars and 5 slaves, meadow for 7 ploughs, [and] pasture for the livestock of the vill. It is and was worth 100s; TRE £7. This manor belonged and belongs to the demesne of the Church of Ely.

The Abbot of Ely holds SUTTON. There are 5 hides. There is land for 10 ploughs. [...]. In demesne [are] 2 hides, and there are 3 ploughs, and there can be a fourth. There are 9 sokemen with 2 hides, who neither could nor can depart without the abbot's leave, and 8 villans, each with 7½ acres, and 15 cottars, all these men with 6 ploughs. There are 7 slaves, meadow for 10 ploughs, [and] pasture for the livestock of the vill. From the fisheries, 44s. [There is] woodland for 5 pigs. In all it is and was worth £12; TRE £16. This manor belonged and belongs to the demesne of the Church of Ely.

VI. The land of St Edmund

THE ABBOT of St Edmundsbury holds in the 2 hundreds of Ely 16 acres in March. There is land for half a plough, and there is [half a plough], with 3 bordars. [There is] meadow for 4 ploughs or oxen, [and] woodland for 4 pigs. It is and always was worth 3s; and pertains and always pertained to the demesne of the Church of St Edmundsbury.

In Wisbech the same abbot has 1 fisherman rendering 5,000 eels.

In Soham the abbot himself holds 6 acres of land. There is 1 fisherman having a seine in the mere of the same vill. It is and was worth 4s; TRE 5s. This land pertains and always pertained to the Church of St Edmundsbury.

[Folio 192V: CAMBRIDGESHIRE]

VII. The land of the Church of Ramsey

IN LONGSTOWE HUNDRED

THE ABBOT of Ramsey holds 1 hide in Bourn, and 2 knights [hold] from him. There is land for 1 plough. There are 2 bordars, [and] meadow for 1 plough. It is and always was worth 10s, and pertains and always pertained to the Church of St Benedict of Ramsey, and is a Berewick of Longstowe.

In LONGSTOWE Guy holds 2 hides under the abbot himself. There is land for 5 ploughs. In demesne are 2 ploughs; and 5 villans and 6 bordars with 3 ploughs. There is 1 cottar, and meadow for 2 ploughs, pasture for the livestock of the vill, [and] a wood for fences and houses. All together it is worth 50s; when received, £4; TRE £6. This manor pertains and pertained to the demesne of the Church of St Benedict of Ramsey.

IN PAPWORTH HUNDRED

The Abbot of Ramsey holds GRAVELEY. There are 5 hides. [There is] land for 7 ploughs. In demesne [are] 2½ hides, and there are 2 ploughs. There are 8 villans and 8 bordars with 5 ploughs. There are 4 slaves, [and] a wood for fences and houses. It is and was worth £6; TRE £8. This manor pertains and always pertained to the Church of St Benedict.

The Abbot of Ramsey holds ELSWORTH. There are 9 hides and 1 virgate and 5 acres. There is land for 22 ploughs. In demesne [are] 4 hides, and there are 3 ploughs, and there can be a fourth. There are 19 villans and 17 bordars, and 1

Frenchman having 3 virgates. These have together 18 ploughs. There are 5 cottars, meadow for 4 ploughs, and 4 slaves, pasture for the livestock of the vill, [and] a wood for the houses of the hall. In all it is worth £16; when received, £14; TRE £20. This manor always pertained and pertains to the demesne of the Church of St Benedict. The Abbot of St Benedict holds KNAPWELL. There are 5 hides. There is land for 8 ploughs. In demesne [are] 1½ hides, and there are 2 ploughs. There are 8 villans and 4 sokemen having 1½ hides, and 4 bordars, each with 5 acres. There are 4 cottars and 4 slaves, a wood for fences, [and] meadow for 2 ploughs. In all it is and was worth £6; TRE £8. This manor pertains and always pertained to the demesne of the Church of St Benedict. The aforesaid 4 sokemen could give and sell their land TRE without the abbot's leave, but the soke remained with the abbot.

In Boxworth the same abbot holds half a hide. There is land for half a plough, [and] meadow for half a plough. It is and was worth 4s. This land pertains and pertained to the demesne of the church.

In Fen Drayton the same abbot holds 3 virgates. There is land for 4 oxen, and there are [4 oxen]. [There is] meadow for 4 oxen. There are 2 slaves. It is and always was worth 3s. This land pertains and always pertained to the demesne of the church.

The Abbot of Ramsey holds OVER. There are 10 hides and 3 virgates. There is land for 10½ ploughs. In demesne [are] 6 hides, and there is 1 plough and there can be another. There are 14 villans and 2 bordars and 3 cottars with 6 ploughs, and there can be 2½ ploughs more. There are 2 slaves, meadow for 10½ ploughs, [and] pasture for the livestock of the vill. From the fen, 6s4d. In all it is worth £8; when received, £6; TRE £10. This manor pertains and always pertained to the demesne of the Church of St Benedict.

IN 'STAPOLE' HUNDRED

The Abbot of Ramsey holds BURWELL. There are 10 hides and 1 virgate. There is land for 16 ploughs. In demesne [are] 3 hides and 40 acres, and there are 4 ploughs. There are 42½ villans with 12 ploughs. There are 8 slaves, meadow for 10 ploughs, pasture for the livestock of the vill, and 2 mills rendering 6s8d. In all it is and was worth £16; TRE £20. This manor pertains and always pertained to the demesne of the Church of St Benedict.

IN 'NORTHSTOWE' HUNDRED

The Abbot of Ramsey holds GIRTON. There are 8 hides and 2½ virgates. There is land for 6 ploughs. In demesne [are] 3 hides, and there is 1 plough, and there can be another. There are 7 villans and 6 bordars with 4 ploughs. There are 2 slaves, [and] meadow for 6 ploughs. In all it is worth £4; when received, £6; TRE £8. This manor pertains and pertained to the Church of St Benedict.

In the Two Hundreds of Ely the Abbot of Ramsey holds 3 hides, less half a virgate, in Chatteris. There is land for 4 ploughs. In demesne [are] 1½ hides, and there is 1 plough; and 10 villans and 5 bordars and 2 slaves with 3 ploughs. [There

is] meadow for 4 ploughs, [and] woodland for 100 pigs. From the fisheries, 3,000 eels, [and] 27d. from gifts [of fish]. It is worth 60s; when received, 20s; TRE £4. This land pertains and pertained to the Church of St Benedict.

In Wisbech the Abbot of Ramsey has 8 fishermen rendering 5,260 eels.

VIII. The land of the Church of Thorney

IN THE TWO HUNDREDS OF ELY

THE ABBOT Of THORNEY holds in WHITTLESEY 4 hides. There is land for 6 ploughs. In demesne [are] 2 hides, and there are 2 ploughs; and 16 villans, each [having] 8 acres, and 6 cottars with 4 ploughs. There is 1 slave, meadow for 6 ploughs, [and] pasture for the livestock of the vill. From the weir, 4s, and from fish 20s besides this. In all it is worth £6; when received, 20s; TRE £7. This manor pertained and pertains to the demesne of the Church of Thorney, but the Abbot of Ely has the soke.

IX. The land of the Church of Crowland

IN 'NORTHSTOWE' HUNDRED

THE ABBOT of CROWLAND holds 7½ hides in OAKINGTON. There is land for 8 ploughs. In demesne [are] 4 hides, and there are 2 ploughs. There are 14 villans and 3 bordars with 6 ploughs. There are 4 cottars and 3 slaves, [and] meadow for 2 ploughs. In all it is and was worth £6; TRE £8. This manor was and is in the demesne of the Church of St | Guthlac. |

IN CHESTERTON HUNDRED

The Abbot of Crowland holds COTTENHAM. There are 11 hides. There is land for 8 ploughs. In demesne [are] 6 hides, and there is 1 plough, and there can be another. There are 12 villans and 8 bordars with 6 ploughs. There is 1 slave, meadow for 8 ploughs, [and] pasture for the livestock of the vill. From the fen, 500 eels, and 12d. from gifts [of fish]. In all it is and was worth £6; TRE £8. This manor always was and is in the demesne of the Church of St Guthlac.

[Folio 193: CAMBRIDGESHIRE]

In Dry Drayton the Abbot of Crowland holds 7½ hides. There is land for 6 ploughs. In demesne [are] 4 hides and 3 virgates, and there is 1 plough, and there can be another. There are 11 villans and 5 bordars with 3 ploughs, and there can be a fourth. There are 4 cottars, [and] meadow for 2 ploughs. It is and was worth £3.10s; TRE 100s. This land pertains and pertained to the demesne of the Church of St Guthlac.

IN THE HUNDRED[S] OF ELY

In Wisbech the Abbot of Crowland has 3 fishermen rendering 4,000 eels.

X. The land of Saint-Wandrille

IN 'RADFIELD' HUNDRED

THE ABBOT OF SAINT-WANDRILLE holds DULLINGHAM from the king. There are 6 hides. There is land for 12 ploughs. In demesne [are] 3 hides, and there are 3 ploughs. There are 17 villans and 10 bordars with 9 ploughs. There are 2 slaves, and meadow for 1 plough, woodland for 100 pigs, [and] pasture for the livestock. In all it is worth £12; when received, £15; TRE £15. Earl Ælfgar held this land.

XI. The land of the Church of Chatteris

IN THRIPLOW HUNDRED

THE ABBESS of CHATTERIS holds 5 hides and 40 acres in FOXTON from the king. There is land for 8 ploughs. In demesne [is] 1 hide and 40 acres, and there are 2 ploughs. There are 16 villans and 11 bordars with 6 ploughs. There is half a mill rendering 10s8d, [and] meadow for all the ploughs. It is and was worth £6; TRE £7. This land always pertained and pertains to the demesne of the church.

IN 'STAPLOE' HUNDRED

In Burwell the nuns of the †Church† of Chatteris hold half a hide. [There is] land for half a plough, and there is [half a plough, and] meadow for 2 oxen. It is and was always worth 10s. This land belonged and belongs to the demesne of the church.

IN 'WETHERLEY' HUNDRED

In Barrington the Church of Chatteris holds 2 hides. There is land for 3 ploughs. In demesne [is] 1 hide, and there is 1 plough. There are 8 bordars and 5 cottars with 2 ploughs. There are 3 slaves, and 1 mill [rendering] 25s4d, [and] meadow for 3 ploughs. It is and was worth £3; TRE £4. This land pertained and pertains to the demesne of the Church of Chatteris.

In Shepreth the same church holds 1 hide and 1½ virgates. There is land for 1½ ploughs. In demesne [is] half a hide, and there is half a plough. There is 1 villan and 3 bordars and 4 cottars with 1 plough. There is 1 slave, and 1 mill rendering 5s4d, [and] meadow for 1½ ploughs. It is and was worth 30s; TRE 40s. This land pertains and always pertained to the demesne of the Church of Chatteris.

In Orwell the same church holds the fourth part of a virgate. There is land for half an ox, and it is worth 12d. It always pertained to the church.

In Over the same church holds 1 hide. There is land for 1 plough, and there is [1 plough], with 4 villans. [There is] meadow for 1 plough, [and] pasture for the livestock. It is and was worth 16s. This land always pertained and pertains to the demesne of the Church of Chatteris.

XII. The land of the Count of Mortain

IN WHITTLESFORD HUNDRED

THE COUNT of Mortain holds 2 hides in Sawston, and the Abbot of Grestain [holds] from him. There is land for 3 ploughs. In demesne is 1 [plough]; and 6 villans and 3 bordars have 2 ploughs. There is 1 mill [rendering] 26s2d, [and] meadow for 3 ploughs. It is and was always worth £6. Ordgar held this land under Earl Harold, and could give it to whom he would.

IN 'WETHERLEY' HUNDRED

In Barton Robert holds 1 hide from the count. There is land for 1 plough, and there is [1 plough], with 2 bordars and 1 slave. [There is] meadow for 1 plough. It is and was worth 40s; TRE 50s. Iudichael, King Edward's huntsman, held this land and could give it to whom he would.

In Grantchester the same Robert holds 1 virgate from the count. There is land for 4 oxen, and there are [4 oxen], with 1 villan. [There is] meadow for 2 oxen. It is and was worth 5s. Iudichael the huntsman held this land and could give it to whom he would.

IN 'NORTHSTOWE' HUNDRED

In Girton Morin holds 2½ hides and half a virgate from the count. There is land for 2½ ploughs. In demesne is 1 plough, and there can be [another] half [-plough]. There is 1 villan and 5 bordars and 3 cottars with 1 plough. [There is] meadow for 1 plough. It is and was worth 40s; TRE £4. Iudichael held this land and could sell it to whom he would.

IN CHESTERTON HUNDRED

In Histon Morin holds 1 virgate and 10 acres from the count. This land is valued in Girton.

XIII. The land of Earl Roger

IN 'ARRINGFORD' HUNDRED

Earl ROGER holds 1 hide and the fourth part of 1 virgate in Steeple Morden. There is land for 2 ploughs. In demesne [is] half a hide and the fourth part of 1 virgate, and there is 1 plough; and 6 bordars with 1 plough. [There is] meadow for 2 ploughs, [and] pasture for the livestock of the vill. It is and was worth 40s; TRE 50s. Goda held this land from Earl Ælfgar, and could give it to whom he would.

In another Morden [Guilden Morden] Earl Roger holds half a hide and half a virgate. There is land for 1 plough and 2 oxen. In demesne [is] 1 virgate of land, and there are 2 oxen. There are 4 bordars with 1 plough. [There is] meadow for 1 plough. It is and always was worth 20s. Goda held this land under Earl Ælfgar, and it pertains to Shingay. Hardwin de Scales usurped 4 acres of this land in defiance of the earl, as the hundred bears witness.

In Croydon Earl Roger holds 3 virgates of land. There is land for 6 oxen, and meadow for as many oxen. It is and was always worth 10s. Almær, the man of Earl Waltheof, held this land and could sell it.

Earl Roger holds SHINGAY. It is assessed at 5 hides. There is land for 6 ploughs. In demesne [are] 3 hides, and there are 2 ploughs. There are 11 bordars and 7 cottars with 4 ploughs, and 1 mill rendering 10s, meadow for 6 ploughs and 2s. from the rent of the meadow, [and] pasture for the livestock of the vill. In all it is and was worth £7;TRE £14. Goda held this land under Earl Ælfgar.

In Abington Pigotts Earl Roger holds 1 virgate of land which pertains to Shingay, his own manor. It is and always was worth 13s4d. Goda held this land under Earl Ælfgar.

[Folio 193V: CAMBRIDGESHIRE]]

In Meldreth the Abbot of Saint-Evroul holds 2 hides from Earl Roger. There is land for 5 ploughs. In demesne [are] 2 ploughs; and 5 villans and 3 bordars with 3 ploughs. There are 2 slaves, and 2 mills rendering 15s4d, [and] meadow for 2 ploughs. All together it is worth £6; when received, 40s.; TRE £8. Goda [held] this land under Earl Ælfgar [and] could sell it.

In Melbourn the same abbot holds from Earl Roger half a hide less the fourth part of a virgate. There is land for half a plough, and there is [half a plough], with 1 villan. [There is] meadow for half a plough. It is and always was worth 5s. Goda held this land from Earl Ælfgar and could sell it.

In Orwell Earl Roger holds 1 hide and 1 virgate and the third part of a virgate. There is land for 1½ ploughs. In demesne [is] half a hide, and there is half a plough; and 2 villans and 3 bordars with 1 plough. There is 1 slave, and meadow for 1 plough, and a wood to repair fences. It is worth 20s; when received, 30s; TRE 50s. 6 sokemen held this land and could give and sell their land. One of them was King Edward's man and provided escort-service for the sheriff. Picot lent 3 of these sokemen to Earl Roger to hold his pleas, but afterwards the earl's men seized them and kept them with their lands without a livery officer and the king neither had nor has their service, as the sheriff himself says.

In 'Ratford' the earl holds 2 hides and 2 parts of a virgate. There is land for 3 ploughs. In demesne [is] 1 hide and 2 parts of 1 virgate, and there is half a plough, and there can be another half. There are 2 cottars and 15 bordars with 2 ploughs. There are 2 slaves, and meadow for 2 ploughs. It is and was worth 40s; TRE 60s. 6 sokemen held this land, and could sell their land to whom they would.

In 'Witewell' Earl Roger holds 1 virgate of land and the third part of a virgate. There is land for 4 oxen. It is and was worth 2s. 3 sokemen held this land and could sell it to whom they would.

In ARRINGTON Earl Roger holds 3½ hides. There is land for 8 ploughs. In demesne [are] 2 hides, and there are 3 ploughs and there can be a fourth. There are 6 villans and 6 cottars with 4 ploughs. There are 3 slaves, and meadow for 2 ploughs, and a wood for fences. All together it is worth £9; when received, £10; TRE £11. Ælfric, King Edward's thegn, held this manor, and there were 3 sokemen, one of them the

man of Earl Waltheof, and another the man of the Abbot of Ely, and the third the man of Robert fitzWimarc, and they could depart whither they would.

IN LONGSTOWE HUNDRED

In Kingston the earl holds 2 parts of a virgate. There is land for 2 oxen. It is and was worth 2s. Almær, the man of Earl Waltheof, held this land and could give it to whom he would.

XIIII. The land of Count Alan

IN FLEAMDYKE HUNDRED

COUNT ALAN holds 8 hides in Fulbourn. There is land for 13 ploughs. In demesne [are] 4 hides, and there are 3 ploughs, and there can be 2 more. There are 16 villans and 10 bordars with 8 ploughs. There are 4 slaves, and 1 mill rendering 20s, [and] meadow for the ploughs. In all it is and always was worth £15. Godwine Cild, the man of Eadgifu the Fair, held this manor; he could not depart.

Count Alan holds CHERRY HINTON. There are 7 hides. There is land for 13 ploughs. In demesne [are] 3½ hides, and there are 4 ploughs. There are 19 villans and 22 bordars with 9 ploughs. There are 4 slaves, and meadow for 3 ploughs, and 4 mills rendering 25s, pasture for the livestock of the vill, and 4 ploughshares. From the fen, 25d, and 6d from the carts. In all it is and was worth £18; TRE £12. Eadgifu the Fair held this manor, and there were 8 sokemen, who provided 2 cartage-dues and 4 watchmen for the sheriff.

In Teversham Count Alan holds 1½ hides. There is land for 2 ploughs, but there are no [ploughs]. This land is valued with Cherry Hinton, the count's manor. 2 sokemen, the men of Eadgifu, held this; they could not depart from her, and they provided 1 cartage-due and 1 watchman for the sheriff.

In the same vill Robert holds 1 hide from Count Alan. There is land for 1 plough, and there is [1 plough], and meadow for 1 plough. It is and was always worth 10s. 5 of Eadgifu's men held this land, and they could not depart from her, and they provided 3 watchmen for the sheriff.

IN CHILFORD HUNDRED

In Horseheath Count Alan holds 2 hides and 2½ virgates. There is land for 5 ploughs, and there are [5 ploughs], with 8 villans and 5 bordars. It is worth 100s; when received, £4; TRE 100s. Eadgifu held this land, and [there were] 2 sokemen, her men; one provided cartage-due, the other escort-service.

In the same vill Alwine holds from Count Alan 1 virgate of land. There is land for 6 oxen. There are 2 bordars, and woodland for 20 pigs. It is and was worth 5s. Godwine, the man of Eadgifu, held this land; he could not depart.

In West Wickham Count Alan holds 2 hides. There is land for 5 ploughs. In demesne [are] 1½ hides, and there are 2 ploughs; and 4 villans and 4 bordars with 3 ploughs. There are 4 slaves, and meadow for 2 ploughs, [and] woodland for 100 pigs. All together it is and was worth £10; TRE £8. Eadgifu held this land, and 2 sokemen, her men, provided 1 cartage-due and 1 watchman. In the same place 1 sokeman holds the fourth part of a virgate under the count. It is worth 12d.

In Barham Ansketil holds 3 hides less half a virgate from Count Alan. There is land for 5 ploughs. In demesne are 3 ploughs; and 6 villans and 4 bordars with 2 ploughs. There are 6 slaves, meadow for 2 ploughs, and 1 mill rendering 5s. All together it is and was worth £9.

In the same vill Morin holds 1½ hides under the count. There is land for 3½ ploughs. In demesne are 2 [ploughs]; and 6 villans and 2 bordars with 1½ ploughs. [There is] meadow for 1 plough, and 1 mill rendering 2s.

[Folio 194: CAMBRIDGESHIRE]

It is and was worth 60s. Eadgifu held these 2 estates. In the same vill 1 sokeman holds 1 virgate under the count. There is land for 4 oxen, and there are [4 oxen]. This land is and was worth 4s. This man held it under Eadgifu, and provided escort-service.

Count Alan holds LINTON. There are 3 hides and 3 virgates. There is land for 8 ploughs. In demesne [are] 2 hides, and there are 3 ploughs. There are 16 villans and 5 bordars with 5 ploughs. There are 6 slaves, and 2 mills rendering 16s, meadow for 2 ploughs, [and] woodland for 30 pigs. All together it is worth £12; when received and TRE, £15. In the same place 1 sokeman holds 1 virgate under the count, and it is valued with Linton. Eadgifu held this land, and there was 1 sokeman who provided cartage-due for the sheriff.

In Cambridge Count Alan has 10 burgesses.

Count Alan holds another LINTON [Little Linton]. There are 2½ hides. There is land for 5 ploughs. In demesne [are] 1½ hides, and there are 2 ploughs. There are 8 villans and 2 bordars with 3 ploughs. There are 4 slaves, and 1 mill rendering 8s, meadow for 1 plough, [and] woodland for 20 pigs. All together it is worth £7; when received and TRE, 100s. Eadgifu the Fair held this manor.

The count himself holds Little Abington. There are 5 hides. There is land for 8 ploughs. In demesne [are] 2½ hides, and there are 3 ploughs. There are 11 villans and 5 bordars with 5 ploughs. There are 4 slaves, and 1 mill rendering 6s8d, meadow for 2 ploughs, [and] woodland for 20 pigs. All together it is and was worth £10. Eadgifu held this manor.

In Babraham Brian holds 2½ hides and 24 acres under Count Alan. There is land for 4 ploughs. In demesne is 1 [plough]; and 17 villans and 3 bordars with 3 ploughs. There is 1 slave, and meadow for 4 oxen. It is and was worth 50s. 6 sokemen held this land under Eadgifu; they could not depart without her leave. These provided 4 cartage-dues and 2 watchmen.

In the same vill Ralph holds 1 hide, less half a virgate, under the count. There is land for 1 plough, and there is [1 plough. There is] meadow for 1 plough, and 3 villans and 3 bordars, and 1 mill rendering 5s4d. It is and was worth 20s. Alric the priest held this land under Eadgifu; he could not depart from her.

In Pampisford 2 knights hold 1 hide and 22 acres under the count. There is land for 2 ploughs and 2 oxen. In demesne [is] 1 plough; and 2 villans and 5 bordars with 1 plough. [There are] 2½ acres of meadow. It is worth 30s; when received, 10s; TRE 30s. Almær held this land under Eadgifu, and could depart, but the soke remained with Eadgifu.

IN WHITTLESFORD HUNDRED

In Whittlesford Gerard holds half a virgate of land from the count. It is and was worth 2s. He himself holds sake and soke of 1½ virgates from the count, which 1½ virgates a man of the count holds. Eadgifu held it.

In Duxford Gerard holds from the count 6 hides from the count. There is land for 6 ploughs. In demesne are 2 [ploughs]; and 4 villans and 5 bordars with 4 ploughs. There is 1 slave, and meadow for 2 ploughs. All together it is and was worth 100s; TRE £7. Eadgifu held this land.

IN THRIPLOW HUNDRED

In Fowlmere 2 knights hold 1 hide from Count Alan. There is land for 1 plough and 2 oxen, [and] meadow for 1 plough. It is and was worth 20s; TRE 25s. Eadgifu held this land, and this land provided 2 watchmen for the sheriff.

In Harston Odo holds 5½ virgates of land from the count. There is land for 1½ ploughs, and there are 1½ ploughs, with 1 villan and 3 bordars. It is worth 20s.; when received, 15[s.] TRE 30s. 4 sokemen held 4½ virgates of this land under Eadgifu and provided 2 watchmen for the sheriff, and yet they could depart; and a priest held 1 virgate under Ordgar, provided 1 watchman, and could depart.

In Little Shelford Hardwin holds 1½ hides and 6 acres from the count. There is land for 2 ploughs, and there are [2 ploughs], with 6 villans and 2 bordars. [There is] meadow for 2 ploughs. It is worth 30s; when received, 20[s]; TRE 40s. 6 sokemen held this land under Eadgifu, provided 4 watchmen, and could depart.

IN 'ARRINGFORD' HUNDRED

In East Hatley Almær holds 1 hide and 3 virgates from the count. There is land for 3 ploughs. In demesne is 1 plough; and 2 villans and 5 bordars with 3 ploughs. There are 3 slaves, meadow for 1 plough, [and] woodland for fences. It is and was worth 40s; TRE 60s. This man held it under Eadgifu TRE, and provided 1 watchman, and could depart.

In Croydon Almær holds 2½ virgates under the count. There is land for 6 oxen, and there are [6 oxen], with 1 bordar and 1 cottar. It is and was worth 10s; TRE 15s. Godgifu held this land under Eadgifu, and could depart.

In the same vill Fulchei holds 1 virgate of land from the count. It is and was worth 5s. Leofgifu held this under Eadgifu, and could depart.

In Wendy Odo holds 4 hides and 3 virgates from Count Alan. There is land for 6 ploughs. In demesne are 2 [ploughs]; and 6 villans and 5 bordars with 4 ploughs. There are 4 slaves, and 2 mills rendering 45s, meadow for 6 ploughs, [and] a wood for fences. All together it is worth £8; when received, £6; TRE

£10. 6 sokemen held 1 hide of this land under Eadgifu, and could depart.

Count Alan himself holds 7 hides and 1½ virgates in BASSINGBOURN. There is land for 18 ploughs. In demesne [are] 4 hides, and there are 5 ploughs, and there can be 2 more. There are 8 villans and 11 bordars and 10 cottars with 11 ploughs. There are 3 slaves, and 2 mills rendering 20s, [and] meadow for 5 ploughs. In all it is worth £30; when received, £26; and as much TRE. Eadgifu held this manor, and there were 10 sokemen; and 8 of them, men of Eadgifu, could sell their land, but the soke remained with her; and the other 2, the men of Earl Ælfgar, provided 4 watchmen for the sheriff, and they themselves could sell their land.

[Folio 194V: CAMBRIDGESHIRE]

In Whaddon Kolsveinn holds half a hide from Count Alan. There is land for 1½ ploughs. In demesne [is] 1 plough; and 1 villan has half a plough. It is and was worth 20s; TRE 40s. This man held it from Eadgifu TRE and could sell it.

In the same vill Ralph holds 2 hides and 1 virgate of land from the count. There is land for 4 ploughs. In demesne are 2 [ploughs]; and 2 villans and 1 bordar with 2 ploughs. There are 4 slaves, and 1 mill rendering 12d, meadow for 1 plough, [and] pasture for the livestock of the vill. All together it is and was worth £6; TRE £8. Leofwig, the man of Esger the staller, held this land, and could give and sell it to whom he would.

In the same [vill] 2 men hold I virgate from the count. There is land for half a plough. It is and was worth 4s; TRE 6s. 2 sokemen held this land; one was the man of Kolsveinn, the other of the soke of St Æthelthryth and he could sell, but the soke remained with the church.

In the same [vill] Odo holds 2 hides and 1 virgate from the count. There is land for 3 ploughs. In demesne are 1½ ploughs; and 2½ villans with 4 bordars have 1½ ploughs. There are 2 slaves, [and] meadow for 1 plough. It is worth 100s; when received, 30; TRE £6. Eadgifu held this land. On this land was and is 1 sokeman holding half a virgate. There is land for 2 oxen. It is and was worth 2s. A man of Eadgifu held it.

In Meldreth Kolsveinn holds 1 virgate from the count. There is land for 1 plough, and there is [1 plough], with 2 cottars, and there are 2 mills rendering 18s, [and] meadow for 2 ploughs. It is worth 30s; when received, 20s; TRE 40s. This man held it under Eadgifu and could give it.

In Melbourn Kolsveinn holds 3 virgates of land from the count. There is land for 1½ ploughs, and there are [1½ ploughs], with 3 bordars and 1 slave. [There is] meadow for 4 oxen. It is worth 20s; when received, 15s; TRE 40s. This man held it under Eadgifu, and could depart from her.

IN 'WETHERLEY' HUNDRED

In Grantchester Gollan holds 1½ virgates under the count. There is land for 1 plough, and there is [1 plough], with 1 villan and 3 cottars and 1 slave. [There is] meadow for 4 oxen. It is and was worth 20s. Godmann, the man of Eadgifu, held this land; he could not depart without her leave.

In this same hundred Count Alan holds 2 mills rendering 100s, which he received at £8; TRE they were worth £6. Eadgifu held them.

In Haslingfield Robert holds 1 hide and half a virgate from the count. There is land for 1½ ploughs. In demesne is 1 plough; and 4 villans with 1 bordar have half a plough. [There is] meadow for 4 oxen. It is worth 20s; when received, 22s; and as much TRE. Ealdræd held this land under Eadgifu; he could not depart without her leave.

In the same vill the count himself holds half a hide in demesne which pertains to Swavesey, his manor. There is land for half a plough. It is and was worth 8s. Eadgifu the Fair held it.

In the same vill Robert holds 12 acres of land from the count. It is and was worth 2s. Merewine held it from Eadgifu and could give it.

In Barrington Picot holds half a virgate from the count. There is land for 2 oxen, and there are [2 oxen], with 2 bordars. [There is] meadow for 2 oxen. It is and was worth 2s; TRE 32d. A man of King Edward held this land; he provided 1 watchman for the sheriff, and could give it to whom he would.

In Shepreth Reginald holds 1½ virgates from the count. There is land for half a plough, and there is [half a plough], with 1 villan, and the sixth part of 1 mill rendering 14d. [There is] meadow for 4 oxen. It is worth 8s; when received, 5s; TRE 8s. Hemming, the man of King Edward, held this land. He provided escort-service and could sell his land.

In Orwell Picot holds 3 virgates and the fourth part of a virgate and 5 acres from the count. There is land for 1½ ploughs, and there are [1½ ploughs], with 6 bordars. [There is] meadow for 1 plough. It is and was worth 20s; TRE 30s. Thorbiorn held this land under Eadgifu, and could depart from her.

In 'Ratford' the count himself holds 1 virgate and the third part of 1 virgate. There is land for half a plough, [and] meadow for 4 oxen, with 1 villan. It is and was worth 8s; TRE 10s. 1 sokeman held this land under Eadgifu, and could give and sell it.

In 'Witewell' Fulcui holds half a hide from the count. There is land for 1 plough, and there is [1 plough], with 3 cottars. [There is] meadow for half a plough, and a wood for fences. It is and was worth 10s; TRE 20s. Godwig held this land under Eadgifu, and could depart from her.

In Wimpole the count himself holds 2 hides and 2½ virgates. There is land for 3 ploughs. In demesne [are] 2 hides, and there is 1 plough, and there can be half [a plough] more. There 2 villans with 1 bordar have 1½ ploughs. There are 6 cottars and 2 slaves, [and] meadow for half a plough. All together it is worth £7; when received, £6; TRE £8. Eadgifu the Fair held this land.

In Arrington Fulcui holds half a hide from the count. There is land for half a plough, and there is [half a plough], with 2 villans. [There is] meadow for 4 oxen, [and] woodland for fences. It is and was worth 10s; TRE 20s. Leofgifu held this land under Eadgifu and could depart from her.

IN LONGSTOWE HUNDRED

In [Great and Little] Eversden Robert and 2 Englishmen hold 1 hide from the count. There is land for 2 ploughs, and there are [2 ploughs], with 2 villans and 3 bordars and 1 cottar. [There is] meadow for 2 ploughs, and a wood for fences. It is worth 25s; when received, 10s; TRE 20s. 2 sokemen, the men of Eadgifu, held this land and could give and sell it.

In Kingston Almæ:r holds 1 virgate from the count. There is land for 2 oxen, and there are [2 oxen. There is] meadow for 2 oxen. It is and was worth 2s. Ælfgeat the man of Earl Ælfgar held this land and could sell it.

In Toft the count holds 2 hides and 1 virgate and 8 acres. There is land for 4 ploughs. In demesne [is] 1 hide and 8 acres, and there is 1 plough. There 5 villans with 2 cottars have 4 ploughs. There are 2 slaves, meadow for 2 ploughs, and a wood for fences. All together it is worth £4; when received, £3; TRE 40. This land is a BEREWICK of Swavesey. Eadgifu held it.

[Folio 195: CAMBRIDGESHIRE]

In Bourn Almær holds 4 hides and 1 virgate from the count. There is land for 5½ ploughs. In demesne is I plough, and there can be half [a plough] more. There 9 villans with 13 bordars have 3 ploughs, and there can be a fourth. There are 2 slaves, meadow for 5½ ploughs, pasture for their livestock, [and] a wood for houses and fences. It is and was worth £4; TRE 100s. Almær who now holds them, held this land and the other 3 which follow. He was the man of Eadgifu and provided 1 watchman, and could depart without leave, and give and sell his land to whom he would.

In Caldecote Almær holds half a hide from the count. There is land for 1½ ploughs. In demesne is 1 plough; and 3 bordars with half a plough. There are 2 slaves, and meadow for 1½ ploughs, [and] a wood for houses and fences. It is and was always worth 30s.

In Longstowe Almær holds 1½ virgates of land from the count. There is land for 6 oxen, and there are [6 oxen]. There are 2 slaves, and meadow for 6 oxen, pasture for the livestock of the vill, [and] a wood for fences and houses. It is worth 30s; when received, 10s; TRE 30s.

In Hatley St George Almæ:r holds 1 virgate from the count. There is land for 2 oxen. It is and always was worth 2s4d.

IN PAPWORTH HUNDRED

The count himself holds PAPWORTH EVERARD. There are 5 hides. There is land for 7 ploughs. In demesne [are] 2½ hides, and there are 2 ploughs. There are 10 villans and 5 bordars with 5 ploughs. There are 4 slaves, meadow for 2 ploughs, [and] a wood for fences and houses. In all it is worth £8; when received, £9; and as much TRE. Goda held this manor under Eadgifu, and could sell it.

In Boxworth 2 sokemen hold 1 hide under the count. There is land for 1 plough, and there is [1 plough, and] meadow for 1 plough. It is and was worth 18d8d; TRE 26s. These men held it under Eadgifu and could sell.

The count himself holds SWAVESEY. There are 13 hides. There is land for 14 ploughs. In demesne [are] 6 hides, and there are 3 ploughs, and there can be a fourth. There are 10 villans with 19 bordars, and 8 sokemen holding 3 hides of this land. These together have 10 ploughs. There are 17 cottars and 2 slaves, and 1 mill rendering 40s. From the fisheries, 4,000 eels, less 250. [There is] meadow for 14 ploughs, [and] pasture for the livestock of the vill. In all it is worth £16; when received, £8; TRE £18. Eadgifu held this manor, and the 8 sokemen themselves could sell their land without her leave.

In Fen Drayton 5 sokemen hold 4½ hides from the count. There is land for 2 ploughs, and there are [2 ploughs], with 1 villan and 5 bordars and 3 cottars. [There is] meadow for 2 ploughs, [and] pasture for the livestock of the vill. It is and was worth 20s TRE 27s. The sokemen themselves held under Eadgifu, and could sell to whom they would.

In Willingham 1 sokeman holds 1 virgate of land from the count. There is land for 2 oxen, [and] meadow for 2 oxen. It is and always was worth 3s. Oswulf, the man of Eadgifu, held this land: he could sell it but the soke remained with the Abbey of Ely.

IN 'NORTHSTOWE' HUNDRED

In Longstanton Picot holds 4 hides and 1½ virgates from the count. There is land for 5 ploughs. In demesne [are] 2 ploughs; and 4 villans and 12 bordars and 6 cottars have 6 ploughs. There is 1 slave, and meadow for 2 ploughs. It is and was worth 100s; TRE £8. 13 sokemen held this land. Of these, one was the man of Bishop Wulfwig, the rest were the men of Eadgifu. All of them could give and sell their land.

In Landbeach Walter holds 4½ hides, less 12 acres, from the count. There is land for 4 ploughs. In demesne [are] 1½ hides and 18 acres, and there is 1 plough. There 3 villans with 13 bordars have 3 ploughs. There are 17 cottars, meadow for 6 ploughs, [and] pasture for the livestock of the vill. [From] the fen, 450 eels. In all it is worth £6.10s; when received, £6; TRE £3. Eadgifu held this manor, and 1 sokeman held 2 hides and 1 virgate there under her. He could give [his land] to whom he would, but the Abbot of Ely had sake and soke of the virgate.

In Dry Drayton the monks of Swavesey hold 3 hides under Count Alan. There is land for 3 ploughs. In demesne is 1 plough; and 5 villans with 2 cottars have 2 ploughs. [There is] meadow for 1 plough. It is and was worth 40s; TRE 60S. Eadgifu held this land.

IN CHEVELEY HUNDRED

Wighen holds WOODDITTON from Count Alan. It was assessed at 5 hides TRE, and now at 3 hides. There is land for 10 ploughs. In demesne [are] 4 ploughs. There 10 villans with 8 bordars have 6 ploughs. There are 4 slaves, pasture for the livestock of the vill, [and] woodland for 150 pigs. In all it is worth £10; when received, £14; TRE 7L. Eadgifu held this manor.

In Cheveley Enisant holds 1½ hides and 20 acres from the count. There is land for 3 ploughs, and there are 2 [ploughs] in demesne; and 4 bordars with 1 plough. There is 1 slave, woodland for 12 pigs, [and] pasture for the livestock of the vill. It is and always was worth 40s. Heoruwulf, the man of Eadgifu, held this land; he could give and sell it.

IN 'STAINE' HUNDRED

In Swaffham Bulbeck Geoffrey holds 1 hide and 3 virgates from the count. There is land for 4 ploughs. In demesne is 1 [plough]; and 3 villans have 3 ploughs. There are 2 slaves, and 1 mill rendering 4s4d. and 100 eels, meadow for 1 plough, [and] pasture for their livestock. It is worth 40s; when received, 20s; TRE the same. 6 sokemen held this land under Eadgifu; they could not depart without her leave, but they provided 3 watchmen and 1 cartage-due a year for the sheriff.

In the same vill 3 knights hold 3 hides and 1 virgate from the count. There is land for 4 ploughs, and there are [4 ploughs], with 3 villans and 2 slaves. [There is] meadow for 2 ploughs. It is worth 100s; when received, 55s; TRE the same. Huscarl, the man of King Edward, held 3 virgates of this land and provided cartage-due. He could give and sell his land, but the soke remained with the king.

[Folio 195V: CAMBRIDGESHIRE]

Eadgifu held 1 hide and 1 virgate of the same land, and Wulfwig, her man, 1 hide and 1 virgate. Eadgifu had its soke.

Odo holds 4 hides from Count Alan [Great Wilbraham]. There is land for 9 ploughs. In demesne are 2 [ploughs]; and 8 villans with 7 bordars have 7 ploughs. There are 6 slaves, and 1 mill [rendering] 5s4d, meddow for 9 ploughs, [and] pasture for the livestock of the vill. In all it is and was worth £12; TRE £10. Ordmær, the man of Eadgifu, held this land, and could give it to whom he would.

Odo holds 1 hide from the count [Stow cum Quy]. There is land for 2 ploughs, and there is [sic] [2 ploughs], with 3 bordars. [There is] meadow for 1 plough, and 1 mill [rendering] 18s. It is worth 40s; when received, 20s; TRE 40s. Grimbald, the man of Eadgifu, held this land; he could neither give nor sell it.

IN 'STAPLOE' HUNDRED

Ordmær holds BADLINGHAM from the count. It was assessed at 3½ hides TRE, and now at 2½ hides. There is land for 6 ploughs. In demesne are 2 [ploughs]; and 9 villans with 6 bordars have 4 ploughs. There are 6 slaves, and 2 mills, one rendering 6s. and the other the milling for the demesne, meadow for 2 ploughs, [and] pasture for the livestock of the vill. In all it is and was worth 60s; TRE 100s. Ordmær held this manor under Eadgifu, and could give it to whom he would.

In Exning [Suffolk] Wihomarc holds 1½ hides from the count. There is land for 3 ploughs. In demesne are 2 ploughs; and 4 villans have 1 plough. There are 8 slaves, and 1 mill [rendering] 5s4d, fisheries [rendering] 1,200 eels, meadow for 2 ploughs, [and] pasture for the livestock of the vill. It is and was worth 50s; TRE 60s. Alsige, the man of Eadgifu, held this land, and could depart without her leave.

In Burwell Alan holds 2½ hides from Count Alan. There is land for 5 ploughs. In demesne are 2 [ploughs]; and 4 villans have 3 ploughs. There are 4 slaves, and 2 mills rendering 6s8d, meadow for 3 ploughs, [and] pasture for the livestock of the vill. It is worth £4; when received, £3; TRE £6. 2 sokemen held this land under Eadgifu; they could depart without her leave. One of them provided escort-service or 4d. for the king's service.

In the same vill Geoffrey holds 1 hide and 1 virgate from Count Alan. There is land for 2 ploughs, and there are [2 ploughs] in demesne, with 3 villans and 2 slaves. [There is] meadow for 1 plough, [and] pasture for the livestock of the vill. It is worth 40s; when received, 30s; TRE 40s. 1 sokeman held this land under Eadgifu; he could depart without her leave.

In Fordham Wihomarc holds 3½ hides from the count. There is land for 4 ploughs. In demesne [is] 1 hide, and 1 plough; and the sokemen have 3 ploughs. [There is] meadow for 1 plough, [and] pasture for the livestock of the vill. It is worth £4; when received, £3; TRE 70s. 3 sokemen held this land, of whom 2 [were] the men of Eadgifu, the third [was] the man of Earl Ælfgar they could depart without their leave. They provided escort-service and cartage-due for the sheriff.

In Isleham Geoffrey holds 40 acres of land from the count. There is land for 4 oxen, meadow for these oxen, and 2 villans. It is worth 10s; when received, 5s. TRE 10s. 2 sokemen held this land. They were the men of King Edward; they could depart. They provided cartage-due or escort-service for the sheriff.

In Soham Adestan holds 1 hide from the count. There is land for 4 ploughs. In demesne [is] 1 plough; and 6 villans with 8 bordars have 2 ploughs, and there can be a third. [There is] meadow for 3 ploughs, pasture for the livestock of the vill, and 1,500 eels, and 1 seine in Soham mere [...] by custom. It is worth 60s; when received, £6; and as much TRE. Alsige held this land under Eadgifu, and could depart without her leave.

The count himself holds WICKEN. It was assessed at 7 hides TRE, and now at 5 hides. [There is] land for 12 ploughs. In demesne [are] 3 hides, and 3 ploughs, and there can be a fourth. There 11 villans with 8 bordars have 8 ploughs. There are 5 slaves, and 3 mills rendering 28s. and 4,250 eels, meadow for 12 ploughs, pasture for the livestock of the vill, and by custom 3 seines in Soham mere. In all it is and was worth £14; TRE £6. Eadgifu the Fair held this manor.

IN 'RADFIELD' HUNDRED

In Dullingham 2 knights hold 2 hides and 10 acres from the count. There is land for 2 ploughs, and there are [2 ploughs], with 2 villans and 9 bordars and 2 slaves. [There is] meadow for 2 oxen. It is and always was worth 44s. 3 sokemen held this land; they could not depart.

In Stetchworth Count Alan holds half a hide. There is land for half a plough, and there is [half a plough]. It is and always was worth 10s. Grim, the man of Eadgifu, held this; he could not depart.

In Westley Waterless 2 knights hold 1 hide from the count. There is land for 2 ploughs, and there are [2 ploughs], with 4 bordars. It is and always was worth 20s. 7 sokemen held this land under Eadgifu. 4 provided cartage-dues in the king's service; they could not depart without the leave of their lady.

The count himself holds BURROUGH GREEN. There are 5 hides. There is land for 8 ploughs. In demesne [are] 3 hides, and there are 4 ploughs. There 7 villans with 10 bordars have 4 ploughs. There are 2 slaves, and 4 acres of meadow, [and] a part for wild beasts. In all it is worth £9; when received, £8; TRE £10. Eadgifu held this land.

In Carlton Wihomarc holds 1 virgate of land from the count. A certain sokeman held it, and provided cartage-due.

The same Wihomarc holds 1½ hides from the count [Weston Colville]. There is land for 3 ploughs. In demesne are 2 [ploughs]; and 3 villans with 3 bordars have 1 plough. There are 3 slaves, meadow for 2 oxen, [and] woodland for 10 pigs. It is and was worth £3. Godwine Cild held this land under Eadgifu; he could not depart.

In West Wratting Almær holds 1½ hides from the count. There is land for 4 ploughs. In demesne are 2 [ploughs]; and 3 villans with 1 bordar have 2 ploughs. There is 1 slave, and woodland for 8 pigs. It is worth 60s; when received, 20s; TRE the same. 2 sokemen held this land under Eadgifu; they could not depart from her. One of them provided cartage-due for the sheriff.

In Balsham Almær holds 40 acres of land from the count. This is valued with the other land. Leofflæd held it under Eadgifu; she could not depart from her.

[Folio 196: CAMBRIDGESHIRE]

XXV. The land of Count Eustace

IN WHITTLESFORD HUNDRED

Count EUSTACE holds ICKLETON. It is assessed at 19½ hides. There is land for 24 ploughs. In demesne [are] 9 hides, and there are 3 ploughs, and there can be a fourth. There 30 villans with 10 bordars have 16 ploughs, and there can be 4 more. There are 3 slaves, and 2 mills [rendering] 30s, [and] meadow for 3 ploughs. All together it is worth £20; when received, £24; and TRE the same. Alsige, King Edward's thegn, held this manor.

In Duxford the count himself holds 5 hides and 3 virgates. There is land for 6 ploughs. In demesne is 1 plough, and there can be 2 more. There 2 villans with 6 bordars have 2 ploughs, and there can be a third. There was 1 mill rendering 12s; [it is] now broken, but can be repaired. [There is] meadow for 2 ploughs. All together it is worth 100s; when received, £7; and as much TRE. Ernulf holds this land from Count Eustace. Heoruwulf held 7 virgates from King Edward, and Archbishop Stigand 3½ hides. Guy holds half a hide of this land and 1 mill at farm from Count Eustace. All together it is worth 25s8d. Ingvar held this land from King Edward, and could sell it.

IN THRIPLOW HUNDRED

In Trumpington Ernulf d'Ardres holds 2 hides and 1½ virgates under the count. There is land for 2½ ploughs. In demesne are 1½ [ploughs]; and 3 villans have 1 plough. There is 1 slave, and meadow for the ploughs. All together it is and was worth £4; TRE 100s. Heoruwulf, King Edward's thegn, held this land; he could give it to whom he would.

IN 'WETHERLEY' HUNDRED

In Grantchester 2 knights hold 2 hides and 3 virgates from the count. There is land for 6 ploughs. In demesne are 3 [ploughs]; and 3½ villans with 13 bordars and 16 cottars have 3 ploughs. There is 1 mill rendering 40s; [and] meadow for 4 ploughs. All together it is worth £8; when received, £10; and as much TRE. 3 sokemen held this land, of whom 2, the men of King Edward, could sell, and the third, the man of Esger the staller, had half a hide and provided cartage-due, yet he could sell his land.

XXVI. The land of the Canons of Bayeux

IN LONGSTOWE HUNDRED

The canons of Bayeux hold 3 hides in Eltisley. There is land for 9 ploughs. In demesne [are] 1½ hides, and there are 3 ploughs; and 6 villans with 10 bordars have 6 ploughs. There are 5 cottars and 6 slaves, meadow for 3 ploughs, [and] woodland for 20 pigs. In all it is and always was worth £13. Earl Ælfgar held this manor.

XXVII. The land of Walter Giffard

IN 'STAINE' HUNDRED

WALTER Gifffard holds BOTTISHAM. It is assessed at 10 hides. There is land for 20 ploughs. In demesne [are] 5 hides, and there are 6 ploughs. There 25 villans with 12 bordars have 14 ploughs. There are 14 slaves, and 4 mills rendering 14s, [and] meadow for 6 ploughs. From the fen, 3 ploughshares and 400 eels. In all it is and was worth £20; TRE £16. Earl Harold held 8 hides of this manor, and Alric the monk had 2 hides which he could not give or sell without the leave of the Abbot of Ramsey, whose man he was.

In Swaffham Bulbeck Hugh holds 7½ hides and 10 acres from Walter. There is land for 11 ploughs. In demesne are 3 [ploughs]; and 12 villans with 4 bordars have 8 ploughs. There are 3 slaves, and 3 mills rendering 30s, less 4d. and 300 eels, meadow for 3 ploughs, [and] pasture for the livestock of the vill. In all it is worth £12; when received, £10; and as much TRE. Alwig the harper held 3 hides and 1 mill of the demesne farm of the monks of Ely [in] this manor; and they themselves [sic] had them both during the life and at the death of King Edward: he could not depart without the leave of the abbot; and 3 sokemen, men of the abbot, held 2½ hides and 10 acres, nor could these men depart without the leave of the abbot; and 19 sokemen, the men of King Edward, held 2 hides: they could not depart without the leave of their lord, but they always provided cartage-due and escort-service for the king's sheriff.

In the same vill Hugh holds 3 virgates from Walter. There is land for 1 plough, and there is [I plough], with 4 bordars. [There is] meadow for 1 plough. It is and was worth 10s; TRE 20s. Wulfwine, the man of the Abbot of Ely, held this land; he could not depart from the church without his leave.

IN 'WETHERLEY' HUNDRED

In Harlton Walter fitzAubrey holds 4 hides from Walter Giffard. There is land for 6 ploughs. In demesne are 2 [ploughs]; and 7 villans with 9 bordars have 4 ploughs. There are 2 slaves, and half a mill rendering 13s4d and 100 eels, [and] meadow for 3 ploughs. All together it renders £7; when received, £6; TRE £8. Aki, the thegn of King Edward, held this land, and there were 5 sokemen, and they provided 5 watchmen and could sell their land.

In Barrington the same Walter holds 40 acres from Walter Giffard. There is land for 6 oxen, and there are [6 oxen], with 2 cottars. [There is] meadow for 6 oxen. It is and always was worth 10s. Aki, Earl Harold's man, held this land and could give and sell it.

In Orwell Walter holds 1 virgate from Walter Giffard. There is land for 2 oxen. There are 3 bordars. It is and always was worth 2s. Aki, Earl Harold's man, held this land. This pertains to Harlton.

XXVIII. The land of William de Warenne

IN 'RADFIELD' HUNDRED

WILLIAM de Warenne holds 2 hides and 7½ acres in Carlton. Walter de Grandcourt holds of him. There is land for 4 ploughs. In demesne are 3 [ploughs]; and 1½ villans with 3 bordars have 1 plough. There are 3 slaves, meadow for 2 oxen, [and] woodland for 12 pigs. It is and always was worth £4. Toki, King Edward's thegn, held this manor.

In the same vill the Abbot of Cluny holds 4 hides and 2 acres from William. There is land for 7 ploughs. In demesne are 3 [ploughs]; and 4 villans with 14 bordars have 3 ploughs. There are 3 slaves, [and] woodland for 100 pigs. It is and always was worth £8. Earl Ælfgar held this land.

William himself holds WESTON COLVILLE. It is assessed at 7 hides. There is land for 15 ploughs. In demesne [are] 4 hides, and there are 2 ploughs, and there can be a third. There 19 villans with 7 bordars have 12 ploughs. There are 5 slaves, and 4 acres of meadow, [and] woodland for 300 pigs. All together.

[Folio 196V: CAMBRIDGESHIRE]

it is worth £16 and 1 ounce of gold; when received, £10; and as much TRE. Toki held this land from the Abbot of Ely on the day on which King Edward was alive and dead, in such a way that he could not alienate it from the church because it was [of] the demesne farm of the abbey, as the men of the hundred bear witness. There were 2 sokemen on this land; one provided cartage-due and the other escort-service. They were the men of Godwine Cild and could not depart from him. Walter holds 1 virgate from William in the same vill.

In West Wratting Lambert holds 3 virgates from William. There is land for half a plough, and there is [half a plough], with 1 villan, and half an acre of meadow. It is and always was worth 5s. Toki held this land from King Edward and provided 1 cartage-due.

IN CHILFORD HUNDRED

In West Wickham Lambert holds 1 hide from William. There is land for 3½ ploughs. In demesne are 2 [ploughs]; and 10 bordars have 1½ ploughs. There are 3 slaves, and meadow for 1 plough, [and] woodland for 12 pigs. It is and always was worth 100s. Toki held this land, and there was 1 sokeman who provided cartage-due.

IN THRIPLOW HUNDRED

In Trumpington William holds 4½ hides. There is land for 5 ploughs. In demesne are 2 [ploughs]; and 9 villans with 4 bordars have 3 ploughs. There is 1 mill rendering 20s, meadow for 5 ploughs, pasture for the livestock of the vill, and 4 ploughshares. It is and was worth £6; TRE £7. Toki held this land from the Church of Ely on the day on which King Edward was alive and dead; he could neither give nor sell it nor alienate it from the church. Afterwards Frederick, William's brother, had this land.

IN 'STAPLOE' HUNDRED'

KENNETT was assessed at 3½ hides TRE, and now at 2½ hides. There is land for 10 ploughs. Nicol holds it from William. In demesne are 5 ploughs; and 7 villans with 5 bordars have 5 ploughs. There are 12 slaves, and 1 mill rendering nothing, meadow for 2 ploughs, [and] pasture for the livestock of the vill. In all it is worth £12; when received, £9; TRE £12. Toki, King Edward's thegn, held this manor, and in the same place 1 sokeman had 1 virgate under him; he provided cartage-due or 8d, yet could give and sell his land.

IN THE HUNDRED [S] OF ELY

In Wisbech William has 6 fishermen rendering 3,500 eels and 5s.

XXV. The land of Richard son of Count Gilbert

IN PAPWORTH HUNDRED

RICHARD, son of Count Gilbert, holds 1 virgate of land in Papworth [?St Agnes], and William [holds] from him. There is land for 4 oxen, and meadow for as many oxen. It is worth 4s; when received, 5s; TRE 8S. Ælfric, a priest, held this land from the Abbot of Ely, and could not depart from him. The soke also always pertained to the church. Richard seized this land in defiance of the king, and took from it 20s. worth of livestock.

IN CHILFORD HUNDRED

In Horseheath Wulfgifu holds half a virgate from Richard. There is land for 4 oxen. It is and was worth 5s.

In West Wickham Wulfgifu holds half a virgate from

Richard, and it is worth 5s; and 1 sokeman [holds] the fourth part of 1 virgate, and it is worth 12d.

IN 'ARRINGFORD' HUNDRED

In Whaddon Hardwin holds I virgate of land from Richard. There is land for 4 oxen. It is and was worth 5s; TRE 15s. Sægifu held this land under Eadgifu the Fair, and could give it to whom she would. This did not pertain to the predecessor of Richard, nor was he ever seised of it, but Ralph Guader held it on the day on which he offended against the king.

The land of Robert de Tosny

IN WHITTLESFORD HUNDRED

ROBERT de Tosny holds 4½ hides in Duxford. Gilbert holds from him. There is land for 5 ploughs. In demesne is 1 [plough], and there can be 2 more; and 4 villans with 5 bordars have 2 ploughs. There are 2 slaves, and 2 mills rendering 20s, [and] meadow for 2 ploughs. It is worth £7.10s; when received, 110s; TRE £8. Ulf, King Edward's thegn, held this land.

The land of Robert Gernon

IN CHILFORD HUNDRED

ROBERT Gernon holds 2 hides in Shudy Camps, and Turstin [holds] of him. There is land for 6 ploughs. In demesne are 2 [ploughs]; and 8 villans with 8 bordars have 4 ploughs. There are 6 slaves, meadow for 2 ploughs, [and] woodland for 12 pigs. It is worth £4; when received, 30s; TRE 40s. Leofsige held this land under Earl Harold, and could depart without his leave.

In Duxford Robert holds half a hide. It is and was worth 5s; TRE 6s. Ælfric held this from King Edward and could depart.

IN THRIPLOW HUNDRED

Robert himself holds Fowlmere. It is assessed at 10 hides. There is land for 11 ploughs. In demesne [are] 5 hides, and there are 2½ ploughs. There 22 villans with 10 bordars have 8½ ploughs. There are 4 slaves, and 1 mill rendering 10s8d, meadow for all the ploughs, [and] pasture for the livestock of the vill, and 1od. In all it is and always was worth £12. Ælfric Cap held this manor from King Edward.

In Harston Ranulph holds 1 hide and 1 virgate from Robert. There is land for 1 plough and 2 oxen, and they are there, with 3 bordars and 1 cottar. [There is] meadow for 1 plough. It is worth 30s; when received, 20s; TRE 30s. 1 sokeman held this land under King Edward [...] and provided 1 watchman, and he could sell his land, but the soke remained with the king.

IN 'WETHERLEY' HUNDRED

In Barrington Robert holds 7 hides and 2½ virgates. There is land for 11 ploughs. In demesne [are] 3½ hides and 2 parts of a virgate, and there is 1 plough, and there can be another. There 20 villans with 7 bordars and 3 cottars have 9 ploughs. There are 2 slaves, and 1½ mills rendering 32s, [and] meadow for 6 ploughs. In all it is worth £12; when received, £8; TRE £16.

On this land there were 15 sokemen holding 4 hides and 1½ virgates from King Edward and providing for the sheriff 12½ cartage-dues and 4 watchmen; and 4 others, the men of Earl Ælfgar, held 2 hides and half a virgate; and 3 others, the men of Esger the staller, held 1 hide. All these men could give and sell their land. Of this land also Eadric Pur held

[Folio 197: CAMBRIDGESHIRE]

3 virgates under King Edward and could sell them, and the same Eadric held half a virgate which on the day of King Edward's death pertained to the Church of Chatteris. Robert Gernon usurped this in defiance of the abbess, as the men of the hundred bear witness.

In Orwell Robert holds I virgate. There is land for 3 oxen, and there are [3 oxen], with 2 bordars. [There is] meadow for 2 oxen, and I mill rendering 12s. It is and always was worth 18s8d 8d. 1 sokeman of King Edward held this land, and he provided I cartage-due, and yet he could sell his land.

IN PAPWORTH HUNDRED

In Conington Picot holds I hide and I virgate from Robert. There is land for I plough, and there is [1 plough], with 3 bordars. [There is] meadow for 1½ ploughs. It is worth 16s; when received, 20s; and as much TRE. 1 man of Earl Waltheof held this land. Its soke pertained to Longstanton.

In Boxworth Picot holds 3½ hides from Robert. There is land for 3 ploughs. In demesne are 2 [ploughs]; and 3 villans with 3 cottars have I plough. There are 2 slaves, [and] meadow for 3 ploughs. It is worth 30s; when received, 10s; TRE 60s. Leofsige, Earl Waltheof's man, held this land and could sell it.

In Swavesey Picot holds I hide from Robert. There is land for I plough, and there are 2 bordars, [and] meadow for I plough. It is and was worth 5s; TRE 20s. Leofsige, Earl Waltheof's man, held this land and could give and sell it. Picot the sheriff holds these lands [...] from Robert Gernon as his wife's dowry.

XX. The land of Geoffrey de Mandeville

IN FLEAMDYKE HUNDRED

GEOFFREY de Mandeville holds 2½ hides in Fulbourn. There is land for 3 ploughs. William holds them from him. There are 3 ploughs, [and] meadow for 1 plough. It is worth 50s; when received, 60s; and as much TRE. Alsige held this land from Esger and could give it without his leave.

IN WHITTLESFORD HUNDRED

In Sawston Roger holds 2 hides from Geoffrey. There is land for 2 ploughs, and there are [2 ploughs], with 6 villans and 4 bordars. There is 1 slave, and meadow for 2 ploughs, and 1 mill rendering 26s8d. It is and always was worth 100s. Sigar held this land from Esger the staller, and could give and sell it without his leave.

IN THRIPLOW HUNDRED

In Thriplow Sigar holds 1½ hides from Geoffrey. There is land for 2 ploughs. In demesne [is] I [plough]; and 4 villans have the other. There is I slave, [and] pasture for the livestock. It is and always was worth 40s. This Sigar held it under Esger and could give or sell it without his leave, but the soke remained with the lord.

In Foxton Sigar holds 3½ hides and 20 acres from Geoffrey. There is land for 5 ploughs. In demesne are 2 [ploughs]; and 5 villans with 10 bordars have 3 ploughs. There is 1 slave, and meadow for 5 ploughs. It is and always was worth £4. This Sigar held it under Esger; he could sell and give it, but the soke remained with the lord.

In the same vill is half a mill rendering 10s8d Robert Gernon usurped in defiance of Geoffrey, as the men of the hundred bear witness.

IN 'STAPLOE' HUNDRED

CHIPPENHAM was assessed at 10 hides TRE, but a certain sheriff reduced them to 5 hides by permission of the same king because its farm was a burden on him, and now it is assessed at 5 hides. There is land for 17 ploughs. Geoffrey holds it from the king. In demesne are 3 hides, and there are 3 ploughs. There 19 villans with 13 bordars have 14 ploughs. There are 6 slaves, meadow for 3 ploughs, [and] pasture for the livestock of the vill. From the fishery, 1,500 eels. In all it is worth £20; when received, £16; TRE £12. Ordgar, King Edward's sheriff, who was afterwards the man of Esger the staller, held this manor. 5 hides of this land were in King Edward's farm, and 2 sokemen had 2 hides from the king and could give their land to whom they would, and yet each one provided 18s8d or 1 horse in the king's service, and paid their forfeitures in Fordham.

Ordgar the sheriff himself had 3 hides if this land, and could give them to whom he would. Ordgar put this land in pledge for 7 marks of gold and 2 ounces, as Geoffrey's men say, but the men of the hundred have seen neither any writ nor any messenger of King Edward concerning it, nor do they produce any testimony.

IN 'ARRINGFORD' HUNDRED

In Guilden Morden Richard holds 3 virgates of land from Geoffrey. There is land for 2 ploughs. In demesne [is] 1 plough; and 1 villan with 5 cottars have 1 plough. There are 3 other cottars, and meadow for 4 oxen, [and] pasture for the livestock. It is worth 20s. when received, 15s; TRE 40s. Godwine held this land from Esger the staller and could sell it.

IN 'WETHERLEY' HUNDRED

In Haslingfield Roger holds 5 hides from Geoffrey. There is land for 6 ploughs. In demesne are 2 [ploughs]; and 8 villans with 18 cottars have 4 ploughs. [There is] meadow for 2 ploughs. All together it is worth £7; when received and TRE, 6. Sigar, the man of Esger the staller, held this land and could give or sell it, but the soke remained with the lord.

In Shepreth Sigar holds 1 hide from Geoffrey. There is land for 1 plough, and there is [1 plough], with 1 villan and 2 bordars, and 2 mills rendering 10s8d, [and] meadow for 1 plough. It is and was worth 20s; TRE 23s. This man held it from Esger and could give or sell it.

In Orwell Sigar holds 1 virgate and the third part of a virgate from Geoffrey. There is land for 4 oxen, and there are [4 oxen. There is] meadow for 2 oxen, with 1 villan. It is and was worth 8s; TRE 10s This man held it under Esger and could sell.

XXI. The land of Gilbert de Ghent

IN PAPWORTH HUNDRED

GILBERT de Ghent holds 1½ virgates in Papworth [?St Agnes]. Alweald holds from him. There is land for 4 oxen, and there are [4 oxen], with 1 villan. [There is] meadow for 4 oxen. It is and was worth 5s; TRE 10s. Ulf, King Edward's thegn, held this land, and it pertains to Fenstanton [Hunts.].

In Elsworth 2 sokemen hold half a hide less 5 acres from Gilbert. There is land for 6 oxen, and there are [6 oxen], and meadow for 6 oxen. It is and always was worth 6s8d. 2 sokemen, the men of Ulf, held this land;

[Folio 197V: CAMBRIDGESHIRE]

one of them provided escort-service for the sheriff, yet both could depart with their land.

In Conington 8 sokemen hold 2 hides and 3 virgates from Gilbert. There is land for 2½ ploughs, and there are [2½ ploughs], with 8 cottars. [There is] meadow for 2½ ploughs. It is and was worth 25s; TRE 30S. These men held from Ulf and could give and sell [their land].

In Boxworth 6 sokemen hold 1 hide and 1 virgate from Gilbert. There is land for 1 plough, and there is [1 plough, and] meadow for 1 plough. It is worth 10s; when received, 16s; TRE 20s. These men held from Ulf and could sell [their land]. Their soke pertained to Fenstanton [Hunts.].

In Swavesey Gilbert holds 1 hide. There is land for 1 plough, and there is [1 plough], with 2 villans and 3 bordars and 2 cottars. From the fen, 225 eels. It is and was worth 10s; TRE 20s. Ulf, King Edward's thegn, held this land.

In Fen Drayton Gilbert holds 3 hides and 1 virgate. There is land for 1½ ploughs. In demesne [is] 1 hide, and 1 sokeman having 1 hide and 1 virgate, and there are 4 villans, meadow for 1½ ploughs, [and] pasture for the livestock of the vill. It is and was worth 10s; TRE 20s. Ulf, King Edward's thegn, held this land, and this 1 sokeman was his man, yet he could give and sell his land without his leave.

XXII. The land of Gilbert fitzTurold

IN 'NORTHSTOWE' HUNDRED

GILBERT fitzTurold holds 4½ hides in Longstanton. There is land for 6 ploughs. Hugh holds of him. In demesne are 2 ploughs; and 7 villans with 9 bordars and 13 cottars have 4 ploughs. There are 3 slaves, [and] meadow for 2 ploughs. From the fen, 3,200 eels and 2s8d. It is and was worth £6; TRE £8. Saxi, King Edward's thegn, held this land and could give or sell it.

XXIII. The land of Eudo fitzHubert

IN CHILFORD HUNDRED

EUDO the steward holds $1\frac{1}{2}$ virgates of land in Babraham, and Pirot holds from him. There is land for half a plough. There are 2 villans. It is and was worth 2 orae. Ælfric held this land and could give and sell it.

In Pampisford Pirot holds 5 acres from Eudo. It is and was worth 6d. Burro held it from Ælfric Campe and could depart.

IN WHITTLESFORD HUNDRED

In Sawston Pirot holds 4 hides from Eudo. There is land for 5 ploughs. In demesne are 2 [ploughs]; and 11 villans with 6 bordars have 3 ploughs. There is 1 slave, and 2 mills rendering 30s8d, [and] meadow for 5 ploughs. It is and always was worth £8. Ælfric held this land from the king, and there were 3 sokemen under him, and they could not depart.

IN 'ARRINGFORD' HUNDRED

In 'Clopton' [in Croydon] Humphrey holds $1\frac{1}{2}$ hides from Eudo. There is land for 2 ploughs, and there are [2 ploughs], with 7 bordars. [There is] meadow for 2 ploughs, and woodland for repairing fences. It is worth £4; when received, 40s; and as much TRE. Earl Gyrth held this land.

In East Hatley Humphrey holds 1 hide and 1 virgate from Eudo. There is land for 1 plough, and there are 2 bordars. [There is] meadow for 1 plough. It is and was worth 20s; TRE 30S. Almær, the man of Robert fitz Wimarc, held this land and could give and sell his land.

In Croydon Humphrey holds 2 hides from Eudo. There is land for 2 ploughs, and there are [2 ploughs], with $6\frac{1}{2}$ villans. [There is] meadow for 2 ploughs. It is and always was worth 40s. Earl Gyrth held this land.

IN 'WETHERLEY' HUNDRED

In Wimpole Humphrey holds I hide and $1\frac{1}{2}$ virgates from Eudo. There is land for 2 ploughs, and there are [2 ploughs] in demesne, and 1 villan and 1 slave, meadow for 1 plough, [and] woodland for fences. It is and always was worth 100s. Earl Gyrth held this land.

IN LONGSTOWE HUNDRED

In Kingston Humphrey holds 10 acres of land from Eudo. There is land for 1 ox. It is and always was worth 8d. Almær the man of Earl Waltheof, held this land and could depart.

In GAMLINGAY Eudo holds 18 hides. There is land for 18 ploughs. In demesne [are] 9 hides, and there are 3 ploughs. There 30 villans with 12 bordars have 15 ploughs. There 1 Frenchman has half a hide, and 12 cottars and [there are] 4 slaves. [There is] meadow for 12 ploughs, woodland for 10 pigs, [and] pasture for the livestock of the vill. In all it is worth £18; when received, £10; and as much TRE. Wulfmær of Eaton Socon held this manor, and there were 9 sokemen who held 4 hides and could give and sell [their land], and besides these hides they held 1 virgate which pertains to Little Gransden, a manor of the Abbot of Ely, [and] which Lisois

de Moutiers seized in defiance of the abbot, so the hundred bears witness.

In Hatley St George Eudo holds 1 hide. There is land for 1 plough, but there is no [plough] recorded there. In demesne are 3 virgates and 10 acres, with 3 bordars with 20 acres. [There is] a wood for fences. It is worth 5s; when received, 10s; TRE 20s. 2 sokemen of Robert fitz Wimarc held this land and could sell it.

XXIIII. The land of Hardwin de Scales

IN 'STAINE' HUNDRED

HARDWIN de Scales holds 1 virgate of land in Swaffham Prior. There is land for 2 oxen. It is and always was worth 5s. 6 sokemen held this land, of whom 3 provided cartage-due and the other 3 escort-service.

In 'Staploe' Hundred Hardwin holds half a hide from the king [Burwell]. There is land for 4 oxen, and there are [4 oxen, and] meadow for these oxen. It is worth 20s; when received, 16s; TRE 20s. Turch, the man of the Abbot of Ramsey, held this land. He could not depart without his leave, and yet provided either escort-service or 4d. in the king's service.

IN 'RADFIELD' HUNDRED

In Dullingham Hardwin holds 2 hides, less 20 acres. There is land for 2 ploughs, and there are [2 ploughs], with 7 villans and 1 bordar. [There is] woodland for 4 pigs. It is and always was worth 40s. 16 sokemen held this land, and they could give and sell their land, and yet they provided cartage-dues.

In Westley Waterless Hardwin holds 15 acres of land. It is and always was worth 16d. 2 sokemen of Earl Harold held them and could not depart.

In Carlton 2 knights hold half a hide, less 3 acres, from Hardwin. There is land for half a plough, and there is [half a plough]. It is and always was worth 10s. 2 sokemen held 38 acres of this land under Harold, and provided 1 watchman for the sheriff. The third held 8 acres from Earl Ælfgar and provided cartage-due, but he could not depart.

[Folio 198: CAMBRIDGESHIRE]

In Weston Colville Durand holds 1 hide from Hardwin. There is land for 1 plough, and there is [1 plough], and meadow for the plough, [and] woodland for 12 pigs. It is worth 20s.; when received, 10s; and as much TRE. Thorger, the man of Earl Ælfgar held this land. He could not depart without his leave.

In the same vill Hardwin holds 1 virgate of land in demesne. There is land for 2 oxen. It is and always was worth 5s. This land provided cartage-due and escort-service; 2 sokemen held this under Earl Harold and could not depart.

In West Wratting Hardwin holds 1 virgate of land. There is land for 2 oxen. There are 2 bordars. It is and was worth 3s. Toki and Wihtgar held this; one provided cartage-due and the other provided escort-service.

IN CHILFORD HUNDRED

In Horseheath 5 villans hold half a hide from Hardwin. There is land for 1 plough, and there is [1 plough], and meadow. [There is] woodland for 24 pigs. It is and always was worth 25s. 4 men held 1½ virgates of this land from the king, and yet provided 1 cartage-due and 2 watchmen, and Leodmær held half a virgate under the predecessor of Aubrey de Vere; he could not depart without his leave.

In West Wickham Hardwin holds 1 virgate from the king. There is land for half a plough, and there is [half a plough], with 3 bordars, and half an acre of meadow. It is and was worth 40d; TRE 5s4d. 3 sokemen held it and provided 1 cartage-due.

In Babraham Durand holds half a hide under Hardwin. There is land for half a plough, and there is [half a plough], with 4 bordars. It is and was worth 18s8d. 4 sokemen held this land; they provided 4 cartage-dues and could not depart. This land is [part] of the king's fief.

In Pampisford Hardwin holds 1 virgate. It is and always was worth 65d. 2 sokemen held it from the king and could not depart.

IN WHITTLESFORD HUNDRED

In Whittlesford Hardwin holds 1 virgate. There is land for 2 oxen. It is and was worth 32d. A man of Earl Gyrth held this; he could not sell it.

In Hinxton Durand holds 1 hide from Hardwin. There is land for 1 plough, and there is [1 plough], with 2 slaves, and meadow for 1 plough. It is worth 20s; when received, 10s; and as much TRE. Eastræd held this land under Earl Ælfgar he could give and sell it to whom he would.

In Ickleton Durand holds half a hide from Hardwin. There is land for 4 oxen. It is worth 32d; when received, 12d; TRE 5s. Eastræd held this under Earl Ælfgar and he could sell it.

In Duxford Payne holds 3 hides and 1 virgate from Hardwin. There is land for 3 ploughs and 2 oxen. In demesne are 2 ploughs; and 1 villan with 4 bordars have 1 plough and 2 oxen. There are 3 slaves, [and] meadow for 1 plough. From the pasture, 1 ploughshare. It is worth 50s; when received, 60s; TRE 100s. 13 sokemen held this land, 11 of whom were the men of King Edward and provided 2 cartage-dues and 9 watchmen for the sheriff, yet they could sell their lands; and the remaining 2 held 1½ hides: one [was] the man of Earl Ælfgar the other the man of Eadgifu, but they could not sell their land.

IN THRIPLOW HUNDRED

In Hauxton Hardwin holds 1½ hides. There is land for 2 ploughs, and there are [2 ploughs], with 4 bordars. In demesne are 1½ hides, and 1 mill rendering 20s, meadow for 2 ploughs, [and] pasture for the livestock of the vill. It is and was worth 60s; TRE £4. Bondi held 3 virgates of this land from the Abbot of Ely, and could sell them, but the soke remained with the abbot; and another sokeman of Earl Ælfgar held 3 virgates and could depart with his land.

In Little Shelford Hardwin holds 6 hides and 1 virgate and 7 acres. There is land for 6 ploughs and 2 oxen, and there are 8 ploughs. In demesne [is] 1 hide, and there is 1 plough; and 13 villans with 4 bordars have 7 ploughs. [There is] meadow for 4 ploughs, [and] pasture for the livestock. It is and was worth £6; TRE £8. 2½ hides and 9 acres of this land and a minster were in the demesne of the Church of Ely, TRE and on the day on which the same king [Edward] died, and now belong to the demesne farm, as the hundred bears witness. Moreover, 7 sokemen held 1½ hides and 6 acres of this land of the soke of the Abbot of Ely: they could not depart with the land, but the soke remained with the Church of Ely. 3 sokemen held half a hide of the same land under Earl Gyrth: they could not depart without his leave; their soke pertained to Whittlesford. Alsige held half a hide from Earl Ælfgar he could give or sell it, but the soke remained with the earl, and he provided 1 watchman. 2 sokemen held 1 virgate and 7 acres from Earl Harold: they could not depart without leave; and 5 sokemen held 3½ virgates under King Edward and provided 1 cartage-due and 2 watchmen for the sheriff: they could sell their land, but their soke remained with the king.

IN 'ARRINGFORD' HUNDRED

In Steeple Morden Hardwin holds 1 hide less the fourth part of 1 virgate. There is land for 2 ploughs, and there are [2 ploughs]. There are 2 mills rendering 2 orae, meadow for 2 ploughs, [and] pasture for the livestock of the vill. It is and was worth 30s; TRE 40s. 7 sokemen now hold this land from Hardwin, and the men themselves held it TRE; they could give and sell their land but the soke remained in Steeple Morden.

In Guilden Morden Alverad holds half a virgate from Hardwin. There is land for half a plough. There is 1 cottar, and 1 acre of meadow. It is and was worth 5s. TRE 10s. Vetrlithr held this land from Earl Ælfgar he could not sell it. This land pertains to Litlington.

In Croydon 2 knights hold 3 hides and 1 virgate from Hardwin. There is land for 4 ploughs. There are 3 ploughs, and there can be a fourth. There are 8 bordars, and meadow for 1 plough. It is and always was worth 65s. Alflæd commended to Archbishop Stigand, held 1 hide of this land, and could give and sell it. 4 sokemen held I hide from King Edward and provided 4 watchmen for the sheriff, but could give or sell their land; and a man of Esger the staller held 5 virgates and could give and sell [his land].

In Wendy Alvred holds 1 virgate from Hardwin. There is land for 3 oxen. It is and always was worth 5s. Goda, commended to Earl Ælfgar held this land; he could give and sell it to whom he would.

In Litlington Adelulf holds 2½ virgates from Hardwin at farm. There is land for 1 plough. There is half a plough, and there can be [another] half [-plough]. There is 1 bordar. It is and was worth 15s; TRE 40s. Algar, the man of Archbishop Stigand, held half a hide of this land, and Alwig, the man of Earl Ælfgar half a virgate, [and] he could not alienate it from Ickleton.

In Abington Pigotts 2 knights hold 1 hide and 1½ virgates from Hardwin. There is land for 2 ploughs, and there are [2 ploughs], with 5 bordars. [There is] meadow for 4 oxen. It is worth 55s; when received, 25s; TRE 60s. A man of King Edward held 1 virgate of this land and provided 1 cartage-due for the sheriff;

[Folio 198V: CAMBRIDGESHIRE]

and 2 other sokemen, the men of Earl Ælfgar; could give and sell their land to whom they would.

In Bassingbourn Lyfing holds 1 hide from Hardwin. There is land for 1 plough, and there is [1 plough], with 2 bordars. [There is] meadow for 2 oxen. It is and was worth 30s; TRE 40s. 2 sokemen of Earl Ælfgar held this land; they could give and sell it to whom they would.

In Whaddon Hardwin holds 1 hide and 3 virgates. There is land for 2 ploughs. In demesne [is] 1 hide, and there is 1 plough; and 3 villans with 5 cottars have 1 plough. [There is] pasture for the livestock of the vill, [and] meadow for 1 plough. It is worth £4I5s; when received, 60s; TRE £4.15s 2 sokemen held this land. One [was] the man of Archbishop Stigand, the other the man of Earl Ælfgar, and they could depart.

In Whaddon Hardwin holds 2½ hides. There is land for 3 ploughs. In demesne [is] 1 hide, and there is 1 plough. There 6 villans and 15 cottars have 1½ ploughs, and there can be half [a plough] more. [There is] meadow for 2 ploughs, [and] pasture for the livestock of the vill. It is and was worth 70s; TRE £4. Thorbiorn held 1 hide of this land under the Abbot of Ely in such a way that he could neither give nor alienate it from the church outside the demesne farm of the monks in the time of king Edward and on the day of his death; and 12 sokemen, the men of the Abbot of Ely, held 1½ hides [and] they could give and sell [their land] to whom they would, but the soke remained with the church.

In the same vill Hardwin holds half a virgate. There is land for 2 oxen. It is and always was worth 2s. Denemund, the man of Esger the staller, held this, and could sell it.

In Meldreth Hardwin holds 1 virgate. There is land for half a plough. It is and always was worth 2s. Almær held this under the Abbot of Ely and could sell it, but the soke remained with the church.

In the same vill Hugh holds 1½ hides from Hardwin. There is land for 2 ploughs, and there are [2 ploughs], with 3 cottars and 1 slave. There is 1 minster, and 1 mill rendering 5s4d, meadow for 2 ploughs, [and] pasture for the livestock of the vill. It is and was worth 40s; TRE £4. This land pertained to the Church of Ely in the demesne of the monks both during the life and at the death of King Edward, as the men of the hundred bear witness.

In Melbourn Durand holds 1 hide and 1 virgate from Hardwin. There is land for 1½ ploughs. There is 1 [plough], and there can be [another] half [-plough]. There is 1 villan with 2 bordars and 3 cottars, meadow for 1 plough, [and] pasture for the livestock. It is worth 25s; when received, 30s;

TRE 40s. Sigeræd, the man of Earl Ælfgar held this land and could give and sell it.

In Shepreth Hardwin holds 2 hides and half a virgate. There is land for 2 ploughs and 2 oxen, and they are there, with 2 villans and 9 cottars and 1 slave. [There is] meadow for all the ploughs. 1 knight holds this land, and 2 Englishmen under him. There is 1 mill rendering 7s, less 2d. It is and was worth 42s; TRE 50s. 5 sokemen held this land. One of them [was] the man of Earl Ælfgar and the others were the men of King Edward, and they provided 2 cartage-dues and 2 watchmen and yet they could sell their land.

In Shepreth Hugh holds half a virgate from Hardwin. There is land for 2 oxen, and meadow for 2 oxen. It is and always was worth 2s. This land pertained to the demesne of the Church of Ely both during the life and at the death of King Edward, as the men of the hundred bear witness.

In Orwell Durand holds 3 virgates and the third part of a virgate from Hardwin. There is land for 1 plough, and there are 6 oxen, with 4 cottars, and 1 mill rendering 8s, [and] pasture for 6 oxen. [There is] a wood to close up [the gaps in] fences. It is and was worth 20s; TRE 40s. 2 sokemen held this land. One, the man of Waltheof, held 3 virgates, the other, the king's man, held the third part of 1 virgate. They provided 2 watchmen and could depart.

In 'Ratford' 2 knights hold 3 virgates from Hardwin. There is land for 1 plough. There are 6 cottars, and meadow for 1 plough. It is and was worth 25s; TRE 50s. 2 sokemen held this land, one of the man of Waltheof and the other the man of Robert fitzWimarc, and they could give and sell [their land].

In 'Witewell' Robert the Bald holds 2 hides from Hardwin. There is land for 2 ploughs. In demesne is 1 plough; and 1 bordar with 4 cottars have 1 plough. [There is] meadow for 1 plough, [and] a wood to close up [the gaps in] fences. It is worth 30s; when received, 20s; TRE 40s. 8 sokemen held this land. 6 of them were the king's men and held 5 virgates and provided 3 cartage-dues and 3 watchmen, and the seventh, the man of Robert fitzWimarc, had half a hide, and the eighth, the man of Earl Ælfgar held 1 virgate. All these men could depart.

IN LONGSTOWE HUNDRED

In [Great and Little] Eversden Durand holds 1 virgate from Hardwin. There is land for 3 oxen, and there are [3 oxen], with 1 villan. [There is] meadow for 3 oxen. It is and always was worth 8s. 1 sokeman of Earl Ælfgar held this land and could depart.

In Kingston 2 knights hold 1 virgate from Hardwin. There is land for 3 oxen, and meadow. It is and always was worth 2s. Goding Thorbert, the man of Eadgifu the Fair, held this land and could depart.

In the same vill Robert the Bald holds 9 acres from Hardwin. There is land for half an ox. It is and always was worth 6d. Wulfmær, the man of Robert fitzWimarc, held this land and could give it.

In Caldecote 2 knights hold 3 virgates and 10 acres from

Hardwin. There is land for 2 ploughs, and there are [2 ploughs], with 6 bordars. [There is] meadow for 2 ploughs. It is and was worth 52s. 2 sokemen held this land under Eadgifu, and could depart.

In Longstowe 1 knight and 2 Englishmen hold 3½ virgates. There is land for 1½ ploughs, and there are [1½ ploughs], with 4 bordars. [There is] meadow for 1½ ploughs, [and] a wood for fences. It is worth 42s; when received, 30s; TRE 42s. 4 sokemen held this land. One of these [was] the man of Archbishop Stigand, and the other 3 [were] the men of the Abbot of Ramsey. They could give and sell [their land].

Hardwin himself holds Caxton. It was assessed at 10 hides TRE, and now at 6 hides. There is land for 12 ploughs. In demesne [are] 5 hides, and there are 4 ploughs. There are 17 villans with 8 bordars and 10 cottars having 8 ploughs. [There is] meadow for 12 ploughs, [and] a wood for fences and houses. All together it is worth 11d; when received, 6d; TRE 14d. Thorger, King Edward's thegn, held this manor, and there were 22 sokemen; 4 of these were King Edward's men: they held 1 hide and half a virgate.

[Folio 199: CAMBRIDGESHIRE]

This half-virgate provided 3 watchmen. These [sokemen] could give and sell their lands. The other 18 were the men of Earl Ælfgar and had 6 hides, less half a virgate, of this land.

In Croxton Adelulf holds 1 hide from Hardwin. There is land for 1½ ploughs, and there are [1½ ploughs]. In demesne [is] 1 plough; and 5 bordars with 2 cottars have half a plough. [There is] meadow for 1½ ploughs, [and] pasture for the livestock. It is worth 20s; when received, 13s; TRE 40s. 2 sokemen, the men of King Edward, held this land and provided 2 cartage-dues for the sheriff.

IN PAPWORTH HUNDRED

In Papworth St Agnes Payne holds 1½ virgates from Hardwin. There is land for 4 oxen, and there are [4 oxen], with 4 bordars, [and] meadow for 4 oxen. It is and always was worth 5s. 2 sokemen, the men of King Edward, held this land, and they provided 2 watchmen and could sell [their land].

In Elsworth Payne holds 1 virgate from Hardwin. There is land for half a plough, and there is [half a plough], with 1 villan, [and] meadow for half a plough. It is and was worth 4s; TRE 5s. 2 sokemen of King Edward held this land, and they provided 1 watchman and could sell [their land].

In Conington Payne holds 2 hides from Hardwin. There is land for 2 ploughs. In demesne [is] 1 plough; and 1 villan with 4 bordars has 1 plough. There are 2 slaves, [and] meadow for 2 ploughs. It is worth 20s; when received, 16s; and as much TRE. 3 sokemen of King Edward held this land, and they provided 2 cartage-dues and 1 watchman and could depart.

In Boxworth Payne holds 4½ hides from Hardwin. There is land for 4 ploughs. In demesne [is] 1 plough; and 8 villans with 6 bordars and 3 cottars have 3 ploughs. There are 2 slaves, and meadow for 4 ploughs. It is and always was worth 60s. 1 thegn of King Edward held 3½ hides [of] this land and could sell them to whom he would; and 7 sokemen of King

Edward had 1 hide and provided 3 cartage-dues and 3 watchmen for the sheriff, and could sell their land.

In Over Ralph holds 2 hides and 1 virgate from Hardwin. There is land for 2½ ploughs, and there are [2½ ploughs], with 3 villans and 1 bordar and 3 cottars. [There is] meadow for 2½ ploughs, [and] pasture for the livestock. It is and was worth 30s; TRE 50s. They held this land [sic]. 1 sokeman held half a hide of this land under the Abbot of Ely: he could not give or sell it outside the church without the abbot's leave; and 2 other sokemen had 3 virgates, [and] could sell [their land, but] the soke remained with the Abbot of Ely; [...] and another 7 had 1 hide: they were the men of the Abbot of Ramsey, [and] could sell without the soke.

IN CHESTERTON HUNDRED

In Dry Drayton Payne holds 5 hides and 3 virgates from Hardwin. There is land for 5 ploughs. In demesne [are] 2 ploughs; and 9 villans with 3 bordars have 2 ploughs, and there can be a third. There are 7 cottars, and meadow for 2 ploughs. This land is worth £4; when received, 100s; TRE £6. 19 sokemen held this land. 6 of these, the men of King Edward, had 2 hides, less half a virgate, and provided 6 watchmen for the sheriff, and could give their land; and 4 others, the men of Eadgifu, had 1½ hides and could depart without the soke; and 5 others were the men of the Abbot of Ely, 4 of whom held 1 hide [...] and could sell it without the soke, the fifth had half a virgate under the abbot but could not sell it; and the other 4 were the men of St Guthlac, [and] held 1 hide and 1 virgate of the demesne farm of the church.

IN 'RADFIELD' HUNDRED

In Stetchworth Hardwin holds 1 virgate. There is land for 2 oxen. It is and always was worth 5s. Godwine, the man of the Abbot of Ely, held this land; he could not sell it.

IN WESTLEY HUNDRED

In West Wratting Hardwin holds 3 hides. There is land for 4 ploughs. In demesne are 2 [ploughs]; and 5 villans with 4 bordars have 2 ploughs. There are 4 slaves, and 4 acres of meadow, [and] woodland for 12 pigs. It is worth £6; when received, 20s; TRE 40s. 10 sokemen, the men of the Abbot of Ely, held this land; they could not sell it.

In BALSHAM Hardwin [...] holds 80 acres of the abbot's land. There is land for 1 plough, and there is [1 plough]. It is and was worth 13s4d. 3 sokemen held this land; they could not sell it.

In Swaffham Prior Hardwin holds 2 hides and 3 virgates. There is land for 3 ploughs. In demesne is 1 [plough]; and 2 villans have 2 ploughs. [There is] meadow for 2 oxen. It is and always was worth 70s. 4 sokemen of the Abbot of Ely held this land; they could not sell it.

IN FLEAMDYKE HUNDRED

In Babraham Hardwin holds half a virgate of the abbot's land from the king. It is and was worth 40d. 2 sokemen held it from the Abbot of Ely. They could not depart.

In Pampisford Hardwin holds 10 acres. There is land for 1 ox.

It is and was worth 12d. Snelling held this land from the Abbot of Ely; he could not depart.

IN THRIPLOW HUNDRED

In Thriplow Hardwin holds from the king 1 hide of the demesne for the sustenance of the monks. There is land for 1 plough, and there is [1 plough]. It is and always was worth 20s. This land belonged to the demesne of the Church of Ely.

In the same vill Hardwin held 2 acres of the abbot's land, for which he does not have a warrantor or a livery officer, but which he has usurped in defiance of the abbot, as the men of the hundred bear witness.

XXV. The land of Hugh de Bernieres

IN LONGSTOWE HUNDRED

HUGH de Bernieres holds 1 hide in [Great and Little] Eversden from the king. There is land for 1 plough, and there is [1 plough], with 1 villan and 1 slave. [There is] meadow for 1 plough, [and] a wood for fences. It is worth 13s; when received, 10s; TRE20s. Eadwig, the man of the Abbot of Ely, held this land: he could give or sell it without his leave but Earl Ælfgar had the soke.

XXVI. The land of Hugh de Port

IN 'STAPLOE' HUNDRED

HUGH de Port holds 1½ hides and 20 acres in Isleham. There is land for 3 ploughs. In demesne is 1 [plough]; and 2 villans with 3 bordars have 2 ploughs. There are 2 slaves, meadow for 1 plough, [and] pasture for the livestock of the vill. It is and was worth 40s; TRE 60S. Ordgar, King Edward's sheriff, held this manor; he could depart without the leave of his lord.

Hugh himself holds Snailwell of the fief of the Bishop of Bayeux. It was always assessed at 5 hides. There is land for 10 ploughs. In demesne are 2 [ploughs], and there can be a third. There are 6 sokemen and 8 villans and 3 bordars and 3 slaves.

[Folio 199V: CAMBRIDGESHIRE]

There are 4 mills rendering 14s4d, meadow for 2 ploughs, [and] woodland for fencing, with 2 carts from the king's woodland of Cheveley. In all it is worth £14; when received, £12; TRE £15. Archbishop Stigand held this manor on the day King Edward was alive and dead; and there were 6 sokemen, the men of the same archbishop, who could depart without his leave and give or sell their land, but the soke remained with the archbishop. TRE this manor pertained to the demesne of the Church of Ely as demesne farm, but the abbot of that time leased it to the archbishop, as the hundred bears witness. Now Abbot Simeon reclaims it by right of his predecessors.

XXVII. The land of Aubrey de Vere

IN CHEVELEY HUNDRED

AUBREY de VERE holds ASHLEY from the king. Everard holds it from him. It was assessed at 3½ hides, TRE, and now at 2 hides. There is land for 4 ploughs. In demesne [are] 2 [ploughs]; and the villans have 2 ploughs. [There is] 1 acre of meadow, woodland for 12 pigs, [and] pasture for the livestock. All together it is worth 100s; when received, 40s; and as much TRE. Wulfwine, King Edward's thegn, held this manor.

Aubrey himself holds Saxon Street, and Everard [holds] of him. It was assessed at 5 hides TRE, and now at 3 hides. There is land for 7 ploughs. In demesne are 3 ploughs; and 10 villans with 4 bordars have 4 ploughs. [There is] meadow for 1 plough, pasture for the livestock of the vill, [and] woodland for 40 pigs. All together it is worth £8; when received, £7; and as much TRE. Wulfwine, King Edward's thegn, held this manor.

Aubrey himself holds SILVERLEY. It was assessed at 6½ hides | in the time of King Edward | and now at 4 hides. There is land for 8 ploughs. In demesne [are] 2 hides, and there are 4 ploughs; and 12 villans with 2 bordars have 4 ploughs. There are 8 slaves, and 1 acre of meadow, woodland for 20 pigs, [and] pasture for the livestock of the vill. In all it is worth 16d; when received, £20; and as much TRE. Wulfwine, King Edward's thegn, held this manor.

In Swaffham Prior Aubrey holds half a hide and 20 acres from the king. There is land for 1 plough, and there is [1 plough], with 1 villan, and 1 mill [rendering] 7s. It is and always was worth 10s. 1 sokeman of King Edward held this land. He could not depart without leave and provided cartage-due for the king's sheriff. Aubrey's predecessor did not have this land, as the men of the hundred bear witness, but Aubrey himself usurped it in defiance of the king.

Aubrey himself holds LITTLE WILBRAHAM from the king. [...] There is land for 8 ploughs. In demesne [are] 2 hides, and there are 4 ploughs; and 8 villans with 5 bordars have 7 ploughs. There are 7 slaves, meadow for 3 ploughs, and 1 mill [rendering] 22s. In all it is worth £12; when received, £10; and as much TRE. Wulfwine, King Edward's thegn, held this manor.

In the same vill Reginald holds half a hide and 30 acres from Aubrey. There is land for 1 plough, and there is [1 plough], with 1 bordar. It is and always was worth 10s. Godric, King Edward's man, held this land: he did not hold it of Aubrey's predecessor, to this the men of the hundred bear witness, but Aubrey usurped it in defiance of the king.

IN CHILFORD HUNDRED

In Castle Camps Aubrey de Vere holds 2½ hides. There is land for 11 ploughs. In demesne [is] 1 hide and 1 virgate, and there are 4 ploughs. There 17 villans with 4 bordars have 7 ploughs. There are 6 slaves, meadow for 3 ploughs, [and] woodland for 500 pigs. From the herbage of the vill, 8s. In all it is worth £15;

when received, £12; and as much TRE. Wulfwine, King Edward's thegn, held this manor.

Norman holds half a hide of this land from Aubrey. There is land for 1 plough, and there is [1 plough]. It is and always was worth £40.

In Horseheath Norman holds 1½ hides from Aubrey. There is land for 3 ploughs. In demesne is 1 [plough]; and 2½ villans with 3 bordars have 2 ploughs. There are 3 slaves, and 4 acres of meadow, [and] woodland for 40 pigs. It is and always was worth 60s. Wulfwine, King Edward's thegn, held this land and had sake and soke, and rendered cartage-due and escort-service.

Aubrey himself holds HILDERSHAM. It is assessed at 5 hides. There is land for 11 ploughs. In demesne [are] 2½ hides, and there are 4 ploughs. There 16 villans have 7 ploughs. There are 4 slaves, and 1 mill rendering 10s, meadow for 3 ploughs, [and] woodland for 20 pigs. All together it is worth £10; when received, £8; TRE £8. Wulfwine, King Edward's thegn, held this land.

Aubrey himself holds Great Abington, and Firmat [holds] from him. It is assessed at 6 hides. There is land for 8 ploughs. In demesne [are] 2 ploughs, and there can be a third. There 9 villans with 5 bordars have 4 ploughs, and there can be a fifth. [There is] meadow for 2 ploughs, woodland for 10 pigs, and 1 mill rendering 9s. From the pasture, 6 ploughshares. It is and was worth £8; TRE £6. The aforesaid Wulfwine, King Edward's thegn, held this manor. A certain priest held 1 hide of this land from Eadgifu the Fair; he could not depart without her leave; and now Count Alan claims it back from Aubrey's men, as the hundred bears witness.

In Babraham Firmat holds half a virgate from Aubrey. It is worth 20d. Godwine held this land under Wulfwine, Aubrey's predecessor; he could not depart.

In [?Little] Abington 1 sokeman has from the king half a hide, which is in the custody of Picot the sheriff, and is worth 12d a year. Almær, King Edward's sokeman, held this and could give or sell it to whom he would TRE, and Aubrey de Vere seized this land from the king's soke, but Picot the sheriff proved his right to it against him, and he still retains 1 plough and 380 sheep which Aubrey has from that land, as the men of the hundred bear witness.

XXVIII. The land of Eustace of Huntingdon

IN PAPWORTH HUNDRED

EUSTACE of Huntingdon holds 1 hide and 3 virgates in Papworth St Agnes. There is land for 3 ploughs. In demesne is 1 [plough]; and 4 villans have 2 ploughs. There is 1 slave, and meadow for 1 plough. It is worth 40s; when received, £4; TRE 50s. Ordnoth, the man of Robert fitzWimarc, held this land; he could give it to whom he would. Now Walter holds it from Eustace.

In the same vill Ordnoth holds 1 hide and 3 virgates from Eustace by the king's command. There is land for 2 ploughs. There are 1½ ploughs, and there can be half [a plough more.

There is] meadow for 1 plough. It is and was worth 20s; TRE 50s. This man held [this land] from Robert fitz Wimarc, and could sell it.

In the same vill Walter holds 1½ virgates from Eustace. There is land for 4 oxen, and meadow for as many oxen. It is and was worth 5s; TRE 10s. Godwine, the man of the Abbot of Ely, held this land and could not sell it.

XXIX. The land of Guy de Raimbeaucourt

GUY de Raimbeaucourt holds 3 hides and 1 virgate from the king in Meldreth. There is land for 5 ploughs, and there are [5 ploughs]. In demesne [is] half a hide, and there is 1 plough; and 15 bordars with 3 cottars have 4 ploughs. There is 1 slave, and 2 mills rendering 10s8d meadow for 5 ploughs, [and] pasture for the livestock. All together it is worth 70s; and as much when received; TRE 100s. This land

[Folio 200: CAMBRIDGESHIRE]

16 sokemen held. Of these, 10 had 2 hides and half a virgate of the soke of St Æthelthryth of Ely, of whom 1 could neither give nor sell his land, the other 9 could, to whom they would, but the soke of all remained with the church; and 5 other sokemen held 1 hide and half a virgate from Earl Ælfgar [and] could give or sell [their land].

In the same vill Guy holds 5 hides and 1½ virgates and the fourth part of a virgate. There is land for 11 ploughs. In demesne [are] 2½ hides, and there are 2 ploughs, and there can be 2 more. There 6 villans with 18 bordars and 10 cottars have 7 ploughs. There is half a mill rendering 2s8d, meadow for 6 ploughs, [and] pasture for the livestock of the vill. All together it is worth 10d10s; when received, £6; TRE £14. Eadric Spur, King Edward's thegn, held 2½ hides of this land [and] could give or sell them; and 8 sokemen, the men of the Abbot of Ely, held 2 hides and half a virgate; and 2 other sokemen, the men of King Edward, held 2 parts of 1 virgate and provided 2 watchmen. All these men could sell their lands, [but] the soke of the 8 sokemen remained with the Abbot of Ely.

IN 'WETHERLEY' HUNDRED

In Barton Humphrey holds 3½ hides from Guy. There is land for 6 ploughs. In demesne [are] 3 ploughs; and 3 villans with 13 bordars have 3 ploughs. There is 1 slave, [and] meadow for 4 ploughs. All together it is worth £6; when received, £10; and as much TRE. There are 3 French knights on this land. 24 sokemen held this land One of these held half a hide under Eadgifu the Fair and could sell it; and all the others were King Edward's sokemen. They held 3 hides, and they could give and sell them, and provided 6 cartage-dues and 17 watchmen for the sheriff.

In Grantchester 2 knights hold 3 virgates from Guy. There is land for 1 plough, but no [plough] is there. [There is] meadow for 4 oxen, and 3 bordars. It is worth 55s; when received, 40s; TRE £4. 5 sokemen, the men of King Edward, held this land and could sell it, and they provided 4 watchmen for the king's sheriff.

In Orwell Ralph holds the third part of 1 virgate from Guy,

and there is an ox. It is and was worth 2s, and he could sell it, and provided the fourth part of a cartage-due for the sheriff.

In 'Ratford' Ralph holds half a hide from Guy. There is land for half a plough, and there is [half a plough], with 2 villans and 2 bordars. [There is] meadow for half a plough, [and] a wood to repair fences. It is worth 20s; when received, 10s; TRE 20s. 2 sokemen of King Edward held this land; and they provided 2 cartage-dues, and could sell it.

IN LONGSTOWE HUNDRED

In [Great and Little] Eversden Guy holds 6 hides and 10 acres of land. There is land for 10 ploughs. In demesne are 4 [ploughs], and there can be a fifth. There 5 villans with 2 bordars and 9 cottars have 5 ploughs. There is 1 slave, meadow for 2 ploughs and 2 oxen, [and] a wood for fences. All together it is worth £9; when received, £6.5s; TR[E] £16. Picot holds half a hide of this land, and Humphrey holds all the other land from Guy. 23 sokemen held this land. 2 of these, the men of Archbishop Stigand, held 1 hide and 3 virgates; and 7, the men of Earl Ælfgar, had 3 virgates; and 1, the man of Eadgifu, had 1 hide; and 14 others, King Edward's men, held 1½ hides and 10 acres, and they provided 9 cartage-dues and 5 watchmen for the sheriff. But all these men could give or sell their lands.

XXX. The land of Picot of Cambridge

IN 'STAINE' HUNDRED

PICOT of Cambridge holds 4½ hides and 10 acres in STOW CUM QUY. There is land for 5 ploughs. In demesne is 1 [plough]; and 8 villans have 4 ploughs. There are 2½ mills rendering 22s, [and] meadow for the ploughs. All together it is and was worth £8. [...] Æthelric the monk and Godric, the men of the Abbot of Ramsey, held 3½ hides of this land, [and] could not depart without his leave; and 4 sokemen, the men of King Edward, held 1 hide and 10 acres [and] could neither give nor sell them without the king's leave.

IN CHILFORD HUNDRED

In Pampisford Ralph holds 3 virgates from Picot. There is land for 1 plough, and there is [1 plough], and 2 acres of meadow. It is and always was worth 10s. Eadric, the man of Ælfric Cild, held this and could depart with the land.

IN WHITTLESFORD HUNDRED

PICOT himself [...] holds HINXTON. It is assessed at 15½ hides. There is land for 13 ploughs. In demesne [are] 7 hides and 3 virgates, and there is 1 plough, and there can be 3 more. There 20 villans with 12 bordars have 9 ploughs. There are 2 mills rendering 21s4d, [and] meadow for 3 ploughs. In all it is worth £10; when received, £16; and as much TRE. Picot received this land as 2 manors, so he says. 20 sokemen held it. One of these, the man of Earl Ælfgar, had half a hide; he could not depart. But the others were the men of King Edward and could depart, and they provided 8 cartage-dues and 8 watchmen and 3 guards for the sheriff.

IN THRIPLOW HUNDRED

In Harston Picot holds 7½ hides. There is land for 9 ploughs. In demesne [are] 3 hides, and there are 2 ploughs, and there can be a third. There 6 villans and 15 cottars have 4 ploughs, and there can be a fifth. There is 1 mill rendering 30s, meadow for 5 ploughs, [and] pasture for the livestock. In all it is worth £8; when received, £4.10s; TRE £10. Ordgar held 4 hides of this land from Earl Harold and could depart; and 6 sokemen, the men of King Edward, held 2 hides and provided 1 cartage-due and 5 watchmen, and could depart with their land.

Fridebert held 1½ hides from the Abbot of Ely and could depart with his land, but the soke remained with the church. Picot serves the abbot for these 1½ hides, and holds them by the king's command.

In Trumpington Hervey holds 2 hides and 1½ virgates from Picot. There is land for 2½ ploughs. In demesne [are] 1½ ploughs; and 3 villans with 1 bordar have 1 plough. There are 3 cottars and 1 slave, [and] meadow for the ploughs. From the weir, 450 eels. It is worth £4; when received, 30s; TRE 100s. Heoruwulf held this land under King Edward and could sell it and depart to whom he would.

IN 'ARRINGFORD' HUNDRED

In Tadlow Picot holds 2 hides and 1½ virgates. There is land for 6 ploughs. In demesne [is] 1 hide and half a virgate, and there is 1 plough, and there can be another; and 2¼ virgates which the villans hold, and 13 bordars have 3 ploughs and there can be a fourth. There is 1 mill rendering 10s, meadow for 6 ploughs, [and] pasture for the livestock of the vill. It is worth 70s; when received, £4; TRE £6. 3 sokemen held this land and provided 1 cartage-due and 1 guard, and could give and sell their land.

In Guilden Morden Picot holds 3½ hides. There is land for 7 ploughs. In demesne is 1 hide, and there is 1 plough, and there can be another. There 8 villans with 11 bordars and 18 cottars have 3½ ploughs, and there can be 1½ [ploughs more]. There is 1 mill rendering 4s, meadow for 7 ploughs, [and] pasture for the livestock of the vill.

In the same place Picot holds 3 hides 3 virgates. There is land for 4 ploughs. In demesne are 2 [ploughs]; and 5 villans have 2 ploughs. There is 1 slave, and meadow for 4 ploughs. It is worth £6; when received it was worth £4; and as much TRE. 2 sokemen of the Abbot of Ely held this land; they could not sell it without his leave. In this vill [there is] half a mill rendering 40d

[Folio 200V: CAMBRIDGESHIRE]

All together it is worth £6.10s; when received, £8; TRE £10. 8 sokemen held this land. 3 of these, the men of Archbishop Stigand, had 1 hide and 3 virgates and could give and sell [their land], but the soke remained in Guilden Morden; and 2 others, the men of Earl Ælfgar, had 3 virgates and could sell [their land], but the soke remained with the earl; and 2 others, the men of King Edward, held 3 virgates and provided 2 watchmen, and could give and sell [their land]; and 1, the man of Eadgifu, had half a virgate and could sell it.

In 'Clopton' [in Croydon] Picot holds a garden of the soke of King Edward which rendered 1 watchman to the king's sheriff.

In East Hatley Picot holds 2 hides. There is land for 3 ploughs. There are 1½ ploughs, and there can be as many [more. There is] meadow for 2 ploughs, and 2 bordars, [and] woodland to repair fences. It is and was worth 40s,; TRE 60s. 8 sokemen held this land and could give and sell it. Of these, 2 were the men of King Edward and provided 2 watchmen; and 3 were the men of Archbishop Stigand, [and] their soke pertained to Guilden Morden; and 1 [was] the man of Earl Gyrth; and 1 the man of Robert fitz Wimarc; and 1 the man of Wulfmær of Eaton Socon. Picot says he has 1 hide of this land in exchange for Eynesbury [Hunts.] and the other in exchange for Rushden [Herts.] because Ilbert of Hertford delivered it to him.

In Croydon Ansketil holds 2 hides less half a virgate from Picot. There is land for 2 ploughs, but there are only oxen [sic], with 1 villan and 2 bordars. It is worth 30s; when received, 40s; and as much TRE. 1 man of Esger the staller held this land; he could give and sell it.

In the same vill Alvred holds 1 hide and 1 virgate from Picot. There is land for 2 ploughs, and there are [2 ploughs]. In demesne [is] 1 [plough]; and 5 bordars with another plough, and 2 cottars. [There is] meadow for 2 ploughs, [and] a wood to repair fences only. It is worth £4; when received, 40s; and as much TRE. 1 man of Robert fitz Wimarc held this land. He could give and sell it but the soke remained with Robert

In Abington Pigotts Picot holds half a virgate. There is land for 2 oxen. It is and always was worth 2s. Asgot, the man of Archbishop Stigand, held this land; it pertains and pertained to Guilden Morden.

IN 'WETHERLEY' HUNDRED

In Comberton 2 men hold 2 hides and 2 acres from Picot. There is land for 4 ploughs. In demesne [are] 2 [ploughs]; and 7 villans with 11 bordars have 2 ploughs. [There is] meadow for 1 plough. It is and was worth 60s TRE £4. 7 sokemen of King Edward held 1 hide and 1 virgate of this land, and provided 5 cartage-dues and 3 watchmen; and 2 other sokemen had 3 virgates and could depart: of these, one was the man of Archbishop Stigand, and the other the man of Earl Waltheof.

In Grantchester Robert holds half a virgate from Picot. There is land for 3 oxen, and there is 1 villan. It is and was worth 5s. Wulfric held this land of the king's soke.

In Haslingfield Seifrid holds 4 hides and 3 virgates from Picot. There is land for 4 ploughs. In demesne [are] 2 ploughs; and 4 villans with 22 bordars have 2 ploughs, and [there is] 1 mill rendering 2s, [and] meadow for 2 ploughs. It is worth £4; when received, 40s; TRE £4. 6 sokemen held this land. Of these, one, the man of Esger, held 1 hide and 3 virgates and could sell [his land]; and the other 5, the men of King Edward, held 3 hides and provided 2 cartage-dues and 3 watchmen. They could give and sell their land.

In Harlton Seifrid holds 1 hide from Picot. There is land for 1 plough, but there is no [plough. There is] meadow for 4 oxen, and 2 bordars. It is and always was worth 20s. Godmann held this land under Esger the staller, and could depart.

In Barrington Ralph holds 20 acres from Picot. There is land for 3 oxen, and there are [3 oxen], with 1 sokeman and 1 bordar. [There is] meadow for 3 oxen. It is and always was worth 5s. Eadsige held this land under Robert fitz Wimarc and could give it.

In 'Ratford' Ralph holds 3 virgates from Picot. There is land for 3 oxen, and there are [3 oxen], with 2 cottars. [There is] meadow for 3 oxen. It is and was worth 3s; TRE 5s. A sokeman of King Edward held this land, and he provided 1 watchman for the sheriff, and could sell his land.

In 'Witewell' Ralph holds 1 hide and 2 parts of 1 virgate from Picot. There is land for 1½ ploughs. In demesne is 1 plough; and 1 villan with 2 cottars have half a plough. [There is] meadow for 2 ploughs, [and] a wood to close up [the gaps in] fences. It is worth 30s; when received, 20s; TRE £4. 3 sokemen held this land. One of these [was] the man of Ælfgar, and another the man of Robert fitz Wimarc, and the third the man of King Edward. The last provided cartage-due and could sell [his land].

IN LONGSTOWE HUNDRED

In Kingston Ralph holds 5½ hides and 16 acres from Picot. There is land for 7½ ploughs. In demesne [are] 2 ploughs; and 9 villans with 2 bordars and 5 cottars have 5½ ploughs. [There is] meadow for 3 ploughs, [and] a wood for fences. There are 4 slaves. All together it is worth £6; when received, £8; TRE £12. 14 sokemen held this land. Of these, 10 had 2 hides and 1½ virgates of the king's soke and provided 7 cartage-dues and 3 watchmen; and 2 others, the men of Earl Ælfgar, had 1 virgate; and 1, the man of Archbishop Stigand, held 3 virgates; and another of them, the man of the Abbot of Ely, had 1 virgate of the abbot's soke; and 2 others, the men of Earl Ælfgar, had 2 hides. They could all depart.

In Toft 2 knights hold 1½ hides and 10 acres from Picot. There is land for 4 ploughs. In demesne are 2 [ploughs], and there can be a third; and 2 villans with 6 cottars have 1 plough. [There is] meadow for 1½ ploughs, [and] a wood for fences. It is worth £4; when received, 20s; TRE £6. 1 of King Edward's men held 1 hide and 4 acres of this land and could give them; and a man of the Abbot of Ely held half a hide and 6 acres and could depart with the land, but the soke remained with the abbot.

Picot himself holds BOURN. It is assessed at 13 hides. There is land for 15 ploughs. In demesne [are] 5 hides, and there are 2 ploughs, and there can be 2 others. There are 8 villans with 4 bordars and 7 sokemen who hold 4 hides. They have 4 ploughs, and there can be 7 more. There are 13 cottars and 6 slaves, meadow for 15 ploughs, pasture for the livestock of the vill, [and] a wood to repair fences and houses. In all it is worth £13; when received, £18; TRE £22. 2 knights hold 2 hides of this land under Picot. There is land for 2 ploughs, and there are [2 ploughs], with 4 cottars. [There is] meadow for 2 ploughs, a wood for fences and houses, [and] pasture for the livestock of the vill. It always was and is worth 40s. A thegn held 3 hides of the land of this manor under King Edward TRE; and 2 priests,

| [in margin] | the men of this thegn, had 1 hide. | They could not withdraw from the church. | And 3 sokemen of Archbishop Stigand [had] 4 hides; and a man of Esger the staller had 1 hide; and 2 men of the Abbot of Ramsey had $1\frac{1}{2}$ hides; and 1 man of Earl Ælfgar had half a hide; and 13 men of King Edward had 2 hides and they themselves provided 6 cartage-dues and 7 watchmen for the sheriff. All 22 could give and sell their lands. Picot says he received this land as 2 manors.

In Hatley St George Roger holds 2 hides from Picot. There is land for 2 ploughs. In demesne is 1 [plough]; and 4 bordars with 6 cottars and 1 villan have half a plough, and there can be half [a plough more. There is] a wood for fences and houses. It is worth 20s; when received, 60s; TRE 100s. Alweard, the man of Robert fitzWimarc, held this land and could sell it.

In the same vill Picot holds 1 hide. There is land for 1 plough. There is half a plough, and there can be half [a plough more. There is] a wood for fences and houses. There are 3 villans. It is worth 10s; when received, 20s; TRE 40s. 3 sokemen of King Edward held this land, and provided 1 cartage-due and 2 watchmen for the sheriff. Picot says he has this [land] in exchange for Rushden [Herts.] which Sigar holds.

IN PAPWORTH HUNDRED

In Papworth [?St Agnes] Picot holds half a virgate. There is land for 2 oxen. It is and was worth 2s. A sokeman of King Edward held this land, and provided 1 watchman for the sheriff.

In Fen Drayton Roger holds 1 hide from Picot. There is land for half a plough, and there are 2 oxen, [and] meadow for 4 oxen. It is and was worth 3s; TRE 5s. 2 sokemen held this land. One of these, the man of the Abbot of Ely, could sell his land without the soke. The other, the man of King Edward, provided 1 watchman for the sheriff and could give his land.

In Over Sæwine holds half a hide from Picot. There is land for half a plough, and there is [half a plough. There is] meadow for half a plough, [and] pasture for the livestock. It is and was worth 5s; TRE 10s. A man of the Abbot of Ramsey held this land, and could sell it without the soke.

In Willingham Roger holds 1 virgate of Picot. There is land for 2 oxen, with meadow, [and] pasture for the livestock. It is and was worth 3s. Golda held this land under the Abbot of Ely; he could not give or sell it.

IN 'NORTHSTOWE' HUNDRED

In Longstanton Guy holds 3 hides from Picot. There is land for 4 ploughs. In demesne are 2 [ploughs]; and 6 bordars with 5 cottars can have 2 ploughs. [There is] meadow for 2 ploughs. It is worth £4; when received, £8; TRE £10. 15 sokemen held this land. Of these, 11, the men of King Edward,

had $1\frac{1}{2}$ hides, and provided 2 cartage-dues and 5 watchmen for the sheriff, and could give and sell their land; and 3 others had 1 hide under the Abbot of Ely and could sell, but the soke remained with the abbot; and 1, the man of Saxi, had half a hide and could not give it.

Roger holds RAMPTON from Picot. It was assessed at 6 hides TRE, and now at $4\frac{1}{2}$ hides. There is land for 6 ploughs. In demesne is 1 plough, and there can be 2 more. There 12 villans with 7 cottars have 3 ploughs. There is 1 slave, and meadow for 6 ploughs, [and] pasture for the livestock. In all it is worth 100s; when received, £8; and as much TRE. 6 sokemen held this manor. One of these, the man of Eadgifu, had $1\frac{1}{2}$ virgates and could depart; and the others were the men of the Abbot of Ely, and 4 could sell their land but the soke remained with the abbot, and the fifth had $1\frac{1}{2}$ virgates and could not depart.

In Lolworth Robert holds from Picot 9 hides as 1 manor. [It is] now [assessed] at 5 hides. There is land for 5 ploughs. In demesne are 2 [ploughs]; and 4 villans with 9 bordars and 3 cottars have 3 ploughs. There 1 Frenchman has $1\frac{1}{2}$ hides, and [there is] 1 slave. [There is] meadow for 1 plough, and 1 mill rendering nothing, [and] a wood for fences. In all it is worth 100s; when received, 40s; TRE £6. An almswoman of King Edward held this manor. She had $3\frac{1}{2}$ hides, and there were 10 sokemen. Of these, 7, the men of King Edward, held $1\frac{1}{2}$ hides and 4 gardens, and provided 2 cartage-dues and 4 watchmen; and 2 others, the men of Eadgifu, had 1 hide; the tenth, however, the man of the Abbot of Ely, held $1\frac{1}{2}$ hides. All these could sell their lands. Only the soke of the Abbot of Ely's man remained with the church.

In Madingley Picot holds 11 hides and $2\frac{1}{2}$ virgates. There is land for 8 ploughs. In demesne [are] 4 hides and 3 virgates, and there are 2 ploughs, and there can be a third. There 7 villans with 4 bordars and 6 cottars have 4 ploughs, and there can be a fifth. There are 3 slaves, meadow for 4 ploughs, [and] a wood for fences. 2 knights hold 3 hides and 3 virgates of this land. In all it is worth £6.5s; when received, £9.10s; and as much TRE. 12 sokemen held this manor. Of these, 7, the men of King Edward, held 8 hides and 1 virgate and provided 5 cartage-dues and 5 watchmen; and the other 5, the men of the Abbot of Ely, had 3 hides and $1\frac{1}{2}$ virgates, and 4 of these could depart, and the fifth held half a hide but could not depart.

In Girton William holds 3 hides and 3 virgates from Picot. There is land for 3 ploughs. In demesne [is] 1 plough, [and] there can be half [a plough more]; and 2 villans with 8 bordars have $1\frac{1}{2}$ ploughs. [There is] meadow for half a plough. It is worth £3; when received, £4; TRE £5. Blæwine, King Edward's sheriff, held this land and could depart.

In Oakington 2 knights hold 3 hides and 1 virgate and 10 acres from Picot, and in the same place a third knight holds half a hide and 9 acres and 3 gardens. There is land for $3\frac{1}{2}$ ploughs. There are 2 [ploughs], and there can be $1\frac{1}{2}$ [more]. There are 12 villans with 3 bordars and 8 cottars. All together it is worth £4.10s; when received, 100s; TRE £8. BLæwine the sheriff held half a hide and 9 acres of this land from the king; and 2 other men of the king held 1 hide and 3 virgates, and provided

1 cartage-due and 1 watchman; and a man of the Abbot of Ely had 1½ hides and 10 acres; he could sell [his land] but the soke remained with the abbot.

In Impington Walter holds 3½ hides from Picot. There is land for 3 ploughs, and there are [3 ploughs], with 4 bordars and 4 cottars. [There is] meadow for 1 plough. All together it is worth 60s; when received, 50s; TRE £4. 3 sokemen of the Abbot of Ely held this land. 2 of these had 1 hide and 1 virgate [and] could sell, but the soke remained with the abbot; the third had 2 hides and 1 virgate, but he could not sell.

[Folio 201V: CAMBRIDGESHIRE]

In Milton Ralph holds 12 hides from Picot. There is land for 7 ploughs. In demesne are 2 [ploughs], and there can be 2 others. There 10 villans with 12 bordars and 9 cottars have 3 ploughs. There are 5 slaves, meadow for 4 ploughs, [and] pasture for the livestock. From the fen, 650 eels and 12d. In all it is worth £7; when received, £8; TRE £12. Æthelbeorht, the abbot's steward, held 6 hides and 3 virgates of this manor in such a way that he could not sell them nor alienate them from the Church, but after his death it was to be restored to the Church of Ely; and 4 sokemen held 4 hides and 2½ virgates under the abbot and could sell them without the soke; and a man of King Edward had 2½ virgates and could sell them where he would.

In Landbeach Osmund holds 1½ hides and 10 acres from Picot. There is land for 1½ ploughs. In demesne is 1 plough, and there can be half [a plough more]. There are 8 bordars and 6 cottars, meadow for 1½ ploughs, [and] pasture for the livestock. From the fen, 1,000 eels and 12d. from the gift [of fish]. It is worth 20s; when received, 30s; and as much TRE. Blæcwine the sheriff held 3 virgates and 12 acres of this land and could give them where he would; and 4 sokemen of King Edward held 3 virgates [and] provided 1 cartage-due and 1 watchman for the sheriff.

In Waterbeach Muceull holds 6 hides from Picot. There is land for 3 ploughs. In demesne is 1 [plough]; and 6 villans with 4 bordars and 9 cottars have 2 ploughs. [There is] meadow for 3 ploughs, [and] pasture for the livestock of the vill. It is worth £4.6s; when received, £3; TRE £4.10s. Blæcwine held 2 hides and 3 virgates of this land from the king; and 4 men of King Edward had 2 hides and provided 3 cartage-dues and 1 watchman for the sheriff; and Albert, the man of the Abbot of Ely, had 1 hide which he could neither sell not alienate from the church; and another man of the abbot had 1 virgate and could sell it but the soke remained with the abbot.

IN CHESTERTON HUNDRED

In Cottenham Roger holds 5 hides from Picot. There is land for 3 ploughs. In demesne is 1 [plough], and there can be another. There 6 villans with 8 cottars have 1 plough. [There is] meadow for 3 ploughs, [and] pasture for the livestock of the vill. From the fen, 150 eels. It is worth 40s; when received, 50s; TRE 60s. 3 sokemen held this land. 1 of these, the man of St Æthelthryth, held 3½ hides, less 14 acres, [and] could not give [his land] because it belonged to the demesne of the

church; and another, the man of the abbot, had 1½ hides and could give them without the soke; and the third, the man of Earl Waltheof, had 14 acres and could give and sell them.

In Cottenham Picot holds 40 acres and 1 garden of the demesne of the Church of Ely.

In the same Cottenham Picot himself holds 40 acres of land and 5 acres of meadow of the demesne of the Church of St Guthlac.

In Westwick Odo holds 3 hides from Picot. There is land for 2 ploughs. In demesne are 1½ [ploughs]; and 2 villans with 1 bordar have half a plough. [There is] meadow for 2 ploughs. It is worth 60s; when received, 70s; TRE 100s. Blæcwine the sheriff, the man of King Edward, held this land and could sell it; and a sokeman of the Abbot of Ely had 40 acres of this land and could depart, but the soke remained with the abbot.

In Childerley Robert holds 2 hides from Picot. There is land for 1 plough. This [land] is valued in Lolworth but is assessed in Childerley. 4 sokemen held this land. 3 of these were the men of King Edward and the fourth the man of Eadgifu the Fair and they could sell.

XXXI. The land of Peter de Valognes

IN LONGSTOWE HUNDRED

PETER de Valognes holds 1 hide and 3 virgates in Bourn. There is land for 2 ploughs, but there are no [ploughs]. There are 2 bordars and 3 cottars, [and] a wood for fences. It is worth 30s; when received, [...]s; TRE 50s. Almær, King Edward's thegn, held this land and could sell it. Now Picot holds it from Peter, the sheriff of Essex.

XXXII.

IN LONGSTOWE HUNDRED

RANULPH the brother of Ilger holds 1 hide of the king in Gamlingay. There is land for 1 plough. It is and always was worth 10s. Ingvar, King Edward's thegn, held this land and could sell it.

XXXIII. The land of John fitzWaleran

IN FLEAMDYKE HUNDRED

JOHN fitzWaleran holds 6 hides in Fulbourn. There is land for 7 ploughs. In demesne [are] 3 hides, and there are 3 ploughs. There 8 villans with 10 bordars and 4 cottars have 3 ploughs. [There is] meadow for 7 ploughs, [and] pasture for the livestock of the vill. It is and always was worth £12. Sigar held 3 hides of this land from King Edward and could sell; and a man of Earl Ælfgar held 2 hides and could give and sell them; and 3 men of Eadgifu had 1 hide from which they provided 2 cartage-dues, and they could not depart from her. Count Alan claims this hide; the men of the hundred bear witness for him.

In Teversham John holds 3½ hides. There is land for 4½ ploughs. In demesne [are] 2 hides, and there are 2 ploughs.

There 5 villans with 17 bordars have 2½ ploughs. There is 1 slave, [and] meadow for 2 ploughs. It is and was worth 3; TRE 4. 2 sokemen held 1½ hides and 20 acres of this land from Earl Ælfgar [and] could not depart from him. The predecessor of Abbot Simeon of Ely bought the third hide of this vill from Earl Ælfgar; and at that time this land provided cartage-due, [but] after it pertained to the church it did not provide it. With this hide belongs a church of that vill, as the men of the hundred bear witness, and 2 men of Godwine Cild provided 1 cartage-due and 2 watchmen.

XXXIIII. The land of William fitzAnsculf

IN 'NORTHSTOWE' HUNDRED

WILLIAM fitzAnsculf holds half a virgate from the king in Longstanton. There is land for 2 oxen, [and] meadow for 2 oxen. It is and was worth 2s; TRE 5s. Hoc held this land under Earl Waltheof; he could not give it. Now Picot holds it from William.

XXXV. The land of William de Keynes

IN 'WETHERLEY' HUNDRED

WILLIAM de Keynes holds 1½ virgates in Comberton. There is land for 1 plough, but there is no plough. [There is] meadow for 1 plough, and 1 villan. It is and always was worth 10s. 1 man of Earl Waltheof held this land and could give and sell it. The Bishop of Bayeux delivered this to William, but the men of the hundred do not know on what grounds.

In Barton William himself holds 2½ hides in the same manner. There is land for 5 ploughs. In demesne are 4 [ploughs]; and 1 villan with 8 bordars have 2 ploughs. There are 2 slaves, [and] meadow for 2 ploughs. It is worth £8; when received, £10; and as much TRE. 4 sokemen, the men of Earl Waltheof, held this land. 2 of these held 1 hide and 2½ virgates but could not depart without his leave. But the other 2 could give and sell their land.

XXXVI. The land of Robert Fafiton

IN CHILFORD HUNDRED

ROBERT Fafiton holds 1 hide and 1 virgate from the king in Babraham. There is land for 2½ ploughs. In demesne are 3 virgates, and there is 1 plough, and there can be another; and 4 villans have half a plough. It is worth 21s; when received, 10s; TRE 26s8d.

[Folio 202: CAMBRIDGESHIRE]

Godgifu held this land under Earl Ælfgar. She provided escort-service, and yet could depart and give her land.

IN THRIPLOW HUNDRED

In Trumpington Robert holds 2 hides. There is land for †3† ploughs. In demesne [is] 1 hide, and 1 plough; and 4 villans with 1 bordar †and† 5 cottars with 2 ploughs. [There is] meadow for 1 plough, [and] pasture for the livestock †of the vill†. It is and was worth 100s; TRE £6. Northmann held 1

hide and 3 virgates of this land from Earl Tosti and could sell them and depart where he would; and a man of King Edward held 1 virgate and provided cartage-due for the sheriff, and yet he could depart with the land. Robert usurped this virgate in defiance of the king, as the hundred bears witness.

IN 'WETHERLEY' HUNDRED

In Grantchester Robert holds 2 hides and 3 virgates. There is land for 4 ploughs. In demesne [is] 1 hide, and there are 2 ploughs. There 4 villans with 7 bordars have 2 ploughs. There are 22 cottars, and 1 mill rendering 40s. From half a weir, half a thousand eels. All together it is and was worth £7; TRE £10. 4 sokemen held this land. One of these, the man of Earl Ælfgar, held 3 virgates; and the others, men of Earl Waltheof, held 2 hides and could give and sell their lands.

IN LONGSTOWE HUNDRED

In Gamlingay 2 men hold 1 hide from Robert. There is land for 1 plough, and there is [1 plough], with 3 cottars. [There is] meadow for 1 plough, [and] a wood for fences. It is and was worth 20s; TRE 40s. 1 man of Earl Ælfgar held this land and could sell it.

IN CHESTERTON HUNDRED

In Dry Drayton Avesgot holds 3 hides from Robert. There is land for 3 ploughs. In demesne is 1 [plough]; and 4 villans with 1 bordar have 2 ploughs. [There is] meadow for 3 ploughs. It is worth 40s; when received, 13s4d; TRE 60s. Sægar, the man of Earl Waltheof, held this land and could depart where he would with the sake [sic].

XXXVII. The land of David d'Argentan

IN LONGSTOWE HUNDRED

DAVID d'Argentan holds 1 virgate and 20 acres in Caldecote. There is land for 1 plough, and there is [1 plough], with 3 bordars and 1 cottar. [There is] meadow for 1 plough. It is and was worth 20s; TRE 30s. Sigar, the man of Earl Waltheof, held this land and could depart.

In Croxton David holds 6 hides. There is land for 9½ ploughs. In demesne [are] 3 hides, and there are 2 ploughs, and there can be a third. There 7 villans with 7 bordars and 2 cottars have 3 ploughs, and there can be 3½ more. [There is] meadow for 9½ ploughs, pasture for the livestock, and from the herbage 16d. From the fen, 500 eels a year. Eustace of Huntingdon usurped this in defiance of David, as the whole hundred bears witness. In all it is and was worth £8; TRE £10. 3 men of Earl Ælfgar and a fourth, the man of Earl Waltheof, held this manor and could sell it.

IN CHESTERTON HUNDRED

In Westwick Robert holds 1 hide from David. There is land for 1 plough, and there is [1 plough, and] meadow for 1 plough. It is worth 20s; when received, 10s; TRE 20s. Guthmund, the man of Earl Waltheof, held this land; the soke remained with the Abbot of Ely.

XXXVIII. The land of Two of the King's Carpenters

IN 'NORTHSTOWE' HUNDRED

In Waterbeach 2 carpenters hold 5 hides from the king. There is land for 2½ ploughs. In demesne [are] 4 hides and 1 virgate, and there are 2 ploughs. There 3 villans with 10 cottars have half a plough. It is worth 110s; when received, £4.10s; TRE £7.10s. 1 man of Waltheof held 1½ hides of this land, and provided 1 cartage-due, and could sell [his land]; and Oswig, the man of the Abbot of Ely, held 3½ hides, [and] could not sell [his land] nor alienate it from the church, as the men of the hundred bear witness.

XXXIX. The land of Countess Judith

IN CHEVELEY HUNDRED

Countess JUDITH holds KIRTLING. It was assessed at 10 hides TRE; and now at 6 hides. There is land for 21 ploughs. In demesne are 4 hides, and there are 4 ploughs. There 28 villans with 17 bordars have 16 ploughs. There are 7 slaves, meadow for 21 ploughs, woodland for 60 pigs, pasture for the livestock of the vill, [and] a park for wild beasts. From the fisheries, 5,500 eels. In all it is and always was worth £18. Earl Harold held this manor.

IN 'RADFIELD' HUNDRED

In Dullingham the countess holds 10 acres, with 1 bordar. It is worth 12d.

In Westley Waterless the countess holds 3 virgates and 10 acres. There is land for 2 ploughs. There is 1 [plough], and there can be another. There is 1 villan with 1 bordar, and 2 acres of meadow. It is and always was worth 20s. 2 men of Earl Harold held this land; they could not depart, and provided cartage-due in the king's service.

In Carlton the countess holds 3 hides. There is land for 8 ploughs. In demesne [are] 1½ hides, and there are 2 ploughs; and 12 villans with 2 bordars have 6 ploughs. There are 2 slaves, and 2 acres of meadow, [and] woodland for 12 pigs. It is and always was worth £6. Earl Harold held this land. 3 sokemen hold 4½ acres of the same land from the countess, and they themselves held them TRE and provided escort-service; and a man of Earl Ælfgar held 2 acres and provided escort-service.

IN CHILFORD HUNDRED

In Babraham the countess holds 1½ virgates. There is land for 4 oxen. It is and was worth 4s. A man of Earl Gyrth held this land and could not depart.

In Pampisford a priest holds half a virgate from the countess. It is and was worth 64d. A certain sokeman of Earl Gyrth held this; he could neither depart nor sell it.

IN WHITTLESFORD HUNDRED

In Whittlesford the countess holds 11 hides and 1 virgate. There is land for 11 ploughs. In demesne [are] 5 hides, and there are 2 ploughs; and 13 villans with 15 bordars have 9 ploughs. There are 5 slaves, and 3 mills rendering 60s, [and] meadow for the ploughs. In all it is worth £16; when received, £15; and as much TRE. Earl Gyrth held this manor.

IN THRIPLOW HUNDRED

In Trumpington Gollam holds half a hide from the countess. There is land for half a plough, and there is [half a plough]. It is and always was worth 10s. A certain sokeman of Earl Waltheof held this land; he could not depart.

IN 'ARRINGFORD' HUNDRED

In Tadlow Picot holds 1 hide and 1½ virgates from the countess. There is land for 2½ ploughs. In demesne there can be 1 plough. There a half-villan with 7 bordars have 1½ ploughs. [There is] woodland to repair fences. It is and was worth 30s; TRE 40s. Thorkil, Earl Tosti's priest, held this land and could sell it.

IN LONGSTOWE HUNDRED

The same Picot holds 3 virgates from the countess. There is land for 1 plough, but there is no [plough], only 1 bordar. [There is] a wood for fences. It is worth 5s; when received, 10s; TRE 20s. 2 sokemen of King Edward held this land and could sell it.

IN PAPWORTH HUNDRED

The same Picot holds 1 hide from the countess. There is land for 1 plough, but there is now [plough. There is] meadow for 1 plough. It is and was worth 7s; TRE 20s. 1 housecarl of Earl Waltheof held this land and could sell it.

IN 'NORTHSTOWE' HUNDRED

The same Picot holds 3 hides from the countess. There is land for 2 ploughs. There is 1 [plough], and there can be another. There are 4 villans and 4 bordars. It is worth 30s; when received, 40s; and as much TRE. 4 men of Earl Waltheof held this land and could sell it.

[Folio 202V: CAMBRIDGESHIRE]

In Oakington Roger holds 1½ hides and 10 acres from the countess. There is land for 1½ ploughs. There is half [a plough], and there can be a plough. There is 1 villan and 6 cottars. It is worth 30s; when received, 20s; TRE £4. Godwine, the man of Earl Waltheof, held this land, and could sell it.

IN PAPWORTH HUNDRED

In Over Roger holds half a hide from the countess. There is land for 4 oxen, and there are [4 oxen], and meadow for the oxen themselves, and 3 cottars, [and] pasture for the livestock of the vill. It is and always was worth 20s. Godwine, the man of Earl Waltheof, held this land and could give it, but the soke remained with the Abbot of Ramsey.

IN CHESTERTON HUNDRED

In Dry Drayton Roger holds 3 virgates from the countess. There is land for 4 oxen, and there are [4 oxen], and meadow for the oxen themselves. There is 1 villan. It is worth 16s; when received, 30s; TRE 20s. 1 man of Earl Waltheof held this land and could sell it.

In Childerley Picot holds 5 hides from the countess. There is land for 5 ploughs. In demesne is 1 [plough]; and 5 villans with 6 bordars and 3 cottars have 4 ploughs. There is 1 slave, [and] a wood for fences. It is worth £4; when received, 70s; TRE 8. 1 man of Earl Waltheof held this land and could sell it.

XL. The land of the wife of Ralph Taillebois

IN 'ARRINGFORD' HUNDRED

AZELINA, the wife of Ralph Taillebois, holds 1 hide and 1 virgate in Tadlow from the king. There is land for 2 ploughs, and there are [2 ploughs], with 5 bordars. [There is] meadow for 2 ploughs, [and] pasture for the livestock of the vill. It is worth 40s; when received, 10s; TRE 40s. Wulfmær of Eaton Socon, King Edward's thegn, held this land; now Walter the monk holds it from the aforesaid Azelina.

XLI. The wife of Boselin de Dives

IN 'NORTHSTOWE' HUNDRED

In Oakington the wife of Boselin de Dives holds 1½ hides which the Bishop of Bayeux delivered to her, but the men of the hundred do not know on what grounds. There is land for 1½ ploughs. There are 6 oxen, and there can be 1 plough. There are 3 villans and 2 cottars. It is and was worth 30s; TRE 60s. Siward, the man of Earl Waltheof, held this land and could sell it, but the soke remained with the Abbot of Ely.

XLII. The land of Erchenger

IN 'WETHERLEY' HUNDRED

ERCHENGER the baker holds 1 hide, less 20 acres, in Comberton from the king. There is land for 2 ploughs. In demesne [is] 1 plough, [and] half a hide less 20 acres. There 4 villans with 8 bordars have 1 plough. There is 1 slave, and meadow for 4 oxen. It is worth 30s; when received, 20s; TRE 40s. 3 sokemen held this land. One of these, the king's man, had 1 virgate and provided half a cartage-due; and another, the man of Archbishop Stigand, 1½ virgates; and the third, the man of Waltheof, 1½ virgates; and they could sell [their land] and depart.

IN LONGSTOWE HUNDRED

In Toft Erchenger holds 1 hide from the king. There is land for 2 ploughs. In demesne there can be 1 plough; and 1 villan with 5 cottars have 1 plough. [There is] meadow for 4 oxen, [and] a wood for fences and for fuel. It is worth 40s; when received, 10s; TRE 60s. 5 sokemen of the Abbot of Ely held this land: they could neither give nor sell it outside the Church of St Æthelthryth TRE and at the death of the king [Edward] himself.

HUNTINGDONSHIRE

IN THE BOROUGH OF HUNTINGDON THERE ARE 4 FERDINGS.

In 2 ferdings there were TRE and are now 116 burgesses rendering all customs and the king's geld, and under them are 100 bordars who help them to pay the geld. Of these burgesses, St Benedict of Ramsey had 10 with sake and soke and every custom, except that they paid geld TRE. Eustace took them away by force from the abbey, and they are now, with the others, in the king's hand.

Ulf Fenman had 18 burgesses; now Gilbert de Ghent has them with sake and soke, except for the king's geld.

The Abbot of Ely has 1 toft with sake and soke, except for the king's geld.

The Bishop of Lincoln had on the site of the castle 1 messuage with sake and soke, which is not there now.

Earl Siward had 1 messuage with a house, with sake and soke, quit of all custom, which Countess Judith has now.

On the site of the castle were 20 messuages [assessed] to all customs, rendering 16s8d a year to the king's farm, which are not there now.

In addition to these, there were and are 60 waste messuages within these ferdings, which gave and give their customs.

And in addition to these, there are 8 waste messuages which TRE were fully occupied, and gave all customs.

In the other 2 ferdings there were and are 140 burgesses, less half a house, [assessed] to all customs and the king's geld, and these had 80 closes for which they gave and give all customs. Of these, St Benedict of Ramsey had †22† burgesses TRE. 2 of these were quit of all customs, and 30 paid 10d a year each. All other customs belonged to the abbot, apart from the king's geld.

In these ferdings, Ælfric the sheriff TRE had 1 messuage, which King William afterwards granted to his wife and sons. Eustace has it now; a poor man, with his mother, claims it. In these 2 ferdings, there were and are 44 waste messuages, which gave and give their customs. And in addition to these, in these 2 ferdings Burgræd and Thorkil TRE had 1 church with 2 hides of land, and 22 burgesses with houses belonging to the same church with sake and soke, all of which Eustace has now. Therefore these men claim the king's mercy. Nevertheless these 22 burgesses give every custom to the king. Bishop Geoffrey has 1 church and 1 house of the aforesaid, which Eustace took away from St Benedict, and

the same saint is still claiming them. In the borough itself, Gos and Hunæf had 16 houses TRE with sake and soke and toll and team. Countess Judith has them now.

The Borough of HUNTINGDON used to be assessed for the king's geld at 50 hides as the fourth part of 'Hurstingstone' Hundred, but now it does not pay geld thus in that hundred, after King William set a geld on the mint of the borough. From this whole borough, £10 came TRE from land-rent, of which the earl had the third part, the king 2 [parts]. Of this rent, 16s8d, [shared] between the earl and the king, now remains upon 20 messuages where the castle is. In addition to these [renders] the king had £20 and the earl £10 from the farm of the borough, or more or less according as [each] could arrange his share. 1 mill renders 40s to the king, 20s to the earl. To this borough there belong 2 hides carucates and 40 acres of land and 10 acres of meadow, of which they divide the rent, the king [having] 2 parts, and the earl the third [part]. The burgesses cultivate this land and lease it through the servants of the king and the earl. Within the aforesaid rent are 3 fishermen paying 3s. In this borough were 3 moneyers paying 40s [shared] between the king and the earl, but now they are not there. TRE it rendered £30; now the same.

In 'HURSTINGSTONE' Hundred, the demesne ploughs are quit of the king's geld. The villans and sokemen pay geld according to the hides written in the return apart from Broughton, where the abbot pays geld for 1 hide with the others.

Here Are Entered the Holders of Lands In Huntingdonshire

I KING WILLIAM
II The Bishop of Lincoln
III The Bishop of Coutances
IIII The Abbey of Ely
V The Abbey of Crowland
VI The Abbey of Ramsey
VII The Abbey of Thorney
VIII The Abbey of Peterborough
IX Count Eustace
X The Count of EU
XI Earl Hugh
XII Walter Giffard
XIII William de Warenne
XIIII Hugh de Bolbec
XV Eudo fitzHubert

XVI Swein of Essex
XVII Roger d'Ivry
XVIII Ernulf de Hesdin
XIX Eustace the sheriff
XX Countess Judith
XXI Gilbert de Ghent
XXII Aubrey de Vere
XXIII William fifzAnsculf
XXIIII Ranulph, Ilger's brother
XXV Robert Fafiton
XXVI William Engaine
XXVII Ralph fiftzOsmund
XXVIII Rohais, Richard's wife
XXIX The king's thegns

[Folio 203V: HUNTINGDONSHIRE]

I. The land of the King

'HURSTINGSTONE' HUNDRED

IN HARTFORD King EDWARD had 15 hides of land to the geld. [There is] land for 17 ploughs. Ranulph, Ilger's brother, has custody of it now. There are now 4 ploughs in demesne; and 30 villans and 3 bordars have 8 ploughs. There is a priest and 2 churches, and 2 mills [rendering] £4, and 40 acres of meadow, [and] woodland pasture I league long and half a league broad. TRE worth £24; now I5.

NORMANCROSS HUNDRED

In BOTOLPH BRIDGE [in Peterborough] King Edward had 5 hides to the geld. [There is] land for 8 ploughs. There the king now has 1 plough in demesne; and 15 villans having 5 ploughs. There is a priest and a church, and 60 acres of meadow, and 12 acres of woodland pasture in Northamptonshire. TRE worth 100s; now £8 Ranulph has custody of it. In this manor of the king and in other manors the sluice of the Abbot of Thorney has flooded 300 acres of meadow.

In Stilton the king's sokemen of Normancross [Hundred] have 3 virgates of land to the geld. [There is] land for 2 ploughs, and 5 oxen ploughing.

In Orton Waterville [in Peterborough] the king has soke over 3½ hides of land in the land of the Abbot of Peterborough which was Godwine's.

TOSELAND HUNDRED

In GREAT GRANSDEN Earl Ælfgar had 8 hides of land to the geld. [There is] land for 15 ploughs. There are now 7 ploughs in demesne; and 24 villans and 8 bordars having 8 ploughs. There is a priest and a church, and 50 acres of meadow and 12 acres of scrubland. From the pasture come 5s4d. TRE worth £40; now £30. Ranulph has custody of it.

'LEIGHTONSTONE' HUNDRED

In ALCONBURY and Great Gidding, a BEREWICK, there were 10 hides to the geld. [There is] land for 20 ploughs. There are now 5 ploughs belonging to the hall, on 2 hides of this land; and 35 villans have 13 ploughs there, and 80 acres of meadow. TRE worth £12; now the same. Ranulph, Ilger's brother, has custody of it.

In KEYSTON King Edward had 4 hides of land to the geld. [There is] land for 12 ploughs. There are now 2 ploughs in demesne; and 24 villans and 8 bordars have 10 ploughs, and [there are] 86 acres of meadow. [There is] woodland, pasture in places, 5 furlongs long and 1½ furlongs broad. TRE, as now, worth £10. Ranulph, Ilger's brother, has custody of it.

In BRAMPTON King Edward had 15 hides to the geld. [There is] land for 15 ploughs. There are now 3 ploughs, and 36 villans and 2 bordars have 14 ploughs. There is a church and a priest, and 100 acres of meadow, woodland pasture half a league long and 2 furlongs broad, and 2 mills rendering 100s. TRE, as now, worth £20. Ranulph, Ilger's brother, has custody of it.

In Grafham are 5 hides to the geld. [There is] land for 8 ploughs. The SOKE [is] in 'Leightonstone' Hundred. There 7 sokeman and 17 villans now have 6 ploughs, and 6 acres of meadow. [There is] woodland pasture 1 league long and 1 broad. TRE worth £5; now 10s less.

In GODMANCHESTER King Edward had 14 hides to the geld. [There is] land for 57 ploughs. There are 2 ploughs now in the king's demesne, on 2 hides of this land; and 80 villans and 16 bordars have 24 ploughs. There is a priest and a church, and 3 mills [rendering] 100s, and 160 acres of meadow and 50 acres of woodland pasture. From the pasture 20s. From the meadows 70s. TRE worth £40; now the same, by tale.

II. The land of the Bishop of Lincoln

TOSELAND HUNDRED

In COTTON the Bishop of Lincoln had 2 hides to the geld. [There is] land for 3 ploughs. There are now 2 ploughs in demesne; and 3 villans having †2 oxen †, and [there are] 20 acres of meadow. TRE, as now, worth 40s. Turstin holds it of the bishop.

In GREAT STAUGHTON the Bishop of Lincoln had 6 hides to the geld. [There is] land for 15 ploughs. There are now 2½ ploughs in demesne; and 16 villans and 4 bordars having 8 ploughs. There is a priest and a church, and 24 acres of meadow and 100 acres of woodland pasture. TRE, as now, worth £10. Eustace holds it of the bishop. The Abbot of Ramsey claims this manor against the bishop.

In DIDDINGTON the Bishop of Lincoln had 2½ hides to the geld. [There is] land for 2 ploughs. There are now 2 ploughs in demesne; and 5 villans having 2 ploughs. There is a church, and 18 acres of meadow, [and] woodland pasture half a league long and a half broad. TRE worth 60s; now 70s. William holds it of the bishop.

In BUCKDEN the Bishop of Lincoln had 20 hides to the geld. [There is] land for 20 ploughs. There are now 5 ploughs in demesne; and 37 villans and 20 bordars having 14 ploughs. There is a church and a priest, and 1 mill [rendering] 30s, and

84 acres of meadow, [and] woodland pasture 1 league long and 1 league broad. TRE worth £20; now £16.10s.

NORMANCROSS HUNDRED

In DENTON Godric had 5 hides to the geld. [There is] land for 2 ploughs. There is now 1 plough in demesne; and 10 villans and 2 bordars have 5 ploughs. There is a church and a priest, and 24 acres of meadow and 24 acres of scrubland. TRE worth 100s; now £4. Turstin holds it of the bishop.

In ORTON WATERVILLE [in Peterborough] Leofric had 3 hides and 1 virgate of land to the geld. [There is] land for 2 ploughs and 1 ox. There is now 1 plough in demesne, and 2 villans, and 9 acres of meadow. TRE worth 20s; now 10s. John holds it of the bishop. The king claims the soke of this land.

In STILTON Tovi had 2 hides to the geld. [There is] land for 2 ploughs and 7 oxen. There is now 1 plough in demesne; and 6 villans with 3 ploughs, and 16 acres of meadow and 5 acres of scrubland. TRE, as now, worth 40s. John holds it of the bishop. This land was given to Bishop Wulfwine [sc. Wulfwig] TRE.

'LEIGHTONSTONE' HUNDRED

In LEIGHTON BROMSWOLD Thorkil the Dane had 15 hides to the geld. [There is] land for 17 ploughs. There are now 6 ploughs in demesne; and 33 villans and 3 bordars having 10 ploughs, and 1 mill [rendering] 3s. 3 knights hold 3 hides, less 1 virgate, of this land. There they have 3 ploughs, and 3 villans with half a plough. There are 30 acres of meadow and 10 acres of scrubland. TRE, as now, the bishop's demesne was worth £20; the land of the knights, 60s. Earl Waltheof gave this manor in alms to ST MARY of Lincoln.

In Pertenhall [Beds.] Alwine had 1 virgate of land to the geld. [There is] land for half a plough. This land is situated in Bedfordshire but renders geld and service in Huntingdonshire. The king's servants claim this [land] for his use. TRE, as now, worth 5s. William holds it of Bishop Remigius and ploughs it there with his own demesne.

[Folio 204: HUNTINGDONSHIRE]

III. The land of the Bishop of Coutances

In HARGRAVE [Northants] Sæmær had 1 virgate of land to the geld. [There is] land for 2 oxen. The SOKE [is] in 'Leightonstone' [Hundred]. The same man himself holds it now of the Bishop of Coutances, and ploughs there with 2 oxen, and has 2 acres of meadow. TRE worth 5s; now the same.

IIII. The land of the Abbey of Ely

| 'HURSTINGSTONE' HUNDRED |

In COLNE the Abbot of Ely had 6 hides to the geld. [There is] land for 6 ploughs, and in demesne [he had] land for 2 ploughs apart from the 6 hides. There are now 2 ploughs in demesne; and 13 villans and 5 bordars having 5 ploughs; and 10 acres of meadow. [There is] woodland pasture 1 league long and a half broad, and as much marsh. TRE worth £6; now 100s.

In BLUNTISHAM the Abbot of Ely had 6½ hides to the geld. [There is] land for 8 ploughs and, apart from these hides, [he] had] land for 2 ploughs in demesne. There are now 2 ploughs in demesne; and 10 villans and 3 bordars with 3 ploughs. There is a priest and a church, and 20 acres of meadow, [and] woodland pasture 1 league long and 4 furlongs broad. TRE, as now, worth 100s.

In SOMERSHAM the Abbot of Ely had 8 hides to the geld. [There is] land for 12 ploughs and, apart from these hides, [he] had] land for 2 ploughs in demesne. There are now 2 ploughs in demesne; and 32 villans and 9 bordars having 9 ploughs. There are 3 fishponds [rendering] 8s, and 20 acres of meadow, [and] woodland pasture 1 league long and 7 furlongs broad. TRE worth £7; now £8.

In SPALDWICK the Abbot of Ely had 15 hides to the geld. [There is] land for 15 ploughs. There are now 4 ploughs in demesne, on 5 hides of this land; and 50 villans and 10 bordars having 25 ploughs. There is 1 mill [rendering] 2s, and 160 acres of meadow and 60 acres of woodland pasture. TRE worth £16; now £22.

In Little Catworth, a BEREWICK of Spaldwick, [there are] 4 hides to the geld. [There is] land for 4 ploughs. There 7 villans have 2 ploughs now.

V. The land of the Abbey of Crowland

In MORBORNE the Abbot of Crowland had 5 hides to the geld. [There is] land for 9 ploughs. There are now 2 ploughs in demesne, on 1 hide of this land; and 16 villans and 3 bordars having 7 ploughs. There is a church and a priest, and 40 acres of meadow and 1 acre of scrubland. TRE, as now, worth 100s.

In Thurning [Northants] [are] 1½ hides to the geld. [There is] land for 1½ ploughs. The SOKE [is] in the king's manor of Alconbury. Eustace holds it now of the Abbot of Crowland, and has 1 plough there, and 1 villan with half a plough, and 6 acres of meadow. TRE, as now, worth 20s.

VI. The land of St Benedict of Ramsey

'HURSTINGSTONE' HUNDRED

In LITTLE STUKELEY the Abbot of Ramsey had 7 hides to the geld. [There is] land for 11 ploughs. Apart from these hides [he had] land for 2 ploughs in demesne. There are now 2 ploughs in demesne; and 16 villan [sic] and 2 bordars having 6 ploughs. There is a church and a priest, and 24 acres of meadow, [and] woodland pasture 4 furlongs long and 3 broad. TRE worth £6; now £4.10s. Richard and Hugh, 2 knights of the abbot, have 3 hides of this land, and have 3 ploughs in demesne there, and [their land] is worth 30s.

In ABBOTS RIPTON the Abbot of Ramsey had 10 hides to the geld. [There is] land for 16 ploughs, and [he had] land for 2 ploughs in demesne, apart from the aforesaid hides. There are now 2 ploughs in demesne; and 27 villans and 6 bordars having 12 ploughs. There is a church and a priest, and 16 acres of meadow, [and] woodland pasture 1 league long and 1 league broad. TRE, as now, worth £8.

In BROUGHTON the Abbot of Ramsey had 4 hides to the geld. [There is] land for 7 ploughs and 2 oxen. The land of the sokemen there is 5 hides to the geld. [There is] land for 8 ploughs and 6 oxen. These sokemen say that they had their fines for fornication and bloodshed and robbery up to 4d, and above 4d the abbot had the forfeiture for robbery. Now the abbot has 4 ploughs in demesne; and 10 sokemen and 20 villans having 10 ploughs. There is a priest and a church, and 1 mill [rendering] 3s, and 10 acres of meadow, [and] woodland pasture 3 furlongs long and 2 broad. TRE worth £9; now £10. Eustace claims 5 hides.

In WISTOW the Abbot of Ramsey had 9 hides to the geld. [There is] land for 16 ploughs, and [he had] land for 3 ploughs in demesne, apart from these hides. There are now 2 ploughs in demesne; and 32 villans having 11 ploughs. There is a priest and a church, and 1 mill [rendering] 2s, and 24 acres of meadow, [and] woodland pasture 1 league long and a half broad. TRE worth £9; now £8.

In UPWOOD the Abbot of Ramsey had 10 hides to the geld. [There is] land for 16 ploughs, and [he had] land for 3 ploughs in demesne, apart from the aforesaid hides. There are now 2 ploughs in demesne; and 32 villans and 2 bordars with 14 ploughs. There is a priest and a church, and 6 acres of meadow, [and] woodland pasture 1½ leagues long and 1 broad. TRE worth £10; now £9.

In HOLYWELL the Abbot of Ramsey had 9 hides to the geld. [There is] land for 9 ploughs, and [he had] land for 2 ploughs in demesne, apart from the aforesaid hides. There are now 2 ploughs in demesne; and 26 villans and 3 bordars with 6 ploughs. There is a church and a priest, and 30 acres of meadow, woodland pasture 1 league long and 4 furlongs and 1 league broad, [and] marsh 1 league long and 1 broad. TRE, as now, worth £8. Alweald has 1 hide of this land of the abbot, and has 1 plough there, and 3 bordars. It is worth 10s.

In ST IVES the Abbot of Ramsey had 20 hides to the geld. [There is] land for 24 ploughs, and [he had] land for 3 ploughs in demesne, apart from the aforesaid hides. There are now 3 ploughs in demesne; and 39 villans and 12 bordars having 20 ploughs. There is a priest and a church, and 60 acres of meadow, [and] woodland pasture 1 league long and a half broad. TRE worth £20; now £16.

[Folio 204V: HUNTINGDONSHIRE]

Of this land, 3 men of the abbot, Everard, Ingelrann, and Pleines, have 4 hides, and they themselves have 3½ ploughs there; and [there are] 5 villans and 6 bordars with 3 ploughs. [They have] a church and a priest. It is worth 45s. Eustace claims 2½ hides.

In HOUGHTON the Abbot of Ramsey had 7 hides to the geld. [There is] land for 10 ploughs, and [he had] land for 2 ploughs in demesne, apart from the aforesaid hides. There are now 2 ploughs in demesne; and 31 villans and 5 bordars with 10 ploughs. There is a church [but] not a priest, and 1 mill

[rendering] 20s, and 60 acres of meadow, [and] woodland pasture 1 league long and half a league broad. TRE, as now, worth £8. Eustace claims 1 hide.

In WYTON the Abbot of Ramsey had 7 hides to the geld. [There is] land for 10 ploughs, and [he had] land for 2 ploughs in demesne, apart from the aforesaid hides. There are now 2 ploughs in demesne; and 24 villans and 5 bordars having 8 ploughs. There is a priest and a church, and 1 mill [rendering] 12s, and 40 acres of meadow. TRE, as now, worth £7.

In Bluntisham there is half a hide to the geld. [There is] land for 5 oxen belonging to Ramsey [Abbey]. There 2 villans have 1 plough. It is worth 5s.

In WARBOYS the Abbot of Ramsey had 10 hides to the geld. [There is] land for 20 ploughs, and [he had] land for 3 ploughs in demesne, apart from the aforesaid hides. There are now 3 ploughs in demesne; and 34 villans and 13 bordars having 16 ploughs. There is a priest and a church, and 3 acres of meadow, woodland pasture 1 league long and 1 league broad, [and] marsh 1 league long and half a league broad. TRE, as now, worth £12.

NORMANCROSS HUNDRED

In SAWTRY the Abbot of Ramsey had 7½ hides and half a virgate of land to the geld. [There is] land for 12 ploughs.[...] There are now 2 ploughs in demesne, on 2 hides of this land; and 12 villans and 3 bordars having 5 ploughs. There is a church and a priest, and 12 acres of meadow, [and] woodland pasture 2 furlongs long and 1 furlong broad. TRE, as now, worth 100s.

In ELTON the Abbot of Ramsey had 10 hides to the geld. [There is] land for 24 ploughs, and [he had] land for 4 ploughs in demesne, apart from the aforesaid hides. There are now 4 ploughs in demesne; and 28 villans having 20 ploughs. There is a church and a priest, and 2 mills [rendering] 40s, and 170 acres of meadow. TRE worth £14; now £16.

In LUTTON [Northants] the Abbot of Ramsey had 2½ hides to the geld. [There is] land for 2 ploughs. There is now half a plough in demesne. Eadric holds it of the abbot. There are 12 acres of meadow. TRE worth 40s; now 20s.

TOSELAND HUNDRED

In YELLING the Abbot of Ramsey had 5 hides to the geld. [There is] land for 7 ploughs. There are now 2 ploughs in demesne; and 10 villans and 2 bordars have 3 ploughs. There are 5 acres of meadow. TRE, as now, worth £4. Swein holds it of the abbot.

In HEMINGFORD ABBOTS the Abbot of Ramsey had 18 hides to the geld. [There is] land for 16 ploughs. There are now 2 ploughs in demesne; and 26 villans and 5 bordars with 8 ploughs. There is a church and a priest, and 1 mill [rendering] 10s8d, and 80 acres of meadow. TRE worth £11; now 10.

In THE SAME PLACE Godric had 1 hide to the geld. He held of the abbot. [He had] land for 1 plough. Now Ralph fitzOsmund has it, but the men of the hundred do not know through whom. TRE worth 10s; now 3s.

In another Hemingford [Hemingford Grey] there are 5 hides to the geld. [There is] land for 5 ploughs. The SOKE [is] in Hemingford Abbots. Aubrey de Vere has it now of the abbot, and a certain knight has 2 hides of this land under him. There is 1 plough in demesne; and 8 villans with 3 ploughs. There are 20 acres of meadow. TRE, as now, worth 60s.

In OFFORD D'ARCY the Abbot of Ramsey had 4 hides to the geld. 1 hide of these was inland, and | in addition to this 2 ploughs in demesne. [There is] land for 4 ploughs. There are now 2 ploughs in demesne; and 4 villans and 2 bordars with 1 plough, and 16 acres of meadow, and 16 acres of woodland pasture. TRE, as now, worth £4.

In DILLINGTON the Abbot of Ramsey had 6 hides to the geld. [There is] land for 12 ploughs. There are now 2 ploughs in demesne; and 16 villans having 10 ploughs. There are 8 acres of meadow, [and] woodland pasture 1 league and 2 furlongs long and 1 league broad. TRE worth £6; now £4.

'LEIGHTONSTONE' HUNDRED

In GREAT GIDDING the Abbot of Ramsey had 1 hide to the geld. [There is] land for 1 plough. This land was in demesne. Now Lunen holds it of the abbot, and has 1 plough there, and 2 villans and 1 bordar with 1 plough, and 6 acres of meadow. TRE, as now, worth 30s.

In BYTHORN the Abbot of Ramsey had 4 hides to the geld. [There is] land for 4 ploughs. There is now 1 plough in demesne, on 1 hide of this land; and 11 villans and 4 bordars with 7 ploughs. There are 30 acres of meadow. TRE worth 100s; now £4. Of this land, 2 knights hold 3½ virgates of land of the abbot, and there they have 1 villan and 3 bordars with 2 ploughs. It is worth 30s.

In BRINGTON the Abbot of Ramsey had 4 hides to the geld. [There is] land for 7 ploughs. There is now 1 plough in demesne, on 1 hide of this land; and 11 villans and 3 bordars have 6 ploughs. There are 40 acres of meadow. TRE, as now, worth £4.

In OLD WESTON the Abbot of Ramsey had 10 hides to the geld. [There is] land for 13 ploughs. There are now 2 ploughs in demesne, on 2 hides of this land; and 20 villans and 1 bordar have 7 ploughs. There is a priest and a church, and 60 acres of meadow. TRE, as now, worth £10.

In STEEPLE GIDDING the Abbot of Ramsey had 7 hides to the geld. [There is] land for 8 ploughs. There is now 1 plough in demesne, on 1 hide of this land; and 18 villans have 7 ploughs. There are 20 acres of meadow, and 2 furlongs of scrubland. TRE, as now, worth 100s.

In ELLINGTON the Abbot of Ramsey had 10 hides to the geld. [There is] land for 16 ploughs. Of these 10 hides, 1 is waste because of the king's woodland.

Folio 205: HUNTINGDONSHIRE]

There are now 2 ploughs in demesne, on 2 hides of this land; and 26 villans and 4 bordars have 12 ploughs; and 60 acres of meadow. There is a church and a priest. TRE worth £10; now

£9. 2 knights hold 1 hide of this land, and have 2 ploughs. It is worth 20s.

VII. The land of St Mary of Thorney

NORMANCROSS HUNDRED

In YAXLEY the Abbot of Thorney had 15 hides to the geld. [There is] land for 20 ploughs. There are now 3 ploughs in demesne; and 38 villans having 18 ploughs. There is a church and a priest, and 24 acres of meadow and 20 acres of scrubland. TRE worth £15; now £12.

In STANGROUND [in Peterborough] the Abbot of Thorney had 8 hides to the geld. [There is] land for 10 ploughs. There are now 2 ploughs in demesne, on 3 hides of this land; and 16 villans and 6 bordars [...]. There is a church and a priest, and 24 acres of meadow and 6 acres of scrubland. TRE, as now, worth £8.

In WOODSTON [in Peterborough] the Abbot of Thorney had 5 hides to the geld. [There is] land for 9 ploughs. There are now 2 ploughs in demesne, on 1½ hides of this land; and 16 villans with 4 ploughs. There is a church and a priest, and 16 acres of meadow and 4 acres of scrubland. TRE worth 100s; now £4.

In HADDON the Abbot of Thorney had 5 hides to the geld. [There is] land for 12 ploughs. There are now 2 ploughs in demesne, on 1½ hides of this land; and 18 villans with 6 ploughs. There is a church and a priest, and 24 acres of meadow and 1 acre of scrubland. TRE, as now, worth 100s.

In WATER NEWTON the Abbot of Thorney had 5 hides to the geld. [There is] land for 8 ploughs. There are now 2 ploughs in demesne, on 1 hide of this land; and 10 villans and 5 bordars having 5 ploughs. There is a priest and a church, and 2 mills [rendering] 32s, and 60 acres of meadow, and 1 customary due of 2s in the woodland of the Abbot of Peterborough. TRE worth £5; now £7.

In SIBSON the Abbot of Thorney had 2½ hides to the geld. [There is] land for 4 ploughs. There is now 1 plough in demesne, on 1 hide of this land; and 4 villans with 1 plough. There is a priest and half a church, and half a mill [rendering] 10s, and 20 acres of meadow. TRE, as now, worth 50s.

In Stibbington there are 5 virgates of land to the geld, belonging to Sibson. [There is] land for 1 plough. There is a church, and 5 villans with 1½ ploughs, and 5 acres of meadow.

In Whittlesey Mere the Abbot of Ramsey has 1 boat, and the Abbot of Peterborough 1 boat, and the Abbot of Thorney 2 boats. The Abbot of Peterborough holds of the Abbot of Thorney 1 of these 2 [boats], and 2 fisheries and 2 fishermen and 1 virgate of land, and for these he gives pasture sufficient for 120 pigs, and if there is not enough pasture, he feeds and fattens 60 pigs with corn. Moreover, he finds timber for 1 house of 60 feet, and stakes for the enclosure around the house. He also repairs the house and the enclosure if they are in decay. This agreement was made between them TRE.

The fisheries and meres of the Abbot of Ramsey in

Huntingdonshire are valued at £10, [those] of the Abbot of Thorney at 60s, [those] of the Abbot of Peterborough at £4.

VIII. The land of St Peter of Peterborough

NORMANCROSS HUNDRED

In OLD FLETTON [in Peterborough] the Abbot of Peterborough had 5 hides to the geld. [There is] land for 8 ploughs. There are now 2 ploughs in demesne, on 1½ hides of this land. There are 14 villans and 3 bordars having 6 ploughs. There is a church and 40 acres of meadow. TRE, as now, worth 100s.

In ALWALTON the Abbot of Peterborough had 5 hides to the geld. [There is] land for 9 ploughs, and in demesne [he had] land for 2 ploughs, apart from these 5 hides. There are now 2 ploughs in demesne; and 20 villans having 7 ploughs. There are 2 mills [rendering] 40s, and 1 fishery [rendering] 500 eels [and] 5s, and 10 acres of meadow. TRE, as now, worth £7.

In Orton Waterville [in Peterborough], a BEREWICK of this manor, there are 5 hides to the geld. [There is] land for 3 ploughs and 2 oxen. This is for the sustenance of the monks. Now Ansgered holds it of the abbot, and has there 3 villans with 1 plough, and 15 acres of meadow.

In the same ORTON WATERVILLE [in Peterborough] Godwine had 3½ hides to the geld. [There is] land for 2 ploughs and 2 oxen. The king had soke over this land. TRE this [land] did not belong to the abbey, but was given to the Church of ST PETER in the days of King William. Ansgered holds it now of the abbot, and has 1 plough there, and 3 villans and 1 bordar with 1 plough, and 9 acres of meadow. TRE worth 40s; now 20s.

IX. The land of Count Eustace

In GLATTON Ulf had 8 hides to the geld. [There is] land for 24 ploughs. There are now 2 ploughs in demesne; and 24 villans and 10 bordars having 14 ploughs. There is a church and a priest, and 60 acres of meadow, and 2 acres of woodland pasture, and 20 acres of scrubland. TRE, as now, worth £10.

In CHESTERTON Ulf had 4½ hides to the geld. [There is] land for 7 ploughs. There is now 1 plough in demesne; and 7 villans and 1 bordar with 3 ploughs. There are 20 acres of meadow, and a customary due of 2s in the woodland of the Abbot of Peterborough. TRE worth £4; now 40s.

In SIBSON Ulf had 2½ hides to the geld. [There is] land for 4 ploughs. There is now 1 plough in demesne; and 3 villans and 1 bordar with 2 ploughs. There is half a church, and half a mill [rendering] 10s, and 20 acres of meadow. TRE, as now, worth 50s.

In Stibbington are 5 virgates of land to the geld, | belonging to Sibson |. [There is] land for 1 plough. There 5 villans now have 1½ ploughs; and [there are] 5 acres of meadow.

Lunen holds all these lands of Count Eustace.

X. The land of the Count of Eu

In BUCKWORTH Tosti had 10 hides to the geld. [There is] land for 18 ploughs. This was a BEREWICK of Great Paxton. Now the Count of EU holds it; and has 2 ploughs in demesne there, on 2 hides of this land; and 16 villans having 10 ploughs, and 1 smith having 5 acres of this land. There is a priest and a church, to which half a hide of this land belongs, with 2 villans and 1 plough. There are 80 acres of meadow and 30 acres of scrubland. TRE, as now, worth £10. A knight holds 2½ hides of this land, and has there 4 villans and 1 bordar with 5 ploughs. It is worth £3.

XI. The land of Earl Hugh

In UPTON Edgar had 4 hides to the geld, with sake and soke. [There is] land for 6 ploughs. There are now 2 ploughs in demesne, on 1 hide of this land; and 14 villans and 5 bordars having 8 ploughs. There is a church and a priest, and 1 mill [rendering] 3s, and 50 acres of meadow. TRE worth £4; now £5. Fulcui holds it of Earl Hugh.

In COPPINGFORD Edgar had 4 hides to the geld, with sake and soke. [There is] land for 5 ploughs. There is now 1 plough in demesne, on half a hide of this land; and 14 villans and 2 bordars have 3 ploughs. There is a church and a priest. TRE, as now, worth £4. Humphrey holds it of Earl Hugh.

XII. The land of Walter Giffard

In FOLKSWORTH Ketilbert had 5 hides to the geld. [There is] land for 5 ploughs. There is now 1 plough in demesne; and 17 villans and 5 bordars with 7 ploughs. There are 20 acres of meadow, [and] woodland pasture 6 furlongs long and 2 furlongs and 6 perches broad. TRE worth 100s; now £4. Hugh holds it of Walter Giffard.

XIII. The land of William de Warenne

In KIMBOLTON Earl Harold had 10 hides to the geld. [There is] land for 20 ploughs. William de Warenne holds it now, and has in demesne there 5 ploughs, on 5 hides; and 84 villans and 36 bordars with 25 ploughs. There is a priest and a church, and 70 acres of meadow, and woodland pasture 1 league long and 1 league broad. There is 1 mill [rendering] 5s. TRE worth £7; now £16.4s. 2 knights have 1 hide of this land, and have 1 plough and 5 oxen there. It is worth 20s.

In Keysoe [Beds.] Ællic [had] 3 virgates of land to the geld. [There is] land for 6 oxen. SOKELAND. There is 1 sokeman and 7 bordars, and 4 acres of meadow and 50 acres of woodland pasture.

In Swineshead [Beds.], 3½ hides to the geld. [There is] land for 4 ploughs. SOKELAND. There is now 1 sokeman and 7 villans and 5 bordars, and 16 acres of meadow, [and] woodland pasture 1 league long and 4 furlongs broad. It is worth 40s. Eustace holds it of William.

In Catworth, 1 hide to the geld. [There is] land for 1 plough. SOKELAND. Eustace holds it of William, and has half a plough there, and 1 bordar with 1 ox, and 1 acre of meadow and 6 acres of scrubland. It is worth 20s.

In another Catworth [Little Catworth], 1 hide to the geld. [There is] land for 1 plough. SOKELAND. Now Thorth holds it of William, and has 1 plough there, and 1 bordar, and 12 acres of meadow. It is worth 30s. All this SOKELAND belongs to Kimbolton.

XIIII. The land of Hugh de Bolbec

NORMANCROSS HUNDRED

In WOODWALTON Saxi had 5 hides to the geld. [There is] land for 7 ploughs. There are now 2 ploughs in demesne, on 1 hide of this land; and 19 villans having 4 ploughs. There is a church, and 16 acres of meadow, [and] woodland pasture 16 furlongs long and 6 furlongs and 2 virgates broad. TRE, as now, worth 100s. Hugh de Bolbec holds it of Earl William.

XV. The land of Eudo fitzHubert

In HAMERTON Wulfheah had 15 carucates hides [sic] of land to the geld. Eudo the Steward has them now of the king, and Ællic and Leofwine [had] 3 hides [of which] the SOKE [was] in 'Leightonstone' Hundred. Eudo has this land, and the king has the soke. Now in the manor there are 4 ploughs in demesne, on 3 hides of this land; and 26 villans having 6 ploughs. There are 60 acres of meadow and 10 acres of scrubland. 2 knights hold 2 hides of this land, and have 2 ploughs there. The whole of this manor was worth £12 TRE; now the same.

XVI. The land of Swein of Essex

TOSELAND HUNDRED

In WARESLEY Robert fitzWimarc had 7 hides to the geld. [There is] land for 9 ploughs. There are now 2 ploughs in demesne; and 17 villans and 4 bordars with 2 ploughs. There are 25 acres of meadow and 16 acres of scrubland. TRE worth £8; now £6. Turold holds it of Swein of Essex.

XVII. The land of Roger d'Ivry

'LEIGHTONSTONE' HUNDRED

In COVINGTON Eskil had 8½ hides to the geld. [There is] land for 13 ploughs. There are now 3 ploughs in demesne, on half a hide of this land; and 18 villans having 8 ploughs. There are 48 acres of meadow. 2 knights hold 2 hides of this land, and have 2 ploughs there. TRE worth £8; now £10. Roger d'Ivry has it of the king.

XVIII. The land of Ernulf de Hesdin

In OFFORD CLUNY Bului had 10 hides to the geld. [There is] land for 10 ploughs. Ernulf de Hesdin holds it now of the king, and the monks of Cluny of him. There are now 5 ploughs in demesne; and 20 villans and 8 bordars having 5 ploughs. There is a church and a priest, and 2 mills [rendering] 50s, and 24 acres of meadow. TRE, as now, worth £10.

[Folio 206: HUNTINGDONSHIRE]

XIX. The land of Eustace the Sheriff

NORMANCROSS HUNDRED

In SAWTRY Tosti had 3 hides and 3½ virgates to the geld. [There is] land for 8 ploughs. There are now 2 ploughs in demesne; and 10 villans and 2 bordars with 4 ploughs. There is a church, and 14 acres of meadow and 30 acres of woodland pasture. TRE worth 100s; now £4. Walter holds it of Eustace the sheriff.

In CALDECOTE Strikr had 5 hides to the geld. [There is] land for 6 ploughs. There is now 1 plough in demesne; and 10 villans and 2 bordars having 4 ploughs. There are 15 acres of scrubland. TRE worth £4; now £3. A knight of Eustace's holds it.

In 'WASHINGLEY' Thorir had 2½ hides to the geld. [There is] land for 4 ploughs. There is now 1 plough in demesne; and 10 villans and 1 bordar have 1½ ploughs. There are 12 acres of meadow, [and] woodland pasture 7 furlongs and 24 perches long and 3 furlongs broad. TRE, as now, worth 50s.

In Orton Longueville [in Peterborough], 8 hides and 1 virgate of land to the geld. [There is] land for 5 ploughs and 3 oxen. There were 7 sokemen. The SOKE [is] the king's, in Normancross [Hundred]. There John has of Eustace 3 oxen in a plough, and 9 acres of meadow. TRE worth 40s; now 20s.

OTHER SOKELAND

In Stilton, 2 hides and 1 virgate of land to the geld. [There is] land for 3 ploughs and 1 ox. John, Eustace's man, has 6 oxen ploughing there, and 2 sokemen and 2 villans with 1 plough. There are 16 acres of meadow and 5 acres of scrubland. TRE, as now, worth 40s.

In ORTON LONGUEVILLE [in Peterborough] Alsige had 7½ hides to the geld. [There is] land for 5 ploughs. There is now 1 plough in demesne; and 12 villans and 2 bordars with 1½ ploughs. There is a church, and 57 acres of meadow. TRE worth £4; now 40s.

In THE SAME PLACE, Ælfric [had] 2½ hides to the geld. [There is] land for 2 ploughs. The SOKE [is] in Normancross [Hundred]. Now Roger, Eustace's man, has 4 bordars, and 5 oxen in a plough there. TRE worth 20s; now 5s.

In CHESTERTON 2 brothers had 4 hides and 2 virgates of land to the geld. [There is] land for 7 ploughs. There are now 2 ploughs in demesne; and 10 villans and 2 bordars having 3 ploughs. There is a church and a priest, and 20 acres of meadow, and 1 customary due in the woodland of the Abbot of Peterborough rendering 2s. TRE worth £4; now the same. 2 knights hold it of Eustace.

In "Botuluesbrige" [in Huntingdon] Burgræd and Thorkil the priests had a church of ST MARY with 2 hides of land to the geld. [There is] land for 2 ploughs. Now they themselves hold it of Eustace, and have 2 ploughs there, and 3 acres of meadow. TRE, as now, worth 40s.

In Great Stukeley [...] Eustace has 1 virgate of land to the geld. It is waste. Herbert holds it of him.

KIMBOLTON HUNDRED

In SWINESHEAD [Beds.] Fursa had half a hide to the geld. [There is] land for half a plough, with sake and soke. There is now 1 villan, and 3 acres of meadow, [and] woodland pasture 1 league long and 1 furlong broad. TRE worth 15s; now 6s. Ralph holds it of Eustace.

In CATWORTH Æfic had 3 hides to the geld. [There is] land for 4 ploughs. There Eustace now has 2 ploughs, and 8 villans and 4 bordars having 4 ploughs, and 1 mill [rendering] 2s. TRE, as now, worth 60s. The king has sake and soke over this land.

In HARGRAVE [Northants] Langfer had 1 virgate of land to the geld. [There is] land for 2 oxen. Herbert, Eustace's man, ploughs there now with half a plough, and has 1 villan, and 6 acres of meadow. TRE, as now, worth 5s. Tovi claims this land [was] unjustly taken from him by Eustace.

In THE SAME PLACE Alwine Cild had 1 hide of land. [There is] land for 1½ ploughs. There is now 1 plough in demesne, and 7 acres of meadow and 2 acres of scrubland. TRE, as now, worth 20s. Herbert and Eadmær hold it of Eustace.

In Great Gidding 6 sokemen, that is, Alweald and his 5 brothers, had 4½ hides to the geld. [There is] land for 6 ploughs. The SOKE [is] in Alconbury, the king's manor. Now Eustace has it, and Ingelrann [holds] of him. There are now 2 ploughs in demesne; and 16 villans and 4 bordars with 6 ploughs. There are 22 acres of meadow. TRE, as now, worth £4. Alweald and his brothers claim that Eustace has unjustly taken this land from them. Of this land William Engaine claims half a virgate and 18 acres of land, with the witness of the whole hundred.

In Winwick Eskil had 2½ hides to the geld, with sake and soke. Eustace has it now, and Oilard [holds] of him.

In the same place Alweald, Leofwine and Elaf had 2½ hides to the geld. [There is] land for 2½ ploughs. The SOKE [is] in Alconbury, the king's manor. Now Eustace has it, and Oilard [holds] of him; and there are now 3 ploughs in demesne; and 15 villans having 6 ploughs, and 20 acres of meadow. TRE, as now, worth £4.

In Thurning [Northants], 5 hides to the geld. [There is] land for 5 ploughs. The SOKE [is] in Alconbury. There are now 1½ ploughs in demesne; and 6 villans and 1 bordar have 2½ ploughs. There are 24 acres of meadow. TRE, as now, worth 60s. Alvred and Joscelin hold it of Eustace. Robert Despenser claims 1 virgate and 1 hide.

In Luddington in the Brook [Northants], 2½ hides to the geld. [There is] land for 3 ploughs. The SOKE [is] in Alconbury, the king's manor. There is now 1 plough in demesne; and 1

villan and 6 bordars with 1 plough, and 4 acres of meadow. TRE worth 60s; now 40s. Ingelrann and Herlwin hold it of Eustace.

In Alconbury Weston, 1 hide to the geld. [There is] land for 2 ploughs. The SOKE [is] in Alconbury. There is now half a plough in demesne; and 4 villans with half a plough. TRE, as now, worth 20s. Gulbert holds it of Eustace.

In Woolley Goda and Wulfric had half a hide of land to the geld. [There is] land for 1 plough. Eustace has it now.

In Grafham Eustace has half a hide, and Oilard the larderer [holds] of him, and ploughs there with 6 oxen. It is worth 10s.

TOSELAND HUNDRED

In HEMINGFORD GREY Ordwig had 4 hides to the geld. [There is] land for 3 ploughs.

[Folio 206V: HUNTINGDONSHIRE]

There is now 1 plough in demesne; and 2 villans and 2 bordars having 2 oxen in a plough. There are 20 acres of meadow. TRE worth 40s; now 20s.

In Papworth St Agnes [Cambs.], 1 hide to the geld. [There is] land for 1 plough. There Eustace has 1 plough in demesne, and 10 acres of meadow. TRE worth 60s; now 20s.

In OFFORD D'ARCY Æthelwine the sheriff had 3 hides to the geld. [There is] land for 3 ploughs. There are now 4 bordars with 2 oxen, and 4 acres of meadow. TRE worth 40s; now 12s. Odo holds it of Eustace.

In Waresley Sumarlithur had half a hide to the geld. [There is] land for half a plough. It is waste. Roger holds it of Eustace. TRE worth 10s; now 2s.

In HAIL WESTON Algeat had 1½ hides to the geld. [There is] land for 1½ ploughs. In demesne is half a hide of this land. There 4 villans have 1 plough now. [There are] 20 acres of woodland pasture. TRE worth 40s; now 20s. Countess Judith claims this land against Eustace.

In THE SAME PLACE Godwine had half a hide to the geld. [There is] land for half a plough. Eustace has half a plough there, and 10 acres of meadow and 10 acres of woodland pasture. TRE worth 10s; now 5s.

In SOUTHOE Dunning had 4½ hides to the geld. [There is] land for 8 ploughs. There is now 1 plough in demesne, on 1½ hides of this land; and 12 villans having 5 ploughs, and 1 fishery [rendering] 1,000 eels and 3 gifts a year worth 49d. There are 20 acres of meadow and 48 acres of woodland pasture. TRE worth 100s; now 70s.

In WEST PERRY Alwine Deule had 1 hide to the geld. [There is] land for 2 ploughs. There are now 1½ ploughs in demesne; and 6 villans with 1 plough. There is a church, and 4 acres of meadow, [and] woodland pasture 1 league long and 4 furlongs broad. TRE, as now, worth 40s.

In Boughton Godric the priest [had] 1 hide to the geld. [There is] land for 2 ploughs. There is now 1 plough; and 5 villans have half a plough. There are 7 acres of meadow. TRE worth 20s; now 10s.

In CATWORTH King Edward had 2 hides to the geld. [There is] land for 3 ploughs. There were 8 thegns having sake and soke under the king. Eustace held this land, and now it is in the king's hand, and there are 8 men, and under them 7 bordars with 3 ploughs. There are 3 acres of meadow. TRE worth 40s; now 30s.

XX. The land of Countess Judith

NORMANCROSS HUNDRED

In CONINGTON Thorkil had 9 hides to the geld. [There is] land for 15 ploughs. Of this land, 2½ hides are in demesne. There are now 2 ploughs, and 26 villans having 13 ploughs. There is a church and a priest, and 40 acres of meadow. TRE, as now, worth £9. Of this land, 6 hides belonged to the Church of ST MARY of Thorney. Thorkil held them of the abbot, and made a voluntary payment from them, but the men of the hundred do not know how much. Countess Judith holds it.

In SAWTRY Thorkil had 10 hides to the geld. [There is] land for 15 ploughs. Of this land, 2½ hides are in demesne. There Countess Judith [has] 2 ploughs now, and 27 villans having 10 ploughs. There is a priest and a church, and 40 acres of meadow, [and] woodland pasture 18 furlongs long and 4 furlongs broad. TRE, as now, worth £10.

'HURSTINGSTONE' HUNDRED

In GREAT STUKELEY Hungifu had 3 hides to the geld. [There is] land for 16 ploughs, and in demesne [she had] land for 2 ploughs, apart from the aforesaid hides. There Countess Judith [has] 3 ploughs now, and 18 villans and 8 bordars with 5 ploughs. There is a church and a priest, and 26 acres of meadow, [and] woodland pasture 9 furlongs long and 8 furlongs broad. TRE, as now, worth £12. Eustace claims it.

KIMBOLTON HUNDRED

In MOLESWORTH Northmann had 4 hides to the geld. [There is] land for 4 ploughs. Of this land, 1 hide is in demesne. There is now 1 plough, and 15 villans and 2 bordars having 5 ploughs. There are 60 acres of meadow. TRE, as now, worth £4. Eustace holds it of the countess.

TOSELAND HUNDRED

In COTTON Earl Tosti had 4 hides to the geld. [There is] land for 8 ploughs. The SOKE belongs to Eynesbury with all customary dues. There Countess Judith now has 12 villans having 2 ploughs, and 20 acres of meadow. The value [is included] under Eynesbury. Of this land, Gilbert the priest has 2 hides of the countess, and has there 1 plough, and 6 villans with 1 plough, and 20 acres of meadow. It is worth 40s.

In EYNESBURY King Edward had 9 hides to the geld. [There is] land for 28 ploughs. There the countess now has 4 ploughs in demesne; and 34 villans and 8 bordars having 28 ploughs. There is a church and a priest, and 2 mills [rendering] 32s, and 60 acres of woodland pasture. In the same vill is

a sheep-fold for 662 sheep, and 60 acres of meadow which the countess gave to St Helen. It is worth 70s.

Of the aforesaid 9 hides, Gilbert the priest holds 2 hides of the countess, and has 2 ploughs in demesne there, and 8 acres of meadow. It is worth 40s. Of the same land, Alan, her steward, has 2 hides of her. There are 2 bordars, and it is worth 10s. TRE the manor was worth £20; now the demesne of the countess is worth £14.12s.

In OFFORD D'ARCY Northmann had 3 hides to the geld.

[Folio 207: HUNTINGDONSHIRE]

[There is] land for 8 ploughs. Hugh holds it of the countess. There is now 1 plough in demesne; and 11 villans and 4 bordars having 6 ploughs. There are 16 acres of meadow. TRE worth £6; now 100s.

In GREAT PAXTON with 3 Berewicks King Edward had 25 hides to the geld. [There is] land for 41 ploughs. There the countess now has 5 ploughs in demesne; and 60 villans and 8 bordars having 34 ploughs. There is a church and a priest, and 3 mills [rendering] 64s, and 80 acres of meadow, woodland pasture half a league long and half a league and 1 furlong broad, and other woodland half a league long and 3 furlongs broad. 1 hide of this land belongs to the church. TRE worth £29.4s; now £33.10s.

In DIDDINGTON Earl Waltheof had 3 hides to the geld. [There is] land for 3 ploughs and 6 oxen. There is now 1 plough in demesne; and 8 villans and 1 bordar with 1 plough. There are 22 acres of meadow, [and] woodland pasture 5 furlongs long and 4 furlongs broad. TRE worth 40s; now 60s. Alan holds it of the countess.

XXI. The land of Gilbert de Ghent

TOSELAND HUNDRED

In FENSTANTON Ulf had 13 hides to the geld. [There is] land for 18 ploughs. There Gilbert de Ghent now [has] 2 ploughs in demesne; and 24 villans and 8 bordars having 11 ploughs. There is a church and a priest, and 80 acres of meadow. TRE worth £17; now £16.

XXII. The land of Aubrey de Vere

TOSELAND HUNDRED

In YELLING Ælfric had 5 hides to the geld. [There is] land for 8 ploughs. There are now 2 ploughs in demesne; and 10 villans and 2 bordars with 3 ploughs. There is a church and a priest, and 40 acres of meadow and 5 acres of scrubland. TRE, as now, worth £4.

In HEMINGFORD GREY Ælfric had 11 hides to the geld. [There is] land for 7 ploughs. There are now 2 ploughs in demesne; and 13 villans and 4 bordars having 5 ploughs. There are 2 mills [rendering] £6, and a fishpond [rendering] 6s, and 50 acres of meadow. TRE, as now, worth £12. Ælfric held these 2 manors of the Abbot of Ramsey TRE; now

Aubrey de Vere holds them of the king, and Ralph fitzOsmund [holds] of him.

XXIII. The land of William fitzAnsculf

TOSELAND HUNDRED

In WARESLEY Magni and Leofa had 2½ hides to the geld. [There is] land for 5 ploughs. There are now 2 ploughs in demesne; and 5 villans and 1 bordar having 2½ ploughs. There is a church and a priest, and 20 acres of meadow, and 5 acres of scrubland. TRE worth 40s; now 50s. Ranulph brother of Ilger holds this manor of William fitzAnsculf.

XXIIII. The land of Ranulph brother of Ilger

TOSELAND HUNDRED

In EVERTON [Beds.] Ingvar had 7 hides to the geld. [There is] land for 18 ploughs. There are now 2 ploughs in demesne; and 19 villans and 2 bordars having 9 ploughs. There is a priest and a church, and 15 acres of meadow and 40 acres of scrubland. TRE worth £10; now £7. Ranulph brother of Ilger holds it of the king.

XXV. The land of Robert Fafiton

TOSELAND HUNDRED

In HAIL WESTON Saxi and Wulfwine had 2 hides to the geld. [There is] land for 6 ploughs. There Robert fitzFafiton now has 2 ploughs in demesne; and 8 villans with 3 ploughs, and 40 acres of woodland pasture. TRE worth £6; now £4.

In SOUTHOE Saxi had 2 hides to the geld. [There is] land for 3 ploughs. There Robert now [has] 1 plough in demesne; and 4 villans with 1 plough, and 10 acres of meadow, and 10 acres of woodland pasture and 5 acres of scrubland. TRE worth 40s; now 20s.

XXVI. The land of William Engaine

'LEIGHTONSTONE' HUNDRED

In [Great and Little] GIDDING Beorhtgifu had 4½ hides to the geld. The SOKE was in the Hundred of "Cresseuuelle". There William Engaine now has 2 ploughs in demesne; and 15 villans and 3 bordars having 5 ploughs, and 22 acres of meadow. TRE worth 40s; now £4.

XXVII. The land of Ralph fitzOsmund

TOSELAND HUNDRED

In HEMINGFORD [?Abbots] Alwine Black had 1 hide to the geld. [There is] land for 1 plough. It is waste. Ralph fitzOsmund has it.

XXVIII. The land of Rohais wife of Richard fitzGilbert

TOSELAND HUNDRED

In EYNESBURY Robert fitzWimarc had 15 hides to the geld. [There is] land for 27 ploughs. There Rohais, Richard's wife, now has 7 ploughs in demesne.

In the same place St Neot has of her 3 ploughs in demesne; and in the same vill 19 villans and 5 bordars having 7 ploughs. There is 1 mill [rendering] 23s, and 1 fishery which is valued with the manor, and 65½ acres of meadow. TRE worth £24; now £21, apart from the sustenance of the monks, which is valued at £4.

William the Breton holds 2 hides and 1 virgate of the same land of her, and has half a plough in demesne; and 3 villans and 4 bordars with 1 plough. It is worth 30s.

[Folio 207V: HUNTINGDONSHIRE]

XXIX. The land of the King's Thegns

In 'WASHINGLEY' Ketilbert had 2½ hides to the geld. [There is] land for 4 ploughs. The same man himself holds of the king, and has 1 plough there, and 10 villans with 4 ploughs. There is a church and a priest, and 12 acres of meadow, [and] woodland pasture 7 furlongs long and 10½ furlongs broad. TRE, as now, worth 10s.

'LEIGHTONSTONE' HUNDRED

In Keysoe [Beds.] Alwine had 1 virgate of land to the geld, with sake and soke. [There is] land for 2 oxen. It belongs to Bedfordshire, but gives geld in Huntingdonshire. The same man himself holds now of the king, and has there 1 villan with 2 oxen in a plough. TRE worth 16d; now the same.

In CATWORTH Æfic had 3 hides to the geld. [There is] land for 4 ploughs. Eric holds it now of the king. And the same man has under the king 1 hide to the geld. [There is] land for 1 plough. He has 2 villans there, and 6 acres of meadow. TRE worth 40s; now 20s.

In Brampton Alric [had] 1 hide and 1 virgate of land to the geld. [There is] land for 10 oxen. There are 3 bordars and 1 plough. It is worth 30s.

In WOOLLEY Golda and Wulfric his son had 3 hides to the geld. [There is] land for 6 ploughs. The same men themselves have it of the king. There is 1 plough in demesne; and 14 villans having 5 ploughs, and 20 acres of meadow. TRE, as now, worth 60s.

In Sawtry Æthelwine [had] half a carucate to the geld. [There is] land for 6 oxen. His wife holds it now of the king, and has 1 plough there, and 2 acres of meadow. TRE, as now, worth 10s.

[Folio 208: [HUNTINGDONSHIRE]

The jurors in Huntingdon say that the Church of ST MARY of the borough and the land which pertains to it belonged to the Church of Thorney, but the abbot gave it in pledge to the burgesses. However, King Edward gave it to Vitalis and Bernard, his priests, and they themselves sold it to Hugh, King Edward's chamberlain. But Hugh sold it to 2 priests of Huntingdon, and they have the seal of King Edward for it. Eustace has it now without livery officer, and without writ, and without seisor.

Eustace took away by force the house of Leofgifu, and gave it to Ogier of London.

They bear witness that the land of Hunæf and Gos was under the hand of King Edward on the day when he was alive and dead, and that they held of him, not of the earl. But [the jurors] say they they had heard that King William should have given it to Waltheof.

Concerning the 5 hides of Broughton, they say that it was the land of sokemen TRE but the same king [Edward] gave the land and the soke over them to St Benedict of Ramsey, in return for a service which Abbot Ælfwine did for him in Saxony, and ever afterwards [the saint] has had it.

The shire bears witness that the land of Beorhtmær Belehorne was reeveland TRE, and belonged to the [king's] farm.

They bear witness that the land of Alwine the priest belonged to the abbot and was both the priest's and the reeve's land.

They bear witness that Ælfric's lands in Yelling and Hemingford Grey belonged to St Benedict and that they were granted to Ælfric for the term of his life on this condition, that after his death they ought to return to the church, and Boxted [Essex] with them. But Ælfric himself was killed in the Battle of Hastings, and the abbot took back his lands [and held them] until Aubrey de Vere disseised him.

Concerning 2 hides which Ralph fitzOsmund holds in Hemingford [?Abbots], they say that 1 of them belonged to the demesne of the Church of Ramsey in King Edward's day, and that he holds it against the abbot's will. Concerning the other hide, they say that Godric held it of the abbot, but when the abbot was in Denmark, Osmund, Ralph's father, seized it from Sæwine the falconer, to whom the abbot had given it for love of the king.

Concerning Sumarlithr, they say that he held his land of Thorulf, who gave it to him, and afterwards of his sons, and that they themselves had sake and soke over him.

They say that the land of Wulfwine Cild of Hail Weston was a manor by itself, and did not belong to Kimbolton, but that nevertheless he was a man of Earl Harold.

Concerning 1½ hides of land which belonged to Algeat, the jurors say that Algeat himself held them of Earl Tosti, with sake and soke, and afterwards of Waltheof.

Godric the priest likewise held 1 hide of land of Earl Waltheof TRE, which Eustace holds now.

They say that the land of Godwine of Hail Weston in no way belonged to Saxi, Fafiton's predecessor.

The men of the shire bear witness that King Edward gave Swineshead [Beds.] to Earl Siward [with] sake and soke, and

so Earl Harold had it, except that [the men] paid geld in the hundred, and went against the enemy with them.

Concerning the land of Fursa, the soke was the king's.

King Edward had soke over 1 virgate of land of Alwine Deule in Pertenhall [Beds.].

They say that the hide of land which Wulfwine Cild had in Catworth was in the king's soke, and that Earl Harold did not have it.

In Little Catworth the same Wulfwine had 1 hide over which King Edward always had sake and soke, but he could give and sell the land to whom he wished. But the men of the countess say that the king gave the land to Earl Waltheof.

The shire bears witness that the third part of half a hide which lies in Easton and pays geld in Bedfordshire belongs to the Abbot of Ely's manor of Spaldwick, and so the abbot had it TRE and for 5 years after the coming of King William. Eustace seized this [land] by force from the church, and kept it.

They say that Keyston was and is [part] of the farm of King Edward, and although Ælfric the sheriff resided in that vill, he nevertheless always paid the king's farm from it, and his sons after him, until Eustace received the shrievalty, nor have they ever seen or heard the sealed writ of King Edward which had put it outside his farm.

Alweald and his brothers claim that Eustace took away their land from them unjustly, and the shire denies that it saw the seal or the seisor who gave him seisin of it.

On that day when King Edward was alive and dead, Great Gidding was a Berewick of Alconbury in the king's farm.

The shire bears witness that Buckworth was a Berewick of Great Paxton TRE.

They say that 36 hides of land in Brampton which Richard Engaine claims belong to the forest were [part] of the king's demesne farm, and did not belong to the forest.

They say that Grafham was and is of the king's soke, and that they have not seen the writ nor the seisor who delivered it to Eustace.

Concerning 6 hides in Conington, they said that they heard

[Folio 208V: [HUNTINGDONSHIRE]]

that they had formerly belonged to the Church of Thorney, and that they had been granted to Thorkil on such a condition that after his death they ought to return to the church with the other 3 hides of the same vill. This they said that they had heard, but had not seen, nor had they been present.

Concerning the land of Tosti of Sawtry, they say that Erik his brother bequeathed it to the Church of Ramsey after his death and that of his brother and sister.

Concerning Old Fletton [in Peterborough], they say that in King Edward's day the whole belonged to the Church of Peterborough, and it ought to belong [to it].

Concerning Leofric's land, they say that it was in the king's soke, but Bishop Remigius has shown the writ of King Edward by which he gave Leofric with all his land into the bishopric of Lincoln, with sake and soke.

BEDFORDSHIRE

BEDFORD was assessed at a half-hundred TRE, and it is so now for military expeditions by land and sea. The land of this vill was never hidated, nor is it now except 1 hide which belonged to the Church of St Paul in alms TRE, and now belongs [to it] as of right. But Bishop Remigius put it outside the almsland of the Church of St Paul, unjustly as the men say, and now holds it and whatever belongs to it. It is worth 100s.

I KING WILLIAM
II The Bishop of Bayeux
III The Bishop of Coutances
IIII The Bishop of Lincoln
V The Bishop of Durham
VI The Abbot of St Edmundsbury
VII The Abbot of Peterborough
VIII The Abbot of Ramsey
IX The Abbot of Westminster
X The Abbot of Thorney
XI The Abbess of Barking
XII The canons of London
XIII The canons of Bedford
XIIII Earnwine the priest
XV Count Eustace
XVI Walter Giffard
XVII William de Warenne
XVIII William de Eu
XIX Miles Crispin
XX Ernulf de Hesdin
XXI Eudo the steward
XXII William Peverel
XXIII Hugh de Beauchamp
XXIIII Nigel d'Aubigny
XXV William Speke
XXVI Robert de Tosny
XXVII Gilbert de Ghent
XXVIII Robert d'Oilly
XXIX Ranulph brother of Ilger
XXX Robert Fafiton
XXXI Alvred of Lincoln
XXXII Walter the Fleming
XXXIII Walter brother of Seiher
XXXIIII Hugh the Fleming
XXXV Hugh the butler
XXXVI Sigar de Chocques
XXXVII Gunfrid de Chocques
XXXVIII Richard son of Count Gilbert

XXXIX Richard Puignant
XL William the chamberlain
XLI William Lovet
XLII William
XLIII Henry fitzAzur
XLIIII Osbern fitzRichard
XLV Osbern fitzWalter
XLVI Osbern the fisherman
XLVII Turstin the chamberlain
XLVIII Gilbert fitzSalomon
XLIX Albert of Lorraine
L David d'Argentan
LI Ralph de l'Isle
LII Joscelin the Breton
LIII Countess Judith
LIIII Adeliza wife of Hugh de Grandmesnil
LV Azelina wife of Ralph Taillebois
LVI The burgesses of Bedford
LVI The king's reeves and beadles and almsmen

The land of the King

LEIGHTON BUZZARD, a demesne manor of the king, is now assessed at 47 hides. TRE there were only 30 hides. Of these 47 hides, 43 hides are in the king's hand. There is land for 52 ploughs. In demesne are 6 ploughs; and the villans have 46 ploughs. There are 82 villans and 30 bordars and 2 slaves, and 2 mills rendering 30s, meadow for 40 ploughs, [and] woodland for 100 pigs. The toll from the market renders £7. All together it renders yearly £22 by weight and half a day to the King's farm [sic] in grain and honey and other things pertaining to the farm. For the queen's use [it renders] 2 ounces of gold, and for 1 pack-horse and [for] customary payment for the dogs 70s, and 100s. by weight and 40s. of blanch silver. Ivo Taillebois imposed this as an additional payment, and 1 ounce of gold for the use of the sheriff yearly.

Of the land of this manor Wynsige the chamberlain held 10 hides of King Edward which Ralph Taillebois added to Leighton Buzzard, where they did not belong TRE. And again the same Ralph added to this manor another 7 hides which were not in it TRE. Starcher, a thegn of King Edward, held these 7 hides.

Bishop Remigius holds the church of this manor, with 4 hides which belong to it, and these 4 [hides] are reckoned in the 47 hides of the manor. There is land for 3 ploughs. In demesne is 1 plough; and the villans [have] 1 plough and there could be another. There are 6 villans and 6 bordars, [and] meadow for

3 ploughs. This land, with the church, is and was worth £4. Bishop Wulfwig held it TRE.

LUTON, a demesne manor of the king, is assessed at 30 hides. There is land for 82 ploughs. In demesne [are] 4 ploughs. The villans [have] 80 ploughs, less 2. There are 80 villans and 47 bordars, and 6 mills rendering 100s, meadow for 4 ploughs, woodland for 2,000 pigs, and from customary dues 10s8d. From the toll and the market 100s.

All together it renders yearly £30 by weight and half a day's [farm] in grain and honey and other customary dues pertaining to the king's farm.

To the queen [it renders] 4 ounces of gold, and from a pack-horse and other small customary dues 70s, and from customary dues for the dogs £6.10s; and from the additional payment which IVO Taillebois imposed £7 by weight and 40s of blanch silver, and 1 ounce of gold for the sheriiff.

William, the king's chamberlain, holds the church of this manor, with 5 hides of land which belong to it. These 5 hides are [part] of the 30 hides of the manor. There is land for 6 ploughs. In demesne [is] 1 plough; and the villans have 5 ploughs. There are 11 villans and 4 bordars and 3 slaves, and 1 mill [rendering] 10s. The church renders 20s a year. [There is] woodland for 50 pigs. All together it is and was worth 60s. Morcar the priest held this church with its land TRE.

[Folio 209V: BEDFORDSHIRE]

HOUGHTON REGIS, a demesne manor of the king, is assessed at 10 hides. There is land for 24 ploughs. In demesne [are] 2 ploughs; and the villans [have] 22 ploughs. There are 38 villans and 12 bordars, meadow for 12 ploughs [and] woodland for 100 pigs. All together it renders yearly £10 by weight, and half a day's [farm] in grain and honey and other things pertaining to the king's farm. From small customary dues and from 1 pack-horse 65s; from customary dues for the dogs 65s; and to the queen 2 ounces of gold; from the additional payment which IVO Taillebois imposed £3 by weight, and 20s of blanch silver, and 1 ounce of gold for the sheriff.

William the chamberlain holds the church of this manor with half a hide which belongs to it, and it is [part] of the 10 hides of the manor. There is land for half a plough, and there is [half a plough]. It is worth 12s a year.

SEWELL was assessed at 3 hides TRE. There is land for 2 ploughs. There are 1½ ploughs, and there can be another half [-plough. There is] meadow for 4 oxen. There is 1 villan and 4 bordars. This land is and was worth 20s. Wælhræfn, a man of Queen Edith, held this and could give it to whom he wished. It belonged to "Odecroft" Hundred TRE but Ralph Taillebois added it to the manor of Houghton Regis with King William's consent, for the additional payment which it gave to him. So state the men of the same Ralph according to what they heard him say.

FLITTON HUNDRED

BISCOT was assessed at 5 hides TRE. There is land for 5 ploughs. There are 2 ploughs in demesne; and 10 villans have 3 ploughs. There are 3 slaves, and meadow for 3 ploughs. In all it is worth 40s; when Ralph Taillebois held it, the same; TRE 60s. Edwin, a man of Esger the staller, held this manor and could do with it what he wished. Ralph Taillebois [...] added this to Luton, the king's manor, for the additional payment which it gave him, and alienated it from the hundred in which it was assessed TRE. On the other hand he took another 5 hides from another hundred and placed them in Flitton Hundred.

II. The land of the Bishop of Bayeux

IN THE HALF-HUNDRED OF STANBRIDGE

THE BISHOP OF BAYEUX holds EATON BRAY. It is assessed at 12 hides and 1 virgate. There is land for 20 ploughs. In demesne [are] 2 hides, and there are 4 ploughs and there can be 2 more. The villans have 8 ploughs and there can be 6 more. There are 20 villans and 13 bordars and 2 slaves, meadow for 6 ploughs, woodland for 300 pigs and from it 12d. In all it is worth £16; when received, £20; TRE the same. Alsige, a man of Queen Edith, held this manor and could give and sell.

In the HUNDRED of 'Manshead' Ansgot of Rochester holds 2 hides in Eversholt of the Bishop of Bayeux's fief. There is land for 2 ploughs. There is 1 [plough] and there can be another. There are 4 villans and 1 bordar, meadow for 1 plough, [and] woodland for 50 pigs. All together it is worth 20s; when received, 30s; TRE 40s 4 thegns held this land TRE and could give and sell.

The same Ansgot holds of the same bishop 4 hides in Milton Bryan. [There is] land for 4 ploughs. In demesne [is] 1 plough and there can be another. The villans [have] 2 ploughs. There are 4 villans and 3 bordars and 8 slaves, meadow for 4 ploughs, [and] woodland for 30 pigs. All together it is worth, and was worth when received, £4; TRE 40s. 7 sokemen held this land and could give and sell it TRE.

In the Hundred of 'Stodden' Tovi the priest holds half a hide of the bishop in Bolnhurst. There is land for 1 plough, and there is [1 plough], and 1 villan and 1 bordar, meadow for half a plough, [and] woodland for 30 pigs. All together it is worth 10s; and as much when received; TRE 12s. Azur, a man of Burgræd, held this land and could sell to whom he wished.

IN THE SAME PLACE 2 sokemen hold of the bishop half a hide. There is land for 1 plough, and there is [1 plough], with 2 bordars. [There is] woodland for 4 pigs. All together it is worth 10s; and as much when received; TR[E] 12s. The same men themselves who hold it held it TRE, and they could sell and give it.

In the Half-Hundred of 'Buckelowe' Herbert fitzIvo holds of the bishop 3 hides and 3 virgates in Stagsden. There is land for 4 ploughs. There are now 3½ ploughs and there can be a half [-plough more]. There are 12 villans and 6 bordars, meadow for 1 plough, [and] woodland for 40 pigs. All together it is worth £7; when received, £9; TRE £12. 12 sokemen held this land. They were King Edward's men and could sell.

In the Hundred of 'Willey' 2 sokemen hold in Carlton 1 hide and 1 virgate of Herbert fitzIvo and he himself [holds] of the bishop. There is land for 1½ ploughs, and there are [1½ ploughs, and] meadow for 1 plough. All together it is worth 26s8d; when received and TRE 30s. The same men themselves held this land who now hold it, and they could give and sell it.

In Turvey Wimund holds of Herbert and he himself [holds] of the bishop 1 hide. There is land for 1 plough, and there is [1 plough, and] meadow for half a plough. All together it is worth 20s; when received and TRE 40s. A man of Æthelweald of Stevington held this land and could sell.

In the Hundred of Barford Herbert [holds] of the bishop, and his nephew Hugh holds of him, 5 hides in Wilden. There is land for 16 ploughs. In demesne there are now no [ploughs], and there can be 3. The villans have 10 ploughs and there can be 3 more. There are 20 sokemen and 12 bordars and 1 slave, meadow for 6 ploughs, [and] woodland for 6 pigs. All together it is worth £9; when received, £12; TRE £20. 24 sokemen held this manor and they could give and sell their land to whom they wished.

III. The land of the Bishop of Coutances

IN 'STODDEN' HUNDRED

THE BISHOP OF COUTANCES holds KNOTTING. It is assessed at 5 hides. There is land for 5 ploughs. In demesne [are] 3 hides, and there are 2 ploughs. The villans have 3 ploughs. There are 8 villans and 5 bordars and 4 slaves, meadow for 2 ploughs, [and] woodland for 400 pigs. It is worth £4; when received, £3; and as much TRE. Burgræd held this manor TRE.

The bishop himself holds MELCHBOURNE. It is assessed at 10 hides. There is land for 10 ploughs. In demesne [are] 3 hides, and 3 ploughs. The villans have 7 ploughs. There are 13 villans and 15 bordars and 3 slaves, meadow for [...] ploughs, [and] woodland for 100 pigs. It is worth £8; when received, 100s; TRE £6. Burgræd held this manor, and there were 6 sokemen, and they could give and sell their land without leave.

The bishop himself holds 4 hides in [Lower and Upper] DEAN. There is land for 5 [?ploughs], and there are [5 ploughs]. There are 6 sokemen and 6 bordars and 2 slaves. It is worth 60s; when received, the same; TRE 40s 6 sokemen held this manor.

[Folio 210: BEDFORDSHIRE]

They were men of Burgræd. 3½ hides of the king's soke they could give and sell and withdraw to another lord without leave of Burgræd. Half a hide, however, they could not give or sell without his his [sic] leave.

GEOFFREY de Trelly holds YELDEN of the Bishop of Coutances. It is assessed at 10 hides. There is land for 15 ploughs. In demesne are 4 ploughs; and the villans have 11 ploughs. There are 17 villans and 1 knight and 12 bordars and 1 slave, meadow for 4 ploughs, [and] woodland for 20 pigs. In all it is worth £9; when received, 100s; [TR] E £8. Burgræd held this manor, and in it were 5 sokemen who held 5 hides of this land and could give or sell them to whom they wished.

Of the bishop himself William, his steward, holds SHELTON [near Swineshead]. It is assessed at 5 hides. There is land for 6 ploughs. In demesne [are] 2 ploughs; and the villans have 4. There are 14 [? villans] and 5 bordars and 3 slaves, and 1 mill [rendering] 3s, meadow for 1 plough, [and] woodland for 4 pigs. It is worth 100s; when received, 60s; TRE £4. Wulfgifu held this manor under Burgræd. She could not give nor sell it without his leave.

In Easton [Hunts.] 4 sokemen hold of the Bishop of Coutances 3 virgates of land. [There is] land for 1 plough, and there is [1 plough]. This land is and was worth 10s; TRE 5s. The same men themselves who hold it held it [TRE]. They were men of Burgraelig;d and could give it to whom they wished. In these 3 virgates the bishop claims against Sigar de Chocques 20 acres of woodland which belonged there TRE and this the men of the hundred attest.

In Riseley 2 Frenchmen and 6 Englishmen hold 6 hides of the bishop. There is land for 7 ploughs, and there are [7 ploughs]. There are 6 villans and 7 bordars and 1 slave, meadow for 3 ploughs, [and] woodland for 200 pigs. It is worth 72s; when received, the same; TRE 100s. Of this land Burgræd held 2 hides in demesne, and 6 sokemen, his men, held 4 hides, which they could give and sell where they wished.

In Bolnhurst the same bishop holds 3 virgates of land in exchange for [?] Bleadon [Som.]. There is land for 1½ ploughs, and there are [1½ ploughs. There is] 1 villan and 4 bordars, meadow for 1 plough, [and] woodland for 20 pigs. It is worth 15s; when received, the same; TRE 20s. Guthmund, a man of King Edward, held this land; he could sell to whom he wished.

In Newton Bromswold [Northants] William, his steward, holds 1 virgate of the bishop. It is and was worth 12d; TRE 16d. Alwine, a man of Burgræd, held this land; he could not give or sell it without his leave.

In the Hundred of 'Willey' Geoffrey de Trelly holds 4 hides of the bishop. There is land for 5 ploughs. In demesne are 2 ploughs; and the villans have 3 ploughs. There are 14 villans and 5 bordars and 4 slaves, [and] meadow for 4 ploughs. It is and was worth 100s. Thorbert, a man of King Edward, held this manor and could sell. The bishop holds this land in exchange for [?] Bleadon [Som.], as his men say.

In TURVEY the same bishop holds 4 hides. There is land for 6 ploughs. In demesne are 2 hides and 3 ploughs. There 3 villans have 3 ploughs, and [there are] 8 bordars and 1 slave, and 1 mill [rendering] 20s, meadow for 2 ploughs, [and] woodland for 40 pigs. It is worth £6; when received, 40s; TRE £6. 3 sokemen, men of King Edward, held this manor and could sell and give. The bishop has this land in exchange for [?] Bleadon [Som.], as his men say.

In Hinwick Turstin holds 1½ hides of the bishop. There is land for 2 ploughs. In demesne is 1 [plough]; and 3 villans have 1 plough, and [there is] 1 bordar. It is worth 20s.

In Sharnbrook a certain Englishman, Thorgisl, holds half a hide of the bishop. There is land for 1 plough, and there is [1 plough], and 1 villan, [and] meadow for 1 plough. It is worth 6s; when received, 3s; TRE 15s. Alwine, a man of Burgræd, held this land and could give it to whom he wished.

In the same vill 7 sokemen hold 3 hides of the bishop. [There is] land for 3 ploughs, and there are [3 ploughs, and] woodland for 24 pigs. It is worth 24s; when received, the same; TRE 6os. The same men themselves held it TRE. They were men of Burgræd and could give and sell it without his leave.

In the same [vill] Humphrey holds half a hide of the bishop. There is land for 1 plough, and there is [1 plough], and 2 bordars, [and] woodland for 30 pigs. It is worth 6s; when received, 10s; TRE 20s. Ælfric, a man of Burgræd, held this land and could give and sell it to whom he wished.

In the same [vill] the bishop holds half a hide. There is land for 6 oxen. There are 4 bordars. It is worth 3s; and as much when received; TRE 5s. Burgræd, a thegn of King Edward, held this land and could do what he wished [with it].

In Rushden [Northants] Alweald holds half a hide of the bishop. [There is] land for 6 oxen. There is half a plough, [and] meadow for 6 oxen. It is worth 5s; and as much when received; TRE 10s. Ælfric held this land; he was a man of Burgræd, and could sell to whom he wished.

IIII. The land of the Bishop of Lincoln

IN 'STODDEN' HUNDRED

Bishop REMIGIUS holds in [Lower and Upper] DEAN 2 hides and half a virgate, and Godfrey [holds] of him. There is land for 3½ ploughs. In demesne are 2 ploughs; and the villans have 1½ ploughs. There are 8 bordars and 2 slaves, [and] meadow for 1 plough. It is worth 40s; when received, 30s; and as much TRE. Godric, a thegn of King Edward, held this land, and he could do what he wished with his land.

In Easton [Hunts.] William de Cairon holds half a hide and half a virgate of the bishop. There is land for 1 plough, and there is [1 plough], and 1 bordar and 3 slaves, meadow for 1 plough, [and] woodland for 100 pigs. It is worth 15s; when received, 10s; and as much TRE. Alwine Deule, a man of the Bishop of Lincoln, held this land and could do with it what he wished. The soke, however, always belonged to the bishop. In this land of the bishopric William de Cairon lays claim to 60 acres, both field and woodland, against Hugh de Beauchamp, of which Ralph Taillebois disseised the father of the same William who held this land TRE, as the men of the hundred say.

In Riseley Godfrey holds 1 hide of the bishop. There is land for 1 plough, and there is [1 plough]. There is 1 villan and 1 bordar, meadow for half a plough, [and] woodland for 20 pigs pigs [sic]. It is and was worth 10s; TRE 20s. Godric, a thegn of King Edward, held this land and could do what he wished [with it].

In the Half-Hundred of 'Buckelowe' Earnwine the priest holds of Bishop Remigius 1 hide and 1 virgate in Biddenham. There is land for 1 plough, and there is [1 plough]. There is 1 villan, and 1 mill rendering 25s a year, [and] meadow for 1 plough. It is and was worth 40s. Leofric, a man of the Bishop of Lincoln, held this land, but he could not give nor sell it without his leave.

In the Hundred of Barford Ivo Taillebois holds of the bishop half a hide in Goldington. There is land for half a plough, and there is [half a plough], with 2 villans. [There is] meadow for half a plough. It is and was worth 6s. Alwine Sac, a man of the Bishop of Lincoln, held it and could do with it what he wished.

In the Hundred of Biggleswade William de Cairon holds of Bishop Remigius 1 hide and 1 virgate and 3 parts of 1 virgate in Tempsford. There is land for 2 ploughs, and there is 1 villan, meadow for 1 plough, and 2 mills rendering 40s and 120 eels. It is worth 60s; when received, 40s; TRE 100s. Alwine Deule held it. He was the king's man and could do with it what he wished.

[Folio 210V: BEDFORDSHIRE]

In the HUNDRED of Clifton William de Cairon [holds] of Bishop Remigius 3 hides and half a virgate in Clifton. There is land for 2 ploughs. There is 1 plough, and there can be another. There are 3 villans and 2 slaves, [and] meadow for 2 ploughs. It is worth 20s; and as much when received; TRE £4. Alwine Deule, a man of King Edward, held this land and could give it to whom he would.

In Chicksands the same William holds half a hide of the same bishop. There is land for half a plough. It is and was worth 12d; TRE 2s. Alwine Deule held it and could give it to whom he would.

The Church of Bedford with what belongs to it is worth 100s.
The Church of Leighton Buzzard is worth £4. Bishop Remigius holds these.

V. The land of the Bishop of Durham

BIGGLESWADE HUNDRED

THE BISHOP OF DURHAM holds 4½ hides of the king in Millow. There is land for 4 ploughs. In demesne [are] 3½ hides, and there is 1 plough and there can be another. The villans have 2 ploughs. There are 4 villans and 1 slave. It is worth 40s; and as much when received; TRE 60s. King Edward gave this land to the Church of HOLY CROSS of Waltham, so the men of the hundred attest.

In the Hundred of Clifton the same bishop holds 8 hides in Arlesey and 2 parts of 1 virgate. There is land for 8 ploughs. In demesne are 3 ploughs; and 8 villans have 4 ploughs, and there can be a fifth. There are 5 bordars and 2 slaves, and 2 mills [rendering] 26s8d, [and] meadow for 3 ploughs. It is and was worth £7; TRE £8. The canons of Holy Cross of Waltham held this manor in alms TRE.

VI. The land of St Edmundsbury [Abbey]

IN THE HALF-HUNDRED OF 'BUCKELOWE'

ABBOT Baldwin of ST EDMUNDSBURY has half a hide in Biddenham, and Ordwig of Bedford holds under him. There is land for half a plough, and there is [half a plough], and 2 slaves, [and] meadow for half a plough. It is and was worth 6s. Wulfmær, a priest of King Edward, held this land. He could give it to whom he wished, but Ordwig, when he was reeve of the borough, took it from him for a certain fine, and now he says he holds it of the Abbot of St Edmundsbury, but the men of the hundred say that he took unjust possession of it.

In the Hundred of Biggleswade the same Abbot of St Edmundsbury holds 'Kinwick' [in Sandy]. It is assessed at 3 hides and 3 virgates. There is land for 4 ploughs. In demesne [is] 1 hide and 3 virgates, and there are 2 ploughs; and 6 villans have 2 ploughs; and [there is] 1 mill rendering 13s4d. [There is] meadow for 1 plough. It is worth 60s; when received, 30s; TRE £4. 2 sokemen held this land and could give it to whom they wished. Earl Waltheof and his wife gave this to St Edmund in alms in the time of King William.

In the Hundred of "Wichestanestou" the same abbot holds 4 hides and 1 virgate in Blunham of the king. There is land for 4 ploughs. In demesne [are] 2 hides and 3 virgates, and there are 2 ploughs. There 8 villans have 2 ploughs, and [there are] 5 bordars and 1 slave, and 1 mill [rendering] 20s, [and] meadow for 4 ploughs. It is worth £4; when received, 70s; TRE £6. 4 sokemen held this land and could give or sell it to whom they wished.

IN 'STODDEN' HUNDRED

The Abbot of PETERBOROUGH holds STANWICK [Northants]. It is assessed at 2½ hides. There is land for 2½ ploughs. There is 1 plough; there can be another [plough] and a half. There are 2 villans and 2 bordars, [and] meadow for 2 ploughs. It is worth 30s; when received, 50s; TRE 40s. PETERBOROUGH [Abbey] held this manor TRE.

VIII. The land of St Benedict of Ramsey

IN 'REDBORNSTOKE' HUNDRED

THE ABBOT OF ST BENEDICT of Ramsey holds CRANFIELD. It is assessed at 10 hides. There is land for 12 ploughs. In demesne [are] 2 hides, and there are 2 ploughs. There 18 villans have 10 ploughs. There are 2 bordars and 5 slaves, meadow for 2 ploughs, [and] woodland for 1,000 pigs and iron for the ploughs. All together it is worth £9; when received, the same; TRE £12. This manor belonged and belongs to the Church of St Benedict.

IN FLITTON HUNDRED

The same abbot holds BARTON-LE-CLAY. It is assessed at 11 hides. There is land for 12 ploughs. In demesne [are] 3 hides, and there are 2 ploughs and there can be a third; and 20 villans have 9 ploughs. There are 7 bordars and 6 slaves, and

1 mill [rendering] 2s, meadow for 6 ploughs, [and] woodland for 200 pigs. All together it is worth £10; and as much when received; TRE £12. This manor has always belonged to the Church of St Benedict. With this manor the abbot claims against Nigel d'Aubigny and Walter the Fleming 12 acres of meadow which belonged to it TRE but John de les Roches disseised him unjustly. The hundred attests this.

The abbot himself holds PEGSDON. It is assessed at 10 hides. There is land for 14 ploughs. In demesne [are] 2 hides, and there are 2 ploughs and there can be a third; and 37 villans have 11 ploughs. There are 7 bordars and 5 slaves, and 2 mills rendering 27s8d, meadow for 3 ploughs, [and] woodland for 60 pigs. It is worth £10; and as much when received; TRE £12. This manor belonged and belongs to the demesne of the Church of St Benedict.

IN BARFORD HUNDRED

In Wyboston Eudo the steward holds 1½ virgates under the Abbot of Ramsey. It is waste, but yet worth 16d. This land belonged to the Church of St Benedict TRE.

IN BIGGLESWADE HUNDRED

In Little Barford Eudo the steward holds 5 hides of the abbot's fief, and Osbern [holds] of him. There is land for 5 ploughs. In demesne [is] 1 plough; and 9 villans have 4 ploughs. There are 4 bordars and 3 slaves, and 1 mill [rendering] 12s and 125 eels, [and] meadow for 2 ploughs. It is worth £4; when received, £3; TRE £4. The Abbot of St Benedict holds this manor, and it was in alms TRE.

IN CLIFTON HUNDRED

In Clifton Leofwine holds 1 hide under the abbot. There is land for half a plough, and there is [half a plough, and] meadow for half a plough. It is and was worth 10s; TRE 20s. The same man held it then, but could not separate it from the church.

The same abbot himself holds SHILLINGTON. It is assessed at 10 hides. There is land for 14 ploughs. In demesne [are] 2 hides, and there are 2 ploughs; and 27 villans have 12 ploughs. There are 5 bordars and 4 slaves, and a broken mill which renders nothing, meadow for 6 ploughs, [and] woodland for 100 pigs. It is worth £12; and was always worth as much. This manor belonged to the demesne of the Church of St Benedict TRE.

The abbot himself holds HOLWELL [Herts.] for 3½ hides. There is land for 4 ploughs. In demesne [is] 1 hide, and there is 1 plough; and 8 villans have 3 ploughs, and [there is] 1 bordar and 2 slaves, [and] meadow for 1 plough. It is worth £4; and was always worth as much. This manor belonged and belongs to the demesne of the Church of St Benedict.

In [Lower and Upper] Stondon the same abbot holds half a hide. There is land for half a plough, and there is [half a plough]. This land belongs and belonged to the demesne of the Church of St Benedict. It is worth 15s.

IX. The land of St Peter of Westminster

IN CLIFTON HUNDRED

THE ABBOT of WESTMINSTER holds 6½ hides in HOLWELL [Herts.]. There is land for 6 ploughs. In demesne [are] 3 hides and half a virgate, and there are 2 ploughs; and 11 villans have 4 ploughs. There are 4 bordars and 3 slaves, and 2 mills [rendering] 20s, [and] meadow for 1 plough. It is and was worth 100s. This manor belonged and belongs to the demesne of the Church of ST PETER.

X. The land of St Mary of Thorney

THE ABBOT of Thorney holds 2 hides and 1 virgate of land in Bolnhurst. There is land for 5 ploughs. In demesne is 1 carucate of land besides the 2 hides and [1] virgate, and there is 1 plough; and 9 villans have 5 ploughs. There are 5 bordars, meadow for 1 plough, [and] woodland for 106 pigs. It is worth 60s; when received, 40s; TRE £6. Alflæd held this manor of King Edward. She could give it to whom she wished. It belonged to the monastery of Thorney on the day on which King Edward was alive and dead. This the men of the hundred attest.

XI. The land of the Church of Barking

IN 'REDBORNSTOKE' HUNDRED

THE ABBESS of Barking holds LIDLINGTON. It is assessed at 10 hides. There is land for 11 ploughs. In demesne [are] 2 hides, and there are 2 ploughs; there can be a third; and 23 villans have 8 ploughs. There are 16 bordars and 7 slaves, meadow for 8 ploughs, [and] woodland for 400 pigs. It is worth £8; and as much when received; TRE £12. This manor belonged and belongs to the demesne of the Church of ST MARY of Barking.

XII. The land of St Paul of London

IN FLITTON HUNDRED

The canons of ST PAUL of London hold CADDINGTON. It is assessed at 5 hides. There is land for 6 ploughs. In demesne [are] 2 hides, and there are 2 ploughs and there can be 4 more. There is 1 villan and 4 bordars and 2 slaves, [and] woodland for 200 pigs. It is worth 40s; when received, 10s; TRE 100s. Leofwine Cild held this manor TRE. The canons have the king's writ in which is recorded that he himself gave this manor to the Church of St Paul.

XIII. [The land] of St Paul of Bedford

IN THE HALF-HUNDRED OF 'BUCKELOWE'

Osmund, a canon of St Paul of Bedford, holds| in Biddenham | of the king 3 virgates. There is land for 1 plough, and there is [1 plough], and 1 villan and 1 bordar, [and] meadow for 1 plough. It is and was worth 10s. Leofgeat the

priest held this land in alms of King Edward and afterwards of King William, which priest on his death-bed gave to the Church of St Paul 1 virgate of this land. Ralph Taillebois added 2 other virgates to the same church in alms.

In the same [vill] Ansfrid the canon holds 1 virgate. There is land for 2 oxen, and there are [2 oxen, and] meadow for 2 oxen. It is and was worth 3s. Mærwynn held this land; she could sell it to whom she wished. This Ralph Taillebois assigned in alms to the Church of St Paul.

The land of Earnwig the Priest

IN "WICHESTANESTOU" HUNDRED

EARNWINE the priest holds 1 hide in HARROWDEN. There is land for 1 plough, and there is half a plough, meadow for half a plough, [and] woodland for 4 pigs. It is worth 10s; when received, 5s; TRE 10s. The father of this aforesaid man held this land. He was a man of King Edward. He has no livery officer nor writ for this land, but he took possession of it to the king's loss, as the hundred attests.

XV. The land of Count Eustace

IN THE HALF-HUNDRED OF 'BUCKELOWE'

Count EUSTACE holds 1½ hides in Bromham. Ernulf d' Ardres holds of him. There is land for 1½ ploughs. There is half a plough and there can be 1 plough [more. There is] meadow for 1½ ploughs. It is worth 10s; when received, 20s; and as much TRE. Æthelweald and Leofric, men of King Edward, held this land and could give and sell it to whom they wished.

In Stevington the same Ernulf holds 3 hides of the count himself. There is land for 24 ploughs. In demesne is 1 plough, and there can be 3 ploughs [more]; and 10 villans have 5 ploughs and there can be 15 more. There are 11 bordars and 2 slaves, meadow for 4 ploughs, [and] woodland for 20 pigs. In all it is worth £14; when received, £20; TRE £30. Æthelweald, a thegn of King Edward, held this manor and could sell to whom he wished.

In Stagsden an Englishman, Godwig, holds 1 virgate of Count Eustace. There is land for half a plough, and 1 ox ploughs there. This land is worth 2s; when received, 5s; TRE 10s.

InPAVENHAM Ernulf d'Ardres holds 2½ hides. There is land for 3 ploughs, but there are no [ploughs]. There is 1 mill [rendering] 20s, and 2 bordars, [and] meadow for 3 ploughs. It is worth 25s; when received, 40s; TRE £4. Æthelweald, a thegn of King Edward, held this manor.

In 'willey' Hundred Ernulf d'Ardres holds 1 hide in Turvey of Count Eustace. There is land for 2 ploughs. In demesne is 1 plough, and there can be another. There is 1 villan and 1 bordar, [and] meadow for 1 plough. It is worth 10s; when received, 20s; and as much TRE. Æthelweald, a thegn of King Edward, held this land; he could give it to whom he wished.

In ODELL Ernulf d'Ardres holds 4½ hides and the third part of 1 virgate as 1 manor of Count Eustace. There is 1 plough in demesne, and there can be another; and 3 villans have 2 ploughs and there can be a third. There are 7 bordars and 2 slaves, meadow for 3 ploughs, [and] woodland for 50 pigs. It is worth 60s; when received, 100s; TRE £8. Æthelweald, a thegn of King Edward, held this land and could sell to whom he wished.

In Sharnbrook Robert fitzRozelin holds 2 hides of Count Eustace. There is land for 4 ploughs. In demesne [are] 2 ploughs; and 4 villans have 2 ploughs. There are 3 bordars and 4 slaves, meadow for 2 ploughs, [and] woodland for 60 pigs. It is worth 40s; and as much when received; TRE £4. Æthelweald, a man of King Edward, held this land and could sell.

XVI. The land of Walter Giffard

IN 'MANSHEAD' HUNDRED

WALTER Giffard holds WOBURN. It is assessed at 10 hides. There is land for 24 ploughs. Hugh de Bolbec holds of him. There are 2 ploughs in demesne, and there can be another 2. There 8 villans have 6 ploughs, and there can be 14 more. There are 7 bordars and 4 slaves, meadow for 6 ploughs, [and] woodland for 100 pigs. It is worth 100s; when received, £12; TRE £15. Ælfric, a thegn of King Edward, held this manor; and in this manor were 6 sokemen: they held 2 hides of this land and could do what they wished [with them].

In BATTLESDEN Richard Talbot holds 9 hides of Walter Giffard. There is land for 8 ploughs. In demesne are 2 ploughs,

[Folio 211V: BEDFORDSHIRE]

and there can be a third. There 7 villans have 5 ploughs. There are 10 bordars, and meadow for 8 ploughs. It is worth 100s; and as much when received; TRE £8. 7 sokemen held this manor TRE, and they could do what they wished with their land.

IN 'REDBORNSTOKE' HUNDRED

In Marston Moretaine Hugh de Bolbec holds of Walter Giffard 2 hides, less half a virgate. There is land for 3 ploughs. In demesne [is] 1 plough; and 6 villans have 2 ploughs. There are 5 bordars, and meadow for 3 ploughs, [and] woodland for 300 pigs. It is worth 50s; when received, 20s; TRE £4. 2 thegns held this land TRE and could give it to whom they wished. In regard to this land Herfast, a man of Nigel d'Aubigny, claims half an enclosure which belonged to the manor of Herfast's predecessor, as the men of the hundred attest.

In Maulden Hugh Bolbec holds 3 hides of the same Walter. There is land for 4 ploughs. In demesne are 2 ploughs; and 5 villans have 2 ploughs. [There is] meadow for 4 ploughs, [and] woodland for 50 pigs. It is worth 50s; and as much when received; TRE £4. Alwine, brother of Bishop Wulfwig, held this manor and could give it to whom he wished.

IN BIGGLESWADE HUNDRED

In Dunton Ralph de Lanquetot holds of Walter Giffard 1 hide and 3 virgates. There is land for 2 ploughs, and there are [2 ploughs], and 4 villans and 2 bordars. It is worth 33s4d; and was always worth as much. 4 sokemen held this land and they could sell their land. They were Archbishop Stigand's men.

In Millow Ralph himself holds 5 hides of the same Walter. There is land for 5 ploughs, and there are [5 ploughs], and 8 villans and 4 bordars. It is and was always worth 100s. 10 sokemen held this manor and they could give or sell their land to whom they wished.

In Stratton Fulcher of Paris holds of Walter Giffard 1 hide and 1½ virgates. There is land for 2 ploughs. In demesne [is] 1 plough; and 1 villan and 5 bordars with 1 plough, [and] meadow for 2 ploughs. It is worth 28s; and as much when received; TRE 30s. 3 sokemen held this land and could give or sell it to whom they wished.

In "Cudessane" Germund holds of Ralph Lanquetot 3½ hides as 1 manor. There is land for 3 ploughs. In demesne is 1 plough; and 1 villan and 3 bordars with 2 ploughs, and 1 slave. [There is] meadow for 3 bordars with [and] woodland for 40 pigs. It is worth 40s; when received, 20s; TRE 60s; and there can be 1 mill. 4 sokemen held this manor and could give and sell.

In Campton Ralph de Lanquetot holds of Walter Giffard 4½ hides and the fourth part of 1 virgate. There is land for 4 ploughs. There is 1 plough in demesne; and 4 villans have 3 ploughs, and [there is] 1 mill [rendering] 3s3d, meadow for 4 ploughs, [and] woodland for 40 pigs. It is worth 60s; when received, 20s; TRE 70s. 6 sokemen held this land and could give it to whom they wished.

XVII. The land of William de Warenne

IN 'STODDEN' HUNDRED

WILLIAM de Warenne holds 2 hides in [Lower and Upper] DEAN, and 3 sokemen [hold] of him. There is land for 3 ploughs, and there are [3 ploughs]. There are 5 bordars and 1 slave. It is and was always worth 30s. This land the same sokemen themselves held who hold it now. One of them could not give or sell his land without his lord's leave. The other 2 could do this.

William Speke was seised by the king and his livery officer of half a hide and half a virgate of this land, but William de Warenne, without the king's writ, disseised him and took away 2 horses from his men and has not yet returned them. This the men of the hundred attest.

William de Warenne himself holds Tilbrook [Hunts.]. It is assessed at 5 hides. There is land for 6 ploughs, and there are [6 ploughs], and 20 sokemen and 4 bordars, [and] meadow for 5 ploughs. It is worth 100s; and as much when received; TRE £4. The same sokemen themselves held this manor who hold [now], and they belonged in such a way to the king's soke and sake that they could give and sell their land to whom they wished and withdraw to another lord without the leave of him under whom they were. Hugh de Beauchamp claims this land of Tilbrook against William, and the men of the hundred bear testimony to it that Ralph Taillebois, his predecessor, was seised of it by the king and held it.

In "Hanefelde" William de Warenne holds 3 virgates of land. There is land for 1 plough, and there is [1 plough]. It is and was always worth 10s. This land always belonged to Kimbolton [Hunts.], but always gave its wara of right in Bedfordshire.

In Easton [Hunts.] William de Warenne holds 1 virgate. There is land for 2 ploughs, and there are [2 ploughs], and 1 villan and 2 bordars, meadow for 1 plough, [and] woodland for 100 pigs. It is worth 20s; when received, 40s; TRE 20s. Authgi, a man of Eskil, predecessor of Hugh de Beauchamp, held this land. He could sell to whom he wished, but the soke Eskil himself retained in his manor of Colmworth. Hugh de Beauchamp claims this land against William de Warenne, and all the sworn men of the shrievalty bear testimony that this land does not belong to William.

In the same vill William de Warenne holds 1 hide and 1 virgate. There is land for 1 plough, and there is [1 plough], and 2 bordars, [and] meadow for 1 plough. It is worth 10s; and as much when received; TRE 15s. Authgi held this land and could give it to whom he wished TRE. King William afterwards granted this to him and by his writ commended him to Ralph Taillebois that he might serve him during his life. On the day on which he died he stated that he was William de Warenne's man and accordingly William was seised of this land.

In the same [vill] the same William holds 1 virgate of land. There is land for 2 oxen, and there are 4 oxen. It is and was worth 2s; TRE 3s. Blæc, a man of Authgi, held this land; he could give it to whom he wished.

In the same [vill] Theodric holds of William 1 virgate and the fourth part of 1 virgate. There is land for 1 plough, and there is [1 plough], meadow for 1 plough, [and] woodland for 24 pigs. It is and was worth 10s; TRE 6s. Godric, a man of the sheriff, held it and could give it to whom he wished.

XVIII. The land of William de Eu

IN FLITTON HUNDRED

WILLIAM de EU holds [Lower and Upper] SUNDON. It is assessed at 10 hides. There is land for 16 ploughs. In demesne [are] 4 hides, and there are 4 ploughs. There 20 villans have 12 ploughs. There are 11 bordars and 12 slaves, meadow for 4 ploughs, [and] woodland for 100 pigs. In all it is worth £10; when received, £8; TRE £20. Ælfstan of Boscombe, a thegn of King Edward, held this manor. In the same vill 1 knight has 1 plough.

[Folio 212: BEDFORDSHIRE]

In Streatley Walter holds 1 hide of William de Eu. There is land for 2 ploughs. In demesne [is] 1 plough; and 2 villans have 1 plough, and [there are] 3 bordars and 3 slaves. [There is] meadow for 1 plough, [and] Woodland for 20 pigs. It is

worth 30s; when received, 20s; TRE 40s. Godwine, a man of Ælfstan, thegn of King Edward, held this land; he could sell it to whom he wished.

IN BIGGLESWADE HUNDRED

In Millow William de EU holds half a hide. There is land for half a plough, and there is [half a plough], with 1 bordar. It is and was worth 10s. Godmær, a man of Ælfstan, held this land and could sell to whom he wished.

In Edworth 2 knights hold of William de EU 7 hides and 3½ virgates. There is land for 8 ploughs. In demesne [are] 3 ploughs; and 8 villans have 5 ploughs. There are 2 bordars and 5 slaves, [and] meadow for 2 ploughs. It is worth £8; when received, £10; and as much TRE. Ælfstan of Boscombe held this manor, and there were 2 sokemen, his men, and they had 1½ hides and could sell them to whom they wished.

In Holme Wulfric holds of William de EU 3 virgates of land. There is land for 1 plough, and there is [1 plough]. It is worth 16s; when received, 12s; TRE 20s. Ælfgifu, a man of Eskil, held this land and could give it to whom she wished.

IN CLIFTON HUNDRED

In Arlesey Bernard holds 5½ hisdes and 2 parts of 1 hide. There is land for 6 ploughs. In demesne [is] 1 plough; and 13 villans have 5 ploughs, and [there are] 10 bordars, and 1 mill [rendering] 10s, [and] meadow for 6 ploughs. There is a market rendering 10s. It is and was always worth £7. Ælfstan of Boscombe held this manor, and there was 1 sokeman, his man, [who] had 2 parts of 1 hide and could give them to whom he wished.

In Campton Fulbert holds half a hide of William de EU. There is land for half a plough, and there is [half a plough], with 1 villan. This land is and was always worth 5s. Alwine, a man of Ælfstan, held this land and could give it to whom he wished.

XIX. The land of Miles Crispin

IN 'STODDEN' HUNDRED

MILES Crispin holds CLAPHAM. It is assessed at 5 hides. There is land for 30 ploughs. Besides these 5 hides there are 10 carucates of land in demesne, and there are 8 ploughs, and there can be 2 more. There 18 villans have 20 ploughs, and [there are] 15 bordars and 4 slaves, meadow for 6 ploughs, and 1 mill [rendering] 40s, [and] woodland for 200 pigs and [rendering] 6d. In all it is worth £24; and when received, as much; TRE £12. Beorhtric, a thegn of King Edward, held this manor of the Abbot of Ramsey. The abbot and monks claim this manor since it is and was, TRE, for their sustenance and the whole hundred bears witness to this.

In Milton Ernest 2 sokemen had 16 acres of land and gave their wara in the same Milton Ernest, but could give or sell their land to whom they wished. These sokemen Robert d'Oilly attached to Clapham, unjustly, as the men of the hundred say, because they never belonged there TRE.

IN 'WILLEY' HUNDRED

In THURLEIGH Leofric holds of Miles 1 virgate of land. There is land for 1 plough, and there is [1 plough]. It is and was always worth 10s. The same man himself held it TRE. He was a man of Beorhtric and could sell and give it.

XX. The land of Ernulf de Hesdin

IN 'MANSHEAD' HUNDRED

ERNULF de Hesdin holds TODDINGTON of the king. It is assessed at 15½ hides. There is land for 30 ploughs. There are 10 carucates of land in demesne, and there are 7 ploughs, and there can be 3 more; [this is] besides the 15½ hides. There 42 villans have 20 ploughs. There are 19 bordars and 19 slaves, meadow for 30 ploughs, [and] woodland for 300 pigs. In all it is worth £25; and when received as much; TRE £30. Wulfweard White held this manor TRE.

In Chalgrave Ernulf holds the third part of 1 virgate of land. It is and was always worth 2s. Edward White held this land TRE.

XXI. The land of Eudo fitzHubert

EUDO the steward holds EATON SOCON. It is assessed at 20 hides. There is land for 16 ploughs. In demesne [are] 7½ hides, and there are 4 ploughs. There 38 villans have 12 ploughs. There are 7 bordars and 8 slaves, and 2 sokemen who could not give or sell their land. There are 2 mills rendering 36s6d and 100 eels, meadow for 12 ploughs, woodland for 400 pigs, and 2 acres of vineyard. All together it is worth £15; when received, £8; TRE £10. Wulfmær of Eaton Socon, a thegn of King Edward, held this manor, and in this manor were 2 sokemen who could sell and give their land. Of this land Theobald, a man of Countess Judith, claims 1 hide, of which Eudo disseised him after he came to this manor.

In WYBOSTON Eudo holds 6 hides and 3 virgates. There is land for 5 ploughs. In demesne [are] 4½ hides, and there are 2 ploughs; and 8 villans have 4 ploughs. There are 8 bordars and 3 slaves, [and] meadow for 2 ploughs. All together it is worth £3; when received, 20s; TRE £10. 4 thegns of King Edward held this land and could sell to whom they wished.

In Chawston Eudo holds 1 hide and 1 virgate. There is land for 1 plough, and there is [1 plough]. There are 4 villans, and meadow for 1 plough. It is and was worth 10s; TRE 20s. 2 men of King Edward held this land and they could give and sell it.

IN BIGGLESWADE HUNDRED

In Tempsford Eudo holds holds [sic] 1 hide and 1 virgate of land. There is land for 2 ploughs. In demesne [is] 1 hide, and there is 1 plough; and 1 villan with 1 plough, and 2 bordars and 1 slave, and 1 mill [rendering] 10s, and meadow for 2 ploughs. It is and was worth 40s; TRE 45s. 2 sokemen held this land and could give it to whom they wished.

In the same vill William de Cairon holds 4 hides and 1 virgate of Eudo the steward. There is land for 4 ploughs. In demesne

[are] 2 ploughs; and 8 villans have 2 ploughs, and [there are] 6 slaves, and 1 mill [rendering] 12s, [and] meadow for 4 ploughs. It is worth 60s; when received, 40s; TRE 60s. 3 sokemen, men of Wulfmær of Eaton Socon, held this land; one of them could not give his land without his lord's leave; the other 2 could do what they wished [with their land].

IN THE HALF-HUNDRED OF 'WENESLAWE'

Eudo the steward holds SANDY. It is assessed at 16 hides and 1 virgate. There is land for 16 ploughs. In demesne [are] 8 hides and 1 virgate, and there are 3 ploughs; and 24 villans have 8 ploughs, and there can be 5 more. There are 6 bordars and 2 slaves, and 2 mills rendering 50s, meadow for 16 ploughs, [and] pasture for the livestock of the vill. All together it is worth £12; when received, £8; TRE £10. Wulfmær of Eaton Socon, a thegn of King Edward, held this manor. Eudo claims here 3 acres of woodland against Hugh de Beauchamp which Wulfmær held; but Ralph, when he was sheriff, disseised him, and accordingly Eudo has refused to give the wara of this woodland. This the same men of the hundred attest.

In Sutton Alwine holds of Eudo 3 virgates of land. There is land for 6 oxen, and there are [6 oxen], and 1 villan, [and] meadow for the oxen. It is worth 6s; when received, 3s; TRE 10s. 2 sokemen held this land and could sell to whom they wished.

IN "WICHESTANESTOU" HUNDRED

In Southill William de Cairon holds half a virgate of Eudo. There is land for 2 oxen, and there are [2 oxen, and] meadow for 2 oxen. It is worth 3s; TRE 4s. Alric held this land and could give it to whom he wished.

[Folio 212V: BEDFORDSHIRE]

In Stanford William de Carion holds 4 hides of Eudo. There is land for 4 ploughs. In demesne [are] 2 ploughs; and 3 villans have 2 ploughs, and [there are] 2 slaves, and 2 mills rendering 29s and 50 eels, meadow for 4 ploughs, [and] woodland for 60 pigs and [rendering] 2s. All together it is worth £4; when recieved, 40s; TR[E] £4. Wulfmær of Eaton Socon, a thegn of King Edward, held this land. In this land was 1 sokeman, a man of this Wulfmær he had half a hide and could sell it.

In the same [vill] are 7 sokemen holding 7 acres of land; they were men of Wulfmær and could give their land. Hugh de Beauchamp holds it now.

In Blunham Domnic holds of Eudo 1 virgate of land. There is land for 2 oxen, and there are [2 oxen, and] meadow for 2 oxen. It is worth 2s; when received, 3s; TRE 5s. 4 sokemen held this land and could sell and give.

In BEESTON Roland holds 3 hides of Eudo. There is land for 3 ploughs, and there are [3 ploughs]. In demesne [are] 2 ploughs; and 4 villans have 1 plough. There are 2 bordars and 1 slave, [and] meadow for 3 ploughs. It is worth 30s; when received, 20s; TRE 40s.

In the same [vill] Northmann holds 4 hides of Eudo. There is land for 4 ploughs. In demesne [is] 1 plough; and 4 villans have 3 ploughs. There are 2 slaves, and 1 mill [rendering] 20s,

[and] meadow for 4 ploughs. It is worth 40s; and when received, as much; TRE 50s. These 4 hides and the 3 above, this Northmann held TRE and in the time of King William. Now Eudo has them of the King, as his men say, but it is not [part] of the fief of Lisois.

In the same [vill] Pirot holds 1 hide of Eudo. There is land for 1 plough, and there is [1 ploughs], with 1 bordar. [There is] meadow for 1 plough. It is worth 10s; when recieved, 5s; TRE 20s. Rawn, a man of Wulfmær of Eaton Socon, held this land and could give it to whom he wished.

In Northill Pirot holds 1½ hides of Eudo. There is land for 1½ ploughs. There is 1 plough, and there can be half [a plough more], and there are 3 villans and 1 bordar, meadow for 1½ ploughs, and 1 mill [rendering] 14s. It is worth 20s; when received, 10s; TRE 25s. Rawn, a man of Wulfmær of Eaton Socon, held this land and could sell.

In the same [vill] Ralph holds 1½ hides of Eudo. There is land for 2 ploughs, and there are [2 ploughs], and 5 bordars and 3 slaves, meadow for 2 ploughs, [and] woodland for 100 pigs. It is worth £3; when received, 40s; TRE 60s. 2 sokemen held this land and could give and sell it.

IN CLIFTON HUNDRED

In CLIFTON William de Cairon holds 6½ hides of Eudo. There is land for 4½ ploughs. In demesne [are] 2 ploughs; and 9 villans have 2½ ploughs. There is 1 bordar and 3 slaves, and 2 mills rendering 40s and 150 eels, [and] meadow for 4½ ploughs. All together it is worth 100s; when received, £4; TRE £6. Wulfmær of Eaton Socon held this manor, and there were 3 sokemen. They had 1 hide and half a virgate and they could sell to whom they wished.

XXII. The land of William Peverel

IN STANBRIDGE HUNDRED

WILLIAM Peverel holds TILSWORTH of the king, and Ambrose [holds] of him. It is assessed at 10 hides. There is land for 8 ploughs. In demesne [is] 1 plough, and there can be another; and 10 villans have 6 ploughs. There are 6 bordars and 3 slaves, meadow for 6 ploughs, [and] woodland for 100 pigs. Oswig took away this woodland and the hundred says that it belonged to this manor TRE. All together it is worth £6; when received, £4; TRE £10. Leofric son of Osmund, a thegn of King Edward, held this manor.

IN 'WILLEY' HUNDRED

In Rushden [Northants] Malet holds of William Peverel 1 virgate of land. There is land for 2 oxen, and there are [2 oxen]. It is and was worth 16d; TRE 2s. Sæmær the priest, a man of Countess Gode, held this land and could give it to whom he wished.

XXIII. The land of Hugh de Beauchamp

IN 'STODDEN' HUNDRED

HUGH de Beauchamp holds KEYSOE. It is assessed at 5 hides, less 1 virgate. There is land for 5 ploughs, and there are [5 ploughs], and 9 villans and 6 bordars and 1 slave, and 1 mill [rendering] 2s, meadow for 4 ploughs, [and] woodland for 200 pigs. In all it is worth 100s; when received, £4; TRE 100s. Eskil, a thegn of king Edward, held this land, and there were 12 sokemen who had 3½ hides, and they could sell and give them to whom they wished.

In Riseley Hugh holds 1 hide and it is a Berewick of Keysoe. There is land for 2 ploughs, and there are [2 ploughs]. Eskil, his predecessor, held this.

IN 'BUCKELOWE' HALF-HUNDRED

Hugh himself holds PUTNOE. It is assessed at 4 hides. There is land for 5 ploughs. In demesne [are] 2 hides, and There are 2 ploughs; and 6 villans have 3 ploughs. There are 4 bordars and 2 slaves, and 1 mill [rendering] 30s. and 100 eels, [and] woodland for 100 pigs. It is worth £4; when received, 40s; and as much TRE. Eskil, a thegn of King Edward, held this manor.

Hugh himself holds STAGSDEN. It is assessed at 5 hides. There is land for 5 ploughs. In demesne [are] 2 hides, and there are 2 ploughs; and 12 villans have 3 ploughs. There are 8 bordars and 2 slaves, meadow for 1 plough, [and] woodland for 100 pigs. # 2 men of King Edward and 1 man of Earl Harold held this manor, and each could give his land to whom he wished.

Hugh himself holds CHANNEL'S END. It is assessed at 5 hides. There is land for 5 ploughs. In demesne [are] 2 hides, and there are 2 ploughs; and 12 villans have 3 ploughs. There are 9 bordars and 5 slaves, meadow for 3 ploughs, and 1 mill [rendering] 40s and 100 eels, [and] woodland for 100 pigs. In all it is worth £8; when recieved, 100s; TRE £7. Eskil, a thegn of King Edward, held this manor.

In the same [vill] Hugh holds half a hide which belongs to Putnoe. There is land for 1 plough, and there are 4 oxen, and 2 bordars. It is and was worth 2s. Eskil, a thegn of King Edward, held this land.

In Goldington Hugh holds 3 hide, and 1 virgate which belongs to Putnoe. There is land for 3 ploughs, and there are [3 ploughs], and 7 villans and 1 bordar, meadow for 1 plough, and 1 mill [rendering] 30s and 100 eels. All together it is worth 60s; and when received, as much; TRE £4. Of this land Ralph Taillebois had 2 hides and 3 virgates in exchange for Ware [Herts.]. 9 sokemen held this land and could give or sell it to whom they wished.

IN "WICHESTANESTOU" HUNDRED

In Southill Hugh holds 2 hides and 1 virgate. There is land for 3 ploughs, and there are [3 ploughs], meadow for 3 ploughs, [and] woodland for 100 pigs. It is and was worth 40s; TRE

50s. 8 sokemen held this land and could do what they wished with it.

In Stanford Hugh holds 1 hide and half a virgate of land. There is land for 1½ ploughs, and there are [1½ ploughs], and 4 villans and 1 bordar, [and] meadow for 1½ ploughs. It is and was always worth 20s. 4 sokemen held this land, of whom 3 were free; the fourth had 1 hide but could neither give nor sell it.

In Cardington Hugh holds 6½ hides, and 2 parts of 1 virgate. There is land for 8 ploughs. In demesne [are] 2½ hides, and there is 1 plough; and 12 villans have 7 ploughs. There are 6 bordars, meadow for 3 ploughs, woodland for 120 pigs, There is a park for wild beasts. All together it is worth 100s; when received, 40s; TRE 100s.

[Folio 213: BEDFORDSHIRE]

and 1 mill [rendering] 40s and 100 eels. All together it is worth £6; when received, 100s; TRE £6. 13 sokemen held this manor and they could withdraw where they wished with their land.

Hugh himself holds WILLINGTON. It is assessed at 10 hides. There is land for 9 ploughs. In demesne [are] 5 hides, and there are 3 ploughs, and there can be a fourth; and 13 villans have 5 ploughs. There are 8 slaves, and 1 mill [rendering] 12s and 100 eels, meadow for 5 ploughs, [and] woodland for 40 pigs. In all it is worth £7; when received, 40s; TRE £6. Eskil, a thegn of King Edward, held this manor, and there were 8 sokemen who could withdraw with their land where they wished. Of this land they had 7 hides.

IN CLIFTON HUNDRED

Hugh himself holds STOTFOLD. It is assessed at 15 hides. There is land for 15 ploughs. In demesne [are] 5 hides, and there are 3 ploughs; and 21 villans have 12 ploughs. There are 14 bordars and 6 slaves, and 4 mills rendering £4 and 400 eels, [and] meadow for 7 ploughs. In all it is worth £25; when received, £12; TRE £20. On the day on which Ralph Taillebois died it was at farm for £30. Eskil, a thegn of King Edward, held this manor. He himself had 9½ hides, and 7 sokemen held the remainder of the land and could sell it to whom they wished. 1 hide of this land belongs to the Church of St Albans, and, as the men of the hundred say, it belonged to it TRE.

IN 'REDBORNSTOKE' HUNDRED

In Maulden Hugh holds half a virgate. There is land for 1 plough, and there is [1 plough], and 1 villan and 1 bordar, meadow for 1 plough, [and] woodland for 20 pigs. It is worth 10s; when received, 5s; TRE 12s. Godwine, a man of Eskil, held this land and could give and sell it.

In HOUGHTON CONQUEST Hugh holds 5 hides. There is land for 6 ploughs, and there are [6 ploughs], and 8 villans and 6 bordars and 2 slaves, meadow for 6 ploughs, [and] woodland for 200 pigs. It is and was worth 100s; TRE £7. 7 sokemen held this manor and could give it to whom they wished.

IN FLITTON HUNDRED

Hugh himself holds HAYNES. It is assessed at 5 hides. There is land for 8 ploughs. In demesne [are] 2½ hides, and there are 3 ploughs; and 14 villans have 5 ploughs. There are 9 bordars and 1 slave, meadow for 1 plough, [and] woodland for 500 pigs. In all it is worth £10; when received, £7; and as much TRE. Aki, a thegn of King Edward, held this manor.

IN BARFORD HUNDRED

Hugh himself holds Salph End. It is assessed at 5 hides. There is land for 8 ploughs and there are [8 ploughs]. 11 sokemen hold this land and the same men themselves held it TRE and could give and sell it to whom they wished. [There is] meadow for 2 ploughs, [and] woodland for 50 pigs. All together it is worth 100s; and when received, as much; TRE £8. Ralph Taillebois had this land in exchange for Ware [Herts.], as his men say; and when received, it was worth £8.

IN 'MANSHEAD' HUNDRED

ASPLEY GUISE is assessed at 10 hides. Acard d'Ivery holds it of Hugh. There is land for 12 ploughs. In demesne [are] 2 ploughs, and there can be a third; and 16 villans have 8 ploughs and there can be ninth. There are 4 bordars and 5 slaves, and 1 mill [rendering] 10s, meadow for 10 ploughs, [and] woodland for 50 pigs. In all it is worth £8; when received, 100s; TRE £10. Leofgifu, [who was] commended to Earl Waltheof, held this manor and she could withdraw where she wished with her land.

SALFORD is assessed at 5 hides. There is land for 5 ploughs. In demesne is 1 plough; and 12 villans have 4 ploughs. There is 1 bordar and 4 slaves. There is 1 mill [rendering] 9s4d, meadow for 5 ploughs, [and] woodland for 150 pigs, and from other customary dues, 10s. In all it is worth £4; when received, 60s; TRE 100s. Thorkil, a thegn of King Edward, held this manor and could give it to whom he wished.

In Eversholt Ralph holds of Hugh 7½ hides as 1 manor. There is land for 8 ploughs. In demesne [are] 2 ploughs; and 15 villans have 6 ploughs. There are 4 slaves, meadow for 8 ploughs, [and] woodland for 100 pigs. It is worth 100s; when received, £3; and as much TRE. Thorgisl, a thegn of King Edward, held this manor and could sell.

In Milton Bryan William Froissart holds of Hugh 6 hides as 1 manor. There is land for 6 ploughs. In demesne [are] 3 ploughs; and 6 villans have 3 ploughs. There are 3 bordars and 4 slaves, meadow for 6 ploughs, [and] woodland for 40 pigs. It is worth £6; when received, £4; TRE £8. Auti, a housecarl of Earl Ælfgar, held this manor and could do with it what he wished.

The same William holds [Lower and Upper] Gravenhurst of Hugh. It is assessed at 3½ hides. There is land for 4 ploughs. In demesne [are] 2 ploughs; and 4 villans have 1 plough, and there can be another. There are 3 bordars and 4 slaves, meadow for 4 ploughs, [and] woodland for 100 pigs. It is worth 60s; and when received, as much; TRE 100s. 5 sokemen held this manor and could give and sell their land to whom they wished.

In Streatley William de Loucelles holds of Hugh 4 hides and 1 virgate as 1 manor. There is land for 6 ploughs. In demesne [is] 1 plough, and there can be another; and 7 villans have 4 ploughs. There are 5 bordars and 1 slave, [and] woodland for 16 pigs. It is worth £4; when received, 40s; TRE 100s. Eskil, a thegn of King Edward, held this manor, and there were *[sic]* 1 sokeman, his man, having 1 hide, and he could give it to whom he wished.

The same William holds Higham Gobion of Hugh. It is assessed at 8 hides. There is land for 11 ploughs. In demesne [are] 4 ploughs; and 14 villans have 7 ploughs. There are 2 bordars and 5 slaves, meadow for 6 ploughs, [and] woodland for 100 pigs. It is worth £8; and when received, as much; TRE £12. 5 sokemen held this manor and they could give their land to whom they wished.

In Easton [Hunts.] Wimund holds half a hide of Hugh. There is land for 3 ploughs, and there are [3 ploughs]. There are 2 villans and 6 bordars, [and] woodland for 40 pigs. It is worth 30s; when received and TRE 20s. Wulfgeat, a man of Eskil, held this land and could give and sell; but the soke always belonged to Colmworth, Eskil's manor.

In Riseley Ælfric the priest holds half a hide of Hugh. There is land for half a plough, and there is [half a plough], and 4 bordars. It is worth 5s; when received, the same; TRE 8s. Wulfnoth, a man of Godric the sheriff, held this land and could give it to whom he wished.

In Milton Ernest William Basset holds of Hugh 2 hides, less half a virgate. There is land for 3 ploughs. In demesne [are] 2 ploughs; and 1 villan has 1 plough. There are 4 bordars and 2 slaves, meadow for 2 ploughs, [and] woodland for 6 pigs. It is worth 30s; and when received, as much; TRE 40s.

IN THE HALF-HUNDRED OF 'BUCKELOWE'

In Bletsoe Osbert de Breuil holds 2½ hides of Hugh. There is land for 4 ploughs. In demesne [is] 1 plough; and 7 villans have 3 ploughs. There are 2 bordars and 2 slaves, and half a mill [rendering] 10s, meadow for 1 plough, [and] woodland for 100 pigs. It is and was always worth 60s. Eskil held this manor,

[Folio 213V: BEDFORDSHIRE]

and 3 sokemen had there 3 virgates and could sell to whom they wished.

In Biddenham Serlo de Rots holds 1 hide of Hugh. There is land for 1 plough, and there is [1 plough], and 1 bordar and 1 slave, [and] meadow for 1 plough. It is and was always worth 10s. Alsige of Bromham, a man of Queen Edith, held this land and he could give it to whom he wished.

In BROMHAM Serlo de Rots holds 6 hides of Hugh. There is land for 6 ploughs. In demesne [are] 2 ploughs; and 16 villans have 4 ploughs. There are 5 bordars and 6 slaves, and 1 mill [rendering] 20s and 125 eels, meadow for 6 ploughs, [and] woodland for 40 pigs. All together it is worth £7; when received, 100s; TRE £4. Alsige, a man of Queen Edith, held this land and could sell.

IN 'WILLEY' HUNDRED

In Turvey Warner holds 1 hide of Hugh. There is land for 2 ploughs. In demesne [is] 1 plough; and 1 villan [has] 1 ploughs. There are 4 bordars. It is worth 10s; and when received, as much; TRE 20s. 2 sokemen held this land and could give it to whom they wished.

In Sharnbrook Osbern de Breuil holds 1½ virgates of Hugh. There is land for 3 oxen. It is and was always worth 2s. 3 sokemen held this land and could give and sell it.

In Thurleigh Leofgeat holds half a hide. There is land for 2 ploughs, and there are [2 ploughs]. There are 4 bordars and 1 slave, [and] woodland for 30 pigs. It is worth 30s; when received, 15s; TRE 30s. Moding, a man of Queen Edith, held this land and could sell.

IN BARFORD HUNDRED

In Wyboston Wimund holds half a virgate of Hugh, and it is and was always worth 2s. Eskil, a thegn of King Edward, held this land.

In Chawston Riwallon holds 4 virgates of Hugh. There is land for 2 oxen. There are 2 bordars, and meadow for 2 oxen, [and] woodland for 60 pigs. It is worth 10s; when received, 15s; TRE 20s. 2 sokemen held this land and could give it to whom they wished.

In Roxton Riwallon holds of Hugh 1 hide and 1 virgate. There is land for 1 plough, meadow for 1 plough, [and] woodland for 4 pigs. There are 2 bordars and 1 slave. It is worth 10s; when received and TRE 20s. 4 sokemen, men of King Edward, held this land and could sell.

In Great Barford Riwallon holds 3 hides of Hugh. There is land for 4 ploughs. In demesne [are] 3 ploughs; and 3 villans have 1 plough. There are 5 bordars and 3 slaves, and 1 mill [rendering] 22s and 80 eels, [and] meadow for 2 ploughs. It is worth £3; when received, 30s; TRE £3. 3 sokemen, men of King Edward, held this land and could sell.

In the same [vill] Wimund de Tessel holds of Hugh 5 hides and 2 parts of 1 hide. There is land for 11 ploughs. In demesne [are] 5 ploughs; and 16 villans have 6 ploughs. There are 6 bordars and 1 slave, [and] meadow for 1 plough. It is worth £10; when received, 20s; 3 sokemen held this manor and could give and sell.

Wimund himself holds COLMWORTH of Hugh. It is assessed at 5 hides. There is land for 10 ploughs. In demesne [are] 2 ploughs; and 12 villans have 8 ploughs. There are 13 bordars and 1 slave, [and] woodland for 200 pigs. It is and was worth 100s; TRE £4. Aki, a thegn of King Edward, held this manor; and there were 8 sokemen, who could give and sell their land to whom they wished.

In Great Barford Ansketil the priest holds 1½ hides of Hugh. There is land for 2 ploughs. In demesne [is] 1 plough; and 1 villan [has] 1 plough. There are 6 bordars and 3 slaves, and 1 mill [rendering] 7s, [and] meadow for 1 plough. It is and was always worth 40s. 2 sokemen held this land and could sell.

In the same [vill] Theobald holds of Hugh 1 hide and 3

virgates and the third part of 1 virgate. There is land for 3 ploughs. In demesne [are] 2 [ploughs]; and 1 villan has 1 plough. There are 8 bordars and 1 slave, [and] meadow for 1 plough. It is worth 40s; when received, 20s; TRE 60s. 3 sokemen held this manor and could give and sell.

In Goldington Roger fitzTheodric holds 2 hides of Hugh. There is land for 3 ploughs. In demesne [are] 2 ploughs; and 3 villans have 1 plough. There are 2 bordars, [and] meadow for 1 plough. It is worth 30s; when received, 20s; TRE 40s. Ralph Taillebois held these 2 hides in exchange for Ware [Herts.]. 3 sokemen, who could give their land to whom they wished, held this land.

In the same [vill] Richard holds of Hugh 3 hides as 1 manor. There is land for 3 ploughs. In demesne [are] 2 ploughs; and 5 villans have 1 plough. There is 1 slave, [and] meadow for 2 ploughs. It is worth 40s; when received, 10s; TRE 60s. Ralph Taillebois held these 3 hides in exchange for Ware [Herts.]. Almær, a man of Eskil, held this manor and could sell.

In the same [vill] Walter holds 1 hide of Hugh. There is land for 1 plough, and there is [1 plough], [and] meadow for half a plough, and there are 2 slaves. It is worth 15s; when received, 10s; TRE 15s. This land is [held in] exchange for Ware [Herts.]. The men of the vill held this land in common and they could sell it.

IN BIGGLESWADE HUNDRED

In Holme Mortving holds 1 virgate of Hugh. [There is] land for 3 oxen, and there are [3 oxen]. It is worth 3s; TRE 5s. 1 sokeman held this land under Eskil and he could sell and give it.

In Astwick Bernard holds of Hugh 1 hide and 1 virgate. There is land for 2½ ploughs. In demesne [is] 1 plough; and 2 villans have 2½ ploughs. There are 3 bordars, and meadow for 4 oxen. It is worth 20s; when received and TRE 10s. 6 sokemen held this manor and could sell.

In the same [vill] Weneline holds half a hide of Hugh. There is land for 1 plough, and there is [1 plough]. There are 3 bordars. It is worth 10s; when received, 5s; TRE 20s - and they could sell it [sic].

In the same [vill] Leodmær holds half a hide. There is land for half a plough, and there is [half a plough]. There are 3 bordars, and 1 mill rendering 9s4d. It is and was always worth 20s. The same man who holds it held it TRE. [He was] a man of Earl Tosti, and he could sell to whom he wished.

IN "WICHESTANESTOU" HUNDRED

In Stanford Roger holds 1 hide of Hugh. There is land for 1½ ploughs, and there are [1½ ploughs], and 4 villans and 1 bordar, meadow for 1½ ploughs, woodland for 16 pigs, and half a mill rendering 5s. All together it is worth 15s; when received, 5s; TRE 10s. Æthelmær of Hoo held this land and could sell to whom he wished.

In Cople Robert holds of Hugh 4 hides as 1 manor. There is land for 4 ploughs. In demesne [are] 2 ploughs; and 6 villans have 2 ploughs. There is 1 bordar and 1 slave, [and] meadow for 1 plough. There is woodland over the whole of Cople for 100 pigs. It is worth 60s; when received, 20s; TRE 60s. 3 sokemen held this land and could sell.

In the same [vill] Reginald holds of Hugh 1 hide and 1 virgate. There is land for 1 plough, and there is [1 plough], and 2 bordars, and meadow for 4 oxen. It is worth 10s; when received, 5s; TRE 10s. 2 sokemen held this land and could sell to whom they wished.

In the same [vill] Gunfrid holds of Hugh 1 hide and half a virgate. There is land for 1 plough, and there is [1 plough]. There is 1 villan and 1 slave, [and] meadow for 4 oxen. It is worth 10s; when received, 5s; TRE 10s. 2 sokemen held this land. They were the king's men and could sell.

In the same [vill] Norman holds 1 hide of Hugh. There is land for 1 plough, and there are 2 oxen, [and] meadow for 4 oxen. It is worth 6s; when received, the same; TRE 8s. Of this land Eskil held 3 virgates.

[Folio 214: BEDFORDSHIRE]

which belonged to Willington, his manor, and Alstan held 1 virgate which he could sell to whom he wished.

In the same [vill] Branting held [sic] 1 hide of Hugh. There is land for 1 plough, and there is [1 plough, and] meadow for 4 oxen. It is and was always worth 10s. 3 sokemen held this land and could sell to whom they wished.

In the same [vill] Robert holds 3 virgates of Hugh. There is land for 1 plough, and there is [1 plough, and] meadow for 4 oxen. It is and was always worth 7½s. 2 sokemen held this land and could sell.

In the same [vill] Roger the priest and Liboret hold half a hide and half a virgate. There is land for 6 oxen, and there are [6 oxen, and] meadow for 4 oxen. It is and was always worth 5s. 3 sokemen held this land and could sell to whom they wished. Ralph Taillebois had 9 hides of this manor of Cople in exchange for Ware [Herts.], as his men say, and when he received them they were worth £4.

In Northill Walter holds half a hide of Hugh. There is land for half a plough, and there is [half a plough, and] meadow for half a plough. It is worth 5s; when received, the same; TRE 10s. Osgeat, a man of King Edward, held this land and could sell to whom he wished.

IN CLIFTON HUNDRED

In "Cudessane" 3 sokemen hold 2 hides of Hugh. There is land for 1½ ploughs, and there are [1½ ploughs], and 1 bordar, meadow for 1½ ploughs, [and] woodland for 4 pigs. It is worth 20s; and when received, as much; TRE 30s. 4 sokemen held this land and could sell to whom they wished.

XXIIII. The land of Nigel d'Aubigny

IN 'MANSHEAD' HUNDRED

In HUSBORNE CRAWLEY Turgis holds of Nigel d'Aubigny 5 hides as 1 manor. There is land for 5 ploughs. In demesne [are] 2 ploughs; and there can be 3 villans' ploughs. There is 1 villan and 7 bordars and 1 slave, [and] meadow for 5 ploughs. All together it is worth 30s; when received, 40s; TRE 100s. 9 thegns held this manor and they could give and sell their land to whom they wished.

In the same hundred Turgis holds 1 hide of Nigel. There is land for 1 plough, and there is [1] plough, and 2 slaves, [and] woodland for 10 pigs. This land is worth 15s; when received, 10s; TRE 20s. Fughle, a man of Ælfric son of Goding, held this land and he could sell to whom he wished.

Turgis holds TINGRITH of Nigel for 2 hides and 1 virgate. There is land for 3 ploughs. In demesne [is] 1 plough; and 4 villans have 2 ploughs. There are 2 bordars, meadow for 3 ploughs, [and] woodland for 150 pigs. It is worth 40s; when received, 30s; TRE 100s. 2 thegns held this manor and could sell to whom they wished.

In Priestley Turgis holds 1½ hides of Nigel. There is land for 2 ploughs, and there are [2 ploughs], meadow for 2 ploughs, [and] woodland for 40 pigs. There is 1 villan and 4 bordars. It is worth 20s; and when received, as much; TRE 60s. 5 thegns held this land and could give and sell it.

NIGEL holds HARLINGTON. It is assessed at 5 hides. There is land for 10 ploughs. In demesne [are] 3½ ploughs, and there can be 2 more. There 12 villans have 5 ploughs. There are 6 bordars and 10 slaves, meadow for 4 ploughs, woodland for 400 pigs, and 1 ram and 1 summa of oats from the woodland. It is worth £6; when received, £4; TRE £9. 4 thegns held this manor and could sell to whom they wished.

IN 'REDBORNSTOKE' HUNDRED

In [Lower and Upper] Shelton Herfast holds 1 hide of Nigel. There is land for 1 plough, and there is [1] plough, meadow for half a plough, [and] woodland for 40 pigs. There is 1 villan and 2 bordars and 1 slave. It is worth 20s; when received, 15s; TRE 20s. Alweard, a man of Ælfric son of Goding, held this land and he could give it to whom he wished.

In the same [vill] Stephen holds half a hide of Nigel. There is land for half a plough, and there is [half a plough], with 2 bordars, meadow for 2 oxen, [and] woodland for 12 pigs. It is worth 6s; when received, 3s; TRE 10s. Fughle, a man of Ælfric son of Goding, held this land and could sell to whom he wished.

In Marston Moretaine Herfast holds of Nigel 8 hides and half a virgate. There is land for 10 ploughs. In demesne [are] 3 ploughs; and 14 villans with 8 ploughs. There are 2 bordars and 4 slaves, meadow for 8 ploughs, [and] woodland for 300 pigs. It is worth £7; when received, 100s; TRE £12. 21 sokemen held this manor, who could sell and give their lands to whom they wished.

Nigel de le Vast holds Millbrook of Nigel d'Aubigny. It is assessed at 5 hides. There is land for 6 ploughs. In demesne [are] 2 ploughs; and 4 villans with 4 ploughs. There are 2 bordars, and 2 mills rendering 6s, meadow for 2 ploughs, [and] woodland for 100 pigs. It is worth £3; when received, 30s; TRE 100s. Godwine son of Leofwine held this manor who could all give or sell their land to whom they wished [sic].

It is assessed at 5 hides. There is land for 8 ploughs. In demesne [are] 2 ploughs; and 6 villans have 4 ploughs, and there can be 2 ploughs more. There are 2 bordars and 1 slave, meadow for 6 ploughs, [and] woodland for 300 pigs. It is worth £4; when received, 40s; TRE £4. 7 sokemen held this manor and they could sell and give their land to whom they wished.

Nigel de le Vast himself holds Ampthill of Nigel d'Aubigny. It is assessed at 5 hides. There is land for 8 ploughs. In demesne [are] 2 ploughs; and 6 villans have 4 ploughs, and there can be 2 ploughs more. There are 2 bordars and 1 slave, meadow for 6 ploughs, [and] woodland for 300 pigs. It is worth £4; when received, 40s.; TRE £4. 7 sokemen held this manor and they could sell and give their land to whom they wished.

In Maulden John de les Roches took unjust possession of 25 acres to the loss of the men who hold the vill, as the men of the hundred attest; and now Nigel d'Aubigny has them.

NIGEL d'Aubigny holds Cotton End. It is assessed at 3 hides, less 1 virgate. There is land for 6 ploughs. There are 5 [ploughs], and there can be a sixth. There are 5 villans and 11 bordars, meadow for 2 ploughs, [and] woodland for 100 pigs and [rendering] iron for the ploughs. It is worth 60s; when received, 40s; TRE £6. 7 sokemen held this manor and they could give and sell their land to whom they wished.

IN FLITTON HUNDRED

Nigel himself holds Clophill. It is assessed at 5 hides. There is land for 8 ploughs. In demesne [are] 3 hides, and there are 2 ploughs; and 5 villans have 6 ploughs. There are 5 bordars and 1 slave, meadow for 4 ploughs, [and] woodland for 200 pigs and [rendering] 12d. It is worth 60s; when received, 30s; TRE £8. 2 thegns, men of Earl Tosti, held this manor. Of these 5 hides Nigel himself claims 1 virgate which his predecessor held TRE. Nigel himself was seised of it after he came into [possession of] the honour, but Ralph Taillebois disseised him.

Nigel himself holds Cainhoe. It is assessed at 4 hides. There is land for 6 ploughs. There are 2 hides and 3 virgates in demesne, and 2 ploughs, and there can be 2 others. There 3 villans have 2 ploughs, and [there is] 1 mill rendering 6s, meadow for 8 ploughs, [and] woodland for 100 pigs and [rendering] 2s. There are 3 bordars and 5 slaves. It is worth 60s; when received, 30s; TRE 100s. Ælfric, a thegn of King Edward, held this manor and could give and sell it without his leave.

In Silsoe a certain concubine of Nigel holds 2 hides. There is land for 4 ploughs. In demesne [is] 1 plough; and 2 villans have 2 ploughs and there can be a third. There are 3 bordars and 1 slave, meadow for 3 ploughs, [and] woodland for 50 pigs. It is worth 30s; and as much when received; and as much TRE Ælfric the Little, a thegn of King Edward, held this land.

Roger and Riwallon hold Nigel d'Aubigny holds [sic] PULLOXHILL. It is assessed at 10 hides. There is land for 13 ploughs. In demesne [are] 2 ploughs, and there can be 2 others; and 11 villans have 9 ploughs. There are 13 bordars and 2 slaves, meadow for 6 ploughs, [and] woodland for 100 pigs. It is worth £10; when received, £8;

TRE £13. 8 sokemen held this manor and they could give and sell their land to whom they wished.

In Streatley Pirot holds of Nigel d'Aubigny 4 hides and the third part of 1 hide as 1 manor. There is land for 6 ploughs. In demesne [are] 2 ploughs; and 4 villans have 1 plough, and there can be 3 more. There are 4 bordars and 1 slave, meadow for 3 ploughs, [and] woodland for 20 pigs. There a certain man has 1 plough. It is worth £4; when received, 40s; TRE £6. Leofwine Cild held this manor, and 3 other thegns of King Edward, and they could sell their land to whom they wished. Pirot holds 3 hides of this land as his wife's marriage portion, and 1 hide and a third part of 1 hide he holds in fee of Nigel d'Aubigny.

In Milton Ernest Turgis holds of Nigel 3 hides, less 1 virgate. There is land for 4 ploughs. In demesne [is] 1 plough; and 4 villans [have] 2½ ploughs and half a plough villans [sic] and 3 bordars. [There is] meadow for 3 ploughs. It is worth 30s; and when received, as much; TRE 40s. 6 sokemen held this land and they could give or sell their land to whom they wished.

IN 'WILLEY' HUNDRED

In Carlton Ketil holds of Nigel 1 hide and the third part of 1 hide. There is land for 1½ ploughs, and there are [1½ ploughs], and 3 villans and 2 bordars, [and] meadow for 1½ ploughs. It is worth 20s; when received, 10s; TRE 15s. Goldrun, a man of Leofnoth, held this land and could give it to whom she wished.

In the same [vill] Bernard holds of Nigel 1 hide and half a virgate. There is land for 1½ ploughs, and there are [1½] ploughs, and 5 bordars, meadow for 1 plough, and 1 mill [rendering] 13s4d. It is worth 40s; when received, 20s; TRE 30s. 3 sokemen held this land and could give it to whom they wished.

In Radwell Nigel de le Vast holds of Nigel d'Aubigny 7 hides and 1½ virgates. There is land for 5 ploughs. In demesne [is] 1 [plough]; and 6 villans have 4 ploughs. There are 6 bordars and 3 slaves, and 1 mill rendering 10s, [and] meadow for 5 ploughs. It is worth £4; and when received, as much; TRE £8. 10 sokemen held this manor and they could give their land to whom they wished.

In Turvey Nigel de le Vast holds of Nigel d'Aubigny 1 hide and half a virgate. There is land for 1½ ploughs, and there are [1½ ploughs], and 5 bordars, meadow for 1 plough, [and] woodland for 20 pigs. It is worth 13s; and when received, as much; TRE 30s. Alweard, a man of Bishop Wulfwig, held this land and could give it to whom he wished.

IN BARFORD HUNDRED

In Wyboston Pirot holds of the king 9 hides and 1 virgate of Nigel's fief. There is land for 9 ploughs. In demesne [are] 4 ploughs; and 12 villans have 5 ploughs. There are 6 bordars, [and] meadow for 2 ploughs. It is worth £6; when received,

£4; TRE £10. 12 sokemen held this manor and could sell to whom they wished.

IN BIGGLESWADE HUNDRED

Fulcher of Paris holds half a hide of Nigel. There is land for 1 plough, and there is [1 plough, and] meadow for 1 plough, and 1 slave. It is worth 52s; when received, 10s; TRE 30s. Sæmær, a man of Leofwine, held this land and could sell.

In Holme Fulcher himself holds of Nigel 1 hide and half a virgate. There is land for 2 ploughs, and there are [2 ploughs], and 3 villans, [and] meadow for 1 plough. It is worth 20s; when received, 10s; TRE 30s. 7 sokemen held this land and could sell and give it.

IN "WICHESTANESTOU" HUNDRED

In Harrowden Nigel holds 6 hides. There is land for 8 ploughs. In demesne [are] 1½ hides and half a virgate, and there is 1 plough; and 14 villans have 7 ploughs. There are 10 bordars and 2 slaves, meadow for 2 ploughs, [and] woodland for 50 pigs. All together it is worth 100s; when received, £4; TRE 100s. 14 sokemen held this manor and they could give and sell their land to whom they wished.

IN CLIFTON HUNDRED

In Clifton William de Cairon holds 2 hides of Nigel. There is land for 1½ ploughs. There is 1 plough, and there can be half [a plough more. There is] meadow for 1 plough. It is worth 15s; when received, 10s; TRE 20s. 4 sokemen held this land and could give and sell it.

In Henlow Herfast holds 5½ hides of Nigel. There is land for 5½ ploughs. In demesne [are] 2 ploughs; and 10 villans have 3½ ploughs. There are 3 slaves, and 1 mill rendering 5s, [and] meadow for 5 ploughs. From pasture 10d. All together it is worth 110s; when received, £4; TRE £7. 9 sokemen held this land and could give and sell it to whom they wished.

Of these 5½ hides Saint-Nicholas of Angers now hold [sic] of Nigel 3 virgates in alms.

In Arlesey Herfast holds of Nigel 3 virgates and the third part of 1 virgate. There is land for 1 plough, and there is [1 plough, and] meadow for 1 plough. It is worth 17s; and when received as much; TRE 20s. 2 sokemen held this land and could sell to whom they wished.

XXV. The land of William Speke

IN 'MANSHEAD' HUNDRED

WILLIAM SPEKE holds in Hulcote 4 hides as 1 manor, and Ralph Passwater [holds] of him. There is land for 3 ploughs. In demesne [is] 1 plough; and 5 villans have 2 ploughs. There are 8 bordars and 1 slave, and 1 mill [rendering] 5s4d, [and] woodland for 50 pigs. All together it is worth 60s; when received, 20s; TRE 40s. Alweard Belrap, a man of Alric, held this manor and could sell to whom he wished. This land is in exchange for Toddington, which he exchanged [for it].

IN 'REDBORNSTOKE' HUNDRED

William fitzReginald holds Steppingley of William Speke. It is assessed at 5 hides. There is land for 7 ploughs. In demesne [are] 1½ ploughs; and 14 villans have 5½ ploughs, and [there are] 2 slaves, meadow for 7 ploughs, [and] woodland for 100 pigs. All together it is worth £4; when received, 40s; TRE £8. Almær, a man of Ælfric of Flitwick held this manor, and there were 2 sokemen, his men, who could sell their land to whom they wished.

IN FLITTON HUNDRED

In Streatley Hugh holds of William 2 parts of 1 virgate. There is land for 2 oxen. It is and was always worth 2s. Ælfric, a man of Ælfric the Little, held this land and could sell to whom he wished.

In Biddenham Ralph and Serlo de Rots hold of William 4 hides, less 1½ virgates. There is land for 4 ploughs. In demesne [are] 2 ploughs; and 6 villans have 2 ploughs. There are 2 bordars and 2 slaves, and 1 mill [rendering] 10s, [and] meadow for 4 ploughs. It is worth 40s; when received, 20s; TRE 40s. 11 sokemen held this manor and they could give and sell their land to whom they wished. William states he has this land in exchange for Toddington.

IN 'WILLEY' HUNDRED

In Hinwick Walter holds 1 hide of William. There is land for 2 ploughs. There is half a plough, and there can be another plough and a half. It is worth 10s; and when received, as much; TRE 20s. Wulfnoth, a man of Wulfsige son of Burgræd, held this land and he could give it to whom he wished.

In Wymington Walter holds 3 virgates of William.

[Folio 215: BEDFORDSHIRE]

There is land for half a plough. It is worth 2s; when received, 10s; TRE 10s. Leofric, a man of Burgræd, held this land and could give it to whom he wished.

IN BARFORD HUNDRED

In Chawston William fitzRaineward holds of William 7 hides and 1 virgate. There is land for 7 ploughs. In demesne [is] 1 plough; and 16 villans have 6 ploughs. There are 2 bordars and 1 slave, and 1 mill rendering 13s4d, meadow for 7 ploughs, [and] woodland for 10 pigs. All together it is worth £6; when received, £4; TRE £9. 12 sokemen held this land and could sell to whom they wished.

Of these 7 hides and 1 virgate the men of William Speke claim 1½ acres of meadow against the men of Eudo the steward; and the hundred attests that his predecessor had it TRE; and the same William claims against a certain man of Hugh de Beauchamp another 7 acres of land of which he himself was disseised, but his predecessor was seised. Of the aforesaid land Eudo the steward claims 1 acre against Riwallon, a man of Hugh de Beauchamp.

In the same [vill] William Gros holds half a hide of William Speke. There is land for half a plough, and there is [half a plough, and] meadow for half a plough. There are 2 villans. It is worth 5s; when received, 5s; TRE 10s. 2 men of King Edward held this land and could sell to whom they wished.

In ROXTON William Speke holds 8 hides and 3 virgates. There is land for 8 ploughs. In demesne [are] 4 hides and 3 virgates, and there are 2 ploughs; and 12 villans have 6 ploughs. There is 1 bordar and 1 slave, and 1 mill rendering 33s and 260 eels, meadow for 3 ploughs, [and] woodland for 20 pigs. It is worth £7; when received, 50s; TRE £10. 12 sokemen held this manor and they could sell their land to whom they wished.

IN BIGGLESWADE HUNDRED

In Eyeworth William Speke holds 9 hides as 1 manor. There is land for 9 ploughs. In demesne [are] 5½ hides, and there are 3 ploughs; and 13 villans have 6 ploughs. There are 2 bordars and 6 slaves, and 1 mill rendering 8s, [and] meadow for 9 ploughs. It is worth £7; when received, the same; TRE £8. 20 sokemen held this manor and they could give or sell their land to whom they wished without leave of their lords.

IN "WICHESTANESTOU" HUNDRED

In Southill 2 Frenchmen hold of William Speke 5 hides and half a virgate. There is land for 7 ploughs. In demesne [are] 4 ploughs; and 8 villans have 3 ploughs. There are 8 bordars and 6 slaves, meadow for 7 ploughs, [and] woodland for 200 pigs. It is worth £4.10s; when received, £4; TRE £3. 16 sokemen held this manor and they could give and sell their land to whom they wished.

In Stanford Hugh holds 1 hide of William Speke. There is land for 1 plough, and there is [1 plough], and half a mill [rendering] 5s. There are 2 slaves, meadow for 1 plough, [and] woodland for 20 pigs. It is worth 15s; when received, 20s; and as much TRE. Lemar, a thegn of King Edward, held this land.

In Old Warden William Speke holds of the king 9 hides as 1 manor. There is land for 9 ploughs. In demesne [are] 3½ hides, and there is 1 plough, and there can be another. There 18 villans have 7 ploughs. There are 4 bordars and 4 slaves, and 1 mill [rendering] 12s, [and] meadow for 6 ploughs. It is worth £6; and when received, as much; TRE £8. 8 sokemen held this manor and they could give their land to whom they wished.

In Beeston William Speke holds 3½ virgates. There is land for 1 plough. There is half a plough, and there can be [another] half. [There is] meadow for half a plough. It is worth 10s; and when received, as much; TRE 20s. This land Leofwine Cild, a king's thegn, held.

In Northill William Speke holds 6½ hides as 1 manor. There is land for 7 ploughs. In demesne [are] 4 hides, and there are 3 ploughs; and 10 villans have 4 ploughs. There are 4 slaves, and half a mill rendering 13s, meadow for 7 ploughs, [and] woodland for 200 pigs. All together it is worth £6; and when received, as much; TRE £8. 6 sokemen held this manor. They could give and sell it to whom they wished TRE.

XXVI. The land of Robert de Tosny

IN STANBRIDGE HUNDRED

ROBERT de Tosny holds Studham of the king, and Baldric [holds] of Robert. It is assessed at 6 hides. There is land for 6 ploughs. In demesne [are] 2 ploughs; and 10 villans have 4 ploughs. There is 1 bordar and 4 slaves, [and] woodland for 100 pigs. It is worth £4; when received, 40s; TRE £8. Oswulf son of Frani, a thegn of King Edward, held this manor.

In Oakley 2 knights hold 4 hides of Robert. There is land for 8 ploughs. In demesne [are] 3 ploughs, and there can be a fourth. There 7 villans have 4 ploughs, and [there are] 3 bordars and 5 slaves, and 1 mill [rendering] 26s and 200 eels, [and] meadow for 4 ploughs. It is worth £4; when received, the same; TRE £4.10s. Oswulf, a thegn of King Edward, held this land.

IN 'WILLEY' HUNDRED

In Turvey 2 knights hold of Robert 2 hides and 1 virgate. There is land for 4½ ploughs. In demesne [are] 2 ploughs; and 3 villans have 2 ploughs and there can be half a plough [more]. There are 6 bordars and 2 slaves, meadow for 1 plough, [and] woodland for 10 pigs. It is worth 40s; when received, 60s; TRE 70s. The aforesaid Oswulf held this land.

XXVII. The land of Gilbert de Ghent

IN THE HALF-HUNDRED OF STANBRIDGE

GILBERT de Ghent holds Edlesborough [Bucks.]. It is assessed at 10 hides. There is land for 7 ploughs. In demesne [are] 5 hides and there are 4 ploughs; and 10 villans have 4 ploughs. In all it is worth 110s; when received, the same; TRE £10. Ulf, a thegn of King Edward, held this manor and could do with it what he wished.

XXVIII. The land of Robert d'Oilly

IN 'WILLEY' HUNDRED

ROBERT d'Oilly holds half a hide in Thurleigh, and Richard Basset [holds] of him. There is land for 2 ploughs. There is now 1 [plough], and there can be another. There is 1 villan and 3 bordars and 2 slaves, [and] woodland for 30 pigs. It is and was always worth 40s. Wulfgeat, a thegn of King Edward, held this land and could sell to whom he wished. The men of Eudo claim this through the predecessor of their lord, all whose lands King William gave to him.

In the same [vill] Salomon the priest holds 1 virgate of Robert d'Oilly. There is land for 1 plough, and there is [1 plough], with 1 bordar. It is and was always worth 10s. Alwine, a man of Bishop Wulfwig, held this land and could sell.

XXIX. The land of Ranulph brother of Ilger

IN THE HALF-HUNDRED OF 'BUCKELOWE'

RANULPH, Ilger's brother, holds 5 hides in Pavenham, and Robert fitzNigel [holds] of him. There is land for 6 ploughs. In demesne [is] 1 plough, and there can be another; and 9 villans have 2 ploughs and there can be another 2. There are 2 bordars and 3 slaves, [and] meadow for 6 ploughs. It is worth £3; when received, £4; TRE £6. Godwine, a thegn of King Edward, held this manor. Of this land Ranulph, Ilger's brother, claims 12 acres of land against Gilbert fitzSalomon, and 4 acres of meadow against Hugh de Grandmesnil, of which Ranulph has been unjustly disseised; and the men of the half-hundred state that this land which Hugh and Gilbert now hold belonged TRE to the land which Ranulph, Ilger's brother, holds.

XXX. The land of Robert Fafiton

IN FLITTON HUNDRED

ROBERT Fafiton holds FLITTON of the king. It is assessed at 5 hides.

[Folio 215V: BEDFORDSHIRE]

There is land for 6 ploughs. In demesne [are] 2 hides, and there are 2 ploughs. There 3 villans have 2 ploughs, and there can be 2 others. There are 3 bordars and 4 slaves, meadow for 6 ploughs, [and] woodland for 50 pigs. All together it is worth 60s; and when received, as much; TRE 100s. Alwine Horne, a thegn of King Edward, held this manor.

XXXI. The land of Alvred of Lincoln

IN 'WILLEY' HUNDRED

ALVRED of Lincoln holds 3 hides in Wymington, and Gleu [holds] of him. There is land for 4 ploughs. In demesne [is] 1 plough and there can be another. There is 1 villan and 6 bordars and 3 slaves with 2 ploughs, [and] meadow for 2 ploughs. It is worth 40s; when received, 50s; TRE 60s. Godwine Frambold held this manor and could sell. With these 3 hides Alvred claims against Walter the Fleming half a hide of which he disseised him unjustly, as the men of the hundred testify, since his predecessor was seised of it TRE, and the same Alvred was afterwards seised of it. With this land, besides, the same Alvred claims against the Bishop of Coutances woodland for 100 pigs, which his predecessor had TRE, but the bishop disseised him unjustly, as the men of the hundred attest.

XXXII. The land of Walter the Fleming

IN THE HALF-HUNDRED OF STANBRIDGE

WALTER the Fleming holds TOTTERNHOE, and Osbert [holds] of him. It was assessed at 15 hides TRE. But after King William came to England it was assessed only at 10 hides, and the men who held and [still] hold the 5 hides kept back all the king's customary dues and rent and [still] keep them back. There is land for 10 ploughs. In demesne [are] 2 ploughs; and 22 villans have 4 ploughs, and there can be 4 others. There are 2 bordars and 4 slaves. There are 3 mills rendering 10s8d, meadow for 4 ploughs, [and] woodland for 150 pigs. All together it is worth £8; when received, £10; TRE £16. Leofnoth, a thegn of King Edward, held this manor and could sell to whom he wished.

IN 'STODDEN' HUNDRED

In Milton Ernest Reginald holds 2 hides of Walter. There is land for 3 ploughs. In demesne is 1 plough; and 2 villans have 1 plough, and there can be another. There is 1 bordar, [and] meadow for 2 ploughs. It is worth 20s; and when received, as much; TRE 25s. 2 sokemen, men of Beorhtric, held this land and could give it to whom they wished.

IN 'WILLEY' HUNDRED

In Turvey Hugh holds 1 hide of Walter. There is land for 2 ploughs. In demesne is 1 [plough]; and 8 bordars and 1 slave with 1 plough. [There is] meadow for 1 plough, [and] woodland for 40 pigs. It is worth 30s; when received, 10s; TRE 40s. Leofnoth, a thegn of King Edward, held this land and could sell to whom he wished.

In Odell Walter the Fleming holds of the king 5 hides and 1 virgate and 2 parts of 1 virgate. There is land for 5 ploughs. In demesne [are] 2 hides, and there are 2 ploughs; and 13 villans with 3 ploughs. There are 5 bordars and 5 slaves, and 1 mill rendering 36s8d and 200 eels, meadow for 5 ploughs, [and] woodland for 60 pigs. It is worth 100s; when received, £8; TRE £10. Leofnoth, a thegn of King Edward, held this manor, and in the same place 1 sokeman had half a hide which he could give to whom he wished.

In Podington Hugh holds of Walter 1 hide and 3 virgates. There is land for 5½ ploughs. In demesne are 2 ploughs; and 4 villans have 3½ ploughs. There are 9 bordars and 2 slaves, meadow for 1 plough, [and] woodland for 20 pigs. It is worth £4.10s; when received, 50s; and as much TRE. Leofnoth, a thegn of King Edward, held this manor.

In Wymington Osbert holds of Walter 4 hides as 1 manor. There is land for 5 ploughs. In demesne [are] 3 ploughs; and there is 1 villan and 8 bordars and 4 slaves with 1 plough. [There is] meadow for 2 ploughs. It is worth £3; and when received, as much; TRE £4. Lant, a man of Leofnoth, a thegn of the king, held this manor, and there 1 sokeman had 1 hide and could give it to whom he wished.

In the same vill the same Osbert holds half a hide of Walter. There is land for half a plough, but there is no [plough] there. It is worth 2s; when received, 4s; TRE 10s. Godwine Frambold held this land and could give it to whom he wished. Alvred of Lincoln claims this same [land] against Walter the Fleming.

In Thurleigh Hugh holds of Walter 3 hides as 1 manor. There is land for 7 ploughs. In demesne [are] 2 ploughs; and 8 villans have 5 ploughs. There are 12 bordars and 3 slaves, [and]

woodland for 150 pigs. It is worth 100s; when received, 60s; TRE £4. Leofnoth, a thegn of King Edward, held this manor.

In the same [vill] Reginald holds half a hide of Walter. There is land for 2 ploughs. In demesne [is] 1 plough; and 4 bordars with 1 plough. It is worth 20s; when received, 10s; TRE 5s. Ordric, a man of Leofnoth, held this land and could sell.

IN BIGGLESWADE HUNDRED

In Stratton he holds 1 hide and 1 virgate. There is land for 1½ ploughs, and there can be 1½ ploughs [more]. There are 3 bordars, [and] meadow for 1 plough. It is and was always worth 10s. Leofwine, a thegn of King Edward, held this land and could give and sell it. This belongs and belonged to Longford, the manor of the same Walter.

In Holme Walter holds 1 hide. There is land for 1½ ploughs. There is 1 plough, and there can be a half [-plough more]. There are 3 bordars, [and] meadow for 1½ ploughs. It is worth 20s; when received, 16s; TRE 20s. 2 sokemen held this land and could give it to whom they wished.

In Astwick Hugh holds 1 virgate of Walter. There is land for 2 oxen, and there are [2 oxen]. There is 1 bordar, and 1 mill rendering 13s. It is and was always worth 16s. Leofwine, a thegn of King Edward, held this land.

Walter himself holds LANGFORD. It is assessed at 10 hides. There is land for 16 ploughs. In demesne [are] 4 hides and 1 virgate, and there are 4 ploughs, and there can be a fifth. There are 12 villans, 7 bordars [and] 5 slaves with 9 ploughs, and there can be 2 [ploughs] more. There are 2 mills rendering 26s8d, meadow for 16 ploughs and [rendering] 2s besides. From pasture 6s, and there is pasture besides for 300 sheep. [There is] woodland for 16 pigs. All together it is worth £15.10s; when received, £10; TRE £15. Leofwine, a thegn of King Edward, held this manor, and there 1 sokemen had 1 hide and he could give it to whom he wished.

IN ''WICHESTANESTOU'' HUNDRED

In Southill Walter holds half a hide of woodland which his predecessor held TRE.

In the same vill Alric holds 1 virgate of Walter. There is land for 4 oxen, and there are [4 oxen], [and] meadow for 4 oxen. It is worth 5s; when received, 3s; TRE 10s. Leofwine, a thegn of the king, held this land in pledge TRE. But after King William came to England, he himself who pledged this land redeemed it, and Seiher took possession of it to the king's loss, as the men of the hundred testify.

IN CLIFTON HUNDRED

In Henlow Hugh holds 3½ hides of Walter. There is land for 3½ ploughs. In demesne [is] 1 plough, and there can be another. There are 4 villans with 2 ploughs, and 4 bordars and 2 slaves, meadow for 3½ ploughs, and 1 mill rendering 34s. All together it is worth 60s; when received, 40s; TRE 70s. 6 sokemen held this land and they could give their land to whom they wished.

XXXIII. The land of Walter brother of Seiher

IN 'REDBORNSTOKE' HUNDRED

WALTER, Seiher's brother, holds SEGENHOE. It is assessed at 10 hides. There is land for 10 ploughs. In demesne [are] 4 hides, and there is 1 plough, and there can be 2 ploughs. There 24 villans have 7 ploughs. There are 4 bordars and 3 slaves, meadow for 8 ploughs, woodland for 300 pigs, and from customary dues of the woodland, 10 rams a year. All together it is worth £6; when received, £10; TRE £16. Leofnoth, a thegn of King Edward, held this manor, and there 1 sokeman had half a hide and could sell it to whom he wished.

IN FLITTON HUNDRED

In SILSOE Hugh holds of Walter 4 hides as 1 manor. There is land for 10 ploughs. In demesne [are] 2 ploughs; and 6 villans and 8 bordars and 4 slaves with 7 ploughs, and there can be an eighth. There is 1 mill rendering 26d, meadow for 6 ploughs, [and] woodland for 100 pigs and [rendering] 2s. All together it is worth £8; when received, 100s; TRE £11. Leofnoth, a thegn of King Edward, held this manor, and there 3 sokemen held half a hide and could give and sell it to whom they wished. Hugh holds this half-hide of the king, as his men say.

XXXIIII. The land of Hugh the Fleming

IN 'WILLEY' HUNDRED

HUGH the Fleming holds of the king in Podington 2 hides and 1 virgate. There is land for $2\frac{1}{2}$ ploughs. In demesne [is] half a hide, and 1 plough; and 3 villans have $1\frac{1}{2}$ ploughs. There are 6 bordars and 1 slave. It is worth 30s; and when received, as much; TRE 40s. 4 sokemen held this land and could sell to whom they wished.

Hugh himself holds in Hinwick $1\frac{1}{2}$ hides of the king. There is land for 3 ploughs. In demesne [are] 2 ploughs; and 1 villan and 4 bordars and 3 slaves with 1 plough. It is worth 30s; when received, 20s; TRE 40s. Alweald, a man of Bishop Wulfwig, held this land and could sell.

In Sharnbrook Robert holds of Hugh half a hide and the fourth part of 1 virgate. There is land for 1 plough, and there is [1 plough], and 1 bordar and 1 slave, [and] meadow for 1 plough. It is worth 10s; when received, 5s; TRE 20s. Leofric, a man of the Abbot of Ramsey, held this land and could give it to whom he wished.

XXXV. The land of Hugh the Butler

IN 'STODDEN' HUNDRED

HUGH the butler holds of the king in Easton [Hunts.] 2 hides and 3 virgates. There is land for 4 ploughs. In demesne [is] 1 hide, and there are 2 ploughs. There are 4 villans and 1 bordar and 1 slave with 2 ploughs, meadow for 1 plough, [and] woodland for 200 pigs. It is worth 40s; when received, 70s;

TRE 40s. Wig, a thegn of King Edward, held this manor, and in the same place 1 sokeman had half a hide and could give it to whom he wished.

In 'Shirdon' [in Sandy] Hugh holds 1 virgate, and it is worth 12d; TRE 2s. Alwine, a man of Earl Harold, held this land and could give it to whom he wished.

XXXVI. The land of Sigar de Chocques

IN 'STODDEN' HUNDRED

SIGAR de Chocques holds in Easton [Hunts.] 2 hides of the king. There is land for 5 ploughs. In demesne [are] 2 carucates of land besides the 2 hides, and there are 2 ploughs; and 6 villans have 3 ploughs. There are 12 bordars and 2 slaves, meadow for 1 plough, [and] woodland for 60 pigs. It is worth £4; when received, £3; TRE £4. Wig, a thegn of King Edward, held this land and could give and sell it to whom he wished.

XXXVII. The land of Gunfrid de Chocques

IN 'WILLEY' HUNDRED

GUNFRID de Chocques holds in Hinwick 1 hide and 3 virgates. Theobald [holds] of him. There is land for 3 ploughs. In demesne [is] 1 plough, and there can be 2 ploughs. There are 3 villans. It is worth 20s; when received, 10s; TRE 40s. 2 sokemen held this land and could give and sell it to whom they wished.

XXXVIII. The land of Richard son of Count Gilbert

IN BARFORD HUNDRED

RICHARD son of Count Gilbert holds in 'Sudbury' [in Eaton Socon] 1 virgate of land which belongs to the Church of St Neot, and belonged [to it] TRE.

In Wyboston the monks of St Neot hold of the aforesaid Richard 2 hides and half a virgate. There is land for half a plough, but there is no [plough] there. [There is] woodland for 100 pigs. It is worth 11s; when received, the same; TRE 21s. This land belonged to the Church of St Neot, TRE, in alms.

XXXIX. The land of Richard Puignant

IN BIGGLESWADE HUNDRED

RICHARD Puignant holds of the king in Dunton 8 hides and a virgate as 1 manor. There is land for 8 ploughs. In demesne [are] 4 hides and 1 virgate, and there are 3 ploughs. There 12 villans have 5 ploughs, and [there are] 2 bordars and 3 slaves, [and] woodland for 60 pigs. All together it is worth £8; when received, £6; and as much TRE. Archbishop Stigand held this manor.

In Tempsford Robert holds of Richard Puignant 2 hides of the king's fief. There is land for 2 ploughs. In demesne [is] 1 plough; and 4 villans with 1 plough, [and] meadow for 1 plough. It is worth 30s; when received, 20s; TRE 20s. 3

sokemen held this land and could give it to whom they wished.

IN "WICHESTANESTOU" HUNDRED

In Southill Richard Puignant holds half a hide of woodland which Archbishop Stigand held TRE.

XL. The land of William the Chamberlain

IN 'MANSHEAD' HUNDRED

WILLIAM the chamberlain holds in Potsgrove 1 hide of the king. There is land for 1 plough, and there is [1 plough, and] meadow for 1 plough. It is worth 15s; when received, the same; TRE 40s. Morcar the priest of Luton held this land and could sell.

In Battlesden Robert holds half a hide of William the chamberlain. There is land for half a plough. It is worth 5s; when received, the same; TRE £7. Morcar the priest held this land and could sell.

IN THE HALF-HUNDRED OF STANBRIDGE

William himself holds Totternhoe of the king. It is assessed at 7 hides less 1 virgate. There is land for 6 ploughs. In demesne [are] 3 hides and 3 virgates, and there is 1 plough. There 4 villans have 3 ploughs. There are 4 bordars and 4 slaves, and 1 mill [rendering] 3s, meadow for 3 ploughs, [and] woodland for 20 pigs. It is worth 50s; when received, the same; TRE £8. Leofwine, a man of Earl Waltheof, held this manor. With this manor William the chamberlain claims 2 hides which his predecessor held TRE, as the hundred testifies, but the Bishop of Bayeux took them from him by force and gave them to Adelulf his chamberlain.

XLI. The land of William Lovet

IN 'MANSHEAD' HUNDRED

WILLIAM Lovet holds in Husborne Crawley of the king 5 hides as 1 manor. There is land for 5 ploughs. In demesne [are] 2 hides and 2 ploughs; and 5 villans have 2 ploughs, and there can be a third. There are 3 bordars and 2 slaves, and 2 mills [rendering] 10s, [and] meadow for 5 ploughs. It is worth 40s; when received, 30s; TRE 100s. Grimbald, a man of King Edward, held this manor and could give it to whom he wished.

IN 'REDBORNSTOKE' HUNDRED

William himself holds Flitwick of the king. It is assessed at 5 hides. There is land for 7 ploughs. In demesne [are] 2 hides, and there are 2 ploughs. There 3 villans have 3 ploughs, and there can be 2 more. There are 7 bordars, and 1 mill [rendering] 4s, meadow for 5 ploughs, [and] woodland for 100 pigs. It is worth 50s; when received, 60s; TRE £8. Alwine, a thegn of King Edward, held this manor.

XLII. The land of William

IN 'WILLEY' HUNDRED

WILLIAM holds 2 hides of the king in Farndish. There is land for 2½ ploughs. In demesne are 2 ploughs; and 3 villans have half a plough. There are 2 bordars and 1 slave, [and] meadow for 1 plough. It is worth 40s; when received, 20s; TRE 40s. 3 sokemen held this land and could give and sell it to whom they wished.

[Folio 216V: BEDFORDSHIRE]

XLIII. The land of Henry fitzAzor

IN 'WILLEY' HUNDRED

HENRY fitzAzor holds 1 hide in Farndish of the king. There is land for 1 plough, and there is [1 plough], and there are 2 villans, [and] meadow for half a plough. It is and was worth 10s; TRE 20s. 2 sokemen held this land and could give it to whom they wished.

XLIIII. The land of Osbern fitzRichard

IN 'STODDEN' HUNDRED

OSBERN fitzRichard holds in Easton [Hunts.] half a hide and half a virgate, and Hugh Hubald [holds] of him. There is land for 1 plough, and there is [1 plough], with 1 slave. [There is] meadow for 1 plough, [and] woodland for 20 pigs. It is worth 10s; when received, the same; TRE 12s. Stori, a man of Earl Tosti, held this land, and there a certain sokeman had half a virgate which he could give and sell.

In Riseley Hugh Hubald holds half a hide of Osbern fitzRichard. There is land for half a plough, and there is [half a plough], with 1 bordar, [and] meadow for half a plough. It is and was worth 5s; TRE 8s. Alwine, a man of Stori, held this land and could give it to whom he wished.

In Keysoe Hugh Hubald holds 1 virgate of Osbern. There is land for 2 oxen. It is and was worth 2s; TRE 4s.

Hugh himself holds of Osbern 'Elvedon' [in Pertenhall]. It is assessed at 1 hide and 1 virgte. [There is] land for 1½ ploughs, and there are [1½ ploughs], meadow for 1 plough, [and] woodland for 34 pigs. It is and was worth 10s; TRE 15s. Alwine, a man of Stori, held this manor and could give it to whom he wished.

XLV. The land of Obsern fitzWalter

IN BIGGLESWADE HUNDRED

OSBERN fitzWalter holds of the king in Little Barford 3 hides as 1 manor. There is land for 3 ploughs. In demesne [are] 2 ploughs; and 4 villans have 1 plough. There are 2 bordars and 5 slaves, [and] meadow for 1 plough. It is worth 60s; when received, 40s; TRE 60s. Wulfmær of Eaton Socon, a thegn of King Edward, held this manor.

XLVI. The land of Osbern the Fisherman

IN 'WILLEY' HUNDRED

OSBERN the fisherman holds in Sharnbrook half a hide of the king. There is land for 1 plough, and there is [1 plough. There is] a mill [rendering] 16d, meadow for half a plough, woodland for 10 pigs, and a fishpond. There is 1 villan and 2 bordars. It is worth 26s; when received, 10s; TRE 40s. Tovi, a housecarl of King Edward, held this land and could sell. With this land the same Osbern claims 1 virgate and the fourth part of 1 virgate which his predecessor held TRE. But after King William came into England he refused to give the rent from this land and Ralph Taillebois gave the rent and took possession of the land itself in forfeiture and handed it over to a certain knight of his.

In Carlton the same Osbern holds of the king 1 hide and 1½ virgates. There is land for 2 ploughs. In demesne [is] 1 plough; and 2 villans have 1 plough. There are 4 bordars, [and] meadow for 2 ploughs. It is and was worth 20s; TRE TRE [sic] 40s. Godwine Frambolt, a thegn of King Edward, held this land and could sell.

XLVII. The land of Turstin the Chamberlain

IN 'BUCKELOWE' HUNDRED

TURSTIN the chamberlain holds of the king in Pavenham 2½ hides as 1 manor. There is land for 3 ploughs. In demesne [is] 1 hide and 1 plough. There are 6 villans with 2 ploughs, and 1 bordar, [and] meadow for 3 ploughs. It is worth 40s; when received, the same; TRE 45s. Alsige, a man of Alli his brother, held this land and could [sell?].

In Hinwick Turstin holds of the king 1 hide and 3 virgates. There is land for 2 ploughs. In demesne [is] 1 hide and 1 plough; and 2 villans with 1 plough, and 1 bordar, [and] meadow for 1 plough. It is worth 30s; when received, 10s; TRE 30s. Godwine Frambolt, a thegn of King Edward, held this land.

IN "WICHESTANESTOU" HUNDRED

In Beeston the aforesaid Turstin holds half a hide of the king. There is land for half a plough, but there is no [plough] there. [There is] meadow for 1 plough. This land has been laid waste, but when Turstin received it, it was worth 10s; TRE 20s. Godwine, a man of Earl Tosti, held this land and could give it.

IN CLIFTON HUNDRED

In Campton Turstin holds of the king 2 hides, and less [sic] the fourth part of 1 virgate. There is land for 1½ ploughs. In demesne [is] 1 hide and 1 virgate and 3 parts of 1 virgate, and there is 1 plough. There 2 villans and 1 bordar have half a plough. [There is] meadow for 1½ ploughs, [and] woodland for 20 pigs. It is and was worth 30s; TRE 40s. 3 sokemen held this land and could give and sell it to whom they wished.

XLVIII. The land of Gilbert fitzSalomon

IN CLIFTON HUNDRED

GILBERT fitzSalomon holds Meppershall of the king. It is assessed at 4 hides in Bedfordshire. There is land for 4 ploughs. In Hertfordshire this vill is assessed at 3 hides and 1 virgate. There is land for 3 ploughs. All together there are 7 ploughs. In demesne [are] 5 hides and 3 ploughs, and there can be 2 more [ploughs]. There 5 villans have 2 ploughs, and [there are] 4 bordars and 2 slaves. [There is] meadow for 7 ploughs, woodland for 200 pigs and from the customary dues of the woodland 10s. It is and was worth £6; TRE £10. Leofwine Cild, a thegn of King Edward, held this manor, and in this manor were 4 sokemen. They held 2 hides and could sell them to whom they wished.

IN 'WILLEY' HUNDRED

In Felmersham Gilbert holds 7½ hides. There is land for 8 ploughs. In demesne [are] 4 hides, and there are 3 ploughs; and 4 villans have 4 ploughs. There are 6 bordars, [and] meadow for 4 ploughs. It is worth 100s; when received, £12; and as much TRE. 6 sokemen held this manor and could sell.

XLIX. The land of Albert of Lorraine

IN 'MANSHEAD' HUNDRED

ALBERT of Lorraine holds CHALGRAVE of the king. It is assessed at 8 hides and 2 parts of 1 virgate. There is land for 10 ploughs. In demesne [are] 3 carucates of land, and there are 2 ploughs. There 13 villans have 8 ploughs. There are 4 bordars and 6 slaves, meadow for 8 ploughs, [and] woodland for 50 pigs. It is worth £7; when received, £6; and as much TRE. The same Albert held this manor TRE and could give it to whom he wished.

IN 'REDBORNSTOKE' HUNDRED

Albert himself holds WOOTTON. It is assessed at 10 hides. There is land for 11 ploughs. In demesne [are] 2 hides, and there are 3 ploughs. There 20 villans have 7 ploughs, and there could be an eighth. There are 6 slaves, meadow for 5 ploughs, [and] woodland for 400 pigs. It is worth £10; when received, £8; TRE £10.15s. Almær, a man of Earl Tosti, held this manor and could sell.

In [Lower and Upper] Shelton Albert holds 3 hides. There is land for 5 ploughs. In demesne [is] 1 hide, and there are 2 ploughs. There are 7 villans with 3 ploughs, and 4 slaves, meadow for 3 ploughs, [and] woodland for 100 pigs. It is worth 40s; when received, 20s; TRE 45s. This manor was and is a member of Wootton. Almær, a man of Earl Tosti, held it.

IN 'WILLEY' HUNDRED

In Sharnbrook Albert holds 2 hides and the fourth part of 1 virgate. There is land for 3 ploughs. In demesne [is] 1 hide, and there are 2 ploughs; and 4 villans with 1 plough. There are 4 bordars and 4 slaves, and 1 mill [rendering] 16s, meadow for 2 ploughs, [and] woodland for 40 pigs. It is worth 50s; when received, 30s; TRE 60s. Algar, a man of Queen Edith, held this land and could give it to whom he wished.

L. The land of David d'Argentan

IN 'STODDEN' HUNDRED

DAVID d'Argentan holds in Riseley 1 hide of the king. There is land for 1 plough, but there is no [plough] there. There is 1 villan and 3 bordars. It is worth 10s; when received, 20s; TRE the same. Homdai, a man of Earl Harold, held this land and could sell to whom he wished.

[Folio 217: BEDFORDSHIRE]

LI. The land of Ralph de l'Isle

IN BIGGLESWADE HUNDRED

RALPH de l'Isle holds of the king in Stratton 4 hides as 1 manor. There is land for 8 ploughs. There are 7 [ploughs], and there can be an eighth. There are 10 villans and 2 bordars, [and] meadow for 4 ploughs. All together it is worth £12; when received, £4; TRE 100s. Archbishop Stigand held this manor.

Ralph himself holds Biggleswade. It is assessed at 10 hides. There is land for 10 ploughs. In demesne [are] 5½ hides, and there are 3 ploughs. There are 7 villans with 7 ploughs, and 10 bordars and 3 slaves, and 2 mills rendering 47s, [and] meadow for 10 ploughs and 5s from the hay. It is worth £17; when received, £15; TRE £10. Archbishop Stigand held this manor, and there 2 sokemen had half a hide which they could give and sell.

In Holme the same Ralph holds 2 hides. There is land for 5 ploughs, and there are [5 ploughs]. There are 6 villans, [and] meadow for 1 plough. It is worth 40s; when received, 30s; TRE 40s. Archbishop Stigand held this manor, and there 3 sokemen had 2 virgates of land and could sell them.

IN "WICHESTANESTOU" HUNDRED

In Old Warden the same Ralph holds 1½ virgates of the king. This land belongs to Biggleswade and it is valued there, and he who held it TRE could neither sell nor give it without the leave of the man who held Biggleswade.

LII. The land of Joscelin the Breton

IN 'MANSHEAD' HUNDRED

JOSCELIN the Breton holds of the king in Potsgrove 7½ hides as 1 manor. There is land for 7½ ploughs. In demesne [are] 3 hides, and there are 3 ploughs. There 3 villans have 2 ploughs, and there can be 2½ others. There are 6 bordars and 3 slaves, [and] meadow for 5 ploughs. It is worth 50s; when received, 100s; TRE £10. 4 thegns held this manor and they could give and sell their land to whom they wished.

IN THE HALF-HUNDRED OF STANBRIDGE

Joscelin himself holds Nares Gladley for 2½ hides. There is land for 1 plough, and there are 4 oxen, and 1 mill [rendering] 16s, meadow for 1 plough, [and] woodland for 100 pigs. It is and was worth 20s; TRE 40s. Vigot, a huntsman of King Edward, held this land and could sell to whom he wished.

LIII. The land of Countess Judith

IN 'REDBORNSTOKE' HUNDRED

Countess JUDITH holds in Maulden 5 hides and 1½ virgates, and the nuns of Elstow hold of her in alms. There is land for 5 ploughs. In demesne [are] 2 ploughs; and 7 villans have 3 ploughs. There are 2 slaves, and 1 mill [rendering] 3s, meadow for 5 ploughs, [and] woodland for 100 pigs. It is worth 60s; when received, £4; TRE £7. Æthelweald, a thegn of King Edward, held this manor, and there 1 sokemen had half a virgate and could give it to whom he wished.

In Houghton Conquest Hugh holds half a hide of Countess Judith. There is land for 1 plough, and there is [1 plough], and 2 bordars, and woodland for 25 pigs. It is and was worth 10s; TRE 12s. Leofsige, a man of Earl Tosti, held this land and could give and sell it to whom he wished.

The countess herself holds WILSTEAD, and nuns hold it of her. It is assessed at 3 hides. [There is] land for 6 ploughs. In demesne [are] 2 ploughs. There 11 villans have 4 ploughs, and [there are] 11 bordars and 1 slave, [and] meadow for half a plough. It is worth £7.6s; when received, 45s; TRE £10.10s. 8 sokemen held this manor and could give and sell it. Countess Judith gave it to ST MARY of Elstow in alms, but the soke has always belonged to Kempston.

ELSTOW is assessed at 3½ hides. The nuns of ST MARY hold it of Countess Judith. There is land for 7 ploughs. In demesne [are] 2 ploughs; and 14 villans have 5 ploughs. There are 11 bordars and 4 slaves, and 1 mill rendering 24s, meadow for 4 ploughs, [and] woodland for 60 pigs. It is worth 100s; when received, 40s; TRE £10. 4 sokemen held this manor. They were men of King Edward; they could give and sell their land, but their soke always belonged to Kempston.

KEMPSTON is assessed at 10 hides. There is land for 20 ploughs. The countess holds it. In demesne [are] 2 hides, and there are 4 ploughs; and 18 villans have 12 ploughs, and there can be 4 more. There are 12 bordars and 8 slaves, and 1 mill rendering 5s, meadow for 20 ploughs, woodland for 200 pigs, and from pasture, 2s. In all it is worth £18; when received, £22; TRE £30. Earl Gyrth held this manor, and in the same place 2 thegns had 2½ hides and 1½ virgates and could give and sell them to whom they wished.

IN 'STODDEN' HUNDRED

In Bolnhurst Hugh holds half a hide of the countess. There is land for 1 plough, and there is [1 plough], with 2 bordars. [There is] meadow for 4 oxen, [and] woodland for 20 pigs. It is worth 10s; when received, 5s; TRE 12s. Almær, a thegn of King Edward, held this land and could give and sell it.

In Oakley Miles Crispin holds 1 hide of the countess. There is land for 1½ ploughs. There is 1 plough, and there can be half [a plough more]. There are 3 bordars, and meadow for 1 plough. It is and was worth 10s; TRE 20s. Godwine, a man of Earl Harold, held this land and could sell.

IN THE HALF-HUNDRED OF 'BUCKELOWE'

In Bletsoe Osbern holds 2½ hides of the countess. There is land for 4 ploughs. In demesne [is] 1 plough; and 6 villans have 3 ploughs. There are 3 bordars and 3 slaves, and half a mill rendering 10s, meadow for 1 plough, [and] woodland for 100 pigs. It is and was always worth 60s. Leofgifu, a man of King Edward, held this manor and could sell and give it to whom she wished.

In Bromham Hugh holds 2 hides of the countess. There is land for 2 ploughs, and there are [2 ploughs], and 5 villans and 2 bordars, and 1 mill rendering 40s and 100 eels. It actually belongs to the fief of the countess, but does not lie in this land. [There is] meadow for 2 ploughs. It is worth 20s; when received and TRE 10s. Godwine, a man of Earl Harold, held this land and could sell.

In Stagsden Hugh holds 1 hide of the countess. There is land for 1 plough, and there is [1 plough], and 2 villans and 2 bordars, [and] woodland for 40 pigs. It is and was worth 10s; TRE 20s. 2 sokemen, men of King Edward, held this land and could sell to whom they wished.

IN 'WILLEY HUNDRED

In Felmersham Gilbert holds 3½ hides of the countess. There is land for 3 ploughs. In demesne [is] 1 plough; and 2 villans with 1 plough, and there can be another. There are 4 bordars, and 1 mill rendering 10s, [and] meadow for 1 plough. It is worth £3; when received, 100s; and as much TRE. Alli, a thegn of King Edward, held this land.

In Radwell Hugh holds 2 hides and 2½ virgates of the fief of the countess. There is land for 1½ ploughs, and there are [1½ ploughs]. There is 1 villan and 1 bordar and 1 slave, [and] meadow for 1 plough. It is worth 20s; when received, 10s; TRE 40s. Tovi, a housecarl of King Edward, held this land.

Gilbert de Blosseville holds Harrold of the countess. It is assessed at 10 hides. There is land for 16 ploughs. In demesne there can be 3 ploughs; there is 1 [plough]; and 10 villans with 7 ploughs, and there can be 6 more. [There is] meadow for 6 ploughs, woodland for 200 pigs, and 1 mill rendering 36s 8d and 200 eels. All together it is worth £6; when received, £16; TRE £20. 3 thegns of King Edward held this manor and could sell to whom they wished.

In Sharnbrook Hugh holds of the countess 3 virgates of land. There is land for 1 plough, and there is [1 plough]. There is 1 villan and 1 bordar, [and] meadow for 1 plough. It is worth 10s; when received, 5s; TRE 20s. Wulfgeat, a man of King Edward, held this land and could give it to whom he wished.

[Folio 217v: BEDFORDSHIRE]

In the HUNDRED of Barford Osbern holds 2 hides and 3 virgates. There is land for 3 ploughs. In demesne [are] 2

ploughs; and 3 villans with 1 plough. There are 2 bordars and 1 slave, meadow for 1 plough, [and] woodland for 200 pigs. It is worth 40s; when received, 10s; TRE 50s. Wulfheah the steersman of King Edward held this land and could sell.

In Potton Hugh holds of the countess half a virgate of land. There is land for 1 plough, and there is [1 plough], with 1 bordar. It is and was worth 5s; TRE 2s. Earl Tosti held this land in his manor of Potton.

IN BIGGLESWADE HUNDRED

In Stratton Fulcher of Paris holds 3½ virgates of the countess. There is land for 2 ploughs. In demesne [is] 1 plough. There is 1 villan and 5 bordars, [and] meadow for 1 plough. It is and was worth 8s; TRE 20s. Alwine, a man of King Edward, held this land and could sell.

In Holme Fulcher holds of the countess half a hide. [There is] land for half a plough, and there is half a plough, [and] meadow for half a plough. There is 1 villan. It is and was worth 7s; TRE 10s. Alwine, a man of King Edward, held this land and could give and sell.

In the same [vill] 2 men hold 1 virgate of the countess. [There is] land for 2 oxen and there are [2 oxen]. It is and was always worth 5s. Godwine, a man of King Edward, held this land and could sell.

IN THE HALF-HUNDRED OF 'WENESLAWE'

Countess JUDITH herself holds POTTON. It is assessed at 10 hides. There is land for 12 ploughs. In demesne [are] 3½ hides, and there are 3 ploughs. There are 18 villans and 2 sokemen with 8 ploughs, and there can be a ninth. There are 13 bordars and 3 slaves, and 1 mill [rendering] 5s, meadow for 12 ploughs, [and] pasture for the livestock of the vill. All together it is worth £12; when received, 100s; TRE £13. King Edward held this manor, and it belonged to Earl Tosti. In the same place were 4 sokemen who had 1 hide and 1 virgate and could give them to whom they wished.

In Sutton Turchil holds 1½ hides. There is land for 1½ ploughs. There is 1 plough, and there can be a half [-plough more]. There are 4 bordars, meadow for 1½ ploughs and [rendering] 16d. It is worth 10s; when received, 8s; TRE 20s. 3 sokemen held this land and could sell.

In the same [vill] Leofgar holds half a hide. There is land for half a plough, and there is [half a plough, and] meadow for half a plough and [rendering] 12d. It is worth 5s; when received and TRE 10s. The same man who holds it now held it [TRE]. He was the king's man and could sell it.

In the same [vill] Robert holds 3½ virgates. There is land for 1 plough, but there are only 2 oxen. # [There is] meadow for 1 plough. It is and was worth 8s; TRE 10s. 2 sokemen held this land and could sell.

In the same [vill] Sweting and Robert hold 1½ virgates of land. [There is] land for 4 oxen and there are [4 oxen], meadow for 1 plough, and 1 bordar. It is and was worth 4s; TRE 5s. Edward, a man of the Abbot of St Albans, held this land and could sell.

IN THE SAME HALF-HUNDRED

In Sutton Turbert holds 2 hides of the countess. There is land for 2 ploughs. In demesne [is] 1 plough; and 4 bordars with 1 plough, [and] meadow for 2 ploughs. It is and was worth 20s; TRE 25s. 2 sokemen held this land and could sell.

In the same [vill] Godwine holds 3 virgates of the countess. There is land for 1 plough, but now there is no [plough]. It is worth 3s; when received, 6s; TRE 10s. Wulfmær, a man of Ordwig, held this land and could sell.

In the same [vill] Eadric holds half a hide. There is land for half a plough, and there is [half a plough], with 1 villan, [and] meadow for half a plough. It is and was worth 5s; TRE 10s. The same man who holds it [now] held it [TRE]. He was the king's man and could sell it.

In Cockayne Hatley Countess Judith holds 3 hides and 2½ virgates as 1 manor. There is land for 6½ ploughs. In demesne [is] 1 hide and half a virgate, and there are 2 ploughs. There are 8 villans with 4½ ploughs. There are 8 bordars, and meadow for 2 ploughs, [and] woodland for 4 pigs. It is worth £6.5s; when received, 100s; TRE £6. Earl Tosti held this manor and it belongs to Potton, the countess's own manor, and there a certain sokeman had 1 virgate. He could give and sell it and withdraw to another lord.

Ranulph, Ilger's brother, holds Everton of the countess. It is assessed at 5 hides. There is land for 5 ploughs. There are 2 ploughs, and there can be 3. There are 4 villans and 5 bordars, [and] meadow for 1 plough. It is worth £3; when received, 100s; and as much TRE. Earl Tosti held this manor, and it belonged to Potton, the countess's own manor.

IN THE HUNDRED OF "WICHESTANESTOU"

In Southill Hugh holds 1 hide of the countess. There is land for 2 ploughs, and there are [2 ploughs]. There are 3 villans and 3 bordars and 1 slave, meadow for 2 ploughs, [and] woodland for 60 pigs. It is worth 30s; when received, 40s; TRE 60s. Tuffa, a man of Earl Waltheof, held this land and could sell.

In Harrowden the canons of Bedford hold 3 hides of the countess. There is land for 3 ploughs, and there are [3 ploughs], and 6 villans and 4 bordars, [and] meadow for 2 ploughs. It is worth 30s; when received, 20s; TRE 40s. Azelin, a man of Earl Tosti, held this land. He could not give nor sell without leave of the man who held Kempston, the earl's manor.

In Cardington Hugh holds of the countess 3 hides and 1 virgate and the third part of 1 virgate. There is land for 4 ploughs, and there are [4 ploughs]. There are 12 villans and 3 bordars and 3 slaves, [and] meadow for 1 plough. It is worth 40s; when received, 20s; TRE 40s. Azelin, a man of Earl Tosti, held this land. He could not give or sell it without leave of the man who held Kempston.

In Cople Hugh holds of the countess 1 virgate of land. This land is and was always worth 30d. Wulfwine, a man of King Edward, held this and could sell to whom he wished.

In Blunham the Abbot of St Edmundsbury holds half a hide of the countess. There is land for 1 plough, and there is [1 plough, and] meadow for 1 plough. It is worth 20s; when received, 10s; TRE 20s. A man of King Edward held this land and could sell.

IN CLIFTON HUNDRED

In Clifton Alwine holds 1 hide of the countess. There is land for half a plough, and there is [half a plough, and] meadow for half a plough. It is and was worth 5s; TRE 10s. Wulfric, a man of King Edward, held this land and could sell.

LIIII. The land of the wife of Hugh de Grandmesnil

IN 'REDBORNSTOKE' HUNDRED

ADELIZA, the wife of Hugh de Grandmesnil, holds of the king half a hide in [Lower and Upper] Shelton. There is land for half a plough, and there is [half a plough], meadow for half a plough, [and] woodland for 6 pigs. There is 1 bordar. It is and was worth 6s; TRE 10s. Godwine, a man of Earl Gyrth, held this land and could give it to whom he wished.

In Houghton Conquest Arnold holds of Adeliza 4½ hides as 1 manor. There is land for 6 ploughs. In demesne [are] 2 ploughs; and 11 villans and 7 bordars with 3½ ploughs, and there can be a half [-plough] more. There are 3 slaves, meadow for 2 ploughs, [and] woodland for 225 pigs. Of this land 1 sokeman holds 1 hide. It is worth £4; when received, 60s; TRE £8. 3 sokemen held this manor who wished [sic] to give and sell their land. In this same [vill] the aforesaid Adeliza claims half a virgate and 30 acres of both woodland and field against Hugh de Beauchamp; and the men of the hundred bear testimony that this land TRE belonged with the other land which Adeliza holds and he who held this land could give or sell it to whom he wished. Ralph took possession of this land unjustly when he was sheriff.

IN "WICHESTANESTOU" HUNDRED

Adeliza herself holds Chalton. It is assessed at 10 hides. There is land for 10 ploughs. In demesne [are] 5 hides, and there are 2 ploughs, and there can be 3 more. There are 16 villans and 9 bordars with 5 ploughs. There are 2 slaves, and 1 mill [rendering] 30s, meadow for 10 ploughs, [and] woodland for 16 pigs. All together it is worth £10; when received, £8; TRE £12. King Edward held this manor and it belonged to Earl Tosti. This land was a Berewick of Potton, | the manor of Countess Judith | TRE, and in such a way that no one could separate it from it.

[Folio 218: BEDFORDSHIRE]

IN 'STODDEN' HUNDRED

In Milton Ernest Ivo, steward of Hugh de Grandmesnil, holds 3 hides and 1 virgate as 1 manor. There is land for 4 ploughs. In demesne [are] 2 ploughs; and 8 villans with 2 ploughs. There is 1 slave, and 1 mill [rendering] 20s, meadow for 2 ploughs, [and] woodland for 40 pigs. It is and was worth 60s; TRE £4. Godwine, a man of Burgræd, held this manor and could sell.

LV. The land of the wife of Ralph Taillebois

IN 'MANSHEAD' HUNDRED

AZELINA, the wife of Ralph Taillebois, holds 1½ hides of the king in Battlesden. There is land for 1½ ploughs. There is 1 [plough], and there can be a half [-plough more]. There are 2 villans and 1 bordar, [and] meadow for 1 plough. It is and was worth 20s; TRE 40s. 2 sokemen, Eskil and Alwine, held this land and could sell to whom they wished.

Azelina herself holds Hockliffe. It is assessed at 10 hides. There is land for 8 ploughs. In demesne [are] 5 hides, and there are 2 ploughs. There are 13 villans and 11 bordars with 6 ploughs, meadow for 4 ploughs, [and] woodland for 100 pigs. All together it is and was worth £8; TRE £12. Eskil held this manor TRE and could sell.

IN FLITTON HUNDRED

In Cainhoe Turstin holds 1 hide of Azelina. There is land for 2 ploughs. In demesne [is] 1 [plough]; and 1 villan has another. There are 3 bordars, and meadow for 1 plough, and woodland for 100 pigs. It is worth 20s; when received, 10s; TRE 20s. Wulfric, a sokeman of King Edward, held this land and could give and sell it to whom he wished.

IN BARFORD HUNDRED

In Wyboston Iudichael holds 5½ virgates of Azelina. There is land for 1 plough, and there is [1 plough], with 1 villan and 2 bordars, [and] meadow for half a plough. It is worth 10s; when received, 5s; TRE 30s. Almær, a man of Wulfmær, held this land and could sell and give it to whom he wished.

IN BIGGLESWADE HUNDRED

In Eyeworth Broddi holds 1 hide of Azelina. There is land for 1 plough, and there is [1 plough], with 1 bordar, [and] meadow for 1 plough. It is and was always worth 10s. This land belongs to [Azelina's] marriage portion. The same Broddi held this [land] and could sell to whom he wished.

IN 'WENESLAWE' HUNDRED

In Cockayne Hatley Azelina holds, [as part] of her marriage portion, 5 hides and 1½ virgates. There is land for 8 ploughs. In demesne [is] 1 hide and 1 virgate, and there are 2 ploughs. There are 8 villans and 4 bordars with 6 ploughs. There is 1 slave, and 1 mill [rendering] 18s, meadow for 2 ploughs, [and] woodland for 4 pigs and from a render 3s. All together it is worth £6; when received, 100s; TRE £6. Wulfmær, a thegn of King Edward, held this manor, and there were 2 sokemen, his men; they had 2½ virgates; and could give and sell them to whom they wished.

IN "WICHESTANESTOU" HUNDRED

In Stanford Roger holds 2 hides of Azelina, and this is [part] of her marriage portion. There is land for 2 ploughs. In demesne [is] 1 plough; and 2 villans and 1 bordar with 1 plough. [There is] meadow for 2 ploughs, woodland for 30 pigs, and 1 mill [rendering] 13s4d. It is worth 60s; when received, 20s; TRE

60s. 2 sokemen held this land and could give it to whom they wished.

In Old Warden Walter, a monk, holds half a hide of Azelina, and this is [part] of her marriage portion. There is land for half a plough, but there is no [plough] there. There is 1 bordar, meadow for half a plough, [and] woodland for 40 pigs. It is worth 10s; when received and TRE 20s. Goding, a man of Eadric the Bald, held this land and could give it to whom he wished.

IN CLIFTON HUNDRED

In Henlow Widrus holds 1 hide and 3 virgates of Azelina. There is land for 2 ploughs, and there are [2 ploughs. There are] 2 villans and 2 bordars and 2 slaves, [and] meadow for 2 ploughs. It is worth 30s; when received, 20s; TRE 30s. Eskil held this land, and it was a Berewick of Stotfold TRE. Hugh de Beauchamp claims this land against Azelina, saying that she has it unjustly and that it was never [part of] her dower.

In the same vill Bernard holds 1 hide of Azelina. There is land for 1 plough, and there is [1 plough], and 3 villans, [and] meadow for 1 plough. It is and was worth 23s; TRE 28s. 2 sokemen, men of Eskil, held this land and could give it to whom they wished.

In Chicksands 3 sokemen hold 3 hides of Azelina, [part] of her dower. There is land for 2 ploughs. There is 1 [plough], and there can be another, meadow for 2 ploughs, [and] woodland for 20 pigs. It is and was worth 20s; TRE 25s. 4 sokemen held this manor and could give and sell it to whom they wished.

In the same vill Walter holds 1 hide of Azelina, and this is [part] of her marriage portion. There is land for 1 plough, and there is [1 plough], meadow for 1 plough, woodland for 50 pigs, and 1 mill rendering 10s. It is and was worth 20s; TRE 30s. Swetmann, a man of Wulfmær of Eaton Socon, held this land and could give it whom he wished.

In [Lower and Upper] Stondon Engeler holds 2½ hides of Azelina. There is land for 2½ ploughs. In demesne [are] 2 ploughs; and 3 bordars with half a plough. There are 2 slaves, [and] meadow for 2½ ploughs. It is worth 60s; when received, 40s; TRE £4. Wulfmær of Eaton Socon, a thegn of King Edward, held this land; and there were 5 sokemen, men of the same Wulfmær, and they could give and sell [their land] to whom they wished.

LVI. The land of the Burgesses of Bedford

IN THE HALF-HUNDRED OF 'BUCKELOWE'

In BIDDENHAM Osgar of Bedford holds 1 virgate of land of the king. There is land for 2 oxen. It is and was always worth 2s. He who now holds it held it TRE and could give it to whom he wished.

In the same vill Godwine, a burgess, holds of the king 1 hide and the fourth part of 1 virgate. There is land for 1 plough, and there is [1 plough, and] meadow for 1 plough. It is and was always worth 10s. He who now holds held TRE half a hide of this land, which he could give to whom he wished. Half a hide and the fourth part of 1 virgate he bought after King William came into England; but neither to the king nor to anyone else has he done service for it, nor has he had a livery officer for it. Against the same man William Speke claims 1 virgate and the fourth part of 1 virgate, which had been delivered to him and [which] he afterwards lost.

In the same vill Ordwig, a burgess, holds of the king 1 hide and the third part of half a hide. There is land for 1 plough, and there is [1 plough]. There are 2 villans and 1 bordar, [and] meadow for 1 plough. It is and was always worth 10s. The same man who now holds half a hide | and the fourth part of 1 virgate | of this land held them TRE, and he could give them to whom he wished. 1 virgate, however, he held in pledge TRE, and still holds it, as the men of this hundred attest. The same man himself bought 1 virgate and the fourth part of 1 virgate after King William came into England and renders service [for it] neither to the king nor to anyone else.

In the same vill Wulfmær, a burgess, holds of the king 2 parts of 1 virgate. There is land for 1 ox. It is and was always worth 12d. The same man held it TRE, and could give it to whom he wished.

IN 'WILLEY' HUNDRED

In Hinwick Edward holds half a hide of the king. There is land for half a plough. There are 2 oxen and 1 bordar. It is and was worth 5s; TRE 10s. This man's father held this land and could sell it TRE. This King William granted to the same man in alms, for which he has the king's writ and the witness of the hundred.

In Sharnbrook Almær holds half a virgate of the king. There is land for half a plough, but there is no [plough] there. It is and was worth 2s; TRE 5s. The father of the same man held this land, and King William gave it to him by his writ.

IN "WICHESTANESTOU" HUNDRED

In Beeston Guthmund holds 3 virgates of the king. [There is] land for 3 oxen, and there are [3 oxen, and] meadow for 3 oxen. It is and was worth 5s; TRE 10s. This man held it TRE and could sell it to whom he wished.

IN CLIFTON HUNDRED

In Henlow Alric holds 1 virgate of the king. There is land for 2 oxen, and there are [2 oxen, and] meadow for 2 oxen. It is and was always worth 2s. This man held it TRE and could sell it.

In Arlesey a certain prebendary of the king, Wulfsige, holds of the king 2 parts of 1 virgate.

[Folio 218V: BEDFORDSHIRE]

The land of the Reeves and Almsmen of the King

IN 'MANSHEAD' HUNDRED

In Eversholt Herbert, the king's reeve, holds half a hide, and in Woburn 3 virgates of land, and in Potsgrove 1 hide. He holds these 3 estates in the king's service which did not belong there TRE, but after Ralph Taillebois was sheriff he states that he had them by grant of the king. There is 1 villan. All together it is worth 6s; when received, 20s; TRE the same. 5 sokemen of King Edward held this land and could sell to whom they wished.

In the same Potsgrove a certain groom of the king holds half a hide. There is land for half a plough, and there is [half a plough]. It is and was worth 5s; TRE 10s. Oswig, a man of Earl Tosti, held this land and could give it to whom he wished.

In Priestley a king's reeve holds 1 hide. There is land for 1 plough. There is 1 villan, meadow for 1 plough, [and] woodland for 20 pigs. It is worth 5s; when received, 10s; TRE 30s. 4 thegns held this land and could give and sell it to whom they wished.

IN 'REDBORNSTOKE' HUNDRED

In Maulden a certain king's reeve holds half a hide. There is land for half a plough, and there is [half a plough], with 2 villans, [and] meadow for half a plough. It is and was worth 3s; TRE 10s. 2 sokemen of King Edward held this land and could give it to whom they wished.

IN BIGGLESWADE HUNDRED

In Tempsford Alwine the reeve holds 1 hide and the fourth part of 1 virgate. There is land for 1 plough, and there is [1 plough], with 3 villans, [and] meadow for half a plough. It is and was worth 20s; TRE 27s. 6 sokemen held this land and could sell to whom they wished.

In Edworth Alwine the king's reeve holds 2½ hides. There is land for 2 ploughs, and there are [2 ploughs], with 2 villans. It is and was always worth 30s. Branting, a man of King Edward, held this manor and could sell.

In Holme Alwine the king's reeve holds 1½ hides. There is land for 1½ ploughs. There is 1 plough and there can be a half [-plough more]. There are 2 villans. It is and was always worth 20s. Ælfric and Lemar, the beadles, held this land and could sell.

In Sutton Alwine holds 1½ virgates. It is and was worth 4s; TRE 5s. 2 sokemen held this land and could give and sell it to whom they wished.

These 6 estates Ralph Taillebois assigned to the king's service when he was sheriff, for they did not belong here TRE. Those who now have them hold them by grant of the king, as they say.

IN FLITTON HUNDRED

In Streatley the reeve of the hundred holds 2 parts of 1 virgate for the king's use, which now belong to Luton, the king's manor, but did not belong there TRE. Bondi the staller assigned them to this manor, and Ralph Taillebois found them assigned there. There is land for half a plough. It is and was worth 5s; TRE 10s. Wulmær the priest held this land and could give to whom he wished.

IN 'WENESLAWE' HUNDRED

In Sutton Alwine holds 1 hide. In demesne [is] 1 plough; and 3 bordars with 1 plough, meadow for 2 ploughs and [rendering] 12d. It is and was worth 20s; TRE 10s. Of this land this man held 3 virgates, and a certain Edward 1 virgate; they could give and sell them to whom they wished.

IN 'WILLEY' HUNDRED

In Carlton Ketilbert holds 3½ virgates. There is land for 1 plough, and there is [1 plough], with 2 villans and 3 bordars, [and] meadow for 1 plough. It is worth 10s; when received, 2 orae; TRE 10s. Of this land this man held 1 virgate. He was a man of Queen Edith and could give it to whom he wished. However, he took possession of 2½ virgates, for which he has produced neither a livery officer nor a warrantor; which land Alli, a thegn of King Edward, held.

In Wymington 5 brothers with their mother hold 3 virgates of her dower. There is land for 1 plough, but there is no [plough] there. It is worth 3s; TRE 20s. Lant, their father, held this land and could give and sell it.

IN BARFORD HUNDRED

In Goldington Alric Wintremelc holds half a hide of the king. There is land for half a plough, and there is [half a plough, and] meadow for 3 oxen. It is and was always worth 5s. He who now holds it held it TRE. He was a man of King Edward, and could give it to whom he wished. He afterwards gave it to the canons of St Paul, under King William, and he granted that they should have it absolutely after his death.

IN "WICHESTANESTOU" HUNDRED

In Stanford Alric holds of the king the fourth part of 1 virgate. There is land for half an ox, and there is half an ox. It is and was worth 12d. The same man who holds it held it TRE, and could give it to whom he wished.

In the same vill Ordwig holds and [sic] the fourth part of 1 virgate. [There is] land for 3 oxen, and there are [3 oxen, and] meadow for 3 oxen. It is and was always worth 4s. This man held it TRE. He was a man of the king, and could sell it to whom he wished.

In Beeston Alwine holds 1½ virgates. There is land for half a plough. There are 2 bordars. It is worth 12d; when received, 4s; TRE 10s. This land was assigned to the king's service to which it did not belong TRE; but Dot, who held it, could give and sell it.

IN 'REDBORNSTOKE' HUNDRED

In Cotton End Ordwig holds 1 virgate of the king. There is land for half a plough. There are 5 oxen, with 1 bordar and 1 slave. It is and was worth 5s; TRE 10s. This man held it then. He was the king's man and could sell it.

IN 'STODDEN' HUNDRED

In [Lower and Upper] Dean 11 sokemen of King William hold 7 virgates of land and the fourth part of 1 virgate. There is land for 3½ ploughs, and there are [3½ ploughs]. It is and was always worth 30s. The same sokemen themselves held this land TRE who now hold it, and they could give it to whom they wished. Ralph assigned this land to the king's service, to which it did not belong TRE.

In the same vill Godwig Dere of Bedford holds half a virgate of the king, and it is and was always worth 12d. This man held it TRE and could do with it what he wished.

In "Hanefeld" sægeat holds 1 virgate of the king's soke. There is land for half a plough, and there is [half a plough]. It is and was worth 5s; TRE 10s. This man held it then, and could do with it what he wished.

In the same Hundred of 'Stodden' Thorgot and his mother hold half a hide of the king. There is land for 1 plough, and there is [1 plough], with 1 villan and 2 bordars, [and] woodland for 4 pigs. It is and was worth 10s; TRE 12s. The father of this Thorgot held this land. He was a king's thegn and could give and sell his land.

In Milton Ernest a certain beadle of the king holds half a virgate of the king. There is land for 2 oxen. It is and was worth 12d. The father of the man who now holds it held this land and he could give it to whom he wished.

IN THE HALF-HUNDRED OF 'BUCKELOWE'

In Bromham Osgeat holds 1 virgate and 2 parts of 1 virgate. There is land for 1 plough, and there is [1 plough, and] meadow for half a plough. It is worth 10s; TRE 5s. This man held it then and could give it.

IN 'WILLEY' HUNDRED

In Turvey Alwine the priest holds of the king the third part of half a hide. There is land for 2 oxen, and there are [2 oxen]. It is and was worth 3s. This man held it TRE and could do with it what he wished. #

In the same hundred Osgeat the king's reeve holds half a hide of the king. There is land for half a plough, and there is [half a plough]. It is and was always worth 3s. 1 sokeman held this land TRE whom King William commended, with this land, to the aforesaid reeve, so that he might supply food and clothing to him as long as he lived.

In Wymington Thorkil holds 1 hide of the king. There is land for 1 plough, and there is [1 plough]. It is and was worth 5s; TRE 10s. This man held it then, and could sell it to whom he wished.

But King William afterwards granted it to him in alms, on which account he performed every week on the second day a mass for the soul of the king and of the queen.

NORTHAMPTONSHIRE

IN THE TIME OF KING EDWARD there were in NORTHAMPTON, in the king's demesne, 60 burgesses, having as many dwellings. Of these, 14 are now waste; 47 are left. Besides these, there are now in the new borough 40 burgesses in King William's demesne.

In the same borough the Bishop of Coutances has 23 houses, rendering 29s4d.

The Abbot of St Edmundsbury [holds] 1 house, rendering 16d.

The Abbot of Peterborough, 15 houses, rendering 14s8d. 2 are waste.

The Abbot of Ramsey, 1 house, rendering 16d.

The Abbot of Coventry, 4 houses, rendering 12d. 3 are waste.

The Abbot of Evesham, 1 house [lying] waste.

The Abbot of Selby, 2 houses, rendering 32d.

The Count of Mortain, 37 [houses], rendering 45s8d. 2 are waste. Of 9 of these houses the king has the soke.

Earl Hugh, 1 house, rendering 4d.

Countess Judith, 16 houses, rendering 12s. 1 is waste.

Robert de Tosny, 4 houses, rendering 4s. 1 is waste.

Henry de Ferrers, 8 houses, rendering 9s4d.

Ansgar, the king's chaplain, 1 house, of which the king ought to have the soke.

William Peverel, 32 houses, rendering 28s8d. 3 of these are waste.

William fitzBoselin, 2 [houses], of the fief of the Bishop of Bayeux and of Countess Judith, rendering 16d.

William Engaine, 1 house of Robert de Bucy, and pays nothing.

Guy de Raimbeaucourt, 4 houses, rendering 64d.

Walter the Fleming, 10 houses, rendering 8s. 1 is waste.

Winemar, 12 houses, rendering 3s. Of these, 4 are waste.

Richard Engaine, 4 houses, rendering 4s.

Robert d'Auvers, 1 house, rendering 12d.

Roger de Bois-Normand, 1 house, rendering 16d.

Geoffrey de la Guerche, 4 houses, rendering 4s.

Geoffrey Alselin and his nephew Ralph, 2 houses, rendering 2s.

Giles, the brother of Ansculf, 3 houses, rendering 32d.

Gunfrid de Chocques, 8 houses, rendering 8s. 3 are waste.

Sigar de Chocques, 1 house, rendering 16d.

Swein, son of Azur, 21 houses, rendering 10s, belonging to Stoke Bruerne.

Ansfrid de Vaubadon, 2 houses, rendering 2s, of the fief of the Bishop of Bayeux.

Baldwin, half a waste tenement. Leofstan, 1 house, rendering 4d.

Osbern Giffard, 1 house, rendering 4d. Godwine the priest, 1 house, rendering 12d.

Durand the reeve, 1 house, rendering 16d, of the fief of Robert de Tosny.

Dodin, 2 houses, rendering 20d. 1 is [held] of Countess Judith, the other of Winemar.

Hugh de Gouville, 2 houses, rendering 32d.

NORTHAMPTONSHIRE renders 3 nights' farm, [that is] £30 by weight. For dogs, £42 blanch at 20[d] to the ora. For a gift to the queen, and for hay, £10 and 5 orae. For a hawk, £10. For a sumpter horse, 20s. For alms, 20s. For a huntsman's horse, 20s. For Queen Edith's manors, £40. For King's Cliffe, £10.

The burgesses of Northampton pay to the sheriff yearly £30.10s. This belongs to his farm.

Countess Judith has £7 of the issues of the same borough.

Here Are Entered the Holders of Lands In Northamptonshire

I KING WILLIAM
II The Bishop of Bayeux
III The Bishop of Durham
IIII The Bishop of Coutances
V The Bishop of Lincoln
VI The Abbey of Peterborough
VII The Abbey of Westminster
VIII The Abbey of St Edmundsbury
IX The Abbey of Ramsey
X The Abbey of Thorney
XI The Abbey of Crowland
XII The Abbey of Coventry
XIII The Abbey of Evesham
XIIII The Abbey of Grestain
XV The Church of St Remy of Rheims
XVI Ansgar the chaplain
XVII Leofwine the priest and other clerks
XVIII The Count of Mortain
XIX The Count of Meulan
XX Count Alan
XXI Earl Aubrey
XXII Earl Hugh
XXIII Hugh de Grandmesnil
XXIIII Hugh d'Ivry

XXV Henry de Ferrers
XXVI Robert de Tosny
XXVII Robert of Stafford
XXVIII Robert d'Oilly
XXIX Robert de Vessey
XXX Robert de Bucy
XXXI Ralph Paynel
XXXII Ralph de Limesy
XXXIII Robert Blund
XXXIIII William de Keynes
XXXV William Peverel
XXXVI William fitzAnsculf
XXXVII William Lovett
XXXVIII Walter d'Aincourt
XXXIX Walter the Fleming
XL Winemar
XLI Guy de Raimbeaucourt
XLII Eudo fitzHubert
XLIII Giles, brother of Ansculf
XLIIII Geoffrey Alselin
XLV Geoffrey de Mandeville
XLVI Gilbert de Ghent
XLVII Geoffrey de la Guerche
XLVIII Gunfrid de Chocques
XLIX Sigar de Chocques
L Swein
LI Sibold
LII Ogier the Breton
LIII Drogo de la Beuvriere
LIIII Mainou the Breton
LV Eustace of Huntingdon
LVI Countess Judith
LVII Gilbert the cook
LVIII David
LIX Richard
LX William and other thegns

The land of the King

IN WITCHLEY WAPENTAKE

THE KING holds KETTON [Rutland]. There are 7 hides.
There is land for 13 ploughs. In demesne are 2 [ploughs], and
3 slaves; and 12 sokemen and 24 villans and 5 bordars, with a
priest, having 11 ploughs. There is a mill rendering 6s8d, and
40 acres of meadow. There are 16 acres of scrubland.

To this manor belongs TIXOVER [Rutland]. There are 2
hides. There is land for 8 ploughs. There 16 sokemen, with 4
bordars, have 6 ploughs. There is a mill rendering 5s, and 8
acres of meadow, and 3 acres of spinney. The whole TRE was
worth 100s; now £10.

The king holds BARROWDEN [Rutland]. There are 4
hides, less 1 virgate. There is land for 10 ploughs. There are
9 villans and 10 sokemen, with 3 bordars, having 6½ ploughs.
There are 16 acres of meadow and 6 acres of spinney. To this
manor belong these members:

In SEATON [Rutland], 1½ hides and 1 bovate of land. There
is land for 6 ploughs, and 4 acres of meadow.

In THORPE BY WATER [Rutland], 1 hide and 1 virgate of
land. There is land for 4 ploughs, and 3 acres of meadow.

In MORCOTT [Rutland], 4 hides. There is land for 8
ploughs, and 6 acres of meadow.

In BISBROOKE [Rutland] and GLASTON [Rutland], 1½
hides. There is land for 4 ploughs, and 8 acres of meadow.

In NORTH LUFFENHAM [Rutland], 4 hides. There is
land for 10 ploughs, and 16 acres of meadow. In these lands
are 15 sokemen and 33 villans and 23 bordars, with a priest,
having 19 ploughs. In Seaton is a mill rendering 36d. [There
is] woodland 1 furlong in length and 1 in breadth. [There is] a
spinney 6 furlongs in length and 2 furlongs in breadth. The
whole TRE was worth £3; now £7.

The king holds SOUTH LUFFENHAM [Rutland] and
'SCULTHORP' [in North Luffenham, Rutland]. There are
7 hides and 1 virgate of land. There is land for 14 ploughs.
There are 12 sokemen and 16 bordars, with a priest, having 12
ploughs. There are 2 mills rendering 40d, and 10 acres of
meadow. TRE it was worth 30s; now 60s. The men labour at
the king's work, which the reeve shall command.

Queen Edith held these lands. Hugh de Port now holds them
of the king at farm.

[Folio 219V: NORTHAMPTONSHIRE]

The king holds [Great or Little] CASTERTON [Rutland].
Earl Morcar held it. There are 3½ hides. There is land for 9
ploughs. In demesne is 1 [plough]; and 24 villans and 2
sokemen and 2 bordars, with a priest, and 2 slaves, have 7
ploughs. There is a mill rendering 16s, and 16 acres of
meadow. [There is] a spinney 3 furlongs in length and 2
furlongs in breadth. It was worth £6; now £10. Hugh
fitzBaldric holds it of the king at farm.

The king has in the demesne of "Portland" [in Stamford] 2
carucates and 2 parts of a third carucate and 12 acres of
meadow. 1 carucate of land belongs to the Church of St Peter,
and half a carucate to the Church of All Saints. "Portland" [in
Stamford], with the meadow, TRE rendered 48s, and 10s for
the rugs of the king's sumpter horses. Besides this the king
ought to have £9.12s for other issues of the borough.

The king holds GREENS NORTON. King Edward held it.
There, with 2 members, Blakesley and Adstone, are 7 hides
and 1 virgate of land. There is land [...]. In demesne are 3
ploughs, and 3 slaves and 2 female slaves; and 19 villans and
15 sokemen and 5 bordars having 21 ploughs. There are 2
mills rendering 15s. [There is] woodland 4 leagues in length
and 3 leagues in breadth. When stocked it is worth 60s and the
honey 4s. The sokemen pay 30s. It was worth £12; now £20.
The smiths paid £7 TRE.

The king holds TOWCESTER. There are 7½ hides. There is
land for 22 ploughs. In demesne are 2 ploughs; and 15 villans
with 10 ploughs. There is a mill rendering 13s4d, and 12 acres
of meadow. [There is] woodland 2 leagues in length and 1 in
breadth. The smiths used to pay 100s, now nothing. There 1
sokeman pays 5s, having half a hide and the fifth part of half a
hide. TRE it was worth £12; now £25.

The king holds KING'S SUTTON. There are 3 hides. There is land for 6 ploughs. In demesne are 2 [ploughs], with 1 slave; and 7 villans and 10 bordars with 2 ploughs. There is a mill rendering 10s8d. From the meadows 20s. From the market 20s. In other land of the same manor are 4 villans with 2 ploughs.

To this manor belongs WHITFIELD. There are 2 hides and inland for 2 ploughs, and for the men land for 5 ploughs. In demesne are 2 [ploughs], with 1 slave; and 8 villans and 3 bordars with 3½ ploughs. [There is] woodland 1 league in length and 7 furlongs in breadth. The whole TRE was worth £19; now £32 at 20[d] to the ora.

IN 'GRAVESEND' HUNDRED

The king holds FAWSLEY. There are 1½ hides and the fifth part of a hide. There is inland for 4 ploughs. There are 2 ploughs; and 6 bordars have 4 ploughs. In the other land outside the demesne are 6 villans, with a reeve, having 4 ploughs. From the meadow come 2s. TRE it was worth £15; now it renders as many pounds at 20[d] to the ora. To this manor belongs the soke of 1 hide less 1 bovate; it renders 4s.

IN COLLINGTREE HUNDRED

The king holds HARDINGSTONE. There are 5 hides, besides the inland. [There is] land for 4 ploughs. There are 2 ploughs; and 4 villans and 10 bordars with 4 ploughs. There are 2 mills rendering 50s. From the meadows and pastures 66d. TRE it was worth £30; now £12. William Peverel and Gunfrid de Chocques have there 2 hides and 60 acres of meadow, by the king's gift, as they say.

IN CORBY HUNDRED

The king holds GRETTON. There are 3 hides and 3 virgates of land. There is land for 14 ploughs. In demesne are 2 [ploughs], and 1 female slave; and 15 villans and 5 bordars, with a priest, have 6 ploughs. There is a mill rendering 3s, and 20 acres of meadow. [There is] woodland 1 league in length and half a league in breadth. It was and is worth £20. Very many things are wanting to this manor which TRE were appendant to it as well in woodland and ironworks as in other renders.

The king holds CORBY. There are 1½ hides. There is land for 9 ploughs. In demesne is 1 [plough]; and 7 villans, with a priest and 3 bordars, have 4 ploughs. [There is] woodland 18 furlongs in length and 4 furlongs in breadth. TRE, as now, worth £10. Many things are wanting to this manor which TRE belonged there in woodland and ironworks and other matters.

The king holds BRIGSTOCK. There are 3½ hides. There is land for 9 ploughs. In demesne are 3 ploughs, and 6 slaves; and 16 villans, with a priest and 4 bordars have 5 ploughs. There is a mill rendering 5s, and 7 acres of meadow. [There is] woodland 15 furlongs in length and 1 league in breadth.

To this manor belong these members: ISLIP. There are 1 hide and 3 virgates of land. In GEDDINGTON, 1 hide. In STANION, 1½ virgates of land. There is land for 8 ploughs.

There are 4 sokemen and 9 villans and 7 bordars. Between them all they have 7 ploughs. In ISLIP are 4 acres of meadow.

The whole manor, with its appendages, TRE was worth £15; now £20.

IN WILLOWBROOK HUNDRED

The king holds DUDDINGTON. There is 1 hide. There is land for 8 ploughs. In demesne is 1 [plough]; and 10 villans, with a priest and 2 bordars, have 3 ploughs. There are 10 acres of meadow. [There is] woodland 1 league in length and 6 furlongs in breadth. There is a mill rendering 4s. This land belongs to the aforesaid manor of Gretton. TRE it was worth £10; and now the same. Many things are wanting to it which belong to the farm, in woods and other matters.

IN ROTHWELL HUNDRED

The king holds ROTHWELL and ORTON. There are 8 hides and 2 parts of 1 hide. There is land for 40 ploughs. In demesne are 4 ploughs; and 19 villans and 45 bordars have 10½ ploughs. There are 2 mills rendering 9s4d, and 8 acres of meadow.

To this manor belong these members:

LODDINGTON, with 1 hide and the third part of 1 hide.

GLENDON, with half a hide and the third part of 1 hide.

DRAUGHTON, with 1 hide and half a virgate of land.

ARTHINGWORTH, with half a virgate of land; DESBOROUGH, [with] half a virgate of land.

KELMARSH, with 2 hides and the third part of 1 virgate.

GREAT OXENDON, with 1 hide and 1 virgate of land; CLIPSTON, with 1½ virgates.

GREAT CRANSLEY, with 2 hides [and] 1 virgate of land; BROUGHTON, with half a hide. There is land for 19 ploughs in all. There are 47 sokemen having 18 ploughs.

This manor of ROTHWELL, with its appendages, TRE was worth £30; now £50.

IN MAWSLEY HUNDRED

The king holds BRIXWORTH. There are 9½ hides. There is land for 35 ploughs. In demesne are 2 [ploughs]; and 14 villans, with a priest and 15 bordars, having 15 ploughs. There are 2 mills rendering 33s4d, and 8 acres of meadow. To this manor belongs a wood which used to render yearly 100s. This is now in the king's forest.

To this manor belongs HOLCOT. There are 2 hides and 2½ virgates of land. There is land for 10 ploughs. There are 11 sokemen with 4 ploughs. The whole TRE rendered £30; now £36.

The king holds FAXTON. There are 2 hides. There is land for 12 ploughs. In demesne are 3 ploughs, and 6 slaves; and 6 villans and 9 bordars with 3 ploughs. There are 16 acres of meadow.

To this manor belong OLD and WALGRAVE. There are 2 hides and 3½ virgates of land. There is land for 7 ploughs.

There are 14 sokemen with 6 ploughs. There are 12 acres of meadow. The whole TRE rendered £15; now £16.

The king holds KINGSTHORPE [near Northampton]. There are 4 hides and 3 virgates of land. There is land for 20 ploughs. In demesne are 2 ploughs; and 16 villans and 8 bordars with 3 ploughs. There are 3 mills rendering 43s4d, and 5 acres of meadow.

To this manor belongs MOULTON. There are 1½ hides and 1 bovate of land, and WESTON FAVELL, with 1 hide, likewise belongs to it. There is land for 5 ploughs in all. There are 10 sokemen with 3 ploughs, and 3 acres of meadow.

The whole TRE rendered £15; now as much.

The king holds UPTON. There are 2 hides. There is land for 10 ploughs. In demesne is 1 [plough]; and 10 villans and 10 bordars have 5 ploughs. There is a mill rendering 12s8d, and 6 acres of meadow.

To this manor belongs HARLESTONE. There is half a hide. There is land for 2 ploughs. There are 2 sokemen with 1 plough. The whole TRE was worth £15; now as much.

The king holds NASSINGTON. There are 6 hides. There is land for 16 ploughs. In demesne are 2 [ploughs]; and 24 villans, with a priest and 2 bordars, have 14 ploughs. There are 2 mills rendering 30s8d, and 40 acres of meadow. [There is] woodland 1 league in length and half a league in breadth. TRE it rendered £26.13s by tale; now £30.

[Folio 220: NORTHAMPTONSHIRE]

In BARFORD is 1 hide. Oslac White held this with 2 sokemen, of whom he himself had the soke. There is land for 2 ploughs. There are 4 villans and 3 bordars with 2 ploughs, and a mill rendering 32d. This land King William granted to Godwine.

In RUSHTON is half a virgate of land. The soke belongs to Barford. There is 1 sokeman having 2 oxen. It is worth 10s.

In APETHORPE are 2 hides belonging to Nassington. There is land for 12 ploughs. In demesne are 2 [ploughs]; and 16 villans and 4 bordars with 10 ploughs. There is a mill rendering 6s, and 6 acres of meadow. [There is] woodland 1 league in length and as much in breadth. TRE it was worth £13.7s.

The king holds TANSOR. There are 6 hides. There is land for 18 ploughs. In demesne are 2 ploughs; and 15 villans and 4 bordars with 14 ploughs. There is a mill rendering 10s, and 12 acres of meadow. [There is] woodland 1 league in length and half a league in breadth. TRE it rendered £20 by tale.

The king holds BARNWELL. There are 6 hides and 1 virgate of land. There is land for 6 ploughs. In demesne are 2 [ploughs]; and 12 villans and 2 bordars with 4 ploughs. There are 24 acres of meadow. TRE it rendered £13.6s6d by tale; now £30 with TANSOR.

The king holds KING'S CLIFFE. There are 1 hide and 2½ virgates. Earl Ælfgar held it. There is land for 14 ploughs. In demesne are 2 ploughs, with 1 slave; and 7 villans, with a priest and 6 bordars, having 5 ploughs. There is a mill ren-

dering 12d, and 4 acres of meadow. [There is] woodland 1 league in length and half a league in breadth. TRE it rendered £7; now £10.

The king holds ROCKINGHAM. There is 1 hide. There is land for 3 ploughs. There are 5 villans and 6 bordars with 3 ploughs. Bovi held this land with sake and soke TRE. It was waste when King William ordered a castle to be made there. It is now worth 26s.

In STOKE ALBANY is 1 hide of the sokeland of CORBY, the king's manor. There is land for 2 ploughs. They are there, with 5 sokemen who render 64d to CORBY.

In WILBARSTON are 3 virgates of land. There is land for 2 ploughs. There are 5 sokemen, with 3 bordars, having 1½ ploughs. It was and is worth 4s.

The king holds PASSENHAM. There is 1 hide. There is land for 12 ploughs. In demesne is 1 [plough], with 1 slave; and 8 villans and 6 bordars, with 1 free man, having 5 ploughs. There is a mill rendering 13s4d, and 30 acres of meadow. [There is] woodland 1 league in length and as much in breadth.

To this manor belongs PUXLEY. There is half a hide. There is land for 1 plough. There is 1 sokeman having half a plough, and he pays 5s.

The whole TRE rendered £8 by tale; now £10.

IN CORBY HUNDRED

The king holds WEEKLEY. Earl Ælfgar held it. There are 2½ hides. There is land for 6 ploughs. In demesne are 2 [ploughs], and 4 slaves; and 12 villans and 6 bordars with 4 ploughs. There is a mill rendering 64d. It was worth £3; now £6.

IN 'NAVISLAND' HUNDRED

The king holds FINEDON. Queen Edith held it. There are, with its appendages, 20 [...] 7 hides. There is land for 54 ploughs. In demesne are 3 hides, and there are 4 ploughs and 7 slaves; and 30 villans and 15 bordars with 11 ploughs, and 50 sokemen with 24 ploughs. There are 2 mills rendering 18s, and a third rendering 16s. There are 50 acres of meadow. [There is] woodland 1 league in length and half a league in breadth. TRE it rendered £20 by tale; now £40 by weight at 20[d] to the ora. The 50 sokemen render yearly for the soke £8.0s10d. The land of this manor lies thus: in Higham Hundred, 10½ hides; in 'Huxloe' Hundred, 1½ hides; in "Geritone" Hundred, 1 hide; in Rothwell Hundred, 3 parts of 1 hide; in Orlingbury Hundred, 4 hides and 1 virgate of land; in 'Navisland' Hundred, 9½ hides.

II. The land of the Bishop of Bayeux

The Bishop of Bayeux holds of the king, and William Peverel of him, half a hide in HULCOTE. There is land for 1 plough. This [plough] is in demesne, with 4 bordars. There is a mill rendering 8d, and 6 acres of meadow. [There is] woodland 1 furlong in length and half a furlong in breadth. It was worth 8s; now 10s. Almær held it with sake and soke.

Of the bishop's fief William holds 1 hide and half a virgate of land in GREAT HOUGHTON. There is land for 4 ploughs. In demesne is 1 [plough], and 2 slaves; and 9 villans and 6 bordars with 3 ploughs. There is a mill rendering 8d, and 20 acres of meadow. [There is] woodland 1 furlong in length and half a furlong in breadth. It was worth 20s; now 40s. Ulf son of Azur held it with sake and soke. Countess Judith claims it.

Of the Bishop of Bayeux's fief, William holds 3 virgates of land in BRAFIELD-ON-THE-GREEN. There is land for 2 ploughs. 5 villans, with 2 bordars, have these [ploughs] there. There are 5 acres of meadow. It was and is worth 20s. Nigel claims it for the use of Countess Judith. Ulf son of Azur held it TRE.

Of the Bishop of Bayeux's fief, William holds 2 hides in GREATWORTH. There is land for 5 ploughs. In demesne is 1 [plough], and 2 slaves; and 10 villans and 5 bordars with 3 ploughs. It was worth £4; now £3. Sæwulf held it freely TRE.

Of the Bishop of Bayeux's fief, William holds 1 virgate of land in BRAUNSTON. The soke of this lies in Fawsley. There is land for 1 plough. This [plough] is there, with 2 villans and 3 bordars. It was and is worth 20s Sæwine held it TRE.

Of the Bishop of Bayeux's fief, William holds 1 virgate of land and the fifth part of 1 virgate in WALTON GROUNDS. The soke of this lies in King's Sutton. There is land for 1 plough. This [plough] is there, with 1 slave and 2 villans. There is a mill rendering 4s. It was worth 10s; now 15s. Wulfric held it of Æthelnoth of Canterbury.

Of the Bishop of Bayeux's fief, the same William holds 4½ hides and the fifth part of half a hide in HARTWELL. There is land for 10 ploughs. In demesne are 2 [ploughs], and 5 slaves; and 11 villans and 9 bordars, with a priest, having 4½ ploughs. There are 12 acres of meadow, and a mill rendering 17s4d. [There is] woodland 8 furlongs in length and 3 in breadth. It was worth £4; now 70s. Eadmær held it freely.

IN CLEYLEY HUNDRED

Of the Bishop of Bayeux's fief, William holds half a hide, less the fifth part of half a hide, in PUXLEY. There is land for 1 plough. There is 1 villan, with 1 bordar, having half a plough. It is worth 4s. Almær held it TRE.

IN 'GRAVESEND' HUNDRED

Of the Bishop of Bayeux's fief, William holds half a hide in GREAT EVERDON. The soke of this land lies in Fawsley. There is land for 1 plough. This [plough] is there, with 2 villans and 2 bordars, and 6 acres of meadow. It was worth 5s; now 10s. Beorn held it TRE.

IN SUTTON HUNDRED

Of the Bishop of Bayeux's fief, Adams holds in CHARLTON 3 virgates of land and the fifth part of 1 virgate. The soke lies in King's Sutton. There is land for 2 ploughs. In demesne is 1 [plough], with 2 bordars. It was and is worth 10s.

IN NOBOTTLE HUNDRED

Of the Bishop of Bayeux's fief, William holds 2 hides and 1½ virgates of land in NETHER HEYFORD. There is land for 4 ploughs. In demesne are 2 ploughs, and 2 slaves; and 7 villans and 2 bordars with 1 plough. There are 10 acres of meadow. It was worth 10s; now 20s. Bisceop and Æthelgeat held it freely TRE.

III. The land of the Bishop of Durham

IN WITCHLEY WAPENTAKE

THE BISHOP OF DURHAM holds 2 hides of the king in HORN [Rutland]. There is land for 4 ploughs. [There is] now in demesne 1 plough; and 12 villans, with a priest and 1 sokeman and 7 bordars and 1 slave, have 4 ploughs. There are 3 mills rendering 20s. [There is] woodland 1 furlong and 12 perches in length and 17 perches in breadth. It was and is worth £4. Langfer held it of King Edward with sake and soke.

[Folio 220V: NORTHAMPTONSHIRE]

IIII. The land of the Bishop of Coutances

THE BISHOP of Coutances holds of the king RAUNDS. There are 6 hides and 1½ virgates. There is land [...]. In demesne are 2 ploughs, and 4 slaves; and 4 villans and 6 bordars with 2 ploughs. There is a mill rendering 34s8d and 100 eels. There are 20 acres of meadow. Of this land, 3 sokemen hold 2 hides; Robert, 1 hide; Geoffrey, 1 hide; Algar, 1½ virgates. There are in demesne 6½ ploughs; and 7 villans and 4 bordars, with 2 slaves, having 2 ploughs, and a mill rendering 12d. It was worth 60s; now 100s. Of this land, William claims against the bishop 1 hide and half a virgate of land. Burgræd held this manor with sake and soke.

The bishop himself holds DENSFORD. There are 5 hides. There is land [...]. In demesne are 4½ ploughs, and 3 slaves; and 12 villans and 18 bordars and 4 sokemen with 12 ploughs. There are 2 mills rendering 50s8d and 250 eels. Burgræd held this manor freely. It was worth 100s; now £8.

IN NAVISFORD HUNDRED

Of the bishop himself, Aubrey holds 2½ hides and 1 bovate in WADENHOE. There is land for 5 ploughs. In demesne are 3 [ploughs], and 4 slaves; and 3 villans and 14 bordars, with a priest, have 2 ploughs. There is a mill rendering 12d, and 11 acres of meadow. It was worth £3; now £4. To this land belong 3 virgates of land in SCALDWELL. There is land for 1 plough. This [plough] is there with 2 villans and 2 bordars. The soke is the king's.

Of the same bishop, the same Aubrey holds 2 hides and half a virgate of land in Wadenhoe. There is land for 6 ploughs. In demesne are 2 ploughs, and 4 slaves; and 9 villans and 3 bordars, with 1 sokeman, having 2½ ploughs. There is a mill rendering 13s4d and 65 eels. There are 16 acres of meadow. [There is] woodland 3 furlongs in length and 1 league in breadth. It was worth 20s; now 60s. Burgræd held it freely TRE.

IN ORLINGBURY HUNDRED

Of the bishop himself, Walkelin holds 2 hides and 3 virgates of land in GREAT HARROWDEN. There is land for 6 ploughs. In demesne are 3 ploughs; and 12 villans and 13 bordars with 1½ ploughs. There is a mill rendering 8s. Of this land, 1 knight holds 3 virgates of land, and has there 1 plough, with 2 villans and 1 bordar. It was worth 60s; now 100s. Edwin held it freely.

Of the bishop himself, Walkelin holds 1½ hides in another HARROWDEN [Little Harrowden]. There is land for 3 ploughs, and these [ploughs] are there in demesne. This land is valued with that above.

Of the fief of the bishop himself, Hardwin, a man of Walkelin, holds 1 hide and 1 virgate of land in the same vill. There is land for 2 ploughs, and these [ploughs] are in demesne, with 1 slave; and 4 villans, with 1 bordar, have half a plough. There are 5 acres of meadow. It was worth 20s; now 40s. Sigefrith held it freely TRE.

Of the bishop himself, Walkelin holds 3 virgates of land in ISHAM. There is land for 1 plough, and this [plough] is in demesne, with 4 bordars who have half a plough. It was worth 5s; now 20s. Burgræd held it with sake and soke.

Of the bishop himself, Walkelin holds 2 hides and 3 virgates of land in BURTON LATIMER. There is land for 5 ploughs. In demesne are 2 [ploughs], with 1 slave and 1 female slave. There 9 villans and 5 bordars have 3½ ploughs. There are 15 acres of meadow. It was worth 20s; now 40s. Burgræd held it with sake and soke.

IN 'STOTFOLD' HUNDRED

Of the bishop himself, Walkelin holds half a hide and 3 parts of 1 virgate in CLIPSTON. There is land for 3 ploughs. In demesne is 1 [plough]; and 4 villans and 2 bordars have 1½ ploughs. To this land belongs 1 virgate of land and 2 parts of 1 virgate. It was worth 10s; now 20s.

IN WARDEN HUNDRED

Of the bishop himself, Walkelin holds 2 hides in EDGCOTE. There is land for 5 ploughs. In demesne are 2 [ploughs], with 2 slaves; and 21 villans and 2 bordars have 3 ploughs. There is a mill rendering 10s, and 6 acres of meadow. It was and is worth £4. Burgræd held it with sake and soke, and likewise the above-mentioned [lands].

IN 'NAVISLAND' HUNDRED

Of the bishop himself, Richard holds 1½ hides in BURTON LATIMER. There is land for 3 ploughs. In demesne is 1 [plough], with 1 slave; and 3 villans, with 1 bordar, have 1 plough. There are 6 acres of meadow. It was and is worth 10s.

Of the bishop himself, Richard holds half a hide in FINEDON. There is land for 2 ploughs. In demesne is 1 [plough], with 3 bordars. There is a mill rendering 5s, and 3 acres of meadow. It was worth 5s; now 20s. Burgræd held both.

Of the bishop himself, Geoffrey holds 1 hide and half a virgate of land in "HANTONE". There is land for 4 ploughs. In demesne are 2 [ploughs], and 3 slaves; and 4 villans and 2 bordars with 2 ploughs. There are 4 acres of meadow. It was worth 20s; now 30s. Alwine Cobbold held it.

IN WYMERSLEY HUNDRED

Of the same bishop, Winemar holds half a hide in HACKLETON. There is land for 1 plough, and this [plough] is there, with 1 slave and 3 bordars. It was worth 16d; now 10s. Burgræd held it.

Of the bishop himself, Winemar holds 1 hide in PRESTON DEANERY, and it was assessed at 1 hide TRE. There is land for 2 ploughs. In demesne is 1 [plough], and 2 slaves; and 4 villans with 1 plough. There are 6 acres of meadow. It was worth 2s; now 20s. Wulfwaru the widow held it TRE.

Of the bishop himself, Robert holds BARTON SEAGRAVE. There are 4½ hides. There is land for 10 ploughs. In demesne are 4 ploughs, and 7 slaves and 1 female slave; and 23 villans, with 3 bordars, have 6 ploughs. There are 2 mills rendering 10s, and 40 acres of meadow, and 8 acres of woodland. It was worth 40s; now 100s. Burgræd held it.

IN 'NAVISLAND' HUNDRED

Of the bishop himself, Robert holds 1 virgate of land in CRANFORD ST JOHN. There is land for 1 plough. There are 5 villans and 1 sokeman, with 2 bordars; they have 2 ploughs. It is worth 10s. It was waste.

IN 'HAMFORDSHOE' HUNDRED

Of the bishop himself, Norgiot holds 1 virgate of land in WELLINGBOROUGH. There is land for half a plough. There are 2 sokemen with this [half-plough]. It is worth 2s. The soke belongs to the bishop's manor of Great Harrowden.

Of the bishop himself, William holds 2 hides, less half a virgate, in NEWTON BROMSWOLD. There is land for 2 ploughs. In demesne are 2 ploughs; and 8 villans and 6 bordars with 2 ploughs. [There is] woodland 2 furlongs in length and 1 furlong in breadth. It was worth 20s; now 40s. Azur held it TRE.

IN 'NAVISLAND' HUNDRED

Of the bishop's fief, Hugh holds 1½ hides in GREAT ADDINGTON. There is land for 2 ploughs. In demesne is 1 [plough]; and 6 villans, with 1 bordar, have 3 ploughs. There is a mill rendering 16d, and 4 acres of meadow. It was worth 10s; now 40s.

Of the bishop's fief, Osmund holds 1 hide and 1 virgate of land in another ADDINGTON [Little Addington]. There is land for 3 ploughs. In demesne is 1 [plough]; and 4 villans have 2 ploughs. There are 2 acres of meadow. It was worth 10s; now 20s. Azur held it of King Edward.

Of the same bishop, Ralph holds 1 hide and 1 virgate of land in WOODFORD. There is land for 2 ploughs. In demesne are 2 ploughs; and 1 villan, with a priest and 5 bordars, have 1½ ploughs. There are 6 acres of meadow, and 1 acre of woodland. It was worth 10s; now 30s. Burgræd held it, but the soke belonged to Peterborough.

Of the same bishop, Odelin holds 3 virgates of land in THRAPSTON. There is land for 2 ploughs. In demesne is 1 [plough], and 2 slaves; and 1 villan, with 4 bordars, has 1 plough. It was worth 12d; now 10s. Burgræd held it freely.

Of the same bishop, Edwin holds 1½ virgates of land in STANION. There is land for 2 ploughs. In demesne is 1 [plough]; and 3 bordars have 1 plough. There is a mill rendering 32d. [There is] woodland 4 furlongs in length and 2 furlongs in breadth. It was worth 2s; now 10s. The same man held it freely TRE.

IN 'HUXLOE' HUNDRED

Of the same bishop, Edwin and Algar hold 2 hides, less 1 virgate, in LOWICK. There is land for 3 ploughs. In demesne is 1 plough, and 1 female slave; and 7 villans and 2 bordars with 2 ploughs. There is a mill rendering 64d. [There is] woodland 5 furlongs in length and 3 furlongs in breadth. It was worth 10s; now 25s.

Of the same bishop, Algar holds 1 hide and 1 virgate of land in ISLIP. There is land for 2 ploughs. In demesne is 1 [plough], and 2 slaves; and 5 villans with 2 bordars have 1 plough.

[Folio 221: NORTHAMPTONSHIRE]

Of the same bishop, Turbern holds 3 virgates of land in HORTON. There is land for 1 plough. This [plough] is there, with 2 villans and 2 bordars. It was worth 6s; now 10s. Frani held it TRE.

IN SUTTON HUNDRED

Of the bishop, Ælfric holds in CROUGHTON 4 parts of half a hide. There is land for half a plough. There are 3 bordars with 1 plough. It is worth 10s. The same man held it of the son of Burgræd and could not leave.

Of the bishop, Robert holds FINMERE [Oxon.]. There are 8 hides. There is land for 9 ploughs. In demesne are 2 [ploughs], and 4 slaves; and 10 villans and 5 bordars with 6 ploughs. There is a mill rendering 14s, and 100 acres of pasture. [There is] woodland 1 furlong in length and 1 in breadth. It was and is worth £8. Wulfweard held it freely TRE.

Of the bishop, Roger holds HETHE [Oxon.]. There are 8 hides. There is land for 8 ploughs. In demesne are 2 [ploughs], with 1 slave; and 8 villans and 5 bordars with 1 plough. There are 20 acres of pasture. It was and is worth £8. Wulfweard held it freely.

Of the bishop, Herlwin holds SHELSWELL [Oxon.]. There are 10 hides. There is land for 7 ploughs. In demesne are 3 ploughs, and 2 slaves; and 7 villans and 7 bordars with 4 ploughs. It was worth 100s; now £10. Edwin son of Burgræd held it.

Of the bishop, William holds GLYMPTON [Oxon.]. There are 10 hides. There is land for 6 ploughs. In demesne are 6 ploughs, and 6 slaves; and 15 villans and 5 bordars with 5 ploughs. There is a mill rendering 5s, and 18 acres of meadow.

[There is] woodland 6 furlongs in length and as much in breadth. It was worth £6; now £8. Wulfweard held it freely of King Edward.

Of the bishop, William and Ilger hold WOOTTON [Oxon.]. There are 5 hides. There is land for 6 ploughs. In demesne are 2 [ploughs], and 2 slaves; and 14 villans and 2 bordars with 5 ploughs. There are 30 acres of meadow, and 13 acres of pasture. It was worth £4; now 100s. Wulfweard held it freely.

Of the bishop, Turstin holds half a hide in [?Over] WORTON [Oxon.]. There is land for half a plough. There are 6 acres of meadow. It was worth 5s; now 10s. Leofgeat held it freely.

Of the bishop, Robert holds 5 hides in [?Upper] HEYFORD [Oxon.]. There is land for 6 ploughs. In demesne are 3 ploughs, and 5 slaves; and 5 villans and 7 bordars with 2 ploughs. There is a mill rendering 20s, and 30 acres of meadow. It was and is worth £6. Edwin son of Burgræd held it freely.

V. The land of the Bishop of Lincoln

IN GUILSBOROUGH HUNDRED AND A HALF

THE BISHOP OF LINCOLN holds of the king HOLLOWELL. There are 1 hide and 2 parts of half a hide. There is land for 3 ploughs. There are 4 villans, with 1 bordar, having 1 plough. It was and is worth 10s. Barthi held it freely.

Of the bishop himself, Walter holds 2 hides in LYDDINGTON [Rutland]. There belong [to it] Stoke Dry [Rutland], Snelston [Rutland], Caldecott [Rutland]. There is land for 16 ploughs in all. In demesne are 6 ploughs, and 4 slaves; and 26 villans and 24 bordars having 9 ploughs. There are 2 mills rendering 8s, and 28 acres of meadow. [There is] woodland 3 furlongs in length and 2 furlongs in breadth. The whole is worth £8. Barthi held it with sake and soke.

Of the same bishop, Walter holds 1 hide in ESSENDINE [Rutland]. There is land for 6 ploughs. In demesne are 2 [ploughs], with 1 slave; and 16 villans and 5 bordars with 4 ploughs. There is a mill rendering 16s, and 3 acres of meadow. [There is] woodland 6 furlongs in length and 4 furlongs in breadth. It was worth £4; now 100s. Barthi held it with sake and soke.

IN 'ALBOLDSTOW' HUNDRED

Of the same bishop, Godfrey holds 4 hides in CHACOMBE. There is land for 10 ploughs. In demesne are 2 [ploughs], and 4 slaves; and 20 villans and 9 bordars with 8 ploughs. There are 3 mills rendering 16s, and 9 acres of meadow. It was worth £10; now £7. Barthi held it freely.

VI. The land of Peterborough [Abbey]

IN STOKE HUNDRED

THE ABBEY OF PETERBOROUGH holds the vill which is called PETERBOROUGH. There are 8 hides. There is land for 16 ploughs. In demesne are 5 [ploughs], and 7 slaves; and 37 villans and 8 bordars with 11 ploughs. There is a mill rendering 5s, and 40 acres of meadow. [There is] woodland 1 league in length and 4 furlongs in breadth. It was worth 20s; now £10.

IN STOKE HUNDRED

The church itself holds COTTINGHAM. There are 7 hides. There is land for 14 ploughs. In demesne are 2 [ploughs], and 4 slaves; and 29 villans and 10 bordars with 10 ploughs. There is a mill rendering 40d, and 12 acres of meadow. [There is] woodland 1 league in length and half a league in breadth. It was worth 10s; now 60s.

The church itself holds LONGTHORPE. There are 2 hides. There is land for 4 ploughs. In demesne are 2 [ploughs], and 4 slaves; and 12 villans and 2 bordars with 2 ploughs. There is meadow 3 furlongs in length and 1 furlong in breadth. [There is] woodland 6 furlongs in length and 4 furlongs in breadth. There are 3 sokemen with 2 ploughs. It was worth 40s; now 50s.

The church itself holds CASTOR. There are 3 hides. There is land for 12 ploughs. In demesne are 2 [ploughs], with 1 slave; and 13 villans and 2 bordars with 3½ ploughs. There is a mill rendering 8s, and 15 acres of meadow. [There is] woodland 6 furlongs in length and 4 furlongs in breadth. It was worth 20s; now 50s.

The church itself holds AILSWORTH. There are 6 hides. There is land for 12 ploughs. In demesne are 2 ploughs; and 17 villans and 2 bordars and 8 sokemen with 12 ploughs. There are 2 mills rendering 12s, and 15 acres of meadow. [There is] woodland 3 furlongs in length and 2 furlongs in breadth. It was worth 20s; now 70s.

The church itself holds 6 hides in PILSGATE. There is land for 6 ploughs. In demesne is 1 [plough], with 1 slave; and 9 villans and 2 bordars and 26 sokemen have 11 ploughs. There is a mill rendering 10s, and 40 acres of meadow, and 5 acres of woodland. It was worth 20s; now £4.

The church itself holds 3 hides in GLINTON. In this [place] with its appendages were 30 ploughs TRE. There is land for 12 ploughs. In demesne are 3 ploughs, and 2 female slaves; and 10 villans and 6 bordars and 8 sokemen with 5 ploughs. There are 100 acres of meadow. [There is] woodland 10 furlongs in length and 9 furlongs in breadth. It was and is worth 60s.

The church itself holds 8 hides and 1 virgate of land in WERRINGTON. There, with its appendages, were 30 ploughs TRE. There is land for 12 ploughs. In demesne are 5 ploughs, and 4 slaves; and 30 villans and 4 bordars and 19 sokemen having 19 ploughs. [There is] woodland 2 leagues in length and 1 league in breadth. It was worth £4; now £7.

The church itself holds in ELTON [Hunts.] 1½ hides. There is land for 3 ploughs. There are 6 sokemen with 3 ploughs, and 8 acres of meadow. It was worth 2s; now 10s.

The church itself holds 6 hides in OUNDLE. There is land for 9 ploughs. In demesne are 3 ploughs, and 3 slaves; and 23 villans and 10 bordars with 9 ploughs. There is a mill rendering 20s and 250 eels, and there are 50 acres of meadow. [There is] woodland 3 leagues in length and 2 leagues in breadth. When stocked it is worth 20s. From the market 25s. It was worth 5s; now £11.

To this manor belongs half a hide in THURNING. There is land for half a plough. There is 1 villan. It was worth 2s; now 40d.

IN WITCHLEY HUNDRED

To the manor itself belong 2 hides and 1 virgate of land in STOKE DOYLE. There is land for 8 ploughs.

[Folio 221V: NORTHAMPTONSHIRE]

In demesne is 1 plough; and 10 villans and 2 bordars with 2½ ploughs. There are 10 acres of meadow. [There is] woodland 1 league in length and 5 furlongs in breadth. It was worth 10s; now 110s.

The church itself holds 7½ hides in WARMINGTON. There is land for 16 ploughs. In demesne are 4 ploughs, and 3 slaves; and 32 villans with 8 ploughs. There is a mill rendering 40s and 325 eels, and 40 acres of meadow, and 1 acre of woodland. It was worth 5s; now £11.

The church itself holds 4½ hides in ASHTON [in Oundle]. There is land for 8 ploughs. In demesne are 2 ploughs, with 1 slave; and 11 villans and 2 bordars with 6 ploughs. There are 2 mills rendering 40s and 325 eels, and 16 acres of meadow, and 4 acres of woodland. It was worth 8s; now £7.

IN WITCHLEY HUNDRED

The church itself holds TINWELL [Rutland]. There are 5 hides and 1 virgate of land. There is land for 8 ploughs. In demesne are 2 [ploughs]; and 24 villans and 11 bordars with 7 ploughs. There are 2 mills rendering 24s, and 20 acres of meadow. It was worth 10s; now £7.

The church itself holds 1 hide and 1 virgate of land in SLIPTON. There is land for 2 ploughs, and these [ploughs] are there, with 6 sokemen. There are 4 acres of woodland. It is worth 5s.

The church itself holds 5 hides and 1 virgate of land in IRTHLINGBOROUGH. There is land for 15 ploughs. In demesne are 2 [ploughs], and 2 slaves; and 9 villans and 8 bordars and 4 sokemen, with 5 ploughs between them all. There is a mill rendering 18s. It was worth £3; now £6.

The church itself holds 1 hide and 1 virgate of land in STANWICK. There is land for 3 ploughs. In demesne are 2 ploughs, with 1 slave; and 8 villans and 4 bordars with 1 plough and 2 oxen. There is a mill rendering 20s, and 8 acres of meadow. It was worth 40s; now 100s.

The church itself holds 10 hides in KETTERING. There is

land for 16 ploughs. In demesne is 1 [plough], and 1 female slave; and 31 villans with 10 ploughs. There are 2 mills rendering 20s, and 107 acres of meadow, and 3 acres of woodland. It was worth £10; now £11.

The land of the Men of the Same Church

In CASTOR 5 knights hold 3 hides of the abbot, and have there 5 ploughs in demesne; and 9 villans and 5 bordars and 3 slaves with 2½ ploughs. It was worth 10s; now 40s.

Roger holds of the abbot MILTON. There are 2 hides. There is land for 3 ploughs. In demesne are 2 [ploughs], with 1 slave; and 5 villans and 6 sokemen with 2 ploughs. [There is] woodland 3 furlongs in length and 1 in breadth. It was worth 20s; now 40s.

In AILSWORTH 3 of the abbot's knights hold 3 hides, and have there 3 ploughs. It is worth £3.

Ansketil holds of the abbot WITTERING. There are 9 hides. There is land for 16 ploughs. TRE there were 30 [ploughs]. In demesne are 3 ploughs, and 5 slaves; and 12 villans and 7 bordars and 20 sokemen with 12 ploughs between them all. There are 3 mills rendering 19s. [There is] woodland 2 leagues in length and 1 in breadth. It was worth £3; now £11.

In BURGHLEY Geoffrey holds 3 virgates of land of the abbot. There is land for 2 ploughs. In demesne is 1 [plough], and 3 slaves; and 7 villans, with 1 bordar, have 1 plough. There are 6 acres of meadow, and 3 acres of woodland. It was worth 10s; now 40s.

In SOUTHORPE Geoffrey and 2 other knights hold 4½ hides of the abbot. There is land for 6 ploughs. TRE there were 12 [ploughs]. In demesne are 3 ploughs; and 4 villans and 2 bordars and 18 sokemen with 7 ploughs. There are 2½ mills rendering 3s, and 20 acres of meadow. [There is] woodland 2 furlongs in length and 1 in breadth. It was worth 40s; now £6.

In GLINTON 3 of the abbot's knights hold 10 hides and 1 virgate of land. They have there 6 ploughs in demesne; and 33 sokemen with 9½ ploughs. There are 2 mills rendering 11s4d. It was worth 40s; now £10.

In WERRINGTON 4 of the abbot's knights hold 3 hides, and have there 4 ploughs and 12 acres of meadow. It was worth 20s; now £4.

In WOTHORPE Alwine holds of the abbot 3 virgates of land which belong to WITTERING. There they have [sic] 3 sokemen with 1½ ploughs, and 4 acres of meadow. It is worth 8s.

In COTTERSTOCK 2 knights hold of the abbot 3 hides. There is land for 6 ploughs. In demesne are 3 [ploughs]; and 10 villans and 4 bordars with 6½ ploughs. There are 24 acres of meadow. [There is] woodland 6 furlongs in length and 4 furlongs in breadth. It was worth 5s; now 60s.

In LUTTON William holds of the abbot 2½ hides. There is land for 6 ploughs. In demesne is 1 [plough], with 1 slave; and 8 villans and 2 bordars with 2 ploughs, and 6 sokemen with 2

ploughs, and 12 acres of meadow. The soke of this land belongs to Oundle. It was worth 10s; now 40s.

In WARMINGTON 2 knights hold of the abbot 1 hide, which belongs to Willowbrook. There is land for 2 ploughs. These [ploughs] are there, with 2 villans and 3 sokemen. It was worth 2s; now 30s.

In POLEBROOK Eustace holds of the abbot 4 hides, less 1 virgate. There is land for 8 ploughs. In demesne is 1 [plough], with 1 slave; and 5 villans and 2 bordars and 3 sokemen, with 8 villans, have 4½ ploughs between them all. There are 5 acres of meadow. It was worth 5s; now 40s. Of this land Geoffrey holds 1 virgate of land.

In ARMSTON and KINGSTHORPE [in Polebrook] 5 knights hold of the abbot 5 hides of sokeland. There is land for 8 ploughs. In demesne are 5 [ploughs]; and 9 villans and 3 bordars and 6 sokemen with 3 ploughs between them all. There are 3 acres of meadow. It was worth 10s; now 40s.

In HEMINGTON 3 knights hold of the abbot 2½ hides, and the soke belongs to Oundle. There is land for 4 ploughs. In demesne are 2 ploughs; and 5 villans with 2 ploughs. There are 10 acres of meadow. It was worth 10s; now 40s.

In LUDDINGTON IN THE BROOK Walter holds of the abbot 1½ hides, which belong to Oundle. There is land for 3 ploughs. In demesne is 1 [plough]; and 7 villans with 1½ ploughs. It was worth 10s; now 30s.

In WINWICK [Hunts.] Eustace holds of the abbot half a hide. The soke belongs to Oundle. There 2 sokemen, with 2 villans, have 2 ploughs. It was worth 5s; now 10s.

Isembard and Rozelin hold 1½ hides of the abbot, and they belong to WARMINGTON. There, with 3 villans, they have 2 ploughs. It was worth 5s; now 40s.

2 knights and 2 sergeants, with 1 sokeman, hold 2 hides and 3 virgates of land, which belong to STOKE DOYLE. There they have 2½ ploughs; and 8 villans and 4 bordars with 3 ploughs. There are 10 acres of meadow. It was worth 5s; now 50s.

In PILTON Roger holds of the abbot 2½ hides. There is land for 5 ploughs. In demesne is 1 [plough]; and 6 villans and 2 bordars and 2 sokemen with 4 ploughs. There are 8 acres of meadow. [There is] woodland 14 furlongs in length and 4 furlongs in breadth. It was worth 5s; now 60s.

In WADENHOE Roger holds of the abbot 1½ virgates of land, and he has there half a plough, with 1 bordar. There are 2 acres of meadow. It is worth 5s.

In ACHURCH Azelin and 2 Englishmen hold of the abbot 6½ hides. There is land for 10 ploughs. In demesne are 3 ploughs, and 3 slaves; and 10 villans and 11 bordars with 5 ploughs. There are 20 acres of meadow, and 6 acres of woodland. It was worth 60s; now 100s.

[Folio 222: NORTHAMPTONSHIRE]

In TITCHMARSH Azelin holds of the abbot 3 hides and 1 virgate of land. There is land for 5 ploughs. In demesne are 2 [ploughs], and 3 slaves; and 7 villans and 3 bordars with 2 ploughs, and 3 sokemen with 1 plough. There are 10 acres of meadow. It was worth 20s; now 55s.

In CLOPTON Eustace holds of the abbot 3 hides and 3 virgates of land and the third part of half a hide. There is land for 5 ploughs. In demesne is 1 [plough]; and 1 knight and 9 villans and 12 bordars and 3 sokemen with 4 ploughs. It was worth 10s; now 40s.

In the same vill Almær holds of the abbot half a hide, and has there 1 plough; and 2 villans and 3 bordars with half a plough. In the whole vill are 26 acres of meadow. This part of Almær's is worth 10s.

In PYTCHLEY Azo holds of the abbot 5 hides and 1 virgate of land. There is land for 13 ploughs. In demesne are 2 [ploughs], and 2 slaves; and 5 villans and as many bordars with 3 ploughs. There is a mill rendering 8s, and 11 acres of meadow.

There also Azo has 1½ hides, and there are 4 sokemen with 1 plough. The whole, when he received it, was worth £8; now 100s. This manor belonged to the monks' farm, and there was a demesne building.

In CATWORTH [Hunts.] Eustace holds 1½ hides. There is land for 3 ploughs. There are 4 sokemen with 1 plough. It was worth 10s; now 5s.

In ALDWINCLE ST PETER are 3 hides. There is land for 10 ploughs. In demesne is 1 [plough]; and 9 villans and 2 bordars and 2 sokemen with 4½ ploughs. There are 20 acres of meadow. [There is] woodland 2 leagues in length and 1 in breadth; it is worth 15s when it is stocked. It was worth 20s; now 30s. If it were well worked it would be worth 100s. This land TRE was for the sustenance of the monks. Ferron holds it by the king's command against the will of the abbot.

In WOODFORD Roger holds of the abbot 7 hides. There is land for 12 ploughs. In demesne are 2½ ploughs, and 4 slaves; and 12 villans and 3 bordars and 12 sokemen with 9½ ploughs. There is a mill rendering 2s, and 20 acres of meadow. It was worth 20s; now 60s.

In the same vill, Roger, Hugh, and Siward hold 3 virgates of land of the abbot, and have there 1 plough; and it is worth 10s. The whole manor was waste when they received it.

In LITTLE ADDINGTON Hugh holds of the abbot 3 hides. There is land for 8 ploughs. In demesne are 2 [ploughs], with 1 slave; and 8 villans and 4 bordars and 1 sokeman with 4 ploughs. There is a mill rendering 12d and 200 eels, and 8 acres of meadow. It was worth 10s; now 40s.

In IRTHLINGBOROUGH 4 knights hold of the abbot 5 hides, less 1 virgate. There they have 6 ploughs in demesne; and 8 villans and 2 bordars with 2 ploughs. There is a mill rendering 5s. It was worth 20s; now 100s. The soke belongs to Peterborough.

In CRANFORD [?St Andrew] Robert holds of the abbot 3 hides, and 1 knight [holds] of him. There is land for 6 ploughs.

There are 15 sokemen having 6 ploughs. it was worth 5s; now 40s.

In CRANFORD [?St Andrew] are 1½ hides. Godric holds of the king. [...] There is land for 3 ploughs. In demesne is 1 [plough]; and 4 bordars have another plough. There is a mill rendering 2s, and 4 acres of meadow, and as many of woodland. It was worth 10s; now 20s.

In DALLINGTON Richard holds of the abbot 4 hides. There is land for 8 ploughs. In demesne are 2 [ploughs], and 3 slaves; and 18 villans, with a priest and 4 bordars, have 6 ploughs. There is a mill rendering 20s, and 5 acres of meadow. It was worth 40s; now 100s.

In ASHTON [in Oundle] Ivo holds of the abbot half a hide. It is worth 4s.

VII. The land of St Peter of Westminster

IN CORBY HUNDRED

THE ABBEY OF ST PETER of WESTMINSTER holds DEENE. There are 2½ hides. There is land for 8 ploughs. In demesne are 2 [ploughs]; and 17 villans, with a priest and 6 bordars, have 6 ploughs; and 2 smiths pay 32s. There is a mill rendering 3s. [There is] woodland 1 league in length and 8 furlongs in breadth. It was and is worth £6. The church always held it.

IN 'HUXLOE' HUNDRED

The church itself holds 3 hides in SUDBOROUGH. There is land for 8 ploughs. In demesne is 1 [plough]; and 12 villans and 5 sokemen, with 2 bordars, have 6 ploughs. There is a mill rendering 6s. [There is] woodland 7 furlongs in length and 6 in breadth. It was and is worth 100s.

VIII. The land of St Edmundsbury [Abbey]

IN ROTHWELL HUNDRED

THE ABBEY OF ST EDMUNDSBURY holds of the king 1 hide of sokeland in BOUGHTON [in Weekley]. There is land for 2 ploughs. There are 6 villans and 2 bordars with 2 ploughs. There is a mill rendering 12d. [There is] woodland 1 furlong in length and 1 in breadth. It was worth 64d; now 12s. Earl Ælfgar held it.

In GEDDINGTON the abbey holds 1 hide and 1 virgate of land of sokeland. There is land for 2 ploughs. These [ploughs] are there, with 5 sokemen and 4 bordars. It was and is worth 6s.

In ARTHINGWORTH the abbey holds half a virgate of sokeland. There is 1 villan, with 2 bordars, having half a plough. It was and is worth 3s.

In SCALDWELL the abbey holds 1 hide and 3 virgates of land. There is land for 3 ploughs. These [ploughs] are there, with 9 sokemen and 9 bordars. It was and is worth 16s. Earl Ælfgar held it. King William gave it to St Edmundsbury for the soul of Queen Matilda.

In HANGING HOUGHTON the abbey holds 1 hide and half a virgate of land. There is land for 2 ploughs. 3 sokemen and 12 bordars have these [ploughs] there. it was and is worth 12s.

In LAMPORT the abbey holds 1 virgate of land and 1 bovate. There is land for 1 plough. 3 sokemen have this [plough] there. It was and is worth 40d.

In BRAYBROOKE the abbey holds half a virgate of land of sokeland. There is land for half a plough. 1 sokeman has this [half-plough] there. It was and is worth 3s.

IN 'STOTFOLD' HUNDRED

In EAST FARNDON the abbey holds half a hide and the third part of 1 virgate of sokeland. There is land for 1 plough. There are 1½ ploughs, with 3 sokemen. It was and is worth 10s. Earl Ælfgar held it.

In HOTHORPE the abbey holds 3½ virgates of land of sokeland. There is land for 1 plough. There is 1 sokeman with half a plough. It was and is worth 2s.

In CLIPSTON the abbey holds 2½ virgates of land. There is land for 1 plough. There are 5 sokemen with 1½ ploughs. It was and is worth 10s.

In KELMARSH the abbey holds half a hide of sokeland. There is land for half a plough. There 5 sokemen have 1 plough. It was and is worth 6s.

In MAIDWELL the abbey holds the third part of 1 virgate. There is 1 sokeman. It was and is worth 6d.

IN 'NAVISLAND' HUNDRED

The abbot himself holds of the king WARKTON. There are 3½ hides. There is land for 9 ploughs. In demesne are 2 ploughs; and 16 villans and 8 bordars with 7 ploughs; and 3 slaves. There is a mill rendering 12s, and 20 acres of meadow. [There is] woodland 3 furlongs in length and 2 furlongs in breadth. It was worth £7; now £8. Ælfgifu the mother of Morcar held it.

IX. The land of St Benedict of Ramsey

IN WILLOWBROOK HUNDRED

THE ABBEY OF RAMSEY holds 1½ virgates of land in HALEFIELD. There is land for 1 plough. This [plough] is there in demesne; and 1 villan and 2 bordars have half a plough. It was and is worth 5s.

In LUTTON the abbey holds half a hide. There is land for half a plough. 1 villan has this [half-plough] there. It was and is worth 2s.

In ELTON [Hunts.] the abbey holds half a hide. There is land for half a plough. Nevertheless, 2 villans have there 1 plough, and 6 acres of meadow. It was worth 3s; it is worth 5s.

IN POLEBROOK HUNDRED

In HEMINGTON the abbey holds 2½ hides. There is land for 4 ploughs. In demesne is 1 [plough]; and 8 villans, with 1 bordar, have 3 ploughs. There are 10 acres of meadow. It was worth 10s; now 20s.

IN 'HUXLOE' HUNDRED

In BARNWELL the abbey holds 6 hides. There is land for 8 ploughs. In demesne are 2 ploughs, and 3 slaves; and 15 villans, with a priest and 6 bordars, have 6 ploughs. There are 2 mills rendering 24s, and 40 acres of meadow. [There is] woodland 6 furlongs in length and 3½ furlongs in breadth. It was worth 30s; now £4.

IN WYMERSLEY HUNDRED

In WISTHON and DENTON the abbey holds 3 hides. There is land for 6 ploughs. In demesne are 2 [ploughs], and 3 slaves; and 20 villans and 8 bordars and 3 sokemen with 5 ploughs.

[Folio 222V: NORTHAMPTONSHIRE]

There is a mill rendering 20s, and 20 acres of meadow. [There is] woodland without pasture, 1 furlong in length and 1 in breadth. It was worth 30s; now £4.

In Brafield-on-the-Green is 1 house belonging to WHISTON, with 5 acres of land. Countess Judith has the soke of half an acre.

X. The land of the Church of Thorney

IN 'HUXLOE' HUNDRED

THE ABBEY of THORNEY holds in TWYWELL 3 hides, less 1½ virgates. There is land for 7 ploughs. In demesne are 2 [ploughs]; and 9 villans and 5 bordars with 5 ploughs. There are 2 mills rendering 7s4d, and 2 acres of woodland. It was worth 10s; now 40s.

IN 'GRAVESEND' HUNDRED

The abbey itself holds half a hide in CHARWELTON, and Baldwin [holds] of it. There is land for 1 plough. In demesne is half [a plough]; and 1 villan with 1 bordar has half a plough. It was worth 12d; now 5s.

In SAWBRIDGE [War.] Turchil holds of the abbot 5 hides. There is land for 5 ploughs. There are 12 villans and 5 bordars, with 4 ploughs, and 8 acres of meadow. It was worth 50s; now 60s.

XI. The land of the Church of Crowland

IN UPTON HUNDRED

THE ABBEY OF CROWLAND holds in WOTHORPE 1½ hides. There is land for 2 ploughs. In demesne is 1 [plough]; and 11 villans and 2 bordars with 2 ploughs. There are 6 acres of meadow, and a mill rendering 5s. It is worth 40s.

In ELMINGTON the abbey holds 1 hide. There is land for 1 plough. This [plough] is there in demesne; and 2 villans and 2 bordars with 1 plough, and there are 6 acres of meadow. It was worth 8s; now 16s.

In ELMINGTON the abbey holds 2 hides. There is land for 3 ploughs. There are 5 villans and 4 bordars with 3 ploughs. There are 12 acres of meadow. It was worth 12s; now 20s.

IN 'NAVISLAND' HUNDRED

In GREAT ADDINGTON the abbey holds 2 hides. There is land for 4 ploughs. In demesne is 1 [plough], and 2 slaves; and 6 villans and 3 bordars, with 1 sokeman, have 3 ploughs. There are 6 acres of meadow, and a mill rendering 13s4d. It was worth 15s; now 40s.

In WELLINGBOROUGH the abbey holds 5½ hides. There is land for 12 ploughs. In demesne is 1 plough, with 1 slave; and 21 villans, with a priest and 7 bordars and 11 sokemen, have 11 ploughs. There are 2 mills rendering 16s, and 30 acres of meadow. It was worth 50s; and afterwards 40s; now £6.

IN 'GRAVESEND' HUNDRED

In BADBY the abbey holds 4 hides. There is land for 10 ploughs. In demesne are 4 ploughs and 8 slaves and 5 female slaves; and 12 villans and 8 bordars with 6 ploughs. There is a mill rendering 2s, and 28 acres of meadow. [There is] woodland 4 furlongs in length and 2 furlongs in breadth. It was and is worth £8.

XII. The land of the Church of Coventry

IN GUILSBOROUGH HUNDRED AND A HALF

THE ABBEY OF COVENTRY holds 3 hides and 1 virgate of land in WINWICK. There is land for 6½ ploughs. There are in demesne 3 ploughs; and 16 villans and 5 bordars, with a priest, have 3 ploughs. It is worth 50s.

In COLD ASHBY the abbey holds 2½ hides, and they belong to Winwick. There is land for 5 ploughs. There are 4 villans and 5 bordars with 2 ploughs. It is worth 10s.

IN 'ALWARDSLEY' HUNDRED

In KILSBY the abbey holds 2 hides. There is land for 5 ploughs. In demesne are 2 [ploughs], and 3 slaves; and 10 villans and 8 bordars with 3 ploughs. There are 8 acres of meadow. It is worth 50s.

In WEST HADDON the abbey holds 2 hides. There is land for 4 ploughs. There are 4 villans, with 2 bordars and 4 sokemen; they have 4 ploughs. It is worth 20s. 1 of these hides renders soke in Winwick.

XIII. The land of the Church of Evesham

IN 'GRAVESEND' HUNDRED

THE ABBEY OF EVESHAM holds 4 hides in LITCHBOROUGH. There is land for 10 ploughs. In demesne are 2 [ploughs]; and 8 villans and 6 bordars with 5 ploughs. It was and is worth 40s. Leofnoth held it freely TRE.

XIIII. The land of the Church of Grestain

THE ABBEY OF ST MARY OF GRESTAIN holds of the king in alms NEWBOTTLE [in Harrington]. There are 2 parts of 1 hide. There is land for 1½ ploughs. In demesne is 1 [plough]; and 3 villans with 1 bordar have half a plough. There is a mill rendering 2s. It was and is worth 6s.

In BRAYBROOKE the church itself holds 2 hides. There is land for 4 ploughs. In demesne is 1 [plough], with 1 slave; and 4 villans and 4 bordars with 3 ploughs. It was worth 6s; now 10s. Ulfkil held these lands.

In GLENDON the church itself holds half a hide and the third part of 1 hide. There is land for 2 ploughs. There are 4 villans and 4 bordars, with 1 slave, having 1 plough. It was worth 5s; now 10s. Ulf held it freely.

In RUSHTON the church itself holds half a virgate of land. There is land for half a plough. There are 2 bordars. It is worth 16d.

IN ROTHWELL HUNDRED

The church itself holds HARRINGTON. There are 5 hides and the third part of 1 hide. There is land for 10 ploughs. In demesne are 3 ploughs; and 12 villans and 13 bordars with 5 ploughs, and 4 sokemen with 2 ploughs. There are 4 mills rendering 2s. It was worth 30s; now £6. Ulf held it.

In WESTON FAVELL the church itself holds 1½ hides. There is land for 3 ploughs. In demesne are 1½ [ploughs], and 2 slaves; and 4 villans and 2 bordars with half a plough. There are 5 acres of meadow. It was worth 20s; now 30s. Ulf held it TRE.

XV. The land of Ansgar the Chaplain

IN 'STOTFOLD' HUNDRED

ANSGAR the clerk holds of the king 1 hide and 3 virgates of land in MAIDWELL, and has there 2 ploughs and 2 slaves; and 5 villans and 2 bordars with 2 ploughs. It is worth 20s. Godric held it TRE.

XVI. The land of St Remy of Rheims

IN CUTTLESTONE HUNDRED

THE CHURCH OF ST REMY holds of the king LAPLEY [Staffs.]. It held it similarly TRE. There are, with its appendages, 3 hides. There is land for 6 ploughs. In demesne are 3 ploughs, and 5 slaves; and 18 villans and 9 bordars with 8 ploughs. There are 16 acres of meadow. [There is] woodland 3 furlongs in length and as many in breadth. It is worth 50s.

In MARSTON [in Church Eaton, Staffs.] 2 men of St Remy hold 1 hide. There is land for 1 plough. It is worth 5s. Godwine held it with soke and sake.

XVII. The land of the King's Almsmen

IN FOXLEY HUNDRED

LEOFWINE the priest holds of the king 1 virgate of land in ADSTONE. Half a plough can be [employed] there. It is worth 6s.

IN 'GRAVESEND' HUNDRED

GODWINE the priest holds of the king 4 parts of half a hide in FAWSLEY. There is land for 1 plough, and there is [1 plough], with 4 bordars. It is worth 10s.

GODWINE the priest and Wulfwine hold of the king 3 virgates of land and the fifth part of 1 virgate in KING'S SUTTON. There is land for 2 ploughs, and there are [2 ploughs], with 9 bordars. There is a mill rendering 32d. It is worth 15s.

IN CLEYLEY HUNDRED

REGINALD holds of the king half a hide in PASSENHAM and has there 1 plough, with 4 bordars. It is worth 10s.

IN 'SPELHOE' HUNDRED

GODWINE the priest holds of the king 1½ virgates of land in BOUGHTON [near Northampton], and has there half a plough. It is worth 5s.

[Folio 223: NORTHAMPTONSHIRE]

XVIII. The land of the Count of Mortain

IN 'HAMFORDSHOE' HUNDRED

THE COUNT OF MORTAIN holds 4 hides in SYWELL. There is land for 10 ploughs. In demesne are 3 ploughs, and 6 slaves; and 18 villans and 2 bordars with 3 ploughs. There are 20 acres of meadow. It was worth 20s; now £6. Osmund son of Leofric held it with soke and sake. 2 hides of this land are in demesne. Countess Judith claims the soke of 1½ virgates.

In LITTLE BILLING the count holds half a hide and half a virgate of land. There is land for 1 plough. There are 3 villans with 2 oxen, and 10[?] acres of meadow. It was worth 2s; now 10s. Osmund held it freely.

IN NOBOTTLE HUNDRED

In BUGBROOKE the count holds 4 hides. There is land for 10 ploughs. In demesne are 3 ploughs, and 4 slaves; and 30 villans and 14 bordars with 10 ploughs. There are 2 mills rendering 40s, and 30 acres of meadow, and 4 acres of woodland.

IN 'SPELHOE' HUNDRED

In WESTON FAVELL the count holds 2½ hides. There is land for 5 ploughs. In demesne are 2 [ploughs], and 4 slaves; and 12 villans and 2 bordars with 3½ ploughs. There are 10 acres of meadow. It was worth 40s; now 60s. Leofric held it freely.

In LITTLE BILLING is sokeland of this manor, 2½ virgates

of land. There is land for 1 plough. There are 2 villans with 1 bordar, and 7 acres of meadow. It was and is worth 10s.

IN NOBOTTLE HUNDRED

In EAST HADDON the count holds 2½ hides. Of these, 1 is in demesne. There is land for 5 ploughs. In demesne are 3 ploughs, and 9 slaves; and 7 villans, with a priest and 7 bordars, have 2 ploughs. There is a mill rendering 10s, and 8 acres of meadow, and 10 acres of scrubland. It was worth 40s; now £4.

In RAVENSTHORPE the count holds half a hide. There is land for 2 ploughs. There is 1 villan, with 2 bordars. It was and is worth 5s. Eadmær held both these estates freely.

In CHURCH BRAMPTON the count holds 4 hides, less 5 acres. There is land for 8 ploughs. In demesne is 1 hide, and there are 2 ploughs and 2 slaves; and 3 villans and 5 bordars and 12 sokemen with 3½ ploughs between them all. There is a mill rendering 28s, and 10 acres of meadow, and 5 acres of scrubland. It was worth 60s; now 100s. Wulfær held half a hide of this land TRE. All the rest lies and lay in Creaton and East Haddon.

In the other HEYFORD [Upper Heyford] the count holds the third part of 1 virgate, which is valued with the capital manor.

IN CLEYLEY HUNDRED

In ALDERTON the count holds 2 hides and half a virgate of land. There is land for 8 ploughs. In demesne are 2 hides and half a virgate, and there are 3 ploughs, with 1 slave; and 3 villans and 3 bordars with 2 ploughs. There are 12 acres of meadow. [There is] woodland 3 furlongs in length and as much in breadth. It was worth 40s; now 50s. Eadmær and Edwin held it freely.

IN 'ALBOLDSTOW' HUNDRED

In HELMDON the count holds 4 hides. There is land for 10 ploughs. In demesne are 2 hides, and there are 5 ploughs and 2 slaves; and 7 villans and 2 bordars with 2 ploughs. There is a mill rendering 12d. It was and is worth £6. Alwine and Godwine held it freely.

IN 'GRAVESEND' HUNDRED

In "CELVERDESCOTE" the count holds 4 hides. There is land for 10 ploughs. In demesne are 2 hides of this land, and ther is 1 slave; and 9 villans and 3 bordars, with a priest, have 4½ ploughs. There are 6 acres of meadow. [There is] woodland 2 furlongs in length and 1½ furlongs in breadth. It was worth 40s; now 60s. Thorbiorn and Alli held it freely.

IN CLEYLEY HUNDRED

In COSGROVE [the count] holds 4 parts of half a hide. There is land for 1 plough, which [plough] is there, with 3 villans. It was worth 5s; now 4s. Godwine held it freely.

IN STOKE HUNDRED

HUMPHREY holds of the Count of Mortain 3 virgates of land in EAST CARLTON. There is land for 3 ploughs. In demesne are 2 [ploughs]; and 7 sokemen, with 6 bordars, have

4 ploughs. There is a mill rendering 16d, and 8 acres of meadow. [There is] woodland 2 furlongs in length and half a furlong in breadth. It was worth 10s; now 20s. Leofric held it freely.

The same man holds 1 hide and the third part of a hide and $1\frac{1}{2}$ bovates in DINGLEY. There is land for 3 ploughs. In demesne is 1 [plough]; and 5 villans have another. There are 4 acres of meadow, and 5 acres of woodland. It was worth 10s; now 20s. Edwin held it freely.

The same man holds 2 hides and 1 virgate of land and 2 parts of 1 virgate in ARTHINGWORTH. There is land for 5 ploughs. In demesne are 2 ploughs, with 1 slave; and 9 villans, with 1 bordar and 8 sokemen, with 3 ploughs. It was and is worth 20s. Ulf and Farthin held it.

In PIPEWELL the same Humphrey holds the third part of 1 hide. There is land for 1 plough, which [plough] 4 bordars have there. It was worth 3s; now 5s. Ulfkil held it freely.

IN 'STOTFOLD' HUNDRED

The same man holds in SIBBERTOFT 3 hides, less 1 virgate. There is land for 9 ploughs. In demesne are 2 [ploughs], and 4 slaves and 5 female slaves; and 8 villans, with a priest, have 2 ploughs. There are 20 acres of meadow. It was worth 5s; now 30s.

The same man holds 3 virgates of land and the third part of 1 virgate in EAST FARNDON. There is land for 2 ploughs. In demesne is 1 [plough]; and 3 villans have another. It was worth 2s; now 5s. Fredegis and Brumage held it.

The same man holds 2 hides and 1 virgate of land and the third part of 1 virgate in LITTLE BOWDEN [Leics.]. There is land for 6 ploughs. In demesne is 1 [plough], with 1 slave; and 11 villans, with 1 bordar, have 2 ploughs. There is a mill rendering 16d, and 8 acres of meadow, and 3 sokemen with 2 ploughs. It was worth 64d; now 30s. Godwine and Wulfsige held it.

The same man holds 1 hide and the third part of 1 virgate in LITTLE OXENDON. There is land for 2 ploughs. In demesne is 1 [plough]; nothing more. It was worth 12d; now 10s. Fredegis held it.

The same man holds 3 hides in HASELBECH. There is land for 9 ploughs. In demesne are 2 [ploughs]; and 9 villans and 10 bordars have 7 ploughs. It was worth 20s; now 40s. Almær and Northmann held it TRE.

The same man holds half a bovate of land in HARLESTONE. There is land for 2 oxen. Eadric held it freely. It is waste.

The same man holds 2 parts of 1 hide in ALTHORP. There is land for 2 ploughs. In demesne he has 1 [plough], with 3 slaves; and 1 knight has another, with 3 bordars. There are 8 acres of meadow and 2 acres of spinney. It was worth 5s; now 20s. Tosti and Snotormann held it freely.

IN CLEYLEY HUNDRED

The same man holds 5 parts of 1 hide in COSGROVE. The soke belongs to Passenham. There is land for $1\frac{1}{2}$ ploughs; and as many [ploughs] are there, with 4 bordars. There are 10 acres of meadow, and 2 furlongs of scrubland. It was and is worth 20s. Æthelric held it freely.

IN 'SPELHOE' HUNDRED

The same man holds 1 virgate of land in PITSFORD. There is land for half a plough, and there is [half a plough], with 1 bordar. There is a mill rendering 2s. It was worth 3s; now 10s. Osmund held it freely.

ALAN holds of the count 1 virgate of land in DESBOROUGH. There is land for 1 plough. There is half a plough, with 2 bordars. It was worth 3s; now 5s. Fredegis held it.

The same man holds 1 hide in WHILTON. There is land for 2 ploughs. In demesne is 1 [plough], and 2 slaves; and 2 villans, with a priest and 6 bordars, have another plough. There are 5 acres of meadow, and a mill rendering 40d. It was worth 10s; now 60s. Bovi held it freely.

The same man holds 2 hides and 4 parts of half a hide in COLD HIGHAM. There is land for 6 ploughs. In demesne is 1 [plough]; and 4 villans, with a priest and 3 bordars, have 1 plough. There are 10 acres of meadow. It was worth 5s; now 20s. Leofric held it freely.

The same man holds half a hide in WEEDON BEC. There is land for $1\frac{1}{2}$ ploughs. There is 1 plough, with 1 villan and 4 bordars, and 6 acres of meadow, and 2 acres of scrubland, and a mill rendering 40d. It was worth 40d; now 10s. Æstan held it freely.

The same man holds 3 hides in STAVERTON. The soke of $1\frac{1}{2}$ hides belongs to Fawsley. There is land for $8\frac{1}{2}$ ploughs. In demesne are 2 [ploughs]; and 6 villans and 12 bordars with 4 ploughs. It was worth 40s; now 60s. Sæwulf, Eadric, and Alwine held it freely.

RALPH holds of the count 2 hides, less 1 virgate, in HANGING HOUGHTON. There is land for 4 ploughs. In demesne are $1\frac{1}{2}$ [ploughs]; and 3 villans, with 2 bordars, have as many [ploughs]. It was worth 3s; now 20s. Fredegis held it freely TRE. The Abbot of St Edmundsbury claims the soke of $2\frac{1}{2}$ virgates of land.

IN WARDEN HUNDRED

The same man holds $1\frac{1}{2}$ hides and 1 bovate of land in WEST FARNDON. There is land for 2 ploughs. There is 1 [plough], with 2 bordars. It was worth 5s; now 20s. Ordric held it of Archbishop Stigand.

The same man holds $1\frac{1}{2}$ hides and the fifth part of 1 hide in TIFFIELD. There is land for 4 ploughs. There is 1 plough, with 1 villan. It was worth 5s; now 10s. Bisceop and Lyfing held it freely.

IN CLEYLEY HUNDRED

The same man holds 2 hides in FURTHO. There is land for 6 ploughs. In demesne is 1 [plough],

[Folio 223V: NORTHAMPTONSHIRE]

and 4 slaves; and 2 villans and 3 bordars with 1 plough. There are 8 acres of meadow. It was worth 10s; now 30s. Godmann and Godgifu held it freely.

The same Ralph holds of the count half a hide and 1 bovate in WALTON GROUNDS. There is land for 1 plough, which [plough] is there, with 3 bordars, and 1 acre of meadow. It was worth 3s; now 10s. Alwine held it freely.

The same man holds 2 hides and 4 parts of half a hide in CHARWELTON. There is land for 6 ploughs. In demesne are 2 [ploughs], with 1 slave; and 7 villans with 3 ploughs. There is a mill rendering 2s. It was worth 6s; now 60s.

IN SUTTON HUNDRED

The same man holds 2 hides in MIDDLETON CHENEY. There is land for 5 ploughs. In demesne are 2 [ploughs], with 1 slave; and 7 villans and 6 bordars with 1 plough. There are 4 acres of meadow. It was worth 50s; now 60s. Almær and Sæwulf held it. The soke of the fifth part of this land belongs to King's Sutton.

The same man holds 1½ hides in CHARLTON. There is land for 3½ ploughs. It is waste. Nevertheless it is and was worth 5s. 4 thegns held it freely.

IN TOWCESTER HUNDRED

The same man holds 4 parts of half a hide in FOXLEY. There is land for 1 plough. It is waste. Nevertheless it is worth 5s. Merefin held it freely.

The same man holds half a hide in SYRESHAM. There is land for 10 oxen. There is 1 villan. [There is] woodland 1 furlong in length and a half in breadth. It was worth 20s; now 5s. Leofnoth held it.

The same man holds 1 virgate of land and 2 parts of 1 virgate in NETHER HEYFORD. The soke belongs to Bugbrooke. There is land for 1 plough, and this [plough] is there, and 1 acre of meadow. It was worth 5s; now 10s. Wulfstan held it.

IN ORLINGBURY HUNDRED

WILLIAM holds of the count half a hide in HANN-INGTON. There is land for 1 plough, and this [plough] is there, with 1 villan and 2 bordars, and 1 acre of meadow. It was worth 12d; now 5s. Edwin held it freely.

IN NOBOTTLE HUNDRED

The same man holds 1½ hides in HARLESTONE. There is land for 3 ploughs. 2 villans and 3 bordars have these [ploughs] there. There is a mill rendering 2s, and 3 acres of meadow. It was worth 5s; now 30s. Leofric and Ordgar held it freely.

The same man holds half a hide in [Great or Little] BRINGTON. There is land for 3 ploughs. In demesne is 1

[plough], and 2 slaves; and 3 villans and 3 bordars with 2 ploughs. It was worth 5s; now 20s. Ælfric held freely 1 virgate of this land. The soke of the other virgate belongs to EAST HADDON, the count's manor.

The same man holds 3 virgates of land in BROCKHALL and MUSCOTT. There is land for 2 ploughs. In demesne is 1 [plough]; and 6 bordars have another. There are 6 acres of meadow. It was and is worth 40s. Leofric and Leofwine held it freely.

The same man holds half a hide in KISLINGBURY. There is land for 1½ ploughs. There is 1 [plough], with 1 villan and 2 bordars and 2 slaves, and 2 acres of meadow. It was worth 10s; now 20s. Leofric held it freely.

The same man holds 3 virgates of land in FLORE. There is land for 2 ploughs. In demesne is 1 [plough], and 4 slaves; and 2 villans and 5 bordars have another. There are 4 acres of meadow, and a mill rendering 10s. It was worth 20s; now 40s. Leofric held it freely, as well as that which follows.

The same man holds 3 virgates of land in GLASS-THORPEHILL, and half a hide in the same vill. There is land for 3 ploughs. In demesne are 2 [ploughs], and 3 slaves; and 1 villan and 1 bordar. It was worth 20s; now 40s. Leofric and Thorbiorn held it freely.

The same man holds 3 virgates of land in YELVERTOFT. There is land for 1½ ploughs, and as many [ploughs] are there, with 1 villan and 4 bordars. There are 2 acres of meadow. It was and is worth 10s. Thorth held it freely.

The same man holds half a hide in COLD ASHBY. There is land for 1 plough. There is half a plough, with 3 villans and 1 bordar. It was and is worth 5s.

The same man holds 1½ hides in the same vill. There is land for 3 ploughs. There are 4 villans with 2 ploughs, and 4 acres of meadow. It was worth 2s; now 10s. Æthelgifu the widow held these 2 estates.

IN FOXLEY HUNDRED

The same man holds 1 hide in SILVERSTONE. There is land for 3 ploughs. In demesne is 1 [plough], with 1 slave. It was worth 10s; now 20s. Leofric held it freely.

IN GUILSBOROUGH HUNDRED

The same William holds half a hide in LITTLE CREATON, and Humphrey [holds] of him. There is land for 1 plough, which [plough] is there, with 2 slaves and 2 bordars, and 10 acres of woodland. It was worth 16d; now 10s.

The same William holds half a hide in TIFFIELD and the fifth part of 1 hide. There is land for 1½ ploughs. There is 1 plough, with 1 villan, and 7 acres of woodland. It was worth 5s; now 10s. Leofwine held it freely. The soke of this land belongs to Towcester.

The same man holds half a hide and 4 parts of half a hide in FURTHO. There is land for 3½ ploughs. In demesne is 1 [plough]; and 2 bordars have half a plough. There are 6 acres of meadow. it was worth 10s; now 30s. Alwine and Oswulf held it freely.

The same man holds 9 parts of 1 hide in the same vill. There is land for 2 ploughs. There is 1 [plough], with 1 villan and 3 bordars. There are 8 acres of meadow. It was worth 10s; now 60s. Godwine held it freely.

The same man holds 3 hides and 1 virgate of land in FARTHINGSTONE. There is land for 8 ploughs. In demesne is 1 [plough], with 2 slaves. There 1 knight holds 1½ hides, and has 2 ploughs, with 2 slaves; and [there are] 6 villans and 3 bordars with 2 ploughs. There are 16 acres of meadow. [There is] woodland 4 furlongs in length and 3 in breadth. It was worth 20s; now £4. Wulfric held freely 1½ hides of this land. Ordgar, Theodgar, and Godric held the remainder. The soke belongs to Fawsley.

The same man holds 3 hides in DODFORD. There is land for 7 ploughs. In demesne are 2 [ploughs], and 4 slaves; and 11 villans, with a priest and 6 bordars, have 5 ploughs. There are 2 mills rendering 10s, and 12 acres of meadow. It was worth 40s; now £4. Thorbiorn held freely 1½ hides of this land. Ordgar, Ælfric, and Leofric held the rest of the land. The soke belongs to Fawsley.

The same man holds 1 hide and 2½ virgates of land in EASTON NESTON. There is land for 6 ploughs. In demesne are 1½ [ploughs], and 2 slaves; and 6 villans with 1½ ploughs. There is a mill rendering 10s, and 3 acres of meadow. [There is] woodland 3½ furlongs in length and 2½ furlongs in breadth. It was and is worth 30s.

IN 'GRAVESEND' HUNDRED

The same man holds 1½ virgates of land in SNORSCOMB. There is land for 1 plough, which [plough] is there, with 1 slave and 1 villan; and 2 acres of scrubland. It was and is worth 10s. Thorbiorn held these 2 estates freely.

IN SUTTON HUNDRED

The same man holds half a hide in LITTLE PURSTON. There is land for 1 plough, which [plough] is there, with 1 bordar; and 2 acres of meadow. It was and is worth 10s. The soke belongs to King's Sutton. Alric held it freely.

The same man holds half a hide in WALTON GROUNDS. There is land for 1 plough, which [plough] is there, with 2 slaves and 2 bordars. It was worth 10s; now 20s. The soke belongs to King's Sutton. 5 thegns held it, and could go where they would.

The same man holds the fifth part of 1 hide in KING'S SUTTON. There is land for half a plough. There is 1 villan. It was and is worth 3s. Alric held it freely.

The same man holds 4 parts of half a hide in CROUGHTON. There is land for 1 plough. There is 1 bordar only. It was worth 20s; now 2s. Leofnoth held it freely. It was a berewick of Evenley.

IN 'ALBOLDSTOW' HUNDRED

The same man holds 1 hide in EVENLEY. There is land for 2½ ploughs. In demesne is 1 [plough]; and 1 villan and 7 bordars with half a plough. There is a mill rendering 12d. It was worth 60s; now 30s. Leofstan held it freely.

IN 'GRAVESEND' HUNDRED

The same man holds half a hide in CHARWELTON. There is land for 1 plough, which [plough] 4 villans and 2 bordars have there. It was worth 10s; now 20s. Wulfric held it freely.

ALVRED holds of the count 2 parts of 1 hide in THRUPP GROUNDS. There is land for 2 ploughs, which [ploughs] are there, with 5 villans and 3 bordars. It was worth 5s; now 20s. Azur son of Leofsige held it freely.

The same man holds 1 virgate of land in 'CHILCOTE' [in Thornby]. There is land for half a plough, which [half-plough] is there, with 2 bordars. It is worth 2s. Thorbiorn held it.

The same man holds 1 hide and 3 virgates of land in ELKINGTON. There is land for 3½ ploughs. In demesne are 2 [ploughs], and 3 slaves; and 10 villans with 1½ ploughs. It was and is worth 40s. Thorbiorn held it freely.

The same man holds 1 virgate of land in LILBOURNE. There is land for 2½ ploughs, and as many [ploughs] are there, with 7 villans and 1 bordar; and 3 acres of meadow. It was worth 12d; now 10s. Thorbiorn held it.

The same man holds 3 virgates of land in YELVERTOFT. There is land for 1 plough. There are 1½ [ploughs], with 1 slave and 4 villans, and 2 acres of meadow. It was worth 5s; now 10s.

[Folio 224: NORTHAMPTONSHIRE]

The same Alvred holds 3 virgates of land in LONG BUCKBY. There is land for 1½ ploughs; and as many [ploughs] are there, with 6 villans and 2 bordars. There are 4 acres of meadow. It was and is worth 30s. Thorbiorn and Alric held it freely.

The same man holds 1 virgate of land and the fifth part of 1 virgate in ADSTONE. There is land for 1 plough, which [plough] is there, and 3 acres of meadow. It was worth 4s; now 6s.

The same man holds 1½ virgates of land in PRESTON CAPES. There is land for 1 plough. It is waste.

The same man holds 3 virgates of land in FARTHINGSTONE. There is land for 1 plough, which [plough] is there in demesne, and 2 slaves. It was worth 10s; now 15s. Ingelrann holds it of him. Leofric held it TRE. The soke of this land belongs to Fawsley.

FULCHER holds of the count 1 hide and the third part of 1 hide in THORPE MALSOR. There is land for 3 ploughs. In demesne is 1 [plough], and 2 slaves; and 10 villans and 8 bordars have 2 ploughs. It was and is worth 30s. Edwin held it freely.

The same man holds 3 virgates of land in PYTCHLEY. There is land for 1½ ploughs. There are 2 ploughs, with 1 sokeman and 2 bordars, and 1 acre of meadow. It was worth 5s; now 10s. Edwin held this also freely.

The same man holds 3 virgates of land in ORLINGBURY. There is land for 1½ ploughs, and as many [ploughs] are there, with 1 villan and 2 bordars. There are 2 acres of meadow. [There is] woodland 1 furlong in length and half a furlong in breadth. It was worth 5s; now 10s.

ROBERT holds of the count half a hide in WALGRAVE. There is land for 2 ploughs. There is 1 [plough], with 1 slave and 1 bordar, and 3 acres of meadow. It was worth 5s; now 10s. Martin held it freely.

The same man holds 2 hides in NORTOFT. There is land for 4 ploughs. In demesne is 1 [plough], with 1 slave; and 4 villans and 3 bordars with 1 plough. There are 8 acres of meadow, and a mill rendering 8d. It was worth 3s; now 30s. A church belongs to this land with 1 virgate of land in GUILS-BOROUGH, and the site of a mill with the third part of 1 virgate in HOLLOWELL. These are waste. Leofwine held them freely.

The same man holds 2½ virgates of land in IRCHESTER. There is land for half a plough. There is 1 villan, and 3½ acres of meadow. It was worth 12d; now 8s. Siward held it freely.

WALTER holds of the count 3 hides in WESTON FAVELL. There is land for 6 ploughs. In demesne is 1 [plough]; and 14 villans and 4 bordars have 5 ploughs. There are 15 acres of meadow. It was worth 40s; now 70s. Lokki, Scotel, and Stenkil and 2 sokemen held it TRE.

IN NOBOTTLE HUNDRED

The same man holds 1 virgate of land and 3 parts of 1 virgate in NETHER HEYFORD. There is land for 1 plough, which [plough] is there, with 2 slaves; and a mill rendering 16s, and 4 acres of meadow. It was worth 10s; now 30s. Bisceop held it. The soke belongs to Bugbrooke.

RALPH holds of the count 1 virgate of land and 2 parts of 1 virgate in NETHER HEYFORD. The soke belongs to Bugbrooke. There is land for 1 plough. There are 1½ [ploughs] with 1 villan. There are 3 acres of meadow. It was worth 5s; now 10s.

The same man holds 4 parts of 1 hide in PRESTON CAPES. There is land for 3 ploughs, and these [ploughs] are there, with 3 slaves and 4 villans and 2 bordars. In demesne is half a plough. It was worth 10s; now 40s. Sawata held it.

RALPH holds 2 hides and 1 virgate of land in HOLDENBY. The soke belongs to EAST HADDON. There is land for 8 ploughs. In demesne are 2 [ploughs], and 4 slaves; and 1 villan and 9 sokemen with 2 ploughs. There are 3 acres of meadow, and 3 acres of woodland. It was worth 20s; now 40s. Siward with 9 sokemen held it freely.

RALPH holds half a hide in EAST HADDON. There is land for 1 plough. 2 villans and 4 bordars have this [plough] there. It was worth 12d; now 5s.

WILLIAM and Durand hold 3 hides, less 1 virgate, in SPRATTON. There is land for 6 ploughs. In demesne are 1½ [ploughs], with 1 slave; and 6 villans and 6 bordars with 3½ ploughs. There is a mill rendering 6s, and 6 acres of meadow. It was worth 20s; now 60s. Osmund held it freely.

IN CLEYLEY HUNDRED

WILLIAM holds 4 parts of 1 hide in GRAFTON REGIS. There is land for 2 ploughs. In demesne is 1 [plough], with 1 bordar. There are 11 acres of meadow, and 20 acres of woodland. It was worth 3s; now 26s. Godwine held it freely.

NIGEL holds of the count 1 hide and half a virgate of land in PRESTON CAPES. There is land for 3 ploughs. In demesne are 2 [ploughs], and 2 slaves; and a priest, with 3 villans, has 1 plough. There is 1 acre of woodland. It was worth 6s; now 40s. Fredegis held it.

In ALDERTON 1 thegn holds of the count 1 hide. There is land for 2 ploughs. There is 1 [plough]. It is worth 10s. He himself held it.

In HOLDENBY Ordmær holds 1 hide and 3 virgates of land. There is land for 4 ploughs. In demesne are 2 [ploughs], and 3 slaves; and 6 villans and 5 bordars with 2 ploughs. There is a mill rendering 8s, and 3 acres of meadow, and 3 acres of scrubland. It was worth 20s; now 40s. Siward held it freely.

In EAST HADDON Alric holds 1½ hides of the count. There is land for 3 ploughs. In demesne is 1 [plough], and 5 slaves; and 4 villans and 7 bordars with 2 ploughs. There are 6 acres of meadow, and 4 acres of scrubland. It was worth 20s; now 40s.

The same man holds the third part of 1 virgate in HOLLOWELL. It is waste.

In BLAKESLEY Segrim holds of the count 1½ hides. The soke is the king's in Greens Norton. There is land for 3½ ploughs. 1 plough only is there, with 2 villans and 2 slaves, and 2 acres of meadow. It was worth 10s; now 20s. He himself held it TRE.

In UPPER BODDINGTON Leofwine holds 2 hides of the count. There is land for 5 ploughs. In demesne are 2 [ploughs], and 4 slaves; and 11 villans and 5 bordars with 3½ ploughs. There are 10 acres of meadow. It was worth 100s; now £4. Thorir held it freely.

In SNORSCOMB Alric holds half a virgate of land of the count. There is land for 1 plough, which [plough] is there, with 1 slave and 1 villan, and 1 acre of scrubland. It is worth 5s. He himself held it.

In WELTON Wulfmær holds of the count half a virgate of land, less 5 acres. There is land for half a plough, and as much is there, with 1 bordar, and 1 acre of meadow. It is worth 5s. He himself held it freely.

In CHURCH BRAMPTON Wulfmær holds of the count half a hide. There is land for 1 plough. This [plough] is there. It is worth 20s. He himself held it.

XIX. The land of the Count of Meulan

IN 'GRAVESEND' HUNDRED

THE COUNT of MEULAN holds of the king in NORTON 2½ hides and the fifth part of half a hide. [There is] land for 7 ploughs. Now in demesne are 2 [ploughs], and 1 hide of land. There 23 villans, with a priest and 9 bordars and 1 slave, have 6 ploughs. There is a mill rendering 10s, and 25 acres of meadow. It was worth £6; now £8. Aghmund held it freely.

XX. The land of Count Alan

IN CLEYLEY HUNDRED

COUNT ALAN holds of the king 4 parts of half a hide in WAKEFIELD and Ralph the steward [holds] of him. There is land for 2 ploughs. In demesne is 1 [plough]; and 3 villans, with 1 bordar, have another plough. There is 1 acre of meadow. [There is] woodland 5½ furlongs in length and 3 furlongs in breadth. It was worth 5s; now 10s.

XXI. The land of Earl Aubrey

IN 'ALBOLDSTOW' HUNDRED

EARL AUBREY held of the king 2 hides in HALSE, and 2 hides in SYRESHAM, and 1 hide in BRACKLEY, with a church and a mill rendering 10s. In these 5 hides there is land for 12½ ploughs. In demesne are 2 [ploughs], and 6 slaves; and 20 villans, with a priest and 10 bordars, have 6 ploughs. There are 20 acres of meadow. [There is] woodland 2½ furlongs in length and 1½ furlongs in breadth. There Osmund holds the third part of 2 hides in SYRESHAM. The whole was worth £12 when he received it; now £9. Azur held it freely.

In BRACKLEY are 2 hides. There is land for 5 ploughs. In demesne are 2 [ploughs], and 6 slaves; and 10 villans and 8 bordars with 3 ploughs. There are 10 acres of meadow. It was worth 100s. When he received it; now £4.

In LILBOURNE are 2 hides and half a virgate of land. There is land for 4 ploughs and 2 oxen. In demesne is 1 [plough]; and 8 villans and 6 bordars and 3 sokemen have 3 ploughs. There are 12 acres of meadow. It was worth 2s; now 30s.

In the same vill are 1½ virgates of land. Ralph holds it of the king. There is land for 6 oxen. There is 1 villan and 2 bordars, and 4 acres of meadow. It is worth 4s.

IN SUTTON HUNDRED

In EVENLEY are 3 virgates of land. Gilbert holds it. There is land for 2 ploughs. There is 1 bordar, with 1 slave. It was worth 10s; now 4s.

In FARTHINGHOE are 4 hides. There is land for 10 ploughs. In demesne are 3 ploughs, and 10 slaves; and 15 villans, with a priest and 8 bordars, have 5 ploughs. There are 20 acres of meadow. It was worth £10 when he received it; now £7.

THESE LANDS BELONGED TO EARL AUBREY [BUT] ARE NOW IN THE KING'S HAND.

The same Count of Meulan holds BERKSWELL [War.] in demesne. There are 4 hides. Of these he has 3 hides in demesne. [There is] land for 8 ploughs. In demesne is 1 [plough], and 4 slaves; and 7 villans, with 3 bordars, have 1 plough. There are 5 acres of meadow. [There is] woodland 1 league in length and 1 league in breadth. It is worth 40s. The same count holds in OVER WHITACRE [War.] half a hide [which is] waste, and it is worth 12d. Leofnoth held these lands freely TRE.

[Folio 224V: NORTHAMPTONSHIRE]

XXXIII [sic]. the land of Hugh de Grandmesnil

HUGH de Grandmesnil holds 1½ virgates of land in WEST FARNDON. There is land for 1 plough. 2 villans have this [plough] there. It was and is worth 5s.

IN 'STOTFOLD' HUNDRED

In MARSTON TRUSSELL and in THORPE LUBEN-HAM Hugh holds of Hugh 2 hides and 1 virgate of land and the third part of 1 virgate. There is land for 4½ ploughs. In demesne are 2 [ploughs], and 2 slaves; and 23 villans and 17 bordars have 7 ploughs. There are 10 acres of meadow. It was worth 15s; now 60s. Oslac held it freely.

IN 'GRAVESEND' HUNDRED

The same man holds 3½ hides in WEEDON BEC in exchange for Watford. There is land for 8½ ploughs. In demesne are 1½ [ploughs]; and 2 villans, with a priest and 3 bordars, have half a plough. There 3 knights, with 6 villans and 3 bordars, have half a 4½ ploughs. There are 17 acres of meadow, and 12 acres of woodland, and a mill rendering 40d. It was worth 40s; now 50s.

The same man holds 4 hides in ASHBY ST LEDGERS. There is land for 10 ploughs. In demesne are 3 ploughs, and 6 slaves; and 15 villans and 3 bordars with 5 ploughs. There are 8 acres of meadow. It was worth 40s; now 60s.

OSBERN holds of Hugh 3 hides, less 1 virgate, in WELTON. There is land for 7 ploughs. In demesne are 2 [ploughs], and 3 slaves; and 5 villans with 4 ploughs. There is a mill rendering 12d, and 8 acres of meadow. It was worth 20s; now 40s. Baldwin held it freely.

The same man holds 1 hide in STAVERTON. There is land for 2½ ploughs. There are 2 ploughs, with 1 villan and 5 bordars. It was worth 15s; now 20s. Leofric held it of Baldwin.

The same man holds 4 parts of half a hide in THRUPP GROUNDS. There is land for 1 plough. This [plough] is there in demesne, with 1 bordar, and 2 acres of meadow. It was worth 12d; now 10s. Alwine held it of Baldwin.

IN FOXLEY HUNDRED

HUGH holds of Hugh in MAIDFORD 2 hides and the fifth part of 1 hide. There is land for 5 ploughs. In demesne is 1 [plough], and 4 slaves; and 9 villans, with a priest and 4 bordars, have 3 ploughs. There is woodland 4 furlongs in length and 1 furlong in breadth. It was worth 20s; now 50s. Willa held it freely.

IN SUTTON HUNDRED

IVO holds of Hugh in NEWBOTTLE [near Brackley] with its appendages 6 hides. There is land for 15 ploughs. In demesne are 3½ ploughs, and 8 slaves. There 1 knight and 12 villans and 4 bordars have 4 ploughs. There are 7 female slaves, and 7 acres of meadow. It was worth £4; now £6. Baldwin held it with soke and sake.

HUGH holds of Hugh in MIDDLETON CHENEY 2 hides. There is land for 5 ploughs. In demesne is 1 [plough]; and 9 villans, with a priest, have 3 ploughs. There are 12 acres of meadow. It was and is worth 40s. Godric held it freely.

HUGH holds of Hugh in KING'S SUTTON 1½ hides and the tenth part of 1 hide. There is land for 4 ploughs. In demesne is 1 [plough], and 2 slaves; and 2 bordars have half a plough. There is a mill rendering 2s. It was worth 10s; now 30s. Willa and Thorbiorn held it.

IN WARDEN HUNDRED

IVO holds of Hugh in BYFIELD 2 hides. There is land for 5 ploughs. In demesne is 1 [plough], with 1 villan and 1 bordar. It was worth 2s; now 10s. 3 thegns held it freely.

RICHARD holds of Hugh in WOODFORD HALSE 2 hides. There is land for 5 ploughs. In demesne are 2 [ploughs], and 4 slaves and 1 female slave; and 11 villans have 3 ploughs. There are 2 acres of meadow, and a mill rendering 8s. It was worth 40s; now 60s. Baldwin held it freely.

HUGH holds of Hugh in EYDON 2 hides. There is land for 5 ploughs. In demesne are 2 [ploughs], and 2 slaves; and 12 villans with 3 ploughs. There is a mill rendering 2s, and 2 acres of meadow. It was worth 40s; now 50s.

WALTER holds of Hugh 1 virgate of land in CHAR-WELTON. There is land for half a plough. It was and is worth 5s. Alwine held it freely.

IN CORBY HUNDRED

XXIIII. HUGH d' Ivry holds of the king half a hide in LITTLE WELDON. There is land for 3 ploughs. In demesne is 1 [plough], with 1 slave; and 11 villans have 2 ploughs. There is woodland 6 furlongs in length and 2 furlongs in breadth. It was worth 10s; now 20s. Wulfric held it freely.

ROGER d'Ivry holds of Hugh COTTISFORD [Oxon.]. There are 6 hides. There is land for 10 ploughs. In demesne are 3 [ploughs], and a fourth would be possible. There are 10 villans and 5 bordars, and 40 acres of pasture. It was worth 100s; now £8.

The same Roger holds of Hugh CHARLTON-ON-OTMOOR [Oxon.]. There are 10 hides. There is land for

15 ploughs. In demesne are 4 ploughs, and 6 slaves; and 15 villans and 11 bordars have 11 ploughs. [There is] meadow 4 furlongs in length and 2 furlongs in breadth. [There is] pasture 3 furlongs in length and 2 furlongs in breadth. It was worth £8; now £10. Baldwin held it freely. 4 hides of this land are in demesne.

HUGH holds 2½ hides in SHIPTON-ON-CHERWELL [Oxon.]. There is land for 4 ploughs. In demesne are 2 [ploughs], and 4 slaves; and 2 villans and 3 bordars have 1 plough. There is a mill rendering 11s, and 4 acres of meadow, and 3 furlongs of pasture. It was worth 40s; now £4. 10s. Ælfric held it freely.

In SIBFORD GOWER [Oxon.] Abba holds 11 hides of Hugh. There is land for 8 ploughs. In demesne are 2 [ploughs], and 4 acres of meadow, and a mill rendering 32d, and 13 furlongs of pasture. It was and is worth £4.10s. Baldwin held it.

XXII. the land of Earl Hugh

IN WARDEN HUNDRED

Earl HUGH holds of the king in BYFIELD 8 hides, and Robert [holds] of him. There is land for 20 ploughs. In demesne are 2 [ploughs], and 5 slaves; and 8 villans and 3 bordars have 3 ploughs. There 1 knight, with 2 villans, has 1 plough, and 2 free men dwell there. [There is] meadow 1 league in length and 7 furlongs in breadth. It was and is worth £8. Eskil held it freely.

The same Robert holds of the earl 1 hide in LOWER BODDINGTON. There is land for 2½ ploughs. In demesne is 1 [plough]; and 6 villans, with a priest and 4 bordars, have 1 plough; and 1 knight has half a plough. There are 5 acres of meadow. It was worth 30s; now 40s. Eskil held it.

IN [...]

The same man holds of the earl 1 hide and 1 virgate of land in TRAFFORD. There is land for 2½ ploughs. In demesne is 1 [plough], and 3 slaves; and 3 villans with 1 plough. There is a mill rendering 6s8d, and 3 acres of meadow. It was and is worth 30s.

IN 'ALBOLDSTOW' HUNDRED

The same man holds 4 hides in MARSTON ST LAWRENCE. There is land for 10 ploughs. In demesne are 4 [ploughs], and 9 slaves; and 26 villans and 10 bordars with 6 ploughs. There is a mill rendering 8s, and 24 acres of meadow. It was and is worth £10.

The same man holds 2 hides in RADSTONE. There is land for 5 ploughs. In demesne are 2 [ploughs], and 6 slaves; and 10 villans and 5 bordars with 3 ploughs. There are 12 acres of meadow, and 6 acres of woodland. It was and is worth 100s.

IN SUTTON HUNDRED

The same man holds in MIDDLETON CHENEY 4 parts of 2 hides. There is land for 4 ploughs. In demesne are 2 [ploughs]; and 8 villans have 1 plough. There are 8 acres of meadow. It was and is worth £3. The soke belongs to King's Sutton.

IN FOXLEY HUNDRED

The same man holds half a hide in BLAKESLEY. There is land for 1½ ploughs. There 2 villans have half a plough. It was and is worth 8s. Ketil held it. The soke belongs to Greens Norton.

IN GUILSBOROUGH HUNDRED AND A HALF

The same man holds 2 hides and 1 virgate of land in YELVERTOFT. There is land for 4 ploughs. In demesne is half a plough; and 8 villans, with a priest and 9 bordars and 2 sokemen, have 1½ ploughs. There are 8 acres of meadow. It was and is worth 20s. Godric held it freely.

IN FOXLEY HUNDRED

JOSCELIN holds of the earl 4 hides in SLAPTON. There is land for 10 ploughs. In demesne are 2 [ploughs], and 3 slaves; and 6 villans, with 1 bordar, have 2 ploughs. There are 8 acres of meadow. It was and is worth £3.

Eskil held these lands with sake and soke. Earl Hugh's men hold them now.

[Folio 225: NORTHAMPTONSHIRE]

XXV. The land of Henry de Ferrers

IN CLEYLEY HUNDRED

HENRY DE FERRERS holds 3 hides and the fifth part of 1 hide in POTTERSPURY. There is land for 10 ploughs. In demesne are 3 ploughs, and 3 slaves; and 20 villans and 7 bordars, with a priest, have 7 ploughs. There is a mill rendering 18s4d, and 16 acres of meadow. [There is] woodland 6 furlongs and 14 perches in length and 2½ furlongs in breadth. It was and is worth £6. Earl Tosti held it.

IN NAVISFORD HUNDRED

SASWALO holds of Henry 10 hides and 2 parts of half a hide less 1 virgate. There is land for 15 ploughs. In demesne are 4 ploughs, and 8 slaves; and 16 villans and 5 bordars have 6½ ploughs, and 7 sokemen with 4½ ploughs. There is a mill rendering 21s4d, and 30 acres of meadow. [There is] woodland 4 furlongs in length and 1 in breadth. It was worth £3; now £7. Bondi held it freely.

IN 'HAMFORDSHOE' HUNDRED

RALPH holds of Henry in ECTON 4 hides. There is land for 8 ploughs. In demesne [are] 1½ hides of this land, and there are 2 ploughs, and 4 slaves; and 8 villans and 9 bordars and 12 sokemen, with 8 bordars, have 6 ploughs. There are 2 mills rendering 14s, and 32 acres of meadow. It was worth £3; now 100s. Bondi held it.

XXVI. The land of Robert de Tosny

ROBERT DE TOSNY [holds] 3 hides in STOKE ALBANY. There is land for 6 ploughs. In demesne are 2

[ploughs], and 3 slaves; and 9 villans and 2 bordars, with 1 sokeman, have 3 ploughs. There is a mill rendering 12d. [There is] woodland 5 furlongs in length and 3 furlongs in breadth. It was worth 60s; now 40s. Oswulf held it freely TRE.

The same man holds 3 hides and 1 virgate of land in WILBARSTON. There is land for 6 ploughs. Of this land 1 hide is in demesne, and there are 2 ploughs, with 1 slave; and 12 villans and 7 bordars have 3 ploughs. [There is] woodland 9 furlongs in length and 5 furlongs in breadth. It was worth 40s; now 30s.

IN WITCHLEY WAPENTAKE

The same man holds 1 hide and 1 bovate of land in SEATON [Rutland]. There is land for 4 ploughs. In demesne are 2 [ploughs], and 2 slaves; and 8 villans and 2 bordars, with a priest, have 1½ ploughs. There are 3 acres of meadow. [There is] woodland 1 furlong in length and another in breadth. Robert has only the third part of the woodland and of the arable land likewise.

To this land belongs 1 virgate of land in BARROWDEN [Rutland]. There are 4 villans with half a plough [...]. It was worth 40s; now 20s.

IN FOXLEY HUNDRED

The same man holds 3 hides in SEAWELL, and 4 parts of 1 virgate. There is land for 7 ploughs. In demesne are 1½ [ploughs], and 2 slaves; and 8 villans and 3 bordars have 3½ ploughs. There is a mill rendering 12d, and 7 acres of meadow. [There is] woodland 2½ furlongs in length and 2 furlongs in breadth. It was worth 10s; now 60s.

IN ROTHWELL HUNDRED

HUGH holds of Robert 1½ hides in RUSHTON. There is land for 4 ploughs. In demesne is 1 [plough], and 2 slaves; and 4 villans and 3 bordars and 3 sokemen with 2½ ploughs between them all. There are 4 acres of meadow, and 15 acres of woodland. It was worth 10s; now 30s. The soke belongs to Great Weldon. Edwin held it.

The same man holds in DESBOROUGH half a hide. There is land for 2 ploughs. In demesne is 1 [plough], and 2 slaves; and 3 bordars. There is half an acre of woodland. It was worth 5s; now 20s. Oswulf held it freely.

Roger holds half a hide of Robert in PIPEWELL. There is land for 2 ploughs. There are 1½ ploughs, with 4 bordars, and 5 acres of woodland. It was worth 5s; now 6s. Edwin held it freely.

Hildwine holds of Robert 2 hides in BRAMPTON ASH. There is land for 5 ploughs. In demesne are 2 [ploughs], and 6 slaves; and 5 villans and 4 bordars with 2½ ploughs. There are 22 acres of meadow. [There is] woodland 5 furlongs in length and 3 furlongs in breadth. It was worth 10s; now 40s. Oswulf held it.

Hildwine holds of Robert 1 hide, less 1½ bovates, in DINGLEY. There is land for 2 ploughs. In demesne are 1½ [ploughs]; and 2 villans and 5 bordars with half a plough.

There are 3 acres of meadow, and 3 acres of woodland. It was worth 10s; now 20s.

Gunfrid and Walkelin hold of Robert 3 hides in ASHLEY. There is land for 6 ploughs. In demesne are 2 [ploughs]; and 7 villans and 9 bordars have 3 ploughs. There is a mill rendering 32d, and 9 acres of meadow, and 2 acres of spinney. [There is] woodland 3 furlongs in length and 8 perches in breadth; and in another place 4 acres of woodland belong to this land. It was worth 20s; now 30s. Frani and Algar held it freely.

Wibert holds of Robert the third part of 1 hide in the same vill. There is land for 1 plough, which [plough] is there, with 2 bordars and 1 slave. It was worth 16d; now 5s. Algar held it freely.

XXVII. The land of Robert of Stafford

IN WARDEN HUNDRED

ROBERT of STAFFORD holds in STONETON [War.] 3 virgates of land, and Hugh [holds] of him. There is land for 3 ploughs. In demesne is 1 [plough], and 3 slaves; and 6 villans and 5 bordars with 2 ploughs. There are 3 acres of meadow. It was worth 10s; now 30s. Æthelgifu held it freely TRE.

XXVIII. The land of Robert d'Oilly

IN CLEYLEY HUNDRED

ROBERT d'OILLY [holds] 1 hide and 1 virgate of land in WICKEN, and Roger [holds] of him. There is land for 10 ploughs. In demesne are 3 ploughs, and 7 slaves; and 7 villans and 3 bordars with 4 ploughs. There are 10 acres of meadow. [There is] woodland 11 furlongs in length and 6 furlongs in breadth. It was worth 40s; now 100s. Azur held it freely TRE.

IN SUTTON HUNDRED

The same man holds of Robert 1 hide in THENFORD. There is land for 3½ ploughs. In demesne is 1 [plough], and 2 slaves; and 7 villans have 2½ ploughs. There is a mill rendering 30d. It was worth 10s; now 30s.

The same man holds half a hide and the fifth part of 1 hide in GREAT PURSTON. There is land for 1½ ploughs, and as many [ploughs] are there, with 4 villans and 2 bordars. There are 8 acres of meadow. It was worth 10s; now 12s. Leofwine held it, and could go where he would. But the king used to have the soke of it.

XXVIIII. The land of Robert de Vessey

IN ROTHWELL HUNDRED

ROBERT de VESSEY holds 1 hide in BRAYBROOKE. There is land for 2 ploughs. 1 [plough] is in demesne; and 4 bordars have another plough. It was worth 5s; now 10s. Æthelric held it freely TRE.

XXX. The land of Robert de Bucy

IN STOKE HUNDRED

ROBERT de BUCY holds 2 parts of 1 hide in ASHLEY. There is land for 1 plough. 6 sokemen have this [plough] there. It was and is worth 10s8d.

The same man holds 2 hides and 2 parts of 1 hide in WESTON BY WELLAND. There is land for 6 ploughs. There 10 sokemen have 3½ ploughs. It was worth 10s; now 42s8d.

The same man holds 1 hide and 2 parts of half a hide in SUTTON BASSETT. There is land for 2½ ploughs. 8 sokemen have these [ploughs] there. It was worth 5s; now 21s4d.

The same man holds in DINGLEY 2 parts of 1 hide and 2 parts of 2 parts of 1 hide. There is land for 4 ploughs. There 11 sokemen have 2½ ploughs. It was worth 10s; now 13s4d.

The same man holds 2 hides in BRAMPTON ASH. There is land for 4 ploughs. There 8 sokemen have 3 ploughs. It was worth 10s; now 8d. more.

IN CORBY HUNDRED

The same man holds 1 hide and 3 virgates of land in GREAT WELDON. There is land for 5 ploughs. In demesne are 2 ploughs; and 8 villans and 4 bordars, with 1 sokeman, have 4 ploughs. [There is] woodland 1 league in length and 3 furlongs in breadth. It was worth 5s; now 30s. Northmann held these lands, and could go where he would.

The same man holds 1 virgate of land in GREAT WELDON. The king claims it.

IN STOKE HUNDRED

WALTER holds of Robert in ASHLEY the third part of 1 hide. The soke belongs to Great Weldon. There is land for half a plough. There 2 sokemen have 1 plough and 2 acres of meadow. It was worth 5s; now 3s. Northmann held it.

HUGH holds of Robert 1 hide in BRAMPTON ASH. There is land for 1 plough. Nevertheless there are in demesne 2 ploughs, and 2 slaves, with 1 bordar. It was worth 2s; now 20s.

[Folio 225V: NORTHAMPTONSHIRE]

Northmann holds of Robert 2 hides in BLATHERWYCKE. There is land for 6 ploughs. Hugh and William hold of him. In demesne are 2 ploughs; and 12 villans and 5 bordars have 4 ploughs. There is a mill rendering 30d, and 6 acres of meadow. [There is] woodland 1 league in length and 3 furlongs in breadth. It is worth 18s.

IN ROTHWELL HUNDRED

HUGH holds of Robert half a hide in BRAYBROOKE. There is land for 1 plough. It was and is worth 16d. Northmann held it.

The same Hugh holds of Robert the third part of 1 hide in the same vill. There is land for half a plough. Nevertheless 1 plough is there, with 1 bordar. It was worth 12d; now 3s. Ulfkil held it.

WILLIAM holds of Robert half a hide in RUSHTON. There is land for 1 plough. Nevertheless 1½ ploughs are there, with 4 villans and 2 bordars. There is half a mill rendering 12d, and 6 acres of woodland. Ulfkil held it. It was worth 12d; now 6s. The soke belongs to Great Weldon.

In the same vill he has half a virgate of waste land.

IN 'SPELHOE' HUNDRED

The same William holds of Robert 2 hides and 1½ virgates of land in MOULTON. There is land for 5 ploughs. In demesne are 3 ploughs, with 1 slave; and 7 villans and 4 bordars have 2 ploughs. There is a mill rendering 8d. It was worth 20s; now 50s. Thorir held it.

Robert holds of Robert 3 virgates of land, less 1 bovate, in BOUGHTON [near Northampton]. There is land for 1 ½ ploughs. 4 bordars, with 1 villan and 1 slave, have 1 [plough] there, and 4 acres of meadow. It was worth 5s; now 10s.

Ralph holds of Robert 1 virgate of land and 1 bovate in SPRATTON. There is land for half a plough. Nevertheless 1 [plough] is there, with 6 bordars. It was and is worth 5s. Wulfmær held it freely.

IN FOXLEY HUNDRED

WILLIAM holds of Robert 1 hide and 4 parts of half a hide in BRADDEN. There is land for 3½ ploughs. In demesne are 2 [ploughs]; and 4 villans have 1 plough. There is 1 acre of meadow. It was worth 60s; now 40s.

IN GUILSBOROUGH HUNDRED AND A HALF

Robert holds of Robert 1 virgate of land in LITTLE CREATON. There is land for 2 oxen. There is 1 Frenchman with 2 oxen. It is worth 2s. Wulfmær held it freely.

Cyneric held Bradden of King Edward.

XXX [sic]. the land of Ralph Paynel

IN STOKE HUNDRED

RALPH Paynel holds of the king 2 hides, and Roger [holds] of him. There is land for 4 ploughs. In demesne is 1 [plough]; and 4 villans and 3 bordars have 1½ ploughs. There are 2 slaves. It was worth 5s; now 10s. Thorkil held it freely.

XXXI [sic]. the land of Ralph de Limesy

IN WILLOWBROOK HUNDRED

RALPH de Limesy holds of the king 2 hides in COLLYWESTON, and Herlwin [holds] of him. There is land for 6 ploughs. In demesne are 2 [ploughs], and 3 slaves; and 16 villans and 3 bordars have 5 ploughs. There is a mill rendering 20s, and 12 acres of meadow. [There is] woodland 3 furlongs in length and 2 furlongs in breadth. It was worth 100s; now £6. Earl Morcar held it.

XXXII [sic]. the land of Robert Blund

IN 'NAVISLAND' HUNDRED

ROBERT Blund holds of the king 3 hides in GRAFTON UNDERWOOD, and Roger [holds] of him. There is land for 8 ploughs. In demesne is 1 [plough], with 1 slave; and 12 villans, with a priest and 6 bordars, have 5 ploughs. There are 2 acres of meadow. [There is] woodland 1 league in length and 4 furlongs in breadth. It was and is worth 40s. Aki held it freely TRE.

XXXIII [sic]. the land of William de Keynes

WILLIAM de KEYNES holds of the king 1 hide in FLORE. There is land for 3 ploughs. In demesne is 1 plough, and 2 slaves; and 4 villans and 3 bordars have 1 plough. There is a mill rendering 5s, and 4 acres of meadow. It is worth 20s. Earnwig held it freely TRE.

XXX [sic]. the land of William Peverel

WILLIAM PEVEREL holds of the king HIGHAM FERRERS. There are 6 hides. There is land for 12½ ploughs. In demesne are 2 hides of this land, and there are 4 ploughs, and 4 slaves; and 16 villans and 9 bordars, with a priest, have 8½ ploughs. There is a market rendering 20s yearly, and a mill rendering 20s, and 10 acres of meadow. [There is] woodland 1 furlong in length and another in breadth.

To this manor belong these MEMBERS:

In RUSHDEN 6 hides. There is land for 12 ploughs. 19 sokemen have these [ploughs] there, and a mill rendering 10s, and 30 acres of meadow.

In Chelveston and Caldecott 1 hide and 3 virgates of land. There is land for 3 ploughs. 6 sokemen have these [ploughs] there, and 3 acres of meadow.

In Knuston 1 hide and 1½ virgates of land. There is land for 2 ploughs. 5 sokemen have these [ploughs] there; and a mill rendering 20s, and 6 acres of meadow.

In Irchester 1 hide and 3 virgates of land of sokeland. There is land for 2 ploughs. 3 sokemen have these [ploughs] there, and 10 acres of meadow. There is 1 Frenchman with 1 plough; and a mill there, rendering 16s, in dispute between the king and William.

In Farndish [Beds.] 3 virgates of sokeland. There is land for 1 plough. 2 sokemen have this [plough] there.

In Podington [Beds.] half a hide of sokeland. There are 4 villans with 1 plough.

In Easton Maudit 1½ virgates of land. It is waste.

In Raunds 7½ hides and half a virgate of land of sokeland, with its appendages. There is land for 14 ploughs. There are 20 villans with 15 ploughs, and 20 acres of meadow.

The whole manor, with its appendages, was worth £10

when he received it; now £18. Gytha held it with sake and soke.

The sokemen of Rushden, Irchester, and Raunds were Burgræd's men, and therefore Bishop Geoffrey [of Coutances] claims their homage.

The same William holds 3½ hides and the fourth part of 1 virgate in CLIPSTON of the soke of Naseby. There is land for 7 ploughs. There is 1 knight with 1 plough; and 19 sokemen, with 7 villans and 3 bordars, have 6 ploughs. It was worth 40s; now 20s.

The same man holds NOBOTTLE. There is 1 hide and half a virgate of land. There is land for 3 ploughs. These [ploughs] he has in demesne, with 1 slave; and 4 villans and 4 bordars have 1 plough. There is a mill rendering 7s, and 6 acres of woodland.

In ALTHORP the same William has the third part of 1 hide and half a virgate. The soke belongs to Nobottle. There is land for 1 plough. 3 sokemen have this [plough] there.

In [Great or Little] BRINGTON the same William has 1½ hides. There is land for 2 ploughs. 6 sokemen, with a priest who holds half a hide of the same land, have these [ploughs] there.

In HARLESTONE are 1½ hides. There is land for 3 ploughs. 3 sokemen, with a priest, have these [ploughs] there.

In GLASSTHORPEHILL is half a hide. There is land for 1 plough. 1 sokeman has this [plough] there.

In FLORE is half a hide. There is land for 1 plough. 3 sokemen have this [plough] there.

When William received these lands they were worth £4; now £7. Gytha held them freely.

The same William holds 4 hides in DUSTON. There is land for 8 ploughs. In demesne are 2 [ploughs], and 2 slaves; and 13 villans and 3 bordars, with 3 sokemen, have 6 ploughs. There is a mill rendering 20s, and 30 acres of meadow, and 11 acres of woodland. It was worth 40s; now 100s.

The same William holds 7 hides in NASEBY. There is land for 14 ploughs. In demesne are 2 [ploughs]; and 8 villans, with a priest and 2 sokemen and 11 bordars, have 3 ploughs. There are 8 acres of meadow. It was worth 20s; now 60s.

IN COLLINGTREE HUNDRED

The same William holds 3½ hides in COURTEENHALL. Of this land 2 hides, less 1 virgate, are in demesne. There is land for 9 ploughs. In demesne are 2 ploughs, with 1 slave; and 12 villans, with 1 bordar and a priest, have 7 ploughs. There is a mill rendering 12d, and 4 acres of meadow. [There is] woodland 2 furlongs in length and 2 furlongs in breadth. It was worth £4; now £5.

The same William holds 3½ hides in BLISWORTH. There is land for 9 ploughs. Of this land 2 hides, less 1 virgate, are in demesne, and there are 2 ploughs; and 12 villans and 6 bordars have 7 ploughs. There is a mill rendering 2s, and 4

acres of meadow. [There is] woodland 12 furlongs in length and 8 furlongs in breadth. It was worth £3; now £4.

Gytha held all these lands TRE with sake and soke.

[Folio 226: NORTHAMPTONSHIRE]

IN 'ALWARDSLEY' HUNDRED

Payne holds of William 2 hides in BARBY. There is land for 5 ploughs. In demesne are 2 [ploughs], with 1 slave; and 10 villans and 8 bordars with 3 ploughs. There are 6 acres of meadow. [There is] woodland 6 perches in length and 4 in breadth. It was worth 30s; now 60s.

IN WITCHLEY HUNDRED

Sasfrid holds of William 2½ hides in EMPINGHAM [Rutland]. There is land for 4 ploughs. In demesne is 1 [plough], with 1 slave; and 8 villans and 4 bordars with 2 ploughs. There are 1½ mills rendering 12s, and 4 acres of meadow, and 6 acres of woodland. It was and is worth 20s. Edward and Fredegis held it with sake and soke.

IN 'GRAVESEND' HUNDRED

The same man holds 4 hides in CATESBY. There is land for 8 ploughs. In demesne are 2 [ploughs], and 2 slaves and 1 female slave; and 17 villans, with a priest and 4 bordars, have 6 ploughs. There are 2 mills rendering 16d, and 4 acres of meadow. 1 knight holds 1 hide of this land, and has 2 ploughs. The whole was worth 40s; now £4. Gytha held it freely.

IN CLEYLEY HUNDRED

The same man holds half a hide, less the fifth part, in ASHTON [in Roade]. It is waste.

IN ROTHWELL HUNDRED

Ambrose holds of William 1 hide and 1 virgate of land in DESBOROUGH. There is land for 3 ploughs. In demesne are 2 [ploughs], and 3 slaves and 1 female slave; and 11 villans and 8 bordars with 1½ ploughs. There is a mill rendering 2s. [There is] woodland 2 furlongs in length and 2 furlongs in breadth. It was and is worth 40s.

The same man holds 1½ hides and the third part of 1 virgate in KELMARSH. There is land for 4 ploughs. In demesne are 2 [ploughs]; and 7 villans and 2 bordars have 2 ploughs. In the same vill he holds 1 virgate of land, which is waste. This renders geld in ARTHINGWORTH. It was worth 5s; now 40s. Osmund held it freely.

Turstin holds of William 1½ virgates of land in BOZEAT. The soke belongs to HIGHAM FERRERS. There is land for half a plough, and as much is there. It is worth 5s.

Eustace holds of William half a hide in HARGRAVE. The soke belongs to HIGHAM FERRERS. There is land for 1 plough. This [plough] is there, with 2 bordars. It is worth 68d. Æthelric held it freely.

Bisceop holds of William in HARPOLE 2½ hides. There is land for 6 ploughs. In demesne are 2 [ploughs], and 7 slaves; and 14 villans, with a priest and 5 bordars, have 4½ ploughs.

There are 10 acres of meadow, and 10 acres of woodland. It was worth 30s; now 40s. The same man held it freely TRE.

Drogo holds 1 hide and 1 virgate of land in RAVENSTHORPE. There is land for 3 ploughs. 3 sokemen and 3 villans and 5 bordars have these [ploughs] there. There are 3 acres of meadow. It was worth 10s; now 20s.

The same man holds 2 hides in TEETON. There is land for 4 ploughs. 4 sokemen and 2 villans and 4 bordars have these [ploughs] there. There is 1 acre of meadow. It was worth 10s; now 20s.

The same man holds 3½ virgates of land in COTON. There is land for 3 ploughs. In demesne are 2 [ploughs], and 3 slaves and 1 female slave; and 1 villan and 4 bordars have half a plough. There is a mill rendering 4s, and 4 acres of meadow.

To this manor belongs 1 hide of sokeland in THORNBY. There is land for 2 ploughs. There is 1 plough and 4 acres of meadow. In WINWICK are 3 virgates of land. There is land for 1 plough. 1 sokeman has this [plough] there.

In WEST HADDON are 1½ virgates of land. There is land for 1 plough. There is 1 sokeman having half a plough. In COLD ASHBY are 1½ virgates of land. There is land for 1 plough. There is 1 sokeman with half a plough. In NORTOFT is half a hide. There is land for 1 plough. 1 sokeman has this [plough] there and 2 acres of meadow. In HOLLOWELL is 1 virgate of land. There is land for half a plough. 1 sokeman has this [half-plough] there.

The whole manor of COTON, with its appendages, was worth 15s when he received it; now 30s.

Robert holds of William half a hide in THORNBY. The soke belongs to Naseby. There is land for half a plough. It is waste.

IN WYMERSLEY HUNDRED

Robert holds of William in GREAT HOUGHTON 1 hide and half a virgate and 2 carucates of land. There is land for 4 ploughs. In demesne are 2 [ploughs], and 4 slaves; and 15 villans and 6 bordars have 2 ploughs. There are 10 acres of meadow. [There is] woodland 3 furlongs in length and 2 furlongs in breadth. It was and is worth 40s. Osmund held it freely.

IN CLEYLEY HUNDRED

Robert holds of William 3½ hides and the fifth part of half a hide in PAULERSPURY. There is land for 9 ploughs. In demesne are 2 [ploughs], and 7 slaves; and 18 villans and 7 bordars, with a priest, have 7 ploughs. There is a mill rendering 26s8d, and 10 acres of meadow. [There is] woodland 6 furlongs in length and 4 furlongs and 2 perches in breadth. It was and is worth £4. Gytha held it freely.

Alvred holds of William 3½ virgates of land in GUILSBOROUGH. There is land for 1½ ploughs. These [ploughs] are there in demesne, and 2 slaves; and 2 villans and 3 bordars with half a plough. There are 4 acres of meadow. It was worth 6s; now 30s. Gytha held it freely.

IN FOXLEY HUNDRED

Walter holds of William 2 hides in BLAKESLEY. There is land for 5 ploughs. In demesne are 2 [ploughs], and 2 slaves; and 5 villans with 2 ploughs. There is a mill rendering 5s, and 1 acre of meadow. [There is] woodland 3 furlongs in length and 1 furlong in breadth. It was worth 10s; now 40s.

Turstin holds of William half a hide and half a virgate of land in COURTEENHALL, and it is sokeland of another Courteenhall, William's manor. There is land for 1 plough. There is half a plough, and it is worth 6s.

Ambrose holds of William 4 hides in MOLLINGTON [Oxon.]. There is land for 4 ploughs. In demesne are 2 [ploughs], and 3 slaves; and 4 villans and 5 bordars with 2 ploughs. There are 16 acres of meadow. It was and is worth £4.

Gytha held these lands freely TRE.

XXXV [sic]. the land of William fitzAnsculf

IN WITCHLEY WAPENTAKE

WILLIAM fitzAnsculf holds half a hide in TOLETHORPE [Rutland], and Robert [holds] of him. There is land for 4 ploughs. The king has the soke of it. In demesne is 1 [plough]; and 12 villans and 15 bordars have 3 ploughs. There are 4 mills rendering 40s, and 20 acres of meadow. 8 sokemen held it. It was worth 40s; now 100s.

IN UPTON WAPENTAKE

Otbert holds of William 3 hides in BARNACK. There is land for 5 ploughs. In demesne is 1 [plough], and 2 slaves; and 15 villans and 2 bordars, with 1 sokeman, have 4 ploughs. There are 12 acres of meadow. [There is] woodland 2 furlongs in length and 1 in breadth. It was worth 20s; now £4. Bondi held it freely.

Ralph holds of William 3 hides in WEST BROMWICH [Staffs.]. There is land for 3 ploughs. In demesne is 1 [plough]; and 10 villans and 3 bordars have 3 ploughs. There is woodland 1 league in length and half a league in breadth. It was and is worth 40s. Beorhtwine held it.

William fitzMauger holds of William 1 hide in CHURCHOVER [War.]. There is land for 2 ploughs. In demesne is 1 [plough], with 1 villan. There are 4 acres of meadow. [There is] woodland 1 furlong in length and half a furlong in breadth. It was and is worth 10s. Wulfwine held it freely TRE, as did the others.

XXXVI [sic]. the land of William Lovett

IN 'STOTFOLD' HUNDRED

WILLIAM Lovett holds of the king the third part of 1 virgate of land. It was and is waste.

XXXVII [sic]. the land of Walter d'Aincourt

IN 'GRAVESEND' HUNDRED

WALTER d'Aincourt holds of the king 3½ hides in BRAUNSTON. There is land for 9 ploughs. In demesne are 3 ploughs; and 13 villans and 4 bordars have 4 ploughs. There is a mill rendering 2s, and 8 acres of meadow, and 1 acre of woodland. It was worth 20s; now £4.10s. Thorir held it freely.

[Folio 226V: NORTHAMPTONSHIRE]

XXXIX. The land of Walter the Fleming

IN ROTHWELL HUNDRED

WALTER the Fleming holds of the king half a hide in PIPEWELL. There is land for 1 plough. Dodin holds it of Walter. There is 1 plough, with 2 bordars, and 5 acres of woodland. It was and is worth 4s. Leofnoth held it.

IN GUILSBOROUGH HUNDRED

The same man holds of Walter 1 hide and 1 virgate of land in COTTESBROOKE. There is land for 2½ ploughs. In demesne is 1 [plough], and 4 slaves and 1 female slave; and a priest and 10 villans and 5 bordars with 1½ ploughs. There is a mill rendering 12d. It was worth 10s; now 30s.

The same man holds of Walter 2 virgates of land and 1 bovate of land in HANGING HOUGHTON. It is worth 4s.

Fulcher holds of Walter 4 hides and 1 virgate of land in LAMPORT. There is land for 2 ploughs. 12 villans and 7 bordars have these [ploughs] there. There are 4 acres of meadow, and an ash spinney 1 furlong in length and 1 furlong in breadth. It is worth £4.

The same man holds of Walter 2½ hides in WYTHEMAIL. There is land for 2 ploughs. He has these [ploughs] there; and 10 villans and 5 bordars, with a priest, have 3 ploughs. There is 1 slave and 1 female slave, and 6 acres of meadow. [There is] woodland 2 furlongs in length and 1½ in breadth. It was and is worth 40s.

IN 'SPELHOE' HUNDRED

The same man holds of Walter 3 hides and 1 virgate of land in PITSFORD. There is land for 7 ploughs. In demesne is 1 [plough], and 2 slaves; and 16 villans and 9 bordars have 6 ploughs. There is a mill rendering 12d. It was and is worth 70s.

Otbert holds of Walter 2 hides in HORTON. There is land for 4 ploughs. In demesne are 2 [ploughs]; and 6 villans and 4 bordars have 2 ploughs. There are 2 slaves, and a mill rendering 12d, and 12 acres of meadow. [There is] woodland 3 furlongs in length and 2 furlongs in breadth. It was worth 10s; now 30s.

IN TOWCESTER HUNDRED

The same man holds of Walter 4 hides in EVENLEY. There is land for 10 ploughs. In demesne are 4 [ploughs], with 1 slave; and 11 villans and 5 bordars have 4 ploughs. There are 2 mills rendering 20s, and 5 acres of meadow. It was worth 40s; now £4.

HUGH holds of Walter 2½ hides in CANONS ASHBY. There is land for 6 ploughs. In demesne is 1 plough, and 4 slaves; and 9 villans and 3 bordars have 3 ploughs, and 12 acres of meadow. It was worth 40s; now £4.

IN 'ALBOLDSTOW' HUNDRED

Otbert holds of Walter 2 hides in EVENLEY. There is land for 5 ploughs. There are 4 ploughs, with 10 villans and 5 bordars. It was worth 30s; now 40s.

IN SUTTON HUNDRED

The same man holds of Walter 1½ hides and the fifth part of half a hide. There is land for 4 ploughs. In demesne are 1½ [ploughs], with 1 slave; and 5 villans and 3 bordars having 1½ ploughs. There is a mill rendering 2s. It was worth 20s; now 40s. This land belongs to EVENLEY.

IN TOWCESTER HUNDRED

Godwine holds of Walter 2 hides [belonging] to the Church of Pattishall in COLD HIGHAM. There is land for 5 ploughs. In demesne is 1 plough; and 9 villans, with a priest and 3 bordars, have 2 ploughs. It was worth 40s; now 20s.

Leofnoth holds of Walter in PLUMPTON 1 hide [...]. There is land for 4 ploughs. In demesne is 1 [plough], and 2 slaves; and 6 villans with 3 ploughs. There are 4 acres of meadow. It was and is worth 40s.

IN 'GRAVESEND' HUNDRED

Hugh holds of Walter 1½ hides and the fifth part of half a hide. There is land for 4 ploughs. In demesne are 2 ploughs, and 2 slaves; and 8 villans and 3 bordars have 2 ploughs. There are 2 acres of spinney. It was and is worth 40s.

Gildre holds of Walter 2 hides in ASTCOTE. He himself has sake and soke of half a hide, and the king of 1½ hides. There is land for 5 ploughs. In demesne are 2 ploughs; and 8 villans, with 1 bordar, have 2 ploughs. It was worth 15s; now 30s.

IN WYMERSLEY HUNDRED

Winemar holds of Walter 2½ hides in WOOTTON. There is land for 7 ploughs. In demesne are 2 [ploughs], and 2 slaves; and 15 villans and 7 bordars with 5 ploughs. There are 4 acres of meadow. It was and is worth £4.

IN CLEYLEY HUNDRED

Hugh holds of Walter 3 hides and the fifth part of 1 hide. There is land for 8 ploughs. In demesne are 2 [ploughs], with 1 slave and a female slave; and 17 villans and 5 bordars have 6 ploughs. There are 36 acres of meadow. [There is] woodland 3 furlongs in length and 3½ furlongs and 10 perches in breadth. It was worth 40s; now 60s.

Leofnoth held all these lands freely TRE, and could go where he would.

The same Walter holds of the king 8 hides in PATTISHALL. Of these he has in demesne 2 hides. There is land for 20 ploughs. In demesne are 2 [ploughs], and 2 slaves and a female slave; and 22 villans and 6 bordars have 12 ploughs. There are 2 mills rendering 32d. It was worth £10 when he received it; now 100s. Leofnoth held it.

XL. The land of Winemar

WINEMAR holds of the king half a hide and the fifth part of 1 virgate of land in COSGROVE. There is land for 1½ ploughs. In demesne is 1 [plough], with 3 bordars. There is a mill rendering 13s, and 5 acres of meadow. [There is] woodland 3 furlongs in length and 2 furlongs in breadth. It was worth 10s; now 20s. Healfdene held it freely.

IN HIGHAM HUNDRED

The same man holds 2 hides and 3 virgates of land. There is land for 5 ploughs. In demesne are 3 ploughs, and 4 slaves; and 10 villans, with a priest and 1 bordar and 1 Frenchman, have 2 ploughs. There is a mill rendering 8d, and 20 acres of meadow. [There is] woodland 4 furlongs in length and 2 furlongs in breadth. It was worth 30s; now 60s. 6 free men held it TRE. 1 of them was called Asgot, whose part of the land Countess Judith claims.

The same Winemar holds 3 virgates of land in "HANTONE". There is land for 1½ ploughs. In demesne is half a plough; and 4 villans with 5 bordars have 1 plough. There are 3 acres of meadow. It was and is worth 10s.

IN CLEYLEY HUNDRED

Dodin holds of Winemar 1 hide and 4 parts of 1 virgate in ASHTON [in Roade]. There is land for 3 ploughs. In demesne is 1 [plough], with 1 slave; and 5 villans and 5 bordars have 2 ploughs. There are 5 acres of meadow. [There is] woodland 6 furlongs in length and 4 furlongs in breadth. It was worth 8s; now 12s. Healfdene held it freely TRE. Dodin has only the tenth part of this land.

Bondi holds of Winemar 4 parts of half a hide in the same vill. There is land for 1 plough. There is 1 bordar. It is worth 4s. The same Healfdene held it freely TRE.

Maiulf holds of Winemar 2½ virgates of land [Easton Neston]. There is land for 1 plough. This [plough] is there in demesne; and 6 villans with half a plough. It was worth 10s; now 20s. Alric and Sigefrith held it freely TRE.

XLI. The land of Guy de Raimbeaucourt

IN 'NAVISLAND' HUNDRED

GUY de Raimbeaucourt holds of the king 8½ hides in BURTON LATIMER. There were 14 ploughs TRE. Of this land 3 hides are in demesne, and there are 3 ploughs, with 1 slave; and 21 villans and 18 bordars have 9 ploughs. There are 2 mills rendering 16s, and 20 acres of meadow, and half an acre of woodland. It was worth 40s; now £6.

IN WARDEN HUNDRED

The same man holds 2 hides and 3 virgates of land. There is land for 6½ ploughs. Of this land 1 hide is in demesne, and there are 3 ploughs; and 15 villans, with a priest and 2 bordars, have 5 ploughs. There are 2 mills rendering 26s, and 20 acres of meadow. It was worth 100s; now £8. Tosti held it freely.

Earl Ralph held Burton Latimer.

IN GUILSBOROUGH HUNDRED AND A HALF

The same Guy holds 2 hides, less half a virgate, in STANFORD ON AVON, and Abbot Benedict bought them of him. There is land for 5 ploughs. There are 17 villans, with a priest and 4 bordars, having 4 ploughs. There are 8 acres of meadow. It was worth 20s; now 40s. Leofric held it freely TRE.

IN ORLINGBURY HUNDRED

NORGIOT holds of Guy 1 hide in GREAT HARROWDEN. There is land for 2 ploughs. In demesne is 1 [plough], with 1 slave and a female slave; and 4 villans, with 1 bordar, have 1 plough. There is a mill rendering 8s, and 2 acres of meadow. It was worth 5s; now 20s. Algar held it freely.

Ralph holds of Guy 1 hide and 2½ virgates of land in ISHAM. There is land for 3 ploughs. In demesne is 1 [plough], with 1 slave; and 7 villans, with 1 bordar, have 2 ploughs. There is a mill rendering 10s, and 5 acres of meadow. It was worth 5s; now 40s. Alwine son of Ulf held it freely TRE. Of this land the Bishop of Coutances claims 1½ virgates and 3 small gardens.

[Folio 227: NORTHAMPTONSHIRE]

IN 'HUXLOE' HUNDRED

Picot, Landric, and Ogier holds of Guy in ALDWINCLE ALL SAINTS 5 hides. There is land for 9 ploughs. In demesne are 3 ploughs, and 3 slaves; and 16 villans and 5 bordars have 5 ploughs. There is a mill rendering 6s, and 10 acres of meadow. [There is] woodland 16 furlongs in length and 8 furlongs in breadth. It is worth 50s. between them all. Leofsige held it freely TRE.

IN 'STOTFOLD' HUNDRED

Walter holds of Guy 2½ hides and the third part of 1 virgate in SULBY. The soke belongs to Stanford on Avon. There he has 1 plough in demesne; and 7 sokemen, with 6 bordars, have 2 ploughs. It was and is worth 40s. Leofric held it freely.

Odelin holds of Guy 3 virgates of land in CRANFORD [?St. Andrew]. There is land for 3 ploughs. In demesne is 1 [plough]; and 1 villan and 5 bordars have 2 ploughs. It is worth 20s.

Norgiot holds of Guy 3½ virgates of land in COGENHOE. There is land for 3 ploughs. In demesne are 2 [ploughs]; and 8 villans have 1 plough. There is a mill rendering 13s, and 10 [?]

acres of meadow. [There is] woodland half a league in length and 1 furlong in breadth. It was worth 10s; now 30s. Edwin held it freely TRE.

IN GUILSBOROUGH HUNDRED AND A HALF

Turchil holds of Guy 3 parts of 1 virgate in ELKINGTON. There is land for 3 oxen. 2 bordars who plough have these [oxen] there. It was and is worth 2s.

XLII. The land of Eudo fitzHubert

IN CORBY HUNDRED

EUDO fitzHubert holds of the king $2\frac{1}{2}$ hides in WAKERLEY. There is land for 6 ploughs. Of this land 1 hide is in demesne, and there are 2 ploughs, and 4 slaves; and 16 villans, with a priest and 4 bordars, have 4 ploughs. There is a mill rendering 5s, and 12 acres of meadow. [There is] woodland 1 league in length and 4 furlongs in breadth. It was worth 20s; now 100s.

IN UPTON HUNDRED

Roland holds of Eudo $1\frac{1}{2}$ hides in EASTON ON THE HILL. There is land for 2 ploughs. 5 sokemen have 3 ploughs there, and 8 acres of meadow. [There is] woodland 3 furlongs in length and 1 in breadth. It was worth 2s; now 30s. This land belongs to Peterborough [Abbey].

IN WILLOWBROOK HUNDRED

Roland holds of Eudo $1\frac{1}{2}$ hides in EASTON ON THE HILL. There is land for 4 ploughs. In demesne are 3 ploughs, and 4 slaves; and 15 villans, with 3 bordars, have 3 ploughs. There is a mill rendering 20s, and 8 acres of meadow. [There is] woodland 3 furlongs in length and 2 furlongs in breadth. It was worth 20s; now £6. Thrond held it freely TRE.

XLIII. The land of Giles, the brother of Ansculf

IN FOXLEY HUNDRED

GILES holds of the king 3 hides in WEEDON LOIS. There is land for $7\frac{1}{2}$ ploughs. In demesne are 3 ploughs, and 9 slaves and 6 female slaves. There 1 knight and 13 villans and 6 bordars have $4\frac{1}{2}$ ploughs. There is a mill rendering 2s, and 6 acres of meadow. It was worth 40s; and now 60s. Fredegis and Siward held it.

Geoffrey holds of Giles $1\frac{1}{2}$ hides in MORETON PINKNEY. There is land for 6 ploughs. In demesne are 3 ploughs, and 5 slaves; and 14 villans and 3 bordars with 3 ploughs. There are 30 acres of meadow. It was worth £8; now £4. Leofric held it freely.

Godwine holds of Giles half a hide in SILVERSTONE. There is land for 1 plough. There are 2 villans, and 3 acres of meadow. [There is] woodland $1\frac{1}{2}$ leagues in length and 1 league in breadth. The fourth part of this woodland belongs to this land. It was worth 2s; now 5s. Siward held it freely.

IN TOWCESTER HUNDRED

Giles himself holds 2 hides in WAPPENHAM. Of this land 3 virgates are in demesne. There is land for 5 ploughs. In demesne are 2 [ploughs], and 9 slaves and 3 female slaves; and 17 villans and 8 bordars, with a priest, have 3 ploughs. There is a mill rendering 4s, and 5 acres of meadow. [There is] woodland 11 furlongs in length and 6 in breadth. It was worth 100s; now £4. Leofric and Siward held it freely.

IN 'ALBOLDSTOW' HUNDRED

Giles himself holds 2 hides in STEANE. There is land for 5 ploughs. Of this land 3 virgates are in demesne; and there are 2 ploughs, and 4 slaves and 2 female slaves; and 11 villans, with a bordar, have 3 ploughs. There is a mill rendering 2s. To this manor belong 4 parts of 1 hide in SUTTON Hundred. There is land for 2 ploughs. There is 1 man having 1 plough. The whole was worth 50s; now 60s.

Landric holds of Giles 2 hides and 4 parts of half a hide in 'BRIME' [?in Culworth]. There is land for 6 ploughs. In demesne are 2 ploughs, and 2 slaves and 3 female slaves; and 6 villans, with a priest, have 2 ploughs. There is a mill rendering 32d, and 4 acres of meadow. It was worth 40s; now 60s. Leofric held it freely.

Ingelrann holds of Giles 2 hides in THORPE MANDEVILLE. There is land for 5 ploughs. In demesne is 1 [plough]; and 6 villans and 3 bordars have 2 ploughs. It was worth 40s; now 50s. Asmund the Dane held it freely.

Hugh and Landric hold of Giles 2 hides in STUCHBURY. There is land for 5 ploughs. In demesne is 1 [plough], and 2 slaves; and 5 villans and 3 bordars and 3 other men with 1 plough. [There is] woodland 3 furlongs in length and 2 furlongs in breadth. It was worth 30s; now 40s. Asmund [? the Dane] held it freely.

Geoffrey and Robert hold 2 hides of Giles in ASTWELL. There is land for 5 ploughs. In demesne are 2 [ploughs], with 1 slave; and 8 villans and 8 bordars have 3 ploughs. There is a mill rendering 12d, and 10 acres of meadow. [There is] woodland 6 furlongs in length and 1 furlong and 5 perches in breadth. It was and is worth 40s. Leofric and Ælfric held it.

Geoffrey holds of Giles half a hide in SYRESHAM. [There is] land for 1 plough and 2 oxen. In demesne is 1 plough; and 3 villans. It was and is worth 10s. Leofric held it freely.

IN WARDEN HUNDRED

Giles himself holds 4 hides in SULGRAVE, and Hugh and Landric and Otbert [hold] of him. There is land for 10 ploughs. In demesne are 3 ploughs, with 1 slave; and 20 villans and 6 bordars have 5 ploughs. There are 8 acres of meadow. It was worth £9; now £7. 4 men held it, but could not depart because the soke of this land belongs to Chipping Warden.

XLIIII. The land of Geoffrey Alselin

IN COLLINGTREE HUNDRED

GEOFFREY Alselin holds of the king 3½ hides in MILTON MALSOR, and William [holds] of him. There is land for 9 ploughs. In demesne is 1 [plough]; and 16 villans, with a priest and 5 bordars, have 7 ploughs. There is a mill rendering 30d, and 10 acres of meadow. [There is] woodland 3 furlongs in length and 2½ furlongs in breadth.

To this manor belong 2 hides, less 1 virgate, in COLLINGTREE. There is land for 4 ploughs. 2 sokemen and 5 villans have these [ploughs] there. There are 3 acres of meadow.

In Rothersthorpe is half a hide belonging to Milton Malsor. There is land for 1 plough, which [plough] is there, with 1 villan. The whole was worth £4; now £6.

Winemar holds half a hide of Geoffrey in the same vill. There is land for 1 plough. This [plough] is there. It was worth 5s; now 8s. Of this half-hide Winemar has only the soke. Toki held all this land with sake and soke.

XLV. The land of Geoffrey de Mandeville

IN SUTTON HUNDRED

GEOFFREY de Mandeville holds of the king AYNHO. There are 3 hides and the fifth part of 1 hide. There is land for 8 ploughs. Of this land 1 hide and the fifth part of 1 hide are in demesne, and there are 3 ploughs, and 8 slaves; and 23 villans and 9 bordars with 5 ploughs. There is a mill rendering 10s, and 20 acres of meadow. It was worth £6; now £8. Esger held it TRE.

Osbern holds of Geoffrey 1 hide and 2 parts of 1 virgate in CROUGHTON. There is land for 3 ploughs. In demesne is 1 [plough], and 3 slaves; and 10 villans with 1½ ploughs, and a mill rendering 2s. It was and is worth 30s. Svartlingr held it, and could not leave.

Swetmann holds of Geoffrey the fifth part of half a hide in CROUGHTON. There is land for 2 oxen. There is 1 villan with half a plough. It is worth 3s. Esger held it freely.

IN WARDEN HUNDRED

Ultbert holds of Geoffrey HINTON. There are 2 hides. There is land for 5 ploughs. In demesne are 2 ploughs, and 2 slaves; and 10 villans and 3 bordars with 3 ploughs. There is a mill rendering 2s, and 3 acres of meadow. It was worth 40s; now 60s.

Mauger holds of Geoffrey 6 hides in ASTON LE WALLS. There is land for 10 ploughs. In demesne are 3 ploughs,

[Folio 227V: NORTHAMPTONSHIRE]

and 5 slaves; and 15 villans and 5 bordars have 6 ploughs. There are 12 acres of meadow. It was worth 100s; now £6.

IN NOBOTTLE HUNDRED

Baldwin holds of Geoffrey half a hide in FLORE. There is land for 1 plough. This [plough] is there, with 1 villan and 2 slaves, and 4 acres of meadow; and of part of a mill he has 5s. The whole was worth 5s; now 15s.

IN FOXLEY HUNDRED

Arnold holds of Geoffrey half a hide in SILVERSTONE. There is land for 1 plough. This [plough] is there, with 2 slaves and 1 villan and 1 bordar. It was worth 10s; now 20s.

The same [Arnold] holds of Geoffrey 2 hides in HINTON-IN-THE-HEDGES. There is land for 5 ploughs. In demesne are 2 ploughs, and 2 slaves; and 11 villans and 5 bordars have 3 ploughs. There is a mill rendering 2s, and 16 acres of meadow. [There is] woodland 2 furlongs in length and half a furlong in breadth. It was worth 30s; now 70s.

IN 'ALBOLDSTOW' HUNDRED

Osbern holds of Geoffrey 1½ hides and 2 parts of 1 virgate in CULWORTH. There is land for 4 ploughs. In demesne are 2 [ploughs], and 4 slaves; and 10 villans, with 1 bordar, have 2 ploughs. There is a mill rendering 40d. It was and is worth £3. Esger held all these lands of Geoffrey's TRE.

XLVI. The land of Gilbert de Ghent

IN NOBOTTLE HUNDRED

GILBERT DE GHENT holds of the king 3½ hides in KISLINGBURY, and Geoffrey holds of him. There is land for 10 ploughs. In demesne are 3 ploughs, and 1½ hides of this land, and 10 slaves; and 22 villans and 7 bordars with 4 ploughs. There are 2 mills rendering 40s, and 14 acres of meadow, and 10 acres of woodland. It was worth £4; now £6.

Sasgar holds of Gilbert 1 hide and 1½ virgates of land in NETHER HEYFORD. There is land for 2 ploughs. In demesne is half a plough; and 3 villans, with 1 bordar, have 1 plough. There are 4 acres of meadow. It was worth 10s; now 20s.

IN 'GRAVESEND' HUNDRED

Gilbert himself holds 4 hides in CHURCH STOWE. There is land for 10 ploughs. In demesne are 3 ploughs, and 7 slaves; and 14 villans and 6 bordars have 7 ploughs. There is a mill rendering 64d. [There is] woodland 7 furlongs in length and 3 furlongs in breadth. It was worth 60s; now 100s.

Gilbert himself holds EMPINGHAM [Rutland]. There are 4 hides. Of these, 3 [are] in demesne. There is land for 8 ploughs. In demesne are 4 ploughs, and 8 slaves; and 15 villans with 4 ploughs. There are 5 mills rendering 42s8d, and 10 acres of meadow. [There is] woodland 1 furlong in length and 10 perches in breadth. It was worth 100s; now £10.

He himself holds in the same vill 7½ hides and 1 bovate of land of the king's sokeland of Rutland, and says the king is his warrantor. There is land for 15 ploughs. 14 sokemen, with 51 villans, have these [ploughs] there. There are 5 mills rendering 24s, and 10 acres of meadow, and 10 acres of woodland. It was and is worth £8.

IN WILLOWBROOK HUNDRED

Gilbert himself gave to [the Abbey of] Saint-Pierre-sur-Dives half a hide in EASTON ON THE HILL. There is land for 2 ploughs. In demesne is 1 [plough]; and 4 villans have another. There are 4 acres of meadow. It was worth 5s; now 10s. Tonni held all these lands with sake and soke.

Robert holds of Gilbert WHICHFORD [War.]. There are 15 hides. There is land for 19 ploughs. In demesne are 4 [ploughs], and 10 slaves; and 33 villans and 21 bordars have 15 ploughs. There are 2 mills rendering 15s, and 3 furlongs of meadow in length and as much in breadth. [There is] woodland 1 furlong in length and as much in breadth. It was worth £10; now £20. Ulf held it freely TRE.

XLVII. The land of Geoffrey de La Guerche

IN GUILSBOROUGH HUNDRED AND A HALF

GEOFFREY DE LA GUERCHE holds of the king 4 hides in WELFORD, and Alvred [holds] of him. There is land for 8 ploughs. In demesne are 2 [ploughs], and 2 slaves and 1 female slave; and 12 villans, with a priest and 2 bordars, have 4 ploughs. There are 20 acres of meadow.

To this manor belong 2½ virgates of land in COLD ASHBY. There is land for 1 plough; and the fourth part of 1 virgate of land in ELKINGTON. There are 2 bordars paying 22d.

IN 'STOTFOLD' HUNDRED

To the same manor belong 2½ hides in SULBY. There is land for 5 ploughs. It is waste. The whole TRE was worth 20s; now 60s. Leofric held it freely TRE.

The same Geoffrey holds in CRICK 4 hides, less 1 virgate of land. There is land for 8 ploughs. In demesne are 3 ploughs, and 4 slaves; and 17 villans, with a priest and 6 bordars, have 5 ploughs. There are 12 acres of meadow. It was worth 30s; now £4.10s. To this land belong 4 sokemen who pay 10d.

XLVIII. The land of Gunfrid de Chocques

IN CORBY HUNDRED

GUNFRID de Chocques holds of the king half a hide in BOUGHTON [in Weekley]. There is land for 1 plough. 2 villans, with 1 bordar, have this [plough] there. It was and is worth 6s.

The same Gunfrid holds in NEWTON 3 virgates of land and 1 bovate and the third part of 1 bovate. There is land for 2 ploughs. In demesne is 1 [plough]; and 4 villans, with 4 bordars, have another. [There is] woodland there half a furlong in length and 5 perches in breadth. It was and is worth 10s. Azur held these 2 lands freely.

IN 'SPELHOE' HUNDRED

The same man holds 3 hides and 1½ virgates of land in LITTLE BILLING. There is land for 7 ploughs. In demesne are 2 [ploughs], and 4 slaves; and 16 villans, with a priest, have 5 ploughs. There is a mill rendering 2s, and 50 acres of meadow. It was worth 40s; now 70s. Swein held it freely.

The same man holds 5 hides in WOLLASTON. There is land for 10 ploughs. In demesne are 4 [ploughs], and 8 slaves; and 22 villans, with a priest and 4 bordars, have 6 ploughs. There is a mill rendering 5s, and 48 acres of meadow. It was worth £3; now £10. 4 thegns held it with sake and soke.

IN ORLINGBURY HUNDRED

The same man holds 1½ hides in GREAT CRANSLEY. There is land for 3 ploughs. In demesne is 1 [plough], and 2 slaves; and 4 villans, with a priest and 10 bordars, have 2 ploughs. There are 5 acres of meadow. It was and is worth 30s.

IN GUILSBOROUGH HUNDRED

The same man holds 2 hides and 1 virgate of land and half a hide of sokeland [?Long Buckby]. There is land for 5½ ploughs. In demesne are 3 ploughs, and 7 slaves; and 13 villans and 5 bordars and 5 sokemen have 2½ ploughs. There are 8 acres of meadow. It was and is worth £4.

The same man holds 1 virgate of land in WEST HADDON. There is land for half a plough, and this [half-plough] is there, with 1 slave. It is worth 4s.

The same man holds 1 hide in CREATON. There is land for 2 ploughs. In demesne is 1 [plough], and 4 slaves; and 3 villans, with 2 bordars, have 1 plough. It was worth 20s; now 30s.

IN COLLINGTREE HUNDRED

The same man holds 2½ hides in ROTHERSTHORPE. There is land for 7 ploughs. In demesne are 2 [ploughs], and 7 slaves; and 14 villans and 5 bordars have 5 ploughs. There is a mill rendering 32d. [There is] woodland 5½ furlongs in length and 1½ furlongs in breadth. It was worth £4; now 100s.

IN 'GRAVESEND' HUNDRED

The same man holds half a hide and the fifth part of half a hide in THRUPP GROUNDS. There is land for 1 plough. This [plough] is there, with 2 bordars. It was worth 2s; now 6s. Swein held all these aforesaid lands with sake and soke.

IN SUTTON HUNDRED

The same man holds 2 hides and the fifth part of 2 hides in OLD GRIMSBURY [Oxon.]. There is land for 6 ploughs. In demesne are 2 [ploughs], and 4 slaves; and 15 villans, with 3 bordars, have 4 ploughs. There is a mill rendering 10s, and 30 acres of meadow. It was worth £4; now £6. This land belongs to 3 lords. Leofnoth held it with sake and soke.

Winemar holds of Gunfrid 1 hide and 3 virgates of land in KNUSTON. There is land for 2 ploughs. In demesne are 1½ [ploughs], with 1 slave; and 6 villans have 1 plough. There is a mill rendering 8d, and 7 acres of meadow. It was worth 5s; now 20s. Wulfgeat held it freely TRE. Eustace claims it.

IN 'SPELHOE' HUNDRED

John holds of Gunfrid half a virgate of land in WESTON FAVELL. There is 1 villan having 3 oxen.

IN NOBOTTLE HUNDRED

Olbald holds of Gunfrid 1 hide and 1 virgate of land in FLORE. There is land for 3 ploughs. In demesne are 2 [ploughs], and 4 slaves; and 5 villans, with 4 bordars, have 1 plough. There are 6 acres of meadow. It was worth 10s; now 25s. 2 thegns held it.

IN CLEYLEY HUNDRED

Theobald holds of Gunfrid 3 virgates of land and the fourth part of 1 virgate in HULCOTE. There is land for 2 ploughs. In demesne is 1 [plough]; and 7 villans have another. There are 5 acres of meadow. It was worth 12s; now 15s.

Bondi holds of Gunfrid 3 virgates of land and the fourth part of 1 virgate in EASTON NESTON. There is land for 2 ploughs. In demesne is 1 [plough]; and 6 villans have another. There are 3 acres of meadow, and from part of a mill 4s. [There is] woodland 5 furlongs in length and in breadth. 2 lords hold it. It is worth 12s. The same Bondi held it freely.

Dodin holds of Gunfrid 4 parts of half a hide in ROADE. There is land for 1 plough. This [plough] is there, with 2 bordars. [There is] woodland half a furlong in length and 4 perches in breadth. It was worth 12d; now 4s. Swein held it freely TRE.

[Folio 228: NORTHAMPTONSHIRE]

XLIX. The land of Sigar de Chocques

IN TOWCESTER HUNDRED

SIGAR de Chocques holds of the king 4 hides and 4 parts of half a hide [?Gayton]. There is land for 10 ploughs. Of this land 1 hide is in demesne, and there are 3 ploughs, and 5 slaves and 3 female slaves; and 21 villans, with a priest and 11 bordars, have 8 ploughs. There are 8 acres of meadow. [There is] woodland 4 furlongs in length and 3 furlongs in breadth. It was and is worth £6. Earl Tosti held it.

L. The land of Swein

IN CLEYLEY HUNDRED

SWEIN holds of the king 4 hides in STOKE BRUERNE. There is land for 10 ploughs. In demesne is 1 [plough]; and 14 villans, with a priest and 7 bordars, have 5 ploughs. There is a mill rendering 13s4d, and 30 acres of meadow. [There is] woodland 3 furlongs in length and 2½ furlongs in breadth. It was and is worth £3.

LI. The land of Sibold

IN 'HUXLOE' HUNDRED

SIBOLD holds of the king 1½ virgates of land in LOWICK. There is land for 1½ ploughs. Of this land 1 virgate is in demesne, and there is 1 plough; and 2 villans and 2 bordars with half a plough. It was worth 4s; now 10s. Leofsige held it freely TRE.

LII. The land of Ogier

IN NAVISFORD HUNDRED

OGIER holds of the king 2½ hides in THRAPSTON. There is land for 5 ploughs. In demesne are 2 ploughs, with 1 slave; and 7 villans and 5 bordars have 1 plough; and 4 sokemen with 1 plough. There is a mill rendering 20s, and 12 acres of meadow. [There is] woodland 6 furlongs in length and as many in breadth. It was and is worth £3.

LIII. The land of Drogo de La Beuvriere

IN WYMERSLEY HUNDRED

DROGO de la Beuvriere holds of the king 1 hide and 3 virgates of land in CHADSTONE. There is land for 5 ploughs. In demesne is 1 plough, with 1 slave; and 9 villans and 4 bordars with 3 ploughs. [There is] woodland 1 furlong in length and as much in breadth. It was worth 20s; now 40s. Ulf, a man of Earl Waltheof, held it. Countess Judith claims it.

LIIII. The land of Mainou

IN SUTTON HUNDRED

MAINOU holds of the king 1 hide in THENFORD. There is land for 2½ ploughs. In demesne is 1 [plough], and 3 slaves; and 6 villans have 1½ ploughs; and from part of a mill 30d. It was and is worth 40s. Algar held it freely TRE.

IN CLEYLEY HUNDRED

The same man holds 3 virgates of land in WICKEN. There is land for 3 ploughs. In demesne are 2 ploughs, with 1 slave; and 5 villans, with 1 bordar, have 2 ploughs. There are 6 acres of meadow. [There is] woodland 10 furlongs in length and 3 furlongs in breadth. It was and is worth 40s. Siward held it freely.

IN 'STOTFOLD' HUNDRED

Berner holds of Mainou 4 hides and 2 parts of 1 virgate in MAIDWELL. There is land for 8 ploughs. In demesne is 1 [plough], with 1 slave; and 8 villans and 4 bordars and 6 sokemen have 6 ploughs. There are 8 acres of meadow. It was worth 5s; now 40s. Leofric held it freely.

IN ROTHWELL HUNDRED

To this manor belongs 1 virgate of land in DRAUGHTON. This is valued with the manor.

LV. The land of Eustace

EUSTACE holds of the king 1 hide and 2½ virgates of land in ISHAM. There is land for 3 ploughs. In demesne is 1 [plough]; and 7 villans and 3 bordars with 2 ploughs. There is a mill rendering 10s, and 5 acres of meadow. It was and is worth 40s. Eustace occupied this land by force, wronging the Church of Ramsey.

Reginald holds of Eustace 3 hides in WOODNEWTON. There is land for 5 ploughs. In demesne is 1 [plough]; and 8 villans and 5 bordars with 3½ ploughs. There is a mill rendering 64d, and 8 acres of meadow. [There is] woodland 4 furlongs in length and 2 furlongs in breadth. It was worth 10s; now 30s. Northmann held these 2 estates.

Alvred holds of Eustace in POLEBROOK 1 hide and 1 virgate of land. There is land for 2 ploughs. In demesne is 1 [plough]; and 4 villans, with a priest and 4 bordars, have 1½ ploughs. It was worth 2s; now 20s. Ordmær held it freely.

Widelard holds of Eustace half a hide in WINWICK [Hunts.]. There is land for 2 ploughs. In demesne is 1 [plough], with 1 slave; and 3 villans with 2 ploughs. There are 3 acres of meadow. It was worth 10s; now 40s. Aki held it.

IN 'NAVISLAND' HUNDRED

Aghmund holds of Eustace half a hide in GRAFTON UNDERWOOD. There is land for 1 plough. This [plough] is there, with certain men. It was and is worth 5s.

IN NAVISFORD HUNDRED

Alvred holds of Eustace 1 hide and 1 virgate of land in CLOPTON. There is land for 2 ploughs. In demesne is 1 [plough]; and 1 villan, with 3 bordars, has half a plough. It was worth 3s; now 10s.

LVI. The land of Countess Judith

IN WITCHLEY WAPENTAKE

Countess JUDITH holds of the king 1½ hides in RYHALL [Rutland]. There is, with its appendages, land for 8 ploughs. In demesne is 1 [plough], and 4 villans and 4 sokemen have 4 ploughs. There are 2 mills rendering 36s. [There is] woodland 4 furlongs in length and 2 furlongs in breadth.

To this manor belongs BELMESTHORPE [Rutland]. There are 1½ hides, and in demesne [are] 2 ploughs; and 14 villans and 6 bordars have 4 ploughs. There is a mill rendering 10s8d, and 16 acres of meadow. The whole was and is worth £6.

[Judith] herself holds the third part of 1 hide in ASHLEY. There are 3 sokemen [who] pay yearly 5s4d.

In SUTTON BASSETT there is half a hide and the third part of half a hide; and 4 sokemen have there 1½ ploughs and pay yearly 10s8d.

In WESTON BY WELLAND there is 1 hide and the third

part of 1 hide; and 5 sokemen have there 1½ ploughs and pay yearly 21s4d.

In DINGLEY there is the third part of 1 hide, and 3 parts of 2 parts of 1 hide; and 5 sokemen with 1½ ploughs there. They pay 6s8d.

In BRAMPTON ASH there is 1 hide; and 4 sokemen have there 2 ploughs, and pay yearly 5s4d.

Earl Waltheof held all this land, and it was worth as much as it is worth now.

IN WILLOWBROOK HUNDRED

The countess herself holds 6 hides in FOTHERINGHAY. There is land for 12 ploughs. Of this land 2 hides are in demesne, and there are 3 ploughs, and 3 slaves; and 19 villans, with a priest and 6 bordars, have 9 ploughs. There is a mill rendering 8s, and 40 acres of meadow. [There is] woodland 1 league in length and 9 furlongs in breadth. When it is stocked and the king does not hunt in it, it is worth 10s. It was worth £8; now £12. Thorkil held it freely TRE.

The countess herself holds 5 hides in HARRINGWORTH. There is land for 16 ploughs. In demesne are 3 ploughs, and 6 slaves and 1 female slave; and 26 villans and 8 bordars and 6 sokemen have 10 ploughs. There is a mill rendering 5s, and 5 furlongs of meadow in length and 2 furlongs in breadth. [There is] woodland 8 furlongs in length and 1 league and 3 furlongs in breadth. It was and is worth £10. Thorkil held it freely.

In LAMPORT is 1 bovate of land, with 1 bordar, rendering 16d.

In BRAYBROOKE is half a virgate of land of sokeland. There 1 villan has half a plough. It was and is worth 4s.

In DRAUGHTON are 2½ virgates of land. 3 sokemen have there 2 ploughs. It was and is worth 10s.

In BROUGHTON are 1½ hides of sokeland. There is land for 3 ploughs. 3 sokemen, with 4 villans and 5 bordars, have these [ploughs] there and 8 acres of meadow.

In GREAT CRANSLEY is 1 hide, and 6 sokemen, with 5 bordars, have there 2 ploughs and 8 acres of meadow.

In HANNINGTON are 3 virgates of land, and 4 sokemen have there 1½ ploughs and 2 acres of meadow. These 3 estates were worth 40s; now 16d more.

The countess herself holds 4 hides in EARLS BARTON. There is land for 8 ploughs. In demesne are 2 [ploughs], and 3 slaves; and 8 villans and 6 bordars and 11 sokemen have 6 ploughs. There are 3 mills rendering 28s8d, and 34 acres of meadow. It was and is worth £4. Bondi held it with sake and soke.

The countess herself holds 4 hides in GREAT DODDINGTON. There is land for 8 ploughs. In demesne are 2 [ploughs], and 2 slaves; and 12 villans and 5 bordars, with 4 sokemen, have 6 ploughs. There are 12 acres of meadow. It was and is worth £4. Bondi held it.

The countess herself holds 4 hides in WILBY. There is land for 7 ploughs. In demesne is 1 [plough]; and 7 sokemen have 6 ploughs. It was and is worth £4. Bondi held it.

The countess herself holds 4 hides in MEARS ASHBY. There is land for 7 ploughs. In demesne is 1 [plough], and 2 slaves; and 6 villans and 6 bordars, with 8 sokemen, have 6 ploughs. It was and is worth £4. Bondi held it. These 3 lands belong to EARLS BARTON.

In BOUGHTON [near Northampton] are 3 virgates of sokeland. There is land for 1½ ploughs. 4 sokemen, with 3 bordars, have these [ploughs] there.

IN WYMERSLEY HUNDRED AND A HALF

The countess herself holds 3½ hides in YARDLEY HASTINGS. There is land for 9 ploughs. Of this land 1 hide is in demesne, and there are 3 ploughs; and 16 villans, with 12 bordars, have 6 ploughs.

[Folio 228V: NORTHAMPTONSHIRE]

There is woodland 13 furlongs in length and 8 furlongs in breadth. This land TRE, as now, was assessed for 3½ hides. To this [manor] belong these following members:

In GRENDON are 3 hides and 1 virgate of land. There is land for 9 ploughs. 12 sokemen have these [ploughs] there and 3 mills rendering 3s, and 30 acres of meadow.

In WHISTON is 1 virgate of land of sokeland. There is land for half a plough. 2 bordars have this [half-plough] there.

In DENTON is 1 hide. There is land for 2 ploughs. 6 sokemen have these [ploughs] there.

In HACKLETON are 2 hides of sokeland. There is land for 6 ploughs. 8 sokemen and 4 bordars have these [ploughs] there and 10 acres of meadow.

In HORTON is 1 virgate of land, and of sokeland 1 hide. There is land for half a plough. It is waste.

In WOLLASTON the countess has the soke of 1 hide.

In BRAFIELD-ON-THE-GREEN are 3 virgates of land. There is land for 2 ploughs. 3 sokemen, with 3 bordars, have these [ploughs] there and 2 acres of woodland.

In QUINTON is half a hide. There is land for 1 plough. 2 sokemen, with 2 villans and 5 bordars, have this [plough] there and 4 acres of meadow.

In HARDINGSTONE are 2 hides. There is land for 4 ploughs. 6 sokemen and 6 bordars have there 3 ploughs and 3 acres of meadow. The whole manor, with its appendages, was worth £12; now £15. Earl Waltheof held it.

The countess herself holds 8 hides in DAVENTRY. There is land for 16 ploughs. In demesne are 3 ploughs, and 3 slaves; and 20 villans, with a priest and 10 bordars, have 7 ploughs. There are 12 acres of meadow. It was worth £3; now £8.

In TWYWELL the countess holds 1½ hides. There is land for 2 ploughs. In demesne is 1 plough, with 2 bordars. It was and is worth 10s. Earl Waltheof held it.

Hugh holds of the countess half a hide in WELLINGBOROUGH, and it was assessed for as much TRE. There is land for 1½ ploughs. In demesne is 1 [plough], with 1 slave; and 2 villans and 2 bordars have half a plough. There is a mill rendering 5s. It was worth 10s; now 20s. Godwine held it freely TRE.

The same man holds of the countess half a hide in [?] WELLINGBOROUGH. There is land for 1 plough. 3 sokemen have this [plough] there. It was worth 2s; now 5s.

Robert holds of the countess 2 hides and 1 virgate of land in BISBROOKE [Rutland]. There is land for 3½ ploughs. In demesne is 1 [plough], and 2 slaves; and 12 villans, with 4 bordars, have 2½ ploughs. There are 20 acres of meadow. [There is] scrubland 1½ furlongs in length and as much in breadth. It was worth 20s; now 30s. Edward held it with sake and soke.

Grimbald holds of the countess 3 hides, less 1 bovate, in TICKENCOTE [Rutland]. There is land for 6 ploughs. In demesne is 1 [plough]; and 8 sokemen, with 12 villans and 1 bordar, have 5 ploughs. There is a mill rendering 24s, and 12 acres of meadow. It was worth 30s; now 50s. Edward held this also.

The same man holds of the countess 1 hide in HORN [Rutland]. There is land for 2 ploughs. In demesne is 1 [plough], and 2 slaves and 2 female slaves; and 9 villans, with 4 bordars, have 2 ploughs. There is a mill rendering 4s8d. It was worth 20s; now 30s.

The same man holds 1 virgate of land of the countess in EAST FARNDON. There is land for 2 oxen. It was and is worth 32d. Thorkil held it freely TRE.

The same man holds of the countess 3 hides and 1 virgate of land in MOULTON. There is land for 6½ ploughs. In demesne is 1 [plough]; and 12 villans, with 4 bordars, have 5½ ploughs. It was and is worth 40s. Æthelric held it freely TRE.

IN CORBY HUNDRED

Thorger holds of the countess in NEWTON 3 virgates of land and 1 bovate and the third part of 1 bovate. There is land for 2 ploughs. In demesne is 1 [plough]; and 4 villans, with 4 bordars, have another. There is half a mill rendering 16d. [There is] woodland 1½ furlongs in length and as much in breadth. It is worth 6s. The same man held it freely.

IN ROTHWELL HUNDRED

Ketilbert holds of the countess 1 hide and 1 virgate of land in BRAYBROOKE. There is land for 2 ploughs. These [ploughs] are there, with 2 villans and 4 bordars. It was and is worth 15s. The same man held it freely TRE.

IN 'STOTFOLD' HUNDRED

Ulf holds of the countess 1 hide of sokeland in GREAT OXENDON. There is land for 2 ploughs. These [ploughs] are there, with 5 sokemen and 6 bordars. It is worth 20s. The same man held it freely TRE.

Bisceop holds of the countess half a hide in MOULTON PARK. There is land for 1 plough. This [plough] is there, with 2 villans and 2 bordars. It is worth 10s.

Turbern holds of the countess half a hide in HORTON. There is land for 1 plough. There is half a plough, with 2 bordars. It was worth 8s; now 10s.

Leofric holds of the countess in WELTON and in THRUPP GROUNDS half a hide and 1 virgate of land, less the fifth part of half a hide. There is land for 1 plough. In demesne is half a plough, with 2 bordars. It is worth 8s. The same Leofric held it TRE. The king has the soke of it.

William holds of the countess 4 hides in GLASTON [Rutland]. There is land for 8 ploughs. In demesne are $1\frac{1}{2}$ ploughs, and 2 slaves; and 5 villans and 3 sokemen, with 2 bordars, have 5 ploughs. There are 10 acres of meadow. It was and is worth 40s. Edward held it with sake and soke.

To this manor belong 6 sokemen in SOUTH LUFFENHAM [Rutland], the king's manor, and 1 in SEATON [Rutland], and 1 in THORPE BY WATER [Rutland], whose stock is noted above.

IN CORBY HUNDRED

Lanzelin holds of the countess in NEWTON 3 virgates of land and 1 bovate and the third part of 1 bovate. There is land for 2 ploughs. In demesne is 1 [plough]; and 8 villans, with 4 bordars, have another. There is a mill rendering 7s8d. [There is] woodland 1 furlong in length and half a furlong in breadth. It was worth 5s; now 16s.

The same Lanzelin holds of the countess $1\frac{1}{2}$ hides and half a virgate of land in GREAT OAKLEY. There is land for 5 ploughs. In demesne is 1 [plough], and 2 slaves; and 19 villans have 3 ploughs. [There is] meadow 4 furlongs in length and 3 perches in breadth. [There is] woodland 1 league in length and half a league in breadth. It was worth 20s; now 30s. Bondi held these lands freely TRE.

The same man holds of the countess 2 hides, less 1 virgate, in BOZEAT. There is land for 4 ploughs. In demesne is 1 [plough], and 2 slaves; and 6 villans with 2 bordars have 3 ploughs. There are 10 acres of meadow. [There is] woodland 2 furlongs in length and 1 furlong in breadth. It was and is worth 40s. Strikr held it of Earl Waltheof.

IN MAWSLEY HUNDRED

Fulcher holds of the countess 3 hides and 3 virgates of land in WALGRAVE. There is land for 7 ploughs. In demesne are 2 [ploughs]; and 14 villans with 9 bordars have 4 ploughs, and 4 sokemen, with 8 bordars, have $1\frac{1}{2}$ ploughs. There are 12 acres of meadow. It was and is worth £3. The countess has the soke. Alsige held it with soke and sake.

Hugh holds of the countess 2 hides and 1 virgate of land in SCALDWELL. There is land for 4 ploughs. 7 sokemen and 4 bordars have these [ploughs] there. It was and is worth 21s4d.

The same Hugh holds of the countess 1 hide and 1 virgate of land in HANGING HOUGHTON. There is land for 2

ploughs. 6 sokemen, with 4 bordars, have these [ploughs] there. It was and is worth 13s4d.

The same man holds of the countess 1 hide and $1\frac{1}{2}$ virgates of land in HOLCOT. There is land for 2 ploughs. 5 sokemen, with 3 bordars, have these there. It is worth 20s.

The same man holds 1 virgate of land in MOULTON PARK. There 1 sokeman has half a plough and pays 33d.

The same man holds of the countess in CASTLE ASHBY 2 hides less 1 virgate; and it was assessed for as much TRE. There is land for 5 ploughs. In demesne are 2 [ploughs]; and 12 villans, with 6 bordars, have 3 ploughs. There is a mill rendering 6s8d, and 12 acres of meadow. [There is] woodland 1 furlong and 11 perches in length and 1 furlong, less 7 perches, in breadth. It was worth 20s; now £4.

To this manor belongs in GRENDON 1 virgate of land of sokeland. 4 sokemen have there 1 plough.

IN ROTHWELL HUNDRED

Eustace holds of the countess $2\frac{1}{2}$ hides and the third part of 1 hide in RUSHTON. There is land for 5 ploughs. In demesne is 1 plough, and 1 female slave;

[Folio 229: NORTHAMPTONSHIRE]

and 19 villans, with 8 bordars, have 4 ploughs. There is 1 sokeman, and a mill rendering 32d, and 4 acres of woodland. It was worth 10s; now 40s.

IN 'HAMFORDSHOE' HUNDRED

Alan holds of the countess 1 hide in HARDWICK. There is land for 2 ploughs. These [ploughs] are there, with 2 slaves and 3 villans and 1 bordar. It was and is worth 20s. Ulf held it with sake and soke.

IN ORLINGBURY HUNDRED

The same man holds of the countess 1 hide in HARDWICK. There is land for 2 ploughs. 7 villans, with 1 bordar, have there 3 ploughs and 7 acres of meadow. It was worth 20s; now 40s.

IN 'HUXLOE' HUNDRED

Walter holds of the countess 5 hides in LILFORD. There is land for 14 ploughs. In demesne are 3 [ploughs], and 4 slaves; and 20 villans and 16 bordars have 12 ploughs. There is a mill rendering 24s, and 50 acres of meadow. It was and is worth £8. Thorkil held it freely TRE.

Rohais holds of the countess 1 hide in SPRATTON. There is land for 2 ploughs. In demesne is 1 [plough]; and 1 villan, with 8 bordars, have $1\frac{1}{2}$ ploughs. There is a mill rendering 64d. It was worth 10s; now 20s.

Corbelin holds of the countess 2 hides in WOLLASTON. There is land for $3\frac{1}{2}$ ploughs. In demesne is 1 [plough], with 1 slave; and 6 villans, with 1 bordar, have $2\frac{1}{2}$ ploughs. There is a mill rendering 6s8d, and 12 acres of meadow. It was worth 16s; now 40s. Strikr held it freely. Winemar of Hanslope claims it.

Dodin holds of the countess 1 virgate of land in EASTON MAUDIT. There is land for half a plough. There are 2 bordars, and 1 acre of meadow. It was worth 12d; now 3s.

Gilbert holds of the countess half a virgate of land in WELLINGBOROUGH. There is land for 1 ox. This land belongs to Great Doddington and is valued there.

Winemar holds of the countess 1 virgate of land in BOZEAT. There are 4 bordars.

The same man holds of the countess half a hide in DENTON. There is land for half a plough, and as much is there.

The same man holds 1 virgate of land of sokeland in BRAFIELD-ON-THE-GREEN. There is land for half a plough. There are 2 bordars ploughing with 2 oxen.

The same man holds of the soke of YARDLEY HASTINGS: in [?Great] HOUGHTON 1 virgate of land; in PRESTON DEANERY 3 virgates of land, and 3 acres of meadow; in QUINTON 3 virgates of land, and 5 acres of meadow; and in the same vill half a hide; in WOOTTON 1 hide; in [?Little] HOUGHTON 1 virgate of land, and 5 acres of meadow. In all, there is land for 6 ploughs. There are 5 sokemen and 9 villans and 2 bordars having 4 ploughs. The whole was worth 30s; now 53s.

Norgiold holds of the countess 3 virgates of land in COGENHOE. There is land for 1½ ploughs, and as many [ploughs] are there, with 6 sokemen, and 10 acres of meadow. It was worth 5s; now 10s.

Robert holds of the countess 3 virgates of land in [?] WOTHORPE. There is land for 1 plough. This [plough] is there in demesne, with 4 villans, and 4 acres of meadow. It was worth 4s; now 10s.

The same man holds of the countess 1 virgate of land in BOUGHTON [near Northampton]. There is land for half a plough, which [half-plough] is there, and it is worth 3s. Ulfkil held it freely.

IN 'SPELHOE' HUNDRED

The countess herself gave to St Wandrille in BOUGHTON [near Northampton], by the king's leave, 3 hides less half a virgate. There is land for 6 ploughs. In demesne are 2½ ploughs; and 14 villans, with 12 bordars, have 3½ ploughs. There are 10 acres of meadow. It was worth 20s; now 40s. 2 thegns held it freely.

Gerard holds of the countess half a virgate of land in BOUGHTON [near Northampton], and it is worth 4s.

Nigel holds of the countess half a virgate of land of sokeland in LITTLE HOUGHTON. There are 2 bordars.

The same man holds of the countess in the same vill 2 hides, and it is assessed for as much. There is land for 5 ploughs. In demesne is 1 [plough]; and 8 villans with 2 bordars have 2 ploughs. There is a mill rendering 13s, and 10 acres of meadow. [There is] woodland 1 furlong in length and half a furlong in breadth. It was worth 40s; now 50s. Ulf held it.

Gilbert holds of the countess 1 hide and 3 virgates of land in PIDDINGTON. There is land for 4 ploughs. In demesne is 1 [plough], with 1 slave; and 4 villans, with 5 bordars and a priest, have 2½ ploughs. There are 20 acres of meadow. [There is] woodland 4 furlongs in length and 2 furlongs in breadth. It was worth 20s; now 40s. 2 men of Burgræd's held it, and could go where they would. Bishop Geoffrey [of Coutances] claims it, and [so does] Winemar of Hanslope.

William Peverel holds of the countess 1 hide and the fifth part of 1 hide in POTTERSPURY. There is land for 3 ploughs. In demesne is 1 [plough], and 2 slaves; and 6 villans, with 3 bordars, have 2 ploughs. There are 5 acres of meadow. [There is] woodland 4 furlongs in length and 2 furlongs in breadth. It was and is worth 30s. Bisceop held it freely.

LVII. The land of Gilbert

IN 'SPELHOE' HUNDRED

GILBERT the cook holds of the king 4 hides in GREAT BILLING. There is land for 8 ploughs. In demesne are 2 ploughs, and 5 slaves and 1 female slave; and 10 villans, with 7 bordars, have 6 ploughs. There is a mill rendering 20s, and 28 acres of meadow. It was worth 40s; now 100s. Thor held it freely TRE.

IN GUILSBOROUGH HUNDRED AND A HALF

The same man holds 2 hides in WATFORD. There is land for 4 ploughs. In demesne are 2 [ploughs], with 1 slave and 1 female slave; and 20 villans, with 5 bordars, have 2 ploughs. There is a mill rendering 12d, and 6 acres of meadow. It was worth 10s; now 40s. Thor held it freely. | The same Gilbert holds 2 parts of 1 virgate of land in HOLLOWELL. There is land for 3 oxen. It is worth 12d. |

The same man holds 1 virgate of land in RAVENSTHORPE. There is land for half a plough. 1 villan and 1 bordar have this [half-plough]. It was worth 3s; now 5s. Northmann held it.

LVIII. The land of David

DAVID holds of the king 3 virgates of land in [Great or Little] CASTERTON [Rutland]. There is land for 1½ ploughs. In demesne, nevertheless, is 1 plough; and 6 villans, with a priest and 3 bordars, have 2 ploughs. There are 2 slaves, and a mill rendering 12s, and 5 acres of meadow. It is worth 40s. Asgot held it with sake and soke.

IN FOXLEY HUNDRED

The same man holds 1 hide and 4 parts of half a hide in BRADDEN. There is land for 3½ ploughs. In demesne is 1 plough, with 1 villan and 1 bordar, and 1 acre of meadow. It was worth 5s; now 10s. Bisceop held it freely TRE.

LIX. The land of Richard

IN UPTON HUNDRED

RICHARD holds of the king 2 hides in STIBBINGTON [Hunts.]. There is land for 2 ploughs. In demesne is 1 [plough]; and 3 villans, with 5 bordars, have another, and they pay 5s. There is a mill rendering 8s, and 12 acres of meadow. [There is] woodland 50 perches in length and 15 perches in breadth. It was worth 2s; now 20s.

IN 'HUXLOE' HUNDRED

The same man holds 3 virgates of land in BENEFIELD. There is land for 2 ploughs. In demesne is 1 [plough]; and 5 villans have another. There are 5 acres of meadow. [There is] woodland 1 league in length and half a league in breadth. It was worth 2s; now 10s.

IN 'SPELHOE' HUNDRED

The same man holds 4 hides in ABINGTON. There is land for 8 ploughs. In demesne is 1 [plough], with 1 slave; and 12 villans, with 5 bordars, have 2 ploughs. There is a mill rendering 20s, and 20 acres of meadow. It was worth 40s; now £4.

IN CORBY HUNDRED

The same man holds 1 virgate of land in KIRBY. There is land for 2 ploughs. This [sic] is in demesne; and 5 villans, with 1 bordar, have another. There are 3 acres of meadow. [There is] woodland 4 furlongs in length and 1½ furlongs in breadth. It was worth 12d; now 6s.

LX. The land of William

IN ORLINGBURY HUNDRED

WILLIAM holds of the king 2 hides in PYTCHLEY. There is land for 4 ploughs. In demesne are 3 ploughs, and 5 slaves; and 7 villans, with 1 bordar, have 1 plough. There are 6 acres of meadow. [There is] woodland 3 furlongs in length and in breadth. It was worth 11s; it is now worth 40s. Alwine the huntsman held these lands of Richard's and William's TRE.

The same William holds LAXTON. There are 1½ hides. There is land for 4 ploughs. In demesne is 1 plough; and 12 villans with 1 sokeman have 2 ploughs. It was worth 10s; now 30s. Thorulf held it freely TRE.

OLAF holds of the king 1 virgate of land in GREAT WELDON. The soke is in the king's [manor of] CORBY. There is land for half a plough. This [half-plough] is there, with 1 bordar. It was worth 2s; now 3s.

DODIN holds of the king half a hide in COTTESBROOKE. There is land for 1 plough. There is 1 villan, with 1 slave. It was worth 12d; now 2s.

IN 'STOTFOLD' HUNDRED

OSLAC holds of the king 3 virgates of land and the third part of 1 virgate in EAST FARNDON. There is land for 1 plough. Nevertheless 2 ploughs are there, with 4 villans and 5 bordars. There is a mill rendering 12d. It was and is worth 16s.

[Folio 229V: [NORTHAMPTONSHIRE]]

Inquisition before William de Sabam and his colleagues among the Ragman Rolls of year the fourth Edward I [SC 5/8/3, m.26: 1275-6]

COUNTY OF NORTHAMPTON

HUNDRED OF SUTTON

How many hundreds, etc. They say that the county of Rutland was once an appurtenance of this county inasmuch as Lord Henry the king, father of our present lord king, gave it to the lord king of Germany, but they do not know of how the Hundred of Spelhoe agreed to this and many other hundreds. Many [areas] contained in Northamptonshire are now in Rutland. [Peter le Neve, 1684-1712]

[Extracted from the Nottinghamshire, Leicestershire and Lincolnshire folios of Great Domesday Book.]

In Rutland

I THE KING II Countess Judith III Robert Malet IIII Ogier V Gilbert de Ghent VI Earl Hugh VII Albert the clerk [Nottinghamshire f.280v]

[Folio 293V: RUTLAND]

In ALSTOE WAPENTAKE are 2 hundreds. In each [are] 12 carucates paying geld, and in each can be 24 ploughs. This wapentake is half in Thurgarton Wapentake and half in Broxtowe Wapentake.

In 'MARTINSLEY' WAPENTAKE is 1 hundred in which [are] 12 carucates of land paying geld, and there can be 48 ploughs, saving the king's 3 demesne manors, in which 14 teams can plough.

THESE 2 WAPENTAKES belong to the sheriffdom of Nottingham for [purposes of] the king's geld.

RUTLAND renders to the king £150 blanch.

ALSTOE WAPENTAKE

In GREETHAM Goda had 3 carucates of land paying geld. [There is] land for 8 ploughs. There the king has 2 ploughs in demesne; and 33 villans and 4 bordars having 8 ploughs, and 1 mill and 7 acres of meadow. [There is] woodland, for pannage in some places, 16 furlongs long and 7 furlongs broad. TRE worth £7; now £10.

In COTTESMORE Goda had 3 carucates of land paying geld. [There is] land for 12 ploughs. There the king has 3 ploughs in demesne; and 3 sokemen on half a carucate of this land; and 40 villans and 6 bordars having 20 ploughs. There are 40 acres of meadow. [There is] woodland 1 league long and 7 furlongs broad. TRE worth £7; now £10.

Of the land of this manor a certain Geoffrey has half a carucate, and has there 1 plough and 8 villans. It is worth 20s.

In MARKET OVERTON and STRETTON, a berewick, Earl Waltheof had 3½ carucates of land paying geld. [There is] land for 12 ploughs. There Countess Judith has 3 ploughs; and 35 villans and 8 bordars having 9 ploughs, and 40 acres of meadow. [There is] woodland, for pannage in places, 1 league long and half a league broad TRE worth £12; now £20. Alvred of Lincoln claims a fourth part of Stretton.

In THISTLETON Erik had half a carucate of land paying geld. [There is] land for 1 plough. There Hugh has of Countess Judith 1 plough; and 6 villans with 1 plough. TRE worth 20s; now 40s.

IN THE SAME PLACE Siward had half a carucate of land paying geld. [There is] land for 1 plough. There Alvred of Lincoln has 1 plough; and 3 villans and 2 bordars with half a plough. TRE worth 20s; now 60s.

In the same hundred, in TEIGH, Godwine had 1½ carucates of land paying geld. [There is] land for 5 ploughs. There Robert Malet has 2 ploughs; and 15 villans with 4 ploughs. [There is] meadow 4 furlongs in length and 3 furlongs in breadth. There is 1 mill [rendering] 2s. TRE worth £4; now the same.

In WHISSENDINE Earl Waltheof had 4 carucates of land paying geld. [There is] land for 12 ploughs. There Hugh de Hotot has of the countess 5 ploughs; and 27 villans and 6 bordars having 8 ploughs. TRE worth £8; now £13.

In EXTON Earl Waltheof had 2 carucates of land paying geld. [There is] land for 12 ploughs. There Countess Judith has 3 ploughs; and 37 villans with 8 ploughs, and 2 mills [rendering] 13s. [There is] meadow 6 furlongs in length. [There is] woodland, for pannage in places, 5 furlongs long and 5 broad. TRE it was worth £8; now £10.

In WHITWELL Besi had 1 carucate of land paying geld. [There is] land for 3 ploughs. There Herbert has of Countess Judith 1 plough; and 6 villans and 4 bordars having 2 ploughs. There is a church and a priest, and 20 acres of meadow and 1 mill [rendering] 12d. [There is] woodland, for pannage in places, 6 furlongs and 6 perches in length and 3 furlongs and 13 perches in breadth. TRE it was worth 40s; now 40[s.].

In 'AWSTHORP' [in Burley] Leofric had 1 carucate of land paying geld. [There is] land for 5 ploughs. There Ogier fitzUngemar has of the king 2 ploughs; and 11 villans and 4 bordars with 4 ploughs, and 16 acres of meadow. [There is] woodland pasture 3 furlongs long and 2 broad. TRE as now, worth 40s.

In BURLEY Ulf had 2 carucates of land paying geld. [There is] land for 7 ploughs. There Geoffrey, the man of Gilbert de Ghent, has 2 ploughs; and 30 villans and 8 bordars having 4 ploughs, and 30 acres of meadow. [There is] woodland, for pannage in places; 1 league long and 3 furlongs broad. TRE worth £4; now 100s.

In ASHWELL Earl Harold had 2 carucates of land paying

geld. [There is] land for 6 ploughs. There Joscelin, Earl Hugh's man, has 2 ploughs; and 13 villans and 3 bordars having 5 ploughs, and 16 acres of meadow. TRE worth 100s; now £6.

'MARTINSLEY' WAPENTAKE

In OAKHAM, with its 5 berewicks, church sokeland, Queen Edith had 4 carucates of land paying geld. [There is] land for 16 ploughs. There the king has 2 ploughs [belonging] to the hall, and nevertheless there can be 4 other ploughs. There are 138 villans and 19 bordars having 37 ploughs, and 80 acres of meadow. There is a priest and a church to which 4 bovates of this land belong. [There is] woodland pasture 1 league long and half a league broad. TRE worth £40.

IN THE SAME PLACE Leofnoth had 1 carucate of land paying geld. Fulcher Malsor has there 5 oxen in a plough and 6 acres of meadow. TRE as now, [worth] 20s.

The whole manor with its berewicks [is] 3 leagues long and 1 league and 8 furlongs broad.

In HAMBLETON, with its 7 berewicks, church sokeland, Queen Edith had 4 carucates of land paying geld. [There is] land for 16 ploughs. There the king has 5 ploughs in demesne; and 140 villans and 13 bordars having 40 ploughs. There are 3 priests and 3 churches to which 1 bovate and 8 acres of land belong. There is 1 mill [rendering] 21s4d, and 40 acres of meadow. [There is] scrubland, bearing mast in places, 3 leagues long and 1½ leagues broad. TRE worth £52.

The whole manor with its berewicks [is] 3 leagues and 8 furlongs long and 2 leagues and 8 furlongs broad.

In RIDLINGTON, with its 7 berewicks, church sokeland, Queen Edith had 4 carucates of land paying geld. [There is] land for 16 ploughs. There the king has 4 ploughs in demesne; and 170 villans and 26 bordars having 30 ploughs and 2 sokemen with 2 ploughs. There are 2 priests and 3 churches and 2 sites for mills, and 40 acres of meadow. [There is] woodland, for pannage in places, 2 leagues long and 8 furlongs broad. TRE worth £40.

The whole manor with its berewicks [is] 3 leagues and 7 furlongs long and 2 leagues and 2 furlongs broad.

[Folio 294: LINCOLNSHIRE]

In the above land Albert the clerk has 1 bovate of land and has there 1 mill [rendering] 16d. The same Albert also has of the king the church of Oakham and of Hambleton and of St Peter of Stamford [Lincs.] which belongs to Hambleton with the lands attached to the same churches, that is, 7 bovates. In this his land there can be 8 ploughs, and nevertheless 16 teams plough there. He himself has there 4 ploughs in demesne; and 18 villans and 6 bordars having 5 ploughs. TRE worth £8; now £10.

[The land of the King]

In Knossington [Leics.] are 3 carucates of land belonging to the soke of OAKHAM. There 17 sokemen with 6 bordars have 6 ploughs, and there is woodland 1 furlong in length and half a furlong in breadth. It is worth 20s. The king has it in demesne. [f.230v]

STAMFORD [Lincs.], A ROYAL BOROUGH, paid geld TRE for 12½ hundreds, for military service by land and sea and for Danegeld. There were and are 6 wards, 5 in Lincolnshire, and the sixth in Northamptonshire which is over the bridge and nevertheless it rendered all customary dues with the others, except for rent and toll, which the Abbot of Peterborough had and has.

Queen Edith had 70 messuages which lay in Rutland with all customary dues except the bakers'. To these belong 2½ carucates of land and 1 plough and 45 acres of meadow outside the vill. Now King William has it, and it is worth £6; TRE worth £4.

Albert [has] 1 church, St Peter's, with 2 messuages and half a carucate of land which lies in Rutland in Hambleton. It is worth 10s. [f.336v]

[The land of Earl Hugh]

In ASHWELL Earl Harold had 2 carucates of land paying geld. [There is] land for 6 ploughs. There Joscelin, Earl Hugh's man, has 2 ploughs; and 13 villans and 2 bordars having 5 ploughs, and 16 acres of meadow. TRE worth 100s; now £6. [f.349v]

[The land of Gilbert de Ghent]

In BURLEY Ulf had 2 carucates of land paying geld. [There is] land for 7 ploughs. There Geoffrey, Gilbert's man, has 2 ploughs; and 30 villans and 7 bordars with 4 ploughs, and 30 acres of meadow. [There is] woodland 1 league long and 3 furlongs wide. TRE worth £4; now 100s. [f.355V]

[The land of Alvred of Lincoln]

In SOUTH WITHAM [Lincs.] Siward had 4 carucates of land paying geld. [There is] land for 4 ploughs. There Gleu, Alvred's man, has 1 plough; and 11 villans and 3 bordars with 3 ploughs, and 100 acres of meadow less 6, and 80 acres of woodland pasture. TRE worth 40s; now 50[s]; from tallage, 10s. This soke is in Thistleton.

In THISTLETON Siward had half a carucate of land paying geld. [There is] land for 1 plough. There Gleu, Alvred's man, has 1 plough; and 3 villans and 2 bordars with half a plough. Its value [is] in [with] South Witham [Lincs.]. Soke.

In another Thistleton [there is] 1 carucate of land paying geld. [There is] land for 1 plough. There 2 sokemen have 3 oxen in a plough. [f.358v]

[The land of Godfrey de Cambrai]

In THISTLETON Thorfridh had 1½ carucates paying geld. [There is] land for 12 oxen. There Gleu, Godfrey's man, has 1 sokeman and 3 bordars with half a plough, and 15 acres of woodland, and 40 acres in Drogo's warnode. TRE worth 20s; now 10[s]. [f.366]

[The land of Countess Judith]

In Uffington [Lincs.] Leofric, Abbot of Peterborough, had 60 acres of land free of geld [...]. Countess Judith has this land. She has no livestock on it but cultivates it in the manor of Belmesthorpe. It is worth 10s. [f.366v]

In MARKET OVERTON and Stretton Earl Waltheof had 3½ carucates of land paying geld. [There is] land for 12 ploughs. There Countess Judith has 3 ploughs in demesne; and 35 villans and 8 bordars with 9 ploughs, [f.366v.] and 40 acres of meadow, and woodland pasture 1 league long and a half wide. TRE worth £12; now £40.

In THISTLETON Erik had half a carucate of land paying geld. [There is] land for 1 plough. There Hugh, the countess's man, has 1 plough; and 6 villans with 1 plough. TRE worth 20s; now 40[s].

In WHISSENDINE Earl Waltheof had 4 carucates of land paying geld. [There is] land for 12 ploughs. There Hugh, the countess's man, has 5 ploughs in demesne; and 27 villans and 7 bordars with 8 ploughs. [There is] meadow 10 furlongs long and 8 furlongs wide. [f.367]

IN RUTLAND

In EXTON Earl Waltheof had 2 carucates of land paying geld. [There is] land for 12 ploughs. There Countess Judith has 3 ploughs; and 37 villans with 8 ploughs, and 2 mills [rendering] 13s. [There is] meadow 6 furlongs long. [There is] woodland, pasture in places, 5 furlongs long and 5 wide. TRE worth £8; now £10.

In WHITWELL Besi had 1 carucate of land paying geld. [There is] land for 3 ploughs. There Herbert, the countess's man, has 1 plough; and 6 villans and 4 bordars with 2 ploughs. There is a church and a priest, and 1 mill [rendering] 12d, and 20 acres of meadow. [There is] woodland pasture 6 furlongs and 6 perches long and 3 furlongs and 13 perches wide. It is worth 40s.

In COLEBY [Lincs.] Arnketil had 5 carucates of land paying geld. [There is] land for 5 ploughs. There Countess Judith has 1 plough; and 1 sokeman with 1 carucate of this land, and 6 villans with 1 plough, and 30 acres of meadow. TRE worth 60s; now 40[s].

In SOUTH WITHAM [Lincs.] [there are] 2 carucates of land paying geld. [There is] land for 2 ploughs. The soke [is] in Market Overton. There 8 sokemen and 2 villans and 1 bordar have 3 ploughs. There is half a church, and 60 acres of meadow, and 100 acres of woodland.

In Thistleton [there are] 6 bovates of land paying geld. [There is] land for 6 oxen. The soke [is] in the same manor. There 2 bordars have 2 oxen in a plough. It is worth 10s. Hugh holds it.

In Bicker [Lincs.] [there are] $1\frac{1}{2}$ bovates of land paying geld. [There is] land for 2 oxen. Demesne in South Witham [Lincs.]. It is waste, except for a salt-pan. [f.367 cont.]

[Claims In Lincolnshire]

The wapentake says that Peterborough [Abbey] had, TRE, 60 acres of land which Countess Judith has and cultivates with the ploughs of Belmesthorpe. The warnode of these 60 acres of land and of 48 acres of meadow lies in Alvred of Lincoln's Uffington [Lincs.], but has been withheld by force.

Archbishop Ealdræd acquired 'Lavington' [Lincs.] and Skillington [Lincs.] with the BEREWICK Hardwick from Ulf Topi's son with his own money which he gave to him in the witness of the wapentake, and afterwards they saw the king's seal, through which he was reseised of these lands, because Ilbod had disseised him of them. [f.376v]

LEICESTERSHIRE

In the time of King EDWARD THE CITY of LEICESTER rendered to the king £30 a year by tale at 20[d] to the ora and 15 sesters of honey.

When the king went with his army by land 12 burgesses from this borough went with him. If, however, he went against an enemy by sea they sent him 4 horses from the same borough as far as London to carry weapons or other things of which there might be need.

King William now has £42.10s. by weight for all the rents of the same city and shire. For a hawk, £10 by tale. For a sumpter horse, 20s. From the moneyers, £20 a year at 20[d] to the ora. Of these £20 Hugh de Grandmesnil has the third penny.

The king has in LEICESTER 39 houses.

The Archbishop of York, 2 houses with sake and soke and pertaining to Tur Langton.

Earl Hugh, 10 houses which pertain to Barrow upon Soar and 6 houses pertaining to Kegworth and 1 house pertaining to Loughborough.

The Abbey of Coventry has 10 houses.

The Abbey of Crowland has 3 houses. From all these the king has his geld.

Hugh de Grandmesnil has 110 houses and 2 churches.

Besides these he has 24 houses in common with the king in the same borough.

Besides these the same Hugh has in Leicester 24 burgesses pertaining to Anstey and 13 burgesses pertaining to Sileby and 3 houses pertaining to Ingarsby and 10 houses pertaining to Belgrave and 4 houses pertaining to Broughton Astley and 9 houses pertaining to Stockerston and 4 houses pertaining to Wigston Magna and 7 houses pertaining to Enderby and 3 houses pertaining to Earl Shilton and 10 houses pertaining to Birstall and 3 houses pertaining to Burton Overy and 1 house pertaining to 'Bromkinsthorpe' [in St Mary, Leicester] and 2 houses pertaining to Desford and 3 houses pertaining to "Legham", which he bought of Osbern, and 1 house pertaining to "Letitone" and 1 house pertaining to Thurcaston.

In the same borough the same Hugh has 2 churches, and 2 houses and 4 waste houses.

Hugh de Gouville holds 5 houses of Hugh himself with sake and soke. These are in exchange for Watford [Northants].

Robert de Vessey has 6 houses with sake and soke pertaining to Newton Harcourt, and 3 others with sake and soke pertaining to Kibworth Harcourt.

Geoffrey de la Guerche [has] 1 house pertaining to Little Dalby and another pertaining to Pickwell.

In Leicester are 4 houses pertaining to Shepshed and 1 pertaining to Saddington and 1 pertaining to Thorpe Acre.

In this borough Henry de Ferrers and Robert Despenser has [sic] 1 burgess.

Countess JUDITH has 28 houses in the same borough, and 5s4d. from half a mill. Outside the borough she herself has 6 carucates of land belonging to the borough, and has there 1 plough, and her men [have] 3 ploughs. There are 8 acres of meadow, [and] woodland 6 furlongs long and 3 furlongs broad. The whole is worth 40s.

The woodland of the whole sheriffdom is called "HERESWODE". It is †4† leagues in length and 1 league in breadth.

Here Are Entered the Holders of Lands In Leicestershire

I KING WILLIAM
II The Archbishop of York
III The Bishop of Lincoln
IIII The Bishop of Coutances
V The Abbey of Peterborough
VI The Abbey of Coventry
VII The Abbey of Crowland
VIII Godwine the priest and other almsmen
IX The Count of Meulan
X Earl Aubrey
XI Countess Godgifu
XII Countess Ælfgifu
XIII Earl Hugh
XIIII Hugh de Grandmesnil
XV Henry de Ferrers
XVI Robert de Tosny
XVII Robert de Vessey
XVIII Roger de Bully
XIX Robert Despenser
XX Robert the usher
XXI Ralph de Mortimer
XXII Ralph fitzHubert
XXIII Guy de Raimbeaucourt
XXIIII Guy de Craon
XXV William Peverel
XXVI William Bonvalet
XXVII William Lovet
XXVIII Geoffrey Alselin

XXIX Geoffrey de la Guerche
XXX Godfrey de Cambrai
XXXI Gunfrid de Chocques
XXXII Humphrey the chamberlain
XXXIII Gilbert de Ghent
XXXIIII Gerbert
XXXV Durand Malet
XXXVI Drogo de la Beuvriere
XXXVII Mainou the Breton
XXXVIII Ogier the Breton
XXXIX Nigel d'Aubigny
XL Countess Judith
XLI Adeliza wife of Hugh
XLII Herbert and other sergeants of the king
XLIIII The men of the Count of Meulan

The land of the King

IN FRAMLAND WAPENTAKE

The king holds CROXTON KERRIAL. There are 24 carucates of land. In demesne are 2 ploughs and 5 slaves; and 22 villans with 2 bordars have 2½ ploughs, and 30 sokemen have 8 ploughs. There are 30 acres of meadow, and 2 mills rendering 8s.

To this manor pertains KNIPTON. There are 8 carucates of land and 6 bovates. In demesne are 2 ploughs and 4 slaves; and 10 villans with 4 bordars and 10 sokemen have 4 ploughs. There are 6 mills rendering 13s4d, and 13 acres of meadow.

To the same manor pertains HARSTON. There are 12 carucates of land. There 20 sokemen with 5 villans and 1 bordar have 6½ ploughs. There are 17 acres of meadow. The whole was worth £10; now £17.

The king holds NETHER BROUGHTON. There are 12 carucates of land. In demesne is 1 plough; and 24 sokemen with 9 villans and 4 bordars have 12 ploughs. There are 100 acres of meadow. It was worth £3; now £8. Earl Morcar held these 2 manors. Now Hugh fitzBaldric holds them at farm of the king.

The king holds ROTHLEY. King Edward held it. There are 5 carucates of land. In demesne are 2 of these and there are 2 ploughs; and 29 villans with a priest and 18 bordars have 6 ploughs. There is a mill rendering 4s, and 37 acres of meadow. [There is] demesne woodland 1 league long and half a league broad, [and] woodland of the villans 4 furlongs long and 3 furlongs broad. This vill is worth 62s. a year.

To this manor belong the following members:

[Folio 230V: LEICESTERSHIRE]

In ALLEXTON are 6 bovates of land. It is waste.

In Barsby, 5 carucates of land, less 1 bovate, and 15 acres of meadow.

In Seagrave, 6 carucates of land, and meadow 3 furlongs in length and 1½ furlongs in breadth.

In Sileby, 2 carucates of land and 2 bovates, and 10 acres of meadow.

In Tugby, 6 carucates of land, and 10 acres of meadow, [and] woodland 2 furlongs long and 1 furlong broad.

In Skeffington, 12 carucates of land, and a mill rendering 12d, [and] woodland 3 furlongs long and 2 furlongs broad.

In Marefield [Marefield or 'North Marefield'], 3 carucates of land, and 8 acres of meadow.

In another Marefield [Marefield or 'North Marefield'], 3 carucates of land, and 8 acres of meadow.

In Halstead, 3 carucates of land, less 2 bovates, and 1 acre of meadow, [and] woodland 1 furlong long and another broad.

In Chadwell and Wycomb, 4 carucates of land, and 2 mills rendering 2s.

In Tilton on the Hill, 2 carucates of land, and 4 acres of meadow and 5 acres of woodland.

In Asfordby, 12 carucates of land, and 2 mills rendering 8s, and 20 acres of meadow.

In Keyham, 4 carucates of land, and 8 acres of meadow.

In Wartnaby, 6 carucates of land, and 10 acres of meadow.

In Twyford, 4½ carucates of land, and 8 acres of meadow.

In Somerby, 1½ carucates of land, and 6 acres of meadow.

In Frisby on the Wreake, 8 carucates of land, and 4 acres of meadow, and 2s. from part of a mill.

In Saxelby, 1 carucate of land, and 5 acres of meadow.

In Grimston, 3 carucates of land, less 1½ bovates.

In Baggrave, 6 carucates of land, less 3 bovates, and 10 acres of meadow.

In Gaddesby, 8 carucates of land and 3 bovates, and 12 acres of meadow.

In these are 204 sokemen with 157 villans and 94 bordars having 82 ploughs, and among them all they pay £31.8s.1d.

The king holds GREAT BOWDEN. King Edward held it. There are 9½ carucates of land. In demesne are 2 ploughs; and 13 sokemen with 8 villans and 16 bordars have 13½ ploughs, and pay 30s. a year. There are [...] acres of meadow. The demesne is worth 40s. a year.

In Medbourne are 2 carucates of land, and 6½ acres of meadow.

In Cranoe, 1 †carucate† of land. In Shangton, 2 carucates of land.

In Carlton Curlieu, 6 bovates of land. In Illston on the Hill, 2 bovates of land.

In Gaulby, 1½ carucates of land, and 4 acres of meadow.

In King's Norton, 3 carucates of land, and 5 acres of meadow.

In Stretton [Little Stretton and 'Stretton Magna'], 9 carucates of land, and 10 acres of meadow. In Smeeton Westerby, 1 carucate of land and 2 bovates.

In Foxton, 2 carucates of land, and 5 acres of meadow.

In these are 60 sokemen with 2 villans and 16 bordars having 13 ploughs, and they pay 150s. and 18d.

The king has the soke of 2 carucates in Blaston, and it belongs to Great Bowden. Robert de Tosny holds this land. This sokeland is worth 11s.0½d.

Humphrey the chamberlain holds at farm 2 carucates of land of the king's sokeland in "ABEGRAVE", and has there

1 plough, with 4 villans and 2 bordars who have 1 plough. There are 6 acres of meadow. It was worth 12d; now 20s.

IN GARTREE WAPENTAKE

The king holds SADDINGTON. There is 1 hide, less 1 carucate. In demesne is 1 plough; and 11 sokemen and 17 villans with 5 bordars having 8 ploughs. There is a mill rendering 2s, and 10 acres of meadow. It was worth £4; now £9.

In WHATBOROUGH are 3 carucates of land. In demesne is half a plough; and 3 villans with 1 sokeman and 11 bordars have 4 ploughs. [There is] meadow 1 furlong long and 1 broad, [and] woodland 5 furlongs long and 3 furlongs broad. It was worth 10s; now 40s.

To Whatborough belong 1½ carucates of land in 'Burfielde' [in Loddington], and there is 1 plough, with 1 villan.

In THORPE ACRE are 5 carucates of land. There 16 villans with 3 sokemen and 8 bordars have 6 ploughs. There are 30 acres of meadow. It was worth £3; now £7.

In DISHLEY is 1 hide. There 16 villans and 16 sokemen with 1 bordar have 8 ploughs. There 2 mills render 5s, and [there are] 10 acres of meadow, [and] woodland 4 furlongs long and as much broad. It was waste; now it is worth 40s.

Queen Edith held these lands. Now Godwine has them of the king at farm. DISHLEY, however, he holds of the king in fief.

The same Godwine holds of the king in fief 2½ hides and 4 carucates of land in SHEPSHED. Asgot held them with sake and soke. In demesne he has 2 ploughs and 2 slaves; and 30 villans with 12 bordars have 15 ploughs, and 20 sokemen with 2 knights and 6 villans and 4 bordars have 21 ploughs. There is a mill rendering 5s, and 50 acres of meadow, [and] woodland 1 league long and 4 furlongs broad. He found this land waste.

From this land come £6 as farm by the order of the Bishop of Bayeux for the service on the Isle of Wight.

In KNOSSINGTON are 3 carucates of land belonging to the sokeland of OAKHAM [Rut.]. There 17 sokemen with 6 bordars have 6 ploughs, and there is woodland 1 furlong in length and half a furlong in breadth. It is worth 20s. The king has it in demesne.

The king holds BITTESBY. Leofwine held it TRE. There are 5 carucates of land. [There is] land for 4 ploughs. In demesne is 1 plough; and 10 villans with 4 bordars have 2 ploughs. There are 20 acres of meadow. It was worth 30s; now 40s.

II. The land of the [Arch] Bishop of York

IN GARTREE WAPENTAKE

THE ARCHBISHOP of York holds TUR LANGTON, and Walkelin [holds] of him. There are 13 carucates of land with [?West] LANGTON which pertains there. In demesne are 3 ploughs and 4 slaves and 2 female slaves; and 20 villans with 4 bordars have 6 ploughs. There are 20 acres of meadow,

[and] woodland 3 furlongs long and 2 furlongs broad. In the same vill Herbert holds of Walkelin 3 carucates of land, and has there 1 plough in demesne; and 5 villans and 2 sokemen with 2 bordars have 3 ploughs. There are 12 acres of meadow. The whole was worth 20s; now 60s.

The same Walkelin holds LUBENHAM of the archbishop, and Robert [holds] of him. There are 8 carucates of land. In demesne are 2 ploughs and 2 slaves and 2 female slaves; and 6 villans with 4 bordars have 3 ploughs.

In the same vill 1 knight holds 3 carucates of land of Robert, and has there 1 plough in demesne; and 5 villans with 1 bordar have 1½ ploughs. There are 36 acres of meadow. The whole was worth 20s; now 40s. Arnketil and Osmund and Oslac held it with sake and soke.

Osbern holds of the archbishop 2 carucates of land in WELHAM. In demesne is 1 plough and 3 slaves; and 4 villans with 1 bordar have 2 ploughs. There are 18 acres of meadow. It was worth 4s; now 20s. Arnketil held it.

The same Osbern holds of the archbishop 2 carucates of land in KEYTHORPE. In demesne he has 1 plough with 1 slave; and 1 Frenchman with 2 villans and 2 bordars have 1 plough. There are 40 acres of woodland. It was worth 4s; now 12s. Arnketil held it with sake and soke.

Hugh holds of the archbishop 1 carucate of land in TILTON ON THE HILL, and Friendai [holds] of him. There is 1 plough, with 4 villans and 2 bordars. It was and is worth 10s. This land belongs to the almsland of ST MARY of Southwell. Gytha held it TRE.

III. The land of the Bishop of Lincoln

THE BISHOP OF LINCOLN holds 10 carucates of land in LEICESTER. In demesne he has there 5 ploughs, and 1½ mills rendering 10s8d, and 2 churches rendering 15s, and 7 burgesses paying 32d. a year. From a part of the land, outside the wall, he has 5s4d, and 3 villans with a priest and 12 bordars have 4 ploughs. There are 20 acres of meadow.

[Folio 231: LEICESTERSHIRE]

The same bishop holds KNIGHTON. There are 2 parts of 1 hide. There is land for 6 ploughs. There 20 villans with 4 sokemen have 6 ploughs. There are 30 acres of meadow.

The same bishop holds 1 carucate of land in LEIRE. There are 2 sokemen with 1 bordar having half a plough.

These lands of ST MARY of Lincoln are worth £6.2s.4d.

Robert holds of the bishop in SHARNFORD 1 carucate of land. There can be 1 plough. There are 2 bordars. It is worth 4s.

Ralph holds of the bishop 2 carucates of land in COTES-DE-VAL. There can be 2 ploughs, and they are there, with 4 sokemen. It was worth 20d; now 10s.

The same Ralph holds of the bishop 4 carucates of land in [Great and Middle] POULTNEY. There is land for 4 ploughs. In demesne are 2 [ploughs] and 4 slaves and 1 female slave; and 9 villans and 9 burgesses in the city with 5 bordars have 2 ploughs. There are 2 acres of meadow. It was worth 20s; now 30s.

The same man holds of the bishop in MISTERTON 3½ carucates of land, and 1 carucate of land which renders soke. There is land for 3 ploughs. There 4 villans with 2 sokemen and 1 villan and 1 bordar have 2 ploughs. There are 6 acres of meadow. It was worth 11s; now 10s.

The same man holds of the bishop in WALCOTE 4 carucates of land, and 2 carucates of land which render soke. There is land for 3 ploughs. In demesne is 1 [plough] with 1 slave; and 3 villans with 1 bordar have 1 plough, and 2 sokemen have 1 plough. There is a mill rendering 10d, and 12 acres of meadow. It was worth 10s; now 20s.

The same man holds of the bishop in KIMCOTE 13½ carucates of land. There is land for 8 ploughs. In demesne is 1 [plough]; and 6 sokemen and 6 villans with 7 bordars have 4 ploughs. There are 10 acres of meadow. It was worth 30s; now 40s.

Ulf holds of the same Ralph 2 bovates of land in SWINFORD, and they are worth 12d. Godric held these lands of Ralph's TRE.

IN GARTREE WAPENTAKE

Ranulph holds of the bishop in HOLYOAKS 3 carucates of land. In demesne are 2 ploughs with 1 slave; and 4 villans with 2 bordars have 1 plough. There is a mill rendering 5s4d, [and] woodland 4 furlongs long and 3 furlongs broad. It was and is worth 20s. Barthi held it.

IN 'GOSCOTE' WAPENTAKE

Godfrey holds of the bishop 8 carucates of land in GREAT DALBY. There is land for 6 ploughs. In demesne are 3 ploughs and 2 slaves; and 7 villans and 16 sokemen have 6 ploughs. There are 6 furlongs of meadow in length and in breadth. It was worth 60s; now 70[s]. Godric held it with sake and soke. In this vill 1 knight holds 1 carucate of land, and it is worth 10s.

Roger holds of the bishop 4 carucates of land in SOUTH CROXTON. In demesne is 1 plough; and 4 villans with 2 bordars have 1 plough. There is a mill rendering 12d, and 6 acres of meadow. It was worth 5s; now 20s. Godric held it.

IN FRAMLAND WAPENTAKE

Ralph holds of the bishop in BRANSTON 7½ carucates of land. In demesne are 2 ploughs and 4 slaves; and 10 villans with 1 bordar and 6 sokemen have 4 ploughs. There are 2 mills rendering 8s, and 16 acres of meadow. It was worth 20s; now 50s. Leofnoth held it.

R[...] fitzWalter holds of the bishop in BUCKMINSTER 9½ carucates of land. There is land for 8 ploughs. In demesne are 2 [ploughs]; and 8 villans and 20 sokemen with 3 bordars have 8 ploughs. There are 52 acres of meadow. It was worth 4s; now £4. Healfdene held it with sake and soke.

Ketilbiorn holds of the bishop 1 carucate of land in

HOLWELL. There is land for 1 plough. 3 villans with 2 bordars have this [plough] there. There are 10 acres of meadow. It was worth 5s; now 6s. Wulfgeat held it with sake and soke.

IIII. The land of the Bishop of Coutances

IN GUTHLAXTON WAPENTAKE

THE BISHOP of Coutances holds in ARNESBY 2½ carucates of land and 1 bovate. Wulfric holds them of him. There is land for 2½ ploughs. In demesne is 1 [plough] with 1 slave; and 3 villans and 2 bordars have 1 plough. It is worth 20s.

V. The land of Peterborough [Abbey]

PETERBOROUGH ABBEY holds in WEST LANGTON 5 carucates of land, less 2 bovates. There is land for 5 ploughs. In demesne is 1 [plough]; and 9 villans with 2 bordars have 3 ploughs. There are 8 acres of meadow and 5 acres of woodland. It was worth 10s; now 40s. Æthelmaer held it freely TRE.

The abbey itself holds in GREAT EASTON 12 carucates of land. There is land for 16 ploughs. In demesne are 2 ploughs; and 10 villans with 5 bordars and 12 sokemen have 8 ploughs. There is woodland half a league long and 4 furlongs broad. There are 30 acres of meadow. It was worth £6; now 100s. Earl Ralph gave it to ST PETER.

Two knights hold in this vill 2 carucates of land of the abbot. There 10 villans have 2 ploughs, and 10 acres of meadow. It was worth 40s; now 100s.

VI. The land of St Mary of Coventry

IN GUTHLAXTON WAPENTAKE

THE ABBEY OF COVENTRY holds BURBAGE. There is 1 hide and the fourth part of 1 hide. There are 22½ carucates of land. In demesne are 2 ploughs; and 20 villans with 2 bordars and 2 slaves have 8 ploughs. There is meadow 1 furlong long and as much broad, [and] woodland half a league long and 4 furlongs broad. It was worth 2s. when the abbey received it; now £4.

The abbey itself holds 3 carucates of land in POTTERS MARSTON. There is land for 2 ploughs. 3 sokemen with 5 bordars have these [ploughs] there. There are 8 acres of meadow. It was worth 12d; now 10s.

The abbey itself holds 4 carucates of land in BARWELL. In demesne is 1 plough; and 14 villans with a priest and 3 bordars have 2 ploughs. There is meadow 1 furlong long and as much broad, [and] woodland 1 league long and 3 furlongs broad. It is worth 30s. In this vill are 8 sokemen having 5 ploughs. To this vill pertains 1 carucate of land in STAPLETON whose resources are here written above.

IN GARTREE WAPENTAKE

The abbey itself holds SCRAPTOFT. There are 12 carucates of land. In demesne are 2 ploughs and 4 slaves; and 7 villans with 6 sokemen and 3 bordars have 5 ploughs. There are 10 acres of meadow. It was worth 2s; now 40s.

IN 'GOSCOTE' WAPENTAKE

The abbey itself holds 8½ carucates of land in PACKINGTON. In demesne is 1 plough; and 3 villans with a priest and 1 bordar and 5 sokemen have 3 ploughs. There is a mill rendering 12d, and 3 acres of meadow. It is worth 20s.

In KIRBY MUXLOE Hugh holds 1½ carucates of land of the abbot. It is worth 2s.

VII. The land of the Church of Crowland

IN GUTHLAXTON WAPENTAKE

CROWLAND ABBEY holds 2 carucates of land in SUTTON CHENEY and 2 carucates of land in STAPLETON. There is land for 5 ploughs. There 6 villans with 2 bordars have 1½ ploughs. It was worth 24s; now 20s.

The abbey itself holds in BEEBY 10½ carucates of land. There is land for 7 ploughs. In demesne is 1 [plough] and 2 slaves; and 21 villans with 5 sokemen and 3 bordars have 6 ploughs. There are 30 acres of meadow. It was worth 60s; now 40s.

VIII. The Almsland of the King

GODWINE the priest holds of the king in PEATLING MAGNA half a carucate of land, and has there half a plough, and 1½ acres of meadow. It was and is worth 5s.

The wife of Quentin holds of the king 2 carucates of land in SHEARSBY and 2 others in SUTTON IN THE ELMS. In these she has 2 bordars. There is land for 2 ploughs. It was worth 15s. now 3s.

Ingald holds of the king in ILLSTON ON THE HILL 2 carucates of land and 1 virgate. There he has 1 plough, and 2 villans with 1 sokeman have half a plough. It was worth 10s; now 5s.

Arnbiorn the priest holds of the king 2½ carucates of land in SWINFORD, and has there 1 plough, with 2 bordars, and 3 acres of meadow. It is worth 5s.

Ælfric the priest holds of the king in WIGSTON PARVA 2 carucates of land belonging to SHARNFORD. There he has 1 plough, and 5 bordars of his have another. There are 4 acres of meadow. It was and is worth 20s.

[Folio 231V: LEICESTERSHIRE]

IX. The land of the Count of Meulan

IN GUTHLAXTON WAPENTAKE

THE COUNT OF MEULAN holds AYLESTONE of the king. There is 1 hide and the sixth part of 1 hide. There were 14 ploughs TRE. In demesne are 2 ploughs and 1 female slave; and 24 villans with 5 bordars have 5 ploughs. There are 4 mills rendering 48s, and 55 acres of meadow. It was worth £3; now £4.

Saxi held, and Leofwine [held] of him, land for 6 ploughs [...], in such a way that with 4 of these he could do what he wished. [But] with 2 [it was] not so.

The count himself holds FROLESWORTH. There is half a carucate of land. There 2 sokemen have half a plough. It was worth 2s; now 5s.

The same count holds 6 carucates of land in HUNCOTE. There is land for 6 ploughs. In demesne are 3 [ploughs] and 2 slaves and 1 female slave; and 20 villans with 8 bordars have 3 ploughs, and there are 2 sokemen with a priest, and a mill rendering 10s, and 15 acres of meadow. [There is] woodland half a league long and 4 furlongs broad. It was worth 15s; now £4.

In COSBY is 1 carucate of land which belongs to HUNCOTE.

The same count holds 6 carucates of land in MARKET BOSWORTH. In demesne are 3 ploughs and 2 slaves; and 7 sokemen with 10 villans and 7 bordars have 2 ploughs. [There is] woodland 1 league long and half a league broad. It was worth £4; now 50s.

Saxi held all these lands and could go where he wished.

X. The land of Earl Aubrey

IN GUTHLAXTON WAPENTAKE

EARL AUBREY held KNAPTOFT. There are 2 parts of 1 hide. There is land for 6 ploughs. In demesne is 1 [plough] and 3 slaves; and 10 villans with a priest and 2 sokemen and 6 bordars have 5 ploughs. There is meadow 3 furlongs long and 2 furlongs broad. It was worth 20s; now 50s.

The same man held SAPCOTE. There are 1½ carucates of land. There are 1½ ploughs, with 2 sokemen and 2 bordars. Wulfric holds it. It was worth 2s; now 10s.

The same earl held HINCKLEY. There are 14 carucates of land. In demesne are 4 ploughs and 8 slaves; and 42 villans with 16 bordars and 3 sokemen have 9½ ploughs. There is meadow 6 furlongs in length and 3 furlongs in breadth, [and] woodland 1 league long and 3 furlongs broad. It was worth £6; now £10.

The same earl held 9 carucates of land in SIBSON. In demesne are 2 ploughs and 1 female slave; and 30 villans and 17 bordars have 7 ploughs. [There is] meadow 3 furlongs long and 2 furlongs broad. In the same vill there are in addition 2 carucates of land. The whole was worth 60s; now 100s.

The same earl held 1 carucate of land in SHENTON. There are 3 bordars. It was worth 12d; now 3s. Hearding held these lands.

Norman holds 4½ carucates of land in SHEARSBY. In demesne are 2 ploughs; and 4 villans with 2 sokemen and 3 bordars have 2 ploughs. [There is] meadow 4 furlongs long and 2 furlongs broad. It was worth 15s; now 40s.

Ralph holds in CROFT 4½ carucates of land and 1 bovate. In demesne is 1 plough and 2 slaves; and 8 villans with 1 sokeman and 4 bordars have 2 ploughs. There is a mill rendering 4s, and 12 acres of meadow. It was worth 68d; now 40s.

To this manor pertains 1 carucate of land. Part of it [is] in Broughton Astley and part in Sutton in the Elms. It was waste; now it is worth 5s.

Almær holds 5½ carucates of land in FENNY DRAYTON. There is land for 5 ploughs. In demesne are 2 [ploughs]; and 14 villans with 8 bordars have 3 ploughs. It was worth 30s; now 40s.

Robert holds 8½ carucates of land in BITTESWELL. There is land for 6 ploughs. In demesne is 1 [plough]; and 2 villans with a priest and 14 bordars have 3 ploughs. [There is] meadow 4 furlongs long and 1 furlong broad. It was worth 10s; now 40s.

The same man holds 1½ carucates of land in SWINFORD. There is land for 2 ploughs. There is a mill rendering 4s, with 1 slave, and 3 acres of meadow. It was worth 2s; now 5s.

Norman holds 4½ carucates of land in WALTON [in Gilmorton]. There is land for 2 ploughs. 10 sokemen have these [ploughs] there. [There is] meadow 1 furlong long and 1 broad. It was worth 10s; now 25s.

The same man holds 6½ carucates of land in THEDDINGWORTH. There is land for 6 ploughs. In demesne are 2 [ploughs]; and 8 villans with 10 bordars have 2 ploughs. There is a mill rendering 2s. It was worth 20s; now 40s.

The same man holds 3 carucates of land and 2 bovates in THEDDINGWORTH. There is land for 3 ploughs. There 7 sokemen have 1½ ploughs. It was worth 10s; now 20s.

Ralph holds 2 carucates of land in LITTLETHORPE. There is land for 2 ploughs. 2 villans with 1 bordar have these [ploughs] there, and there is a mill rendering 2s. It was worth 10s; now 20s.

Ralph de Chartres holds 4 carucates of land in WANLIP. There is land for 4 ploughs. In demesne is 1 [plough]; and 8 villans with 3 bordars have 3 ploughs. There is a mill rendering 8s, and 32 acres of meadow. It was worth 10s. now 25s.

The same man holds 11 carucates of land in SHOBY. There is land for 11 ploughs. In demesne is 1 [plough]; and 4 villans and 8 sokemen with 2 bordars have 9 ploughs. [There is]

meadow 5 furlongs long and 3 furlongs broad. It was worth 20s; now 30s.

The same man holds 7 carucates of land in WALTON ON THE WOLDS. In demesne is 1 plough; and 7 sokemen with 2 villans and 1 bordar have 4 ploughs. There are 30 acres of meadow. It was worth 32d; now 30s.

Hearding with his men held all these lands, and Earl Aubrey had them afterwards; now they are in the king's hand.

XI. The land of Countess Godgifu

COUNTESS GODGIFU held NORTON JUXTA TWYCROSS. There are 6 carucates of land. There is land for 7 ploughs. In demesne are 3 ploughs. There a priest with 1 villan and 2 bordars have 1 plough. There are 8 acres of meadow. It was worth 5s; now 6s.

The countess herself held 3 carucates of land in APPLEBY [?Parva]. There is land for 3 ploughs. In demesne are 2 ploughs; and 8 villans with 6 bordars have 2 ploughs. It was and is worth 20s.

The countess herself held 1½ carucates of land in BILSTONE. There are 3 sokemen with 1 plough. TRE 2 ploughs were there. It was and is worth 5s.

XII. The land of Countess Ælfgifu

COUNTESS ÆLFGIFU held 5 carucates of land in AYLESTONE. TRE 12 ploughs were there. In demesne there are now 2 [ploughs] with 1 slave; and 18 villans with 1 sokeman and 8 bordars have 6 ploughs. It was and is worth 110s.

IN 'GOSCOTE' WAPENTAKE

The countess herself held CASTLE DONINGTON. There are 22½ carucates of land. TRE 20 ploughs were there. Now in demesne there are 3 [ploughs]; and 30 villans with a priest and 5 sokemen and 11 bordars have 12 ploughs. There is a mill rendering 10s8d, [and] woodland 12 furlongs long and 8 broad. It was worth 100s; now £11.

[Folio 232: LEICESTERSHIRE]

XIII. The land of Hugh de Grandmesnil

IN GUTHLAXTON WAPENTAKE

HUGH de Grandmesnil holds WIGSTON MAGNA of the king. There is 1 hide and the third part of 1 hide. There is land for 16 ploughs. Of this land the third part of 1 hide is in demesne, and there are 4 ploughs and 2 slaves and 1 female slave; and 32 villans with a priest and 12 bordars have 5 ploughs. There 31 sokemen with 1 clerk and 2 knights and 4 Frenchmen have 8 ploughs. There are 50 acres of meadow. It was and is worth £8. Earl Ralph held it.

The same man holds 1 carucate of land in SAPCOTE. There is land for 2 ploughs. In demesne is 1 [plough]; and 3 villans with 3 sokemen and 2 bordars have half a plough. There are 2 acres of meadow. It is worth 10s.

1 carucate of land in FROLESWORTH belongs there. There is land for half a plough. There are 3 bordars. It is worth 5s.

The same man holds of the queen's fief, as he says, 2 carucates of land in SHARNFORD. There is land for 1 plough. There 1 sokeman with 3 bordars has half a plough. It was worth 12d; now 10s. Alwine held it with sake and soke.

The same man holds 5 carucates of land in EARL SHILTON. In demesne are 3 ploughs with 1 slave; and 10 villans with a priest and 4 sokemen and 5 bordars have 3 ploughs. There are 12 acres of meadow, and a mill rendering 16d, [and] woodland 8 furlongs long and 3 broad. It was worth 5s; now 70s.

The same man holds in RATBY 6 carucates of land, less 3 bovates. There is land for 6 ploughs. In demesne are 2 ploughs with 1 slave; and 10 villans with a priest and 5 bordars have 4 ploughs. There is a mill rendering 28d. It was worth 20s; now 60s.

Of the soke of these [lands] 2 carucates of land are in 'Bromkinsthorpe' [in St Mary, Leicester] and 3 in Desford and half [a carucate] in Glenfield and half [a carucate] in Braunstone.

The same man holds in GROBY 6 carucates of land, less 3 bovates. There is land for 4 ploughs. In demesne are 2 [ploughs]; and 10 villans with 1 sokeman and 5 bordars have 3 ploughs. There is woodland 2 leagues long and half a league broad. It was worth 20s; now 60s. Ulf held these 2 estates with sake and soke.

The same man holds in KIRKBY MALLORY 2 carucates of land. There is land for 1 plough. This [plough] is there in demesne, with 1 villan and 5 bordars, and 4 acres of meadow. It was worth 5s; now 10s.

The same man holds 3 carucates of land, less 3 bovates, in DESFORD. There is land for 4 ploughs. There 1 villan has 1 plough, and there are 4 acres of meadow, [and] woodland half a league long and as much broad. It was worth 5s; now 20s.

The same man holds in STAPLETON 1 carucate of land. There is land for 1 plough. There 2 villans with 3 bordars have half a plough. It was worth 5s; now 10s.

The same man holds 2½ carucates of land in KIRKBY MALLORY. There is land for 1 plough. There 2 villans and 2 sokemen have 1½ ploughs. It was worth 12d; now 10s.

The same man holds of the queen's fief 2 carucates of land in NEWBOLD VERDON and BRASCOTE. There is land for 3 ploughs. There 3 villans have 1 plough. It was worth 5s; now 20s.

The same man holds 6 carucates of land in PECKLETON. There is land for 4 ploughs. In demesne is 1 [plough], with 1 slave and 3 bordars. It was worth 5s; now 60s.

IN GARTREE WAPENTAKE

The same man holds in ILLSTON ON THE HILL 9 carucates of land, less 1 virgate. There is land for 6 ploughs. There 13 sokemen with 1 villan and 2 bordars have 4 ploughs. There are 20 acres of meadow. It was worth 20s; now 30s.

The same man holds in THORPE LANGTON half a carucate of land. There is land for half a plough. There are 2 men. It is worth 3s.

The same man holds STOCKERSTON. There are 28 carucates of land. There is land for 22 ploughs. In demesne are 3 ploughs and 4 slaves; and 19 villans and 33 sokemen with 5 bordars have 22 ploughs. There are 60 acres of meadow. It was worth £8; now £9. Earl Ralph held it.

The same Hugh holds 12 carucates of land in BURTON OVERY. There is land for 8 ploughs. In demesne are 3 ploughs and 8 slaves; and 15 villans and 6 sokemen with 5 bordars have 6 ploughs. There are 14 acres of meadow. It was worth £4; now £6.

The same man holds 11 carucates of land and 1 bovate in CARLTON CURLIEU. There is land for 7 ploughs. In demesne are 3 ploughs and 5 slaves; and 9 villans with a priest and 8 bordars and 1 Frenchman have 5 ploughs. There are 16 acres of meadow. It was worth £3; now £4.

The same man holds 12 carucates of land in NOSELEY. There is land for 8 ploughs. In demesne are 2 [ploughs] and 3 slaves; and 16 villans with a priest and 8 bordars have 6 ploughs. There are 20 acres of water-meadow. It was worth 30s; now 60s.

IN 'GOSCOTE' WAPENTAKE

The same man holds 9 carucates of land in THURCASTON. There is land for 4 ploughs. In demesne are 2 [ploughs] and 4 slaves; and 22 villans with 4 bordars have 6 ploughs. There is a mill rendering 3s, [and] woodland 2 leagues long and half a league broad. It was worth 30s; now £4. Leofwine held it freely.

The same man holds 7 carucates of land in BELGRAVE. There is land for 6 ploughs. In demesne are 3 ploughs and 3 slaves; and 8 villans with 5 bordars and 7 sokemen have 4 ploughs. There is a mill rendering 12s, and 24 acres of meadow, [and] woodland 5 furlongs long and 3 furlongs broad. It was worth 60s; now 100s.

The same man holds 6 carucates of land in BIRSTALL. There is land for 5 ploughs. In demesne is 1 [plough] with 1 slave; and 3 villans and 9 sokemen with 11 bordars have 3 ploughs. There is a mill rendering 10s, and 36 acres of meadow, [and] woodland 3 furlongs long and 2 furlongs broad. It was worth 40s; now 5 ounces of gold. Alwine pbochestan [sic] held it, but Hugh says that the king gave it to him.

The same man holds 2 carucates of land in ANSTEY. There is land for 4 ploughs. In demesne is 1 [plough] and 4 slaves; and 13 villans with 4 bordars have 2 ploughs. There are 8 acres of meadow, woodland 1 league long and half a league broad, and other woodland 2 furlongs long and 1 furlong broad. It was worth 10s; now 40s.

The same man holds 10 carucates of land in THUR-MASTON. There is land for 7 ploughs. In demesne are 3 ploughs and 5 slaves; and 15 villans with 2 sokemen and 7 bordars have 4½ ploughs. There is a mill rendering 6s8d, and 24 acres of meadow. It was and is worth 60s. Hugh has this [land] as 1 manor, but the shire denies it.

The same man holds 9 carucates of land in HUM-BERSTONE. The soke belongs to Earl Shilton. There is land for 6 ploughs. There 14 sokemen with 6 bordars have 7½ ploughs. There are 12 acres of meadow. It was worth 20s; now 40s.

The same man holds 5 bovates of land in SWINFORD. There is land for half a plough. 1 villan with 2 bordars has this [half-plough] there. It was worth 5s; now 10s.

The same man holds 6 carucates of land in BRUNTINGTHORPE. There is land for 4 ploughs. In demesne is 1 [plough] and 3 slaves; and 6 villans with 3 bordars have 2 ploughs. There is a mill rendering 20s. To this manor belong 4 sokemen in SMEETON WESTERBY. These have 1 plough, and 8 acres of meadow. [There is] woodland 3 furlongs long and 3 furlongs broad. It was worth 20s; now 40s. This land with all its customary dues belongs to Leicester.

Robert de Bucy holds of Hugh 6 carucates of land in "LESTONE". There is land for 4 ploughs. In demesne is 1 plough with 1 slave; and 9 villans with 1 bordar have 3 ploughs. It was worth 20s; now 40s.

The same Robert holds 6 carucates of land in the same vill. There is land for 4 ploughs. In demesne is 1 [plough] with 1 slave; and 6 villans have 2 ploughs. There are 20 acres of meadow. It was and is worth 20s. Baldwin and Alwine held it.

The same man holds 5 carucates of land, less 1 bovate, in SMEETON WESTERBY. There is land for 3 ploughs. In demesne is 1 plough; and 2 sokemen with 1 villan and 3 bordars have 1 plough. It was and is worth 20s.

[Folio 232V: LEICESTERSHIRE]

The same Robert holds of Hugh 2 carucates of land in TWYFORD. There is land for 1 plough. This [plough] is there in demesne, with 3 bordars, and 5 acres of meadow. It was worth 5s4d; now 20s.

Roger holds of Hugh in OADBY 1½ carucates of land. There is land for 1 plough. It was and is worth 5s.

Huard holds of Hugh in another PEATLING [Peatling Parva] 3½ carucates of land. There is land for 2 ploughs. In demesne is 1 [plough]; and 8 villans with 2 bordars have another. There is a mill rendering 16d, and 2 sokemen with half a plough, and 5 acres of meadow. It was and is worth 20s.

The same Huard holds 1 carucate of land in SHEARSBY of the king's alms which he has in pledge. There is land for half a plough. 1 knight has this [plough] there. It was and is worth 5s.

Fulbert holds 2 carucates of land in SAPCOTE of Hugh. There is land for 2 ploughs. In demesne is 1 [plough]; and 2 villans with 2 bordars and 2 sokemen have 1½ ploughs. There is a mill rendering 3s, and 16 acres of meadow. It was worth 5s; now 25s.

IVO holds of Hugh in WILLOUGHBY WATERLESS 3 carucates of land. There is land for 1½ ploughs. In demesne is 1 plough; and 3 sokemen with 1 villan and 4 bordars and 1 slave have 1 plough. It was worth 64d; now 20s.

Ulf holds of Hugh in the same vill 1 carucate of land. There is land for half a plough. It was worth 3s; now 5s.

The wife of Robert holds of Hugh in CROFT 5½ carucates of land, less 1 bovate. There is land for 3½ ploughs. In demesne is 1 plough with 1 slave; and 4 villans and 4 bordars and 3 sokemen with 3 Frenchmen have 3 ploughs. There is a mill rendering 3s. It was worth 5s; now 40s.

Osbern holds of Hugh 3 carucates of land in BROUGHTON ASTLEY. There is land for 3 ploughs. In demesne are 2 [ploughs]; and 6 villans with 2 bordars have 1 plough. There is a mill rendering 2s, and 7 acres of meadow. It was worth 10s; now 30s.

Ulf holds of Hugh in ENDERBY 6 carucates of land, less 3 bovates. There is land for 4 ploughs. In demesne are 2 [ploughs] with 1 slave; and 10 villans with 1 bordar have 2 ploughs. There is a mill rendering 5s, and 20 acres of meadow, [and] woodland 6 furlongs long and 4 furlongs broad. It was worth 20s; now 55s.

Erneis holds of Hugh in GLENFIELD 6 carucates of land, less 3 bovates. There is land for 4 ploughs. In demesne are 2 [ploughs] and 2 slaves; and 3 villans with a priest and 2 bordars and 4 sokemen have 3 ploughs. There is a mill rendering 16d, and 8 acres of meadow, [and] woodland 8 furlongs long and 4 furlongs broad. It was worth 10s; now 40s.

The son of Robert Burdet holds of Hugh in BRAUNSTONE 6 carucates of land, less 5 bovates. There is land for 4 ploughs. In demesne is 1 [plough] and 4 slaves; and 2 sokemen and 4 villans with 1 bordar have 2 ploughs. There are 5 acres of meadow, [and] woodland 5 furlongs long and 3 furlongs broad. It was worth 20s; now 60s.

Serlo holds of Hugh 5 bovates of land in KIRKBY MALLORY. There is land for half a plough. There is 1 bordar, [and] woodland half a league long and 3 furlongs broad. It was worth 2s; now 3s.

Arnold holds of Hugh 1 carucate of land in SUTTON CHENEY. There is land for half a plough. This [plough] is there in demesne. It was worth 3s; now 10s.

IVO holds of Hugh 2 carucates of land in CADEBY. There is land for 1 plough. Yet in demesne is 1 plough; and 7 villans with a priest and 3 bordars have 1 plough. There is woodland 3 furlongs long and 2 furlongs broad. It was worth 5s; now 20s.

Arnold holds of Hugh 1 carucate of land in "NEULEBI", and

it belongs to the queen's fief. There is land for half a plough. There are 3 villans, [and] woodland 3 furlongs long and 2 furlongs broad. It was worth 2s; now 10s.

Ralph and Arnold hold of Hugh in BARLESTONE 3 carucates of land, less 1 virgate. There is land for 2 ploughs. 6 villans with 4 bordars have these [ploughs] there. [There is] woodland 3 furlongs long and 2 furlongs broad. It was worth 10s; now 40s.

Walter holds of Hugh 1 carucate of land in SHEEPY PARVA. There is land for 1 plough. In demesne is 1 [plough]; and 3 villans with 2 bordars have 1 plough. There is a mill rendering 10s. It was worth 2s; now 20s.

Gilbert holds of Hugh 9 carucates of land in COTESBACH. There is land for 6 ploughs. In demesne is 1 [plough]; and 10 villans with 2 bordars have 4 ploughs. There is a mill rendering 3s. It was worth 20s; now 30s.

Edwin holds of Hugh in the same vill 1½ carucates of land. There is land for 1 plough. There 2 men have half a plough. It is worth 10s.

IN GARTREE WAPENTAKE

IVO holds of Hugh in EVINGTON 10½ carucates of land. There is land for 7 ploughs. In demesne are 3 ploughs and 6 slaves; and 25 villans with 2 bordars have 5½ ploughs. There is a mill rendering 2s, and 20 acres of meadow. It was worth 40s; now 100s.

The same man holds of Hugh in INGARSBY 12 carucates of land. There is land for 8 ploughs. In demesne are 2 [ploughs] and 4 slaves and 1 female slave; and 16 villans with 7 bordars, and 1 knight with 3 Frenchmen have 5 ploughs. There is a mill rendering 4s. It was worth 40s; now £4.

Huard and Erneis hold of Hugh 4 carucates of land in STOUGHTON. There is land for 2 ploughs. There are 2½ ploughs. It was worth 15s; now 20s.

The son of Robert Burdet holds of Hugh in GAULBY 13 carucates of land and 2 bovates. There is land for 10 ploughs. In demesne is 1 plough and 5 slaves and 2 female slaves; and 14 villans with 2 bordars and 11 sokemen have 7 ploughs, and [there is] 1 Frenchman with 1 plough. There is a mill rendering 2s, and 30 acres of meadow. It was and is worth £3.

Of this land 2 knights hold 1 carucate of land and 3 bovates, and have there 1½ ploughs. It is worth 20s.

Fulk holds of Hugh 2 carucates of land in FRISBY [near Billesdon]. There is land for 1 plough. In demesne is 1 [plough] with 1 slave; and 2 villans with 1 sokeman and 3 bordars have 1 plough. There are 5 acres of meadow. It was worth 10s; now 20s.

Hugh holds of Hugh 4 carucates of land in SHANGTON. There is land for 3 ploughs. In demesne are 2 [ploughs] with 1 slave; and 4 villans and 4 bordars with 2 sokemen have 1½ ploughs. There are 10 acres of meadow. It was worth 16s; now 40s.

The same man holds of Hugh 6 carucates of land in

STONTON WYVILLE. There is land for 4 ploughs. In demesne are 2 [ploughs] and 2 slaves; and 15 villans with a priest and 2 bordars have 4 ploughs. There are 2 mills rendering 5s 4d, and 8 acres of meadow, [and] woodland 6 furlongs long and 4 furlongs broad. It was worth 40s; now 60s.

Osbern holds of Hugh 11 carucates of land in EAST LANGTON. There is land for 8 ploughs. In demesne are 2 [ploughs] and 3 slaves; and 12 villans with a priest and 1 knight and 5 bordars and 1 sokeman have 7 ploughs. There is a mill rendering 2s, and 12 acres of meadow. It was and is worth 40s.

Lovet holds of Hugh in GREAT GLEN 17 carucates of land and 2 bovates. There is land for 12 ploughs. In demesne are 3 ploughs and 2 slaves and 3 female slaves; and 12 villans with 6 bordars and 20 sokemen have 6 ploughs. There is a mill rendering 3s, and 30 acres of meadow. It was and is worth £6.

Alwine holds of Hugh 1 carucate of land in the same vill. There is land for half a plough. This [plough] is there, with 2 villans. It was worth 2s; now 5s.

IN 'GOSCOTE' WAPENTAKE

Swein holds of Hugh in SYSTON 9 carucates of land. There is land for 6 ploughs. In demesne is 1 [plough]; and 17 villans with a priest and 1 bordar and 11 sokemen have 6 ploughs. There is a mill rendering 8s, and 30 acres of meadow. It was worth 30s; now 40s.

Widard holds of Hugh 2 carucates of land in BIRSTALL. There is land for 1 plough. In demesne is 1 [plough] and 2 slaves; and 8 villans with 4 bordars have 1 plough. There is a mill rendering 12d, and 16 acres of meadow. It was worth 10s; now 3 ounces of gold.

William holds of Hugh in THURMASTON 3½ carucates of land. There is land for 2½ ploughs. In demesne is 1 [plough]; and 3 villans have another. There are 7 acres of meadow. It was worth 10s; now 40s.

Robert and Serlo hold of Hugh 9 carucates of land and 5 bovates in WYMESWOLD. There is land for 6 ploughs. In demesne are 2 ploughs with 1 slave; and 11 villans and 4 sokemen with 4 bordars and 9 French

[Folio 233: LEICESTERSHIRE]

sergeants have 10 ploughs among them all. There are 15 acres of meadow. It was worth 20s; now 100s. 2 brothers held this land as 2 manors and afterwards one bought from the other his share and made 1 manor out of the 2 [that were there] TRE.

Arnold holds of Hugh in SILEBY 8½ carucates of land. There is land for 5 ploughs. In demesne are 3 ploughs and 4 slaves; and 18 villans with 4 sokemen and 4 bordars have 6 ploughs. There are 2 mills rendering 30s, and 60 acres of meadow. It was worth 60s; now 110s.

IVO holds of Hugh 14 carucates of land in ASHBY DE LA ZOUCH. There is land for 10 ploughs. In demesne is 1 [plough] and 2 slaves; and 8 villans with a priest and 6 sokemen and 4 bordars have 6 ploughs. [There is] woodland 1 league long and 4 furlongs broad for 100 pigs. It was worth 10s; now 40s.

Arnold holds of Hugh 6½ carucates of land in ALTON. There is land for 4 ploughs. In demesne are 2 [ploughs] and 4 slaves; and 25 villans with 1 knight and 4 bordars have 8 ploughs. There is a mill rendering 2s, and 4 acres of meadow, [and] woodland 1 league long and half a league broad. It was worth 10s; now 60s.

The same man holds 2 carucates of land of Hugh in STAUNTON HAROLD. There is land for 1 plough. In demesne is 1 [plough]; and 6 villans with 1 bordar have 1 plough. [There is] woodland 5 furlongs long and 3 furlongs broad, and on the other side 4 acres of woodland. It was worth 2s; now 10s. These 2 estates of Arnold's belong to the fief of Earl W[altheof]. Swein held them both freely TRE.

Hugh holds of Hugh half a carucate of land in WHITWICK. There is land for half a plough. There is 1 bordar, [and] woodland 1 furlong long and half a furlong broad. It is worth 2s.

Walter holds of Hugh 16½ carucates of land in WALTHAM ON THE WOLDS. There is land for 11 ploughs. In demesne are 2 ploughs; and 24 sokemen with 1 villan and 1 bordar have 6 ploughs. There 1 knight with 7 bordars and 3 slaves and 1 female slave has 1½ ploughs. There are 100 acres of meadow. It was worth £3; now £6.

The same man holds of Hugh in THORPE ARNOLD 15 carucates of land. There is land for 10 ploughs. In demesne are 5 ploughs and 2 slaves; and 16 villans with 11 sokemen and 8 bordars have 7 ploughs. There is a mill rendering 5s 4d, [and] meadow 4 furlongs long and as much broad. It was worth 20s; now £7.

The same man holds of Hugh 3 carucates of land in the same vill. There is land for 2 ploughs. 8 villans with 3 bordars have these [ploughs] there. It was worth 3s; now 20s.

Hugh holds of Hugh 2 carucates of land in MARKET BOSWORTH. There is land for 1 plough. A priest with a deacon and 4 bordars and 2 slaves has this [plough] there. There are 12 acres of meadow, [and] woodland 1 furlong long and half a furlong broad. It was worth 10s; now 20s.

The same man holds of Hugh the third part of 1 carucate of land in BARTON IN THE BEANS. There is land for half a plough. He has this [half-plough] there, with 1 villan and 2 bordars. There are 2 acres of meadow. It was worth 12d; now 3s.

These 2 estates belong to the queen's fief. Alwine held them freely TRE.

Huard holds in NEWBOLD VERDON 2 carucates of land. There is land for 2 ploughs. Now there is 1 plough in demesne, with 2 bordars. It is worth 10s.

XIIII. The land of Henry de Ferrers

HENRY de Ferrers holds STAPLEFORD of the king. There are 14 carucates of land. TRE 17 ploughs were there. Of this land 4 carucates are in demesne, and there are 5 ploughs and 4 slaves. There 23 villans with 4 bordars and 23 sokemen have 13 ploughs. There are 2 mills rendering 8s, and 130 acres of meadow. It was worth £4; now £10.

The same Henry holds TONGE with all its appendages. There are 21½ carucates of land. TRE 11 ploughs were there, Of this land 3 carucates are in demesne. [...] There 27 villans with 2 sokemen and 8 bordars have 13 ploughs. There are 6 acres of meadow, [and] woodland 1 league long and half a league broad. It was worth 5s; now £6.

In WORTHINGTON are 4 carucates of land. TRE 5 ploughs were there. There 4 sokemen with 6 villans and 2 bordars have 3 ploughs. [There is] woodland 4 furlongs long and 1 furlong broad. It was worth 12d; now 20s. Alwine claims the soke of 1 carucate of this land, saying that it belongs to SHEPSHED, [a manor] of the king.

In SAXBY are 5 carucates of land belonging to STAPLEFORD. There 9 villans have 3 ploughs, and a mill rendering 2s, and 60 acres of meadow. The value of it [is included] in [that of] STAPLEFORD.

The same Henry holds 9 carucates of land in COSTON. TRE 10 ploughs were there. In demesne are 1½ ploughs and 2 slaves; and 12 sokemen and 10 villans with 1 bordar have 7 ploughs. There is a mill rendering 10s, and 100 acres of meadow. It was worth 40s; now £7.

The same Henry holds EDMONDTHORPE and WYMONDHAM. There are 27½ carucates of land. TRE 16 ploughs were there. Of this land 2 carucates are in demesne, and there are 7 ploughs and 4 slaves; and 28 villans with a priest and 15 sokemen and 4 bordars have 14 ploughs. There are 300 acres of meadow. It was worth £4; now £13.

In SEAGRAVE is half a carucate of land. There 1 villan with 1 bordar have 1 plough, and [there are] 4 acres of meadow. It was worth 6d; now 2s.

In WYFORDBY is half a carucate of land [which is] waste. Yet it is worth 8d.

The same Henry holds 6 carucates of land in ORTON ON THE HILL. [...] TRE 6 ploughs were there. In demesne are 4 ploughs with 1 slave; and 15 villans with 13 bordars have 5 ploughs. It was worth 40s; now 100s.

NIGEL holds of Henry 6 carucates of land in TWYCROSS. TRE 6 ploughs were there. In demesne is 1 plough with 1 slave; and 11 villans with 6 bordars have 6 ploughs. It was worth 3s; now 40s.

Roald holds of Henry 3 carucates of land in GOPSALL. TRE 3 ploughs were there. In demesne is 1 plough; and 8 villans with 5 bordars have 2 ploughs. It was worth 12d; now 30s.

Henry himself holds 2 carucates of land in SHEEPY MAGNA. TRE 3 ploughs were there. 8 villans with 6 bordars have these [ploughs] there. There is a mill rendering 2s, and 6 acres of meadow. It was worth 2s; now 30s.

Roger holds of Henry in CONGERSTONE 2 carucates of land. TRE 2 ploughs were there. In demesne is 1 plough; and 10 villans with 6 bordars have 2 ploughs. There is a mill, and 3 acres of meadow. It was worth 2s; now 20s.

Wazelin holds in SMOCKINGTON 1½ carucates of land of Henry. TRE 2 ploughs were there. In demesne is 1 plough with 1 slave; and 6 villans with 2 bordars have 2 ploughs. There are 4 acres of meadow. It was worth 2s; now 20s.

Roger holds of Henry in SHENTON 2 bovates of land. There is 1 villan. It is worth 2s.

IN GARTREE WAPENTAKE

Godric holds of Henry 9 carucates of land in HOUGHTON ON THE HILL. TRE 5 ploughs were there. In demesne is half a plough and 2 slaves; and 5 villans with 3 bordars have 3½ ploughs. There are 20 acres of meadow. It was and is worth 20s. Earl Waltheof held it. Countess Judith claims it.

Hugh holds of Henry 1 carucate of land in ASHBY FOLVILLE, and it belongs to 'Newbold Folville'. TRE 1 plough was there. There are 2 villans. It was and is worth 3s.

[Folio 233V: LEICESTERSHIRE]

Meginta holds of Henry in COLEORTON 1 carucate of land. There she has 1 plough, with 1 villan and 2 bordars. [There is] woodland 1 furlong long and another in breadth. It was worth 6d; now 5s.

Robert holds SEAL [Netherseal or Overseal, Derby.] of Henry. There are 7 carucates of land. TRE 5 ploughs were there. There 4 sokemen with 2 villans have 2 ploughs. [There is] woodland 6 furlongs long and 4 furlongs broad. It was and is worth 20s.

The same man holds of Henry another SEAL [Netherseal or Overseal, Derby.]. There are 6 carucates of land. TRE 3 ploughs were there. In demesne are 3 ploughs; and 21 villans with 12 bordars have 3 ploughs. There is a mill rendering 5s, and 12 acres of meadow. It was worth 20s; now 60s.

The same man holds of Henry 1 carucate of land in BOOTHORPE. There 1 villan has 1 plough. It was worth 8d; now 4s.

The same man holds of Henry 1 carucate of land in APPLEBY PARVA. There 4 sokemen have 2 ploughs, and 3 acres of meadow. It was worth 12d; now 10s.

Nigel holds of Henry 10 carucates of land in SWEPSTONE. TRE 10 ploughs were there. In demesne are 2 ploughs; and 15 villans with a priest and 3 bordars have 6 ploughs. There are 12 acres of meadow. It was worth 12d; now 40s.

Of this land, TRE, Esbiorn held 2 carucates of land and could go where he wished. The remaining land Leofric held, whose land Bishop Osmund holds of the king.

Glædwine holds of Henry in NEWTON BURGOLAND

half a carucate of land. In demesne is 1 plough, with 1 bordar, and 2 acres of meadow.

Roger holds of Henry 1 carucate of land in the same vill. It is worth 2s.

John holds of Henry in WOODCOTE 2 carucates of land. TRE 2 ploughs were there. In demesne is 1 [plough]. [There is] woodland 3 furlongs long and 3 broad. It was worth 12d.; now 10s.

Eardwulf holds of Henry 1 carucate of land in OSGATHORPE. In demesne he has half a plough; and 3 villans with 5 bordars have 1 plough. It was worth 12d; now 5s.

Roger holds of Henry in STRETTON EN LE FIELD 1 waste carucate of land, and another in DONISTHORPE, likewise waste, and a third in COLEORTON, likewise waste. Yet they are worth 2s. Ælfric and Leofnoth held 2 of these [carucates] freely; Kari held the third, but he could not depart with it.

Robert holds of Henry 1 carucate of land and 1 bovate in BURTON LAZARS. There is 1 plough in demesne; and 1 villan with half a plough. There are 2 acres of meadow. It was worth 5s; now 10s.

Nigel holds of Henry in "WINDESERS" 3 waste carucates of land. TRE 2 ploughs were there. Ælfric held it freely.

Roger holds of Henry in SOMERBY 3 carucates of land and 2 bovates. TRE 4 ploughs were there. In demesne is 1 [plough]; and 5 villans with a priest and 2 bordars have 2 ploughs. There are 20 acres of meadow. It was worth 15s; now 40s.

To this manor belong 5 carucates of land in LITTLE DALBY. TRE 4 ploughs were there. There 16 sokemen with a priest have 6 ploughs. There are 40 acres of meadow. It was worth 10s; now 20s. Alweald held it freely.

The same Roger holds of Henry in BURROUGH ON THE HILL 2 carucates of land and 3 bovates. TRE 4 ploughs were there. In demesne is 1 plough; and 4 villans have 1 plough with 1 bordar. There are 20 acres of meadow. It was worth 5s; now 20s. Alweald held it freely.

Hugh holds of Henry 3 carucates of land in NEWBOLD [near Melton Mowbray]. TRE 4 ploughs were there. In demesne are 1½ ploughs; and 4 villans have 2 ploughs. There are 8 acres of meadow, and a mill rendering 12d. It was worth 3s; now 10s. Gamal held it freely.

Nigel holds of Henry in LINTON [Derby.] 1 waste carucate of land.

XV. The land of Robert de Tosny

IN GARTREE WAPENTAKE

ROBERT DE TOSNY holds of the king in HORNINGHOLD 3 carucates of land. TRE 5 ploughs were there. In demesne are 2 ploughs. There 8 villans and 3 sokemen with 2 bordars have 3 ploughs. There are 12 acres of meadow, [and] woodland 2 furlongs long and 1 furlong broad. It was worth 10s; now 30s.

The same Robert holds 4 carucates of land in MEDBOURNE. TRE 8 ploughs were there. In demesne are 3 ploughs and 3 slaves; and 13 villans with 6 bordars have 4 ploughs.

To this manor pertain 2 carucates of land in BLASTON. There 15 sokemen have 3 ploughs.

In the manor are 20 acres of meadow, [and] woodland 3 furlongs long and 2 furlongs broad. It was worth 30s; now £4.

The same Robert holds 17 carucates of land in HARBY. TRE 14 ploughs were there. In demesne are 3 [ploughs] and 8 slaves; and 24 sokemen with 7 villans and 3 bordars have 13 ploughs. There is meadow 5 furlongs long and 4 furlongs broad. It was worth £4; now 100s.

The same Robert holds 15 carucates of land in BARKESTONE. TRE 15 ploughs were there. In demesne are 3 ploughs and 7 slaves; and 14 villans with 2 bordars and a priest and 4 other villans and 25 sokemen have 11 ploughs. It was worth £4; now 100s.

The same Robert holds 9 carucates of land in BOTTESFORD. TRE 25 ploughs were there. In demesne are 5 ploughs and 6 slaves; and 12 villans and 60 sokemen with 5 bordars have 15 ploughs. There is a priest with 1 plough. There are 4 mills rendering 40s. It was worth £12; now £15.

The same Robert holds 3 carucates of land in REDMILE. TRE 4 ploughs were there. This pertains to Bottesford. There 2 sokemen with 2 bordars have half a plough. It was and is worth 20s.

To the same manor of Bottesford pertain 3 carucates of land and 2 bovates in KNIPTON. TRE 3 ploughs were there. There 5 sokemen have 2 ploughs, and a mill rendering 5s, and 4 acres of meadow. It is worth 20s.

Four thegns, Oswulf, Osmund, Rolf and Leofric, held these lands and could go with them where they wished.

Walter holds 2 carucates of land of Robert in LAUGHTON. TRE 3 ploughs were there. In demesne is 1 plough and 2 slaves; and 3 villans with 2 bordars have 1 plough. There are 8 acres of meadow. It was worth 6s; now 20s.

Osbern holds of Robert 2 carucates of land in LUBENHAM. There is land for 3 ploughs. In demesne are 1½ ploughs; and 6 villans with 2 bordars have 1 plough. There are 10 acres of meadow. It was worth 10s; now 20s.

William holds of Robert 18 carucates of land in BARKBY. There is land for 16 ploughs. In demesne are 3 ploughs and 3 slaves; and 7 villans with 3 bordars and 10 sokemen and 4 Frenchmen have 10 ploughs.

Of this land 1 knight holds 6 carucates in HUNGARTON, and has there 1 plough in demesne and 2 slaves; and [there are] 7 sokemen with 3 ploughs. There are 16 acres of meadow. It was worth 30s; now £4.

Roger holds of William 5 carucates of land in SOUTH

CROXTON and Walter [holds] 2½ carucates of land in QUENBY, and in demesne they have 3 ploughs and 4 slaves; and 7 villans with 4 bordars having 1 plough. There are 24 acres of meadow. It was worth 15s; now 30s.

In the same vill 1 Frenchman holds land for 1 plough. It is worth 5s.

IN FRAMLAND WAPENTAKE

IVO holds of Robert 17 carucates of land, less 3½ bovates, in LONG CLAWSON. There is land for 17 ploughs. In demesne are 4 ploughs and 12 slaves; and 14 villans with 2 bordars and 30 sokemen have 12 ploughs. There are 20 acres of meadow. It was and is worth £6.

Gilberd holds 6 carucates of land of Robert in HOSE. There is land for 7 ploughs. In demesne are 2 ploughs and 2 slaves; and 5 villans and 8 sokemen with 1 Frenchman have 2½ ploughs. There are 18 acres of meadow. It was and is worth 40s.

[Folio 234: LEICESTERSHIRE]

Osmund and Roger hold of Robert 4 carucates of land. [...] There is land for 4 ploughs. In demesne are 3 ploughs and 4 slaves; and 4 villans with 3 bordars have half a plough. It was and is worth 40s.

Odard holds of Robert 1 carucate of land in BOTTESFORD and Baldric 2 carucates of land and Clarebald 2 carucates of land and Robert 1 carucate of land, Helduin 1½ carucates of land, Gilbert 1 carucate of land and 4 other Frenchmen 3½ carucates of land. All together [there are] 12 carucates of land. There is land for 12 ploughs. In demesne are 9 ploughs and 4 slaves; and 7 sokemen with 2 villans and 13 bordars having 2 ploughs among them all. Some have nothing. There are 2½ mills rendering 5s6d.

The whole was worth £6 when they received it; now £16. Leofric held it and could go where he wished.

In STATHERN William holds of Robert 4½ carucates of land | and 3 bovates | and Roger [holds] 4 carucates of land and 7 bovates. There is land for 9 ploughs. In demesne are 2 ploughs; and 12 sokemen with 2 villans and 3 bordars have 5 ploughs. There are 40 acres of meadow. It was worth 40s; now 50s. The said Leofric held it freely. The soke and sake pertains to BOTTESFORD.

XVI. The land of Robert de Vessey

IN GUTHLAXTON WAPENTAKE

ROBERT de VESSEY holds GILMORTON of the king, and Godfrey [holds] of him. There are 14 carucates of land. TRE 9 ploughs were there. In demesne are 2 ploughs with 1 slave; and 24 sokemen and 4 Frenchmen have 5 ploughs. It was worth 10s; now 40s.

Norman holds of Robert 6 carucates of land, less 2 bovates, in SHENTON. TRE 5 ploughs were there. In demesne is 1 [plough]; and 7 villans with 3 bordars have 2 ploughs. It was worth 12d; now 30s.

Durand holds of Robert 4 carucates of land in [North or

South] KILWORTH. TRE 5 ploughs were there. In demesne are 3 ploughs and 2 slaves; and 5 villans with 3 bordars have 1 plough. There are 12 acres of meadow. It was worth 6s; now 30s.

IN GARTREE WAPENTAKE

Geoffrey holds of Robert 4 carucates of land in GUMLEY. TRE 2 ploughs were there. In demesne is 1 [plough] and 2 slaves; and 3 sokemen have another. There are 8 acres of meadow. It was worth 12d; now 10s.

Geoffrey holds of Robert 2 carucates of land in SHANGTON. There is land for 1 plough, which [plough] is there in demesne with 2 slaves. It was worth 12d; now 5s.

Moriland holds of Robert 3 carucates of land and 6 bovates in THORPE LANGTON. TRE 4 ploughs were there. In demesne are 2 ploughs and 6 slaves; and 7 villans with 3 bordars have 1½ ploughs. There are 3 acres of meadow. It was worth 4s; now 20s.

Robert himself holds of the king 4 carucates of land in HUSBANDS BOSWORTH, and Laurence [holds] of him. TRE 3 ploughs were there. In demesne are 3 ploughs and 3 slaves; and 4 villans with 1 bordar have 1 plough. There is a mill rendering 3s, and 16 acres of meadow. It was worth 4s; now 30s. In this vill 20 sokemen with 5 bordars have 6 ploughs, and 20 acres of meadow. It is worth 20s.

Robert himself holds 12 carucates of land in KIBWORTH HARCOURT. TRE 10 ploughs were there. In demesne are 3 ploughs and 6 slaves; and 10 villans with 6 sokemen and 6 bordars and 1 Frenchman have 5 ploughs. There are 16 acres of meadow. It was worth 40s; now 60s.

Robert himself holds NEWTON HARCOURT. There are 10 carucates of land. In demesne are 3 ploughs; and 11 villans with 8 sokemen and a priest and 5 bordars and 6 slaves have 5 ploughs. Of this land 1 knight has 2 carucates of land, and has there 1 plough. There are 12 acres of meadow, and a mill rendering 2s. It was worth 30s; now 60s.

Æthelric son of Mærgeat held these lands of Robert's TRE and he was a free man.

XVII. The land of Robert de Bucy

IN GUTHLAXTON WAPENTAKE

ROBERT de BUCY holds of the king 3 carucates of land in PEATLING MAGNA. There is land for 2 ploughs. There is 1 villan, and 8 acres of meadow. It was worth 2s; now 5s.

The same Robert holds 2 carucates of land in LEIRE. There is land for 2 ploughs. 8 villans with 1 bordar have these [ploughs] there. It was worth 2s; now 15s.

The same Robert holds half a carucates of land in FROLESWORTH. There is land for half a plough. There is 1 bordar. It was worth 12d; now 2s. Alwine held these lands freely TRE.

The same Robert holds 7½ carucates of land in DUNTON BASSETT. TRE 6 ploughs were there. In demesne are 2

[ploughs]; and 7 villans and 9 sokemen with 4 bordars have 4½ ploughs. There are 16 acres of meadow. It was worth 20s; now 60s. Leofwine held it freely.

The same Robert holds 2 carucates of land in ASHBY PARVA. TRE 2½ ploughs were there. There 6 villans with 1 bordar have 1 plough. There are 8 acres of meadow. It was worth 6s; now 10s. Godwine held it freely.

IN GARTREE WAPENTAKE

The same Robert holds 1 carucate of land in EVINGTON. There he has half a plough in demesne; and 4 villans have 1 plough. It was and is worth 5s.

IN GUTHLAXTON WAPENTAKE

Hugh holds of Robert 2½ carucates of land in SWINFORD. In demesne is 1 plough; and the villans have half a plough. It was worth 6s; now 10s.

The same Hugh holds of Robert in WALCOTE 2 carucates of land. There is land for 2 ploughs. In demesne is 1 [plough]; and Ulf with his men has another. It was worth 20d; now 6s. Oslac held these 2 estates freely.

Robert holds of Robert 3 carucates of land in COSBY. There is land for 3 ploughs. In demesne is 1 [plough] with 1 slave; and 3 villans with 3 Frenchmen and 5 bordars have 2 ploughs. It was worth 5s; now 20s.

Geoffrey holds of Robert 1 carucate of land and 1 virgate in BARLESTONE. There is land for 1½ ploughs. There are 2 villans with 3 bordars having 1 plough. It was worth 8s; now 10s.

Warin holds of Robert 3½ carucates of land in SWINFORD. TRE 4½ ploughs were there. There 2 men of his have 2 ploughs. It was worth 21s; now 20s. 3 thegns held it.

Hugh holds of Robert 3½ carucates of land, less 1 virgate. TRE 5 ploughs were there. In demesne is 1 plough with 1 slave; and 3 villans with 3 bordars have 1 plough. It was worth 10s; now 20s.

Lambert holds of Robert in the same vill 3 carucates of land and the fourth part of 1 virgate. TRE 3 ploughs were there. In demesne is 1 plough; and 3 villans with 3 bordars have 1 plough. It was worth 2s; now 20s.

Of the above-mentioned 8 carucates of land Alsige holds 1½ carucates of land and the fourth part of a virgate. In demesne is 1 plough, with 1 villan and 1 bordar. There are 15 acres of meadow. It is worth 5s.

Suavis holds of Robert 2 carucates of land and 2 bovates in HUSBANDS BOSWORTH. There is land for 2 ploughs. There he has 1 villan and 2 bordars with 1 plough. It was worth 2s; it is worth 5s.

Ingeld holds of Robert half a carucate of land in ILLSTON ON THE HILL. There is 1 plough, with 1 sokeman and 2 bordars. There are 2 acres of meadow. It was worth 2s; now 5s.

The same man holds of Robert in SLAWSTON 1 waste virgate of land. It was and is worth 4d.

Roger holds of Robert 3 carucates of land and 2 bovates in THORPE LANGTON. TRE 3 ploughs were there. In demesne is 1 plough with 1 slave; and 2 villans with 8 bordars have 2 ploughs. There are 4 acres of meadow. It was worth 8s; now 10s.

Gilbert holds 6 carucates of land of Robert in WELHAM. TRE 5 ploughs were there. In demesne are 2 [ploughs]; and 7 villans with a priest have 2 ploughs. There is a mill rendering 3s, and 42 acres of meadow. It was worth 3s; now 25s. Earl Ralph held it.

Godwine and Frani hold 2½ carucates of land in SLAWSTON. TRE 5 ploughs were there. In demesne is 1 [plough]; and 4 villans with 4 bordars have 1 plough. It was worth 3s; now 16[s].

[Folio 234V: LEICESTERSHIRE]

IN 'GOSCOTE' WAPENTAKE

Ingald holds of Robert in REARSBY 2 carucates of land, less 2 bovates. TRE 2 ploughs were there. In demesne is 1 [plough], and half a mill rendering 2s, and 8 acres of meadow. It was worth 3s; now 10s. Alnoth held it with sake and soke.

Gerard holds of Robert 3 carucates of land in GRIMSTON. TRE 3½ ploughs were there. In demesne is 1 plough; and 5 villans with 2 sokemen have 3 ploughs. It was worth 3s; now 10s.

Robert holds of Robert 2 carucates of land in SEAGRAVE. TRE 2 ploughs were there. In demesne is 1 [plough], and 3 villans with 3 bordars. There are 7 acres of meadow. It was worth 12d; now 5s.

The same man holds of Robert 12 carucates of land in LODDINGTON. TRE 12 ploughs were there. In demesne is 1 [plough]; and 5 sokemen with 3 villans and 3 bordars have 1½ ploughs. There is a mill rendering 16d.

Gerard holds half of this land, and has there 1 plough in demesne; and 4 sokemen and 4 villans with 4 bordars have 2½ ploughs. There are 20 acres of meadow, [and] woodland half a league long and 4 furlongs broad. It was worth 5s; now 20s.

Ansfrid holds 1 carucate of land in GREAT DALBY of Robert. There is land for 1 plough. There are 3 villans with 1 bordar, and 10 acres of meadow. It was worth 12d; now 3s.

Hugh holds of Robert 6 carucates of land in RAGDALE. TRE 6 ploughs were there. In demesne is 1 [plough]; and 4 sokemen have another. There are 30 acres of meadow. It was worth 16d; now 20s.

The same Hugh holds 2 carucates of land in 'WILLOWES' [in Ragdale]. They are waste, and yet they are worth 12d.

Warin holds of Robert 4 carucates of land in COLEORTON. TRE 6 ploughs were there. In demesne is 1 [plough]; and 2 villans with 1 bordar have 1 plough. [There is] woodland 2 furlongs long and 1 furlong broad. It was worth 12d; now 4s.

The wife of Robert Burdet holds of Robert 2 carucates of land in RATCLIFFE ON THE WREAKE. TRE 4 ploughs were there. There 3 villans with 2 bordars have 1 plough. There is a mill rendering 3s, and 12 acres of meadow.

IN FRAMLAND WAPENTAKE

Gerard holds of Robert 5 carucates of land in HOLWELL and in AB KETTLEBY 6 carucates of land. TRE 10 ploughs were there. In demesne are 2 ploughs; and 7 villans with 4 bordars with a priest and 6 sokemen have 5 ploughs. There is meadow 3 furlongs long and half a furlong broad. It was worth 8s; now 60s.

The same Gerard holds of Robert in HARBY 1 carucate of land. There is land for 1 plough. 2 sokemen with 3 bordars have this [plough] there. It is worth 5s.

Ansfrid holds of Robert 3½ carucates of land in WYMONDHAM. TRE 3 ploughs were there. In demesne is 1 [plough]; and 5 villans and 4 sokemen with 2 bordars have 3 ploughs. There are 30 acres of meadow. It was worth 2s; now 30s.

Ralph Pippin holds of Robert 6 carucates of land in GOADBY MARWOOD and half a carucate of land in SCALFORD. TRE 6½ ploughs were there. In demesne is 1 plough; and 6 sokemen with 1 bordar have 2 ploughs. It was worth 6s; now 22s. There are 26 acres of meadow.

Those who held these lands TRE could go where they wished, except one called Særic, who held 3 carucates of land in Ragdale, but he could not withdraw anywhere with it.

XVIII. The land of Roger de Bully

IN GARTREE WAPENTAKE

ROGER DE BULLY holds of the king 2 carucates of land in KNOSSINGTON. TRE 2 ploughs were there. There 4 sokemen with 2 villans and 2 bordars have 2 ploughs. There are 4 acres of meadow. [There is] woodland 2 furlongs long and 1 furlong broad. The fourth part of this woodland belongs to a certain sokeman of the king. It was worth 10s; now 8s.

IN 'GOSCOTE' WAPENTAKE

Roger holds of Roger 2 carucates of land in WYMESWOLD. TRE 3 ploughs were there. 6 villans with 2 Frenchmen have these [ploughs] there. There are 30 acres of meadow. It is worth 10s.

IN FRAMLAND WAPENTAKE

Roger himself holds SALTBY. There are 2 hides and 3 carucates of land. TRE 28 ploughs were there. In demesne are 6 ploughs and 16 slaves; and 24 villans and 23 sokemen with 14 bordars have 20 ploughs. There are 2 mills rendering 8s, and 40 acres of meadow. It was worth £9; now £10. Morcar held it.

Richard holds WYFORDBY of Roger. There are 5 carucates of land and 4½ bovates. TRE 5 ploughs were there. In demesne is 1 [plough] and 7 slaves; and 12 villans with 8 bordars have 5½ ploughs. There are 14 acres of meadow, and 2 mills rendering 10s. It was and is worth 40s.

The same man holds of Roger 3 carucates of land in BURTON LAZARS. TRE 4 ploughs were there. In demesne is 1 [plough]; and 5 villans with 4 bordars have 2 ploughs. There are 3 acres of meadow. It was and is worth 20s.

XIX. The land of Robert Despenser

IN GUTHLAXTON WAPENTAKE

ROBERT Despenser holds of the king 5 carucates of land in LEIRE. There is land for 3 ploughs. In demesne are 1½ [ploughs]; and 4 villans with a priest and 2 bordars have 1½ ploughs. There are 48 acres of meadow. It was and is worth 20s.

The same man holds 6 carucates of land in STONEY STANTON. There is land [...]. There 7 villans with 3 bordars have 3 ploughs, and there are 4 free men, and 12 acres of meadow. [There is] woodland 3 furlongs long and 1 furlong broad. It was and is worth 20s.

The same man holds 1 carucate of land in PRIMETHORPE. There is land for 1 plough. There 3 villans with 3 bordars have half a plough. There are 6 acres of meadow. It was and is worth 5s. Æthelmær held it freely.

The same man holds 1 carucate of land in SUTTON IN THE ELMS. There is land [...]. There 2 sokemen have half a plough. [There is] woodland 3 furlongs long and 2 furlongs broad. It was and is worth 2s.

The same man holds 2 carucates of land in RATCLIFFE CULEY. There is land [...]. In demesne is 1 [plough] and 2 slaves; and 6 villans with 2 bordars have 1 plough. It was and is worth 20s.

The same man holds 1½ carucates of land in SHACKERSTONE. There is land [...]. There 5 villans have 1 plough. [...] There Robert seized 1½ carucates of land. Henry de Ferrers claims them against him. There are 10 acres of meadow. It was and is worth 5s.

The same man holds half a carucate of land in CONGERSTONE. There 1 villan with 1 bordar has half a plough. It was and is worth 2s.

The same man holds 1 carucate of land in SNARESTONE. This is waste.

The same man holds 1 carucate of land in ODSTONE. There is land [...]. There 3 sokemen have 1 plough. There are 6 acres of meadow. It was and is worth 10s. Henry de Ferrers claims this land. The soke of these 2 carucates belongs to the above-mentioned vill.

The same man holds 1 carucate of land in FLECKNEY. It is waste, and yet it is worth 12d.

The same man holds 3 carucates of land in SMEETON WESTERBY. There is land [...]. In demesne is 1 plough;

and 3 sokemen with 2 villans and 1 bordar have 1 plough. There is 1 acre of meadow. It was and is worth 10s.

IN GARTREE WAPENTAKE

The same man holds 3 carucates of land in FLECKNEY. There is land [...]. In demesne is 1 plough; and 2 villans with 1 bordar have 1 plough. There is meadow 2 furlongs long and 1 furlong broad. It is worth 20s.

The same man holds 11 carucates of land and 3 bovates in WISTOW. TRE 8 ploughs were there. In demesne are 2 [ploughs] with 1 slave; and 5 villans with 5 bordars and 9 sokemen have 4 ploughs; and there are 2 Frenchmen and a mill rendering 2s, and 10 acres of meadow. It was worth 20s; now 50s.

The same man holds 5 carucates of land and 6 bovates in KIBWORTH BEAUCHAMP. TRE 5 ploughs were there. There 8 villans with 6 bordars have 2 ploughs. There are 12 acres of meadow. It was worth 10s; now 30s. Edwin Alfrith held these 3 estates freely with sake and soke.

[Folio 235: LEICESTERSHIRE]

The same Robert holds 6 carucates of land in KIBWORTH BEAUCHAMP. TRE 3 ploughs were there. In demesne are 2½ ploughs and 3 slaves; and 9 villans with 2 bordars have 2½ ploughs. There are 12 acres of meadow. It was worth 30s; now 40s.

The same man holds 1 carucate of land and 2 bovates in WISTOW. It is waste, and yet it is worth 2s.

The same man holds 3 carucates of land in TILTON ON THE HILL. In demesne are 2 ploughs; and 13 villans with a priest and 1 bordar have 3 ploughs. There are 8 acres of meadow. It was and is worth 20s. Almær held these lands with sake and soke.

The same man holds in EAST NORTON 4½ carucates of land. In demesne is 1 plough; and 6 villans with 2 sokemen and 3 bordars have 2½ ploughs. There is a mill rendering 2s, and 2 acres of meadow and 3 acres of woodland. It was and is worth 20s.

IN FRAMLAND WAPENTAKE

The same man holds 5 carucates of land and 3 bovates in SOMERBY. In demesne is 1 plough; and 6 villans with 3 bordars have 1 plough. There are 10 acres of meadow. It was and is worth 10s. Wulfnoth held it freely.

The same man holds in WITHCOTE 1½ carucates of land. This is waste. There are 2 acres of meadow, [and] woodland 1½ furlongs long and 1 furlong broad. It is worth 12d.

XX. The land of Robert the Usher

ROBERT the usher holds of the king 2 carucates of land in HOSE. There is land for 3 ploughs. In demesne is 1 plough and 3 slaves; and 8 villans with 1 bordar have 2 ploughs. There are 7 acres of meadow. It was and is worth 20s.

Turstin holds of Robert 2½ carucates of land in HOSE. There

is land for 2 ploughs. In demesne is 1 [plough] and 2 slaves; and 6 villans with 2 bordars have 1½ ploughs. There are 9 acres of meadow. It was and is worth 20s.

The same man holds of Robert 4 carucates of land in LONG CLAWSON. There is land for 2 ploughs. 3 sokemen with 2 villans and 2 bordars have these [ploughs] there. There are 8 acres of meadow. It was and is worth 10s.

Theobald holds of Robert 2 carucates of land in LONG CLAWSON. In demesne is 1 plough with 1 slave; and 3 villans with 1 bordar have 1 plough. There are 6 acres of meadow. It was and is worth 10s.

XXI. The land of Ralph de Mortimer

RALPH de Mortimer holds OSBASTON of the king, and Roger [holds] of him. There are 4 carucates of land. [There is] land for 4 ploughs. In demesne is 1 [plough] and 2 slaves; and 10 villans with 2 ploughs. [There is] woodland 7 furlongs long and 3 furlongs broad. It was worth 30s; now 40s.

The same Roger holds 'WESTON' [in Sheepy Magna] of Ralph. There are 5½ carucates of land. There is land for 5 ploughs. In demesne are 2 [ploughs] and 4 slaves; and 12 villans with 1 sokeman have 3½ ploughs. It is worth 70s; it was waste. Eadric and Edith held these 2 estates freely.

XXII. The land of Ralph fitzHubert

IN 'GOSCOTE' WAPENTAKE

RALPH fitzHubert holds of the king 9 carucates of land in OLD DALBY, and Robert [holds] of him. There is land for 12 ploughs. In demesne is 1 [plough]; and 1 knight with 2 sokemen and 13 villans and 8 bordars have 7 ploughs. There is meadow 1 league long and half a league broad, [and] spinney 2 furlongs long and 1 furlong broad. It was worth £3; now £4.

XXIII. The land of Guy de Raimbeaucourt

IN 'GOSCOTE' WAPENTAKE

GUY de Raimbeaucourt holds of the king 18 carucates of land in THRUSSINGTON. There is land for 12 ploughs. In demesne are 2 ploughs; and 30 sokemen with 4 villans and 3 bordars have 11 ploughs. There is a mill rendering 8s, and 16 acres of meadow. It was worth 20s; now £4.

IN GUTHLAXTON WAPENTAKE

Abbot Benedict holds of Guy 9 carucates of land in 'STORMSWORTH' [in Westrill]. There is land for 6 ploughs. There 12 sokemen have 2 ploughs. This land belongs to STANFORD ON AVON [Northants] in Northamptonshire. It was worth 30s; now 60s. Leofric held it TRE.

The same abbot holds of Guy 1 carucate of land in MISTERTON. There is land for 1½ ploughs. It is waste. Yet it is worth 2s.

IN GARTREE WAPENTAKE

The same abbot holds 2 carucates of land and 2 bovates in HUSBANDS BOSWORTH of Guy. There is land for 1 plough. Yet in demesne is 1 [plough]; and 4 villans with 3 bordars have 1 plough. There are 8 acres of meadow. It was worth 6s; now 20s. Abbot Benedict bought these lands from Guy.

Robert holds of Guy 2½ carucates of land in [North or South] KILWORTH. There is land for 1½ ploughs. There 7 sokemen with 4 bordars have 2 ploughs. There are 6 acres of meadow. It was worth 5s; now 10s.

The same man holds of Guy 11½ carucates of land in HUSBANDS BOSWORTH. There is land for 12 ploughs. There 20 sokemen with 5 bordars have 6 ploughs. There are 20 acres of meadow. It was worth 30s; now 20s. These 2 estates belong to STANFORD ON AVON [Northants]. Leofric held them.

XXIIII. The land of Guy de Craon

IN FRAMLAND WAPENTAKE

GUY DE CRAON holds of the king 8 carucates of land in STONESBY. TRE 8 ploughs were there. In demesne are 3 ploughs and 7 slaves; and 4 villans with 5 bordars and 11 sokemen have 6 ploughs. There are 60 acres of meadow. It was worth 20s; now 60s.

The same man holds in WALTHAM ON THE WOLDS 2½ carucates of land with sake and soke and half a carucate of land without soke and sake. The resources of this land are assessed above.

Warin holds of Guy in SPROXTON 3 carucates of land. There is land for 3 ploughs. In demesne is 1 [plough] and 2 slaves; and 7 sokemen with 1 villan have 2 ploughs. There is a mill rendering 4s, and 15 acres of meadow. It was worth 20s; now 40s.

XXV. The land of William Peverel

IN GUTHLAXTON WAPENTAKE

WILLIAM PEVEREL holds FOSTON of the king. There is half a hide. There is land for 5 ploughs. In demesne are 2 [ploughs] and 2 slaves and 1 female slave; and 11 sokemen with 8 villans and 4 bordars have 5 ploughs. There are 16 acres of meadow. It was worth 40s; now 50s.

The same William holds half a hide and 3 bovates of land in ARNESBY. There is land for 7 ploughs. There 2 of William's men with 14 villans and 3 bordars have 7 ploughs. There is meadow 4 furlongs long and as much broad. It was worth 20s; now 50s. In Leicester is 1 burgess belonging to this vill.

Payne holds of William 6 carucates of land and 5 bovates in 'LUBBESTHORPE'. There is land for 4 ploughs. In demesne are 2 [ploughs]; and 10 villans and 6 bordars, who with 2 sokemen dwelling in 'Bromkinsthorpe' [in St Mary, Leicester] have 2 ploughs and 5 oxen ploughing. These 2 sokemen have 5 bovates of land. There are 40 acres of meadow. [There is] unproductive woodland 6 furlongs long and 1 furlong broad. It was worth 50s; now £4.

Ricolf holds of William in KIRBY MUXLOE 3 carucates of land, less 3 bovates, and they belong to 'Lubbesthorpe'. There is land for 2 ploughs. In demesne is 1 [plough]; and 6 villans with 2 bordars have 1 plough. There are 8 acres of meadow, [and] woodland 4 furlongs long and 2 furlongs broad. It was worth 5s; now 30s.

Sasfrid holds of William in ASHBY MAGNA 16 carucates of land, less 2 bovates. There is land for 7 ploughs. In demesne are 3 ploughs and 2 slaves; and 13 sokemen with 1 villan and 10 bordars have 4½ ploughs. There are 40 acres of meadow. It was worth 20s; now 60s.

XXVI. The land of William Bonvalet

IN 'GOSCOTE' WAPENTAKE

WILLIAM Bonvalet holds 2 carucates of land in RAVENSTONE. It was and is waste.

[Folio 235V: LEICESTERSHIRE]

XXVII. The land of William Lovet

WILLIAM Lovet holds of the king 3 carucates of land of DISEWORTH. There is land for 3 ploughs. In demesne is 1 [plough]; and 6 villans with 6 bordars have 2 ploughs. It was worth 10s; now 30s;

The same William holds THEDDINGWORTH. TRE 2 ploughs were there. There 2 sokemen with 2 other men have 1 plough. There are 10 acres of meadow. It was worth 3s; now 10s. The soke of this land belongs to the king's manor of Great Bowden.

The same William holds 5 carucates of land in SEWSTERN. TRE 5 ploughs were there. In demesne is 1 plough; and 6 villans with 1 sokeman have 1½ ploughs. It was worth 3s; now 10s. This land is IN FRAMLAND WAPENTAKE.

XXVIII. The land of Geoffrey Alselin

IN GARTREE WAPENTAKE

GEOFFREY ALSELIN holds of the king 6 carucates of land in HALLATON, and Norman [holds] of him. TRE 8 ploughs were there. In demesne are 2 ploughs and 2 slaves; and 19 villans with 1 sokeman and 1 free man and 3 bordars have 6 ploughs. There is woodland 4 furlongs long and 2 furlongs broad. It was worth 60s; now 100s.

The same Norman holds of Geoffrey in GOADBY [near Noseley] 3 carucates of land. TRE 2 ploughs were there. In demesne is half a plough with 1 slave; and 4 villans with 2 bordars have 1 plough. [There is] woodland 4 furlongs long and 2 furlongs broad. It was and is worth 20s.

The same Norman holds of Geoffrey in KEYTHORPE 1 carucate of land. TRE 1 plough was there. There 1 sokeman with 2 villans and 1 bordar have 1 plough. There are 10 acres of woodland. It was worth 5s; now 6s.

The same Norman holds of Geoffrey 12 carucates of land in BILLESDON. TRE 12 ploughs were there. In demesne there [neither] was nor is anything. There 4 sokemen with 3 villans and 2 bordars have 2 ploughs. There are 10 acres of meadow.

Of this land 3 knights hold 7½ carucates, and in demesne they have 3 ploughs; and 11 villans with 2 bordars having 2½ ploughs. The whole was worth 55s; now 60s.

The same Norman holds of Geoffrey 10 carucates of land in ROLLESTON. TRE 6 ploughs were there. In demesne is 1 plough; and 1 knight with 7 villans and 1 bordar have 3 ploughs. There are 8 acres of meadow. It was worth 20s; now 25s. Toki held all this land with sake and soke.

XXIX. The land of Geoffrey de La Guerche

GEOFFREY DE LA GUERCHE holds of the king 3 carucates of land in STANTON UNDER BARDON. TRE 4 ploughs were there. In demesne is 1 plough; and 13 villans with 5 bordars have 3 ploughs. There is woodland 1 league long and half a league broad. It was and is worth 20s. King William gave this land to Geoffrey in exchange for the vill which is called Thurcaston, and likewise this following [land].

The same Geoffrey holds 4½ carucates of land in EAST NORTON TRE 3 ploughs were there. In demesne are 1½ ploughs; and 3 villans with 1 sokeman and 1 bordar have 1 plough. There is a mill rendering 2s, and 3 acres of meadow and 3 acres of woodland. It was and is worth 10s. Alwine and Ulf held it freely.

IN FRAMLAND WAPENTAKE

Geoffrey himself holds MELTON MOWBRAY. There are 7 hides and 1 carucate of land and 1 bovate. In each hide are 14½ carucates of land. In demesne are 4 ploughs and 4 slaves; and 20 villans with 2 priests and 14 bordars have 6½ ploughs. The merchants render 20s, and 2 mills 25s. There are 20 acres of meadow, [and] woodland 1 furlong long and 1 furlong broad. It was worth 100s; now £8. To this manor belong these members;

In Freeby, 10 carucates of land, and 30 acres of meadow.

In Wyfordby, 1½ carucates of land and half a bovate, and 6 acres of meadow.

In Burton Lazars, 12 carucates of land, less 1 bovate, and 12 acres of meadow.

In Eye Kettleby, 8 carucates of land, and 6 acres of meadow.

In Kirby Bellars, 17 carucates of land. In Sysonby, 2½ carucates of land.

In Eastwell, 6 carucates of land, and 10 acres of meadow. In Goadby Marwood, 6 carucates of land, and 20 acres of meadow.

In these lands TRE were 48 ploughs.

Now there are 100 sokemen with 10 villans and 13 bordars

having 43 ploughs. The whole was worth £4.10s. when received; now £15.10s.

Leofric son of Leofwine held this land TRE with sake and soke.

In WELBY are 8 carucates of land, less 2 bovates, which belong to Melton Mowbray. There were 5 ploughs. Now 16 sokemen have 5 ploughs there, and 6 acres of meadow. It was worth 10s; now 40s.

IN GUTHLAXTON WAPENTAKE

Walter holds of Geoffrey 8 carucates of land in ULLESTHORPE. There were 6 ploughs. In demesne are 2 [ploughs] and 4 slaves; and 9 villans and 4 bordars with 2 ploughs. There is a mill rendering 16d, and 16 acres of meadow. It was worth 10s; now 30s.

Alvred holds of Geoffrey 2 carucates of land in "LILINGE". There were 4 ploughs. In demesne is 1 plough and 2 slaves; and 9 villans with 3 bordars have 2 ploughs. It was worth 10s; now 20s.

Robert holds of Geoffrey in BITTESWELL 1 carucate of land. There is 1 bordar. It was and is worth 12d.

Alwine holds of Geoffrey in 'STORMSWORTH' [in Westrill] 1 carucate of land. There was 1 plough, and now there is the same, with 2 villans and 1 bordar. It was and is worth 5s.

Alwine holds of Geoffrey in SWINFORD 1 carucate of land. It is waste. Yet it is worth 2s.

IN GARTREE WAPENTAKE

Buter holds of Geoffrey 14 carucates of land in PICKWELL and LEESTHORPE. There were 10 ploughs. In demesne are 4 ploughs and 14 slaves; and 7 villans with a priest and 26 sokemen and 9 bordars have 13 ploughs. There is a mill rendering 4d, and 50 acres of meadow. It was worth 40s; now £4. Ordmær held it freely TRE.

IN FRAMLAND WAPENTAKE

In "Godtorp" are 3½ carucates of land. The soke [belongs] to Pickwell and to Somerby. There were 3 ploughs. There is now 1 plough, with 2 bordars, and 3 acres of meadow. It was and is worth 10s.

In Burrough on the Hill is 1 carucate of land. There was 1 plough. The soke [belongs] to Pickwell. It was and is worth 5s.

IN 'GOSCOTE' WAPENTAKE

William holds of Geoffrey in QUENIBOROUGH 9 carucates of land. There were 8 ploughs. In demesne are 2 [ploughs]; and 28 villans with 7 bordars have 7 ploughs. There is a mill rendering 10s, and 40 acres of meadow. It was worth £3; now £4.

The same man holds of Geoffrey Burton on the Wolds with soke and sake. There are 5 carucates of land. There were 3 ploughs. There 9 sokemen have 4 ploughs. There are 40 acres of meadow. It was worth 5s; now 20s. Leofwine held it freely.

Aubrey holds of Geoffrey in COLD NEWTON 6 carucates of land. There were 4 ploughs. In demesne is 1 [plough]; and 5 sokemen with 2 villans and 2 bordars have 3 ploughs. There are 16 acres of meadow. It was worth 12s; now 20s. This land also is [part] of the exchange for Thurcaston.

Ralph holds of Geoffrey in KIRBY BELLARS 7 carucates of land, and he has in demesne 3 ploughs; and 6 villans with 4 bordars having 1 plough. There are 20 acres of meadow. It is worth £7.

Rainer holds of Geoffrey in SYSONBY 2 carucates of land, and he has in demesne 1½ ploughs; and 2 sokemen with 4 villans have 1½ ploughs. There are 10 acres of meadow. It is worth 20s.

William and Roger hold of Geoffrey 8 carucates of land and 2 bovates in STATHERN, and it belongs to Melton Mowbray. There were 5 ploughs. In demesne is half a plough; and 16 sokemen with 2 bordars have 5 ploughs. There are 30 acres of meadow. It was worth 30s; now 40s. Leofric son of Leofwine held it freely.

IN FRAMLAND WAPENTAKE

Robert holds of Geoffrey in LITTLE DALBY 4½ carucates of land. There were 3½ ploughs. In demesne is 1 plough; and 4 sokemen with 5 villans and 1 bordar have 2 ploughs. There are 10 acres of meadow. It was worth 5s; now 20s.

Alweald holds of Geoffrey in WITHCOTE 1½ carucates of land. There was 1 plough. Now there is 1 villan, and 2 acres of meadow and 5 acres of woodland. It was and is worth 5s. These 2 estates are [part] of the exchange for Thurcaston, as Geoffrey's men say. Alweald held them freely.

In LITTLE DALBY are 2½ carucates of land, and there are 2 sokemen. The soke [belongs] to Pickwell. It is worth 10s.

XXX. The land of Godfrey de Cambrai

IN FRAMLAND WAPENTAKE

GODFREY de Cambrai holds of the king 2 carucates of land in SPROXTON. There were 2 ploughs. There 7 sokemen with 1 villan and 1 bordar have 1 plough. There is a mill rendering 5s4d, and 4 acres of meadow. It was worth 8s; now 12s.

XXXI. The land of Gunfrid de Chocques

IN GARTREE WAPENTAKE

GUNFRID de Chocques holds of the king 3 carucates of land in MOWSLEY. There he has 1 plough in demesne with 1 slave; and 4 villans with 2 bordars have 1 plough. There are 8 acres of meadow. It is worth 20s. It was waste. Theodbert holds it of Gunfrid.

XXXII. The land of Humphrey the Chamberlain

IN 'GOSCOTE' WAPENTAKE

HUMPHREY the chamberlain holds of the king in GREAT DALBY 1 carucate of land. There were 2½ ploughs. In demesne is 1 [plough]; and 3 villans have half a plough. There are 6 acres of meadow.

The same man holds in BARSBY 1 carucate of land. There were 2½ ploughs. In demesne is 1 [plough]; and 3 villans have half a plough. There are 6 acres of meadow. These 2 estates were worth 8s; now 20s. Alwine held them freely.

XXXIII. The land of Gilbert de Ghent

IN GARTREE WAPENTAKE

GILBERT de Ghent holds of the king 5 carucates of land in HUSBANDS BOSWORTH, and William Peverel [holds] of him. There were 3 ploughs. In demesne is 1 plough, and 1 villan with 2 bordars. There are 16 acres of meadow. It was worth 6d. when received; now 20s.

XXXIIII. The land of Gerbert

IN GUTHLAXTON WAPENTAKE

GERBERT holds of the king 4½ carucates of land in ASHBY MAGNA. There were 3 ploughs. In demesne is 1 plough, with 3 villans dwelling there. It was worth 15s; now 10s.

The same man holds 4 carucates of land in MOWSLEY. There were 3 ploughs. There is now 1 villan, and 10 acres of meadow. It was worth 5s; now 12d.

XXXV. The land of Durand Malet

DURAND Malet holds of the king in BURTON ON THE WOLDS 5 carucates of land. There were 4 ploughs. In demesne is 1 plough; and 2 sokemen with 2 villans and 1 bordar have 1 plough. There are 40 acres of meadow. It was worth 3s; now 10s. To this land belong 1½ carucates of land, less 1 bovate, in PRESTWOLD. There was half a plough. There is 1 sokeman. It is worth 2s.

The same Durand holds 1 carucate of land in WYMESWOLD. It is waste. There are 5 acres of meadow. Rolf and Edwin held it.

XXXVI. The land of Drogo de La Beuvriere

IN FRAMLAND WAPENTAKE

DROGO de la Beuvriere holds of the king 12 carucates of land in COLD OVERTON, and Fulk [holds] of him. There were 12 ploughs. In demesne is 1 plough; and 8 villans with a priest and 4 sokemen and 4 bordars have 5 ploughs. There are

30 acres of meadow and as many of woodland. It was and is worth 50s.

IN 'GOSCOTE' WAPENTAKE

Adelelm holds of Drogo 4 carucates of land and 2 bovates in HOBY. There were 4 ploughs. In demesne is 1 plough; and 8 villans with 4 bordars have 1 plough. There are 6 acres of meadow. It was worth 2s; now 20s. Ulf held it with soke and sake.

XXXVII. The land of Mainou the Breton

MAINOU the Breton holds LUTTERWORTH of the king. There are 13 carucates of land. There were 9 ploughs. In demesne are 3 ploughs and 2 slaves and 1 female slave; and 6 villans with 7 bordars and 12 sokemen have 4 ploughs. There are 12 acres of meadow. It was and is worth £7. Earl Ralph held these 3 estates.

The same man holds 2 carucates of land in MISTERTON. There were 2 ploughs. Now 1 sokeman with 1 bordar has there 1 plough. It was and is worth 20s.

The same man holds in CATTHORPE 2 carucates of land. There were 2 ploughs. Now in demesne he has 1½ ploughs, and a mill rendering 2s. It was and is worth 20s.

XXXVIII. The land of Ogier the Breton

IN GUTHLAXTON WAPENTAKE

OGIER the Breton holds in KILBY of the king 2 parts of 1 hide, that is 12 carucates of land. There were 8 ploughs. In demesne are 2 ploughs and 2 slaves; and 9 villans with 7 bordars and 10 sokemen have 4 ploughs. There is a mill rendering 2s, and 12 acres of meadow. It was and is worth 40s. Eur held it freely TRE.

XXXIX. The land of Nigel d'Aubigny

IN 'GOSCOTE' WAPENTAKE

NIGEL d'AUBIGNY holds of the king in SEAL [Netherseal or Overseal, Derby.] 2 carucates of land, and Humphrey [holds] of him. There is 1 plough in demesne. It was worth 12d; now 5s.

Turchil holds of Nigel 3 hides in DONINGTON LE HEATH. [There is] land for 6 ploughs. There is 1 villan, and 4 acres of meadow, [and] woodland half a league long and 4 furlongs broad. It was worth 20s; now 2s. He received it waste.

XL. The land of Countess Judith

IN GUTHLAXTON WAPENTAKE

Countess JUDITH holds in OADBY 9 carucates of land and 2 bovates. There were 9 ploughs; and 46 sokemen with 11 bordars and 3 slaves have as many ploughs there. There are 30 acres of meadow. It was worth 40s; now 60s.

The same countess holds in PEATLING MAGNA 4 carucates of land. There were 2 ploughs. Now 4 sokemen with 2 bordars have there 1 plough. There are 8 acres of meadow.

The same countess holds in COSBY 8 carucates of land. There were 6 ploughs. Now 26 sokemen have there 5 ploughs. There are 20 acres of meadow. It was worth 30s. Now these 2 estates are worth 100s.

In FROLESWORTH the countess holds 6 carucates of land. There were 6 ploughs. Now 14 sokemen have there 5 ploughs, and 8 acres of meadow. It is worth 40s.

In SHARNFORD the countess holds 1 carucates of land. It was and is worth 32d.

In WILLOUGHBY WATERLESS the countess holds 5 carucates of land, less 1 virgate. There were 5 ploughs. Now 13 sokemen have there 3 ploughs, and 12 acres of meadow. It was worth 30s; now 40s.

In HEATHER the countess holds 4 carucates of land. There were 2 ploughs. Now 4 villans have there 1 plough. It was worth 16d; now 20s. Earl Waltheof and Esbiorn, a free man, held all this land.

IN GUTHLAXTON WAPENTAKE

HUGH de Grandmesnil holds of Countess Judith 4 carucates of land in BROUGHTON ASTLEY. There were 2 ploughs. Now 8 sokemen with 2 bordars have there 3 ploughs. It was worth 10s; now 20s.

The same man holds 2 carucates of land in MARKFIELD. There were 2 ploughs. Now there are 2 bordars. [There is] woodland 6 furlongs long and 4 furlongs broad. The whole was worth 2s; now 10s. Ulf held it freely TRE.

The same Hugh holds 2 carucates of land in "ELVELEGE". There were 2 ploughs. Now in demesne he has 1 plough with 2 slaves, and there are 2 villans. [There is] woodland 4 furlongs long and 2 furlongs broad. It was worth 2s; now 10s.

The same Hugh holds in 'RINGLETHORP' [in Scalford] 2 carucates of land and 2 bovates. There were 2 ploughs. Now there are 2 villans, and a mill rendering 4s, and 8 acres of meadow. It was and is worth 10s.

Hugh Burdet holds of the countess 2½ carucates of land in REARSBY. There is 1 plough in demesne, and a priest with 1 villan and 3 bordars, and a mill rendering 2s, and 10 acres of meadow. It was worth 10s; now 20s.

The same man holds 6½ carucates of land in WELBY. There were 4 ploughs. Now in demesne there are 1½ ploughs; and 7 villans with 2 sokemen and 3 bordars have 1½ ploughs. From part of a mill 3s, and [there are] 12 acres of meadow. It was worth 10s; now 20s.

The same man holds half a carucate of land in SYSONBY. There 1 sokeman has 1 plough. It was worth 8d; now 2s. Healfdene held it freely.

IN GARTREE WAPENTAKE

Robert de Bucy holds of the countess 7 carucates of land in LUBENHAM. There were 6 ploughs. Now there are 2 ploughs in demesne and 3 slaves; and 8 villans with 3 bordars and 2 Frenchmen have 4 ploughs. There are 20 acres of meadow. It was worth 10s; now 60s.

The same Robert holds 7½ carucates of land in FOXTON. There were 6 ploughs. Now there are 2 ploughs in demesne and 5 slaves and 1 female slave; and 3 sokemen with a priest and 18 villans and 3 bordars have 9 ploughs. There are 20 acres of meadow. It was worth 20s; now £4.

The same man holds 9 carucates of land in GUMLEY. There were 6 ploughs. Now there is in demesne 1 plough and 2 slaves; and 6 villans with a priest and 5 bordars and 1 free man have 5 ploughs. There are 20 acres of meadow. It was worth 10s; now 40s. 3 thegns held it freely.

The same man holds 3 carucates of land in GREAT BOWDEN. There were 4 ploughs. Now in demesne [there is] 1 plough; and 4 villans with 8 bordars have 2 ploughs. There are 15 acres of meadow. It was worth 10s; now 20s.

The same man holds 2½ carucates of land in OTHORPE. There were 3 ploughs. Now in demesne there are 2 ploughs; and 8 villans with 2 sokemen and 4 bordars have 2 ploughs.

[Folio 236V: LEICESTERSHIRE]

There are 9 acres of meadow, [and] woodland 2 furlongs long and 1 furlong broad. It was worth 8s; now 40s.

The same Robert holds of the countess 1 carucate of land in BLASTON. There is 1 villan. It was worth 10d; now 2s. Robert de Tosny has the soke of this land.

The same man holds 3 carucates of land in STOCKERSTON. There were 4 ploughs. Now in demesne [there is] 1 plough; and 2 villans with 1 sokeman have 1 plough. There is a mill rendering 2s, and 8 acres of meadow, [and] woodland 5 furlongs long and 2 furlongs broad. It was worth 7s; now 20s.

Hugh de Grandmesnil holds of the countess 3 carucates of land in GLOOSTON. There were 3 ploughs. Now in demesne [there is] 1 plough; and 6 villans with 2 bordars have 2 ploughs. There are 4 acres of meadow, [and] woodland 3 furlongs long and 1 furlong broad. It was worth 3s; now 30s.

Robert holds of the countess 11 carucates of land in SCALFORD. There were 12 ploughs. Now in demesne [there are] 1½ ploughs; and 5 villans with 11 sokemen and 13 bordars have 6 ploughs. There are 30 acres of meadow. It was worth 10s; now 60s. 5 thegns held it freely TRE.

Hugh Burdet holds of the countess 9 carucates of land in LOWESBY. There were 6 ploughs. Now in demesne [there are] 2 ploughs; and 7 sokemen with a priest and 6 villans and 5 bordars have 5 ploughs. There is a mill rendering 2s, and 24 acres of meadow, [and] woodland 1 furlong long and 1 broad. It was and is worth 40s.

Robert holds of the countess 2 carucates of land, less 2

bovates, in OADBY and WIGSTON MAGNA. There were 1½ ploughs. Now there is 1 bordar. It was and is worth 2s.

Grimbald holds of the countess 7 carucates of land in OWSTON. There were 12 ploughs. Now in demesne [there are] 2 ploughs; and 15 villans with 3 bordars have 6 ploughs. There 1 Frenchman has 1 plough, with 3 bordars. There are 30 acres of meadow, [and] woodland 5 furlongs long and 1 furlong broad. It was worth 50s; now £3. Thorkil held it with sake and soke.

Grimbald holds of the countess 5 carucates of land in ALLEXTON. There were 5 ploughs. Now in demesne [there is] 1 plough; and 4 villans with 4 bordars have 1 plough. There is a mill rendering 2s. It was worth 10s; now 20s.

Osbern holds of the countess 2 carucates of land in STONTON WYVILLE. There was 1 plough. Now in demesne [there is] half a plough, and 10 acres of meadow. It is worth 4s.

Azo holds of the countess 2 carucates of land in CRANOE. There were 3 ploughs. Now in demesne [there is] 1 plough; and 4 villans have another. There are 4 acres of meadow, [and] woodland 4 furlongs long and 2 furlongs broad. It was worth 8s; now 20[s];

Gilbert holds 1 carucate of land in WELHAM. It is waste, and yet it is worth 3s.

Gunduin holds 2 carucates of land in THEDDINGWORTH. There was 1 plough. Now 1 villan has there half a plough. There are 2½ acres of meadow. It was worth 12d; now 10s.

Ralph holds of the countess 4 carucates of land in ASHBY FOLVILLE. There were 8 ploughs. Now in demesne [there are] 2 ploughs and 2 slaves; and 24 villans with a priest and 3 bordars have 6 ploughs. There is a mill rendering 4s, and 40 acres of meadow, [and] spinney 1 furlong long and 1 broad. It was and is worth £4.

The same man holds of the countess 1½ carucates of land in 'NEWBOLD FOLVILLE'. There was 1 plough. Now in demesne [there is] 1 plough; and 1 villan with 4 bordars has another. There are 3 acres of meadow. It was and is worth 20s.

Feigr holds of the countess 1½ carucates of land in GADDESBY. There was 1 plough. Now in demesne [there is] 1 plough, with 1 bordar. There is a mill rendering 12d, and 3 acres of meadow. It was and is worth 5s.

Othenkar holds of the countess half a carucate of land in GADDESBY. There was half a plough, and there is now, and 2 acres of meadow, and half a mill rendering 2s. It was and is worth 5s.

Wulfsige holds of the countess in BROOKSBY 6 bovates of land. There was 1 plough. Now in demesne [there is] 1 plough, with 2 bordars, and 4 acres of meadow. It was and is worth 4s.

Godwine holds 1 carucate of land and 2 bovates in WELBY. It is waste; yet it is worth 3s.

Ralph holds of the countess half a carucate of land in WELBY. It is waste; yet it is worth 2s.

IN 'GOSCOTE' WAPENTAKE

Grimbald holds of the countess half a carucate of land in ALLEXTON. In demesne is half a plough, and a mill rendering 16d. It is worth 5s.

IN FRAMLAND WAPENTAKE

Hugh Musard holds of the countess 5 carucates of land in SAXBY. There were 6 ploughs. Now in demesne [there is] 1 plough; and 2 villans with 6 sokemen have 3 ploughs. There are 60 acres of meadow, and a mill rendering 4s. It was and is worth 20s.

The same man holds of the countess 8 carucates of land in SPROXTON. There were 6 ploughs. Now in demesne [there is] 1 plough; and 16 sokemen with 5 villans and a priest have 4 ploughs. There is a mill rendering 4s, and meadow 2 furlongs long and as much broad. It was worth 20s; now 50s. Algar held it with soke and sake.

XLI. The land of Adeliza, wife of Hugh de Grandmesnil

ADELIZA, Hugh's wife, holds of the king 1 carucate of land in BELGRAVE. There is land for half a plough. 3 villans have this [half-plough] there. It was worth 5s; now 4s.

Leofric holds of her 8¼ carucates of land in another PEATLING [Peatling Parva]. There is land for 4 ploughs. Now in demesne [there is] 1 plough; and 9 villans with a priest and 4 sokemen and 7 bordars have 4½ ploughs. There is a mill rendering 16d, and 10 acres of meadow. It was and is worth 40s.

The same man holds of the same woman in BARKBY 1½ carucates of land. There is land for 2 ploughs. Now in demesne [there is] 1 plough with 1 slave; and 6 villans with 5 bordars have 2 ploughs. There is a mill [rendering] 12d, and 5 acres of meadow. It was and is worth 30s. Siward held it freely.

XLII. The Lands of the King's Sergeants

IN GARTREE WAPENTAKE

HERBERT holds of the king 4 carucates of land in BURROUGH ON THE HILL. There were 5 ploughs. Now in demesne [there are] 1½ ploughs and 4 slaves; and 6 bordars with 1 sokeman have 3 ploughs. There are 20 acres of meadow, [and] woodland 13 furlongs long and 4 broad. It was worth 10s; now 30s.

The same man holds half a carucate of land in COLD NEWTON. In demesne he has there half a plough, and 2 villans, and 2 acres of meadow. It was worth 2s; now 5s.

The same man holds 3 carucates of land in COLD NEWTON. There were 3½ ploughs. Now in demesne [there are] 2 ploughs, and Herbert's brother has there 2 ploughs with 1 slave; and 9 villans have 2 ploughs. There are 8 acres of meadow. It was worth 5s; now 20s.

IN FRAMLAND WAPENTAKE

The same man holds of sokeland 6 bovates of land in BURROUGH ON THE HILL. It is waste. It was and is worth 2s.

ROBERT de Jort holds of the king 5 carucates of land in HOTON. There were 4 ploughs. There are now 2 villans, and meadow 1 furlong long and half a furlong broad. Robert occupies it by force.

The same man holds 2 carucates of land in WYMESWOLD. Now 1 villan with 1 bordar has half a plough there. There are 5 acres of meadow. These 2 estates are worth 7s.

ASKELL holds of the king in EASTWELL 5 carucates of land and 2 bovates. There is land for 4 ploughs. Now in demesne [there is] 1 plough; and 7 villans with 3 bordars have 3 ploughs. There are 20 acres of meadow. It was and is worth 24s.

RAWN holds of the king in 'RINGLETHORP' [in Scalford] 2 carucates of land, less 2 bovates. There is land for 2 ploughs. There 1 villan with 1 bordar has half a plough. There are 6 acres of meadow. It was worth 8s; now 10s.

Ralph Framen holds of the king in commendation 3½ carucates of land in ASFORDBY. There are 2 villans having 6 ploughs [...]. It is worth 10s.

Turchil holds of the king half a carucate of land in SHARNFORD. There are 3 bordars having 6 oxen. It is worth 4s.

[Folio 237: LEICESTERSHIRE]

XLIII. The land of Earl Hugh

IN GUTHLAXTON WAPENTAKE

EARL HUGH holds BARROW UPON SOAR of the king. There are 15 carucates of land. In demesne he has 4½ ploughs and 2 slaves with 1 female slave; and 40 villans with 13 bordars have 11 ploughs. There are 3 mills rendering 30s, [and] woodland 1 league long and 4 furlongs broad which renders 5s.

Earl Harold held this manor with the appendages written below:

In Castle Donington, 5 carucates of land, and meadow 3 furlongs long and 1 furlong broad.

In Cossington, 6 carucates of land. In Hoton, 6 carucates of land.

In Seagrave, 2 carucates of land, and 10 acres of meadow. In Sileby, 1 carucate of land.

In Rearsby, 2 carucates of land, less 1 bovate, and 8 acres of meadow.

In Brooksby, 2 carucates of land, and 7 acres of meadow, and a mill [rendering] 5s.

In Frisby on the Wreake, 1½ carucates of land, and 4 acres of meadow.

In Prestwold, 2 carucates of land, meadow 3 furlongs long and 1 furlong broad, [and] woodland 6 furlongs long and 5 furlongs broad.

In Charley, 4 carucates of land. It is waste.

In Gaddesby, 1 carucate of land, and 4 acres of meadow, and a mill [rendering] 3s.

In Rotherby, 3 carucates of land, less 2 bovates, and 3 acres of meadow.

In Frisby on the Wreake, 1½ carucates of land, and 4 acres of meadow, and a mill [rendering] 28d.

Of these lands 4 knights hold of the earl 12 carucates of land.

In these the earl himself has in demesne 4½ ploughs; and 30 sokemen and 25 villans and 13 bordars having 15½ ploughs with 1 slave.

His knights have in demesne 3 ploughs; and 12 villans with 1 sokeman and 2 bordars having 3 ploughs.

In LOUGHBOROUGH Roger holds of the earl 8 carucate of land, Ralph 3½ carucates of land, Hugh #[1] 3½ carucates of land, Godric †3½† carucates of land, Roger half a carucate of land.

In demesne are 5 ploughs; and 8 villans with 15 sokemen and 16 bordars have 12½ ploughs. There are 2 mills rendering 10s, and 45 acres of meadow, [and] woodland 7 furlongs long and 3 furlongs broad. 5 thegns held it freely.

Leofwine holds of the earl 1 hide in BURTON ON THE WOLDS. The soke belongs to Loughborough. In demesne is 1 plough, and 1 villan with 2 bordars, and 20 acres of meadow;

In the same vill Godric holds of the earl 2 carucates of land, and has there 1 plough in demesne, and 20 acres of meadow. Hugh de Grandmesnil claims the soke of this land.

Roger holds 5 carucates of land of Earl Hugh in THEDDINGWORTH. There he has 1 plough in demesne; and 4 villans with 4 bordars have 2 ploughs. There is a mill [rendering] 6d, and 6 acres of meadow. This land is among the king's claims. Earl Harold held it.

Robert holds of Earl Hugh 15 carucates of land in KEGWORTH. There he has 5 ploughs in demesne with 1 slave and 2 female slaves; and 25 villans with 13 bordars have 10 ploughs. Earl Harold held it.

To this manor belong 3 carucates of land in HATHERN and in DISHLEY. There are 20 acres of meadow, [and] woodland 1½ furlongs long and 1 furlong broad.

In all these above-written lands there were 80 ploughs TRE. The whole was and is worth £40; when the earl received it, it was worth £10.

In BURTON ON THE WOLDS Hugh #[1] holds of the earl 2 carucates of land, less 1 bovate. It is waste. This is reckoned with the above [lands].

Roger de Bully holds of Earl Hugh in [...] 1 carucate of land. There is half a plough in [...]; and 4 villans with 2 bordars have †1½† ploughs. Alnoth held it.

ROBERT the son of William the usher holds of the king in HOSE 2 carucates of land. There he has 1 plough in demesne and 3 slaves; and 8 villans with 1 bordar having 2 ploughs. There are 7 acres of meadow. It was and is worth 20s.

Turstin holds of Robert in HOSE 2½ carucates of land. There he has 1 plough and 2 slaves; and 6 villans and 2 bordars with 1½ ploughs. There are 9 acres of meadow. It was and is worth 20s.

The same Turstin holds of Robert in LONG CLAWSON 4 carucates of land, and Theobald 2 carucates of land. There is 1 plough in demesne; †and 3† sokemen and 5 villans and 4 bordars with 3 ploughs and 1 slave. There are 14 acres of meadow. The whole was and is worth 20s.

TRE Auti and Earnwig held these lands with sake and soke.

XLIIII. The land of the Men of the Count of Meulan

IN GUTHLAXTON WAPENTAKE

OF THE COUNT OF MEULAN Turold holds the land of 4 villans, and has there in demesne land for 1 plough; and 5 sokemen with 1 villan and 2 bordars having 2 ploughs. There are 5 acres of meadow. It is worth 20s. This land belongs to AYLESTONE.

Wulfnoth holds of the count 4 carucates of land belonging to AYLESTONE. In demesne he has 1 plough; and 2 villans with 3 bordars have 1 plough. There are 2 acres of water-meadow of which William Peverel has the soke [which renders] 2d a year. The whole is worth 20s. Leofwine held it TRE.

William holds of the count half a hide and 1½ carucates of land | in BLABY |. There were 9 ploughs. Now in demesne [there is] 1 plough with 1 slave; and 28 sokemen and 4 villans with 4 bordars have 6 ploughs. There is a mill rendering 2s, and 30 acres of meadow. It was worth 30s; now 50s. Beorhtmær and Ulf held it.

Ralph holds WHETSTONE of the count. There is half a hide and 1 carucate of land. There are 6 ploughs. Now in demesne [there are] 2 ploughs and 2 slaves; and 24 sokemen and 11 villans with 5 bordars have 5 ploughs. There is 1 knight, and a mill rendering 2s, and 16 acres of meadow. It was worth 25s; now 60s.

Robert holds of the count 4½ carucates of land in PEATLING MAGNA. There was 1 plough. There 3 sokemen have half a plough. There are 10 acres of meadow. It was worth 4s; now 5s. Osmær held it freely.

The same man holds BRUNTINGTHORPE of the count.

There are 2 parts of 1 hide, that is 12 carucates of land. There were 6 ploughs. Now in demesne [there are] 2 ploughs and 2 slaves; and 9 sokemen and 3 villans with 6 bordars have 3 ploughs. There are 16 acres of meadow. Of this land Osbern holds 3 carucates of land, and has there 1 plough. It was worth 30s; now 40s. Bovi held it freely.

Fulk holds of the count 8 carucates of land in CLAYBROOKE [Magna and Parva]. There were 9 ploughs. Now in demesne [there is] 1 plough and 2 slaves; and 9 sokemen and 9 villans and 2 knights with 6 bordars have 5 ploughs. It was worth 10s; now 55s.

Robert holds SHAWELL of the count. There are 9 carucates of land. There were 7 ploughs, and 6 slaves, and 23 villans with 11 bordars have 6 ploughs. There is a mill rendering 2s, and 60 acres of meadow. It was worth 40s; now 60s. Saxi held it freely TRE.

Robert holds of the count in "PLOTELEI" 4 carucates of land. There were 4 ploughs. Now in demesne [there are] 2 ploughs and 2 slaves; and 4 villans with 1 bordar have 1 plough. There are 2 acres of meadow. It was worth 10s; now 30s. Leofric held it.

Ralph holds of the count 9 carucates of land in BAGWORTH. There were 7 ploughs. Now in demesne there are 2 [ploughs] with 1 slave; and 24 villans and 3 sokemen with 7 bordars have 5 ploughs. [There is] woodland 1 league long and half a league broad. It was worth 40s; now £4. Saxi held it freely.

Ingulf holds of the count 6 carucates of land in IBSTOCK. There were 4 ploughs. Now in demesne [there is] 1 plough; and 10 sokemen with 11 bordars have 3 ploughs. It was worth 5s; now 40s. The soke belongs to the above vill of Bagworth.

Ralph holds of the count 2½ carucates of land in [North or South] KILWORTH. There were 2 ploughs. Now [there is] 1 plough in demesne with 1 slave; and 2 villans with 5 bordars have 1 plough. There are 8 acres of meadow. It was and is worth 20s. Ulfkil held it freely.

The same man holds of the count †2† carucates of land and 2 bovates in the same vill. There was half a plough, and there is as much in demesne, with 1 sokeman and 2 bordars and 1 female slave. There is a mill rendering 2s, and 4 acres of meadow. It was worth 2s; now 10s. The same Ulfkil held it.

[Folio 237V: [LEICESTERSHIRE]]

[Blank in MS]

WARWICKSHIRE

IN THE BOROUGH OF WARWICK the king has in his demesne 113 houses and the king's barons have 112, from all of which the king has his geld.

The Bishop of Worcester has 9 messuages; the Bishop of Chester 7; the Abbot of Coventry 36, and 4 [of these] are waste on account of the site of the castle. The Bishop of Coutances has 1 house. The Count of Meulan [has] 12 messuages. Earl Aubrey had 4, which belong to the land which he held. Hugh de Grandmesnil [has] 4, and the monks of Pillerton Priors have 1 from him. Henry de Ferrers has 2; Harold 2; Robert of Stafford 6; Roger d'Ivry 2; Richard the huntsman 1; Ralph de Limesy 9; the Abbot of Malmesbury 1; William Bonvalet 1; William fitzCorbucion 2; Geoffrey de Mandeville 1; Geoffrey de la Guerche 1; Gilbert de Ghent 2; Gilbert de Bouille 1; Nicholas the crossbowman 1; Stephen the steersman 1; Thorkil 4; Harold 2; Osbern fitzRichard 1; Christina 1; Leofgyth the nun 2.

These messuages belong to the lands which the barons themselves hold outside the borough and are valued there.

Besides these above-mentioned messuages there are in the borough itself 19 burgesses, who have 19 messuages with sake and soke and all customs and had them thus TRE.

IN THE TIME of King Edward the shire of Warwick with the borough and with the royal manors rendered £65 and 36 sesters of honey, or £24.8s. in place of all [dues] pertaining to honey.

Now, including the farm of the royal manors and the pleas of the shire, it renders £145 a year by weight, and £23 for the customary payment for dogs, and 20s. for a sumpter horse, and £10 for a hawk, and 100s. to the queen for a benevolence.

Besides these it renders 24 sesters of honey by the greater measure and from the borough 6 sesters of honey, that is, a sester for 15d. From these the Count of Meulan has 6 sesters and 5s.

The custom of Warwick was that when the king went by land on an expedition 10 burgesses of Warwick went on behalf of all the others.

He who did not go when summoned paid a 100s. fine to the king.

If, however, the king went against his enemies by sea [the burgesses] sent him either 4 boatswains or £4 of pennies.

Here Are Entered Those Holding Lands In Warwickshire

I KING WILLIAM
II The Bishop of Chester
III The Bishop of Worcester
IIII The Bishop of Bayeux
V The Bishop of Countances
VI The Abbey of Coventry
VII The Abbey of Abingdon
VIII The Abbey of Burton
IX The Abbey of Malmesbury
X The Abbey of Winchcombe
XI The Abbey of Evesham
XII Earl Roger
XIII Earl Hugh
XIIII Earl Aubrey
XV Countess Godgifu
XVI The Count of Meulan
XVII Thorkil of Warwick
XVIII Hugh de Grandmesnil
XIX Henry de Ferrers
XX Roger d'Ivry
XXI Robert d'Oilly
XXII Robert of Stafford
XXIII Robert Despenser
XXIIII Robert de Vessey
XXV Ralph de Mortimer
XXVI Ralph de Limesy
XXVII William fitzAnsculf
XXVIII William fitzCorbucion
XXIX William Bonvalet
XXX Geoffrey de Mandeville
XXXI Geoffrey de la Guerche
XXXII Gilbert de Ghent
XXXIII Gilbert fitzTurold
XXXIIII Gerwy
XXXV Urse d'Abetot
XXXVI Stephen
XXXVII Osbern fitzRichard
†XXXVIII† Harold son of Earl Ralph
XXXVIIII Hascoit Musard
†XL† Nicholas the crossbowman
XLI Nigel d'Aubigny
XLII Christina
XLIII Leofgifu and Edith

XLIIII Richard and other thegns and sergeants of the king
XLV Adeliza, wife of Hugh

The land of the King

IN "FEXHOLE" HUNDRED

The king holds [Lower and Upper] BRAILES. Earl Edwin held it. There are 46 hides. There is land for 60 ploughs. In demesne are 6 [ploughs], and 12 slaves and 3 female slaves; and 100 villans and 30 bordars with 46 ploughs. There is a mill rendering 10s., and 100 acres of meadow, [and] woodland 3 leagues long and 2 leagues broad. TRE it rendered £17.10s.; now it is worth £55 and 20 summae of salt.

The king holds KINETON and WELLESBOURNE [Hastings and Mountford]. King Edward held them. There are 3 hides. There is land [...]. In demesne are 6 ploughs, and 3 slaves and 2 female slaves; and 100 villans, less 7, and 18 bordars with 32 ploughs. [...] There are 130 acres of meadow, [and] woodland half a league and 2 furlongs long and 4 furlongs broad. This is [shared] between the manor and the Berewick.

The king holds BIDFORD-ON-AVON. King Edward held it. There are 5 hides. There is land [...]. In demesne are 5 ploughs, and 8 slaves and 5 female slaves; and 28 villans and 13 bordars with 16 ploughs. There are 4 mills rendering 43s4d., and 150 acres of meadow, [and] woodland 4 leagues long and 1 league broad.

The king holds STONELEIGH. King Edward held it. There are 6 hides. There is land [...]. In demesne are 5 ploughs, and 1 slave and 1 female slave; and 68 villans and 4 bordars with 2 priests have 30 ploughs. There are 2 mills rendering 35s4d., and 20 acres of meadow, [and] woodland 4 leagues long and 2 leagues broad, [and] pasture for 2,000 pigs.

The king holds COLESHILL. King Edward held it. [...] There are 3 hides. There is land [...]. There 30 villans with a priest and 13 bordars have 16 ploughs. There is a mill rendering 40d., and in Tamworth 10 burgesses belong to this manor, [and] woodland 3 leagues long and 2½ leagues broad.

The king holds 'COTEN'[in Warwick]. Earl Edwin held it. There is 1 hide. There is land for 20 ploughs. In demesne is 1 [plough], and 4 slaves; and 10 villans and 6 bordars with 3 ploughs. There are 2 mills rendering 100s., and 80 acres of meadow, woodland 3 furlongs long and as much broad, [and] from meadows and pastures, £4. Outside the borough 100 bordars with their garden- plots pay 50s. [rent]. This land, with the borough of Warwick and the third penny of the pleas of the shire, rendered £17 TRE. When Robert received it at farm, it was worth £30; now as much, with everything that belongs to it.

The king holds SUTTON COLDFIELD. Earl Edwin held it. There are 8 hides and 1 virgate of land. There is land for 22 ploughs. In demesne is 1 plough, and 2 slaves; and 20 villans and 4 bordars with 7 ploughs. There are 10 acres of meadow. [There is] woodland 2 leagues long and 1 broad; when it is

stocked, it is worth 30s. The whole manor was and is worth £4.

In "OPTONE" Albert the clerk holds 3 hides of the king in alms. There are 2 priests with 2 ploughs, and 10 villans and bordars with 4 ploughs. [There is] woodland half a league long and 3 furlongs broad.

In KENILWORTH Richard the forester holds 3 virgates of land of the king. There are 10 villans and 7 bordars with 3 ploughs. [There is] woodland half a league long and 4 furlongs broad. These 2 members belong to Stoneleigh, a manor of the king.

[Folio 238V: WARWICKSHIRE]

II. The land of the Bishop of Chester

IN 'HUNESBERI' HUNDRED

THE BISHOP OF CHESTER holds of the king 3 hides in FARNBOROUGH. Stori held them TRE and was a free man. There is land for 14 ploughs. In demesne is 1 [plough], and 2 slaves; and 18 villans and 1 bordar with 9 ploughs. There are 60 acres of meadow. TRE it was worth 100s.; when received, 60s.; now 100s.

IN COLESHILL HUNDRED

The same bishop holds 2 hides in CALDECOTE. There is land for 6 ploughs. In demesne is 1 [plough], and 2 slaves; and 7 villans with a priest have 5 ploughs. There is a mill rendering 2s., and 12 acres of meadow, [and] woodland 3 leagues long and as much broad. TRE it was worth 40s.; and afterwards, as now, 60s. Tonni held this land, but could not go where he would with the land.

IN 'TREMLOWE' HUNDRED

The same bishop holds 7 hides in BISHOP'S TACHBROOK. There is land for 12 ploughs. In demesne are 2 ploughs, and 9 slaves; and 11 villans with a priest and 7 bordars have 9 ploughs. [...] There are 2 mills rendering †16†s. 8d., and 12 acres of meadow. TRE it was worth £3; now £7; and as much when he received it. This land belongs to the Church of ST CHAD.

III. The land of the Bishop of Worcester

IN PATHLOW HUNDRED

THE BISHOP of WORCESTER holds HAMPTON LUCY. There are 12 hides. There is land for 22 ploughs. In demesne are 2 [ploughs], and 4 slaves; and 22 villans and 9 bordars with a priest having 24 ploughs. There is a mill rendering 6s8d., and meadow 15 furlongs in length and 1 furlong in breadth.

In Warwick, 3 houses rendering 16d. [There is] woodland 1 league long and another broad. TRE it was worth £4; and afterwards as much; now it is worth £20.

The same bishop holds and held STRATFORD-UPON-AVON. There are 14½ hides. There is land for 31 ploughs. In demesne are 3 ploughs; and 21 villans with a priest and 7 bordars have 28 ploughs. There is a mill rendering 10s. and 1,000 eels, and meadow 5 furlongs long and 2 furlongs broad. TRE, and afterwards, it was worth 100s.; now £25.

The same bishop holds ALVESTON. There are 15 hides. There is land for 24 ploughs. In demesne are 2 [ploughs]; and 28 villans and 15 bordars and 1 female slave: these have 22 ploughs. There are 3 mills rendering 40s. and 12 sticks of eels and 1,000 [eels]. In Warwick, 4 houses rendering 16d. [There is] meadow 6 furlongs long and 1 furlong broad. TRE, and afterwards, it was worth £8; now £15.

The same bishop holds 1 hide in LOXLEY. There is land for 3 ploughs. In demesne is 1 [plough]; and 4 villans with 1 plough. TRE, and afterwards, it was worth 20s.; now 25s.

The same bishop holds SPELSBURY [OXON.], and Urse [holds] of him. There are 10 hides. There is land for 16 ploughs. In demesne are 4 ploughs, and 5 slaves; and 25 villans and 12 bordars with 12 ploughs. There is a mill rendering 50d., and 32 acres of meadow, and 36 acres [of] pasture, [and] woodland 1 league and 1 furlong long and 7 furlongs broad. It was and is worth £10.

The same bishop holds in FLECKNOE 2 hides and half a virgate of land, and Leofwine [holds] of him. There is land for 2 ploughs. There are 2 villans and 1 bordar with 1 plough. There are 6 acres of meadow. TRE, and afterwards, it was worth 10s.; now 20s.

Beorhtwine TRE held 7½ hides in ALVESTON. Of this land Archbishop Ealdraed had soke and sake and toll and team and church-scot and all other forfeitures except those 4 which the king has throughout his whole kingdom. His sons Leofwine, Eadmaer, and 4 others testify to this, but they do not know from whom he held this land, whether from the church, or from Earl Leofric, whom he served. They say, however, that they themselves held it from Earl Leofric and could turn where they would, with the land. The remaining 7½ hides Beorhtnoth and Alwig held TRE. But the shire knows not from whom they may have held. Bishop Wulfstan says that he made good his claim to this land before Queen Matilda in the presence of 4 shire courts, and thereof he has the writs of King William and the testimony of the shire of Warwick.

IIII. The land of the Bishop of Bayeux

THE BISHOP of Bayeux holds ARROW of the king, and Stephen [holds] of him. Leofwine held it and was a free man. There are 7½ hides. There is land for 8 ploughs. In demesne are 2 [ploughs]; and 8 villans and 10 bordars with 4 ploughs. There is a mill rendering 6s8d., and 30 acres of meadow, [and] woodland 1 league long and 2 furlongs broad. TRE it was worth 60s.; and afterwards 40s.; now £4.

IN 'TREMLOWE' HUNDRED

The same bishop holds 4 hides in ATHERSTONE ON STOUR, and Corbin [holds] of him. Esbiorn held them and was a free man. There is land for 7 ploughs. In demesne are 2

[ploughs]; and 4 villans with a priest and 4 bordars and 4 slaves have 3 ploughs. There is a mill rendering 10s. and 10 sticks of eels. There are 3 acres of meadow. TRE, as now, worth £4; when received, £4.

IN "FERNECUMBE" HUNDRED

The same bishop holds half a hide in BEAUSALE, and Wadard [holds] of him, and Gerald under him. Edwin the sheriff held it and was a free man. There is land for 1 plough. There are 7 villans and 4 bordars with 3 ploughs. There are 4 acres of meadow and 2 furlongs of woodland. It was worth 5s.; now 20s.

The same bishop holds 1½ hides in WOLFORD[Wolford or Little Wolford], and Wadard [holds] of him, and Gerald under him. Ælfric held them and was a free man. There is land for 1 plough. There are 3 villans with half a plough, and there are 6 acres of meadow. It was worth 10s.; now 20s.

The same bishop holds in BIDFORD-ON-AVON 2½ virgates of land, and Robert d'Oilly [holds] of him. Earnwulf and Arngrim held them and were free men. There is land [...]. There is 1 free man and 1 slave and 1 bordar with 1 plough, and 14 acres of meadow. [There is] woodland 2 furlongs long and 1 broad. It was worth 12d.; now 10s.

The same bishop holds 4½ hides in BROOM, and Stephen [holds] of him. 5 free men held them TRE. There is land for 4 ploughs. In demesne are 2 [ploughs]; and 4 villans and 10 bordars with 2 ploughs. There are 14 acres of meadow. TRE it was worth 40s.; and afterwards 30s.; now 60s.

V. The land of the Bishop of Coutances

THE BISHOP of Coutances holds half a hide in FILLONGLEY, and Leofwine [holds] of him. There is land for 2 ploughs. In demesne is 1 [plough], with 2 slaves; and 5 villans with 2 bordars have 1 plough. There are 2 acres of meadow, [and] woodland 2 furlongs long and 1 furlong broad. It was worth 10s.; now 30s. Alwine held it freely.

VI. The land of the Church of Coventry

IN COLESHILL HUNDRED

THE ABBEY OF COVENTRY holds half a hide in FILLONGLEY. There is land for 2 ploughs. There are 8 villans and 6 bordars with 2 ploughs. There is the fourth part of a league of woodland; when it is stocked it is worth 10s. TRE it was worth [...] 10s.; now 30s.

IN MARTON HUNDRED

The church itself [holds] GRANDBOROUGH. There are 8 hides and 1 virgate of land. There is land for 17 ploughs. In demesne are 2 [ploughs]; and 27 villans and 11 bordars and 4 slaves with 14 ploughs. There is a mill rendering 16d., and 32 acres of meadow. TRE it was worth £6; and afterwards 100s.; now £8.

The church itself holds 'SURLAND'. There are 6 hides. There is land for 12 ploughs. In demesne are 2 [ploughs], and 4 slaves; and 26 villans and 9 bordars with 8 ploughs. There are 40 acres of meadow. TRE it was worth £7; and afterwards £4; now £6.

The church itself holds BIRDINGBURY. There are 2 hides. There is land for 4 ploughs. In demesne are 2 [ploughs], and 3 slaves; and 4 villans and 6 bordars with 1 plough. There are 6 acres of meadow. TRE it was worth 40s.; and afterwards 20s.; now 35s.

IN STONELEIGH HUNDRED

The church itself holds BINLEY. There are 3 hides. There is land for 8 ploughs. In demesne is 1 plough, and 4 slaves; and 10 villans and 6 bordars with 5 ploughs. There are 8 acres of meadow, [and] woodland half a league long and 1 furlong broad. TRE, as now, worth 60s.

Ealdgyth wife of Gruffydd held this land. The abbot bought this from Osbern fitzRichard.

The church itself holds in COUNDON 3 virgates of land. There is land for 2 ploughs. There are 4 villans and 6 bordars with 2 ploughs, and 1 slave. [There is] woodland 3 furlongs and 30 perches long and 3 furlongs broad. It was and is worth 20s.

The church itself holds 2 hides in CUBBINGTON. There is land for 4 ploughs. In demesne is half a plough, and 2 slaves; and 5 villans and 1 bordar with 1 plough. There are 8 acres of meadow. It was worth 20s.; now 30s.

The church itself holds 4 hides in SOUTHAM. There is land for 12 ploughs. In demesne are 2 ploughs, and 7 slaves; and 20 villans and 8 bordars with 8 ploughs. There are 2 mills rendering 4s., and 10 acres of meadow. [There is] woodland 1 league long and half a league broad; this woodland is in the king's hand. TRE, as now, worth 100s.; when received, 60s.

To this church Æthelwine the sheriff gave CLIFTON UPON DUNSMORE by grant of King Edward and of his [own] sons, for his soul, and with the testimony of the shire. Earl Aubrey wrongfully seized this and took it from the church.

[Folio 239: WARWICKSHIRE]

The church itself holds 3½ hides in WALSGRAVE ON SOWE. There is land for 5 ploughs. In demesne is 1 [plough], and 4 slaves; and 10 villans with 5 ploughs. There is a mill rendering 2s., [and] woodland half a league long and 4 furlongs broad. TRE it was worth 40s.; now 60s.

The church itself holds 4 hides in UFTON. There is land for 8 ploughs. In demesne are 2 [ploughs], and 7 slaves; and 12 villans and 2 bordars with 6 ploughs. There is 1 acre of meadow. TRE it was worth £4; and afterwards 40s.; now 100s.

The church itself holds BISHOP'S ITCHINGTON. There are 5 hides. There is land for 16 ploughs. In demesne are 2 [ploughs], and 6 slaves; and 30 villans and 7 bordars with 13 ploughs. There are 50 acres of meadow. TRE it was worth £10; and afterwards £3; now £12.

The church itself holds in HARBURY 1 hide and 1 virgate of land. There is land for 1 plough. It has been laid waste by the king's army. There are 2 acres of meadow. It was worth 10s.; now 2s.

IN 'HUNESBERI' HUNDRED

The church itself holds PRIORS HARDWICK. There are 15 hides. There is land for 16 ploughs. In demesne are 2 [ploughs], and 4 slaves; and 43 villans and 2 bordars with 13 ploughs. There are 40 acres of meadow. TRE it was worth £9; and afterwards £4; now £10.

IN "FEXHOLE" HUNDRED

The church itself holds HONINGTON. There are 5 hides. There is land for 16 ploughs. In demesne are 3 ploughs; and 36 villans and 13 bordars and 4 slaves with 10 ploughs. There are 4 mills rendering 54s4d., and 40 acres of meadow. TRE it was worth £10; and afterwards £7; now £10.

IN 'TREMLOWE' HUNDRED

The church itself holds CHADSHUNT. There are 5 hides. There is land for 16 ploughs. In demesne are 2 [ploughs], and 6 slaves; and 18 villans and 12 bordars with 8 ploughs. There are 12 acres of meadow. TRE it was worth £6; and afterwards £3; now £7.

The church itself holds 1½ hides in CHESTERTON. There is land for 4 ploughs. In demesne are 2 [ploughs], and 3 slaves; and 5 villans and 9 bordars with 2 ploughs. There are 10 acres of meadow. TRE it was worth 40s.; and afterwards 20s.; now 50s.

The church itself holds WASPERTON. There are 5 hides. There is land for 11 ploughs. In demesne is 1 [plough], and 2 slaves; and 18 villans and 1 bordar with 7 ploughs. There is a mill rendering 20s. and 4 summae of salt and 1,000 eels. There are 30 acres of meadow, [and] woodland half a league long and 2 furlongs broad. TRE it was worth £4; and afterwards 50s.; now 70s.

IN "FERNECUMBE" HUNDRED

The church itself holds NEWNHAM [in Aston Cantlow]. There are 5 hides. There is land for 14 ploughs. In demesne are 2 [ploughs], and 4 slaves; and 15 villans and 5 bordars with 8 ploughs. It was and is worth £6.

IN 'HUNESBERI' HUNDRED

The church itself holds 3 hides in RADWAY, and Ermenfrid [holds] of the abbot. There is land for 6 ploughs. In demesne is 1 [plough], and 4 slaves; and 13 villans and 6 bordars have 5½ ploughs. There are 16 acres of meadow. It was worth 20s.; now 50s.

VII. The land of the Church of Abingdon

IN MARTON HUNDRED

THE ABBEY OF ABINGDON has in HILL 2 hides which the abbot bought of the fief of Thorkil, and Warin holds them of the abbot. There is land for 3 ploughs. In demesne [there are] now 2 ploughs; and 5 villans with 7 bordars have 1 plough. There are 12 acres of meadow. It was worth 30s.; now 40s.

VIII. The land of the Church of Burton

IN COLESHILL HUNDRED

THE ABBEY OF BURTON holds 2½ hides in AUSTREY. There is land for 4 ploughs. In demesne is 1 [plough]; and 6 villans and 4 bordars with 2 ploughs. TRE it was worth 40s.; and afterwards 10s.; now 30s. Earl Leofric gave this land to the same church.

IX. The land of the Church of Malmesbury

THE ABBEY OF MALMESBURY holds 3 hides in NEWBOLD [in Leamington Spa]. [There is] land for 6 ploughs. [There are] now in demesne 2 ploughs, and 4 slaves; and 8 villans with 3 bordars have 3 ploughs. There is a mill rendering 8s., and 16 acres of meadow. It was worth 30s.; now 50s. Wulfwine, a monk, held it, and himself had given it to the church when he became a monk.

X. The land of the Church of Winchcombe

THE ABBEY OF WINCHCOMBE holds 6 hides in GREAT ALNE. [There is] land for 6 ploughs. In demesne is 1 plough, and 3 slaves; and 11 villans with 4 bordars have 5 ploughs. There is a mill rendering 5s., [and] woodland half a league long and 4 furlongs broad. It was worth £3; now £4.

XI. The land of the Church of Evesham

IN "FERNECUMBE" HUNDRED

THE ABBEY OF EVESHAM holds 5 hides in WIXFORD. There is land for 6 ploughs. In demesne are 2 [ploughs], and 3 slaves and 2 female slaves; and 4 villans and 6 bordars with 2 ploughs. There is a mill rendering 10s. and 20 sticks of eels. There are 24 acres of meadow, [and] woodland 1 furlong long and a half broad. TRE it was worth 40s.; and afterwards 30[s.]; now 50s. Vigot held this land TRE.

The church itself holds 3 hides in SAMBOURNE. There is land for 4 ploughs. In demesne is 1 [plough], and 2 slaves; and 2 villans and 4 bordars with 3 ploughs. [There is] woodland 1 league long and half a league broad. It was worth 20s.; now 30s.

The church itself holds 2 hides in ABBOT'S SALFORD. There is land for 6 ploughs. In demesne is 1 [plough], and 2 slaves; and 9 villans and 5 bordars with 7 ploughs. There is a mill rendering 10s. and 20 sticks of eels, and meadow 6½ furlongs long and 1½ furlongs broad. It was worth 40s.; now 60s.

The church itself holds 3 hides in KINWARTON, and Ranulph [holds] of the abbot. There is land for 5 ploughs. In demesne is 1 [plough], and 3 slaves; and 3 villans and 2 bordars with 1 plough. There is a mill rendering 3s., [and] meadow 1 furlong long and 12 perches broad. It was worth 40s.; and afterwards 5s.; now 20s.

The church itself holds 3 hides in WEETHLEY. There is land for 4 ploughs. They are there.

XII. The land of Earl Roger

IN STONELEIGH HUNDRED

EARL ROGER holds LEAMINGTON SPA of the king. There are 2 hides. There is land for 8 ploughs. In demesne are 2 [ploughs], and 3 slaves; and 5 villans with a priest and 3 bordars have 4 ploughs. There are 2 mills rendering 24s., and 26 acres of meadow. It was worth 50s.; and afterwards 25s.; now £4. Wulfwine held it freely TRE.

The same earl holds in FRANKTON 4 hides, less 1 virgate. There is land for 6 ploughs. In demesne are 3 ploughs; and 8 villans and 6 bordars with 3½ ploughs. There are 15 acres of meadow. It was and is worth 60s. Wulfwine held it freely TRE.

Of the fief of Earl Roger Reginald holds 5 hides in STRETTON- ON-DUNSMORE. There is land for 7 ploughs. In demesne are 3 ploughs, and 8 slaves; and 20 villans and 6 bordars with 14 ploughs. There are 5 acres of meadow, [and] woodland 3 furlongs long and 1 broad. It was worth £3; and afterwards 100s.; now £6.

The same Reginald holds of the earl 5 hides in WOLSTON. There is land for 12 ploughs. In demesne are 4 [ploughs], and 6 slaves; and 18 villans with a priest and 19 bordars have 12 ploughs. There is a mill rendering 6s4d., and 5 acres of meadow. It was worth 60s.; and afterwards 20s.; now 100s. Æthelmund held | these 2 manors |.

The same man holds of the earl 5 hides in CHURCH LAWFORD. There is land for 7 ploughs. In demesne is 1 [plough], with 2 slaves; and 9 villans and 17 bordars and 2 Frenchmen with 6 ploughs. There is a mill rendering 10s6d., and 11 acres of meadow. It was worth 40s.; and afterwards 10s.; now 50s. Ketilbiorn held it.

William holds of the earl in BILTON 5 hides, less 1 virgate. There is land for 11 ploughs. In demesne are 2 [ploughs]; and 23 villans with a priest and 9 bordars have 8½ ploughs. There are 8 acres of meadow. It was worth £4; and afterwards 10s.; now £3. Wulfwine held it.

IN STONELEIGH HUNDRED

Reginald holds of the earl in WOLSTON 1 virgate of land. There is land for half a plough. There is 1 villan. It is worth 5s. Æthelmund held it.

Auti holds of the earl 3 hides in QUATT [Shrops.]. There is land for 12 ploughs. In demesne are 4 [ploughs], and 5 slaves; and 19 villans and 14 bordars with 10 ploughs. There is 1 acre of meadow, woodland 2 leagues long and 1 broad, and a mill rendering 2s. It was worth £6; now 100s. The same Auti held it freely.

Walter holds of the earl 1 hide in ROMSLEY [Shrops.].

There is land for 7 ploughs. In demesne is 1 [plough], and 2 slaves; and 7 villans and 7 bordars with 3 ploughs. [There is] woodland 1 league long and half a league broad. It was worth 30s.; now 40s. Aki held it freely.

Ralph holds of the earl 5 hides in RUDGE [Shrops.]. There is land for 7 ploughs. In demesne is 1 [plough], with 1 slave; and 3 villans and 4 bordars with 2 ploughs. It was worth 60s.; now 40s. Eadric held it freely of Earl Leofric.

The same Ralph holds of the earl 1 hide in SHIPLEY [Shrops.]. There is land for 3 ploughs. There are 2 villans; and 1 furlong of oaks in length and breadth. It is worth 5s. Alsige held it freely TRE.

XIII. The land of Earl Hugh

IN 'TREMLOWE' HUNDRED

EARL HUGH holds 1 hide and 3 virgates of land in PILLERTON PRIORS, and Waleran [holds] of him. There is land for 2 ploughs. In demesne is 1 [plough], with 1 slave; and 2 villans and 2 bordars with 1 plough. It was worth 20s.; now 30s. Hugh the chamberlain held it freely.

[Folio 239V: WARWICKSHIRE]

XIIII. The land of Earl Aubrey

IN COLESHILL HUNDRED

EARL AUBREY held NUNEATON of the king. Hearding held it TRE. There is land for 26 ploughs. In demesne are 3 [ploughs], and 3 slaves; and 44 villans and 6 coliberts and 10 bordars with 16 ploughs. There is a mill rendering 32d., and 20 acres of meadow, [and] woodland 2 leagues long and 1½ leagues broad. TRE it was worth £4; and afterwards £3; now 100s.

IN MARTON HUNDRED

The earl himself held CLIFTON UPON DUNSMORE. Æthelwine the sheriff held it TRE and he was free, with the land. There are 5 hides. There is land for 16 ploughs. In demesne are 2 ploughs; and 12 villans with a priest and 20 bordars have 7 ploughs. There are 2 mills rendering 11s., and 8 acres of meadow. TRE, and afterwards, it was worth 40s.; now £4.

IN 'BUMBELOWE' HUNDRED

The earl himself held 'SMEETON' [in Combe Fields]. Hearding held it TRE and was a free man. There are 6 hides. There is land for 25 ploughs. In demesne are 2 ploughs; and 22 villans and 23 bordars with 12 ploughs. There are 2 free men. [There is] woodland half a league long and as much broad, and there are 50 acres of meadow. It was worth 40s.; now £6.

The earl himself held 1½ hides in BRAMCOTE. There is land for 3 ploughs. Salo held them and was a free man. There is 1 villan. It was worth 5s.

The earl himself held 2½ hides in [?] CHURCHOVER.

There is land for 3 ploughs. Alric held them and he was free, with the land. There is 1 villan and 2 bordars. It was worth 5s.; now 4d. more.

IN 'HUNESBERI' HUNDRED

The earl himself held 2 hides in RADWAY. There is land for 3 ploughs. Hearding held it, and he, with it, was free. There are 4 villans and 1 bordar with 1 plough. There are 8 acres of meadow. It was and is worth 20s.

THESE LANDS OF EARL AUBREY ARE IN THE KING'S HAND. Geoffrey de la Guerche has charge of them.

XV. The land of Countess Godgifu

IN COLESHILL HUNDRED

COUNTESS GODGIFU held ALSPATH TRE. There are 4 hides. There is land for 8 ploughs. There are 8 villans and 1 bordar with 2½ ploughs. The woodland is 1½ leagues long and 1 league broad. TRE it was worth 40s.; and afterwards, as now, 30s.

The countess herself held 3 hides in ATHERSTONE [near Nuneaton]. There is land for 5 ploughs. There are 11 villans and 2 bordars and 1 slave with 4 ploughs. There are 6 acres of meadow, [and] woodland 2 leagues long and 2 leagues broad. It was worth 40s.; now 60s.

The countess herself held 2 hides in HARTSHILL and ANSLEY. There is land for 7 ploughs. There are 13 villans with 5 ploughs. There are 6 acres of meadow. It was worth £4; now 100s.

The countess herself held KINGSBURY. There are 6 hides. There is land for 7 ploughs. In demesne are 2 ploughs, and 1 slave; and 33 villans and 3 bordars with 2 priests having 16 ploughs. There is a mill rendering 9s4d., and 12 acres of meadow, [and] woodland 1 league long and as much broad. TRE it was worth £6; and afterwards £7; now £13 by weight.

IN 'BUMBELOWE' HUNDRED

The countess herself held ANSTY and FOLESHILL. There are 9 hides. There is land for 7 ploughs. In demesne are 3 [ploughs], and 2 slaves; and 30 villans and 6 bordars with 11 ploughs. TRE, and afterwards, it was worth £10; now £12.

The countess herself held COVENTRY. There are 5 hides. There is land for 20 ploughs. In demesne are 3 ploughs, and 7 slaves; and 50 villans and 12 bordars with 20 ploughs. There is a mill rendering 3s., [and] woodland 2 leagues long and as much broad. TRE, and afterwards, it was worth £12; now £11 by weight.

NICHOLAS holds THESE LANDS of Countess GODGIFU at farm from the king.

XVI. The land of the Count of Meulan

IN STONELEIGH HUNDRED

THE COUNT OF MEULAN holds MYTON of the king. There are 2 hides. There is land for 8 ploughs. Earl Ælfgar held it. In demesne is 1 [plough], and 2 slaves; and 6 villans and 11 bordars with 3 ploughs. There are 2 mills rendering 70s., and 12 acres of meadow. TRE it was worth £3; and afterwards 40s.; now £6.

The count himself holds in OLD MILVERTON 2 hides, less 1 virgate. Leofwine held them and was a free man. There is land for 8 ploughs. In demesne is 1 [plough], and 2 slaves; and 1 villan and 5 bordars with 1 plough. There is a mill rendering 50s., and 30 acres of meadow. It was worth 10s.

The count himself holds WOODCOTE [Woodcote and Little Woodcote]. There is 1 hide. [There is] land for 2 ploughs. Centwine and Thorbiorn held it and were free. There are 4 villans and 5 bordars with 1 plough. TRE it was worth 10s.; now 30s.

The count himself holds 1 hide in ROUNDSHILL. It is waste. [...] There is woodland half a league long and 2 furlongs broad; when it is stocked, it is worth 10s.

The count himself holds 10 hides in AVON DASSETT. 3 thegns held them and were free. There is land for 12 ploughs. In demesne are 3 ploughs, and 10 slaves; and 12 villans with a priest and 5 bordars have 7 ploughs. There are 50 acres of meadow. TRE it was worth £10; and afterwards 40s.; now £8.

The count himself holds 13 hides in WARMINGTON. Azur held them and was a free man. There is land for 14 ploughs. In demesne are 4 [ploughs], and 12 slaves; and 36 villans and 8 bordars with 14 ploughs. There are 69 acres of meadow. TRE it was worth £10; now as much.

The count himself holds 4½ hides in HARBURY. Leofwine and Alric held them and could sell them, but not withdraw with the land. There is land for 10 ploughs. In demesne is 1 plough, with 1 slave; and 9 villans and 6 bordars with 4 ploughs. TRE it was worth 100s.; and afterwards 60s.; now 100s.

IN 'TREMLOWE' HUNDRED

The count himself holds MORETON MORRELL. Deormann held it, and a free man held it [sic]. There are 5 hides. There is land for 8 ploughs. In demesne are 4 ploughs, and 18 slaves; and 20 villans with a priest and 1 bordar have 7 ploughs. There are 40 acres of meadow. TRE, and afterwards, it was worth £6; now £11.

The count himself holds WALTON. Saxi held it and was a free man. There are 5 hides. There is land for 6 ploughs. In demesne are 3 [ploughs], and 6 slaves; and 9 villans and 1 bordar with 4 ploughs. There is a mill rendering 6s. TRE, and afterwards, it was worth £3; now £7.

The count himself holds WALTON. Gytha and Sægyth held it and were free. There are 10 hides. There is land for 10

ploughs. In demesne are 2 ploughs, and 9 slaves; and 32 villans and 3 bordars with 10 ploughs. There are 2 mills rendering 12s., and 8 acres of meadow, [and] woodland 4 furlongs long and 2 broad. TRE it was worth 100s.; and afterwards £4; now £10.

The count himself holds COMPTON VERNEY. Wulfweard and Centwine held it and were free. There are 7 hides. There is land for 8 ploughs. In demesne are 3 [ploughs], and 7 slaves; and 14 villans with a priest and 3 bordars with 5 ploughs. There are 10 acres of meadow. TRE it was worth 100s.; and afterwards the same; now £6.

The count himself holds CHARLECOTE. Saxi held it and was a free man. There are 3 hides. There is land for 5 ploughs. In demesne are 2 [ploughs], and 7 slaves; and 14 villans and 2 bordars with 5 ploughs. There are 2 mills rendering 21s., and 12 acres of meadow. TRE, and afterwards, it was worth 50s.; now £4.

IN "FERNECUMBE" HUNDRED

The count himself holds SHERBOURNE. Eadric and Leofgeat held it and [...] were free. There are 2½ hides. There is land for 6 ploughs. In demesne are 1½ ploughs, and 4 slaves; and 9 villans with a priest and 2 bordars have 2 ploughs. There are 16 acres of meadow. TRE it was worth 60s.; and afterwards 40s.; now 50s.

The count himself holds [Lower and Upper] FULBROOK. Alflæd held it and was free. There are 2½ hides. There is land for 8 ploughs. In demesne are 1½ ploughs, and 4 slaves; and 10 villans and 3 bordars with 5 ploughs. There is a mill rendering 12s., and 8 acres of meadow. TRE it was worth 60s.; and afterwards 40s.; now 60s.

[Folio 240: WARWICKSHIRE]

The count himself [holds] SNITTERFIELD. Saxi held it and was a free man. There are 4 hides. There is land for 14 ploughs. In demesne are 2 [ploughs], and 10 slaves; and 11 villans with a priest and 4 bordars have 6 ploughs. There are 12 acres of meadow. TRE, and afterwards, it was worth £4; now 100s.

The count himself holds CLAVERDON. Bovi held it and was a free man. There are 3 hides. There is land for 5 ploughs. In demesne is 1 [plough]; and 12 villans with a priest and 14 bordars have 5 ploughs. There are 3 slaves, and 16 acres of meadow, and 1 league of woodland, when it is stocked, is worth 10s. It was worth 40s.; now £4.

The count himself holds [?] HONILEY. Alweald held it and was a free man. There is 1 hide. [There is] land for 2 ploughs. There are 6 villans and 2 bordars with 2 ploughs. There is an enclosure which is half a league long and as much broad. It was worth 20s.; now 30s.

The count himself holds PRESTON BAGOT. Thorbiorn held it and was a free man. There are 5 hides. There is land for 3 ploughs. In demesne is 1 plough, and 2 slaves; and 7 bordars with 1 Frenchman have 1 plough. There is a mill rendering 16s. [There is] woodland 1 league long and half a league broad; when it is stocked, it is worth 10s. It was worth 30s.; now 50s.

The same count holds KINGTON GRANGE. Beorhtnoth held it and was a free man. There are 1½ hides. [There is] land for 1 plough. It is waste. It is worth 5s. The woodland is worth 10s. a year. It was worth as much TRE.

The count himself holds ILMINGTON. 3 thegns held it and †were† free. There are 7 hides, less half a virgate of land. There is land for 12 ploughs. In demesne are 3 ploughs, and 9 slaves; and 24 villans and 3 bordars with a priest have 8 ploughs. There are 40 acres of meadow. TRE it was worth £7; and afterwards 100s.; now £10.

The count himself holds WHITCHURCH as 2 manors. Alwine held it and could go where he would. There are 7 hides. There is land for 12 ploughs. In demesne are 3 ploughs, and 7 slaves; and 16 villans and 1 free man and 2 bordars with a priest have 8 ploughs. There are 2 mills rendering 20s., and 30 acres of meadow. It was worth £6; now £8.10s.

IN COLESHILL HUNDRED

The count himself holds 2½ hides in SHUTTINGTON, and Leofwine [holds] of him. Ceolræd and Godric held them and were free men. There is land for 3 ploughs. In demesne is 1 [plough], and 2 slaves; and 7 villans and 4 bordars with 2 ploughs. There is half a mill rendering 5s., and 8 acres of meadow, [and] woodland half a league long and 3 furlongs broad. It is worth 20s.

The count himself holds 2½ hides in the same vill, and Godric [holds] of him. The same man held them TRE and was free. There is land for 5 ploughs. In demesne is 1 [plough], and 2 slaves; and 3 villans and 3 bordars with 1 plough. There is half a mill rendering 5s., and 8 acres of meadow, [and] woodland half a league long and 3 furlongs broad. It is worth 20s.

The count himself holds 3 hides in WILNECOTE, and Ingulf and Arnulf [hold] of him. Leofnoth held them and was a free man. There is land for 6 ploughs. There are 11 villans and 5 bordars with 2 smiths having 3½ ploughs. [There is] woodland 1 league long and a half broad; it is worth 5s., and the forge 5s. It is worth 30s.

The count himself holds 2½ hides in SECKINGTON, and Ingulf and Arnulf [hold] of him. Godric held them and was a free man. There is land for 5 ploughs. In demesne are 2 ploughs; and 6 villans and 5 bordars with 3 ploughs. It is worth 40s.

The count himself holds 3 hides in WEDDINGTON, and Hereweard [holds] of him. The same man held them TRE and was free. There is land for 7 ploughs. In demesne are 1½ [ploughs], and 4 slaves; and 12 villans and 5 bordars with 4 ploughs. There are 20 acres of meadow, [and] woodland 2 furlongs long and 1 furlong broad. It is worth 30s.

The count himself holds 1 hide in BERKSWELL, and Walter [holds] of him. Leofnoth held it and was free. There is 1 villan with half a plough. It is worth 5s.

The count himself holds in "WERLAVESCOTE" 3 virgates of land. Saxi held them freely TRE. There is land for 1 plough. This [plough] is there, with 2 villans, and 3 acres of meadow. It is worth 2s.

The count himself holds in FRANKTON 1 hide and 1 virgate of land, and Ranulph [holds] of him. There is land for 3 ploughs. In demesne is 1 [plough], and 2 slaves; and 4 villans and 1 bordar with 1 plough. There are 10 acres of meadow. It was and is worth 20s. Centwine held it freely TRE.

The count himself holds 5 hides in BOURTON ON DUNSMORE, and Ingulf [holds] of him. There is land for 8 ploughs. In demesne are 3 [ploughs], and 7 slaves; and 13 villans and 11 bordars with 3½ ploughs; and 1 knight has there 1½ ploughs. There are 50 acres of meadow. It was worth 60s.; now 70s. Leofwine held it freely TRE.

The count himself holds in NAPTON ON THE HILL 3 hides and 3 virgates of land, and Robert [holds] of him. There is land for 8 ploughs. In demesne are 2 [ploughs], and 4 slaves; and 11 villans with a priest and 8 bordars have 4½ ploughs. There are 10 acres of meadow and as many of pasture. It was worth £4; now £3. Leofnoth and Bondi held it freely TRE.

The count himself holds 4 hides in UPPER SHUCKBURGH, and Herluin [holds] of him. There is land for 4 ploughs. In demesne are 2 [ploughs], and 2 slaves; and 8 villans and 6 bordars with 3½ ploughs. There are 6 acres of meadow. It was worth 40s.; and afterwards 30s.; now 50s. Leofwine held it freely TRE.

The count himself holds 2½ hides in THURLASTON, and Robert [holds] of him. There is land for 6 ploughs. In demesne is 1 [plough], and 2 female slaves; and 4 villans and 1 bordar with 2 ploughs. There are 50 acres of meadow, and 2 furlongs of pasture. It was worth 40s.; and afterwards 30[s.]; now 35s. Wulfgar held it freely TRE.

The count himself holds 4 hides in HODNELL, and Gilbert [holds] of him. There is land for 4 ploughs. In demesne is 1 [plough]; and 1 knight with 6 villans and 3 bordars has 3 ploughs. There are 20 acres of meadow. It was worth 20s.; and afterwards 40[s.]; now 60[s.]. Ordric held it freely TRE.

The count himself holds 1½ hides in [?] MARTON, and Merewine [holds] of him. There is land for 6 ploughs. In demesne is 1 [plough], and 1 slave; and 5 villans and 6 bordars with 3 ploughs. There are 12 acres of meadow. It was worth 30s.; and afterwards 35s.; now 30s. Merewine and Skrauti and Waltheof held it freely.

The count himself holds in the same vill 1 hide and 1 virgate of land, and Waltheof [holds] of him. There is land for 6 ploughs. In demesne is 1 [plough], with 1 slave; and 10 villans and 7 bordars with 4 ploughs. There are 12 acres of meadow. It was worth 50s.; and afterwards, as now, 45s. Skrauti held it freely TRE.

The count himself holds half a hide in [?] MARTON, and

Waltheof [holds] of him. There is land for 2 ploughs. There are 3 villans with 1 bordar and 1 slave [who] have 1 plough, and there are 6 acres of meadow. It was worth 15s.; now 10s. The same Waltheof held it freely TRE.

IN 'BUMBELOWE' HUNDRED

The count himself holds 2 hides in WESTON IN ARDEN, and Fulk [holds] of him. There is land for 7 ploughs. In demesne is 1 [plough]; and 6 villans and 7 bordars with 3 ploughs. There are 8 acres of meadow. It was and is worth 40s.

The count himself holds half a hide in WIBTOFT and in WILLEY, and Fulk [holds] of him. There is land for 4 ploughs. In demesne are 2 [ploughs]; and 3 villans and 4 bordars with 2 ploughs. There are 40 acres of meadow. It was and is worth 30s.

The count himself holds 2½ hides in the same vill, and Robert [holds] of him. There is land for 5 ploughs. In demesne are 2 [ploughs]; and 5 villans and 3 bordars with 2 Frenchmen have 3 ploughs. There are 30 acres of meadow. It was and is worth 50s.

These 3 estates Saxi held freely TRE.

The count himself holds in BULKINGTON 4 hides and 1 virgate of land, and Salo [holds] of him. There is land for 8 ploughs. In demesne is 1 [plough], and 2 slaves; and 5 villans with 1 plough. There are 100 acres of meadow. It was and is worth 20s. Algeat and Alsige held it freely.

The count himself holds 1 hide in ASTLEY, and Godric [holds] of him. There is land for 2 ploughs.

[Folio 240V: WARWICKSHIRE]

In demesne is 1 plough; and 5 villans and 3 bordars with 1 plough. [There is] woodland 1 league long and half a league broad; when it is stocked, it is worth 10s. It was and is worth 20s. Alsige held it freely TRE.

The count himself [holds] 1 hide in 'SMERCOTE' [in Bedworth] and in SOLE END, and Godric [holds] of him. There is land for 2 ploughs. There are 2 villans. [There is] woodland 1 league long and half a league broad; when it is stocked, it is worth 10s. It was worth 15s.; now 5s. Saxi held it freely TRE.

The count himself holds 4 hides in BEDWORTH, and Ulfkil [holds] of him. There is land for 6 ploughs. In demesne is 1 [plough], and 2 slaves; and 5 villans and 3 bordars with 2 ploughs. There are 16 acres of meadow, [and] woodland 1 league long and half a league broad; it is worth 10s., when it is stocked. It was and is worth 40s. Earl Edwin held it.

The count himself holds 2 hides in SHILTON, and Waltheof [holds] of him. There is land for 3 ploughs. In demesne is 1 plough; and 6 villans and 2 bordars with 2 ploughs. There are 4 acres of meadow, [and] woodland 2 furlongs long and 1 furlong broad. It was and is worth 40s. The same Waltheof held it freely TRE.

The count himself holds 1 hide in MARSTON JABBETT,

and Hereweard [holds] of him. There is land for 4 ploughs. In demesne are 2 [ploughs], and 1 female slave; and 12 villans and 8 bordars with 4 ploughs. There are 6 acres of meadow. It was and is worth £3. The same Hereweard held it freely TRE.

IN MARTON HUNDRED

The count himself holds 2 hides in LADBROKE. There is land for 3 ploughs. In demesne is 1 [plough]. William holds from him. There are 4 villans and 1 bordar with 2 ploughs, and 10 acres of meadow. It was worth 20s.; now 50s.

The count himself holds in BARNACLE 3 virgates of land, and Hereweard [holds] of him. There is land for 2 ploughs. There are 2 villans and 2 bordars with 1 plough. [There is] woodland 4 furlongs long and 3 broad. It was and is worth 20s. The same Hereweard held it freely TRE.

The count himself holds, and Gilbert [holds] of him, 2 hides and 1 virgate of land which belong to the count's manor of Stoneleigh. There is 1 plough in demesne. It is worth 20s.

The count himself holds 4 hides in LILLINGTON, and Warin and Roger [hold] of him. There is land for 4 ploughs. In demesne is 1 [plough], and 4 slaves; and 2 villans and 3 bordars with 1 plough. There is a mill rendering 6s8d. There are 9 acres of meadow, [and] woodland 1 league long and a half broad. It was worth 20s.; now 40s. Eadric held it freely TRE.

The count himself holds 1 hide in WOODCOTE [Woodcote and Little Woodcote], and Gilbert [holds] of him. There is land for 1 plough. There 1 knight with 2 villans and 9 bordars has 1½ ploughs. The woodland is 1 league long and a half broad. It was worth 10s.; now 20s. Leofric held it freely TRE.

The count himself holds in WESTON UNDER WETHERLEY 3 hides, less the third part of a virgate, and Robert [holds] of him. There is land for 5 ploughs. In demesne are 2 [ploughs], and 2 female slaves. There is 1 knight and 3 villans and 7 bordars with 2 ploughs, and 12 acres of meadow. [There is] a spinney 2 furlongs long and 1 broad. It was worth 30s.; now 50s. Ulf held it freely TRE.

The count himself holds 3 hides in CUBBINGTON, and Boscher [holds] of him. There is land for 3 ploughs. In demesne is 1 plough, with 3 bordars. There are 8 acres of meadow. It was worth 40s.; now 30s. Leofwine and Ketilbiorn held it freely TRE.

IN 'HUNESBERI' HUNDRED

The count himself holds 1½ hides in WORMLEIGHTON. There is land for 5 ploughs. Gilbert holds of him. In demesne are 2 ploughs, and 6 slaves; and 15 villans and 2 bordars with 7 ploughs and with a priest. There are 9 acres of meadow. It was worth 30s.; and afterwards 20s.; now £4.10s. Leofric held it freely TRE.

The count himself holds 2½ hides in WARMINGTON, and a certain knight [holds] of him. Azur held them freely TRE. It is worth 20s. What this knight has there is included with the stock of the men who are in the count's manor.

The count himself holds 5 hides in ARLESCOTE, and

SAINT-PIERRE of Preaux [holds] of him. There is land for 5 ploughs. In demesne are 1½ ploughs, and 2 slaves; and 4 villans and 3 bordars with 2 ploughs. There are 12 acres of meadow. It was and is worth £3. Bovi held it freely TRE.

The count himself holds in FENNY COMPTON 4 hides and 3 virgates of land, and Gilbert [holds] of him. There is land for 6 ploughs. In demesne are 2 ploughs, and 7 slaves; and 8 villans with a priest and 6 bordars with 4 ploughs. There are 40 acres of meadow. It was worth 60s.; now £4. Ælfric held it freely TRE.

The count himself holds in TACHBROOK MALLORY 8 hides, less 1 virgate, and Roger [holds] of him. There is land for 6 ploughs. In demesne is half a plough; and 5 villans and 7 bordars with 3 ploughs. There are 12 acres of meadow. It was worth 60s.; now 40[s.]. Baldwin held it freely TRE.

The count himself holds 2 hides in NEWBOLD [in Leamington Spa], and Gilbert [holds] of him. There is land for 4 ploughs. In demesne are 2 [ploughs]; and 6 villans and 4 bordars with 4 ploughs. There are 12 acres of meadow. It was worth 30s.; now 50s. Alsige, Æthelræd and Tubbi held it freely TRE.

IN PATHLOW HUNDRED

The count himself holds 12 hides in LUDDINGTON, and 4 knights [hold] of him. There is land for 9 ploughs. In demesne are 5 ploughs; and 20 villans and 9 bordars with 5 ploughs. There are 42 acres of meadow. It was worth £8; now £6. 4 thegns held it freely TRE as 2 manors.

The count himself holds in LOXLEY 4 hides, less 1 virgate, and Hugh [hold] of him. There is land for 8 ploughs. In demesne are 2 [ploughs], and 3 slaves; and 11 villans with a priest and 11 bordars have 6 ploughs. It was worth 30s.; now £4.10s. Æstan held it freely TRE.

The count himself holds 5 hides in PRESTON BAGOT, and Hugh [holds] of him. There is land for 3 ploughs. In demesne is half a plough, and 2 slaves; and 1 villan and 3 bordars with 1 plough. It was worth 30s.; now 40[s.]. Beorthnoth held it freely TRE.

The count himself holds 3 hides in OVERSLEY, and Fulk [holds] of him. There is land for 4 ploughs. In demesne is 1 [plough]; and 5 villans and 5 bordars with 2 ploughs. There is a mill rendering 4s., and 6 acres of meadow, [and] woodland 3 furlongs long and 1 broad. It was and is worth 40s. Beorhtmær held it freely TRE.

IN BARCHESTON HUNDRED

The count himself holds in ILMINGTON 1 hide and half a virgate, and Odard [holds] of him. He has there in demesne 2 ploughs, and 6 slaves; and [there are] 6 villans with half a plough. It is worth 40s. This land is in the count's manor of ILMINGTON.

In WHITCHURCH, the count's manor, Walter holds of him 1 hide, and has there 1 plough; and it is worth 10s. Alwine held it freely TRE.

The count himself holds 4½ hides in WOLFORD [Wolford or

Little Wolford], and Ralph [holds] of him. There is land for 4 ploughs. In demesne is 1 [plough], and 2 slaves; and 3 villans and 5 bordars with 1 plough. It was worth 30s.; now 40s. Ælfric held it freely TRE.

XVII. The land of Thorkil of Warwick

IN COLESHILL HUNDRED

THORKIL holds CURDWORTH of the king. There are 4 hides. There is land for 7 ploughs. In demesne are 3 ploughs, and 3 slaves; and 12 villans and 7 bordars with 5 ploughs. There are 16 acres of meadow, [and] woodland half a league long and as much broad. It was worth 40s.; now 50s. Wulfwine held it freely TRE.

The same Thorkil holds BICKENHILL [Bickenhill or Middle Bickenhill]. There are 2 hides. There is land for 4 ploughs. In demesne is half a plough; and 7 villans and 4 bordars with 3 ploughs. There are 3 acres of meadow, [and] woodland 4 furlongs long and as much broad. It was and is worth 30s. Alweard held it freely TRE.

The same Thorkil holds another BICKENHILL [Bickenhill or Middle Bickenhill]. There are 2 hides. There is land for 4 ploughs. There are 8 villans with 2 ploughs. There is woodland 12 furlongs long and 6 broad. It was worth 20s.; now 10s. Ælfric held it freely TRE.

The same Thorkil holds 1 hide in MINWORTH. There is land for 1 plough. There is 1 villan with half a plough, and 5 acres of meadow. [There is] woodland half a league long and 3 furlongs broad. It was and is worth 5s. Godric held it freely TRE.

IN MARTON HUNDRED

The same Thorkil holds WOLFHAMPCOTE. There are 4½ hides. There is land for 3 ploughs. In demesne is 1 [plough], and 4 slaves; and 7 villans with a priest and 10 bordars have 4 ploughs. There are 5 acres of meadow. It was and is worth 40s. Eskil held it freely TRE.

IN STONELEIGH HUNDRED

The same Thorkil holds 3½ hides in RYTON-ON-DUNSMORE. There is land for 10 ploughs. There are 23 villans with a priest and 8 bordars having 8 ploughs, and there is a mill rendering 12s., and 12 acres of meadow. [There is] woodland half a league long and 2 furlongs broad. It was worth 100s.; now 60s. Æthelwine, his father, held it freely TRE.

[Folio 241: WARWICKSHIRE]

From Thorkil, Guthmund his brother holds PACK-INGTON [Packington and Little Packington]. There are 4 hides. There is land for 3 ploughs. In demesne is 1 [plough]; and 7 villans and 8 bordars with 3 ploughs. There are 2 mills rendering 2s., and 10 acres of meadow, [and] woodland 1 league long and 1 broad, worth 20s. when it is stocked. The whole was and is worth 30s. Alweard held it; he was free.

From Thorkil, Almær holds LONGDON [in Solihull]. There

are 2½ hides. There is land for 2 ploughs. In demesne is half [a plough]; and 6 villans and 3 bordars have 1½ ploughs. There are 6 acres of meadow, [and] woodland 1 league long and a half broad. It was and is worth 20s. Earnwulf held it TRE.

From Thorkil, Alnoth holds 'MACKADOWN' [in Sheldon]. There are 5 hides, less 1 virgate. There is land for 5 ploughs. There are 10 villans and 4 bordars with 3 ploughs, and 2 acres of meadow. [There is] woodland 1 league long and a half broad. It was worth 20s.; now 40s. Æthelmund held it freely TRE.

From Thorkil, Roger holds MARSTON GREEN [in Bickenhill]. There are 3 hides. There is land for 3 ploughs. In demesne is 1 [plough]; and 4 villans and 2 bordars with 3 ploughs. There are 2 acres of meadow. It was worth 20s.; now 30[s.]. Edwin the sheriff held it freely.

From Thorkil, the same Roger holds half a hide in ELMDON. There is land for half a plough, yet there is there 1 plough in demesne, and 5 acres of meadow. [There is] woodland 1 furlong long and another broad. It was and is worth 5s. Toki held it freely.

From Thorkil, Bruning holds in WIGGINS HILL 3 virgates of land. There is land for 1 plough. This [plough] is there in demesne, and 8 acres of meadow. [There is] woodland 2 furlongs long and as much broad. It was and is worth 5s. The same man held it freely.

From Thorkil, Robert d'Oilly holds in DOSTHILL 2 hides in pledge. There is land for 3 ploughs. There are 7 villans with 2 ploughs, and 2 slaves, and a mill rendering 32d., and 10 acres of meadow. [There is] woodland 2 furlongs long and as much broad. It was worth 30s.; now 40s. Untan held it.

From Thorkil, Edwin holds in [?Nether] WHITACRE 2 hides, less 1 virgate. There is land for 1 plough. This [plough] is in demesne, with 2 villans and 5 bordars, and there are 2 acres of meadow. [There is] woodland 1 league long and a half broad. It was and is worth 10s. Two Wulfrics held it freely TRE.

From Thorkil, Robert d'Oilly holds BARSTON in pledge. There are 9 hides. There is land for 11 ploughs. In demesne is 1 plough; and 6 free men with 9 villans and 4 bordars have 10 ploughs. There is a mill rendering 4s., [and] woodland half a league long and 3 furlongs broad. It was and is worth 100s. Æthelmær held it, and by the king's licence sold it to Æthelwine the sheriff, the father of Thorkil.

From Thorkil, William holds BADDESLEY ENSOR. There are 2 hides. There is land for 2 ploughs. There are 3 villans and 5 bordars and 2 slaves with 1 plough. [There is] woodland 1½ leagues long and half a league broad. It was and is worth 10s.

This William seized upon a fifth part of this land to King William's loss; and a certain Beorhtric who held it TRE dwells there. Arnketil and Ceolræd, Thorkil's men, held the rest of the land.

From Thorkil, 4 brothers hold in WOLFHAMPCOTE 1 hide and half a virgate of land. There is land for 2 ploughs,

and yet there are 3 ploughs, and 3 acres of meadow. It was and is worth 20s. The same men themselves held it, and were free.

From Thorkil, Ermenfrid holds in LADBROKE 1 hide and 1 virgate of land. There is land for 2 ploughs. There are 3 men having 2 ploughs and 6 acres of meadow. It was worth 15s.; now 20s. Edwin held it.

From Thorkil, Ermenfrid holds half a hide in CALCUTT. There is land for 2 ploughs. In demesne is 1 [plough], and 8 acres of meadow. It was worth 4s.; now 8s.

From Thorkil, Richard holds half a hide in CALCUTT. There is land for 1 plough. This [plough] is there, with 2 men, and 8 acres of meadow. It was and is worth 4s.

From Thorkil, Almær holds 1½ hides in LADBROKE and [Lower and Upper] RADBOURN. There is land for 4 ploughs. In demesne are 3 [ploughs], and 6 slaves; and 9 villans and 2 bordars with 3 ploughs, and there are 6 acres of meadow. It was worth 30s.; now 40s.

From Thorkil, Almær holds 1½ hides in CAWSTON. There is land for 3 ploughs. In demesne is 1 [plough], with 1 slave; and 4 villans and 2 bordars have 1 plough. It was worth 10s.; now 16s. 4

From Thorkil, William holds in LADBROKE 2 hides and 1 virgate of land. There is land for 2 ploughs. There are 4 villans and 3 bordars and 2 slaves and 1 knight with 2 ploughs among them all. There are 2 acres of meadow. It was worth 20s.; now 40s.

From Thorkil, 1 priest holds 1 virgate of land in the vill itself. There is 1 plough, with 1 villan, and there are 2 acres of meadow. It was worth 5s.; now 10s.

From Thorkil, Eadwulf holds 2½ hides in RUGBY. There is land for 6 ploughs. In demesne is 1 plough, and 2 slaves; and 11 villans and 5 bordars with 5 ploughs. There is a mill rendering 13s4d., and 16 acres of meadow. It was worth 50s.; now 40s.

From Thorkil, Ulf holds 1 hide in CAWSTON. There is land for 1 plough. This [plough] is in demesne, and 4 villans and 1 bordar and 1 slave. It was worth 10s.; now 12s.

Edwin held these 9 estates mentioned above and could go where he would.

From Thorkil, Joscelin holds in BIRDINGBURY 1 hide and half a virgate of land. There is land for 3 ploughs. There are 3 free men with 4 villans and 3 bordars having 3 ploughs. It was worth 20s.; now 40s. The free men themselves held it freely TRE.

IN MARTON HUNDRED

From Thorkil, Robert holds in NAPTON ON THE HILL 3 virgates of land. There is land for 5 ploughs. In demesne is 1 [plough]; and 4 villans and 5 bordars have 2 ploughs. There are 8 acres of meadow. It was worth 10s.; now 30s. Edwin held it.

From Thorkil, Oslac holds 2½ hides in FLECKNOE. There is land for 4 ploughs. In demesne are 1½ [plough], and 3 slaves;

and 10 villans and 3 bordars with 3½ ploughs. It was and is worth 30s. Edwin held it.

From Thorkil, Hearding holds 4 hides in HODNELL. There is land for 4 ploughs. In demesne is 1 [plough]; and 11 villans and 2 bordars with 2 ploughs, and 20 acres of meadow. It was and is worth 40s. Wulfnoth held it freely TRE.

From Thorkil, Godwine holds 1 hide in the same vill. There is land for 1 plough. This [plough] is in demesne, with 1 slaves; and 4 bordars with half a plough, and 4 acres of meadow. It was worth 10s.; now 20s. Ordric held it freely TRE.

From Thorkil, Æthelric holds in FLECKNOE 1 hide and half a virgate of land. There is land for 2 ploughs. In demesne is 1 [plough]; and 1 villan and 4 bordars with 1 plough. There are 4 acres of meadow. It was worth 20s.; now 30s. Æthelwine, the father of Thorkil, held it.

From Thorkil, Gilbert holds in LADBROKE 3 virgates of land. There is land for half a plough. In demesne, however, is 1 plough, and 2 slaves, and 2 acres of meadow. It was worth 5s.; now 10s. Hereweard held it.

From Thorkil, Wulfric holds in WILLOUGHBY 1½ virgates of land. There is land for 1 plough. This [plough] is in demesne, and 2 villans with 1 bordar, and 1 acre of meadow. It was and is worth 10s. The same Wulfric held it freely.

From Thorkil, Wulfsige holds 3½ virgates of land. There is land for 1½ ploughs. In demesne is half [a plough]; and 2 villans and 3 bordars with 1 plough, and 4 acres of meadow. It was and is worth 10s.

From Thorkil, Gilbert holds in "BENTONE" 1 virgate of land. There is land for half a plough. It was worth 5s.; now 2s.

From Thorkil, Ordric holds 2 hides in 'WALCOTE' [in Frankton] and WILLOUGHBY and CALCUTT. There is land for 1 plough. In demesne, however, is 1 plough, and 2 slaves; and 4 villans and 6 bordars with 1½ ploughs. There are 6 acres of meadow. It was worth 20s.; now 30s. The same Ordric held it freely.

From Thorkil, Ufkil holds half a hide in NAPTON ON THE HILL. There is land for 3 ploughs. In demesne is half a plough; and 4 villans and 2 bordars with 1½ ploughs, and 6 acres of meadow. It was worth 20s.; now 30s. The same Ufkil held it freely.

From Thorkil, Alwine holds in UPPER SHUCKBURGH half a virgate of land. There is land for half a plough. There is [half a plough] in demesne, with 2 bordars, and 2 acres of meadow. It was and is worth 5s. Wulfwine held it freely.

From Thorkil, Leofgeat and Godwine hold half a hide in WILLOUGHBY. There is land for 1 plough. This [plough] is in demesne, and 2 acres of meadow. It was and is worth 10s. The same men themselves held it.

From Thorkil, Godric holds 2 hides in NEWTON. There is land for 2 ploughs. In demesne is 1 [plough], and 4 villans and 2 bordars, and 2 acres of meadow. It was and is worth 20s. Wulfstan held it freely TRE.

From Thorkil, Healfdene holds half a hide in NEWTON. There is land for half a plough; yet there is 1 plough, with 2 bordars. It was and is worth 10s. Godgifu | held it freely | .

From Thorkil, Ralph holds half a hide in NEWTON. There is land for 1 plough. There are 2 villans, and half an acre of meadow. It was and is worth 2s.

From Thorkil, Wulfric holds 1 hide in 'BIGGIN' [in Stoke]. There is land for half a plough; yet there is 1 plough, with 2 villans and 1 bordar and 1 slave, and 3 acres of meadow. It was worth 5s.; now 10s. The same Wulfric held it freely.

[Folio 241V: WARWICKSHIRE]

From Thorkil, Ralph holds 1 hide in 'BIGGIN' [in Stoke]. There is land for 1 plough. There is 1 bordar with half a plough, and 3 acres of meadow. It was worth 5s.; now 3s. Wulfstan held it freely TRE.

From Thorkil, the same Ralph holds half a hide in [?] CHURCHOVER. There is land for half a plough. There is 1 villan, and half an acre of meadow. It was and is worth 3s.

From Thorkil, Leofgifu holds 2 hides in LITTLE LAWFORD. There is land for 1½ ploughs. There are 6 villans with 1 plough and 1 slave, and a mill rendering 4s., and 1½ acres of meadow. It was worth 20s.; now 10s8d. Alwine held it freely TRE.

From Thorkil, Robert d'Oilly holds 1 hide in [?] MARSTON [in Wolston]. There is land for 1 plough. It is waste. There are 3 acres of meadow. It was worth 10s.; now 16d. Earl Ælfgar held it.

From Thorkil, Ermenfrid holds 2 hides in ASHOW. There is land for 4 ploughs. There are 9 villans and 13 bordars with 4 ploughs, and 2 mills rendering 20s., and 16 acres of meadow. [There is] woodland half a league long and 3 furlongs broad. It was worth 20s.; now 40s. Thorkil held it freely.

From Thorkil, William holds 4 hides in HARBURY. There is land for 9 ploughs. There are 12 villans with a priest and 5 bordars having 4 ploughs. There are 6 acres of meadow. It was and is worth 60s. Ordric held it freely.

From Thorkil, Alwine holds 4 hides in BAGINTON. There is land for 4 ploughs. In demesne are 2 [ploughs]; and 7 villans and 8 bordars with 2 ploughs. There is a mill rendering 10s8d., and 27 acres of meadow. It was worth 30s.; now 50s. Arnketil held it freely TRE.

From Thorkil, Eadwulf holds 2 hides in BINLEY. There is land for 3 ploughs. In demesne is 1 [plough]; and 5 villans and 7 bordars with 2 ploughs. There are 2 slaves, and a mill rendering 40d., and 8 acres of meadow, [and] woodland 4 furlongs long and 2 furlongs broad. It was worth 20s.; now 35s. The same man held it who now holds it.

From Thorkil, Robert holds in WESTON UNDER WETHERLEY 1½ virgates of land. There is land for half a plough. It is waste. There are 4 acres of meadow. It was worth 6s.; now it renders nothing. Wulfwig held it freely.

From Thorkil, Wulfsige holds half a hide in BRANDON.

There is land for 4 ploughs. There are 10 villans with 1 slave; they have 3 ploughs. There is a mill rendering 26d., and 16 acres of meadow, [and] woodland 4 furlongs long and 2 furlongs broad. It was worth 20s.; now 25s. Thorkil held it freely.

From Thorkil, Robert d'Oilly holds half a hide in LILLINGTON. There is land for half a plough, yet there is 1 [plough], with 6 bordars and 1 female slave who have another plough. There are 4 acres of meadow. It was worth 10s.; now 20s. Bruning held it freely.

From Thorkil, Ermenfrid holds 5 hides in RADFORD SEMELE. There is land for 13 ploughs. In demesne are 3 ploughs, and 8 slaves; and 19 villans and 8 bordars with 9 ploughs. There is a mill rendering 6s8d., and 12 acres of meadow. It was worth 100s.; and afterwards 40s.; now £6. Edwin held it freely TRE. Ermenfrid bought it from Ketilbert by [the king's] leave and holds it of the king in fief, as the king's writ testifies.

IN 'HUNESBERI' HUNDRED

From Thorkil, Almær holds 5 hides in RATLEY. There is land for 7 ploughs. In demesne are 2 [ploughs], and 6 slaves; and 18 villans and 7 bordars with 7 ploughs. There are 24 acres of meadow. It was worth £3; and afterwards £4; now 100s. Ordric held it freely TRE.

From Thorkil, Almær holds 2 hides in FENNY COMPTON. There is land for 2 ploughs. In demesne are 1½ ploughs, and 4 slaves; and 6 villans and 2 bordars with 1½ ploughs. There are 16 acres of meadow. It was worth 20s.; now 40s.

From Thorkil, Roger holds in the same vill 3 hides and 1 virgate of land. There is land for 6 ploughs. In demesne are 2 [ploughs], with 1 slave; and 8 villans and 4 bordars with 4 ploughs. There are 34 [acres] of meadow. It was worth 40s.; now 50s. Ordric and Alwine and Wulfsige held it freely TRE.

Of the fief of Thorkil, the Count of Meulan holds MYTON. There are 2 hides. There is land for 2 ploughs. In demesne is 1 [plough], and 2 slaves; and 7 villans and 7 bordars with 3 ploughs. There are 2 mills rendering 70s., and 8 men paying 32d. It was worth 100s.; and afterwards 40s.; now £6. Earl Edwin held it. R. Halebold bought this land.

From Thorkil, Warin holds 3 hides in WORMLEIGHTON. There is land for 8 ploughs. In demesne are 4 [ploughs]; and 15 villans and 4 bordars and 2 Frenchmen, among them all, have 7 ploughs. There are 36 acres of meadow. Of this land, 2 knights hold 1 hide and 1 virgate, and have 2 ploughs, with 3 bordars. The whole was worth TRE £4; and afterwards as much; now £10. Ordric and Wulfwine and Wulfric held it freely.

IN STONELEIGH HUNDRED

From Thorkil, Tonni holds 2 hides in BERICOTE. There is land for 3 ploughs. In demesne is 1 [plough], and 2 slaves; and 4 villans and 3 bordars with 2 ploughs. There is a mill rendering 4s., and 6 acres of meadow. It was worth 20s.; now 40s. Æthelwine, the father of Thorkil, held it.

From Thorkil, the Church of ST MARY of Warwick holds 1 hide in MYTON. There is land for 1 plough. There are 3 bordars with 1 plough, and 1 female slave. There are 4 acres of meadow. It was worth 5s.; now 10s. Earl Edwin held it.

From Thorkil, Algar holds 1½ hides. There is land for 3 ploughs. In demesne are 2 ploughs, and 6 slaves; and 4 villans and 4 bordars with 1 plough. There are 12 acres of meadow. It was worth 30s.; now 40s. Ælfric held it freely.

IN 'TREMLOWE' HUNDRED

From Thorkil, Ermenfrid holds 1 hide in FULREADY and another in ETTINGTON. There is land for 1 plough. This [plough] is in demesne, with 1 bordar. It was worth 10s.; now 25s. Almær held it freely TRE.

From Thorkil, Alwine holds 3 hides in COMPTON [?Verney]. There is land for 6 ploughs. In demesne are 2 [ploughs], and 4 slaves; and 9 villans and 10 bordars with 5 ploughs. There are 30 acres of meadow. It was and is worth £4.

From Thorkil, the Abbot of Abingdon holds 1 hide in KINGSTON. There is land for 7 ploughs, and 2 slaves; and 10 villans and 8 bordars with 6 ploughs. There are 16 acres of meadow. It was worth 60s.; now 100s. Alweald held it.

From Thorkil, the same abbot holds in KINGSTON 1 hide in pledge. There is land for 2 ploughs. There are 5 English knights having 4½ ploughs. There are 8 acres of meadow. It was worth 20s.; now 50s. Alnoth, Beorhtwine and Thorir held it freely TRE.

IN "FERNECUMBE" HUNDRED

From Thorkil, William holds 4 hides in COUGHTON. There is land for 6 ploughs. There are 2 free men and 7 bordars and 4 slaves with 3 ploughs. There is a mill rendering 32d., and in Warwick 1 house rendering 8d. There are 10 acres of meadow, woodland 6 furlongs long and 4 furlongs broad, [and] pasture for 50 pigs. It was worth 40s.; and afterwards 20s.; now 50s. Unton held it freely.

From Thorkil, Robert d'Oilly holds 3 hides in [?] NUNEATON. There is land for 5 ploughs. In demesne are 3 ploughs, and 5 slaves; and 9 villans and 8 bordars with 8 ploughs. There are 5 acres of meadow, [and] woodland 1 league in length and bredth. It was worth 40s.; now £4. Alwine held it freely TRE.

[Folio 242: WARWICKSHIRE]

XVIII. The land of Hugh de Grandmesnil

Hugh de Grandmesnil holds of the king, in charge, 1 hide and the sixth part of 1 hide in HILLMORTON and in WILLOUGHBY. There is land for 2 ploughs. There are 5 villans with 1 bordar having 2 ploughs. It was worth 20s.; now 30s. Grimkel and Swein held it.

IN 'TREMLOWE' HUNDRED

The same Hugh holds 10 hides in BUTLERS MARSTON. There is land for 10 ploughs. In demesne are 3 [ploughs], and 6 slaves and 2 female slaves; and 30 villans and 2 bordars with a priest have 7 ploughs. There are 2 mills rendering 11s., and there are 2 Frenchmen, and 2 burgesses in Warwick pay 16d. It was worth £10; now £15. Baldwin held it freely.

The same Hugh holds 10 hides in PILLERTON HERSEY. There is land for 10 ploughs. In demesne are 3 [ploughs], and 8 slaves and 4 female slaves; and 23 villans with a priest and 1 knight and 5 bordars having 9 ploughs. There is a mill rendering 5s., [and] woodland 1 league long and 1 broad, and in Warwick 1 messuage rendering 4d., and 20 acres of meadow. It was worth £10; now £17. Baldwin held it freely.

The same Hugh holds 4 hides in MIDDLETON. There is land for 4 ploughs. In demesne are 1½ ploughs, and 3 slaves; and 12 villans with a priest and 5 bordars have 2½ ploughs. There is a mill rendering 20s., and 6 acres of meadow. It was worth £4; now £6. Palli held it freely TRE.

IN "FEXHOLE" HUNDRED

The same Hugh holds OXHILL. There are 10 hides. There is land for 8 ploughs. In demesne are 3 [ploughs], and 11 slaves; and 20 villans and 11 bordars with 7 ploughs. There is a mill rendering 16d., and 20 acres of meadow. It was worth £10; now £11. Toli held it freely TRE.

The same Hugh holds 3 hides in SHREWLEY. There is land for 12 ploughs. In demesne is 1 [plough], and 3 slaves; and 8 villans and 6 bordars with 2½ ploughs. There are 10 acres of meadow, [and] woodland 1 league long and a half broad. It was worth 20s.; now 30s. Toli held it freely.

The same Hugh holds half a hide in LAPWORTH. There is land for 1 plough. There are 3 villans. [There is] woodland 2 leagues long and 1 league broad. It was worth 10s.; now 20s. Baldwin held it freely.

From HUGH himself, Hubert holds 2½ hides in THURLASTON. There is land for 7 ploughs. In demesne are 2 [ploughs]; and 9 villans and 4 bordars with 3 ploughs. There are 40 acres of meadow, and 1 furlong of pasture. It was worth 40s.; now 60s. Baldwin held it.

From Hugh, William holds 3 virgates of land in LADBROKE. There is land for 1 plough. There a priest and 1 villan with 2 bordars have half a plough, and [there is] a mill rendering 3s., and 3 acres of meadow. It was worth 5s.; now 10s.

From Hugh, Robert holds 1 hide in ETTINGTON. [...] There is land for 1 plough. There 1 villan with 1 bordar has half a plough. It was and is worth 10s. Baldwin held it.

From Hugh, the Abbey of Saint-Evroul holds 6 hides and 1 virgate of land in PILLERTON PRIORS. There is land for 10 ploughs. In demesne are 3 [ploughs]; and 13 villans and 23 bordars with 1 Frenchman and 3 thegns have 8 ploughs. There are 12 acres of meadow. It was worth £6; now £10. 4 thegns held it freely TRE.

From Hugh, Roger holds 5 hides in WHATCOTE. There is land for 5 ploughs. In demesne are 4 [ploughs]; and 7 villans with a priest and 19 bordars have 3 ploughs. It was worth 100s.; now £7. Toli held it freely.

From Hugh, the same Roger holds 3 hides in ROWINGTON. There is land for 8 ploughs. There 27 villans with a priest and 24 bordars have 9 ploughs. [There is] woodland 1½ leagues long and 8 furlongs broad. It was and is worth 100s. Baldwin held it freely TRE.

From Hugh, Osbern holds 5 hides in BILLESLEY. There is land for 8 ploughs. In demesne are 3 ploughs, and 8 slaves; and 8 villans with a priest and 9 bordars having 4 ploughs, [and] in Warwick 1 house rendering 8d. It was and is worth 100s. Baldwin held it.

From Hugh, Hugh fitzConstantius holds 1 virgate of land in LOXLEY. There is land for half a plough. There is 1 villan. It was and is worth 5s. Manegot held it freely.

IN COLESHILL HUNDRED

From Hugh, Walter holds half a hide in [?Over] WHITACRE. There is land for half a plough. There is 1 villan ploughing with 2 oxen. It was and is worth 2s. Baldwin held it.

XIX. The land of Henry de Ferrers

IN COLESHILL HUNDRED

HENRY de Ferrers holds 5½ hides in GRENDON, and Turstin [holds] of him. There is land for 16 ploughs. There are 24 villans and 16 bordars with 8 ploughs. There is a mill rendering 5s., and 36 acres of meadow, [and] woodland 1½ leagues long and 1 league broad. It was and is worth 40s. Siward Barn held it.

IN 'BUMBELOWE' HUNDRED

From Henry, Ralph holds 4 hides in BURTON HASTINGS. There is land for 8 ploughs. In demesne are 2 [ploughs]; and 13 villans with a priest and 7 bordars have 6 ploughs. There are 2 mills rendering 7s8d. It was worth £4; now 40s. Siward held it.

IN STONELEIGH HUNDRED

From Henry, Wazelin holds 2 hides in HARBURY. There is land for 5 ploughs. In demesne are 2 [ploughs], and 2 slaves; and 4 villans with 1 plough. It was worth 40s.; now £4. Siward held it.

IN 'TREMLOWE' HUNDRED

From Henry, Saswalo holds 17 hides in ETTINGTON. There is land for 12 ploughs. In demesne are 4 ploughs, and 10 slaves; and 32 villans with a priest and 25 bordars and 1 knight and 2 thegns have 16½ ploughs. There is a mill rendering 18s., and 30 acres of meadow. It was worth £6; and afterwards £4; now £20.

From Henry, Wazelin holds half a hide in CHESTERTON.

There is land for 1½ ploughs. There is 1 plough, with 1 oxman, and 1 acre of meadow. It was and is worth 10s. [...]

From Henry, Nigel holds 2½ hides in AUSTREY. There is land for 2 ploughs. In demesne is 1 [plough]; and 7 villans and 3 bordars have 2 ploughs. It was and is worth 20s.

XX. The land of Roger d'Ivry

IN STONELEIGH HUNDRED

ROGER d'IVRY holds of the king, as he says, 5 hides in CUBBINGTON. There is land for 4 ploughs. In demesne are 2 [ploughs], and 3 slaves; and 2 villans and 2 bordars with 1 plough. There are 15 acres of meadow. It was and is worth 40s. Thorbiorn held it freely TRE. This is of the fief of the Bishop of Bayeux.

XXI. The land of Robert d'Oilly

IN COLESHILL HUNDRED

ROBERT d'OILLY holds 2 hides in [?] MARSTON [in Bickenhill], and Robert the huntsman [holds] of him. [There is] land for 2 ploughs. In demesne is 1 [plough], and 2 slaves; and 4 villans have 2 ploughs. There are 6 acres of meadow, [and] woodland 4 furlongs long and 1 furlong broad. It was worth 10s.; now 20s. Ælfric held it freely TRE. Robert bought this land from him by leave of King William.

[Folio 242V: WARWICKSHIRE]

XXII. The land of Robert of Stafford

IN 'BUMBELOWE' HUNDRED

ROBERT of Stafford holds of the king 7 hides in [?] CHURCHOVER. There is land for 12 ploughs. In demesne are 4 [ploughs]; and 14 villans and 5 bordars have 5 ploughs. There is a mill rendering 2s., and 4 acres of meadow. It was worth 20s.; now 100s. Vagn held it freely TRE.

The same Robert holds 7 hides in WOLFORD [Wolford or Little Wolford]. There is land for 10 ploughs. In demesne are [...] and 4 slaves; and 8 villans and 8 bordars with a priest have 6 ploughs. There is a mill rendering 20d. It was worth 20s.; now 100s. Vagn held it freely.

The same Robert holds 5 hides in BURMINGTON. There is land for 8 ploughs. In demesne are 2 [ploughs]; and 12 villans and 8 bordars with 6 ploughs. There is a mill rendering 10s., and 12 acres of meadow. It was worth 60s.; now 100s.

IN "FEXHOLE" HUNDRED

The same Robert holds [Lower, Middle and Upper] TYSOE. There are 23 hides. There is land for 32 ploughs. In demesne are 11 [ploughs], and 9 slaves; and 53 villans with a priest and 28 bordars have 23 ploughs. There are 16 acres of meadow, and in Warwick 3 houses rendering 18d. It was worth £20; now £30. Vagn held it freely.

The same Robert holds 5 hides in IDLICOTE. There is land for 9 ploughs. In demesne are 3 ploughs, and 7 slaves; and 26

villans and 3 bordars with 8 ploughs. It was worth £4; now £8. Hafgrimr and Ordheah held it freely.

IN "FERNECUMBE" HUNDRED

The same Robert holds 1 hide in ULLENHALL. There is land for 15 ploughs. There are 17 villans and 11 bordars with 6 ploughs. [There is] woodland half a league long and 1 furlong broad. It was and is worth £3. Vagn held it.

The same Robert holds 5 hides in 'OFFORD' [in Wootton Wawen]. There is land for 6 ploughs. There are 3½ ploughs, with 3 slaves and 10 bordars. There is a mill rendering 4s., [and] woodland 1 league long and half a league broad. It was worth £3; now £4. Vagn held it freely TRE.

The same Robert holds 5 hides in EDSTONE. There is land for 5 ploughs. In demesne are 2 [ploughs], and 2 slaves; and 4 villans and 6 bordars with 1 plough, and in Warwick 1 house rendering 5d. [There is] woodland half a league long and half a furlong broad. It is worth £3. Æthelric and Wulfwine held it freely.

IN PATHLOW HUNDRED

The same Robert holds 7 hides in WOOTTON WAWEN. There is land for 9 ploughs. There are 23 villans with a priest and 22 bordars having 6 ploughs. There are 2 mills rendering 11s. and 8 sticks of eels, [and] woodland 2 leagues long and 1 broad. It is worth £4. Vagn held it freely.

IN STONELEIGH HUNDRED

From the same Robert, Ælfric holds 5 hides in BUBBENHALL. There is land for 5 ploughs. In demesne are 1½ ploughs, with 1 slave; and 6 villans and 2 bordars with 2½ ploughs. There is a mill rendering 4s., [and] woodland 2 furlongs long and as much broad. It is worth 50s. The same man held it freely.

From Robert, Grim holds half a hide in BARTON-ON-THE-HEATH. There is land for 1 plough. This [plough] is there in demesne, and 5 slaves, and 2 villans and 3 bordars. It was and is worth 20s. This land is IN BARCHESTON HUNDRED

From Robert, Ordwig holds 2 hides in WOLFORD [Wolford or Little Wolford]. There is land for 6 ploughs. In demesne are 2 [ploughs]; and 4 villans and 4 bordars with 1 plough. It is worth 50s. Alwig held it freely.

From Robert, Alwine holds 2 hides in the same vill. There is land for 2 ploughs. In demesne is 1 [plough], with 1 slave; and 4 villans and 3 bordars with 1 plough. It was worth 20s.; now 30s. Alwine held it freely.

From Robert, Iwein holds 1½ hides in WILLINGTON. There is land for 2 ploughs. In demesne is 1 [plough], and 2 slaves, with 1 villan and 1 bordar. It was and is worth 20s. Dodda and Leofric held it freely.

From Robert, Brian holds 2 hides in DITCHFORD. There is land for 7 ploughs. In demesne are 2 [ploughs], and 9 slaves; and 8 villans and 3 bordars with 3 ploughs. There is a mill rendering 68d. It was worth 40s.; now £4. Leofric held it freely TRE.

From Robert, Warin holds 5 hides in COMPTON [?Scorpion]. There is land for 6 ploughs. In demesne are 3 ploughs, and 8 slaves; and 8 villans and 2 bordars with 6 ploughs. There are 6 acres of meadow. It was worth 60s.; now 100s. Beorhtric holds [sic] held it freely.

From Robert, Alwine holds 1 hide in COMPTON [?Wynyates]. There is land for 1 plough. There are 2 bordars. It was and is worth 10s. 2 brothers held it freely.

IN "FERNECUMBE" HUNDRED

From Robert, Hugh holds 2 hides in MORTON BAGOT. There is land for 4 ploughs. In demesne is 1 [plough], and 2 slaves; and 5 villans and 5 bordars with 2 ploughs. There is meadow 3 furlongs long and 6 perches broad, [and] woodland half a league long and 1 furlong broad. It was worth 30s.; now 50s. Grimulf held it freely.

IN BARCHESTON HUNDRED

From Robert, Æthelric holds 1 hide in [?] ADMINGTON. There is land for 1 plough. This [plough] is there in demesne, with 2 slaves and 1 villan. It was worth 10s.; now 15s. Æthelric held it freely.

IN PATHLOW HUNDRED

From Robert, Hugh holds 1 hide and 1 virgate of land in 'RUIN CLIFFORD' [in Old Stratford]. There is land for 2 ploughs. In demesne is 1 [plough], and 2 slaves; and 3 villans and 3 bordars with 1 plough. It was and is worth 30s. Sæweard held it freely TRE.

From Robert, William holds 5 hides in CLOPTON [in Old Stratford]. There is land for 3 ploughs. In demesne is 1 [plough], with 1 slave; and 7 villans and 3 bordars with 2 ploughs. It was and is worth 60s. Old and Æthelgifu held it freely TRE.

From Robert, Hervey holds 1 hide in NORTON LINDSEY. There is land for 2 ploughs. In demesne, however, are 2 [ploughs], and 4 slaves; and 5 villans and 2 bordars with 2 ploughs. It was worth 20s.; now 40s. Vagn held it freely TRE.

From Robert, Urfer holds 1 hide and 1 virgate and the third part of 1 virgate in WOLVERTON. There is land for 2 ploughs. In demesne is 1 [plough], with 1 slave and 2 villans, and 1 furlong of meadow. It was worth 10s.; now 20s. Sigmund the Dane held it freely TRE.

From Robert, Drogo holds 3 hides in WHITLEY. There is land for 6 ploughs. In demesne is 1 [plough], and 2 slaves; and 3 villans and 6 bordars with 2 ploughs. There is a mill rendering 2s., and 10 acres of meadow, [and] woodland half a league long and 2 furlongs broad. It was worth 20s.; now 40s. 3 brothers held it.

From Robert, Iudichael holds 1½ hides in LANGLEY. There is land for 2 ploughs. In demesne are 2 [ploughs], with 1 slave; and 3 villans and 4 bordars with 2 ploughs. There are 12 acres

of meadow, [and] woodland 1 league long and half a league broad. It was worth 30s.; now 40s. Earnwig held it freely.

From Robert, Æthelric holds 1 hide in BEARLEY. There is land for 1 plough. There is 1 villan and 1 slave, and 1 acre of meadow. It was worth 20s.; now 10s. The same man held it.

Lyfing holds in 'OFFORD' [in Wootton Wawen] land for 1 plough of inland and there he has 1 plough. It was and is worth 10s.

XXIII. The land of Robert Despenser

IN COLESHILL HUNDRED

ROBERT Despenser holds of the king 9 hides in MARSTON [near Kingsbury]. There is land for 8 ploughs. In demesne are 2 [ploughs], and 2 slaves; and 24 villans with 6 ploughs. There is a mill rendering 10s., and 6 acres of meadow. It was and is worth £4. Æthelmær held it freely TRE. In the same way [he held] this land following.

The same Robert holds half a hide in FILLONGLEY. There is land for 2 ploughs. There are 4 villans with a priest and 1 bordar having 2 ploughs. There is 1 acre of meadow, [and] woodland 2 leagues long and 1 league broad. It was worth 10s.; now 20s.

The same Robert holds 1 hide in LEA MARSTON. There is land for 1 plough. There is 1 knight with 1 plough; and 4 villans and 1 bordar and 2 slaves with 1 plough. There are 2 acres of meadow. It was worth 10s.; it is worth 15s. Alwine held it freely.

The same Robert holds 10 hides in BARSTON. There is land for 10 ploughs. There are 6 free men and 9 villans and 4 bordars with 10 ploughs. There is a mill rendering 4s., [and] woodland half a league long and 3 furlongs broad. It was and is worth 100s. Æthelmær held it freely and, with the leave of King William, sold it to Æthelwine the sheriff.

XXIIII. The land of Robert de Vessey

IN 'BUMBELOWE' HUNDRED

ROBERT de Vessey holds of the king 5½ hides in WOLVEY. There is land for 8 ploughs. In demesne are 2 [ploughs], and 4 slaves; and 15 villans with a priest and 2 bordars have 7 ploughs. There are 50 acres of meadow, [and] pasture half a league in length and breadth. It was worth †£3†; now 50s. Æthelric son of Mærgeat held it freely TRE.

The same Robert holds 3 virgates of land in [?Nether] WHITACRE. There is land for 1 plough, and there is [1 plough], with 1 villan, and 2 acres of meadow. It was worth 10s.; now 2s. Æthelric held it freely.

XXV. The land of Ralph de Mortimer

IN 'BUMBELOWE' HUNDRED

RALPH de Mortimer holds STRETTON [near Nuneaton], and Roger [holds] of him. There are 3 hides. There is land for 6 ploughs. In demesne are 2 [ploughs]; and 8 villans and 4 bordars with 4 ploughs. There are 5 acres of meadow. It was worth 40s.; now 30s. Eadric held it freely.

XXVI. The land of Ralph de Limesy

RALPH de Limesy holds of the king 5 hides in BUDBROOKE. There is land for 12 ploughs. In demesne are 3 ploughs, and 7 slaves; and 22 villans and 13 bordars with 6 ploughs. There is a mill rendering 2s., and 30 acres of meadow, [and] woodland 1 league long and 3 furlongs broad. In Warwick 7 houses render 7s. a year. It was and is worth £8. Earl Edwin held it.

XXVII. The land of William fitzAnsculf

WILLIAM fitzAnsculf holds of the king ASTON [in Birmingham], and Godmund [holds] of him. There are 8 hides. There is land for 20 ploughs. In demesne is land for 6 ploughs, but the ploughs are not there. There 30 villans with a priest and 1 slave and 12 bordars have 18 ploughs. There is a mill rendering 3s., [and] woodland 3 leagues long and half a league broad. It was worth £4; now 100s. Earl Edwin held it.

From William, Stenkil holds 1 hide in WITTON. There is land for 4 ploughs. In demesne is 1 [plough], and 2 slaves; and 1 villan and 2 bordars with 2 ploughs. It was worth 10s.; now 20[s.]. The same Stenkil held it freely.

From William, Peter holds 3 hides in ERDINGTON. There is land for 6 ploughs. In demesne is 1 [plough], and 2 slaves; and 9 villans and 3 bordars with 4 ploughs. There is a mill rendering 3s., and 5 acres of meadow. [There is] woodland 1 league long and a half broad, but it is in the king's preserve. It was worth 20s.; now 30[s.]. Earl Edwin held it.

From William, Drogo holds 2 hides in EDGBASTON. There is land for 4 ploughs. In demesne are 1½ ploughs; and 3 villans and 7 bordars with 5 ploughs. [There is] woodland 3 furlongs broad and half a league long. It was worth 20s.; now 30[s.]. Aski and Alwig held it freely.

From William, Richard holds 4 hides in BIRMINGHAM. There is land for 6 ploughs. In demesne is 1 [plough]; and 5 villans and 4 bordars with 2 ploughs. [There is] woodland half a league long and 2 furlongs broad. It was and is worth 20s. Wulfwine held it freely TRE.

IN CUTTLESTONE HUNDRED

From William, Roger holds 2 hides in ESSINGTON[Staffs.]. There is land for 6 ploughs. In demesne is 1 [plough], and 2 slaves; and 15 villans and 2 bordars with 3 ploughs. [There is] woodland 1 league long and as much broad. In Bushbury [Staffs.] is 1 virgate of land belonging to this land, but it is waste. It was and is worth 20s.

XXVIII. The land of William fitzCorbucion

WILLIAM fitzCorbucion holds "ERMENDONE" of the king, and Robert [holds] of him in pledge. There are 4 hides. There is land for 5 ploughs. In demesne are 2 [ploughs], and 6 slaves; and 6 villans and 3 bordars with 2½ ploughs. There are 10 acres of meadow, [and] woodland 4 furlongs long and 2 furlongs broad. It was and is worth 50s. Thorkil Batoc held it freely.

From William, Æthelmær holds 2 hides in KINETON GREEN [in Solihull]. There is land for 2 ploughs. There are 5 villans having these. [There is] woodland half a league long and 4 furlongs broad. It was and is worth 10s. Thorkil held it freely TRE.

From William, Juhell holds 2½ hides in SECKINGTON. There is land for 4 ploughs. In demesne is 1 [plough]; and 6 villans and 4 bordars with 2 ploughs. There are 1½ acres of meadow. It was and is worth 30s. Earnwig held it.

From William, Ordric holds 2 hides in WISHAW. There is land for 2 ploughs. There are 3 villans with a priest and 4 bordars. [There is] woodland 3 furlongs long and 1 broad. It was worth 30s.; now 10s. The same Ordric held it freely.

IN MARTON HUNDRED

From William, Roger holds 1 hide in HODNELL. There is [land] for 1 plough. This [plough] is there, with 2 villans and 2 bordars. There are 6 acres of meadow. It was worth 10s.; now 20s. Alwig held it freely.

From William, Osmund holds 2 hides in HUNNINGHAM. There is land for 4 ploughs. In demesne is 1 [plough], and 2 slaves; and 4 villans and 2 bordars with 1 plough. There are 6 acres of meadow. It was worth 40s.; now 30s. Earnwig held it freely TRE.

From William, Ketil holds 1½ hides in the same vill and half a virgate of land. There is land for 3 ploughs. In demesne is 1 [plough], with 1 slave; and 3 villans and 5 bordars with 2 ploughs. There are 6 acres of meadow. It was and is worth 30s. Sæwulf held it freely.

IN STONELEIGH HUNDRED

From William, Johais holds 2½ virgates of land in WESTON UNDER WETHERLEY. There is land for 1½ ploughs. In demesne is 1 [plough], with 1 villan and 1 bordar. There are 10 acres of meadow. It was and is worth 10s. Sæweald held it freely.

From William, Roger holds 1 virgate of land in COUNDON. There is land for 1 plough. There are 2 bordars. [There is] woodland half a league long and 4 furlongs broad. It was worth 5s.; now 4s.

IN BARCHESTON HUNDRED

From William, Johais holds 2½ hides in BARCHESTON. There is land for 3½ ploughs. In demesne are 2 [ploughs]; and 5 villans and 7 bordars with 1½ ploughs. There is a mill rendering 100d., and 12 acres of meadow. It was worth 40s.; now 50s. Viking held it freely TRE.

From William, Geoffrey holds 1 hide in MAPPLEBOROUGH. There is land for 3 ploughs. In demesne is 1 [plough], with 1 slave; and 2 villans with 1 plough. There are 10 acres of meadow, [and] woodland 1 furlong long and 1 broad. It was worth 20s.; now 15s. Leofgeat held it freely.

From William, Turchil holds 1½ hides in EXHALL. There is land for 1 plough. There are 2 bordars, and 10 acres of meadow. It was worth 10s.; now 5s. Swein held it freely TRE.

From William, Leofric and Æthelgifu hold 3 hides and 1 virgate of land in [?Ardens] GRAFTON. There is land for 2 ploughs. In demesne is 1 [plough], and 2 slaves; and 1 villan and 3 bordars with 1 plough. There are 4 acres of meadow. It was worth 40s.; now 30s. The same men themselves held it freely.

From William, William holds 2 hides in BINTON. There is land for 2 ploughs. In demesne is 1 [plough], with 1 slave, and 5 bordars. There are 3 acres of meadow. From part of a mill, 4 summae of corn and 8 sticks of eels, and from Droitwich [Worcs.] 3 summae of salt. It was worth 20s.; now 30s. Eadric held it freely TRE.

IN 'TREMLOWE' HUNDRED

William himself holds 1 hide in BARFORD of the king. There is land for 2 ploughs. There are 2 slaves, and 9 acres of meadow. It was worth 20s.; now 5s. Sæwulf held it TRE.

IN "FERNECUMBE" HUNDRED

The same William holds 4 hides in STUDLEY. There is land for 11 ploughs. In demesne are 2 [ploughs], and 3 slaves; and 19 villans with a priest and 12 bordars have 9 ploughs. There is a mill rendering 5s., and 24 acres of meadow. A salt-pan renders 19 summae of salt. [There is] woodland 1 league long and half a league broad. It was and is worth 100s. Swein held it freely.

The same William holds 2½ hides and 2 parts of 1 virgate in WOLVERTON. There is land for 5 ploughs. In demesne is 1 [plough], and 4 slaves; and 10 villans and 7 bordars with 5 ploughs. There are 20 acres of meadow, [and] woodland 1 furlong long and a half broad. In Warwick 1 house renders 8d. It was worth 30s.; now 60s. Earnwine held it freely TRE.

The same William holds 4 hides in BEARLEY. There is land for 4 ploughs. In demesne is 1 [plough], and 2 slaves; and 9 villans and 6 bordars with 5 ploughs. There are 4 acres of meadow. In Warwick 1 house renders 8d. It was worth 60s.; now 40s. Earnwine and his mother held it freely.

IN CUTTLESTONE HUNDRED

The same William holds CHILLINGTON [Staffs.]. There are 3 hides. There is land for 6 ploughs. In demesne is 1 plough, and 9 slaves; and 13 villans and 6 bordars with 5 ploughs. There are 2 acres of meadow, [and] woodland 2 leagues long and half a league broad. It was worth £4; now 30s. The Bishop of Chester claims this land.

XXIX. The land of William Bonvalet

IN 'TREMLOWE' HUNDRED

WILLIAM Bonvalet holds LIGHTHORNE of the king. There are 5 hides besides inland. There is land for 18 ploughs. In demesne are 2 ploughs, and 7 slaves; and 19 villans and 9 bordars with a priest have 6 ploughs. There are 30 acres of meadow, and 1 grove 2 furlongs long and 20 perches broad. It was worth 100s.; now £7. Earl Ralph held it.

[Folio 243V: WARWICKSHIRE]

IN STONELEIGH HUNDRED

The same William holds 3 virgates of land in HARBURY. There is land for 2 ploughs. There are 2 villans. It was worth 10s.; now 5s. Alwine held it freely TRE.

IN "FERNECUMBE" HUNDRED

From William, Roger holds 4½ hides in UPTON. There is land for 8 ploughs. In demesne are 1½ [ploughs], and 4 slaves; and 10 villans and 5 bordars with 4 ploughs. There are 30 acres of meadow, [and] woodland 10 furlongs and 18 perches long and 5 furlongs broad. It is worth 70s.; it was worth 10s. 3 men of Earl Leofric held it freely.

From William, Hugh holds 2 hides in SPERNALL. There is land for 4 ploughs. In demesne is 1 [plough]; and 4 villans and 7 bordars with 3 ploughs. There is a mill rendering 4s. and 7 sticks of eels, and 8 acres of meadow, [and] woodland 3 furlongs long and 1 broad. It is worth 40s.

From William, William holds 1 hide in STUDLEY. There is land for 2 ploughs. In demesne is 1 plough, and 4 acres of meadow. [There is] woodland 3 furlongs long and 2 furlongs broad. It is worth 10s. Godric held it freely.

XXX. The land of Geoffrey de Mandeville

GEOFFREY de Mandeville holds LONG COMPTON of the king. There are 30 hides. There is land for 20 ploughs. In demesne are 7 [ploughs], and 25 slaves; and 45 villans with a priest and 13 bordars and 2 knights have 10 ploughs. There is a mill rendering 10s., and meadow 3 furlongs long and as much broad, [and] woodland 2 furlongs in length and breadth. It was worth £15; now £30. Esger the staller held it.

IN 'HUNESBERI' HUNDRED

From the same Geoffrey, William holds half a hide and the fourth part of a hide in WORMLEIGHTON. There is land for 1½ ploughs. In demesne is 1 plough, with 2 bordars. It was worth 20s.; now 15s.

XXXI. The land of Geoffrey de La Guerche

IN 'BUMBELOWE' HUNDRED

GEOFFREY de la Guerche holds MONKS KIRBY of the king. There are 15 hides. There is land for 20 ploughs. In demesne are 7 [ploughs], and 6 slaves and 2 female slaves; and 41 villans and 2 bordars with 2 priests having 21 ploughs. There are 40 acres of meadow.

In this manor the monks of Saint-Nicholas have 2 ploughs, and 22 villans and 6 bordars with 5 ploughs.

The whole was worth 100s.; and afterwards 40s.; now £10. Leofwine held it freely.

The same Geoffrey holds NEWBOLD ON AVON. There are 8 hides. There is land for 16 ploughs. In demesne are 3 [ploughs], and 2 slaves; and 25 villans and 8 bordars with 11 ploughs. It was and is worth 100s. Leofwine held it freely.

The same Geoffrey holds NEWBOLD REVEL. There are 8 hides. There is land for 16 ploughs. In demesne are 4 ploughs, and 8 slaves; and 26 villans and 3 bordars with 10 ploughs. There are 10 acres of meadow. It was and is worth £7. Leofwine held it freely.

IN MARTON HUNDRED

The same Geoffrey holds 5 hides in LONG LAWFORD. There is land for 14 ploughs. In demesne is 1 [plough]; and 14 villans and 7 bordars have 7 ploughs. There is a mill rendering 14s. It was worth 40s.; now 50s.

The same Geoffrey holds WAPPENBURY. There are 5 hides. There is land for 15 ploughs. In demesne are 3 ploughs, and 6 slaves; and 19 villans and 6 bordars with 10 ploughs. There is a mill rendering 6s8d., [and] woodland half a league long and 2 furlongs broad. It was and is worth 110s.

The same Geoffrey holds HAMPTON IN ARDEN. There are 10 hides. [...] There is land for 22 ploughs. In demesne are 2 [ploughs], and 2 slaves and 2 female slaves; and 50 villans with a priest and 16 bordars have 13 ploughs. There is a mill rendering 40d., and 10 acres of meadow, [and] woodland 3 leagues long and 3 broad. It was and is worth 100s.

From the same Geoffrey, Sot holds SHUSTOKE. There are 4 hides. There is land for 8 ploughs. In demesne is 1 plough, and 3 slaves; and 10 villans with 3 ploughs. There are 16 acres of meadow, [and] woodland 1 league long and half a league broad. It was and is worth 40s.

From Geoffrey, Ansgot the priest holds 1 hide in BENTLEY in alms. There is land for 2 ploughs, and there are [2 ploughs], with 4 villans. [There is] woodland half a league long and 3 furlongs broad. It was and is worth 64d.

From Geoffrey, Bruno holds 2 hides in BROWNSOVER. There is land for 2 ploughs, and there are [2 ploughs], with 4 villans and 3 bordars and 2 slaves. There are 2 acres of meadow. It was and is worth 20s.

From Geoffrey, Robert holds 5 hides in [?] CESTERSOVER. There is land for 8 ploughs. In demesne are 2 [ploughs], with 1 slave; and 9 villans and 2 bordars with 5 ploughs. There is a mill rendering 2s., and 10½ acres of meadow. It was and is worth 40s.

From Geoffrey, Ansegis holds 1 hide in NEWNHAM PADDOX. There is land for 8 ploughs. In demesne is 1 [plough], and 3 slaves; and 16 villans and 5 bordars with 6 ploughs. There are 20 acres of meadow. It was worth 20s.; now 60s.

From Geoffrey, Wulfric holds 3 hides in HOPSFORD. There is land for 3 ploughs, and there are [3 ploughs], with 6 villans and 2 slaves. There are 5 acres of meadow. It was worth 20s.; now 30s. The same Wulfric held it freely.

All the above-mentioned lands Leofwine held, and could go where he would.

XXXII. The land of Gilbert de Ghent

GILBERT de Ghent holds of the king 1 hide and 1½ virgates of land in WILLINGTON, and Fulbric [holds] of him. There is land for 1 plough. There is 1 villan and 2 bordars and 4 slaves with 1 plough. There is a mill rendering 5s., and 15 acres of meadow. It was and is worth 20s. Alweard held it freely.

XXXIII. The land of Gilbert fitzTurold

IN BARCHESTON HUNDRED

GILBERT fitz Turold holds of the king 6 hides in STRETTON ON FOSSE, and Walter [holds] of him. There is land for 8 ploughs. In demesne are 1½ ploughs, and 4 slaves; and 8 villans and 3 bordars with a priest and 1 knight have 5 ploughs. There are 23 acres of meadow, and pasture 40 perches long and as much broad. It was worth 70s.; now 110s. Cyneweard and Beorhtric held it freely.

XXXIIII. The land of Gerwy

GERWY holds of the king 5 hides in BINTON. There is land for 4 ploughs. In demesne are 2 [ploughs], with 1 slave; and 5 villans and 5 bordars with 1 plough. There is a mill rendering 4s., and 15 acres of meadow. It was worth 40s.; now 60s. Grim held it freely TRE.

XXXV. The land of Urse d'Abetot

IN "FERNECUMBE" HUNDRED

URSE d'Abetot holds of the king 1½ hides in HILLBOROUGH. There is land for 2 ploughs. In demesne is 1 [plough], and 2 slaves; and 3 bordars with half a plough. There are 9 acres of meadow, and a salt-pan in Droitwich [Worcs.] rendering 3s. It was worth 16s.; now 20s. Earnwig held it freely TRE.

The same Urse holds 2 hides in BINTON. There is land for 2 ploughs. In demesne is 1 [plough]; and 3 villans and 1 bordar with 1 plough. There is a mill rendering 2s. It was worth 16s.; now 40s. Earnwig held it freely.

XXXVI. The land of Stephen

STEPHEN holds of the king 1 hide in LITTLE DORSINGTON. There is land for 2 ploughs. In demesne are 2 [ploughs]; and 1 free man with 8 bordars with 1 plough. There are 4 acres of meadow. It was worth 20s.; now 30[s.]. Ordwig held it freely.

IN PATHLOW HUNDRED

The same Stephen holds 3 hides in UPPER MILCOTE. There is land for 4 ploughs. In demesne are 2 [ploughs]; and 6 villans and 6 bordars with 3 ploughs. There are 15 acres of meadow. It was worth 40s.; now 50s. Bishop Wulfstan and Alstan held it freely.

[Folio 244: WARWICKSHIRE]

XXXVII. The land of Osbern fitzRichard

OSBERN fitzRichard holds ASTON CANTLOW of the king. There are 5 hides. There is land for 10 ploughs. There are 9 Flemings and 16 villans with a priest and 10 bordars having 12 ploughs. There is a mill rendering 8s. and 5 sticks of eels, and 40 acres of meadow, [and] woodland 1 league in length and breadth. It was worth 100s.; now £6. Earl Ælfgar held it.

IN PATHLOW HUNDRED

From the same Osbern, Urse holds 3 hides in WILMCOTE MANOR. There is land for 4 ploughs. In demesne are 2 [ploughs], and 2 slaves; and 2 villans and 2 bordars with 2 ploughs. There are 24 acres of meadow. It was worth 30s.; now 60s. Leofwine Dodda held it freely TRE.

IN MARTON HUNDRED

From Osbern, William holds 5 hides in DUNCHURCH. There is land for 9 ploughs. In demesne is 1 [plough], and 3 slaves; and 12 villans with a priest and 11 bordars have 5 ploughs. There are 30 acres of meadow. It was and is worth 100s. Wulfmær held it.

IN 'TREMLOWE' HUNDRED

From Osbern, Hugh holds 4 hides in BARFORD. There is land for 12 ploughs. In demesne is 1 [plough], and 2 slaves; and 2 knights with a priest, and 4 villans and 11 bordars have 3 ploughs. There is a mill rendering 2s. and 13 sticks of eels, and 60 acres of meadow. It was and is worth 40s.

IN "FERNECUMBE" HUNDRED

From Osbern, the same Hugh holds 3½ hides in HILLBOROUGH and in BINTON. There is land for 4 ploughs. In demesne is 1 [plough], and 4 slaves; and 7 villans and 2 bordars with 2 ploughs. There is a mill rendering 12d., and 20 acres of meadow. It was and is worth 40s. Ludric held it freely TRE.

From Osbern, the same Hugh holds 3 hides in IPSLEY [Worcs.]. There is land for 7 ploughs. In demesne is 1 [plough], and 2 slaves; and 7 villans with a priest and 13 bordars with 4 ploughs. There is a mill rendering 16d., [and] woodland 1 league long and half a league broad. It was worth 30s.; now 40s. Earl Ælfgar held it.

From Osbern, Gilbert holds 5 hides in TEMPLE GRAFTON. There is land for 5 ploughs. In demesne are 2 [ploughs], and 4 slaves; and 6 villans and with [sic] a priest and 6 bordars with 5 ploughs. There are 24 acres of meadow. It was worth £3; now £4. Merewine and Skrauti and Toti and Tosti held it freely TRE.

IN BARCHESTON HUNDRED

From Osbern, Walter holds 2 hides in STRETTON ON FOSSE. He has there half a plough in demesne; and 2 villans with 1 plough. It was worth 20s.; now 30s. Beorhtric held it freely.

From Osbern, William holds MOLLINGTON [Oxon.]. There are 5 hides. There is land for 5 ploughs. In demesne is 1 [plough]; and 4 villans and 5 bordars with 1 plough. There are 20 acres of meadow. It was worth 40s.; now 60s. The mother of Leofwine of Newnham Paddox held it freely TRE.

XXXVIII. The land of Harold son of the Earl

IN COLESHILL HUNDRED

HAROLD son of Earl Ralph holds CHILVERS COTON of the king. There are 8 hides. There is land for 10 ploughs. In demesne is half a plough, and 9 slaves; and 15 villans and 7 bordars with 7 ploughs. [There is] meadow 3 furlongs long and 1 broad, [and] woodland 1½ leagues long and 1 league broad. It was worth 40s.; now 50s. His father held it.

IN 'HUNESBERI' HUNDRED

The same Harold holds 15 hides in BURTON DASSETT. There is land for 23 ploughs. In demesne is 1 plough, and 4 slaves; and 46 villans with a priest and 9 bordars have 26 ploughs. There 3 knights have 12 villans with 3 ploughs. There are 27 acres of meadow. It was worth £16; now £20. Harold held it TRE.

XXXIX. The land of Hascoit

IN MARTON HUNDRED

HASCOIT Musard holds of the king in LEAMINGTON HASTINGS 12½ hides and half a virgate of land. There is land for 27 ploughs. In demesne are 7 ploughs, and 15 slaves; and 33 villans with a priest and 24 bordars have 18 ploughs. There is a mill rendering 2s., and 20 acres of meadow. It was worth £10; now £12. Azur held it freely TRE.

From Hascoit, Humphrey holds 2 hides in WHITNASH. There is land for 8 ploughs. In demesne are 2 [ploughs], and 5 slaves; and 11 villans and 8 bordars with 6 ploughs. There are 10 acres of meadow. It was worth 60s.; now 100s. Alfred held it freely TRE.

IN 'TREMLOWE' HUNDRED

From Hascoit, the same Humphrey holds 5 hides in NEWBOLD PACEY. There is land for 9 ploughs. In demesne are 4 ploughs, and 5 slaves; and 11 villans and 11 bordars with 8½ ploughs. There are 10 acres of meadow. It was worth 60s.; now 100s. Alfred held it freely TRE.

IN "FERNECUMBE" HUNDRED

From Hascoit, the same Humphrey holds HASELEY. There are 3 hides and half a virgate of land. There is land for 2 ploughs. In demesne is 1 [plough]; and 3 villans with a priest and 7 bordars have 2 ploughs. There is a mill rendering 4s., and 6 acres of meadow, [and] woodland 1 league long and 2 furlongs broad. It was worth 20s.; now 30s. Azur held it freely.

XL. The land of Nicholas the Crossbowman

IN 'TREMLOWE' HUNDRED

NICHOLAS the crossbowman holds of the king 3 hides and 1 virgate of land in AILSTONE. There is land for 5 ploughs. In demesne are 2 [ploughs], and 4 slaves and 3 female slaves; and 9 villans and 3 bordars with 3 ploughs. It was and is worth 60s. Leofric held it freely.

IN "FERNECUMBE" HUNDRED

The same Nicholas holds 5 hides and 1 virgate of land in HASELOR. There is land for 9 ploughs. In demesne are 2 ploughs, and 5 slaves and female slaves; and 16 villans with 1 bordar have 7 ploughs. There is a mill rendering 6s8d., and a salt-pan rendering 4s. and 2 summae of salt. There 2 Frenchmen and 1 burgess pay 7½d. It was worth £4; now £6. Wulfgeat and Ælfric held it freely.

XLI. The land of Nigel d'Aubigny

NIGEL d'Aubigny holds AUSTREY of the king. There are 5½ hides and 1 virgate of land. There is land for 10 ploughs. In demesne are 2 [ploughs]; and 12 villans with a priest and 8 bordars have 5 ploughs. There is meadow 1 furlong long and another broad. It was worth £6; now £3. 8 thegns held it freely TRE.

The same Nigel holds 2½ hides in "ALTONE". There is land for 4 ploughs. There are 3 villans with 1 bordar having 2½ ploughs. It was and is worth 20s. Wulfwine and Leofric held it freely.

XLII. The land of Christina

IN COLESHILL HUNDRED

CHRISTINA holds of the king 8 hides in ULVERLEY GREEN. There is land for 20 ploughs. In demesne is 1 [plough], and 3 slaves; and 22 villans with a priest and 4 bordars have 7 ploughs. There are 12 acres of meadow. [There is] woodland 4 leagues long and half a league broad; when it is stocked, it is worth 12s. It was worth £10; now £4. Earl Edwin held it.

With this is valued also the following land.

Christina herself holds 1 hide in ARLEY. There are 4 villans having 2 ploughs. [There is] woodland 1½ leagues long and in breadth 1 league; when it is stocked, it is worth 60s.

IN MARTON HUNDRED

Christina herself holds LONG ITCHINGTON. There are 24 hides. There is land for 21 ploughs. In demesne are 5 ploughs, and 10 slaves; and 83 villans with 2 priests and 4 bordars have 17 ploughs. There are 2 mills rendering 6s8d., and 16 acres of meadow, [and] pasture 2 furlongs long and 1 furlong broad. It was worth £12; now £20. When the king gave it to Christina it rendered £36.

XLIII. The King's Alms[Men]

LEOFGIFU the nun holds SALFORD PRIORS of the king in alms. There are 3 hides. There is land for 10 ploughs. In demesne are 2 [ploughs], and 7 slaves; and 8 villans and 8 bordars with a priest having 8 ploughs. There is a mill rendering 5s., and 12 acres of meadow, [and] woodland 2 furlongs long and half a furlong broad. It was worth 40s.; now £6. Godgifu, the wife of Earl Leofric, held it.

IN "FERNECUMBE" HUNDRED

Edith holds of the king 5 hides in BICKMARSH [Worcs.]. There is land for 9 ploughs. In demesne are 3 ploughs, and 4 slaves; and 13 villans and 3 bordars with 6 ploughs. It was worth £4; now 100s. She herself held it TRE.

[Folio 244V: WARWICKSHIRE]

XLIIII. The land of Richard the Forester

IN 'BUMBELOWE' HUNDRED

RICHARD the forester holds HARBOROUGH [Magna and Parva] of the king. There are 4½ hides. There is land for as many ploughs. There are 4 villans and 4 bordars with 1 plough. There are 20 acres of meadow. It was worth 10s.; now 20s. 4 thegns held it freely.

The same Richard holds half a hide in BRAMCOTE. There is land for 1 plough. There is 1 villan with half a plough. It is worth 2s. Saxi held it freely.

IN MARTON HUNDRED

Richard holds of the king 2 hides in GRANDBOROUGH. There is land for 4 ploughs. In demesne are 2 [ploughs], and 3 slaves; and 6 villans and 2 bordars with 2 ploughs. There are 20 acres of meadow. It was worth 20s.; now 50s.

The same Richard holds half a hide in LOWER SHUCKBURGH. There is land for 1 plough, and there is [1 plough], with 5 villans. It was worth 10s.; now 20s. Eadric held it freely.

Bondi held it freely.

The same Richard holds 1 hide in HILLMORTON. There is land for 2 ploughs. In demesne is half a plough; and 3 villans and 3 bordars with 1 plough. There are 10 acres of meadow. It was and is worth 20s. Viking held it freely.

IN 'HUNESBERI' HUNDRED

From the same Richard, Ermenfrid holds 1 hide at farm in RADWAY. There is land for 3 ploughs. In demesne are 2 [ploughs], with 1 slave; and 1 villan and 3 bordars with 1 plough. There are 3 acres of meadow. It was worth 20s.; now 25[s.]. Earl Ralph held it TRE.

IN STONELEIGH HUNDRED

Richard the huntsman holds of the king 1 hide in WALSGRAVE ON SOWE. There is land for 2 ploughs. In demesne is 1 [plough]; and 2 villans and 2 bordars with half a plough. There are 3 acres of meadow. The woodland there, between himself and the king and the abbot, is 3 leagues long and 1 league broad. It was worth 20s.; now 60s. Kolbrand held it freely TRE.

IN 'TREMLOWE' HUNDRED

Richard the huntsman holds 3 hides in CHESTERTON. There is land for 6 ploughs. In demesne are 3 ploughs; and 6 villans and 4 bordars with 3 ploughs. There are 30 acres of meadow. It was worth 40s.; now 100s. 4 thegns held it freely.

IN BARCHESTON HUNDRED

ÆLFRIC holds of the king 1 hide and half a virgate of land in BARCHESTON. There is land for 2 ploughs. In demesne is 1 [plough]; and 4 villans have 2 ploughs. There are 10 acres of meadow. It was worth 20s.; now 40s. Viking held it freely.

IN COLESHILL HUNDRED

ALSIGE holds of the king half a hide in FILLONGLEY. There is land for 1 plough, and this [plough] is in demesne, with 1 slave; and 7 villans with 1 bordar have 1 plough. [There is] woodland rendering 10s. When it is stocked. It is worth 30s. The same man himself held it.

IN MARTON HUNDRED

LEOFWINE holds of the king 1½ hides in FLECKNOE. There is land for 2 ploughs. In demesne is 1 [plough], and 3 slaves; and 3 villans with 1 bordar have 1 plough. It was worth 10s.; now 30s. This Leofwine bought it from Alwine his brother.

The same Leofwine holds 2 hides and half a virgate of land in FLECKNOE. There is land for 2 ploughs. There is 1 [plough], with 2 villans and 1 bordar, and 6 acres of meadow. It was worth 10s.; now 20s.

Leofwine said that he holds this land of Bishop Wulfstan; but the bishop failed him in [his] plea, whereby Leofwine himself is at the king's mercy.

ORDRIC holds of the king 1 hide in ETTINGTON. This is waste.

GODWINE holds of the king 1 hide in CORLEY. There is land for 2 ploughs. In demesne is 1 [plough], and 3 slaves; and 4 villans and 2 bordars with 2 ploughs. There are 6 acres of meadow, [and] woodland having in length the fourth part of a league, and in breadth the fourth part of half a league. It was worth 10s.; now 30s. The same Godwine held it freely TRE.

XLV. The land of the wife of Hugh de Grandmesnil

ADELIZA wife of Hugh, holds of the king 4 hides in MIDDLETON. There is land for 4 ploughs. In demesne are 1½ ploughs, and 3 slaves; and 12 villans and 5 bordars with 3½ ploughs. It was worth £4; now £6. Thorgot held it freely TRE.

Robert holds of the king half a hide in BARSTON, and there he has 1 plough, and a mill rendering 20d. It is worth 20s. Thorkil held it freely.

ANSEGIS holds of the king 4 hides in HARBOROUGH [Magna and Parva]. [There is] land for 4 ploughs. Now in demesne [there is] 1 plough; and 8 villans with a priest and 7 bordars have 2 ploughs. There is a mill rendering 16d. It was worth 10s.; now 20s. Bruning held it freely TRE.

[Folio 245: [WARWICKSHIRE]]

[Blank in MS]

[Folio 245V: WARWICKSHIRE]

[Blank in MS]

STAFFORDSHIRE

IN THE BOROUGH OF STAFFORD the king has in his demesne 18 burgesses and 8 waste messuages. In addition to these the king has there 22 messuages of the honour of the earls; 5 of these are waste, the others are inhabited.

The Bishop of Chester has 14 messuages; 1 is waste.

The Abbey of Burton upon Trent has 5 messuages.

Earl Roger has 3 messuages which belong to Sheriffhales [Shrops.]. The earl himself has 31 messuages within the walls; 10 of these are waste.

Hugh, his son, holds 5 messuages of the earldom and they belong to Worfield [Shrops.].

Robert of Stafford has 13 messuages of the honour of the earls, and they belong to Bradley [near Stafford]; 6 of these are waste.

The same Robert has 41 messuages of his own fief; 17 of these are waste.

William fitz Ansculf has 4 messuages of the earldom which belong to Upper Penn, a manor of the earl; 1 only of these is occupied.

Henry de Ferrers has 1 waste messuage. The priests of the borough have 14.

All of these have sake and soke. The king has the geld from all each year.

In the time of King Edward the borough of Stafford rendered £9 in pennies for all customary dues. 2 parts were the king's, the third [part] the earl's.

Now King William has £7 from the renders of the borough as his share and as that of the earl. Robert has half the king's own share, by the king's gift, as he says.

Here Are Entered the Landholders In Staffordshire

I KING WILLIAM
II The Bishop of Chester
III The Abbey of Westminster
IIII The Abbey of Burton upon Trent
V The Church of Saint-Remi of Rheims
VI The canons of Stafford and of Wolverhampton
VII Samson the clerk
VIII Earl Roger
IX Hugh de Montgomery
X Henry de Ferrers
XI Robert of Stafford
XII William fitz Ansculf

XIII Richard the forester
XIIII Reginald de Bailleul
XV Ralph fitz Hubert
XVI Nigel
XVII Cynewine and other thegns

The land of the King

IN SEISDON HUNDRED

The king holds KINGSWINFORD. King Edward held it. There are 5 hides. There is land for 6 ploughs. In demesne is 1 [plough], and 1 slave; and 14 villans and 4 bordars with 6 ploughs. There is a mill rendering 2s, and 4 acres of meadow, [and] woodland half a league long and 3 furlongs broad. It is worth 70s.

To this manor belongs half a hide waste in 'Crockington' [in Trysull].

The king holds TETTENHALL. There is 1 hide. There is land for 2 ploughs. There are [2 ploughs] in demesne; and 4 villans and 3 bordars with 1 plough. There is woodland half a league in length and breadth. In Compton is 1 hide belonging to Tettenhall. TRE it was worth 20s; now 30s.

In Wightwick is half a hide and it belongs to Tettenhall. There is half a plough, with 1 villan. It was and is worth 4s.

In BILSTON are 2 hides. There is land for 4 ploughs. There are 8 villans and 3 bordars with 3 ploughs. There is 1 acre of meadow, [and] woodland half a league long and a half broad. It was worth 20s; now 30s.

In BESCOT is 1 carucate of land, waste.

The king holds WEDNESBURY with its appendages. [...] There are 3 hides. There is land for 9 ploughs. In demesne is 1 [plough], and 1 slave; and 16 villans and 11 bordars with 7 ploughs. There is a mill rendering 2s, and 1 acre of meadow, [and] woodland 2 leagues long and 1 broad.

BLOXWICH [Bloxwich and Little Bloxwich] is a member of the same manor. There is woodland 3 furlongs long and 1 broad. And in Shelfield is 1 waste hide belonging to the same manor.

The king holds PENKRIDGE. King Edward held it. [...] There is 1 hide. There is land for 4 ploughs. In demesne are 2 [ploughs], and 2 slaves; and 2 villans and 2 bordars with 2 ploughs. There is a mill rendering 5s, and 16 acres of meadow. The woodland is 1 league long and 1 broad. It is worth 40s.

To this manor belong these members:

In WOLGARSTON is 1 hide. There is land for 3 ploughs.

In DRAYTON [in Penkridge], 1 hide; it is waste. There is land [...].

In CONGREVE, 1 hide. There is land for 3 ploughs.

In DUNSTON, 2 hides. There is land for 4 ploughs.

In [Lower and Upper] COWLEY and BEFFCOTE, 1½ hides. There is land for 3 ploughs.

In demesne are 2 ploughs, and 1 thegn and there are 16 villans and 12 bordars. Among them all they have 6 ploughs, and [there are] 18 acres of meadow, [and] woodland half a league long and 3 furlongs broad.

TRE the whole was worth 65s; now 100s.

IN PIREHILL HUNDRED

The king holds TRENTHAM. There is 1 hide. There is land for 3 ploughs. In demesne is 1 [plough]; and 5 villans with 1 bordar and a reeve have 3½ ploughs. There a priest and 1 free man have 2 ploughs, and [there are] 3 villans and 6 bordars with 1 plough. There is woodland 1 league long and a half broad. TRE it was worth 100s; now 115s.

The king holds WIGGINTON. There are 2 hides. There is land for 6 ploughs. There are 8 villans and 1 slave and 1 bordar, and 4 burgesses in Tamworth. Among them all they have 6 ploughs. There is meadow 6 furlongs in length and 2 furlongs broad.

The king holds WILLENHALL. There are 3 hides. There is land for 4 ploughs. There are 5 villans and 3 bordars with 3 ploughs. There is 1 acre of meadow. It was and is worth 20s.

IN OFFLOW HUNDRED

The king holds ALREWAS. Earl Ælfgar held it. There are 3 hides. There is land for 8 ploughs. In demesne are 2 [ploughs], and 1 slave; and 20 villans and 6 bordars with a priest have 6 ploughs. There are 24 acres of meadow. A fishery renders 1,500 eels. [There is] woodland 1 league long and a half broad. TRE it was worth £10; now £11.

The king holds KING'S BROMLEY. Earl Harold held it. There are 3 hides. There is land for 5 ploughs. In demesne are 2 ploughs, and 2 slaves; and 11 villans and 2 bordars with 6 ploughs. There are 25 acres of meadow, [and] woodland 1 league long and a half broad. It was and is worth 100s.

The king holds SANDON. Earl Ælfgar held it, with its appendages. There is 1 hide. There is land for 15 ploughs. In demesne are 2 [ploughs]; and 18 villans and 8 bordars with 8 ploughs. There are 8 acres of meadow. The woodland is 1 league long and a half broad. TRE it was worth 100s; now £6.

Folio 246v: STAFFORDSHIRE]

The king holds CHARTLEY. Earl Ælfgar held it. There is 1 hide. There is land [...]. In demesne are 2 ploughs; and 9 villans and 6 bordars with 8½ ploughs. There are 10 acres of meadow, [and] woodland 1 league long and a half broad. TRE it was worth 100s; now 10s. more

The king holds WOLSTANTON. Earl Ælfgar held it. There are 2 hides with the appendages. There are 2 ploughs in demesne; and 14 villans and 2 bordars with a priest have 8 ploughs. [There is] woodland 1 league long and 1 furlong broad. TRE it was worth 100s; now £6.

The king holds PENKHULL. Earl Ælfgar held it. There are 2 hides with the appendages. There is land for 11 ploughs. In demesne are 2 [ploughs]; and 17 villans and 6 bordars with 8 ploughs. There are 2 acres of meadow, [and] woodland 1 league long and 2 furlongs broad. It is worth £6.

The king holds ROCESTER. Earl Ælfgar held it. There is 1 hide with the appendages. There is land for 9 ploughs. In demesne are 2 [ploughs]; and 18 villans and 10 bordars with 9 ploughs. There is a mill rendering 10s, and 20 acres of meadow, [and] woodland 1 furlong long and as much broad. TRE it was worth £4; now £8.

The king holds CRAKEMARSH. Earl Ælfgar held it. There is half a hide with the appendages. There is land for 6 ploughs. There are 2 villans and 4 bordars with 2 ploughs, and 6 acres of meadow. [There is] woodland 1 league long and as much broad. There is a mill rendering 10s. It is worth 10s.

The ing holds UTTOXETER. Earl Ælfgar held it. There is half a hide. There is land for 10 ploughs. In demesne are 2 [ploughs], with 1 slave; and 24 villans and 11 bordars with 11 ploughs. There are 16 acres of meadow, [and] woodland 2 leagues long and as many broad. TRE it was worth £7; now £8.

The king holds BARTON-UNDER-NEEDWOOD. Earl Ælfgar held it. There are 3 hides with the appendages. There is land for 18 ploughs. In demesne are 2 [ploughs], and 2 slaves; and 17 villans and 8 bordars with 9 ploughs. There are 20 acres of meadow. The woodland is 2 leagues long and 1 broad. There is a mill rendering 6s. TRE it was worth £6; now £7.

The king holds LEEK. Earl Ælfgar held it. There is 1 hide with the appendages. There is land for 12 ploughs. There are 15 villans and 13 bordars with 6 ploughs. There are 3 acres of meadow, [and] woodland 4 leagues long and as many broad. TRE it was worth £4; now 100s.

The king holds RUGELEY. Earl Ælfgar held it. There is the fifth part of a hide. There is land for 5 ploughs. There are 9 villans with 3 ploughs, and a mill rendering 30d, and 3 acres of meadow. [There is] woodland 3 leagues long and 2 broad. TRE it was worth 20s; now 30s.

The king holds MAYFIELD. Earl Ælfgar held it. There is 1 hide with the appendages. There is land for 12 ploughs. In demesne is 1 [plough]; and 9 villans and 3 bordars with a priest have 3 ploughs. There are 8 acres of meadow, [and] woodland 4 furlongs long and 2 furlongs broad. TRE it was worth 40s.

The king holds MERETOWN. Earl Ælgar held it. There are 4 hides with the appendages. There is land for 10 ploughs. In demesne is 1 [plough], and 2 slaves; and 18 villans with 10 ploughs. There is a mill rendering 3s and 4,000 eels, [and]

woodland half a league long and 2 furlongs broad. TRE it was worth £4; now 10s more.

The king holds CANNOCK. Earl Ælfgar held it. There is 1 hide with the appendages. There is land for 15 ploughs. There are 8 villans and 3 bordars with 3 ploughs. [There is] woodland 6 leagues long and 4 leagues broad. TRE it rendered nothing; now it is worth 20s.

The king holds ELFORD. Earl Ælfgar held it. There are 3 hides. There is land for 11 ploughs. In demesne are 3 [ploughs]; and 24 villans and 8 bordars with 8 ploughs. There are 24 acres of meadow, and 2 mills rendering 20s. TRE it was worth £11; now 12[l].

The king holds KINVER. Earl Ælfgar held it. There are 5½ hides with the appendages. There is land for 16 ploughs. In demesne is 1 [plough], and 3 slaves; and 17 villans and 7 bordars with a priest having 10 ploughs. There are 2 mills rendering 20s, and 6 acres of meadow, [and] woodland 3 leagues long and 1 broad. It was and is worth 100s.

The king holds PATTINGHAM. Earl Ælfgar held it. There are 2 hides. There is land for 8 ploughs. There are 3 villans with a priest and 10 bordars having 3 ploughs. There is woodland 1 league long and half a league broad. It was and is worth £3.

The king holds CLIFTON CAMPVILLE. There are 8 hides with the appendages. There is land for 4 ploughs. In demesne are 2 [ploughs], and 2 slaves; and 33 villans and 7 bordars with a priest have 11 ploughs. There are 2 mills rendering 10s, and 50 acres of meadow. TRE it was worth £11; now £12.

The king holds DRAYTON BASSETT. There are 2 hides with the appendages. There is land for 4 ploughs. There are 9 villans and 3 bordars with 4½ ploughs; and 8 burgesses in Tamworth belong to this manor and work there like the other villans. In the manor the king has 2 mills rendering 21s, and 20 acres of meadow. [There is] woodland 2 leagues long and half a league broad. It was and is worth £4.

The king holds HOPWAS. There are 3 hides. There is land for 6 ploughs. In demesne is a mill rendering 13s4d; and 11 villans and 2 bordars with 5 ploughs. There are 30 acres of meadow, [and] woodland 6 furlongs [long] and 3 furlongs broad. It was and is worth 40s.

The king holds HARLASTON. There are 4 hides. There is land for 8 ploughs. In demesne are 2 [ploughs]; and 16 villans and 5 bordars have 4 ploughs. There is a mill rendering 4s, and 2 slaves. It was and is worth £6.

Earl Ælfgar held these 4 manors as well as those above.

IN CUTTLESTONE HUNDRED

In BIDDULPH [Biddulph and Over Biddulph] is 1 hide with the appendages. Gruffydd held it. There is land for 3 ploughs.

In BUCKNALL, the third part of a hide. Ketil held it. There is land for 3 ploughs.

In OAKLEY [in Mucklestone], 1 hide. Aki held it. There is land for 3 ploughs.

In HEIGHLEY is half a virgate of land. Alweard held it. There is land for 1 plough.

In MILLMEECE [...] Wulfhere held it. There is land for 2 ploughs.

In SHELTON UNDER HARLEY is 1 virgate of land. Ælfgeat held it. There is There is land for 2 ploughs.

In [Lower and Upper] HATTON is half a hide. Ælfgeat held it. There is land for 2 ploughs.

In FULFORD is 1 virgate of land. Almær held it. There is land for 2 ploughs.

In MILWICH is 1 virgate of land. Rafwin held it. There is land for 2 ploughs.

In [?] COTON [in Milwich] is 1 virgate of land with the appendages. Ylving held it. There is land for 1 plough.

In ENSON is 1 virgate of land. Wulfheah held it. There is land for 2 ploughs.

In HILDERSTONE is half a virgate of land. Wulfric held it. There is land for half a plough.

In COTWALTON is 1 virgate of land. Rafwin and Alwine held it. There is land for 2 ploughs.

In HILCOTE There is half a virgate of land. thorbiorn held it. There is land for 1 plough.

In ASTON [in Stone] is 1 carucate of land and 1 virgate of land. Oda held it. There is land for 1 plough.

IN PIREHILL HUNDRED

In WOOTTON [in Ellastone] is land for 2 or 3 ploughs. Swein held it.

In STANTON, land for 1 plough. Arnketil held it.

In MUSDEN [Musden Grange and Upper Musden], land for 1 plough. Uhtræligd held it.

In SHEEN, land for 2, or 1, ploughs. Alweard held it.

In STANSHOPE, land for 1 or 2 ploughs. Wudia held it.

In FARLEY, land for 1 or 2 ploughs. Alweard held it.

In ALTON, land for 2 ploughs. Iwar held it.

In DENSTONE, land for 2 ploughs. Iwar held it.

In CONSALL, 1 carucate of land. Wulfheah held it.

In CHEADLE, 1 carucate of land. Wulfheah held it.

In NEWTON [in Draycott-in-the-Moors], 2 carucates of land. Wulfgeat and Alweard held it.

In "LUFAMESLEG", land for 1 plough. Wulfgeat held it.

In FORSBROOK, land for 1 plough. Swein held it.

In ENDON, land for 1 or 2 ploughs. Dunning held it.

In ROWNALL, land for 1 plough. Wulfmær held it.

In RUDYARD, land for 1 or 2 ploughs. Wulfmær held it.

In RUSHTON [in Leek and Lowe], land for 2 ploughs. Wulfgeat held it.

All this land of the KING is waste.

[Folio 247: STAFFORDSHIRE

II. The land of the Bishop of Chester

IN CUTTLESTONE HUNDRED

THE BISHOP OF CHESTER holds BREWOOD. The church held it TRE. There are 5 hides. There is land for 20 ploughs. In demesne are 3 ploughs, and 8 slaves; and 24 villans and 18 bordars with a priest have 14 ploughs. There are 2 mills rendering 4s, and 4 acres of meadow, [and] woodland 1½ leagues long and 1 league broad. TRE it was worth £10; now 100s.

The bishop himself holds BASWICH. The church held it TRE. There are 5 hides. There is land for 4 ploughs. In demesne is 1 [plough], and 2 villans with a priest.

To this manor belongs WALTON-ON-THE-HILL. There are 4 bordars having 2 ploughs, and there are 4 acres of meadow, [and] woodland 1½ leagues long and 1 league broad. TRE it was worth 10s; now 15s.

The bishop himself holds ACTON TRUSSELL, and Robert [holds] of him. There is [...]. There is land for 4 ploughs. In demesne is 1 [plough]; and 10 villans and 8 bordars with 4 ploughs. There is a mill rendering 2s, and 8 acres of meadow, [and] woodland 3 furlongs long and 2 furlongs broad. TRE it was worth 5s; now 20s.

IN PIREHILL HUNDRED

The bishop himself holds BROCTON [in Baswich] and BEDNALL. They belong to Baswich and are waste.

The bishop himself holds [Great and Little] HAYWOOD. St CHAD held it TRE. There is half a hide. This is land for 10 ploughs. In demesne are 2 [ploughs]; and 9 villans and 5 bordars with a priest have 6½ ploughs. There is a mill rendering 5s. It was and is worth 40s. These lands entered below belong to [Great and Little] Haywood.

The bishop himself holds HIXON, and Picot [holds] of him, and Nigel [holds] of Picot. There is [...]. There are 5 villans with 2 ploughs, and 3 acres of meadow. It was and is worth 10s9d.

The bishop himself holds WOLSELEY, and Nigel [holds] of him. There is half a hide belonging to [Great and Little] Haywood. There are 4 villans and 2 bordars with 1 plough, and 3 acres of meadow. It was and is worth 40d.

The bishop himself holds FRADSWELL, and Ælfhelm [holds] of him. There is [...] belonging to [Great and Little] Haywood. There is land for 5 ploughs. There are 3 villans and 2 bordars with 2 ploughs. There is 1 acre of meadow, [and] woodland half a league long and 2 furlongs broad. TRE it was worth 3s; now 13s4d.

In the manor of [Great and Little] HAYWOOD are 6 acres of meadow. [There is] woodland 2 leagues long and 1 broad.

IN PIREHILL HUNDRED

The bishop himself holds ECCLESHALL. ST CHAD held it. There are 7 hides. There is land [...]. In demesne are 4 ploughs, and 2 slaves; and 14 villans with a priest and 2 bordars have 7 ploughs. There are 4 acres of meadow, and 2 mills rendering 4s. It is worth £4.

To this manor belongs BISHOP'S OFFLEY. Leofnoth holds it of the bishop. In demesne he has land for 3 ploughs; and 3 villans and 1 bordar with 1 plough. There is 1 acre of meadow. It was and is worth 10s. To THE SAME MANOR belong these members:

In Flashbrook is land for 2 ploughs. In Charnes is land for 1 plough. In Chatcull is land for 1 plough. In 'Doresley' [in Eccleshall] is land for half a plough. In Hill Chorlton is land for 2 ploughs. In Chapel Chorlton is land for 1 plough. In Cotes is land for 1 plough. In Coldmeece is land for 2 ploughs. In Baden Hall is land for half a plough. In Slindon is land for 2 ploughs. In Brockton [in Eccleshall] is land for 1 plough. All these lands are waste.

In BROUGHTON the bishop has half a carucate of land. This is waste.

The bishop himself has 4 villans and 4 bordars with 2 ploughs in Aspley. There is land for 2 ploughs, and it belongs to Eccleshall. There is 1 acre of meadow. It is worth 10s.

In Croxton is land for 3 ploughs. There the bishop has 2 villans and 8 bordars with 2 ploughs. It belongs to Eccleshall. It is worth 20s.

IN TOTMONSLOW HUNDRED

The bishop himself holds ELLASTONE. St Chad held it TRE. There is the fourth part of 1 hide. There is land for 5 ploughs. In demesne are 2 [ploughs]; and 8 villans and 5 bordars with 3 ploughs. There are 3 acres of meadow, [and] woodland 1 league long and a half broad. It is worth 12s; TRE it was worth 9s.

IN OFFLOW HUNDRED

The bishop himself holds LICHFIELD with its appendages. The church itself held it. There are 25½ hides and 1 virgate of land. There is land for 73 ploughs. In demesne are 10 ploughs, and 10 slaves; and 42 villans and 12 bordars having 21 ploughs; and 5 canons have 3 ploughs there. There are 35 acres of meadow, and 2 mills rendering 4s. It was and is worth £15.

To this manor belong these members; Packington, land for 4 ploughs; and the two Hammerwiches [Hammerwich], 5 carucates of land; and Stychbrook, land for 1 plough; and Norton Canes and Little Wyrley, 4 carucates of land; and Rowley, 1 carucate of land. All these lands are waste.

The bishop himself holds COLEY, and Nigel [holds] of him. There are 2 carucates of land. In demesne is 1 plough; and 8 villans and 2 bordars with 1 plough. There is 1 acre of meadow. It is worth 10s.

The bishop himself holds MORETON [Moreton and Upper Moreton, in Colwich], and Nigel [holds] of him. There are 2 carucates of land. In demesne is 1 plough; and 2 villans and 4 bordars with half a plough. There are 2 acres of meadow. It is worth 5s.

The bishop himself holds DROINTON, and Nigel [holds] of him. There is 1 villan with half a plough. It was and is worth 30d.

The bishop himself holds SUGNALL, and Frani and Fargrimr [hold] of him. There is land for 2 ploughs. There are 3 villans and 1 slave and 6 bordars with 3 ploughs. There are 3 acres of meadow. It was and is worth 10s. These members belong to the same manor:

In Gerrard's Bromley and Podmore is land for 3 ploughs.

In Tunstall, land for 2 ploughs. In Swinchurch is land for 4 ploughs. In Ellenhall is land for 3 ploughs. In Walton [in Eccleshall] is land for 4 ploughs. In Adbaston is land for 2 ploughs. In Wootton [in Eccleshall] is land for 3 ploughs. In Knighton [in Adbaston] is land for 2 ploughs.

Four thegns and 4 Frenchmen hold these 8 Berewicks, and other men [hold] of them.

There are in demesne 3 ploughs; and 14 villans and 34 bordars having 10 ploughs among them all, and [there are] 12 acres of meadow.

The whole was worth 62s. TRE; now, among them all, the same.

The bishop himself holds SEIGHFORD: there is land for 3 ploughs; and Aston [in Seighford] and Doxey: there is land for 3 ploughs; and [Great and Little] Bridgeford: there is land for 2 ploughs; and Coton Clanford: There is land for 2 oxen. 2 Frenchmen and 1 thegn hold these lands of the bishop. They belong to Eccleshall. There are 10 villans and 6 bordars with 5 ploughs, and they have 5 acres of meadow. The woodland of this manor of Eccleshall is 4 leagues long and 2 leagues broad.

The bishop himself holds LICHFIELD, and it has already been described above. Woodland belongs there $8\frac{1}{2}$ leagues and 7 furlongs long and $6\frac{1}{2}$ leagues and 8 furlongs broad. To this manor belong these members:

"Hortone", land for 2 ploughs. Alwine holds it. Packington, land for 4 ploughs. Ulfkil holds it. Tamhorn, land for 4 ploughs. Nigel holds it. Handsacre, land for 5 ploughs. Robert holds it. Hints, land for 7 ploughs. Osweald holds it. Yoxall, land for 4 ploughs. Rawn and Alwine hold it. Pipe Ridware, land for 1 plough. Alric holds it. Weeford and "Burouestone" and "Litelbech", land for 4 ploughs. Ralph holds them. Freeford, land for 6 ploughs. Ranulph holds it. 'Tymmor' [in Lichfield], land for 1 plough. Ranulph holds it. Harborne [War.], land for 1 plough. Robert holds it. Smethwick, land for 2 ploughs. Tipton, land for 5 ploughs. William holds them.

In these lands or Berewicks are 7 ploughs in demesne; and 60 villans and 22 bordars with 25 ploughs. Among them all [are] 52 acres of meadow, and a mill.

The value is reckoned in [that of] the manor.

[Folio 247V: STAFFORDSHIRE]

III. The land of St Peter of Westminster

THE ABBEY OF ST PETER of Westminster holds PERTON. There are 3 hides. There is land for 6 ploughs. In demesne is 1 [plough]; and 13 villans and 2 bordars and 1 free man with 5 ploughs. There are 8 acres of meadow, [and] woodland half a league long and as much broad. It was and is worth 40s.

IIII. The land of St Mary of Burton

THE ABBEY OF ST MARY of Burton upon Trent holds $1\frac{1}{2}$ hides in the vill of Stafford. There is land for 2 ploughs. There are [2 ploughs] in demesne; and 9 villans have 2 ploughs there. There are 16 acres of meadow, [and] woodland half a league long and as much broad. TRE it was worth 60s; now 70s.

The abbey itself holds BRANSTON. Countess Godgifu held it TRE. There are $1\frac{1}{2}$ hide. There is land for 5 ploughs. In demesne are $1\frac{1}{2}$ [ploughs]; and 5 villans and 3 bordars with 3 ploughs. There are 24 acres of meadow, [and] woodland half a league long and as much broad. It was worth 60s; now 40s.

The abbey itself holds WETMORE. There are $1\frac{1}{2}$ hides with its appendages. There is land for 7 ploughs. In demesne are 2 [ploughs]; and 6 villans have 2 ploughs. There are 4 acres of meadow, [and] woodland 1 league long and another broad. TRE it was worth £4; and afterwards 20s; now 50s.

The abbey itself holds STRETTON [in Burton-upon-Trent]. There are $1\frac{1}{2}$ hides. There is land for 2 ploughs. In demesne is 1 [plough]; and 8 villans and 2 bordars have 5 ploughs. There are 28 acres of meadow. TRE it was worth 60s; and afterwards 20s; now 40s.

The abbey itself holds ABBOTS BROMLEY. There is half a hide with [the] appendages. There is land for 1 plough. This [plough] is in demesne; and a priest with 1 villan and 1 bordar have 1 plough. There is woodland 2 leagues long and 1 broad. It was worth 10s; now 20s.

The abbey itself holds DARLASTON, and 2 men [hold] of it. There are 3 virgates of land. There is land for 2 ploughs. There are 2 villans [...]. There are 6 acres of meadow, [and] woodland 2 furlongs long and 1 furlong broad. TRE it was worth 30s; and afterwards 10s; now 27s4d.

The abbey itself holds CHURCH LEIGH. There are 3 virgate of land. There is land for 3 ploughs. In demesne is 1 [plough]. There is 1 free man and 10 villans having 5 ploughs. There is woodland 1 league long and as much broad. It was and is worth 40s.

The abbey itself holds OKEOVER. There are 3 virgates of land with its appendages. There is land for 2 ploughs. Eadwulf holds it at rent. There is 1 mill, [and] woodland half a league long and 3 furlongs broad. It is worth 20s.

The abbey itself holds WHISTON, and Nawen [holds] of it. There is 1 hide. There is land for 1 plough. This [plough] is there, with 1 villan and 2 bordars. It is worth 4s.

The abbey itself holds 'BEDINTONE' [in Penkridge]. There is half a hide. There is land for 2 ploughs. There is 1 villan. [...] [There is] woodland half a league long and as much broad. It was worth 13s; now 7s4d.

V. The land of Saint-Remi

IN PIREHILL HUNDRED

THE CHURCH OF SAINT-REMI holds half a hide in MEAFORD, and Nawen holds of the church. There is land for 2 ploughs. In demesne is 1 [plough]; and 4 villans and 3 bordars with 2 ploughs. There are 3 acres of meadow, [and] woodland 3 furlongs long and 1 broad. It is worth 13s.

IN OFFLOW HUNDRED

The church itself holds 1 virgate of land in HAMSTALL RIDWARE. There is land for 1 plough. Godric holds of the church. He has there half a plough; and 2 villans [have] half [a plough]. There is a mill rendering 2s, and 2 acres of meadow. It is worth 5s.

Earl Ælfgar gave these 2 estates to Saint-Remi.

VI. [The land of the Canons of Stafford]

In the city of STAFFORD the king has 13 prebendary canons, and they hold 3 hides from the king in alms. There is land for 9 ploughs. There are 4 villans and 8 bordars and 4 slaves having 2 ploughs. There is a mill rendering 4s, and meadow 2 furlongs in length and 1 furlong broad. It was worth 20s TRE; now 60s.

VII. The land of the Clerks of Wolverhampton

THE CANONS OF WOLVERHAMPTON hold 1 hide of Samson [Wolverhampton]. There is land for 3 ploughs. TRE there were 8 ploughs. Now there are 10 [ploughs], and 14 slaves; and 6 villans and 30 bordars with 9 ploughs. There are 2 acres of meadow.

The canons themselves hold 2 hides in UPPER ARLEY [Worcs.]. There is land for 6 ploughs. In demesne is 1 plough, and 2 slaves; and 7 villans and 3 bordars with 4 ploughs. There are 3 free men, [and] woodland 6 furlongs long and 4 furlongs broad.

To this land belongs half a hide in another Arley [Upper Arley, Worcs.] which Osbern fitz Richard has taken away by force from the canons. There is land for 1 ploughs. There is [1 plough], with 4 villans. It is worth 10s.

In BUSHBURY the canons themselves have 1 virgate of land. There is land for half a plough. There is 1 free man with 1 plough. It is worth 12d.

In TRESCOTT they have 1 virgate of land. There is land for half a plough. 1 free man has this [plough] there; and it is worth 12d.

In TETTENHALL they have 1 hide. There is land for 2½ ploughs; and there are 3 ploughs, with 1 villan and 3 bordars.

This land does not belong to Wolverhampton, but it is [part of] the king's alms to the church of the same vill.

From the same alms the priests of Tettenhall have 1 hide in BILBROOK. There are 2 free men with 1 villan and 2 bordars having 2½ ploughs.

The canons themselves have 5 hides in "HASWIC". There is land for 8 ploughs. Now it is waste on account of the king's forest. Half the woodland, which is in the forest, belonged there.

The canons themselves have 5 hides in WEDNESFIELD. There is land for 3 ploughs. There are 6 villans and 6 bordars having 6 ploughs. [There is] woodland pasture half a league long and 3 furlongs broad.

The canons themselves hold 2 hides in WILLENHALL. There is land for 1 plough. There are 3 villans and 5 bordars having 3 ploughs.

They themselves hold half a hide in PELSALL. There is land for 1 plough. This is waste.

They themselves hold 3 virgates of land in HILTON [in Shenstone]. There is land for 1 plough. There 2 free men and 4 bordars have 2 ploughs. In "HOCINTURE" [is] 1 hide, waste.

All this land of the canons is worth £6 a year.

IN CUTTLESTONE HUNDRED

SAMSON holds of the king, and Edwin and Alric, priests, [hold] of him, 3 hides of land in HATHERTON. There is land for 2 ploughs. In demesne is 1 [plough], and 1 slave. There 1 knight and 3 villans with 7 bordars have 3 ploughs. There is woodland half a league long and 4 furlongs broad. It was worth 2s; now 10s.

They themselves hold 1 hide in KINVASTON. There is land for 1 plough. In demesne are 2 ploughs, and 3 slaves, and 3 bordars. There is a mill rendering 3s, and 8 acres of meadow. TRE it was worth 12d; now it is worth 10s.

[The Church of] ST MARY of Wolverhampton held these 2 estates TRE.

They themselves hold 2 hides in HILTON [near Featherstone]. There is land for 2 ploughs. In demesne is 1 [plough], with 1 slave; and 1 free man with 2 bordars has 1½ ploughs, and 3 villans have 1 plough there. It was worth 12d; now 10s.

They themselves have 1 hide, waste, in FEATHERSTONE.

IN CUTTLESTONE HUNDRED

In PENKRIDGE 9 clerks hold 1 hide of the king. There is land for 4 ploughs. In demesne are 5 ploughs, and 6 slaves; and 7 villans with 3 ploughs. It was worth 3s; now 10s.

The clerks themselves hold 2 hides and 3 virgates of land in GNOSALL. There is land for 2 ploughs. In demesne are 4 ploughs; and 8 villans and 4 bordars with 2 ploughs. There is a mill rendering 12d. It was worth 2s; now 15s.

[Folio 248: STAFFORDSHIRE]

VIII. The land of Earl Roger

EARL Roger holds CLAVERLEY [Shrops.]. There are 20 hides. Earl Ælfgar held it. There is land for 32 ploughs. In demesne are 5 ploughs; and 32 villans and 13 bordars having 23 ploughs. There is a mill rendering 5s, and 12 acres of meadow, [and] woodland 2 leagues long and half a league broad. TRE it was worth £7.10s; now £10.

The earl himself holds KINGSNORDLEY [Shrops.]. Earl Ælfgar held it. There are 2 hides. There is land for 12 ploughs.

In demesne are 3 ploughs; and 7 villans and 2 bordars have 5 ploughs. There is a mill rendering 2s, [and] woodland 1½ leagues long and a half broad. TRE it was worth £8; now £4.

The earl himself holds ALVELEY [Shrops.]. Earl Ælfgar held it There is 1 hide. There is land for 9 ploughs. In demesne are 2 [ploughs]; and 8 villans with a priest and 4 bordars with 6 ploughs. There are 6 acres of meadow, [and] woodland 2 leagues long and a half broad. TRE it was worth £6; now 100s.

The earl himself holds "COBINTONE", and Reginald [holds] of him. [...] There are 2 hides. There is land for 4 ploughs. In demesne are 2 [ploughs], and 5 slaves; and 3 villans and 2 free men with 2½ ploughs. There are 12 acres of meadow. TRE it was worth 40s; and afterwards 2s; now 40s. Almund held this land and he was a free man.

IN CUTTLESTONE HUNDRED

The earl himself holds SHERIFFHALES [Shrops.], and Reginald [holds] of him. Earl Ælfgar held it. There are 2 hides. There is land for 15 ploughs. In demesne are 4 ploughs, and 2 slaves; and 26 villans and 14 bordars and 1 knight having 10 ploughs. There is a mill rendering 3s, and 8 acres of meadow, [and] woodland 1½ leagues long and 1 league broad.

In this vill Saint-Evroul has 1 plough, with a priest who has 2 oxen. It is worth £8.

The sheriff claims this manor for the king's farm, and the shire attests that Earl Edwin held it.

The earl himself holds KNIGHTLEY, and Reginald [holds] of him. Beornwulf held it as a free man. There is 1 hide. There is land for 4 ploughs. In demesne is half a plough; and 6 villans and 5 bordars have 2 ploughs. There is woodland 1 league long and half a league broad. It is worth 10s.

The earl himself holds MORETON [in Gnosall], and Benedict [holds] of him.[...] Ælfgeat held it without soke and sake. There are 2 hides. There is land for 3 ploughs. In demesne is 1 plough, with 1 slave; and 1 knight with 1 Englishman have 1 plough, and 4 bordars. There is a mill rendering 16d.

The Church of SAINT-EVROUL holds HIGH ONN of the earl. [...] There are 2 hides. There is land for 5 ploughs. In demesne are 3 ploughs, and 1 slave; and 7 villans with 1 plough. There is 1 acre of meadow, [and] woodland 1 league long and a half broad. Swein, a free man, held this land TRE. It is worth £4.

The church itself holds MARSTON [near Stafford] of the earl. Wulfgar held it, and he was free. There is 1 hide. There is land for 10 ploughs. In demesne are 4 ploughs, and 2 slaves; and 4 villans with 1 plough. There are 12 acres of meadow. 18 burgesses in Stafford belong to this manor. A certain Walter has 1 plough there. It is worth 100s.

The earl himself holds NORBURY, and Reger [holds] of him. Auti held it as a free man. There are 2½ hides. There is land for 8 ploughs. In demesne are 2 ploughs, with 1 slave; and 2 priests and 14 villans and 4 bordars with 6 ploughs.

There is 1 acre of meadow, [and] woodland 1 league long and a half broad. It is worth £3.

The earl himself holds WALTON GRANGE [in Gnosall], and Roger [holds] of him. Almund held it. There are 2 hides. There is land for 3 ploughs. In demesne are 2 [ploughs], and 3 slaves; and 5 villans with 1 plough. There is half an acre of meadow. It is worth 10s.

IN PIREHILL HUNDRED

The earl himself holds YARLET, and Robert [holds] of him. There is 1 hide with [the] appendages. There is land for 6 ploughs. In demesne are 2 ploughs, and 2 slaves; and 4 villans and 4 bordars with 1 plough. There are 5 acres of meadow. It is worth 30s.

The earl himself holds GAYTON Amerton, and Gosbert and Wulfric [hold] of him. There is 1 hide. There is land for 4 ploughs. In demesne is 1 [plough]; and 10 villans have 4 ploughs with 6 bordars. There are 6 acres of meadow, [and] woodland 1 league long and a half broad. It is worth 30s. Almær and Alric held it.

The earl himself holds 'COTON' [in St Mary, Stafford], and Azelin [holds] of him. There are 2 hides. There is land for 4 ploughs. There is 1 plough and 6 oxen, with 1 slave and 1 villan. There are 4 acres of meadow. It is worth 20s. Almund held it and he was free.

The earl himself holds COLTON, and Azelin [holds] of him. There is 1 hide. There is land for 4 ploughs. Almund held it, and he was free. In demesne are 2 ploughs, and 4 slaves; and 14 villans with a priest have 3 ploughs. There are 19 acres of meadow, [and] woodland 1 league long and a half broad. It is worth 40s.

In "COLT" is half a hide and it belongs to Colton. Almær held it.

The earl himself holds MAVESYN RIDWARE, and Azelin [holds] of him. There are 1½ hides. There is land for 4 ploughs. In demesne is 1 [plough], and 2 slaves, with 1 villan. There are 16 acres of meadow, [and] woodland 1½ leagues long and as much broad. It is worth 20s. 5 Englishmen held it TRE, and they still have land for 2½ ploughs.

The earl himself holds LOXLEY [Loxley and Lower Loxley], and Azelin [holds] of him. There is the fourth part of a hide. There is land for 4 ploughs. It was and is waste. There are 4 acres of meadow, [and] woodland 1½ leagues long and half a league broad. It is worth 20s. Edmund held it, and he was a free man.

The earl himself holds CRESWELL, and William Pantulf [holds] of him. There is 1 hide. There is land for 6 ploughs. There are 4 villans and 4 bordars with 2 ploughs. There is a mill rendering 5s, and 40 acres of meadow. And in Stafford, 1 waste messuage. It is worth 20s. Godwine held it, and he was a free man.

The earl himself holds DERRINGTON, and William [holds] of him. There is 1 hide. There is land for 6 ploughs. There are 3 villans with 1 plough. There are 2 acres of meadow, [and] woodland 4 furlongs long and 3 furlongs broad. It is worth 20s. Swein held it, and he was a free man.

The earl himself holds MODDERSHALL, and William [holds] of him. There is half a hide. There is land for 5 ploughs, and in Cotwalton, which belongs there [...]. There are 3 villans and 2 bordars with 1 plough, and 3 acres of meadow. [There is] woodland half a league long and broad. It is worth 10s. Godgifu held it.

The earl himself holds ALMINGTON, and William [holds] of him. There are 3 hides with [the] appendages. There is land for 6 ploughs. In demesne is 1 [plough]; and 4 villans and 4 bordars with 1 plough. There are 2 acres of meadow, [and] woodland 2 leagues long and 1 broad. It is worth 30s. Godwine held it, and he was a free man.

The earl himself holds TIXALL, and Henry de Ferrers [holds] of him. There is half a virgate of land. There is land for 4 ploughs. In demesne is 1 plough, with 1 villan. There are 2 acres of meadow, [and] woodland 3 furlongs long and 2 broad. It is worth 10s. Almund held it.

The earl himself holds MEAFORD, and Helgot [holds] of him. There is half a hide. There is land for 4 ploughs. In demesne is 1 [plough], with 1 slave; and 5 villans and 2 bordars with 1 plough. There are 2 acres of meadow. It is worth 30s. Swein held it; he was free.

The earl himself holds ASHLEY, and Geoffrey [holds] of him. There are 2 hides. There is land for 3 ploughs. In demesne is 1 [plough]; and 2 villans and 2 bordars. There is woodland 1 league long and a half broad. It is worth 15s. Wulfmær held it; he was free.

The earl himself holds HAMSTALL RIDWARE, and Walter [holds] of him. There is 1 virgate of land. There is land for 1½ ploughs. There are 2 slaves and 4 villans, and 4 acres of meadow, [and] woodland 1 league long and a half broad. It is worth 5s. Edmund held it, and he was a free man.

The earl himself holds BLITHFIELD, and Roger [holds] of him. There is 1 hide. There is land for 4 ploughs. In demesne are 2 ploughs, and 4 slaves; and 7 villans with a priest and 1 bordar have 2 ploughs. There are 6 acres of meadow. The woodland is 3 furlongs long and 1 furlong broad. It is worth 20s. Edmund held it, and he was a free man.

The earl himself holds ALSTONEFIELD, and William [holds] of him. There are 3 virgates of land. There is land for 3 ploughs. In demesne is 1 [plough]; and 1 villan with 1 plough.

In Warslow, which belongs to this manor, there is land [...]. There are 4 villans and 2 bordars with 1 plough. There are 8 acres of meadow. There is woodland 1 league long and a half broad. It is worth 40s. Godwine held it.

The earl himself holds CHEDDLETON, and William [holds] of him. There is half a hide. There is land for 4 ploughs. In demesne is half a plough; and 3 villans and 1 bordar with half a plough.

[There is] woodland half a league long and 3 furlongs broad.

In BASFORD, which belongs to this manor, is half a hide. There are 4 villans and 1 bordar with 1 plough. There is 1 acre of meadow, [and] woodland 2 leagues long and 1½ leagues broad. The whole is worth 15s. Godwine held it, and he was free.

IN OFFLOW HUNDRED

The same Earl Roger holds SHENSTONE, and Robert d'Oilly [holds] of him. There are 3 hides. There is land for 12 ploughs. In demesne are 2 ploughs, with 1 slave; and 21 villans and 4 bordars with 14 ploughs. There is a mill rendering 66d, and 1 acre of meadow, [and] woodland 3 leagues long and 1½ leagues broad. It is worth 100s. Godwine held it, and he was a free man.

VIII. The land of Hugh de Montgomery

HUGH de Montgomery holds WORFIELD [Shrops.] of the king. Earl Ælfgar held it. There are 30 hides. There is land for 30 ploughs. In demesne are 4 [ploughs], and 5 slaves; and 67 villans with a priest and 10 bordars have 25 ploughs. There are 3 mills rendering 40s, and a fishery rendering 15s, and 16 acres of meadow, [and] woodland 3 leagues long and 1 broad. There 3 Englishmen have 5 ploughs, with 18 villans and 5 bordars. It was worth £3; now £18. Of this land 3 hides are waste.

IX. The land of Henry de Ferrers

IN PIREHILL HUNDRED

HENRY de Ferrers has the castle of TUTBURY.

In the borough around the castle are 42 men living only from his market, and with the market they pay £4.10s.

In "BURTONE" he has half a hide on which is situated his castle, on which [half-hide] were 12 ploughs TRE. Now there are 4 ploughs in demesne. It is worth 24s a year.

IN OFFLOW HUNDRED

Henry himself holds ROLLESTON. Earl Morcar held it. There are 2½ hides. There is land for 8 ploughs. In demesne are 4 ploughs, and 1 female slave; and 18 villans and 16 bordars with a priest having 14 ploughs. There is a mill rendering 5s. There are 50 acres of meadow, woodland pasture 3 leagues long and 2 leagues broad, [and] arable land 2 leagues long and 1 broad. It is worth £10.

Henry himself holds MARCHINGTON. There are 2 hides, and in Agardsley, 1 virgate of land. Wulfric held it, and he was a free man. There is land for 7 ploughs. In demesne are 2 [ploughs], with 1 slave; and 18 villans and 9 bordars with 3 ploughs. There are 40 acres of meadow, [and] woodland pasture 3 leagues long and 1½ leagues broad. It is worth 100s.

Henry himself holds DRAYCOTT IN THE CLAY. There is half a hide. There is land for 1 plough. This plough is in demesne; and 4 villans and 4 bordars have 1 plough. There are 12 acres of meadow, [and] woodland half a league long and as much broad. It is worth 15s.

Henry himself holds FAULD, and Hubert [holds] of him. There is half a hide [...]. There is land for 1 plough. This [plough] is in demesne; and there are 6 bordars. It is worth 15s.

In the same vill Roger holds of Henry half a hide. There is land for half a plough. There a priest has 1 plough, and there are 2 bordars. There is 1 hide which these 2 hold. There are 50 acres of meadow, [and] woodland pasture 3 leagues long and 1 league broad. It is worth 15s.

TRE St Werburh of Chester held this whole vill of FAULD.

Henry himself holds MORETON [in Hanbury], and Ealhhere [holds] of him. There is 1 virgate of land. There is land for half a plough. There are 3 villans with 1 plough. There are 12 acres of meadow, [and] woodland 1 league in length and breadth. 3 free men held it.

Henry himself holds CHEBSEY, and Humphrey [holds] of him. There are 5 hides. There is land for 12 ploughs. In demesne are 3 [ploughs], and 8 slaves; and 20 villans with a priest and 9 bordars have 8 ploughs. There are 20 acres of meadow, [and] woodland pasture 2 furlongs long and 1 broad. It is worth £4.

To this manor belonged the land of Stafford on which the king ordered a castle to be built which has now been demolished.

In the vill of "Burtone" Ralph, a knight of Henry, has 1 plough in demesne; and 3 bordars with 1 plough. There are 20 acres of meadow, [and] woodland 4 furlongs long and as much broad.

XI. The land of Robert of Stafford

IN PIREHILL HUNDRED

ROBERT OF STAFFORD holds TILLINGTON. Tholf held it, and he was a free man. There are 3 hides. [There is] land for 4 ploughs. There are 5 villans and 2 bordars with 2 ploughs. There are 4 acres of meadow. It is worth 30s.

IN TOTMONSLOW HUNDRED

Robert himself holds [Lower and Upper] TEAN. Wulfgeat and Wulfmær held it, and they were free. There is half a hide. There is land for 6 ploughs. There are 6 villans and 6 bordars with 3 ploughs, and 3 slaves. There are 6 acres of meadow, [and] woodland 1 league long and a half broad. It is worth 30s.

Robert himself holds the third part of 1 hide in GRINDON. It is waste. Wulfgeat held it TRE.

Robert himself holds 1 virgate of land in CAULDON. There is land for 1 plough. It is waste. Godgifu held it TRE.

Robert himself holds in BROUGH HALL 1 virgate of land which belongs to HAUGHTON. There is land for 1 plough.

Wulfmær held it, and he was a free man. There are 2 villans with 1 plough, and 2 acres of woodland. It is worth 5s.

Robert himself holds BRADLEY [near Stafford] with [the] appendages. Earl Edwin held it. There is land for 44 ploughs among all the Berewicks. In Bradley [there is] only 1 hide. In demesne is 1 plough and 2 slaves; and 12 villans and 4 bordars with 11 ploughs. There is a mill rendering 5s, and 12 acres of meadow, [and] woodland 1 league long and a half broad.

In Barton [in Bradeley], [is] 1 hide. In Apeton, 2 hides. In Littywood, 1 hide. In Billington, 2 hides. In Burton [in Castle Church], 2½ hides. In 'Silkmore' [in Stafford], 1 hide. In Longnor, 1 hide. In Mitton, 2 hides. In Alstone, 1 hide. In [Lower and Upper] Woollaston, 2 hides. These lands belong to Bradley [near Stafford].

In these are 48 villans and 26 bordars having 17 ploughs. And in demesne is 1 [plough] in Alstone, and a certain knight, and 15 acres of meadow.

The whole manor with the members is worth £7.

In the Borough of STAFFORD Robert has 70s from half of the king's share.

IN PIREHILL HUNDRED

Robert himself holds WALTON [in Stone], and Arnold [holds] of him. There are 3 hides. There is land for 6 ploughs. In demesne is 1 [plough]; and 7 villans and 2 bordars and 5 slaves with a priest having 4 ploughs. [There is] woodland 2 furlongs long and 1 broad; and meadow of the same amount. It is worth 60s. Aki, a free man, held it and gave 1 carucate of this land to his sister.

Robert himself holds 3 parts of 1 hide in ASTON [in Stone] and Stoke [Stoke and Little Stoke, in Stone]. 6 thegns held them, and they were free. There is land for 8 ploughs. In demesne are 2 ploughs; and 7 villans and 4 bordars with 1 slave having 5 ploughs. [There is] woodland 2 furlongs long and 1 furlong broad, and as much meadow. It is worth 70s. Cadio holds of Robert.

Robert himself holds 1 virgate of land in 'Little SANDON', and the same Cadio [holds] of him. Alwine and Alwine and Wihtric held this. 2 of them were free; Wihtric could not depart with the land. In this virgate is land for 4 ploughs. In demesne is 1 [plough]; and 4 villans and 2 bordars with 2 ploughs. There are 14 acres of meadow. It is worth 10s.

Robert himself holds 2 hides in HOPTON. Alweard held them, and he was a free man. There is land for 6 ploughs. In demesne are 2 ploughs; and 6 villans and 4 bordars and 2 slaves with 3½ ploughs. There are 4 acres of meadow, [and] scrubland 2 furlongs long and a half broad. It is worth 40s. Gilbert holds of Robert.

Robert himself holds 2 hides in SALT, and Gilbert [holds] of him. Bishop Leofwine and Ordmær held these, but the king had the sake and soke of this Ordmaær. There is land for 4 ploughs. There is 1 plough; and 6 villans and 4 bordars and 2 [...]. There is a mill rendering 3s, and 12 acres of meadow and 4 acres of woodland. It is worth 10s.

Robert himself holds 2 hides in CHESWARDINE [Shrops.]

and in Chipnall [Shrops.], and Gilbert holds of him. There is land for 6 ploughs. In demesne are 2 ploughs; and 12 villans and 8 bordars with $3\frac{1}{2}$ ploughs. There is 1 acre of meadow, [and] woodland 2 leagues long and a half broad. It is worth 40s. Godgifu held it but paid 2s from Chipnall [Shrops.] to the Church of St Chad.

Robert himself holds 1 hide in HIGH OFFLEY, and Urfer [holds] of him. Wulfric held it and he was free. There is land for 4 ploughs. In demesne are 2 [ploughs], with 1 slave; and 4 villans and 4 bordars with 2 ploughs. There are 8 acres of meadow. The woodland is 1 league long and a half broad. It is worth 40s.

Robert himself holds 2 hides in STANDON and in RUDGE, and Brian [holds] of him. Siward held them, and he was a free man. There is land for 6 ploughs. In demesne is 1 [plough]; and 11 villans and 3 bordars and 3 slaves with 5 ploughs. There is a priest, and a mill rendering 5s. There are 2 acres of meadow and 14 acres of grove. It is worth 40s.

Robert himself holds 1 virgate of land in WESTON [in Standon], and Brian [holds] of him. Godwine held it, and he was free. There is land for 2 ploughs. In demesne is 1 plough, and 6 slaves; and 4 villans and 2 bordars with 1 plough. [There is] woodland half a league long and 2 furlongs broad. It is worth 20s.

[Folio 249: STAFFORDSHIRE]

Robert himself holds 1 virgate of land in MAER, and Wulfgeat [holds] of him. He himself held it, and he was a free man. There is land for 2 ploughs. There are 4 villans and 1 bordar with 1 plough. [There is] woodland 1 league long and another broad. It is worth 10s.

The same Robert holds 2 hides in SWYNNERTON, and Aslen [holds] of him. Brothir held them, and he was a free man. There is land for 8 ploughs. In demesne is 1 [plough]; and 10 villans and 5 bordars with 6 ploughs. There are 10 acres of meadow, [and] woodland 1 league long and 1 broad. It is worth 40s.

Robert himself holds 2 hides in NORTON IN THE MOORS, and in [the] appendages. Godric and Wulfgeat held them, and they were free. There is land for 4 ploughs. There are 6 villans and 3 bordars with 3 ploughs. [There is] woodland 3 leagues long and 2 leagues broad. It is worth 40s.

Robert himself holds 1 hide in MADELEY [near Stoke-on-Trent], and Wulfgeat [holds] of him. Swein held it, and he was a free man. There is land for 4 ploughs. In demesne is 1 plough; and 5 villans and 7 bordars with 2 ploughs. [There is] woodland $1\frac{1}{2}$ leagues long and 1 league broad. It is worth 30s.

The same Robert holds the third part of 1 hide in ABBEY HULTON and in 'RUSHTON' [in Burslem], and Wulfgeat holds of him. He himself held it TRE. There is land for 3 ploughs. There are 3 villans and 3 bordars with 1 plough. [There is] woodland 1 league long and a half broad. It is worth 10s.

Robert himself holds the third part of 1 hide in BURSLEM. Alweard held it, and he was a free man. There is land for 2

ploughs. There is 1 villan and 4 bordars with 1 plough. There are 2 acres of alder-grove. It is worth 10s. Wulfgeat held it.

Robert himself holds 1 hide in ASTON [in Stone] and [the] appendages, and Algot [holds] of him. Godgifu and Eadric held it, and they were free. There is land for 3 ploughs. There are 3 bordars with 1 plough. [There is] woodland 1 league long and half a league broad. It is worth 10s.

The same Robert holds half a hide in BARLASTON, and Helgot [holds] of him. Augustine held it, and he was a free man. There is land for 6 ploughs. In demesne is 1 [plough], with 1 slave; and 4 villans and 3 bordars with 1 plough. There are 6 acres of meadow and 3 acres of woodland. It is worth 40s.

The same Robert holds half a hide in RANTON, and Godric, who also held it as a free man, [holds] of him. There is land for 2 ploughs. In demesne is 1 [plough]; and 6 villans and 5 bordars have 3 ploughs. There are 3 acres of meadow, [and] woodland 1 league long and a half broad. It is worth 20s.

Robert himself holds half a hide in COOKSLAND, and Helio [holds] of him. Toki and Ælfric held it, and they were free. There is land for 2 ploughs. There is 1 villan and 2 bordars, and 5 acres of meadow, [and] woodland 2 furlongs long and 1 broad. It is worth 6s.

Robert himself holds the fifth part of 1 hide in HILDERSTONE. Dunning and Wulfric held it, and they were free men. There is land for 3 ploughs. In demesne is 1 [plough]; and 2 villans and 2 bordars and 2 slaves with 1 plough, and 1 acre of meadow. [There is] woodland 1 league long and a half broad. It is worth 10s. Vitalis holds it of Robert.

The same Robert holds half a hide in "BRADELIE", and Tanio [holds] of him. Wulfgeat and Alweard held it, and they were free. There is land for 4 ploughs. In demesne is 1 [plough], and 3 slaves; and 3 villans and 6 bordars with 2 ploughs. There are 4 acres of meadow, [and] woodland 2 leagues long and 1 broad. It is worth 40s.

The same Robert holds 1 hide in COLTON, and Geoffrey [holds] of him. Oda and Wulfric held it, and they were free. There is land for 6 ploughs. In demesne is 1 [plough]; and 10 villans and 1 slave with 3 ploughs. There is a mill rendering 12d, and 16 acres of meadow, [and] woodland 1 league long and 3 furlongs broad. It is worth 50s.

The same Robert holds 3 parts of 1 hide in MILWICH, and Osbern [holds] of him. Swein and Rafwin held them, and they were free. There is land for 4 ploughs. In demesne is 1 [plough]; and 4 villans and 4 bordars with 3 ploughs. There is 1 acre of meadow, [and] woodland 1 league long and a half broad. It is worth 20s.

The same Robert holds 3 parts of 1 hide in TIXALL, and Hugh [holds] of him. Alric and Ordmær held them, and they were free. There is land for 6 ploughs. In demesne is 1 [plough], and 3 slaves; and 7 villans and 2 bordars with 2 ploughs. There are 6 acres of meadow, [and] woodland 1 league long and 3 furlongs broad. It is worth 30s.

The same Robert holds 3 hides in INGESTRE, and Hugh [holds] of him. Godwine and Vithgripr held them, and they were free. There is land for 4 ploughs. There are 9 villans and 2 bordars with 2 ploughs. There are 9 acres of meadow, and 10d from 1 part of a mill, [and] woodland half a league long and 1 furlong broad. It is worth 15s.

The same Robert holds 3 hides in TITTENSOR, and Stenulf [holds] of him. Wulfgeat and Godric held them, and they were free. There is land for 3 ploughs. In demesne is half a plough; and 8 villans and 2 bordars and 1 slave with $1\frac{1}{2}$ ploughs. There are 4 acres of meadow, and a mill rendering 8d, [and] woodland 6 furlongs long and as much broad. It is worth 30s.

Robert himself holds 1 virgate of land in WESTON COYNEY, and Ernulf de Hesdin [holds] of him. Wulfric held it. There is land for 3 ploughs. There are 5 villans with 2 ploughs. [There is] woodland 1 league long and half a league broad. It is worth 10s.

IN TOTMONSLOW HUNDRED

Robert himself holds 1 virgate of land in GRATWICH, and Wulfheah [holds] of him. Goding held it, and he was a free man. There is land for 3 ploughs. There are 4 villans and 4 bordars and 1 slave with 3 ploughs. There is a mill rendering 4s, and 1 acre of meadow, [and] woodland half a league long and a half broad. It is worth 24s.

Robert himself holds 1 virgate of land in CAVERSWALL, and Ernulf [holds] of him. Wulfgeat held it, and he was a free man. There is land for 4 ploughs. In demesne is 1 [plough]; and 10 villans and 2 bordars with 3 ploughs. There are 6 acres of meadow, and woodland 1 league long and a half broad; and half the church of Stoke-on-Trent with half a carucate of land. It is worth 30s.

Robert himself holds half a hide in MADELEY [in Checkley], and Wulfheah [holds] of him. Godgifu held this even after the coming of King William into England, but she could not withdraw with the land. There is land for 6 ploughs. In demesne is 1 [plough], and 5 slaves; and 10 villans and 8 bordars with 3 ploughs. There are 2 acres of meadow, [and] woodland 1 league long and 4 furlongs broad.

In the same vill 2 Englishmen hold $1\frac{1}{2}$ carucates of land of the same land, and there they have 5 bordars and 2 villans with 1 plough.

The whole manor is worth £4.

Robert himself holds 1 virgate of land in BRAMSHALL of which virgate half, as the road divides it, belongs to the king. But Robert seized the same part belonging to the king and makes himself warrantable [for it]. Bagot holds of him. Wulfgeat held it, and he was a free man. There is land for 3 ploughs. In demesne is 1 [plough], and 2 slaves. There are 4 villans and 1 bordar with 1 plough. [There is] woodland half a league long and 4 furlongs broad. It is worth 20s.

Robert himself holds 1 virgate of land in ELLASTONE, and Wudumann and Alsige [hold] of him. 6 thegns held it TRE, and they were free men. There is land for 6 ploughs. In demesne are $1\frac{1}{2}$ ploughs, with 1 slave; and 11 villans and 4

bordars with $1\frac{1}{2}$ ploughs. There are 12 acres of meadow, and a mill rendering 32d, [and] woodland 1 league long and a half broad. It is worth 30s.

Robert himself holds 1 virgate of land in BLORE, and Eadric [holds] of him. 4 thegns held it, and they were free men. There is land for 5 ploughs. In demesne is 1 plough; and 2 villans with 1 plough. There are 2 furlongs of spinney. It is worth 5s.

Robert himself holds 1 virgate of land in DILHORNE, and Walbert [holds] of him. Godwine held it, and he was a free man, with 2 other men similarly free. There is land for 4 ploughs. In demesne is half a plough; and 5 villans and 5 bordars with $3\frac{1}{2}$ ploughs. There is 1 acre of meadow, [and] woodland 1 league long and a half broad. It is worth 20s.

Robert himself holds 1 virgate of land in CHEADLE, and Robert [holds] of him. Godgifu held it, and she was free. There is land for 4 ploughs. In demesne is 1 [plough]; and 7 villans and 1 bordar with $1\frac{1}{2}$ ploughs. There is a mill rendering 12d, and 1 acre of meadow, [and] woodland 2 leagues long and 1 broad. It is worth 20s.

IN SEISDON HUNDRED

Robert himself holds 5 hides in BOBBINGTON, and Helgot [holds] of him. Vithfari held them with sake and soke. There is land for 6 ploughs. In demesne are 2 ploughs, and 4 slaves; and 5 villans and 3 bordars with 1 plough. [There is] woodland pasture 1 league long and a half broad. It is worth 40s.

Robert himself holds 3 hides in PATSHULL, and Hugh [holds] of him. Brothir held them with sake and soke, and he was a free man. There is land for 6 ploughs. In demesne are 2 ploughs, with 1 slave; and 12 villans and 6 bordars with 4 ploughs. There is a mill rendering 12d, [and] woodland half a league long and 4 furlongs broad. It is worth 30s.

Robert himself holds 5 hides in OAKEN, and Hugh [holds] of him. Brothir held them, and he was a free man. There is land for 3 ploughs. In demesne is 1 [plough]; and 4 villans and 4 bordars with $1\frac{1}{2}$ ploughs. [There is] woodland half a league long and 2 furlongs broad. It is worth 8s.

Robert himself holds 2 hides in WROTTESLEY, and Glædwine [holds] of him. Hunta held them, and he was a free man. There is land for 2 ploughs. In demesne is 1 [plough], and 1 villan and 1 bordar. [There is] woodland half a league long and 2 furlongs broad. It is worth 4s.

Robert himself holds 2 hides in OAKLEY [near Alrewas], and Helio [holds] of him. Wulfwine held them, and he was a free man. There is land for 4 ploughs. In demesne is 1 [plough]; and 2 villans and 6 bordars with 1 plough. There are 4 acres of meadow. It is worth 20s.

Robert himself holds 2 hides in SYERSCOTE, and Turchil [holds] of him. 4 thegns held them. This land was subject to customary payment as regards the king's toll only, but they had the rest of the soke and they could go where they would with their lands. There can be ploughs. In demesne is 1 plough; and 2 villans with 1 plough; and 2 Englishmen have there $1\frac{1}{2}$ ploughs, with 1 slave. It is worth 16s.

Robert himself holds 2 hides in WYCHNOR, and Robert [holds] of him. 4 thegns held them, and they were free. There is land for 4 ploughs. In demesne is 1 plough, and 4 villans and 2 bordars. There is a mill rendering 18d. There are 20 acres of meadow, [and] woodland half a league long and 5 furlongs broad. It is worth 15s.

[Folio 249V: STAFFORDSHIRE]

The same Robert holds 3 virgates of land in HAMSTALL RIDWARE, and Herman [holds] of him. 3 thegns held them, and they were free men. There is land for 4 ploughs. In demesne is 1 [plough], with 1 slave. There 1 free man holds 1 virgate of this land, and there he has 2 villans with half a plough. There is a mill rendering 2s, and 8 acres of meadow, [and] woodland 1½ leagues long and 1 league broad. It is worth 15s.

IN CUTTLESTONE HUNDRED

Robert himself holds 2 hides, and Urfer [holds] of him. Wulfric held them, and he was a free man. There is land for 2 ploughs; and 7 villans and 5 bordars with 2 ploughs. There is a mill rendering 12d, and 1 furlong of woodland. It is worth 16s.

Robert himself holds 3 hides in HAUGHTON, and Urfer [holds] of him. Wulfric, a free man, held them. There is land for 4 ploughs. In demesne are 2 ploughs, with 1 slave; and 6 villans and 7 bordars with 3 ploughs. There are 6 acres of meadow, [and] woodland 1 furlong long and half a furlong broad. It is worth 30s.

Robert himself holds half a hide in LOYNTON, and Gilbert [holds] of him. Æthelric and Ordmær held it, and they were free. There is land for 1 plough. It is waste. It is worth 2s.

Robert himself holds 3 hides in WILBRIGHTON, and Laurence [holds] of him. 3 thegns held them, and they were free. There is land for 5 ploughs. In demesne are 2 ploughs, and 2 slaves; and 2 villans and 3 bordars with 1 plough. There are 3 acres of meadow, [and] woodland half a league long and as much broad. It is worth 15s.

Robert himself holds 2 hides in BRINETON, and Warin [holds] of him. 5 thegns held them, and they were free. There is land for 3 ploughs. There are 3 villans and 2 bordars with 2 ploughs. There are 8 acres of meadow, [and] woodland 2 furlongs long and as much broad. It is worth 10s.

Robert himself holds 1 hide in BLYMHILL. Warin [holds] of him. 5 brothers held it, and they were free. There is land for 4 ploughs. In demesne is 1 [plough], with 1 slave; and 7 villans and 4 bordars with 6 ploughs. There are 2 acres of meadow, [and] woodland 1 league long and 1 furlong broad.

In "Ruscote" is 1 hide belonging to the same manor. The whole is worth 20s.

Robert himself holds 3 hides in STRETTON [in Penkridge], and Hervey [holds] of him. 3 thegns held them, and they were free. There is land for 6 ploughs. In demesne is 1 [plough]; and 4 villans and 8 bordars with 1 plough. There 1 knight holds 1 carucate of land, and he has there 1 plough. There is a mill

rendering 4s, and 6 acres of meadow. The woodland is half a league long and 3 furlongs broad. It is worth 16s.

Robert himself holds 1 hide in WATER EATON, and Hervey [holds] of him. Ordmær held it, and he was free. There is land for 3 ploughs. In demesne is 1 plough, and 3 slaves; and 3 villans and 4 bordars with 1 plough. There is a mill rendering 3s. It is worth 8s.

Robert himself holds 1 hide in GAILEY, and Hervey [holds] of him. Bodin held it, and he was a free man. There is land for 2 ploughs. There is 1 villan, and 1 acre of meadow. It is worth 2s.

Robert himself holds 1 hide in OTHERTON, and Clodoan [holds] of him. Æthelric held it, and he was a free man. There is land for 2 ploughs. In demesne is 1 [plough], and 2 slaves; and 2 bordars with 1 plough. It is worth 3s.

Robert himself holds 2 hides in GREAT SAREDON, and Hervey [holds] of him. 4 free thegns held it. There is land for 2 ploughs. In demesne is 1 [plough], with 1 slave; and 2 villans and 4 bordars with 1 plough. It is worth 5s.

Robert himself holds 1 hide in COVEN, and Burgræd [holds] of him. Alric held it, and he was free. There is land for 2 ploughs. In demesne is 1 [plough], and 4 slaves; and 2 villans and 2 bordars with 1 plough. There are 3 acres of meadow, [and] woodland half a league long and 1 furlong broad. This woodland is in the king's demesne. The land is worth 16s.

Robert himself holds 1 hide in COPPENHALL, and Burgræd [holds] of him. 3 free men held it. There is land for 4 ploughs. In demesne is 1 [plough]; and 8 villans and 6 bordars with 3 ploughs. It is worth 12s.

Robert himself holds 3 hides in SHARESHILL, and Hervey [holds] of him. 2 free men held them. There is land for 3 ploughs. There are 2 villans and 5 bordars with 1 plough. [There is] woodland half a league long and a half broad. It is worth 10s.

Robert himself holds 3 hides in CHURCH EATON, and Godric [holds] of him. Vilgrip held them as a free man. There is land for 7 ploughs. In demesne is 1 [plough], and 3 slaves; and 8 villans and 8 bordars with a priest have 3 ploughs. There are 4 acres of meadow, [and] woodland 1 furlong long and as much broad. It is worth 20s.

Robert himself holds 3 hides in LEVEDALE, and Brian and Drogo [hold] of him. 3 free men held them. There is land for 7 ploughs. In demesne is 1 plough; and 5 villans and 2 bordars with 1 slave have 3 ploughs. There are 2 acres of meadow. It is worth 10s.

Robert himself holds 2½ hides in RICKERSCOTE, and Robert [holds] of him. Earl Edwin held it, and it belongs to Bradley [near Stafford]. There is land for 4 ploughs. In demesne is 1 [plough]; and 3 villans and 3 bordars with 1 plough. There are 2 acres of meadow. It is worth 20s.

Robert himself holds 1 hide in "MONETVILE", and Walter and Ansgar [holds] of him. Earl Edwin held it. There is land for 2 ploughs. There are [2 ploughs] in demesne, with 8 bordars. There are 2 acres of meadow. It is worth 10s.

XII. The land of William fitzAnsculf

IN SEISDON HUNDRED

WILLIAM fitz Ansculf holds SEDGLEY of the king. Earl Ælfgar held it. There are 6 hides. There is land for 12 ploughs. In demesne is 1 plough, and 3 slaves; and 45 villans with a priest and 2 bordars have 18 ploughs. There are 16 acres of meadow, [and] woodland 2 leagues long and 1 league broad. TRE it was worth £10; now the same.

The priests of Wolverhampton claim part of the woodland of this manor.

The same William holds MORFE. There are 5 hides. There is land for 6 ploughs. It is waste. 3 free men held it TRE. The woodland is 2 leagues long and as much broad.

The same William holds 1 hide in CHASEPOOL. There is land for 2 ploughs. It is in the king's forest and is waste.

The same William holds 2 hides in SEDGLEY, and Geoffrey [holds] of him, and there he has 1 plough in demesne; and 9 villans with 2 ploughs, and 2 acres of meadow. It is worth 20s.

The same William holds 3 hides in LOWER PENN, and Gilbert [holds] of him. Countess Godgifu held them. There is land for 6 ploughs. In demesne is 1 [plough]; and 6 villans with 1 free man have 1½ ploughs. There are 4 acres of meadow. It is worth 20s.

The same William holds 5 hides in UPPER PENN, and Robert [holds] of him. Earl Ælfgar held them. There is land for 6 ploughs. In demesne is 1 [plough], with 1 slave; and 8 villans and 2 bordars with 1 plough. There is a mill rendering 2s. It was and is worth 30s.

The same William holds 3 hides in ORTON, and Walbert [holds] of him. Wulfstan held them, and he was a free man. There is land for 4 ploughs. In demesne are 2 [ploughs], and 2 slaves; and 7 villans and 2 bordars with 2 ploughs. There are 4 acres of meadow. It was and is worth 40s.

The same William holds 7 hides in WOMBOURN, and Ralph [holds] of him. Thorsten held them with sake and soke. There is land for 8 ploughs. In demesne are 2 [ploughs], and 8 slaves; and 14 villans with a priest and 3 bordars have 4 ploughs. There are 2 mills rendering 4s, and 4 acres of meadow. It was and is worth £3.

The same William holds 1 hide in OXLEY, and Robert [holds] of him. Godwine and Alric held it, and they were free. There is land for 2 ploughs. In demesne is 1 [plough]; and 4 villans with 1 plough. There are 2 acres of meadow. It was and is worth 15s.

William himself holds 3 hides in ENVILLE, and Gilbert [holds] of him. Alric, a thegn of King Edward, held them with the soke. There is land for 4 ploughs. In demesne is 1 [plough], with 1 slave; and 5 villans and 1 bordar have 1½ ploughs. There are 4 acres of meadow, [and] woodland 1

league long and a half broad. The king holds it in the forest. It was and is worth 24s.

The same William holds 3 hides in "CIPPEMORE", and Roger [holds] of him. Edwin held them as a free man. There is land for 4 ploughs. In demesne are 2 [ploughs], and 3 slaves, and 5 bordars. [There is] woodland 1 league in length and breadth. The king has it in the forest. It was and is worth 10s.

The same William holds 2 hides less half a virgate of land in HIMLEY, and Arni [holds] of him. Wulfstan and Ramkel held them, and they were free. There is land for 3 ploughs. In demesne is 1 [plough]; and 8 villans and 3 bordars with 2 ploughs. There are 2 acres of meadow, and woodland. It was and is worth 24s.

In the same vill Gilbert holds 1 hide of William. Lovet held it, and he was a free man. There is land for 2 ploughs. In demesne is 1 [plough]; and 3 villans and 2 bordars with 1 plough. There is 1 acre of meadow. It was and is worth 10s.

The same William holds 1 hide in AMBLECOTE, and Payne [holds] of him. 2 [...] men of Earl Ælfgar held it without soke. There is land for 2 ploughs. There are 4 villans and 2 bordars and 1 slave with 2 ploughs. There are 4 acres of meadow, and woodland. It was and is worth 10s.

[Folio 250: STAFFORDSHIRE]

William himself holds 2 hides in TRYSULL, and Baldwin [holds] of him. Thorgot held them with sake and soke, and he was a free man. There is land for 3 ploughs. In demesne are 2 ploughs, and 5 slaves; and 4 villans and 1 bordar with 2 ploughs. There is a mill rendering 4s, and 4 acres of meadow. It was and is worth 30s.

William himself holds 1½ hides in 'CROCKINGTON' [in Trysull], and Baldwin [holds] of him. 3 free men held them, but the soke belonged to the king. There is land for 2 ploughs. It is waste.

William himself holds 5 hides in SEISDON, and Walbert [holds] of him. 4 free men held them, but their soke belonged to the king. There is land for 6 ploughs. In demesne is 1 [plough], and there are 2 sergeants, and there are 4 acres of meadow. It was and is worth 8s.

The same William holds 2 hides in ETTINGSHALL, and Robert [holds] of him. Thorsten held them with sake and soke. There is land for 4 ploughs. In demesne are 2 [ploughs]; and 9 villans and 3 bordars with 2 ploughs. There are 5 acres of meadow. The woodland is 3 furlongs in length and breadth. It was and is worth 30s.

The same William holds 2 hides and 2½ virgates in BUSHBURY, and Robert [holds] of him. Wulfric held them with sake and soke. There is land for 5 ploughs. There are 3 villans and 4 bordars with 2 ploughs. There are 6 acres of meadow. It was and is worth 20s.

The same William holds 2 hides in PENDEFORD, and Almær [holds] of him. Wulfstan and Godwine held them, and they were free men. There is land for 3 ploughs. In demesne is 1 [plough], and 3 slaves; and 4 villans and 5 bordars with 1 plough. There are 4 acres of meadow. It was and is worth 20s.

The same William holds 1 hide in MOSELEY, and Roger [holds] of him. Countess Godgifu held it. There is land for 2 ploughs. In demesne is 1 [plough]; and 1 villan and 2 bordars with 1 plough, and there is 1 acre of meadow. [There is] woodland 2 furlongs long and 1 broad. It was and is worth 8s.

IN CUTTLESTONE HUNDRED

Roger holds of William 2 hides of land in ESSINGTON. There is land for 6 ploughs. In demesne is 1 [plough], and 2 slaves; and 15 villans with 2 bordars have 3 ploughs. [There is] woodland 1 league long and as much broad. In Bushbury is 1 virgate of land belonging to this manor, but it is completely waste. It was and is worth 20s. Countess Godgifu held it.

IN OFFLOW HUNDRED

Walbert holds of William 1 hide in BRADLEY [Bradley and Lower Bradley, in Bilston]. There is land for 2 ploughs. There 4 villans have 1 plough. [There is] woodland 3 furlongs long and 1 furlong broad. It was and is worth 64d. Untan held it with sake and soke. There are 2 acres of meadow.

Robert holds of William 3 hides in ALDRIDGE. There is land for 3 ploughs. In demesne are 2 [ploughs], with 1 slave; and 5 villans with 1 bordar have 2 ploughs. There is 1 acre of meadow, and woodland pasture 5 furlongs long and 3 furlongs broad. It was and is worth 15s. 2 thegns held it freely, and the king had the soke.

The same man holds of William 3 hides in GREAT BARR. There is land for 3 ploughs. There is nothing in demesne; but there is only 1 villan with 1 bordar. [...] [There is] woodland pasture 1 league long and 4 furlongs broad. It was and is worth 5s. Vagn held it.

Turchil holds William 1 hide in RUSHALL. There is land for 2 ploughs. In demesne is half a plough; and 6 villans with 2 bordars have 1½ ploughs. There is a mill rendering 4d, and 1 acre of meadow, [and] woodland pasture 5 furlongs long and 2 furlongs broad. It was and is worth 10s. Vithfari held it with sake and soke.

Drogo holds of William 3 hides in PERRY [War.]. There is land for 3 ploughs. In demesne is 1 plough; and there are 4 villans and 3 bordars. There is a mill rendering 16d. There are 4 acres of meadow, [and] woodland 1 league long and half a league broad. It was and is worth 20s. Leofwaru held it with sake and soke.

The same man holds of William 3 hides in [?] 'LITTLE BARR'. There is land for 3 ploughs. In demesne is 1 [plough]; and 2 villans with 1 bordar have 1 plough. There is 1 acre of meadow, [and] woodland 4 furlongs long and as much broad. It was and is worth 5s. Alfred held it with sake and soke.

The same Drogo holds of William 1 hide in HANDSWORTH [War.]. There is land for 2 ploughs. In demesne is 1 [plough]; and 6 villans with 4 bordars have 2 ploughs. There is a mill rendering 2s, and 2 acres of meadow, [and] woodland half a league long and as much broad. It was

and is worth 20s. Æthelfrith and Alwine held it with sake and soke.

WILLIAM fitz Corbucion holds 10 hides in SIBFORD GOWER [Oxon.], and Ralph [holds] of him. There is land for 7 ploughs. In demesne is 1 [plough], and 2 slaves; and 6 villans with 3 ploughs. There is a mill [rendering] 32d, and 4 acres of meadow, [and] pasture 7 furlongs long and broad. It was and is worth £4.

THORSTEN holds 5 hides in DRAYTON [Oxon.]. [There is] land for 5 ploughs. In demesne [are] 3 ploughs, and 2 slaves; and 12 villans and 4 bordars with 3 ploughs. There is a mill [rendering] 4s. It was worth 100s; now £8.

[Folio 250V: STAFFORDSHIRE]

XIII. The land of Richard the Forester

IN PIREHILL HUNDRED

RICHARD the forester holds THURSFIELD of the king, and Nigel [holds] of him. Beornwulf held it, and he was a free man. There is 1 virgate of land. There is land for 2 ploughs. There is 1 [plough], with 2 villans and 1 bordar. [There is] woodland 1 league long and as much broad. It is worth 10s.

The same Richard holds Whitmore, and Nigel [holds] of him. Wulfheah held it, and he was a free man. There is half a hide. There is land for 3 ploughs. In demesne is 1 [plough]; and 3 villans and 2 bordars with 1 plough. There is 1 acre of meadow, [and] woodland 1 league long and a half broad. It is worth 10s.

The same Richard holds NORMACOT, and Almær and Wulfric [hold] of him. Wulfmær held it, and he was a free man. There is 1 virgate of land. There is land for 1 plough. In demesne is 1 [plough]. [There is] woodland 3 furlongs long and 2 furlongs broad. It is worth 2s.

The same Richard holds HANFORD, and Nigel [holds] of him. There is 1 virgate of land. There is land for 1 plough. It is waste. Tholf held it. [There is] scrubland 20 perches in length and breadth. It is worth 2s.

The same Richard holds HANCHURCH. Pata held it, and he was a free man. There are 3 parts of half a hide. There is land for 2 ploughs. There are 2 villans and 7 bordars with 1½ ploughs, and there is 1 acre of meadow. [There is] woodland 2 furlongs long and 1 broad. It is worth 5s.

The same Richard holds CLAYTON, and Nigel [holds] of him. Segrim held it, and he was a free man. There is half a hide. There is land for 3 ploughs. In demesne is half a plough; and 4 villans and 6 bordars with 1½ ploughs. There is woodland 1 league long and a half broad. It is worth 10s.

The same Richard holds 1 virgate of land in DIMSDALE. Glædwine and Godwine held it, and they were free. There is land for 2 ploughs. There are 5 villans and 2 bordars with 2 ploughs, and 4 acres of meadow. [There is] woodland 12 furlongs long and 6 broad. It is worth 10s.

The same Richard holds KNUTTON. Godwine held it, and he was a free man. There is 1 virgate of land. There is land for 2 ploughs. There are 4 villans with 1 bordar; they have 1 plough, and [there are] 4 acres of meadow. It is worth 5s.

IN CUTTLESTONE HUNDRED

The same Richard holds 3 hides in RODBASTON. There is land for 3 ploughs. Alli held them, and he was a free man. In demesne is 1 plough, with 4 bordars. It was worth 2s; now 15s.

The same Richard holds 1 waste hide in "ESTENDONE".

XIIII. The land of Reginald de Bailleul

IN CUTTLESTONE HUNDRED

REGINALD de Bailleul holds of the king 4 hides in WESTON UNDER LIZARD and BEIGHTERTON and BROCKTON GRANGE [near] Blymhill]. 9 thegns held them TRE as 9 manors. There were 11 ploughs. There is land for 6 ploughs. In demesne are 3 ploughs, and 2 slaves; and 10 villans with 2 ploughs. The woodland of these lands is 1 league long and half a league broad. It is worth 40s.

Of this land Amerland holds 1 hide of Reginald. There he has 3 slaves and 1 bordar. It is worth 5s.

IN PIREHILL HUNDRED

The same Reginald holds NEWTON [in Blithfield]. Godwine held it, and he was a free man. There is half a hide. There is land for 4 ploughs. In demesne is half a plough; and 8 villans and 5 bordars with 3 ploughs. There is 1 slave, and a mill rendering 4s, and 2 acres of meadow, [and] woodland 1 furlong long and 1 broad. It is worth 40s.

XV. The land of Ralph fitzHubert

IN TOTMONSLOW HUNDRED

RALPH fitzHubert holds of the king 2 hides in BRADLEY IN THE MOORS, and Robert de Bucy [holds] of him. Leofric held them, and he was a free man. There is land for 3 ploughs. In demesne is 1 [plough]; and 6 villans and 4 bordars with 2 ploughs. There is 1 acre of meadow, [and] woodland 1 league long and a half broad. It was worth 5s; now 10s.

The same Robert de Bucy holds in KINGSLEY 1 hide of Ralph, and Nigel [holds] of him. Leofric held it, and he was a free man. There is land for 1 plough. This [plough] is in demesne, and [there are] 2 acres of meadow. There is woodland 1 league long and 4 furlongs broad. It was worth 6s; now 10s.

XVI. The land of Nigel

NIGEL holds THORPE CONSTANTINE. There are 3 hides. There is land for 6 ploughs. In demesne is 1 [plough]; and 7 villans and 6 bordars have 4 ploughs. There are 8 acres of meadow. It was worth 20s; now 40s. Wulfwine held it.

Nicholas claims this land [as belonging] to the king's farm in Clifton Campville.

XVII. The land of the King's Thegns

IN SEISDON HUNDRED

CYNEWINE holds of the king 3 hides in CODSALL. He himself held them TRE. There is land for 3 ploughs. There are 6 villans with 2 ploughs.

UDI holds of the king 1 hide in LITTLE SAREDON. Gamal held it, but his soke belonged to the king. There is land for 2 ploughs. There are 3 villans with 1 plough, and 1 acre of meadow.

ALRIC holds of the king 3 virgates of land in BICKFORD. He himself held them TRE, and he was a free man. There is land for 1 plough.

These 3 men pay the sheriff 12s. a year.

ÆLFRIC holds 1 carucate of land in CANNOCK. There is land for 1 plough. There he has 3 bordars; and it is worth 5s.

ALMÆR holds 1 carucate of land in BISHTON. Earnwig held it, and he was a free man. There is land for 1 plough. There is [1 plough] in demesne, with 2 bordars. There are 3 acres of meadow. It is worth 2s.

IN PIREHILL HUNDRED

DUNNING holds KNIGHTON [in Mucklestone], and he himself held it TRE. [...] There is land for 1 plough. This [plough] is there, with 2 slaves, and half an acre of meadow. [There is] woodland 2 furlongs long and 2 furlongs broad. It is worth 2s.

LYFING holds MUCKLESTONE. Alric and Eadric held it TRE. There is 1 hide. There is land for 3 ploughs. There a priest and 3 villans have 1 plough. There is 1 acre of meadow, [and] woodland 2 furlongs long and as much broad. It is worth 5s.

The same Lyfing holds WINNINGTON. There is 1 virgate of land. There is land for 1 plough. There are 2 villans with 1 bordar, and half an acre of meadow. [There is] woodland 3 furlongs long and 2 furlongs broad. It is worth 2s.

WULFWINE holds BETLEY. Godric and Wulfgeat held it, and they were free. There is half a hide. [There is] land for 1 plough. This [plough] is there, with 2 villans and 1 bordar. There is 1 acre of meadow, [and] woodland 1 league long and a half broad. It is worth 4s.

The same Wulfwine holds BALTERLEY. Godwine held it, and he was a free man. There is half a virgate of land. There is land for 1 plough. There are 2 villans with 1 bordar, and half an acre of meadow. [There is] woodland 1 league long and a half broad. It is worth 4s.

GAMAL holds BALTERLEY of the king. Wulfric held it. There is half a virgate of land. There is land for 2 ploughs. There is 1 villan with 3 bordars and half a plough, and half an acre of meadow. [There is] woodland 6 furlongs long and 3 furlongs broad. It is worth 4s.

The same Gamal holds AUDLEY. Wulfric and Godric held it, and they were free. There is half a hide. There is land for 3 ploughs. In demesne is 1 plough; and 4 villans and 3 bordars with 1 plough. There is 1 acre of meadow, [and] woodland 2 leagues long and 1 broad. It is worth 10s.

The same Gamal holds TALKE. Godric held it, and he was a free man. There is 1 virgate of land. There is land for 1 plough. This [plough] is there, with 4 villans, and 1 acre of meadow. [There is] woodland 1 league long and as much broad. It is worth 3s.

SPERRIR holds WESTON [near Stafford]. Wulfhelm held it. There is half a virgate of land. There is land for 1 plough. There is 1 villan, and 3 acres of meadow. It is worth 2s.

RICHARD holds LITTLE ONN. Æthelric held it. There is half a hide. There is land for 2 ploughs.

ALRIC holds STRAMSHALL. He himself held it, and he was a free man. There are 2 carucates and 1 virgate of land. There are 2 villans and 5 bordars with 1 plough, and 2 acres of meadow. [There is] woodland 40 perches long and as much broad. It is worth 5s.

ALWEALD holds CROXDEN. He himself held it TRE, and he was a free man. There is half a virgate of land. There is land for 2 ploughs. In demesne is half a plough; and 4 bordars have 1 plough. There is 1 acre of meadow. It is worth 5s.

OTTO holds CHECKLEY. Wulfgeat held it. There is half a hide. There is land for 3½ ploughs. In demesne is half a plough, and 3 villans [...]. There are 2 acres of meadow, [and] woodland 1 league long and as much broad. It is worth 5s.

IN CUTTLESTONE HUNDRED

LEOFHILD holds SHUSHIONS. There is half a hide. There is land for 3 ploughs. There 3 villans with 1 bordar have half a plough. There are 2 acres of meadow. It is worth 4s.

ALWEARD holds FENTON. There is 1 virgate of land. There is land for 3 ploughs. It is waste.

The same Nigel holds of the king 3 hides in KINGSLEY. There is land for 3 ploughs. Leofric held them freely TRE. There are 4 villans and 7 bordars with 1½c ploughs, and 1 acre of meadow.

Of this land Ligulf holds 2 hides of Nigel. The whole is worth 17s. The same Nigel holds 1 hide in MORETON [Moreton and Upper Moreton, in Colwich]. [There is] land for 2 ploughs. Wulfric held it freely TRE. There is 1 plough in demesne; and 2 villans and 2 bordars with 1 plough. It is worth 10s.

[Folio 251: [STAFFORDSHIRE]]

[Blank in MS]

[Folio 251V: [STAFFORDSHIRE]]

[Blank in MS]

SHROPSHIRE

IN THE CITY OF SHREWSBURY IN THE TIME OF KING EDWARD there were 252 houses, and as many burgesses in these houses, rendering £7.16s8d of rent a year. There King Edward had these undermentioned customs.

If any person wittingly broke the king's peace imposed by [the king's] own hand he was made an outlaw; he who broke the king's peace imposed by the sheriff paid a fine of 100s; and he who committed highway robbery or housebreaking gave as much. King Edward had these 3 forfeitures in demesne all over England over and above the farms.

When the king stayed in this city, 12 of the better citizens mounted watch for his protection, and likewise when he went hunting there the better [among the] burgesses possessing horses guarded him with arms. For heading off [game] the sheriff sent 36 men on foot as long as the king was there. [For hunting] in the park of [?] Marsley, however, [the sheriff] found 36 men for 8 days by custom.

When the sheriff wished to march into Wales, anyone who after being summoned by him did not go gave a fine of 40s.

A woman taking a husband in any way, gave to the king 20s if she was a widow, 10s if an unmarried woman, in whatever way she took the man.

Should the house of any burgess be burnt by misfortune or accident or by negligence he gave 40s to the king by way of fine and 2s to each of his 2 nearest neighbours.

When a burgess who was in the king's demesne died, the king had 10s by way of relief.

If any burgess broke the due date which the sheriff fixed for him, he paid a 10s fine. Whosoever shed blood paid a 40s fine.

When the king was leaving the city the sheriff sent 24 horses for him [from] Leintwardine [Herefs.], and the king took these [with him] as far as the first house in Staffordshire.

The king had there 3 moneyers, who, after they purchased the money-dies, like other moneyers of the kingdom, on the fifteenth day gave to the king 20s each, and this was done when the coinage was changed.

All together this city rendered £30 a year. The king had 2 parts, and the sheriff the third. In the year before this survey it rendered £40 to Earl Roger.

TRE this city paid geld for 100 hides. Of these St Alkmund had 2 hides; St Juliana half a hide; St Milburh 1 hide; St Chad 1½ hides; ST MARY 1 virgate; the Bishop of Chester 1 hide; Edith 3 hides, which Ralph de Mortimer [now] has.

The English burgesses of Shrewsbury say that it is very hard on them that they themselves render as much geld as they rendered TRE, although the earl's castle has occupied [the site of] 51 messuages and another 50 messuages are waste, and 43 French burgesses hold messuages paying geld TRE, and the earl himself has granted to the abbey which he is building there 39 burgesses formerly paying geld in the same way as the others. All together there are 200 messuages, less 7, which do not pay geld.

Here Are Set Down Those Holding land of the King In Shropshire

I The Bishop of CHESTER II The Bishop of Hereford III The Church of Saint-Remi [of Rheims]

IIII EARL ROGER. What remains he holds with his men. V Osbern fitzRichard VI Ralph de Mortimer VII Roger de Lacy VIII Hugh l'Asne IX Nigel the physician

I. The land of the Bishop of Chester

THE BISHOP OF CHESTER had in SHREWSBURY 16 messuages, and as many burgesses paying geld with the other burgesses. Now 10 of these messuages are waste and the remaining 6 render 4s7d.

The same bishop had in this city 16 canons. They did not pay geld, nor is it known how much they rendered to the bishop.

IN THE HUNDRED OF THE CITY

The same bishop has a manor, MEOLE BRACE. It is not and was not inhabited, TRE it rendered 20s; now 17s4d.

IN THE SAME HUNDRED

The same bishop holds SHELTON, and the Church of St Chad [holds] of him. There are 1½ hides. In demesne is half a plough, and there might be 2 more ploughs. There 4 villans have 1½ ploughs. It was and is worth 12s. This land pays geld.

IN WROCKWARDINE HUNDRED

The same bishop holds LONGNER, and Vigot [holds] of him. There is 1 hide [...]. There is land for 2 ploughs. In demesne is 1 [plough] and 2 slaves; and 2 villans have 1 plough. It was and is worth 8s.

IN CONDOVER HUNDRED

The same bishop holds BETTON [Abbots and Strange], and he held it TRE. There are 2 hides paying geld. In demesne are $1\frac{1}{2}$ ploughs; and 4 villans with $2\frac{1}{2}$ ploughs. There are 3 slaves. It was worth 15s; now 16s.

The same bishop holds BUILDWAS, and held it TRE. There is 1 hide paying geld. In demesne are 2 ploughs; and 3 villans with a reeve have 3 ploughs. There are 5 slaves, and a mill, and woodland for 200 pigs. TRE it was worth 45s; and afterwards 40s; now 45s.

IN HODNET HUNDRED

The same bishop holds PREES, and held it TRE. There are 8 hides paying geld. In demesne are 3 ploughs; and 10 villans and a priest and 3 bordars with 5 ploughs. There are 6 oxmen, and woodland for 60 pigs. Ansketil holds of the bishop half a hide of this manor, and Fulcher 2 hides. In demesne they have 2 ploughs; and 2 villans with 1 plough, and 3 other men ploughing there render 10s, and there are 2 oxmen. The whole TRE was worth 50s; and afterwards it was waste; now what the bishop has is worth 40s; what his men [have] 28s. 6 ploughs more might be there.

IN WROCKWARDINE HUNDRED

The same bishop holds 'CHATSALL' [in Stoke upon Tern], and he held it. There is 1 hide and 1 virgate of land. There is land for 2 ploughs. It was worth 8s; now it is waste.

Ii. The land of the Bishop of Hereford

IN "RINLAU" HUNDRED

THE BISHOP of Hereford holds of the king LYDBURY NORTH, and he held it TRE. There are 53 hides paying geld. In demesne are 4 ploughs; and 38 villans and 4 bordars and 8 radmen with 28 bordars. They have among them all 23 ploughs. There are 2 slaves, and a mill serving the hall, [and] woodland for fattening 160 pigs.

Of this manor a certain Franco and William the clerk hold of the bishop a member, and the church of the same manor with the priests and with the land pertaining there, and there is 1 plough. In this manor there might be 92 ploughs more than there are. It was worth £35 TRE; and afterwards £10; now £12.

Of this land $32\frac{1}{2}$ hides are waste.

IN "CULVESTAN" HUNDRED

The same bishop held ONIBURY TRE, and now Roger de Lacy holds of him. There are 3 hides paying geld. In demesne is 1 plough; and 4 whole villans and 6 half [-villans] and a priest and 1 cotset with 3 ploughs. There is 1 slave. 1 knight holds 1 hide there, and has 1 plough, and 5 villans. TRE there were in this manor 9 ploughs, and it was worth 40s; now 20s.

III. The land of Saint-Remi [Of Rheims]

IN 'OVERS' HUNDRED

THE CHURCH OF SAINT-REMI held and holds of the king 1 manor of 1 hide, and there were and are 2 ploughs. It was and is worth 10s8d.

[Folio 252V: SHROPSHIRE]

IN SHREWSBURY city Earl Roger is building an abbey and has given to it the minster of ST PETER, where there was a parish church of the city; and [has given] to the monks as much [in dues] from his burgesses and mills as renders £12.

IN WROCKWARDINE HUNDRED

The church itself holds EYTON ON SEVERN. Earl Leofric held it TRE. There are $8\frac{1}{2}$ hides. In demesne are 4 ploughs, and there might be 2 [ploughs] more. There are 16 villans and 14 bordars with 16 ploughs. There are 8 slaves and 4 female slaves, and 2 fisheries. One renders 16s, the other is for the sustenance of the monks. TRE it was worth £21; and when the earl gave it to the church it rendered £14.

IN CONDOVER HUNDRED

The church itself holds EMSTREY. Earl Edwin held it. There are 9 hides paying geld. In demesne are 4 ploughs; and 22 villans and 5 bordars and 1 Frenchman with 12 ploughs among them all. There are 20 slaves, and woodland for fattening 40 pigs. In the city [is] 1 messuage rendering 2s. TRE it was worth 100s; and afterwards £4; now £11.

The church itself holds BORETON, and held it TRE. There is 1 hide paying geld. In demesne is 1 plough; and 6 bordars with 1 plough, and there are 2 oxmen. It was worth 5s; now 8s.

In this vill Ælfric held TRE 1 hide paying geld, and could go where he would, and this land was worth 5s. Now St Peter holds it and it is waste.

What the Church of St Milburh Holds

IN PATTON HUNDRED

Earl Roger has made the CHURCH OF ST MILBURH into an abbey. The church itself holds MUCH WENLOCK, and held it TRE. There are 20 hides. Of these, 4 were quit of geld in King Cnut's time, and the others pay geld. In demesne are $9\frac{1}{2}$ ploughs; and 9 villans and 3 radmen and 46 bordars. Among them all they have 17 ploughs, and another 17 [ploughs] might be there. There are 15 slaves, and 2 mills serving the monks. There is 1 fishery, and woodland for fattening 300 pigs, and there are 2 enclosures. TRE it was worth £15; now £12.

The church itself holds TICKLERTON, and held it TRE. There are 7 hides paying geld, and 3 other hides quit of geld. In demesne is 1 plough; and 6 villans and 6 bordars and 1 radman with 5 ploughs, and 6 ploughs more might be there. There are 3 slaves, and woodland for fattening 60 pigs. TRE it was worth 100s; now 50s.

The church itself holds MADELEY, and held it TRE. There is 1 hide not paying geld and 3 other hides paying geld. In demesne are 2 ploughs; and 6 villans and 4 bordars with 4 ploughs. There are 4 slaves, and 6 ploughs more might be there. [There is] woodland for fattening 400 pigs. TRE it was worth £4; now 50s.

The church itself holds LITTLE WENLOCK, and held it TRE. There is 1 hide not paying geld and 2 others paying geld. In demesne is 1 plough; and 4 villans and 2 bordars with 3 ploughs. There are 2 oxmen, and woodland for fattening 300 pigs, in which are 2 enclosures and a hawk's eyrie. TRE it was worth 70s; now 40s.

The church itself held and holds SHIPTON. There is half a hide not paying geld and 3 other hides paying geld. In demesne is 1 plough; and 5 villans and 5 bordars with 5 ploughs, and 2 slaves. It was worth 30s; now 4d more.

The church itself held and holds PERKLEY. There is half a hide not paying geld. In demesne is 1 plough; and 3 bordars with 1 plough, and 2 slaves, and woodland for fattening 40 pigs, and there is 1 enclosure. It was worth 8s; now 6s.

The church itself held and holds BOURTON, and Eadric [holds] of it. Ælfric, his father, held it and could not withdraw from the church. There are 2 hides and 3 virgates of land paying geld. In demesne is half a plough; and 4 villans and 4 radmen and 3 bordars with $3\frac{1}{2}$ ploughs, and 1 slave, and a mill serving the court, and 1 enclosure. TRE it was worth 50s; now 40s; and there can be 2 ploughs more.

The church itself held STOKE ST MILBOROUGH. Earl Roger gave it to his chaplains, but the church ought to have it. There are 20 hides. Of these, 3 do not pay geld; the others pay geld. In demesne are 2 ploughs; and 25 villans and 5 bordars with 9 ploughs, and 4 oxmen, and 19 ploughs more might be there. TRE it was worth £13; now £9.

IN "ALNODESTREU" HUNDRED

The church itself held and holds DEUXHILL. There is half a hide paying geld. In demesne is 1 plough; and 2 bordars and 1 cottar with 1 plough, and there is 1 slave. It was worth 10s; now 20s.

The church itself held and holds PICKTHORN. There is half a hide paying geld. In demesne is 1 plough; and 1 villan and 2 bordars with 2 ploughs, and 2 slaves. It was and is worth 7s.

IN SHREWSBURY HUNDRED

The church itself held and holds SUTTON [near Shrewsbury]. There is 1 hide. [...] There are 8 men, both free men and villans, with 4 ploughs. It was worth 12s; now 16s.

IN "CULVESTAN" HUNDRED

The church itself held and holds CLEESTANTON. There are 2 hides. [...] There is 1 man and 1 plough, and there might be 6 other ploughs. It was worth 18s; now 6s.

IN CONDOVER HUNDRED

St WIHTBURH [sic] holds half a hide paying geld, and Ælfric's son [holds] of it. There is 1 villan with 1 plough, and another [plough] might be there. It is worth 3s.

What the Church of St Mary Holds

IN BASCHURCH HUNDRED

THE CHURCH OF ST MARY held and holds BROUGHTON. There are 5 hides paying geld. A priest there has half a plough, and [there are] 7 villans with $2\frac{1}{2}$ ploughs, and 3 ploughs more might also be there. There is woodland for fattening 24 pigs. TRE it was worth 10s; now 15s.

The church itself held and holds ASTLEY. There are 3 hides paying geld. A priest with 9 villans and 2 bordars has 3 ploughs, and there might be 2 ploughs more. [There is] woodland for fattening 50 pigs. It was worth 20s; now 25s.

IN SHREWSBURY HUNDRED

The church itself held and holds 1 virgate of land in MEOLE BRACE, a manor of Ralph de Mortimer. It was and is worth 4s.

IN 'OVERS' HUNDRED

The church itself held and holds half a hide. It was and still is waste.

IN BASCHURCH HUNDRED

The church itself held and holds MYTTON, and Picot [holds] of it. There are 2 hides paying geld. There are 4 villans with 2 ploughs. It was worth 12s; now it is at farm for 11s.

The church itself holds BROMFIELD, and it is situated there. There are now 10 hides, and in demesne 6 ploughs and 12 oxmen; and 15 villans and 12 bordars with 8 ploughs. It is worth 50s to the canons, and Nigel the physician has out of this manor 16s.

In this manor, TRE, there were 20 hides, and 12 canons of this church had the whole. One of them, Spirites by name, alone held 10 hides, but when he was banished from England, King Edward gave these 10 hides to Robert fitzWimarc as to a canon. Robert, however, gave the same land to his son-in-law. When the canons pointed this out to the king, he forthwith ordered that the land revert to the church, only delaying until, at the court at the coming Christmas, he should order Robert to provide other land for his son-in-law. But the king himself died during those feast-days, and from that time until now the church has lost the land. This [land] Robert now holds of Earl Roger and it is waste and was found waste. All together there is land for 54 ploughs.

What St Michael Holds

THE CHURCH OF ST MICHAEL holds of the earl LESSER POSTON. Ketil held it. There is 1 virgate of land. [There is] land for half a plough. 1 man renders thence a bundle of box on Palm Sunday.

The church itself holds SOULTON. Beorhtric held it freely. There is 1 hide paying geld. [There is] land for 1 plough. There is half a plough. It was worth 5s; now 4d more.

[Folio 253: SHROPSHIRE]

What St Chad Holds

IN CONDOVER HUNDRED

THE CHURCH OF ST CHAD holds and held 'LITTLE ETON' [in Pitchford], and Turold [holds] of it. There is half a hide paying geld. It rendered 8s; now 4s.

IN WITTERY HUNDRED

The church itself holds and held MARTON. Alweard holds it of the church. There are 2 hides paying geld. In demesne is half a plough; and 3 villans and 3 radmen and 1 bordar with 3½ ploughs, and there might also be 2 ploughs more. [There is] woodland for fattening 50 pigs. TRE it rendered 8s; now it is worth 10s, but renders no more than 6s2d.

IN BASCHURCH HUNDRED

The church itself held BICTON. Wiger holds of it. There are 2 hides paying geld. In demesne is 1 plough; and 4 villans and 1 free man with 2 ploughs, and there might be another 2 [ploughs]. It was worth 10s; now 15s.

The church itself held and holds YORTON. There are 2 hides paying geld. There is land for 4 ploughs. There is a priest and 1 villan with 1 plough. It was worth 8s; now 5s.

The church itself held and holds BROUGHTON. There are 2 hides paying geld. There is land for 5 ploughs. There 3 villans have 2 ploughs. It was worth 10s; now 11s4d.

The church itself held and holds ROSSALL. There is 1 hide paying geld. 2 radmen with 7 bordars have 3½ ploughs. It was worth 8s; now 15s.

The church itself held and holds ONSLOW. There is 1 hide paying geld. It was waste. There 3 villans have 1 plough. It is worth 4s.

What St Alkmund Holds

THE CHURCH OF ST ALKMUND holds in SHREWSBURY 21 burgesses, besides 12 houses for canons. These burgesses pay 8s8d.

The same church has 2 hides of the 100 hides which are reckoned in the geld of the city. 2 canons hold these, and have there 1½ ploughs, and 4 villans having 2½ ploughs. It is worth 15s.

IN WROCKWARDINE HUNDRED

The church itself held and holds LILLESHALL. There are 10 hides [...]. In demesne are 2 ploughs; and 10 villans and 5 bordars and 3 French sergeants with 8 ploughs among them all, and there might be 9 ploughs more. There are 4 oxmen,

and a mill, but it renders nothing. [There is] 1 league of woodland. TRE it was worth £6; now £4. Godebold the priest holds it.

The church itself held and holds LONGDON UPON TERN. There are 2 hides [...]. In demesne is 1 plough; and 4 bordars with 1 plough, and there might be 3 ploughs more. There are all together 6 slaves and female slaves, and a mill rendering 5s. TRE it was worth 21s; now 9s4d.

The church itself held and holds UCKINGTON, and Godebold [holds] of it. There are 4 hides paying geld. In demesne are 3 ploughs; and 2 radmen and 3 bordars with 1 plough, and there might be 3 ploughs more. There are 6 oxmen. TRE it was worth 24s; now 30s.

The church itself held and holds ATCHAM, and Godebold [holds] of it. There is 1 hide [...]. In demesne are 1½ ploughs; and 2 villans and 3 bordars with 3 ploughs. It was worth 10s; now it renders 6s8d.

The church itself held and holds ALBRIGHTLEE. There is 1 hide. [...] In demesne is 1 plough; and 2 villans and 1 bordar with 1 plough. There is 1 league of woodland, but Earl Roger has taken it from the church. It was and is worth 12s.

IN BASCHURCH HUNDRED

The church itself held and holds PRESTON GUBBALS, and Godebold [holds] of it. There are 4 hides [...]. In demesne is 1 plough; and 2 villans and 3 bordars and 2 Frenchmen with 2 ploughs, and there might be another 2 ploughs more. It was waste; now it is worth 10s.

IN "CULVESTAN" HUNDRED

The church itself held and holds 'CHARLTON' [in Shawbury]. There is 1 hide. 1 radman was and is there. It rendered 4s; now 5s.

IN "REWESET" HUNDRED

The church itself held and holds PRESTON MONTFORD. There is 1 hide paying geld. In demesne is 1 plough; and 2 villans with 1 plough. It was worth 8s; now 5s. Alweard holds it.

The church itself held and holds DINTHILL. There is 1 hide paying geld. In demesne is 1 plough; and 1 villan and 1 bordar with half a plough. It was and is worth 8s.

What St Juliana Holds

THE CHURCH OF ST JULIANA holds half a hide, and it has there 1 plough, and 2 burgesses labouring on this land pay 3s. It was and is worth 8s.

IIII. The land of Earl Roger

IN WROCKWARDINE HUNDRED

Earl ROGER holds WROCKWARDINE. King Edward held it. To this manor pertain 7½ Berewicks. There are 5 hides paying geld. In demesne are 4 ploughs; and 13 villans and 4 bordars and a priest and 1 radman. Among them all they have

12 ploughs. There are 8 oxmen, and a mill rendering 12s, [and] woodland 1 league long and a half broad.

The Church of ST PETER holds the church of this manor with 1 hide, and has there 1 plough, and there might be another. It is worth 5s.

To this manor pertained TRE 2 pennies of Wrockwardine Hundred. The earl had the third penny. TRE it rendered £6.13s8d; now it renders £12.10s of farm.

IN CONDOVER HUNDRED

The earl himself holds CONDOVER. King Edward held it. To this manor pertain 10 Berewicks. There are 13 hides paying geld. In demesne are 7 hides, and there are 4 ploughs; and 12 villans and a priest with 7 ploughs, and 3 ploughs more might be there. There are 8 oxmen, and a mill rendering 8s6d.

To this manor pertained 2 pennies of Condover Hundred TRE. It rendered £10; now with the hundred it renders £10.

Roger the huntsman holds 1 hide of the land of this manor, Osbern 1 hide, [and] Alweard 4 hides. There is 1 plough, and 4 villans and 2 bordars and 3 radmen and 2 oxmen. Among them all they have 3 ploughs, and there might be 8 ploughs more. The whole is worth 41s.

IN BASCHURCH HUNDRED

The earl himself holds BASCHURCH. King Edward held it. There are 3½ hides [...]. One of these is in demesne, and there are 4 ploughs; and 6 villans and 2 bordars with 2 ploughs. There are 8 oxmen, and 3 fisheries rendering 22d. To this manor pertained 2 pennies of this hundred. All together it rendered £7; now the demesne of the earl is worth £6.

Of this manor the Church of ST PETER holds of the earl 2½ hides and the church of the vill. There is land for 5 ploughs, [and] there are [2 ploughs], with 13 bordars. It is worth 26s8d.

The earl himself holds HODNET. King Edward held it. There are 1½ hides. [...] In demesne are 3 ploughs; and 12 villans and 2 bordars and a priest and a reeve with 7 ploughs, and 9 ploughs more might be there. There is a little wood rendering nothing. The Church of ST PETER holds the church of this manor. TRE this manor rendered £3.6s8d; now, with the hundred which pertains to the manor, it renders £8.

The earl himself holds MORVILLE with 18 Berewicks. King Edward held it. There are 12 hides. One of these Berewicks, Chawson [Worcs.], at 1 hide, is in Worcestershire.

Four hides of this land are in demesne, and there are 2 ploughs, and there might be another 6 ploughs. There are 9 villans and 6 bordars with 3 ploughs, and there might also be another 2. There are 4 oxmen.

To this manor pertains the whole of "ALNODESTREU" Hundred. 2 pennies belonged to King Edward and the third to the earl. All together it rendered £10; now what the earl has is worth £3.

The church of this manor is in honour of St Gregory, which [church] had TRE 8 hides of this land, and 8 canons served there.

The Church of ST PETER holds this church of the earl with 5 hides of land. In demesne are 2 ploughs, and there might be another 4 [ploughs]. There are 9 villans and 1 bordar and 3 priests with 9 ploughs, and 4 oxmen; and 1 knight | holds 1 hide | rendering 4s to the monks. The whole of this is worth 67s.

The chaplains of the earl hold the remaining 3 hides, and 5 men [hold] of them. There is land for 6 ploughs. There are 2 ploughs. The whole is worth 60s and | 18d. |

Richard the butler holds 2 hides of this land of this manor, and has there 1 plough and 2 slaves, and 7 villans with 1 plough, and a mill rendering 10 summae of corn. There might be 9 ploughs more there. It is worth 20s.

[Folio 253V: SHROPSHIRE]

The earl himself holds 'CORFHAM' [in Diddlebury]. King Edward held it [...] with 4 Berewicks. There are 4 hides paying geld. In demesne are 5 ploughs, and there might be a sixth. There 3 villans and 3 bordars have 3 ploughs, and there might be 2 ploughs more. There are 10 oxmen.

Of this land 1 knight of the earl holds half a hide, and has there 1 plough, and 2 slaves and 2 villans with 1 plough. It is worth 5s.

The Church of ST PETER holds the church of this manor with 1 hide. There is land for 3 ploughs. It renders 18s to the monks.

To this manor pertains the whole of "CULVESTAN" Hundred and PATTON Hundred. It rendered TRE with the 2 pennies of the hundred £10 of farm. Now with the hundreds it renders to the earl £6.

The earl himself holds MINSTERLEY, and Roger [holds] of him. King Edward held it. There are 6 hides paying geld. In demesne are 2 ploughs, and there might be another 2 [ploughs]. There are 8 villans and 4 bordars with 8 ploughs. There are 4 oxmen, [and] 2 leagues of woodland. TRE it was worth 60s; now 5s more.

The earl himself holds TREWERN [Wales], and Roger [holds] of him. King Edward held it. There are 20 hides paying geld. There is land for 40 ploughs. With the exception of 2 hides it was waste. In demesne is 1 plough; and 5 villans with 1 free man have 3 ploughs, and certain Welshmen labouring there pay 16s. [There are] 2 leagues of woodland. There is waste land for 31 ploughs.

In this manor 5 of Roger's knights have 6½ ploughs in demesne, and 2 villans and 6 bordars and 2 Welshmen and 1 radman with 3 bordars and 6 oxmen. Among them all they have 3 ploughs. TRE it rendered 8s; now all together £4.

The earl himself holds ALBERBURY, and Roger [holds] of him. King Edward held it. There is 1 hide.[...] In demesne is 1 plough; and 8 bordars with 2 ploughs, and there are 2 oxmen. To this manor pertains "REWESET" Hundred. TRE it was worth 5s; now 20s.

The earl himself holds CHIRBURY. King Edward held it. [...] In demesne are 4 ploughs; and 13 villans with a reeve have 5 ploughs. There are 8 oxmen. There are 2 churches with a priest, who has 1 plough. To this manor pertains WITTERY Hundred. TRE it was waste; now it is worth 40s.

The earl himself holds MAESBURY with 5 Berewicks, and Reginald [holds] of him. King Edward held it. There are 7 hides paying geld, and there Reginald has built the castle of OSWESTRY. In demesne he has 2 ploughs; and 10 Welshmen with a priest having 8 ploughs, and there might be 6 ploughs more. There is a church. There are 4 oxmen. There is a little wood rendering nothing.

Of this land Robert holds half a hide and Hengebald 2 hides, and they have 2 ploughs. To this manor pertains "MERSET" Hundred. TRE it was waste; now it is worth 40s.

The earl himself holds WHITTINGTON with $8\frac{1}{2}$ Berewicks. King Edward held it. There are 18 hides paying geld. There is land for 25 ploughs. In demesne are 6 ploughs; and 15 villans and 6 bordars with 12 ploughs. There are 12 oxmen, and some Welshman pay 20s, and there is a mill rendering 5s. [There is] 1 league of woodland. TRE it was waste; now it renders £15.15s. In the time of Æthelræd, father of King Edward, these 3 manors rendered half a knight's farm.

TEWDWR, a certain Welshman, holds of the earl 1 district of Welsh land and pays £4.5s for it.

The earl himself holds LYDHAM. TRE Eadric the Wild held it. There are 15 hides paying geld. In demesne are 4 ploughs; and 14 villans with a reeve and a priest and 6 bordars have 10 ploughs, and there might be 16 ploughs more. There are 6 radmen, and a mill rendering 1 pig, [and] 2 leagues of woodland. TRE it was worth £10; now £14.

At the castle of Montgomery [Wales] the earl himself has 4 ploughs, and he has £6 of pence from a certain district of Wales belonging to the jurisdiction of this castle. Roger Corbet has there 2 ploughs, and with his brother he has 40s from Wales.

The earl himself holds FORD. Earl Edwin held it with 14 Berewicks. There are 15 hides [...]. In demesne are 10 ploughs, and 20 slaves and 6 female slaves; and 50 villans and 14 bordars with 29 ploughs. There is a mill rendering 3 orae, and half a fishery [rendering] 2s. TRE it rendered £9; now £34.

The earl himself holds GREAT NESS. Earl Morcar held it with 4 Berewicks. There are 5 hides. [...] In demesne are 5 ploughs and 10 oxmen; and 15 villans and 5 bordars with 6 ploughs, and there might be 3 ploughs more. 6 Welshmen there render 20s. [There is] 1 league of woodland.

The Church of ST PETER holds the church of this manor with 1 virgate of land. A certain Robert has 4 villans who pay 5s. TRE it rendered £3; now £13.10s.

The earl himself holds LOPPINGTON. Eadric the Wild held it. There are 5 hides paying geld. In demesne are 2 ploughs and 4 slaves; and 15 villans with 6 ploughs, and there might be 2 ploughs more. TRE it was worth £3; now £6.10s.

The earl himself holds ELLESMERE. Earl Edwin held it.

There are $4\frac{1}{2}$ hides. In demesne are 5 ploughs and 10 oxmen; and 36 villans and 14 bordars with 2 priests have 14 ploughs. There is a mill. TRE it rendered £10 of farm; now £20.

Of the same manor Mundret holds 1 hide and Reginald 1 hide. They have there 2 ploughs and 4 slaves, and 4 villans and 7 bordars with $3\frac{1}{2}$ ploughs. It is worth 23s.

The earl himself holds BERWICK [Berwick and Upper Berwick, in St Alkmond, Shrewsbury]. Eadric the Wild held it. There are $1\frac{1}{2}$ hides. In demesne are 2 ploughs and 4 slaves and 1 female slave; and 11 villans with 5 ploughs. TRE it was worth 30s; now £9.

The earl himself holds HIGH ERCALL. Earl Edwin held it with 5 Berewicks. There are 7 hides.[...] In demesne are 6 ploughs and 12 oxmen. There 29 villans and 12 bordars have 15 ploughs. There 2 mills render 12 summae of corn, and [there is] a fishery rendering 1,502 large eels, [and] 1 league of woodland. TRE it was worth £20; now as much. As a customary due whenever the countess visited the manor 18 orae of pence were brought to her.

The earl himself holds WELLINGTON. Earl Edwin held it [...], with 5 Berewicks. There are 14 hides paying geld. In demesne are 6 ploughs and 12 oxmen; and 12 villans and 8 bordars with a priest have 9 ploughs, and there might be another 9 ploughs. There is a mill rendering 12s, and 2 fisheries rendering 8s. TRE it was worth £20; now £18.

Of the land of this manor William holds of the earl 1 hide, DAWLEY MAGNA, as a manor. Grim held it before. There is 1 plough, and 7 villans have 1 plough. It was worth 30s; now 10s.

The earl himself holds EDGMOND. Leofwine Cild held it with 6 Berewicks. There are 14 hides paying geld. In demesne are 6 ploughs and 12 oxmen and 1 female slave; and 33 villans and 8 bordars with 2 Frenchmen have 11 ploughs. There a mill with a fishery renders 10s; and 11 ploughs more might be there. TRE it rendered £14; now £15.

The earl himself holds TONG. Earl Morcar held it. There are 3 hides paying geld. In demesne are 4 ploughs and 8 slaves; and 3 villans and 2 bordars with 3 ploughs. There is 1 league of woodland. TRE it was worth £11; now £6.

The earl himself holds DONINGTON. Earl Edwin held it. There are 3 hides. In demesne are 4 ploughs and 8 oxmen and 2 female slaves; and 12 villans and 2 bordars with 3 ploughs, and 7 ploughs more might be there. There is a mill rendering 5 summae of corn, and woodland 1 league long and a half broad. 5 salt-pans in Droitwich [Worcs.] render 20s. TRE it rendered £20; now £9.

The earl himself holds DITTON PRIORS. Earl Edwin held it with 4 Berewicks. There are 12 hides paying geld. In demesne are 5 ploughs and 10 slaves; and 20 villans and 8 bordars with 6 ploughs, and another 13 ploughs might be there. 1 salt-pan in Droitwich [Worcs.] renders 2s. TRE it rendered £10; now £1.

The earl himself holds CHURCH STRETTON. Earl Edwin held it with 4 Berewicks. There are 8 hides [...]. In demesne are 3 ploughs, and 6 slaves and 2 female slaves; and 18 villans and 8 bordars with a priest having 12 ploughs. There is a mill, and a church, and in the woodland 5 enclosures, and there might be 6 ploughs more. TRE it was worth £13; now 100s.

The same earl himself holds SIEFTON. Eadric held it. There are 5 hides. [...] In demesne are 3 ploughs and 2 female slaves; and 3 villans and 3 bordars with 1 plough, and there can be 7 ploughs more. TRE it was worth £6; now 100s.

The same earl himself holds CULMINGTON. Eadric held it. There are 5 hides paying geld, with 3 Berewicks. In demesne are 2 ploughs and 4 slaves; and 12 villans with 3 ploughs, and 7 ploughs more might be there. TRE it was worth £4; now £6.

The same earl himself holds STOTTESDON. Earl Edwin held it with 7 Berewicks. There are 9 hides [...]. In demesne are 4 ploughs and 8 slaves and 3 female slaves; and 18 villans and 5 bordars and 6 coliberts with 11 ploughs. There is a mill rendering 10s, and 2 leagues of woodland. TRE it was worth £20; now £10.

The Church of ST PETER holds the church of this manor with 2½ hides. There are 10 villans with 2 ploughs, and another 2 ploughs might be there. It is worth 20s.

The same earl himself holds CHETTON. Countess Godgifu held it TRE. There is 1 hide paying geld. In demesne are 3 ploughs and 6 slaves and 2 female slaves; and 4 villans and 1 bordar with a priest and a reeve have 3 ploughs, and there might be 2 ploughs more. There is a new mill, and 1 league of woodland. TRE it was worth 100s; now 45s.

The earl himself holds EARDINGTON. St Milburh held it TRE. There are 5 hides. [...] In demesne is 1 plough and 4 slaves; and 9 villans and 2 bordars with 3 ploughs, and there might be 8 ploughs more. There is a mill rendering 3 orae, and a new house, and a borough called QUATFORD, rendering nothing. TRE it was worth 40s; now 30s.

The earl himself holds "BOLEBEC". Stenulf held it TRE. There is half a hide paying geld. There is land for 1 plough. It was and is waste. In OVERS, half a hide paying geld. It is worth 3s. Siward held it TRE.

IN WITTERY HUNDRED

The earl himself has built a castle called MONTGOMERY [Wales] to which belongs 52½ hides which Siward, Oslac [and] Azur held of King Edward quit of all geld. They had these for the chase.

In [Lower and Upper] Edenhope 1 hide; in Aston [Wales] 2 hides; in "Stantune" [?Wales] 7 hides; in Castlewright [Wales] 2 hides; in Mellington [Wales] 3 hides; in "Goseford" [?Wales] 3 hides; in Hopton [Wales] 2 hides; in "Benehale" [?Wales] 7 hides; in Dudston 1 hide; in Pen-y-lan [Wales] 3 hides; in Hockleton half a hide; in Walcot 1 hide; in Trelystan [Wales] 3 hides.

The 3 above-mentioned thegns held these lands. Now Earl Roger holds them. They are and were waste, and of the above 50 hides, 3 hides are in his demesne.

The same 3 thegns themselves held Weston Madoc [Wales] at 3 hides and 'Starcote' [in Montgomery, Wales] at 1 hide and 'Horsewall' [in Montgomery, Wales] at half a hide and The Gaer [Wales] at 1 hide and [Great and Little] Hem [Wales] at 3 hides and Edderton [Wales] at 1 hide and Forden [Wales] at half a hide and 'Wropton' [in Forden, Wales] at 1 hide and Ackley [Wales] at 1 hide.

These lands Roger Corbet holds of the earl, except Ackley [Wales], which Æthelweard holds. In these 9½ ploughs are in demesne; and 15 villans and 14 bordars with 3 radmen and 8 slaves have 12½ ploughs.

They were waste; now they are worth 100s.

In [Great and Little] Hem [Wales] are 3 fisheries and woodland with an enclosure. In Edderton [Wales] [is] woodland for fattening 60 pigs, [and] in Ackley [Wales] 1 enclosure.

Earl ROGER himself holds of the king the city of SHREWSBURY and the whole shire, and all the demesne which King Edward had there, with 12 manors which the king himself held, with 57 Berewicks pertaining there, and the same earl has 11 other manors in the same shire.

All together, that id the city and the manors and the hundreds and the pleas of the shire, they render £300 and 115s of farm.

Earl HUGH holds of Earl Roger in Wales the land of Ial. This land extends 5 leagues in length and 1½ leagues in breadth. TRE it was waste, and likewise when Hugh received it [...]. In demesne are 3 ploughs; and 2 priests and 33 men having among them 8 ploughs, and 1 plough more might be there. There is a mill rendering nothing. The whole now is worth 40s.

IN HODNET HUNDRED

REGINALD the sheriff holds MARCHAMLEY of the earl. Siward and Ælfric held it | as 2 manors | TRE and were free. There are 5½ hides paying geld. In demesne are 2 ploughs and 4 slaves and 6 villans and 7 bordars and 2 radmen having 3 ploughs among them all. There is a mill rendering 5s; and there might be 10 ploughs more. There is woodland for fattening 100 pigs, and an enclosure.

Of this land Walter holds 1½ hides, and has there 1 plough and 1 slave, and 1 villan and 1 bordar with half a plough. The whole TRE was worth 100s; and afterwards it was waste; now it is worth 46s4d.

The same Reginald holds HIGH HATTON of the earl, and Richard [holds] of him. Alric, Wulfheah, Wulfgeat and Leofric held it as 4 manors TRE. There are 2 hides paying geld. In demesne is 1 plough and 4 slaves; and 2 villans and 2 cottars with 2 ploughs, and 5 ploughs more might be there. The men who held these lands were free. TRE it was worth 60s; and afterwards [it was] waste; now [worth] 10s.

The same Reginald holds STANTON UPON HINE HEATH of the earl, and Richard [holds] of him. Sæweard held it and was free with this land. There is 1 hide paying geld. In demesne is 1 plough and 4 slaves. [There is] a church and a priest and 6 bordars and a smith. Among them all they have 2 ploughs, and there might be a third. There is a mill rendering 10s8d. TRE it was worth 35s; and afterwards it was waste; now it is worth 22s.

The same Reginald holds GREAT WYTHEFORD, and Ealhhere [holds] of him. Sten and Vilgrip held it and were free with that land. There are 2½ hides paying geld. In demesne are 2 ploughs and 8 slaves; and 5 villans and 1 radman and 1 Frenchman with 3½ ploughs. There is a mill rendering 8s. TRE it was worth 28s; and afterwards [it was] waste; now [worth] 40s.

The same Reginald holds in the same vill 1 hide paying geld, and Albert [holds] of him. Wulfric and Karli held it as 1 manor. There is 1 plough, and 2 slaves and 2 bordars, and there might be another plough. It was worth 7s; and afterwards it was waste; now [worth] 7s.

IN PATTON HUNDRED

The same Reginald holds ACTON ROUND of the earl. There are 4 hides paying geld. Wulfgeat held it and was free with this land. In demesne are 2 ploughs and 7 slaves; and 9 villans and 4 bordars with 4 ploughs, and there might be 3 ploughs more. There is a mill rendering 32d. TRE it was worth 60s; now 40s.

The same Reginald holds ABDON, and Azo [holds] of him. Wulfwine held it and was free with this land. There are 3 hides paying geld. There is 1 plough and 3 slaves; and 1 Frenchman and 2 villans and 1 radman and 2 bordars with 1 plough, and there might be 3 ploughs more. It was worth 20s; now 12s.

The same Reginald gave TUGFORD to the church of ST PETER for the soul of Warin his predecessor. Alwine held it and was free with the land. There are 3½ hides. In demesne are 3 ploughs and 3 slaves and 3 oxmen; and 3 villans and 8 bordars with 5 ploughs. There is a mill rendering 4s. It was worth 20s; now 40s.

Of this land Rayner holds 1 hide of Reginald. There he has 1 plough and 1 oxman, and 3 villans and 1 bordar with 1 plough. It is worth 8s.

The same Reginald holds STANWAY [in Rushbury] of the earl, and Odo [holds] of him. Ælfric held it and was a free man. There are 2 hides paying geld. In demesne are 2 ploughs and 4 slaves; and 3 villans and 1 bordar with 2 ploughs, and there might be 3 ploughs more. TRE it was worth 40s; now 30s. It was waste when he received it.

The same Reginald with a certain Robert holds GRETTON of the earl, and Odo [holds] of them. Alric and Ottar held it as 2 manors. There are 2 hides paying geld. These thegns were free. There are 5 villans with 2 ploughs, and another 2 might be there. TRE it was worth 32s; now 10s; when received, it was waste.

The same Reginald holds EASTHOPE of the earl, and Fulcher [holds] of him. †Earnwig† and Wulfric held it and were free. There are 2 hides paying geld.

In demesne is 1 plough and 4 slaves; and 1 villan and 5 bordars with 1 plough, and 2 ploughs more might be there. TRE it was worth 15s; now 20s; when received it, he found it waste.

The same Reginald holds LUTWYCHE, and Richard [holds] of him. Godwine held it and was a free man. There is 1 hide paying geld. In demesne is 1 plough and 2 oxmen; and 1 villan and 1 bordar with half a plough. It was and is worth 8s.

The same Reginald holds BROCKTON [in Long Stanton], and Richard [holds] of him. Sæmær and Algeard and Edwin held it and were free with this land. There are 2 hides paying geld. In demesne is half a plough and 2 slaves; and 3 villans and 2 bordars and 1 Frenchman with 1 plough among them all, and 4 ploughs more might be there. TRE it was worth 28s; now 15s; when he received it, he found it waste.

IN CONDOVER HUNDRED

The same Reginald holds BERRINGTON, and Azo [holds] of him. Thorth held of St Andrew by service half a hide in this vill. Besides this half-hide, he himself held 2 hides paying geld. [...] In demesne are 2 ploughs and 7 slaves; and 6 villans with 1 plough, and there can be 2 ploughs more.

Of this vill ST PETER in Shrewsbury holds the church and the priest. TRE it was worth 30s; and afterwards 14s; now 40s.

The same Reginald holds [?] LONGNOR, and Azo [holds] of him. Ealdræd held it and could go where he would. There are 2 hides paying geld. In demesne is 1 plough and 1 slave; and 5 villans with 2 ploughs, and there can be 6 ploughs more. Roger the huntsman holds of Earl Roger the head of this manor, and the 2 hides which Azo holds acquit his land, which is inland, from geld. In Roger's demesne are 2 ploughs and 3 slaves and 2 oxmen; and 9 bordars with 1 plough, and 3 ploughs more might be there. There is woodland for fattening 600 pigs, and there are 3 secure enclosures, and a mill. TRE the whole was worth £8; and afterwards 20s; now 64s.

The same Reginald holds COUND [Cound and Upper Cound]. Earl Morcar held it. There are 4½ hides paying geld. In demesne are 2 ploughs and 6 slaves and 4 female slaves; and 6 villans and 6 bordars with 4 ploughs. There are 2 mills rendering 20s, and woodland for fattening 50 pigs. TRE it was worth £4.7s; now £10.

The same Reginald holds GOLDING, and Odo [holds] of him. Swein, a free man, held it. There is half a hide paying geld. In demesne is 1 plough, and 3 slaves and 1 bordar, and another plough might be there. It was worth 8s; now 5s.

The same Reginald holds ACTON PIGOTT, and Odo [holds] of him. Geri held it and could give and sell it. There are 3 hides paying geld. In demesne is 1 plough and 3 slaves; and 4 villans with 1 plough. [There is] woodland for fattening 20 pigs. TRE it was worth 20s; and afterwards 12s; now 13s4d.

The same Reginald holds KENLY, and Odo [holds] of him. Eadric held it and was a free man. There is 1 hide paying geld. In demesne is 1 plough, and another 4 ploughs might be there. There is woodland for fattening 400 pigs. TRE it was worth 30s; and afterwards it was waste; now it is worth 4s.

The same Reginald holds EATON MASCOTT, and Fulcher [holds] of him. Thorth held it and was a free man. There are 3 hides paying geld. In demesne is 1 plough and 4 slaves; and 3 villans and 4 bordars with 1 plough, and there can be another 2 ploughs. There is a mill rendering 4s. TRE it was worth 20s; and afterwards 24s; now 20s.

IN WROCKWARDINE HUNDRED

The same Reginald holds EATON CONSTANTINE of the earl. Wynsige held it TRE. There are 2 hides [...]. In demesne are 2 ploughs and 4 slaves and 2 female slaves; and 1 villan and 5 bordars with 1 plough, and there might be 2 ploughs more. There is a fishery on the Severn rendering nothing, and scrubland rendering 5d. TRE it was worth 50s; now 40s. He found it waste.

The same Reginald holds LEIGHTON [near Wellington]. Leofwig held it TRE. There are 3 hides [...]. In demesne are 3 ploughs and 6 oxmen; and 4 villans and 7 bordars with a priest and 1 Frenchman have 5 ploughs. There is a mill rendering 4s, and half a league of woodland rendering 11d. TRE it was worth 20s; now 40s. He found it waste.

The same Reginald holds CHILD'S ERCALL of the earl. Siward held it. There are 3 hides [...]. In demesne are 2 ploughs and 4 oxmen; and 7 villans and 10 bordars and a priest and a smith and a Frenchman. Among them all they have 7½ ploughs, and 1 more might be there. There is half a league of woodland rendering 3d. TRE it was worth 45s; now 60s. He found it waste.

The same Reginald holds UPTON MAGNA. Siward held it TRE. There are 5 hides paying geld. In demesne are 3 ploughs and 7 slaves; and 25 villans and 1 free man with 12 ploughs, and there can be 8 ploughs more. There is a mill rendering 16s, and a fishery rendering what it can, and half a league of woodland. TRE it was worth £10; now £7.

The same Reginald holds BERWICK [in Atcham]. Wulfgeat held it TRE. There is half a hide [...]. In demesne are 2 ploughs and 4 oxmen; and 4 villans and 3 bordars with 2 ploughs. There is 1 league of woodland rendering 16d; and 1 plough more might be there.

The same Reginald holds WROXETER. Thorth held it and was a free man. There is 1 hide paying geld. In demesne are 1½ ploughs and 7 slaves and female slaves together. There are 7 villans and 4 bordars and 4 priests and 1 radman. Among them all they have 4 ploughs. There is a church, and 1 league of woodland. TRE it was worth 40s; and now as much.

The same Reginald holds HADLEY, and Geoffrey [holds] of him. Wihtric and Alric held it as 2 manors. There are 2 hides. In demesne is 1 plough and 2 slaves; and 8 bordars with half a plough, and 2½ ploughs more might be there. There is a mill rendering 2s, and 1 league of woodland. TRE it was worth 37s; now 15s. He found it waste.

The same Reginald holds DAWLEY PARVA, and Benedict [holds] of him. Sighsten held it. There is 1 hide. [...] In demesne is half a plough and 1 slave; and 1 villan and 2 bordars with half a plough, and there might be 2 ploughs more. [There is] 1 league of woodland. The earl has this in demesne. TRE it was worth 24s; now 5s.

The same Reginald holds of the earl 2 hides and 2 parts of 1 hide as a manor. Wicga held them TRE. Richard holds them of Reginald, and has 1 plough in demesne and 2 slaves; and 3 villans with 2 ploughs.

Of this land a free man holds half a hide and 2 parts of 1 virgate, and has there, with his 3 bordars, 6 oxen ploughing. TRE it was worth 25s; now 20s. 1½ ploughs [more] might be there.

The same Reginald holds LEEGOMERY, and Thorth [holds] of him. He himself held it TRE. There are 3 hides [...]. In demesne is 1 plough, and 5 slaves and female slaves together, and 2 villans and 4 radmen with 2 ploughs, and there might be another 2 ploughs. [There are] 2 leagues of woodland. TRE it was worth 20s; now 15s.

The same Reginald holds RODINGTON, and Thorth [holds] of him. The same man held it TRE. There are 4 hides and 1 virgate [...]. In demesne is 1 plough and 2 slaves and 3 female slaves. [There is] a church and a priest, and 2 villans and 3 bordars and 3 radmen. Among them all they have 2½ ploughs, and there might be 3 ploughs more. There is a mill rendering 6d. TRE it was worth 27s; now 20s.

IN "MERSET" HUNDRED

The same Reginald holds HALSTON. Eadric held it with 3 Berewicks. There are 7 hides paying geld. There is land for 8½ ploughs. There 2 Welshmen and 1 Frenchman with 2 men have 1½ ploughs. It is worth 4s. It was waste, and he found it waste.

The same Reginald holds WESTON RHYN. Siward held it. There are 5 hides paying geld, with 5 Berewicks. There is land for 15 ploughs. There are 2 Welshmen with 2 ploughs.

Of this land Robert holds 1 hide, and has there 1 plough, with 3 villans. It was waste, and he found it waste; now it is worth 10s.

The same Reginald holds MORTON and "AITONE". Siward held them as 2 manors. There are 5 hides. There is land for 8 ploughs. 5 men there have 2 ploughs. There is a small laund of woodland. It was waste; now it renders 64d.

The same Reginald holds MAESBROOK. Leofnoth held it TRE. There are 2 hides. There is land for 4 ploughs. There is 1 Welshman with 1 plough, and he pays 5s.

The same Reginald holds 'TIBETONE'. Wulfgeat held it TRE. There is 1 hide. There is land for 2 ploughs. 2 Welshmen there have 1 plough and pay 4s. These 2 manors were waste, like many others.

The same Reginald holds MELVERLEY. Eadric held it TRE. There is 1 hide. There is land for 2 ploughs. 2 Welshmen there have 1 plough, and they pay 32d.

The same Reginald holds WESTON COTON. Siward held it TRE. There is 1 hide paying geld. There is land for 3 ploughs. In demesne are 2 ploughs and 4 oxmen; and 4 Welshmen with 1 plough, and they pay 4s. The whole is worth 10s; and these were waste.

The same Reginald holds WOOTTON of the earl, and Robert [holds] of him. Eadric held it with 2 Berewicks. There are 2 hides. [...] There is land for 4 ploughs. In demesne is 1 plough and 2 oxmen; and 8 Welshmen with 1 plough. It is worth 15s. There are 2 leagues of woodland.

The same Reginald holds WOOLSTON [in West Felton], and a knight [holds] of him. Wulfric held it TRE with 1 Berewick. There are 1½ hides. There is land for 3 ploughs. 4 Welshmen there have 1 plough. It is worth 6s.

The same Reginald holds WEST FELTON, and a knight [holds] of him. Siward held it. There is half a hide. There is land for 1 plough. It was and is waste.

The same Reginald has in Wales 2 districts, CYNLLAITH and EDEIRNION. From one he has 60s as farm and from the other 8 cows from the Welshmen.

The same Reginald holds OSBASTON and KYNASTON. Siward and Alwig held them as 2 manors. There are 2 hides. There is land for 6 ploughs. There are 2 leagues of woodland. They were and are waste.

IN "CULVESTAN" HUNDRED

The same Reginald holds CARDINGTON. Austin and another Austin held it TRE as 2 manors. There are 5 hides. In demesne is 1 plough and 5 slaves; and 15 villans and 1 radman with 7 ploughs. among them all, and 8 ploughs more might be there. There are 2 leagues of woodland. TRE it was worth 40s; now as much.

The same Reginald holds MUNSLOW ASTON. Almund held it TRE. There are 8½ hides paying geld. In demesne are 2 ploughs and 6 slaves; and 5 villans and 8 bordars and a priest and 1 Frenchman and 1 radman, with 5 ploughs among them all, and 9 ploughs more might be there. There is a mill rendering 3 measures of wheat. TRE it was worth 65s; now 40s. He found it waste.

IN LEINTWARDINE HUNDRED

The same Reginald holds CLUNGUNFORD, and Fulk [holds] of him. Gunnvarthr held it TRE. There are 2 hides paying geld. There are 5 villans and 1 bordar with 2 ploughs, and 6 ploughs more might be there. There are 3 enclosures. The whole is worth 12s.

The same Reginald holds STREFFORD, and Azo [holds] of him. Almund held it. There are 2 hides paying geld. There is land for 4 ploughs. There are no men there, and yet he has 20s from it. TRE it was worth 30s; and afterwards it was waste.

IN 'OVERS' HUNDRED

The same Reginald holds HENLEY, and Roger [holds] of him. Almund held it and was free with this land. There is 1 hide paying geld. In demesne is half a plough and 4 slaves and female slaves together; and 2 villans and 1 bordar with 1 plough. There is a mill rendering 4s. It was and is worth 12s.

IN BASCHURCH HUNDRED

The same Reginald holds ENGLISH FRANKTON, and Robert [holds] of him. Ealdgyth held it TRE. There are 2 hides. In demesne is 1 plough and 2 oxmen; and 3 villans with 1 plough. TRE it was worth 10s; now 15s.

The same Reginald holds SHRAWARDINE. Æli held it TRE. There are 2 hides [...]. In demesne are 2 ploughs and 4 oxmen; and 3 villans and 4 bordars with 2½ ploughs. It was and is worth 40s.

The same Reginald holds ALBRIGHT HUSSEY. Siward held it. There are 2 hides not paying geld. There are 3 villans and 1 radman and 1 Frenchman with 4 bordars and they have 2½ ploughs. It is and was worth 15s.

The same Reginald holds LITTLE NESS. Siward held it TRE. There are 3 hides [...]. In demesne are 2 ploughs; and 4 villans and 3 bordars with 2 ploughs, and there might also be another 2 [ploughs]. There is a mill rendering 20s and 600 eels. TRE it was worth £3; and afterwards £4; now 10s more.

The same Reginald holds MYDDLE. Siward held it TRE. There are 8 hides [...]. In demesne is 1 plough, and 8 bordars and a priest and 2 Frenchmen.

There is woodland for fattening 40 pigs. There is land for 20 ploughs. TRE it was worth £6; and afterwards £4; now 70s.

The same Reginald holds WELSHAMPTON. Ealdgyth held it TRE. There are 3 hides [...]. Albert holds it of Reginald. In demesne is 1 plough and 3 slaves; and 6 villans and 4 bordars with 2 ploughs, and another 2 ploughs might be there. TRE it was worth 15s; now 30s.

The same Reginald holds YEATON, and Albert [holds] of him. Leofric held it TRE. There are 2 hides. [...] In demesne is 1 plough and 4 slaves; and 2 villans and 3 bordars with 1 plough. There is a mill rendering 10s. It was worth 15s; now 25s.

The same Reginald holds ROSSALL, and Albert [holds] of him. Hunning held it TRE. There is 1 hide. [...] In demesne is 1 plough and 4 slaves; and 2 villans and 4 bordars with 1 plough, and there might also be another. It was worth 20s; now 12s.

The same Reginald holds ALBRIGHT HUSSEY, and Herbert [holds] of him. Siward, a free man, held it. There are 2 hides [...]. In demesne is 1 plough; and 8 villans and 4 bordars with 2 ploughs. It was worth 14s; now 25s.

The same Reginald holds HADNALL, and Osmund [holds] of him. Godwine held it. There are 4 hides paying geld. In demesne is 1 plough and 2 oxmen; and 6 villans and 1 bordar and 2 Frenchmen with 3 ploughs, and there might be 4 ploughs more. There is woodland for fattening 40 pigs. TRE it was worth 60s; and afterwards 10s; now 20s.

The same Reginald holds ACTON REYNALD, and Richard [holds] of him. Siward held it TRE and was a free man. There are 3 hides paying geld. There is land for 5 ploughs. There 2 knights have 1 plough. There is woodland for fattening 30 pigs. It was worth £4; and now 10s.

IN "ALNODESTREU" HUNDRED

The same Reginald holds ASTON EYRE, and Ealhhere [holds] of him. Saxi held it TRE and was a free man. There are 2 hides paying geld. In demesne are 3 ploughs and 8 slaves; and 9 villans and 2 bordars with 5 ploughs, and a mill rendering nothing. It was worth 15s; now 30s.

The same Reginald holds EUDON BURNELL. Alweard held it and was a free man. There are 2 hides paying geld. In demesne are 3 ploughs and 6 slaves; and 1 villan and 5 bordars and 1 Frenchman with 2 ploughs. [There is] woodland for 60 pigs. It was worth 30s; now 40s.

The same Reginald holds in HATTON [in Shifnal] half a hide. Thorgot held it as 1 manor, and it pays geld.

The same Reginald holds UPTON CRESSETT. Almund held it and was a free man. There are 3 hides paying geld. In demesne are 2 ploughs and 3 slaves; and 1 free oxman and 6 villans and 4 bordars and 1 radman with 4 ploughs, and there might also be another 4 [ploughs]. There is woodland for fattening 30 pigs. TRE it was worth 40s; and afterwards 10s; now 25s.

The same Reginald holds GLAZELEY, and Azo [holds] of him. Alweard held it and was free with his land. There are 2 hides paying geld. In demesne is 1 plough and 7 slaves; and 4 villans and 5 bordars and 1 radman and a priest with 3 ploughs, and there might be 2 ploughs more. There is a mill rendering 5s. It was worth 25s; now 20s.

The same Reginald holds MIDDLETON SCRIVEN, and Ealhhere and Albert [holds] of him. Eadric, a free man, held it as 2 manors. There are 2 hides paying geld. In demesne are 2 ploughs and 5 slaves; and 6 villans and 5 bordars with 3 ploughs, and there might be another 3 more [ploughs]. TRE it was worth 13s; now 28s. They were waste.

The same Reginald holds ASTON BOTTERELL, and Tochil [holds] of him. Alric held it and was free with this land. There is 1 hide paying geld. In demesne is 1 plough and 6 slaves; and 2 villans and 3 bordars and 3 radmen with 2 ploughs among them all, and a third plough might be there. It was worth 14s; now 15s.

The same Reginald holds 'FOUSWARDINE' [in Sidbury], and Ralph [holds] of him. Almund held it and was a free man. There is half a hide paying geld. In demesne is 1 plough and 4 slaves; and 1 villan and 1 bordar with 1 plough, and 1 plough more might [be] there. TRE it was worth 16s; and afterwards 6s; now 10s.

The same Reginald holds OLDBURY, and Ralph [holds] of him. Alweard held it and was free. There is 1 hide and 3

virgates paying geld. In demesne is 1 plough and 7 slaves; and 3 Frenchmen and 2 cottars and 1 bordar with 2 ploughs, and there might be another 2 [ploughs]. There is a mill rendering 2s, and woodland for fattening 100 pigs. TRE it was worth 30s; now 13s. He found it waste.

[Folio 255V: SHROPSHIRE]

IN 'CONDITRE' HUNDRED

REGINALD himself holds NORTON [in Aston Botterell], and Thorth [holds] of him. He himself held it freely TRE. There are 2 hides paying geld. In demesne is 1 plough and 6 slaves; and 5 villans with 2 ploughs, and another 2 [ploughs] might be there. TRE it was worth 20s; now 15s.

The same Reginald holds DETTON, and Robert [holds] of him. Alweard and Alric held it as 2 manors and were free. There are 2 hides paying geld. In demesne are 2 ploughs and 7 slaves; and 1 villan and 4 bordars and 1 radman with 1 plough only. TRE it was worth 24s; now 15s. He found it waste.

IN BASCHURCH HUNDRED

EALHHERE held of Warin, who was the predecessor of Reginald, ALBRIGHTON [in St Alkmond, Shrewsbury]. Geri held it and was a free man. There are 3 hides paying geld. There is land for 6 ploughs. In demesne are 2 [ploughs] and 4 slaves; and 1 Frenchman and 6 villans and 1 bordar with 3 ploughs. TRE it was worth 20s; and afterwards 15s; now 30s.

IN CONDOVER HUNDRED

ROGER fitzCorbet holds WELBATCH of Earl Roger, and Ranulph [holds] of him. Hunning held it and was free with this land. There is 1 hide paying geld. In demesne is 1 plough and 2 slaves, and 2 bordars. There is a mill for winter, not for summer, use. TRE it was worth 20s; now 5s.

The same Roger holds, and Ranulph [holds] of him, 1 manor, [?] STAPLETON, at 1½ virgates, and it pays geld. Hunning held it and was free. There is land for 1 plough. There is 1 villan. It was worth 16d; now 12d.

The same Roger holds ACTON BURNELL, and a certain Roger [holds] of him. Godric held it and was a free man. There are 3½ hides paying geld. In demesne is 1 plough and 2 slaves; and 1 villan and 4 bordars and 1 radman with 1½ ploughs. TRE it was worth 30s; and afterwards 15s; now 20s. 1 plough more might be there.

IN "RINLAU" HUNDRED

The same Roger holds WENTNOR. Eadric held it and was a free man. There are 2½ hides and they pay geld. In demesne are 3 ploughs and 15 slaves; and 5 villans and 11 bordars with 8 ploughs. [...] There are 4 enclosures. TRE it was worth £6; and afterwards 40s; now £4.

IN "REWESET" HUNDRED"

The same Roger holds WINSLEY. Siward, a free man, held it. There are 2 hides paying geld. In demesne are 2 ploughs; and 1 villan and 1 radman with 1½ ploughs. It was and is worth 15s.

IN THIS HUNDRED

The same Roger holds half a hide which Earl Morcar held. There is 1 villan with half a plough. It was and is worth 32d.

The same Roger holds WOLLASTON. Wulfgeat held it and was a free man. There is half a hide paying geld. It was and is waste; and yet it renders 12d.

The same Roger holds BAUSLEY [Wales]. Siward held it. There is 1 hide not paying geld. There are 2 Welshmen with 1 plough. It was and is worth 2s; and yet it is at farm for 6s8d.

The same Roger holds EYTON [in Alberbury]. Almær held it There is 1 hide and 3 virgates. There are 2 bordars with 5 oxen ploughing. It is worth 3s. There is land for 2 ploughs.

The same Roger holds LOTON. Eadric held it. There is 1 hide paying geld. In demesne is 1 plough and 1 slave, and 1 enclosure. It is worth 5s, and 2 ploughs more might also be there.

The same Roger holds YOCKLETON. Eadric held it and was a free man. There are 6 hides paying geld. In demesne are 3 ploughs and 8 slaves; and 19 villans and †6† bordars with 8 ploughs. There is a mill rendering 1 summa of malt, and woodland for fattening 100 pigs. TRE it was worth £8; now £6.

The same Roger holds PONTESBURY. Earnwig held it, and still holds it of Roger. There are 4½ hides paying geld, and 1½ hides not paying geld. In demesne are 4 ploughs and 7 slaves; and 10 villans and 5 bordars. and 1 radman with 5 ploughs, and there can be 3 ploughs more. There is a mill rendering corn, and woodland for fattening 40 pigs. TRE it was worth £8; now £6.

The same Roger holds FARLEY, and Earnwine [holds] of him. He himself held it TRE and was free with the land. There is 1 hide paying geld. In demesne is 1 plough and 3 slaves; and 3 bordars, and there can be 2 ploughs more. It was worth 4s; now 3s.

The same Roger holds GREAT HANWOOD. Eadric held it and was a free man. There are 2 hides paying geld. In demesne is half a plough and 5 slaves; and 3 villans and 2 bordars with 2½ ploughs, and 1 plough more might be there. It was and is worth 10s.

The same Roger holds WESTBURY. Earnwig held it and was free. There are 2 hides paying geld. In demesne is 1 plough and 1 slave; and 2 priests and 5 villans with 3 ploughs. It was worth 20s; now 25s.

The same Roger holds WATTLESBOROUGH. Eadric held it. There are 2 hides paying geld. In demesne are 3 ploughs and 3 oxmen; and 2 villans and 1 bordar and 1 radman with 5 oxen, and there might be 2 ploughs more. TRE it was waste; now it is worth 20s.

The same Roger holds MARCHE. Leofgeat and Dainz and Wyngeat held it as 3 manors and were free. There are 3 virgates paying geld. In demesne is 1 plough and 2 oxmen. It was worth 9s; now 5s.

The same Roger holds CARDESTON, and Gilbert [holds] of him. Leofnoth held it and was a free man. There is 1 hide paying geld. In demesne is 1 plough and 4 slaves; and 1 villan and 1 bordar, and 3 ploughs more might be there. TRE it was worth 30s; now 20s.

The same Roger holds WHITTON. Leofnoth and Leodmær and Ulfkil held it and were free. There are 1½ hides paying geld. In demesne is 1 plough and 2 oxmen; and 1 villan and 5 bordars and 1 radman with 1 plough only, and another 2 ploughs might be there. TRE it was worth 9s; now 15s.

IN WITTERY HUNDRED

The same Roger holds WORTHEN. Earl Morcar held it. There are 14½ hides paying geld, with 13 Berewicks. In demesne are 2 ploughs and 2 slaves; and 13 villans and 6 bordars and 3 radmen with 10½ ploughs. 2 mills there render 3 summae of wheat, and [there is] woodland 2 leagues long in which are 4 enclosures, and it is sufficient for fattening 200 pigs.

Of the land of this manor Picot holds of Roger 3 hides, and Reinfrid 3½ hides, and Geoffrey 1½ hides, and Grento half a hide. In demesne they have 4½ ploughs, and [there are] 4 slaves; and 7 villans and 8 bordars with 4 ploughs and 3 oxmen. In this manor is land for 41 ploughs. On Roger's demesne there might be 4 ploughs. The whole TRE was worth £10; and afterwards 10s; now what he holds, 100s, what the knights [holds] £4.10s.

The same Roger holds RORRINGTON, and Oswulf [holds] of him. Alweard held it and was a free man. There is 1 virgate not paying geld. In demesne is half a plough; and 6 bordars with half a plough. There is woodland for fattening 15 pigs, and half an enclosure. It was worth 7s; and afterwards 16d; now 6s.

The same Roger holds LEIGHTON [Wales]. Siward held it and was free. There is 1 hide not paying geld. In demesne is 1 plough and 2 oxmen, and 1 radman. There is woodland 2 leagues long and sufficient for fattening 200 pigs. It was and is worth 5s.

IN BASCHURCH HUNDRED

Roger holds MONTFORD of the earl. Almær held it. There are 3 hides. [...] In demesne are 1½ ploughs; and 13 villans with 6 ploughs, and there might be 3½ ploughs more. There is half a fishery, and woodland for fattening 24 pigs. TRE it was worth £4; and afterwards 20s; now £4.10s. Bishop R. claims this manor.

Roger holds PRESTON MONTFORD of the earl. Godric held it and was a free man. There is 1 virgate of land. In demesne is half a plough. It was and is worth 3s. [There is] woodland for fattening 10 pigs.

IN WROCKWARDINE HUNDRED

Roger holds [?] CHERRINGTON of the earl. Wulfric held it. There is 1 hide. 2 sergeants have half a plough there, and there might be 1½ ploughs more. It was waste; now it renders 5s.

[Folio 256: SHROPSHIRE]

IN CONDOVER HUNDRED

ROBERT fitzCorbet holds WOOLSTASTON of Earl Roger. Ketil and Ælfric held it as 2 manors. There are 2 hides; and these men were free. In demesne is 1 plough; and 7 villans with 1½ ploughs, and 3 ploughs more might be there. There is woodland for fattening 12 pigs. TRE it was worth 40s; now 12s.

The same Robert holds RATLINGHOPE. Siward held it. There are 2 hides. They are and were waste.

The same Robert holds WOMERTON. Auti and Einulf and Arngrim and Arnketil held it as 4 manors. There are 2½ hides paying geld. These thegns were free. There are 2 villans with half a plough. The greater part of this manor is waste. TRE it was worth all together 68s; now 10s. There is land for 5 ploughs.

The same Robert holds OAKS. Earnwig held it and was a free man. There are 2 hides paying geld. In demesne is half a plough and 2 slaves; and 1 radman and 1 villan and 1 bordar with 1 plough, and 4 ploughs more might be there. TRE it was worth 40s; and afterwards 10s; now 8s.

Robert holds BROMPTON of the earl. Siward held it. There is half a hide. It was and is waste.

IN "RINLAU" HUNDRED

Robert holds CHOULTON of the earl. Gunnfrothr held it and was a free man. There are 2 hides paying geld. In demesne are 2 ploughs and 1 slave; and 7 villans with 2 ploughs, and another 2 [ploughs] might also be there. It was and is worth 20s.

IN "REWESET" HUNDRED

Robert holds ONSLOW of the earl, and Earnwig [holds] of him. He himself held it and was a free man. There is 1 hide paying geld. In demesne is 1 plough; and 3 villans with 1 plough. It was worth 10s; now 12[s].

The same Robert holds WOODCOTE [in Bicton]. Wulfric held it and was a free man. There are 1½ hides paying geld. In demesne is 1 plough; and 1 villan and 1 bordar with 1 plough, and there might be 1 more, and 1 burgess pays 8s. It was worth 8s TRE; now it is worth 15s.

The same Robert holds LONGDEN. Leofric held it and was a free man. There are 3 hides paying geld. In demesne are 2 ploughs and 4 slaves, and 1 villan and 9 bordars and 3 radmen and 6 cottars. Among them all they have 2 ploughs, and 3 ploughs more might be there. [There is] woodland for fattening 60 pigs. TRE it was worth £4; and afterwards 30s; now 40s.

The same Robert holds MARCHE. Ælfric held it and was a free man. There are 2 hides paying geld. In demesne are 2 ploughs and 6 slaves, and 1 bordar and 1 radman. There might be 4 ploughs. TRE it was worth 15s; now 12s.

The same Robert holds [Lower and Upper] WIGMORE. Ælfric held it and was a free man. There is 1 hide paying geld.

There are 4 villans with 1 plough, and there might also be another [plough]. It was and is worth 5s.

IN WITTERY HUNDRED

The same Robert holds RORRINGTON. Ælfric held it. There is 1 virgate not paying geld. In demesne is 1 plough and 7 slaves, and 2 bordars. There is woodland for fattening 15 pigs, and there is half an enclosure. It was worth 3s; now 6s. Leofric holds it of Robert.

The same Robert holds MIDDLETON [in Chirbury]. Eadric the Wild held it. There are 3 virgates paying geld. There is 1 radman and 1 villan and 2 bordars with half a plough, and there might be 1 plough more. It was worth 4s; now 5s.

The same Robert holds PRIESTWESTON. 6 thegns held it as 6 manors and were free. Each had 1 virgate of land and it paid geld. [...] Now there are 7 radmen with 3 ploughs, and they pay 20s. The land of 2 thegns was worth 10s, but [that] of the others was waste.

The same Robert holds MARRINGTON. Alweard and Ælfric held it as 2 manors, and were free man. There is half a hide paying geld. There are 2 radmen and 3 bordars with 2 ploughs, and woodland for fattening 15 pigs. It was worth 7s; and afterwards 5s; now 4d more.

IN BASCHURCH HUNDRED

ROBERT the butler holds WALFORD of Earl Roger, and Sturmid [holds] of him. Siward held it TRE. There are 2 hides. [...] In demesne is half a plough and 1 oxman; and 2 villans and 2 bordars with 1½ ploughs. TRE it was worth 15s; and afterwards it was waste; now it is worth 20s.

The same Robert holds STANWARDINE IN THE FIELDS. Ealdræd held it. There are 2 hides. There is 1 villan and 1 bordar and a smith with half a plough, and 2 ploughs more might be there. It was and is worth 10s.

The same Robert holds PETTON, and Ralph [holds] of him. Leofnoth held it. There are 1½ hides. [...] In demesne is 1 plough; and 2 villans and 2 bordars with 1 plough. It was worth 5s; now 10s.

The same Robert holds EYTON [in Baschurch], and another Robert [holds] of him. Leofwig held it. There is 1 hide. [...] There is 1 villan and 3 bordars with 1½ ploughs. It was waste; now it is worth 5s.

The same Robert holds CRUDGINGTON. Earl Edwin held it. There are 1½ hides. In demesne is 1 plough and 2 slaves and 1 female slave; and 9 villans and 2 bordars and 1 free man with 3 ploughs. There are 4 fisheries rendering 13s4d. TRE it rendered as farm 73s4d; now £4 and | 1,000 eels. |

The same Robert holds [?] ASTON [in Oswestry]. Wulfric held it. [...] There are 2 hides [...]. There is land for 4 ploughs. There 12 Welshmen have 2 ploughs. It was worth 3s; now 10s.

IN WROCKWARDINE HUNDRED

ROGER de Courseulles holds of Earl Roger SUTTON [near Market Drayton]. Countess Godgifu held it. There are 4 hides paying geld. In demesne is 1 plough and 2 oxmen; and 9 bordars with 1 radman have 2 ploughs, and there can also be 4 ploughs more. There is a mill rendering 8 summae of corn. It was and is worth 25s.

The same Roger holds TIBBERTON. Wulfgar held it. There are 5 hides paying geld. In demesne is 1 plough and 2 oxmen; and 4 bordars with 1 plough, and there might be 7 ploughs more. TRE it was worth 60s; and afterwards it was waste; now it is worth 10s.

IN HODNET HUNDRED

The same Roger holds EDGELEY of the earl. Ælfric held it and was a free man. There is 1 hide paying geld. There is 1 radman and 1 villan and 5 bordars with 1 plough, and 5 ploughs more might be there. There is 1 slave. TRE it was worth 40s; now 12s. He found it waste.

The same Roger holds 'DODINGTON' [in Whitchurch]. Earl Edwin held it. There is 1 hide paying geld. There are 4 villans and 1 radman with 2 ploughs, and there might be another 2 [ploughs]. [There is] woodland for fattening 60 pigs. It was worth 16s; now 9s.

The same Roger holds STEEL. Algar, Kollungr, Beorhtric and Thorger held it and were free men. There is 1 hide as 4 manors. There are 4 villans and 1 bordar with 1 plough, and there might be 2 ploughs more. There is woodland for fattening 30 pigs. TRE it was worth 13s; now 6s.

IN HODNET HUNDRED

ROGER de Lacy holds MORETON SAY of Earl Roger, and William [holds] of him. Almund held it and was a free man. There are 3 hides paying geld. In demesne is 1 plough and 8 slaves; and 4 villans and 4 bordars with 2 ploughs, and 6 ploughs more might be there. [There is] woodland for fattening 100 pigs. TRE it was worth 40s; and afterwards it was waste; now it is worth 30s.

The same Roger holds [?] LOWE [in Wem], and William [holds] of him. There is 1 hide paying geld. Alwig held it and was a free man. 1 free man there has half a plough, and 1 plough more might be there. It was worth 6s; now 2s. It was waste.

[Folio 256V: SHROPSHIRE]

In this HUNDRED Eadric held 1 Berewick, Hopton [in Hodnet], at half a hide and it paid geld, and this land could not be alienated from the manor of STOKE UPON TERN which Roger de Lacy holds. This land is assessed in that manor in Wrockwardine Hundred.

IN PATTON HUNDRED

The same Roger holds PATTON of the earl. Alwine held it and was a free man. There is 1 hide paying geld. Herbert holds it of Roger. In demesne he has 1 plough and 2 slaves; and 1 villan and 1 radman with 1 plough, and there might be 3 ploughs more. There is a priest, and 1 bordar. TRE it was worth 10s; and afterwards was waste; now [worth] 24s.

The same Roger holds RUSHBURY, and Odo [holds] of him. Alwine held it and was a free man. There are 5 hides

paying geld. In demesne are 2 ploughs and 4 slaves; and 1 villan and 3 radmen and 2 bordars with 5 ploughs. There is a mill, and woodland for fattening 40 pigs, and a hawk's eyrie. TRE it was worth 60s; and afterwards it was waste; now [worth] 35s; and 2 ploughs more might be there.

The same Roger holds STANTON LONG, and Herbert [holds] of him. Alwine held it and was a free man. There are 3 hides paying geld. In demesne are 1½ ploughs and 2 slaves; and 1 bordar with half a plough. It was worth 6s; now 12s.

IN WROCKWARDINE HUNDRED

The same Roger holds STOKE UPON TERN. Edmund held it. There are 7 hides [...]. In demesne are 3 ploughs and 6 slaves and 3 female slaves. [There is] a church, and a priest and 11 villans and 3 radmen and 1 Frenchman with 10 ploughs among them all, and there might also be 5 ploughs more. There is a mill rendering 12s, and the third part of a league of woodland. TRE it was worth £6; and afterwards it was waste; now it is worth £7.

The same Roger holds LITTLE WYTHEFORD, and Robert [holds] of him. Leofnoth held it. There is half a hide [...], and half a plough, and there might be another half [-plough]. It was wroth 2s. Now it is assessed in the farm of Stoke upon Tern

The same Roger holds WATERS UPTON, and Siward [holds] of him. Gamal held it. There are 3 hides [...]. In demesne are 2 ploughs and 4 oxmen; and 4 villans and 1 bordar and 1 radman with 2 ploughs, and there might be another 2 [ploughs]. There is a mill rendering 12s1d. TRE it was worth 40s4d; and afterwards it was waste; now it is worth 30s2½d.

IN "CULVESTAN" HUNDRED

The same Roger holds CORFTON, and Herbert [holds] of him. Alsige held it. There are 3 hides paying geld. In demesne are 2 ploughs and 4 oxmen; and 4 villans and 1 bordar with 2 ploughs, and there might be another 2 [ploughs]. There is an enclosure for catching roe-deer. It was worth 16s; now 12s.

The same Roger holds MIDDLEHOPE, and Herbert [holds] of him. Alsige held it. There is 1 hide paying geld. In demesne are 2 ploughs and 4 slaves; and 2 villans and 4 bordars and 1 radman with 2 ploughs. TRE it was worth 7s; and afterwards 2s; now 20s.

IN LEINTWARDINE HUNDRED

The same Roger holds PLAISH, and Berner [holds] of him. Godwine held it. There is 1 hide paying geld. In demesne is 1 plough; and 1 villan and 1 slave with half a plough. It was worth 3s; now 5s.

IN 'OVERS' HUNDRED

The same Roger holds BITTERLEY. Godwine held it and was a free man. There are 3 hides paying geld. In demesne is 1 plough and 4 slaves and female slaves together. [There is] a church, and a priest and 6 villans and 1 bordar with 3 ploughs, and another 3 [ploughs] might be there. There are 2 enclosures. TRE it was worth 60s; and afterwards it was waste; now [worth] 40s.

IN BASCHURCH HUNDRED

The same Roger holds FORTON, and Osbern [holds] of him. Eadmær held it. There are 3 hides. In demesne is 1 plough and 2 oxmen; and 1 villan and 13 bordars with 2½ ploughs, and another 2 [ploughs] might be there. There is woodland for fattening 100 pigs. TRE it was worth 20s; and afterwards as much; now 25s.

The same Roger holds HIGFORD. Godwine held it and was a free man. There are 3 hides paying geld. Berner holds it of Roger. In demesne he has 3 ploughs and 9 slaves; and 7 villans and 7 bordars and 2 radmen with 5 ploughs. There is a mill rendering 8s, [and] woodland for fattening 100 pigs. It was worth 40s; now 60s.

IN 'CONDITRE' HUNDRED

The same Roger holds WHEATHILL of the earl. Almund held it. There are 3 hides [...]. In demesne are 2 ploughs and 10 slaves; and 4 villans with a reeve have 2 ploughs. TRE it was worth 40s; now it is worth 60s and renders 1 hawk.

IN BASCHURCH HUNDRED

ROBERT fitzTheobald holds SHIFNAL of Earl Roger. Earl Morcar held it. There are 7½ hides paying geld. In demesne are 9 ploughs and 26 slaves; and 37 villans and 3 bordars and 3 radmen with 27 ploughs. There is woodland for fattening 300 pigs. TRE it was worth £15; and afterwards 6s; now it renders £15.

The same Robert holds KEMBERTON. Ælfric, Almær, and Wulfwine and Eadmær held it as 4 manors, and were free. There are 3 hides paying geld. In demesne are 2 ploughs and 4 slaves; and 3 villans and 3 bordars and 1 radman with 1½ ploughs among them all, and 8 ploughs more might be there. There is woodland for fattening 30 pigs. TRE it was worth 28s; now 15s.

IN WROCKWARDINE HUNDRED

The same Robert holds WOODCOTE [in Newport], and Toki [holds] of him. Ælfric held it. There are 3 hides [...]. In demesne is 1 plough and 2 oxmen; and 1 villan and 3 bordars and 3 free men with 2 ploughs among them all, and there might be 3 ploughs more. It was worth 20s; now 10s.

The same Robert holds 1 manor at 1 virgate of land in the same hundred, and Toki [holds] of him. There is land for 1 plough. There is 1 villan and 2 slaves, and they have nothing. It was worth 5s.

IN CONDOVER HUNDRED

RANULPH Peverel holds CRESSAGE of Earl Roger. Eadric held it and was a free man. There are 1½ hides paying geld. In demesne are 3 ploughs and 8 slaves; and 7 villans and 11 bordars and 4 cottars have 4 ploughs, and there might be 2 [ploughs] more. There is a fishery rendering 8s, and woodland for fattening 200 pigs. TRE it was worth 110s; now £10; when received, it was worth £6.

IN HODNET HUNDRED

The same Ranulph holds LACON. Alnoth held it and was a free man. There are 2½ virgates of land paying geld. In demesne is half a plough with 1 bordar, and there might be half a plough more. It was worth 5s; now 3s.

The same Ranulph holds WESTON [near Wem]. Eadric the Wild held it. There are 3 hides paying geld. In demesne are 2 ploughs and 8 slaves; and 3 villans and 1 radman and 9 bordars with 1 plough, and 5 ploughs more might be there. TRE it was worth 60s; and afterwards 5s; now 40s.

The same Ranulph holds WHIXALL. Ealdgyth held it and was a free man. There is 1 hide paying geld. In demesne is 1 plough and 2 oxmen, and 2 bordars, and 1 plough more might be there. TRE it was worth 8s; now 5s.

IN CONDOVER HUNDRED

RALPH de Mortimer holds SHEINTON of Earl Roger, and Helgod [holds] of him. Azur, Algar and Sæwulf held it as 3 manors and were free men with the lands. There are 2 hides paying geld. In demesne are 1½ ploughs and 2 slaves; and 1 Frenchman with 9 bordars have 2 ploughs, and there might be a third. There is a mill rendering 10s, and woodland for fattening 100 pigs. It was worth 17s; now 20s.

IN "CULVESTAN" HUNDRED

The same Ralph holds HUNTINGTON, and Turstin [holds] of him. Ludi held it. There are 1½ hides paying geld. In demesne are 2 ploughs and 4 oxmen; and 2 villans and 2 bordars and 1 radman with 1 plough, and there might be another plough. There is a mill rendering 400 eels. It was worth 10s; and afterwards 5s; now 10s.

The same Ralph holds in the same place 1 manor, and Richard [holds] of him. Azur held it. There are 1½ hides paying geld. In demesne are 1½ ploughs and 4 slaves; and 2 villans and 2 bordars with 1 plough. It was worth 5s; now 10s.

IN 'OVERS' HUNDRED

The same Ralph holds CAYNHAM. Earl Morcar held it. There are 8 hides paying geld. In demesne are 4 hides, and there are 2 ploughs and 2 slaves; and 10 villans and 5 bordars with 4 ploughs. There is a mill, and 4 summae of salt from Droitwich [Worcs.], [and] woodland for fattening 200 pigs, and there are 3 enclosures. In the whole manor there is land for 19 ploughs.

Of this land of this manor Robert de Vessey holds 3 hides and Walter 1 hide of Ralph. In demesne they have 2 ploughs and 7 slaves; and 4 villans and 4 bordars with 1 plough only. The whole manor TRE was worth £8; and afterwards 60s; now what Ralph holds [is worth] 40s; what the knights [holds] 38s.

[Folio 257: SHROPSHIRE]

IN BASCHURCH HUNDRED

The same Ralph holds EUDON GEORGE. Eadric held it and was a free man. There are 2 hides paying geld. In demesne are 2 ploughs and 6 slaves; and 1 villan and 2 bordars with 1 plough, and there might be 2 ploughs more. TRE it was worth 25s; and afterwards it was waste; now it is worth 15s.

The same Ralph holds CHELMARSH. Earl Edwin held it. There are 5 hides paying geld. In demesne are 3 ploughs and 6 slaves; and 13 villans and 8 bordars with 6 ploughs. TRE it was worth £6; and afterwards it was waste; now [worth] 40s.

The same Ralph holds SIDBURY. Wicga held it and was a free man. There is 1 hide paying geld. In demesne are 2 ploughs and 6 slaves; and 6 villans and 3 bordars with 2 ploughs, and there might be another 2 [ploughs] more. TRE it was worth 20s; and afterwards it was waste; now [worth] 18s.

The same Ralph holds NEENTON, and Roger [holds] of him. Azur held it and was a free man. There is half a hide. [...] In demesne are 2 ploughs and 2 slaves; and 2 villans and 2 bordars with 1 plough, and 2 ploughs more might be there. TRE, as now, worth 17s.

The same Ralph holds BURWARTON, and Helgot [holds] of him. Azur held it. There is half a hide paying geld. There is land for 3 ploughs. 2 villans there have 1 plough. It was waste; now it is worth 2s.

Ralph holds COSFORD. Thorgot held it and was a free man. There is 1 hide paying geld. There is land for 3 ploughs. In demesne is 1 [plough]. TRE it was worth 40s; and afterwards it was waste; now [worth] 5s.

IN 'CONDITRE' HUNDRED

The same Ralph holds HIGHLEY. Countess Godgifu held it. There are 3 hides paying geld. In demesne are 1½ ploughs; and 6 villans and 6 bordars and 1 radman have 2½ ploughs, and there might be 2 ploughs more. There is woodland for fattening 36 pigs. TRE it was worth 15s; and afterwards 3s; now 18s.

The same Ralph holds WALTON, and Ingelrann [holds] of him. Eadric held it and was a free man. There is half a hide paying geld. In demesne is 1 plough and 4 slaves, and 6 bordars. It was worth 10s; now 8s. He found it waste.

The same Ralph holds LOWER BAVENEY, and Fech [holds] of him. Alsige and Fech held it as 2 manors. There is half a hide. 1 virgate of these 2 [virgates] lay in Cleobury Mortimer. Now 2 radmen and 2 bordars have 1 plough there. It was worth 10s; now 6s.

The same Ralph holds WALL TOWN, and Richard [holds] of him. Wulfric held it. There is 1 hide. There is land for 2 ploughs. There is 1 [plough] with 2 oxmen. It was worth 6s; now 8s.

The same Ralph holds CATSLEY, and Ulf [holds] of him. Eadric held it. There is half a hide. [...] In demesne is 1 plough and 2 oxmen; and 1 villan and 2 bordars with 1 plough. It was worth 6s6d; now 8s.

The same Ralph holds OVERTON, and Ingelrann [holds] of him. Eadric held it. There are 2 hides. [...] In demesne is 1 plough and 2 oxmen; and 3 villans and 2 bordars with 1 plough. It was and is worth 20s.

IN WROCKWARDINE HUNDRED

Ralph holds PRESTON UPON THE WEALD MOORS of Earl Roger. Burrer held it. There is 1 hide paying geld. There is land for 4 ploughs. In demesne is 1 [plough] and 2 oxmen; and 3 villans with 1 plough. There is half a league of woodland. It was worth 40s; now 20s.

Ralph holds ISOMBRIDGE of Earl Roger. Ulf held it. There are 2 hides paying geld. There is land for 4 ploughs. In demesne is 1 [plough] and 2 oxmen; and 4 villans and 3 bordars with 2 ploughs. There is a mill rendering 3 summae of corn. 1 knight there has half a hide of this land. It was and is worth 20s.

Ralph holds PEPLOW of Earl Roger. Ordgrim and Wulfric held it as 2 manors. There are 3 hides paying geld. There is land for 7 ploughs. In demesne is 1 plough and 2 slaves; and 5 villans with 3 ploughs. TRE it was worth 46s; now 12s4d. He found it waste.

RICHARD holds of the earl half a hide in BROCKTON [in Longford]. There is land for 1 plough. Aisil held it as 1 manor. There is 1 free man. It renders 16d.

IN HODNET HUNDRED

WILLIAM de Warenne holds WHITCHURCH of Earl Roger. Earl Harold held it. There are 7½ hides paying geld. In demesne are 4 ploughs and 2 slaves and 6 oxmen; and 23 villans and 9 bordars and 1 radman with 8 ploughs, and 14 ploughs more might be there. There is woodland for fattening 400 pigs, and there are 3 enclosures. TRE it was worth £8; now £10.

IN HODNET HUNDRED

WILLIAM Pantulf holds WOLVERLEY of Earl Roger. Wicga and Almær held it as 2 manors and were free man. There are 3 hides paying geld. There is land for 4 ploughs. There are 3 villans with 1 plough, and 1 radman. TRE it was worth 17s; now 8s. He found it waste.

The same William holds GREAT WYTHEFORD. Karli held it. There is half a hide paying geld. There is land for 2 ploughs. 1 villan and 1 bordar have 1 plough there. TRE it was worth 10s; and afterwards 8s; now 10s.

The same William holds HORTON [in Wem]. Ælfgifu held it and was a free woman. There are 2 hides paying geld. There is land for 4 ploughs. In demesne is half a plough and 2 slaves; and 3 bordars with half a plough. There is woodland for fattening 60 pigs. It was and is worth 10s.

The same William holds WEM. Wicga and Leofwine and Ælfgifu and Ælfgifu held it as 4 manors and were free. There are 4 hides paying geld. There is land for 8 ploughs. In demesne is 1 plough and 2 slaves; and 4 villans and 8 bordars with 1 plough. There is a hawk's eyrie, and woodland for fattening 100 pigs, and 1 enclosure. TRE it was worth 27s; now 40s. He found it waste.

The same William holds TYRLEY [Staffs.]. Wulfric and Hrafnsvartr held it as 2 manors and were free. There is 1 hide paying geld. There is land for 2 ploughs. There are 4 villans and 1 slave with 1 plough. It was worth 17s; now 20s.

The same William holds EDSTASTON. Ordwig and Ælfgifu held it and were free. There are 2 hides paying geld. There is land for 2 ploughs. 3 villans have 1 plough there. [There is] woodland for fattening 60 pigs. TRE it was worth 7s; now 20s. He found it waste.

The same William holds COTON [in Wem]. Wicga and Grimkel held it and were free man. There are 2 hides, as 2 manors, and they pay geld. There is land for 3 ploughs. 2 radmen with 1 villan have 1 plough there. TRE it was worth 20s; now 12s. There is woodland for fattening 60 pigs, and 1 enclosure.

The same William holds ALKINGTON. Almær held it and was a free man. There is 1 hide and 1 virgate paying geld. There is land for 5 ploughs. In demesne is half a plough and 1 slave; and 2 villans and 1 bordar with half a plough. [There is] woodland for fattening 100 pigs. TRE it was worth £4.3s; and afterwards the same; now 10s only.

The same William holds 1 Berewick, MARKET DRAYTON. Godwine held it and was a free man. There are 2 hides paying geld. There is land for 8 ploughs. In demesne is 1 [plough] and 2 oxmen; and a priest and 2 bordars with 1 plough. It was worth 20s; now 10s.

The same William holds HARCOURT [in Stanton upon Hine Heath]. Thorsten held it and was a free man. There is half a hide paying geld. There is land for 1½ ploughs. 1 radman has half a plough there. It was worth 8s; now 2s.

The same William holds ASTON [in Wem], and Walter [holds] of him. Wulfgeat and Almær held it as 2 manors and were free. There is 1 hide paying geld. There is land for 3 ploughs. In demesne is 1 plough and 1 slave and 1 oxman, and 2 bordars. [There is] woodland for fattening 40 pigs. It was worth 20s; now 10s.

IN CONDOVER HUNDRED

The same William holds BAYSTON [Baystonhill and Lower Bayston]. Eadric held it of the Bishop of Hereford and could not alienate it from him, because it was for his sustenance, and he had leased it to him only for his lifetime. There is 1 hide paying geld. There is land for 3 ploughs. In demesne is 1 [plough] and 4 slaves, and 2 bordars. It was worth 10s; now 25s.

The same William holds NORTON [in Condover]. Wulfric held it and was a free man. There is 1 hide paying geld. There is land for 2 ploughs. 3 villans with 1 bordar have 1 plough there. TRE it was worth 30s; and afterwards 9s; now 25s.

IN WROCKWARDINE HUNDRED

The same William holds HINSTOCK, and Sasfrid [holds] of him. Algar held it. There are 2½ hides paying geld. There is land for 5 ploughs. In demesne is 1 [plough] and 2 oxmen, and 1 bordar. [There is] 1 league of woodland. It was worth 40s; now 8s.

The same William holds CROSS HILLS, and Sasfrid [holds] of him. Godwine held it. There are 2 hides paying geld. There is land for 4 ploughs. There is 1 bordar having nothing. TRE it was worth 20s; and afterwards 40s; now 12d.

[Folio 257V: SHROPSHIRE]

The same William holds BESLOW. Godwine held it. There is half a hide paying geld. There is land for 2 ploughs. In demesne is half a plough and 1 slave, and 1 free man with 2 bordars. It was worth 11s; now 5s.

The same William holds BUTTERY. Thorkil held it. There is 1 hide paying geld. There is land for 2 ploughs. There are only 3 oxen. It was worth 6s; now 2s.

The same William holds EYTON UPON THE WEALD MOORS, and Warin [holds] of him. Wicga and Wulfgeat held it as 2 manors. There are 3 hides paying geld. In demesne are 2 ploughs and 4 oxmen; and 2 villans and 1 bordar with half a plough, and there might be 1½ ploughs more. TRE it was worth 33s; now 20s.

The same William holds BRATTON. Earngeat held it. There are 1½ hides paying geld. There is land for 4 ploughs. There are 5 bordars and they have nothing. TRE it was worth 24s; now it is almost waste. Warin holds it.

The same William holds HORTON [in Wellington], and Warin [holds] of him. Earngeat held it. There are 3 virgates of land paying geld. There is land for 1 plough. It is waste. There is half a league of woodland and 1 enclosure.

The same William holds LAWLEY. Earngeat held it. There is half a hide paying geld. There is land for 1 plough. It was and is waste.

IN "CULVESTAN" HUNDRED

The same William holds UPPER LEDWYCHE, and Berner [holds] of him. Wulfric held it. There are 2 hides paying geld. There is land for 4 ploughs. In demesne is 1 plough and 2 oxmen; and 2 villans and 4 bordars with 1 plough. TRE it was worth 13s4d; now 10s. He found it waste.

The same William holds MIDDLETON. [in Bitterley], and Berner [holds] of him. Wulfric held it and Edwin [also] as 2 manors. There are 2 hides paying geld. There is land for 8 ploughs. In demesne are 2 ploughs and 4 oxmen; and 1 villan and 8 bordars with 1 plough, and a mill rendering 2s. It was worth 20s; now 14s.

The same William holds LITTLE SUTTON. Ælfric held it. There is half a hide paying geld. There is land for 2 ploughs. In demesne is 1 [plough] with 2 oxmen, and 1 bordar. It was worth 3s; now 9s. He found it waste.

The same William holds 'MARSTON' [in Diddlebury].

Gamal and Wulfric held it. [...] There are 1½ hides paying geld. There is land for 3 ploughs. In demesne is 1 plough and 2 slaves, and 3 bordars. It was worth 15s; now 10s.

The same William holds SLEAP. Wulfric held it; he was a free man. There is half a hide paying geld. There is land for 1 plough. There is 1 free man with 1 plough. [There is] woodland for fattening 6 pigs. It was and is worth 5s.

The same William holds "SUDTELCH". Aski held it and was a free man. There is half a hide paying geld. There is land for 2 ploughs. It was worth 5s; now it renders 2s.

IN HODNET HUNDRED

WILLIAM Malbank holds GRAVENHUNGER of Earl Roger. Ælfric and Wulfgar held it as 2 manors and were free. There is 1 hide of land paying geld. There is land for 4 ploughs. 2 radmen have 1 plough there. There is 1 enclosure. TRE it was worth 13s; now 12s. He found it waste.

The same William holds WOORE. Leofwine and Eadric held it as 2 manors and were free. There is 1 hide paying geld. There is land for 3 ploughs. 2 radmen have 1 plough with 3 bordars there. [There is] woodland for fattening 60 pigs. TRE it was worth 23s; now 10s. He found it waste.

The same William holds DORRINGTON. Leofwine and Eadric held it as 2 manors and were free. There is 1 hide paying geld. There is land for 3 ploughs. There is 1 radman with 1 plough and 1 bordar. [There is] woodland for fattening 100 pigs. TRE it was worth 14s; now 8s. He found it waste.

The same William holds ONNELEY. Eadric held it. There is 1 virgate of land paying geld. TRE it was worth 5s; now it is waste.

IN BASCHURCH HUNDRED

WALKELIN holds GRINSHILL of Earl Roger. Leofgeat and Godric and Siward and Algar held it as 3 manors and were free. There are 2 hides paying geld. There is land for 2 ploughs. There are 3 free men and they pay 7s a year. This land was worth 32s TRE.

IN "ALNODESTREU" HUNDRED

The same Walkelin holds FAINTREE [Faintree and Lower Faintree]. Ulfkil, Arnketil, Wulfgeat, Alwig, Ordwig and Ordric held it as 6 manors,

The same William holds INGARDINE. Edwin held it and was a free man. There is 1 virgate of land paying geld. There is land for half a plough. In demesne is [half a plough] with 1 slave. It was and is worth 5s.

IN PATTON HUNDRED

William holds "BUCHEHALE". Almær held it. There is 1 virgate. There is land for half a plough. It was and is waste. and these thegns were free. There are 2 hides paying geld. There is land for 5 ploughs. In demesne are 1½ ploughs and 1 slave; and 2 villans and 5 bordars with 2 ploughs. TRE it was worth 27s; now 20s. He found it waste.

IN "ALNODESTREU" HUNDRED

OSBERN holds BADGER of Earl Roger, and Robert [holds] of him. Bruning held it and was a free man. There is half a hide paying geld. There is land for 2 ploughs. In demesne is 1 plough; and 4 bordars with 1 plough. [There is] woodland for fattening 30 pigs. It was worth 7s; now 10s.

The same Osbern holds BROCKTON [in Sutton Maddock]. The above Bruning held it. There is 1 virgate of land and 8 acres. There is land for 1 plough. [...] There is 1 bordar with 2 oxen. It was worth 8s; now 12d. He found it waste.

The same Osbern holds RYTON. Vithfari and Beorhtweald held it as 2 manors. There are 5 hides paying geld. There is land for 8 ploughs. In demesne are 2 ploughs and 3 slaves, with 3 bordars. There is a mill rendering 8 sesters of rye. TRE it was worth 30s; now 20s. He found it waste.

IN BASCHURCH HUNDRED

ODO holds HARDLEY of Earl Roger. Algar and Dunning held it as 2 manors and were free. There are 2 hides paying geld. There is land for 3 ploughs. There are 5 villans and 5 bordars with 2 ploughs. [There is] woodland for fattening 60 pigs. TRE it was waste; now it renders 15s.

The same Odo holds "UDEFORD" and RUYTON-XI-TOWNS. Leofnoth held it as 2 manors. There are 1½ hides paying geld. There is land for 4 ploughs. 4 villans and 2 bordars have 2 ploughs there. In demesne is 1 plough and 2 oxmen. [There is] woodland for fattening 40 pigs, and 5 fisheries rented by the villans. TRE it was waste; and afterwards it was worth 13s; now 20s.

The same Odo holds WYKEY. Earl Edwin held it. There are 7 hides with 3 Berewicks. There is land for 10 ploughs, and it pays geld. In demesne are 3 ploughs and 6 oxmen; and 4 bordars with 1 plough. There is a fishery rendering nothing, and woodland in which is 1 enclosure. It was waste; now it is worth 15s.

IN WROCKWARDINE HUNDRED

TUROLD holds LONGFORD of Earl Roger. Earl Edwin held it. There are 6 hides, with 4 Berewicks, and they pay geld. In demesne are 2 hides; and 8 villans have 3 ploughs there. 2 knights hold of him 4 hides and have 3 ploughs and 4 oxmen there, and 7 villans and 3 bordars and 1 radman with 3½ ploughs, and there might be 4 ploughs more. There is a mill. TRE the whole manor was worth £9; now 44s. He found it waste.

The same Turold holds CHETWYND. Countess Godgifu held it. There are 3 hides paying geld. There is land for 8 ploughs. In demesne are 3 [ploughs] and 6 oxmen; and 2 villans and 3 bordars with 1 plough. There is a priest, and a mill with 2 fisheries rendering 5s and 64 sticks of eels. There is a small wood. TRE it was worth 25s; now 50s. He found it waste.

The same Turold holds PULESTON. Earl Edwin held it. There is 1 hide paying geld. There is land for 4 ploughs. TRE it was worth 8s. He found it waste and it is [so now].

The same Turold holds SAMBROOK. Wulfgar held it. There are $1\frac{1}{2}$ hides [...]. There is land for 7 ploughs. 1 knight holds it of him and has 1 plough, and 5 bordars with 2 ploughs; and a mill rendering 64d. TRE it was worth 45s; now 16s. He found it waste.

The same Turold holds HOWLE, and Walter [holds] of him. Batsveinn held it. There are 2 hides paying geld. There is land for 5 ploughs. In demesne are 2 ploughs and 4 oxmen, and a mill rendering 64d. TRE it was worth 20s; now 16s. He found it waste.

[Folio 258: SHROPSHIRE]

The same Turold holds LAWLEY, and Hunning [holds] of him. There is 1 hide paying geld. There is land for 2 ploughs. In demesne is 1 [plough] and 4 slaves, and there is 1 villan. It was worth 12s; now 10s.

IN HODNET HUNDRED

The same Turold holds BEARSTONE. Wulfgar held it and was a free man. There is 1 hide paying geld. There is land for 5 ploughs. In demesne is 1 [plough] and 2 oxmen; and 3 bordars with 1 plough. There is a mill rendering 3s, [and] woodland for fattening 60 pigs. TRE it was worth 20s; now 10s. He found it waste.

The same Turold holds LITTLE DRAYTON. Countess Godgifu held it. There is 1 hide paying geld. There is land for 5 ploughs. In demesne is 1 [plough] with 2 oxmen and 1 villan. TRE it was worth 8s; now 6s8d. He found it waste.

IN BASCHURCH HUNDRED

Turold himself holds MORETON CORBET, and Hunning with his brother [hold] of him and they were free men. There is 1 hide paying geld. There is land for 2 ploughs. There are [2 ploughs] with 5 slaves and 1 bordar. It was worth 10s; now 16s. They themselves held it TRE.

The same Turold holds PRESTON BROCKHURST, and Hunning [holds] of him. Hunning himself and Wulfgeat held it and were free. There are $1\frac{1}{2}$ hides as 2 manors and they paid geld. There is land for 2 ploughs. In demesne is 1 [plough] and 2 slaves, and 3 villans. It was and is now worth 13s.

IN "ALNODESTREU" HUNDRED

The same Turold holds WILLEY, and Hunning [holds] of him. He himself held it and was free. There is half a hide paying geld. There is land for 2 ploughs. There are [2 ploughs], with 2 villans and 2 bordars. It was and is worth 5s.

IN CONDOVER HUNDRED

The same Turold holds PITCHFORD. Eadric and Leofric and Wulfric held it as 3 manors and were free. There are 3 hides paying geld. There is land for 5 ploughs. In demesne are 3 [ploughs] and 3 slaves and 3 oxmen; and 1 villan and 3 bordars and a smith and 1 radman with 2 ploughs. There is woodland for fattening 100 pigs. TRE it was worth 8s; and afterwards 16s; now 40s.

The same Turold holds WIGWIG. Almær held it and was a free man. There is 1 hide paying geld. There is land for 2 ploughs. There is [sic] [2 ploughs] in demesne and 4 slaves; and 2 villans and 1 bordar with half a plough. [There is] woodland for fattening 50 pigs. TRE it was worth 15s; and afterwards 3s; now 10s.

IN CONDOVER HUNDRED

PICOT holds BROMPTON of Earl Roger. Earnwig and Almaær held it as 2 manors and were free men. There are 3 hides paying geld. There is land for 6 ploughs. In demesne are $1\frac{1}{2}$ [ploughs] and 3 oxmen; and 7 villans and 2 bordars with $2\frac{1}{2}$ ploughs. TRE it was worth 25s; and afterwards 20s; now 40s.

IN "RINLAU" HUNDRED

The same Picot holds MYNDTOWN, and Leofric [holds] of him. He himself held it and was a free man. There are $1\frac{1}{2}$ hides paying geld. There is land for $3\frac{1}{2}$ ploughs. In demesne are $1\frac{1}{2}$ ploughs and 2 slaves; and 4 villans and 4 bordars with 2 ploughs. There is 1 enclosure. TRE it was worth 60s; now 30s.

The same Picot holds CLUNTON. Almund and Wulfric and Almund held it as 3 manors and were free. There are 4 hides paying geld. There is land for 12 ploughs. In demesne are 2 ploughs and 6 slaves; and 4 villans and 8 bordars and 1 radman with 2 ploughs. There were 5 enclosures. TRE it was worth £7.14s; and afterwards 5s; now 40s.

The same Picot holds CLUNBURY. Swein held it. This manor has never paid geld, nor has it been assessed in hides. TRE it was worth £4. There were 6 ploughs.

The same Picot holds KEMPTON. The same Swein held it. There are 4 hides paying geld. There is land in these 2 manors for 14 ploughs. In demesne are 4 [ploughs] and 13 slaves; and 8 villans and 2 bordars with 5 ploughs, and 2 Welshmen pay 14d. There is woodland for fattening 100 pigs, and there are 3 enclosures.

These 2 manors were worth TRE £8; and afterwards £3; now £6.

The same Picot holds HOPESAY. Eadric held it and was a free man. There are 7 hides paying geld. There is land for 14 ploughs. In demesne are 2 ploughs and 6 slaves; and 14 villans and a smith and a reeve with 6 ploughs. There are 2 enclosures. TRE it was worth £10; and afterwards £3; now £7.

The same Picot holds SIBDON CARWOOD. Swein held it and was a free man. There are 2 hides paying geld. There is land for 3 ploughs. In demesne is 1 [plough] and 4 slaves; and 2 radmen with 1 plough. There is woodland for fattening 100 pigs. TRE it was worth 20s; and now 30s.

The same Picot holds CLUN. Eadric held it and was a free man. There are 15 hides paying geld. There is land for 60 ploughs. In demesne are 2 [ploughs] and 5 slaves; and 10 villans and 4 bordars with 5 ploughs, and a mill serving the court, and 4 Welshmen pay 2s4d.

Walter holds of Picot 2 hides of this land, and a knight [named] Picot 3 hides and Gislold 2 hides. These men have 3 ploughs and 2 slaves and 2 oxmen; and 8 villans and 4 bordars and 2 Welshmen with 2 ploughs among them all. There 2 radmen render 2 beasts as rent. The whole manor TRE was worth £25; and afterwards £3; now what Picot has, £6.5s; what the knights [have], £4 less 5s.

The same Picot holds PURSLOW. Wulfric held it and was a free man. There is 1 hide paying geld. There is land for 2 ploughs. TRE it was worth 15s. It is waste.

The same Picot holds BARLOW. Wulfric held it. There is half a hide.

The same Picot holds OBLEY. Almund held it. There are 2 hides. These lands were and are waste.

The same Picot holds HOPTON CASTLE. Eadric held it and was a free man. There are 2 hides paying geld. There is land for 4 ploughs. TRE it was worth 40s; now it is waste.

The same Picot holds COSTON. Swein held it and was a free man. There is 1 hide paying geld. There is land for 3 ploughs. In demesne is 1 [plough]; and 2 villans and 1 bordar with 1 plough. TRE it was worth 20s; now the same.

The same Picot holds EDGTON. Swein held it and was a free man. There are 2 hides paying geld. There is land for 9 ploughs. In demesne are 2 [ploughs] and 6 slaves; and 5 villans and 1 bordar with 2 ploughs. TRE it was worth 60s; and afterwards 15s; now 30s.

| IN BASCHURCH HUNDRED |

The same Picot holds FITZ. Hunning held it and was a free man. There are 3 hides paying geld. There is land for 5 ploughs. In demesne are 2 ploughs and 9 slaves; and 4 villans and 1 radman and a smith with 2 ploughs among them all. TRE it was worth 40s; and afterwards 60s; now £6.

The same Picot holds MERRINGTON. Hunning held it. There are 2 hides paying geld. There is land for 5 ploughs. In demesne is 1 [plough] and 4 slaves; and 3 villans and 4 bordars and 1 radman with 2 ploughs among them all. There is woodland for fattening 24 pigs. TRE it was worth 15s; and afterwards as much; now 40s.

The same Picot holds WESTHOPE. Almund held it. [...] There are 2 hides paying geld. There is land for 4 ploughs. In demesne are 2 [ploughs] and 6 slaves; and 4 villans with 1 plough. TRE it was worth 15s; and afterwards 6s; now 25s.

IN LEINTWARDINE HUNDRED

The same Picot holds WOOLSTON [in Wistanstow], and 2 knights [hold] of him. Spirites the priest held it. There are 2 hides paying geld. There is land for 8 ploughs. There are 6 villans and a priest and 3 bordars and 1 radman with 4 ploughs. It is worth 20s.

The same Picot holds "CAURTUNE". The Church of St Alkmund held it in alms. There is half a hide paying geld. There is land for 1 plough. It was and is waste. TRE it was worth 3s. Picot holds it unjustly.

The same Picot holds of the earl 3 virgates of land in LEINTWARDINE [Herefs.], and Fulk [holds] of him. There is land for 2 ploughs. It renders 5s.

The same Picot holds "CHINBALDESCOTE". The Church of ST MARY of Bromfield held it. There are 5 hides paying geld with 1 Berewick. There is land for 7 ploughs. It was and is waste. There are 3 enclosures.

The same Picot holds MENUTTON. Eadric held it. There is 1 hide paying geld. There is land for 2 ploughs. It was and is waste. There is 1 enclosure.

The same Picot holds [?] LURKENHOPE. Eadric held it. There are 2 hides and 1 virgate paying geld. There is land for 6 ploughs. It was and is waste. There are 2 enclosures.

The same Picot holds CLUNGUNFORD. Gunnvarthr held it. There are 6 hides paying geld. There is land for 15 ploughs. In demesne are 3 [ploughs] and 8 slaves; and 8 villans and 4 bordars with 4 ploughs. There is a mill rendering 54d.

Fulk holds of Picot 1½ hides of this land, and has 2 ploughs in demesne and 4 oxmen; and 3 villans and 3 bordars with 3 ploughs, and a mill rendering 32d. The whole TRE was worth £12; and afterwards 30s; now £4 all together.

[Folio 258V: SHROPSHIRE]

The same Picot holds BEDSTONE, and Fulk [holds] of him. Wulfric held it. There are 2 hides paying geld. There is land for 4 ploughs. It was and is waste.

The same Picot holds ADLEY MOOR [Herefs.], and Bernard [holds] of him. There are 3 hides and 3 virgates paying geld. There is land for 8 ploughs. In demesne is 1 plough with 2 oxmen. It is worth 6s. There is 1 league of woodland. It was and is waste for a great part.

The same Picot holds SELLEY, and Fulk [holds] of him. Ulfkil held it. There is 1 virgate of land paying geld. There is land for 1 plough. There is [1 plough], with 2 bordars. It is worth 4s.

IN HODNET HUNDRED

HELGOT holds NORTON IN HALES of Earl Roger. Azur held it and was a free man. There are 3 hides paying geld. There is land for 6 ploughs. There is 1 radman with 1 plough, and 4 villans with 2 ploughs. [There is] woodland for fattening 200 pigs. TRE it was worth 30s; now 20s.

IN PATTON HUNDRED

The same Helgot holds CLEE ST MARGARET. Ælfric held it and was a free man. There is 1 hide paying geld. There is land for 4 ploughs. In demesne is 1 [plough] and 4 slaves; and 2 villans with 1 plough, and 2 bordars, and a mill serving the court. It was worth 8s; now 10s.

The same Helgot holds UPPER MILLICHOPE. Gamal held it and was free. There is 1 hide paying geld. There is land for 3 ploughs. In demesne is 1 [plough] and 4 slaves. It was worth 50s; now 15s.

The same Helgot holds [Great and Little] OXENBOLD. Eadric and Siward held it as 2 manors and were free. There is 1 hide paying geld. There is land for 4 ploughs. In demesne is half [a plough] and 1 oxman; and 1 villan and 1 bordar and 1 Frenchman with $1\frac{1}{2}$ ploughs. It was worth 11s; now 8s.

The same Helgot holds HOLDGATE. Ketil held it and was a free man. There are 2 hides paying geld. [There is] land for 3 ploughs. There is 1 radman with half a plough, and 1 slave and 1 bordar [...]. It was worth 8s; now 3s.

The same Helgot holds HOLDGATE. Genust and Alweard, Dunning and Ælfgifu [held it] as 4 manors and were free with their lands. There are 3 hides paying geld. There is land for 6 ploughs. There Helgot has a castle, and 2 ploughs in demesne and 4 slaves; and 3 villans and 3 bordars and 1 Frenchman with $3\frac{1}{2}$ ploughs. There is a church and a priest. TRE it was worth 18s; now 25s. He found it waste.

IN CONDOVER HUNDRED

The same Helgot holds CHURCH PREEN, and Richard [holds] of him. Edwin held it and was a free man. There are 3 hides paying geld. There is land for 3 ploughs. In demesne is 1 plough and 4 slaves. Godebold has 1 hide of this land, and has there 1 plough and 1 slave, and 1 villan and 1 bordar with 1 plough. [There is] woodland for 100 pigs. TRE it was worth 20s; now 10s. He found it waste.

The same Helgot holds HARLEY. Eadric, Wulfmær, Almund and Eadric held it as 4 manors and were free man. There are 4 hides paying geld. There is land for $4\frac{1}{2}$ ploughs. In demesne are $1\frac{1}{2}$ ploughs and 3 slaves, and 1 villan and 1 bordar. There is a mill [...], and woodland for fattening 100 pigs. TRE it was worth 21s; now 40s. He found it waste.

The same Helgot holds BELSWARDYNE. Almund held it and was a free man. There is half a hide paying geld. There is land for 2 ploughs. In demesne is half a plough and 1 slave; and 2 bordars with half a plough. It was worth 10s; now 4s.

IN BASCHURCH HUNDRED

The same Helgot holds FELTON BUTLER. Ælfric, Alweard and Alchen held it and were free men; [they held it] as 3 manors. There are 3 virgates of land paying geld. There is land for 5 ploughs. In demesne is 1 plough and 3 slaves; and 3 villans with 1 plough. Bernard holds it of Helgot. TRE it was worth 14s; now 15s.

IN "ALNODESTREU" HUNDRED

The same Helgot holds "BOSLE". Gethne held it and was a free man. There is 1 hide paying geld. There is land for 2 ploughs. In demesne is 1 [plough] and 4 slaves; and 4 bordars and 1 radman with 1 plough. TRE it was worth 16s1d; now 12s. He found it waste.

The same Helgot holds MEADOWLEY. Austin held it. There is half a hide paying geld. He was free. Richard holds it of Helgot. There is land for 6 ploughs. In demesne is 1 plough and 3 slaves; and 1 radman with half a plough, and 2 bordars. TRE it was worth 30s; now 11s; when received, 2s.

IN WROCKWARDINE HUNDRED

The same Helgot holds CHARLCOTTE. Alsige held it and was free. There is half a hide paying geld. There is land for 2 ploughs. It is and was waste. It was worth 10s.

The same Helgot holds UFFINGTON. Genust and Ælfgifu [...] held it as 2 manors and were free. There are 5 hides paying geld. There is land for 12 ploughs. In demesne are $1\frac{1}{2}$ ploughs and 3 slaves and 4 female slaves; and 3 villans and 2 bordars and 2 Frenchmen with 2 ploughs. There is half a league of woodland. TRE it was worth 30s; now the same.

IN "CULVESTAN" HUNDRED

The same Helgot holds GREAT SUTTON, and Herbert [holds] of him. Ælfric held it and was free. There are 2 hides paying geld. There is land for 5 ploughs. In demesne are 2 [ploughs] and 4 oxmen; and 4 villans and 1 bordar with 3 ploughs. There is a mill rendering 3s. TRE it was worth 20s; now 25s. He found it waste.

The same Helgot holds STEVENTON. Hrafnsvartr held it and was a free man. There is 1 hide paying geld. There is land for 4 ploughs. In demesne are 2 [ploughs] and 4 slaves and 2 female slaves; and 3 villans with 2 ploughs. TRE it was worth 12s; now 15s.

The same Helgot holds GREATER POSTON. Ælfric held it. There is 1 virgate of land paying geld. There is land for half a plough. It was and is waste.

The same Helgot holds BOULDON. Siward and Almund held it as 2 manors and were free. There are 2 hides paying geld. There is land for 3 ploughs. In demesne are 2 ploughs and 4 oxmen. It was worth 8s; now 15s. He found it waste.

IN LEINTWARDINE HUNDRED

The same Helgot holds ALCASTON. Eadric held it. There is 1 hide paying geld. There is land for 4 ploughs. In demesne is 1 [plough] and 2 slaves; and 5 villans with 1 plough. It was worth 20s; now 8s.

IN LEINTWARDINE HUNDRED

HUGH fitz Turgis holds CHELMICK of Earl Roger. Eadric held it with 1 Berewick. There are 4 hides paying geld. There is land for 6 ploughs. There 9 villans have 3 ploughs. TRE it was worth 12s; now 8s. It was waste.

IN CONDOVER HUNDRED

Hugh holds WILDERLEY of the earl. Ketil held it and was free. There are 2 hides paying geld. There is land for 4 ploughs. In demesne is 1 [plough] and 4 slaves; and 3 villans with 1 plough. There is woodland for fattening 100 pigs. TRE it was worth 30s; now 20s; when received, 10s.

IN "CULVESTAN" HUNDRED

The same Hugh holds HOPE BOWDLER. Eadric the Wild held it. There are 3 hides paying geld. There is land for 6 ploughs. In demesne are 2 [ploughs] and 4 slaves and 2 female slaves; and 2 villans with 1 plough. [There are] 2 leagues of woodland. TRRE [sic] it was worth 25s; now 15s.

IN WROCKWARDINE HUNDRED

GERARD holds KYNNERSLEY of Earl Roger. Vilgrip held it. There is 1 hide paying geld. There is land for 4 ploughs. In demesne is 1 plough and 3 slaves; and 4 villans and 3 bordars with 2 ploughs. TRE it was worth 21s; now 18s.

The same Gerard holds UPPINGTON. Godwine held it. There are 2 hides paying geld. There is land for 5 ploughs. In demesne are 3 ploughs and 6 oxmen; and 5 villans and 4 bordars with 2 ploughs. [There is] woodland 1 league long, and there is 1 enclosure. TRE it was worth 25s; now 31s. He found it waste.

The same Gerard holds SHAWBURY. Eadric and Algeat held it as 2 manors. There are 1½ hides paying geld. There is land for 8 ploughs. In demesne is 1 [plough] and 2 slaves. [There is] a church, and a priest and 3 bordars and 1 free man, and a mill rendering 5s. TRE it was worth 12s; now 16s.

The same Gerard holds CHERRINGTON. Wulfgeat held it. There are 3 hides paying geld. There is land for 6 ploughs. In demesne are 1½ [ploughs] and 3 oxmen; and 2 villans and 3 bordars with 1 plough. TRE it was worth 23s; now 22s. He found it waste.

The same Gerard holds 'CHATSALL' [in Stoke upon Tern]. Ledwi held it. There is 1 hide and 3 virgates paying geld. There is land for 5 ploughs. In demesne is 1 [plough] and 2 slaves; and 2 bordars and 1 radman with 1 plough. TRE it was worth 15s; now the same.

IN HODNET HUNDRED

The same Gerard holds SANDFORD. Wulfgeat held it and was free. There are 3 hides paying geld. There is land for 3 ploughs. In demesne are 1½ [ploughs] and 2 slaves; and 4 villans with 1 plough. There is woodland for fattening 30 pigs, and an enclosure. TRE it was worth 15s; now 10s. He found it waste.

The same Gerard holds ELLERDINE. Dodda held it and was a free man. There is 1 hide and the third part of another hide paying geld.

The same Gerard holds COLD HATTON. Godric held it and was free. There is half a hide and 2 parts of 1 virgate paying geld. There is land for 3 ploughs in these 2 manors. In demesne are 2 [ploughs] and 4 slaves and 2 oxmen; and 6 bordars with 1 plough. TRE it was worth 38s; now 20s. He found it waste.

[Folio 259: SHROPSHIRE]

The same Gerard holds BETTON [in Norton in Hales]. Ulfkil held it and was a free man. There are 3 hides paying geld. There is land for 6 ploughs. In demesne are 2 ploughs and 2 slaves and 2 oxmen; and 3 bordars with 1 plough. There is a mill, and woodland for fattening 60 pigs, and there are 2 enclosures. TRE it was worth 40s; now 30s.

The same Gerard holds LONGSLOW. Wulfgeat held it and was a free man. There are 3 hides paying geld. There is land

for 5 ploughs. In demesne is 1 plough and 2 slaves; and 1 man there pays 40d. TRE it was worth 10s; now 12s.

The same Gerard holds IGHTFIELD. Wulfgeat held it and was a free man. There are 2 hides paying geld. There is land for 4 ploughs. There is a priest and 2 bordars with 1 plough. There is woodland for fattening 60 pigs, and 2 enclosures. It was worth 15s; now 10s.

The same Gerard holds WOLLERTON. Eskil held it and was a free man. There is 1 hide paying geld. There is land for 4 ploughs. In demesne are 2 [ploughs] and 7 slaves; and 3 villans and 2 bordars and 1 radman with 1 plough. There is a mill rendering 10s, and woodland for fattening 80 pigs. TRE it was worth 15s; now 25s. He found it waste.

IN PATTON HUNDRED

The same Gerard holds RUTHALL, and Gerelm [holds] of him. Eskil held it and was a free man. There is half a hide paying geld. There is land for 2 ploughs. In demesne is half a plough and 2 oxmen; and 3 bordars with half a plough. TRE it was worth 6s; now 8s.

IN BASCHURCH HUNDRED

The same Gerard holds BESFORD, and Robert [holds] of him. Eskil and Dodda held it as 2 manors and were free men. There are 3 hides paying geld. There is land for 3 ploughs. In demesne is 1 [plough] and 3 slaves; and 3 villans and 2 widows with 1 plough. TRE it was worth 7s; and afterwards 5s; now 20s.

The same Gerard holds PRESTON BROCKHURST, and Robert [holds] of him. Beorhthun held it and was a free man. There is 1 virgate of land. There is land for half a plough. It was and is waste.

IN "ALNODESTREU" HUNDRED

The same Gerard holds SUTTON MADDOCK. Earl Morcar held it. There are 4 hides paying geld. There is land for 12 ploughs. In demesne are 2 ploughs and 6 slaves; and 12 villans and 4 bordars with 7 ploughs; and a certain knight has there 1 plough and 2 slaves. TRE it was worth 40s; now the same.

The same Gerard holds HATTON [in Shifnal], and William [holds] of him. Thorgot held it and was a free man. There is half a hide paying geld. There is land for 3 ploughs. In demesne is 1 [plough] and 1 slave, and 4 bordars, and 1 settler pays 2s. TRE it was worth 12s; now 11s. He found it waste.

The same Gerard holds STOCKTON, and Hugh [holds] of him. Edwin and Ordwig held it as 2 manors and were free men. There is 1 hide paying geld. There is land for 3 ploughs. In demesne is half a plough and 1 slave; and 1 villan and 1 bordar with half a plough. TRE it was worth 12s; now 4s.

IN HODNET HUNDRED

NIGEL holds ADDERLEY of Earl Roger. Eadric held it and was a free man. There are 3 hides paying geld. There is land for 6½ ploughs. In demesne is 1 [plough] and 2 oxmen; and 4 villans with 1 plough. There are 2 enclosures. It was and is worth 15s.

The same Nigel holds SHAVINGTON. Dodda held it and was free. There is half a hide paying geld. There is land for 4 ploughs. In demesne is half [a plough] and 2 slaves; and 3 bordars with half a plough. It was worth 12s; now 15s. He found it waste.

The same Nigel holds SPOONLEY. Dunning held it and was free. There is 1 hide paying geld. There is land for 2 ploughs. It was and is waste. TRE it was worth 20s.

The same Nigel holds CALVERHALL. Eadmær and Alwig held it as 2 manors and were free with these lands. There is 1 hide and 3 virgates. There is land for 6 ploughs. This land pays geld. In demesne is 1 [plough] and 2 oxmen; and 4 villans with 1 plough. [There is] woodland for fattening 20 pigs. TRE it was worth 18s; now 20s and it renders 1 hawk.

IN CONDOVER HUNDRED

NORMAN holds CANTLOP of Earl Roger. Eadric held it and was a free man. There is 1 hide paying geld. There is land for 4 ploughs. In demesne are 2 [ploughs] and 6 slaves; and 4 villans with 1 plough. There is a mill rendering 10s. TRE it was worth 20s; and afterwards £4.10s; now 110s.

The same Norman holds LEE BROCKHURST. Wulfgeat and Wihtric and Ælfheah held it as 3 manors and were free. There is 1 hide paying geld. There is land for 2 ploughs. These [ploughs] are in demesne with 4 oxmen, and 1 bordar. There is a mill rendering 6s. TRE it was worth 13s; now £3. He found it waste.

IN BASCHURCH HUNDRED

The same Norman holds COLEMERE. Ealdgyth held it. There are 2 hides paying geld. There is land for 4½ ploughs. In demesne is 1 [plough]; and 2 villans and 2 bordars with half a plough, and 4 settlers there pay 40d. TRE it was worth 10s; now 30s. He found it waste.

The same Norman holds "ESTONE", and Fulcher [holds] of him. Alnoth held it. There are 2½ hides paying geld. There is land for 7 ploughs. It was waste; now it is at farm for 36s.

In "CHENELTONE" is 1 hide which TRE was and [still] is waste.

IN "ALNODESTREU" HUNDRED

The same Norman holds ALBRIGHTON [in Shifnal]. Algar and Godgyth held it as 2 manors. There are 1½ hides paying geld. There is land for 4 ploughs. In demesne are 3 [ploughs] and 13 slaves; and 3 villans and 3 bordars with 1 plough. There is woodland for fattening 100 pigs. But now it is in the king's hand. TRE it was worth 21s; now 16s. He found it waste.

The same Norman holds BISHTON. Thorgot held it and was a free man. There is 1 hide paying geld. There is land for 6 ploughs. There 2 Frenchmen with 4 villans and 2 bordars have 3 ploughs. There is woodland for fattening 10 pigs. TRE it was worth 30s; now 10s.

IN BASCHURCH HUNDRED

ROGER the huntsman holds 'SLACKBURY' of Earl Roger. Ælfgeat held it. There is 1 hide paying geld. TRE it was worth 5s; now it is waste.

In that HUNDRED lies BROOM [in Ellesmere] at 1 hide, and it belongs to Welshampton, Albert's vill. The earl's men are litigating about this.

IN CONDOVER HUNDRED

The same Roger holds WRENTNALL. Earnwig and Ketil held it as 2 manors. There are 2 hides. There is land for 5 ploughs. [...] In demesne are 3 ploughs and 5 slaves; and 3 villans and 1 radman with 1 plough. There is woodland for fattening 100 pigs, and 1 enclosure. TRE it was worth 60s; now 30s; when received, it was worth 5s.

Of this land the Church of ST CHAD claims 1½ hides, and the shire has decided that they belonged to the church before King Edward [sic], but they do not know how they were lost.

The same Roger holds [Castle and Church] PUL-;VERBATCH. Hunning and Wulfgeat held it as 3 manors. There are 2 hides paying geld. There is land for 5 ploughs. In demesne are 2 [ploughs] and 4 slaves, and 7 villans with 5 ploughs. There is woodland for fattening 100 pigs. There are 2 radmen. TRE it was worth £6; now 30s; when received, it was worth 20s.

IN PATTON HUNDRED

The same Roger holds BECKBURY. Azur held it and was a free man. There is 1 hide paying geld. There is land for 2 ploughs. 1 knight there pays 20d. TRE it was worth 12s.

The same Roger holds MOSTON. Dodda and Wulfgar held it as 2 manors and were free. There are 2 hides paying geld. There is land for 4 ploughs. 1 radman has 1 plough with 2 villans there. TRE it was worth 40s; now 15s. He found it waste.

RALPH the cook and Toki hold of Earl Roger [?] COTTON [in Stoke upon Tern]. Dunning and Sæwine held it and were free. There are 2 hides paying geld. There is land for 3 ploughs. In demesne are 1½ ploughs and 2 oxmen and 5 slaves, and 1 bordar. TRE it was worth 8s; now 16s. It was partly waste.

IN WROCKWARDINE HUNDRED

FULCO holds WITHINGTON of Earl Roger. Wulfwine and Wulfric held it as 2 manors. There are 2½ hides [...]. There is land for 4 ploughs. In demesne are 2 ploughs and 4 slaves and 1 female slave; and 3 villans and 1 bordar with 1½ ploughs. TRE it was worth 15s; now 21s. [He found it] waste.

The same Fulco holds LITTLE WYTHEFORD. Godric held it. There is half a hide [...]. There is land for 2 ploughs. There is 1 plough, and it renders 3s as farm. TRE it was worth 8s.

IN "MERSET" HUNDRED

ERNUCION holds KINNERLEY of the earl. Dunning and Algar held it as 2 manors. There is 1 hide paying geld. There is land for 2 ploughs. 1 Welshman there renders 1 hawk as farm, and there is half a league of woodland.

IN WROCKWARDINE HUNDRED

Roger the huntsman holds HAUGHTON. Eadwig held it. There is 1 hide paying geld. There is land for 2 ploughs. There is 1 man rendering 6s as farm.

IN CONDOVER HUNDRED

THEODULF holds of earl 'HAWKSLEY' [in Langley]. Alric held it and was a free man. There is half a hide paying geld. It was and is waste. There is woodland for fattening 40 pigs. This manor is at farm for 6d.

The same Theodulf holds PULLEY. Edith held it. There are 3 virgates of land paying geld. There is land for 1 plough. This [plough] is there, with 1 slave and 2 bordars. It was and is worth 6s.

[Folio 259V: SHROPSHIRE]

IN WITTERY HUNDRED

GODEBOLD holds THE LACK of the earl. Leofric held it. There are 1½ virgates of land paying geld. It was waste; now it renders 16d.

IN CONDOVER HUNDRED

AVENEL holds COTHERCOTT of the earl. Hunning held it. There is half a hide. There is land for 1 plough. This [plough] is there with 2 slaves. It was waste; now it is worth 3s.

ALWEARD holds STAPLETON of the earl. Alric held it. There is 1 hide and half a virgate. There is land for 2½ ploughs. In demesne is half a plough; and 1 radman and 1 villan with 1 plough. It was worth 3s; now 4[s].

TORET holds LANGLEY of the earl. Swein held it and was free. There is half a hide paying geld. There is land for 1 plough. This [plough] is there with 4 slaves. It was and is worth 5s.

SIWARD holds FRODESLEY of the earl. He himself held it and was free. There is 1 hide paying geld. There is land for 4 ploughs. 3 villans and 3 bordars have 1 plough there. There is woodland for fattening 100 pigs, and there are 3 enclosures. It was worth 10s; now 8s.

AUTI holds of the earl 'LYDLEY HAYES' [in Cardington]. He himself held it and was a free man. There is 1 hide paying geld. There is land for 2 ploughs. There are [2 ploughs], with 2 radmen. There is woodland for fattening 30 pigs. It was worth 10s; now 8s.

The same Auti holds LEEBOTWOOD. He himself held it and was a free man. There is half a hide paying geld. There is land for 1 plough. This [plough] is there, with 2 radmen. It was and is worth 5s.

SIWARD holds OVERS of the earl. He himself held it. There is half a hide paying geld. There are 2 villans with half a plough. It was and is worth 3s.

EDMUND holds SMETHCOTE of the earl, and Ealdræd [holds] of him. He himself held it. There is 1 hide paying geld. There is land for 3 ploughs. There are 2 radmen and 1 bordar with 1 plough. [There is] woodland for fattening 50 pigs. It was worth 4s; now 4s.

IN "REWESET" HUNDRED

ALRIC holds EYTON [in Alberbury] of the earl. Siward and Wulfric held it as 2 manors. There are 3 virgates of waste land.

ALMUND and ALWEARD his son hold 'AMASTON' [in Cardeston] of the earl. [Almund] himself held it and was free. There are 2 hides paying geld. There is land for 3½ ploughs. 4 villans and 3 bordars have 1½ ploughs there. It was worth 10s; now 7s.

The same son of Almund holds ROWTON [in Alberbury]. Before him, 4 thegns held it as 4 manors and they were free. There are 2 hides paying geld. There is land for 4 ploughs. There are 2 radmen. TRE it was worth 9s; now 3s. They were waste and are still nearly so.

The same man holds POLMERE, and Ordmær [holds] of him. Leodmær and Almær held it and were free men. There is half a hide as 2 manors, and it pays geld. There is land for 1½ ploughs. In demesne is half a plough, with 1 slave and 1 bordar. It was worth 4s; now 2s.

The same man holds BENTHALL. Almær held it and was a free man. There is 1 hide paying geld. There is land for 3 ploughs. There is 1 radman and 2 villans and 2 bordars with 1 plough. It was worth 13s8d; now 5s.

IN WITTERY HUNDRED

The same man holds WOTHERTON. Almund held it and was a free man. There are 3 hides paying geld. There is land for 14 ploughs. In demesne is half a plough; and 6 villans and 1 bordar and a priest and 4 radmen with 12 ploughs. There is a mill rendering 24 measures of wheat. TRE it was worth £4; and now the same.

ERTEIN holds MIDDLETON [in Chirbury] of the earl. He himself held it [and] was a free man. There are 3 virgates of land paying geld. There is land for 1 plough. There is [1 plough] in demesne with 2 slaves. It was worth 9s; now 12s.

ALWEARD holds [?] 'MUNTON' [in Worthen]. Godric held it and was a free man. There is 1 virgate of land paying geld. There is land for 1 plough. There is [1 plough] in demesne with 2 slaves. It was and is worth 5s.

ALWEARD holds RHISTON. Siward held it and was a free man. There are 3 hides paying geld. There is land for 4 ploughs. 1 radman has 1 plough with 3 slaves there, and [there are] 2 villans with 1 plough. [There is] woodland for fattening 30 pigs. It was worth 10s; now 12s.

ALWEARD holds CHURCH STOKE [Wales]. Siward

held it and was free. There are 5 hides paying geld. There is land for 7 ploughs. 1 Welshman has 1 plough there. There is woodland for fattening 100 pigs. It was worth 10s; now 64d.

IN HODNET HUNDRED

EDITH holds ROWTON [in Ercall Magna] of the earl. Morcar and Dot held it as 2 manors and were free. There are 2 hides paying geld. There is land for 4 ploughs. In demesne is 1 [plough] and 3 slaves; and a priest and 4 bordars with 1 plough. It was worth 25s; now 15s.

IN BASCHURCH HUNDRED

ANSKETIL holds LEATON of the earl. Hunning held it and was a free man. There is 1 hide paying geld. There is land for 2 ploughs. In demesne is 1 [plough], and there are 2 settlers paying 4s8d. It was worth 8s; now 10s.

EALDWINE holds 'YAGDONS' [in St Alkmond, Shrewsbury] of the earl. He himself held it and was a free man. There is half a hide paying geld. There is land for 1 plough. There is [1 plough], with 2 bordars. It was and is worth 5s.

IN WROCKWARDINE HUNDRED

WULFGEAT holds POYNTON and "TUNESTAN" of the earl. He himself held them as 2 manors. There are 1½ hides [...]. There is land for 3 ploughs. In demesne is 1 [plough] and 2 slaves. It was worth 11s; now 12s.

RICHARD holds BROCKTON [in Longford] of the earl. Aisil held it. There is half a hide paying geld. There is land for 1 plough. There 1 free man pays 16d as farm.

IN "MERSET" HUNDRED

MADOC holds HALSTON and

"BURTONE" of the earl. Siward held them. There are 2 hides paying geld. There is land for 4 ploughs. It is waste.

IN LEINTWARDINE HUNDRED

SIWARD holds CHENEY LONGVILLE of the earl. He himself held it. There are 1½ hides paying geld. There is land for 7 ploughs. There 1 villan and 3 bordars have 2 ploughs. It was worth 20s; and afterwards was waste; now it is worth 5s.

EALDRÆD holds ACTON SCOTT of the earl. Eadric held it. There are 3 hides paying geld. There is land for 4 ploughs. 2 villans and 2 radmen have 3 ploughs there. There is 1 enclosure. It was worth 10s; now 15s.

IN "MERSET" HUNDRED

IWARD holds "NEWETONE" of the earl. Thorgot held it. There is half a hide paying geld. There is land for 2 ploughs. 2 villans and 2 bordars have half a plough there. It was worth 7s; now 5s.

IN 'CONDITRE' HUNDRED

EALHHERE holds [Lower and Upper] HARCOURT [in Stottesdon] of the earl. Alweard held it, and was a free man. There is 1 hide paying geld. There is land for 5 ploughs. In

demesne is 1 plough and 3 slaves; and 6 bordars with 4 ploughs. It was worth 7s; and afterwards 5s; now 12s.

IN CONDOVER HUNDRED

EARL Roger holds BROOME [in Cardington]. Thorsten and Austin held it. There is half a hide paying geld. There is land for 2 ploughs. Of this land Reginald has half a virgate of land.

The earl himself holds NETLEY. Almær held it and was a free man. There is 1 hide paying geld. There is land for 2 ploughs. It is and was waste. It was worth 12s.

IN BASCHURCH HUNDRED

The earl himself holds FENEMERE. Siward held it and was a free man. There is half a hide paying geld. There is land for 1 plough. It was and is waste.

In LEINTWARDINE hundred Earl Leofric had 2 manors, MINTON and WHITTINGSLOW. There are 4 hides paying geld. These 2 manors belong to the farm of Earl Roger at Church Stretton.

IN 'CONDITRE' Hundred Widard has 1 manor, FARLOW, at 1 hide and 3 virgates of land. It belongs to LEOMINSTER [Herefs.], the king's manor in Herefordshire, and is valued there. He holds of the king.

IN "MERSET" HUNDRED

Earl Roger holds "WLFERESFORDE". King Edward held it. There are 2 hides [...]. There is land for 6 ploughs. It was and is waste. There is a little wood.

[Folio 260: SHROPSHIRE]

V. The land of Osbern fitzRichard

IN 'OVERS' HUNDRED

OSBERN fitzRichard holds BURFORD of the king. His father Richard held it. There are 6½ hides paying geld. There is land for 29 ploughs. Osbern has there 2 mills rendering 12 summae of corn, and there are 6 slaves and 12 villans and 3 radmen and 24 bordars and 7 coliberts, and a church with 2 priests. Among them all they have 23 ploughs. There is woodland for fattening 100 pigs, and there is 1 enclosure. TRE it was worth 100s; now £4.

The same Osbern holds TETSTILL. Saelig;weard held it and was a free man. There is 1 hide paying geld. There is land for 3½ ploughs. In demesne is 1 plough and 3 slaves; and 3 bordars with half a plough. [There is] woodland for fattening 40 pigs. TRE it was worth 6s; now 10s.

IN "CULVESTAN" HUNDRED

The same Osbern holds ASHFORD CARBONEL. Ledhe held it. There are 2 hides paying geld. There is land for 4 ploughs. 1 Frenchman and 4 villans have 2 ploughs there. There is a mill rendering 3 summae of corn. TRE it was worth 16s; now 8s. He found it waste.

IN LEINTWARDINE HUNDRED

The same Osbern holds "HUMET". He himself held it of King Edward. There are 5 hides paying geld. There is land for 20 ploughs. 2 knights have 1 plough there in demesne; and [there are] 5 villans and 5 bordars and 1 radman with 3 ploughs. This land was and is waste, excepting the demesne, which is worth 10s.

The same Osbern holds STANAGE [Wales]. There are 6 hides. There is land for 15 ploughs. It was and is waste. There are 3 enclosures.

The same Osbern holds and held CASCOB [Wales]. There is half a hide. There is land for 2 ploughs. It was and is waste. There is woodland and 1 enclosure.

The same Osbern holds ACKHILL [Wales]. Eadric held it. There are 3 hides. There is land for 6 ploughs. It was and is waste. There is half a league of woodland.

IN 'CONDITRE' HUNDRED

The same Osbern holds NEEN SOLLARS, and Siward [holds] of him. Siward himself held it, and was a free man. This manor has never been assessed in hides, nor has it paid geld. There is land for 5 ploughs. In demesne is 1 [plough] and 10 slaves; and a mill rendering a measure of wheat. TRE it was worth 40s; now 18s.

IN 'OVERS' HUNDRED

To this manor pertains 1 Berewick, MILSON. There are 3½ hides paying geld. There is land for 6 ploughs. 3 radmen and 3 villans have 3 ploughs there. TRE it was worth 14s; now 10s. He found it waste.

VI. The land of Ralph de Mortimer

IN 'OVERS' HUNDRED

RALPH de Mortimer holds CORELEY of the king. Siward held it as 2 manors and was a free man. There are 2 hides paying geld. There is land for 4 ploughs. In demesne is 1 [plough] and 4 slaves; and 1 villan and 2 bordars and 1 radman with half a plough. TRE it was worth 48s; now 10s; when received, 3s.

IN 'CONDITRE' HUNDRED

The same Ralph holds CLEOBURY MORTIMER. Edith held it. There are 4 hides paying geld. There is land for 24 ploughs. In demesne are 4 ploughs and 14 slaves; and 20 villans and a priest and 2 radmen and 8 bordars. Among them all they have 20 ploughs. There is a mill rendering 2 summae of corn. Woodland for fattening 500 pigs renders 40s. TRE it was worth £8; and afterwards the same; now £12.

The same Ralph holds MAWLEY at 1 hide and "LEL" at 1 virgate and "FECH" at 1 virgate of land. These were 3 manors and paid geld. 3 thegns held them, and were free men. When Turstin of Wigmore received them from Earl William he linked them to the above manor of Cleobury Mortimer and then as now, they were valued with it.

And in 'OVERS' HUNDRED there is 1 hide, EARLSDITION, which is also valued with it.

IN 'CONDITRE' HUNDRED

The same Ralph holds LOWE [in Farlow], and Richard [holds] of him. The Church of ST PETER held it. There is 1 hide paying geld. There is land for 2 ploughs. In demesne is 1 plough; and 2 villans and 1 bordar with 1 plough. It was worth 5s; now 10s. He found it waste.

The same Ralph holds NEEN SAVAGE, and Richard [holds] of him. Wulfric held it and was a free man. There are 1½ hides paying geld. There is land for 3½ ploughs. There is 1 slave and 1 villan with half a plough. TRE it was worth 15s; and afterwards 3s; now the same, 3s.

The same Ralph holds NEEN SAVAGE, and Ingelrann [holds] of him. Hunning held it and was free. There are 4 hides paying geld. There is land for 5 ploughs. In demesne is 1 plough and 4 slaves; and 3 villans and 3 bordars with 1 plough. There is a mill rendering 2s.

The same Ralph holds STEPPLE [Stepple and Little Stepple], and Geoffrey [holds] of him. Godric held it and was free. There are 1½ hides paying geld. There is land for 4 ploughs. In demesne is 1 plough and 3 slaves; and 6 bordars with 1 plough. TRE it was worth 12s; and afterwards, as now, 7s.

The same Ralph holds KINLET, and Richard [holds] of him. Edith held it. There are 4 hides. [...] There is land for 8 ploughs. In demesne are 2 [ploughs] and 6 slaves; and 8 villans and 2 radmen and 6 bordars and 1 Frenchman with 6 ploughs. TRE it was worth 60s; and afterwards 30s; now 40s.

IN "CULVESTAN" HUNDRED

The same Ralph holds SHEET, and Ingelrann [holds] of him. Leofnoth held it with 1 Berewick. There are 2 hides paying geld. There is land for 4 ploughs. In demesne are 2 ploughs and 4 oxmen; and 2 villans with half a plough. TRE it was worth 5s; and afterwards 2s; now 10s.

IN LEINTWARDINE HUNDRED

The same Ralph holds LEINTWARDINE [Herefs.]. King Edward held it. There are 4 hides and 1 virgate. There is land for 14 ploughs. In demesne are 3 ploughs and 6 oxmen; and 10 villans and 8 bordars and a reeve and 2 radmen with a priest. Among them all they have 8 ploughs. There is a church, and a mill rendering 6s8d and 6 sticks of eels.

Of this land 1 knight holds 1½ hides, and has there 1 plough and 5 slaves; and 5 villans and 3 bordars with 2 ploughs. 2 men there pay 4s for leasing the land. There is 1 league of woodland. TRE it was worth 40s; and afterwards 30s; now £4.

The same Ralph holds 'STANWAY' [in Leintwardine, Herefs.]. Almær held it. There is 1 hide paying geld. There is land for 3 ploughs. In demesne are 2 [ploughs] and 6 slaves; and a reeve with half a plough. It was worth 10s; now 12s.

The same Ralph holds ADFORTON [Herefs.]. Eadric held it. There are 3 hides paying geld. There is land for 6 ploughs. There are 5 villans and 6 bordars and 1 radman with 4 ploughs among them all. It was worth 8s; now 5s.

The same Ralph holds LINGEN [Herefs.], and Turstin [holds] of him. Gunnfrothr and Eadric held it as 2 manors. There are 1½ hides paying geld. There is land for 7 ploughs. In demesne is 1 [plough] and 2 oxmen; and 1 villan and 4 bordars with 2 ploughs. There is half a league of woodland, and 3 enclosures for taking roe-deer. TRE it was waste; and afterwards was worth 6s; now 10s.

The same Ralph holds SHIRLEY [Herefs.], and Turstin [holds] of him. There is half a hide. Almær held it. There is land for 1 plough. There is [1 plough] with 2 slaves and 1 bordar. It was waste; now it is worth 2s.

The same Ralph holds UPPER LYE [Herefs.], and 1 knight [holds] of him. Almær held it. There is 1 hide. There is land for 2 ploughs. In demesne is 1 [plough] and 2 oxmen; and 3 bordars with 1 plough. There are 2 enclosures. TRE it was worth 5s; now 7s. He found it waste.

The same Ralph holds 'TUMBERLAND' [in Leintwardine, Herefs.]. Ealdræd held it. There are 1½ hides. There is land for 5 ploughs. It was and is waste.

The same Ralph holds LETTON [Herefs.], and Ingelrann [holds] of him. Siward held it. There are 1½ hides. There is land for 6 ploughs. 6 villans with 1 knight have 3 ploughs there. It was waste; and afterwards was worth 5s; now 10s.

The same Ralph holds WALFORD [Herefs.], and ST MARY of Wigmore [holds] of him. Alsige held it. There is half a hide. There is land for 2 ploughs. In demesne is 1 [plough] with 2 oxmen. It was worth 12s; now 8s. He found it waste.

[Folio 260V: SHROPSHIRE]

The same Ralph holds WALFORD [Herefs.], and Ingelrann [holds] of him. Wulfweard and Blær and Dunning held it as 3 manors. There are 2½ hides. There is land for 5 ploughs. In demesne are 2 [ploughs] and 4 oxmen; and 3 villans with 1 plough. TRE it was worth 11s; and afterwards 12s; now 15s.

The same Ralph holds BUCKTON [Herefs.], and Oidelard [holds] of him. Saxi held it. There are 5 hides. There is land for 10 ploughs. In demesne are 2 [ploughs] and 4 oxmen; and 2 villans and 1 bordar with half a plough. There is a mill rendering 8s. TRE it was worth 30s; and afterwards 20s; now 21s.

The same Ralph holds LLANVAIR WATERDINE. Eadwig held it. There are 5 hides. There is land for 12 ploughs. It was and is waste.

The same Ralph holds BRAMPTON BRYAN [Herefs.], and Richard [holds] of him. Gunnvarthr held it. There are 2½ hides. There is land for 6½ ploughs. In demesne are 1½ [ploughs] and 3 oxmen, and 1 villan and 3 bordars. There is half a league of woodland. TRE it was waste; and afterwards it was worth 5s; now 10s.

The same Ralph holds PEDWARDINE [Herefs.], and Richard [holds] of him. Alric held it. There are 3 virgates of land. There is land for 2 ploughs. In demesne is 1 [plough] and 2 oxmen, and 1 bordar. It is worth 3s; it was waste.

The same Ralph holds PEDWARDINE [Herefs.], and Richard [holds] of him. Earngeat held it. There is 1 hide. There is land for 2 ploughs. In demesne is 1 [plough] and 2 oxmen, and 1 bordar. TRE and afterwards, as now, worth 10s.

The same Ralph holds PEDWARDINE [Herefs.], and Richard [holds] of him. Arngrim held it. There are 3 virgates. There is land for 2 ploughs. There are 2 villans with half a plough. TRE it was waste; and afterwards, as now, worth 5s.

The same Ralph holds ADLEY MOOR [Herefs.], and Helgot [holds] of him. Hrafnsvartr held it. There is half a hide. There is land for 2 ploughs. It was and is waste.

The same Ralph holds BUCKNELL, and Helgot [holds] of him. There are 2 hides. There is land for 6 ploughs. It was and is waste. There is 1 league of woodland. Alwig held it.

IN CONDOVER HUNDRED

The same Ralph holds PULLEY. Edith held it. There is 1 hide and 1 virgate paying geld. There is land for 5 ploughs. There are 3 radmen and 4 villans and 5 bordars with 7 ploughs. TRE it was worth 30s; and afterwards, as now, 40s.

The same Ralph holds [Lower and Upper] EDGEBOLD. Edith held it. There is 1 hide paying geld. There is land for 2 ploughs. There is 1 free man, who pays 8s as farm. [There is] woodland for fattening 20 pigs. TRE it was worth 40s; and afterwards it was waste.

IN SHREWSBURY HUNDRED

The same Ralph holds MEOLE BRACE. Edith held it. There are 3 hides paying geld. In demesne are 3 ploughs and 6 slaves and 4 female slaves; and 6 villans and 3 bordars with 3 ploughs, and 1 radman with half a plough. To this manor pertain 9 burgesses in the city, and [there is] a mill rendering 20s. TRE, and afterwards, it was worth £7; now £13.5s6d.

The same Ralph holds SHEINTON, and Helgot [holds] of him. Azur and Algar and Sæwulf held it as 3 manors. There are 2 hides paying geld. There is woodland for 100 pigs, and a mill [rendering] 10s. The whole is worth 20s.

The same Ralph holds half a virgate of land in ADLEY MOOR [Herefs.]. It is waste.

VII. The land of Roger de Lacy

IN BASCHURCH HUNDRED

ROGER de Lacy holds of the king CLEOBURY NORTH, and Wulfweard [holds] of him. Siward held it and was a free man. There are 2½ hides paying geld. There is land for 4 ploughs. In demesne is 1 [plough] and 1 slave; and 4 villans and 4 bordars with 3 ploughs. There is a mill rendering 4s. TRE it was worth 12s; and afterwards 7s; now 20s.

IN 'CONDITRE' HUNDRED

The same Roger holds HOPTON WAFERS, and Widard [holds] of him. Siward, a free man, held it. There are 3 hides paying geld. There is land for 4 ploughs. In demesne is 1 plough and 1 slave; and 1 radman and 2 villans and 3 bordars with 1 plough. TRE it was worth 10s; and afterwards 12s; now 9s2d.

IN "CULVESTAN" HUNDRED

The same Roger holds STANTON LACY. Siward held it and was a free man. There are 20½ hides paying geld. There is land for 50 ploughs. In demesne are 10 ploughs and 28 slaves and female slaves together; and 67 villans and 2 smiths and 5 bordars and 4 cotsets. Among them all they have 23 ploughs. There is a church having 1½ hides, and 2 priests with 2 villans have 3 ploughs. There are 2 mills rendering 26s. ST PETER of Hereford has 1 villan there.

Of this land of this manor Richard holds 1½ hides, Azelin 1½ hides,

The same Roger holds [?] EARLSDITTON, and it pertains to Cleobury [? North]. There is 1 hide, and it is valued there. Roger 1½ hides. These men have in demesne 6 ploughs and 6 slaves; and 2 half-villans and 5 bordars and 2 cotsets with 1 plough, and a mill rendering 10s.

Of the same manor 4 sergeants have land for 3 ploughs and 1 ferding and 10 acres of land; and they themselves have 4 ploughs. There are 3 radknights having land for 2½ ploughs, and there they have as many ploughs, and 1 man, Auti, holds 1 member of this manor, in which are 3 hides, and he has there 1 plough with a half-villan. TRE the whole manor was worth £24; now £25.

The same Roger holds STOKESAY. Ealdræd held it and was a free man. There are 7 hides paying geld. There is land for 14 ploughs. In demesne were 5 ploughs and 16 slaves and female slaves together; and 20 villans with 8 ploughs, and 9 female cottars. There is a mill rendering 9 summae of wheat, and there is a miller and a bee-keeper. TRE it was worth £10.

The same Roger holds ALDON. Siward held it and was a free man. There are 2½ hides paying geld. There is land for 15 ploughs. [...] In demesne are 2 ploughs and 8 slaves and female slaves together; and 24 villans and 2 bordars and 1

cotset with 8 ploughs among them all. There is a mill rendering 5s.

Of the land of this manor Richard holds 1 hide and Ealdræd a member of the land. There is 1 plough, and 12 villans and 7 bordars and 3 slaves with 3 ploughs.

The church has half a hide, and a priest 1 plough with 1 cotset. The whole manor TRE was worth 105s; now what Roger holds [is worth] £8, what the men [hold] 16s, what the priest [holds] 5s.

VIII. The land of Hugh l'Asne

IN LEINTWARDINE HUNDRED

HUGH l'Asne holds of the king KNIGHTON [Wales]. Leofflæd held it TRE. There are 5 hides. [...] There is land for 12 ploughs. It was and is waste. There is a great wood.

The same Hugh holds NORTON [Wales]. Leofflæd held it TRE. There are 5 hides. [...] There is land for 12 ploughs. It was and is waste. There is a great wood.

IX. The land of Nigel the Physician

IN LEINTWARDINE HUNDRED

NIGEL the physician holds WISTANSTOW of the king. Spirites the priest held it of St Alkmund, and TRE it was for the sustenance of the canons. There are 4 hides [...]. There is land for 15 ploughs. There are 7 villans with 7 ploughs, and 1 Frenchman having a mill which renders 5 summae of corn. TRE it was worth 30s; now 20s. He found it waste.

The same Nigel holds "CLEU". Spirites held it. There is 1 hide paying geld. There is land for 4 ploughs. In demesne is half a plough and 1 slave; and 1 radman and 4 bordars with 1 plough. TRE it was worth 12s; now 10s. He found it waste.

[Folio 261: [SHROPSHIRE]]

[Blank in MS]

[Folio 261V: [SHROPSHIRE]]

[Blank in MS]

CHESHIRE

[Folio 262: CHESHIRE]

[Blank in MS]

[Folio 262V: CHESHIRE]

THE CITY OF CHESTER paid geld in the time of King Edward for 50 hides. [There are] 3½ hides which are outside the city, that is 1½ hides beyond the bridge, and 2 hides in Newton [in Chester] and 'Redcliff' [in Chester] and in the bishop's borough; these paid geld with the city.

There were in the city itself TRE 431 houses paying geld, and besides these the bishop had 56 houses paying geld.

This city then rendered 10½ marks of silver. 2 parts belonged to the king and the third to the earl. And these were the laws there:

If the peace given by the hand of the king or by his writ or through his commissioner had been broken by anyone, the king had 100s for it.

But if this peace of the king, given at his command by the earl, had been broken, the earl had the third penny of the 100s which were given for this.

If, however, the same peace given by the king's reeve or by the earl's officer had been broken, a fine of 40s was paid and the third penny belonged to the earl.

If any free man, breaking the king's peace that had been given, killed a man in a house, his land and all his chattels belonged to the king and he himself became an outlaw. The earl had the same only from his own man making this forfeiture. But no one could restore peace to any outlaw except through the king.

He who shed blood from the morning of Monday to noon on Saturday paid a fine of 10s.

But from noon on Saturday to Monday morning a fine of 20s was paid for bloodshed. Similarly, he paid 20s who did this during the 12 days of Christmas, and at Candlemas, and on the first day of Easter, and on the first day of Whitsun, and on Ascension Day, and on [the day of] the Assumption or of the Nativity of ST MARY, and on the feast of All Saints.

He who killed a man on these holy days paid a fine of £4, but on the other days of 40s. Similarly, he who committed housebreaking or highway robbery on these feast-days and on Sunday paid £4, on other days 40s.

He who incurred the fine for wrongfully hanging a thief in the city gave 10s, but a reeve of the king or of the earl incurring this forfeiture paid a fine of 20s.

He who committed robbery or theft or raped a woman in a house was fined 40s for each of these.

If a widow had unlawful intercourse with any man, she paid a fine of 20s, but an unmarried woman [paid] 10s for the same offence.

He who seized the land of another in the city and could not prove it to be his paid a fine of 40s; similarly, too, he who made claim to it, if he could not prove that it ought to be his.

He who wished to take up his land or that of his kinsman gave 10s.

He who did not pay his rent at the term it was due paid a fine of 10s.

But if he could not or would not, the reeve took his land into the king's hand.

If fire broke out in the city the man from whose house it started paid a fine of 3 orae of pennies and to his nearest neighbour he gave 2s.

Two parts of all these forfeitures belonged to the king and the third [part] to the earl.

If ships were to arrive at or depart from the port of the city without the king's leave, the king and the earl had 40s from each man who was on the ships.

If a ship were to come against the king's peace and in spite of his prohibition, the king and earl had both [the ship] itself and the men with all that was in it.

But if it were to come in the king's peace and with his leave, those who were on board sold what they had undisturbed. When it left, however, the king and the earl had 4d from each load. If the king's reeve were to order those who had marten pelts not to sell to anyone until [they had] first [been] shown to him [and] he had bought, whoever did not observe this paid a fine of 40s.

A man or woman caught giving false measure in the city paid a fine of 4s. Similarly, the brewer of bad beer was either put in the cucking-stool or gave 4s to the reeves.

The officers of the king and of the earl took this forfeiture in the city in whosesoever land it arose, whether the bishop's or that of another man. Similarly [they took] toll; if anyone withheld it beyond 3 nights he paid a fine of 40s.

TRE there were in the city 7 moneyers who gave £7 to the king and earl over and above the farm when the coinage was changed.

There were then 12 lawmen in the city and these were [chosen] from the men of the king and of the bishop and of the earl. If any of them absented himself without obvious excuse from the hundred [court] on a day on which it sat, he paid a fine of 10s [divided] between the king and the earl.

For the repair of the city wall and bridge the reeve called up

1 man from each hide in the shire. The lord of any man whose man did not come paid a fine of 40s to the king and the earl; this forfeiture was over and above the farm.

This city then rendered at farm £45 and 3 timbers of marten pelts. The third part belonged to the earl and 2 [parts] to the king.

When Earl Hugh received it, it was only worth £30, for it had been greatly wasted. There were 205 fewer houses than there had been TRE.

There are now as many there as he found.

Mundret held this city from the earl for £70 and 1 mark of gold. He himself had at farm for £50 and 1 mark of gold all the earl's pleas in the shire and the hundreds except 'Englefield'.

The land on which the Church of ST PETER stands, which Robert of Rhuddlan claimed as thegnland, never belonged to a manor outside the city, as the shire proved, but belongs to the borough and always paid customary dues to the king and earl like [the land] of other burgesses.

IN CHESHIRE the bishop of the same city holds of the king what belongs to his bishopric.

Earl Hugh with his men holds of the king all the rest of the land of the shire.

Roger de Poitou held the LAND BETWEEN THE RIBBLE AND THE MERSEY; the king holds it now.

[Folio 263: CHESHIRE]

THE BISHOP OF CHESTER has these customs in the city itself: if any free man works on a holy day, the bishop has 8s for it, but from a slave or female slave breaking a holy day the bishop has 4s.

If a merchant coming to the city and bearing a bale [of goods] opens it without leave of the bishop's officer from Saturday noon to Monday, or on any other feast-day, the bishop has for it 4s as forfeiture. If a man of the bishop finds any man loading within the territory of the city, the bishop has for it as forfeiture 4s or 2 oxen.

IN 'DUDDESTON' HUNDRED

The bishop himself holds FARNDON and held it TRE. There are 4 hides paying geld. There is land for 5 ploughs. In demesne are 2 [ploughs]; and 7 villans with 1 plough. There is woodland 1 league long and a half wide.

Of this land 2 priests hold 1½ hides of the bishop. There is 1 plough in demesne; and 2 Frenchmen and 2 villans and 1 bordar with 1½ ploughs and 4 slaves. A priest of the vill has half a plough, and 5 bordars with 1 plough. The whole was worth TRE 40s; now 60s. It was waste.

IN RUSHTON HUNDRED

The same bishop held and holds TARVIN. There are 6 hides paying geld. There is land for 22 ploughs. In demesne are 3 ploughs and 6 oxmen; and 3 radmen and 7 villans and 7 bordars with 6 ploughs. [There is] woodland 1 league in length and a half in width.

Of this land of this manor William holds 2 hides of the bishop, and has there half a plough, and 4 villans and 3 bordars with

3½ ploughs. The whole was worth TRE £8; now £4.10s. It was waste.

IN WILLASTON HUNDRED

The bishop himself held and holds GUILDEN SUTTON. There is 1 hide paying geld. There is land for 3 ploughs. In demesne is 1 [plough]; and 5 villans and 2 bordars with 1 plough. There are 6 acres of meadow. TRE it was worth 40s; now 20s.

IN "EXESTAN" HUNDRED

ST CHAD held [?] 'EYTON' [in Holt, Wales] TRE. There is 1 hide. [...]

In [the same] 'EYTON' the same saint has 1 villan, and half a fishery, and half an acre of meadow and 2 acres of woodland. It was worth 5s.

King Edward gave to King Gruffydd all the land that lay beyond the water which is called the DEE. But after Gruffydd himself wronged him, he took this land from him, and restored it to the Bishop of Chester and to all his men who formerly held it.

IN "WARMUNDESTROU" HUNDRED

The bishop himself holds WYBUNBURY and held it TRE, and now William holds it of him. There is half a hide paying geld. There is land for 2 ploughs. There is 1 priest and 2 villans and 2 bordars with 1 plough. There is woodland half a league long and as much wide, and there are 2 enclosures. TRE it was worth 64d; now 4s. It was waste.

IN RUSHTON HUNDRED

The bishop himself holds [?] BURTON [in Tarvin] and held it TRE. There are 3 hides paying geld. There is land for 7 ploughs. In demesne are 2 ploughs; and 7 villans and 4 bordars and a priest and 1 radman with 3 ploughs. There is 1 acre of meadow. TRE it was worth 40s; now as much; when received, 15s.

The bishop himself held and holds in 'Redcliff' [in Chester] 2 parts of 1 hide paying geld. TRE it was worth 13s; now it is worth 2d more. It belongs to the Church of St John.

In the Minster of ST MARY which is next to the Church of St John lie 2 bovates of land which were waste and are now waste.

The Church of St John has in the city 8 houses quit of every customary due. One of these belongs to the dean of the church, the others belong to the canons.

In a manor of Robert fitzHugh, BETTISFIELD [Wales], the Bishop of Chester claims 2 hides which belonged to the bishopric in the time of King Cnut, and [...] the shire testifies for him that St Chad lost them unjustly.

IN THE CITY OF CHESTER the Church of ST WERBURH has 13 houses quit of every customary due. One belongs to the warden of the church, the others belong to the canons.

IN 'DUDDESTON' HUNDRED

The church itself holds SAIGHTON and held it TRE. There are 2 hides paying geld. There is land for 8 ploughs. In demesne is 1 plough and 1 slave; and 9 villans with 5 ploughs. It was and is worth 40s.

The church itself holds CHEAVELEYHALL, and held it TRE. There are 3 hides paying geld. There is land for 5 ploughs. In demesne are 2 [ploughs] and 3 slaves; and 3 villans and 1 bordar with 2 ploughs. There is a small boat and a net. TRE it was worth 30s; now 20s.

The church itself holds HUNTINGTON and held it TRE. There are 3 hides paying geld. There is land for 6 ploughs. In demesne are 2 [ploughs] and 4 slaves; and 2 villans and 2 bordars with 1 plough. There is 1 acre of meadow, and a small boat and a net. TRE it was waste; now it is worth 16s.

The church itself holds BOUGHTON [in Chester] and held it TRE. There are 3 hides paying geld. There is land for 5 ploughs. In demesne are 2 [ploughs] and 4 slaves; and 5 villans and 4 bordars with 3 ploughs. TRE it was worth 20s; now 16s.

IN RUSHTON HUNDRED

The church itself holds 'IDDENSHALL' and held it TRE. There is 1 hide paying geld. There is land for 1 plough. In demesne is half a plough and 1 slave. There is woodland half a league long and 1 acre wide. TRE it was worth 8s; now 5s.

IN WILLASTON HUNDRED

The church itself holds WERVIN and held it TRE. There is 1 hide and 2 parts of 1 hide [...]. There is land for 3 ploughs. [...] There 4 villans and 2 bordars have 1½ ploughs. There is half an acre of meadow. TRE it was worth 30s; now 20s.

The church itself holds CROUGHTON and held it TRE. There is 1 hide paying geld. There is land for 1 plough. There 1 radman and 2 villans and 1 bordar have 1 plough. There is 1 acre of meadow. It was and is worth 10s.

The church itself held and holds LEA [in Backford]. There is 1 hide paying geld. There is land for 3 ploughs. In demesne is 1 [plough] and 2 slaves; and 2 villans and 2 bordars with 1 plough, and 1 acre of meadow. TRE it was worth 10s; now as much.

The church itself holds [Great and Little] SUTTON and held it TRE. There is 1 hide paying geld. There is land for 5 ploughs. In demesne is half a plough; and 5 villans and 9 bordars with 2 ploughs. TRE it was worth 40s; now 30s.

The church itself held and holds SAUGHALL. There is 1 hide paying geld. There is land for 1 plough. There is [1 plough] in demesne and 2 slaves, and 1 villan and 1 bordar. TRE it was worth 16s; now as much.

The church itself held and holds SHOTWICK. There is 1 hide paying geld. There is land for 3 ploughs. There are 4 villans and 2 bordars with 1 plough, and 1 acre of meadow. TRE it was worth 16s; now 13s3d.

The church itself held and holds NESTON, and William

[holds] of it. There is a third part of 2 hides paying geld. There is land for 1 plough. It rendered and renders at farm 17s4d.

The church itself held and holds RABY, and William [holds] of it. There is half a hide paying geld. There is land for 1 plough. It rendered and renders at farm 6s8d.

IN RULOE HUNDRED

The church itself held and holds BRIDGE TRAFFORD. There is 1 hide paying geld. There is land [...]. In demesne is 1 plough and 4 slaves and 1 female slave, and 1 bordar, and 1 acre of meadow, and a man paying 20d. TRE it was worth 5s; now 8s.

The church itself held and holds INCE. There are 3 hides paying geld. There is land for 5 ploughs. In demesne is 1 plough and 2 slaves; and 8 villans and 1 bordar with 1 plough. TRE it was worth 30s; now 15s. There are 2 acres of meadow.

IN "TUNENDUNE" HUNDRED

The church itself held and holds MIDDLETON, and William [holds] of it. There is 1 hide paying geld. There is land for 3 ploughs. In demesne is half a plough and 1 oxman; and 3 villans with half a plough, and 1 bordar. There are 2 acres of woodland. TRE it rendered 16s; now it is worth 10s.

IN "EXESTAN" HUNDRED

The church itself held and holds HOSELEY [Wales]. There is half a hide paying geld. There is land for 1 plough. There is 1 villan paying 8d. It is worth 3s. It was waste.

[Folio 263V: CHESHIRE]

IN 'DUDDESTON' HUNDRED

The church itself holds PULFORD and held it TRE. There is half a hide paying geld. There is land for 1 plough. There is [1 plough], with 1 villan and 1 bordar. It was worth 4s; now 5s.

IN ATI'S CROSS HUNDRED

The church itself held and holds WEPRE [Wales]. There are 2 parts of 1 hide paying geld. There is land for 1 plough. There is [1 plough], with 2 villans and 2 bordars. William holds it of the church. There is woodland 1 league long and half a league wide.

The church itself held LACHE [in Chester]. There is 1 virgate paying geld. There is land for half a plough. It was and is waste.

IN RULOE HUNDRED

EARL HUGH holds WEAVERHAM in demesne. Earl Edwin held it. There are 13 hides paying geld. There is land for 18 ploughs. In demesne are 2 [ploughs] and 2 oxmen and 2 slaves; and 10 villans and 1 bordar, and 1 radman with 1 villan. Among them all they have 3 ploughs. There is a church and a priest, and a mill serving the hall, and 1 acre of meadow, woodland 2 leagues long and 1 league wide, and there are 2 enclosures for [catching] roe-deer.

To this manor belong 10 burgesses in the city. Of these, 6 pay 10s8d and 4 pay nothing. A Frenchman holds them of the earl.

In Wich [Middlewich, Nantwich or Northwich] were 7 salt-pans belonging to this manor. One of these now supplies the hall with salt, the others are waste.

In another hundred 1 virgate of land called Antrobus belongs to this manor and is waste.

Of this land of this manor Joscelin holds 4 hides of the earl, and has there 1 plough and 3 slaves, and 5 villans and 1 radman with 2 ploughs, and half a fishery. The earl has placed 3 hides of this land in the forest.

The whole manor was at farm TRE for £10. The earl found it waste. Now his demesne [is worth] 50s; Joscelin's [land] 10s.

The earl himself holds 'CONERSLEY' [in Whitegate]. Wulfheah, a free man, held it. There is 1 hide paying geld. There is land for 2 ploughs. It is all in the forest. [There is] woodland 1 league long and half a league wide. TRE it was worth 6s. It was waste.

The earl himself holds DUNHAM-ON-THE-HILL. Æscwulf held it in parage as a free man. There are 3 hides paying geld. There is land for 9 ploughs. In demesne is half a plough; and 7 villans and a smith and 3 bordars with 1½ ploughs. There are 2 acres of meadow, [and] woodland half a league long and a fourth part [of a league] wide. TRE it was worth 40s; now 16s. It was waste.

The earl himself holds ELTON. Toki and Grim held it as 2 manors as free men. There are 2 hides paying geld. There is land for 7 ploughs. In demesne is 1 [plough] and 2 oxmen; and 6 villans and 1 bordar with 1 plough. TRE it was worth 38s; now 6s. It was waste.

The earl himself holds WIMBOLDS TRAFFORD. Leofric and Guthlac held it as 2 manors as free men. There is 1 hide paying geld. There is land for 1 plough. There is [1 plough], with 1 radman and 2 bordars. TRE it was worth 10s; now 2s. He found it waste.

The earl himself holds MANLEY. Toki held it as a free man. There is half a hide paying geld. There is land for 1 plough. It renders at farm a mark of silver. TRE it was worth 10s.

The earl himself holds HELSBY. Earnwig Fot held it as a free man. There is 1 hide paying geld. There is land for 3 ploughs. 3 villans with 1 bordar have 1 plough there. There is 1 acre of meadow, and woodland half a league long and as much wide. TRE it was worth 12s; now 10s.

The earl himself holds FRODSHAM. Earl Edwin held it. There are 3 hides paying geld. There is land for 9 ploughs. In demesne are 2 [ploughs] and 1 slave; and 8 villans and 3 bordars with 2 ploughs.

The earl himself holds OLLERTON. Godric held it. There is 1 virgate of land paying geld. There is land for half a plough. It was and is waste. There a priest and a church have 1 virgate of land, and there is a winter mill, and 2½ fisheries, and 3 acres of meadow, and woodland 1 league long and half a league wide, and there are 2 enclosures, and in Wich [Middlewich, Nantwich or Northwich] half a salt-pan serving the hall.

The third penny of the pleas of this hundred belonged to this manor TRE. It was then worth £8; now £4. It was waste.

The earl himself holds 'ALDERLEGH' [in Frodsham]. Karli held it. [...] There are 3 hides paying geld. There is land for 6 ploughs. It was waste, and is now in the earl's forest. TRE it was worth 30s.

The earl himself holds "DONE". Wulfgeat held it as a free man. There are 2 hides paying geld. There is land for 2 ploughs. It was waste, and is now in the earl's forest. TRE it was worth 10s.

The earl himself [holds] EDDISBURY. Godwine held it as a free man. There are 2 hides paying geld. There is land for 6 ploughs. It was and is waste. This land is 1 league long and as much wide.

IN 'DUDDESTON' HUNDRED

The earl himself holds EATON. Earl Edwin held it. There are 1½ hides paying geld. There is land for 2 ploughs. In demesne is 1 [plough] and 2 oxmen; and 2 villans with 1 plough. There is a fishery rendering 1,000 salmon, and 6 fishermen, and 1 acre of meadow. TRE it was worth £10; and afterwards £8; now £10.

The earl himself holds LEA [near Aldford]. Godwine, a free man, held it. There are 1½ hides paying geld. There is land for 4 ploughs. In demesne is 1 [plough] and 2 oxmen; and 8 villans with 1 plough. There is 1 acre of woodland. TRE it was worth 30s; and afterwards 5s; now 10s.

The earl himself holds CODDINGTON. Earnwig and Asgot and Dot held it as 3 manors. There are 2 hides paying geld. There is land for 4 ploughs. In demesne is 1 [plough] and 2 oxmen; and 5 villans and 1 bordar and 1 radman and 1 Frenchman with 2 ploughs. There is a mill, and 12 acres of meadow. TRE it was worth 9s6d; now 12s. He found it waste.

The earl himself holds LEA [near Aldford]. Sten held it as a free man. There is half a hide paying geld. There is land for 1 plough. It is waste.

The earl himself holds RUSHTON. Cypping held it as a free man. There is half a hide paying geld. There is land for 2 ploughs. It is waste.

The earl himself holds "OPETONE". Arni, a free man, held it. There is 1 hide paying geld. There is land for 2 ploughs. It is waste. There is woodland 1 league long and 2 acres wide.

The earl himself holds LITTLE BUDWORTH. Dedol, a free man, held it. There is half a hide paying geld. There is land for 2 ploughs. It is waste. [There is] woodland 1 league long and a half wide.

The earl himself holds "ALRETONE". Sten held it. He was a free man. There is 1 hide paying geld. There is land for 2 ploughs. It is waste.

The earl himself holds OVER. 4 free men held it as 4 manors. There is 1 hide paying geld. There is land for 5 ploughs. There is 1 radman with 1 plough. There is woodland half a league long and as much wide. It was worth 6s; now 5s.

IN WILLASTON HUNDRED

The earl himself holds EASTHAM. Earl Edwin held it. There are 22 hides paying geld. There is land for as many ploughs. In demesne are 2 ploughs and 4 slaves; and 14 villans and 10 bordars with 6 ploughs. There is a mill, and 2 radmen and 1 priest.

Of the land of this manor Mundret holds 2 hides, and Hugh 2 hides, and William 1 hide, Hamo 7 hides, Robert 1 hide, [and] Robert half a hide. In demesne are 4 ploughs and 8 oxmen; and 22 villans and 11 bordars and 5 radmen and 2 Frenchmen with 9 ploughs. The whole manor TRE was worth £24; and afterwards £4; now the earl's demesne is worth £4, his men's [land] 112s.

The earl himself holds MICKLE TRAFFORD. Ordm held it. He was a free man. There are 2 hides paying geld. There is land for 6 ploughs. In demesne are 2 [ploughs] and 2 slaves; and 4 villans and 2 bordars with 1 plough. TRE it was worth 100s; now 40s. He found it waste.

The earl himself holds 'HADLOW' [in Neston]. Earl Edwin held it. There is 1 hide paying geld. There is land for 1 plough. It was waste. Now a certain man ploughs there and pays 2s.

IN "HAMESTAN" HUNDRED

The earl himself holds MACCLESFIELD. Earl Edwin held it. There are 2 hides paying geld. There is land for 10 ploughs. In demesne is 1 plough and 4 slaves. There is a mill serving the court, woodland 6 leagues long and 4 wide, and there were 7 enclosures. [There is] meadow for the oxen. The third penny of the hundred belongs to this manor. TRE it was worth £8; now 20s. It was waste.

[Folio 264: CHESHIRE]

The same earl holds ADLINGTON. Earl Edwin held it. There are 4½ hides paying geld. There is land for 10 ploughs. There are 2 radmen and 6 villans and 3 bordars with 3 ploughs. There are 21 acres of meadow, woodland 11 leagues long and 2 wide, and there are 7 enclosures and 4 eyries of hawks. TRE it was worth £8; now 20s. He found it waste.

The earl himself holds GAWSWORTH. Beornwulf, a free man, held it. There is 1 hide paying geld. There is land for 6 ploughs. It is waste. TRE it was worth 20s. There is woodland 2 leagues long and 2 leagues wide, and 2 enclosures.

The earl himself holds MARTON. Godric held it. He was a free man. There is 1 virgate of land paying geld. There is land for 1 plough. It was and is waste. There are 20 perches of woodland.

The earl himself holds "HUNGREWENITUNE" [in Prestbury]. Godwine held it. There is half a hide paying geld. It was and is waste.

The earl himself holds CHELFORD. Brun held it. There is half a hide paying geld. There is land for 2 ploughs. It was and is waste.

The earl himself holds HENBURY at half a hide, [...] CAPESTHORNE at half a hide, and HENBURY at 1

hide paying geld, and "HOFINCHEL" at 1 hide, and TINTWISTLE at 1 virgate of land, and HOLLINGWORTH at 1 virgate, and WERNETH at 1 virgate, and ROMILEY at 1 virgate, and 'LEIGHTON' [in Stockport] at 1 virgate of land. All paid geld. 8 free men held these lands as manors. In all there is land for 16 ploughs. The whole was and is waste.

In "Hofinghel" is woodland 2 leagues long and 2 wide. In TINTWISTLE is woodland 4 leagues long and 2 wide. In WERNETH is woodland 3 leagues long and 2 wide. TRE this hundred was worth 40s; now 10s.

IN MIDDLEWICH HUNDRED

The earl himself holds ALSAGER. Wulfric, a free man, held it. There is half a hide paying geld. There is land for 1 plough. It is waste. TRE it was worth 3s.

The earl himself holds SANDBACH at 2½ virgates paying geld, [...] and CLIVE at 1 virgate paying geld, and SUTTON [in Middlewich] at 4 bovates of land paying geld, and WIMBOLDSLEY at 1 virgate paying geld, and WEAVER at 1 virgate of land paying geld, and OCCLESTONE GREEN at 1 hide paying geld.

Six free men held these lands as 6 manors. In all there is land for 7 ploughs.
   The whole was and is waste. In Wimboldsley is 1 acre of meadow, and the fourth part of a wood which is 1 league long and 4 perches wide. In Weaver, half an acre of meadow, and the fourth part of a wood which is 1 league long and as much wide.

IN WILLASTON HUNDRED

The earl himself holds UPTON [in Chester]. Earl Edwin held it. There are 4½ hides paying geld. There is land for 12 ploughs. In demesne is 1 [plough] and 2 oxmen; and 12 villans and 2 radmen with 5 ploughs.

Of this land of this manor Hamo holds 2 parts of 1 hide, and Herbert half a hide, and Mundret 1 hide. There are in demesne 4 ploughs and 8 oxmen; and 2 villans and 2 bordars with 1 plough. There is 1 acre of meadow. The whole manor TRE was worth 60s; now the earl's demesne is worth 45s, [the land] of his men 40s.

The earl himself holds STANNEY [Stanney and Little Stanney], and Restald [holds] of him. Regnvald held it as a free man. There is 1 hide paying geld. There is land for 2 ploughs. In demesne is 1 [plough] and 2 oxmen, and 2 villans and 2 bordars, and 1 fishery. TRE it was worth 12s; now 14s. Of this land the fifth acre belonged and ought to belong to the Church of ST WERBURH, by witness of the shire. The canons claim it because they have lost it unjustly.

IN "TUNENDUNE" HUNDRED

The earl himself holds ANTROBUS. Leofnoth held it and was a free man. There are 1½ virgates of land paying geld. There is land for 1 plough. It was and is waste. There is woodland 1 league long and a half wide. TRE it was worth 4s.

IN 'DUDDESTON' HUNDRED

ROBERT fitzHugh holds BETTISFIELD [Wales] of Earl Hugh. Earl Edwin held it. There are 7 hides paying geld. There is land for 8 ploughs. In demesne is 1 [plough] and 2 slaves; and 3 villans with 1 plough. There is half an acre of meadow, [and] woodland 3 leagues long and 2 wide. In this land 3 knights have 3 ploughs in demesne; and 9 villans and 5 bordars and 2 slaves and 3 other men. Among them all they have 3 ploughs. A priest has 1 plough. The whole was worth £18.17s4d. TRE; it was waste; now it is worth all together £3. Besides woodland this manor is 2 leagues long and as much wide.

Of this manor the Bishop of Chester claims 2 hides which ST CHAD held in the time of King Cnut, but he complains that he has lost them from that time until now.

The same Robert holds "BURWARDESTONE" [Wales]. Earl Edwin held it. There are 5 hides paying geld. There is land for 14 ploughs. In demesne is 1 [plough]; and 12 villans and 2 bordars with 3 ploughs, and 1 knight has 1 plough there, and another knight holds half a hide which renders 12s to him. There is a salt-pan rendering 24s. TRE it was worth £6.4s; now 54s. He found it waste. This manor is 2 leagues long and 1 wide.

Of this manor the Bishop of Chester claims 1½ hides and 1 salt-pan.

The same Robert holds WORTHENBURY [Wales]. Earl Edwin held it. There are 5 hides paying geld. There is land for 10 ploughs. In demesne is 1 [plough] and 1 slave; and 3 villans and 3 Frenchmen and 1 radman with 4 ploughs. There is a new mill, and 1 acre of meadow.

Of this manor a knight holds 1½ hides, and has there 1 plough with his men. TRE it was worth 12 orae which the villans paid; now it is worth 30s. He found it waste. It is 2 leagues in length and 1 in width.

The same Robert holds MALPAS. Earl Edwin held it. There are 8 hides paying geld. There is land for 14 ploughs. In demesne are 3 [ploughs], and 1 bordar, and half an acre of meadow. Of this land 5 knights hold 5½ hides of Robert, and have there 3 ploughs, and 7 villans with 2½ ploughs. There are 2 acres of meadow. TRE the whole was worth £11.4s; afterwards it was waste; now, all together, it is worth 52s. It is 2 leagues long and 1 wide.

The same Robert holds TILSTON. Earl Edwin held it. There are 4 hides paying geld. There is land for 8 ploughs. In demesne is 1 [plough] and 2 slaves; and 4 villans and 2 bordars and 4 radmen and a reeve and a smith and a miller with 4 ploughs among them all. There is a mill rendering 8s.

Of this land Ranulph holds half a hide of Robert, paying 6s8d. TRE the whole was worth £6; now 30s. He found it waste. It is 1 league long and another wide. Of the land of this manor the Bishop of Chester claims half a hide, but the shire does not testify [that] it [belongs] to his bishopric.

The same Robert holds CHRISTLETON. Earl Edwin held it. There are 7 hides paying geld. There is land for 14 ploughs.

In demesne is 1 plough and 2 female slaves; and 12 villans and 5 bordars and 2 reeves with 8 ploughs. There is a mill rendering 12s, and there are 2 radmen. Of this manor Ranulph holds 2 hides of Robert; he pays 12d to him. The whole TRE was worth £6; now it is worth £3. He found it waste. It is 2 leagues long and 1 wide.

The same Robert holds CHOLMONDELEY. Edwin and Dot, free men, held it as 2 manors. There are 2 hides paying geld. There is land for 4 ploughs. Edwin and Drogo hold it of Robert. In demesne is 1 plough and 5 slaves; and 1 villan and 3 bordars and 1 reeve and a smith with 1 plough, and there is woodland 1½ leagues long and 1 wide. There are 3 enclosures. TRE it was worth 13s; now 6s3d. It has half a league of open land.

The same Robert holds EDGE. Edwin held it and still holds it of Robert. He was a free man. There are 2½ hides paying geld. There is land for 1 plough. There are moors. In demesne is 1 plough and 3 slaves. [There is] woodland 2 acres long and 1 wide. It was waste and he found it [so]; now [it is worth] 4s.

The same Robert holds HAMPTON, and Edwin and Drogo [hold] of him. Edwin himself held it as 2 manors and was a free man. There are 2 and a half hides paying geld. There is land for 4 ploughs. There are 3 settlers having nothing. There is woodland 5 acres long and 2 wide. The whole TRE was worth 5s; now it renders 2s and a sparrow-hawk.

[Folio 264V: CHESHIRE]

The same Robert holds LARKTON, and Edwin and Drogo [hold] of him. The same Edwin held it. He was a free man. There is 1 hide paying geld. There is land for 3 ploughs. There is 1 man and he pays 12d, and 1 bordar pays 2s. TRE it was worth 8s. It is 4 leagues long and 4 wide.

The same Robert holds DUCKINGTON, and Edwin [holds] of him. He himself held it as a free man. There is 1 hide paying geld. There is land for 2 ploughs. It is waste.

The same Robert holds EDGE, and Edwin [holds] of him and held it as a free man. There is half a hide paying geld. There is land for 1 plough. It is waste. There is woodland 2 acres long and 1 wide. It is worth 12d.

The same Robert holds CHOWLEY, and Mundret [holds] of him. Wulfgifu held it and was free. There is 1 hide paying geld. There is land for 1 plough. There is [1 plough], with 2 radmen. [There is] woodland half a league long and 1 acre wide, and 2 enclosures. TRE it was worth 10s; now 5s. He found it waste.

The same Robert holds BROXTON, and Roger and Picot [hold] of him. Beorhtmær and Rawn, 2 free men, held it as 2 manors. There are 5 hides paying geld. There is land for 6 ploughs. In demesne is 1 plough; and 3 villans with 1 plough. [There is] 1 league of woodland. TRE it was worth 10s8d; now 18s8d.

The same Robert holds OVERTON. Wulfwig held it. He was a free man. There are 1½ hides paying geld. There is land for 2 ploughs. In demesne is 1 [plough]. [There is] woodland 2 acres long and 1 wide. It was worth 5s; now 6s.

The same Robert holds CUDDINGTON. The above Wulfwig held it. There is half a hide paying geld. There is land for 1 plough. There are 2 bordars ploughing with 2 oxen. It is worth 16d. It was waste.

The same Robert holds SHOCKLACH, and Drogo [holds] of him. Dot, a free man, held it. There are 3 hides paying geld. There is land for 4 ploughs. In demesne are 2 [ploughs] and 2 oxmen; and 2 villans with 1 plough. There is half an acre of meadow. TRE it was worth 8s; now 12s.

The same Robert holds TUSHINGHAM, and Humphrey [holds] of him. Earnwine, a free man, held it. There is 1 hide paying geld. There is land for 2 ploughs. In demesne is 1 [plough], with 1 bordar. [There is] half a league of woodland. TRE it was worth 10s; now 4s. | It was | waste.

The same Robert holds BICKLEY, and Fulk [holds] of him. Wudumann held it and was a free man. There is 1 hide paying geld. There is land for 2 ploughs. In demesne is 1 plough; and a reeve and 2 bordars with 1 plough. TRE it was worth 5s; now 8s. He found it waste.

The same Robert holds BICKERTON, and Drogo [holds] of him. Dot and Edwin and | Earnwine |, 3 thegns, free men, held it as 3 manors. There are 3 hides paying geld. There is land for 4 ploughs. There are 2 villans with 1 plough. [There is] half a league of woodland. TRE it was worth 18s; now 11s. It was and is for the most part waste.

The same Robert holds BURWARDSLEY [Burwardsley and Higher Burwardsley], and Humphrey [holds] of him. Ælfric, and Colbert and Ramkel held it and were free men. There are 3 hides paying geld. There is land for 3 ploughs. There are 3 bordars with 1 plough, and woodland 1 league long and a half wide. TRE it was worth 2s; now 5s. It was waste. Of this land 1 hide was taken from the Church of ST WERBURH. The reeves of Earls Edwin and Morcar sold this to a certain Ramkel.

The same Robert holds CREWE [in Farndon], and Eli [holds] of him. He himself held it and was a free man. There is 1 hide paying geld. There is land for 1 plough. There is [1 plough] in demesne, with 2 bordars, and half a fishery. It is worth 10s. It was waste and he found it [so].

IN RUSHTON HUNDRED

The same Robert holds TILSTONE FEARNALL, and William [holds] of him. Stenulf held it and was a free man. There are 2 hides paying geld. There is land for 2 ploughs. In demesne is 1 [plough], with 1 bordar. There is a little woodland. TRE it was worth 6s8d; now 4s. He found it waste.

The same Robert holds BEESTON. Wulfwig held it and was a free man. There is 1 hide paying geld. There is land for 2½ ploughs. In demesne is 1 [plough], with 2 oxmen. TRE it was worth 10s; now 5s. He found it waste.

The same Robert holds BUNBURY [Bunbury and Lower Bunbury]. Dedol held it and was a free man. There is 1 hide paying geld. There is land for 2 ploughs. In demesne is 1 [plough]; and a priest with 2 villans have 1 plough. [There is]

woodland 1 league long and 1 acre wide. It was worth 4s; now 13s.

The same Robert holds TIVERTON. Dedol and Hundolfr held it as 2 manors and were free men. There are 2 hides paying geld. There is land for 2 ploughs. There 3 villans and 2 bordars have 1 plough. [There is] woodland 1 league long and another wide. It was worth 10s; now 25s.

The same Robert holds SPURSTOW. Wulfric held it and was a free man. There are 1½ hides paying geld. There is land for 3 ploughs. There 2 radmen and 3 bordars have 1 plough. There is woodland 1½ leagues long and half a league wide, and 1 acre of meadow. TRE it was worth 16s; now 6s. He found it waste.

The same Robert holds PECKFORTON. Wulfric, a free man, held it. There is 1 hide paying geld. There is land for 2 ploughs. There is 1 villan with 1 plough. It was worth 8s; now it renders 20s.

IN WILLASTON HUNDRED

The same Robert holds [?] GUILDEN SUTTON. Toki held it and was a free man. There is 1 hide paying geld. There is land for 3 ploughs. In demesne is 1 [plough], and 3 bordars with 1 villan. There are 6 acres of meadow. TRE it was worth 40s; and afterwards 6s; now it renders as farm 64d.

IN "HAMESTAN" HUNDRED

Robert holds BUTLEY of the earl. Hundingr held it and was a free man. There is 1 hide paying geld. There is land for 5 ploughs. It is waste except for 12 sown acres. TRE it was worth 30s; now 2s. There are 2½ acres of meadow. There is woodland 3 leagues long and 1 wide, and 1 enclosure there.

Robert holds CRANAGE of the earl. Godric held it and was a free man. There is 1 hide paying geld. There is land for 1½ ploughs. There 1 radman and 1 villan have half a plough. There is woodland half a league long and 40 perches wide, and 1 enclosure there. It was waste; now it is worth 3s.

IN WILLASTON HUNDRED

ROBERT of Rhuddlan holds MOLLINGTON of Earl Hugh. Godwine held it and was a free man. There are 1½ hides paying geld. There is land for 3 ploughs. In demesne is 1 [plough] and 3 slaves, and 3 villans and 3 bordars, and 2 acres of meadow, and 2 acres of woodland. TRE it was waste; when received, it was worth 20s; now 15s.

The same Robert holds MOLLINGTON, and Lambert [holds] of him. Gunnar and Ulf held it as 2 manors and were free men. There is 1 hide paying geld. There is land for 2 ploughs. There is 1 [plough] in demesne with 2 slaves, and there are 2 acres of meadow. It is worth 14s. It was waste and he found it waste.

The same Robert holds LEIGHTON [in Neston], and William [holds] of him. Leofnoth held it and was a free man. There is 1 hide paying geld. There is land for 2 ploughs. In demesne is 1 plough with 1 slave, and 1 Frenchman and 2 bordars, and 2 fisheries. It was and is worth 15s.

The same Robert holds THORNTON HOUGH, and William [holds] of him. Ulfkil held it and was a free man. There is half a hide paying geld. There is land for 2 ploughs. There 1 radman and 1 villan and 1 bordar have half a plough. It was worth 10s; and afterwards, as now, 5s.

The same Robert holds GAYTON, and William [holds] of him. Leofnoth, a free man, held it. There is 1 hide paying geld. There is land for 2 ploughs. There 2 villans and 3 bordars have 1 plough, and there are 2 fisheries. It was worth 15s; and afterwards 2s; now 3s.

The same Robert holds HESWALL, and Herbert [holds] of him. Ulfkil held it and was a free man. There are 2 hides paying geld. There is land for 4 ploughs. In demesne is 1 plough and 2 oxmen; and 3 villans and 1 bordar with 1 plough. TRE it was worth 16s; and afterwards 20s; now 22s.

The same Robert holds THURSTASTON, and William [holds] of him. Leofnoth held it. He was a free man. There are 2 hides paying geld. There is land for 4 ploughs. In demesne is 1 [plough] and 2 oxmen; and 4 villans and 4 bordars with $1\frac{1}{2}$ ploughs. TRE it was worth 30s; and afterwards 8s; now 16s.

The same Robert holds CALDY. Leofnoth held it. He was a free man. There are 3 hides paying geld. There is land for 10 ploughs. There 5 villans and 5 bordars have 2 ploughs; and 1 Frenchman with 1 sergeant has 2 ploughs [...]. In demesne [are] 2 oxen, and 2 acres of meadow. TRE it was worth 50s; and afterwards 10s; now 24s.

The same Robert holds MEOLS. Leofnoth held it. There is 1 hide paying geld. There is land for $1\frac{1}{2}$ ploughs. There 1 radman and 2 villans and 2 bordars have 1 plough. TRE it was worth 15s; now 10s. He found it waste.

The same Robert holds MEOLS. Leofnoth held it. There is 1 hide paying geld. There is land for 3 ploughs. There 1 radman and 3 villans and 3 bordars have 1 plough. TRE it was worth 10s; and afterwards 8s; now 12s.

The same Robert holds WALLASEY. Uhtræd held it and was a free man. There are $1\frac{1}{2}$ hides paying geld. There is land for 4 ploughs. There is 1 villan and 1 bordar with half a plough, and 1 Frenchman has 1 plough with 2 oxmen, and 1 radman and 1 bordar.

Robert the cook holds LITTLE NESTON of the earl. Asgot held it and was a free man. There is 1 hide paying geld. There is land for 3 ploughs. In demesne are 2 [ploughs] and 1 slave; and 2 villans and 4 bordars with 1 plough, and there is 1 Frenchman. TRE it was worth 13s4d; now 16s. He found it waste.

The same Robert holds HARGRAVE. Asgot held it. There is 1 hide paying geld. There is land for 2 ploughs. There 3 villans and 2 bordars have 1 plough. TRE it was worth 6s8d; now 10s; when received, it was worth [folio 265: CHESHIRE]

IN RUSHTON HUNDRED

RICHARD de Vernon holds ASHTON. Thorth held it and was a free man. There are 4 hides paying geld. There is land for 5 ploughs. In demesne is 1 [plough] and 2 slaves; and 5 villans and 2 radmen and 3 bordars with 2 ploughs. There is woodland half a league long and 1 acre wide. TRE it was worth 16s; now 20s. He found it waste.

IN WILLASTON HUNDRED

The same Richard holds PICTON. Toki held it and was a free man. There is 1 hide paying geld. There is land for 3 ploughs. In demesne is 1 [plough] and 2 oxmen; and 1 radman and 3 bordars with 1 plough. There is half an acre of meadow. TRE it was worth 40s; and afterwards 5s; now 20s.

The same Richard holds HOOTON. Toki held it. There is 1 hide and 2 parts of 1 hide paying geld. There is land for 3 ploughs. There are 4 radmen and 1 villan and 4 bordars with 2 ploughs. TRE it was worth 30s; and afterwards 5s; now 16s.

IN "TUNENDUNE" HUNDRED

The same Richard holds COGSHALL, and Payne [holds] of him. Leofnoth and Dedol held it as 2 manors and were free men. There is half a hide paying geld. There is land for 1 plough. There is [1 plough], with 1 radman and 1 bordar. [There is] woodland 1 league long and a half wide. TRE it was worth 2s; now 5s.

IN MIDDLEWICH HUNDRED

The same Richard holds SHIPBROOKHILL. Osmær held it. He was a free man. There are 2 hides paying geld. There is land for 5 ploughs. In demesne is 1 [plough] and 2 slaves; and 2 villans with 2 ploughs. There are 3 acres of meadow and 2 acres of woodland. TRE it was worth 20s; now 10s. He found it waste.

The same Richard holds [Higher and Lower] SHURLACH. Alweard and Bersi held it as 2 manors and were free. There is 1 hide paying geld. There is land for 2 ploughs. In demesne is 1 plough and 2 slaves; and 2 villans with half a plough, and 1 bordar, and 1 fishery, and 3 acres of meadow. TRE it was worth 8s; now 7s. He found it waste.

The same Richard holds LEFTWICH. Osmær and Alsige held it as 2 manors and were free. There is 1 hide paying geld. There is land for 3 ploughs. In demesne is 1 [plough] and 2 slaves; and 3 villans with 1 plough, and 4 acres of meadow. TRE it was worth 12s; now 6s.

The same Richard holds MOULTON. Leofnoth held it and was a free man. There is 1 hide paying geld. There is land for 2 ploughs. There 1 villan and 1 bordar have half a plough. There is 1 acre of meadow, [and] woodland 1 league long and 1 wide. There is 1 enclosure. It was and is worth 5s.

The same Richard holds WHARTON. Arngrim and Alsige held it as 2 manors. They were free men. There is half a hide paying geld. There is land for 1 plough. There is [1 plough] in demesne and 2 slaves, and 2 bordars. TRE it was worth 4s; now 6s. He found it waste.

The same Richard holds DAVENHAM. Osmær held it. He was a free man. There is half a hide paying geld. There is land for 2 ploughs. In demesne is 1 plough and 2 slaves; and a priest with a church, and 1 villan and 1 bordar with half a plough. It was worth 8s; now 5s.

The same Richard holds BOSTOCK. Osmær held it. There is 1 hide paying geld. There is land for 2 ploughs. There are [2 ploughs], with 3 radmen and 2 slaves, and 2 acres of meadow, and 2 acres of woodland. TRE it was worth 3s; now 10s. He found it waste.

IN "WARMUNDESTROU" HUNDRED

The same Richard holds AUDLEM. Osmær held it. There are 2 hides paying geld. There is land for 5 ploughs. In demesne is 1 [plough] and 1 slave; and 1 villan and 1 radman and 1 bordar with 1 plough. There are 2 acres of meadow, [and] woodland 2 leagues long and 1 league wide, and 2 enclosures and a hawk's eyrie. TRE it was worth 20s; now 8s. He found it waste.

The same Richard holds CREWE [in Barthomley]. Osmær held it. There is 1 hide paying geld. There is land for 2 ploughs. There is 1 radman and 1 villan and 2 bordars with 1 plough. There are 1½ acres of meadow, [and] woodland 1 league long and a half wide. TRE it was worth 10s; now 5s. He found it waste.

RICHARD the butler holds POULTON [in Pulford] of the earl. Edwin held it and was a free man. There is 1 hide paying geld. There is land for 5 ploughs. In demesne are 3 ploughs and 6 oxmen; and a reeve and 3 bordars with 2 ploughs. There are 8 acres of meadow. TRE it was worth 40s; and afterwards as much; now £4.

The same Richard holds "CALUINTONE". Dot held it and was a free man. There are 2 hides paying geld. There is land for 2 ploughs. It was waste and he found it waste; now it is at farm for 60s.

IN "HAMESTAN" HUNDRED

The same Richard de Vernon holds BREDBURY, and Wulfric [holds] of him, who also held it as a free man. There is 1 hide paying geld. There is land for 3 ploughs. There 1 radman and 6 villans and 2 bordars have 1 plough. There is woodland 1 league long and half a league wide, and 3 enclosures and 1 hawk's eyrie. TRE it was worth 10s; now the same.

IN RUSHTON HUNDRED

WALTER de Vernon holds WILLINGTON of Earl Hugh. Earngeat held it and was a free man. There is 1 hide paying geld. There is land for 2 ploughs. There 2 villans have 1 plough. There is woodland half a league long and 1 acre wide. TRE it was worth 8s; now 10s. He found it waste.

IN WILLASTON HUNDRED

The same Walter holds NESS. Earngeat held it. There are 1½ hides paying geld. There is land for 2 ploughs. In demesne is 1 [plough] and 2 oxmen; and 5 villans and 3 bordars with 2 ploughs. There is half an acre of meadow. TRE it was worth 20s; now 16s.

The same Walter holds LEDSHAM. Earngeat held it. There is 1 hide paying geld. There is land for 2 ploughs. In demesne is half a plough and 1 slave; and 1 radman and 1 bordar with half a plough among them all. TRE it was worth 5s; and afterwards 8s; now 10s.

The same Walter holds PRENTON. Wulfgeat, Eadric and Luvede held it as 3 manors and were free. There are 1½ hides paying geld. There is land for 3 ploughs. In demesne is 1 [plough] and 2 oxmen, and 2 bordars. There is a mill serving the court, [and] woodland 1 league long and 1 wide. It was worth 7s; now 5s.

IN 'DUDDESTON' HUNDRED

WILLIAM Malbank holds TATTENHALL of Earl Hugh. Earnwine held it and was a free man. There are 5 hides paying geld. There is land for 6 ploughs. In demesne is 1 [plough]; and 2 villans and 2 bordars have another, and 1 Frenchman a third. There is 1 league of woodland. TRE it was worth 20s; now 26[s]. It was waste.

The same William holds 'GOLBORNE BELLOW' [in Tattenhall]. Lothæn held it. There is half a hide paying geld. There is land for 1 plough, which [plough] is there in demesne, and 2 oxmen, with 1 villan and 3 bordars. There is a winter mill. It was worth 5s; now 6s. He found it waste.

IN RUSHTON HUNDRED

The same William holds "ULURE". Wulfheah held it and was a free man. There are 2 hides paying geld. There is land for 4 ploughs. There 1 radman and 2 villans and 3 bordars have 2 ploughs. There are 2 acres of meadow, [and] woodland 1 league long and a half wide. TRE it was worth 40s; now 10s. He found it waste.

IN WILLASTON HUNDRED

The same William holds WERVIN. Colbert held it and was a free man. There is a third part of 1 hide paying geld. There is land for 1 plough. There are 2 villans with half a plough. It was worth 8s; now 4s.

The same William holds POOL ['Netherpool' and Overpool, in Eastham]. Earnwine held it as a manor. There is land for 4 oxen paying geld. There 1 villan and 1 bordar have half a plough. It was and is worth 4s.

The same William holds SAUGHALL. Lyfing held it and was a free man. There are 6 hides paying geld. There is land for 6 ploughs. In demesne are 1½ [ploughs] and 1 slave; and 7 villans and 1 radman and 4 bordars with 3½ ploughs. There is a fishery. TRE it was worth 20s; and afterwards 22s; now 45s.

The same William holds LANDICAN. æscwulf held it and was a free man. There are 7 hides paying geld. There is land for 8 ploughs. In demesne is 1 [plough]; and a priest and 9 villans and 7 bordars and 4 Frenchmen with 5 ploughs among them all. TRE it was worth 50s; now 40s. He found it waste.

The same William holds UPTON [in Overchurch], and Colbert [holds] of him, who also held it as a free man. There are 3 hides paying geld. There is land for 5 ploughs. In demesne is 1 [plough] and 4 slaves; and 2 villans and 1 radman and 4 bordars with 1 plough. There are 2 acres of meadow. TRE it was worth 25s; now 20s.

The same William holds THINGWALL, and Durand [holds] of him. Vetrlithr held it and was a free man. There is 1 hide paying geld. There is land for 2 ploughs. In demesne is 1 [plough] and 2 slaves; and 1 villan and 1 bordar have another [plough]. TRE it was worth 8s; now 5s.

The same William holds NOCTORUM, and Richard [holds] of him. Colbert held it and was a free man. There is half a hide paying geld. There is land for 1 plough, which [plough] is there in demesne, with 2 oxen and 2 villans. It was worth 15s; now 10s. It was waste.

IN MIDDLEWICH HUNDRED

The same William holds HASSALL. Auti held it and was a free man. There is half a hide paying geld. There is land for 2 ploughs. There is 1 radman with half a plough and 1 slave, and 1 radman and 2 villans and 3 bordars with 1 plough. [There is] woodland 1 league long, and there is an enclosure and a hawk's eyrie. TRE it was worth 4s; now 5s.

The same William holds HASSALL. Godric held it and was a free man. There is half a hide paying geld. There is land for 2 ploughs. There 1 radman with 1 bordar has half a plough. TRE it was worth 5s; now 5s. It was waste.

[Folio 265V: CHESHIRE]

The same William holds 'MINSHULL VERNON' [in Middlewich]. Leofnoth held it and was a free man. There is 1 hide paying geld. There is land for 1 plough. There 1 radman and 2 slaves and 2 bordars have 1 plough. There is 1 acre of meadow, woodland 1 league long and 1 wide, and 4 enclosures and a hawk's eyrie. It was and is worth 4s. It was waste.

The same William holds CHURCH MINSHULL. Deorc and Arngrim held it as 2 manors and were free men. There is 1 hide paying geld. There is land for 2 ploughs. There are [2 ploughs], with 3 radmen and 2 bordars. There is 1 acre of meadow, and woodland half a league long and a half wide, and an enclosure and a hawk's eyrie. It was worth 4s; now 8s.

The same William holds SPROSTON. Almær held it and was free. There is half a hide paying geld. There is land for 1 plough. There is [1 plough], with 1 radman and 1 slave, and 2 villans and 2 bordars. There is half an acre of meadow, [and] woodland 2 furlongs long. TRE it was worth 5s; now 4s. He found it waste.

IN "WARMUNDESTROU" HUNDRED

The same William holds ACTON. Earl Morcar held it. There are 8 hides paying geld. There is land for 30 ploughs. In demesne are 3 [ploughs] and 2 slaves; and 13 villans and 15 bordars with 7 ploughs. There is a mill serving the court, and 10 acres of meadow, woodland 6 leagues long and 1 wide, and 1 hawk's eyrie. There are 2 priests with 1 plough, and 2 Frenchmen having 1½ ploughs and 1 slave and 6 villans and 7 bordars with 4 ploughs.

This manor has its court in the hall of its lord, and in Wich [Nantwich] 1 house quit for the making of salt. The whole TRE was worth £10; now £6.

The same William holds ASTON [in Wrenbury]. Dot held it and was a free man. There is 1 hide paying geld. There is land for 2 ploughs. In demesne is 1 [plough] and 2 oxmen; and 2 villans and 3 bordars have another plough. There is woodland 1 league long and as much wide. TRE it was worth 10s; now 5s. He found it waste.

The same William holds WILLASTON. Wulfgeat, a free man, held it. There is 1 virgate paying geld. There is land for half a plough. There is 1 bordar. It was worth 5s; now 2s.

The same William holds WRENBURY. Karli held it and was a free man. There are 1½ hides paying geld. There is land for 2 ploughs. In demesne is 1 [plough] and 2 oxmen, and 1 bordar. There is woodland 2 leagues long and 1 wide, and 2 enclosures and a hawk's eyrie. It was and is worth 5s. He found it waste.

The same William holds CHORLTON. Frani held it and was a free man. There is half a hide paying geld. There is land for half a plough. There is 1 villan with 2 oxen. It was and is worth 2s. He found it waste.

The same William holds MARBURY at 1½ hides, and NORBURY [in Marbury] at 1½ hides, and WIRSWALL at 1 hide. These lands pay geld. They were Berewicks. They lay in WHITCHURCH [Shrops.]. Earl Harold held them. There is land for 5 ploughs. In demesne is 1 [plough] and 2 oxmen; and 2 villans and 3 bordars with 1 plough. [There is] woodland 2 leagues long and 1 league and 40 perches wide. The whole TRE was worth 21s; now 10s. Wirswall is waste.

The same William holds WALGHERTON. Gunningr and Healfdene held it as 2 manors and were free men. There is 1 hide and 1 virgate paying geld. There is land for 2 ploughs. There is 1 [plough], with 1 oxman, and 1 radman and 2 bordars. TRE it was worth 9s; now 5s. He found it waste.

The same William holds SHAVINGTON. Godwine and Dot held it as 2 manors and were free. There are 3 virgates paying geld. There is land for 1 plough. There 1 radman has half a plough, and 2 bordars. TRE it was worth 4s; now 3s. He found it waste.

The same William holds BUERTON. Siward held it and was a free man. There is 1 hide paying geld. There is land for 3 ploughs. In demesne are 2 [ploughs] and 1 oxman. There is woodland half a league long and as much wide, and 3 enclosures and a hawk's eyrie. It is worth 10s.

The same William holds HATHERTON. Ulfkil held it and was a free man. There is 1 hide paying geld. There is land for 5 ploughs. In demesne is 1 [plough] and 2 oxmen; and 2 villans and 1 bordar with 1 plough. There is woodland half a league long and as much wide. There is 1 enclosure.

The same William holds WISTASTON. Wulfric held it and was a free man. There is 1 hide paying geld. There is land for 5 ploughs. In demesne is 1 [plough] and 2 oxmen; and 2 villans and 1 radman and 2 bordars with 1 plough. There is half an acre of meadow, woodland 1 league long and a half wide, and 2 enclosures. TRE it was worth 30s; now 10s.

The same William holds BASFORD. Owine, Erlekin and Leofric held it as 3 manors and were free men. There is 1 hide paying geld. There is land for 2 ploughs. There 3 radmen and 2 villans and 3 bordars have 1 plough. There is 1 virgate of meadow, [and] woodland 4 furlongs long and 1 wide. It was worth 5s; now the same. They were waste.

The same William holds BATHERTON. Healfdene and Deorc held it as 2 manors and were free men. There is half a hide paying geld. There is land for 2 ploughs. In demesne is 1 [plough] and 2 oxmen; and 1 villan and 2 bordars. There are 40 perches of woodland. TRE it was worth 6s; now 3s. He found it waste.

The same William holds WORLESTON. Hakun, Alweard and Alric held it as 3 manors and were free. There is half a hide paying geld. There is land for 2 ploughs. In demesne is 1 [plough] and 2 oxmen; and 1 villan and 1 radman and 2 bordars with 1 plough. There is woodland half a league long and a half wide, and 1 enclosure. TRE it was worth 7s4d; now 8s. It was waste.

The same William holds BARTHOMLEY. Siward held it and was a free man. There is 1 hide paying geld. There is land for 3 ploughs. In demesne is 1 [plough] and 2 oxmen; [and] a priest and 1 radman and 1 villan and 2 bordars with 2 ploughs. There is 1 acre of meadow, [and] woodland 1 league long and a half wide, and 1 enclosure and a hawk's eyrie. It was and is worth 20s. He found it waste.

The same William holds [?] AUSTERSON. Osmær and Owine held it as 2 manors and were free men. There are 3 virgates paying geld. There is land for 5 ploughs. In demesne is 1 [plough] and 2 oxmen; and 3 bordars with 1 plough. There is 1 acre of meadow, [and] woodland 1 league long and a half wide. There are 3 enclosures and 1 hawk's eyrie. TRE it was worth 20s; now 10s. He found it waste.

The same William holds WILKESLEY. Dot and Godric held it as 2 manors and were free men. There is 1 hide and 1 virgate paying geld. There is land for 3 ploughs. There 1 radman and 1 villan and 6 bordars have 1 plough. There is 1 acre of meadow, woodland 1 league long and as much wide, and 5 enclosures and 1 hawk's eyrie. TRE it was worth 18s; now 5s.

The same William holds TITTENLEY [Shrops.]. Eadric held it and was a free man. There are 3 virgates paying geld. There is land for 1 plough. There is [1 plough], with 2 villans and 2 bordars. There is woodland half a league long and as much wide. It was worth 4s; now 5s.

The same William holds STAPELEY. Ælfric and Dot held it as 2 manors and were free men. There is half a hide paying geld. There is land for 2 ploughs. There is [1 plough], with 2 oxmen and 1 villan and 1 bordar. There are 1½ acres of meadow, [and] woodland half a league long and as much wide. TRE it was worth 10s; now 6s. He found it waste.

The same William holds 'WISTERSON' [in Nantwich]. Leofwine and Osmær held it as 2 manors and were free.

There are 3 virgates paying geld. There is land for 2 ploughs. In demesne are 1½ [ploughs] and 3 oxmen; and 1 villan with half a plough, and 1 bordar. There is 1 perch of meadow, [and] woodland half a league long and as much wide. It was worth 8s; now 10s.

The same William holds BROOMHALL GREEN. Eadric and Eadric held it as 2 manors and were free. There is half a hide paying geld. There is land for 1 plough. In demesne is half [a plough] with 1 oxman. There is woodland 1 league long and a half wide, and there is an enclosure. TRE it was worth 4s; now 2s. He found it waste. 1 virgate lay in Poole manor.

The same William holds POOLE. Hakun held it and was a free man. There is half a hide paying geld. There is land for 1 plough. This [plough] is in demesne with 2 oxmen, and 3 bordars. There is half an acre of meadow. It was worth 5s; now 8s.

The same William holds FRITH. Leofwine and Osmær held it as 2 manors and were free men. There is 1 virgate paying geld. There is land for 2 ploughs. There 3 villans have 1 [plough], and there are 4 acres of meadow, and woodland half a league long and 3 furlongs wide. TRE it was worth 7s; now 5s.

The same William holds CHORLEY. Ælfric, a free man, held it. There are 3 virgates paying geld. There is land for 1½ ploughs. There are 2 villans and 1 bordar with half a plough. [There is] woodland half a league long and 2 furlongs wide. There is an enclosure. It is worth 3s.

The same William holds BADDILEY. Ælfric, a free man, held it. There is half a virgate paying geld. There is land for 1 plough, which [plough] is there in demesne. [There is] woodland half a league long and as much wide. There is an enclosure. It was worth 10s; now 5s.

The same William holds 1 Berewick, STONELEY GREEN. This belonged to WHITCHURCH [Shrops.]. Earl Harold held it. There is half a virgate paying geld. There is land for 2 oxen. There is 1 radman, [and] woodland half a league long and a half wide. There is an enclosure. It was and is worth 2s.

The same William holds COPPENHALL. Healfdene and Wulfheah held it as 2 manors and were free. There is 1 hide paying geld. There is land for 4 ploughs. In demesne is 1 [plough] and 2 oxmen; and 1 radman and 1 villan and 1 bordar with 1 plough. There are 3 acres of meadow, [and] woodland 1 league long and 1 wide. There are 2 enclosures. TRE it was worth 24s; now 12s.

[Folio 266: CHESHIRE

The same William holds POOLE. Wulfgifu held it and was free. There is 1 virgate paying geld. There is land for 1 plough. There is 1 villan and 3 bordars with half a plough. There are 2 acres of meadow, and 1 acre of scrubland. It was and is worth 3s.

The same William holds ASTON JUXTA MONDRUM. Ramkel held it and was free. There is 1 virgate paying geld. There is land for 1 plough. There 1 radman has half a plough, with 2 bordars. There are $1\frac{1}{2}$ acres of meadow, [and] woodland 1 league long and a half wide. It was worth 5s; now 3s. It was waste.

The same William holds CHOLMONDESTON. Wulfgifu held it and was free. There is 1 hide paying geld. There is land for 2 ploughs. There is 1 radman having 1 plough, and 3 villans with 1 plough. TRE it was worth 10s; now 6s.

IN CHESTER HUNDRED

WILLIAM fitzNigel holds of Earl Hugh NEWTON [in Chester]. Arni held it. There is 1 hide paying geld. There is land for 3 ploughs. In demesne are 2 [ploughs] and 4 oxmen; and 6 villans with 1 plough. TRE it was worth 20s; and afterwards 10s; now 20s.

The same William holds NETHERLEIGH [in Chester]. Arni held it. There is 1 virgate paying geld. There is land for half a plough. There is [half a plough], with 3 villans. It was worth 5s; now 8s.

The same William holds 1 carucate of land in HANDBRIDGE [in Chester] paying geld. Arni held it as a manor. There are 3 bordars having half a plough. It was worth 10s; now 4s.

IN 'DUDDESTON' HUNDRED

The same William holds CLUTTON. Edward and Wulfwine Cild held it as 2 manors and were free men. There is 1 hide paying geld. There is land for 2 ploughs. In demesne is half a plough; and 1 Frenchman with 3 villans has half a plough. There is half an acre of meadow, [and] half a league of woodland. TRE it was worth 20s; now 8s.

IN RUSHTON HUNDRED

The same William holds [Great and Little] BARROW. Thorth held it and was a free man. There are 3 hides paying geld. There is land for 8 ploughs. There is 1 [plough] in demesne and 2 oxmen; and 2 villans and 4 bordars and 2 Frenchmen. Among them is 1 plough. There are 2 mills rendering 10s, and 1 acre of meadow, [and] woodland 1 league long and a half wide. TRE it was worth 30s; now as much. He found it waste.

IN WILLASTON HUNDRED

The same William holds NESTON. Arni held it and was a free man. There are 2 parts of 2 hides paying geld. There is land for 4 ploughs. In demesne are 2 ploughs and 1 slave. A priest and 4 villans and 2 bordars have 3 ploughs there. TRE it was worth 20s; and afterwards as much; now 25s.

The same William holds RABY, and Hardwin [holds] of him. Arni held it. There is half a hide paying geld. There is land for 1 plough. In demesne is [1 plough] and 1 slave; and 2 villans and 2 bordars with 1 plough. TRE it was worth 10s; and afterwards 14s; now 20s.

The same William holds CAPENHURST, and David [holds] of him. There is half a hide paying geld. Arni held it. There is land for 1 plough. There is [1 plough], with 1 villan and 2 bordars. TRE, and afterwards, it was worth 5s; now 8s.

The same William holds BARNSTON, and Ralph [holds] of him. Hrafnsvartr and Leofgeat held it as 2 manors and were free men. There is 1 hide paying geld. There is land for 2 ploughs. In demesne is 1 [plough] and 2 oxmen, and 3 bordars. It is worth 10s. He found it waste.

IN BUCKLOW HUNDRED

The same William holds WARBURTON. Earnwig held it and was free. There is half a hide paying geld. There is land for 1 plough. There is 1 radman with 2 oxen. It was worth 5s; now 2s.

The same William holds MILLINGTON. Dot [held it and] was a free man. There is half a hide paying geld. There is land for 1 plough. It was and is waste.

The same William holds KNUTSFORD, and Erchenbrand [holds] of him, who also held it as a free man. There is half a hide paying geld. There is land for 2 ploughs. It was and is waste. [There is] woodland half a league long and 2 acres wide. It was worth 10s.

The same William holds OVER TABLEY. Leofwine held it and was free. There is the third part of 1 hide paying geld. There is land for 1 plough. It was and is waste. There is woodland half a league long and 40 perches wide. It was worth 10s.

The same William holds in the vill itself 1 bovate of land and the third part of 1 hide paying geld. Sigrith and Wulfsige held them as 2 manors and were free. There is land for 1 plough. It was and is waste. TRE it was worth 7s.

The same William holds LOWER PEOVER. Edward held it. There are 2 parts of 1 hide paying geld. And he was a free man. There is land for 1 plough. It was and is waste. There is woodland 1 league long and 1 acre wide. It was worth 5s; now 12d.

The same William holds TATTON. Erchenbrand, a free man, held it. There is 1 hide paying geld. There is land for $3\frac{1}{2}$ ploughs. There are 3 villans and 4 bordars. It is worth 4s.

IN "TUNENDUNE" HUNDRED

The same William holds HALTON. Orm held it and was a free man. There are 10 hides. Of these, 5 pay geld and the others do not pay geld. There is land for 20 ploughs. In demesne are 2 ploughs and 4 oxmen; and 4 villans and 2 bordars and 2 priests with 5 ploughs among them all. 2 fishermen there pay 5s, and [there is] 1 acre of meadow, [and] woodland 1 league long and a half wide. There are 2 enclosures. In Wich [Middlewich, Nantwich or Northwich], 1 waste house.

Of this land of this manor Odard holds half a hide, Geoffrey 2 hides, Aitard $1\frac{1}{2}$ hides, Humphrey $1\frac{1}{2}$ hides, Odard half a hide, [and] Hardwin half a hide.

There are in demesne 3 ploughs; and 12 villans and 1 radman and 5 bordars with 5 ploughs among them all, and 6 oxmen, and half an acre of meadow, and 18 acres of woodland.

The whole manor TRE was worth 40s; and afterwards it

was waste; now what William holds is worth 50s, what his knights [hold] is worth 54s.

The same William holds WESTON. Gruffydd held it as a free man. There are 2 hides paying geld. There is land for 5 ploughs. Odard and Beorhtric hold it of William, and there they have 2 ploughs in demesne and 3 oxmen; and 5 villans and 3 bordars with 3 ploughs, and 2 fishermen, and 2 acres of meadow, and woodland 1 league long and a half wide, and an enclosure. TRE it was worth 8s; now 35s. He found it waste.

The same William holds ASTON [in Runcorn], and Odard [holds] of him. Leofric, a free man, held it. There is 1 hide paying geld. There is land for 2½ ploughs. In demesne are 1½ ploughs and 3 oxmen; and 1 villan and 1 bordar with 1 plough. There is a mill serving the court, and a fisherman, and 1 acre of woodland. TRE it was worth 5s; now 20s.

The same William holds NORTON, and Ansfrid [holds] of him. Uhtræd and Toki held it as 2 manors and were free men. There are 2 hides paying geld. There is land for 6 ploughs. In demesne is 1 [plough] and 2 slaves; and 3 villans with 1 plough. There is 1 fisherman, and 3 acres of meadow, and 4 acres of woodland and 2 enclosures. TRE it was worth 16s; now 9s4d. He found it waste.

The same William holds EANLEYWOOD. Wicga held it. There is half a hide paying geld. There is land for half a plough. It was and is waste.

The same William holds DUTTON. Edward held it as a free man as 1 manor. There is half a virgate paying geld. There is land for 2 oxen. There is 1 radman and 1 villan. It is worth 6d. It was waste.

The same William holds LITTLE LEIGH. Edward held it as a free man. There is 1 hide paying geld. There is land for 1 plough. There is [1 plough], with 1 radman and 1 slave and 2 villans and 1 bordar. It is worth 4s; it was worth 5s. Of this land Earl Hugh has 1 virgate which renders 3s.

The same William holds ASTON PARK, and Payne [holds] of him. Leofnoth held it as a free man. There are 2½ virgates paying geld. There is land for 1 plough, which [plough] is there in demesne, and 2 oxmen, and 1 radman and 1 bordar and 1 slave. There is woodland 1 league long and 40 perches wide and there are 2 enclosures.

The same William holds GREAT BUDWORTH, and Payne [holds] of him. Edward held it as a free man. There is 1 hide paying geld. There is land for 2 ploughs. In demesne are half a plough and 1 slave; and a priest and 2 villans and 1 bordar with 1 plough, and a mill serving the hall. There are 1½ acres of meadow. TRE it was worth 6s; now 8s.

The same William holds [Higher and Lower] WHITLEY, and Payne and Odard [hold] of him. Leofnoth held it as a free man. There are 2 hides paying geld. There is land for 2 ploughs. In demesne is 1 [plough], with 1 slave. There is 1 acre of meadow, [and] woodland 1 league long and a half wide. It is worth 6s.

The same William holds GOOSTREY, and Ralph [holds] of

him. Kolben held it as a free man. There is 1 virgate paying geld. There is land for 2 oxen. It was and is waste.

IN "HAMESTAN" HUNDRED

WILLIAM holds of the earl 'OVER ALDERLEY'. Brun held it and was a free man. There is 1 hide paying geld. There is land for 4 ploughs. It was and is waste. [There is] woodland 2 leagues long and 2 wide. TRE it was worth 20s.

IN MIDDLEWICH HUNDRED

WILLIAM holds of the earl LACH DENNIS. Hasten held it and was a free man. There is half a hide paying geld. There is land for 1 plough. It was and is waste.

[Folio 266V: CHESHIRE]

IN CHESTER HUNDRED

HUGH Delamere holds of Earl Hugh 'OVERLEIGH' [in Chester]. Leofwine held it. There is 1 virgate of land paying geld. There are 2 villans and 1 bordar with half a plough. TRE it was worth 10s; now 8s. He found it waste.

The same Hugh holds HANDBRIDGE [in Chester]. Leofwine held it. There is 1 carucate of land paying geld. There 2 bordars have half a plough. It was and is worth 3s.

The same Hugh holds 'REDCLIFF' [in Chester]. Gunwor held it. There is the third part of 1 hide paying geld. There is 1 plough in demesne, with 2 oxmen. It was waste when he received it. TRE it was worth 10s; now 6s8d.

IN WILLASTON HUNDRED

The same Hugh holds GRANGE. Earngeat held it and was a free man. There is 1 hide paying geld. There is land for 3 ploughs. In demesne is 1 [plough], with 1 bordar. It was worth 5s; now 10s.

IN MIDDLEWICH HUNDRED

Hugh holds of the earl CHURCH LAWTON. Godric held it and was a free man. There is 1 hide paying geld. There is land for 3 ploughs. It is waste. There is woodland 1 league long and 1 wide, and 1 acre of meadow. TRE it was worth 16s.

Hugh holds [?] BUGLAWTON of the earl. Godric held it. There is half a hide paying geld. There is land for 3 ploughs. It is waste. There is woodland 2 leagues long and 1 wide. TRE it was worth 20s.

Hugh holds BYLEY of the earl. Godric and Godwine and Arnketil held it as 3 manors, and were free. There is 1 hide paying geld. There is land for 2 ploughs. There 2 radmen and 2 bordars have 1 plough. There are 2 acres of meadow, and 2 acres of woodland. TRE it was worth 10s; now as much.

Hugh holds GOOSTREY of the earl. Godric held it and was a free man. There are 3 virgates of land [...] paying geld. There is land for 1½ ploughs. It always was and is waste.

Hugh fitzOsbern holds of the earl in HANDBRIDGE [in Chester] 1 carucate of land paying geld. Wulfnoth held it. There are 2 bordars with 3 oxen. It is worth 3s.

IN 'DUDDESTON' HUNDRED

The same Hugh holds CALDECOTT. Wulfgar the priest and 3 other thegns held it as 3 manors and were free. There is 1 hide paying geld. There is land for 2 ploughs. These [ploughs] are there, with 1 radman and 2 villans and 3 oxmen. There is half a fishery. TRE it was waste, yet it rendered 2s; now 15s.

The same Hugh holds PULFORD. Wulfric held it as a free man. There are $1\frac{1}{2}$ hides paying geld. There is land for 1 plough, and there is [1 plough], with 2 radmen and 1 villan and 2 bordars. This land was waste; now it is worth 5s.

IN RUSHTON HUNDRED

The same Hugh holds WARDLE. Alweald held it as a free man. There is half a hide paying geld. There is land for 1 plough. There 1 villan has half a plough. There is woodland half a league long and 1 acre wide. It was and is worth 3s.

IN "HAMESTAN" HUNDRED

Hugh holds BOSLEY of the earl. Godric held it and was a free man. There is half a hide paying geld. There is land for 4 ploughs. It is waste. There is woodland 2 leagues long and half a league wide. TRE it was worth 20s.

Hugh holds MARTON of the earl. Godric held it and was a free man. There is 1 virgate of land paying geld. It was always waste. There is woodland 20 perches long and as much wide.

Hugh holds of the earl 1 Berewick, KERMINCHAM. Godric held it. There is half a hide paying geld. There is land for 2 ploughs. It was and is waste. It was worth 5s.

Hugh holds SOMERFORD of the earl. Godric held it as a free man. There is half a hide paying geld. There is land for 1 plough. It was and still is waste.

IN "WARMUNDESTROU" HUNDRED

HAMO holds PUDDINGTON of Earl Hugh. Wulfric held it and was a free man. There are $2\frac{1}{2}$ hides paying geld. There is land for 3 ploughs. In demesne is 1 [plough] and 1 slave; and 4 villans and 4 bordars and 1 radman with 1 plough. It is worth 20s. It was waste.

IN BUCKLOW HUNDRED

The same Hamo holds DUNHAM [in Bowden]. Alweard held it and was a free man. There is 1 hide paying geld. There is land for 3 ploughs. In demesne is 1 [plough] and 2 oxmen, and 2 villans and 1 bordar, and 1 acre of woodland, and in the city 1 house. TRE it was worth 12s; 10s. It was waste.

The same Hamo holds BOWDON. Alweard held it and was a free man. There is 1 hide paying geld. There is land for 2 ploughs. There 2 Frenchmen have 1 plough. There is a priest and a church to which half of this hide belongs. There is a mill rendering 16d. It is worth 3s. It was waste and he found it so.

The same Hamo holds HALE. Alweard held it. There is 1 hide paying geld. There is land for $2\frac{1}{2}$ ploughs. There 3 villans with 1 radman have 2 ploughs. There is woodland 1 league long and a half wide, and an enclosure, and a hawk's eyrie, and

half an acre of meadow. TRE it was worth 15s; now 12s. He found it waste.

IN "HAMESTAN" HUNDRED

The same Hamo holds BRAMHALL. Brun and Hakun held it as 2 manors and were free men. There is 1 hide paying geld. There is land for 6 ploughs. There 1 radman and 2 villans and 2 bordars have 1 plough. There is woodland half a league long and as much wide, and half an enclosure, and 1 acre of meadow. TRE it was worth 32s; now 5s. He found it waste.

IN BUCKLOW HUNDRED

The same Hamo holds ASHLEY. Alweard held it and was a free man. There is 1 virgate of land paying geld. There is land for 2 oxen. It was and is waste.

The same Hamo holds 'ALRETUNSTALL' [in Bowdon]. Alweard held it. There are $1\frac{1}{2}$ virgates of land paying geld. There is land for 6 oxen. It was and is waste.

IN 'DUDDESTON' HUNDRED

BIGOD holds FARNDON of Earl Hugh. Earl Edwin held it. There are 4 hides paying geld. [There is] land for 8 ploughs. In demesne are 2 [ploughs]; and 7 villans and 3 bordars with 2 ploughs. There is a mill, and a fishery with 2 fishermen, and 1 acre of meadow. TRE it was worth 40s; now £6. He found it waste.

The same Bigod holds LEA [near Aldford]. Asgot held it as a free man. There is 1 hide paying geld. There is land for 2 ploughs. There are 2 bordars, and 1 acre of meadow. It is worth 2s. It was waste.

The same Bigod holds THORNTON-LE-MOORS. Stenkil held it and was a free man. There are 2 hides paying geld. There is land for 2 ploughs. In demesne is half [a plough]; and 2 villans and a bordar have half a plough. There is a church and a priest, and 1 acre of meadow. TRE it was worth 20s; now 10s. He found it waste.

IN BUCKLOW HUNDRED

The same Bigod holds MOBBERLEY. Dot held it and was a free man. There are $1\frac{1}{2}$ hides paying geld. There is land for 4 ploughs. There a thegn has half a plough and 1 slave, and 1 villan and 2 bordars. There is 1 acre of meadow, and woodland 2 leagues long and as much wide, and 2 enclosures. TRE it was worth 12s; now 5s. He found it waste.

IN "HAMESTAN" HUNDRED

The same Bigod holds NORBURY [in Stockport]. Brun held it and was a free man. There is 1 hide paying geld. There is land for 4 ploughs. There 1 radman with 3 bordars has 1 plough. There is 1 acre of meadow, woodland 5 leagues long and 3 leagues wide, and 3 enclosures there. TRE it was worth 10s; now 3s. He found it waste.

The same Bigod holds NETHER ALDERLEY. Godwine held it as a free man. There is 1 hide paying geld. There is land for 8 ploughs. In demesne is 1 [plough], with 2 oxmen; and 3 villans and 1 radman with 1 plough. There is 1 acre of meadow, woodland $1\frac{1}{2}$ leagues long and 1 league wide, and

2 enclosures there. TRE it was worth 20s; now 10s. He found it waste.

The same Bigod holds SIDDINGTON. Brun held it and was a free man. There are $1\frac{1}{2}$ hides paying geld. There is land for 7 ploughs. There a Frenchman has half a plough, and 1 villan and 1 bordar with half a plough. There is woodland 1 league long and a half wide. TRE it was worth 20s; now 5s.

The same Bigod holds NORTH RODE. Beornwulf held it and was a free man. There is half a hide paying geld. There is land for 2 ploughs. It is waste and he found it so. TRE it was worth 8s. [There is] woodland 1 league long and half a league wide.

IN MIDDLEWICH HUNDRED

The same Bigod holds CONGLETON. Godwine held it. There is 1 hide paying geld. There is land for 4 ploughs. There are 2 [ploughs], with 2 villans and 4 bordars. There is woodland 1 league long and 1 wide, and 2 enclosures there. It was waste and he found it so; now it is worth 4s.

The same Bigod holds SANDBACH. Dunning held it and was free. There is 1 hide paying geld, and $1\frac{1}{2}$ virgates likewise paying geld. There is land for 2 ploughs. There is 1 Frenchman with half a plough and 3 slaves, and 2 villans with half a plough. There is a priest and a church, [and] woodland half a league long and 40 perches wide. TRE it was worth 4s; now 8s.

The same Bigod holds SUTTON [in Middlewich]. Alstan and Beollán held it as 2 manors and were free men. There are 3 virgates and 16 acres of land paying geld. There is land for $1\frac{1}{2}$ ploughs. In demesne is half a plough and 2 oxmen; and 2 villans have half a plough. TRE it was worth 4s; now 3s. It was waste.

The same Bigod holds WIMBOLDSLEY. Leofwine held it and was free. There is 1 virgate of land paying geld. There is land for 1 plough. There 1 radman has half a plough and 2 slaves, with 1 villan. It is worth 2s. It was waste and he found it so.

The same Bigod holds WEAVER. Stenulf held it and was free. There is 1 virgate of land paying geld. There is land for half a plough. There is [half a plough], with 1 radman and 1 villan and 2 bordars. [There is] woodland 1 furlong long and as much wide, and an enclosure there. It was worth 2s; now 3s.

IN RUSHTON HUNDRED

BALDRIC holds "COCLE" of Earl Hugh. Wulfheah held it and was a free man. There is 1 hide paying geld. There is land for 1 plough. This [plough] is there in demesne, and 1 slave. TRE it was worth 40s; now the same. He found it waste.

IN "EXESTAN" HUNDRED

Thorth, a free man, held TREVALYN [Wales]. There are 3 hides paying geld.

In [?] 'EYTON' [in Holt, Wales] St Chad held 1 hide, and in SUTTON GREEN [Wales] the same saint held 1 hide

paying geld. When Earl Hugh received these 3 manors, they were waste. Now Hugh fitzOsbern holds them of him, and has half a plough in demesne and 3 slaves; and 7 villans and 5 bordars and 2 Frenchmen. They have $1\frac{1}{2}$ ploughs among them all. There is a mill rendering 4s, and half a fishery, and 4 acres of meadow, [and] woodland 2 leagues long and a half wide. There are 2 enclosures. It is worth 30s. There could be 4 ploughs more. TRE it was worth 20s.

[Folio 267: CHESHIRE]

IN 'DUDDESTON' HUNDRED

GILBERT de Venables holds ECCLESTON of Earl Hugh. Edwin held it and was a free man. There are 5 hides paying geld. There is land for 6 ploughs. In demesne is 1 [plough] and 2 slaves; and 4 villans and 1 bordar with 1 plough. There is a boat and a net, and half an acre of meadow. TRE it was worth 10s; now 50s. It was waste.

The same Gilbert holds ALPRAHAM. Earl Edwin held it. There are 2 hides paying geld. There is land for 4 ploughs. There 3 villans with 6 bordars have 1 plough. There is woodland 2 leagues long and 1 wide, and 2 acres of meadow. TRE it was worth 20s; now 8s.

IN RUSHTON HUNDRED

The same Gilbert holds TARPORLEY. Wulfgeat held it and was a free man. There are 2 hides paying geld. There is land for 4 ploughs. In demesne is 1 [plough] and 2 slaves; and 4 villans and 2 bordars with 1 plough. [There is] woodland 1 league long and 1 wide, and 1 acre of meadow. TRE it was worth 20s; now 10s. He found it waste.

The same Gilbert holds WETTENHALL. Glewin held it and was a freeman. There is 1 hide paying geld. There is land for 2 ploughs. There 1 radman with 1 villan and 2 bordars has 1 plough. There are 2 acres of meadow, [and] woodland $1\frac{1}{2}$ leagues long and 1 league wide. It was and is worth 5s. He found it waste.

IN RULOE HUNDRED

The same Gilbert holds HARTFORD. Dodda held it # as a free man. There are 2 hides paying geld. There is land for 2 ploughs. There are 4 villans and 2 bordars and a smith having 1 plough. In Wich [Middlewich, Nantwich or Northwich] 1 salt-pan renders 2s, and another half salt-pan [is] waste. There is 1 acre of meadow. Of this land a knight holds half a hide, and has there 1 plough, and 2 oxmen and 3 bordars. TRE it was worth 20s; now 10s.

IN BUCKLOW HUNDRED

The same Gilbert holds LYMM. Wulfgeat held it and was free. There is 1 hide paying geld. There is land for 2 ploughs. There are 3 bordars. There is half a church with half a virgate of land. [There is] woodland half a league long and as much wide. TRE it was worth 10s; now 12d. He found it waste.

The same Gilbert holds HIGH LEGH. Wulfgeat and Dot held it as 2 manors and were free men. There is 1 hide paying geld. There is land for 2 ploughs. There 1 man of his has half a plough and 3 slaves. There is a priest and a church with 1 villan and 2 bordars having half a plough. There is woodland 1 league long and half a league wide, and an enclosure there. TRE it was worth 10s; now 5s.

The same Gilbert holds WINCHAM. Dot held it and was a free man. There are 1½ hides paying geld. There is land for 2 ploughs. In demesne is 1 plough, with 1 slave. There is 1 acre of woodland, and a hawk's eyrie, and 1 house in Wich [Middlewich, Nantwich or Northwich], and 1 bordar. It is worth 10s. It was waste and he found it so.

The same Gilbert holds MERE. Wulfgeat held it and was a freeman. There is 1 hide paying geld. There is land for 2 ploughs. It was and is waste. There is woodland half a league long and 40 perches wide. There are 2 acres of meadow. TRE it was worth 8s.

The same Gilbert holds PEOVER [Peover or Lower Peover]. Dot held it. There are 2 bovates of land paying geld. It was and is waste.

The same Gilbert holds ROSTHERNE. Wulfgeat held it. There is 1 virgate of land paying geld. There is land for 1 plough. It was waste. There are 2 acres of woodland. TRE it was worth 4s.

IN "EXESTAN" HUNDRED

The same Gilbert holds HOPE [Wales]. Edwin held it and was a free man. There is 1 hide paying geld. There is land for 1 plough, and there is [1 plough], with 2 villans, and 2 acres of woodland. It is worth 7s. It was waste and he found it so.

IN MIDDLEWICH HUNDRED

Gilbert the huntsman holds of the earl 'NEWBOLD' [in Astbury]. Wulfgeat held it and was a free man. There are 1½ hides paying geld. There is land for 5 ploughs. There 1 radman has 1 plough, and a priest 1 plough, and [there are] 3 villans and 2 bordars. There is 1 acre of meadow, and woodland 1 league long and as much wide, and 2 enclosures there. TRE it was worth 20s; now 8s.

The same Gilbert holds BRERETON. Wulfgeat held it. There are 2 hides paying geld. There is land for 4 ploughs. In demesne is 1 [plough] and 2 oxmen, and 2 villans and 3 bordars. There is 1 acre of meadow, woodland 1 league long and a half wide, and a mill rendering 12d. Of this land 2 of his men hold 1 hide, and they have 1 plough, with 2 slaves and 2 villans and 4 bordars. The whole TRE was worth 20s; now the same. He found it waste.

The same Gilbert holds KINDERTON. Godwine held it and was a free man. There are 3 hides paying geld. There is land for 5 ploughs. In demesne is 1 [plough] and 2 slaves, and 3 bordars. There is 1 acre of meadow, woodland half a league long and as much wide, and 1 enclosure there. It is worth 10s. It was waste and he found it [so].

The same Gilbert holds DAVENPORT. Godwine held it. There is half a hide paying geld. There is land for 1 plough. There is [1 plough], with 1 radman and 2 oxmen and 3 bordars, and 1 acre of woodland. It is worth 3s. He found it waste.

The same Gilbert holds WITTON. Dot held it and was a free man. There are 1½ hides paying geld. There is land for 2 ploughs. There 1 Frenchman has 1 plough, and 2 oxmen and 1 bordar. There is a mill rendering 3s. It is worth 7s. He found it waste.

IN "WARMUNDESTROU" HUNDRED

The same Gilbert holds BLAKENHALL. Godwine held it and was a free man. There are 4 hides, less 1 virgate, and they pay geld. There is land for 5 ploughs. There 4 radmen and 2 bordars have 2 ploughs. There is woodland 2 leagues long and 1 league wide. There is an enclosure and a hawk's eyrie. TRE it was worth 10s; now 12s.

IN MIDDLEWICH HUNDRED

JOSCELIN holds of Earl Hugh 'NEWTON' [in Middlewich]. Gruffydd held it and was a free man. There is 1 hide paying geld. There is land for 3 ploughs. In demesne is 1 [plough] and 2 oxmen. A priest with 1 bordar has 1 plough. There is half an acre of meadow. TRE it was worth 4s; now 10s.

The same Joscelin holds CROXTON. Godwine held it and was a free man. There is 1 hide paying geld. There is land for 1 plough, which [plough] is there, with 1 radman and 2 slaves and 2 villans and 1 bordar. It was worth 4s; now 10s.

IN BUCKLOW HUNDRED

The same Joscelin holds TABLEY. Uhtbrand held it and was a free man. There are 2 bovates of land paying geld. There is land for half a plough. It was and is waste.

IN WILLASTON HUNDRED

RANULPH holds of Earl Hugh BLACON [in Chester]. Thorth held it and was a free man. There are 2 hides paying geld. There is land for 4 ploughs. In demesne are 2 [ploughs] and 4 oxmen; and 4 villans and 4 bordars have 1 plough. There is a fishery. TRE it was worth 14s; now 40s.

IN RULOE HUNDRED

Ranulph holds WINNINGTON. Leofnoth held it and was a free man. There is half a hide paying geld. There is land for half a plough. There is 1 radman and 1 villan. It is worth 2s.

IN BUCKLOW HUNDRED

Ranulph holds TATTON of the earl. Leofwine held it. There is the sixth part of a hide paying geld. There is land for half a plough. This [half-plough] is there, with 1 radman and 2 slaves and 2 villans and 4 bordars. There is woodland 1 league long and as much wide. In Wich [Middlewich, Nantwich or Northwich], 1 waste house. It is worth 3s.

The same Ranulph holds PEOVER. Earngeat held it and was free. There is half a hide paying geld. There is land for 1 plough. There a certain man of his has 2 oxen, and 2 slaves and 2 villans [...]. There is woodland half a league long and 40 perches wide, and a hawk's eyrie. TRE it was worth 15s; now 4s. It was waste.

Ranulph himself holds WARFORD, and Godgyth [holds] of

him. She held it herself and was free. There is half a hide paying geld. There is land for 1 plough. There she has 2 oxen, and 4 slaves and 2 female slaves. It is worth 3s. It was waste.

The same Ranulph holds PEOVER [Peover or Lower Peover] at 2 bovates of land paying geld. There is land for half a plough.

The same Ranulph holds 'CHAPMONSWICHE' [in Rostherne] at half a hide paying geld. There is land for half a plough. Godyth held it and was a free woman. This land was and is waste.

The same Ranulph holds OLLERTON at half a virgate of land paying geld. Godgyth held it. There is land for 2 oxen. It was and is waste.

The same Ranulph holds SNELSON. Leofnoth held it. There is 1 virgate of land paying geld. There is land for half a plough. It was and is waste.

IN "TUNENDUNE" HUNDRED

The same Ranulph holds COGSHALL. Wulfgeat held it and was a free man. There is half a hide paying geld. There is land for 1 plough. From the pasture comes 3s. The land is waste.

IN MIDDLEWICH HUNDRED

The same Ranulph holds WHEELOCK. Earl Morcar held it. There are 3 hides paying geld. There is land for 4 ploughs. In demesne is 1 [plough] and 4 slaves; and 2 radmen with 1 plough. There is woodland 3 leagues long and 1 wide. TRE, and afterwards, it was waste; now it is worth 20s.

The same Ranulph holds TETTON. Godgyth held it. There is 1 hide and 1 virgate paying geld. There is land for 2 ploughs. There 1 Frenchman has 1 plough and 2 oxmen, and 1 radman with half a plough, and 3 bordars. There is woodland 40 perches long and 1 acre wide, and an enclosure there. TRE, and afterwards, it was waste; now it is worth 10s.

IN 'DUDDESTON' HUNDRED

RALPH the huntsman holds STAPLEFORD of Earl Hugh. Wulfsige held it and was a free man. There are 2 hides paying geld. There is land for 3 ploughs. In demesne is 1 [plough]; and a radman and 2 villans and 5 bordars with 3 ploughs. There is woodland 2 acres long and 1 wide. There is a mill. It was and is worth 16s.

[Folio 267V: CHESHIRE]

IN "EXESTAN" HUNDRED

REGINALD holds of Earl Hugh GRESFORD [Wales]. Thorth held it and was a free man. There are 1½ hides paying geld. There is land for 2 ploughs. There 1 villan with 2 bordars has 1 plough. It is worth 20s. Of woodland which is 4 leagues long and 2 wide he has as much as belongs to 1½ hides.

The same Reginald holds ERBISTOCK [Wales]. Rhys held it as a free man. There is half a hide paying geld. There is land for 1 plough. This [plough] is there, with 1 radman and 1 villan and 1 bordar. TRE it was waste; and afterwards it was worth 10s; now 9s.

IN 'DUDDESTON' HUNDRED

ILBERT holds WAVERTON of Earl Hugh. Earnwine held it and was a free man. There are 3 hides paying geld. There is land for 4 ploughs. In demesne is 1 [plough]; and 3 Frenchmen with 3 villans have 3 ploughs. TRE it was worth 20s; and afterwards 6s; now 16s.

The same Ilbert holds HATTON. Alnoth and Earnwine held it as 2 manors and were free men. There are 2 hides paying geld. There is land for 3 ploughs. There is 1 villan with 1 plough. TRE it was worth 20s; now 9s4d. It was waste.

IN RUSHTON HUNDRED

The same Ilbert holds CLOTTON. Stenulf held it and was a free man. There are 3 hides paying geld. There is land for 6 ploughs. There are 6 villans and 2 bordars and 4 radmen having 5 ploughs. It was and is worth 12s.

IN 'DUDDESTON' HUNDRED

OSBERN fitzTezzo holds HANDLEY of Earl Hugh. Grimkel held it and was a free man. There is 1 hide paying geld. There is land for 4 ploughs. In demesne are 1½ ploughs with 1 slave; and 2 villans and 1 bordar have half a plough. TRE it was worth 13s3d; now 15s.

The same Osbern holds GOLBORNE [in Handley]. Edwin held it and was a free man. There is 1 hide paying geld. There is land for 3 ploughs. In demesne is 1 [plough], and 1 villan and 1 bordar. There is half an acre of meadow. It was and is worth 16s.

IN WILLASTON HUNDRED

The same Osbern holds POULTON [in Bebington], and Roger [holds] of him. Gamal held it and was a free man. There are 2 hides paying geld. There is land for 4 ploughs. In demesne is 1 [plough] and 2 slaves; and 1 radman and 1 villan and a priest and 4 bordars with 1 plough among them all. TRE it was worth 25s; and afterwards it was waste; now it is worth 25s.

IN RULOE HUNDRED

The same Osbern holds WINNINGTON. Hundingr held it and was a free man. There is half a hide paying geld. There is land for half a plough. There is 1 radman with 1 villan. It is worth 2s.

IN BUCKLOW HUNDRED

The same Osbern holds LYMM. Edward held it and was a free man. There is 1 hide paying geld. There is land for 4 ploughs. Edward holds it of him. He has there 1 plough and 2 oxmen, and 2 villans and 4 bordars, and [there is] half a church with a priest with half a virgate of land quit. [There is] woodland half a league long and as much wide. TRE it was worth 10s; now 8s. He found it waste.

The same Osbern holds WARBURTON. Rawn held it and was a free man. There is half a hide paying geld. There is land for 1 plough. There is 1 radman and 2 villans and 1 bordar with half a plough. It was worth 5s; now 2s. It was waste.

IN "TUNENDUNE" HUNDRED

The same Osbern holds DUTTON. Edward held it. He was a free man. There is half a hide paying geld. Edward holds it of Osbern. There is 1 radman and 1 villan and 3 bordars with $1\frac{1}{2}$ ploughs. TRE it was worth 12d; now 2s.

The same Osbern holds APPLETON THORN. Dot held it and was a free man. There is 1 hide paying geld. There is land for 4 ploughs. It was and is waste. TRE it was worth 16s. There is woodland half a league long and 40 perches wide.

The same Osbern holds GRAPPENHALL, and Edward [holds] of him. He himself and Dot held it as 2 manors and were free men. There is 1 hide and half a virgate of land paying geld. There is land for 2 ploughs. In demesne are $1\frac{1}{2}$ [ploughs] and 2 slaves, and 1 villan and 3 bordars. There is woodland 1 league long and 40 perches wide. There are 2 enclosures. TRE it was worth 5s; now 6s. It was waste.

IN RUSHTON HUNDRED

NIGEL holds OULTON of Earl Hugh. Dunning held it and was a free man. There is half a hide paying geld. There is land for 1 plough. It renders at farm 5s4d. TRE it was worth 20s. He found it waste.

IN WILLASTON HUNDRED

The same Nigel holds GREASBY. Dunning held it. There are 2 hides paying geld. There is land for 3 ploughs. In demesne is 1 [plough] and 2 slaves; and 3 villans and 2 Frenchmen and 1 bordar with 1 plough among them all. TRE it was worth 25s; and afterwards 10s; now 20s.

The same Nigel holds STORETON. Dunning held it. There are 2 hides paying geld. There is land for 3 ploughs. In demesne is half a plough and 1 slave; and 5 villans and 3 bordars with $1\frac{1}{2}$ ploughs. TRE it was worth 15s; now 20s. It was waste.

TEZELIN holds of Earl Hugh SOMERFORD [?Booths]. Hrafnsvartr and Ketil and Morfari held it as 3 manors. 2 were free men; Morfari could not withdraw from his lord. There is 1 virgate of land paying geld. It was divided into 3 portions. There is land for 3 ploughs. There is 1 radman having 1 plough and 2 slaves. There is woodland 40 perches long and as much wide. It was worth 6s; now 4s.

IN "TUNENDUNE" HUNDRED

ODARD holds DUTTON of the earl. Rawn held it and was a free man. There are $1\frac{1}{2}$ virgates of land paying geld. There is land for 1 plough. There is 1 radman with 1 slave. [There is] woodland 1 league long and a half wide. There is a hawk's eyrie. TRE it was worth 5s; now 12d.

MUNDRET holds BARTINGTON of the earl. Dunning held it. There is half a hide paying geld. There is land for 1 plough. This [plough] is there, with 1 radman and 1 slave and 1 bordar. TRE it was worth 3s; now 64d.

WULFGEAT holds BARTINGTON of the earl. Leofnoth held it. There is half a hide paying geld. There is land for 1 plough. It is waste. It was worth 2s.

A sergeant of the earl holds a piece of land in this HUNDRED OF "TUNENDUNE". This land has never been assessed in hides. He has there 1 plough, with 1 oxman. It is worth 4s.

IN RULOE HUNDRED

DUNNING holds KINGSLEY of the earl. He himself held it as a free man. There is 1 hide paying geld. There is land for 2 ploughs. In demesne is 1 [plough] and 5 slaves, and 1 villan and 3 bordars. There are $1\frac{1}{2}$ fisheries. There is woodland 1 league long and 1 wide. The earl put this into his forest, and there is a hawk's eyrie and 4 enclosures for [catching] roe-deer. TRE it was worth 30s; now 6s.

LEOFRIC holds ALVANLEY of the earl. Earnwig held it and was a free man. There is half a hide paying geld. There is land for 4 ploughs. In demesne is 1 [plough], with 1 villan and 2 bordars. [There is] woodland half a league long and a half wide.

IN "HAMESTAN" HUNDRED

WULFRIC holds BUTLEY. He himself held it as a free man. There is 1 hide paying geld. There is land for 5 ploughs. It is waste except for 7 sown acres. There is woodland 3 leagues long and 1 wide, and an enclosure there, and $2\frac{1}{2}$ acres of meadow. TRE it was worth 30s; now 2s.

GAMAL holds CHEADLE of the earl. His father held it as a free man. There are 2 hides paying geld. There is land for 6 ploughs. In demesne is 1 [plough] and 2 oxmen; and 4 villans and 3 bordars with 2 ploughs. There is woodland 1 league long and a half wide, and an enclosure and a hawk's eyrie, and 1 acre of meadow. It was and is worth 10s. The whole manor is 2 leagues long and 1 wide.

The same Gamal holds MOTTRAM ST ANDREW. His father held it. There are $1\frac{1}{2}$ hides paying geld. There is land for 4 ploughs. It is waste. There is woodland 3 leagues long and 2 wide, and 2 enclosures and a hawk's eyrie.

WULFRIC holds OLLERTON of the earl. He himself held it as a free man. There are 2 parts of a hide paying geld. There is land for 3 ploughs. There is 1 [plough], with 1 oxman and 1 villan and 2 bordars. There is 1 acre of meadow and 3 acres of woodland. It is worth 5s; it was waste TRE.

IN MIDDLEWICH HUNDRED

MORAN holds of the earl LACH DENNIS. Kolben held it as a free man. There is half a hide paying geld. There is land for 1 plough. There is [1 plough] in demesne and 2 oxmen, and 1 bordar. There is half an acre of meadow. It is worth 8s; it was waste TRE.

[Folio 268: CHESHIRE]

IN BUCKLOW HUNDRED

RANULPH and Bigod hold of the earl NORTHENDEN [Lancs.]. Wulfgeat held it as 1 manor and was a free man. There is 1 hide paying geld. There is land for 2 ploughs. It is waste. There is a church and 2 furlongs of woodland. It is worth 3s; TRE it was worth 10s.

GILBERT and Ranulph and Hamo hold SINDERLAND GREEN and BAGULEY [Lancs.]. Alweard and Sucga and Wudumann and Pat held it as 4 manors and were free men. There is 1 hide paying geld. There is land for $1\frac{1}{2}$ ploughs. The whole is waste; TRE it was worth 3s.

IN "EXESTAN" HUNDRED

HUGH and Osbern and Reginald hold GRESFORD [Wales]. Thorth held it as a free man. There are 13 hides paying geld. There is land for 12 ploughs. Hugh has 5 hides, Osbern $6\frac{1}{2}$ hides, Reginald $1\frac{1}{2}$ hides. In demesne are $1\frac{1}{2}$ ploughs. There is a church and a priest and 7 villans and 12 bordars and 1 Frenchman. Among them all they have $2\frac{1}{2}$ ploughs.

In the whole manor [is] woodland 4 leagues long and 2 wide and 2 eyries of hawks. Osbern has a mill grinding corn for his court. The whole was waste TRE; and they received it waste; now it is worth 65s among them all.

Of this land of this manor 1 hide lay in the Church of ST CHAD TRE, half [a hide] in "Chespuic" [Wales], and half [a hide] in "Radenoure" [Wales]. To this the shire testifies, but it does not know how the church lost it.

IN MIDDLEWICH HUNDRED

HUGH and William hold of the earl RODE [in Astbury]. Godric and Hrafnsvartr held it as 2 manors and were free men. There is 1 hide paying geld. There is land for 3 ploughs. It is waste except that 1 radman has under them [...] $\frac{1}{2}$ plough *[sic]*. It is worth 2s; TRE it was worth 20s. There is woodland 2 leagues long and 1 wide, and 2 enclosures and a hawk's eyrie.

In the same MIDDLEWICH HUNDRED there was a third Wich which is called NORTHWICH and it was at farm for £8. These laws and customs were there, as there were in the other Wiches, and the king and earl similarly divided the renders.

All the thegns who had salt-pans in this Wich did not give boilings of salt on Fridays throughout the year. Anyone who brought a cart with 2 or more oxen from another shire gave 4d in toll. A man from the same shire gave 2d for a cart within the third night after he returned whence he had come. If the third night passed [without payment], he paid a fine of 40s. A man from another shire gave 1d for a horse-load, but [one] from the same shire [gave] a mite within the third night as aforesaid.

If a man living in this hundred carted salt about the same shire to sell, he gave 1d for each cart every time he loaded it. If he carried salt on a horse to sell, he gave 1d at MARTINMAS. Anyone who did not pay at that date paid a fine of 40s. All the other [customs] in these Wiches are the same.

This one was waste when Earl Hugh received it; now it is worth 35s.

IN THE TIME OF King EDWARD there was in "WARMUNDESTROU" HUNDRED a Wich [Nantwich] in which there was a brine-pit for making salt, and there were 8 salt-pans between the king and Earl Edwin so that of all the issues and renders of the salt-pans the king had 2 parts and the earl the third. But besides these the earl himself had a salt-pan of his own which belonged to his manor of ACTON. From this salt-pan the earl had sufficient salt for his own house throughout the year. If, however, any was sold from that source, the king had 2d in toll and the earl the third [penny].

In the same Wich very many men of the country had salt-pans, from which there was the following custom: from the Ascension of Our Lord to Martinmas anyone having a salt-pan could carry his own salt to his house [without toll], but if he sold any of it either there or in the whole shire of Chester, he gave toll to the king and earl. After Martinmas anyone who might carry salt thence, whether his own or purchased, gave toll, the above-mentioned salt-pan of the earl excepted, as having its own custom.

In the week in which these aforesaid 8 salt-pans of the king and earl were employed in boiling [salt], on the Friday they rendered 16 boilings, of which 15 made a summa of salt. Other men's salt-pans did not give these boilings on Fridays from the Ascension of Our Lord to MARTINMAS, but when Martinmas was over, up to the Ascension of Our Lord, they all gave the boiling custom like the salt-pans of the king and earl.

All these salt-pans, both common and demesne, were bounded on one side by a certain stream and on the other side by a certain ditch.

Anyone who incurred a forfeiture within this boundary could pay a fine of 2s or 30 boilings of salt, except for homicide or theft where the thief was sentenced to death. If these [offences] were committed here, they were fined as throughout the whole shire.

If anyone had taken the toll beyond the aforesaid boundary of the salt-pans to anywhere else in the whole shire, if proved, he returned it and paid a fine there of 40s if he were a free man, of 4s if he were not free. But if he took this toll to another shire, he paid a fine where it was claimed.

TRE this Wich rendered £21 as farm, including all the pleas of the same hundred. When Earl Hugh received it, it was waste, except for only 1 salt-pan. William Malbank now holds the same Wich of the earl with all the customs belonging to it, and the whole of that HUNDRED, which is valued at 40s, of which sum 30s is charged upon the land of William himself, the remaining 10s upon the land of the bishop and upon the lands of Richard and Gilbert which they have in the same hundred; and [this] Wich is at farm for £10.

In MIDDLEWICH HUNDRED there was another Wich [Middlewich] between the king and the earl. There were no demesne salt-pans there, however, but the same laws and customs were in force there as have been mentioned under the above Wich, and the king and the earl took their shares in the same way. This Wich was at farm for £8, and the hundred in which it lay for 40s. The king [took] 2 parts; the earl the third. It was waste when Earl Hugh received it; now the earl holds it himself and it is at farm for 25s and 2 cart-loads of salt. The hundred is, however, worth 40s.

Whoever carried away in a cart salt he had bought from these two Wiches gave 4d in toll if he had 4 oxen or more to the cart; if 2 oxen, he gave 2d toll if there were 2 summae of salt. A man from another hundred gave 2d for a horse-load. But a man from the same hundred gave only ½d for a summa of salt.

Anyone who so overloaded his cart that the axle broke within a league of either Wich gave 2s to the officer of the king or of the earl, if he could overtake him within the league.

Similarly he who overloaded a horse so that its back broke gave 2s, [if] overtaken within a league; beyond a league, nothing.

Anyone who made 2 summae of salt out of 1 paid a fine of 40s, if the officer could overtake him. If he was not found, he paid no fine through any other person.

Men on foot from another hundred buying salt there gave 2d for 8 men's loads; men of the same hundred [gave] 1d for 8 loads.

[Folio 268V: [CHESHIRE: NORTH WALES]]

Flintshire & North Wales [mid 18th century, perhaps Abraham Farley]

IN ATI'S CROSS HUNDRED

Earl HUGH holds HAWARDEN in demesne. Earl Edwin held it. There are 3 hides paying geld. There is land for 4½ ploughs. In demesne are 2 ploughs and 4 slaves. There is a church to which half a carucate of land belongs, and there are 4 villans and 6 bordars with 2 ploughs. There is half an acre of meadow, [and] woodland 2 leagues long and 1 wide. It is worth 40s. 2 waste messuages in the city belong there.

The earl himself holds 'RADINGTON' [in Holywell]. Earl Edwin held it. There is 1 hide paying geld. There is land for 1 plough. It was and is waste.

Robert of Rhuddlan holds BROUGHTON of the earl. Leofnoth held it and was a free man. There are 1½ virgates paying geld. There is land for half a plough, which [half-plough] is there, with 1 villan. [There are] 1½ virgates of meadow. It is worth 3s, and has a third part of woodland 1 league long and wide.

The same Robert holds there 1 manor at half a hide paying geld. Wulfmær, a free man, held it. There is land for half a plough. There 1 radman has this [half-plough], with 1 villan and 1 bordar. It is worth 3s.

The same Robert holds GOLFTYN, and Azelin [holds] of him. Leofnoth held it. He was a free man. There is 1 hide paying geld. There is land for 1 plough. There are 2 villans and 1 bordar with 6 oxen. [There is] woodland 1 league long and as much wide. It is worth 10s.

The same Robert holds LEADBROOK. Leofnoth and Wulfbert held it as 2 manors and were free. There is half a hide paying geld. There is land for 1 plough. There 2 radmen have this [plough], with 2 bordars. [There is] woodland 1 league long and as much wide. It is worth 10s.

The same Robert holds BAGILLT, and Roger [holds] of him.

Arni held it. There is 1 hide paying geld. There is land for 1 plough. There 2 villans and 4 bordars have this [plough]. It is worth 8s.

The same Robert holds COLESHILL, and Edwin, who also held it as a free man, [holds] of him. There is 1 hide paying geld. There is land for 1 plough. This [plough] is there, with 1 radman and 4 villans and 2 bordars. It is worth 10s; it was worth 6s.

WILLIAM Malbank holds 'CLAYTON' [? in Hawarden], and Richard [holds] of him. Ramkel held it and was a free man. There is 1 hide paying geld. There is land for 1 plough. There is [1 plough] in demesne, with 2 bordars. There is 1 acre of meadow, [and] woodland 1 league long and as much wide. It is worth 10s.

The same William holds WEPRE. Earnwig held it and was free. There is the third part of a hide paying geld. There is land for the third part of a plough. There 1 radman has this [third part of a plough], with 1 villan. It is worth 10s.

William fitzNigel holds MARLSTON HEYES [Ches.]. Arni held it. Ansgar holds it of William, and has there half a plough. There is 1 virgate of land paying geld. There is 1 slave. It was waste; now it is worth 4s.

HUGH fitzOsbern holds BROUGHTON. Hrafnsvartr held it and was free. There are 1½ virgates of land paying geld. There is land for half a plough. There 1 radman has this [half-plough], with 1 villan and 2 bordars. [There is] woodland 1 league long and 1 wide. It is worth 5s.

The same Hugh holds 'CLAVERTON' [in St Mary on the Hill, Chester]. Osmær held it and was a free man. There are 2 hides paying geld. There is land for 2 ploughs. 1 [plough] is in demesne and 2 oxmen; and 4 villans have the other with 3 bordars. To this manor belong 8 burgesses in the city and 4 over the river, and they pay 9s4d, and in Northwich [is] 1 salt-pan rendering 12d. There are 3 acres of meadow. It was and is worth 40s. He found it waste.

The same Hugh holds "EDRITONE" [? Wales], and Richard [holds] of him. Almær and Ramkel held it as 2 manors and were free men. There are 1½ hides paying geld. There is land for 1 plough. This [plough] is there, with 2 radmen and 3 bordars. There is 1 acre of meadow. It is worth 10s. Of this land, Osbern fitzTezzo holds 1 hide and Hugh fitzNorman half a hide.

OSBERN fitzTezzo holds DODLESTON [Ches.]. Earl Edwin held it. There are 2 hides paying geld. There is land for 2 ploughs. In demesne are 1½ [ploughs] with 3 oxmen; and 4 villans with 3 bordars have half a plough. To this manor belong 15 burgesses in the city and they pay 8s. [There is] woodland 1 league long and as much wide. It is worth 40s.

HAMO holds ASTON [in Hawarden]. Edwin and Thorth held it as 2 manors and were free. There is 1 hide paying geld. There is land for 1 plough. This [plough] is there, with 2 radmen and 2 villans and 3 bordars. There is woodland 1 league long and as much wide. It is worth 10s. Of this land Ranulph holds 1 virgate.

The same Hamo holds [?] 'LLYS EDWIN' [in Northop], and Osmund [holds] of him. Edwin held it as a free man. There is half a hide paying geld. There is land for 1 plough. There 2 villans have half [a plough], with 1 bordar. [There is] woodland 1 league long and as much wide. It is worth 5s.

RALPH the huntsman holds BROUGHTON of the earl. Wulfheah held it and was a free man. There is 1 virgate of land paying geld. There is land for 1 plough. This [plough] is there in demesne, with 2 slaves. There is 1 virgate of meadow. It is worth 5s.

Ralph holds SOUGHTON. Esbiorn held it and was a free man. There is 1 hide paying geld. There is land for 1 plough. This [plough] is there, with 1 radman and 4 bordars. It is worth 5s. There is woodland half a league long and 4 acres wide.

Of these 20 hides the earl has placed all the woods in his forest, whereby the manors are much depreciated.

This forest is 10 leagues long and 3 leagues wide. There are 4 eyries of hawks.

[Folio 269: [CHESHIRE: NORTH WALES]]

IN ATI'S CROSS HUNDRED

EARL HUGH holds RHUDDLAN of the king. 'ENGLEFIELD' lay there TRE and the whole was waste. Earl Edwin held it. When Earl Hugh received it, it was likewise waste. Now he has in demesne half of the castle which is called RHUDDLAN and it is the chief place of this district. He has there 8 burgesses, and half of the church and mint, and half of [every] iron-mine wherever discovered in this manor, and half of the river Clwyd and of the mills and fisheries which shall be made there, that is to say, in that part of the river which belongs to the earl's fief, and half of the forests which did not belong to any vill of this manor, and half of the toll, and half of the vill which is called BRYN. There is land for 3 ploughs, and there are [3 ploughs] in demesne, with 7 slaves. To BRYN belong these 5 lands: Cwybr, 'Cefndy' [in Rhuddlan], Bryn Hedydd, Llewerllyd, and half Pentre. It is worth £3.

To this manor of Rhuddlan belong these Berewicks: [?] Dyserth, Bodeugan, Cil Owen, and Maen Efa. In these there is land for only 1 plough, and woodland 1 league long and a half wide. There 1 Frenchman and 2 villans have 1 plough.

Also "Widhulde", The Blorant, Tremeirchion, and Bryngwyn. There is land for 1 plough, which [plough] 2 villans and 1 sergeant of the earl have there. [There is] woodland 1 league long and a half wide.

In Trellyniau and Ysceifiog there is land for 1 plough, which [plough] 3 villans have there. [There is] woodland 40 perches long and as much wide.

In Glust and [?] 'Mechlas' [in Cilcain] and 'Llys-y-Coed' [in Cilcain] there is land for 1 plough, which [plough] 3 villans have there, and 1 acre of woodland.

In Brynford and Halkyn and "Ulchenol" there is land for 1 plough, which [plough] 5 villans have there. [There is] woodland 1 league long and 2 acres wide.

In Greenfield there is land for 1 plough, which [plough] 3 villans and 2 bordars have there. [There is] woodland half a league long and 40 perches wide.

In Mertyn and Calcoed and a third part of Whitford there is land for 1 plough, which [plough] a priest with 6 villans have there, and a church. [There is] woodland half a league long and 20 perches wide. Odin holds [this land] of the earl.

In Axton and Gelli Loveday there is land for 1 plough. Marcud holds it of the earl, and there are 3 villans and 1 bordar ploughing with 10 oxen.

All these Berewicks were waste TRE and when Earl Hugh received them. Among them all they are now worth 110s.

ROBERT of RHUDDLAN holds of Earl Hugh half of the same castle and borough, in which Robert himself has 10 burgesses, and half of the church and mint, and of [every] iron-mine found there, and half of the river Clwyd and of the fisheries and mills made or to be made there, and half of the toll, and of the forests which do not belong to any vill of the aforesaid manor, and half of the vill which is called Bryn, with these Berewicks: Llewerllyd, "Penegors" [in Rhuddlan], Rhydorddwy, "Tredueng", and Cwybr Bach. In these there is land for only 3 ploughs, and there are [3 ploughs] in demesne with 6 slaves, and there is a mill rendering 3 modii of corn. It is worth £3.

In Dyserth and Bodfari and "Ruargor" there is land for 1 plough. There is [1 plough] in demesne and 2 slaves, and a church with a priest, and 2 villans, and a mill rendering 3s, and 2 bordars. [There is] woodland 1 league long and a half wide, and there is a hawk's eyrie. It is worth 30s.

In Hiraddug and "Pengdeslion" there is land for 1 plough. There is [1 plough] in demesne, with 3 villans. It is worth 10s.

In Trelawnyd there is land for 1 plough, and there is [1 plough] in demesne, with 2 slaves, and 5 bordars. It is worth 20s.

In Caerwys and Llanelwy and Cyrchynen there is land for 1 plough, and this [plough] is there, with 1 slave, and 6 bordars. [There is] woodland 40 perches long and 40 wide. It is worth 15s.

In "Meincatis" and Trefraith and [?] Marian Trefedwen there is land for 1 plough, and there is [1 plough] in demesne, with 2 slaves and 4 bordars and 2 villans. It is worth 25s.

In "Inglecroft" and Brynford and Halkyn there is land for 1 plough. There is [1 plough] in demesne, with a church and a priest and 3 bordars. There is a mill rendering 5s, [and] woodland half a league long and 40 perches wide. It is worth 10s.

In Whitford and Bychton there is land for 1 plough. There is [1 plough], with 2 villans and 12 slaves and female slaves. There is a fishery, and woodland half a league long and 40 perches wide. It is worth 20s.

In MOSTYN there is land for 1 plough. There is [1 plough], with 4 villans and 8 bordars. [There is] woodland 1 league long and 40 perches wide. It is worth 20s.

In PICTON and "Melchanestone" there is land for 1 plough, and there is [1 plough], with 2 villans and 2 bordars.

[There is] woodland half a league long and 40 perches wide. It is worth 15s.

In [?] Tan-y-Fron, Kelston, and Gwespyr there is land for 1 plough. There are 2 radmen and Tual, a certain Frenchman, with 7 bordars, and 1 church. It is worth 15s.

In Carn-y-chain and Gwaenysgor there is land for 1 plough, and there is [1 plough] in demesne, with 2 Frenchmen and 2 villans, and 1 waste church. It is worth 15s.

In Gronant and Golden Grove there is land for 1 plough. This [plough] is there, with 2 villans and 5 bordars. It is worth 16 ploughs [sic].

In "Wenfesne" there is land for 1 plough, and there is [1 plough] in demesne, with 2 slaves. It is worth 40s.

In Prestatyn and Meliden there is land for 1 plough, and there is [1 plough] in demesne, with 2 oxmen and 2 villans and 4 bordars. There is a church. It is worth 20s.

In Dincolyn and "Rahop" and "Witestan" there is land for 1 plough, and this [plough] is there, with 2 villans and 2 bordars. There is woodland 1 league long and a half wide. It is worth 12s.

All these aforesaid Berewicks of 'Englefield' lay in Rhuddlan TRE and were then waste, and when Earl Hugh received them they were waste.

The land of this manor of Rhuddlan and 'Englefield' or of the other aforesaid Berewicks belonging there has never paid geld, nor has it been hidated.

In this manor of RHUDDLAN a castle, likewise called Rhuddlan, has lately been built. There is a new borough and in it 18 burgesses [are divided] between the earl and Robert, as has been said above. To these burgesses they have granted the laws and customs which are [enjoyed] in Hereford and Breteuil [Eure, France], that is to say that throughout the year they shall give only 12d. for any forfeiture, except homicide and theft and premeditated housebreaking. In the very year of this survey the toll of this borough was let at farm at 3s.

The payment to Earl Hugh from Rhuddlan and 'Englefield' is valued at £6.10s., Robert's share at £17.3s.

IN ATI'S CROSS HUNDRED

BISTRE was a manor of Earl Edwin TRE. It has never paid geld nor has it been hidated. It was then waste and [was] also waste when Earl Hugh received it. Now Hugh fitzNorman holds of the earl half of this manor and the whole of [?] Leeswood and "Sudfell". There is land for 1 plough, which [plough] is there in demesne, with 2 bordars, and there is 1 acre of meadow. It is worth 10s.

The other half of this manor and half of "Mulintone" and the whole of "Wiselei" Odin holds of the earl. There is land for 1 plough, which [plough] is there, with 2 slaves, and 1 bordar. It is worth 10s.

BEREWICKS OF THE SAME MANOR

Hugh fitzNorman holds of the earl 'Hendrebifa' [in Mold] and "Weltune" and "Munentone" and 2 "Horsepol"'s and half "Mulintone". There is land for 2 ploughs. These 2 ploughs are there, with 3 villans and 2 bordars. It is worth 18s.

Warmund the huntsman holds Broncoed of the earl. There is land for 1 plough. There is 1 villan with half a plough and 2 oxen. It is worth 10s.

Ralph holds of the earl [?] Rhos Ithel. There is land for 1 plough. This [plough] is there, with 4 bordars. It is worth 8s.

William holds Gwysaney of the earl. There is land for 1 plough. This [plough] is there, with a priest and 2 villans. There is woodland 1 league long and a half wide. It is worth 10s. All this land belongs to Bistre and was waste. It has never paid geld nor has it been hidated.

In this same manor is a wood 1 league [in] length and half a league [in] width. There is a hawk's eyrie. The earl has put this woodland in his forest.

In the same hundred of ATI'S CROSS King Gruffydd had 1 manor, Bistre, and had 1 plough in demesne; and his men [had] 6 ploughs. When the king himself came there, every plough rendered him 200 loaves and 1 vat full of beer and 1 firkin of butter.

ROBERT of Rhuddlan holds of the king 'NORTH WALES' [? Gwynedd] at farm for £40, except for that land which the king gave him in fief, and except for the lands of the bishopric.

The same Robert claims a HUNDRED [called] ARWYSTLI which Earl Roger holds. The Welsh testify that this HUNDRED is [one] of those of 'NORTH WALES' [? Gwynedd].

In the fief which Robert himself holds of the king, RHOS and RHUFONIOG are 12 leagues of land long and 4 leagues wide. There is land for only 20 ploughs. It is valued at £12. All the rest of the land consists of woods and moors; it cannot be ploughed.

[Folio 269V: BETWEEN THE RIBBLE AND THE MERSEY]

ROGER DE POITOU HELD THE UNDER-MENTIONED LAND BETWEEN THE RIBBLE AND THE MERSEY

IN WEST DERBY HUNDRED

THERE King EDWARD had 1 manor called WEST DERBY, with 6 Berewicks. There are 4 hides. There is land for 15 ploughs. [There is] forest 2 leagues long and 1 broad and a hawk's eyrie.

Uhtræd held 6 manors, Rody, Knowsley, Kirby [near Liverpool], Little Crosby, Maghull [and] Aughton. There are 2 hides. [...] [There is] woodland 2 leagues long and broad and 2 eyries of hawks.

Dot held Huyton and Tarbock. There is 1 hide quit of every customary due except geld. There is land for 4 ploughs. It was worth 20s.

Beornwulf held Toxteth. There is 1 virgate of land and half a carucate of land. It rendered 4s.

Stenulf held Toxteth. There is 1 virgate of land and half a carucate of land. It was worth 4s.

Five thegns held Sefton. There is 1 hide. It was worth 16s.

Uhtræd held Kirkdale. There is half a hide quit of every customary due except geld. It was worth 10s.

Wynstan held Walton [in Liverpool]. There are 2 carucates of land and 3 bovates. It was worth 8s.

Almær held Litherland [in Walton-on-the-Hill]. There is half a hide. It was worth 8s.

There thegns held Ince Blundell as 3 manors. There is half a hide. It was worth 8s.

Aski held Thornton [in Sefton]. There is half a hide. It was worth 8s.

Three thegns held RAVEN MEOLS as 3 manors. There is half a hide. It was worth 8s.

Uhtræd held Woolton. There are 2 carucates of land and half a league of woodland. It was worth 64d.

Æthelmund held 'SMITHDOWN' [in Walton-on-the-Hill]. There is 1 carucate of land. It was worth 32d.

Three thegns held Allerton as 3 manors. There is half a hide. It was worth 8s.

Uhtræd held Speke. There are 2 carucates of land. It was worth 64d.

Four radmen held Childwall as 4 manors. There is half a hide. It was worth 8s. There was a priest having half a carucate of land in alms.

Wulfbert held "Wibaldeslei" [? in Woolton]. There are 2 carucates of land. It was worth 64d.

Two thegns held Woolton as 2 manors. There is 1 carucate of land. It was worth 30d.

Lyfing held Wavertree. There are 2 carucates of land. It was worth 64d.

Four thegns held Bootle as 4 manors. There are 2 carucates of land. It was worth 64d. A priest had 1 carucate of land [belonging] to the Church of Walton [in Liverpool].

Uhtræd held Aughton. There is 1 carucate of land. It was worth 32d.

Three thegns held Formby as 3 manors. There are 4 carucates of land. It was worth 10s.

Three thegns held Ainsdale. There are 2 carucates of land. It was worth 64d.

Stenulf held Up Holland. There are 2 carucates of land. It was worth worth 64d.

Uhtræd held Dalton [in Upholland]. There is 1 carucate of land. It was worth 32d.

The same Uhtræd [held] SKELMERSDALE. There is 1 carucate of land. It was worth 32d.

The same Uhtræd held 'Litherland [in Aughton]. There is 1 carucate of land. It was worth 32d.

Wigbeorht held 'ARGARMELES' [in Southport]. There are 2 carucates of land. It was worth 8s. This land was quit except of geld.

Five thegns held Meols [near Southport]. There is half a hide. It was worth 10s.

Uhtræd held LATHOM with 1 Berewick. There is half a hide. [There is] woodland 1 league long and a half broad. It was worth 10s8d.

Uhtræd held Hurlston and half Martin [in Burscough Bridge]. There is half a hide. It was worth 10s8d.

Godgifu held Melling [near Liverpool]. There are 2 carucates of land. [There is] woodland 1 league long and half a league broad. It was worth 10s.

Uhtræd held Lydiate. There are 6 bovates of land. [There is] woodland 1 league long and 2 furlongs broad. It was worth 64d.

Two thegns held 6 bovates of land as 2 manors in Downholland. It was worth 2s.

Uhtræd held [Great and Little] Altcar. There is half a carucate of land. It was waste.

Teos held Barton [in Halsall]. There is 1 carucate of land. It was worth 32d.

Ketil held Halsall. There are 2 carucates of land. It was worth 8s.

All this land paid geld, and 15 manors rendered nothing to King Edward except geld.

This manor of West Derby with these aforesaid hides rendered to King Edward £26.2s at farm. Of these, 3 hides were free, the rent of which he pardoned to the thegns who held them. These rendered £4.14s8d.

All these thegns had by custom to render 2 orae of pennies for each carucate of land, and by custom they made the king's houses and whatever belonged to them, like villans, and the fisheries and the enclosures in the woodland, and the deer hays; and the man who did not go to these [works] when he ought paid a fine of 2s, and afterwards came to the work and laboured until it was completed.

Each one of them sent his reapers 1 day in August to cut the king's crops. If not he paid a fine of 2s.

If any free man committed theft, or highway robbery, or housebreaking, or broke the king's peace, he paid a fine of 40s.

If any committed bloodshed, or rape of a woman, or if he remained away from the shiremoot without reasonable excuse, he paid a fine of 10s. If he remained away from the hundred [court] or did not go to a plea when the reeve ordered, he paid a fine of 5s.

If [the reeve] ordered anyone to go upon his service and he did not go, he paid a fine of 4s.

If anyone wished to withdraw from the king's land, he gave 40s. and went where he would.

If anyone wished to have the land of his deceased father, he paid a relief of 40s; the king had both the land and all the chattels of the deceased father [of] the man who would not [pay the relief].

Uhtræd held Little Crosby and Kirkdale as 1 hide, and it was quit of every custom except these 6: breach of the peace, highway robbery, housebreaking, and fighting which continued after the oath was made, and [non-] payment of debt to anyone [when] bound by the reeve's judgement, and non-observance of the due date given by the reeve; for these he paid a fine of 40s. But he paid the king's geld like the men of the country.

In Meols [near Southport], and Halsall and Hurlston there were 3 hides quit of the geld on the carucates of land and of the forfeiture of bloodshed and rape of a woman. But they rendered all other customary dues.

These men now hold land of this manor of WEST DERBY by the gift of Roger de Poitou: Geoffrey 2 hides and half a carucate, Roger 1½ hides, William 1½ hides, Warin half a hide, Geoffrey 1 hide, Theobald 1½ hides, Robert 2 carucates of land, Gilbert 1 carucate of land.

These have in demesne 4 ploughs, and 46 villans and 1 radman and 62 bordars and 2 slaves and 3 female slaves. Among them all they have 24 ploughs.

Their woodland [is] 3½ leagues long and 1½ leagues and 40 perches broad, and there are 3 eyries of hawks. The whole is worth £8.12s. In each hide are 6 carucates of land.

The demesne of this manor which Roger held is worth £8. There are now in demesne 3 ploughs and 6 oxmen, and 1 radman and 7 villans.

IN NEWTON HUNDRED

In NEWTON-LE-WILLOWS there were 5 hides TRE. Of these, 1 was in demesne. The church of this manor had 1 carucate of land, and St Oswald of this vill had 2 carucates of land quit in all things.

The rest of the land of this manor 15 men whom they called drengs held as 15 manors, but they were Berewicks of this manor, and among them all they rendered 30s. There is woodland 10 leagues long and 6 leagues and 2 furlongs broad, and there are eyries of hawks.

The free men of this HUNDRED, except 2, were [subject] to the same customs as the men of West Derby, and in addition to these they reaped on 2 days in August in the king's ploughlands. These 2 men had 5 carucates of land and the forfeiture of bloodshed, and of a woman who had been raped, and the pannage of their own men. The king had the other [forfeitures].

This whole manor rendered £10.10s at farm to the king. Now there are 6 drengs and 12 villans and 4 bordars. Among them all they have 9 ploughs. This demesne is worth £4.

IN WARRINGTON HUNDRED

King Edward held WARRINGTON with 3 Berewicks. There is 1 hide. To this manor belonged 34 drengs, and they had as many manors, in which there were 42 carucates of land and 1½ hides. St Elfin held 1 carucate of land quit of every customary due except geld. The whole manor with the HUNDRED rendered at farm to the king £15, less 2s.

Now there are in demesne 2 ploughs; and 8 men with 1 plough. These men hold land there: Roger 1 carucate of land, Theobald 1½ carucates, Warin 1 carucate, Ralph 5 carucates, William 2 hides and 4 carucates of land, Adelard 1 hide and half a carucate, Osmund 1 carucate of land. The whole of this is worth £4.10s. The demesne is worth £3.10s.

•lio 270: [BETWEEN THE RIBBLE AND THE MERSEY]]

IN BLACKBURN HUNDRED

King Edward held BLACKBURN. There are 2 hides and 2 carucates of land. The church had had [sic] 2 bovates of this land, and the church of ST MARY had 2 carucates of land in Whalley quit of every customary due. In the same manor [is] woodland 1 league long and as much broad, and there was a hawk's eyrie.

To this manor or HUNDRED belonged 28 free men holding 5½ hides and 40 carucates of land as 28 manors. There is woodland 6 leagues long and 4 leagues broad, and they were [subject] to the above customary dues.

In the same HUNDRED King Edward had Huncoat at 2 carucates of land, and Walton-le-Dale at 2 carucates of land, and Pendleton at half a hide.

The whole manor with the HUNDRED rendered at farm to the king £32.2s.

Roger de Poitou gave the whole of this land to Roger de Bully and Albert Greslet, and there are as many men who have 11½ ploughs, [to] whom they themselves have granted quittance [from rent] for 3 years, and therefore it is not now valued.

IN SALFORD HUNDRED

King Edward held SALFORD. There are 3 hides and 12 carucates of waste land and forest 3 leagues long and as much broad and there are several enclosures and a hawk's eyrie.

King Edward held Radcliffe as a manor. There is 1 hide and another hide belonging to Salford.

The Church of ST MARY and the Church of St Michael held in Manchester 1 carucate of land quit of every customary due except geld.

To this manor or HUNDRED belonged 21 Berewicks which as many thegns held for as many manors, in which there were 11½ hides and 10½ carucates of land.

There is woodland 9½ leagues long and 5 leagues and 1 furlong broad.

One of them, Gamal, holding 2 hides in Rochdale was quit of his customs except these 6: theft, housebreaking, highway robbery, breach of the king's peace, breach of a due date set by the reeve, continuance of fighting after the oath was made. For these he paid a fine of 40s.

Some of these lands were quit of every customary due except for geld and some are quit of geld.

The whole manor of Salford with the HUNDRED rendered £37.4s

Now there are in demesne in the manor 2 ploughs and 8 slaves; and 2 villans with 1 plough. This demesne is worth 100s.

Of this land of this manor [these] knights hold by the gift of Roger de Poitou: Nigel 3 hides and half a carucate of land, Warin 2 carucates of land, and another Warin 1½ carucates, Geoffrey 1 carucate of land, [and] Gamal 2 carucates of land. In these [lands] are 3 thegns and 30 villans and 9 bordars and a priest and 10 slaves. Among them all they have 22 ploughs. It is worth £7.

IN LEYLAND HUNDRED

King Edward held LEYLAND. There is 1 hide and 2 carucates of land. [There is] woodland 2 leagues long and 1 broad, and a hawk's eyrie.

To this manor belonged 12 carucates of land [sic] which 12 free men held for as many manors. In these [are] 6 hides and 8 carucates of land. There is woodland 6 leagues long and 3 leagues and 1 furlong broad.

The men of this manor and of Salford did not work by custom at the king's hall nor reaped in August. They only made 1 enclosure in the woodland and had the forfeiture for bloodshed and for a woman who had been raped. In respect of the other customs they had the same arrangements as the other manors mentioned above.

The whole manor of Leyland with the HUNDRED rendered at farm to the king £19.18s2d.

Of this land of this manor Gerard holds 1½ hides, Robert 3 carucates of land, Ralph 2 carucates of land, Roger 2 carucates of land, [and] Walter 1 carucate of land. There are 4 radmen, a priest, and 14 villans and 6 bordars and 2 oxmen. Among them all they have 8 ploughs. [There is] woodland 3 leagues long and 2 leagues broad, and there are 4 eyries of hawks. The whole is worth 50s. In part it is waste.

King Edward held [Higher and Lower] PENWORTHAM. There are 2 carucates of land and they rendered 10d.

Now there is a castle, and there are 2 ploughs in demesne; and 6 burgesses and 3 radmen and 8 villans and 4 oxmen. Among them all they have 4 ploughs. There is half a fishery. [There is] woodland, and eyries of hawks as TRE. It is worth £3.

In these 6 HUNDREDS, West Derby, Newton, Warrington, Blackburn, Salford and Leyland, there are 188 manors, in which there are 80 hides, less 1, paying geld.

TRE it was worth £145.2s2d. When Roger de Poitou received it from the king, it was worth £120. Now the king holds it and has in demesne 12 ploughs; and 9 knights holding a fief. Among them and their men there are 115 ploughs and 3 oxen.

The demesne which Roger held is valued at £23.10s, what he gave to the knights is valued at £20.11s.

[Folio 270V: [BETWEEN THE RIBBLE AND THE MERSEY]]

[Blank in MS]

[Folio 271: [BETWEEN THE RIBBLE AND THE MERSEY]]

[Blank in MS]

[Folio 271V: [BETWEEN THE RIBBLE AND THE MERSEY]]

[Blank in MS]

DERBYSHIRE

[Folio 272: DERBYSHIRE]

Look [for] the town of Derby in the first leaf of Nottinghamshire. [f.280] [Arthur Agarde 1570-1615]

Here Are Entered Those Who Hold Lands In Derbyshire

I KING WILLIAM II The Bishop of Chester III The Abbey of Burton IIII Earl Hugh V Roger de Poitou VI Henry de Ferrers VII William Peverel VIIII Walter d'Aincourt IX Geoffrey Alselin X Ralph fitzHubert XI Ralph de Buron XII Hascoit Musard XIII Gilbert de Ghent XIIII Nigel of Stafford XV Robert fitzWilliam XVI Roger de Bully XVII The king's thegns

I. The land of the King

'SCARSDALE' WAPENTAKE

In NEWBOLD [Newbold and Upper Newbold], with 6 BEREWICKS - Old Whittington, Brimington, Tapton, Chesterfield, Boythorpe, Eckington-there are 6 carucates of land and 1 bovate to the geld. [There is] land for 6 ploughs. There the king has 16 villans and 2 bordars and 1 slave having 4 ploughs. To this manor belong 8 acres of meadow. [There is] woodland pasture 3 leagues long and 3 leagues broad. TRE worth £6; now £10.

THE SOKELAND of this manor

In Wingerworth [are] 2 carucates of land to the geld. [There is] land for 2 ploughs. There 14 sokemen have 4 ploughs.

In 'Greyhurst' [in Wingerworth] and ''Padinc'' [are] 4 bovates of land to the geld. It is waste.

In Temple Normanton [is] the fifth part of 1 carucate of land to the geld. [There is] land for 1 plough. There 1 sokeman has 2 oxen in a plough.

In Unstone [is] the third part of 1 carucate of land to the geld. [There is] land for 2 oxen.

In Dronfield [is] 1 carucate of land to the geld. [There is] land for 1 plough. There 3 villans and 1 bordar have 2 ploughs.

In ''Ravenesholm'' and 'Upton' [in Dronfield] [is] 1 carucate of land to the geld. [There is] land for 1 plough. There 4 sokemen have 1 plough.

In Old Tupton and Norton [in Sheffield, Yorks.] [are] 2 bovates of land to the geld.

To these lands of the sokemen belong 7 acres of meadow. [There is] woodland pasture 5 leagues long and 3 leagues broad, [and] 60 acres of open land.

In UNSTONE and Temple Normanton Leofwine and Edwin had 7 bovates of land and 4 acres to the geld. [There is] land for 12 oxen. There is now 1 plough in demesne; and 6 villans and 4 bordars having 4 ploughs. There is a church and a priest, and 2 mills [rendering] 4s, and 2½ acres of meadow, [and] woodland pasture half a league long and a half broad. TRE worth 13s; now 20s.

In WALTON Hundolfr had 2 carucates of land to the geld. [There is] land for 3 ploughs. It is waste. [There is] woodland pasture 1 league long and 1 broad. TRE [it was worth] 20s.

HAMSTON WAPENTAKE

In DARLEY King Edward had 2 carucates of land to the geld. In Farley and 'Cotes' [in Darley] and Burley Fields [is] 1 carucate of land and 2 bovates to the geld. [There is] land for 3 ploughs. There the king has 1 plough, and 7 villans having 3 ploughs. There is a priest and a church, and 12 acres of meadow, [and] woodland pasture 2 leagues long and 2 broad. TRE worth 40s and 2 sesters of honey; now £4.

In MATLOCK [?Bridge] King Edward had 2 carucates of land exempt from geld. It is waste. There are 8 acres of meadow, and 1 lead-mine, [and] woodland, pasture in places, 3 leagues long and 2 broad. To this manor belong these Berewicks: Matlock, Snitterton, Wensley, Bonsall, Ible, Tansley. In these [are] 7 carucates of land to the geld. [There is] land for 7 ploughs. There 11 villans and 12 bordars have 6 ploughs, and 22 acres of meadow. [There is] woodland pasture 2 leagues long and 1 league broad, [and] as much scrubland.

[Folio 272V: DERBYSHIRE]

In WIRKSWORTH are 3 carucates of land to the geld. [There is] land for 4 ploughs. There is a priest and a church, and 16 villans and 9 bordars having 4 ploughs. There are 3 lead-mines, and 26 acres of meadow, [and] woodland pasture 2 leagues long and 2 leagues broad.

BEREWICKS of this manor

In Cromford, 2 carucates, and Middleton [in Wirksworth], 2 carucates, and Hopton, 4 carucates, and ''Welledene'', 2 carucates, and Carsington, 2 carucates, and Callow, 2 carucates, and Kirk Ireton, 4 carucates, [are] 18 carucates of land to the geld. [There is] land for as many ploughs. In these are 36 villans and 13 bordars having 14½ ploughs. There are 14 acres of meadow, [and] woodland pasture and scrubland 3 leagues long and 2 broad.

In ASHBOURNE are 3 carucates of land to the geld. [There is] land for 3 ploughs. It is waste; nevertheless it renders 20s. There is a priest and a church with 1 carucate of land to the geld, and he has there 2 villans and 2 bordars having half a plough. He himself [has] 1 plough, and 1 man who pays 16d, and [there are] 20 acres of meadow, [and] woodland pasture 1 league long and half a league broad.

BEREWICKS of this manor

In Mapleton, 2 carucates, and Broadlowash, 2 carucates, and Thorpe, 2 carucates, and Fenny Bentley, 2 carucates, and Offcote, 2 carucates, and Hognaston, 4 carucates, [are] 14 carucates of land to the geld. [There is] land for as many ploughs. They are waste, except for 11 villans and 17 bordars having 6½ ploughs. There are 25 acres of meadow.

In PARWICH are 2 carucates of land to the geld. [There is] land for 2 ploughs. It is waste. Kolli holds it of the king, and has there 6 villans and 2 bordars with 3 ploughs. There are 12 acres of meadow.

To this manor belong 3 BEREWICKS: Alsop en le Dale, Hanson Grange, [and] Coldeaton. There are 2 carucates of land to the geld. [There is] land for 2 ploughs. It is waste.

These 5 manors, Darley, Matlock [?Bridge], Wirksworth, Ashbourne, and Parwich, with their BEREWICKS, rendered TRE £32 and 6½ sesters of honey; now £40 of pure silver.

In WALTON-ON-TRENT and Rosliston Earl Ælfgar had 6 carucates of land to the geld. [There is] land for 7 ploughs. There the king has 2 ploughs in demesne; and 3 sokemen and 33 villans and 10 bordars having 12 ploughs. There is a church and a priest, and 1 mill [rendering] 6s8d, and 40 acres of meadow, [and] woodland, pasture in places, 7 furlongs long and 5 furlongs broad. TRE worth £6; now £10.

In NEWTON SOLNEY and Bretby Ælfgar had 7 carucates of land to the geld. [There is] land for 5 ploughs. There the king has 1½ ploughs; and 19 villans and 1 bordar having 5 ploughs. There are 12 acres of meadow, [and] woodland pasture 2 leagues long and 3 furlongs broad. TRE, as now, worth 100s.

In MELBOURNE King Edward had 6 carucates of land to the geld. [There is] land for 6 ploughs. There the king has 1 plough; and 20 villans and 6 bordars having 5 ploughs. There is a priest and a church, and 1 mill [rendering] 3s, and 24 acres of meadow, [and] woodland pasture 1 league long and half a league broad. TRE worth £10; now £6; nevertheless it renders £10. BEREWICKS of this manor [sic].

THIS SOKELAND belongs to Melbourne in 'Scarsdale' Wapentake.

In Barrow upon Trent 12½ bovates. In Swarkestone 1 carucate. In Chellaston 1½ carucates. In Osmaston [in Derby] 2 carucates and 2 bovates, and Cottons, 4 bovates 2 carucates and 6 bovates. In Normanton [in Derby] 1 carucate. [There is] land for 12 ploughs. [There are] 8 carucates and 2 bovates to the geld.

In REPTON and Milton Earl Ælfgar had 6 carucates of land to the geld. [There is] land for 8 ploughs. There the king has 2 ploughs in demesne; and 37 villans and 3 bordars having 12 ploughs. There is a church and 2 priests with 1 plough. There are 2 mills, and 42 acres of meadow, [and] woodland pasture 1 league long and half a league broad. TRE worth £15; now £8.

SOKELAND

In Willesley [Leics.] [are] 2 carucates of land to the geld. [There is] land for 2 ploughs. There 2 sokemen and 7 villans and 1 bordar have 2½ ploughs. There are 16 acres of meadow, [and] woodland pasture 1 furlong long and 1 furlong broad.

In Ticknall [are] 2 carucates of land and 2 bovates and 2 parts of 1 bovate to the geld. [There is] land for 2 ploughs. There 2 sokemen have 1 plough, and [there are] 22 acres of meadow.

In ''Trangesbi'' [?Leics.] [is] half a carucate of land to the geld. [There is] land for 4 oxen.

In Measham [Leisc.] [are] 2 carucates of land to the geld. [There is] land for 3 ploughs. It is waste. There are 20 acres of meadow, [and] scrubland 1 furlong long and 1 furlong broad.

In Chilcote [Leics.] [are] 3 carucates of land to the geld. [There is] land for 3 ploughs. There 3 villans have 2 ploughs, and 12 acres of meadow. TRE worth 40s; now 10s. This belongs to Clifton Campville [Staffs.] in Staffordshire.

In Ingleby [are] 3 bovates of land to the geld. [There is] land for 4 oxen. THE SOKE [belongs] to Repton. There 3 sokemen have 1 plough, and 4 acres of meadow, and [there is] 1 acre of water-meadow.

[There is] woodland pasture in Ticknall 1 league long and half a league broad.

In BAKEWELL, with 8 Berewicks, King Edward had 18 carucates of land to the geld. [There is] land for 18 ploughs. There the king has now 7 ploughs in demesne, and 33 villans and 9 bordars. There are 2 priests and a church, and under them 2 villans and 5 bordars, all these having 11 ploughs. There 1 knight has | 16 acres of land |, and 2 bordars. There is 1 mill [rendering] 10s8d, and 1 lead-mine, and 80 acres of meadow, [and] scrubland 1 league long and 1 broad. Of this land 3 carucates belong to the church. Henry de Ferrers claims 1 carucate in Haddon [Haddon or Over Haddon].

These are THE BEREWICKS of this manor: Haddon [Haddon or Over Haddon], Holme [in Bakewell], Rowsley, Burton [in Bakewell], Conksbury, One Ash, Monyash, Haddon [Haddon or Over Haddon].

In ASHFORD IN THE WATER-with its BEREWICKS, Rowland, [?Little] Longstone, Hassop, Calver, Baslow, Bubnell, Birchills, Sheldon, Taddington, Flagg, Priestcliffe, [and] Blackwell-King Edward had 22 carucates of land to the geld and 1 carucate of land exempt from geld. There the king has now in demesne 4 ploughs; and 18 villans have 5 ploughs.

[There is] land for 22 ploughs. There is 1 mill [rendering] 12d, and the site of 1 mill, and 1 lead-mine, and 40 acres of meadow, [and] woodland, not for pasture, 2 leagues long and 2 broad.

In HOPE-with its BEREWICKS, Edale, Aston [in Hope], Shatton, half of Offerton, Tideswell, 'Stoke' [in Eyam], [and] "Muchedesuuelle"-King Edward

[Folio 273: DERBYSHIRE]

had 10 carucates of land to the geld. [There is] land for 10 ploughs. There now 30 villans and 4 bordars have 6 ploughs. There is a priest and a church to which belongs 1 carucate of land. There is 1 mill [rendering] 5s4d, and 30 acres of meadow, [and] woodland, pasture in places, 4 leagues and 2 furlongs long and 2 leagues broad.

TRE these 3 manors rendered £30, and 5½ sesters of honey and 5 cartloads of lead [each] consisting of 50 sheets; now they render £10.6s. William Peverel has charge [of them].

In LONGDENDALE and in Thornsett Ligulf had 4 bovates of land to the geld. In 'Ludworth' [in Mellor, Ches.] Brun [had] 4 bovates of land. In Charlesworth and Chisworth [Chisworth and Higher Chisworth] Swein [had] 1 carucate of land. In Chunal Æthelmær [had] 4 bovates of land. In Hadfield [are] 4 bovates. In Padfield Lyfing [had] 1 carucate of land. In [Higher and Lower] Dinting Leofnoth [had] 2 bovates of land. In Old Glossop Lyfing [had] 4 bovates of land. In Whitfield [are] 4 bovates of land. In Hayfield Æthelmær [had] 4 bovates of land. In Kinder Godric [had] 2 bovates of land. All together [they had] 6 carucates of land to the geld and 12 manors. The whole of Longdendale is waste. There is woodland, not for pasture [but] suitable for hunting. The whole [is] 8 leagues long and 4 leagues broad. TRE [it was worth] 40s.

In BEELEY Godric had 6 bovates of land to the geld. [There is] land for 6 oxen. There 3 villans and 5 bordars have 1 plough, and [there is] 1 acre of meadow.

In 'LANGLEY' [in Edensor] and Chatsworth Leofnoth and Ketil had 10 bovates of land to the geld. [There is] land for 10 oxen. This belongs to Edensor. William Peverel has charge [of it] for the king. There 5 villans and 2 bordars have 2 ploughs, and [there is] 1 acre of meadow, woodland pasture 1 league long and 1 broad, and a little scrubland. TRE worth 20s; now 16s.

In EYAM Karski had 2 carucates of land to the geld. [There is] land for 2 ploughs. There 12 villans and 7 bordars have 5 ploughs. [There is] woodland pasture 1 league long and 1 broad. TRE, as now, worth 20s.

In STONEY MIDDLETON Godgyth had 4 bovates of land to the geld. [There is] land for 4 oxen. There 8 villans and 1 bordar have 2 ploughs, and 4 acres of meadow and a little scrubland. TRE, as now, worth 6s.

In MAPPERLEY Stapolwine had 4 bovates of land to the geld. [There is] land [...]. William Peverel has charge [of it] for the king. It is waste. There is half an acre of meadow, [and] woodland pasture 4 furlongs long and 4 broad. TRE it was worth 16s. In the same place is half a carucate of land of [this] SOKE, belonging to Henry's manor of Spondon.

In TIBSHELF Ligulf had 3 carucates of land to the geld. [There is] land for 3 ploughs. William Peverel has charge [of it] for the king. There is now half a plough in demesne; and 9 villans have 2 ploughs. There is 1 acre of meadow, [and] woodland pasture 1 league long and 1 broad. TRE worth 40s; now 10s. Robert holds it.

In WESTON-ON-TRENT with its Berewicks Earl Ælfgar had 10 carucates of land and 2½ bovates to the geld. [There is] land for as many ploughs. There are now 3 ploughs in demesne; and 24 villans and 6 bordars having 12 ploughs, and 4 rent-paying tenants paying 16s. There are 2 churches and a priest, and 1 mill [rendering] 19s4d, and a fishpond, and a ferry [rendering] 13s4d, and 51 acres of meadow, [and] pasture half a league long and 3 furlongs broad. TRE worth £8; now £16.

BEREWICKS of this manor

In Aston-on-Trent and Shardlow [are] 6½ bovates of land to the geld. There is 1 plough in demesne; and 4 villans and 2 bordars with 1 plough, and 4 acres of meadow. Uhtbrand holds it of the king. It is worth 5s.

II. The land of the Bishop of Chester

'MORLEYSTONE' WAPENTAKE, SAWLEY HUNDRED

In SAWLEY and Draycott and Hopwell the Bishop of Chester had 12 carucates of land to the geld. [There is] land for as many ploughs. There the bishop has 3 ploughs; and 29 villans and 13 bordars having 13 ploughs. There is a priest and 2 churches, and 1 mill [rendering] 20s, and 1 fishery, and 30 acres of meadow, woodland pasture 3 furlongs long and 1 furlong broad, and a little water-meadow. Ralph fitzHubert holds Hopwell.

In Long Eaton [are] 12 carucates of land to the geld. [There is] land for 12 ploughs. There 22 sokemen and 10 bordars under them have 9 carucates of this land, and 13 ploughs. The other 3 carucates of land belong to the villans. There are 2 mill-sites, and 40 acres of meadow and a little scrubland. TRE worth £8; now the same.

In BUPTON and in its members [are] 5 carucates of land to the geld and 2 bovates. [There is] land for 5 ploughs. There the Bishop of Chester has 1 plough; and 12 villans and 3 bordars having 7 ploughs. There is a priest and a church, and 1 mill [rendering] 10s, and 60 acres of meadow. TRE worth £7; now £4.

III. The land of the Abbey of Burton

In MICKLEOVER king EDWARD had 10 carucates of land to the geld. [There is] land for 15 ploughs. 3 BEREWICKS belong there: Littleover, Findern, [and] Potlock. There the Abbot of Burton has now in demesne 5½ ploughs; and 20 villans and 10 bordars having 8 ploughs.

There are 2 mill-sites, and 73 acres of meadow, woodland pasture half a league long and a half broad, and as much scrubland. TRE worth £25; now £10. SOKELAND of the same manor: Snelston 12 bovates, Bearwardcote 4 bovates, Dalbury 3 bovates, Hoon 3 bovates, Rodsley 12 bovates, Sudbury 4 bovates, Hilton 4 bovates, Sutton on the Hill 1 carucate. All together [there are] 6 carucates and 2 bovates of land to the geld.

In APPLEBY MAGNA [Leics.] the Abbot of Burton had 5 carucates of land to the geld. [There is] land for 5 ploughs. Of this land Abbot Leofric leased 1 carucate of land to Countess Gode which the king has now. In the same vill [are] now 2 ploughs in demesne; and 8 villans and 1 bordar with 1 plough. TRE worth 20s; now 60s.

In WINSHILL [Staffs.] the Abbot of Burton had 2 carucates of land to the geld. [There is] land for 3 ploughs. There are now 2 ploughs in demesne; and 10 villans having 1½ ploughs. There King William placed 6 sokemen belonging to Repton who have 1 plough. There is 1 mill [rendering] 5s4d, and 8 acres of meadow, [and] scrubland 1 league long and 1 furlong broad. TRE worth 20s; now 60s.

In COTON IN THE ELMS Ælfgar had 2 carucates of land to the geld. [There is] land for 3 ploughs. Now the abbot has it of the king. There is now 1 plough in demesne; and 6 villans and 3 bordars having 2 ploughs. TRE worth 40s; now 30[s].

In STAPENHILL [Staffs.] the Abbot of Burton had 4 carucates of land and 2 bovates to the geld. [There is] land for 4 ploughs. There are now 2 ploughs in demesne; and 12 villans having 2 ploughs. There are 4 acres of meadow, [and] woodland pasture 1 league long and 3 furlongs broad. TRE, as now, worth 60s.

In CALDWELL Ælfric had 2 carucates of land to the geld. [There is] land for 2 ploughs. There is now 1 plough in demesne; and 6 villans with 1 plough. TRE, as now, worth 20s. King William gave this manor to the monks as their benefice.

In Ticknall the Abbot of Burton has 5 bovates of land and the third part of 1 bovate to the geld. There he has 1 plough in demesne; and 4 villans with 1 plough, and 8 acres of meadow, and the fifth part of the woodland pasture of this manor. It is worth 10s.

[Folio 273V: DERBYSHIRE]

IIII. The land of Earl Hugh

In MARKEATON Earl Siward had 9½ carucates of land to the geld. [There is] land for 9 ploughs. There Earl Hugh has 2 ploughs in demesne; and 15 villans and 7 bordars having 5 ploughs. There is a priest and a church, and 1 mill [rendering] 6s8d, and 1 fishery, and 24 acres of meadow, [and] woodland pasture 1 league long and half a league broad. TRE worth £4; now £3.

BEREWICKS

In Kniveton [near Hognaston] and Mackworth and Allestree [are] 4 carucates of land to the geld. [There is] land for 4 ploughs. It is waste. There are 30 acres of meadow, and woodland pasture 1 league long and half a league broad. 1 carucate of these 4 belongs to Henry's manor of Ednaston. Joscelin holds it of the earl, and Kolli pays Joscelin 10s8d. for it.

V. The land of Roger de Poitou

In SUTTON SCARSDALE Stenulf had 4 carucates of land to the geld. [There is] land for 5 ploughs. The lord has there 1 plough; and 6 villans and 1 bordar with 1 plough. There is 1 mill [rendering] 2s, and 8 acres of meadow, [and] woodland pasture half a league long and 3 furlongs broad. TRE worth 40s; now 20[s].

SOKELAND

In Beighton [Yorks.] [are] 5½ bovates of land to the geld. [There is] land for 6 oxen. There 2 villans have 1 plough, and [there is] 1 acre of meadow, [and] woodland pasture 1 league long and half a league broad. TRE [worth] 5s; now 6s4d.

In the two 'LOWNES' ['Lowne' in Heath] Stenulf had 2 carucates of land to the geld. [There is] land for 2 ploughs. There 8 villans have 3 ploughs, and [there are] 10 acres of meadow, [and] woodland pasture 4 furlongs long and 4 broad. TRE worth 40s; now 10s.

In STAINSBY and in 'Tunstall' [in Ault Hucknall] Stenulf had 12 bovates of land to the geld. [There is] land for 2 ploughs. There are now 2 ploughs in demesne; and 8 villans and 5 bordars having 4 ploughs. There is a priest with 3 bordars, and 1 acre of meadow. [There is] woodland pasture 6 furlongs long and 4 furlongs broad. TRE worth 40s; now 30[s].

In BLINGSBY GATE and Hardstoft Stenulf had 1 carucate of land to the geld. [There is] land for 2 ploughs. There is 1 sokeman and 1 villan and 3 bordars having 1 plough. There are 3 acres of meadow, [and] woodland, not for pasture, 2 furlongs long and 2 broad. TRE worth 20s; now 8s.

Roger de Poitou had these lands; now they are in the king's hand.

In [?South] WINGFIELD Alnoth [had] 2 carucates of land to the geld. [There is] land for 3 ploughs. Robert holds it of Count Alan under william Peverel, and has 1 plough. There is a priest and 8 villans and 2 bordars with 3 ploughs. There are 4 acres of meadow. It was and is worth 20s.

[Folio 274: DERBYSHIRE]

VI. The land of Henry de Ferrers

HAMSTON WAPENTAKE

In IVONBROOK GRANGE Ketil had 5 bovates of land to the geld. [There is] land for 1 plough. It is waste. TRE it was worth 20s.

In WINSTER Lyfing and Rawn had 12 bovates of land to the geld. [There is] land for 12 oxen. There Cola, Henry's man, has 7 villans and 12 bordars having 4 ploughs. [There is] scrubland half a league long and 4 furlongs broad. TRE, as now, worth 20s.

In COWLEY Swein and Uhtræd had 2 bovates [each] of land to the geld. [There is] land for 4 oxen. There 2 villans and 1 bordar have 1 plough. There are 4 acres of meadow, [and] scrubland half a league long and 2 furlongs broad. TRE, as now, [worth] 10s. Swein holds it.

In ELTON Karski and Uhtræd [had] 2 carucates of land to the geld. [There is] land for 2 ploughs. There is now 1 plough in demesne; and 9 villans and 10 bordars having 4 ploughs, and 12 acres of meadow. [There is] scrubland 3 furlongs long and 3 furlongs broad. TRE, as now, worth 40s.

In BRASSINGTON Siward had 4 carucates of land to the geld. [There is] land for 4 ploughs. There are now 3 ploughs in demesne; and 16 villans and 2 bordars have 6 ploughs, and 30 acres of meadow. [There is] scrubland 3 furlongs long and 1 broad. TRE worth £6; now £3.

In BRADBOURNE Ælfric had 4 carucates of land to the geld. [There is] land for 4 ploughs. Now in demesne [are] 2 ploughs; and 12 villans and 4 bordars have 4 ploughs. There is a priest and a church, and 12 acres of meadow, [and] scrubland 3 furlongs long and 2 broad. TRE worth £4; now 30s.

In TISSINGTON Ulfkil, Eadric, Gamal, Wulfgeat, Wihtric, Leofric [and] Godwine had 4 carucates of land to the geld. [There is] land for 4 ploughs. There are now 3 ploughs in demesne; and 12 villans and 8 bordars having 4 ploughs, and 1 mill [rendering] 3s, and 30 acres of meadow. [There is] scrubland 1 league long and 4 furlongs broad. TRE worth £4; now 40s.

In NEWTON GRANGE Osmær had 4 carucates of land to the geld. [There is] land for 4 ploughs. It is waste. There are 8 acres of meadow. TRE it was worth 20s.

In HARTINGTON Godwine and Ligulf had 2 carucates of land to the geld. [There is] land for 2 ploughs. It is waste. There are 16 acres of meadow, [and] scrubland 3 furlongs long and 2 broad. TRE it was worth 40s.

In 'SOHAM' [in Hartington] Cola had 2 carucates of land to the geld. [There is] land for 2 ploughs. It is waste. There are 16 acres of meadow, [and] scrubland half a league long and a half broad. TRE it was worth 40s.

In PILSBURY and Ludwell Alsige had 2 carucates of land to the geld. [There is] land for 2 ploughs. It is waste. There are 12 acres of meadow. TRE it was worth 10s.

In SHOTTLE and Wallstone Gamal had 6 carucates of land to the geld. [There is] land for as many ploughs. There is now 1 plough in demesne; and 3 villans and 3 bordars have 1 plough, and 5 acres of meadow. [There is] woodland pasture 3½ leagues long and 2½ leagues broad. TRE worth 60s; now 10s. Godric holds it.

In ATLOW Ælfric had 3 carucates of land to the geld. [There is] land for 2 ploughs. There are 4 acres of meadow, woodland pasture half a league long and 3 furlongs broad, [and] as much scrubland. TRE worth 20s; now 2s.

"WALECROS" WAPENTAKE

In CROXALL [Staffs.] Siward had 3 carucates of land to the geld. [There is] land for 8 ploughs. There are now 2 ploughs in demesne; and 35 villans and 11 bordars having 8 ploughs. There are 2 mills [rendering] 18s, and 22 acres of meadow, [and] scrubland 2 furlongs long and 1 furlong broad. TRE worth £3; now £4. Roger holds it.

In Edingale [Staffs.] [is] 1 carucates of land to the geld. [There is] land for 1 plough. There 4 villans have 1 plough. [There is] scrubland 3 furlongs long and 1 furlong broad.

In STRETTON EN LE FIELD [Leics.] Ælfric had 1 carucate of land to the geld. [There is] land for 1 plough. There 4 villans have 2 ploughs, and 1 mill [rendering] 5s, and [there are] 10 acres of meadow. TRE worth 20s; now 15s. Roger holds it.

In CATTON Siward had 3 carucates of land to the geld. [There is] land for 3 ploughs. There are now 3 ploughs in demesne; and 14 villans and 2 bordars have 4 ploughs, and 24 acres of meadow. [There is] scrubland 1 furlong long and 1 furlong broad. TRE, as now, worth 60s. Nigel holds it.

In "BOLUN" Ælfric had 4 carucates of land to the geld. [There is] land for 4 ploughs. There are now 4 ploughs in demesne; and 8 villans and 8 bordars having 3 ploughs, and 18 acres of meadow. [There is] woodland pasture 1 furlong long and 1 broad. TRE worth 100s; now £4.

In LINTON Leofric had 2 carucates of land to the geld. [There is] land for 12 oxen. It is waste. [There is] scrubland 1 furlong long and a half broad. TRE [it was worth] 20s.

In WILLESLEY [Leics.] Ælfric had 1 carucates of land to the geld. [There is] land for 1 plough. It is waste. There 3 villans have 5 oxen ploughing. TRE worth 20s; now 16s.

In STANTON [near Burton upon Trent] Alwine had half a carucates of land to the geld. [There is] land for 4 oxen. There 1 sokeman and 1 bordar have 1 plough, and 10 acres of meadow. TRE worth 20s; now 10s.

In HARTSHORNE Ælfric had 4 carucates of land to the geld. [There is] land for 4 ploughs. [There is] woodland pasture half a league long and a half broad, [and] as much arable land. TRE worth £4; now 10s.

In another HARTSHORNE Ælfric had 2 carucates of land to the geld. [There is] land for 2 ploughs. It is waste. [There is] woodland pasture half a league long and half a league broad, [and] as much arable land. TRE [worth] 40s; now 10s.

In MARSTON ON DOVE Brun and Alric had 2 carucates of land to the geld. [There is] land for 3 ploughs. There are now 2 ploughs in demesne; and 18 villans and 5 bordars having 5 ploughs. There is a priest and a church, and 1 mill [rendering] 6s5d. There are 50 acres of meadow and 1 acre of scrubland. It is worth 100s. The monks hold it of Henry.

In DOVERIDGE Earl Edwin had 4 carucates of land to the geld. [There is] land for 6 ploughs. There are now 3 ploughs in demesne; and 30 villans and 10 bordars having 7 ploughs. There is a church and a priest, and 1 mill [rendering] 10s, and 48 acres of meadow, [and] woodland pasture 1 league long and half a league broad. TRE worth £8; now 100s. The monks hold it of Henry.

[Folio 274V: DERBYSHIRE]

In FOSTON Leofnoth, Wulfmær, Baldric and Wulfric had 2½ carucates of land to the geld. [There is] land for 20 oxen. There now 12 villans and 8 bordars have 3 ploughs, and 10 acres of meadow. It is worth 40s.

In SCROPTON with 3 BEREWICKS Toki had 6 carucates of land to the geld. [There is] land for 7 ploughs. There now 32 villans and 26 bordars have 12 ploughs. There is a priest and a church, and 1 mill and the site of another mill. In demesne [are] now 4 ploughs; and a certain knight [has] 3 ploughs, and 120 acres of meadow. [There is] woodland pasture 4 furlongs long and 2 furlongs broad. TRE worth £8; now £10. Geoffrey Alselin claims it.

In ASTON [in Sudbury] Leofnoth had 2 carucates of land to the geld. [There is] land for 2 ploughs. There are now 3 ploughs in demesne; and 8 villans and 4 bordars having 2 ploughs, and 24 acres of meadow. [There is] woodland pasture half a league long and a half broad. TRE worth 60s; now 40[s.]. Ealhhere holds it.

In SAPPERTON Godric and Leofwine Cild had 1 carucate of land to the geld. [There is] land for 12 oxen. There now 5 villans have 1 plough. [There is] woodland pasture 3 furlongs long and 2 broad. TRE, as now, worth 20s Roger holds it.

In SUDBURY Godric and Wulfric and Almær had 2 carucates, | less half a bovate | [...] to the geld. [There is] land for 2 ploughs. There now 14 villans and 4 bordars have 3 ploughs. There is a priest and a church, and 1 mill [rendering] 6s and 100 eels, and 22 acres of meadow and a little scrubland. TRE it was worth 60s; now 20[s.]. Ealhhere holds it.

In the same place [is] half a bovate of land and the sixth part of 1 bovate to the geld. THE SOKE [belongs] to Scropton. A certain old woman held it. Now Ealhhere holds it.

In CHURCH BROUGHTON Wulfric had 2 carucates of land to the geld. [There is] land for 2 ploughs. There is now 1 plough in demesne; and 10 villans and 2 bordars have 3 ploughs, and 18 acres of meadow and 4 acres of pasture.

In [?Potter] SOMERSALL Ordmær and Earngeat had 2 carucates of land to the geld. [There is] land for 2 ploughs. There is now 1 plough in demesne; and 5 villans and 1 bordar have 2 ploughs, and 14 acres of meadow and 4 acres of pasture. [There is] woodland pasture half a league long and a half broad. TRE, as now, worth 60s. Ealhhere holds it.

In another SOMERSALL [?Somersall Herbert] Alric had 1 carucate of land to the geld. [There is] land for 1 plough. There 6 bordars have 1 plough, and [there are] 24 acres of meadow, [and] woodland pasture 1 league long and 1 broad. TRE worth 20s; now 1 mark of silver. Alric holds it.

In BARTON Godric and another Godric, Eadric, Leofnoth, Ælfheah, Leodmær, Dunning and Edward had 4 carucates of land to the geld. [There is] land for 4 ploughs. There are now 3 ploughs in demesne, and 19 villans and 11 bordars having 7 ploughs. There is a priest and a church, and 2 mills [rendering] 20s, and 64 acres of meadow. TRE, as now, worth £4. Ralph holds it.

In ALKMONTON Wulfgeat had 1½ carucates of land to the geld. [There is] land for 2 ploughs. There are now 2 ploughs in demesne; and 8 villans and 7 bordars having 2 ploughs, and 12 acres of meadow. [There is] woodland pasture 1 league long and a half broad. TRE worth 60s; now 40s. Ralph holds it.

In BENTLEY [in Longford] wulfgeat and Ulfkil had 1 carucate of land to the geld. [There is] land for 1 plough. It is waste. TRE worth 20s; now 11s. Ralph holds it.

In ASHE Ulfkil and Æfic and Hakon had 16 bovates of land to the geld. [There is] land for 2 ploughs. There are now 2 ploughs in demesne; and 7 villans having 1 plough. There are 18 acres of meadow. TRE worth 40s; now 30[s.]. Robert holds it.

In "TOXENAI" Ulfkil and Æfic had 12 bovates of land to the geld. [There is] land for 2 ploughs. There is now 1 plough in demesne; and 4 villans and 5 bordars having 2½ ploughs. There 5 rent-paying tenants pay 5s, and 2 sokemen 5s. There are 33 acres of meadow, [and] woodland pasture 1 league long and 4 furlongs broad. TRE worth 40s; now 30s. Hugh holds it.

In SUTTON ON THE HILL Thorir, Alweald, Ubeinn, Leofwine and Eadric had 2 carucates of land to the geld. [There is] land for 3 ploughs. There are now 3 ploughs in demesne; and 9 villans having 7 ploughs. There is a church and a priest, and 1 mill [rendering] 10s, and 24 acres of meadow. TRE, as now, worth 60s. Wazelin holds it.

In BRAILSFORD Earl Waltheof had 2 carucates of land to the geld. [There is] land for 2 ploughs. There are now 2 ploughs in demesne; and 24 villans and 3 bordars have 5 ploughs. There is a priest and half a church, and 1 mill [rendering] 10s 8d, and 11 acres of meadow, [and] woodland pasture 1 league long and 1 league broad. TRE worth 60s; now 40s. Elfin holds it.

In Hollington and Shirley [are] 3 bovates of land to the geld. [There is] land for half a plough.

In HOLLINGTON Leofsige and Ælfheah, Æfic and 3 other thegns had 1½ carucates of land to the geld. [There is] land for 12 oxen. There 11 villans and 7 bordars have 7 ploughs, and 8 acres of meadow and a little scrubland. TRE, as now, worth 40s.

In SHIRLEY Ketil and Wulfmær, Thorgisl, Alric, Algar, Wulfgeat and Leofsige had 2 carucates of land, less half a bovate, to the geld. [There is] land for 2 ploughs. There are now 2 ploughs in demesne; and 6 villans and 7 bordars having 3 ploughs. There is a priest and a church, and 1 mill [rendering] 2s, [and] woodland pasture 1 league long and 1 broad. TRE worth 60s; now 40[s.].

In BRADLEY [near Ashbourne] Ælfric and Leofwine had 1 carucate of land to the geld. [There is] land for 2 ploughs. There 11 villans and 6 bordars have 4 ploughs, and [there is] 1 acre of meadow, [and] woodland pasture 1 league long and 1 broad. TRE worth 40s; now 20[s.].

In YELDERSLEY Ulfkil and Godwine had 2 carucates of land to the geld. [There is] land for 2 ploughs. There are now 2½ ploughs in demesne; and 1 villan having half a plough. [There is] woodland pasture 1 league long and 1 broad. TRE worth 60s; now 20s. Cola holds it.

In HILTON Wulfric and Ulf and Ubbi and Alric had 3 carucates of land to the geld. [There is] land for 4 ploughs. There are now 2 ploughs in demesne; and 12 villans and 7 bordars having 4 ploughs. There are 2 mills [rendering] 10s, and 60 acres of meadow. TRE worth £6; now £3. Robert holds it.

In HOUGHPARK Wulfsige and Godwine and Wulfsige had 2 carucates of land [...] to the geld. [There is] land for 2 ploughs and 2 oxen. There are now 2 ploughs in demesne; and 11 villans and 5 bordars having 2 ploughs, and 1 mill [rendering] 9s, and 40 acres of meadow. TRE worth 60s; now 40[s.]. Saswalo holds it.

In Hatton [are] 6½ bovates of land of sokeland and 1½ bovates of thegnland. This belongs to Scropton.

[Folio 275: DERBYSHIRE]

In HATTON Eadric and Kollungr and Baldric had 1 carucate of land to the geld. [There is] land for 1 plough. There 5 villans and 5 bordars have 2 ploughs, and 20 acres of meadow. TRE worth 40s; now 20[s.] Saswalo holds it.

In EATON DOVEDALE and Sedsall Wulfric had 1 carucate of land to the geld. [There is] land for 2 ploughs. There 5 villans and 5 bordars have 3 ploughs, and 1 mill [rendering] 4s, and [there are] 16 acres of meadow, [and] woodland pasture 1 league long and a half broad. TRE worth 40s; now 30s. Ealhhere holds it.

In MARKEATON Ealdgyth had 4 carucates of land to the geld. [There is] land for 4 ploughs. There are now 2 ploughs in demesne; and 18 villans and 5 bordars have 3 ploughs, and 12 acres of meadow. [There is] woodland pasture 1 league long and 1 broad. TRE, as now, [worth] 60s.

In BUPTON Ulfkil had 6 bovates of land to the geld. [There is] land for 1 plough. There 3 bordars and 1 slave have 1½ ploughs, and 20 acres of meadow. [There is] woodland pasture half a league long and half a league broad, and as much scrubland. TRE worth 40s; now 20s. Elfin holds it.

In SNELSTON Leofnoth, Ælfric and Sæwulf had 2 carucates of land and 2 bovates and the third part of 2 bovates to the geld.

In the same place [is] half a carucate of land [of which] the soke [belongs] to Mickleover, and 3 bovates of land [of which] the soke [belongs] to Rocester [Staffs.], and 5 bovates of land

and 2 parts of 2 bovates which belong to Norbury. [There is] land for 4 ploughs all together. There now 9 villans and 9 bordars and 1 slave have 6 ploughs, and 50 acres of meadow. [There is] woodland pasture 1 league long and a half broad. TRE worth £8; now 40s. Ralph holds it.

In [Great and Little] CUBLEY Siward had 2 carucates of land to the geld. [There is] land for 2 ploughs. There are now 2 ploughs in demesne; and 4 villans and 4 bordars and 1 slave have 1 plough. There is a priest and a church, and 1 mill [rendering] 12d, and 8 acres of meadow, [and] woodland pasture 1 league long and 1 league broad. TRE worth 100s; now 40s. Ralph holds it.

In BOYLESTONE Godric and Leofnoth had 2 carucates of land to the geld. [There is] land for 2 ploughs. There are now 2 ploughs in demesne; and 8 villans and 8 bordars having 3 ploughs, and 1 mill [rendering] 12d, and 6 acres of meadow. [There is] woodland pasture 1 league long and half a league broad. TRE worth 40s; now 30s. Roger holds it.

In [?] 'KNIVETON' [in Ashbourne] and Sturston [Sturston and Nether Sturston] Ulfkil and Wudia had 2 parts of 1 carucate of land to the geld. [There is] land for 6 oxen. There now 11 villans and 10 bordars have 6 ploughs, and 1 mill [rendering] 8s, and [there are] 8 acres of meadow, [and] woodland pasture 4 furlongs long and 4 broad. TRE worth 40s; now 20s.

In NORBURY and Roston Siward had 3 carucates of land to the geld. [There is] land for 3 ploughs. There are now 2 ploughs in demesne; and 17 villans and 7 bordars having 4 ploughs. There is a priest and a church, and 1 mill [rendering] 10s, and 24 acres of meadow, [and] woodland pasture 1 league long and 1 broad. TRE worth 100s; now 60[s]. Henry holds it.

In Roston itself [is] 1 carucate of land to the geld belonging to Rocester [Staffs.]. There are now 2 villans.

In OSMASTON [near Ashbourne] Waltheof and Æthelgeat had 2 carucates of land to the geld. [There is] land for 2 ploughs. There 8 villans and 4 bordars have 5 ploughs, and 2 acres of meadow. [There is] woodland pasture 1 league long and 1 league broad. TRE worth £4; now 40s. Elfin holds it.

In WYASTON and Edlaston Earl Edwin had 2 carucates of land to the geld. [There is] land for 2 ploughs. There 9 villans and 4 bordars have 2 ploughs, and 2 acres of meadow. [There is] woodland pasture 2 leagues long and 1 league broad. TRE worth 60s; now 20s. Ormr holds it. These 2 vills belong to the king's farm in Rocester [Staffs.], except 1 bovate which belongs to Osmaston [near Ashbourne].

In THURVASTON and in Bupton Ulfkil had 5 bovates of land to the geld. [There is] land for 1 plough. There 3 villans and 3 bordars have 1½ ploughs, and 20 acres of meadow and a little scrubland. TRE worth 40s; now 20s. Elfin holds it.

In YEAVELEY the 2 Ligulfs had 12 bovates of land to the geld. [There is] land for 12 oxen. There 7 villans and 3 bordars have 3 ploughs. [There is] woodland pasture 1 league long and 1 broad. TRE worth £4; now 40s. Alsige holds it.

In RODSLEY Brune had 12 bovates of land to the geld. [There is] land for 12 oxen. There is now 1 plough in demesne; and 6 villans and 2 bordars have 2 ploughs, and 2 acres of meadow. [There is] woodland pasture 2 leagues long and half a league broad. TRE worth £4; now 20s. John holds it. The abbot claims the soke of this vill.

In OSLESTON Earnwig and Leofwine had 12 bovates of land to the geld. [There is] land for 3 ploughs. There are now 2 ploughs in demesne; and 12 villans and 4 bordars having 3 ploughs. [There is] woodland pasture half a league long and 4 furlongs broad. TRE worth 60s; now 40s. John holds it.

In THURVASTON Eadwulf had 12 bovates of land to the geld. [There is] land for 3 ploughs. There are now 2 ploughs in demesne; and 6 villans and 3 bordars have 2 ploughs, and 12 acres of meadow. [There is] woodland pasture half a league long and 4 furlongs broad. TRE worth £4 now 40s. Robert holds it.

In BREASTON Leofnoth Sterre had 3 bovates of land to the geld. [There is] land for 1 plough. There is now 1 plough in demesne; and 2 villans have 5 oxen in a plough, and 3 acres of meadow. TRE worth 10s; now 4s. Herbert holds it.

In DUFFIELD and 'Bradley' [in Belper] and Holbrook, waste, and Milford, waste, and Makeney, waste, and in "Herdebi", Siward had 7 carucates of land to the geld and the sixth part of 1 carucate. [There is] land for 7 ploughs and the sixth part of 1 plough. There are now 3 ploughs in demesne; and 32 villans and 8 bordars and 10 slaves having 8 ploughs, and 20 acres of meadow. [There is] woodland pasture 4 leagues long and 2 broad. There is a priest and a church, and 2 mills [rendering] 8s. TRE worth £9; now £7. In "Herdebi" Henry has the sixth part of 1 carucate.

In SPONDON Stori had 5 carucates of land to the geld. [There is] land for 5 ploughs. There are now 3 ploughs in demesne; and 14 villans and 2 bordars have 4 ploughs. There is a priest and a church, and 1 mill [rendering] 5s4d.

In Chaddesden [are] 4½ carucates of land to the geld and 2 parts of 1 bovate. [There is] land for as many ploughs. There now 11 sokemen and 10 villans and 5 bordars have 6 ploughs, and 28 acres of meadow. [There is] woodland pasture half a league long and 5 furlongs broad, [and] as much scrubland. TRE worth £4; now £3.

[Folio 275V: DERBYSHIRE]

In BREADSALL Siward had 5 carucates of land to the geld. [There is] land for 5 ploughs. There are now 2 ploughs in demesne; and 21 villans and 7 bordars having 8 ploughs. There 1 knight has 1 plough. There is a priest and a church, and 1 mill [rendering] 13s4d, and 12 acres of meadow, [and] woodland pasture 8 furlongs long and 8 broad. TRE, as now, worth £4. Robert holds it.

IN THE SAME PLACE [sic], | in | MORLEY, Siward had the third part of 2 carucates to the geld. There Henry has 4 villans with 1 plough. [There is] woodland pasture 4 furlongs long and 3 broad.

In PILSLEY [in Edensor] Dunning had 2 carucates of land to the geld. [There is] land for 2 ploughs. It is waste. There are 2 acres of meadow, and scrubland 3 furlongs long and 2 broad. TRE it was worth 20s.

In [?Great] LONGSTONE Kolli had 3 carucates of land to the geld. [There is] land for 3 ploughs. It is waste. There are 6 acres of meadow, [and] scrubland 2 leagues long and 1 league broad. TRE it was worth 30s.

In STANTON IN PEAK Godric and Rawn had 1 carucate of land to the geld. [There is] land for 1 plough. There 4 villans and 6 bordars have 3 ploughs. There are 24 acres of meadow, [and] woodland pasture 1 league long and 1 league broad. TRE worth 10s; and now the same.

BEREWICK

In Birchover [is] 1 carucate of land to the geld. [There is] land for 1 plough. It is waste. There are 8 acres of meadow, [and] scrubland half a league long and 3 furlongs broad, the third part for pasture. TRE [it was worth] 8s.

In HARTHILL Ketil had 4 bovates of land to the geld. It is waste. There are 3 acres of meadow. TRE it was worth 5s4d.

In YOULGREAVE Kolli and Ketil had 12 bovates of land to the geld. [There is] land for 3 ploughs. There are now 3 ploughs in demesne; and 1 villan with 1 plough, and 1 mill [rendering] 5s4d, and 4 acres of meadow. TRE worth 32s; now 16s.

In MIDDLETON [in Youlgreave] Dunning and Ylving had 2 carucates of land to the geld. [There is] land for 2 ploughs. It is waste. There are 2 acres of meadow. TRE it was worth 20s.

In GRATTON Ketil had 1 carucate of land to the geld. [There is] land for 2 ploughs. There is now 1 plough in demesne; and 4 villans and 2 bordars have 2 ploughs. There are 3 acres of meadow. TRE it was worth 10s.

In Wormhill and "Muchedesuuelle" Siward had 4 carucates of land to the geld. [There is] land for 4 ploughs. It is waste. There are 20 acres of meadow, [and] scrubland 1 league long and 3 furlongs broad.

In KEDLESTON Wulfsige and Godwine had 2 carucates of land to the geld. [There is] land for 2 ploughs. There are now 2 ploughs in demesne; and 5 villans and 5 bordars with 1 plough, and 1 mill [rendering] 5s, and a little scrubland. TRE worth 40s; now 20[s]. Gulbert holds it.

In Thulston Geoffrey Alselin holds 1 carucate of land of Henry. It is waste; nevertheless it is worth 3s.

In BARROW UPON TRENT Godwine and Kolgrimr had 3½ bovates of land to the geld. It is waste. There 1 villan has 4 oxen, and 8 acres of meadow. TRE worth 13s4d; now 2s.

In SWARKESTONE Gamal and Wulfstan and Ulf and Wulfgeat had 1 carucate of land to the geld. [There is] land for 1 plough. There is now 1 plough in demesne; and 6 villans having 1 plough. There are 68 acres of meadow, and 1 mill-site. TRE, as now, worth 20s.

In CHELLASTON Wulfsige had 4 bovates of land to the

geld. [There is] land for half a plough. It is waste. There are 4 acres of meadow. TRE worth 12s; now 3s. Amalric holds it.

In ARLESTON Kolgrimr and Ramkel had 1 carucate of land to the geld. [There is] land for 1 plough. There are now 2 ploughs in demesne; and 7 villans with 1 plough. There are 20 acres of meadow. TRE worth 20s; now 40s.

In TWYFORD and Stenson Leofric had 4 carucates of land to the geld. [There is] land for 3 ploughs. There are now 2 ploughs in demesne; and 4 villans and 5 bordars with 1 plough, and 1 mill [rendering] 5s, and 24 acres of meadow. [There is] woodland pasture 1 furlong long and 1 broad. TRE worth £8; now £4.

IN THE SAME PLACE Godwine and Wulfstan had 1 carucate of land to the geld. [There is] land for 1 plough. It is waste.

In OSMASTON [in Derby] Osmund had 3 bovates of land to the geld. [There is] land for 1 plough. There is now 1 plough in demesne, and 1 villan paying 2s8d. There are 20 acres of meadow. TRE worth 40s; now 20[s]. Of this money 2 parts are the king's, the third Henry's.

In COTTONS Osmund had 4 bovates of land to the geld. [There is] land for 1 plough. There 2 villans have 1 plough, and 3 acres of meadow. TRE worth 5s; now 2s6d.

In Osmaston [in Derby] [are] 3 bovates of land to the geld, belonging to Cottons.

In SINFIN Ulfkil had 2 carucates of land to the geld. [There is] land for 1 plough. There is now 1 plough in demesne; and 2 villans have 1 plough, and 6 acres of meadow. TRE worth 10s; now 10s. William holds it.

In NORMANTON [in Derby] Leofric, Gamal and Theodric had 6 bovates of land to the geld. [There is] land for 1 plough. There is now 1 plough in demesne, and 1 villan pays 12d. There are 12 acres of meadow and a little scrubland. TRE worth 20s; now 10s. Amalric holds it. In the same place [are] 2 bovates of land to the geld, belonging to Twyford.

In IRETON Godwine had 1 carucate of land to the geld. [There is] land for 2 ploughs. There is now 1 plough in demesne; and 6 villans and 6 bordars have 2 ploughs. There are 6 acres of meadow, and 1 mill [rendering] 16d, [and] woodland pasture half a league long and a half broad. TRE worth 40s; now 20s. Orm holds it.

In ASTON-ON-TRENT Uhtbrand had 1 carucate of land and 2½ bovates, sokeland, to the geld, and [there are] 5 acres of meadow. TRE worth 6s; now 8s.

In BURNASTON and Bearwardcote Gamal 10 bovates, Ælfric 2 bovates, Alric 2 bovates, Leodmær 1 bovate, [and] Lyfing 1 bovate had all together 2 carucates of land to the geld. [There is] land for 3 ploughs. There are now 3 ploughs in demesne; and 8 villans and 1 bordar have 4 ploughs. There are 36 acres of meadow and a little scrubland. TRE worth 40s; now 30s. Henry holds it.

In MUGGINTON Gamal had 2 carucates of land to the geld. [There is] land for 3 ploughs. There is now 1 plough in

demesne; and 8 villans and 8 bordars have 2 ploughs. There is a church and a priest, and 1 mill [rendering] 3s, and 3 acres of meadow, [and] woodland pasture 1½ leagues long and 1 broad. TRE worth 40s; now 20s. Ketil holds it.

[Folio 276: DERBYSHIRE]

In MERCASTON Gamal had 4 carucates of land to the geld. [There is] land for 6 ploughs. There is now 1 plough in demesne; and 6 villans and 4 bordars have 1 plough. There are 14 acres of meadow, and the site of 1 mill, [and] woodland pasture half a league long and 4 furlongs broad. TRE [worth] 40s; now 30s. Robert and Roger hold it.

In DALBURY Godric had 2 carucates of land to the geld. [There is] land for 4 ploughs. There are now 2 ploughs in demesne; and 6 villans and 1 bordar with 2 ploughs. There is a priest and a church, and 20 acres of meadow, [and] woodland pasture 1 league long and half a league broad. TRE worth 40s; now 60s. Robert holds it.

In ETWALL Gamal, Eadric, Wulfgeat, Ælfric [and] Alwine had 5 carucates of land to the geld. [There is] land for 5 ploughs. There are now 3 ploughs in demesne; and 14 villans and 8 bordars having 8 ploughs. There is a priest and a church, and 30 acres of meadow. TRE, as now, worth 100s. Saswalo holds it.

In RADBOURNE Wulfsige had 3 carucates of land to the geld. [There is] land for 4 ploughs. There are now 3 ploughs in demesne; and 6 villans and 5 bordars having 3 ploughs. There are 12 acres of meadow, [and] woodland pasture half a league long and 4 furlongs broad. TRE worth 40s; now 30s. Ralph fitzHubert claims the third part of Radbourne and the wapentake bears witness for him.

In MORLEY [is] the third part of 2 carucates of land to the geld. Siward had it. Now Henry has it.

In EDENSOR Leofnoth and Ketil had 2 carucates of land as 2 manors. Henry now [has] 4 carucates to the geld and as many ploughs for ploughing. There are 10 villans and 7 bordars with 6 ploughs, and 1 acre of meadow. Formerly [worth] 40s; now 20s.

VII. The land of William Peverel

In BOLSOVER Leofric had 3 carucates of land to the geld. [There is] land for 4 ploughs. There are now 2 ploughs in demesne; and 14 villans and 3 bordars having 4 ploughs, and 8 acres of meadow. [There is] woodland pasture 2 leagues long and 1 broad. TRE worth 40s; now 60[s]. Robert holds it.

In GLAPWELL Leofric had 1 carucate of land to the geld. [There is] land for 1 plough. There 8 villans have 2 ploughs. TRE worth 20s; now 10s. Serlo holds it.

In 'SNODSWICK' [in Morton] Healfdene had half a carucate of land to the geld. [There is] land for 1 plough. There is now 1 plough in demesne; and 6 villans and 1 bordar have 3 ploughs. There is the site of 1 mill, and woodland pasture 1 league long and 4 furlongs broad. TRE worth 40s; now 20s. Drogo holds it.

In SOUTH NORMANTON Ælfheah had 2 carucates of land to the geld. [There is] land for 2 ploughs. There is now 1 plough in demesne; and 6 villans and 1 bordar with 1 plough. There are 5 acres of meadow, [and] woodland pasture 1 league long and 4 furlongs and 2 furlongs broad [sic]. TRE worth 20s; now 10[s]. Edwin holds it.

In SHIRLAND and in Ufton Fields Leofric had 2½ carucates of land to the geld. [There is] land for as many ploughs. There now 5 villans and 1 bordar have 2 ploughs. [There is] woodland pasture 9 furlongs long and 4 broad. TRE worth 16s; now 10s8d. Warner holds it.

In CODNOR and Heanor and Langley [in Heanor] and 'Smithycote' [in Codnor Park] 8 thegns had 7 carucates of land to the geld. [There is] land for as many ploughs. There are now 3 ploughs in demesne; and 11 villans and 2 bordars and 3 sokemen having 5½ ploughs. There is a church, and 1 mill [rendering] 12d, and 35 acres of meadow, [and] woodland pasture 2 leagues long and 3 furlongs broad. TRE worth £4; now 41s4d. Warner holds it.

Arnbiorn and Hundingr held the land of William Peverel's castle in Castleton. These men had there 2 carucates of land to the geld. There is land for 2 ploughs. There are now 4 ploughs in demesne; and 3 villans with 1 plough, and 8 acres of meadow. TRE worth 40s; now 50s.

In BRADWELL Lyfing and Sprot and Owine had 2 carucates of land to the geld. [There is] land for 2 ploughs. There are now 4 ploughs in demesne; and 8 villans have 2 ploughs. TRE worth 20s; now 30s.

In HAZELBADGE and Litton Leofwine had 3½ carucates of land to the geld. [There is] land for as many ploughs. There is now 1 plough in demesne; and 3 villans with half a plough. There are 2 acres of meadow and a little scrubland. TRE worth 20s; now 4s.

In [Great and Little] HUCKLOW Earnwig, Hundolfr [and] Wulfric [had] 2 carucates of land to the geld. [There is] land for 2 ploughs. It is waste.

In ABNEY Swein had 1 carucate of land to the geld. [There is] land for 1 plough. It is waste.

In [?] NETHER WATER Leofwine had 1 carucate of land to the geld. [There is] land for 1 plough. It is waste.

[Folio 276V: DERBYSHIRE]

VIII. The land of Walter D'Aincourt

In MORTON and Ogston and Wessington Swein Cild had 11½ bovates of land and 8 acres of land to the geld. [There is] land for 3 ploughs. There are now 2 ploughs in demesne; and 14 villans having 5½ ploughs, and 4 slaves. There is a priest and a church, and 1 mill [rendering] 6s8d with a mill-keeper, and 8 acres of meadow, [and] woodland pasture 1½ leagues long and as much broad. TRE, as now, worth £4. Walter d'Aincourt holds it.

In OLD BRAMPTON and Wadshelf Wada had 3½ bovates of land and 4 acres to the geld. [There is] land for half a

plough. There Walter has now 1 plough in demesne; and 1 villan and 3 bordars having half a plough, and 2 acres and 1 perch of meadow. [There is] woodland pasture 1½ leagues long and 1½ furlongs broad. TRE, as now, worth 5s4d. Of this land Walter vouches the king as warrantor and Henry de Ferrers as livery officer.

In PILSLEY [in North Wingfield] and [?] Owlcotes and Williamthorpe Swein Cild had 2 carucates of land, less half a bovate, to the geld. [There is] land for 4 ploughs. There Walter has now 2 ploughs in demesne; and 12 villans and 3 bordars having 6 ploughs. To this manor belong 2 bovates of land to the geld. THE SOKE [belongs] to [?North] Wingfield, and there are 5 sokemen and a priest and a church. And in Old Tupton [is] 1 bovate of land and the third part of 1 bovate to the geld, and there is 1 sokeman and 8 villans and 1 bordar with 3½ ploughs. There are 3 acres of meadow, [and] woodland pasture 1 league long and 1 broad. TRE, as now, worth £4.

In HOLMESFIELD Swein had 1 carucate of land to the geld. [There is] land for 2 ploughs. There now 10 villans have 3 ploughs, and [there is] 1 acre of meadow, [and] woodland pasture 2 leagues long and 1 broad. TRE worth 40s; now 20s.

In ELMTON Swein Cild had 1 carucate of land to the geld. [There is] land for 3 ploughs. There Walter has now 1 plough in demesne; and 36 villans and 2 bordars having 9 ploughs. There is a priest and a church, [and] scrubland 1 league long and a half broad. TRE worth 40s; now £7.

In STONY HOUGHTON Swein Cild had 3 bovates of land to the geld. [There is] land for 2 ploughs. There 18 villans and 6 bordars have 8 ploughs. TRE worth 10s; now 60[s].

IX. The land of Geoffrey Alselin

In ALVASTON and Ambaston [and] Thulston and Elvaston Toki had 10 carucates of land to the geld. [There is] land for 14 ploughs. There Geoffrey Alselin has now 2 ploughs in demesne; and a certain knight of his [has] 1 plough. There 32 villans have 15 ploughs. There is a priest and a church, and 1 mill [rendering] 12s, and 1 smith, and 52 acres of meadow and a little scrubland. TRE worth £12; now £10.

In ETWALL Dunstan had 1 carucate of land to the geld. [There is] land for 1 plough. There now 1 villan has 2 oxen in a plough. There are 6 acres of meadow. TRE worth 20s; now 4s4d. Azelin holds it.

In EDNASTON and Hulland Toki had 3 carucates of land to the geld. [There is] land for 3 ploughs. There is now 1 plough in demesne, and 2 villans and 2 bordars, and half a church, and 2 acres of meadow. [There is] woodland pasture 1 league long and 1 broad, and other woodland half a league long and a half broad. TRE worth £4; now 35s.

To this manor belong 2½ bovates of land to the geld. The soke belongs to Hollington. [There is] land for 2½ oxen.

In EGGINTON Toki had 4 carucates of land to the geld. [There is] land for 6 ploughs. There is now 1 plough in demesne; and 2 villans and 5 bordars having 1 plough.

There is a priest and a church, and 1 mill [rendering] 5s, and 6 rent-paying tenants pay 14s4d. There are 200 acres of meadow and a little scrubland. TRE worth £8; now 60s. Azelin holds it.

SOKELAND

In Breaston [is] 1 bovate of land to the geld. [There is] land for 1 ox, and it is waste and renders 2 spurs. There is 1 acre of meadow. There Gilbert de Ghent has 2 carucates of land 1 league long and 3 furlongs broad.

In OCKBROOK Toki had 4 carucates of land to the geld. [There is] land for 4 ploughs. There now 10 villans and 2 bordars have 3 ploughs, and 4 rent-paying tenants pay 14s. There are 5 acres of meadow, [and] woodland pasture 1 league long and a half broad. TRE worth £4; now 40s. Geoffrey holds it.

[Folio 277: DERBYSHIRE]

X. The land of Ralph fitzHubert

In ECKINGTON Leofnoth had 4 carucates of land to the geld. [There is] land for 5 ploughs. There Ralph fitzHubert has now 1 plough in demesne; and 14 villans having 5 ploughs. There is a priest, and 1 slave, and 1 mill [rendering] 3s, and 8 acres of meadow, [and] woodland pasture 2 leagues and 1 furlong long and 1 league and half a furlong broad. TRE worth £7; now 60s.

SOKELAND

In Mosborough [Yorks.] [are] 2 carucates of land to the geld. [There is] land for 3 ploughs. There now 13 sokemen have 5 ploughs, and [there are] 3 acres of meadow, [and] woodland pasture 1½ leagues long and 1 league broad.

SOKELAND

In Beighton [Yorks.] [are] 4 bovates of land to the geld. [There is] land for as many oxen. It is waste.

In BARLBOROUGH and Whitwell Leofnoth had 6 carucates of land to the geld. [There is] land for 8 ploughs. There are now 3 ploughs in demesne; and 10 sokemen and 10 villans and 36 bordars having 8 ploughs. There is a priest and a church, and 1 slave, and 2 mills [rendering] 3s. There are 3 acres of meadow, woodland pasture 2 leagues long and 1 broad, [and] scrubland 1 league long and 1 broad. TRE, as now, worth £6. Robert holds it. In CLOWNE [are] 2 bovates of land to the geld. They belong to this manor.

In PALTERTON and Scarcliffe and 'Tunstall' [in Ault Hucknall] Leofnoth had 6 carucates of land and 2 bovates to the geld. [There is] land for 8 ploughs. There are now 2 ploughs in demesne; and 10 villans and 1 sokeman and 2 bordars having 3 ploughs, and 1 rent-paying tenant with 1 plough. There is 1 mill [rendering] 4s, and 8 acres of meadow, [and] woodland pasture 1 league long and half a league broad. TRE worth £6; now 50s. Reynard holds it.

In DUCKMANTON Leofnoth had 4 carucates of land and 2 bovates to the geld. [There is] land for 5 ploughs. There now

18 rent-paying tenants have 5 ploughs. There are 8 acres of meadow, [and] woodland pasture 1 league long and 1 league broad. TRE worth £4; now 19s. Geoffrey holds it.

In STRETTON and Egstow and Handley [in North Wingfield] Leofnoth had 1 carucate of land to the geld. [There is] land for 2 ploughs. There are now 1½ ploughs in demesne; and 6 villans and 4 bordars having 3 ploughs, and 8 acres of meadow. [There is] woodland pasture 2 leagues long and 1 broad. TRE worth 60s; now 20s. Robert holds it.

In another STRETTON [Stretton Hall] Leofric had 2½ bovates of land to the geld. [There is] land for 4 oxen. There now 2 villans and 4 bordars have 2 ploughs, and 2 acres of meadow. [There is] woodland pasture 3 furlongs long and 1 broad. TRE, as now, worth 3s. Robert holds it.

In ASHOVER Leofric and Leofnoth had 2 carucates of land to the geld. [There is] land for 2 ploughs. There now 3 rent-paying tenants and 14 bordars have 3 ploughs. There is now 1 plough in demesne, and a priest and a church, and 1 mill [rendering] 16d. [There is] woodland pasture 2 leagues long and 2 broad. TRE worth £4; now 30s. Serlo holds it.

In NEWTON Leofric and Leofnoth had 3 carucates of land to the geld. [There is] land for 5 ploughs. There is now 1 plough in demesne; and 13 villans and 4 bordars having 5 ploughs. There is a priest having 1 bordar, and 7 acres of meadow. [There is] woodland pasture 1 league long and a half broad. TRE worth £4; now 30s. Ralph holds it.

In CRICH and Shuckstonfield Leofric and Leofnoth had 4 bovates of land to the geld. [There is] land for 1 plough. There is now 1 plough in demesne; and 10 villans and 2 bordars having 3 ploughs. There are 3 acres of meadow, woodland pasture 3 leagues long and 1 league broad and 1 lead-mine. TRE worth 40s; now 30s. Ralph holds it.

In Wessington [are] 3½ bovates of land to the geld. [There is] land for 1 plough. THE SOKE [belongs] to Crich. There now 1 villan and 6 bordars have 2 ploughs. [There is] woodland pasture 1 league long and a half broad. TRE worth 10s; now 5s. Lyfing holds it.

In Ogston [are] 2 bovates of land to the geld. [There is] land for 4 oxen. [There is] woodland pasture half a league long and 4 furlongs broad. THE SOKE [belongs] to Crich, and it is waste.

In Ufton Fields [are] 4 bovates of land to the geld. [There is] land for half a plough. [It is] a BEREWICK [belonging] to Pentrich. It is waste. There are 2 acres of meadow, [and] woodland pasture half a league long and 4 furlongs broad. Nigel holds it.

In STONEY MIDDLETON Leofnoth and his brother had 1 carucate of land to the geld. [There is] land for 1 plough. It is waste. This manor is 1 league long and 4 furlongs broad.

In HATHERSAGE Leofnoth and Leofric had 2 carucates of land to the geld. [There is] land for 2 ploughs. To this manor belong 4 Berewicks: Bamford, [Nether and Upper] Hurst, half of Offerton, and 2 parts of Stoney Middleton. In these [are] 2 carucates of land to the geld. [There is] land for 2 ploughs. There now 8 villans and 2 bordars have 5 ploughs. [There is] woodland, pasture in places, 2 leagues long and 2 leagues broad. TRE worth 60s; now 30s.

In HARTHILL Leofnoth had 2 carucates of land to the geld. [There is] land for 2 ploughs. There now 5 villans and 3 bordars have 3 ploughs. There are 8 acres of meadow and a little scrubland. TRE worth 20s; now 12s. Kolli holds it.

In BOULTON Leofnoth had 1 carucate of land to the geld. [There is] land for 2 ploughs. There is now 1 plough in demesne; and 2 sokemen and 3 villans have 1 plough. There are 10 acres of meadow, [and] pasture 4 furlongs long and 3 furlongs broad. TRE worth 40s; now 20s.

In WILLINGTON Leofric had 3 carucates of land to the geld. [There is] land for 4 ploughs. There now 4 villans and 2 bordars have 4 ploughs, and [there are] 30 acres of meadow. TRE worth 40s; now 20s.

In KIRK LANGLEY Leofnoth had 4 carucates of land to the geld. [There is] land for 6 ploughs. There is now 1 plough in demesne; and 2 villans and 4 bordars have 2 ploughs. [There is] woodland pasture 1 league long and 3 furlongs broad, and a little scrubland. TRE worth 100s; now 40s.

In BALLIDON Leofric and Leofnoth had 4 carucates of land to the geld. [There is] land for 4 ploughs. There is now 1 plough in demesne; and 6 villans have 1 plough. There are 16 acres of meadow, [and] scrubland half a league long and 1 furlong broad. TRE worth 60s; now 12s6d.

In INGLEBY he had 1 carucate of land and the sixth part of 1 carucate to the geld. [There is] land for 1½ ploughs. There is now 1 plough in demesne; and 3 villans and 2 bordars have 1 plough. There are 7 acres of meadow and 1 mill-site. | It is worth 10s. |

In Wirksworth and Lea and Tansley [are] 4 bovates of land to the geld. [There is] land for 1 plough. There now 3 villans and 7 bordars have 1 plough, and 2½ acres of meadow. [There is] woodland pasture half a league long and as much broad. TRE worth 10s; now 7s. This land belongs to Crich, but it pays geld in Hamston Wapentake.

[Folio 277V: DERBYSHIRE]

In CLIFTON Leofric and Leofnoth had 3 carucates of land to the geld. [There is] land for 3 ploughs. There now 8 villans and 5 bordars have 4 ploughs, and [there are] 4 acres of meadow. TRE worth 40s; now 10s.

In RIPLEY and Pentrich Leofnoth had 2 carucates of land to the geld. [There is] land for 2 ploughs. There are now 3 ploughs in demesne; and 13 villans and 3 bordars have 3 ploughs. There are 3 acres of meadow, [and] woodland pasture 2 leagues long and 1 broad. TRE worth £4; now 50s.

In Barrow upon Trent [are] 12 bovates of land to the geld. THE SOKE [belongs] to Melbourne. There is a priest and a church, and 1 sokeman with half a plough, and 18 acres of meadow.

In "Werredune" Leofnoth [had] 2 bovates of land to the geld. [There is] land for 4 oxen. There now 6 villans have 1 plough,

and [there is] 1 acre of meadow, and scrubland. TRE, as now, worth 5s.

XI. The land of Ralph de Buron

In WESTON UNDERWOOD Wulfsige had 1 carucate of land to the geld. [There is] land for 1 plough. There is now 1 plough in demesne; and 6 villans and 6 bordars have 2 ploughs. There are 8 acres of meadow, [and] woodland pasture 1 league long and a half broad. TRE worth 40s; now 20s. Gulbert holds it of Ralph de Buron.

In HORSLEY Thorger had 3 carucates of land to the geld. [There is] land for 4 ploughs. There are now 2 ploughs in demesne; and 19 villans and 4 bordars having 6 ploughs. There are 60 acres of meadow, [and] woodland pasture 1 league long and 1 broad. TRE worth 100s; now 60s. Ralph holds it.

In DENBY Osmund had 2 carucates of land to the geld. [There is] land for 4 ploughs. There now 7 villans and 1 bordar have 3 ploughs. There are 12 acres of meadow, and the site of 1 mill, [and] woodland pasture 1 league long and 1 broad. TRE worth 100s; now 20s. A knight of Ralph's holds it.

In KIRK HALLAM Dunstan had 1 carucate of land to the geld. [There is] land for 2 ploughs. There is now 1 plough in demesne; and 5 villans and 4 bordars have 2 ploughs. There are 16 acres of meadow, [and] woodland pasture 7 furlongs long and 6 furlongs broad. TRE, as now, worth 20s.

In "HERDEBI" Thorger had 5 parts of 1 carucate of land to the geld. [There is] land for 1 plough. It is waste. There are 6 acres of meadow, [and] woodland pasture 1 league long and a half broad. TRE worth 30s; now 8s.

XII. The land of Hascoit Musard

In BARLOW Hakon had 2 parts of 1 carucate of land to the geld. [There is] land for half a plough. There now 6 villans and 1 bordar have 1 plough. There are 2 acres of meadow, [and] woodland pasture 1½ leagues long and 8 furlongs broad. TRE, as now, worth 10s. Hascoit Musard holds it.

In STAVELEY Hakon had 4 carucates of land to the geld. [There is] land for 4 ploughs. There Hascoit has now 3 ploughs in demesne; and 21 villans and 7 bordars have 4 ploughs. There is a priest and a church, and 1 mill [rendering] 5s4d. There are 60 acres of meadow, [and] woodland pasture 1½ leagues long and as much broad. TRE, as now, worth £6.

In 'HOLME' [in Brampton] and Wadshelf and Old Brampton Dunning had 10½ bovates of land to the geld. [There is] land for 12 oxen. There now 8 villans and 5 bordars have 3 ploughs. There are 3 acres of meadow, [and] woodland pasture 1½ leagues and 1 furlong long and 2½ furlongs broad. TRE worth 20s; now 10s. Hascoit holds it.

In OLD BRAMPTON and Wadshelf Brandwin had 7 bovates of land and 4 acres to the geld. [There is] land for 1 plough. There is now 1 plough in demesne; and 3 villans and 1 bordar have 1 plough. There are 5 acres of meadow, [and] woodland pasture 1½ leagues long and 3 furlongs broad. TRE, as now, worth 10s. Hascoit holds it.

In KILLAMARSH Alweald had half a bovate of land to the geld. It is waste. There is half an acre of meadow, [and] woodland pasture 1 league long and 30 perches broad. TRE [worth] 16d; now 12[d].

XIII. The land of Gilbert de Ghent

In ILKESTON and West Hallam and Stanton-by-Dale Ulf Fenman had 6 carucates of land and 6 bovates to the geld, and in Breaston, SOKELAND, 2 carucates of land to the geld. [There is] land for 8 ploughs and 6 oxen. There are now 3 ploughs in demesne; and 10 sokemen on 2 carucates of this land and 18 villans and 7 bordars having 12 ploughs. There is the site of 1 mill, and 70 acres of meadow, woodland pasture 1 league long and 3 furlongs broad, and scrubland 5 furlongs long and 2 broad. TRE worth £8; now 100s. Mauger holds it.

In SHIPLEY Brun and Othenkar had 2 carucates of land to the geld. [There is] land for 2 ploughs. There now 7 villans and 1 sokeman and 1 bordar have 5 ploughs. There are 3 acres of meadow, [and] woodland pasture 7 furlongs long and 3 broad. TRE worth 40s; now 30s. Mauger holds it. The jurors say this land did not belong to Ulf Fenman TRE, but those 2 thegns held it in such a way that they could give and sell it to whom they wished.

[Folio 278: DERBYSHIRE]

XIIII. The land of Nigel of Stafford

In DRAKELOWE and Hearthcote Alric had 4 carucates of land to the geld. [There is] land for 4 ploughs. There now Nigel of Stafford has 4 ploughs in demesne; and 6 villans having 3 ploughs. There is the site of 1 mill, and 12 acres of meadow, [and] woodland pasture 2½ leagues long and 2 leagues broad. TRE worth 60s; now 40[s].

In STAPENHILL [Staffs.] Godric had 6 bovates of land to the geld. [There is] land for 1 plough. There is now 1 plough in demesne; and 4 villans and 3 bordars have 1 plough. There are 3 acres of meadow, [and] scrubland 1 furlong long and 1 broad. TRE, as now, worth 10s.

In SWADLINCOTE Godric had 1 carucate of land to the geld. [There is] land for 1 plough. There is now 1 plough in demesne; and 4 villans and 2 bordars have 1 plough, and 1 rent-paying tenant has 1 plough. There is 1 acre of meadow, [and] woodland pasture 4 furlongs long and 4 broad. TRE worth 20s; now 30[s].

In FOREMARK Ulfkil had 2 carucates of land to the geld. [There is] land for 2 ploughs. There is now 1 plough in demesne; and 5 villans and 3 bordars have 1 plough. There is 1 mill [rendering] 2s, and 24 acres of meadow, [and] woodland pasture half a league long and as much broad. TRE worth 40s; now 15s.

THE SOKELAND OF THE SAME MANOR

In Ingleby [are] 3 bovates of land to the geld. [There is] land for 4 oxen. There is 1 villan and 2 bordars with half a plough, and 4 acres of meadow.

In Ticknall [is] 1 carucate of land to the geld. [There is] land for 1 plough. THE SOKE belongs to the king's manor of Repton. There Nigel has 1 plough in demesne; and 1 villan and 1 bordar with 1 plough. There are 10 acres of meadow. It is worth 3s. The fourth part of the woodland pasture of the same vill, whose length is 1 league and breadth half a league, belongs to Nigel.

In SMISBY Edwin had 2 carucates of land to the geld. [There is] land for 2 ploughs. There is now 1 plough in demesne; and 5 villans with 1 plough. [There is] woodland pasture half a league long and 6 furlongs broad. TRE worth 40s; now 20s.

In RAVENSTONE [Leics.] Godric had 1 carucate of land to the geld. [There is] land for 1 plough. It is waste. There are 8 acres of meadow. TRE worth 15s; now 12d.

In DONISTHORPE [Leics.] Karli had 1 carucate of land to the geld. [There is] land for half a plough. It is waste. TRE worth 5s; now 12d.

In OAKTHORPE [Leics.] Earnwine had 6 bovates of land to the geld. [There is] land for half a plough. It is waste. TRE worth 5s; now 4d.

In "TRANGESBY" [?Leics.] Alnoth had half a carucate of land to the geld. It is waste. TRE worth 5s; now 2d.

XV. The land of Robert fitzWilliam

In STANLEY Ulvar had 2 carucates of land to the geld. [There is] land for 2 ploughs. There Robert fitzWilliam has 2 villans and 2 bordars with 1 plough. There are 6 acres of meadow, [and] woodland pasture 1 league long and a half broad. TRE worth 20s; now 10s.

XVI. The land of Roger de Bully

In BREASTON Ligulf and Leofwine Cild had 3 carucates of land to the geld. [There is] land [...]. There Fulk, the man of Roger de Bully, has 5 villans with 2 ploughs, and 10 acres of meadow. TRE worth 40s; now 21s. This Ligulf had half a carucate of sokeland which Fulk de Lisors has, having seized it to the loss of Gilbert de Ghent.

In RISLEY Wulfsige had 5 bovates of land and the third part of 1 bovate to the geld, and Godric [had] 5 bovates and the third part of 1 bovate to the geld. [There is] land [...]. There now 5 villans have 2 ploughs, and 20 acres of meadow. [There is] woodland pasture 9 furlongs long and 3 furlongs broad. TRE worth 21s4d; now 22s8d. Fulk holds it of Roger. Earnwine claims it.

In BEIGHTON [Yorks.] Swein had 6½ bovates to the geld. There is land for 1½ ploughs. There are nevertheless 4 ploughs, and 11 villans and 2 bordars. Formerly [worth] 20s; now 32s. Roger holds it, and Leofwine [holds] of him.

In DORE [Yorks.] Edwin [had] 2 bovates of land to the geld. There is land for half a plough.

In the same place Leofwine [had] 2 bovates of land to the geld. There is land for 1 plough. Formerly [worth] 20s; now 64d.

In NORTON [in Sheffield, Yorks.] Godgifu and Bada had 12½ bovates of land and 8 acres of land. [There is] land for 2 ploughs. There 3 villans have 1 plough. Ingram holds it of Roger. Formerly [worth] 20s; now 18d.

In ALFRETON Morcar had as a manor 4½ bovates and 4 acres of land to the geld. There is land for 1 plough. There are 9 villans and 3 bordars with 2 ploughs. There are 5 acres of meadow. Formerly [worth] 20s; now 30s. Ingram holds it of Roger.

In ROWTHORNE Wulfsige and Stenulf had 1 carucate of land to the geld as a manor, and in Bramley Vale 2 bovates of land of the sokeland of Rowthorne. There is land for 2 ploughs. There 6 villans with 1 bordar have 1 plough. In demesne [is] 1 plough, and 2½ acres of meadow. Formerly [worth] 20s; now 16s.

[Folio 278V: DERBYSHIRE]

XVII. The land of the King's Thegns

In BARLOW Leofric and Uhtræd had 2½ bovates of land to the geld. [There is] land for 5 oxen. There now 3 villans and 4 bordars have 1 plough. [There is] woodland pasture 3 leagues long and 4 furlongs broad. TRE, as now, worth 6s8d.

In KILLAMARSH Godric [...] and Eadric and Thorgisl had 7½ bovates of land to the geld. [There is] land for 1 plough. There now 5 villans have 1 plough. There are 7 acres of meadow, [and] woodland pasture 3 leagues and 5 furlongs and 70 perches broad. TRE worth 18s; now 9s.

In OLD TUPTON Dolgfinnr had 2 bovates of land to the geld. It is waste. TRE worth 8s; now 5s.

In TOTLEY [Yorks.] Tholf had 4 bovates of land to the geld. [There is] land for 1 plough. It is waste. [There is] woodland pasture 1 league long and half a league broad. TRE worth 10s; now 12d.

In COAL ASTON Tholf had 5½ bovates of land to the geld. [There is] land for 1 plough. There are now 2 sokemen and 6 villans and 1 bordar having 3 ploughs. There are 2 acres of meadow, [and] woodland pasture 7 furlongs long and 4 furlongs broad. TRE, as now, worth 20s. Leofwine holds it of the king.

In [Middle, Nether and West] HANDLEY Godric had 7 bovates of land to the geld. [There is] land for 1 plough. There is now 1 plough in demesne; and 2 sokemen and 4 villans and 2 bordars have 3½ ploughs. There are 2 acres of meadow. TRE worth 10s; now 20s. Leofwine holds it of the king.

IN THE SAME PLACE Rawn had 1 bovate of land to the geld. It is waste. Sedret holds it of the king.

In TAPTON Bada had 1 bovate of land and 4 acres to the geld. [There is] land for 2 oxen. There now 4 villans have 1

plough, and [there is] woodland 1 acre in length and 1 acre in breadth. TRE worth 10s; now 2s8d. Dolgfinnr holds it of the king.

In CALOW Esbiorn and Hakon had 1 carucate of land to the geld. [There is] land for 12 oxen. There now Stenulf and Dunning have 2½ ploughs, and 17 villans and 1 bordar with 2 ploughs. There are 3 acres of meadow, [and] woodland pasture 1 furlong long and 1 broad. TRE worth 30s; now 20s. Dolgfinnr claims it.

In CLOWNE Earnwig had 6 bovates of land to the geld. [There is] land for 1 plough. There is now half a plough in demesne; and 8 villans with 1 plough. TRE worth 20s; now 8s. Earnwig holds it of the king.

In LULLINGTON Auti had 5 carucates of land to the geld. [There is] land for 5 ploughs. There now Edmund has of the king 21 villans and 3 bordars with 4 ploughs. There is a priest, and 1 mill [rendering] 6s8d, and 12 acres of meadow. TRE, as now, worth £4.

In EDINGALE [Staffs.] Algar had 2 carucates of land to the geld. [There is] land for 3 ploughs. There now 12 villans have 8 ploughs, and [there are] 4 acres of meadow, [and] scrubland 3 furlongs long and 1 broad. TRE, as now, worth 40s.

In ILKESTON Osmund Benz had 3 bovates of land to the geld. The same man himself holds them of the king.

IN THE SAME PLACE Toli had 3 bovates of land to the geld. [There is] land for as many oxen. There now 2 villans have 5 oxen in a plough. There are 5 acres of meadow. This land belongs to Sandiacre.

In SANDIACRE Toli, Knut and Glædwine had 4 carucates of land [...] to the geld. [There is] land for 5 ploughs. Now Toli holds it of the king. There are 2 ploughs in demesne; and 10 villans and 6 bordars have 5 ploughs. There is a priest and a church, and 1 mill [rendering] 5s4d, and 30 acres of meadow and a little scrubland. TRE, as now, worth 40s.

IN THE SAME PLACE Osmund had 1 carucate of land to the geld. [There is] land for 1 plough. Now it is waste. There are 6 acres of meadow and a little scrubland.

IN THE SAME PLACE Toki had 2 bovates of land to the geld.

In "CELLESDENE" Osmund had 4 bovates of land and 3 parts of 1 bovate to the geld. [There is] land for 6 oxen. The same man himself holds it of the king, and has there 3 villans with half a plough, and [there are] 2½ acres of meadow, [and] woodland pasture 3 furlongs long and 2 broad. TRE worth 10s; now 5s.

In "ULVRITUNE" Alun had 1 carucate of land to the geld. [There is] land for 2 ploughs. Now Healfdene holds it of the king. There are 12 acres of meadow, [and] woodland pasture 1 league long and a half broad. TRE worth 10s; now 2s.

In RISLEY Leofwine had 5 bovates of land and the third part of 1 bovate to the geld. His son holds it now of the king. There are 10 acres of meadow, [and] woodland pasture 9 furlongs long and 1½ furlongs broad. TRE worth 10s8d; now 5s4d.

In [?] MARSH Leofnoth had 4 bovates of land to the geld. [There is] land for 4 oxen. It is waste.

In STANTON BY BRIDGE Edward had 1½ carucates of land to the geld. [There is] land for 2 ploughs. There are nevertheless 4½ ploughs, and 4 sokemen and 4 villans, and 40 acres of meadow, and a mill [rendering] 2s. Earnwig holds it. It was and is worth 20s.

In INGLEBY [are] 2 parts of 1 bovate of land. It belongs to Stanton by Bridge.

[Folio 279: [DERBYSHIRE]]

[Blank in MS]

[Folio 279V: [DERBYSHIRE]]

[Blank in MS]

[Folio 280: NOTTINGHAMSHIRE]

THERE WERE IN THE BOROUGH OF NOTT-INGHAM TRE 173 burgesses and 19 villans. To this borough belong 6 carucates of land to the king's geld, and 1 meadow, and scrubland 6 furlongs long and 5 broad. This land was divided among 38 burgesses, and rendered 75s7d from the rent of the land and the services of the burgesses and 40s. from 2 moneyers. In it Earl Tosti had 1 carucate of land, from the soke of which land the king used to have the 2 pennies and the earl himself the third.

Hugh fitzBaldric, the sheriff, found 136 men dwelling [there], now there are 16 less. Nevertheless, Hugh himself built 13 houses, which did not exist before, on the earl's land in the new borough, adding them to the rent of the old borough.

In Nottingham there is 1 church in the king's demesne, to which belong 3 messuages of the borough and 5 bovates of land of the above-mentioned 6 carucates with sake and soke, and to the same church belong 5½ acres of land of which the king has sake and soke. The burgesses have 6 carucates of arable land, and 20 bordars and 14 ploughs. They were accustomed to fish in the river Trent, and now they make complaint that they are forbidden to fish. TRE Nottingham rendered £18; now it renders £30 and £10 from the mint.

In Nottingham Roger de Bully has 3 messuages on which are established 11 houses rendering 4s7d.

William Peverel has 48 merchants' houses rendering 36s, and 12 horsemen's houses, and 8 bordars.

Ralph de Buron has 13 horsemen's houses; in 1 of these 1 merchant dwells. Gulbert [has] 4 houses.

Ralph fitzHubert has 11 houses; in these dwell 3 merchants.

Geoffrey Alselin has 21 houses, and Aitard the priest 2 houses.

In the priest's croft are 65 houses and in these the king has sake and soke. The church with everything that pertains to it is worth 100s a year. Richard Frail has 4 houses.

In the borough ditch are 17 houses and 6 other houses.

The king granted to William Peverel 10 acres of land for making an orchard.

In Nottingham King Edward had 1 carucate of land with the geld. [There is] land for 2 ploughs. There the king has now 11 villans having 4 ploughs, and 12 acres of meadow. In demesne [is] nothing. TRE worth £3; now the same.

In Nottingham the river Trent and the ditch and the road towards York are so guarded that if anyone impedes the passage of boats, or if anyone ploughs or makes a ditch within 2 perches of the king's road, he has to pay a fine of £8.

IN THE BOROUGH OF DERBY, TRE, there were 243 burgesses dwelling, and there belong to this borough 12 carucates of land to the geld, which 8 teams can plough. This land was divided among 41 burgesses who also had 12 ploughs. To the king [belonged] 2 parts, and to the earl the third, of rent and toll and forfeiture and of every customary due. In the same borough there was 1 church in the king's demesne, with 7 clerks who held 2 carucates of land freely in Little Chester. There was also another church, similarly the king's, in which 6 clerks held 9 bovates of land, likewise freely, in Quarndon and Little Eaton.

In the vill itself there were 14 mills.

Now there are 100 burgesses and 40 other lesser ones. 103 messuages are waste which used to pay rent. There are now 10 mills and 16 acres of meadow.

[There is] scrubland 3 furlongs long and 2 broad.

TRE it rendered £24 all together; now with the mills and the vill of Litchurch it renders £30.

In Litchurch the king has 2 carucates of land to the geld. [There is] land for 3 ploughs. There| 1 sokeman| and 9 villans have |2 ploughs, and 12 acres of meadow.|

In Derby the Abbot of Burton has 1 mill, and 1 messuage with sake and soke, and 2 messuages of which the king has the soke, and 13 acres of meadow.

Geoffrey Alselin has 1 church which belonged to Toki.

Ralph fitzHubert, 1 church which belonged to Leofric |with 1 carucate of land.|

Norman of Lincoln, 1 church which belonged to Brun.

Eadric has there 1 church which belonged to Kolli his father.

Earl Hugh has 2 messuages and 1 fishery with sake and soke.

Henry de Ferrers, 3 messuages, similarly with sake and soke.

Osmær the priest has 1 bovate of land with sake and soke.

Godwine the priest, 1 bovate of land similarly.

At the feast of St Martin the burgesses render to the king 12 thraves of corn of which the Abbot of Burton has 40 sheaves.

There are in addition in the same borough 8 messuages with sake and soke. These belonged to Ælfgar; now they belong to the king.

The king's 2 pennies and the earl's third which come out of 'Appletree' Wapentake in Derby [shire] are in the sheriff's hand, or rent, by the witness of the 2 shires.

Of Stori, Walter d'Aincourt's predecessor, they say that without anyone's leave he could build himself a church on his own land and in his own soke and assign his tithes where he wished.

[Folio 280V: [NOTTINGHAMSHIRE]]

In Nottinghamshire and in Derbyshire if the king's peace, given under his hand or seal, is broken a fine is paid by 18 hundreds, each hundred [paying] £8. The king has 2 parts of this fine, the earl the third. That is, 12 hundreds pay the fine to the king and 6 to the earl.

In anyone is exiled according to law for any crime none but the king can restore peace to him.

A thegn having more than 6 manors does not give relief for his land except £8 to the king alone.

If he has only 6 or less he gives 3 marks of silver to the sheriff as relief wherever he dwells, in the borough or without.

If a thegn having sake and soke forfeits his land, the king and earl between them have half his land and resources, and his lawful wife with his legitimate heirs, if there are any, have the other half.

Here are noted those who had soke and sake and toll and team and the king's customary dues of the 2 pennies.

The Archbishop of York over his manors, and Countess Godgifu over Newark Wapentake, and Ulf Fenman over his land; the Abbot of Peterborough over Collingham [Notts.]; the Abbot of Burton; Earl Hugh over Markeaton; the Bishop of Chester; Toki; Swein son of Svavi; Siward Barn; Azur son of Svala; Wulfric Cild; Alsige [of] Illing; Leofwine son of Alwine; Countess Ælfgifu; Countess Gode; Alsige son of Karski over Worksop [Notts.]; Henry de Ferrers over Ednaston and Doveridge and Brailsford; Walter d'Aincourt over Granby [Notts.] and Morton and Pilsley [in North Wingfield].

None of all these could have the earl's third penny except by his grant, and that for as long as he should live, except the Archbishop and Ulf Fenman and Countess Godgifu.

Over the soke which belongs to Clifton [in Nottingham] the earl ought to have the third part of all customary dues and services.

NOTTINGHAMSHIRE

THERE WERE IN THE BOROUGH OF NOTT-INGHAM TRE 173 burgesses and 19 villans. To this borough belong 6 carucates of land to the king's geld, and 1 meadow, and scrubland 6 furlongs long and 5 broad. This land was divided among 38 burgesses, and rendered 75s7d from the rent of the land and the services of the burgesses and 40s. from 2 moneyers. In it Earl Tosti had 1 carucate of land, from the soke of which land the king used to have the 2 pennies and the earl himself the third.

Hugh fitzBaldric, the sheriff, found 136 men dwelling [there], now there are 16 less. Nevertheless, Hugh himself built 13 houses, which did not exist before, on the earl's land in the new borough, adding them to the rent of the old borough.

In Nottingham there is 1 church in the king's demesne, to which belong 3 messuages of the borough and 5 bovates of land of the above-mentioned 6 carucates with sake and soke, and to the same church belong 5½ acres of land of which the king has sake and soke. The burgesses have 6 carucates of arable land, and 20 bordars and 14 ploughs. They were accustomed to fish in the river Trent, and now they make complaint that they are forbidden to fish. TRE Nottingham rendered £18; now it renders £30 and £10 from the mint.

In Nottingham Roger de Bully has 3 messuages on which are established 11 houses rendering 4s7d.

William Peverel has 48 merchants' houses rendering 36s, and 12 horsemen's houses, and 8 bordars.

Ralph de Buron has 13 horsemen's houses; in 1 of these 1 merchant dwells. Gulbert [has] 4 houses.

Ralph fitzHubert has 11 houses; in these dwell 3 merchants.

Geoffrey Alselin has 21 houses, and Aitard the priest 2 houses.

In the priest's croft are 65 houses and in these the king has sake and soke. The church with everything that pertains to it is worth 100s a year. Richard Frail has 4 houses.

In the borough ditch are 17 houses and 6 other houses.

The king granted to William Peverel 10 acres of land for making an orchard.

In Nottingham King Edward had 1 carucate of land with the geld. [There is] land for 2 ploughs. There the king has now 11 villans having 4 ploughs, and 12 acres of meadow. In demesne [is] nothing. TRE worth £3; now the same.

In Nottingham the river Trent and the ditch and the road towards York are so guarded that if anyone impedes the passage of boats, or if anyone ploughs or makes a ditch within 2 perches of the king's road, he has to pay a fine of £8.

IN THE BOROUGH OF DERBY, TRE, there were 243 burgesses dwelling, and there belong to this borough 12 carucates of land to the geld, which 8 teams can plough. This land was divided among 41 burgesses who also had 12 ploughs. To the king [belonged] 2 parts, and to the earl the third, of rent and toll and forfeiture and of every customary due. In the same borough there was 1 church in the king's demesne, with 7 clerks who held 2 carucates of land freely in Little Chester [Derby]. There was also another church, similarly the king's, in which 6 clerks held 9 bovates of land, likewise freely, in Quarndon [Derby.] and Little Eaton [Derby.].

In the vill itself there were 14 mills.

Now there are 100 burgesses and 40 other lesser ones. 103 messuages are waste which used to pay rent. There are now 10 mills and 16 acres of meadow.

[There is] scrubland 3 furlongs long and 2 broad.

TRE it rendered £24 all together; now with the mills and the vill of Litchurch [Derby]. it renders £30.

In Litchurch [Derby.] the king has 2 carucates of land to the geld. [There is] land for 3 ploughs. There | 1 sokeman | and 9 villans have | 2 ploughs, and 12 acres of meadow. |

In Derby the Abbot of Burton has 1 mill, and 1 messuage with sake and soke, and 2 messuages of which the king has the soke, and 13 acres of meadow.

Geoffrey Alselin has 1 church which belonged to Toki.

Ralph fitzHubert, 1 church which belonged to Leofric | with 1 carucate of land. |

Norman of Lincoln, 1 church which belonged to Brun.

Eadric has there 1 church which belonged to Kolli his father.

Earl Hugh has 2 messuages and 1 fishery with sake and soke.

Henry de Ferrers, 3 messuages, similarly with sake and soke.

Osmær the priest has 1 bovate of land with sake and soke.

Godwine the priest, 1 bovate of land similarly.

At the feast of St Martin the burgesses render to the king 12 thraves of corn of which the Abbot of Burton has 40 sheaves.

There are in addition in the same borough 8 messuages with sake and soke. These belonged to Ælfgar; now they belong to the king.

The king's 2 pennies and the earl's third which come out of 'Appletree' Wapentake in Derby [shire] are in the sheriff's hand, or rent, by the witness of the 2 shires.

Of Stori, Walter d'Aincourt's predecessor, they say that without anyone's leave he could build himself a church on his own land and in his own soke and assign his tithes where he wished.

[Folio 280V: [NOTTINGHAMSHIRE]]

In Nottinghamshire and in Derbyshire if the king's peace, given under his hand or seal, is broken a fine is paid by 18 hundreds, each hundred [paying] £8. The king has 2 parts of this fine, the earl the third. That is, 12 hundreds pay the fine to the king and 6 to the earl.

If anyone is exiled according to law for any crime none but the king can restore peace to him.

A thegn having more than 6 manors does not give relief for his land except £8 to the king alone.

If he has only 6 or less he gives 3 marks of silver to the sheriff as relief wherever he dwells, in the borough or without.

If a thegn having sake and soke forfeits his land, the king and earl between them have half his land and resources, and his lawful wife with his legitimate heirs, if there are any, have the other half.

Here are noted those who had soke and sake and toll and team and the king's customary dues of the 2 pennies.

The Archbishop of York over his manors, and Countess Godgifu over Newark Wapentake, and Ulf Fenman over his land; the Abbot of Peterborough over Collingham; the Abbot of Burton; Earl Hugh over Markeaton [Derby.]; the Bishop of Chester; Toki; Swein son of Svavi; Siward Barn; Azur son of Svala; Wulfric Cild; Alsige [of] Illing; Leofwine son of Alwine; Countess Ælfgifu; Countess Gode; Alsige son of Karski over Worksop; Henry de Ferrers over Ednaston [Derby.] and Doveridge [Derby.] and Brailsford [Derby.]; Walter d'Aincourt over Granby and Morton [Derby.] and Pilsley [in North Wingfield, Derby.].

None of all these could have the earl's third penny except by his grant, and that for as long as he should live, except the Archbishop and Ulf Fenman and Countess Godgifu.

Over the soke which belongs to Clifton [in Nottingham] the earl ought to have the third part of all customary dues and services.

Here Are Entered the Holders of Lands In Nottinghamshire

I King WILLIAM
II Count Alan
III Earl Hugh
IIII The Count of Mortain
V The Archbishop of York
VI The Bishop of Lincoln
VII The Bishop of Bayeux
VIII The Abbey of Peterborough
IX Roger de Bully
X William Peverel
XI Walter d'Aincourt
XII Geoffrey Alselin
XIII Ralph fitzHubert
XIIII Ralph de Limesy
XV Ralph de Buron
XVI Roger de Poitou
XVII Gilbert de Ghent
XVIII Gilbert Tison
XIX Geoffrey de la Guerche
XX Ilbert de Lacy
XXI Berengar de Tosny
XXII Hugh fitzBaldric
XXIII Hugh de Grandmesnil
XXIIII Henry de Ferrers
XXV Robert Malet
XXVI Durand Malet
XXVII Osbern fitzRichard
XXVIII Robert fitzWilliam
XXIX William the usher
XXX The king's thegns
IN RUTLAND I THE KING
II Countess Judith
III Robert Malet
IIII Ogier
V Gilbert de Ghent
VI Earl Hugh
VII Albert the clerk

[Folio 281: NOTTINGHAMSHIRE]

The land of the King

'BASSETLAW' WAPENTAKE

In DUNHAM ON TRENT, with its 4 Berewicks, Ragnall, Whimpton, Darlton [and] 'Swanston' [in Dunham], King Edward had 5½ carucates of land to the geld. [There is] land for 12 ploughs. Now the king has there 2 ploughs in demesne; and 50 villans and 3 bordars having 10 ploughs, and 1 mill [rendering] 3s, and 1 fishery [rendering] 10s8d, and 120 acres of meadow. [There is] woodland pasture 6 furlongs long and 4 broad. TRE it rendered £30 and 6 sesters of honey; now £20 with everything that belongs to it.

SOKELAND OF THIS MANOR

In East Drayton [are] 2 carucates of land and 3 bovates and the fifth part of 1 bovate to the geld. [There is] land for 5 ploughs. There 16 sokemen and 17 villans have 13 ploughs, and 20 acres of meadow. [There is] woodland pasture 1 furlong long and a half broad.

In East Markham [are] 3½ carucates of land to the geld. [There is] land for 10 ploughs. There 25 sokemen and 15 villans have 10 ploughs. There is a church and a priest, and 40 acres of meadow and a little scrubland.

In Little Gringley [are] 2 bovates of land and the sixth part of 1 bovate to the geld. [There is] land for 2 ploughs. There 5 sokemen and 1 bordar have 2 ploughs. [There is] woodland pasture 4 furlongs long and 4 broad.

In Ordsall [is] 1 bovate of land to the geld. [There is] land for 1 plough. There 2 sokemen have 1 plough, and 3 acres of meadow and 3 acres of woodland.

In Headon [Headon and Nether Headon] [is] half a bovate of land to the geld. [There is] land for 1 ox, and 2 acres of meadow. It is waste.

In Upton [is] 1 bovate of land to the geld. [There is] land for 1 plough. There 4 sokemen and 2 bordars have 1½ ploughs, and 3 acres of meadow. [There is] woodland pasture 2 furlongs long and 1 broad.

In Normanton [in Bothamsall] [are] 1½ bovates of land to the geld. Half of this land belongs to Dunham on Trent, the other [half] to Bothamsall. It is waste. [There is] woodland pasture 3 furlongs long and 2 broad.

In BOTHAMSALL Earl Tosti had 12 bovates of land to the geld. [There is] land for 8 ploughs. Now the king has there 5 villans and 1 bordar with 2 ploughs, and 1 mill [rendering] 8s, and 40 acres of meadow. [There is] woodland pasture half a league long and 4 furlongs broad. TRE worth £8; now 60s.

SOKELAND OF THIS MANOR

In Elkesley [are] 4 bovates of land to the geld. [There is] land for 2 ploughs. There is a church and a priest and 6 sokemen with 1½ ploughs, and 1 mill [rendering] 4s, and a little scrubland.

In Morton [in Babworth] and the other [?Little] Morton [in Babworth] [are] 10 bovates of land to the geld. [There is] land for 4 ploughs. There 7 sokemen and 1 bordar have 4 ploughs. [There is] woodland pasture 2 furlongs long and 1 broad.

In Babworth [are] 2½ bovates, and "Odestorp" 4½ bovates, and Ordsall 1 bovate. All together [there are] 7½ bovates of land to the geld. [There is] land for 3 ploughs. It is waste except for 1 villan and 2 bordars with half a plough. There are 10 acres of meadow.

In Ranby 3 bovates, and Ordsall 3 bovates, [are] 5 bovates of land to the geld. [There is] land for 1½ ploughs. It is waste.

In Ranby [are] 2 carucates of land to the geld. [There is] land for 4 ploughs. It is waste.

In Mattersey [are] 11 bovates of land to the geld. [There is] land for 3 ploughs. There 12 sokemen and 2 villans and 3 bordars have 6½ ploughs. [There is] meadow 3 furlongs long and 1 broad, [and] woodland pasture 1 league long and 1½ furlongs broad.

In Lound and Barnby Moor [are] 6 bovates of land and half [a bovate] and the third part of 1 bovate to the geld. There 3 sokemen have 1 plough, and 3½ acres of meadow. [There is] woodland pasture 2 furlongs long and a half broad.

In GRIMSTON HILL [are] 4 bovates of land […] to the geld. [There is] land for 2 ploughs. [This manor is] a BEREWICK of Mansfield. There 3 sokemen and 3 bordars have 2 ploughs,

and 2 acres of meadow. [There is] woodland pasture half a league long and 4 furlongs broad.

SOKELAND OF THIS MANOR

In the same place [are] 1½ bovates of land to the geld. [There is] land for 2 oxen. There 2 sokemen have half a plough.

In [?] Kirton [is] half a bovate to the geld.

In Willoughby [in Walesby] and Walesby [are] 2 bovates of land to the geld. [There is] land for 1 plough. There 4 sokemen have 1 plough. [There is] woodland pasture 4 perches long and 4 broad.

In Beesthorpe 2 [bovates], and Carlton-on-Trent 2 [bovates, are] 4 bovates of land to the geld. [There is] land for 1 plough. There 4 sokemen and 3 bordars have 2 ploughs, and 30 acres of woodland pasture.

In Farnsfield the king has 1 bovate of land to the geld near to Nottingham.

BROXTOWE WAPENTAKE

In MANSFIELD and Skegby [in Sutton in Ashfield], a Berewick, and Sutton in Ashfield, a Berewick, King Edward had 3 carucates of land and 6 bovates to the geld. [There is] land for 9 ploughs. There the king has 2 ploughs in demesne; and 5 sokemen on 3 bovates of this land and 35 villans and 20 bordars with 19½ ploughs, and 1 mill and 1 fishery [rendering] 21s, and 24 acres of meadow. [There is] woodland pasture 2 leagues long and 2 broad. There are 2 churches and 2 priests.

In Warsop 1 bovate. In 'Clown' [in Welbeck] 4 bovates. In Carburton 2 carucates. In Clumber 3 bovates. In Budby 2 carucates. In Thoresby 6 bovates. In Scofton and Perlethorpe and Rayton 2 carucates. In Edwinstowe 1 carucate. In Grimston Hill half a carucate. In Eakring 3½ bovates. In Maplebeck 2 bovates. In Beesthorpe 2 bovates. In Carlton-on-Trent 2 bovates. In [?] Kirton 1½ bovates. In Willoughby [in Walesby] 1½ bovates. In Ompton 1 bovate and half a bovate. In Carlton in Lindrick 4 carucates.

All together 13 carucates of land and 6½ bovates to the geld.

In Warsop [is] 1 bovate of land which a certain blind man holds of the king in alms, where he has 1 bordar with 6 oxen in a plough.

In Perlethorpe [is] the fourth part of 1 bovate of land. It is waste. It belongs to Mansfield.

BEREWICK

In Grimston Hill [are] 4 bovates of land to the geld. [There is] land for 2 ploughs. There the king has 1 plough, and 8 villans and 1 bordar having 2 ploughs. [There is] woodland pasture 6 furlongs long and 4 broad.

BEREWICK

In Edwinstowe [is] 1 carucate of land to the geld. [There is] land for 2 ploughs. There is a church, and a priest and 4 bordars have 1 plough. [There is] woodland pasture half a league long and a half broad.

In Maplebeck [are] 2 bovates of land to the geld. [There is] land for 4 oxen. There 3 sokemen have 1 plough.

In Carlton in Lindrick [are] 2 carucates. In Scofton and Rayton and Perlethorpe, 2 carucates. In Ranby from Bothamsall, 2 carucates of land. That is 4 [carucates] to the geld. The soke [belongs] to Mansfield. They are waste.

ALSO SOKELAND IN OSWALDBECK WAPENTAKE

In Tiln [are] 2 bovates of land and the fourth part of 1 bovate to the geld. [There is] land for 1 plough. There 2 sokemen and 1 villan and 1 bordar have 6 oxen in a plough. There are 2 mills [rendering] 32s, and 6 acres of meadow. It is worth 40s.

[Folio 281V: NOTTINGHAMSHIRE]

In South Leverton [are] 12 bovates of land to the geld. [There is] land for 4 ploughs. There 22 sokemen and 11 villans have 9 ploughs. TRE these sokeman paid 20s as a customary due. In Fenton [is] half | a carucate to the geld. |

In Littleborough [are] 4 bovates of land to the geld. [There is] land for 1 plough. There 14 sokemen and 2 villans and 4 bordars have 5 ploughs. [There is] meadow 3 furlongs and 10 virgates long and 2 furlongs broad. This sokeland is worth 10s.

In Sturton le Steeple [are] 2 carucates of land to the geld. [There is] land for 6 ploughs. There 24 sokemen and 11 villans and 7 bordars have 8 ploughs. [There is] meadow 1 league long and 1 furlong broad, [and] woodland pasture 1 league long and 5 furlongs broad. This sokeland is worth 40s.

In [North and South] Wheatley [are] 2 bovates of land to the geld. [There is] land for 2 ploughs. There 6 sokemen and 1 villan have 2 ploughs. [There is] woodland pasture 1 league and 1 furlong long and 1½ broad. TRE worth 3s; now 7s.

In Walkeringham [are] 12½ bovates of land to the geld. [There is] land for 4 ploughs. There 13 sokeman and 2 villans and 3 bordars have 4 ploughs. [There is] meadow 6 furlongs long and 4 broad, [and] woodland 8 furlongs long and 4 broad. It is worth 20s.

In Misterton [are] 5 bovates of land and the fourth part of 1 bovate to the geld. [There is] land for 1 plough. There 5 sokemen and 6 villans and 1 bordar have 1 plough. [There is] meadow 1 furlong long and half a furlong broad. It is worth 7s.

In Wiseton [is] 1 carucate of land to the geld. [There is] land for 2 ploughs. There 7 sokemen and 7 villans and 4 bordars have 6 ploughs. [There is] meadow 2 furlongs long and 2 broad, [and] woodland pasture 14 furlongs long and 4 broad. It is worth 10s.

In Clayworth [is] 1 carucate of land and 6 bovates to the geld. [There is] land for 3 ploughs. There 12 sokemen and 1 villan and 18 bordars have 10 ploughs. [There is] meadow 2 furlongs long and 1½ furlongs broad, [and] woodland pasture 10 furlongs long and 6 furlongs broad. It is worth 26s4d.

In Clarborough and Tiln [are] 2 bovates of land and the fourth part of 1 bovate to the geld. [There is] land for 1 plough. There are 2 sokemen and 1 villan and 1 bordar having 6 oxen in a plough, and 2 mills [rendering] 32s, and 6 acres of meadow. It is worth 40s.

In Welham and "Simentone" [are] 5 bovates of land and the third part of 1 bovate to the geld. [There is] land for 2 ploughs. There 5 sokemen and 1 villan and 1 bordar have 2 ploughs. [There is] meadow 1½ furlongs long and 1 furlong and 10 perches broad, [and] woodland pasture 9 furlongs long and 2½ furlongs broad. It is worth 10s8d.

In Little Gringley [are] 2½ bovates of land to the geld. [There is] land for 1 plough. There 6 sokemen and 1 villan and 1 bordar have 2 ploughs. [There is] woodland pasture 6 furlongs long and 4 broad. It is worth 10s.

In Saundby 1 villan holds 1 garden; he renders salt for the king's fish from Bycarrs Dyke.

In ARNOLD [in Nottingham] King Edward had 3 carucates of land to the geld. [There is] land for 3 ploughs. There the king has 1 plough, and 20 villans and 4 bordars having 7 ploughs. [There is] woodland, pasture in places, 3 leagues long and 3 broad. TRE worth £4 and 2 sesters of honey; now £8 and 6 sesters of honey.

SOKELAND OF THIS MANOR

In Bramcote | [are] 6 bovates of land to the geld. [There is] land for 6 oxen.

In Wollaton [in Nottingham] [is] 1 carucate of land to the geld. [There is] land for 1 plough. [It is] a BEREWICK. It is waste.

In Lenton [in Nottingham] [are] 4 bovates of land to the geld. The soke [belongs] to Arnold [in Nottingham]. It is waste.

In Broxtowe [in Nottingham] [is] 1 bovate of land to the geld. It is waste. The soke [belongs] to Arnold [in Nottingham].

In Bilborough [in Nottingham] [is] 1 bovate of land to the geld.

BINGHAM WAPENTAKE

In ORSTON King Edward had 3 carucates of land to the geld. [There is] land for 10 ploughs. There the king has 3 ploughs, and 3 sokemen on 1 carucate of this land and 19 villans and 11 bordars having 14 ploughs. There is a church and 2 priests having 1 plough and 1 ox, and 180 acres of meadow. TRE worth £30 by tale; now £20.

BEREWICK OF THIS MANOR

In Scarrington [are] 2 carucates of land to the geld. [There is] land for 3 ploughs. There the king has 2 ploughs, and 23 villans and 4 bordars having 5½ ploughs. In STAUNTON IN THE VALE [are] 7 bovates and 3 acres of land to the geld.

In Thoroton [are] 12 bovates of land to the geld. [There is] land for 4 ploughs. There is 1 sokeman and 18 villans and 1 bordar having 7 ploughs. There is a priest.

In Screveton [is] 1 carucate of land to the geld. [There is] land for 3 ploughs. There 3 sokemen and 2 villans and 1 bordar have 1½ ploughs, and 8 acres of meadow.

In Car Colston [are] 4 bovates and 4 acres of land to the geld. [There is] land for 1 plough. There 5 sokemen have 1½ ploughs.

In Aslockton [is] 1 bovate of land to the geld; 1 villan ploughs there.

In 'NEWBOLD' [in Kinoulton] Earl Morcar had 3 carucates of land to the geld. [There is] land for 8 ploughs. There the king has 3 ploughs, and 13 sokemen and 13 villans and 3 bordars having 7 ploughs, and 2 acres of scrubland. There is a priest and a church. TRE worth £4; now £10.

In UPPER BROUGHTON Earl Ælfgar had 2 carucates of land to the geld. [There is] land for 7 ploughs. There the king has 2 ploughs, and 23 villans and 4 bordars having 7 ploughs, and 1 mill [rendering] 5s, and 100 acres of meadow. TRE worth £3; now 4[l].

BEREWICK

In 'Thorpe le Glebe' [are] 10 bovates of land to the geld. [There is] land for 10 oxen. It is waste. There are 12 acres of meadow. It is worth 2s; TRE 40s.

In FLINTHAM Alwine had 14 bovates of land and 3 parts of 1 bovate to the geld. [There is] land for 5 ploughs. There the king has 2 ploughs in demesne; and 5 sokemen and 4 villans and 5 bordars having 3 ploughs. There is a church and a priest having half a plough, and 60 acres of meadow. [There is] scrubland 3½ furlongs long and 1 furlong broad. TRE worth 60s; now 40[s].

In Kneeton [are] 3 bovates of land to the geld. [There is] land for 4 oxen. There 1 sokemen has half a plough, and 1 acre of meadow.

In Sneinton [in Nottingham] the king has 1 carucate of land to the geld. [There is] land for 2 ploughs. There 11 villans have 4 ploughs, and 12 acres of meadow. It is worth £3.

In 'MEERING' William had 6½ bovates to the geld.
    In MISSION the king has 3 bovates to the geld. Tosti had them. There are 6 villans with 3 ploughs. The soke [belongs] to KIRTON IN LINDSEY [Lincs.].
    In the same place [is] half a bovate to the geld. It belongs to Laughton [near Blyton, Lincs.]. There is 1 villan. Guy hold it, and Alvred [holds] of him.

[Folio 282: [NOTTINGHAMSHIRE]]

[Blank in MS]

[Folio 282v: NOTTINGHAMSHIRE]

II. The land of Count Alan

In SIBTHORPE Ospak had 2½ bovates of land to the geld. [There is] land for 1 plough. Count Alan has it. Fredegis holds of him, and has there 1 plough, and 4 sokemen on 1 bovate of land and 2 bordars having 1 plough. There is a priest and a church, to which the fourth part of the land belongs. There are 10 acres of meadow. TRE [worth] 20s; now 12s.

IN THE SAME PLACE Osbern had 1 bovate of land and 3

acres to the geld. [There is] land for half a plough. There is a priest and 2 bordars, and 4 acres of meadow. TRE worth 10s; now 4s.

In SUTTON on TRENT William son of Skialdvarthr had 2 carucates of land and 6 bovates to the geld. [There is] land for 5 ploughs. There Hervey, Count Alan's man, has 2 ploughs, and 13 sokemen on half of this land, and 17 villans and 3 bordars having 8 ploughs. There is a priest and a church, and 3 fisheries, and 100 acres of meadow, [and] woodland pasture 1 league long and half a league broad. TRE, as now, worth £4.

In RUDDINGTON Leofgeat had 12 bovates of land to the geld. [There is] land for 4 ploughs. There Count Alan has in demesne 1 plough; and 6 sokemen and 7 villans having 3 ploughs. There are 55 acres of meadow. TRE worth 60s; now 30s.

In KNEETON Alsige had 1 carucate of land to the geld. [There is] land for 12 oxen. There Count Alan has 1 plough, and 3 sokemen and 5 villans having 2 ploughs. There is a priest and half a church, and 1 mill [rendering] 10s, and 5 acres of meadow. TRE worth 20s; now 40[s].

IN THE SAME PLACE Wulfric had 1 carucate of land to the geld. [There is] land for 12 oxen. There is 1 villan and 1 bordar.

In TRESWELL Wulfmær had 6 bovates of land and the third part of 1 bovate to the geld. [There is] land for 4 ploughs. Robert de Moutiers, Count Alan's man, has 1 plough; and 8 villans and 5 bordars having 4 ploughs, and 40 acres of meadow. [There is] woodland pasture 4 furlongs long and 1½ furlongs broad. TRE, as now, worth 40s.

III. The land of Earl Hugh

In SUTTON BONINGTON Harold had 1½ carucates of land to the geld. [There is] land for 1 plough. Earl Hugh has it now. Robert fitz William holds it of him, and has there 1½ ploughs, and 3 sokemen and 6 villans having 3½ ploughs, and 1 mill [rendering] 20s, and 15 acres of meadow. TRE, as now, worth 40s.

In Normanton on Soar, sokeland, [are] 2 bovates of land and 2 parts of 1 bovate to the geld. [There is] land for 1 plough. It is waste. There are 3 acres of meadow. TRE worth 5s; now 3s.

In SUTTON BONINGTON Harold had 6 bovates of land to the geld. [There is] land for 2 ploughs. There Robert, the earl's man, has 3 sokemen and 5 villans having 2½ ploughs. There are 10 acres of meadow. TRE, as now, worth 20s.

In KINGSTON ON SOAR Leofwine and Ricard had 3½ bovates of land to the geld. [There is] land for 10 oxen. There 1 sokeman now has half a plough, and 9 acres of meadow under Earl Hugh. TRE worth 30s; now 10s.

IIII. The land of the Count of Mortain

In NORMANTON ON SOAR Stori had 10 bovates of land to the geld. [There is] land for 2 ploughs. Now the Count of Mortain has it. Healfdene holds it of him, and has there 1 plough, and 2 sokemen and 2 villans and 3 bordars having 2 ploughs. There are 15 acres of meadow. TRE worth 40s; now 30[s].

In SUTTON BONINGTON Stori had half a carucate of land to the geld. [There is] land for 12 oxen. There is now 1 plough in demesne, and 5 acres of meadow. TRE worth 30s; now 20[s].

In GOTHAM Stori had 2 carucates of land and 3½ bovates to the geld and │5 acres.│ [There is] land for 6 ploughs. There Count Robert has 3 ploughs in demesne; and 3 sokemen and 20 villans and 2 bordars having 9 ploughs, and 80 acres of meadow. TRE worth 60s; now 40s.

In [East and West] Leake [are] 2 bovates of land to the geld. There is nothing there.

SOKELAND OF THIS MANOR

In STANTON-ON-THE-WOLDS Stori had 3½ bovates of land to the geld. [There is] land for 1 plough. There Alvred, the count's man, has 1 plough, and 6 villans and 3 bordars with 2 ploughs. There are 20 acres of meadow. TRE worth 40s; now 20[s].

In KEYWORTH Stori had 3 bovates of land and the third part of 1 bovate to the geld. [There is] land for 1 plough. There Alvred, the count's man, has 2 sokemen and 1 villan and 1 bordar with 1½ ploughs. TRE worth 20; now 10s.

In the same Stanton-on-the-Wolds Frani had 1 bovate of land and 3 parts of 1 bovate to the geld. [There is] land for half a plough. There 3 villans now have 1 plough.

In NEWTHORPE Alwine had 1 bovate of land to the geld. [There is] land for 2 oxen. There is woodland pasture 8 furlongs long and 2½ furlongs broad. TRE worth 2s; now 12d.

[Folio 283: NOTTINGHAMSHIRE]

V. The land of the Archbishop of York

THURGARTON WAPENTAKE

In SOUTHWELL with its Berewicks are 22½ carucates of land to the geld. [There is] land for 24 ploughs. There Archbishop Thomas has 10 ploughs in demesne; and 10 sokemen and 75 villans and 23 bordars having 37 ploughs. There are 2 mills [rendering] 40s, and a fishpond, and a ferry [rendering] 6s.

Of the same land 6 knights hold 4½ carucates of land. 3 clerks have 1½ carucates of land; 2 bovates of it are in a prebend. 2 Englishmen have 3 carucates of land and 5 bovates.

The knights have 7 ploughs in demesne; and 35 villans and 28 bordars having 21 ploughs, and 1 mill [rendering] 8s.

The clerks have 1½ ploughs in demesne; and 7 villans and 5 bordars having 3 ploughs.

The Englishmen have 4 ploughs in demesne; and 20 villans and 6 bordars having 6½ ploughs.

To Southwell belong 188 acres of meadow. [There is] woodland pasture 8 leagues long and 2½ furlongs broad, [and] arable land 5 leagues long and 3 broad.

TRE worth £40; now £40.15s.

In Southwell there are reckoned 12 Berewicks.

In North Muskham [are] 1½ carucates to the geld.

BINGHAM WAPENTAKE

In CROPWELL BISHOP and Hickling, a Berewick, ST MARY of Southwell had 2½ carucates of land to the geld. [There is] land for 7 ploughs. The canons have 2 ploughs there in demesne; and 5 sokemen and 15 villans and 4 bordars having 6 ploughs and 2 oxen, and 20 acres of meadow. TRE worth 60s; now 50[s]..

In LANEHAM [Church Laneham and Laneham] with these Berewicks - Askham, Beckingham, Saundby, Bole, 'West Burton', [North and South] Wheatley [and] North Leverton with Habblesthorpe- [are] 9 carucates of land and 2 bovates to the geld. [There is] land for 27 ploughs. In the demesne of the hall are 10 bovates of this land. The remainder is sokeland. Now Archbishop Thomas has there 4½ ploughs, and 35 villans and 6 bordars having 16 ploughs. There is a church and a priest, and 2 fisheries [rendering] 8s, and 1 mill [rendering] 16s, woodland pasture 3 leagues long and 1½ leagues broad, [and] 100 acres of meadow.

In the BEREWICKS mentioned above belonging to the manor itself are 38 sokemen and 17 villans and 20 bordars having 14½ ploughs. There are also 33 other sokemen and 6 villans and 18 bordars having 15 ploughs. 2 knights hold these with their land of the archbishop.

In SUTTON [near East Retford] and Scrooby, a Berewick, and Lound, a Berewick, [is] 1 carucate of land and 6 bovates to the geld. [There is] land for 6 ploughs. Archbishop Thomas has there 2 ploughs in demesne; and 14 villans and 6 bordars having 6 ploughs. There are 7 acres of meadow, [and] woodland pasture half a league and 8 furlongs long and 8½ furlongs broad. TRE worth £8; now the same.

SOKELAND OF THIS MANOR

In Eaton 2 carucates to the geld. In Tiln 2 bovates and the fourth part of 1 bovate. In Welham and "Simenton" 5 bovates and the fourth part of 1 bovate. In Little Gringley 1 bovate and the fourth part of 1 bovate. In Scaftworth 1 carucate. In Everton 1 carucate and the third part of 1 bovate. This land is [sufficient] for 12 ploughs. There 38 sokemen with 18 villans and 20 bordars now have 25 ploughs. In Tiln 1 mill belonging to Laneham [Church Laneham and Laneham] renders 30s. In [East or West] Retford 1 mill belongs to Sutton [near East Retford]. In Clarborough │6½│ bovates. [There is] meadow 4½ furlongs long and as much broad and 45 acres in addition, [and] woodland pasture 2½ leagues long and 2 leagues broad.

In BLIDWORTH the Archbishop of York had 9 bovates of land to the geld. [There is] land for 3 ploughs. Archbishop Thomas has there 5 villans having 2 ploughs, and 1 mill which is in Lowdham. [There is] woodland pasture 3 leagues long and 1 broad.

BEREWICK

In Calverton [are] 6 bovates of land to the geld. [There is] land for 12 oxen. There 7 villans and 2 bordars have 2 ploughs. There is a church and a priest, and 2 acres of meadow, [and] woodland pasture 8 furlongs long and 3 broad. TRE, as now, worth 40s.

In OXTON Alnoth had 6 bovates of land to the geld. [There is] land for 2 ploughs. There Archbishop Thomas has 1 plough in demesne; and 1 sokeman and 1 villan and 1 bordar having 2 ploughs. The king has 1 bovate of this land. The remainder belongs to Blidworth. TRE worth 40s; now 20[s]..

| In RANSKILL | [are] 4½ bovates to the geld. There is land for 1 plough. It was and is waste. Godric held it. The archbishop holds it.

In NORWELL, ST MARY of Southwell had 12 bovates of land to the geld. [There is] land for 6 ploughs. There are now 2 ploughs in demesne; and 22 villans and 3 bordars having 7 ploughs. There is a church and a priest, and 1 mill [rendering] 12d, and 1 fishery, and 73 acres of meadow, [and] woodland pasture 2 leagues long and 1 broad. TRE worth £6; now 100s.

SOKELAND OF THIS MANOR

In Osmanthorpe [are] 4 bovates of land to the geld. [There is] land for 2 ploughs. There 4 sokemen have 2 ploughs. [There are] 8 acres of meadow, [and] woodland pasture 4 furlongs long and 3 broad.

In Willoughby [in Norwell] [are] 3½ bovates of land to the geld. [There is] land for 1 plough. There 4 sokemen and 3 villans have 2 ploughs, and 16 acres of meadow.

In Caunton [are] 2 bovates of land to the geld. [There is] land for 4 oxen. There 1 sokeman and 5 bordars have 1½ ploughs, and 2 acres of meadow. [There is] woodland pasture 3 furlongs long and 2 broad.

In Hockerton [is] 1 bovate of land to the geld. There is 1 villan and 1 bordar, and 2 acres of meadow.

In Woodborough [are] 7 bovates of land to the geld. [There is] land for 2 ploughs. There is half a plough in demesne; and 2 villans and 1 bordar have 1 plough. It belongs to Southwell.

In the same place 1 clerk has 1 bovate of land to the geld under the archbishop.

In South Muskham and Little Carlto [are] 4 carucates of land and 5 bovates to the geld. [There is] land for 9½ ploughs. Archbishop Thomas has there 2 ploughs in demesne; and 20 sokemen and 7 villans and 16 bordars having 6 ploughs. There is 1 mill [rendering] 2s, and 66 acres of meadow and 80 acres of scrubland. TRE worth 16s, now 10[s]..

In ROLLESTON Ælfric had as a manor 4½ bovates to the geld. [There is] land for 1 for plough, which [plough] 5 villans have there. There are 12 acres of meadow. Formerly 20s; now it is worth 10s.

VI. The land of the Bishop of Lincoln

In NEWARK-ON-TRENT with its 2 Berewicks, Balderton and Farndon, Countess Godgifu had 7 carucates of land and 2 bovates to the geld. [There is] land for 26 ploughs. There Bishop Remigius has 7 ploughs in demesne; and 56 burgesses and 42 villans and 4 bordars having 20½ ploughs. There are 10 churches and 8 priests having 5 ploughs. There 7 free men have 5½ ploughs. There is 1 mill [rendering] 5s4d, and 1 fishery. To Newark-on-Trent belong all the customary dues of the king and the earl from the wapentake itself. TRE it rendered £50; now £34.

SOKELAND OF THIS MANOR

In Balderton [are] 6½ bovates of land to the geld. [There is] land for 3 ploughs. There 26 sokemen and 3 bordars have 9 ploughs.

In Kilvington 1 bovate, Syerston 1½ bovates, Elston 1 bovate, East Stoke 1½ bovates, Hawton 2½ bovates, Coddington 1 carucate, Barnby in the Willows 2½ bovates, [and] Winthorpe 6½ bovates. Together [there are] 3 carucates and half a bovate to the geld. [There is] land for 10½ ploughs.

There 77 sokemen with 4 bordars have 15½ ploughs. In these [sokelands are] 163 acres of meadow.

In South Scarle 2½ carucates, Girton 1½ carucates, Spalford 3½ bovates, Thorney 1 carucate and Wigsley 7 bovates, Harby 1 bovate, [and] Cotham 1 bovate. Together [there are] 6½ carucates and half a bovate to the geld. [There is] land for 21 ploughs and 3 oxen. There 71 sokemen and 7 bordars have 21½ ploughs. There are 280 acres of meadow, [and] woodland pasture 5 furlongs long and 4 furlongs broad.

In ELSTON Leofwine and Pilwine had 2 bovates of land to the geld. [There is] land for 4 oxen. There 1 villan and 3 bordars have 1 plough. There are 12 acres of meadow. TRE, as now, worth 10s. Hrafnsvartr and Arngrim hold it of the bishop.

In Coddington Wulfric had 1 bovate of land to the geld. [There is] land for 2 oxen. The bishop has there half a plough, and 1 acre of meadow. TRE worth 40s; now 20[s].

In the same place Buggi had 1½ bovates of land to the geld. [There is] land for half a plough. It is waste. Bothild holds it, and it is worth 2s. There are 2 acres of meadow.

In [North and South] CLIFTON Wulfgeat had 6½ bovates of land to the geld. [There is] land for 3 ploughs. Bishop Remigius has there 3 sokemen on 3 bovates of this land and 1 bordar with 1 plough. There are 30 acres of meadow, [and] woodland pasture half a league long and 3 furlongs broad. TRE worth 20s; now 10s. Ralph holds it.

In HARBY Godwine had 6 bovates of land to the geld. [There is] land for 2 ploughs. There 5 villans now have 2 ploughs, and 12 acres of meadow. [There is] woodland pasture half a league long and a half broad. TRE worth 40s; now 20[s].

In [North and South] CLIFTON Frani had 3½ bovates of land to the geld. [There is] land for 12 oxen. Bishop Remigius has there 1 plough, and 6 villans and 2 bordars having 1½ ploughs. There are 14 acres of meadow. TRE worth 40s; now 20[s]. Siwate holds it.

In the same place Wulfgeat had 1½ bovates of land to the geld. [There is] land for 1 plough.

[Folio 284: NOTTINGHAMSHIRE]

It is waste. Ralph holds it. There is the fourth part of 1 church, and 8 acres of meadow. TRE worth 10s; now 5s.

In the same place Aghmund had 2½ bovates of land to the geld. [There is] land for 1 plough. The same Aghmund holds it of the bishop, and has 2 oxen in a plough, and 2 villans likewise [have] 2 oxen in a plough, and 8 acres of meadow. TRE worth 10s; now 6s.

IN 'BASSETLAW' WAPENTAKE

In FLEDBOROUGH Countess Godgifu had 1 carucate and 3½ bovates to the geld. [There is] land for 4 ploughs. There Nigel, the bishop's man, has 2½ ploughs, and 16 villans and 5 sokemen on 1 bovate of this land having ploughs. There is a priest and a church, and 1 mill [rendering] 12d, [and] woodland pasture 1 league long and half a league broad. TRE worth £8; now 5[l]

SOKELAND

In Normanton on Trent [are] 6 bovates of land to the geld. [There is] land for 12 oxen. There 11 sokemen have 3 ploughs, and 6 acres of meadow.

In STOKEHAM Countess Godgifu had 6 bovates of land and a third part and a fifteenth to the geld. [There is] land for 12 oxen. There Nigel, the bishop's man, has 5 sokemen and 4 bordars; they have 3 ploughs, and 6 acres of meadow and scrubland. TRE worth 20s; now 10s

VI. The land of the Bishop of Bayeux

In COTHAM Leofric had 3 bovates of land to the geld. [There is] land for 12 oxen. There Wazelin, the man of the Bishop of Bayeux, has 1 plough, and villans and 1 bordar having half a plough, and 20 acres of meadow. TRE worth 40s; now 30[s].

In BARNBY IN THE WILLOWS Wulfric had 7 bovates of land to the geld. [There is] land for 3 ploughs. There Losoard, the man of the Bishop of Bayeux, has 1 plough, and 4 sokemen on 2 bovates of this land and 9 villans and 6 bordars having 4½ ploughs. There is a priest and a church to which belongs half a bovate of this land, and 1 mill [rendering] 5s4d, and 30 acres of meadow, and scrubland. TRE, as now, worth 40s.

In CODDINGTON Wulfric had 3½ bovates of land to the geld. [There is] land for 12 oxen. There Losoard, the bishop's man, has 2 villans and 4 bordars with 1 plough, and 3 acres of meadow. TRE worth 20s; now 10[s].

In CODDINGTON Leofric had bovates of land to the geld. [There is] land for 2 ploughs. There Audkil has under the bishop half a plough, and 4 sokemen on 4 bovates of this land and 3 bordars with half a plough, and 5 acres of meadow.

In ROLLESTON Godwine had 2½ carucates of land to the geld and the fourth part of 1 bovate. [There is] land for 6 ploughs. There Losoard, the bishop's man, has 1 plough, and 11 villans and 9 bordars having 4½ ploughs. There is 1 mill [rendering] 27s, and 68 acres of meadow. TRE worth £8; now £4.10s. To this manor belong 7 sokemen in Upton and Collingham.

In SCREVETON Toti had 12 bovates of land to the geld. [There is] land for 3 ploughs. There Hugh, kinsman of Herbert [and] the bishop's man, has 5 sokemen and 4 villans and 1 bordar having 3 ploughs and 6 oxen, and 12 acres of meadow. TRE worth 20s; now 32s.

VII. The land of Peterborough [Abbey]

In COLLINGHAM Peterborough [Abbey] had 4 carucates of land and half a bovate to the geld. [There is] land for 14 ploughs. In demesne there are now 2 ploughs; and 37 sokemen on 2 carucates and 3 bovates of this land and 8 villans and 20 bordars having 14 ploughs. There is a priest and 2 churches, and 2 mills [rendering] 20s , and 200 acres of meadow, [and] scrubland 2 furlongs long and 1 broad. TRE worth £9; now the same.

In NORTH MUSKHAM Peterborough [Abbey] had 10 bovates of land to the geld. [There is] land for 4 ploughs. In demesne there is now 1 plough; and 2 sokemen on 2½ bovates of land and 5 villans and 3 bordars having 1½ ploughs, and 2 mills [rendering] 20s, and 1 waste [mill], and half a fishery, and 30 acres of meadow. TRE worth 60s; now 40s.

[Folio 284V: NOTTINGHAMSHIRE]

VIII. The land of Roger de Bully

NEWARK WAPENTAKE

In ELSTON Othenkarhad 2 bovates of land to the geld. [There is] land for half a plough. There Norman the priest has of Roger de Bully 5 villans having 5 oxen in a plough. TRE, as now, worth 10s.

In SHELTON and FLAWBOROUGH Alsige had 7½ bovates of land to the geld. [There is] land for 2½ ploughs. There Robert, Roger's man, has 1 plough, and 6 villans and 2 bordars have 2 ploughs. There is a church, and the site of 1 mill, and 30 acres of meadow. TRE worth 40s; now 30[s].

In [North and South] CLIFTON Ødhgrim had 6 bovates of land to the geld. [There is] land for 3 ploughs. There Roger, Roger's man, has 1 plough, and 1 sokeman on 1 bovate of this land and 7 villans with 3 ploughs, and the fourth part of a church, and 30 acres of meadow. [There is] woodland pasture 2 furlongs long and a half broad. TRE worth 40s; now 30[s].

SOKELAND

In Spalford [are] 4 bovates of land to the geld. [There is] land for 1 plough. There 2 sokemen have half a plough, and 12 acres of meadow.

In BROADHOLME OR [North and South] CLIFTON

Alwig had 3 bovates of land to the geld. [There is] land for 12 oxen. There are 4 sokemen on 2 bovates of this land and 3 villans having 4 ploughs, and 12 acres of meadow. Roger de Bully holds it. TRE worth 40s; now 30[s].

'BASSETLAW' WAPENTAKE

In EAST MARKHAM Eadwig had 9 bovates of land to the geld. [There is] land for 4 ploughs. There Geoffrey, Roger's man, has 1 plough, and 9 villans and 5 bordars have 3 ploughs. There is a church, and 1 mill [rendering] 16s. TRE [worth] £3; now £4.

In the same place Frani had 3½ bovates of land to the geld. [There is] land for 2 ploughs. There Turold, Roger's man, has 1 plough, and 1 villan with 2 oxen in a plough. TRE, as now, worth 20s.

In the same place Godwine and Ulfkil had 7½ bovates of land to the geld. [There is] land for 3½ ploughs. There Ulfkil and 4 sokemen and 2 bordars have 1½ ploughs. TRE, as now, worth 16s.

In TUXFORD Alwig and Wulfmær had 12 bovates of land to the geld. [There is] land for 10 ploughs. There Roger has 4 ploughs, and 32 villans and 2 bordars having 14 ploughs, and 1 mill [rendering] 10s8d. TRE worth £10; now £8.

SOKELAND OF THIS MANOR

In [?] Kirton and Walesby [are] 2 bovates of land to the geld. [There is] land for 6 oxen. There 5 sokemen and 1 bordar have 2 ploughs.

In Egmanton [are] 1½ bovates of land to the geld. [There is] land for 1 plough. There 1 sokeman and 3 villans have 2 ploughs. [There is] woodland pasture 1 league long and half a league broad.

In EGMANTON Thorkil and Wulfmær had 4½ bovates of land and the third part of 1 bovate to the geld. [There is] land for 3 ploughs. There Roger has 4 ploughs, and 13 villans and 9 bordars having 8 ploughs. There are 2 mills [rendering] 30s. TRE worth £4; now the same.

In BOUGHTON Eadwig had 3 bovates of land to the geld. [There is] land for 3 ploughs. There is now 1 plough in demesne; and 2 villans and 1 bordar with 1 plough. TRE worth 20s; now 10s.

In OLLERTON Alweald had 2½ bovates of land to the geld. [There is] land for 1 plough. There now 5 sokemen and 1 villan have 2 ploughs, and 1 mill [rendering] 6s8d. TRE, as now, it was worth 20s.

In COTTAM Heardwulf had 4 bovates of land to the geld. [There is] land for 2 ploughs. There Fulk, Roger's man, has 8 villans with 2 ploughs. TRE, as now, it was worth 16s.

In ORDSALL Osweard, Thorsten, Ordric and Thorsten had 4 bovates of land to the geld. [There is] land for 4 ploughs. There 2 men of Roger have 3 ploughs, and 5 villans and 2 bordars having 2 ploughs. There are 16 acres of meadow, [and] woodland pasture 1 furlong long and a half broad. TRE worth 28s; now 24s.

In EATON 10 thegns each had his hall. Among them [they had] 6½ bovates of land and the sixth part of 1 bovate to the geld. [There is] land for 4 ploughs. There Fulk, Roger's man, has 1 plough, and 14 villans and 9 bordars having 7 ploughs, and 2 mills [rendering] 20s, and 60 acres of meadow. [There is] woodland pasture 5 furlongs long and 3 broad. TRE worth £6; now 3[l].

In GROVE Alwig and Osmund had 4½ bovates of land to the geld. [There is] land for 3 ploughs. There Robert, Roger's man, has 1½ ploughs, and 6 villans and 3 bordars and 1 sokeman having 2½ ploughs. There is a priest and a church, and 8 acres of meadow, [and] woodland pasture 1 league long and a half broad. TRE worth 40s; now the same.

In Ranby [are] 2½ bovates of land to the geld. [There is] land for 1 plough. The SOKE [belongs] to Grove to Grove [sic]. It is waste. In Ranby [is] 1 bovate to the geld. The SOKE [belongs] to Eaton.

In HEADON [Headon and Nether Headon] Godric and 6 other thegns each had a hall. Among them [they had] 8 bovates of land and the third part of 1 bovate to the geld. [There is] land for 5½ ploughs. There William, Roger's man, [has] 2 ploughs, and 14 sokemen and 9 villans and 6 bordars having 16 ploughs. There are 26 acres of meadow, [and] woodland pasture 5 furlongs long and 4 broad. TRE worth £4; now the same.

In Upton [is] half a bovate of land to the geld. [There is] land for 2 oxen. There are 3 sokemen and 2 bordars with 1 plough, and 2 acres of meadow.

In WEST MARKHAM Godric had 4 bovates of land to the geld. [There is] land for 2 ploughs. There Roger has 2 ploughs, and 4 villans and 2 bordars having 2 ploughs, and 16 acres of meadow. [There is] woodland pasture 5 furlongs long and 3 broad. TRE worth 40s; now the same. Claron holds it.

In Headon [Headon and Nether Headon] [is] 1 bovate of land to the geld. [There is] land for 2 oxen. The SOKE [belongs] to East Markham, and [there are] 2 acres of meadow. There 1 sokeman has 2 oxen. In Upton [are] 2½ bovates of land to the geld. [There is] land for 2 ploughs. The soke [belongs] to East Markham. There 9 sokemen and 2 bordars have 4 ploughs, and 6 acres of meadow. In Gamston [in Eaton] 1 garden and 1 sokeman belong to East Markham and 1 garden belongs to Eaton.

In Mission [is] 1 bovate of land to the geld. It belongs to Eaton.

[Folio 285: NOTTINGHAMSHIRE]

In West Markham [are] 6 bovates of land to the geld. [There is] land for 3 ploughs. The SOKE [belongs] to Tuxford. There 6 sokemen and 5 villans have 4½ ploughs. There are 16 acres of meadow.

In the same place [is] 1 bovate of land to the geld [of which] the SOKE [belongs] to Grove, and 1 bovate to the geld [of which] the SOKE [belongs] to Eaton, and 1 bovate to the geld [of which] the SOKE [belongs] to West Drayton. [There is] land for half a plough. There 3 sokemen have 2 ploughs.

In WEST DRAYTON Swein and Wulfstan had 4 bovates of land and 2 parts of 1 bovate to the geld. [There is] land for 2 ploughs. There 2 of Roger's men have 1 plough, and 8 villans and 1 bordar having 2 ploughs. There are 3 mills rendering 50s, and 7 acres of meadow, [and] woodland pasture 3 furlongs long and half a furlong broad. TRE worth 30s; now 17s4d.

In ELKESLEY Locre and Ulfkil had 4 bovates of land to the geld. [There is] land for 2 ploughs. There Claron has 1 plough, and 3 villans and 1 bordar have 1½ ploughs. TRE, as now, [worth] 2s.

In BABWORTH Wulfmær had 2½ bovates of land to the geld. [There is] land for 2 ploughs. There Geoffrey, Roger's man, has 1 plough, and 1 bordar with half a plough. [There is] woodland pasture 2 furlongs long and 1 broad. TRE worth 40s; now 10s.

In MORTON [in Babworth] Asfrith and Leofketel had 2 bovates of land to the geld. [There is] land for 2 ploughs. It is waste. [There is] woodland pasture 1 furlong long and half a furlong broad. TRE it was worth 16s.

In "CALDECOTES" Karski had 1 bovate of land to the geld. [There is] land for 4 oxen. It is waste. There are 6 acres of meadow, and 2 mills [rendering] 20s. TRE it was worth 30s.

In CUCKNEY Alric and Wulfsige had 1 carucate of land to the geld. [There is] land for 2 ploughs. There Geoffrey, Roger's man, has 1 plough, and 9 villans having 3 ploughs. [There is] woodland pasture 2 furlongs long and 2 broad. TRE worth 20s; now 2s less.

In PERLETHORPE Thorsten and Wulfmær had 10 bovates of land to the geld. [There is] land for 3 ploughs. There Richard, Roger's man, has 4 ploughs, and 5 villans and 4 bordars having 2½ ploughs, and 7 acres of meadow. [There is] woodland pasture [...] furlongs long and 4 broad. TRE worth 40s; now 26s.

SOKELAND of the same place

In Gleadthorpe [are] 4 bovates of land [...] to the geld. [There is] land for 6 oxen. There 4 sokemen have 2 ploughs. [There is] woodland pasture 1 furlong long and 1 broad.

In OLD CLIPSTONE Osbern and Wulfsige had 1 carucate of land to the geld. [There is] land for 2 ploughs. There Roger has in demesne 1½ ploughs; and 12 villans and 3 bordars having 3½ ploughs, and 1 mill [rendering] 3s. [There is] woodland, pasture in places, 1 league long and 1 broad. TRE worth 60s; now 40[s].

In WARSOP Godric and Leofgeat and Ulfkil had 3 carucates of land to the geld. [There is] land for 6½ ploughs. There Roger has in demesne 3½ ploughs; and 6 sokemen on 2 bovates of this land and 15 villans and 11 bordars having 3 ploughs. There is a priest and a church, and 1 mill [rendering] 16d, and half the site of a mill, [and] woodland pasture 5 furlongs long and 4 broad. TRE [worth] 64s; now 4s less.

In CLUMBER Æthelweald and Ulfkil had 5 bovates of land to the geld. [There is] land for 2 ploughs. Part (2 bovates) is waste, which Fulk holds. In the other [part] Ulfkil has under Roger 1 plough, and 1 mill [rendering] 12d. [There is] woodland pasture 2 furlongs long and 1 broad. TRE worth 20s; now 4s.

In "Odestorp" and [East or West] Retford [are] 1½ bovates of land to the geld. [There is] land for 4 oxen. The soke [belongs] to Clumber. It is waste.

In WORKSOP Alsige had 3 carucates of land to the geld. [There is] land for 8 ploughs. There Roger has 1 plough in demesne; and 22 sokemen on 12 bovates of this land and 24 villans and 8 bordars having 22 ploughs, and 7 acres of meadow. [There is] woodland pasture 2 leagues long and 3 furlongs broad. TRE worth £8; now 7[l].

In 'ROOLTON' [in Worksop] Wulfsige and Arnketil had 1 carucate of land to the geld. [There is] land for 2 ploughs. There Roger, Roger's man, has 1 plough, and 4 sokemen on 2 bovates of this land and 1 bordar with 1 plough. There are 2 acres of meadow, [and] woodland pasture 6 furlongs long and 3 broad. TRE worth 20s; now 10s. In the same place [is] 1 bovate of land to the geld. SOKELAND. It is waste.

In BILBY Grimkel had 6 bovates of land to the geld. [There is] land for 3 ploughs. There Ingram, Roger's man, has 1 plough, and 9 villans and 1 bordar having 3 ploughs, and 6 acres of meadow. TRE worth 40s; now 20[s].

In HODSOCK Wulfsige had 2 carucates of land to the geld. [There is] land for 4 ploughs. There Turold, Roger's man, has 2 ploughs, and 3 sokemen on 4 bovates of this land and 12 villans having 9 ploughs. There are 2 mills [rendering] 16s4d, and 8 acres of meadow, [and] woodland pasture 1 league long and half a league broad. TRE, as now, [worth] 60s.

SOKELAND OF THIS MANOR

In Blyth [is] 1 bovate of land and the fourth part of 1 bovate to the geld. [There is] land for 1 plough. There 4 villans and 4 bordars have 1 plough, and 1 acre of meadow.

In CARLTON IN LINDRICK 6 thegns each had a hall. Among them all [they had] 2 carucates of land to the geld. [There is] land for 4 ploughs. There Turold, Roger's man, has 2 ploughs, and 2 sokemen and 16 villans and 3 bordars having 4 ploughs. There is a church, and 2 mills [rendering] 21s, and 20 acres of meadow, [and] woodland pasture 1½ leagues long and half a league broad. TRE worth £4; now 3[l].

In LOUND Ulfkil had 2 bovates of land and 2 parts of 1 bovate to the geld. [There is] land for 1 plough. In demesne is 1 plough; and 6 villans with 2 ploughs, and 5 acres of meadow. [There is] woodland pasture 6 furlongs long and 2 broad. TRE worth 20s; now 10[s].

In SERLBY Ælfric had 1½ bovates of land to the geld. [There is] land for 4 oxen. There Gilbert, Roger's man, has 1 plough, and 5 villans and 8 bordars with 3 ploughs, and 1 mill [rendering] 3s. TRE, as now, worth 20s.

In TORWORTH Beorhtsige and Karski had 6 bovates of land to the geld. [There is] land for 2 ploughs. I [sic] Azo the priest has it of Roger, and it is waste. [There is] woodland pasture 1 league long and 1 furlong broad. TRE worth 20s; now 3s.

In BARNBY MOOR Thorfridh and Swarti had 1½ bovates of land to the geld. [There is] land for 4 oxen. It is waste. There is 1 acre of meadow, [and] woodland pasture 1 furlong long and half a furlong broad. TRE worth 10s; now 12d.

In HARWORTH Wada, Wulfgeat, and Wulfstan had 1 carucate of land to the geld. [There is] land for 2 ploughs. There Fulk, Roger's man, [has] in demesne 1 plough; and 8 villans and 1 bordar with 3 ploughs. There is a church, [and] woodland pasture 1 league long and 1 broad. TRE worth 40s; now 30s.

SOKELAND OF THE SAME PLACE

In Martin [is] 1 carucate of land to the geld. [There is] land for 2 ploughs. There 10 villans have 5 ploughs. [There is] woodland pasture 1 league long and half a league broad.

In STYRRUP Lyfing, Thorkil and Leofric had 7 bovates of land to the geld. [There is] land for 4 ploughs. There Bernard, Roger's man, has 1 plough, and 9 sokemen on half a carucate of this land and 7 villans and 5 bordars having 3½ ploughs. There are 6 acres of meadow and 10 acres of woodland pasture. TRE worth 50s; now 25s.

In the same place [is] 1 bovate of land to the geld. It is SOKELAND. It is waste.

IN 'LYTHE' WAPENTAKE

In KELHAM Thorkil and Godric had 10 bovates of land and the third part of 1 bovate to the geld. [There is] land for 3 ploughs. There Turold, Roger's man, has 1 plough, and 7 sokemen on 5 bovates of this land and 3 villans and 3 bordars having 2½ ploughs. There are 22 acres of meadow, [and] scrubland 16 furlongs long and 74 virgates broad. TRE worth 60s; now 28s.

In HOCKERTON Wulfsige and Thorkil had 1 carucate of land to the geld. [There is] land for 2½ ploughs. There Roger has in demesne 2 ploughs; and 11 villans and 4 bordars having 4 ploughs. There are 36 acres of meadow. There is a church, [and] woodland pasture 1 league long and 4 furlongs and 4 virgates broad. TRE worth £4; now 3[l].

In Carlton-on-Trent Roger has 12 acres of meadow.

In GRASSTHORPE Dunning and Grim had 6½ bovates of land and the fourth part of 1 bovate to the geld. [There is] land for 2 ploughs. There Roger, Roger's man, has 2 ploughs, and 4 sokemen and 12 villans and 1 bordar having 5 ploughs. There are 3 mills [rendering] 20s, and 12 acres of meadow and 4 acres of woodland pasture. TRE, as now, worth £3.

In Sutton on Trent [is] 1 bovate of land to the geld. [It is] SOKELAND. It is waste. There are 6 acres of meadow.

In [? High] MARNHAM Ælfric and Dene had 6½ bovates of land and the fourth part of 1 bovate to the geld. [There is] land for 2 ploughs. There Fulk, Roger's man, has 1 plough, and there 1 sokeman has 12 acres of land, and [there are] 10 villans

and 4 bordars having 4½ ploughs. There are 40 acres of meadow. TRE worth 40s; now 20[s].

In another [? Low] MARNHAM Wulfsige had 2 carucates of land to the geld. [There is] land for 4 ploughs. There Roger has in demesne 4 ploughs; and 2 sokemen on 40 acres of land and 20 villans having 7 ploughs, and 1 mill [rendering] 4s, and 1 fishery, and 24 acres of meadow. [There is] scrubland half a league long and as much broad. TRE worth £4; now £3.

In SKEGBY [in Marnham] Alweald and Ulfkil had 1 carucate of land to the geld. [There is] land for 2½ ploughs. There 2 of Roger's men have in demesne 3 ploughs; and 7 villans and 2 bordars having 3 ploughs. There are 16 acres of meadow, [and] woodland pasture half a league long and 3 furlongs broad. TRE worth 48s; now 40s.

SOKELAND

In Sutton on Trent [is] 1 bovate of land to the geld. [There is] land for half a plough. There 1 sokeman has 1 plough.

In Normanton on Trent [is] half a bovate of land to the geld. There 2 villans and 2 bordars have 1 plough.

In NORMANTON ON TRENT 5 thegns, Iusten, Aslak, Durand, Alweard, Wulfmær [and] Aslak, each had his hall and each 1 bovate of land and the fifth part of 1 bovate to the geld. [There is] land for 12 oxen. There Roger, Roger's man, has 9 sokemen and 4 bordars having 3 ploughs, and 12 acres of meadow. TRE worth 10s; now 6s.

In WESTON Almær, Alwig, Osbern, Grim, Eadric [and] Stenulf each had his hall and each [had] 1 bovate of land. Among them all [they had] 6½ bovates to the geld. [There is] land for 4 ploughs. There Fulk, Robert and Turold, Roger's men, have 4½ ploughs, and 1 sokeman and 14 villans and 3 bordars having 3½ ploughs. There is a church, and 1 mill, and 30 acres of meadow, [and] woodland pasture half a league long and as much broad. TRE worth 70s; now 50s.

SOKELAND OF THE SAME PLACE

In "Odestorp" and [East or West] Retford [is] half a bovate of land to the geld. [There is] land for 4 oxen. There is 1 villan, and the fourth part of 1 mill, and 4 acres of meadow.

IN THURGARTON WAPENTAKE

In GEDLING [in Nottingham] Dunstan had 9½ bovates of land and the third part of 1 bovate to the geld. [There is] land for 2 ploughs. There Roger has 2 ploughs, and 9 villans and 1 bordar having 2 ploughs, and 10 acres of meadow. [There is] woodland pasture 2 furlongs long and 1 furlong broad. TRE worth 32s; now 40s.

In EPPERSTONE and WOODBOROUGH Wulfgeat had half a carucate of land to the geld. [There is] land for 12 oxen. There Roger has 1 plough, and 2 sokemen on 1 bovate of this land and 3 villans having 1½ ploughs. There is 1 mill [rendering] 5s4d, and 3 acres of meadow. TRE worth 5s; now 1 mark of silver.

In GUNTHORPE Morcar had 3 carucates of land and 3 bovates to the geld. [There is] land for 6 ploughs. There Roger has in demesne 4 ploughs; and 5 sokemen on 1½ bovates of this land and 40 villans and 7 bordars having 16 ploughs. There is a toll and a [ferry] boat rendering 30s8d, and 2 fisheries [rendering] 25s, and 180 acres of meadow, [and] woodland pasture 6 furlongs long and 5 broad. TRE worth £15; now £10. Tallage 30s.

In Burton Joyce and Lowdham [are] 12 bovates of land to the geld. [There is] land for 1 plough. The SOKE [belongs] to Gunthorpe. There 4 sokemen and 2 villans have 1 plough. There are 4 acres of meadow.

In OXTON Thorsten and Othenkar had 1 carucate of land to the geld. [There is] land for 2½ ploughs. There Roger has

[Folio 286: NOTTINGHAMSHIRE]

2 ploughs, and 5 villans and 6 bordars having 2 ploughs, and 1 mill [rendering] 5s4d. TRE worth 40s; now 60s.

IN RUSHCLIFFE WAPENTAKE

In STANFORD ON SOAR Alsige had 10 bovates of land to the geld. [There is] land for 2 ploughs. There Roger has 1 plough, and 5 sokemen and 3 villans and 2 bordars having 2 ploughs. There is half a mill [rendering] 6s8d, and 11 acres of meadow. TRE worth 30s, now 40s.

In Normanton on Soar [are] 3 bovates of land to the geld. [There is] land for 1 plough. [It is] SOKELAND. It is waste. There are 4 acres of meadow. TRE, as now, worth 4s.

In THRUMPTON Leofwine and Alnoth had 7 bovates of land to the geld. [There is] land for 2 ploughs. There Roger has 1 plough, and 3 sokemen and 2 villans and 2 bordars having 1½ ploughs. TRE worth 40s; now 20s.

In HOLME PIERREPONT Thorth had 12 bovates of land to the geld. [There is] land for 3 ploughs. There Roger has 2 ploughs, and 14 villans and 2 bordars having 5 ploughs, and 1 mill [rendering] 5s, and 80 acres of meadow. TRE, as now, worth £6.

In PLUMTREE Wulfheah and Godric had on [sic] 12 bovates of land to the geld. [There is] land for 3 ploughs. There Roger has in demesne 3 ploughs; and 33 villans having 5 ploughs. There is a church, and 23 acres of meadow. TRE, as now, worth 60s.

SOKELAND OF THE SAME PLACE

In Ruddington [are] 10 bovates of land and 2 parts of 1 bovate to the geld. [There is] land for 2 ploughs. There 18 sokemen have 3 ploughs, and 33 acres of meadow.

In NORMANTON-ON-THE-WOLDS Ufagr had 6 bovates of land to the geld. [There is] land for 3 ploughs. There Roger has in demesne 2 ploughs; and 6 villans and 3 bordars and 4 sokemen with 3 ploughs. TRE worth 40s; now 30[s].

IN THE SAME PLACE [are] 4½ bovates of land to the geld. [There is] land for half a plough. There 2 villans and 1 bordar have half a plough. It belongs to Plumtree.

In Stanton-on-the-Wolds [is] half a bovate of land to the geld. There 1 villan has 5 oxen in a plough. It belongs to Plumtree.

In Keyworth [are] 2 bovates of land to the geld. There 2 villans have half a plough. It belongs to Plumtree.

In KEYWORTH Harold, Ricard and Frani had 6 bovates of land and 2 parts of 1 bovate to the geld. [There is] land for 2 ploughs. There Roger has 4 sokemen and 3 villans and 2 bordars having 3 ploughs. There are 16 acres of meadow. TRE worth 30s; now 17s.

In [East and West] LEAKE Godric had 2 bovates of land and the third part of 1 bovate to the geld. [There is] land for 4 oxen. There Ernulf, Roger's man, has 2 ploughs, and 2 villans with half a plough, and 8 acres of meadow. TRE worth 40s; now 10s.

IN BROXTOWE WAPENTAKE

In WYSALL Æstan, Alsige [and] Glædwine had 3 carucates of land to the geld. [There is] land for 3 ploughs. There Roger, Roger's man, has 3 ploughs in demesne; and 15 villans and 5 sokemen on 6 bovates of this land and 1 bordar having 10 ploughs. There is a church. TRE [worth] 45s; now 48s.

In WILLOUGHBY-ON-THE-WOLDS Othenkar had 6 bovates of land to the geld. [There is] land for 6 oxen. There 2 sokemen on 1 bovate of this land and 3 villans and 15 bordars have 4 ploughs, and 13 acres of meadow. TRE [worth] 20s; now 10[s].

In 'Thorpe le Glebe', the king's [land], 7 bovates of land to the geld belong to Wysall. [It is] sokel-and. It is waste. There are 6 acres of meadow, and it is worth 2s.

In Willoughby-on-the/Wolds [is] the fourth part of 1 bovate of land to the geld. It is waste.

In COSTOCK and Rempstone Godric and Algar had 13 bovates of land to the geld. [There is] land for 13 oxen. There Roger has 2 sokemen on 2 bovates of this land and 3 villans with 2 ploughs. 1 carucate of this land is waste. There are 30 acres of meadow. TRE worth 40s; now 12s.

IN BINGHAM WAPENTAKE

In TOLLERTON Alsige had 2 carucates of land to the geld. [There is] land for 4 ploughs. There Roger has in demesne 1½ ploughs; and 11 villans and 1 bordar having 3 ploughs, and 8 sokemen with 3½ ploughs, and 2 mills [rendering] 3s. There is a church, and 30 acres of meadow. TRE worth 40s; now 60[s].

In LAMCOTE Frani and Othenkar had 7½ bovates of land and the third part of 1 bovate to the geld. [There is] land for 1 plough. There Roger has 1½ ploughs, and 1 villan, and 2 acres of meadow. TRE, as now, it was worth 15s.

In BINGHAM Tosti had 3 carucates of land and 2½ bovates to the geld. [There is] land for 5 ploughs. There Roger has in demesne 4 ploughs; and 26 villans and 5 bordars and 14 sokemen having 12½ ploughs. [There is] woodland pasture 1 league long and 8 furlongs broad. TRE, as now, worth £10. In Newton [are] 3 bovates to the geld.

IN THE SAME PLACE [Bingham] Hoga and Helghi had 5

bovates of land and 2 parts of 1 bovate to the geld. [There is] land for 1 plough. There is 1 sokemen and 8 villans and 1 bordar having 1 plough, and 24 acres of meadow. TRE worth 20s; now 13[s].

In Shelford [are] 3 bovates of land to the geld. [There is] land for 1 plough. The SOKE [belongs] to Bingham. There 3 sokemen have 1 plough.

In EAST BRIDGFORD Othenkar had 4 carucates of land to the geld. [There is] land for 6 ploughs. There Roger has in demesne 3 ploughs; and 20 sokemen on 10 bovates of this land and 15 villans and 3 bordars having 11 ploughs. There is a priest and a church, and 12 acres of meadow. TRE worth £3; now £5.

IN THE SAME PLACE Thorsten and Hrosskell and Iusten had 6 bovates of land to the geld. [There is] land for 1 plough. There are 3 acres of meadow. The land is not cultivated. TRE worth 8s; now 3s.

In KNEETON Wulfgeat had 5 bovates of land and the third part of 1 bovate to the geld. [There is] land for 1 plough. There Roger has 1 plough, and 2 villans with 1 plough, and 4 acres of meadow. TRE, as now, worth 10s.

In SAXONDALE Wulfgeat and Ospak had 12 bovates of land to the geld. [There is] land for 4 ploughs. There Roger has in demesne 2 ploughs; and 5 sokemen and 5 villans and 3 bordars having 2 ploughs. There is a church, and 1 acre of meadow. TRE, as now, worth 25s.

In CLIPSTON Wulfgeat had 3 carucates of land to the geld. [There is] land for 3 ploughs. There Roger has in demesne 2 ploughs; and 3 sokemen and 12 villans and 1 bordar having 6 ploughs. There are 20 acres of meadow. TRE worth 60s; now 40[s].

In 'WARBY' [in Plumtree] Godric had 12 bovates of land to the geld. [There is] land for 12 oxen. It is waste. There are 10 acres of meadow. TRE worth 20s; now 5s.

In SCREVETON Othenkar had 5 bovates of land to the geld. [There is] land for 1 plough. There 1 sokeman with 1 bordar has 1 plough. TRE worth 5s; now 8s.

In Bassingfield [are] 10 bovates of land to the geld and 2 parts of 1 bovate. [There is] land for 2 ploughs. The soke [belongs] to Holme Pierrepont. There 8 sokemen have 3 ploughs, and [there are] 15 acres of meadow.

[Folio 286V: NOTTINGHAMSHIRE]

In CAR COLSTON Wulfgeat had 6 bovates of land and 1 acre to the geld. [There is] land for 5 ploughs. There Roger, Roger's man, has 2 ploughs in demesne; and 13 sokemen and 3 villans and 7 bordars having 8 ploughs. There are 17 acres of meadow. TRE worth 30s; now 40[s].

In FLINTHAM Othenkar had 6 bovates of land to the geld. [There is] land for 2 ploughs. There Roger, Roger's man, has 1 plough, and 2 sokemen and 3 villans and 4 bordars having 2 ploughs. TRE, as now, worth 20s.

In the same place [are] 1½ bovates of land to the geld. [There

is] land for 4 oxen. The SOKE [belongs] to Kneeton. Earnwine the priest has it of Roger. There 2 sokemen and 1 bordar have 1 plough. There are 8 acres of meadow.

In Elton Morcar had 7 bovates of land to the geld. [There is] land for 4 ploughs. There Ralph, Roger's man, has 3 ploughs, and 3 sokemen and 11 villans having 6 ploughs. There is a church, and 12 acres of meadow. TRE, as now, [worth] £4.

In OWTHORPE Helghi had half a carucate of land to the geld. [There is] land for 3 ploughs. There William, Roger's man, has 1 plough, and 4 sokemen and 8 villans having 3 ploughs. There are 12 acres of meadow. TRE, as now, it was worth 30s.

IN OSWALDBECK WAPENTAKE

In FENTON Wulfheah and Leofric and Grim had 1 bovate of land and the third part of 1 bovate to the geld. The land is waste except for 1 bordar. There are 30 acres of woodland pasture. TRE it was worth 5s.

In the same place Spearhafoc had 2 bovates of land and 2 parts of 1 bovate to the geld. [There is] land for 1 plough with sake and soke [but] without a hall. It is waste. There are 60 acres of woodland pasture. TRE, as now, worth 10s8d.

In STURTON LE STEEPLE Spearhafoc and Arnketil had 4½ bovates of land to the geld. [There is] land for 2½ ploughs. There are now 2 villans and 2 sokemen and 2 bordars having 7 oxen in a plough, and 8 acres of meadow. [There is] woodland pasture 6 furlongs long and 3½ furlongs broad. TRE worth 2 marks of silver; now the same.

In [North and South] WHEATLEY 5 thegns had 9 bovates of land to the geld. [There is] land for 8 ploughs. There Roger has in demesne 4 ploughs; and 4 sokemen and 25 villans having 12½ ploughs, and [there are] 5 acres of meadow. [There is] scrubland 1 league long and 1 furlong broad. TRE, as now, worth £8.

In 'WEST BURTON' Spearhafoc had 6 bovates of land to the geld. [There is] land for 2 ploughs. There Geoffrey, Roger's man, has 1 plough, and 1 sokeman and 1 villan and 2 bordars have 1½ ploughs. There is 1 fishery [rendering] 200 eels, [and] scrubland 1 furlong long and 1 broad. TRE worth 20s; now 40[s].

SOKELAND OF THE SAME PLACE

In Everton and Harwell [are] 2 bovates of land and 3 parts of 1 bovate to the geld. [There is] land for 1 plough. There 1 sokeman has half a plough, and 1½ acres of meadow. [There is] woodland pasture 1 furlong long and 1 broad.

In BOLE Thorfridh had 7 bovates of land to the geld. [There is] land for 2 ploughs. There now 4 sokemen and 4 bordars have 3 ploughs. To this manor belong 6 bovates of land to the geld, of which the soke belongs to Saundby. [There is] land for 2 ploughs. There Geoffrey, Roger's man, has 1 plough, and 2 sokemen and 4 villans and 3 bordars having 1½ ploughs. [There is] meadow 8 furlongs long and 2 broad, [and] woodland pasture 1 league long and 3 furlongs broad. TRE worth 40s; now 50s.

In BECKINGHAM Osbern had 3 bovates of land to the geld. [There is] land for 1 plough. There Geoffrey, Roger's man, has 1 plough, and 15 acres of meadow. [There is] woodland pasture 7 furlongs long and 1 broad. TRE worth 10s; now 16s.

In WALKERINGHAM Æthelstan had 10½ bovates of land to the geld. There Roger, Roger's man, has 4 sokemen and 1 villan and 5 bordars having 2 ploughs. [There is] meadow 2 furlongs long and 1 broad, [and] woodland 4 furlongs long and 1 broad. TRE worth 20s; now 15s.

In MISTERTON 5 thegns had 13½ bovates of land to the geld. [There is] land for 2½ ploughs. There Roger has 8 villans and 5 bordars having 2½ ploughs. There is a church, and meadow 3 furlongs long and 1½ furlongs broad, [and] woodland pasture 12½ furlongs long and 2 furlongs broad. TRE worth 20s; now 2s more.

In GRINGLEY ON THE HILL 7 thegns had 3 carucates of land to the geld. [There is] land for 8 ploughs. There Roger, Roger's man, has 3 ploughs, and 10 villans and 6 bordars having 8 ploughs. There is a church, and 1 fishery [rendering] 1,000 eels, and 40 acres of meadow, [and] woodland pasture 1 league long and 3 furlongs broad. TRE worth £10; now £4.

SOKELAND OF THE SAME PLACE

In Misterton [are] 7½ bovates of land to the geld. [There is] land for 12 oxen. There 5 sokemen and 1 villan and 5 bordars have 1½ ploughs. [There is] meadow 4 furlongs long and a half broad, [and] woodland pasture 4 furlongs long and 1½ furlongs broad.

In Harwell and Everton [are] 3 bovates of land and 3 parts of 1 bovate to the geld. [There is] land for 1 plough. There 1 sokeman and 1 villan have half a plough, and 3 acres of meadow. [There is] woodland pasture 5 furlongs long and 2 broad.

In BOLE Wulfmær had 1½ bovates of land to the geld. [There is] land for 1 plough. There Roger has 1 plough, and the fourth part of a church, and 2 mills [rendering] 32s, and 10 acres of meadow. TRE worth 40s; now the same.

In CLAYWORTH Grimkel had 2 bovates of land to the geld. [There is] land for 4 oxen. There Fulk, Roger's man, has 3 sokemen and 3 bordars with 3½ ploughs. [There is] meadow 2½ furlongs long and 18 perches broad, [and] woodland pasture 3 furlongs and 10 perches long and as much broad. TRE worth 4s; now 5s.

In CLARBOROUGH Regnvald had 2 bovates of land to the geld. [There is] land for 2 ploughs. There Fulk, Roger's man, has half a plough, and 8 villans and 1 bordar with 1½ ploughs, and 7 acres of meadow. [There is] woodland pasture 4 furlongs long and 2 broad. TRE worth 6s; now 20s.

[Folio 287: NOTTINGHAMSHIRE]

IN THE SAME PLACE Ulfkil had half a bovate of land to the geld with sake and soke. [There is] land for 2 oxen. The same Ulfkil himself holds it of Roger, and has there 2 bordars with 2 oxen and 1 acre of meadow. [There is] woodland pasture 2 furlongs long and 1 broad. TRE, as now, worth 16d.

In TRESWELL Godric had 6 bovates of land and the third part and the fifteenth part of 1 bovate to the geld. [There is] land for 4 ploughs. There Roger, Roger's man, has 2 ploughs, and 14 villans and 5 bordars having 5 ploughs. [There is] meadow 4 furlongs long and 1 furlong broad, [and] woodland pasture 4 furlongs long and 1½ furlongs broad. TRE, as now, worth 50s

In South Leverton [are] 3½ bovates of land and half a fifth part of 1 bovate to the geld. Roger has this land, and there he has 7 villans having 1½ ploughs. There is half a church. There is woodland pasture 1½ furlongs long and 1 furlong broad, and meadow 1½ furlongs long and 1 furlong broad. Roger has half of this woodland and meadow. It is worth 10s. [There is] land for 1 plough.

In RAMPTON 7 thegns had 2 carucates of land and 3 bovates and the fifth part of 1 bovate to the geld. [There is] land for 7½ ploughs. There Roger de Bully with his 4 men has 3 ploughs, and 11 sokemen and 8 villans and 6 bordars having 5½ ploughs. There is a church, and 3½ fisheries [rendering] 3s6d. There are 65 acres of meadow. TRE worth 54s; now 4s less.

SOKELAND

In Mattersey [is] 1 bovate of land to the geld. There is 1 sokeman, and 2 acres of meadow.

IX. The land of William Peverel

In COLWICK [in Nottingham] Godric had 7 bovates of land to the geld. [There is] land for 1 plough. There William Peverel has 1 plough in demesne; and 7 villans and 6 bordars having 3 ploughs. There is a priest and a church, and 2 slaves, and 1 mill [rendering] 5s, and half a fishery, and 30 acres of meadow and 15 acres of scrubland. TRE worth 20s; now 40[s]. Walan holds it.

In SIBTHORPE Leofwine and Thorbiorn had 4 bovates of land to the geld. [There is] land for 13 oxen. There Robert, William's man, has 1 plough, and 5 villans with 1 plough, and 1 mill [rendering] 20d, and 17 acres of meadow. TRE worth 40s; now 24s.

In GONALSTON and Milton Wulfsige Cild had 2 carucates of land and 2 bovates and 2 parts of 1 bovate to the geld. [There is] land for 3 ploughs. There William has in demesne 1 plough; and 2 sokemen on 3 bovates of this land and 7 villans and 2 bordars and 2 rent-paying tenants having 3 ploughs, and 2 mills [rendering] 40s, and 10 acres of meadow. [There is] woodland pasture 5 furlongs long and 3 broad. TRE worth £4; now 60s.

In THRUMPTON Stapolwine had 3 bovates of land and 3 parts of 1 bovate to the geld. [There is] land for 1 plough. There 4 sokemen have 1 plough, and 5 acres of meadow. TRE, as now, worth 5s4d.

In CLIFTON [in Nottingham] Countess Gode had 2½ carucates of land to the geld. [There is] land for 5 ploughs. There William has 2 ploughs in demesne; and 4 sokemen and 19 villans and 8 bordars having 9 ploughs. There is a priest and a church, and 1 mill [rendering] 12d, and 12 acres of meadow. TRE worth £16; now £9.

In the same place Ulfkil had and has 1 bovate of land to the geld, and 1 villan with 2 oxen and 1 acres of meadow.

In Wilford, SOKELAND, [are] 3 carucates of land to the geld. [There is] land for 6 ploughs. There 23 sokemen have 7 ploughs. There is a priest, and 18 acres of meadow and half a fishery.

In West Bridgford, SOKELAND, [are] 12 bovates of land to the geld. [There is] land for 3 ploughs. There William has half a plough in demesne; and 3 sokemen and 4 villans and 2 bordars having 4½ ploughs, and 12 acres of meadow.

In Normanton-on-the-Wolds [are] 1½ bovates. In Keyworth the third part of 1 bovate. In Willoughby-on- the-Wolds 2½ bovates. In Stanton-on-the-Wolds 2 bovates and the fourth part of 1 bovate to the geld. [There is] land for 2 ploughs. The SOKE [belongs] to Clifton [in Nottingham]. There are 4 sokemen and 1 villan and 1 bordar having 3 ploughs. There William has in demesne in Stanton-on-the-Wolds 1 plough, and 2 acres of meadow.

In Costock [is] 1 bovate of land to the geld. There 1 sokeman has 1 plough, and 2 acres of meadow. [There is] land for 1 ox. In Adbolton [are] 6 bovates to the geld.

In Bassingfield [are] 5 bovates of land and 3 parts of 1 bovate to the geld. [There is] land for 1 plough. There 2 sokemen and 2 bordars have 1 plough, and 5 acres of meadow.

In Gamston [in West Bridgford] [are] 6 bovates of land to the geld. [There is] land for 1 plough. There 2 sokemen have 1 plough, and 7 acres of meadow.

In RADFORD [in Nottingham] Ælfric had 3 carucates of land to the geld. [There is] land for 3 ploughs. There William has in demesne 2 ploughs; and 11 villans and 4 bordars having 4 ploughs.

[Folio 287V: NOTTINGHAMSHIRE]

There are 4 mills [rendering] £3, and 30 acres of meadow, and 3 acres of scrubland and half a fishery. TRE, as now, it was worth £4.

Of the same land Wulfnoth holds 1 bovate in the thegnland.

In STAPLEFORD Wulfsige Cild and Stapolwine and Godwine and Glædwine had 2 carucates of land and 6 bovates to the geld. [There is] land for 3 ploughs. Robert holds of him. There William has in demesne 3 ploughs; and 6 villans and 2 slaves with 6 ploughs. There is a priest and a church, and 58 acres of meadow. TRE worth 60s; now 40[s].

In 'MORTON' [in Lenton, Nottingham] Bovi had 1½ carucates of land to the geld. [There is] land for 12 oxen. There William has 1½ ploughs, and 5 sokemen on 3 bovates of this land and 12 villans and 1 bordar having 9½ ploughs. TRE, as now, worth 20s.

In NEWBOUND Morcar had 12 bovates of land to the geld. [There is] land for 2 ploughs. There William has in demesne 1½ ploughs; and 9 villans having 3 ploughs, and 40 acres of meadow. TRE, as now, worth 60s.

In Lenton [in Nottingham] [are] 2 carucates of land to the geld. The SOKE [belongs] to Newbound. [There is] land for 2 ploughs. There 4 sokemen and 4 bordars have 2 ploughs, and 1 mill.

In LINBY 3 brothers had 1½ carucates of land to the geld. [There is] land for 2 ploughs. There William has 3 ploughs, and 12 villans and 2 bordars having 5 ploughs. There is a priest, and 1 mill [rendering] 10s, [and] woodland pasture 1 league long and 1 league broad. TRE worth 26s8d; now 40s.

In Papplewick 5 bovates of land belong to this manor.

In OLD BASFORD [in Nottingham] Alwine had 10 bovates of land to the geld. [There is] land for 12 oxen. There Sasfrid, William's man, has 1 plough, and 2 villans and 5 bordars and 1 sokeman having 2½ ploughs. There is a priest, and 1 acre of meadow and 1 acre of woodland. TRE, as now, worth 20s.

IN THE SAME PLACE Skuli had 1 bovate of land to the geld. Now it is in William's custody.

In LENTON [in Nottingham] Olaf had 4 bovates of land to the geld. [There is] land for half a plough. Now [it is] in the custody of William. There the same Olaf has 1 plough, and 1 villan and 1 bordar having 1 plough, and 1 mill [rendering] 10s, and 10 acres of meadow and 10 acres of scrubland. TRE worth 10s; now 15[s].

In TOTON Healfdene had 3 carucates of land to the geld. [There is] land for 3½ ploughs. There Warner, William's man, has 3 ploughs, and 4 sokemen on 3 bovates of this land and 16 villans and 3 bordars having 6 ploughs. There is half a church and a priest, and 2 mills [rendering] 8s, and 100 acres of meadow and a little plantation of willows. TRE, as now, it was worth 60s.

SOKELAND OF THIS MANOR

In Chilwell [are] 3 bovates of land to the geld.

In STRELLEY Godric had 6 bovates of land to the geld. [There is] land for 6 oxen. There Godwine the priest has of William 1 plough, and 3 villans and 2 bordars having 2 ploughs. TRE, as now, worth 10s.

IN THE SAME PLACE Brun had 3 bovates of land to the geld. Ambrose now holds them of William. TRE worth 3s; now 12d.

In GREASLEY Wulfsige had 4 bovates of land to the geld. [There is] land for 1 plough. There William has 1 plough, and 5 villans and 2 bordars having 3 ploughs. There is a priest and a church, [and] woodland pasture 9 furlongs long and 6 furlongs broad. TRE worth 16s; now 10s.

IN THE SAME PLACE Wulfsige had 4 bovates of land to the geld. the geld. [There is] land for 1 plough. It is waste. Æthelric holds it of William.

In BRINSLEY Brun had 4 bovates of land to the geld. [There

is] land for half a plough. There Æthelric has under William 1 plough, and 1 villan having 1 plough, and 2 acres of meadow. [There is] woodland pasture 6 furlongs long and 3½ furlongs broad. TRE worth 6s8d; now 4s.

In EASTWOOD Ulfkil had 4 bovates of land to the geld. [There is] land [...]. It is waste. William has the custody of it. [There is] woodland pasture 3 furlongs long and 3 broad. TRE it was worth 5s.

In NEWTHORPE Grimkel had 7 bovates of land to the geld. [There is] land for half a plough. It is waste. TRE worth 5s; now 2s.

In BEESTON Ælfheah, Alwine and Ulfkil had 3 carucates of land to the geld. [There is] land for 4 ploughs. There William has in demesne 2 ploughs; and 17 villans and 1 sokeman having 9 ploughs. There are [...] 24 acres of meadow. TRE, as now, worth 30s.

In WOLLATON [in Nottingham] Wulfsige Cild had 1½ carucates to the geld. [There is] land for 12 oxen. There Warner, William's man, has 1 plough, and 7 sokemen and 4 villans having 4 ploughs. [There is] scrubland 1 league long and 1 furlong broad. TRE worth 100s; now 60s.

In COSSALL, A BEREWICK, [are] 6 bovates of land to the geld. [There is] land for 6 oxen. There is in demesne 1 plough, and 2 villans, and 1 acre of meadow. [There is] woodland pasture 4 furlongs long and 2 broad.

In Bramcote, SOKELAND, [are] 6 bovates of land to the geld. It is waste.

In 'Sutton Passeys' [in Wollaton, Nottingham], SOKELAND, [are] 12 bovates of land to the geld. [There is] land for 3 ploughs. | It is waste. |

In BILBOROUGH [in Nottingham] Æthelric and Wulfsige [and] Swein had 7 bovates of land to the geld. [There is] land for as many oxen. There Ambrose, William's man, has 1 plough, and 2 sokemen and 3 villans and 4 slaves with 1 plough. There are 8 acres of meadow, and scrubland. TRE worth 30s; now 20s

In NUTHALL Healfdene had 4½ bovates of land to the geld. [There is] land for as many oxen. There William has 1½ ploughs, and 3 villans and 4 bordars having 1 plough. [There is] scrubland 5 furlongs long and 1 broad. TRE, as now, worth 10s.

In Broxtowe [in Nottingham] belong 5 acres.

In Watnall, SOKELAND, [are] 2 bovates of land to the geld.

In WATNALL Grimkel had 1 carucate of land to the geld. [There is] land for 1 plough. There William has 3 ploughs in demesne. [There is] woodland pasture 5 furlongs long and 2 broad.

In WATNALL Siward had 2 bovates of land to the geld.

In the same place Grim [had] 2 bovates of land to the geld. The SOKE [belongs] to Watnall.

In the same place Almær [had] 2 bovates of land to the geld.

The SOKE [belongs] to Bulwell [in Nottingham]. [There is] land for 1 plough. There is 1 plough in demesne; and 1 sokeman and 2 villans and 2 bordars have 2 ploughs. [There is] woodland pasture 5 furlongs long and 3 furlongs broad. TRE

worth 40s; now the same. Joscelin and Grimkel hold it.

In KIMBERLEY Azur had 4 bovates of land to the geld and Grimkel 4 bovates of land to the geld. [There is] land for 1 plough. There 2 sokemen and 1 villan and 5 bordars have 3½ ploughs. [There is] scrubland 4 furlongs long and 2 broad. TRE, as now, worth 10s.

IN THE SAME PLACE, in AWSWORTH, Alwine had 4 bovates of land to the geld. It is waste. William has the custody of it.

In HUCKNALL 2 brothers had 4 bovates of land to the geld. [There is] land for half a plough. There 3 villans have 1 plough. TRE worth 8s; now 4[s].

In Hempshill [are] 6½ bovates of land to the geld. [There is] land for 1 plough. There 2 sokemen and 2 villans and 2 bordars have 2 ploughs, and 4 acres of scrubland. This SOKELAND belongs to Bulwell [in Nottingham] and Watnall.

In OLD BASFORD [in Nottingham] Ælfheah and Algot had 2 carucates of land and 3 bovates to the geld. [There is] land for as many ploughs and oxen. There Payne and Sasfrid, William's men, have 1 plough, and 2 villans and 5 bordars having 2 ploughs, and 3 mills [rendering] 25s4d, and 6 acres of meadow, and scrubland. TRE worth 40s; now the same.

In the same place [is] 1 bovate to the geld. Skuli held it.

In COSTOCK Fredegis had 2 bovates of land to the geld. [There is] land for 2 oxen. There Godwine under William has 1 plough, and 2 villans [have] 1 plough, and 3 acres of meadow. TRE worth 10s; now 5s4d.

In REMPSTONE Fredegis had 6 bovates of land to the geld. [There is] land for 6 oxen. There 5 villans have 1 plough, and 15 acres of meadow. TRE worth 10s; now 5s4d.

In RADCLIFFE ON TRENT Fredegis had 1½ carucates of land to the geld. [There is] land for 3 ploughs. Now Fredegis and Wulfgeat under William have there 2 ploughs, and 15 villans and 6 bordars having 4 ploughs, and 18 acres of meadow, and the site of half a fishery and the third part of a fishery. TRE worth 60s; now 32[s].

In ADBOLTON Godwine the priest had 6 bovates of land to the geld. [There is] land for 1 plough. There William has in demesne 1 plough; and 6 villans and 1 bordar having 2 ploughs. There is a church, and 7 acres of meadow. TRE worth 10s; now 20[s].

In TYTHBY Wulfric had 4 bovates of land and 3 parts of 1 bovate to the geld. [There is] land for 1 plough. Now Fredegis under William holds it. There 1 sokeman and 5 villans and 4 bordars have $2\frac{1}{2}$ ploughs, and 20 acres of meadow. TRE worth 20s; now 10s.

In WIVERTON Wulfric had 1 bovate of land and 3 parts of 1 bovate to the geld. [There is] land for half a plough. There 3 villans and 1 bordar have 1 plough, and 6 acres of meadow. TRE, as now, worth 10s.

In LANGAR Godric had 2 carucates of land and $4\frac{1}{2}$ bovates to the geld. [There is] land for 6 ploughs. There William has in demesne 3 ploughs; and 15 sokemen on 6 bovates of this land and 19 villans and 6 bordars having 11 ploughs, and 2 mills [rendering] 5s, and 50 acres of meadow. There 1 free man has 1 plough. TRE worth 100s; now £10.

In Wiverton, SOKELAND, [are] $3\frac{1}{2}$ bovates of land to the geld. [There is] land for 1 plough. There 7 sokemen and 1 bordar have 3 ploughs and 2 oxen, and 8 acres of meadow.

In BARNSTONE Godric and Azur each had a hall and each [had] 4 bovates of land and 7 parts of 1 bovate to the geld. [There is] land for 4 ploughs. There William has in demesne 3 ploughs; and 7 sokemen on 4 bovates of this land and 7 villans and 6 bordars having $4\frac{1}{2}$ ploughs. There are 36 acres of meadow. TRE worth 10s; now £4.

In NEWTHORPE Grimkel had 5 bovates of land to the geld. [There is] land for half a plough.

In the same place [are] 2 bovates of land to the geld. [There is] land for 2 oxen. [It is] a BEREWICK of Kimberley. Each [of these estates] is waste.

In MANTON Alwine and Wulfgeat [had] 1 carucate to the geld, as 2 manors. [There is] land for 2 ploughs. There are 3 sokemen with 3 ploughs. It was and is worth 10s.

In SELSTON Wulfmær, Glædwine and Wulfric had 3 bovates of land as 3 manors. There is land for 1 plough. There 4 villans and 2 bordars have 2 ploughs. There is a church, and 3 acres of meadow. Formerly 8s; now it is worth | 10s |.

In BULWELL [in Nottingham] Godric had 2 carucates of land as a manor. [There is] land for 2 ploughs. There is 1 plough, and 1 villan and 1 bordar, and 2 acres of meadow. Formerly 12s; now it is worth 5s.

In FLINTHAM Thorir had 6 bovates of land to the geld. [There is] land for 2 ploughs. There 1 sokeman and 7 villans and 1 bordar have 2 ploughs, and 24 acres of meadow. Reynold, Walter's man, has 1 plough. [There is] scrubland

[Folio 288V: NOTTINGHAMSHIRE]

X. The land of Walter D'Aincourt

In FLAWBOROUGH Wulfric had 2 bovates of land to the geld. [There is] land for 1 plough. There Walter d'Aincourt has 1 plough, and 4 villans with 1 plough. TRE, as now, worth 20s.

In STAUNTON IN THE VALE Thorir had 10 bovates of land to the geld. [There is] land for 3 ploughs. There are now 3 ploughs in demesne; and 4 sokemen on $1\frac{1}{2}$ bovates of this land and 11 villans and 2 bordars having 2 ploughs. There is a

priest and a church, and 1 mill [rendering] 5s4d, and 80 acres of meadow. TRE worth £4; now 100s.

SOKELAND OF THIS MANOR

In Alverton and Flawborough and 'Dallington' [in Flawborough] [are] 6 bovates of land to the geld. [There is] land for 2 ploughs. There 12 sokemen have 3 ploughs, and 100 acres of meadow. Mauger holds it.

In COTHAM Swein and Thorir had 9 bovates of land to the geld. [There is] land for 6 ploughs. There Walter has in demesne 1 plough; and 10 villans and 8 bordars having 3 ploughs. There is a priest and a church, and 60 acres of meadow. TRE worth 100s; now £6.

SOKELAND

In Flawborough [are] $1\frac{1}{2}$ bovates of land to the geld. [There is] land for 1 plough. There are 24 acres of meadow. There 5 sokemen have $1\frac{1}{2}$ ploughs, and 24 acres of meadow.

In EAST STOKE Thorir had 6 bovates of land to the geld. [There is] land for 2 ploughs. There is in demesne 1 plough; and 3 villans and 5 bordars having half a plough, and 60 acres of meadow. TRE worth 60s; now 40[s]. Osbert holds it.

In Hawton [are] 2 bovates of land to the geld. [There is] land for 1 plough. There 6 sokemen have 2 ploughs, and 20 acres of meadow.

In HOCKERTON Thorir had 3 bovates of land to the geld. [There is] land for 1 plough. There Walter has 1 plough, and 5 villans and 5 bordars having half a plough, and 16 acres of meadow. [There is] woodland pasture 1 league long and $1\frac{1}{2}$ furlongs broad. TRE worth 20s; now 15[s].

In KNAPTHORPE Thorir had $4\frac{1}{2}$ bovates of land to the geld. [There is] land for 1 plough. There is in demesne 1 plough; and 5 villans and 3 bordars having $1\frac{1}{2}$ ploughs, and 2 acres of meadow. [There is] woodland pasture 8 furlongs long and 2 broad. TRE, as now, [worth] 20s.

In BULCOTE Swein Cild had 2 carucates of land and 2 bovates to the geld, and in the same place $15\frac{1}{2}$ bovates of land to the geld, SOKELAND of the same manor. [There is] land for $5\frac{1}{2}$ ploughs. There is in demesne 1 plough; and 8 sokemen and 11 villans and 12 bordars and 2 slaves with 3 ploughs. There are 76 acres of meadow, [and] woodland, pasture in places, 1 league long and 8 furlongs broad. TRE, as now, worth £4.

In OXTON Thorir had 4 bovates of land to the geld. [There is] land for 12 oxen. There is 1 sokeman on the third part of 1 bovate of this land, with 1 bordar, having half a plough, and 4 acres of meadow. TRE worth 16s; now 5s4d.

In THURGARTON and in 'Horsepool' [in Thurgarton] Swein had 3 carucates of land and 3 bovates to the geld. [There is] land for 6 ploughs. There Walter has in demesne 2 ploughs; and 10 sokemen on 9 bovates of this land

In Tythby [are] 2 bovates to the geld. and 12 villans and 2 bordars having 6 ploughs. There is a priest and a church, and

40 acres of meadow, [and] woodland pasture 1 league long and a half broad. TRE worth £3; now £4.

In HOVERINGHAM Swein had 2 carucates of land and 2 bovates to the geld. [There is] land for 4 ploughs. There Walter has in demesne 2 ploughs; and 6 sokemen on 3 bovates and the third part of 1 bovate of this land and 9 villans and 3 bordars having 4 ploughs. There is a priest and a church, and 2 mills [rendering] 40s, and 2 fisheries [rendering] 8s, and 40 acres of meadow. TRE worth £4; now the same and 10s more.

In Fiskerton Walter has half a carucate of land to the geld, of which the SOKE belongs to Southwell. There he himself has 1 plough, and 3 villans with 1 plough.

In Morton [near Southwell] Walter has half a carucate of land to the geld, of which the SOKE belongs to Southwell. There he himself [has] 1 plough, and 3 villans have 1 plough.

In Farnsfield Walter has 2 bovates of land to the geld. One is in the SOKE of Southwell and the other in the king's [soke], but nevertheless it belongs to the hundred of Southwell. There is 1 plough in demesne. TRE worth 5s; now 8s.

In ROLLESTON Thorir had 11 bovates of land and the fourth part of 1 bovate to the geld. [There is] land for 2 ploughs. There is 1 plough in demesne; and 8 villans and 6 bordars having 3 ploughs and 3 oxen. There is a priest and a church, and 32 acres of meadow, [and] woodland pasture 4 furlongs long and 2 broad. TRE worth 40s; now 60[s].

SOKELAND OF THIS MANOR

In Kelham [are] 9 bovates of land and the third part of 1 bovate to the geld. [There is] land for 2½ ploughs. There 18 sokemen and 3 bordars have 7½ ploughs, and 16 acres of meadow. [There is] scrubland 9 furlongs long and 50 virgates broad.

In FISKERTON Thorir had 2 carucates of land and 2 bovates to the geld. [There is] land for 5 ploughs. There Walter has in demesne 1 plough; and 11 villans having 4 ploughs. There are 2 mills, and 1 fishery, and 1 ferry [rendering] 46s8d, and 42 acres of meadow, [and] woodland pasture 2 furlongs long and 1 furlong broad. TRE worth £3; now 4[l].

In this Fiskerton Walter has 6 bovates of land of which the archbishop has the soke.

In ASLOCKTON Thorir had 1 carucate of land to the geld. [There is] land for 3 ploughs. There Walkelin, Walter's man, has 2 ploughs, and 1 sokeman on 1 bovate of this land and 6 villans and 2 bordars with 1½ ploughs, and [there are] 24 acres of meadow. TRE, as now, worth 30s.

SOKELAND

In Hawksworth [is] 1 bovate of land to the geld. [There is] land for 2 oxen. There 2 sokemen and 1 bordar have 2 oxen in a plough, and 2 acres of meadow.

In CAR COLSTON Thorir had 2½ bovates of land and 1 acre of land to the geld. [There is] land for 1 plough. There 1 bordar ploughs with 1 ox. There are 3 acres of meadow. TRE worth 10s; now 5s. Walkelin holds it.

1 furlong long and 1 furlong broad. TRE, as now, worth 20s.

In GRANBY Hemming had 1½ carucates of land to the geld. [There is] land for 12 ploughs. There Walter has in demesne 4 ploughs; and 44 villans and 9 bordars having 10 ploughs. There is a priest and a church, and 1 mill [rendering] 2s, and 200 acres of meadow. TRE worth £12; now £20.

SOKELAND OF THIS MANOR

In Barnstone [is] half a carucate of land to the geld. [There is] land for 2 ploughs. There 5 sokemen and 1 bordar have 2 ploughs and 2 oxen ploughing, and 11 acres of meadow.

In Langar [are] 4½ bovates of land to the geld. [There is] land for 2 ploughs. There 8 sokemen have 2 ploughs and 6 oxen ploughing. There is half a church, and 13 acres of meadow.

In Wiverton [are] 6½ bovates of land to the geld. [There is] land for 1 plough. There 5 sokemen have 2 ploughs and 2 oxen ploughing, and 20 acres of meadow.

In Hickling [are] 2 carucates of land to the geld. [There is] land for 4 ploughs. There 8 sokemen and 1 villan and 10 bordars have 5 ploughs. There is a mill [rendering] 16s, and 80 acres of meadow.

In Kinoulton [are] 7 bovates of land to the geld. [There is] land for 2 ploughs. There are 9 sokemen and 4 bordars having 3 ploughs and 7 oxen ploughing, and 20 acres of meadow.

In Cropwell Butler and Wiverton [are] 4 bovates of land to the geld. [There is] land for 1 plough. There 4 sokemen and 7 bordars have 2 ploughs, and 13 acres of meadow.

In RADCLIFFE ON TRENT Swein had 1½ carucates of land to the geld. [There is] land for 3 ploughs. There in demesne are 2 ploughs; and 14 villans and 3 bordars having 2 ploughs, and 19 acres of meadow. TRE, as now, it was worth 40s.

XII. The land of Geoffrey Alselin

In LAXTON Toki had 2 carucates of land to the geld. [There is] land for 6 ploughs. There Walter, a man of Geoffrey Alselin, has 1 plough, and 22 villans and 7 bordars having 5 ploughs, and 5 slaves and 1 female slave, and 40 acres of meadow. [There is] woodland pasture 1 league long and a half broad. TRE worth £9; now £6.

SOKELAND OF THIS MANOR

In [?] Kirton [are] 2 bovates of land to the geld. [There is] land for 4 oxen. There 3 sokemen have 1 plough. In Willoughby [in Walesby] is 1 garden belonging to Laxton.

In Walesby [are] 2 bovates of land to the geld. [There is] land for 4 oxen. There 2 sokemen have 1 plough.

In Eakring [is] half a bovate of land to the geld. It is waste.

In Ompton [are] 2 bovates of land to the geld. It is waste.

In Knapthorpe [is] 1 bovate of land to the geld. It is waste. [There is] land for 2 oxen.

In Caunton [are] 6 bovates of land to the geld. [There is] land for 3 ploughs. There 8 sokemen and 10 bordars have 5 ploughs. There is 1 mill [rendering] 2s, and 8 acres of meadow, [and] woodland pasture 1 league long and 4 furlongs broad.

In Beesthorpe [are] 2 bovates of land to the geld. [There is] land for half a plough. There 2 sokemen and 1 bordar have half a plough, and half an acre of meadow. [There are] 10 acres [of] woodland pasture.

In Carlton-on-Trent [is] 1 carucate of land to the geld. [There is] land for 1 plough. There 4 sokemen have 2 ploughs, and 20 acres of meadow. [There is] woodland pasture 4 furlongs long and 4 broad.

In NORTH MUSKHAM Wulfric had 3 bovates of land to the geld. [There is] land for 4 ploughs. There in demesne is 1 plough; and 4 villans and 7 bordars having 1½ ploughs. There is 1 mill [rendering] 10s, and 12 acres of meadow. TRE worth 40s; now 30[s].

In the same place [are] 4 bovates of land to the geld. [There is] land for 1 plough. [It is] SOKELAND. It is waste. There are 12 acres of meadow.

In Little Carlton [is] 1 bovate of land to the geld. There are 2 sokemen having nothing.

In WILLOUGHBY [in Norwell] Toki had 1½ bovates of land to the geld. [There is] land for 4 oxen. It is waste. There is half a mill, and 12 acres of meadow.

In STOKE BARDOLPH and Gedling [in Nottingham] Toki had 3 carucates and 2 bovates and 2 parts of 1 bovate to the geld. [There is] land for 4 ploughs. There in demesne Geoffrey has 2 ploughs; and [there are] 15 villans and 6 slaves and 21 bordars having 8 ploughs. There is a priest and a church, and 1 fishery, and 2 mills [rendering] 20s, and 30 acres of meadow, [and] woodland pasture 3 furlongs long and 3 furlongs broad. TRE worth 110s; now £6.

In Carlton [in Nottingham] and Gedling [in Nottingham] and Colwick [in Nottingham] [are] 15 bovates of land to the geld. [There is] land for 4 ploughs. There 30 sokemen have 10½ ploughs, and 20 acres of meadow. [There is] scrubland 3 furlongs long and 1 broad.

In BURTON JOYCE Swein had 1 carucate of land and the fourth part of 1 bovate to the geld. [There is] land for 2 ploughs. There Geoffrey has 1 sokeman on 5 acres of land, and 5 villans and 1 bordar and 1 slave and 1 female slave. Together they have 3 ploughs. There is a church and a priest, and 16 acres of meadow, [and] woodland pasture 2 furlongs long and 1 broad. TRE, as now, worth 1 mark of silver.

In SHELFORD Toki had 4 carucates of land to the geld. [There is] land for 8 ploughs. There are now 36 villans and 12 bordars having 9 ploughs,

and 1 mill [rendering] 4s, and 1 fishery. There is a priest and a church. TRE worth £8; now £4.

SOKELAND OF THIS MANOR

In Newton [are] 9 bovates of land to the geld. [There is] land for 3 ploughs. There are 9 sokemen and 4 bordars having 4 ploughs, and 4 acres of meadow.

In Owthorpe Toki had 1 carucate of land to the geld. Nothing is reckoned there.

In KNAPTHORPE [is] half a bovate to the geld. It belongs to NORWELL.

In CARLTON-ON-TRENT [are] 2 bovates of land to the geld. [There is] land for half a plough. There are 4 sokemen, and 3 acres of meadow. Formerly [worth] 8s; now 3s.

XIII. The land of Ralph fitzHubert

In BARTON IN FABIS Leofric had 13 bovates of land to the geld. [There is] land for 3 ploughs. There Ralph fitzHubert has 2 ploughs, and 18 villans and 5 bordars having 5½ ploughs. There are 48 acres of meadow, [and] scrubland 2 furlongs long and half a furlong broad. TRE worth £6; now 100s, with the 2 Chilwells, in which [are] 7 sokemen and half a church.

IN THE SAME PLACE Wulfric had 2 bovates of land to the geld. [There is] land for 1 plough. There Ralph has 1 plough, and 2 villans and 1 bordar with 1 plough. TRE, as now, worth 20s.

In Clifton [in Nottingham] 2 bovates of land to the geld belong to Barton in Fabis.

In Chilwell and 'Eastern' Chilwell [are] 3 carucates of land and 3 bovates to the geld. The SOKE [belongs] to Barton in Fabis. [There is] land for 4½ ploughs. There Ralph has 1 plough, and 2 sokemen and 5 villans and 13 bordars having 6 ploughs and 2 oxen ploughing. There are 70 acres of meadow, and half a church, and 4 acres of scrubland and 4 acres of willow plantation. In Chilwell [are] 5 bovates of sokeland to the geld [belonging] to Toton.

In BUNNY Leofnoth had 2 carucates of land to the geld. [There is] land for 6 ploughs. There Ralph has in demesne 2 ploughs; and 18 villans and 7 sokemen and 2 bordars having 7 ploughs. There is a church and a priest, and 1 mill [rendering] 12d, and 160 acres of meadow, and scrubland 10 furlongs long and 1 broad. TRE [worth] £4; now 60s.

In KEYWORTH Frani had 5 bovates of land to the geld. [There is] land for 1 plough. There Ralph has 1½ ploughs, and 3 acres of meadow. TRE [worth] 20s; now 10s.

In TEVERSAL Leofric had 6 bovates of land to the geld. [There is] land for 1½ ploughs. There Ralph has 2 ploughs, and 1 sokeman on 1 bovate of land and 9 villans having 3½ ploughs. There is 1 mill [rendering] 16d, and 8 acres of meadow, and scrubland 1 league long and 1 broad. TRE worth 60s; now 30[s]. Geoffrey holds it.

In KIRKBY IN ASHFIELD Leofnoth had 10 bovates of land to the geld. [There is] land for 2 ploughs. There Ralph has in demesne 3 ploughs; and 1 sokeman on 1 bovate of land and 20 villans and 6 bordars having 12 ploughs. There is a church and a priest, and 2 mills [rendering] 3s, and 3 acres of meadow, [and] woodland, pasture in places, 2 leagues long and 1 broad. TRE worth £4; now £3.

In WANSLEY Leofric had 5 bovates of land to the geld. [There is] land for 1 plough. There Ralph has half a plough, and 3 villans and 2 bordars. There is a priest and half a church, and 4 acres of meadow, [and] woodland pasture 4 furlongs, long and 4 broad. TRE worth 8s; now 10s.

In ANNESLEY Leofnoth had 1 carucate of land to the geld. [There is] land for 12 oxen. There Ralph has 1 plough, and 19 villans and 1 bordar having 7 ploughs, and 3 acres of meadow. [There is] woodland pasture 1 league long and 1 league broad. TRE, as now, worth 40s. Richard holds it.

In COSSALL Leofnoth had 6 bovates of land to the geld. [There is] land for as many oxen. There are 3 ploughs with 3 villans, and 5 acres of meadow. Formerly 16s; now it is worth 10s.

In GIBSMERE and Morton [near Southwell] [is] 1 carucate of land and 3 bovates to the geld. The soke [belongs] to Southwell. [There is] land for 3½ ploughs. It was and is worth 28s.

In WIDMERPOOL [is] 1 bovate of land to the geld and it belongs to BUNNY.

XIIII. The land of Ralph de Limesy

In HAWTON Thorth had 4½ bovates of land to the geld. [There is] land for 2 ploughs. There Ralph de Limesy has 2 ploughs, and 4 sokemen on 2½ bovates of land and 5 villans and 5 bordars having 3 ploughs. There is a priest and 2 churches, and 1 mill [rendering] 5s4d.

IN THE SAME PLACE Buggi, Regnvald, Thorfridh and Buggi had 6½ bovates of land to the geld. [There is] land for 2½ ploughs.

SOKELAND

In the same place [are] 5 bovates of land to the geld. [There is] land for 2 ploughs. On these lands are 18 sokemen and 2 villans and 10 bordars having 6 ploughs. Alvred holds these 5 manors of Ralph. TRE worth 100s; now £4.10s.

SOKELAND

In Danethorpe [is] 1 bovate of land to the geld. [There is] land for 2 oxen. There 5 sokemen and 6 bordars have 2 ploughs. There is a church and a priest with 1 plough, and 80 acres of meadow.

In EPPERSTONE and Woodborough Wulfric, and Alsige [who had] no hall, had 3 carucates of land and 4 bovates to the geld. [There is] land for 6 ploughs. There Ralph has in demesne 3 ploughs; and 14 sokemen on 6 bovates and a fourth of 1 bovate of this land and 12 villans and 10 bordars having 6 ploughs. There is a church and a priest, and 4 mills [rendering] 77s, and 8 acres of meadow, [and] woodland pasture 2 leagues long and 9 furlongs broad. TRE worth £5; now £7.

In Gonalston Ralph de Limesy has 4 carucates of land 5 bovates and the third part of 1 bovate to the geld.

In THORPE [near Newark-on-Trent] Wulfric had 6½ bovates of land to the geld. [There is] land for 4 ploughs. There Mainfrid, Ralph's man, has 1 plough, and 9 villans and 5 bordars having 3 ploughs, and 72 acres of meadow.

In Shelton and Collingham [are] 5½ bovates of land to the geld. [There is] land for †3† ploughs. There are 8 sokemen and 5 villans having 3 ploughs, and 60 acres of meadow, and 2 acres and 1 virgate of woodland, not for pasture. TRE worth £4; now 40s.

[Folio 290: NOTTINGHAMSHIRE]

XV. The land of Ralph de Buron

'BASSETLAW' WAPENTAKE

In OSSINGTON Osmund had 6 bovates of land to the geld. [There is] land for 3 ploughs. There Ralph de Buron has 3 ploughs, and 4 sokemen on half a bovate of this land and 16 villans and 6 bordars having 6 ploughs, and 28 acres of meadow. [There is] woodland pasture 2 leagues long and 1 league broad. TRE worth 60s; now 40[s].

In Ompton [are] 3 bovates of land to the geld. [There is] land for 1 plough. There 2 bordars have 1 plough.

In KELHAM Osmund had 2 bovates of land and the third part of 1 bovate to the geld. There William, Ralph's man, has 1 plough, and 3 bordars with 2 oxen ploughing, and 9 acres of meadow. [There is] scrubland 8 furlongs long and 12 virgates broad. TRE worth 40s; now 16s;

BROXTOWE WAPENTAKE

In HUCKNALL Ulfkil had 12 bovates of land to the geld. [There is] land for 2 ploughs. There Osmund, Ralph's man, has 1 plough, and 5 villans having 3½ ploughs. [There is] woodland pasture 1 league long and a half broad. TRE worth 30s; now 15s.

In COSTOCK Særic and his 2 brothers had 14 bovates of land to the geld. [There is] land for 14 oxen. There William, Ralph's man, has 3 ploughs, and 1 sokeman on 2 bovates of land and 9 villans and 4 bordars having 5 ploughs. There are 30 acres of meadow. TRE worth 40s; now 30s.

In REMPSTONE Ulfkil had 6 bovates of land to the geld. [There is] land for 6 oxen. It is waste. TRE worth 10s; now 2s. There are 10 acres of meadow.

BINGHAM WAPENTAKE

In LAMCOTE Ulfkil had 5 bovates of land to the geld. There Osmund, Ralph's man, has 1 plough, and 1 villan, and 6 acres of meadow. TRE, as now, worth 10s.

In COTGRAVE Oghe had 2 carucates of land to the geld. [There is] land for 3 ploughs. There in demesne are 3 ploughs; and 7 sokemen and 4 villans and 4 bordars having 4½ ploughs. There is half a church. [There is] scrubland 1 furlong long and 1 furlong broad. TRE worth 40s; now 60[s].

IN THE SAME PLACE Thorkil had 1 carucate of land to the geld. [There is] land for 1 plough. There Joscelin, Ralph's man, has half a plough, and 5 villans and 1 bordar having 2 ploughs. There are 30 acres of meadow, [and] scrubland half a furlong long and a half broad. TRE, as now, worth 10s.

In Cotgrave Warner has 6 bovates of the land of the same manor.

XVI. The land of Roger de Poitou

'BASSETLAW' WAPENTAKE

In GAMSTON [in Eaton] Gamal and Swein had 1 carucate of land to the geld. [There is] land for 8 ploughs. There Roger de Poitou has in demesne 2 ploughs; and 7 sokemen on 2 bovates of this land and 3 villans and 1 bordar having 3½ ploughs. There are 2 mills [rendering] 40s, and 20 acres of meadow and 20 acres of scrubland. TRE worth £4; now the same.

In THE SAME PLACE Ketilbiørn had 1 bovate of land to the geld. [There is] land for 1 plough. The same Ketilbiørn has it of Roger, and there he has 1 plough, and 2 bordars, and 3 acres of woodland, pasture in places. TRE worth 20s8d; now 10s

THURGARTON WAPENTAKE

In CALVERTON Wulfric had 3 bovates of land to the geld. [There is] land for 1 plough. There are now 2 villans, and 1 virgate of meadow. TRE worth 20s; and now 5s4d.

RUSHCLIFFE WAPENTAKE

In EDWALTON Stiupi had 6 bovates of land to the geld. [There is] land for 12 oxen. There is now in demesne 1 plough, and 1 villan, and 16 acres of meadow. TRE worth 30s; now 10s.

In WILLOUGHBY-ON-THE-WOLDS Godric and Earnwig had 6½ bovates of land and 2 parts of 1 bovate to the geld. [There is] land for 12 oxen. There are now in demesne 1½ ploughs; and 2 sokemen and 6 villans and 2 bordars having 2½ ploughs. There are 9 acres of meadow. TRE worth 50s; now 22s.

BINGHAM WAPENTAKE

In CROPWELL BUTLER Wulfric had 2 carucates and 6 bovates of land to the geld. [There is] land for 6 ploughs. There Roger has 3 ploughs, and 8 sokemen and 17 villans having 6 ploughs. There are 20 acres of meadow, [and] woodland pasture half a league long and 4 furlongs broad. TRE worth £8; now 100s.

In COTGRAVE Wulfric had 3 carucates of land to the geld. [There is] land for 4 ploughs. There Roger has 1 plough in demesne; and 6 sokemen and 10 villans and 1 bordar having 5 ploughs. There are 30 acres of meadow, [and] scrubland 2 furlongs long and 1 broad. TRE worth £4; now 40s.

In 'WARBY' [in Plumtree] Fredegis had 13½ bovates of land to the geld. [There is] land for 2 ploughs. There Roger has 1 plough, and 2 sokemen and 1 bordar having 1 plough, and 10 acres of meadow. TRE worth 10s; now 12s.

In HAUGHTON Baldric had 12 bovates of land to the geld.

[There is] land for 4 ploughs. It is waste. There are 16 acres of meadow, and woodland pasture 1 furlong long and 8 perches broad. TRE worth 60s; now 20s.

SOKELAND

In Walesby [is] half a bovate of land to the geld. [There is] land for 4 oxen. It is waste.

In [?West] DRAYTON Swein had 2 bovates of land and the third part of 1 bovate to the geld. [There is] land for 1 plough. Now Wulfsige holds it of Roger, and there he has half a plough, and 1 villan and 1 bordar with half a plough. There are 3 acres of meadow, [and] woodland pasture 1 furlong long and half a furlong broad. TRE worth 10s; now 5s4d.

In WILLOUGHBY-ON-THE-WOLDS Earnwig had 5 bovates of land as a manor. [There is] land for as many oxen. There are 2 ploughs, with 1 villan and 6 bordars, and 4 acres of meadow. Formerly 20s; now it is worth 10s.

[Folio 290V: NOTTINGHAMSHIRE]

XVII. The land of Gilbert de Ghent

NEWARK WAPENTAKE

In BOUGHTON Ulf [...] had 3 bovates of land to the geld. [There is] land for 3 ploughs. There Gilbert de Ghent has 3 villans and 1 sokeman and 1 bordar having 3½ ploughs. There are 4 acres of meadow, [and] woodland pasture 3 furlongs long and 3 broad. TRE worth 20s; now 10s.

In [?] KIRTON Regnvald had 2 bovates of land to the geld. [There is] land for half a plough. There 4 villans have 2 ploughs. [There is] woodland pasture 1 furlong long and 1 broad. TRE worth 20s; now 10s.

In OLLERTON Wada had 5½ bovates of land to the geld. [There is] land for 3 ploughs. There William, Gilbert's man, has 1 plough, and 6 sokemen on 2 bovates of land and 3 villans having 6 ploughs. There are 2 mills [rendering] 16s, [and] woodland pasture 1 league long and 4 furlongs broad. TRE worth 40s; now 30s.

In RUFFORD Ulf had 12 bovates of land to the geld. [There is] land for 4 ploughs. There Gilbert has in demesne 1 plough; and 10 villans having 3 ploughs. There are 20 acres of meadow, [and] woodland pasture 1½ leagues long and 1 league broad. TRE worth £6; now 60s.

SOKELAND OF THE SAME PLACE

In Bilsthorpe [are] 2 carucates of land to the geld. [There is] land for 6 ploughs. There 13 sokemen and 6 bordars have 6 ploughs, and 4 acres of meadow. [There is] woodland pasture 1 league long and 4 furlongs broad.

In Inkersall [is] 1 carucate of land to the geld. [It is] a BEREWICK. It is waste.

In EAKRING Ingulf had 6 bovates of land to the geld. [There is] land for 2 ploughs. There William, Gilbert's man, has 1 plough, and 3 sokemen on 3 bovates of this land and 2 villans and 3 bordars having 2 ploughs. There is a priest and a church, and 3 acres of meadow, [and] woodland pasture 6 furlongs long and 4 broad. TRE worth 20s; now 16s.

In THE SAME PLACE Egbrand had 6 bovates of land to the geld. [There is] land for 2 ploughs. The same Egbrand holds it of Gilbert, and has there 1 plough, and 6 sokemen on 4 bovates of land and 2 villans and 2 bordars having $2\frac{1}{2}$ ploughs. There are 3 acres of meadow, [and] woodland pasture 6 furlongs long and 4 broad. TRE worth 20s; now 16s.

In KNEESALL and Kersall Ulf [...] had 12 bovates of land to the geld. [There is] land for 4 ploughs. There Gilbert has in demesne 3 ploughs; and 8 sokemen on 3 bovates of land and 16 villans and 4 bordars having 12 ploughs. There are 22 acres of meadow, [and] woodland pasture 1 league long and a half broad. TRE worth £8; now £6.

SOKELAND OF THE SAME PLACE

In Ompton [are] $1\frac{1}{2}$ bovates of land to the geld. [There is] land for 2 oxen. There 2 sokemen and 1 bordar have 2 ploughs.

In Maplebeck [are] 14 bovates of land to the geld. [There is] land for 4 ploughs. There Gilbert has 1 plough, and 9 sokemen on $10\frac{1}{2}$ bovates of this land and 5 bordars having 4 ploughs, and 30 acres of meadow. [There is] woodland pasture 1 league long and 3 furlongs broad.

[?] Wellow Ulf [...] had $2\frac{1}{2}$ carucates of land to the geld. [There is] land for 4 ploughs. There Gilbert has 2 ploughs, and 22 villans and 2 bordars having 9 ploughs, and 26 acres of meadow. [There is] woodland pasture half a league long and a half broad. TRE worth £6; now £3.

In Kirklington Ulf [...] had $4\frac{1}{2}$ bovates of land to the geld. [There is] land for 2 ploughs. The SOKE belongs to the archbishop's manor of Southwell. There Gilbert has 1 plough, and 4 villans †having† 2 ploughs, and 1 mill [rendering] 16s. TRE worth 40s; now 8s.

In Normanton [in Southwell] Ulf had $3\frac{1}{2}$ bovates of land to the geld. [There is] land for 1 plough. There Gilbert has 4 villans with 1 plough. The SOKE [belongs] to Southwell. TRE worth 16s; now 8s.

In RUDDINGTON Ulf had half a carucate of land to the geld. [There is] land for 1 plough. There is now in demesne 1 plough; and 4 sokemen and 5 villans and 2 bordars having 3 ploughs. There are 33 acres of meadow. TRE worth 20s; now 8s.

BINGHAM WAPENTAKE

In WHATTON Ulf [...] had $2\frac{1}{2}$ carucates of land to the geld. [There is] land for 9 ploughs. There Robert, Gilbert's man, has 3 ploughs, and 28 villans and 12 bordars having 9 ploughs, and 1 mill [rendering] 4s, and 80 acres of meadow. There is 1 stone-pit where millstones are quarried rendering 3 marks of silver. TRE worth £20; now £16.

SOKELAND OF THE SAME MANOR

In Hawksworth [are] 13 bovates of land to the geld. [There is] land for 3 ploughs. There 20 sokemen and 1 bordar have $4\frac{1}{2}$ ploughs, and 20 acres of meadow.

In Aslockton [is] half a carucate of land to the geld. [There is] land for $1\frac{1}{2}$ ploughs. There 9 sokemen have 4 ploughs.

[Folio 291: NOTTINGHAMSHIRE]

XVIII. The land of Gilbert Tison

In AVERHAM Swein had 3 carucates of land to the geld. [There is] land for 6 ploughs. There Gilbert Tison has in demesne 2 ploughs; and 8 sokemen on 6 bovates of land and 21 villans and 22 bordars having 12 ploughs. There is a church and a priest, and 1 mill [rendering] 5s, and 80 acres of meadow, [and] scrubland 8 furlongs long and 4 broad. TRE worth 6[l]; now £10 and 12d. To this manor belong 5 sokemen in other hundreds.

In Cromwell [are] 2 bovates of land to the geld. [There is] land for 4 oxen. There 2 sokemen have 1 plough.

In FINNINGLEY Swein had 6 bovates of land to the geld. [There is] land for 3 ploughs. There Gilbert has half a plough, and 15 villans and 4 bordars having $5\frac{1}{2}$ ploughs. [There is] woodland pasture 2 leagues long and 2 broad. TRE worth 40s; now 45s.

In KELHAM Ælfric had 2 bovates of land to the geld. [There is] land for 6 oxen. There is 1 sokeman and 1 bordar with half a plough, and 6 acres of meadow. [There is] scrubland 8 furlongs long and 14 virgates broad. TRE worth 16s; now 3s.

In WINKBURN Swein had 12 bovates of land to the geld. [There is] land for 3 ploughs. There Gilbert has 2 ploughs in demesne; and 15 sokemen on 4 bovates of land and 7 villans and 5 bordars having 7 ploughs. There is a church, and 16 acres of meadow, [and] woodland pasture 1 league long and half a league broad. TRE worth 100s; now 60s.

5 thegns held 2 bovates of this land. One of them was the senior of the others. This [land] did not belong to Swein.

In "ALWOLDESTORP" Æthelstan had 4 bovates of land to the geld. [There is] land for 1 plough. There Gilbert has 1 plough in demesne, and 4 bordars. There are 10 acres of meadow. TRE worth 20s; now 10s.

BLIDWORTH HUNDRED

In STAYTHORPE Swein had 9 bovates of land to the geld. [There is] land for 2 ploughs. There Gilbert has 1 plough, and 12 villans and 4 bordars having $4\frac{1}{2}$ ploughs, and 1 mill [rendering] 5s, and 60 acres of meadow. TRE worth 60s; now the same.

XIX. The land of Geoffrey de La Guerche

In LANGFORD Leofric had 2 carucates of land and 3 bovates and the fifth part of 1 bovate to the geld. [There is] land for 8 ploughs. There Ranulph, the man of Geoffrey de la Guerche, has 2 ploughs and half a plough, and 16 sokemen and 17 villans and 4 bordars having 7 ploughs. There is a priest and a church, and 2 mills [rendering] 12s, and 1 fishery and 100 acres of meadow. TRE worth £4; now the same and 10s more.

XX. The land of Ilbert de Lacy

In SIBTHORPE Pilwine had 2½ bovates of land to the geld. [There is] land for 1 plough. Now Ilbert de Lacy has it. Arngrim holds it of him. There is 1 plough in demesne; and 3 sokemen on half a bovate of land and 16 bordars having 3 ploughs, and the third part of 1 mill [rendering] 10d, and 10 acres of meadow. The fourth part of this land belongs to the church of the same manor. There is a priest. TRE, as now, worth 30s.

SOKELAND

In Shelton and Alverton and Kilvington and Thoroton [are] 3 bovates of land to the geld. [There is] land for 1 plough. There 6 villans and 1 bordar have 2 ploughs, and 30 acres of meadow.

In EAST STOKE Thorkil had 5 bovates of land to the geld. [There is] land for 2 ploughs. Mainfrid holds it of Ilbert, and has there half a plough, and 3 sokemen and 5 bordars having 1 plough and 2 oxen ploughing, and 64 acres of meadow. TRE worth 20s; now 15[s].

In Elston Ilbert has 3 messuages in which are 2 sokemen and 1 bordar belonging to East Stoke. They have no land.

Ilbert claims the priest's land against Bishop Remigius and in East Stoke he claims the fourth part of the vill.

In ELSTON Godwine had 6 bovates of land to the geld. [There is] land for 3 ploughs. Arngrim holds it of Ilbert, and has there 1 plough, and 3 sokemen on 2 bovates of land and 1 villan and 5 bordars having 2 ploughs. There are 30 acres of meadow. TRE worth 40s; now 25s.

In ASLOCKTON Lyfing had 1 bovate of land to the geld with sake and soke. [There is] land for half a plough. Wulfric holds it of Ilbert, and there he has 2 oxen ploughing, and 2 sokemen and 1 bordar having half a plough, and 8 acres of meadow. TRE worth 5s4d; now the same.

In CROPWELL BUTLER Wulfgeat and Godric had 4 bovates of land to the geld. [There is] land for 2 ploughs. Ilbert de Lacy was seised of this land, but when Roger de Poitou received [his] land he took possession of this manor to Ilbert's wrong. The wapentake bears witness that Ilbert had been seised [of it]. Now it is in the king's hand except the third part and the thegn [land] which is the head of the manor, which Ilbert holds. There is now 1 plough in demesne; and 4 sokemen having 9 oxen ploughing, and 6 acres of meadow. TRE worth 16s; now 10s.

In HICKLING [are] 3½ carucates of land to the geld. Thorkil and Godwine held them as 2 manors. [There is] land for 8 ploughs. In demesne are 3 ploughs; and 4 sokemen and 23 villans with 1 bordar have 6 ploughs. There are 200 acres of meadow. Formerly £6; now it is worth £4.

[Folio 291V: NOTTINGHAMSHIRE]

XXI. The land of Berengar de Tosny

In EAST STOKE Esbiorn Croc had 2½ bovates of land to the geld. [There is] land for 1 plough. Berengar de Tosny has it. Ralph, his man, holds it. There he has 1 plough, and 2 villans and 3 bordars ploughing with 2 oxen. There are 40 acres of meadow. TRE worth 12s; now 10s.

In SYERSTON Esbiorn Croc had 2½ bovates of land to the geld. [There is] land for 1 plough. Godwine holds it of Berengar, and has there 1 plough, and 1 sokeman and 2 villans with half a plough. There are 10 acres of meadow. TRE worth 30s; now 20s.

In Broadholme Thorgot and Healfdene had 5 bovates of land to the geld. [There is] land for 2 ploughs. It is waste. Now Berengar de Tosny and William de Percy have it. The land belongs to Newark-on-Trent but the service of the villans belongs to Saxilby [Lincs.] in Lincolnshire. There are 30 acres of meadow, [and] woodland pasture 1 furlong long and another broad.

XXII. The land of Hugh fitzBaldric

In KILVINGTON and Alverton Kolgrimr had 3 bovates of land to the geld. [There is] land for 2 ploughs. Hugh fitzBaldric has it. Ansger holds it of him, and has there 2 ploughs, and 1 sokeman on half a bovate of land and 3 villans and 2 bordars having 2 ploughs, and 20 acres of meadow. TRE worth 30s; now 20s.

In CUCKNEY Swein had 2 carucates of land to the geld. [There is] land for 4 ploughs. Richard holds it of Hugh, and has there 2 ploughs in demesne; and 3 sokemen on 2 bovates of land and 10 villans and 5 bordars having 3 ploughs. There is a priest and a church, and 2 mills [rendering] 8s, [and] woodland pasture 4 furlongs long and 4 furlongs broad. TRE, as now, worth 30s.

XXIII. The land of Hugh de Grandmesnil

In EDWALTION Gode had 6 bovates of land to the geld. [There is] land for 2½ ploughs. There Hugh de Grandmesnil has in demesne 2 ploughs; and 6 sokemen and 1 villan having 1½ ploughs, and 20 acres of meadow. TRE worth 10s; now 20s. It belongs to Stockerston [Leics.].

In THRUMPTON [are] 1½ bovates to the geld. [There is] land for 1 plough. There are 2 sokemen and 2 bordars with 2 ploughs, and 3 acres of meadow. It belongs to SANDIACRE [Derby.].

XXIIII. The land of Henry de Ferrers

In [East and West] LEAKE Siward had 2 carucates of land to the geld. [There is] land for 6 ploughs. There Henry de Ferrers has in demesne 4 ploughs; and 16 sokemen and 16 villans having 17 ploughs. There is a priest and a church, and 1 mill [rendering] 2s, and 50 acres of meadow, and scrubland 2 furlongs long and 1 broad. TRE worth £6; now £7.

To this manor belongs the BEREWICK of [East and West] Leake, where there are 2 carucates of land to the geld. This lies in Plumtree Hundred.

In SUTTON BONINGTON Siward had 1½ bovates of land to the geld. [There is] land for 4 oxen. There 3 villans have 1½ ploughs, and 3 acres of meadow. TRE worth 6s; now the same.

In Willoughby-on-the-Wolds [is] 1 bovates of land to the geld. [There is] land for 3 oxen. The SOKE [belongs] to Bathley. It is waste. There are 6 acres of meadow.

XXV. [The land] of Robert Malet

In BRADMORE Azur had 12 bovates of land to the geld. [There is] land for 3 ploughs. There Robert Malet has in demesne 3 ploughs; and 16 villans and 8 bordars having 5 ploughs. TRE, as now, worth 6os.

In Ruddington [is] 1 bovate of land and the third part of 1 bovate to the geld. [There is] land for 2 oxen. The SOKE [belongs] to Bradmore.

XXVI. [The land] of Durand Malet

In OWTHORPE Rolf had half a carucate of land to the geld. [There is] land land [sic] for 3 ploughs. There Durand Malet has 1 plough, and 4 sokemen and 3 villans having 2 ploughs. There are 12 acres of meadow. TRE worth 30s; now 20s.

[Folio 292: NOTTINGHAMSHIRE]

XXVII. The land of Osbern fitzRichard

In GRANBY Earl AElig;lfgar had 3 carucates of land to the geld. [There is] land for 10 ploughs. Osbern fitzRichard has it now. Robert d'Oilly holds it of him, and has there 4 ploughs, and 22 sokemen and 14 villans and 8 bordars having 10 ploughs. There is a priest and a church, and 2 mills [rendering] 10s, and 10 acres of meadow. TRE worth £8; now £15.

In Wiverton [are] 3½ bovates of land to the geld. [There is] land for 1 plough. There 7 sokemen have 2 ploughs. The SOKE [belongs] to Colston Basset.

In Salterford [are] 6 bovates of land to the geld. It is waste. [It is] a BEREWICK of Colston Basset. [There is] woodland pasture 1 league long and 4 furlongs broad.

XXVIII. [The land] of Robert fitzWilliam

In STANFORD ON SOAR Ælfheah had 10 bovates of land to the geld. [There is] land for 4 ploughs. There Robert fitzWilliam has 1 plough, and 4 sokemen and 7 villans and 2 bordars having 7 ploughs. There is the site of a mill, and 15 acres of meadow. TRE it was worth 40s.

SOKELAND OF THE SAME PLACE

In [East and West] LEAKE [is] 1 bovate of land to the geld. [There is] land for 4 oxen. There 2 sokemen have 1 plough. It belongs to Stanford on Soar.

In BROXTOWE [in Nottingham] Godric had 3 bovates of land to the geld. [There is] land for 3 oxen. There Robert has 1 plough, and 1 villan. [There is] scrubland 1 furlong long and 1 broad. TRE worth 16s; now 8s.

XXIX. [The land] of William the Usher

In BRAMCOTE Ulfkil, Godric, Ælfric and Leofric had 12 bovates of land to the geld. [There is] land for 12 oxen. There William the usher has 1 plough, and 4 villans and 1 bordar having 3½ ploughs. TRE worth 6os; now 20[s].

In TROWELL Uhtbrand had 1½ carucates of land to the geld. [There is] land for 12 oxen. There William the usher has 1 plough, and 6 villans with 4 ploughs. There is a priest and half a church, and 6 acres of meadow. TRE worth 100s; now 20s.

[Folio 292V: NOTTINGHAMSHIRE]

XXX. The land of the Thegns

'BASSETLAW' WAPENTAKE

In OSBERTON Alwine and Wulfgeat had 1 carucate of land to the geld. [There is] land for 4 ploughs. Now Swein and Wulfgeat hold it of the king, and have there 5 sokemen having 4 ploughs, and a church, and 20 acres of meadow. [There is] woodland pasture 6 furlongs long and 3 broad. TRE worth 6os; now 10s.

In CARLTON-ON-TRENT Ulfkil had 3 bovates of land to the geld. [There is] land for 6 oxen. Healfdene has it of the king. There 2 bordars have 3 oxen ploughing, and 10 acres of meadow. [There is] woodland pasture 2 furlongs long and a half broad. TRE worth 10s; now 5s4d.

In KNAPTHORPE Healfdene holds of the king 2 bovates of land to the geld. [There is] land for 6 oxen. There he has 1 plough, and 4 bordars having 1 ox in a plough, and 4 acres of meadow. [There is] woodland pasture 2 furlongs long and 1 broad. TRE, as now, worth 10s8d.

In CROMWELL Healfdene holds of the king 2 carucates of land and 6 bovates to the geld. [There is] land for 4 ploughs. There he has 1 plough, and 5 sokemen on 1 carucate of this land and 8 villans and 2 bordars having 4½ ploughs. There is a church, and 1 mill [rendering] 12d, and 1 fishery, [and] meadow 6 furlongs long and 3 broad. TRE worth 6os; now 40[s].

In LAMBLEY Ulfkil had 2 carucates of land and 2 bovates to the geld. [There is] land for 3 ploughs. Healfdene holds it of the king, and has there 1 plough, and 20 villans and 3 bordars having 4 ploughs, and 3 sokemen on half a carucate of land with 1 plough. There are 2 mills [rendering] 20s, and 20 acres of meadow, [and] woodland pasture 1 league long and 4 furlongs broad. TRE, as now, it was worth 6os.

In WOODBOROUGH Ulfkil had 3 bovates of land to the geld. [There is] land for 1 plough. There Healfdene has 3 villans having half a plough. TRE, as now, worth 5s4d.

In NORTH MUSKHAM Siward had 3 bovates of land to

the geld. [There is] land for 3 ploughs. There the same Siward has 2 bordars, and 1 mill [rendering] 10s, and 12 acres of meadow. TRE worth 40s; now 16s.

In COLWICK [in Nottingham] Ælfric, 3 [bovates], and Buggi, 2 [bovates, had] 5 bovates of land to the geld. [There is] land for 1 plough. They themselves hold it of the king, and have there 2 ploughs, and 1 sokeman on 1 bovate and 6 villans and 1 bordar with 2 ploughs. There are 31 acres of meadow and 8 acres of scrubland. TRE it was worth 25s4d.

In WOODBOROUGH Ulfkil had 3 bovates of land to the geld. [There is] land for 2 ploughs. The same man holds it of the king, and has there 1 plough, and 3 villans and 1 bordar with 1½ ploughs, and 1 mill [rendering] 20s, and 1 virgate of meadow. [There is] woodland pasture 2 leagues long and 5 furlongs broad. TRE worth 20[...]; now 30s.

In NORMANTON [in Southwell] Earnwig the priest had 5 bovates of land to the geld. [There is] land for 2 ploughs. It is waste.

In "ODESTORP" Wulfmær had 2½ bovates of land to the geld. [There is] land for 1 plough. There is in demesne 1 plough, and half a mill [rendering] 4s, and 10 acres of meadow. TRE worth 40s; now 4s.

In CALVERTON Ælfric [had] 3 bovates of land to the geld. There is and for 1 plough. There 2 sokemen and 4 villans have 2 ploughs. Formerly 16s; now it is worth 10s. The same man holds it.

RUSHCLIFFE WAPENTAKE

In NORMANTON ON SOAR Asgot had 3½ bovates of land to the geld. [There is] land for 1 plough. There are 2 villans, and 2 acres of meadow. TRE [worth] 20s; now 6s.

In Sutton Bonington [are] 1½ bovates of land to the geld. [There is] land for half a plough. It belongs to Normanton on Soar. There are 5 villans with 1 plough, and 3 acres of meadow. TRE, as now, [worth] 6s.

In the same Normanton on Soar Rawn, 2 bovates of land to the geld.

In SUTTON BONINGTON Leofweard had 3 bovates of land to the geld. Siward holds them of the king.

IN THE SAME PLACE Coleman, 1½ bovates of land to the geld.

In KINGSTON ON SOAR Algar had 3 bovates of land to the geld. [There is] land for 2 ploughs. Sæwine holds it of the king, and has there 2 villans with 1 plough, and the site of a mill, and [there are] 10 acres of meadow. TRE [worth] 20s; now 10s.

In RATCLIFFE ON SOAR Asgot had 10 bovates of land and 4 parts of 1 bovate to the geld. [There is] land for 6 ploughs. Sæwine holds it of the king, and has there 2 ploughs, and 9 villans and 3 bordars having 2 ploughs. There is a priest and a church, and 1 mill [rendering] 10s, and 6 acres of meadow. TRE worth 100s; now 60s.

In Kingston on Soar [is] 1 carucate of land to the geld. [There

is] land for 2 ploughs. There 8 sokemen and 3 villans have 3 ploughs.

IN THE SAME PLACE Ulfkil had 1½ bovates of land to the geld. [There is] land for 1 plough. Godric holds it now, but the men of the neighbourhood do not know through whom [or] how. There is 1 villan, and 6 acres of meadow. TRE worth 20s; now 3s.

In BARTON IN FABIS Algar had 1½ bovates of land and the fourth part of 1 bovate to the geld. [There is] land for 1 plough. There Sæwine has 1 villan and 2 bordars with 3 oxen ploughing, and [there are] 3 acres of meadow. TRE worth 10s; now 3s.

In GOTHAM Godric had 3½ bovates of land and 1 acre to the geld. [There is] land for 1 plough. It is waste. Sæwine has it. There are 12 acres of meadow. TRE worth 10s; now 2s.

In CLIFTON [in Nottingham] Ulfkil has of the king 1 bovate of land to the geld. There he has 1 villan with 2 oxen ploughing, and [there is] 1 acre of meadow.

In Willoughby-on-the-Wolds Algar, 2½ bovates of land to the geld. The SOKE [belongs] to 'Thorpe le Glebe'. There are 2 sokemen with 3 ploughs, and 3 acres of meadow.

In KIRKBY IN ASHFIELD Ælfric had 2 bovates of land to the geld. [There is] land for 2 oxen. The same man holds it of the king, and has there 1 plough. TRE [worth] 5s; now 2s.

In Old Basford [in Nottingham] Ælfric had 1 bovate to the geld: it is waste; and Skuli 1 bovate: it is waste.

In PAPPLEWICK Ælfric and Ælfheah and Alric had 2 carucates of land and 3 bovates to the geld. These are waste. There is woodland pasture 1 league long and a half broad. TRE it was worth 20s.

In TROWELL Ulfkil had half a carucate of land to the geld. [There is] land for 4 oxen. It is waste. Healfdene has it. There are 2 acres of meadow. TRE worth 10s; now 5s4d.

In STRELLEY Ulfkil had 3 bovates of land to the geld.

[Folio 293: NOTTINGHAMSHIRE]

[There is] land for 3 oxen. Now Wulfsige and Godwine hold it of the king, and have there 4 villans and 1 bordar. TRE worth 4s; now 3s.

In NUTHALL Eskil had 3½ bovates of land to the geld. [There is] land for 3½ oxen. Ælfric holds it of the king, and has there 6 villans with 2 ploughs. TRE worth 10s; now 6s8d.

In AWSWORTH Ulfkil had half a carucate of land to the geld. Healfdene holds it.

In OLD BASFORD [in Nottingham] Ælfric had 4 bovates of land to the geld. [There is] land for half a plough. The same man holds it of the king, and has there 1 villan with 1 plough, and 1 acre of meadow, and 2 mills [rendering] 16s, and 1 acre of scrubland. TRE, as now, it was worth 20s.

In WILLOUGHBY-ON-THE-WOLDS Esbiorn and Wulfmær had 3 bovates of land to the geld. [There is] land for 3 oxen. Alwine and Earnwine hold it of the king. It is waste.

There are 5 acres of meadow, and 5 bordars. TRE worth 10s4d; now 4s.

BINGHAM WAPENTAKE

In LAMCOTE Ulfkil had 5 bovates of land and the third part of 1 bovate to the geld. Healfdene holds it of the king, and has there 1 plough in demesne, and 6 acres of meadow. TRE worth 10s; now 5s.

In ASLOCKTON Leofric had 1 bovate of land to the geld. [There is] land for 4 oxen. Wulfric holds it of the king, and has there 2 oxen in a plough, and 2 sokemen and 1 bordar with half a plough. There are 8 acres of meadow. TRE, as now, worth 5s4d.

In KINOULTON Azur had 1 bovate of land to the geld. [There is] land for 3 oxen. Now Azur's son holds it of the king, and has there 3 villans with 3 oxen ploughing, and 3 acres of meadow. TRE worth 10s; now 2s8d.

In CLARBOROUGH Wulfmær had 1½ bovates of land to the geld with sake and soke without a hall. [There is] land for 3 oxen. The same man holds it of the king, and has there 2 villans and 3 bordars with half a plough, and 3 acres of meadow. [There is] woodland pasture 6 furlongs long and 3 broad. TRE worth 3s; now 2s.

NEWARK WAPENTAKE

In SYERSTON-it is the king's-Thorfridh had 2 bovates of land to the geld. [There is] land for 5 oxen. There 2 villans and 1 bordar have 1 plough, and 5 acres of meadow. TRE worth 10s; now 5s.

In ELKESLEY Eskil had 4 bovates of land to the geld. [There is] land for 2 ploughs. Earnwine the priest holds it of the king. There 4 villans have 1½ ploughs. TRE worth 8s; now 10s. In MORTON [in Babworth] [are] 3 bovates to the geld. Eskil held it. Earnwine holds it. It is waste.

In MISSON Knut had 1½ bovates of land to the geld. [There is] land for 3 oxen. Earnwine has there 4 villans with half a plough, and 2 sokemen with 1 plough, and a fishery [rendering] 3s. [There is] woodland pasture 1 furlong long and 1 broad. It is worth 8s.

In the same place [are] 3 bovates of land to the geld. The SOKE [belongs] to Kirton in Lindsey [Lincs.]. There 6 villans have 3 ploughs.

In KELHAM Ulfkil had 1 bovate of land and 2 parts of 1 bovate to the geld. [There is] land for 6 oxen. There Healfdene has 2 villans and 2 bordars with 1 plough, and 6 acres of meadow. [There is] scrubland 8 furlongs long and 8 virgates broad. TRE [worth] 20s; now 10[s].

In SOUTH MUSKHAM Svartbrandr had 6 bovates of land to the geld. [There is] land for 1½ ploughs. Særic holds it of the king, and has there 1 sokeman and 2 bordars with 2 oxen in a plough, and 12 acres of meadow. [There is] woodland pasture 1 furlong long and 1 broad. TRE worth 16s; now 5s.

In WIDMERPOOL William had 11 bovates of land to the geld. [There is] land for 2 ploughs. Healfdene has there 14 sokemen and 2 villans and 2 slaves with 6 ploughs, and 20 acres of meadow. TRE worth 40s; now 30s.

IN THE SAME PLACE 4 thegns had 6 bovates of land to the geld. [There is] land for 1 plough. Healfdene has there 1 sokeman with 3 oxen in a plough, and 6 acres of meadow. TRE worth 21s; now 6s.

In Gonalston Earwhine the priest with 4 sokemen had 5 bovates of land to the geld. [There is] land for 12 oxen. The SOKE [belongs] to Arnold [in Nottingham]. There 4 sokemen have 1 plough, and 5 acres of meadow and 16 acres of scrubland.

In TROWELL Ælfric had half a carucate of land to the geld. [There is] land for 4 oxen. The same man holds it of the king, and has there 3 villans with 2 ploughs, and 2 acres of meadow. TRE, as now, worth 9s.

In the same place Wulfric had half a carucate of land to the geld. [There is] land for half a plough. Earnwine has 1 bordar and 1 villan with 1 plough, and 2 acres of meadow. TRE worth 10s; now 5s4d. 1 bovate of land belongs there. [It is] SOKELAND. It is waste.

In 'EASTERN' CHILWELL Dunning had 5 bovates of land to the geld. [There is] land for 5 oxen. Earnwine has there 1 villan with half a plough, and 12 acres of meadow. TRE [worth] 5s4d; now 3s4d.

In WARSOP a certain blind man holds 1 bovate in alms of the king.
    In CLARBOROUGH [are] 2 bovates of land to the geld. [There is] land for 2 ploughs. Arnketil held it. Earnwine holds it. There are 2 villans, and 6 acres of meadow. It was worth 4s; now 2s.
    In 'SUTTON PASSEYS' [in Wollaton, [Nottingham] Ælfric and Brun held 12 bovates of land to the geld, as 2 manors, and Wulfsige 1½ carucates to the geld. The soke belongs to Wollaton [in Nottingham]. There is land for 3 ploughs. It is waste.
    In ORDSALL [is] 1 bovate to the geld. [There is] land for 4 oxen. Earnwig holds it.

[Folio 293V: RUTLAND]

Look for those who hold lands in Rutland at the beginning of the County of Nottingham among those who hold lands there. [Arthur Agarde 1570-1615]

In ALSTOE WAPENTAKE are 2 hundreds. In each [are] 12 carucates to the geld, and in each can be 24 ploughs. This wapentake is half in Thurgarton Wapentake and half in Broxtowe Wapentake.

In 'MARTINSLEY' WAPENTAKE is 1 hundred in which [are] 12 carucates of land to the geld, and there can be 48 ploughs, saving the king's 3 demesne manors, in which 14 teams can plough.

THESE 2 WAPENTAKES belong to the sheriffdom of Nottingham for [purposes of] the king's geld.
    RUTLAND renders to the king £150 blanch.

ALSTOE WAPENTAKE

In GREETHAM Goda had 3 carucates of land to the geld. [There is] land for 8 ploughs. There the king has 2 ploughs in demesne; and 33 villans and 4 bordars having 8 ploughs, and 1 mill and 7 acres of meadow. [There is] woodland, pasture in places, 16 furlongs long and 7 furlongs broad. TRE worth £7; now £10.

In COTTESMORE Goda had 3 carucates of land to the geld. [There is] land for 12 ploughs. There the king has 3 ploughs in demesne; and 3 sokemen on half a carucate of this land and 40 villans and 6 bordars having 20 ploughs. There are 40 acres of meadow. [There is] woodland 1 league long and 7 furlongs broad. TRE worth £7; now £10.

Of the land of this manor a certain Geoffrey has half a carucate, and has there 1 plough, and 8 villans. It is worth 20s.

In MARKET OVERTON and STRETTON, a BEREWICK, Earl Waltheof had 3½ carucates of land to the geld. [There is] land for 12 ploughs. There Countess Judith has 3 ploughs, and 35 villans and 8 bordars having 9 ploughs, and [there are] 40 acres of meadow. [There is] woodland, pasture in places, 1 league long and half a league broad. TRE worth £12; now £20. Alvred of Lincoln claims a fourth part of Stretton.

In THISTLETON Erik had half a carucate of land to the geld. [There is] land for 1 plough. There Hugh has of Countess Judith 1 plough, and 6 villans with 1 plough. TRE worth 20s; now 40s.

IN THE SAME PLACE Siward had half a carucate of land to the geld. [There is] land for 1 plough. There Alvred of Lincoln has 1 plough, and 3 villans and 2 bordars with half a plough. TRE worth 20s; now 60s.

In the same hundred, in TEIGH, Godwine had 1½ carucates of land to the geld. [There is] land for 5 ploughs. There Robert Malet has 2 ploughs, and 15 villans with 4 ploughs. [There is] meadow 4 furlongs in length and 3 furlongs broad. There is 1 mill [rendering] 2s. TRE worth £4; now the same.

In WHISSENDINE Earl Waltheof had 4 carucates of land to the geld. [There is] land for 12 ploughs. There Hugh de Hotot has of the countess 5 ploughs, and 27 villans and 6 bordars having 8 ploughs. TRE worth £8; now £13.

In EXTON Earl Waltheof had 2 carucates of land to the geld. [There is] land for 12 ploughs. There Countess Judith has 3 ploughs, and 37 villans with 8 ploughs, and 2 mills [rendering] 13s. [There is] meadow 6 furlongs in length. [There is] woodland, pasture in places, 5 furlongs long and 5 broad. TRE worth £8; now £10.

In WHITWELL Besi had 1 carucate of land to the geld. [There is] land for 3 ploughs. There Herbert has of Countess Judith 1 plough, and 6 villans and 4 bordars having 2 ploughs. There is a church and a priest, and 20 acres of meadow, and 1 mill [rendering] 12d. [There is] woodland, pasture in places, 6 furlongs and 6 perches in length and 3 furlongs and 13 perches in breadth. TRE worth 40s; now 40[s].

In 'AWSTHORP' [in Burley] Leofric had 1 carucate of land to the geld. [There is] land for 5 ploughs. There Ogier fitzUngemar has of the king 2 ploughs, and 11 villans and 4 bordars with 4 ploughs, and 16 acres of meadow. [There is] woodland pasture 3 furlongs long and 2 broad. TRE, as now, it was worth 40s.

In BURLEY Ulf had 2 carucates of land to the geld. [There is] land for 7 ploughs. There Geoffrey, the man of Gilbert de Ghent, has 2 ploughs, and 30 villans and 8 bordars having 4 ploughs, and 30 acres of meadow. [There is] woodland, pasture in places, 1 league long and 3 furlongs broad. TRE worth £4; now 100s.

In ASHWELL Earl Harold had 2 carucates of land to the geld. [There is] land for 6 ploughs. There Joscelin, Earl Hugh's man, has 2 ploughs, and 13 villans and 3 bordars having 5 ploughs, and 16 acres of meadow. TRE worth 100s; now £6.

'MARTINSLEY' WAPENTAKE

In OAKHAM, with its 5 Berewicks, church sokeland, Queen Edith had 4 carucates of land to the geld. [There is] land for 16 ploughs. There the king has 2 ploughs [belonging] to the hall, and nevertheless there can be 4 other ploughs. There are 138 villans and 19 bordars having 37 ploughs, and 80 acres of meadow. There is a priest and a church to which 4 bovates of this land belong. [There is] woodland pasture 1 league long and half a league broad. TRE it was worth £40.

IN THE SAME PLACE Leofnoth had 1 carucate of land to the geld. Fulcher Malsor has there 5 oxen in a plough, and 6 acres of meadow. TRE, as now, [worth] 20s. The whole manor with its BEREWICKS [is] 3 leagues long and 1 league and 8 furlongs broad.

In [Middle, Nether and Upper] HAMBLETON, with its 7 Berewicks, church sokeland, Queen Edith had 4 carucates of land to the geld. [There is] land for 16 ploughs. There the king has 5 ploughs in demesne; and 140 villans and 13 bordars having 40 ploughs. There are 3 priests and 3 churches to which 1 bovate and 8 acres of land belong. There is 1 mill [rendering] 21s4d, and 40 acres of meadow. [There is] scrubland, bearing mast in places, 3 leagues long and 1½ leagues broad. TRE it was worth £52.

The whole manor with its BEREWICKS [is] 3 leagues and 8 furlongs long and 2 leagues and 8 furlongs broad.

In RIDLINGTON, with its 7 Berewicks, church sokeland, Queen Edith had 4 carucates of land to the geld. [There is] land for 16 ploughs. There the king has 4 ploughs in demesne; and 170 villans and 26 bordars having 30 ploughs, and 2 sokemen with 2 ploughs. There are 2 priests and 3 churches, and 2 sites for mills, and 40 acres of meadow. [There is] woodland, pasture in places, 2 leagues long and 8 furlongs broad. TRE it was worth £40. The whole manor with its BEREWICKS [is] 3 leagues and 7 furlongs long and 2 leagues and 2 furlongs broad.

[Folio 294: [RUTLAND]]

Again look in the counties of Northamptonshire and

Leicestershire for other manors and lands than are represented here. [Arthur Agarde 1570-1615]

In the above land Albert the clerk has 1 bovate of land, and has there 1 mill [rendering] 16d. The same Albert also has of the king the church of Oakham and of [Middle, Nether and Upper] Hambleton and of St Peter of Stamford [Lincs.] which belongs to [Middle, Nether and Upper] Hambleton with the lands attached to the same churches, that is, 7

bovates. In this same land of his there can be 8 ploughs, and nevertheless 16 teams plough there. He himself has there 4 ploughs in demesne; and 18 villans and 6 bordars having 5 ploughs.

TRE worth £8; now £10.

[Folio 294V: [NOTTINGHAMSHIRE]]

[Blank in MS]

YORKSHIRE

[Folio 297: YORKSHIRE]

[Blank in MS]

[Folio 297V: [YORKSHIRE]]

[Blank in MS]

[Folio 298: [YORKSHIRE]]

IN THE CITY OF YORK IN THE TIME OF KING EDWARD, besides the shire of the archbishop, there were 6 shires. One of these has been laid waste for the castles. In 5 shires there were 1, 418 inhabited messuages. Of 1 of these shires the archbishop still has a third part. In these no one else had customary dues unless as a burgess, except Mærle-Sveinn in a house which is within the castle, and except the canons wherever they dwelt; and except 4 judges, to whom the king gave this gift by his writ and for so long as they lived. But the archbishop had full customary dues from his shire. Of all the above-mentioned messuages there are now inhabited 400, less 9, both great and small, in the hand of the king rendering customary dues; and 400 messuages not inhabited, the better ones [of] which render 1d and the others less; and 540 messuages so empty that they render nothing at all; and Frenchmen hold 145 messuages. St Cuthbert has 1 house which he always had, as many say, quit of every customary due; but the burgesses say that it was not quit in the time of King Edward, unless as a [house] of the burgesses, save only that on account of it he had his own toll and [that] of the canons. Besides this, the Bishop of Durham has as the gift of the king the Church of All Saints and what belongs to it, and the whole land of Uhtræd, and the land of Earnwine which Hugh the sheriff has delivered to Bishop Walcher by the king's writ and the burgesses who dwell in it say that they hold it under the king.

The Count of Mortain has there 14 messuages, and 2 stalls in the Shambles, and the Church of St Cross. Osbern fitzBoso received these and whatsoever belongs to them. These messuages belonged to these men: Sunulf the priest, 1; Morulf, 1; Sterri, 1; Snarri, 1; Gamal with 4 drengs, 1; Arnketil, 5; Lyfing the priest, 2; Thorfinnr, 1; Ligulf, 1.

Nigel de Muneville has 1 messuage of a certain moneyer.

Nigel Fossard has 2 messuages of Modgifu, and he holds of the king.

Waldin has usurped 2 messuages of Ketil the priest in exchange for 1 messuage of Sterri.

Hamelin has 1 messuage in the ditch of the city; and Waldin 1 messuage of Einulf and 1 messuage of Alwine.

Richard de Sourdeval [has] 2 messuages of Thorkil and Ramkel. Nigel Fossard has usurped 2 messuages, but he said that he had returned them to the Bishop of Coutances.

William de Percy has 14 messuages of these men: Beornwulf, Gamal Barn, Swart, Ecgbeorht, Selakollr, Alfgrimr, Northmann, Dunstan, Othulf, Weleret, Ulfkil, Godelind, Sunngifu, Odbert; and the Church of St Mary. Of Earl Hugh, the same William has 2 messuages of 2 reeves of Earl Harold; but the burgesses say that 1 of them had not been the earl's, and that the other had been forfeited to him. Also the same William avows [that he holds] the Church of St Cuthbert of Earl Hugh, and 7 very small messuages measuring 50 feet in breadth. Concerning a messuage of a certain Uhtræd, moreover, the burgesses say that William de Percy had removed it for himself into the castle after he returned from Scotland. William himself, however, denies that he had the land of the same Uhtræd but says that through Hugh the sheriff he had taken the house of [Uhtræd] himself into the castle, in the first year after the destruction of the castles.

Hugh fitzBaldric has 4 messuages of Ealdwulf, Hedned, Thorkil and Gospatric, and 29 very small lodgings, and the Church of St Andrew which he bought. Robert Malet has 9 messuages of these men: Tumi, Grim, Grimkel, Earnwig, Alsige, and another Earnwig, Gluniairnn, Healfdene [and] Ramkel. Erneis de Buron has 4 messuages of Grim, Alwine, Gospatric, and Gospatric, and the Church of St Martin. 2 of these messuages render 14s. Gilbert Maminot has 3 messuages of Murdac. Berengar de Tosny has 2 messuages of Gamal-Karli and Alwine, and 8 messuages for lodgings. Half of these are in the ditch of the city. Osbern d'Arques has 2 messuages of Brun the priest and his mother, and 12 messuages of lodgings, and 2 messuages [held] of the Bishop of Coutances. Odo the crossbowman has 3 messuages of Forne and Orm, and 1 lodging of Elaf, and 1 church. Richard fitzErfast [has] 3 messuages of Ealhmund and Gospatric and Beornwulf, and the Church of HOLY TRINITY. Hubert de Mont-Canisy [has] 1 messuage, [namely] of Bondi. Landric the carpenter has 10½ messuages, which the sheriff leased to him.

TRE the city was worth to the king £53; now £100 by weight.

In the shire of the archbishop there were TRE 200 inhabited messuages, less 11; now there are 100 inhabited [messuages], both great and small, besides the court of the archbishop and the houses of the canons. In this shire the archbishop has as much as the king has in his shires.

In the geld of the city are 84 carucates of land, and each

paid as much geld as 1 house in the city, and were [assessed] with the citizens for the 3 works of the king. Of these the archbishop has 6 carucates, which 3 ploughs could plough. These belong to the farm of his hall. This [land] was not inhabited TRE, but tilled in places by the burgesses; now it is the same. Of this land, the king's pool destroyed 2 new mills worth 20s, and fully 1 carucate of arable land and meadows and gardens. TRE worth 16s; now 3s.

In Osbaldwick [is] land of the canons of 6 carucates, where there could be 3 ploughs. There the canons now have 2½ ploughs, and 6 villans and 3 bordars having 2½ ploughs. Also the canons have in Murton [in Osbaldwick] 4 carucates of land, where there could be 2 ploughs, but it is waste. These 2 vills are 1 league broad and 1 long.

In Stockton on the Forest are 6 carucates, where there could be 3 ploughs. They are waste. Of these, 3 belong to the canons and 3 to Count Alan. It is half a league long and a half broad. In these [is] neither meadow nor woodland.

In Sandburn are 3 carucates where there could be 1½ ploughs. It is waste. Ralph Paynel holds it. The canons say that they had it TRE.

In Heworth, Orm had 1 manor of 6 carucates of land, which 3 ploughs could plough. Now Hugh fitzBaldric has 1 man and 1 plough. TRE worth 10s; now 5s.

In the same vill Waltheof had 1 manor of 3 carucates of land. Now Richard has it of the Count of Mortain. TRE worth 10s; now 10s8d. This vill [is] 1 league long and a half broad.

In Gate Fulford, Morcar had 1 manor of 10 carucates of land. Now Count Alan has it. There could be 5 ploughs. In demesne there are now 2 ploughs; and 6 villans there have 2 ploughs. It is in length

[Folio 298V: YORKSHIRE]

1 league and half a league broad. TRE worth 20s; now 16[s].

Within the circuit of the city Thorfinnr had 1 carucate of land, and Thorkil 2 carucates of land. 2 ploughs could plough these.

In Clifton [near York] are 18 carucates of land paying geld. 9 ploughs could plough this. Now it is waste; TRE it was worth 20s.

Of these, Morcar had 9½ carucates of land paying geld, which 5 ploughs could plough. Now Count Alan has 2 ploughs there, and 2 villans and 4 bordars with 1 plough. In it are 50 acres of meadow. Of these, 29 belong to St Peter and the others belong to the count. Besides these, the archbishop has there 8 acres of meadow. This manor [is] 1 league long and another broad. TRE worth 20s; now the same. The canons have 8½ carucates. They are waste.

In Rawcliffe are 3 carucates of land paying geld which 2 ploughs could plough. Of these, Seaxfrith the deacon had 2 carucates with a hall, now St Peter [has them], and they were worth 10s; and Thorbiorn had 1 carucate with a hall, now the king [has them], and they were worth 5s. Now each is waste. There are 3 acres of meadow. All together [it is] half a league long and as much broad.

In Overton are 5 carucates of land to the geld, which 2½ ploughs could plough. Morcar had a hall there. Now Count

Alan has 1 plough there, and 5 villans and 3 bordars with 3 ploughs, and [there are] 30 acres of meadow, and woodland pasture 1 league long and 2 furlongs broad. All together [it is] 1 league long and 2 furlongs broad. TRE, as now, [worth] 20s.

In Skelton [near York] are 9 carucates of land to the geld, which 4 ploughs could plough. Of these, St Peter had TRE, and has, 3 carucates, and it was worth 6s; now it is waste. Of this land, Thorbiorn held 2 carucates, with a hall, and 6 bovates. Now 1 rent-paying tenant has it under the king, and there are 2 ploughs, and 6 villans. TRE [worth] 6s; now 8[s]. Of the same land, 2 carucates and 6 bovates belong to Overton. Count Alan has 1 man there with 1 plough. All together [it is] half a league long and a half broad.

In 'Mortona' [in Overton] are 3 carucates of land to the geld, which 1 plough could plough. Arnketil held this land, and it was worth 10s; now it is waste.

In Wigginton are [sic] 1 carucate to the geld, which 1 plough could plough. Seaxfrith the deacon held this; now St Peter has it. It was and is waste. There is scrubland. All together [it is] half a league long and a half broad.

These had soke and sake and toll and team and all customary dues TRE: Earl Harold, Mærle-Sveinn, Ulf Fenman, Thorgot Lag, Toki son of Auti, Edwin and Morcar upon the land of Ingeld only, Gamal son of Osbeorht upon Cottingham only, Kofse upon Coxwold only, and Knut. Of these, he who transgressed paid a fine to no one, except to the king and the earl.

In the demesne manors the earl had nothing at all, nor the king in the manors of the earl, except what pertains to the spiritual jurisdiction, which belongs to the archbishop.

In all the land of St Peter of York, and St John, and St Wilfrid, and St Cuthbert, and of HOLY TRINITY, in like manner, [neither] the king, nor the earl, nor anyone else, had any customary dues there.

The king has 3 ways by land and a fourth by water. In these every forfeiture belongs to the king and the earl wherever the ways lead, whether through the land of the king, or of the archbishop, or of the earl.

If peace, given by the hand of the king or by his seal, be broken, a fine is paid to the king alone by 12 hundreds, each hundred £8.

[If] peace [is] given by the earl, and broken by anyone, a fine is paid to the earl himself by 6 hundreds, each hundred £8.

[If] anyone be exiled according to law, none but the king shall give him peace. But if the earl or the sheriff should have sent anyone out of the kingdom, they themselves can recall him and give him peace, if they will.

Those thegns who have had more than 6 manors give relief for [their] lands to the king only. The relief is £8.

But if he has had only 6 manors or less he gives 3 marks of silver to the sheriff for relief.

But the burgesses of the city of York do not give relief.

I THE LAND OF THE KING. IN YORKSHIRE

II The Archbishop of York, and the canons, and his men
III The Bishop of Durham and his men
IIII The Abbot of York
V Earl Hugh
VI Robert, Count of Mortain
VII Count Alan
VIII Robert de Tosny
IX Berengar de Tosny
X Ilbert de Lacy
XI Roger de Bully
XII Robert Malet
XIII William de Warenne
XIIII William de Percy
XV Drogo of Holderness
XVI Ralph de Mortimer
XVII Ralph Paynel
XVIII Walter d'Aincourt
XIX Gilbert de Ghent
XX Gilbert Tison
XXI Hugh fitzBaldric
XXII Erneis de Buron
XXIII Osbern d'Arques
XXIIII Odo the crossbowman
XXV Richard fitzErfast
XXVI Geoffrey Alselin
XXVII Aubrey de Coucy
XXVIII Gospatric
XXIX The land of the king's thegns

[Folio 299: YORKSHIRE]

The land of the King In Yorkshire

IN EASINGWOLD are 12 carucates of land to the geld, which 7 ploughs could plough. Morcar held these as 1 manor TRE. Now it is in the king's hand, and there are 10 villans having 4 ploughs. [There is] a church with a priest. [There is] woodland pasture 2 leagues long and 2 broad. All together [it is] 3 leagues long and 2 broad. Then worth £32; now 20s.

To this manor belongs the soke of these lands: in Huby, 4 carucates; in Moxby, 3 carucates; in Murton [in Sutton-on-the-Forest], 2½ carucates; in 'Thorpe' [in Sutton-on-the-Forest], Sutton-on-the-Forest, Kelsit and Cold Kirby, 17 carucates; in Thormanby, 1½ carucates; in Sandhutton, 6 carucates; in Sowerby [near Thirsk], 3 carucates, and 2 others belonging to the hall, with a mill which renders 20s. All together there are 39 carucates to the geld, which 20 ploughs could plough. There are only 2 villans and 4 bordars having 1½ ploughs. The remaining land is waste. Yet there is woodland, pasture in some [places], 1½ leagues in length and the same in breadth.

IN NORTHALLERTON are 44 carucates of land to the geld, which 30 ploughs could plough. Earl Edwin held this as 1 manor TRE, and had 66 villans with 35 ploughs. To this manor belong 11 Berewicks: Birkby, Great Smeaton, Sowerby [in Kirby Sigston], Little Smeaton [in Birkby], Kirby Wiske, East Cowton, Landmoth, Borrowby [in Leake], Thornton-le-Beans, Romanby, Yafforth. It is now in the king's hand, and is waste; it was then worth £80. There is a meadow of 40 acres, [and] woodland and open land 5 leagues long and the same broad.

To this manor belongs the soke of these lands: Newsham [near Northallerton], "Westhuse" [? in Newsham, near Northallerton], Maunby, Warlaby, Ainderby Steeple, Yafforth, Lazenby [near Northallerton], Over Dinsdale, West Rounton, Irby, 'West Harlsey' [in Osmotherley], Kirby Sigston, Cowesby, Thimbleby, Leake, Knayton, Ravensthorpe, Thornton-le-Street, Crosby, North Otterington, Romanby, Brompton [near Northallerton], North Kilvington, Knayton. All together there are 85 carucates to the geld, which 45 ploughs could plough. There are 60 acres of meadow. There were 116 sokemen. Now it is waste.

In FALSGRAVE and Northfield, a Berewick, are 15 carucates of land to the geld, which 8 ploughs could plough. Tosti held this as 1 manor. Now it belongs to the king. There are 5 villans having 2 ploughs. [There is] woodland pasture 3 leagues long and 2 leagues broad. All together [it is] 6 leagues long and 4 broad. TRE worth £56; now 30s.

To this manor belongs the soke of these lands: Osgodby [near Scarborough], 4 carucates; Lebberston, Gristhorpe, "Scagetorp" [in Gristhorpe], "Eterstorp" [in Gristhorpe], "Rodebestorp" [in Gristhorpe], Filey, 'Burton Dale' [in Scarborough], [High, Low and Middle] Deepdale, West Ayton, "Neuuetun" [in West Ayron], 'Preston' [in Hutton Buscel], Hutton Buscel, Martin Garth, Wykeham [near Ruston], Ruston, Thirley Cote, Staintondale, Burniston, Scalby, Cloughton.

All together there are 84 carucates to the geld, which 42 ploughs could plough. In these were 108 sokemen with 46 ploughs. Now there are 7 sokemen and 15 villans and 14 bordars having 7½ ploughs. The rest are waste.

In PICKERING are 37 carucates of land to the geld, which 20 ploughs could plough. Morcar held this as 1 manor, with its Berewicks, Barton-le-Street, Newton-on-Rawcliffe, Blansby and Easthorpe [in Appleton-le-Street]. Now the king has it. There is 1 plough; and 20 villans with 6 ploughs. [There is] meadow half a league long and as much broad. But all the woodland which belongs to the manor is 16 leagues long and 4 broad. This manor was worth TRE £88; now 20s4d.

To this manor belongs the soke of these lands: Brompton [near Snainton], 3 carucates; "Odulfesmare" [in Marishes], Ebberston, Allerston, Wilton [near Thornton Dale], 'Farmanby' [in Thornton Dale], 'Roxby' [in Thornton Dale], Kingthorpe, "Chiluesmares" [in Marishes], "Aschilesmares" [in Marishes], "Maxudesmares" [in Marishes], Snainton, "Chigogemers" [in Thornton Dale], Ellerburn, Thornton Dale, Levisham, Middleton [near Pickering], Barton-le-Street. All together there are 50 carucates to the geld, which 27 ploughs could plough. There are now only 10 villans having 2 ploughs. The rest [is] waste; nevertheless there are 20 acres of meadow. All together [it is] 16 leagues long and 4 broad.

In HEMINGBROUGH are 3 carucates to the geld, which 2 ploughs could plough. Tosti held this as 1 manor. Now the king has there 5 villans and 3 bordars with 2 ploughs. There is a priest and a church, 7 acres of meadow, [and] woodland pasture half a league long and as much broad. All together [it is] 1 league long and a half broad. TRE worth 40s; now 16s.

In MARKET WEIGHTON, with a Berewick Shiptonthorpe, are 30 carucates to the geld, in which there could be 30 ploughs. Morcar held this as 1 manor. Now the king has 1 plough there; and 8 villans with 4 ploughs, and 5 bordars. [There is] meadow 1 league long and a half broad. The whole [is] 4 leagues long and 3 broad. TRE worth £30; now 60s.

To this manor belongs the soke of 1 carucate in North Cliffe, which 1 plough could plough; and in Goodmanham, sokeland, 1½ carucates to the geld; in Houghton, sokeland, 4½ carucates to the geld.

In WARTER, with 3 Berewicks, Harswell, 'Thorp' [in Thorpe le Street] [and] Nunburnholme, are 29 carucates to the geld, which 15 ploughs could plough. Morcar held this as 1 manor. Now the king has there 10 villans with 2 ploughs. There is a priest and a church, a mill rendering 2s, [and] 20 acres of meadow. The whole [is] 2 leagues long, and as much broad. TRE worth £40; now 30s.

To this manor belongs the soke of 8 carucates in Duggleby and "Turodebi" [in Kirby Grindalythe], where there could be 4 ploughs. They are waste.

[Folio 299V: YORKSHIRE]

IN GREAT DRIFFIELD, with 4 Berewicks, Kilham, Elmswell, Little Driffield [and] Kelleythorpe, are 23 carucates of land to the geld, which 12 ploughs could plough. Morcar held this as 1 manor TRE, and it was worth £40. Now the king has it, and it is waste.

To this manor belongs the soke of these lands: Great Kendale, 6 carucates; Kelleythorpe, 3 carucates; Eastburn [in Kirkburn], 6 carucates; Kirkburn, 5 carucates; Southburn, 7 carucates; Kilnwick, 5 carucates; Tibthorpe, 8½ [carucates]; Skerne, 1½ carucates; Cranswick, 1 carucate; Kilham, 6 carucates. In all, there are 50 carucates to the geld, and there could be 25 ploughs. It is waste.

In BESWICK are 2½ carucates to the geld and another half [carucate] which belonged to Iuli, which 2 ploughs could plough. The soke of this land belongs to Great Driffield, and yet Morcar had a manor there TRE, and it was worth 20s. Now it is waste. In the above-mentioned manor of Great Driffield there were 8 mills and 2 churches. The whole manor [is] 3 leagues long and 2 leagues broad.

IN POCKLINGTON, with 3 Berewicks, Hayton, Millington [and] Bielby, are 25 carucates to the geld, and there could be 15 ploughs. Morcar held this as 1 manor. Now the king has there 13 villans and 5 bordars having 5 ploughs, and 4 rent-paying tenants who pay 30s. There is a church and a priest, and 2 mills rendering 5s. The whole manor [is] 4 leagues long and 3 broad. TRE worth £56; now £8.

To this manor belongs the soke of these lands:

Nunburnholme, 1 carucate; Meltonby, 8 carucates; Grimthorpe, 4 carucates; Millington, 13 carucates; Burnby, 1½ carucates; Allerthorpe [near Pocklington], 6 carucates; Waplington, 2 carucates; Fangfoss, 8 carucates; Barmby Moor, 6 bovates; Great Givendale [near Pocklington], 8 carucates; Ousethorpe, 3 carucates. In all, there are 55½ carucates of land to the geld, and there could be 30 ploughs. Now, in the king's hand, there are 15 burgesses having 7 ploughs, and a mill rendering 2s. Moreover, in Kilnwick Percy there are 16 carucates of land to the geld, where there could be 8 ploughs. Of these carucates, 6 belong to the hall, and 10 are in the soke of Pocklington. [There is] woodland pasture 4 furlongs long and as much broad. The whole of Kilnwick Percy [is] 1 league long and half a league broad.

IN BRIDLINGTON, with 2 Berewicks, Hilderthorpe and Wilsthorpe, are 13 carucates to the geld, which 7 ploughs could plough. Morcar held this as 1 manor. Now it is in the king's hand, and there are 4 burgesses paying rent. [There are] 8 acres of meadow, [and] 1 church. The whole manor [is] 2 leagues long and half a league broad. TRE worth £32; now 8s.

To this manor belongs the soke of these lands: Marton [in Sewerby], 6 carucates; Bessingby, 8 carucates; Easton, 5 [carucates]; Boynton, 2 [carucates]; and another Boynton [Boynton Hall], half a carucate; Grindale, 8 [carucates]; Speeton, 4 [carucates]; Buckton, 5 [carucates]; Flixton, 4 [carucates]; Staxton, 1 [carucate]; Foxholes, 2 [carucates]; "Elestolf" [in Brigham], 1 [carucate]; Ganton, 7 [carucates]; Willerby [near Staxton], 5 [carucates]. In all, there are 58½ carucates to the geld, which 30 ploughs could plough. Now there are 3 villans and 1 sokeman with 1½ ploughs. The rest [is] waste.

In HENSALL [are] 4 carucates of land to the geld. [There is] land for 2 ploughs. There are 5 sokemen and 12 bordars with 1 plough, and 1 acre of meadow. Barth held it TRE, and it was worth £4; now 10s.

In "SANTONE" [in Woolley] and Woolley [are] 12 carucates of land to the geld. [There is] land for 8 ploughs. There is 1 villan and 1 sokeman and 1 bordar with 2 ploughs, and 1 acre of meadow. Thorkil held it TRE, and it was worth £3; now 10s.

IN BURTON AGNES, with 3 Berewicks, Gransmoor, Harpham [and] Boythorpe, are 25 carucates of land to the geld, which 15 ploughs could plough. Morcar held this as 1 manor TRE, and it was then worth £24. Now 1 rent-paying tenant pays 10s to the king. The whole manor [is] 1 league long and as much broad.

To this manor belongs the soke of these lands: Langtoft, 3 carucates; Haisthorpe, 4 carucates; Thwing, 8 carucates; Potter Brompton, 3 carucates; Thornholme, 7 carucates. In all, there are 25 carucates to the geld, which 14 ploughs could plough. Now it is waste.

In WAKEFIELD, with 9 Berewicks, Sandal Magna, Sowerby [near Halifax], Warley, Midgley, 'Wadsworth' [in Heptonstall], 'Cruttonstall' [in Erringden], Longfield [and] Stansfield, are 60 carucates of land and 3 bovates and the third part of 1 bovate to the geld. 30 ploughs could plough this land. This manor was in the demesne of King Edward; now, in the king's hand, there are 4 villans, and 3 priests and 2 churches, and 7 sokemen and 16 bordars. Together, they have 7 ploughs. [There is] woodland pasture 6 leagues long and 4 leagues broad. The whole [is] 6 leagues long and 6 leagues broad. TRE worth £60; now £15.

To this manor belongs the soke of these lands: Crigglestone, 10 bovates; West Bretton, 1 carucate; Horbury, 2 [carucates] and 7 bovates; Ossett, 3½ carucates; Earlsheaton, 1 carucate; Stanley, 3 carucates; 'Shitlington' [in Thornhill], 6 bovates; Emley, 3 carucates; Cartworth, 6 carucates; Kirkburton, 3 carucates; Shepley, 2 carucates; Shelley, 1 carucate; Lower Cumberworth, 1 carucate; 'Northcrosselande' [in Huddersfield], 1 carucate. In all, there are 30 carucates to the geld, which 20 ploughs could plough. Now they are waste, except Crigglestone and Horbury, where there are 4 sokemen and 1 villan and 3 bordars with 4 ploughs, and in Ossett, 4 villans and 3 bordars with 2 ploughs. In West Bretton is woodland pasture 1 league long and a half broad. In Horbury, woodland pasture 3 furlongs long and 3 broad, [and] in Ossett, woodland pasture half a league long and as much broad.

Besides this there are 2 carucates to the geld in Holme [near Holmfirth], and the other Holme [Yateholm], and Austonley and Upperthong. 1 plough could plough this land. It is waste. [There is] woodland in places. Some say this is thegnland, others, sokeland of Wakefield.

In NORMANTON are 10 carucates to the geld, which 5 ploughs could plough. 2 thegns had 2 manors there TRE. Now, in the king's hand, there are 6 villans and 3 bordars, a priest and a church with 3 ploughs. [There are] 3 acres of meadow, [and] woodland pasture 6 furlongs long and 1 furlong broad. The whole of this land lies in the soke of Wakefield, except the church. TRE worth 12s; now 10s.

Also in Dewsbury are 3 carucates to the geld, which 2 ploughs could plough. This land belongs to Wakefield; nevertheless, King Edward had a manor in it. Now it is in the king's hand, and there are 6 villans and 2 bordars with 4 ploughs. [There is] a priest and a church. The whole manor [is] 4 furlongs long and as much broad. TRE worth 10s; now the same.

In ALDBOROUGH, with 3 Berewicks, Clareton, "Hiltone" [? in Copgrove] and Burton Leonard, are 34 carucates to the geld, which 18 ploughs could plough. King Edward had a manor there. Now, under the king's hand, there are 6 villans with 5 ploughs. [There are] 8 acres of meadow. The whole manor [is] 1 league long and as much broad. TRE worth £10; now 55s.

[Folio 300: YORKSHIRE]

To this manor belongs this sokeland: Ellenthorpe [in Aldborough], 6 carucates; Milby, 6 carucates; Felliscliffe, 3 carucates; Killinghall, 1 carucate; 'Clifton' [in Norwood], 1 carucate; Timble, 1 carucate; Whipley, 1 carucate; South Stainley, 2 carucates. Together, to the geld, [there are] 21 carucates of land. [There is] land for 12 ploughs. They are all waste.

In KNARESBOROUGH, 6 carucates, with 11 Berewicks: Walkingham Hill, 3 carucates less 2 bovates; Ferrensby, 3 carucates less 2 bovates; Scriven, 6 carucates; 'Beeston' [in Fewston], 4 carucates; Fewston, 3 carucates; Brearton, 6 carucates; Susacres, 1 carucate; Cayton [in South Stainley], 2 carucates; Farnham, 3 carucates; South Stainley, 2 carucates; [...]. Together there are to the geld 42 carucates of land, less half [a carucate]. There is land for 24 ploughs. King Edward had this manor in demesne. Now it is under the king's hand and is waste. TRE worth £6; now it renders 20s. In 'Beeston' [in Fewston] only is woodland pasture half a league long and a half broad.

In FERRENSBY is sokeland of this manor, 3 carucates and 3 bovates. [There is] land for 2 ploughs. It is waste.

NORTH RIDING

LANGBAURGH WAPENTAKE

In NORMANBY [in Fylingdales], Ligulf had 2 carucates of land. Land for 2 ploughs. 1 league long and a half broad. TRE it was worth 16s.

In Roxby [near Loftus], Northmann, 1 carucate of land. Land for 1 plough.

In Ugthorpe, Ligulf, 2 carucates of land to the geld. Land for 2 ploughs. 2 leagues long and 1 broad. TRR [sic] [it was worth] 10s. Within this boundary, Gamal, 2 carucates to the geld. Land for 2 ploughs.

In Boulby, Ketilbert, 1 carucate of land to the geld. Land for 1 plough. 8s.

In LOFTUS 2 thegns had 4 carucates of land to the geld. Land for 3 ploughs. 8 acres of meadow, and scrubland there. 3 leagues long and 1 broad. TRE [it was worth] 20s.

In "Steintun" [in Stanghow] is 1 bovate of land to the geld.

In Moorsholm, half a carucate of land to the geld. Land for 2 oxen. 8s.

In KILTON THORPE, Thorkil, 2½ carucates of land to the geld. Land for 1 plough.

In KILTON THORPE, Thorkil, 3 carucates of land to the geld. Land for 2 ploughs. 8 acres of meadow there.

In Guisborough, Ulfkil, 1 carucate of land to the geld. Land for half a plough.

In Thornton Fields, Ulfkil, 2 carucates of land to the geld. Land for 1 plough. Half a league long and a half broad.

In Kirkleatham, Leysingr, 3 carucates of land to the geld. Land for 1½ ploughs. 4 acres of meadow there. TRE [it was worth] 10s.

In Lazenby [in Ormesby], Leofnoth, 3½ carucates of land to the geld. Land for 1½ ploughs. 3 acres of meadow there. TRE [it was worth] 10s.

In Upsall [in Ormesby], Northmann, 1 carucate to the geld. Land for half a plough.

In Pinchinthorpe, Ulfkil, 3 carucates of land to the geld. Land for 1½ ploughs. 4 acres of meadow there. TRE [it was worth] 10s.

In Aireyholme, Ealdræd, 2 carucates to the geld. Land for 1 plough.

In Little Ayton, Ulfkil, 2 carucates to the geld. Land for 1 plough. 16s.

In Newton under Roseberry, Magbanec, 6 carucates to the geld. Land for 3 ploughs. 1 carucate is sokeland of Little Ayton. TRE [it was worth] 10s.

In Morton [in Ormesby] and NUNTHORPE, Magbanec and Alfred, 9 carucates of land to the geld. Land for 5 ploughs. 4 acres of meadow there. TRE [it was worth] 20s.

In Dunsley, Thorulf, 3 carucates to the geld. Land for 1 plough. 32s.

In Thornaby-on-Tees, Ulfkil, 1½ carucates to the geld. Land for 1 plough.

In Great Ayton, Hawarth, 2 carucates of land to the geld. Land for 1 plough. 10s.

In Easby [near Ingleby Greenhow], Hawarth, 2 carucates to the geld. Land for 1 plough.

In Battersby, Hawarth, 2 carucates to the geld. Land for 1 plough.

In Marton [in Middlesbrough], Ulfkil, 1 carucate to the geld. Land for half a plough.

In Newham, Leysingr, 2 carucates and 2 bovates to the geld. Land for 1 plough. 10s.

In Tollesby, Leysingr, 2 carucates to the geld. Land for 1 plough.

In Acklam [in Middlesbrough], Leysingr [and] Ulfkil, 3 carucates to the geld. Land for 2 ploughs. 20s.

In Tunstall [in Nunthorpe], Leysingr, 3 carucates of land to the geld. Land for 2 ploughs.

In Tanton, Leysingr, 2½ carucates to the geld. Land for 1 plough. 20s.

In "Berguluesbi" [in Seamer, near Stokesley], Arnketil, 1 carucate to the geld. Land for half a plough.

In Skutterskelfe, Gamal, 2 bovates of land to the geld.

In Thoraldby, Arnketil, 1 carucate to the geld. Land for half a plough. 16d.

In Hilton [near Stokesley], Alvar, 3 carucates to the geld. Land for 1½ ploughs.

In "Camisedale" [in Ingleby Greenhow], Ulfkil, 5 carucates to the geld. Land for 2 ploughs. 10s.

In Great Broughton, Siward, 4 carucates to the geld. Land for 2 ploughs. 10s.

In Great Busby, Leysingr, 1½ carucates to the geld. Land for 1 plough.

In Faceby, Arnketil and Leysingr, 8 carucates to the geld. Land for 4 ploughs. Now there is 1 villan and 3 bordars [who] have 1 plough, and 10 acres of meadow. 2 leagues long and a half broad. TRE [worth] 30s; now 5s.

In Goulton, Arnketil, 1 carucate to the geld. Land for half a plough.

In Crathorne, Ulf, 5 carucates to the geld. Land for 3 ploughs. 40s.

In East Rounton, Thor and Karli, 8 carucates to the geld. Land for 4 ploughs. 40s.

In Cayton [near Scarborough], Hundgrimr and Gospatric, 4 carucates to the geld. Land for 2½ ploughs. 15s.

In Martin Garth and Wykeham [near Ruston], half a carucate to the geld.

In Brompton [near Snainton], Ulf, 1 carucate and 6 bovates to the geld. Land for 1 plough.

In Troutsdale, Arnketil, 2 carucates to the geld. Land for 1 plough.

In Allerston, Gospatric, 3 carucates to the geld. Land for 2 ploughs. 20s.

In Loft Marishes, Arnketil, 1½ carucates to the geld. Land for 1 plough.

In Thornton Dale, Thorbrandr, Gospatric and Thor, 3 carucates to the geld. Land for 2 ploughs.

In Ellerburn, Gospatric, 3 bovates of land to the geld.

In Low Dalby, Gospatric, 2 carucates to the geld. Land for 1 plough.

In 'Chetelestorp' [in Thornton Dale], Gospatric, 1 carucate to the geld. Land for half a plough.

In Lockton, Ulfkil, 5 carucates to the geld. Land for 4 ploughs. 40s.

In Aislaby [near Pickering], Gospatric, 4 carucates to the geld. Land for 2 ploughs.

In Wrelton, Gospatric, 1½ carucates to the geld. Land for 1 plough. Now there is 1 plough in demesne; and 7 villans with 2 ploughs, and 4 acres of meadow. Woodland pasture 3 furlongs. The whole manor, 1 league long and 3 furlongs broad. TRE worth 10s; now 6s8d.

In Cawthorne [in Middleton, near Pickering], Gospatric, 1 carucate to the geld. Land for half a plough.

In Cropton, Gospatric, 5 carucates to the geld. Land for 3 ploughs. In these 2 manors, woodland pasture 3 leagues long and 1 broad. The whole 4 leagues long and 1 league broad. 20s.

In "Baschebi" [in Lastingham], Gamal, 1 carucate to the geld. Land for half a plough.

In 'Thornton Riseborough' [in Normanby, near Salton], Gamal, 4 carucates to the geld. Land for 2 ploughs. 10s.

In [Great and Little] Habton, Ulf and Knut, 6½ carucates to the geld. Land for 2 ploughs. 6s.

In Ryton, Knut, 2½ carucates to the geld. Land for 1 plough. 2s.

In 'Newsham' [in Amotherby], Eadne, 10 bovates of land to the geld. Land for 1 plough.

[Folio 300V: YORKSHIRE]

In Amotherby, Knut, 2½ carucates to the geld. Land for 1 plough.

In Wykeham [in Malton], Siward, 1 carucate to the geld. Land for half a plough.

In another Wykeham [Wykeham Hill], Thorkil, 2 carucates to the geld. Land for 1 plough.

In Old Malton, Siward and Thorkil, 8 carucates to the geld. Land for 2 ploughs. There are now 1½ ploughs in demesne; and 7 villans and 5 bordars with 3½ ploughs. There is a church, and the site of 1 mill. TRE worth 20s; now 10s.

In Old Malton, Kolbrand, 3 carucates to the geld. Land for 1½ ploughs. There is 1 villan with half a plough, and 16 acres of meadow. 1 league long and 1 broad. TRE worth 10s; now 5s. There are 2 bovates of land to the geld, sokeland of the same manor.

In Broughton [in Appleton-le-Street], Gamal and Ligulf, 8 carucates and 2 bovates to the geld. Land for 5 ploughs. TRE it was worth 15s.

In Swinton [in Appleton-le-Street], Knut and Gamal, 11 carucates to the geld. Land for 5 ploughs. 1 league long and half a league broad. TRE [it was worth] 10s.

In Appleton-le-Street, Knut, 5 carucates to the geld. Land for 3 ploughs. 20s.

In Great Barugh, Ligulf, 2 carucates to the geld. Land for 1 plough.

In another Barugh [Little Barugh], Esbiorn, 1½ carucates to the geld. Land for 1 plough.

In High Northolme, Gamal, 1½ carucates to the geld. Land for 1 plough.

In Welburn [in Kirkdale], Grim, 1 carucate to the geld. Land for half a plough.

In Normanby [near Salton], Gamal, 3 carucates to the geld. Land for 1 plough.

In West Newton [in Oswaldkirk], Northmann and Grim, 2 carucates to the geld. Land for 1 plough.

In East Newton [in Stonegrave], Brune, 2 carucates to the geld. Land for 1 plough. Woodland pasture 4 furlongs long and 2 broad. 10s.

In Sproxton, Thorløgh, Northmann and Svartkollr, 4 caru-cates and 2 bovates to the geld. Land for 2 ploughs. TRE [it was worth] 10s.

In GRIFF, Grim, 2 carucates to the geld. Land for 1 plough.

In Stiltons, Fredegæst, 1 carucate to the geld. Land for half a plough.

In Helmsley, 3 thegns, 3½ carucates to the geld. Land for 2 ploughs.

In Harome, Svartkollr, 1½ carucates to the geld. Land for 1 plough.

In Riccal, Gamal, 2 carucates to the geld. Land for 1 plough.

In Nunnington, Gamal, half a carucate to the geld.

In Coulton, Øthulf, 1 carucate to the geld. Land for half a plough.

In Low Hutton, Knut [and] Thorkil, 8½ carucates to the geld. Land for 4 ploughs. TRE [it was worth] 10s.

In Scackleton, Gamal, half a carucate to the geld. Soke in Dalby.

In Sheriff Hutton, Thorkil, Thorulf [and] Thorsten, 4 caru-cates to the geld. Land for 2 ploughs. TRE it was worth 10s.

In Ganthorpe, Gamal, half a carucate to the geld.

In Wiganthorpe, Knut, 1 carucate to the geld. Land for half a plough.

In Hildenley, Knut, 2 carucates to the geld. Land for 1 plough.

In [East and West] Lilling, 4 thegns, 4 carucates to the geld. Land for 2 ploughs.

In Crambe, Sumarlithr, 4 carucates to the geld. Land for 2 ploughs. Now [there are] in demesne 5 villans with 2 ploughs, and half a church.

In Harton, Gospatric, 12 carucates to the geld. Land for 7 ploughs. There are now 4 villans with 2 ploughs. TRE [worth] 40s; now 8s.

In Claxton, Gospatric and Arnger, 3 carucates to the geld. Land for 2 ploughs. TRE [it was worth] 10s.

In Sand Hutton, Gospatric, 1 carucate to the geld. Land for half a plough.

In "Diche" [in Haxby], Gospatric and Uhtræd, 2 carucates to the geld. Land for 1 plough.

In Sutton-on-the-Forest, 1½ carucates to the geld, soke in "Caldenesche" [in Huby].

In Sutton-on-the-Forest, Ligulf and Egelfride, 1½ carucates to the geld. Land for 1 plough.

In Holtby [near York], 3 thegns, 6 carucates to the geld. Land for 3 ploughs.

In [East and West] Lilling, Ulf, 14 bovates of land to the geld. Land for 1 plough.

[...]

In Huntington, Fredegæst and Arngrim, 2 carucates and 6 bovates to the geld. Land for 2 ploughs.

In Flaxton, 3 thegns, 2½ carucates to the geld. Land for 2 ploughs.

In Raskelf, Knut, 8 carucates to the geld. Land for 4 ploughs.

[...]

In Myton-on-Swale, Gospatric and Aluerle, 3 carucates and 2 bovates to the geld. Land for 1½ ploughs.

In Brafferton, Gospatric, 5 carucates to the geld. Land for 2 ploughs. Now there is a church and a priest with 1 plough, and 3 villans with 1 plough. Half a league long and a half broad. TRE worth 40s; now 10s.

In the same manor Gospatric, 1 carucate to the geld. Land for half a plough. 1 villan there with 1 plough pays 2s.

In Oulston, Gospatric, 6 carucates to the geld. Land for 3 ploughs.

In Thorpe [near Ampleforth], 3 carucates to the geld. Land for 1 plough. Soke in Oulston.

In Carlton Miniott, Ulfkil, 4 carucates to the geld. Land for 2 ploughs.

In Newsham [in Kirkby Wiske], 2 Ligulfs, 2½ carucates to the geld. Land for 1 plough. 10s.

In Sowerby [near Thirsk], Orm, 2 carucates to the geld. Land for 1 plough.

In Thirsk, Orm, 8 carucates to the geld. Land for 4 ploughs. 20s.

In South Otterington, Egelfride and Haldor, 6 carucates to the geld. Land for 3 ploughs. 20s.

In Romanby, 3 thegns, 5 carucates and 1 bovate to the geld. Land for 2 ploughs. 16s.

In Hutton Bonville, 3 thegns, 6 carucates to the geld. Land for 3 ploughs. 20s.

In Little Smeaton [in Birkby], Madalgrim, 5 carucates to the geld. Land for 2 ploughs. 20s.

In High Worsall, Haldor and Alsige, 4 carucates to the geld. Land for 2 ploughs.

In another Worsall [Low Worsall], Hawarth, 3 carucates to the geld. Land for 2 ploughs.

In Appleton Wiske, Orm, 6 carucates to the geld. Land for 3 ploughs. 20s.

In Kirklevington, Hawarth, 6 carucates to the geld. Land for 3 ploughs. 40s.

In Yarm, Hawarth, 3 carucates to the geld. Land for 1 plough. 4s.

In another Levington ['Castlelevington', in Kirklevington], Hawarth, 4 carucates to the geld. Land for 2 ploughs. 5s.

In Welbury, Fredegæst and Maelmaedhog, 6 carucates to the geld. Land for 3 ploughs.

In 'West Harlsey' [in Osmotherley], Ligulf, 3½ carucates to the geld. Land for 2 ploughs.

In another Harlsey [East Harlsey], Madalgrim, 6 carucates to the geld. Land for 3 ploughs. 20s.

In Morton [in East Harlsey], 3 carucates to the geld. Land for 1 plough. Madalgrim.

In Ingleby Arncliffe, Madalgrim, 6 carucates to the geld. Land for 3 ploughs. 20s.

In Arncliffe [in Ingleby Arncliffe], Madalgrim, 2 carucates to the geld. Land for half a plough.

In 'Brodeby' [in Osmotherley], Madalgrim, 2 carucates to the geld. Land for 1 plough.

In Ellerbeck, Ligulf, 5 carucates to the geld. Land for 2 ploughs. 30s.

In Osmotherley, Ligulf and Elaf, 5 carucates to the geld. Land for 2 ploughs.

In Over Silton, Arnketil, 3 carucates to the geld. Land for 1½ ploughs.

In Sowerby [in Kirby Sigston], Dubhghall and Ulfkil, 2 carucates to the geld. Land for 1 plough. 10s.

In Crosby, Thor, 1 carucate to the geld. Land for half a plough. 5s.

In Kepwick, Arnketil and Gillemicel, 5 carucates to the geld. Land for 2 ploughs.

In Dale Town, Ulf and Eskil and Fredegæst, 3 carucates to the geld. Land for 2 ploughs. 8s.

In Hawnby, Fredegæst, 1½ carucates to the geld. Land for 1 plough.

EAST RIDING

In Anlaby, Forne, 9 bovates of land to the geld. Land for half a plough.

In Belby, Orm and Basinc, 4 bovates to the geld.

In Cleaving, Thorkil, 10 bovates to the geld. Land for 4 oxen. 6s.

In the same place Ligulf, Brune [and] Forne, 1 carucate and 6 bovates to the geld. Land for 1 plough. 16s.

In Old Sunderlandwick, Vifli and Siward, 1½ carucates to the geld. 7s.

In Tibthorpe, Vifli, 1 carucate to the geld. Land for 4 oxen. 10s.

In "Torp" [in Tibthorpe], Ulf, 2 carucates of land to the geld. Land for 1 plough. 20s.

In Naburn, Thorkil, 2 carucates to the geld. Land for 1 plough. 5s.

In Huggate, Barth $8\frac{1}{2}$ carucates to the geld. Land for 8 ploughs. 40s.

In Haywold, Grim and Ingrith, 5 carucates to the geld. Land for 2 ploughs. 20s.

In Yapham, Ulf and Wulfstan, 10 carucates and 6 bovates to the geld. Land for 2 ploughs. 40s.

In Bridlington, Karli, 4 carucates to the geld. Land for 2 ploughs. 20s.

In Auburn, Karli, half a carucate to the geld.

In Easton, Elaf, 1 carucate to the geld. Land for 4 oxen. 10s.

In Boynton, Ulf and Arnketil and Knut, 3 carucates to the geld. Land for 1 plough. 20s.

In Reighton, Tholf and Gamal, 5 carucates to the geld. Land for 2 ploughs. 16s.

In Flixton, Ottar and Karli, 10 carucates to the geld. Land for 5 ploughs. 50s.

In Staxton, Karli and Thorfinnr, 5 carucates to the geld. Land for 3 ploughs. 40s.

In Muston, Healfdene, 2 carucates to the geld. Land for 1 plough. 20s.

In Wold Newton, Ketilbert, 3 carucates to the geld. Land for $1\frac{1}{2}$ ploughs. 10s.

In the same place Ligulf, 1 carucate to the geld. Land for 4 oxen.

In Fordon and "Ledemare" [in Fordon], a Berewick, Karli, 6 carucates to the geld. Land for 3 ploughs. 20s.

In Burton Fleming, Karli, $14\frac{1}{2}$ carucates to the geld. Land for 7 ploughs. £4.

In the same place Ketilbert, $1\frac{1}{2}$ carucates to the geld. Land for 1 plough. 20s.

In Folkton, Karli and Ottar, 9 carucates to the geld. Land for 4 ploughs. 30s.

In Argam, Karli, 1 carucate to the geld. It belongs to Burton Fleming.

In Nafferton, Bark, 6 bovates to the geld.

In Little Kelk, Uhtræd, 2 carucates to the geld. Land for 1 ploughs. 4s.

In Kilham †3† thegns, 3 carucates and 2 bovates to the geld. Land for 3 ploughs. 40s.

In Ruston Parva, Ecgfrith, 3 carucates to the geld. Land for 2 ploughs. 20s.

In Lowthorpe, Ecgfrith, $1\frac{1}{2}$ carucates to the geld. Land for 1 plough. 10s.

In Low Caythorpe, Ketilbert and Ecgfrith, 5 carucates to the geld. Land for 3 ploughs. 20s.

In Thwing, Ketilbert and Grimkel, 2 carucates and 2 bovates to the geld. Land for 2 ploughs. 60s.

In "Fornetorp" [in Thwing], Thorulf, 1 carucate to the geld. Land for half a plough.

In the same place and in Octon, 3 carucates to the geld. It belongs to Thwing.

In Langtoft, Ottar, 3 carucates to the geld. Land for 2 ploughs. 10s. [...]

In Sutton [near Malton], Osweard, 2 carucates and 2 bovates to the geld. Land for 1 plough. 10s.

In the same place Ulfkil, half a carucate to the geld. It belongs to Norton [near Malton].

In Norton [near Malton], Ulfkil, 1 carucate and 1 bovate to the geld. 10s.

In Towthorpe [in Wharram Percy], Lagman and Sunulf, 3 carucates and 3 bovates to the geld. Land for 2 ploughs. 30s.

In the same place Karli, 2 carucates and 6 bovates to the geld. Land for 1 plough.

In Burdale, Ingifrith, 10 bovates to the geld. Land for 4 oxen.

In Scampston, 4 carucates to the geld. Soke in Rillington.

In the same place Orm, $1\frac{1}{2}$ carucates to the geld. Land for 1 plough. 6s.

In Thorpe Bassett, Ulfkil and Gamal and Knut, 5 carucates to the geld. Land for 3 ploughs. 20s.

In Rillington, Gilli, 2 carucates to the geld. Land for 1 plough. 10s.

In Menethorpe, Northmann, 2 carucates to the geld. Land for 1 plough. 5s.

In Eddlethorpe, Øthulf, 4 carucates to the geld. Land for 2 ploughs. 10s.

In Burythorpe, Ulf and Sprot, 2 carucates to the geld. Land for 1 plough. 5s.

In Kirby Underdale, 3 thegns, 4 carucates and 2 bovates to the geld. Land for 2 ploughs. 30s.

In Uncleby, Thorkil, 2 carucates to the geld. Land for 1 plough. 5s.

In Painsthorpe, 4 thegns, 4 carucates to the geld. Land for 2 ploughs. 20s.

In North Grimston, 5 thegns, 4 carucates to the geld. Land for 2 ploughs. 40s.

In Wharram Percy, Lagman and Karli, 8 carucates to the geld. Land for 4 ploughs. 60s.

In Fridaythorpe, Arnbiorn, 1 carucate to the geld. Land for half a plough. 5s.

In Raisthorpe, Hundingr and Grim, 3 carucates to the geld. Land for 2 ploughs. 40s.

In Kirby Grindalythe, Uglu-Barthr, half a carucate to the geld. Land for 1 plough. 10s.

In Croome, Mylnu-Grimr, 2 carucates to the geld. Land for 1 plough. 20s.

In the same place Uglu-Barthr and Alfrith, 2 carucates to the geld. Land for 1 plough. 20s.

In Cowlam, Ketilbert and his brother, 6 carucates to the geld. Land for 3 ploughs. 40s.

WEST RIDING

In Rawcliffe, Thorbiorn, 1 carucate to the geld. Land for half a plough. 5s.

In Skelton [near York], Thorbiorn, 2 carucates and 6 bovates to the geld. Land for 1 plough. 8s.

In Wothersome, Ligulf, 4 carucates to the geld. Land for 2 ploughs. 20s.

In Bardsey, Ligulf, 2 carucates to the geld. Land for 1 plough. 20s.

In [East and West] Morton, Eardwulf, 4 carucates to the geld. Land for 2 ploughs. 30s.

In Riddlesden, Eardwulf, 1 carucate to the geld. Land for half a plough. 16s.

In Shadwell, Ketil, 6 carucates to the geld. Land for 3 ploughs. 40s.

In "Mortune" [in Harewood], Arnketil, 3 carucates to the geld. Land for 2 ploughs. 10s.

In Harewood, with a Berewick, Thor, Sprot and Grim, 10 carucates to the geld. Land for 5 ploughs. 40s.

In East Keswick, Thor, 5 carucates to the geld. Land for 3 ploughs. 20s.

In Stockton, Hrosskell, 5 carucates and 6 bovates to the geld. Land for 4 ploughs. 20s.

In 'Newhall' [in Harewood], 1carucate to the geld. Sokeland [...]. Land for half a plough.

In Wike, Ligulf and Gluniairnn, 6 carucates to the geld. Land for 3 ploughs. 18s.

In Lofthouse [in Harewood], Alsige and Hrosskell, 2 carucates to the geld. Land for 1 plough. 10s.

In Stub House, Karli, 1 carucate to the geld. Land for half a plough. 10s.

In Alwoodley, Hrosskell, 5 carucates to the geld. Land for 3 ploughs. 20s.

In Horsforth, 3 thegns, 6 carucates to the geld. Land for 3 ploughs. 30s.

In Rawdon, Gluniairnn, Gamal and Sande, 3 carucates to the geld. Land for 2 ploughs. 10s.

In Yeadon, Gamal and Gluniairnn, 4 carucates to the geld. Land for 2 ploughs. 20s.

In Sprotbrough, Svartkollr, 1 carucate to the geld. Land for half a plough.

In Goldthorpe, Siward, 10 bovates to the geld. Land for half a plough. 20s.

In 'Waldershelf' [in Bolsterstone] and Onesacre, Godric, 1 carucate to the geld. Land for half a plough. 16s.

In Penistone, Alric, 10 bovates to the geld. Land for 1 plough. 20s.

In Darton, Arnbiorn, 1 carucate to the geld. Land for half a plough. 5s.

In Normanton, Godric and Cniht, 5 carucates of land to the geld. Land for 4 ploughs. Now there is a priest and a church and 6 villans and 3 bordars with 3 ploughs, and 3 acres of meadow. Woodland pasture 6 furlongs long and 1 broad. TRE worth 12s8d; now 10s8d. The whole of this land belongs as sokeland to Wakefield, except the church and 4 bovates of land.

In Holme [near Holmfirth], Dunstan, 2 carucates to the geld. Land for 1 plough. This land, some say, [is] inland, others, sokeland of Wakefield.

In Old Lindley, Godwine, half a carucate to the geld.

In Rastrick, Godwine, half a carucate to the geld. [...] [Folio

In Bishopthorpe, Gluniairnn, 9 bovates to the geld. Land for 1 plough.

In Great Ouseburn, Alfred, Ramkel, Orm, Thorbrandr and Rawn, 12 carucates to the geld. Land for 6 ploughs. 1 league long and 1 broad. TRE [worth] £4; now 5s. 3 carucates are sokeland of Aldborough.

In Little Ouseburn, 5 carucates to the geld. Land for 3 ploughs. Inland, and sokeland of Knaresborough.

In Branton Green, Ulfkil, 1 carucate to the geld. Land for half a plough. 10s.

In Grafton, Orm and Suneman, 3 carucates to the geld. Land for 2 ploughs. 20s.

In the same place there is of the king ['s land] 1 carucate of land to the geld. Land for half a plough. 10s.

In Ribston ['Great Ribston' and Little Ribston], Gunnar, 1½ carucates to the geld. Land for 1 plough. 20s.

In Hopperton, Thorbiorn, 1½ carucates to the geld. Land for 1 plough. 10s.

In Allerton Mauleverer, Thorgrim, Ketil, Thorbiorn, Gunnar [and] Leysingr, 4 carucates to the geld. Land for 3 ploughs. TRE it was worth 30s.

In Arkendale, Claman, 1 carucate of land to the geld. Land for half a plough. 5s.

In Minskip, Gamal and Orm, 4 carucates to the geld. Land for 2 ploughs. 40s. Now there are 3 villans with 2 ploughs, paying 5s4d.

In Aldfield, Dolgfinnr, half a carucate to the geld.

In Laverton, Flotmann, half a carucate to the geld. Land for 4 oxen. 3s.

In 'Poppleton' [in Fountains Earth], Gospatric and Gamal Barn, 4 carucates to the geld. Land for 2 ploughs. 30s.

In Birstwith, Gamal Barn, 1 carucate to the geld. Land for half a plough. 5s.

In Rowden, Gamal Barn, 2 carucates to the geld. Land for 1 plough. 8s.

In Beamsley, Gamal Barn, 6 bovates to the geld. Land for half a plough. 5s.

In Addingham, Gamal Barn, 1 carucate to the geld. Land for half a plough. 5s.

In Leathley, 4 thegns, $2\frac{1}{2}$ carucates to the geld. Land for 1 plough. 40s.

In Weeton [near Harewood], Ketil, 3 carucates to the geld. Land for $1\frac{1}{2}$ ploughs. 16d.

In Addlethorpe, Egbrand, 1 carucate to the geld. Land for 4 oxen. 3s.

In Sicklinghall, Egbrand and Wulfric, 6 carucates to the geld. Land for 3 ploughs. 25s.

In Stainburn, 4 thegns, 5 carucates to the geld. Land for 2 ploughs. 40s.

In Rossett Green, Ulf, $1\frac{1}{2}$ carucates to the geld. Land for 1 plough. 10s.

In Castley, Alwine, 1 carucate to the geld, and Biarni and Alflæd, 1 carucate to the geld. Land for 2 ploughs. Everard, the man of William de Percy, tills it, but William does not acknowledge it. TRE worth 10s; now 16d.

In Kirby Hill, Gospatric, 6 carucates to the geld. Land for 3 ploughs. 20s.

In Brampton [in Kirby Hill], Thor, 4 carucates to the geld. Land for 2 ploughs. 20s.

In Grassington, Gamal Barn, 3 carucates to the geld.

In Threshfield, Gamal Barn, 4 carucates to the geld.

In Cononley, Thorkil, 2 carucates to the geld.

In [High and Low] Bradley, Arnketil, Thorkil and Gamal, 7 carucates to the geld.

In Farnhill, Gamal, 2 carucates to the geld.

In Kildwick, Arnketil, 2 carucates to the geld, and 1 church.

In Eastburn [in Kildwick], Gamal Barn, 2 carucates of land and 2 bovates to the geld.

In Utley, William, 1 carucate to the geld.

In Keighley, Ulfkil and Toli and Hrafnsvartr and William, 6 carucates to the geld.

In Wilsden, Gamal Barn, 3 carucates and [...] to the geld.

In Oakworth, Gamal Barn and William, 1 carucate to the geld.

In Newsholme [in Keighley], William, 1 carucate to the geld.

In Laycock, Hrafnsvartr, 2 carucates to the geld.

In Sutton-in-Craven, Ramkel, 2 carucates to the geld.

In Melling [near Carnforth, Lancs.] and Hornby [Lancs.] and Wennington [Lancs.], Ulf, 9 carucates to the geld.

In the same place Orm had $1\frac{1}{2}$ carucates to the geld.

In Thornton in Lonsdale and in [Nether or Over] Burrow [Lancs.], Orm, 6 carucates to the geld.

In BOLTON ABBEY, Earl Edwin had 6 carucates of land to the geld.

In Halton East, 6 carucates. In Embsay, 3 carucates inland and 3 carucates sokeland.

In Draughton, 3 carucates; [High and Low] Skibeden, 3 carucates; Skipton, 4 carucates; Low Snaygill, 6 carucates; Thorlby, 10 carucates; Addingham, 2 carucates.

Beamsley, 2 carucates; Holme [in Stirton], 3 carucates; Gargrave, 3 carucates; Stainton [in Bank Newton], 3 carucates.

Otterburn, 3 carucates; Scosthrop, 3 carucates; Malham, 3 carucates; Coniston Cold, 3 carucates; Hellifield, 3 carucates.

Anley, 2 carucates; Hanlith, 3 carucates. Together, to the geld, 77 carucates. They are waste.

AMOUNDERNESS

In PRESTON [Lancs.], Earl Tosti, 6 carucates to the geld. These lands belong there; Ashton [in Preston, Lancs.], 2 carucates; Lea Town [Lancs.], 1 carucate; Salwick [Lancs.], 1 carucate; Clifton [Lancs.], 2 carucates; Newton [in Kirkham, Lancs.], 2 carucates; Freckleton [Lancs.], 4 carucates; Ribby [Lancs.], 6 carucates; Kirkham [Lancs.], 4 carucates; Treales [Lancs.], 2 carucates; Westby [Lancs.], 2 carucates; [Great and Little] Plumpton [Lancs.], 2 carucates; Weeton [Lancs.], 3 carucates; Preese [Lancs.], 2 carucates; Warton [in Kirkham, Lancs.], 4 carucates; Lytham [Lancs.], 2 carucates; [Great and Little] Marton [in Poulton-le-Fylde, Lancs.], 6 carucates; Layton [Layton and Little Layton, Lancs.], 6 [carucates]; Staining [Lancs.], 6 carucates; Carleton [Carleton and Little Carleton, Lancs.], 4 carucates; Bispham [Lancs.], 8 carucates; Rossall [Lancs.], 2 carucates; Burn [Lancs.], 2 carucates; Thornton [Thornton and Little Thornton, in Poulton-le-Fylde, Lancs.], 6 carucates; Poulton [Poulton-le-Fylde and Little Poulton, Lancs.], 2 carucates; Singleton [Singleton and Little Singleton, Lancs.], 6 carucates; Greenhalgh [Lancs.], 3 carucates; [Great or Little] Eccleston [Lancs.], 4 carucates; another Eccleston [Great Eccleston or Little Eccleston, Lancs.], 2 carucates; Elswick [Lancs.], 3 carucates; Inskip [Lancs.], 2 carucates; Sowerby [in St Michael on Wyre, Lancs.], 1 carucate; "Aschebi" [Lancs.], 1 carucate; St Michael's on Wyre [Lancs.], 1 carucate; Catterall [Lancs.], 2 carucates; Claughton [in Garstang, Lancs.], 2 carucates; Newsham [Lancs.], 1 carucate; Woodplumpton [Lancs.], 5 carucates; Broughton [Lancs.], 1 carucate; Whittingham [Lancs.], 2 carucates; Barton [in

Preston, Lancs.], †3† carucates; Goosnargh [Lancs.], 1 carucate; Haighton [Lancs.], 1 carucate; 'Threlfall' [in Kirkham, Lancs.], 1 carucate; Wheatley [Lancs.], 1 carucate; Chipping [Lancs.], 3 carucates; 'Aighton' [in Mitton, Lancs.], 1 carucate; Fishwick [Lancs.], 1 carucate; Grimsargh [Lancs.], 2 carucates; Ribchester [Lancs.], 2 carucates; Dilworth [Lancs.], 2 carucates; Swainshead [Swainshead and Lower Swainshead, Lancs.], 1 carucate; Forton [Lancs.], 1 carucate; [Great and Little] Crimbles [Lancs.], 1 carucate; Garstang [Lancs.], 6 carucates; 'Upper Rawcliffe' [in St Michael on Wyre, Lancs.], 2 carucates; another Rawcliffe [Rawcliffe, Lancs.], 2 carucates; a third Rawcliffe [Out Rawcliffe, Lancs.], 3 carucates; Hambleton [Lancs.], 2 carucates; Stalmine [Lancs.], 4 carucates; Preesall [Lancs.], 6 carucates; Mythop [Lancs.], 1 carucate.

All these vills and 3 churches belong to Preston [Lancs.]. Of these [vills], 16 are inhabited by a few people; but it is not known how many the inhabitants are. The rest are waste, Roger de Poitou had them. [...]

In HALTON [Lancs.], Earl Tosti had 6 carucates of land to the geld.

In Aldcliffe [Lancs.], 2 carucates; [Lower and Upper] Thurnham [Lancs.], 2 carucates; Hillam [Lancs.], 1 carucate; Lancaster [Lancs.], 6 carucates; "Chercaloncastre" [In Lancaster, Lancs.], 2 carucates; 'Hutton' [in Lancaster, Lancs.], 2 carucates; 'Newton' [in Lancaster, Lancs.], 2 carucates; Overton [Lancs.], 4 carucates; Middleton [Lancs.], 4 carucates; Heaton [Lancs.], 4 carucates; [Higher and Lower] Heysham [Lancs.], †3† carucates; Oxcliffe [Lancs.], 2 carucates; 'Poulton' [in Morecambe, Lancs.], 2 carucates; Torrisholme [Lancs.], 2 carucates; Skerton [Lancs.], 6 carucates; Bare [Lancs.], 2 carucates; Slyne [Lancs.], 6 carucates; Bolton-le-Sands [Lancs.], 4 carucates; [Nether and Over] Kellet [Lancs.], 6 carucates; 'Stapleton Terne' [in Bolton-le-Sands, Lancs.], 2 carucates; "Neuhuse" [Lancs.], 2 carucates; Carnforth [Lancs.], 2 carucates.

All these vills belong to Halton.

In WHITTINGTON [Lancs.], Earl Tosti had 6 carucates of land to the geld.

In Newton [in Whittington, Lancs.], 2 carucates; Arkholme [Lancs.], 6 carucates; Gressingham [Lancs.], 2 carucates; Hutton Roof [Westm.], 3 carucates; Cantsfield [Lancs.], 4 carucates; Ireby [Lancs.], 3 carucates; [Nether or Over] Burrow [Lancs.], 3 carucates; Leck [Leck and Over Leck, Lancs.], 3 carucates; Burton in Lonsdale, 4 carucates; Barnoldswick [in Burton in Lonsdale], 1 carucate; Ingleton, 6 carucates; Casterton [Westm.], 3 carucates; Barbon [Westm.], 3 carucates; Sedbergh, 4 carucates; 'Thirnby' [in Whittington, Lancs.], 2 carucates.

All these vills belong to Whittington [Lancs.].

In AUSTWICK and "Heldetune" [?Yorks.], Clapham, Middleton [Westm.], Mansergh [Westm.], Kirkby Lonsdale [Westm.], Lupton [Westm.], Preston Patrick [Westm.], Holme [Westm.], Burton-in-Kendal [Westm.], Priest Hutton [Lancs.], Warton [near Carnforth, Lancs.],

Claughton [near Lancaster, Lancs.], Caton [Lancs.], Thorfinnr had these as 12 manors. In these there are 43 carucates to the geld.

In [High and Low] BENTHAM, Wennington [Lancs.], Tatham [Lancs.], Farleton [Lancs.], [and] Tunstall [Lancs.], Ketil had 4 manors, and in them are 18 carucates to the geld and 3 churches.

In "HOUGUN" [?Lancs.], Earl Tosti had 4 carucates of land to the geld.

In 'Killerwick' [in Dalton-in-Furness, Lancs.], †3† carucates; Sowerby [in Dalton-in-Furness, Lancs.], 3 carucates; "Hietun" [?Lancs.], 4 carucates; Dalton-in-Furness, [Lancs.], 2 carucates; "Warte" [?Lancs.], 2 carucates; Newton [in Dalton-in-Furness, Lancs.], 6 carucates; 'Walton' [in Dalton-in-Furness, Lancs.], 6 carucates; "Suntun" [?Lancs.], †2† carucates; 'Fordbottle' [in Dalton-in-Furness, Lancs.], 2 carucates; Roose [Lancs.], 6 carucates; 'Hart' [in Aldingham, Lancs.], 2 carucates; Leece [Lancs.], 6 carucates; another Leece [Lancs.], 2 carucates; Gleaston [Lancs.], 2 carucates; Stainton [Lancs.], 2 carucates; 'Crivelton' [in Dalton-in-Furness, Lancs.], 4 carucates; Orgrave [Lancs.], 3 carucates; Marton [in Dalton-in-Furness, Lancs.], 4 carucates; Pennington [Lancs.], 2 carucates; "Gerleuuorde" [?Lancs.], 2 carucates; "Borch" [?Lancs.], 6 carucates; Bardsea [Lancs.], 4 carucates; Whicham [Cumb.], †4† carucates; Bootle [Cumb.], 4 carucates; Kirksanton [Cumb.], 1 carucate; "Hougenai" [?Lancs.], 6 carucates. All these vills belong to "Hougun" [? Lancs.].

[Folio 302: [YORKSHIRE]]

In 'STRICKLAND [ketel and Roger]' [in Kendal, Westm.], Mint [Westm.], Kendal [Westm.], Helsington [Westm.], Stainton [Westm.], 'Bothelford', [in Kendal, Westm.], Old Hutton [Westm.], Burton-in-Kendal [Westm.], Dalton [Westm.], Patton [Westm.], Gillemicel had these [vills]. In these there are 20 carucates of land to the geld.

In [?] Kirkby [near Ulverston, Lancs.], Dubhan, 6 carucates to the geld.

In Aldingham [Lancs.], Earnwulf, 6 carucates to the geld.

In Ulverston [Lancs.], Thorulf, 6 carucates to the geld.

In Bolton [Lancs.], 6 carucates. In [?] Dendron [Lancs.], 1 carucate.

The land of the Archbishop of York

In PATRINGTON, with 4 Berewicks, Winestead, Halsham, Thorpe [in Welwick] [and] | 'Thurlesthorp' [in Patrington] |, are 35½ carucates and 2 bovates and 2 parts of 1 bovate to the geld. There is land for 35 ploughs. This manor belonged and belongs to the Archbishop of York.

Now there are in demesne 2 ploughs; and 8 villans and 63 bordars having 13 ploughs. There 6 sokemen with 2 villans and 20 bordars have 5½ ploughs. There are 32 acres of meadow.

Of the land of this manor 2 knights have 6 carucates, and 2

clerks [have] 2 carucates and 3 bovates and the third part of 1 bovate. They have there 4 sokemen and 5 villans and 3 bordars with 5 ploughs. TRE it was worth £30; now £10.5s. The arable land [is] 3 leagues long and 1½ leagues broad.

In SWINE, with 4 Berewicks, are 10 carucates of land and 2 bovates to the geld. [There is] land for 8 ploughs. This manor belonged and belongs to the Archbishop of York. Now he has in demesne there 1 plough; and 8 villans and 6 bordars having 3½ ploughs. There is a priest with half a plough. There are 30 acres of meadow. [It is] 3 leagues long and 1 broad. TRE worth 100s; now 40s.

In BURNBY [are] 4 carucates to the geld. [There is] land for 4 ploughs. This manor belonged and belongs to the Archbishop of York. Now Geoffrey, the man of the archbishop, has in demesne 2 ploughs; and 14 villans and 4 bordars with 6 ploughs, and 1 mill [rendering] 6s. TRE it was worth [...].

In COULTON, the king's vill, the archbishop has half a carucate of land, the soke of which belongs to Helmsley, a manor of the king.

[Folio 302V: YORKSHIRE]

II. The land of the Archbishop of York

IN SHERBURN IN ELMET, with its Berewicks, there are, to the king's geld, 96 carucates of land, in which there could be 60 ploughs. This manor was and is in the demesne of the Archbishop of York. In it he now has 7 ploughs in demesne; and 30 villans and 8 bordars with 10½ ploughs, and 6 sokemen and 15 bordars having 6½ ploughs. There are 2 churches, and 2 priests with 1 bordar having 1 plough. 1 mill renders 10s. In the whole manor [there are] 350 acres of meadow. [There is] woodland pasture 8 leagues long and 3 leagues broad, and scrubland 4 leagues long and 1 broad, [and] open land 5 leagues long and 2 [leagues] and1 furlong broad.

Of this land the archbishop's knights have 52 carucates, where they have in demesne 16 ploughs; and 60 villans and 75 bordars having 34 ploughs. Of this land 1 thegn has 5 carucates and 1 bovate, where he has 2 sokemen and 6 villans and 18 bordars having 7 ploughs. Of this land 2 clerks have 6 carucates, where they have in demesne 2½ ploughs; and 5 villans and 5 bordars having 4 ploughs. Of the same land the Abbot of Selby has 7 carucates.

This manor TRE was worth £34.6s; now the same; and it is in Barkston WAPENTAKE.

The archbishop has near the city 15 carucates to the geld, which 15 ploughs could plough. He has there in demesne 2 ploughs, and 60 acres of meadow. This land is 1 league long and 1 broad. This, and all that which he has in the city, TRE was worth £8; now £10.

IN ELLOUGHTON and in WAULDBY are 17 carucates of land to the geld, where there could be 9 ploughs. Archbishop Ealdræd held this as 1 manor. Now Archbishop Thomas has it, and Godwine [holds] of him. He has there 1 plough; and 36 villans and 3 bordars having 11 ploughs. Of this land 1 knight

has 2 carucates, and there is 1 plough. There is a priest and a church, [and] meadow 5 furlongs long and 1 furlong broad. The whole manor [is] 2 leagues long and 1 broad. TRE worth £7; now 100s.

IN WALKINGTON are 8 carucates and 1 bovate to the geld, where there could be 4 ploughs. Archbishop Ealdræd held this as 1 manor. Now the canons of St Peter have it under Archbishop Thomas. In demesne [is] 1 plough; and 14 villans and 8 bordars with 6 ploughs. TRE worth 40s; now 30s.

In NORTH CAVE there is 1 carucate and 6 bovates to the geld, where there could be 1 plough. Archbishop Ealdræd held this as 1 manor. Now the canons of St Peter have it under Archbishop Thomas, and it is waste, except that 1 rent-paying tenant pays 10s8d.

In [North and South] NEWBALD are 28 carucates and 2 bovates to the geld, where there could be 16 ploughs. Archbishop Ealdræd held this as 1 manor. Now, under Archbishop Thomas, the canons of St Peter have in demesne 2 ploughs; and 7 villans with 2½ ploughs, and 4 mills rendering 30s. There is a church and a priest. The whole manor [is] 3 leagues long and 2 leagues broad. TRE worth £24; now £10.

In RICCALL are 2 carucates to the geld, and there could be 2 ploughs. Archbishop Ealdræd held this as 1 manor. Now, under Archbishop Thomas, the canons of St Peter [have] in demesne 2 ploughs; and 20 villans having 4 ploughs. [There is] meadow half a league long and as much broad, [and] woodland pasture 1 league long and a half broad. The whole manor [is] 1 league long and 1 broad. TRE worth 100s; now 30s.

IN DUNNINGTON [near York] are 4 carucates to the geld, and there could be 2 ploughs. 2 thegns, Slettan and Edwin, had 2 manors there. Now the canons of St Peter have there 2 villans with 1 plough. TRE worth 10s; now 15s.

In EVERINGHAM, with its Berewicks, Londesborough, 'Towthorpe' [in Londesborough] [and] Goodmanham, are 17 carucates to the geld, and there could be 10 ploughs. Archbishop Ealdræd held this as 1 manor. Now, under Archbishop Thomas, 2 clerks and 1 knight have this land, having among themselves 3 ploughs; and 22 villans having 6 ploughs, and 2 mills, [and] 10 acres of meadow. The whole manor [is] 1 league long and half a league broad. TRE worth £14; now £6.

IN WETWANG are 13½ carucates to the geld, and there could be 7 ploughs. Archbishop Ealdræd held this as 1 manor. Now Archbishop Thomas has it and it is waste. TRE it was worth £4. This manor is 2 leagues long and 1½ leagues broad.

IN BISHOP WILTON, with these Berewicks, Bolton [in Bishop Wilton], Gowthorpe, Youlthorpe, Greenwick [and] Fridaythorpe, there are 30 carucates and 7 bovates to the geld, and there could be 18 ploughs. Archbishop Eldræd held this as 1 manor. Now Archbishop Thomas has there 15 rent-paying tenants having 7 ploughs. There is a church and a priest, [and] meadow half a league long and 3 furlongs broad. The whole manor [is] 3 leagues long and 1 league broad. TRE worth £14; now £4.

In Fridaythorpe are 1½ carucates to the geld, of which the soke belongs to Bishop Wilton. It is waste.

IN GRINDALE are 4 carucates to the geld, and there could be 2 ploughs. St Peter of York held this as 1 manor. Now it is waste. TRE it was worth 30s.

IN BARMBY MOOR and Millington are 10 carucates and 2 bovates to the geld, and there could be 6 ploughs. Archbishop Ealdræd held this as 1 manor. Now, under Archbishop Thomas, there are 15 villans having 9 ploughs. The whole manor [is] 1 league long and a half broad. TRE worth 100s; now 40s.

In AIKE [are] 6 bovates to the geld, and there could be half a plough. Archbishop Thomas has there 2 villans with half a plough.

[Folio 303: YORKSHIRE]

IN LOW CAYTHORPE are 4 carucates to the geld, and 2 ploughs could plough it. This land belonged and belongs to St Peter. TRE worth 10s; now 8s.

IN LANGTOFT are 9 carucates to the geld, and there could be 5 ploughs. Ulf held this as 1 manor. Now St Peter has it, and it is waste. TRE it was worth 40s.

IN COTTAM are 9 carucates to the geld, and there could be 5 ploughs. Ulf had 1 manor there. Now St Peter has it and it is waste. It is 1 league in length and a half in breadth. TRE it was worth 40s.

IN WEAVERTHORPE, 18 carucates, with these Berewicks: Low Mowthorpe [in Kirby Grindalythe], 5 carucates, [and] Sherburn, 3 carucates, there are 26 carucates to the geld, and there could be 15 ploughs. Archbishop Ealdræd held this as 1 manor. Now Archbishop Thomas has it, and it is waste. TRE it was worth £14.

To this manor belongs Helperthorpe, where there are 12 carucates to the geld: 6 under soke, and 6 with sake and soke. It is waste.

To the same manor belongs the soke of these lands: North Grimston, 3½ carucates; Sutton [near Malton], half a carucate; Birdsall, 2½ carucates; Croome, 4 carucates; Thirkleby [in Kirby Grindalythe], 1 carucate; [East and West] Lutton, 8 carucates; "Ulchiltorp" [in West Lutton], 1 carucate. In these there are 2 sokemen and 3 bordars having 1 plough, and paying 10s. Walkelin the knight has North Grimston under the archbishop. The Church of Cowlam belongs to Archbishop Thomas, with half a carucate of land.

IN BUGTHORPE are 4½ carucates to the geld, and there could be 2 ploughs. Clibert had 1 manor there. Now St Peter has 2 rent-paying tenants there, who pay 20s4d. There are 8 acres of meadow. TRE it was worth 5s.

NORTH RIDING

IN WYKEHAM HILL is half a carucate to the geld. St Peter had and has it, and it is waste.

IN SALTON are 9 carucates to the geld, and there could be 5 ploughs. Ulf had 2 manors there. Now St Peter has in demesne half a plough; and 4 villans with 1½ ploughs. [There are] 12 acres of meadow, and a mill rendering 5s. This manor TRE was worth 20s; now 10s.

In BRAWBY are 6 carucates to the geld, and there could be 3 ploughs. Ulf had 2 manors there. Now St Peter has it, and it is waste. [There are] 6 acres of meadow. The whole manor [is] 1 league long and 1 broad. TRE it was worth 10s.

IN GREAT BARUGH and another BARUGH [Little Barugh] are 3½ carucates to the geld, and there could be 3 ploughs. Ulf had 3 manors there. Now St Peter has it and it is waste. There are 7 acres of meadow. TRE [it was worth] 11s4d. The whole [is] half a league long and 3 furlongs broad.

In EAST NEWTON [in Stonegrave] are 4 carucates to the geld, and there could be 2 ploughs. Gamal gave it to St Peter TRE; now it is waste. It was a manor.

IN NAWTON are 4 carucates to the geld, and there could be 2 ploughs. Ulf had it, and now St Peter has it. It is waste.

IN OLD MALTON [is] 1 carucate to the geld. Ulf had 1 manor.

IN WOMBLETON is 1 carucate to the geld. Ulf had 1 manor.

IN POCKLEY, 1 carucate to the geld. Ulf had 1 manor.

IN AMPLEFORTH, 3 carucates to the geld. Ulf had 1 manor.

IN FLAXTON, 6 bovates to the geld. Ulf had 1 manor.

IN MURTON [in Sutton-on-the-Forest], 2½ carucates to the geld. Ulf had 1 manor.

IN 'BAXBY' [in Husthwaite], 6 carucates and 1 bovate to the geld. Ulf had 1 manor.

IN CARLTON HUSTHWAITE, 4½ carucates to the geld. Ulf had 1 manor.

In all, [there are] 19 carucates and 7 bovates; and there could be 10 ploughs. Now St Peter has them. They are waste, except that 4 villans, having 2 ploughs, pay 2s. TRE they were worth 60s.

In Ampleforth are 8 acres of meadow. [There is] woodland pasture half a league long and as much broad. 'Baxby' [in Husthwaite], both woodland and open land, [is] 1 league long and another broad.

In STONEGRAVE Ulf held 6 bovates. The same man gave it to St Peter. [...]

IN HIGH BELTHORPE are 4 carucates to the geld.

IN GATE HELMSLEY, 4 carucates and 2 bovates to the geld.

In WARTHILL, 3 carucates to the geld.

In CARLTON [in Stockton on the Forest], 3 carucates to the geld.

In all, [there are] 14 carucates, and 8 ploughs could plough them. St Peter of York had and has these; and there are 8 villans in them, having 5 ploughs. The rest are waste. TRE worth 15s; now 20s.

IN MARTON [in Sewerby] [are] 3 carucates to the geld, and there could be 2 ploughs. St Peter had and has it, with sake and soke. TRE worth 10s; now 8s4d.

In STILLINGTON [are] 10 carucates to the geld, and there could be 6 ploughs. St Peter had and has it. [There are] 6 villans with 2 ploughs, and 1 mill [rendering] 3s. [There are] 8 acres of meadow, [and] woodland pasture 1½ leagues long and half a league broad. TRE worth 40s; now 10s.

In HAXBY [are] 6 carucates and 1 bovate to the geld, and there could be 4 ploughs. St Peter had and has it. There are 7 villans with 3 ploughs. TRE worth 20s; now 10s.

In TOLLERTON [are] 8 carucates to the geld, and there could be 4 ploughs. St Peter had and has it. Now [there are] in demesne 2 ploughs; and 6 villans and 2 bordars with 2 ploughs.

IN ALNE [are] 8 carucates to the geld, and there could be 4 ploughs. St Peter had and has it, but it is waste. These 2 estates are 1 league long and 1 broad. TRE they were worth 50s; now 40[s].

In HELPERBY [are] 5 carucates to the geld, and there could be 3 ploughs. St Peter had and has it, but it is waste. TRE it was worth 10s; now a certain Rayner holds it and pays 6s.

To this vill belongs the soke of these lands: Youlton, Tholthorpe and Wide Open, [and] Myton-on-Swale. In all, [there are] 11 carucates and 2 bovates to the geld, and there could be 7 ploughs. [There is] woodland pasture 1 league long and a half broad. The rest are waste.

[Folio 303V: YORKSHIRE]

In the same Helperby, St Peter had and has 3 carucates of land to the geld. [There is] land for 1½ ploughs. Seaxfrith held it of St Peter. It is waste.

In Strensall, Seaxfrith and Thorkil held of St Peter 5 carucates to the geld. [There is] land for 2 ploughs. It is waste.

In Towthorpe [in Huntington], Seaxfrith held of St Peter 3 carucates to the geld.

In Earswick, Seaxfrith and Godric held of St Peter 3 carucates to the geld.

In 'Corburn' [in Wigginton] the same Seaxfrith held of St Peter 3 carucates of land. All these are waste.

WEST RIDING

IN WARMFIELD [are] 9 carucates to the geld, and there could be 6 ploughs. St Peter had and has it. Ilbert holds it and has in demesne 1 ploughs; and 13 villans and 1 bordar with 5 ploughs, and [there are] 2 acres of meadow. [There is] woodland pasture 8 furlongs long and 5 broad. The whole manor [is] 1 league long and 1 broad. TRE worth £7; now 45s. It belongs to Osbaldwick; but, nevertheless, it was a manor.

IN UPPER POPPLETON [are] 8 carucates to the geld, and there could be 4 ploughs. St Peter had it as 1 manor. Now, under Archbishop Thomas, there are 2 villans with 1½ ploughs, and 1 prebendary. [There are] 12 acres of meadow,

[and] woodland pasture 4 furlongs long and 3 broad. TRE worth 40s; now 18s8d.

In ACOMB [are] 14½ carucates to the geld, and there could be 8 ploughs. St Peter had and has it as 1 manor. There are now 14 rent-paying tenants having 7 ploughs. [There are] 6 acres of meadow, [and] scrubland 2 furlongs long and 2 broad. The whole [is] 1 league long and a half broad. TRE worth 30s; now the same.

In OTLEY, with these Berewicks: 'Stublham' [in Ilkley], Middleton [in Ilkley], Denton, Clifton [near Newall], 'Bikerton' [in Newall with Clifton], Farnley [in Otley], Nether Timble, "Ectone" [in Lindley], Pool, Guiseley, Hawksworth, another Hawksworth [Thorpe, in Hawksworth], Baildon, Menston, Burley in Wharfedale, Ilkley.

In all, there are 60 carucates and 6 bovates to the geld, in which there could be 35 ploughs. Archbishop Ealdræd had this as 1 manor. Now Archbishop Thomas has in demesne 2 ploughs; and 6 villans and 10 bordars having 5 ploughs; and there are 5 sokemen having 4 villans and 9 bordars with 5 ploughs. [There is] a church and a priest with 1 villan and 1 plough. [There are] 4 acres of meadow, woodland pasture 2 leagues and 3 furlongs long and as much broad, scrubland 9 leagues long and as much broad, arable land 2 leagues long and 2 broad, [and] moor 2 leagues long and 1 broad. The greatest part of this manor is waste. TRE worth £10; now £3.

In GRAFTON [are] 3 carucates to the geld, and there could be 2 ploughs. This belongs to the sustenance of the canons, but it is waste. TRE [it was worth] 10s.

In ULLESKELF, with its Berewicks, are 13 carucates, less 1 bovate, to the geld, and 8 ploughs could plough it. Archbishop Ealdræd held this as 1 manor. Now, under Archbishop Thomas, William de Verly has 2 ploughs in demesne; and 8 villans and 9 bordars having 4 ploughs; and [there are] 3 sokemen with 2 villans and 5 bordars having 2½ ploughs. There is a church, 60 acres of meadow, woodland pasture 8 furlongs long and as much broad, water meadows 1 furlong long and 1 broad, [and] arable land 10 furlongs long and as much broad. TRE [worth] 100s; now £4.

In RIPON, [of] ST WILFRID'S LEAGUE, there could be 10 ploughs. Archbishop Ealdræd held this manor. Now Archbishop Thomas has in demesne 2 ploughs, and 1 mill [rendering] 10s, and 1 fishery [rendering] 3s; and 8 villans and 10 bordars having 6 ploughs. [There are] 10 acres of meadow, [and] scrubland. Of this land the canons have 14 bovates. The whole [extends] 1 league around the church. To this manor belong these Berewicks; Littlethorpe, "Estuinc" [in Newby, near Ripon], Westwick, Bishop Monkton, Nidd, Killinghall, Bishop Thornton, Sawley, Eavestone, Wilsill, 'Knayser' [in Skelding], Grantley, 'How' [in Markington] [and] Markington. Together, there are 43 carucates to the geld, and there could be 30 ploughs. All this land is waste, except that in Markington there is 1 plough in demesne; and 2 villans and 3 bordars with 1 plough, and 1 sokeman with 1 plough. In Bishop Monkton 1 thegn has 5 villans and 5 bordars with 4 ploughs. In 'How' [in Markington] [are] 3 villans and 3 bordars with 2 ploughs. There are 75 acres of meadow, [and] woodland pasture belonging to these lands contains 1 league. The whole [is] 6 leagues long and 6 broad.

In ALDFIELD [are] 2 bovates to the geld. It belongs to Ripon, and it is waste. To Ripon belongs the soke of these lands: "Estanlai" [in North Stainley] and Sutton Grange, another Studley [Studley Roger], North Stainley, Sleningford [and] "Sutheuuic".

In all, there are 21½ carucates to the geld, and there could be 15 ploughs. There are now 5 villans and 3 bordars having 3 ploughs. [There are] 2 acres of meadow in "Suthewic", [and] scrubland 1½ leagues long and 1 league broad.

TRE Ripon was worth £32; now £7.10s.

In NUNWICK, to the geld, [are] 4½ carucates inland, and half a carucate in the soke of Ripon. There could be 4 ploughs. Reginald holds it of the archbishop, and has 1 villan and 2 bordars and 1 sokeman with 2 ploughs. [It is] half a league long and as much broad.

In BRIDGE HEWICK [are] 3 carucates to the geld, and there could be 3 ploughs. [There is] 1 acre of meadow.

In COPT HEWICK [are] 2 carucates to the geld, and there could be 2 ploughs. There are 2 bordars with 1 plough. TRE worth 5s; now 8s.

IN GREAT GIVENDALE [near Ripon] [are] 11 carucates to the geld, and in Skelton [near Boroughbridge], a Berewick, 8 carucates to the geld, and there could be 12 ploughs. Now there are 2 villans and 4 bordars with 3 ploughs. [There are] 6 acres of meadow. The whole manor [is] 1 league long and a half broad. TRE worth £12; now 10s.

In HOWGRAVE, 2 carucates. In Hutton Conyers, 2 bovates. In "Hashundebi" [in Sharow], 2 carucates. In Markington and South Stainley, 1 carucate. This land of St Peter is free from the king's geld. It is waste. TRE it was worth 20s.

[Folio 304: YORKSHIRE]

IN BEVERLEY, St John's carucate was always free from the king's geld. The canons have there in demesne 1 plough; and 18 villans and 15 bordars having 6 ploughs, and 3 mills [rendering] 13s, and a fishery [rendering] 7,000 eels. [There is] woodland pasture 3 leagues long and 1½ leagues broad. The whole [is] 4 leagues long and 2½ leagues broad. TRE it was worth £24 to the archbishop; now £14. Then it was worth to the canons £20; now the same. To this manor belong these Berewicks: Skidby [and] Bishop Burton. In these there are 31 carucates to the geld, and there could be 18 ploughs. The canons have in demesne there 4 ploughs; and 20 villans with 6 ploughs, and 3 knights [with] 3 ploughs.

IN SOUTH DALTON [are] 12 carucates to the geld, and there could be 6 ploughs. Archbishop Ealdræd held this as 1 manor. Now St John has in demesne 1 plough; and 12 villans with 7 ploughs. The whole [is] 1 league long and a half broad. TRE worth £4; now 40s.

In [East and West] FLOTMANBY the clerks of Beverley have 1 bovate of land.

IN RISBY [are] 6 carucates to the geld, and there could be 3 ploughs. It is waste.

IN LOCKINGTON [are] 2½ carucates to the geld, and there could be 2 ploughs. St John had and has it. TRE worth 10s; now 8[s].

In ETTON [are] 8 carucates to the geld, and there could be 4 ploughs. This was and is a manor of St John's. There 8 villans have 5 ploughs. TRE worth 10s; now 8s.

In 'RAVENTHORPE' [in Cherry Burton] [are] 3 carucates to the geld, and there could be 2 ploughs. St John had and has it. Now in demesne [is] 1 plough; and 3 villans [have] 1 plough. TRE worth 10s; now 12s.

IN CHERRY BURTON [are] 12 carucates and 6 bovates to the geld, and there could be 7 ploughs. Wulfgeat had 1 manor there. Now St John has in demesne 3 ploughs; and 12 villans with 3 ploughs. TRE worth 50s; now 40s.

In MOLESCROFT [are] 3 carucates to the geld, and there could be 2 ploughs. One half belongs to the archbishop and the other to St John 2 villans have 1 plough there.

In KELLEYTHORPE, St John has 2 bovates to the geld, and 1 mill.

In KIPLING [are] 2½ carucates to the geld, and there could be 2 ploughs. St John had and has it. It is waste. Ketil holds it.

In MIDDLETON-ON-THE-WOLDS [are] 5 carucates and 6 bovates to the geld, and there could be 3 ploughs. Archbishop Ealdæd held this as 1 manor. Now St John has it. In demesne [is] 1 plough; and 8 villans [with] 2½ ploughs. There is a church and a priest. TRE worth 40s; now 20s.

In Leconfield, St John has 2 bovates of land.

IN GREAT KELK, with these Berewicks, Gembling [and] Reighton, there are 13 carucates to the geld, and there could be 7 ploughs. Wulfgeat held this as 1 manor. Now St John has it, and it is waste, except that 3 villans have 1 plough there. TRE worth 40s; now 12d. The whole manor [is] 1 league long and a half broad.

In GARTON-ON-THE-WOLDS [are] 9 carucates to the geld, and there could be 5 ploughs. St John had 1 manor there, and Wulfgeat another manor. Now St John has both, and they are waste. TRE it was worth 45s.

In LOWTHORPE, with the Berewicks Ruston Parva [and] Haisthorpe, there are 12½ carucates to the geld, and there could be 7 ploughs. St John held this as 1 manor, and [holds it] now. It is waste, except that a rent-paying tenant pays 8s.

In BENTLEY [near Beverley] [are] 2 carucates to the geld, and 1 plough could plough it. St John had 1 manor there. Now it is waste; yet there is woodland pasture 1 league long and 4 furlongs broad. TRE it was worth 20s.

BEREWICKS IN BEVERLEY AND HOLDERNESS BELONGING TO THE ARCHBISHOP.

In Wawne [are] 2 carucates of land and 2 bovates to the geld. [There is] land for 1 plough. 11 villans and 2 bordars have 3 ploughs there.

In Weel [are] 2 carucates of land to the geld. [There is] land for 6 oxen. 6 villans and 1 bordar have 1 plough there.

In Tickton [are] 12 bovates of land to the geld. [There is] land for 6 oxen. 3 villans have half a plough there.

In Eske [are] 2 carucates of land to the geld. [There is] land for 1 plough. 6 villans and 1 bordar have 2 ploughs there.

In Stork Hill [is] 1 carucate of land to the geld. [There is] land for 2 oxen. 2 villans have 1 plough there. THIS IS NOT IN HOLDERNESS.

THESE BEREWICKS BELONG TO ST JOHN, AND ARE IN HOLDERNESS.

SOUTH HUNDRED

In Welwick [are] 4 carucates of land to the geld, and in Weeton [in Welwick], 2 carucates of land and 5 bovates to the geld. [There is] land for 6 ploughs. There are in demesne 1½ ploughs; and 32 villans and 13 bordars having 9 ploughs. There is a church and a priest, and 20 acres of meadow.

In Grimston [in Garton] [are] 2 carucates of land to the geld. It is waste.

In Monkwith [are] 2 carucates of land to the geld. [There is] land for 2 ploughs. 6 villans have 3 ploughs there, and they pay 10s.

In Ottringham [are] 6½ carucates of land to the geld. There is a church and a priest. A certain knight rents it, and pays 10s.

MIDDLE HUNDRED

In Bilton [near Hull] [are] 3 carucates of land to the geld. [There is] land for 2 ploughs. 13 villans have 2 ploughs and 5 oxen there.

In Burton Constable [are] 5 carucates of land to the geld. [There is] land for 5 ploughs. 1 knight has 1 plough in demesne there.

In West Newton [in Aldbrough] [are] 3 carucates of land to the geld. [There is] land for 2 ploughs. There are 20 acres of meadow.

In Flinton [are] 6 bovates of land to the geld. [There is] land for 4 oxen. 3 villans and 1 bordar have 1 plough there.

In Danthorpe [is] 1 carucate of land to the geld. [There is] land for 1 plough. There is 1 bordar.

In Withernwick [is] 1 carucate of land to the geld. 4 villans have 1 plough there, and [there are] 20 acres of meadow.

In Routh [are] 15 bovates of land to the geld. 7 villans have 2 ploughs there. There are 12 acres of meadow. In the same vill Drogo has taken away from St John 2 carucates of land which is also waste.

In Sutton-on-Hull [are] 9 bovates of land to the geld. There 1 free man has 3 villans with 1½ ploughs.

In Southcoates [is] 1 carucate of land to the geld. In Drypool, 3 bovates, and soke over 5 bovates. This is waste.

NORTH HUNDRED

In Great Cowden [are] 9 carucates of land to the geld. [There is] land for 7 ploughs. There 1 knight has 1 plough; and 12 villans with 3 ploughs. In Rise [is] half a carucate of land to the geld. It is waste.

In Sigglesthorne [are] 8 carucates of land to the geld. [There is] land for 5 ploughs. There is 1 plough in demesne; and 14 villans and 5 bordars having 6 ploughs. There is a priest and a church, and 16 acres of meadow.

In Catwick [is] 1 carucate of land to the geld. There 1 knight has 1 plough, and 3 villans and 4 bordars.

In Brandesburton [is] 1 carucate of land to the geld. There 1 clerk has 1 plough, and 1 villan, and 8 acres of meadow.

In Leven [are] 6 carucates of land to the geld. [There is] land for 4 ploughs. There is 1 plough in demesne; and 15 villans and 1 bordar with 3 ploughs. There is a priest and a church.

[Folio 304V: YORKSHIRE]

III. The land of the Bishop of Durham

In WELTON, 18 carucates, with these Berewicks: Ellerker, 8 carucates; Walkington, 9 carucates; [High and Low] Hunsley, 2½ carucates; Yokefleet [near Blacktoft], 1½ carucates; there are 39 carucates to the geld, and there could be 20 ploughs. Morcar held this as 1 manor. Now the Bishop of Durham has it. In demesne [are] 6 ploughs; and [he has] 33 villans and 3 bordars having 9 ploughs, and 10 sokemen with 6 ploughs, and 3 mills rendering 18s. [There is] meadow 1 league long and 4 furlongs broad, [and] scrubland 4 furlongs long and 3 broad. There whole manor [is] 2 leagues long and half a league broad. TRE worth £20; now £13.

To this manor belongs this sokeland: Brantingham, 2 carucates; and another Brantingham [Brantinghamthorpe], 5 bovates; Hotham, 3 carucates; South Cliffe, 4 carucates; Scorborough, 1 carucate; 'Newton' [in Cherry Burton], 1 carucate; Gardham, 6 carucates.

In all, [there are] 17 carucates and 5 bovates to the geld, and there could be 12 ploughs. They are waste, except that in Brantingham there are 3 villans and 1 sokeman with 1 plough. [There is] meadow 1 league long and 3 furlongs broad, [and] scrubland 2 furlongs long and as much broad.

William de Percy holds Scorborough of the bishop, where he has a mill, and 3 villans with half a plough.

In LUND [near Beverley] [are] 12 carucates to the geld, and there could be 6 ploughs. Morcar held this as 1 manor; nevertheless the soke is in Welton. Now the Bishop of Durham has it, and it is waste. [There is] scrubland 2 furlongs long and 1 broad. The whole manor [is] 2 leagues long and 1 broad.

In "PERSENE" [in Scorborough] [are] 6 bovates to the geld, and there could be 1 plough. It belongs to Lund [near Beverley]. William de Percy holds it of the bishop.

IN HOWDEN, 15 carucates, with the Berewicks: Hive, 1 carucate; Owsthorpe, 1½ carucates; Portington, 2 carucates and 3 bovates; Cavil, 2 carucates and 2 bovates; Eastrington, 1 carucate; Kilpin, 3 carucates and 2 bovates; Belby, 3 carucates and 2 bovates; Yokefleet [near Blacktoft], half a carucate; Cotness, half a carucate; Saltmarshe, 6 carucates; Laxton, 1 carucate; Skelton [in Howden], 3 carucates and 2 bovates; Barnhill, 1 carucate; Thorpe Lidget, 1½ carucates; Knedlington, 6 carucates; Asselby, 1 carucate; Barmby on the Marsh, 1 carucate; Babthorpe, 2 bovates. In all, there are 51 carucates and 6 bovates to the geld, and there could be 30 ploughs. King Edward had this manor. Now the Bishop of Durham has it. In demesne [is] 1 plough; and [he has] 65 villans and 23 bordars having 16 ploughs, and 3 sokemen with 2 ploughs. In the manor there is a priest and a church. [There is] woodland pasture 3 leagues long and 1 league broad. The whole manor [is] 6 leagues long and 2 broad. TRE worth £40; now £12. All the Berewicks [are] waste. To this manor belongs this sokeland: Eastrington, 5 carucates; Belby, half a carucate; Knedlington, 1 carucate; Asselby, 4 carucates; Barmby on the Marsh, 5 carucates; Babthorpe, 3 carucates and 2 bovates; Barlby, 1 carucate. In all, [there are] 19 carucates and 6 bovates to the geld, and there could be 10 ploughs. Now there are 4 sokemen and 3 bordars with 2 ploughs. The rest [is] waste.

In BELBY [is] 1 carucate and 6 bovates to the geld, and there could be 1 plough. Muli had 1 manor there. Now the bishop has there 1 bordar. TRE it was worth 20s.

In RICCALL [is] 1 carucate to the geld. The soke belongs to Howden. The king had it. Now the bishop has there 2 sokemen and 3 villans and 2 bordars with 2 ploughs.

In 'NEWTON' [in Cherry Burton] [is] 1 carucate to the geld. Basinc had 1 manor there,

and it was worth £6 TRE. Now the bishop has it, and it is waste.

In HOLME ON THE WOLDS [are] 12 carucates to the geld, and there could be 6 ploughs. The soke of this land belongs to Welton. Of these, Nigel has 6 carucates of the bishop. The whole [is] 1½ leagues long and 1 broad.

In HUTTON CONYERS and HOWGRAVE [are] 14 carucates to the geld, and there could be 7 ploughs. The Bishop of Durham had and has it as 1 manor. He has there in demesne 2 ploughs; and 4 villans and 6 bordars with 4 ploughs. The whole manor [is] 4 leagues long and 4 broad. TRE worth £10; now 50s. To this manor belongs this sokeland: Norton Conyers, 6 carucates; Sutton Howgrave, 3 carucates; Holme [in Pickhill], 5 carucates; "Torp" [in Pickhill], 1 carucate. In all, there are 15 carucates to the geld, and there could be 8 ploughs. There are 2 sokemen and 6 villans and 3 bordars having 6½ ploughs. [There are] 10 acres of meadow. Robert holds this land of the bishop.

In Crayke [are] 6 carucates to the geld, and there could be 4 ploughs. Bishop Æthelwine held this as 1 manor. Now Bishop William has in demesne 1 plough; and 9 villans with 3 ploughs. There is a church and a priest, [and] a little woodland pasture. The whole [is] 2 leagues long and 2 broad. TRE [worth] 40s; now 20s.

IN SESSAY [are] 5 carucates to the geld, and there could be 3 ploughs. St Cuthbert had and has it as 1 manor. There 8

villans have 3 ploughs. [There is] a little woodland pasture. The whole [is] 1 league long and a half broad. TRE [worth] 60s; now 20s. [In] "Horebodebi" [are] 3 carucates to the geld, and there could be 2 ploughs. The soke of this land is in Sessay, and it is waste.

In KNAYTON [are] 4 carucates to the geld, and there could be 2 ploughs. St Cuthbert had and has it as 1 manor. Now in demesne [is] 1 plough; and 4 villans with 3 ploughs. TRE worth 20s; now the same.

In Foxton [are] 2 carucates to the geld, and there could be 1 plough. [It is] a Berewick of the above-mentioned manor, and it is waste.

In BROMPTON [near Northallerton] [are] 14 carucates to the geld, and there could be 7 ploughs. St Cuthbert had it as 1 manor. Now it is waste. [There are] 6 acres of meadow. The whole [is] 2 leagues long and 2 broad. TRE it was worth 40s.

In GIRSBY the Bishop of Durham had 6 carucates of land to the geld. [There is] land for 3 ploughs. Now it is waste. TRE it was worth 10s.

In DEIGHTON [near Welbury] the Bishop of Durham had 6 carucates of land to the geld. [There is] land for 3 ploughs. Now it is waste. TRE it was worth 20s. [It is] 1 league long and broad.

In WINTON the Bishop of Durham had 6 carucates of land to the geld. [There is] land for 3 ploughs. Now it is waste. TRE it was worth 30s. [It is] 1 league long and broad.

[Folio 305: YORKSHIRE]

IIII. The land of Earl Hugh

In WHITBY and SNEATON, a Berewick, are 15 carucates to the geld, and there could be 15 ploughs. Earl Siward held this as 1 manor. Now Earl Hugh has it, and William de Percy [holds] of him. In demesne [are] 2 ploughs; and 10 villans and 3 bordars having 1 plough. [There is] woodland pasture 7 leagues long and 3 leagues broad. The whole of the open land [is] 3 leagues long and 2 broad. TRE worth £112; now 60s.

To this manor belongs this sokeland: Fyling, 1 carucate; Fylingthorpe, 5 carucates; Gnipe Howe, 3 carucates; 'Prestebi' [in Whitby], 2 carucates; Ugglebarnby, 3 carucates; 'Sourebi' [in Whitby], 4 carucates; 'Brecca' [in Whitby], 1 carucate; 'Bauldbyes' [in Whitby], 1 carucate; 'Flowergate' [in Whitby], 2 carucates; High Stakesby, 2 carucates and 6 bovates; Newholm, 4 carucates.

In all, [there are] 28 carucates and 6 bovates to the geld, and there could be 24 ploughs. Earl Hugh has this, and William [holds] of him. Nearly all [are] waste. Only in 'Prestebi' [in Whitby] and 'Sourebi' [in Whitby], which the Abbot of York has of William, are there 2 ploughs in demesne; and 8 sokemen with 1 plough, and 30 villans with 3 ploughs, and 1 mill [rendering] 10s, and 26 acres of meadow, in places.

In SOUTH LOFTUS [are] 4 carucates to the geld, and there could be 4 ploughs. Earl Siward held this as 1 manor. Now Earl Hugh has it, but it is waste. [There is] barren woodland

and 8 acres of meadow. The whole manor [is] 3 leagues long and 1 broad. TRE worth £48; now nothing.

To this manor belongs this sokeland: "Roscheltorp" [in Loftus], 1 carucate; Hinderwell, 10 bovates; Boulby, 2 carucates; Easington [near Loftus], 8 carucates; Liverton, 6 carucates; Guisborough, 6 bovates; Rawcliff Banks, 2 carucates; Upleatham, 10 carucates; Marske-by-the-Sea, 2 carucates; Kirkleatham, 2 carucates; Lazenby [in Ormesby], half a carucate; Lackenby, 1 carucate and 6 bovates.

In all, [there are] 46½ carucates to the geld, and there could be 30 ploughs. All are waste, except Easington [near Loftus], in which there is 1 villan with 1 plough. [There is] a church without a priest, [and] woodland pasture 1 league long and 2 furlongs broad. The whole [is] 4 leagues long and a half broad.

IN ACKLAM [in Middlesbrough] and BARWICK, a Berewick, [are] 11 carucates to the geld, and there could be 7 ploughs. Earl Siward held this as 1 manor. Now Earl Hugh has it, and Hugh fitzNorman [holds] under him. In demesne [are] 3 ploughs; and 12 villans with 3 ploughs. [There is] a church and a priest. The whole manor [is] 2 leagues long and 1 broad. TRE worth £48; now 40s.

To this manor belongs this sokeland: Coulby, 1 carucate; Hemlington, 3 carucates; Stainton [near Thornaby-on-Tees], 2 carucates; Thornton [near Hemlington], 3 carucates; Maltby [near Middlesbrough], 3 carucates; Ingleby, 6 carucates; Thornaby-on-Tees, 3 carucates; Stainsby, 3 carucates. All together, [there are] 25 carucates to the geld, and there could be 15 ploughs. All [are] waste, except Ingleby, where there are 3 sokemen with 3 ploughs.

In FLAMBOROUGH [are] 15 carucates to the geld, and there could be 8 ploughs. Earl Harold had 1 manor there. Now Earl Hugh [has it], and under him Hugh fitzNorman [has] in demesne 1 plough, and 1 bordar. The whole manor [is] 1 league long and a half broad. TRE worth £24; now 10s.

In Sewerby there is sokeland of this manor, 1½ carucates to the geld. It is waste.

In [High and Low] CATTON [are] 40 carucates to the geld, and there could be 24 ploughs. Earl Harold had 1 manor there. Now Earl Hugh [has it], and William [holds] of him. In demesne [is] 1 plough; and 32 villans and 6 sokemen with 17 ploughs, and 1 mill [rendering] 10s. [There is] woodland pasture 2 leagues long and 1 broad. The whole manor [is] 4 leagues long and 4 broad. TRE worth £28; now 100s.

V. The land of the Count of Mortain

In LYTHE [are] 2 carucates to the geld, and 1 plough could plough them. Swein had 1 manor there. Now the Count of Mortain has it, and Nigel [holds] of him. There are 6 villans with 1 plough, and 6 acres of meadow. [There is] woodland pasture 1 league long and 2 furlongs broad. The whole manor [is] 1½ leagues long and half a league broad. TRE worth 20s; now 5s6d.

In HUTTON MULGRAVE [are] 3 carucates to the geld,

and there could be 3 ploughs. Swein had 1 manor there. Now Nigel has it of the count. It is waste. [There is] woodland pasture 3 leagues long and 1 broad. The whole manor [is] 4 leagues long and 1 broad. TRE it was worth 20s.

In EGTON [are] 3 carucates to the geld, and there could be as many ploughs. Swein had 1 manor there. Now Nigel has it of the count. [There is] woodland pasture 3 leagues long and 2 broad. The whole manor [is] 4 leagues long and 2 broad. TRE it was worth 20s; now it is waste.

In MULGRAVE CASTLE [are] 6 carucates to the geld, and there could be 3 ploughs. Swein had 1 manor there. Now Nigel has it of the count. The whole manor [is] 1 league long and 1 broad. TRE it was worth 20s; now it is waste.

In GOLDSBOROUGH [in Lythe] [are] 2 carucates to the geld, and there could be 2 ploughs. Swein had 1 manor there. Now Nigel has it of the count. There are 16 acres of meadow. The whole manor [is] 1 league long and a half broad. TRE it was worth 10s; now it is waste.

In ELLERBY [are] 6 carucates to the geld, and there could be 4 ploughs. Siward and Swein had 2 manors there. Now Nigel has it of the count. There are 6 acres of meadow. The whole manor [is] 1 league long and a half broad. TRE it was worth 40s; now it is waste.

In MICKLEBY [are] 4 carucates to the geld, and there could be 2 ploughs. Swein had 1 manor there. Now Nigel has it of the count. There are 6 acres of meadow, and scrubland. The whole [is] 1½ leagues long and a half broad. TRE it was worth 20s; now it is waste.

In BORROWBY [in Ugthorpe] and ROXBY [near Loftus], a Berewick, [are] 6 carucates to the geld, and there could be 4 ploughs. Swein had 1 manor there. Now Nigel has it of the count. There are 8 acres of meadow. [There is] woodland, not pasture, half a league long and 1 furlong broad. The whole manor [is] 2 leagues long and 1 broad. TRE [it was worth] †40†s; now it is waste. To this manor belongs sokeland in Newton Mulgrave of 3 carucates to the geld, and there could be 3 ploughs. It is waste.

In AISLABY [near Whitby] [are] 3 carucates to the geld, and there could be 2 ploughs. Uhtræd had 1 manor there. Now Richard Sourdeval has it of the count. There are 6 acres of meadow, [and] woodland pasture 1 league long and 1 broad. The whole manor [is] 1½ leagues long and 1 league broad. TRE [it was worth] 10s8d; now it is waste.

In "GRIMESBI" [in Ugthorpe] [are] 2 carucates to the geld, and 1 plough could plough them. Swein had 1 manor there. Now the count has it, and it is waste.

In SEATON [in Hinderwell] [are] 3 carucates to the geld, and there could be 2 [ploughs]. Uhtræd had 1 manor there. Now Richard has it of the count. In demesne [is] 1 plough; and 6 villans with 2 ploughs, and half a church. The whole manor [is] 1 league long and a half broad. TRE worth 10s; now the same. To this manor belongs sokeland in Roxby [near Loftus] of 2 carucates to the geld, and there could be 2 ploughs. [There is] woodland pasture 1 league long and 4 furlongs broad. The whole of Roxby [near Loftus] [is] 2 leagues long and half a league broad. Uhtræd holds it.

In "STEINTUN" [in Stanghow] [are] 7 bovates to the geld, and there could be 1 plough. Uhtræd had 1 manor there. Now Richard has it of the count, and it is waste.

[Folio 305V: YORKSHIRE]

In MOORSHOLM [are] 3 carucates to the geld, and there could be 2 ploughs. Uhtræd had 1 manor there. Now Richard has it of the count, and it is waste.

In another MOORSHOLM [Little Moorsholm] [is] 1 carucate to the geld, and half a plough could plough it. Uhtræd had 1 manor there. Now Richard has it of the count, and it is waste. The whole [is] half a league long and 2 furlongs broad.

In KILTON THORPE [are] 1½ carucates to the geld, and there could be 1 plough. Uhtræd had 1 manor there. Now the count has it, and it is waste.

In KILTON [is] 1 carucate to the geld, and half a plough could plough it. Uhtræd had 1 manor there. Now Count Robert has it, and it is waste.

In BROTTON [are] 12 carucates to the geld, and there could be 6 ploughs. Uhtræd had 1 manor there. Now Richard has it of the count. In demesne [is] 1 plough; and 8 villans with 4 ploughs. There are 12 acres of meadow. The whole manor [is] 1½ leagues long and 1 broad. TRE worth 20s; now 13s4d.

To this manor belongs sokeland in Marske-by-the-Sea of 10 carucates to the geld, and 5 ploughs to plough them. There is 1 villan ploughing with 2 oxen, and 10 acres of meadow.

In SKELTON [near Saltburn] [are] 13 carucates to the geld, and there could be 7 ploughs. Uhtræd had 1 manor there. Now Richard has it of the count. In demesne [is] 1 ploughs; and 12 villans with 3 ploughs, and 20 acres of meadow. [There is] Woodland pasture 2 leagues long and 2 furlongs broad. The whole manor [is] 5 leagues long and 2 broad. TRE worth 40s; now 16s.

In GUISBOROUGH and [in Guisborough] and HUTTON LOWCROSS [are] 25 carucates to the geld, and there could be 14 ploughs. Uhtræd had 3 manors there. Now the count has in demesne 1 plough; and 10 villans with 4 ploughs. There is a priest and a church, and 1 mill [rendering] 4s. TRE worth 40s; now 16s.

In TOCKETTS [are] 2 carucates to the geld, and 1 plough could plough them. Uhtræd had 1 manor there. Now Richard has it of the count, and it is waste. TRE it was worth 5s4d.

In KIRKLEATHAM [are] 9 carucates to the geld, and there could be 5 ploughs. Uhtræd had 1 manor there. Now the count has it, and it is waste. There are 14 acres of meadow. TRE it was worth 16s.

In WILTON [in Ormesby] [are] 4 carucates to the geld, and there could be 2 ploughs. Northmann had 1 manor there. Now Nigel has it of the count. There are 2 bordars, and 6 acres of meadow. TRE worth 16s; now 16d. In the same vill are 4 bovates to the geld, the soke belonging to the land of Nigel.

In LACKENBY [are] 2 carucates to the geld, and there could be 1 plough. Northmann had 1 manor there. Now Nigel has it of the count, and it is waste. TRE it was worth 13s4d.

In ESTON [are] 9 carucates to the geld, and there could be 5 ploughs. Waltheof had 1 manor there. Now Count Robert has it, and it is waste. Richard [holds it] of the count. TRE it was worth 40s.

In NORMANBY [in Eston] [are] 7 carucates to the geld, and there could be 4 ploughs. Uhtræd had 1 manor there. Now the count has it, and it is waste. TRE it was worth 20s.

In BARNABY [are] 6 carucates to the geld, and there could be 3 ploughs. Uhtræd had 1 manor there. Now Richard has it of the count, and it is waste. There are 5 acres of meadow. TRE it was worth 5s4d. The whole manor [is] 1 league long and as much broad.

In LITTLE AYTON [are] 6 carucates to the geld, and there could be 3 ploughs. Northmann had 1 manor there. Now Nigel has it of the count. In demesne [is] 1 plough; and 8 villans with 2 ploughs. [There is] a church, and 6 acres of meadow. TRE worth 40s; now 30s.

In SEAMER [near Stokesley] and TANTON [are] 13 carucates to the geld, and there could be 8 ploughs. Gospatric had 1 manor there. Now Richard has it of the count. In demesne [is] 1 plough; and 5 villans with 2 ploughs. The whole manor [is] 2 leagues long and a half broad. TRE worth 40s; now 20s.

To this manor belongs this sokeland: Hilton [near Stokesley], 6 carucates; Middleton-on-Leven, 8 carucates; High Foxton, 3 carucates; Carlton in Cleveland, 8 carucates; that is, 25 carucates to the geld, and there could be 13 ploughs. They are waste, except that in Middleton-on-Leven there are 3 villans with 3 ploughs.

In HUTTON RUDBY [are] 6 carucates to the geld, and there could be 4 ploughs. Gospatric had 1 manor there. Now Count Robert has it. There is a church and a priest. The whole manor [is] 1½ leagues long and 1 league broad. TRE worth £24; now 26s8d.

To Hutton Rudby belongs this sokeland: Rudby, Skutterskelfe, 'Blaten Carr' [in Great Busby], Whorlton, Goulton, Crathorne. In all, [there are] 20 carucates to the geld, and there could be 12 ploughs. All are waste, except Whorlton, in which there are 20 villans with 8 ploughs.

In Great BROUGHTON [are] 5 carucates to the geld, and there could be 3 ploughs. Northmann had 1 manor there, and Ulfkil 1 manor. Now Nigel has it of the count, and it is waste. TRE it was worth 25s. The whole manor [is] 2 leagues long and 1 broad.

In CLOUGHTON, Gunwor had 1 manor of 2 bovates to the geld. Now the count has it, and it is waste.

In "STEMANESBI" [in Scalby], Uhtræd had 1 manor of 2½ carucates to the geld, and there could be 1 plough. Now Nigel has it of the count, and it is waste. In the same vill are 1½ carucates to the geld, of which the soke belongs to Falsgrave, [which] is the king's. The whole manor [is] 1 league long and 3 furlongs broad. TRE it was worth 10s8d.

In LOFT MARISHES [in Thornton Dale], Thorfinnr had 1 manor of 1½ carucates.

In "GHIGOGESMERSC" [in Thornton Dale], Thorfinnr [had] 1 manor of 1 carucate and 2 bovates.

In [Great and Little] HABTON, Ulfkil and Orm [had] 1 manor of half a carucate. There was no hall.

In 'NEWSHAM' [in Amotherby], Waltheof [had] 1 manor of 1½ carucates.

In OLD MALTON, Otfrida [had] 1½ carucates.

In OSWALDKIRK, Uhtræd [had] 1 manor of 1 carucate.

In SCAWTON, Uhtræd [had] 1 manor of 2 carucate.

In POCKLEY, Uhtræd [had] 1 manor of 1 carucate.

In BEADLAM, Uhtræd [had] 1 manor of 4 carucate.

In HAROME, Uhtræd [had] 1 manor of 5 carucate.

In CAWTON, Waltheof [had] 1 manor of 3 carucate.

In SCACKLETON, Waltheof [had] 1½ carucate. [...]

Count Robert has these, and they are waste.

In BARTON-LE-STREET [are] 8 carucates to the geld, and there could be 4 ploughs. Waltheof had 1 manor there. Now Richard has it of the count. In demesne [is] 1 plough; and 8 villans with 3 ploughs, and a church. The whole manor [is] 1 league long and a half broad. TRE worth 20s; now 10s.

In FADMOOR [are] 5 carucates to the geld, and there could be 3 ploughs. Waltheof had 1 manor there. Now Count Robert has it, and it is waste. [There is] woodland pasture and field 10 leagues long and a half broad. TRE it was worth 10s.

In NUNNINGTON [are] 6 carucates of land to the geld. [There is] land for 3½ ploughs. 2 thegns had it as 2 manors. There is 1 plough in demesne; and 4 villans with 3 ploughs, and 12 acres of meadow. It was and is worth 20s.

In SLINGSBY [are] 14 carucates of land to the geld. [There is] land for 7 ploughs. 2 thegns held it as 2 manors. Now a priest with 18 villans have 10 ploughs there, and [there are] 20 acres of meadow. It was worth 70s; now 30s.

In STILTONS, Uhtræd had 1 manor of 2 carucates to the geld, and there could be 2 ploughs. Now Count Robert has it, and it is waste. [There is] woodland pasture and field 1 league long and 1 broad. TRE it was worth 20s.

In HELMSLEY, Uhtræd had 1 manor of 8 carucates to the geld, and there could be 4 ploughs. Now the count has there 6 villans with 2 ploughs. There is a priest and a church, [and] woodland pasture and arable field 6 leagues long and 1½ leagues broad. TRE worth 32s; now 10s.

In FRYTON and COULTON is sokeland belonging to this manor of 2 carucates to the geld. It is waste.

In BEADLAM, Uhtræd had 1 manor of 4 carucates to the geld, and there could be 2 ploughs. Now the count has it, and it is waste. [There is] woodland pasture and open land 2 leagues long and 2 broad.

In BULMER and in HIGH STITTENHAM, Ligulf and Northmann had 2 manors of 15 carucates to the geld, and there could be 8 ploughs. Now Nigel has them of the count. In demesne [are] 2 ploughs; and 25 villans with 8 ploughs. There is a priest and a church, and a mill [rendering] 2s, and 20 acres of meadow, [and] woodland pasture 7 furlongs long and 2 broad. The whole [is] 1½ leagues long and 4 furlongs [broad]. TRE worth 100s; now 40s.

In SHERIFF HUTTON, 11 carucates, and WELBURN [in Bulmer], 5 carucates, and GANTHORPE, and TERRINGTON, 3 carucates and 5 bovates, is sokeland belonging to this manor. In all, [there are] 19 carucates and 5 bovates to the geld, and there could be 12 ploughs. Nigel has 1 plough there in demesne; and 11 sokemen and 5 villans and 4 bordars with 4 ploughs. [There is] woodland pasture 1 league long and 2 furlongs broad.

In TERRINGTON and WIGANTHORPE, Waltheof had 1 manor of 3 carucates and 6 bovates to the geld. Now Count Robert has it, and it is waste. TRE it was worth 10s.

In CONEYSTHORPE, Thorkil had 1 manor of 3 carucates to the geld.

In SKEWSBY, Guthrothr had 2 manors of 8 carucates to the geld. Now Count Robert has them, and they are waste. TRE they were worth 30s.

In MARTON-IN-THE-FOREST, Northmann had 1 manor of 6 carucates to the geld, and there could be 3 ploughs. Now Nigel has it of the count. In demesne [is] half a plough; and 20 villans with 6 ploughs. [There is] a church, and 8 acres of meadow, [and] woodland pasture half a league long and a half broad. The whole manor [is] 1 league long and 1 broad. TRE worth 20s; now 16s.

In FARLINGTON and "FORNETORP" [? in Cornborough], Ligulf had 2 manors of 7 carucates to the geld, and there could be 4 ploughs. Now Nigel has them of the count. In demesne [is] 1 plough; and 5 villans with 1 plough, and 12 acres of meadow. [There is] woodland pasture 2 furlongs long and 2 broad. The whole [is] 8 furlongs long and 3 broad. TRE worth 20s; now 10s.

In CORNBOROUGH, Ligulf had 1 manor of 9 carucates to the geld, and there could be 6 ploughs. Now Nigel has it of the count. There is 1 villan with 1 plough, and 6 acres of meadow. The whole [is] 1 league long and 5 furlongs broad. TRE [worth] 20s; now 2s.

In [East and West] LILLING, 2 bovates, and THORNTON-LE-CLAY, 3 carucates, and CLAXTON, 1 carucate, and UPPER HELMSLEY, 4 carucates, and [East and West] LILLING, 1 carucate and 4 bovates. In all, [there are] 9½ carucates and 2 bovates to the geld, the soke belonging to

Bulmer, and there could be 4 ploughs. Nigel has these of the count, and they are waste, except for 3 villans ploughing with 1 plough.

In CRAMBE, Waltheof had 1 manor of 4 carucates to the geld, and there could be 2 ploughs. Now the count has 5 villans with 2 ploughs, and 1 priest, and a church. In demesne [is] 1 plough. TRE [worth] 10s; now 20s.

In BARTON-LE-WILLOWS, Thorkil, Gamal [and] Skænkil had 3 manors of 8 carucates to the geld. Now Count Robert has in demesne 1 plough; and 11 villans with 4 ploughs, and [there are] 12 acres of meadow. The whole manor [is] half a league long and a half broad. TRE [worth] 40s; now 20s.

In WARTHILL, Swarthøfthi had 1 manor of 2 carucates to the geld. Now Count Robert has it, and it is waste; yet 2 villans have 2 ploughs, and pay 2s.

In WHITWELL-ON-THE-HILL, Waltheof had 1 manor of 5 carucates to the geld, and there could be 3 ploughs; and Orm 1½ carucates; and Arnketil 10 bovates; and Northmann 1 carucate and 6 bovates; this is 4 carucates to the geld, and there could be 2 ploughs. Now Count Robert has 1 man there, who pays 2s, and [there are] 10 acres of meadow and 11 acres of woodland. The whole manor [is] 1 league long and 1 broad. TRE worth £3; now 4s8d.

In HUNTINGTON, Thorkil and Thormoth had 2 manors of 5 carucates to the geld, and there could be 3 ploughs. Now Nigel has of the count in demesne half a plough; a priest and a church, and 8 villans with 1 plough. The whole manor [is] 7 furlongs long and 7 broad. TRE [worth] 20s; now 12s.

In LINTON-ON-OUSE, Thorfinnr and Thorn had 2 manors of 5 carucates to the geld, and there could be 3 ploughs. Now Count Robert has in demesne 1 plough; and 5 villans and 3 bordars with 3 ploughs, and [there are] 20 acres of meadow. [There is] woodland and open land 1 league long and 1 broad. TRE [worth] 20s; now the same.

In "Waruelestorp" [in Tollerton] is sokeland of 2 carucates to the geld belonging to Linton-on-Ouse.

In MYTON-ON-SWALE, Ligulf had 1 manor of 4½ carucates. It is waste.

In ALDWARK, Ligulf had 1 manor of 8 carucates. It is waste.

In BRECKENBROUGH, Thorfinnr had 1 manor of 6 carucates. It is waste.

In NORTH KILVINGTON, Waltheof had 1 manor of 2 carucates. It is waste.

In LEAKE, Gamal had 1 manor of 3 carucates. It is waste. [...] and there could be 12 ploughs.

In BRAFFERTON, Haldor had 1 carucate without a hall. Now there is, under the count, 1 villan with half a plough, and he pays 3s.

In NORTH KILVINGTON and UPSALL [in South Kilvington] and HUNDULFTHORPE, Waltheof had 1

manor of 11 carucates to the geld, and there could be 6 ploughs. It is waste. In Upsall [in South Kilvington], 3 villans have 1 plough. Richard has them of the count. [There is] woodland and open land 1½ leagues long and as much broad.

In NORTH CAVE, Basinc and Ulf and Thorkil had 2 manors of 6 carucates and 2 bovates to the geld, and there could be 4 ploughs. Now Nigel has it of the count. In demesne [is] 1 plough; and 5 villans with 2 ploughs. TRE worth 40s; now the same.

In ANLABY, Siward and Thorkil had 5 bovates to the geld.

In NORTH FERRIBY, Siward had half a carucate to the geld, and there could be 1 plough. In these, Nigel has 3 villans having half a plough.

In SEATON ROSS, Gamal had 1 manor of 4 carucates to the geld, and there could be 2 ploughs. Now Nigel has it of the count, and it is waste.

[Folio 306V: YORKSHIRE]

In HOTHAM, Thorkil had 1 manor of 4 carucates and 5 bovates to the geld, and there could be 4 ploughs. Now Nigel has of the count in demesne 1 plough; and 4 villans and 3 bordars with 1 plough, and 1 mill [rendering] 4s. TRE worth £3; now 30s. In the same vill is sokeland of Welton of 7 bovates to the geld. Nigel has it.

In AUGHTON [near Bubwith], Earnwig had 1 manor of 6 carucates to the geld, and there could be 3 [ploughs]. Now Nigel has it of the count. There 6 villans and 4 bordars have 3 ploughs. [There is] woodland pasture 1 league long and a half broad. The whole manor [is] 1 league long and 1 broad. TRE worth 100s; now 20s.

In Spaldington, 3 carucates and 1½ bovates, and Willitoft, 5 bovates, and Foggathorpe, 1½ carucates, and Laytham, 2 carucates and 5 bovates, and East Cottingwith, 2 carucates and 6 bovates, there is sokeland of this manor of 10 carucates to the geld, and there could be 5 ploughs. Nigel has there 6 sokemen and 1 bordar with 1 plough.

In Brantingham, Ulfkil had 7 bovates which belong to "Toschetorp" [in Brantingham]. Nigel has there 2 sokemen with half a plough.

In EAST COTTINGWITH, Knut had 1 manor of 2 carucates to the geld, and there could be 1 plough. Now Nigel has it of the count. In demesne [is] half a plough; and 8 villans with 1½ ploughs.

In SOUTH DUFFIELD were 2 manors [belonging] to 5 brothers, of 7 carucates and 5 bovates to the geld, and there could be 4 ploughs. Now Nigel has it of the count. In demesne [is] 1 plough, and woodland pasture 2 leagues long and a half broad. TRE worth £4; now 40s. In the same vill [are] 1½ carucates to the geld. Soke in Howden.

In NORTH DUFFIELD [are] 7 carucates and 2 bovates to the geld, and there could be 4 ploughs.

In CLIFFE [near Hemingbrough] [are] 3 carucates to the geld, and there could be 2 ploughs.

In Osgodby [in Hemingbrough] [are] 2½ carucates and half a bovate to the geld, and there could be 2 ploughs. The soke of these lands belongs to Howden, the Bishop of Durham's manor. Now Nigel has in demesne 1 plough; and 9 villans with 2 ploughs, and 6 sokemen and 4 villans and 2 bordars with 2 ploughs. TRE worth 40s; now 20s. In Hotham [are] 7 bovates to the geld. The soke [is] in Welton.

In OSGODBY [in Hemingbrough], Northmann and Toki had 2 manors of 3 bovates to the geld. Nigel has there 1 plough in demesne. [There are] 20 acres of meadow, [and] woodland pasture half a league long and as much broad. The whole [is] 1 league long and 1 broad. TRE worth 12s; now 5s.

In GOODMANHAM, Kolgrimr and Orm had 2 manors of 5 carucates and 6 bovates to the geld, and there could be 3 ploughs. Now Nigel has it of the count. In demesne [is] 1 plough; and 2 villans with 1 plough, and [he has] 1 man paying 32d. TRE worth £4; now 12s.

In EASTHORPE [in Londesborough], Kolgrimr had 1 manor of 2 carucates and 6 bovates to the geld, and there could be 2 ploughs. Nigel has it, and it is waste. TRE it was worth 30s.

In KIPLING, Kolgrimr had 1 manor of 2 carucates to the geld, and there could be 1 plough. Richard has it, and it is waste. TRE it was worth 20s.

In MIDDLETON-ON-THE-WOLDS, Gamal had 1 manor of 3 carucates to the geld, and there could be 2 ploughs. Nigel has it, and it is waste, except for 1 man having 3 oxen. TRE worth 30s; now 5s.

In the same vill [is] half a carucate and the third part of 1 bovate to the geld; the soke is in Great Driffield, the king's manor. Nigel has there 2 villans with 3 oxen.

In KIRK ELLA, Siward and Thorkil had 2 manors of 4 carucates to the geld, and there could be 2 ploughs. Nigel has there 5 villans with 1 plough, and they pay 10s.

In ELLERTON [near Bubwith], a Berewick of Aughton [near Bubwith], [are] 6 bovates to the geld; and in the same vill are 10 bovates to the geld, sokeland of Aughton [near Bubwith]. Nigel has 2 villans and 2 bordars there.

In ASSELBY, Thorkil had 1 manor of 1 carucate to the geld. Its soke [is] in Howden. Nigel has there 1 man with 2 oxen, and 5 fisheries rendering 2,400 eels.

In North Duffield and South Duffield [are] 14 bovates to the geld. The soke [is] in Howden.

In MIDDLETON-ON-THE-WOLDS, Edith had 1 manor of 3 carucates and 5 bovates to the geld, and there could be 2 ploughs. Richard has it of the count, but the predecessor of the count did not have it. In demesne is 1 plough. TRE worth 20s; now 20s. In the same vill is sokeland of Great Driffield, the king's manor, of 6 bovates. Richard has the land, but the king does not have the soke.

In WATTON, Thorkil and Mula-Grimr, Orm and Gamal, had 4 manors of 13 carucates to the geld, and there could be 7 ploughs. Nigel has 3 villans with 2 ploughs there. [There is] a priest and a church, [and] meadow half a league long and as much broad. The whole [is] 2 leagues long and 1 broad. TRE worth £6; now 6s.

In KILNWICK, Ealdwif and Mula-Grimr had 2 manors of 5 carucates to the geld, and there could be 3 ploughs. Nigel has it, and it is waste. TRE worth 30s; now 6[s.].

In BESWICK, Gamal had [1 manor] of 3 carucates to the geld, and there could be 2 ploughs. The soke is in Great Driffield. Nigel has 1 plough in demesne; and 7 villans with 2 ploughs, and 1 mill [rendering] 10s. TRE worth 20s; now the same.

In LOCKINGTON, Gamal, Orm, Uhtræd, Wulfstan, Thorkil [and] Sprot had each 1 manor of 9½ carucates to the geld, and there could be 5 ploughs. Now Nigel has 1 plough in demesne; and 9 villans with 3 ploughs, and 1 mill [rendering] 13s. This is worth 30s. TRE it was worth £6. Of 1 carucate of this land, the soke is in Welton, and of another the soke is in Warter.

In AIKE are 6 bovates to the geld. The soke is in Welton. Nigel has there 2 men paying 2s.

In "STEITORP" [in Etton] and ETTON, Thorkil had 2 manors of 7 carucates and 6 bovates to the geld, and there could be 5 ploughs. Nigel has in demesne 1 plough; and 7 villans and 1 bordar with 1½ ploughs. [There is] woodland pasture half a league long and as much broad. TRE worth 50s; now 20s.

In LECONFIELD, Gytha had 1 manor of 10 bovates to the geld, and 1 plough could plough it. Nigel has 1 plough there in demesne; and 4 villans with half a plough. [There is] a fishery [rendering] 4,000 eels, [and] woodland pasture 1 league long and as much broad. TRE worth 30s; now the same.

In 'RAVENTHORPE' [in Cherry Burton], Gytha, Osbern, Thorkil [and] Siward had 4 manors of 5 carucates and 2 bovates to the geld, and there could be 3 ploughs. Nigel has in demesne there 1 plough; and 10 villans and 1 bordar with 2 ploughs. [There is] woodland pasture half a league long and 3 furlongs broad. TRE worth 44s; now 30s.

[Folio 307: YORKSHIRE]

In CHERRY BURTON there is sokeland of Welton, of 1 carucate to the geld. Nigel held it, but now he relinquishes it.

In GRIMSTON [in Dunnington, near York], Sunulf had 1 manor of 2 carucates to the geld, and there could be 1 plough. Nigel has in demesne 1 plough; and 3 villans with half a plough. TRE worth 20s; now 10s.

In CRANSWICK and HUTTON CRANSWICK [are] 9½ carucates to the geld, and there could be 4 ploughs. Eadwulf, Northmann and Knut had 3 manors there. Nigel has there 5 villans with 2 ploughs. TRE worth 60s; now 10s.

In NESWICK, Northmann and Uhtræd had 1 manor of 9 carucates to the geld, and there could be 5 ploughs. It is waste. Nigel has it.

In "NEUSON" [in Leconfield], Uhtræd had 1 manor of 1 carucate to the geld. It is waste. Nigel has it.

In BAINTON [are] 13 carucates to the geld, and there could be 7 ploughs. Northmann, 7 carucates, and Gamal, 6 carucates, had 3 manors there. Nigel has 2 ploughs there; [and] a priest and 10 villans with 3 ploughs. TRE worth £7; now 40s.

In NORTH DALTON, Northmann and Orm and Arnketil had 3 manors of 8 carucates to the geld, and there could be 4 ploughs. Nigel has there 3 men [paying] 8s. TRE it was worth 50s.

In SUTTON UPON DERWENT [are] 7 carucates to the geld, and there could be 3 ploughs. Orm, 1 carucate, Kolgrimr, 3 carucates, Ulf, 1 carucate, [and] Gamal, 1 carucate, had 2 manors there. Nigel has 1 plough there; and 6 villans and 4 bordars with 3 ploughs. TRE worth 20s; now the same.

In SEWERBY, Karli and Thorkil had 2 manors of 6½ carucates. Richard has it, and it is waste.

In MARTON [in Sewerby], Karli had 1 carucate without geld, with sake and soke. Count Robert has it.

In BRIDLINGTON, Thorkil had 1 manor of 5 carucates to the geld.

In FRAISTHORPE, Ligulf had 1 manor of 7 carucates to the geld.

In BOYNTON, Thorkil had 1 manor of 4 carucates to the geld.

In SPEETON, Ligulf had 1 manor of 6 carucates to the geld.

In BUCKTON, Leofwine had 2 manors of 3 carucates and 6 bovates.

In BEMPTON, Ligulf had 1 manor of 6 carucates to the geld.

In BRIGHAM, Gunwor had 1 manor of 3½ carucates to the geld.

In RUDSTON, Gunwor had 1 manor of 8 carucates to the geld.

Richard has all this land of Count Robert, but it is altogether waste.

In GARTON-ON-THE-WOLDS, Asulf had 1 manor of 4 carucates to the geld, and there could be 2 ploughs. Count Robert has 1 plough there; and 4 sokemen and 2 villans with 3 ploughs. There is a priest and a church.

In the same vill, Muli, Orm, Sunulf [and] Thorkil had 7 carucates to the geld, and there could be 10 ploughs. Now the count has it, but it is waste.

In BINNINGTON, Ketilbert had 1 manor of 6 carucates to the geld.

In BIRDSALL, Ketilbert had 1 manor of 13 carucates to the geld. Nigel has this of the count, but it is waste.

In WHARRAM LE STREET, Ketilbert had 1 manor of 12 carucates to the geld. Nigel has it of the count, and it is waste.

There are 30 acres of meadow. The whole manor [is] 2 leagues long and 1 broad. TRE it was worth 100s.

In TOWTHORPE [in Wharram Percy], Orm had 3 carucates to the geld. The soke is in Howsham. Count Robert has it, and it is waste.

In SCAGGLETHORPE [in Settrington] is 1 carucate to the geld, sokeland of Menethorpe. The count has there 1 man paying 2s.

In RILLINGTON are 2 carucates and 2 bovates to the geld. The soke belongs to Kirkham. The count has it, and it is waste.

In ACKLAM [near Leavening], Orm had 2½ carucates to the geld. The soke belongs to Howsham. The count has it, and it is waste.

In BARTHORPE, Waltheof had 6 carucates to the geld. The soke belongs to Howsham. The count has it, and it is waste.

In HOWSHAM and "SUDNICTON" [in Westow], a Berewick, are 14 carucates to the geld, and there could be 8 ploughs. Waltheof had 1 manor there. Now Count Robert has in demesne there 2 ploughs; and 8 villans and 1 sokeman having 2½ ploughs, and 1 mill [rendering] 8s. [There are] 14 acres of meadow. The whole manor [is] 1 league long and 1 broad. TRE worth £4; now the same.

In KIRKHAM [are] 8 carucates to the geld, and there could be 4 ploughs. Waltheof had 1 manor there. Now Count Robert has in demesne 2 ploughs; and 12 villans with 4 ploughs, and 1 mill [rendering] 8s. There is a church and a priest. [There is] woodland pasture 1 league long and 10 perches broad. The whole manor [is] 1 league long and a half broad. TRE worth £3; now 40s.

In THIXENDALE, Gamal had 5 carucates and 6 bovates to the geld. The soke belongs to Howsham. The count has it, and it is waste.

In THIRKLEBY [in Kirby Grindalythe], Ketilbert had 1 manor of 4 carucates to the geld, and there could be 2 ploughs. Nigel has it, and it is waste.

In KIRBY GRINDALYTHE, Ketilbert had 1 manor of 4½ carucates. Nigel has it, and it is waste.

In the same vill, Thorfinnr had 1 manor of 12 carucates to the geld. The count has it, and it is waste.

In LOW MOWTHORPE [in Kirby Grindalythe], Ketilbert had 1 manor of 1 carucate to the geld, and there could be 2 ploughs. Nigel has it, and it is waste.

[Folio 307V: YORKSHIRE]

In SLEDMERE, Ketilbert Thorfinnr had 1 manor of 9 carucates to the geld, where there could be 4 ploughs. Nigel has it of the count, and it is waste. TRE it was worth 20s.

In CROOME, Mylnu-Grimr had 1 manor of 2 carucates to the geld. Nigel held it until now, but it belongs to the king.

IN THE WEST RIDING

In ARTHINGTON, Alweard had 1 manor of 3 carucates and 2½ bovates to the geld, where now there could be 3 ploughs. Richard has it of the count. There is 1 villan ploughing with 2 oxen, and there are 2 acres of meadow. [There is] woodland pasture 2 furlongs long and 2 broad. The whole manor [is] 1 league long and 4 furlongs broad. TRE worth 30s; now 5s.

In ADEL, Alweard himself had 1 manor of 1½ carucates to the geld, where there could be 2 ploughs. Richard has it, and it is waste. [There is] woodland pasture 1 league long and 1 broad. The whole manor [is] 1½ leagues long and 1 league broad. TRE it was worth 10s.

In COOKRIDGE, Alweard himself had 1 manor of 3 carucates to the geld, where now there could be 2 ploughs. Richard has it. [There is] woodland pasture 3 furlongs long and as much broad. The whole manor [is] half a league long and 3 furlongs broad. TRE it was worth 20s; now it is waste.

In BURDEN HEAD, Alweard himself had 1 manor, without a hall, of 2 carucates to the geld, and there could be 2 ploughs. Richard has it. [There are] 3 acres of meadow, and scrubland. The whole manor [is] 4 furlongs long and as much broad. TRE it was worth 20s; now it is waste.

In ECCUP, Alweard himself had 1 manor, without a hall, of 1 carucate to the geld, which 1 plough could plough. Richard has 3 acres of meadow there. [There is] woodland, not pasture, 3 furlongs long and 2 broad. The whole manor [is] 1 league long and half a league broad. TRE it was worth 10s; now it is waste.

BARKSTON WAPENTAKE

In CLIFFORD, Ligulf had 1 manor of 6 carucates to the geld, where there could be 4 ploughs. Nigel has it of Count Robert. In demesne [are] 2 ploughs; and 3 villans with 2 ploughs, and 1 mill [rendering] 2s. [There is] scrubland 4 furlongs long and 3 broad. The whole manor [is] 1 league long and a half broad. TRE worth 40s; now 10s.

In BRAMHAM, Ligulf had 1 manor of 12 carucates to the geld, and there could be 8 ploughs. Nigel has 3 ploughs there; and 15 villans with 5½ ploughs. There is the site of a mill, a church and a priest, [and] woodland pasture 2 leagues long and a half broad. The whole manor [is] 2 leagues long and 1½ leagues broad. TRE worth £8; now 50s. To this manor belongs sokeland in 'Monk Hay' [in Barwick in Elmet], 1 carucate; in Toulston, 3 carucates; in Oglethorpe, 1 carucate; and in Newton Kyme, 1 carucate. Together, [there are] 6 carucates to the geld.

In HEXTHORPE, Earl Tosti had 1 manor of 3 carucates to the geld, and there could be 4 ploughs. Nigel has it of Count Robert. In demesne [is] 1 plough; and 3 villans and 2 bordars with 2 ploughs. There is a church and a priest having 5 bordars and 1 plough, and 2 mills [rendering] 32s. [There are] 4 acres of meadow, [and] woodland pasture 1½ leagues long and 1 league broad. The whole manor [is] 2½ leagues long and 1½ leagues broad. TRE worth £18; now £12.

To this manor belongs this sokeland: in Doncaster, 2 carucates; in Warmsworth, 1 carucate; in Balby, 2 carucates; and Loversall, 2 carucates; Littleworth, 4 carucates; Austerfield, 2 carucates; Auckley, 2 carucates. Together, [there are] 15 carucates to the geld, where there could be 18 ploughs. Now in demesne [is] 1 plough; and 24 villans and 27 bordars and 40 sokemen. These have 27 ploughs. [There is] woodland, in places pasture [and] in places barren.

In MARR, Ulfkil had 1 manor of 5 bovates to the geld, where there could be 1 plough. Count Robert has there now 1 villan and 1 bordar with 5 oxen. TRE worth 40s; now 6s.

In BARNBY DUN, Ulfkil had 1 manor of carucates and 2 bovates to the geld, where there could be 2 ploughs. Now Count Robert has 1 plough in demesne; and 3 villans and 5 bordars [with] half a plough.

In LONG SANDALL, Skotkollr had 1 manor of 6 carucates and 5 bovates to the geld, where there could be 3 ploughs. Nigel has there 2 villans and 3 bordars and 2 sokemen with 2 ploughs. [There is] woodland pasture 4 furlongs long and 2½ furlongs broad. The whole manor [is] 1 league long and 1 broad. TRE worth 40s; now 10s.

In HOOTON LEVITT, Buggi had 1 manor of 3 carucates and 6 bovates to the geld, where there could be 2 ploughs. Now Count Robert has in demesne 1 plough; and 8 villans and 3 bordars with 3 ploughs, and 1 mill [rendering] 28d. The whole [is] 6 furlongs long and as much broad. Now it is worth 20s.

In ROTHERHAM, Hakun had 1 manor of 5 carucates to the geld, where there could be 3 ploughs. Nigel has 1 plough there in demesne; and 8 villans and 3 bordars having 2½ ploughs, and 1 mill [rendering] 10s. [There is] a priest and a church, 4 acres of meadow, [and] 7 acres of woodland pasture. The whole [is] 10 furlongs long and 5½ furlongs broad. TRE worth £4; now 30s.

In HOOTON PAGNELL and Bilham, Earl Edwin had 1 manor of 10 carucates to the geld, and there could be 10 ploughs. Richard has now in demesne 3 ploughs; and 12 villans with 6 ploughs, and 1 mill [rendering] 4s. [There is] woodland pasture half a league long and 3 furlongs broad. The whole [is] 10 furlongs long and 8 broad. TRE worth £8; now 100s.

[Folio 308: YORKSHIRE]

In BRODSWORTH or PICKBURN, Asi had 1 manor of 2½ carucates to the geld, and there could be 2 ploughs. Nigel has there now 1 plough, and 6 bordars. [There are] 1½ acres of meadow. TRE worth 20s; now 15s.

In TODWICK, Regnvald had 1 manor of 12 carucates to the geld, where there could be 6 ploughs. Richard has now 1 plough there; and 11 villans and 2 sokemen and 5 bordars with 5½ ploughs. There is a church, and 3 acres of meadow, [and] woodland pasture half a league long and 4 furlongs broad. The whole manor [is] 1 league long and a half broad. TRE worth 40s; now 15s.

In GREAT HOUGHTON, 3 sons of Hundingr had 3 of 5

carucates and 2 bovates to the geld, and Godhyse 1 manor of 6 bovates to the geld. 5 ploughs could plough this land. Now Richard has 1 plough there; and 6 villans and 5 bordars with 5 ploughs. [There is] woodland pasture half a league long and 6 furlongs broad. The whole manor [is] 1 league long and half a league broad. TRE worth 40s; now 20s.

In THURNSCOE, Ligulf had 1 manor, without a hall, of 7 bovates to the geld. In the same vill is sokeland of 9 bovates to the geld belonging to Shafton, and in 'Deightonby'[in Thurnscoe] 2 carucates and $5\frac{1}{2}$ acres, and in Clayton [near Thurnscoe] 1 carucate, and [in] Stotfold 1 carucate, the soke likewise belonging to Shafton. There could be 4 ploughs. Now Richard has there 3 sokemen and 1 bordar with 2 ploughs, and [there are] 6 acres of meadow. [There is] woodland pasture half a league long and 3 furlongs broad. The whole manor [is] 1 league long and a half broad. TRE worth 60s; now 30s.

In WHISTON and HANDSWORTH, $4\frac{1}{2}$ carucates of sokeland, Thorkil had 1 manor of 5 carucates to the geld, and there could be 7 ploughs. Now Richard has there 1 ploughs; and 11 villans and 4 bordars and 6 sokemen with $7\frac{1}{2}$ ploughs. [There is] woodland pasture 3 leagues long and 1 broad. The whole manor [is] $2\frac{1}{2}$ leagues long and 2 leagues broad. TRE worth £8; now 40s.

In TREETON, Ulfkil, 1 carucate, and Morcar, 2 carucates, had 2 manors of 3 carucates to the geld, and there could be 2 ploughs. Now Richard has there 1 plough; and 4 villans and 13 bordars with 4 ploughs, and half a mill [rendering] 5s, and the sites of 2 mills, a church and a priest. [There is] woodland pasture half a league long and 1 furlong broad. The whole manor [is] 1 league long and 1 broad. TRE worth 40s; now 20s.

In AUGHTON [near Aston], Leofsige, 6 bovates, and Grim, half a carucate, and Leofketel, 4 bovates, had 3 manors of 1 carucate and 6 bovates to the geld; and in the same place 3 sokemen had 1 carucate to the geld. In this land there could be 2 ploughs. Now Richard has there 4 villans and 3 bordars with $1\frac{1}{2}$ ploughs. [There is] woodland pasture 1 league long and 11 furlongs broad. The whole manor [is] 16 furlongs long and 1 league broad. TRE [worth] 40s; now 10s.

In ASTON, Leofsige had 1 manor of 2 carucates and 2 bovates to the geld, and there could be 2 ploughs. Now Richard has there 5 villans and 1 sokeman with 2 ploughs. There is a church, and a priest, [and] woodland pasture half a league long and as much broad. The whole manor [is] 1 league long and a half broad. TRE [worth] 20s; now 8s.

In WALES, Morcar had 1 manor of 1 carucate to the geld, which half a plough could plough. [There is] woodland pasture half a league long and 2 furlongs broad. The whole [is] 10 furlongs long and 6 broad. TRE it was worth 10s; now it is waste. Richard has it

In ULLEY, Morcar had 1 manor of 2 carucates to the geld, and 2 brothers 2 carucates belonging to Aughton [near Aston]. These 4 [carucates] 2 ploughs could plough. The

whole [is] 1 league long and a half broad. TRE it was worth 40s; now it is waste. Richard has it.

In BRAMPTON EN LE MORTHEN, Andor, Morcar and Ulfkil had 3 manors, each [having] 2 carucates to the geld. These 6 carucates 2 ploughs could plough. There is woodland pasture 2 furlongs long and 2 broad. The whole [is] 1 league long and a half broad. TRE it was worth 40s; now it is waste. Richard has it.

In WHEATLEY, Wulfsige and Regnvald had 2 manors, each [having] $10\frac{1}{2}$ bovates to the geld, where there could be 2 ploughs.

In the same Wheatley, a Berewick, Regnvald had $10\frac{1}{2}$ bovates of land to the geld. [There is] land for 1 plough.

In 'LANGTHWAITE' [in Adwick le Street], Arulf had 1 manor of 11 bovates to the geld. There is land for 1 plough. [...]

In the same vill Ulfkil had 1 manor of 4 carucates to the geld. There is land for 3 ploughs.

In 'SKYNYTHORP' [in Sprotbrough], Wulfsige and Arnketil had 2 manors of 2 carucates and 5 bovates to the geld. There is land for 2 ploughs. Now there is in demesne 1 plough, and 2 bordars. These 6 manors TRE were worth £6; now £4. Nigel has them of Count Robert.

This sokeland belongs to Wheatley; Doncaster, 3 bovates; Bentley [near Doncaster], 3 bovates; 'Langthwaite' [in Adwick le Street], 1 carucate and 7 bovates; Adwick le Street, half a carucate; Kirk Sandall, half a carucate. Together, [there are] 4 carucates to the geld. Now there is 1 plough in demesne; and 1 sokeman and 7 villans and 8 bordars having 5 ploughs. [There is] scrubland 7 furlongs long and 7 broad.

'OSGODCROSS' WAPENTAKE

In ADWICK LE STREET are 2 bovates to the geld. The soke is in Marr. Now Nigel has 1 plough there. TRE worth 5s; now 5s.

STAINCROSS WAPENTAKE

In PILLEY, Alric had 1 manor of 2 carucates to the geld, and there could be 1 plough. [There is] woodland pasture 1 league long and 1 broad. The whole [is] 1 league long and 1 broad. TRE worth 10s; now 6s8d. Richard has

[Folio 308V: YORKSHIRE]

there 1 plough in demesne; and 3 villan and 3 bordars with 2 ploughs.

In TANKERSLEY, Leodwine had 1 manor of $1\frac{1}{2}$ carucates to the geld, where there could be 2 ploughs. Now Richard has there 3 villans and 2 bordars with 2 ploughs. There is a church and a priest, [and] woodland pasture 1 league long and 1 broad. The whole manor [is] $1\frac{1}{2}$ leagues long and 1 league broad. TRE worth 20s; now 7s.

In WORTLEY, Alric had 1 manor of 1 carucate to the geld, and there could be 1 plough. Now Richard has 1 plough there; and 3 villans and 3 bordars with 2 ploughs. [There is] woodland pasture half a league long and a half broad. The whole [is] 1 league long and 1 broad. TRE worth 10s; now 8s8d.

AINSTY WAPENTAKE

In PALLATHORPE, Alwine had 1 manor of 6 bovates to the geld, and there could be 1 plough. Nigel has it. TRE it was worth 10s; now it is waste.

BURGHSHIRE WAPENTAKE

In HUNSINGORE, Ligulf had 1 manor of 4 carucates and 3 bovates to the geld, where there could be 2 ploughs. Now Richard has it. TRE it was worth 30s; now it is waste.

In Ingmanthorpe [are] 1½ carucates [of] sokeland.

HALLIKELD WAPENTAKE

In CUNDALL, and Norton-le-Clay, a Berewick, and Leckby, a Berewick, Waltheof had 1 manor of 21 carucates to the geld, where there could be 12 ploughs. Count Robert has it now, and it is waste. Alvred holds it of him. To this manor belongs this sokeland: in Leckby, 4 carucates; in Brampton [in Kirby Hill], 2 carucates; in Cundall, 2 carucates; in North Stainley, 1 carucates; in East Tanfield, 1 carucates; in 'Caldewell' [in Marton-le-Moor] 4 carucates. Together, [there are] 14 carucates to the geld, where there could be 8 ploughs. All [are] waste, except that in 'Caldewell' [in Marton-le-Moor] there is 1 villan with half a plough. The whole manor [is] 2 leagues long and 1 broad. TRE worth £4; now 20s. In the above-mentioned manor of Cundall there are 4 villans with 2 ploughs.

[Folio 309: YORKSHIRE]

VI. The land of Count Alan

In GILLING, Earl Edwin had 1 manor of 4 carucates to the king's geld, in which there could be 16 ploughs. Now Count Alan has 2 ploughs there in demesne; and 7 villans with 2 ploughs. [He has] a church, and [there are] 12 acres of meadow, [and] scrubland 1 league long and 1 broad.

To this manor belong these Berewicks: Hartforth, 3 carucates; Newton Morrell, 6 carucates; South Cowton, 3 carucates; and another Cowton [North Cowton], 3 carucates; Eryholme, 6 carucates; Low Hail, 2½ carucates; Stapleton [near Cleasby], 3 carucates; Forcett, 8 carucates; Barforth, 3 carucates.

Together, [there are] 37½ carucates to the geld, and there could be 37 ploughs. All [are] now waste, except that in Hartforth there is 1 man having 3 ploughs, and in South Cowton, Godric the steward has, under the count, 1 plough in demesne; and 5 villans and 2 bordars with 3 ploughs.

To this manor also belongs this sokeland in Moulton, 16 carucates to the geld, and there could be 12 ploughs. Ulf had 1 manor there. Now Count Alan has in demesne 3 ploughs; and 4 villans and 4 bordars with 1½ ploughs.

In Barton, 2½ carucates; in Eppleby, 7 carucates; in Cliffe [in Manfield], 3 carucates; in Carlton [in Stanwick-St-John], 2 carucates; in Barforth, 1 carucate; in Ovington, 3 carucates; in Girlington, 3 carucates; in Wycliffe, 12 carucates; in

Thorpe [in Wycliffe], 3 carucates; in Mortham, 3 carucates; in Egglestone, 3 carucates; in Brignall, 12 carucates; in Scargill, 3 carucates; in Barningham, 4 carucates; in West Layton, 3 carucates; in East Layton, 3 carucates; in Stanwick-St-John, 3 carucates; in another Stanwick [Stanwick-St-John], 1 carucate. Together, [there are] 71½ carucates to the geld, and there could be as many ploughs. Now they are altogether waste.

Besides there is also sokeland of this manor in Manfield of 16 carucates to the geld, where there could be as many ploughs. Now Count Alan has there 3 sokemen having 1 carucate and 6 bovates of this land, and there are 3 ploughs. The rest is waste. There is 1 fishery rendering 10s. There is a church.

In Hutton Magna there is also sokeland of the above-mentioned manor of 6 carucates to the geld, where there could be 6 ploughs. Thor has there under the count 1 plough in demesne; and 7 villans and 4 bordars with 2 ploughs. In these lands there are meadows in some places, also scrubland. For the most part [they are] waste. TRE they were worth £56; now they render £4. The whole manor [is] 2 leagues long and 2 broad.

In MIDDLETON TYAS, Ulf had 1 manor, with sake and soke, of 6 carucates to the geld, and there could be as many ploughs. [...] Uhtræd has it now of Count Alan. In demesne [is] 1 plough; and 5 villans with 4 ploughs. TRE worth 40s; now 20s. The whole manor [is] 2 leagues long and 4 furlongs broad.

In Kneeton, Ulf had 1 manor, with sake and soke, of 8 carucates to the geld, and there could be 6 ploughs. Now Uhtræd has it of the count. TRE it was worth 40s; now it is waste. The whole [is] 2 leagues long and a half broad.

In STAPLETON [near Cleasby], Thor had 1 manor of 5 carucates to the geld, and there could be as many ploughs. Now Enisant has it of the count. TRR [sic] it was worth 10s; now it is waste. The whole [is] 1 league long and a half broad.

In BARNINGHAM, Thor had a hall and 2 carucates of land to the geld, and there could be 2 ploughs. Now Enisant has it of the count. It is waste. The whole [is] 2 leagues long and 1 broad. But there is scrubland 1 league long and a half broad.

In EAST LAYTON, Thorfinnr had 3 carucates of land to the geld, with sake and soke, and there could be 3 ploughs. Now Bodin has it of the count. TRE it was worth 3s; now it is waste. The whole [is] 1 league long and 1 broad

In STANWICK-ST-JOHN, Thor had 3 carucates, with sake and soke, and there could be 3 ploughs. Now Enisant has of the count in demesne 1 plough; and 3 villans with 2 ploughs. TRE worth 3s; now 12s. The whole [is] half a league long and a half broad.

In the same vill is 1 carucate to the geld, and the soke [is] in Gilling.

In OVER DINSDALE, Alsige had 1 manor of 3 carucates to the geld, and there could be 3 ploughs. Now Count Alan has it, and it is waste. [It is] half a league long and as much broad.

TRE it was worth 10s. The soke of this manor belongs to Northallerton.

In GREAT SMEATON [are] 6 carucates to the geld, and there could be 6 ploughs. Madalgrim had 1 manor there. Now Count Alan has it, and it is waste. The king has 2 carucates of this land. The whole [is] 1½ leagues long and 1 league broad.

In GREAT LANGTON [are] 9 carucates to the geld, and there could be 9 ploughs. Thorfinnr, 3½ carucates, and Finnghall, 2 carucates, had 2 halls there. Thorfinnr with sake and soke; and a third man, Thor by name, [had] the remaining land, with sake and soke, but not a hall. Now Bodin and Hervey have it of the count. TRE it was worth 22s; now it is waste. The whole [is] 1 league long and 1 broad. [There are] 12 acres of meadow.

[Folio 309V: YORKSHIRE]

In CALDWELL [are] 6 carucates to the geld, and there could be 6 ploughs. Thor had 1 manor there. Now Enisant has it of Count Alan. In demesne [is] 1 plough, and 1 acre of meadow. The whole [is] 1 league long and 1 broad. TRE worth 20s; now the same.

In ALDBROUGH ST JOHN [are] 8 carucates to the geld, and there could be 8 ploughs. Thor had 1 manor there. Now Enisant has it of Count Alan. In demesne [is] 1 plough; and 11 villans and 3 bordars with 6 ploughs. [There are] 4 acres of meadow, a mill, and a church. The whole [is] 1 league long and 1 broad. TRE worth 40s; now £4. In Carlton [in Stanwick-St-John] are 2 carucates to the geld, and it is inland of Aldbrough St John.

In CLEASBY [are] 6 carucates to the geld, and there could be 6 ploughs. Thor had 1 manor there. Now Enisant has it. In demesne [is] 1 plough; and 2 villans with 1 plough. [There are] 2 acres of meadow. The whole [is] 1 league long and a half broad. TRE worth 10s; now the same.

In CROFT-ON-TEES [are] 14 carucates to the geld, and there could be 12 ploughs. He [sic] had 1 manor there. Now Enisant [has it] of Count Alan. [There are] 5 acres of meadow. The whole [is] 1 league long and 1 broad. TRE it was worth 40s; now it is waste.

In "TORP" [in Croft-on-Tees] [are] 2 carucates to the geld, and there could be 2 ploughs. Rawn had 1 manor there. Now Enisant has it, and it is waste. [There is] 1 acre of meadow. The whole [is] 6 furlongs long and 1 broad. TRE it was worth 5s.

In STARTFORTH [are] 6 carucates to the geld, and there could be 6 ploughs. Thor, 2 carucates, and Thorfinnr, 4 carucates, were there; the former had a manor; the other not. Now Enisant has the land of Thor, and Bodin the land of Thorfinnr. They are waste; but there is only a church. TRE it was worth 12s. The whole [is] 1 league long and 1 broad.

In RICHMOND [are] 5 carucates to the geld, and there could be 3 ploughs. Thor had 1 manor there. Now Enisant has it. In demesne [is] 1 plough; and 6 villans and 2 bordars with 3 ploughs. There is a church and a priest. [There is] scrubland 1

league long and a half broad. The whole [is] 1½ leagues long and half a league broad. TRE worth 10s; now 16s.

In EASBY [near Richmond] [are] 6 carucates to the geld, and there could be 5 ploughs. Thor had 1 manor there. Now Enisant has in demesne 1 plough; and 7 villans with 4 ploughs. The whole [is] 1 league long and a half broad. TRE worth 10s; now |13s|.

In BROMPTON-ON-SWALE [are] 10 carucates to the geld, and there could be 10 ploughs. Thor had 1 manor there. Now Enisant has 2 ploughs there; and 14 villans and 2 bordars with 5 ploughs, and 1 mill [rendering] 5s4d. [There are] 8 acres of meadow. The whole [is] 1 league long and 1 broad. TRE worth 40s; now 32s.

In SKEEBY [are] 6 carucates to the geld, and there could be 4 ploughs.

In "NEUTONE" [in Scorton] [are] 6 carucates to the geld, and there could be 3 ploughs. Thor had 1 manor there. Now Enisant [has it] and both are waste. The whole [is] 1 league long and 1 broad.

In BOLTON-ON-SWALE [are] 6 carucates to the geld, and there could be 4 ploughs. Thor had 1 manor there. Now Enisant has 2 ploughs there, and 4 villans and 1 bordar with 1 plough. The whole [is] 1 league long and a half broad. TRE worth 40s; now 20s.

In KIPLIN [are] 9 carucates to the geld, and there could be 6 ploughs. Thor had 1 manor there. Now Enisant has 2 ploughs there; and 9 villans and 2 bordars with 3 ploughs. The whole [is] 1 league long and 1 broad. TRE worth 40s; now 32s.

In LITTLE LANGTON [are] 7½ carucates to the geld, and there could be 6 ploughs. Odil, 1½ carucates, and Alfkil, 1½ carucates, and Gernand, 3½ carucates, and Sprot, 1 carucate, had there 3 manors. Now Count Alan has it, and it is waste. The whole [is] 1 league long and a half broad. TRE it was worth 20s. This land is in the soke of Kirkby Fleetham, which is noted below.

In THRINTOFT [are] 5 carucates to the geld, and there could be 4 ploughs. This is likewise sokeland of Kirkby Fleetham, 3 carucates. Grim, 1 carucate and 1 bovate, and Ketil, 7 bovates, had 2 manors there, and Hundgrimr had 6 bovates in the same vill, and the soke is in Morton-on-Swale. Now Picot has in demesne 2 ploughs; and 4 villans with 2 ploughs. [There are] 3 acres of meadow. The whole [is] 1 league long and a half broad. TRE worth 16[s.] now 16s.

In SOLBERGE [are] 4 carucates to the geld, and there could be 2 ploughs. Haldor, 2 carucates, and Gillepatric, 2 carucates, each had a hall there. Now Picot has half of the land and the count the other half. [It is] waste. In demesne Picot [has] 1 plough; and 4 villans with 1 plough. The whole [is] 1 league long and 2 furlongs broad. TRE worth 8s; now 13s.

In MAUNBY [are] 10 carucates to the geld, and there could be 8 ploughs. Of these, Gilli had 8 carucates and 5 bovates and 1 manor there. Of these 8 carucates, 4 lie in the soke of Northallerton. Of the remaining land of the manor, Haldor had 6 bovates and Ligulf 5 bovates with sake and soke. Now

Picot has this land, and there are 6 villans with 2 ploughs. The whole [is] 1 league long and 1 broad. TRE worth 20s; now 8s.

In KIRBY WISKE [are] 8 carucates to the geld, and there could be 4 ploughs. Ulfkil, 1½ carucates, had 1 manor there. Ligulf and Thor and Gamal and Siward had the remaining land with 1 hall. Now Picot has it of Count Alan, and it is waste. TRE it was worth 10s. The whole [is] 1 league long and 1 broad. The soke of 2 carucates of this land is in Northallerton.

In MORTON-ON-SWALE [are] 11 carucates to the geld, and there could be 6 ploughs. Gospatric had there 1 manor of 9 carucates, and Grim and Gospatric 3 carucates of which the soke is in Kirkby Fleetham. Now Gospatric has it of the count. In demesne [are] 2 ploughs; and 4 villans with 1 plough. A certain Walter has the land of Grim, 2 carucates, and 2 villans with 1 plough there.

[Folio 310: YORKSHIRE]

There is the site of a fishery. The whole [is] 1 league long and a half broad. TRE worth 40s; now 36s.

In ELLERTON [in Bolton-on-Swale] [are] 9 carucates to the geld, and there could be 6 ploughs. Gospatric had 1 manor there, and the same man has it now of Count Alan. In demesne [are] 2½ ploughs; and 6 villans with 1½ ploughs, and 1 mill [rendering] 6s. [There are] 6 acres of meadow. The whole [is] 2 leagues long and 4 furlongs broad. TRE worth 40s; now 50s

In YAFFORTH [are] 8 carucates to the geld, and there could be 4 ploughs. This land is a Berewick of Northallerton. There is a meadow of 8 acres. The whole [is] 1 league long and 5 furlongs broad.

In AINDERBY STEEPLE, 9 carucates to the geld, is sokeland of Northallerton, 3 carucates, and there could be 6 ploughs. Thorkil had 1 manor there of 6 carucates, and Ulfkil 3 caurcates. Now Ansketil has it of the count, and has there 1 plough, and a church. The whole [is] half a league long and a half broad. TRE worth 20s; now 8s

In WARLABY [are] 6 carucates to the geld, and there could be 4 ploughs. Siward had 1 manor there of 4 carucates of this land, and 2 sokemen 2 carucates belonging to Northallerton. Now Hervey has 1 plough there. The whole [is] half a league long and a half broad. TRE worth 20s; now 5s

In DANBY WISKE [are] 10 carucates to the geld, and there could be 5 ploughs. Kofse had 1 manor there. Now Landric, the man of Count Alan, has it. In demesne [is] 1 plough; and 3 villans with 1 plough. [There are] 6 acres of meadow. The whole [is] 1 league long and a half broad. TRE worth 40s; now 10s

In EAST COWTON [are] 6 carucates to the geld, and there could be 3 ploughs. Thorkil had 1 manor there. Now Landric has it of the count, and it is waste. TRE it was worth 20s. The whole [is] 1 league long and 1 broad.

In LONTON [is] 1 carucate to the geld, and there could be 1 plough. Thorfinnr had this land; now Bodin has it, and it is

waste. [There is] scrubland 3 leagues long and 1 league broad. TRE it was worth 10s

In MICKLETON [are] 6 carucates to the geld, and there could be 3 ploughs. Thorfinnr had this; now Bodin has it, and it is waste. TRE it was worth 16s. The whole [is] 1 league long and a half broad.

In ROMALDKIRK [is] 1 carucate to the geld, and there could be 2 ploughs. Thorfinnr had it; now Bodin has it, and it is waste. TRE it was worth 5s

In HUNDERTHWAITE [is] 1 carucate to the geld, and there could be 1 plough.

In LARTINGTON [are] 3 carucates to the geld, and there could be 2 ploughs.

In COTHERSTONE [are] 6 carucates to the geld, and there could be 3 ploughs.

In ROKEBY [are] 3 carucates to the geld, and there could be 2 ploughs. Thorfinnr had these; now Bodin has them and they are waste. TRE they were worth 50s. [There is] scrubland 2 leagues long and 1 broad.

In 'BROGHTON' [in Newsham, near Barningham] [are] 5 carucates to the geld, and there could be 3 ploughs. Ulfkil had 1 manor there. Now Bodin has it, and it is waste. TRE it was worth 8s. The whole [is] 1 league long and a half broad.

In NEWSHAM [near Barningham] [are] 7 carucates to the geld, and there could be 5 ploughs. Ulfkil, 5 carucates, and Sprot, 2 carucates, had halls there. Now Count Alan has the land of Sprot, and Bodin the land of Ulfkil, and 10 villans and 4 bordars with 4 ploughs. [There are] 4 acres of meadow, [and] scrubland half a league long and as much broad. The whole [is] 1 league long and a half broad. TRE worth 20s.; now 16s

In DALTON [in Ravensworth] [are] 8 carucates to the geld, and there could be 4 ploughs. Gospatric, 3½ carucates, and Thorfinnr, 4½ carucates, had this land; now Bodin has the land of Thorfinnr, and the count the land of Gospatric. They are waste. TRE worth 20s; now 3s. The whole [is] 1 league long and 4 furlongs broad.

In another DALTON [Dalton in Ravensworth] [are] 4 carucates to the geld, and there could be 2 ploughs. Gospatric had 1 manor there. Now the same man has it, and it is waste. TRE it was worth 20s. The whole [is] 1 league long and a half broad.

In RAVENSWORTH [are] 12 carucates to the geld, and there could be 8 ploughs. Thorfinnr had 1 manor there. Now Bodin has half a plough there; and 16 villans and 4 bordars with 8 ploughs. There is a church, and a priest, [and] 4 acres of meadow. The whole [is] 1 league long and a half broad. TRE worth 40s; now 30s

In MELSONBY and 'Didirston' [in Melsonby], a Berewick, [are] 11 carucates to the geld, and there could be 10 ploughs. Thorfinnr had 1 manor there. Now Bodin has 1 plough there; and 15 villans and 3 bordars with 7 ploughs. There is a church and a priest. The whole [is] 1 league long and 1 broad. TRE worth 40s; now 30s

In this vill there are 4 carucates to the geld, of which the soke belongs to Gilling.

In SCORTON [are] 16 carucates to the geld, and there could be 16 ploughs. Thorfinnr had 1 manor there. Now Bodin has 3 ploughs there; and 9 villans with 3 ploughs, and 1 mill [rendering] 3s. [There are] 12 acres of meadow. The whole [is] 2 leagues long and 1 broad. TRE worth 5s; now 50s.

[Folio 310V: YORKSHIRE]

In CATTERICK [are] 10 carucates to the geld, and there could be 10 ploughs. Earl Edwin had 1 manor there. Now Count Alan has it. In demesne [are] 6 ploughs; and 14 villans and 6 bordars with 4 ploughs. There is a church and a priest with half a plough.

To this manor belong these Berewicks: Killerby [in Catterick], 5 carucates; Ainderby Mires, 2½ carucates; Tunstall [near Catterick], 3 carucates and 6 bovates. Together, [there are] 11 carucates and 2 bovates to the geld, and there could be 10 ploughs. Now there are 3 ploughs in demesne; and 16 villans and 10 bordars with 7 ploughs. The whole manor with the Berewicks [is] 1½ leagues long and and [sic] 1 broad. TRE worth £8 now the same.

In AINDERBY MIRES [are] 2½ carucates to the geld, and there could be 2 ploughs. Beornwulf had this land, with sake and soke. Now Landric, the man of the count, has it. In demesne [are] 3 ploughs; and 8 villans and 4 bordars with 2 ploughs. TRE worth 5s; now 40s

In TUNSTALL [near Catterick] [are] 2 carucates to the geld, and there could be 1 plough. Northmann had 1 manor there. Now Count Alan has it. In demesne [are] 2 ploughs; and 3 villans with 1 plough. TRE worth 10s; now 10s

In KIRKBY [near Great Langton] [are] 3 carucates to the geld, and there could be 2 ploughs. Ealdræd had 1 manor there. Now the same man has of the count 1 plough in demesne; and 6 villans with 2 ploughs. The whole [is] 1 league long and 2 furlongs broad. TRE worth 10s; now 16s.

In KIRKBY FLEETHAM [are] 8 carucates to the geld, and there could be 6 ploughs. Gamal and Uhtræd had 2 manors there. Now Odo, the man of the count, has 2 ploughs in demesne; and 16 villans and 2 bordars with 4 ploughs. There is a church and a priest, [and] 8 acres of meadow.

To this manor belong 2 Berewicks, and they are called the Fencotes [Great Fencote and Little Fencote]. In these [are] 9 carucates to the geld, and there could be 9 ploughs. Odo has in demesne there 1 plough; and 10 villans with 2½ ploughs. The whole manor with the Berewicks [is] 1 league long and a half broad. TRE worth 40s; now 40s and 1 sore hawk.

In ASKE [are] 6 carucates to the geld, and there could be 4 ploughs. Thor had 1 manor there. Now Wihomarc, the man of the count, has in demesne 1 plough; and 5 villans and 3 bordars with 2 ploughs. The whole [is] 1 league long and a half broad. TRE worth 20s; now the same.

In SCRUTON [are] 14 carucates to the geld, and there could be 10 ploughs. Knut, 8 carucates, and Thorfinnr, 3½ carucates, had 2 manors there, and Gernand, 2½ carucates. Now Picot, the man of the count, has in demesne 2 ploughs; and 6 villans and 4 bordars with 3 ploughs. The whole [is] half a league long and a half broad. TRE worth 40s; now 50s

In LANGTHORNE [are] 3 carucates to the geld, and there could be 1½ ploughs. Uhtræd had 1 manor there. Now Odo has there 3 villans with 2 ploughs. [There are] 4 acres of meadow. The whole [is] half a league long and a half broad. TRE worth 16s; now 5s

In HACKFORTH [are] 6 carucates to the geld, and there could be 3 ploughs. Arnketil, 5 carucates, and Uhtræd, 1 carucate, had this land. Now Geoffrey has the land of Arnketil, and there are 2 ploughs; and 6 villans with 3 ploughs. TRE worth 14s; now 16s. But Odo has the land of Uhtræd, and it is waste. TRE it was worth 8s. The whole [is] half a league long and as much broad.

In HORNBY [near Hackforth] [are] 8 carucates to the geld, and there could be 6 ploughs. Arnketil had a manor there. Now Gospatric has it of Count Alan. It is waste. The whole [is] 1 league long and 1 broad. TRE it was worth 40s

In HOLTBY [near Ainderby Mires] [are] 3 carucates to the geld, and there could be 2 ploughs. Arnketil had a manor there. Now Gospatric holds it of the count, and it is waste. The whole [is] half a league long and a half broad. TRE it was worth 20s

In EAST APPLETON [are] 12 carucates to the geld, and there could be 8 ploughs. Thorkil had 1 manor there. Now Count Alan has 2 ploughs. The whole [is] 1 league long and 1 broad. TRE [worth] 32s; now 5s

In BROUGH [near Catterick] [are] 9 carucates to the geld, and there could be 6 ploughs. Thor had a manor there. Now Enisant [has] there 3 villans with 2 ploughs. The whole [is] 1 league long and 1 broad. TRE worth 32s; now 8s

In COLBURN [are] 5 carucates to the geld, and there could be 3 ploughs. Gospatric had 1 manor there. Now the same man has it of the count. There are 5 villans and 2 bordars with 2 ploughs. The whole [is] half a league long and 3 furlongs broad. TRE [worth] 20s; now 13s

In HIPSWELL [are] 3 carucates to the geld, and there could be 2 ploughs. Thor had 1 manor there. Now Enisant has there 4 villans and 2 bordars with 3 ploughs. The whole [is] 1 league long and a half broad. TRE worth 16s; now 10s

In SCOTTON [near Richmond] [are] 9 carucates to the geld, and there could be 6 ploughs. Gospatric and Thorfinnr had 2 manors there. Now the same Gospatric has what he had. Bodin has the land of Thorfinnr. Both are waste. The whole [is] 1 league long and 1 broad. TRE it was worth 30s

[Folio 311: YORKSHIRE]

In HUDSWELL [are] 6 carucates to the geld, and there could be 3 ploughs. Thor had this land. Now Enisant has it, and it is waste. The whole [is] 1 league long and 1 broad. TRE it was worth 16s

In RICHMOND [is] 1 carucate to the geld, and there could be 1 plough. Thor had it. Now the count has it, and it is waste. There is a fishery, and scrubland. The whole [is] 1 league long and 1 broad. TRE worth 10s; now 16d

In DOWNHOLME [are] 3 carucates to the geld, and there could be 2 ploughs. Gospatric had a manor there. Now the same man has it of the count, and it is waste. The whole [is] 1 league long and 1 broad. TRE it was worth 10s

In ELLERTON ABBEY [are] 2 carucates to the geld, and there could be 2 ploughs. Gamal had a manor there. Now the count has it, and it is waste. [There is] scrubland. The whole [is] 2 leagues long and 1 broad. TRE it was worth 13s

In MARRICK [are] 5 carucates to the geld, and there could be 2 ploughs. Arnketil had a manor there. Now Gospatric has it, and it is waste. [There is] scrubland. The whole [is] 1 league long and a half broad. TRE it was worth 20s

In GRINTON [is] 1 carucate to the geld, and there could be 1 plough. Thorfinnr had a manor there. Now Bodin has it, and it is waste. The whole [is] 1 league long and a half broad. TRE it was worth 5s.

In FREMINGTON [is] 1 carucate to the geld, and there could be 1 plough. Crin had a manor there. Now Count Alan has it, and it is waste. The whole [is] 1 league long and a half broad. TRE it was worth 5s

In REETH [are] 6 carucates to the geld, and there could be 3 ploughs. Thorfinnr had a manor there. Now Bodin has it, and it is waste. The whole [is] 1 league long and 1 broad. TRE it was worth 14s

In "DENTONE" [in Low Abbotside] [are] 4 carucates to the geld, and there could be 2 ploughs. Thorfinnr had a manor there. Now Bodin has it. The whole [is] 1 league long and 1 broad. TRE it was worth 5s

In 'BROUGH' [in Bainbridge] [are] 3 carucates to the geld, and there could be 2 ploughs. Arnketil had a manor there. Now Count Alan has it, and it is waste. The whole [is] 1 league long and 1 broad. TRE it was worth 8s

In 'FORS' [in Low Abbotside] [are] 4 carucates to the geld, and there could be 2 ploughs. Thorfinnr had this land. Now Bodin has it, and it is waste. The whole [is] 1 league long and a half broad. TRE it was worth 7s

In ASKRIGG [are] 10 carucates to the geld, and there could be 5 ploughs. Arnketil had a manor there. Now Gospatric has it, and it is waste. The whole [is] 1 league long and 1 broad. TRE it was worth 10s

In WORTON [are] 6 carucates to the geld, and there could be 4 ploughs. Thorfinnr had a manor there. Now Bodin has it, and it is waste. The whole [is] 1 league long and 1 broad. TRE it was worth 16s

In THORNTON RUST [are] 6 carucates to the geld, and there could be 4 ploughs. Thor had a manor there. Now Count

Alan has it, and it is waste. The whole [is] 1 league long and 1 broad. TRE it was worth 10s

In AYSGARTH [are] 3 carucates to the geld, and there could be 2 ploughs. Knut had a manor there. Now Geoffrey has it of the count. The whole [is] 1 league long and a half broad. TRE it was worth 8s

In 'CROOKSBY' [in Newbiggin] [are] 3 carucates to the geld, and there could be 1 plough. Beornwulf had a manor there. Now the same man has it of the count, and it is waste. The whole [is] 2 leagues long and a half broad. There are moors. TRE it was worth 5s

In THORALBY [in Aysgarth] [are] 6 carucates to the geld, and there could be 4 ploughs. Beornwulf had a manor there. Now the same man has it, and it is waste. The whole [is] 1 league long and 1 broad. TRE it was worth 20s

In WEST BURTON [are] 6 carucates to the geld, and there could be 4 ploughs. Thorkil had this land. Now Geoffrey has it, and it is waste. In Eshington, a Berewick of West Burton, [are] 3 carucates to the geld, and there could be 2 ploughs. The whole of West Burton [is] 2 leagues long and 1 broad. TRE [it was worth] 20s

In CARPERBY [are] 9 carucates to the geld, and there could be 6 ploughs. Thor had a manor there. Now Enisant has it, and it is waste. TRE it was worth 20s. The whole [is] 1 league long and 1 broad.

In WEST BOLTON [are] 6 carucates to the geld, and there could be 4 [ploughs]. Gillepatric had a manor there. Now Ribald has it, and it is waste. The whole [is] 2 leagues long and 1 broad. TRE it was worth 20s

In another BOLTON [Castle Bolton] [are] 6 carucates to the geld, and there could be 3 ploughs. The 4 sons of Beald had 4 manors there. Now Count Alan has it, and it is waste. The whole [is] 1 league long and 1 broad. TRE it was worth 20s

In [High and Low] THORESBY [is] 1 carucate to the geld, and there could be 1 plough. Gospatric had this, and now has it again of the count, and it is waste.

In REDMIRE [are] 5 carucates to the geld, and there could be 3 ploughs. There were 2 manors of Gillepatric and Gamal. Now Count Alan has it, and Ribald [holds] of him, and it is waste. The whole [is] 1 league long and 1 broad. TRE it was worth 18s

In PRESTON-UNDER-SCAR [are] 3 carucates to the geld, and there could be 2 ploughs. Thorfinnr had 1 manor there. Now Bodin has it, and it is waste. The whole [is] 1 league long and 1 broad. TRE it was worth 10s

In EAST WITTON [are] 12 carucates to the geld, and there could be 8 ploughs. Gluniairnn had 1 manor there. Now Count Alan has it.

[Folio 311V: YORKSHIRE]

In demesne [are] 2 ploughs; and 11 villans and 2 bordars with 5 ploughs. [There is] meadow 1 league long and 1 furlong broad, [and] scrubland. The whole [is] $1\frac{1}{2}$ leagues long and as much broad. TRE worth £4; now 20s.

To this manor belong [these] Berewicks: [High and Low] Thoresby, 2 carucates; West Witton, 5 carucates; Wensley, 4 carucates; and another Wensley, 3 carucates. Together, [there are] 14 carucates to the geld, and there could be 10 ploughs. They are waste. The whole [is] 2 leagues long and 2 broad.

In CARLTON [near Middleham] [are] 6 carucates to the geld, and there could be 4 ploughs. Beornwulf had a manor there. Now the same man has it of the count, and it is waste. [There is] scrubland, with open land, 4 leagues long and a half broad. TRE it was worth 16s

In WEST SCRAFTON [are] 3 carucates to the geld, and there could be 2 ploughs. Gillepatric had a manor there. Now Ribald has it, and it is waste. [There is] scrubland and open land 4 leagues long and a half broad. TRE it was worth 10s.

In MELMERBY [in Coverham] [are] 6 carucates to the geld, and there could be 4 ploughs. Ealdæd had a manor there. Now the same man has it of the count, and it is waste. The whole [is] 1 league long and 1 broad. TRE it was worth 8s.

In AGGLETHORPE [are] 3 carucates to the geld, and there could be 2 ploughs. Thorkil had a manor there. Now the same man has it of the count, and it is waste. The whole [is] 1 league long and a half broad. TRE it was worth 8s.

In CALDBERGH [are] 5 carucates to the geld, and there could be 3 ploughs. Orm had a manor there. Now the same man has it of the count, and it is waste. The whole [is] 1 league long and 1 broad. TRE it was worth 7s.

In COVERHAM [are] 4 carucates to the geld, and there could be 3 ploughs. Thor and Egbrand had 2 manors there. Now Count Alan has it, and it is waste. The whole [is] 1 league long and 1 broad. TRE it was worth 20s.

In MIDDLEHAM [are] 5 carucates to the geld, and there could be 3 ploughs. Gillepatric had a manor there. Now Ribald has it, and it is waste. The whole [is] 1 league long and 1 broad. TRE it was worth 20s.

In LEYBURN [are] $7\frac{1}{2}$ carucates to the geld, and there could be 5 ploughs. Eskil and Othulf had 2 manors there. Now Wihomarc has them, and they are waste. The whole [is] 1 league long and 1 broad. TRE it was worth 20s.

In HARMBY [are] 9 carucates to the geld, and there could be 6 ploughs. Thor had a manor there. Now Wihomarc has in demesne 1 plough; and 12 villans and 8 bordars with 5 ploughs. The whole [is] 1 league long and a half broad. TRE worth 30s; now the same.

In SPENNITHORNE [are] $8\frac{1}{2}$ carucates to the geld, and there could be 6 ploughs. Gillepatric had a manor there. Now Ribald has there 12 villans and 6 bordars with 6 ploughs. There is a church, [and] 6 acres of meadow. The whole [is] 1 league long and a half broad. TRE worth 20s; now 16s.

In DANBY [in Thornton Steward] [are] 4 carucates to the geld, and there could be 3 ploughs. Gamal had a manor there. Now his sons have it of the count. In demesne [are] 2 ploughs;

and 5 villans and 3 bordars with 2 ploughs. The whole [is] 5 furlongs long and 3 broad. TRE worth 10s; now now the same.

In BELLERBY [are] 6 carucates to the geld, and there could be 6 ploughs. Thor had a manor there. Now Enisant has 1 plough there; and 13 villans and 2 bordars with 4 ploughs. [There are] 8 acres of meadow. The whole [is] 1 league long and 1 broad. TRE worth 32s; now the same.

In BARDEN [are] 5 carucates to the geld, and there could be 4 ploughs. Gamal had a manor there. Now Count Alan has it, and it is waste. [There are] 5 acres of meadow. The whole [is] 1 league long and 1 broad. TRE it was worth 20s.

In EAST HAUXWELL [are] 6 carucates to the geld, and there could be 4 ploughs. Gunnar had a manor there. Now Ribald has it, and it is waste. The whole [is] 1 league long and a half broad. TRE it was worth 20s.

In another HAUXWELL [West Hauxwell] [are] 6 carucates to the geld, and there could be 4 ploughs. Gunnar and Gamal had 2 manors there. Now Count Alan has it, and it is waste. The whole [is] 1 league long and a half broad. TRE it was worth 10s.

In GARRISTON [are] 3 carucates to the geld, and there could be 2 ploughs. Thorkil had a manor there. Now Geoffrey has it, and it is waste. The whole [is] 5 furlongs long and 4 broad. TRE it was worth 5s4d

In CONSTABLE BURTON [are] 12 carucates to the geld, and there could be 10 ploughs. Thor had a manor there. Now Enisant has 2 ploughs there; and 12 villans and 8 bordars with 4 ploughs. The whole [is] 1 league long and a half broad. TRE worth 20s; now 25s4d

In THORNTON STEWARD [are] 6 carucates to the geld, and there could be 3 ploughs. In ASCAM'' [in East Witton], a Berewick of this manor, [are] 4 carucates to the geld, and there could be 5 ploughs. Of these, 1 carucate lies in the soke of East Witton. In Thornton Steward, Gospatric had a manor. Now the same man has it himself of the count. In demesne [is] 1 plough; and 5 villans and 2 bordars with 2 ploughs. There is a church. The whole [is] 1 league long and 1 broad. TRE worth 30s; now 20s

In [High and Low] ELLINGTON [are] 6 carucates to the geld, and there could be 4 ploughs. Gospatric, 2 carucates, and Northmann, 3 carucates and 2 bovates, and Thorkil, 6 bovates, had 3 manors there. Now the same Gospatric has of the count what he had. In demesne [is] 1 plough;

[Folio 312: YORKSHIRE]

and 2 villans and 3 bordars with 1 plough. In the remaining land the count has 6 villans with 3 ploughs. [There are] 6 acres of meadow. The whole [is] $1\frac{1}{2}$ leagues long and half a league broad. TRE worth 40s; now 30s.

In 'SWARTRUPS' [in High Ellington] [is] 1 carucate to the geld, and there could be 1 plough. Half is inland of Masham. Thorkil had it. Now the count has it, and it is waste.

In HIGH SUTTON [is] 1 carucate to the geld, and there

could be 1 plough. Northmann had a manor there. Now Count Alan has it, and it is waste. The whole [is] half a league long and a half broad. TRE it was worth 10s.

In FEARBY [are] 3 carucates to the geld, and there could be 2 ploughs. Gospatric and Ealdræd had 2 manors there. Now the count has them, and Gospatric [holds] of him. 8 villans and 1 bordar have 2½ ploughs there. The whole [is] half a league long and 4 furlongs broad. TRE worth 10s; now 16s.

In ILTON [are] 2 carucates to the geld, and there could be 2 ploughs. Arnketil had a manor there. Now Gospatric has 1 plough there, and 3 villans and 2 bordars. The whole [is] half a league long and a half broad. TRE worth 16s; now 8s.

In MASHAM [are] 12 carucates to the geld, and there could be 8 ploughs. Gospatric had 1 manor there. Now Ernegis has 1 plough there; and 10 villans and 3 bordars with 5 ploughs. There is a church.

To this manor belong the Berewicks: 'Twistlebro' [in Masham], 3 carucates; Swinton [in Masham], 3½ carucates; and High Sutton, 1 carucate; 7½ carucates to the geld, and there could be 4 ploughs. They are waste. The whole manor, with the Berewicks, [is] 1 league long and 1 broad. TRE worth £6; now 16s.

In CLIFTON CASTLE [are] 3 carucates to the geld, and there could be 2 ploughs. Knut had a manor there. Now Donewald has 1 plough there; and 3 villans with 1½ ploughs. The whole [is] half a league long and a half broad. TRE worth 8s; now 5s.

In WELL [are] 8 carucates to the geld, and there could be 6 ploughs. Thorkil had a manor there. Now Beornwulf has 2 ploughs there; and 6 villans and 6 bordars with 3 ploughs. There is a church and a priest. The whole [is] 1 league long and 1 broad.

To this manor belong the Berewicks: High Burton, 4 carucates; "Opetone" [in Snape], 4 carucates; "Achebi" [in Snape], 4 carucates. Together [there are] 12 carucates to the geld, and there could be 8 ploughs. There are now 26 villans and 4 bordars with 14 ploughs. [There are] 4 acres of meadow, [and] scrubland. The whole [is] half a league long and a half broad. The whole manor TRE was worth 40s; now 60s.

In FIRBY [in Bedale] [are] 5 carucates to the geld, and there could be 4 ploughs. Ødhvidh had a manor there. Now Count Alan has there 7 villans and 3 bordars with 4 ploughs. The whole [is] half a league long and a half broad. TRE worth 10s; now 13s.

In BEDALE [are] 6 carucates to the geld, and there could be 4 ploughs. Thorir had a manor there. Now Bodin has there 2 ploughs; and 17 villans and 5 bordars with 5 ploughs. [There is] a church, and a mill [rendering] 5s, [and] 6 acres of meadow. The whole [is] 1 league long and a half broad. TRE worth 20s; now 30s.

In AISKEW is sokeland belonging to Masham, 10 carucates to the geld, and there could be 7 ploughs. Count Alan has there 5 villans and 1 bordar with 3 ploughs. [There is] scrubland. The whole [is] 1 league long and a half broad.

In BURRILL is sokeland belonging to East Witton, 5 carucates to the geld, and there could be 3 ploughs. The count has there 2 villans having 6 oxen. The whole [is] half a league long and 3 furlongs broad.

In THORNTON WATLASS [are] 6 carucates to the geld, and there could be 4 ploughs. Wulfweard had a manor there, and another man, Sten, [held there] without a hall. Now Ribald has there 1 plough, and 1 villan and 5 bordars. [There are] 3 acres of meadow. The whole [is] 1 league long and 1 broad. TRE worth 10s; now 5s.

In WATLASS [are] 3 carucates to the geld, and there could be 2 ploughs. Sigrith had a manor there. Now Ribald has it, and it is waste. The whole [is] 1 league long and a half broad. TRE it was worth 16s.

In THORP PERROW is sokeland of Well, 4 carucates to the geld, and there could be 3 ploughs. It is waste.

In COWLING [in Bedale] [are] 4 carucates to the geld, and there could be 3 ploughs. Edwin had this land. Now Robert has it, and it is waste.

In THIRN [are] 3 carucates to the geld, and there could be 2 ploughs. Beornwulf had a manor there. Now the same man has it himself of the count. In demesne [is] 1 plough; and 13 villans and 7 bordars have 6 ploughs. The whole [is] 4 furlongs long and as much broad. TRE worth 5s; now 20s.

In ROOKWITH [are] 6 carucates to the geld, and there could be 4 ploughs. Stenulf had a manor there. Now Count Alan has it, and it is waste. [It is] half a league long and a half a league broad. TRE it was worth 8s.

In HUTTON HANG [are] 5 carucates to the geld, and there could be 4 ploughs. Gilli had a manor there. Now Landric has there 1 villan and 2 bordars with 1 plough. TRE worth 20s; now 4s.

In FINGHALL [are] 6 carucates to the geld, and there could be 4 ploughs. Gamal had a manor there. Now Count Alan has there 13 villans having 7 ploughs. [It is] half a league long and a half broad. TRE worth 10s; now 20s

[Folio 312V: YORKSHIRE]

In RUSWICK [are] 2 carucates to the geld, and there could be 2 ploughs. Asulf and Ulfkil had 1 manor there. Now the count has it, and it is waste. TRE it was worth 5s.

In NEWTON-LE-WILLOWS [are] 12 carucates to the geld, and there could be 7 ploughs. Arnketil, Thorkil and Asulf had 3 manors there. Now 4 knights have them of the count. In demesne [are] 3 ploughs; and 12 villans having 4 ploughs. [There is] scrubland. The whole [is] 1 league long and a half broad. TRE worth 20s; now 28s.

In HUNTON [are] 12 carucates to the geld, and there could be 8 ploughs. Gospatric and Thorfinnr had 2 manors there. Now Gospatric has what he had, and there are 2 villans with 1 plough. Bodin has the land of Thorfinnr. He himself [has] 2 ploughs there; and 13 villans and 1 bordar with 5 ploughs. The whole manor [is] 1 league long and a half broad. TRE worth 26s; now 28s.

In HESELTON [are] 6 carucates to the geld, and there could be 4 ploughs. Thorfinnr and Orm had 2 manors there. Now 3 knights have them of Count Alan. In demesne [is] 1 plough; and 7 villans and 3 bordars with 7 ploughs. [There are] 6 acres of meadow, [and] scrubland and open land half a league long and a half broad. TRE worth 24s; now 15s.

In PATRICK BROMPTON [are] 13 carucates to the geld, and there could be 7 ploughs. [...] Gilli and Thorfinnr were there, having halls, and Arnketil without a hall. Now 3 knights have it of Count Alan. They themselves [have] 2 ploughs; and 22 villans and 5 bordars with 7 ploughs, and a mill [rendering] 5s. [There are] 4 acres of meadow. The whole [is] 1 league long and 1 broad. TRE worth 36s; now 46s.

In GREAT CRAKEHALL [are] 12 carucates to the geld, and there could be 7 ploughs. Of these, 1 carucate [is] sokeland of Masham. Gilli and Ulfkil had 2 manors there. Now 2 knights have them of the count, and there are 2 ploughs in demesne; 8 villans and 6 bordars with 5 ploughs, and 1 mill [rendering] 4s. [There are] 8 acres of meadow, [and] woodland pasture 2 furlongs long and as much broad. The whole manor [is] 1 league long and 1 broad. TRE worth 40s; now 38s.

In EAST TANFIELD [are] 5 carucates to the geld, and there could be 3 ploughs. Arnketil had a manor there. Now Gospatric has it. There is 1 plough. [There is] scrubland and open land 1 league long and 1 broad. TRE worth 20s; now 5s.

In another TANFIELD [West Tanfield] [are] 8 carucates to the geld, and there could be 4 ploughs. Thorkil had a manor there. Now the count has there 5 villans with 3 ploughs. [There is] scrubland and open land 1 league long and a half broad. TRE worth 20s; now 10s.

In UPSLAND [are] 3 carucates to the geld, and there could be 2 ploughs. Arnketil and Thorfinnr had 2 manors there. Now the count has it, and it is waste. [There is] woodland pasture 4 furlongs long and 2 broad. The whole [is] half a league long and a half broad. TRE it was worth 8s.

In HOWGRAVE [are] 5 carucates to the geld. The Archbishop of York has 2, the Bishop of Durham 2, [and] Count Alan 1. They are waste.

In SUTTON HOWGRAVE [are] 4 carucates to the geld, and there could be 3 ploughs. Of these carucates, 3 belong to the Bishop of Durham and 1 to Count Alan. Flotmann had a manor there. Now the count has there 9 villans having 4 ploughs. The whole manor [is] 5 furlongs long and 4 broad. TRE worth 20s; now 8s.

In WATH [near East Tanfield] [are] 6 carucates to the geld, and there could be 4 ploughs. Arnketil and Hrosskell had a manor there. Now the count has it, and it is waste. TRE it was worth 20s.

In MELMERBY [near Middleton Quernhow] [are] 6 carucates to the geld, and there could be 4 ploughs. Arnketil and Thor had a manor there. Now the count has it, and it is waste. TRE it was worth 20s.

In MIDDLETON QUERNHOW [are] 5 carucates to the geld, and there could be 3 ploughs. Thor had a manor there. Now Enisant has 1 plough there; and 8 villans and 2 bordars with 2 ploughs. The whole manor [is] 5 furlongs long and 3 broad. TRE worth 20s; now 15s.

In KIRKILINGTON [are] 9 carucates to the geld, and there could be 6 ploughs. Hrosskell had a manor there. Now Robert, the man of the count, has $1\frac{1}{2}$ ploughs there; and 4 villans [with] $2\frac{1}{2}$ ploughs. The whole manor [is] half a league long and a half broad. TRE worth 20s; now 16s.

In 'YARNWICK' [in Kirklington] [are] 3 carucates to the geld, and there could be 2 ploughs. Gernand had a manor there. Now Robert has it, and it is waste. TRE it was worth 20s.

In "NORMANEBI" [in Carthorpe] [are] 6 carucates to the geld, and there could be 4 ploughs. Arnketil had this land. Now Gospatric has it, and it is waste. TRE it was worth 20s.

In CARTHORPE [are] 4 carucates to the geld, and there could be 2 ploughs. Arnketil had a manor there. Now Gospatric has 1 plough there. TRE worth 30s; now 5s.

[Folio 313: YORKSHIRE]

In BURNESTON, 8 carucates, and THEAKSTON, 12 carucates, and EXELBY, $8\frac{1}{2}$ carucates, and 'Newton Picot' [in Leeming], 6 carucates, and Gatenby, 3 carucates, and "Ounesbi" [in Gatenby], 3 carucates [...] [there are] 40 carucates to the geld, and there could be 20 ploughs. Mæle-Sveinn had 3 manors there. Now Robert, the man of Count Alan, has them. All [are] waste, except that 1 man has 1 plough there. [They are] 3 leagues long and $1\frac{1}{2}$ leagues broad. TRE they were worth £6.

In LOW SWAINBY [are] 6 carucates to the geld, and there could be 4 ploughs. Eskil had a manor there. Now Ribald has 1 plough there; and 3 villans and 5 bordars with 1 plough. The whole [is] 1 league long and a half broad. TRE worth 20s; now 10s.

In ALLERTHORPE [in Pickhill] [are] 2 carucates to the geld. Eskil had it. Ribald has it.

In "SEUENETORP" [in Low Swainby] [are] 3 carucates to the geld. Eskil had it. The count has it.

In PICKHILL [are] 12 carucates to the geld. Thor and Sprot [had] 2 manors. The count has them.

In SINDERBY [are] 6 carucates to the geld. Flotmann [had] a manor. The count has it.

In AINDERBY QUERNHOW [are] 6 carucates to the geld. Flotmann [had] a manor. The count has it.

In HOWE [are] 3 carucates to the geld. Sprot [had] a manor. Robert has it.

In BALDERSBY [are] 3 carucates to the geld. Arnketil [had] a manor. The count has it.

In 'ESEBY' [in Baldersby] [are] 4 carucates to the geld. Thorkil had it. The count has it.

In RAINTON [are] 9 carucates to the geld. Thorkil [had] a manor. The count has it.

All these are waste, except that in Pickhill there is 1 villan with 1 plough, and he pays 3s. In all, TRE they were worth £8. Together, [there are] 50 carucates to the geld, and there could be 30 ploughs.

WEST RIDING

In ASKHAM BRYAN [are] 8 carucates to the geld, and there could be 4 ploughs. Earl Edwin had 1 manor there. Now Count Alan has 2 ploughs there; and 8 villans having 4 ploughs. [There are] 3 acres of meadow, [and] woodland 1 league long and a half broad. The whole [is] 1 league long and 1 broad. TRE [worth] £3; now the same.

In OVERTON and SKELTON [near York], a Berewick, [are] 7 carucates and 6 bovates to the geld, and there could be 4 ploughs. Morcar had 1 manor there. Now Count Alan has 2 ploughs there; and 6 villans and 3 bordars having 4 ploughs. [There are] 30 acres of meadow, [and] woodland pasture 1 league long and 2 furlongs broad. TRE worth 26s; now the same.

In ACASTER SELBY [are] 6 bovates to the geld, and there could be half a plough. Godwine had 1 manor there. Now Count Alan has there 4 bordars and 1 villan with 1½ ploughs. TRE worth 5s; now 6s8d.

In STOCKTON ON THE FOREST [are] 3 carucates to the geld, and there could be 2 ploughs. Count Alan has it, and it is waste.

In GATE FULFORD [are] 10 carucates to the geld, and there could be 5 ploughs. Morcar had 1 manor there. Now Count Alan has 2 ploughs there; and 6 villans with 2 ploughs. [There are] 20 acres of meadow. The whole [is] 1 league long and a half broad. TRE worth 20s; now 16s. To this manor belongs the soke of 2 bovates to the geld in Stillingfleet, which is in the EAST RIDING.

In CLIFTON [near York] [are] 9½ carucates to the geld, and there could be 5 ploughs. Morcar had 1 manor there. Now Count Alan has 2 ploughs there; and 2 villans and 4 bordars with 1 plough. [There are] 21 acres of meadow. TRE worth 20s; now 16s. [...]

IN THE EAST RIDING

To the above-mentioned manor of CLIFTON [near York] belongs this sokeland: Water Fulford, 1 carucate and 3 bovates; Escrick, 4 carucates; "Chetelstorp" [in Escrick], 4 carucates; Langwith, 1½ carucates; Moreby, 1 carucates; Deighton [in Escrick], 4 carucates. These 3 were manors, yet they are in the soke of Clifton [near York]. Together, [there are] 15 carucates, less 1 bovate, to the geld, and there could be 8 ploughs. Now Count Alan has †3† sokemen and 9 villans having 5 ploughs. [There are] 26 acres of meadow, [and] woodland pasture 2 leagues long and 2 broad.

IN THE NORTH RIDING

In FOSTON [are] 8 carucates to the geld, and there could be 4 [ploughs]. Morcar had 1 manor there. Now Count Alan has there 12 villans with 6 ploughs, and 1 church. [There is] woodland pasture 3 furlongs long and 3 broad. The whole manor [is] half a league long and a half broad. TRE worth 40s; now the same.

To this manor belongs this sokeland: Terrington, 1½ carucates; Thornton-le-Clay, 2 carucates; Huntington, 1 carucate and 2 bovates; Flaxton, 1½ carucates. Together, [there are] 6 carucates and 2 bovates to the geld, and there could be 5 ploughs. They are waste.

[Folio 313V: [YORKSHIRE]]

[Blank in MS]

[Folio 314: YORKSHIRE]

VII. The land of Robert de Tosny

In NORTH DALTON [are] 15 carucates and 2 bovates to the geld. Thorgot had 1 manor there. There could be 15 ploughs. Now Robert de Tosny has it, and Berengar, his son, [holds] of him. In demesne [are] 4 ploughs; and 22 villans and 3 bordars having 5 ploughs. There is a priest and a church.

In the same vill is sokeland belonging to this manor of 6 carucates and 6 bovates to the geld. There is 1 sokeman now. TRE the manor was worth £4; now £3

In NABURN [are] 4 carucates to the geld, and there could be 4 ploughs. Thorgot had 1 manor there. Now Berengar has it of his father Robert. There are 3 oxen ploughing. [There are] 30 acres of meadow, [and] scrubland 1 league long and 1 broad. TRE worth 10s; now 7s

VIII. The land of Berengar de Tosny

IN THE NORTH RIDING

In KIRBY MISPERTON, Thorbrandr had 2 carucates and 6 bovates to the geld. [There is] land for 2 ploughs. Now Berengar de Tosny has it, and the Abbot of York [holds] of him. In demesne [are] 3 ploughs, and 13 villans, and [he has] half a church, with a priest, and 1 mill rendering 5s4d, and [there are] 12 acres of meadow. TRE worth 3s; now 20s.

In another KIRBY [Kirby Misperton], Gamal had 1 manor of 4 carucates and 2 bovates to the geld. [There is] land for 2 ploughs. Now the abbot has it of Berengar, and it is waste. TRE it was worth 8s. The whole [is] 1 league long and 1 broad.

In LASTINGHAM, Gamal had 1 manor with 1 carucate of land to the geld. [There is] land for 1 plough. Of Berengar the abbot now has there 1 villan with 1 plough.

In SPAUNTON, Gamal had 1 manor with 6½ carucates of land to the geld. [There is] land for 6 ploughs. Now the abbot has it of Berengar. In demesne [are] 2 ploughs; and 9 villans with 2 ploughs. [There is] woodland pasture half a league long and 4 furlongs broad. TRE worth 10s; now the same.

In DALBY, Gamal had 1 manor with 3 carucates to the geld. [There is] land for 3 ploughs. Now the abbot has it of Berengar. In demesne [is] 1 plough; and 6 villans with 2 ploughs, and 1 mill [rendering] 2s, and 12 acres of meadow. [There is] woodland pasture 5 furlongs long and 3 broad. The whole manor [is] 1 league long and a half broad. TRE worth 10s; now the same.

To this manor belongs 1 carucate of land in "Fornetorp" [?in Cornborough].

In BROMPTON [near Snainton], Gamal had 6 carucates to the geld. [There is] land for 3 ploughs. Now Berengar has 1 plough there; and 9 villans with 5 ploughs, and 1 mill [rendering] 5s. [He has] a priest and a church, and [There are] 8 acres of meadow, and [he has] scrubland 2 furlongs long and 2 broad. TRE worth 10s; now 20s.

In "LEIDTORP" [in Thornton Dale], Gamal had 3½ carucates to the geld. [There is] land for 2 ploughs. Now Berengar has 1 plough there, and 15 villans and 9 bordars and 7 rent-paying tenants, and [there are] 4 acres of meadow. The whole manor [is] 2 leagues long and 1 broad. TRE worth 10s8d; now 16s4d

In SINNINGTON, Thorbrandr had 3 carucates of land to the geld. [There is] land for 2 ploughs. Now Berengar has 1 plough there; and 8 villans and 6 bordars with 3 ploughs, and 8 acres of meadow. [There is] woodland pasture 1 league long and 1 broad. The whole manor [is] 1½ leagues long and 1 broad. TRE worth 8s; now 10s.

In LOW HUTTON, Thorbrandr had 5½ carucates of land to the geld. [There is] land for 5 ploughs. Now Berengar has there 2 villans with half a plough, and 3 rent-paying tenants and 14 other villans and 12 bordars with 6 ploughs. TRE worth 20s; now 8s.

In 'HENDERSKELFE' [in Bulmer], Thorbrandr had 4 carucates of land to the geld. [There is] land for 4 ploughs. Now Berengar has there 3 rent-paying tenants with 2 ploughs, and 4 acres of meadow. The whole [is] 1 league long and a half broad. TRE worth 10s; now 5s

In EAST AYTON, Gamal had 2 carucates to the geld. [There is] land for 1 plough.

In NEWTON-ON-RAWCLIFFE [is] 1 carucate to the geld. [There is] land for half a plough.

In SNAINTON [are] 5 carucates to the geld. [There is] land for 3 ploughs.

In 'Little MARISH' [in Ebberston] [are] 2 carucates to the geld. [There is] land for 1 plough.

In THORNTON DALE [is] 1 carucate to the geld. [There is] land for half a plough.

In MARTON [in Sinnington] [are] 5 carucates to the geld. [There is] land for 3 ploughs.

In BROUGHTON [in Appleton-le-Street] [is] 1 carucate to the geld. [There is] land for half a plough.

In HIGH NORTHOLME [are] 1½ carucates to the geld. [There is] land for 1 plough.

In OSWALDKIRK [is] 1 carucate to the geld. [There is] land for half a plough.

In TERRINGTON [are] 2 bovates to the geld. [There is] land for 2 oxen.

In WIGANTHORPE [is] 1 carucate to the geld. [There is] land for half a plough.

Gamal had these lands, and now Berengar has them, but they are all waste.

In GREAT EDSTONE, Gamal had 8 carucates to the geld. [There is] land for 4 ploughs. Now Berengar has it, and it is waste. [He has] 8 acres of meadow. [There is] woodland, pasture in places, 2 furlongs long and 1 broad. The whole [is] 1 league long and 1 broad. TRE it was worth 20s.

In Little EDSTONE, Thorbrandr had 3 carucates to the geld. [There is] land for 2 ploughs. Now Berengar has it, and it is waste. [There are] woodland pasture 2 furlongs long and 1 broad. The whole manor [is] half a league long and a half broad. TRE it was worth 10s

[Folio 314V: YORKSHIRE]

In NAWTON [are] 2 carucates to the geld.

In SINNINGTON [are] 2 carucates to the geld.

In WELBURN [in Kirkdale] [is] 1 carucate to the geld.

In "WALETUNE" [in Kirdale] [is] 1 bovate to the geld.

In HAROME [are] 2 bovates to the geld. Thorbrandr had these lands. Now Berengar has them, and they are waste.

WEST RIDING

In WESTON, Thorbrandr had 5 carucates of land to the geld. [There is] land for 5 ploughs. Now Berengar has there 4 villans with 1 plough. [He has] a church and a priest, and 2 acres of meadow. [There is] woodland pasture half a league long and a half broad. The whole [is] 1 league long and 1 broad. TRE worth 30s; now 10s.

In ASKWITH, Gamal had 1 carucate of land to the geld.

In Bank Newton and Broughton [near Skipton], Thorbrandr had 8 carucates of land to the geld.

EAST RIDING

In 'BUCKTON HOLMS' [in Settrington], Thorbrandr had 10 carucates of land to the geld. [There is] land for 10 ploughs. Now Berengar has there in demesne 4 ploughs, and 1 mill [rendering] 6s. [He has] a church and a priest. In this vill is sokeland of 12 carucates and 6 bovates to the geld. There are now 7 sokemen having 12 villans and 6 bordars with 9 ploughs, and 1 mill [rendering] 2s. TRE the manor was worth 4; now 8 To the same manor belongs also this sokeland: Uncleby, 4 carucates; East Heslerton, 1½ carucates; Croome,

1 carucate; Cowlam, 6 carucates. All these are waste. Together, [there are] 12½ carucates to the geld. [There is] land for as many ploughs.

In MENETHORPE, Gamal had 6 carucates to the geld. [There is] land for 6 ploughs. Now Berengar has 2 ploughs there; and 9 villans and 9 bordars with 4 ploughs, and 1 mill [rendering] 12s. [It is] half a league long and 4 furlongs broad. TRE worth 40s; now the same.

In SETTRINGTON, Thorbrandr had 9 carucates of land to the geld. [There is] land for 9 ploughs. Now Berengar has there 2 ploughs in demesne; and 16 villans and 2 bordars with 6 ploughs. [There are] 20 acres of meadow. TRE worth 30ss. [sic]; now 40s.

In DUGGLEBY, Thorbrandr and Gamal had 8 carucates to the geld. [There is] land for 8 ploughs. Now Berengar has 1 plough there, and 5 villans and 2 bordars with 2 ploughs, and it is worth 10s. TRE [...].

In HEATHFIELD, Gamal had 2 carucates to the geld. [There is] land for 2 ploughs. Now Berengar has it, and it is waste. [There is] woodland pasture 1 league long and a half broad. The whole manor [is] 1 league long and 1 broad. TRE it was worth 20s.

In BURYTHORPE, Thorbrandr had 3 carucates to the geld. [There is] land for 3 ploughs. Now Berengar has it, and it is waste. TRE it was worth 10s.

[Folio 315: YORKSHIRE]

IX. The land of Ilbert de Lacy

WEST RIDING

'SKYRACK' WAPENTAKE

In KIPPAX and LEDSTON, Earl Edwin had 18 carucates to the geld, and there could be 10 ploughs. To this manor belongs land which is properly called Barwick in Elmet, in which there are 8 carucates to the geld, and there could be 4 ploughs.

Ilbert de Lacy has this land now, where he has in demesne 12 ploughs; and 48 villans and 12 bordars with 16 ploughs, and 3 churches and 3 priests, and 3 mills [rendering] 10s. [There is] woodland pasture 2 leagues long and 1 broad. The whole manor [is] 5 leagues long and 2 broad. TRE worth £16; now the same.

To this manor belongs this sokeland: Allerton Bywater, 6 carucates; [Great and Little] Preston, 6 carucates; Swillington, 3 carucates; Garforth, 1½ carucates; 'Skelton' [in Leeds], 3 carucates; Coldcotes, 2 carucates; Colton [in Temple Newsam], 2 carucates; Austhorpe, 4 carucates; Manston, 4 carucates; Kiddal, 3 carucates; Potterton, 2 carucates; Gipton, 1 carucate; Parlington, 6 carucates; | 'Cowthwaite' [in Aberford], 2 carucates. Together, [there are] 45½ carucates to the geld, and there could be 24 ploughs. These are waste. In this manor are 30 acres of meadow.

In GARFORTH, Earnwig had 7 carucates of land to the

geld, and there could be 4 ploughs. Now Ilbert has there 2 ploughs in demesne; and 4 villans and 1 bordar with 1 plough. [He has] a church and a priest, [and] 4 acres of meadow. [There is] woodland pasture 2 furlongs long and 2 broad. The whole manor [is] half a league long and a half broad. TRE worth 60s; now 30s.

In the same vill, William and Warin, men of Ilbert, have 3 ploughs.

In SWILLINGTON, Dunstan and Oda had 9 carucates of the geld, and there could be 5 ploughs. Now Ilbert has there 2 villans and 2 bordars with 1 plough. There is a church, and 4 acres of meadow, [and] woodland pasture 4 furlongs long and 1 furlong broad. The whole manor [is] half a league long and a half broad. TRE worth £4; now 10s.

In SHIPPEN and Sturton, Godric and Earnwig had 4 carucates of land to the geld, and there could be 2 ploughs. Ilbert has it, and Ranulph [holds] of him. It is waste. [He has] 4 acres of meadow. [There is] woodland pasture 4 furlongs long and 1 broad. The whole manor [is] half a league long and 4 furlongs broad. TRE it was worth 20s.

In STURTON, Grimkel had 5 carucates to the geld, and there could be 3 ploughs. Now Ralph has it of Ilbert. There are 5 ploughs; and 5 villans and 3 bordars with 1 plough. [He has] 3 acres of meadow. The whole manor [is] half a league long and a half broad. TRE worth 30s; now 40s.

In KIDDAL and Parlington, Ulfkil had 3 carucates of land [to] the geld, where there could be 2 ploughs. Now Ilbert has there 3 bordars with 1 plough. There is woodland pasture 4 furlongs long and 4 broad. TRE worth 30s; now s

In HALTON [in Temple Newsam], Morfari had 6 carucates of land to the geld, where there could be 3 ploughs. Now Ilbert has it, and it is waste. TRE it was worth 20s; now it renders 2s.

In SEACROFT, Oda and Nivelung, Wulfmær, Stenulf [and] Regnild had 7 carucates of land to the geld, and there could be 4 ploughs. Now a certain Robert has it of Ilbert, and it is waste. [There is] woodland pasture 4 furlongs long and 3 broad. TRE worth £4; now 20d.

In THORNER, Ulfkil, Ulvar, Bergulf and Wulfstan had 8 carucates of land to the geld, and there could be 4 ploughs. Now Ilbert has there 2 villans and 1 bordar with 2 ploughs. [There is] woodland pasture half a league long and as much broad. TRE worth 4; now 10s.

In BIRKBY HILL and 'Wetecroft' [in Thorner], Alweard had 2 carucates of land to the geld, and there could be 1 plough. Now Robert has it of Ilbert, and it is waste. TRE it was worth 20s.

In CHAPEL ALLERTON, Gluniairnn had 6 carucates of land to the geld, where there could be 3 ploughs. Now Ilbert has it, and it is waste. TRE it was worth 40s. [There is] woodland pasture 1 league long and a half broad.

In GIPTON and Colton [in Temple Newsam], Gospatric had 4½ carucates of land to the geld, and there could be 3 ploughs.

Now Ilbert has it, and it is waste. TRE worth 40s; now 2s. There is a church, and woodland pasture half a league long and a half broad.

In NEWSAM GREEN, [...] Dunstan and Gluniairnn had 8 carucates of land to the geld, and there could be 4 ploughs. Now Ansfrid has it of Ilbert, and there are 8 villans and 2 sokemen with 3 ploughs. [He has] 3 acres of meadow. [There is] woodland pasture half a league long and a half broad. TRE worth 60s; now 6s.

In 'THORPE STAPLETON' [in Leeds], Oda had 4 carucates of land to the geld, and there could be 2 ploughs. Now Gilbert has it of Ilbert, and there are 2 villans and 3 bordars with 2 ploughs, and 5 acres of meadow. [There is] woodland pasture 1 furlong long and as much broad. TRE worth 20s; now 5s4d.

In "SNITERTUN", Nivelung, Mabon, Morfari [and] Uhtræd had 8 carucates of land to the geld, and there could be 6 ploughs. Now Ilbert has it, and it is waste. TRE it was worth 60s. There are 2 acres of meadow.

In LEAD, Gunnar had 2 carucates of land to the geld, and there could be 3 ploughs. Now William has it of Ilbert. In demesne [are] 2 ploughs; and 3 villans and 2 bordars with 1 plough, and [he has] 2 acres of meadow. TRE worth 20s; now 30s.

In LEEDS [are] 10 carucates of land and 6 bovates to the geld. [There is] land for 6 ploughs. 7 thegns held it TRE as 7 manors. There now 27 villans and 4 sokemen and 4 bordars have 14 ploughs. There is a priest and a church, and a mill [rendering] 4s, and 10 acres of meadow. It was worth £6; now £7. In HEADINGLEY [are] 7 carucates of land to the geld. [There is] land for 3½ ploughs. 2 thegns held it as 2 manors. There are 2 villans with 1 plough. It was worth 40s; now 4s. In SAXTON [are] 6 carucates of land to the geld. [There is] land for 4 ploughs, and in 4 Berewicks belonging there [are] 9 carucates of land and 2 bovates to the geld. [There is] land for 8 ploughs. Now there are in demesne 3 ploughs; and 7 villans and 7 bordars with 6 ploughs. There is a church and 3 parts of a church, and 2 mills [rendering] 10s, and 10 acres of meadow. It was worth £7; now 100s. 3 thegns held it as 3 manors.

In BURTON and Brayton, a Berewick, and Thorpe Willoughby, a Berewick, [there are] 3½ carucates to the geld. [There is] land for 2 ploughs. There is a church, and a priest with 2 ploughs. Bath held it TRE.

In "HUNCHILHUSE" [in Sherburn in Elmet], Hunchil had 1 carucate of land to the geld. [There is] land for half a plough. Now Ilbert has it, and it is waste. TRE it was worth 10s8d.

In BARKSTON, Saxulf had 1 carucate of land to the geld. [There is] land for half a plough. Now Ilbert has there 1 sokeman with 1 plough. TRE worth 10s; now the same.

In [Church and Little] FENTON, Asmund had 3 bovates to the geld. [There is] land for half a plough. Now the same man has it of Ilbert. In demesne [is] 1 plough, and 1 acre of meadow. TRE worth 10s; now 10s.

In RYTHER, Arnketil and Gamal and Hrosskell had 2 carucates of land to the geld, and there could be 2 ploughs. Now Hugh has it of Ilbert, In demesne [is] 1 plough; and 6 villans and 4 bordars with 1 plough. [There is] a priest and a church, 18 acres of meadow, [and] woodland pasture 1½ leagues long and 1 league broad. The whole [is] 2 leagues long and 1 league broad. TRE worth 40s; now 30s.

In HAMBLETON, Alfkil had 3 carucates of land to the geld, and there could be 2 ploughs. Now Earnwig has it of Ilbert. In demesne [is] 1 plough; and 6 villans and 1 bordar and 2 sokemen, but they have no ploughs. [There is] woodland pasture 1 league long and 1 broad. The whole manor [is] 2 legues long and 1½ leagues broad. TRE worth 30s; now 20s.

In BIRKIN, Ælfric had 1 carucate of land to the geld, and there could be 1 plough. Now Gamal has it under Ilbert. In demesne [is] 1 plough; and 4 villans and 2 bordars with 2 ploughs, and 1 mill [rendering] 3s. [There are] 2 acres of meadow, [and] woodland pasture 1 league long and a half broad. TRE worth 10s; now the same. This land is said to belong to Snaith.

In NEWTON [in Ledsham], Alweard had 3 carucates of land to the geld, and there could be 2 plough. Now Ilbert has it, and Humphrey [holds] of him. In demesne [is] 1 plough; and 2 villans and 1 bordar with 1 plough, and 5 acres of meadow. TRE worth 20s; now 20s.

In FAIRBURN, Ligulf had 2½ carucates of land to the geld, and there could be 2 ploughs. Now the same man has it of Ilbert. In demesne [is] 1 plough; and 4 villans and 3 bordars with 1 plough, and 5 acres of meadow. TRE worth 20s; now the same.

To this manor belongs Ledsham, where there are 2 carucates of land to the geld, and there could be 1 plough. Now there are 2 villans and 3 bordars with 2 ploughs.

In GRIMSTON [in Kirkby Wharfe], Wulfsige had 1 carucate and 5 bovates of land to the geld, and there could be 1 plough. Now Ilbert has it, and it is waste. TRE it was worth 10s.

In KIRKBY WHARFE, Forne had half a carucate of land to the geld, and there could be half a plough. Now Ilbert has it, and it is waste. TRE it was worth 5s.

In "NIUUESHUSUM" [in Ulleskelf], Ketil had 2 carucates of land to the geld, and there could be 1 plough. Now Ilbert has it, and it is waste. TRE it was worth 5s. There are 2 acres of meadow, and the site of a mill.

In NORTH MILFORD, Wulfstan had 2 carucates of land to the geld, where there could be 1 plough. Now Turstin has it of Ilbert. There are 4 villans and 5 bordars, but they do not plough. TRE worth 10s; now 10s.

In SOUTH ELMSALL and MOORTHORPE and SOUTH KIRKBY and FRICKLEY, Swein and Arnketil had 11 carucates of land to the geld, where there could be 6 ploughs. Now Ilbert has 3 ploughs there; and 11 villans and 5 bordars having 7 ploughs. There is a church and a priest, and 3 acres of meadow, and the site of a mill, [and] woodland pasture 1 league long and 1 broad. The whole manor [is] 1 league long and ½ long *[sic]* and 1 broad. TRE worth 100s; now £4.10s8d; and from the shire £6.

In NORTON [near Campsall], Alsige and Orm had 5 carucates of land to the geld, where there could be 3 ploughs. Now Ilbert has it, and the same men themselves [hold] under him. In demesne [are] 2 ploughs; and 10 villans and 15 bordars with 6 ploughs, and 1 mill [rendering] 5s. [There is] woodland pasture 1 league long and a half broad. The whole manor [is] 1 league long and 11 furlongs broad. TRE worth £6; now 70s.

In CAMPSALL, Alsige had 2½ carucates of land to the geld, and there could be 5 ploughs. Now Ilbert has 2 ploughs there; and 16 villans and 3 bordars with 5 ploughs. [There is] woodland pasture 1 league long and a half broad. The whole manor [is] 3 leagues long and a half broad. TRE worth £4 now the same.

In BURGHWALLIS, Toki had 3 carucates of land to the geld, and there could be 3 ploughs. Now William has it of Ilbert. In demesne [is] 1 plough; and 3 villans and 3 bordars having 2½ ploughs, and 2 acres of meadow. [There is] woodland pasture half a league long and as much broad. The whole manor [is] 1 league long and a half broad. TRE worth 40s; now 30s.

In CAMPSALL, Barth had 2½ carucates to the geld, where there could be 5 ploughs. Now Ilbert has 4 ploughs there; and 2 villans and 3 bordars with 2 ploughs, and [there are] 2 acres of meadow. [There is] woodland pasture 1 league long and a half broad. The whole manor [is] 3 leagues long and a half broad. TRE worth £4; now the same.

In SKELLOW, Gluniairnn, Northmann, Alsige, Adelo [and] Leofkoll had 4 carucates of land to the geld. [There is] land for 3 ploughs. Now William has it of Ilbert. In demesne [is] 1 plough; and 10 villans and 5 bordars having 3 ploughs. There are 8 acres of meadow, [and] woodland pasture half a league long and 4 furlongs broad. TRE worth 60s; now 40s.

In OWSTON, Gluniairnn, Ulfkil and Skotkollr had 4 carucates of land to the geld, where there could be 3 ploughs. Now Alvred has it of Ilbert. He himself [has] 1 plough; and 12 villans and 5 bordars having 4 ploughs. There are 8 acres of meadow, [and] woodland pasture half a league long and a half broad. TRE worth 60s; now 40s.

In "NEUUOSE" [in Campsall] and Sutton [near Campsall], Alsige had 2 carucates of land to the geld, where there could be 2 ploughs. Now the same man has it of Ilbert, and it is waste. TRE worth 60s; now 1 mill which is there renders 6s.

[Folio 316: YORKSHIRE]

In SKELBROOKE, Godric and Alwine had 3 carucates of land to the geld, where there could be 4 ploughs. Now Hervey has it of Ilbert. He himself [has] 2 ploughs there; and 9 villans and 2 bordars having 4 ploughs, and [there are] 5 acres of meadow. TRE worth £4; now 3

In STUBBS, Godric had 1 carucate of land without geld, where there could be 1 plough. Now Ansgot has it of Ilbert. He

himself [has] 1 plough there, and half a mill rendering 3s, and [there are] 4 acres of meadow. TRE worth 20s; now the same.

In WALDEN STUBBS, Alsige, Arnketil and Edward had 3 carucates of land and half a bovate to the geld, where there could be 2 ploughs. Now Robert has it of Ilbert. He himself [has] 2 ploughs there; and 3 sokemen and 1 villan and 3 bordars having 2 ploughs. TRE worth 40s; now 30s.

In BADSWORTH and Upton [in Badsworth] and Rogerthorpe, 2 brothers had 9 carucates of land and 5 bovates to the geld, where there could be 6 ploughs. Now Ilbert has 1½ ploughs; and 13 villans and 11 bordars having 5 ploughs. There is a church and a priest, and 1½ acres of meadow, [and] woodland pasture 1 league long and 3 furlongs broad. TRE worth 3; now the same.

In THORPE AUDLIN, Alsige had 6 carucates of land and 3 bovates to the geld, where there could be 5 ploughs. Now Ralph has it of Ilbert. He himself [has] there 1½ ploughs; and 8 villans and 6 bordars having 3½ ploughs. There is the site of 1 mill, and 1 acre of meadow. TRE worth £4; now 40s

In [Kirk and Little] SMEATON [in Womersley], Gamal, Ulfkil and Morcar had 5 carucates of land to the geld, and there could be 5 ploughs. Now Robert has it under Ilbert. He himself [has] there 2 ploughs, and 7 villans and 6 bordars and 2 free men. There is a priest and a church. All these [have] 1 plough, and 1 mill [rendering] 2s. TRE worth 4; now 40s

In [Kirk and Little] SMEATON [in Womersley], Barth and Andor and Gamal and Ulfkil and Morcar had 9 carucates of land to the geld, where there could be 13 ploughs. Now Robert has it of Ilbert, and the same men themselves have under him 6 ploughs; and 23 villans and 20 bordars having 8 ploughs, and 2 mills rendering 9s4d. [There is] scrubland in places. The whole manor [is] 1 league long and a half broad. TRE worth £6; now £6.14s.

In WOMERSLEY, Wege had 6 carucates of land to the geld, and there could be 6 ploughs. Now Ilbert has 3 ploughs there; and 14 villans and 4 bordars having 8 ploughs. There is a priest and a church, and 3 acres of meadow, [and] woodland pasture 1 league long and a half broad. The whole manor [is] 1 league long and 1 broad. TRE worth £6; now £5

In STAPPLETON [in Darrington], Barth and Ulfkil had 4 carucates of land to the geld, where there could be 5 ploughs. Now Gilbert has it of Ilbert. He himself [has] there 2½ ploughs; and 4 villans and 12 bordars with 4 ploughs, and [there is] 1 acre of meadow. The whole manor [is] 1 league long and a half broad. TRE worth £4; now £3.

In DARRINGTON, Barth and Alsige had 6 carucates of land to the geld, where there could be 8 ploughs. Now Ilbert has 3 ploughs there; and 16 villans and 6 bordars having 12 ploughs. There is a priest and a church, and 1 mill [rendering] 3s. TRE worth £8; now 100s.

In [High and Low] ACKWORTH, Eadwulf and Oswulf had 6 carucates of land to the geld, where there could be 5 ploughs. Now Humphrey has it of Ilbert. He himself [has] there 1½ ploughs; and 14 villans and 2 bordars with 6 ploughs. There is a church and a priest, and a mill [rendering] 16d. TRE worth £4; now £3.

In HESSLE [in Wragby], Alweard had half a carucate of land to the geld, and there could be half a plough. Now Mauger has it of Ilbert. There are 6 iron workers and 3 bordars with 1 plough. TRE worth 5s; now 8s.

In NORTH FEATHERSTONE and Purston Jaglin and West Hardwick and Nostell, Ligulf had 16 carucates of land to the geld, and there could be 6 ploughs. Now Ralph and Ernulf have them of Ilbert. In demesne [are] 3 ploughs; and 20 villans and 15 bordars with 7 ploughs. There are 2 churches and 2 priests, [and] woodland pasture 1 league long and 1 broad. TRE worth 100s; now 60s

In GLASS HOUGHTON, Leofwine had 6 carucates of land to the geld, and there could be 4 ploughs. Now Ilbert has 3 ploughs there; and 14 villans and 4 bordars having 6 ploughs. TRE worth 100s; now 4

In WHELDALE and WATER FRYSTON, Gamal had 7 carucates of land to the geld, where there could be 5 ploughs. Now Gherbod has it of Ilbert. He himself [has] 3 ploughs there; and 4 villans and 1 bordar having 4½ ploughs. There is a church and a priest, and 24 acres of meadow. TRE worth £4; now 30s

In FERRYBRIDGE, Swein had 5 carucates of land to the geld, where there could be 4 ploughs. Now Hamelin has it of Ilbert. He himself [has] 2 ploughs there; and 3 villans with 2 ploughs, and [there are] 3 acres of meadow. TRE worth 50s; now 20s.

In KNOTTINGLEY, Barth had 4 carucates of land to the geld, and there could be 4 ploughs. Now Ranulph has it of Ilbert. He himself [has] 1½ ploughs there; and 6 villans and 2 bordars with 1½ ploughs. [There is] woodland pasture half a league long and 4 furlongs broad. TRE worth £4; now 40s.

In BEAL, Barth had 4 carucates of land to the geld, where there could be 2 ploughs. Now a certain thegn has it of Ilbert. He himself [has] 2 ploughs there; and 2 villans and 2 bordars with 2 ploughs, and [there are] 6 acres of meadow. [There is] woodland pasture half a league long and a half broad. TRE worth 60s; now 20s.

In KELLINGTON, Barth had 2 carucates of land to the geld, where there could be 1 plough. Now Alric has it of Ilbert. He himself [has] half a plough there, and 1 villan and 2 bordars. [There is] woodland pasture half a league long and 3 furlongs broad, and 3 acres of meadow.

[Folio 316V: YORKSHIRE]

TRE worth 20s; now 5s.

In ROALL and [High and Low] Eggborough, Barth had 4 carucates of land to the geld, where there could be 2 ploughs. Now the same man has it of Ilbert. He himself [has] 1 plough there; and 2 villans and 3 bordars with 1 plough. There are 4 acres of meadow, and 1 mill rendering 3s. TRE worth 60s.; now 20s.

In KELLINGTON, Barth had 2 carucates of land to the geld,

where there could be 1 plough. Now the same man has it of Ilbert. He himself [has] 1 plough there; and 2 villans with 1 plough. TRE worth 20s; now 15s. To this manor belongs [High and Low] Eggborough, sokeland, 2 carucates of land to the geld, where there are 2 villans and 1 bordar with 1 plough.

In NORTH ELMSALL, Siward and Alsige had 8 carucates of land to the geld, where there could be 5 ploughs. Now Alric has it of Ilbert. He himself [has] 2 ploughs there; and 1 villan and 5 bordars with 1 plough. [There is] woodland pasture 3 furlongs long and 3 broad. TRE worth £3; now 20s.

In TANSHELF are 16 carucates of land, without geld, where there could be 9 ploughs. The king had this manor. Now Ilbert has 4 ploughs there; and 60 lesser burgesses and 16 cottars and 16 villans and 8 bordars having 18 ploughs. There is a church and a priest, and 1 fishery, and 3 mills rendering 42s, and 3 acres of meadow, [and] woodland pasture 1 league long and a half broad. The whole manor [is] 1½ leagues long and a half broad. TRE worth 20; now 15. within this boundary is contained the alms [land] of the poor.

To the same manor belongs this sokeland: Minsthorpe, 2 carucates; Barnby [in Cawthorne, near Barnsley], 2 carucates; Silkstone, 1½ carucates. Together, [there are] 5½ carucates of land to the geld, where there could be 5 ploughs. There are 9 villans and 3 bordars having 4 ploughs.

STAINCROSS WAPENTAKE

In KINSLEY, Alsige had 3 carucates of land to the geld, where there could be 2 ploughs. Now Gamal has it of Ilbert. He himself [has] 1 plough there; and 2 villans and 3 bordars with 1 plough. [There is] woodland pasture 1 league long and a half broad. TRE worth 40s; now 10s.

In HEMSWORTH, Ulf and Siward had 4 carucates of land to the geld, where there could be 3 ploughs. Now Gamal has it of Ilbert. He himself [has] 2 ploughs there; and 3 villans and 1 bordar with 1 plough, and [there are] 4 acres of meadow. [There is] woodland pasture half a league long and a half broad. TRE worth 60s; now 20s.

In BRIERLEY and SOUTH HIENDLEY, Earnwig had 6 carucates of land to the geld, and there could be 3 ploughs. Now Alric has it of Ilbert. He himself [has] 2 ploughs there; and 3 villans and 6 bordars with 2 ploughs, and [there are] 2 acres of meadow. [There is] woodland pasture 1 league long and 1 broad. TRE worth 40s; now 20s.

In ROYSTON, Wulfheah and Northmann had 4 carucates of land to the geld, where there could be 2 ploughs. Now Ulfkil has it of Ilbert. He himself [has] there 2 villans and 3 bordars with 1 plough, and [there is] 1 acre of meadow. [There is] woodland pasture 6 furlongs long and 4 broad. TRE worth 40s; now 10s.

In DODWORTH, Swein had 5 carucates of land to the geld, where there could be 3 ploughs. Now the same man has it of Ilbert. He himself [has] 1 plough there; and 2 villans and 2 bordars with 1 plough. [There is] woodland pasture 1 league long and half a league broad. TRE worth 20s; now 10s.

In CAWTHORNE [near Barnsley], Alric had 3 carucates of

land to the geld, and there could be 2 ploughs. Now the same man has it of Ilbert. He himself [has] 2 ploughs there; and 4 villans with 2 ploughs. There is a priest and a church, [and] woodland pasture 2 leagues long and 2 broad. The whole manor [is] 3 leagues long and 2 broad. TRE worth 40s; now 20s. To this manor belongs Silkstone, 1½ carucates; Hoyland Swaine, 6 bovates; "Clactone" [in Oxspring], 6 bovates. That is, 3 carucates of land to the geld, and there could be 2 ploughs.

In PENISTONE, Alric had 10 bovates of land to the geld, and there could be 1 carucate of land *[sic]*. Now the same man has it of Ilbert, and it is waste. TRE it was worth 20s.

In BARUGH, Arnbiorn had 3 carucates of land to the geld, where there could be 2 ploughs. Now the same man has it of Ilbert. He himself [has] half a plough there; and 3 villans and 2 bordars with 2 ploughs. TRE worth 20s; now 10s.

In DARTON, Arnbiorn had 1 carucate of land to the geld, and there could be half a plough. Now the same man has it of Ilbert, and it is waste. TRE it was worth 5s.

In KEXBROUGH, Godric had 2½ carucates of land to the geld, and there could be 1 plough. Now Swein has it of Ilbert. He himself [has] 1 plough there; and 2 villans with 1 plough, and [there are] 2 acres of meadow. [There is] woodland pasture 6 furlongs long and as much broad. TRE worth 10s; now the same.

In HIGH HOYLAND, Oswulf had 2 carucates of land to the geld, and there could be 2 ploughs. Now the same man has it of Ilbert. He himself [has] 1 plough there. [There is] woodland pasture 1 league long and 1 broad. TRE worth 20s; now 5s.

In SHAFTON and Carlton [near Barnsley], Alsige had 18 carucates of land to the geld, and there could be 12 ploughs. Now Gamal and Alric have them of Ilbert. They themselves [have] 1 plough; and 9 villans and 3 bordars with 7 ploughs, and [there are] 4 acres of meadow. [There is] woodland pasture 6 furlongs long and 5 broad. TRE worth £4; now 30s.

[Folio 317: YORKSHIRE]

In WORSBOROUGH, Arnbiorn and Healfdene had 5½ carucates of land to the geld, where there could be 4 ploughs. Now Gamal and Ketilbiørn have it of Ilbert. They themselves [have] 2 ploughs, and 4 bordars, and 1 mill rendering 2s. [There is] woodland pasture half a league [long] and a half broad. TRE worth £4; now 30s.

In THURGOLAND, Ælfric and Gamal had 4½ carucates of land to the geld, where there could be 2 ploughs. The soke belongs to Tanshelf. Now Ilbert has it, and it is waste. TRE it was worth 20s. [There is] woodland pasture 1 league long and a half broad.

In STAINBOROUGH is other sokeland belonging to Tanshelf, of 2 carucates of land to the geld, and there could be 1 plough. Now Ilbert has 1 plough there, and 1 villan and 1 bordar, and [there is] 1 acre of meadow. [There is] woodland pasture 1 league long and 2 furlongs broad.

In 'KERESFORTH' [in Barnsley] and Barnsley there is

likewise sokeland belonging to Tanshelf, of 5 carucates of land to the geld, and there could be 3 ploughs. Now there is 1 villan with 2 ploughs, and 1 acre of meadow. [There is] woodland pasture half a league long and as much broad.

In DARTON are 4 carucates of land to the geld, and there could be 2 ploughs. This belongs to Tanshelf. Now Ilbert has there 4 villans and 1 bordar with 2 ploughs. [There is] woodland pasture 1 league long and 1 broad.

In NOTTON are 6 carucates of land to the geld, where there could be 4 ploughs. Of this land, 4 carucates are in the soke of Tanshelf, and 2 carucates inland. Yet Godric had a hall there. Now Ilbert has there 2 sokemen and 3 bordars with half a plough. [There is] woodland pasture half a league long and a half broad. TRE it was worth 20s.

In CHEVET are 4 carucates of land to the geld, where there could be 3 ploughs. 2½ carucates are in the soke of Tanshelf, and 1½ carucates inland. Yet Northmann had a hall there. Now, under Ilbert, there are 3 sokemen with 2 ploughs, and 6 acres of woodland pasture. TRE it was worth 10s.

In COLD HIENDLEY are 4 carucates of land to the geld, where there could be 2 ploughs. 3 carucates are in The soke of Tanshelf, and 1 inland. The whole is waste.

In HUNSHELF, Alric had 3 carucates of land to the geld, where there could be 2 ploughs. Now the same man has it of Ilbert, and it is waste. TRE it was worth 10s. [There is] woodland pasture 1 league long and 1 broad.

In THURLSTONE and INGBIRCHWORTH and SKELMANTHORPE, Alric and Healfdene had 9 carucates of land to the geld, and there could be 5 ploughs. Now Ilbert has it, and it is waste. TRE it was worth £4. [There is] woodland pasture 1½ leagues long and as much broad.

In [Lower and Upper] DENBY [near Penistone], Eadwulf and Godric had 3 carucates of land to the geld, where there could be 1½ ploughs. Now Alric has it of Ilbert. There is woodland pasture 1 league long and 1 broad. TRE worth 10s; now 6s. There is a dairy farm.

In UPPER CUMBERWORTH, Leofwine and Alric had 1 carucate of land to the geld. Now Ilbert has it, and it is waste. TRE it was worth 6s.

In CLAYTON WEST, Alsige had 3 carucates of land to the geld, and there could be 2 ploughs. Now Ilbert has it, and it is waste. TRE it was worth 20s. [There is] woodland pasture half a league long and a half broad.

In MONK BRETTON, Wulfmær had 1½ carucates of land to the geld. There could be 1 plough. Now Ilbert has it, and it is waste. TRE it was worth 20s. [There is] woodland pasture half a league long and a half broad.

In OXSPRING and ROUGHBIRCHWORTH, Swein had 2 carucates of land to the geld, and there could be 2 ploughs. Ilbert has it, and it is waste. TRE it was worth 20s. [There is] woodland pasture 6 furlongs long and 3 broad.

In HOYLAND SWAINE, Thorbiorn had 10 bovates of land to the geld, where there could be 1 plough. Ilbert has it, and it is waste. TRE it was worth 8s. [There is] woodland pasture 1 league long and a half broad.

In RYHILL are 4 carucates of land to the geld, where there could be 3 ploughs. This belongs to Shafton. There are 5 villans with 2 ploughs. [There is] woodland pasture half a league long and a half broad.

AGBRIGG WAPENTAKE

In METHLEY, Oswulf and Knut had 8 carucates of land to the geld, where there could be 5 ploughs. Ilbert has there 17 villans and 5 bordars with 5 ploughs. [There is] woodland pasture 1 league long and 1 broad. There is a church and a priest. TRE worth 60s; now 40s.

In ACKTON, Ligulf had 3 carucates of land to the geld, where there could be 2 ploughs. Now William has it of Ilbert. He himself [has] half a plough there; and 2 villans and 6 bordars with 1½ ploughs. [There is] woodland pasture half a league long and 4 furlongs broad. TRE worth 10s; now the same.

In "WESTREBI" [in Altofts], Swein, Healfdene and Orm had 6 carucates of land to the geld, and there could be 3 ploughs. Of these, 1 carucate is in the soke of Tanshelf. Now Ilbert has it, and Roger [holds] of him. [He has] 1 plough there; and 5 villans and 4 bordars with 5 ploughs, and 1 mill [rendering] 12d, and 3 acres of meadow. [There is] woodland pasture 1 league long and 1 broad. TRE worth £3; now 16s.

In OLD SNYDALE, Earnwine had 6 carucates of land to the geld, where there could be 4 ploughs. Now Humphrey has it of Ilbert. He himself [has] 1 plough there; and 9 villans and 3 bordars with 3 ploughs. [There is] woodland pasture half a league long and 2 furlongs broad. TRE worth £3; now 30s.

In CROFTON, Arnbiorn and Alweard had 4 carucates of land to the geld, where there could be 2 ploughs. Now Gherbod has it of Ilbert. He himself [has] 1 plough there; and 4 villans and 2 bordars with 2 ploughs, and [there are] 6 acres of meadow. [There is] woodland pasture 6 furlongs long and 6 broad. TRE worth 40s; now 20s.

[Folio 317V: YORKSHIRE]

In WHITWOOD, Ligulf had 8 carucates of land to the geld, where there could be 4 ploughs. Now Roger has it of Ilbert. He himself [has] 2 ploughs there; and 4 villans and 1 bordar with 1 plough, and 3 acres of meadow. TRE worth 40s; now 20s.

In FLOCKTON, Alric and Gamal had 3 carucates of land to the geld, where there could be 2 ploughs. Ilbert now has it, and it is waste. TRE it was worth 20s.

In UPPER DENBY [in Upper Whitley], Healfdene had 3 carucates of land to the geld, and there could be 2 ploughs. Ilbert has it, and it is waste. TRE it was worth 20s. [There is] woodland pasture 1 league long and 1 broad.

In LEPTON, Arnbiorn had 3 carucates of land to the geld, and there could be 3 ploughs. Ilbert has it, and it is waste. [There is] woodland pasture 1 league long and 1 broad. TRE it was worth 20s.

In KIRKHEATON 2 brothers had 3 carucates of land to the geld, and there could be 3 ploughs. Ilbert has it, and Gamal [holds] of him, but it is waste. TRE it was worth 20s. [There is] woodland pasture 1½ leagues long and 1 league broad.

In ALMONDBURY, Ketil and Swein had 4 carucates of land to the geld, and there could be 4 ploughs. Now Leysingr has it of Ilbert, and it is waste. TRE it was worth £3. [There is] woodland pasture 1 league long and 1 broad.

In FARNLEY TYAS, Godwine and Swein had 3 carucates of land to the geld, and there could be 3 ploughs. Ilbert has it now, but it is waste. TRE it was worth 40s. [There is] woodland pasture 6 furlongs long and 6 broad.

In HONLEY and MELTHAM, Cola and Sweine had 4 carucates of land to the geld, where there could be 3 ploughs. Ilbert has it, and it is waste. TRE it was worth 40s. [There is] woodland pasture 2 leagues long and 1½ leagues broad.

In UPPER HOPTON, Alric had 2 carucates of land to the geld, and there could be 1 plough. Now the same man has it of Ilbert, and it is waste. TRE it was worth 6s. There are 2 acres of meadow, and 20 acres of woodland.

In HUDDERSFIELD, Godwine had 6 carucates of land to the geld, where there could be 8 ploughs. Now the same man has it of Ilbert, but it is waste. [There is] woodland pasture 1 league long and 1 broad. TRE it was worth 100s.

In BRADLEY Godwine and Dolgfinnr had 2 carucates of land to the geld, and there could be 2 ploughs. Now Ketil has it of Ilbert, but it is waste. TRE it was worth £3. [There is] woodland pasture 1½ leagues long and 1 broad.

In LINDLEY, Godwine had 2 carucates of land to the geld, and there could be 2 ploughs. Now Ulfkil has it of Ilbert, but it is waste. TRE it was worth 20s. [There is] woodland pasture 5 furlongs long and 2 broad.

In QUARMBY, Gamal and Godwine had 2 carucates of land to the geld, and there could be 2 ploughs. Ilbert has it, but it is waste. TRE it was worth 10s. [There is] woodland pasture 1 league long and a half broad.

In GOLCAR, Lyfing had half a carucate of land to the geld, and there could be half a plough. Now Dunstan has it of Ilbert, and it is waste. TRE it was worth 10s. [There is] woodland pasture 1 league long and half a league broad.

In SOUTH CROSLAND, Swein had 2 carucates of land to the geld, and there could be 2 ploughs. Ilbert has it, but it is waste. TRE it was worth 10s. [There is] woodland pasture 2 leagues long and 1 broad.

In THORNHILL, Arnbiorn, Healfdene and Gamal had 4 carucates of land to the geld, and there could be 3 ploughs. Now Arnbiorn has there 3 villans and 3 bordars with 2 ploughs. There is a priest and a church, [and] woodland pasture 6 furlongs long and 6 broad. TRE worth 40s; now 10s.

In WHITLEY LOWER, Arnbiorn had 5 carucates of land to the geld, where there could be 2 ploughs. Now Gamal and Alric have there 4 villans with 4 ploughs. There are 4 acres of meadow, [and] woodland pasture 1 league long and 1 broad. TRE worth 40s; now [...].

In DALTON [near Huddersfield], Alric had 2 carucates of land to the geld, and there could be 2 ploughs. Now Swein has it of Ilbert. He himself [has] 1 plough there; and 2 villans with 1 plough. [There is] woodland pasture 5 furlongs long and 4 broad. TRE worth 20s; now 10s.

MORLEY WAPENTAKE

In MORLEY, Dunstan had 6 carucates of land to the geld, and there could be 6 ploughs. Ilbert has it, but it is waste. There is a church, [and] woodland pasture 1 league long and 1 broad. TRE it was worth 40s.

In ROTHWELL, and Lofthouse [near Wakefield], Carlton [in Lofthouse, near Wakefield], Thorpe on the Hill and Middleton [in Leeds] are 24 carucates of land and 1 bovate to the geld, and there could be 12 ploughs. Harold, 14 carucates, Barth, $7\frac{1}{2}$ carucates, Alric, $10\frac{1}{2}$ bovates, and Stenulf, $10\frac{1}{2}$ bovates, had halls there. Now Ilbert has 2 ploughs there; and 16 villans and 1 bordar with 8 ploughs, and 1 mill [rendering] 2s, and 9 acres of meadow. [There is] woodland pasture 2 leagues long and 1 broad. The whole manor [is] 2 leagues long and 2 broad. TRE worth £8; now 65s.

In ARDSLEY EAST, Alric and Arnbiorn had 5 carucates of land and 3 bovates to the geld, where there could be 3 ploughs. Now Swein has it of Ilbert. He himself [has] 1 plough there. [There is] woodland pasture 1 league long and 1 broad. TRE worth 30s; now 10s.

In 'REESTONES' [in Armley] and ARMLEY, Morfari and Arnketil had 6 carucates of land to the geld, where there could be 3 ploughs. Now Ligulf has it of Ilbert, and there are 8 villans with 3 ploughs. [There are] 6 acres of meadow, [and] woodland pasture half a league long and 4 furlongs broad. TRE worth 20s; now 10s.

In PUDSEY, Dunstan and Stenulf had 8 carucates of land to the geld, where there could be 4 ploughs. Ilbert has it now, but it is waste. TRE it was worth 40s. [There is] woodland pasture half a league long and a half broad.

[Folio 318: YORKSHIRE]

In BRAMLEY [in Armley], Arnketil had 4 carucates of land to the geld, and there could be 2 ploughs. Ilbert has it now, and it is waste. [There is] woodland pasture half a league long and a half broad. TRE it was worth 20s.

In BEESTON [in Leeds], Thorsten and Morfari had 6 carucates of land to the geld, where there could be 4 ploughs. Now Ilbert has it, and it is waste. TRE it was worth 40s. [There is] woodland pasture half a league long and a half broad.

In HUNSLET are 6 carucates of land to the geld, where there could be 3 ploughs. The soke is in Beeston [in Leeds]. There are 8 villans having 3 ploughs, and 6 acres of meadow. [There is] woodland pasture 5 furlongs long and 4 broad.

In CALVERLEY and FARSLEY, Arnketil had 3 carucates

of land to the geld, and there could be 2 ploughs. Ilbert has it, and it is waste. TRE it was worth 20s. [There is] woodland pasture half a league long and a half broad.

In TONG, Stenulf had 4 carucates of land to the geld, where there could be 2 ploughs. Ilbert has it, but it is waste. TRE it was worth 20s. [There is] woodland pasture half a league long and a half broad.

In DRIGHLINGTON, Dunstan had 4 carucates of land to the geld, where there could be 2 ploughs. Ilbert has it, and it is waste. TRE it was worth 20s. [There is] woodland pasture 4 furlongs long and as much broad.

In GOMERSAL, Dunstan and Gamal had 14 carucates of land to the geld, where there could be 7 ploughs. Ilbert has it, and it is waste. TRE it was worth 40s. [There is] woodland pasture 1 league long and 1 broad.

In BRADFORD, with 6 Berewicks, Gamal had 15 carucates of land to the geld, where there could be 8 ploughs. Ilbert has it, and it is waste. TRE it was worth £4. [There is] woodland pasture half a league long and a half broad.

In BOLTON [in Bradford], Arnketil had 4 carucates of land to the geld, where there could be 2 ploughs. Ilbert has it, and it is waste. TRE it was worth 10s. To this manor belongs this land: Chellow, Allerton, Thornton [near Bradford], Clayton [near Bradford], [and] Wibsey. Together, [there are] 10 carucates of land to the geld, and there could be 6 ploughs. It is waste. TRE it was worth 40s.

In BOWLING, Sindi had 4 carucates of land to the geld, where there could be 2 ploughs. Ilbert has it, and it is waste. TRE it was worth 5s.

In SHIPLEY, Ramkel had 3 carucates of land to the geld, where there could be 2 ploughs. Ilbert has it, and it is waste. TRE it was worth 10s. [There is] woodland pasture 1 league long and a half broad.

In 'NORTH BIERLEY' [in Bradford], Stenulf had 4 carucates of land to the geld, where there could be 2 ploughs. Ilbert has it, and it is waste. TRE it was worth 10s. [There is] woodland pasture half a league long and a half broad.

In WYKE, Stenulf and Vestarr had 4 carucates of land to the geld, where there could be 2 ploughs. Ilbert has it, and it is waste. TRE it was worth 20s. [There is] woodland pasture 4 furlongs long and 4 broad.

In CLECKHEATON, Dunstan and Ramkel had 6 carucates of land to the geld, where there could be 3 ploughs. Ilbert has it now, and it is waste. TRE it was worth 20s.

In CLIFTON [near Brighouse], Escelf had 7 carucates of land to the geld, where there could be 4 ploughs. Ilbert has it, and it is waste. TRE it was worth £3. [There is] woodland pasture half a league long and 3 furlongs broad.

In MIRFIELD, Arnbiorn, Healfdene and Gamal had 6 carucates of land to the geld, where there could be 3 ploughs. Now 3 Englishmen have it of Ilbert. They themselves [have] 2 ploughs; and 6 villans and 3 bordars with 2 ploughs. [There is] woodland pasture half a league broad and 1 league long. TRE worth £3; now 10s.

In BATLEY, Dunstan, Stenulf and Vestarr had 5 carucates of land to the geld, where there could be 2 ploughs. Now Ilbert has there 6 villans and 4 bordars with 5 ploughs. There is a priest and a church, and 2 acres of meadow. [There is] woodland pasture 3 furlongs long and 3 broad. TRE worth 20s; now the same.

In LIVERSEDGE, Leofnoth and Arnbiorn had 4 carucates of land to the geld, where there could be 2 ploughs. Now Ralph has it of Ilbert. There are 5 villans and 4 bordars with 2 ploughs. [There is] woodland pasture 1 league long and a half broad. TRE worth 20s; now 10s.

In HARTSHEAD, Arnbiorn had 2 carucates of land to the geld, where there could be 1 plough. Now Alsige has it of Ilbert. 3 villans have 1 plough there. [There is] woodland pasture 3 furlongs long and 3 broad. TRE worth 10s; now 5s.

In ELLAND, Gamal had $3\frac{1}{2}$ carucates of land to the geld, where there could be 2 ploughs. Ilbert has it now, and it is waste. TRE it was worth 20s. [There is] woodland pasture half a league long and 4 furlongs broad. and 4 acres of meadow.

In SOUTHOWRAM, Gamal had 3 carucates of land to the geld, where there could be 2 ploughs. Ilbert has it, and it is waste. TRE it was worth 20s. [There is] woodland pasture 3 furlongs long and 3 broad.

[Folio 318V: [YORKSHIRE]]

[Blank in MS]

[Folio 319: YORKSHIRE]

X. The land of Roger de Bully

In LAUGHTON-EN-LE-MORTHEN and THROAP-HAM are 18 carucates of land to the geld, where there could be 9 ploughs. Earl Edwin had a hall there. Now Roger de Bully has there in demesne 5 ploughs; and 33 villans and 6 bordars having 10 ploughs. [There is] woodland pasture 1 league long and 2 furlongs and 8 furlongs [sic] broad. The whole manor [is] $2\frac{1}{2}$ leagues long and 8 furlongs broad.

To this manor belongs this sokeland: Dinnington, 4 carucates; South Anston, 6 carucates; North Anston, 10 carucates; Thorp Salvin, 6 carucates; Wales, $3\frac{1}{2}$ carucates; Slade Hooton, 3 carucates; Newhall, $3\frac{1}{2}$ carucates. Together, [there are] 36 carucates to the geld, where there could be 20 ploughs. There are now 50 villans and 17 bordars and 23 sokemen having 18 ploughs. Roger has there in demesne 5 ploughs; and 2 of his knights [have] 2 ploughs.

The whole manor, with the members, TRE was worth £24; now £15.

In WADWORTH, Sæweard and Toki had 12 carucates of land to the geld, where there could be 4 ploughs. Now Roger has 4 ploughs there in demesne; and 24 [villans] and 1 bordar with 11 ploughs. [There is] woodland pasture half a league long and $3\frac{1}{2}$ furlongs broad. TRE worth £8; now £5.

In DADSLEY, STAINTON [near Tickhill] and HELLABY, Alsige and Sæweard had 8 carucates of land to the geld, and there could be 8 ploughs. Now Roger has in demesne there 7 ploughs; and a certain knight of his [has] $2\frac{1}{2}$ ploughs. There are 54 villans and 12 bordars having 24 ploughs, and 31 burgesses, and 3 mills rendering 40s. There is a priest and a church, and 2 acres of meadow, [and] woodland pasture 3 furlongs long and 1 broad. TRE worth £12; now £14.

In MALTBY [near Rotherham] and HELLABY, Alsige had 4 carucates of land to the geld, where there could be 6 ploughs. Now Roger has in demesne there 5 ploughs; and 13 villans and 18 bordars with 18 ploughs, and 3 mills rendering 16s. [There is] woodland pasture 16 furlongs long and 5 broad. The whole manor [is] 2 leagues long and a half broad. TRE worth £8; now £6.

In STAINTON [near Tickhill], Sæweard had $2\frac{1}{2}$ carucates of land to the geld, where there could be 1 plough. Now Roger has 1 plough there; and 2 villans and 3 bordars ploughing with 2 oxen. TRE worth 20s; now 16s.

In WICKERSLEY, Healfdene and Æstan had 4 carucates of land to the geld, where there could be 3 ploughs. Roger has it, and it is waste. TRE it was worth 40s. [There is] woodland pasture half a league long and a half broad.

In BRINSWORTH, Godric had 11 bovates of land to the geld, where there could be $1\frac{1}{2}$ ploughs. Roger has it, and it is waste. TRE it was worth 15s.

In TINSLEY, Ulfkil, Aghmund and Arnketil had 5 carucates of land to the geld, where there could be 4 ploughs. Roger has there now 1 villan and 3 sokemen with 1 plough, and the site of 1 mill, and 10 acres of meadow. [There is] woodland pasture 1 league long and 8 furlongs broad. TRE worth £4; now 20s.

In ORGREAVE is sokeland of this manor, 4 carucates of land to the geld, where there could be 2 ploughs.

In GREASBROUGH, Godric had 3 carucates of land to the geld, where there could be 2 ploughs. Roger has now 1 plough there; and 3 villans and 3 bordars with 1 plough. [There is] woodland pasture 3 furlongs long and 2 broad. TRE worth 40s; now 20s.

In "GRIMESHOU" [? in Grimesthorpe], Wulfheah had $3\frac{1}{2}$ carucates of land to the geld, where there could be 2 ploughs. Now Roger has 1 plough there; and 3 villans and 3 bordars with 1 plough. [There is] woodland pasture 3 furlongs long and 2 broad. TRE worth 40s; now 20s.

In NEWHILL and Hooton Roberts and Old Denaby, Wulfheah, Ulfkil [and] Ulfkil had 6 carucates of land to the geld, where there could be 4 ploughs. Roger has now 1 plough there, and 6 villans and 6 bordars with 3 bordars [sic], and the site of a mill. [There is] woodland pasture 9 furlongs long and 2 broad. TRE worth £4; now 30s. To these manors belongs sokeland in Maltby [near Rotherham] of half a carucate of land to the geld.

In MEXBOROUGH, Wulfheah, Ulfkil [and] Ulfkil had 5 carucates of land to the geld, where there could be 4 ploughs,

Roger has now 1 plough there; and 8 villans and 4 bordars with 3 ploughs, and 1 mill [rendering] 8s. TRE worth £6; now 40s.

In ADWICK UPON DEARNE, Wulfheah and Regnvald had 2½ carucates of land to the geld, where there could be 2 ploughs. Roger has now 1 plough there; and 16 villans with 4 ploughs, and 1 mill [rendering] 5s. [There is] woodland pasture 7 furlongs long and 3 broad. TRE worth 40s; now 30s.

In BARNBURGH and Bilham, Oswulf had 6 carucates of land to the geld, where there could be 3 ploughs. Roger has now 1½ ploughs there; and 9 villans and 20 bordars with 5 ploughs, and 2 acres of meadow, and 200 acres of scrubland. TRE worth 60s; now 40s.

In ECCLESFIELD, Wulfheah, Alsige, Godric, Dunning, Almær and Northmann had 4 carucates of land to the geld, where there could be 3 ploughs. Roger has now 1 plough there; and 2 villans and 2 bordars with 1 plough. [There is] woodland pasture 1½ leagues long and as much broad. TRE worth £3; now 10s.

[Folio 319V: YORKSHIRE]

In WATH UPON DEARNE, Rethar had 6 carucates of land to the geld, where there could be 3 ploughs. Roger has now 1 plough there; and 4 villans and 8 bordars with 1 plough. TRE worth 40s; now 10s.

To this manor belongs sokeland in Swinton [near Rotherham] and Wentworth, 2 carucates of land and 2 bovates to the geld. This land is waste. [There is] woodland pasture 14 furlongs long and 5 broad.

In HOYLAND NETHER, Rethar had 2 carucates to the geld, and there could be 2 ploughs. Roger has it now, and it is waste. [There is] woodland pasture 1 league long and 6 furlongs broad. TRE it was worth 20s.

In WOMBWELL, Ketilbert had 14 bovates of land to the geld, where there could be 1 plough. Roger has now 1 plough there; and 8 villans and 4 bordars with 3 ploughs. TRE worth 20s; now the same. To this manor belongs sokeland in "Toftes" [in Wombwell], 1 bovate, and [in] West Melton, 2 bovates.

In HIGH MELTON, Swein had 8 carucates of land to the geld, and there could be 3 ploughs. Roger has now 3 ploughs there; and 8 villans and 1 bordar with 3 ploughs. [There is] scrubland 4 furlongs long and 4 broad. TRE worth £4; now 60s and 16d.

In 'WILDTHORPE' [in Sprotbrough], Ketilbert had 2 carucates of land to the geld, and there could be 2 ploughs. Roger has now 1 plough there. There is a priest. TRE worth 40s; now 10s8d.

In CADEBY, Swein had 3 carucates of land to the geld, where there could be 2 ploughs. Roger has now 1 plough there; and 3 villans and 2 sokemen with 2 ploughs. TRE worth 40s; now 20s.

In SPROTBROUGH and Cusworth and Balby, Swein had 8 carucates of land to the geld, where there could be 4 ploughs.

Roger has now 3 ploughs there; and 12 villans and 10 bordars and 8 sokemen having 8 ploughs. [There is] scrubland 1 league long and 2½ furlongs broad. TRE worth £4; now £3.

In LITTLE HOUGHTON, Oswulf had 2 carucates of land to the geld, where there could be 1 plough. Roger has it now, and it is waste. TRE worth 20s; now 4s. There are 2 acres of meadow, and scrubland 3 furlongs long and 1½ furlongs broad.

In BILLINGLEY, Swein had 5 carucates of land to the geld, and there could be 3 ploughs. Roger has it now, and it is waste. TRE worth 40s; now 10s. There are 20 acres of meadow.

In BOLTON UPON DEARNE, Oswulf had 2½ carucates of land to the geld, where there could be 2 ploughs. Roger has there now 8 villans and 1 bordar having 4½ ploughs, and 1 mill [rendering] 5s. There is a priest and a church, [and] woodland pasture 1 league long and 1 furlong broad. TRE worth 40s; now 20s.

In MARR, Wulfstan had 2 carucates of land and 3 bovates to the geld, and Ulfkil 9 bovates of land to the geld. In these there could be 2 ploughs. Roger has now 1 plough there; and 7 villans with 3 ploughs. [There is] scrubland 8 furlongs long and 4 broad. TRE worth 40s; now 20s. These 9 bovates of land are in the soke of Hexthorpe. | Fulk holds them of Roger. |

In GOLDTHORPE and in THURNSCOE, Oswulf had 5 carucates of land to the geld, where there could be 4 ploughs. Roger has there now 3 villans with 3 ploughs, and 7 acres of meadow. [There is] woodland pasture 6 furlongs long and 2 broad. TRE worth 30s; now 16s.

In KIRK BRAMWITH, Swein had 1½ carucates of land to the geld, where there could be 1 plough. Half a carucate is sokeland of another Bramwith [South Bramwith]. Now Roger has there 9 villans and 2 bordars with 3½ ploughs. [There is] woodland pasture 3 furlongs long and 1 furlong and 1 virgate broad. TRE worth 50s; now 11s.

In BARNBY DUN, Ketilbert had 9 bovates of land to the geld, where there could be 1 plough. Now Roger has there 4 villans and 1 bordar with 1 plough, and 3 waste fisheries. [There is] woodland pasture 1 league long and 1 furlong broad. TRE worth 40s; now 20s.

In KIMBERWORTH, Alsige had 6 carucates of land to the geld, where there could be 3 ploughs. Roger has now 2 ploughs there, and 8 villans and 12 bordars [...], and 6 acres of meadow. [There is] woodland pasture 13 furlongs long and 1 league broad. TRE worth £4; now 30s.

In HAMPOLE, Swein had 3 carucates of land to the geld, where there could be 2 ploughs. Roger has now 1 plough there; and 3 villans and 2 bordars with 1 plough, and half a mill [rendering] 40d. [There is] scrubland 5 furlongs long and 2½ furlongs broad. TRE worth 40s; now 10s.

In FRICKLEY and Stotfold, Swein had 6 bovates of land to the geld, and there could be 1 plough. Roger has it now, and it is waste. Fulk holds it of Roger.

In BRODSWORTH, Alsige had 5½ carucates of land to the geld, where there could be 4 ploughs. Roger has now 2 ploughs there; and 3 villans and 9 bordars with 3 ploughs. There is a priest and a church. TRE worth £4; now 50s.

In HOLDWORTH, Healfdene had 2 carucates of land to the geld, where there could be 1 plough. Roger has it now, and it is waste. [There is] woodland pasture 1 league long and 1 broad. TRE it was worth 20s.

In UGHILL and Worrall and Wadsley, Healfdene had 14 bovates of land to the geld, where there could be 2 ploughs. Roger has it now, and it is waste. TRE worth 20s. [There is] woodland pasture 1 league long and 1 broad.

In ARKSEY, Godric had 2 carucates of land and 6 bovates to the geld, where there could be 2 ploughs. Roger has now half a plough there; and 5 villans and 6 bordars with 5½ ploughs. [There is] woodland pasture 7 furlongs long and 2 broad. TRE worth 40s; now 20s.

[Folio 320: YORKSHIRE]

In BENTLEY [near Doncaster], Oswulf had 2 carucates of land and 2 bovates of the geld, where there could be 2½ ploughs. Roger has there now 12 villans and 2 bordars with 6 ploughs, and 8 acres of meadow. [There is] woodland pasture 1 league long and 4 furlongs broad. TRE worth 40s; now 20s.

In ADWICK LE STREET, Swein and Gluniairnn and Arnketil had 6 carucates of land to the geld, where there could be 3 ploughs. Roger has now 2 ploughs there; and 12 villans and 11 bordars with 5 ploughs, and 9 acres of meadow. [There is] scrubland 8 furlongs long and 2 broad. TRE worth 40s; now the same. Fulk holds it of Roger.

In MARR is sokeland of this manor, 11 bovates of land to the geld, where there could be 1 plough.

In 'HALLAM', with 16 Berewicks, are 29 carucates of land to the geld. Earl Waltheof had a hall there. There could be 20 ploughs. Roger has this land of Countess Judith. He himself [has] 2 ploughs there; and 33 villans having 12½ ploughs. There are 8 acres of meadow. [There is] woodland pasture 4 leagues long and 4 broad. The whole manor [is] 10 leagues long and 8 broad. TRE worth 8 marks of silver; now 40s.

In ATTERCLIFFE and SHEFFIELD, Swein had 5 carucates of land to the geld, where there could be 3 ploughs. This land is said to have been inland of 'HALLAM'.

In SCAWSBY, Alsige had 5 carucates of land to the geld, where there could be 3 ploughs. This land belongs to Brodsworth, 2 carucates inland and 3 carucates sokeland.

Roger has now 2 ploughs there; and 8 villans and 5 bordars with 3 ploughs. [There is] scrubland 4 furlongs long and 4 broad. This valued in the manor to which it belongs.

[Folio 320V: YORKSHIRE]

XI. The land of Robert Malet

EAST RIDING

CAVE HUNDRED

In SOUTH CAVE, Gamal had 24 carucates of land to the geld, where there could be 12 ploughs. Now Robert Malet has there 4 ploughs in demesne; and 30 villans having 8 ploughs. There is a church and a priest, and the sites of 2 mills. [There is] woodland pasture and scrubland 1 league long and 1 broad. The whole manor [is] 7 leagues long and 1 broad. TRE worth £12; now 100s.

In another CAVE [North Cave], Thorth, 2 carucates, Basinc, 2 carucates, Muli, 10 bovates, Ealdræd, 4 bovates, Thorsten, 1 carucate, [and] Wulfgeat, half a carucate, had 7 carucates of land and 2 bovates to the geld, where there could be 4 ploughs. Now Robert has there 2 ploughs; and 6 villans and 4 bordars having 1½ ploughs. TRE worth 70s; now 13s. The greatest part [is] waste.

In DREWTON, Ketil and Northmann had 4 carucates of land to the geld, where there could be 2 ploughs. Now Robert has there 2 ploughs; and 6 villans and 5 bordars with 2 ploughs. TRE worth 40s; now 32s.

In KETTLETHORPE, Ketil had 2 carucates of land to the geld, and there could be 1 plough. Robert has it, and it is waste. TRE it was worth 30s. In the same vill Thorth had 1 carucate of land to the geld. Robert has this, and it is waste.

In HOTHAM, Orm and Basinc had 1½ carucates of land to the geld, where there could be 1 plough. Now Robert has it, and it is waste. TRE it was worth 30s. To this manor belongs 1 carucate of land which is in Yokefleet [near Blacktoft]. It is waste.

NORTH RIDING

LANGBAURGH WAPENTAKE

In GUISBOROUGH, Leysingr had 3 carucates of land and 2 bovates to the geld, where there could be 2 ploughs. Now Robert has 1 plough there; and 3 villans with 1 plough. TRE worth 5s4d; now the same.

In NORMANBY [in Eston], Leysingr had half a carucate of land to the geld. Robert has it, and it is waste. TRE it was worth 5s4d.

In PINCHINTHORPE, Edmund had 3 carucates of land to the geld, where there could be 2 ploughs. Robert has it, and it is waste. TRE it was worth 10s.

In LITTLE AYTON, Ealdræd, Edmund [and] Thorormr had 4 carucates of land to the geld, where there could be 2 ploughs. Now Robert has there 1 plough; and 9 villans with 2 ploughs, and 3 acres of meadow. TRE worth 20s; now 25s4d.

In another AYTON [Great Ayton], Eskil had 2 carucates of land to the geld, and there could be 1 plough. Robert has it, and it is waste. TRE it was worth 10s.

In MARTON [in Middlesbrough], Edmund had 5 carucates

of land to the geld, where there could be 3 ploughs. Robert has it now, and it is waste. TRE it was worth 20s.

In NEWHAM, Edmund had 10 bovates of land to the geld, where there could be 1 plough. Robert has it, and it is waste. TRE it was worth 10s.

In TOLLESBY are 3 carucates of land to the geld, which belong to Marton [in Middlesbrough]. They are waste.

In ACKLAM [in Middlesbrough], Edmund had 1 carucate of land to the geld. Robert has it, and it is waste. [There is] land for half a plough.

In STAINTON [near Thornaby-on-Tees], Edmund had 2 carucates of land to the geld.

In THORNABY-ON-TEES, Edmund had 1½ carucates of land to the geld. Robert Malet has these, and they are waste. [...]

In THORNTON [near Hemlington] is 1 carucate of land to the geld, the soke belonging to Stainton [near Thornaby-on-Tees]. It is waste. [...]

In GREAT BUSBY, Ealdræd had half a carucate of land to the geld. Robert has it, and it is waste.

"MANESHOU" WAPENTAKE

In SCAWTON, Eskil had 3 carucates of land to the geld, where there could be 2 ploughs. Now Robert has it, and it is waste. TRE it was worth 10s.

'BULFORD' WAPENTAKE

In THORNTON-LE-CLAY, Arnketil had 2 carucates of land to the geld, where there could be 1 plough. Robert has it, and it is waste. TRE it was worth 10s.

'YARLESTRE' WAPENTAKE

In THORMANBY, Eskil had 4 carucates of land to the geld, where there could be 2 ploughs. Robert has it, and it is waste. TRE it was worth 10s. In the same vill, Gamal had half a carucate to the geld.

In OLD BYLAND, Eskil had 6 carucates of land to the geld, where there could be 3 ploughs. Now Robert has 1 plough there; and 7 villans with 2 ploughs. There is a priest and a wooden church. TRE it was worth 20s; now 16s.

In "BERNEBI" [in Birdforth], Eskil had 4 carucates of land to the geld. [There is] land for | 2 ploughs |.

In "HORENBODEBI", Eskil had 2 carucates of land and 2 bovates.

ALLERTON WAPENTAKE

In THORNTON-LE-MOOR, Edmund had 5 carucates of land to the geld.

In MURTON [near Hawnby], Eskil had 6 carucates of land to the geld.

In DALE TOWN, Ulf and Eskil had 1½ carucates of land to the geld.

In HAWNBY, Ulf had 1½ carucates of land to the geld.

Robert Malet has these lands, but they are all waste. [...] and in these there could be | 10 ploughs |.

WEST RIDING

'SKYRACK' WAPENTAKE

In EAST CARLTON, Arnketil had 3 carucates of land to the geld, where there could be 2 ploughs. Robert has it, and it is waste. TRE it was worth 20s. [There is] scrubland half a league long and 3 furlongs broad. The whole manor [is] 1 league long and a half broad.

[Folio 321: YORKSHIRE]

In MIDDLETHORPE, Christ's Church, Gamal [had] 1 carucate to the geld. [There is] land for half a plough. Now Robert has it, and it is waste. TRE worth 20s; now 3s.

In ACASTER MALBIS, Alsige [had] 4 carucates of land to the geld. [There is] land for 2 ploughs. Now Robert has there 2 ploughs, and 3 villans. TRE worth 20s; now 15s.

In the other ACASTER [Acaster Selby], Wulfstan had 6 bovates to the geld, and half a carucate to the geld. [It is] sokeland. [There is] land for 1 plough. Now Robert has 1 villan and 2 bordars with 1 plough. TRE worth 12s; now 5s.

In Stainforth [in Hatfield] are 7 sokemen with 4 ploughs. [There is] woodland pasture 1 furlong long and as much broad.

In Kirk Bramwith [are] 5 sokemen and 2 bordars with 1 plough. [There is] woodland pasture 1 furlong long and 1 broad.

In Fishlake [are] 11 sokemen and 6 villans and 7 villans [sic]] with 4 ploughs. [There is] woodland pasture 5 furlongs long and 5 broad.

In Thorne [are] 5 sokemen and 11 villans with 4 ploughs.

In Tudworth Green [are] 7 sokemen and 7 villans with 3 ploughs. There are 20 fisheries rendering 20,000 eels.

In Hatfield [are] 12 sokemen with 6 ploughs. There is a church and a priest, [and] woodland pasture 6 furlongs long and 6 broad.

In Edenthorpe [are] 2 sokemen and 1 bordar with 1 plough. [There is] woodland pasture half a league long and as much broad.

In Long Sandall [is] 1 sokeman and 3 villans with 2 ploughs.

TRE worth £18; now £30, and from tallage £10.

XII. The land of William de Warenne

In CONISBROUGH, Earl Harold had 5 carucates of land to the geld. There is land for 5 ploughs. There William de Warenne has now 5 ploughs in demesne; and 21 villans and 11 bordars having 11 ploughs. There is a church and a priest, and 2 mills worth 32s, [and there is] woodland pasture 1 league long and 1 broad.

To this manor belongs this sokeland: Ravenfield, 1½ carucates; Clifton [in Conisbrough], 3 carucates; Braithwell, 11 carucates; Barnburgh, 6 carucates; Hoyland Nether, 1 carucate; Bilham, 1 carucate; Dalton [in Rotherham], 3 carucates; Wilsic, 15 acres; Harthill and Kiveton Park, 13½ carucates; Aston, 6 bovates; Kirk Sandall, 2 carucates; Greasbrough, 3 carucates; Cusworth, 3 carucates; Bramley [in Braithwell], 3 carucates; Aughton [near Aston], 2 bovates; Whiston, 3 carucates; Warmsworth, 1 carucate and 6 bovates; Dinnington, 2 carucates; North Anston, 2 carucates; Stainforth [in Hatfield], 3 carucates; Kirk Bramwith, 6 bovates; Fishlake, 5 carucates; Thorne, 4 carucates; Tudworth Green, 1 carucate; Hatfield, 8 carucates; Edenthorpe, 2 carucates; Long Sandall, 1 carucate and 3 bovates.

Together, [there are] 86 carucates [...] and 15 acres to the geld. There is land for 54 ploughs.

In Ravenfield is 1 plough in demesne; and 2 villans and 4 bordars with 1 plough. [There is] woodland pasture 2 furlongs long and as much broad.

In Clifton [in Conisbrough] [are] 4 ploughs in demesne; and 1 sokeman with 1 plough. [There is] woodland pasture 3 furlongs long and as much broad.

In Braithwell are 16 sokemen and 20 bordars with 16 ploughs. There is a church and a priest, [and] woodland pasture 1 furlong long and 1 broad.

In Barnburgh [are] 4 sokemen having 3½ ploughs, and a mill [rendering] 5s. [There is] woodland pasture 2 furlongs long and 2 broad, and 6 acres of meadow.

In Hoyland Nether [are] 4 sokemen with 1 plough. [There is] woodland pasture 3 furlongs long and broad.

In Bilham [is] 1 sokeman and 1 bordar with half a plough.

In Wilsic [are] 3 bordars with 1 plough. [There is] woodland pasture 1 furlong long and broad.

In Harthill [are] 13 sokemen and 11 villans with 12 ploughs. [There is] woodland pasture 4 furlongs long and 4 broad.

In Dalton [in Rotherham] [are] 5 sokemen and 13 bordars with 4 ploughs. [There is] woodland pasture 1 furlong long and 1 broad.

In Aston [is] 1 sokeman and 4 bordars with 1 plough. [There is] woodland pasture 4 furlongs long and half a furlong broad.

In Kirk Sandall [is] 1 plough in demesne, a church and a priest, and 4 bordars. [There is] woodland pasture 2 furlongs long and a half broad.

In Greasbrough [are] 6 sokemen and 3 bordars with 1 plough. [There is] woodland pasture 4 furlongs long and 3 broad.

In Cusworth [are] 7 sokemen with 3 ploughs. [There is] woodland 3 furlongs long and 2 broad.

In Bramley [in Braithwell] [is] 1 sokeman and 7 villans with 3 ploughs. [There is] woodland pasture 3 furlongs long and 2 broad.

In Aughton [near Aston] [is] 1 sokeman and 3 bordars with 1 plough. [There is] woodland pasture 1 furlong long and 2 perches broad.

In Whiston [are] 2 sokemen and 7 bordars with 2 ploughs. [There is] woodland pasture 5 furlongs long and 5 broad.

In Warmsworth, William has 5 ploughs in demesne; and 1 sokeman and 4 villans and 16 villans [sic] with 1 plough.

In Dinnington [are] 3 sokemen and 6 bordars with 3 ploughs. [There is] woodland pasture 8 furlongs long and 3 broad.

In North Anston [are] 4 sokemen with 1 plough. [There is] woodland pasture 1 furlong long and half a furlong broad.

[Folio 321V: YORKSHIRE]

XIII. The land of William de Percy

In TADCASTER, Dunstan and Thorkil had 8 carucates of land to the geld, where there could be 4 ploughs. Now William de Percy has 3 ploughs there; and 19 villans and 11 bordars having 4 ploughs, and 2 mills [rendering] 10s, and 1 fishery [rendering] 5s. There are 16 acres of meadow. The whole manor [is] 5 furlongs long and 5 broad. TRE worth 40s; now 100s.

In Stutton, Arnketil and Wulfstan had 1½ carucates of land to the geld, where there could be 1 plough. Now Mauger has them of William. He himself [has] there 1 plough; and 4 villans with 2 ploughs, and 1 mill [rendering] 5s. There are 5 acres of meadow, [and] woodland pasture 5 furlongs long and 1 broad. The whole manor [is] 6 furlongs long and 3 broad. TRE worth 40s; now 15s.

In HAZELWOOD, Gamal and Ulf had 3 carucates of land to the geld, where there could be 2 ploughs. Now Mauger has them of William. He himself [has] there 1 plough; and 3 bordars with 2 ploughs. [There is] scrubland half a league long and 4 furlongs broad. The whole manor [is] 1 league long and a half broad. TRE it was worth [...].

In "SAXHALLA", Gamal had 4 carucates of land to the geld, where there could be 3 ploughs. Now Mauger has it of William, but it is waste. [There is] scrubland half a league long and 2 furlongs broad. The whole manor [is] half a league long and a half broad. TRE it was worth 20s.

In ILKLEY, Gamal had 3 carucates of land to the geld, where there could be 2 ploughs. Now William has it, and it is waste. TRE it was worth 20s. There is a church and a priest, and woodland pasture 1 league long and 4 furlongs broad. The whole manor [is] 1 league long and 8 furlongs broad.

In BRINSWORTH, Northmann had 3 carucates and 5 bovates of land to the geld, where there could be 3 ploughs. Now Roscelin has it of William, but it is waste. There are 6 acres of meadow, [and] woodland pasture 1 league long and 1 furlong broad. The whole manor [is] 1 league long and 4 furlongs broad. TRE it was worth 40s.

In BOLTON UPON DEARNE, Northmann had 2½ carucates of land to the geld, where there could be 2 ploughs. Now

Picot has it of William. He himself [has] 1 plough there; and 3 villans and 1 bordar with 1 plough. There is the site of a mill, and 10 acres of meadow. The whole manor [is] 9 furlongs long and 2 broad. TRE worth 60s; now 15s.

To this manor belongs this sokeland: in Thurnscoe, 6 bovates; in Steeton [in Bolton Percy], 1 carucate. In this land there could be 1 plough.

In BARNBY DUN, Oswulf had 9 bovates of land to the geld, and there could be half a plough. Now Mauger has it of William. He himself [has] half a plough; and 4 villans and 1 bordar with 1 plough. There is a priest and a church.

In OLD EDLINGTON and Braithwell and Doncaster, Northmann had 3 carucates and 5 bovates of land to the geld, where there could be 3 ploughs. Now Mauger has them of William. He himself [has] 2 ploughs there; and 8 villans and 4 bordars having 4½ ploughs. There is 1 acre of meadow, [and] woodland pasture 1 league long and a half broad. The whole manor [is] 1 league long and 1 broad. TRE worth £4; now 30s.

In THRYBERGH, Northmann had 4 carucates of land to the geld, where there could be 2 ploughs. Now Roscelin has it of William. He himself [has] there 2 villans with 2 ploughs, and 4 acres of meadow. The whole [is] 1 league long and a half broad. TRE worth £4; now 8s.

In DALTON [in Rotherham], Northmann had 2 carucates and 6 bovates of land to the geld, where there could be 2 ploughs. Now Roscelin has it of William. He himself [has] 1 plough there, and 3 acres of meadow. [There is] woodland pasture half a league long and a half broad. The whole manor [is] 1 league long and a half broad. TRE worth 20s; now 10s.

In BOLTON PERCY, Ligulf, Thorkil [and] Earnwig had 8 carucates of land to the geld, where there could be 4 ploughs. Now Roscelin has it of William. He himself [has] 2 ploughs there; and 6 villans with 2 ploughs, and 20 acres of meadow. There is a priest and a church, [and] woodland half a league long and a half broad. The whole [is] 1 league long and a half broad. TRE worth 40s; now 30s.

In PALLATHORPE, Gamal Barn had 2 carucates of land to the geld, and there could be 1 plough. Now Fulk has it of William. There are 2 villans and 2 bordars with 1 plough. TRE worth 20s; now 20s.

In OUSTON are 2½ carucates of land to the geld. This is inland; and half a carucate [is] sokeland in Healaugh. There could be 2 ploughs. It is waste. There are 4 acres of meadow. The whole [is] half a league long and a half broad. TRE it was worth 5s4d.

In "MALCHETONE" [in Tadcaster East], Ligulf had 4 carucates of land to the geld, where there could be 2 ploughs. Now William has it, and it is waste. There are 4 acres of meadow, and half a fishery. TRE worth 20s; now the same.

In 'HACKERBY' [in Healaugh], Arnketil had 3 carucates of land to the geld, where there could be 2 ploughs. The soke is in Heaulaugh. Now Everard has it of William. He himself [has] 1 plough there; and 2 villans and 1 bordar with 1 plough, and

[there are] 4 acres of meadow. [There is] woodland pasture half a league long and a half broad. The whole manor [is] 1 league long and 1 broad. TRE worth 20s; now 24s.

In HORNINGTON, Gamal Barn and Healfdene had 3 carucates of land to the geld, where there could be 2 ploughs. Now Godfrey has it of William. There are 5 villans with 1 plough, and 12 acres of meadow. [There is] woodland pasture half a league long and as much broad. The whole [is] 6 furlongs long [and] 6 broad. TRE worth 10s; now 15s.

In COWTHORPE is sokeland of Whixley, 4 carucates to the geld, where there could be 2 ploughs. Now Godfrey has it of William. There are 4 villans with 2 ploughs, and 1 acre of meadow. [There is] woodland pasture 1 league long and a half broad. The whole manor [is] 1 league long and 1 broad. TRE worth 20s; now 5s4d.

BURGHSHIRE WAPENTAKE

[Folio 322: YORKSHIRE]

In RIBSTON ['Great Ribston' and Little Ribston], Thorbiorn had 1½ carucates of land to the geld, where there could be 1 plough. Now Godfrey has it of William. He himself [has] 1 plough there. TRE worth 20s; now 10s.

In MARKENFIELD, Grim had 5 carucates of land to the geld, where there could be 3 ploughs. Now Beornwulf has it of William. He himself [has] there 2 villans with 2 ploughs. TRE worth 20s; now 10s.

In 'AISMUNDERBY' [in Littlethorpe], Grim had 2 carucates of land to the geld, and there could be 1 plough. Now Beornwulf has it of William. There are 3 villans with 2 ploughs. TRE worth 20s; now 10s.

In STUDLEY ROYAL, Leodwine had 13 bovates of land to the geld, and there could be 1 plough. Now Arnketil has it of William, and it is waste. TRE it was worth 10s.

In CLOTHERHOLME, Wulfwine had 1½ carucates to the geld, and there could be 1 plough. It was worth 20s.

In NESFIELD, Gamal Barn had 3 carucates of land to the geld, where there could be 2 ploughs.

In ASKWITH, Ulfkil and Gamal and Beornwulf had 3 carucates of land to the geld, where there could be 2 ploughs.

William de Percy has these, but they are waste, except that in Askwith there are 4 villans with 2 ploughs, and it is worth 10s.

In LEATHLEY, Arnketil had 4 carucates of land to the geld, where there could be 2 ploughs. Now Everard has it of William. He himself [has] 2 ploughs there; and 5 villans and 3 bordars with 2 ploughs, and 1 mill [rendering] 2s, and [there are] 2 acres of meadow. TRE worth 40s; now 24s.

In KEARBY, Wigbeorht had 4 carucates of land to the geld, where there could be 2 ploughs. Now William has it. There is woodland pasture 2 furlongs long and 1 broad. The whole [is] 1 league long and 1 broad. TRE worth 20s; now 16d.

In KIRKBY OVERBLOW, and 'Tetherfield' [in Kirkby Overblow], Gamal Barn had 6 carucates of land to the geld, where there could be 3 ploughs. Now William has 2 ploughs there; and 11 villans and 4 bordars with 4 ploughs, and [there are] 2 acres of meadow. [There is] woodland pasture 1 league long and 1 broad. TRE worth 40s; now 24s. The whole manor [is] 2 leagues long and 2 broad. There is sokeland of this manor in 'Walton Head' [in Kirkby Overblow], of 1 carucate of land to the geld.

In BARROWBY [is] likewise sokeland of Kirkby Overblow, of 1 carucate of land to the geld, and there could be 1 plough. There are 5 villans with 1 plough.

In RUDFARLINGTON, Gamal Barn had 2 carucates and 2 bovates of land to the geld, and there could be 1 plough. Now Ealdræd has it of William. There are 3 villans and 5 bordars with 2 ploughs. [There is] woodland pasture 1 league long and 9 furlongs broad. TRE worth 20s; now 10s.

In PLOMPTON, Gamal Barn had 2 carucates of land to the geld, and there could be 1 plough. Now Ealdræd has it of William. There are 8 villans and 10 bordars with 3 ploughs, and 2 acres of meadow. TRE worth 20s; now the same.

In "GREAT" BRAHAM, Gamal Barn had 4 carucates of land to the geld, where there could be 2 ploughs. Now William has 1 plough there; and 8 villans and 3 bordars with 2 ploughs, and 1 mill [rendering] 5s4d. Godfrey holds it. TRE worth 40s; now 30s.

In SPOFFORTH, Gamal Barn had 3 carucates of land, and there could be 2 ploughs. Now William has 4 ploughs there; and 9 villans and 10 bordars with 4 ploughs, and 1 mill [rendering] 2s, and [there are] 4 acres of meadow. [There is] woodland pasture 1 league long and 1 broad. The whole [is] 16 furlongs long and 12 broad. TRE worth 20s; now 60s.

In 'CRAUWEL' [in Spofforth], Thorbiorn had 2 carucates of land to the geld, and there could be 1 plough. William has it now, but it is not inhabited. [There is] woodland pasture half a league long and a half broad. The whole [is] 1 league long and 1 broad. TRE worth 20s; now 5s4d.

In LINTON [in Spofforth], Wigbeorht, Ulf, Ramkel, Hrosskell, Ber [and] Ulfkil had 8½ carucates of land to the geld, where there could be 4 ploughs. Now Everard has it of William. He himself [has] 1 plough there; and 3 villans and 2 bordars with 1 plough, and 1 mill [rendering] 16s. [There are] 12 acres of meadow, [and] woodland pasture 1 league long and a half broad. The whole [is] 1 league long and 1 broad. TRE worth 60s; now 40s.

In WETHERBY, Wigbeorht had 2 carucates of land to the geld, and there could be 2 ploughs. Now William the knight has it of William de Percy. He himself [has] 1 plough there; and 3 villans and 1 bordar with 1 plough. TRE worth 20s; now the same.

In this vill itself is 1 carucate of land to the geld, the soke belonging to Knaresborough. William has it. There could be half a plough.

In COWTHORPE are 3 carucates of land to the geld, where there could be 2 ploughs. The soke is in Whixley. Now Godfrey has it of William. There are 3 villans with 1 plough.

There is a church, [and] woodland pasture half a league long and a half broad. The whole manor [is] 1 league long and a half broad. TRE worth 20s; now 5s4d.

HALLIKELD WAPENTAKE

In DISHFORTH, Thorkil had 6 carucates of land to the geld, where there could be 3 ploughs. Now William has it, and it is waste. [It is] half a league long and a half broad. TRE it was worth 20s.

IN CRAVEN

In RIMINGTON, 8 carucates to the geld; Crooks, 1 carucate; Little Middop, 1 carucate; 'Starkeshergh' [in Rimington], 1 carucate.

In BOLTON-BY-BOWLAND and RAYGILL MOSS and HOLME [in Bolton-by-Bowland], 8 carucates to the geld.

In PAINLEY and Gisburn and Paythorne, Newsholme [in Gisburn] [and] Ellenthorpe [in Gisburn], 12½ carucates to the geld.

In NAPPA, 2 carucates to the geld. In HORTON [in Gisburn], 4½ carucates to the geld.

In THORNTON-IN-CRAVEN, 6 carucates to the geld. In KELBROOK, 2½ carucates.

In SWINDEN and Hellifield and Malham and Coniston Cold, 13½ carucates to the geld.

These manors belonged to Beornwulf. Now William de Percy has them, and they are waste.

In Glusburn and "Cheldis" [in Glusburn], Gamal had 3 carucates. William has them.

[Folio 322V: YORKSHIRE]

IN THE EAST RIDING

WEIGHTON HUNDRED

In GOODMANHAM, Northmann had 2 carucates of land to the geld, and there could be 1 plough. William de Colleville has it of William de Percy. He himself [has] 2 ploughs there. TRE worth 20s; now 10s.

In EASTHORPE [in Londesborough], Beornwulf and Northmann had 6 carucates of land and 6 bovates to the geld, where there could be 5 ploughs. Now Geoffrey has it of William. He himself [has] 2 ploughs there; and 5 villans with 2 ploughs, and 2 mills [rendering] 6s. TRE worth 70s; now 16s.

In KIPLING is 1 carucate of land to the geld; the soke [is] in Warter. Beornwulf had it. William has it now, and it is waste. There could be 1 plough.

"SNECULFCROS" HUNDRED

In LECONFIELD, Osbern and Wulfgeat and Osbern had 3 carucates of land and 5 bovates to the geld, where there could be 3 ploughs. Now William has 2 ploughs there; and 8 villans with 1½ ploughs, and 10 fisheries rendering 2,400 eels. [There is] woodland pasture 2 leagues long and 2 broad. TRE worth 30s; now 40s.

In SCOREBY, Cille (a manor), Alwine (a manor), Asa (a manor), Forne [and] Fargrimr had 6 carucates of land to the geld, where there could be 3 ploughs. Now Osbern has them of William. He himself [has] 2 ploughs there; and 4 villans and 2 bordars with 2 ploughs. [There is] meadow 3 furlongs long and 1 broad, [and] woodland pasture half a league long and a half broad. The whole manor [is] 1 league long and a half broad. TRE worth 30s; now 40s.

In "IANULFESTORP" [in Dunnington, near York] are 2 carucates of land to the geld; the soke [is] in Clifton [near York]. Healfdene had it. William has it, and it is waste. There could be 1 plough.

In DUNNINGTON [near York], Northmann and Healfdene had 5 carucates of land and 6 bovates to the geld, where there could be 3 ploughs. Now Geoffrey has them of William. He himself [has] 1 plough there; and 2 villans with half a plough. TRE worth 24s; now 10s.

In GRIMSTON [in Dunnington, near York], Ulfkil had 1 carucate of land to the geld, and there could be 1 plough. William has it, and it is waste. TRE it was worth 10s.

WARTER HUNDRED

In WARTER, Northmann had 4 carucates of land to the geld, where there could be 2 ploughs. Geoffrey has it of William, and it is waste.

POCKLINGTON HUNDRED

In HAYTON, Northmann and Asa had $2\frac{1}{2}$ carucates of land to the geld, and there could be $1\frac{1}{2}$ ploughs. This belongs to Burnby.

In BURNBY, Beornwulf and Asa had 2 carucates and 7 bovates to the geld, and there could be $1\frac{1}{2}$ ploughs. William has this, and it is waste.

In SUTTON UPON DERWENT, Beornwulf and Northmann had 5 carucates of land to the geld, and there could be 3 ploughs. Now Picot has it of William. He himself [has] 1 plough there; and 11 villans with 3 ploughs. TRE worth 36s; now 20s. In the same vill Sigrith had 1 carucate of land to the geld, which half a plough could plough. There William has now 3 fisheries rendering 4s. TRE it was worth 20s.

In WHELDRAKE, Northmann had 6 carucates of land and 6 bovates to the geld, where there could be 4 ploughs. Now William de Colleville has it of William. He himself [has] 1 plough there; and 3 villans and 3 bordars with 1 plough, and 3 fisheries rendering 2,000 eels. There is a church, and 20 acres of meadow, [and] woodland pasture $1\frac{1}{2}$ leagues long and 1 broad. The whole manor [is] $2\frac{1}{2}$ leagues long and 1 broad. TRE worth 20s; now the same.

In ELVINGTON, Ulfkil had 6 carucates of land to the geld, where there could be 3 ploughs. Now Æthelwulf has it of William. He himself [has] 1 plough there; and 3 villans with 1 plough. There is a church, and 2 fisheries rendering 1,000

eels, and [he has] 10 acres of meadow. [There is] woodland pasture 1 league long and a half broad. The whole [is] 1 league long and 1 broad. TRE worth 40s; now 10s.

"TORBAR" HUNDRED

In FOSTON ON THE WOLDS, Karli had 5 carucates of land to the geld, where there could be 3 ploughs. Now Hugh holds it of William. He himself [has] 1 plough there; and 2 villans with 1 plough. There is a church, and 1 mill [rendering] 5s. The whole [is] half a league long and a half broad. TRE worth 40s; now 15s.

In NAFFERTON, Karli had 23 carucates of land and 2 bovates to the geld, where there could be 15 ploughs. Now William has 3 ploughs there, and 13 villans have 3 ploughs, and 1 mill [rendering] 5s. [There is] meadow 2 leagues long and a half broad. TRE worth £8; now 50s. To this manor belongs sokeland in Pockthorpe, 5 carucates to the geld, where there could be $2\frac{1}{2}$ ploughs.

IN THE NORTH RIDING LANGBAURGH WAPENTAKE

In FYLING, Merewine had 1 carucate of land to the geld, which half a plough could plough. William has it, and it is waste. TRE it was worth 5s4d.

In HINDERWELL, Northmann had 4 carucates of land and 6 bovates to the geld, where there could be $2\frac{1}{2}$ ploughs. William has it, and it is waste. [There are] 13 acres of meadow. TRE it was worth 20s.

In "ARNODESTORP" [in Hinderwell] is sokeland belonging to Hinderwell, 10 bovates of land to the geld, and there could be 1 plough.

In MARSKE-BY-THE-SEA, Northmann had 8 carucates of land to the geld, where there could be 4 ploughs. Now William has there 16 villans with 5 ploughs, [and] 8 acres of meadow. TRE worth 10s; now 20s.

In KIRKLEATHAM, Northmann had 4 carucates of land to the geld, where there could be 2 ploughs. Now William has there 1 sokeman.

[Folio 323: YORKSHIRE]

and 7 bordars with 1 plough. There is a priest and a church, and 6 acres of meadow. TRE worth 10s; now 5s4d.

In NORMANBY [in Eston] is sokeland, half a carucate of land to the geld, belonging to Marske-by-the-Sea. It is waste.

"DIC" WAPENTAKE

In CLOUGHTON, Ligulf had 1 carucate of land to the geld, where there could be half a plough. Now Richard has it of William, and it is waste. TRE it was worth 5s4d.

In KILLERBY [in Cayton], Blæc and Sprot had 2 carucates of land to the geld, where there could be 1 plough. Now William has it, and it is waste.

In SEAMER [near Scarborough], Karli had 6 carucates of land to the geld, where there could be 3 ploughs. Now William has 5 ploughs there, and 15 villans with 3 ploughs. There is a church and a priest, [and] woodland pasture 3 furlongs long and 2 broad. The whole [is] 1 league long and 1 broad. TRE worth 20s; now £4.

In "TORP" [in Irton] and IRTON, Karli and Blacre had 4½ carucates of land to the geld, where there could be 2 ploughs. Now William has it, and it is waste. TRE worth 16s; now 16d.

In 'HILL GRIPS' [in East Ayton], Karli had 1 carucate of land to the geld, and there could be half a plough. Now William has it, and it is waste. [There is] woodland pasture 3 furlongs long and 2 broad.

In EAST AYTON, Blacre, Gilleandrais and Thorbrandr had 6 carucates of land to the geld, where there could be 4 ploughs. Now William has there 1 mill [rendering] 5s, and 18 villans with 6 ploughs, [and] 40 acres of meadow. [There is] woodland pasture 9 furlongs long and 9 broad. TRE worth 30s; now 40s.

In HACKNESS and SUFFIELD and EVERLEY are 8 carucates of land to the geld, where there could be 5 ploughs. Of this land, 2 carucates are in the soke of Falsgrave, and the others are of the land of St Hilda. Now William has 2 ploughs there; and 14 villans and 4 bordars with 4 ploughs. There are 3 churches and a priest, [and] woodland pasture 2 leagues long and 1 broad. The whole manor [is] 6 leagues long and 2 broad. TRE worth £7; now 20s.

In SNAINTON, Blacre had 1½ carucates of land to the geld, and there could be 1 plough. Now Fulk has it of William. He himself [has] 1 plough there; and 5 villans [with] half a plough, and 2 acres of meadow. TRE worth 16s; now the same.

In 'INGOLFTWAYT' [in Easingwold], Gamal had 8 carucates of land to the geld, where there could be 4 ploughs. Now Fulcher has it of William, and it is waste. TRE worth 20s; now 8s. [There is] woodland half a league long and as much broad.

'YARLESTRE' WAPENTAKE

In "BERGHEBI" [in Topcliffe], Knut had 8 carucates of land to the geld, where there could be 4 ploughs. William has it, and it is waste. TRE it was worth 20s. [There is] woodland pasture 4 furlongs long and as much broad.

In TOPCLIFFE and Crakehill, Dalton [near Topcliffe], Asenby [and] Skipton on Swale, Beornwulf had 26 carucates of land to the geld, where there could be 15 ploughs. Now William has 3 ploughs there; and 35 villans and 14 bordars with 13 ploughs. There is a church, and 2 priests having 1 plough, and 1 mill [rendering] 5s, [and] woodland pasture 4 furlongs long and 4 broad. The whole manor [is] 3 leagues long and 2 broad. TRE [worth] £4; now 100s.

In RAINTON or Rainton [sic], Eardwulf and Arnketil had 3 carucates of land to the geld, where there could be 2 ploughs. Now William has there 3 villans with 1 plough, and 4 acres of meadow. The whole [is] half a league long and a half broad. TRE worth 20s; now 2s.

In CATTON, Beornwulf, Thorn, karli and Ulfgrimr had 6 carucates of land to the geld, where there could be 3 ploughs.

Now William has 2 ploughs there, and 3 villans with 1 plough. TRE worth 30s; now 10s.

[Folio 323V: YORKSHIRE]

XV. The land of Drogo de La Beuvriere

In BURSTWICK, Earl Tosti had 4 carucates of land to the geld, where there could be 6 ploughs. Now Drogo has there 1 plough, and 1 bordar, and 30 acres of meadow. [There is] woodland pasture 4 furlongs long and as much broad.

To this manor belong these Berewicks: Paull, 1 carucate; Newton Garth, 1 carucate; Paull Holme, 1 carucate; Nuthill, 2 carucates; Skeckling, 6 bovates. Together, [there are] 4 carucates of land to the geld, where there could be [...] ploughs. Now Drogo has there 2 ploughs; and 26 villans and 4 bordars having 7 ploughs.

To the same manor belongs this sokeland: Sutton-on-Hull, 2 carucates; Skeckling, 2½ carucates; Camerton, 6 carucates; Thorngumbald, 2 carucates; Paull Holme, 1 carucate; Lelley Dyke, 4 carucates; Sproatley, 1 carucate; Preston [near Hedon], 11 bovates. Together, [there are] 20 carucates and 3 bovates of land to the geld, where there could be 20 ploughs. There Drogo has now 5 ploughs, and 6 sokemen and 16 villans, but they do not plough.

The whole manor, with appurtenances, was worth TRE £56; now £10.

In KILNSEA, Morcar had 13 carucates of land to the geld, †where† there could be 12 ploughs. Now Drogo has 1 plough there; and 25 villans and 2 bordars with 7 ploughs, and 12 acres of meadow.

To this manor belongs this sokeland: Tunstall [near Withernsea], 7 carucates; Roos, 3 carucates #; Owstwick, 3 carucates; Elstronwick, 4 carucates; Tansterne, 1 carucate; Etherdwick, 2 carucates; Ringbrough, 1 carucate; Humbleton, 1 carucate; "Fostun" [in Humbleton], 3 carucates; Flinton, 3½ carucates; Winestead, half a carucate. [...] Together, [there are] 29 carucates of land to the geld, where there could be 32 ploughs. Now Drogo has there 2½ ploughs; and 20 villans having 6 ploughs, and 6 sokemen and 1 bordar. In "Fostune" [in Humbleton] there is a church and a priest. TRE worth £56; now £10.

In HILSTON and OWSTWICK, Murdac had 7 carucates of land to the geld, and there could be 7 ploughs. Now Drogo has it, and it is waste. TRE it was worth 55s.

In WITHERNSEA, Morcar had 18 carucates of land and 6 bovates to the geld, where there could be 15 ploughs. Now Drogo has there 1 plough; and 4 villans and 5 bordars and 2 priests. All these together [have] 2 ploughs, and 100 acres of meadow.

To this manor belongs this sokeland: "Andrebi" [in Roos], 2 carucates; Burton Pidsea, 7 carucates; Danthorpe, 2 carucates and 6 bovates; Fitling, 6 carucates; Sproatley, 5 bovates; Grimston [in Garton], 4 carucates; Waxholme, 6 bovates; Tunstall [near Withernsea], 1 carucate; Owthorne, 5 bovates; Hollym, 1 carucate; 'Redmere' [in Owthorne], 3 bovates. Together, [there are] 32 carucates of land to the geld, where there could be 25 ploughs. Now Drogo has there 10 sokemen and 10 villans and 2 bordars having 7 ploughs. TRE worth £56; now £6.

In MAPPLETON, Morcar had 13 carucates of land to the geld, and there could be 13 ploughs. Now Drogo has there 1 plough; and 4 villans have 1 plough, and 100 acres of meadow.

To this manor belongs this sokeland: Rolston, 5 carucates and 2 bovates; "Arnestorp" [in Great Hatfield], 1½ carucates; 'Little Cowden' [in Mappleton], 3 carucates; Withernwick, 6 carucates. Together, [there are] 16 carucates of land, less 2 bovates, to the geld, where there could be 15 ploughs.

Now Drogo has there 4 sokemen and 6 villans and 9 bordars having 3 ploughs.

Also other sokeland belonging to Mappleton: Thirtleby, 4 carucates; Wyton, 4 carucates; Marfleet, 4 carucates; Coniston, 4 carucates; Routh, 4 carucates; Great Hatfield, 2 carucates and 2 bovates; Goxhill, 3 carucates and the third part of 1 bovate. Together, [there are] 26 carucates to the geld, where there could be †27† ploughs. Now Drogo's men have there 4 ploughs; and 19 villans and 9 sokemen and 6 bordars having 6 ploughs.

TRE worth £56; now £6.

In HORNSEA, Morcar had 27 carucates of land to the geld, and there could be as many ploughs. Now Drogo has 1 plough there, and Wizo, his man, 1 plough, and 9 villans and 3 bordars with 1½ ploughs. There is a church and a priest, and [he has] 60 acres of meadow.

To this manor belongs this sokeland: Hornsea Burton, 2 carucates; Southorpe, 1½ carucates; Long Riston, 2 carucates and 6 bovates; North Skirlaugh, 6 bovates; High Skirlington, 5 carucates.

Together, [there are] 11½ carucates of land to the geld, where there could be 12 ploughs. Now Drogo has there 2 sokemen and 3 villans with 2 ploughs. TRE worth £56; now £6.

In 'CLEETON', Harold had 28 carucates of land and 1½ bovates to the geld, where there could be 28 ploughs. Now Drogo has there 2 ploughs; and 6 villans with 1 plough, and 100 acres of meadow. To this manor belongs sokeland in Dringhoe and Upton [in Skipsea] of 5½ carucates of land to the geld, where there could be 5½ ploughs. Now there is 1 villan having 2 oxen. The whole manor, with appurtenances, [is] 5½ leagues long and 1 league broad. TRE worth £32; now £6.

In EASINGTON [near Kilnsea], Morcar had 15 carucates of land to the geld, and there could be as many ploughs. Now Drogo has there 1 plough;

[Folio 324: YORKSHIRE]

and 13 villans and 4 bordars having 3 ploughs, and 100 acres of meadow. To this manor belongs this sokeland: Garton and Ringbrough, 8 carucates of land to the geld, and there could be as many ploughs. Now Baldwin has it of Drogo. He

himself [has] there 1 plough. There is a priest and a church, and [he has] 60 acres of meadow.

In DIMLINGTON are 5 carucates of land to the geld, and as many [ploughs] to plough them. It belongs to Easington [near Kilnsea]. TRE worth £32; now £8.

In ALDBROUGH, Ulf had 9 carucates of land to the geld, where there could be 10 ploughs. In East Newton [in Aldbrough] and South Skirlaugh and Totleys are 2 carucates of land and 6 bovates to the geld, where there could be 3 ploughs. Now Drogo has 1 plough there; and a certain knight of his 1 plough, and 14 villans with 2 ploughs. There are 100 acres of meadow, [and] woodland pasture 4 furlongs long and 3 broad.

To this manor belongs this sokeland: Wawne, 7 carucates; Meaux, 2 carucates; Benningholme, 2 carucates and 5 bovates; Rowton, 2 carucates; South Skirlaugh, 4 carucates; Dowthorpe, 3 carucates; Marton [in South Skirlaugh], 2 carucates; Low Fosham, 3 carucates; Bewick, 6 carucates; East Newton [in Aldbrough], 1½ carucates; Ringbrough, 1 carucate; Waxholme, 2 carucates and 2 bovates; Totleys, 5 carucates and 6 bovates; Ottringham, half a carucate. [...] Together, [there are] 41 carucates of land to the geld, where there could be 40 ploughs.

Now Drogo has 2 ploughs there; and 6 sokemen and 13 villans and 3 bordars having 7 ploughs. 3 of Drogo's knights have there 2 ploughs, and 2 villans and 3 bordars.

To these belong 174 acres of meadow. The whole manor with appurtenances [is] 9 leagues long and 6½ leagues broad. TRE worth £40; now £6.

In KEYINGHAM, Thorfridh had 8 carucates of land to the geld, where there could be 8 ploughs. Now Drogo has there 30 villans †having† 3 ploughs. There is a priest and a church, and 24 acres of meadow. [It is] 2 leagues long and 1 broad. TRE worth £8; now 30s.

In OTTRINGHAM, Thor and Thorkil had 4 carucates of land, and there could be 4 ploughs. Now Henry has there, of Drogo, 1 plough; and 6 villans and 6 bordars with 1½ ploughs. There is a priest and a church, and 1 mill, and 20 acres of meadow. [It is] 2 leagues long and a half broad. TRE worth 100s; now 20s.

HALSHAM belongs to this manor. There are 6 bovates of land to the geld and there could be 1 plough. Now Gummar has there, of Drogo, 4 villans and 1 bordar with 1 plough, and [there are] 4 acres of meadow. [It is] 4 furlongs long and as much broad.

In [Great and Little] NEWSOME, Earnwine had 5 carucates of land and 2 bovates to the geld, where there could be 5 ploughs. Now Drogo has there 1 sokeman and 9 villans and 7 bordars with 3 ploughs, and [there are] 20 acres of meadow. [It is] 1 league long and 1 broad. TRE worth 60s; now 40s.

In RIMSWELL, Oda had 5 carucates of land and 2 bovates to the geld, where there could be 5 ploughs. Now Baldwin and Guntard have it of Drogo. They themselves [have] 2 ploughs, and 20 acres of meadow. [It is] 1 league long and 1 broad. TRE worth 60s; now 40s.

In WAXHOLME, Thorkil and Thor had 2 carucates of land to the geld, and there could be 2 ploughs. Now Alelm has it of Drogo. There are 6 villans and 4 bordars with 2 ploughs, and [he has] 16 acres of meadow. [It is] 1 league long and 4 furlongs broad. TRE worth 20s; now 10s.

In 'REDMERE' [in Owthorne], Ramkel and Karli had 1½ carucates of land to the geld, and there could be 1½ ploughs. It is waste. There are 20 acres of meadow. [It is] half a league long and a half broad. TRE [it was worth] 20s.

In HOLMPTON, Oda, Hwelp, Siward, Alstan, Azur [and] Grimkel had 8 carucates of land to the geld, and there could be as many ploughs. Now Walter has it of Drogo. He himself [has] 1 plough there; and 4 villans and 5 bordars with 2 ploughs, and [there are] 16 acres of meadow. [It is] 1 league long and 1 broad. TRE worth £8; now 20s.

In OUT NEWTON, Ligulf had 5 carucates of land to the geld, and there could be 6 ploughs. Now Drogo has 1 plough there; and 4 villans with 1 plough, and [there are] 20 acres of meadow. [It is] 1 league long and a half broad.

In RYSOME GARTH, Thorgot had 2 carucates of land to the geld, and there could be 2 ploughs. Now Drogo has 1 bordar there, and [there are] 10 acres of meadow. [There is] woodland pasture 3 furlongs long and 2 broad. The whole [is] half a league long and a half broad. TRE worth 20s; now 12d.

In "TORP" [in Easington, near Kilnsea], Thorgot had 3 carucates of land to the geld, and there could be as many ploughs. Now Walter has there 12 villans and 2 bordars having 3 ploughs, and [there are] 20 acres of meadow. [It is] 2 leagues long and a half broad. TRE worth 40s; now the same.

In LISSETT, Ulf had 3 carucates of land to the geld, and there could be 3 ploughs. It is waste. [There are] 30 acres of meadow. [It is] 1 league long and a half broad. TRE it was worth 60s.

In BEEFORD, Ulf had 12½ carucates of land to the geld, and there could be 12 ploughs. Now Drogo has 1 plough there. There is a priest and a church, [and] 30 acres of meadow. [It is] 1 league long and 1 broad.

To this manor belongs this sokeland: Dunnington [in Beeford], 6 carucates; 'Winton' [in Barmston], 5 carucates and 2 bovates; Nunkeeling, 2 carucates. Together, [there are] 13 carucates of land and 2 bovates to the geld, and there could be as many ploughs. Now the priest of Drogo has 1 plough there. [There are] 52 acres of meadow. TRE worth £20; now 10s.

In NORTH FRODINGHAM, Ulf had 12 carucates of land to the geld, and there could be 12 ploughs. Now Drogo has 1 plough there; and 5 villans with 4 ploughs. There is a church and a priest, and 3 fisheries, and 30 acres of meadow. [It is] 1½ leagues long and 1 broad. TRE worth £14; now 10s.

In BARMSTON, Thorkil, Siward, Bondi and Alfkil had 8 carucates of land to the geld, and there could be as many ploughs. It is waste.

TRE it was worth 60s.

In ULROME, Thorkil and Thorsten had 2½ carucates of land to the geld, and there could be 2 ploughs. Now Erenbald has it of Drogo. He himself [has] 1 plough there, and 2 bordars, and [there are] 22 acres of meadow. TRE worth 40s; now 10s.

In NUNKEELING, 2 Ketilberts had 4 carucates of land to the geld, and there could be as many ploughs. Now Baldwin has 1 bordar there, and [there are] 16 acres of meadow. [It is] 2 leagues long and 1 broad. TRE it was worth 30s.

In BEWHOLME, Northmann, Ketilbert and Thorkil had 5 carucates of land and 6 bovates to the geld. Now Manbodo has it of Drogo. He himself [has] 1 plough there, and [there are] 20 acres of meadow. [There is] woodland pasture 3 furlongs long and 1 broad. The whole [is] 3 leagues long and half a league broad. TRE worth £4; now 10s.

In ARRAM, Thorkil had 1 carucate of land to the geld, and there could be 1 plough. Now Rayner, Drogo's man, has 1 plough there, and 2 villans, and 6 acres of meadow. [It is] 1 league long and 3 furlongs broad. TRE worth 20s; now the same.

In BRANDESBURTON, Swein, Ulf, Ulfkil, Veikr, and the other Ulf, Ketilbert [and] Earnwig had 12½ carucates of land to the geld, and there could be as many ploughs. Now Drogo has 1 plough there, and 6 villans [have] 1 plough, and 1 knight, 1 plough. TRE worth £40; now 40s.

In SEATON [in Sigglesthorne], Ulf and Svartgeirr had 6½ carucates of land to the geld, and there could be 6 ploughs. Now Robert, Drogo's man, has 1 plough there, and 2 villans, and 20 acres of meadow. [It is] 1 league long and a half broad. TRE worth £9; now 10s.

In CATFOSS, Knut had 6 carucates of land to the geld, and there could be as many ploughs. Now Franco, Drogo's man, has 1 plough there; and 10 villans and 4 bordars with 2 ploughs, and 24 acres of meadow. [It is] 1 league long and a half broad. TRE worth 60s; now 20s.

In CATWICK, Swein and Murdac had 5 carucates of land to the geld, and there could be 5 ploughs. Now 2 of Drogo's knights have 2 ploughs there; and 2 villans and 2 bordars with 1 plough. There is a church, and 1 mill, and 40 acres of meadow. [It is] 1 league long and 1 broad. TRE worth 60s; now 30s.

In "CHENECOL" [in Long Riston], Gamal had 1 carucate of land to the geld, and there could be 1 plough. It is waste. TRE it was worth 10s.

In LONG RISTON, Ulf and Huna had 3 carucates of land to the geld, and there could be 3 ploughs. Now Gherbod, Drogo's man, has there 1½ ploughs, and 20 acres of meadow. [It is] 1 league long and 3 furlongs broad. TRE worth 30s; now the same.

In RISE, Knut had 5½ carucates of land to the geld, and there could be 6 ploughs. Now Franco, Drogo's man, has 2 ploughs there; and 7 villans and 6 bordars with 1 plough, and 1 mill, and 30 acres of meadow. [There is] woodland pasture 2 furlongs long and 2 broad. TRE worth 60s; now 30s.

In WASSAND, Swein had 2 carucates of land to the geld, and there could be 2 ploughs. Now Turstin, Drogo's man, has 1 plough there, and 1 villan and 3 bordars, and 6 acres of meadow. [It is] half a league long and a half broad. TRE worth 20s; now 10s.

In GREAT HATFIELD, Ramkel and Ketilbert had 3 carucates of land to the geld, and there could be 3 ploughs. Now Rayner, Drogo's man, has 1 plough there, and 3 villans and 1 bordar, and 30 acres of meadow. [It is] half a league long and a half broad. TRE worth 40s; now | 20s |.

In WITHERNWICK, Thor had 1 carucate of land to the geld, and there could be 1 plough. Now Wazelin, Drogo's man, has half a plough there, and 2 bordars, and 6 acres of meadow. TRE worth 10s; now 5s.

In LANGTHORPE [near Old Ellerby], Thor had 1 carucate of land to the geld, and there could be 1 plough.

In LITTLE HATFIELD, Redhe had 2 carucates of land and 3 bovates to the geld, and there could be 2 ploughs. Now Walter has [sic], Drogo has 1 plough there; and 8 villans and 7 villans [sic] with 2 ploughs, and 4 acres of meadow. [It is] half a league long and a half broad. TRE it was worth 50s.

In OLD ELLERBY, Frani, Elaf, Mann, Thorbiorn and Ramkel had 4 carucates of land to the geld, and there could be 4 ploughs. Now Theobald, Drogo's man, has 1 plough there, and 2 villans and 3 bordars, and [there are] 20 acres of meadow. [It is] 1 league long and a half broad. TRE worth 40s; now 10s.

In OUBROUGH, Thorfridh had 2 carucates of land to the geld, and there could be 2 ploughs. Now Frumold, Drogo's man, has 1 plough there; and 5 villans and 3 bordars with 1 plough, and 10 acres of meadow. [It is] half a league long and a half broad. TRE worth 30s; now 20s.

In GANSTEAD, Frani and Healfdene had 4 carucates of land to the geld, and there could be 4 ploughs. Now Albert, Drogo's man, has 1 plough there; and 7 villans and 4 bordars with 2 ploughs, and 20 acres of meadow. [It is] 1 league long and a half broad. TRE worth 40s; now 20s.

In SUTTON-ON-HULL, Grimkel had 3 carucates of land and 2 bovates to the geld. Now Lambert, Drogo's man, has 2 ploughs there, and 4 villans and 9 bordars, and 60 acres of meadow. [There is] woodland pasture 2 furlongs long and 1 broad. [It is] 2 leagues long and a half broad. TRE worth 40s; now 40s.

In BILTON [near Hull], Healfdene had 1 carucate of land to the geld, and there could be 1 plough. Now Franco, Drogo's man, has there 4 villans

[Folio 325: YORKSHIRE]

having 1 plough, and [there are] 10 acres of meadow. [It is] 1 league long and 2 furlongs broad. TRE worth 10s; and now the same.

In PRESTON [near Hedon], Frani and the other Frani, Basinc, Maccus, Thor, Gamal, Thorbiorn and Thorfridh had 10 carucates of land to the geld and 2 bovates. There could be 10 ploughs. Now Baldwin, Drogo's man, has 1 plough there; and 45 villans and 3 bordars having 9 ploughs. There is a priest and a church. 3 of Drogo's knights have there 11 villans and 4 bordars with 3 ploughs, and 200 acres of meadow. [It is] 2 leagues long and 2 broad. TRE worth £12; now £6.

In SOUTHCOATES and DRYPOOL, Otti and Ramkel had 13 bovates of land to the geld, and there could be 2 ploughs. It is waste. TRE it was worth 30s.

In WEST CARLTON, Swein had 2 carucates of land to the geld. There could be 2 ploughs. Now Ralph, Drogo's man, has 1 plough there, and 20 acres of meadow. [It is] half a league long and a half broad. TRE worth 20s; now 5s.

In MARTON [in South Skirlaugh], Swein had 1 carucate to the geld. There is land for 1 plough. Now Franco, Drogo's man, has there 1 villan with 1 plough, and [there are] 8 acres of meadow. [It is] half a league long and a half broad. TRE worth 10s; now 5s.

In SPROATLEY, Basinc, Forne and Thor had 4 carucates of land to the geld. There is land for 4 ploughs. Now Roger, Drogo's man, has 1 plough there; and 4 villans with 1 plough, and 40 acres of meadow. [It is] 1 league long and 7 furlongs broad. TRE worth 50s; now 20s.

In ROOS, Murdac and Svartgeirr had 3 carucates of land and 5 bovates to the geld. There is land for 4 ploughs. Now Fulk, Drogo's man, has 1 plough there; and 1 villan with 1 plough. There is a priest and a church, and [he has] 30 acres of meadow. [It is] half a league long and a half broad. TRE worth 60s; now 20s.

In WILSTHORPE, a Berewick of 'Cleeton', [are] 2 carucates of land to the geld. [There is] land for 1 plough. Harold had it. Now Drogo has it, and it is waste. [It is] half a league long and 3 furlongs broad.

XVI. The land of Ralph de Mortimer

EAST RIDING

HESSLE HUNDRED

In KIRK ELLA, Eadgifu had 10 carucates of land to the geld. [There is] land for 5 ploughs. Now Ralph de Mortimer has 3 ploughs there, and 20 villans with 3 ploughs. TRE worth 100s; now £4.

In NORTH FERRIBY, Eadgifu had 10 carucates of land to the geld. There is land for 5 ploughs. Ralph has there now 14 villans with 3 ploughs. There is a priest and a church. TRE worth 100s; now 60s. To this manor belong these Berewicks: Anlaby, 2 bovates; Wauldby, 1 carucate; Riplingham, 10 bovates; ''Totfled'' [in Hull], 1 carucate; 'Myton', 1½ carucates; 'Wolfreton' [in Kirk Ella], half a carucate; Hessle [near Hull], 1 carucate. Together, [there are] 6½ carucates of land to the geld. There is land for 4 ploughs. These are waste, except that in Hessle [near Hull] are 4 villans with 1 plough.

In NEWSHOLME [in Wressle], Eadgifu had 6 carucates of land and 1 bovate to the geld. There is land for 4 ploughs. 6 bovates of this land are in the soke of Spaldington. Ralph has there now half a plough; and 1 villan with 2 oxen. TRE worth 20s; now 10s. To this manor belongs sokeland in Wressle, 1 carucate and 6 bovates, and Gribthorpe, 2 carucates; this is 3 carucates and 6 bovates to the geld. There is land for 3 ploughs. Ralph has 1 plough there, and it is worth 6s8d.

In BREIGHTON, Eadgifu had 2 carucates of land to the geld. There is land for 1 plough. Now Ralph has there 5 sokemen and 2 villans with 2 ploughs, and it is worth 12s. [It is] 1 league long and 4 furlongs broad.

In 'LUND' [in Breighton] is land belonging to Breighton, $2\frac{1}{2}$ carucates of land to the geld. There is land for 1 plough. It is waste.

In WILLITOFT, $2\frac{1}{2}$ carucates, and FOGGATHORPE, 2 carucates, is sokeland of Breighton. [There is] land for $2\frac{1}{2}$ ploughs.

In "CHETELESTORP" [in Storwood], Eadgifu had 1 carucate of land to the geld. Ralph has it, and it is waste.

In MELBOURNE, Eadgifu had 6 carucates of land to the geld. There is land for 3 ploughs. Ralph has it, and it is waste. TRE it was worth 20s. [There is] woodland pasture 2 leagues long and 2 furlongs broad.

In THORNTON [near Pocklington], Eadgifu had 6 carucates of land to the geld. There is land for 3 ploughs. Ralph has it, and it is waste. TRE it was worth 14s.

"SCARD" HUNDRED

In WELHAM, Eadgifu had 5 carucates of land and 5 bovates to the geld. There is land for 3 ploughs. Ralph has it, and it is waste. TRE it was worth 40s.

In SUTTON [near Malton] and NORTON [near Malton] [are] 5 carucates of land to the geld. There is land for 3 ploughs. It belongs to WELHAM.

In WINTRINGHAM, Eadgifu had 20 carucates of land to the geld. There is land for 12 ploughs. Ralph has now 2 ploughs there; and 18 villans with 6 ploughs.

[Folio 325V: YORKSHIRE]

[It is] 3 leagues long and 1 broad. TRE worth 60s; now 40s.

In SCAMPSTON, Orm had 4 carucates of land to the geld. There is land for 2 ploughs. Now Ralph has it, and it is waste. TRE it was worth 10s. [It is] $1\frac{1}{2}$ leagues long and 1 broad.

In KNAPTON [in Wintringham], Eadgifu had 6 carucates of land to the geld. There is land for 3 ploughs. Ralph has it, and it is waste. TRE [it was worth] 40s. There are 20 acres of meadow. [It is] $1\frac{1}{2}$ leagues long and 1 broad.

In THIRKLEBY [in Kirby Grindalythe], Eadgifu had 8 carucates of land to the geld. There is land for 4 ploughs.

Ralph has it, and it is waste. TRE it was worth 30s. [It is] 2 leagues long and 1 broad.

In DALBY, Eadgifu had 1 carucate of land to the geld. There is land for half a plough. Ralph has it, and it is waste.

In GILLING EAST, Orm had 4 carucates of land to the geld. There is land for 2 ploughs. Ralph has 1 rent-paying tenant there, who pays 10s8d. TRE it was worth 10s. [There is] woodland pasture half a league long and a half broad. The whole manor [is] 1 league long and 1 broad.

XVII. The land of Ralph Paynel

EAST RIDING

In THORGANBY, Mærle-Sveinn had 3 carucates of land to the geld. There is land for 2 ploughs. Now Ralph Paynel has 1 plough there; and 4 villans with 1 plough, and 8 fisheries [rendering] 4s. [There is] woodland pasture 1 league long and a half broad. TRE worth 20s; now 12s.

In WEST COTTINGWITH, a BEREWICK of Thorganby, [are] 10 bovates of land to the geld. There is land for 1 plough. It is waste.

In BARLBY, Mærle-Sveinn had 1 carucate of land to the geld. There is land for half a plough. Ralph has it, and it is waste. There are 5 acres of meadow, [and] woodland pasture 4 furlongs long and 2 broad.

In PLACE NEWTON, Mærle-Sveinn had 18 carucates of land to the geld. There is land for 9 ploughs. Ralph has it, and it is waste. There are 10 acres of meadow. [It is] $1\frac{1}{2}$ leagues long and 1 broad. TRE it was worth £4.

In RUDSTON, Mærle-Sveinn had 8 carucates of land to the geld. There is land for 4 ploughs. Ralph has it, and it is waste. TRE it was worth 60s.

NORTH RIDING

In NUNNINGTON, Mærle-Sveinn had 6 carucates of land to the geld. There is land for 3 ploughs. Ralph has it, and it is waste. TRE it was worth 40s.

To this manor belongs this sokeland: Wykeham Hill, 6 bovates; Stonegrave, 5 carucates and 2 bovates; [East and West] Ness, 3 carucates; South Holme, 1 carucate. Together, [there are] 10 carucates of land to the geld, in which there could be 5 ploughs. Ralph now has 1 plough there; and 7 villans with 4 ploughs. There is a church and a priest, and 1 mill [rendering] 3s, and 10 acres of meadow. [It is] 1 league long and 1 broad. It is worth 20s.

In NEWTON-ON-OUSE and "TORESBI" [in Newton-on-Ouse], Mærle-Sveinn had 9 carucates of land to the geld. There is land for 5 ploughs. Ralph has there now 1 plough; and 16 villans with 4 ploughs. [There is] woodland pasture half a league long and 3 furlongs broad. The whole manor [is] 1 league long and 1 broad. TRE worth 40s; now 26s8d.

WEST RIDING

In Drax, Little Airmyn, Camblesforth and Barlow, Mærle-Sveinn had 5 carucates of land and 1 bovate to the geld. There is land for 3 ploughs. Ralph has now 1 plough there; and 6 villans and 2 sokemen with 2 ploughs. There is a church and a priest, [and] woodland, pasture in places, 5 leagues long and 3 furlongs broad. The whole manor [is] 5 leagues long and 1½ leagues broad. TRE worth 40s; now 20s.

In RIBSTON ['Great Ribston' and Little Ribston], Mærle-Sveinn had 4 carucates of land to the geld. [There is] land for 2 ploughs. Ralph has it, and it is waste. TRE it was worth 20s.

In GOLDSBOROUGH [near Knaresborough], Mærle-Sveinn had 8 carucates of land to the geld. [There is] land for 4 ploughs. Now Hubert, Ralph's man, has 1 plough there; and 7 villans with 2 ploughs, and half a fishery rendering 5s4d. [There is] woodland pasture 12 furlongs long and 4 broad. The whole manor [is]

[Folio 326: YORKSHIRE]

1 league long and 1 broad. TRE worth £4; now 40s.

In RIPLEY, Mærle-Sveinn had 4½ carucates to the geld. [There is] land for 3 ploughs. Ralph has it, and it is waste. TRE it was worth 20s.

In [Kirk and North] DEIGHTON, Mærle-Sveinn had 12 carucates of land to the geld. There is land for 6 ploughs. Ralph has it now. There is a church, [and] woodland pasture half a league long and a half broad. TRE worth 60s; now 4s.

In THORPE UNDERWOOD is sokeland of Newton-on-Ouse, 1½ carucates of land to the geld. There is land for 1 plough. [There is] woodland pasture half a league long and 4 furlongs broad. Ralph has it, and it is waste. There are 4 acres of meadow.

XVIII. The land of Geoffrey de La Guerche

WEST RIDING

In ADLINGFLEET, Siward Barn had 6 carucates of land to the geld. There is land for 3 ploughs. Now Geoffrey de la Guerche has 1 plough there; and 13 villans and 1 bordar with 3 ploughs. There is a church and a priest, and 1 mill [rendering] 10s, [and] scrubland 1 league long and 1 furlong broad. The whole manor [is] 2 leagues long and 1 broad. TRE worth £4; now 30s.

XIX. The land of Geoffrey Alselin

WEST RIDING

In BRANTON and CANTLEY, Toki had 14 carucates of land and 1½ bovates to the geld. [There is] land for 15 ploughs. Now Geoffrey Alselin has 2 ploughs there; and 6 villans and 2 sokemen and 5 bordars having 6½ ploughs. There is a priest and a church.

In the same vill Alsige had 1 carucate of land to the geld. [There is] land for half a plough. [There is] woodland pasture

1 league long and 1 broad. The whole manor [is] 2 leagues long and 2 broad. TRE worth £8; now 30s.

In HEALAUGH and the two Wighills [Wighill and Wighill Park], Toki had 18 carucates of land to the geld. There is land for 9 ploughs. Now Geoffrey has 2 ploughs there; and 18 villans and 1 bordar with 7 ploughs. [There is] woodland pasture 2 leagues long and 1 broad. The whole manor [is] 2 leagues long and 2 broad. TRE worth £8; now 60s.

XX. The land of Walter d'Aincourt

WEST RIDING

In WOMBWELL, Thorir had 3½ carucates of land to the geld. There is land for 4 ploughs. Walter d'Aincourt has it, and it is waste. There are 4 acres of meadow, [and] woodland pasture 5½ furlongs long and as much broad. TRE worth 60s; now 10s8d.

In WEST MELTON and "TOFTES" [in Wombwell] is sokeland of this manor, 6 bovates to the geld. [There is] land for half a plough.

In RAWMARSH, Store had 4 carucates of land to the geld. [There is] land for 2 ploughs. Now Walter has 1 plough there; and 4 villans and 1 bordar and 2 sokemen having 2 ploughs. There are 12 acres of meadow, and 1 mill [rendering] 10s, [and] woodland pasture 1 league long and a half broad. The whole manor [is] 1½ leagues long and 1 league broad. TRE worth 60s; now 30s.

XXI. The land of Gilbert de Ghent

EAST RIDING

In HUNMANBY, Karli had 23 carucates of land to the geld. There is land for 13 ploughs. Now Gilbert de Ghent has 3 ploughs there; and 8 villans and 6 bordars having 4 ploughs. There is a priest and a church, and meadow 1 league long and a half broad.

In the same vill Ketilbert had 1 carucate of land to the geld. [There is] land for half a plough. Gilbert has it, and it is waste. TRE it was worth 4s.

In "RICSTORP" [in Muston] is a Berewick of this manor, 4 carucates of land to the geld. [There is] land for 3 ploughs. Gilbert has there 5 villans and 2 bordars with 2 ploughs. To this manor belongs this sokeland: Muston, 4 carucates; "Scolfstona" [in Muston], 3 carucates; [East and West] Flotmanby, 6 carucates. Together, [there are] 14 carucates of land to the geld. [There is] land for 7 ploughs. Gilbert has there 16 villans and 4 bordars having 4 ploughs.

In WOLD NEWTON, a Berewick of this manor, [are] 7 carucates of land to the geld. There is land for 4 ploughs. The whole of Hunmanby [is] 3 leagues long and 2 broad. TRE worth £12; now 60s.

XXII. The land of Gilbert Tison

EAST RIDING

In KIRK ELLA, Alwine, Ketil [and] Knut had 23 carucates of land to the geld. There is land for 12 ploughs. Now Gilbert Tison has 3 ploughs there; and 29 villans and 16 bordars having 6 ploughs. There is a church and a priest. TRE worth £8; now £6.

In HESSLE [near Hull], Alwine and Ketil had 7 carucates of land to the geld. There is land for 4 ploughs. Now Gilbert has 1 plough there; and 17 villans and 2 bordars with 3 ploughs. There is a church and a priest. [It is] 1 league long and a half broad. TRE worth 60s; now 50s.

In ANLABY, Knut had 3½ carucates of land to the geld. There is land for 2 ploughs. Now Gilbert has 1 plough there; and 7 villans with 1 plough. TRE worth 40s; now 50s. Richard holds it.

In "CHRACHETORP" [in Hessle, near Hull], Knut had 3 carucates to the geld. There is land for 2 ploughs. Fulk, Gilbert's man, has it, and it is waste. TRE it was worth 30s.

In WRESSLE and "Siuuarbi" [in Wressle], Alwine had 8 carucates of land to the geld. There is land for 4 ploughs. Now Gilbert has 1 plough there; and 16 villans and 5 bordars with 5 ploughs. There is a priest and a church, [and] woodland pasture 1 league long and 1½ furlongs broad. The whole manor [is] 2 leagues long and 1 broad. TRE worth 40s; now 60s.

To this manor belongs [this] sokeland: in Spaldington, 6 carucates of land, and in 'Lund' [in Breighton], 1½ carucates of land. There is land for 4 ploughs. Now there are 2 sokemen with half a plough.

To the same manor belongs other [sokeland]: in Willitoft, 7 bovates; and Gribthorpe, 2 carucates; and Laytham, 11 bovates. Together, to the geld, [there are] 4 carucates of land and 2 bovates to the geld. There is land for 3 ploughs. Gilbert has there 4 villans and 1 bordar with 1½ ploughs. In NORTH DUFFIELD [is] 1 carucate of land which belongs to Wressle.

In GUNBY, Alwine had 1 carucate of land and 3 bovates to the geld. There is land for 1 plough. Now Gilbert has 1 plough there; and 1 sokeman and 2 villans with 1 plough. [It is] 1 league long and 4 furlongs broad. TRE worth 20s; now 60s.

In BUBWITH, Alwine had 6 carucates of land and 2 bovates to the geld. There is land for 9 ploughs. In the same vill, Ketil had 2 carucates and 2 bovates; the soke of this sokeland belongs to Breighton. There is land for 1½ ploughs. Now Richard, Gilbert's man, has half a plough there; and 5 villans with 1 plough. [There is] woodland pasture half a league long and 2 furlongs broad. TRE worth 20s; now 12s.

In FOGGATHORPE, Ketil had 3 carucates of land to the geld. There is land for 2½ ploughs. Gilbert has it, and it is waste. TRE it was worth 20s.

In HOLME-ON-SPALDING-MOOR, Alwine had 8 carucates of land to the geld. There is land for 4 ploughs. Now Geoffrey, Gilbert's man, has half a plough there; and 12 villans and 8 bordars with 3 ploughs. There is a priest and a church, [and] woodland pasture 2 leagues long and 3 furlongs broad. The whole manor [is] 3 leagues long and 3 leagues broad. TRE worth £10; now 60s.

In SANCTON, Northmann had 15 carucates of land to the geld. There is land for 8 ploughs. Now 3 knights have it of Gilbert. They themselves [have] 1½ ploughs there; and 6 villans and 5 bordars having 2½ ploughs. There is a priest and a church, and 6 acres of meadow. [It is] 3 leagues long and 1 broad. TRE worth £8; now 50s.

In HOUGHTON, Thorkil had half a carucate to the geld. [There is] land for half a plough. Now Humphrey, Gilbert's man, has 1 plough there; and 3 villans and 2 bordars with half a plough, and 2 acres of meadow. The whole [is] 1 league long and 1 broad. TRE worth 10s; now 20s.

In THORPE LE STREET, Alwine had 6 bovates of land to the geld. There is land for half a plough. And, in the same vill, [are] 2 carucates and 2 bovates to the geld. [There is] land for 1½ ploughs. The soke [is] in Pocklington. Now Gilbert has it, and it is waste. TRE it was worth 20s.

WEST RIDING

In BRAMHOPE, Ulfkil had 8 carucates to the geld. There is land for 4 ploughs. Now the same man has it of Gilbert, but it is waste. [There is] scrubland half a league long and 2 furlongs broad. The whole manor [is] 1 league long and 1 broad. TRE it was worth 40s.

In SWINTON [near Rotherham], Æthelstan had 3½ carucates to the geld. There is land for 2 ploughs. Now Gilbert has there 8 villans with 2 ploughs. [There is] woodland pasture 1 league long and 1 furlong broad. The whole manor [is] 1 league long and 1 broad. TRE worth 60s; now 15s.

In SCOTTON [in Farnham] is sokeland belonging to ALDBOROUGH, 4 carucates of land to the geld. [There is] land for 2 ploughs. Gilbert has 1½ ploughs there; and 1 sokeman with 1 plough. In Beamsley, Gilbert has 6 bovates.

In ADDINGHAM, Gamal Barn had 2 carucates of land to the geld. There is land for 1 plough. Gilbert has 1 plough there. [There is] woodland pasture 1 league long and a half broad. TRE worth 10s; now the same.

In LEATHLEY, Ulfkil had 1 carucate of land to the geld. There is land for half a plough. Now Gilbert has there 3 villans and 1 bordar with 2 ploughs, and 2 acres of meadow. TRE worth 10s; now 5½s.

In BRIMHAM, Gamal Barn had 2 bovates of land to the geld.

In NORTH RIGTON, Gamal Barn had 2 carucates to the geld. [There is] land for 1 plough.

In BECKWITH, Gamal Barn had 3 carucates to the geld. [There is] land for 2 ploughs.

In ROSSETT GREEN, Gamal Barn and Ulf had 2 carucates to the geld. [There is] land for 1 plough.

In BILTON [near Harrogate], Gamal Barn had 3½ carucates to the geld. [There is] land for 2 ploughs. Gilbert Tison has these lands, but they are all waste;

[Folio 327: YORKSHIRE]

only Bilton [near Harrogate] renders 3s of rent.

In RUDFARLINGTON, Gamal Barn had 14 bovates to the geld. There is land for 1 plough. Now it is cultivated, and renders 5s. [There is] woodland pasture 1½ leagues long and 9 furlongs broad. The whole [is] 2 leagues long and 11 furlongs broad. TRE it was worth 8s.

In PLOMPTON, Gamal Barn had 2 carucates to the geld. There is land for 1 plough. [It is] half a league long and 3 furlongs broad. Now it is cultivated, and renders 5s. TRE it was worth 20s.

In "GREAT" BRAHAM, Gamal Barn had 4 carucates of land to the geld. There is land for 2 ploughs. It is waste. TRE it was worth 20s. [There is] woodland pasture 5 furlongs long and 5 broad. The whole manor [is] 11 furlongs long and 11 broad.

IN CRAVEN

In Grassington, 3 carucates; in Linton [near Hebden], 2 carucates; in Threshfield, 2 carucates; in Eastburn [in Kildwick], 2 carucates and 2 bovates; in Steeton [in Kildwick], 3 carucates. Gamal Barn had these; now Gilbert Tison has them.

In Glusburn and "Chelchis" [in Glusburn], 3 carucates. Gamal had them. Gilbert has them.

In Oakworth, Gamal Barn [had] 1 carucate. Gilbert has it.

XXIII. The land of Richard fitzErfast

In MIDDLETHORPE, Christ's Church, [are] 2 carucates of land to the geld. [There is] land for 1½ ploughs. Richard fitzErfast has it, and it is waste. Nevertheless it renders 8s.

In BILBROUGH, Christ's Church, [are] 8 carucates of land to the geld. [There is] land for 4 ploughs. Richard has 1 plough there; and 6 villans and 2 bordars with 2 ploughs. [There is] woodland, pasture in places. The whole [is] 1 league long and a half broad. TRE worth 44s; now 22s.

In MOOR MONKTON, Christ's Church, [are] 9 carucates to the geld. [There is] land for as many ploughs. Richard has there now 4 villans and 2 bordars with 4 ploughs, and 6 acres of meadow. [There is] woodland pasture 6 furlongs leagues [sic] long and 4 broad. The whole [is] 1 league long and a half broad. TRE worth 40s; now 20s.

In HESSAY, Healfdene [had] 2 carucates, less 2 bovates, to the geld. [There is] land for 2 ploughs. Richard has there 3 bordars and 2 ploughs. TRE worth 10s8d; now 5s4d.

In KNAPTON [near York], Christ's Church, [are] 3 car-

ucates to the geld. There is land for 3 ploughs. Richard has there 4 villans with 2 ploughs. TRE worth 16s; now the same.

In Christ's Church, near the city of York, [is] half a carucate of land and 3 tofts to the geld. Richard has it, and it is cultivated. From the church and the land he has 30s.

XXIIII. The land of Hugh fitzBaldric

WEST RIDING

'YARLESTRE' WAPENTAKE

In COXWOLD, Kofse had 10 carucates of land to the geld; in "Iretone" [in Coxwold], 3 carucates; Yearsley, 3 carucates; Ampleforth, 1 carucate; Osgoodby, 3 carucates; Thirkleby [near Thirsk], 8 carucates; 'Baxby' [in Husthwaite], 15 bovates. Together, [there are] 20 carucates of land, less 1 bovate, to the geld. There is land for 15 ploughs.

Hugh fitzBaldric has there now 4 ploughs; and 54 villans having 29 ploughs. [There is] woodland 8 leagues long and 3 leagues and 4 furlongs broad. The whole manor [is] 9 leagues long and 4 leagues broad. TRE worth £6; now £12.

In KILBURN, Arnketil had 6 carucates of land to the geld. [There is] land for 3 ploughs. Now Hugh has there 1 villan, and 2 ploughs. [It is] 1 league long and a half broad. TRE worth 10s; now 6s.

In WILDON is sokeland of this manor, 3 carucates of land to the geld. [There is] land for 2 ploughs. There are now 11 villans having 8 ploughs.

In CAWTON, Thorbrandr and Salomon had 4 carucates of land to the geld. [There is] land for 2 ploughs. Hugh has there now 3 villans, and 3 ploughs, and 4 acres of meadow. [It is] 1 league long and 3 furlongs broad. TRE worth 16s; now 20s. Gerard holds it.

In THIRSK, Thor had 12 carucates of land to the geld. There is land for 6 ploughs. Hugh has there 10 villans having 2 ploughs, and 8 acres of meadow. TRE worth £4; now 10s.

In THORPEFIELD and NEWSHAM [in Kirkby Wiske] [are] 8 carucates of land to the geld. There is land for 4 ploughs. Now they are waste. The whole manor [is] 2 leagues long and 1 league broad.

In BAGBY, Orm had 5 carucates of land to the geld. There is land for 2½ ploughs. Hugh has there now half a plough; and 4 villans with 1 plough, and 10 acres of meadow. [There is] woodland pasture half a league long and as much broad. The whole [is] 1 league long and 1 league broad. TRE worth £8; now 40s.

These belong to Bagby: Kirby Knowle, 3 carucates; Carlton Miniott, 3 carucates; Islebeck, 1 carucate; Sutton-under-Whitestonecliffe, 1 carucate; Arden, 3 carucates; Kepwick, 1 carucate. Together, [there are] 12 carucates of land to the geld. [There is] land for 6 ploughs. Now there are 2 villans and 1 bordar with 1 plough, and a priest. [There is] woodland pasture 5 leagues long and 5 furlongs broad. The whole [is] 9½ leagues long and 3½ leagues broad.

In SUTTON-UNDER-WHITESTONECLIFFE, Ligulf had 5 carucates of land to the geld. There is land for 2 ploughs. Gerard, Hugh's man, has 1 plough there; and 8 villans with 2 ploughs. There is a priest, and a mill, [and] woodland pasture 1½ leagues long and 5 furlongs broad. The whole manor [is] 2 leagues long and 5 furlongs broad. TRE worth 26s; now 20s.

In MARDERBY, Gamal had 3 carucates of land to the geld. There is land for 1 plough. There Gerard, Hugh's man, has 1 plough;

[Folio 327V: YORKSHIRE]

and 7 villans with 4 ploughs. There is a priest, and woodland, without pasture, 4 furlongs long and 2 furlongs broad. The whole manor [is] 6 furlongs long and 4 broad. TRE worth 26s; now 20s.

In FELIXKIRK, Ligulf and Gamal had 3 carucates of land to the geld. There is land for 1 plough. Gerard, Hugh's man, has 2 ploughs there; and 1 villan with 1 plough. [There is] woodland 8 furlongs long and 4 broad. The whole manor [is] 1 league long and half a league broad. TRE worth 26s; now 5s.

This belongs to Felixkirk: Ravensthorpe, 1 carucate to the geld. [There is] land for half a plough.

In BOLTBY, Sumarfugl had 3 carucates of land to the geld. [There is] land for 1 plough. Gerard, Hugh's man, has 2 ploughs there; and 5 villans with 2 ploughs, and 6 acres of meadow. [There is] scrubland 4 furlongs long and as much broad. The whole manor [is] 1 league long and 1 broad. TRE, as now, worth 20s.

This belongs to Boltby: Ravensthorpe, 1 carucate of land to the geld. [There is] land for half a plough. It is waste.

In COWESBY, Gamal had 3 carucates of land to the geld. There is land for 1 plough. Gerard, Hugh's man, has there 7 villans having 4 ploughs. [There is] scrubland 4 furlongs long and as much broad. The whole manor [is] 1 league long and 4 furlongs broad. TRE worth 5s; and now the same.

In ELLERBECK, Gamal had 1 carucate of land to the geld. [There is] land for half a plough. Gerard, Hugh's man, has there 4 villans with 1 plough, and 5 acres of meadow. The whole [is] half a league long and 2 furlongs broad. TRE worth 8d; now 3s.

In 'CRUNKLY' [in Glaisdale], Orm had 5 carucates of land to the geld. [There is] land for 2 ploughs. Hugh fitzBaldric has there now 1 villan and 5 bordars with 1 plough.

These belong to this manor: Danby [near Castleton], Lealholm, Great Broughton, "Camisedale" [in Ingleby Greenhow]. In these are 11 carucates of land to the geld. [There is] land for 5 ploughs. [There is] woodland pasture 3 leagues long and 3 leagues broad. The whole manor [is] 7 leagues long and 3 leagues and 4 furlongs broad. TRE worth 60s; now 3s.

In KIRKBYMOORSIDE, Orm had 5 carucates of land to the geld. There is land for 2 ploughs. Hugh fitzBaldric has 2 ploughs there; and 10 villans with 3 ploughs. There is a priest and a church, and 1 mill [rendering] 4s.

These belong to Kirkbymoorside: "Waletun" [in Kirkdale], Hutton-le-Hole, Gillamoor, 'Hoveton' [in Kirkdale]. In these are 24 carucates of land to the geld. There is land for 7 ploughs. Now there are 15 villans with 5 ploughs, and [he has] 29 acres of meadow. [It is] 12 leagues long and 2 leagues broad.

These belong to Kirkbymoorside: Welburn [in Kirkdale], "Middelham" [in Muscoates], Harome, Nawton, Great Baurgh, Normanby [near Salton], Kirby Misperton, Ryton, Marton [in Sinnington], Little Baurgh. In these are 27½ carucates to the geld. There is land for 12 ploughs. Now there are 21 villans having 7 ploughs. There are 40 acres of meadow. The whole manor, with appurtenances, was worth TRE £12; now 100s.

IN CRAVEN

In HOLKER [Lancs.], Orm had 8 carucates of land to the geld.

In HOVINGHAM, Orm had 8 carucates of land to the geld. There is land for 4 ploughs. Hugh fitzBaldric has now 2 ploughs there; and 10 villans having 4 ploughs. There is a church and a priest.

These belong to this manor: Wath [in Hovingham], Fryton, Howthorpe, Scackleton, "Hauuade" [in Hovingham], Coulton, Grimston [in Gilling East], East Newton [in Stonegrave], [East and West] Ness, South Holme, Slingsby, Butterwick, Amotherby, Broughton [in Appleton-le-Street], 'Newsham' [in Amotherby].

Together, [there are] 32 carucates of land to the geld. There is land for 15 ploughs. Now 2 of Hugh's men have there 2½ ploughs. Now there are 43 villans having 14 ploughs, and [there are] 32 acres of meadow. The whole manor, with appurtenances, TRE was worth £12; now 100s.

Woodland [...].
The whole [...].

In LAYSTHORPE, Orm had 2 carucates of land to the geld. [There is] land for 1 plough. Hugh fitzBaldric has now 1 plough there; and 2 villans with 1 plough, and 5 acres of meadow. [It is] half a league long and a half broad.

In GILLING EAST, Bark had 4 carucates of land to the geld. [There is] land for 2 ploughs. Hugh fitzBaldric has 2 ploughs there; and 3 villans with 2 ploughs. [There is] woodland pasture 3 furlongs long and 3 broad. The whole manor [is] half a league long and a half broad. TRE worth 20s; now 8s.

In BRANDSBY and Stearsby, Knut had 11 carucates of land to the geld. [There is] land for 6 ploughs. Hugh fitzBaldric has there 11 villans having 6 ploughs. There is a church and a priest, [and] woodland pasture 8 furlongs long and as much broad. The whole manor [is] 1 league long and 1 broad. TRE worth 40s; now 20s.

In BENINGBROUGH, Asfrith had 3 carucates of land to the geld. There is land for 1½ ploughs. Ralph, Hugh's man, has there now 5 villans with 2 ploughs, and 6 acres of meadow. [There is] woodland pasture 3 furlongs long and 1 broad. The whole manor [is] 6 furlongs long and 3 broad. TRE [...].

In HESLINGTON and 'Thorpe Hill' [in Sand Hutton] and Buttercrambe, Fulcher and Orm had 5 carucates of land to the geld. There is land for 2 ploughs. Hugh fitzBaldric has there now 3 villans with 2 ploughs, and 2 acres of meadow. [It is] 1 league and 4 furlongs long and 8 furlongs broad. TRE worth 42s; now 20s.

In SAND HUTTON, Sprot had 7 carucates. There is land for 3½ ploughs. Gulbert, Hugh's man, has 1 plough there; and 11 villans with 2 ploughs. [It is] 2 leagues long and 7 furlongs broad. TRE worth 32s; now 30s.

In SCRAYINGHAM, Thorkil had 8 carucates of land to the geld. There is land for 4 ploughs. Walo, Hugh's man, has 3 ploughs there; and 10 villans with 3½ ploughs, and 12 acres of meadow. [It is] 1 league long and 1 broad.

These belong to this manor: Barnby [in Bossall], Bossall and Buttercrambe. In these [are] 7 carucates of land to the geld. [There is] land for 3½ ploughs. Now there are 19 villans having 12 ploughs. There is a church and a priest, and 20 acres of meadow. The whole manor, with appurtenances, TRE was worth 50s; now 60s.

In BUTTERCRAMBE and Scrayingham and Flaxton, Egelfride had

[Folio 328: YORKSHIRE]

6 carucates of land and 2 bovates to the geld. [There is] land for 3 ploughs. Hugh fitzBaldric has now 2 ploughs there, and 2 villans, and 1 mill [rendering] 20s, and 6 acres of meadow. TRE worth 21s; now 60s.

EAST RIDING HESSLE HUNDRED

In KIRK ELLA, Ketil had 2 carucates of land to the geld. [There is] land for half a plough. Hugh has there 1 villan with 2 oxen.

In COTTINGHAM and PILLWOOD, Gamal had 16 carucates of land, and 2 parts of 1 carucate, to the geld. There is land for 8 ploughs. Now Hugh has 4 ploughs there; and 20 villans and 3 bordars having 7 ploughs, and 2 mills [rendering] 8s. [There is] woodland pasture 7 furlongs long and 3 broad. The whole manor [is] 4 leagues long and 1 broad; and [there are] 5 fisheries [rendering] 8,000 eels. TRE worth £4; now £7.

In LITTLE WEIGHTON and North Cave, Gamal had 5 carucates of land and 2 bovates to the geld. There is land for 3 ploughs. Hugh has now 2 ploughs there; and 16 villans with 4 ploughs. There is a church and a priest, and 2 mills [rendering] 16s. [It is] 1 league long and 1 broad. TRE worth 40s; now 50s.

In [High and Low] HUNSLEY, Gamal had 2½ carucates of land to the geld. There is land for 1 plough. Hugh has 2 ploughs there; and 6 villans with 2 ploughs. [It is] 1 league long and 2 furlongs broad. This vill belongs to Little Weighton.

In SKIPWITH, Gamal had 3 carucates of land to the geld. There is land for 2 ploughs. Hugh has 1 plough there; and 12 villans with 3 ploughs. There is a church and a priest, [and]

woodland pasture 2 leagues long and 1 broad. The whole manor [is] 2 leagues long and 1½ leagues broad. TRE worth 40s; now 20s.

In ETTON, Gamal had 9 carucates of land and 2 bovates to the geld. There is land for 5 ploughs. Hugh, Hugh's man, has now 2 ploughs there; and 10 villans and 2 bordars with 1 plough. TRE worth 40s; now the same.

In "TORP" [in Etton], Thorth had 1 carucate of land to the geld. There is land for half a plough. It is waste. TRE it was worth 10s.

In SKERNE and CRANSWICK or HUTTON CRANSWICK, Gamal had 8 carucates of land to the geld. There is land for 4 ploughs. Hugh has now 1 plough there; and 12 villans with 2 ploughs. [It is] 1 league long and 1 broad. TRE worth 60s; now 20s.

In BAINTON, Gamal and Thorkil had 11 carucates of land to the geld. There is land for 6 ploughs. William, Hugh's man, has 1 plough there; and 9 villans with 2 ploughs. TRE worth 45s; now †5†s.

In KELFIELD, Gamal had 1 carucate of land and 7 bovates to the geld. There is land for 1 plough. Hugh has there 4 villans with 1 plough, [...] and [there are] 8 acres of meadow. [There is] woodland pasture 1 league long and a half broad. TRE worth 20s; now the same.

In STILLINGFLEET, Ramkel had 1½ carucates of land to the geld. There is land for 1 plough. Hugh has now half a plough there; and 7 villans with 2 ploughs. TRE worth 10s; now the same.

In MOREBY, Fulcric had 1 carucate of land to the geld. There is land for half a plough. Hugh has there 4 villans with 1 plough, and 20 acres of meadow. [There is] woodland pasture 1 league long and a half broad. The whole [is] 1 league long and 1 broad. TRE worth 5s; now 3s.

In FRAISTHORPE, Gamal had 1 carucate of land to the geld. [There is] land for half a plough. It belongs to Sherburn. It is waste.

In LANGTON and Kennythorpe and Burdale, Raisthorpe, Sherburn [and] East Heslerton, Orm had 39 carucates of land to the geld. There is land for 20 ploughs. Hugh has now 3 ploughs there, and Geoffrey his man 3 ploughs. There are 43 villans and 4 bordars and 1 sokeman having 15 ploughs. There are 2 churches and 2 priests, and 1 mill [rendering] 5s, and 30 acres of meadow. [It is] 2 leagues long and 2 broad. TRE worth £12; now £6.

In NORTON [near Malton] and WELHAM, Gamal had 4 carucates of land and 3 bovates to the geld. There is land for 2 ploughs. Hugh has 2 ploughs there; and 12 villans with 4 ploughs. There is a church and a priest, and a mill [rendering] 10s. TRE worth 60s; now the same.

In 'BUCKTON HOLMS' [in Settrington], Gamal had 3 carucates of land to the geld. There is land for 1½ ploughs. Hugh has it. It is waste.

In NORTH GRIMSTON, Gamal had 2 carucates of land

and 2 bovates to the geld. [There is] land for 1 plough. Hugh has 2 ploughs there; and 6 villans with 1 plough. TRE worth 20s; now 30s.

In SCRAYINGHAM, Skialdfrithr and Thorkil had 12 carucates of land to the geld. There is land for 6 ploughs. Hugh has now 5 ploughs there; and 15 villans having 6½ ploughs, and 1 mill [rendering] 20s, and 18 acres of meadow. TRE worth 60s; now 100s. [It is] 2 leagues long and 1 broad.

In BISHOPTHORPE, Orm had 14 bovates of land to the geld. [There is] land for 1 plough. Hugh has there 4 villans with 1 plough, and 30 acres of meadow. TRE worth 20s; now the same.

NORTH RIDING

In 'CRUNKLY' [in Glaisdale] and LEALHOLM and DANBY [near Castleton], Orm had 12 carucates of land to the geld. There is land for 4 ploughs. Hugh has it, and it is waste. [There is] woodland pasture 3 leagues long and 3 broad. The whole manor [is] 7 leagues long and 3 broad.

In "CAMISEDALE" [in Ingleby Greenhow], Orm had 1 carucate of land to the geld. There is land for half a plough. Hugh has there 1 villan with 1 plough.

In HEWORTH, Orm had 3 carucates of land to the geld. [There is] land for 1 plough. Hugh has there 1 man with 1 plough. TRE worth 10s; now 5s.

[Folio 328V: YORKSHIRE]

XXXV. The land of Erneis de Buron

WEST RIDING

'SKYRACK' WAPENTAKE

In BINGLEY, Gospatric had 4 carucates of land to the geld. There is land for 2 ploughs. Erneis de Buron has it, and it is waste. TRE it was worth £4. [There is] woodland pasture 2 leagues long and 1 broad. The whole manor [is] 4 leagues long and 2 broad.

Within this boundary is contained this sokeland: Baildon, 2 carucates; Cottingley, 2 carucates; Eldwick, 1 carucate; Micklethwaite, 1 carucate; Marley, 1 carucate; 'Halton' [in Bingley], 1 carucate. Together, [there are] 8 carucates to the geld. There is land for 4 ploughs. They are all waste.

In COPMANTHORPE, Gospatric had 2 carucates and 2 bovates to the geld. [There is] land for 1 plough. Erneis has there now 2 ploughs; and 3 villans and 2 bordars with 1 plough. TRE worth 20s; now 40s.

In ACASTER SELBY, Grim had 5 bovates of land to the geld. Now Wulfric has it of Erneis, and it is waste.

BURGHSHIRE WAPENTAKE

In [Lower and Upper] DUNSFORTH, Gospatric had 3 carucates of land to the geld. [There is] land for 2 ploughs. Ranulph, the man of Erneis, has it, but it is waste. TRE worth 20s; now 3s. There are 6 acres of meadow.

In BRANTON GREEN and GRAFTON, Gospatric had 7 carucates of land to the geld. [There is] land for 4 ploughs. Erneis has them, and they are waste. TRE they were worth 30s.

In OLD THORNVILLE, Gospatric had 3 carucates to the geld. [There is] land for 2 ploughs. Erneis has 1 plough there; and 5 villans and 3 bordars with 2 ploughs. [It is] half a league long and a half broad. TRE worth 30s; now the same.

In HUNSINGORE, Gospatric had 4 carucates of land and 3 bovates to the geld. [There is] land for 2 ploughs. Erneis has 1 plough there; and 9 villans and 3 bordars with 3 ploughs. [There is] woodland pasture 2 furlongs long and 1 broad. TRE worth 30s; now 50s.

In the same vill are 10 bovates of land to the geld; the soke [is] in Knaresborough. Erneis has it, and it is cultivated.

In RIBSTON ['Great Ribston' and Little Ribston] and HOPPERTON, Thorgot and Arnketil had 2 carucates to the geld. There is land for 1 plough. TRE worth 20s; now 5s4d.

In FLAXBY [are] 4 carucates of land to the geld. [There is] land for 2 ploughs. The soke [is] in ALDBOROUGH. Erneis has 1 plough there; and 5 villans and 2 bordars with 1 plough. [It is] half a league long and a half broad. TRE worth 30s; now 25s.

In ARKENDALE and LOFTUS HILL, Gamal had 5 carucates of land to the geld. [There is] land for 2½ ploughs. The same man has it of Erneis, and it is cultivated. TRE worth 43s; now 6s.

In COPGROVE, Gospatric had 6 carucates of land to the geld. There is land for 3 ploughs. Turstin, the man of Erneis, has 1 plough there; and 7 villans with 1 plough. There is a church. [It is] 1 league long and a half broad. TRE worth 20s; now 16s.

In BRIMHAM, Gospatric had 3 carucates and 6 bovates to the geld. There is land for 2 ploughs. Erneis has it, and it is waste. TRE it was worth 23s.

In WHIPLEY and BEAMSLEY, Gospatric had 1 carucate of land to the geld. There is land for half a plough. Erneis has it, and it is waste.

In BEWERLEY and DACRE, Gospatric had 6 carucates of land to the geld. [There is] land for 4 ploughs. Erneis has it, and it is waste. TRE it was worth 50s. [There is] woodland pasture 2 leagues long and 2 broad. The whole [is] 4 leagues long and 3 broad.

In "LITTLE" BRAHAM, Gospatric had 4 carucates of land to the geld. There is land for 2 ploughs. Erneis has 1 plough there; and 3 villans with 1 plough. [It is] half a league long and a half broad. TRE worth 20s; now the same. Picot holds it of Ernegis.

This belongs to this manor: "Great" Braham, 1 carucate of land to the geld. It is waste, but it renders 16d.

In NEWSOME, Arni had 2 carucates of land to the geld.

[There is] land for 1 plough. John, the man of Erneis, has it, but it is waste. [There is] woodland pasture 4 acres long and 4 broad. [It is] half a league long and a half broad. TRE it was worth 20s.

In WETHERBY are 2 carucates of land to the geld. The soke [is] in Knaresborough. [There is] land for 1 plough. Erneis has there 1 sokeman and 4 villans with 2 ploughs. [There is] woodland pasture half a league long and a half broad.

In BARROWBY, 3 carucates, and [Kirk and North] DEIGHTON, 4 carucates, and INGMANTHORPE, 1½ carucates. The soke [is] in Hunsingore. Together, [there are] 8½ carucates to the geld. There is land for 4 ploughs. Erneis has there 1 sokeman and 4 villans and 2 bordars with 2 ploughs. TRE worth 28s; now 5s.

IN CRAVEN

In MARLEY, 1 carucate; 'Halton' [in Bingley], 2 carucates; Cottingley, 2 carucates; Cullingworth, 2 carucates; Hainworth, half a carucate. Together, [there are] 6½ carucates of land to the geld. [There is] land for 3 ploughs. Erneis has them, and they are waste.

EAST RIDING CAVE HUNDRED

In EAST COTTINGWITH, Grim had 1 carucate of land to the geld. [There is] land for half a plough. Erneis has it, and it is waste. [There is] woodland pasture 2 furlongs long and 2 broad.

In STILLINGFLEET, Grim had 2 carucates to the geld. [There is] land for 2 ploughs. Humphrey, the man of Erneis, has 2 ploughs there, and and [sic] 2 villans and 1 bordar. TRE worth 10s; now 15s.

[...]

[Folio 329: YORKSHIRE]

XXXVI. The land of Osbern D'Arques

WEST RIDING

AINSTY WAPENTAKE

In STEETON [in Bolton Percy], Arnketil, Godwine and Godwine and Alwine had 6 carucates of land to the geld. There is land for 6 ploughs. Now Osbern d'Arques has 1 plough there; and 2 villans and 4 bordars with 1 plough, and 3 acres of meadow. [It is] 1 league long and a half broad. TRE worth 20s; now 40s.

In APPLETON ROEBUCK, Farthin, Alwine and Tonni had 12 carucates of land to the geld. There is land for 12 ploughs. 2 of Osbern's men have there now 7 villans with 5 ploughs, and the site of a mill, and 20 acres of meadow. [There is] woodland pasture 1 league long and a half broad. The whole [is] 2 leagues long and 1 broad. TRE worth £4; now 32s.

In COLTON [near York], Arnketil, Godwine and Godwine, Thor and Wulfstan had 4½ carucates to the geld. There is land for 4 ploughs. Of this land, 9 bovates are in the soke of

"Rodouuelle". Now 2 of Osbern's men have there 5 bordars with 1 plough. [There is] woodland pasture half a league long and a half broad. The whole [is] 1 league long and a half broad. TRE worth 40s; now 12s.

In PALLATHORPE are 2 bovates of land to the geld. Osbern has it, and it is waste.

In OXTON is sokeland of Long Marston, 4 carucates of land to the geld. There is land for 2 ploughs. Osbern has it, and it is waste.

In CATTERTON, 5 thegns had 2 carucates of land to the geld. [There is] land for 2 ploughs. Fulk, Osbern's man, has there 4 villans and 1 bordar with 2 ploughs, and 6 acres of meadow. [There is] woodland pasture 1 league long and 4 furlongs broad. The whole [is] 1 league long and a half broad. TRE worth 16s; now 17s.

In HORNINGTON, the same Osbern has 1 bovate of land to the geld.

In THORPE ARCH, Orm, Godwine and Thor had 3 carucates of land to the geld. There is land for 3 ploughs. Now Osbern has there 3 ploughs; and 6 villans and 7 bordars with 2 ploughs. There is a priest and a church, and the site of a mill. [It is] 1 league long and a half broad. TRE worth £4; now 10s less.

In WALTON [near Wetherby], 6 thegns had 9 carucates of land to the geld. There is land for 9 ploughs. Osbern has 1 plough there; and 1 of his men 1 plough, and 6 villans with 2 ploughs, and 14 acres of meadow. [It is] 1 league long and 1 broad. There is scrubland. TRE worth £4; now 30s.

In BILTON [near Wetherby], 7 thegns had 9 carucates of land to the geld. There is land for 9 ploughs. Now Osbern has there 8 villans with 4 ploughs, and 2 acres of meadow. [There is] scrubland 1 league long and 3 furlongs broad. The whole [is] 1 league long and 1 broad. TRE worth £3; now 15s.

In LONG MARSTON, Alwine had 23 carucates of land to the geld. There is land for as many ploughs. Of these, 11 carucates are in its soke. It belongs to Tockwith and Wilstrop. Now 2 of Osbern's men have there 1½ ploughs; and 9 villans with 3 ploughs. [There is] woodland pasture 2 leagues long and 1 broad. The whole [is] 2 leagues long and 2 broad. TRE worth £6; now 42s4d.

In HUTTON WANDERSLEY, Alwine had 6 carucates of land to the geld. There is land for 6 ploughs. Now the same man has it of Osbern. He himself [has] 1 plough; and 5 villans and 2 bordars with 2 ploughs, and 7 acres of meadow. [There is] woodland pasture 4 furlongs long and 2 broad. The whole [is] 1 league long and a half broad. TRE worth 40s; now 36s.

In UPPER POPPLETON, Earnwine had 3½ carucates of land to the geld. There is land for as many ploughs. Ermenfrid, Osbern's man, has there 3 villans with 1 plough. TRE worth 20s; now 8s.

In the other POPPLETON [Nether Poppleton], Oda the deacon had 2½ carucates to the geld. There is land for as many ploughs. This was the land of St Everild. Osbern has 1 plough there; and 2 villans with 1 plough. [There is] woodland pasture 1 league long and 3 furlongs broad. TRE worth 40s; now 28s.

In ASKHAM RICHARD, Ealdræd and Svartkollr had 6 carucates of land to the geld. There is land for 6 ploughs. Osbern has there now 1 plough; and 5 villans and 2 bordars with 2 ploughs, and 7 acres of meadow. [There is] woodland pasture 4 furlongs long and 2 broad. The whole [is] 1 league long and a half broad. TRE worth £4; now 30s.

In 'SCAGGLETHORPE' [in Moor Monkton], Earnwine had 3 carucates of land to the geld. There is land for 3 ploughs. Ermenfrid, Osbern's man, has 1 villan and 4 bordars there, and 3 acres of meadow. [There is] woodland pasture half a league long and 4 acres broad. The whole [is] 1 league long and a half broad. TRE worth 10s8d; now 6s.

In HESSAY, Ragne had 2 carucates of land and 2 bovates to the geld. There is land for as many ploughs. Ealdræd has there of Osbern 2 bordars with 1 plough. [There is] woodland pasture 3 furlongs long and 3 broad. TRE worth 10s8d; now 4s.

In KNAPTON [near York], Alwine had 2 carucates of land to the geld. There is land for 2 ploughs. Now the same man has it of Osbern. There is 1 sokeman with 1 plough, and 3 acres of meadow. [There is] woodland pasture 3 furlongs long and 2 broad. TRE [worth] 2s2d; now the same.

In RUFFORTH, Alwine and Ealdwulf had 4 carucates of land to the geld. There is land for 4 ploughs. Now Osbern, Osbern's man, has 1 plough there; and 3 villans and 5 bordars with 1 plough, and 3 acres of meadow. [There is] woodland pasture half a league long and a half broad. The whole [is] 1 league long and 1 broad. TRE worth 40s; now 30s.

BURGHSHIRE WAPENTAKE

In NUN MONKTON, 5 thegns had 8 carucates of land to the geld. There is land for as many ploughs. Hugh, Osbern's man, has there 10 villans with 4 ploughs, and 4 acres of meadow, and half a fishery. [There is] woodland pasture 1 league long and 3 furlongs broad. The whole [is] 1 league long and a half broad. TRE worth 40s; now 25s.

[Folio 329V: YORKSHIRE]

In KIRBY [in Little Ouseburn], Northmann had 2 carucates of land to the geld. [There is] land for 2 ploughs. Osbern has it now, and it is worth 20d.

In WHIXLEY, Barth had 13 carucates of land to the geld. There is land for as many ploughs. Osbern has it now, and it is waste. There are 2 churches, and 3 acres of meadow. TRE worth £3; now 21d.

In GREEN HAMMERTON, 3 thegns had 6 carucates of land to the geld. There is land for 6 ploughs. Osbern has it, and it is waste.

In the other HAMMERTON [Kirk Hammerton], Thorkil, Gamal [and] Haldor had 6½ carucates of land to the geld. There is land for 6 ploughs. John, Osbern's man, has 2 ploughs there; and 5 villans with 1 plough. There is a priest

and a church, and 1 mill [rendering] 2s, and 1 fishery [rendering] 3s. The whole [is] half a league long and a half broad. TRE worth £4; now 45s.

In HOPPERTON, Gamal had 1 carucate of land to the geld. [There is] land for 1 plough. Osbern has it, and it is waste. TRE it was worth 10s.

In SUSACRES, Northmann had 1 carucate of land to the geld. [There is] land for 1 plough. Osbern has it, and it is waste. TRE it was worth 10s.

BARKSTON WAPENTAKE

In STUTTON, Thorkil had 1½ carucates of land to the geld. There is land for as many ploughs. There 2 of Osbern's men have 2 villans and 2 bordars with 1 bordar [sic] with 1 plough, and 10 acres of meadow. [There is] woodland pasture 1½ furlongs long and as much broad. TRE worth 30s; now 10s.

In TOULSTON and Newton Kyme and Oglethorpe, 4 thegns had 7 carucates of land and 7 bovates to the geld. Now Fulk, Osbern's man, has 1 plough there; and 5 villans with 1 plough, and 8 acres of meadow. The whole [is] 1 league long and 1 broad. TRE worth 40s; now 20s.

In NEWTON KYME and Toulston, 5 thegns had 3 carucates of land to the geld. There is land for 4 ploughs. Fulk, Osbern's man, has 1 plough there; and 7 villans with 2 ploughs, and 16 acres of meadow, and the site of 1 mill. The whole manor [is] 6 furlongs long and as much broad. TRE worth 60s; now 20s.

IN CRAVEN

In SILSDEN, 5 thegns had 8 carucates of land to the geld.

In HEBDEN and Thorpe [near Hebden], Dreng had 4 carucates of land and 2 bovates to the geld.

In BURNSALL and Drebley, Dreng had 2 carucates and 2 bovates to the geld.

Osbern d'Arques has these lands, but they are all waste.

In CATTAL are 5 carucates of land to the geld. There is land for 2 ploughs. The soke is in Aldborough, the king's manor. Osbern has it, and it is waste.

XXXVII. The land of Odo the Crossbowman

EAST RIDING

In BUGTHORPE, Forne had 4½ carucates of land to the geld. There is land for as many ploughs. Odo the crossbowman has 1 plough there; and 3 villans with 1 plough, and 8 acres of meadow. TRE worth 20s; now 10s.

In BARTHORPE, Forne had 2 carucates of land to the geld. [There is] land for 2 ploughs. Odo has it, and it is waste. TRE it was worth 10s.

In YOULTHORPE, sokeland of Pocklington, [are] 4 carucates of land to the geld. [There is] land for as many ploughs. Odo has it, and it is waste.

In FRIDAYTHORPE, Forne and Gamal had †18† carucates of land to the geld. [There is] land for as many ploughs. Odo has it, and it is waste. TRE [it was worth] | 20s |.

In THIXENDALE, Gamal and Orm had 4 carucates of land and 2 bovates to the geld. Odo has it, and it is waste. TRE it was worth 45s.

In FRIDAYTHORPE are 5 carucates of land to the geld, belonging to Thixendale. [It is] inland. There is land for 5 ploughs. It is waste.

In RAISTHORPE, Orm had 2 carucates of land to the geld. [There is] land for 2 ploughs. Odo has it, and it is waste. TRE it was worth 20s.

In "SCRADIZTORP" [in Skirpenbeck], Orm and Forne had 3 carucates of land to the geld. [There is] land for 3 ploughs. Odo has there 4 villans with 1 plough. [It is] half a league long and a half broad. TRE worth 10s; now 5s.

In SWAYTHORPE, Forne had 9 carucates of land to the geld. There is land for 9 ploughs. Odo has it, and it is waste. TRE it was worth 20s.

In SKIRPENBECK, Forne had 5 carucates and 6 bovates of land to the geld. [There is] land for as many ploughs. Odo has 1 plough there; and 27 villans with 6 ploughs, and 1 mill [rendering] 2s. [It is] 1 league long and 1 broad. TRE worth £3; now £4.

In HANGING GRIMSTON, Odo has 4½ carucates of land to the geld. [There is] land for as many ploughs. This renders 3s. There are 8 acres of meadow.

In KILHAM, Forne and Gamal had 7 carucates of land to the geld. [There is] land for as many ploughs. Odo has it, and it is waste. TRE it was worth 20s.

XXXVIII. The land of Aubrey de Coucy

In HICKLETON, Swein and Andor had 5 carucates of land and 5 bovates to the geld. [There is] land for 4 ploughs. Aubrey de Coucy has 2 ploughs there; and 4 villans and 13 bordars having 3 ploughs. TRE worth †70†s; now 40s.

In CADEBY, Swein had 2 carucates and 1 bovate to the geld. [There is] land for 1 plough. Aubrey has 1 plough there; and 4 villans and 2 bordars and 2 sokemen with 1 plough. TRE worth 40s; now 20s.

[Folio 330: YORKSHIRE]

XXXVIIII. The land of Gospatric

WEST RIDING

In MARTON [near Boroughbridge], Gospatric had 12 carucates of land to the geld. [There is] land for 6 ploughs. The same man himself has there now 1 plough; and 2 villans and 2 bordars with 2 ploughs. [It is] 1 league long and 1 broad. TRE worth 40s; now 20s.

In "CADRETONE" [in Allerton Mauleverer], Gospatric has half a carucate of land to the geld.

In ALLERTON MAULEVERER, likewise half a carucate of land to the geld. In these [is] land for 1 plough.

In THORPE HILL [near Whixley], he has 1 carucate of land to the geld. This renders 5s.

In 'THORNBOROUGH' [in Allerton Mauleverer], Gospatric has 3 carucates of land to the geld. [There is] land for 1 plough. [It is] half a league long and a half broad. It is waste.

In STAVELEY, Gospatric has 8 carucates of land to the geld. [There is] land for 4 ploughs. Now there is 1 plough, and 1 villan. [It is] half a league long and a half broad. TRE worth †20†s; now 10s.

In FARNHAM, Gospatric [has] 3 carucates of land to the geld. [There is] land for 1 plough. Now there is a priest and a church, and 1 plough. TRE worth 10s; now 5s.

In CLARETON, Gospatric [has] 3 carucates of land to the geld. [There is] land for 1½ ploughs. The same man has there now 2 ploughs, and 1 villan. TRE [worth] 10s; now the same.

In LAVERTON, Gospatric [has] 2½ carucates to the geld. [There is] land for 1 plough. Now there is 1 villan and 1 bordar. TRE [worth] 20s; now 4s.

In KIRKBY MALZEARD, Gospatric [has] 5 carucates of land to the geld. [There is] land for 3 ploughs. Now he has 1 plough there; and 8 villans with 1 plough. [There is] scrubland 1 league long and 1 broad. The whole manor [is] 1½ leagues long and as much broad. TRE worth 30s; now 20s.

In GREWELTHORPE, Gospatric [has] 7 carucates of land to the geld. [There is] land for 3 ploughs. He himself [has] there now 1 plough; and 3 villans and 2 bordars with 1 plough. [There is] scrubland half a league long and 4 furlongs broad. The whole [is] 1 league long and a half broad. TRE worth 20s; now 10s.

In STUDLEY ROYAL, Gospatric [has] 2½ carucates of land to the geld. [There is] land for 1 plough. It is waste.

In WINKSLEY, Gospatric [has] 3 carucates of land to the geld. [There is] land for 2 ploughs. He himself has it now, but does not cultivate it. There is scrubland. The whole [is] 1½ leagues long and as much broad. TRE worth 20s; now 10s.

In AZERLEY, Gospatric [has] 5 carucates of land to the geld. [There is] land for 3 ploughs. He himself [has] there now 1 plough; and 1 villan and 2 bordars with 1 plough. TRE worth 20s; now 10s.

In [High and Low] BRAMLEY [are] 2 carucates of land to the geld. [There is] land for 1 plough.

In CARLESMOOR [are] 2 carucates of land to the geld. [There is] land for 1 plough.

In KEX MOOR [are] 2 carucates of land to the geld. [There is] land for 1 plough.

In SWETTON [are] 2 carucates of land to the geld. [There is] land for 1 plough.

In 'POPPLETON' [in Fountains Earth] [are] 3 carucates of land to the geld. [There is] land for 2 ploughs.

In BRIMHAM [are] 3 carucates of land and 2 bovates to the geld. [There is] land for 2 ploughs.

In ADDLETHORPE [are] 4 carucates of land to the geld. [There is] land for 2 ploughs.

In KIRBY HILL [are] 6 carucates of land to the geld. [There is] land for 3 ploughs.

In BIRSTWITH [is] 1 carucate to the geld. [There is] land for half a plough.

In SKELTON [near Boroughbridge] [is] 1 carucate to the geld. [There is] land for half a plough.

In "HEUUORDE" [in Conistone] [is] 1 carucate of land to the geld. [There is] land for half a plough.

In OLD SUNDERLANDWICK [are] 1½ carucates to the geld. [There is] land for 1 plough.

In SNAINTON [is] 1 carucate of land to the geld. [There is] land for half a plough.

Gospatric had and has all these, but now they are waste.

In ASKWITH, Gospatric [has] 2 carucates of land to the geld. There is land for 1 plough. He himself has there now 4 villans with 1 plough. TRE worth 20s; now 10s.

In WEETON [near Harewood], Gospatric [has] 2½ carucates of land to the geld. [There is] land for 2 ploughs. Now there are 2 villans and 1 bordar with 1 plough, and it renders 7s.

In WEARDLEY, Ligulf and Saxulf had 5 carucates of land to the geld. Now Gospatric has it, and it is waste. TRE it was worth 25s. [It is] half a league long and a half broad.

In LANGTHORPE [in Kirby Hill], Gospatric [has] 6 carucates of land to the geld. [There is] land for 3 ploughs. He himself [has] now 1 plough there, and 1 villan and 3 bordars. [It is] half a league long and a half broad. TRE worth 30s; now 10s.

In THORNTON [in Brafferton], Gospatric [has] 6 carucates of land to the geld. [There is] land for 3 ploughs. He himself [has] now 1 plough there; and 7 villans with 3 ploughs. [It is] 1 league long and a half broad. TRE worth 20s; now the same.

In HUMBERTON, Arnketil had 4 carucates of land and 2 bovates to the geld. [There is] land for 2 ploughs. Now Gospatric has 1 plough there; and 7 villans with 2 ploughs, and 4 acres of meadow. [There is] scrubland 2 furlongs long and 2 broad. TRE worth 16s; now 8s.

In BRAFFERTON, Gospatric [has] 1 carucate of land to the geld. [There is] land for half a plough. He himself has there now 1 villan with half a plough. It is worth 2½s.

In OULSTON, Gospatric [has] 6 carucates of land to the geld. [There is] land for 3 ploughs. Now there are 4 villans, but they do not plough. [It is] 1 league long and a half broad. TRE worth 20s; now 10s.

In HUMBERTON [are] 4 carucates, sokeland, in Aldborough, a manor of the king, and 2 carucates inland. [There is] land for 2 ploughs. It is waste. Gospatric holds it.

In BICKERTON, Arnketil had 8 carucates of land to the geld. [There is] land for 3 ploughs. Gospatric has there now 4 villans with 1½ ploughs. [There is] half a league of woodland pasture. The whole [is] 1 league long and 1 broad. TRE worth 40s; now 10s.

In ALDFIELD, Arnketil had 2 carucates of land to the geld. [There is] land for 1 plough. Now Gospatric has it, and it is worth 10s. TRE it was worth the same.

In "MIDDELTUN" [in Appleton Wiske], Gospatric [has] 4 carucates of land to the geld. [There is] land for 2 ploughs. He himself has 1 plough there; and 4 villans and 3 bordars with 2 ploughs. There is a church and a priest, and 6 acres of meadow. TRE worth 20s; now 10s.

In SLEDMERE, Gospatric [has] 9 carucates of land to the geld. [There is] land for 5 ploughs. He himself has it, and it is waste. TRE it was worth 40s. [He has] 100 acres of meadow there.

In 'KNAYSER' [in Skelding], Gospatric [has] half a carucate of land to the geld. The same man himself has it, and it is waste.

[Folio 330V: YORKSHIRE]

XL. The land of the King's Thegns

WEST RIDING

'SKYRACK' WAPENTAKE

In CARLTON [near Snaith], Wicga had 6 carucates of land to the geld. There is land for 2 ploughs. Now Ulfkil has 2 ploughs there; and 7 villans and 5 bordars with 4 ploughs. [There are] 1½ leagues of woodland pasture. The whole [is] 1 league long and 1 broad. TRE worth 40s; now 20s.

In CAMBLESFORTH, Grucan had 1 carucate of land to the geld. [There is] land for half a plough. Now Earnwine the priest has it, and it is waste. There are 1½ leagues of woodland pasture. The whole [is] 1½ leagues long and a half broad. TRE it was worth 10s.

In DARFIELD, Alsige and Ketilbert had 4 carucates of land to the geld. There is land for 2 ploughs. Now Alsige has 2 ploughs there; and 5 villans and 10 bordars with 3 ploughs. [There is] 1 league and 3 furlongs of woodland pasture. The whole [is] 1 league and 1 furlong long and 1 league broad. TRE worth 40s; now 32s.

In WOMBWELL and WEST MELTON, Thor had 2 carucates of land and 1 bovate to the geld. [There is] land for 1½ ploughs. Half a carucate is sokeland. He himself has now 1 plough there; and 5 villans and 3 bordars and 2 sokemen with 2 ploughs. [There are] 5 furlongs of woodland pasture. The whole [is] 5 furlongs long and 5 broad. TRE worth 40s; now 20s.

In WEST MELTON, with 4 Berewicks, Swein had 5 carucates of land to the geld. [There is] land for 3 ploughs. He himself has now 1 plough there; and 9 villans with 3 ploughs. [There is] 1 league of woodland pasture. The whole manor [is] 1 league long and 1 broad. TRE worth 30s; now 15s.

In WATH UPON DEARNE, with 3 Berewicks, Wulfsige had 7 carucates of land and 5 bovates to the geld. [There is] land for 4 ploughs. He himself has now 1 plough there, and 1 villan and 3 bordars, and 2 acres of meadow. [There are] 1½ leagues of woodland pasture. The whole manor [is] 1½ leagues long and 1 league broad. TRE worth 30s; now 15s.

In WEST MELTON and BRAMPTON [in Wath upon Dearne] and with [sic] 4 Berewicks, Andor the priest had 6 carucates of land [and] 2 bovates to the geld. [There is] land for 5 ploughs. He himself has now 2 ploughs there; and 3 villans and 1 bordar with 2 ploughs, and 6 acres of meadow. [There are] 1½ leagues of woodland pasture. The whole manor [is] 2 leagues long and 1 broad.

In ARMTHORPE, Ulfkil had 5 carucates of land to the geld. [There is] land for 3 ploughs. Now Earnwine the priest has half a plough there; and 1 villan and 3 bordars and 4 sokemen having 2½ ploughs. [There are] 2 leagues of woodland pasture. The whole manor [is] 2 leagues long and 10 furlongs broad. TRE worth 40s; now 20s.

In WHITLEY, Regnvald and Wicga had 2 carucates of land to the geld. The soke belongs to Snaith. [There is] land for 1 plough. Alric has there 2 villans and 6 bordars with 2 ploughs. [There is] 1 league of woodland pasture. The whole manor [is] 1 league long and 1 broad. TRE worth 40s; now 20s.

In "MULEDE", 3 thegns had 1 carucate of land to the geld. [There is] land for half a plough. The same men themselves have it of the king, and it is waste.

In BISHOPTHORPE, Thorkil had half a carucate of land to the geld. [There is] land for 2 oxen. He himself has there half a plough, and it is worth 3s.

In ACOMB, Ulfkil had 2 carucates of land to the geld. [There is] land for 1 plough. He himself has there half a plough. [There are] 10 furlongs of woodland. It is worth 4s.

In LITTLE OUSEBURN, Maccus and Orm had 3 carucates of land to the geld. Now Maelcolumban has there 3 villans having 2 ploughs, and 4 acres of meadow. TRE [worth] 20s; now 5s.

In HOPPERTON, Ketil had 1½ carucates of land to the geld. [There is] land for 1 plough. He himself has half a plough there, and it is worth 10s.

In ALLERTON MAULEVERER, Ulfkil had 1½ carucates of land to the geld. [There is] land for 1 plough. He himself has half a plough there, and it is worth 10s.

In LOFTUS HILL, 3 thegns had 4 carucates of land to the geld. [There is] land for 2 ploughs. They themselves still have it and cultivate it. It renders 5s.

In SCOTTON [in Farnham], Ramkel [had] 2 carucates of land to the geld. [There is] land for 1 plough. He himself has there 1 plough, and 1 villan. It is worth 10s.

In 'THORPE JUXTA SCOTTON' [in Farnham], Ramkel and Thorkil [had] 2 carucates of land to the geld. [There is] land for 1 plough. They themselves still have it, but it is waste.

In LAVERTON, Ulfkil and Wulfric [had] 3 carucates of land to the geld. [There is] land for 2 ploughs. They themselves have 1 plough there. It is worth 11s.

In WIDDINGTON, Alfred [had] 1 carucate of land to the geld. [There is] land for half a plough. He himself has it, and it is waste. TRE it was worth 5s4d.

In WEETON [near Harewood], Ulfkil [had] 2½ carucates of land to the geld. [There is] land for 1 plough. He himself has 3 villans there, and 2 ploughs. It is worth 5s.

In AZERLEY, Orm [had] half a carucate of land to the geld. [There is] land for half a plough. The same man himself has it, and it is waste.

In EAST RIGTON, Ligulf [had] 3 carucates of land to the geld. [There is] land for 2 ploughs. He himself has half a plough there; and 7 villans and a priest. [It is] 1 league long and 1 broad. TRE worth 16s; now 10s.

EAST RIDING

HESSLE HUNDRED

In ANLABY, Skuli had 2 carucates of land to the geld. [There is] land for 1 plough. Now Thorkil has 1 plough there, and 7 villans and 2 bordars with 1 plough. It is worth 20s.

In TIBTHORPE, Gamal [had] 2 carucates of land and 2 bovates to the geld. [There is] land for 1 plough. He himself has it under the king, and it is waste.

In NORTH DALTON, Odbert [had] 1 carucate of land to the geld. [There is] land for half a plough. He himself has 1 plough there, and 1 villan. It is worth 10s.

In NUNBURNHOLME, Morcar, Thorfridh and Thorkil had 11 carucates of land to the geld. [There is] land for 6 ploughs. 1 carucate is sokeland of Pocklington. Forne has it of the king, and it is waste.

In BOLTON [in Bishop Wilton], Karli [had] 1 carucate of land to the geld. [There is] land for half a plough. The same man himself has 1 plough there, and 2 acres of meadow. It is worth 4s.

In FLAMBOROUGH, Clibert [had] 1½ carucates to the geld. [There is] land for 1 plough. The same man himself has it, and it is waste.

In HUGGATE, Ingrith [had] 8 carucates to the geld. [There is] land for 4 ploughs. Earnwine the priest has it now, and it is waste.

[Folio 331: YORKSHIRE]

In MARTON [in Sewerby], Clibert [had] 2 carucates of land to the geld. [There is] land for 1 plough. The same man himself has it, and it is waste.

In HILDERTHORPE, Clibert [had] half a carucate of land

to the geld. [There is] land for 2 oxen. The same man himself has there 6 villans with 1 plough. It is worth 10s.

In FRAISTHORPE, Karli had 1 carucate of land to the geld. [There is] land for half a plough. Uhtræd has now 1 plough there; and it is worth 5s.

In ELMSWELL, Northmann [had] 10 carucates of land to the geld. [There is] land for 5 ploughs. The same man himself has it, and it is waste. [It is] 1. league long and a half broad.

In KILHAM, and Gransmoor and Harpham, Earnwine the priest had 40 carucates of land to the geld. [There is] land for 20 ploughs. The same man himself has it now, and it is waste. TRE it was worth £15.

In LOWTHORPE, Northmann and Asa [had] 4 carucates of land to the geld. [There is] land for 2 ploughs. Gamal has there 6 villans with 1 plough, and a church. It is worth 8s.

In RUDSTON, Ligulf [had] 8 carucates of land to the geld. [There is] land for 4 ploughs. Uhtræd has 1 plough there; and 5 villans with 1 plough. It is worth 10s.

In BIRDSALL and Sutton [near Malton], Ulfkil [had] $3\frac{1}{2}$ carucates of land to the geld. [There is] land for 2 ploughs. The same man himself has half a plough there, and 2 bordars. It is worth 2s.

In HANGING GRIMSTON, Gudhridh and Ødhvidh had 4 carucates of land to the geld. Now Osweard and Hrothmund have it of the king, and it is waste.

In KIRBY UNDERDALE, Arngrim [had] 6 bovates, and Siward 1 carucate, of land to the geld. [There is] land for 1 plough. The same men themselves still have it, and it is worth 2s.

In PAINSTHORPE, Arngrim [had] 1 carucate of land to the geld. [There is] land for half a plough. The same man himself has it, and it is waste.

In GARROWBY, Gamal [had] 3 carucates of land to the geld. [There is] land for $1\frac{1}{2}$ ploughs. He himself has there now 2 villans with 2 ploughs. It is worth 8s.

In THORALBY [in Bugthorpe], Gamal, with his mother and brother, had 4 carucates of land to the geld. [There is] land for 2 ploughs. The same man himself has it, and he lets it. It is worth 5s.

In WHARRAM PERCY, Ketilbert has 1 carucate of land of the king which renders 10s. [There is] land for half a plough.

In EAST HESLERTON, Gospatric [had] $3\frac{1}{2}$ carucates of land to the geld. [There is] land for $5\frac{1}{2}$ ploughs. Uhtræd has it now, and it is waste.

In another HESLERTON [West Heslerton], Osweard [had] 5 carucates of land to the geld. [There is] land for $2\frac{1}{2}$ ploughs. The same man himself has it, and it is waste.

In WALKINGTON, Gamal had 1 carucate of land to the geld. [There is] land for half a plough. The same man himself has it, and it is waste. TRE it was worth 5s.

In NORTH CLIFFE, Northmann [had] 1 carucate of land to

the geld. [There is] land for half a plough. Now there are 4 villans and 1 bordar with 1 plough. TRE worth 10s; now 8s.

In WATTON, Thorth [had] 3 carucates to the geld. The same man himself has it. [There is] land for 2 ploughs.

NORTH RIDING

In WILTON [in Ormesby], Haldor had 3 carucates of land and 6 bovates to the geld. [There is] land for 2 ploughs. There Maldred has 1 plough there sic; and 8 villans and 10 bordars with 3 ploughs, and 6 acres of meadow. TRE worth 20s; now the same.

In Wilton [in Ormesby] and Lazenby [in Ormesby] [is] 1 carucate of land to the geld. [There is] land for half a plough. The soke belongs to Wilton [in Ormesby].

In ORMESBY, 4 thegns had 12 carucates of land to the geld. [There is] land for 8 ploughs. Orm has 1 plough there; and 2 villans and 16 bordars with 3 ploughs. There is a priest and a church. [It is] 1 league long and 1 broad. TRE worth £4; now 40s.

In UPSALL [in Ormesby] [are] 2 carucates of land to the geld. The soke belongs to Ormesby. [There is] land for 1 plough.

In KILDALE, Ligulf had 6 carucates of land to the geld. [There is] land for 3 ploughs. Orm has 1 plough there; and 8 bordars with 2 ploughs. There is a priest and a church. [It is] 2 leagues long and 1 broad. TRE worth 16s; now 20s.

In MARTON [in Middlesbrough], Arnketil [had] 3 carucates of land to the geld. [There is] land for 2 ploughs. The same man himself has 1 plough there; and 14 villans and 6 bordars with 3 ploughs. TRE worth 40s; now 20s.

In Tollesby [are] 4 carucates of land to the geld belonging to Marton [in Middlesbrough]. [There is] land for 2 ploughs. It is waste.

In STOKESLEY, Hawarth had 6 carucates of land to the geld. [There is] land for 3 ploughs. Uhtræd has 1 plough there; and 8 villans with 4 ploughs. There is a priest and a church, and 1 mill [rendering] 10s, and 8 acres of meadow. [It is] 1 league long and a half broad. TRE worth £24; now £8.

In Skutterskelfe, 2 carucates and 2 bovates; Thoraldby, 2 carucates; Ingleby Greenhow, 7 carucates; 'Little Broughton', 8 carucates; | Tanton, $1\frac{1}{2}$ carucates; | Kirby [near Stokesley], 3 carucates; Dromonby, 3 carucates; Great Busby, 5 carucates; and another Busby [Busby], 3 carucates. Together, to the geld, [there are] $34\frac{1}{2}$ carucates. [There is] land for 16 ploughs. There are now 9 sokemen and 18 villans having 10 ploughs.

In "STEMANESBI" [in Scalby] [are] 2 carucates of land to the geld. [There is] land for 1 plough. Uhtræd has it, and it is waste.

In [East and West] LILLING, Ulf [had] 14 bovates to the geld. [There is] land for 1 plough. Gamal has it there, and it is waste.

In 'NEWSHAM' [in Amotherby], Thorbiorn and Uhtræd

[had] 2½ carucates to the geld. [There is] land for 1 plough. They themselves have now 2 ploughs; and 6 villans and 1 bordar with 1 plough, and 12 acres of meadow. TRE worth 3s; now 5s.

In HUBY, Seaxfrith and Siward [had] 2 carucates of land to the geld. [There is] land for 1 plough. Now in demesne there is half a plough; and 6 villans with 1 plough. TRE worth 4s; now 3s.

ALSO IN THE EAST RIDING

In SEWERBY, Clibert [had] 1½ carucates to the geld. [There is] land for 1 plough. The same man himself has it, and it is waste. TRE it was worth 10s.

In CARNABY, Ketilbert [had] 13 carucates to the geld. [There is] land for 7 ploughs. 2 rent-paying tenants there have 9 villans with 3 ploughs. They hold of the king. [It is] 1 league long and 1 broad.

[Folio 331V: YORKSHIRE]

In ACKLAM [near Leavening], Siward had †10½† carucates of land. [There is] land for 4 ploughs. Now 2 men have it of the king. They themselves [have] 2 ploughs there, and a church. It is worth 10s.

In Leavening, Sprot, Kolbrand, Odfrid [and] Gillebride had 5 carucates of land to the geld. [There is] land for 3 ploughs. now 2 men have it of the king. They themselves [have] 5 villans and 5 bordars there. TRE [worth] 40s; now 30s.

In HENSALL, Barth [had] 4 carucates of land to the geld. [There is] land for 2 ploughs. The soke is in Snaith. Now there is 1 plough in demesne, and 5 sokemen and 12 bordars, and 4 acres of meadow. TRE worth £4; now 10s.

In WORTLEY, Wulfsige and Alric had 4 carucates of land to the geld. [There is] land for 2 ploughs. Now Alric holds it of the king, but it is waste. TRE it was worth 40s. [There is] woodland pasture 1 league long and 1 broad. The whole [is] 2 leagues long and 2 broad.

In BISHOPSTHORPE, Basinc [had] half a carucate to the geld. [There is] land for 2 oxen. Now Landri has half a plough there. TRE worth 20s; now 6s.

In ACASTER SELBY, Ketil had 6 bovates of land to the geld. [There is] land for half a plough. Now Landric has there 3 villans with half a plough. TRE worth 12s; now 5s4d.

In the same place Thorkil had 5 bovates of land to the geld. [There is] land for 2 oxen. Now Tonni holds it of the king, and it is worth 2s.

In [Lower and Upper] DUNSFORTH, Thorbiorn had 3 carucates of land to the geld. [There is] land for 2 ploughs. The same man has it, and it is waste. TRE it was worth 16s.

In BRANTON GREEN, Thorbiorn had 4 carucates of land to the geld. [There is] land for 2 ploughs. The same man has it of the king, and it is waste. TRE it was worth 20s.

In GRAFTON, Thorbiorn had 2 carucates of land to the geld.

[There is] land for 1 plough. The same man has it, and it is waste. TRE it was worth 10s.

In STUDLEY ROYAL, Snæbiorn had 7 bovates of land to the geld. [There is] land for half a plough. The same man has it now of the king, but it is waste. TRE it was worth 10s.

In WHIPLEY, Arnketil had half a carucate of land to the geld. [There is] land for 2 oxen. The same man has it, and it is waste. TRE it was worth 2s8d; [...] 2s.

In RIPLEY, Ramkel and Arnketil [had] 1½ carucates of land to the geld. [There is] land for 1 plough. They themselves still have it. TRE it was worth 13s. It is waste.

In DUNKESWICK, Ulfkil [had] 4 carucates of land to the geld. [There is] land for 2 ploughs. Now the same man and his wife have 1 plough there, and 1 villan, and 2 acres of meadow. TRE worth 8s; now 5s.

In NORTH RIGTON, Arnketil [had] 2 carucates of land to the geld. [There is] land for 1 plough. The same man himself has it now, and it is waste. TRE it was worth 10s.

In BILTON [near Harrogate], Arnketil [had] 3½ carucates of land to the geld. [There is] land for 2 ploughs. The same man himself has it now, and it is waste. TRE it was worth 10s.

IN CRAVEN

In RYLSTONE, Almund [had] 4 carucates of land to the geld. Dolgfinnr has them.

In HARTLINGTON, Almund [had] 1 carucate of land to the geld. Dolgfinnr has it.

In APPLETREEWICK [are] 1½ carucates of land to the geld. Dolgfinnr has them.

In BURNSALL and Thorpe [near Hebden], Heardwulf [had] 3½ carucates to the geld. The same Heardwulf has them of the king.

In HARTLINGTON, Northmann [had] 3 carucates of land to the geld. The same man has them.

In RYLSTONE, Ramkel [had] 1½ carucates to the geld. The same man himself has them.

In APPLETREEWICK, Ketil [had] 2½ carucates to the geld. Orm has them.

In "HOLEDENE" [in Hartlington], Ketil [had] 2 carucates of land to the geld. Orm has them.

In the same place Gospatric and Ulfkil [had] 4 carucates of land to the geld. The same men themselves have them.

In KILNSEY, Gamal [had] 6 carucates of land to the geld. Ulf has them.

In "HEUURDE" [in Conistone], Gospatric [had] 1 carucate to the geld. The same man himself has it.

In CONISTONE, Arnketil [had] 3 carucates to the geld. Ketil has them.

In [...]

[Folio 332: YORKSHIRE]

The land of Roger de Poitou

In GIGGLESWICK, Fech had 4 carucates to the geld. Stainforth [near Settle], 3 carucates; Rathmell, 2 carucates; Kirkby Malham, 2 carucates; Litton, 6 carucates. These Berewicks belong to the above-mentioned manor. Roger de Poitou has them now.

In Coniston Cold [are] 2 carucates. William de Percy held them, but Roger de Poitou has them.

In Barnoldswick [near Gisburn], Gamal [had] 12 carucates to the geld. Berengar de Tosny held it, but now it is in the jurisdiction of the castle of Roger de Poitou.

In Long Preston, Ulf had 3 carucates to the geld, and 1 church. Stainforth [near Settle], 3 carucates; Wigglesworth, 1 carucate; Hellifield, 1½ carucates; Newsholme [in Gisburn], half a carucate; Painley, 1 carucate; Gisburn, 2 carucates; Horton [in Gisburn], 1½ carucates; Kelbrook, 6 bovates; Crooks, 2 bovates; to the geld.

In KETTLEWELL, Ulf had 1 carucate to the geld; Hubberholme, half a carucate; Starbotton, half a carucate.

In Anley, Bo had 3 carucates of land to the geld; Settle, 3 carucates to the geld.

In WINTERBURN, Thorfinnr had 3 carucates of land to the geld; "Leuetat" [in Flasby], 3 carucates; Flasby, 4 carucates; Gargrave, 2 carucates; Little Newton, 2 carucates; Horton in Ribblesdale, 2 carucates; Selside, 1 carucate.

In the same place Thorfinnr had 2 carucates of land to the geld.

In Rathmell, Karli had 1 carucate to the geld; Wigglesworth, 10 bovates; Hellifield, 2½ carucates.

In Arnford, Almund had 2 carucates to the geld; Wigglesworth, 2 carucates; "Caretorp" [in Wigglesworth], 2 carucates.

In Paythorne, Gamal Barn had 2 carucates; [in] Ellenthorpe [in Gisburn], half a carucate.

In Otterburn, Gamal Barn [had] 3 carucates to the geld.

In Gargrave, Gamal had 8 carucates to the geld.

In Carleton and Lothersdale [are] 10 carucates to the geld. Gamal had them.

In Bracewell, Ulfkil and Arnketil had 6 carucates to the geld.

In Stock, Arnketil had 4 carucates to the geld.

In Broughton [near Skipton], 4 thegns [had] 12 carucates to the geld.

In Cowling [near Glusburn], Arnketil [had] 2 carucates and 2 bovates to the geld.

In Thornton-in-Craven, Alcolm had 3 carucates to the geld.

In Earby, Alcolm had 3 carucates to the geld.

In another Earby, Alcolm [had] 2 carucates and 6 bovates to the geld.

In Elslack, Gospatric and Ketil [had] 8 carucates to the geld.

In Bank Newton, Gospatric [had] 4 carucates to the geld.

In Hetton, Svartkollr [had] 4 carucates to the geld.

In Stainton [in Bank Newton], Sten had 3 carucates to the geld.

In [East and West] Marton, Arnketil and Orm and Arnbrandr [had] 6 carucates to the geld.

In Ingthorpe, Uhtræd and Arnketil [had] 2 carucates to the geld.

In Airton, Arnbrandr [had] 4 carucates to the geld.

In Scosthrop, Arnketil and Orm [had] 3 carucates to the geld.

In Calton, Gospatric and Gluniairnn [had] 4 carucates to the geld. Erneis had it, but now it is in the jurisdiction of Roger's castle.

In Langcliffe, Fech [had] 3 carucates to the geld.

In Stackhouse, Arnketil [had] 3 carucates to the geld.

In Eshton, Arnketil and Uhtræd [had] 6 carucates to the geld.

In Bordley, Svartkollr [had] 2 carucates to the geld.

In Arncliffe [near Litton], Thorfinnr [had] 4 carucates to the geld.

In Hawkswick, Gamal [had] 3 carucates to the geld. [...]

In GRINDLETON, Earl Tosti had 4 carucates of land to the geld. In West Bradford, 2 carucates; Waddington, 2 carucates; Bashall Eaves, 4 carucates; Great Mitton, 4 carucates; Hammerton, 2 carucates; Slaidburn, 4 carucates; Dunnow, 2 carucates; Newton [in Slaidburn], 4 carucates; "Bogeuurde" [in Slaidburn], 2 carucates; Easington [in Slaidburn], 3 carucates; Radholme Laund, 2 carucates; Lees, 3 carucates. These lands belong to Grindleton.

In "LANESDALE" [Lancs.] and COCKERHAM [Lancs.], Ulf and Machel had 2 carucates to the geld.

In ASHTON [in Lancaster, Lancs.], Clibert, Machern and Gillemicel had 6 carucates to the geld. In Ellel [Lancs.], 2 carucates. In Scotforth [Lancs.], 2 carucates.

In BEETHAM [Westm.], Earl Tosti had 6 carucates to the geld. Now Roger de Poitou has them, and Earnwine the priest [holds] under him. In Yealand [Conyers and Redmayne, Lancs.], 4 carucates; Farleton [Westm.], 4 carucates; 'Preston Richard' [in Heversham, Westm.], 3 carucates; Borwick [Lancs.], 2 carucates; Hincaster [Westm.], 2 carucates; Heversham [Westm.], 2 carucates; Levens [Westm.], 2 carucates.

[Folio 332V: [YORKSHIRE]]

THIS IS THE FIEF of Robert de Bruis which was given after the book of Winchester was written, namely:

In the East Riding. In BURTON AGNES and in its soke

this Robert holds 44 carucates of land: this is in HARPHAM and in Gransmoor and in Haisthorpe and in Thornholme and in Foxholes and in Thwing. And in this same Thwing he himself holds 10 carucates; and in Rudston, 8 carucates; and in the two Heslertons [East and West Heslerton], 10 carucates and 6 bovates; and in Scampston, 5 carucates.

In Kirkburn and in Tibthorpe, 32 carucates and 2 bovates; but part of that land is of the fief of Robert Fossard.

In Brantingham and in North Cave and in Hotham, 9 carucates and 1 bovate.

In South Cliffe, 2 bovates. In Kilnwick Percy, 16 carucates. In Millington, 6 bovates.

In Birdsall, 2 carucates. In Garrowby, 6 carucates. In Eddlethorpe, 4 carucates.

In Thornthorpe, 1 carucate and 6 bovates.

In Firby [in Westow], 2 carucates. In North Grimston, 4 carucates and 2 bovates. In Burythorpe, 3 carucates.

IN THE WEST RIDING the same Robert holds in Allerton Mauleverer 6 carucates of land.

In Widdington, 1 carucate. In Great Ouseburn, 12 carucates. In Hopperton, 4 carucates.

In [Lower and Upper] Dunsforth, 2½ carucates. In Branton Green, 3 carucates and 3 bovates. In Grafton, 4 carucates and 6 bovates. In 'Thorpe juxta Scotton' [in Farnham], 2 carucates. In Scotton [in Farnham], 2 carucates. In Susacres, 1 carucate. In Laverton, 4½ carucates. In Azerley, 6 carucates of land. In Leathley, 2 carucates. In Rawdon, 6 bovates. In Horsforth, 2 carucates. In Grewelthorpe, 2 carucates. In Carlton [near Snaith], 6 carucates. In Camblesforth, 1 carucate.

IN THE NORTH RIDING the same Robert holds in Appleton Wiske 6 carucates of land.

In Hornby [in Great Smeaton], 2 carucates. In Low Worsall, 3 carucates. In Yarm, 3 carucates.

In South Otterington, 6 carucates. In East Harlsey, 6 carucates. In Welbury, 6 carucates.

In Kirklevington, 6 carucates. In another Levington ['Castlelevington', in Kirklevington], 4 carucates. In Morton [in East Harlsey], 3 carucates.

In 'Brodeby' [in Osmortherley], 2 carucates. In Arncliffe [in Ingleby Arncliffe], 2 carucates. In Ingleby Arncliffe, 6 carucates. In Busby, 2 carucates. In Crathorne and in High Foxton, 9 carucates. In Hilton [near Stokesley], 3 carucates. In Thornaby-on-Tees, 1½ carucates. In Marton [in Middlesbrough], 4 carucates. In Newham, 2 carucates and 2 bovates. In Tollesby, 3 carucates. In Acklam [in Middlesbrough], 2 carucates. In Faceby, 8 carucates. In Tanton, 2½ carucates. In Goulton, 1 carucate. In "Bergolbi" [in Seamer, near Stokesley], 1 carucate. In Nunthorpe, 6 carucates. In Morton [in Ormesby], 3 carucates. In Newton under Roseberry, 4 carucates and 6 bovates. In Upsall [in Ormesby], 3 carucates. In Pinchinthorpe, 3 carucates.

In Kildale, 6 carucates. In Ormesby, 12 carucates. In Lazenby [in Ormesby], 1½ carucates. In Guisborough, 1 carucate.

In "Esteintona" [in Stanghow], 1 bovate. In Moorsholm, half a carucate. In Cawthorne [in Middleton, near Pickering], 1 carucate. In Crambe, 4 carucates. IN 'Newsham' [in Amotherby], 10 bovates. In Amotherby, 2½ carucates. In

Low Hutton, 3 carucates. In Ganthorpe, half a carucate. In Brompton [near Snainton],

14 bovates. In Thornton Dale, 11 bovates.

In Wykeham [near Ruston], half a carucate. In Cayton [near Scarborough], 2 carucates of land.

In HARPHAM, Robert de Bruis holds 8 carucates of land which he has exchanged with the king. And in Gransmoor, 2 carucates. And in 'Eskdale' [in Whitby], 12 carucates and 2 bovates, namely in Danby [near Castleton], 6 carucates, and in 'Crunkly' [in Glaisdale], 3 carucates, and in the two 'Hangtons' [in Glaisdale], 2 carucates, and in Lealholm, 10 bovates. [inscribed probably between 1120 and 1129]

[Blank in MS]

[Blank in MS]

[Blank in MS]

Clamores of Yorkshire

IN THE NORTH RIDING

In Langbaurgh Wapentake, Earl Hugh claims against William de Percy 1 carucate of land in Fyling, saying it belongs to Whitby, but he has no witness.

In "Maneshou" Wapentake, Ralph Paynel claims 6 bovates of land in Stonegrave of the land of Ulf; but the jurors say it belongs to St Peter of York.

They testify that William Malet held the land of Hawarth in Yorkshire before the castle was taken.

They say that William Malet bought 7 carucates of the land of Sprot in Sand Hutton for 10 marks of silver.

Nigel Fossard held unjustly the land of Thorulf and Thorkil and Thorsten in Sheriff Hutton, that is, 3 manors of 4 carucates of land; but he has given them up and they are in the king's hand.

EAST RIDING

The same Nigel has relinquished 2 carucates of land, 1 manor, in South Cliffe, which belonged to Basinc.

Nigel has relinquished 2 carucates of land in Ellerton [near Bubwith], which belonged to Barn and Ulf.

In Middleton-on-the-Wolds the same Nigel held 1 carucate of land which belonged to Mula-Grimr, but now he has given it up.

The same Nigel has retained by force until now the soke of half a carucate of land and of the third part of 1 bovate in the same vill, and it belongs to the king's manor of Great Driffield.

In like manner, Hamelin has detained by force until now 2 carucates of land and 5 bovates in the same vill with soke belonging to Great Driffield.

In the same vill, Richard de Sourdeval holds 3 carucates of land and 5 bovates which belonged to Ealdgyth, whose land was not delivered to Count Robert.

Also in the same vill, the same Richard holds 6 bovates of land, the soke of which belongs to Great Driffield, but as yet it has not been returned.

In North Dalton the same Nigel held 2 carucates of land and 1 bovate, which land belonged to Northmann. This he is also now giving up.

In Naburn, Robert Malet has given up 2 carucates of land which belonged to Thorkil and [which] Geoffrey de Beauchamps held of the same Robert.

In Croome, Nigel Fossard has given up 2 carucates of land which belonged to Mylnu-Grimr. This is in "Toreshou" Wapentake; now it is in the king's hand.

In Cherry Burton, the manor of St John of Beverley, Nigel Fossard held 1 carucate of land which belonged to Morcar and the soke is in Welton. Now he has relinquished it.

In Belby are 4 bovates of land which belonged to Orm and Basinc, and they had halls there. The Bishop of Durham has held them until now, but no one claims them now, neither the sheriff nor the bishop.

The jurors say that William Malet had in demesne the land of Northmann son of Ulf in Brantingham, which Nigel Fossard has. In like manner they say concerning the land of Ulf the deacon, which he had in North Cave, [that] Nigel has it, but William Malet had it.

On the testimony of the jurors, the 3½ bovates of land which Ralph de Mortimer claims in 'Lund' [in Breighton] belonged to Alwine, the predecessor of Gilbert Tison, not to Eadgifu, whose land Ralph de Mortimer has.

Concerning all the land of Asa, they testify that it ought to belong to Robert Malet, because she herself had her land separate and free from the rule and control of Beornwulf, her husband, even when they were together, in such a way that he himself could make neither gift nor sale of it, nor forfeit it. After their separation, she herself withdrew with all her land, and possessed it as its lady. But the men of the shire have seen William Malet seised both of that [land] and of all her land, until the castle was attacked. This they testify concerning all the land of Asa which she had in Yorkshire.

They say that the soke which Gilbert Tison claims in Burland ought to belong to the Bishop of Durham in Howden.

They say that 14 bovates of land which the Bishop of Durham claims against Robert Malet in Belby belonged to Muli and Egbrand and Basinc and Orm, with sake and soke, and William Malet had this land.

They say that the land which Earnwine the priest claims in Aughton [near Bubwith] ought to be his; but Nigel Fossard calls the king as warrantor, concerning this land, for the use of Count Robert.

Concerning 7 carucates of land in North Driffield, which Nigel has, they say that William Malet was seised of them, and had the land and the service until the castle was destroyed.

They say that 2 carucates of land which Nigel has in South Driffield belong to the king's demesne in Pocklington. But William Malet had the remaining 6 carucates in the same place, so long as he held the castle of York, and the men rendered service to him.

[Concerning] 3 carucates of land in Cliffe [near Hemingbrough] and 3 carucates in Osgodby [in Hemingbrough], Nigel holds them, but the jurors say that William Malet had this land in demesne so long as he held land in Yorkshire.

They testify that William Malet had in demesne 7½ carucates of land in Sancton, that is, half of the vill, and that he was seised of them.

The whole shire testifies that William Malet held in his demesne, so long as he held land in Yorkshire, the whole land which Northmann son of Maelcolumban had in the East Riding.

They say that the soke which the Bishop of Durham claims, of 5 carucates of land and 2 bovates, really belonged to Welton; but the canons of Beverley claim it as the gift and confirmation of King William. Likewise concerning the soke of 1 carucate of land in 'Newton' [in Cherry Burton], which the Bishop of Durham claims [as belonging] to Welton, they say that it was so TRE; but the clerks claim it of the king in the same manner.

They say that the soke of 2 bovates in "Ianulfestorp" [in Dunnington, near York], which William de Percy has, ought to belong to the archbishop.

They testify that the whole vill of Scoreby, that is, 6 carucates of land, belonged to William Malet, and that he possessed it in demesne.

They testify that, in like manner, 14 bovates of land in "Ianulfestorp" [in Dunnington, near York] and in Dunnington [near York], the land of Northmann and Healfdene, belonged to William Malet, and that he held them in demesne.

Concerning the land of Sunulf in Grimston [in Dunnington, near York] which Nigel holds, and William de Percy claims, they know not which of them ought to have it. Earnwine the priest claims the same land.

[Folio 373V: [CLAMORES]]

They testify that 6 bovates of land in Thorpe le Street, which the archbishop claims, ought to belong to Gilbert Tison.

They testify that 6 carucates of land of Ulfkil in Elvington, which William de Percy has, [ought to be] for Robert Malet's use, because his father had them like the above lands.

[Concerning] land for 4 ploughs in Wheldrake, which William de Percy holds, of which the soke belongs to Clifton [near York], the jurors testify that William Malet held in demesne not only those 4 carucates but also the whole vill of Wheldrake, and was seised of it.

In Lowthorpe, Richard de Sourdeval claims the land of Northmann and Asa, but the jurors say it ought to belong to the king.

Odo the crossbowman has the land in Skirpenbeck and "Scardiztorp" [in Skirpenbeck] of Orm and Bondi, but by the testimony of the jurors it ought to belong to the king.

In Risby, Gamal had 4 carucates of land which he sold to Archbishop Ealdræd TRW. Of this land, the soke formerly belonged to Welton; but Archbishop Thomas has the writ of King William, by which he granted that soke quit to St John of Beverley. Likewise, the soke of 4 carucates of land in Walkington belonged to Welton, but King William gave it quit to Archbishop Ealdræd, according to the testimony of the wapentake which saw and heard the king's writ for it.

IN THE WEST RIDING

The men of Barkston Wapentake and of 'Skyrack' Wapentake attribute to Osbern d' Arques the testimony that Wulfbert, his predecessor, had all Thorner, by whose gift they do not know, that is, 4 manors of 8 carucates of land. But all Thorner is situated within the boundary of the castle of Ilbert according to the first measurement, and according to the newest measurement it is situated without.

They state that William Malet had these lands: the land of Gamal in Yeadon, 1 manor of 2 carucates; and in Oglethorpe, 2 manors of 1 carucate of the land of Grim and Esger, but the soke belonged to Bramham. [...] In Hazelwood, 3 manors of 12 bovates of the land of Gamal son of Osmund, and 1 carucate of the land of Arnketil and his brother in the same vill. This aforesaid vill is within the boundary of Ilbert according to the first measurement, and without, according to the newest. And William Malet had, as they say, all Stutton, 3 manors of 3 carucates of land and 1 mill; and in Tadcaster, 2 manors of 2 carucates and 2 bovates and 1 strip of ploughland of the land of Thorkil. In North Milford, 1 manor of 2 carucates of the land of Wulfstan. This vill is within the boundary of Ilbert, as is stated above of the others. And in "Neuhuse" [in Ulleskelf], 1 manor of 2 carucates of the land of Ketil. In Toulston, 1 carucate of the land of Thorkil, in like manner, within the limits of Ilbert. In Ryther, 2 manors of 2 carucates of the land of Ketil and his brothers; and this is within the boundary of Ilbert, as is stated above of the others. In "Saxehale", 1 manor of 2 carucates of the land of Ketil, within the boundary of the castle. In Lead, 2 carucates of sokeland, which belongs to Hazelwood. In Newton Kyme, 1 manor of 2 carucates of the land of Ligulf and Thorn.

They say that William Malet was seised of all these.

According to their testimony, Gilbert de Ghent has 1 carucate of the land of Ulf in Birkin.

They say that Dunstan did not have the land of Thorkil in Tadcaster TRE.

They say that the land of Ligulf belonged to Weardley and East Rigton, the land of Richard de Sourdeval to Compton.

The men of Strafforth Wapentake testify to the use of William de Warenne 2 carucates of the land of Siward in Clifton [in Conisbrough], which Roger de Bully claimed.

They testify to the use of the king in demesne 4 bovates of land in Clifton [in Conisbrough] of the land of Brune, which William de Warenne had.

They testify to the use of William de Warenne 6 carucates of land in Barnburgh, which belong to Conisbrough.

They testify to the use of the same William 15 acres of land in Wilsic. This belongs to Barnburgh, and all that belongs to it.

They say that Nigel Fossard ought to have in Kirk Sandall 7 bovates of land of Alwine's land, the soke of which belongs to Conisbrough; and in the same vill 1 church of Skotkollr's of which the soke belongs to Conisbrough.

They say that the same Nigel ought to have 3 bovates of the land of Ulfkil, and the soke is in Conisbrough; and in Kirk Bramwith, 1 bovate of the land of Ulfkil [of which] the soke likewise is in Conisbrough.

In Tudworth Green and Stainforth [in Hatfield], Nigel has 1 bovate of land and 3 tofts of the land of Ulfkil [of which] the soke belongs to Conisbrough; and in Fishlake, the land of Northmann, 1 toft and the fourth part of 1 bovate. The soke [belongs] to Conisbrough.

Fulk de Lisors has in Loversall 2 bovates of the land of Wulfmær, the soke [of which] belongs to Hexthorpe, the land of Nigel; and in Edenthorpe, 1 carucate of the land of Swein, the soke [of which] belongs to Conisbrough.

Roger de Bully [has] 1 carucate of land in Cantley of the land of Alsige.

Geoffrey Aselin [...] [has] in Loversall 4 bovates of the land of Toki. The soke belongs to Hexthorpe.

Two marshals took possession of the land of Northmann, [...] and held it. The men of the wapentake know not how, nor for whose use, but they have seen them holding it.

Nigel Fossard [has] in Wadworth 1 manor of 14 bovates of land of the land of Siward [...]. In Stancil, 1 manor of 1 carucate of the land of Siward.

Geoffrey Aselin [has] in Wadworth [...] 10½ carucates of land of the land of Toki.

But Roger de Bully holds this land; they know not how.

In Great Houghton the king has 1 manor of 6 bovates of land, of the land of Godhyse.

Concerning the claims of Nigel in Hexthorpe, they said that in King Edward's day it was as it is now.

They say that after the death of King Edward, Archbishop Ealdræd purchased the land of Swein of Adwick le Street, and had it quit.

To the loss of the Church of ST MARY, which is in the woodland of Morley, the king has half of the alms of the 3 feasts of ST MARY, which belongs to Wakefield. By the judgement of the men of Morley Wapentake, Ilbert has all the other [half], and [so does] the priest who serves the church.

The men of Ainsty Wapentake testify that 1 manor, in Steeton [in Bolton Percy] and Colton [near York] and Catterton, of 3 carucates of land and 5 bovates of the land of Arnketil the son of Wulfstan [is] for William Malet's use. Osbern d'Arques holds these.

They say that William Malet had 3 carucates of land in 'Hackerby' [in Healaugh] of the land of Arnketil son of Ulf, which William de Percy holds. One of those carucates belongs to the soke of Healaugh.

Likewise they testify that 4½ carucates of the land of Northmann son of Maelcolumban, which Osbern d'Arques holds [are] for the same William's use; and in Colton [near York] and Steeton [in Bolton Percy] they testify that 13 bovates of the land of Godwine son of Eadric which the same Osbern holds [are] for William Malet's use.

And they say that William Malet ought to have 1 carucate of land in Askham Richard, which belonged to Ulf the deacon, which Osbern d'Arques holds.

And the same Osbern holds 7 bovates in Colton [near York] of the land of Wulfstan the priest; and they say that William Malet ought to have them.

In Pallathorpe [is] 1 carucate of land, and in "Mulehale" half a carucate of the land of Northmann, which Landric holds; they testify that they ought to belong to William Malet.

In Hornington [are] 10 bovates of land of the land of Healfdene, and, in the same vill, 5 bovates of the land of Oda and Alwine. William de Percy holds these, but the men of the wapentake say that Malet ought to have them.

They testify that 1 manor in 'Scagglethorpe' [in Moor Monkton], and 1 manor in the two Poppletons [Nether Poppleton and Upper Poppleton], 6½ carucates of land of the land of Earnwine [...] Catenase, which Osbern d'Arques holds, [is] for Malet's use and they say that Earnwine the priest ought to have them of Robert Malet.

They testify thus that they have seen William Malet seised of and holding them, and the men of the land did service to him and were his men; but they do not know how he had them.

In Bolton Percy, William de Percy has 5 carucates of the land of Ligulf. The soke belongs to Healaugh, the land of Geoffrey Alselin.

The soke of 12 bovates of land in Walton [near Wetherby], of the land of Godwine, belongs to Healaugh, the land of Geoffrey Alselin.

William de Percy calls on his peers to witness that when William Malet was living and holding the shrievalty in York, he himself was seised of Bolton Percy and held it.

Osbern d'Arques confirms that Wulfbert, his predecessor, had Appleton Roebuck and all other lands quit.

Ulfkil suabrodre [had] in Steeton [in Bolton Percy], 2 carucates; in Hornington, half a carucate; in Oxton, 1 caruate; in Pallathorpe, 6 bovates; in Colton [near York], 7 bovates. Count Robert has them. Nigel Fossard holds them of him.

The men of Burghshire Wapentake testify that 4 bovates of land in Nun Monkton of the land of Mærle-Sveinn, which Osbern d'Arques holds, [are] for Ralph Paynel's use.

It is testified by the men of the Riding that all the land which Drogo claimed against St John [of Beverley] is for the use of the same St John, by the gift of King William, which he gave to St John in the time of Archbishop Ealdræd. The canons

have the seal of King Edward and of King William for this.

The jurors of Holderness have testified that these lands noted below [are] for William Malet's use, because they saw them seised in the hand of the same William, and saw him having and holding them until the Danes took him; but they have not seen the king's writ or seal for this.

In Brandesburton, 11 carucates of land which belonged to Ealdwif and Ulf and his brother and Ulfkil.

In "Luuetotholm" [in Leven], 1 carucate of land which belonged to Luvetote.

In "Chenuthesholm" [in Long Riston], 1 carucate of land which belonged to Knut.

In Catfoss, 6 carucates of land which belonged to Knut.

In Rise, 7½ carucates of land which belonged to Knut.

In Catwick, 4 carucates of land which belonged to Ealdwif.

In Old Ellerby, 4 carucates of land which belonged to Frani son of Thor.

In Langthorpe [near Old Ellerby], 1 carucate of land which belonged to Ecgfrith.

In Sproatley, 6 carucates of land which belonged to Thorsten.

In Keyingham, 8 carucates of land which belonged to Thorfridh.

In Preston [near Hedon], 16 carucates of land which belonged to Frani and his brother.

In "Andrebi" [in Roos], 2 carucates of land which belonged to Ramkel.

In Waxholme, 5 carucates of land which belonged to Brandulfr.

In 'Redmere' [in Owthorne], 1 carucate of land which belonged to Ramkel.

In Holmpton, 8 carucates of land [which] belonged to Oda the priest, Æthelstan and Siward.

In Rysome Garth, 2 carucates of land which belonged to Thorgot.

In "Torp" [in Easington, near Kilnsea], 3 carucates of land which belonged to Grimkel.

In Southcoates, 1 carucate of land which belonged to Oda the deacon.

Drogo has this land.

This land belongs to Healaugh: in Bolton Percy, 5 carucates of land; in 'Hackerby' [in Healaugh], 1 carucate; Acaster Selby, 1 bovate; Ouston, 2½ carucates, inland, and 4 bovates, sokeland. William de Percy holds these. In Walton [near Wetherby], 12 bovates of land; in Rufforth, 1 carucate. Osbern d'Arques holds these. In Askham Bryan, 1 carucate of land. Count Alan has this.

[Blank in MS]

The Clamores which are in the SOUTH RIDING of Lincoln, and their settlement [...] by the jurors.

In Tathwell Hundred, the Bishop of Bayeux's men claim 1 carucate of land against Robert Despenser; and the men of the wapentake say that the bishop himself ought by right to have it.

In the same hundred, the men of the same bishop claim 3

bovates of land against Earl Hugh; and the wapentake says that the bishop himself ought to have them.

In the same hundred, the wapentake says that Robert Despenser ought to have with his land the mill which belonged to Aghmund, and which after him, Lambert and Joscelin his son had.

In LOUTH Hundred, the Bishop of Lincoln claims 1 mill against Count Alan; and the wapentake bears witness that it ought to belong to the same bishop.

Those lands which Alsige and Ulfgrimr had in Lindsey they placed in the Church of St Mary of Lincoln, and in the mercy of Bishop Wulfwig; and therefore Bishop Remigius claims them because they had £160 for these lands TRE.

In Burwell Hundred, the king's officers claims against Earl Hugh in Haugham and Maidenwell the lands of 2 brothers, Godric and Eadric; and the men of the wapentake have adjudged them for the king's use.

In [Great and Little] Carlton Hundred, William de Percy claims half a carucate of land against Kolsveinn; and the wapentake bears witness for the same William.

In [North and South] Somercotes Hundred, Alvred of Lincoln claims half a carucate of land against the king in Yarburgh; but the Riding says that he has nothing there except $9\frac{1}{2}$ acres and 1 toft of which the soke belongs to the king's manor of Gayton le Wold.

In the same hundred, Siward Buss claims 1 mill against Alvred; and the men of the Riding [say] that Alvred has a half belonging to Rayner de Brimeux's [manor of] Keddington, and the Bishop of Durham has the other half [of which] the soke [belongs] to Keddington.

In Skidbrooke Hundred, Alvred claims 3 bovates of land in Stewton against Ilbert; the men of the Riding say that Alvred himself ought to have them.

In Withcall Hundred, Rayner claims the whole of the church; and the men of the Riding say that it belonged to his predecessor, as [did] a third part of the soke, and [that] Ilbert de Lacy [has] 2 parts of the soke over the church and the land which belongs to it.

In Swaby Hundred, Robert Despenser claims against Earl Hugh 1 carucate of land in Claythorpe. The men of the Riding say that the soke belongs to Greetham, and belonged to Vighlak, and [that] he himself departed from the land, and made forfeiture; and they say that Robert Despenser has nothing there.

In Rigsby Hundred, Losuard claims 1 carucate of land in Well against Gilbert de Ghent. The men of the Riding say that TRE Thorulf had it with sake and soke, and afterwards Tonni had it; and [that] this land was delivered to Bishop Odo by charter, but they have not seen the king's writ for it, and [that] he himself had it on the day on which he was taken, and afterwards he was disseised.

In the same hundred, Rayner de Brimeux claims 2 bovates of land in Ulceby [near Well] against Earl Hugh; and the men of the Riding say that he ought to have nothing except the soke [which belongs] to Cumberworth, and the earl the land.

In Theddlethorpe [All Saints and St Helen] Hundred, the Bishop of Durham claims 2 bovates against Earl Hugh in Mablethorpe. The men of the Riding say that he has only 1 bovate which belonged to Bærghthor, and [that] the soke belongs to Earl Hugh in Greetham. And in the same place William Blund [has] 3 bovates which belonged to Sumarlithr and Godric and Siward; and the soke belongs to Greetham by the testimony of the whole Riding.

In Huttoft Hundred, Alvred claims 2 bovates of land; and the men of the Riding say that he ought he has [sic] to have one with sake and soke, and [that] the other is his in the same way, but Earl Hugh has the soke in Greetham.

In the same hundred, the Riding says that the same Alvred ought to have the soke of 1 bovate which Alvred claims against Ketilbiørn in Sutton on Sea.

In Mumby Hundred, Count Alan claims 2 bovates of land against Gilbert de Ghent; but the Riding says that Gilbert's predecessor had the sake and soke of it TRE, and [that] it ought to be his.

In Willoughby Hundred, the Bishop of Durham claims the land of Alnoth the priest against Gilbert de Ghent; and the men of the Riding say that they never saw the bishop's predecessor seised of it, either by writ or by officer and they testify [it is] for Gilbert's use.

In the same hundred, the men of the Riding testify that Ketilbiørn ought to have 20 acres of woodland in 'Hanby' [in Welton le Marsh], and Ivo Taillebois the soke.

Touching the dispute between the Bishop of Durham and Eudo fitzSpirewic, the men of Horncastle Wapentake bore witness, with the assent of the whole Riding, that 3 brothers, Harold and Guthfrith and Ælfric, divided their father's demesne land equally and in parage; and [that] Harold and Guthfrith only, without the third brother, divided their father's soke, and [that] they held it TRE equally and in parage.

Touching the soke of 6 bovates, about which there is a dispute between the bishop and Eudo, in Langton by Wragby and [?] Tattershall Thorpe, the men of 'Wraggoe' Wapentake say that the aforesaid 2 brothers had the soke TRE equally and in parage; but in the year in which the same king [Edward] died, the sons of Guthfrith had the whole soke, but they know not on what ground they had it, whether by force or by the gift of their uncle.

Touching the claim which Robert Despenser makes against Gilbert de Ghent about woodland which is in Low Langton, 'Wraggoe' Wapentake, with the assent of the whole Riding, says that Tonni had it TRE with sake and soke in Baumber; and therefore [that] Gilbert de Ghent has it by right.

Touching the scrubland which Robert Despenser claims against the king in Hainton, and against Erneis de Buron in Wragby, he has nothing there according to the testimony of the wapentake. But, by the testimony of the men of the wapentake and Riding, he has the soke over 12 acres of Earl Hugh's and over 8 acres of the Bishop of Bayeux's.

[In respect of] the claims which Rayner de Brimeux made against Alvred of Lincoln touching the soke of $3\frac{1}{2}$ bovates, he ought to have nothing there as the men of the wapentake and Riding testify; but Roger de Poitou ought to have it as belonging to the house of his predecessor Klak in Hainton.

Touching the claim which Erneis de Buron makes against William de Percy.

concerning the soke of 4 bovates in Legsby, the wapentake says that the same Erneis ought by right to have it.

Touching the claim which Archbishop Thomas made, that is, that he ought to have the soke over the land of Siward, the predecessor of Ivo Taillebois, the wapentake says, and the Riding, that Siward held his land with sake and soke in just the same way as Godwine, the archbishop's predecessor, held [his], and therefore he does not claim it rightly.

Archbishop Thomas ought to have the soke over Eskil's land which the Bishop of Bayeux has in South Willingham, because, as the whole shire testifies, the archbishop's predecessor had sake and soke over the same land, and the bishop's men unjustly took away the same soke from the same archbishop.

TRE Almær, Archbishop Thomas's predecessor, was seised of the soke of 10 bovates in South Wiilingham. This land belonged to Koddi, and now it belongs to Rayner de Brimeux; and it was given in pledge for £3; TRE; and now the men of the Riding assert that the archbishop ought by right to have this soke until the £3 are repaid to him.

Gilbert de Ghent and Norman d'Arcy claim against William de Percy the soke of 12 bovates in Stainfield [near Lincoln] which belongs to Barlings, and belonged to Tonni. But the wapentake says, and the shire, that Gilbert ought to have it, not Norman. William de Percy, however, holds it by the king's gift, in the same way as Robert fitzStigand held it.

They put forward the same argument touching the soke of 7 bovates in Apley, because it belongs to Barlings, and Tonni held it TRE

In the same Apley, the Bishop of Durham claims the soke of 2 bovates against William de Percy; and the wapentake says that the same Bishop's predecessor had it, and [that] he himself ought to have it as belonging to Bullington.

The Wapentake of Horncastle says that Robert Despenser unjustly makes a claim against Gilbert de Ghent touching half a carucate of land in Baumber and Touching another half-carucate in Edlington. Tonni had this land TRE.

Robert Despenser ought to have the soke over a fishery and over a toft which Ketilbiørn holds in Coningsby, because Aki, Robert's predecessor, had it TRE.

'Candlehoe' Wapentake says that Ivo Taillebois ought to have in Ashby by Partney what he claims against Earl Hugh, that is, 1 mill and 1 bovate of land, but the soke belongs to Greetham.

Touching 2 carucates of land which Robert Despenser claims against Gilbert de Ghent in Scremby through Vighlak his predecessor, the wapentake says that he [Vighlak] had only 1 carucate, and the soke of that belonged to Bardney; but Vighlak forfeited that land to the loss of Gilbert his lord and therefore, by the testimony of the Riding, Robert has nothing there.

In the same Scremby, Ketilbiørn claims 1 carucate through Godric against Gilbert de Ghent; but they say that he [Godric] had only half a carucate, and its soke belonged to Bardney, and Ketilbiørn claims unjustly, as the wapentake says, because his predecessor forfeited it.

The men of 'Candleshoe' Wapentake testify, with the consent of the whole Riding, that TRE Sighwat and Alnoth and Fenkell and Eskil divided their father's land amongst themselves equally and in parage, and held it in such a way that if they were needed in the king's military expedition, and Sighwat could go, the other brothers assisted him. After him, another went, and Sighwat with the rest assisted him; and thus with respect to them all. Sighwat, however, was the king's man.

[The men] of Bolingbroke [Wapentake] bear witness to the same with the above-mentioned, the South Riding assenting.

In Saltfleet and in 'Mare' [in South Somercotes] and in 'Swine' [in Grainthorpe] a new toll has been established, and Ansgar of Skidbrook has been receiving it, and Reginald and Humphrey and Geoffrey; and 'Louthesk' Wapentake says this, and [so does] the whole South Riding, that this toll did not exist TRE. Godric gave a toll of 1d, according to the testimony of Ulfkil of Asterby who saw it, and Arnketil of Withern testifies this, that he himself saw Ansgar receive the toll from 24 ships from Hastings [Sussex].

In Saltfleet, Hugh the sergeant receives the customary dues of ships which come there, willingly and unwillingly [paid], which [dues] did not exist there TRE; and they began this as a new practice, and the men of the Riding say this, that they saw the claim made for it.

CLAMORES IN THE NORTH RIDING

In Barton-upon-Humber and in South Ferriby, Gilbert de Ghent's men are receiving a different toll to the one they received TRE, in respect of bread, fish, hides, and very many other things, for which nothing was ever given.

In Caistor the king's men do the same.

In [Great or Little] Limber, Ivo Taillebois claims 6 bovates of land against the king. The men of the shire say that he himself ought to have the land, and the king the soke.

Instead of 30 acres of meadow which Alvred claims in Ulceby [near Wootton], he ought to have 1 strip of ploughland in the same vill.

Yarborough Wapentake bears witness that Morcar gave Hugh 4 bovates of land in Goxhill with sake and soke which Drogo de la Beuvriere claims. Alvred claims 1 bovate of this land. The wapentake says that the land belongs to Hugh, and the soke belongs to Alvred.

The wapentake bears witness that King William gave the church of Caistor to ST MARY of Lincoln in alms; to which church belong 2 bovates of land in demesne, and 2 villas, and 1 mill, and in Hundon the soke of 1 carucate.

Joscelin claims 3 bovates of land in Searby against Count Alan. The shire says that Joscelin ought to have them, not Alan.

Hugh fitzBaldric claims half a bovate of land in Brocklesby. The men of the Riding say that the land ought to belong to him, and the soke to Norman, through their predecessors.

In Stallingborough, the wapentake says [of] Elaf's 2 manors that Rayner the deacon held them on the day on which he departed from this country.

Rayner de Brimeux ought to have in Great Limber the soke of half a bovate of land which Archbishop Thomas has in Stallingborough.

Touching 1 manor of Elaf's, which Archbishop Thomas now has in Keelby, Rayner the deacon was seised of it on the very day on which he departed from this land.

In Great Coates [in Great Grimsby], Alvred ought to have the land of 2 bovates, and Durand Malet the soke, with 3 villans who belong to it.

Rayner the deacon was seised of 1 carucate of land in Swallow when he departed

[Folio 376: [CLAMORES]]

from this land.

Likewise the same Rayner the deacon was seised of Erik's land which is in Great Grimsby Hundred. Now the Bishop of Bayeux has it.

Ralph de Mortimer's men and Losoard's men are receiving a new toll in Great Grimsby, which did not exist TRE; but Losoard denies that his men did it on his account.

The Bishop of Bayeux and the Bishop of Lincoln ought to have the soke over 2½ bovates of land which belongs to the church of 'Winghale' [in South Kelsey].

In [North and South] Owersby Hundred, the Bishop of Bayeux has the soke over half a carucate of land which belonged to Earnwine the priest, and now belongs to Siward the priest.

In Osgodby [near West Rasen], Joscelin fitzLambert ought to have the soke over half a bovate of land.

In Tealby Hundred, Rayner the deacon had Erik's land with all that belongs to it there. Joscelin holds it, and Rayner claims it. The Riding bears witness that Count Alan's predecessor had the soke, but they know not of what sort.

In Claxby [near Walesby], Joscelin fitzLambert ought to have 1 mill which Geoffrey, Ivo Taillebois's man, seized from him.

In Croxby, William Blund ought to have 1 garden on Ivo Taillebois's land; but he is obstructed on account of a mill which was not there TRE.

In Fulstow, the Bishop of Durham ought to have 40 acres of land-meadow-and 4 tofts, and Count Alan the soke of them, as the wapentake says.

In the same vill they adjudge that Count Alan has the soke over 1 carucate of land in Robert Depenser's land. And Drogo ought to have there 1 salt-pan which he claims, and Count Alan the soke of it.

Rayner the deacon was seised of Fulcric's land in Cuxwold when he departed from this land. Now Archbishop Thomas holds it. Rayner de Brimeux claims it.

In the same Cuxwold, in the land of Hugh fitzBaldric, William de percy ought to have 2 bovates of land which he claims. The wapentake bears witness for him.

The wapentake says that Count Alan ought to have soke over the hall of Grimkel, whose land the Bishop of Durham has in Wold Newton.

Kolsveinn did not deliver the land of Ingimund and his brothers to Count Alan, but the same Ingimund made it subject to the count himself because of other land which he held of him.

The North Riding and the whole shire bear witness that the land of Ulf of North Ormsby, that is 4½ carucates of land, was sold to ST MARY of Stow TRE, and it belonged to that

[church] on the very day on which the same king died; and afterwards Bishop Remigius was seised of it.

In Scemund [North Ormsby] in the land of Ivo Taillebois, Drogo claims 3 messuages which, by the testimony of the wapentake, he ought to have with sake and soke.

In Fotherby, the land of Berengar de Tosny, the Bishop of Durham ought to have 5 bovates of land, and Berengar the soke of them.

The Wapentake and the whole shire bear witness that the Bishop of Durham ought to have the land of 3 brothers with sake and soke, and Eudo fitzSpirewic the land of the fourth brother with sake and soke likewise. Their names [are] Sighwat-orGodwine- Alnoth, Fenkell, and Eskil.

CLAMORES IN THE WEST RIDING

'LAWRESS' WAPENTAKE bears witness that Alnoth had soke and sake over his land, 3 carucates in Burton. Svartbrandr now has it after him.

The Abbot of Peterborough claims 4 bovates of land in Riseholme, Kolsveinn's land; and the wapentake bears witness that TRE they belonged to the Church of All Saints in Lincoln.

Three burgesses of Lincoln, Guthrøthr and Leofwine and Sigewine, TRE held in pledge from Aghmund the land in 'Middle Carlton' [in North Carlton] which Joscelin fitzLambert claims against Norman Crassus.

In Scampton, Norman Crassus added £3 and 1 mark of gold, and he pledged this to Ivo the sheriff.

In Scothern Hundred, Godric, Norman's predecessor, had 4½ bovates of land TRE, as the wapentake bears witness.

In the same hundred Gilbert de Ghent claims 1 carucate of land against the Abbot of Peterborough. The wapentake, however, bears witness that St Peter had this land with its soke on the day on which King Edward was alive and dead.

In Nettleham Hundred, Bishop Remigius claims 2 bovates of land, and the wapentake bears witness that he himself ought to have them.

The wapentake says that St Peter of Peterborough ought to have the fourth part of woodland in Reepham which Ranulph and Kolsveinn claim.

The wapentake bears witness that Ulfkil and Asfrith and Restelf and Wulfmær had sake and soke over their lands and over their men in Sturton by Stow Hundred.

And touching forfeiture in the wapentake, ST MARY has 2 parts of the soke, and the earl the third. Now the king [has the third part]. Likewise with respect to heriot. And if they had forfeited their land, ST MARY would have had two parts, and the earl the third.

The shire bears witness that Gunnhvati's land, 1 manor, [having] 1 carucate in demesne, was forfeited, 2 parts to ST MARY and the third part for the earl's use. Likewise with respect to all the soke which belongs to Gate Burton or "Broctone". Likewise also with respect to Steingrimr's land, 18 bovates of land.

With respect to all the thegns who have land in 'Well' Wapentake, ST MARY has 2 parts of [their] forfeiture, and the earl the third. Likewise with respect to heriot. Likewise if they had forfeited their land, 2 parts [would have belonged] to ST MARY, and the third part [would have been] in the earl's hand. Now the king has [the third part]. Neither Gilbert de Ghent nor Robert de Tosny nor Ralph de Mortimer, through their predecessors, are subject to this custom.

Grimkel had sake and soke over his land TRE, but in the year in which the same king died, he forfeited it, and he gave it to Mærle-Sveinn the sheriff because he stood accused before the king and made him heir to that.

In Owmby-by-Spital, Joscelin has 9 bovates of Aghmund's land, and Ivo 1 bovate. Bishop Remigius ought to have the soke of these.

In [?] Northorpe [near Kirton in Lindsey] Hundred, Siward Rufus had 1 carucate of land with sake and soke TRE; and Ralph de Neville lately held it of Abbot Turold, but he did not have a livery officer for it. Now it is adjudged for the king's use.

In the same hundred in the vill [of] Laughton [near Blyton], Guy de Craon, through his predecessor Wilgrim, claims soke over Swein's land; and the wapentake bears witness that TRE this Wilgrim had sake and soke over the same Swein.

The shire bears witness that, on the day on which King Edward was alive and dead and afterwards, Eskil had of King Edward these 3 manors, Scotton, Scotter, and 'Raventhorpe' [in Broughton], in his own jurisdiction. In like manner he had North Muskham in Nottinghamshire, and he held 1 manor, Manton, of his brother Brand the monk in leasehold.

The WEST RIDING bears witness that the claims which are [put forward] in Epworth Wapentake are rightly made: Norman Crassus claims 7 bovates of land against Geoffrey de la Guerche in Haxey. Gilbert de Ghent claims 4 carucates of land and 6 bovates against this Geoffrey. This is Ulf Fenman's land in Belton [near Epworth]. Henry de Ferrers claims 3 bovates of land against this Geoffrey. This is Siward Barn's land in Amcotts. Also Gilbert de Ghent claims against the same Geoffrey half a carucate of sokeland in Belton [near Epworth], which belonged to Ulf Fenman.

The wapentake bears witness that in Winteringham Hundred Erneis de Buron ought to have Wege's land, that is 6 bovates of land and 1 toft in the soke of Gilbert de Ghent, and another toft with sake and soke.

In Thealby Hundred, Ralph Paynel claims 1 toft. The Wapentake says that he himself ought to have it, and the king [its] soke in Kirton in Lindsey.

Norman d'Arcy claims 3 bovates of land in Normanby against Drogo. The wapentake says that the land ought to belong to him, and the soke to Drogo.

CLAMORES IN KESTEVEN

'NESS' WAPENTAKE and the whole Riding have borne witness that the land of Wulfgeat and his mother Wulfflæd did not belong to Arnbiorn his sister's relative and that he only had it in wardship until Wulfgeat could hold land; that is, in Uffington 7 carucates, in Tallington 6½ carucates, in Casewick 6 bovates, [and] in Deeping [Deeping St James or Market Deeping] 4 bovates: half a carucate.

The wapentake says that TRE Peterborough [Abbey] had 60 acres of land which Countess Judith has and tills with the ploughs of Belmesthorpe [Rut.].

The warnode of these 60 acres of land and of 48 acres of meadow belongs to Uffington, Alvred of Lincoln's [manor], but it is forcibly withheld.

The wapentake says that Azur's half carucate of land in Barholm ought to belong to Gunfrid de Chocques.

The wapentake says that Hereweard did not have Asfrith's land in Barholm Hundred on the day on which he fled.

Ralph Paynel has 6 bovates of land of Morcar's land in Burton-le-Coggles Hundred; but Mærle-Sveinn did not have them TRE.

The Abbot of Peterborough claims 1 bovate of land against Drogo in Witham on the Hill Hundred; the wapentake says that the land ought to belong to St Peter, and the soke to Gilbert de Ghent in Edenham.

In Little Bytham Hundred, Ratbod ought to have 1 carucate of land which he claims; but the soke belongs to Peterborough [Abbey].

They say that the warnode of 4d from 60 acres of woodland, which lies at Skillington, belongs to Castle Bytham.

They say that Arnbiorn had 13 acres of woodland and 25 acres of arable land in Irnham; and that they belong to Aslackby, which Robert de Tosny has.

Archbishop Ealdræd acquired Lenton and Skillington with the BEREWICK [of] Hardwick [Northants] from Ulf son of Topi with his own money, which he gave him in the sight of the wapentake; and afterwards they saw the king's seal by which he was re-seised of those lands, because Hilbold had disseised him of them.

The wapentake says that Eskil was the king's thegn, and that he never had his land under Mærle-Sveinn.

Robert of Stafford unjustly held the soke [of] 6 bovates of Arnketil's land in [North or South] Rauceby Hundred, as the wapentake says.

They say that the claim which Bishop Remigius makes with respect to Arnketil's soke in [North or South] Rauceby Hundred is unjust, because he himself had only 10 bovates of the demesne of the same Arnketil's land in exchange, and the whole of the rest of the land was delivered to the Bishop of Durham.

The wapentake says that the 9 bovates of land which Walter d'Aincourt claims, are sokeland of Branston, the land of Alsige the deacon which Walter now has, and therefore he claims justly.

The men of Navenby forcibly withhold 16s of customary dues of the pastures which are in Scopwick and Kirkby Green; and they did not give them in King Edward's day.

Robert of Stafford claims that the land of Auti, Archbishop Thomas's man, |ought| to belong to the soke of his predecessor Leofsige; but the wapentake says that they never saw Auti give the soke to Leofsige.

Touching Earl Hugh's claim they say that Øthin had the land TRE, and the soke belonged to Potterhanworth.

In Canwick, Svartbrandr claims 140 acres. The wapentake bears witness in his favour because his father Ulf gave for this land 1 mark of gold, in pledge.

In [Great and Little] Ponton, Countess Judith holds 2

manors which belonged to Almær and his brothers. Robert de Tosny claims them; and the wapentake bears witness in his favour that they were delivered to him in exchange for Marston.

In 'Casthorpe' [in Barrowby], Robert de Tosny claims 2 bovates and 2 tofts against Robert Malet; and the wapentake says that they ought to belong to Woolsthorpe.

Touching 1 garden in the same vill, they say that it ought to belong to Robert of Stafford's [manor of] 'Casthorpe' [in Barrowby].

They say that Northmann son of Merewine had 7 gardens in Grantham of which the soke belongs to the same place, but the gardens themselves belong to Gonerby [Great Gonerby or 'Little Gonerby' in Grantham].

They say the same with respect to 2 bovates of land which pertain to Gonerby [Great Gonerby or 'Little Gonerby' in Grantham], and the soke belongs to Grantham.

Ivo Taillebois claims 2 carucates of land, less 30 acres, in Stenwith against Robert de Tosny for which he himself pays the geld. Concerning this, they say that it is right that they themselves should go over the land itself and divide it rightly according to the geld they pay.

In Stoke Rochford Half-Hundred, Robert of Stafford claims Karli's land, 3 carucates of land. The wapentake says that this land belonged to Ralph the staller, and the aforesaid Robert has nothing there.

They say that the tithes and customary church dues of 'Winnibriggs' Wapentake and 'Threo' Wapentake, in respect of all the sokes and inlands which the king has there, belong to the church of Grantham.

Osbern, the king's messenger, claims 1 carucate of land in Thurlby [near Norton Disney] which, by the witness of the wapentake, he ought to have and to render soke for in Eagle, Countess Judith's manor.

Drogo de la Beuvriere claims the soke [of] 10 bovates of land in Thurlby [near Norton Disney] against Osbern d'Arques; but the wapentake says that he claims unjustly.

Touching the claim which the Abbot of Westminster makes against Baldwin with respect to the land and soke of Æthelric son of Mærgeat, they say that they had heard that the same Æthelric gave it to St Peter, but they do not know whether [he gave] the whole or the half.

They say, however, that in Haddington there are 8½ carucates of land, sokeland and inland of Doddington; and in South Hykeham 4 carucates of land, sokeland of Doddington; and in Skellingthorpe 12 carucates, sokeland of Doddington; and in Whisby 6 carucates of land, inland and sokeland of Doddington. The Abbot of Westminster claims the whole of this because the capital manor was given to St Peter. All the shire bears witness in St Peter's favour.

The wapentake says that Kofse had 10 bovates of land and 1 church in the soke of Thorpe on the Hill.

The wapentake says that Siward, not Ulf, Svartbrandr's father, had a manor of 4 carucates of land in North Hykeham; and therefore his [Svartbrandr's] claim is wrong.

They say that 6 bovates of land in Ewerby Thorpe which belonged to Godric, and now belongs [sic] to Martin, ought to be inland of Ewerby.

Ralph Paynel claims against Kolsveinn in Heckington 6 bovates, the land which belonged to Algar the deacon. The wapentake says that Mærle-Sveinn, Ralph's predecessor, did not have it.

In Quarrington, Waldin the Breton claims 14 bovates of land against the Abbot of Ramsey; but the wapentake says that he claims them unjustly.

In the same Quarrington, Bishop Remigius claims that he held Arnketil's land in pledge; but [Arnketil] himself denies this, and he holds of the king.

Kolsveinn claims against the king in Kirkby la Thorpe 2 bovates of land and 1 garden of Earl Morcar's land, which Thorkil held; the wapentake says both that the soke belonged to Earl Morcar, and that this land did not belong to another manor.

In Ingoldsby, Robert Malet claims the soke over 4 bovates of land which Gilbert de Ghent has. The wapentake says that Robert himself ought to have it through Azur his predecessor.

In Caythorpe Hundred, Gilbert de Ghent claims against Robert de Vessey the meadow which belonged to his predecessor Ætherlric; but the wapentake says that the same Æthelric had the whole meadow, and Gilbert's predecessor had nothing there except by renting it for money.

The wapentake bears witness that the tithe and other customary dues of Carlton Scroop belong to the church of the same vill.

In Long Bennington, Count Alan claims 10 bovates of land; but the wapentake says that they belong to Carlton Scroop, William de Warenne's manor, and [that] Earl Harold, his predecessor, had them in this way.

The Bishop of Durham claims 2 bovates of land in Marston of Thorfridh's land; and touching this they say that TRE Northmann gave Thorfridh himself 3 marks of gold for this land, and after the same king's death, he gave him a fourth mark.

The men of 'Aveland' Wapentake bear witness that TRE the manor [of] Bourne belonged to Earl Morcar. Now Ogier has it of the king. Drogo claims it, but unjustly.

The wapentake says that 3½ bovates which Ogier has in Dyke belong to Haconby, and rightly belong to Heppo the crossbowman.

They say that 1 carucate of land in Morton [near Hanthorpe], inland, and 1½ bovates in Hanthorpe, sokeland, belong to Haconby, and were there TRE; and [that] Leofric had these.

They say that in the same Morton [near Hanthorpe], St Benedict of Ramsey ought to have half a carucate of land with sake and soke. Ogier holds this unjustly.

They say that Ogier holds 9 bovates of land in Haconby unjustly because Gilbert de Ghent ought to have them through Ulf Fenman, his predecessor, who had them TRE.

The wapentake says that Healfdene's land in Dunsby [near Bourne], which Bishop Remigius holds and the Abbot of Peterborough claims, did not belong to St Peter TRE.

In Rippingale, Ogier holds 1 carucate of land, which the wapentake says belonged to Robert de Tosny's predecessor.

They say that Osfram's land in Kirkby Underwood was not in Arnbiorn's soke. They say that St Guthlac's land, which Ogier holds in Rippingale, was the monk's demesne farm, and that Abbot Ulfkil granted it to Hereweard at farm, as might be agreed between them each year;

but the abbot took possession of it again before Hereweard fled the country, because he had not kept the agreement.

They say that the soke of 3 carucates of land in Dowsby, which Osfram had in pledge, and [which] was afterwards redeemed, ought to belong to Rippingale, St Guthlac's manor, and they say that it was thus TRE, and afterwards until Guy de Craon took possession of it.

The claims which Drogo de la Beuvriere makes upon Morcar's lands they leave to the king's decision.

They say that Robert of Stafford claims Karli's land in Billingborough unjustly, because the same Karli held it of Ralph the staller.

They say that Wulfric Wild's land in Walcot [near Folkingham] Hundred ought to belong half to the Bishop of Durham, and half to a certain man, Wulfgeat, who has it by the king's alms.

Ralph Paynel claims soke and soke [sic] over Ælfric's land which Guy de Craon has in Osbournby. The wapentake says that the same Ralph ought to have 1 horse from this land when he goes on a military expedition.

In Pickworth are 2 carucates of land which belonged to Auti, and now belong to Kolsveinn. These are not enumerated in any hundred, nor have they [their] like in Lincolnshire.

Touching Thorir's land in Old Somerby, which Walter d'Aincourt has, they say that TRE they saw that the same Thorir had it, but in the very year in which the same king died, Northmann held it in pledge. The men of the wapentake do not know on what condition, for they did not see him do any service for it.

They say that the tithe and other customary dues of the church in respect of Thorir's land in Ropsley Hundred belong to the Church of St Peter.

Walter d'Aincourt claims the service of Guy de Raimbeaucourt's men as belonging to the manor [of] Syston, but he does not have a just claim.

In Welby Hundred, Drogo claims 4 carucates of land against Guy de Craon; but the Wapentake bears witness in Guy's favour that they are rightly his.

They say that Walter d'Aincourt ought not to have the half-carucate of land which he claims against the king in Belton [near Grantham], but [that] the king [ought to have it].

In the same Belton [near Grantham], Kolgrimr ought to have 1 bovate of land of Algar's land which Guy de Craon has, but the soke belongs to Guy in 'Towthorpe' [in Londonthorpe].

They say that TRE Leofric Cild withheld the warnode of 10 acres of meadow in the same Belton [near Grantham]. Kolgrimr claims the soke of these 10 acres.

They say that the whole of the customary dues of the church and tithe of 'Westhorpe' [in Old Somerby] belong to the Church of Grantham, as Bishop Osmund claims.

In Honington Hundred, Gilbert claims the soke of 2½ carucates of land through Ulf his predecessor; but the wapentake says that Ivo ought to have the soke just as Azur his predecessor had it of Ulf.

Robert of Stafford claims 2 mills which are in Barkston, and Kolsveinn claims the same. The wapentake says that they belong to Marston, and their soke to Grantham. In Drayton Hundred, Count Alan has 1 carucate of land of St Benedict of Ramsey. Bishop Remigius claims it, and the wapentake bears witness in his favour that Wulfwig his predecessor held it of St Benedict TRE.

Guy de Craon holds 4 bovates of land in Drayton and 10 bovates in Bicker Hundred of the land of Æthelstan son of Godram. Count Alan claims these, and Algar his man has given to the king's barons a pledge to prove by ordeal or by combat that Æthelstan himself was not seised of these 14 bovates TRE. On the other hand, Ælfstan of Frampton, Guy's man, has given his pledge to prove that he was seised of them with sake and soke, and Guy was seised of them from the time of Ralph the staller until now, and holds them now.

The men of Holland bear witness that in 'Stenning' [in Swineshead] Healfdene, the predecessor of Bishop Remigius, had 3 carucates of land quit, which Count Alan has now, and unjustly, because the bishop was seised of them.

Alvred of Lincoln claims 1 carucate of land in Quadring against Count Alan. The men of Holland agree with the same Alvred, both because it belonged to his predecessor and [because] he himself was seised of it in the time of Earl Ralph.

Gyrth, Count Alan's man, has given a pledge to maintain that Count Alan's predecessor had 6 bovates of land with sake and soke | in Gosberton |, and therefore Guy de Craon does not claim them justly.

The men of Holland bear witness [that] the soke of Ketil's church of Long Sutton belongs to the king's manor of Tydd St Mary.

Six carucates of land which the king's officers claim in Holbeach belonged to the king's manor of Gedney. Count Alan has them now as 1 manor by the king's gift.

[Blank in MS]

[Blank in MS]

In the geld of the city of York are 84 carucates of land, which TRE paid, each of them, as much geld as 1 house in the city. Of these, the archbishop has 6 carucates [belonging] to the farm of his hall.

In Osbaldwick, the archbishop 6 carucates. In Murton [in Osbaldwick], 4 carucates.

In Stockton on the Forest, the archbishop 3 carucates. In the same place, 3 carucates. In Sandburn, 3 carucates.

In Heworth, 3 carucates. In the same place, Count Alan 3 carucates. In Gate Fulford, Count Alan 10 carucates.

In Clifton [near York], the archbishop 8½ carucates. In the same place, Count Alan 9½ carucates. In the same place, the archbishop 37 acres of meadow.

In Rawcliffe, Seaxfrith had 2 carucates. In the same place, the king 1 carucate. In Overton, Count Alan 5 carucates.

In Skelton [near York], the archbishop 3½ carucates. In the

same place, the king 2 carucates and 6 bovates. In the same place, Count Alan 2 carucates and 6 bovates.

In 'Mortona' [in Overton], Arnketil had 3 carucates. In Wiggington, the archbishop 3 carucates. Within the circuit of the city, 3 carucates. Thorfinnr and Thorkil held them.

'SKYRACK' WAPENTAKE

In OTLEY, a manor, Pool, Guiseley, Hawksworth, and another Hawksworth [Thorpe, in Hawksworth], Baildon, Menston, Burley in Wharfedale [and] Ilkley, the archbishop 60 carucates and 6 bovates.

Also in "GEREBURG" WAPENTAKE are these BERE-WICKS of Otley: 'Stubham' [in Ilkley], Farnley [in Otley], Middleton [in Ilkley], Nether Timble, Denton, "Estone" [in Lindley], Clifton [near Newall] [and] 'Bikerton' [in Newall with Clifton]. All together, 20 |carucates|. The archbishop [has] these.

In East Rigton, 3 carucates. In Weardley, 4 carucates. Half of these belongs to Gospatric.

In Kippax and Ledston, Allerton Bywater, [Great and Litle] Preston, Swillington, Garforth, 'Skelton' [in Leeds], Coldcotes, Colton [in Temple Newsam], Austhorpe, Manston, Barwick in Elmet, Kiddal, Potterton, Parlington [and] Gipton, Ilbert [has] all together 69½ carucates of land.

In Garforth, Ilbert 7 carucates. In Swillington, the same Ilbert 9 carucates. In Sturton, Ilbert 5 carucates.

In Shippen and Sturton, Ilbert 4 carucates. In Kiddal and Parlington, Ilbert 3 carucates.

In 'Cowthwaite' [in Aberford], Ilbert 2 carucates. In Halton [in Temple Newsam], Ilbert 6 carucates. In Seacroft, Ilbert 8 carucates.

In Thorner, Ilbert 8 carucates. In Birkby Hill and 'Wetecroft' [in Thorner], Ilbert 2 carucates.

In Chapel Allerton and Gledhow, Ilbert 6 carucates. In Gipton and Colton [in Temple Newsam], Ilbert 4½ carucates.

In Shadwell, the king 6 carucates. In Newsam Green, Ilbert 8 carucates. In 'Thorpe Stapleton' [in Leeds], Ilbert 4 carucates.

In Leeds, Ilbert 10 carucates and 6 bovates. In Headingley, Ilbert 7 carucates. In [East and West] Morton, the king 4 carucates.

In "Snitertun", Ilbert 8 carucates. In Wothersome, the king 4 carucates. In Bardsey, the king 2 carucates.

In Riddlesden, the king 1 carucate. In Harewood and 'Newhall' [in Harewood], the king 10 carucates.

In East Keswick, the king 5 carucates. In Stockton and 'Newhall' [in Harewood], the king 6 carucates and 6 bovates.

In Lofthouse [in Harewood], the king 2 carucates. In Stub House, the king 1 carucate. In Alwoodley, the king 5 carucates.

In Wike, the king 6 carucates. In Bramhope, Gilbert Tison 8 carucates. In East Carlton, Robert Malet 3 carucates.

In Horsforth, the king 6 carucates. In Rawdon, the king 3 carucates. In Yeadon, the king 4 carucates.

In Bingley and Baildon, Eldwick, Marley, Cottingley, 'Halton' [in Bingley] [and] Micklethwaite, Erneis 12 caru-

cates. In Ilkley, William de Percy 3 carucates. In Adel, the Count of Mortain 1½ carucates.

In Arthington, the Count of Mortain 3 carucates and 2½ bovates. In Cookridge, the Count of Mortain 3 carucates.

In Burden Head, the Count of Mortain 2 carucates. In Eccup, the Count of Mortain 1 carucate.

BARKSTON WAPENTAKE

In Sherburn in Elmet, with [its] Berewicks, the archbishop 100 carucates of land, less 4.

In Ulleskelf, with [its] Berewicks, the archbishop 13 carucates, less 1 bovate.

In Clifford, the Count of Mortain 6 carucates. In Bramham and 'Monk Hay' [in Barwick in Elmet], Toulston, Newton Kyme [and] Oglethorpe, the Count of Mortain 18 carucates. In Hazelwood, William de Percy 3 carucates.

In "Saxhale", William de Percy 4 carucates. In Stutton, William de Percy 1½ carucates. In the same place, Osbern d'Arques 1½ carucates.

In Saxton, Stutton, Grimston [in Kirby Wharfe], Towton and Kirkby Wharfe, Ilbert 15 carucates and 2 bovates. In Lead, the same man 2 carucates. In Burton, Brayton and Thorpe Willoughby, the same man 3 carucates and 6 bovates. In "Hunchilhuses" [in Sherburn in Elmet], Ilbert 1 carucate. In Barkston, the same man 1 carucate.

In [Church and Little] Fenton, the same man 3 bovates. In Ryther, the same man 2 carucates. In Hambleton, the same man 3 carucates.

In Birkin, the same man 1 carucate. In Carlton [near Snaith], the king 6 carucates. In Camblesforth, Earnwine 1 carucate.

In Newton [in Ledsham], Ilbert 3 carucates. In Toulston, Newton Kyme and Oglethorpe, Osbern d'Arques 7 carucates and 6 bovates. In Grimston [in Kirkby Wharfe], Ilbert 1 carucate and 5 bovates. In "Neuhuse" [in Ulleskelf], Ilbert 2 carucates.

In Kirkby Wharfe, Ilbert half a carucate. In North Milford, Ilbert 2 carucates. In Drax, Little Airmyn, Camblesforth and Barlow, Ralph Paynel 5 carucates and 1 bovate.

In Conisbrough, with [its] Berewicks, William de Warenne 91 carucates of land and 3 bovates and 15 acres.

In Laughton-en-le-Morthen, Throapham, Dinnington, South Anston, North Anston, Thorpe Salvin, Wales, Slade Hooton [and] Newhall, Roger de Bully 54 carucates of land.

In Wadworth, Roger de Bully 12 carucates. In Stainton [near Tickhill], Roger de Bully 1½ carucates.

In Dadsley, Stainton [near Tickhill] and Hellaby, Roger de Bully 8 carucates. In Wickersley, the same man 4 carucates.

In Maltby [near Rotherham] and Hellaby, the same Roger 4½ carucates. In Brinsworth, Roger de Bully 1 carucate and 3 bovates.

In the same place, William de Percy 3 carucates and 5 bovates. In Tinsley, Roger de Bully 8 carucates and 1 bovate.

In the same place, the king 7 bovates. In Greasbrough, Roger de Bully 3 carucates. In "Grimeshou" [? in Grimesthorpe], Roger de Bully 3½ carucates.

In Mexborough, Roger de Bully 5 carucates. In Newhill,

Hooton Roberts [and] Old Denaby, Roger de Bully 6 carucates.

In Adwick upon Dearne, Roger de Bully 2½ carucates. In Barnburgh and Bilham, Roger de Bully 6 carucates.

In Ecclesfield, Roger de Bully 4 carucates. In Wath upon Dearne, Swinton [near Rotherham] and Wentworth, Roger de Bully 7 carucates and 2 bovates.

In Hoyland Nether, the same Roger 2 carucates. In Wombwell and West Melton and "Toftes" [in Wombwell], the same Roger 2 carucates.

In the same place, the king 2 carucates and 1 bovate. In the same place, Walter d'Aincourt 4 carucates and 2 bovates. In Rawmarsh, Walter d'Aincourt 4 carucates.

In Hickleton, Earl Aubrey 5 carucates and 5 bovates. In the same place, the same Aubrey 1 carucate and 5 bovates. In Darfield, the king 4 carucates.

In High Melton, Roger de Bully 8 carucates. In 'Wildthorpe' [in Sprotbrough], the same Roger 2 carucates. In Cadeby, Roger de Bully 3 carucates.

In the same place, Earl Aubrey 2 carucates and 1 bovate. In Sportbrough and Cusworth and Balby,. 8 carucates.

In the same place, the king 1 carucate. In West Melton, Hoyland Nether, Thorpe Hesley, Wentworth and Brampton [in Wath upon Dearne], the king 5½ carucates. In Wath upon Dearne, West Melton, Wentworth and "Eldeberge" [in Wath upon Dearne], the king 7 carucates and 5 bovates. In West Melton, the king 1 carucate and 5 bovates.

In Brampton [in Wath upon Dearne], Thorpe Hesley and "Eldeberge" [in Wath upon Dearne], the king 3 carucates and 1 bovate. In Billingley, the king half a carucate.

In Wentworth, the king 1 carucate and 2 bovates. In Little Houghton, Roger de Bully 2½ carucates.

In Billingley, Roger de Bully 5 carucates. In Bolton-upon-Dearne, the same man 2½ carucates. In the same place, William de Percy 2½ carucates.

In Goldthorpe and Thurnscoe, Roger de Bully 4 carucates and 6 bovates. In Marr, the same man 4½ carucates.

In the same place, the Count of Mortain 5 bovates. In Hexthorpe, Doncaster, Balby, Littleworth, Warmsworth, Loversall, Austerfield, Auckley [and] Auckley [sic], the Count of Mortain 22½ carucates. In Branton and Cantley, Geoffrey Alselin 14 carucates and 1½ bovates.

In Armthorpe, Earnwine 5 carucates. In Kirk Bramwith, Roger de Bully 1½ carucates.

In Barnby Dun, the Count of Mortain 2 carucates and 2 bovates. In the same place, William de Percy 1 carucate and 1 bovate. In the same place, Roger de Bully 1 carucate and 1 bovate.

In Long Sandall, the Count of Mortain 6 carucates and 5 bovates. In Hooton Levitt, the Count of Mortain 3 carucates and 6 bovates.

In Old Edlington, Braithwell and Doncaster, William de Percy 3 carucates and 6 bovates.

In Thrybergh, William de Percy 4 carucates. In Dalton [in Rotherham], William de Percy 2 carucates and 6 bovates. In Rotherham, the Count of Mortain 5 carucates.

In Kimberworth, Roger de Bully 6 carucates. In Swinton [near Rotherham], Gilbert Tison 3 carucates and 6 bovates.

In Hampole, Roger de Bully 3 carucates. In Frickley and Stotfold, Roger de Bully 6 bovates. In Hooton Pagnell, the Count of Mortain 10 carucates.

In Brodsworth and Pickburn, Roger de Bully 5½ carucates. In the same place, the Count of Mortain 2½ carucates.

In Todwick, the Count of Mortain 12 carucates. In Great Houghton, the Count of Mortain 6 carucates. In Thurnscoe, Clayton [near Thurnscoe], 'Deightonby' [in Thurnscoe] and Stotfold, the Count of Mortain 6 carucates and 5½ acres. In the same place, William de Percy 6 bovates.

In Goldthorpe, the king 1 carucate and 2 bovates. In Whiston and Handsworth, the Count of Mortain 9½ carucates.

In Treeton, the Count of Mortain 3 carucates. In AUGHTON [near Aston], the Count of Mortain 2 carucates and 6 bovates. In Wales, the Count of Mortain 1 carucate.

In Aston, the Count of Mortain 2 carucates and 2 bovates. In Ulley, the Count of Mortain 4 carucates. In Brampton en le Morthen, the Count of Mortain 6 carucates.

In Wheatley, Doncaster, Adwick le Street, 'Skynythorp' [in Sprotbrough], 'Langthwaite' [in Adwick le Street], Bentley [near Doncaster] and Kirk Sandall, the Count of Mortain 15 carucates. [In Holdworth, Roger de Bully 2 carucates. *Tickhill and Strafforth [c.1300]*

[Folio 379V: WEST RIDING]

In 'Hallam', Countess Judith 29 carucates. In Attercliffe, the same countess 3 carucates. In Sheffield, the same countess 3 carucates.

In 'Waldershelf' [in Bolsterstone], the king 1 carucate. In Ughill and Worrall and Wadsley, Roger de Bully 1 carucate and 6 bovates.

In South Elmsall and Frickley, Moorthorpe and South Kirkby, Ilbert 11 carucates of land.

'OSGODCROSS' WAPENTAKE

In Arksey, Roger de Bully 2 carucates and 6 bovates. In Bentley [near Doncaster], Roger de Bully 2 carucates and 2 bovates.

In Adwick le Streer, Roger de Bully 7 carucates and 2 bovates. In the same place, the Count of Mortain 2 bovates. In Norton [near Campsall], Ilbert 5 carucates.

In Scawsby, Roger de Bully 5 carucates. In Campsall, Ilbert 2½ carucates.

In Skellow, Ilbert 4 carucates. In Burghwallis, Ilbert 3 carucates. In Owston, Ilbert 4 carucates.

In "Neuhuse" [in Campsall] and Sutton [near Campsall], Ilbert 2 carucates. In Skelbrooke, Ilbert 3 carucates. In Stubbs, Ilbert 1 carucate.

In Walden Stubbs, Ilbert 3 carucates and half a bovate. In Thorpe Audlin, Ilbert 6 carucates and 3 bovates.

In Badsworth, Upton [in Badsworth] and Rogerthorpe, Ilbert 9 carucates and 5 bovates.

In [Kirk and Little] Smeaton [in Womersley], Ilbert 4 carucates. In Womersley, Ilbert 6 carucates.

In Stapleton [in Darrington], Ilbert 4 carucates. In Darrington, Ilbert 6 carucates. In Hessle [in Wragby], Ilbert half a carucate.

In [High and Low] Ackworth, Ilbert 6 carucates. In Glass

Houghton, Ilbert 6 carucates. In Ferrybridge, Ilbert 5 carucates.

In North Featherstone and Purston Jaglin, West Hardwick and Nostell, Ilbert 16 carucates.

In Wheldale and Water Fryston, Ilbert 7 carucates. In Knottingley, Ilbert 4 carucates.

In Beal, Ilbert 4 carucates. In Kellington, Ilbert 2 carucates. In North Elmsall, Ilbert 8 carucates.

In Roall and [High and Low] Eggborough, Ilbert 4 carucates. In Kellington and [High and Low] Eggborough, Ilbert 4 carucates.

In Tanshelf and Pontefract, the king 16 carucates, and, in alms, 2 carucates of land.

In Hensall, the king 4 carucates. In Whitley, the king 2 carucates. In Minsthorpe, Ilbert 2 carucates.

STAINCROSS WAPENTAKE

In Kinsley, Ilbert 3 carucates. In Hemsworth, Ilbert 4 carucates. In Barnby [in Cawthorne, near Barnsley], the king 2 carucates.

In Silkstone, the king 1½ carucates. In Adlingfleet, Geoffrey de la Guerche 6 carucates.

In Brierley and South Hiendley, Ilbert 6 carucates. In Royston, Ilbert 4 carucates.

In Dodworth, Ilbert 5 carucates. In Cawthorne [near Barnsley], Ilbert 3 carucates. In Silkstone, Ilbert 3 carucates.

In Penistone, 1 carucate and 2 bovates. In Darton, 1 carucate. In Barugh, Ilbert 3 carucates.

In Kexbrough, Ilbert 2½ carucates. In High Hoyland, Ilbert 2 carucates.

In "Sactun" [in Woolley], the king 12 carucates. In Shafton and Carlton [near Barnsley], Ilbert 18 carucates.

In Worsborough, Ilbert 5½ carucates. In Pilley, the Count of Mortain 2 carucates. In Wortley, the king 4 carucates.

In Wortley, the Count of Mortain 1 carucate. In Tankersley, the Count of Mortain 1½ carucates.

In Thurgoland, Ilbert 4½ carucates. In Stainborough, Ilbert 2 carucates. In Hunshelf, Ilbert 3 carucates.

In Thurlstone and Ingbirchworth, Ilbert 6 carucates. In Upper Cumberworth, Ilbert 1 carucate.

In [Lower and Upper] Denby [near Penistone], Ilbert 3 carucates. In Skelmanthorpe, Ilbert 3 carucates. In Clayton West, Ilbert 3 carucates.

In Monk Bretton, Ilbert 1½ carucates. In Oxspring and Roughbirchworth, Ilbert 2 carucates.

In Hoyland Swaine, Ilbert 1 carucate and 1 bovate. In Darton, Ilbert 4 carucates. In Notton, Ilbert 6 carucates.

In 'Keresforth' [in Barnsley] and Barnsley, 5 carucates. In Chevet, Ilbert 1½ carucates.

In Cold Hiendley, Ilbert 4 carucates. In the same place and [in] Ryhill, Ilbert 4 carucates.

AGBRIGG WAPENTAKE

In Warmfield and [its] Berewick, the archbishop 9 carucates. In Methley, Ilbert 8 carucates.

In Whitwood, Ilbert 8 carucates. In Ackton, Ilbert 3 carucates. In "Westrebi" [in Altofts], Ilbert 6 carucates.

In Normanton, the king 10 carucates. In Old Snydale,

Ilbert 6 carucates. In Walton [near Wakefield], the king 8 carucates.

In Crofton, Ilbert 4 carucates. In Sandal Magna, the king 6 carucates. In Flockton, Ilbert 3 carucates.

In Upper Denby [in Upper Whitley], Ilbert 3 carucates. In Emley, 3 carucates. In Thornhill, Ilbert 4 carucates.

In Lower Whitley, Ilbert 5 carucates. In Lepton, Ilbert 3 carucates. In Kirkheaton, Ilbert 3 carucates.

In Dalton [near Huddersfield], Ilbert 2 carucates. In Almondbury, Ilbert 4 carucates. In Farnley Tyas, Ilbert 3 carucates.

In Honley and Meltham, Ilbert 4 carucates. In Shepley and Shelley, 3 carucates.

In Wakefield, the king 40 carucates and 3 bovates of land and the third part of 1 bovate. In Crigglestone, the king 1 carucate and 2 bovates.

In West Bretton, the king 1½ carucates. In Horbury, the same man 2 carucates and 7 bovates. In Earlsheaton, the same man 1 carucate.

In Ossett, the same man 3½ carucates. In Stanley, the same man 3 carucates. In 'Shitlington' [in Thornhill], the same man 3 carucates.

In the two Holmes [Holme, near Holmfirth, and Yateholm] and Austonley and Upperthong, the king 2 carucates. In Lower Cumberworth, the same man 1 carucate.

In Kirkburton, the same man 3 carucates. In 'Northcrosselande' [in Huddersfield], the same man 1 carucate. In Upper Hopton, Ilbert 2 carucates. In Huddersfield, Ilbert 6 carucates.

In Cartworth and Hepworth, Wooldale, Foulston and Thurstonland, the king 6 carucates.

In Bradley, Ilbert 2 carucates. In Lindley, Ilbert 2 carucates. In Golcar, Ilbert half a carucate. In Quarmby, Ilbert 2 carucates.

In the other Crosland [South Crosland], Ilbert 2 carucates.

MORLEY WAPENTAKE

In Morley, Ilbert 6 carucates. In Ardsley East, Ilbert 5 carucates and 3 bovates. In Beeston [in Leeds], Ilbert 6 carucates.

In Rothwell and Carlton [in Lofthouse, [near Wakefield], Thorpe on the Hill and Middleton [in Leeds], Ilbert 24 carucates.

In Hunslet, Ilbert 6 carucates. In 'Reestones' [in Armley] and Armley, Ilbert 6 carucates. In Bramley [in Armley], Ilbert 4 carucates.

In Calverley and Farsley, Ilbert 3 carucates. In Pudsey, Ilbert 8 carucates. In Tong, Ilbert 4 carucates.

In Drighlington, Ilbert 4 carucates. In Gomersal and 2 Berewicks, Ilbert 14 carucates.

In Bolton [in Bradford], Ilbert 4 carucates. In Bradford and 6 Berewicks, Ilbert 15 carucates. In Bowling, Ilbert 4 carucates.

In Chellow, Thornton, Allerton, Clayton [near Bradford] and Wibsey, Ilbert 10 carucates.

In Shipley, Ilbert 3 carucates. In 'North Bierley' [in Bradford], Ilbert 4 carucates. In Wyke, Ilbert 4 carucates. In Cleckheaton, Ilbert 6 carucates.

In Clifton [near Brighouse], Ilbert 12 carucates. In Mirfield, Ilbert 6 carucates. In Dewsbury, the king 3 carucates. In Batley, Ilbert 5 carucates.

In Liversedge, Ilbert 4 carucates. In Hartshead, Ilbert 2 carucates. In Elland, Ilbert 3 carucates. In Southowram, Ilbert 3 carucates.

In Hipperholme, the king 2 carucates; in Northowram, 2 carucates; in Shelf, 1 carucate; in Stainland, 2 carucates.

In Old Lindley, half a carucates; in Fixby, 1 carucate; in Rastrick, 1 carucate; in Eccleshill, 3 carucates.

In Franley [in Armley], 3 carucates; in West Ardsley, 4 carucates and 5 bovates; in Greetland, half a carucate.

In Hanging Heaton, 1 carucate. All these [belong] to the soke of Wakefield.

AINSTY WAPENTAKE

In Bishopthorpe, Hugh fitzBaldric 5 carucates and 7 bovates. In the same place, the king 2 carucates and 1 bovate. In Middlethorpe, Christ's Church, Richard fitzErfast 2 carucates. In the same place, Robert Malet 1 carucate.

In Copmanthorpe, Erneis 2 carucates and 2 bovates. In the same place, Count W. 3 carucates and 6 bovates.

In Acaster Malbis, Robert Malet 4 carucates. In another Acaster [Ascaster Selby], Count Alan 6 bovates. In the same place, Robert Malet 1 carucate and 2 bovates. In the same place, Erneis 5 bovates.

In the same place, the king 11 bovates. In Appleton Roebuck, Osbern d'Arques 12 carucates. In Bolton Percy, William de Percy 8 carucates. In Steeton [in Bolton Percy], Osbern d'Arques 6 carucates.

In the same place, Earnwine 1 carucate. In Pallathorpe, William de Percy 2 carucates. In the same place, Osbern d'Arques 2 carucates. In the same place, the Count of Mortain 6 bovates. In Oxton, Osber d'Arques 4 carucates.

In Colton [near York], Osbern d'Arques 4½ carucates. In Ouston, William de Percy 3 carucates. In "Malchetone" [in Tadcaster East], William de Percy 4 carucates.

In 'Hackerby' [in Healaugh] and Healaugh, William de Percy 3 carucates. In Hornington, William de Percy 3 carucates. In the same place, Osbern d'Arques 1 bovate.

In Catterton, Osbern d'Arques 2 carucates. In Bilbrough, Christ's Church, Richard fitzErfast 8 carucates. In Thorpe Arch, Osbern d'Arques 3 carucates.

In Healaugh and the two Wighills [Wighill and Wighill Park], Geoffrey Alselin 18 carucates. In Walton [near Wetherby], Osbern d'Arques 9 carucates.

In Bilton [near Wetherby], Osbern d'Arques 9 carucates. In Long Marston and Wilstrop, Osbern d'Arques 23 carucates.

In Hutton Wandersley, Osbern d'Arques 6 carucates. In Askham Richard, Osbern d'Arques 6 carucates. In Nether Poppleton, Osbern d'Arques 2½ carucates.

In another Poppleton [Upper Poppleton], the archbishop 8 carucates. In the same place, Osbern d'Arques 3½ carucates. In 'Scagglethorpe' [in Moor Monkton], Osbern d'Arques 3 carucates.

In Moor Monkton, Christ's Church, Richard fitzErfast 9

carucates. In Hessay, Osbern d'Arques 2 carucates and 2 bovates.

In the same place, Richard fitzErfast 1 carucate and 6 bovates. In Knapton [near York], Christ's Church, Richard fitzErfast 3 carucates. In the same place, Osbern d'Arques 2 carucates.

In Acomb, the archbishop 14½ carucates. In the same place, the king 2 carucates. In Rufforth, Osbern d'Arques 4 carucates.

In Christ's Church near the city, Richard fitzErfast half a carucate and 3 crofts. In "Mulhede", the king 1 carucate.

In "Bithen" [in Middlethorpe], 1 bovate. In Cowthorpe, William de Percy 4 carucates. In Bickerton, Gospatric 8 carucates.

In Askham Bryan, Count Alan 8 carucates. Near the city, the archbishop 15 carucates of land and 60 acres of meadow.

BURGHSHIRE WAPENTAKE

In Nun Monkton, Osbern d'Arques 8 carucates. In Thorpe Underwood, Ralph Paynel 1 carucate. In Thorpe Hill [near Whixley], Hugh fitzBaldric 7 carucates.

In the same place, Gospatric 1 carucate. In Widdington, the king †1† carucate. In Kirby [in Little Ouseburn], Osbern d'Arques 6 carucates.

In Great Ouseburn, the king 12 carucates. In another Ouseburn [Little Ouseburn], the king 8 carucates. In [Lower and Upper] Dunsforth, Erneis 3 carucates.

In the same place, the king 3 carucates. In Branton Green, Erneis 4 carucates. In the same place, the king 5 carucates. In Marton [near Boroughbridge], Gospatric 12 carucates.

In Grafton, the archbishop 3 carucates. In the same place, Erneis 3 carucates. In the same place, the king 6 carucates. In 'Thornborough' [in Allerton Mauleverer], Gospatric 3 carucates.

[Folio 380: WEST RIDING]

In Whixley, Osbern d'Arques 13 carucates. In the same place, Gospatric 5 carucates. In Elwicks, the king 4 carucates. In Cattal, Osbern d'Arques 5 carucates.

In Green Hammerton, Osbern d'Arques 6 carucates. In another Hammerton [Kirk Hammerton], Osbern d'Arques 8 carucates. In another Cattal [Old Thornville], Erneis 3 carucates.

In Hunsingore, the Count of Mortain 4 carucates and 3 bovates. In the same place, Erneis 5 carucates and 3 bovates. In Goldsborough [near Knaresborough], Ralph Paynel 8 carucates.

In Ribston ['Great Ribston' and Little Ribston], Ralph Paynel 4 carucates. In the same place, the king 1½ carucates. In the same place, Erneis 1 carucate. In the same place, William de Percy 1½ carucates.

In Hopperton, the king 3 carucates. In the same place, Erneis 1 carucate. In the same place, Osbern d'Arques 1 carucate. In Allerton Mauleverer, the king 3½ carucates.

In the same place, Gospatric 1½ carucates. In Flaxby, Erneis 4 carucates. In Clareton, the king 2 carucates.

In the same place, Gospatric 3 carucates. In Arkendale, the

king 1 carucate. In the same place Erneis 4 carucates. In Loftus Hill, the king 4 carucates.

In the same place, Erneis 1 carucate. In Aldborough, the king 20 carucates. In Minskip, the king 8 carucates.

In Staveley, Gospatric 8 carucates. In "Hilton" [? in Copgrove], the king 6 carucates. In Copgrove, Erneis 6 carucates.

In Burton Leonard, the king 6 carucates. In Farnham, the king 3 carucates. In the same place, Gospatric 3 carucates. In 'Thorpe juxta Scotton' [in Farnham], the king 2 carucates.

In Walkingham Hall, the king 3 carucates. In Ferrensby, the king 6 carucates. In Scriven, the king 6 carucates.

In Knaresborough, the king 6 carucates. In Scotton [in Farnham], Gilbert Tison 4 carucates. In Scotton [in Farnham], the king 2 carucates.

In Brearton, the king 6 carucates. In Susacres, Osbern d'Arques 2 carucates. In South Stainley, the king 4 carucates.

In Cayton [in South Stainley], the king 2 carucates. In Markenfield, William de Percy 5 carucates. In 'Aismunderby' [in Littlethorpe], William de Percy 2 carucates.

In Aldfield, Gospatric 2 carucates. In the same place, the king half a carucate. In the same place, the archbishop 2 bovates. In Clotherholme, William de Percy 1½ carucates.

In Studley Royal, Gospatric 2½ carucates. In the same place, the king 7 bovates. In the same place, William de Percy 13 bovates.

In Winksley, Gospatric 3 carucates. In Laverton, the same Gospatric 2½ carucates. In the same place, the king 3½ carucates.

In Kirkby Malzeard, Gospatric 5 carucates. In Grewelthorpe, the same Gospatric 5 carucates. In Grewelthorpe, the same place Gospatric 2 carucates. In Azerley, the same Gospatric 5 ½ carucates.

In the same place, the king half a carucate. In [High and Low] Bramley, Gospatric 2 carucates. In Carlesmoor, the same Gospatric 2 carucate. In Swetton, the same Gospatric 2 carucates.

In Kex Moor, the same Gospatric 2 carucates. In 'Poppleton' [in Fountains Earth], the king 1 carucate. In the same place, Gospatric 3 carucates. In Whipley, Erneis half a carucate. In the same place, the king 1½ carucates.

In Brimham, Gospatric 3 carucates and 2 bovates. In the same place, Gilbert Tison 2 bovates. In the same place, Erneis half a carucate.

In Ripley, Ralph Paynel 4½ carucates. In the same place, the king 1½ carucates. In Heathfield, Berengar de Tosny 2 carucates.

In Bewerley, Erneis 3 carucates. In Dacre, Erneis 3 carucates. In 'Beeston' [in Fewston], the king 4 carucates.

In Fewston, the king 3 carucates. In 'Ellesworth' [in Norwood], 'Clifton' [in Norwood] and Timble, the king 5½ carucates.

In Birstwith, the king 1 carucate. In the same place, Gospatric 1 carucate. In Felliscliffe, the king 3 carucates. In Rowden, the king 2 carucates.

In Killinghall, the king 1 carucate. In Beamsley, Erneis half a carucate. In the same place, the king 6 bovates. In the same place Gilbert Tison 6 bovates.

In Nesfield, William de Percy 3 carucates. In Addingham, the king 1 carucate. In the same place, Gilbert Tison 1 carucates. In Askwith, Gospatric 2 carucates.

In the same place, William de Percy 3 carucates. In the same place, Berengar de Tosny 1 carucate. In Weston, Berengar de Tosny 5 carucates. In Leathley, William de Percy 3 carucates and 7 bovates.

In the same place, the king 2½ carucates. In the same place, Gilbert Tison 1 carucate. In Weeton [near Harewood], the king 5½ carucates. In the same place, Gospatric 2½ carucates.

In Dunkeswick, the king 4 carucates. In Kearby, William de Percy 4 carucates. In Barrowby, Erneis 3 carucates. In the same place, William de Percy 1 carucate.

In Kirkby Overblow, William de Percy 3 carucates. In 'Walton Head' [in Kirkby Overblow] and 'Tetherfield' [in Kirkby Overblow], William de Percy 4 carucates. In Sicklinghall, the king 6 carucates.

In Addlethorpe, Gospatric 4 carucates. In the same place, the king 1 carucate. In North Rigton, the king 2 carucates. In the same place, Gilbert Tison 2 carucates.

In Stainburn, the king 5 carucates. In Beckwith, Gilbert Tison 3 carucates. In Rossett, the king and Gilbert Tison 3 carucates.

In Bilton [near Harrogate], the king 3½ carucates. In the same place, Gilbert Tison 3½ carucates. In Rudfarlington, William de Percy 2 carucates and 2 bovates.

In the same place, Gilbert Tison 2 carucates and 6 bovates. In Plompton, William de Percy 2 carucates. In the same place, Gilbert Tison 2 carucates. In "Little" Braham, Erneis 4 carucates.

In "Great" Braham, William de Percy 4 carucates. In the same place, Gilbert Tison 4 carucates. In the same place, Erneis 1 carucate. In Spofforth, William de Percy 3 carucates.

In 'Crauwel' [in Spofforth], William de Percy 2 carucates. In Newsome, Erneis 2 carucates. In Linton [in Spofforth], William de Percy 8½ carucates.

In Wetherby, William de Percy 3 carucates. In the same place, Erneis 2 carucates. In [Kirk and North] Deighton, Ralph Paynel 12 carucates. In the same place, Erneis 4 carucates.

In Ingmanthorpe, the Count of Mortain 1½ carucates. In the same place, Erneis 1 ½ carucates. In Cowthorpe, William de Percy 3 carucates.

In RIPON, the League of St Wilfrid, the archbishop. In Littlethorpe, the archbishop 4 carucates; in "Estuuic" [in Newby, near Ripon], 2 carucates; in Nidd, 5 carucates.

In Westwick, 4 carucates; in Bishop Monkton, 8 carucates; in Killinghall, 1 carucate; in Bishop Thornton, 2 carucates.

In Sawley, 2 carucates; in Eavestone, 2 carucates; in Wilsill, 2 carucates; in 'Knayser' [in Skelding], 1½ carucates; in Studley Roger, 4 carucates.

In Grantley, 2½ carucates; in 'How' [in Markington], 3 carucates; in Markington, 4 ½ carucates; in "Stanlai" [in North Stainley] and Sutton Grange, 8 carucates; in North Stainley and Sleningford, 6½ carucates.

In 'Knayser' [in Skelding], Gospatric half a carucate. In Castley, Everard, a man of William de Percy, 2 carucates.

HALLIKELD WAPENTAKE

In Nunwick, the archbishop 5 carucates; in "Suthauuic", 5 carucates; in Great Givendale [near Ripon], 11 carucates.

In Skelton [near Boroughbridge], 8 carucates; in Howgrave, 2 carucates; in Copt Hewick, 2 carucates; in "Hashundebi" [in Sharow], 2 carucates.

In Hutton Conyers, 2 bovates; in Markington and South Stainley, 1 carucate; in Bridge Hewick, 3 carucates. The archbishop [has] these.

In HUTTON CONYERS, the Bishop of Durham 12 carucates; in Norton Conyers, 6 carucates; in Sutton Howgrave, 3 carucates; in Howgrave, 2 carucates.

In Holme [in Pickhill], 6 carucates; in "Torp" [in Pickhill], 1 carucate. These [are] the Bishop of Durham's [and belong] to Hutton Conyers.

In Skelton, Gospatric 1 carucate. In Langthorpe [in Kirby Hill], 6 carucates; in Kirby Hill, 6 carucates; in Thornton [in Brafferton], 6 carucates; in Humberton, 6 carucates. Gospatric [has] these.

In Ellenthorpe [in Aldborough], the king 6 carucates. In Milby, the king 6½ carucates. In Brampton [in Kirby Hill], the king 4 carucates.

In CUNDALL, the Count of Mortain 12 carucates; in Norton-le-Clay, 7 carucates; in Leckby, 6 carucates; in Brampton [in Kirby Hill], 2 carucates; in Cundall, 2 carucates; in North Stainley, 1 carucate; in East Tanfield, 1 carucate; in 'Caldewell' [in Marton-le-Moor], 4 carucates. All these [belong] to Cundall.

CRAVEN

In BOLTON ABBEY, 6 carucates; in Halton East, 6 carucates; in Embsay, 6 carucates; in Draughton, 3 carucates.

In [High and Low] Skibeden, 3 carucates; in Skipton, 4 carucates; in Low Snaygill, 6 carucates; in Thorlby, 10 carucates.

In Addingham, 2 carucates; in Beamsley, 2 carucates; in Holme [in Stirton], 3 carucates; In Gargrave, 3 carucates.

In Stainton [in Bank Newton], 3 carucates; in Otterburn, 3 carucates; in Scosthrop, 3 carucates; in Malham, 3 carucates; in Anley, 2 carucates.

In Coniston Cold, 3 carucates; in Hellifield, 3 carucates; in Hanlith, 3 carucates. All these [belong] to Bolton Abbey.

[Folio 380v: NORTH RIDING]

LANBAURGH WAPENTAKE

In FLYING, William de Percy 1 carucate of land. In the same place, Earl Hugh 1 carucate. In Flyingthorpe, Earl Hugh 5 carucates.

In Gnipe Howe, Earl Hugh 3 carucates. In Whitby, Earl Hugh 10 carucates. In 'Prestebi' [in Whitby], Earl Hugh 2 carucates.

In Normanby [in Fylingdales], the king 2 carucates. In Sneaton, Earl Hugh 5 carucates. In Ugglebarnby, Earl Hugh 3 carucates.

In 'Sourebi' [in Whitby], Earl Hugh 4 carucates. In 'Brecca'

[in Whitby], Earl Hugh 1 carucate. In 'Bauldbyes [in Whitby], Earl Hugh 1 carucate. In 'Flowergate' [in Whitby], Earl Hugh 2 carucates.

In High Stakesby, Earl Hugh 2 carucates and 6 bovates. In the same place, the Count of Mortain 2 bovates. In Newholm, Earl Hugh 4 carucates. In Lythe, the Count of Mortain 2 carucates.

In Dunsley, the king 3 carucates. In the same place, Berengar de Tosny 1 carucate. In Hutton Mulgrave, the Count of Mortain 3 carucates. In Egton, the Count of Mortain 3 carucates.

In Mulgrave Castle, the Count of Mortain 6 carucates. In [East and West] Barnby, the king 4 carucates. In Goldsborough [in Lythe], the Count of Mortain 2 carucates.

In Ellerby, the Count of Mortain 6 carucates. In Mickleby, the Count of Mortain 4 carucates. In Newton Mulgrave, the Count of Mortain 3 carucates.

In "Grimesbi" [in Ugthorpe], the Count of Mortain 2 carucates. In Borrowby [in Ugthorpe], the Count of Mortain 5 carucates. In Roxby [near Loftus], the Count of Mortain 3 carucates. In the same place, the king 1 carucate.

In Ugthorpe, the king 4 carucates. In "Roscheltorp" [in Loftus], Earl Hugh 1 carucate. In Aislaby [near Whitby], the Count of Mortain 3 carucates.

In "Arnodestorp" [in Hinderwell], William de Percy 1 carucate and 2 bovates. In Hinderwell, William de Percy 4 carucates and 6 bovates.

In the same place, Earl Hugh 1 carucate and 2 bovates. In Seaton [in Hinderwell], the Count of Mortain 3 carucates. In Boulby, the king 1 carucate. In the same place, Earl Hugh 2 carucates.

Easington [near Loftus], Earl Hugh 8 carucates. In Liverton, Earl Hugh 6 carucates. In South Loftus, Earl Hugh 4 carucates.

In another Loftus [Loftus], the king 4 carucates. In 'Crunkly' [in Glaisdale], Lealholm and Danby [near Castleton], Hugh fitzBaldric 12 carucates.

In "Steintun" [in Stanghow], the Count of Mortain 7 bovates. In the same place, the king 1 bovate. In Moorsholm, the Count of Mortain 3½ carucates. | In the same place, the king half a carucate. |

In another Moorsholm [Little Moorsholm], the Count of Mortain 1 carucate. In Kilton Thorpe, the Count of Mortain 1½ carucates. In the same place, the king 2½ carucates.

In Kilton, the Count of Mortain 1 carucate. In the same place, the king 3 carucates. In Brotton, the Count of Mortain 12 carucates. | In Skelton [near Saltburn], the Count of Mortain 13 carucates. |

In Guisborough, "Mideltune" [in Guisborough] and Hutton Lowcross, the Count of Mortain 25 carucates. In the same place, the king 1 carucate.

In the same place, Robert Malet 3 carucates and 2 bovates. In the same place, Earl Hugh 6 bovates. In Rawcliff Banks, Earl Hugh 2 carucates.

In Tocketts, the Count of Mortain 2 carucates. In Thornton Fields, the king 2 carucates. In Upleatham, Earl Hugh 10 carucates.

In Marske-by-the-Sea, the Count of Mortain 10 carucates.

In the same place, William de Percy 8 carucates. In the same place, Earl Hugh 2 carucates. In Kirkleatham, the king 3 carucates.

In the same place, William de Percy 4 carucates. In the same place, Earl Hugh 2 carucates. In the same place, the Count of Mortain 9 carucates. In Wilton [in Ormesby], the king 4½ carucates.

In the same place, the Count of Mortain 4½ carucates. In Lazenby [in Ormesby], the king 3 carucates and 6 bovates. In the same place, Earl Hugh half a carucate.

In Lackenby, Earl Hugh 1 carucate and 5 bovates. In the same place, the Count of Mortain 2 carucates. In Eston, the Count of Mortain 9 carucates.

In Normanby [in Eston], the Count of Mortain 7 carucates. In the same place, Robert Malet half a carucate. In the same place, William de Percy half a carucate.

In Ormesby, the king 12 carucates. In Upsall [in Ormesby], the king 4 carucates. In Barnaby, the Count of Mortain 6 carucates.

In Pinchinthorpe, Robert Malet 3 carucates. In the same place, the king 3 carucates. In Aireyholme, the king 2 carucates. In Little Ayton, Robert Malet 3 carucates.

In the same place, the king 2 carucates. In the same place, the Count of Mortain 6 carucates. In Newton under Roseberry, the king 6 carucates. In Morton [in Ormesby], the king 3 carucates.

In Nunthorpe, the king 6 carucates. In Great Ayton, Robert Malet 2 carucates. In another Ayton [Great Ayton], the king 2 carucates. In Easby [in Ingleby Greenhow], the king 2 carucates.

In Battersby, the king 2 carucates. In Kildale, the king 6 carucates.

In Marton [in Middlesbrough], Robert Malet 5 carucates. In the same place, the king 4½ carucates. In Newham, the king 2 carucates and 2 bovates.

In the same place, Robert Malet 6 bovates. In Tollesby, the king 6 carucates. In the same place, Robert Malet 3 carucates. In Acklam [in Middlesbrough], the king 3 carucates.

In the same place, Earl Hugh 8 carucates. In the same place, Robert Malet 1 carucate. In Coulby, Earl Hugh 1 carucate. In Hemlington, Earl Hugh 3 carucates.

In Stainton [near Thornaby-on-Tees], Earl Hugh 2 carucates. In the same place, Robert Malet 2 carucates. In Thornton [near Hemlington], Earl Hugh 3 carucates. In the same place, Robert Malet 1 carucate.

In Maltby [near Middlesbrough], Earl Hugh 3 carucates. In Ingleby, Earl Hugh 6 carucates. In Barwick, Earl Hugh 3 carucates.

In Thornaby-on-Tees, the king 1½ carucates. In the same place, Robert Malet 1½ carucates. In the same place, Earl Hugh 3 carucates.

In Stainsby, Earl Hugh 3 carucates. In Tunstall [in Nunthorpe], the king 3 carucates. In Tanton, the king 4 carucates.

In the same place, the Count of Mortain 2 carucates. In Seamer [near Stokesley], the Count of Mortain 11 carucates. In "Berguluesbi" [in Seamer, near Stokesley], the king 1 carucate. In Hilton [near Stokesley], the Count of Mortain 6 carucates.

In Middleton-on-Leven, the Count of Mortain 8 carucates. In High Foxton, the Count of Mortain 3 carucates. In Thoraldby, the king 3 carucates.

In Stokesley, the king 6 carucates. In Ingleby Greenhow, the king 7 carucates. In "Camisedale" [in Ingleby Greenhow], the king 5 carucates.

In the same place, the Count of Mortain 3 carucates. In the same place, Hugh fitzBaldric 1 carucate.

In 'Little Broughton', the king 8 carucates. In another Broughton [Great Broughton], the Count of Mortain 5 carucates.

In the same place, the king 4 carucates. In Kirkby [near Stokesley], the king 3 carucates. In Dromonby, the king 3 carucates. In Hutton Rudby, the Count of Mortain |6 carucates. |

In the two Busbys [Busby and Great Busby], the king 9½ carucates. In the same place, Robert Malet half a carucate. In Carlton in Cleveland, the Count of Mortain 8 carucates.

In Faceby, the king 8 carucates. In 'Blaten Carr' [in Great Busby], Goulton, and Whorlton, [and] Crathorne, the Count of Mortain 16 carucates and 3 bovates.

In the same place, the king 6 carucates. In East Rounton, the king 8 carucates.

"DIC" WAPENTAKE

In Falsgrave, the king 10 carucates. In Northfield, the king 5 carucates. In Osgodby [near Scarborough], the king 4 carucates.

In Thirley Cote, Staintondale, Burniston and Scalby, the king 14 carucates.

In Cloughton, the king 4 carucates. In the same place, William de Percy 1 carucate. In the same place, the Count of Mortain 2 bovates. In "Stemainesbi" [in Scalby], the Count of Mortain 2½ carucates.

In Lebberston, "Scagestorp" [in Gristhorpe], Gristhorpe, "Roudelvestorp" [in Gristhorpe], "Eterstorp" [in Gristhorpe] and Filey, the king 18 carucates.

In Killerby, William de Percy 2 carucates. In Cayton [near Scarborough], the king 4 carucates. In 'Burton Dale' [in Scarborough] and [High, Low and Middle] Deepdale, the king 12 carucates.

In Seamer [near Scarborough], William de Percy 6 carucates. In "Torp" [in Irton] and Irton, William de Percy 4½ carucates. In 'Hill Grips' [in East Ayton], William de Percy 1 carucate.

In East Ayton, William de Percy 6 carucates. In the same place, Berengar de Tosny 2 carucates. In another Ayton [West Ayton] and "Neuuetone" [in West Ayton] and 'Preston' [in Hutton Buscel] and Hutton Buscel, the king 22 carucates.

In Martin Garth, Wykeham [near Ruston] and Ruston, the king 10 carucates. In Suffield and Everley, William de Percy 6 carucates.

In Hackness, William de Percy 4 carucates.

In Brompton [near Snainton], the king 9 carucates. In the same place, Berengar de Tosny 6 carucates. In Newton-on-

Rawcliffe, Berenger de Tosny 1 carucates. In 'Little Marish' [in Ebberston], Berengar de Tosny 2 carucates.

In Pickering, Barton-le-Street, Blansby, Newton-on-Rawcliffe and Easthorpe, the king 37 carucates.

In "Ouduluesmersc" [in Marishes], Allerston, Ebberston, 'Farmanby' [in Thornton Dale], Kingthorpe, "Aschelemersc" [in Marishes], Wilton [near Thornton Dale], 'Roxby' [in Thornton Dale], "Chiluesmersc" [in Thornton Dale], [and] "Maxudesmersc" [in Marishes], the king 37 carucates and 6 bovates.

In Snainton, Berengar de Tosny 5 carucates. In the same place, the king $3\frac{1}{2}$ carucates. In the same place, William de Percy $1\frac{1}{2}$ carucates. In Troutsdale, the king 2 carucates.

In Allerston, the king 3 carucates. In Loft Marishes, the Count of Mortain $1\frac{1}{2}$ carucates. In the same place, the king $1\frac{1}{2}$ carucates.

In "Chigomersc" [in Thornton Dale], the Count of Mortain 1 carucate and 2 bovates. In the same place, the king 1 carucate and 2 bovates. In Thornton Dale, the king $5\frac{1}{2}$ carucates.

In the same place, Berengar de Tosny 1 carucate. In "Liedtorp" [in Thornton Dale], Berengar de Tosny $3\frac{1}{2}$ carucates. In Ellerburn, the king 1 carucate. In Low Dalby, the king 2 carucates.

In 'Chetelstorp' [in Thornton Dale], the king $1\frac{1}{2}$ carucates. In the same place, the Count of Mortain 1 carucate. In Lockton, the king 5 carucates.

In Levisham, the king 2 carucates and 6 bovates. In Middleton [near Pickering], the king 5 carucates. In Aislaby [near Pickering], the king 4 carucates.

In Wrelton, the king $1\frac{1}{2}$ carucates. In Barton-le-Street, the king half a carucate. In Cawthorne [in Middleton, near Pickering], the king 1 carucate.

In Cropton, the king 5 carucates. In Lastingham, the abbot 2 carucates. In the same place, Berengar de Tosny 1 carucate. In "Baschesbi" [in Lastingham], the king 1 carucate.

In Appleton-le-Moors, the abbot 2 carucates. In Sinnington, Berengar de Tosny 3 carucates. In Marton [in Sinnington], Berengar de Tosny 5 carucates.

"MANESHOU" WAPENTAKE

In 'Thornton Riseborough' [in Normanby, near Salton], the king 4 carucates. In Kirby Misperton and another Kirby [Kirby Misperton], Berengar de Tosny, and the abbot of him, 7 carucates.

In [Great and Little] Habton, the king $6\frac{1}{2}$ carucates. In the same place, the Count of Mortain half a carucate. In "Salescale" [in Ryton], the king 6 bovates.

In Ryton, the king $2\frac{1}{2}$ carucates. In 'Newsham' [in Amotherby] and Amotherby, the king 3 carucates and 6 bovates. In Wykeham [in Malton], the king 1 carucate.

In Amotherby, the king $2\frac{1}{2}$ carucates. In the same place, the Count of Mortain $1\frac{1}{2}$ carucates. In another Wykeham [Wykeham Hill], the king 2 carucates.

In the same place, the archbishop half a carucate. In the same place, Ralph Paynel 6 bovates. In Old Malton, the archbishop 1 carucate. In the same place, the king $11\frac{1}{2}$ carucates.

In the same place, the Count of Mortain $1\frac{1}{2}$ carucates. In Broughton [in Appleton-le-Street], the king 8 carucates and 2 bovates. In the same place, Berengar de Tosny 1 carucate.

In Swinton [in Appleton-le-Street], the king 11 carucates. In Appleton-le-Street, the king 5 carucates. In Salton, the archbishop 9 carucates. I [sic]

In Brawby, the archbishop 6 carucates. In Great Barugh, the archbishop 3 carucates. In the same place, the king 2 carucates. In another Barugh [Little Barugh], the archbishop half a carucate.

In the same place, the king $1\frac{1}{2}$ carucates. In Great Edstone, Berengar de Tosny 8 carucates. In another Edstone [Little Edstone], Berengar de Tosny 3 carucates.

In High Northolme, the king $1\frac{1}{2}$ carucates. In the same place, Berengar de Tosny $1\frac{1}{2}$ carucates. In Sinnington, Berengar de Tosny 2 carucates.

In Nawton, the archbishop 4 carucates. In the same place, Berengar de Tosny 2 carucates.

In Welburn [in Kirkdale], Berengar de Tosny 1 carucate. In the same place, the king 1 carucate. In Wombleton, the archbishop 1 carucate.

In "Waleton" [in Kirkdale], Berengar de Tosny 1 bovate. In Spaunton, Berengar de Tosny, and the abbot of him, $6\frac{1}{2}$ carucates. In the same place, the king, and the abbot of him, 1 carucate.

In Appleton-le-Moors, the abbot, of the king, 2 carucates. In Normanby [near Salton], the king 3 carucates. In the same place, the abbot, of the king, 3 carucates. In Barton-le-Street, the Count of Mortain 8 carucates.

In Oswaldkirk, Berengar de Tosny 1 carucate. In the same place, the Count of Mortain 1 carucate. In East Newton [in Stonegrave], the archbishop 4 carucates. In the same place, the king 2 carucates.

In Gilling East, Ralph de Mortimer 4 carucates. In West Newton [in Oswaldkirk], the king 2 carucates. In Sproxton, the king 5 carucates.

In Fadmoor, the Count of Mortain 5 carucates. In Scawton, Robert Malet 4 carucates. In Griff, the Count of Mortain 2 carucates. In the same place, the king 2 carucates.

In Stiltons, the king 1 carucate. In the same place, the Count of Mortain 3 carucates. In Helmsley, the king $3\frac{1}{2}$ carucates. In the same place, the Count of Mortain 7 carucates.

In Pockley, the archbishop 1 carucate. In the same place, the Count of Mortain 1 carucate. In Beadlam, the Count of Mortain 4 carucates. In Harome, the Count of Mortain 5 carucates.

In the same place, the king $1\frac{1}{2}$ carucates. In the same place, Berengar de Tosny 2 bovates. In Riccall, the king 2 carucates. In Nunnington, Ralph Paynel 6 carucates.

In the same place, the Count of Mortain 6 carucates. In Stonegrave, the archbishop 6 bovates. In the same place, Ralph Paynel 5 carucates and 2 bovates. In [East and West] Ness, Ralph Paynel 3 carucates.

In South Holme, Ralph Paynel 1 carucate. In Ampleforth, the archbishop 3 carucates. In Coulton, the king 1 carucate. In Coulton, the archbishop half a carucate.

In the same place, the Count of Mortain $1\frac{1}{2}$ carucates. In

Cawton, the Count of Mortain 3 carucates. In Slingsby, the Count of Mortain 14 carucates.

In Fryton, the Count of Mortain half a carucate.

'BULFORD' WAPENTAKE

In Low Hutton, Berengar de Tosny 5½ carucates. In the same place, the king 8½ carucates. In 'Henderskelfe' [in Bulmer], Berengar de Tosny 4 carucates.

In Dalby, Berengar, and the abbot of him, 3 carucates. In Scackleton, the king half a carucate. In the same place, the Count of Mortain 1½ carucates.

In Bulmer and Stittenham, the Count of Mortain 15 carucates. In Sheriff Hutton, the Count of Mortain 11 carucates. In the same place, the king 4 carucates.

In Welburn [in Bulmer], the Count of Mortain 3½ carucates. In Ganthorpe, the Count of Mortain 2½ carucates.

In the same place, the king half a carucate. In Terrington, the Count of Mortain 6 carucates and 3 bovates. In the same place, Berengar de Tosny 2 bovates.

In the same place, Count Alan 1½ carucates. In Wiganthorpe, the Count of Mortain 1 carucate. In the same place, the king 1 carucate. In the same place, Berengar de Tosny 1 carucate.

[Folio 381: NORTH RIDING]

In Hildenley, the king 2 carucates. In Coneysthorpe, the Count of Mortain 3 carucates. In Marton-in-the-Forest, the Count of Mortain 6 carucates.

In Farlington and "Fornetorp" [? in Cornborough], the Count of Mortain 7 carucates. In the same place, Berengar de Tosny 1 carucate. In Cornborough, the Count of Mortain 9 carucates.

In Skewsby, the Count of Mortain 8 carucates. In [East and West] Lilling, the king 3 carucates. In the same place, the Count of Mortain 2 bovates. In Thornton-le-Clay, the Count of Mortain 3 carucates,

In the same place, Count Alan 2 carucates. In the same place, 2 carucates. In Crambe, the Count of Mortain 4 carucates. In the same place, the king 4 carucates. In Barton-le-Willows, the Count of Mortain 8 carucates.

In Harton, the king 12 carucates. In Claxton, the king 3 carucates. In the same place, the Count of Mortain 1 carucate. In Sand Hutton, the king 1 carucate.

In "Dic" [in Haxby], the king 2 carucates. In Upper Helmsley, the Count of Mortain 4 carucates. In Sutton-on-the-Forest, the king 3 carucates. In Holtby [near York], the king 6 carucates.

In another Helmsley [Gate Helmsley], the archbishop 4 carucates and 2 bovates. In Warthill, the archbishop 3 carucates. In the same place, the Count of Mortain 2 carucates.

In Carlton [in Stanwick-st-John], the archbishop 3 carucates. In Whitwell-on-the-Hill, the Count of Mortain 9½ carucates. In [East and West] Lilling, the king 1 carucate and 6 bovates.

In the same place, the Count of Mortain 1 carucate and 2 bovates. In Strensall, 5 carucates. In Towthorpe [in Huntington], 3 carucates. In the same place, the Count of Mortain 1 carucate.

In Earswick, 3 carucates. In Huntington, the Count of Mortain 5 carucates. In the same place, the king 2 carucates and 6 bovates. In the same place, Count Alan 1 carucate and 2 bovates.

In Flaxton, the king 2½ carucates. In the same place, the archbishop 6 bovates. In the same place, Count Alan 1½ carucates. In Huby, the king 6 carucates.

In Whenby, the king 8 carucates. In Foston, Count Alan 8 carucates. In Stillington, the archbishop 10 carucates.

In Moxby, the king 3 carucates. In Murton [in Sutton-on-the-Forest], the archbishop 2½ carucates. In the same place, the king 2 carucates.

In 'Thorpe' [in Sutton-on-the-Forest], Kelsit, Sutton-on-the-Forest, and Cold Kirby 17 carucates.

In Easingwold, the king 12 carucates. In Raskelf, the king 8 carucates. In 'Corburn' [in Wigginton], 3 carucates.

In Newton-on-Ouse and "Toresbi" [in Newton-on-Ouse], Ralph Paynel 9 carucates. In 'Ingolftwayt' [in Easingwold], William de Percy 8 carucates.

In Haxby, the archbishop 6 carucates and 1 bovate. In Tollerton, 8 carucates; in Alne, 8 carucates; in Youlton, 4 carucates; in Myton-on-Swale, 2 bovates.

In Tholthorpe and Wide Open, 7 carucates; in Helperby, 6 carucates. These [belong] to the archbishop.

In Helperby, the archbishop 4 carucates. In Myton-on-Swale, the archbishop 4½ carucates. In the same place, the king 3 carucates and 2 bovates.

In Aldwark, the Count of Mortain 8 carucates. In Brafferton, the king 6 carucates. In the same place, the Count of Mortain 1 carucate. In Stearsby, the Count of Mortain 2 carucates.

In Low Mowthorpe [in Terrington], the Count of Mortain 3 carucates. In Shipton, Count Alan 6 carucates. In Bossall, 2½ bovates.

'YARLESTRE' WAPENTAKE

In Thormanby, the king 1½ carucates. In the same place, half a carucate; Gamal held it. In the same place, Robert Malet 4 carucates. In Crayke, the Bishop of Durham 6 carucates.

In 'Baxby' [in Husthwaite], the archbishop 6 carucates and 1 bovate. In Carlton Husthwaite, the archbishop 4½ carucates. In Thorpe [near Ampleforth], Gospatric 3 carucates.

In Oulston, Gospatric 6 carucates. In Old Byland, Robert Malet 6 carucates. In "Bernebi" [in Birdforth], Robert Malet 4½ carucates.

In Sessay, the Bishop of Durham 5 carucates. In "Horenbodebi", the Bishop of Durham 3 carucates. In Topcliffe, with 4 Berewicks, William de Percy 26 carucates.

In "Bergebi" [in Topcliffe], William de Percy 8 carucates. In Rainton, William de Percy 4 carucates. In Catton, William de Percy 6 carucates.

In Carlton Miniott, the king 4 carucates. In Sand Hutton, the king 6 carucates. In Breckenbrough, the Count of Mortain 6 carucates. In Thirsk, the king 8 carucates.

In Newsham [in Kirby Wiske], the king 2½ carucates. In Sowerby [near Thirsk], the king 5 carucates. In Knayton, the Bishop of Durham 4 carucates. In the same place, the king 2 carucates.

In North Kilvington, the king 8 carucates. In the same place and in Upsall and Hundulfthorpe, the Count of Mortain 13 carucates.

ALLERTON WAPENTAKE

In Northallerton, Birkby, Sowerby [in Kirby Sigston], Kirby Wiske, Landmoth, Thornton-le-Beans, Great Smeaton and Little Smeaton [in Birkby], East Cowton, Borrowby [in Leake], Romanby and Yafforth, the king 42 carucates of land. In Newsham [near Northallerton], 'West Harlsey' [in Osmotherley], "Westhuse" [? in Newsham, near Northallerton], Maunby, Kirby Sigston, Cowesby, Warlaby, Thimbleby, Ainderby Steeple, Yafforth, Leake, Knayton, Lazenby, Ravensthorpe, Over Dinsdale, Thornton-le-Street, Crosby, West Rounton, North Otterington, Romanby, Brompton [near Northallerton] [and] Irby, the king 75 carucates.

In South Otterington, the king 6 carucates. In Romanby, the king 5 carucates and 1 bovate.

In Hutton Bonville, the king 6 carucates.

In Little Smeaton [in Birkby], the king 5 carucates. In Girsby, the Bishop of Durham 6 carucates. In the two Worsalls [High and Low Worsall], the king 7 carucates.

In Appleton Wiske, the king 6 carucates. In Kirklevington, the king 6 carucates. In another Levington ['Castlelevington', in Kirklevington], the king 4 carucates.

In Yarm, the king 3 carucates. In Welbury, the king 6 carucates. In the two Harlseys [East Harlsey and 'West Harlsey'], the king 9 carucates.

In Deighton [near Welbury], the Bishop of Durham 6 carucates. In Winton, 6 carucates. In Foxton, 2 carucates. In Brompton [near Northallerton], 14 carucates. The Bishop of Durham [has] these.

In Morton [in East Harlsey], the king 3 carucates. In Ingleby Arncliffe, the king 6 carucates. In Arncliffe, the king 1 carucate. In 'Brodeby' [in Osmotherley], the king 2 carucates.

In Ellerbeck, the king 5 carucates. In Osmotherley, the king 5 carucates. In Over Silton, the king 3 carucates. In another Silton [Nether Silton], the Count of Mortain 3 carucates.

In Sowerby [in Kirby Sigston], the king 2 carucates. In Crosby, the king 1 carucate. In Thornton-le-Moor, Robert Malet 5 carucates. In Leake, the Count of Mortain 3 carucates.

In Kepwick, the king 5 carucates. In Murton [near Hawnby], Robert Malet 6 carucates. In Dale Town, the king 1½ carucates. In the same place, Robert Malet 1½ carucates.

In Hawnby, the king 1½ carucates. In the same place, Robert Malet 1½ carucates.

[The land] of Count Alan

In GILLING, 4 carucates of land. In Hartforth, 3 carucates. In Newton Morrell, 6 carucates.

In South Cowton, 3 carucates. In another Cowton [North Cowton], 3 carucates. In Eryholme, 6 carucates. In Low Hail, 2½ carucates.

In Stapleton [near Cleasby], 3 carucates. In Forcett, 8 carucates. In Barforth, 3 carucates.

In MOULTON, 16 carucates. In Barton, 2½ carucates. In Eppleby, 7 carucates. In Cliffe [in Manfield], 3 carucates. In Carlton [in Stanwick-St-John], 2 carucates.

In Barforth, 1 carucate. In Ovington, 3 carucates. In Girlington, 3 carucates. In Wycliffe, 12 carucates. In Thorpe [in Wycliffe], 3 carucates.

In Mortham, 3 carucates. In Egglestone, 3 carucates. In Brignall, 12 carucates. In Scargill, 3 carucates.

In Barningham, 4 carucates. In West Layton, 3 carucates. In East Layton, 3 carucates. In the two Stanwicks [Stanwick-St-John], 4 carucates.

In Manfield, 16 carucates. In Great Hutton, 6 carucates. In Middleton Tyas, 6 carucates. In Kneeton, 8 carucates. In Stapleton [near Cleasby], 5 carucates.

In Barningham, 2 carucates. In East Layton, 3 carucates. In Stanwick-St-John, 4 carucates. In Over Dinsdale, 3 carucates.

In Great Smeaton, 6 carucates. In Great Langton, 9 carucates. In Caldwell, 6 carucates. In Aldbrough St John, 8 carucates. In Carlton [in Stanwick-St-John], 2 carucates.

In Cleasby, 6 carucates. In Croft-on-Tees, 14 carucates. In "Torp" [in Croft], 2 carucates. In Startforth, 6 carucates. In Richmond, 5 carucates. In Easby [near Richmond], 6 carucates.

In Brompton-on-Swale, 10 carucates. In Skeeby, 6 carucates. In "Neutone" [in Scorton], 6 carucates. In Bolton-on-Swale, 6 carucates. In Kiplin, 8 carucates.

In Little Langton, 7½ carucates. In Thrintoft, 5 carucates. In Solberge, 4 carucates. In Maunby, 10 carucates. In Kirby Wiske, 8 carucates.

In Morton-on-Swale, 11 carucates. In Ellerton [in Bolton-on-Swale], 9 carucates. In Yafforth, 8 carucates. In Ainderby Steeple, 9 carucates. In Warlaby, 6 carucates.

In Danby Wiske, 10 carucates. In East Cowton, 6 carucates. In Lonton, 1 carucate. In Mickleton, 6 carucates. In Romaldkirk, 1 carucate.

In Hunderthwaite, 1 carucate. In Lartington, 3 carucates. In Cotherstone, 6 carucates. In Rokeby, 3 carucates.

In 'Broghton' [in Newsham, near Barningham], 5 carucates. In Newsham [near Barningham], 7 carucates. In Dalton [in Ravensworth], 8 carucates. In another Dalton [Dalton in Ravensworth], 4 carucates. In Ravensworth, 12 carucates.

In Melsonby, 11 carucates. In 'Didirston' [in Melsonby], 4 carucates. In Scorton, 16 carucates.

[The land] of the Same Count

In CATTERICK, 10 carucates. In Killerby [near Catterick], 5 carucates. In Ainderby Mires, 2½ carucates. In Tunstall [near Catterick], 3 carucates and 6 bovates.

In Ainderby Mires, 2½ carucates. In Tunstall [near Catterick],

2 carucates. In Kirkby [near Great Langton], 3 carucates. In Kirkby Fleetham, 8 carucates. In Aske, 6 carucates.

In the two Fencotes [Great and Little Fencote], 9 carucates. In Scruton, 14 carucates. In Langthorne, 3 carucates.

In Hackforth, 6 carucates. In Hornby [near Hackforth], 8 carucates. In Holtby [near Ainderby Mires], 3 carucates. In East Appleton, 12 carucates. In Brough [near Catterick], 9 carucates.

In Colburn, 5 carucates. In Hipswell, 3 carucates. In Scotton [near Richmond], 8 carucates. In Hudswell, 6 carucates.

In Richmond, 1 carucate. In Downholme, 3 carucates. In Ellerton Abbey, 2 carucates. In Marrick, 5 carucates. In Grinton, 1 carucate.

In Fremington, 1 carucate. In Reeth, 6 carucates. In "Denon" [in Low Abbotside], 3 carucates. In 'Brough' [in Bainbridge], 3 carucates. In 'Fors' [in Low Abbotside], 4 carucates. In Askrigg, 10 carucates.

In Worton, 6 carucates. In Thornton Rust, 6 carucates. In Aysgarth, 3 carucates. In 'Crooksby' [in Newbiggin], 1 carucate. In Thoralby [in Aysgarth], 6 carucates.

In West Burton, 6 carucates. In Carperby, 9 carucates. In West Bolton, 6 carucates. In another Bolton [Castle Bolton], 6 carucates. In [High and Low] Thoresby, 1 carucate.

In Redmire, 5 carucates. In Preston-under-Scar, 3 carucates. In East Witton, 12 carucates. In [High and Low] Thoresby, 2 carucates. In West Witton, 5 carucates. In West Scrafton, 3 carucates.

In the two Wensleys, 7 carucates. In Carlton [near Middleham], 6 carucates. In Melmerby [in Coverham], 6 carucates. In Agglethorpe, 3 carucates.

In Caldbergh, 5 carucates. In Coverham, 4 carucates. In Middleham, 5 carucates. In Leyburn, 7½ carucates. In Harmby, 9 carucates.

In Spennithorne, 8½ carucates. In Danby [in Thornton Steward], 4 carucates. In Bellerby, 6 carucates. In Barden, 5 carucates. In Garriston, 3 carucates.

In East Hauxwell, 6 carucates. In another [Hauxwell] [West Hauxwell], 6 carucates. In Constable Burton, 12 carucates. In Thornton Steward, 6 carucates. In "Ascham" [in East Witton], 4 carucates.

In [High and Low] Ellington, 6 carucates. In 'Swartrups' [in High Ellington], 1 carucate. In High Sutton, 1 carucate. In Fearby, 3 carucates. In Ilton, 2 carucates.

In Masham, 12 carucates. In 'Twistlebro' [in Masham], 3 carucates. In Swinton [in Masham], 3 carucates. In High Sutton, 1 carucate. In Clifton Castle, 3 carucates.

In Well, 8 carucates. In High Burton, 4 carucates. In "Opetune" [in Snape], 4 carucates. In "Achebi" [in Snape], 4 carucates. In Firby [in Bedale], 5 carucates. In Bedale, 6 carucates.

In Aiskew, 10 carucates. In Burrill, 5 carucates. In Thornton Watlass, 6 carucates. In Watlass, 3 carucates. In Thorp Perrow, 4 carucates. In Cowling [in Bedale], 4 carucates.

In Thirn, 3 carucates. In Rookwith, 6 carucates. In Hutton Hang, 5 carucates. In Finghall, 6 carucates. In Ruswick, 2 carucates. In Newton-le-Willows, 12 carucates.

In Hunton, 12 carucates. In Heselton, 6 carucates. In Patrick Brompton, 13 carucates. In Great Crakehall, 12 carucates. In East Tanfield, 5 carucates.

In another Tanfield [West Tanfield], 8 carucates. In Upsland, 3 carucates. In Howgrave, 5 carucates. In Sutton Howgrave, 4 carucates. In Wath [near East Tanfield], 6 carucates.

In Melmerby [near Middleton Quernhow], 6 carucates. In Middleton Quernhow, 5 carucates. In Kirklington, 9 carucates. In 'Yarnwick' [in Kirklington], 3 carucates.

In "Normanebi" [in Carthorpe], 6 carucates. In Carthorpe, 4 carucates. In Burneston, 8 carucates. In Theakston, 12 carucates. In Exelby, 8 carucates.

In 'Newton Picot' [in Leeming], 6 carucates. In Gatenby, 3 carucates. In "Ounesbi" [in Gatenby], 3 carucates. In Low Swainby, 6 carucates. In Pickhill, 12 carucates.

In Allerthorpe [in Pickhill], 2 carucates. In "Seuenetorp" [in Low Swainby], 3 carucates. In Sinderby, 6 carucates. In Ainderby Quernhow, 6 carucates.

In Howe, 3 carucates. In Baldersby, 3 carucates. In 'Eseby' [in Baldersby], 4 carucates. In Rainton, 9 carucates.

Count Alan has within the jurisdiction of his castle 200 manors, less 1. Of these, 108 are waste; and of these, his men hold 133 manors. In all, there are to the geld 1,153 carucates of land. [There is] land for 853 ploughs. The value [is] £80.

Besides the jurisdiction of the castle, he has 43 manors. Of these, 4 are waste. In all, there are to the geld 161 carucates of land and 5 bovates. [There is] land for 170½ ploughs. Of these his men hold 10 manors. They are appraised at £110.11s8d.

[Folio 381V: EAST RIDING]

HESSLE HUNDRED

In HESSLE [near Hull], Gilbert Tison 7 carucates of land. In the same place, Ralph de Mortimer 1 carucate. In "Cracetorp" [in Hessle, near Hull], Gilbert Tison 3 carucates.

In Anlaby, the king 3 carucates and 1 bovate. In the same place, Gilbert Tison 3½ carucates. In the same place, the Count of Mortain 5 bovates.

In the same place, Ralph de Mortimer 3 bovates. In Kirk Ella, Gilbert Tison 22½ carucates. In the same place, Ralph de Mortimer 10 carucates.

In the same place, the Count of Mortain 4 carucates. In the same place, Hugh fitzBaldric 2 carucates. In North Ferriby, Ralph de Mortimer 10 carucates. In the same place, the Count of Mortain half a carucate.

In Wauldby, Ralph de Mortimer 1 carucate. In 'Myton', Ralph de Mortimer 1½ carucates. In Riplingham, Ralph de Mortimer 1 carucate and 2 bovates.

In "Totfled" [in Hull], Ralph de Mortimer 1 carucate. In 'Wolfreton' [in Kirk Ella], Ralph de Mortimer half a carucate. In Wressle, Gilbert Tison 14 carucates.

In the same place, Ralph de Mortimer 1 carucate and 6 bovates. In Newsholme [in Wressle], Ralph de Mortimer 6 carucates and 1 bovate. In Spaldington, the Count of Mortain 3 carucates and 1½ bovates.

In 'Lund' [in Breighton], Gilbert Tison 1½ carucates. In the same place, Ralph de Mortimer 2½ carucates. In Breighton, Ralph de Mortimer 2 carucates.

In Gunby, Gilbert Tison 1 carucate and 3 bovates. In the same place, the Count of Mortain 5 bovates. In Bubwith, Gilbert Tison 8½ carucates.

In the same place, Ralph de Mortimer 1 carucates and 3 bovates. In Willitoft, the Count of Mortain 5 bovates. In the same place, Ralph de Mortimer 2½ carucates.

In the same place, Gilbert Tison 7 bovates. In Willerby [near Hull], the king 2 carucates.

WELTON HUNDRED

In Welton, the Bishop of Durham 26 carucates. In Brantingham, 2 carucates. In Walkington, 9 carucates.

In Lund [near Beverly], 18 carucates. In Brantinghamthorpe, 2 carucates and 7 bovates. The Bishop of Durham [has] all these.

In Cottingham, HughfitzBaldric 14 carucates and 2 parts of 1 carucate. In Little Weighton, Hugh fitzBaldric 5 carucates.

In Skidby, the archbishop 14 carucates and the third part of 1 carucate. In Elloughton, 10 carucates. In Wauldby, 7 carucates.

In Walkington, 8 carucates and 1 bovate. In Bentley [near Beverley], 2 carucates. In Risby, 6 carucates. The archbishop [has] all these.

In Brantigham, the Count of Mortain 1 carucate and 6½ bovaetes. In the same place, Robert Malet 2 carucates and 7½ bovates.

In Waldkington, the king 1 carucate. In Pilwood, Hugh fitzBaldric 2 carucates.

CAVE HUNDRED

In South Cave, Robert Malet 24 carucates. In another Cave [North Cave], Robert Malet 7 carucates and 2 bovates.

In the same place, the archbishop 1 carucate and 6 bovates. In the same place, the Count of Mortain 6 carucates and 2 bovates. In the same place, Hugh fitzBaldric 2 bovates. In Everthorpe, the Count of Mortain 5 carucates.

In Drewton, Robert Malet 4 carucates. In [High and Low] Hunsley, the Bishop of Durham 2½ carucates. In the same place, Hugh fitzBaldric 2½ carucates.

In [North and South] Newbald, the archbishop 28 carucates and 2 bovates. In Kettlethorpe, Robert Malet 3 carucates. In Hotham, the Bishop of Durham 3 carucates.

In the same place, the king 1 carucate. In the same place, the Count of Mortain 5½ carucates. In the same place, Robert Malet 3 carucates. In South Cliffe, the Bishop of Durham 3½ carucates. In the same place, the king 2 carucates.†N

In Seaton Ross, the king 4 carucates. In the same place, the Count of Mortain 4 carucates. In Foggathorpe, the Count of Mortain 1½ carucates. In the same place, Ralph de Mortimer 2 carucates.

In the same place, Gilbert Tison 3 carucates. In Gribthorpe, Gilbert Tison 2 carucates. In the same place. Ralph de Mortimer 2 carucates. in Laytham, the Count of Mortain 2 carucates and 5 bovates.

In the same place, Gilbert Tison 1 carucate and 3 bovates. In Aughton [near Bubwith], the Count of Mortain 6 carucates. In Ellerton [near Bubwith], the Count of Mortain 2 carucates. In the same place, the king 2 carucates.†N

In East Cottingwith, the Count of Mortain 2 carucates. In another Cottinwith [East Cottingwith], the Count of Mortain 2 carucates and 6 bovates. In the same place, Erneis 1 carucate.

In Melbourne, Ralph de Mortimer 6 carucates. In Thornton [near Pocklington], Ralph de Mortimer 6 carucates. In Yokefleet [near Blacktoft], the Bishop of Durham 1½ carucates. In the same place, Robert Malet 1 carucate.

HOWDEN HUNDRED

In Howden, the Bishop of Durham 15 carucates. In Hive, 1 carucate. In Owsthorpe, 1½ carucates. In Portington, 1½ carucates.

In Burland, 1 carucate. In Cavil, 2 carucates and 2 bovates. In Eastrington, 6 carucates. In Kilpin, 3 carucates and 2 bovates. In Yokefleet [near Blacktoft], half a carucate.

In Cotness, half a carucate. In Saltmarshe, 6 carucates. In Laxton, 1 carucate. In Skelton [in Howden], 3 carucates and 2 bovates. In Barnhill, 1 carucate.

In Belby, 4 carucates and 6 bovates. In Thorpe Lidget, 1½ carucates. In Knedlington, 6 carucates. In Asselby, 5 carucates.

In Barnby on the Marsh, 6 carucates. In Babthorpe, 1 carucate. In Brackenholme, 1 carucate and 6 bovates. In Hagthorpe, 1 carucate. In Bowthorpe, 4 carucates.

In Barlby, 1 carucate. In Ricall, 1 carucate. All these the Bishop of Durham [has] in Howden.

In Belby, the king half a carucate. In Asselby, the Count of Mortain 1 carucate. In Brackenholme, Gilbert Tison 5 bovates. In Cliffe [in Hemingbrough], the Count of Mortain 3 carucates.

In Hagthorpe, Gilbert Tison half a carucate. In South Duffield, the Count of Mortain 7 carucates and 5 bovates. In North Duffield. the Count of Mortain 7 carucates and 2 bovates.

In the same place, Gilbert Tison 1 carucate. In Skipwith, HughfitzBaldric 5 carucates. In Brackenholme, Earnwine 2 bovates. In Osgodby [in Hemingbrough], the Count of Mortain 3 carucates.

In Hemingbrough, the Bishop of Durham 3 carucates. In Barlby, the king 1 carucate. In the same place, the Bishop of Durham 1 carucate. In West Cottinwith, Ralph Paynel 1 carucate and 2 bovates.

In Riccall, the archbishop 2 carucates. In Thorganby, Ralph Paynel 3 carucates.

WEIGHTON HUNDRED

In Market Weighton, the king 24 carucates. in Shiptonthorpe, the king 6 carucates. In Houghton, the king or Robert Malet 3½ carucates. In North Cliffe, the king 1 carucate.†N

In Holme-on-Spalding-Moor, Gilbert Tison 8 carucates. In Goodmanham, Gilbert Tison 1½ carucates. In the same place, the king 1 carucate and 5 bovates. In the same place, the Count of Mortain 1 carucate and 2 bovates.

In Sancton, Gilbert Tison 15 carucates. In Houghton, the king $4\frac{1}{2}$ carucates. In the same place, Gilbert Tison half a carucate. In North Cliffe, the king 1 carucate.†N

In Goodmanham, the archbishop 4 carucates. In the same place, the Count of Mortain 5 carucates and 6 bovates. In the same place, William de Percy 2 carucates. In the same place, half a carucate; no one has it.

In Easthorpe [in Londesborough],William de Percy 7 carucates and 2 bovates. In the same place, the Count of Mortain 2 carucates and 6 bovates. In Lodesborough, the archbishop $7\frac{1}{2}$ carucates.

In 'Towthorpe' [in Londesborough], the archbishop 3 carucates. In Harswell, the king 1 carucate. In 'Thorp' [in Thorpe Street], the king 4 carucates. In Cleaving, the king 3 carucates.

In Kipling, the archbishop $2\frac{1}{2}$ carucates. In the same place, the Count of Mortain 2 carucates. In the same place, William de Percy 1 carucate. In Bishop Burton, the archbishop 17 carucates.

"SNECULFCROS" HUNDRED

In Middleton-on-the-Wolds, the archbishop 5 carucates and 6 bovates. In the same place, the Count of Mortain and his men 12 carucates and 1 bovates and the third part of 1 bovate.

In Bracken, Erneis 6 carucates. In Watton, the king 3 carucates. In the same place, the Count of Mortain 13 carucates. In Kilnwick, the king 5 carucates.

In the same place, the Count of Mortain 5 carucates. In Beswick, the Count of Mortain 3 carucates. In the same place, the king 3 carucates. In Lockington, the Count of Mortain $9\frac{1}{2}$ carucates. In the same place, the archbishop $2\frac{1}{2}$ carucates.

In Aike, the archbishop 6 bovates. In the same place, the Count of Mortain 6 bovates. In "Persene" [in Scorborough], William de Percy 4 bovates. In the same place, the Bishop of Durham 2 bovates. In Scorborough, the Bishop of Durham 1 carucate.

In the same place, William de Percy half a carucate. In Etton, Hugh fitzBaldric 9 carucates and 2 bovates. In "Torp" [in Etton], Hugh fitzBaldric 1 carucate. In "Steintorp" [in Etton], the Count of Mortain 1 carucate. In Etton, the archbishop 8 carucates.

In the same place, the Count of Mortain 6 carucates and 6 bovates. In Leconfield, William de Percy 3 carucates and 5 bovates. In the same place, the Count of Mortain 1 carucate and 2 bovates. In "Neuson" [in Leconfield], the Count of Mortain 1 carucate.

In 'Raventhorpe' [in Cherry Burton], the archbishop 3 carucates. In the same place, the Count of Mortain $4\frac{1}{2}$ carucates. In Cherry Burton, the archbishop 14 carucates and 2 bovates. In the same place, the king 1 carucate.†N

In 'Newton' [in Cherry Burton], the Bishop of Durham 3 carucates. In Molescroft, the archbishop 3 carucates. In Gardham, the Bishop of Durham 6 carucates. In South Dalton, the archbishop 12 carucates.

In Holme on the Wolds, the Bishop of Durham 12 carucates. In Scoreby, William de Percy 6 carucates. In

"Ianulfestorp" [in Dunnungton, near York], William de Percy 2 carucates. In Dunnington [near York], the archbishop 4 carucates.

In the same place, William de Percy 5 carucates and 6 bovates. In Grimston [in Dunnington, near York], the Count of Mortain 2 carucates. In the same place, William de Percy 1 carucate. In Beverley, St John 1 carucate of land, quit.

DRIFFIELD HUNDRED

In GREAT DRIFFIELD, the king $32\frac{1}{2}$ carucates. In Elmswell, the king 2 carucates. In Kelleythorpe, the archbishop 2 bovates.

In the same place, the king $4\frac{1}{2}$ carucates. In Great Kendale, the king 6 carucates. In Eastburn [in Kirkburn], the king 6 carucates. In Kirkburn, the king 5 carucates.

In Southburn, the king 7 carucates. In Tibthorpe, the king $8\frac{1}{2}$ carucates. In Skerne and Cranswick, the king $2\frac{1}{2}$ carucates.

In Great Driffield, the Count of Mortain 6 bovates. In Rotsea, the Count of Mortain 2 carucates. In Skerne, Hugh fitzBaldric 6 carucates. In Neswick, the Count of Mortain 9 carucates.

In Cranswick and Hutton Cranswick, the Count of Mortain 8 carucates and 3 bovates. In the same place Hugh fitzBaldric 2 carucates. In Bainton, the Count of Mortain 13 carucates. In the same place, Hugh fitzBaldric 11 carucates.

In Old Sunderlandwick, the king $1\frac{1}{2}$ carucates. In the same place, Gospatric $1\frac{1}{2}$ carucates. In Tibthorpe, the king 3 carucates and 2 bovates. In "Torp" [in Tibthorpe], the king 2 carucates.

WARTER HUNDRED

In Warter, the king 20 carucates. In the same place, William de Prcy 4 carucates. In Naburn, Robert de Tosny 4 carucates. In the same place, the king 2 carucates.

In North Dalton, the Count of Mortain 6 carucates. In the same place, the king 3 carucates and 5 bovates. In the same place, Robert de Tosny 22 carucates and 1 bovate. In Nunburnholme, the king 11 carucates.

In Wetwang, the archbishop $13\frac{1}{2}$ carucates. In Huggate, the king $8\frac{1}{2}$ carucates. In the same place, Earnwine 8 carucates.

In Haywold, the king 5 carucates. In the same place, the archbishop 1 carucate. In Kilnwick Percy, the king 16 carucates. In Meltonby, the king 8 carucates. In Ousethorpe, the king 3 carucates.

In Yapham, the king 10 carucates. In Great Givendale [near Pocklington], the king 8 carucates. In another Givendale [Little Givendale], the king 4 carucates. In the same place, the archbishop 2 carucates.

In Grimthorpe, the king 4 carucates. In Millington, the king 15 carucates. In the same place, the archbishop 3 carucates. In Water Fulford, the archbishop 1 carucate and 2 bovates.

In the same place, Count Alan 1 carucate and 3 bovates. In the same place, Erneis 1 carucate and 3 bovates. In Heslington, the archbishop 4 carucates. In the same place,

Count Alan 5 carucates. In the same place, Hugh fitzBaldric 3 carucates.

In Langwith, Count Alan 1½ carucates. In the same place, Hugh fitzBaldric half a carucate.

POCKLINGTON HUNDRED

In POCKLINGTON, the king 13 carucates. In Bielby, the king 3 carucates. In Hayton, the king 9½ carucates. In the same place, William de Percy 2½ carucates.

In Burnby, the king 1½ carucates. In the same place, the archbishop 4 carucates. In the same place, Robert Malet 2 carucates. In the same place, William de Percy 2½ carucates. In Waplington, the king 2 carucates.

In Allenthorpe [near Pocklington], the king 6 carucates. In Thorpe le Street, Gilbert Tison 3 carucates. In Everingham, the archbishop 3 carucates. In Sutton upon Derwent, the Count of Mortain 6 carucates.

In the same place, William de Percy 6 carucates. In [High and Low] Catton, Earl Hugh 40 carucates. In Kelfield, Count Alan 2 carucates and 1 bovate. In the same place, Hugh fitzBaldric 1 carucate and 7 bovates.

In Stillingfleet, the king 2 bovates. In the same place, Count Alan 2 bovates. In the same place, Erneis 2 carucates. In the same place, Hugh fitzBaldric 1½ carucates. In Escrick, Count Alan 4 carucates.

In Morby, Count Alan 1 carucate. In the same place, Hugh fitzBaldric 1 carucate. In Deighton [in Escrick], Count Alan 4 carucates. In "Chetelstorp" [in Escrick], Count Alan 4 carucates. In Bishop Wilton, the archbishop 15 carucates.

In Wheldrake, William de Percy 6 carucates and 6 bovates. In Elvington, William de Percy 6 carucates. In Bolton [in Bishop Wilton], the king 1 carucate. In the same place, the archbishop 4 ½ carucates.

In Fangfoss, the king 8 carucates. In Gowthorpe, the archbishop 4 carucates. In Youlthorpe, Odo the crossbowman 4 carucates. In the same place, the archbishop 2 carucates.

In Greenwick, the archbishop 3 carucates. In High Belthorpe, the archbishop 4 carucates. In Barmby Moor, the archbishop 7 carucates and 2 bovates. In the same place, the king 6 bovates.

HUNTOW HUNDRED

In Flamborough, Earl Gugh 15 carucates. In Sewerby, Earl Hugh 1½ carucates. In the same place, the Count of Mortain 6½ carucates.

In the same place, the king 1½ carucates. In Marton [in Sewerby], the king 5 carucates. In the same place, the archbishop 3 carucates. In the same place, the Count of Mortain 1 carucate. In Bridlington, the king 13 carucates.

In the same place, the Count of Mortain 5 carucates. In Hilderthorpe, the king 2½ carucates. In the same place, the Count of Mortain 3½ carucates. In Wilsthorpe, the king 2 carucates.

In the same place, Drogo 2 carucates. In Bessingby, the king 8 carucates. In Fraisthorpe, the king 1 carucate. In the same place, the Count of Mortain 7 carucates. In the same place, Hugh fitzBaldric 1 carucate.

In Auburn, the king half a carucate. In Easton, the king 6 carucates. In Boynton, the king 8½ carucates. In the same place, the Count of Mortain 5½ carucates.

In Grindale, the archbishop 4 carucates. In the same place, the king 8 carucates. In Reighton, the archbishop 3 carucates. In the sale place, the king 5 carucates. In Bempton, the Count of Mortain 6 carucates.

[Folio 382: EAST RIDING]

In Speeton, the king 4 carucates. In the same place, the Count of Mortain 6 carucates. In Buckton, the king 5 carucates and 6 bovates. In the same place, the Count of Mortain 3 carucates and 6 bovates.

In the same place, Earl Hugh 2½ carucates. In Flixton, the king 14 carucates. In Staxton, the king 6 carucates. In Foxholes, the king 8 carucates.

"TORBAR" HUNDRED

In Hunmanby, Gilbert de Ghent 24 carucates. In "Ricstorp" [in Muston], Gilbert de Ghent 4 carucates. In Muston, the same Gilbert 4 carucates.

In "Scloftone" [in Muston], the same Gilbert 3 carucates. In Wold Newton, the same Gilbert 7 carucates. In [East and West] Flotmanby, the same Gilbert 5 carucates and 7 bovates.

In the same place, the archbishop 1 bovate. In Muston, the king 2 carucates. In Wold Newton, the king 4 carucates. In Fordon, the king 5 carucates.

In "Ledemare" [in Fordon], the king 1 carucate. In Burton Fleming, the king 16 carucates. In Folkton, the king 9 carucates. In Great Kelk, the archbishop 5 carucates.

In another Kelk [Little Kelk], the king 2 carucates. In Argam, the king 1 carucate. In the same place, the Count of Mortain 1 carucate. In Brigham, the Count of Mortain 3½ carucates.

In the same place, the king half a carucate. In "Estolf" [in Bringham], the king 1 carucate. In Foston on the Wolds, William de Percy 5 carucates. In Gembling, the archbishop 5 carucates.

In Nafferton, William de Percy 23 carucates. In the same place, the king 6 bovates. In Pockthorpe, William de Percy 5 carucates. In the same place, the Count of Mortain 1 carucate.

In Elmswell, the king 10 carucates. In Garton-on-the-Wolds, the archbishop 9 carucates. In the same place, the Count of Mortain 25 carucates.

BURTON HUNDRED

In Burton Agnes, the king 12 carucates. In Gransmoor, the king 4 carucates. In the same place, Earnwine 2 carucates. In Harpham, the king 4 carucates.

In the same place, Earnwine 8 carucates. In Kilham, Earnwine 30 carucates. In the same place, the king 11 carucates. In the same place, Odo the crossbowman 7 carucates.

In Ruston Parva, the archbishop 9 carucates. In the same place, the king 3 carucates. In Lowthorpe, the archbishop 1½ carucates. In the same place, the king 5½ carucates.

In Thornholme, the king 7 carucates. In Haisthorpe, the king 4 carucates. In the same place, the archbishop 2 carucates. In Thorpe [in Rudston], the Count of Mortain 3 carucates.

In Carnaby, the king 13 carucates. In Caythorpe, the king 5 carucates. In the same place, the archbishop 4 carucates. In the same place, the Count of Mortain 3 carucates.

In Rudston, the king 8 carucates. In the same place, the Count of Mortain 8 carucates. In the same place, Ralph Paynel 8 carucates. In Thwing, the king 17 carucates and 2 bovates.

In Swaythorpe, Odo the crossbowman 9 carucates. In "Fornetorp" [in Thwing] and Octon, the king 4 carucates. In the same place, the Count of Mortain 14 carucates. In Butterwick, the Count of Mortain 12 carucates.

In Langtoft, the archbishop 9 carucates. In the same place, the king 6 carucates. In Boythorpe, the king 5 carucates. In Potter Brompton, the king 3 carucates.

In Ganton, the king 8 carucates. In Binnington, the Count of Mortain 6 carucates. In Willerby, the king 5 carucates.

"SCARD" HUNDRED

In Langton, Hugh fitzBaldric 18 carucates. In Kennythorpe, the same Hugh 2 carucates and 5 bovates. In Birdsall and Sutton [near Malton], the Count of Mortain 13½ carucates. In the same place, the king 3½ carucates. In the same place, the archbishop 2½ carucates.

In Welham, Ralph de Mortimer 5 carucates and 5 bovates. In the same place, Hugh fitzBaldric 1 carucate and 3 bovates. In Sutton [near Malton], the king 2 carucates and 6 bovates.

In the same place, the archbishop half a carucate. In the same place, Ralph de Mortimer 4 carucates. In the same place, Hugh fitzBaldric 1½ carucates. In Norton [near Malton], the king 1 carucate and 1 bovate.

In the same place, Ralph de Mortimer 1 carucate. In the same place, Hugh fitzBaldric 3 carucates. In Settrington, Berengar de Tosny 9 carucates. In Wharram le Street, the Count of Mortain 12 carucates.

In 'Buckton Holms' [in Settrington], Berengar de Tosny 22 carucates and 6 bovates. In the same place, Hugh fitzBaldric 3 carucates. In North Grimston, the king 4 carucates and 2 bovates.

In the same place, the archbishop 3½ carucates. In the same place, Hugh fitzBaldric 2 carucates and 2 bovates. In Duggleby, Berengar de Tosny 8 carucates. In the same place, the king 2 carucates.

In Towthorpe [in Wharram Percy], the king 6 carucates. In the same place, the Count of Mortain 3 carucates. In Burdale, Hugh fitzBaldric 6 carucates. In the same place, the king 10 bovates.

In Wintringham, Ralph de Mortimer 20 carucates. In Linton [in Wintringham], the same Ralph 4 carucates. In Scampston, the same Ralph 4 carucates.

In the same place, the king 5½ carucates. In Thorpe Bassett, the king 5 carucates. In the same place, the Count of Mortain 6 bovates. In Rillington, the king 2 carucates.

In the same place, the Count of Mortain 2 carucates and 2 bovates. In the same place Berengar de Tosny 5 carucates. In Scagglethorpe [in Settrington], Berengar de Tosny 2½ carucates. In the same place, the Count of Mortain 1 carucate.

ACKLAM HUNDRED

In Menethorpe, Berengar de Tosny 6 carucates. In the same place, the king 2 carucates. In Eddlethorpe, the king 4 carucates.

In Burythorpe, Berengar de Tosny 3 carucates. In the same place, the king 2 carucates. In Kirby Underdale, the king 6 carucates. In Painsthorpe, the king 5 carucates. In the same place, Gilbert Maminot 1 carucate.

In Uncleby, Berengar de Tosny 4 carucates. In the same place, the king 2 carucates. In Hanging Grimston, the king 4½ carucates. In the same place, Odo the crossbowman 4½ carucates.

In Acklam [near Leavening], the king 6½ carucates. In the same place, the Count of Mortain 2½ carucates. In Garrowby, the king 3 carucates.

In the same place, the Count of Mortain 3 carucates. In Leavening, the king 5 carucates. In another Leavening, the Count of Mortain 7 carucates. In Howsham, the Count of Mortain 8 carucates.

In Bugthorpe, the archbishop 4½ carucates. In the same place, Odo the crossbowman 4½ carucates. In Thoralby [in Bugthorpe], the king 4 carucates.

In Skirpenbeck, Odo the crossbowman 9 carucates. Of these, the Count of Mortain has 3 carucates and 2 bovates. In Scrayingham, Hugh fitzBaldric 12 carucates.

In "Scardiztorp" [in Skirpenbeck], Odo the crossbowman 3 carucates. In Barthorpe, the Count of Mortain 6 carucates. In the same place, Odo the crossbowman 3 carucates.

In Leppington, the Count of Mortain 8 carucates. In "Sudcniton" [in Westow], the Count of Mortain 6 carucates. In Kirkham, the Count of Mortain 8 carucates.

In Wharram Percy, the king 9 carucates. In Fridaythorpe, the archbishop 6 carucates and 3 bovates. In the same place, the king 1 carucate. In the same place, the Count of Mortain 1½ carucates.

In the same place, Odo the crossbowman 7½ carucates. In Thixendale, the Count of Mortain 5 carucates and 6 bovates. In the same place, Odo the crossbowman 4 carucates and 2 bovates.

In Raisthorpe, the king 3 carucates. In the same place, Odo the crossbowman 2 carucates. In the same place, Hugh fitzBaldric 1 carucate.

"TORESHOU" HUNDRED

In Sherburn, the archbishop 3 carucates. In the same place, the Count of Mortain 6 carucates. In the same place, Hugh fitzBaldric 9 carucates. In place Newton, Ralph Paynel 18 carucates.

In East Heslerton, the king 3½ carucates. In the same place, the Count of Mortain 2 carucates. In the same place, Hugh fitzBaldric 3 carucates. In the same place, Berengar de Tosny 1½ carucates.

In another Heslerton [West Heslerton], the king 5 carucates. In the same place, the Count of Mortain 5 carucates. In Knapton, Ralph de Mortimer 6 carucates.

In Weaverthorpe, the archbishop 18 carucates. In [East

and West] Lutton, the archbishop 8 carucates. In Helperthorpe, the archbishop 12 carucates.

In Thirkleby [in Kirby Grindalythe], Ralph de Mortimer 8 carucates. In another Thirkleby [Thirkleby, in Kirby Grindlaythe], the Count of Mortain 4 carucates. In "Turodebi" [in Kirby Grindalythe], the king 6 carucates.

In Kirby Grindalythe, the Count of Mortain $16\frac{1}{2}$ carucates. In the same place, the king $1\frac{1}{2}$ carucates. In Low Mowthorpe [in Kirby Grindalythe], the archbishop 6 carucates.

In the same place, the Count of Mortain 1 carucate. In Sledmere, the king 9 carucates. In the same place, the Count of Mortain 9 carucates. In Cowlam, the archbishop half a carucate.

In Croome, the king 4 carucates. In the same place, Berengar de Tosny 1 carucate. In the same place, Hugh fitzBaldric 3 carucates. In Cottam, the archbishop 9 carucates.

In Cowlam, the king 6 carucates. In the same place, Berengar de Tosny 6 carucates.

In Patrington, the archbishop 15 carucates and 2 bovates. In Winestead, $7\frac{1}{2}$ carucates.

In Halsham, 7 carucates and 2 bovates and 2 parts of 1 bovate. In Thorpe [in Welwick], 3 carucates.

In "Thurlesthorp" [in Patrington], 2 carucates and 6 bovates. In Swine, 7 carucates and 7 bovates.

In North Skirlaugh, 9 bovates. In Marfleet, 1 bovate. In Sproatley, 1 bovate. In Danthorpe, 1 carucate. The archbishop [has] these.

In Wawne, the archbishop 2 carucates and 6 bovates. In Weel, 2 carucates. In Tickton, $1\frac{1}{2}$ carucates. In Eske, 2 carucates. In Stork Hill, 1 carucate.

IN SOUTH HUNDRED

In Welwick, 4 carucates. In Weeton [in Welwick], 2 carucates and 5 bovates.

In Grimston [in Garton], 2 carucates. In Monkwith, 2 carucates. In Ottringham, $6\frac{1}{2}$ carucates.

MIDDLE HUNDRED

In Bilton [near Hull], 3 carucates. In Burton Constable, 5 carucates. In West Newton [in Aldbrough], 3 carucates. In Flinton, 6 bovates.

In Danthorpe, 1 carucate. In Withernwick, 1 carucate. In Routh, 1 carucate and 7 bovates. In Sutton-on-Hull, 1 carucate and 1 bovate.

In Southcoates, 1 carucate. In Drypool, 1 carucate.

IN NORTH HUNDRED

In Great Cowden, the archbishop 9 carucates. In Rise, half a carucate. In Sigglesthorne, 8 carucates. In Catwick, 1 carucate.

In Brandesburton, 1 carucate. In Leven, 6 carucates.

Holderness

In BURSTWICK, 4 carucates of land. In Paull, 1 carucate. In Sutton-on-Hull, 2 carucates. In Paull Holme, 1 carucate.

In Newton Garth, 1 carucate. In Nuthill, 2 carucates. In Skeckling, 2 carucates and 2 bovates. In Camerton, 6 carucates.

In Thorngumbald, 2 carucates. In Paull Holme, 1 carucate. In Lelley Dyke, 4 carucates. In Sproatley, 1 carucate. In Preston [near Hedon], 1 carucate and 3 bovates.

In Kilnsea, $13\frac{1}{2}$ carucates. In Tunstall [near Withernsea], 7 carucates. In Roos, 3 carucates and the third part of 1 carucate.

In Hilston, 2 carucates. In Owstwick, 5 carucates and the third part of 1 carucate. In Elstronwick, 4 carucates. In Tansterne, 1 carucate.

In Etherdwick, 2 carucates. In Ringbrough, 1 carucate. In Humbleton, 1 carucate. In "Fostun" [in Humbleton], 3 carucates. In Flinton, $3\frac{1}{2}$ carucates.

In Winstead, half a carucate. In Withernsea, 18 carucates and 6 bovates. In "Andrebi" [in Roos], 2 carucates. In Burton Pidsea, 7 carucates.

In Danthorpe, 2 carucates and 6 bovates. In Fitling, 6 bovates. In Sproatley, 5 bovates. In Grimston [in Garton], 4 carucates. In Waxholme, 6 bovates.

In Tunstall [near Withernsea], 1 carucate. In Owthorne, 5 bovates. In Hollym, 1 carucate. In 'Redmere' [in Owthorne], 3 bovates. In Mappleton, 13 carucates.

In Rolston, 5 carucates and 2 bovates and 2 parts of 1 bovate. In "Arnestorp" [in Great Hatfield], $1\frac{1}{2}$ carucates. In 'Little Cowden' [in Mappleton], 3 carucates.

In Withernwick, 6 carucates. In Thirtleby, 4 carucates. In Wyton, 4 carucates. In Marfleet, 2 carucates. In Coniston, 4 carucates.

In Routh, 3 carucates. In the same place, St John [of Beverley], 1 carucate. In Hornsea, 27 carucates. In Hornsea Burton, 2 carucates. In Southorpe, $1\frac{1}{2}$ carucates.

In Long Riston, 2 carucates and 6 bovates. In North Skirlaugh, 6 bovates. In High Skirlington, 5 carucates. In 'Cleeton', 28 carucates and $1\frac{1}{2}$ bovates.

In Easington [near Kilnsea], 15 carucates. In Garton, 6 carucates. In Ringbrough, 2 carucates. In Aldbrough, 9 carucates.

In East Newton [in Aldbrough], $1\frac{1}{2}$ carucates. In South Skirlaugh, 1 carucate. In Totleys, 2 bovates. In Wawne, 7 carucates. In Meaux, 2 carucates.

In Benningholme, 2 carucates and 5 bovates. In Rowton, 2 carucates. In South Skirlaugh, 4 carucates. In Dowthorpe, 3 carucates. In Marton [in South Skirlaugh], 2 carucates.

In Low Fosham, 3 carucates. In Bewick, 6 carucates. In East Newton [in Aldbrough], $1\frac{1}{2}$ carucates. In Ringbrough, 1 carucate. In Waxholme, 2 carucates and 2 bovates.

In Ottringham, half a carucate. In Totleys, 5 carucates and 6 bovates. In Keyingham, 8 carucates. In Ottringham, 4 carucates. In Halsham, 6 bovates.

In [Great and Little] Newsome, 5 carucates and 2 bovates.

In Rimswell, 5 carucates and 2 bovates. In Waxholme, 2 carucates. In 'Redmere' [in Owthorne], 1½ carucates. In Holmpton, 8 carucates.

In Out Newton, 5 carucates. In Rysome Garth, 2 carucates. In "Torp" [in Easington, near Kilnsea], 3 carucates. In Lissett, 3 carucates. In Beeford, 12½ carucates. In Dunnington [in Beeford], 6 carucates.

In 'Winkton' [in Barmston], 5 carucates and 2 bovates. In Nunkeeling, 2 carucates. In North Frodingham, 12 carucates. In Barmston, 8 carucates. In Ulrome, 2½ carucates.

In Nunkeeling, 4 carucates. In Bewholme, 5 carucates and 6 bovates. In Arram, 1 carucate. In Brandesburton, 12½ carucates. In Seaton [in Sigglesthorpe], 6 carucates. In Catfoss, 6 carucates.

In Catwick, 5 carucates. In "Chenucol" [in Long Riston], 1 carucate. In Long Riston, 3 carucates. In Rise, 5½ carucates. In Wassand, 2 carucates. In Great Hatfield, 3 carucates.

In Withernwick, 1 carucate. In Langthorpe [near Old Ellerby], 1 carucate. In Little Hatfield, 2 carucates and 2 parts of 1 carucate. In Old Ellerby, 4 carucates. In Oubrough, 2 carucates.

In Ganstead, 4 carucates. In Sutton-on-Hull, 3 carucates and 2 bovates. In Bilton [near Hull], 1 carucate. In Preston [near Hedon], 12 carucates and 1 bovate. In Southcoates, 1 carucate. In Drypool, 5 bovates.

In West Carlton, 2 carucates. In Marton [in South Skirlaugh], 1 carucate. In Sproatley, 4 carucates. In Roos, 3 carucates and 5 bovates.

[Folio 382V: [YORKSHIRE]]

[Blank in MS, apart from gathering signature at foot of page.]

LINCOLNSHIRE

[Folio 335: LINCOLNSHIRE]

[Blank in MS]

[Folio 335V: [LINCOLNSHIRE]]

[Blank in MS]

[Folio 336: [LINCOLNSHIRE]]

IN THE CITY OF LINCOLN in the time of King Edward there were 970 inhabited messuages. This number is reckoned according to the English method, that is 100 for 120. In the city itself were 12 lawmen, that is men having sake and soke: Harthaknut; Swærting son of Grimbald; Ulf's son, Svartbrandr, who had toll and team; Wælhræfn; Alweald; Beorhtric; Guthrothr; Wulfbert; Godric son of Eadgifu; Siward the priest; Leofwine the priest; Healfdene the priest.

Now there are as many there having sake and soke in like manner: (1) Swærting in the place of his father Harthaknut; (2) Swærting;(3) Svartbrandr in the place of his father Ulf; (4) Aghmund in the place of his father Wælhræfn; (5) Alweald; (6) Godwine son of Beorhtric; (7) Norman Crassus in the place of Guthrothr; (8) Wulfbert, brother of Ulf, [who] is still living; (9) Peter de Valognes in the place of Godric son of Eadgifu; (10) Wulfnoth the priest in the place of Siward the priest; (11) Burgweald in the place of his father Leofwine who is now a monk; (12) Leodwine son of Rawn in the place of Healfdene the priest.

Toki son of Auti had in the city 30 messuages besides his hall and 2½ churches, and he had his hall quit of every custom, and with respect to another 30 messuages he had rent; and besides this [he had] from each [messuage] 1d, that is landgafol. In respect of these 30 messuages the king had toll and forfeiture, as the burgesses testified. But Wulfgeat the priest gainsays their sworn testimony, and offers himself to undergo the ordeal that it is not as they say. Geoffrey Alselin holds this hall, and his nephew Ralph. Bishop Remigius holds the above-mentioned 30 messuages in respect of the Church of ST MARY, in such a way that Geoffrey Alselin has nothing therein either by way of exchange or other render. The same Geoffrey has 1 messuage outside the wall, from which he has landgafol, as Toki had.

Ralph Paynel has 1 messuage, which was Mærle- Sveinn's, quit of every custom.

Earnwine the priest has 1 messuage, Earl Morcar's, with sake and soke, and he holds it of the king in the same way as Morcar had it, as he himself says.

Gilbert de Ghent has 1 messuage, Ulf's, with sake and soke; and another messuage from which he had 1d; and yet again, 1 messuage, [which was] Siward's, quit of every custom.

Earl Hugh has 1 messuage, Earl Harold's, with sake and soke; and 2 messuages from which he has landgafol.

Roger de Bully has 1 messuage, Swein the son of Svavi's, with sake and soke.

Countess Judith has 1 messuage, Stori's, without sake and soke; and Ivo Taillebois claims this through the burgesses.

Bishop Remigius has 1 little manor with 1 carucate in near [sic] the city of Lincoln with sake and soke and with toll and team; and likewise over 3 messuages, and over 2 churches, and likewise over 78 messuages, except for the king's geld which they give with the burgesses. Of these, 20 messuages are waste. Of the 3 messuages above, 1 is quit of all things, but 2 pay geld with the burgesses.

In the fields of Lincoln outside the city are 12½ carucates of land, besides the carucate of the bishop of the city. Of this land the king and the earl have 8 carucates in demesne. Of these, King William gave 1 to a certain Ulfkil for a ship which he bought from him. But he who sold the ship is dead, and no one has this carucate of land unless the king grant it. Besides these 8 carucates the king and the earl has [sic] 231 acres of arable land, inland, and 100 acres of meadow.

Of the rest of the land, that is 4½ carucates, Ulf had TRE 1 carucate; now his son Svartbrandr has it.

Siward the priest and Auti had another carucate TRE, and 6 acres of land which Wulfgeat the priest holds. Now Ælfnoth has half of this carucate, and Northmann son of Siward the priest the other half. But Olaf the priest seized this aforesaid half of this land and Siward the priest's wife, while it was in the seisin of the king on account of 40s which the king himself had laid upon Siward the priest.

Peter de Valognes has the third carucate, which TRE Godric had.

The fourth carucate belonged to the Church of All Saints TRE, and 12 tofts and 4 crofts. Godric son of Garwine had this church, and the church's land, and whatever belonged to it; but, now he has become a monk, the Abbot of Peterborough [...] has possession of them. But all the burgesses of Lincoln say that he has them unjustly, because neither Garwine nor his son Godric nor anyone else could give them outside the city nor outside their kindred, except by grant of the king.

This church and what belongs to it Earnwine the priest claims [...] by inheritance from his kinsman Godric.

ST MARY of Lincoln, in which the bishopric is now, had and has the remaining half-carucate of land.

The churches of Lincoln and the burgesses had among them 36 crofts in Lincoln, excepting the $12\frac{1}{2}$ carucates of land which have been enumerated above.

Of the aforesaid messuages which were inhabited TRE, there are now waste 200, by English reckoning that is 240; and by the same reckoning 760 are now inhabited.

Those written below have not paid the king's geld as they ought:

The land of ST MARY on which Theodbert dwells in the high street has not paid geld, nor has the bishop's land situated at St Laurence's paid geld in respect of 1 house.

The Abbot of Peterborough has not paid geld in respect of 1 house and of 3 tofts.

Earl Hugh has not paid geld in respect of any of his land, nor [has] Turold of 'Greetwell', nor Losuard, nor Ketilbert.

Hugh fitzBaldric has not paid geld in respect of 2 tofts, nor Geoffrey Alselin likewise in respect of 2 tofts.

Nor has Gilbert paid geld in respect of 3 houses, nor Peter de Valognes in respect of his house, nor Countess Judith in respect of her house, nor Ralph Paynel in respect of 1 house, nor Ralph de Bapaume in respect of his house, nor Ertald in respect of his house.

This house, in respect of which the Abbot of Peterborough has not, as has been said, paid geld,

[Folio 336V: [LINCOLNSHIRE]]

Norman Crassus claims as of the king's fief, for Guthrothr his predecessor had this in pledge for $3\frac{1}{2}$ marks of silver.

Kolsveinn has in the city of Lincoln 4 tofts of his nephew Cola's land; and outside the city he has 36 houses and 2 churches to which nothing belongs, which he built on the wasteland that the king gave him, and that was never before built upon. Now the king has all the customs from them.

Alvred, Turold's nephew, has 3 tofts from Sibbi's land, which the king gave him, in which he has all customs except the king's geld from the mint-tax.

The Abbot of Ely has half a messuage from Eadstan's land.

Hugh fitzBaldric has 2 tofts which the king gave him.

Of the aforesaid waste messuages, 166 had been destroyed on account of the castle. The remaining 74 have been destroyed outside the castle boundary, not because of the oppression of the sheriffs and officers, but because of misfortune and poverty and the ravages of fire.

TRE the city of Lincoln rendered to the king £20 and to the earl £10. Now it renders £100 by tale between the king and the earl. The mint, however, [...] renders £75.

The customary dues of the king and the earl in South Lincolnshire render £28.

In the North Riding the customary dues of the king and the earl render £24.

In the West Riding the customary dues of the king and the earl render £12.

In the South Riding the customary dues of the king and the earl render £15.

If the peace given by the king's hand or by his seal [is] broken, a fine is paid by 18 hundreds.

Each hundred pays £8. 12 hundreds pay the fine to the king, and 6 to the earl.

If anyone for any crime is outlawed by the king and by the earl and by the men of the shire, no one but the king can give him peace.

THE KING'S BOROUGH OF STAMFORD paid geld TRE for $12\frac{1}{2}$ hundreds for military service by land and sea and for danegeld. There were and are 6 wards, 5 in Lincolnshire, and the sixth in Northamptonshire which is beyond the bridge; and yet this [sixth ward] rendered every custom together with the others except [land] gafol and toll, which the Abbot of Peterborough had and has.

In these 5 wards TRE were 141 messuages and half a mill, which rendered all customs. But there are also as many [messuages] now, except 5 which are waste on account of the work of the castle.

In these wards are 6 messuages which TRE gave all customs, but now they do not give them. Brand has 4, and Ulfkil son of Merewine 2.

In these wards are 77 messuages of sokemen, who have their lands in demesne, and who seek lords where they will, over whom the king has nothing else except the fine of their forfeiture, and heriot, and toll. And [there is] 1 mill rendering 30s, which Eustace of Huntingdon took away. It belonged to one of the sokemen.

In Stamford TRE were 12 lawmen who had sake and soke within their houses and over their men, excepting geld, and heriot, and forfeiture of their bodies at 40 orae of silver, and excepting larceny. The same men have this now, but there are only 9 [of them]. One of them has 17 messuages under him, and half a mill [rendering] 15s; the second 14 messuages: one of these is waste; the third 2 messuages; the fourth $2\frac{1}{2}$ the fifth 5; the sixth 4; the seventh 3; the eighth 1; the ninth 3, but Hugh Musard has taken 2 away from him.

In these wards there are still 22 messuages and 2 churches with 12 acres of land rendering 14s, which Earnwine the priest had TRE; and Eadsige had 1 messuage. Eudo the steward has these 23 messuages now. The king had every custom over them; now he does not have them.

In the same vill Azur had 7 messuages and half a mill TRE. Now Gunfrid de Chocques has them. To these belong 70 acres outside the vill.

Edward Cild had 14 messuages and 70 acres outside the vill. Now Countess Judith has them.

Queen Edith had 70 messuages which belonged to Rutland, with all customs except those for bread. To these belong 2½ carucates of land, and 1 ploughing team, and 45 acres of meadow outside the vill. Now King William has it, and it is worth £6; TRE it was worth £4.

In Stamford, the Abbot of Peterborough had and has 10 messuages belonging to Lincolnshire, and 1 mill [rendering] 40s; and 5s in respect of houses and of 8 acres.

Leofwine had 9 messuages; now Alvred has them. Leofwine also [had] 1 messuage with every custom except geld, which [messuage] Guy de Raimbeaucourt has now.

Fastulf had 1 church of the king, quit, with 8 acres.

Albert [has] 1 church, St Peter's, with 2 messuages, and half a carucate of land which belongs to Upper Hambleton in Rutland. It is worth 10s.

The king has 600 acres [of] arable land outside the vill in Lincolnshire.

The lawmen and burgesses have 272 acres without every custom.

TRE Stamford gave £15; now it gives at farm £50. In respect of every king's custom it now gives £28.

[Folio 337: [LINCOLNSHIRE]]

In TORKSEY TRE there were 213 burgesses. They all had the same customs as the people of Lincoln, and [this] in addition, that whoever of them had a messuage in the same vill gave neither toll nor customary due either coming in or going out. This, however, was their [duty], that if the king's messengers should come thither, the men of the same town should conduct them to York with their ships and other means of navigation, and the sheriff should find the messengers' and sailors' provisions out of his farm. But if any of the burgesses should wish to go elsewhere, and to sell [his] house which was in the same vill, he could do it, if he wished, without the knowledge and licence of the reeve.

Queen Edith had this small town of Torksey and the manor of Hardwick [in Torksey] adjoining it in demesne, and she had 2 carucates of land without geld outside the city. Now the king has them in demesne, and there are 102 burgesses dwelling there, but 111 messuages are waste. To this vill belong 20 acres of meadow, and 60 acres of scrubland, and 11 fisheries. 1 of these belongs to Berengar de Tosny. TRE it was worth £18 between the king and the earl; now £30.

TRE Torksey and Hardwick [in Torksey] rendered in Lincoln the fifth penny of the city's geld. Towards this fifth part Torksey gave 2 pennies and Hardwick [in Torksey] the third. From this Torksey Morcar had the third penny of all customs.

In Hardwick [in Torksey], Swein and Godric had 1 carucate of land, and 12 men dwelt there. Now Roger de Bully has a half, and the Bishop of Lincoln the other half in respect of St MARY of Stow. On this there falls the third part of the king's geld which the king does not have from that which belongs to Torksey.

Here are written those who had sake and soke and toll and team in Lincolnshire: the Bishop of Lincoln, Queen Edith, the Abbot of Peterborough, the Abbot of Ramsey, the Abbot of Crowland, Earl Harold, Earl Morcar, Earl Waltheof, Earl Ralph, Ulf Fenman, Mærle-Sveinn, Thorgot Lag, Toki son of Auti, Stori, Ralph the staller, Siward Barn, Harold the staller, Fiacc, Ralph son of Skialdvor, Godric son of Thorfridh, Aki son of Siward and Vighlak his brother in respect of their father's land, Leofwine son of Alwine, Azur son of Svala, Æthelric son of Mærgeat, Auti son of Azur, Æthelstan son of Godram, Thorir son of Roald, Toli son of Alsige, Azur son of Burg, Wulfweard White, Ulf, Hemming, Barthi, Swein son of Svavi.

XLIIII Durand Malet
XLV Martin
XLVI Waldin the Breton
XLVII Waldin Engaine
XLVIII Odo [...] the crossbowman
XLVIX William Blund
L Restold
LI Godfrey de Cambrai
LII Gunfrid de Chocques
LIII Osbern the priest and
LIIII Ralph the steward
LV Ansgot
LVI Countess Judith
LVII Guy de Craon
LVIII Robert Malet
LIX Robert of Stafford
LX Peter de Valognes
LXI Heppo [...] the crossbowman
LXII Ralph fitzHubert
LXIII Geoffrey de la Guerche
LXIIII Geoffrey Alselin
LXV Baldwin the Fleming
LXVI William Taillebois
LXVII Kolgrimr
LXVIII Svartbrandr
LXIX Ketilbiørn and others
LXX The king's thegns

[Folio 337V: LINCOLNSHIRE]

The land of the King

'ASWARDHURN' WAPENTAKE

In KIRKBY LA THORPE, Earl Morcar had 5 carucates of land to the geld. There is land for 4 ploughs. Now the king has there 1 plough, and 14 sokemen with 2 ploughs, and 5 villans and 5 bordars with 1 plough. There is half a church. TRE worth £4; now £8 weighed and assayed.

Evedon belongs to the above-mentioned manor, 10 bovates of land to the geld. [There is] land for 1 plough. There 2 sokemen and 2 villans have 1 plough. There is a mill [rendering] 5s4d, and the site of 1 mill, and 6 acres of meadow.

To the same manor belongs this sokeland: Ewerby Thorpe, 1 carucate; Howell, 2½ bovates; Heckington, 1 bovate; Quarrington, 1 bovate. All together, 1½ carucates and half a bovate to the geld. [There is] land for 1½ ploughs. In these the king has 7 sokemen having 1 plough. There is 1 mill [rendering] 12s, and 13 acres of meadow, and 11 acres of scrubland, and 20 acres of marsh.

In SOUTH KYME, Earl Morcar had 4 carucates of land and 2 bovates to the geld. [There is] land for 2 ploughs. Now the king has half a plough there, and 12 villans and 3 bordars with 2 ploughs. There are 2 churches, and 1 priest, and 2 acres of meadow, and 6 fishponds [rendering] 4s; 210 acres of woodland, pasture in places, and 700 acres of marsh. TRE worth 40s; now 60s weighed and assayed.

In BOOTHBY GRAFFOE, Earl Morcar had 8 carucates of land to the geld. [There is] land for 9 ploughs. The king has 2 ploughs there, and 20 villans and 2 bordars having 4 ploughs, and 11 sokemen on 3 carucates having 3 ploughs. There is a church and a priest; 1 carucate of land belongs to the church. There is 1 mill [rendering] 3s, and 120 acres of meadow. TRE worth £20; now likewise £20 by weight.

In WELLINGORE, Earl Morcar had 18 carucates of land to the geld. [There is] land for as many ploughs. Now the king has 2 ploughs there, and 7 villans and 7 bordars with 1 plough, and 28 sokemen with 7 ploughs. There is a church, and a priest having 2 carucates and 2 bovates of the same land, and this church belongs to the Church of St Peter in Lincoln. There are 129 acres of meadow, and another 14 acres belonging to the church. TRE worth £30; now £15 by weight.

In COLEBY [near Boothby Graffoe], Siward had 7 carucates of land to the geld. [There is] land for as many ploughs. Now the king has 1 plough there, and 5 villans and 6 bordars with 1 plough, and 10 sokemen with 2 ploughs, and 30 acres of meadow. TRE it was worth £4. King William, however, placed this land in Washingborough, and it is valued there. [There is] a priest, and a church having 1 bovate of this land.

In Coleby [near Boothby Graffoe] itself are 12 carucates of land to the geld. [There is] land for as many ploughs. Of these, 1 carucate is inland of Washingborough; but 11 are sokeland. Ralph the staller had this land. Now the king has there 14 sokemen and 7 villans with †8† ploughs, and 60 acres of meadow. The value of this is in Washingborough.

In GRANTHAM, Queen Edith had 12 carucates to the geld. There is no arable land outside the vill. No one had sake or soke there except Alswith the nun, who gave it to Peterborough Abbey; and now Kolgrimr has this with sake and soke. Queen Edith had a hall, and 2 carucates and land for 3 ploughs without geld. [There were] 111 burgesses, [and] 80 tofts, less 3, of the sokemen of the thegns. Now the king has the like [number]. Ivo found 1 plough, and it is still [there], and 72 bordars. [He has] 1 church with 8 tofts, and 4 mills rendering 12s, and 8 acres of meadow without geld. Of the above tofts the Bishop of Durham claims 7 tofts which Earnwine the priest has, and the hundred bears testimony in the bishop's favour. TRE the whole of Grantham was sokeland [farmed] at £52; now it renders £100 by weight. The church was then [farmed] at £8; now it is at £10; but it is only worth 100s.

In GREAT GONERBY are 7 carucates of land to the geld. [There is] land for 9 ploughs. 3 carucates are inland, and 4 sokeland of Grantham. Now the king has 1 plough there, and 21 sokemen and 1 villan and 1 bordar having 6 ploughs, and [there are] 105 acres of meadow.

In HARLAXTON are 12 carucates of land to the geld. [There is] land for 16 ploughs. 9 [carucates] are sokeland, and 3 [belong] to the hall of Grantham. Now the king has there 10 villans and 2 bordars with 2 ploughs, and 58 sokemen having 14 ploughs. There are 2 mills [rendering] 2s, and 60 acres of meadow, and 60 of spinney.

In Stoke Rochford, 6, and North Stoke, 3, are 9 carucates of land to the geld. [There is] land for 12 ploughs. Now the king has 1 plough there, and 16 villans with 3 ploughs, and 10 sokemen with 2 ploughs, and 2 mills rendering 21s4d. [There is] meadow 9 furlongs long and 3 broad and 20 acres.

In [?] Spittlegate [in Grantham] are 3 carucates of land and 5½ bovates to the geld. [There is] land for as much. [It is] sokeland of Grantham. The king has there 13 sokemen and 6 villans with 4 ploughs, and 1 mill [rendering] 13s4d, and 3 acres of meadow.

In GREAT PONTON, Queen Edith had 12 carucates of land to the geld. [There is] land for 10 ploughs. Now this land is sokeland of Grantham. There are now 10 villans and 3 bordars and 12 sokemen, and half a plough. Ivo found as much there. [There is] scrubland 8 furlongs long and 3 broad.

To GRANTHAM belongs this sokeland: Old Somerby, 2 carucates and 2 bovates; Sapperton, 5 carucates; and Braceby, 5 carucates; Welby, 8 carucates; Belton [near Grantham], 5 carucates; Harrowby, 4 carucates; 'Dunsthorpe' [in Grantham], 2 carucates; Londonthorpe, 5 carucates and 6 bovates; Barkston, 8 carucates; Denton, 10 carucates. All together 55 carucates to the geld. [There is] land for 60 ploughs. This land is all in 'Aswardhurn' WAPENTAKE.

[Folio 338: LINDSEY]

In Old Somerby the king has 2½ carucates and 2 bovates and 8 sokemen with 2½ ploughs.

In Sapperton and Braceby are 24 sokemen and 5 villans and 2 bordars with 9 ploughs, and 140 acres of meadow, and 46 acres of woodland pasture, and 64 acres of scrubland, and 1 church.

In Welby are 37 sokemen and 7 villans and 4 bordars with 10 ploughs, and 160 acres of meadow, and 150 acres of scrubland, and a church with a priest.

In Belton [near Grantham] are 18 sokemen and 14 bordars with 4 ploughs, and 68 acres of meadow.

In Harrowby are 16 sokemen with 4 ploughs, and 34 acres of meadow.

In 'Dunsthorpe' [in Grantham] are 5 villans and 1 bordar and 8 sokemen with 2 ploughs, and 20 acres of meadow.

In Londonthorpe are 21 sokemen and 6 villans with 5 ploughs, and 44 acres of meadow, and 1 mill [rendering] 10s.

In Barkston are 35 sokemen and 10 bordars with 6 ploughs, and 70 acres of meadow, and 2 mills which Thorfridh son of Wulffrith had. Their soke [belongs] to Grantham.

In Denton are 80 acres of meadow.

In Skillington [is] sokeland of Grantham, 3 carucates of land to the geld. [There is] land for 3 ploughs. 14 villans and 2 bordars and 1 sokeman have 3 ploughs there, and 10 acres of meadow, and 140 acres of scrubland. Its value [is] in Grantham.

In BASSINGHAM, Earl Morcar had 24 carucates of land to

the geld. [There is] land for 16 ploughs. The king has 2 ploughs there, and 35 villans and 8 bordars and 1 sokeman having 6 ploughs, and 2 mills rendering 32s. There is a church, and a priest, and 420 acres of meadow. The whole [is] 16½ furlongs long and 15 furlongs broad. TRE worth £25; now £16.

In Thorpe on the Hill is sokeland of this manor, 6 bovates of land to the geld. [There is] land for 5 oxen. There is 1 sokeman with half a plough, and 5 acres of meadow.

In TYDD ST MARY, Earl Ælfgar had 5 carucates of land and 1 bovate to the geld. [There is] land for 3 ploughs. The king has 1 plough there, and 16 villans and 5 bordars and 1 sokeman having 8 ploughs, and 80 acres of meadow. TRE it was worth £8, and 1 fishery with woodland rendered 70s, less 4d; now the whole is worth £15.

In LUTTON, Earl Ælfgar had 4 carucates of land to the geld. [There is] land for 2 ploughs. The king has 6 oxen there, and 16 villans with 4 ploughs, and 1 fishery [rendering] 12d, and 60 acres of meadow. TRE worth £8; now the same.

In Tydd St Mary is a Berewick of this manor, 2 carucates and 1 bovate of land to the geld. Now there are 8 villans and 1 sokeman having 1 plough and 2 oxen, and 30 acres of meadow.

In GEDNEY, Earl Ælfgar had 8 carucates of land to the geld. [There is] land for 4 ploughs. The king has 6 oxen there, and 18 villans with 3 ploughs, and 30 acres of meadow, and a fishery [rendering] 12d. [It is] 20 furlongs long and 12 broad. TRE worth £8; now £6.

In Holbeach is sokeland of this manor, 8 carucates of land and 6 bovates to the geld. The king has there 26 sokemen and 5 bordars with 11 ploughs, and 80 acres of meadow. This sokeland is valued at 17 in addition to the above-mentioned amount.

In the same Holbeach and Whaplode are 5 carucates of land to the geld, which Count Alan held; now they are in the king's hand.

In Fleet, Earl Ælfgar had 6 carucates of land to the geld. [There is] land for 4 ploughs. The king has there 6 oxen, and 8 villans with 2½ ploughs, and 1 fishery [rendering] 16d, and 2 salt-pans [rendering] 2s, and [there are] 500 acres of meadow. [It is] 1 league long and 1 broad. TRE worth £4; now 50s.

[Entries erased.]

In NETTLEHAM, Queen Edith had 12 carucates of land to the geld. [There is] land for 16 ploughs. The king has there 3 ploughs, and 28 villans and 12 bordars and 1 sokeman having 11 ploughs. The whole [is] 20 furlongs long and 20 broad. TRE worth £24; now £30.

In Dunholme is sokeland of this manor, 8 carucates of land to the geld. [There is] land for as many ploughs. There are 18 sokemen with 6 ploughs, and 50 acres of meadow. Of this land Odo the crossbowman has 2½ carucates.

In Swinthorpe, 6 bovates, and Wickenby, 1 carucate,

[there is] sokeland of Nettleham. In Reasby, 2 bovates, sokeland of the same place.

In KIRTON IN LINDSEY, Earl Edwin had 8 carucates of land to the geld. [There is] land for 16 ploughs. Now the king has 4 ploughs there in demesne; and 80 villans and 37 bordars with 18 ploughs, and 1 mill [rendering] 12d, and 200 acres of meadow. [It is] 2 leagues long and 20 furlongs broad. TRE worth £24; now £80.

To this manor belongs this sokeland: Glentworth, 6 carucates and 2½ bovates; Hemswell, 4 carucates and 2 bovates; Harpswell, 2 carucates and 6½ bovates; Snitterby, 4 bovates; Saxby, 1 carucate; Grayingham, 4 carucates; Corringham, 1 carucate; Aisby [in Corringham], 1 carucate; Heapham, 2½ carucates; Springthorpe and Corringham, 6 carucates; Somerby [in Corringham], 2 carucates; Blyton, 3 carucates; Pilham, 1 carucate; Northorpe [near Kirton in Lindsey], 2 carucates; Ashby [in Scunthorpe], 1 carucate; Hibaldstow, 2½ carucates; 'Stainton' [in Waddingham], 6 bovates; Redbourne, 9 bovates; Brumby [in Scunthorpe], 5 carucates; Ashby [in Scunthorpe], 13 bovates; Bottesford, 2 carucates; Yaddlethorpe, 1 carucate; Winterton, 4 carucates; Scunthorpe, 3 carucates and 6 bovates and 2 parts of 1 bovate. All together 59 carucates of land to the geld. [...] There is land for 69 ploughs.

[Folio 338V: [LINCOLNSHIRE]]

In Glentworth are 24 sokemen and 6 bordars with 5 ploughs, and 212 acres of meadow.

In Hemswell are 17 sokemen and 1 villan and 7 bordars with 3 ploughs, and 173 acres of meadow.

In Harpswell are 6 sokemen with 2½ ploughs, and 150 acres of meadow.

In Snitterby are 9 sokemen with 2 ploughs.

In Saxby are 4 sokemen with 1 plough, and 6 acres of meadow.

In Grayingham are 7 sokemen and 14 villans with 4 ploughs.

In Corringham are 4 sokemen and 1 bordar with 2 ploughs.

In Aisby [in Corringham] are 7 sokemen and 1 bordar with 2 ploughs.

In Heapham are 16 sokemen with 4 ploughs, and 120 acres of meadow.

In Springthorpe and Corringham are 41 sokemen with 10 ploughs, [and] a church and a priest.

In Somerby [in Corringham] are 6 sokemen with 1½ ploughs, and 45 acres of meadow.

In Blyton, nothing.

In Pilham, 8 sokemen with 2 ploughs, and 16 acres of meadow.

In Northorpe [near Kirton in Lindsey], 6 sokemen with 2½ ploughs, and 60 acres of meadow.

In Ashby [in Scunthorpe], 9 sokemen with 1½ ploughs.

In Hibaldstow is 1 plough in demesne; and 16 villans and 2 bordars with 2 ploughs, and 222 acres of meadow, and 120 acres of scrubland.

In 'Stainton' [in Waddingham] and Waddingham are 3 sokemen having 5 oxen, and 16 acres of meadow.

In Redbourne are 4 sokemen with 1 plough, and 30 acres of meadow.

In Brumby [in Scunthorpe], 14 sokemen with 3 ploughs, and 80 acres of meadow.

In Ashby [in Scunthorpe], 7 sokemen with 1½ ploughs.

In Bottesford, 2 sokemen with 2 oxen, and 30 acres of meadow.

In Yaddlethorpe [there is] nothing except 15 acres of meadow and 12 acres of scrubland.

In Winterton, 9 sokemen and 1 bordar with 5 oxen.

In Scunthorpe, 20 sokemen with 2 ploughs and 2 oxen, and 80 acres of meadow.

All together 223 sokemen, 16 bordars [and] 15 villans with 50 ploughs.

In Thealby and 'Derby' [in Burton upon Stather] and Burton upon Stather the king has 6 tofts, and half a market belonging to Kirton in Lindsey.

Hibaldstow is a Berewick, not sokeland; and in Grayingham are 2 carucates of inland; and in Springthorpe half a carucate is inland. All the rest is sokeland.

In CAISTOR and Hundon, Earl Morcar had 3 carucates of land to the geld. [There is] land for 6 ploughs. The king has 1 plough there in demesne; and 40 villans and 12 sokemen with 3 ploughs. There is a church and a priest, which the Bishop of Lincoln claims. There are 4 mills [rendering] 13s4d, and 60 acres of meadow. TRE worth £30; now £50.

To the hall of this manor belong Cadney and Howsham, 4 carucates of land to the geld. [There is] land for 8 ploughs. There are 2 ploughs in demesne; and 20 villans and 15 sokemen and 10 bordars having 9 ploughs. There are 360 acres of meadow.

To the same manor belongs this sokeland:

In [Great or Little] Limber 4½ carucates of land and half a bovate. There is 1 plough in demesne; and 33 sokemen and 5 villans with 3 ploughs, and 30 acres of meadow.

In North Kelsey 5 carucates of land. There are 50 sokemen and 2 villans with 6 ploughs, and 700 acres of meadow.

In Fonaby 1½ carucates of land. There are 18 sokemen with 3 ploughs, and 3 acres of meadow.

In Clixby 1½ carucates of land [which is] in land and sokeland. There is 1 plough in demesne; and 14 villans and 2 sokemen with 3 ploughs, and 30 acres of meadow.

In Kirmington 4 carucates of land and 6 bovates. There are 20 sokemen and 1 villan and 14 bordars with 3½ ploughs.

In Croxton 2 bovates of land. There are 3 sokemen with half a plough.

In [Great or Little] Limber 3 bovates of land. There are 3 sokemen.

In Grasby half a carucate of land belonging to the church of Caistor, with 1 villan having 1 ox. This is valued at 6s8d.

In Owmby 5 bovates of land [which is] inland. There is nothing except 10 acres of meadow.

In Searby 1 bovate of land [which is] inland. There is 1 villan with 2 oxen.

In Habrough and Newsham 2 carucates of land and 2 bovates and 2 parts of 1 bovate. There are 8 sokemen and 2 bordars with 1½ ploughs, and 1 salt-pan [rendering] 12d, and 200 acres of meadow.

In Keelby 15 bovates of land to the geld. There 13 sokemen and 3 bordars have 2 ploughs.

In South Kelsey 3 carucates of land. There 35 sokemen and 12 bordars have 5½ ploughs. [There is] meadow 1 league long and 2½ furlongs broad.

In Holton le Moor 2½ carucates of land. There 26 sokemen have 3½ ploughs, and [there are] 60 acres of meadow. Of this sokeland Ivo Taillebois has 1 carucate.

All together 28 carucates of land and 1 bovate to the geld. [There is] land for 58 ploughs. All together 211 sokemen and 24 villans and 28 bordars with 30 ploughs.

In GAYTON LE WOLD Queen Edith had 3 carucates of land to the geld. [There is] land for 4 ploughs. There the king has 1½ ploughs in demesne; and 18 sokemen and 4 bordars with 5 ploughs. There is a church, and 50 acres of meadow. [It is] 7½ furlongs long and 7 broad. TRE worth £15; now £45.

SOKELAND OF THIS MANOR.

In Saltfleetby [All Saints, St Clement or St Peter] 2 carucates of land. There are 40 sokemen and 9 bordars having 4 ploughs, and 120 acres of meadow.

In Manby [near Grimoldby] 3 carucates of land. There are 20 sokemen with 4 ploughs.

In Grimoldby 4 carucates of land. There 6 sokemen and 5 bordars have 3 ploughs, and [there are] 100 acres of meadow.

In Grainthorpe 2 carucates of land. There 13 sokemen and 6 villans have 2 ploughs, and 6 salt-pans [rendering] 6s.

In [North or South] Somercotes 3 carucates of land. There 30 sokemen and 7 villans and 8 bordars have 6 ploughs, and [there are] 80 acres of meadow.

In Yarburgh 2½ carucates of land and 1 bovate and the third part of 1 bovate.

[Folio 339: [LINCOLNSHIRE]]

In Alvingham 1 carucate of land. There are 14 sokemen and 7 villans and 5 bordars with 2 ploughs, and 40 acres of meadow.

In Skidbrooke 3 carucates of land. There 24 sokemen and 3 villans have 8½ ploughs, and [there are] 60 acres of meadow.

In Welton le Wold 4 carucates of land. There 20 sokemen and 14 villans have 5½ ploughs, and [there are] 40 acres of meadow.

All together 25½ carucates and 1 bovate and the third part of a bovate to the geld. [There is] land for 38 ploughs.

In these are 167 sokemen and 37 villans and 27 bordars having 34 ploughs.

In HORNCASTLE, Queen Edith had 3 carucates of land without geld. [There is] land for 4 ploughs. The king has 2 ploughs there in demesne; and 29 villans and 12 bordars having 3 ploughs. There are 2 mills [rendering] 26s, and 100 acres of meadow. TRE worth £20; now £44.

SOKELAND OF THIS MANOR

In Thimbleby 4 carucates of land [...]. There 22 sokemen and 18 villans have 4½ ploughs, and [there are] 240 acres of meadow.

In [High or Low] Toynton 3 carucates of land. There 23 sokemen and 2 villans and 7 bordars have 4 ploughs, and 300 acres of meadow.

In Langton [near Horncastle] and "Torp" [in Woodhall] 3 carucates of land. There 13 sokemen and 24 villans have 4 ploughs, and 1 mill [rendering] 9s, and 120 acres of meadow, and 250 acres of woodland pasture.

In 'Fulsby' [in Tumby] half a carucate of land. There 3 sokemen have half a plough, and 8 acres of meadow, and 120 acres of woodland, pasture in places.

In Coningsby 1½ carucates of land [which are] inland. There are 8 villans and 3 bordars with 1½ ploughs, and 5 fisheries [rendering] 5s, and 12 acres of meadow, and 60 acres of scrubland.

In Haltham 2 carucates and 6 bovates of land. There 7 sokemen have 1½ ploughs, and 32 acres of meadow, and 20 acres of woodland pasture.

In 'Fulsby' [in Tumby] 1 carucate of land. There 1 sokemen has 1 plough.

In Roughton 12 bovates of land. There 8 sokemen have 1½ ploughs, and 15 acres of meadow, and 40 acres of woodland pasture.

In Scrivelsby 3 carucates and 7 bovates of land. There 20 sokemen and 12 bordars have 6 ploughs, and 200 acres of meadow, and 6 acres of scrubland.

In Moorby 3 carucates of land. There 8 sokemen and 10 bordars have 4 ploughs. There is a church, and 240 acres of meadow, and 6 acres of scrubland.

In Mareham le Fen 3 carucates of land. There 21 sokemen and 11 bordars have 4 ploughs. There is a church, and a priest, and 60 acres of meadow, and 300 acres of scrubland.

In Wood Enderby 3 carucates of land. There 16 sokemen and 6

bordars have 4 ploughs, and 60 acres of meadow, and [there are] 450 acres of woodland pasture.

In Wilksby 1½ carucates of land. There 4 sokemen and 5 bordars have 1 plough, and 20 acres of scrubland.

In West Ashby 6 carucates of land. There 45 sokemen and 5 villans and 13 bordars have 8 ploughs, and [there are] 500 acres of meadow and pasture.

In [High or Low] Toynton 4 carucates of land. There 21 sokemen and 8 villans and 3 bordars have 8 ploughs, and [there are] 400 acres of meadow.

All together [there are] 42 carucates of land to the geld. T[sic] [There is] land for 58 ploughs.

In these are 212 sokemen and 66 villans and 70 bordars having 55 ploughs.

[Folio 339V: LINCOLNSHIRE]

II. The land of the Archbishop of York

In SOUTH WILLINGHAM, Almær had 3 carucates of land to the geld. There is land for 4 ploughs. Archbishop Thomas has it now, and William [has it] of him. In demesne [are] 2½ ploughs; and 11 villans and 2 bordars having 2 ploughs, and 77 acres of meadow. TRE worth £4.10s; now the same.

In East Barkwith is sokeland of this manor, 6 bovates of land to the geld. [There is] land for 1½ ploughs. There 7 sokemen and 1 bordar have 1 plough. There are 13 acres of meadow.

In PANTON, Ælfric had 2 carucates of land to the geld. [There is] land for 3 ploughs. Now Gilbert, the archbishop's man, has in demesne 1½ ploughs; and 1 villan and 12 sokemen with 1½ ploughs, and 17 acres of meadow. TRE worth 30s; now 40s.

In West Barkwith is sokeland of this manor, 6 bovates of land to the geld. [There is] land for 1 plough. It is waste. There are 15 acres of meadow.

In GIRSBY, Almær had 2 carucates of land and 2 bovates to the geld. [There is] land for 4½ ploughs. Now William, the archbishop's man, has 2 ploughs in demesne; and 8 villans and 7 bordars and 18 sokemen having 4½ ploughs, and 20 acres of meadow. TRE worth £3; now the same; and tallage 20s.

In STALLINGBOROUGH, Elaf had 1 carucate of land and 2 bovates to the geld. [There is] land for 2½ ploughs. Herbert, the archbishop's man, has there 1 plough in demesne; and 5 villans and 3 sokemen and 1 bordar with 1 plough. There is half a mill [rendering] 32d, and 2 salt-pans, and 80 acres of meadow. TRE worth 30s; now 50s.

SOKELAND OF THIS MANOR: Healing, 1 bovate; Old Clee [in Great Grimsby], 3 bovates; 'Thrunscoe' [in Clee-thorpes], 2 bovates; that is, 6 bovates of land to the geld. [There is] land for 1 plough and 2 oxen. There 5 sokemen and 3 villans have 1 plough, and [there are] 25 acres of meadow.

In KEELBY, Elaf had 4½ bovates of land to the geld. [There is]

land for 1 plough and 1 ox. William, the archbishop's man, has half a plough there, and 2 sokemen and 2 bordars, and half a mill [rendering] 3s4d. TRE worth 10s; now the same.

In CUXWOLD, Fulcric had 7 bovates and 3 parts of 1 bovate of land to the geld. [There is] land for 1 plough and 6 oxen. William, the archbishop's man, has 1 plough there, and 1 villan and 1 bordar and 1 sokeman. They themselves [have] 1 plough. TRE worth 20s; now the same.

In Swallow is sokeland and inland of this manor, 1 carucate of land to the geld. [There is] land for 2 ploughs. There are 3 sokemen and 1 bordar with half a plough.

In LISSINGTON, Lambkarl had 4 carucates of land to the geld. [There is] land for 10 ploughs. Herbert, the archbishop's man, has 2 ploughs there in demesne; and 16 villans and 8 bordars and 4 sokemen having 5 ploughs. There are 80 acres of meadow, and 80 acres of scrubland. TRE worth £4; now £7.10s; tallage 40s. INLAND AND SOKELAND of this manor

In Swinthorpe 1½ carucates of land [to] the geld. [There is] land for 2 ploughs. There is 1 plough in demesne, and 2 villans, and 12½ acres of meadow.

In Snelland 2 bovates of land to the geld. [There is] land for half a plough. It is waste. There are 3 acres of meadow.

In Holton cum Beckering 1 carucate of land to the geld. [There is] land for 2 ploughs. There 5 sokemen and 5 villans have 3 ploughs, and [there are] 13 acres of meadow.

In Beckering 2 bovates of land to the geld. [There is] land for half a plough. There 4 sokemen have 1 plough and 6 oxen ploughing.

In BENNIWORTH, Godwine had 2½ carucates of land to the geld. [There is] land for 3½ ploughs. Now Osbern the priest has it of the archbishop. In demesne [are] 2 ploughs; and 7 villans and 2 bordars and 6 sokemen having 1½ ploughs. There is a church, and the site of 1 mill, and 60 acres of meadow. TRE worth 30s; now 70s.

In HACKTHORN, Alwine had 1 carucate and 5 bovates of land to the geld, and Auti 3 bovates of land to the geld. [There is] land for 3½ ploughs. William, the archbishop's man, has 1 plough there, and 6 villans and 7 bordars and 2 sokemen have 3 ploughs and 5 oxen. There is half a church, and 2 mills [rendering] 4s, and 60 acres of meadow. TRE worth 60s; now 40s.

In the soke of this manor Archbishop Thomas has 3 bovates to the geld.

In RIGSBY, Healfdene had 6 bovates of land to the geld. [There is] land land [sic] for 1 plough and 2 oxen. Herbert, the archbishop's man, has 1 plough there, and 3 villans and 4 bordars with 2 oxen. There is a church, and a priest, and 90 acres of woodland pasture, and 60 acres of scrubland. TRE worth 60s; now the same.

In Sutton on Sea and Trusthorpe and Addlethorpe is inland of this manor, half a carucate of land to the geld. [There is] land for 1 plough. There 6 villans have half a plough, and [there are] 40 acres of meadow.

SOKELAND of the same manor: Rigsby, 4 bovates; Ailby, 3 bovates; 'Tatebi' [in Ulceby], 1 carucate: this was a manor; that is, 15 bovates of land to the geld. [There is] land for 3½ ploughs. In them, 7 sokemen and 2 villans and 1 bordar have 1½ ploughs, and †20† acres of meadow, and [there are] 12 acres of woodland, and 20 acres of †scrubland†. This sokeland TRE was worth £4; now 40s.

In TETFORD, Almær and Earnwig had 3 carucates of land to the geld. [There is] land for 4 ploughs. There Gilbert, the archbishop's man, has 2 ploughs and 1 ox, and 8 villans and 7 sokemen with 2 ploughs. There is a church, and 1 mill [rendering] 4s, and 120 acres of meadow, and 6 acres of scrubland. TRE worth 30s; now £4.

In South Ormsby is sokeland of this manor, half a carucate of land to the geld. [There is] land for 6 oxen. There is 1 sokeman and 1 villan with half a plough, and 20 acres of meadow.

[Folio 340: LINDSEY]

In Hainton is sokeland of "Torp", 1½ carucates of land to the geld. [There is] land for 3 ploughs. There 3 sokemen and 3 bordars have 5 oxen ploughing, and [there are] 80 acres of meadow. Almær had it. William has it of THE ARCHBISHOP.

In the SOKE of Great Limber the archbishop has 3 bovates of land to the geld. [There is] land for 1 plough.

In Stallingborough is inland of Great Limber, half a bovate of land to the geld. [There is] land for 1 ox. The archbishop [has] there 1 villan ploughing with 1 ox, and the site of a mill, and half a †salt-pan†.

In Newton on Trent the archbishop has 100 acres of meadow belonging to Laneham [Church Laneham and Laneham, Notts.].

In HARPSWELL, Alwine had 5½ bovates of land to the geld. [There is] land for 1 plough. William, the archbishop's man, has there 1 villan and 5 sokemen ploughing with 6 oxen, and 39 acres of meadow. TRE worth 16s; now 10s.

In WORLABY [near Tetford], Ælfric had 2 carucates of land and 2 bovates to the geld. [There is] land for 3 ploughs. Now the archbishop has there 1 plough, and 1 villan and 10 sokemen with 1 plough, and 20 acres of meadow. TRE worth £3; now 40s.

In DOWSBY, Healfdene had 3 carucates of land to the geld. [There is] land for 3 ploughs. Now Hugh, the archbishop's man, has there 1 plough, and 9 villans and 3 bordars and 1 sokeman having 2 ploughs, and 1 mill [rendering] 3s, and [there are] 32 acres of meadow, and 20 acres of scrubland. TRE worth £3; now £4; tallage 20s.

In Bicker is inland of this manor, 1½ bovates of land to the geld. [There is] land for as much. It is waste. There is 1 waste salt-pan.

In GRABY is sokeland of the same manor, 1 carucate of land.

[There is] land for 1 plough. There 6 sokemen have 1 plough and 1 ox.

In BILLINGBROUGH, Thorkil had 5 bovates of land to the geld. [There is] land for 5 oxen. Now Walter d'Aincourt has it of the archbishop. There is half a plough, and 1 villan and 1 bordar, and 7 acres of meadow, and 1 site of a mill. | It is worth 10s. |

In HORBLING, Thorkil had 4 carucates of land to the geld. [There is] land for as many ploughs. Now Walter has it of the archbishop. In demesne [is] 1 plough; and 9 villans and 1 bordar and 8 sokemen having 3 ploughs. There is a church, and 20 acres of meadow. The arable land [is] 1 league long and 1 broad. TRE worth £6; now 40s; tallage 20s.

In NORTH WITHAM, Baca had 1 carucate of land to the geld. [There is] land for 1 plough. And Wulfwine [had] 1 carucate to the geld. [There is] land for 1 plough. Now Walkelin, the archbishop's man, has there 2 ploughs, and 4 villans and 2 bordars with 1 plough. There is a church of which Edward Cild has the third part, and 1 site of a mill, and 27 acres of meadow. TRE worth 40s; now 50s; tallage 11s.

In 'Twyford' [in Colsterworth] is sokeland of North Witham, half a carucate of land to the geld. [There is] land for half a plough. There are 2 bordars ploughing with 2 oxen. There are 3 acres of meadow, and 27 acres of scrubland.

In NORTH WITHAM, Alwine had 2 carucates of land to the geld. [There is] land for 2 ploughs. Walkelin, the archbishop's man, [has] 2 ploughs there, and 6 villans and 2 sokemen and 1 rent-paying tenant. There are 89 acres of meadow, and 120 acres of woodland in Drogo's warnode, and 40 acres of scrubland. TRE worth 20s; now 25s; tallage 5s.

In SKILLINGTON, Earl Morcar had 3 carucates of land to the geld, and Fredegæst and Beorhtmær 1 carucate of land to the geld. [There is] land for 5½ ploughs. [It is] free sokeland of Skillington. Walkelin, the archbishop's man, [has] 2 ploughs there, and 13 villans and 5 sokemen having 4 ploughs. There are 121½ acres of meadow, and 60 acres of woodland pasture in the warnode of Bishop Remigius. TRE worth £4; now the same; tallage 20s.

In the same place [sic] in EASTON, Siward had 3 carucates of land to the geld. [There is] land for 3 ploughs and 6 oxen. Osbern, the archbishop's man, has 1 plough there , and 12 villans and 6 bordars. There is half a church, and 1 mill [rendering] 8s, and 10 acres of meadow, and 200 acres of woodland and pasture, and 240 acres of scrubland. TRE worth 40s; now 40s.

In WOOLSTHORPE-BY-COLSTERWORTH, Earl Morcar had 3 carucates of land to the geld. [There is] land for 3 ploughs. [It is] sokeland of Skillington. 4 sokemen and 4 villans have 2 ploughs there, and [there are] 120 acres of woodland, pasture in places.

In BILLINGHAY, Swein had 12 carucates of land to the geld. [There is] land for 4 ploughs. Walkelin, the archbishop's man, and the 2 sons of Swein [have] 2 ploughs there, and 3 villans and 15 sokemen having 4 ploughs. There are 16 acres of meadow, and 3 sites of fisheries. TRE worth £4; now the same, and 5s more.

In Walcot [in Billinghay] is inland of this manor, 8 carucates of land to the geld. [There is] land for 6 ploughs. 15 sokemen and 1 villan have 6 ploughs there, and 4 acres of meadow, and [there are] 46 acres of scrubland.

In LENTON, Ulf had 4 carucates of land to the geld. [There is] land | for 5 ploughs |. [...] Ranulph, the archbishop's clerk, has 2 ploughs there in demesne; and 12 villans and 1 sokeman and 4 bordars having 6 ploughs. There are 36 acres of meadow, and 110 acres of scrubland in Guy de Craon's warnode. [There is] arable land and pasture 2 leagues long and 6 furlongs broad. TRE worth £4; now 60s.

[Folio 340V: LINCOLNSHIRE]

III. The land of the Bishop of Durham

In BRATTLEBY, Stiupi had 5 bovates of land to the geld. The soke [belongs to] the same place. [There is] land for 6 oxen. Now the Bishop of Durham has this land, and Kolsveinn [has it] of him, and cultivates it. TRE [worth] 3s; now 4s.

In Snarford, Siward had 2 carucates of land and 2 bovates to the geld. [There is] land for 2 ploughs and 6 oxen. Now the Bishop of Durham, and of him Kolsveinn, has 1 plough, and 14 sokemen with 2 ploughs, and 60 acres of meadow. TRE [worth] 20s; now 30s; and tallage 10s.

In BARLINGS, Dene had 9 bovates of land to the geld. [There is] land for 1½ ploughs. Now Kolsveinn [has it] of the bishop. In demesne [is] 1 plough; and 2 villans and 1 bordar with 1 plough, and 20 acres of meadow, and 20 acres of scrubland. TRE worth 16s; now 20s.

In BLYBOROUGH, Redhulf had 7 bovates of land to the geld. [There is] land for 2 ploughs. Now the monks of Durham have 2 ploughs there, and 3 villans and 1 bordar and 1 sokeman with 1 plough, and 20 acres of meadow, and half a church between the bishop and Joscelin fitzLambert. TRE worth 20s; now 30s.

NORTH RIDING

In BROCKLESBY, Godwine had 1 carucate of land to the geld. [There is] land for 2 ploughs. There Nigel, the bishop's man, has 3 villans with 1 ox, and 30 acres of meadow. TRE worth 40s; now 10s.

In FULSTOW, Healfdene and Almær had 1 carucate of land and 2 bovates to the geld. [There is] land for 2½ ploughs. Walbert, the bishop's man, has there 16 villans and 10 bordars with half a plough, and 1 plough in demesne, and 11 salt-pans [rendering] 2s, and 60 acres of meadow. TRE worth 60s; now £4.

In WOLD NEWTON, Grimkel had 11 bovates of land to the geld. [There is] land for 2 ploughs. Walbert, the bishop's man, has 1 plough there, and 2 villans and 2 bordars with half a plough. There is a church, and 40 acres of meadow; and in Thorganby 1 mill which Norman d'Arcy holds unjustly and 10 acres of meadow. TRE worth 100s; now 30s. There is a hall with a toft and soke and sake.

SOUTH RIDING

In BULLINGTON, Æfric had 3½ bovates of land to the geld. [There is] land for 1 plough. Nigel, the bishop's man, has half a plough there, and 6 villans with 1 plough, and 10 acres of meadow, and [there are] 160 acres of scrubland. TRE worth 20s; now 10s.

In 'HARDWICK' [in Panton], Ælfric had 2 bovates of land and the third part of a bovate to the geld. [There is] land for 5 oxen. Nigel has it of the bishop, and it is waste. There are 27 acres of meadow. TRE worth 10s; now 3s.

In Langton by Wragby are 3 bovates of land to the geld. [There is] land for 6 oxen. It is sokeland of 'Little Sturton' [in Baumber], and there are 65 acres of scrubland.

In Wispington [are] 2 carucates of land to the geld. [There is] land for 4 ploughs. [It is] inland and sokeland of 'Little Sturton' [in Baumber] and Kirkby on Bain. There are 9 sokemen and 6 bordars with 3 ploughs.

In Waddingworth [are] 6 carucates of land to the geld. [There is] land for 6 ploughs. It is sokeland of 'Little Sturton' [in Baumber] and in Kirkby on Bain. There are 20 sokemen with 4 ploughs, and 20 acres of meadow, and 25 acres of scrubland.

In KIRKBY ON BAIN, Harold had 10 bovates of land to the geld. [There is] land for 13 oxen. The Bishop of Durham has there 3 villans and 2 bordars with half a plough, and [there are] 12 acres of meadow, and 170 acres of woodland, pasture in places. TRE worth 100s; now the same.

In Martin [near Horncastle] is sokeland of this manor, 12 bovates to the geld. [There is] land for 2 ploughs. There 3 sokemen and 2 bordars have 1 plough, and [there are] 34 acres of meadow, and 33 acres of woodland pasture, and 60 acres of scrubland.

In Tattershall Thorpe is inland and sokeland of the same manor, 2 carucates of land to the geld. [There is] land for 2 ploughs. 16 villans and 1 sokeman and 4 bordars have 1 plough there, and the third part of 2 mills rendering 8s, and 3 fisheries rendering 7s6d, and [there are] 15 acres of meadow, and 120 acres of woodland pasture. Eudo claims it.

In COVENHAM ST MARY, Esbiorn had 2½ carucates of land to the geld. [There is] land for 3 ploughs and 6 oxen. Now [the Abbey of] Saint-Carilef has from the bishop there 2½ ploughs, and 12 villans and 6 sokemen with 1½ ploughs. There is a church, and 60 acres of meadow, and 2 salt-pans [rendering] 3s. TRE worth 60s; now £4; tallage 20s.

In Little Grimsby is sokeland of this manor, 2 bovates of land to the geld. [There is] land for 3 oxen. It was waste; now it is cultivated.

In FOTHERBY, Sumarlithr and Arnketil had 7 bovates to the geld. [There is] land for 2 ploughs and 5 oxen. Turstin, the bishop's man, has there 1 sokeman [and] 6 villans having 1 plough, and [there are] 42 acres of meadow. TRE worth £4; now 20s.

In MAVIS ENDERBY and Raithby [near Spilsby], Alnoth had 4½ bovates to the geld. [There is] land for 5 oxen. Now there is half a plough, and 1 villan, and half the site of a mill, and 10 acres of meadow. TRE worth 10s; now the same.

In SPILSBY and 'Eresby' [in Spilsby] and Thorpe St Peter, Eskil had 6 carucates of land to the geld. [There is] land for 6 ploughs. The bishop has 1 plough there, and 5 villans and 5 sokemen and 1 bordar having 1 plough, and 2 mills [rendering] 9s, and [there are] 12 acres of meadow. TRE worth 20s; now the same.

In the same places is sokeland of Grebby and East Keal, 2 carucates of land to the geld. [There is] land for 3 ploughs. 12 sokemen have 2 ploughs there.

In EAST KEAL, Alnoth had 6 bovates of land to the geld. [There is] land for 6 oxen. 2 villans plough there with 2 oxen. There are 5 acres of meadow. TRE worth 10s; now the same. Eudo claims the soke.

In Toynton [All Saints or St Peter] is sokeland of Spilsby, 2 bovates of land to the geld. [There is] land for 2 oxen. There is 1 sokeman, and 6 acres of meadow.

In Skidbrooke is inland of Covenham St Mary, 7 bovates of land to the geld. [There is] land for 9 oxen. [The Abbey of] Saint-Carilef has there 6 men with 2 ploughs, and 9 acres of meadow.

In Grainthorpe is sokeland of Covenham St Mary, 4½ bovates of land to the geld. 6 villans have 1 plough and 2 oxen there, and [there are] 50 acres of meadow.

[Folio 341: LINDSEY]

SOUTH RIDING

In KEDDINGTON, Harold and Andor had 9½ bovates of land to the geld. [There is] land for 1½ ploughs. Turstin, the bishop's man, has 1 plough there, and 15 sokemen and 12 villans with 4 ploughs, and 3½ mills [rendering] 20s, and 12 acres of meadow. TRE worth 40s; now 60s.

In Saltfleetby [All Saints, St Clement or St Peter] is sokeland of this manor, 1 bovate of land to the geld. [There is] land for 2 oxen. There are 3 sokemen and 1 villan with 4 oxen.

In [North or South] Cockerington is other sokeland, half a bovate of land to the geld. [There is] land for 1 ox. There is 1 villan ploughing with 1 ox.

'WINNIBRIGGS' WAPENTAKE

In GREAT GONERBY, Morcar had 1½ carucates of land to the geld. [There is] land for 2 ploughs. Lambert, the bishop's man, has 1 plough there, and 5 villans and 2 bordars with 1 plough, and 2 mills [rendering] 16s, and 22½ acres of meadow. TRE worth 40s; now the same.

'AVELAND' WAPENTAKE

In NEWTON, Wulfric Wild had 7 bovates of land to the geld. [There is] land for 2 ploughs. The Bishop of Durham has half, and Wulfgeat and his wife have the other of the king. The whole of this land belonged to his wife's mother. The bishop has half a plough there, and 3 villans with half a plough, and 6 acres of meadow, and 35 acres of scrubland. Wulfgeat has half a plough, and 3 villans with half a plough, and 6 acres of meadow, and 35 acres of scrubland. The whole TRE was worth 40s; now the bishop's part [is worth] 25s; and Wulfgeat's part 25s; the bishop claims it.

HACEBY HUNDRED

In PICKWORTH, Swein and Aghmund had 1 carucate and 5 bovates of land to the geld. [There is] land for 2 ploughs and 2 oxen. Now Joscelin, the bishop's man, has 1 plough there, and 5 villans and 3 bordars ploughing with 5 oxen. There is half a church, and 16 acres of meadow, and 33 acres of woodland, pasture in places. TRE worth 40s; now the same.

'THREO' WAPENTAKE

In Braceby Hundred is sokeland of this manor, 1 carucate of land to the geld. [There is] land for 1 plough. 1 sokeman has half a plough there, and [there are] 30 acres of meadow, and 21 acres of woodland, pasture in places.

'ASWARDHURN' WAPENTAKE

'LAYTHORPE' [IN KIRKBY LA THORPE] HUNDRED

In KELBY, Aslak, Beorhtric and Arnketil had 6 carucates of land and 3 bovates to the geld. [There is] land for 8 ploughs. Now Almod, the bishop's man, has 2 ploughs there, and 7 villans and 3 sokemen and 3 bordars with 2 ploughs. TRE worth 70s; now £6. There are 70 acres of meadow, and 90 acres of scrubland, which Bishop Remigius and Kolgrimr and their fellows hold. The bishop has the soke.

'FLAXWELL' WAPENTAKE

ASHBY DE LA LAUNDE HUNDRED

In EVEDON, Thorfridh had 2½ carucates to the geld. [There is] land for 3 ploughs. Kolsveinn, the bishop's man, has 1 plough there, and 4 villans and 2 bordars with 1 plough and 2 oxen, and 20 acres of meadow. TRE worth £4; now 20s.

In North Rauceby Hundred and the other Rauceby Hundred [South Rauceby Hundred] is sokeland of Silk Willoughby or Kirkby la Thorpe, 3 carucates of land and 1 bovate to the geld. [There is] land for 4 ploughs. Almod, the bishop's man, has there 15 sokemen and 6 bordars having 5 ploughs, and half a church. These are valued in the above-mentioned manor.

In Evedon is sokeland of Kirkby la Thorpe, 1 bovate of land to the geld. There is 1 villan and 2 bordars, and 2 acres of meadow.

NORTH RIDING

BRADLEY WAPENTAKE

AYLESBY HUNDRED

In AYLESBY, Habeinn had 6 bovates of land and the third part of 1 bovate to the geld. [There is] land for 1 plough. Nigel, the bishop's man, has half a plough there, and 3 sokemen and 1 villan and 1 bordar with half a plough, and the site of 1 mill. TRE worth 40s; now 20s.

'HAVERSTOE' WAPENTAKE

'FENBY' [IN ASHBY CUM FENBY] HUNDRED

In WEST RAVENDALE, Grimkel had 2 bovates of land to the geld. [There is] land for half a plough. Walbert, the bishop's man, ploughs it with 3 oxen. TRE worth 20s; now 5s.

SOUTH RIDING

'WRAGGOE' WAPENTAKE

In BISCATHORPE, Godric and his 2 brothers had 3 carucates of land to the geld. 2 served the third. Now 2 of the bishop's men have 2 ploughs there, and 3 villans and 7 bordars and 9 sokemen with 2½ ploughs, and 2 mills [rendering] 5s, and [there are] 24 acres of meadow. TRE worth 60s; now the same.

In TATTERSHALL THORPE, Godwine and Gunnhvati had 5 bovates of land and the third part of 1 bovate to the geld. [There is] land for 6 oxen. The bishop has 1 plough there, and 5 villans and 1 bordar with 1 plough, and the fourth part of a mill [rendering] 12d, and 1½ fisheries [rendering] 3s; and the third part of a church, and 8 acres of meadow, and 46 acres of woodland pasture. TRE worth £3; now 33s4d.

'CANDLESHOE' WAPENTAKE

In SCREMBY, Fenkell had 1 carucate of land to the geld. [There is] land for 1 plough. Now the same man has it of the bishop. There is 1 plough, and 4 villans ploughing with 5 oxen. TRE worth 40s; now 20s.

In Ashby by Partney is sokeland of this manor, 1 carucate of land to the geld. [There is] land for 1 plough. There are 2 villans, and 5 acres of meadow.

In Scremby is sokeland of East Keal, 2 bovates of land to the geld.

In Addlethorpe is inland of East Keal and Orby and Grebby, 6 bovates of land to the geld. [There is] land for 6 oxen. 6 villans and 1 sokeman have 1 plough and 1 ox ploughing there, and 120 acres of meadow.

In WAINFLEET [All Saints or St Mary] 3 brothers had 7½ bovates of land to the geld. [There is] land for 1 plough. This is inland of the above-mentioned manor. Now Bondi and Ralph have there 10 villans and 1 bordar with 1 plough and 2 oxen, [...] and 2 salt-pans [rendering] 8d, and 83 acres of meadow.

'LOUTHESK' WAPENTAKE

In 'SOUTH CADEBY' [in Calcethorpe], Sumarlithr and Asgot had 4½ bovates of land to the geld.

In Saltfleetby [All Saints, St Clement or St Peter] [is] 1 bovate to the geld.

[Folio 341V: LINCOLNSHIRE]

[There is] land for 1 plough and 2 oxen. There Turstin, the bishop's man, has 1 plough there, and 3 villans and 1 bordar ploughing with 2 oxen, and 10 acres of meadow. TRE worth 20s; now 18s.

In Welton le Wold is sokeland of this manor, 1 carucate of land to the geld. [There is] land for 1 plough. 2 sokemen have half a plough there, and the third part of the site of 1 mill, and 10 acres of meadow.

'CALCEWATH' WAPENTAKE

In HAUGH and Calceby, Healfdene had 2 bovates of land to the geld. [There is] land for 3 oxen. Now William, the bishop's man, has half a plough there, and 1 bordar. TRE worth 10s; now 10s.

In BONTHORPE, Thorir had 1 carucate of land to the geld. [There is] land for 2 ploughs. Nigel, the bishop's man, has 1 plough there, and 6 villans and 4 bordars with 1 plough, and [there are] 9 acres of meadow. TRE worth 60s; now 60s.

In Sloothby [is] inland, half a carucate of land to the geld. [There is] land for 7 oxen. There are 6 villans and 2 bordars with half a plough, and 20 acres of meadow.

In FULLETBY, Siward and Eadric had 3 carucates of land and 6 bovates to the geld. [There is] land for 5 ploughs. William, the bishop's man, has 2 ploughs there, and 5 villans and 19 sokemen having 2 ploughs and 2 oxen. There are 50 acres of meadow. TRE worth £4; now 100s.

In Oxcombe and Worlaby [near Tetford] is sokeland of this manor, 1½ carucates of land to the geld. [There is] land for 2 ploughs. 11 sokemen have 2 ploughs there, and 60 acres of meadow.

In Threekingham is inland of Newton, 5 bovates of land and the sixth part of 2 bovates to the geld. There is 1 sokeman and 3 villans having half a plough. The Bishop of Durham has the twelfth part of a church of St Peter there, and the sixth part of a church of St Mary, and the sixth part of 4 bovates of land which belong to the Church of ST MARY.

In the same hundred and in this same vill a certain Wulfgeat has of the king's alms as much land and [as many] parts of the churches and of the ploughs and of the men as it is said above that the bishop has, for they divide Newton and what belongs to it in half.

[Folio 342: LINDSEY]

IIII. The land of the Bishop of Bayeux

In SOUTH CARLTON, Ealdormann had 1 carucate of land to the geld. [There is] land for 1 plough. The Bishop of Bayeux has there 4 sokemen with 1½ ploughs, and 1 church. TRE worth 10s8d; now the same; tallage 13s4d.

Ralph the steward and Gilbert de Ghent have this land by the seal of the Bishop of Bayeux. Earnwine the priest says that it ought to belong to the king.

In INGLEBY, Ketil and Ulfkil had 3 carucates of land and 6 bovates to the geld. [There is] land for 4 ploughs. Kolsveinn and Wadard, the Bishop of Bayeux's men, have 2 ploughs there, and 12 villans and 2 sokemen and 4 bordars having 1½ ploughs, and 90 acres of meadow, and 110 acres of scrubland. TRE worth 30s; now 50s; tallage 20s.

In STURTON BY STOW, Ulfkil, Asfrith, Restelf and Wulfmær had 8 carucates of land to the geld. [There is] land for 8 ploughs. Ilbert, the bishop's man, has 4 ploughs there, and 16 villans with 2 ploughs, and 30 acres of meadow, and 80 acres of scrubland. TRE worth £7; now £4; tallage 40s.

In WILLINGHAM BY STOW, Arnketil had 1½ carucates to the geld. [There is] land for 12 oxen. Now Ilbert, the bishop's man, has 1 plough there, and 2 villans and 3 sokemen with 1 plough. TRE worth 20s; now the same.

In INGHAM, Gamal had 1 carucate of land to the geld. [There is] land for 12 oxen. Now Ilbert has 2 ploughs there, and 2 villans and 3 bordars and 3 sokemen having 1 plough, and 10 acres of meadow. TRE worth 5s; now 20s; tallage 10s

In GLENTWORTH, Æstan had 7 bovates of land to the geld. In the same place [are] 4 bovates of land to the geld. [It is] sokeland of Glentham. [There is] land for 10 ploughs. Now Wadard, the bishop's man, has half a plough, and 6 sokemen and 1 villan [with] half a plough, and †50† acres of meadow. TRE worth 15s4d; now 40s8d.

In HEMSWELL, Alnoth had 4 bovates of land to the geld. [There is] land for 1 plough. Now Losoard, the bishop's man, has there 1 villan and 2 bordars with 1 plough, and 27½ acres of meadow. TRE worth 20s; now 10s.

In GLENTHAM, Æthelstan and Wulfmær had 10 bovates of land to the geld. [There is] land for 10 oxen. Wadard has there 2 villans and †2† sokemen with 1 plough. He himself [has] 1 plough, and 40 acres of meadow. TRE worth 15s4d; now 60s.

In NORMANBY-BY-SPITAL, Thor had 1 carucate of land to the geld. [There is] land for 2 ploughs. Now Ilbert, the bishop's man, has 2 sokemen with 1 plough, and 10 acres of meadow. TRE worth 10s; now 12s.

In [East and West] FIRSBY, Alwig and Eskil had 3 carucates of land and 5 bovates to the geld. Now Ilbert, the bishop's man, has 2 ploughs there, and 8 villans and 8 bordars and 6 sokemen with 2 ploughs. There is a church, and 30 acres of meadow. TRE worth 60s; now the same; tallage 10s.

In NORTHORPE [near Kirton in Lindsey], Eskil had 10 bovates to the geld. [There is] land for 2 ploughs. Now Ilbert, the bishop's man, has 1 plough there, and 5 villans and 3 bordars with 1 plough, and 10 acres of meadow. TRE worth 20s; now 20s.

In CLEATHAM, Eskil had 6 bovates of land to the geld.

[There is] land for 12 oxen. Ilbert, the bishop's man, has 1 plough, and 3 villans and 2 bordars with 1 plough, and 6 acres of meadow. TRE worth 30s; now 40s.

In 'STAINTON' [in Waddingham] and Waddingham, Harthgripr had 6 bovates of land to the geld. [There is] land for 1 plough. Ilbert, the bishop's man, has himself 1 plough there, [and] 6 villans and 2 bordars with 1 plough, and [there are] 16 acres of meadow. TRE worth 20s; now †15†s.

In ELSHAM, Ketilbiørn had 7 bovates of land to the geld. [There is] land for 2 ploughs. Ilbert, the bishop's man, has there 6 villans and 1 bordar with 1 plough, and [there are] 47 acres of meadow. TRE worth †15†s; now 15s.

In AUDLEBY, Tosti, Thorfridh and Earnwig had 10 bovates of land to the geld. [There is] land for 3 ploughs. Now [there are] 3 ploughs in demesne; and 15 villans and 3 sokemen and 6 bordars with 2 ploughs, and 60 acres of meadow. TRE worth 100s; now £8. The whole [is] 15 furlongs long and 6 broad.

SOKELAND OF THIS MANOR

In Newton by Toft [are] 10 bovates of land to the geld. [There is] land for 3 ploughs. 10 sokemen have 3 ploughs there.

In Sumarlithr [Osgodby near West Rasen] [are] 5 bovates of land to the geld. [There is] land for 1½ ploughs. 8 sokemen have 1 plough and 2 oxen ploughing there.

In Risby [is] 1 carucate of land to the geld. [There is] land for 2 ploughs. 14 sokemen and 4 villans have 3 ploughs there, and [there are] 31 acres of meadow, and 12 acres of scrubland. [It is] 3 leagues long and 3 furlongs broad.

In Kingerby [are] 5 bovates of land to the geld. [There is] land for 2 ploughs. 8 sokemen have 1 plough and 2 oxen ploughing there.

In COATES is inland of Ingham, half a carucate of land to the geld. [There is] land for half a plough. Ilbert has there 3 villans and 2 bordars [who] have 1 plough.

In Osgodby [near West Rasen] [are] 5 bovates of land to the land geld. [There is] land for 10 oxen. 9 sokemen have 1 plough and 2 oxen ploughing there. [It is] sokeland of Audleby.

In NETTLETON, Ketilbiørn and Gamal had 1 carucate and 6 bovates of land to the geld. [There is] land for 3½ ploughs. Now Erneis and Wadard, the bishop's men, have 2 ploughs there, and 13 villans and 5 bordars with 1 plough and 2 oxen, and 2 mills [rendering] 3s, and 60 acres of meadow. TRE worth 60s; now £4.

In North Thoresby and 'Audby' [in North Thoresby] is sokeland of this manor, 2 bovates of land to the geld. There are 4 villans, and 3 salt-pans, and 20 acres of meadow.

In Rothwell [is] 1 bovate of land to the geld. 1 sokeman has 1 ox there.

In Newton by Toft is sokeland of [East and West] Firsby, 6 bovates of land to the geld. [There is] land for 2 ploughs. Ilbert has there 5 sokemen [...] with 1½ ploughs, and 20 acres of meadow.

In GRASBY, Ulfkil had 2 carucates of land to the geld. [There is] land for 4 ploughs. Now there are 2 ploughs in demesne; and 6 villans and 6 bordars and 11 sokemen having 2 ploughs. There is a church and a priest, and 1 mill [rendering] 3s, and 40 acres of meadow. TRE worth 60s; now 100s.

In Swallow is sokeland of this manor, 1 carucate of land to the geld. [There is] land for 2 ploughs. There are 8 sokemen with 1 plough.

In KEELBY, Sigar had 4½ bovates of land to the geld. [There is] land for 9 oxen. Wadard, the bishop's man, has 1 plough there, and 2 villans and 3 sokemen ploughing with 2 oxen. TRE worth 30s; now the same.

In [?] 'Houfleet' [in Stallingborough] [are] 2 bovates to the geld. [There is] land for 2 oxen.

In Stallingborough is sokeland inland of this manor, 5½ bovates of land to the geld. [There is] land for 11 oxen. 8 villans and 2 sokemen have 1 plough there, and 180 acres of meadow, and half a mill [rendering] 3s.

In HEALING, Sigar had 7 bovates of land to the geld. [There is] land for 1 plough and 6 oxen. Wadard, the bishop's man, has 1 plough there, and 3 villans and 5 bordars and 2 sokemen with 1 plough, and 5 acres of meadow. TRE worth 30s; now 40s; tallage 20s.

In Old Clee [in Great Grimsby] is sokeland of this manor, 3 bovates of land to the geld. [There is] land for half a plough. 4 sokemen and 2 villans and 1 bordar have 5 oxen ploughing there, and 25 acres of meadow.

In 'Thrunscoe' [in Cleethorpes] [are] 2 bovates of land to the geld. [There is] land for half a plough. 1 villan and 3 sokemen have half a plough there.

In LITTLE COATES [in Great Grimsby], Azur had 15 bovates of land to the geld. [There is] land for 4 ploughs. Now there are 16 sokemen having 3 ploughs, and 40 acres of meadow. TRE worth 20s; now 40s.

In Great Coates [in Great Grimsby] [are] 6 or 3 bovates of land to the geld. [There is] land for 6 oxen. [It is] sokeland of Little Coates [in Great Grimsby]. 2 sokemen have 2 oxen ploughing there, and 100 acres of meadow.

In OLD CLEE [in Great Grimsby], Algar had half a carucate of land to the geld. [There is] land for 1 plough. Now Ilbert has it of the bishop, and it is waste. There are 40 acres of meadow. TRE worth 10s; now 20s.

In 'Itterby' [in Cleethorpes] is inland and sokeland of this manor, 1 carucate of land to the geld. [There is] land for 1½ ploughs. Ilbert has 5 sokemen and 2 villans having 1½ ploughs there.

In [? West] RASEN, Rolf had 5 bovates of land to the geld and 2 parts of a bovate. [There is] land for 1½ ploughs. Wimund, the bishop's man, has 1 plough there, and 7 villans and 3 bordars with 1 plough, and 2 mills [rendering] 6s, and [there are] 61 acres of meadow. TRE worth 20s; now 30s.

In MIDDLE RASEN, Ulfgrimr, Broklauss, Ulf, Godwine, Alwine and Leofric had 2 carucates and 1 bovate of land to the geld. [There is] land for 5 ploughs. Wadard, the bishop's man, has 18 villans and 11 bordars having 5 ploughs there. There is a church and a priest, with 2 bordars. 1 bovate of this land belongs to the church. There are 120 acres of meadow. TRE worth 70s; now £4.

In TOFT NEXT NEWTON, Azur had 14 bovates of land and the third part of a bovate to the geld. [There is] land for 4 ploughs. Wadard, the bishop's man, has 1 plough there, and 3 villans and 11 sokemen having 5 ploughs, and 60 acres of meadow. TRE worth 10s; now 60s; tallage 20s.

In TEALBY, Rolf had half a carucate of land to the geld. [There is] land for 1 plough. Losoard, the bishop's man, has 1 plough there, and 3 villans ploughing with 3 oxen, and 1 mill [rendering] 2s, and another mill which belongs to Grasby. TRE worth 20s; now the same.

In NORTH THORESBY and 'AUDBY' [in North Thoresby], Thorfridh had 4 carucates of land and 3 bovates and the sixth part of a bovate to the geld. [There is] land for 6 ploughs. Ilbert, the bishop's man, has 2 ploughs there, and 23 villans and 5 bordars with 2 ploughs and 5 oxen, and 27 sokemen having 5 ploughs, less 2 oxen. There are 80 acres of meadow, and turbary rendering 10s, and 16 salt-pans rendering 16s. TRE worth £8; now the same; tallage 40s. Edward exchanged this land with the bishop of Bayeux.

In GREAT STURTON, Grimkel had 3 carucates of land and 2 bovates and 2 parts of 1 bovate to the geld. [There is] land for 4 ploughs. Now Ilbert, the bishop's man, has 1 plough there, and 3 villans and 3 bordars and 23 sokemen having 4 ploughs. There is a church, and 1 mill [rendering] 8s, and 120 acres of meadow. TRE worth 40s; now 50s; tallage 10s.

In Ranby is inland and sokeland of this manor, 9 bovates of land to the geld. [There is] land for 2 ploughs. Now there is 1 plough in demesne; and 3 villans and 1 bordar and 4 sokemen having 1 plough, and 200 acres of meadow. There is a church to which belong 40 acres of land, and 5 acres of meadow. There is a priest having half a plough.

In 'Burreth' [in Tupholme] is sokeland, 3 bovates of land to the geld. [There is] land for half a plough. There is 1 villan and 1 bordar having 1 ox ploughing, and [there are] 15 acres of meadow, and 120 acres of woodland pasture, and 100 acres of scrubland.

In HAINTON, Rolf had 15 bovates of land to the geld. [There is] land for 3 ploughs and 6 oxen. Ilbert, the bishop's man, has half a plough there, and 9 villans and 2 bordars and 1 sokeman having 2 ploughs, and [there are] 100 acres of meadow. TRE worth 40s; now the same.

In Strubby [in Langton by Wragby] [are] 2 bovates of land to the geld. [There is] land for half a plough. It is sokeland. 3 sokemen have half a plough there.

In East Barkwith [are] 3 bovates of land to the geld. [There is] land for 6 oxen. 3 sokemen have half a plough there.

In SOTBY, Wulfnoth had 4 carucates of land to the geld. [There is] land for 6 ploughs. Ralph, the bishop's man, has there 16 sokemen and 3 villans with 4 ploughs. [There is] nothing in demesne. There is a church, and 150 acres of meadow. TRE worth £3; now £4.

In LANGTON [near Horncastle] and in "TORP" [in Woodhall], Leofsige had 1 carucate of land to the geld. [There is] land for 1½ ploughs. There a man of the bishop has

In Southrey [is] inland of Hainton, 2 bovates of land to the geld. [There is] land for half a plough. 2 villans have half a plough there, and [there are] 4 acres of meadow, and 20 acres of woodland.

[Folio 343: LINDSEY]

1 plough, and 26 villans and 3 sokemen having 5 oxen ploughing, and 60 acres of meadow, and 80 acres of woodland, pasture in places. TRE worth 40s; now the same.

In Thimbleby is inland and sokeland of this manor, 10 bovates of land to the geld. [There is] land for 14 oxen. 5 villans and 3 sokemen have 2 ploughs there, and [there are] 12 acres of meadow, and 30 acres of scrubland.

In SOUTH WILLINGHAM, Eskil had 6½ bovates of land to the geld. [There is] land for 13 oxen. Wadard has 1 plough there, and 4 villans and 1 bordar with 1 plough, and [there are] 36 acres of meadow. TRE worth 20s; now 40s.

In KIRKBY ON BAIN, Wulfmær had 10 bovates of land to the geld. [There is] land for 1½ ploughs. Ilbert, the bishop's man, has 1 plough there, and 10 villans and 4 bordars with 1 plough, and the site of a mill, and 12 acres of meadow, and 160 acres of woodland, pasture in places. TRE worth 40s; now 20s.

In SIXHILLS, Guthmund had 6½ bovates of land to the geld. [There is] land for 9 oxen. Ilbert, the bishop's man, has 1 plough there, and 3 villans and 1 bordar and 2 sokemen having half a plough. There is a church, and 25 acres of meadow. TRE worth 20s; now 20s.

In [North or South] COCKERINGTON, Eskil and Ulfgrimr had 3 carucates of land and 1 bovate to the geld. [There is] land for 6 ploughs. Ilbert, the bishop's man, has 2 ploughs there, and 7 villans and 4 bordars and 27 sokemen having 3 ploughs. There are 80 acres of meadow, and 60 acres of scrubland, and 2 parts of a mill [rendering] 2s. TRE worth 60s; now the same; tallage 20s.

In Alvingham [are] 4 bovates of land and 2 parts of a bovate to the geld. [There is] land for 1 plough. [It is] sokeland of [North or South] Cockerington. 4 sokemen have 1 plough there, and [there are] 7 acres of meadow.

In ABY, Wulfstan and Eskil had 14 bovates of land to the geld. [There is] land for 2 ploughs and 6 oxen. Wadard, the bishop's man, has 1 plough there, and and [sic] 12 villans and 4 sokemen and 2 bordars having 2½ ploughs, and 80 acres of meadow, and 27 acres of woodland pasture, and 300 acres of scrubland. TRE worth £3; now £4.

In Strubby [near Maltby le Marsh] [is] 1 carucate and 2

bovates of land to the geld. [There is] land for 2½ ploughs. 5 sokemen and 4 villans have 2 ploughs there. [It is] sokeland of Aby.

In RIGSBY, Thorulf and Odbert had 10 bovates of land to the geld. [There is] land for 2 ploughs. Losoard, the bishop's man, has 1 plough there, and 5 villans and 3 bordars with half a plough, and [there are] 120 acres of woodland pasture, and 60 acres of scrubland. TRE worth †60†s; now the same.

In Well [is] 1 bovate of land to the geld. [There is] land for 3 oxen. [It is] sokeland of Rigsby. There is 1 sokeman and 2 villans.

In Ailby [are] 5 bovates of land to the geld. [There is] land for 10 oxen. [It is] sokeland of Rigsby. In TATTERSHALL THORPE, Wulfmær had 2 carucates of land to the geld as a manor. [There is] land for 2 ploughs. There are 18 villans and 4 bordars with 1 plough, and 16 acres of meadow, and 120 acres of woodland pasture, and the third part of 2 mills rendering 7s, and 3 fisheries rendering 30d. It was and is worth 20s. Eudo holds it of the king. 3 sokemen and 2 bordars have 1 plough there, and 12 acres of meadow, and 12 acres of woodland pasture, and 40 acres of scrubland.

In Tothby [is] half a carucate of land to the geld. [There is] land for 10 oxen. [It is] sokeland [of] Rigsby. There are 3 sokemen ploughing with 3 oxen, and 20 acres of meadow, and 12 acres of woodland.

In ASHBY PUERORUM, Othenkar and Ketilbert had 4 carucates of land to the geld. [There is] land for 5 ploughs. Now the bishop has 1 plough there in demesne; and 9 villans and 2 bordars and 14 sokemen having 3 ploughs, and 2 mills [rendering] 3s6d, and [there are] 31 acres of meadow. TRE worth £3; now £7.

In Bag Enderby, 3 bovates, and Markby, 4 bovates, [are] 7 bovates of land to the geld. [There is] land for 1 plough. [It is] sokeland [of] Ashby Puerorum. 14 sokemen and 10 villans and 1 bordar have 2 ploughs there, and [there are] 12 acres of meadow.

In ASHBY CUM FENBY, Algar had 9 bovates of land to the geld. [There is] land for 2 ploughs and 2 oxen. Ilbert, the bishop's man, has half a plough there, and 2 villans and 2 bordars and 8 sokemen with 1 plough, and 1 mill [rendering] 3s, and 30 acres of meadow, and 6 acres of scrubland. TRE worth 30s; now 40s; tallage 20s.

In Brigsley and Waithe and East Ravendale [are] 2 carucates of land and 5½ bovates to the geld. [There is] land for 4 ploughs and 6 oxen. [It is] sokeland of Ashby cum Fenby. 13 sokemen and 10 villans have 4 ploughs there, and [there are] 25 acres of meadow.

In LACEBY and Bradley and Scartho, Swein, Erik and Tosti had 9 carucates of land to the geld. [There is] land for 16 ploughs. The Bishop of Bayeux has 3 ploughs there in demesne; and 4 villans and 5 bordars and 85 sokemen having 13½ ploughs. There are 3 churches with priests, and 2 mills [rendering] 8s, and 360 acres of meadow, and 100 acres of scrubland.

In Great Grimsby the customary dues and the ferry render 40s. TRE worth £12; now £30.

In Great Grimsby, 11 bovates, and Old Clee [in Great Grimsby], 3 bovates and the third part of a bovate, and 'Itterby' [in Cleethorpes], 4 bovates, and 'Thrunscoe' [in Cleethorpes], 7 bovates, [there is] sokeland of this manor. To the geld, 3 carucates and 1 bovate of land to the geld [sic]. [There is] land for 5 ploughs and 7 oxen. 55 sokemen and 1 villan have 6 ploughs there, and 54 acres of meadow.

In WITHCALL, Eskil and ødhgrim had 3½ carucates of land, less the third part of 1 bovate, to the geld. [There is] land for 6 ploughs. Ilbert, the bishop's man, has 1 plough there, and 4 villans and 42 sokemen having 6 ploughs, and 2 parts of a mill [rendering] 26d, and 56 acres of meadow. TRE worth £4; now the same; tallage 20s.

In STEWTON, Eskil had 3 bovates of land to the geld. [There is] land for 6 oxen. Ilbert has 1 plough there, and 1 bordar, and 3 acres of meadow, and 60 acres of woodland pasture. TRE worth 20s; now 15s.

In [North or South] OWERSBY, Gamal had 2 carucates of land to the geld. [There is] land for 4 ploughs. Wadard, the bishop's man, has 1 plough there, and 5 villans and 4 bordars and 26 sokemen having 5 ploughs, and 130 acres of meadow. TRE worth 40s; now 60s; tallage 20s.

In THORGANBY, Ælfric had 15 bovates of land to the geld.

[Folio 343V: LINCOLNSHIRE]

[There is] land for 3 ploughs and 6 oxen. The bishop has 1 plough there, and 8 acres of meadow. TRE worth 40s; now 20s.

In DRY DODDINGTON, Glædwine had 6 bovates of land to the geld. [There is] land for 6 oxen. Baldric, the bishop's man, has there 2 villans and 2 bordars with 1 plough, and half a mill [rendering] 3s, and 10 acres of meadow. It is worth 10s.

In CLAYPOLE, Thorfridh had 3 carucates of land and 1 bovate to the geld. [There is] land for 3 ploughs. The bishop has 1 plough there, and 6 villans and 3 bordars with 1½ ploughs, and [there are] 15 acres of meadow. TRE [worth] 40s; now 30s.

In 'CASTHORPE' [in Barrowby], Thorfridh had 1½ carucates of land to the geld. [There is] land for 14 oxen. Swein, the bishop's man, has there 5 villans and 1 bordar with 1 plough, and 10 acres of meadow. TRE worth 40s; now 30[s].

In STAPLEFORD, Thorfridh had 2 carucates of land to the geld. [There is] land for 1 plough. Thor, the bishop's man, has 1 plough there, and 3 villans and 1 bordar ploughing with 6 oxen. [There are] 1½ furlongs of meadow. TRE worth 20s; now the same.

In CANWICK, Skuli had 1½ carucates to the geld. [There is] land for 12 oxen. Ilbert has 2 ploughs there, and 2 [...] and 1 bordar, and 27 acres of meadow.

In OWMBY-BY-SPITAL, Rolf and Siward had 5 bovates of land to the geld. [There is] land for 5 oxen. Ilbert and

Wadard have 5 oxen in a plough there, and 9 acres of meadow. TRE worth 15s; now 20s8d.

V. The land of Bishop Osmund

In LONDONTHORPE are 15 bovates of land to the geld. [There is] land for 2 ploughs. This land belongs to the church of Grantham, and it is quit from all services. Bishop Osmund has there 7 villans with 1 plough, and 13 acres of meadow.

In [?] Spittlegate [in Grantham], St Wulfram of Grantham has half a carucate of land to the geld. [There is] land for 4 oxen. 1 villan ploughs there with 2 oxen.

In Great Gonerby, St Wulfram of Grantham has 1 carucate of land to the geld with sake and soke. [There is] land for 12 oxen.

The value of this land is reckoned with [that of] the church of Grantham.

VI. [The land] of Bishop Geoffrey

In CANWICK and Bracebridge [in Lincoln], Ulf had 6 carucates of land to the geld. [There is] land for as many ploughs. Bishop Geoffrey has 1½ ploughs there, and 2 sokemen on 11 bovates of this land, and 12 villans and 11 bordars having 2½ ploughs, and 3 fisheries rendering 3s, and 80 acres of meadow. TRE, as now, worth 60s; tallage 10s.

[Folio 344: LINDSEY]

VII. The land of the Bishop of Lincoln

In STOW [near Torksey] are 4 carucates of land to the geld. There is land for 4 ploughs. Bishop Remigius [has] 1 plough there in demesne; and 20 villans and 3 sokemen having 3½ ploughs. There is a church and a priest, and 3 forges. TRE worth £32; now £30. Of this land 2 knights have as much as is worth 30s.

In Willingham by Stow is inland of this manor, 10 bovates of land and the third part of 2 bovates. [There is] land for as much. There are 2 bovates of which Joscelin has the soke.

In Caenby [is] inland of Stow [near Torksey], 4 carucates of land to the geld. [There is] land for 4 ploughs. 20 sokemen and 15 bordars have 5 ploughs there. There is a church, and 1 mill [rendering] 4s, and 20 acres of meadow.

In Bishop Norton [are] 6 carucates of land to the geld. [There is] land for 6 ploughs. [It is] inland and sokeland of Stow [near Torksey]. There are 3 ploughs in demesne; and 25 sokemen and 4 villans and 21 bordars have 5 ploughs. One of the bishop's men has 1 plough there. There is the site of a mill, and 430 acres of meadow.

In Glentham [are] 3 carucates of land and 6 bovates to the geld. [There is] land for 3 ploughs and 6 oxen. [It is] sokeland of Stow [near Torksey]. 16 sokemen and 11 bordars have 5 ploughs there, and [there are] 110 acres of meadow.

In Owmby-by-Spital [are] 4 carucates of land and 3 bovates to the geld. [There is] land for as much. 17 sokemen have 5½ ploughs there, and [there are] 21 acres of meadow.

In Upton and Kexby and Normanby by Stow [is] sokeland of Stow [near Torksey], 11 carucates of land and 6 bovates and 4 parts of 2 bovates and 2 parts of half a bovate to the geld. [There is] land for 10 ploughs [...]. 20 sokemen and 7 bordars have 6½ ploughs there, and 171 acres of meadow, and 162 acres of scrubland.

In WELTON, Swein had 12 carucates of land to the geld. [There is] land for 16 ploughs. Now 6 canons of Lincoln have 5 ploughs there in demesne; and 48 sokemen and 4 bordars having 11 ploughs, and 5 mills [rendering] 40s, and 150 acres of meadow, and 40 acres of scrubland. TRE worth £16; now £11; tallage 40s. [It is] 3 leagues long and 1 broad.

In Burton [is] sokeland of this manor, 1 carucate of land to the geld. [There is] land for 1 plough. 6 sokemen have 1 plough there.

In BRAMPTON, ST MARY [of] Stow had 4 carucates of land to the geld. [There is] land for 4 ploughs. Now there are 4 ploughs in demesne; and 4 villans and 1 sokeman with 2 ploughs, and 40 acres of meadow, and scrubland 10 furlongs long and 4 broad. The whole manor [is] 16 furlongs long and 9 broad. TRE worth £12; now the same.

In KNAITH [are] 12 bovates and 2 parts of a bovate to the geld. [There is] land for 13 oxen. ST MARY has there 3 sokemen with 2 ploughs, and 25 acres of meadow, and 26 acres of woodland.

In STOW [near Torksey] [is] sokeland of Brampton, 1 carucate and 2 parts of 2 bovates to the geld. [There is] land for as much.

In the same place Alsige [had] 1 toft belonging to the soke of Bishop Remigius; William de Percy holds it.

In INGHAM, Hakun had 6 bovates of land to the geld. [There is] land for 1 plough. Erchenold, the bishop's man, has 5 oxen ploughing there, and 1 villan and 1 sokeman ploughing with 6 oxen, and 12 acres of meadow. TRE worth 20s; now 25s; tallage 5s.

In COATES, Hakun had half a carucate of land to the geld. [There is] land for as much. Erchenold has 1 plough there. TRE worth 20s; now 30s.

In Grayingham, Healfdene had 1 carucate of land to the geld. [There is] land for 1½ ploughs. Mauger, the bishop's man, has 1 plough there, and 8 villans with 1 plough, and 20 acres of meadow. TRE worth 40s; now 30s.

In MESSINGHAM, Rolf had 2 carucates of land and 2 bovates to the geld. [There is] land for as much. Mauger has 1 plough there, and 1 villan, and 1 mill [rendering] 5s, and 10 acres of meadow. TRE worth 40s; now 15s; tallage 5s.

In BIGBY, Healfdene Topi had 1 carucate of land to the geld. [There is] land for 2 ploughs. Ranulph, the bishop's man, has 1½ ploughs there, and 11 villans and 1 sokeman with 1½ ploughs. There is a priest and a church. TRE worth 50s; now 40s; tallage 10s.

In ELSHAM, Wulfmær had 2 carucates of land and 2 bovates to the geld. [There is] land for 9 ploughs. Joscelin, the bishop's man, has 3 ploughs there, and 10 villans and 5 bordars and 2 sokemen having 2 ploughs, and 100 acres of meadow, and the site of a mill. TRE worth £6; now 70s; tallage 10s.

In Worlaby [near Elsham], Wulfmær and Healfdene had 2½ carucates of land to the geld. [There is] land for 5 ploughs. Joscelin has 4 ploughs there, and 10 villans and 5 bordars with 2 ploughs. TRE worth 100s; [now] £3.10s; tallage 10s.

In WOOTTON, Wulfmær had 2 carucates of land to the geld. [There is] land for 4 ploughs. Roger, the bishop's man, has 2 ploughs there, and 4 villans and 6 sokemen with 1½ ploughs. TRE worth 40s; now the same; tallage 10s.

In ULCEBY [near Wootton], Healfdene had 6 bovates of land to the geld. [There is] land for 2 ploughs. Ranulph, the bishop's man, has 1 plough there. TRE worth 10s; now the same.

In GOXHILL, Auti had 1 carucate of land to the geld. [There is] land for 2 ploughs. Roger, the bishop's man, has 2 ploughs there, and 8 villans and 8 sokemen with 1 plough, and 80 acres of meadow. TRE worth 32s; now 40s; tallage 10s.

In WYHAM, Rolf had 2 carucates of land to the geld. [There is] land for 3 ploughs. Mauger has 1 plough there, and 1 villan and 1 bordar and 11 sokemen having 2 ploughs, and 4 acres of meadow, and 10 acres of scrubland. TRE worth 30s; now 40s; tallage 20s.

In North Ormsby [is] sokeland of this manor, 13 bovates of land to the geld. [There is] land for 3 ploughs. 5 sokemen have 1 plough there, and 8 acres of meadow, and 4 acres of scrubland.

In CROXTON, Auti had 2 bovates of land to the geld, belonging to Grimkel's soke. [There is] land for half a plough. Joscelin has 1 plough there, and 2 villans. TRE worth 20s; now 5s.

[Folio 344V: LINCOLNSHIRE]

In KEELBY, Healfdene had 5 bovates of land and the third part of a bovate to the geld. [There is] land for 11 oxen. Ranulph, the bishop's man, has 1 plough there, and 4 villans and 1 bordar with 2 oxen, and 1 mill [rendering] 6s8d, and [there are] 6 acres of meadow. TRE worth 30s; now the same; tallage 10s.

In [North or South] OWERSBY, Auti had 2 carucates of land to the geld. [There is] land for 4 ploughs. Joscelin, the bishop's man, has 2 ploughs there, and 3 villans and 6 bordars and 20 sokemen with 3 ploughs, and 1 mill [rendering] 3s, and 110 acres of meadow. TRE worth £3; now 40s; tallage 20s.

In Southrey [is] inland of Cherry Willingham, 2 bovates of land to the geld. [There is] land for half a plough. Osbern, the bishop's clerk, has there 2 villans with half a plough.

In DUNSBY [near Bourne], Healfdene had 5 carucates of land to the geld. [There is] land for as many ploughs. Ralph, the bishop's man, has 2 ploughs there, and 6 villans and 6 bordars and 13 sokemen having 7 ploughs. There is a priest and a church, and 100 acres of meadow, and 100 acres of woodland, pasture in places. TRE worth 60s; now £4; tallage 20s.

In Haconby [is] sokeland of this manor, and 4½ bovates to the geld. [There is] land for as much. 5 sokemen have 1 plough there, and 10 acres of meadow, and 10 acres of scrubland.

In 'RINGSTONE' [in Rippingale], Healfdene had 2 carucates of land and 2 bovates to the geld. [There is] land for as much. Adam, the bishop's man, has 1 plough there, and 10 villans and 6 bordars with 2 ploughs. There is a priest and the third part of a church, and 20 acres of meadow, and 60 acres of scrubland. TRE [worth] £3; now 40s; tallage 20s.

In Dunsby [near Bourne] [is] inland of this manor, 1 carucate of land to the geld. [There is] land for 1 plough. 2 villans have half a plough there, and 20 acres of meadow, and 43 acres of woodland.

In GOSBERTON CHEAL, Azur and his brothers had 2 carucates of land and 2 bovates to the geld. [There is] land for as much. Mauger, the bishop's man, has 1 plough there, and 6 villans with 2½ ploughs, and 8 acres of meadow, and [there is] 1 salt-pan [rendering] 8d. Its value [is] in Gosberton.

In Quadring [is] inland of this manor, 1 carucate of land to the geld. [There is] land for 1 plough. Mauger has there 8 villans with 1 plough.

In GOSBERTON, Asli had 1 carucate of land and 6 bovates to the geld. [There is] land for 1 plough and 6 oxen. Mauger has 1 plough there, and 12 villans and 9 bordars with 3 ploughs, and [there is] 1 salt-pan [rendering] 4d, and 12 acres of meadow, and 1 sokeman on his garden. TRE worth £6; now £4; tallage 20s.

In Quadring [is] inland, | 1½ carucates to the geld. |

In CARLBY, Barthi had 1 carucate of land and half a bovate to the geld. [There is] land for as much. Erchenold, the bishop's man, has 1 plough there, and 10 villans and 11 bordars with 2 ploughs, and 10 acres of meadow, and 40 acres of woodland, pasture in places. TRE worth 30s; now 50s; tallage 10s.

In CORBY GLEN, Barthi had 8 carucates of land to the geld. [There is] land for 8 ploughs. Walter, the bishop's man, has 2 ploughs there, and 17 villans and 17 villans [sic], 12 bordars and 22 sokemen having 5 ploughs, and 1,100 acres of woodland pasture. TRE worth £7; now £7; tallage 40s.

In Bitchfield [is] sokeland of this manor, 2 carucates of land and 2 bovates to the geld. [There is] land for 3 ploughs. Walter, the bishop's man, has 2 ploughs there, and 3 villans and 8 bordars and 6 sokemen having 3 ploughs. There is a church and a priest, and 1 mill [rendering] 12d, and 13 acres of meadow, and 700 acres of woodland, pasture in places. TRE worth 20s; now 60s; now [sic] 20s.

In Swayfield [is] sokeland of Corby Glen, 2 carucates to the geld. [There is] land for 2 ploughs. 10 sokemen have 3 ploughs there, and 8 acres of woodland.

In Swinstead [are] 2 carucates to the geld. [There is] land for 2 ploughs.

In SLEAFORD, Barthi had 11 carucates of land to the geld. [There is] land for 11 ploughs. The bishop has 3 ploughs there in demesne; and 29 villans and 6 sokemen and 11 bordars having 14 ploughs. There is a priest and a church, and 8 mills rendering £10, and 320 acres of meadow, and 1 acre of scrubland, [and] 330 acres of marsh. TRE worth £20; now £25.

In Lobthorpe [are] 2 carucates to the geld. [There is] land for 2 ploughs. It is worth 20s.

In Ewerby [are] 13 bovates of land to the geld. [There is] land for 10 oxen. [It is] sokeland of Sleaford. There 2 sokemen plough with 2 oxen, and [there are] 16 acres of meadow, and 13 acres of scrubland.

In Howell [are] 5 carucates of land and 3 bovates to the geld. [There is] land for 4 ploughs. [It is] sokeland in like manner. There are 10 sokemen and 7 bordars having 4½ ploughs. There is a priest and a church, and 32 acres of meadow.

In Heckington [is] sokeland, 2 bovates of land to the geld. There is 1 villan having 2 oxen, and 3 acres of meadow.

In Quarrington, Barthi had 9 carucates of land and 2½ bovates. [There is] land for 9 ploughs and as many oxen. There are 32 sokemen and 15 bordars with 7½ ploughs, and 2 mills [rendering] 16s, and 60 acres of meadow. In this sokeland Osmund has 2 ploughs in demesne, and it is worth 60s. Also in this sokeland Hugh Rufus has 1 carucate of land and 1 plough in demesne, and it is worth 25s.

In 'Laythorpe' [in Kirkby la Thorpe] [is] sokeland, 2 carucates of land to the geld, and land for 11 oxen. There are 5 sokemen and 2 bordars with 2 ploughs.

In Evedon [are] 4 carucates of land and 3 bovates to the geld. [There is] land for 4 ploughs. The bishop has there 13 sokemen with 5 ploughs, and [there are] 20 acres of meadow, and 100 acres of marsh, and 16 acres of scrubland.

Of this sokeland Osmund has 11 bovates of land, and 1½ ploughs in demesne. It is worth 30s.

In CANWICK, Wælhræfn had sokeland, 2 carucates of land and 1½ bovates to the geld. [There is] land for 2 ploughs and 1½ oxen. William, the bishop's man, has 1 plough there, and 3 villans and 3 bordars with 1 plough, and 55 acres of meadow. TRE worth 60s; now 20s.

In LEASINGHAM, Barni had 6 carucates of land to the geld. [There is] land for 6 ploughs. Adam, the bishop's man, has 2 ploughs there, and 16 villans

[Folio 345: LINDSEY]

and 1 sokeman and 4 bordars having 4 ploughs, and 30 acres of meadow. TRE worth £6; now 100s.

In SILK WILLOUGHBY, Arnketil had 1 carucate of land to the geld. [There is] land for 2 ploughs. Ralph, the bishop's man, has 2 ploughs there, and 5 villans and 2 sokemen having 2 ploughs, and 30 acres of meadow. TRE worth 30s; now 50s.

In HOUGHAM, Thorir had 14 carucates of land to the geld. [There is] land for 9½ ploughs. Hugh, the bishop's man, has 2 ploughs there, and 21 villans and 4 sokemen and 1 bordar have 9 ploughs. There is a church and a priest, and 2 mills [rendering] 13s4d, and †40† acres of meadow. TRE worth £4; now £7.

In this vill Robert the priest had 1 carucate of land of the king in alms, and now, with the same land, he has been made a monk in ST MARY'S, Stow; but it is not permissible for anyone to have the land except by grant of the king. TRE worth 10s; now the same.

In LOUTH, the Bishop of Lincoln had 12 carucates of land to the geld. [There is] land for 12 ploughs. Now the bishop has 3 ploughs there in demesne, and 80 burgesses, and 1 market rendering 29s, and 40 sokemen and 2 villans. Among them all they have 13 ploughs, and 13 mills rendering 60s. 2 knights have 2 ploughs there, and 21 acres of meadow, and 400 acres of woodland, pasture in places. [It is] 1 league and 8 furlongs long and 10 furlongs broad. TRE worth £12; now £22; tallage £3.

In REDBOURNE, Arnketil had 1 carucate of land to the geld. [There is] land for 2 ploughs. Now Bishop Remigius and the canons of ST MARY have 2 villans ploughing with 3 oxen, and 24 acres of meadow. TRE worth 20s; now 10s.

In KINGERBY, Joscelin holds of the bishop 2 carucates of land to the geld. [There is] land for 6 ploughs. Auti held it TRE. There are 2 ploughs, a priest and a church, and 20 villans and 5 bordars with 5 ploughs, and a mill [rendering] 4s, and [there are] 400 acres of meadow. It was and is worth £4.

In CHERRY WILLINGHAM [are] 10 bovates of land to the geld. [There is] land for 10 oxen. There are 8 villans and 1 sokeman with 1½ ploughs, and [there are] 20 acres of meadow. Formerly 20s; now it is worth 30s.

[Folio 345V: LINCOLNSHIRE]

VIII. The land of Peterborough [Abbey]

In FISKERTON [are] 3 carucates of land to the geld. [There is] land for 3 ploughs. This manor belonged and belongs to Peterborough [Abbey]. There are 3 ploughs in demesne; and 18 villans and 3 bordars having 4 ploughs. There is a church and a priest, and 3½ fisheries rendering 21d, and 120 acres of meadow, [and] woodland pasture 10 furlongs long and 9 broad. The whole [is] 20 furlongs long and 9 broad. TRE worth £14; now £17; tallage £3.

In Scothern and 'Holme' [in Sudbrooke] and Sudbrooke [is] sokeland of this manor, 5½ carucates of land to the geld. [There is] land for 6 ploughs. St Peter has there 32 sokemen having 8 ploughs.

In Reepham [is] inland of this manor, 4 carucates and 6 bovates of land to the geld. [There is] land for 4 ploughs and 6 oxen. 12 villans and 2 bordars have 4 ploughs there, and 60 acres of meadow. [There is] scrubland 8 furlongs long and 4 broad.

In THURLBY [near Bourne], Peterborough [Abbey] had and has 3 carucates of land and 5 bovates to the geld. [There is] land for as many ploughs and oxen. There is 1 plough in demesne; and 10 villans and 2 sokemen have 1½ ploughs. Of this land 2 of the abbot's men have 2 carucates, and there are 1½ ploughs, and 7 villans and 2 sokemen with 1 plough. There are 20 acres of meadow, and 80 acres of woodland, pasture in places. TRE worth 60s; now the same; tallage 10s.

In "ADEWELLE" [in Careby], Peterborough [Abbey] had and has 5 carucates of land to the geld. [There is] land for 5 ploughs. Now there are 2 ploughs in demesne; and 10 villans and 2 bordars and 2 sokemen having 3½ ploughs, and 18 acres of meadow. [There are] 180 acres of woodland pasture, and 60 acres of scrubland. TRE worth 60s; now the same; tallage 12s.

In WHITHAM ON THE HILL and Manthorpe [in Witham on the Hill] and Toft [and] Lound is a Berewick, half a carucate of land to the geld. [There is] land for 4 oxen. 2 villans have half a plough there, and 8 acres of meadow, and 40 acres of scrubland. TRE worth 5s4d; now the same. Ansfrid holds it.

In Little Bytham is a Berewick of "Adewelle" [in Careby], 4 carucates of land to the geld. [There is] land for 4 ploughs. This land is demesne of Peterborough [Abbey]. Now 6 villans have there 2 ploughs and 2 oxen. There Saswalo, the abbot's man, has of this land 2 carucates of land, and in demesne half a plough; and 3 villans with 1 plough, and 25 acres of meadow, and 100 acres of scrubland. TRE this sokeland was worth 30s; now 20s.

In OSGODBY [in Lenton], Peterborough [Abbey] had and has 5 carucates of land to the geld. [There is] land for 5 ploughs. Now Ansketil, the abbot's man, has 2 ploughs there, and 13 villans with 4 ploughs, and 14 acres of meadow. [There is] woodland pasture 13 furlongs long and 4 broad. TRE worth 60s; now 100s; tallage 20s.

The arable land [is] 14 furlongs long and 6 broad. 2 carucates of this manor belong to Lenton Hundred.

In WALCOT [near Folkingham], Peterborough [Abbey] had and has 5 carucates of land to the geld. [There is] land for 6 ploughs. Now Gilbert, the abbot's man, has 1 plough there, and 6 villans and 5 bordars with 2 ploughs, and a church, and 14 sokemen on 2 carucates having 4 ploughs. One half of the soke belongs to St Peter, and the other to Gilbert de Ghent [and] belongs in Folkingham. There are 30 acres of meadow. TRE worth £8; now £4; #

In DONINGTON, Peterborough [Abbey] had and has 3 carucates of land to the geld. [There is] land for 3 ploughs. Now there is 1 plough in demesne; and 12 villans and 20 bordars with 2 ploughs, and 16 salt-pans [rendering] 20s, and 12 acres of meadow. TRE worth 60s; now the same.

In 'Haythby' [in West Halton] [is] SOKELAND of Walcot [in Alkborough], 2 bovates of land to the geld. [There is] land for 1½ oxen. 1 sokeman ploughs there with 2 oxen. Ivo. holds it.

In 'HOUGHTON' [in Grantham], Peterborough [Abbey] has half a carucate of land to the geld, with sake and soke. 3 villans have 1 plough there. Kolgrimr holds it.

In RISEHOLME, Alnoth had 4 bovates of land to the geld. [There is] land for half a plough. Now Kolsveinn has it [...] of Abbot Turold, and he himself [has] 2 bordars there. TRE worth half a mark of silver; and now the same.

In YAWTHORPE, Rolf had half a carucate of land to the geld. [There is] land for 4 oxen. Abbot Turold has 1 plough there, and 3 acres of meadow. TRE worth 12s; now 5s.

In SCOTTON, Eskil had 6 carucates of land to the geld. [There is] land for 6 ploughs. Richard, the abbot's man, has there under the abbot 3 ploughs, and 22 villans and 5 bordars and 17 sokemen having 2 ploughs. In Lincoln [are] 3 burgesses rendering 5s, and [he has] 50 acres of meadow, and 36 acres of scrubland. TRE worth 100s; now £4; tallage 40s.

In Northorpe [near Kirton in Lindsey] [is] SOKELAND of this manor, 1 carucate of land to the geld. [There is] land for 1½ ploughs. 4 sokemen have there 2 villans and 1 bordar with 1 plough.

In SCOTTER, Alnoth and Eskil had 8 carucates of land to the geld. [There is] land for 12 ploughs. Now Abbot Turold has 4 ploughs there, and 32 villans and 13 bordars with 4 ploughs, and 15 sokemen with 3 ploughs, and 1 mill and a half of 2 [mills] rendering 8s, and 2 fisheries [rendering] 15s, and 120 acres of meadow, and [there are] 28 acres of woodland pasture. TRE [worth] £11; now £10. [It is] 3 leagues long and 1 broad.

In Scotterthorpe is SOKELAND of this manor, 3 carucates of land to the geld. [There is] land for 2 ploughs. 8 sokemen and 4 villans have 4 ploughs there,

[Folio 346: LINDSEY]

and 30 acres of meadow.

In CLEATHAM, Alnoth had 7 bovates of land to the geld. [There is] land for 1½ ploughs. Roger, the abbot's man, has 1 plough there, and 4 villans ploughing with 5 oxen, and 7 acres of meadow. TRE worth 40s; now 30s.

In MANTON, Rolf had 2 carucates of land to the geld. [There is] land for 4 ploughs. Ralph, the abbot's man, has 1 plough there, and 5 villans and 4 bordars with 1 plough, and 20 acres of meadow. TRE worth £12; now 60s; tallage 20s. [It is] 2 leagues long and 1 broad.

In Cleatham [is] SOKELAND of this manor, 1 bovate of land to the geld. There is 1 sokeman ploughing †with 1 ox†.

In HIBALDSTOW, Rolf had 10 bovates of land to the geld. [There is] land for 3 ploughs. Gilbert, the abbot's man, has 2 ploughs there, and 11 villans and 1 sokeman and 3 bordars have 2½ ploughs, and 1 mill [rendering] 4s, and 111 acres of meadow, and 60 acres of scrubland. TRE worth £6; now 70s; tallage 20s.

In 'RAVENTHORPE' [in Broughton], Eskil had 2 carucates of land to the geld. [There is] land for 4 ploughs. Ralph, the

abbot's man, has 1 plough there, and 5 villans and 4 bordars with 1 plough, and 12 acres of meadow. TRE worth £6; now 30s; tallage 10s.

In CLEATHAM [are] 2 bovates to the geld.

In Holme [in Bottesford] [is] SOKELAND of this manor, 3 carucates of land to the geld. [There is] land for 3 ploughs. 6 sokemen have 2 ploughs there, and 1 mill [rendering] 4s, and 12 acres of scrubland.

In Ashby [in Scunthorpe] [is] other SOKELAND, 3 bovates of land to the geld. [There is] land for 3 oxen. 1 sokeman has 1 plough there, and [there are] 3 acres of scrubland.

In APPLEBY and [High or Low] RISBY and 'SAWCLIFFE' [in Roxby]. Eskil had 3 bovates of land to the geld. [There is] land for 6 oxen. Ralph, the abbot's man, has 1 plough there, and 12 acres of meadow. TRE worth 20s; now 16s.

In WALCOT [in Alkborough], Eskil had 6 carucates of land and 5 bovates to the geld. [There is] land for as many ploughs and oxen. Now Ivo has it of the abbot. There is 1 plough, and 7 villans and 2 bordars and 10 sokemen with 2 ploughs, and 380 acres of meadow, and 60 acres of scrubland. TRE worth £6; now 40s; tallage 10s.

In Alkborough [is] a BEREWICK of this manor, 1 carucate of land to the geld. [There is] land for 1½ ploughs. 3 villans plough there with 3 oxen.

In 'Haythby' [in West Halton] [is] SOKELAND, 2 bovates of land to the geld. [There is] land for 1½ oxen. 1 sokeman ploughs there with 2 oxen.

In MESSINGHAM, Alnoth had 5 carucates of land to the geld. [There is] land for 5 ploughs and 2 oxen. William, the abbot's man, has 2 ploughs there, and 5 villans and 4 bordars and 18 sokemen having 3 ploughs, and 20 acres of meadow. TRE worth £4; now the same; tallage 20s.

In Scunthorpe [is] a BEREWICK of this manor, 1 bovate of land and the third part of 1 bovate to the geld. [There is] land for 1 ox. 1 villan has 2 oxen there in a plough.

In Uffington, Peterborough [Abbey] has 48 acres of meadow without geld. Geoffrey holds these, and [also] the abbot's villans. TRE worth 20s; now the same.

In WITHAM ON THE HILL and Manthorpe [in Witham on the Hill] and Toft [and] Lound, Hereweard had 12 bovates of land to the geld. [There is] land for 1½ ploughs. Ansfrid, Abbot Turold's man, has there 6 villans and 4 bordars and 2 sokemen with 2 ploughs, and 20 acres of meadow, and 40 acres of woodland. TRE worth 40s; now the same.

In Barholm and 'Stowe' [in Barholm and Stowe] [is] a BEREWICK of this manor, 1 carucate of land to the geld. [There is] land for 1 plough. Ansfrid has there 2 villans and 2 bordars with 1 plough.

In the same places [is] 1 carucate of land to the geld. [There is] land for 1 plough. [It is] sokeland of Peterborough

[Northants]. Now Godfrey, the abbot's man, has 9 sokemen and 1 villan and 2 bordars with 2 ploughs. Robert holds half. TRE worth 20s; now likewise 20[s].

In 'STOWE' [in Barholm and Stowe] [is] sokeland of Witham on the Hill, 4½ bovates of land to the geld. [There is] land for as much. Ansfrid has of the abbot there 1 villan and 2 sokemen with half a plough.

In the same place [are] 2 bovates of land to the geld. [There is] land for 2 oxen. [It is] sokeland for the use of Peterborough Abbey. Godfrey has there of the abbot 1 villan and 2 sokemen with half a plough. TRE worth 3s; now the same.

In THURLBY [near Bourne], Alnoth had 1½ carucates to the geld. [There is] land for 1½ ploughs. [It was] free sokeland under Aslak. Geoffrey has there under the abbot 1 plough, and 1 villan and 4 bordars, and 30 acres of scrubland. TRE worth 20s; now likewise 20s.

IX. The land of St Peter of Westminster

In DODDINGTON, Æthelric had 6 carucates of land to the geld. [There is] land for 4 ploughs. ST PETER of Westminster has 1 plough there, and 14 villans and 6 bordars with 4 ploughs. There is a priest and a church, meadow half a league long and a half broad, [and] woodland pasture 1½ leagues long and half a league broad. TRE, with all things belonging to this manor, it was worth £20; now what St Peter has is worth £4.

In Thorpe on the Hill [are] 6 carucates of land and 2 bovates to the geld. [There is] land for 6 ploughs. [It is] SOKELAND of the same manor. 30 sokemen have 7½ ploughs there. [There is] meadow 2 furlongs long and 2 broad.

[Folio 346V: LINCOLNSHIRE]

X. The land of St Benedict of Ramsey

In QUARRINGTON, St Benedict of Ramsey had and has 1 carucate of land and 6 bovates to the geld. [There is] land for as many ploughs and oxen. Now there is 1 plough in demesne; and 3 villans and 1 bordar and 1 sokeman with 1 plough. There are 2 churches, and 1 mill [rendering] 21s4d, and 14 acres of meadow. TRE worth 40s; now £4.

In Old Sleaford [is] SOKELAND of this manor, 1 carucate of land to the geld. [There is] land for 1 plough. 1 sokeman and 2 villans have 1 plough there, and [there are] 27 acres of meadow.

In Cranwell [is] other SOKELAND, 6 carucates of land to the geld. [There is] land for as many ploughs. Now 11 sokemen and 3 bordars have 3 ploughs there, and 6 acres of meadow.

In THREEKINGHAM, St Benedict of Ramsey had and has half a carucate of land to the geld. [There is] land for 4 oxen. 1 villan has half a plough there, TRE worth 5s; now the same.

In 'Coteland' [in Ruskington], St Benedict has half a carucate of meadow to the geld in Cranwell.

XI. The land of St Guthlac of Crowland

In HOLBEACH and WHAPLODE, St Guthlac had and has 1 carucate of land to the geld. [There is] land for 6 oxen. Now there is 1 plough in demesne; and 3 villans with half a plough, and 12 acres of meadow. TRE worth 20s; now the same.

In Spalding [is] a BEREWICK of Crowland, 2 carucates of land to the geld. [There is] land for 1½ ploughs. 7 villans and 4 bordars have 3 ploughs there. TRE worth 20s; now the same.

In LANGTOFT, St Guthlac had and has 6 carucates of land to the geld. [There is] land for 6 ploughs. Now there is 1 plough in demesne; and 8 villans and 4 bordars and 20 sokemen having 5 ploughs, and 100 acres of meadow. [There is] woodland [rendering] 2s, marsh 2 leagues long and 2 broad, [and] arable land 15 furlongs long and 9 broad. TRE worth £4; now 60s; tallage 10s.

In BASTON, St Guthlac had and has 4 carucates of land to the geld. [There is] land for 4 ploughs. Now there is 1 plough in demesne; and 5 villans and 2 bordars and 7 sokemen with 2 ploughs. There is a church, and half a mill, and 45 acres of meadow, marsh 16 furlongs long and 8 broad, [and] arable land 8 furlongs long and 8 broad. TRE worth 40s; now the same.

In DOWDYKE, St Guthlac had and has 2 carucates of land to the geld. [There is] land for 2 ploughs, with sake and soke. Now there is 1 plough in demesne; and 13 villans with 1 plough, and 20 acres of meadow. TRE worth 40s; now the same. Kolgrimr holds it.

In Drayton [is] a BEREWICK of this manor, 1 carucate of land to the geld. [There is] land for 1 plough. 5 villans there do not plough. There are 4 salt-pans [rendering] 5s4d, and 6 acres of meadow.

In Algarkirk [is] another Berewick, 12 bovates of land to the geld. [There is] land for 10 oxen. Now it is waste. Kolgrimr holds it of the abbot.

In Burtoft, St Guthlac had and has 1 bovate of land which belongs to Dowdyke. The king has the soke of it.

In BUCKNALL, Gamal had 10 bovates of land to the geld. [There is] land for 10 oxen. In the same place [is] SOKELAND of Belchford, 10 bovates of land to the geld. [There is] land for 10 oxen. Now St Guthlac has 1 plough there in demesne; and 5 villans and 2 bordars and 8 sokemen having 1 plough. There are 120 acres of meadow, and 50 acres of woodland pasture, and 70 acres of scrubland. TRE worth 30s; now the same. Thorald the sheriff gave this land to St Guthlac for his soul.

[Folio 347: LINDSEY]

XII. The land of Count Alan

In GATE BURTON, Gunnhvati and Godric had 4 carucates of land and 6 bovates to the geld. [There is] land for 5 ploughs. Now Count Alan has there 1 plough, and 10 sokemen having

3 ploughs, and 40 acres of meadow, and 70 acres of water-meadow. TRE worth £3; now 30s; tallage 10s.

In Marton [is] SOKELAND of this manor, 6 bovates of land to the geld. [There is] land for 1 plough. It is waste.

In WILLINGHAM BY STOW, Steingrimr had 12 bovates of land to the geld. [There is] land for 12 oxen.

In the same place Gunnhvati had 6 bovates of land and the third part of 2 bovates to the geld. [There is] land for as many oxen. Count Alan has 1 plough there in demesne; and 5 villans and 2 sokemen with 1 plough. TRE worth 40s; now 20s.

In LEA, Fulcric and his 2 brothers had 3½ carucates of land to the geld. In the same place Ulfkil had half a carucate of land to the geld. [There is] land for 5 ploughs. Now Robert, the count's man, has 1 plough there, and 16 villans and 2 sokemen with 3 ploughs, and half a fishery rendering 10d, and 1 ferry rendering 12d, and 115 acres of meadow, and 100 acres of scrubland. TRE worth 100s; now 30s; tallage 20s.

In Heapham [is] a BEREWICK of this manor and SOKELAND, 4 bovates of land to the geld. [There is] land for half a plough. Now 4 sokemen plough there with 2 oxen. There are 20 acres of meadow.

In Somerby [in Corringham] [is] other SOKELAND, half a carucate of land to the geld. [There is] land for 4 oxen. 2 sokemen plough there with 3 oxen. There are 10 acres of meadow, and 10 acres of scrubland.

In [North and South] KILLINGHOLME, Ralph, Wilgrim, Eskil, Arnketil, Segrim and Earnwine the priest had 2½ carucates of land to the geld. [There is] land for 6 ploughs. Now Landric, the count's man, has 2 ploughs there, and 11 villans with 1 plough, and 100 acres of meadow. TRE worth £4; now 30s; tallage 10s.

In KIRMINGTON, Eskil Barn had 4 bovates of land to the geld. [There is] land for 1½ ploughs. Now there is 1 plough in demesne; and 1 villan and 4 sokemen with 1 plough. TRE worth 40s; now 20s.

In NORTH KELSEY, Grimbald Crac had 1 carucate of land to the geld. [There is] land for 2 ploughs. Now there is 1 villan with 6 oxen, and 1 mill [rendering] 7s. TRE worth 20s; now the same.

In Searby [is] a BEREWICK of this manor, 3 bovates of land to the geld. [There is] land for 6 oxen. 1 villan ploughs there with 3 oxen.

In Cadney and Howsham [is] another BEREWICK, 5 bovates of land to the geld and the third. part of 1 bovate to the geld, and as much land for ploughing. 5 villans have 2 ploughs there, and [there are] 100 acres of meadow. It is worth 40s.

In Owmby [is] another BEREWICK, 3 bovates of land to the geld. 1 villan ploughs there with 3 oxen. There are 8 acres of meadow.

In CADNEY and HOWSHAM, Grimbald Crac had 5 bovates of land and the third part of a bovate to the geld.

[There is] land for as many oxen. There 6 [men] with the lord have 3½ ploughs. TRE worth 60s; now 40s.

In AYLESBY, Orm had 2 carucates of land and 6 bovates and 2 parts of a bovate to the geld. [There is] land for 5 ploughs. Now Picot, the count's man, has 2 ploughs there, and 6 villans and 3 bordars and 20 sokemen having 2 ploughs and 2 oxen. There is a church and a priest, and 1½ mills [rendering] 9s. TRE worth £5; now £4; tallage 20s.

In Swallow [is] SOKELAND of this manor, 3 bovates of land to the geld. [There is] land for 6 oxen. Now there is 1 bordar.

In [Great of Little] Coates [in Great Grimsby] [is] other SOKELAND, 1 bovate of land to the geld. It is waste.

In SWALLOW, Esbiorn had 1½ carucates to the geld. [There is] land for 3 ploughs. Picot has half a plough there, and 5 villans and 1 bordar and 9 sokemen with 1½ ploughs. TRE worth 20s; now 60s; tallage 20s.

In HOLTON LE CLAY, Thorgot had 2 bovates of land and 5 acres and 2 virgates to the geld. Wimund, the count's man, has there 2 villans ploughing with 5 oxen, and 5 acres of meadow. TRE worth 3s; now 8s.

In FULSTOW, Rolf and Esbiorn had 2 carucates of land and 2 bovates to the geld. [There is] land for 3½ ploughs. Picot has of the count 2 ploughs there, and 14 villans and 7 bordars and 2 sokemen with 2 ploughs, and 8 salt-pans rendering 8s, and 260 acres of meadow. TRE worth 40s; now £4; tallage 20s.

In GRAINSBY, Spillir, Æthelstan and Leofsige had 3 carucates of land to the geld. [There is] land for 5 ploughs. Wimund, the count's man, has 1½ ploughs there, and 12 villans and 4 bordars and 13 sokemen having 3½ ploughs, and [there are] 51 acres of meadow, and turbary [rendering] 5s4d. TRE worth 70s; now £4; tallage 20s.

In WALTHAM, Ralph the staller had 6 carucates of land to the geld. [There is] land for 12 ploughs. Now Count Alan has 4 ploughs there, and 12 villans and 1 bordar and 18 sokemen having 9½ ploughs. There is a church and a priest, and 68 acres of meadow. TRE worth £20; now £45; tallage £15. The whole [is] 15 furlongs long and 9 broad.

In Waithe [is] SOKELAND of this manor, 11 bovates of land to the geld. [There is] land for 11 oxen. 12 sokemen have 1½ ploughs there, and 20 acres of meadow.

In Ashby cum Fenby [is] other SOKELAND, 6 bovates of land to the geld. [There is] land for 12 ploughs. 5 sokemen have 1 plough there, and 25 acres of meadow, and [there are] 5 acres of scrubland.

In Barnoldby le Beck [is] SOKELAND, 6 carucates of land to the geld. [There is] land for 12 ploughs.

[Folio 347V: LINCOLNSHIRE]

There are 26 sokemen and 9 bordars having 9½ ploughs, and 200 acres of meadow.

In 'FENBY' [in Ashby cum Fenby] [is] sokeland, 3 carucates of land to the geld. [There is] land for 6 ploughs. There are 15 sokemen and 2 bordars having $3\frac{1}{2}$ ploughs, and 40 acres of meadow.

In [East and West] Ravendale and the other Ravendale [East and West Ravendale] [is] sokeland, 3 carucates of land to the geld. [There is] land for 6 ploughs. 14 sokemen have 2 ploughs there.

In North Cadeby [is] sokeland, 3 carucates of land to the geld. [There is] land for 4 ploughs. 14 sokemen have 3 ploughs there.

In 'Beesby' [in Hawerby] [is] sokeland, 3 carucates of land to the geld. [There is] land for 4 ploughs. Count Alan has 1 plough there, and 1 sokeman, and 16 acres of meadow, and 6 acres of scrubland.

In the same BEESBY [in Hawerby], Ingimund and One, Eadric and Ecgwulf had 3 carucates and 3 bovates of land and 3 parts of a bovate and also the third part of a bovate. [There is] land for 4 ploughs.

Now the count has there 1 sokeman and 8 villans with $1\frac{1}{2}$ ploughs, and [there are] 16 acres of meadow, and 6 acres of scrubland. TRE [worth] 20s; now 30s. William Blund had Ecgwulf's land, $5\frac{1}{2}$ bovates, on that day on which Earnwine the priest was taken, and before.

In Wold Newton [is] SOKELAND, 3 carucates of land and half a bovate to the geld. [There is] land for 5 ploughs. 20 sokemen and 2 bordars have 4 ploughs there.

In the same WOLD NEWTON, Ingimund and his 3 brothers had 3 bovates of land to the geld. [There is] land for 1 plough. Wimund, the count's man, has 1 plough there.

SOKELAND OF WALTHAM

In Hawerby [is] sokeland, 2 carucates of land and 3 bovates to the geld. [There is] land for 4 ploughs. There are 14 sokemen and 1 villan and 1 bordar with 3 ploughs.

In Swinhope [is] sokeland, 15 bovates of land and the fourth part of 1 bovate to the geld. [There is] land for 4 ploughs. 16 sokemen have 2 ploughs there.

In Gunnerby [is] sokeland, 2 carucates of land to the geld. [There is] land for 4 ploughs. 6 sokemen and 5 bordars have 4 ploughs there, and 1 mill [rendering] 6s, and 10 acres of meadow.

In Hatcliffe [is] sokeland, 4 carucates of land to the geld. [There is] land for 7 ploughs. 9 sokemen and 9 bordars have 4 ploughs there, and 2 mills [rendering] 8s, and 20 acres of meadow.

In Beelsby [is] sokeland, 4 carucates of land to the geld. [There is] land for 8 ploughs. 24 sokemen and 7 bordars have 7 ploughs there, and $2\frac{1}{2}$ mills [rendering] 12s, and [there are] 30 acres of meadow.

In WELTON LE WOLD, Siward had 1 carucate of land to the geld. [There is] land for 2 ploughs. Landric, the count's man, has 2 ploughs there, and 11 villans and 2 sokemen with $1\frac{1}{2}$ ploughs, and 1 mill [rendering] 10s, and 20 acres of

meadow, and the fourth part of a church. TRE worth £4; now £3.

In North Thoresby [is] sokeland of Waltham, $9\frac{1}{2}$ bovates of land to the geld. [There is] land for 14 oxen. 14 sokemen and 2 bordars have 2 ploughs there, and 2 salt-pans [rendering] 2s, and 16 acres of meadow.

In Brigsley [is] sokeland of Waltham, $1\frac{1}{2}$ carucates of land to the geld. [There is] land for 3 ploughs. 17 sokemen and 1 bordar have 3 ploughs there, and [there are] 10 acres of meadow.

BOLINGBROKE WAPENTAKE

In HALTON HOLEGATE Hundred and Little Steeping, Alric had 3 bovates of land to the geld. [There is] land for 3 ploughs. Eudo, the count's man, has 1 plough there, and 80 acres of meadow. TRE worth 10s; now the same.

In STOW [near Torksey], Count Alan has half a carucate of land to the geld. It is SOKELAND. [There is] land for half a plough. 2 sokemen have half a plough there.

In SPRIDLINGTON, Knut had 2 carucates of land and $1\frac{1}{2}$ bovates to the geld. [There is] land for 3 ploughs and 2 oxen. The count has 1 plough there in demesne; and 6 villans and 6 bordars and 6 sokemen having 3 ploughs and 2 oxen, and 8 acres of meadow. TRE worth 30s; now the same; tallage 10s.

'LOVEDEN' WAPENTAKE

HOUGH ON THE HILL HUNDRED

In HOUGH ON THE HILL, Ralph the staller had 7 carucates and 6 bovates to the geld. [There is] land for 12 ploughs. Count Alan has 4 ploughs there, and 17 villans and 14 sokemen and 7 bordars having 12 ploughs. There is a priest and a church, and 4 mills [rendering] 30s, and 100 acres of meadow. TRE worth £12; now £16; tallage £4; for horse-feed 50s.

HUNDRED

In Gelston [is] a BEREWICK of this manor, 12 carucates of land to the geld. [There is] land for 16 ploughs. Now 18 villans and 6 bordars and 2 sokemen have 6 ploughs there, and 146 acres of meadow, and [there are] 200 acres of scrubland, and a hare warren.

In Carlton Scroop is 1 carucate of land to the geld. [It is] SOKELAND of HOUGH ON THE HILL.

In BRANT BROUGHTON HUNDRED, Ralph the staller had 13 carucates of land to the geld in demesne, and 5 carucates of land to the geld of sokeland. [There is] land for 18 ploughs. Count Alan has 3 ploughs there in demesne; and 36 villans and 9 bordars and 15 sokemen and 11 other bordars having together 15 ploughs. There is a priest and a church, and 1 mill [rendering] 12s, and 200 acres of meadow. Of the above-mentioned sokeland Cadio holds 6 bovates of land and has there 6 oxen ploughing. TRE worth £15; now £18; tallage 100s; for horse-feed 50s.

FOUR HUNDREDS

In FULBECK and LEADENHAM, Ralph the staller had 24 carucates of land to the geld in demesne, and 15 carucates of sokeland to the geld. [There is] land for 24 ploughs. Count Alan has 6 ploughs there in demesne; and 69 villans and 4 bordars and 44 sokemen having together 28 ploughs. There are 2 churches and 2 priests, and half a mill [rendering] 10s. Of this land Kolgrimr and Deoring have 5 carucates and 6 bovates, and they have 2½ ploughs there. TRE worth £30; now £32; tallage £8; for horse-feed 100s.

In Marston [is] 1 carucate of land to the geld. [It is] sokeland of Hough on the Hill. [There is] land for 12 oxen.

[Folio 348: LINDSEY]

In the 2 HUNDREDS of LONG BENNINGTON, Ralph the staller had 14 carucates of land to the geld in demesne, and 7 carucates and 6 bovates of land to the geld of sokeland. Count Alan has 5 ploughs there in demesne; and 19 villans and 5 bordars and 20 sokemen having together 12 ploughs. There is a priest and a church, and 300 acres of meadow. Of this land Hervey holds 1 carucate and 3 bovates, and he has 1 plough there. TRE worth £26; now £32; tallage £8; for horse-feed 100s. There are 4 mills rendering £4.

In Foston HUNDRED [is] a BEREWICK of this manor, 12 carucates of land to the geld in demesne, and 7 carucates of land to the geld of sokeland.. Now the count has 2 ploughs there, and 10 villans and 5 bordars and 46 sokemen having together 11 ploughs, and 100 acres of meadow. [There is] arable land for 14 ploughs.

In the same FOSTON, Thorfridh had 1 carucate of land to the geld. [There is] land for 2 ploughs. Hervey, the count's man, has 1 plough there, and 2 villans and 1 bordar with half a plough. TRE worth 16s; now 10s.

'BELTISLOE' WAPENTAKE

BURTON-LE-COGGLES HUNDRED

In WESTBY, Karli had 6 bovates of land to the geld. [There is] land for 6 oxen. Kolgrimr, the count's man, has there 1 villan and 1 bordar with 1 plough, and 7½ acres of meadow, and 29 acres of scrubland. TRE worth 10s; now 12s.

In KIRKBY UNDERWOOD, Withar had 5 bovates of land to the geld. [There is] land for 5 oxen. Godric, the count's man, has there 2 villans and 1 bordar ploughing with 2 oxen, and 4 acres of meadow, and 60 acres of scrubland. TRE worth 20s; now 10s.

HUNDRED

In Pointon [is] SOKELAND of this manor, half a carucate of land to the geld. [There is] land for 4 oxen. 1 sokeman and 2 bordars have half a plough there.

In BILLINGBOROUGH HUNDRED, Karli had 1 carucate of land to the geld. [There is] land for 1 plough. Kolgrimr, the count's man, has 1 plough there in demesne; and †2† villans and 2 bordars with half a plough, and 15 acres of meadow. TRE worth 20s; now the same.

HUNDRED

In HORBLING, Greifi had 4 carucates of land to the geld. [There is] land for 4 ploughs. Stephen, the count's man, has 2 ploughs there, and 9 villans and 1 bordar and 3 sokemen having 3 ploughs, and 20 acres of meadow. TRE worth 40s; now the same.

'THREO' WAPENTAKE

In HARROWBY [and] HORBLING, Withar had 1 carucate of land to the geld. [There is] land for 1 plough and 2 oxen. Godric, the count's man, has half a plough there in demesne; and 4 villans having 5 oxen ploughing, and 2 mills [rendering] 10s, and 10 acres of meadow. TRE worth 12s; now 16s.

In DRAYTON HUNDRED, Greifi had 6 bovates of land to the geld. [There is] land for 6 oxen. Toli, the count's man, has 1 plough there in demesne; and 4 villans and 4 bordars with 1 plough, and [there are] 10 acres of meadow, and half a salt-pan [rendering] 8d. TRE worth 16s; now the same.

In the same Drayton, Bishop Wulfwig had 1 carucate of land to the geld. [There is] land for 1 plough. This belonged to St Benedict of Ramsey according to the witness of the men of the wapentake, who say that they do not know through whom the bishop held it. Count Alan has 2 bordars there, and 8 acres of meadow, and [there is] 1 salt-pan rendering 16d. TRE worth 3s; now 2s.

DRAYTON HUNDRED

In DRAYTON itself Ralph the staller had 8 carucates of land and 2 bovates to the geld. [There is] land for 8 ploughs. This land is sokeland of the vill itself. Now Count Alan has there 6 villans and 6 sokemen and 1 bordar having 5 ploughs. There are 4½ salt-pans [rendering] 6s, and 40 acres of meadow. TRE Drayton with all things belonging to it was worth £30; now £70; tallage £20.

KIRTON WAPENTAKE

In Donington [is] a BEREWICK of this manor, 5 carucates of land and 6 bovates to the geld. [There is] land for as many ploughs and oxen. Count Alan has 3 ploughs there in demesne; and 26 villans with 5 ploughs, and 9 salt-pans [rendering] 12s, and 60 acres of meadow.

'WOLMERSTY' WAPENTAKE

In Wrangle [is] SOKELAND of Drayton, 10 carucates of land to the geld. [There is] land for 5 ploughs. 7 sokemen have 1 plough there.

OLD LEAKE HUNDRED

In Old Leake [is] SOKELAND [of] Drayton, 12 carucates of land to the geld. [There is] land for 10 ploughs. 32 sokemen and 30 villans and 15 bordars have 11 ploughs there, and 26 salt-pans, and 34 acres of meadow. Of this sokeland 2 of the count's men have 2 carucates, and 2 ploughs there, and 1 bordar, and 15 salt-pans, and 10 villans with 1 plough.

LEVERTON HUNDRED

In Leverton [is] SOKELAND [of] Drayton, 12 carucates of land to the geld. [There is] land for as many ploughs. 25 sokemen and 15 villans and 24 bordars have 12 ploughs there. There is a priest and a church, and 60 acres of meadow. Of this sokeland 2 of the count's men have 2 carucates of land and 3 bovates, and they have 3 ploughs ploughing there.

FISHTOFT HUNDRED

In FISHTOFT [is] SOKELAND [of] Drayton, 3 carucates of land to the geld. [There is] land for 3 ploughs. 17 sokemen have $5\frac{1}{2}$ ploughs there, and 20 acres of meadow.

In Skirbeck HUNDRED [is] a BEREWICK [of] Drayton, 2 carucates of land to the geld, and in the same place [is] SOKELAND [of] Drayton, 9 carucates of land and 6 bovates to the geld. [There is] land for 8 ploughs. 19 sokemen and †13† villans have 8 ploughs there. The count himself [has] 1 plough in demesne. There are 2 churches and 2 priests, and 2 fish-ponds [rendering] 10s, and 40 acres of meadow.

In Wyberton HUNDRED [is] SOKELAND [of] Drayton, 9 carucates of land and 3 bovates to the geld. [There is] land for $12\frac{1}{2}$ ploughs. 34 sokemen have 11 ploughs there. There is a church, [and] 12 acres of meadow.

FRAMPTON HUNDRED

In Frampton [is] a BEREWICK [of] Drayton, 7 carucates of land and 6 bovates to the geld. [There is] land for 10 ploughs. Count Alan has 2 ploughs there in demesne; and 12 sokemen and 16 villans and 2 bordars having 8 ploughs. There are 15 salt-pans rendering 20s, and 100 acres of meadow.

HUNDRED

In Kirton [is] SOKELAND [of] Drayton, 10 carucates of land and 1 bovate

[Folio 348V: LINCOLNSHIRE]

and the third part of a bovate to the geld. [There is] land for 12 ploughs. Count Alan has there 30 sokemen and 16 bordars having 10 ploughs, and [there are] 2 salt-pans [rendering] 16d. There is a church, and 60 acres of meadow.

In 'Riskenton' [in Kirton] HUNDRED [is] SOKELAND, 12 carucates of land to the geld. [There is] land | for as many ploughs. | 29 sokemen and 12 bordars have 6 ploughs there, and [there are] 30 acres of meadow.

In Algarkirk HUNDRED [is] SOKELAND [of] Drayton, 10 carucates of land and 5 bovates to the geld. [There is] land for 9 ploughs. 42 sokemen have 6 ploughs there, and 5 acres of meadow.

"RICHE" [IN WIGTOFT] HUNDRED

In "RICHE [in Wigtoft] [is] SOKELAND [of] Drayton, 10 carucates of land to the geld. [There is] land for 10 ploughs. 35 sokemen and 28 bordars have 7 ploughs there, and [there are] 12 acres of meadow.

BICKER HUNDRED

In BICKER [is] SOKELAND [of] Drayton, 5 carucates of land and 7 bovates to the geld. [There is] land for as many ploughs and oxen. There are 19 sokemen and 18 villans and 1 bordar having 5 ploughs. There is a church and a priest, and 20 salt-pans [rendering] 30s, and 20 acres of meadow.

HUNDRED

In Gosberton [is] SOKELAND [of] Drayton, 3 carucates of land and 2 bovates to the geld. [There is] land for 3 ploughs and 2 oxen.

Of this land Wulfbert has 6 bovates. There is 1 ploughs, and 2 villans and 10 bordars with 1 plough, and 6 acres of meadow, and 2 salt-pans [rendering] 12d. The other 2 carucates and 4 bovates belong to the soke [of] Drayton. Æthelstan held 6 bovates, and Earl Ralph had the soke, and TRE these 6 were worth 4s; now 40s.

In "Tric" [in Skegness] [is] SOKELAND [of] Drayton, half a carucate of land to the geld. [There is] land for 4 oxen. There is 1 bordar, and 60 acres of meadow.

In Burgh le Marsh [is] SOKELAND [of] Drayton, $1\frac{1}{2}$ carucates to the geld. [There is] land for 12 oxen. 3 sokemen and 2 villans and 3 bordars have $1\frac{1}{2}$ ploughs there.

In Addlethorpe [is] SOKELAND [of] Drayton, 1 bovate of land to the geld. [There is] land for 1 ox. There 2 villans plough with 2 oxen, and [there are] 20 acres of meadow.

In the same ADDLETHROPE, Alnoth had 1 carucate of land to the geld. [There is] land for 1 plough. Eudo, the count's man, has there 3 sokemen with half a plough, and 100 acres of meadow. TRE worth 20s; now 2s8d.

In Candlesby [is] SOKELAND of this manor, 2 bovates of land to the geld. [There is] land for 3 oxen. 2 villans have half a plough there, and [there are] 100 acres of marsh.

In Hagworthingham [is] other SOKELAND, 6 bovates of land to the geld. [There is] land for 9 oxen. Eudo, the count's man, [has] there 4 sokemen and 2 villans having 1 plough, and 30 acres of meadow.

'ELLOE' WAPENTAKE

In Holbeach and Whaplode, Earl Ælfgar had 1 carucate of land to the geld. [There is] land for 6 oxen. [It is] a BEREWICK of Fleet. Count Alan has it, but the king's officers claim it for the use of the king. There are 3 villans with 3 oxen | in a plough. |

In the same places Earl Æfgar had 13 carucates of land and 6 bovates to the geld. [There is] land for 9 ploughs and 2 oxen. [It is] SOKELAND of Gedney. Of this land Count Alan has 5 carucates. Landric holds them of him. He has 2 ploughs there, and 29 villans with 5 ploughs, and 80 acres of meadow. It is worth £8. This is adjudged for the use of the king.

'HILL' WAPENTAKE

In HAGWORTHINGHAM, Holmkell had half a carucate of land to the geld. [There is] land for 1 plough. Eudo, the count's man, has 16 acres of meadow there. Of this land, 30 acres are sokeland of Beesby in the Marsh. Its value [is assessed] in other manors.

'CALCEWATH' WAPENTAKE

In MALTBY LE MARSH, Broklauss had 6 bovates of land to the geld. [There is] land for 6 oxen. Eudo has there under the count 3 sokemen and 4 villans with 1 plough, and 20 acres of meadow. TRE worth 10s; now the same.

In Strubby [near Maltby le Marsh] [is] SOKELAND of Legbourne, 2½ bovates of land to the geld. [There is] land for 5 oxen. 2 sokemen have half a plough there, and 10 acres of meadow.

KIRTON WAPENTAKE

In KIRTON, Eadric had 10 bovates of land to the geld. [There is] land for 1 plough and 5 oxen. Toli, the count's man, has 1 plough there, and 4 villans have 1 plough, and [there are] 8 acres of meadow. TRE worth 40s; now 20s.

In 'Stenning' [in Swineshead], Healfdene had 3 carucates of land to the geld. [There is] land for 3 ploughs. Geoffrey de Tournai, the count's man, has 2 ploughs there, and 8 villans having half a plough, and 6 salt-pans [rendering] 8S, and 50 acres of meadow. TRE worth 20s; now the same.

In QUADRING, Thorkil had 1 carucate of land to the geld. [There is] land for 1 plough, with sake and soke, except 2 bovates over which the count has the soke. Gyrth, the count's man, holds this land, but the men of the wapentake do not know through whom. There are 3 villans, and 6 acres of meadow, and 2 salt-pans [rendering] 12d. TRE worth 10s; now the same.

In STOKE ROCHFORD, Ralph the staller had 3 carucates of land to the geld. [There is] land for 3 ploughs. Kolgrimr, the count's man, has 2 ploughs there belonging to [his] hall, and 7 villans and 1 bordar with 2 ploughs, and 2 mills [rendering] 7s4d, and [there are] 30 acres of meadow, and 140 acres of woodland pasture and 6 perches. TRE worth 30s; now 60s.

In NORTH HYKEHAM HUNDRED, Siward had 4 carucates of land to the geld. [There is] land for 2 ploughs. Kolgrimr, the count's man, has 1 plough there, and 2 villans ploughing with 2 oxen, and 1 mill [rendering] 5s, and [there are] 26 acres of meadow. TRE worth 20s; now the same.

MUMBY HUNDRED

In MUMBY, Earnwig had 3 carucates of land to the geld. [There is] land for 4 ploughs. Eudo, the count's man, has 3 ploughs there, and 16 villans and 8 bordars have 1½ ploughs, and [there are] 200 acres of meadow.

In Claxby [near Alford], a BEREWICK of this manor, Count Alan has 15 acres of land.

In Theddlethorpe [All Saints or St Helen] [is] SOKELAND of Mumby, 3 bovates of land to the geld. [There is] land for 3 oxen. 5 sokemen and 1 bordar have half a plough there, and [there are] 30 acres of meadow.

In HAGWORTHINGHAM MUMBY, Ormkil, Sigefrith, Alric, Swein, Svavi [and] Holmkell had 8 carucates of land to the geld. [There is] land for †11† ploughs and 5 oxen. Eudo, the count's man, has 3 ploughs there in demesne; and 40 villans and 4 sokemen and 12 bordars having 5 ploughs and 6 oxen ploughing, and [there are] 310 acres of meadow. TRE these 7 manors were worth £10; now £16.

HUTTOFT HUNDRED

In Sutton on Sea [is] 1 bovate of land to the geld. 2 villans have 20 acres of meadow there. [It is] SOKELAND of Cumberworth.

[Folio 349: LINDSEY]

XIII. The land of Earl Hugh

In GREETHAM, Earl Harold had 2 carucates of land without geld. [There is] land for 6 ploughs. 2 bovates of this land [are] SOKELAND. Earl Hugh has 4 ploughs there in demesne; and 46 villans and 8 bordars and 1 sokeman having 8 ploughs. There is a priest and a church, and 1 mill [rendering] 8s, and 300 acres of meadow. [It is] 1 league and 1 furlong long and 1 league broad. TRE worth £40 and half a mark of gold; now £60; tallage £70.

In Legbourne [is] SOKELAND, 10 carucates of land to the geld. [There is] land for 12 ploughs. There are 31 sokemen and 18 villans and †19† bordars having 16 ploughs, and 40 acres of meadow, and 80 acres of woodland, pasture in places.

In Swaby and Belleau and South Thoresby and Claythorpe and Tothill [is] SOKELAND, 12 carucates of land to the geld. [There is] land for 18 ploughs. There are 46 sokemen and 22 villans and 38 bordars having 31 ploughs, and 6 mills rendering £4 and 16d, and 20 acres of meadow, and 600 acres of woodland pasture.

In Withern and Aby and Haugh and Calceby [is] SOKELAND, 7 carucates of land and a half to the geld. [There is] land for 6½ ploughs. 17 sokemen and 10 villans have 6½ ploughs there, and 16 acres of meadow, and [there are] 92 acres of woodland pasture and scrubland.

In Sutterby and Dalby and Dexthorpe [is] SOKELAND, 15 carucates of land to the geld. [There is] land for 16 ploughs. There are 47 sokemen and 8 villans and 11 bordars having 11 ploughs. In Dalby the earl has 1 plough in demesne, and 2 churches, and 80 acres of meadow.

In Fordington and Ashby by Partney and Bratoft and 'Langene' [in Irby in the Marsh] [is] SOKELAND, 18½ carucates of land to the geld. [There is] land for 18 ploughs. Now 49 sokemen and 26 villans and 22 bordars have 18 ploughs there. There are 3 churches, and 620 acres of meadow.

In Wainfleet [All Saints or St Mary] and Haugh and Calceby and Theddlethorpe [All Saints or St Helen] and Mablethorpe [is] SOKELAND, 20 carucates of land and 2 bovates to the geld. [There is] land for as many ploughs. 83 sokemen and 33 villans and 35 bordars have 18½ ploughs there, and 1,000 acres of meadow, and 20 salt-pans [rendering] 10s, and 80 acres of scrubland.

In Huttoft and Thurlby [in Bilsby] and Sutton on Sea and Trusthorpe and Bilsby and Markby [is] SOKELAND, 18 carucates of land to the geld. [There is] land for 20 ploughs. 69 sokemen and 19 villans and 23 bordars have 16 ploughs there, and 780 acres of meadow.

'HILL' WAPENTAKE

In Langton [near Spilsby] and Hagworthingham and Salmonby and Tetford and Brinkhill and Winceby and Claxby Pluckacre [is] SOKELAND, 29 carucates of land to the geld. [There is] land for 33 ploughs. There are 150 sokemen and 20 bordars and 12 villans having 39 ploughs, and 9 mills rendering 20s, and 350 acres of meadow.

All this land or SOKELAND belongs to Greetham. All together [there are] 131 carucates to the geld. [There is] land for 144 ploughs. [There are] 376 sokemen, 148 villans [and] 168 bordars, having 156 ploughs.

In WEST HALTON, Earl Harold had 8 carucates of land to the geld. [There is] land for 6 ploughs. Of this land, 4 carucates are sokeland. Now Earl Hugh has them, and William fitzNigel [holds] of him. [There are] 4 ploughs in demesne; and 3 villans and 9 bordars and 14 sokemen having 2 ploughs, and 30 acres of meadow. TRE worth £19; now £10; tallage £5.

In Walcot [in Alkborough] [is] a BEREWICK of this manor, 3 bovates of land to the geld. [There is] land for 3 oxen.

In Winterton [is] SOKELAND, 4 carucates of land to the geld. [There is] land for 4 ploughs. 16 sokemen and 7 bordars have 2½ ploughs there.

In Coleby [in West Halton] [is] SOKELAND, 15 bovates of land to the geld. [There is] land for 2 ploughs. 3 sokemen plough there with 1 ox, and [there are] 9 acres of meadow.

In 'Haythby' [in West Halton] [is] SOKELAND, 3 carucates of land to the geld. [There is] land for 2 ploughs. Now 9 sokemen and 1 bordar have 2 ploughs there, and 80 acres of meadow, and 20 acres of scrubland.

In Thealby [is] SOKELAND, 10½ carucates of land to the geld. [There is] land for 9 ploughs. Now 16 sokemen and 15 bordars have 4½ ploughs there, and 50 acres of meadow, and 70 acres of scrubland.

In Crosby [in Scunthorpe] and 'South Conesby' [in Crosby] [is] SOKELAND, 6 carucates of land and 6 bovates to the geld. [There is] land for 6 ploughs and 6 oxen. Now 25 sokemen and 10 bordars have 6 ploughs there, and 80 acres of meadow.

NORTH RIDING

In BARNETBY LE WOLD, Earl Harold had 6 carucates of land to the geld. [There is] land for 12 ploughs. 3 carucates are SOKELAND. William, Earl Hugh's man, has 3 ploughs

there in demesne; and 4 villans and 60 sokemen and 10 bordars having 7½ ploughs. TRE worth £14; now £20; tallage £10.

In Barton-upon-Humber, 2 bovates, and Bigby, 1 carucates, and Worlaby [near Elsham], 2 carucates, and Somerby [near Howsham], half a carucate, and Habrough, 1 bovate and 2 parts of a bovate to the geld. [There is] land for 7 ploughs. There are 36 sokemen and 1 villan having 4½ ploughs, and 40 acres of meadow. This SOKELAND belongs to Barnetby le Wold.

Also in 'Lobingham' [in Killingholme], 4 carucates and 1 bovate, and Irby upon Humber, 1½ carucates, and Riby, 4½ carucates, all together [there are] 10 carucates of land and 1 bovate to the geld. [There is] land for 20 ploughs and 2 oxen. [It is] SOKELAND of Barnetby le Wold. There are 52 sokemen and 11 villans and 7 bordars having 11 ploughs, and 315 acres of meadow.

In Riby, Erneis, the earl's man, has 2 ploughs in demesne. He himself holds that sokeland of the earl. William, Ralph and Azelin, the earl's men, hold the others.

In FULSTOW, Godric had 6 bovates of land to the geld. [There is] land for 11 oxen. Rozelin, the earl's man, has 1 plough there, and 7 villans and 1 bordar with 1 plough, and 100 acres of meadow. TRE worth 20s; now 40s.

[Folio 349V: LINCOLNSHIRE]

In HEMINGBY, Lambkarl had 6 bovates of land to the geld. [There is] land for 6 oxen. Baldric, the earl's man, has 1 plough there, and 2 villans and 2 bordars and 7 sokemen having 2 ploughs, and half a mill [rendering] 7s, and 30 acres of meadow. TRE worth 30s; now 25s.

In Bucknall and Horsington [is] SOKELAND of this manor, 9 bovates of land to the geld. [There is] land for 1 plough and 2 oxen. 10 sokemen and 3 bordars have 2 ploughs there, and 62 acres of meadow, and 20 acres of woodland, pasture in places.

SOUTH RIDING

In STAINTON BY LANGWORTH, Godric had 3 carucates of land to the geld. [There is] land for 4 ploughs. Half a carucate [belongs] to the sokemen. Osbern, the earl's man, has 2 ploughs there, and 5 villans and 4 bordars and 4 sokemen with 2 ploughs, and 1 mill [rendering] 12d, and 80 acres of meadow, and 140 acres of scrubland. TRE worth £3; now the same.

In Reasby [is] a BEREWICK of this manor, 6 bovates of land to the geld. [There is] land for 6 oxen.

In BULLINGTON, Lambkarl had 3½ bovates of land to the geld. [There is] land for 1 plough. Kolsveinn, the earl's man, has 1 plough there, and 2 villans and 3 bordars having half a plough, and 10 acres of meadow, and 160 acres of scrubland. TRE worth 20s; now the same.

In Coningsby [is] inland of [High or Low] Toynton, 1 bovate of land to the geld. 1 villan ploughs there with 2 oxen, and [there is] 1 fishery [rendering] 30d, and 2 acres of meadow, and 20 acres of woodland.

In TATHWELL, Earl Harold had 5 carucates of land to the geld. [There is] land for 20 ploughs. 2 carucates [are] sokeland. Earl Hugh has 6 ploughs there in demesne; and 12 villans and 4 bordars and 24 sokemen having 3 ploughs. There is a church, and 1 mill [rendering] 16d, and 8 acres of meadow, and 80 acres of woodland pasture. TRE worth £15; now £20; tallage 100s.

In Hallington and Kelstern and Raithby [near Louth] and Maltby, is SOKELAND of this manor, 9 carucates of land and 2 bovates to the geld. [There is] land for 9½ ploughs. 41 sokemen and 20 villans have 6 ploughs there, and 10 acres of meadow.

In RUCKLAND, Godric had 1 carucate of land to the geld. [There is] land for 3 ploughs. Brisard, the earl's man, has 1 plough there, and 6 villans and 3 bordars with 1 plough. There is a church, and 1 mill [rendering] 2s, and 30 acres of meadow. TRE worth £4; now 40s.

In FARFORTH, Lambkarl had 1½ carucates of land to the geld. [There is] land for 2 ploughs. 1 bovate [is] sokeland. Baldric, the earl's man, has 1 plough there, and 10 villans and 2 sokemen and 6 bordars with 2 ploughs. There is a church, and 1 mill [rendering] 3s, and 8 acres of meadow. TRE worth £3; now the same.

In MAIDENWELL, Aleifr, Eadric and Godric had 2 carucates of land, less 1 bovate, to the geld. [There is] land for 3 ploughs. Half a bovate [is] sokeland. Osbern, the earl's man, has 3 ploughs there, and 8 villans and 2 sokemen with 1 plough, and 1 salt-pan, and 34 acres of meadow, and 5 acres of scrubland. TRE worth 100s; now £4; | tallage 5s. |

In Oxcombe [is] SOKELAND of Farforth, 1½ carucates of land to the geld. [There is] land for 2 ploughs. 12 sokemen and 1 villan have 2 ploughs there, and 60 acres of meadow. TRE, as now, [worth] 40s.

In WADDINGTON, Earl Harold had 24 carucates of land to the geld. [There is] land for as many ploughs. 9 carucates and 2 bovates [are] SOKELAND. Earl Hugh has 4 ploughs there in demesne; and 15 villans and 9 bordars and 24 sokemen having 11 ploughs. There is a church and a priest, and 2 mills rendering 11s, and 270 acres of meadow. TRE worth £100, less £4; now £20; tallage £10.

In Metheringham [is] a BEREWICK of this manor, 8½ carucates of land to the geld. [There is] land for 4 ploughs and 2 oxen. The earl has 2 ploughs there, and 10 villans and 6 bordars with 2 ploughs, and 1 mill [rendering] 8s, and 190 acres of meadow, and 120 acres of scrubland.

In Timberland [is] a BEREWICK, 6 bovates of land to the geld. [There is] land for 4 oxen. 2 bordars have half a plough there, and 50 acres of scrubland.

In Harmston [is] SOKELAND of Waddington, 20½ carucates of land to the geld. [There is] land for as many ploughs. 38 sokemen and 11 bordars have 10 ploughs there. There is a church and a priest, and 1 fishery rendering 75,000 eels.

In ASHWELL [Rut.], Earl Harold had 2 carucates of land to the geld. [There is] land for 6 ploughs. Joscelin, Earl Hugh's man, has there 2 ploughs, and 13 villans and 2 bordars having 5 ploughs, and [there are] 16 acres of meadow. TRE worth 100s; now £6.

In FULLETBY, Earl Harold had 2 carucates of land to the geld. [There is] land for 3 ploughs. Baldric, the earl's man, has 1 plough there, and 9 sokemen and 5 villans and 4 bordars having 1½ ploughs, and [there are] 60 acres of meadow. TRE worth 40s; now the same.

The priest of the same vill has of the king 2 bovates of land to the geld, and 12 acres of meadow.

In SOUTH ORMSBY, Godric had 3 carucates of land to the geld. [There is] land for 4 ploughs. Hugh, the earl's man, has 2 ploughs there, and 7 villans and 1 bordar and 11 sokemen having 2 ploughs, and 1 mill [rendering] 32d, and [there are] 80 acres of meadow. TRE worth 70s; now £4.

In KETSBY, Godric had 3 carucates of land to the geld. [There is] land for 4 ploughs. Hugh, the earl's man, has 3 ploughs there, and 6 villans and 1 bordar and 11 sokemen having 2½ ploughs, and 1 mill [rendering] 32d, and 60 acres of meadow. TRE worth £4; now 100s.

In Walmsgate [is] SOKELAND of this manor, 1 carucate of land to the geld. [There is] land for 14 oxen.

In HAUGHAM, Ælfgifu, Godric and Eadric had 2 carucates of land to the geld. [There is] land for 6 ploughs. The monks of Saint-Sever have 3 ploughs there, and 29 villans and 3 bordars with 6 ploughs, and 46 acres of meadow, and woodland, pasture in places, 1 league long and 3 furlongs broad. TRE worth £6; now £8.

In NEWBALL, Godric had 3 carucates of land to the geld. [There is] land for 3 ploughs. Osbern, the earl's man, has 2 ploughs there, and 13 villans and 2 bordars with 2 ploughs, and 120 acres of meadow, and 500 acres of woodland pasture. TRE worth 60s; now 100s.

[Folio 350: LINDSEY]

XIIII. The land of Ivo Taillebois

In TETNEY, Thorgisl and Swein had 4 carucates of land to the geld. [There is] land for 8 ploughs. 1 carucate and 2 bovates and the third part of 2 bovates of this land [are] SOKELAND. Now IVO Taillebois has 6 ploughs there in demesne; and 25 villans and 7 bordars and 12 sokemen having 6 ploughs. There is 1 mill [rendering] 16s, and 13 salt-pans [rendering] 12s, and 140 acres of meadow. TRE it was worth £10; now £20; tallage £20.

In Holton le Clay [is] SOKELAND of this manor, 2 carucates of land to the geld. [There is] land for 4 ploughs. 14 sokemen have 3 ploughs there. It is worth 40s.

In the same place Esbiorn had 1 carucate of land to the geld. [There is] land for 2 ploughs. Hermer, Ivo's man, has there 5 villans and 2 bordars ploughing with 5 oxen. There is the site of a mill, and 14 acres of meadow. TRE, as now, worth 40s.

In Humberstone [is] sokeland of Tetney, 6 carucates of land to the geld. [There is] land for 12 ploughs. 67 sokemen have 18 ploughs there, and 200 acres of meadow.

In OLD CLEE [in Great Grimsby], Grimbald had 2 bovates of land and 2 parts of a bovate to the geld. [There is] land for half a plough. Wimund, Ivo's man, has half a plough there, and 16 acres of meadow. TRE worth 20s; now 10s.

In 'THRUNSCOE' [in Cleethorpes], Grimkel had 5 bovates of land to the geld. [There is] land for 10 oxen. Wimund has 1 plough there, and 5 villans with 1 ox, and 12 acres of meadow. TRE, as now, worth 20s.

'WALSHCROFT' WAPENTAKE

In North Willingham, IVO has half a carucate of land of the soke of Erik.

In CLAXBY [near Walesby] and NORMANBY LE WOLD, Godwine had 10 bovates of land to the geld. [There is] land for 2½ ploughs.

In the same places Godric, Siward, Ulfkil and Godwine had 12 bovates of land to the geld, and 1 toft with sake and soke. [There is] land for 3 ploughs. Hugh, IVO's man, has 2 ploughs there, and 48 sokemen and 4 bordars with 6 ploughs. There are 2 churches, and 100 acres of meadow, and 40 acres of scrubland. TRE worth 40s; now £4; tallage £4.

In Osgodby [near West Rasen] and Tealby [is] inland, 2 bovates, and SOKELAND, 1 bovate, of this manor: 3 bovates of land to the geld. [There is] land for 6 oxen. 4 sokemen and 1 villan plough there with 6 oxen, and there is 1 mill [rendering] 3s, and 3 acres of meadow.

In CLAXBY [near Walesby], Alwine had 3 bovates of land to the geld. [There is] land for 6 oxen. Geoffrey, Ivo's man, has 1 plough there, and 2 villans who do not plough, and [there is] 1 mill [rendering] 2s, and 13 acres of meadow, and 6 acres of scrubland. TRE worth 15s; now 13s.

In THORGANBY, Grimbald had 2 bovates of land to the geld. [There is] land for 5 oxen. Odo, Ivo's man, has 1 plough there, and 2 villans, and 3 parts of a mill [rendering] 5s, and 9 acres of meadow. TRE worth 20s; now 30s.

In WALESBY, and Otby, Grimbald had 1 carucate of land to the geld. [There is] land for 2 ploughs. Geoffrey, Ivo's man, has 1 plough there, and 20 villans with 2 ploughs, and 1 mill [rendering] 16d, and 20 acres of meadow, and 5 acres of scrubland. TRE worth 40s; now the same; tallage 10s.

In THORESWAY, Grimbald has 2 bovates of land to the geld. [There is] land for 6 oxen. Odo, Ivo's man, has there 1 villan ploughing with 1 ox, and [there are] 15½ acres of meadow. TRE worth 20s; now 9s4d.

In CROXBY, Siward had 5 bovates of land to the geld. [There is] land for 2 ploughs. 5 acres of land [are] SOKELAND. Odo, Ivo's man, has 1½ ploughs there, and 6 villans and 1 bordar with 1 plough, and 3 mills [rendering] 8s, and [there are] 18 acres of meadow. TRE worth 30s; now 40s.

In BLYBOROUGH, Gamal had 5½ bovates to the geld. [There is] land for 11 oxen. Nigel, Ivo's man, has 2 ploughs

there, and 7 villans and 5 bordars with 1 plough, and 1 mill [rendering] 12d, and 20 acres of meadow. TRE worth 26s8d; now 50s; tallage 20s.

In GLENTHAM, Thorgisl had 3 carucates of land to the geld. [There is] land for 4 ploughs. 2 carucates of land and 2 bovates of this land [are] SOKELAND. Rainfrid, Ivo's man, has 2 ploughs there, and 2 villans and 13 bordars and 19 sokemen with 2½ ploughs, and 90 acres of meadow. TRE worth 30s; now 60s; tallage 20s.

In NORMANBY-by-SPITAL, Koddi had 5 carucates of land to the geld. [There is] land for 8 ploughs. 1½ carucates [are] SOKELAND. Now Ivo has 4 ploughs there, and 15 villans and 14 sokemen having 5 ploughs. There is a church and a priest, and 2 mills [rendering] 5s4d, and 67½ acres of meadow. TRE worth 50s; now 100s; tallage 20s.

In Snitterby [is] SOKELAND of this manor, 1 bovate of land. There are 3 sokemen ploughing with 6 oxen, and 40 acres of meadow.

In OWMBY-by-SPITAL, Koddi had 4 bovates of land to the geld. [There is] land for half a plough. Peter, Ivo's man, has 1 plough there, and 2 villans, and 10 acres of meadow. TRE worth 10s; now 20s.

In the same place Ivo has 1 bovate of land of the soke of Bishop Remigius.

In SOMERBY [in Corringham] [are] 7 bovates of land to the geld. [There is] land for 7 oxen. Ivo has 1 bordar there, and 20 acres of woodland pasture. TRE worth 20s; now 5s.

In 'DUNSTALL' [in Corringham], Gamal had 2 carucates of land to the geld. [There is] land for 2½ ploughs. 10 bovates of this land [are] SOKELAND. Ivo has 2 ploughs there in demesne; and 2 villans and 11 sokemen and 1 bordar with 2 ploughs. There is a church and a priest, and 1 mill [rendering] 2s, and 7 acres of meadow. TRE worth 40s; now £4.

In MORTON [in Gainsborough], Gamal had 3 bovates of land to the geld. [There is] land for 6 oxen. Ivo has there 4 villans ploughing with 2 oxen, and 10 acres of meadow. [There are] moors and scrubland half a league long and a half broad. TRE worth 4s; now 10s.

In SCOTTON, Gamal had 2½ carucates of land to the geld. [There is] land for 2½ ploughs. Half a carucate of this land [is] SOKELAND. Joscelin, Ivo's man, has 2 ploughs there, and 15 villans and 3 bordars and 6 sokemen with 2 ploughs, and [there are] 31 acres of meadow, and 18 acres of scrubland, and the site of a mill.

TRE worth 30s; now 50s; tallage 10s.

[Folio 350V: LINCOLNSHIRE]

'MANLEY' WAPENTAKE

In HIBALDSTOW, Gamal had 1½ carucates of land to the geld. [There is] land for 3 ploughs. Ivo has 4 ploughs there, and 18 villans and 2 bordars with 2 ploughs, and 1 mill [rendering] 5s, and 111 acres of meadow, and 60 acres of scrubland. TRE worth 100s; now 100s; tallage 20s.

In Hibaldstow [and] 'GAINSTHORPE' [in Hibaldstow], Wulfgar had 2 bovates of land. He has this in exchange for 1 bovate, and 2 fisheries of Crowle. There is 1 plough. TRE, as now, [worth] 10s.

In STURTON [in Scawby] and Scawby [is] inland, 3 bovates of land to the geld. One of Ivo's men [has] 1 plough there, and 1 villan. TRE worth 5s4d; now 20s.

In ALKBOROUGH, William Malet had 5 carucates of land to the geld. [There is] land for 6 ploughs. 3 carucates of this land [are] SOKELAND. Ivo has 3 ploughs there, and 8 villans and 20 sokemen with 5 ploughs. TRE worth 100s; now £4; tallage 40s.

In SAXBY ALL SAINTS, Siward and Thorgisl had 4 carucates of land to the geld. [There is] land for 7½ ploughs. Roger, Ivo's man, has 2 ploughs there, and 8 villans and 2 sokemen with 3 ploughs, and 3 fisheries [rendering] 3s. TRE worth £4; now 50s; tallage 10s.

In [North and South] KILLINGHOLME, Beorhtfrith, Siward and Thorgisl [had] 2 carucates of land and 7 bovates to the geld. [There is] land for 3 ploughs. 1 carucate and 1 bovate and 2 tofts [are] SOKELAND. Odo, Ivo's man, has 3 ploughs there, and 4 villans and 19 sokemen with 3 ploughs, and half a mill [rendering] 3s, and [there are] 212 acres of meadow. TRE worth £5; now £3; tallage 20s.

In LITTLE LIMBER, Alwine had 9 bovates of land to the geld. [There is] land for 4 ploughs. 1 bovate of this land [is] SOKELAND. Nigel, Ivo's man, has 3 ploughs there, and 1 villan. TRE worth 40s; now 60s.

In NEWSHAM, Alwine had 5 bovates of land to the geld. [There is] land for 10 oxen. Roger, Ivo's man, has 1 plough there, and 6 villans with 1 plough, and 1 mill [rendering] 2s, and 30 acres of meadow. TRE worth 22s; now 40s.

In IRBY UPON HUMBER, Sæweard had 1 carucate of land to the geld. [There is] land for 2 ploughs. Odo, Ivo's man, has 1 plough there, and 5 villans and 10 bordars ploughing with 3 oxen. TRE worth 10s8d; now 20s.

In HOLTON LE MOOR, Ivo has 1 carucate of land to the geld, [which he has] in exchange. [There is] land for 2 ploughs. There is 1 plough. Odo has it, and it is worth 15s.

In HABROUGH, Thorgisl had 3 bovates and the third part of a bovate to the geld. [It is] SOKELAND of East Halton. It is waste.

In BROCKLESBY, Alwine had 3 bovates of land to the geld. [There is] land for 1 plough. 1 bovate [is] SOKELAND. Nigel, Ivo's man, has there 2 sokemen ploughing with 2 oxen. TRE worth 16s; now 3s.

In WAITHE [are] 2 bovates to the geld. [There is] land for 2 oxen. 4 villans and 1 sokeman have half a plough there, and 5 acres of meadow.

In CABOURNE, Olaf had 1 carucate of land and 3 bovates to the geld. [There is] land for 3 ploughs. Roger, Ivo's man, has 2 ploughs there, and 3 villans and 5 bordars and 11

sokemen with 2½ ploughs, and 100 acres of meadow. TRE worth 30s; now 60s; tallage 20s.

In CUXWOLD, Alwine had 1½ bovates of land to the geld. [There is] land for half a plough. Joscelin, Ivo's man, has 1 plough there. TRE worth 20s; now 16s.

In REDBOURNE, Gamal had 1 carucate of land and half a bovate to the geld. [There is] land for 1 plough and half an ox. Peter, Ivo's man, has 1 plough there, and 5 villans and 1 sokeman and 1 bordar with 1 plough, and 24 acres of meadow. TRE worth 21s; now 30s; tallage 10s.

In the same place Healfdene had 3 bovates of land to the geld. Ivo has there 1 villan with 1 ox, and [there are] 8 acres of meadow. It is worth |5s.|

In 'WESTLABY' [in Wickenby], Harold had 7 bovates of land to the geld. [There is] land for 14 oxen. Odo, Ivo's man, has half a plough there, and 2 villans and 2 bordars with half a plough, and 20 acres of meadow. TRE worth 20s; now 16s.

In 'LOBINGHAM' [in Killingholme], Alwine had 6 bovates of land to the geld. [There is] land for 12 oxen. Odo, Ivo's man, has there 1 bordar ploughing with 1 ox, and 30 acres of meadow. TRE worth 20s; now 12s.

In KEELBY, Alwine had 2 bovates of land to the geld. [There is] land for 4 oxen. Nigel, Ivo's man, has half a plough there, and 2 villans and 1 bordar ploughing with 1 ox. There is the site of a mill, and 27 acres of meadow. TRE worth 10s; now 20s.

'HAVERSTOE' WAPENTAKE

In BELCHFORD, Stori had 6 carucates of land to the geld. [There is] land for 8 ploughs. 2 carucates of this land [are] sokeland. Ivo has 5 ploughs there in demesne; and 9 villans and 15 bordars and 45 sokemen having 9 ploughs. There are 2 mills rendering 18s8d, and 360 acres of meadow, and 3 acres of scrubland. [It is] 1 league long and 1 broad. TRE worth £15; now £33; tallage £27. SOKELAND OF THIS MANOR

In Goulceby [are] 3 carucates of land to the geld. [There is] land for 3 ploughs. 16 sokemen and 2 villans have 6 ploughs there, and 1 mill [rendering] 4s, and [there is] a priest and a church, and 120 acres of meadow.

In Hemingby [are] 3 carucates to the geld. [There is] land for 3 ploughs. 22 sokemen and 7 villans and 6 bordars have 7 ploughs there, and [there are] 120 acres of meadow.

In Scamblesby [are] 6 carucates of land to the geld. [There is] land for 7 ploughs. Ivo has 1 plough there, and 27 sokemen and 11 villans and 3 bordars have 5 ploughs, and [there are] 240 acres of meadow.

In Cawkwell [are] 1½ carucates of land to the geld. [There is] land for as much. 12 sokemen and 1 villan have 2 ploughs there, and 60 acres of meadow.

In Donington on Bain [are] 6 carucates of land to the geld. [There is] land for 8 ploughs. Ivo has 3 ploughs there, and 28 sokemen and 6 bordars have 6 ploughs, and [there are] 2 mills [rendering] 17s4d, and 240 acres of meadow.

In Stenigot [are] 3 carucates of land to the geld. [There is] land for 3 ploughs. Ivo has 2 ploughs there, and 23 sokemen and 5 villans have 4 ploughs,

[Folio 351: LINDSEY]

and [there are] 120 acres of meadow, and 20 acres of scrubland.

In Asterby [are] 3 carucates of land to the geld. [There is] land for 3 ploughs. There are 9 sokemen and 2 villans and 7 bordars having 3 ploughs, and 120 acres of meadow.

In the two Mintings [Minting and 'Little Minting'] [are] 7 carucates of land to the geld, and 5 bovates and the fifth part of a bovate to the geld. [There is] arable land for twice [as many ploughs and oxen]. Ivo has 2 ploughs there in demesne; and 27 sokemen and 10 villans and 20 bordars having 9 ploughs, and [there are] 260 acres of meadow, and 1,010 acres of woodland pasture, and 100 acres of scrubland.

In Stixwould [are] 2 carucates of land and 2 bovates to the geld. [There is] land for 2 ploughs and 2 oxen. 10 sokemen and 3 villans and 4 bordars have 3 ploughs there, and [there are] 40 acres of meadow, and 80 acres of woodland pasture.

In Horsington [is] 1 carucate of land to the geld. [There is] land for 1 plough. 4 villans and 4 sokemen have 1 plough there, and [there are] 50 acres of meadow, and 25 acres of scrubland.

In 'Burreth' [in Tupholme] and 'Thorley' [in Minting and Gautby] [is] 1 carucate of land and 3 bovates and the third part of a bovate to the geld. [There is] arable land for as much. 9 sokemen have 3 ploughs there, and [there are] 175 acres of meadow, and 180 acres of woodland pasture, and 500 acres of scrubland.

In BULLINGTON, Lambi had 5 bovates of land to the geld. [There is] land for 2 ploughs. Odo, Ivo's man, has 1 plough there, and 13 villans and 1 villan [sic] and 2 bordars with 1 plough, and [there are] 5 acres of meadow, and 80 acres of scrubland. TRE worth 16s; now 20s; tallage 10s.

In BENNIWORTH, Siward and Thorgot had 3½ carucates of land to the geld. [There is] land for 6 ploughs. Of this land half a carucate [is] sokeland. Odo, Ivo's man, has 3 ploughs there, and 11 villans and 10 bordars and 18 sokemen having 6 ploughs, and 140 acres of meadow. TRE worth £4; now £5; tallage 20s.

In KINGTHORPE, Bærghthor had 2½ bovates and the third part of half a bovate to the geld. [There is] arable land for twice [as many ploughs and oxen]. Odo has 2 villans ploughing there with 2 oxen, and [there are] 5 acres of meadow, and 80 acres of woodland, pasture in places. TRE worth 10s; now the same.

In Strubby [in Langton by Wragby] [are] 2 bovates to the geld.

In LUDFORD, Thorald had 5 bovates of land to the geld.

[There is] land for 10 oxen. Odo has 1 plough there, and 8 villans with 1 plough, and 1 mill [rendering] 12d, and 10 acres of meadow. TRE worth 40s; now 30s.

In EDLINGTON, Gamal had 2 carucates of land to the geld. [There is] land for 2 ploughs. Walter, Ivo's man, has 2 ploughs there, and 4 villans and 6 sokemen and 3 bordars with 1 plough, and 1 mill [rendering] 8s, and 30 acres of meadow, and 30 acres of scrubland, and a church. TRE worth 40s; now 60s.

In WYHAM, Alwine had 2 carucates of land to the geld. [There is] land for 3 ploughs. Wimund, Ivo's man, has 2 ploughs there, and 4 villans and 4 sokemen with 1 plough, and [there are] 8 acres of meadow. TRE worth 40s; now the same; tallage 20s.

In NORTH ORMSBY, Alwine had 2 carucates of land and 2 bovates to the geld. [There is] land for 3½ ploughs. Wimund, Ivo's man, has 2 ploughs there, and 13 sokemen and 2 villans with 2 ploughs, and [there are] 16 acres of meadow, and 8 acres of scrubland. TRE worth 50s; now 40s; tallage 20s.

In BOLINGBROKE, Stori had 2 carucates of land to the geld. [There is] land for 2 ploughs. 1 carucate of this land [is] SOKELAND. Now Ivo has 2 ploughs there, and 12 villans and 8 bordars and 12 sokemen with 3 ploughs. There is a church, and a new market, and 3 mills [rendering] 10s, and 70 acres of meadow. TRE worth £30; now £40; tallage £80 with all things belonging to it.

SOKELAND OF THIS MANOR

In Hareby [are] 4 carucates of land to the geld. [There is] land for 4 ploughs. 33 sokemen and 5 villans and 5 bordars have 4 ploughs there, and [there are] 100 acres of meadow.

In Miningsby [are] 6 carucates of land to the geld. [There is] land for 6 ploughs. 36 sokemen and 8 villans and 4 bordars have 6 ploughs there, and [there are] 40 acres of meadow.

In Asgarby [near Spilsby] [are] 3 carucates of land to the geld. [There is] land for 3 ploughs. 20 sokemen and 2 villans have 3 ploughs there, and 80 acres of meadow.

In Mavis Enderby [are] 5 carucates of land to the geld. [There is] land for 5 ploughs. 24 sokemen and 5 bordars have 5 ploughs there, and 100 acres of meadow.

In Raithby [near Spilsby] [are] 3 carucates of land and 7 bovates to the geld. [There is] land for as much [sic] ploughs and oxen. 18 villans and 3 villans [sic] and 5 bordars have 4 ploughs there. There is a church, and a mill [rendering] 12s, and 40 acres of meadow.

In Hundleby [are] 4 carucates of land to the geld. [There is] land for 4 ploughs. 25 sokemen and 12 villans have 4 ploughs there. There is a church, and a mill [rendering] 5s, and 80 acres of meadow. In this land Thor had 4 acres of land which belong to the Bishop of Durham's manor of Spilsby.

In Halton Holegate and Little Steeping [are] 9 carucates of land to the geld. [There is] land for 9 ploughs. Ivo has 1 plough there, and 58 sokemen and 4 villans with 9 ploughs. There is a church, and 4 mills [rendering] 24s, and 120 acres of meadow.

In Thorpe St Peter [are] 2 carucates of land and 5 bovates to the geld. [There is] land for as many ploughs and oxen. 18 sokemen and 8 villans have 3 ploughs there. There is a church, and 280 acres of meadow.

In Toynton [All Saints or St Peter] [are] 3 carucates of land to the geld. [There is] land for 3 ploughs. 14 villans and 13 sokemen have 3 ploughs there. There is a church, and 30 acres of meadow, and 5½ acres of scrubland.

In Stickney [are] 3 carucates of land to the geld. [There is] land for 3 ploughs. 33 sokemen and 5 villans have 3 ploughs there. There is a church, and 40 acres of meadow.

In Sibsey [are] 6 carucates of land to the geld. [There is] land for 6 ploughs. 51 sokemen and 16 villans and 10 bordars have 6 ploughs there. Ivo himself has 1 plough there, and [there is] a church, and 120 acres of meadow.

In Stickford [are] 2½ carucates of land to the geld. [There is] land for as many ploughs. 28 sokemen and 2 villans have 3 ploughs there. There is a church, and 30 acres of meadow.

In East Keal [are] 4½ carucates of land to the geld. [There is] land for as many ploughs. Ivo has 1 plough there, and 7 sokemen and 12 villans and 4 bordars with 4½ ploughs. There is half a church, and 20 acres of meadow.

[Folio 351V: LINCOLNSHIRE]

Sumarlithr had a manor there, and it was worth 20s. TRE; now the same.

In West Keal [are] 4 carucates of land to the geld. [There is] land for 5 ploughs. 35 sokemen and 8 villans and 6 bordars have 6 ploughs there, and 100 acres of meadow.

In Toynton [All Saints or St Peter] [are] 5 carucates and 2 bovates of land to the geld. [There is] land for 6 ploughs. 40 sokemen and 7 villans and 3 bordars have 6 ploughs there. There is a church, and 70 acres of meadow, and 10 acres of scrubland.

In Hagnaby [are] 2 carucates of land and 5 bovates to the geld. [There is] land for as many ploughs and oxen. 14 sokemen and 4 villans and 2 bordars have 3 ploughs there, and [there are] 73 acres of meadow.

In East Kirkby and Revesby [are] 12 carucates of land to the geld. [There is] land for 12 ploughs. 54 sokemen and 14 villans have 12 ploughs there. Ivo has 1 plough there, and 2 churches, and 180 acres of meadow.

The whole manor with all things appertaining to it [is] 6 leagues long and 6 broad.

In NORTH ELKINGTON, Esbiorn had 4 carucates of land to the geld. [There is] land for 8 ploughs. Of this land 2½ carucates [are] SOKELAND. Geoffrey, Ivo's man, has 2 ploughs there, and 19 sokemen and 5 villans with 3 ploughs. There is half a church, and half the site of a mill, and 60 acres of meadow. TRE worth 60s; now £6; tallage 40s.

In Little Grimsby [is] SOKELAND, 1½ carucates of land to the geld. [There is] land for 2 ploughs. Geoffrey has 1 plough

there, and 5 villans and 6 sokemen with 1 plough, and [there are] 10 acres of meadow.

In Sloothby [are] 7 bovates of land to the geld. [There is] land for 1½ ploughs. [It is] inland, 6 bovates, of 'Hanby' [in Welton le Marsh], and sokeland, 1 bovate, of Claxby [near Alford]. 8 villans and 3 bordars have 1 plough there, and 15 acres of meadow.

In 'AUSTERBY' [in Bourne], Seuen had †3† bovates of land to the geld. [There is] land for 3 oxen. Odo, Ivo's man, has there 3 villans and 1 bordar with half a plough, and the sixth part of a mill [rendering] 20d, and 3 fishponds [rendering] 8d, and and [sic] 3½ acres of meadow, and 15 acres of scrubland. TRE worth 6s; now 10s.

In BRACEBY and Sapperton [is] 1 carucate of land to the geld. [There is] land for 1 plough. [It is] SOKELAND of Barrowby. 2 villans and 1 bordar have 1 plough there, and 16 acres of meadow, and 30 acres of woodland pasture, and 5 acres of scrubland.

In Honington [are] 9 carucates of land to the geld. [There is] land for 9 ploughs. [It is] SOKELAND of Barrowby. Ivo has 2 ploughs there, and 16 villans and 4 bordars and 10 sokemen having 3½ ploughs. There is a church and a priest, and the site of a mill, and 105 acres of meadow. TRE worth £6; now £5; tallage 20s.

In Barkston [are] 10 bovates of land to the geld. [There is] land for 10 oxen. [It is] SOKELAND of Honington. There is 1 plough in demesne; and 1 sokeman and 1 villan and 3 bordars with 1 plough, and 13 acres of meadow.

In Syston [are] 2 bovates of land to the geld. [It is] SOKELAND [of] Honington. It is waste.

In KINGTHORPE, Bærghthor and Thorulf had 7½ bovates and the third part of half a bovate to the geld. [There is] arable land for twice [as many ploughs and oxen]. Odo, Ivo's man, has 1 plough there, and 10 villans with 1 plough, and [there are] 15 acres of meadow, and 80 acres of woodland, pasture in places. TRE worth 50s; now 40s.

In Wilsthorpe, Beornheah and Boli had 4 carucates of land to the geld. [There is] land for 4 ploughs. Of this land 2 carucates [are] SOKELAND. Odo, Ivo's man, [has] 1 plough there, and 10 sokemen and 10 villans having 2½ ploughs, and 2 mills [rendering] 20s, and 40 acres of meadow, and 12 acres of scrubland. TRE worth 40s; now 80s; now [sic] 30s.

SOKELAND

In Obthorpe [are] 2 bovates of land to the geld. [There is] land for 2 oxen. There are 2 sokemen with half a plough, and 4 acres of meadow.

In BURTON-LE-COGGLES and Bassingthorpe, he had 14 bovates of land to the geld. [There is] land for 14 oxen. Azur, Ivo's man, has there 3 villans and 2 bordars with 2 ploughs, and 300 acres of scrubland, and 13 acres of meadow. TRE worth 30s; now 20s. This belongs to Barrowby.

In Helpringham [are] 6 bovates of land to the geld. [There is] land for 6 oxen. [It is] SOKELAND belonging to Wilsthorpe.

There are 3 sokemen and 1 bordar with 1 plough, and 1 acre of meadow.

In SPALDING, Earl Ælfgar had 9 carucates of land to the geld. [There is] land for as many ploughs. Ivo has 4 ploughs there in demesne; and 40 villans and 33 bordars having 13 ploughs. There is a market [rendering] 40s, and 6 fisheries [rendering] 30s, and 20s, from salt-pans, and a wood of alders [rendering] 8s. TRE worth £23.2s8d; now £30; tallage £30.

In Long Sutton [are] 3 carucates of land and 2 bovates to the geld. [There is] land for 2 ploughs. [It is] a BEREWICK of Spalding. 9 villans and 1 bordar have 3 ploughs there. Ivo has 2 ploughs there in demesne, and a church.

In Pinchbeck [is] SOKELAND, 10 carucates of land to the geld. [There is] land for 10 ploughs. 22 sokemen and and *[sic]* 16 villans and 12 bordars have 9 ploughs there, and [there are] 4 fisheries [rendering] | 1,500 eels. | | [partly in margin] |

In Weston and Moulton [is] SOKELAND, 10 carucates of land and 1 bovate to the geld. [There is] land for as many ploughs and oxen. 26 sokemen and 31 villans and 20 bordars have 20 ploughs there.

In Welton le Marsh and 'Boothby' [in Welton le Marsh] [are] 2 carucates of land and 2 bovates to the geld. [There is] land for 3 ploughs. [It is] SOKELAND of 'Hanby' [in Welton le Marsh]. 7 sokemen and †2† villans and 5 bordars have 4 ploughs there, and 1 mill [rendering] 2s. Wimund has it.

XV. The land of William de Warenne

In CARLTON SCROOP, Earl Harold had 5 carucates of land to the geld. [There is] land for 7 ploughs. Aldelin, William de Warenne's man, has 3 ploughs there in demesne; and 21 sokemen on 2 carucates of this land and 11 villans and 6 bordars with 5 ploughs. There is a priest and a church, and 50 acres of meadow. TRE worth £6; now £10.

In Long Bennington [are] 2 carucates of land and 2 bovates to the geld. [There is] land for 3 ploughs. [It is] inland, 10 bovates, and sokeland, 1 carucate, of the same manor. There is 1 plough in demesne; and 3 sokemen and 1 bordar have 1 plough, and 20 acres of meadow.

[Folio 352: LINDSEY]

XVI. The land of Roger de Poitou

In RIBY, Stenkil had 12 bovates of land to the geld. [There is] land for 3 ploughs. Earnwine, Roger de Poitou's man, has 1 plough there, and 5 villans and 5 sokemen with 1 plough, and 12 acres of meadow. TRE worth 30s; now the same; tallage 10s.

In SWALLOW, Stenkil and Earnwine had 1 carucate of land to the geld. [There is] land for 2 ploughs. Wimund, Roger's man, has half a plough there, and 3 villans and 3 sokemen with 1 plough. TRE worth 40s; now 20s.

In MIDDLE RASEN [are] 3 bovates of land to the geld.

[There is] land for 7 oxen. Mainard, Roger's man, has there 4 villans with half a plough. TRE worth 10s; now 22s.

In SOUTH KELSEY, Earnwig had 3 carucates of land to the geld. [There is] land for 6 ploughs. Roger, Roger de Poitou's man, has 1½ ploughs there, and 4 villans and 6 bordars and 20 sokemen having 3 ploughs. TRE worth 100s; now 60[s].

In THORNTON LE MOOR, Grimbald had 2 bovates of land to the geld. [There is] land for 6 oxen. Roger de Poitou has 1 plough there, and 1 villan. TRE worth 10s; now 5[s].

In the same place Roger has 11 bovates of land to the geld. [There is] land for 14 oxen, and [he has] 364 acres of meadow.

In HOLTON LE MOOR, Earnwig had half a carucate of land to the geld. [There is] land for 1 plough. Roger, Roger de Poitou's man, has 1 plough there, and 4 sokemen with half a plough, and 5 acres of meadow. TRE, as now, worth 10s.

In [North or South] OWERSBY, Earnwig had 1½ carucates of land to the geld. [There is] land for 3 ploughs. This land belongs to the church of 'Winghale' [in South Kelsey]. 2 bordars plough there with 2 oxen. There are 76 acres of meadow. Roger de Poitou has it. TRE worth 30s; now 10s.

In OSGODBY [near West Rasen], Ingimund had 2½ bovates of land to the geld. [There is] land for 5 oxen. Groffrey, Roger' Roger's man, has there 4 villans and 1 bordar and 1 sokeman with half a plough, and 1 mill [rendering] 3s. of which Bishop Remigius has the soke, and 20 acres of meadow. TRE worth 20s; now 5s.

In TEALBY, Swein and Beorhtnoth had 1½ carucates of land to the geld. [There is] land for 2½ ploughs. Roger, Roger de Poitou's man, has 1 plough there, and 4 villans and 5 bordars and 3 sokemen ploughing with 5 oxen. There are 4 mills [rendering] 16s4d, and 78 acres of meadow.

SOKELAND OF THIS MANOR: in Market Rasen, 8½ bovates; in Osgodby [near West Rasen], 1 bovate; in Walesby, 1 carucate; in Otby, 1 carucate: 3 carucates of land and 1½ bovates to the geld. [There is] land for 7 ploughs. There are 41 sokemen having 4 ploughs, and 60 acres of meadow, and 1 mill [rendering] 3s.

In HAINTON, Othin had 9 bovates of land to the geld. [There is] land for 2 ploughs and 2 oxen. Hakun, Roger's man, has 1 plough there, and 8 villans and 2 bordars with 1½ ploughs, and 60 acres of meadow. TRE worth 30s; now 40s.

In Strubby [in Langton by Wragby] [is] SOKELAND of this manor, 2 bovates of land to the geld. [There is] land for 4 oxen. 1 sokeman and 2 bordars plough there with 2 oxen.

In HAINTON, Klak and Siundi had 1 carucate and half a bovate to the geld. [There is] land for 2 ploughs. Albert, Roger's man, has 1 plough there, and 3 villans ploughing with 3 oxen, and 54 acres of meadow. TRE worth 50s; now 60s.

In [East or West] Barkwith and Southrey [is] inland, 2 bovates, and SOKELAND, 3 bovates, of this manor to the geld. 6 sokemen and 2 villans have 2 ploughs there. There is 1 fishery, and 16 acres of meadow, and 20 acres of woodland pasture.

In BECKERING, Alric had 2 bovates of land to the geld. [There is] land for 4 oxen. 3 villans and 4 bordars plough there with 3 oxen. There are 3 acres of meadow. TRE worth 10s; now 20s.

In West Torrington [is] SOKELAND, 5 bovates of land to the geld. [There is] land for 10 oxen. 3 sokemen and 3 villans and 1 bordar have 1 plough and 1 ox ploughing there, and 8 acres of meadow.

WEST RIDING

In SNARFORD, Ulfkil had 3 bovates of land to the geld. [There is] land for 4 oxen. Now Mainard and Turold have it of Roger, and it is waste. There are 16 acres of meadow. TRE it was worth 10s.

In NORTHORPE [near Kirton in Lindsey], Sperrir had 6 bovates of land to the geld. [There is] land for 1 plough. And Frani and Alnoth [had] 6 carucates of land to the geld. [There is] land for 2 ploughs. Roger de Poitou has there 4 villans and 8 sokemen having 3 ploughs. He himself [has] 5 oxen ploughing, and 24 acres of meadow. TRE worth £4; now 60s; tallage 10s.

In 'Thonock' [in Gainsborough] in Wharton, [are] 1½ carucates to the geld. [There is] land for 2 ploughs. [It is] inland and SOKELAND. 6 sokemen and 4 villans and 1 bordar have 1½ ploughs there, and 20 acres of meadow. [There is] woodland pasture 1 league long and a half broad.

In 'Dunstall' [in Corringham] [is] 1 carucate of land and 2 bovates to the geld. [There is] land for 12 oxen. [There is] inland, 4 bovates, and SOKELAND, 6 bovates. There is 1 villan and 1 sokeman with half a plough. Ivo has 2 bovates and renders soke.

In the other Thorpe ['Southorpe' in Northorpe] [are] 2 bovates of land to the geld. [It is] inland of the above manor of Northorpe [near Kirton in Lindsey]. Roger de Poitou has nothing there.

In Yawthorpe [is] half a carucate to the geld. [It is] SOKELAND.

In THORPE [Northorpe near Kirton in Lindsey or 'Southorpe' in Northorpe], Godric had 1½ carucates of land to the geld. [There is] land for 2 ploughs. Roger, Roger de Poitou's man, has 2 ploughs there, and 1 villan and 6 bordars ploughing with 2 oxen. TRE worth 40s; now 20s.

In LAUGHTON [near Blyton], Swein had 1½ carucates of land to the geld. [There is] land for 2 ploughs. Blanchard, Roger de Poitou's man, has 1 plough there, and 3 villans ploughing with 3 oxen, and half a mill [rendering] 12d, and [there is] half a fishery [rendering] 2s, and 15 acres of meadow. TRE worth 30s; now 20s.

In Scotton [are] 2 bovates of land to the geld. [It is] SOKELAND of Laughton [near Blyton].

In the same LAUGHTON [near Blyton], Leodwine had 10 bovates of land to the geld. [There is] land for 12 oxen. 5

sokemen have 6 oxen ploughing there, and 8 acres of meadow. TRE worth 30s; now 10s.

In Blyton [are] 2 bovates of land to the geld. [It is] SOKELAND of this manor.

In 'STAINTON' [in Waddingham], Gamal had 6 bovates of land to the geld. [There is] land for 6 oxen. Roger, Roger's man, has half a plough there, and 6 villans with 1 plough, and 16 acres of meadow. TRE worth 20s; now 10s.

In ELSHAM, William had 9 bovates of land to the geld. [There is] land for 2½ ploughs. Earnwig, Roger's man, has 1 plough there, and 5 villans and 1 bordar ploughing with 2 oxen, and [there are] 60 acres of meadow. TRE worth 60s; now 20s; tallage 10s.

In Cadney [is] inland of this manor, 5 bovates of land and 3 parts of 1 bovate to the geld. 5 villans have 1 plough there.

In Bleasby are 2 bovates of the woodland which belongs to Hainton.

In Sixhills [is] SOKELAND of Hainton, 2½ carucates of land and half a bovate to the geld. [There is] land for 3 ploughs. 30 sokemen have 3 ploughs there, and 320 acres of meadow.

In AUDLEBY, Grimkel had 5 bovates of land to the geld. [There is] land for 1 plough. Blanchard, Roger de Poitou's man, has half a plough there, and 5 villans and 4 bordars.

[Folio 352V: LINCOLNSHIRE]

In 'SOUTH CADEBY' [in Calcethorpe], Godric and Siward had 4½ bovates of land to the geld. [There is] land for 1 plough. Now Roger has half a plough there, and 2 villans and 1 sokeman with 1 plough, and 10 acres of meadow. TRE worth 30s; now the same.

In East Wykeham [is] half a bovate of land. [It is] inland [of] 'South Cadeby' [in Calcethorpe].

In Welton le Wold [is] half a carucate of land to the geld. [There is] land for 12 oxen. [It is] SOKELAND of this manor. 4 sokemen and 3 villans have 1½ ploughs there, and 2 parts of a site of a mill.

In LEGBOURNE, Hambe had 1 carucate of land to the geld. [There is] land for 1½ ploughs. Gerard, Roger's man, has there 8 sokemen and 11 bordars with 1 plough, and 20 acres of meadow, and 142 acres of scrubland. TRE worth 30s; now 20s.

In [North or South] Somercotes [are] 3 parts of a carucate to the geld. [There is] land for half a plough. 3 sokemen plough there with 2 oxen.

In INGHAM, Alwig had 4 bovates of land to the geld. [There is] land for 6 oxen. Roger has there 3 sokemen and 2 bordars and 1 villan with 1 plough, and 10 acres of meadow. TRE worth 10s; now the same. Mainard holds it.

In Coates [is] 1 bovate of land to the geld. [It is] inland of Ingham.

In FILLINGHAM, Thorgot had 2 carucates of land and 1 bovate to the geld. [There is] land for 3½ ploughs. Ansketil,

Roger's man, has 2 ploughs there, and 9 sokemen and 2 villans with 2½ ploughs, and [there are] 80 acres of meadow. TRE worth 30s; now 40s; tallage 10s.

In NETTLETON, Grimkel had 5 bovates of land to the geld. [There is] land for 2 ploughs. Blanchard, Roger's man, has there 5 villans and 4 bordars and 1 sokeman with 1 plough, and 2 mills [rendering] 10s, and 40 acres of meadow. TRE worth 40s; now 30s.

In CROXTON, Eskil had 6 bovates of land [to] the geld. [There is] land for 12 oxen. Ansketil, Roger's man, has 1 plough there, and 5 villans and 7 sokemen with 1 plough. TRE worth 40s; now the same.

In BLOXHOLM, Thorfridh had 9 carucates of land and 5 bovates to the geld. [There is] land for as many ploughs and oxen. Roger de Poitou has 1½ ploughs there in demesne; and 18 sokemen and 2 villans having 5 ploughs, and 13 acres of meadow. TRE worth £4; now £3.

In CANWICK and Bracebridge [in Lincoln], Strui had 2 carucates of land to the geld. [There is] land for 2 ploughs. Earnwine, Roger's man, has there 1 plough, and 4 sokemen and 5 villans and 1 bordar ploughing with 6 oxen. There is a church and a priest, and 40 acres of meadow, and 2 fisheries [rendering] 2s. TRE worth 30s; now 40s.

In the same places [is] 1 carucate of land to the geld. [There is] land for 1 plough. It belongs to [?] Branston.

In EAGLE, Arnketil Barn had 13 bovates of land to the geld. [There is] land for 10 oxen. There are 5 villans, and 16 acres of meadow. TRE, as now, worth 20s.

In Cold Hanworth [are] 3 bovates of land to the geld. [There is] land for 1 plough. [It is] SOKELAND of Snarford. Turold the priest has there 1 sokeman and 2 bordars ploughing with 2 oxen.

XVII. The land of Roger de Bully

In 'GREETWELL', Swein had 3 carucates of land to the geld. [There is] land for 5 ploughs. Turold, Roger de Bully's man, has 3 ploughs there, and 15 villans and 6 bordars with 4 ploughs. There is a church and a priest, and 2 fisheries [rendering] 15d, and 1 mill [rendering] 5s, and [there are] 16 acres of meadow. TRE worth £8; now the same.

In APPLEBY and [High or Low] RISBY and 'SAWCLIFFE' [in Roxby], Gamal had 9 carucates of land and 5 bovates to the geld. [There is] land for 19 ploughs and 2 oxen. Roger de Bully has 4 ploughs there in demesne; and 31 villans and 2 bordars with 6 ploughs, and 31 sokemen with 6 ploughs. There is a church and a priest. [There is] woodland pasture half a league long and 1 furlong broad, and 20 acres of meadow. TRE worth £8; now £10; tallage £3.

In Santon [is] SOKELAND, 1 carucate of land to the geld. [There is] land for 1 plough. 12 sokemen have 2 ploughs there, and 6 acres of meadow.

XVIII. The land of Robert de Tosny

In INGLEBY, Thorgot Lag had 4 carucates of land to the geld. [There is] land for 4 ploughs. Berengar has of Robert de Tosny 2 ploughs there, and 5 sokemen and 8 villans with 2 ploughs, and 180 acres of meadow. [There is] woodland pasture 6 furlongs long and 3 broad. TRE worth £8; now £10; tallage 40s. Of this land 1½ carucates [are] SOKELAND.

In Broxholme [are] 10 carucates of land to the geld. [There is] land for 10 ploughs. [There is] SOKELAND, 9 carucates, and inland, 1 carucate. There is 1 plough in demesne; and 24 sokemen and 2 villans with 8½ ploughs. There is a church, and 200 acres of meadow.

In BUSLINGTHORPE, Thorgot had 2 carucates of land to the geld. [There is] land for 3 ploughs. Berengar has of Robert 1½ ploughs there, and 12 villans and 2 sokemen with 3 ploughs, and 60 acres of meadow, and 33 acres of woodland pasture. Half a carucate [is] SOKELAND. TRE worth 40s; now the same; tallage 10s.

In BRANSBY, Thorgot had 2 carucates of land to the geld. [There is] land for 2 ploughs. Berengar has of Robert 1 [plough] there, and 6 villans and 3 sokemen with 1½ ploughs, and 14 acres of meadow, and 50 acres of scrubland. TRE worth 60s; now 50[s]. #

In CORRINGHAM, Thorgot had 2 carucates of land to the geld. [There is] land for 2 ploughs. Berengar has of Robert 1 plough there, and 5 villans and 3 bordars with 1½ ploughs. [There is] woodland pasture 5 furlongs long and 5 broad. TRE worth 50s; now 30[s].

In Burton [is] 1 carucate of land to the geld. [There is] land for 1 plough. [It is] inland [of] Bransby. 2 bordars have 1 plough there.

In BINBROOK, Thorgot Lag had 8 carucates of land and 4½ bovates to the geld. [There is] land for 24 ploughs. Now Robert de Tosny has it, and Berengar of him. In demesne [are] 4 ploughs; and 6 villans and 4 bordars and 44 sokemen with 8 ploughs. There is a church, and a priest, and 2 mills [rendering] 20s, and 100 acres of meadow. TRE worth £7; now £15; tallage £10. Of this land 4 carucates and 4½ bovates belong to the SOKEMEN.

In Ludborough [are] 8 carucates of land to the geld. [There is] land for 12 ploughs. [It is] SOKELAND of the above manor. Berengar has 3 ploughs there, and 38 sokemen with 5 ploughs, and 200 acres of meadow.

In Fotherby, 4 carucates and 5 bovates, and Thorganby, 1 carucate, [are] 5 carucates of land and 5 bovates to the geld. [There is] land for 9 ploughs. Berengar has 1 plough there, and 33 sokemen and 2 bordars with 6 ploughs, and 120 acres of meadow, and 4 salt-pans [rendering] 2s.

In Croxby [is] 1 carucate of land to the geld. [There is] land for

3 ploughs. 14 sokemen and 4 bordars have 3 ploughs there, and 3 acres of meadow.

In UFFINGTON, Arnbiorn had 2 carucates of land to the geld. [There is] land for 2 ploughs. Robert de Tosny has 2 ploughs there, and 8 villans and 2 bordars with 2 ploughs, and 10 acres of meadow. TRE, as now, worth 40s; tallage 10s.

In TALLINGTON, Alwine and Arnbiorn had 5½ carucates of land to the geld. [There is] land for as many ploughs. William and Roger, Robert's men, have 1½ ploughs there, and 5 villans with 1 plough, and 17 acres of meadow. TRE worth 40s; now 30[s].

In GREATFORD, Thorgot Lag had 5½ carucates of land to the geld. [There is] land for as many ploughs. Berengar had of Robert 2 ploughs there, and 10 villans and 10 sokemen and 2 bordars with 3½ ploughs, and 2 mills [rendering] 10s, and 60 acres of meadow, and 20 acres of woodland, pasture in places. TRE worth £8; now £9; tallage £3.

In Braceborough and 'Banthorpe' [in Braceborough] [are] 5½ carucates of land to the geld. [There is] land for as many ploughs. 17 sokemen and 6 villans have 5½ ploughs there, and 40 acres of meadow.

In 'RINGSTONE' [in Rippingale], Aslak and Dene had 4 carucates of land and 7 bovates and 2 parts of 1 bovate to the geld. [There is] land for as many ploughs and oxen. IVO, Robert's man, has 2 ploughs there, and 9 villans and 6 sokemen and 1 bordar with 1½ ploughs, and 46 acres of meadow, and 120 acres of scrubland, and the third part of a church. TRE worth 50s; now 60[s].

In KIRKBY UNDERWOOD [are] 2 bovates of land to the geld. [There is] land for 2 oxen. 2 villans plough there with 3 oxen, and [there are] 2 acres of meadow, and 40 acres of scrubland. [It is] inland.

In 'WEST GRABY' [in Aslackby], Arnbiorn had 2 carucates of land and 2 bovates to the geld. [There is] land for as many ploughs and oxen. Gunfrid, Robert's man, has 2 ploughs there, [and] 3 sokemen and 1 bordar ploughing with 2 oxen. There are 11 acres of meadow, and 209 acres of woodland pasture. TRE worth £4; now 40s.

In SCOTTLETHORPE, Arnbiorn had 10 bovates of land to the geld. [There is] land for as many oxen. Now it is waste. TRE worth 100s; now, however, 10s.

In ASLACKBY, Arnbiorn had 6 carucates of land and half a bovate to the geld. [There is] land for as many ploughs. Now Robert has there 7 villans and 1 bordar having 2 ploughs, and 40 acres of meadow, and 24 acres of scrubland. Of 2 carucates Gilbert de Ghent has the SOKE in Folkingham.

In 'AVETHORPE' [in Aslackby], Arnbiorn had 2½ carucates of land to the geld. [There is] land for 3 ploughs. Gunfrid, Robert's man, has half a plough there, and 4 sokemen and 1 bordar with 1 plough. There are 12 acres of meadow, and 130 acres of meadow [sic]. TRE worth £6; now 40s; tallage 20s.

In Laughton [in Folkingham] [are] 5 bovates of land and the third part of 1 bovate to the geld. [There is] land for as many oxen. 11 sokemen have 1 plough there, and half a church, and 8 acres of scrubland.

In Aslackby [are] 6½ bovates of land to the geld. [There is] land for 1 plough. 6 sokemen have 2 ploughs there, and 6 acres of meadow, and 12 acres of scrubland.

In 'Sempringham' [is] 1 carucate of land to the geld. [There is] land for 1 plough. 4 sokemen have 1 plough there, and 10 acres of meadow, and 6 acres of scrubland.

In ROPSLEY, Thorir had 8 carucates of land to the geld. [There is] land for 9 ploughs. IVO, Robert's man, has 2 ploughs there, and 2 villans and 29 sokemen with 8½ ploughs. There is a church, and 120 acres of woodland pasture, and 450 acres of scrubland. TRE worth £6; now 100s; tallage 40s. [There is] SOKELAND of 6 bovates.

In DENTON or Wyville, Eadgifu had 6 carucates of land to the geld. [There is] land for as many ploughs. Robert has 3 ploughs there in demesne; and 13 villans with 4 ploughs. TRE worth £4.5s4d; now 100s; tallage 20s.

In Hungerton [are] 6 carucates of land to the geld. [There is] land for 6 ploughs. It is inland. 13 villans have 6 ploughs there, and 50 acres of meadow, and 87 acres of scrubland. This woodland belongs to the SOKE of Grantham.

In WOOLSTHORPE, Leofric had 4 carucates of land to the geld. [There is] land for as many ploughs. Robert has 1 plough there in demesne; and 6 villans and 3 bordars and 8 sokemen having 3 ploughs, and 3 mills [rendering] 15s. TRE, as now, worth 40s.

In the same place Godwine and Arnketil had 4 carucates of land to the geld. [There is] land for as many ploughs. Robert has 1½ mills there [rendering] 8s6d, and 11 villans with 1 plough. There is a church, and a priest having half a carucate of this land. There are 30 acres of meadow and 3 virgates. TRE, as now, worth 40s.

In AUBOURN, Thorgot Lag had 12 carucates of land to the geld. [There is] land for as many ploughs. Berengar has of Robert 2 ploughs there in demesne; and 14 villans and 4 bordars and 1 sokeman with 4 ploughs. There is a church and a priest, and 1 mill [rendering] 20s, and 1 fishery [rendering] 1,000 eels, and 100 acres of meadow. TRE worth £5; now £6.

[Folio 353V: LINCOLNSHIRE]

In Haddington [are] 3½ carucates of land to the geld. [There is] land for 2 ploughs. [It is] a BEREWICK of Aubourn. 2 villans have half a plough there, and [there are] 6 acres of meadow, and 3 acres of scrubland.

In WEST ALLINGTON, Godwine had 3 carucates of land to the geld. [There is] land for 6 ploughs. Robert has 2 ploughs there in demesne; and 14 sokemen and 5 villans and 5 bordars with 4 ploughs. There is a church, and 140 acres of meadow. Warin, his man, has 1 carucate there, and 1 bordar having 2 bovates of land. TRE worth £3; now £6.

In NORTH KYME, Mere had 6 carucates of land to the geld. [There is] land for 8 ploughs. Ivo, Robert's man, has 3 ploughs there, and 12 villans and 2 bordars with 4 ploughs, and 56 acres of meadow, and 30 acres of woodland pasture. TRE worth £3.13s8d; now £7.

XIX. The land of Berengar de Tosny

In WEST ALLINGTON. Ulfkil and Godwine had 6 carucates of land to the geld. [There is] land for 5 ploughs. Berengar de Tosny has 1 plough there, and 14 sokemen and 5 villans and 5 bordars having 4 ploughs. There is a church having half a carucate of this land, and 140 acres of meadow. TRE worth £3; now £6.

XX. The land of Ilbert de Lacy

In DUNHOLME, Alric had 2 carucates of land to the geld. [There is] land for 2 ploughs. Now Ilbert de Lacy has it. A knight of his [has] of him 1 plough in demesne; and 2 sokemen and 2 villans with 1 plough, and 17 acres of meadow. TRE worth 20s; now 16[s]; tallage 4s.

In Scothern [are] 7 bovates of land to the geld. [There is] land for 9 oxen.

In Stow [near Torksey] [is] half a carucate of land to the geld. [There is] land for half a plough. [It is] inland and SOKELAND.

In WILLINGHAM BY STOW, Deincora had 12 bovates of land to the geld. [There is] land for 12 oxen. On this land dwells 1 knight of Ilbert's. TRE, as now, worth 20s.

XXI. The land of Henry de Ferrers

In WHITTON, Siward Barn had 12 carucates of land to the geld. [There is] land for 8 ploughs. Saswalo, Henry's man, has 2 ploughs there, and 10 villans and 4 bordars and 30 sokemen having 5 ploughs, and [there are] 300 acres of meadow. TRE worth £10; now £7; tallage £3.

In Winterton [are] 2 bovates of land to the geld. [There is] land for 2 oxen. It is inland, and it is waste.

XXII. The land of William de Percy

In IMMINGHAM, Alwine had 4 carucates of land and 1½ bovates to the geld. [There is] land for 8 ploughs. William de Percy has 4 ploughs there in demesne; and 12 villans and 14 bordars and 13 sokemen having 4 ploughs, and 80 acres of meadow. TRE worth £8; now the same; tallage 40s.

In Laceby [is] half a bovate of land to the geld. [It is] SOKELAND.

In HABROUGH, Alcude had 6 bovates of land to the geld. [There is] land for 12 oxen. Norman, William's man, has half a plough there, and 2 villans and 4 bordars and 5 sokemen ploughing with 1 plough and 2 oxen, and 60 acres of meadow. TRE worth 14s; now 20s; tallage 4s.

In 'Lobingham' [in Killingholme] [are] 1½ bovates of land to

the geld. [There is] land for 3 oxen. There is 1 sokeman ploughing with 2 oxen, and 20 acres of meadow.

In THORNTON LE MOOR, Alwine had 2 carucates of land and 6 bovates to the geld. [There is] land for 4 ploughs. There are 12 sokemen and 3 bordars and 2 villans with 1½ ploughs. And besides these 11 bovates of land, Roger de Poitou has 11 bovates similarly, like William, which the same William ought to have by the witness of the men of the wapentake. There are 364 acres of meadow. [It is] SOKELAND of [North or South] Owersby.

In [North or South] OWERSBY, Alwine had 7 bovates of land and 2 parts of a bovate to the geld. [There is] land for 2 ploughs. William has 2 ploughs there in demesne; and 3 villans and 10 sokemen with 1 plough. There is a church and a priest, and 1 mill [rendering] 3s, and 80 acres of meadow. TRE worth 40s; now 50s; tallage 10s.

In CABOURNE, Grimkel had 1 carucate of land to the geld. [There is] land for 2 ploughs. Norman, William's man, has 1 plough there, and 1 villan and 1 bordar, and 12 acres of meadow belonging to [?] North Kelsey. TRE worth 30s; now 26s.

In Cuxwold [is] 1 bovate of land to the geld. [It is] inland of Cabourne.

In WICKENBY, Thorgot had 2 carucates of land to the geld. [There is] land for 3 ploughs. Osbern, William's man, has 2 ploughs there, and 8 villans and 2 sokemen with 2 ploughs, and 15 acres of meadow. [There is] scrubland 1 league long and 5 furlongs broad. TRE, as now, worth £3. SOKELAND of this manor

In 'Westlaby' [in Wickenby] [are] 9 bovates of land to the geld. [There is] land for 18 oxen. Ralph, William's man, has there 6 sokemen with 2 ploughs, and 30 acres of meadow.

In Beckering [are] 1½ bovates of land to the geld. [There is] land for 3 oxen. Robert, William's man, has there 1 sokeman and 1 bordar [who] plough with 2 oxen, and [there is] 1 acre of meadow.

In Reasby [is] half a carucate of land to the geld. [There is] land for 4 oxen. Norman, William's man, has there 1 sokeman with half a plough, and [there are] 10 acres of meadow.

In Snelland [are] 4 bovates of land to the geld. [There is] land for 1 plough. Waldin, William's man, has there 3 sokemen with 1 plough, and [there are] 6 acres of meadow, and 6 acres of scrubland.

In Reasby [are] 4 bovates of land to the geld. [There is] land for 4 oxen. It belongs to Snelland.

In STAINFIELD [near Lincoln], Siward had 1½ carucates of land to the geld. [There is] land for 1 plough. William has 1 plough there, and 8 villans and 6 bordars and 4 sokemen with 4 ploughs, and 40 acres of meadow, and [there are] 264 acres of woodland pasture.

In Barnetby le Wold [are] 2 bovates of land to the geld. [There is] land for 4 oxen. It is waste. [It is] inland of Thornton le Moor.

TRE worth 30s; Now 60s.

In the same place Tonni had 1½ carucates of land to the geld. [It is] SOKELAND of Barlings. William has there 4 sokemen and 1 bordar with 2 ploughs, and 20 acres of meadow, and 117 acres of woodland pasture.

In Apley [are] 7 bovates of land to the geld. [There is] land for 12 oxen. 10 sokemen have 3 ploughs there, and 15 acres of meadow, and 110 acres of scrubland.

In the same place Tonni had 7 bovates of land to the geld. [There is] land for 12 oxen. [It is] SOKELAND of Barlings. William has there 10 sokemen with 3 ploughs, and 10 acres of meadow, and 110 acres of scrubland.

In the same place Ælfric had 2 bovates of land to the geld. [It is] SOKELAND of Bullington. William has there 2 sokemen ploughing with 1 ox.

In LUDFORD, Alsige had 1 carucate of land and 6 bovates to the geld. [There is] land for 3½ ploughs. And in the same place Vaghlak and Siward had 3 carucates of land to the geld. [There is] land for 6 ploughs. William de Percy has 3½ ploughs there in demesne; and 28 villans and 8 sokemen with 4 ploughs, [and] 60 acres of meadow. TRE, as now, worth £4; tallage 20s.

In the same place Tonni had 2 bovates of land to the geld. [There is] land for 4 oxen. [It is] SOKELAND of Baumber. It is waste. There are 4 acres of meadow.

In KIRMOND LE MIRE, Alsige had 3 carucates of land to the geld. [There is] land for 6 ploughs. William has 4 ploughs there in demesne; and 18 villans and 4 bordars and 2 sokemen having 4 ploughs. There is a church, and 1 mill [rendering] 2s, and 20 acres of meadow. TRE worth £3; now 4[l].

In LITTLE GRIMSBY, Alric had 1 carucate of land and 2 bovates to the geld. [There is] land for 3 ploughs. Fulk, William's man, has 1 plough there, and 3 villans and 5 sokemen with 1 plough. There is a church, and 11 acres of meadow, and 1 salt-pan [rendering] 6d. TRE worth 30s; now 25s; tallage 5s.

In COVENHAM ST BARTHOLOMEW, Alsige and Ketil and Thorfridh had 3½ carucates of land to the geld. [There is] land for 4 ploughs. William has 3 ploughs there in demesne; and 18 villans and 17 sokemen with 5½ ploughs, and 5 salt-pans [rendering] 2s, and 150 acres of meadow. TRE worth 110s; now £4; tallage 30s. Ketil and Thorfridh were brothers, and after their father's death they divided the land, in such wise, however, that when Ketil was doing the king's service he should have his brother Thorfridh's aid. William de Percy has Ketil's and Alsige's land from the king; but he, the same William, bought Thorfridh's land from Ansketil, a certain cook, in the time of King William.

In SOUTH ELKINGTON, Alsige had 8 carucates of land to the geld. [There is] land for 16 ploughs. Fulk, William's man, has 2 ploughs there, and 38 sokemen with 7½ ploughs. There is a church, and a mill [rendering] 3s, and the site of another

mill, and 20 acres of meadow. TRE worth £3; now 4[l]; tallage 40s. 6½ carucates of this land. are SOKELAND.

In Grainthorpe [are] 3½ bovates of land to the geld. [There is] land for as many oxen. [It is] SOKELAND of Covenham St Bartholomew. 3 sokemen have 1 plough there, and 50 acres of meadow.

In 'Holtham' [in Legsby] [is] SOKELAND of Legsby, 10 bovates of land to the geld. [There is] land for 2 ploughs. Everard, William's man, has there 6 sokemen and 4 villans and 2 bordars with 2 ploughs, and 30 acres of meadow.

In NORTH RESTON and LITTLE CARLTON, Alsige had 3 carucates of land to the geld. [There is] land for 4 ploughs. Osbern, William's man, has 2 ploughs there, and 4 villans and 4 bordars and 18 sokemen with 4 ploughs. There is a church, and 2 mills [rendering] 5s, and 30 acres of meadow, and 100 acres of woodland pasture. TRE it was worth, and now it is worth, 40s; tallage 20s. Half this land belongs to the sokemen.

In SAXILBY, Gunnhvati had 2 carucates of land and 2 bovates to the geld. [There is] land for as many ploughs and oxen. William has 1 plough there, and 5 villans and 1 sokeman with half a plough. There is a priest, and 50 acres of meadow, and 50 acres of scrubland. TRE worth 20s; now 25[s]; tallage 5s.

In OWMBY, Grimkel had 2 carucates of land and 3 bovates to the geld. [There is] land for 4 ploughs and 6 oxen. William, William's man, has 3 ploughs there, and 7 villans and 11 sokemen with 3 ploughs, and 1 mill [rendering] 2s, and 40 acres of meadow. TRE worth 40s; now 60[s]; tallage 20s. Of this land 9 bovates [are] SOKELAND.

In STAINTON LE VALE, Grimkel had 4 bovates of land to the geld. [There is] land for 12 oxen. Æthelwulf, William's man, has 2 ploughs there, and 6 villans with 1 plough, and 1 mill [rendering] 12d, and [there are] 26 acres of meadow. TRE worth 30s; now 50[s].

In FOTHERBY, Esbiorn had half a carucate of land to the geld. [There is] land for 12 oxen. Fulk, William's man, has it and tills it. There are 4 acres of meadow. TRE worth 10s; now 3s.

In WICKENBY, Godric had 5 bovates of land to the geld. [There is] land for 7 oxen. Robert, William's man, has 1 plough there, and 1 villan with 1 ox, and 10 acres of meadow. TRE, as now, worth 20s.

In LEGSBY, Alsige had 1 carucate of land to the geld. [There is] land for 2 ploughs. Everard, William's man, has 2 ploughs there, and 6 villans and 1 bordar with 1 plough, and 1 mill [rendering] 6d, and [there are] 12 acres of meadow, and 12 acres of woodland, pasture in places. TRE worth 30s; now 40[s].

In the same place [are] 4 bovates of land to the geld. [It is] SOKELAND of Wragby. It is waste.

In Somerby [near Howsham], Salecoc had 2½ carucates of land to the geld. [There is] land for 5 ploughs. [It is]

SOKELAND of Burnham. 14 sokemen have 5 ploughs there, and 80 acres of meadow, and 20 acres of scrubland.

XXIII. The land of Gilbert Tison

In SOUTH FERRIBY, Godwine had 2 carucates of land and 7 bovates and the eighth part of a bovate to the geld. [There is] land for 4 ploughs. Ansketil, Gilbert Tison's man, has 1 plough there, and 6 sokemen on 9 bovates of this land and 17 villans having 4½ ploughs. There is a church, and 1 mill [rendering] 10s, and 1 ferry [rendering] 60s, and 210 acres of meadow. TRE worth £8; now the same.

[Folio 354V: LINCOLNSHIRE]

XXIIII. The land of Gilbert de Ghent

In SCAMPTON, Ulf Fenman had 6¼ carucates of land to the geld. [There is] land for 10 ploughs. Gilbert de Ghent has 4 ploughs there in demesne; and 16 villans and 12 sokemen and 6 bordars with 7 ploughs. There is a church and a priest, and 1 mill [rendering] 2s, and 166 acres of meadow. TRE worth £6; now £8; tallage £4.

In Riseholme [are] 1½ carucates to the geld. [There is] land for 1½ ploughs. [It is] a BEREWICK of Scampton. Kolsveinn, Gilbert's man, has 1 plough there, and 1 mill [rendering] 12d, and 36 acres of meadow.

In Burton [are] 3 carucates of land to the geld. [There is] land for 2 ploughs. There are 11 sokemen and 9 bordars with 3 ploughs.

In [?] 'Middle Carlton' [in North Carlton] [are] 6 bovates of land to the geld. [There is] land for as many oxen. 2 sokemen plough there with 5 oxen, and [there are] 4 acres of meadow.

In CHERRY WILLINGHAM, Ulf had 14 bovates of land to the geld. [There is] land for as many oxen. Gilbert has 2 ploughs there, and 12 villans and 1 sokeman with 2 ploughs. There is a church and a priest, and 2 fisheries [rendering] 32d, and 40 acres of meadow. TRE worth 100s; now £4.

SOKELAND of Scampton

In Brattleby and Thorpe le Fallows [are] 3 carucates of land to the geld. [There is] land for 3 ploughs. 5 sokemen and 2 bordars have 3 ploughs and 2 oxen there, and 8 acres of meadow. ASLO:

In Thorpe le Fallows and Aisthorpe [are] 5 carucates of land and 2 bovates to the geld. [There is] land for 6 ploughs. There are 10 sokemen and 1 bordar with 3½ ploughs. One of Gilbert's men has there 6 sokemen and 5 bordars with 1 plough, and [there are] 101 acres of meadow.

In Nettleham [are] 2 bovates of land to the geld. [It is] inland of Cherry Willingham.

In Stow [near Torksey], Ulf [had] 4 tofts with sake and soke belonging to Scampton.

In APPLEBY and [High or Low] Risby and 'Sawcliffe' [in Roxby], Ulf had 2 carucates of land to the geld. [There is] land for 4 ploughs. Robert, Gilbert's man, has 2 ploughs there, and 10 villans and 2 bordars with 2 ploughs. There is a priest and a church, and 12 acres of meadow. TRE worth 50s; now 40[s]; tallage 10s.

In Roxby [are] 2 bovates of land to the geld. [There is] land for 3 oxen. 1 villan has 2 oxen there.

In WINTERINGHAM, Ulf had 12 carucates of land to the geld. [There is] land for as many ploughs. Robert, Gilbert's man, has 4 ploughs there in demesne; and 40 villans and 5 sokemen and 10 bordars with 7 ploughs. There is a priest and a church, and 3 mills [rendering] 37s4d, and 1 ferry [rendering] 13s, and the site of a fishery. TRE, as now, worth £10; tallage | 40s |.

In BARTON-UPON-HUMBER, Ulf had 13 carucates of land to the geld. [There is] land for 27 ploughs. Gilbert has 7 ploughs there in demesne; and 63 villans and 16 bordars with 9 ploughs, and 42 sokemen and 67 bordars with 10 ploughs. There is a church and a priest, and 2 mills [rendering] 40s, and 1 market and a ferry rendering £4.

In South Ferriby [are] 3 carucates of land, less 1 bovate, to the geld and the eighth part of a bovate to the geld. [It is] SOKELAND of Barton-upon-Humber. [There is] land for 5½ ploughs. There are now 34 sokemen and 13 bordars with 8 ploughs, and 1 ferry [rendering] £3, and 210 acres of meadow, and 260 acres of marsh. TRE worth £38.16s; now £30; tallage £10.

In "Sudtone" [in Great Sturton] [are] 2 bovates of land to the geld. [There is] land for 3 oxen. Gilbert has a flock of sheep there.

In Horkstow [are] 4 carucates of land to the geld. [There is] land for 7 ploughs. [It is] SOKELAND and inland of Barton-upon-Humber. Gilbert has 1½ ploughs there, and 7 villans and 20 sokemen with 8½ ploughs.

In Low Langton, Gilbert has 140 acres of woodland pasture.

In BARDNEY, Ulf had 2 carucates of land to the geld. [There is] land for 3 ploughs. Gilbert has 1 plough there, and 16 villans and 5 bordars and 6 sokemen with 2 ploughs, and 1 mill [rendering] 8s, and 5 fisheries [rendering] 5s4d, and 20 acres of meadow, and [there are] 500 acres of woodland pasture. TRE, as now, worth £20; tallage £30.

In 'Osgodby' [in Bardney] [is] SOKELAND of this manor, 2 carucates of land to the geld. [There is] land for 3 ploughs. 16 sokemen have 3 ploughs there, and [there are] 60 acres of meadow, and 240 acres of woodland, pasture in places.

In Southrey [is] inland of Cherry Willingham, 2 bovates of land to the geld. There are 3 villans ploughing with 6 oxen, and 1 fishery, and 4 acres of meadow, and 20 acres of woodland pasture.

In BAUMBER, Ulf had had [sic] 12 carucates of land to the geld. [There is] land for 10 ploughs. Gilbert has 5 ploughs there, and 21 villans and 6 bordars and 20 sokemen and their 16 bordars. Among them all [they have] 7 ploughs, and 1 mill [rendering] 8s, and 140 acres of woodland pasture. TRE worth £10; now £12; tallage £3. Of this land 6 carucates [are] SOKELAND.

In EDLINGTON, Ulf had 10 carucates of land to the geld. [There is] land for 10 ploughs. Ecgbeorht, Gilbert's man, has 4 ploughs there, and 25 sokemen and 7 villans and 14 bordars with 6 ploughs, and 1 mill [rendering] 16s, and [there are] 90 acres of meadow, and 210 acres of scrubland. TRE worth £10; now £11; tallage £3.

In Santon [is] inland of [High or Low] Risby, 1 bovate of land to the geld. It is waste.

In LUSBY, Tonni had 3 carucates of land to the geld. [There is] land for 4 ploughs. William, Gilbert's man, has 5 ploughs there, and 17 sokemen and 8 villans having 9 ploughs. There is a church, and a priest, and 1 mill [rendering] 3s, and 180 acres of meadow. TRE worth £14; now £10; tallage 100s.

In EDENHAM, Ulf had 12 carucates of land to the geld. [There is] land for 12 ploughs. Gilbert has 5 ploughs there, and 32 villans and 24 sokemen and 4 bordars with 9 ploughs, and 29 acres of meadow, and 400 acres of woodland, pasture in places. TRE worth £10; now £18; tallage £6.

In Osfram [?Keisby] [is] a BEREWICK, 3½ carucates of land to the geld. [There is] land for 5 ploughs. There are 2 ploughs in demesne; and 5 villans with 3 ploughs, and 80 acres of meadow, and 120 acres of scrubland.

In Baston [is] a BEREWICK, 2 carucates of land to the geld. [There is] land for 2 ploughs. Ivo, Gilbert's man, has half a plough there, and 8 sokemen on 1 carucate of this land and 4 villans and 3 bordars with 2 ploughs, and 40 acres of meadow. It is worth 50s.

In Greatford [are] 2 bovates of land to the geld. [It is] SOKELAND. There are 4 sokemen with 1 plough.

In Barholm [is] half a carucate of land to the geld. [There is] land for 4 oxen. [It is] SOKELAND of Edenham. There are 4 sokemen ploughing with 2 oxen. And it is worth 8s.

[Folio 355: LINDSEY]

In Braceborough and 'Banthorpe' [in Braceborough] [is] half a carucate to the geld. [There is] land for 4 oxen.

In Obthorpe [are] 13 bovates of land to the geld. [There is] land for as many oxen. 17 sokemen have 3 ploughs there, and [there are] 20 acres of meadow, and 20 acres of woodland pasture.

In Witham on the Hill and Manthorpe [in Witham on the Hill] and Toft and Lound [are] 8 carucates of land and the third part of a carucate. [There is] land for as many ploughs. 45 sokemen and 10 bordars have 10 ploughs there. There is a church, and 40 acres of meadow, and 40 acres of woodland pasture, and 1 mill [rendering] 20s. Of this land Berewold holds 1 carucate of land, and has 1 plough there, and 1 mill [rendering] 12s, and 2 villans and 4 bordars | with | half a plough. TRE worth 20s; now 40[s].

In Carlby [are] 15 bovates of land to the geld. 8 sokemen and 1 bordar have 2 ploughs there. TRE worth 20s; now the same;

tallage 7s. Ivo has this land, and Berewold under him, and he himself [has] half a plough there.

In 'Stowe' [in Barholm and Stowe] [are] 6½ bovates of land to the geld. 5 sokemen have half a plough there.

In Barholm [is] half a carucate of land to the geld. [There is] land for 4 oxen. [It is] SOKELAND of Casewick.

In CRANWELL, Ulf had 12 carucates of land to the geld. [There is] land for as many ploughs. Geoffrey, Gilbert's man, has 1 plough there in demesne; and 21 sokemen on 9 carucates of this land and 2 villans and 5 bordars with 8 ploughs, and 29 acres of meadow. [There is] arable land 22 furlongs long and 7½ broad, [and] pasture 10 furlongs long and 7½ broad. TRE worth 100s; now £7.

In CULVERTHORPE, Tunni had 3 carucates of land and 3 bovates to the geld. [There is] land for 4 ploughs. Gilbert has 5 ploughs there, and 8 villans with 2 ploughs. There is a priest, and a church, and 120 acres of meadow. TRE worth £18; now £25.

SOKELAND of this manor

In Ewerby Thorpe and Ewerby [are] 3 carucates of land to the geld. [There is] land for 2 ploughs. 9 sokemen and 9 bordars have 4 ploughs there. There is a church, and a priest, and 24 acres of meadow, and 20 acres of scrubland.

In Howell [is] 1 carucate and half a bovate. [There is] land for 1 plough. 3 sokemen have there 1 plough and 2 oxen ploughing, and 8 acres of meadow.

In Heckington [is] inland, 3 carucates, and sokeland, 5 carucates: 8 carucates of land to the geld. [There is] land for as many ploughs. Gilbert has 2 ploughs there in demesne; and 22 sokemen and 7 villans and 15 bordars with 8 ploughs. There is a priest and a church, and 100 acres of meadow, and 3 fisheries [rendering] 5s4d.

In [Great and Little] Hale [are] 8½ carucates to the geld. [There is] land for 10 ploughs. 38 sokemen have 12 ploughs there. Ralph, Gilbert's man, has 3 ploughs there in demesne. [It is] SOKELAND.

In Hagworthingham [are] 6 bovates of land to the geld. [There is] land for 10 oxen. It is SOKELAND of Greetham. And [there are] 10 acres of meadow.

In the same place [is] 1 carucate of land to the geld. [There is] land for 12 ploughs. [It is] a BEREWICK of Lusby. There is 1 plough in demesne; and 1 villan, and 1 bordar ploughing with 1 ox, and 20 acres of meadow, and 1 mill [rendering] 12d.

In the same place [is] 1 carucate of land to the geld. [There is] land for 2 ploughs. [It is] SOKELAND of Lusby. There are 2 bordars with 1 ox, and 30 acres of meadow.

SOKELAND OF BARDNEY

In Partney [is] SOKELAND, 5 carucates of land to the geld. [There is] land for as many ploughs. Gilbert has there 17 sokemen and 27 bordars with 5 ploughs. There is a market [rendering] 10s, and 100 acres of meadow.

In Skendleby [are] 6 carucates of land to the geld. [There is] land for 6 ploughs. Gilbert has 3 ploughs there in demesne, and a church, and 2 mills [rendering] 13s, and 40 acres of meadow. He found there 28 sokemen and 9 bordars with 9 ploughs.

In Scremby [are] 4½ carucates of land to the geld. [There is] land for 4 ploughs. There are 15 sokemen and 8 bordars with 5 ploughs, and 100 acres of meadow, and 1 church.

In Great Steeping [are] 11½ carucates of land to the geld. [There is] land for as many ploughs. 61 sokemen and 11 bordars have 10 ploughs there, and 2 churches, and [there are] 80 acres of meadow.

In Candlesby [is] 1 carucate of land to the geld. [There is] land for 1 plough. 13 sokemen and 6 bordars have 2 ploughs there.

In Burgh le Marsh [are] 8 carucates of land to the geld. [There is] land for 8 ploughs. 21 sokemen and 11 villans and 3 bordars have 6 ploughs there, and [there is] 1 church, and 500 acres of meadow.

In Addlethorpe [are] 4 carucates of land and 2 bovates to the geld. [There is] land for as many ploughs. 18 sokemen and 17 villans have 4 ploughs there, and [there are] †440† acres of meadow.

In Wainfleet [All Saints or St Mary] [is] 1 bovate of land to the geld. It is waste. It is inland.

In Hagworthingham, Joscelin fitzLambert has a church, and half a carucate of land to the geld, of which Gilbert de Ghent has the soke.

In WILLOUGHBY, Tunni had 2 carucates of land to the geld. [There is] land for 4 ploughs. Roger, Gilbert's man has 2 ploughs there 4 sokemen on half a carucate of land have 2 ploughs there, and 40 acres of meadow, and 40 acres of marsh, and [there are] 120 acres of woodland pasture, and 60 acres of scrubland. TRE worth £4; now £8.

In Mumby [is] a BEREWICK, 2 bovates of land to the geld. [There is] land for 3 oxen. Gilbert has there 1 villan ploughing with 1 ox.

In the same place [is] a BEREWICK, 4 bovates of land to the geld. [There is] land for 6 oxen. There are 6 villans and 8 bordars with 1 plough, and 30 acres of meadow. The lord [has] 80 acres of meadow.

In Hasthorpe [is] 1 carucate of land to the geld. [There is] land for 2 ploughs. There are 4 sokemen on half a carucate of land and 2 villans and 2 bordars plough with 6 oxen. Roger has 1 plough there, and [there are] 30 acres of marsh.

In Sloothby [are] 3 bovates of land to the geld. [There is] land for 6 oxen. Roger has there 2 villans ploughing with 3 oxen, and 10 acres of marsh.

In Willoughby [are] 3 bovates of land with sake and soke to the geld. [There is] land for 5 oxen. There is 1 church having half a carucate. TRE [worth] 20s; now 10s.

In CLAXBY [near Alford], Tonni had 6 bovates of land to the geld. [There is] land for 12 oxen. Rademer, Gilbert's man, has

2 ploughs there, and 6 villans with 1 plough. There are 660 acres of scrubland. TRE, as now, worth £8.

In the same vill Gilbert has 80 acres of scrubland and another 120 acres of scrubland. Of 3 parts of these acres Guy de Craon has the soke.

In Sloothby [is] inland of Claxby [near Alford], half a carucate of land to the geld.

In Welton le Marsh and 'Boothby' [in Welton le Marsh] [is] 1 carucate of land to the geld. [There is] land for 1 plough. [It is] SOKELAND of Willoughby.

[Folio 355V: LINCOLNSHIRE]

[There is] land for 1 plough. There are 6 villans and 1 bordar with 1 plough, and 60 acres of meadow.

In Beesby in the Marsh [is] SOKELAND, 3 carucates of land to the geld. [There is] land for as many ploughs. 20 sokemen and 8 bordars have 5½ ploughs there, and [there are] 90 acres of meadow, and 180 acres of scrubland.

In Maltby le Marsh [are] 2 carucates of land and 6 bovates to the geld. [There is] land for 3 ploughs. 14 sokemen have 2 ploughs there, and 60 acres of meadow, and 5 acres of scrubland.

In Saleby [is] half a carucate of land to the geld. [There is] land for 4 oxen. There are 2 villans ploughing with 1 ox, and 10 acres of meadow, and 30 acres of scrubland.

In Withern [are] 3½ carucates of land to the geld. [There is] land for 4 ploughs. Rauemer, Gilbert's man, has 2 ploughs there, and 20 sokemen and 13 villans with 3 ploughs, and 1 mill [rendering] 15s, and 180 acres of meadow. There is a priest, and a church. The soke belongs to Hugh fitzBaldric.

In Strubby [near Maltby le Marsh] [are] 2½ bovates to the geld. [There is] land for 5 oxen. 2 villans have half a plough there, and 10 acres of meadow.

In WELL, Tonni had 1 carucate of land to the geld. [There is] land for 3 ploughs. Rauemer, Gilbert's man, has 2 ploughs there, and 4 sokemen on 2 bovates of this land and 12 villans with 1 plough, and 1 mill [rendering] 15s, and [there are] 1½ acres of meadow, and 22 acres of woodland. TRE worth £8; now £7.

In Ulceby [near Well] [are] 2 bovates of land to the geld. [There is] land for 4 oxen. There is 1 sokeman with 1 plough.

In Alford [are] 6½ bovates of land to the geld. [There is] land for 12 oxen. There are 2 sokemen and 3 villans and 1 bordar with 1 plough, and 10 acres of meadow.

In Mablethorpe [is] half a carucate of land to the geld. [There is] land for 1 plough. 4 villans have 1 plough there, and 20 acres of meadow.

In WEST ASHBY, Siward had 1½ carucates to the geld. [There is] land for 2 ploughs. Roger, Gilbert's man, has 2 ploughs there, and 5 villans and 5 bordars with half a plough, and 100 acres of meadow, and 6 acres of scrubland. TRE worth 30s; now 40[s]; tallage 3s.

In DRIBY, Siward had $5\frac{1}{2}$ carucates of land to the geld. [There is] land for 5 ploughs. Ivo, Gilbert's man, has 4 ploughs there in demesne; and 7 sokemen on 2 carucates of land and 3 villans and 5 bordars [with] 3 ploughs, and 1 mill [rendering] 12d, and 60 acres of meadow. TRE worth £6; now 100s; tallage 20s.

In CROFT, Othenkar had 2 carucates of land and 2 bovates to the geld. [There is] land for 2 ploughs and 2 oxen. Ralph, Gilbert's man, has 2 ploughs there, and 9 sokemen and 3 villans and 3 bordars with 3 ploughs, and [there is] 1 salt-pan [rendering] 6d, and 120 acres of meadow. TRE worth 20s; now £4.

In Wainfleet [All Saints or St Mary] [is] a BEREWICK, 2 bovates of land to the geld. There are 6 villans with 2 oxen, and 6 salt-pans [rendering] 3s.

In SOUTH KYME, Tunni had 14 bovates of land to the geld. [There is] land for $1\frac{1}{2}$ ploughs. Ecgbeorht, Gilbert's man, has half a plough there, and 6 villans with half a plough, and 1 acre of meadow, and 82 acres of scrubland, and 3 fisheries [rendering] 2s. TRE worth 20s; now 40[s].

In Morton [near Hanthorpe] and Hanthorpe [are] $2\frac{1}{2}$ carucates of land and the fourth part of 1 carucate and the fourth part of 1 bovate to the geld. [There is] land for as many ploughs and oxen. [It is] SOKELAND of Edenham. There were 14 sokemen and 5 bordars with 3 ploughs. There are 45 acres of meadow, and 40 acres of woodland pasture.

In 'HOLME' [in Beckingham], Ulf had 12 carucates of land in demesne and 12 carucates of land to the geld. [There is] land for as many ploughs. Gilbert has 4 ploughs there in demesne; and 28 sokemen and 28 villans and 3 bordars having 14 ploughs. There are 2 priests, and 2 churches, and 1 mill [rendering] 13s4d. TRE worth £10; now the same; tallage £3.

In Scott Willoughby, Gilbert has the fourth part of a church, sokeland of Aswarby.

In BURLEY [Rut.], Ulf had 2 carucates of land to the geld. [There is] land for 7 ploughs. Geoffrey, Gilbert's man, has 2 ploughs there, and 30 villans and 7 bordars with 4 ploughs, and [there are] 30 acres of meadow. [There is] woodland 1 league long and 3 furlongs broad. TRE worth £4; now 100s.

In BOOTHBY PAGNELL, Sighwat had 5 carucates of land to the geld. [There is] land for 5 ploughs. Roger, Gilbert's man, has 1 plough there in demesne; and 4 villans and 2 bordars and 12 sokemen on 3 carucates of this land having 3 ploughs. There is a church, and 6 acres of meadow, and 40 acres of woodland pasture, and 60 acres of scrubland. TRE worth 60s; now the same. Guy de Craon renders soke in respect of $3\frac{1}{2}$ bovates of this land.

In FOLKINGHAM, Ulf had 12 carucates of land to the geld. [There is] land for as many ploughs. Gilbert has 5 ploughs there in demesne; and 24 villans and 5 sokemen and 9 bordars with 7 ploughs. There is a church, and 1 mill [rendering] 10s8d, and 100 acres of meadow, and 80 acres of scrubland. TRE worth £50; now £40; tallage £50.

In Cranwell [is] inland of this manor, $1\frac{1}{2}$ carucates of land to the geld. Azur had the soke of this land. Geoffrey, Gilbert's man, has there 6 villans and 1 bordar with 1 plough, and $17\frac{1}{2}$ acres of meadow. TRE [worth] 20s; now 10[s].

SOKELAND OF THIS MANOR

In Honington [are] 3 carucates of land to the geld. [There is] land for 3 ploughs. Fulbert, Gilbert's man, has there 12 sokemen and 1 bordar with 3 ploughs, and 35 acres of meadow.

In Oasby [are] 5 carucates of land to the geld. [There is] land for 7 ploughs. 18 sokemen and 3 bordars have 6 ploughs there, and 40 acres of meadow, and 30 acres of scrubland.

In 'Little Lavington' [in Lenton] [are] 4 carucates of land to the geld and the third part of 1 carucate to the geld. Azelin, Gilbert's man, has 2 ploughs there in demesne; and 10 villans and 3 bordars with 3 ploughs, and 30 acres of meadow. It is worth 100s.

In Pickworth [are] 2 carucates of land and half a bovate to the geld. [There is] land for $2\frac{1}{2}$ ploughs. Gilbert has there 21 sokemen with 4 ploughs, and 16 acres of meadow, and 50 acres of scrubland, and 20 acres of woodland pasture.

In Haceby [is] 1 carucate of land to the geld. [There is] land for 12 oxen. 12 sokemen and 5 bordars have 3 ploughs there, and 5 acres of meadow.

In Dembleby [is] 1 carucate of land to the geld. [There is] land for 12 oxen. 20 sokemen and 3 bordars have 3 ploughs there, and 18 acres of meadow, and 12 acres of scrubland.

In Osbournby [are] 4 carucates of land to the geld. [There is] land for $5\frac{1}{2}$ ploughs.

[Folio 356: LINDSEY]

16 sokemen and 8 bordars have 8 ploughs there; and there is 1 church.

In Threekingham [is] 1 carucate of land to the geld. [There is] land for 1 plough. There is a market rendering 40s, and 11 sokemen and 8 bordars.

In Stow [in Threekingham] [are] $5\frac{1}{2}$ carucates of land to the geld. [There is] land for as many plough. Robert, Gilbert's man, has there 21 sokemen and 14 bordars having 5 ploughs. There is 1 plough in demesne, and 1 church, and 16 acres of meadow. The value [is] 100s.

In Walcot [near Folkingham] [are] 4 carucates of land to the geld. [There is] land for 5 ploughs. There are 22 sokemen and 4 bordars, and half a church, and 26 acres of meadow.

In Billingborough, Gilbert has the soke over half a carucate of land.

In Birthorpe [are] 15 bovates of land to the geld. [There is] land for 2 ploughs. 8 sokemen and 8 bordars have 3 ploughs there, and 27 acres of meadow.

In Laughton [in Folkingham] [are] 4 carucates of land to the geld. [There is] land for 4 ploughs. 14 sokemen and 4 bordars have 3½ ploughs there, and 9 acres of meadow, and 13 acres of scrubland.

In Aslackby, half a carucate, and 'Sempringham' 2 carucates and 6 bovates, [are] 3 carucates of land and 2 bovates to the geld. [There is] land for 3½ ploughs. There are 13 sokemen and 1 bordar having 3 ploughs, and half a church, and the sixth part of another church, and 24 acres of meadow, and 40 acres of scrubland.

In Pointon [are] 2 carucates of land and 2 bovates to the geld. [There is] land for as many ploughs and oxen. 16 sokemen have 6 ploughs there, and [there are] 32 acres of meadow, and 40 acres of scrubland.

In Ingoldsby [are] 3 carucates of land and 1 bovate to the geld. [There is] land for 3 ploughs. 17 sokemen and 2 bordars have 5 ploughs there, and 25 acres of meadow, and 100 acres of scrubland.

In Hough on the Hill and Brandon [are] 3 carucates of land and 3 bovates to the geld. [There is] land for 5 ploughs. 13 sokemen have 6 ploughs there, and 6 acres of meadow. The whole of this Deoring holds of Gilbert, and he has half a plough there in demesne. It is worth | 40s. |

In Kirkby la Thorpe [are] 7 carucates of land to the geld. [There is] land for 5 ploughs. 31 sokemen and 6 bordars have 6 ploughs there.

In Silk Willoughby [are] 5 carucates of land to the geld. [There is] land for 10 ploughs. 29 sokemen and 1 bordar have 6 ploughs there. There is a priest and a church, and 140 acres of meadow, and 24 acres of meadow [sic].

In Aswarby [are] 4½ carucates of land and 1 bovate to the geld. [There is] land for 9 ploughs. 41 sokemen and 3 bordars have 18 ploughs there. There is a priest and a church, and 2 parts of a church, and 180 acres of meadow. Ralph the priest has 3½ carucates of this land, and he has 4 ploughs there in demesne.

In Scredington [are] 10½ carucates of land to the geld. [There is] land for 9 ploughs. 40 sokemen and 1 villan have 14 ploughs there. There is a priest and a church, and 21 acres of meadow.

In Helpringham, 3 carucates and 2 bovates, and Burton Pedwardine, 2 carucates, [are] 5 carucates of land and 2 bovates to the geld. [There is] land for 8 ploughs. 35 sokemen and 7 bordars have 10 ploughs there, and 26 acres of meadow.

XXXV. The land of Hugh fitzBaldric

In BONBY, Grimkel and Merdo and Healfdene and 3 other thegns had 3 carucates of land to the geld. [There is] land for 6 ploughs. Hugh fitzBaldric has 3 ploughs there in demesne; and 14 villans and 7 bordars with 4 ploughs. TRE worth £4; now 6[l]; tallage 20s. 3 bovates of this land [are] sokeland.

In WORLABY [near Elsham], Grimkel had half a carucate of land to the geld. [There is] land for 1 plough. Ralph, Hugh's man, has 1 plough there, and 2 villans having 2 oxen in a plough. TRE, as now, worth 20s.

In [Great or Little] LIMBER, Siward and Ulf had 2½ carucates of land to the geld. [There is] land for 5½ ploughs. Hugh fitzBaldric has 2 ploughs there, and 10 villans and 4 bordars and 20 sokemen on 5 bovates of this land. Among them all [are] 4 ploughs and 2 oxen in a plough. TRE worth 100s; now the same; tallage 20s.

In Cabourne [is] half a bovate of land. [It is] sokeland of [Great or Little] Limber.

In KIRMINGTON, Topi had 2 bovates of land to the geld. [There is] land for 2 ploughs. Hamelin, Hugh's man, has 1 plough there, and 5 villans and 8 bordars and 10 sokemen with 1 plough having 18 tofts. TRE worth 40s; now 30[s]; tallage 10s.

In CROXTON, Siward had 10 bovates of land to the geld. [There is] land for 2½ ploughs. Hamelin, Hugh's man, [has] 1 plough there, and 6 villans and 3 bordars and 2 sokemen with 1½ ploughs. 1 bovate [is] SOKELAND. There are 8 acres of meadow. TRE, as now, worth 40s.

In STALLINGBOROUGH, Siward and Gamal and Ulfkil had 1 carucate of land to the geld. [There is] land for 2 ploughs. Hugh has 1 plough there, and 2 sokemen on 5 tofts, and 2 villans and 1 bordar, and 2½ mills [rendering] 10s, and 2½ salt-pans [rendering] 2s, and [there are] 200 acres of meadow. TRE, as now, worth 30s.

In STAINTON LE VALE, Baelig;rghthor had 1 carucate of land to the geld. [There is] land for 3 ploughs. Hugh has 1 plough there, and 4 sokemen on 1 bovate of land and 11 villans and 3 bordars with 1 plough and 2 oxen in a plough, and [there are] 55 acres of meadow. TRE worth £3; now 40s; tallage 10s.

In CABOURNE, Grimkel had 2 carucates of land and 3½ bovates to the geld. [There is] land for 5 ploughs. Hugh has 2 ploughs there, and 12 sokemen on 1 carucate of land and 1 villan and 3 bordars with 3 ploughs, and 20 acres of meadow. TRE worth 30s; now 60[s]; tallage 20s.

In Cuxwold [is] a BEREWICK, 3 bovates of land to the geld. [There is] land for 6 oxen. There are 4 villans and 3 sokemen with 1 plough.

In CROXTON, Grimkel had half a carucate of land to the geld. [There is] land for 1 plough. Hamelin, Hugh's man, has 1 plough there, and 9 sokemen on 2 bovates of land and 6 villans and 1 bordar having 1½ ploughs, and 8 acres of meadow. TRE, as now, worth 40s.

In North Thoresby and 'Audby' [in North Thoresby] [is] 1 bovate and 5 parts of 1 bovate to the geld. [There is] land for 2 oxen. [It is] SOKELAND of Cabourne. There are 2 villans, and 2 salt-pans [rendering] 2s, and 15 acres of meadow.

[Folio 356V: LINCOLNSHIRE]

In 'KETTLEBY THORPE' [in Bigby], Klak and Leofwine had 10 bovates of land to the geld. [There is] land for 2½ ploughs. Gilbert, Hugh's man, has 1½ ploughs there, and 2 sokemen on 5½ bovates of land and 12 villans and 5 bordars with 1½ ploughs, and 60 acres of meadow. TRE worth 60s; now 50[s]; tallage 10s.

In Bigby [is] a BEREWICK, 5½ bovates of land to the geld. [There is] land for 1 plough. 1 villan and 1 bordar have 1 ox in a plough there.

In HEMINGBY, Eadric had 6 bovates of land to the geld. [There is] land for 6 oxen. Hugh has 2 ploughs there, and 13 sokemen on 2 bovates of land and 3 villans with 2 ploughs, and 60 acres of meadow. TRE worth 60s; now 100[s]; tallage 20s.

In Bucknall [is] SOKELAND, 6½ bovates of land to the geld. [There is] land for as many oxen. 5 sokemen and 2 villans have 1 plough there, and 65 acres of meadow, and 9 acres of woodland pasture, and 5 acres of scrubland.

In Horsington [are] 2 carucates of land and 6½ bovates to the geld. [There is] land for 3 ploughs. 16 sokemen and 2 bordars have 3 ploughs there, and [there are] 153 acres of meadow, and 15 acres of scrubland.

In Ludford [is] SOKELAND of 'West Wykeham' [in Ludford], 2 bovates of land to the geld. [There is] land for 4 oxen. 2 sokemen have half a plough there, and [there are] 4 acres of meadow.

In CLAXBY [near Alford], Dene had 1 carucate of land to the geld. [There is] land for 14 oxen. Guy, Hugh's son-in-law, has 2 ploughs there, and 1 sokeman on 3 bovates of land and 5 villans with 1½ ploughs. There is a church and a priest, and 1 mill [rendering] 2s, and 120 acres of scrubland. Gilbert de Ghent has 2 parts of it and Guy the other 3 parts. TRE worth £8; now 9[l].

SOKELAND OF THIS MANOR

In Withern [are] 6 bovates of land to the geld. [There is] land for 1 plough. 8 sokemen and 2 villans have 2 ploughs there, and 12 acres of meadow, and 60 acres of scrubland.

In Woodthorpe [are] 2½ carucates of land to the geld. [There is] land for 5 ploughs. 19 sokemen and 9 bordars have 4 ploughs there. [There is] scrubland half a league long and as much broad.

In Strubby [near Maltby le Marsh], 5 bovates, and Maltby le Marsh, 2 [bovates], [are] 7 bovates of land to the geld. [There is] land for 12 oxen. 5 sokemen have 5 oxen in a plough there, and 30 acres of meadow.

In Saleby [are] 2 carucates of land to the geld. [There is] land for 2 ploughs. 2 sokemen and 2 villans have 2 ploughs there.

In Thoresthorpe [are] 2 carucates of land to the geld. [There is] land for 2 ploughs. 5 sokemen and 2 bordars have 2½ ploughs there, and [there are] 40 acres of meadow, and 40 acres of scrubland.

In SLOOTHBY, Dene had 3 bovates of land to the geld. [There is] land for 1 plough. Guy, Hugh's son-in-law, has there 4 villans and 3 bordars with half a plough, and 4 acres of meadow. TRE worth 20s; now 6s.

XXXVI. The land of Kolsveinn

In BRATTLEBY, Ketil had 3 carucates of land to the geld. [There is] land for 3½ ploughs. Kolsveinn has 2 ploughs there in demesne; and 9 sokemen on 7 bovates of this land and 6 villans and 1 bordar with 4 ploughs. TRE worth 40s; now 60[s]; tallage 20s.

In RISEHOLME, Leofsige had 1 carucate of land to the geld. [There is] land for 1 plough. Kolsveinn has 2 ploughs there, and 3 villans and 1 bordar with 1 plough, and 1 mill [rendering] 2s. TRE worth 20s; now 60[s].

In FALDINGWORTH, Esbiorn had half a carucate of land to the geld. [There is] land for 4 oxen. 3 villans of Kolsveinn have half a plough there, and 8 acres of meadow. TRE [worth] 10s; now 5[s]4d.

In SCOTHERN and 'Holme' [in Sudbrooke] and Sudbrooke, Thorulf had 3 carucates of land and 5 bovates to the geld. [There is] land for 4 ploughs. Kolsveinn has 1 plough there, and 11 sokemen on 2½ carucates of land and 1 villan and 1 bordar with 3 ploughs, and 64 acres of meadow. TRE worth 40s; now 60[s]; tallage 20s.

In the same places Godric had 4½ bovates of land to the geld. [There is] land for 1 plough. 1 villan and 1 bordar having have 2 oxen in a plough there. TRE, as now, worth 5s.

In the same places Kolsveinn has 1 carucate of land of the king, as he says; and from it he renders customary dues in Fiskerton to Peterborough [Abbey]. He has 1 mill there, and 3 villans with 1 plough. TRE, as now, it rendered 10s.

In BARLINGS, Koll had 6 bovates of land to the geld. [There is] land for 1 plough. Kolsveinn has 1 plough there, and 3 villans with half a plough, and 1 church. TRE worth 10s; now £4.

In Reepham [are] 6 bovates of land to the geld. [There is] land for 1 plough. [It is] a BEREWICK. Kolsveinn [has] 1 plough there, and 4 villans [with] half a plough, and 18 acres of meadow.

In CAMMERINGHAM, Knut and Alnoth and Ulfkil and Esbiorn had 4½ carucates of land to the geld. [There is] land for 5 ploughs. Kolsveinn has 4 ploughs there in demesne; and 8 sokemen on half a carucate of this land and 11 villans and 2 bordars with 3 ploughs, and [there are] 70 acres of meadow. TRE worth £3; now 4[l]; tallage 20s.

In INGHAM, Frani and Sumarlithr had 1 carucate of land to the geld. [There is] land for 1½ ploughs. Roger and Ansketil, Kolsveinn's men, have 1½ ploughs there, and 4 villans and 1 bordar with 3 oxen in a plough, and 16 acres of meadow. TRE worth 50s; now 30[s]; tallage 10s.

In Friesthorpe [are] 3 carucates of land to the geld. [There is] land for 3 ploughs. [It is] SOKELAND of Ingham, 7 bovates, and Fillingham, 17 bovates. 10 sokemen and 3 bordars have 3 ploughs there, and 50 acres of meadow, and 20 acres of scrubland.

In Faldingworth [are] 2 carucates of land to the geld. [There is] land for 2½ ploughs. [It is] SOKELAND of Fillingham, 6 bovates, and Spridlington, 1 carucate, and Ingham, 2 bovates. 9 sokemen have 1 plough there, and 26 acres of meadow, and [there is] 1 acre of woodland.

In COLD HANWORTH, Frani had 6 bovates of land to the geld. [There is] land for 12 oxen. Turold the priest has 1 plough there, and 6 villans and 1 bordar having 1 plough, and 10 acres of meadow. TRE worth 20s; now 30s[].

In Hackthorn [is] a BEREWICK, 3 bovates of land to the geld and the fourth part of 1 bovate. [There is] land for 4 oxen.

[Folio 357: LINDSEY]

In the same HACKTHORN, Knut had 3 bovates of land to the geld. [There is] land for 4 oxen. Kolsveinn has there 2 oxen in a plough, and 8 acres of meadow. TRE worth 5s4d; now the same.

In SCAWBY and Sturton [in Scawby], Thorulf had 11 bovates of land to the geld. [There is] land for 2 ploughs. Alfred, Kolsveinn's man, has has [sic] 1 plough there, and 5 sokemen on 1 carucate of this land and 3 villans with 1½ ploughs. TRE worth 10s; now 20[s]; tallage 5s.

In Redbourne [are] 2 bovates of land and 4 parts of 1 bovate to the geld. [There is] land for 5½ oxen. Kolsveinn has it, and it is waste.

In Hibaldstow [is] the third part of 2 bovates to the geld. [It is] SOKELAND of Scawby.

In SOUTH RESTON and Great Carlton, Alsige had half a carucate of land to the geld. [There is] land for 6 oxen. Matthew, Kolsveinn's man, has 1 plough there, and 4 villans with half a plough, and 20 acres of meadow, and 160 acres of woodland pasture. TRE worth 15s; now 30[s].

In [North or South] COCKERINGTON, Alnoth had 1 bovate of land to the geld. [There is] land for 2 oxen. Matthew has half a plough there. TRE, as now, [worth] 3s.

In BARLINGS, Asgot had 6 bovates of land to the geld. [There is] land for 1 plough. Kolsveinn has 1 plough there, and 2 villans and 3 bordars with half a plough, and 20 acres of meadow, and 20 acres of scrubland. TRE worth 30s; now 40[s].

In KEXBY, Eskil had 3 carucates of land and 3½ bovates to the geld. [There is] land for as many ploughs and oxen. Adelelm, Kolsveinn's man, has 2 ploughs there, and 9 villans and 3 bordars with 1½ ploughs, and 1 mill [rendering] 16d, and 58 acres of meadow, and 40 acres of scrubland. TRE, as now, worth 40s; tallage 10s.

In Coates [are] 2 bovates of land to the geld. [There is] land for 2 oxen. [It is] SOKELAND of Ingham.

In FILLINGHAM, Frani and Alnoth and Eskil and Alnoth and Godric had 7 carucates of land and 1 bovate to the geld. [There is] land for 11 ploughs. Kolsveinn has 4 ploughs there, and 32 sokemen on 4½ ploughs of this land and 12 villans with 3½ ploughs. There is a church, and 240 acres of meadow. TRE worth £4; now 5[l]; tallage 40s.

In SPRIDLINGTON, Ebrard and his 2 brothers had 2 carucates of land and 5½ bovates to the geld. [There is] land for 3 ploughs. Kolsveinn has 2 ploughs there, and 4 sokemen on 1 bovate of this land and 16 villans and 4 bordars with 2 ploughs, and 8 acres of meadow. TRE worth 21s; now 40[s]; tallage 10s.

In EWERBY THORPE, Eadgifu had 3½ carucates of land and 1 bovate to the geld. [There is] land for 3 ploughs. Kolsveinn has 2 ploughs there, and 8 villans with 1 plough, and 44 acres of meadow, and 23 acres of scrubland. TRE worth 30s; now 60[s].

In HECKINGTON, Thorkil and Algar had 1 carucate of land and 6 bovates to the geld. [There is] land for 1 plough and 5 oxen. Conded, Kolsveinn's man, has 1 villan there, and 18 acres of meadow. TRE worth 36s; now 30s.

In Helpringham [are] 2 bovates of land to the geld. [There is] land for 2 oxen. There is 1 villan, and 2 acres of meadow. This land is almost waste.

In HOWELL Hundred [are] 2½ bovates to the geld. [There is] land for 2 oxen. [It is] SOKELAND of Kirkby la Thorpe.

In 'LAYTHORPE' [in Kirkby la Thorpe], Thor and Eskil had 5½ carucates of land to the geld. Conded and Ansketil, Kolsveinn's men, has [sic] 4 ploughs there, and 7 villans and 10 bordars and 1 sokeman with 1½ ploughs, and half a church, and with [sic] half a priest. TRE worth £4; now the same; tallage 20s.

In DRY DODDINGTON, Auti had 6 bovates of land to the geld. [There is] land for as many oxen. Kolsveinn has there 2 villans and 2 bordars with half a plough, and half a mill [rendering] 3s, and 10 acres of meadow. TRE, as now, worth 10s.

In the same place [are] 6 bovates of land to the geld. [There is] land for 6 oxen. [It is] SOKELAND of Marston. 2 sokemen and 2 bordars have 2 oxen there. The lord [has] half a plough, and 10 acres of meadow.

In MARSTON, Alsige had 1 carucate of land to the geld in demesne and 10 bovates of SOKELAND. [There is] land for 3 ploughs. Walter, Kolsveinn's man, has 1 plough there, and 4 sokemen and 5 bordars with 1 plough and 1 ox, and the site of 1 mill, and 32 acres of meadow. TRE worth 30s; now 50[s.].

In Hougham [are] 2 carucates of land to the geld. [There is] land for 12 oxen. [It is] SOKELAND of Marston. 4 sokemen and 1 bordar have half a plough there, and 4 acres of meadow.

In HOUGHAM, Azur had 2 carucates of land to the geld. [There is] land for 3 ploughs. William, Kolsveinn's man, has 1 plough there, and 5 villans and 5 bordars with 1 plough and 2 oxen, and 2½ acres of meadow. TRE, as now, worth 30s.

In BILLINGBOROUGH, Swein had 2 carucates of land and 7 bovates to the geld. Brunel, Kolsveinn's man, has 1½ ploughs there, and 8 villans and 2 bordars with 1½ ploughs. There is half a church, and 1 mill [rendering] 5s4d, and 27 acres of meadow, and 26 acres of scrubland. TRE worth 40s; now 60[s].

In 'OUSEBY' [in Billingborough], Alsige had 2 carucates of land and 1½ bovates to the geld. [There is] land for 18 oxen. Brunel, Kolsveinn's man, has 1½ ploughs there, and 8 villans with 2 ploughs. There is half a church, and 1 mill [rendering] 5s4d. TRE, as now, worth 60s.

In Pointon [is] half a carucate of land to the geld. [There is] land for 4 oxen. Conded, Kolsveinn's man, has 1 plough there, and 3 bordars, and 4 acres of meadow.

In Spanby [are] 2 carucates of land to the geld. [There is] land for 3 ploughs. 12 sokemen have 2 ploughs there, and 20 acres of meadow.

In NEWTON, Thorkil and Godwine had 10 bovates of land to the geld. [There is] land for 2 ploughs. Ralph, Kolsveinn's man, has 1 plough there, and 4 villans and 4 bordars with half a plough, and [there are] 18 acres of meadow, and 72 acres of scrubland. TRE, as now, [worth] 70s; tallage 20s.

In 'Ouseby' [in Billingborough] [are] 6 bovates of land and the third part of 1 bovate to the geld. [There is] land for 1 plough. [It is] inland of Newton. There is now 1 bordar, and the site of a mill, and 9 acres of meadow.

In Threekingham [are] 14 bovates and the third part of 1 bovate to the geld. [There is] land for 2½ ploughs. [It is] inland. There is 1 sokeman and 5 villans and 3 bordars with 1½ ploughs.

In DEMBLEBY, Gunnkil had 1 carucate of land to the geld. [There is] land for 10 oxen. Reginald, Kolsveinn's man, has 1 plough there, and 4 sokemen and 1 bordar with 1 plough, and 16 acres of meadow, and 20 acres of scrubland. TRE, as now, [worth] 20s.

[Folio 357V: LINCOLNSHIRE]

In SWATON, Auti had 7 carucates of land to the geld. [There is] land for 9 ploughs. Kolsveinn has 3 ploughs there, and 40 sokemen on 5 carucates of this land and 7 villans and 2 bordars with 10 ploughs, and 80 acres of meadow. TRE worth £8; now 4[l]; tallage 40s.

In the same vill Alsige and Æthelstan had 1 carucate of land to the geld. [There is] land for 10 oxen. Ælfric their brother had the soke over them in Haceby only in respect of the king's service. Kolsveinn has half a plough there, and 3 villans with half a plough, and 13 acres of meadow. TRE, as now, [worth] 10s.

In HORBLING, Swein had 3 carucates of land and 2 bovates to the geld. [There is] land for as many ploughs and oxen. Matthew, Kolsveinn's man, has 1 plough there, and 11 sokemen on 1 carucate of this land and 3 villans with 3 ploughs, and 15 acres of meadow. TRE, as now, worth 40s; tallage 20s.

In AISBY [in Heydour], Aslak had 3 carucates of land to the geld. [There is] land for 4 ploughs. William, Kolsveinn's man, has there 9 sokemen and 2 bordars having 4 ploughs, and 100 acres of meadow. TRE worth 60s; now the same; tallage 20s.

In BURTON-LE-COGGLES and Bitchfield, Leodflæd had 6 bovates of land to the geld. [There is] land for 1 plough. William, Kolsveinn's man, has half a plough there, and 3

villans and 2 bordars with half a plough, and [there are] 4 acres of meadow, and 150 acres of woodland, pasture in places. TRE worth 16s; now 20s.

In ASHBY DE LA LAUNDE, Auti and Eskil had 3½ carucates of land to the geld. [There is] land for 4 ploughs. Kolsveinn has 1½ ploughs there, and 12 villans and 2 sokemen on 1 bovate of this land and 1 bordar with 2 ploughs, and 15 acres of meadow. TRE worth 50s; now 70s.

In NORTH KYME, Auti had 5 carucates of land and 2 bovates to the geld. [There is] land for 2 ploughs. Kolsveinn has 1 plough there, and 1 fishery [rendering] 8d, and 20 acres of meadow, and 5 acres of scrubland. TRE worth 40s; now £4.

In Westby [are] 10 bovates of land to the geld. [There is] land for 10 oxen. [It is] free sokeland of Heydour. 1 sokeman and 6 villans have 2 ploughs there, and [there are] 12 acres of meadow, and 50 acres of woodland, pasture in places.

In Evedon [are] 2 carucates of land to the geld. [There is] land for 2 ploughs. [It is] inland of Kirkby la Thorpe. There are 6 acres of meadow, and 8 acres of scrubland, and 40 acres of marsh.

In PICKWORTH, Auti had 2 carucates of land to the geld. [There is] land for 3 ploughs. These 2 carucates are not enumerated in any hundred nor have they [their] like in Lincolnshire. William, Kolsveinn's man, has 1 plough there, and 6 villans and 2 bordars with 1 plough. There is a priest, and half a church. In this land a certain free man has 1 carucate.

And in the same vill are 2½ bovates of land to the geld. [There is] land for 3½ oxen. [It is] SOKELAND of Pickworth. 2 villans have 2 oxen there. TRE, as now, worth 40s.

XXVII. The land of Alvred of Lincoln

In GOXHILL, Siward had 1 carucate of land and 2 bovates to the geld. [There is] land for 2½ ploughs. Ralph, Alvred's man, has 1 plough there, and 16 sokemen on 2 bovates of this land and 6 villans with 2 ploughs, and 60 acres of meadow. TRE worth 30s; now 40[s]; tallage 10s.

In HABROUGH, Alwine had 5 bovates of land to the geld. [There is] land for 10 oxen. Ralph, Alvred's man, has 1 plough there, and 1 villan and 2 bordars with 2 oxen, and 1 mill [rendering] 2s, and 30 acres of meadow. TRE, as now, [worth] 30s.

In GREAT COATES [in Great Grimsby], Morcar had 5 bovates of land to the geld. [There is] land for 10 oxen. Bernard, Alvred's man, has there 2 villans and 2 bordars and 8 sokemen on 1 bovate of this land with 2 ploughs, and 100 acres of meadow. TRE worth 30s; now 24[s].

In Aylesby [is] half a bovate of land to the geld. [There is] land for 2 oxen. 1 villan has 1 ox there. [It is] SOKELAND of Great Coates [in Great Grimsby].

In HEALING, Morcar had 2 carucates of land to the geld. [There is] land for 4 ploughs. Bernard, Alvred's man, has 2 ploughs there, and 13 sokemen on half a carucate of this land and 2 villans and 2 bordars with 2½ ploughs, and half a mill [rendering] 3s, and 26 acres of meadow. TRE worth 40s; now 50[s]; tallage 10s.

In Swallow [are] 3 bovates of land to the geld. [There is] land for 6 oxen. [It is] inland of this manor. 1 villan has 1 ox in a plough there.

In LINWOOD, William and Grimkel and Asfrith had 1½ carucates of land to the geld. [There is] land for 4 ploughs. Alvred has 2 ploughs there in demesne; and 20 villans and 5 bordars with 4 ploughs, and 2 parts of a mill [rendering] 2s, and 280 acres of meadow. TRE worth 65s; now 50s; tallage 10s.

In Middle Rasen [are] 4 bovates of land to the geld. [There is] land for 12 oxen. [It is] inland of this manor. 3 villans have 2 oxen in a plough there.

In the other Rasen [Market Rasen] [are] 4½ bovates of land to the geld. [There is] land for 1 plough. [It is] SOKELAND. 10 sokemen have 1 plough there, and 1 mill [rendering] 12d, and 10 acres of meadow.

In THORESWAY, Rolf and Koddi had 5 carucates of land and 7 bovates to the geld. [There is] land for 13 ploughs. Alvred has 2 ploughs there, and 56 sokemen and 5 villans with 5 ploughs, and 2 mills [rendering] 3s, and 40 acres of meadow in the soke of William de Percy's manor of Caistor. TRE worth £4; now 100s; tallage 40s.

In Tealby, Alvred has 1 mill in the soke of the Bishop of Bayeux.

In CUXWOLD, Leodwine had 3 bovates of land to the geld. [There is] land for 6 oxen. Gleu, Alvred's man, has 1 plough there, and 2 villans and 1 bordar. TRE, as now, worth 20s.

In Cabourne [is] 1 bovate of land to the geld. [It is] SOKELAND of Cuxwold. 1 villan and 1 bordar have 1 ox in a plough there.

In ROTHWELL, Grimkel and William had 4 carucates of land and 1 bovate and 2 parts of 1 bovate to the geld. [There is] land for 8 ploughs. Gleu, Alvred's man, has 1½ ploughs there, and 12 sokemen on 7 bovates of this land and 7 villans and 1 bordar with 2½ ploughs, and 2 mills [rendering] 3s, and 46 acres of meadow, and 1 church. TRE worth £4; now 3[l]; tallage 10s.

In ROTHWELL, Thorkil had half a carucate of land to the geld. [There is] land for 1 plough. Alvred has there 1 sokeman and 2 bordars with half a plough. TRE, as now, worth 6s.

In North Thoresby and 'Audby' [in North Thoresby], Alvred has 1 salt-pan belonging to Rothwell.

[Folio 358: LINDSEY]

In Cuxwold [is] 1 bovate of land to the geld. 3 sokemen have 1 plough there.

In Cabourne [are] 2½ bovates of land to the geld. It is waste.

In STIXWOULD, Siward had 6 bovates of land to the geld.

[There is] land for 12 oxen. The same man has there of Alvred 4 villans with 1 plough, and 20 acres of meadow, and 40 acres of woodland pasture. TRE, as now, worth 10s.

In West Torrington, Rolf had 3½ bovates of land to the geld. [There is] land for 1 plough. [It is] SOKELAND of the vill itself. Joscelin, Alvred's man, has there 2½ sokemen having 2½ oxen in a plough, and 11 acres of meadow.

In the same place Klak had 3½ bovates of land to the geld. [There is] land for 1 plough. [It is] SOKELAND of Hainton. 2½ sokemen have 2½ oxen in a plough there. Joscelin holds it of Alvred.

In ALVINGHAM, Eadric had 5½ bovates of land and the sixth part of a bovate to the geld. [There is] land for 1½ ploughs. Joscelin, Alvred's man, has 1 plough there, and 5 villans with half a plough. 2 bovates of this land are SOKELAND, and [there are] 20 acres of meadow. TRE worth 20s; now 30[s].

In Brackenborough [is] 1 bovate of land to the geld. [There is] land for 2 oxen. Ranulph, Alvred's man, has 1 plough there, and 4 villans with half a plough. [It is] SOKELAND of Alvingham, and [there are] 10 acres of meadow.

In the vill itself Eadric and Hoc had 6 bovates of land to the geld. [There is] land for 14 oxen. Ranulph, Alvred's man, has [sic] there 1 villan and 10 sokemen with 2 ploughs, and 4 parts of a mill [rendering] 2s, and [there are] 18 acres of meadow. TRE worth 16s; now 40[s].

In [North and South] COCKERINGTON, Eadric and Maccus had 7 bovates of land to the geld. [There is] land for 14 oxen. Alvred and Joscelin his man have half a plough there, and 1 sokeman on a toft and 2 villans with half a plough, and half a mill [rendering] 3s, and [there are] 70 acres of meadow, and 58 acres of scrubland. TRE worth 21s; now 30s.

In STEWTON, Almær had 13 bovates of land to the geld. [There is] land for 3 ploughs and 2 oxen. Alvred has 2 ploughs there, and 10 sokemen on half a carucate of land and 8 villans with 1 plough, and [there are] 200 acres of woodland pasture. TRE worth 20s; now 60s.

In 'SOUTH CADEBY' [in Calcethorpe], Maccus had 7 bovates of land to the geld. [There is] land for 14 oxen. Alvred has 1 plough there, and 1 sokeman on 4 bovates of this land and 4 villans with 1 plough, and 13 acres of meadow. TRE worth 30s; now 20[s].

In Grimoldby [is] 1 bovate of land to the geld. [It is] SOKELAND of 'South Cadeby' [in Calcethorpe]. Alvred has two parts and William the third. It is waste.

In Saltfleetby [All Saints, St Clement or St Peter] [is] 1 bovate of land to the geld. [There is] land for 1½ oxen. [It is] SOKELAND of 'South Cadeby' [in Calcethorpe]. Alvred has two parts, William the third.

In 'CALCETHORPE' [or] 'SOUTH CADEBY' [in Calcethorpe], Rolf had 5 bovates of land to the geld. [There is] land for 10 oxen. Alvred has 1 plough there, and 1 sokeman on $2\frac{1}{2}$ bovates of this land and 3 villans having 2 oxen in a plough, and 6 acres of meadow. TRE worth 30s; now 60[s].

In East Wykeham [is] half a bovate of land to the geld. [There is] land for 1 ox. [It is] SOKELAND OF 'Calcethorpe'. It is waste.

In the same East Wykeham [are] 5 bovates of land to the geld. [There is] land for 10 oxen. [It is] SOKELAND of 'South Cadeby' [in Calcethorpe]. 5 sokemen have half a plough there, and 10 acres of meadow.

In KELSTERN, Rolf and Maccus had 2 carucates of land and 6 bovates to the geld. [There is] land for $5\frac{1}{2}$ ploughs. Alvred has 1 plough there, and 9 sokemen on 15 bovates of this land and 4 villans with 2 ploughs. TRE worth 30s; now 40[s].

In UFFINGTON, Arnbiorn had 7 carucates of land to the geld. [There is] land for as many ploughs. Alvred has 2 ploughs there in demesne; and 16 sokemen on 4 carucates of this land and 31 villans with 7 ploughs, and $3\frac{1}{2}$ mills rendering 40s. There is a church and a priest, and 100 acres of meadow. TRE worth £7; now 11[l]; tallage £3.

In the same vill Leodwine had 1 carucate of land to the geld. [There is] land for 1 plough. Alvred has there 4 sokemen on 4 bovates of this land and 3 villans with 1 plough, and 9 burgesses of Stamford pay 4s, and [he has] 20 acres of meadow. TRE, as now, worth 30s.

In 'Stowe' [in Barholm and Stowe] [are] $1\frac{1}{2}$ bovates to the geld. [There is] land for $1\frac{1}{2}$ oxen. Alvred has a church there which belongs to Uffington.

In CASEWICK, Wulfgeat had 6 bovates of land to the geld. [There is] land for 6 oxen. Boso, Alvred's man, has 1 plough there, and 2 villans and 1 bordar with 2 oxen in a plough. TRE worth 10s; now 20s.

In TALLINGTON, Wulfgeat had $6\frac{1}{2}$ carucates of land to the geld. [There is] land for as many ploughs. He has 2 ploughs there, and 14 sokemen on 4 carucates of land and 9 villans with 4 ploughs, and 1 mill [rendering] 12s, and [there are] 80 acres of meadow. TRE worth £3; now 4[l]; tallage 20s.

In Deeping [Deeping St James or Market Deeping] [are] 4 bovates of land to the geld. [There is] land for half a plough. [It is] SOKELAND of this manor. 6 villans and 2 bordars have $1\frac{1}{2}$ ploughs there, and 20 acres of meadow, and 1 fishery [rendering] 5d.

In CREETON, Thorkil had 6 bovates of land and 3 parts of 2 bovates to the geld. [There is] land for as many oxen. Ralph, Alvred's man, has half a plough there, and 2 villans, and 2 acres of meadow, and 30 acres of scrubland. TRE, as now, [worth] 20s.

In IRNHAM and Hawthorpe and 'Little Bulby' [in Irnham], Healfdene had 2 carucates of land and 7 bovates to the geld. [There is] land for as many ploughs and oxen. Alvred has 2 ploughs there, and 4 sokemen on 10 bovates of this land and 2 villans with 2 ploughs, and 8 acres of meadow, and 320 acres

of woodland, pasture in places. TRE worth 30s; now 40[s]; tallage 20s.

In ELSTHORPE, Siward had 2 carucates of land to the geld. [There is] land for 2 ploughs. Alvred has 1 plough there, and 5 sokemen on 6 bovates of this land and 5 villans with 2 ploughs, and 18 acres of meadow, and 240 acres of woodland. TRE worth 30s; now 40[s]; tallage 20s.

In STAINBY, Siward had 6 carucates of land to the geld. [There is] land for 8 ploughs. Alvred has 2 ploughs there, and 2 mills [rendering] 2s, and $8\frac{1}{2}$ acres of meadow and 40 acres of scrubland. 4 carucates of the same land there are SOKELAND. TRE worth 20s; now 40[s]; tallage 20s.

In 'ROXHOLM' [in Ruskington], Healfdene had 2 carucates of land and 6 bovates to the geld. [There is] land for as many ploughs and oxen. Ralph, Alvred's man, has $1\frac{1}{2}$ ploughs there, and 8 villans with 2 ploughs, and 40 acres of meadow. TRE worth 40s; now 50s.

[Folio 358V: LINCOLNSHIRE]

In BRAUNCEWELL, Healfdene had 2 carucates of land and 6 bovates to the geld. [There is] land for as many ploughs and oxen. Alvred has there 3 villans and 2 bordars with 3 oxen in a plough. TRE [worth] 20s; now 10s.

SOKELAND of this manor

In Bloxholm [are] 2 carucates of land and 3 bovates to the geld. [There is] land for as many ploughs and oxen. There are 2 sokemen with half a plough.

In SOUTH WITHAM, Siward had 4 carucates of land to the geld. [There is] land for 4 ploughs. Gleu, Alvred's man, has 1 plough there, and 11 villans and 3 bordars with 3 ploughs, and 100 acres of meadow less 6, and 80 acres of woodland pasture. TRE worth 40s; now 50[s]; tallage 10s. This SOKELAND belongs to Thistleton [Rut.].

In THISTLETON [Rut.], Siward had half a carucate of land to the geld. [There is] land for 1 plough. Gleu, Alvred's man, has 1 plough there, and 3 villans and 2 bordars with half a plough. Its value [belongs] to South Witham.

SOKELAND

In another "Tisteltune" [in South Witham] [is] 1 carucate of land to the geld. [There is] land for 1 plough. 2 sokemen have there 3 oxen in a plough.

In MARSTON, Wulfsige had 1 carucate of land in demesne, and 1 carucate of land [which is] sokeland. [There is] land for 3 ploughs. Walefrid, Alvred's man, has 1 plough there, and 8 villans and 2 bordars and 1 sokeman with 3 ploughs, and 2 mills [rendering] 8s, and 32 acres of meadow. TRE worth 20s; now 40[s].

In 'AUSTERBY' [in Bourne], Thorkil had 6 bovates of land to the geld. [There is] land for 6 oxen. Dodin, Alvred's man, has 1 plough there, and 2 villans and 4 bordars with 1 plough, and the third part of 1 mill [rendering] 3s4d, and 6 fisheries [rendering] 16d, and 6 acres of meadow, and 30 acres of woodland pasture. TRE, as now, worth 20s.

In Thurlby [near Bourne] [is] half a carucate of land to the geld. [There is] land for 4 oxen. 4 villans have half a plough there. [It is] inland of 'Austerby' [in Bourne].

In RIPPINGALE, Thorkil had 15 bovates of land and 2 parts of a bovate to the geld. [There is] land for as many oxen. Dodin, Alvred's man, has half a plough there, and 7 villans and 3 bordars with 1½ ploughs. There is a priest and the third part of a church, and 20 acres of meadow, and 60 acres of scrubland. TRE, as now, worth 30s.

In KIRKBY UNDERWOOD, Thorfridh had 1½ carucates of land to the geld. [There is] land for 12 oxen. Alvred has half a plough there, and 4 sokemen on 4 bovates of this land and 4 villans and 2 bordars with 1 plough, and 16 acres of meadow, and 60 acres of scrubland. TRE, as now, [worth] 30s.

In the same place Osfram had 5 bovates of land to the geld. [There is] land for as many oxen. The same Osfram has there, of Alvred, 2 oxen in a plough, and 2 villans, and 5 acres of meadow, and 60 acres of scrubland. TRE worth 20s; now 10[s].

In 'AVETHORPE' [in Aslackby], Osfram had half a carucate of land to the geld. [There is] land for 6 oxen. Swein, Alvred's man, has 1 plough there, and 2 villans and 1 bordar, and 4 acres of meadow. TRE worth 5s; now the same.

In 'SEMPRINGHAM', Morcar had 4 carucates of land and 2 bovates to the geld. [There is] land for as many ploughs and oxen. Josceliln, Alvred's man, has 1 plough there, and 14 sokemen on 2½ carucates of this land, and 8 villans and 2 bordars, and the fourth part of a church, and 11 acres of meadow, and 7 acres of scrubland. TRE, as now, worth 40s; tallage 20s.

In BILLINGBOROUGH, Toli had 1 carucate of land to the geld. [There is] land for 1 plough. Joscelin, Alvred's man, has 1 plough there, and 2 villans and 1 bordar with 2 oxen in a plough, and [there are] 14 acres of meadow. TRE, as now, [worth] 10s.

In BOOTHBY GRAFFOE and 'Somerton' [in Boothby Graffoe], Healfdene and Osfrith had 4 carucates of land to the geld. [There is] land for 4 ploughs and 6 oxen. Joscelin, Alvred's man, has 2½ ploughs there, and 6 sokemen on 1 carucate of this land and 4 villans and 6 bordars with 2 ploughs, and [there are] 55 acres of meadow. TRE worth 30s; now 40[s].

In HUTTOFT, Stiupi had 1 bovate of land to the geld. [There is] land for 1½ oxen. Dodo, Alvred's man, has half a plough there, and 1 villan, and 40 acres of meadow. TRE, as now, worth 10s.

In the same place Siward had 1 bovate of land to the geld. [There is] land for 1½ oxen. Bernard, Alvred's man, has there 2 oxen in a plough, and 40 acres of meadow. TRE, as now, worth 5s4d.

In Theddlethorpe [All Saints or St Helen] [is] half a carucate of land to the geld. [There is] land for 4 oxen. 4 sokemen and 1 villan have there 2 oxen in a plough, and 40 acres of meadow.

In Habrough [is] 1 bovate of land to the geld. [There is] land for 2 oxen. [It is] SOKELAND of Newsham. Alvred has it and it is waste.

In Brocklesby [are] 1½ bovates of land to the geld. [There is] land for 3 oxen. [It is] SOKELAND of Newsham. Alvred has there 1 sokeman with 2 oxen in a plough, and 11 acres of meadow.

[Folio 359: LINDSEY]

XXVIII. The land of Joscelin fitzLambert

In BLYBOROUGH, Tovi had 6 bovates of land to the geld. [There is] land for 2 ploughs. Joscelin fitzLambert has 2 ploughs there in demesne; and 1 sokeman on a bovate of this land and 8 villans with 1 plough, and 20 acres of meadow. TRE worth 20s; now 33[s]; tallage 7s.

In GLENTWORTH, Godric had 7 bovates of land to the geld. [There is] land for 12 oxen. Joscelin has there 4 sokemen on 4 bovates of this land with half a plough. Ansketil, his man, has 1 plough there, and 30 acres of meadow. TRE worth 10s8d; now 20s.

In NORMANBY-BY-SPITAL and Owmby-by-Spital, Aghmund had half a carucate of land to the geld. [There is] land for 4 oxen. Kolsveinn, Joscelin's man, has half a plough there, and 1 villan, and 4 acres of meadow. TRE worth 8s; now 10s.

In the same places Joscelin has 9 bovates of land to the geld of which Bishop Remigius has the soke. [There is] land for 9 oxen.

In WILLINGHAM BY STOW, Aslak and Earnwig had 5 carucates of land to the geld and the third part of a carucate. [There is] land for as many ploughs. Walo, Joscelin's man, has 1 plough there, and 5 sokemen on 3 carucates and 3 bovates of this land and 1 bordar with 1 plough. TRE worth 60s; now 40[s].

In STOW [near Torksey] [is] 1 carucate of land to the geld. [There is] land for 1 plough. [It is] SOKELAND of Willingham by Stow. 4 sokemen have 1 plough there.

In INGHAM, Alnoth and Aslak had 1 carucate of land to the geld. [There is] land for 12 oxen. Ansketil, Joscelin's man, has 1 plough there, and 1 sokeman on 2 bovates of this land and 1 bordar with 1 ox in a plough, and 6 acres of meadow. TRE worth 20s; now 10s.

In COATES, Aslak had half a carucate of land to the geld. [There is] land for 4 oxen. 1 villan has there 1 ox in a plough. TRE worth 20s; now 5[s].

In the same place [is] 1 bovate of land to the geld. [It is] SOKELAND of Ingham. It is waste.

In Snitterby [is] 1 bovate of land to the geld. [It is] SOKELAND of Waddingham. [It is] waste.

In HARPSWELL, Aghmund and Sighet and 2 other brothers had 2½ carucates of land to the geld. [There is] land for 3 ploughs. Joscelin has 2 ploughs there, and 13 villans with 3 ploughs, and half a church, and 109 acres of meadow. TRE worth 9s; now 50[s]; tallage 10s.

In HACKTHORN and Cold Hanworth, Sighet and Beorhtgifu had 2 carucates of land and 1 bovate to the geld. [There is] land for 4 ploughs.

In the same places [are] 4 bovates of land to the geld, SOKELAND of Harpswell, and another 2 bovates of land to the geld, inland of Owmby-by-Spital. [There is] land for 1 plough. Joscelin has 2 ploughs there in demesne; and 11 sokemen on 13 bovates of this land and 3 villans and 11 bordars with 3 ploughs, and 1 mill [rendering] 16d, and 40 acres of meadow. TRE, as now, worth 60s; tallage 20s.

In WADDINGHAM and 'Stainton' [in Waddingham], Steingrimr and Aghmund had 6 bovates of land to the geld. [There is] land for 6 oxen. Joscelin has 1 plough there, and 20 villans with 1 plough and 2 oxen in a plough, and 20 acres of meadow. TRE worth 40s; now 30[s]; tallage 10s.

In REDBOURNE, Aghmund and Brunhyse and Skuli had 7 carucates of land and 1 bovate to the geld. [There is] land for 14 ploughs and 2 oxen. Joscelin, and a certain man of his, has [sic] 3 ploughs there in demesne; and 6 sokemen on 10 bovates of this land and 21 villans and 4 bordars with 3½ ploughs, and 1 mill [rendering] 3s, and 140 acres of meadow. TRE worth £13; now 100s; tallage 20[s].

In SCAWBY and Sturton [in Scawby], Aghmund had 13 bovates of land to the geld. [There is] land for 2½ ploughs. Baldric, Joscelin's man, has 1 plough there, and 6 sokemen on 3 bovates of this land and 1 villan and 3 bordars with 1 plough. TRE worth 20s; now 30[s]; tallage 10s.

In BOTTESFORD, Aghmund had 1 carucate of land to the geld. [There is] land for 1 plough. Joscelin and a certain knight of his have 2 ploughs there, and 1 sokeman and 6 villans and 4 bordars with 1 plough, and the site of 1 mill, and a church, and 15 acres of meadow, and 30 acres of scrubland. TRE worth £4; now 30s; now tallage 10s.

In Cleatham [are] 2 bovates of land to the geld. [It is] inland of this manor. 1 villan has 1 ox there.

In MIDDLE RASEN, Thor had 3 bovates of land to the geld. [There is] land for 5 ploughs. Walo, Joscelin's man, has there 2 oxen in a plough, and 1 sokeman on half a bovate of this land and 4 villans with half a plough. TRE worth 10s; now 24[s].

In TEALBY, Eadric had 1 carucate of land to the geld. [There is] land for 12 oxen. Godard, Joscelin's man, has 1 plough there, and 4 sokemen on 1 bovate of this land and 10 villans with 1½ ploughs, and 3 mills [rendering] 16s, and [there are] 61 acres of meadow. TRE worth 60s; now 100[s]; tallage 60s.

In North Willingham [is] SOKELAND of this manor, 15 bovates of land to the geld. [There is] land for 3½ ploughs. 28 sokemen and 10 bordars have 2½ ploughs there, and 200 acres of meadow. Ivo has half a carucate there.

In Sumarlithr [Osgodby near West Rasen] [is] 1 bovate of land to the geld. There is 1 bordar.

In Claxby [near Walesby] and Normanby le wold [are] 9

bovates of land to the geld. [There is] land for 2 ploughs and 2 oxen. 14 sokemen have there 11 oxen in a plough, and 40 acres of meadow, and 40 acres of scrubland.

In Osgodby [near West Rasen] [is] 1 bovate of land to the geld. [There is] land for 2 oxen. There is 1 bordar.

In SNELLAND, Aghmund had 1 carucate of land to the geld. [There is] land for 2 ploughs. Rayner, Joscelin's man, has 1 plough there, and 3 sokemen on 2 bovates of this land and 1 villan with half a plough, and 10 acres of meadow, and 14 acres of scrubland. TRE, as now, worth 30s.

In Reasby [are] 1½ carucates of land to the geld. [It is] SOKELAND of this manor. [There is] land for 12 oxen. 4 sokemen have 1 plough there, and 5 acres of meadow, and 10 acres of scrubland. Of this sokeland William de Percy holds 4 bovates.

In Swinthorpe [are] 6 bovates of land to the geld. [There is] land for 1 plough. There is 1 sokeman, and 6 acres of meadow.

In Wickenby [are] 3 bovates of land to the geld. [There is] land for 5 oxen. There are 4 sokemen, and 6 acres of meadow.

In BLEASBY, Aghmund had 14½ bovates of land to the geld. [There is] land for 3 ploughs. Herman, Joscelin's man, has 1½ ploughs there, and 2 sokemen on 2½ bovates of this land, and 2 villans and 2 bordars with 1 plough and 2 oxen, and 120 acres of meadow, and 120 acres of scrubland. TRE [worth] 22s; now 40s.

In Beckering [is] half a bovate of land to the geld. [There is] land for 1 ox. 1 sokeman ploughs there with 1 ox, and [there is] half an acre of meadow.

[Folio 359V: LINCOLNSHIRE]

In Holton cum Beckering [is] 1 carucate of land to the geld. [There is] land for 2 ploughs. There are 4 sokemen with 9 oxen in a plough, and 10 acres of meadow. Herman has it under Joscelin.

In BEESBY IN THE MARSH and Maltby le Marsh, Aghmund had 6 bovates of land to the geld. [There is] land for 6 oxen. Eurold, Joscelin's man, has half a plough there, and 1 sokeman on 4 tofts of this land and 1 villan with 2 oxen in a plough, and [there is] a church. TRE, as now, worth 10s.

In BAG ENDERBY, Leysinger had 1 carucate of land to the geld. [There is] land for 12 oxen. Baldric, Joscelin's man, has 1 plough there, and 3 sokemen and 5 villans with 5½ ploughs, and 1 mill [rendering] 2s. TRE worth 40s; now 30s.

In Hagworthingham, Joscelin has 1 mill [rendering] 2s.

In TETFORD, Beorhtnoth had 2 carucates of land and 2 bovates to the geld. [There is] land for 3 ploughs. Walter, Joscelin's man, has 1 plough there, and 5 sokemen on 6 bovates of this land and 3 villans with 1½ ploughs. TRE worth 20s; now 30s.

SOKELAND OF HAMERINGHAM

In SOMERSBY Aghmund had 1 carucate of land to the geld. [There is] land for 12 oxen. 5 sokemen have 1½ ploughs there, and half a mill [rendering] 10d.

In the same place Snarri had 1 carucate of land to the geld. [There is] land for 12 oxen. Rayner, Joscelin's man, has there 6 sokemen with 1 plough, and half a mill [rendering] 10d. TRE worth 10s; now 16s.

In BAG ENDERBY, Leofsige had 6 bovates of land to the geld. [There is] land for 1 plough. Lambert, Joscelin's man, has there 3 oxen in a plough, and 6 sokemen and 1 villan and 1 bordar with 1 ox in a plough. TRE worth 8s; now 10s.

In the same place [is] 1 bovate of land to the geld. [There is] land for 2 oxen. [It is] SOKELAND of Ashby Puerorum. 1 sokeman and 1 villan have there 1 ox in a plough. Also SOKELAND

In Markby [is] 1 bovate of land to the geld. 1 sokeman has there 1 ox in a plough.

In Wainfleet [All Saints or St Mary] [are] 2 bovates of land to the geld. [There is] land for 2 oxen. 2 villans have there 2 oxen in a plough, and 20 acres of meadow, and 1 salt-pan [rendering] 8d.

In WINCEBY and Claxby Pluckacre, Aghmund had 1 carucate of land to the geld. [There is] land for 1 plough. Walter, Joscelin's man, has 1 plough there, and 1 villan, and 1 mill [rendering] 4s. TRE, as now, worth 20s.

In Welton le Marsh and 'Boothby' [in Welton le Marsh] [are] 2 carucates of land and 2 bovates to the geld. [There is] land for 3 ploughs. [It is] SOKELAND of Claxby Pluckacre. Rayner, Joscelin's man, has half a plough there, and 14 sokemen have 3 ploughs.

XXVIIII. The land of Eudo fitzSpirewic

SOUTH RIDING

In 'LITTLE STURTON' [in Baumber], Godwine and Gunnhvati had 2 carucates of land to the geld. [There is] land for 5 ploughs. Eudo fitzSpirewic has 5 ploughs there in demesne; and 16 villans with 2 ploughs, and 1 mill [rendering] 10s8d, and 200 acres of meadow less 10. TRE worth 100s; now £8; tallage 40s.

In ''Sudtone'' [in Great Sturton] [is] a BEREWICK, 3 bovates of land and the fourth part of 1 bovate to the geld. [There is] land for 4 oxen. There are 2 villans.

In the same place Godwine [had] 1½ bovates of land to the geld. [There is] land for 2 oxen. Eudo has there 3 sokemen and 3½ villans with 1 plough, and 25 acres of meadow. TRE, as now, worth 10s.

In KIRKBY ON BAIN, Godwine and Gunnhvati had half a carucate of land to the geld. [There is] land for 5 oxen. Eudo has 1 plough there, and 8 acres of meadow, and 80 acres of woodland, pasture in places. TRE, as now, worth 10s.

In Martin [near Horncastle] [are] 1½ carucates of land to the geld. [There is] land for 2 ploughs. 2 sokemen and 3 bordars have 1 plough there, and 34 acres of meadow, and 34 acres of woodland pasture, and 200 acres of scrubland less 10. [It is] SOKELAND of the above manor.

In Waddingworth [are] 6 carucates of land to the geld. [There is] land for 6 ploughs. [It is] SOKELAND of 'Little Sturton' [in Baumber] and of Kirkby on Bain. Half belongs to the Bishop of Durham, and half to Eudo. 40 sokemen have 8 ploughs there, and [there are] 80 acres of meadow, and 100 acres of scrubland.

In Wispington [are] 4 carucates of land to the geld. [There is] land for 8 ploughs. [It is] SOKELAND of 'Little Sturton' [in Baumber] and of Kirkby on Bain. likewise divided between the bishop and Eudo. 18 sokemen and 16 bordars have 6 ploughs there, and 140 acres of meadow. Eudo claims † both parts of the land † against the bishop.

In TATTERSHALL THORPE, Godwine and Gunnhvati had 2 carucates of land to the geld. [There is] land for 2 ploughs. Now there are 2 ploughs in demesne; and 16 villans and 4 bordars have 2 ploughs. There is a church, and 4½ fisheries [rendering] 10s, and the third part of 2 mills rendering 7s, and 24 acres of meadow, and 140 acres of woodland pasture. TRE, as now, worth 100s. Of this vill the Bishop of Durham has the third part, Eudo two [parts].

In TUMBY, Godwine and Gunnhvati had 2½ carucates of land to the geld. [There is] land for 3 ploughs. Eudo has 1 plough there, and 10 villans and 5 bordars and 2 sokemen on 2 bovates of this land with 2 ploughs. There are 20 acres of meadow, and 1½ fisheries [rendering] 2s, and 2 mills [rendering] 20s, and 370 acres of woodland, pasture in places. TRE worth 40s; now 60[s].

In EAST KEAL, Sighwat had 6 bovates of land to the geld. [There is] land for 6 oxen. Eudo has half a plough there, and 2 villans, and 5 acres of meadow. TRE, as now, [worth] 10s.

In WEST KEAL, Godwine had 6 bovates of land to the geld. [There is] land for 1 plough. Eudo has 1 plough there, and 3 bordars. There is a church, and 1 mill [rendering] 3s, and 24 acres of meadow. TRE worth 60s; now 10s.

In Hagnaby [are] 3 bovates of land to the geld. [There is] land for as many oxen. [It is] a BEREWICK. 3 villans have there 3 oxen in a plough, and 7 acres of meadow.

In Scremby [are] 2 bovates of land to the geld. [There is] land for 2 oxen. 1 villan has 1 ox there, and [there are] 4 parts of half a church.

In Sutton on Sea [are] 5 bovates of land and the fourth part of a bovate to the geld. [There is] land for 7 oxen. [It is] SOKELAND of Burgh le Marsh. 4 sokemen and 2 villans and 2 bordars have there 6 oxen in a plough, and 80 acres of meadow.

In the same place [are] 3 bovates of land and the fourth part of a bovate to the geld. [There is] land for 4 oxen. [It is] a BEREWICK of 'Little Sturton' [in Baumber].

In the same place [are] 1½ bovates of land to the geld. [There is] land for 2 oxen. 3 sokemen and 3½ villans have 1 plough there, and 25 acres of meadow. TRE, as now, worth 10s.

In Wainfleet [All Saints or St Mary] [are] 2½ bovates of land to the geld. [There is] land for as many oxen. [It is] a BEREWICK of [East or West] Keal. 2 villans and 1 bordar have half a plough there.

In Addlethorpe [are] 2 bovates of land to the geld. [There is] land for 2 oxen. [It is] a BEREWICK of [East or West] Keal. 1 villan has 1 ox in a plough there.

'CANDLESHOE' WAPENTAKE

In BURGH LE MARSH, Godwine and Toki and Godric had †10† bovates of land to the geld. [There is] land for as many oxen. Eudo and 2 men of his have 1 plough there, and 5 villans and 4 bordars and 3 sokemen with 1 plough, and 85 acres of meadow. TRE worth 40s; now 23s.

In Addlethorpe [is] 1 carucate of land and 1 bovate to the geld. [There is] land for 9 oxen. Of these, 4 bovates are waste. [It is] inland of Burgh le Marsh. 1 sokeman has 6 oxen in a plough there. There are 160 acres of meadow.

In Wainfleet [All Saints or St Mary] [is] 1 bovate of land to the geld. [There is] land for 1 ox. [It is] inland of Burgh le Marsh. 3 villans have 2 oxen in a plough there, and 4 acres of meadow, and 2 salt-pans [rendering] 16d.

In "Tric" [in Skegness] [are] 2 bovates of land to the geld. [There is] land for 2 oxen. [It is] SOKELAND of Burgh le Marsh. 1 man has 1 ox in a plough there, and 30 acres of meadow. [...]

In CANDLESBY, Grimkel and Klak had 4 carucates of land and 2 bovates to the geld. [There is] land for 5 ploughs and 3 oxen. Eudo has 5½ ploughs there, and 10 sokemen on 1 carucate of this land and 4 villans and 11 bordars with 2½ ploughs, and 2 churches. TRE worth 108s; now £8 and 12d.

In Addlethorpe [is] a BEREWICK, 1 carucate of land to the geld. [There is] land for 1 plough. 3 villans have 2 oxen in a plough there, and 100 acres of meadow.

In "Tric" [in Skegness] [is] SOKELAND, 2 bovates of land to the geld. [There is] land for 2 oxen. 2 villans have 2 oxen in a plough there, and 30 acres of meadow.

In Burgh le Marsh [is] SOKELAND, 1 carucate of land to the geld. [There is] land for 1 plough. 1 sokeman has 1 plough there.

In the same places Svartbrandr [had] 1 bovate of land to the geld. [There is] land for 1 ox. [It is] SOKELAND of Gunby [near Candlesby]. 1 sokeman has 2 oxen in a plough there. Eudo has it.

In DEXTHORPE 2 brothers had 1 carucate of land and 5 bovates to the geld. [There is] land for 13 oxen. Ivo, Eudo's man, has there 1 sokeman with 2 oxen, and 3 acres of scrubland. TRE worth 10s; now 8s.

In TATTERSHALL THORPE, Godwine and Gunnvhati had 10 bovates of land and 2 parts of 1 bovate to the geld. [There is] land for as many oxen. Eudo has 1 plough there, and 10 villans and 2 bordars with 1 plough. He has 2 parts of a church there, and the fourth part of 2 mills rendering 6s, and 3 fisheries [rendering] 6s8d, and 16 acres of meadow, and 100 acres, less 8, of woodland pasture. TRE worth £6; now 66s8d.

'ASLACOE' WAPENTAKE

In SAXBY, Eskil had 2½ carucates of land to the geld. [There is] land for 3 ploughs. Eudo has 2 ploughs there, and 1 sokeman on 2 bovates of this land and 12 villans with 2 ploughs, and 2 mills [rendering] 3s, and [there are] 6 acres of meadow. TRE, as now, worth 40s.

NORTH RIDING

BOLINGBROKE WAPENTAKE

In MAVIS ENDERBY, Godwine had half a carucate of land to the geld. [There is] land for 4 oxen. Eudo has 1 plough there, and 1 bordar, and 10 acres of meadow. TRE, as now, worth 10s.

In Raithby [near Spilsby] [is] a BEREWICK, half a bovate of land to the geld, and half the site of a mill.

In Mumby [are] 6 bovates of land to the geld. [There is] land for 1 plough. 1 villan and 1 bordar have there 2 oxen in a plough, and [there are] 10 acres of meadow.

In Skirbeck Quarter [in Boston] [are] 2 bovates of land to the geld. [There is] land for 1 ox. 8 villans have 1 plough there. [It is] SOKELAND of Tattershall.

In TATTERSHALL THORPE, Wulfmær had 2 carucates of land to the geld. [There is] land for 2 ploughs, which are there, with 18 villans and 4 bordars. It is worth 20s.

XXX. The land of Drogo de La Beuvriere

WEST RIDING

In BARROW UPON HUMBER, Earl Morcar had 9 carucates of land and 2 bovates to the geld. [There is] land for 18½ ploughs. Drogo de la Beuvriere has 4 ploughs there, and 50 sokemen on 2 carucates of this land and 7 villans with 8 ploughs, and 1 mill [rendering] 13s4d. TRE worth £32; now £15; tallage 100s. SOKELAND of this manor

In Goxhill [are] 2 carucates of land to the geld. [There is] land for 4 ploughs. 20 sokemen have 3 ploughs there, and 300 acres of meadow.

In NORMANBY 3 brothers had 5 carucates of land to the geld. [There is] land for 5 ploughs. Joscelin, Drogo's man, has 1 plough there, and 16 sokemen and 4 villans and 3 bordars with 4 ploughs and 2 oxen, and the site of 1 mill, and 100 acres of meadow, and 72 acres of scrubland. TRE [...].

In Thealby [is] 1 carucate of land to the geld. [There is] land for 1 plough. [It is] SOKELAND of Normanby. There are 3 sokemen with 1 plough, and 8 acres of meadow.

In BARROW UPON HUMBER, Earnwine and Siward

had 2 carucates of land to the geld. [There is] land for 4 ploughs. Theobald, Drogo's man, with 4 villans, has 1 plough there. TRE worth 40s; now it is valued in the above manor.

In 'KETTLEBY' [in Bigby], Ulf had 3 bovates of land and the third part of 1 bovate to the geld. [There is] land for 1 plough. Rayner, Drogo's man, has 1 plough there, and 5 villans having 5 oxen in a plough, and 13 acres of meadow. TRE worth 40s; now 30s.

In KIRMINGTON, Ulf had 4 bovates of land to the geld. [There is] land for 12 oxen. Robert, Drogo's man, has 1 plough there, and 1 villan. TRE worth 40s; now 20s.

In [Great or Little] LIMBER, Ulf had 1 carucate of land to the geld. [There is] land for 4 ploughs. It is waste. TRE it was worth 40s.

In KEELBY or 'COTON' [in Brocklesby], Rolf had 1 carucate of land to the geld. [There is] land for 3 ploughs. Robert, Drogo's man, has 1 plough there, and 10 villans and 1 bordar with 2 ploughs, and 1 salt-pan [rendering] 12d, and 40 acres of meadow. TRE worth 40s; now 30[s]; tallage 10s. #

In 'Lobingham' [in Killingholme] [are] 3 bovates of land to the geld. [There is] land for 6 oxen. [It is] SOKELAND of 'Coton' [in Brocklesby]. 1 sokeman has there 1 ox in a plough, and [there are] 30 acres of meadow.

In WEELSBY [in Great Grimsby], Rolf had 4 carucates of land to the geld. [There is] land for 6 ploughs. Robert, Drogo's man, has there 2 villans and 15 sokemen on 2 carucates of this land and 5 bovates and the third part of 1 bovate. They themselves have 2 ploughs, and 80 acres of meadow. TRE worth £6; now 100s. SOKELAND of this manor

In Little Coates [in Great Grimsby] [are] 7 bovates of land to the geld. [There is] land for 14 oxen. 6 sokemen have 1 plough there, and 30 acres of meadow.

In Great Grimsby [is] 1 bovate of land to the geld. [There is] land for 2 oxen. [It is] a BEREWICK. 4 villans have 1 ox in a plough there, and [there is] 1 acre of meadow.

In Laceby [is] 1 bovate of land to the geld. [There is] land for 2 oxen. [It is] SOKELAND. 1 villan has 1 ox in a plough there.

In 'Itterby' [in Cleethorpes] [is] 1 bovate of land to the geld. [There is] land for 1½ oxen. 1 villan has 1 ox in a plough there.

In [North and South] Killingholme [is] half a carucate of land to the geld. [There is] land for 10 oxen. [It is] a BEREWICK of 'Coton' [in Brocklesby]. It is waste. There are 30 acres of meadow.

[Folio 360V: LINCOLNSHIRE]

In STAINTON LE VALE, Rolf had 6 bovates of land to the geld. [There is] land for 2 ploughs and 2 oxen. Geoffrey, Drogo's man, has 1 plough there, and 1 sokeman on 1 toft and 7 villans with 1 plough, and the site of the mill, and 45 acres of meadow. TRE worth 50s; now 26s.

In THIMBLEBY, Osmund had 3 carucates of land and 6 bovates to the geld. [There is] land for 5 ploughs. Geoffrey,

Drogo's man, has 1 plough there, and 15 sokemen on 2 carucates and 6 bovates of this land and 4 villans with 2 ploughs and 2 oxen ploughing, and 1 mill [rendering] 9s4d, and [there are] 240 acres of meadow, and 240 acres of scrubland. TRE worth £4; now £3; tallage 20s.

In LANGTON [near Horncastle], Arnketil and Ælfric had 2 carucates of land to the geld. [There is] land for 3 ploughs. Geoffrey, Drogo's man, has 1 plough there, and 5 sokemen on 2 bovates of this land and 10 villans with 1½ ploughs, and 160 acres of meadow, and 200 acres of woodland pasture, and 500 acres of scrubland. TRE, as now, [worth] 40s.

In NORTH ORMSBY, Ulf and Scemund had 4 carucates of land and 7 bovates to the geld. [There is] land for 8 ploughs. Geoffrey, Drogo's man, has 1 plough there, and 10 sokemen on 2 carucates and 2 bovates of this land and 1 bordar with 1 plough, and 40 acres of meadow, and 10 acres of scrubland. TRE worth 70s; now 45s; tallage 10s.

In the same place Alwine had 2 bovates of land to the geld. [There is] land for 1 plough.

In STROXTON HUNDRED, Earl Morcar had 2 carucates of land to the geld. [...] Guy, Drogo's man, has there 2 ploughs in demesne; and 4 sokemen and 9 villans and 1 bordar having 3 ploughs. There is a church and a priest, and 30 acres of meadow; Archbishop Thomas has 15, and Hugh de Grandmesnil 15. TRE worth £6; now 100s.

In Great Ponton [is] a Berewick of this manor, 4 carucates of land to the geld. [There is] land for 3 ploughs. There is 1 bordar, and 1 mill [rendering] 6s. [There is] woodland of thorn, 8 furlongs long and 1 broad.

In another Ponton [Little Ponton] [are] 2 carucates of land to the geld. [There is] land for 2 ploughs. [It is] a BEREWICK. There are 2 bordars.

In STOKE ROCHFORD HALF-HUNDRED, SOKELAND of Grantham, Morcar had 1½ carucates of land to the geld. [There is] land for 12 oxen. Kolgrimr, Drogo's man, has half a plough there, and 3 villans with 1 plough, and 2 mills [rendering] 10s.

In NORTH STOKE, Earl Morcar had 10 bovates of land to the geld. [There is] land for 1 plough. Kolgrimr has it of Drogo, and the rent-paying tenants plough there [and] pay 7s. [There are] 16 acres of meadow.

In CARLTON LE MOORLAND HUNDRED, Morcar had 12 carucates of land to the geld. [There is] land for 16 ploughs. Drogo has 2 ploughs there, and 9 sokemen on 12 bovates of this land and 9 villans and 10 bordars with 5 ploughs. There is a church and a priest, and 255 acres of meadow. TRE worth £10; now £9.

'BELTISLOE' WAPENTAKE

In HOLYWELL HUNDRED, Earl Morcar had 7 carucates of land to the geld. [There is] land for 7 ploughs. [It is] SOKELAND of Castle Bytham. The men, Ingelrann and Earnwulf, have 1 plough there, and 6 sokemen and 1 villan and 5 bordars with 2 ploughs. There is 1 mill [rendering] 4s, and 200 acres of scrubland. TRE worth £4; now 40s; tallage 12s.

In CASTLE BYTHAM, Morcar had 9 carucates of land to the geld. [There is] land for as many ploughs. Drogo has there 3 ploughs in demesne; and 24 sokemen on half of this land and 7 villans with 8 ploughs. 7 Frenchmen have 2 ploughs there, and 3 iron-works rendering 40s8d. [There is] woodland, pasture in places, 1½ leagues long and as many broad, and 60 acres of meadow. TRE worth £19.10s; now £10. SOKELAND of this manor

In 'Counthorpe' [in Castle Bytham] [are] 6 carucates of land to the geld. [There is] land for 6 ploughs. Walter, Drogo's man, has 2 ploughs there, and 12 sokemen and 6 bordars with 3 ploughs. TRE worth £10; now £6. Ulric, another of his men, has there 5 sokemen with half a plough. TRE worth 20s; now 10s.

In LITTLE BYTHAM HUNDRED. Edward had 7 carucates of land to the geld. [There is] land for 7 ploughs. Drogo has 2 ploughs there, and 6 sokemen on 1 carucate of this land and 18 villans and 3 bordars with 5 ploughs, and 1 mill [rendering] 3s, and an iron-works [rendering] 40s, and 7 acres of meadow, and 300 acres of woodland, pasture in places. TRE, as now, worth £6; tallage 40s.

In WITHAM ON THE HILL Hundred. Ulf had 5 bovates of land to the geld. [There is] land for 5 oxen. Drogo has 1 plough there, and 6 villans and 2 bordars with 1 plough, and 30 acres of meadow, and 40 acres of woodland pasture. TRE worth 30s; now 40[s]. Kolgrimr holds it. The Abbot of Peterborough claims 1 bovate in the SOKE of Gilbert.

In HAGWORTHINGHAM, Æthelstan had 1 carucate of land to the geld. [There is] land for 14 oxen. Robert, Drogo's man, has 1 plough there, and 8 villans with 1 plough, and 1 mill [rendering] 18d, and 40 acres of meadow. TRE worth 50s; now 30[s].

In the vill itself Drogo has a hall with sake and soke, and 1 toft.

In Anwick he has 5½ bovates of land to the geld. It is worth 25s.

In Ruskington he has 6 bovates of land to the geld, and he has 1 plough there, and it is worth 20s.

'WALSHCROFT' WAPENTAKE WALESBY HUNDRED

In CLAXBY [near Walesby] and Normanby le Wold, Ulf had 6 bovates of land to the geld. [There is] land for 12 oxen. Kolsveinn, Drogo's man, has 1 plough there, and 2 sokemen on 1 bovate of this land and 5 villans and 2 bordars with 1 plough, and the fourth part of a mill [rendering] 8d, and 32½ acres of meadow, and 40 acres of scrubland. TRE, as now, worth 30s.

In Coningsby [is] 1 bovate of land to the geld. [It is] SOKELAND of Hagworthingham. There is 1 bordar and 1 villan with 1 ox in a plough, and 2 acres of meadow, and 20 acres of scrubland.

XXXI. The land of Walter d'Aincourt

In BELTON [near Grantham] HUNDRED, Thorir had 4 carucates of land to the geld. [There is] land for 4 ploughs. Walter d'Aincourt has 2 ploughs there in demesne; and 8 villans and 5 bordars with 1 plough. There is a church, and 3 mills [rendering] 30s, and 60 acres of meadow. TRE worth £3; now 4[l]; tallage 20s.

In GREAT GONERBY HUNDRED, Siward and Alwig had 1½ carucates of land to the geld. [There is] land for 2 ploughs. Alwig, Walter's man, has 1½ ploughs there, and 6 villans and 4 bordars with 2 ploughs, and 2 mills [rendering] 16s, and 22½ acres of meadow. TRE, as now, worth 40s.

In OLD SOMERBY, Thorir had 2 carucates of land and 2 bovates to the geld. [There is] land for 18 oxen. Reginald, Walter's man, has 2 ploughs there, and 5 villans with 1½ ploughs. There is a church and a priest with 1 plough, and 180 acres of woodland, pasture in places. Walter has the wara. TRE worth £4; now 3[l]; tallage 20s. Thorir held this manor TRE, and Northmann after him in the same time, but the men of the neighbourhood and of the wapentake do not know on what basis he had it, because they have not seen him do any service for it.

In Humby [are] 4 carucates of land to the geld. [There is] land for 4 ploughs and 6 oxen. [It is] SOKELAND of Old Somerby. There are 15 sokemen and 1 villan and 1 bordar with 5 ploughs, and 20 acres of woodland pasture, and 220 acres of scrubland.

In 'WESTHORPE' [in Old Somerby], Thorir had 2 carucates of land to the geld. [There is] land for 2½ ploughs. Reginald, Walter's man, has 2 ploughs there, and 1 villan and 9 bordars with 1 ox in a plough, and 3 mills [rendering] 40s, and [there are] 19 acres of meadow. TRE, as now, worth £4.

In 'Houghton' [in Grantham] [is] 1 carucate of land to the geld. [There is] land for 1 plough. [It is] a BEREWICK of 'Westhorpe' [in Old Somerby]. There is 1 bordar.

'BELTISLOE' WAPENTAKE

In "SUDWELLE" [in Swayfield], Thorir had 2 carucates of land to the geld. [There is] land for 2 ploughs. Walter has 2 ploughs there, and 7 sokemen and 6 villans and 1 bordar with 3 ploughs, and 4 acres of meadow, and 130 acres of woodland, pasture in places. TRE worth 40s; now 60[s]; tallage 10s.

In Swinstead HUNDRED [is] half a carucate of land to the geld. [It is] a BEREWICK of "Suduuelle" [in Swayfield]. Odo, Walter's man, has half a plough there, and 1 villan, and half an acre of meadow, and 15 acres of scrubland. TRE worth 10s; now 15[s].

In BURTON-LE-COGGLES HUNDRED, Arnketil and Leofric had 3 carucates of land to the geld. [There is] land for 3 ploughs. Walter has there 4 villans and 3 bordars with 1 plough. Of this land 2 of his men have half, and they have there 2 ploughs, and 6 villans and 3 bordars with 2 ploughs, and 31½ acres of meadow, and 323 acres of woodland pasture, and 1 mill [rendering] 2s. TRE, as now, worth 60s.

| 'ASWARDHURN' WAPENTAKE |

In INGOLDSBY, Siward had 4 bovates of land and the third part of 1 bovate to the geld. [There is] land for 6 oxen. It is waste. TRE [worth] 10s; now 3[s]. There are 3½ acres of meadow, and 16 acres of scrubland.

In BRANSTON HUNDRED, Hemming had 12 carucates of land to the geld. [There is] land for 10 ploughs. Walter has 5 ploughs there in demesne; and 2 sokemen on 2 carucates of this land and 48 villans and 23 bordars with 8 ploughs. There is a church, and a priest, and 4 mills rendering 27s, and 3 fisheries rendering 30d, and 60 acres of meadow, and woodland pasture 7½ furlongs long and 5½ furlongs broad. TRE worth £20; now £26.

In Walcot [in Billingham] HUNDRED [are] 4 carucates of land to the geld. [There is] land [...]. [It is] SOKELAND of this manor. 7 sokemen and 2 bordars have 4 ploughs there, and 16 acres of meadow.

In Timberland HUNDRED [are] 5 carucates of land and 6 bovates to the geld and the fourth part of a bovate. [There is] land for 4 ploughs. 18 sokemen and 3 bordars have 7½ ploughs there.

In Kirkby GREEN HUNDRED and Scopwick HUNDRED [are] 7½ carucates of land to the geld. [There is] land for 6 ploughs. 14 sokemen and 2 bordars have 5 ploughs there, and 4 mills rendering 21s4d, and 25 acres of meadow.

In THE SAME PLACES Godric had 10 carucates of land to the geld. [There is] land for 9 ploughs. Walter has 2 ploughs there, and 32 sokemen on 6 carucates and 2 bovates of this land and 7 villans and 2 bordars with 13 ploughs. There is a church, and a priest, and 2 mills [rendering] 20s, and 26½ acres of meadow. TRE worth 70s; now £4.

In the two hundreds of BLANKNEY, Hemming had 24 carucates of land to the geld. [There is] land for 13 ploughs. Walter has 3 ploughs there, and 22 sokemen and 10 villans and 4 bordars with 10 ploughs. There is a church, and a priest, and 60 acres of meadow, and scrubland 7 furlongs long and 3 broad. TRE worth £6; now 7[l]. The tallage [belongs] to Branston. Of this land his knights hold 2 carucates, and they have 1 plough there, and 2 bordars; and it is worth 10s.

In POTTERHANWORTH HUNDRED, Healfdene and his 2 brothers had 12 carucates of land to the geld. [There is] land for 6 ploughs. Walter has 2 ploughs there in demesne; and 9 sokemen on 3 carucates of this land and 22 villans and 11 bordars having 9½ ploughs. There is a church, and a priest, with 1 carucate. Of this land a certain knight of his holds 2 carucates, and has 1 plough there, and 2 villans with half a plough; and it is worth 20s. There are 150 acres of meadow, and 150 acres of woodland pasture. TRE worth £3; now £4.

In Metheringham [are] 8½ carucates of land to the geld. [There is] land for 4 ploughs and 2 oxen. Wintrehard, Walter's man, has 2 ploughs there, and 10 sokemen and 8 villans and 16 bordars with 6 ploughs, and 2 mills [rendering] 12s, and [there are] 150 acres of meadow, and 60 acres of scrubland. TRE worth £3; now 4[l]. [It is] SOKELAND of Branston.

[Folio 361V: LINCOLNSHIRE]

XXXII. [The land of] Norman d'Arcy

NORTH RIDING

In STALLINGBOROUGH, Ulf and Styr had 2½ carucates of land to the geld. [There is] land for 4 ploughs. Norman d'Arcy has 2 ploughs there in demesne; and 1 sokeman and 18 villans and 1 bordar with 2 ploughs. There is half a church and the site of a mill, and 2 salt-pans [rendering] 3s, and 400 acres of meadow. TRE worth £4; now 7[l]; tallage 20s.

In Brocklesby [are] 1½ bovates of land to the geld. [There is] land for 3 oxen. There is 1 sokeman and 2 villans and 1 bordar with 1 plough, and 10 acres of meadow.

In 'LOBINGHAM' [in Killingholme], Fulcric had 4½ bovates of land to the geld. [There is] land for 9 oxen. Berewold, Norman's man, has 1 plough there, and 2 villans with 3 oxen in a plough, and half a mill [rendering] 4s, and 40 acres of meadow. TRE worth 20s; now 30[s].

In KEELBY, Grimkel had 5 bovates of land and the third part of a bovate to the geld. [There is] land for 10½ oxen. Geoffrey, Norman's man, has 1 plough there, and 4 villans and 2 bordars with 2 oxen in a plough. TRE worth 40s; now the same.

In [North or South] OWERSBY Ingimund had 2 bovates of land and the third part of a bovate to the geld. [There is] land for 4½ oxen. Geoffrey, Norman's man, has half a plough there, and 1 sokeman and 4 villans and 2 bordars with 1 plough, and 60 acres of meadow. TRE, as now, worth 20s.

In THORGANBY, Grimkel had 14 bovates of land to the geld. [There is] land for 3½ ploughs. Gamelin, Norman's man, has 1 plough there, and 8 villans and 2 bordars with 1 plough, and 1½ mills [rendering] 8s, and 13 acres of meadow. TRE, as now, worth 40s; tallage 10s.

In CLAXBY [near Walesby], Ketil had 2 bovates of land and Godwine 1 bovate of land, inland, to the geld. [There is] land for 5 oxen. Geoffrey, Norman's man, has half a plough there, and 2 villans with 1 ox in a plough, and 15 acres of meadow, and 15 acres of scrubland. TRE, as now, [worth] 8s.

In CROXBY, Fulcric had 3 bovates of land to the geld. [There is] land for 9 oxen. Odo, Norman's man, has half a plough there, and 3 villans and 1 bordar with 3 oxen in a plough, and [there is] 1 acre of meadow. TRE, as now, [worth] 20s. 1 bovate belongs to the soke of Berengar de Tosny.

In Swinhope [is] 1 bovate of land to the geld. [It is] inland of Croxby. There is 1 villan having 1 ox in a plough.

In CAWKWELL, Ketil had 1½ carucates of land to the geld. [There is] land for 12 oxen. Roger, Norman's man, has 1 plough there, and 5 villans and 6 bordars with 1 plough. There is a priest and a church, and 70 acres of meadow. TRE worth 40s; now 60[s].

SOUTH RIDING

In BECKERING, Thorulf had 2 bovates of land to the geld. [There is] land for 4 oxen. Herbert, Norman's man, has there 2 oxen in a plough, and 1 sokeman on 1 toft having likewise 2 oxen in a plough, and 2 acres of meadow. TRE, as now, [worth] 8s.

WEST RIDING

In WINTERTON, Fulcric had 12 bovates of land to the geld. [There is] land for 12 oxen. Norman has 2 ploughs there, and 1 sokeman on 2 bovates of this land and 10 villans with 1 plough. TRE worth £4; now 3[l]; tallage 20s.

In Roxby [are] 4 bovates of land to the geld. [There is] land for 4 oxen. [It is] SOKELAND. 1 sokeman has 3 oxen in a plough there, and 7 acres of meadow.

In WALCOT [in Alkborough], Fulcric had 10 bovates of land to the geld. [There is] land for 10 oxen. Robert, Norman's man, has there 3 villans with 1 plough, and 40 acres of meadow, and 10 acres of scrubland. TRE worth 20s; now 16[s]; tallage 4s.

In 'Haythby' [in West Halton] [are] 2 bovates of land to the geld. [There is] land for 2 oxen. [It is] inland of Walcot [in Alkborough]. There is 1 villan with 1 ox in a plough, and 4 acres of meadow.

In FLIXBOROUGH, Fulcric had 11 carucates of land and 7 bovates to the geld. [There is] land for as many ploughs and oxen. Norman has 4½ ploughs there in demesne; and 3 sokemen on 2 carucates of this land and 29 villans and 6 bordars with 4½ ploughs. There are 2 sites of mills, and 205 acres of meadow, and 120 acres of scrubland. TRE, as now, worth £8; tallage 40s.

In Thealby [is] half a carucate of land to the geld. [There is] land for 4 oxen. [It is] inland. 3 villans have there 3 oxen in a plough, and 7 acres of meadow.

In WOOTTON, Aghete had 6 bovates of land to the geld. [There is] land for 12 oxen. Norman has 1 plough there, and 2 sokemen and 2 bordars. TRE worth 40s; now 20[s]; tallage 5s.

In ULCEBY [near Wootton], Ulfkil had 6 bovates of land to the geld. [There is] land for 2 ploughs and 2 oxen. Norman has, [and] Odo of him, 1 plough there, and 4 sokemen on 3 bovates of this land, and 2 villans with half a plough, and 9 acres of meadow. TRE, as now, [worth] 20s; tallage 5s.

In [North and South] KILLINGHOLME, Fulcric had 4 carucates of land and 7 bovates to the geld. [There is] land for 10 ploughs. Norman has 3 ploughs there, and 32 sokemen

on 3 carucates of this land, and 1 bordar with 4 ploughs, and [there are] 200 acres of meadow. TRE worth £5; now 6[l]; tallage 40s.

In Immingham [are] 5 bovates of land to the geld. [There is] land for 2 ploughs. [It is] SOKELAND. 3 sokemen have there 3 oxen in a plough, and 15 acres of meadow. [It is] SOKELAND.

In Habrough [are] 3 bovates of land and 2 parts of a bovate to the geld. [There is] land for 7 oxen. 1 sokeman has 1 plough there.

In KIRKBY GREEN HUNDRED and Scopwick HUNDRED, Gardulf had 6 bovates of land to the geld. [There is] land for half a plough. Norman has there 2 oxen in a plough, and 1 sokeman and 2 bordars having 2 oxen in a plough, and 2½ acres of meadow. TRE, as now, worth 20s.

'LANGOE' WAPENTAKE

In Martin [in Timberland] [are] 2 carucates of land and 3 bovates and the fifth part of 1 bovate to the geld. [There is] land for 12 oxen. 7 sokemen and 2 bordars have 2 ploughs there. It is SOKELAND.

In STUBTON, Toki had 5½ bovates of land to the geld. [There is] land for 1 plough. Now it is waste, except for 1 bordar, and 34 acres of meadow. TRE [worth] 10s; now 5[s].

IN THE SAME PLACE Ulfkil had 1 carucate of land to the geld. [There is] land for 1 plough. Gamelin, Norman's man, has half a plough there, and 3 bordars, and 5 acres of meadow. TRE, as now, [worth] 10s.

YARBOROUGH WAPENTAKE

In LITTLE LIMBER, Styr had half a carucate of land to the geld. [There is] land for 2 ploughs. Herbert, Norman's man, has there 4 villans with half a plough. TRE worth 20s; now 10s.

In [Great or Little] Coates [in Great Grimsby] [are] 4½ bovates of land to the geld. [There is] land for 9 oxen. [It is] SOKELAND of Keelby. Richard has there 2 villans and 4 sokemen with 1½ ploughs, and 100 acres of meadow.

[Folio 362: LINDSEY]

In SCOTHERN, Godric had 9 bovates of land to the geld. [There is] land for 12 oxen. Norman has 1 plough there, and 5 villans and 3 bordars having 6 oxen in a plough, and 23 acres of meadow. TRE, as now, worth 20s; tallage 5s.

In CROSBY [in Scunthorpe] and 'South Conesby' [in Crosby] [are] 9½ bovates of land to the geld. [There is] land for as many oxen. [It is] inland of 'North Conesby' [in Flixborough]. 4 villans have 1 plough there.

In SOUTH ORMSBY, Eadric and Gamal had 2½ carucates of land to the geld. [There is] land for 3½ ploughs. Herbert, Norman's man, has 1 plough there, and 5 sokemen and 3 villans and 1 bordar with 1 plough, and 70 acres of meadow. TRE worth 40s; now the same.

In NOCTON, Ulf had 23 carucates of land to the geld.

[There is] land [...]. Norman has 5 ploughs there in demesne; and 26 sokemen and 9 villans and 3 bordars with 9 ploughs and 2 oxen in a plough. There is a church, and a priest, and 100 less 5 acres of meadow, and 40 acres of scrubland. TRE worth £6; now £10; tallage 40s.

IN THE SAME PLACE Oswulf had 1 carucate of land to the geld. Norman has there 1 villan, and 5 oxen in a plough. This is valued in the above manor.

In Dunston, Ulf had 12 carucates of land to the geld. [There is] land [...]. [It is] SOKELAND of Nocton. Norman found there 3 villans and 31 sokemen and 13 bordars having 9 ploughs, and 6 mills [rendering] 24s, and 12 acres of meadow, and 80 acres of scrubland. There is a church and a priest.

The men of Coleby [near Boothby Graffoe] Withhold 6s 10d of the customary dues.

The men of [sic] Harmston withhold 8s of the customary dues.

XXXIII. The land of Norman Crassus

In 'MIDDLE CARLTON' [in North Carlton], Aghmund had 2 carucates of land and 2 bovates to the geld. [There is] land for 18 oxen. Norman Crassus has there 10 sokemen on 12 bovates of this land and 2 villans and 3 bordars with 1 plough and 2 oxen in a plough, and 15 acres of meadow. TRE worth 16s; now 20[s]; tallage 40s.

In CANWICK, Wælhræfn had 1 carucate of land [...] to the geld. [There is] land for 6 oxen. Norman has 1 plough there, and 25 acres of meadow. TRE worth 20s; now the same.

XXXIIII. The land of Erneis de Buron

In MELTON ROSS, Eadgifu had 3 carucates of land to the geld. [There is] land for 7 ploughs. Erneis de Buron has 5 ploughs there, and 3 sokemen on 1 bovate of this land, and 30 villans and 9 bordars with 4 ploughs. There is a church and a priest, and 78 acres of meadow. TRE worth £6; now 8[l]; tallage 40s.

In ULCEBY [near Wootton], Grim and Siward had 4 carucates of land to the geld. [There is] land for 10 ploughs. Erneis has 4 ploughs there, and 30 sokemen on 1 carucate of this land and 8 villans and 10 bordars with 9 ploughs. There is a church and a priest, and half a mill [rendering] 10s and 500 eels, and 60 acres of meadow. TRE worth £5; now 8[l]; tallage 40s.

In MESSINGHAM, Eadgifu had 10½ bovates of land to the geld. [There is] land for 12 oxen. Turstin, Erneis' man, has 1 plough there, and 8 villans with 1½ ploughs, and 1 mill [rendering] 5s, and 10 acres of meadow. TRE worth 60s; now 20[s]; tallage 10s.

In BARNETBY LE WOLD, Grim and Ulf and Fin had 7 bovates of land to the geld. [There is] land for 14 oxen. Wulfric, Erneis' man, has 1 plough there, and 12 sokemen on 1 bovate of this land and 5 tofts and 5 villans with 1 plough, and half a church. TRE worth 20s; now 16[s]; tallage 4s.

In THORNTON CURTIS and Burnham, Grim had 2 bovates of land to the geld. [There is] land for 4 oxen. Wulfric, Erneis' man, has there 3 oxen in a plough, and 1 sokeman on 1 toft and 7 villans with 3 oxen in a plough. TRE worth 16s; now 8s; tallage 2s.

In GOXHILL, Grim had 10 bovates of land to the geld. [There is] land for 2½ ploughs. Wulfric, Ernei's man, has half a plough there, and 25 sokemen and 5 villans with 2½ ploughs, and 60 acres of meadow. TRE worth 30s; now 40s[s]; tallage 10s.

In NETTLETON, Gamal had 5 bovates of land to the geld. [There is] land for 15 oxen. There are 3 villans and 3 bordars with 2 oxen in a plough, and 1 mill. [rendering] 12d, and 20 acres of meadow. TRE, as now, [worth] 20s.

In 'KETTLEBY' [in Bigby], Eadgifu had 3 bovates of land and the third part of 1 bovate to the geld. [There is] land for 1 plough. Turstin, Erneis' man, has there 3 oxen in a plough, and 1 sokeman on 5 acres of this land, and 6 villans and 1 bordar with 1 plough, and [there are] 14 acres of meadow, and 3 acres of scrubland. TRE worth 40s; now 20[s].

In BROCKLESBY, Eadgifu had 3 bovates of land to the geld. [There is] land for 6 oxen. Ranulph, Erneis' man, has 1 plough there, and 2 sokemen on 1 bovate of this land and 1 villan with 5 oxen in a plough, and 80 acres of meadow. TRE, as now, [worth] 20s.

In Habrough and Newsham [are] 2 bovates of land to the geld. [There is] land for 4 oxen. [It is] SOKELAND of this manor. 2 villans have there 5 oxen in a plough, and 30 acres of meadow.

In the same places [are] 2 bovates of land to the geld. [There is] land for 4 oxen. Ulfkil had it. Now it is waste.

In WRAGBY, Countess Judith had 6½ bovates of land to the geld. [There is] land for 12 oxen. Erneis has 1 plough there, and 10 villans with 1½ ploughs. There is a church and a priest, and half a mill [rendering] 12d, and 24 acres of meadow. [There is] woodland pasture 4 furlongs long and 4 broad, [and] scrubland 5 furlongs long and 5 broad. TRE worth £14; now £10; tallage £10.

[Folio 362V: LINCOLNSHIRE]

SOKELAND [OF] WRAGBY

In Hatton [are] 5 carucates of land to the geld. [There is] land for 8 ploughs. There are 15 sokemen and 10 bordars with 4 ploughs, and 100 acres of meadow, and 230 acres of scrubland.

In Collow [are] 1½ carucates of land to the geld. [There is] land for 4 ploughs. There are 2 sokemen and 4 bordars having 2 oxen in a plough. In demesne Erneis [has] 1 plough, and 2 sites of mills, and [there are] 8 acres of meadow.

In Panton [are] 2 carucates of land to the geld. [There is] land for 3 ploughs. There are 2 ploughs in demesne; and 13 sokemen and 6 bordars with 2 ploughs. There is a church, and 40 acres of meadow.

In 'Hardwick' [in Panton] [are] 5 bovates of land and the third part of 1 bovate to the geld. [There is] land for 11 oxen. 6 sokemen have 1 plough there, and 53 acres of meadow.

In West Barkwith [are] 2 carucates and 2 bovates of land to the geld. [There is] land for 3 ploughs. 10 sokemen have 1 plough there. Erneis [has] 1 plough in demesne, and [there is] a church, and 33 acres of meadow.

In East Torrington [are] 2½ carucates of land to the geld and the third part of 1 bovate to the geld. [There is] land for 4 ploughs. Erneis has 1 plough there, and 12 sokemen having nothing.

In Langton by Wragby [are] 2 bovates of land to the geld. [There is] land for 4 oxen. 1 villan has there 2 oxen in a plough, and [there are] 21 acres of scrubland.

In Fulnetby [are] 3 carucates of land to the geld. [There is] land for 5 ploughs. 12 sokemen have 3 ploughs there, and 100 acres of meadow, and [there are] 120 acres of scrubland.

In Rand [are] 3 carucates of land to the geld. [There is] land for 5 ploughs. 8 sokemen and 5 bordars have there 2 ploughs and 5 oxen in a plough, and [there are] 40 acres of meadow, and 20 acres of scrubland.

In Girsby and Burgh on Bain [are] 6 bovates of land to the geld. [There is] land for 12 oxen. 3 sokemen have 1½ ploughs there, and [there are] 12 acres of meadow.

In Kingthorpe [are] 2 bovates of land and 2 parts of half a bovate to the geld. [There is] land for 5 oxen. 1 villan has there 1 ox in a plough, and [there are] 4 acres of meadow, and 80 acres of woodland, pasture in places.

In COLEBY [in West Halton], Wege and Barth had 2 carucates of land and 1 bovate to the geld. [There is] land for 17 oxen. John, Erneis' man, has 2 ploughs there, and 1 sokeman on 1 toft and 5 villans and 2 bordars with 2 ploughs, and [there are] 10 acres of meadow. TRE worth 40s; now 50[s]; tallage 10s.

BEREWICKS

In Walcot [in Alkborough] [are] 6 bovates of land to the geld. [There is] land for 4 oxen. 1 villan has there 2 oxen in a plough, and [there are] 24 acres of meadow, and 4 acres of scrubland.

In Winterton [is] 1 bovate of land to the geld. [There is] land for 1 ox. It is waste.

In GRAYINGHAM, Eadgifu had 1 carucate of land to the geld. [There is] land for 12 oxen. Erneis has 2 ploughs there, and 8 villans and 1 bordar with 1½ ploughs, and [there are] 10 acres of meadow. TRE, as now, worth 40s.

XXXV. The land of Ralph Paynel

In BROUGHTON, Maerle-Sveinn had 10 carucates of land and 6 bovates to the geld. [There is] land for 12 ploughs. Ralph Paynel has 2 ploughs there, and 29 sokemen on 5 carucates and 3 bovates of this land and 34 villans and 8 bordars with 13 ploughs. There is a church and a priest, and 1 mill [rendering] 2s, and 240 acres of meadow, and scrubland 2

leagues long and 1 broad. TRE worth £10; now 7[l]; but in the past year it was worth £10.

IN THE SAME PLACE Grimkel had 7 bovates of land to the geld. [There is] land for 1 plough. Ralph has 1 plough there, and 5 rent-paying tenants with 1 plough, and 10 acres of meadow. TRE worth 40s; now [...].

In DUNHOLME, Maerle-Sveinn had 2 carucates of land to the geld. [There is] land for 2 ploughs. A certain knight of Ralph's has half a plough there, and 4 sokemen on 1 carucate of this land and 4 villans with 1½ ploughs, and [there are] 17 acres of meadow. TRE worth 10s; now 16[s]; tallage 4s.

In ROXBY, Maerle-Sveinn had 5 carucates of land and 2 bovates. [There is] land for 6 ploughs. Ralph has there 2 ploughs and 2 oxen in a plough, and 23 sokemen on 21 bovates of this land and 8 villans and 4 bordars with 6 ploughs, and [there are] 44 acres of meadow, and 6 acres of scrubland. TRE worth £6; now 4[l]; tallage 20s. Herbert holds it.

In Winterton [are] 2 bovates of land to the geld. [There is] land for 2 oxen. 2 villans have there 2 oxen in a plough.

In [Middle or West] RASEN, Maerle-Sveinn had 6 carucates of land and 6 bovates to the geld. [There is] land for 9 ploughs. Ralph has 4 ploughs there in demesne; and 37 sokemen on 4 carucates and 7 bovates of this land and 15 villans with 9 ploughs, and 1 mill [rendering] 2s, and [there are] 300 acres of meadow. TRE worth £16; now £10; tallage £6.

In the other Rasen [Middle Rasen or West Rasen] [are] 14 bovates of land to the geld. [There is] land for 3 ploughs. [It is] SOKELAND of this manor. 16 sokemen have 2½ ploughs there, and 160 acres of meadow.

In North Willingham [are] 9 bovates of land to the geld. [There is] land for 18 oxen. 19 sokemen have 2 ploughs there.

In TEALBY, Maerle-Sveinn had 14 bovates of land to the geld. [There is] land for 2½ ploughs. Ralph has †10† sokemen there on 3 bovates and 10 villans with 1 plough, and 3 mills [rendering] 12s, and 89 acres of meadow, and 3 sites of mills. TRE worth £12; now 50s; tallage 9s.

In WITHAM ON THE HILL, Maerle-Sveinn had 1 carucate of land to the geld. [There is] land for 1 plough. Hakun, Ralph's man, has there 2 oxen in a plough, and 4 villans and 1 bordar with 1 plough, and 10 acres of meadow, and 84 acres of woodland. TRE worth 20s; now 10s8d.

In Swinstead, Maerle-Sveinn had 5 carucates of land to the geld. [There is] land for 5 ploughs. There was 1 thegn whom King Edward gave to Maerle-Sveinn, as the men of the hundred bear witness. Ralph has there 22 sokemen and 4 villans with 6 ploughs, and [there are] 18 acres of meadow, and 200 acres of scrubland.

In BURTON-LE-COGGLES, Earl Morcar had 6 bovates of land to the geld. [There is] land for 6 oxen. Ogier, Ralph's man, has 1 plough there, and 5 villans with half a plough, and [there are] 12 acres of meadow. [There is] woodland 7 furlongs long and 5½ furlongs broad. Besides this [there are] 280 acres of woodland, pasture in places. TRE worth 20s; now 30[s].

In Osgodby [near West Rasen] [is] 1 bovate of land to the geld. [There is] land for 2 oxen. 2 sokemen have half a plough there belonging to Tealby.

[Folio 363: LINDSEY]

In IRNHAM, Mærle-Sveinn had 7 carucates of land to the geld. [There is] land for 7 ploughs. Ralph has 3½ ploughs there, and 7 sokemen on 2 carucates of this land and 29 villans and 9 bordars with 7 ploughs. There is a church and a priest, and 50 acres of meadow. [There is] woodland pasture 1 league long and 10 furlongs broad. Besides this [there are] 200 more acres of woodland, pasture in places. TRE worth £12; now 10[l]; tallage 40s.

In ASHBY DE LA LAUNDE, Mærle-Sveinn had 6 carucates of land to the geld. [There is] land for 6 ploughs. Ralph has 2 ploughs there, and 17 sokemen and 2 villans and 2 bordars with 8 ploughs, and [there are] 50 acres of meadow. TRE worth £4; now 100s.

In SCAWBY and Sturton [in Scawby], Grimkel had 3 carucates of land and 2 bovates to the geld. [There is] land for 5 ploughs. Ralph has 2 ploughs there, and 5 sokemen on 4 bovates of this land and 7 villans and 3 bordars with 2 ploughs. TRE worth 60s; now 40[s]; tallage 10s.

In Snarford [are] 3 bovates of land to the geld. [There is] land for 2 oxen. 4 sokemen have half a plough there, and 12 acres of meadow. [It is] SOKELAND of [Middle or West] Rasen.

XXXVI. The land of Ralph de Mortimer

In GREAT GRIMSBY and Swallow, Eadgifu had 2 carucates of land and 2 bovates to the geld. [There is] land for 4½ ploughs. Richard, Ralph de Mortimer's man, has 2 ploughs there in demesne; and 7 sokemen on 8 tofts and 11 villans and 10 bordars having 1½ ploughs. There is a church, and a priest, and 1 mill [rendering] 4s, and 1 ferry [rendering] 5s, and 30 acres of meadow. TRE worth £8; now 100s.

In THORNTON CURTIS and "Bodebi" [in Thornton Curtis] and Wootton, Eadgifu had 10 carucates of land to the geld. [There is] land for 20 ploughs. Ralph de Mortimer had 3 ploughs there in demesne; and 58 sokemen on 4 carucates of this land and 7 villans and 7 bordars having 7 ploughs, and half a mill [rendering] 3s[...] TRE worth £10; now 15[l]; tallage £5. Of this land Odo, Ralph's man, has 2 carucates, and he has 2 ploughs there, and 13 sokemen on 1 carucate of this land and 1 villan with 1½ ploughs; and it is worth 50s.

In BONBY, Kofse had 1 carucate of land to the geld. [There is] land for 2 ploughs. William, Ralph's man, has 2 ploughs there, and 2 villans and 1 bordar with 1 ox in a plough. TRE, as now, worth 20s; tallage 10s.

In HARMSTON, Kofse had 3½ carucates of land to the geld. [There is] land for as many ploughs. Ralph has 1 plough there in demesne; and 1 sokeman and 4 villans with 1 plough, and

35 acres of meadow. TRE, as now, worth 40s. Over this land Earl Hugh has soke belonging to Waddington.

In STOW [near Torksey], Eadgifu had 3 messuages with sake and soke. Ralph has them.

XXXVII. The land of Robert de Vessey

In HELPRINGHAM, Æthelric had 7 carucates of land and 3 bovates to the geld. [There is] land for as many ploughs and oxen. Robert de Vessey has 3 ploughs there in demesne; and 13 villans and and [sic] 9 bordars with 4 ploughs, and 15 acres of meadow. TRE worth £3; now 12[l].

In CAYTHORPE, Æthelric had 19 carucates of land and 2 bovates in demesne, and 28 carucates of land and 6 bovates of sokeland to the geld. [There is] land for as many ploughs, that is 48. Three hundreds, Frieston [in Caythorpe], Normanton, West Willoughby, belong to it. Robert de Vessey has 3 ploughs, there in demesne; and 113 sokemen with 32 ploughs, and 50 villans and 7 bordars with 13 ploughs. There are 2 churches, and 2 priests, and half a mill [rendering] 10s, and 880 acres of meadow.

Of the above-mentioned land and sokeland 3 of Robert's men have 12 carucates and 7 bovates, and they have 4½ ploughs there. 1 Englishman also has 1 carucate and 5 bovates, and he has 1 plough there. TRE worth £30; now £50.

SOKELAND OF THIS MANOR

In Brandon [are] 7 bovates of land to the geld. [There is] land for 11 oxen. 8 sokemen have 2 ploughs and 2 oxen there.

In 'Hanbeck' [in Wilsford] [are] 3 carucates of land to the geld. [There is] land for 4 ploughs. 19 sokemen have 3 ploughs there.

In Swaton [is] half a carucate of land to the geld. [There is] land for 6 oxen. [It is] a BEREWICK. 1 villan and 2 bordars have there 3 oxen in a plough, and 5 acres of meadow.

In 'STENNING' [in Swineshead], Æthelric had 6 bovates of land to the geld. [There is] land for 6 oxen. Robert has 1 villan there, and 2 salt-pans rendering 2s8d, and 1 fishery rendering 200 eels, and [there are] 18 acres of meadow. TRE, as now, worth 20s.

SOKELAND OF CAYTHORPE

In Heckington [are] 6½ bovates of land to the geld. [There is] land for 5½ oxen. 1 villan and 2 bordars have there 6 oxen in a plough, and [there are] 6 acres of meadow.

[Folio 363v: LINCOLNSHIRE]

XXXVIII. The land of Robert Despenser

In THORNTON, Aki had 3 carucates of land to the geld. [There is] land for 6 ploughs. Robert Despenser has 3 ploughs there in demesne; and 9 sokemen on 10 bovates of this land and villans and bordars having 4 ploughs, and 2 mills [rendering] 20s, and 80 acres of meadow, and 30 acres of woodland in places. TRE worth £5; now 4[l]; tallage 20s.

In Roughton [are] 12 bovates of land to the geld. [There is] land for 12 oxen. [It is] SOKELAND. 3½ sokemen have 2 ploughs and 3 oxen ploughing there, and [there are] 1 acres of meadow, and 1 fishery [rendering] 2s, and 40 acres of woodland, pasture in places.

In SCRIVELSBY, Siward had 7 carucates of land and 5 bovates to the geld. [There is] land for 8½ ploughs. Robert has 6 ploughs there in demesne; and 30 sokemen on 3 carucates of this land and 16 villans and 11 bordars with 6 ploughs. There is a church, and 1 mill [rendering] 13s 4d, and 200 acres of meadow, and 100 acres of woodland, pasture in places. TRE worth £12; now £14.

In Coningsby [are] 9 bovates of land to the geld. [There is] land for 9 oxen. [It is] a BEREWICK. 15 villans and 3 bordars have 1½ ploughs there, and 10 fisheries [rendering] 8s4d, and [there are] 60 acres of meadow, and 60 acres of woodland pasture.

In Wilksby [are] 1½ carucates of land to the geld. [There is] land for 2 ploughs. [It is] a BEREWIC K. Robert has 1 plough there in demesne; and villans have 2 oxen in a plough, and 20 acres of meadow, and 40 acres of scrubland.

In Mareham on the Hill [is] 1 bovate of land to the geld. [There is] land for 2 oxen. [It is] SOKELAND of Scrivelsby. There is 1 villan with 1 ox in a plough.

In Wood Enderby, Siward had 9 acres of arable land and 8 acres of woodland with sake and soke. Robert Despenser has them now.

In ADDLETHORPE, Vighlak had 3 carucates of land to the geld. [There is] land for 3 ploughs. Robert has 3 ploughs there in demesne; and 32 sokemen on half of this land and 12 villans with 6 ploughs. There are 2 churches, and 400 acres of meadow. TRE worth £8; now £10.

SOKELAND of [?]lngoldmells

In Partney and Great Steeping and "Tric" [in Skegness] and Burgh le Marsh [are] 2½ carucates of land to the geld. [There is] land for as many ploughs. 5 sokemen and 2 villans have half a plough there, and 30 acres of meadow.

In 'BUTYATE' [in Bardney], Vighlak had 1 carucate of land to the geld. [There is] land for 12 oxen. Robert has 1 plough there, and 5 sokemen on half a carucate of this land and 10 villans having 3 ploughs, and [there are] 15 acres of meadow, and 200 acres of woodland, half [of which is] for pasture. TRE worth 40s; now 50[s].

In Low Langton [are] 1½ carucates of land to the geld. [There is] land for 4 ploughs. Robert has 1 plough there, and 8 sokemen on half a carucate of this land and 4 villans with 2 ploughs, and [there are] 24 acres of meadow, and 280 acres of woodland pasture.

In TATHWELL, Siward had 1 carucate of land to the geld. [There is] land for 4 ploughs. Robert has 1 plough there, and 8 villans with 1 plough, and 2 mills [rendering] 14s, and 100 acres of meadow. TRE, as now, worth 40s.

In HALTHAM, Aki had 2 carucates of land and 2 bovates to the geld. [There is] land for as many ploughs and oxen. Robert has 1 plough there, and 3 sokemen on half a carucate of this land and 5 villans with 1 plough, and 2 mills [rendering] 13s 4d, and [there are] 24 acres of meadow, and 80 acres of woodland pasture. TRE, as now, worth 30s.

In FULSTOW, Eskil had 14 bovates of land to the geld. [There is] land for 3 ploughs. Robert has 1 plough there, and 3 sokemen on 9 bovates of this land and 4 villans and 2 bordars with 1½ ploughs, and 6 salt-pans [rendering] 6s. TRE worth 100s; now 20s; tallage 10s.

XXXIX. The land of Guy de Raimbeaucourt

In SCOTT WILLOUGHBY, Leofric had 3 carucates of land and 2 bovates to the geld. [There is] land for 4 ploughs. Guy de Raimbeaucourt has 2 ploughs there in demesne; and 10 sokemen on 10 bovates of this land and 3 bordars having 2½ ploughs. There is a priest having 37½ acres of land rendering 16d in customary dues. Over a fourth part of the church of the same vill Guy has soke, and [he has] 30 acres of meadow, and 28 acres of scrubland. TRE worth £7; now 4[l]; tallage 20s.

In Aunsby [are] 3½ carucates of land to the geld. [There is] land for 7 ploughs. [It is] SOKELAND of the same manor, and 2 bovates are inland. 25 sokemen have 6½ ploughs there, and [there are] 70 acres of meadow, and 6 acres of scrubland.

In SYSTON, Leofric had 11 carucates of land and 6 bovates to the geld. [There is] land for as many ploughs and oxen. There is now 1 plough in demesne; and 27 sokemen on 8 carucates and 6 bovates of this land and 10 villans with 12 ploughs. There is a priest and a church to which belongs 1 bovate of land. There are †6† mills rendering 50s, and 21 acres of meadow. TRE worth £6; now 4[l]; tallage 40s.

In Belton [near Grantham], Guy de Raimbeaucourt has 10 acres of meadow.

Ingelrann his son holds all these lands of him.

[Folio 364: LINDSEY]

XL. The land of Rainer de Brimeux

In GREAT LIMBER, Iolfr and Thorfridh had 2 carucates of land to the geld. [There is] land for 5 ploughs. Rayner de Brimeux has 1 plough there, and 2 sokemen on 2 tofts and 2 villans and 11 bordars with half a plough. TRE worth £4; now 30s.

In INGHAM, Iolfr had half a carucate of land. [There is] land for 6 oxen. Kolsveinn, Rainer's man, has half a plough there, and 3 villans and 2 bordars with 5 oxen in a plough, and [there are] 8 acres of meadow. TRE, as now, [worth] 10s.

In Newton by Toft [are] 3 bovates of land to the geld. [There is] land for 1 plough. [It is] SOKELAND of the same manor. 2 sokemen have 3 oxen in a plough there, and 10 acres of meadow.

In HOLTON LE CLAY, Iolfr had 5 bovates of land and 14 acres of land and 1 virgate to the geld. [There is] land for 10 oxen. Roger, Rayner's man, has there 5 oxen in a plough, and 4 villans and 1 bordar having 5 oxen in a plough, and 13 acres of meadow. TRE worth 30s; now 20[s].

In STAINTON LE VALE, Iolfr had 6 bovates of land to the geld. [There is] land for 18 oxen. Rayner has half a plough there, and 4 sokemen on 1 bovate of this land and 1 villan and 2 bordars having 5 oxen in a plough, and the site of a mill, and 45 acres of meadow. TRE worth 60s; now 20[s]; tallage 5s.

In WALESBY, Iolfr had 1 carucate of land to the geld. [There is] land for 12 oxen. Baldwin, Rayner's man, has 1 plough there, and 7 villans with half a plough, and 20 acres of meadow, and 5 acres of scrubland. TRE, as now, worth 30s.

In [East or West] BARKWITH, Koddi had 4 bovates of land to the geld. [There is] land for 1 plough. Gerard, Rayner's man, has there 5 oxen in a plough, and 1 villan with 1 ox in a plough, and 9 acres of meadow. TRE, as now, worth los.

In South Willingham [are] 10 bovates of land to the geld. [There is] land for 2½ ploughs. [It is] SOKELAND of the same manor. 13 sokemen have 3 ploughs there, and [there are] 40 acres of meadow.

In HAINTON, Koddi had 3½ bovates of land to the geld. [There is] land for 7 oxen. Now Rayner has it, and it is waste. There are 26 acres of meadow. TRE worth 20s; now 30s.

In KINGTHORPE, Iolfr had 3 bovates of land to the geld. [There is] land for 6 oxen. Rayner has there 1 villan and 1 bordar with 3 oxen in a plough, and [there are] 8 acres of meadow, and 100 acres of woodland, pasture in places. TRE, as now, worth 10s.

In Strubby [in Langton by Wragby] [are] 2 bovates of land to the geld. [It is] SOKELAND of this manor. 2 sokemen have 2 oxen in a plough there.

In SIXHILLS, Iolfr had 5 bovates of land to the geld. [There is] land for 1 plough. Rayner has 1 plough there, and 2 sokemen and 1 bordar having 3 oxen in a plough, and 80 acres of meadow. TRE, as now, worth 30s.

In 'Holtham' [in Legsby] [are] 2 parts of a bovate of land to the geld. [It is] SOKELAND. It is waste.

In TEALBY, Rayner has 1 mill, and 4 acres of land, and 1 villan who belongs to Sixhills.

In 'WEST WYKEHAM' [in Ludford], Iolfr had 1 carucate of land to the geld. [There is] land for 2 ploughs. There Rayner has 10 men who do not plough. TRE worth 30s; now 15[s].

In LUDFORD [is] 1 bovate of land to the geld. [There is] land for 2 oxen. [It is] SOKELAND of 'West Wykeham' [in Ludford]. 2 sokemen have half a plough there, and [there is] 1 acre of meadow.

In KEDDINGTON, Iolfr had 4½ bovates of land to the geld | and the fourth part of 1 bovate |. [There is] land for 1 plough. Baldwin has 1 plough there, and 7 sokemen on 1½ bovates and the fourth part of 1 bovate have 5 oxen in a plough, and 1 mill [rendering] 8s, and 6 acres of meadow.

There is a church and a priest, with 1 mill [rendering] 11s TRE worth 20s; now 25[s].

In [North or South] Cockerington [is] half a bovate of land to the geld. [There is] land for 2 oxen. [It is] SOKELAND. 1 man has there 1 ox in a plough.

In Saltfleetby [All Saints, St Clement or St Peter] [is] half a bovate of land to the geld. [There is] land for half an ox. [It is] SOKELAND. It is waste.

In CUMBERWORTH, Iolfr had 6 bovates of land to the geld. [There is] land [. . .]. Rayner has 1 plough there, and 9 villans with 1 plough, and 20 acres of meadow. TRE, as now, worth 50s.

In Mablethorpe [is] half a carucate of land to the geld. [There is] land for 10 oxen. [It is] a BEREWICK. 5 villans have 1 plough there, and 20 acres of meadow.

In Ulceby [near Well] [are] 2 bovates of land to the geld. [There is] land for 1 plough. [It is] SOKELAND. It is waste.

In [North or South] COCKERINGTON he had 14 bovates of land to the geld. [There is] land for 3½ ploughs. Rayner has 1 plough there, and 8 sokemen on 1 carucate of land and 2 villans and 4 bordars with 1 plough, and the site of a mill, and 60 acres of meadow, and 20 acres of scrubland. TRE, as now, worth 40s; tallage 10s.

In [North or South] Somercotes [is] the third part of 1 carucate to the geld. [There is] land [. . .]. 3 men held this land. Ilbert de Lacy has the land of 2 [men] from the Bishop of Bayeux. Rayner has the land of the third man from the king; and there he has 1 man with 1 ox.

In Alvingham [are] 2 bovates of land and the sixth part of a bovate to the geld. [There is] land for half a plough. There is 1 sokeman, and 7 acres of meadow.

In WITHCALL, Iolfr had 15 bovates of land and the third part of 1 bovate to the geld. [There is] land for 3 ploughs. Rayner has 1 plough there, and 12 sokemen on 13 bovates of this land and the third part of 1 bovate and 2 villans with 1½ ploughs, and 1 mill and the third part of a mill [rendering] 4s, and [there are] 12 acres of meadow. TRE, as now, worth 60s. He has the third part of 1 church there, and he claims the other 2 parts by the witness of the wapentake.

XLI. The land of Osbern d'Arques

In SCAWBY and Sturton [in Scawby], [. . .] and Grimbald had 2 carucates of land and 3 bovates to the geld. [There is] land for 4 ploughs. Alvred, Osbern's man, has 1 plough there, and sokemen on 1 carucate of this land and 5 villans with 1 plough and 1 ox. TRE worth 30s; now 25s; tallage 5s.

In Redbourne [are] 2½ bovates of land and the fourth part of a bovate to the geld. [There is] land for twice [as many] oxen. [It is] a BEREWICK of Scawby. There are 12 acres of meadow. It is waste.

XLII. The land of Ogier the Breton

In BOURNE, Earl Morcar had 2½ carucates of land to the geld. [There is] land for 2½ ploughs. Ogier the Breton has 2 ploughs there in demesne; and 4 sokemen on 4 bovates of this land and 14 villans and 4 bordars with 5 ploughs. There is half a church and a priest, and 3 mills [rendering] 30s, and 6 fisheries rendering 2½ thousand eels, and 19 acres of meadow. [There is] woodland pasture 1 league and 8 furlongs long and 1 furlong broad. TRE worth 100s; now £8; tallage 40s.

IN THE SAME PLACE Leofwine had 7 bovates of land to the geld. [There is] land for 7 oxen. Ogier has there 3 sokemen on 4 bovates of this land and 4 villans and 2 bordars with 2 ploughs. There is half a church, and 6 fisheries [rendering] 24d, and 2 parts of a mill [rendering] 5s, and 9 acres of meadow. [There is] woodland pasture 1 league and 8 furlongs long and 4 furlongs broad. TRE, as now, [worth] 60s; tallage 20s.

In Dyke [is] 1 carucate of land to the geld. [There is] land for 1 plough. [It is] a BEREWICK of Bourne. 2 villans and 2 bordars have half a plough there, and 9 acres of meadow, and 20 acres of woodland pasture.

In Cawthorpe [are] 2½ carucates of land to the geld. [There is] land for as many ploughs. [It is] SOKELAND. 10 sokemen have 5 ploughs there, and 16 acres of meadow, and 24 acres of woodland pasture.

Also in Dyke and Cawthorpe [are] 1½ carucates of land. [There is] land for 12 oxen. There are 9 sokemen with 1 plough and 2 oxen in a plough, and 6 acres of meadow, and 12 acres of woodland pasture.

In the same places [are] 3½ bovates of land to the geld. [There is] land for as many oxen. [It is] SOKELAND of Haconby.

In Spanby [are] 4 bovates of land to the geld. [There is] land for 6 oxen. [It is] a BEREWICK of Bourne. Ogier has 1 plough there, and 18 acres of meadow. TRE, as now, worth 10s.

In Laughton [in Folkingham], Ogier has 1 carucate of land to the geld. Gilbert de Ghent has SOKE over it.

In the same LAUGHTON [in Folkingham], Toli and Hereweard had 4 bovates of land to the geld. [There is] land for half a plough. Ogier has 2 ploughs there in demesne; and 4 villans having half a plough, and the fourth part of 2 churches, and 10 acres of meadow, and 6 acres of scrubland. TRE, as now, worth 40s.

In Aslackby and 'Avethorpe' [in Aslackby] [are] 6 bovates of land to the geld. [There is] land for 1 plough. [It is] a BEREWICK of Laughton [in Folkingham]. 2 villans have half a plough there, and 6 acres of meadow, and 2 acres of scrubland.

In 'Ringstone' [in Rippingale] and Rippingale, Ogier has 1 carucate of land to the geld. [There is] land for 1 plough.

In 'Ringstone' [in Rippingale] [is] 1 carucate of land to the geld. [There is] land for 1 plough. Ogier has it.

In RIPPINGALE, St Guthlac had for the sustenance of the monks 3 carucates of land to the geld. [There is] land for 3 ploughs. Ogier has 2 ploughs there, and 3 sokemen on 6 bovates of this land. [...] There are 60 acres of meadow. TRE worth 40s; now 60[s].

In HACONBY and Stainfield [in Haconby], Ulf Fenman had 9 bovates of land to the geld. [There is] land for as many oxen. [It is] SOKELAND of Edenham. Ogier has there 2 sokemen on 4 bovates of this land and 3 villans with 1 plough, and 12 acres of meadow, and 20 acres of woodland. TRE, as now, worth 20s.

In MORTON [near Hanthorpe] and Hanthorpe, Ulf Fenman had 5 carucates and half a carucate. of land and half a bovate to the geld. [There is] land for as many ploughs. [It is] SOKELAND of Edenham. Ogier has half of this land, and he has there 14 sokemen and 3 bordars with 6 ploughs, and 45 acres of meadow, and 40 acres of woodland pasture. It is worth 40s.

In the same Morton [near Hanthorpe], Cwenleofu had 2 carucates of land and half a bovate to the geld. [There is] land for as many ploughs. Ogier has 2 ploughs there, and 2 sokemen on 2 bovates of this land, and 8 villans and 4 bordars with 2 ploughs. There is a church, and a priest, and 18 acres of meadow, and 16 acres of scrubland. TRE worth 40s; now 60[s].

In the same Morton [near Hanthorpe] [is] 1 carucate of land to the geld. [There is] land for 1 plough. [It is] inland of Haconby. 4 villans have 1 plough there, and 9 acres of meadow, and 16 acres of scrubland. TRE, as now, worth 10s.

In the same place [are] 1½ bovates of land to the geld. [There is] land for 2½ oxen. [It is] SOKELAND of Haconby.

In the same Morton [near Hanthorpe] [is] half a carucate of land to the geld. [There is] land for 4 oxen. [It is] SOKELAND of Quarrington. There are 4 villans with half a plough, and 5 acres of meadow, and 8 acres of scrubland.

XLIII. [The land] of Ranulph de Saint-Valery

In RANBY, Godric had 13 bovates of land to the geld. [There is] land for 5 ploughs. Ranulph de Saint-Valery has 3 ploughs there in demesne; and 14 sokemen on 7 bovates of this land and 3 villans and 2 bordars with 2 ploughs. There is a church and a priest, and 1 mill [rendering] 10s8d, and 270 acres of meadow. TRE worth 40s; now £6; tallage 40s.

In Great Sturton [is] 1 carucate of land to the geld. [There is] land for 1 plough. [It is] inland of the same manor. There is 1 plough in demesne; and 3 villans and 3 bordars with 1 ox in a plough, and 60 acres of meadow.

In Market Stainton [are] 4 carucates of land to the geld. [There is] land for 7 ploughs. [It is] SOKELAND of the same manor. There is 1 plough in demesne; and 16 sokemen and 9 villans and 3 bordars having 4 ploughs and 2 oxen in a plough, and 2 mills [rendering] 5s8d, and 80 acres of meadow.

In 'Burreth' [in Tupholme] [are] 3 bovates of land and the third part of a bovate to the geld. [There is] land for as many oxen. [It is] SOKELAND of the same manor. 3 sokemen and 1 villan have 3 oxen in a plough there, and [there are] 15 acres of meadow, and 220 acres of woodland, pasture in places.

In REEPHAM, Godric had half a carucate of land to the geld. [There is] land for 4 oxen. Ranulph has 1 plough there, and 2 villans with 2 oxen in a plough, and [there are] 12 acres of meadow. TRE worth 10s; now 20[s].

In Scothern [are] 2½ bovates of land to the geld. [There is] land for 4 oxen. [It is] SOKELAND of the same manor. There is a church, and a priest having 1 plough.

[Folio 365: LINDSEY]

XLIIII. The land of Durand Malet

In CAMMERINGHAM, Siward had half a carucate of land to the geld. [There is] land for 6 oxen. And Alnoth [had] half a carucate of land to the geld, SOKELAND of the same manor. Durand Malet has 1 plough there, and 8 sokemen and 2 villans having 5 oxen in a plough. TRE worth 20s; now 10[s]; tallage 3s.

In SCAWBY and Sturton [in Scawby], Edwin had 9 bovates of land to the geld. [There is] land for 2 ploughs. Alvred, Durand's man, has 1 plough there, and 3 sokemen and 1 villan and 2 bordars with 1 plough. TRE worth 15s; now 20[s]; tallage 5s.

SOKELAND of the same manor

In Winterton [are] 4 bovates of land to the geld. [There is] land for half a plough. 1 sokeman has half a plough there.

In BROUGHTON and 'Manby' [in Broughton] and Castlethorpe, Edwin had 3 bovates of land to the geld. [There is] land for 1 plough. It is waste. There are 10 acres of meadow and 10 acres of scrubland. TRE worth 10s; now 4s.

In NETTLETON, Rolf had 14 bovates of land to the geld. [There is] land for 5 ploughs. 2 of Durand's men have 2 ploughs there, and 10 villans and 5 bordars with 1 plough, and 3 mills [rendering] 5s, and a church, and 60 acres of meadow, and 60 acres of scrubland. TRE, as now, worth £4.

In North Thoresby and 'Audby' [in North Thoresby], Durand has 1 salt-pan which belongs to Rothwell.

In SEARBY, Rolf had 2½ carucates of land to the geld. [There is] land for 5 ploughs. Durand has 2 ploughs there, and 15 sokemen on 1 carucate of this land and 4 villans and 2 bordars with 3 ploughs. There is a church, and 1 mill [rendering] 2s, and 80 acres of meadow. TRE worth 10s; now 50s; tallage 10s.

In GREAT COATES [in Great Grimsby], Rolf had 10½ bovates of land to the geld. [There is] land for 2 ploughs and 5 oxen. Richard, Durand's man, has 1 plough there and

10 sokemen on 1½ bovates of this land and 6 villans with 2 ploughs. There is a church, and a priest, and 1 mill [rendering] 12s, and 500 acres of meadow. TRE, as now, worth 60s; tallage 20s.

In IRBY UPON HUMBER, Rolf had 3½ carucates of land to the geld. [There is] land for 7 ploughs. Durand has 2 ploughs there, and 17 sokemen and 15 villans with 4 ploughs. There is a church and a priest. TRE worth 40s; now 50[s]; tallage 30s.

In LINWOOD, Rolf had half a carucate of land to the geld. [There is] land for 2 ploughs. Durand has 1 plough there, and 7 villans and 1 bordar with 1½ ploughs, and the third part of a church, and the third part of a mill [rendering] 8d, and 40 acres of meadow, and 100 acres of scrubland. TRE worth 30s; now 20[s]; tallage 5s.

In ROTHWELL, Rolf had 13½ bovates of land and the third part of a bovate to the geld. [There is] twice [as much] land for ploughing. Durand has 1 plough there, and 3 sokemen on 2½ bovates of this land and 6 villans and 1 bordar with 1 plough. There are 18 acres of meadow. TRE worth 40s; now 30[s].

In Cuxwold [is] 1 bovate and 3 parts of a bovate to the geld. [There is] land for 3½ oxen. [It is] SOKELAND of the same manor. 2 sokemen have half a plough there.

In Cabourne [is] 1 bovate of land to the geld. [It is] SOKELAND of the same manor. It is waste.

In 'Audby' [in North Thoresby] is 1 salt-pan which belongs to Rothwell. Durand has it.

In Claxby [near Walesby] [are] 5 bovates of land to the geld. [There is] land for 10 oxen. [It is] SOKELAND of 'Wykeham' [in Nettleton].

In NAVENBY, Rolf had 1 carucate of land to the geld. [There is] land for 10 oxen. Durand has 2 ploughs there in demesne; and 2 villans with 2 oxen in a plough, and 8 acres of meadow. TRE worth 32s; now 50s.

In Wellingore [are] 3 carucates of land to the geld. [There is] land for 3 ploughs. [It is] a BEREWICK of this manor. There are 2 sokemen on 1½ bovates of land, and 1 villan, and 11 acres of meadow.

In Eagle [are] 3 bovates of land to the geld. [There is] land for 2 oxen. 1 sokemen has 2 oxen in a plough there, and [there are] 4 acres of meadow. [It is] SOKELAND of Navenby.

In MIDDLE RASEN, Durand has the third part of half a carucate of land, and he has there 3 villans with 1 ox in a plough.

XLV. The land of Martin

In GLENTWORTH, Gamal had 6 bovates of land to the geld. [There is] land for 10 oxen. Martin has there 4 sokemen and 1 villan with 5 oxen in a plough, and 30 acres of meadow. TRE worth 8s; now 10s.

In HEMSWELL, Sperrir had 10 bovates of land to the geld. [There is] land for 14 oxen. Martin has 1 plough there, and 1 sokemen on 2 bovates of this land and 4 villans and 4 bordars with 1 plough. TRE [worth] 40s; now 20s.

In HACKTHORN, Swein had 3 bovates of land and 4 parts of a bovate to the geld. [There is] land for 4 oxen. Martin has there 2 villans having 3 oxen in a plough, and 10 acres of meadow. TRE, as now, [worth] 5s.

In EWERBY THORPE, Godric had 6 bovates of land to the geld. [There is] land for 5 oxen. [It is] a BEREWICK of Ewerby. There are 2 villans, and 8 acres of meadow, and 1 acre of scrubland. TRE worth 10s; now 8s.

XLVI. The land of Waldin the Breton

In HACEBY, Wulfgeat had 11 bovates of land to the geld. [There is] land for 2 ploughs. Godwine, Waldin the Breton's man, has there 2 villans and 2 bordars having 2 oxen in a plough, and 8½ acres of meadow, and 17 acres of scrubland. TRE worth 20s; now 10s.

In Horbling [are] 6 bovates of land to the geld. [There is] land for 6 oxen. [It is] SOKELAND of Haceby. Waldin has 1 bordar there, and and [sic] 2½ acres of meadow. TRE worth 10s; now 4[s]. Guy de Craon has the soke.

In Silk Willoughby, Wulfgeat had 15 bovates of land to the geld. [There is] land for 3 ploughs and 6 oxen. Waldin has 2 ploughs there, and 8 villans with 2 ploughs, and 56 acres of meadow. TRE worth 40s; now 20s.

In STIXWOULD, Wulfgeat had 1 carucate of land to the geld.

[Folio 365V: LINCOLNSHIRE]

[There is] land for 10 oxen. He has 1 plough there, and 2 fisheries [rendering] 4s, and [there are] 40 acres of meadow, and 80 acres of scrubland. TRE, as now, [worth] 20s.

XLVII. The land of Waldin Engaine

In WILLOUGHTON, Grimkel had 17½ bovates of land to the geld, and Esbiorn 2 bovates of land to the geld. [There is] land for 3½ ploughs. Waldin Engaine has 2 ploughs there, and 17 sokemen on 10½ bovates of this land and 7 bordars with 2 ploughs, and 80 acres of meadow. TRE worth 70s; now 60[s]; tallage 20s.

In HACKTHORN, Earnwig had 1½ carucates of land to the geld. [There is] land for 2 ploughs. Waldin has 1 plough there, and 3 villans and 7 bordars with 10 oxen in a plough, and half a church, and 1 mill [rendering] 12d, and [there are] 30 acres of meadow. TRE, as now, worth 40s.

In KEELBY, Erik had 3 bovates of land and the third part of a bovate to the geld. [There is] land for 6½ oxen. William, Waldin's man, has there 1 ox in a plough, and 1 sokeman on 2 tofts, and 2 bordars, and 14 acres of meadow. TRE, as now, [worth] 10s.

In 'ITTERBY' [in Cleethorpes], Elaf had 2½ bovates of land to the geld. [There is] land for 5 oxen. William, Waldin's man,

has there 2 oxen in a plough, and 14 acres of meadow. TRE worth 20s; now 16[s].

In THORGANBY, Elaf had 5 bovates of land to the geld. [There is] land for 10 oxen. William, Waldin's man, has there 1 bordar and 2 sokemen on 2 tofts, and 4 parts of a mill [rendering] 2s, and 9 acres of meadow. TRE [worth] 20s; now 10[s].

In [East or West] RAVENDALE, Elaf had 2 bovates of land to the geld. [There is] land for 4 oxen. William, Waldin's man, has 1 plough there, and 2 villans having 2 oxen in a plough. TRE worth 20s; now 10[s].

In BEELSBY, Elaf had 1 carucate of land to the geld. [There is] land for 2 ploughs. William, Waldin's man, has 1 plough there, and 8 villans with 1 plough, and half a mill [rendering] 3s, and 10 acres of meadow. TRE, as now, worth 40s.

In WRAGBY, Guthfrith had 5½ bovates of land to the geld. [There is] land for 2 ploughs. Waldin has 1 plough there, and 3 sokemen on 2 bovates of this land and 4 villans and 5 bordars with 1½ ploughs, and the site of a mill, and 16 acres of meadow, and 240 acres of woodland, pasture in places. TRE worth 30s; now 35s; tallage 5s.

In Langton by Wragby [are] 4 bovates of land to the geld. [There is] land for 1 plough. [It is] SOKELAND of Wragby. 6 sokemen have 1 plough there, and 43 acres of scrubland.

In KELSTERN, Klak had 2 bovates of land to the geld. [There is] land for 4 oxen. Waldin has there 3 oxen in a plough, and 8 acres of meadow. TRE worth 20s; now 5s8d.

XLVIII. The land of Odo the Crossbowman

In WILLOUGHTON, Alstan and Othenkar had 3 carucates and 3 bovates of land to the geld. [There is] land for 4½ ploughs. Odo the crossbowman has 2 ploughs there in demesne; and 18 sokemen on 13½ bovates of this land and 6 villans with 2½ ploughs, and [there are] 108 acres of meadow. TRE worth £4; now 3[l]; tallage 60s.

In SCAWBY, Esbiorn and Grimbald had 2 carucates of land and 3 bovates to the geld. [There is] land for 3 ploughs. Alvred, Odo's man, has 1 plough there, and 5 sokemen on 1 carucate of this land and 4 villans with 1 plough. TRE worth 30s; now 25[s]; tallage 5s.

In Redbourne [are] 2½ bovates of land to the geld. [It is] a BEREWICK of Scawby. It is waste.

In SWINHOPE, Enar and his stepmother had 3 carucates of land and half a bovate and the fourth part of a bovate to the geld. [There is] land for 6½ ploughs. Odo has 2 ploughs there, and 10 sokemen on 10 tofts and 8 villans and 2 bordars with 3½ ploughs, and 12 acres of meadow, and 1 mill [rendering] 5s. TRE worth £3; now 4[l]; tallage 20s.

In NEWTON, Alsige had 7 bovates of land to the geld. [There is] land for 10 oxen. Odo has 1 plough there, and 1 sokeman on 1 bovate of this land and 5 villans and 4 bordars with 1½ ploughs. There is a church, and 12 acres of meadow, and 70 acres of woodland, pasture in places. TRE worth £4; now the same; tallage 40s.

In 'Ouseby' [in Billingborough] [are] 6 bovates of land and the third part of 1 bovate to the geld. [There is] land for as many oxen. [It is] a BEREWICK of Newton. William, Odo's man, has 3 bordars there, and half a mill [rendering] 3s, and 9 acres of meadow.

In Threekingham [are] 10 bovates of land and the third part of 2 bovates to the geld. [There is] land for as many oxen. [It is] a BEREWICK of Newton. Odo has there 2 sokemen on 2 bovates of this land and 5 villans and 1 bordar with 1 plough and 2 oxen in a plough. There belongs the sixth part of a church of St Peter, and the third part of 1 church of St Mary, and the third part of half a carucate which belongs to the church of ST MARY.

In HACEBY, Gunnkil had 2 bovates of land to the geld. [There is] land for 2 oxen. Odo has 2 oxen in a plough there, and 2 acres of meadow, and 8 acres of scrubland. TRE worth 10s; now 3s.

In Thorganby [are] 2 carucates of land to the geld. [There is] land for 4 ploughs. [It is] SOKELAND of Bleasby. Herbert, Odo's man, has there 12 sokemen with 2 ploughs, and 30 acres of meadow, and 1 mill [rendering] 3s.

In BEELSBY, Eadric had half a carucate of land to the geld. [There is] land for 1 plough. Odo has 1 bordar there, and 6 acres of meadow. TRE worth 10s; now 2s.

In BLEASBY, Alstan had 5 bovates of land and the third part of a bovate to the geld. [There is] land for 12 oxen. Herbert, Odo's man, has 1 plough there, and 1 villan and 3 bordars, and 40 acres of meadow, and 42 acres of scrubland. TRE, as now, worth 20s; tallage 20s.

[Folio 366: LINDSEY]

In SWARBY, Godmann had 3½ bovates of land to the geld. [There is] land for 6 oxen. Odo has there 2 sokemen with 10 oxen in a plough, and the third part of a church, and 20 acres of meadow, and 12 acres of scrubland. TRE, as now, worth 10s.

In SILK WILLOUGHBY, Regnvald had 2 bovates of land to the geld. [There is] land for 4 oxen. Kolgrimr, Odo's man, has there 1 bordar, and 1 ox in a plough, and 8 acres of meadow. TRE worth 10s; now 5s.

In THURLBY [near Norton Disney], Bothild had 4½ carucates of land to the geld. [There is] land for 3 ploughs. Odo has there 3 sokemen and 4 villans and 1 bordar with 2 ploughs, and 3 acres of meadow. TRE worth 20s; now 16[s.].

In EAGLE, Gunnkil had 7 bovates of land to the geld. [There is] land for 5 oxen. Odo has there 2 villans and 2 bordars with half a plough, and 10 acres of meadow. TRE, as now, worth 10s.

In Dunholme, Odo the crossbowman has 2 carucates of land to the geld. [There is] land for 2 ploughs. [It is] SOKELAND of Nettleham.

XLIX. The land of William Blund

In FALDINGWORTH, Oswulf had 2 carucates of land and 3 bovates to the geld. [There is] land for as many ploughs and oxen. William Blund has 1 plough there, and 2 sokemen on 5 bovates of this land and 6 villans and 2 bordars having 6 oxen in a plough, and 40 acres of meadow, and 12 acres of scrubland. TRE worth £4; now 20s; tallage 5s.

In CROXBY, Asfrith had 1 carucate of land to the geld. [There is] land for 3 ploughs. William has 1 plough there, and 1 sokeman on 2 bovates of this land and 5 villans and 1 bordar with 1 plough, and 9 acres of meadow. TRE worth 60s; now 40[s.].

In Thorganby, William has 1 mill [rendering] 3s. which belongs to Croxby, in Thorgot's SOKE.

In WITHCALL, Godric and Siward had 2 bovates of land to the geld. [There is] land for 6 oxen. William has 1 plough there, and 3 villans with 3 oxen in a plough, and 8 acres of meadow. TRE, as now, worth 20s.

In 'SOUTH CADEBY' [in Calcethorpe], Alnoth had 2½ bovates of land to the geld. [There is] land for 5 oxen. William has them. TRE worth 20s; now 5s.

In Saltfleetby [All Saints, St Clement or St Peter] and Skidbrooke [are] 2 bovates of land to the geld. [There is] land for 3 oxen. [It is] SOKELAND of 'South Cadeby' [in Calcethorpe]. It is waste.

L. The land of Restold

In GLENTWORTH, Soti had 7 bovates of land to the geld. [There is] land for 12 oxen. Restold has half a plough there, and 4 sokemen on 3 bovates of this land and 1 bordar with 1 plough, and 25 acres of meadow. TRE worth 20s; now 10s.

LI. The land of Godfrey de Cambrai

In WEST DEEPING, Azur had 2½ carucates of land to the geld. [There is] land for as many ploughs. And Almær had as much land, 2½ carucates, to the geld. [There is] land for as many ploughs. Godfrey de Cambrai has there 10 villans having 3 ploughs, and 4 mills [rendering] 40s, and 100 acres of meadow, and 8 acres of scrubland. TRE worth £8; now 6[l]; tallage 10s.

In DEEPING [Deeping St James and Market Deeping], Almær and Arnbiorn and Fredegæst had 3 carucates of land and 6 bovates to the geld. [There is] land for as many ploughs and oxen. 2 of Godfrey's men have 2 ploughs there, and 19 villans and 4 bordars having 7 ploughs, and [there are] 93 acres of meadow. TRE, as now, worth 100s; tallage 35s.

IN THE SAME PLACE Peterborough [Abbey] had 5 sokes [sic] over 5 manors of 2 carucates of land and 6 bovates to the geld. [There is] land for as many ploughs and oxen. 2 of Godfrey's men have 1½ ploughs there, and 12 villans with 3½ ploughs, and 1 fishery [rendering] 12d, and 70 acres of meadow. TRE worth 60s; now 50[s.]; tallage 12s.

In BARHOLM, Eskil had 1 carucate of land to the geld. [There is] land for 1 plough. 2 of Godfrey's men have half a plough there, and 5 sokemen on the third part of this land, free sokeland, having 2 oxen in a plough, and 1 acre of meadow. TRE worth 20s; now 12[s.]; tallage 12s. likewise.

In 'Stowe' [in Barholm and Stowe] [are] 1½ bovates of land to the geld. [There is] land for as many oxen. 5 sokemen have 5 oxen in a plough there. [It is] SOKELAND of Barholm. It is worth 2s.

In Greatford [are] 2 bovates of land to the geld. [There is] land for 2 oxen. Euremar, Godfrey's man, has 3 sokemen there, and 4 oxen in a plough, and 4 acres of meadow. Its value [...].

In CREETON, Ulf Cild had 2½ carucates of land to the geld. [There is] land for as many ploughs. Godfrey has there 10 villans with 1 plough, and 7 acres of meadow, and 100 acres of scrubland. TRE worth 60s; now 20[s.].

In Little Bytham [are] 4 bovates of land to the geld. [There is] land for 4 oxen. [It is] SOKELAND. 1 villan has 2 oxen in a plough there, and 1 acre of meadow.

In the wood of Castle Bytham Godfrey has 40 acres for 8d warnode.

In "TISTELTUNE" [in South Witham], Thorfridh had 1½ carucates to the geld. [There is] land for 12 oxen. Gleu, Godfrey's man, has there 1 sokeman and 3 bordars with half a plough, and 15 acres of woodland, and 40 acres belonging to Drogo's warnode. TRE worth 20s; now 10[s.].

In Helpringham, Azur had 1 church to which belong 4 bovates of land and 4 acres of meadow. Godfrey has it and it belongs to Deeping [Deeping St James, West Deeping or Market Deeping].

In WILSFORD, Siward had 9 carucates of land to the geld. [There is] land for 12 ploughs. Of this land Azur his brother had 6 bovates, and 1 mill quit of every service except the host. Godfrey has 3 ploughs there, and 12 sokemen on 3 carucates of this land and 6 villans and 2 bordars having 6 ploughs. There is a church to which belong 2 bovates of this land, and 45 acres of meadow, and 20 acres of scrubland. TRE, as now, worth £4; tallage 20s.

Bishop Remigius bought this manor of Godfrey for the Church of ST MARY of Lincoln.

[Folio 366V: LINCOLNSHIRE]

LII. The land of Gunfrid de Chocques

In CASEWICK, Azur had 10 bovates of land to the geld. [There is] land for 10 oxen. Gunfrid de Chocques has 1 plough there, and 5 villans and 5 bordars with 1 plough, and half a mill [rendering] 12s, and [there are] 6 acres of meadow. TRE, as now, worth 40s.

In POINTON, Arnbiorn had 2 bovates of land to the geld. [There is] land for 2 oxen. There is 1 villan, and 3 acres of meadow, and 40 acres of scrubland. TRE worth 10s; now 3s.

LIII. The land of Osbern the Priest

In FALDINGWORTH, Thorfridh had 10 bovates of land to the geld. [There is] land for as many oxen. Osbern the priest has 1 plough there, and 2 sokemen on 2 bovates of this land and 2 villans and 1 bordar, and 12 acres of meadow, and [there is] 1 acre of scrubland. TRE, as now, worth 20s.

In BINBROOK, Ketilbiørn had 9 bovates of land and 3 parts of 1 bovate to the geld. [There is] land [...] Osbern the priest has 1 plough there, and 4 sokemen on 1 bovate of this land and 13 villans and 7 bordars with 1½ ploughs. There is a church, and 1 mill [rendering] 5s, and 12 acres of meadow. TRE, as now, worth 50s.

LIIII. [The land] of the Same Osbern and of Ralph

In MARSTON, Thorfridh and another Thorfridh had 6 carucates of land to the geld. [There is] land for 8 ploughs. Ralph the steward and Osbern the priest have 2½ ploughs there, and 3 sokemen on 4½ bovates of this land and 10 villans and 5 bordars with 2 ploughs, and [there are] 2 mills [rendering] 22s, and 80 acres of meadow. TRE, as now, worth £4.

In Barkston [is] 1 carucate of land to the geld. [There is] land for 1 plough. [It is] SOKELAND of this manor. There are 7½ acres of meadow.

LV. The land of Ansgot

In BURWELL, Godric had 2 carucates of land to the geld. [There is] land for 8 ploughs. Ansgot has 3 ploughs there in demesne; and 23 villans and 6 bordars with 6 ploughs. There is a church, and 1 mill [rendering] 3s, and woodland pasture 1 league long and 1 broad. TRE worth £16; now 15[l]; tallage 40s.

In Authorpe [are] 2 carucates of land to the geld. [There is] land for 3 ploughs. [It is] SOKELAND of the same manor. There are 4 sokemen and 5 villans and 1 bordar with 2 ploughs, and 8 acres of meadow.

In MUCKTON, Thorfridh had 12 bovates of land to the geld. [There is] land for 3 ploughs. Ansgot has 1 plough there, and 2 sokemen and 5 villans and 2 bordars with 1½ ploughs. There is a church, and 7 acres of meadow, [and] scrubland 1 league long and 4 furlongs broad. TRE worth 30s; now 20[s].

In Welton le Wold, Ansgot has 1 villan with half a plough. There is land [assessed] to the geld, 2 bovates. [There is] land for 5 oxen. It is worth 5s.

LVI. The land of Countess Judith

In [North and South] WITHAM, Edward Cild had 5 carucates of land to the geld. [There is] land for 5 ploughs. Countess Judith, and Bernard under her, has 2 ploughs there, and 2 salt-pans [rendering] †10†s, and [there are] 41 acres of meadow. TRE worth £6; now £8; tallage 20s.

In 'Twyford' [in Colsterworth] [are] 5½ carucates of land to the geld. [There is] land for 7 ploughs. [It is] SOKELAND. 8 sokemen and 6 villans have 4 ploughs there, and 16 acres of meadow. [There is] woodland, pasture in place, 9 furlongs and 9 perches long and 6 furlongs broad.

In Swinstead [are] 2 carucates of land to the geld. [There is] land for 2 ploughs. [It is] SOKELAND. 8 sokemen have 2 ploughs there, and 4 acres of meadow, and [there are] 100 acres of woodland pasture less 4.

In Uffington, Leofric, Abbot of Peterborough, had 60 acres of land without geld. [...] Countess Judith has this land. On it she has no livestock, but tills it with the manor of Belmesthorpe [Rut.]. It is worth 10s.

In HOUGHAM, Stori had 5 carucates of land to the geld. [There is] land for 3 ploughs. Bishop Remigius has this manor of her, and he has there 9 villans and 2 bordars, and 1 mill [rendering] 5s4d, and the site of a mill [rendering] 13s4d, and 10 acres of meadow. TRE worth 20s; now 50s.

In Great PONTON, Grimbert and Almær had 8 carucates of land to the geld. [There is] land for 6 ploughs. Nigel, the countess' man, [has] 1 plough there, and 3 villans and 1 bordar with half a plough, and 5 mills [rendering] 44s. [There is] scrubland 16 furlongs long and 4 furlongs broad, and 3 acres of meadow. TRE worth 100s; now the same.

In Little PONTON, Thorfridh had 10 carucates of land to the geld. [There is] land for 10 ploughs. Nigel has of the countess 1 plough there, and 8 sokemen on 3 carucates of this land and 12 villans and 3 bordars with 5 ploughs, and 4 mills rendering 63s. [There is] scrubland 6 furlongs long and 5½ furlongs broad. TRE, as now, worth £6.

In 'GANTHORPE' [in Great Ponton], Thorfridh and Grimbert had 1 carucate of land and 6 bovates to the geld. [There is] land for 2 ploughs. Nigel has of the countess half a plough there, and 11 villans with 1½ ploughs, and 3 mills rendering 25s4d, and 16 acres of meadow, and 30 acres of scrubland. TRE worth 50s; now 40s.

In STAPLEFORD, Morcar had 10 carucates of land to the geld. [There is] land for 5 ploughs. Osbern has of the countess 2 ploughs there, and 27 sokemen on 6 carucates and 6 bovates of this land and 3 villans and 3 bordars with 7 ploughs. There is a priest and a church with half a carucate of this land, and meadow 5 furlongs long and 60 perches broad. TRE worth £7; now £8; tallage 40s.

In Norton Disney [are] 12 carucates of land to the geld. [There is] land for 7 ploughs. Judith has there 7 sokemen and 11 villans with 5 ploughs, and 12 acres of meadow. [There is] scrubland 6 furlongs long and 1 broad.

In MARKET OVERTON [Rut.] and Stretton [Rut.], Earl Waltheof had 3½ carucates of land to the geld. [There is] land for 12 ploughs. Countess Judith has 3 ploughs there in demesne; and 35 villans and 8 bordars with 9 ploughs,

and 40 acres of meadow, and woodland pasture 1 league long and a half broad. TRE worth £12; now 40s.

In THISTLETON [Rut.], Erik had half a carucate of land to the geld. [There is] land for 1 plough. Hugh, the countess' man, has 1 plough there, and 6 villans with 1 plough. TRE worth 20s; now 40[s].

In WHISSENDINE. [Rut.], Earl Waltheof had 4 carucates of land to the geld. [There is] land for 12 ploughs. Hugh, the countess' man, has 5 ploughs there in demesne; and 27 villans and 7 bordars with 8 ploughs. [There is] meadow 10 furlongs long and 8 furlongs broad.

In EAGLE, Earl Waltheof had 8 carucates of land to the geld. [There is] land for 6 ploughs. Countess Judith has 2 ploughs there, and 18 villans and 1 bordar with 4 ploughs. There is a church and a priest, and meadow 15 furlongs long and 1 broad, [and] woodland 14 furlongs long and 4 broad. TRE worth £10; now £12.

In Thurlby [near Norton Disney] [are] 7½ carucates of land to the geld. [There is] land for 3 ploughs and 6 oxen. [It is] inland and SOKELAND of Eagle. There are 14 sokemen with 4 ploughs.

In Swinderby [are] 11 carucates to the geld. [It is] SOKELAND of Eagle. [There is] land for 6 ploughs. Countess Judith has there 49 sokemen having 13 ploughs. [There is] woodland pasture 8 furlongs long and 5 broad, half of it pasture and the other half scrubland.

IN RUTLAND

In EXTON [Rut.], Earl Waltheof had 2 carucates of land to the geld. [There is] land for 12 ploughs. Countess Judith has 3 ploughs there, and 37 villans with 8 ploughs, and 2 mills [rendering] 13s. [There is] meadow 6 furlongs long, [and] woodland, pasture in places, 5 furlongs long and 5 broad. TRE worth £8; now £10.

In WHITWELL [Rut.], Besi had 1 carucate of land to the geld. [There is] land for 3 ploughs. Herbert, the countess' man, has 1 plough there, and 6 villans and 4 bordars with 2 ploughs. There is a church, and a priest, and 1 mill [rendering] 12d, and 20 acres of meadow, [and] woodland pasture 6 furlongs and 6 perches long and 3 furlongs and 13 perches broad. It is worth 40s.

In COLEBY [near Boothby Graffoe], Arnketil had 5 carucates of land to the geld. [There is] land for 5 ploughs. Countess Judith has 1 plough there, and 1 sokeman on 1 carucate of this land and 6 villans with 1 plough, and 30 acres of meadow. TRE worth 60s; now 40[s].

In South Witham [are] 2 carucates of land to the geld. [There is] land for 2 ploughs. [It is] SOKELAND of Market Overton [Rut.]. 8 sokemen and 2 villans and 1 bordar have 3 ploughs there. There is half a church, and 60 acres of meadow, and 100 acres of woodland.

In ''Tisteltone'' [in South Witham] [are] 6 bovates of land to the geld. [There is] land for 6 oxen. [It is] SOKELAND of the same manor. 2 bordars have 2 oxen in a plough there. It is worth 10s. Hugh holds it.

In Bicker [are] 1½ bovates of land to the geld. [There is] land for 2 oxen. [It is] inland of North Witham. It is waste except for 1 salt-pan.

In MINTING [Minting or 'Little Minting'], William the priest has 2½ bovates and the sixth part of 1 bovate to the geld. [There is] land for 6 oxen. It is worth 2s.

LVII. The land of Guy de Craon

In ASHBY CUM FENBY, Aslak had 9 bovates of land to the geld. [There is] land for 2½ ploughs. Alvred, Guy de Craon's man, has 2 ploughs there, and 9 sokemen on 3 bovates of this land and 3 villans with 1 plough, and 30 acres of meadow, and 9½ acres of scrubland. TRE worth 40s; now £4; tallage 40s.

SOKELAND OF THIS MANOR

In East Ravendale [are] 10 bovates of land to the geld. [There is] land for 2½ ploughs. 10 sokemen have 2½ ploughs there.

In Brigsley [are] 6 bovates of land to the geld. [There is] land for 12 oxen. 8 sokemen and 1 bordar have 1 plough there, and 5 acres of meadow.

In Waithe [are] 5½ bovates of land to the geld. [There is] land for as many oxen. 6 sokemen have 1 plough there, and 10 acres of meadow.

In Normanby and Santon, Esbiorn and Ketil had 7 bovates of land to the geld. [There is] land for as many oxen. Alvred, Guy's man, has 1½ ploughs there, and 2 villans and 2 bordars with half a plough, and [there are] 60 acres of meadow. TRE worth 20s; now 15[s]; tallage 5s.

In BINBROOK and 'Orford' [in Stainton le Vale], Edward had 10 bovates of land to the geld. [There is] land for 3½ ploughs. Alvred, Guy's man, has 2 ploughs there, and 1 mill [rendering] 5s, and 12 acres of meadow. TRE, as now, [worth] 40s.

In LAUGHTON [near Blyton], Ulfgrimr had 2 carucates of land and 2 bovates to the geld. [There is] land for 3 ploughs. Alvred, Guy's man, has 2 ploughs there, and 9 sokemen on 10 bovates of this land and 8 villans and 4 bordars with 3 ploughs, and 17 acres of meadow, and 12 acres of scrubland. TRE worth 60s; and now the same; tallage 40s.

SOKELAND OF THIS MANOR

In Blyton [are] 14 bovates of land to the geld. [There is] land for 2 ploughs.

In Scotton, Guy has 2 bovates of land.

In RIPPINGALE, Æthelstan had 3 carucates of land to the geld. [There is] land for 3 ploughs. Now Widald, Guy's man, has 1 plough there, and 10 villans and 2 bordars with 5 ploughs, and 60 acres of meadow, and 16 acres of scrubland. TRE worth £4; now 3[l].

SOKELAND OF THIS MANOR

In Laughton [in Folkingham] [are] 5 bovates of land and the third part of a bovate to the geld. [There is] land for as many oxen. Warner, Guy's man, has 3 bordars there, and 10 acres of scrubland. TRE, as now, worth 10s.

In DOWSBY, Osfram had in pledge 3 carucates of land to the geld. [There is] land for 3 ploughs. Hernald fitzAnsgot redeemed this land before Guy was seised of Osfram's land, and afterwards Guy always had the service. There is 1 plough in demesne; and 3 villans with 1 plough, and 31 acres of meadow. TRE, as now, worth 30s.

In POINTON, Æthelstan had 1 carucate of land to the geld. [There is] land for 1 plough. Warner, Guy's man, has 1 plough there, and 20 acres of scrubland. TRE worth 20s; now 30[s].

In SCOTTLETHORPE, Æthelstan had 1 carucate of land to the geld.

[Folio 367V: LINCOLNSHIRE]

[There is] land for 1 plough. Guy until now held it in soke, and now it is adjudged as a capital manor for the king's use. There is 1 plough in demesne; and 1 villan and 2 bordars having 2 oxen in a plough. There is 1 acre of meadow and 1 acre of scrubland. TRE worth 20s; now 10[s].

In OSBOURNBY, Ælfric had 2 carucates of land to the geld. [There is] land for 3 ploughs. Vitalis, Guy's man, has 1 plough there, and 1 sokeman on 1 carucate of this land and 5 villans and 3 bordars with 1½ ploughs, and [there are] 24 acres of meadow. TRE worth 40s; now £6.

In Dembleby [are] 6 bovates of land to the geld. [There is] land for 2 ploughs. [It is] SOKELAND of Osbournby. 1 sokeman and 2 villans have 1 plough there, and 14 acres of meadow, and 20 acres of scrubland.

In Scott Willoughby, Guy has the soke over half a church and over a priest who belongs to Osbournby.

In HACEBY, Ælfric had 11 bovates of land to the geld. [There is] land for 2 ploughs. Godwine, Guy's man, has 1 plough there, and 1 sokeman and 1 villan and 1 bordar having 2 oxen in a plough. There is a priest and a church, and 8½ acres of meadow, and 18 acres of scrubland. TRE worth 20s; now 30[s].

Waldin claims this land by gift of the king. Guy has soke over 11 bovates of Waldin's land, as the wapentake bears witness.

In SWATON, Æthelstan had 1 carucate of land to the geld. [There is] land for 11 oxen. Warner, Guy's man, has 1 plough there, and 1 villan with 2 oxen in a plough, and 8 acres of meadow. TRE worth 40s; now 10s.

In Horbling, Guy has soke over 6 bovates of Waldin's land.

In Heydour [are] 4 carucates of land to the geld. [There is] land for 5 ploughs. [It is] SOKELAND of Osbournby. 24 sokemen and 3 bordars have 6 ploughs there, and [there are] 80 acres of meadow, and 16 acres of scrubland. There is a priest and a church.

In WELBY, Æthelstan had 4 carucates of land to the geld. [There is] land for 4 ploughs. Ranulph, Guy's man, has 2 ploughs there in demesne; and 5 sokemen on 3 carucates and 2 bovates of this land and 3 villans with 2 ploughs, and 53 acres of meadow, and 80 acres of scrubland. TRE worth 40s; now 60[s].

In HARROWBY, Algar had 1 carucate of land to the geld. [There is] land for 10 oxen. The same Algar has there of Guy 1 plough in demesne, and 1 mill rendering 4s, and 9 acres of meadow. TRE as now, worth 10s.

In 'TOWTHORPE' [in Londonthorpe], Algar had 2½ carucates of land to the geld. [There is] land for as many ploughs. Ranulph, Guy's man, has 1 plough there in demesne; and 2 sokemen on 2 bovates of this land and 5 villans and 6 bordars with 1 plough. There is a priest and a church, and 3 mills [rendering] 40s, and 17 acres of meadow. TRE, as now, worth 60s.

SOKELAND OF THIS MANOR

In Belton [near Grantham] [is] half a carucate of land to the geld. [There is] land for 4 oxen. There is 1 sokeman with half a plough, and 9 acres of meadow.

In Great Gonerby [are] 3 bovates of land to the geld and half a bovate of land to the geld. [There is] land for 3 oxen. 2 sokemen and 1 villan have 1½ ploughs there, and 7½ acres of meadow, and a mill [rendering] 5s.

In 'TYTTON' [in Wyberton], Æthelstan had 11 bovates to the geld. [There is] land for 14½ oxen. Guy has 2 ploughs there in demesne, and 10 acres of meadow, and 2 bordars. TRE worth 60s; now 50s.

In FRAMPTON, Æthelstan had 4 carucates of land and 2 bovates to the geld. [There is] land for 5½ ploughs. Guy has 2 ploughs there in demesne; and 2 sokemen on 4 bovates of this land and 10 villans and 1 bordar having 2½ ploughs. There is a church and a priest, and 60 acres of meadow. TRE worth 70s; now the same; tallage 10s.

In KIRTON, Ælfric had 14 bovates of land and 2 parts of a bovate to the geld. [There is] land for 17 oxen. Guy has 1 plough there in demesne; and 2 sokemen on 1 bovate of this land having 3 oxen in a plough, and [there are] 16 acres of meadow. TRE worth 20s; now 30s.

In BURTON PEDWARDINE, Æthelstan had 10 carucates of land to the geld. [There is] land for 17 ploughs. Guy has 5 ploughs there, and 30 sokemen and 9 villans and 12 bordars having 11½ ploughs. There is a priest and a church, and 1 mill [rendering] 2s, and 120 acres of meadow. TRE worth £6; now £8; tallage 40s.

In Heckington [are] 4 bovates of land to the geld. [There is] land for 4 oxen. [It is] SOKELAND. There are 2 villans and 1 bordar having 3 oxen in a plough, and 3 acres of meadow.

In Aswarby [are] 4 bovates of land to the geld. [There is] land for 1 plough. [It is] SOKELAND of 'Cold Mareham' [in Burton Pedwardine]. 1 sokeman and 1 bordar have half a plough there, and 20 acres of meadow.

In SWARBY, Ælfric had 2 bovates of land to the geld. [There is] land for 4 oxen. Vitalis, Guy's man, has 1 plough there, and 16 sokemen and 3 villans having 2½ ploughs, and 80 acres of meadow, and 80 acres of scrubland. TRE worth 20s; now the same.

SOKELAND OF THIS MANOR

In Kelby [is] 1 bovate of land to the geld. [There is] land for 2 oxen. There Eskil the priest has under Guy 2 villans having 3 oxen in a plough.

In Marston [are] 6 bovates of land to the geld. [It is] a BEREWICK of Haceby. Osbert has 3 oxen in a plough there, and 12 acres of meadow. It is worth 10s.

In WRANGLE, Æthelstan had 2 carucates of land to the geld. [There is] land for 1 plough. Guy has it, and it is waste on account of the sea flooding.

In FISHTOFT, Æthelstan had 9 carucates of land to the geld. [There is] land for as many ploughs. Guy has 3 ploughs there, and 1 sokeman and 9 villans and 1 bordar having 4 ploughs. There is a church and a priest, and 1 mill [rendering] 10s, and 60 acres of meadow. TRE worth £8; now 10[l].

In BUTTERWICK, Wulfweard had 12 carucates of land to the geld. [There is] land for 12 ploughs. Guy has 2 ploughs there, and 36 sokemen on 9 carucates of this land and 6 villans and 10 bordars having 15 ploughs. There are 2 churches and 2 priests, and 100 acres of meadow. TRE, as now, worth £10; tallage 100s.

SOKELAND OF THIS MANOR

In Freiston [near Boston] [are] 12 carucates of land to the geld. [There is] land for as many ploughs. 20 sokemen and 26 villans and 15 bordars have 15 ploughs there. Of this sokeland 2 of Guy's men have 5 carucates and 1 bovate, and they have 2½ ploughs there, and 5 sokemen and 12 villans having 1½ ploughs.

In Threekingham, Guy has 2 bovates of Gilbert de Ghent's land of which the soke belongs to Folkingham.

[Folio 368: LINDSEY]

In KEISBY, Osfram had 2 carucates of land to the geld. [There is] land for 3 ploughs. Guy has 1 Plough there, and 2 villans and 4 bordars having 1½ ploughs, and 24 acres of meadow, and 60 acres of scrubland. TRE worth 40s; now 30[s].

In 'Avethorpe' [in Aslackby] [are] 4 bovates of land to the geld. [There is] land for 6 oxen. [It is] a BEREWICK of the same manor. 2 villans have 1 plough there, and 8 acres of meadow. It is worth 10s.

In Old Somerby, Æthelgyth [had] 6 bovates of land to the geld. [There is] land for 6 oxen. This SOKELAND was such that it rendered nothing, but provided service in the king's host by land and sea. Guy has there 5 oxen in a plough, and 5 acres of scrubland. TRE, as now, worth 5s.

In BICKER, Æthelstan had 10 bovates of land to the geld. [There is] land for as many oxen. Guy has 1 plough there, and

4 villans and 4 bordars with half a plough, and [there is] 1 salt-pan [rendering] 16d, and 20 acres of meadow. TRE, as now, worth 20s.

In 'SOUTHORPE' [in Edenham], Osfram had 2 carucates of land to the geld. [There is] land for 2 ploughs. Guy has 2 ploughs there, and 10 villans and 6 bordars with 2 ploughs, and 1 mill [rendering] 2s, and 16 acres of meadow, and 200 acres of woodland pasture. TRE worth 40s; now 50[s]; tallage 10s.

In SKILLINGTON, Colbert had 1 carucate of land to the geld. [There is] land for 12 oxen. Guy has there 5 villans with 1 plough, and 20 acres of meadow, and 20 acres of woodland pasture belonging to Algar's warnode, and 20 acres of scrubland belonging to the warnode of the archbishop. TRE, as now, worth 20s.

In 'CASTHORPE' [in Barrowby], Algar had 1 carucate of land to the geld. [There is] land for 10 oxen. The same Algar has it of Guy. There is 1 plough, and 3 villans and 2 bordars have 5 oxen in a plough, and 8 acres of meadow. TRE worth 16s; now 20[s].

In 'HOUGHTON' [in Grantham], Alstan had 3 carucates of land and 2½ bovates to the geld. [There is] land for as many ploughs and oxen. Vitalis, Guy's man, has 1 plough there, and 1 sokeman on 1 bovate of this land and 10 villans and 4 bordars having 2½ ploughs, and 2 mills [rendering] 26s8d, and 3 acres of meadow. TRE worth £4; now 3[l].

SOKELAND OF 'HOUGHTON' [IN GRANTHAM]

In 'Towthorpe' [in Londonthorpe] [are] 2 bovates of land to the geld. [There is] land for 2 oxen. There are 3 acres of meadow.

In HOLBEACH and WHAPLODE, Alstan had 2 carucates of land and 2 bovates to the geld. [There is] land for 12 pence [sic]. Guy has 1 plough there, and 4 villans and 1 bordar with 1 plough, and 10 acres of meadow. TRE worth 100s; now £8.

SOKELAND OF THIS MANOR

In Long Sutton [are] 12 bovates of land to the geld. [There is] land for 1 plough. There is 1 sokeman and 1 villan having 2 oxen in a plough.

In Pinchbeck [are] 2 carucates of land to the geld. [There is] land for 2 ploughs. Guy has 7 villans with 1 plough there.

In Weston and Moulton [are] 15 bovates of land to the geld. [There is] land for 15 ploughs. 6 villans have half a plough there.

In SPALDING, Alstan had 11 bovates of land to the geld. [There is] land [...]. Guy has 1 plough there, and 5 villans and 2 bordars with 1 plough, and a drying-place with salt-pans rendering 4d. TRE, as now, worth 40s.

In BOOTHBY PAGNELL and Old Somerby, Alstan had 1 carucate of land to the geld. [There is] land for 1 plough. Godwine, Guy's man, has 1 plough there, and 3 villans with half a plough, and [there are] 2 acres of meadow, and 30 acres

of pasture, and 80 acres of scrubland. To this manor belong 3½ bovates of land of which Sighwat has the soke. TRE worth 20s; now the same.

In DRAYTON, Alstan had half a carucate of land to the geld. [There is] land for 4 oxen. This land was delivered to Guy as 1 manor. He has 1 villan and 4 bordars with half a plough there, and 2 acres of meadow. TRE worth 5s; now 3s.

In Elsthorpe and in Bulby, Osfram had 2 bovates of land to the geld. Guy has them, and they are vacant, but nonetheless they are tilled.

LVIII. The land of Robert Malet

In WELBOURN, Godwine had 12 carucate of land to the geld. [There is] land for 16 ploughs. Robert Malet has 3 ploughs there in demesne; and 35 sokemen on 7 carucates of this land and 12 villans and 8 bordars having 12 ploughs and 2 oxen. There is a priest, and a church to which belong 5 bovates of land, and 1 mill [rendering] 2s, and 200 acres of meadow. TRE, as now, worth £16; tallage 40s.

In BARROWBY, Godwine had 8 carucates of land to the geld. [There is] land for 15 ploughs. Robert has 5 ploughs there, and 2 sokemen on 10 bovates of this land and 50 villans and 2 bordars having 10 ploughs, and 1 mill [rendering] 3s. There is a church, and a priest, and 60 acres of meadow. TRE worth £12; now 16[l].

SOKELAND OF THIS MANOR

In Ingoldsby [are] 6 bovates of land to the geld. 4 sokemen have 1 plough and 2 oxen there, and 7 acres of meadow, and 52 acres of scrubland.

In 'Casthorpe' [in Barrowby] [are] 6 bovates of land to the geld. [There is] land for 1 plough. Ivo holds this SOKELAND of Robert, and he has there 6 sokemen with 1 plough and 2 oxen, and 2 mills [rendering] 4s, and 7 acres of meadow.

In Stenwith [are] 4 carucates of land to the geld. [There is] land for as many ploughs. 19 sokemen and 2 bordars have 4 ploughs there, and 1 mill [rendering] 4s, and 15 acres of meadow.

In SEDGEBROOK, Godwine had 4 carucates of land to the geld. [There is] land for 9 ploughs. Robert has 4 ploughs there, and 27 villans and 5 bordars having 6 ploughs, and 3 mills [rendering] 16s, and [there are] 60 acres of meadow, and 8 acres of scrubland. TRE worth £9; now 8[l]; tallage 40s.

In Wilsford [are] 3 carucates of land to the geld. [There is] land for 4 ploughs. [It is] SOKELAND of this manor. 9 Sokemen and 2 bordars have 3 ploughs there, and 15 acres of meadow.

In East Allington [are] 6 carucates of land to the geld. [There is] land for 5 ploughs. Godric has of Robert Malet 2 ploughs there in demesne; and 11 sokemen and 10 villans and 3 bordars having 4 ploughs, and 140 acres of meadow.

[Folio 368V: LINCOLNSHIRE]

LIX. The land of Robert of Stafford

In DENTON, Uhtbrand had 1 carucate of land and 6 bovates to the geld. [There is] land for as many ploughs and oxen. [It is] SOKELAND belonging to Grantham. Robert of Stafford, and Geoffrey of him, has half a plough there, and 3 villans and 2 bordars with 1 plough, and 28 acres of meadow. TRE worth 40s; now 20[s].

In 'CASTHORPE' [in Barrowby], Ulfkil had 6 bovates of land to the geld. [There is] land for 6 oxen. Hugh, Robert's man, has half a plough there, and 1 villan and 2 bordars with 1 ox in a plough, and [there are] 7 acres of meadow. TRE worth 20s; now 10[s].

In BOULTHAM [in Lincoln], Osmund had 9 bovates of land to the geld. [There is] land for 6 oxen. Now there is 1 villan with 1 ox, and 8 acres of meadow. Tre worth 13s4d; now 6s.

In CARLBY, Dene and Karli had 1 carucate of land and twice the fourth part of a bovate to the geld. [There is] land for as many ploughs and oxen. The land of Karli was free soke-land under Dene. Geoffrey, Robert's man, has 1 plough there, and 10 villans with 2 ploughs, and 10 acres of meadow, and 40 acres of scrubland. TRE worth 40s; now 50[s]; tallage 10s.

In BRACEBOROUGH and 'Banthorpe' [in Brace-borough], Dene and Karli and Leodflæd had 20 bovates of land to the geld. [There is] land for as many oxen. The land of 2 of these was free sokeland under Dene. Geoffrey, Robert's man, has 1 plough there, and 4 villans with half a plough, and 2 mills [rendering] 20s, and the third part of a church, and 7 acres of meadow, and 55 acres of scrubland. TRE worth 60s; now 40[s].

In the same places Karli and Dene [had] 4 bovates of land to the geld. [There is] land for 4 oxen. It is SOKELAND of Thorgot Lag's manor of Greatford. It is waste.

In 'AUSTERBY' [in Bourne], Healfdene had 6 bovates of land to the geld. [There is] land for 6 oxen. Geoffrey, Robert's man, has half a plough there, and 3 villans and 3 bordars with 1 plough, and the third part of a mill [rendering] 3s4d, and 6 fishponds [rendering] 16d, and 7 acres of meadow, and 30 acres of scrubland. TRE, as now, worth 20s.

In Thurlby [near Bourne] [is] half a carucate of land to the geld. [There is] land for 4 oxen. [It is] a BEREWICK. 2 villans and 2 bordars have half a plough there, and 4 acres of meadow, and 30 acres of scrubland.

In CREETON, Fredegæst and Beorhtmær had 12 bovates of land and 2 parts of 2 bovates to the geld. [There is] land for as many oxen. The land of Beorhtmær [was] free sokeland under Fredegæst. Basuin, Robert's man, has half a plough there, and 5 sokemen and 4 villans with 1½ ploughs. TRE worth 40s; now 30[s]; tallage 10s.

In Little Bytham [is] half a carucate of land to the geld. [There is] land for 4 oxen. [It is] SOKELAND of Creeton. It is waste. There is 1 acre of meadow.

In BITCHFIELD and Westby, Almær had 12 bovates of land to the geld. [There is] land for 12 oxen. Basuin, Robert's man, has there 2 villans and 1 bordar with 6 oxen in a plough, and 14 acres of meadow, and 300 acres of woodland, pasture in places. TRE worth 30s; now 20[s].

In SOUTH RAUCEBY, Wulfsige had 3 carucates of land and half a bovate to the geld, and Osmund, 3½ bovates, and Siward, 1 carucate, had 11½ bovates of land to the geld. [There is] land for as many ploughs and oxen. Siward's land [was] free sokeland under Osmund. Edelo, Robert's man, has there 7 sokemen on 2 carucates and 5 bovates of this land and 1 villan with 4 ploughs.

And in the other Rauceby [North Rauceby], Thorfridh had 3½ bovates of land to the geld. [There is] land for as many oxen. 6 villans and 1 rent-paying tenant have 2 ploughs there, and half a church. TRE worth 60s; now 70s.

In [North or South] RAUCEBY, Thorfridh had 9 carucates of land to the geld. [There is] land for 9 ploughs. Brian, Robert's man, has 1½ ploughs there, and 2 villans and 1 bordar. In the same place 5 bovates of land belong to the hall.

In the same place Osmund had 3 carucates of land and 1 bovate to the geld. [There is] land for as many ploughs. 3½ bovates belonged to his hall. The rest was SOKELAND of the same manor. Brian, Robert's man, has there 20 sokemen and 4 bordars having 4 ploughs and 3 oxen in a plough. TRE worth 40s; now the same; tallage 10s.

In SCREDINGTON, Leofric had 12 bovates of land to the geld. [There is] land for as many oxen. Gulfered, Robert's man, has 1 plough there, and half a sokeman and 1 villan having 3 oxen in a plough, and 3 acres of meadow. TRE worth 20s; now 10[s.]..

In HACONBY, Wulfgeat had 1 carucate of land to the geld. [There is] land for 1 plough, Gulfer, Robert's man, has 1 plough there, and 5 villans and 1 bordar with 1 plough, and 16 acres of meadow, and 35 acres of woodland meadow [sic] TRE, as now, worth 30s.

In SKINNAND, Wulfgifu had 3 carucates of land to the geld. [There is] land for 3 ploughs. Kolgrimr, Robert's man, has there 7 villans having 4 ploughs and 1 ox in a plough, and 50 acres of meadow. TRE worth 60s; now 20[s].

In METHERINGHAM, Leofsige had 1 carucate of land to the geld. [There is] land for half a plough. Ehelo, Robert's man, has 30 acres of meadow there, and 3 acres of scrubland. TRE worth 16s; now 10[s.].

In [Scott or Silk] WILLOUGHBY, Osmund had 6 bovates of land to the geld. [There is] land for 12 oxen. Godwine, Robert's man, has half a plough there, and 1 sokeman on 3 bovates of this land and 1 villan with 5 oxen in a plough, and 24 acres of meadow, and 12 acres of scrubland. TRE, as now, worth 10s.

In 'Counthorpe' [in Castle Bytham], Robert has 2 sokemen on 2 acres and 3 perches of land. [It is] SOKELAND of Creeton.

LX. The land of Peter de Valognes

In Burton, Godric had 2 carucates of land to the geld. [There is] land for 2 ploughs. [It is] SOKELAND of Scampton, but nevertheless there was a hall there. Now Peter de Valognes has there 1 villan and 4 bordars with half a plough, and 5 acres of meadow. The demesne is tilled and leased. TRE worth 15s; now 11s.

[Folio 369: LINDSEY]

LXI. The land of Heppo the Crossbowman

In HACONBY and in STAINFIELD [in Haconby], Leofric had 3 carucates of land and $2\frac{1}{2}$ bovates to the geld. [There is] land for as many ploughs and oxen. Heppo the crossbowman has 2 ploughs there, and 3 sokemen on 12 bovates of this land and 13 villans and 6 bordars with 6 ploughs. There is a priest, and a church, and 1 mill [rendering] 12d, and 40 acres of meadow, and 80 acres of scrubland. TRE, as now, worth 100s; tallage 20s.

In Dyke [are] 3 bovates of land to the geld. [There is] land for 3 oxen. [It is] SOKELAND of the same manor.

In Morton [near Hanthorpe] [are] $9\frac{1}{2}$ bovates of land to the geld. [There is] land for as many oxen. 9 sokemen have 1 plough there, and 10 acres of meadow, and 12 acres of scrubland.

In HANTHORPE, Thorfridh had 1 carucate of land to the geld. [There is] land for 1 plough. Simund, Heppo's man, has 1 plough there, and 9 acres of meadow, and 20 acres of scrubland. TRE worth 20s; now 30[s].

In SURFLEET, Alsige had $4\frac{1}{2}$ carucates of land to the geld. [There is] land for as many ploughs. Heppo has 1 plough there, and 11 villans and 6 bordars with $2\frac{1}{2}$ ploughs, and 2 salt-pans [rendering] 12d. TRE worth £4; now 66s.

In KIRKBY GREEN and Scopwick, Healfdene had 5 carucates of land and 6 bovates to the geld. [There is] land for 4 ploughs. Heppo has 2 ploughs there, and 13 sokemen on 4 carucates and 2 bovates of this land and 3 villans and 2 bordars with $5\frac{1}{2}$ ploughs, and half a mill [rendering] 5s, and 20 acres of meadow. TRE worth 20s; now 50[s.]; tallage 10s.

In Martin [in Timberland] [are] 3 carucates of land to the geld. [There is] land for 2 ploughs. [It is] a BEREWICK. Simund, Heppo's man, has half a plough there, and 11 sokemen on 2 carucates of this land and 1 bordar with 2 ploughs. TRE worth 20s; now 30s.

In Scopwick [are] 12 bovates of land to the geld. [There is] land for 12 oxen. 1 sokeman has 1 plough there, and 4 acres of meadow. TRE worth 10s; now 6s.

In SNITTERBY, Godwine had 10 bovates of land to the geld. [There is] land for 12 oxen. Heppo has 1 plough there, and 75 acres of meadow. TRE worth 20s; now the same; tallage 10s.

SOKELAND

In Redbourne [are] 3 bovates of land to the geld, and in 'Stainton' [in Waddingham] and Waddingham half a bovate of land to the geld. [There is] land for as many oxen. There are 2 villans with half a plough, and 6 acres of meadow.

LXII. The land of Ralph fitzHubert

In GUNBY [near North Witham], Godwine had 4 carucates of land to the geld. [There is] land for 4 ploughs. Ralph fitzHubert has 2 ploughs there, and 1 mill [rendering] 12d, and 63 acres of meadow. TRE worth 40s; now 70s; tallage 10s.

In the same place Wulfwine had 1 carucate of land to the geld. [There is] land for 1 plough. Ansfrid, Ralph's priest, seized this. On it [there are] 2 villans, and 10 acres of meadow. A certain William leases it for 6s. [It is] SOKELAND and a Berewick of [?] North Witham.

LXIII. The land of Geoffrey de La Guerche

In BLYBOROUGH, Leofric Cild had 2 carucates of land and 3 bovates to the geld. [There is] land for 6 ploughs. Robert, Geoffrey de la Guerche's man, has 2 ploughs there, and 13 sokemen on 10 bovates of this land and 4 villans with $2\frac{1}{2}$ ploughs. There is half a church, and 1 mill [rendering] 2s, and 60 acres of meadow. TRE, as now, worth 40s; tallage 20s.

In GAINSBOROUGH, Leodwine had 8 carucates of land to the geld. [There is] land for 12 ploughs. Reginald, Geoffrey's man, has 2 ploughs there, and 12 sokemen on 4 carucates of this land and 4 villans with 6 ploughs, and 40 acres of meadow, and 80 acres of scrubland. TRE worth £6; now 3[l]; tallage 20s.

In Somerby [in Corringham] [are] 4 bovates of land to the geld. [It is] a BEREWICK. [There is] land for 4 oxen. There is half a plough in demesne; and 1 villan having 2 oxen in a plough, and 10 acres of meadow, and 10 acres of scrubland.

In Yawthorpe [is] 1 carucate of land to the geld. [There is] land for 1 plough. [It is] inland and SOKELAND. There is 1 plough in demesne; and 6 sokemen have 1 plough.

In EPWORTH, Leodwine had 8 carucates of land to the geld. [There is] land for 12 ploughs. Geoffrey de la Guerche has 2 ploughs there, and 8 sokemen on 2 carucates and 5 bovates of this land and 13 villans and 9 bordars with 6 ploughs, and 11 fisheries [rendering] 5s, and [there are] 16 acres of meadow. [There is] woodland pasture 1 league long and 1 broad. TRE worth £8; now 5[l]; tallage 20s.

In OWSTON FERRY, Gytha had 4 carucates of land to the geld. [There is] land for 4 ploughs. Geoffrey has 1 plough there, and 9 villans and 6 bordars with 3 ploughs, and 3 fisheries [rendering] 3s, and 6 acres of meadow. [There is] woodland pasture 1 league long and 1 broad. TRE worth £6; now 30s; tallage 10s.

In HAXEY, Siward Barn had 3 carucates of land to the geld. [There is] land for 6 ploughs. Wazelin, Geoffrey's man, has $2\frac{1}{2}$

ploughs there, and 16 villans and 8 bordars with 3½ ploughs, and 9 fisheries [rendering] 7s, and 3 acres of meadow. [There is] woodland, pasture in places, 5 furlongs long and 1 furlong broad. TRE, as now, worth 100s; tallage 20s.

In EAST LOUND and the other LOUND [Graizelound], Fulcric and Wege had 14 bovates of land to the geld. [There is] land for 7 oxen.

In the same places [are] 9 bovates of land to the geld. [It is] SOKELAND of Epworth.

In the same places [is] 1 bovate of land to the geld. [It is] a BEREWICK of Belton [near Epworth]. [There is] land for 5 oxen. There are 4 sokemen and 4 villans and 2 rent-paying tenants having 3½ ploughs, and 1 fishery [rendering] 12d. TRE worth 20s; now 16s.

In High Burnham and the other Burnham [Low Burnham] [are] 6 carucates of land to the geld. [There is] land for 6 ploughs. [It is] SOKELAND of Epworth. 18 sokemen have 7 ploughs there.

In BELTON [near Epworth], Ulf and Alnoth had 5 carucates of land to the geld. [There is] land for 5 ploughs. Geoffrey has 1 plough there, and 17 sokemen and 20 villans and 6 bordars having 4 ploughs and 6 oxen, and 11 fisheries [rendering] 7s. [There is] woodland, pasture in places, 2 leagues long and 2 broad. TRE worth £7; now 4[l]5s4d; tallage 20s.

In Beltoft [is] 1 carucate of land to the geld. [There is] land for 1 plough. 4 sokemen and 16 bordars have 3 ploughs there. [There is] woodland, pasture in places, 4 furlongs long and 4 broad.

In Althorpe [is] 1 carucate of land to the geld. [There is] land for 1 plough. 6 sokemen have 1 plough there.

[Folio 369V: LINCOLNSHIRE]

In CROWLE, Alwine had 6 carucates of land less 1 bovate to the geld. [There is] land for as many ploughs; and in the same place 1 bovate of land to the geld, inland of Upperthorpe. Now a certain abbot of St German of Selby has it of Geoffrey. There is 1 plough in demesne; and 15 villans and 19 bordars have 7 ploughs, and 31 fisheries [rendering] 31s, and [there are] 30 acres of meadow. There is a church, and woodland pasture 1 league long and 1 league broad. TRE worth £12; now £8; tallage 40s.

SOKELAND OF THIS MANOR

In Amcotts [are] 2 carucates of land to the geld. [There is] land for 1 plough. 2 sokemen and 6 villans have 1 plough there.

In the same place [are] 3 bovates of land to the geld. [There is] land for 3 oxen. [It is] inland of Westwoodside.

In the same place [are] †6† bovates of land to the geld. [There is] land for 5 oxen. [It is] SOKELAND of Garthorpe.

In Garthorpe and Luddington [are] 4½ carucates of land to the geld. [There is] land for 1½ ploughs. [It is] SOKELAND of Crowle. Now 12 sokemen have 2 ploughs there.

IN THE SAME PLACES Fulcric had 1 carucate of land to the geld. [There is] land for half a plough; and in the same places Ulf had half a carucate of land to the geld. [It is] SOKELAND of Belton [near Epworth]. This land is waste; yet it renders 3s. TRE it was worth 10s.

In West Butterwick [are] 3 carucates of land to the geld. [It is] SOKELAND and inland of Owston Ferry. [There is] land for 1 plough. 1 sokeman and 6 villans have 1 plough there, and 1 mill [rendering] 4s.

In LUDDINGTON and Garthorpe and 'The Marshes' [in Luddington] and 'Waterton' [in Luddington] [are] 6 carucates of land to the geld. [There is] land for 2 ploughs. Of this land 4½ carucates are in the SOKE of Crowle. Now 12 sokemen have 2 ploughs there.

THERE Fulcric had 1 carucate of land with a hall. Now it is waste.

There Ulf Fenman [had] half a carucate. [It is] SOKELAND of Belton [near Epworth]. Gilbert claims it. Geoffrey has it; and it is waste. TRE worth 10s; now 3s.

To this island belong marshes 10 leagues long and 3 broad.

SOKELAND OF RUSKINGTON

In 'Roxholm' [in Ruskington] [are] 3 carucates of land and 6 bovates to the geld. [There is] land for as many ploughs and oxen.

In Leasingham [are] 6 carucates of land to the geld. [There is] land for 6 ploughs. There are 30 acres of meadow.

In 'Coteland' [in Ruskington] [are] 5 carucates of meadow to the geld. [There is] marsh 10 furlongs long and 6 furlongs broad.

In Stubton [are] 5 carucates and 2½ bovates to the geld. [There is] land for 7 ploughs. [It is] SOKELAND of Westborough. There are 20 sokemen and 5 bordars with 7 ploughs. There is a priest and a church, and 120 acres of meadow. Of this land 1 knight of his has 6 bovates, and has 1 plough there.

LXIIII. The land of Geoffrey Alselin

'FLAXWELL' WAPENTAKE

In RUSKINGTON, Toki had 12 carucates of land to the geld. [There is] land for as many ploughs. Geoffrey Alselin and Ralph his nephew have 2 ploughs there, and 22 sokemen on 3 carucates and 2 bovates of this land and 8 villans and 8 bordars having 8 ploughs, and 60 acres of meadow, and 240 acres of woodland, pasture in places. TRE worth £25; now £50; tallage £10. There is a church and a priest, and 3 mills [rendering] £4.12s8d.

A certain Drogo holds 6 bovates of land in Ruskington, and has 1 plough there. It is worth 20s.

In Anwick [are] 6 carucates of land to the geld. [There is] land for as many ploughs. [It is] a BEREWICK of Ruskington. Ralph, Geoffrey's nephew, has there 21 sokemen and 4 villans having 7 ploughs. Drogo, his man, holds 5½ bovates of the same land, and has 6 oxen in a plough there, and 1 villan and 3 bordars with 1 ox. It is worth 25s.

SOKELAND OF THIS MANOR

In Dorrington [are] 12 carucates of land to the geld. [There is] land for 12 ploughs. Geoffrey has 1 plough there in demesne; and 28 sokemen and 8 bordars with 7 ploughs. A man of his has there 9 bovates of land with 1 plough. It is worth 20s. There are †160† acres of meadow, and 50 acres of scrubland.

In Digby [are] 12 carucates of land to the geld. [There is] land for as many ploughs. 35 sokemen have 12 ploughs there, and 100 acres of meadow, and 10 acres of scrubland.

In Rowston [are] 12 carucates of land to the geld. [There is] land for 12 ploughs. 32 sokemen have 10 ploughs there. 2 of Geoffrey's knights hold 1 carucate of this land, and have there 1½ ploughs, and 2 bordars, and 150 acres of meadow. It is worth 20s.

In Brauncewell [is] sokeland, 9 carucates of land, and inland, 2 bovates, to the geld. [There is] land for as many ploughs and oxen. Geoffrey has 1 plough there, and 13 sokemen and 3 bordars with 4 ploughs. 2 of his men hold 13 bovates of this land, and have 1 plough there, a church, and a priest, and 4½ acres of meadow, and 14 acres of scrubland. It is worth 20s.

In 'Dunsby' [in Brauncewell] [are] 6 carucates of land to the geld. [There is] land for 6 ploughs. Geoffrey and his nephew have 2 ploughs there, and 13 sokemen and 1 bordar with 1 plough, and 6 acres of meadow.

In [North or South] Rauceby [are] 6 carucates of land to the geld and 2½ bovates. [There is] land for as many ploughs and oxen. There Geoffrey's nephew has 25 sokemen and 8 villans and 5 bordars with 8 ploughs.

In the other Rauceby [North Rauceby or South Rauceby] [is] 1 carucate of land to the geld. [There is] land for 12 oxen. There are 7 sokemen and 2 bordars with 1 plough and 3 oxen.

In Evedon [are] 2 carucates of land to the geld. [There is] land for 14 oxen. [It is] a BEREWICK. Geoffrey and his nephew have 1 mill there [...], and 40 acres of marsh.

In WESTBOROUGH, Toki had 12 carucates of land to the geld. [There is] land for 12 ploughs. Geoffrey Aselin and Ralph his nephew have 4 ploughs there, and 5 sokemen on 12 bovates of this land and 12 villans

[Folio 370: LINDSEY]

and 6 bordars with 2 ploughs. There is a priest, and a church, and 2 mills [rendering] 30s, and 200 acres of meadow.

Of this land 2 of their men hold 11 bovates, and they have 1 plough and 2 oxen there, and 6 bordars with 1 ox. TRE worth £15; now 25[l].

SOKELAND OF THIS MANOR

In Dry Doddington [are] 9 carucates of land and 6 bovates to the geld. [There is] land for as many ploughs and oxen. 5 sokemen and 12 villans have 7 ploughs there, and 200 acres of meadow, and 10 acres of scrubland.

In Claypole [are] 7 carucates of land and 7 bovates to the geld. [There is] land for as many ploughs and oxen. 34 sokemen and 6 bordars have 8 ploughs there. There is a church, and a priest, and 1 mill [rendering] 10s, and 40 acres of meadow. Of this land Ealdwine has 2½ carucates of land, and has 1½ ploughs there. It is worth 40s.

In WRAWBY, Toki had 2 carucates of land and 3 bovates and 5 parts of 1 bovate to the geld. [There is] land for 7 ploughs. Now there are 2 ploughs in demesne; and 16 villans and 15 bordars have 4 ploughs. There is a church, and a priest, and 100 acres of meadow, and 100 acres of woodland, pasture in places. TRE worth £10; now £6; tallage 20s. Ralph holds it of Geoffrey.

In Elsham [are] 2 carucates of land and 2 bovates to the geld. In 'Kettleby' [in Bigby] [are] 3 bovates of land and the third part of 1 bovate to the geld. [There is] land for 6 ploughs. [It is] SOKELAND and inland of Wrawby. Now there is 1 plough in demesne; and 11 sokemen and 4 villans and 8 bordars with 2 ploughs, and 114 acres of meadow.

LXV. The land of Baldwin

In Haddington, Æthelric had 8½ carucates of land to the geld; 7 carucates and 3 bovates sokeland and 9 bovates inland of Doddington. [There is] land for 4 ploughs and 2 oxen. Baldwin has there 13 sokemen having 3½ ploughs. It is worth 20s.

In Whisby [are] 6 carucates of land to the geld. [There is] land for 3 ploughs. [It is] SOKELAND 4 carucates, and inland, 2 carucates, of the same manor. 7 sokemen have 2 ploughs there, and meadow 5 furlongs long and 1 broad. It is worth 20s.

In South Hykeham [are] 4 carucates of land to the geld. [There is] land for 3 ploughs. [It is] inland, 3 carucates, and sokeland, 1 carucate, of the same manor. There is 1 plough in demesne; and 2 sokemen and 10 villans and 2 bordars with 3 ploughs, and 2 fisheries [rendering] 3s, and meadow 2 furlongs long and 2 broad, and as much scrubland. It is worth 40s.

In Skellingthorpe [are] 12 carucates of land to the geld. [There is] land for 6 ploughs. 18 villans and 2 sokemen and 4 bordars have 6 ploughs there. [There is] meadow 1 league long and 2½ furlongs broad, and as much scrubland. It is worth 40s.

In North Hykeham [are] 8 carucates of land to the geld. [It is] SOKELAND, 7 carucates, and inland, 1 carucate, of the same manor. 13 sokemen have 3½ ploughs there, and 52 acres of meadow. It is worth 20s.

All this land belongs to Doddington, St Peter of Westminster's manor. Baldwin holds this of the king, but the abbot claims it for the use of St Peter by the testimony of the men of the whole shire.

LXVI. The land of William Taillebois

In WEST ASHBY, Thorfrith had 3 bovates of land to the geld. [There is] land for 5 oxen. William Taillebois has there 2 oxen in a plough, and 40 acres of meadow. TRE worth 10s; now 5[s].

In ALFORD, Thorfridh had 4 bovates of land to the geld. [There is] land for 6 oxen. William has there 1 villan with 2 oxen in a plough, and 6 acres of meadow. TRE worth 30s; now 5s.

LXVII. The land of Kolgrimr

In EWERBY, Kolgrimr had and has 2 carucates of land to the geld. [There is] land for 14 oxen. Roald, Kolgrimr's man, has 1 plough there, and 2 sokemen and 4 villans with 1 plough, and 21 acres of meadow, and 9 acres of scrubland. TRE worth 20s; now 40s.

SOKELAND OF THIS MANOR

In Howell [are] 4 bovates of land to the geld. [There is] land for 4 oxen. There are 4 acres of meadow.

In "Burg" [in Kirkby la Thorpe] [are] 6 bovates of land to the geld. [There is] land for 4 oxen. There is a church.

In Evedon [are] 2 bovates of land to the geld. [There is] land for 2 oxen. There is a church, and 2 acres of meadow, and 1 acre of scrubland, and 5 acres of marsh.

In "BURG"[in Kirkby la Thorpe], Arnketil had 6½ bovates of land to the geld. [There is] land for as many oxen. The same man has 1 plough of the king there, and 2 villans and 5 bordars with 2 oxen, and 1 mill [rendering] 20s, and 8 acres of meadow, and 3 acres of scrubland. TRE worth 30s; now 40[s].

In Heckington [are] 2½ bovates of meadow belonging to "Burg" [in Kirkby la Thorpe]. [It is] inland.

In INGOLDSBY, Kolgrimr had 4 bovates of land and the third part of a bovate to the geld in demesne, and as much land in soke to the geld. [There is] land for 2 ploughs. Now he himself has 1 plough there, and 2 sokemen and 6 villans with 2 ploughs, and 9 acres of meadow, and 63 acres of woodland, pasture in places, and a church. TRE, as now, worth 10s.

In THE SAME PLACE Ingulf had 4 bovates of land to the geld. [There is] land for 6 oxen. Now Eskil has them of the king in alms, and he has there 2 villans with 5 oxen, and 4 acres of meadow, and 16 acres of scrubland. TRE, as now, worth 5s.

In 'AUSTERBT' [in Bourne], Wulfric had 3 bovates of land to the geld. [Thre is] land for 3 oxen. Now Seuen has them of the king. There are 5 villans and 1 bordar with 1 plough and 1 ox in a plough, and 6 parts of a mill [rendering] 18d, and 3 fisheries [rendering] 8d, and 4½ acres of meadow, and 15 acres of scrubland. TRE worth 10s; now 16s.

In NEWTON, Wulfric Wild had 3½ bovates of land to the geld. [There is] land for as many oxen. Now Wulfgeat has them of the king, and [has] half a plough there, and 3 villans with half a plough, and 6 acres of meadow, and 35 acres of scrubland. TRE worth 20s; now 25s.

In Threekingham [are] 5 bovates of land and the sixth part of

2 bovates to the geld. [There is] land for as many oxen. Now Wulfgeat has them of the king, and [has] there 1 sokeman on 1 bovate and the sixth part of a bovates and 3 villans with half a plough, and the twelfth part of a church of St Peter, and the sixth part of a church of ST MARY and the sixth

[Folio 370V: LINCOLNSHIRE]

part of 4 bovates which belong to the church of St Mary.

In Old Somerby, Wulfsige had 6 bovates of land to the geld. [There is] land for 6 oxen. Now Thorkil has them of the king, and has there 1 ox in a plough, and 1 bordar, and 8 acres of scrubland. TRE, as now, [worth] 5s.

In BELTON [near Grantham], Roald had 2½ carucates of land to the geld. [There is] land for as many ploughs. Kolgrimr has 1 plough there, and 1 sokeman on 1 bovate of this land and 7 villans and 4 bordars with 2 ploughs, and 2 mills [rendering] 12s, and [there are] 36 acres of meadow, and 16 acres of scrubland. TRE worth 30s; now the same.

In 'Towthorpe' [in Londonthorpe] [are] 6 bovates of land to the geld. [There is] land for 6 oxen. [It is] a BEREWICK of Belton [near Grantham]. Kolgrimr has there 1 villan and 1 bordar with half a plough, and 5 acres of meadow.

In Barkston [are] 6 bovates of land to the geld. [There is] land for 6 oxen. There is half a plough in demesne, and 2 mills of which the soke belongs to Grantham.

In the same [vill is] 1 carucate of land to the geld. [There is] land for 1 plough. [It is] SOKELAND of Belton [near Grantham]. 2 sokemen and 2 villans have half a plough there, and [there are] 35 acres of meadow.

In Londonthorpe [are] 6 bovates of land to the geld. [There is] land for 6 oxen. [It is] a BEREWICK of Belton [near Grantham]. Kolgrimr has there 1 villan and 1 bordar with half a plough.

In Drayton, Withar had half a carucate of land to the geld. [There is] land for half a plough. [It is] SOKELAND of Count Alan's manor of Drayton. Godric has 3 bordars there, and 2 acres of meadow.

In Bicker, Withar [had] 1 carucate of land to the geld. [There is] land for 1 plough. Godric has 1 plough there in demesne, and 12 villans. TRE worth 20s; now 40[s.].

In 'HOUGHTON' [in Grantham], Kolgrimr had 14 bovates of land to the geld. [There is] land for as many oxen. Fredegæst, Kolgrimr's man, has there 2 villans and 3 bordars with 1 plough, and 2 mills [rendering] 30s, and 3 acres of meadow. TRE, as now, worth 40s.

In the same place [are] 10 bovates of land to the geld. [There is] land for 10 oxen. Abbot Turold holds this land of Kolgrimr, and ploughs it with his demesne. There are 6 acres of meadow. It is worth 6s.

In 'OUSEBY' [in Billingborough], Wulfric had 6 bovates of land to the geld. [There is] land for 6 oxen. Now Swein has it of the king, and has 1 plough there, and 3 villans with half a plough, and half a mill [rendering] 3s, and [there are] 9 acres of meadow. TRE it was worth 10s.

In DOWSBY, Osfram had 3 carucates of land to the geld. [There is] land for 3 ploughs. Now he himself has 1 plough there, and 6 villans with 1 plough, and 31 acres of meadow. TRE, as now, worth 30s.

In [?] 'LITTLE GONERBY' [in Grantham], Kolgrimr had 4 bovates of land to the geld. [There is] land for 6 oxen. Now the same man has 1 plough there and 2 sokemen and 3 villans with 6 oxen, and 8 acres of meadow. TRE, as now, worth 16s.

In Swinderby [is] 1 carucate of land to the geld. [There is] land for 6 oxen. Kolgrimr has it with 1 plough there, and 100 acres of meadow. [There is] scrubland 9 furlongs long and 3 furlongs broad.

In Canwick, Aghmund had 1 carucate of land to the geld. [There is] land for 1 plough. There are 2 villans with 1 plough, and 3 bordars, and 55 acres of meadow. TRE, as now, worth 15s.

In the same place Cwenthryth the nun [had] half a carucate of land to the geld. [There is] land for 4 oxen. It is worth 8s.

LXVIII. The land of Svartbrandr and Other Thegns

In BURTON, Eadnoth had 3 carucates of land to the geld. [There is] land for 3 ploughs. Svartbrandr has 2 ploughs there in demesne; and 8 villans and 3 bordars with 1 plough, and 4 rent-paying tenants paying 8s. There are 8 acres of meadow. TRE worth 21s; now 40s.

In SOUTH CARLTON, Gunnhvati had 6 carucates of land to the geld. [There is] land for 6 ploughs. Svartbrandr has 6 oxen in a plough there, and a certain man of his 1 plough, and [he has] 8 sokemen and 6 villans and 4 bordars with 2½ ploughs, and 30½ acres of meadow, and 100 acres of meadow in Nottingham [shir]. TRE, as now, worth 40s; tallage 40s.

In North Carlton [is] 1 carucate of land to the geld. [There is] land for 1 plough. 3 sokemen and 3 bordars have 1½ ploughs there. There is a priest, and a church and 22 acres of meadow.

In METHERINGHAM, Regnvald had 5½ carucates of land to the geld. [There is] land for 2½ ploughs. Svartbrandr has 1 plough there, and 2 sokemen and 10 villans and 4 bordars having 4 ploughs. There is a church, and 100 acres of meadow, and 8 acres of scrubland. TRE, as now, worth 40s.

In WEST KEAL, Sigeric had 12 bovates of land to the geld. [There is] land for 14 oxen. Ketilbiørn has [sic] 1 plough there, and 8 villans with half a plough, and 56 acres of meadow. TRE worth 40s; now 50s.

In Coningsby [is] 1 bovate of land to the geld. [There is] land for 1 ox. [It is] inland of West Keal. Ketilbiørn has 1 villan there, and 1 fishery [rendering] 40d, and 20 acres of scrubland.

In [?] West Ashby, Ketilbiørn has 1 mill [rendering] 12s.

In Candlesby, Svartbrandr had half a carucate of land to the geld. [There is] land for 5 oxen. Ketilbiørn has half a plough there. TRE worth 20s; now 10s.

In Bratoft, Svartbrandr [had] 2 bovates of land to the geld. [There is] land for 2 oxen. 2 villans have 1 plough there, and [there are] 60 acres of meadow.

In Addlethorpe [are] 2 bovates of land to the geld. [There is] land for 2 oxen. Ketilbiørn has 4 villans there who do not plough, and [there are] 80 acres of meadow.

In Friskney, Svartbrandr [had] 2 bovates of land to the geld. [There is] land for 2 oxen. Ketilbiørn has 3 villans there who do not plough, and [there are] 4 acres of meadow.

In Theddlethorpe [All Saints or St Helen], Sigeric [had] 3 bovates of land to the geld. [There is] land for 3 oxen. Ketilbiørn has there 4 sokemen having 2 oxen in a plough, and [there are] 24 acres of meadow.

In SUTTON ON SEA, Sigeric had 5½ bovates of land to the geld. [There is] land for 7 oxen. Ketilbiørn has 1 plough there, and 4 sokemen and 6 villans and 6 bordars with 1 plough, and [there are] 50 acres of meadow. TRE, as now, worth 40s.

In the same place Siward [had] 1 bovate of land to the geld. [There is] land for 1½ oxen. [It is] SOKELAND of Huttoft. Ketilbiørn has there 4 sokemen with half a plough, and [there are] 4 acres of meadow. It is worth 5s.

In GRASBY, had half a carucate of land to the geld. [There is] land for 1 plough. 4 sokemen and 4 bordars have 1 plough there, and 10 acres of meadow. TRE, as now, worth 20s.

[Folio 371: LINDSEY]

In CREETON, Leofric had 1 carucate of land to the geld. [There is] land for 1 plough. The same man himself has 1 plough there, and 2 acres of meadow. TRE, as now, worth 30s.

In SWINSTEAD, Regnvald had half a carucate of land to the geld. [There is] land for 4 oxen. The same man himself has there 2 villans with half a plough, and 1½ acres of meadow, and 15 acres of scrubland. TRE, as now, worth 10s.

In CORBY GLEN, Beorhtgifu had 1 carucate of land to the geld. [There is] land for 1 plough. The same man himself [sic] has 1 plough there, and 3 bordars, and 1 acre of meadow, and 30 acres of woodland pasture. TRE, as now, worth 20s.

In WESTBY, Toki had 1 carucate of land to the geld. [There is] land for 1 plough. Kolgrimr has 5 oxen in a plough there, and 1 villan, and 12 acres of meadow, and 30 acres of scrubland. TRE worth 20s; now 10[s].

In LOBTHORPE, Algar had 1 carucate of land to the geld. [There is] land for 1 plough. He himself [has] 1 plough there, and 2 villans, and [there are] 8 acres of meadow, and 20 acres of woodland pasture. TRE, as now, worth 20s.

In HANBY [in Lenton], Osfram had 2 carucates of land to the geld. [There is] land for 2 ploughs. He himself pledged 1 carucate of this land for 9 years for 20s, and [there are] 14 acres of meadow. TRE [worth] 20s; now 5s.

In KEISBY, Osfram had 4 bovates of land to the geld. [There is] land for 4 oxen. It is waste, except for 3 villans with 6 oxen. The men of the hundred say that the soke belongs to Osgodby [in Lenton]. There are 4 acres of meadow and 2 acres of scrubland. TRE, as now, worth 10s.

In SKILLINGTON, Karli had 1 carucate of land to the geld. [There is] land for 1 plough. The same man still has it in alms, and has there 4 villans with 1 plough, and 20 acres of meadow. TRE, as now, worth 20s.

In COLSTERWORTH a thegn of the queen's had 4 carucates of land to the geld. [There is] land for 4 ploughs. The same man himself has there 3 sokemen and 3 villans and 7 bordars with 2 ploughs, and 2 mills [rendering] 2s, and 1 acre of meadow, and 80 acres of woodland pasture. TRE, as now, worth 20s.

In [North or South] WITHAM, Earnwine the priest has of the king in alms 6 bovates of land to the geld. [There is] land for 6 oxen. He has there 3 villans and 2 bordars with 1½ ploughs, and 21 acres of meadow, and 1 rent-paying tenant with 1 plough paying 4s. TRE, as now, [worth] 10s.

In "BURG" [in Kirkby la Thorpe], Arnketil has 5 bovates of land to the geld. [There is] land for 6 oxen. There are 2 sokemen with 1 plough. TRE, as now, worth 3s.

WEST RIDING

In THORPE LE FALLOWS and Aisthorpe, Swein had 6 bovates of land to the geld. [There is] land for 1 plough. Wulfgeat has them of the king. 1 villan and 2 bordars have 1 plough there, and 13½ acres of meadow. TRE worth 8s; now 20s.

There Healfdene the priest has of the king 1 church to which belongs 1 bovate of land. Now it is waste. TRE it was worth 5s4d.

In Kexby, Leodwine has of the king 6 bovates of land to the geld. [There is] land for 6 oxen. It is waste. There are 32 acres of meadow, and 6½ acres of scrubland.

In INGHAM, Swein had 2 bovates of land to the geld. [There is] land for 3 oxen. Earnwine [has it] of the king and queen. Now there is 1 sokeman and 1 villan having 2 oxen in a plough, and 4 acres of meadow. TRE, as now, worth 10s.

In FILLINGHAM, Godric the deacon had 2 bovates of land to the geld. [There is] land for 3 oxen. Earnwine the priest held it of the queen. Now it belongs to the king. Roger de Poitou took it without a livery officer. Ansketil holds it. 2 sokemen and 1 bordar have 3 oxen in a plough there. TRE, as now, worth 4s.

In CLEATHAM, Arnketil had 6 bovates of land to the geld. [There is] land for 12 oxen. Healfdene has 1½ ploughs there, and 3 villans with 1 plough, and 6 acres of meadow. TRE, as now, worth 20s.

In HIBALDSTOW, Brunier had 2 bovates of land to the geld. [There is] land for 6 oxen. Auti has 1 ox in a plough there, and 15 acres of meadow. It is worth 2s.

In WADDINGHAM, Arnketil [had] 2 bovates of land to the geld. [There is] land for 2 oxen. Healfdene has half a plough there, and 2 villans and 2 bordars with 2 oxen in a plough, and 1 mill [rendering] 2s, and 12 acres of meadow. TRE, as now, worth 5s4d.

IN THE SAME PLACE Godric the deacon had 3 bovates of land to the geld. [There is] land for 3 oxen. Elfin has there 3 villans and 2 bordars with 1 plough, and 14 acres of meadow. TRE worth 10s; now 20[s].

In the same place Elfin has 2 bovates of land to the geld. [There is] land for 2 oxen. [It is] SOKELAND of the same manor. 2 sokemen have half a plough there.

In YADDLETHORPE, Ketil had 1 carucate of land to the geld. [There is] land for 1 plough. It is waste. Waldin had it but the king gave it back to an Englishman. There are 16 acres of meadow, and 13 acres of scrubland. TRE [it was worth] 20s.

In Winterton, Grimbald and Fulcric had 11 bovates of land to the geld. [There is] land for as many oxen. Siward the priest has there 1 villan and 1 bordar having 2 oxen in a plough. TRE worth 50s; now 15[s].

In ULCEBY [near Wootton], Hugh had 4 bovates of land to the geld. [There is] land for 11 oxen. The same man himself has 1 plough there. TRE, as now, worth 10s.

In GOXHILL, Hugh had 4 bovates of land to the geld. [There is] land for 1 plough. The same man has there 4 villans with 1 plough, and 60 acres of meadow. TRE worth 20s; now the same.

In NEWTON BY TOFT, Iusten had 3 bovates of land to the geld. [There is] land for 1 plough. The same man has it, and it is waste. TRE it was worth 5s4d.

In [North or South] OWERSBY, Earnwine the priest had half a carucate of land to the geld. [There is] land for 1 plough. Siward the priest has half a plough there, and 2 sokemen on 2 bovates of this land and 2 villan with 3 oxen in a plough, and 1 mill [rendering] 3s, and 20 acres of meadow. TRE worth 40s; now 10s.

In OSGODBY [near West Rasen], Abba had 2½ bovates of land to the geld. [There is] land for 5 oxen. It is waste. Siward has it. There are 6 acres of meadow. TRE [worth] 10s; now 3s.

In CUXWOLD, Stenkil had 6 bovates of land to the geld. [There is] land for 10 oxen. Siward has there † 3 † sokemen and 2 bordars with 6 oxen in a plough. TRE worth 20s; now 5s.

In BEELSBY, Aghmund had 4 bovates of land to the geld. [There is] land for 1 plough. Godric his son has there 2 oxen in a plough, and 6 acres of meadow. TRE it was worth and now it is worth 5s.

In OSGODBY [near West Rasen], Sumarlithr [had] 1 bovate of land to the geld. [There is] land for 2 oxen. Siward the priest has there 1 villan and 1 bordar with 1 ox. TRE worth 5s; now 2s.

[Folio 371V: LINDSEY]

In [North or South] RESTON, Aghmund the priest [had] half a carucate of land to the geld. [There is] land for 4 oxen. The same man himself has 1 plough there. This belongs to the Church of St Michael [of Burwell]. TRE worth 10s; now 20[s.].

In NETTLETON, Leofgifu [had] 5 bovates of land to the geld. [There is] land for 2 ploughs. She herself has there half a plough, and 2 villans and 1 bordar and 1 sokeman with half a plough, and 1 mill [rendering] 12d, and 20 acres of meadow. TRE worth 20s; now 5s.

[Folio 372: [LINDSEY]]

[Blank in MS]

[Folio 372V: [LINDSEY]]

[Blank in MS]

[Folio 375: [CLAMORES]]

The Clamores which are in the SOUTH RIDING of Lincoln, and their settlement [...] by the jurors.

In Tathwell Hundred, the Bishop of Bayeux's men claim 1 carucate of land against Robert Despenser; and the men of the wapentake say that the bishop himself ought by right to have it.

In the same hundred, the men of the same bishop claim 3 bovates of land against Earl Hugh; and the wapentake says that the bishop himself ought to have them.

In the same hundred, the wapentake says that Robert Despenser ought to have with his land the mill which belonged to Aghmund, and which after him, Lambert and Joscelin his son had.

In LOUTH Hundred, the Bishop of Lincoln claims 1 mill against Count Alan; and the wapentake bears witness that it ought to belong to the same bishop.

Those lands which Alsige and Ulfgrimr had in Lindsey they placed in the Church of St Mary of Lincoln, and in the mercy of Bishop Wulfwig; and therefore Bishop Remigius claims them because they had £16 for these lands TRE.

In Burwell Hundred, the king's officers claim against Earl Hugh in Haugham and Maidenwell the lands of 2 brothers, Godric and Eadric; and the men of the wapentake have adjudged them for the king's use.

In [Great and Little] Carlton Hundred, William de Percy claims half a carucate of land against Kolsveinn; and the wapentake bears witness for the same William.

In [North and South] Somercotes Hundred, Alvred of Lincoln claims half a carucate of land against the king in Yarburgh; but the Riding says that he has nothing there except 9½ acres and 1 toft of which the soke belongs to the king's manor of Gayton le Wold.

In the same hundred, Siward Buss claims 1 mill against Alvred; and the men of the Riding [say] that Alvred has a half belonging to Rayner de Brimeux's [manor of] Keddington, and the Bishop of Durham has the other half [of which] the soke [belongs] to Keddington.

In Skidbrooke Hundred, Alvred claims 3 bovates of land in Stewton against Ilbert; the men of the Riding say that Alvred himself ought to have them.

In Withcall Hundred, Rayner claims the whole of the church; and the men of the Riding say that it belonged to his predecessor, as [did] a third part of the soke, and [that] Ilbert de Lacy [has] 2 parts of the soke over the church and the land which belongs to it.

In Swaby Hundred, Robert Despenser claims against Earl Hugh 1 carucate of land in Claythorpe. The men of the Riding say that the soke belongs to Greetham, and belonged to Vighlak, and [that] he himself departed from the land, and made forfeiture; and they say that Robert Despenser has nothing there.

In Rigsby Hundred, Losuard claims 1 carucate of land in Well against Gilbert de Ghent. The men of the Riding say that TRE Thorulf had it with sake and soke, and afterwards Tonni had it; and [that] this land was delivered to Bishop Odo by charter, but they have not seen the king's writ for it, and [that] he himself had it on the day on which he was taken, and afterwards he was disseised.

In the same hundred, Rayner de Brimeux claims 2 bovates of land in Ulceby [near Well] against Earl Hugh; and the men of the Riding say that he ought to have nothing except the soke [which belongs] to Cumberworth, and the earl the land.

In Theddlethorpe [All Saints and St Helen] Hundred, the Bishop of Durham claims 2 bovates against Earl Hugh in Mablethorpe. The men of the Riding say that he has only 1 bovate which belonged to Bærghthor, and [that] the soke belongs to Earl Hugh in Greetham. And in the same place William Blund [has] 3 bovates which belonged to Sumarlithr and Godric and Siward; and the soke belongs to Greetham by the testimony of the whole Riding.

In Huttoft Hundred, Alvred claims 2 bovates of land; and the men of the Riding say that he ought he has [sic] to have one with sake and soke, and [that] the other is his in the same way, but Earl Hugh has the soke in Greetham.

In the same hundred, the Riding says that the same Alvred ought to have the soke of 1 bovate which Alvred claims against Ketilbiørn in Sutton on Sea.

In Mumby Hundred, Count Alan claims 2 bovates of land against Gilbert de Ghent; but the Riding says that Gilbert's predecessor had the sake and soke of it TRE, and [that] it ought to be his. In Willoughby Hundred, the Bishop of Durham claims the land of Alnoth the priest against Gilbert de Ghent; and the men of the Riding say that they never saw the bishop's predecessor seised of it, either by writ or by officer and they testify [it is] for Gilbert's use.

In the same hundred, the men of the Riding testify that Ketilbiørn ought to have 20 acres of woodland in 'Hanby' [in Welton le Marsh], and Ivo Taillebois the soke.

Touching the dispute between the Bishop of Durham and Eudo fitzSpirewic, the men of Horncastle Wapentake bore witness, with the assent of the whole Riding, that 3 brothers, Harold and Guthfrith and Ælfric, divided their father's demesne land equally and in parage; and [that] Harold and Guthfrith only, without the third brother, divided their father's soke, and [that] they held it TRE equally and in parage.

Touching the soke of 6 bovates, about which there is a

dispute between the bishop and Eudo, in Langton by Wragby and [?] Tattershall Thorpe, the men of 'Wraggoe' Wapentake say that the aforesaid 2 brothers had the soke TRE equally and in parage; but in the year in which the same king [Edward] died, the sons of Guthfrith had the whole soke, but they know not on what ground they had it, whether by force or by the gift of their uncle.

Touching the claim which Robert Despenser makes against Gilbert de Ghent about woodland which is in Low Langton, 'Wraggoe' Wapentake, with the assent of the whole Riding, says that Tonni had it TRE with sake and soke in Baumber; and therefore [that] Gilbert de Ghent has it by right.

Touching the scrubland which Robert Despenser claims against the king in Hainton, and against Erneis de Buron in Wragby, he has nothing there according to the testimony of the wapentake. But, by the testimony of the men of the wapentake and Riding, he has the soke over 12 acres of Earl Hugh's and over 8 acres of the Bishop of Bayeux's.

[In respect of] the claim which Rayner de Brimeux made against Alvred of Lincoln touching the soke of 3½ bovates, he ought to have nothing there as the men of the wapentake and Riding testify; but Roger de Poitou ought to have it as belonging to the house of his predecessor Klak in Hainton.

Touching the claim which Erneis de Buron makes against William de Percy

[Folio 375V: [CLAMORES]]

concerning the soke of 4 bovates in Legsby, the wapentake says that the same Erneis ought by right to have it.

Touching the claim which Archbishop Thomas made, that is, that he ought to have the soke over the land of Siward, the predecessor of Ivo Taillebois, the wapentake says, and the Riding, that Siward held his land with sake and soke in just the same way as Godwine, the archbishop's predecessor, held [his], and therefore he does not claim it rightly.

Archbishop Thomas ought to have the soke over Eskil's land which the Bishop of Bayeux has in South Willingham, because, as the whole shire testifies, the archbishop's predecessor had sake and soke over the same land, and the bishop's men unjustly took away the same soke from the same archbishop.

TRE Almær, Archbishop Thomas's predecessor, was seised of the soke of 10 bovates in South Willingham. This land belonged to Koddi, and now it belongs to Rayner de Brimeux; and it was given in pledge for £3 TRE; and now the men of the Riding assert that the archbishop ought by right to have this soke until the £3 are repaid to him.

Gilbert de Ghent and Norman d'Arcy claim against William de Percy the soke of 12 bovates in Stainfield [near Lincoln] which belongs to Barlings, and belonged to Tonni. But the wapentake says, and the shire, that Gilbert ought to have it, not Norman. William de Percy, however, holds it by the king's gift, in the same way as Robert fitzStigand held it.

They put forward the same argument touching the soke of 7 bovates in Apley, because it belongs to Barlings, and Tonni held it TRE.

In the same Apley, the Bishop of Durham claims the soke of 2 bovates against William de Percy; and the wapentake

says that the same bishop's predecessor had it, and [that] he himself ought to have it as belonging to Bullington.

The Wapentake of Horncastle says that Robert Despenser unjustly makes a claim against Gilbert de Ghent touching half a carucate of land in Baumber and touching another half carucate of Edlington. Tonni had this land TRE.

Robert Despenser ought to have the soke over a fishery and over a toft which Ketilbiørn holds in Coningsby, because Aki, Robert's predecessor, had it TRE.

Candleshoe' Wapentake says that Ivo Taillebois ought to have in Ashby by Partney what he claims against Earl Hugh, that is, 1 mill and 1 bovate of land, but the soke belongs to Greetham.

Touching 2 carucates of land which Robert Despenser claims against Gilbert de Ghent in Scremby through Vighlak his predecessor, the wapentake says that he [Vighlak] had only 1 carucate, and the soke of that belonged to Bardney; but Vighlak forfeited that land to the loss of Gilbert his lord and therefore, by the testimony of the Riding, Robert has nothing there.

In the same Scremby, Ketilbiørn claims 1 carucate through Godric against Gilbert de Ghent; but they say that he [Godric] had only half a carucate, and its soke belonged to Bardney, and Ketilbiørn claims unjustly, as the wapentake says, because his predecessor forfeited it.

The men of 'Candleshor' Wapentake testify, with the consent. of the whole Riding, that TRE Sighwat and Alnoth and Fenkell and Eskil divided their father's land amongst themselves equally and in parage, and held it in such a way that if they were needed in the king's military expedition, and Sighwat could go, the other brothers assisted him. After him, another went, and Sighwat with the rest assisted him; and thus with respect to them all. Sighwat, however, was the king's man.

[The men] of Bolingbroke [Wapentake] bear witness to the same with the above-mentioned, the South Riding assenting.

In Saltfleet and in 'Mare' [in South Somercotes] and in 'Swine' [in Grainthorpe] a new toll has been established, and Ansgar of Skidbrook has been receiving it, and Reginald and Humphrey and Geoffrey; and 'Louthesk' Wapentake says this, and [so does] the whole South Riding, that this toll did not exist TRE. Godric gave a toll of 1d, according to the testimony of Ulfkil of Asterby who saw it, and Arnketil of Withern testifies this, that he himself saw Ansgar receive the toll from 24 ships from Hastings [Sussex].

In Saltfleet, Hugh the sergeant receives the customary dues of ships which come there, willingly and unwillingly [paid], which [dues] did not exist there TRE; and they began this as a new practice, and the men of the Riding say this, that they saw the claim made for it.

CLAMORES IN THE NORTH RIDING

In Barton-upon-Humber and in South Ferriby, Gilbert de Ghent's men are receiving a different toll to the one they received TRE, in respect of bread, fish, hides, and very many other things, for which nothing was ever given.

In Caistor the king's men do the same.

In [Great or Little] Limber, Ivo Taillebois claims 6 bovates of land against the king. The men of the shire say that he himself ought to have the land, and the king the soke.

Instead of 30 acres of meadow which Alvred claims in Ulceby [near Wootton], he ought to have 1 strip of ploughland in the same vill.

Yarborough Wapentake bears witness that Morcar gave Hugh 4 bovates of land in Goxhill with sake and soke which Drogo de la Beuvriere claims. Alvred claims 1 bovate of this land. The wapentake says that the land belongs to Hugh, and the soke belongs to Alvred.

The wapentake bears witness that King William gave the church of Caistor to ST MARY of Lincoln in alms; to which church belong 2 bovates of land in demesne, and 2 villans, and 1 mill, and in Hundon the soke of 1 carucate.

Joscelin claims 3 bovates of land in Searby against Count Alan. The shire says that Joscelin ought to have them, not Alan.

Hugh fitzBaldric claims half a bovate of land in Brocklesby. The men of the Riding say that the land ought to belong to him, and the soke to Norman, through their predecessors.

In Stallingborough, the wapentake says [of] Elaf's 2 manors that Rayner the deacon held them on the day on which he departed from this country.

Rayner de Brimeux ought to have in Great Limber the soke of half a bovate of land which Archbishop Thomas has in Stallingborough.

Touching 1 manor of Elaf's, which Archbishop Thomas now has in Keelby, Rayner the deacon was seised of it on the very day on which he departed from this land.

In Great Coates [in Great Grimsby], Alvred ought to have the land of 2 bovates, and Durand Malet the soke, with 3 villans who belong to it.

Rayner the deacon was seised of 1 carucate of land in Swallow when he departed

[Folio 376: [CLAMORES]]

from this land.

Likewise the same Rayner the deacon was seised of Erik's land which is in Great Grimsby Hundred. Now the Bishop of Bayeux has it.

Ralph de Mortimer's men and Losoard's men are receiving a new toll in Great Grimsby, which did not exist TRE; but Losoard denies that his men did it on his account.

The Bishop of Bayeux and the Bishop of Lincoln ought to have the soke over 2½ bovates of land which belongs to the church of 'Winghale' [in South Kelsey].

In [North and South] Owersby Hundred, the Bishop of Bayeux has the soke over half a carucate of land which belonged to Earnwine the priest, and now belongs to Siward the priest.

In Osgodby [near West Rasen], Joscelin fitzLambert ought to have the soke over half a bovate of land.

In Tealby Hundred, Rayner the deacon had Erik's land with all that belongs to it there. Joscelin holds it, and Rayner claims it. The Riding bears witness that Count Alan's predecessor had the soke, but they know not of what sort.

In Claxby [near Walesby], Joscelin fitzLambert ought to

have 1 mill which Geoffrey, Ivo Taillebois's man, seized from him.

In Croxby, William Blund ought to have 1 garden on Ivo Taillebois's land; but he is obstructed on account of a mill which was not there TRE.

In Fulstow, the Bishop of Durham ought to have 40 acres of land-meadow-and 4 tofts, and Count Alan the soke of them, as the wapentake says.

In the same vill they adjudge that Count Alan has the soke over 1 carucate of land in Robert Despenser's land. And Drogo ought to have there 1 salt-pan which he claims, and Count Alan the soke of it.

Rayner the deacon was seised of Fulcric's land in Cuxwold when he departed from this land. Now Archbishop Thomas hold it. Rayner de Brimeux claims it.

In the same Cuxwold, in the land of Hugh fitzBaldric, William de Percy ought to have 2 bovates of land which he claims. The wapentake bears witness for him.

The wapentake says that Count Alan ought to have soke over the hall of Grimkel, whose land the Bishop of Durham has in Wold Newton.

Kolsveinn did not deliver the land of Ingimund and his brothers to Count Alan, but the same Ingimund made it subject under the count himself because of other land which he held of him.

The North Riding and the whole shire bear witness that the land of Ulf of North Ormsby, that is 4½ carucates of land, was sold to ST MARY of STOW TRE, and it belonged to that [church] on the very day on which the same king died; and afterwards Bishop Remigius was seised of it.

In Scemund [North Ormsby] in the land of Ivo Taillebois, Drogo claims 3 messuages which, by the testimony of the wapentake, he ought to have with sake and soke.

In Fotherby, the land of Berengar de Tosny, the Bishop of Durham ought to have 5 bovates of land, and Berengar the soke of them.

The wapentake and the whole shire bear witness that the Bishop of Durham ought to have the land of 3 brothers with sake and soke, and Eudo fitzSpirewic the land of the fourth brother with sake and soke likewise. Their names are Sighwat-or Godwine-Alnoth, Fenkell, and Eskil.

CLAMORES IN THE WEST RIDING

'LAWRESS' WAPENTAKE bears witness that Alnoth had soke and sake over his land, 3 carucates in Burton. Svartbrandr now has it after him.

The Abbot of Peterborough claims 4 bovates of land in Riseholme, Kolsveinn's land; and the wapentake bears witness that TRE they belonged to the Church of All Saints in Lincoln.

Three burgesses of Lincoln, Guthrøthr and Leofwine and Sigewine, TRE held in pledge from Aghmund the land in 'Middle Carlton' [in North Carlton] which Joscelin fitzLambert claims against Norman Crassus.

In Scampton, Norman Crassus added £3 and 1 mark of gold, and he pledged this to Ivo the sheriff.

In Scothern Hundred, Godric, Norman's predecessor, had 4½ bovates of land TRE, as the wapentake bears witness.

In the same hundred Gilbert de Ghent claims 1 carucate of

land against the Abbot of Peterborough. The wapentake, however, bears witness that St Peter had this land with its soke on the day on which King Edward was alive and dead.

In Nettleham Hundred, Bishop Remigius claims 2 bovates of land, and the wapentake bears witness that he himself ought to have them.

The wapentake says that St Peter of Peterborough ought to have the fourth part of woodland in Reepham which Ranulph and Kolsveinn claim.

The wapentake bears witness that Ulfkil and Asfrith and Restelf and Wulfmær had sake and soke over their lands and over their men in Sturton by Stow Hundred.

And touching forfeiture in the wapentake, ST MARY has 2 parts of the soke, and the earl the third. Now the king [has the third part]. Likewise with respect to heriot. And if they had forfeited their land, ST MARY would have had two parts, and the earl the third.

The shire bears witness that Gunnhvati's land, 1 manor, [having] 1 carucate in demesne, was forfeited, 2 parts to ST MARY and the third part for the earl's use. Likewise with respect to all the soke which belongs to Gate Burton or "Broctone". Likewise also with respect to Steingrimr's land, 18 bovates of land.

With respect to all the thegns who have land in 'Well' Wapentake, ST MARY has 2 parts of [their] forfeiture, and the earl the third. Likewise with respect to heriot. Likewise if they had forfeited their land, 2 parts [would have belonged] to ST MARY, and the third part [would have been] in the earl's hand. Now the king has [the third part]. Neither Gilbert de Ghent nor Robert de Tosny nor Ralph de Mortimer, through their predecessors, are subject to this custom.

Grimkel had sake and soke over his land TRE, but in the year in which the same king died, he forfeited it, and he gave it to Mærle-Sveinn the sheriff because he stood accused before the king and made him heir to that.

In Owmby-by-Spital, Joscelin has 9 bovates of Aghmund's land, and Ivo 1 bovate. Bishop Remigius ought to have the soke of these.

[Folio 376V: [CLAMORES]]

In [?] Northorpe [near Kirton in Lindsey] Hundred, Siward Rufus had 1 carucate of land with sake and soke TRE; and Ralph de Neville lately held it of Abbot Turold, but he did not have a livery officer for it. Now it is adjudged for the king's use.

In the same hundred in the vill [of] Laughton [near Blyton], Guy de Craon, through his predecessor Wilgrim, claims soke over Swein's land; and the wapentake bears witness that TRE this Wilgrim had sake and soke over the same Swein.

The shire bears witness that, on the day on which King Edward was alive and dead and afterwards, Eskil had of King Edward these 3 manors, Scotton, Scotter, and 'Raventhorpe' [in Broughton], in his own jurisdiction. In like manner he had North Muskham in Nottinghamshire, and he held 1 manor, Manton, of his brother Brand the monk in leasehold.

The WEST RIDING bears witness that the claims which are [put forward] in Epworth Wapentake are rightly made: Norman Crassus claims 7 bovates of land against Geoffrey de la Guerche in Haxey. Gilbert de Ghent claims 4 carucates

of land and 6 bovates against this Geoffrey. This is Ulf Fenman's land in Belton [near Epworth]. Henry de Ferrers claims 3 bovates of land against this Geoffrey. This is Siward Barn's land in Amcotts. Also Gilbert de Ghent claims against the same Geoffrey half a carucate of sokeland in Belton [near Epworth], which belonged to Ulf Fenman.

The wapentake bears witness that in Winteringham Hundred Erneis de Buron ought to have Wege's land, that is 6 bovates of land and 1 toft in the soke of Gilbert de Ghent, and another toft with sake and soke.

In Thealby Hundred, Ralph Paynel clamis 1 toft. The wapentake says that he himself ought to have it, and the king [its] soke in Kirton in Lindsey.

Norman d'Arcy claims 3 bovates of land in Normanby against Drogo. The wapentake says that the land ought to belong to him, and the soke to Drogo.

CLAMORES IN KESTEVEN

'NESS' WAPENTAKE and the whole Riding have borne witness that the land of Wulfgeat and his mother Wulfflæd did not belong to Arnbiorn his sister's relative and that he only had it in wardship until Wulfgeat could hold land; that is, in Uffington 7 carucates, in Tallington $6\frac{1}{2}$ carucates, in Casewick 6 bovates, [and] in Deeping [Deeping St James or Market Deeping] 4 bovates: half a carucate.

The wapentake says that TRE Peterborough [Abbey] had 60 acres of land which Countess Judith has and tills with the ploughs of Belmesthorpe [Rut.].

The warnode of these 60 acres of land and of 48 acres of meadow belongs to Uffington, Alvred of Lincoln's [manor], but it is forcibly withheld.

The wapentake says that Azur's half carucate of land in Barholm ought to belong to Gunfrid de Chocques.

The wapentake says that Hereweard did not have Asfrith's land in Barholm Hundred on the day on which he fled.

Ralph Paynel has 6 bovates of land of Morcar's land in Burton-le-Coggles Hundred; but Mærle-Sveinn did not have them TRE.

The Abbot of Peterborough claims 1 bovate of land against Drogo in Witham on the Hill Hundred; the wapentake says that the land ought to belong to St Peter, and the soke to Gilbert de Ghent in Edenham.

In Little Bytham Hundred, Ratbod ought to have 1 carucate of land which he claims; but the soke belongs to Peterborough [Abbey].

They say that the warnode of 4d from 60 acres of woodland, which lies at Skillington, belongs to Castle Bytham.

They say that Arnbiorn had 13 acres of woodland and 25 acres of arable land in Irnham; and that they belong to Aslackby, which Robert de Tosny has.

Archbishop Ealdræd acquired Lenton and Skillington with the BEREWICK [of] Hardwick [Northants] from Ulf son of Topi with his own money, which he gave him in the sight of the wapentake; and afterwards they saw the king's seal by which he was re-seised of those lands, because Hilbold had disseised him of them.

The wapentake says that Eskil was the king's thegn, and that he never had his land under Mærle-Sveinn.

Robert of Stafford unjustly held the soke [of] 6 bovates of Arnketil's land in [North or South] Rauceby Hundred, as the wapentake says.

They say that the claim which Bishop Remigius makes with respect to Arnketil's soke in [North or South] Rauceby Hundred is unjust, because he himself had only 10 bovates of the demesne of the same Arnketil's land in exchange, and the whole of the rest of the land was delivered to the Bishop of Durham.

The wapentake says that the 9 bovates of land which Walter d'Aincourt claims, are sokeland of Branston, the land of Alsige the deacon which Walter now has, and therefore he claims justly.

The men of Navenby forcibly withhold 16s of customary dues of the pastures which are in Scopwick and Kirkby Green; and they did not give them in King Edward's day.

Robert of Stafford claims that the land of Auti, Archbishop Thomas's man, | ought | to belong to the soke of his predecessor Leofsige; but the wapentake says that they never saw Auti give the soke to Leofsige.

Touching Earl Hugh's claim they say that Øthin had the land TRE, and the soke belonged to Potterhanworth.

[Folio 377: [CLAMORES]]

In Canwick, Svartbrandr claims 140 acres. The wapentake bears witness in his favour because his father Ulf gave for this land 1 mark of gold, in pledge.

In [Great and Little] Ponton, Countess Judith holds 2 manors which belonged to Almær and his brothers. Robert de Tosny claims them; and the wapentake bears witness in his favour that they were delivered to him in exchange for Marston.

In 'Casthorpe' [in Barrowby], Robert de Tosny claims 2 bovates and 2 tofts against Robert Malet; and the wapentake says that they ought to belong to Woolsthorpe.

Touching 1 garden in the same vill, they say that it ought to belong to Robert of Stafford's [manor of] 'Casthorpe' [in Barrowby].

They say that Northmann son of Merewine had 7 gardens in Grantham of which the soke belongs to the same place, but the gardens themselves belong to Gonerby [Great Gonerby or 'Little Gonerby' in Grantham].

They say the same with respect to 2 bovates of land which pertain to Gonerby [Great Gonerby or 'Little Gonerby' in Grantham], and the soke belongs to Grantham.

Ivo Taillebois claims 2 carucates of land, less 30 acres, in Stenwith against Robert de Tosny for which he himself pays the geld. Concerning this, they say that it is right that they themselves should go over the land itself and divide it rightly according to the geld they pay.

In Stoke Rochford Half-Hundred, Robert of Stafford claims Karli's land, 3 carucates of land. The wapentake says that this land belonged to Ralph the staller, and the aforesaid Robert has nothing there.

They say that the tithes and customary church dues of 'Winnibriggs' Wapentake and 'Threo' Wapentake, in respect of all the sokes and inlands which the king has there, belong to the church of Grantham.

Osbern, the king's messenger, claims 1 carucate of land in Thurlby [near Norton Disney] which, by the witness of the wapentake, he ought to have and to render soke for in Eagle, Countess Judith's manor.

Drogo de la Beuvriere claims the soke [of] 10 bovates of land in Thurlby [near Norton Disney] against Osbern d' Arques; but the wapentake says that he claims it unjustly.

Touching the claim which the Abbot of Westminster makes against Baldwin with respect to the land and soke of Æthelric son of Mærgeat, they say that they had heard that the same Æthelric gave it to St Peter, but they do not know whether [he gave] the whole or the half.

They say, however, that in Haddington there are 8½ carucates of land, sokeland and inland of Doddington; and in South Hykeham 4 carucates of land, sokeland of Doddington; and in Skellingthorpe 12 carucates, sokeland of Doddington; and in Whisby 6 carucates of land, inland and sokeland of Doddington. The Abbot of Westminster claims the whole of this because the capital manor was given to St Peter. All the shire bears witness in St Peter's favour.

The wapentake says that Kofse had 10 bovates of land and 1 church in the soke of Thorpe on the Hill.

The wapentake says that Siward, not Ulf, Svartbrandr's father, had a manor of 4 carucates of land in North Hykeham; and therefore his [Svartbrandr's] claim is wrong.

They say that 6 bovates of land in Ewerby Thorpe which belonged to Godric, and now belongs [sic] to Martin, ought to be inland of Ewerby.

Ralph Paynel claims against Kolsveinn in Heckington 6 bovates, the land which belonged to Algar the deacon. The wapentake says that Mærle-Sveinn, Ralph's predecessor, did not have it.

In Quarrington, Waldin the Breton claims 14 bovates of land against the Abbot of Ramsey; but the wapentake says that he claims them unjustly.

In the same Quarrington, Bishop Remigius claims that he held Arnketil's land in pledge; but [Arnketil] himself denies this, and he holds of the king.

Kolsveinn claims against the king in Kirkby la Thorpe 2 bovates of land and 1 garden of Earl Morcar's land, which Thorkil held; the wapentake says both that the soke belonged to Earl Morcar, and that this land did not belong to another manor.

In Ingoldsby, Robert Malet claims the soke over 4 bovates of land which Gilbert de Ghent has. The wapentake says that Robert himself ought to have it through Azur his predecessor.

In Caythorpe Hundred, Gilbert de Ghent claims against Robert de Vessey the meadow which belonged to his predecessor Æthelric; but the wapentake says that the same Æthelric had the whole meadow, and Gilbert's predecessor had nothing there except by renting it for money.

The wapentake bears witness that the tithe and other customary dues of Carlton Scroop belong to the church of the same vill.

In Long Bennington, Count Alan claims 10 bovates of land; but the wapentake says that they belong to Carlton Scroop, William de Warenne's manor, and [that] Earl Harold, his predecessor, had them in this way.

The Bishop of Durham claims 2 bovates of land in Marston of Thorfridh's land; and touching this they say that TRE

Northmann gave Thorfridh himself 3 marks of gold for this land, and, after the same king's death, he gave him a fourth mark.

The men of 'Aveland' Wapentake bear witness that TRE the manor [of] Bourne belonged to Earl Morcar. Now Ogier has it of the king. Drogo claims it, but unjustly.

The wapentake says that 3½ bovates which Ogier has in Dyke belong to Haconby, and rightly belong to Heppo the crossbowman.

They say that 1 carucate of land in Morton [near Hanthorpe], inland, and 1½ bovates in Hanthorpe, sokeland, belong to Haconby, and were there TRE; and [that] Leofric had these.

They say that in the same Morton [near Hanthorpe] St Benedict of Ramsey ought to have half a carucate of land with sake and soke. Ogier holds this unjustly.

They say that Ogier holds 9 bovates of land in Haconby unjustly because Gilbert de Ghent ought to have them through Ulf Fenman, his predecessor, who had them TRE.

The wapentake says that Healfdene's land in Dunsby [near Bourne], which Bishop Remigius holds and the Abbot of Peterborough claims, did not belong to St Peter TRE.

In Rippingale, Ogier holds 1 carucate of land, which the wapentake says belonged to Robert de Tosny's predecessor.

They say that Osfram's land in Kirkby Underwood was not in Arnbiorn's soke.

They say that St Guthlac's land, which Ogier holds in Rippingale, was the monks' demesne farm, and that Abbot Ulfkil granted it to Hereweard at farm, as might be agreed between them each year;

[Folio 377V: [CLAMORES]]

but the abbot took possession of it again before Hereweard fled the country, because he had not kept the agreement.

They say that the soke of 3 carucates of land in Dowsby, which Osfram had in pledge, and [which] was afterwards redeemed, ought to belong to Rippingale, St Guthlac's manor, and they say that it was thus TRE, and afterwards until Guy de Craon took possession of it.

The claims which Drogo de la Beuvriere makes upon Morcar's lands they leave to the king's decision.

They say that Robert of Stafford claims Karli's land in Billingborough unjustly, because the same Karli held it of Ralph the staller.

They say that Wulfric Wild's land in Walcot [near Folkingham] Hundred ought to belong half to the Bishop of Durham, and half to a certain man, Wulfgeat, who has it by the king's alms.

Ralph Paynel claims soke and soke [sic] over Ælfric's land which Guy de Craon has in Osbournby. The wapentake says that the same Ralph ought to have 1 horse from this land when he goes on a military expedition.

In Pickworth, are 2 carucates of land which belonged to Auti, and now belong to Kolsveinn. These are not enumerated in any hundred, nor have they [their] like in Lincolnshire.

Touching Thorir's land in Old Somerby, which Walter d'Aincourt has, they say that TRE they saw that the same Thorir had it, but in the very year in which the same king died, Northmann held it in pledge. The men of the wapentake do

not know on what condition, for they did not see him do any service for it.

They say that the tithe and other customary dues of the church in respect of Thorir's land in Ropsley Hundred belong to the Church of St Peter.

Walter d'Aincourt claims the service of Guy de Raimbeaucourt's men as belonging to the manor [of] Syston, but he does not have a just claim.

In Welby Hundred, Drogo claims 4 carucates of land against Guy de Craon; but the wapentake bears witness in Guy's favour that they are rightly his.

They say that Walter d'Aincourt ought not to have the half-carucate of land which he claims against the king in Belton [near Grantham], but [that] the king [ought to have it].

In the same Belton [near Grantham], Kolgrimr ought to have 1 bovate of land of Algar's land which Guy de Craon has, but the soke belongs to Guy in 'Towthorpe' [in Londonthorpe].

They say that TRE Leofric Cild withheld the warnode of 10 acres of meadow in the same Belton [near Grantham]. Kolgrimr claims the soke of these 10 acres.

They say that the whole of the customary dues of the church and tithe of 'Westhorpe' [in Old Somerby] belong to the Church of Grantham, as Bishop Osmund claims.

In Honington Hundred, Gilbert claims the soke of 2½ carucates of land through Ulf his predecessor; but the wapentake says that Ivo ought to have the soke just as Azur his predecessor had it of Ulf.

Robert of Stafford claims 2 mills which are in Barkston, and Kolsveinn claims the same. The wapentake says that they belong to Marston, and their soke to Grantham.

In Drayton Hundred, Count Alan has 1 carucate of land of St Benedict of Ramsey. Bishop Remigius claims it, and the wapentake bears witness in his favour that Wulfwig his predecessor held it of St Benedict TRE.

Guy de Craon holds 4 bovates of land in Drayton and 10 bovates in Bicker Hundred of the land of Æthelstan son of Godram. Count Alan claims these, and Algar his man has given to the king's barons a pledge to prove by ordeal or by combat that Æthelstan himself was not seised of these 14 bovates TRE. On the other hand, Ælfstan of Frampton, Guy's man, has given his pledge to prove that he was seised of them with sake and soke, and Guy was seised of them from the time of Ralph the staller until now, and holds them now.

The men of Holland bear witness that in 'Stenning' [in Swineshead] Helfdene, the predecessor of Bishop Remigius, had 3 carucates of land quit, which Count Alan has now, and unjustly, because the bishop was seised of them.

Alvred of Lincoln claims 1 carucate of land in Quadring against Count Alan. The men of Holland agree with the same Alvred, both because it belonged to his predecessor and [because] he himself was seised of it in the time of Earl Ralph.

Gyrth, Count Alan's man, has given a pledge to maintain that Count Alan's predecessor had 6 bovates of land with sake and soke | in Gosberton |, and therefor Guy de Craon does not claim them justly.

The men of Holland bear witness [that] the soke of Ketil's church of Long Sutton belongs to the king's manor of Tydd St Mary.

Six carucates of land which the king's officers claim in Holbeach belonged to the king's manor of Gedney. Count Alan has them now as 1 manor by the king's gift.

[Folio 378: [CLAMORES]]

[Blank in MS]

[Folio 378V: [CLAMORES]]

[Blank in MS]

Little Domesday

ESSEX

[Holders of Lands]

I W[ILLIAM] King of the English
[II] Holy Trinity, Canterbury
[III] The Bishop of London
[IV] The fief of the same bishop
V The Canons of St Paul's
VI The Abbey of Westminster
VII The Bishop of Durham
VIII The Canons of Waltham
IX The Abbey of [Bark]ing
X The Abbey of Ely
XI The Abbey of St Edmund
XII The Canons of St Martin of London
XIII The Abbey of Battle
XIIII [The Abbey of] Saint Valéry
XV The Abbey of La Trinité, Caen
XVI The Abbey of Saint-Etienne of the same [Caen]
XVII The Abbey of Saint-Ouen
XVIII The Bishop of Bayeux
[XIX] The Bishop of Hereford
[XX] Count Eustace
[XXI] Count Alan
XXII W[illiam] de Warenne
[XXIII] Richard, son of Count G[ilbert]
[XXIV] Swein of Essex
XXV Eudo the steward
XXVI Roger d'Auberville
XXVII Hugh de Montfort
XXVIII Hamo the steward
[XXVIIII] Henry de Ferrers
XXX Geofrey de Mandeville
XXXI The Count of Eu
XXXII Robert Gernon
XXXIII Ralph Baynard
XXXIIII Ranulf Peverel
XXXV Aubrey de Vere
XXXVI Peter de Valognes
XXXVII Ranulf, brother of Ilger
XXXVIII Tihel the Breton
XXXVIIII Roger de Rames
XL John fitzWaleran
XLI Robert fitzCorbucion
XLII Walter the deacon
XLIII Roger Bigod

XLIIII Robert Malet
XLV W[illiam] d'Ecouis
XLVI Roger de Poitou
XLVII Hugh de Gournai
XLVIII W[illiam] Peverel
XLIX Ralph de Limesy
L Robert de Tosny
LI Ralph de Tosny
LII Walter de Douai
LIII Mathew de Mortagne
LIIII The Countess of Aumale
LV Countess Judith
LVI Frodo, brother of the abbot
LVII Sasselin
LVIII Gilbert fitzTurold
LIX William Leofric
LX Hugh de Saint-Quentin
LXI Edmund, son of Algot
LXII Roger the marshal
LXIII Adam fitzDurand
LXIIII Goscelin the lorimer
LXV John, nephew of Waleram
LXVI W[illiam] the deacon
LXVII Walter the cook
LXVIII Modwin
LXIX Ilbod
LXX Hagebern
LXXI Theodoric Point[el]
[LXXII] R[oger] God-save-the-ladies
LXXIII G[ilbert] fitzSalomon
LXXIIII W[illiam] fitzConstantine
LXXV Ansgar the cook
LXXVI Robert fitzRoscelin
LXXVII Ralph Pinel
LXXVIII Robert fitzGosbert
LXXIX Reginald the crossbowman
LXXX Gundwin
LXXXI Otto the goldsmith
LXXXII Gilbert the priest
LXXXIII Grim
LXXXIIII Wulfgifu
LXXXV Edward
LXXXVI Thorkil
LXXXVII Stanheard
LXXXVIII Godwine
[LXXXVIV] The King's free men
[XC] Annexations

I. Essex Lands of the King.

HUNDRED OF BARSTABLE.

Harold held [North and South] Benfleet TRE as 1 manor and as 8 hides. Ranulf, brother of Ilger now has custody of this manor [which is] in the king's hands. [There were] then 12 villans; now 21. Then as now [there were] 6 bordars. [There were] then 3 slaves and now 3. In demesne [there were] then 3 ploughs; now 2. Then the men [had] 11 ploughs; now 5, and 30 acres of woodland. [There is] pasture for 130 sheep [and there is] half a mill. Then it was assessed at £8. Now it renders £12, but it is assessed at only £8. In this manor there was at that time a certain free man with half a hide who has now become one of the villans; and he is included above. From this manor half a hide was given TRE to a certain church of another manor, but after that manor came into the king's hands it was taken away from the church and belongs again to [this] manor. In the whole of this Hundred the king has 18 free men holding half a hide and 49 acres and [there is] pasture for 20 sheep. It is assessed at 10s. In the demesne of the manor there is 1 horse, 1 ass, 30 pigs [and] 70 sheep.

HALF-HUNDRED OF WITHAM.

Harold held Witham TRE as 1 manor and as 5 hides. Peter the sheriff now has custody of this manor [which is] in the king's hands. [There were] then 2 ploughs in demesne; now 3. [There were] then 21 villans; now 15. [There were] then 9 bordars; now 10. [There were] then 6 slaves; now 9. [There were] then 23 sokemen and now the same. Then the men [had] 18 ploughs; now 7 and this loss was in the time of the sheriffs Swein and Baynard and through the cattle plague. [There is] woodland for 150 pigs [and there are] 30 acres of meadow. The pasture which then rendered 6d. now [renders] 14d. Then as now [there was] 1 mill. The said sokemen [are] holding 2 hides and 1 virgate, having 2 ploughs. Then it was worth in total £10, now £20, but the sheriff,

among his customary dues and [profits of] the pleas of the half Hundred, receives from it £34 and £4 in exactions. In the demesne of this manor Peter took over 4[...], 24 head of cattle, 136 pigs [and] 101 sheep; now the same number. 34 free men belonged to this manor TRE, who then rendered 10s. 11d. in customary dues. Of these, Ilbod holds 2 with 45 acres and they are worth 6s. and they render to the manor their customary dues. Theodoric Pointel [holds] 8 with half a hide and 22½ acres, rendering customary dues, and they are worth 20s. Ranulf Peverel [holds] 10 with 2 hides and 45 acres, not rendering customary dues, and they are worth 15s. William fitzGross [holds] 5 with 1 hide and 15 acres, only one of whom renders customary dues and they are worth £3. 13s. Ralph Baynard [holds] 6 with half a hide and 35 acres; one renders customary dues and they are worth 20s. Hamo the steward [holds] 1 with half a hide and he is worth 20s. Goscelin the lorimer has the land of one and does not render customary dues, namely 1 hide which the monks of St. Æthelthryth of Ely

claim, and the Hundred testifies in their favour concerning half of it and as to the other half they know nothing. It was then worth 100s., now 60, and when Goscelin received [it] 100s. It was worth in all TRE £14 less 2s.; now £12. 9s.

HALF-HUNDRED OF HARLOW.

Harold held Hatfield [Broad Oak] TRE as 1 manor and as 20 hides. [There were] then 51 villans; now 60. [There were] then 19 bordars; now 30. [There were] then 20 slaves; now 22. [There were] then 9 ploughs in demesne; now 8 and 3 horses, 40 head of cattle, 195 pigs and 200 sheep less 7. The men [had] then 40 ploughs, now 31½, and this loss was in the time of all the sheriffs and through the plague. [There is] woodland for 800 pigs [and there are] 120 acres of meadow. [There is] pasture which renders 9 wethers

to the manor and 41 acres for ploughing. To the church of this manor belonged 1 hide and 30 acres which Swein took away from it after he lost the shrievalty, and this land rendered customary dues to this manor. There also belonged to this manor 1 sokeman with half a hide TRE, which G[eoffrey] de Mandeville took away from it. To this land belongs 1 villan with 1 acre which Count E[ustace] holds and [which is] worth 4d., and 30 acres which a smith, who was put to death for theft, held TRE and [thereupon] the king's reeve added that land to this manor. And [there are] 40 acres of woodland which King Edward's reeve held, and Osmund d'Anjou disseised the king's reeve and the manor of the land and the woodland. Robert Gernon now holds [them]. Half a hide which 1 sokeman held TRE R[obert] Gernon now holds. In addition to this, 3 berewicks were attached to this manor TRE, Hertford, Amwell and Hoddesdon, lying in Hertfordshire which Ralph de Limésy now holds. And [there is] 1 sokeman with 30 acres always belonging to this manor and the manor was then worth £36, now £60; the sheriff receives from it £80 and 100s. in exactions. And the 3 berewicks were then worth £12 and the lands of the sokemen [are worth] 45s. [There is] woodland for 40 pigs. Later we recovered half a hide which 1 sokeman of Harold's held TRE; now Ralph de Marcy holds it in the fief of Hamo. Then it was worth 10s.; now 7.

HUNDRED OF BECONTREE.

Harold held Havering [-atte-Bower] TRE as 1 manor and as 10 hides. [There were] then 41 villans; now 40. Then as now [there were] 41 bordars and 6 slaves and 2 ploughs in demesne. The men [had] then 41 ploughs; now 40. [There is] woodland for 500 pigs [and there are] 100 acres of meadow. [There is] now 1 mill and 2 horses, 10 head of cattle, 160 pigs and 269 sheep. To this manor were attached 4 free men with 4 hides TRE,

The King

rendering customary dues. Now [...] Robert fitzCorbucion holds 3 hides and Hugh de Montfort a fourth hide and they have not rendered customary dues since they have had them. And moreover the same Robert holds 4½ hides which 1 free man held in this manor TRE. [There was] also appurtenant 1 sokeman with 30 acres, rendering customary dues, and now John fitzWaleran holds [him]. This manor was worth £36 TRE; now 40, and Peter the sheriff receives from it £80 in rent and £10 in exactions. To this manor belongs 20 acres lying in Loughton which Harold's reeve held TRE. Now the king's reeve holds [them] and they are worth 40d.

HUNDRED OF DUNMOW.

In Shellow Bowells [there are] 3 sokemen with 35 acres and they are worth 3s. 10d.

HUNDRED OF 'WIBERTSHERNE'.

In Latchingdon Alwine, a free man, held half a hide and 30 acres TRE. Later Theodoric Pointel appropriated them and now the king has [them]. Then as now [there was] half a plough and it is worth 15s. Of the same land, 1 villan holds 30 acres at "Studly" and they are worth 5s., and another villan [holds] 15 acres and they are worth 3s. And 3 men hold half a hide and 10 acres and half a plough. [This] was then worth 8s., now 5s. 4d. In Latchingdon Leofwine, a free man, [held] 30 acres TRE. [There was] then half a plough, now [there is] none. It was then worth 8s., now 5s. 4d. In the same [there were] 8 free men TRE; now 4 with 52 acres. [It was] then worth 8s.; now 4s. 4d. In Roding Golstan, a sokeman of King William, holds 1 hide and has never rendered service nor customary dues for it, and therefore he has given a pledge. In this hide there is 1 plough in demesne and 1 bordar and 3 slaves. [There is] woodland for 10 pigs [and there are] 10 acres of meadow. It was worth then 20s.; now 30.

[Folio 3v: ESSEX]

HUNDRED OF UTTLESFORD.

Earl Edgar held [Great and Little] Chesterford TRE as 1 manor and as 10 hides. Picot the sheriff now [has custody of it] in the king's hands. Then as now [there were] 4 ploughs in demesne. Then the men [had] 18 ploughs; later and now 14. Then as now [there were] 24 villans and 13 bordars and 6 slaves. [There is] woodland for 1,000 pigs [and there are] 15 acres of meadow. Then as now [there were] 2 mills. Belonging to this manor are 1½ hides which are in Cambridgeshire. Then as now [there were] 7 villans and 3 bordars and a mill and the men [have] 3 ploughs. All this [was] worth then £24; later and now 30. In the demesne of this manor [there are] 2 horses, 7 head of cattle, 61 pigs, 81 sheep and 87 goats. Attached to this manor TRE [there were] 1½ hides which Hardwin de Scales held, by what right the Hundred knows not. The half hide, on which 1 man dwelt, was of the demesne, and the other hide was held by 1 sokeman, who rendered his soke dues in the king's manor. Picot holds the half a hide which 1 sokeman held TRE. In these 2 hides [there are] 2 ploughs and they are worth 40s.

Heoruwulf held Birchanger TRE. Now Tascelin the priest holds [it] in the alms of the king as 1 hide. Then as now [there was] 1 plough and 2 bordars and 2 slaves. [There is] wood-

land for 40 pigs [and there are] 5 acres of meadow and 1 mill. It was then and later worth 20s.; now 30.

HUNDRED OF HINKFORD.

Earl Ælfgar held Shalford TRE as 1 manor and 5 hides and 30 acres. Later the queen held it. Now Otto the goldsmith rents it from the king. Then as now [there were] 3 ploughs in demesne. Then the men [had] 6 ploughs; later and now 5. Then and later [there were] 13 villans; now 12. Then as now [there were] 6 bordars. [There were] then 12 slaves; later and now 8. [There is] woodland for 100 pigs [and there are] 20 acres of meadow [and] 1 mill. It was then worth £12; later and now 22. In demesne [there are] 4 horses. [There were] then 65 head of cattle (now 56) and 52 sheep, 118 pigs (now 80) and 40 goats. From this manor are lacking 30 acres of woodland which the queen gave to Richard fitzGilbert. To this manor belonged half a hide of soke TRE which Walter fitzGilbert holds.

The King

[Folio 4: ESSEX]

The same Ælfgar held Finchingfield TRE and later the queen[held it]. Now the same Otto [the goldsmith] rents [it] as 2½ hides. Then as now [there were] 3 ploughs in demesne and the men [had] 5 ploughs and [there were] 10 villans and 9 bordars. [There were] then 6 slaves; later 4 [and] now 2. [There is] woodland for 60 pigs [and there are] 16 acres of meadow, 1 mill, 25 head of cattle and 2 horses. [There were] then 63 pigs; now 61, and 100 sheep. It was then worth £9; later and now, 18.

The same Ælfgar held Wethersfield TRE as 1 manor and as 2 hides 15 acres. Now Picot [has custody of it] for as much, in the king's hands. [There were] then 4 ploughs in demesne; later 2 [and] now 3. Then and later the men [had] 15 ploughs now 10. [There were] then and later 24 villans; now 28. [There were] then 7 bordars; later 15 [and] now 24. [There were] then 7 slaves; later 14 [and] now 7. [There was] then woodland for 800 pigs; later and now 500 and [there are] 24 acres of meadow. [There was] then and later 1 mill; now 2. [There were] then 17 head of cattle; now 10, and 100 sheep. [There were] then 100 pigs; now 40. [There were] then 61 goats; now 40. To this manor 6 sokemen belonged TRE; now 8, holding 1 hide and 14 acres. Then as now [there were] 2 ploughs, 1 bordar and 5 acres of meadow. It was then worth £20; later and now 28. To this manor belonged 30 acres of land TRE which 1 priest held in alms and he rendered soke, and 8½ acres belonging to another church. Gilbert fitzWarin holds these 2 lands . There belonged to this manor 7½ acres which Count Alan now holds, and 45 acres of demesne which Swein holds of the fief of Richard, son of Count G[ilbert], and they are worth 8s. In that Hundred the king has 18 sokemen holding 26½ acres, and they have never rendered the customary dues except the king's service.

HUNDRED OF DENGIE 'WIBERTSHERNE'.

Leofweard, a free man, held [North and South] Benfleet TRE [and] later Theodoric Pointel [held it] as 1 hide. Then as now [there was] 1 bordar. [There was] then 1 plough; now none. [There was] pasture for 40 sheep. [There was] then 1 fishery; now none, and it is worth 20s.

Ælfric, a free man, held Steeple TRE as 1 hide. [There was] then 1 bordar; now none. [There was] then 1 plough; now half. It was then worth 20s.; now 16. In "Ulwinescherham" 4 free men [held] 1 hide less 6 acres TRE; now they are not there. It was then worth 20s.; now 10. This land is claimed by Theodoric Pointel [as his] by exchange. Free men held 51 acres and they are not included in the king's farm. They were then worth 8s.; now 5. A servant of the king holds this land and does not render geld. In Maldon [there are] 2 free men with 10 acres. Of these, Ranulf Peverel has 5 acres and Hugh de Montfort [has] 5 acres. They were then worth 10d.; now 12. Two free men held 6 acres TRE and they belonged to the king's Hundred, and now Baynard has [them].

IN THE HUNDRED OF ROCHFORD

Grim the reeve held then as now 10 acres and they are worth 16d.

HUNDRED OF LEXDEN.

Harold held Stanway TRE as 1 manor and as 5½ hides; now the king has [it] for as much. [There were] then 12 villans; later and now 9. [There were] then 6 bordars; later and now 9. Then as now [there were] 6 slaves and 3 ploughs in demesne. The men [had] then 13 ploughs; later and now 2½. Then as now [there was] 1 mill. [There is] woodland for 100 pigs [and there are] 12 acres of meadow and 20 head of cattle, 59 pigs, 260 sheep and 11 horses. There is also 1 berewick of 2½ hides and 13 acres which is called Layer, and it belongs to this manor. Then as now [there were] 7 villans, 2 bordars, 4 slaves and 2 ploughs in demesne. The men [had] then 2 ploughs; later and now 1½. There also belongs 1 berewick of 4 hides which is called Lexden. [There were] then 6 villans; later and now 5. [There were] then 10 bordars; later and now 12. [There were] then 4 slaves; later and now 5. Then as now [there were] 2 ploughs in demesne. The men [had] then 4 ploughs; later and now 3. [There is] woodland for 100 pigs [and there are] 18 acres of meadow. [There are] now 2 mills. And [there are] 16 sokemen with 2 hides and 36 acres. Then as now [they had] 2½ ploughs. The whole [manor] was then worth £22. Now Peter receives from it £33 and

The King

£3 in exactions. From this manor Raymond Gerald took 1 villan with half a hide and he rendered the customary dues. Then as now there is there half a plough and it was worth 10s. Northmann held this land and rendered the customary dues, but Raymond took it away and Roger likewise. Roger de Poitou also took 1 villan holding 1 acre, and Engelric took

away 1 woman, Beorhtgifu, holding 18 acres and she rendered 32d. to this manor every year.

HUNDRED OF ONGAR.

Harold held Woolston as a manor and as 3 hides and 40 acres; now King William [holds it]. Then as now [there were] 4 villans. [There were] then 2 bordars; now 6. [There was] then among the men 1 plough; now the same. [There is] woodland for 60 pigs [and there are] 4 acres of meadow. It was worth 20s. then; now 40. A certain free man held 20 acres TRE. [He had] then half a plough; now none, and it is worth 3[...]. He was always in lordship, but now he is in the sheriff's hands in the king's farm.

HUNDRED OF CHAFFORD.

The king has Fingrith, which Harold held TRE. Then as now [there was] 1 plough in demesne and 6 villans and 8 bordars. They have 2 ploughs in demesne [and] 24 head of cattle. [There is] woodland for 1,000 pigs [and] 3 acres of meadow. It was then worth £4; now 14. In [North and South] Ockendon the king has 1 sokeman with 25 acres. It was then worth 32d. [and] now 52.

Fridebert held Margaretting and Mountnesling TRE as a manor and as 3½ hides. Then as now [there were] 6 villans and 3 bordars. [There were] then 2 slaves; now [there is] 1. Then as now [there were] 2 ploughs in demesne and the men [had] 1 plough and 4 acres of meadow and 88 pigs. [It is] assessed in Fingrith. Harold held Childerditch. Later the queen [held it]. Now the sheriff of Surrey [holds it] as 1½ hides. [There were] then 3 villans; now 5. [There were] then 3 bordars; now 4. [There is] 1 slave. [There was] then 1 plough in demesne; now 1½. Then the men [had] 2 ploughs;

HUNDRED OF CHELMSFORD.

Harold held Writtle as a manor and as 16 hides TRE. Now King William [holds it] as 14 hides. [There were] then 100 villans less 3; later and now 73. [There were] then 36 bordars; later and now 60. [There were] then 24 slaves; later and now 18.

[There were] then 12 ploughs in demesne; later and now 9. [There were] then among the men 64 ploughs; later and now 45. [There was] then woodland for 1,500 pigs; now 1,200 [and there are] 80 acres of meadow. [There was] then 1 mill; now 2. Then as now [there were] 9 horses, 5 colts, 40 head of cattle, 318 sheep and 172 pigs. This manor then rendered 10 nights' farm and £10. Now it renders £100 by weight and 100s. in exactions. Engelric obtained 2 hides of the land of Harold's reeve, rendering all the customary dues of this manor, namely £12, after the king came into England. And now Count E[ustace] holds [it] since his predecessor was seised of it. In the time of Harold there was 1 swineherd, rendering the customary dues to this manor [and] residing on 1 virgate of land and 15 acres, but after the king came [into England] Robert Gernon took him from the manor and made him [a] forester of the king's woodland. And Harold gave 1 hide to a certain priest of his; the Hundred does not know if he gave [it to be held] freely or in alms. Now R[obert], Bishop of

Hereford holds [it]. And [there is] half a hide which 1 sokeman held freely, rendering soke in the manor, he could go where he would with his land. Count Eustace added him to his land. To this manor then as now belonged 2 sokemen with half a hide and 10 acres, having then as now half a plough. [There are] four acres of meadow. [This] is included in the above £100.

In Writtle the same bishop holds 2 hides and 20 acres, of which 1 hide belonged to the church TRE and the other [was] in the king's fief. Then as now [there were] 3 villans and 1 priest. [There were] then 2 bordars; now 8. [There were] then 2 slaves. Then as now [there was] 1 plough in demesne and the men [had] 2 ploughs. [There is] woodland for 100 pigs [and there are] 8 acres of meadow and it is worth 50s.

HALF-HUNDRED OF MALDON.

In Maldon the king has 1 house and pasture for 100 sheep and 1 sokeman with 49 acres, having 1 bordar. [There was] 1 plough TRE; now a half. It was then worth 10s.; now 5. In the same the king has 180 houses which burgesses hold and 18 derelict messuages, 15 of whom hold half a hide and 21 acres and the other

The King

[Folio 6: ESSEX]

men do not hold more than their houses in the borough. And among them they have 12 horses, 140 head of cattle, 103 pigs and 336 sheep. From the king's hall has always issued 6s. 8d., and from the land of Swein 4s., and from the 2 houses of Eudo the steward 16d., which the king has not received since he came into this land. From the said sokeman, Ranulf Peverel had customary dues every year of 3s., but TRE his predecessor had commendation only. The whole together rendered £13. 2s. TRE and when Peter received it £24; now £16 by weight.

HUNDRED OF TENDRING.

Harold held Brightlingsea as a manor and as 10 hides. Now King William [holds it]. Then as now [there were] 24 villans. [There were] then 10 bordars; later 11, now 16, and 10 bordars not holding land. [There were] then 4 slaves; now 5. [There were] then 3 ploughs in demesne; later and now 2. The men [had] 16 ploughs then; later and now 11. [There is] woodland for 100 pigs [and] now [there is] 1 mill. [There is] pasture for 600 sheep. Then as now [there were] 16 head of cattle, 5 horses, 166 sheep and 62 pigs. Then Brightlingsea and Harkstead rendered between them 2 nights' farm and when P[eter] received [them] £25; now £22. But that berewick lies in Suffolk. In demesne [there are] 4 head of cattle and 5 pigs.

Harold held Lawford as 1 manor and as 10 hides; now King William [holds it] as so much. Then as now [there were] 15 villans and 24 bordars. [There were] then 7 slaves; now 6. Then as now [there were] 4 ploughs in demesne. [There were] then among the men 20 ploughs, and when Baynard held [it] 16 ploughs. When P[eter] received [it] 9, and now the same. [There is] woodland for 15 pigs [and there are] 12 acres of meadow. [There was] then 1 mill; now 2. [There is] pasture for 300 sheep. [There is] now 1 salt-pan. It rendered then 2 nights'

farm, and when Baynard held [it] £14; now 11. To this manor belonged 17 sokemen TRE with 1 hide, all rendering customary dues. After the king came to this land and [when] Baynard was sheriff, Theodoric Pointel acquired this land, and when he received it, 17 sokemen, having 9 ploughs, dwelt on it.

[Folio 6v: ESSEX]

They are now in the king's hands and 13 men hold this land, having 4 ploughs. [There is] woodland for 15 pigs [and there are] 2½ acres of meadow. It was then worth £4, and when Theodoric Pointel held [it] £4; now 40s. In the demesne of this manor, Peter took over 21 head of cattle, 4 horses, 45 pigs and 200 sheep less 10. To this manor belonged TRE 1 berewick with 4 hides, which Engelric appropriated. Count E[ustace] holds it. Twenty-one sokemen also belonged here, holding 1 hide and 2 virgates and 5 acres, whom Roger de Rames has by exchange, as he says, and he vouches Swein to warranty. And there were 4 sokemen TRE in this manor, rendering all customary dues, whom Richard, son of Count Gilbert, appropriated when Swein was sheriff, holding half a hide and 15 acres, which are now in the king's hands because there was no one on his part who would say how he had them. Then as now [there was] 1 plough and TRE it was worth 13s. and thereafter R[ichard] had that rent. Waleran appropriated 1 sokeman with 30 acres. [There was] then 1 plough; now [there is] none. It is worth 10s., and until now Waleran had this rent. Hagebert holds 30 acres which 1 sokeman held, and he vouches Swein to warranty. [There was] then 1 plough; now a half. It was then worth 5s. 4d.; now 32d. Count E[ustace] holds 1½ hides and 45 acres, which Engelric appropriated, and 8 sokemen held that land. The Bishop of Bayeux holds half a hide, which Ralph fitzTurold holds under him. Ranulf, brother of Ilger holds 15 acres; Hugh de Montfort [holds] 30 acres; Ralph Baynard [holds] half a hide and 35 acres; Eudo the steward [holds] 37½ acres; Roger, a man of the Bishop of London, [holds] 1 hide and 30 acres; Walter the deacon [holds] 5 acres. All this land rendered all customary dues to this manor TRE.

The King

[Folio 7: ESSEX]

HUNDRED OF UTTLESFORD.

Harold held Newport TRE as a manor and as 8½ hides; now King William [holds it]. [There were] then 18 villans; later 15 [and] now 26. [There were] 8 bordars; later 6 [and] now 13. [There were] then 4 slaves; later and now 2. [There were] then 2 ploughs in demesne; later and now 1. Then and later [there were] 8 ploughs among the men; now 10. [There is] woodland for 100 pigs [and there are] 24 acres of meadow. Then as now [there were] 2 mills and 10 head of cattle, 1 horse, 79 pigs and 102 sheep. Then it rendered 2 nights' farm. There is also 1 berewick which lies in Cambridgeshire and is called Shelford, with 3 hides and 46 acres. Then as now [there were] 8 villans, 5 bordars and 1 plough in demesne, and the men [had] 2 ploughs and 15 acres of meadow. [There was] then 1 horse; now [there is] none. Then as now [there were] 10 head of cattle. [There were] then 80 pigs; now 50. [There were] then 80 sheep; now 87. [There were] then 13 goats; now 24. This berewick was included in the above farm TRE, but now it renders £25. 16s. Robert Gernon holds 2 sokemen with 2½ hides belonging to this manor , whom he received when Swein was sheriff, and rendering all customary dues, and the Hundred knows not how he had them, since there came into the Hundred neither writ nor officer on the king's behalf [to say] that the king had given him that land. A certain clerk of Count E[ustace] had appropriated 42 acres and held those of the earl's fief, but the Hundred testifies that they [belong] to Newport, and so the king now has [them]. The clerk is adjudged to be in the king's mercy as to all his possessions and his body. In that land there was then 1 plough; now [there is] none [and] 1 acre of meadow. [There is] woodland for 6 pigs and it is worth 6s.

Harold held Rickling as a manor and as 8 hides; now King William [holds it] as so much. [There were] then 13 villans; later 16 [and] now 20. Then and later [there were] 6 bordars; now 10. Then as now [there were] 4 slaves and 2 ploughs in demesne. Then and later the men [had] 8 ploughs; now 10. [There is] woodland for 30 pigs

[Folio 7v: ESSEX]

and [there are] 3 acres of meadow. It was then worth £8; now £12. 16s. In demesne [there are] 7 head of cattle and 70 sheep.

HALF-HUNDRED OF FRESHWELL.

Eadgifu held Great and Little] Sampford; later Earl Ralph [held it and] now Godric the steward [has custody of it] in the king's hands as a manor and as 7 hides and 30 acres. [There were] then 26 villans; later 13 [and] now 16. [There were] then 9 bordars; later 6 [and] now 5. Then as now [there were] 4 slaves and 2 ploughs in demesne. Then [there were] 22 ploughs among the men; later 15 [and] now 14. [There is] woodland for 150 pigs [and there are] 30 acres of meadow. Then as now [there was] 1 mill. It was then worth £20; later 26 [and] now 30.

. King William has 4 salt-pans in this Hundred which are in the sheriff's custody and 3 men with 10 acres, and it is worth 20d.

[Folio 8: ESSEX]

II. Lands of Holy Trinity, Canterbury,

for the sustenance of the monks.

HUNDRED OF WITHAM.

In [Great and Little] Coggeshall, Holy Trinity held 3 virgate of land TRE and now the same. Then as now [there were] 2 ploughs. [There was] then 1 bordar; now 8. [There were] then 3 slaves; now 1. [There are] 8 acres of meadow [and] 1 mill, and it is worth 60s. In demesne [there are] 4 horses, 3 head of cattle, 20 sheep [and] 7 pigs.

Holy Trinity has always held Bocking as a manor and as 4½ hides and 2 ploughs in demesne. The men [had] then 35 ploughs; now 29. [There were] then 19 villans; now 18. [There were] then 25 bordars; now 44. [There were] then 4 slaves; now 2. [There is] woodland for 300 pigs, pasture for 60 sheep,

[and there are] 22 acres of meadow and 1 mill and 6 head of cattle, 100 sheep and 54 pigs. To this manor belongs now as then 2 hides in Mersea. [There is] 1 plough in demesne and the men [have] 1 plough, and [there are] 2 villans and 1 bordar. [There is] pasture for 50 sheep. Then the whole was worth £24; now 28.

Holy Trinity held Stisted as a manor and as half a hide. [There were] then 4 ploughs in demesne; now 3. The men [had] then 5 ploughs; now 6. [There were] then 8 villans; now 13. [There were] then 11 bordars; now 25. [There were] then 6 slaves; now 4. [There is] woodland for 800 pigs [and there are] 27 acres of meadow and 1 mill and 3 horses, 40 head of cattle, 120 sheep, 77 pigs. It was then worth £10; now 15.

HUNDRED OF DENGIE.

Holy Trinity held Lawling as a manor and as 14 hides. [There were] then 14 villans; now 21. [There were] then 16 bordars; [There were] then 3 slaves; now 4. [There were] then 2 ploughs in demesne; now 3. The men [had] 17 ploughs then; now 16½. Then as now [there was] 1 mill. [There is] woodland for 800 pigs, and [there are] 3 horses and 1 mule and 16 head of cattle and 60 pigs and 200 sheep and 18 goats. It was then worth £12; now 16.

Holy Trinity held Latchingdon as a manor and as 2 hides, and [there was] 1 plough in demesne. [There are] now 2 villans and 1 slave. [There is] pasture for 30 sheep and [there are] 6 head of cattle and 60 sheep and 16 pigs. It was then worth 20s.; now 25.

Holy Trinity held St Lawrence as a manor and as 3 hides. [There was] then 1 villan; now 3. Then as now [there were] 2 slaves.

[Folio 8v: ESSEX]

[There were] then 2 ploughs; now 1. [There were] then 24 sheep and now the same. It was then worth 20s. [and] now 40.

HUNDRED OF ROCHFORD.

Holy Trinity held Milton as a manor and 2 hides. Then as now [there were] 8 villans. [There were] then 13 bordars; now 15. Then as now [there is] 1 slave and 2 ploughs in demesne and the men [had] 6 ploughs. [There is] woodland for 60 pigs and [there are] 8 head of cattle and 2 horses and 25 pigs and 124 sheep. It was then worth 100s.; now £8.

Holy Trinity held Southchurch as a manor and as 4 hides. Then as now [there were] 14 villans and 5 bordars. [There were] then 2 slaves; now 1. Then as now [there were] 2 ploughs in demesne and the men [had] 6 ploughs. [There is] pasture for 200 sheep. [There is] woodland for 40 pigs and [there are] 2 fisheries and 4 horses and 8 head of cattle and 13 pigs and 150 sheep and 16 goats. It was then worth 100s.; now £7.

Holy Trinity held [Great and Little] Stambridge as a manor and 1 hide TRE. Now Ralph Baynard [holds it] of the church. Then as now [there was] 1 plough in demesne. [There were] then 3 bordars; now 7; and 1 acre of meadow. [There is] pasture for 200 sheep and [there are] 4 head of cattle and 10 pigs and 58 sheep. It was then worth 30s.; now .

[Folio 9: ESSEX]

The BISHOP of London
The FIEF of the same bishop
The CANONS of St Paul in London
ST PETER'S [Abbey] of Westminster
The BISHOP OF DURHAM
The CANONS of The Holy Cross of Waltham

[Folio 9v: ESSEX]

III. Land of the Bishop of London.

HUNDRED OF BARSTABLE.

The bishop holds Laindon which Ælfthryth, a certain woman, held TRE as 1 manor and 9 hides. [There were] then 2 ploughs in demesne; now 3. The men [had] then 7 ploughs; now 6. [There were] then 8 villans; now 3. [There are] now 14 bordars. Then as now [there were] 6 slaves. [There is] woodland for 100 pigs, pasture for 100 sheep. It was then worth £9; now 10, but the bishop receives from it £14. Of this manor Ralph and William hold 3 hides and 80 acres and [there is] 1 plough in demesne and the men [have] 2 , and it is worth 100s. in the same valuation. The bishop received in desmesne 100 sheep less 3 and 10 pigs.

The bishop holds Orsett which Bishop William held TRE as a manor and 13 hides, but Count Eustace holds 1 of these, which is not [one] of his 100 manors. Then and now [there were] 2 ploughs in demesne. The men [had] then 34 ploughs; now 22. [There were] then 34 villans; now 22. [There were] then 6 bordars; now 36. [There were] then 4 slaves; now 2. [There is] woodland for 1,000 [pigs] and [there are] 6 head of cattle and 115 sheep and 40 pigs. It was then worth £35; now 28. Of this same manor, Tidbald, Ansketil, William [and] Gilbert hold 4½ hides and 40 acres and [there are] 6 ploughs and it is worth £8 [which is included] in the above valuation.

William holds Ramsden [Bellhouse and Crays] of the bishop as a manor and 3 hides. Then as now [there was] 1 plough in demesne and the men [had] half a plough. [There were] then 6 bordars; now 8. [There is] 1 slave. [There is] woodland for 100 pigs. [There is] now 1 mill. It was then worth 60s.; now 40.

HUNDRED OF WITHAM.

In Slampseys Roger holds of the bishop 15 acres and it is worth 30d.

HUNDRED OF BECONTREE.

St Paul held Wanstead; now Ralph fitzBrian [holds it] of the bishop as 1 manor and 1 hide. [There was] then 1 plough in demesne; now 1½. Then as now the men [had] 2 ploughs and [there are] 3 villans. [There were] then 7 bordars; now 8. [There were] then 2 slaves; now none. [There is] woodland for 300 pigs. [There is] now 1 mill. Then as now [there was] 1 salt-pan and it is worth 40s.

The Bishop

[Folio 10: ESSEX]

HUNDRED OF WINSTREE.

Two free men held Layer TRE. Now Roger [holds it] of the bishop as 3 hides. Then as now [there were] 1½ ploughs in demesne and the men [had] 2 ploughs. [There were] then 5 villans; now 4. [There were] then 4 bordars; now 6. [There were] then 3 slaves; now 4. [There is] woodland for 150 pigs and [there are] 2 acres of meadow. It was then worth 70s.; now £4.

The same R[oger] holds Layer, of the bishop, which 1 free woman held TRE as 3 hides. Then as now [there were] 2 ploughs in demesne; now the men [have] half a plough. Now [there is] 1 villan. [There was] then 1 bordar; now 4. [There were] then 3 slaves; now 4. [There is] woodland for 150 pigs. [There is] 1 mill. Then as now [there was] 1 salt-pan. It was then worth 70s.; now £4. Bishop W[illiam] proved his right to these 2 manors, for the use of his church, after the death of King Edward, by command of King William.

HUNDRED OF HINCKFORD.

Bishop W[illiam] held Rayne TRE as 4 hides and 30 acres. Then as now [there were] 2 ploughs in demesne. The men [had] then 5 ploughs; now 4. [There were] then 16 villans; now 10. [There were] then 9 bordars; now 8. [There were] then 4 slaves; now 3. [There is] woodland for 200 pigs [and there are] 16 acres of meadow. [There is] now 1 mill and 10 head of cattle, 45 sheep, 24 pigs. To this manor have been added 15 acres TRW which 1 free man held TRE, as the Hundred testified. It was then worth £10; now 14. In this manor Roger holds 3 virgates of the bishop and [there is] 1 plough and 2 slaves. It is worth 50s.

HUNDRED OF DENGIE.

In Southminster [there are] 30 hides which are held by 14 knights of the bishop , and TRE [there were] 22 villans; now 11. [There were] then 23 bordars; now 25. Then as now [there were] 5 slaves and 3 ploughs in demesne. The men [had] then 18 ploughs; now 11. [There is] pasture for 1,000 sheep. It was then worth £24; now 16. In this manor TRE there were 15 free men holding 18 hides and 30 acres. Now there are 14 men who hold them of the bishop. [There were] then 4 bordars; now 16. [There were] then 4 slaves; now 8. [There were] then 12 ploughs; now 7. [There is] pasture for 300 sheep. It was then worth £12; now 8. In the demesne of this manor there are 11 head of cattle and 700 sheep less 4 and 20 pigs. King Cnut took away this land, but

[Folio 10v: ESSEX]

Bishop William recovered it TRW. The bishop holds Copford in demesne as 1½ hides and 18 acres. [There were] then 16 bordars; now 14. [There were] then 5 slaves; now 3. Then as now [there were] 2 ploughs in demesne. The men had [then] 7 ploughs; now 5. [There is] woodland for 100 pigs, [and there are] 16 acres of meadow and 6 head of cattle and 12 pigs and 37 sheep. Then as now it was worth £8. To this manor TRE belonged 12 sokemen [and] now [there are] 10, holding 1 hide and 2½ acres, and they cannot withdraw, as the Hundred testifies. [There were] then between them 2 ploughs; now 1½. It is included in the above valuation. Of this land, Roger holds 25 acres of the bishop and [there is] half a plough and it is worth 15s. In this manor were 17 acres which the bishop held TRE, but now Robert Gernon holds them of the king's gift. Robert also held 1 virgate of land which the bishop held, and a certain free man so held it that he could go where he would, but the soke remained in the manor.

HUNDRED OF CHAFFORD.

Gyrth held [Great and Little] Warley as a manor and 4 hides less 15 acres; now Humphrey [holds it] of the bishop. Then as now [there were] 5 villans and 2 bordars [and] now [there are] 2 slaves. [There were] then 3 ploughs in demesne; now 2. Then as now the men [had] 3 ploughs. [There is] woodland for 700 pigs, pasture for 100 sheep. Then and later it was worth £6; now £7. Of this manor Tascelin the priest holds 15 acres. King William gave this manor to Bishop William after he had crossed the sea because it was of old of the church of St Paul.

Bishop William held TRE. Now the bishop [holds it] in demesne as a manor and 8 hides. [There were] then 5 villans; now 4. [There were] then 2 ploughs in demesne; now 3. Among the men [there were] then 5 ploughs; now 1. [There is] woodland for 300 pigs, 30 acres of meadow. Then as now [there was] 1 mill and 2 head of cattle and 27 pigs and 100 sheep and it is worth £8.

HUNDRED OF THURSTABLE.

The bishop holds Wickham [Bishops] in demesne which Bishop William held TRE as a manor and 3 hides. [There were] then 7 villans; now 5. [There was] then 1 bordar; now 4. Then as now [there were] 4 slaves and 2 ploughs in demesne. The men [had] then 4 ploughs; now 2½. [There is] woodland for 30 pigs [and there are] 31 acres of meadow. Then as now [there was] 1 mill and 6 head of cattle and 50 sheep, 10 pigs, 20 goats and it is worth £6.

The Bishop

[Folio 11: ESSEX]

In the same [Wickham Bishops] [there is] 1 free man with 5 acres and [he] is worth 12d.

HUNDRED OF TENDRING.

The bishop holds St Osyth in demesne as a manor and 7 hides and TRE [there were] 18 villans; now 9. Then as now [there were] 5 bordars. [There were] then 3 ploughs in demesne; now 2. Then among the men [there were] 9 ploughs; now 5. [There are] 4 acres of meadow, pasture for 200 sheep and [there are] 6 head of cattle, 150 sheep and 16 [sic] and 30 pigs. Then it was worth £18; now 12.

[Great and Little] Clacton was always in the bishopric as a manor and 20 hides. [There were] then 50 villans; now 45. [There were] then 20 bordars; now 50. [There were] then 13 slaves; now 7. [There were] then 4 ploughs in demesne; now 3. Among the men were then 50 ploughs; now 20. [There is]

woodland for 400 pigs [and there are] 20 acres of meadow. Then as now [there was] 1 fishery. Now [there is] 1 mill. [There is] pasture for 100 sheep and [there is] 1 horse and 7 head of cattle and 30 pigs and 41 sheep. It was then worth £40; now 26. Of this same manor, 5 knights hold 4 hides and [there are there] 6 ploughs and [there are] 2 villans and 45 bordars and 3 slaves, having 3 ploughs, and it is worth £8. 2s. [and is included] in the above valuation. In Colchester the bishop has 14 houses and 4 acres, which render no customary dues, save scot, to any one but the bishop. In the same Hugh holds of the bishop 2 hides and 1 acre and renders customary dues. Then as now [there were] 2 ploughs in demesne and the men [had] 1 plough and [there were] 2 villans and 11 bordars and 1 slave and 6½ acres of meadow. [There is] now 1 mill. It was then and later worth 40s. [and] now 50s.

IIII. The Fief of the Bishop of London

HUNDRED OF CHAFFORD.

Ælfric held Cranham TRE as a manor and 3 hides and 40 acres. Now Hugh holds [it] of the bishop. [There were] then 6 villans; now 8. [There were] then 5 bordars; now 15. [There were] then 6 slaves; now 4. Then as now [there were] 3 ploughs in demesne and the men [had] 4 ploughs. [There is] woodland for 500 pigs [and there are] 20 acres of meadow and 4 colts, 144 sheep, 20 head of cattle. Then and later it was worth £4; now 6.

William fitzBrian holds of the bishop [Great and Little] Totham which Eadweald held as a manor and half a hide and 30 acres. [There is] now 1 villan. Then as now [there are] 6 bordars and 2 slaves and 1 plough in demesne. [There is] woodland for 60 pigs [and there are] 4 acres of meadow and 1 fisherman. [There is] pasture for 40 sheep, and 1 salt-pan. [There are] now 4 head of cattle and 4 pigs, 60 sheep. Then as now it was worth 30s.

[Folio 11V: ESSEX]

William Balt holds of the bishop [Great and Little] Totham which Ælfric held as a manor and half a hide and 30 acres. Now [there are] 3 bordars. Then as now [there is] 1 plough and 1 salt-pan and 2 acres of meadow. [There is] woodland for 30 pigs. Then as now it was worth 30s.

Eadweald held Alresford as a manor and 2 hides of land. Now Humphrey holds [it] of the bishop. Then as now [there were] 2 villans. [There were] then 2 bordars; now 6. [There were] then 3 slaves; now 2. [There were] then 2 ploughs in demesne; now [there are] none. Then as now the men [had] 1 plough. It was then worth 40s.; now 20.

Roger holds Tendring of the bishop, which Alweard held, as one hide and 45 acres TRE. Then as now [there were] 5 bordars. [There were] then 4 slaves; now 3. [There were] 2 ploughs in demesne and 3 acres of meadow. [There is] pasture for 50 sheep. [There were] then 3 horses; now 4. [There are] now 3 head of cattle. Then [there were] 6 pigs; now 16. Then [there were] 36 sheep; now 66. Then as now it is worth 30s.

HUNDRED OF BARSTABLE.

Ansketil holds [Little] Thurrock of the bishop which Wulfwine, a free man, held under King Edward as 1 manor and 2 hides and 2 acres. Then as now [there were] 2 ploughs in demesne. [There was] then 1 bordar; now 6. [There were] then 6 slaves; now 1. [There is] woodland for 50 pigs, pasture for 50 sheep. [There was] then 1 fishery; now [there are] none. [There were] then 4 head of cattle; now 5. [There are] now 2 horses and 2 colts. Then [there were] 12 pigs; now 16. [There were] then 80 sheep; now 128. Then as now it was worth 30s. 4d.

Ralph and Turold hold Well of the bishop, which the same Wulfwine held TRE as a manor and as 1 hide and 30 acres. Then as now [there was] 1 plough. [There was] then 1 villan; now [there are] none. Then as now [there were] 2 bordars. [There is] woodland for 40 pigs and it is worth 20s. Walter holds [Great and Little] Burstead of the bishop, which Godwine held TRE as a manor and as 3 hides. Then as now [there were] 2 ploughs in demesne and the men [had] 1 plough and [there were] 2 villans. [There was] then 1 bordar; now 6. [There were] then 4 slaves; now 1. [There is] woodland for 60 pigs and [there are] 30 acres more claimed from TRE. [There are] now 2 colts and 4 head of cattle. [There were] then 5 pigs; now 24. [There were] then 50 sheep; now 88 and [there are] 44 goats. It was then worth 60s.; now 50.

William holds Corringham of the bishop, which Sigar, a free man, held as 1 manor and 4

The Fief

[Folio 12: ESSEX]

hides and 10 acres. [There are] now $3\frac{1}{2}$ hides and 10 acres. The Bishop of Bayeux holds the half a hide which was taken from it. [There were] then 3 ploughs in demesne; now $2\frac{1}{2}$. Then as now the men [had] 4 ploughs. [There were] then 3 villans; now 2. [There were] then 7 bordars; now 25. [There were] then 5 slaves; now 3. [There is] woodland for 300 pigs, pasture for 400 sheep; Then as now [there was] 1 mill. [There were] then 2 horses; now none. [There were] then 3 head of cattle; now 6. [There were] then 8 pigs; now 10. [There were] then 400 sheep; now 500 and [there are] 21 goats. It was then worth £7; now £7 and 6s.

The same [William] holds Horndon [on the Hill] of the bishop, which Godwine, a free man, held as 1 manor and $1\frac{1}{2}$ hides. Then as now [there was] 1 plough in demesne and 4 bordars and 1 slave. [There is] woodland for 10 pigs [and there is] an eighth part of 1 fishery. Then as now it was worth 20s. From this manor half a hide was taken away, which the Bishop of Bayeux holds.

Hugolin holds Chadwell of the bishop, which Ælfric, a thegn of King Edward, held as a manor and 2 hides. Then as now [there were] 2 ploughs in demesne and the men [had] $1\frac{1}{2}$ ploughs. [There was] then 1 priest and 3 bordars; now 1 priest and 7 bordars. Then as now [there were] 4 slaves. [There is] pasture for 100 sheep. [There was] then 1 fishery; now none. [There are] 2 horses, 10 head of cattle, 81 sheep. Then and later it was worth 40s.; now 30.

William holds Ramsden [Bellhouse and Crays] of the

bishop, which Godric held as 1 manor and 1 hide and 10 acres. Then as now [there was] 1 plough in demesne and 4 bordars. [There is] woodland for 25 pigs. [There are] 8 pigs, 50 sheep, 12 goats. It is worth 20s.

Ralph holds Laindon of the bishop, which Wulfmær held as a manor and half a hide TRE. [There was] then 1 slave; now [there is] none and it is worth 6s.

HUNDRED OF WITHAM.

Hugolin holds [Great and Little] Braxted of the bishop, which Ælfric, a free man, held as a manor and as 1 hide. Then as now [there were] 2 ploughs in demesne. The men had [then] 2 ploughs; now none. [There were] then 4 villans; now none. [There were] then 3 bordars; now 8 and 1 priest. [There were] then 4 slaves; now 2. [There is] woodland for 40 pigs [and there is] 1 mill, 1 horse, 4 head of cattle, 13 pigs, 130 sheep. Then as now it was worth 60s.

Ralph fitzBrian holds Howbridge, which Alwine, a free man, held as 1 manor and half a hide. Then as now [there was] 1 plough in demesne and the men [had] 1 plough and [there was] 1 villan and 10 bordars. [There were] then 2 slaves; now none. [There is] woodland for 100 pigs. [There are] 12 acres of meadow, 16 head of cattle, 100 sheep, 20 goats, 14 pigs, and it is worth 40s.

[Folio 12v: ESSEX]

HALF-HUNDRED OF HARLOW.

In [Great and Little] Hallingbury Eadgifu held 30 acres TRE. Then as now [there was] half a plough and 2 acres of meadow. It is worth 5s.

HUNDRED OF DENGIE.

Hugh holds Ulehams of the bishop, which Godhere, a free man, held TRE as a manor and as 2 hides and 20 acres. [There were] then 3 villans; now none. [There were] then 3 bordars; now 1. [There were] then 4 slaves; now 2. Then as now [there were] 2 ploughs in demesne. The men [had] then 1 plough; now none. [There is] pasture for 30 sheep. [There are] 3 horses, 140 sheep. Then and later it was worth 60s.; now 40.

Ralph fitzBrian holds Bassets of the bishop, which Alwine, a free man, held TRE as a manor and half a hide and 14 acres. [There were] then 2 villans; now none. Then as now [there were] 3 bordars. [There was] then 1 slave; now 2. Then as now [there was] 1 plough. [There is] woodland for 20 pigs [and there are] 8 acres of meadow. It is worth 20s.

V. Land of the Canons of St Paul In Essex

HUNDRED OF BARSTABLE.

Eadgifu held Lee Chapel freely TRE as a manor and half a hide and 30 acres. [There were] then 2 ploughs in demesne and the men [had] 2 ploughs; now none. [There were] then 2 villans; now 6. [There were] then 6 bordars; now 5. [There were] then 2 slaves; now 3. [There is] woodland for 25 pigs [and] pasture for 100 sheep. [There is] 1 cow, 1 pig, 7 sheep. It was then worth 40s.; now 20. This land is claimed for the king's use.

HUNDRED OF WALTHAM.

St Paul held Chingford TRE as 1 manor and as 6 hides. Then as now [there were] 2 ploughs in demesne. The men [had] then 3 ploughs; now 4. [There were] then 7 villans; now 8. [There were] then 3 bordars; now 6. Then as now [there were] 4 slaves. [There is] woodland for 500 pigs [and there are] 50 acres of meadow and 2 fisheries, 9 head of cattle, 2 horses, 27 pigs, 100 sheep. It was then worth £4; now 100s. From this manor Peter de Valognes took away 1 hide and 8 acres of meadow, which belonged to the manor TRE, with woodland for 50 pigs. It is worth 10s. From this same manor Geoffrey de Mandeville took away 10 acres of meadow.

HUNDRED OF HINCKFORD.

St Paul held Belchamp TRE as a manor and 5 hides.

The Canons

[Folio 13: ESSEX]

Then as now [there were] 2 ploughs in demesne and the men [had] then 12 ploughs. [There were] 24 villans, 10 bordars, 5 slaves. [There is] woodland for 60 pigs. [There are] 30 acres of meadow, 9 head of cattle, 2 horses, 40 pigs, 100 sheep, 5 goats. Then as now it was worth £16.

St Paul held Wickham [St Pauls] TRE as a manor and 3 hides less 1 virgate. [There was] then 1 plough in demesne; now 2. The men [had] then 4 ploughs; now 3. [There were] then 6 villans; now 5. [There were] then 4 bordars; now 10. [There was] then 1 slave; now 3. [There is] woodland for 200 pigs. [There are] 10 acres of meadow, 2 horses, 4 head of cattle, 23 pigs, 50 sheep, 24 goats and 2 hives of bees. It was then worth 40s.; now £4.

HUNDRED OF DENGIE.

St Paul held Tillingham as a manor and 20 hides and 6 acres. Then as now [there were] 20 villans and 8 bordars and 4 slaves. [There were] then 3 ploughs in demesne; now 4. Then as now the men [had] 10 ploughs. [There is] pasture for 400 sheep. [There is] now 1 mill and 1 fishery, 15 head of cattle, 30 pigs, 340 sheep. In addition to this land, 10 acres, which belong to this manor, were given to the church. The whole was then worth £10; now 15.

HUNDRED OF ONGAR.

Godgyth, a certain woman, held Norton [Mandeville] TRE as half a hide; now St Paul [holds it]. Then as now [there was] 1 plough and 2 bordars. [There is] woodland for 40 pigs [and there are] 4 acres of meadow, 1 horse, 5 head of cattle. It is worth 20s. Godgyth gave this land to St Paul after the king came into England, but [the canons] do not show the king's writ or permission.

Howard and Wulfsige, 2 free men, held Navestock as 2 manors and as 5 hides less 20 acres. Now St Paul has [it] as the same since the king came into this land and [the canons] say that they had it by the king's gift. Then as now [there

were] 12 villans and 11 bordars. [There were] then 4 slaves; now 2. Then as now [there were] 4 ploughs in demesne and the men [had] 4 ploughs. [There is] woodland for 600 pigs [and there are] 44 acres of meadow. Then as now [there were] 13 head of cattle, 2 horses, 116 sheep, 24 pigs, 24 goats, 4 hives of bees. Then as now it was worth £10.

Thorsten the Red held the other Navestock as a manor and as 1 hide and 40 acres. Now St Paul has appropriated [it] and it is with the other land, and he holds [it] as the same. [There was] then 1 bordar; now 2. Then as now [there were] 2 ploughs. [There is] woodland for 100 pigs. Then as now it is worth 30s. In the same vill

[Folio 13v: ESSEX]

7 free men held 2 hides, which St Paul holds as the same and now [there are] in this land 12 men. [There are] now 3 bordars. Then as now [there were] 4 ploughs. [There is] woodland for 210 pigs [and there are] 7 acres of meadow. Then as now it is worth 40s. In Navestock 1 priest holds half a hide and 20 acres, but the Hundred bears testimony that it is St Paul's. Then as now [there were] 2 bordars. [There was] then 1 plough; now half [a plough]. Then as now it was worth 10s.; now it is in the king's hands.

HUNDRED OF CHELMSFORD.

St Paul holds Runwell now as then as 8 hides. Then as now [there were] 8 villans and 8 bordars. [There were] then 2 slaves; now 1. [There were] then 3½ ploughs in demesne and now the same. Among the men then [there were] 2½ ploughs. [There is] woodland for 200 pigs. [There are] 2 horses, 1 cow, 8 pigs, 100 sheep. Then as now it is worth £8.

HUNDRED OF THURSTABLE.

St Paul holds 'Tidwoldington' [Heybridge] now as then as 8 hides and as 1 manor, but Ralph Baynard holds half a hide and the Hundred does not know how he should have it. Then as now [there were] 16 villans and 4 bordars and 4 slaves. [There were] then 2 ploughs in demesne; now 1½. The men [had] then 8 ploughs; now 3. [There is] woodland for 60 pigs [and there are] 30 acres of meadow. [There is] pasture for 160 sheep. Then as now [there was] 1 mill and 1 salt-pan, 1 horse, 8 head of cattle, 12 pigs, 150 sheep, 3 hives of bees. Then as now it was worth £8.

HUNDRED OF TENDRING.

St Paul holds The Naze now as then as a manor and as 27 hides. [There were] then 86 villans; now 63. [There were] then 40 bordars; now 50. Then as now [there were] 6 and 6 ploughs in demesne. Among the men [there were] then 60 ploughs; now 30. [There is] woodland for 300 pigs. [There are] 9 acres of meadow. [There are] now 2 mills. [There were] then 3 salt-pans; now 2. [There is] pasture for 300 sheep. [There are] 22 head of cattle, 30 pigs, 200 sheep, 4 hives of bees. It was then worth £26; now 30 and 1 mark of silver.

HUNDRED OF ROCHFORD.

St Paul holds Barling now as then as 1 manor and as 2½ hides less 15 acres. [There were] then 2 villans; now none. [There were] then 5 bordars; now 9. Then as now [there was] 1 slave and 1 plough in demesne and the men [had] 2 ploughs. [There is] pasture for 40 sheep. [There are] 2 horses, 2 head of cattle, 4 pigs, 160 sheep. It was then worth £4. 10s.; now £6. In the same [Barling] 1 free man held

The Canons

half a hide and 10 acres TRE; now St Paul [holds it]. Then as now [there was] 1 plough and it is worth 20s. The canons obtained possession of this land after the king came into England.

VI. Land of St Peter, Westminster.

HUNDRED OF BARSTABLE.

In [North and South] Benfleet St Peter has 7 hides and 30 acres, which belonged to the church of St Mary TRE, but King William gave the church with the land to St Peter of Westminster, in which land there are 2 ploughs in demesne and the men [have] 5 ploughs. Then as now [there were] 15 villans. [There were] then 7 bordars; now 12. [There is] pasture for 200 sheep. Now [there is] half a mill It was then worth £4; now 6. Engelric gave the eighth hide of the same church of St Mary to [the Church of] St Martin, [London] and it still belongs to it, as the Shire testifies, without the king's command. In Fanton [there are] 4 hides and 30 acres. Then as now [there was] 1 plough in demesne. The men [had] then 4 ploughs; now 1. [There were] then 6 villans; now 1. [There were] then 4 slaves. [There was] then 1 bordar; now 9 and in the same vill can be employed 2 more ploughs in demesne. [There are] 30 acres of waste woodland, 2 horses, 30 sheep. It was then worth 60s.; now £6. In Bowers [Gifford] St Peter has 50 acres, which 1 Englishman holds of him. Then as now [there was] 1 villan and it is worth 50d.

Æthelstan Stric held Fanton TRE as a manor and 1 hide. [There was] then 1 plough; now none. Then as now [there was] 1 bordar. Then and later it was worth 20s.; now 10. This land is claimed for the king's use because it came to the church by a forged writ. In demesne [there are] 2 horses [and] 30 sheep.

HUNDRED OF WITHAM.

In Kelvedon TRE [there were] 5 hides, which St Peter held. Then as now [there were] 2 ploughs in demesne. Then the men [had] 8 ploughs; now 4. [There were] then 20 villans; now 18. [There were] then 3 bordars; now 7. Then as now [there were] 3 slaves. [There is] woodland for 50 pigs and [there are] 25 acres of meadow and 1 mill. It was then worth 100s.; now £8 and the abbot has £12 from it. In demesne [there are] 2 horses, 6 head of cattle, 35 pigs, 35 sheep.

HUNDRED OF BECONTREE.

St Peter held [East and West] Ham TRE as a manor and 2 hides. Then as now [there was] 1 plough. [There were] then 3 bordars; now 5. [There is] woodland for 8 pigs. It was then

worth 20s.; now 60. In Leyton Ralph Baynard holds 1 hide of the abbot, which Tostig held TRE. [There was] then 1 plough; now half a plough. [There are] now 5 bordars, 20 acres of meadow, 1 mill. It was then worth 30s.; now 40.

HUNDRED OF LEXDEN.

Harold held Feering TRE as 4 hides and 30 acres. Now St Peter holds [it]. [There were] then 34 villans; now 27. [There were] then 10 bordars; now 24. Then as now [there were] 6 slaves and 4 ploughs in demesne. The men [had] then 15 ploughs; now 10. [There is] woodland for 500 pigs. [There are] 20 acres of meadow, 3 mills. In addition to this above mentioned land, [there were] 12 sokemen dwelling on 2½ hides, who could not withdraw. Then as now, under them [were] 6 bordars and 2½ ploughs. [There is] woodland for 20 pigs. [There are] 12 acres of meadow and 2 houses in Colchester which belong to this manor. In demesne [there are] 5 horses, 16 head of cattle, 60 pigs, 84 sheep. It was then worth £22. 10s.; now £34. 10s. Roger de Rames holds 85 acres of the abbot and each renders 10s. to the abbot every year as his service. Mauger, a man of the archbishop, appropriated to the king's wrong 1 free man, holder of half a virgate, who belonged to St Peter's manor TRE, and now he is in the king's hand. Then as now [there was] half a plough and it was worth 5s.

HUNDRED OF ONGAR.

Æthelric held Kelvedon [Hatch] TRE as a manor and 2 hides; now St Peter [holds it]. Then as now [there was] 1 villan. [There were] then 5 bordars; now 10. Then as now [there were] 2 slaves and 2 ploughs in demesne and the men [had] 1 plough. [There is] woodland for 200 pigs. [There are] 16 acres of meadow. Now [there is] 1 mill. It was then worth 40s.; now 60. This abovesaid Æthelric went away to a naval battle against King William and when he returned he fell ill. Then he gave this manor to St Peter, but none of the men from the Shire knows this but one, and since then St Peter has thus held this manor and [the monks] have had neither a writ nor delivery by a servant of the king

St Peter

since the king came into this land.

In [North and South] Ockenden William the chamberlain holds 1 hide of the abbot and [there is] 1 plough in demesne and the men [have] 1 plough. [There are] 4 villans. It is worth 40s.

HUNDRED OF CHAFFORD.

Harold held [North and South] Ockendon as a manor and 2 hides less 40 acres TRE; now St Peter holds [it]. [There were] then 8 villans; now 7. [There were] then 5 bordars; now 8. Then as now [there were] 4 slaves and 2 ploughs in demesne. The men [had] then 6 ploughs; now 4. [There is] woodland for 300 pigs. [There is] 1 horse, 6 head of cattle, 30 pigs, 110 sheep. It was then worth £4; now 10. This land [has been acquired] by exchange since the king crossed the sea.

St Peter held Wennington as a manor and $2\frac{1}{2}$ hides then and now. [There were] then 3 villans; now 2. [There were] then 3 bordars; now 1. [There were] then 2 slaves; now none. [There was] then 1 plough in demesne; now half a plough. The men [had] then 1 plough; now half a plough. [There is] 1 horse, 1 cow, 4 pigs, 60 sheep. It was then worth 40s.; now 60. A free man gave St Peter half a hide, but Robert the pervert, a man of Robert Gernon, took possession [of it] and it renders 20d. a year.

St Peter holds "Geddesduna" as 1 hide. Then as now [there was] 1 villan and 1 bordar. [There was] then half a plough; now 1. Then as now it was worth 20s.

HUNDRED OF CHELMSFORD.

St Peter holds Moulsham now as then as 5 hides less 30 acres. [There were] then 8 villans; now 3. [There were] then 4 bordars; now 21. [There are] now 2 slaves. Then as now [there were] 3 ploughs in demesne and the men [had] 4 ploughs. [There is] woodland for 400 pigs. [There are] 30 acres of meadow, 1 mill, 1 horse, 2 cows, 36 pigs, 100 sheep. It was then worth £9; now 12.

HUNDRED OF ROCHFORD.

St Peter holds Paglesham as a manor and as $1\frac{1}{2}$ hides. [There were] then 2 bordars, now 11. [There were] then 4 slaves. [There were] then 2 ploughs in demesne; now 1. Then as now the men [had] 1 plough. [There is] pasture for 20 sheep [and there is] 1 horse, 4 head of cattle, 100 sheep. It was then worth £4; now 6. One thegn gave this land to the church when he went to the battle in York with Harold

[Folio 15v: ESSEX]

VII. Lands of the Bishop of Durham In Essex

HALF-HUNDRED OF WALTHAM.

Harold held Waltham [Holy Cross] TRE as a manor and 40 hides. Then as now [there were] 80 villans and 24 bordars. [There were] then 6 slaves; now 7. [There were] then 7 ploughs in demesne; now 6. Then as now the men [had] 37 ploughs. [There is] woodland for 202 pigs. [There are] 80 acres of meadow, 2 horses, 20 head of cattle, 80 sheep, 12 goats, 40 pigs. There is pasture there which is worth 18s. [There was] then 1 mill; now 3. [There are] 5 fisheries, and [there were] then 20 rent-paying tenants; now 36, and 1 plough more could be employed on the manor. To this manor belong 2 sokemen, [who were] holding 6 hides TRE; now 5, and [the church of] Holy Cross holds half of the sixth hide and William de War[enne] took the other half, and [there belonged] 4 sokemen with 2 hides and half a virgate. And to this manor also belonged 1 hide less 15 acres, which the same William took away from it. And Ranulf, brother of Ilger [has taken] 30 acres of land and 4 of meadow. All those sokemen who are now there have [between them] 7 hides and 15 acres, and they had in their demesne TRE 4 ploughs; now $4\frac{1}{2}$. Then as now [there was] 1 villan. [There were] then 6 bordars; now 8. [There were] then 2 slaves; now none. [There is] woodland for 180 pigs. [There are] $16\frac{1}{2}$ acres of meadow and 4 of pasture. >From all this Harold had TRE £36, and the bishop's men assess [it] at £63. 5s. 4d. But now, as the other men of the Hundred testify, it is worth £100. And in London there are 12 houses belonging to the manor, which render 20s. and a gate which the king gave to the bishop's predecessor which also renders 20s.

VIII. Lands of the Canons of the Holy Cross of Waltham.

HUNDRED OF WALTHAM.

Holy Cross held Epping then as now as a manor and 2 hides and 15 acres. Then as now [there were] $1\frac{1}{2}$ ploughs in demesne and 2 bordars and 2 slaves. [There is] woodland for 50 pigs. [There are] 3 acres of meadow, 10 head of cattle

Holy Cross

[Folio 16: ESSEX]

1 horse, 20 pigs, 20 sheep, 8 goats and it is worth 15s.

Holy Cross held Nazeing then as now as 5 hides. [There was] then 1 plough in demesne; now $1\frac{1}{2}$. The men [had] then 1 plough; now $1\frac{1}{2}$. Then as now [there were] 5 villans. Now [there are] 2 bordars. [There were] then 2 slaves; now none. [There is] woodland for 50 pigs. [There are] 13 acres of meadow, half a fishery, 1 horse, 4 head of cattle, 10 pigs, . It was then worth 40s.; now 60.

HUNDRED OF BECONTREE.

Holy Cross then as now holds Woodford [...], TRE [as] 5 hides. Then as now [there were] 2 ploughs in demesne. The men [had] then 13 ploughs; now 7. [There were] then 4 slaves, now none. Then as now [there were] 13 villans. [There were] then 4 bordars; now 7. [There is] woodland for 500 pigs [and] 26 acres of meadow . [There was] then 1 mill, now none. [There was] then 1 ox; now 6 [head of cattle]. [There are] 100 sheep, 50 pigs, 40 goats. Then as now it was worth 100s.

Holy Cross held Loughton then as now as a manor and 4 hides and 20 acres. [There were] then 2 ploughs in demesne; now 1. Then as now the men [had] 1 plough and 2 villans. [There were] then 2 bordars; now 5. [There is] woodland for 100 pigs [and there are] 5 acres of meadow. One plough more could be employed. [There are] 5 head of cattle, 5 sheep. It is worth 40s.

Holy Cross holds Loughton as a manor and $2\frac{1}{2}$ hides. Then as now [there was] 1 plough in demesne. [There were] then 2 bordars; now 4. [There is] woodland for 40 pigs. [There are] 4 acres of meadow, 9 head of cattle, 10 pigs, 20 sheep. It is worth 20s.

HUNDRED OF ONGAR.

Holy Cross held Paslow then and now as a manor and as 2 hides less 30 acres. [There were] then 6 villans; now 5. [There are] now 4 bordars. [There were] then 7 slaves; now 3. [There were] then 2 ploughs in demesne; now 3. Then the men [had] 3 ploughs, now 2. [There is] woodland for 700 pigs. [There are] 8 acres of meadow. [There were] then 3 head of cattle; now 6. [There were] then 20 pigs; now 30 [and] 50 sheep. [There were] then 16 goats; now 36. Now [there is] 1 horse. Then as now it was worth £6.

Holy Cross held Alderton then as now as a manor and 4½ hides and 10 acres. [There were] then 7 villans; now 9. [There were] then 2 bordars; now 6. [There were] then 5 slaves; now 3. Then as now [there were] 2 ploughs in demesne. The men [had] then 3 ploughs; now 2. [There is] woodland for 400 pigs. [There are] 15 acres of meadow, 2 head of cattle, 8 sheep, 10 pigs, 15 goats. Then as now it is worth £4.

Holy Cross held Debden then as now as a manor and 3 hides and 40 acres. Then as now [there were] 4 villans and 7 bordars. [There were] then 4 slaves; now none. [There were] then 2 ploughs in demesne; now 1. The men [had] then 2 ploughs; now 1.

[Folio 16v: ESSEX]

[There is] woodland for 300 pigs. [There are] 6 acres of meadow, 2 head of cattle, 8 pigs, 9 sheep. Then as now it is worth 40s. A certain free man held 40 acres which the church appropriated after the king came into this land and holds still. [There was] then 1 plough; now none, and when it received [the land] half [a plough]. [There are] 4 acres of meadow. It was then worth 6s. 8d.; now 5s. 4d.

HUNDRED OF CHAFFORD.

Holy Cross held [South] Weald then as now as 1 manor and TRE as 2 hides; now as 1½. Geoffrey de Mandeville has the other half [a hide], but the Hundred does not know why he has [it]and G[eoffrey] says that he has it by exchange. Then as now [there were] 10 villans and 6 bordars and 3 slaves and 2 ploughs in demesne. The men [had] then 6 ploughs; now 4. [There is] woodland for 200 pigs. [There are] 1½ acres of meadow. Now [there are] 4 head of cattle. [There were] then 10 pigs; now 25. [There were] then 25 sheep; now 65 and it is worth £6. To this manor belonged 1 sokeman who held 1 carucate of land, but now Robert Gernon has [it] of the king's gift, as he says.

Holy Cross holds Upminster as 2½ hides and 40 acres. [There were] then 8 villans; now 6. [There were] then 2 bordars; now 4. [There were] then 4 slaves; now 3. Then as now [there were] 2 ploughs in demesne and the men [had] 4 ploughs. [There is] woodland for 300 pigs. [There are] 6 acres of meadow [and] 2 head of cattle. [There were] then 20 sheep; now 50. [There were] then 11 pigs; now 30. Then as now it was worth £4. To this manor belongs 1 sokeman with 30 acres and half a plough and [it] is worth 20d.

The church [Holy Cross] held Walter then as now as 4 hides less 40 acres. [There were] then 4 bordars; now 10. [There were] then 6 slaves; now 3. Then as now [there were] 2 ploughs in demesne and the men [had] 1 plough. [There is] woodland for 30 pigs. [There are] 18 acres of meadow. [There is] now 1 horse. Then as now [there were] 5 head of cattle, 5 pigs, 40 sheep, 2 hives of bees. It is worth 40s.

[Folio 17: ESSEX]

ST MARY of Barking in Essex
ST Æthelthryth of Ely
ST Edmund
ST Martin, London
ST Martin of Battle
SAINT-Valéry
La TRINITÉ, Caen
SAINT-Étienne, Caen
SAINT-Ouen
The BISHOP of Bayeux

[Folio 17v: ESSEX]

IX. land of St Mary of Barking

HUNDRED OF BARSTABLE.

St Mary holds Mucking for 7 hides, and Turold of Rochester took 30 acres away from it and they [now] belong to the fief of the Bishop of Bayeux. And TRE [there was] 1 plough in demesne; now 2. Then as now the villans [had] 9 ploughs and [there were] 12 villans. [There were] then 14 bordars; now 25. [There were] then 4 slaves; now none. [There is] woodland for 300 pigs. [There is] pasture for 300 sheep. [There are] 40 acres of meadow. Now [there is] 1 mill, 1 fishery, 10 head of cattle, 2 horses, 18 pigs, 250 sheep. Then as now it was worth £10.

St Mary holds Bulphan as 7 hides. [There was] then 1 plough in demesne; now 2. The men [had] then 7 ploughs; now 10. [There were] then 10 villans; now 16. [There were] then 5 bordars; now 16. [There are] 3 slaves. [There is] woodland for 500 pigs. [There are] 8 head of cattle, 15 pigs, 1 horse, 80 sheep. It was then worth £8; now 10. Ravengar took away from this land 24 acres. In Fanton 1 villan holds 40 acres of land. Then as now [there is] half a plough and it is worth 40d. Of the abovesaid manor, that is, Mucking, William holds half a hide and 30 acres, and [there are] 3 bordars, and it is worth 18s. [and is included] in the above valuation of the same manor. In this Hundred are 6 free men holding 2 hides and 50 acres. Then as now [there were] 2 ploughs. [There were] then 3 bordars; now 6. [There was] then 1 slave; now none. [There was] then woodland for 100 pigs; now 55. [There is] a thirteenth part of 1 fishery. The whole is worth 30s. These free men belonged to Barking, but now the king can do with them what he likes. Robert Gernon has woodland from this land for 50 pigs. And of the abovesaid land, Godwine Woodhen holds 3 virgates and it is worth 10s.

HALF-HUNDRED OF HARLOW.

In [Great and Little] Parndon St Mary holds now as then half a hide. [There is] half a plough, 1 bordar, woodland for 10 pigs [and there are] 5 acres of meadow. It is worth 10s.

HUNDRED OF BECONTREE.

St Mary holds Barking now as then as 30 hides. [There were] then 4 ploughs in demesne; now 3, and a fourth [plough] could be [employed]. The men [had] then 70 ploughs; now 68. [There were] then 100 villans; now 140. [There were] then 50 bordars; now 90. [There were] then 10 slaves; now 6. [There is] woodland for 1,000 pigs. [There are] 100 acres of meadow, 2 mills, 1 fishery, 2 horses, 34 head of cattle, 150 pigs, 114 sheep, 24 goats, 10 hives of bees. In London [there are] 28 houses which render 13

St Mary

[Folio 18: ESSEX]

13s. 8d. and a moiety of a church which TRE rendered 6s. 8d. and now does not render [anything]. This manor was worth £80 TRE and now the same, as the Englishmen say, but the Frenchmen assess [it] at £100. To this manor belonged TRE 24 acres, which Goscelin the lorimer has taken away from it and 3 knights hold 2 hides, and [there are] 3 ploughs

HUNDRED OF WINSTREE.

St Mary holds [Great and Little] Wigborough now as then as 11½ hides and 13 acres. [There were] then 2½ ploughs in demesne; now 2. The men [had] then 10 ploughs; now 9. [There were] then 9 villans; now 10. [There were] then 24 bordars; now 33. Then as now [there were] 8 slaves. [There is] woodland for 100 pigs. [There is] pasture for 100 sheep, which renders 16d. [There are] 6 salt-pans. [There were] then 12 head of cattle and now the same. [There are] 2 horses, 14 pigs, 230 sheep. it was then worth £12; now 10. To this manor belong 3 houses in Colchester.

HUNDRED OF CHAFFORD.

St Mary holds [Great and Little] Warley now as then as 3 hides. Then as now [there were] 9 villans. [There were] then 8 bordars; now 10. [There were] then 3 slaves; now 5. Then as now [there were] 2 ploughs in demesne. The men [had] then 8 ploughs; now 6. [There is] woodland for 200 pigs. [There is] pasture for 100 sheep. [There are] 8 head of cattle, 11 pigs, 150 sheep, 1 hive of bees. Then as now it was worth £7. In Stifford St Mary has 40 acres. [There was] then 1 villan; now 2, and [there are] 2 bordars [and] 1 acre of meadow. [There was] then 1 plough; now half [a plough] and it is worth 3s. There were also 30 acres [belonging] to this land, which William de War[enne] has by exchange, as he says. There are also 30 acres more and 2½ acres of meadow, and [this] is worth 3s.

HUNDRED OF CHELMSFORD.

St Mary holds Fryerning and Ingatestone now as then as 3½ hides and 10 acres. Then as now [there are] 2 villans. [There were] then 6 bordars; now 7. Then as now [there is] 1 slave and 1 plough in demesne. The men [had] then 1½ ploughs; now 1. [There is] woodland for 500 pigs, and [there is] 1 sokeman with 30 acres, 1 horse, 9 head of cattle, 20 pigs, 16 sheep. It was then worth 70s.; now 60.
[...] St Mary holds Fristling as 1½ virgates. [There were] then 3 bordars; now 4. [There was] then 1 slave; now none. Then as now [there was] 1 plough. [There is] woodland for 200 pigs. [There are] 4 head of cattle, 37 sheep, 10 goats. It was then worth 8s.; now 10.

[Folio 18v: ESSEX]

HUNDRED OF ROCHFORD.

St Mary holds Hockley now as then as a manor and 7½ hides. [There were] then 24 villans; now 27. Then as now [there were] 12 bordars. [There were] then 3 slaves; now none. Then as now [there were] 2 ploughs in demesne and the men [had]

15 ploughs. [There is] pasture for 200 sheep. [There is] 1 mill, 2 horses, 8 head of cattle, 151 sheep, 26 pigs. Then as now it was worth £10. Of this manor, William de Boursigny holds 3 virgates of the [abbey], and [there is] 1 plough, and it is worth 21s. [and is included] in the above valuation.

HUNDRED OF THURSTABLE.

St Mary holds Tollesbury now as then as a manor and 8 hides. [There were]then 11 villans; now 12 and [there were] 14 bordars; now 16. [There were] then 5 slaves; now 7. Then as now [there were] 2 ploughs in demesne. The men [had] then 8 ploughs; now 7. [There is] woodland for 500 pigs. [There is] pasture for 400 sheep. [There is] now 1 mill and 1 fishery and 2 salt-pans and 2 horses, 10 head of cattle, 28 pigs, 300 sheep. Then as now it was worth £10. Ranulf Peverel holds 1 hide which Siward held of the abbey and he is willing to do such service as his predecessor did, but the abbess is not willing because [the land] was for the sustenance of the [nuns]. Odo, a man of Swein, has obtained 10 acres which [belonged] to the [abbey] and the Hundred testifies to this, but he vouches his lord to warranty for them. Now as then they are worth 16d.

X. Lands of St Æthelthryth of Ely.

HUNDRED OF DUNMOW.

St Æthelthryth holds Broxted now as then as a manor and 3 hides. Then as now [there were] 2 ploughs in demesne and the men [had] 4 ploughs. [There are] 16 villans. [There were] then 2 bordars; now 5. [There are] 5 slaves. [There is] woodland for 250 pigs. [There are] 30 acres of meadow. Then and now [there were] 16 head of cattle, 2 horses, 70 sheep, [...] 2 hives of bees. It was then worth £10; now 8. From this manor 9 acres of land were taken away TRW, which Eudo the steward holds, and moreover 2 carucates of land from the demesne, which the same Eudo [holds], and [this] is worth £4.

St Æthelthryth

[Folio 19: ESSEX]

St Æthelthryth holds Roding now as then; [she held it] TRE as 3 hides and 45 acres [and] now as 2 hides and 45 acres. William de Warenne took away the third hide from the demesne, which belonged there TRE. Then as now [there were] 8 villans and 1 priest, 2 bordars, 4 slaves. [There were] then 3 ploughs in demesne; now 2. Then as now the men [had] 4 ploughs. [There is] woodland for 100 pigs. [There are] 20 acres of meadow, 2 horses, 9 head of cattle, 28 pigs, 15 sheep, and 3 sokemen belong to this manor and 11 bordars and 3 slaves. It was then worth £4; now 6.
St Æthelthryth held Rettendon TRE as 1 manor and as 20 hides. Now they hold [it] as 16½ hides. Then as now [there were] 26 villans and 6 bordars. [There were] then 7 slaves; now 6. Then as now [there were] 3 ploughs in demesne and the men [had] 12 ploughs. [There is] woodland for 300 pigs. [There are] 9 head of cattle, 41 pigs, 164 sheep. It was then worth £17; now 20. And Siward held 1 hide and 30 acres of St Æthelthryth; now Ranulf Peverel holds [it] of the king, but the Hundred testifies that [they are] of the abbey. And [there

are] 2 hides and 30 acres which the [abbey] held and Leofsunu [held them] from the same TRE. Now Eudo holds [the land] of the abbey because his predecessor held it, but the Hundred testifies that he cannot sell them without the abbot's licence.

HALF-HUNDRED OF FRESHWELL.

St Æthelthryth holds Hadstock now as then as 1 manor and 2 hides. [There were] then 8 villans; now 12. [There were] then 4 bordars; now 13. [There were] then 4 slaves; now 2. Then as now [there were] 2 ploughs in demesne. The men [had] then 3 ploughs; now 4. [There is] woodland for 100 pigs. [There are] 6 acres of meadow. [There was] then 1 mill; now none. [There is] 1 horse, 4 head of cattle, 16 pigs, 36 sheep, 8 goats. It was then worth £6; now 10.

HUNDRED OF UTTLESFORD.

St Æthelthryth holds Littlebury now as then as 1 manor and 25 hides. Then as now [there were] 39 villans and 19 bordars [and] 7 slaves. [There were] then 5 ploughs in demesne; now 4. The men [had] then 17 ploughs; now 15. [There is] woodland for 160 pigs. [There are] 55 acres of meadow. Then as now [there were] 4 mills, 2 horses, 32 pigs, 80 sheep, 3 hives of bees. It is worth £20. There is also 1 berewick which is called Strethall [and] which 2 men, William and Alwig held as 5 hides and they could not withdraw

[Folio 19v: ESSEX]

from the land without licence of the abbot. Now Hugh holds [it] under the abbot. [There were] then 7 villans; now 6. [There were] then 4 bordars; now 7. Then as now [there were] 6 slaves and 3 ploughs in demesne. The men [had] then 4 ploughs; now 5. [There is] woodland for 10 pigs. [There are] 12 acres of meadow. [There is] 1 mill. It was then worth £7; now 8. In demesne [there are] 7 head of cattle, 100 sheep, 22 pigs, 2 hives of bees.

There is also 1 berewick which is called Heydon, which Alwig [held] as half a hide and 15 acres. [There were] then 2 ploughs in demesne; now 1. [There were] then 4 slaves; now none. [There were] then and now 55 sheep. It was worth then 60s.; now 30. From this manor, William Cardon, a man of Geoffrey de Mandeville, acquired 24 acres of woodland when Swein was sheriff, as the Hundred testifies.

XI. Land of St Edmund. Hundred of Witham.

William fitzGross holds Benton of the abbot as 1 hide and 15 acres. [There were] then 2 ploughs in demesne; now 1. Then as now the men [had] 1 plough [and] 4 villans, 3 bordars. [There is] now 1 mill. [There is] woodland for 50 pigs. [There are] 20 acres of meadow, 2 horses, 6 head of cattle, 12 pigs, 5 goats. It is worth 50s.

HALF-HUNDRED OF HARLOW.

St Edmund holds Harlow now as then as 1 manor and 1½ hides. Then as now [there were] 2 ploughs in demesne and the men [had] 6 ploughs and [there were] 12 villans, 15 bordars and 4 slaves. [There is] woodland for 150 pigs. [There are] 30 acres of meadow, 1 mill, 4 horses, 25 head of cattle, 3 colts, 50 pigs, 60 sheep, 5 hives of bees. To this manor were added 3

hides TRW, which 5 free men held TRE. In these [hides] are now as then 6 ploughs in demesne, 8 bordars, 4 slaves. [There is] woodland for 100 pigs. [There are] 14 acres of meadow. Then as now the manor was worth £8 and the 3 hides were then worth 70s.; now £4.

St Edmund holds Latton as a manor and as 4½ hides, which Thorgot, a free man, held TRE. Then as now [there were] 2 ploughs in demesne and the men [had] 1 plough [and there were] 4 villans. [There were] then 4

St Edmund

[Folio 20: ESSEX]

bordars; now 5. Then as now [there were] 4 slaves. [There is] woodland for 200 pigs. [There are] 35 acres of meadow, 4 head of cattle, 50 pigs, 30 sheep, 25 goats. Then as now it was worth £6.

HUNDRED OF HINCKFORD.

In Alphamston St Edmund holds half a hide. [There is] 1 plough in demesne. [There was] then 1 slave. [There are] now 3 bordars [and] 2 acres of meadow. It was then worth 10s.; now 20.

Hundred of Lexden. In Colne, St Edmund holds 36 acres. [There were] then 3 bordars; now 4. Then as now [there was] half a plough. [There is] woodland for 40 pigs. [There are] 3 acres of meadow. It is worth 20s.

HUNDRED OF ONGAR.

St Edmund holds Stapleford [Abbotts] now as then as 3½ hides and 6½ acres. [There were] then 8 villans; now 9. Then as now [there were] 5 bordars and 2 slaves and 1 plough in demesne. The men [had] then 4 ploughs; now 3. [There is] woodland for 250 pigs. [There are] 12 acres of meadow, 20 head of cattle, 1 horse, 48 sheep, 43 pigs [and] 3 colts and in the soke of the manor are 2 free men with 36½ acres, 1 plough, woodland for 40 pigs [and] 2 acres of meadow. It was then worth 45s.; now 50.

HUNDRED OF CHELMSFORD.

Albert holds Waltham of the abbot, which Stanheard held TRE, as 1 manor and 2 hides less 15 acres, and St Edmund [has it] of the king's gift. Then as now [there was] 1 villan and 7 bordars and 2 slaves and 2 ploughs in demesne and the men [had] 1 plough. [There is] woodland for 30 pigs. [There are] 7 acres of meadow, 1 ox, 50 sheep, 2 pigs, 10 goats. It was then worth 40s.; now 60.

HUNDRED OF TENDRING.

St Edmund holds Wrabness now as then as 1 manor and as 5 hides. Then as now [there were] 6 villans, 8 bordars, 6 slaves. [There were] then 3 ploughs in demesne; now 2. The men [had] then 6 ploughs; now 5½. [There is] 1 acre of meadow. Now [there is] 1 mill and 1 salt-pan, 2 colts, 30 pigs, 200 sheep, 5 hives of bees. It is worth £6.

XII. Land of St Martin of London.

Æthelmær, a thegn of King Edward, held [Good] Easter and Count Eustace gave [it] to St Martin as 1 manor and 4 hides and 50 acres. [There were] then 3 ploughs in demesne; now 2. Then as now the men [had] 8 ploughs [and there were] 8 villans. [There were] then 16 bordars; now 21. [There were] then 8 slaves; now 3. [There is] woodland for 60 pigs. [There are] 20 acres of meadow. [There is] now 1 mill. It was then worth £8; now 10. To this manor belonged 1 berewick with half a hide and 20 acres TRE, but Count E[ustace] has retained it for himself and it belongs to the Hundred of Chelmsford.

XIII. Land of St Martin of Battle.

HUNDRED OF BARSTABLE.

Goti, a free man, held Hutton TRE as 1 manor and 3 hides less 20 acres. Then as now [there were] 2 ploughs in demesne and the men [had] 3 ploughs. [There was] then 1 villan; now 2. [There were] then 10 bordars; now 15. [There are] 4 slaves. [There is] woodland for 1,000 pigs. [There was] then 1 fishery; now none. [There were] then 2 horses; now 3. [There were] then 4 head of cattle; now 19. [There are] 100 sheep. [There were] then 60 pigs; now 100 less 8. [There are] 4 hives of bees and 3 sokemen with 1 hide and 30 acres. Then as now [there was] 1 plough and 15 acres of free land. It was then worth 100s.; now £6 and these 15 acres are worth 30d.

HUNDRED OF HINCKFORD.

Ordgar, a free man, held Horseham TRE as a manor and as 1 hide. Then as now [there were] 2 ploughs in demesne and the men [had] 1 plough. [There were] then and later 5 villans; now 3. [There was] then 1 bordar; now 3. [There were] then 3 slaves; now 2. [There are] 13 acres of meadow, 8 head of cattle, 10 pigs. [There were] then 30 sheep; now 25. [There are] 3 hives of bees. It is worth 40s.

XIIII. Land of Saint-Valéry.

HUNDRED OF HARLOW.

Godric, a free man, held Matching TRE as 40 acres. [There was] then 1 plough; now none. It is worth 10s. 8d.

Heoruwulf, a free man, held Lindsell TRE as 1 manor and as 1 hide.

Saint-Valéry

Now Saint-Valéry [holds it]. Then as now [there were] 2 ploughs in demesne and the men [had] 3 ploughs. [There were] then 8 villans; now 9. [There were] then 4 bordars; now 15. [There were] then 4 slaves; now none. [There is] woodland for 50 pigs [...] [and there are] 6 acres of meadow, 4 head of cattle, 40 pigs, 28 sheep, 5 hives of bees. Then and later [...] it was worth 100s.; now £6.

HUNDRED OF UTTLESFORD.

[...] Saint-Valéry holds Takeley, which Thorkil, a free man, held [...] TRE as half a hide. Then as now [there were] 2 ploughs [...] in demesne [...] and the men [had] 3 ploughs. [There are] 8 villans. Then and later [there were] 3 bordars; now 5. Then as now [there are] 2 slaves. Then and later [there was] woodland for 1,000 pigs; now 600. [There are] 24 acres of meadow. Then and later [there was] 1 mill; now half a mill. [There are] 3 horses, 4 head of cattle, 30 pigs, 28 sheep, 50 goats, 5 hives of bees. Then and later it was worth £6; now 7.

The same Thorkil held Birchanger as 2 hides and as 1 manor. Then and later [there were] 2 ploughs in demesne; now 1. Then as now the men [had] 2 ploughs [and there was] 1 villan [and] 5 bordars. [There were] then 2 slaves. [There was] then woodland for 100 pigs; now 50. [There are] 6 acres of meadow, 1 mill, 2 horses, 6 head of cattle, 28 pigs, 36 goats. Then and later it was worth 60s.; now 50.

The same Thorkil held Widdington as a manor and 4½ hides. Then and later [there were] 3 ploughs in demesne; now 2. Then as now the men [had] 6 ploughs. Then and later [there were] 8 villans; now 11. [There are] 20 sheep [and] 6 slaves. [There is] woodland for 10 pigs. [There are] 12 acres of meadow, 5 head of cattle, 24 pigs, 50 sheep. Then as now it was worth £7. To this land belong 2 hides which now as then 4 sokemen hold and [this] is worth 30 s.

HUNDRED OF DENGIE.

Thorkil, a free man, held St Peter's Chapel [Bradwell] TRE as 1½ hides and 20 acres. [There were] then 2 bordars; now 3. Then as now [there were] 2 slaves and 1 plough. [There is] pasture for 300 sheep. [There is] 1 fishery, 3 head of cattle, 20 pigs, 216 sheep. It was then worth 40s.; now 70. In the same [vill] are 3 free men with 1½ hides [and] 1 plough. It is worth 20s.

The same held Dengie as 2½ hides. [There are] 4 villans. [There was] then 1 bordar; now 8. Then as now [there were] 4 slaves, 2 ploughs in demesne and the men [had] 2 ploughs. [There is] pasture for 200 sheep. Then [it was worth] £4; now 100s. In the same vill

4 free men hold 50 acres and [this] is worth 5s.

XV. Land of La Trinité of Caen.

HUNDRED OF HINCKFORD.

Earl Ælfgar held Felstead TRE as 5 hides; now La Trinité holds [it] as 4 hides. Then as now [there were] 3 ploughs in demesne and the men [had] 16 ploughs. [There were] then 22 villans; later and now 20. Then and later [there were] 23 bordars; now 33. Then as now [there were] 11 slaves. [There is] woodland for 600 pigs. [There are] 36 acres of meadow, 2 mills, 21 head of cattle, 200 pigs, 58 sheep, 30 goats, 1 horse. To this manor belonged 55 acres TRE which 3 sokemen held [and] now 4 [hold]. [There were] then 2 ploughs; now 3.

[There are] now 2 bordars. [There is] woodland for 30 pigs. [There are] 12 acres of meadow. It was then worth £20; later 30 [and] now 32. The fifth hide is not [now] in this manor, for King William gave 3 virgates to Roger God-save-the-ladies and the fourth to Gilbert fitzSalomon.

HUNDRED OF CHELMSFORD.

Earl Ælfgar held as 1 manor and as 8 hides. Now La Trinité [holds it] for as much. Then as now [there were] 16 villans. [There were] then 8 bordars; now 15. Then as now [there were] 6 slaves and 3 ploughs in demesne. The men [had] then 8 ploughs; now 12. [There is] woodland for 400 pigs. [There are] 45 acres of meadow, 1 mill, 1 horse and 1 colt and 14 head of cattle, 100 pigs less 4, 38 sheep, 13 goats, and [there are] 3 sokemen with 1 virgate and 20½ acres, who could not withdraw. It then rendered 8 nights'

Saint-Étienne

[Folio 22: ESSEX]

farm; now £17.

XVI. Land of Saint-Étienne of Caen.

HUNDRED OF HINCKFORD.

One free woman held Panfield TRE as 1 hide and 3 virgates TRE. [There were] then 4 ploughs in demesne; now 3. The men [had] then 2 ploughs; when received none, now half. [There were] then 4 villans; now none. Then as now [there were] 8 bordars. [There were] then 8 slaves; now 7. [There is] woodland for 200 pigs. [There are] 12 acres of meadow, 2 horses, 12 head of cattle, 165 sheep, 37 pigs. It was then worth £10; later 100s. [and] now £10.

XVII. Land of Saint-Ouen.

HUNDRED OF WINSTREE.

Saint-Ouen held [East and West] Mersea TRE as 20 hides. [There were] then 4 ploughs in demesne; now 6. Then as now the men [had] 16 ploughs, and [there were] 36 villans, 62 bordars. Then [there were] 10 slaves; now 3. [There are] 11 horses and 2 colts, 16 head of cattle, 34 pigs, 300 sheep. To this manor belonged half a hide which 1 priest held then as now and it is worth 10s., and [there is] woodland for 200 pigs. [There is] pasture for 300 sheep. [There was] then 1 fishery. It was then worth £26; now 22. There is also in Colchester 1 house which belonged to this land, but Waleran took it away. And in the Hundred of Winstree[there are] 8 sokemen of the king, holding 107 acres and worth 10s. Of these, Saint-Ouen has 2 parts. And Engelric took away 2 sokemen with half a hide and 30 acres; now Count E[ustace] has them. And [there were] 2 sokemen who have been added to Layer, a manor of the king in another Hundred. And of all this soke, Saint-Ouen has 2 thirds and the king has one third. And [Saint-Ouen has] now as then 2 thirds of the forfeitures of the Hundred.

[Folio 22V: ESSEX]

XVIII. Lands of the Bishop of Bayeux in Essex.

HUNDRED OF BARSTABLE.

[Ralph] fitzTurold holds of the Bishop Vange, which 2 free men held, as 5½ hides. Then as now [there were] 2 ploughs in demesne and the men [had] 4 ploughs [and there were] 6 villans, 9 bordars, 1 slave, half a hide of woodland, pasture for 120 sheep, 1 fishery. [There is] now 1 mill, 2 horses, 4 head of cattle, 4 pigs. [There were] then 67 sheep; now 270. Of this land, 1 free man held 30 acres which were added to the aforesaid land TRW and it is not known how. It was then worth 100s.; now £8.

The bishop holds [Great and Little] Burstead in demesne, which Ingvar the thegn held TRE as 1 manor and 10 hides. Then as now [there were] 3 ploughs in demesne. Then the men [had] 12 ploughs; now 11. [There were] then 20 villans; now 22. [There were] then 5 bordars; now 10. [There is] half a hide of woodland, pasture for 150 sheep, 2 horses, 11 head of cattle, 106 pigs, 219 sheep. It is worth £200. To this manor have been added TRW 28 free men holding 28 hides and 5 acres on which there were then 16 ploughs; now 13. [There are] 5 hides of woodland, 23 acres of meadow, pasture for 250 sheep, 54 bordars, 4 slaves. This addition was then worth £20; now 16.

The bishop holds Dunton in demesne, which 1 priest, a free man, held TRE as 7 hides and 40 acres. [There were] then 4 ploughs in demesne; now 2. Then as now the men [had] 4 ploughs. [There were] then 7 villans; now 2, [and] 6 bordars. [There were] then 5 slaves; now 2. [There are] 2 horses, 2 head of cattle, 15 pigs, 34 sheep. It was then worth £12; now 7.

[Ralph] fitzTurold holds Barstable of the bishop, which 1 free man held as 5½ hides and 30 acres, Then as now [there were] 3 ploughs in demesne and [the men had] 2 ploughs [and there were] 6 villans, 11 bordars. It was then worth £4; now 100s. In demesne [there were] 2 horses, 5 head of cattle, 18 pigs, 36 sheep; now 1 horse, 9 head of cattle, 24 pigs, 80 sheep.

[Ralph] fitzTurold holds Ingrate of the bishop, which 1 free man held TRE as 2 hides. Then as now [there was] 1 plough in demesne and the men [had] 1 plough. [There is] 1 villan. [There was] then 1 bordar; now 5. [There are] 3 slaves and 1½ hides of woodland,

The Bishop of Bayeux

[Folio 23: ESSEX]

3 horses, 8 head of cattle. [There were] then 30 pigs; now 58. [There were] then 40 sheep; now 76. [There were] then 32 goats; now 14. It was then worth 60s.; now 70. To this manor have been added 7 free men with hides TRW. Then as now [there were] 5 ploughs, 1½ hides of woodland, 11 bordars, 4 acres of meadow. It was then worth £4; now 40s.

Two knights hold Ramsden [Bellhouse and Crays] of the bishop, which 2 free men held as 3 hides. As the English say, Ravengar took away the land from one of them and Robert fitzWymarc [took away] the land from the other. Now they do not know how it came to the bishop. Then [these men] had 2 ploughs; now there are none there. [There were] then 5 bordars; now 7. [There is] half a hide of woodland, pasture for 100 sheep. It was then worth £3; now 4.

In Wheatley and in Wickford Pointel and Osbern hold 2 hides which 2 free men held TRE. [There were] then 2 ploughs; now 1. [There are] 4 bordars, 1 hide of woodland, 25 acres of meadow. [There is] pasture for 40 sheep. It was then worth 40s.; now 30. And Ravengar took this land away from them and now the English do not know how it came into the bishop's hands.

[Ralph] fitzTurold holds Wickford of the bishop, which 5 free men held TRE, as 2 hides and 48 acres. Then as now [there were] 2 ploughs, 5 bordars, 2 slaves. [There is] woodland for 30 pigs. It is worth 40s. Teher holds Wickford of the bishop, which Godric, a free man, held TRE as 1 hide. Then as now [there was] 1 plough. [There was] then 1 bordar; now 2. [There is] woodland for 30 pigs. [There are] 8 acres of meadow. It is worth 20s.

[Ralph] fitzTurold holds Hassenbrook, which 16 free men held TRE, as 12 hides and 13½ acres. [There were] then 11 ploughs; now 7. [There are] now 14 bordars, 20 sokemen. [There is] woodland for 200 pigs. [There are] 16 acres of meadow. [There is] pasture for 400 sheep. It is worth £10.

The same [Ralph] holds of the bishop, which Eadweald, a reeve of King Edward, held, as 1½ hides. Then as now [there were] 1½ ploughs in demesne [and] the men [had] half a plough. [There were] then 6 bordars; now 7. [There were] then 2 slaves; now 1. [There is] a certain sokeman with 30 acres. [There is] woodland for 80 pigs, pasture for 100 sheep.

[Folio 23v: ESSEX]

[There was] then 1 fishery; now [there is] none, but there could be. Of this land, 30 acres [belonged to] another land TRE. It was then worth 40s.; now the whole altogether is worth 30s. In [East and West] Horndon the bishop has 20 acres which 1 free man held TRE. It is worth 30d.

HUNDRED OF WITHAM.

In Hatfield Peverel [are] 15 acres which 1 sokeman held. It was then worth 3s.; now 4.

HUNDRED OF ROCHFORD.

Swein holds [Great and Little] Stambridge of the bishop, which Osweard held TRE as 3½ hides and 30 acres. [There were] then 7 villans; now none. [There were] then 6 bordars; now 10. [There were] then 3 slaves; now none. Then as now [there were] 2 ploughs in demesne. The men [had] then 3 ploughs; now 4. [There is] pasture for 300 sheep [and there is] 1 mill. [There is] now 1 horse. [There were] then 4 head of cattle; now 2. [There were] then 15 pigs; now 25. [There were] then 100 sheep; now 58. Then as now it was worth £6.

Ravengar held Beckney; now the bishop [holds it] in demesne as half a hide. [There was] then 1 slave; now 1 bordar. Then as now [there was] 1 plough in demesne. [There is] pasture for 30 sheep. It was then worth 20s.; now 30. In this valuation are [included] 30 acres and 1 bordar and half a plough.

The bishop holds Barling in demesne, which 1 free man held as half a hide. Then as now [there was] 1 bordar. [There was] then 1 plough; now none, but there could be [one employed there]. It is worth 10s.

The bishop holds [North and South] Shoebury in demesne, which 1 free man held as 1 hide and 30 acres. Then as now [there were] 2 villans. [There were] then 2 bordars; now 3. [There was] then 1 plough in demesne; now 2 oxen. Then as now the men [had] 1 plough. [There is] pasture for 40 sheep. It was then worth 40s.; now 55.

Hundred of Dengie. Swein holds Creeksea of the bishop, which Eadric, a free man, held TRE as 1 manor and as 1 hide. [There were] then 2 bordars; now 3. Then as now [there were] 2 slaves and 1 plough in demesne. [There is] woodland for 20 pigs, pasture for 20 sheep. [There were] then 4 head of cattle and now the same. Then and later it was worth 13 s.; now 30.

Pointel holds Creeksea of the bishop, which Leofric held TRE, as half a hide. [There was] then half a plough; now none. It was then worth 10s.; now 5.

The Bishop of Bayeux

[Folio 24: ESSEX]

HUNDRED OF WINSTREE.

Ralph fitzTurold holds Sampsons of the bishop, which 2 free men held as half a hide and 30 acres. Then as now [there was] half a plough. Now [there are] 2 bordars. It was then worth 16s.; now 15.

HUNDRED OF HINCKFORD.

The wife of Aubrey holds "Napstead" [in Little Maplestead] of the bishop, which 8 free men held TRE as 22½ acres. Then as now [there was] 1 plough. [There is] woodland for 20 pigs. [There are] 6 acres of meadow. Then as now it was worth 30s. In this Hundred Tihel de Helléan holds 22 free men with 2 hides and 13½ acres. Then as now [there are] 5 ploughs. Then and later [there was] 1 bordar; now 9. Then as now [there was] 1 slave. [There is] woodland for 4 pigs. [There are] 31 acres of meadow. Then and later it was worth 60s.; now £4.

HUNDRED OF DENGIE.

One of the bishop's knights holds Dengie, which Sigeric held TRE as 2½ hides. Then as now [there were] 2 villans. [There are] now 6 bordars. Then as now [there were] 3 slaves and 2 ploughs in demesne and the men [had] 1 plough. [There is] pasture for 160 sheep. It was then worth £4; now 100s. In the demesne [there are] 150 sheep, 1 horse, 13 pigs. To this manor TRE [belonged] 2 free men with 47 acres, of whom the same bishop's knight has taken possession. Then as now it was worth 4s. One of the bishop's knights holds [...] 'Hackfleet' [Bradwell Quay], which Alweard, a free man, held as 2 hides and 30 [...] acres. [There were] then 4 bordars; now 10. Then as now [there is] 1 plough. [There is] pasture for 260 sheep. [There is] 1 fishery. The church holds 40 acres. It was then worth 60s.; [...] now £4. 11s. In this vill was 1 free man with 30 acres [who] [...] was outlawed. Now Swein's men have taken the land and hold [it] still.

HUNDRED OF LEXDEN.

Leofgifu [...] held Aldham as 1 hide less 5 acres TRE. Now the wife of Aubrey holds [it] of the bishop. [There was] then 1 villan; now none. Then as now [there were] 4 slaves and 2 ploughs in demesne. [There is] woodland for 12 pigs. [There are] 3 acres of meadow, 1 horse, 6 head of cattle. Then and later it was worth 30s.; now 60.

HUNDRED OF ONGAR.

Hugh, nephew of Herbert holds Kelvedon [Hatch] of the bishop, which Algar, a free man, held as half a hide and 20 acres. Then as now [there were] 4 bordars and 1 plough. [There is] woodland for 60 pigs.

[Folio 24v: ESSEX]

[There are] 7½ acres of meadow, 1 ox, 5 pigs, 47 sheep. It is worth 20s.

HUNDRED OF CHAFFORD.

Mauger holds Upminster of the bishop, which Wulfwine held as 1½ hides. [There were] then 2 bordars and now the same. Then as now [there was] 1 plough. It was then worth 20s.; now 30.

The same Mauger holds Aveley, which Edward, a free man, held as 1 hide and 30 acres. Then as now [there were] 6 bordars and 1 plough in demesne and the men [had] 1 plough. It was then worth 20s.; now 30.

Hugh holds Thurrock [Grays and West], of the bishop, which Alweard, a free man, held as 1 hide and 40 acres. Then as now [there were] 2 bordars. [There were] then 2 ploughs; now 1. [There is] woodland for 10 pigs. [There are] 8 acres of meadow. [There is] pasture for 50 sheep. It was then worth 30s.; now 40. [There was] then 1 horse. [There was] then 1 cow; now 2 [head of cattle]. [There were] then 25 pigs; now 9. [There were] then 50 sheep; now 48.

Ansketil holds Thurrock [Grays and West], of the bishop, which Manni, a free man, held TRE as 2½ hides and 40 acres. [There are] now 2 villans. [There were] then 3 bordars; now 8. [There were] then 6 slaves; now none. Then as now [there was] 1 plough in demesne and the men [had] 1 plough and [there are] 8 acres of meadow. It was then worth £3; now 4.

Hugh holds Rainham of the bishop, which Alsige, a free man, held as a manor and as 4 hides TRE. Then as now [there were] 8 villans. [There were] then 3 bordars; now 5. [There were] then 4 slaves; now none. [There were] then 3 ploughs in demesne and when [the manor was] received 2; now none. Then and later the men [had] 3 ploughs; [...] now 2. Then and later it was worth £6; now 40s. In Thurrock [Grays and West], Wulfwine [...] held half a hide. Now Hugh [holds it] of the bishop. [...] [There was] then 1 plough; now none. [There is] woodland for 5 pigs. [There are] 8 acres of meadow. [There is] pasture for 50 sheep. It is worth 20s.

[...] Ælfric, a free man, held Stifford as 1 hide and 30 acres. [...] Now the same Hugh holds [it]. Then as now [there was] 1 bordar and 1 plough [and] 5 acres of meadow. It is worth 30s. Of this land, [...] 15 acres are in the soke of William Peverel of Thurrock [Grays and West], as the Shire testifies. To the

church of this manor belong 30 acres which the neighbours gave in alms.

Hugh holds Cranham of the bishop, which Alwine, a free man, held as a manor and as 1½ hides. Then as now [there was] 1 villan and 1 bordar. [There was] then 1 plough; now half a plough. [There is] woodland for 100 pigs. [There are] 1½ acres of meadow. Then and later it was worth 50s.; now 20. In Stifford Gilbert, a man of the Bishop of Bayeux,

The Bishop of Bayeux

[Folio 25: ESSEX]

held 1½ hides which [Ralph] fitzTurold holds of the bishop. Then as now [there were] 3 villans and 4 bordars and 2 ploughs in demesne. It was worth 30s. The Hundred testifies that this hide belonged TRE to Thurrock [Grays and West], a manor of William Peverel, except for 10 acres.

Hugh holds "Limpwella" of the bishop, which Eadric, a free man, held as 1 manor and half a hide. [There was] then 1 bordar; now 2. [There was] then 1 plough; now half a plough. [There is] woodland for 20 pigs, pasture for 20 sheep. It was then worth 10s.; now 20.

HUNDRED OF CHELMSFORD.

Fridebert held Hanningfield as 1 manor and as 9 hides TRE; now Ralph fitzTurold holds [it] of the bishop. Then as now [there were] 3 villans. [There were] then 2 bordars; now 5. [There were] then 4 slaves; now 8. [There were] then 2 ploughs in demesne; now 3. Then as now the men [had] 2 ploughs. [There is] woodland for 60 pigs. [There are] 3 horses, 16 head of cattle, 32 pigs. [There were] then 117 sheep; now 810. It was then worth 100s.; now 7. In the same [vill] 23 free men held 14 hides, who could withdraw from the same manor without licence of the king. The bishop holds these [men], but the shire does not know how he came to have them. Then as now [there was] 1 villan and 18 bordars and 8 slaves. [There were] then 11 ploughs; now 10. [There is] woodland for 150 pigs. It was then worth £8; now £7. 2s. Turold of Rochester appropriated these hides and the abbey of Ely claims 2 hides and 3 virgates, which 2 men held and the Hundred testifies that they held their land freely and were only commended to the abbey of Ely.

Othin the Dane, a free man, held "Berewic" TRE. Now Turold [holds it] of the bishop as 6 hides and 37 acres. [There were] then 4 villans; now 6. [There were] then 4 bordars; now 6. [There were] then 3 slaves; now 5. Then as now [there were] 3 ploughs in demesne and the men [had] 2 ploughs. [There is] woodland for 100 pigs. [There are] 3 acres of meadow. [There were] then 3 horses; now 5. [There were] then 4 head of cattle; now 18. [There were] then 16 pigs; now 61. [There were] then 60 sheep; now 126. It was then worth £4; now 6.

Thorkil held Lawn as a manor [and] as 2½ hides and 6 acres TRE. Now [Ralph] fitzTurold [holds it] of the bishop as the same. [There were] then 2 villans; now 1. Then as now [there were] 5 bordars and 2 slaves and 1 plough in demesne and the men [had] 1 plough. [There is] woodland for 100 pigs. [There are] 17 acres of meadow. [There were] then 3 horses; now 1. [There were] then 5 head of cattle; now 9. [There were] then 19 pigs; now 40. [There were] then 45 sheep; now 110. Then and later it was worth 40s; now 60.

Anund the Dane held Walter TRE as a and as 1½ hides now [Ralph] fitzTurold [holds it] of the bishop. Then as now [there were] 2 bordars and 1 slave and 1 plough. [There is] woodland for 60 pigs. [There are] 15 acres of meadow, 1 horse. [There were] then 5 head of cattle; now 4. [There were] then 15 sheep; now 50. [There were] then 11 pigs; now 17. [There is] 1 goat. It was then worth 20s.; now 30.

Sægar held Patching as a manor and as 2 hides and 30 acres TRE; now [Ralph] fitzTurold holds it of the bishop. [There was] then 1 villan; now 3. Then as now [there were] 4 bordars and 1 slave and 1 plough in demesne and the men [had] 1 plough. [There is] woodland for 15 pigs. [There are] 8 acres of meadow. [There is] 1 mill. [There were] then 3 horses; now 4. [There were] then 2 head of cattle; now 4. [There were] then 11 sheep; now 23. It is worth 40s.M [sic]

Godric held Moulsham as a manor and as 2½ hides and 30 acres. Now [Ralph] fitzTurold holds it of the bishop. [There was] then 1 villan; now 2. [There was] then 1 bordar; now 6. [There were] then 4 slaves; now 3. Then as now [there were] 2 ploughs in demesne. The men [had] then 1½ ploughs; now 1. [There is] now woodland for 60 pigs. [There are] 10 acres of meadow. Then as now [there is] 1 mill. [There were] then 3 horses and 1 colt; now [there are] 2 horses and 4 colts. [There were] then 9 head of cattle; now 28. [There were] then 47 sheep; now 140. It was then worth 50s.; now £4.

Wulfmær, a free man, held the other Moulsham as a manor and as 1 hide and 40 acres. Now [Ralph] fitzTurold [holds it] of the bishop. [There was] then 1 bordar. Then as now [there were] 2 slaves and 1 plough. [There is] woodland for 40 pigs. [There are] 10 acres of meadow. It is worth 20s.

HUNDRED OF TENDRING.

Æthelstan held Thorrington as 1 manor and as 4 hides. Now Ralph [fitzTurold] holds it of the bishop as the same, and Turold of Rochester appropriated this land. Then as now [there were] 3 villans and 9 bordars and 5 slaves. [There were] then 2 ploughs in demesne; now 1½, but a third could be [employed]. Among the men [there were] then 2½ ploughs; now 1½. [There is] woodland for 100 pigs. [There is] 1 acre of meadow, pasture for 100 sheep. [There is] now 1 mill, 1 salt-pan. Then as now it was worth £4. A certain free man held half a hide in Alresford, which Turold appropriated like the other land, and when he received [it], [there was] half a plough. Now [there is] none, but there could be, and the Hundred does not know how he had this land and since neither an officer nor any other man came on his behalf to prove his right to this land, it has been taken into the king's hands with the rest. Then and later it was worth 10s.; now 5[s.] 4d.

HUNDRED OF THURSTABLE.

Aslak, a free man, held Tolleshunt as 1 hide; now the bishop [holds it]

The Bishop of Bayeux

as the same. [There were] then 2 bordars; now 3. [There is] now 1 slave. [There was then 1 plough; now half a plough. [There is] woodland for 30 pigs, pasture for 60 sheep. It was then worth 20s. Later and now [it is worth] 30[s.]

XIX. Land of the Bishop of Hereford.

In Writtle the bishop holds 2 hides and 20 acres, of which 1 was in [the lands of] the church TRE and the other [was in] the fief of Harold. Then as now [there were] 3 villans and 1 priest. [There were] then 2 bordars; now 8. [There were] then 2 slaves; now none. Then as now [there is] 1 plough in demesne and the men [had] 2 ploughs. [There is] woodland for 100 pigs. [There are] 8 acres of meadow. It is worth 50s.

XX. Lands of Count Eustace in Essex.

HUNDRED OF BARSTABLE.

Beorhtmær, a thegn of King Edward, held Fobbing as 5 hides and as 1 manor. Now Count E[ustace holds it] in demesne. Then as now [there were] 4 ploughs in demesne and the men [had] 5 ploughs. [There were] then 8 villans; now 3. [There were] then 8 bordars; now 22. [There were] then 12 slaves; now 6. [There is] woodland for 700 pigs, pasture for 700 sheep, half a fishery, 31 pigs, 717 sheep. Turold took away 30 acres from this land, which are in the fief of the Bishop of Bayeux. Besides this, Engelric added to this manor 22 free men holding 15½ hides and 15½ acres, in which land there were then as now 12 ploughs and 20 bordars and 3 slaves. [There is] woodland for 50 pigs. [There are] 10 acres of meadow. [There is] pasture for 400 sheep. [There is] the third part of 1 fishery and there could be added 3½ ploughs. The manor was then worth £20 and the land of the sokemen £12. Now the whole together [is worth] £36.

Warner holds Horndon [on the Hill] of the count, which Wulfric, a free man, held as 1 manor and as 2 hides and 50 acres. Then as now [there were] 2 ploughs in demesne. [There were] then 2 villans; now none. [There were] then 7

bordars; now 12. [There were] then 2 slaves; now 3. [There are] 12 acres of meadow. [There is] pasture for 60 sheep. [There are] 2 cows, 10 pigs, 110 sheep. Besides this, [there are] 15 acres [belonging to] the church in alms. It was then worth 60s.; now 50.

Roger holds Shenfield of the count, which Bodda, a free man, held TRE as 1 manor and as 2 hides. [There were] then 2 ploughs in demesne; now 1. Now the men [have] half a plough. [There was] then 1 bordar; now 6. [There were] then 2 slaves; now none. [There is] woodland for 40 pigs. [There are] 2 head of cattle, 20 pigs, 15 goats. It is worth 60s.

The count holds Orsett which the Bishop of London held TRE as 1 hide and which Engelric held of [the bishop's] church. Then as now [there was] 1 plough in demesne and 1 priest had 1 plough there. It is worth 20s. This hide does not belong to his 100 manors.

Harold held "Gravesend" [in Tilbury] and Engelric [held it] of him as a manor and as 1 hide. Then as now [there was] 1 plough. [There was] then 1 villan; now 2. It was then worth 10s.; now 20 and this hide does not belong to his 100 manors.

HUNDRED OF WITHAM.

Ælfric the thegn holds [Black and White] Notley of the count as 1 manor, which Harold held TRE. Then and later [there were] 3 ploughs in demesne; now 2. Then and later the men [had] 5 ploughs; now 3. Then and later [there were] 10 villans; now 6. [There were] then 3 bordars; later and now 16. [There were] then 9 slaves; now 4. [There was] then woodland for 200 pigs; now 100. [There are] 30 acres of meadow. [There is] pasture for 100 sheep. [There are] now 2 mills, 5 cows, 14 pigs, 100 sheep, 7 goats, 3 horses. From this manor Ralph de Marcy took 30 acres, and they belong to the fief of [Hamo] fitzHamo. Then as now it was worth £10.

The count holds [Great and Little] Coggeshall in demesne, which Cola, a free man, held TRE as 1 manor and as 3½ hides and 33 acres. Then as now [there were] 3 ploughs in demesne and when received [there was] 1 plough. The men [had] then 16 ploughs; later and now [There were] then 11 villans; later and now 9. [There were] then 22 bordars; now 31. [There are] now 4 slaves. [There was] then woodland for 600 pigs; now 500. [There are] 38 acres of meadow. [There is] as much pasture as is worth 10d. Then as now [there was] 1 mill, 1 horse, 15 pigs, 4 goats, 4 hives of bees. To this manor belong 11 sokemen and 1 priest and 1 swineherd and 1 hired servant. To this land have been added 38 acres,

Count Eustace

[Folio 27: ESSEX]

which 1 free man holds of the king. This manor was then worth £10; now 14, but it renders £20, and the abovesaid 38 acres are worth 10s.

The count holds Rivenhall in demesne, which Queen Edith held TRE as 1 manor and as 2½ hides. [There were] then 3 ploughs in demesne; now 2. The men [had] then 8 ploughs; now 6. [There were] then 12 villans; now 13. [There were] then 8 bordars; now 14. Then as now [there were] 6 slaves. [There was] then woodland for 400 pigs; now 350. [There are] 30 acres of meadow. [There is] pasture from which are received 3s. [There was] then 1 mill; now half a mill. [There is] 1 sokeman with 15 acres, 1 burgess at Colchester, and Richard de Sackville took away half of the mill. [There is] 1 horse, 6 head of cattle, 40 pigs, 8 goats, 2 hives of bees. It was then worth £9; now 12, but it renders £20.

The count holds Rivenhall in demesne, which Harold held as 1 manor and as 1 hide and 15 acres. [There were] then 2 ploughs in demesne; now 1. Then as now the men [had] 1 plough. [There were] then 2 villans; now 5. [There was] then 1 bordar; now 2. [There were] then 5 slaves; now 4, and [there are] 21 acres of meadow. [There is] pasture [worth] 6d. [There are] 10 pigs, 27 sheep. It was then worth 60s.; now 30.

The count holds Blunt's Hall in demesne, which 1 free woman held TRE as 1 manor and half a hide. Then as now [there was] 1 plough in demesne and 1 bordar. [There are] 6 acres of meadow. It was then worth 20s.; now 10.

Richard holds Witham of the count, which Harold held as 51 acres. Then as now [there was] 1 plough and 1 bordar. [There are] 2½ acres of meadow. It is worth 20s.

HUNDRED OF HARLOW.

Iwain holds [Great and Little] Parndon of the count, which Ulf, a thegn of the king, held TRE as 1 manor and as 3½ hides. Then as now [there were] 2 ploughs in demesne and the men [had] 2 ploughs. [There were] then 4 villans; now 3. [There were] then 4 bordars; now 5. Then as now [there were] 2 slaves. [There is] woodland for 200 pigs. [There are] 14 acres of meadow. It is worth £4.

Adelulf [de Marck] holds Latton of the count, which Ernulf, a free man, held TRE

[Folio 27v: ESSEX]

as 1 manor and as 1½ hides and 30 acres. [There were] then 2 ploughs in demesne; now 1. Then as now [there is] 1 villan and 2 bordars. [There were] then 4 slaves; now 2. [There is] woodland for 300 pigs. [There are] 35 acres of meadow and 1 priest who holds half a hide [belonging] to a church. It was then worth 50s.; now 60.

Geoffrey holds Harlow of the count, which Beorhtmær, a free man, held TRE for half a hide. Then as now [there was] half a plough. [There is] woodland for 40 pigs. [There are] 3 acres of meadow. It is worth 11s.

HUNDRED OF DUNMOW.

Adelulf [de Marck] holds [Great and Little] Dunmow of the count, which Eadmær, a free man, held TRE as 1 manor and as 2 hides and 30 acres. [There were] then 3 ploughs in demesne; now 2. The men [had] then 1 plough; now 3. [There were] then 3 villans; now 13. [There are] now 9 bordars. [There were] then 10 slaves; now 4. [There is] woodland for 300 pigs. [There are] 36 acres of meadow and 1 plough [more] could be restored. [There are] 12 head of cattle, 50 pigs, 100 sheep, 1 horse, 4 hives of bees. It is worth £8.

HUNDRED OF DENGIE.

The count holds Iltney in demesne, which Engelric held TRE as 1 manor and as 2 hides. [There was] then 1 slave. [There are] now 2 bordars. Then as now [there was] 1 plough in demesne. [There is] pasture for 50 sheep. It is worth 30s. Eadgifu held Purleigh TRE as 1 manor and as 1 hide and 30 acres, but it was not of the fief of Engelric and now Count Eustace has [it]. It was then worth 16s. 8d.; now 23s. Then 2 men dwelt there; now 1 priest.

HUNDRED OF DUNMOW.

Bernard holds "Plesingho" [in Willingale] of the count, which 1 free man held TRE as half a hide. Then as now [there was] half a plough. [There were] then 2 bordars. [There is] now 1 slave. [There is] woodland for 20 pigs. [There are] 5 acres of meadow. It is worth 10s.

HUNDRED OF WINSTREE.

Engelric held Langenhoe TRE as 1 manor and as 7 hides. [...] Now the count holds [it] in demesne. [There were] then 5 ploughs in demesne; later 4 [and] now 3. Then and later the men [had] 1½ ploughs; now 2. [There were] then 5 villans; now 9. Then as now [there were] 7 bordars. [There were] then 12 slaves; now 8. [There is] woodland for 200 pigs.

Count Eustace

[Folio 28: ESSEX]

[There is] 1 acre of meadow, pasture for 500 sheep, 1 mill, 1 salt-pan. [There are] 2 head of cattle, 300 sheep, 13 pigs and 3 horses. To this manor Engelric added TRW 2 hides, which 1 free man held TRE, and half a hide, which 3 free men held TRE. In these [2] hides and a half were then as now 2 ploughs. [There are] now 4 bordars. [There is] pasture for 100 sheep. The whole together was then worth £17; now [£]17. 5s., and when received, the same.

Ralph de Marcy holds Abberton, which Siward, a free man, held TRE as 1 manor and as 1½ hides and 1 virgate. Then as now [there was] 1 plough in demesne. The men [had] then half a plough and now the same. [There were] then 4 bordars; now 3. [There was] then 1 slave; now none. [There is] woodland for 100 pigs. [There are] 4 acres of meadow, 4 head of cattle, 100 sheep, 30 pigs, 2 horses. It is worth 60s.

Alric, a free man, held Layer, TRE as 2½ hides and 1 virgate. [There were] then 1½ ploughs in demesne; now 2. [There was] then 1 bordar; now 3. [There were] then 2 slaves; now 1. [There is] woodland for 40 pigs. [There is] now 1 mill. [There was] then 1 horse; now 2. [There were] then 3 head of cattle; now 5. [There were] then 38 sheep; now 146. [There are] 6 hives of bees. It was then worth £4; now 3.

HUNDRED OF UTTLESFORD.

One free man held Shortgrove TRE. Now Adelulf [de Marck] holds [it] of the count as 1 manor and as 1 hide and 30 acres. Then and later [there was] 1 plough in demesne; now 2. Then and later [there was] 1 villan; now none. Then and later [there was] 1 bordar; now 3. [There was] then 1 slave; now none. [There are] 9 acres of meadow, 3 head of cattle, 2 horses, 11 pigs, 90 sheep. It is worth 40s. Engelric appropriated this land TRW.

HUNDRED OF HINCKFORD.

A free man named Godwine held Ridgewell TRE as 1 manor and as 2 hides and 3 virgates. [There were] then 5 ploughs in demesne; later and now 4. [There are] 14 villans, 14 slaves, 3 bordars. [There is] woodland for 80 pigs. [There are] 36 acres of meadow, 22 head of cattle, 44 pigs, 102 sheep, 30 goats and 2 horses. To this manor belonged then as now 14 sokemen with 67½ acres, having 1½ ploughs. [There are] 6 acres of meadow. The whole was then worth £18; later and now 24. The count holds this in demesne.

[Folio 28v: ESSEX]

Adelulf [de Marck] holds Shortgrove of the count, which 1 free man held TRE, as 1 manor and as 1 hide and 30 acres.

[There was] then 1 plough in demesne; now none. Then as now [there was] 1 villan and 1 bordar and 1 acre of meadow. Then and later it was worth 30s.; now 33.

Leodmær, a free man, held Claret TRE as 1½ hides and 35 acres. [There were] then 5 ploughs in demesne; later and now 3. Then as now the men [had] 2 ploughs. [There were] then 7 villans; later and now 4. Later and now [there were] 12 bordars. [There were] then 10 slaves; later and now 4. [There are] 27 acres of meadow, 1 mill, 3 horses, 8 head of cattle, 40 pigs, 239 sheep. To this manor belonged then as now 1 berewick, which is called [Great and Little] Yeldham, with 2 hides and 18 acres. [There were] then 3 ploughs in demesne; later and now 2. Then as now the men [had] 2 ploughs. [There were] then 8 villans; later and now 6. Later and now [there were] 8 bordars. [There were] then 8 slaves; later and now 6. [There are] 18 acres of meadow. To this manor also belong 7 sokemen with 35 acres of land, having 1 plough. This manor was then worth £18; later and now 22. To this manor Engelric added also 1 free man TRW, and he had 15 acres and 1 plough and it is worth 10s. The count holds this manor in demesne.

Leodmær, a free man, held Belchamp TRE as 1 hide and 45 acres. Now Ulmar holds [it] of the count. Then as now [there were] 2 ploughs in demesne and the men [had] 2 ploughs and [there were] 4 villans. Then and later [there were] 4 bordars; now 5. Then and later [there were] 4 slaves; now 2. [There is] woodland for 20 pigs. [There are] 8 acres of meadow. To this manor belong 5 sokemen, 2 of whom Engelric appropriated TRW, who were then free men having 35 acres of land. In demesne [there are] 9 head of cattle, 2 horses, 20 pigs, 100 sheep. It was then worth 40s.; later and now £4.

Adelulf [de Marck] holds [Steeple] Bumpstead of the count, which 1 free man held TRE as a manor and as half a hide. [There were] then 3 ploughs in demesne; later and now 2. Then as now the men [had] 2 ploughs [and there were] 7 villans, 11 bordars, 4 slaves, 15 acres of meadow, 1 horse, 3 head of cattle. It was then worth £4; later and now 100s.

Count Eustace

[Folio 29: ESSEX]

Bernard holds Belchamp, of the count, which Eadnoth, a free man, held held TRE as half a hide and 10 acres. Then as now [there was] 1 plough in demesne. [There are] now 2 bordars, 2 slaves, 4 acres of meadow, 1 sokeman with 20 acres, 1 horse, 4 cows. [There were] then 14 pigs; now none. Then as now [there were] 50 sheep. It is worth 30s.

Adelulf [de Marck] holds holds Weston of the count, which 1 free man held TRE as 30 acres. Then as now [there was] 1 plough and 4 acres of meadow. It was then worth 20s.; now 25.

Guy holds Finchingfield of the count, which Northmann held TRE as a manor and as half a hide and 10 acres. Then as now [there was] 1 plough in demesne and 1 bordar and 1 slave. [There is] woodland for 20 pigs. [There are] 9 acres of meadow, 3 head of cattle, 20 [...] less 1. It was then worth 20s.; now 40.

Wulfric, a free man, held Finchingfield TRE. Now the same Guy [holds it] of the count as 37 acres. Then as now [there was] 1 plough. [There was] then 1 slave. [There were] then 2 bordars. [There was] then woodland for 20 pigs; now 5. [There are] 4 acres of meadow. [There is] 1 mill. It is worth 16s.

Rainer holds Smeetham of the count, which 1 free woman held TRE as 1 manor and as 3 hides. [There were] then 4 ploughs in demesne; later and now 2. Then and later the men [had] 1½ ploughs; now 1. Then and later [there were] 4 villans; now 3. Then as now [there were] 14 bordars and 2 slaves. [There is] woodland for 20 pigs. [There are] 20 acres of meadow. It was then worth £7; now 8. Engelric held these manors.

Bernard holds Toppesfield of the count, which 1 free man held as 15 acres TRE. Then as now [there was] 1 plough in demesne and 1 villan and 1 bordar. [There was] then 1 slave; now none. [There is] woodland for 10 pigs. [There are] 6 acres of meadow. It is worth 20s.

HUNDRED OF DENGIE.

St Martin of London holds Maldon of the count, which 1 free man held TRE as 1½ hides and 30 acres. Later Engelric held [it]. Then as now [there were] 6 bordars and 2 slaves and 2 ploughs. [There is] woodland for 30 pigs, pasture for 100 sheep. It was then worth £4 now 100s. In demesne [there are] 2 cows, 14 pigs,

[Folio 29v: ESSEX]

100 sheep. It was then worth £4; now 100s. One free man held 30 acres TRE in the same, which Engelric appropriated. Now St Martin holds [it] of the count and another free man with 30 acres. Engelric put these men in his hall. In their land there was then as now 1 plough and it is worth 20s.

Robert holds Ulehams of the count, which 1 free man held TRE. Later Engelric [held it] as 1 hide. It was then worth 8s. 4d.; now 14s.

HUNDRED OF LEXDEN.

One free man held Tey TRE as 3½ hides; now Count Eustace [holds it]. [There were] then 6 villans; now 2. [There were] then 16 bordars; now 35. [There were] then 9 slaves; now 10. [There were] then 4 ploughs in demesne; now 2. Among the men [there were] then 6 ploughs; now 4. [There is] woodland for 160 pigs. [There are] 20 acres of meadow, 3 horses, 7 head of cattle, 68 pigs, 80 sheep, 34 goats. To this manor belongs a berewick of 1½ hides less 10 acres. Then as now [there was] 1 bordar and 2 slaves. [There were] then 2 ploughs in demesne; now 1. [There is] woodland for 24 pigs and [there are] 17 sokemen holding 2 hides and 5 acres in this manor. Now 16 sokemen hold this land. Then as now [there were] 6 bordars under them. [There were] then 2 slaves; now none. [There were] then 6 ploughs among them; now 4. [There is] woodland for 30 pigs. [There are] 12 acres of meadow. Then as now [there was] 1 mill and those sokemen could not withdraw from this manor. And there also belongs to this manor 1 house in Colchester. This manor was then worth £16 and when received, the same. It is now worth £22 blanch.

In the same, 5 free men, who did not [belong] to this manor, held 60 acres and 28 acres, whom the count now has, because

his predecessor was seised [of them], and this land was assessed TRE in the above valuation.

Ælfric held Boxted as 4½ hides. Now the count [holds it] in demesne. Then as now [there were] 5 villans and 18 bordars. [There were] then 2 slaves; now none. [There were] then 2 ploughs in demesne; now the same. Then as now the men [had] 6 ploughs. [There is] woodland for 300 pigs. [There are] 8 acres of meadow. [There was] then 1 mill; now none. And [there is] 1 sokeman who could not withdraw, holding half a hide. [There was] then half a plough; now none. [There are] 2 acres of meadow, 13 head of cattle, 35 pigs and 140 sheep and 25 goats and 2 horses.

Count Eustace

[Folio 30: ESSEX]

Then and later it was worth £8; now [£]12 blanch.

Eadric held [East] Donyland as a manor and as 1½ hides. Now the count holds [it] in demesne. Then as now [there were] 10 bordars. [There were] then 4 slaves; now 1. [There were] then 2 ploughs in demesne; now 1. The men [had] then 2 ploughs; now 1. [There is] woodland for 100 pigs. [There are] 6 acres of meadow. [There is] pasture for 100 sheep. Then and later it was worth 40s.; now £3. In demesne [there are] 80 sheep. In the same 1 free man held half a hide, which now the count holds, but Engelric had it and the Hundred does not know how he came to have it. It is worth 5s.

Hugh holds [Great and Little] Birch of the count, which Eadric held as 1 manor and as 3 hides and later Engelric held [it]. [There were] then 13 villans; now 6. [There were] then 5 bordars; now 17. [There were] then 6 slaves; now 4. [There were] then 3 ploughs in demesne; now 2½. The men [had] then 8 ploughs; now 6. [There is] woodland for 100 pigs. [There are] 16 acres of meadow and 2 houses in Colchester, which belong to this manor, and 1 sokeman with 13 acres, who could not recede. Then as now he had half a plough. In demesne then [there was] 1 horse; now 3. [There were] then 20 head of cattle; now 10. [There were] then 35 pigs; now 34. [There were] then 140 sheep; now 120. [There were] then 40 goats; now 20. Then and later it was worth £6; now 100s.

The same [Hugh] holds Easthorpe of the count, which Eadric, a free man, held TRE as a manor and as 1 hide and 25 acres. [There were] then 2 bordars; now 8. [There were] then 4 slaves; now 2. [There were] then 2 ploughs in demesne; now 1. Among the men [there was] then 1 plough; now 3. [There is] woodland for 30 pigs. [There are] 6 acres of meadow. [There was] then 1 horse and 16 head of cattle and 15 pigs and 30 sheep. [There are] now 10 pigs and 1 horse. It was then worth 40s.; now 30.

Robert holds Colne of the count, which Ælfric Bigga held as 1 virgate and 10 acres TRE. [There was] then 1 bordar; now 3. Then as now [there were] 2 ploughs in demesne. Among the men now [there is] 1 plough. [There were] then 5 slaves; now 3. [There are] 13 acres of meadow. [There is] woodland for 40 pigs. It was then worth 30s.; now 40. This Ælfric held this land freely, but Engelric had it after the king came and the Hundred does not know how.

The same [Robert] holds [East] Donyland, which Godric of Colchester held as 25 acres. It is worth 12d.

HUNDRED OF ONGAR.

Leofwine held Stanford [Rivers] TRE and later Engelric [held it] as 1 manor and as 9 hides. Now the count holds [it] in demesne as the same. Then as now [there were] 24 villans. [There were] then 2 bordars; now 17. [There were] then 22 slaves; now 16. [There were] then 10 ploughs in demesne and when received 7; [...] now 5. Then as now the men [had] 15 ploughs. [There is] woodland for 400 pigs. [There are] 50 acres of meadow. Then as now [there was] 1 mill. [There are] 4 horses, 40 head of cattle, 11 pigs, 233 sheep. It was then worth £24 and when received the same; now £40 blanch.

In the same, a certain free man held 40 acres, but Engelric took him, adding [him] to this land. Then as now there was half a plough there. [There is] woodland for 20 pigs. Then as now And Beorhtwine held 20 acres, which Engelric added to his land and it is assessed in the above £[40].

The father of Ælfric held Little Stanford Rivers TRE as 1 manor and as 1 hide and 80 acres. Now the count holds [it] as the same, as of Engelric's fief. [There were] then 3 villans and when received 5; now the same. Then as now [there were] 3 slaves. [There were] then 2 ploughs in demesne; now none. Then as now the men [had] 1 plough. [There is] woodland for 100 pigs. [There are] 6 acres of meadow, 6 head of cattle, 213 sheep. It was then worth 40s. Of this manor, Ælfric holds half a hide of the count and it is worth 10s. in the above valuation.

Leofwine held Laver, TRE as 1 hide and 40 acres and Alwine held the other part of that manor as 1 hide and 40 acres as a manor, but Engelric added [it] to his own manor. Now Count Eustace holds [it] in demesne. Then as now [there were] 7 villans and 10 bordars and 15 slaves and 5½ ploughs in demesne and the men [had] 5 ploughs. [There is] woodland for 200 pigs. [There are] 37½ of meadow, 2 head of cattle, 11 pigs, 80 sheep, 3 horses. Then and later it was worth £16; now 20 blanch. Of this manor, Ralph holds 80 acres and 1 villan and 3 bordars and 1 plough and it is worth 20s. in the above valuation.

A certain free man held 40 acres in the same [vill], which Engelric added to this land. Now Ralph holds [it] of the count and it is [included] in the same valuation and is worth 10s.

Æthelgyth held Ongar [Chipping and High], as 1 hide and as 1 manor. Now the count [holds it] in demesne. Then as now

Count Eustace

[there were] 8 villans and 8 bordars and 3 slaves and 2 ploughs in demesne and the men [had] 3 ploughs. [There is] woodland for 1,000 pigs. [There are] 28 acres of meadow, 2 horses, 10 head of cattle, 36 pigs, 112 sheep. It was then worth 100s.; now £8.

In the same, 1 free man held half a hide which [belonged] to this manor. Now Ralph Baynard holds [it].

Richard holds Laver, of the count, which Beorhtmær held

as 40 acres and as 1 manor. Then as now [there was] 1 slave and 1 plough. [There are] 6 acres of meadow. It is worth 10s.

David holds Lambourne of the count, which Leofsige held as 1 manor and as 2 hides and 80 acres. Then as now [there was] 1 villan. [There were] then 10 bordars; now 12. Then as now [there was] 1 slave and 2 ploughs in demesne and the men [had] 1 plough. [There is] woodland for 100 pigs. [There are] 20 acres of meadow. It was then worth 40s.; now 60. In demesne [there are] 9 head of cattle and 80 sheep.

Richard holds Fyfield of the count, which Beorhtmær held as 40 acres TRE and as 1 manor. Then as now [there were] 3 slaves and 1 plough in demesne. [There is] woodland for 24 pigs. [There are] 20 acres of meadow. It was then worth 10s.; now 20. A certain free man holds 10 acres, but Engelric appropriated [him]. Then as now [there were] 3 slaves. [There is] woodland for 24 pigs.

Iwain holds Fyfield of the count, which Alwine held TRE as 1 manor and as 80 acres. Then as now [there was] 1 villan. [There were] then 4 bordars; now 6. Then as now [there were] 2 slaves and 1 plough in demesne and the men [had] 1 plough. [There is] woodland for 50 pigs. [There are] 10 acres of meadow. It was then worth 30s.; now 40.

HUNDRED OF CHELMSFORD.

Mauger holds Newland of the count, which Harold held TRE as 1 manor and as 3 hides. Then as now [there were] 15 villans and 7 bordars and 2 slaves and 2 ploughs in demesne and the men [had] 2 ploughs. [There is] woodland for 100 pigs. [There are] 20 acres of meadow. It was then worth 100s.; now £7. Engelric appropriated this manor and the Hundred testifies that it belonged

Leofwine held [Great and Little] Baddow as 5 hides TRE. Now Lambert holds [it] of the count as the same. Engelric also appropriated this land after the king arrived. Then and later [there were] 3 villans; now none. Then and later [there were] 4 bordars; now 8. Then and later [there were] 6 slaves; now 3.

Then as now [there were] 3 ploughs in demesne. Then and later the men [had] 1 plough; now none. [There is] woodland for 100 pigs. [There are] 24 acres of meadow, 1 horse, 15 head of cattle, 50 pigs, 135 sheep. Then and later it was worth 100s.; now £6.

The same Lambert holds Runwell of the count, which Leofstan held TRE as a manor and as 1 hide, and Engelric appropriated it. [There were] then 2 bordars; now 3. Then as now [there was] 1 plough. [There is] woodland for 50 pigs. [There are] 2 acres of meadow, 13 head of cattle, 20 pigs, 36 sheep. It is worth 20s.

Adelulf [de Marck] holds Runwell of the count, which Eadgifu held TRE as 1 manor and as 4 hides, and Engelric appropriated this. [There were] then 4 bordars; now 5. [There were] then 2 slaves; now 1. Then and later [there was] half a plough in demesne; now 2½. Then as now the men [had] half a plough. [There is] woodland for 80 pigs. Then and later it was worth 100s.; now £6.

Lambert holds [Great and Little] Waltham of the count, which Leofstan held TRE as 1 manor and as 2 hides and 1 virgate, and Engelric appropriated this. Then and later [there were] 4 bordars; now 7. [There were] then 2 slaves; now 1. Then and later [there were] 2 ploughs in demesne; now 1½. Then as now the men [had] half a plough. [There is] woodland for 10 pigs. [There are] 12 acres of meadow, 1 horse, 8 head of cattle, 100 sheep. Then and later it was worth 50s.; now 60.

The same Lambert holds Boreham of the count, which 14 free men held as 8 hides and 23 acres, and Engelric appropriated this after the king came into this land. Under them [were] then 4 bordars; now 8. Then as now [there were] 3 slaves and 2 ploughs in demesne. Among the men [were] then 13 ploughs; when received and now, 2. [There is] woodland for 10 pigs. [There are] 54 acres of meadow. [There is] now 1 mill, 1 horse. [There are] 15 head of cattle, 132 sheep. It was then worth £12 and when received £6; now 8.

In the same, 1 free man holds 5 acres and it is worth 10d.

Ranulf Peverel claims half a hide and 18 acres, which belong to the church of this manor, and half of the church, and Engelric was not seised [of it], but Count Eustace gave [it] to a certain knight of his who vouches him to warranty for it,

Count Eustace

[Folio 32: ESSEX]

and [he] claims 30 acres which used to render 12d. a year to Ranulf Peverel's predecessor, as the Hundred testifies.

HUNDRED OF THURSTABLE.

Adelulf [de Marck] holds Tolleshunt of the count, which Thorbiorn held as a manor and as 8½ hides. [There were] then 5 villans; now 3. [There were] then 16 bordars; now 14. [There were] then 8 slaves; now 4. [There were] then 4 ploughs in demesne; now 3. The men [had] then 4 ploughs; now 2. [There is] woodland for 60 pigs, pasture for 300 sheep. [There were] then 12 salt-pans; now 5. [There are] 2 horses, 16 head of cattle, 40 pigs, 400 sheep. Then and later it was worth £10; now 100s. In the same [vill], 3 free men hold half a hide and 1 acre and it is worth 10s.

The same Adelulf [de Marck] holds Goldhanger of the count, which Alric held as 1 hide and 15 acres. [There are] now 4 bordars. [There were] then 2 slaves; now none. Then as now [there is] 1 plough in demesne. Now the men [have] half a plough. [There is] woodland for 40 pigs. [There are] 3½ acres of meadow. [There is] pasture for 50 sheep. It was then worth 20s.; now 30.

The count holds Tolleshunt in demesne, which Almær held as 2 hides and 5 acres. [There were] then 3 bordars; now 5. Then as now [there were] 2 slaves and 1 plough in demesne and the men [had] 1 plough. [There is] woodland for 100 pigs, pasture for 160 sheep. [There are] 50 sheep. It was then worth 40s. and when received 15s.; now 20.

St Martin holds Tolleshunt of the count, which Wulfric, a free man, held as 1 manor and as 1 hide and 35 acres. Then as now [there were] 2 bordars and 1 plough. [There is] woodland for 30 pigs. [There is] 1 cow. It is worth 30s.

In "Blatchams" 4 free men held half a hide and could sell it. Now Count Eustace holds [it]. Then as now [there was] 1 plough. It is worth 10s. and when received 10s.; now 7s.

Amalfrid holds of the count, which Guthmund, a free man,

held freely as 1 manor and as 3 hides TRE, and this is of the fief of Engelric. [There were] then 4 bordars; now 3. [There were] then 4 slaves; now 2. In demesne then [there were] 3 ploughs; now 2. Then as now the men [had] half a plough. [There is] pasture for 100 sheep. [There is] 1 salt-pan. It was then worth £4; later and now 3.

[Folio 32v: ESSEX]

HUNDRED OF TENDRING.

The Count holds St Osyth in demesne, which Edward held as 1 manor and as 3 hides and 40 acres TRE. Later Engelric [held it]. [There were] then 9 villans; later and now 7. [There are] now 2 bordars. [There were] then 8 slaves; later and now 2. [There was] then 1 plough in demesne, and when received none; now 1. The men [had] then 6 ploughs; later and now 3. [There is] woodland for 400 pigs. [There are] 6 acres of meadow, 1 cow, 11 sheep. It was then worth £12, and when received 40s.; now £10. To this manor belongs 1 berewick which is called Frating, with 40 acres, [and there is] now half a plough. It is assessed above. And at "Burna" [there are] 30 acres, [where there was] then 1 plough; now half a plough. It is worth 20s. And in Frowick [there are] 50 acres, and then as now [there were] 3 bordars and 1 slave and 1½ acres of meadow. [There is] now 1 plough, woodland for 12 pigs. It is worth 10s.

Frewin held Tendring TRE as 1 manor and as half a hide. Now the count holds [it] in demesne as the same. Then as now [there was] 1 villan and 2 bordars and 2 slaves. [There were] then 2 ploughs in demesne; later and now 1. Then as now the men [had] 1 plough. [There is] woodland for 30 pigs. [There are] 2 acres of meadow. [There were] then 2 horses; now 4. [There were] then 4 head of cattle; now 7. Then as now [there were] 20 pigs. [There were] then 40 sheep; now 100. [There were] then 14 goats; now 20. It was then worth 40s.; now 60.

Hato holds Alresford of the count, which Edward held as 1 manor and as 2 hides and 50 acres. [There were] then 4 bordars; now 7. [There were] then 6 slaves; now 2. [There were] then in demesne 2 ploughs, and when received, none; now half a plough. The men [had] then 1 plough; now half a plough. [There is] woodland for 100 pigs. [There are] 3 acres of meadow. [There is] pasture for 20 sheep. It is worth 60s.

Ralph de Marcy holds Frinton of the count, which Harold held as 1 manor and as 3 hides TRE. Later Engelric held [it]. [There were] then 6 villans; now 4. [There were] then 3 bordars; now none. [There were] then 2 slaves; now 1. Then as now [there was] 1 plough in demesne. The men [had] then 2 ploughs; now half a plough. [There is] pasture for 60 sheep. [There are] 2 head of cattle, 7 pigs, 20 sheep. It was then worth 60s.; now £4. 10s.

Robert holds Birch of the count, which Engelric held of St Paul

Count Eustace

[Folio 33: ESSEX]

of London as 1 manor and as 3 hides. [There were] then 6 bordars; now 8. [There were] then 2 slaves; now 1. [There were] then in demesne 2 ploughs; now none. Among the men [there was] then 1 plough; now 2. [There is] woodland for 10 pigs, pasture for 100 sheep. [There were] then 2 horses; now none. [There were] then 8 head of cattle; now none. [There were] then 13 sheep; now none. [There were] then 6 pigs; now none. It was then worth 60s.; now £4. 7s.

Adelulf [de Marck] holds [Great and Little] Holland of the count, which Leofstan held as 1 manor and as 4 hides TRE. Later Engelric held [it]. [There were] then 11 villans; now 8. Then as now [there were] 5 bordars. [There were] then 2 slaves; now 1. [There were] then 2 ploughs in demesne; now 1. Among the men [there were] then 6 ploughs; now 2. [There is] woodland for 50 pigs, 100 sheep. [There are] 13 pigs, 14 sheep. It was then worth £6; now 4.

The same holds Lawford of the count, which Ælfric, a free man, held TRE. Later Engelric [held it] as a manor and as 2 hides. [There were] then 4 villans; now 1. [There were] then 7 bordars; now 10. [There were] then 4 slaves; now 1. [There were] then in demesne 2 ploughs; now 1. Among the men [there were] then 4 ploughs; now 2. [There is] woodland for 20 pigs. [There are] 6 acres of meadow. [There is] pasture for 200 sheep. [There are] 4 head of cattle, 80 sheep, 1 horse, 8 pigs. Then as now it was worth £10. In the same [Lawford] 3 sokemen held half a hide and 30 acres, whom Engelric appropriated and now Count Eustace holds them and the same Adelulf [holds them] of him. Among them [there were] then 2 ploughs; now 1. [There are] 2 acres of meadow. It is worth 20s.

Bernard holds Tendring of the count, which Eadnoth held as a manor and as 1 hide less 15 acres and this is of the fief of Engelric. [There were] then 8 villans; now 6. [There are] now 6 bordars. [There were] then 6 slaves; now 1. Then as now [there were] 2 ploughs in demesne and the men [had] 3 ploughs. [There is] woodland for 200 pigs. [There are] 2 acres of meadow. Then as now it is worth £4.

HUNDRED OF UTTLESFORD.

Ingvar held Chrishall as 1 manor and as 6 hides TRE. Now Count Eustace holds [it] in demesne of the fief of Engelric. Then as now [there were] 32 villans. [There were] then 6 bordars; now 13.

Then as now [there were] 6 slaves and 3 ploughs in demesne and the men [had] 16 ploughs. [There is] woodland for 200 pigs and [there are] 8 acres of meadow, 1 horse, 40 pigs, 150 sheep, 24 goats, 4 hives of bees. Then as now it was worth £15. To this manor belong 2 sokemen with 8 acres and 1 sokeman with 8 acres, whom Engelric appropriated TREW. On these 8 acres are 3 bordars and [this] is worth 16d. To this manor belonged 1 sokeman with 3 virgates TRE, whom William Cardon now holds of the fief of G[eoffrey] de Mandeville, and [who] paid 2d. a year.

Guy holds [Great and Little] Chishill of the count, which Siward, a free man, held TRE as a manor and as 6 hides and 30 acres. [There were] then 5 villans; now 6. [There were] then 3 bordars; now 5. Then as now [there were] 6 slaves and 3 ploughs [...] in demesne and the men [had] 5 ploughs and 8 acres of meadow. [There are] 24 pigs, 250 sheep. Then and later it was worth 100s. [...] and now £6.

Godric, a free man, held [Great and Little] Chishill TRE.

Now the same Guy holds [it] of the count as 1 manor and as $2\frac{1}{2}$ hides. It is worth 60s. In the same 1 free man held half a hide, which Engelric appropriated TRW, and now Anselm holds [it] of the count. In that land then as now were 2 bordars and 1 plough and 2 acres of meadow. It is worth 10s.

Roger de Sommery holds Elmdon of the count, which Almær, a free man, held TRE and Engelric appropriated this manor TRW. Now as then there are 14 hides and 26 villans and 15 bordars. [There were] then 12 slaves; now none. [There were] then 6 ploughs in demesne, and when received 3; now 4. Then as now the men [had] 10 ploughs. [There is] woodland for 250 pigs. [There are] 7 acres of meadow, 20 pigs, 200 sheep and 88 sheep [sic]. It was then worth £16, and when received and now £20.

Beorhtwulf, a free man, held [Elmdon] Lee TRE as a manor and as $2\frac{1}{2}$ hides.

Count Eustace

Later Engelric held [it]. Now the same Roger [holds it] of the count. Then as now [there were] 5 villans. [There was] then 1 bordar; later and now 8. [There were] then 4 slaves; now none. [There were] then 3 ploughs in demesne; later and now 2. The men [had] then 4 ploughs, and when received 3, and now the same. [There is] woodland for 50 pigs. Then and later it was worth £4; now 100s.

The same [Roger] holds Crawley of the count, which Leofsige, a free man, held TRE as 30 acres, and Engelric appropriated [it] TRW. Then as now [there were] 2 bordars. [There was] then 1 slave. Then as now [there was] 1 plough [and] 2 acres of meadow. It is worth 10s.

HALF-HUNDRED OF FRESHWELL.

Leodmær the priest held Bendysh TRE as a manor and as $4\frac{1}{2}$ hides. Later Engelric held [it]. Now the count holds [it] in demesne. Then as now [there were] 8 villans and 3 bordars and 8 slaves and 4 ploughs in demesne. Among the men [there were] then 4 ploughs; later and now 3. [There is] woodland for 100 pigs. [There are] 8 acres of meadow, 28 pigs, 112 sheep and 1 sokeman held 1 acre and 1 rood, whom Engelric appropriated. Now the count holds [him]. The whole was then worth £11; now 12.

Alsige held Newnham as 1 hide TRE. Later Engelric held [it]. Now the count holds [it] in demesne. [There were] then 6 villans; now 9. [There were] then 2 bordars; later and now 7. Then as now [there were] 6 slaves and 3 ploughs in demesne. The men [had] then 4 ploughs; later and now 3. [There is] woodland for 20 pigs. [There are] 5 acres of meadow, 14 pigs, 56 sheep, 1 horse. To this manor [belonged] 5 sokemen holding half a hide and 35 acres, remaining with the soke. [There were] then 3 ploughs; later and now 2. [There are] 5 acres of meadow. It was then worth £11; now 12.

Adelulf [de Marck] holds [Great and Little] Bardfield of the count, which Northmann held TRE as 2 hides and 1 virgate. Later Engelric held it and appropriated him. Then as now [there were] 6 villans. Then and later [there was] 1 bordar; now 12. Then as now [there were] 4 slaves and 3 ploughs in demesne and the men [had] 2 ploughs. [There is] woodland for 200 pigs. [There are] 49 acres of meadow, 5 head of cattle, 25 pigs, 2 hives of bees,

30 goats, 1 horse. Then as now [there was] 1 mill. [There is] now 1 fishery. It was then worth £8; now £10.

HUNDRED OF ROCHFORD.

One free man held Shopland TRE as 5 hides. Later Engelric held [it]; now Count Eustace holds it] in demesne. Then as now [there were] 5 villans and 2 sokemen and the lord had soke and sake of them. Then as now [there were] 9 bordars and 2 ploughs in demesne and the men [had] 5 ploughs. [There is] woodland for 40 pigs, pasture for 400 sheep. [There are] 2 head of cattle, 54 sheep, 14 pigs, 13 goats, 3 horses. It was then worth £6; now 10. In the same 1 free man held half a hide and 30 acres, which Engelric appropriated. Then as now [there was] 1 plough and [there were] 3 bordars and this is assessed in [the above] £10.

XXI. Land of Count Alan

HUNDRED OF HARLOW.

Wihtgar, a free man, held Epping TRE as 1 manor and as 1½ hides and half a virgate. Then as now [there was] 1 plough in demesne and the men [had] half a plough and 2 villans and 2 bordars. [There is] woodland for 100 pigs. [There are] 8 acres of meadow. It was then worth 20s.; now 30. Osbern now holds this manor of the count.

HUNDRED OF DUNMOW.

Hervey [d'Épaignes] holds Willingale [Doe and Spain] which Eadgifu held TRE as 1 manor and as 1 hide and 1½ virgates. Then as now [there were] 3 ploughs in demesne and the men [had] 1½ ploughs and [there were] 4 villans and 8 bordars and 4 slaves. [There is] woodland for 250 pigs. [There are] 12 acres of meadow. It was then worth 60s.; now 100.

Aubrey de Vere holds [Great and Little] Canfield of the count, which Eadgifu held TRE as 1 hide and 30 acres. Then as now [there] was 1 plough in demesne and the men [had] 1 plough. [There were] then 3 villans; now 1. [There were] then 5 bordars; now 10. [There is] woodland for 100 pigs. [There are] 48 acres of meadow, among meadow and marsh. Then as now it was worth 60s.

HUNDRED OF HINCKFORD.

Hervey [d'Épaignes] holds Finchingfield of the count, which 3 free men held TRE as 2½ hides under Eadgifu. Then as now [there were] 5 ploughs in demesne and the men [had] 7 ploughs and [there were] 3 villans and 50 bordars, 5 slaves. [There is] woodland for 160 pigs. [There are] 16 acres of meadow. It was then worth 100s.; now £8.

In [Steeple] Bumpstead 1 knight holds 7½ acres, which 1 sokeman held under Eadgifu TRE and 1½ acres of meadow. It was then worth 2s.; now 3. In Yeldham [there are] 42 acres, which 1 free man held TRE.

Then as now [there was] 1 plough and 3 bordars. [There were] then 2 slaves; now 1. [There is] woodland for 15 pigs. [There are] 5 acres of meadow. [There is] now 1 mill. It was then worth 20s.; now 25.

In Finchingfield the count holds 38½ acres in demesne, which 2 sokemen and 1 free man held TRE. Then as now [there was] half a plough and 2 bordars. [There are] 2 acres of meadow. It is worth 5s.

HUNDRED OF ONGAR.

Aubrey de Vere holds [Abbess and Beauchamp] Roding of the count, which Leofwine and Eadsige held as a manor TRE and as 1½ hides. Then as now [there were] 2 villans and 13 bordars and 3 ploughs in demesne and the men [had] 1 plough. [There is] woodland for 200 pigs. [There are] 50 acres of meadow. It was then worth £4; later and now 100s.

HUNDRED OF TENDRING.

Hervey [d'Épaignes] holds [Great and Little] Bentley of the count, which Alwine held freely as 42½ acres. Earl R[alph] held this land. Then as now [there were] 3 villans and half a plough and 1 acre of meadow. [There is] woodland for 6 pigs. It is worth 3s. The same held half a hide. Then as now [there were] 4 villans and 1 plough. [There is] woodland for 6 pigs. [There is] half an acre of meadow. It is worth 10s.

HUNDRED OF UTTLESFORD.

The same H[ervey d'Épaignes] holds Emanuel Wood of the count, which Siward held as 1 hide. Then as now [there were] 2 villans. [There was] then 1 slave; now none. [There is] now 1 bordar. Then as now [there was] half a plough. [There are] 7 acres of meadow and 2 parts of a mill. It is worth 20s.

HALF-HUNDRED OF FRESHWELL.

In Rothend the same holds 30 acres, which Eadgifu held. Then as now [there was] half a plough. [There is] woodland for 8 pigs. [There are] 2½ acres of meadow. It was then worth 5s.; now 10. In Stevington Eadgifu held 5 acres which Hervey [d'Épaignes] holds. It is worth 2s.

XXII. Land of William de Warenne in Essex.

HUNDRED OF BARSTABLE.

A certain woman, Eadgifu, held "Upham" TRE as half a hide and 30 acres. Now William holds [it] in demesne. It is worth 10s.

Ranulf holds [East and West] Tilbury of William, which Sweting, a free man, held TRE as 30 acres. Then as now [there was] 1 bordar. [There is] pasture for 40 sheep. [There is] 1 acre of meadow. It was then worth 7s.; now 14.

HALF-HUNDRED OF HARLOW.

Richard holds Housham of William, which Holdfæst, a free man, held TRE as 1 manor and as 1 hide and 3 virgates. [There were] then 2 ploughs in demesne; now 1. The men

[had] then 3½ ploughs; now 5. [There were] then 6 villans; now 10. Then as now [there were] 3 bordars. [There were] then 3 slaves; now 1. [There is] woodland for 50 pigs. [There are] 10 acres of meadow. When received, [there were] 5 head of cattle and 1 calf and 40 pigs, 40 sheep. [There are] now 6 head of cattle and 50 pigs, 90 sheep, 3 hives of bees. Added to this manor TRW [was] 1 virgate, which Wulfric, a free man, held TRE. [There was] then half a plough; now none. Then as now [there is] 1 bordar. [There is] woodland for 10 pigs. [There are] 2 acres of meadow. It was then worth 4s.; now 6, and the manor was then worth £6; now 7.

The same Richard holds Quicksbury of William, which Alwine Gotton held TRE as 3 hides. Then as now [there were] 2 ploughs in demesne. The men [had] then 3½ ploughs; now 3. [There were] then 7 villans; now 6. [There are] now 6 bordars. [There were] then 5 slaves; now 2. [There are] 20 acres of meadow. Then as now [there was] 1 mill. [There were] then 47 sheep; now 52. And [there are] 2 colts. It is worth 100s.

HUNDRED OF DUNMOW.

Dufa, a free woman, held [Great and Little] Easton TRE as a manor and as 2 hides. Now William [holds it] in demesne. Then as now [there were] 2 ploughs in demesne. The men [had] then 4 ploughs; now 2. Then as now [there were] 4 villans. [There were] then 3 bordars; now 8. [There were] then 3 slaves; now 2. [There was] then woodland for 200 pigs; now 150. [There are] 52 acres of meadow. [There was] then 1 horse and 7 head of cattle and 60 pigs and 60 sheep. [There is] now 1 horse, 23 head of cattle, 20 pigs, 70 sheep, 4 hives of bees. It is worth 100s.

[Folio 36v: ESSEX]

Two free men held [Great and Little] Canfield TRE as 2 hides less 8 acres. Now William [holds it] in demesne. [There were] then 4 ploughs in demesne; now 2. The men [had] then 8 ploughs; now 6. [There was] then 1 priest and villans; now 1 priest and 7 villans. [There were] then 3 bordars; now 17. Then as now [there were] 2 slaves. [There is] now 1 mill. [There was] then woodland for 160 pigs; now 120. [There are] 70 acres of meadow. [There was] then 1 horse and 8 head of cattle and 100 pigs and 200 sheep. [There is] now 1 horse, 15 head of cattle, 50 pigs, 70 sheep, 9 goats. It was then worth £8; now 9.

William de Vatteville holds [High] Roding of William, which the Abbot of Ely held TRE as 1 manor and as 2½ hides. Then as now [there were] 3 ploughs in demesne and the men [had] 3 ploughs and [there was] 1 priest and 8 villans. [There were] then 12 bordars; now 11. Then as now [there are] 7 slaves. [There is] woodland for 300 pigs. [There are] 42 acres of meadow. Then as now [there were] 3 horses, 8 head of cattle and 120 sheep. [There are] now 7 pigs. It was then worth £10 and when received 12; now 18.

Walter holds [High] Roding of William, which a free woman held TRE as 1 manor and as 2½ hides, and now

there are 3½ hides. [There were] then 3 ploughs in demesne; now 2 and when received 3. Then as now the men [had] 1 plough. [There were] then 3 villans. [There is] now 1 priest and [there are] 4 villans. [There were] then 4 bordars; now 13. [There were] then 4 slaves; now 2. [There is] woodland for 50 pigs. [There are] 30 acres of meadow. [There are] now 4 head of cattle and 40 pigs, 83 sheep, 1 hive of bees. It is worth £8. And that hide which has been added to this manor belonged TRE to the abbey of Ely, as the Hundred testifies.

Guibert holds [Great and Little] Dunmow of William, which Earl Ælfgar held TRE as half a hide. Then as now [there was] half a plough in demesne. [There are] now 3 bordars. [There were] then 3 slaves; now none. [There is] woodland for 40 pigs. [There are] 7 acres of meadow. [There were] then 10 pigs, 30 sheep. [There are] now 9 head of cattle, 30 pigs, 80 sheep, 12 goats, 8 hives of bees. It was then worth 20s. and when received 30s. It is now worth 35s.

William de Warenne

[Folio 37: ESSEX]

HALF-HUNDRED OF CLAVERING.

Sigemond holds Peyton of William, which 1 free man held as a manor and as 1 hide and 30 acres TRE. Then as now [there was] 1 plough in demesne and the men [had] 1 plough. Then and later [there were] 3 villans; now 2. Then and later [there were] 3 bordars; now 7. [There are] 7 acres of meadow. [There was] then 1 horse and 9 pigs. Now [there is] 1 horse, 9 pigs, 40 sheep. It was then worth 20s.; now 25.

HUNDRED OF HINCKFORD.

In Halstead William de Warenne holds 2 hides less 4 acres, which 30 free men held TRE, in which land there is now as then 10 ploughs in demesne and the men [have] 3 ploughs and [there are] 8 villans and 23 bordars and 6 slaves. [There is] woodland for 140 pigs. [There are] 46 acres of meadow, 2 mills. [There were] then 6 head of cattle, 40 sheep, 12 pigs; now 14 head of cattle, 36 sheep, 20 pigs, 2 horses, 2 hives of bees. Then and later it was worth £10; now £13. 17s. 4d. Of this land, Richard holds 34 acres and it is worth 10s. in the same valuation.

In [Steeple] Bumpstead Guibert holds 3 hides and 18 acres, which 12 free men held TRE. In that land there are now as then 9 ploughs and 3 villans and 18 bordars and 5 slaves. [There is] woodland for 20 pigs. [There are] 40 acres of meadow. [There was] then 1 horse, 40 sheep, 30 pigs. [There is] now 1 horse, 16 head of cattle, 100 pigs, 100 sheep, 4 hives of bees. Then and later it was worth £10; now 12.

In 'Pooley' [Hunts Hall] William holds 3½ hides and 13 acres. Of this land, Richard holds 25 acres and Gladiou [holds] 3 virgates. Twenty-three men held all this land TRE. They had then 10 ploughs. Later and now there are 8 ploughs. [There are] now 6 bordars. [There were] then 7 slaves; now none 5. [There is] now 1 mill. [There was] then woodland for 60 pigs; now 40. [There were then] 30 acres of meadow, 8 head of cattle, 20 pigs, 20 sheep. [There are] now

12 head of cattle, 30 pigs, 60 sheep, 2 hives of bees. It was then worth £10; now £14.

[Folio 37v: ESSEX]

16s. William claims these lands by exchange.

HUNDRED OF CHAFFORD.

Three free men held Kenningtons as 4 hides TRE. Now William holds [it] as the same by exchange, as he says, and Guibert [holds it] of him. [There was] then 1 villan; now 7. [There is] now 1 bordar. [There were] then 3 slaves; now 1. [There were] then in all 3 ploughs; now 1½. [There is] woodland for 100 pigs. [There are] 8 acres of meadow. [There were] then 2 head of cattle and 15 pigs, 20 sheep. Now [there are] 2 head of cattle, 15 pigs, 50 sheep. It was then worth [..]s., and when received 30; now 100s. less 3s. Ranulf also has half a hide which Wulfwine, a free man, held TRE. [There was] then 1 plough; now half a plough. It is worth 6s.

HUNDRED OF CHELMSFORD.

Three free men held Hanningfield as 3 manors and as 4 hides and 27 acres. Now William [holds it] for the same by his exchange and Guibert [holds it] of him. Then as now [there were] 3 bordars and 2 slaves. [There were] then 3 ploughs in demesne; now 4. [There is] woodland for 40 pigs. [There are] 2 acres of meadow. [There is] pasture for 100 sheep. [There were] then 2 horses and 12 head of cattle, 60 sheep, 40 pigs. [There are] now 2 horses, 30 head of cattle, 100 sheep, 15 pigs. It was then worth 60s.; now £4.

Ranulf holds Hanningfield of William, which Godric Scipri held TRE as 1 manor and as 2 hides less 30 acres. [There were] then 2 slaves; now none. Then as now [there was] 1 plough. [There are] 3 acres of meadow. It was then worth 30s.; now 40.

William holds Boreham in demesne, which Eskil held as a manor and as half a hide. Then as now [there was] 1 bordar. [There was] then 1 slave; now none. [There was] then 1 plough; now half a plough. [There are] 5 acres of meadow. [There is] woodland for 20 pigs. It is worth 10s.

Richard holds Belstead of William, which Godric Poinc held as a manor and as 1 hide less 10 acres. [There were] then 2 slaves; now 1. [There were] then 2 ploughs in demesne; now 1. [There are] 6 acres of meadow. [There is] woodland for 20 pigs. It is worth 40s.

William de Warenne

[Folio 38: ESSEX]

HUNDRED OF UTTLESFORD.

Richard holds Wendens [Ambo and Lofts] of William, which Wulfmær held as a manor and as 1½ hides and 30 acres, and this is [William's] by exchange. Then as now [there were] 2 villans and 7 bordars. Then and later [there was] 1 plough in demesne; now 1½. Then as now the men [had] 1½ ploughs. [There are] 16 acres of meadow. [There were] then 17 pigs; now none. Then as now [there were] 50 sheep. It was then worth 40s.; now 60.

The same R[ichard] holds Chardwell, which Wulfmær

held as a manor and as 2½ hides. [There were] then 4 villans; now 3 . [There were] then [...] bordars; now 8. [There were] then 2 slaves. [There were] then 1½ ploughs in demesne, and when received none; now 1½ ploughs. Then as now the men [had] 1½ ploughs. [There are] 10 acres of meadow. There was no stock when received; now 32 pigs, 52 sheep, 2 head of cattle, 3 hives of bees. It was then worth 40s.; now 60. In [Great and Little] Chishill 8 free men held 1 hide and 45 acres. Now William de Warenne has [it] by exchange and the same R[ichard holds it] of him. [There were] then 3 ploughs; now 2 and when received none. [There are] 2 acres of meadow. It is worth 30s.

HUNDRED OF ROCHFORD.

In Paglesham William de Warenne holds 1 hide in demesne, which 1 free man held TRE. Then as now [there was] 1 plough in demesne. [There were] then 4 slaves; now 3 3. [There is] pasture for 100 sheep. It is worth 20s.

In Plumberow Ranulf holds 30 acres of William, which 1 free man held TRE. [There was] then half a plough; now 1. Then [it was worth] 5s.; now 10. He claims these lands in exchange for [lands in] Normandy.

HUNDRED OF LEXDEN.

In Fordham Ælfric held freely 25 acres. Now William [holds them] by the same exchange. Then as now [there was] half a plough [and] 1½ acres of meadow. It was then worth 10s.; now 6s. 8d. This land is of the soke of the king.

[Folio 38v: ESSEX]

XXIII. land of Richard, son of Count Gilbert.

HUNDRED OF HARLOW.

Richard holds Wallbury in demesne, which Toti, a free man, held TRE as 1 manor and as 1 hide. [There were] then 2 ploughs in demesne; now 1. Then as now the men [had] 1 plough. [There were] then 2 bordars; now 6. [There were] then 2 slaves; now none. [There is] woodland for 100 pigs. [There are] 24 acres of meadow. It was then worth 30s.; now 40.

HUNDRED OF DUNMOW.

Wihtgar held Thaxted TRE; now R[ichard holds it] in demesne as 1 manor and as 9½ hides. [There were] then 8 ploughs in demesne; now 7. The men [had] then 34 ploughs; now 18. [There were] then 55 villans; now 52. Then as now [there are] 24 bordars and 16 slaves. [There was] then woodland for 1,000 pigs; now 800. [There are] 120 acres of meadow. [There was] then 1 mill; now 2. And 16 ploughs [more] could be restored. Then as now [there were] 4 horses and 36 head of cattle, 128 pigs. [There were] then 200 sheep; now 320. [There were] then 10 hives of bees; now 16. It was then worth £30, and when received the same. Now it is worth £50, as the French and English say, but Richard gave it to a certain Englishman for £60 in rent, but [the rent] is deficient by at least £10 each year. To this manor belong now as then 3 sokemen with 2 hides and 15 acres, whom Warner holds of R[ichard]. [There were] then 4 ploughs; now 3½. [There were] then 10 villans; now 2. [There were] then 2 bordars; now 10.

[There were] then 4 slaves; now none. [There is] woodland for 50 pigs. [There are] 34 acres of meadow. It is worth £6, and of this land 1 sokeman of the king held TRE 7½ acres, which have been added to this manor TRW and have not paid the customary dues of the king.

Wihtgar held [Great and Little] Dunmow TRE as 1 manor and as 2 hides and 30 acres. Then as now [there were] 2 ploughs in demesne and the men [had] 2 ploughs and [there were] 5 villans. [There were] then 4 bordars; now 7. Then as now [there were] 4 slaves. [There was] then woodland for 500 pigs; now 300. [There are] 15 acres of meadow. Then as now [there was] 1 mill. Then and later it was worth 60s.; now 100, and Vital, a knight, claims this land, which, as

Richard

[Folio 39: ESSEX]

he testifies, 1 free man held TRE. In this manor now as then 1 priest holds half a hide in alms and then as now [there was] half a plough and 2 bordars. Arnold holds the manor.

HUNDRED OF HINCKFORD.

W[illiam] Pecche holds Gestingthorpe of R[ichard], which Leodmær the priest held TRE as half a hide. Then as now [there were] 3 ploughs in demesne and the men [had] 3 ploughs and [there were] 8 villans. [There are] now 9 bordars. Then as now [there were] 6 slaves. [There is] woodland for 20 pigs. [There are] 20 acres of meadow. [There was] then 1 mill; now none. To this land belongs now as then 1 sokeman with 15 acres and he has half a plough and 2 bordars and 1 acre of meadow. It was then worth 100s.; now £7.

Two sokemen held Finchingfield TRE as 48 acres. Now Elinant holds [it] of R[ichard]. Then as now [there were] 1½ ploughs. Then and later [there were] 4 bordars; now 7. [There is] woodland for 6 pigs and [there are] 6½ acres of meadow. [There was] then 1 horse and now none. [There were] then 10 head of cattle; now 8. [There were] then 20 pigs; now 26. [There were] then 100 sheep; now 127. It was then worth 10s.; now 30.

Robert holds Panfield of R[ichard], which Wihtgar held TRE as 1 manor and as 1½ hides and 30 acres. [There were] then 4 ploughs in demesne; later and now 2. Then as now the men [had] 5 ploughs. Then and later [there were] 10 villans; now 8. Then and later [there were] 8 bordars; now 15. Then and later [there were] 8 slaves; now 7. [There is] woodland for 120 pigs. [There are] 13 acres of meadow and 2 ploughs [more] could be restored. Then and later it was worth £8; now 10.

In [Great and Little] Yeldham Goismer holds 1 hide and 5 acres [of Richard], which 8 sokemen held TRE under Wihtgar. Then as now [there were] 3½ ploughs in demesne and the men [had] half a plough. Then and later [there were] 5 bordars; now 8. Then and later [there were] 5 slaves; now 2. [There is] woodland for 20 pigs. [There are] 23 acres of meadow. [There was] then 1 mill. Then and later it was worth 60s.; now 100s.

In Wickham [St Paul's] Arnold held half a hide and 10 acres of R[ichard], which 2 sokemen held under Wihtgar

TRE. Then as now [there were] 2 ploughs in demesne. Then and later [there were] 5 bordars; now 10. Then and later [there was] 1 slave; now none. [There was] then woodland for 40 pigs; now 20. [There are] 10 acres of meadow.

[Folio 39v: ESSEX]

Then and later it was worth 30s.; now 40. In Finchingfield the same Arnold holds 38 acres which 2 sokemen held under Wihtgar TRE. Then as now [there was] 1 plough. [There are] now 3 bordars and 1 slave and 4½ acres of meadow. It is worth 10s.

In "Binsley" [in Bulmer] Widelard holds 1 hide which 1 sokeman held under Wihtgar. Then as now [there was] 1 plough in demesne and the men [had] half a plough and [there were] 2 villans. Then and later [there were] 16 bordars; now 7. [There were] then 2 slaves; now none. [There is] woodland for 20 pigs. [There are] 4 acres of meadow. It was then worth 20s.; later and now 40. In Alderford 2 knights hold 36 acres, which 3 sokemen held under Wihtgar. Then as now [there were] 2 ploughs and 4 bordars. [There is] woodland for 12 [pigs]. [There are] 9 acres of meadow, 30 sheep. It was then worth 40s.; later and now 60.

At Ashen Richard holds half a hide and 40 acres in demesne, which 2 sokemen held TRE under Wihtgar. Then as now [there was] 1 plough. Then and later [there were] 2 bordars; now 6. [There are] 9 acres of meadow. [There is] now 1 mill. It was then worth 20s.; later and now 35.

At Finchingfield 2 knights hold 36 acres of R[ichard], which 3 sokemen held under Wihtgar TRE. Then as now [there were] 2 ploughs and 4 bordars. [There were] then 4 slaves; later and now 2. [There is] woodland for 10 pigs. [There are] 7 acres of meadow. Then and later it was worth 40s.; now 65.

In Bulmer Mascerel holds half a hide and 30 acres, which 1 sokeman held under Wihtgar. Then as now [there were] 2 ploughs; now 1. [There is] woodland for 5 pigs. [There are] 2 acres of meadow and it is worth 22s. 2d.

At Howe Germund holds 32½ acres, which 3 sokeman held under Wihtgar. Then as now [there were] 2 ploughs and 5 bordars and 3 slaves. [There is] woodland for 30 pigs. [There are] 8 acres of meadow. [There were] then 5 head of cattle; now 8. Now [there are] 4 pigs. [There were] then 20 sheep; now 83. [There are] now 32 goats. Then and later it was worth 30s.; now 50.

In Bures Richard has 13 sokemen with 35 acres in demesne. Then as now [there are] 4 ploughs.

Richard

[Folio 40: ESSEX]

[There were] then 9 bordars; now 16. [There was] then 1 slave; now none. [There is] woodland for 20 pigs. [There are] 11 acres of meadow. In Foxearth [there are] 19 sokemen with 1½ hides and 15 acres. Then as now [there were] 5 ploughs and 10 bordars and 1 slave. [There are] 22 acres of meadow. In Pebmarsh [there are] 18 sokemen with half a hide and 12 acres. Then as now [there were] 3 ploughs and 3 bordars and 3 acres of meadow.

In Alphamstone now as then 15 sokemen hold 1 hide less 5 acres and they have 2 ploughs and 3 bordars. [There is] woodland for 5 pigs. [There are] 4 acres of meadow.

In Middleton [there are] 13 sokemen with 1½ hides and 30 acres. Then as now [there were] 3 ploughs and 8 bordars. [There is] woodland for 8 pigs. [There are] 13 acres of meadow.

In [Steeple] Bumpstead [there are] 3 sokemen who hold now as then 25 acres. Then as now [there was] 1 plough and 2 bordars and 6 acres of meadow. In Finchingfield [there are] 11 sokemen with half Then as now [there was] 1 plough and 3 acres of meadow.

In Coupals [there are] 5 sokemen with half a hide less 5 acres. Then as now [there is] 1 plough. [There are] 2 acres of meadow.

In Twinstead [there are] 18 sokemen with half a hide and 15 acres. Then as now [there are] 2 ploughs and 7 bordars. [There is] woodland for 8 pigs. [There are] 3 acres of meadow. In "Cheneboltuna" [there are] 15 sokemen [with] half a hide and 5 acres. Then as now [there were] 1½ ploughs, 3 bordars, 4 acres of meadow.

In Halstead 22 sokemen hold half a hide and 11 acres. Then as now [there were] 5 ploughs and 1 villan, 15 bordars, 2 slaves. [There is] woodland for 50 pigs. [There are] 19 acres of meadow, 1 mill.

In Sudbury [there are] 5 burgesses holding 2 acres. These, with all [those] aforesaid, render £15. 6s. 6d., and all this [it] is in the demesne of Richard.

In Boyton Colsege, a free man, held half a hide and 10 acres TRE. Then as now [there were] 2 ploughs in demesne. The men [had] then 3 ploughs; later and now 2. Then as now [there was] 1 villan. [There were] then 7 bordars; later and now 8. Then and later [there were] 4 slaves; now 2. [There is] woodland for 30 pigs. [There are] 8 acres of meadow. It was then and later worth 40s.; later and now £4. To this manor have been added 45 acres TRW, which belonged to Wethersfield, the king's manor. [There was] then half a plough; now none.

[Folio 40v: ESSEX]

Then and later [there was] 1 bordar; now 2. [There is] woodland for 10 pigs. [There are] 2 acres of meadow. It is worth 8s.

In Bures Leofgifu, a free woman, held 40 acres. Then as now the men [had] 1½ ploughs and [there was] 1 villan. Then and later [there were] 2 bordars; now 3. Then as now [there were] 2 slaves. [There is] woodland for 20 pigs. [There are] 5 acres of meadow. It is worth 30s. Richard has this land, namely Boyton and Bures, by exchange, as his men [say].

Colman held ['Morrell'] Roding [in White Roding], TRE as 3 virgates; now R[ichard holds it] as the same in demesne. And Colman was so free that he could go where he would with soke and sake, but yet he was the man of Wihtgar, predecessor of Richard. Then as now [there was] 1 villan and 2 bordars. [There were] then 4 slaves; now 1. Then as now [there were] 2 ploughs in demesne and the men [had] half a plough. [There is] woodland for 200 pigs. [There are] 20 acres of meadow. It was then worth 60s.; later 40, now £4.

HUNDRED OF TENDRING.

Wihtgar held [Great and Little] Bentley as 1 hide and as 1 manor. Now Roger holds [it] of Richard. Then as now [there were] 3 villans and 4 bordars. [There was] then 1 slave; now none. Then as now [there was] 1 plough in demesne and the men [had] 1 plough. [There is] woodland for 100 pigs. [There are] 3 acres of meadow. It was then worth 40s.; now 50.

Alwine held [Great and Little] Bromley as 1 manor and as half a hide, and he was commended to Wihtgar, [but] being able to sell his land. Now R[oger] holds [it] under Richard. Then as now [there was] 1 villan. [There are] now 2 bordars. [There was] then 1 plough in demesne; now none. [There is] woodland for 100 pigs. [There are] 2 acres of meadow. [There are] now 11 sheep. It is worth 40s.

Algar held Alresford as 37 acres TRE. Now he holds [it] under R[ichard] and this is of the king's soke of Lawford, as the Hundred testifies. [There was] then 1 plough; now none. [There is] pasture for 40 sheep. It was then worth 10s.; now 6.

HUNDRED OF LEXDEN.

In TRE [there] were 5 sokemen whom Wihtgar held, [namely] Wulfwine and his two sisters in Colne, holding

Richard

[Folio 41: ESSEX]

holding 64 acres, and Leofric, holding 30 acres in the same town, and they could not withdraw from the soke of Wihtgar. Under them, [there were] then as now 2 bordars and 1 plough. [There is] woodland for 12 pigs. [There are] 9 acres of meadow. It is worth 20s. In Fordham Wulfmær held 40 acres under Wihtgar

In [West] Bergholt Leofcild held 31½ acres. Now Goding holds [them] under R[ichard]. [There were] then 2 bordars; now 6. [There is] now 1 slave. Then as now [there was] half a plough. [There is] woodland for 16 pigs. [There are] 3 acres of meadow. [There was] then 1 mill; now none. It is worth 10s.

In "Witesworda" Algar held 12½ acres under Wihtgar [and] could not withdraw from the soke. [There is] now 1 bordar and 1 acre of meadow. It is worth 3s.

Walter Tirel holds Langham of R[ichard], which Fin the Dane held as 2½ hides and as 1 manor. [There were] then 22 villans; now 17. [There were] then 9 bordars; now 27. [There were] then 4 slaves; now none. Then as now [there was] 1 plough in demesne. The men [had] then 11 ploughs; now 7. [There is] woodland for 1,000 pigs. [There are] 40 acres of meadow. [There was] then 1 mill; now 2. [There were] then 6 horses; now none. Then as now [there were] 22 head of cattle. [There were] then 46 pigs; now 80. [There were] then 54 sheep; now 200. [There were] then 62 goats; now 80. [There were] then 3 hives of bees; now none. It was then worth £12; now 15.

HALF-HUNDRED OF FRESHWELL.

Wihtgar held [Great and Little] Bardfield as 1 manor and as 4 hides. Now Richard holds [it] in demesne. [There were] then 24 villans; now 20. Then and later [there were] 7 bordars; now 22. Then as now [there were] 8 slaves. Then as now [there were] 4 ploughs in demesne. Then and later [the men had] 21 ploughs; now 9. [There is] woodland for 800 pigs. [There are] 32 acres of meadow. Then as now [there were] 2 mills. [There were] then 4 horses; now 5. [There were] then 28 head of cattle; now 41. [There were] then 60 pigs; now 107. [There were] then 100 sheep; now 200. Then as now it was worth £16.

Wihtgar held [Great and Little] Sampford as 1 manor and as 5 hides. Now Richard holds [it] in demesne. [There were] then 23 villans; now 14. [There were] then 2 bordars; now 18. [There were] then 6 slaves; now 4. Then as now [there were] 3 ploughs in demesne. The men [had] then 21 ploughs; now 10.

[There is] woodland for 60 pigs. [There are] 22 acres of meadow. [There was] then 1 mill; now none. It was then worth £12; now 17. When Richard received this manor, he then found there 3 horses; now [there are] 2. [There were] then 19 head of cattle; now 9. [There were] then 50 pigs; now 30. [There were] then 100 sheep; now 88. [There were] then 3 hives of bees; now 1. Of this manor and of the abovesaid 5 hides, 2 Frenchmen hold 1½ hides and [there are] 9 bordars and 2 ploughs and 16 acres of meadow. It is assessed above.

Wihtgar held Hempstead as 1 manor and as 4 hides less 30 acres TRE. Now Robert de Vatteville [holds it] of R[ichard]. Then as now [there were] 22 villans. [There were] then 6 bordars; now 10. [There were] then 8 slaves; now 7. [There were] then 4 ploughs in demesne; now 3. The men [had] then 14 ploughs; now 10. [There is] woodland for 200 pigs. [There are] 15 acres of meadow. It was then worth £12; now 16.

In [Great and Little] Bardfield Widelard holds 1 hide, which 2 servants of Wihtgar held and they did not then render customary dues or geld to the king, nor could they withdraw without the licence of their lord, as the Hundred testifies. Then as now [there is] 1 plough in demesne. It is worth 20s.

HUNDRED OF ROCHFORD.

Fin the Dane held Barrow [as] 1½ hides; now R[ichard holds it] in demesne. Then as now [there were] 3 bordars and 3 slaves and 2 ploughs. [There is] woodland for 30 pigs. It was then worth 40s.; now £4.

XXIIII. Land of Swein of Essex.

HUNDRED OF BARSTABLE.

Alwine, a thegn of King Edward, held [East and West] Horndon TRE and King William gave [it] to Robert. Now Swein holds [it] and Sigeric [holds it] of him as 1 manor and as 5 hides and 15 acres. Then as now [there were] 2 ploughs in demesne and the men [had] 3 ploughs and [there were] 3 villans. [There were] then 7 bordars; now 10. [There were] then 4 slaves; now 1. [There are] 2 hides of woodland and 2 sokemen with 50 acres, having now as then half a plough. In this manor Swein received a horse, 8 head of cattle, 20 pigs, 60 sheep. Now [there are] 4 head of cattle, 12 pigs, 50 sheep. It was then worth 100s.

Walter holds Langdon of Swein, which Alric, a thegn of King E[dward], held as a manor and as 5 hides. Then as now

[there were] 2 ploughs in demesne and the men [had] 3 ploughs and [there were] 5 villans. [There were] then 4 slaves; now 4 and [there is] 1 hide of woodland. [There is] pasture for 100 sheep. [There were] then 5 head of cattle and 10 pigs, 60 sheep; now [there are] 10 pigs, 42 sheep. It was then worth 100s.; now £6.

2 Frenchmen, namely Osbern and Ralph, hold [East and West] Tilbury of Swein, which Ælfric the priest, a free man, held TRE as 1 manor and as 2 hides. Then as now [there were] 2 ploughs in demesne and the men [had] 4 ploughs and [there was] 1 villan and 11 bordars and 2 slaves and 4 hides of woodland. [There is] pasture for 300 sheep and [there is] 1 fishery. [There was] then 1 horse and 60 sheep. Now [there is] 1 horse and 12 colts and 31 head of cattle, 9 pigs and 260 sheep. It was then worth £8; now 100s.

Osbern holds Childerditch of S[wein], which Alwynn, a free woman, held TRE and it is not known how it came to Robert fitzWymarc. Then as now there is there 1 hide and 40 acres. Then as now [there is] 1 plough in demesne. The men [had] then half a plough; now nothing. [There was] then 1 villan; now none. [There was] then 1 bordar; now 4. [There were] then 2 slaves; now 1. [There is] woodland for 100 pigs. [There is] pasture for 100 sheep. [There was] then 1 cow; now 10 head of cattle. It is worth 40s.

Ælfric the priest, a free man, held Horndon [on the Hill] TRE as 1 manor and as 2 hides and 30 acres. Then as now [there was] 1 plough in demesne and the men [had] half a plough and 11 bordars

and [there were] 3 slaves. Of this land, Ælfric the priest gave to a certain church half a hide and 30 acres, but Swein took [it] from the church. Then as now [there was] 1 horse and 2 head of cattle. It was worth 30s. Pain holds the manor of Swein.

Turold holds Hassenbrook of Swein, which Leofstan, a free man, held TRE as 1 hide and 30 acres. Then as now [there was] 1 plough in demesne. [There were] then 2 bordars; now 3. [There were] then 2 slaves; now none. [There are] 6 acres of meadow. [There were] then 10 sheep; now 13 and [there are] 5 pigs. It is worth 20s.

The same Turold holds Basildon of S[wein], which the same Leofstan held TRE as 1 hide and as a manor and 15 acres. Then as now [there was] 1 plough. [There were] then 3 bordars; now 1. Then as now [there were] 2 slaves. [There is] pasture for 100 sheep. [There were] then 2 horses and 7 pigs and 15 sheep. [There is] now 1 horse and 1 cow and 1 pig and 95 sheep. It was then worth 20s.; now 25.

W. holds Basildon, which Godgyth, a certain free woman, held TRE as a manor and as 3 hides. [There were] then 3 ploughs in demesne; now 2½. The men [had] then 1 plough; now 1½. [There were] then 2 villans; now 1. [There were] then 4 bordars; now 3. [There were] then 4 slaves; now none. [There is] woodland for 40 pigs, pasture for 100 sheep. [There was] then 1 horse and 17 sheep. Now [there are] 5 head of cattle and 16 pigs and 39 sheep. It is worth 60s.

Turchil holds Wickford, which Leofstan held freely as a manor and as half a hide and 35 acres. Then as now [there was] 1 plough and 1 bordar. [There was] then 1 slave; now none. [There are] 30 acres of woodland [and] 3 acres of meadow. [There were] then 2 horses and 16 head of cattle and 3 pigs and 100 sheep. Now [there are] 3 horses and 8 head of cattle and 11 pigs and 60 sheep. Besides this land, Beorhtgifu, a free woman held half a hide and 15 acres, which Swein added to the aforesaid land, in which [there] was then 1 plough; now none. Then as now [there were] 2 bordars and 1 villan. [There are] 20 acres of woodland. He also added 3 free men with 45 acres, in which [there] was then 1 plough; now half a plough. He also added 1 free man with 9 acres. The whole was then worth TRE 60s.; now 50.

Swein holds Wickford in demesne, which Godwine, a thegn of the king, held

Swein of Essex

as 1 manor and as 10 hides. Then as now [there were] 2 ploughs in demesne. The men [had] then 6 ploughs; now 4. Then as now [there were] 7 villans. [There were] then 2 bordars; now 12. [There were] then 6 slaves; now none. [There were] then 12 hides of woodland; now 6 acres. [There was] then 1 horse and 12 sheep and 17 goats and 2 hives of bees. Now [there is] 1 cow and 20 sheep and 2 colts and 3 hives of bees. It was then worth £16; now 9.

William fitzOdo holds Wickford, which Dot, a free man, held TRE as a manor and half a hide and 45 acres. [There was] then 1 plough in demesne and 1 bordar. [There is] woodland for 10 pigs. It is worth 10s. Mainard holds Wickford, which Godric held TRE as 30 acres. It is worth 5s.

Swein holds [North and South] Benfleet in demesne, which Alwine, a free man, held TRE as a manor and as 2 hides. [There were] then 3 ploughs in demesne; now 1, and 1 plough [more] could be restored. [There are] now 5 bordars and 2 slaves. [There is] pasture for 250 sheep. It is worth 40s.

Walter holds Wheatley of Swein, which Eadric held TRE as a manor and as half a hide. Then as now [there was] 1 plough. [There is] now 1 bordar and 15 acres of pasture. It was worth 10s.

Swein holds Wheatley in demesne, which Leofcild, a thegn of the king, held TRE as 1 manor and as 5 hides. [There were] then 2 ploughs and the men [had] 1 plough and now the same. [There was] then 1 villan; now none. [There were] then 10 bordars; now 11. [There is] half a hide of waste woodland, pasture for 100 sheep. [There was] then 1 fishery; now 2. [There were] then 3 horses and 5 head of cattle and 20 pigs and 100 sheep. [There is] now 1 horse and 1 colt and 7 head of cattle and 70 sheep. It was then worth 60s.; now £4.

Swein holds Thundersley in demesne, which Godric, a thegn of the king, held TRE as 1 manor and as 5 hides and 15 acres. Then as now [there were] 2 ploughs in demesne and the men [had] 2 ploughs and [there were] 5 villans and 5 bordars. [There were] then 4 slaves; now 2. [There is] pasture for 200 sheep, woodland for 50 pigs. [There were] then 2 horses and 7 head of cattle and 16 pigs and 200 sheep and 2 hives of bees. [There are] now 3 horses and 1 horse, 14 head of cattle, 36 pigs, 200 sheep, 2 hives of bees. It was then worth 102s.; now 100s.

HUNDRED OF ROCHFORD.

Swein holds Rayleigh in demesne as 1 manor and as 5 hides. [There were] then 2 ploughs in demesne; now 3. Then as now the men [had] 10 ploughs. [There were] then 21 villans; now 6. [There were] then 6 bordars; now 15. Then as now [there were] 2 slaves. [There are] 10 acres of meadow. [There is] woodland for 40 pigs, 1 park and 6 arpents of vineyard, and it renders 20 muids of wine if it does well. [There were] then 4 horses and 13 head of cattle, 25 pigs, 105 sheep. [There are] now 5 horses and 2 colts and 20 head of cattle and 11 pigs and 80 sheep and 11 goats. It was then worth £10; now the same, besides the wine, and Swein built his castle in this manor. Of this manor, 4 Frenchmen hold 2 hides [in which there are] 4 ploughs and 4 bordars and this is worth 60s. in the above valuation.

Swein holds Rayleigh in demesne, which 1 free man held TRE as a manor and as 2½ hides. Then as now [there were] 2 ploughs in demesne. [There were] then 3 villans; now 2. [There were] then 5 bordars; now 6, having then 2½ ploughs in demesne; now only half a plough. [There was] then 1 horse and 2 head of cattle and 15 sheep. [There are] now 2 horses, 9 head of cattle, 9 pigs, 20 sheep. Then and later it was worth 30s.; now 40.

Two Frenchmen hold Hockley of Swein. Godbald [holds] 1 hide and Odo [holds] 30 acres and 1 free man held this manor TRE. Then as now [there were] 2½ ploughs in demesne. [There were] then 3 bordars; now 5. [There were] then 5 slaves; now 3. [There is] pasture for 100 sheep. Then as now [there was] 1 mill. [There were] then 5 head of cattle and 10 pigs and 100 sheep and 7 goats. [There is] now 1 horse and 13 head of cattle and 22 pigs and 100 sheep and 4 hives of bees. It was then worth 30s.; later and now 40.

Swein holds Eastwood in demesne, which his father held TRE as 1 manor and as 3½ hides. Then as now [there were] 3 villans and 2 ploughs in demesne. The men [had] then 8 ploughs; now 5. [There were] then 21 bordars; now 30. Then as now [there were] 2 slaves [and] 4 acres of meadow. [There was] then woodland for 50 pigs; now 30. [There is] now 1 mill, pasture for 300 sheep. [There were] then 2 horses and 6 head of cattle, 30 pigs, 300 sheep. [There are] now 2 horses and 2 colts and 33 head of cattle, 40 pigs, 136 sheep. It was then worth £6; now 10. Of this manor

Swein of Essex

Geoffrey holds half a hide and 1 bordar and 1 plough and it is worth 20s. in the above valuation.

Swein holds [Great and Little] Wakering in demesne as 1 manor and as 5½ hides. Then as now [there were] 2 villans and 18 bordars and 2 ploughs in demesne and [there] could be a third. The men [had] then 3 ploughs; now 5. [There is] woodland for 40 pigs, pasture for 300 sheep. [There were] then 4 horses, 9 head of cattle, 38 pigs, 115 sheep. [There are] now 4 horses, 2 head of cattle, 110 sheep, 27 pigs. It was then worth £9; now 10. of this manor, Warner and W. hold 1 hide and 2 ploughs and it is worth 30s. in the above valuation.

Swein holds Prittlewell in demesne as $7\frac{1}{2}$ hides. [There were] then 7 villans; now 4. [There were] then 14 bordars; now 23. [There were] then 2 ploughs in demesne; now 3. The men [had] then 7 ploughs; now 9. [There is] pasture for 12 pigs, pasture for 200 sheep. [There were] then 2 horses, 8 head of cattle, 30 pigs, 100 sheep. [There is] now 1 horse, 3 colts, 13 head of cattle, 65 pigs, 200 sheep less 4, 66 goats, 9 hives of bees. Of this land, 1 free man holds 1 virgate, which he could sell, but the soke belonged to this manor. And to the church of this manor 2 men added 30 acres of another land. Then as now it was worth £12. Of this manor Grapinel holds half a hide and 2 bordars and 1 plough and it is worth 10s. in the above valuation.

Robert fitzWymarc held [North and South] Shoebury after the death of King Edward. Now Swein [holds it] in demesne as 1 manor and as 5 hides. Then as now [there were] 9 villans. [There were] then 4 bordars; now 6. Then as now [there were] 2 ploughs in demesne and the men [had] 8 ploughs. [There are] 3 acres of meadow. [There is] woodland for 20 pigs. [There were] then 2 horses, 4 head of cattle, 12 pigs, 100 sheep. [There are] now 2 horses, 16 pigs, 64 sheep. Then and later it was worth £6; now 10.

Swein holds Canewdon in demesne as $6\frac{1}{2}$ hides and 30 acres. [There were] then 22 villans; now 16. [There were] then 2 bordars; now 8. [There were] then 3 slaves; now 1. [There were] then 2 ploughs in demesne; now 3 and [there] could be a fourth. The men [had] then 10 ploughs; now 6. [There is] pasture for 600 sheep. [There were] then 4 horses, 10 head of cattle, 24 pigs, 336 sheep. [There are] now 3 horses and 5 head of cattle,

20 pigs, 342 sheep. It was then worth £12; now 13. In this manor Hugh de Montfort has 1 hide and it is worth 20s. Of this manor 2 Frenchmen hold [as follows]: Gerald 1 hide and John 30 acres, and [there are] 3 bordars and 1 plough and it is worth 40s. in the above valuation. S[wein] has also [here] 1 hide and 4 bordars and 1 plough, which 1 free man held TRE with soke. It is worth 20s.

Odo holds [Little] Thorpe of S[wein], which Godric, a thegn of King Edward, held, and Robert fitzWymarc had [it] after the death of King Edward as 1 manor and as 1 hide and 30 acres. [There was] then 1 villan; now 2. [There were] then 4 bordars; now 6. [There were] then 4 slaves; now 1. Then as now [there were] 2 ploughs in demesne and the men [had] 1 plough. [There is] pasture for 100 sheep. [There was] then 1 horse and 7 head of cattle, 19 pigs, 60 sheep; now 6 head of cattle, 34 pigs, 160 sheep, 2 hives of bees. It was then worth 40s.; later and now 60.

Alvred holds Rochford of S[wein], which 1 free man held TRE as a manor and as $2\frac{1}{2}$ hides. Then as now [there were] 5 villans. [There were] then 4 bordars; now 12. [There were] then 2 slaves; now 3. [There were] then 2 ploughs in demesne; now 3. The men [had] then 3 ploughs; now 4. And 1 free man holds 30 acres and [there] also belongs to this manor 2 acres of meadow. [There is] woodland for 20 pigs, 1 mill. [There was] then 1 horse and 8 pigs and 11 sheep. [There are] now 3 horses

and 2 colts and 10 head of cattle and 21 pigs and 160 sheep and 23 sheep. It was then worth 100s.; now £7.

Wiard holds [Great and Little] Stambridge of S[wein], which 1 free man held TRE as 1 manor and as $1\frac{1}{2}$ hides and $7\frac{1}{2}$ acres. Then as now [there were] 2 bordars and 1 slave and [there was] then half a plough; now 1. [There is] pasture for 100 sheep. It was then worth 10s.; now 25.

Walter holds [North and South] Shoebury of S[wein], which 1 free man held TRE as 1 manor and as 4 hides. Then as now [there were] 4 villans. [There were] then 6 bordars; now 8. [There were] then 2 slaves; now none. [There were] then 2 ploughs in demesne; now 3. Then as now the men [had] 2 ploughs. [There is] woodland for 12 pigs. One free man holds the fourth hide of these [4 hides]. [There is] pasture for 100 sheep.

Swein of Essex

[There was] then 1 horse and 2 head of cattle and 40 sheep. [There is] now 1 horse and 6 head of cattle, 1 pig, 115 sheep. Then and later it was worth £6; now 8.

S[wein] holds [Great and Little] Wakering, which 1 free man held TRE as a manor and as 2 hides and Robert fitzWymarc held this after the death of King Edward. [There was] then 1 bordar and 15 slaves; now [there are] 10 bordars. Then as now [there were] 2 ploughs in demesne and the men [had] 1 plough. [There is] pasture for 300 sheep. [There were] then 2 head of cattle and 100 sheep. [There is] now 1 horse and 2 head of cattle, 115 sheep, 1 hive of bees. It was then worth £3; later and now 4. Of this same manor, Robert holds 1 hide and Godric [holds] half [a hide], and [this] is worth 40s. in the above valuation.

Ascelin holds Sutton of S[wein], which 2 free men held TRE as a manor and as $1\frac{1}{2}$ hides and 30 acres. [There are] now 8 bordars. [There were] then 4 slaves; now none. Then as now [there were] 2 ploughs in demesne and the men [had] half a plough. [There is] pasture for 300 sheep. [There were] then 2 horses and 40 pigs, 200 sheep. [There are] now 7 head of cattle, 160 sheep. Then and later it was worth 60s.; now £4.

The same A[scelin] holds Plumberow of S[wein], which Robert fitzWymarc held as a manor and as 1 hide. [There was] then 1 bordar and 1 slave; now [there are] 8 bordars. [There were] then $1\frac{1}{2}$ ploughs in demesne; now 1. The men [have] half a plough. [There is] woodland for 30 pigs, pasture for 100 sheep. [There is] now 1 mill. [There was] then 1 horse, 7 head of cattle, 30 pigs, 100 sheep, 40 goats. [There are] now 2 horses and 1 colt, 3 head of cattle, 20 pigs, 100 sheep, 23 goats. It was then worth 20s.; now 40.

The same Ascelin holds Pudsey of S[wein], which 1 free man held TRE as a manor and 52$\frac{1}{2}$ acres. Then as now [there were] 2 bordars and 1 plough. [There is] pasture for 30 sheep. [There is] now 1 mill. [There was] then 1 horse and 1 colt and 1 cow and 3 pigs and 80 sheep; now the same. Then and later it was worth 20s.; now 30.

Pain holds Hockley of S[wein] as 1 manor and as 1 hide. Then as now [there were] 12 bordars and 1 plough in demesne. The men [had] then 2 ploughs; now 1. [There is] woodland for 30 pigs, pasture for 200 sheep. [There is] now 1 mill. [There were] then 2 horses and 2 head of cattle and 12 pigs and 160 sheep and 30 goats. [There are] now 4 horses, 10 head of cattle, 24 pigs, 300 sheep, 53 goats,

[Folio 45v: ESSEX]

6 hives of bees. It was then worth £3; now 4.

John holds Pudsey of S[wein], which 1 free man held TRE as a manor and as 1½ hides and 30 acres. Then as now [there were] 8 bordars. [There is] pasture for 50 sheep. [There was] then 1 horse and 8 pigs and 25 sheep. [There are] now 11 pigs, 86 sheep. It is worth 40s.

Ælfgyth, a certain Englishwoman, holds Sutton of S[wein], which Robert fitzWymarc held after the death of King Edward as 1 manor and as 1 hide and 15 acres. Then as now [there were] 3 bordars. [There were] then 2 slaves; now none. Then as now [there is] 1 plough in demesne. [There were] then 2 horses and 10 head of cattle and 11 pigs and 100 sheep. [There are] now 10 head of cattle, 10 pigs, 63 sheep. It is worth 30s.

Almær holds Pudsey of S[wein], which 1 sokeman of Robert [fitzWymarc] held as a manor and as half a hide and 15 acres. Then as now [there were] 3 bordars and 1 plough in demesne. [There is] pasture for 50 sheep. [There was] then 1 horse and 8 pigs and 25 sheep. [There are] now 11 pigs and 86 sheep. It is worth 30s.

Hugh holds Pudsey of S[wein], which 1 free man held TRE and Robert [fitzWymarc] had the soke, as a manor and 38 acres. [There was] then 1 villan; now 2. Then as now [there is] half a plough. [There is] pasture for 30 sheep. [There was] then 1 horse and 2 head of cattle and 10 pigs, 75 sheep. [There is] now 1 horse and 1 cow and 114 sheep. It is worth 10s.

In Ashingdon Roger holds half a hide of S[wein], which Robert [fitzWymarc] held. Then as now [there was] 1 bordar. [There is] pasture for 40 sheep. [There was] then 1 plough; now half a plough and a whole one could be employed. It is worth 10s.

In Sutton Roger holds half a hide, which Robert [fitzWymarc] held TRE. Then as now [there was] 1 plough. [There is] pasture for 40 sheep. It is worth 20s.

In Hawkwell Godfrey holds 15 acres, and [there is] half a plough and 1 bordar. It is worth 10s.

In Eastwood [...] Robert holds 30 acres of S[wein]and [there are] 5 bordars. [There was] then half a plough; now 1. It was then worth 10s.; now 20. And in the aforesaid Hundred Swein has 100s. from the pleas.

HUNDRED OF DENGIE.

Ralph holds Iltney of Swein,

Swein of Essex

[Folio 46: ESSEX]

which Leofstan held freely as a manor and as half a hide and 40 acres. Then as now [there was] 1 villan and 1 bordar. [There were] then 2 slaves; now 1. Then as now [there was] 1 plough in demesne and the men [had] half a plough. [There is] pasture for 50 sheep. [There were] then 5 head of cattle and 40

sheep. [There are] now 5 head of cattle and 60 sheep and 26 pigs and 2 horses. Then and later it is worth 20s.; now 26.

Warner holds Asheldham of S[wein], which Godric held freely TRE as a manor and as half a hide and 37 acres. [There were] then 3 bordars; now 2. Then as now [there was] 1 plough. [There are] 5 acres of meadow. [There was] then nothing; now 3 head of cattle, 4 pigs, 11 goats. It is worth 20s. R[obert] fitzWymarc held this manor after the arrival of King William.

HUNDRED OF WITHAM.

Clarenbold holds Rivenhall of S[wein], which Leofstan, a free man, held as 30 acres TRE. Then as now [there was] 1 plough in demesne and the men [had] half a plough. [There were] then 5 bordars; now 6. Then as now [there were] 2 slaves. [There are] 10 acres of meadow. [There is] pasture worth 4s. and 1 sokeman with 5 acres. [There were] then 2 head of cattle and 2 horses and 15 sheep. [There are] now 2 head of cattle, 2 horses, 100 sheep, 6 pigs, 8 goats, 2 hives of bees. It was then worth 40s.; now 30.

Godbald holds [Black and White] Notley as half a hide and 30 acres, which Aki, a free man, held TRE as 1 manor. [There were] then 2 ploughs in demesne; now 1. The men [had] then 2 ploughs; now 1. [There were] then 4 villans; now 2. [There were] then 4 bordars; now 5. [There were] then 2 slaves; now none. [There was] then woodland for 40 pigs; now 30. [There are] 10 acres of meadow. [There was] then 1 horse and 2 cows. [There are] now 2 horses and 8 head of cattle, 30 pigs, 11 sheep, 10 hives of bees. It was then worth 40s.; now 60.

HUNDRED OF HARLOW.

Walter holds [Great and Little] Hallingbury of S[wein], which Godric, a free man, held as 1 manor and as 2½ hides. Then as now [there were] 2 ploughs in demesne. The men [had] then 3 ploughs; now 4. [There were] then 8 villans; now 10. [There are] now 17 bordars. [There were] then 4 slaves. [There was] then woodland for 150 pigs; now 100. [There are] 30 acres of meadow. [There is] now half a mill. [There were] then 2 horses and 6 head of cattle and 24 pigs, 30 sheep, 30 goats. [There are] now 2 colts and 7 head of cattle and 13 pigs, 50 sheep, 32 goats, 7 hives of bees.

[Folio 46v: ESSEX]

It was then worth 100s.; now £6.

HUNDRED OF DUNMOW.

Warner holds Willingale [Doe and Spain] of Swein, which 1 free man held TRE as 20 acres. It was then worth 4s.; now 8.

Eadmær holds [Great and Little] Dunmow of S[wein], which 1 free man held TRE as 37 acres, and of which 7 acres were added after the arrival of King William, which [belonged] to a certain other free man. [There was] then half a plough; now 1. [There were] then 2 bordars; now 3. Then as now [there was] 1 slave. [There is] woodland for 30 pigs. [There are] 5 acres of meadow. [There is] now 1 mill. [There were] then 4 head of cattle, 9 pigs, 11 sheep, 5 goats. [There are] now 5 head of cattle, 8 pigs, 13 sheep, 7 goats. It was then worth 10s.; now 20.

HUNDRED OF WINSTREE.

Swein holds [East and West] Mersea in demesne, which Robert fitzWymarc held TRE as a manor and as 6 hides. Then as now [there were] 2 ploughs in demesne. [The men had] then 8 ploughs; now 6. [There were] then 9 villans; now 8. [There were] then 12 bordars; now 14. [There were] then 3 slaves; now none. [There was] then woodland for 40 pigs. [There are] 5 acres of meadow, 4 fisheries. [There was] then 1 horse, 9 head of cattle, 25 pigs, 107 sheep. [There are] now 3 horses, 12 head of cattle, 10 pigs, 100 sheep, 1 hive of bees. It is worth £10.

Odo holds Peldon of Swein, which 1 free man held TRE as a manor and as half a hide. Then as now [there was] half a plough. It is worth 10s.

The same holds Abberton as 15 acres, which 1 free man held TRE. [There was] then 1 free man. [There is] now 1 bordar. [There are] 5 acres of meadow. It is worth 5s.

THE HALF-HUNDRED OF CLAVERING

belongs to Swein, and the pleas of this Hundred render to him 25s. a year.

HALF-HUNDRED OF CLAVERING.

Swein holds Clavering in demesne, which Robert fitzWymarc held TRE as 1 manor and as 15 hides. Then and later [there were] 4 ploughs in demesne; now 5. Then as now the men [had] 25 ploughs and [there were] 17 villans. Then and later [there were] 9 bordars; now 37. Then and later [there were] 8 slaves; now 12.

Swein of Essex

[There was] then woodland for 800 pigs; now 600. [There are] 35 acres of meadow. [There was] then 1 mill and 1 plough [more] could be restored in this manor. [There were] then 3 horses and 25 head of cattle, 50 pigs, 40 sheep, 15 goats, 12 hives of bees. [There are] now 2 horses and 1 colt, 14 head of cattle, 21 pigs, 90 sheep, 23 goats, 5 hives of bees. It was then worth £20; now 30.

Godmann, a sokeman of Robert [fitzWymarc], held Berden TRE. Now Alvred holds [it] of S[wein] as a manor and as 2 hides. Then as now [there was] 1 plough in demesne and the men [had] 2 ploughs and [there were] 4 villans and 5 bordars. Then and later [there were] 4 slaves; now none. [There is] woodland for 10 pigs. [There are] 2 acres of meadow. [There were] then 14 pigs and 25 sheep. [There are] now 3 horses and 2 colts and 13 head of cattle and 21 pigs, 122 sheep, 8 goats, 1 hive of bees. It was then worth 30s.; now 40.

HUNDRED OF DENGIE.

Ralph holds Asheldham of S[wein] as a manor and as half a hide and 37 acres, which 1 free man held TRE. Then as now [there was] 1 plough. [There were] then 3 bordars; now 2. [There are] 5 acres of meadow. It is worth 20s. Robert fitzWymarc had this land after the arrival of King William.

Of the abovesaid manor, namely Clavering, Ansgot holds

half a hide and 30 acres of Swein, and Wiard [holds] 3 virgates, and Robert [holds] half a hide and 15 acres, and Ralph [holds] 15 acres. And among them all [there are] 14 bordars and 3½ ploughs, and the whole is worth £4 in the above valuation.

HUNDRED OF LEXDEN.

R[obert fitzWymarc] held Nayland as 1 manor and as 5½ hides. Now S[wein] holds [it] in demesne. Then as now [there were] 18 villans. [There were] then 33 bordars; now 42. Then as now [there were] 7 slaves and 2 ploughs in demesne and the men [had] 10 ploughs. [There is] woodland for 600 pigs. [There are] 24 acres of meadow. Then as now [there was] 1 mill. It was then worth £10; now 12. Of this manor, Godbald holds of Swein 1½ hides and 30 acres and [there are] 2 villans and 8 bordars and 2 ploughs in demesne and the men [have] 2 ploughs. It is worth 60s. in the above valuation. The same holds also 37 free men dwelling on 3 hides of land, whom Robert had TRE and Swein later. [There were] then among them 4 [ploughs]:

now 5. [There is] now 1 mill. [There is] woodland for 60 pigs. [There are] 14 acres of meadow. It was then worth £4; now 100s. and a certain free man [who] was commended to Robert held 7½ acres and he could go where he would. And Swein has that land. It is worth 5s.

HUNDRED OF CHELMSFORD.

Osbern held Boreham of Swein, which Thorkil held as 1 manor and as 1 hide. Then as now [there was] 1 bordar. [There is] now 1 slave. [There was] then 1 plough; now none. [There are] 8 acres of meadow. It is worth 20s.

HUNDRED OF ONGAR.

Sigeric holds Stapleford [Tawney] of Swein, which Godric held as 1 manor and as 5 hides, and of which 5 hides he gave to his 10 free men freely 4 hides and retained 1 in demesne. And after the king arrived, Robert held [the] 1 hide of the king's gift and Swein his son added the 4 hides to it after the death of his father. In the 1 hide then [there] were no bordars and in the 4 hides then [there were] 6 bordars. [There are] now 2 villans and 18 bordars. [There is] woodland for 300 pigs. [There are] 20 acres of meadow. Then as now [there was] 1 mill. It was then worth £8; now 10. In demesne [there was] then 1 cow and 13 sheep. [There are] now 8 head of cattle and 17 pigs, 118 sheep, 2 hives of bees.

Robert holds Theydon of S[wein], which Godric held as 1 manor and as 3 hides and 80 acres, and S[wein] holds this manor of the gift of King William, which he gave to his father Robert. [There were] then 5 villans; now 1. [There were] then 3 bordars; now 17. [There were] then 4 slaves; now none. [There were] then 2 ploughs in demesne; now 3. Among the men [there were] then 4 ploughs; now 3. [There is] woodland for 500 pigs. [There are] 28 acres of meadow. [There was] then 1 horse and 12 head of cattle, 60 pigs, 100 sheep. [There are] now 3 horses, 3 colts, 13 head of cattle, 39 pigs, 148 sheep. It was then worth £6, and when received the same; now it is worth 9.

HUNDRED OF CHAFFORD.

Godric held [Great and Little] Warley freely as 1 manor and as 2 hides TRE. Now S[wein holds] similarly in his demesne. [There were]then 2 villans; now 3. [There were] then 2 bordars; now 8. [There were] then 3 slaves; now 1. Then as now [there were] 2 ploughs in demesne. Among the men [there was] then 1 plough; now 2½. [There is] woodland for 150 pigs. [There are] 3 acres of meadow. [There were] then 2 horses and 7 head of cattle and 17 pigs.

Swein of Essex

[Folio 48: ESSEX]

It was then worth [...] £4, and when received the same; now £6.

Leofwine holds Kenningtons of S[wein], which Wulfstan held freely as a manor and as 1 hide TRE. [There were] then 3 bordars; now 4. And [there is] 1 plough, 1 cow and 2 head of cattle, 16 pigs, 30 sheep. It is worth 20s.

HALF-HUNDRED OF MALDON.

In Maldon Robert [fitzWymarc] held half a hide. Now S[wein] holds [it], and Gunnar of him. And in this land the king has 4s. of customary dues and [these] provide aid with the other burgesses to find a horse for the host and in building a ship, but Swein has the other customary dues. Then as now [there was] 1 bordar and 1 plough and it is worth 20s.

HUNDRED OF TENDRING.

Robert fitzWymarc held Elmstead. Now Swein [holds it] and Sigeric of him, as 1 manor and as 8 hides. Then as now [there were] 14 villans; now 13. [There were] then 31 bordars; now 36. [There were] then 6 slaves; now 1. [There were] then in demesne 3 ploughs; now 4. The men [had] then 19 ploughs; now 18. [There is] woodland for 500 pigs. [There are] 22 acres of meadow. [There is] pasture for 60 sheep. Then as now [there was] 1 mill and 1 salt-pan. [There were] then 3 horses and 18 head of cattle and 30 pigs, 150 sheep, 40 goats, 5 hives of bees. [There are] now 5 horses, 10 head of cattle, 32 pigs, 190 sheep, 80 goats, 2 hives of bees. It was then worth £9; now 10.

Odard holds Foulton of S[wein], which Beorhtsige held as 1 hide less 10 acres and as 1 manor. [Beorhtsige] held this land freely, and when the king came into this land he was outlawed and R[obert fitzWymarc] received his land. Later S[wein] had [it]. Then as now there is 1 bordar and 1 slave and 1 plough and 2 acres of meadow. [There is] pasture for 100 sheep. He received nothing then; now [there are] 6 head of cattle and 10 pigs and 20 sheep and 2 hives of bees. It was then worth 10s.; now 20.

HUNDRED OF THURSTABLE.

Odo holds Tolleshunt of Swein, which Brun held as a manor and as 1½ hides and 40 acres, but Robert had [it]

[Folio 48v: ESSEX]

after the king came into this land, and now S[wein] has [it]. There are now [...] 4 bordars. [There were] then 2 slaves; now

1. [There is] woodland for 12 pigs, pasture for 20 sheep. [There were] then 2 head of cattle and 1 horse and 20 sheep. [There are] now 12 head of cattle, 2 horses, 12 pigs, 80 sheep. It was then worth 20s.; now 25.

Gunnar held [Great and Little] Totham TRE and he still holds [it] under Swein as 30 acres. Then as now [there were] 3 bordars. [There was] then half a plough; now the same. [There is] woodland for 20 pigs, pasture for 60 sheep. It is worth 10s.

[Folio 49: ESSEX]

XXV. Land of Eudo the Steward

HUNDRED OF WITHAM.

Richard holds [Great and Little] Braxted of E[udo], which a thegn of the king held as 1 manor and as 2 hides less 15 acres. Then as now [there were] 2 ploughs in demesne and the men [had] 3 ploughs. [There were] then 5 villans; now 6. [There were] then 4 bordars; now 6. [There were] then 2 slaves; now none. [There is] woodland for 300 pigs. [There are] 30 acres of meadow. [There is] now half a mill [and] 1 sokeman with 4 acres. [There were] then 2 horses and 14 head of cattle, 40 pigs, 80 sheep. [There is] now 1 horse, 6 head of cattle, 46 pigs, 110 sheep, 4 hives of bees. It is worth £8.

HALF-HUNDRED OF HARLOW.

Turgis holds Harlow of Eudo, which Godwine, a free man, held TRE as a manor and as 1 hide and 3 virgates. [There were] then 2 ploughs in demesne; now 1. The men [had] then 1 plough; now none. [There were] then 3 villans; now none. [There are] now 2 bordars. [There were] then 2 slaves; now 1. [There is] woodland for 50 pigs. [There are] 10 acres of meadow. [There was] then 1 cow and 30 sheep. [There are] now 18 head of cattle, 4 horses, 19 pigs, 75 [...], 2 hives of bees. Of this land [there] are 50 acres, which were added TRW and Lisois added them to this land. Then as now it was worth 40s.

HUNDRED OF DUNMOW.

Turgis holds Roding of Eudo, which Sæmær, a free man, held TRE as 1½ hides and 45 acres. Then as now [there were] 2 ploughs in demesne. The men [had] then 2 ploughs; now 1. [There were] then 9 villans; now 3. [There was] then 1 bordar; now 3. [There were] then 3 slaves; now 1. [There is] woodland for 100 pigs. [There are] 19 acres of meadow. [There was] then 1 horse; now 7. [There were] then 10 head of cattle; now 25. [There were] then 6 pigs; now 89. [There were] then 50 sheep; now 225. [There are] now 55 goats and 8 hives of bees. It was then worth 100s.; now 6. The Abbot of Ely claims this manor, [as] the Hundred attests.

Eudo holds Lindsell in demesne, which Wulfmær, a free man, held TRE as 1 manor and as 1 hide. Then as now [there were] 2 ploughs in demesne and the men [had] 3 ploughs and [there were] 9 villans and 1 priest. [There was] then 1 bordar; now 9. [There were] then 4 slaves; now 1. [There is] woodland for 30 pigs. [There are] 6 acres of meadow. [There is] now 1 mill. [There was] then 1 horse and 5 head of cattle and 60 pigs. [There is] now 1 horse and

[Folio 49v: ESSEX]

it was then worth 100s.; now £6. And this manor was [worth the same] when [he] received [it].

HUNDRED OF DENGIE.

Godwine, a thegn of the king, held Mundon as 1 manor and as 10 hides. Now Eudo holds [it] in demesne. [There were] then 10 villans; now 15. [There were] then 8 bordars; now 14. [There were] then 9 slaves; now 7. And [there were] 2 Frenchmen holding half a hide, which Lisois appropriated, because one of them was outlawed. In this manor [there] are 4 ploughs in demesne. The men [had] then 8 ploughs; now 10, and [there are] 2 arpents of vineyard. [There is] woodland for 24 pigs, pasture for 200 sheep. [There were] then 4 horses and 8 head of cattle, 40 pigs, 250 [...]. [There are] now 4 horses and 15 head of cattle and 65 pigs, 354 sheep, 4 hives of bees. It was then worth £10; now 17. To this manor belong 30 acres. They were worth 30d.; now 36. There also belong 20 acres of "Wringehala", which 1 sokeman holds. They were then worth 20d.; now 3s.

Richard holds Lawling of E[udo], which Wulfric Cave held as a manor and as 3½ hides TRE. [There were] then 4 slaves; now 3. [There is] now 1 bordar. [There were] then 2 ploughs in demesne; now 1. [There was] then 1 horse; now none. [There were] then 87 sheep; now 63. It was then worth 60s.; when received 40s. [and] now £4.

The same R[ichard] holds Steeple of E[udo], which Northmann held TRE as a manor and as 3 hides and 35 acres. Then as now [there was] 1 bordar and 2 slaves and 2 ploughs. [There is] woodland for 10 pigs. [There were] then 6 head of cattle; now 27. Then as now [there was] 1 horse and 15 pigs. [There were] then 120 sheep; now 160. It is worth £4.

The same R[ichard] holds Down of E[udo], which Moding held TRE as a manor and as 2 hides and 20 acres. Then as now [there were] 2 bordars and 2 slaves and 1 plough. [There is] pasture for 100 sheep. [There was] then 1 horse; now 3. [There are] now 3 head of cattle. [There were] then 120 sheep; now 160 less 1. It is worth 60s.

The same R[ichard] holds "Landuna" of E[udo], which 4 free men held TRE as half a hide and 20 acres. Then as now [there was] half a plough. It is worth 10s. The same holds "Acleta" of E[udo], which Moding held as a manor and as 1½ [hides] and 10 acres. Then as now [there was] 1 bordar and 1 plough.

Eudo the Steward

[Folio 50: ESSEX]

[There is] pasture for 100 sheep. Then as now [there were] 2 head of cattle and 80 sheep and 9 pigs. Then and later it was worth 40s.; now 50.

HUNDRED OF ROCHFORD.

Pirot holds Hawkwell of Eudo, which Wulfmær held TRE as a manor and as 3½ hides less 15 acres. [There were] then 11 villans; now 8. Then as now [there were] 5 bordars. [There were] then 2 slaves; now 3. Then as now [there were] 2 ploughs in demesne. The men [had] then 6 ploughs; now 5.

[There are] 4 acres of meadow. [There is] woodland for 10 pigs. [There were] then 2 horses and 5 head of cattle, 102 sheep, 20 pigs. [There are] now 16 head of cattle, 106 sheep, 20 pigs, 2 hives of bees. Then and later it was worth £6; now 7.

In the abovesaid Hundred of [Great and Little] Dunmow Richard holds of Eudo 1 manor with 9 acres, which is called Broxted [and] which 2 sokemen held TRE of the abbot of Ely. [There were] then 3 ploughs in demesne; now 2½. The men [have] now 1 plough and 2 villans. [There were] then 3 bordars; now 5. [There were] then 3 slaves; now 1. [There is] woodland for 100 pigs. [There are] 6 acres of meadow. [There was] then 1 horse and 3 head of cattle and 16 pigs. [There are] now 5 head of cattle, 33 pigs. Then and later it was worth 60s.; now £4.

Eudo holds Shellow [Bowells] in demesne, which Wulfmær, a free man, held TRE as a manor and as half a hide. Then as now [there was] half a plough in demesne. [There are] now 2 bordars. [There is] woodland for 16 pigs. [There are] 4 acres of meadow. Then as now it was worth 10s.

Ralph holds Dunmow of E[udo], which 1 free man held TRE as a manor and as 37½ acres. Then as now [there was] half a plough in demesne and the men [had] half a plough and [there were] 2 villans. [There are] now 2 bordars. [There was] then 1 slave; now none. [There is] woodland for 15 pigs. [There are] 4 acres of meadow. Then and later it was worth 10s.; now 20. And in the same vill [are] another 30 ½ acres, which another free man held, in which there is the same as in the others, and they are worth the same amount.

HUNDRED OF UTTLESFORD.

E[udo] holds Takeley in demesne, which Wulfmær, a free man, held TRE as a manor and as 1 hide and 15 acres. Then as now [there were] 2 ploughs in demesne and the men [had] 2 ploughs. [There were] then 3 villans; now 5 and [there is] 1 priest. [There were] then 3 bordars; later and now 10. Then as now [there were] 2 slaves. [There was] then woodland for 1,000 pigs; later and now 600. [There are] 16 acres of meadow. [There was] then 1 horse and 14 head of cattle, 30 pigs, 30 goats, 80 sheep. [There are] now 2 horses, 20 head of cattle, 43 pigs, 103 sheep,

[Folio 50v: ESSEX]

40 goats. Then and later it was worth £8; now 10.

HUNDRED OF CLAVERING.

Richard holds Pledgdon of E[udo], which 2 free men held TRE as a manor and as 5 hides less 20 acres. [There were] then 4 ploughs in demesne; later and now 2. Then and later the men [had] 1 plough; now 3. Then and later [there were] 2 villans; now 6. Then and later [there were] 2 bordars; now 16. Then and later [there were] 2 slaves; now none. [There is] woodland for 20 pigs. [There are] 20 acres of meadow. [There were] then 2 horses; now none. [There were] then 2 head of cattle. [There are] now 66 pigs. [There were] then 300 sheep; now 200. [There are] 6 hives of bees. Then and later it was worth 100s.; now £8. Of this land, G[eoffrey] de Mandeville claims 20 hides less 20 acres and the Hundred testifies to this.

HUNDRED OF LEXDEN.

Arthur holds Boxted of E[udo], which Grim held as a manor and as 1 hide. [There was] then 1 villan; now none. [There were] then 2 bordars; now 9. Then as now [there was] 1 plough in demesne. The men [had] then 2 ploughs; now 1. [There is] woodland for 42 pigs. [There are] 2 acres of meadow. [There were] then 6 head of cattle; now 4. [There were] then 30 sheep; now 64. [There were] then 10 pigs; now 13. [There are] now 13 goats and 1 hive of bees. It was then worth 20s.; now 40. And a certain free [man] held [there] 5 acres; now the same Arthur holds [it] of E[udo]. Then as now [there was] half a plough. It is worth 5s.

HUNDRED OF ONGAR.

Eudo holds Theydon in demesne, which Wulfmær held as 1 hide and 40 acres TRE. [There were] then 4 villans; now 6. [There were] then 2 bordars; now 4. [There were] then 4 slaves; now 1. Then as now [there were] 2 ploughs in demesne and the men [had] 2 ploughs. [There is] woodland for 400 pigs. [There are] 5 acres of meadow. Then as now [there were] 2 horses. [There were] then 8 head of cattle; now 13. [There were] then 35 pigs; now 66. [There were] then 87 sheep; now 100 and [there are] 15 goats. [There were] then 2 hives of bees; now 6. Then and later it was worth 40s.; now £4. And 1 sokeman held 6 acres, who could sell his land, but the soke remained in the manor. [This] is worth 12d.

Eudo holds Roding, in demesne, which Wulfmær held as a manor and as 3 hides TRE. Then as now [there were] 7 villans. [There are] now 2 bordars. Then as now [there were] 4 slaves and 2 ploughs in demesne and the men [had] 3 ploughs. [There is] woodland for 20 pigs. [There are] 20 acres of meadow. [There was] then 1 horse; now 3. [There were] then 10 head of cattle; now 14. [There were] then 40 pigs; now 60. [There were] then 100 sheep; now 131. And [there is] 1 sokeman who could

Eudo the Steward

sell his land, but the soke remained in the manor, holding half a virgate and 8½ acres. Then and later [there was] 1 plough; now half a plough. Then as now [there was] 1 slave. Then and later the whole was worth £8; now 12.

HUNDRED OF CHELMSFORD.

Richard holds Rettendon of E[udo], which Leofsunu held as a manor and as 2 hides and 30 acres TRE, and the Abbey of Ely claims this land and the Hundred bears witness [to this]. Then as now [there were] 4 bordars and 2 slaves and 1 plough in demesne and the men [had] 1 plough. [There were] then 2 horses; now 4. [There were] then 4 head of cattle; now 7. [There were] then 10 pigs; now 33. [There were] then 80 sheep; now 100 less 3. It was then worth 40s.; now 70.

Richard holds [Great and Little] Leighs of E[udo], which Eadric held as a manor and as 2 hides. Then as now [there were] 3 villans. [There were] then 2 bordars; now 9. [There were] then 7 slaves; now 2. [There were] then in demesne 2 ploughs; now 1½. [There is] woodland for 800 pigs. [There

are] 16 acres of meadow. [There is] now 1 mill. [There were] then 3 horses; now 1. [There were] then 10 head of cattle; now 9. [There were] then 40 pigs; now 35. [There were] then 50 sheep; now 63. And [there are] 11 goats. It was then worth 60s.; now £4.

HUNDRED OF TENDRING.

Godwine held Weeley as a manor and as 3 hides and 38 acres. Now E[udo] holds [it] in demesne. [There were] then 13 villans; now 11. [There were] then 4 bordars; now 9. [There were] then 8 slaves; now 4. [There is] woodland for 200 pigs. [There are] 6 acres of meadow. [There is] pasture for 100 sheep, and 2 sokemen, who belonged to this manor, held 2 hides and 45 acres. Then as now [there were] 5 bordars and 2 ploughs. [There is] woodland for 30 pigs. [There are] 3 acres of meadow. [There is] pasture for 60 sheep. [There were] then in demesne 15 head of cattle; now 16. [There were] then 60 pigs; now 30. Then as now [there were] 240 sheep. [There were] then 5 hives of bees; now 2. The whole together was then worth £8; now £19 and 1 ounce of gold.

HUNDRED OF UTTLESFORD.

Richard holds Quendon of E[udo], which Ealdræd held as a manor and as 2 hides. [There were] then 6 villans; later and now 3. [There are] now 4 bordars. Then as now [there were] 3 slaves and 2 ploughs in demesne and among the men [there were] then 3 ploughs; now 2. [There is] woodland for 40 pigs. [There are] 6 acres of meadow. [There were] then [...] horses; now 5. [There were] then 6 head of cattle; now 9. [There were] then 32 pigs; now 50. [There were] then 80 sheep; now 200. [There are] now 44 goats. [There were] then 4 hives of bees; now 17. It was then worth

£8; now 6.

HALF-HUNDRED OF FRESHWELL.

In Radwinter Richard holds 15 acres, which Ælfric Wand held. Then as now [there was] 1 villan and 1 bordar and 1 slave and 1 plough. [There are] 5 acres of meadow. [There were] then 5 head of cattle; now 8. [There are] now 2 horses. [There were] then 5 sheep and 3 pigs; now none. It was then worth 10s.; now 30.

HUNDRED OF ROCHFORD.

E[udo] holds Hawkwell in demesne, which Wulfmær, a free man, held as a manor and as 3½ hides less 15 acres TRE. [There were] then 11 villans; now 8. Then as now [there were] 5 bordars. [There were] then 2 slaves; now 3. Then as now [there were] 2 ploughs in demesne. The men [had] then 6 ploughs; now 5. [There are] 4 acres of meadow. [There is] woodland for 10 pigs. [There were] then 2 horses; now 6. [There were] then 5 head of cattle; now 16. [There were] then 102 sheep; now 106. Then as now [there were] 20 pigs. [There are] now 2 hives of bees. It was then worth £6; now 7.

HUNDRED OF UTTLESFORD.

E[udo] holds Arkesden in demesne, which Ælfric Wand held as a manor and as 2 hides less 15 acres. Then as now [there were] 2 villans and 7 bordars and 2 slaves. Then and later [there were] 2 ploughs in demesne; now 1. Then as now the men [had] 2 ploughs. [There is] woodland for 20 pigs. [There are] 10 acres of meadow. It is worth 100s.

[Folio 52: ESSEX]

XXVI. Land of Roger d'Auberville.

HUNDRED OF HARLOW.

Two free men held [Great and Little] Hallingbury TRE as a manor and as 3 hides and 38 acres. [There were] then 6 ploughs in demesne; now 3. The men [had] then 10½ ploughs; now 2½. [There were] 18 villans; now 8. [There were] then 4 bordars; now 5. [There was] then 1 slave; now none. [There is] woodland for 600 pigs. [There are] 25 acres of meadow. [There is] pasture [worth] 28d., 1 mill and 9 ploughs [more] could be restored. And 1 of these manors was worth TRE £8 and when received 100s.; now £4. And the other was then worth 60s.; now 40. In demesne Roger [took over] 1 horse and 3 head of cattle and 30 sheep and 40 pigs. [There is] now 1 horse and 8 head of cattle and 80 pigs and 120 sheep and 3 hives of bees.

HUNDRED OF DUNMOW.

Thorkil, a free man, held Roding, TRE as a manor and as 2 hides. In demesne [there were] then [... ploughs]; now 1½. [There were] then 3 villans. [There is] now 1 priest and 2 villans. [There were] then 2 bordars; now 5. [There were] then 4 slaves; now 3, having 1 plough. [There is] woodland for 30 pigs. [There are] 24 acres of meadow. It was then worth £6; now 100s., and when received [it], he found there only the land [itself] and 1 plough.

HUNDRED OF UTTLESFORD.

Leofwine held Arkesden freely as a manor and as 1 hide, and Roger [holds it by] exchange. [There were] then 2 villans; later and now 1. Then as now [there were] 3 bordars. [There was] then 1 plough in demesne, [and] when received none; now 1. Then and later the men [had] 1 plough; now none. [There are] 7 acres of meadow. [There is] woodland for 10 pigs. [There was] then 1 cow and 19 sheep. [There is] now 1 colt, 14 pigs, 90 sheep. It was then worth 40s.; now 50.

In the same vill Ulf held 1 hide freely TRE and Roger [holds it] by exchange. [There were] then 2 villans; later and now 1. Then as now [there were] 3 bordars. [There was] then 1 plough in demesne, and when received none; now 1. Then and later the men [had] 1 plough; now none. [There are] 7 acres of meadow. [There is] woodland for 10 pigs. It was then worth 40s.; now 50.

[Folio 52v: ESSEX]

Eadric held [Great and Little] Chishill as a manor and as 3½ hides. [There were] then 8 villans; later and now 6. Then as now [there were] 2 bordars. [There were] then 2 slaves; now 1.

Then and later [there were] 2 ploughs in demesne; now 1. Then and later the men [had] 3 ploughs; now 2. [There is] woodland for 40 pigs. [There are] 6 acres of meadow. [There was] then 1 horse and 2 pigs and 213 sheep. [There are] now 2 horses and 1 cow, 32 pigs, 200 sheep. Then and now it was worth £4.

XXVII. Land of Hugh de Montfort.

HUNDRED OF BARSTABLE.

Osbern holds Ramsden [Bellhouse and Crays], of Hugh, which 3 free men held TRE as a manor and as 2 hides and 40 acres. Then as now [there was] 1 plough in demesne. The men [had] then half a plough; now 1. [There were] then 3 bordars; now 5. [There was] then 1 slave; now none. [There is] woodland for 60 pigs. [There are] 3 acres of meadow. [There were] then 2 head of cattle and 3 pigs and 60 sheep. [There is] now 1 horse and 2 head of cattle and 9 pigs and 70 sheep. It is worth 40s. In the same vill are 30 acres which belong to the church and they are worth 30d.

HUNDRED OF WITHAM.

William fitzGross holds Kelvedon of Hugh, which Guthmund, a thegn of the king, held as a manor and as 3½ hides. Then as now [there were] 2 ploughs in demesne. The men [had] then 4 ploughs; now 1. Then as now [there were] 9 villans and 3 slaves and 5 bordars. [There is] woodland for 50 pigs. [There are] 25 acres of meadow, 1 mill. [There was] then 1 horse and 4 head of cattle and 7 pigs and 40 sheep. [There are] now 2 horses, 140 sheep. It was then worth £6; now 7.

HUNDRED OF BECONTREE.

Hugh holds Leyton in demesne, which Alsige held

Hugh de Montfort

[Folio 53: ESSEX]

TRE as a manor and as 3 hides and 30 acres. [There were] then 2 ploughs in demesne; now 1. The men [had] then 1 plough; now 1½. [There were] then 6 villans. [There is] now 1 priest and 1 villan. [There were] then 4 bordars; now 3. [There were] then 2 slaves; now none. [There is] woodland for 150 pigs. [There are] 30 acres of meadow. [There were] then 60 sheep. [There are] now 4 pigs and 60 sheep. It was then worth 30s.; now 40. And one of those hides rendered customary dues TRE to Havering-atte-Bower, a manor of the king, and now does not render [them].

HUNDRED OF DENGIE.

Hugh holds Purleigh in demesne, which Guthmund, a free man, held TRE as a manor and as 4 hides. Then as now [there were] 5 villans. [There were] then 6 bordars; now 7. [There were] then 6 slaves; now 5. Then as now [there were] 2 ploughs in demesne. The men [had] then 3 ploughs; now 2, and a third could be employed. [There is] woodland for 700 pigs. Then as now [there were] 3 horses and 16 head of cattle. [There were] then 300 sheep; now 306. [There were] then 30 pigs; now 35. It was then worth £8; later and now 7.

Guthmund held Latchingdon as a manor and as $3\frac{1}{2}$ hides and 20 acres. Then as now [there were] 2 villans. [There were] then 2 bordars; now 4. [There were] then 5 slaves; now 4. Then as now [there were] 2 ploughs in demesne and the men [had] half a plough. [There is] pasture for 200 sheep, woodland for 100 pigs. It was then worth £7; later and now 100s. Of this same manor Humphrey holds 2 hides of Hugh and Wulfmær [holds] 1 hide, and they are worth 60s. in the above valuation.

In Purleigh 10 free men held 7 hides, which Hugh received as 2 manors, but the Hundred knows nothing of this. There were then in this land 4 bordars; now 8. [There was] then 1 slave; now none. [There were] then 8 ploughs; now 6. [There is] woodland for 15 pigs, pasture for 100 sheep. Then and later it was worth £6; now 100s.

Hugh holds also in Purleigh 1 manor with $1\frac{1}{2}$ hides and $8\frac{1}{2}$ acres, which 3 free men held TRE with the soke. Then as now [there were] $1\frac{1}{2}$ ploughs. [There is] pasture for 40 sheep. Then as now it was worth 20s. The whole abovesaid [land] was worth £30 when [he] received [it].

[Folio 53v: ESSEX]

Hugh holds "Halesduna" in demesne, which Alwine, a thegn, held TRE as a manor and as 2 hides. [There was] then 1 bordar and 1 villan; now the same. Then as now [there was] 1 slave and 1 plough in demesne. [There is] pasture for 40 sheep. It was then worth 30s.; when received 20s. [and] now 30.

Hugh holds "Studly" [in Woodham Ferrers] in demesne, which 2 villans hold then as now. [There were] then 2 bordars and now the same. And [there were then] $1\frac{1}{2}$ ploughs and now the same. It is worth 30s.

HUNDRED OF WINSTREE.

Hugh holds Layer, in demesne, which Leofwine, a free man, held TRE as a manor and as $1\frac{1}{2}$ hides and 18 acres. Then as now [there were] $1\frac{1}{2}$ ploughs in demesne. The men [have] now half a plough. [There are] now 3 bordars. [There were] then 3 slaves; now none. Then as now [there were] 3 cows. [There were] then 20 sheep; now 60. [There are] now 14 pigs and 1 horse and 7 goats. It was then worth 50s. and when received 20s.; now 40s.

HUNDRED OF HINCKFORD.

Ealhhere holds Rayne of Hugh, which Guthmund held as a manor and as 2 hides less 20 acres. Then as now [there were] 3 ploughs in demesne. Then and later the men [had] 7 ploughs; now $2\frac{1}{2}$. Then and later [there were] 18 villans; now 5. Then and later [there were] 6 bordars; now 7. Then and later [there were] 6 slaves; now 4. [There is] woodland for 150 pigs. [There are] 16 acres of meadow. Then as now [there was] 1 mill and 1 horse. [There were] then 18 head of cattle; now 17. Then as now [there were] 70 sheep and 10 goats. Then and later it was worth £6; now 7.

HUNDRED OF DENGIE.

Wulfmær holds St Peter's Chapel [Bradwell] of Hugh, which Ingulf, a free man, held TRE as a manor and as $1\frac{1}{2}$ hides. Then as now [there were] 2 bordars. [There was] then 1 slave; now none. [There is] 1 plough in demesne and the men [have] half a plough. [There is] pasture for 200 sheep. It is worth 30s.

HUNDRED OF LEXDEN.

Nigel holds Markshall of Hugh, which Guthmund held TRE as 1 manor and as half a hide and 13 acres. Then as now [there were] 2 villans. [There were] then 7 bordars; now 8. Then as now [there were] 5 slaves. [There were] then 2 ploughs in demesne; now $1\frac{1}{2}$. Then as now the men [had] $1\frac{1}{2}$ ploughs. [There is] woodland for 200 pigs. [There is] 1 acre of meadow. Then as now

Hugh de Montfort

[Folio 54: ESSEX]

[there was] 1 horse. [There were] then 2 head of cattle; now 10. [There were] then 30 sheep; now 80. Then as now [there were] 12 pigs. [There are] now 3 hives of bees. It was then worth 40s.; now 60.

HUNDRED OF CHELMSFORD.

Robert holds "Bensted" [in Sandon] of Hugh, which Guthmund held TRE as a manor and as 4 hides. [There was] then 1 villan; now none. [There were] then 9 bordars; now 10. Then and later [there were] 6 slaves; now 1. Then and later [there were] 2 ploughs in demesne; now 1. Then as now the men [had] 1 plough. [There are] 5 acres of meadow. [There were] then 3 horses; now none. [There were] then 25 head of cattle. [There is] now 1 cow. [There were] then 100 pigs; now 14. [There were] then 108 sheep; now 24. [There were] then 60 goats; now none. It was then worth £8, and when received the same; now £4. And 5 free men held $1\frac{1}{2}$ hides and 23 acres, which the same Robert holds of Hugh. Then as now [there were] 5 bordars and $2\frac{1}{2}$ ploughs. [There is] woodland for 40 pigs. [There are] 4 acres of meadow. Then as now it was worth 50s. The monks of Ely claim that this manor was in the abbey's demesne, and the Hundred testifies [to] this.

HUNDRED OF TENDRING.

Queen Edith held Wix TRE as a manor. Roger holds [it] now of Hugh. Then as now [there were] 2 villans. [There were] then 2 bordars; now 8. [There were] then 2 slaves; now none. Then as now [there was] 1 plough. [There is] woodland for 10 pigs. [There are] 3 acres of meadow. It is worth 10s. Roger holds this land and the Hundred does not know how and the queen had the soke.

HUNDRED OF THURSTABLE.

Hugh fitzMauger holds [Great and Little] Totham of Hugh, which Cola, and later Richard, held as a manor and 2 hides and 32 acres. [There were] then 4 bordars; now 3. [There were] then 4 slaves; now 5. [There were] then 2 ploughs in demesne; now 1. [There is] woodland for 20 pigs, pasture for 100 sheep. [There are] 3 acres of meadow. [There was] then 1 salt-pan; now 3. [There were] then 3 horses; now 2. [There were] then 16 pigs; now 20. [There were] then 48 goats; now 93. [There are] now 18 goats. It was then worth 40s. and when received 10s. Now it is worth 40s.

The same holds Goldhanger of Hugh, which Leofwine held after Hager [held it] as a manor and as 1 hide and 15 acres. Then as now [there was] 1 villan and 6 bordars and 4 slaves.

[There was] then 1 plough; now half a plough. [There is] woodland for 60 pigs. [There are] 7 acres of meadow. [There is] pasture for 60 sheep. [There was] then half a salt-pan; now 1½. It was then worth 30s. and when received 10s. Now it is worth 20s. And 9 free men dwelt on half a hide and 1 man, a thegn, held 30 acres and 2 other free men held 10 acres. [There was] then 1 plough; now half a plough. It was then worth 26s. 8d.; now 8s. A certain knight of Hugh de Montfort named Hugh fitzMauger received 15 acres from a free thegn and put [them] with his own land, and did not have livery, as the Hundred testifies, and so [this land] is in the king's hands.

Humphrey holds Tolleshunt of Hugh, which Wulfsige held TRE as a manor and as half a hide and 30 acres. Then as now [there were] 2 bordars and 1 plough. [There is] woodland for 30 pigs. [There are] 2½ acres of meadow. It is worth 20s.

XXVIII. Land of Hamo the Steward.

HUNDRED OF BARSTABLE.

Serlo holds "Ateleia" of Hamo, which Goti held of Harold TRE as a manor and as 1 hide. Then as now [there was] 1 plough and 1 bordar and 1 slave. It is worth 20s.

HUNDRED OF WITHAM.

Ralph holds Faulkbourne of Hamo, which Thorbiorn held TRE as a manor and as 1½ hides and 7½ acres. Then as now [there were] 2 ploughs in demesne. [There are] now 8 bordars. [There were] then 6 slaves; now 3. [There are] 5 acres of meadow. [There was] then 1 mill; now none. It is worth 50s.

Hamo the Steward

Ralph [de Marcy] holds [Black and White] Notley of H[amo], which Æthelstan, a free man, held as a manor and as half a hide and 30 acres. Then as now [there was] 1 plough. [There is] now 1 bordar. [There were] then 2 slaves; now 1. [There is] 1½ acres of meadow. It is worth 30s. In the same land the same holds 30 acres, which Ælfric held TRE. Then as now [there was] half a plough and it is worth 5s.

The same R[alph] holds Rayne of H[amo], which Goding held as a manor and as half a hide. Then as now [there was] 1 plough and 1 bordar and [there are] 2 acres of meadow. It is worth 20s.

Guthmund holds [Great and Little] Braxted as a manor and as 1 hide and 35 acres, which Thorbiorn held TRE. [There were] then 2 ploughs in demesne; now 1. The men [had] then 1 plough; now none. [There were] then 3 villans; now 1. [There were] then 4 bordars; now 6. [There were] then 4 slaves; now 2. [There was] then woodland for 100 pigs; now 80. [There are] 15 acres of meadow. [There were] then 20

sheep; now 50. [There were] then 16 pigs; now 11. It was then worth 100s. and when he received it £4; now 60s.

HUNDRED OF HARLOW.

Ralph [de Marcy] holds Ryes of Hamo, which Harold held as belonging to the manor of Hatfield [Broad Oak] TRE as half a hide. [There was] then 1 plough in demesne; now half a plough. [There was] then 1 slave. [There is] now 1 villan. [There is] woodland for 20 pigs. [There are] 3½ acres of meadow. It was then worth 10s.; now 7.

HUNDRED OF DUNMOW.

Serlo holds [Great and Little] Dunmow of Hamo, which 1 free man held TRE as 30 acres. And 7½ acres were added TRW. Then as now [there was] half a plough in demesne and 2 bordars. [There is] woodland for 40 pigs. [There are] 4 acres of meadow. It is worth 16s.

Serlo holds Roding [Marci], of Hamo, which Vithi held of Harold TRE as a manor and as 1½ hides; now [as] 1 hide and 15 acres. Then as now [there were] 2 ploughs in demesne and the men [had] 1 plough. [There were] then 4 villans; now 3. [There were] then 2 bordars; now 11. [There were] then 2 slaves; now 1. [There is] woodland for 100 pigs. [There are] 16 acres of meadow. It was then worth £4 and when received 40s.; now 100s. Of this land, Eudo the Steward holds 45 acres,

which Hamo claims.

HUNDRED OF WINSTREE.

Vitalis holds [Great and Little] Wigborough of Hamo, which Goti, a free man held TRE as a manor and as 7 hides of land and 1 of woodland. Then as now [there were] 2 ploughs in demesne. The men [had] then 2 ploughs; now 1. Then as now [there were] 3 villans and 1 bordar. [There were] then 6 slaves; now 4. [There is] pasture for 200 sheep. [There were] then 10 head of cattle; now 14. [There were] then 60 sheep; now 260. Then as now [there were] 6 horses and 10 pigs. Then as now it was worth £7. Of this land, Bernard took away the abovesaid hide of woodland and he holds [it] of the fief of Baynard. And Engelric took away half a hide of land, which Count Eustace [now] holds.

HUNDRED OF CLAVERING.

In Farnham Serlo holds half a hide of Hamo, which a free man held TRE. It is worth 10s.

HUNDRED OF HINCKFORD.

In Stambourne and in Toppesfield Hamo holds 1 hide in demesne and as a manor, which Goti held TRE. Then and later [there were] 4 ploughs in demesne; now 3. Then as now the men [had] 3 ploughs [and there were] 14 villans and 10 bordars and 6 slaves. [There is] woodland for 40 pigs. [There are] 15 acres of meadow. Then as now [there were] 3 horses. [There were] then 24 head of cattle; now 13. [There were] then 40 pigs; now 20. [There were] then 120 sheep; now 100. [There are] 4 hives of bees. And 15 sokemen now as then belong to this manor, holding half a hide less 10 acres and having 3 ploughs and [there are] 12 acres of meadow and 5 bordars, 1 arpent of vineyard. This land was in 2 manors TRE. Stambourne was then worth 100s.; later and now £6. And Toppesfield was then worth £7; later and now £8. Of this manor 5 knights hold 58 acres and [they] are worth 20s. in the above valuation.

HUNDRED OF DENGIE.

Richard holds 'Carseia' [Northey Island] of Hamo, which Thorbiorn, a free man, held as a manor and as 4 hides and 40 acres. [There were] then 2 villans; now 3. Then as now [there were] 4 slaves and 2 ploughs in demesne and the men [had] 1 plough. [There is] pasture for 60 sheep. It was then worth 60s.; now £4.

Hamo the Steward

[Folio 56: ESSEX]

HUNDRED OF ONGAR.

Hamo holds Greensted in demesne, which Gotild held as a manor and as 2 hides TRE. Then as now [there were] 10 villans. [There were] then 4 bordars; now 9. [There were] then 6 slaves; now 4. [There were] then 3 ploughs in demesne, and when received 2; now 1. Then and later the men [had] 5½ ploughs; now 3½. [There is] woodland for 400 pigs. [There are] 16 acres of meadow. [There is] now 1 mill. [There were] then 2 horses; now 1. [There were] then 4 head of cattle; now 3. [There were] then 30 pigs; now 14. [There are] now 40 goats and 20 sheep. It was then worth £4, and when received 40s. is now worth 100s. Of this manor, Serlo holds 40 acres and it is worth 10s. in the above valuation. In the same [manor] 3 free men held half a hide and 45 acres. [There were] then under them 10 bordars; now 16. [There were] then 3 slaves; now 2. Then as now [there were] 3½ ploughs. [There is] woodland for 120 pigs. [There are] 19 acres of meadow. It was then worth 35s.; now 60. Of this land, Ralph holds half a hide and 5 acres and they are worth 40s. in the above valuation.

The same holds Navestock of Hamo, which Gotild held as a manor and as 80 acres TRE. [There were] then 2 bordars; now 5. [There was] then 1 plough; now none, but there could be [one] there. [There is] woodland for 50 pigs. [There are] 2 acres of meadow. It was then worth 12s., and when received 8s.; now 15.

Ralph holds Kelvedon [Hatch] of Hamo, which Leofgifu held as 1 hide and 45 acres as 1 manor. And Hamo says [that] he has that land [as part of] his fief. [There were] then 2 villans; now 1. [There were] then 2 bordars; now 7. [There were] then 2 slaves; now 1. [There were] then 2 ploughs in demesne; now 1½. Among the men [there was] then 1 plough; now half a plough. [There is] woodland for 20 pigs. [There are] 17 acres of meadow. It was then worth 30s., when received 20; now 35s.

Wimund holds Norton [Mandeville] of Hamo, which Gotild held as a manor and as 1½ hides and 15 acres. [There were] then 4 villans; now 6. Then as now [there were] 4 bordars and 4 slaves. [There were] then 2 ploughs in demesne; now 1. Among the men [there was] then 1 plough; now 1½. [There is] woodland for 200 pigs. [There are] 10 acres of meadow. Then as now [there were] 2 head of cattle. [There is]

now 1 horse and 40 sheep and 20 goats. [There were] then 16 pigs; now 26. Then and later it was worth 40s.; now £4.

HUNDRED OF THURSTABLE.

Richard holds Totham of Hamo,

[Folio 56v: ESSEX]

which Thurbert held as 1 manor and as 5 hides TRE. [There were] then 10 villans; now 9. Then as now [there were] 16 bordars. [There were] then 12 slaves; now 13. [There were] then 4 ploughs in demesne; now 3. Then as now the men [had] 5 ploughs. [There is] woodland for 100 pigs. [There are] 16 acres of meadow, 2 salt-pans. Then as now [there were] 20 head of cattle and 40 pigs. [There were] then 5 horses; now 2. [There were] then 100 sheep; now 150. Then as now [there were] 40 goats. Then and later it was worth 100s.; now £6. In the same [land] 8 free men held 1½ hides, which the same Richard holds. Then as now [there were] 2 ploughs. [There are] 3 acres of meadow. It is worth 20s.

The same Richard holds Osea [Island], which Thurbert held TRE as a manor and as 4 hides. [There was] then 1 bordar; now none. Then as now [there were] 3 slaves, 1 fishery. [There is] pasture for 60 sheep. It is worth 60s.

XXIX. Land of Henry de Ferrers.

HUNDRED OF DUNMOW.

Henry holds Tilty in demesne, which Doding held TRE as a manor and as half a hide. Then as now [there were] 2 ploughs in demesne and the men [had] 1 plough. Then as now [there were] 3 villans. [There were] then 2 bordars; now 6. [There were] then 3 slaves and now the same. [There are] 30 acres of meadow, 20 acres of marsh. [There are] now 40 head of cattle. It was then worth 100s.; now £7.

HUNDRED OF HINCKFORD.

[...] H[enry] holds Stebbing in demesne, which Siward held as a manor and as 2 hides and 30 acres. Then and later [there were] 2 ploughs in demesne; now 3. Among the men [there were] then 4 ploughs; now 6½. [There were] then 6 villans; now 8. [There were] then 16 bordars; now 33.

Henry de Ferrers

[Folio 57: ESSEX]

[There were] then 2 slaves; now 1. [There is] woodland for 150 pigs. [There were] then 9 acres of meadow. When he received [it], [there was] half a mill; now none. Then as now 1 priest is there. [There were] then 7 head of cattle and 40 sheep and 60 [...] pigs and 1 horse. [There are] now 18 head of cattle and 140 sheep and 80 pigs and 1 horse. It was then worth £10; now 12. And TRE it was all the same and was worth as much when received.

HUNDRED OF DENGIE.

H[enry] holds Steeple in demesne, which Bondi, a free man, held TRE as a manor and as 3½ hides. Then as now [there were] 2 bordars. [There were] then 4 slaves; now 3. Then as now [there was] 1 plough in demesne and the men [had] half a plough. [There were] then 100 sheep; now 130. Now as then it is worth 60s.

HUNDRED OF CHELMSFORD.

H[enry] holds Woodham [Ferrers] in demesne, which Bondi held as 1 manor and as 14 hides. Then as now [there were] 24 villans. [There were] then 8 bordars; now 31. [There were] then 6 slaves; now 4. Then as now [there were] 3 ploughs in demesne and the men [had] 16 ploughs. [There is] woodland for 800 pigs. [There is] now 1 mill. He received then 20 head of cattle and 13 horses and 300 sheep and 60 pigs. [There are] now 28 head of cattle and 15 horses and 300 sheep and 100 pigs and 35 goats. It was then worth £20; now 28.

Henry's steward holds Buttsbury of [Henry], which Bondi held as a manor and as 5½ hides. [There were] then 6 villans; now 4. [There were] then 8 bordars; now 12. [There were] then 4 slaves; now 3. Then as now [there were] 2 ploughs in demesne and the men [had] 4 ploughs. [There is] woodland for 500 pigs, pasture for 100 sheep. [There were] then 20 head of cattle and 50 pigs and 60 sheep. [There are] now 7 head of cattle and 100 sheep and 40 pigs. Then as now it is worth £7.

[Folio 57v: ESSEX]

XXX. Land of Geoffrey de Mandeville.

HUNDRED OF LEXDEN.

G[eoffrey] holds Tey in demesne, which Wulfric held TRE as a manor and as 1½ hides and 20 acres. [There were] then 11 bordars; now 15. Then as now [there were] 4 slaves and 2 ploughs in demesne. Among the men [there were] then 3 ploughs; now 2½. [There is] woodland for 100 pigs. [There are] 20 acres of meadow. Then G[eoffrey] received 250 sheep and 8 head of cattle and 6 calves and 2 horses, 28 pigs, 2 hives of bees. [There are] now 67 sheep and 8 head of cattle and 6 calves and 2 horses and 21 pigs. In the same [land] 20 sokemen held 1½ hides and 31 acres. Now 30 sokemen hold that land and they cannot withdraw from that manor. Now as then they have 3 ploughs [and there are] 6 acres of meadow. Then and when received it was worth £7; now 10. And there were 3 free men holding 12 acres, but they were not of that manor which G[eoffrey] has, but he vouches [to warranty] him who gave him livery of seisin. Then as now there was 1 plough and it is worth 40s.

HUNDRED OF ONGAR.

Reginald holds Shelley of Geoffrey, which Leofdæg held as a manor and as 80 acres, and it was not of the fief of Esger, for he was only his man. [There were] then 4 villans; now 5. [There are] now 5 bordars. [There were] then 2 slaves; now 3. Then and later [there were] 2 ploughs in demesne; now 1. Among the men then [there was] 1 plough; now 2. [There is] woodland for 150 pigs. [There are] 20 acres of meadow. Then and later 60s.; now £4.

Geoffrey Martel holds [Abbess] Roding of G[eoffrey], which Leofhild held as a manor and as 3 virgates. Then as now [there was] 1 villan and 2 bordars. [There was] then 1 slave; now none. Then as now [there was] 1 plough in

demesne and the men [had] half a plough. [There is] woodland for 40 pigs. [There are] 15 acres of meadow. Then and later it was worth 30s.; now 40. And this land, which G[eoffrey] now holds, was in [the possession of] the abbey of Barking, as the Hundred testifies, but he who held this land was only the man of Geoffrey's predecessor and could not put this land in the possession of anyone but the abbey.

HUNDRED OF CHAFFORD.

Turold holds [North and South] Ockendon of G[eoffrey], which Fridebert, a thegn, held freely as 1 manor and as 10½ hides and 20 acres,

Geoffrey de Mandeville

[Folio 58: ESSEX]

and Geoffrey has [it] by exchange, as he says. Then as now [there were] 3 villans, 34 bordars. [There were] then 3 slaves; now none. [There were] then 2 ploughs in demesne; now 3. Among the men [there were] then 7 ploughs; now 8. [There is] woodland for 150 pigs. [There are] 8 acres of meadow. [There is] pasture for 100 sheep. Now [there is] 1 mill. [There were] then 5 head of cattle and 18 sheep. [There are] now 18 head of cattle and 1 horse, 35 pigs, 220 sheep, 1 hive of bees. Then and when received it was worth £7. Now it is worth £16. On this land [there] are 13 sokemen, who freely hold 8½ hides and 20 acres and they have 12 bordars [under them], and they belong to this farm of £16. And [there] are also 40 acres and 4 bordars [who hold them].

HUNDRED OF CHELMSFORD.

G[eoffrey] holds [Great and Little] Waltham in demesne, which Esger held as a manor and as 8 hides TRE. Then as now [there were] 72 villans and 28 bordars. [There were] then 14 slaves; now 13. [There were] then 6 ploughs in demesne; now 5. Among the men [there were] then 42 ploughs; now 36. [There is] woodland for 1,200 pigs. [There are] 44 acres of meadow. Then as now [there were] 2 mills. [There are] now 10 arpents of vineyard. [There were] then 5 horses, 12 cows, 50 pigs, 80 goats. [There are] now 3 horses, 11 cows, 60 pigs, 132 sheep, 7 goats, 20 acres hives of bees. It was then worth £50; now 60. Of this manor Hubert holds 1 virgate and half a plough and it is worth 5s. in the above valuation and Walter [holds] 1 virgate and half a plough and it is worth 5s. in the above valuation. Turchil [holds] 1 virgate and 2 bordars and half a plough and it is worth 5s. in the above valuation, and Walter [holds] 30 acres and Turchil [holds] 30 acres and Hubert [holds] 30 acres.

In [Great and Little] Waltham Wulfwine held freely with the soke 1 hide and 50 acres. Roger now holds [it] of G[eoffrey] as a manor and as the same. Then as now [there were] 3 villans. [There were] then 4 bordars; now 6. [There were] then 2 ploughs in demesne; now 1½. Then as now the men [had] 1 plough and [there was] 1 slave. [There are] 7 acres of meadow and 1 mill. It was then worth 40s.; now 60.

Edward held Chatham as a manor and as 2 hides and 30 acres. Walter now holds [it] of Geoffrey as the same. Then as now [there were] 2 villans. [There were] then 2 bordars; now

5. Then as now [there were] 6 slaves and 2 ploughs in demesne and the men [had] 1 plough. [There is] woodland for 100 pigs. [There are] 6 acres of meadow.

Then and later it was worth 40s.; now 60.

The same E[dward] held Patching TRE as a manor and as 2 hides. Now Walter holds [it] of G[eoffrey]. Then as now [there was] 1 slave and 1 plough. [There is] woodland for 30 pigs. [There are] 9 acres of meadow. It is worth 20s.

Sæwulf held Broomfield as a manor and as 4 hides. The same Walter now [holds it] of G[eoffrey]. Then as now [there were] 9 villans. [There were] then 4 bordars. [There were] then 5 slaves; now 4. Then as now [there were] 2 ploughs in demesne and the men [had] 4 ploughs. [There is] woodland for 50 pigs. [There are] 14 acres of meadow. Then as now [there was] 1 mill. Then and later it was worth 100s.; now £6.

Three free men held Chignall TRE as 1 hide and 15 acres. Richard now [holds it] of G[eoffrey] as a manor and as the same. [There were] then 2 bordars; now 10. [There are] now 3 villans. Then as now [there were] 3 slaves. Then and later [there were] 2 ploughs in demesne; now 1. Among the men [there is] now 1 plough. [There is] woodland for 10 pigs. [There are] 15 acres of meadow. It was then worth 30s.; now 45.

Godwine the deacon held Chignall TRE as a manor and as 1½ hides less [...] 5 acres. Now Richard Garnet holds [it] as a manor and as the same. Then as now [there was] 1 villan. [There was] then 1 bordar; now 3. [There were] then 3 slaves; now 2. Then as now [there was] 1 plough in demesne. Among the men [there was] 1 plough in demesne. [There is] woodland for 12 pigs. [There are] 16 acres of meadow. It was then worth 30s.; now 40.

In the same vill Wulfwine held 45 acres TRE. Now Ralph holds [it] of G[eoffrey] as a manor and as the same. Then as now [there were] 3 bordars and 1 plough and 3 acres of meadow. It is worth 10s. In the same vill Leofsunu holds 1 virgate of G[eoffrey], which the same held TRE. Then as now [there was] 1 plough. [There are] 5 acres of meadow. It is worth 5s. And Leofric held and holds 30 acres of G[eoffrey]. [There was] then half a plough; now none. [There are] 7 acres of meadow. It is worth 3s. and Leofwine held and holds 15 acres [of land] and 2 acres of meadow. It is worth 30d. And Æthelstan holds now as then 10 acres [of land] and 3 acres of meadow. It is worth 2s.

In Mashbury Edwin held and holds 45 acres under G[eoffrey]. Then as now [there were] 3 bordars. [There was] then half a plough; now none. It is worth 10s.

Geoffrey de Mandeville

Erling held Danbury as a manor and as 2½ hides. Now William [holds it] of G[eoffrey] as the same. Then as now [there was] 1 villan. [There were] then 3 bordars; now 9. [There were] then 4 slaves; now 1. Then as now [there was] 1 plough in demesne and the men [had] 1 plough. [There is]

woodland for 100 pigs. [There are] 16 acres of meadow. It was then worth 30s.; now 40.

In Chignall Sæwine the priest held 15 acres. Now Richard [holds it] of G[eoffrey]. [There was] then half a plough; now nothing. It is worth 5s. In the same vill Eadsige held 15 acres. Now the same R[ichard holds them]. [There are] 2 acres of meadow. It is worth 3s. The abovesaid were free to the extent that they could sell the land with soke and sake to whom they would, as the Hundred testifies.

Esger held [Great and Little] Leighs as a manor and as 2½ hides and 15 acres. Now W. [holds it] of G[eoffrey] as the same. [There were] then 4 villans; now 2. Then as now [there were] 8 bordars; now 12. [There were] then 3 slaves; now 4. [There were] then 2 ploughs in demesne; now 3. Then as now the men [had] 2 ploughs. [There is] woodland for 40 pigs. [There are] 6 acres of meadow. Then as now [there was] 1 mill. [There are] now 10 head of cattle, 10 pigs, 100 sheep. Then and later it was worth £4; now £4. 10s. Esger gave this manor TRE to Harold, and Harold in turn gave [it] to a certain housecarl of his named Skalpi, and this Skalpi gave [it] in dower to his wife in the sight of 2 men, namely Roger the marshal and a certain Englishman. And the [men of the] Hundred testify that they heard [the right of] Skalpi recognised, and after the king came into this land, Skalpi held [it] until he went where he died, [namely] in York, in outlawry.

Toli held Cuton as a manor and as 2 hides and 1 virgate. Now Osbert [holds it] of G[eoffrey] in exchange, as he says. Then as now [there was] 1 villan. [There were] then 6 bordars; now 4. Then as now [there were] 3 slaves and 2 ploughs in demesne. Among the men [there was] then 1 plough; now half a plough. [There are] 18 acres of meadow. Then as now [there was] 1 mill. [There were] then 2 cows, 13 sheep, 12 pigs. [There are] now 8 head of cattle, 32 sheep, 20 pigs, 14 goats, 2 horses, 5 hives of bees. It was then worth 40s.; now 60.

HUNDRED OF TENDRING.

Leofsunu held Moze as a manor and as 4 hides. Now Geoffrey [holds it] in demesne. Then as now [there were] 14 villans. [There are] now 13 bordars.

[There were] then 13 slaves, and when received 11; now 3. Then and later [there were] 4 ploughs in demesne; now 2. Then and later the men [had] 6 ploughs; now 4. [There is] woodland for 150 pigs. [There are] 6½ acres of meadow. [There was] then 1 mill; now none. [There is] pasture for 150 sheep. [There are] 3 salt-pans. And the king gave this manor to G[eoffrey] when he stayed in London. [There were] then 2 horses and 9 head of cattle, 180 sheep, 14 pigs. [There are] now 2 horses, 14 head of cattle, 15 pigs, 160 sheep, 50 goats, 3 hives of bees. It was then worth £8, and when received the same. Now it is worth £9.

Rainhelm holds Frinton of G[eoffrey], which Leofsunu held as a manor and as 3 hides. Then and later [there were] 3 villans; now 1. Then and later [there were] 4 slaves; now 3. Then as now [there were] 2 ploughs in demesne and the men [had] 2 ploughs then, and when received 1½; now only half a plough. [There are] 3½ acres of meadow. [There is] pasture for 50 sheep. [There were] then 49 sheep. [There are] now 2 horses and 4 pigs and 40 sheep. Then and later it was worth £7; now 4.

William holds Ardleigh of G[eoffrey], which 2 free men, Bondi and Alric, brothers, held as 2 hides and as 2 manors, but they could not withdraw without the licence of that Algar. Then as now [there were] 5 villans and 8 bordars. [There was] then 1 slave; now none. Then as now [there were] 2 ploughs in demesne. Then and later the men [had] 5 ploughs; now 4. [There is] woodland for 100 pigs. [There are] 12 acres of meadow. [There is] pasture for 50 sheep. Then and later it was worth £4; now 40s.

In the Hundred of Barstablewere 6 free men TRE, whom G[eoffrey] appropriated [at the expense of] King William, holding 12 hides of land, which 5 knights hold of [Geoffrey]. Then as now [there were] 9½ ploughs. [There was] then 1 villan; now none. [There were] then 10 bordars; now 36. [There were] then 14 slaves; now 7. [There was] then woodland for 100 pigs; now 50. [There is] pasture for 300 sheep. [There are] 10 acres of meadow, 1 fishery. >From these 12 hides, Ravengar took away 12 acres of land and added [them] to his fief and Swein took away thence 30 acres and put [them] in his manor of [East and West] Tilbury. The whole together was then worth £7, and now the same.

[...]HUNDRED OF WITHAM.

Walter holds [Black and White] Notley of G[eoffrey].

Geoffrey de Mandeville

which Esger held as a manor and as 1½ hides and 45 acres. Then as now [there were] 2 ploughs in demesne and the men [had] 4 ploughs. Then as now [there were] 10 villans and 5 bordars and 4 slaves. [There is] woodland for 100 pigs. [There is] now 1 mill. And [there are] 2 free men with 40 acres, and he vouches the king to warranty for them. [There were] then 6 head of cattle and 1 horse and 12 pigs and 60 sheep. [There are] now 8 head of cattle, 16 pigs, 100 sheep, 1 horse. It was then worth 100s.; now £6.

Walter holds Ridley of G[eoffrey], which Esger held TRE as a manor and as 1 hide. Then as now [there was] 1 plough in demesne and the men [had] half a plough. [There are] now 3 bordars. [There were] then 3 slaves; now 1. [There is] woodland for 10 pigs. [There are] 4 acres of meadow. And 30 acres belonged TRE to this land, of which G[eoffrey] de Mandeville has 20 acres and Richard son of Count Gilbert [has] 10 acres, but the Hundred testifies that the whole rightly belongs to Geoffrey's land. The whole together is worth 30s.

HUNDRED OF HARLOW.

Martel holds [Great and Little] Hallingbury of G[eoffrey], which Esger held TRE as a manor and as 1 hide. [There were] then 2 ploughs in demesne; now 1. [There was] then 1 priest and 1 villan with 20 acres, which belonged to the church, but they do not [belong] to the church now. [There are] now 4 bordars. [There were] then 3 slaves; now 2. [There is] woodland for 100 pigs. [There are] 20 acres of meadow. [There is] now half a mill. Now as then it is worth 40s.

Esger held Matching as a manor and as 40 acres, which

G[eoffrey] holds in demesne. Then as now [there was] 1 plough. [There was] then 1 slave; now none. [There is] woodland for 10 pigs. [There are] 3 acres of meadow. It is worth 10s.

Hugh holds [Great and Little] Hallingbury of G[eoffrey], which Godgyth, a free woman, held TRE as a manor and as half a hide less 8 acres. [There was] then half a plough; now none. [There were] then 2 villans; now none. [There are] 5 acres of meadow. It is worth 5s.

HUNDRED OF DUNMOW.

Esger held [High] Easter TRE as a manor and as 2 hides. Now G[eoffrey] holds [it] in demesne. Then as now [there were] 4 ploughs in demesne and the men [had] 12 ploughs. [There were] then 46 villans; now 47. [There were] then 14 bordars; now 33. Then as now [there were] 9 slaves. [There is] woodland for 600 pigs. [There are] 30 acres of meadow, and a fifth plough [more] could be [employed] in demesne.

[There were] then 3 horses and 7 head of cattle and 60 pigs and 60 sheep, 30 goats, 10 hives of bees. [There are] now 3 horses and 7 cows, 27 pigs, 50 sheep and 4 goats, 17 hives of bees. Then and later it was worth £20; now 30.

To this manor belong now as then 6 sokemen with 1½ hides. [There were] then 2 ploughs; now 1. [There are] now 3 bordars, 8 acres of meadow. It was then worth 20s.; now 30. To this manor also belong 2 hides and 1 virgate, which 2 sokemen held TRE, in which [there] are now as then 4 ploughs in demesne and the men [have] 1½ ploughs. [There were] then 8 villans; now 7. [There were] then 6 bordars; now 7. Then as now [there were] 3 slaves. [There is] woodland for 60 pigs. [There are] 24 acres of meadow. Then and later it was worth 100s.; now £10. Four of Geoffrey's knights hold this. And [there] also belongs to that manor half a hide which belonged to the church of the manor TRE, and now Gutbert holds it of G[eoffrey]. Then as now [there] was 1 plough. [There was] then 1 bordar; now 3 and [there is] 1 slave. [There is] woodland for 20 pigs. [There are] 5 acres of meadow. It was then worth 20s.; now 30. And the abbot of Ely claims this aforesaid manor, and the Hundred testifies that it was in [the possession of] the abbey TRE, but [that] Esger held this manor on the day that King Edward was alive and dead.

Hugh de Bernières holds Newton of G[eoffrey], which Wulfric Cave held TRE as a manor and as 2 hides and 1 virgate. [There were] then 2 ploughs in demesne; now 1½. Then as now the men [had] 1 plough and [there were] 5 villans. [There was] then 1 bordar; now 5. Then as now [there were] 2 slaves. [There is] woodland for 160 pigs [and there are] 12 acres of meadow. It was then worth 60s., and when received 40s.; now £4.

The same holds Barnston, which Wulfwine held TRE as a manor and as 2 hides and 30 acres. Then as now [there were] 2 ploughs in demesne and the men [had] 3 ploughs. [There were] then 6 villans; now 7. [There were] then 5 bordars; now 7. Then as now [there were] 2 slaves. [There is] woodland for 200 pigs. [There are] 20 acres of meadow. It was then worth £4; now 100s., and when received the same.

The same holds [Berners] Roding, which Wulfric held

TRE as a manor and as $2\frac{1}{2}$ hides. Then as now [there were] 2 ploughs in demesne and the men [had] $1\frac{1}{2}$ ploughs. Then as now [there were] 4 villans and 3 bordars

Geoffrey de Mandeville

[Folio 61: ESSEX]

and 4 slaves. [There is] woodland for 100 pigs. [There are] 27 acres of meadow. Then as now [there is] 1 mill. Then and later it was worth 100s.; now £7. And the king commanded, through Robert d'Oilly, that Hugh should hold these 3 manors of G[eoffrey] de Mandeville if the same G[eoffrey] could prove that they belonged to his fief, and before G[eoffrey] proved that they belonged to his fief, Hugh held them of Geoffrey.

Martel held Bigods of G[eoffrey], which Esger held TRE as 1 manor and as 4 hides and 10 acres. Then as now [there were] 3 ploughs in demesne and the men [had] 2 ploughs. [There were] then 11 villans; now 7. [There were] then 6 bordars; now 24. [There were] then 6 slaves; now 4. [There was] then woodland for 400 pigs; now 350. [There are] 36 acres of meadow. Then as now [there was] 1 mill. Then and later it was worth £7; now £10.

The same holds [Great and Little] Dunmow of G[eoffrey], which the same Esger held TRE as a manor and as $1\frac{1}{2}$ hides. Then as now [there were] 2 ploughs in demesne and the men [had] 2 ploughs. [There were] then 13 villans; now 5. [There were] then 7 bordars; now 6. [There was] then 1 slave; now 3. [There is] woodland for 200 pigs. [There are] 26 acres of meadow. It was then worth 100s.; now £7.

Lambert holds Shellow Bowells of G[eoffrey], which E[sger] held TRE as a manor and as $1\frac{1}{2}$ hides. Then as now [there were] 2 ploughs in demesne. [There were] then 2 villans; now 1. [There were] then 5 bordars; now 8. [There were] then 2 slaves; now 1. [There is] woodland for 150 pigs. [There are] 10 acres of meadow, 3 head of cattle, 3 pigs, 25 sheep. [There is] now 1 hive of bees. Then and later it was worth 40s.; now 60.

G[eoffrey] holds Shellow Bowells in demesne, which Wulfric, a free man, held of Harold TRE as a manor and as 2 hides. Then as now [there were] 2 ploughs in demesne. The men [had] then 1 plough; now half a plough. [There were] then 2 villans; now 1. [There were] then 2 bordars; now 4. [There were] then 4 slaves; now 6. [There is] woodland for 150 pigs. [There are] 12 acres of meadow and 1 plough more could be [employed]. It was then worth £4; now 100s. To this land belongs half a hide of land, which now as then 1 sokeman holds. [There was] then 1 plough in demesne; now half a plough. Then as now [there was] 1 bordar and $1\frac{1}{2}$ acres of meadow and half a plough could be restored. It is worth 10s.

[Folio 61v: ESSEX]

Martel holds [White] Roding, of G[eoffrey], which Esger held as a manor and as 2 hides TRE. Then as now [there were] 2 ploughs in demesne. The men [had] then 3 ploughs now 2 and a third was able to be restored. [There were] then 6 villans; now 8. [There was] then 1 bordar; now 5. [There was] then 1 slave; now none. [There is] woodland for 20 pigs.

[There are] 20 acres of meadow. Then and later it was worth 100s.; now £6.

William holds [Great and Little] Dunmow as a manor and as half and 15 acres, which the same E[sger] held TRE. Then as now [there was] 1 plough in demesne. [There were] then 4 villans; now 1 and [there are] 4 bordars. [There is] woodland for 50 pigs. [There are] 16 acres of meadow. Then and later it was worth 20s.; now 60.

Richard holds [Great and Little] Easton of G[eoffrey], which 1 free man held TRE as a manor and as half a hide. Then as now [there was] 1 plough in demesne. [There was] then 1 slave. [There is] now 1 bordar. [There are] 12 acres of meadow. Then and later it was worth 10s.; now 30.

Richard holds [Great and Little] Canfield of G[eoffrey], which E[sger] held TRE as a manor and as half a hide and 16 acres. [There were] then 2 ploughs in demesne; now 1. The men [have] now 1 plough. [There are] now 2 villans. [There were] then 8 bordars; now 4. [There is] woodland for 30 pigs. [There are] 16 acres of meadow. It was then worth 40s., and when received the same; now 60.

Rainhelm holds Roding, of G[eoffrey], which E[sger] held TRE as a manor and as 2 hides less 10 acres. Then as now [there were] 2 ploughs in demesne. [There are] now 8 bordars. Then as now [there were] 2 slaves. [There is] woodland for 20 pigs. [There are] 32 acres of meadow. Then and later it was worth 60s.; now 100, and 1 plough more could be restored. To this land were added 10 acres, which 1 free man held TRE, and now the whole Hundred testifies [that] they [are] of the demesne of King William.

William holds Roding, which 1 free man held TRE as a manor and as 1 hide and 3 virgates. Half of this land rendered soke to Esger and the other part, which the king gave to G[eoffrey], was free, as his men say. [There were] then $1\frac{1}{2}$ ploughs in demesne; now 1. The men now [have] 1 plough. Then as now [there were] 4 villans. [There are] now 2 bordars. [There were] then 2 slaves; now none, nor when received. [There is] woodland for 30 pigs. [There are] 16 acres of meadow. Then and later it was worth

Geoffrey de Mandeville

[Folio 62: ESSEX]

40s.; now £4.

William holds Shellow [Bowells] of G[eoffrey], which 1 free man held as 35 acres TRE. [There is] woodland for 20 pigs. [There are] 4 acres of meadow. It was then worth 5s.; now 10. This land belonged to the manor of Eudo the Steward at Roding, TRE and the abbot of Ely claims both the land and the manor of Roding, with the witness of the Hundred.

In [Great and Little] Dunmow Geoffrey holds in demesne 30 acres, which 1 sokeman held of Esger. Then as now [there was] half a plough. [There was] then 1 bordar; now 3. [There is] woodland for 10 pigs. [There are] 4 acres of meadow. It was then worth 7s.; now 10.

Martel holds [White] Roding, which Esger held TRE and Leofgyth, a certain woman, under him as half a hide. [There are] 4 acres of meadow. It was then worth 10s.; now 12.

HUNDRED OF DENGIE.

Hugh holds Stow Maries of G[eoffrey], which Fridebern, a free man, held TRE as a manor and as 4 hides TRE. Then as now [there were] 4 villans. [There were] then 2 bordars; now 7. [There were] then 2 slaves; now none. Then as now [there were] 2 ploughs in demesne. The men [had] then 1½ ploughs. [There is] woodland for 40 pigs, pasture for 30 sheep. Now as then it is worth 60s. The same Hugh also has 1 hide, which a free man held. It is worth 20s. And the same [Hugh] has 30 acres, which 1 free man held. [There was] then half a plough; now none. It is worth 5s.

HUNDRED OF UTTLESFORD.

G[eoffrey] holds [Saffron] Walden in demesne, which Esger held TRE as a manor and as 19½ hides. Then and later [there were] 8 ploughs in demesne; now 10. Then as now the men [had] 22 ploughs. Then and later [there were] 66 villans; now 46. Then and later [there were] 17 bordars; now 40. Then and later [there were] 16 slaves; now 20. Then and later [there was] woodland for 1,000 pigs; now 800, and [there are] 80 acres of meadow. Then as now [there was] 1 mill. To this manor belonged TRE 13 sokemen; now 14, holding 6 and ½ a hide.

[Folio 62v: ESSEX]

Then and later [there were] 8½ ploughs; now 8. Then and later [there were] 10 bordars; now 14. Then and later [there was] woodland for 50 pigs; now 30. [There are] 20 acres of meadow [and] the third part of a mill. [There were] then 6 horses, 11 [...] head of cattle, 200 sheep, 110 pigs, 40 goats, 4 hives of bees. [There are] now 9 horses, 10 head of cattle, 243 sheep, 100 pigs, 20 goats, 30 hives of bees. Then and later it was worth £36. It is now worth 50.

Of this manor Odo holds 1 hide and 1 virgate and Reginald [holds] 1 hide less 12 acres and [there are] 2 ploughs and 13 bordars and [this] is worth 50s. in the above valuation. William Cardon holds [Great and Little] Chishill of G[eoffrey], which Wulfheah, a free man, held TRE as a manor and as 2½ hides. [There were] then 3 ploughs in demesne; later and now 2. Then and later the men [had] 3 ploughs; now none. Then and later [there were] 9 villans; now none. Then as now [there were] 6 bordars. Then and later [there were] 6 slaves; now 1. [There is] woodland for 30 pigs. [There are] 6 acres of meadow. [There were] then 200 sheep and 10 pigs. [There are] now 220 sheep, 30 pigs, 66 goats, 3 head of cattle. Then and later it was worth £6; now 100s.

In the same vill the same [Odo] holds 3 hides and 17 acres, which 5 free men held TRE. [There were] then 5 ploughs, and when received 2; now none. [There is] now 1 villan and 3 bordars. [There are] 4 acres of meadow. Then and later it was worth 100s.; now 40. G[eoffrey] claims [to have] these lands by exchange.

In Emanuel a certain Englishman holds 3 virgates of G[eoffrey], which a free man held TRE and TRW he became Geoffrey's man by his own wish. And the men of Geoffrey say that afterwards the king granted them to Geoffrey in exchange, but neither that man nor the Hundred bear witness for Geoffrey. In that land [there] was then 1 plough; now half

a plough. Then as now [there were] 3 bordars. [There are] 7 acres of meadow. It is worth 10s.

Germund holds Birchanger of G[eoffrey], which 1 sokeman held of Esger as half a hide TRE. Then as now [there was] 1 plough in demesne and 3 bordars. Then and later [there was] woodland for 40 pigs; now 30. It was then worth 20s.; now 10.

HUNDRED OF CLAVERING.

In Pledgdon Richard holds [of Geoffrey] 1 hide and 20 acres, [which] a sokeman [held] of Esger TRE. [There was] then 1 plough; now none. Then as now [there were] 3 bordars. [There is] woodland for 10 pigs.

Geoffrey de Mandeville

[Folio 63: ESSEX]

[There are] 10 acres of meadow. Then as now it was worth 21s.

HUNDRED OF DENGIE.

Hugh de Verly holds Stow Maries, which Fridebern held as a manor and as 3 . Then as now [there were] 2 villans. [There were] then 2 bordars; now 7. [There were] then 2 slaves; now none. Then as now [there were] 2 ploughs in demesne. The men [had] then 1 plough; now half a plough. [There is] woodland for 40 pigs, pasture for 30 sheep. [There were] then 5 pigs, 30 sheep and [there are] now 70 pigs. It is worth 60s. In the same [vill] the same holds 37 acres. [There was] then half a plough; now none. It is worth 5s.

Esger held "Wenesuuic" TRE as a manor and as 5 hides and 40 acres, which Godfrey and Everard held. Then as now [there were] 2 villans. [There were] then 4 bordars; now 7. Then as now [there were] 3 slaves and 2 ploughs in demesne. The men [had] then 2 ploughs; now 1½. It is worth £4. In the same [vill] 6 free men held 1 hide and 40 acres, which the same Godfrey and Everard hold. It was then worth 20s.; now 10.

XXXI. Land of the Count of Eu.

The count holds [Grays and West] Thurrock in demesne, which Harold held as a manor and as 13 hides. [There were] then 12 villans; now 17. [There were] then 16 bordars; now 45. [There were] then 16 slaves; now 8. [There were] then 6 ploughs in demesne; now 5. The men [had] then 10 ploughs; now 13. [There is] woodland for 200 pigs. [There are] 40 acres of meadow. [There is] pasture for 500 sheep. [There was] then 1 fishery; now 2. Then as now [there were] 5 cows, 3 horses, 16 pigs, 550 sheep. It was then worth £12; now 30. And [there] are 7 houses in London which belong to this manor and [are included] in this farm.

XXXII. Lands of Robert Gernon.

HUNDRED OF BARSTABLE.

Robert holds Ramsden [Bellhouse and Crays] in demesne, which 3 free men held TRE as a manor and as 3½ hides and 30 acres. Then as now [there were] 2 ploughs in demesne and the men [had] 1 plough. [There were] then 3 villans; now 2. [There were] then 3 bordars; now 13. [There were] then 3 slaves; now 4. [There is] woodland for 90 pigs. [There was] then 1 horse; now 2. [There were] then 2 head of cattle; now 10. Then as now [there were] 60 sheep and 40 pigs. [There are] now 2 hives of bees. It is worth 50s.

Ansketil holds Ramsden [Bellhouse and Crays] of Robert, which Ælfric held freely as a manor and as 2 hides. Then as now [there was] 1 plough in demesne and the men [had] half a plough. [There were] then 2 villans; now 1. Then as now [there were] 6 bordars. [There were] then 2 slaves; now none. [There is] woodland for 40 pigs. Then as now [there was] 1 horse. [There were] then 7 pigs; now 20. [There are] now 6 head of cattle. [There were] then 20 sheep; now 80. [There are] 2 hives of bees. It is worth 30s.

Hundred of Witham. Hugh holds Witham of R[obert], which Burgheard, a free man, held TRE as 1 manor and as 4 hides. [There were] then 4 ploughs in demesne; now 2. The men [have] now 2 ploughs, and [there are] 2 villans and 6 bordars. [There were] then 6 slaves; now 3. [There are] 6 acres of meadow, 1 mill. [There was] then 1 horse and 2 head of cattle and 80 sheep and 12 pigs. [There is] now 1 horse and 4 head of cattle and 100 sheep and 20 pigs and 3 hives of bees. Then as now it was worth £4.

Richard holds Howbridge of R[obert], which Beorhtmær held TRE as a manor and as 2½ hides. Then as now [there were] 2 ploughs in demesne and the men [had] 1 plough and [there were] 2 villans and 6 bordars. [There were] then 6 slaves; now none. [There is] woodland for 40 pigs. [There are] 11 acres of meadow, 1 mill. [There were] then 2 head of cattle; now 4. [There was] then 1 horse; now none. [There were] then 12 pigs; now 40. [There were] then 30 sheep; now 54. [There are] now 24 goats. It is worth 40s.

Ascelin holds Rivenhall of R[obert], which Æthelstan, a free man, held TRE as a manor and as half a hide. Then as now [there was] 1 plough in demesne. [There was] then 1 bordar; now 8. [There was] then 1 slave; now none. [There is] woodland for 10 pigs. [There are] 8 acres of meadow. [There are] now 8 pigs. It is worth 20s.

Robert Gernon

HUNDRED OF HARLOW.

Hugh holds Matching of Robert, which Ælfric Cild, a free man, held TRE as a manor and as 1 hide. Then as now [there was] 1 plough in demesne. The men [had] then half a plough; now none. [There was] then 1 villan; now none. [There was] then 1 bordar; now 4. [There were] then 3 slaves; now none.

[There is] woodland for 40 pigs. [There are] 8 acres of meadow. [There was] then 1 horse and 8 pigs. [There are] now 16 pigs and 12 sheep and 8 goats and 4 head of cattle. It was then worth 20s.; now 30.

HUNDRED OF WALTHAM.

Ordgar the thegn holds Chingford of Robert, which 1 free man held TRE and it renders 10d. to Waltham as soke. [There were] then 2 ploughs in demesne; now 1. The men [had] then 3 ploughs; now 2. Then as now [there were] 7 villans and 6 bordars and 4 slaves. [There is] woodland for 500 pigs. [There are] 50 acres of meadow. Then as now [there was] 1 mill and 4 fisheries and 2 ploughs more could be restored, one in demesne and the other for the villans. [There were] then 11 head of cattle; now none. [There were] then 30 pigs; now 21. It was then worth 70s.

HUNDRED OF BECONTREE.

Robert holds [East and West] Ham in demesne, which Æthelstan, a free man, held TRE as a manor and as 8 hides and 30 acres. And King William [gave] this manor to Ranulf Peverel and Robert Gernon. [There were] then 5 ploughs in demesne; now 4. The men [had] then 8 ploughs; now 12. [There were] then 32 villans; now 48. [There were] then 16 bordars; now 80 less 1. Then as now [there were] 3 slaves. [There is] woodland for 100 pigs. [There are] 60 acres of meadow. [There were] then 9 mills then; now 8. It was then worth £16, and when received £12. Now it is worth £24. And of this manor, R[anulf] Peverel has a moiety. And in the demesne of Robert, R[obert] received 1 horse and it is similarly now there. [There was] then 1 cow. [There are] now 9 head of cattle. [There were] then 6 sheep; now 12. [There were] then 5 pigs; now 11. Of this manor, Osbern holds 30 acres of Robert and half a plough and it is worth 10s. in the above valuation.

Robert holds [East and West] Ham in demesne, which Leofræd, a free man, held TRE as a manor and as 7 hides. Then as now [there were] 3 ploughs in demesne. The men [had] then 7 ploughs; now 13. [There were] then 34 villans; now 38. [There were] then 3 bordars; now 26. [There were] then 19 slaves;

now 3. [There is] woodland for 700 pigs. [There are] 50 acres of meadow. [There were] then 8 head of cattle; now 15. [There were] then 20 pigs; now 34. [There are] now 200 sheep less 20. [There are] now 4 horses and 3 hives of bees. And to this land were added 3 virgates TRW, which Edwin, a free priest, held TRE. [There was] then 1 plough; now half a plough. [There are] now 2 bordars. [There is] woodland for 10 pigs. [There are] 9 acres of meadow, and this manor was worth TRE £10, and when received £7; now £18. And to this manor belong 30 acres, which 1 sokeman holds. Of this manor, Ilger holds 40 acres and [has] 2 bordars and 1 plough and it is worth 15s. in the above valuation.

In Leyton Robert holds in demesne half a hide, which 1 free man held TRE. Then as now [there was] half a plough and 2 bordars. [There are] 5 acres of meadow. It is worth 5s.

In Loughton W. de Corbon holds 44 acres of R[obert], which 1 free man held TRE. Then as now [there was] half a plough. [There are] now 2 bordars. [There is] woodland for 20 pigs. [There is] 1 acre of meadow. It is worth 10s.

HUNDRED OF DENGIE.

Richard holds Purleigh of R[obert], which Algar, a free man, held as a manor and as 2 hides and 15 acres. [There was] then 1 slave. [There is] now 1 bordar. Then as now [there was] 1 plough. It was then worth 10s., and when received 20; now 30. In demesne [there] are now 34 sheep and [there was] nothing [when] he received [it].

Ansketil holds [Great] Whitmane of R[obert], which Leofstan, a free man, held TRE as a manor and as 1½ hides. [There were] then 2 villans; now none. [There were] then 4 bordars; now 8. Then as now [there was] 1 slave and 2 ploughs in demesne. The men [had] then 1½ ploughs; now 1. [There is] woodland for 150 pigs. [There were] then 2 cows. [There are] now 8 head of cattle. [There were] then 100 sheep; now 140. [There were] then 16 pigs; now 20. Then as now [there was] 1 horse. It was then worth 40s., and when received 30. Now it is worth £4.

HUNDRED OF WINSTREE.

Robert de Verly holds "Lega" of Robert, which Gotar, a free man, held TRE as a manor and as 4½ hides. [There were] then 3 ploughs in demesne; now 2. Then as now the men [had] 3 ploughs. [There were] then 7 villans; now 5. [There were] then 5 bordars; now 12. [There were] then 7 slaves; now 3. [There is] woodland for 100 pigs. [There is] now 1 mill.

Robert Gernon

[Folio 65: ESSEX]

[There was] then 1 horse; now 8. [There were] then 160 sheep; now 80. [There were] then 20 pigs; now none. Then as now it was worth £4.

The same R[obert de Verly] holds Virley of the same [Robert], which 1 free man held TRE as a manor and as 1½ hides. Then as now [there was] 1 plough in demesne. [There were] then 4 bordars; now 3. Then as now [there was] 1 slave. [There was] then nothing; now [there are] 2 horses, 20 pigs, 80 sheep, 2 head of cattle. It was then worth 26s.; now 30.

HUNDRED OF UTTLESFORD.

Robert holds Stansted [Mountfitchet] in demesne, which a free man held TRE as a manor and as 6 hides. [There were] then 4 ploughs in demesne; later 2 [and] now 3. Then as now the men [had] 10 ploughs and 11 villans and 1 priest. Then and later [there were] 4 bordars; now 18. [There were] then 8 slaves; later 4 [and] now 3. [There is] woodland for 1,000 pigs. [There are] 20 acres of meadow. Then as now [there is] 1 mill. [There were] then 8 head of cattle; now 16. [There were] then 140 sheep; now 120. [There were] then 20 pigs; now 60. [There were] then 40 goats; now 24. [There are] now 2 horses and 5 asses. To this manor belongs 1 berewick, which is called Manuden, with 1 hide. Then as now [there was] 1 plough in demesne and 2 bordars. [There is] woodland for 10 pigs. Then and later it was worth £8; now 11.

R[obert] holds Takeley in demesne, which 1 free man held

TRE as a manor and as 3 hides and 15 acres. Then as now [there were] 2 ploughs in demesne and the men [had] 3 ploughs and [there were] 3 villans. [There are] now 8 bordars. Then and later [there were] 3 slaves; now 2. [There is] woodland for 20 pigs. [There are] 20 acres of meadow. [There were] then 2 horses; now 1. [There were] then 12 head of cattle; now 3. [There were] then 16 sheep; now 10. [There were] then 20 pigs; now 38. Then as now it was worth 100s. Peter holds half a hide and 1 ox of R[obert]. It is worth 12s.

Hugh holds Wendens [Ambo and Lofts], of R[obert], which 1 free man held TRE as a manor and as 7 hides less 6 acres. Then as now [there were] 3 ploughs in demesne. The men [had] 4 ploughs then and when received; now 5. Then and later [there were] 8 villans; now 9. [There are] now 5 bordars. Then and later [there were] 6 slaves; now 5. [There are] 24 acres of meadow. Then and later [there was] 1 mill; now 2. [There were] then 5 sheep and 7 pigs. [There are] now 3 colts and 30 pigs and 67 sheep. Then and later it was worth £7; now 8.

HALF-HUNDRED OF CLAVERING.

R[obert] holds Bentfield [Bury] in demesne,

[Folio 65v: ESSE

which a free man held TRE as a manor and as 5 hides. Then as now [there were] 3 ploughs in demesne. The men [had] then 7 ploughs; later 6 [and] now 4. [There were] then 10 villans; later and now 9. Then and later [there were] 2 bordars; now 11. Then and later [there were] 7 slaves; now 4. [There is] woodland for 200 pigs. [There are] 16 acres of meadow, 1 mill. [There were] then 2 horses; now 3. [There was] then 1 ox; now 14. [There were] then 80 sheep; now 30. [There were] then 50 pigs; now 40. Then and later it was worth 100s.; now £7. To this land belongs now as then 1 sokeman with 30 acres.

In Bollington Robert holds 1 hides and 15 acres in demesne. [There were] then 1½ ploughs; later and now 1. Then as now [there were] 2 bordars. [There were] then 10 pigs and 28 sheep. [There is] now 1 cow and 2 pigs and 4 sheep. Then as now it was worth 25s. In this manor Robert holds of R[obert] half a hide and half a plough and it is worth 10s. in the above valuation.

Robert holds Farnham in demesne, which 1 free man held TRE as a manor and as 2 hides. Then as now [there were] 2 ploughs in demesne and the men [had] 2 ploughs. Then and later [there were] 2 villans; now 1. Then as now [there were] 8 bordars. Then and later [there were] 8 slaves; now 1. Then and later [there was] woodland for 200 pigs; now 150. [There are] 10 acres of meadow. [There were] then 4 horses; now 2. [There were] then 15 head of cattle; now none. [There were] then 40 pigs; now 17. [There were] then 60 sheep; now 30. [There are] now 39 goats and 3 hives of bees. It was then worth 40s.; now 50.

Four free men held Manuden TRE as a manor and as 4 hides. Now 4 knights hold [it] of R[obert]. Then as now [there were] 3 ploughs and 2 villans and 5 bordars and 1 slave. [There is] woodland for 30 pigs. [There are] 13 acres of meadow. [There were] then 8 head of cattle and 80 sheep and 20 goats and 20 pigs. [There are] now 5 head of cattle and

33 pigs and 1 colt and 44 sheep and 8 goats. It was then worth 50s.; now 60.

HUNDRED OF HINCKFORD.

Ilger holds [Great and Little] Maplestead of R[obert], which Wulfwine, a free man, held TRE as a manor and as half a hide. Then as now [there were] 2 ploughs in demesne and the men [had] 3 ploughs and [there were] 5 villans. Then and later [there were] 2 bordars; now 6. Then and later [there were] 4 slaves; now 2.

Robert Gernon

[Folio 66: ESSEX]

[There was] then woodland for 100 pigs; now 60. [There are] 26 acres of meadow. [There was] then 1 horse and 8 head of cattle and 10 pigs and 20 sheep and 20 goats. [There is] now 1 horse and 14 head of cattle and 18 pigs and 80 sheep and 23 goats and 2 hives of bees. It is worth 60s.

HUNDRED OF LEXDEN.

Ilger holds Wormingford of R[obert], which Godwine held as a manor and as 1½ hides and 10 acres. [There were] then 3 villans; now 4. [There were] then 2 bordars; now 8. Then as now [there were] 4 slaves. [There were] then 3 ploughs in demesne; now 4. Then as now the men [had] 2 ploughs. [There is] woodland for 100 pigs. [There are] 16 acres of meadow. [There is] now 1 mill, 1 fishery. [There was] then 1 horse; now 6. [There were] then 5 head of cattle; now 33. [There were] then 40 pigs; now 60. [There were] then 6 sheep; now 200. [There were] then 15 goats; now 47. [There are] now 7 hives of bees. It was then worth £4; now 6. And [there were] 19 sokemen TRE holding 2½ hides less 6 acres, whom R[obert] has by exchange, as he says, [and] whom the same Ilger [holds] of him, and they have 8 bordars. Then as now [there were] 2 ploughs, 4 acres of meadow. [There is] woodland for 16 pigs. Then as now it was worth 40s. And these sokemen, as the Shire testifies, could not withdraw from that manor and Raymond Gerald took away 1 villan, of whom Robert was seised. And Roger of Poitou has [him] still.

Nigel holds Wivenhoe of R[obert], which Ælfric held as a manor and as 5 hides less 15 acres. Then as now [there were] 5 villans. [There were] then 6 bordars; now 20. [There was] then 1 slave; now 2. Then as now [there were] 2 ploughs in demesne. Among the men [there were] 3 ploughs then; now 2. [There is] woodland for 100 pigs. [There are] 12 acres of meadow. [There is] pasture for 60 sheep. [There is] now 1 mill. [There were] then 8 head of cattle; now 10. [There was] then 1 horse; now 2. [There were] then 60 sheep; now 87. [There were] then 30 goats; now 20. [There were] 20 pigs; now 24. Then as now it was worth 40s. And a free man held 20 acres, which Robert holds of the gift of the king, and Nigel [holds it] of him. Then as now [there was] half a plough. It is worth 3s. And another free [man] held 20 acres, which the reeve of the Hundred has. It is worth 3s. [and] the same Nigel [now] holds [it].

Robert holds [Great and Little] Birch of R[obert], which Wulfwine held as a manor and as 2 hides

[Folio 66v: ESSEX]

less 4½ acres. Then as now [there were] 12 bordars. [There were] then 6 slaves; now 5. Then as now [there were] 2 ploughs in demesne and the men [had] 2 ploughs. [There is] woodland for 40 pigs. [There are] 12 acres of meadow. Then as now [there was] 1 mill. [There were] then 2 head of cattle; now 7. [There were] then 38 sheep; now 80. [There are] now 33 goats. [There were] then 5 pigs; now 33. [There are] now 2 horses. Then as now it was worth 60s.

HUNDRED OF ONGAR.

R[obert] holds Stapleford [Abbotts] in demesne, which 5 free men held as 2½ hides and 6½ acres. [There were] then 8 bordars; now 14. Among the men [there were] 5 ploughs; now 4. [There is] woodland for 200 pigs. [There are] 21 acres of meadow. Then and later it was worth 50s.; now 60. Of this manor, Nigel holds 1½ hides and [there are] 3 villans and 6 bordars and 2 ploughs and it is worth 28s. in the above valuation.

HUNDRED OF CHAFFORD.

Robert holds Rainham of R[obert], which Alweard held as a manor and as 3½ hides. [There were] then 4 villans; now 5. Then and later [there were] 6 bordars; now 4. [There were] then 2 slaves; now none. Then as now [there were] 2 ploughs in demesne. Among the men [there were] then 2½ ploughs; now 1. [There were] then 3 horses and 14 head of cattle and 6 pigs and 100 sheep. [There are] now 4 horses and 11 head of cattle and 24 pigs and 80 sheep and 12 hives of bees. It was worth £6 then and when received. Now it is worth £4. And 1 free man held 1 hide, who later forfeited it because he committed theft, and [it] was in the king's hands, but Robert the pervert appropriated [it], as the Hundred testifies. [There was] then 1 plough; later and now, none. Then as now it was worth 20s. The same Robert holds this [now] of R[obert].

Ralph holds [South] Weald of R[obert], which Sprot held as a manor and as 1 hide. [There is] now 1 villan and 6 bordars and 1 plough. [There is] woodland for 40 pigs. It is worth 20s. R[obert] has this land, as he says, by exchange, by [the livery of] Hubert de Port, and it has never rendered geld and did not [pay] the last [geld].

HUNDRED OF CHELMSFORD.

Robert holds Fryerning and Ingatestone in demesne, which Siward held as a manor and as 3 hides TRE. Then as now [there was] 1 villan. [There were] then 3 bordars; now 9. [There was] then 1 slave; now 3. Then as now [there was] 1 plough in demesne. The men [had] then half a plough; now 1. [There is] woodland

Robert Gernon

[Folio 67: ESSEX]

for 400 pigs. [There were] then 5 head of cattle; now 4. [There were] then 28 sheep; now 26. [There were] then 12 pigs; now 17. It was then worth 30s.; now 20.

Edwin Groats held Fryerning and Ingatestone as a manor and as 1 hide and 33 acres. Now Ilger holds [it] of Robert.

Then as now [there was] 1 bordar and 1 plough. [There is] woodland for 40 pigs. [There are] 2 acres of meadow. It is worth 20s. R[obert] has this land by exchange.

Ansketil holds Chignall of R[obert], which Dot held as a manor and as 2 hides. Then as now [there was] 1 villan and 2 bordars and 2 ploughs in demesne and the men [had] 1 plough. [There is] woodland for 30 pigs. [There are] 20 acres of meadow. Then as now [there was] 1 horse and 6 head of cattle and 12 sheep and 14 pigs. It was then worth 40s.; now £4.

Corp holds Springfield of R[obert], which Godric held as a manor and as 2 hides and 40 acres. Then as now [there were] 4 villans and 7 bordars and 2 ploughs in demesne and the men [had] 1 plough. [There is] woodland for 30 pigs. [There are] 20 acres of meadow, 1 fishery. [There was] then 1 horse; now 10. [There were] then 5 head of cattle; now 30. [There were] then 4 sheep; now 100. [There were] then 13 pigs; now 40. It was then worth 40s.; now 60.

William holds Fryerning of R[obert], which Sylvi and Topi held as a manor and as 2½ hides and 31 acres, and Robert has [it] by exchange. Then as now [there was] 1 villan and 14 bordars and 1½ ploughs in demesne and the men [had] 1½ ploughs. [There is] woodland for 100 pigs. [There are] 4 acres of meadow. [...][There were] then 10 head of cattle; now the same. [There was] then 1 horse; now 5. Then as now [there were] 20 sheep. [There were] then 30 pigs; now 16. [There are] now 2 hives of bees. Then as now it was worth £4. And Brorda held 30 acres; now R[ichard holds them]. Then as now [there was] half a plough and 2½ acres of meadow. It is worth 10s.

Picot holds Patching, which Brorda held as a manor and as 2½ hides TRE. [There was] then 1 villan; now none. [There are] now 6 bordars. [There were] then 4 slaves; now none. [There were] then 2 ploughs in demesne; now 1. Then as now the men [had] half a plough. [There is] woodland for 50 pigs. [There are] 10 acres of meadow. [There were] then 4 head of cattle and 20 pigs and 20 sheep; now nothing. Then as now it was worth 40s. R[obert] has this land by exchange. Of the fief of Culverts Azo holds of R[obert] what Godwine held

as a manor and as 1½ hides. [There was] then 1 villan and 1 slave. [There are] now 2 bordars. Then as now [there were] 1½ ploughs in demesne and 10 acres of meadow. Then as now [there was] 1 mill. Then as now it was worth 30s.

In Tolleshunt [D'Arcy] Robert de Verly holds 40 acres which belong to this Hundred and they are assessed in [his] manor.

HUNDRED OF TENDRING.

R[obert] holds [Great and Little] Oakley in demesne, which Ælfric Cempa held as a manor and as 10 hides TRE. Then and later [there were] 12 villans; now 11. Then and later [there were] 20 bordars; now 30. Then and later [there were] 10 slaves; now 5. Then as now [there were] 3 ploughs in demesne. Among the men [there were] 10 ploughs; now 9. [There is] woodland for 100 pigs. [There are] 8 acres of meadow. [There is] now 1 mill, 2 salt-pans, pasture for 20 sheep. [There were] then 10 horses; now 4. [There were] then 10 head of cattle; now 5. Then as now [there were] 200 sheep

less 20. [There were] then 20 pigs; now 15. It was worth £11 then and when received. Now it is worth £16. Of this manor Ralph holds 2 hides and 10 acres and [there are] 13 bordars and 1 plough and it is worth 30s. in the above valuation. And Robert holds of a certain free man land which is called Tendring [and] which Walter holds of [Robert] as a manor and as 1 hide less 15 acres. [There were] then 5 villans; now 2. [There were] then 3 bordars; now 7. [There were] then 3 slaves; now none. Then as now [there was] 1 plough in demesne. Among the men [there were] then 3 ploughs; now 2. [There is] woodland for 20 pigs. [There is] 1 acre of meadow. [There were] then 2 horses; now 4. [There were] then 2 head of cattle; now 10. [There were] then 20 pigs; now 27. [There were] then 49 sheep; now 60. [There were] then 24 goats; now 37. [There are] now 3 hives of bees. It was then worth 20s.; now 30. R[obert] received this in exchange.

Nigel holds Dickley of R[obert], which Æthelstan held as a manor and as 1 hide and 37½ acres. Then as now [there were] 8 bordars. [There was] then 1 slave; now none. [There were] then 2 ploughs in demesne; now 1½. Then as now the men [had] 2 ploughs. [There is] woodland for 10 pigs. [There are] 2 acres of meadow. [There were] then 7 head of cattle; now 8. [There was] then 1 horse; now 4. [There were] then 37 sheep; now 51. [There were] then 7 pigs; now 15. Then as now [there were] 20 goats. It is worth 20s.

William holds Ardleigh of R[obert], which Skalpi held as a manor and as half a hide

Robert Gernon

and 30 acres. And it belongs to a certain manor in Suffolk, but pertains to this Hundred. [There was] then 1 villan; now none. Then as now [there was] 1 slave. [There were] then 2 ploughs in demesne [and] when received 1; now none. [There were] then 2 bordars; now none. [...][There is] 1 acre of meadow. It was then worth 40s. and when received 20; now 5.

HUNDRED OF UTTLESFORD.

Robert holds Widdington of R[obert], which Ingulf held as a manor and as 3 hides and 1 virgate. And Robert [Gernon] has [it] by exchange, as he says. [There were] then 5 villans; now 4. [There were] then 3 bordars; now 5. Then as now [there were] 5 slaves and 2 ploughs in demesne. The men [had] then 4 ploughs; now 2. [There are] 10 acres of meadow. [There were] then 3 sheep; now 65. [There were] then 24 pigs; now 49. It was then worth 60s.; now £4.

The same R[obert] holds Shortgrove, which Wulfwine and Grimkel held as a manor and as 2 hides. And Robert [Gernon] has [it] by exchange. Then and later [there were] 6 slaves; now 3. [There were] then 3 ploughs in demesne; later and now 2. [There are] 12 acres of meadow. [There was] then 1 mill; now none. [There were] then 3 horses; now none. [There were] then 3 cows; now none. Then as now [there were] 100 sheep. [There were] then 60 pigs; now none. [There were] then 23 hives of bees; now 11. It was then worth £4, and when received 50s.; now 60.

Picot holds Arkesden of R[obert], which Grimkel held as a

manor and as 1 hide less 8 acres. And Robert has [it] by exchange. [There are] now 4 bordars. Then as now [there were] 2 slaves and 1 plough, 6 acres of meadow. [There are] now 2 head of cattle. Then as now [there were] 12 pigs and 32 sheep. [There are] now 2 hives of bees. It is worth 20s.

Peter holds Elsenham of R[obert], which Leofstan held as a m anor and as 1 hide. And Robert has [it] by exchange. [There were] then 4 villans; later and now 3. Then and later [there are] 3 bordars; now 6. [There were] then 4 slaves; now none. Then and later [there were] 2 ploughs in demesne; now 1. Then and later the men [had] 2 ploughs; now 3. [There is] woodland for 100 pigs. [There are] 20 acres of meadow. Then as now [there was] 1 horse. [There were] then 7 head of cattle. Now [there is] 1 calf. [There were] then 16 sheep; now none. [There were] then 8 pigs; now 18. [There were] then 20 goats; now none. Now as then it is worth 40s.

HUNDRED OF THURSTABLE.

Robert de Verly holds Tolleshunt [D'Arcy] of R[obert],

[Folio 68v: ESSEX]

which Gotar held as a manor and as 5½ hides. [There were] then 4 villans; now 7. [There were] then 6 bordars; now 14. [There were] then 3 slaves; now 5. Then as now [there were] 2 ploughs in demesne and the men [had] 2 ploughs. [There is] woodland for 200 pigs. [There is] 1 acre of meadow, pasture for 40 sheep, 1 salt-pan. [There were] then 3 horses; now none. [There were] then 14 head of cattle; now none. [There were] then 40 pigs; now 20. [There were] then 100 sheep; now 60. [There were] then 30 goats; now 20. [There are] now 8 hives of bees. Then and later it was worth £4; now 100s. And 2 free men held 30 acres. [There was] then 1 plough; now none. Then as now it was worth 10s. and he says that he has this land by exchange.

XXXIII. land of Ralph Baynard.

HUNDRED OF WITHAM.

Gerard holds Ulting of Ralph Baynard, which Hakon held TRE as a manor and as 1 hide and 40 acres. Then as now [there were] 4 ploughs in demesne. The men [had] then 3 ploughs; now 1½. [There were] then 7 villans; now 4. [There are] now 12 bordars. [There were] then 6 slaves; now none. [There is] woodland for 100 pigs. [There are] 20 acres of meadow. Then as now [there were] 2 mills and 5 acres of land were added TRW and are [required to render him] his customary dues. [There were] then 5 horses, 20 head of cattle, 7 pigs, 70 sheep. [There are] now 4 horses, 9 head of cattle, 24 pigs, 35 sheep, 2 hives [of bees]. It was worth £4 then and when received. It is now worth 100s.

In Langford Geoffrey holds 5 free men of R[alph] with 3 virgates of land

Ralph Baynard

[Folio 69: ESSEX]

and 1 acre, who rendered to the king 15d. of customary dues TRE. Then as now they had 1½ ploughs and 1 bordar. [There are] 3 acres [of meadow]. It was then worth 10s.; now 20.

HUNDRED OF DENGIE.

R[alph] holds [Cold] Norton in demesne, which Wulfric, a free man, held TRE as a manor and as 8 hides. Then as now [there were] 5 villans and 11 bordars. [There were] then 2 slaves; now none. [There were] then 2 ploughs in demesne; now 3. The men [had] then 4 ploughs; now 3. Of these hides, 2 are of woodland. [There is] pasture for 40 sheep. [There is] now 1 mill. [There were] then 4 horses and 15 head of cattle, 20 pigs, 150 sheep. [There are] now 6 horses, 8 head of cattle, 20 pigs and 60 sheep. It was then worth £6; now 7. R[alph] has also a manor, 3 hides and 45 acres, which 6 free men hold now as then. [There were] then 5 ploughs; now 3. It was then worth 40s.; now 30. [This] was delivered [to Ralph] in exchange. Of this manor, Walcher holds half a hide and [this] is worth 10s. in the above valuation.

Pointel holds Woodham [Mortimer and Walter] of R[alph], which Leofgifu held as a manor and as 7 hides. [There were] then 12 villans; now 6. Then as now [there were] 4 bordars. [There were] then 6 slaves; now 4. Then as now [there were] 3 ploughs in demesne. The men [had] then 4 ploughs; now 1. [There are] 24 acres of meadow. [There is] woodland for 500 pigs. [There was] then 1 mill; now 2. [There were] then 2 head of cattle and 7 pigs, 37 sheep. [There are] now 8 head of cattle, 21 pigs, 6 asses, 130 sheep, 13 hives of bees. It was then worth £8 and when received 40s. Now it is worth £7.

The same holds Curling Tye [Green], which Grim held TRE as a manor and as 1 hide. [There were] then 2 villans; now 4. Then as now [there were] 9 bordars. [There were] then 4 slaves; now none. Then as now [there were] 2 ploughs in demesne and the men [had] 1 plough. [There are] 22 acres of meadow. [There is] woodland for 40 pigs. [There was] then 1 mill; now none. Then and later it was worth 40s.; now £4. Godric also [holds] of R[alph] half a hide, which [Ralph] has by exchange, as he says, but the Hundred does not know [of it]. Then as now [there was] half a plough. It is worth 10s.

HUNDRED OF DUNMOW.

R[alph] holds [Great and Little] Dunmow in demesne, which Æthelgyth, a certain free woman, held as a manor and as 4½ hides. Then as now [there were] 3 ploughs in demesne. The men [had] then 7 ploughs; now 6. Then as now [there were] 15 villans and 1 priest. [There were] then 12 bordars; now 16.

[Folio 69v: ESSEX]

Then as now [there were] 10 slaves. [There is] woodland for 150 pigs. [There are] 50 acres of meadow. [There is] now 1 mill. [There were] then 3 horses, 11 head of cattle, 40 pigs, 15 sheep, 23 goats. [There are] now 11 horses, 21 head of cattle, 30 pigs, 104 sheep, 53 goats, 8 hives of bees. Then and later it was worth £8; now 10. To this land has been added 1 hide, which 1 free man held TRE. Then as now [there was] 1 plough and 1 villan and 1 bordar and 1 slave. [There is] woodland for 24 pigs. [There are] 10 acres of meadow. It is worth 20s. And to this manor further belongs half a hide, which 1 sokeman held of [Ralph] Baynard's predecessor and he still holds [it]. [There were] then 1½ ploughs in demesne; now 1. Then as now [there was] 1 villan and 1 slave and [there is] woodland for 20 pigs. [There are] 9 acres of meadow. Now as then it is worth 20s.

R[alph] holds Wimbish in demesne, which Æthelgyth held TRE as a manor and as 8 hides. Then as now [there were] 3 ploughs in demesne. The men [had] then 21 ploughs; now 15. Then as now [there were] 26 villans and 1 priest. [There were] then 19 bordars; now 55. [There were] then 6 slaves; now none. [There was] then woodland for 500 pigs; now 400. [There are] 40 acres of meadow. [There were] then 2 horses and 4 head of cattle, 60 pigs, 120 sheep, 4 hives of bees. [There are] now 2 horses, 4 head of cattle, 28 pigs, 80 sheep, 4 hives of bees. It was then worth £12; now 20.

HUNDRED OF WINSTREE.

Modbert holds Barn Hall of R[alph], which Ælfric, a free man, held TRE as a manor and as 1 hide. Then as now [there was] 1 plough in demesne. [There were] then 3 bordars; now 4. [There is] woodland for 20 pigs. [There were] then 2 horses, 1 cow, 1 pig, 15 sheep. [There are] now 2 horses, 1 cow, 2 pigs, 33 sheep, 34 goats. It is worth 30s.

Bernard holds Messing of R[alph], which a free woman held as a manor and as half a hide TRE. [There is] now 1 bordar. [There is] woodland for 12 pigs. It was then worth 10s.; now 3.

HUNDRED OF CLAVERING.

In Manuden 1 free man held TRE 30 acres, which Amalfrid now holds of R[alph]. Then as now [there was] 1 plough. It was then worth 5s.; now 10.

HUNDRED OF HINCKFORD.

A free woman held Pentlow TRE as a manor and as 4 hides and 3 virgates. Then as now [there were] 3 ploughs in demesne and the men [had] 5 ploughs

Ralph Baynard

[Folio 70: ESSEX]

and [there were] 8 villans. Then and later [there was] 1 bordar; now 8. [There were] then 8 slaves; now none. [There is] woodland for 200 pigs. [There are] 30 acres of meadow. Then as now [there was] 1 mill. [There were] then 2 horses, 22 head of cattle, 48 pigs, 10 sheep, 8 hives of bees. [There are] now 3 horses, 24 head of cattle, 20 pigs, 80 sheep, 8 hives of bees. And [there are] 18 sokemen with 2 hides and 30 acres, and they have 5 ploughs. [There were] then 4 slaves; now 1. [There are] now 4 bordars. [There is] woodland for 10 pigs. [There are] 10 acres of meadow. This whole [estate] was worth £10 TRE; now 16. Of this manor, Walcher holds 30 acres and [this] is worth 10s. in the above valuation.

HUNDRED OF DENGIE.

R[alph] holds Burnham in demesne, which Alweard, a free man, held TRE as a manor and as 4 hides and 12 acres. Then as now [there was] 1 villan. [There were] then 6 bordars; now 12. [There were] then 4 slaves; now none. Then as now [there were] 2 ploughs in demesne and the men [had] 1 plough. [There is] pasture for 300 sheep. [There were] then 2 horses, 4 head of cattle, 12 pigs, 200 sheep. [There are] now 6 horses, 13 head of cattle, 16 pigs, 336 sheep. It was then worth £4; now 100s. In the same vill [there were] 10 free men TRE, holding 8 hides and 28 acres, which R[alph] holds in demesne. [There were] then 10 bordars; now 16. Then as now [there were] 7 slaves and 8 ploughs. [There is] now 1 mill. [There is] pasture for 600 sheep. Then and later it was worth £7; now £8. Ralph Baynard claims this land by exchange.

HUNDRED OF CHELMSFORD.

Germund holds [Great and Little] Baddow of R[alph], which Leofwine held as a manor and as 4 hides. Then as now [there were] 2 villans and 2 bordars. [There were] then 9 slaves; now 7. Then as now [there were] 4 ploughs in demesne. Among the men [there was] then 1 plough; now none. [There is] woodland for 100 pigs. [There is] 1 acre of meadow. Then as now [there were] 7 horses, 47 head of cattle, 108 pigs, 80 sheep. [There are] now 10 horses, 53 head of cattle, 163 sheep. Then and later it was worth 100s.; now £6. And 5 free men held 2 hides and 31 acres, who could go where they would. The same Germund and 4 Frenchmen now hold [it]. Then as now [there were] 3 bordars and 1 slave. [There were] then 2 ploughs; now 1. [There is] woodland for 26 pigs. [There are] 13 acres of meadow.

[Folio 70v: ESSEX]

Then as now it is worth 20s.

Berengar holds Hanningfield of R[alph], which Northmann held as a manor and as 3 hides. [There were] then 3 villans; now none. [There are] now 9 bordars. Then as now [there were] 2 slaves. [There were] then 2 ploughs in demesne; now 1. The men [had] then 1 plough; now half a plough. [There is] woodland for 200 pigs. [There are] now 3 head of cattle, 23 pigs, 47 sheep, 4 goats. Then and later it was worth 50s.; now £4.

HUNDRED OF TENDRING.

Germund holds [Great and Little] Oakley of R[alph], which Eadnoth held as a manor and as 5½ hides. [There were] then 7 villans; now 17. Then as now [there were] 4 bordars and 8 slaves and 3 ploughs in demesne and the men [had] 3 ploughs. [There is] woodland for 33 pigs. [There are] 2 acres of meadow, 1 fishery. [There is] pasture for 100 sheep. [There were] then 2 horses and 13 head of cattle, 50 pigs, 50 sheep. [There are] now 3 horses, 4 head of cattle, 27 pigs, 118 sheep. Then and later it was worth £7; now 9.

Roger holds Ramsey, which Ælfric Cempa held as a manor and as 7 hides and 35 acres. Then as now [there were] 18 villans. [There were] then 6 bordars; now 9. Then as now [there were] 6 slaves and 3 ploughs in demesne. Among the men [there were] 7 ploughs; now 5. [There is] woodland for 60 pigs. [There are] 8 acres of meadow. [There is] now 1 mill, 1 salt-pan. It was then worth £12; now 15. [There was] then 1 horse and 20 head of cattle, 22 pigs, 115 sheep. [There are] now 2 horses, 20 head of cattle, 49 pigs, 309 sheep, 8 hives of bees.

Bernard holds Michaelstow of R[alph], which Alric held as a manor and as 2½ hides. [There were] then 3 bordars; now 1. [There were] then 3 slaves; now none. Then as now [there were] 2 ploughs in demesne. Among the men [there was] then half a plough; now none. [There are] 4 acres of meadow. [There were] then 2 horses, 6 head of cattle, 27 pigs, 150 sheep. [There are] now 25 pigs, 83 sheep. It was then worth 70s.; now £4. And R[alph] holds 2 sokemen by exchange, as his men say, but the others do not testify [to it], only [his men] alone, of the manor which is called Lawford, holding half a hide and 35 acres. The same B[ernard] holds this of R[alph]. [There was] then 1 plough; now half a plough. It was then worth 8s.; now 10. And in "Witelebroc" Roger holds 1 hide of R[alph], which Ælfric held as a manor. Then as now [there was] 1 bordar and 1 plough and 1 acre of meadow. It is worth 10s., and this

Ralph Baynard

[Folio 71: ESSEX]

land did not belong to the other lands. These 3 manors are worth [...] £20.

HUNDRED OF UTTLESFORD.

Amalfrid holds Wendon [Ambo and Lofts], which 1 free man, Alwine Still held as a manor and as 1½ hides and 30 acres, and R[alph] has [it] by exchange. Then as now [there were] 5 villans and 3 bordars and 2 slaves and 2 ploughs in demesne and the men [had] 1 plough. [There is] woodland for 80 pigs. [There are] 3 acres of meadow. It was then worth £4; now 5.

HALF-HUNDRED OF FRESHWELL.

R[alph] holds Henham in demesne, which Æthelgyth held as a manor and as 13½ hides less 10 acres. Then and later [there were] 18 villans; now 8. Then and later [there were] 5 bordars; now 38. Then and later [there were] 8 slaves; now none. Then as now [there were] 4 ploughs in demesne and the men [had] 8 ploughs. [There is] woodland for 200 pigs. [There are] 16 acres of meadow. [There were] then 3 horses, 8 head of cattle, 80 pigs, 160 sheep, 16 hives of bees. [There are] now 8 horses, 7 head of cattle, 100 pigs, 80 sheep, 10 hives of bees. It was then worth £12; now 20.

R[alph] holds Ashdon in demesne, which Æthelgyth held as a manor and as 2 hides. [There were] then 14 villans; now 20. [There were] then 3 bordars; now 9. [There were] then 2 slaves; now none. Then as now [there were] 2 ploughs in demesne and the men [had] 4 ploughs. [There is] woodland for 100 pigs. [There are] 6 acres of meadow, 1 acre of vineyard. [There were] then 2 horses, 5 head of cattle, 60 pigs, 200 sheep, 10 hives of bees. [There is] now 1 horse, 7 head of cattle, 60 pigs, 65 sheep, 3 hives of bees. It was then worth £6; now 8. And [there are] 2 sokemen holding 15 acres freely. R[alph] received these in exchange. They are worth 3s.

HUNDRED OF ROCHFORD.

In Paglesham Theodoric Pointel holds half a hide and 15 [acres], which 1 free man held. [There were] then 2 bordars; now 5. Then as now [there is] 1 plough. [There is] pasture for 50 sheep. Then as now it was worth 20s. R[alph] claims this in exchange.

HUNDRED OF THURSTABLE.

Cola and Æthelmær held Langford as a manor and as 3½ hides. And Æthelmær held this half a hide paying rent to St Paul, but R[alph] is seised of it [now]. And Geoffrey holds the whole [of it] of R[alph]. Then as now [there was] 1 villan. [There were] then 4 bordars; now 9. [There were] then 4 slaves; now 3. [There were] then 3 ploughs in demesne; now 2.

[Folio 71V: ESSEX]

[There is] woodland for 20 pigs. [There are] 25 acres of meadow. Then as now [there was] 1 mill. [There were] then 3 horses, 5 head of cattle, 24 pigs, 40 sheep. [There are] now 2 horses, 4 head of cattle, 40 pigs, 80 sheep. It was then worth 100s., and when received the same; now £4. [There were] then 5 free men with 1½ hides; now 4 men. [There were] then 1½ ploughs; now 1. [There was] then 1 bordar; now 3. [There was] then 1 slave; now none. It was then worth 30s.; now 20.

Bernard holds Tolleshunt of R[alph], which Æthelmær held as a manor and as 3 hides and 8 acres. [There were] then 4 villans; now 8. Then as now [there were] 5 bordars. [There were] then 4 slaves; now 1. Then as now [there were] 1½ ploughs in demesne and the men [had] 2 ploughs. [There is] woodland for 200 pigs, pasture for 20 sheep, 5 salt-pans. [There were] then 2 horses, 6 head of cattle, 20 pigs, 100 sheep. [There are] now 2 horses, 5 head of cattle, 20 pigs, 100 sheep, 28 goats. Then as now it was worth 60s. In the same vill are 8 free men with 1½ hides and 14 acres. Then as now [there were] 2 bordars and 2 ploughs. It is worth 20s. R[alph] Baynard has this land by exchange.

XXXIIII. Lands of Ranulf Peverel.

HUNDRED OF BARSTABLE.

In Bowers [Gifford] Serlo holds of Ranulf [with] 1 plough and 1 slave, which Æthelstan, a free man, held. [There is] pasture for 120 sheep. [There was] then 1 horse, 100 sheep, 14 pigs, 4 calves. [There are] now 2 horses, 100 sheep, 14 pigs, 4 calves. It was then worth 20s.; now 40.

The same Serlo holds Vange of R[anulf], which a free man, who became the man of Ranulf Peverel's predecessor TRW, held as a manor and as 1 hide, but he did not give him his land. When the king gave the land to Ranulf, he took seisin of it with

Ranulf Peverel

[Folio 72: ESSEX]

the rest. In which [land there] was 1 plough; now none. [There is] pasture for 300 sheep. It was then worth 20s.; now 10. The same Serlo holds Ingrave, which Ælfgyth held TRE as a manor and as 1 hide and 20 acres. Then as now [there was] 1 plough. [There were] then 3 bordars; now 4. [There is] woodland for 30 pigs. It was then worth 20s.; now 10.

HUNDRED OF WITHAM.

R[anulf] holds Hatfield [Peverel] in demesne, which Æthelmær held TRE as a manor and as 9 hides and 82 acres. Then as now [there were] 5 ploughs in demesne. The men [had] then 13 ploughs; now 11. [There were] then 12 villans; now 13. [There were] then 12 bordars; now 38. [There were] then 10 slaves; now 7. [There is] woodland for 700 pigs. [There are] 50 acres of meadow. [There were] then 2 mills; now 1. [There were] then 6 horses and 4 colts and 6 cows and 8 calves, 150 sheep, 100 pigs. [There are] now 5 horses, 4 colts, 5 cows, 7 calves, 57 sheep, 39 pigs, 20 goats. It was then worth £16; now 20. And he received this manor at as much value as now. Of this manor, Serlo and Ernulf and Richard hold 3 hides and 20 acres, and it is worth £4 in the above valuation. And 5 knights hold 4 hides and 15 acres of R[anulf], which 13 free men held TRE. Then as now [there were] 7 ploughs, 16 bordars, 2 villans and 2 slaves and 1 mill. It is worth £4.

Humphrey holds Blunt's Hall of R[anulf], which Beorhtmær held TRE as a manor and as 2½ hides. Then as now [there were] 2 ploughs in demesne. The men [had] then 1 plough; now 1½. Then as now [there were] 2 villans. [There were] then 3 bordars; now 5. [There were] then 6 slaves; now 4. [There are] 18 acres of meadow, and [there is] 1 mill and 1 sokeman with 15 acres. [There was] then 1 horse, 4 head of cattle and 4 calves, 60 sheep, 16 pigs. [There are] now 2 horses, 4 cows and 4 calves, 80 sheep, 36 pigs. Then as now it is worth £4.

Richard holds Terling of R[anulf], which Æthelmær, a thegn of the king, held TRE as a manor and as 2½ hides and 30 acres. Then as now [there were] 2 ploughs in demesne and the men [had] 3 ploughs. [There were] then 11 villans; now 5. [There are] now 11 bordars. [There were] then 5 slaves; now none. [There is] woodland for 150 pigs.

[There are] 20 acres of meadow. [There is] pasture for 100 sheep. [There was] then 1 mill; now 2. And [there are] 2 houses in Colchester; one renders 6d. and the other 14[d.]. [There is] 1 free man with 5 acres and he rendered 10d. to Ranulf's predecessor and now similarly to R[anulf]. [There were] then 12 head of cattle, 180 sheep, 50 goats, 40 pigs. [There are] now 2 horses and 2 colts, 8 head of cattle, 75 sheep, 16 goats, 34 pigs. It was then worth £8, and when received the same; now £6.

Turold holds Fairstead, which Beorhtmær held TRE as a manor and as 55 acres. Then as now [there were] 2 ploughs in demesne and the men [had] 2 ploughs and [there were] 4 villans. [There were] then 7 bordars; now 10. [There were] then 4 slaves; now 3. [There is] woodland for 100 pigs. [There are] 40 acres of meadow. [There is] pasture [worth] 4d. [There is] now 1 mill. [There was] then 1 horse, 13 sheep, 6 pigs. [There are] now 2 horses, 124 sheep, 32 pigs, 4 cows, 100 calves, 3 hives of bees. And 15 acres belonged there TRE, of which Saswalo disseised [him], and they belong [now] to the

fief of G[eoffrey] de Mandeville. It was then worth £4; now 100s.

HUNDRED OF BECONTREE.

R[anulf] holds [East and West] Ham in demesne, which Æthelstan, a free man, held TRE as a manor and as 8 hides and 30 acres. And King William gave this manor to R[anulf] Peverel and Robert Gernon. [There were] then 5 ploughs in demesne; now 4. The men [had] then 8 ploughs; now 12. [There were] then 32 villans; now 48. [There were] then 16 bordars; now 80 less 1. Then as now [there were] 3 slaves. [There is] woodland for 100 pigs. [There are] 60 acres of meadow. [There were] then 9 mills; now 8. [There was] then 1 horse, 1 cow, 3 pigs. [There are] now 2 horses, 2 colts, 2 cows with calves, 20 pigs, 60 sheep. It was then worth £16, and when they received [it] £12. Now it is worth £23, and R[obert] Gernon has a moiety of this manor.

HUNDRED OF DUNMOW.

Warin holds Chickney of R[anulf], which Siward, a thegn of King Edward, held as a manor and as 2½ hides. Then as now [there were] 3 ploughs in demesne and the men [had] 2 ploughs. [There were] then 2 villans; now none. [There were] then 7 bordars. [There is] now 1 priest and 14 bordars. [There is] woodland for 60 pigs. [There are] 20 acres of meadow. [There were] then 2 horses, 3 cows, 100 calves, 60 sheep, 20 pigs, 24 goats. [There are] now 3 horses, 6 cows [with] calves, 100 sheep, 30 pigs,

Ranulf Peverel

30 goats. It was then worth 100s.; now £7.

Ravenot holds Willingale [Doe and Spain] of R[anulf], which Siward held TRE as a manor and as 1 hide and 1½ virgates. Then as now [there were] 3 ploughs in demesne. The men [had] then half a plough; now 1. [There was] then 1 villan; now 3. Then as now [there were] 6 bordars. [There were] then 6 slaves; now 4. [There is] woodland for 120 pigs. [There are] 12 acres of meadow. [There were] then 3 horses, 16 head of cattle, 30 pigs. [There are] now 3 horses, 4 colts, 16 head of cattle, 100 sheep, 165 pigs, 5 hives of bees. It was then worth 100s., and when received £6; now 10.

To this land has been added 1 sokeman, whom R[anulf] Peverel held, and R[anulf] still holds [him] and Ravenot of [Ranulf]. And 30 acres have also been added to this land TRW, which a free man held TRE. They are worth 10s.

HUNDRED OF DENGIE.

R[anulf] holds Woodham [Mortimer and Walter] in demesne, which Siward held as a manor and as 5 hides. Then as now [there] were 4 villans. [There were] then 9 bordars; now 8. [There were] then 5 slaves; now 2. Then as now [there were] 2 ploughs in demesne. The men [had] then 4 ploughs; now 1½. [There are] 3 acres of meadow. [There is] woodland for 200 pigs. [There were] then 2 horses, 6 cows, 4 calves, 60 sheep, 20 pigs, 45 goats. [There are] now 3 horses, 2 colts, 4 cows, 4 calves, 135 sheep, 46 pigs, 5 goats. Then as now it was worth 100s.

R[anulf] holds Maldon in demesne, which Siward held TRE as a manor and as 5½ hides and 10 acres. [There were] then 16 villans; now 9. [There are] now 10 bordars. Then as now [there were] 3 slaves and 2 ploughs in demesne. The men [had] then 10 [ploughs]; now 5. [There are] 10 acres of meadow. [There is] woodland for 50 pigs, 1 mill. [There were] then 2 horses; now the same. And [there are] now 3 cows, 4 calves, 140 sheep, 29 pigs. Then as now it was worth £12.

Serlo holds Hazeleigh of R[anulf], which the same S[iward] held as a manor and as 4½ hides. Then as now [there were] 4 villans. [There were] then 4 slaves; now 3. [There were] then 2 ploughs; now 1. The men [had] then 1 plough; now half a plough. [There is] woodland for 60 pigs. [There were] then 2 horses, 2 cows, 2 calves, 60 sheep, 5 pigs. [There are] now 2 horses, 4 cows, 100 sheep, 9 pigs. It is worth £4.

[Folio 73v: ESSEX]

Godric holds Hazeleigh of R[anulf], which Æthelmær, a free man, held TRE as a manor and as half a hide and 20 acres. Then as now [there was] 1 villan. [There were] then 2 bordars; now none. Then as now [there was] 1 plough in demesne. [There is] woodland for 80 pigs. It is worth 20s.

HUNDRED OF WINSTREE.

Turold holds Layer of R[anulf], which Æ[thelmær] held TRE as a manor and as 1 hide less 12½ acres. Then as now [there was] 1 plough in demesne. The men [have] now half a plough. [There was] then 1 bordar; now 4. [There were] then 4 slaves; now 1. [There is] woodland for 16 pigs. [There was] then 1 horse, 5 cows, 5 calves, 100 sheep. [There are] now 2 horses, 4 cows, 5 calves, 103 sheep. It was then worth 30s.; now 20.

R[anulf] holds Abberton in demesne, which 1 free man held TRE as a manor and as 1½ hides and 1 virgate. Then as now [there was] 1 plough in demesne and the men [had] half a plough and 4 bordars and 1 slave. [There is] woodland for 60 pigs. [There are] 4 acres of meadow. It was then worth 60s.; now 50.

Algar holds [Great and Little] Wigborough of R[anulf], which 1 free man held TRE as a manor and as half a hide. Then as now [there was] 1 plough. [There was] then 1 bordar; now 2. It is worth 10s.

HUNDRED OF UTTLESFORD.

R[anulf] holds Debden in demesne, which Siward held as a manor and as 16½ hides. Then as now [there were] 6 ploughs in demesne and the men [had] 11 ploughs and [there were] 36 villans. Then and later [there was] 1 bordar; now 17. Then as now [there were] 12 slaves. [There is] woodland for 1,000 pigs. [There are] 40 acres of meadow. Then as now [there was] 1 mill. [There are] now 2 arpents of vineyard in bearing [fruit] and 2 others not [yet] bearing. [There were] then 6 horses, 28 head of cattle, 150 sheep, 250 pigs, 6 hives of bees. [There are] now 7 horses, 2 colts, 10 head of cattle, 168 sheep, 110 pigs, 3 hives of bees. Then and later it was worth £24; now 30. Of this

manor, Vital[is] holds 15 acres of R[anulf], and [this] is worth 10s. in the above valuation.

R[anulf] holds Amberden in demesne, which Siward held as a manor and as 5 hides. Then as now [there were] 3 ploughs in demesne and the men [had] 6 ploughs. Then and later [there were] 13 villans;

Ranulf Peverel

[Folio 74: ESSEX]

now 19. [There was] then 1 bordar; later 2; now 7. Then as now [there were] 6 slaves. Then and later [there was] woodland for 250 pigs; now 200. [There are] 30 acres of meadow. [There were] then 2 horses, 6 head of cattle, 40 sheep, 40 pigs, 5 hives of bees. [There are] now 3 horses, 1 colt, 14 head of cattle, 68 sheep, 30 pigs, 1 hive of bees. Then as now it was worth £12, but R[anulf] had £18 a year for 3 years. The Abbot of Ely claims this vill and the Hundred testifies that it belonged to the [abbey].

HUNDRED OF HINCKFORD.

R[anulf] holds Stebbing in demesne, which Siward held TRE as a manor and as 3 hides and 30 acres. [There was] then 1 plough in demesne, and when received 6; now 5. Then as now the men [had] 11 ploughs. Then and later [there were] 18 villans; now 19. Then and later [there were] 14 bordars; now 31. Then and later [there were] 13 slaves; now 11. [There is] woodland for 200 pigs. [There are] 24 acres of meadow. [There was] then 1 mill, and when received 1½; now 2. [There are] now 2½ arpents of vineyard and only the half is bearing. [There were] then 5 horses, 5 cows, 100 sheep, 50 pigs, 5 hives of bees. It was then worth £10; later 12 [and] now £16. Of this manor, Vitalis [holds] 35 acres and [this] is worth 10s. in the above valuation.

Turold holds [Great and Little] Henny of R[anulf], which Wulfwine, a free man, held TRE as a manor and as 2½ hides and 45 acres. Then as now [there were] 2 ploughs in demesne and the men [had] 3 ploughs and [there were] 5 villans and 11 bordars. Then and later [there were] 2 slaves; now none. [There is] woodland for 80 pigs. [There are] 12 acres of meadow. Then as now [there was] 1 mill. [There were] then 2 horses, 5 cows with calves, 50 sheep, 14 pigs, 3 hives of bees. [There is] now 1 horse, 9 cows, 100 calves, 134 sheep, 36 pigs. And to this manor belongs 22d. in customary dues from Sudbury. It was then worth 40s.; now £4.

Turold holds Lamarsh of R[anulf], which Algar held TRE as a manor and as 3½ hides. Then as now [there were] 2 ploughs in demesne. Then and later the men [had] 2½ ploughs; now 2. Then as now [there were] 4 villans. [There are] now 8 bordars. [There is] woodland for 70 pigs. [There are] 13 acres of meadow. [There were] then 6 cows, 100 calves, 54 sheep, 11 pigs. [There are] now 7 horses, 5 colts, 10 cows, 8 calves, 20 sheep, 54 pigs, 60 goats, 6 hives of bees. It was then worth £4;

[Folio 74v: ESSEX]

now 6. In Lamarsh Alweard held 1½ hides as a manor TRE. Now the same T[urold] holds [it] of Ranulf. Then as now [there was] 1 plough in demesne and the men [had] 1 plough and [there were] 2 villans. [There were] then 3 bordars; now 9. [There is] woodland for 30 pigs. [There are] 7 acres of meadow. It was then worth 40s.; now 60. These two lands were thus divided between two brothers TRE. Later they were given to Ranulf as 1 manor, as his men say.

HUNDRED OF DENGIE.

R[anulf] holds Down in demesne, which Siward held as a manor and as 14 hides. [There were] then 2 villans; now 4. [There were] then 3 bordars; now 15. [There were] then 12 slaves; now 6. Then as now [there were] 5 ploughs in demesne. The men [had] then 2 ploughs; now 3. [There is] woodland for 50 pigs, pasture for 50 sheep. Then and later it was worth £10; now 13. Of this manor, Ascelin holds 1½ hides of R[anulf] and [this] is worth 20s. in the above valuation.

R[anulf] holds Lawling in demesne, which Brun, a free man, held TRE as a manor and 2½ hides and 35 acres. Then as now [there were] 2 slaves and 2 ploughs. [There is] woodland for 20 pigs, pasture for 50 sheep. [There is] now 1 fishery. Then and later it was worth £4; now £3. 15s.

In Down 8 free men held 5 hides less 6 acres, which R[anulf] holds in demesne. Then as now [there were] 6 bordars and 2½ ploughs. Then and later it was worth 60s.; now £4. 10s.

Ralph fitzBrian holds Stansgate, which Siward held as a manor and as 9½ hides TRE. Then as now [there were] 2 villans. [There were] then 22 bordars; now 18. [There were] then 8 slaves; now 3. [There were] then 4½ ploughs in demesne; now 4. Then as now the men [had] 3 ploughs. [There is] woodland for 60 pigs, pasture for 60 sheep. Then and later it was worth £10; now 8.

HUNDRED OF LEXDEN.

The same R[alph fitzBrian] holds Prested, which Beorhtmær held TRE as a manor and as 1½ hides. [There were] then 5 bordars; now 10. [There were] then 4 slaves; now none. Then as now [there were] 2 ploughs in demesne. [There is] woodland for 100 pigs. [There are] 8 acres of meadow. [There were] then 2 horses, 10 head of cattle, 80 sheep, 15 pigs, 20 goats, 2 hives of bees. [There is] now 1 horse

Ranulf Peverel

[Folio 75: ESSEX]

and 1 colt, 60 sheep, 20 pigs, 9 goats, 2 hives of bees. Then as now it was worth £4. And 1 free man held then as now 5 acres and was commended to the predecessor of R[anulf], but he could go where he would with his land and now R[anulf] has [him]. [There was] then 1 plough; now half a plough. It was then worth 16s.; now 12.

HUNDRED OF ONGAR.

Ravenot holds Plunker's [Green] of R[anulf], which Wulfric the priest held freely of Harold as 14 acres, and now R[anulf] has [it] because his predecessor was seised of it, but it did not belong to him, as the Shire testifies. Then as now [there was] 1

villan and half a plough. [There is] woodland for 20 pigs. [There are] 1½ acres of meadow. It is worth 5s.

HUNDRED OF CHELMSFORD.

Robert holds Springfield of R[anulf], which Æthelstan held as a manor and as 5 hides and 20 acres. [There were] then 6 villans; now 4. [There were] then 3 bordars; now 10. [There were] 8 bordars; now 6. Then as now [there were] 3 ploughs in demesne. Then and later the men [had] 3 ploughs; now 2. [There is] woodland for 30 pigs. [There are] 25 acres of meadow. Then as now [there was] 1 mill. [There were] then 2 horses, 12 head of cattle, 100 sheep, 50 pigs. [There are] now 4 horses, 5 colts, 26 head of cattle, 40 sheep, 25 pigs, 12 goats, 2 asses, 1 hive of bees. It was then worth £5; now 6. And 2 free men held 13 acres, which R[anulf] has. It is worth 2s.

Ralph fitzBrian holds Rettendon, which Siward held as a manor and as 1 hide and 30 acres. Then as now [there was] 1 bordar and 1 plough in demesne. [There is] woodland for 6 pigs. Then as now it was worth 25s. and the Abbey of Ely claims [it].

HALF-HUNDRED OF MALDON.

In Maldon R[anulf] holds half a hide and 24 acres in demesne, which Siward held TRE as a manor. [There was] then 1 bordar; now 3. It is worth 5s. and this land is [included] in the £12 from Maldon.

HUNDRED OF TENDRING.

R[anulf] holds Tendring in demesne, which Wulfwig held freely as a manor and as half a hide and 30 acres, and R[anulf] has [it] by exchange. [There were] then 2 slaves; now 1. [There were] then 2 ploughs; later and now 1. [There is] woodland for 30 pigs.

[Folio 75v: ESSEX]

[There are] 2 acres of meadow. Then and later it was worth 20s.; now 60.

Turold holds St Osyth of R[anulf], which Siward held as a manor and as 2½ hides. Then and later [there were] 9 villans; now 6. Then and later [there were] 12 bordars; now 11. Then as now [there were] 7 slaves. Then and later [there were] 4 ploughs in demesne; now 3. Then and later the men [had] 7 ploughs; now 5. [There is] woodland for 800 pigs. [There are] 4 acres of meadow. [There is] pasture for 200 sheep. Then as now [there was] 1 mill. [There were] then 6 horses, 50 head of cattle, 300 sheep, 40 pigs, 6 hives of bees. [There are] now 4 horses, 4 head of cattle, 68 sheep, 37 pigs, 18 goats. Then and later it was worth £9; now 8.

The same T[urold] holds Frating of R[anulf], which Ketil held as a manor and as 2 hides. [There were] then 2 bordars; now 3. [There were] then 3 slaves; now 2. [There were] 2 ploughs in demesne; now 1. Then as now the men [had] 1 plough. [There is] woodland for 150 pigs. [There are] 4 acres of meadow. [There was] then 1 horse, 4 head of cattle, 4 calves, 100 sheep, 40 pigs. [There is] now 1 horse, 2 cows, 2 calves, 66 sheep, 20 pigs, 6 hives of bees. It was then worth 40s.; now 60.

HUNDRED OF ROCHFORD.

R[anulf] holds Leigh in demesne, which 1 free man held as a manor and as 1 hide. Then as now [there were] 2 villans and 2 bordars and 1 plough in demesne and the men [had] half a plough and 5 bordars by the water, who do not hold land. [There is] pasture for 100 sheep. [There was] then 1 horse, 5 cows, 5 calves, 100 sheep. [There are] now 2 horses, 4 cows, 5 calves, 103 sheep. It was then worth 40s.; now 100.

HUNDRED OF THURSTABLE.

Humphrey holds Tolleshunt [D'Arcy] of R[anulf], which Siward held as a manor and as $3\frac{1}{2}$ hides and 30 acres. [There were] then 9 villans; now 10. [There were] then 3 bordars; now 13. [There were] then 10 slaves; now 6. Then as now [there were] 3 ploughs in demesne and the men [had] 3 ploughs, 1 salt-pan. [There are] 5 acres of meadow. [There is] pasture for 30 sheep. [There is] woodland for 150 pigs. [There were] then 3 horses, 20 head of cattle, 80 sheep, 60 pigs. [There are] now 3 horses, 20 head of cattle, 160 sheep, 37 pigs, 18 goats. Then as now it was worth 100s. In this manor 4 free men held half a hide and 5 acres, but Ralph

Ranulf Peverel

[Folio 76: ESSEX]

Baynard has it and Hugh de Montfort.

Richard holds Goldhanger of R[anulf], which Leofwine and Wulfweard the priest held as a manor and as $2\frac{1}{2}$ hides and 25 acres. [There were] then 3 bordars; now 14. Then as now [there are] 2 slaves. [There were] then 2 ploughs in demesne; now 1. The men [have] now 1 plough. [There is] woodland for 80 pigs, pasture for 50 sheep. [There are] $3\frac{1}{2}$ acres of meadow. [There were] then 51 sheep, 8 pigs. [There is] now 1 horse, 1 cow, 3 sheep, 3 pigs. Then as now it was worth 40s. In the same [vill are] 2 free men with $7\frac{1}{2}$ acres and it is worth 20d.

XXXV. Land of Aubrey de Vere.

HUNDRED OF DUNMOW.

Aubrey holds [Great and Little] Canfield in demesne, which Wulfwine held TRE as a manor and as 2 hides. Then as now [there were] 2 ploughs in demesne. The men [had] then 4 ploughs; now 3. Then as now [there were] 10 villans. [There were] then 4 bordars; now 9. Then as now [there were] 4 slaves. [There is] woodland for 160 pigs. [There are] 51 acres of meadow, 1 mill. [There were] then 7 head of cattle, 2 horses, 20 pigs, 80 sheep, 3 hives of bees. [There are] now 8 head of cattle, 3 horses, 30 pigs, 100 sheep, 3 hives of bees. Then as now it was worth £6.

Aubrey holds "Udecheshale" in demesne, which Wulfwine held as a manor and as 1 hide. Then as now [there were] 2 ploughs in demesne. The men [had] then 3 ploughs; now 1. [There were] then 11 villans; now 6. [There were] then 2 bordars; now 4. Then as now [there were] 4 slaves. [There is] woodland for 100 pigs. [There are] 48 acres of meadow. [There were] then 6 head of cattle, 2 horses, 20 pigs, 60 sheep, 3 hives of bees. [There are] now 8 head of

cattle, 2 horses, 30 pigs, 80 sheep, 3 hives of bees. Then as now it was worth 60s.

[Folio 76v: ESSEX]

To this land have been added 1 virgate and 8 acres, which a free man held TRE. Now Ralph holds [it] of A[ubrey]. Then as now [there was] 1 plough in demesne. [There was] then 1 bordar; now 3. [There is] woodland for 30 pigs. [There are] 9 acres of meadow. It was then worth 16s.; now 30.

HUNDRED OF UTTLESFORD.

Ralph holds Thunderley of A[ubrey], which Æthelmær, a free man, held TRE as a manor and as 5 hides. Then and later [there were] 2 ploughs in demesne; now 3. Then as now the men [had] 3 ploughs and [there was] 1 priest and 11 villans and 5 bordars. Then and later [there was] woodland for 100 pigs; now 80. [There are] 12 acres of meadow. [There were] then 120 sheep, 40 pigs, 60 goats, 8 head of cattle, 3 horses, 5 hives of bees. [There are] now 140 sheep, 60 pigs, and the rest the same. Then and later it was worth £6; now 7.

HALF-HUNDRED OF CLAVERING.

Ralph holds Ugley of A[ubrey], which Wulfwine held as a manor and as 5 hides. Then as now [there were] 3 ploughs in demesne and the men [had] 4 ploughs. [There were] then 10 villans; later and now 7. Then and later [there was] 1 bordar; now 10. Then and later [there were] 6 slaves; now 2. Then and later [there was] woodland for 200 pigs; now 160. [There are] 25 acres of meadow. [There were] then 5 head of cattle, 50 pigs, 160 sheep, 2 horses, 50 goats, 2 hives of bees. [There are] now 3 head of cattle, 22 pigs, 80 sheep, 4 horses, 20 goats, 2 hives of bees. It was then worth £6; now 8.

HUNDRED OF HINCKFORD.

Aubrey holds Hedingham [Castle and Sible] in demesne, which Wulfwine held as a manor and as 2 hides. Then as now [there were] 4 ploughs in demesne and the men [had] 6 ploughs and [there were] 15 villans and 7 bordars and 8 slaves. [There is] woodland for 200 pigs. [There are] 30 acres of meadow. [There was] then 1 mill; now none. [There are] now 6 arpents of vineyard. [There were] then 11 head of cattle, 140 sheep, 80 pigs, 4 horses. [There are] now 160 sheep, 100 pigs, 1 horse, 100 goats. And [there are] 13 sokemen, who could not withdraw, holding 1 hide and 10 acres. Then as now [there were] 5 ploughs. [There were] then 15 villans; now 18. [There are] now 22 bordars. [There were] then 6 slaves; now 2, having 3 ploughs. [There is] woodland for 60 pigs. [There are] 43 acres of meadow. Then as now [there was] 1 mill. It was then worth £13; now 20. To this manor belong 15 burgesses in Sudbury and they are assessed in those £20. Of this manor Robert Blund holds 35 acres, Warin [holds] 25 acres, Pinceon [holds] 15 acres, Godwine [holds] 15 acres, having

Aubrey de Vere

[Folio 77: ESSEX]

5 ploughs and [this] is worth £7. in the above valuation.

HALF-HUNDRED OF THUNRESLAU.

A[ubrey] holds Belchamp in demesne, which Wulfwine held TRE as a manor and as 2½ hides. Then as now [there were] 4 ploughs [in demesne] and the men [had] 7 ploughs. Then and later [there were] 13 villans; now 15. Then and later [there were] 9 bordars; now 14. Then and later [there were] 6 slaves; now 8. [There is] woodland for 20 pigs. [There are] 60 acres of meadow. [There are] now 11 arpents of vineyard, [of which] 1 [is] bearing. [There were] then 24 head of cattle, 160 sheep, 80 pigs, 2 horses. [There are] now 28 head of cattle, 200 sheep, 100 pigs, 2 horses. To this manor belong now as then 7 sokemen with 1½ hides and 15 acres. Then as now [there were] 3½ ploughs. [There are] now 4 bordars. [There are] 10½ acres. Then and later it was worth £14; now 18. Of this manor Enisant holds of A[ubrey] half a hide and 30 acres, William Pecche [holds] half a hide, Suadus [holds] 30 acres, and [these] are worth £4 in the above valuation.

HUNDRED OF HINCKFORD.

Adelelm holds Horseham of A[ubrey], which 2 sokemen held of Aubrey's predecessor in such a way that they could not withdraw without his licence. Then as now [there were] 1½ ploughs. [There were] then 5 bordars; now 10. [There was] then woodland for 40 pigs; now 30. [There are] 7 acres of meadow. It is worth 20s.

HUNDRED OF LEXDEN.

A[ubrey] holds Colne, in demesne, which Wulfwine held as a manor and as 5 hides. Then as now [there were ...] villans and 13 bordars and 6 slaves. [There were] then 3 ploughs in demesne; now 5. Among the men [there were] then 3 ploughs; now 4. [There is] woodland for 400 pigs. [There are] 40 acres of meadow, 2 mills. [There were] then 20 cows and 19 head of cattle, 120 sheep, 60 pigs, 60 goats, 3 horses. [There are] now 45 head of cattle, 160 sheep, 80 pigs, 80 goats, 4 horses and 6 asses and 20 horses. And 4 sokemen dwelt on these 5 hides and [had] 10 bordars and 4 slaves. Then and later it was worth £10; now 12. Of this manor, Demiblanc holds 1 hide and [there are] 7 bordars and 2 ploughs in demesne and the men [have] 1 plough, and [this] is worth 45s. in the above valuation.

[Folio 77v: ESSEX]

HUNDRED OF TENDRING.

A[ubrey] holds [Great and Little] Bentley in demesne, which Wulfwine held as a manor and as 3 hides. Then and later [there were] 7 villans; now 6. [There were] then 5 bordars; now 10. Then as now [there were] 4 slaves. [There were] then 4 ploughs in demesne; now 3. Among the men [there were] then 5 ploughs; now 4. [There is] woodland for 150 pigs. [There are] 6 acres of meadow. [There is] pasture for 150 sheep, 1 salt-pan. [There were] then 3 horses, 100 sheep, 20 head of cattle, 40 pigs, and now 100 sheep, and 3 horses, 26 head of cattle, 40 pigs. It was then worth £6; now 10s.

A[ubrey] holds Dovercourt in demesne which Wulfwine held as a manor and 6 hides. [There were] then 8 villans; now 6. [There were] then 6 bordars; now 12. Then and now [there are] 6 slaves and 3 ploughs in demesne and the men [had] 6 ploughs. [There are] 3 acres of meadow. [There is] pasture for 200 sheep. [There were] then 3 horses, 12 head of cattle, 200 sheep, 40 pigs and now the same. It was then worth £6; now 12.

Edward holds Beaumont of A[ubrey], which Wulfwine held as a manor and as 2 hides. Then as now [there were] 17 villans. [There were] then 3 bordars; now 1. [There were] then 3 slaves; now none. [There were] then 2 ploughs in demesne; now 1. Then as now the men [had] 5 ploughs. [There is] woodland for 15 pigs. [There are] 10 acres of meadow, 2 salt-pans. [There were] then 12 head of cattle, 150 sheep, 30 pigs, 2 horses. [There are] now 4 head of cattle, 100 sheep, 30 pigs, 1 horse, 3 hives of bees. It was then worth 100s.; now £8. To this manor belongs 1 sokeman, who could not withdraw from the land without the licence of Aubrey's predecessor, holding 2 hides less 15 acres. [There were] then 2 villans; now none. [There were] then 2 bordars; now 3. [There was] then 1 slave; now none. Then as now [there was] 1 plough in demesne. Among the men then [there was] 1 plough; now none. [There is] woodland for 50 pigs. [There are] 2 acres of meadow. It was then worth 20s.; now 40.

HALF-HUNDRED OF FRESHWELL.

Adelelm holds [Helions] Bumpstead of A[ubrey], which Wulfwine held as a manor and as 2 hides. Then as now [there were] 7 villans and 3 bordars and 4 slaves. Then and later [there were] 2 ploughs in demesne; now 2½. Then and later the men [had] 2 ploughs; now 1½. [There is] woodland for 20 pigs. [There are] 5 acres of meadow. [There were] then 7 head of cattle, 8 pigs, 1 horse, 5 sheep, 15 goats, 3 hives of bees. [There are] now 12 head of cattle, 40 pigs, 5 horses, 80 sheep, 40 goats, 5 hives of bees. It was then worth £5; now 8.

Aubrey de Vere

[Folio Folio78: ESSEX]

Demiblanc holds Radwinter of A[ubrey], which Ælfric, a sokeman, held as a manor and as half a hide and 15 acres. And he could sell the land, but soke and sake remained with Aubrey's predecessor. [There were] then 4 villans; now 2. [There was] then 1 bordar; now 5. [There was] then 1 slave; now 2. [There was] then 1 plough in demesne; now 2. The men [had] then 2 ploughs; now 1. [There is] woodland for 30 pigs. [There are] 9 acres of meadow. It was then worth 20s.; now 60.

In Stevington Reginald holds 30 acres of A[ubrey], which Alwine held, and Ordric held 15 acres. And these 2 [men] were in the king's soke, but he gave them to Aubrey. Then as now [there were] 3 villans and 2 bordars and 1 plough. [There is] woodland for 10 pigs. [There are] 3 acres of meadow. It was then worth 20s.; now 30. In the same [vill], a certain Englishman holds 40 acres of A[ubrey], which Ælfric the sokeman held, being able to sell the land, but the soke and sake remained [with Aubrey's predecessor]. Then as now [there were] 2 bordars and 1 plough. It is worth 10s.

XXXVI. Land of Peter de Valognes.

HUNDRED OF HARLOW.

Peter holds Sheering in demesne, which 3 free men held TRE as a manor and as 5 hides and 30 acres. Then as now [there were] 5 ploughs in demesne and the men [had] 1 plough and [there were] 3 villans. [There were] then 3 bordars; now 6. Then as now [there were] 8 slaves. [There is] woodland for 100 pigs. [There are] 32 acres of meadow. [There is] 1 mill. [There were] then 8 cows, 100 calves and 1 horse, 35 sheep, 16 pigs. [There are] now 2 horses and 1 mule and 1 ass, 84 sheep, 56 pigs, 3 hives of bees. Then and later it was worth 100s.; now £6.

Turgis holds Latton of P[eter], which a free man held TRE as a manor

[Folio 78v: ESSEX]

and as 2½ hides and 30 acres of land. [There were] then 2 ploughs in demesne; now 1. The men [have] half a plough. Then as now [there was] 1 villan and priest. [There are] now 4 bordars. [There were] then 4 slaves; now none. [There is] woodland for 350 pigs. [There are] 35 acres of meadow. Then as now it was worth 60s.

Roger holds [Great and Little] Parndon of P[eter], which 1 free man held TRE as a manor and as 3 hides. [There were] then 2 ploughs in demesne; now 1, and the men now [have] half a plough. [There was] then 1 bordar; now 5. Then as now [there were] 3 slaves. [There is] woodland for 100 pigs. [There are] 45 acres of meadow and marsh. Then as now [there was] 1 mill. And 5 acres of land have been added, which a free man held TRE. [There were] then 8 head of cattle and 41 sheep. [There are] now 14 sheep and 1 horse and 76 sheep and 26 pigs and 3 hives of bees. Then and later it was worth 40s.; now 60.

In [North] Weald [Basset] Ralph holds 30 acres of P[eter], which a free man held TRE as a manor. Then as now [there was] 1 plough and 2 slaves and 1 bordar. [There is] woodland for 100 pigs. [There are] 2 acres of meadow. It is worth 20s.

HUNDRED OF BECONTREE.

P[eter] holds Leyton in demesne, which Swein Swart held as a manor and as 3 hides. Then as now [there was] 1 plough in demesne and the men [had] then 1 plough; now 2. [There were] then 7 villans; now 10. Then as now [there were] 2 bordars. [There is] woodland for 30 pigs. [There are] 24 acres of meadow. [There was] then 1 mill, which was taken away from there TRW; now [there is] none. [There were] then 2 fisheries; now none. [There is] now 1 horse and 11 pigs. It was then worth 20s. and when he received [it], there was nothing there but the land, and now it is worth 40s.

P[eter] holds Higham in demesne, which Halfdan, a free man, held TRE as a manor and as 5 hides. Then as now [there were] 2 ploughs in demesne and the men [had] 4 ploughs. [There were] then 8 villans; now 10. [There were] then 2 bordars; now 3. Then as now [there were] 4 slaves. [There is] woodland for 300 pigs. [There are] 18 acres of meadow. [There were] then 3½ fisheries; now none. [There was] then 1 ox. Now [there are] 15 head of cattle and 1 horse and 37 pigs and 2 hives of bees. It was then worth 60s.; now £4. 10s. And

when he received this manor, he did not find [there] more than 1 ox and 1 acre sown. And of these 5 hides, which I mentioned above, 2 free men held 1 TRE,

Peter de Valognes

[Folio 79: ESSEX]

which was added to this manor TRW, and was worth TRE 10s.; now 20. And William holds this of Peter de Valognes.

Ralph holds Loughton of P[eter], which Wulfric, a free man, held TRE as a manor and as 1 hide and 30 acres. Then as now [there was] 1 plough in demesne. [There are] now 5 bordars. [There is] woodland for 80 pigs. [There are] 6 acres of meadow. It was then worth 10s.; now 20.

HALF-HUNDRED OF THUNRESLAU.

Ralph Fatatus holds Ballingdon of Peter, which Ælfric, a free man, held TRE as a manor and as 3½ hides. Then as now [there were] 2 ploughs in demesne and the men [had] 1 plough. Then and later [there were] 3 bordars; now 9. Then as now [there were] 4 slaves. [There are] 33 acres of meadow. [There were] then 5 cows with calves and 30 pigs. [There are] now 33 head of cattle and 28 pigs. It was then worth 40s.; now 100.

Peter holds "Binsley" [in Bulmer] in demesne, which Wulfwine held TRE as 1 hide. Then as now [there was] 1 plough in demesne and the men [had] half a plough and [there were] 13 bordars. Then and later [there were] 2 slaves; now 1. [There is] woodland for 20 pigs. [There are] 4 acres of meadow. It is worth 20s. P[eter] [holds] this land in pledge by order of the king, yet he does not lose his customary dues, [as] the Bishop of Bayeux witnesses.

P[eter] holds Loughton in demesne, which Leofcild held as a manor and as 1 hide. [There were] then 3 bordars; now 2. [There were] then 2 slaves; now none. Then as now [there was] 1 plough. [There is] woodland for 30 pigs. [There are] 4 acres of meadow. Then as now [there was] 1 mill. It was then worth 20s., and when he received [it] 30. Now it is worth 20s.

P[eter] holds Theydon in demesne, which Hakon held as a manor and as 3½ hides and 80 acres. [There were] then 7 villans; now 12. [There were] then 3 bordars; now 4. Then as now [there were] 5 slaves. [There is] woodland for 400 pigs. [There are] 16 acres of meadow, 1 mill. [There were] then 2 cows and 3 horses and 54 pigs and 47 sheep. [There are] now 2 horses and 92 pigs and 157 sheep and 12 hives of bees. It was then worth 60s.; now 100. And 7 free men held 2 hides and 1½ virgates, which now Peter holds. Then as now [there were] 2 slaves and 1 bordar. Then and later [there were] 6 ploughs;

[Folio 79v: ESSEX]

now 4. [There is] woodland for 140 pigs. [There are] 20 acres of meadow. Then as now it was worth 46s. And this [he holds] by exchange, as P[eter] himself says. And Walter holds half a hide and 40 acres of P[eter], which Wulfwine held, and Peter has [it] in pledge, as he says, by grant of the king. [There was] then 1 villan; now none. [There are] now 3 bordars. [There was] then 1 slave; now none. [There were] then 2 ploughs;

later and now 1. [There is] woodland for 100 pigs. [There are] 7 acres of meadow. It was then worth 16s.; now 20.

Ralph Fatatus holds [North] Weald [Basset] of P[eter], which 2 free men held TRE as 2 manors and as 2 hides and 40 acres. And Peter has [it] by exchange. Then and later [there were] 7 villans; now 13. Then and later [there were] 3 bordars; now 8. Then and later [there were] 9 slaves; now 7. [There were] then 5 ploughs in demesne; later 3 [and] now 2. Then and later the men [had] 2½ ploughs; now 5. [There is] woodland for 1,500 pigs. [There are] 40 acres of meadow. [There were] then 3 cows and 1 horse and 35 pigs and 5 sheep and 3 goats. Now 17 head of cattle and 1 horse, 28 pigs, 70 sheep and 5 hives of bees. It was then worth £7, and when he received [it] £6. Now it is worth £12. And a certain man held freely 40 acres, whom P[eter] has by exchange. Then as now [there were] a now 2 bordars. [There is] woodland for 60 pigs. [There are] 5 acres of meadow. Then as now [there was] 1 plough and it is worth 20s.

XXXVII. Land of Ranulf, brother of Ilger.

HUNDRED OF BARSTABLE.

W. holds Ingrave of R[anulf], which Aslak held TRE . Then as now [there was] 1 plough in demesne and the men [had] 1 plough. [There were] then 5 bordars; now 9. [There were] then 2 slaves; now none. [There is] woodland for 100 pigs. [There were] then 14 head of cattle, 60 sheep, 60 pigs. [There are] now 8 head of cattle, 100 sheep, 20 pigs, 3 hives of bees. It was then worth 40s.; now 30.

Humphrey holds Ramsden [Bellhouse and Crays] of R[anulf], which Sigeric held freely as 2 hides

Ranulf

and 30 acres. [There were] then 2 ploughs in demesne; now 1½. The men [have] now half a plough. And [there is] 1 free man. Then as now [there were] 3 slaves and 1 bordar. [There is] woodland for 100 pigs. [There are] 2 acres of meadow. [When he received it], he found nothing. Now [there are] 4 head of cattle, 2 horses, 58 sheep, 21 pigs. It was then worth 60s.; now 40.

HUNDRED OF HARLOW.

R[anulf] holds Roydon in demesne, which Ingvar, a free man, held TRE as a manor and as 6 hides. Then as now [there were] 3 ploughs in demesne and the men [had] 4 ploughs. [There were] then 12 villans; now 8. [There were] then 2 bordars; now 12. [There were] then 8 slaves; now 3. [There is] woodland for 120 pigs. [There are] 60 acres of meadow. [There is] pasture [worth] 2s., 1 mill. [There were] then 6 head of cattle, 60 sheep, 30 pigs. [There are] now 10 head of cattle, 60 sheep, 30 pigs, 10 horses. It was then worth £6; now 9. To this manor belongs 1 berewick, Harlow, which Richard holds of R[anulf] as 1 hide and 1 virgate. Then as now [there was] 1 plough. [There were] then 2 villans; now 1. [There is] woodland for 50 pigs. [There are] 7 acres of meadow. Then and later it was worth 25s.; now 30. To this land were added 4 hides of land, which 5 free men

held TRE. Then as now [there were] 4 ploughs. [There were] then 3 villans; now 2. [There were] then 5 bordars; now 7. [There was] then 1 slave; now none. [There is] woodland for 60 pigs. [There are] 25 acres of meadow. It was then worth £4.

Roger holds [Great and Little] Parndon of R[anulf], which Alsige Bolla, a free man, held TRE as a manor and as 2 hides. [There was] then 1 plough in demesne; now 1½. [There was] then 1 villan. [There are] now 5 bordars. Then as now [there was] 1 slave. [There is] woodland for 140 pigs. [There are] 18 acres of meadow. [There were] then 12 head of cattle; now 8. [There are] 34 pigs, 80 sheep. It was then worth 30s.; now 40.

Alvred holds [Great and Little] Parndon of R[anulf], which Ælfgifu, a free woman, held as a manor and as half a hide. Then as now [there was] half a plough and 1 bordar. [There is] woodland for 30 pigs. [There are] 5 acres of meadow. It is worth 11s.

In [Great and Little] Parndon Roger holds 35 acres of R[anulf], which Thorsten, a free man, held TRE. Then as now [there was] half a plough. [There is] woodland for 20 pigs. [There are] 2 acres of meadow. It is worth 6s.

Richard holds [North] Weald [Basset] of R[anulf], which Godwine, a free man, held TRE as a manor and as half a hide and 15 acres. Then as now [there was] 1 plough in demesne and the men [had] half a plough.

[There was] then 1 villan; now 2. Then as now [there was] 1 bordar. [There were] then 2 slaves; now 1. [There is] woodland for 200 pigs. [There are] 2 acres of meadow. [There were] then 20 pigs; now 60. [There are] now 17 head of cattle, 65 sheep and 3 horses. It was then worth 20s.; now 30.

In Nazeing Odo holds 1 hide of R[anulf], and [there is] 1 villan and 4 bordars and 1 plough and it is worth 20s.

HUNDRED OF WALTHAM.

Two free men held Nazeing and Epping TRE as a manor and as 4½ hides less 15 acres. [There were] then 3 ploughs in demesne; now 2. Then as now the men [had] 3 ploughs. [There were] then 11 villans; now 7. [There are] now 9 bordars. [There were] then 3 slaves; now none. [There is] woodland for 100 pigs. [There are] 54 acres of meadow. [There is] pasture [worth] 32d. [There was] then 1 mill; now none. [There were] then 7 head of cattle and 30 pigs. [There are] now 2 head of cattle and 18 pigs; this is in Nazeing. And in Epping [there are] 2 head of cattle and 26 sheep and 6 pigs. Then as now they were worth £4; Nazeing [is worth] 60s. and Epping [is worth] 20s. And in addition to this, there has been added to this land 1 hide which a free man held TRE and he still holds [it]. [There was] then 1 plough; now half. [There were] then 2 bordars; now 3. [There is] woodland for 20 pigs. [There are] 12 acres of meadow. It was then worth 10s.; now 20. And [there is] further 1 virgate of land, which has been added TRW and belonged to Waltham [Holy Cross] TRE, [and] which R[anulf], brother of Ilger took from it, as the Hundred testifies. And it is worth 3s. R[anulf] holds all this in demesne.

HUNDRED OF ROCHFORD.

Odo holds Thorpehall of R[anulf], which Ingvar held TRE as a manor and as 2½ hides. Then as now [there were] 4 villans and 4 bordars and 4 slaves and 2 ploughs in demesne and the men [had] 3 ploughs. [There is] woodland for 60 pigs, pasture for 100 sheep. [There were] then 2 head of cattle and 2 horses and 100 sheep and 30 pigs. [There are] now 2 head of cattle and 1 horse and 100 sheep and 7 pigs and 18 goats and 4 hives of bees. Then and later it was worth £4; now 6.

HUNDRED OF HINCKFORD.

R[anulf] holds Birdbrook in demesne, which 1 free man held TRE as a manor and as 2 hides. [There were] then 3 ploughs in demesne; later 2 [and] now 3. Then as now the men [had] 3 ploughs. Then and later [there were] 7 villans; now 6. Then and later [there was] 1 bordar; now 9. Then as now [there were] 4 slaves. [There is] woodland for 16 pigs. [There are] 22 acres of meadow. [There were] then 15 head of cattle

Ranulf

[Folio 81: ESSEX]

and 50 pigs and 80 sheep and 13 [sheep] and 25 goats. [There are] now 4 head of cattle and 10 pigs and 55 sheep and 2 horses. Then and later it was worth £8; now 9.

R[anulf] holds Baythorne [End] in demesne, which Ingvar held as a manor and as 2 hides TRE. Then as now [there were] 2 ploughs in demesne and the men [had] 4 ploughs and [there were] 6 villans. [There are] now 7 bordars. Then and later [there were] 2 slaves; now 3. [There are] 31 acres of meadow. Then as now [there was] 1 mill. Then and later it was worth £7; now 8. To these 2 manors belong now as then 2 sokemen with 5 acres.

Walter holds [Great and Little] Yeldham of R[anulf], which a free man held TRE as a manor and as half a hide. [There was] then 1 plough; later none [and] now 1. [There are] 9 acres of meadow. [There was] then nothing. Now [there are] 2 head of cattle and 1 horse and 30 sheep and 2 pigs. It is worth 20s.

HUNDRED OF DENGIE.

W. holds St Lawrence of R[anulf], which Ingvar held TRE as a manor and as 1½ hides and 35 acres. [There are] now 4 bordars. Then as now [there was] 1 slave and 1 plough in demesne. It was then worth 20s.; later and now 30. And [there are] 7½ acres, which 1 free man held, and it is worth 7d.

Richard holds Bobbingworth of R[anulf], which 2 free men held TRE as 1 hide and 30 acres. [There was] then 1 bordar; now 2. [There were] then 4 slaves; now 2. [There were] then 2 ploughs in demesne; later and now 1. [There is] woodland for 80 pigs. [There are] 4 acres of meadow. Then as now [there was] 1 cow and 3 pigs and 107 sheep. It was then worth 40s.; now 60.

HUNDRED OF CHELMSFORD.

R[anulf] holds Margaretting and Mountnessing in demesne, which Ingvar held as a manor and as 9 hides. [There were] then 18 villans; now 16. [There were] then 8 bordars; now 20.

[There were] then 5 slaves; now 7. [There were] then 2 ploughs in demesne; now 1. Among the men [there were] then 12 ploughs; now 9. [There is] woodland for 700 pigs. [There are] now 7 head of cattle and 60 sheep. It was then worth £8; now 10. And 1 free man holds 20 acres and they are worth 3s. In the same [vill] William de Bosc [holds] 2 hides and 26 acres of R[anulf], which Ælfheah and Algar held TRE, and he has [it] by exchange. [There are] now 3 bordars. [There were] then 2 slaves; now 1.

[Folio 81v: ESSEX]

[There were] then 2 ploughs in demesne; now 1. [There is] woodland for 60 pigs, pasture for 100 sheep. It is worth 40s.

William holds Cowbridge of R[anulf], which Alwine held as a manor and as half a hide and 6½ acres. And half a plough can be [employed there]. [There is] 1 acre of meadow, woodland for 20 pigs. It is worth 10s.

Two free girls held Margaretting and Mountnessing as 80 acres. Now R[anulf] [holds it] by exchange and W. of him. Then as now [there was] 1 plough. It is worth 15s.

HUNDRED OF TENDRING.

In "Derleigh" [in Little Bromley] Eadric of Easthorpe held 1 manor with 2½ hides. Now R[anulf] holds [it] as 1½ hides and Roger [holds it] of him. [There were] then 2 villans; now 1. [There was] then 1 slave; now none. Then and later [there was] 1 plough in demesne; now half a plough. Then and later the men [had] 1 plough; now none, and [there] could be 3 ploughs [more]. [There is] woodland for 20 pigs. [There are] 4 acres of meadow. Then and later it was worth 30s.; now 10. R[anulf] has this land by exchange. He also has in the soke of Lawford 15 acres and 1 man dwells there, who renders 7s. 8d.

XXXVIII. Land of Tihel the Breton.

HUNDRED OF UTTLESFORD.

Two free men held Yardley TRE as a manor and as 1 hide. Then as now [there was] 1 plough in demesne and [there were] 2 bordars; now 7. [There was] then woodland for 40 pigs; later and now 30. [There are] 10 acres of meadow. [There were] then 5 head of cattle, 14 sheep and 26 pigs and 32 goats and 1 horse and 1 hive of bees. [There are] now 4 head of cattle and 14 pigs and 38 sheep and 3 hives of bees and 1 horse. Serlo holds this of Tihel. Tihel claims this land of the king's gift. It was then worth 16s.; now 20.

Tihel the Breton

[Folio 82: ESSEX]

Hundred of Freshwell. Tihel holds Stevington in demesne, which Aslak, a free man, held TRE as a manor and as 42½ acres. Then as now [there were] 2 ploughs in demesne. Then and later [there was] 1 bordar; now 3. Then as now [there were] 4 slaves. [There are] 5 acres of meadow. [There were] then 5 head of cattle and 5 pigs and 10 sheep and 2 hives of bees. [There are] now 5 cows and 1 horse and 30 pigs and 50 sheep and 1 hive of bees. Then and later it was worth 60s.; now 100s. and 1 ounce of gold.

Guthred holds Redwinter of T[ihel], which Leofsige held TRE as a manor and as half a hide and half a virgate. Then as now [there were] 2 ploughs in demesne and the men [had] 1 plough and 4 villans. [There were] then 5 bordars; now 7. [There is] woodland for 60 pigs. [There are] 8 acres of meadow. [There were] then 6 head of cattle; now 4. And [there were then] 18 pigs; now the same. [There were] 49 sheep; now 32. [There were] 4 hives of bees. [There were] then 20 goats; now none. It was then worth 20s.; now 60. Tihel claims [to hold] this of the king's gift.

T[ihel] holds [Helions] Bumpstead in demesne, which Leofwine Cild held TRE as a manor and as 4 hides. Then as now [there were] 4 ploughs in demesne. The men [had] then 4 ploughs; now 2. [There were] then 9 villans; now 7. Then as now [there were]8 bordars and 8 slaves. [There is] woodland for 100 pigs. [There are] 7 acres of meadow. Then as now [there were] 6 head of cattle. [There were] then 24 pigs; now 40. [There were] then 40 sheep; now 115. [There was] then 1 horse; now 1 [horse] and 1 colt. [There were] then [...] hives of bees; now 3. It was then worth £6; now 9.

HUNDRED OF HINCKFORD.

T[ihel] holds [Steeple] Bumpstead in demesne, which a free man held TRE as a manor and as 1 virgate. Then as now [there were] 3 ploughs in demesne and the men [had] 2 ploughs and [there were] 5 villans and 13 bordars and 6 slaves. [There is] woodland for 20 pigs. [There are] 15 acres of meadow. Then as now [there was] 1 mill. Then and later it was worth 60s.; now £6.

[...] T[ihel] holds Sturmer in demesne, which a free woman held TRE as a manor and 1½ hides and 15 acres. Then as now [there were] 2 ploughs in demesne and the men [had] 1 plough and [there were] 2 villans [and] 3 bordars. Then and later [there was] 1 slave; now 2. [There are] 16 acres of meadow. [There were] then [...] cows and 2 horses and 60 pigs and 3 hives of bees. [There are] now 4 head of cattle and 1 horse

and 1 colt and 44 pigs and 72 sheep and 3 hives of bees. It was then worth 40s.; now 60.

T[ihel] holds Surmer in demesne, which a free man held TRE as a manor and as [...] 1½ hides. Then as now [there were] 2 ploughs in demesne and 1 villan and 6 slaves. [There are] 20 acres, 1 mill. [There were] then 6 head of cattle and 1 horse and 12 pigs and 60 sheep. [There are] now 12 head of cattle and 30 pigs and 100 sheep less 2 and 1 horse and 3 colts. Then and later it was worth 40s.; now 60.

T[ihel] holds Tilbury [-Juxta-Clare] in demesne, which 1 free man held TRE as a manor and as 1 hide and 38 acres. Then as now [there were] 3 ploughs in demesne and the men [had] 1 plough and [there were] 5 villans and 1 bordar and 6 slaves. [There is] woodland for 20 pigs. [There are] 19 acres of meadow. [There were] then 15 head of cattle and 40 pigs and 80 sheep and 6 hives of bees. [There are] now 5 head of cattle and 1 horse and 36 pigs and 63 sheep. Then and later it was worth 60s.; now 100.

XXXIX. Land of Roger de Rames.

HUNDRED OF HINCKFORD.

Roger holds Rayne in demesne, which Alwine, a free man, held TRE as a manor and as 1 hide and 20 acres. Then as now [there were] 2 ploughs in demesne. Then and later the men [had] 4 ploughs; now 3. Then and later [there were] 9 villans; now 8. Then as now [there were] 5 bordars. Then and later [there were] 4 slaves; now 3. [There is] woodland for 100 pigs , 1 mill. [There were] then 8 cows; now 3. [There was] then 1 horse; now none. Then as now [there were] 100 sheep. [There were] then 30 pigs; now 40. Then as now it was worth £4.

Of this manor, Roger holds 30 acres of R[oger] and Wiburh [holds] 30 acres. And [this] is worth 20s. in the above valuation.

Roger de Rames

R[oger] holds Rayne in demesne, which Eadric, a free man, held TRE as a manor and as 1 hide. [There were] then 2 ploughs in demesne; later and now 1. The men [have] now half a plough and [there are] 3 bordars. Then and later [there were] 6 slaves; now 3. [There is] woodland for 40 pigs. [There are] 13 acres of meadow. Then as now it was worth 60s.

Warengar holds Hedingham [Castle and Sible] of R[oger], which Godwine, a free man, held TRE as a manor and as half a hide. Then as now [there were] 2 ploughs in demesne and the men [had] 3 ploughs and [there were] 8 villans. Then and later [there was] 1 bordar; now 3. [There were] then 4 slaves; later and now 2. Then and later [there was] woodland for 600 pigs; now 500. [There are] 18 acres of meadow. To this manor belongs now as then 2 sokemen with 3 acres. Then and later it was worth £4; now 100s.

HUNDRED OF LEXDEN.

R[oger] holds Messing in demesne, which Ordmær, a free man, held TRE as a manor and as half a hide. [There were] then 6 villans; now 3. [There were] then 12 bordars; now 18. [There were] then 6 slaves; now 4. Then as now [there were] 2 ploughs in demesne. Among the men [there were] then 5 ploughs; now 3. [There is] woodland for 40 pigs. [There are] 20 acres of meadow. [There is] now 1 mill. Then as now [there were] 2 horses and 2 cows with calves and 100 sheep. [There were] then 30 pigs; now 20. Then as now [there were] 35 goats. Then as now it was worth 100s. Of this manor, Ansketil holds of R[oger] 16 acres and they are worth 5s. in the above valuation. And 3 sokemen holding freely 18 acres belong to this manor, whom Gerald holds of R[oger], and Roger says that he has them by exchange. Then as now [there was] half a plough. Then and later it was worth 10s.; now 3.

R[oger] holds Dedham in demesne, which Ælfric Cempa [...] held as a manor and as 2½ hides. [There were] then 7 villans; now 5. Then as now [there were] 24 bordars. [There were] then 4 slaves; now 3. [There were] then 2 ploughs in demesne; now 3. Among the men [there were] then 10 ploughs; now 5. [There is] woodland for 250 pigs. [There are] 40 acres of meadow. [There was] then 1 mill; now 2. [There were] then 2 horses; now 10. [There were] then 5 cows; now 3. [There were] then 40 sheep; now 100. [There were] then 25 pigs; now 30. Then as now it was worth £12. Of this manor Gerald holds 30 acres and [this] is worth 10s. in the above valuation. In [Mount] Bures R[oger] has 25 acres. Then as now [there were] 3 bordars and half a plough. [There is] woodland for 15 pigs.

[Folio 83v: ESSEX]

[There is] 1 acre of meadow. It is worth 7s.

HUNDRED OF TENDRING.

R[oger] holds Bradfield in demesne, which Ælfric Cempa held as a manor and as 4½ hides. [There were] then 7 villans; later and now 4. Then as now [there were] 10 bordars and 2 slaves and 2 ploughs in demesne. Then and later the men [had] 7 ploughs; now 3. [There is] woodland for 30 pigs. [There is] 1 salt-pan. [There were] then 4 cows, 100 calves; now none. Then as now [there were] 100 sheep. [There were] then 20 pigs; now 33. Then and later it was worth £7; now 60s. Of this manor, a certain wife of a knight of his holds half a hide and it is worth 10s. in the above valuation.

R[oger] holds Ardleigh in demesne, which Bondi held as a manor and as 1 hide. Then as now [there was] 1 villan. [There were] then 11 bordars; now 10. [There was] then 1 slave; now none. Then as now [there were] 2 ploughs in demesne. Then and later the men [had] 9 ploughs; now 1. [There is] woodland for 40 pigs. [There are] 4½ acres of meadow. [There were] then 40 sheep; now 100. [There were] then 2 cows and 3 horses; now none. Then and later it was worth £4; now 30s. Of this manor, Ralph of Hastings holds 30 acres and [this] is worth 10s. in the above valuation.

R[oger] holds Jacques Hall in demesne, which Ælfhelm held TRE as a manor and as 1 hide and 25 acres. Then as now [there was] 1 villan. Then and later [there were] 4 bordars; now 3. Then as now [there was] 1 slave. Then and later [there were] 2 ploughs in demesne; now 1. Among the men [there was] then 1 plough; now none. [There is] woodland for 15 pigs. [There are] 1½ acres of meadow. [There is] pasture for 15 sheep. [There is] now 1 salt-pan. Then and later it was worth £4; now 20s.

The wife of Aubrey holds Mistley of R[oger], which Ælfric held as a manor and as 1 hide. Then as now [there was] 1 bordar. [There were] then 2 ploughs; now none. It was then worth 20s.; now 2s.

In Cliff R[oger] holds in demesne 8 free men with 30 acres and 1 plough and [this] is worth 5s.

In Ardleigh R[oger] holds in demesne 6 free men with 1 hide and 2 ploughs and [this] is worth 40s. Of this, Ralph holds 10 acres and Restald [holds] 40 acres, and [this] is worth 20s. in the above valuation. This is [acquired] by exchange.

[Folio 84: ESSEX]

HUNDRED OF WITHAM.

XL. Land of John fitzWaleran.

John fitzErnucion holds [Black and White] Notley of John, which Harold held TRE as a manor and as 4 hides and 30 acres. [There were] then 5 ploughs in demesne; now 3. The men [had] then 4 ploughs; now 2. [There were] then 7 villans; now 5. [There were] then 13 bordars; now 11. [There were] then 4 slaves; now none. [There was] then woodland for 330 pigs; now 200. [There are] 24 acres of meadow. Then as now [there was] 1 mill. [There is] pasture [worth] 6d. [There was] then 1 horse and 2 cows; now nothing. It was then worth £7; now 6.

HUNDRED OF HINCKFORD.

Turstin holds [Great] Saling of John, which 1 free man held TRE as a manor and as half a hide. [There were] then 2 ploughs in demesne; later none [and] now 1. The men [had] then 1½ ploughs; later none [and] now half a plough. [There were] then 3 villans and 1 priest; later 1 [and] now 2 villans and 1 priest. Then and later [there were] 3 bordars; now 5. [There were] then 4 slaves; later and now 3. Then and later [there was] woodland for 250 pigs; now 200. [There are] 10 acres of meadow. It is worth 60s.

Osmund holds [Great and Little] Maplestead of John, which Grim, a free man, [held] TRE as a manor and as half a hide. [There were] then 2 ploughs in demesne; later none [and] now 1. [There were] then 2 bordars; later 1 [and] now 5, and 1 priest. Then as now [there were] 2 slaves. [There was] then woodland for 60 pigs; later and now 16. [There are] 3 acres of meadow. [There was] then 1 mill, which now William de Warenne holds as pledge. Then he received nothing; now [there are] 2 cows and 14 pigs and 57 sheep. It was then worth 40s.; later and now 30.

Roger holds [Great and Little] Henny of John, which a free man held TRE as a manor and as 2½ hides. [There were] then 2 ploughs in demesne; later 1 [and] now 2. Then as now the men [had] 1 plough. Then and later [there was] 1 villan; now none. Then as now [there were] 3 bordars and 2 slaves. [There was] then woodland for 60 pigs;

[Folio 84v: ESSEX]

later and now 30. [There are] 12 acres of meadow. [There were] then 6 head of cattle and 15 pigs and 11 sheep. [There are] now 5 horses and 8 head of cattle and 30 pigs and 66 sheep and 15 goats. To this manor belongs a customary due of 22½d., which is [payable] from Sudbury. It was then worth 40s.; later and now 50.

In Bures Hugh holds of J[ohn] 15 acres, which Tostig, a free man, held. Then as now [there was] half a plough and 2 villans and 2 bordars. [There is] woodland for 4 pigs. [There is] 1 acre of meadow. It is worth 6s. This land is in the shire of Suffolk.

HUNDRED OF ONGAR.

Roger holds Fyfield of John, which Leofric held TRE as a manor and as 1½ hides and 30 acres. [There were] then 12 villans; now 7. Then and later [there were] 2 bordars; now 10. Then as now [there were] 4 slaves and 2 ploughs in demesne. Then and later the men [had] 4 ploughs; now 3. [There is] woodland for 400 pigs. [There are] 10 acres of meadow. [There is] now 1 mill. [There are] now 11 cows and 11 pigs and 60 sheep and 1 hive of bees. Then and later it was worth £5; now 7.

The same holds the other Fyfield of the same, which Æthelstan held as a manor and as 30 acres. Then as now [there were] 3 bordars. [There was] then 1 plough; now none. [There is] woodland for 40 pigs. [There are] 6 acres of meadow. Then as now it was worth 20s.

The same holds Ongar [Chipping and High] of the same, which Leofric held as a manor and as 3 virgates. Then as now [there were] 6 bordars and 1 slave and 1 plough in demesne. [There is] woodland for 200 pigs. [There are] 8 acres of meadow. [There are] now 30 pigs and 40 sheep. It was then worth 40s. and when he received [it] 20s. Now it is worth 40s.

HUNDRED OF CHAFFORD.

Swein held Aveley freely TRE as a manor and as 3½ hides. Now John holds [it] in demesne as the same. [There were] then 8 villans; now 6. [There were] then 3 bordars; now 5. [There were] then 4 slaves; now 1. [There were] then 2 ploughs in demesne; now 1. Among the men then [there were] 3 ploughs; now 2. [There are] 60 acres of meadow. Then and later it was worth £8; now 100s. And a certain free man, Wulfsige, held half a hide, which he could sell, but Waleran, father of John, added him to this manor. Then as now [there was] 1 villan and 1 bordar. [There was] then half a plough; now nothing. It was then worth

[Folio 85: ESSEX]

10s., and when received the same. Now it is worth 7s.

XLI. Land of Robert fitzCorbucion.

HUNDRED OF BARSTABLE.

Gerard holds Doddinghurst of R[obert], which Ælfric held freely TRE as a manor and as 1 hide and 17 acres. Then as now [there was] 1 plough. [There is] woodland for 20 pigs. It is worth 20s.

HUNDRED OF WITHAM.

Nigel holds Smallands of R[obert], which Earl Ælfgar held as a manor and as 2 hides. Then as now [there was] 1 plough and 1 bordar and 1 slave. [There are] 9 acres of meadow. [There are] now 2 parts of a fishery. [There were] then 2 head of cattle; now 4. [There was] then 1 pig; now 25. [There are] now 2 colts. [There were] then 6 sheep; now 35. [There were] then 6 goats; now none. Then as now it was worth 20s.

HUNDRED OF BECONTREE.

R[obert] holds Leyton in demesne, which Harold held TRE as a manor and as 4½ hides. [There were] then 2 ploughs in demesne; now none. Then as now the men [had] 1 plough. [There were] then 3 villans; now 5, and 1 priest. [There were] then 4 bordars; now 6. [There were] then 4 slaves; now none. [There is] woodland for 300 pigs. [There are] 40 acres of meadow. [There were] then 7 fisheries; now none. [There was] then 1 mill; now none. And [there] could be restored 2 ploughs more. It was then worth £4; now 20s.

In Leyton R[obert] holds 3 hides, which 8 sokemen held TRE.

[There were] then 4 ploughs; now none. [There are] now 6 villans and 1 bordar. [There is] woodland for 10 pigs.

[There are] 30 acres of meadow. [There was] half a fishery then; now none. It was then worth 60s.; now 20. And those sokemen rendered customary dues TRE to Havering[-atte-Bower], a manor of the king, and they [still] render [it] now.

W. holds Lawling of R[obert], which Lyfing, a free man, held TRE as a manor

[Folio 85v: ESSEX]

and as 4½ hides. [There were] then 3 bordars; now 5. Then as now [there were] 4 slaves and 2 ploughs. [There is] pasture for 40 sheep. [There were] then 2 horses; now 3. [There were] then 7 head of cattle; now 9. [There were] then 107 sheep; now 124. [There were] then 6 goats; now none. It was then worth £3; now 4.

HUNDRED OF CHELMSFORD.

Ranulf holds Hanningfield of R[obert], which Æthelstan, a free man, held TRE as a manor and as 1½ hides. [There is] now 1 bordar and 1 slave. And then as now [there was] 1 plough. [There are] 2 acres of meadow. [There is] woodland for 12 pigs. Then as now it was worth 30s.

W. holds [Great and Little] Waltham of R[obert], which Wulfsige held as a manor and as 1 hide and 30 acres. [There was] then 1 villan; now none. [There were] then 9 bordars; now 11. Then as now [there was] 1 slave and 1 plough. [There is] woodland for 30 pigs. [There are] 8 acres of meadow. Then as now [there was] 1 mill. It was then worth 30s.; now 40.

In the same [vill] Ranulf holds of R[obert] 1 free man with 30 acres, whom R[obert] appropriated. Then as now [there was] half a plough. It is worth 4s.

Nigel holds "Bensted" [in Sandon], which Starcher held as a manor and as 3½ hides. [There were] then 2 villans; now none. Then as now [there were] 7 bordars and 2 slaves and 1 plough in demesne and the men [had] 1 plough. [There is] woodland for 100 pigs. [There are] 1½ acres of meadow. [There was] then 1 horse and 4 cows with calves; now none. [There were] then 40 sheep; now 30. [There were] then 16 pigs; now 7. It was then worth 40s.; now 50. And a certain free man held half a hide, which R[obert] appropriated. Now Godfrey holds [it] of him. Then and later [there was] half a plough; now none. [There is] woodland for 10 pigs. It is worth 10s.

HUNDRED OF TENDRING.

Gerard holds Foulton
of R[obert], which Eadnoth, a free man, held TRE
as a manor and as 2½ hides and 20 acres. [There was]
then 1 villan; now 4. Then as now [there were] 2 bordars
and 2 slaves and 2 ploughs in demesne. The men [had]
then 1 plough; now none. [There are] 3 acres of
meadow. [There is] pasture for 60 sheep.

Robert fitzCorbucion

[Folio 86: ESSEX]

[There were] then 4 head of cattle; now 3. [There was] then 1
horse; now none. [There were] then 10 pigs; now 20. [There
were] then 40 sheep; now 20. It was then worth 50s., and when
received 20s. Now it is worth 50s.

HUNDRED OF ROCHFORD.

The same G[erard] holds Paglesham of R[obert], which a free
man held as a manor and as half a hide and 30 acres. Then as
now [there were] 2 bordars and 1 plough in demesne. It was
then worth 40s.; now [...] 5.

HUNDRED OF THURSTABLE.

Mauger holds Tolleshunt [Major] of R[obert], which Starcher
held as a manor and as 1 hide. [There were] then 5 villans;
now 4. [There was] then 1 bordar; now 6. [There were] then 5
slaves; now 2. Then and later [there were] 2 ploughs; now 1, in
demesne. Then and later the men [had] 2 ploughs; now 1.
[There is] woodland for 100 pigs. [There is] 1 acre of meadow,
pasture for 60 sheep. [There were] then 15 head of cattle.
[There are] now 2 cows and 1 calf. [There were] then 50 sheep;
now 25. [There was] then 1 horse; now none. [There were]
then 2 hives of bees; now none. It was then worth £4; later 3
[and] now 40s.

And 7 free men held 4 hides and 2 acres and could go where
they would, whom Robert appropriated and now 4 knights
hold [them] of R[obert]. [There were] then 4 slaves; now 2.
Then as now [there were] 2 ploughs. [There is] woodland for
120 pigs, pasture for 60 sheep, 1 salt-pan. It is worth 50s.

XLII. Land of Walter the Deacon.

HUNDRED OF BARSTABLE.

In Bowers [Gifford] Walter holds 2 hides of the land of
Theodoric his brother, and a certain knight holds [it] of him.
Then as now [there was] 1 plough and 1 bordar and 1 slave
and 30 acres of waste woodland. [There is] pasture for 60
sheep. To this manor were added 40 acres TRW, which a free
man held TRE and Theodoric had those. And the aforesaid
hides were then worth 40s. and now the same. And the 40
acres are worth 8s. 4d. In demesne Walter received 4 head of
cattle;

[Folio 86v: ESSEX]

[there are] now the same [number]. [There were] then 2

horses; now 1. [There were] then 100 sheep less 2; now 55.
[There were] then 10 pigs; now 11.

HUNDRED OF DENGIE.

Walter holds Purleigh in demesne, which Leofwine held TRE
as a manor and as 3½ hides. Then as now [there were] 2
villans. [There is] now 1 bordar. [There were] then 3 slaves;
now 1. [There were] then 2 ploughs in demesne; now 1½. Then
as now [there was] half a plough. [There is] woodland for 60
pigs. Then as now [there were] 8 head of cattle. [There were]
then 5 horses; now 4. [There were] then 152 sheep; now 80.
[There were] then 62 pigs; now 47. [There are] now 23 goats.
Then as now it was worth 60s.

Walter holds [Great and Little] Easton in demesne, which
Doding held TRE as a manor and as 2 hides. [There were]
then 6 ploughs in demesne; now 4. [There were] then 5 villans
and 1 priest; now 1 priest and 3 villans. [There were] then 2
bordars; now 25. [There were] then 7 slaves; now 1. [There
was] then woodland for 800 pigs; now 400. [There are] 26
acres of meadow. [There is] 1 mill. Then as now [there were] 6
cows, 4 calves. [There are] now 25 head of cattle. [There were]
then 2 horses; now 6. [There were] then 80 sheep; now 120.
[There were] then 74 pigs; now 62. [There were] then 24 goats;
now 34. [There are] 2 hives of bees. It was then worth £7; now
8.

Walter holds Purleigh in demesne, which Leofwine Cild
held as a manor and as 5 hides TRE. [There were] then 10
villans; now 5. [There was] then 1 bordar; now 6. Then as now
[there were] 4 slaves and 3 ploughs in demesne and the men
[had] 4 ploughs. [There is] woodland for 100 pigs, pasture for
100 sheep. It was then worth £7; now it is worth £6.

One knight holds Stow Maries of W[alter], which a free
man held as a manor and as 2 hides. Then as now [there were]
2 bordars and 1 slave and 1 plough and it is worth 50s.

HUNDRED OF LEXDEN.

One knight holds Colne, of W[alter], which Leofwine held as a
manor and as half a hide and 13 acres. Then as now [there
were] 12 bordars and 2 slaves and 2 ploughs in demesne and
the men [had] 1 plough. [There is] woodland for 100 pigs.
[There are] 13 acres of meadow. Then as now [there was] 1
mill. [There were] then 6 head of cattle; now 2. [There were]
then 2 horses; now none. [There were] then 12 sheep; now 24.
[There were] then 16 pigs; now 14. [There are] now 13 goats
and 3 hives of bees. Then as now it was worth 40s.

Walter the Deacon

[Folio Folio87: ESSEX]

HUNDRED OF TENDRING.

Walter holds Wix in demesne, which Queen Edith held as a
manor and as 4 hides. Then as now [there were] 14 villans.
[There were] then 18 bordars; now 28. [There were] then 4
slaves; now 3. Then as now [there were] 4 ploughs in
demesne. Then and later the men [had] 12 ploughs; now 8.
[There is] woodland for 100 pigs. [There are] 8 acres of
meadow. [There were] then 12 head of cattle; now 14. Then
as now [there were] 2 horses. [There were] then 100 sheep;

now 84. [There were] then 40 pigs; now 71. [There were] then 30 goats; now 34. [There were] then 7 hives of bees; now 10. Then and later it was worth £6. 10s.; now it is worth £10. And Queen E[dith] gave this land to Walter after the arrival of King William.

One knight holds [Great and Little] Bromley of Walter, which Queen E[dith] held as a manor and as 2 hides less 20 acres. Then as now [there was] 1 villan. [There were] then 17 bordars; now 15. [There were] then 4 slaves; now 3. Then as now [there were] 2 ploughs in demesne. Among the men then [there were] 6 ploughs; now 4. [There is] woodland for 40 pigs. [There are] 4 acres of meadow. [There were] then 9 head of cattle; now 7. [There were] then 2 horses; now 4. [There were] then 100 sheep; now 200. [There were] then 12 pigs; now 30. [There are] now 2 hives of bees. It was then worth £5; now 4.

HUNDRED OF UTTLESFORD.

One knight holds [Great and Little] Chesterford of Walter, which Queen E[dith] held as a manor and as 5 hides. Then as now [there were] 10 villans. [There were] then 4 bordars; now 16. [There were] then 4 slaves; now 1. Then as now [there were] 2 ploughs in demesne and the men [had] 3 ploughs. [There is] woodland for 20 pigs. [There are] 8 acres of meadow. Then as now [there is] 1 mill. [There were] then 2 head of cattle; now 4. [There was] then 1 horse; now none. [There were] then 36 sheep; now 43. [There were] then 16 pigs; now 34. [There are] now 23 goats. It was then worth 100s.; now £6.

[Folio 87v: ESSEX]

XLIII. Land of Roger Bigod.

HUNDRED OF HINCKFORD.

Warengar holds Hedingham [Castle and Sible] of R[oger] as 25 acres, which 15 free men held TRE. Then as now [there were] 5½ ploughs and 1 villan and 2 slaves. [There is] woodland for 70 pigs. [There are] 11 acres of meadow. It was then worth 40s.; now £4. In the same vill 3 free men held 48½ acres TRE. Now the same W[arengar] holds [it] of R[oger]. Then as now [there were] 2 ploughs in demesne and the men [had] 2 ploughs and [there were] 5 villans. [There were] then 6 slaves; now 4. [There was] then woodland for 200 pigs; now 160. [There are] 24 acres of meadow. [There is] now 1 mill. It was then worth 40s.; now 60. Of these 48 acres, the Hundred does not testify that R[oger] is seised of them by the king's act. Warengar holds these 2 lands and Roger de Rames claims them, but the Hundred does not testify to it.

The same W[arengar] holds Pebmarsh of R[oger], which 3 free men held TRE. Then as now [there were] 1½ ploughs and 1 bordar. [There is] woodland for 8 pigs. [There are] 3½ acres of meadow. It was then worth 40s.; now £4.

R[oger] holds Ovington in demesne, which a free man held TRE as a manor and as 1 hide and 30 acres. Then as now [there were] 2 ploughs in demesne and the men [had] 2 ploughs. [There were] then 4 villans; later and now 3. [There were] then 6 bordars; later and now 5. Then as now

[there were] 2 slaves. [There are] 24 acres of meadow. It was then worth 40s.; now £4.

Robert de Vaux holds Belchamp of R[oger], which 6 free men held

TRE as 1 hide and 38½ acres. Then as now [there were] 3 ploughs in demesne. Then and later the men [had] 1 plough; now half a plough. [There were] then 3 villans; later and now 2. Then and later [there were] 9 bordars; now 12. [There were] then 4 slaves; now and later 1. [There is] woodland for 30 pigs. [There are] 15 acres of meadow. It was then worth 60s.; now 100.

The same R[obert de Vaux] holds [Great and Little] Henny of R[oger], which 5 free men held

Roger Bigod

[Folio 88: ESSEX]

TRE as 1½ hides less 4 acres. Then as now [there were] 4 ploughs in demesne. [There were] then 4 villans; later and now 1. Then and later [there were] 2 bordars; now 3. Then as now [there were] 2 slaves. Then and later [there was] woodland for 30 pigs; now 20. [There are] 18 acres of meadow. Then and later it was worth 40s.; now 64.

Hugh de Houdain holds Weston, which 4 free men held TRE, who were of the soke of [Earl] Ælfgar, as 1 hide and 50 acres. Then as now [there were] 5 ploughs in demesne. Then and later [there were] 5 bordars; now 10. Then and later [there were] 9 slaves; now 4. [There is] woodland for 6 pigs. [There are] 24 acres of meadow. [There is] now 1 mill. Then and later it was worth 60s.; now £4.

XLIII. Land of Robert Malet

HUNDRED OF HINCKFORD.

Hubert holds Stanstead of Robert, which Godwine, a free man, held TRE as a manor and as 1 hide. Then as now [there were] 2 ploughs in demesne. Then and later the men [had] 5 ploughs; now 4. [There were] then 10 villans; later 8 [and] now 4. Then as now [there were] 7 bordars. [There were] then 7 slaves; now 6. [There was] then woodland for 500 pigs; now 400. [There are] 10 acres of meadow. [There was] then 1 mill; now 2. To this manor belong 1½ hides and 52 acres, which sokemen held TRE. [There were] then 4 ploughs; now 4½. Then and later [there were] 6 bordars; now 24. [There were] then 4 slaves; now 1. [There is] woodland for 30 pigs. [There are] 16 acres of meadow. [There were] then 16 head of cattle, 5 horses, 60 sheep, 50 goats, 40 pigs, 10 hives of bees. [There are] now 10 head of cattle, 50 sheep, 26 goats, 40 pigs, 8 hives of bees. It was then worth £6; now 9. And [there is] 1 sokeman, who could not withdraw from the land, holding 20 acres and it is worth 2s.

The same Hubert holds Goldingham of R[obert], which Godwine, a free man, held TRE as a manor and as 2 hides. [There were] then 3 ploughs in demesne; later and now 2. Then as now

[Folio 88v: ESSEX]

[there were] 6 villans and 5 bordars. Then and later [there were] 6 slaves; now 2. Then as now [there were] 16 acres of meadow. To this manor belonged 4 sokemen with 17 acres and 1 acre of meadow. [There were] then 10 head of cattle and 2 horses, 50 sheep, 40 goats. [There are] now 12 head of cattle, 1 horse, 260 sheep, 65 pigs, 5 hives of bees. It was then worth 60s.; now £6.

HUNDRED OF LEXDEN.

R[obert] holds Colne [Wakes], in demesne, which Azur held as a manor and as 1 hide and 30 acres. Then as now [there were] 7 villans and 15 bordars. [There were] then 4 slaves; now 3. And then as now [there were] 3 ploughs in demesne. Among the men [there were] then 5 ploughs; now 4. [There is] woodland for 400 pigs. Then as now [there was] 1 mill. [There are] 13 acres of meadow. [There were] then 12 head of cattle, 3 horses, 60 pigs, 40 goats, 20 sheep. [There are] now 6 head of cattle, 20 pigs, 30 sheep, 3 hives of bees. Then as now it was worth £6. And [there] was then 1 sokeman who held freely 1 virgate. Now R[obert] has [it]. Then as now [there was] half a plough. It was then worth 8s.; now 7.

Walter holds Colne [Engaine] of R[obert], which Godwine held as a manor and as 1 hide and 1 virgate. [There were] then 8 bordars; now 17. [There were] then 4 slaves; now 1. [There is] woodland for 30 pigs. [There are] 11 acres of meadow. [There is] 1 mill. It was then worth 40s.; now 60 and it is [included] in the assessment of Stanstead for £9.

HUNDRED OF ONGAR.

XLV. Land of William d'Écouis.

William holds Moreton in demesne, which Saxi held as a manor and as 1 hide and 20 acres. [There were] then 4 villans; now 3. Then as now [there were] 16 bordars. [There were] then 6 slaves; now 4. Then and later [there were] 3 ploughs in demesne; now 2. Then and later the men [had] 2 ploughs; now 1½. [There is] woodland for 400 pigs. [There are] 20 acres of meadow. [There were] then [...] horses; now 4. [There were] then 8 cows and 6 calves. [There are] now 11 head of cattle. [There are] now 36 sheep. [There were] then 60 pigs; now 14. [There were] then 30 goats; now 60. It was then worth £8; now 10. And 1 free man held 43½ acres. Now W[illiam] has appropriated [him] and he did not belong to that manor which Ralph holds of him. Then as now [there was] 1 villan and 2 bordars and 1 slave

William d'ÉCouis

[Folio 89: ESSEX]

and 1 plough in demesne and the men [had] half a plough. Then as now it was worth 20s., but he has had thus far 30s.

XLVI. Land of Roger de Poitou.

HUNDRED OF LEXDEN.

Wulfmær held [Mount] Bures as a manor and as 1 hide. Now R[oger holds it] as the same. [There were] then 6 villans, and when received the same; now 5. Then as now [there were] 9 bordars. Then and later [there were] 6 slaves; now 4. Then and later [there were] 3 ploughs in demesne; now 2. Then and later the men [had] 3 ploughs; now 1½. [There is] woodland for 300 pigs. [There are] 12 acres of meadow. Then as now [there was] 1 mill. And then as now [there were] a further 3 villans and 2 bordars, having 1 plough. [There were] then 2 horses, 14 head of cattle, 80 sheep, 28 pigs, 26 goats. [There are] now 7 head of cattle, 54 sheep, 6 pigs. It was then and later worth £7; now 11, and when received the same. And 8 free men held half a hide and 30 acres. Then as now [there were] 3 ploughs and 3 acres of meadow. [There is] woodland for 30 pigs. This is assessed above.

Leofwine Crook held [West] Bergholt as a manor and as 1 hide and 25 acres. Now Roger [holds it] as the same. [There were] then 7 villans; later and now 5. [There were] then 5 bordars, and when received 7; now 5. Then as now [there were] 2 slaves. Then and later [there were] 2 ploughs in demesne; now 1. Then and later the men [had] 2 ploughs; now 1. [There is] woodland for 300 pigs. [There are] 8 acres of meadow. Then as now [there was] 1 mill. To this manor belongs 1 berewick, which is called Bradfield, as half a hide and 30 acres. Then and later [there was] 1 plough in demesne; now none. R[oger] received then in demesne 1 horse and 14 head of cattle and 48 sheep and 100 sheep and 6 pigs, 32 goats. [There are] now 4 head of cattle, 80 sheep, 11 pigs. It was then worth £6, and when received 7; now it is worth 60s. And 7 free men held half a hide and 11½ acres. Then and later [there were] 2 ploughs; now 1. [There are] 2 acres of meadow, and it is assessed in the abovesaid pounds.

HUNDRED OF TENDRING.

In Bradfield Leofwine held half a hide and 15 acres. [There was] then 1 bordar and 1 slave; now none. Then and later [there was] 1 plough; now none. It was then worth 40s.,

[Folio 89v: ESSEX]

and when received 30s.; now it is worth 5s.

XLVII. Land of Hugh de Gournai.

HUNDRED OF HINCKFORD.

Geoffrey Talbot holds Liston, which a free man held as a manor and as half a hide and 30 acres. Then as now [there were] 2 ploughs in demesne and the men [had] 1 plough. Then and later [there were] 6 bordars; now 5. Then and later [there were] 3 slaves; now none. [There are] 30 acres of meadow. [There is] half a mill. [There were] then 3 cows with calves, 12 sheep, 7 pigs. Now [there are] 3 cows with calves, 22 sheep, 8 hives of bees. Then as now it was worth 68s.

HUNDRED OF TENDRING.

Osbert held Ardleigh as a manor and as $2\frac{1}{2}$ hides. Now Agnes holds [it]. [There were] then 16 villans; later and now 7. [There were] then 4 bordars; now none. [There were] then 4 slaves; now none. Then as now [there were] 2 ploughs in demesne. Among the men [there were] then 8 ploughs, and when received 6; now 3. [There is] woodland for 40 pigs. [There are] 3 acres of meadow. [There are] now 2 mills. [There were] then 30 sheep, 5 pigs. [There are] now 44 sheep, 8 pigs, 7 head of cattle, 10 goats, 3 hives of bees. It was then worth £6; later and now 4.

HUNDRED OF LEXDEN.

Geoffrey holds Fordham of Hugh, which Esbiorn held as a manor and as 2 hides. [There were] then 10 villans; now 7. [There were] then 5 bordars; now 11. [There were] then 5 slaves; now 4. Then as now [there were] 3 ploughs in demesne. The men [had] then 5 ploughs; now 3. [There is] woodland for 100 pigs. [There are] 12 acres of meadow. Then as now [there was] 1 mill. [There were] then 2 horses and 3 cows with calves, 60 sheep, 12 goats, 8 pigs, 10 hives of bees. [There are] now 2 horses, 8 head of cattle, 80 sheep, 25 goats, 10 pigs, 6 hives of bees. And 3 free men hold 13 acres. Then as now [there was] half a plough. Then as now it was worth £7. And Roger de Poitou took 10 acres from this manor, as the Hundred testifies.

[Folio 90: ESSEX]

XLVIII. Land of William Peverel.

Drogo holds [East and West] Horndon of William, which Æthelmær, a free man, held TRE as a manor and as $1\frac{1}{2}$ hides. Now [there] are $3\frac{1}{2}$ hides and 21 acres. Then as now [there were] 2 ploughs in demesne. The men [had] then 2 ploughs; now 3. [There was] then 1 villan; now none. [There were] then 4 bordars; now 11. [There were] then 3 slaves; now 2. [There was] then 1 cow, 60 sheep, 11 pigs. [There are] now 5 cows, 15 pigs, 60 sheep. [There were] then 4 sokemen and now the same, holding $2\frac{1}{2}$ hides and 21 acres of the same land. And 56 acres of it have been taken away. Then as now there is woodland for 100 pigs, pasture for 60 sheep. It was then worth 60s.; now 100.

HUNDRED OF CHAFFORD.

W[illiam] holds [Grays and West] Thurrock in demesne, which Æthelmær held TRE as a manor and as 3 hides and 42 acres. [There were] then 2 villans; now 3. [There were] then 11 bordars; now 18. Then as now [there were] 2 slaves and 2 ploughs in demesne. The men [had] then 4 ploughs; now 5. [There is] pasture for 100 sheep. Then as now [there was] 1 fishery. [There were] then 2 villans, 58 sheep, 1 horse. [There are] now 5 cows, 4 calves, 85 sheep, 8 pigs. It was worth £6 then and when received; now £12 and an ounce of gold. To this manor belonged 9 sokemen TRE, holding 3 hides. Now [there] are 5 sokemen and they hold $1\frac{1}{2}$ hides. And Gilbert, a man of the Bishop of Bayeux, holds $1\frac{1}{2}$ hides less 10 acres, and the Hundred does not know how [he holds it]. And also Ansketil, a man of the Bishop of London, holds 20 acres

which belonged to this manor TRE, and the Hundred similarly does not know [how].

XLIX. Land of Ralph de Limésy.

Ralph holds Brundon in demesne, which a free man held TRE as a manor and as $2\frac{1}{2}$ hides less 15 acres. Then as now [there were] 2 ploughs in demesne and the men [had] 3 ploughs and [there were] 7 villans

[Folio 90v: ESSEX]

and 7 bordars and 4 slaves. [There is] woodland for 10 pigs. [There are] 32 acres of meadow, 1 mill. It was then worth £4; later and now 6. To this manor Hardwin added 20 acres TRW. Then as now [there was] half a plough. [There is] now 1 bordar. [There was] then woodland for 20 pigs; now 6. It is assessed above.

In "Niuetuna" 1 sokeman belongs [there], holding now as then half a plough, and [this] is worth 3s.

HUNDRED OF ONGAR.

R[alph] holds Chigwell in demesne, which Harold held of King Edward as a manor and as 7 hides. Then as now [there were] 19 villans and 2 bordars and 2 ploughs in demesne. The men [had] then 16 ploughs; now 11. [There is] woodland for 800 pigs. [There are] 31 acres of meadow. Then as now [there was] 1 mill. It was then worth £8; now 10. And 6 free men dwelt on 2 hides and 15 acres, whom Robert Gernon now has of the king's gift, so he says. And they had then 3 ploughs; now 2. [There is] woodland for 40 pigs. [There are] 8 acres of meadow. [There was] then 1 mill; now none. Then as now it was worth 40s. And a certain free man, whom Peter the sheriff now has, holds and held 30 acres. [There was] then 1 plough; now half a plough. [There is] woodland for 30 pigs. [There are] 2 acres of meadow worth 5s. P[eter] had livery of this land with his fief.

In the abovesaid manor of Brundon, R[alph] received 3 head of cattle, 15 sheep, 15 pigs, 1 horse. [There are] now 6 head of cattle, 24 sheep, 18 pigs, 1 horse. And in Chigwell he received 6 head of cattle and 17 sheep and 11 pigs. [There are] now 10 head of cattle, 60 sheep, 20 pigs. Ralph de Limésy holds 6 acres of the king's soke, but his predecessor appropriated [it].

L. Land of Robert de Tosny.

HUNDRED OF UTTLESFORD.

One free man held Chiswick TRE as a manor and as $1\frac{1}{2}$ hides. Then as now [there was] 1 plough in demesne and the men [had] 2 ploughs. Then and later [there were] 4 villans; now 3. [There are] now 2 bordars. [There is] woodland for 100 pigs. [There are] 4 acres of meadow. It is worth 40s.

[Folio 91: ESSEX]

LI. Land of Ralph de Tosny.

HUNDRED OF HARLOW.

In Housham Roger holds half a hide of R[alph], which Eadmær held. Then as now [there was] 1 plough. [There is] woodland for 12 pigs. It was then worth 10s.; now 15.

Roger holds Laver of R[alph], which Saxi held as a manor and as 1 hide. [There were] then 4 villans; now 3. [There are] now 7 bordars. [There were] then 4 slaves; now 3. [There were] then 2 ploughs in demesne; now 1. [There is] woodland for 30 pigs. [There are] 16 acres of meadow. Then as now [there were] 13 pigs and 60 sheep and 4 cows. Then as now it was worth 70s.

LII. Land of Walter de Douai.

HUNDRED OF CHAFFORD.

Walter holds Upminster in demesne, which Swein Swart held as a manor and as 6½ hides and 30 acres. Then as now [there were] 8 villans. [There were] then 5 bordars; now 7. Then as now [there were] 4 slaves and 2 ploughs in demesne. The men [had] then 5 ploughs; now 4. [There is] woodland for 200 pigs. [There are] 8 acres of meadow. [There was] then 1 colt; now none. [There are] now 85 sheep and 25 sheep [sic]. It was then worth £7; now 8. And 10 acres belonged to this manor, which G[eoffrey] de Mandeville holds by exchange, as he says.

Walter holds Rainham in demesne, which Leofstan the reeve held TRE as a manor and as 8 hides. [There were] then 3 ploughs in demesne; now 2. The men [had] then 6 ploughs; now 5. Then as now [there were] 12 villans. [There were] then 2 bordars; now 9. [There were] then 5 slaves; now 4. [There are] 105 sheep, 20 pigs, 1 horse. Then as now it was worth £10. To this manor was added half a hide, which 3 free men held TRE.

And after King William came, Walter added them to his manor, to which they did not belong TRE, as the earldom testifies. And they had then 1 plough; now half a plough, and when received half. It is worth 20s.

HUNDRED OF TENDRING.

Leofstan holds [Great and Little] Holland as 6½ hides. Then as now [there were] 17 villans. Then and later [there were] 10 bordars; now 11.

[Folio 91v: ESSEX]

Then and later [there were] 5 slaves; now 3. Then and later [there were] 4 ploughs in demesne; now 3. Then and later the men [had] 11 ploughs; now 8. [There is] woodland for 100 pigs. [There are] 14 acres of meadow. Then as now it was worth £14.

LIII. Land of Matthew de Mortagne.

HUNDRED OF DUNMOW.

M[atthew] holds [Great and Little] Easton in demesne, which Aki, a free man, held TRE as a manor and as 5 hides. [There were] then 5 ploughs in demesne, and when received 4; now 3. The men [had] then 10 ploughs; now 7. [There were] then 11 villans and 1 priest; now 15 villans and 1 priest. [There were] then 10 bordars; now 16. [There were] then 10 slaves; now 9. [There was] then woodland for 200 pigs; now 150. [There were] then 67 acres of meadow. Then as now [there was] 1 mill and 1 horse and 8 head of cattle, [...]120 pigs and 60 sheep and 10 goats and 3 hives of bees. It was then worth £10, and when received the same; now it is worth £15.

HUNDRED OF CHELMSFORD.

M[atthew] holds Margaretting and Mountnessing, which Eskil held as a manor and as 5 hides. Then as now [there were] 7 villans and 8 bordars and 4 slaves and 2 ploughs in demesne and the men [had] 3 ploughs. [There is] woodland for 300 pigs and 1 horse and 5 head of cattle, 20 pigs, 30 sheep. It was then worth [...]s.; now £6.

LIIII. Land of the Countess of Aumale.

HUNDRED OF HINCKFORD.

[She] holds Borley in demesne, which Leofwine, a free man, held TRE as a manor and as 2 hides and 30 acres. [There were] then 3 ploughs in demesne; later and now 2. Then as now the men [had] 5 ploughs and [there were] 10 villans and 5 bordars. [There is] woodland for 30 pigs. [There are] 40 acres of meadow and 7 head of cattle and 25 sheep and 24 goats, 28 pigs, 2 hives of bees. Then and later it was worth £8; now 12.

HUNDRED OF TENDRING.

[She] holds Old Hall in demesne, which Ælfric held as a manor and as 2 hides. Then as now [there were] 15 bordars. [There were] then 4 slaves;

Countess Judith

[Folio 92: ESSEX]

later and now 1. [There were] then 2 ploughs in demesne; later and now 1. The men [had] then 4 ploughs; later and now 2. [There is] woodland IIII [sic] for 40 pigs. [There are] 6 acres of meadow. [There was] then 1 mill and 1 fishery; now none. [There is] pasture for 40 sheep. [There were] then 3 cows, 3 calves, 40 sheep, 2 horses, 30 pigs. [There is] now 1 horse, 3 head of cattle, 48 sheep. Then as now it was worth 60s.

LV. Land of Countess Judith.

HUNDRED OF BECONTREE.

Earl Waltheof held Walthamstow TRE as a manor and as 10½ hides. Then as now [there were] 2 ploughs in demesne. The men [had] then 15 ploughs; now 22. [There were] then 25 villans; now 36. [There was] then 1 bordar; now 25. Then as now [there were] 4 slaves. [There is] woodland for 300 pigs. [There are] 80 acres of meadow. [There is] pasture [worth] 8s. Then as now [there was] 1 mill. [There were] then 6 fisheries; now 1. [There are] now 8 head of cattle, 1 horse, 35 pigs, 60 sheep, 20 goats. It was then worth £15; now £28 and 2 ounces of gold.

LVI. Land of Frodo, brother of the Abbot.

F[rodo] holds Radwinter in demesne, which Ordgar held as a manor and as 1 hide and 1 virgate. Then as now [there were] 15 villans and 6 bordars and 3 and 3 [sic] ploughs in demesne and the men [had] 6 ploughs. [There is] woodland for 100 pigs. [There are] 30 acres of meadow. [There were] then 10 head of cattle, 60 sheep, 50 pigs, 25 goats, 1 hive of bees. [There are] now 18 head of cattle, 140 sheep, 37 pigs, 30 goats, 4 hives of bees. It was then worth £8; now 15. Of this manor Algar holds 30 acres of Frodo and they are worth 10s. in the above assessment.

[Folio 92v: ESSEX]

LVII. Land of Sasselin.

HUNDRED OF BARSTABLE.

S[asselin] holds 'Stanmer' and 'Cray's Hill' [in Ramsden, Bellhouse and Crays], which Ælfric and Wulfwine held as a manor and as 2 hides and 30 acres. Then as now [there were] 2 ploughs and the men [had] 2 oxen. [There is] woodland for 40 pigs. [There was] then 1 horse and 7 pigs and 15 sheep. [There is] now 1 horse, 70 sheep, 18 pigs, 20 goats. Then as now it was worth 50s.

HUNDRED OF WITHAM.

In [Black and White] Notley, S[asselin] holds half a hide and 22 acres, which Leofcild held TRE. [There was] then 1 plough; now half a plough. [There was] then 1 ox; now 4 [head of cattle]. And [there are] 12 sheep, 6 pigs, 1 horse. It is worth 10s.

HUNDRED OF WINSTREE.

S[asselin] holds Layer, which 2 free men held TRE as a manor and as 8 hides. [There were] then 4 ploughs in demesne; now 2. Then as now the men [had] 2 ploughs and 1 villan and 17 bordars. [There were] then 8 slaves; now 3. [There was] then woodland for 100 pigs; now 60. [There are] 7 acres of meadow. [There were] then 24 head of cattle, 200 sheep, 23 pigs, 3 horses, 4 hives of bees. [There are] now 7 head of cattle, 125 sheep, 9 pigs, 3 horses, 4 hives of bees. Then as now it was worth £7.

HALF-HUNDRED OF CLAVERING.

S[asselin] holds Pinchpools, which a free man held as a manor and as 1 hide. Then as now [there was] 1 plough. [There are] now 3 bordars and 1 slave and 4 acres of meadow and 18 sheep and 18 pigs. It is worth 20s.

HUNDRED OF CHAFFORD.

In Childerditch S[asselin] holds 1 manor with 1½ hides and 30 acres, which Ordgar, a free man, held TRE. [There was] then 1 plough in demesne; now 1½. Then as now the men [had] 2 ploughs. [There were] then 3 villans; now 4. Then as now [there were] 6 bordars. [There were] then 2 slaves; now none. [There is] woodland for 100 pigs, pasture for 60 sheep. [There were] then 50 sheep, 24 pigs, 4 horses, 12 head of cattle. [There are] now 4 head of cattle, 12 sheep, 6 pigs, 1 horse. It was then worth 60s.; now £4. And 1 sokeman was in this land with 15 acres, which he could sell, but the soke belonged to the land of St Paul in [Great and Little] Warley. Then as now [there was] half a plough and

Sasselin

[Folio 93: ESSEX]

it is worth 3s.

HUNDRED OF UTTLESFORD.

S[asselin] holds Bonhunt as a manor, which Ælfric, a free man, held TRE as a manor and as 2 hides. When he received [it], [there were] 4 bordars and now [the same]. Then as now [there was] 1 plough in demesne. The men [have] now half a plough. [There are] 10 acres of meadow. [There was] then 1 cow and 1 pig. [There are] now 30 sheep, 2 head of cattle, 1 horse. Then and later it was worth 40s.; now 55.

LVIII. Land of Gilbert fitzTurold.

HUNDRED OF UTTLESFORD.

Saxi, a free man, held Wicken TRE as a manor and as 3 hides and 13 acres. Then and later [there were] 8 villans; now 9. Then and later [there were] 8 bordars; now 11. Then as now [there were] 3 slaves and 2 ploughs in demesne and the men [had] 3 ploughs. Then and later [there was] woodland for 100 pigs; now 60. [There are] 10 acres of meadow. Then as now it was worth £7. [There was] then 1 horse, 50 sheep, 30 pigs, 36 goats. [There is] now 1 horse, 40 sheep, 30 goats, 26 pigs, 2 head of cattle.

LIX. Land of William Leofric.

Asgot, a free man, held "Scilcheham" TRE as a manor and as 8 hides. Then as now [there were] 6 villans. [There were] then 8 bordars; now 10. Then as now [there were] 3 slaves and 2 ploughs in demesne and the men [had] 3 ploughs. [There is] pasture for 100 sheep. Then as now it was worth £6.

LX. Land of Hugh de Saint-Quentin.

Winge held Horndon [on the Hill] TRE as a manor and as 1½ hides. Then as now [there was] 1 plough in demesne. [There were] then 3 bordars; now 4. [There is] woodland for 10 pigs. [There is] the eighth part of a fishery. Then as now [there was] 1 horse, 1 cow, 30 sheep, 1 pig. It is worth 20s. Godwine [Woodhen] took 2 places away from this land.

HUNDRED OF WINSTREE.

Ælfric, a free man, held [Great and Little] Wigborough

[Folio 93v: ESSEX]

as a manor and as 2 hides. Then as now [there was] 1 plough in demesne. [There was] then 1 bordar; now 2. [There were] then 2 slaves; now 3. [There was] then 1 mill; now none. Then as now [there was] 1 horse and 7 head of cattle and 1 pig. [There were] then 55 sheep; now 45. Then as now it was worth 30s.

HUNDRED OF LEXDEN.

Wulfweard held [Great and Little] Birch TRE as a manor and as half a hide and 15 acres. Now Hugh holds [it] of the queen's gift as the same. [There is] woodland for 10 pigs. [There are] 4 acres of meadow. [There was] then 1 bordar and 1 slave and now the same. Then as now [there was] 1 horse, 7 head of cattle, 25 pigs, 53 sheep. Then and later it was worth 20s.; now 16.

HUNDRED OF BARSTABLE.

LXI. Land of Edmund son of Algot.

Two free men held Horndon [on the Hill] TRE as a manor and as 2½ hides and 15 acres. [There were] then 3 ploughs in demesne; now 2. The men [had] then 2 ploughs; now 1. Then as now [there was] 1 villan. [There were] then 14 bordars; now 16. [There were] then 3 slaves; now none. [There is] pasture for 50 sheep. [There are] 12 acres of meadow. [There was] then 5 head of cattle, 1 horse, 20 pigs, 150 sheep. [There are] now 35 sheep. It is worth 50s. In the same vill [there] is a certain deacon having 30 acres and the fourth part of the church, and [this] belongs to the alms of the king.

E[dmund] holds Matching, which Almær Holdfæst held TRE as 1½ hides and as a manor. [There were] then 2 ploughs in demesne; now 1. The men [had] then 3½ ploughs; now 3. [There were] then 7 villans; now 9. [There are] now 4 bordars. [There were] then 4 slaves; now none. [There is] woodland for 50 pigs. [There are] 8 acres of meadow. [There were] then 7 cows, 1 pig, 100 sheep less 5, 40 goats, 1 horse, 6 hives of bees. [There are] now 4 head of cattle, 9 pigs, 24 sheep,

[Folio 94: ESSEX]

2 hives of bees. Then as now it was worth 100s.

T [sic]

LXII. Land of Roger the marshal.

HUNDRED OF BARSTABLE.

Alweard Dore held Nevendon as a manor and as 40 acres. Now R[oger] holds [it]. [There was] then half a plough; now none. Then as now it was worth 4s. And in [Black and White] Notley [there are] 5 acres, which Cola, a free man, held and they are worth 4s.

Wulfwine Hapra held "Byrton" [in Stanway] as a manor and as half a hide. Now R[oger] holds [it]. [There was] then 1

plough; now half a plough. [There is] 1 acre of meadow. It was then worth 10s.; now 5.

Alwine held "Lohou" as a manor and as 40 acres. Now R[oger holds it]. Then as now [there was] half a plough. [There is] woodland for 3 pigs [and] it is worth 5s.

LXIII. Land of Adam fitzDurand Malzor; Hundred of Dunmow.

Five free men held Willingale [Doe and Spain] TRE as a manor and as half a hide. [There were] then 2 ploughs; now 1. [There are] now 6 bordars. It is worth 10s.

HUNDRED OF HINCKFORD.

Godric, a free man, held Stebbingford as 15 acres TRE. Now A[dam] holds [it]. Then and later [there was] 1 plough in demesne; now half a plough. Then as now [there were] 5 bordars. [There is] woodland for 11 pigs. [There are] 3 acres of meadow. It was then worth 10s.; now 13.

LXIIII. Land of Goscelin the lorimer.

HUNDRED OF BECONTREE.

Two free men held Ilford TRE as a manor and as 3 hides less 30 acres. [There were] then 2 ploughs in demesne; now 1. The men [had] then ½ ploughs; now 1. [There were] then 7 villans; now 4.

[Folio 94v: ESSEX]

[There were] then 4 bordars; now 6. [There was] then 1 slave; now none. [There is] woodland for 20 pigs. [There are] 20 acres of meadow. [There is] now 1 mill and 1 fishery. Then as now it was worth £4.

LXV. Land of John, nephew of Waleran.

HUNDRED OF UTTLESFORD.

Mærwynn, a free woman, held Elsenham TRE as a manor and as 4 hides. Then as now [there were] 2 ploughs in demesne. Then and later the men [had] 7 ploughs; now 6. Then as now [there were] 8 villans. Then and later [there was] 1 bordar; now 12. Then as now [there were] 5 slaves. [There was] then woodland for 1,300 pigs, and when received 1,100; now 1,000. [There are] 12 acres of meadow. Then as now [there was] 1 mill and 220 sheep and 8 cows and 60 pigs and 1 horse and 1 colt. Then and later it was worth £6; now 8.

LXVI. Land of William the deacon.

HUNDRED OF WINSTREE.

Thorkil, a free man, held Peldon TRE as a manor and as 5 hides. Then as now [there were] 2 ploughs in demesne and the men [had] 2 ploughs. [There were] then 4 villans; now 3. [There were] then 9 bordars; now 10. [There were] then 2 slaves; now 4. [There is] woodland for 60 pigs, 1 salt-pan and 1 church with 30 acres. Then as now [there was] half a plough and 1 sokeman with 17 acres. Of these 5 hides, Hamo the steward took away 80 acres of arable land and 200 acres of marsh, all of which belonged to this manor TRE and after the arrival of King William, as the Hundred testifies. And we have received this appropriation into the king's hands. The abovesaid manor with all this was then and when received worth £6, and now it is worth 100s. And that which was taken away from it is worth 20s.

HUNDRED OF HINCKFORD.

Godhere, a free man, held Shalford as a manor and as half a hide TRE. Then and later [there was] 1 plough; now 1½ ploughs. [There were] then 3 slaves. [There is] now 1 bordar.

[Folio 95: ESSEX]

[There is] woodland for 12 pigs. [There are] 7 acres of meadow. It was then worth 40s.; now 50.

LXVII. Land of Walter the cook.

HUNDRED OF HINCKFORD.

A free man held Shalford TRE as a manor and as half a hide. Then and later [there were] 1½ ploughs; now 1. Then as now [there was] 1 villan and 3 bordars. Then and later [there were] 2 slaves; now 1. [There is] woodland for 8 pigs. [There are] 11 acres of meadow. [There were] then 2 horses and 12 head of cattle and 60 pigs and 53 sheep and 3 goats. [There are] now 10 head of cattle and 8 pigs and 53 sheep and 20 goats and 5 hives of bees. It was then worth 40s.; now 50.

In Ashwell Felagi held half a hide as a manor. Now Walter [holds it]. [There were] then 3 bordars; now 7. [There were] then 1½ ploughs; now 1. [There is] woodland for 60 pigs. [There are] 11 acres of meadow. [There was] then 1 cow and 30 pigs and 5 sheep. [There are] now 4 head of cattle and 8 pigs and 53 sheep. It was then worth 40s.; now 60.

HUNDRED OF BARSTABLE.

LXVIII. Land of Modwin.

Edwin Groats held Wickford freely as a manor and as half a hide. Then as now [there was] 1 plough and 1 bordar. [There are] 4 acres of meadow. It is worth 10s.

HUNDRED OF WITHAM.

[...] In Witham M[odwin] holds 1 hide, which Harold held. Then as now [there was] 1 plough. [There was] then 1 bordar; now 2. [There is] woodland for 12 pigs. [There were] then 8 acres of meadow; now 4, and Geoffrey Baynard took the others. [There were] then 4 pigs; now 7. [There were] then 20 sheep; now 40. [There were] then 4 head of cattle; now 10. [There are] now 2 horses. It is worth 20s.

HUNDRED OF DENGIE.

Alweard held Creeksea TRE as a manor and as 1 hide. [There were] then 2 bordars; now 1. Then as now [there was] 1 plough. [There is] pasture for 40 sheep; now 85 sheep. Then as now it was worth 30s.

HUNDRED OF WINSTREE.

A free man held Layer TRE as a manor

[Folio 95v: ESSEX]

and as 2 hides. Then as now [there were] 2 ploughs in demesne. [There were] then 5 bordars; now 4. Then as now [there were] 2 slaves. [There is] woodland for 20 pigs. [There were] then 32 sheep; now 100. [There was] then 1 cow with a calf. [There are] now 10 head of cattle. [There are] now 40 goats and 2 horses. [There were] then 7 pigs; now 10. Then as now it was worth 60s.

HUNDRED OF LEXDEN.

Alweard held Crepping as 1 virgate of land. Now Modwin holds [it]. [There was] then 1 plough; now half a plough. [There were] 2 acres of meadow. [There is] woodland for 40 pigs. It is worth 10s. One free man held this.

In [East] Donyland Lagman held 1 virgate. Now Modwin holds [it]. Then as now [there was] 1 bordar. Then and later [there was] half a plough; now none. It was then worth 10s.; now 6.

HUNDRED OF TENDRING.

Ælfric held Tendring as 15 acres. Now Modwin [holds it] as a manor and as the same. [There were] then 2 slaves; now 1. Then as now [there was] 1 plough. It is worth 20s. Then as now [there was] 1 horse. [There are] now 4 pigs and 4 goats and 10 sheep and 6 head of cattle. This is in demesne.

Godwine the priest held "Derleigh" [in Little Bromley] as a manor and as 1 hide and 5 acres. Now M[odwin] holds [it]. [There was] then 1 plough; now none. It was then worth 10s.; now 30d.

HUNDRED OF BARSTABLE.

LXIX Land of Ilbod.

Two free men held Wickford TRE as 40 acres. Now Ilbod holds [it] as the same. Then as now [there was] half a plough and 2 free men. It is worth 40d.

HUNDRED OF HINCKFORD.

Ilbod holds Liston, which a free man held TRE as a manor and as half a hide and 1 virgate. Then as now [there were] 2 ploughs in demesne and the men [had] 1 plough and [there were] 5 bordars and 4 slaves and 30 acres of meadow and half a mill. Then as now [there were] 5 head of cattle and 1 horse and 43 sheep and 15 pigs and it is worth 60s. And Ilbod holds 7 free men holding half a hide TRE. Then and when received [there were] 2 ploughs; now half a plough and 4 bordars. It was then worth 20s.; now 15s. 6d.

Ilbod

[Folio 96: ESSEX]

Four free men held [East] Donyland as 1½ hides and 8 acres. Now I[lbod] holds [it]. Among the men [there were] then 2 ploughs; now 1 plough. [There are] now 3 bordars, 2 acres of meadow. It was then worth 10s.; now 7.

LXX. Land of Hagebern.

HUNDRED OF BARSTABLE.

Tovi, a free man, held Nevendon TRE as 54 acres. [There was] then 1 plough; now none. It was then worth 10s.; now 3s. 4d.

Modwin held [East] Donyland as half a hide and 12 acres. Now Hagebern holds [it] as the same. Then as now [there were] 2 bordars. [There was] then 1 plough; now none. It was then worth 14s.; now 10. One priest held Rainham freely as half a hide. Now Hagebern holds [it]. [There was] then half a plough; now none. It is worth 10s.

LXXI. Land of Theodoric Pointel.

Hunald holds [East and West] Tilbury of Theodoric, which a free man held TRE as a manor and 45 acres. Then as now [there was] half a plough and 1 bordar and 4 acres of meadow. [There is] pasture for 50 sheep. It was then worth 7s.; now 8.

HUNDRED OF DENGIE.

Godric, a free man, held [North] Fambridge TRE as a manor and as 8 hides. Now T[heodoric holds it] in demesne. [There were] then 12 villans; now 2. [There are] now 10 bordars. [There were] then 10 slaves; now 5. Then as now [there were] 2 ploughs in demesne. The men [had] then 4 ploughs; now 2. [There is] woodland for 200 pigs. Two free men were here, having 50 acres in addition to the abovesaid hides. [There were] 2 horses, 10 head of cattle, 10 pigs, 150 sheep. [There are] now 2 horses, 5 asses, 8 head of cattle, 20 pigs, 200 sheep. Then as now it was worth £7.

Theodoric holds 1½ hides by exchange for [Great and Little] Coggeshall, which Tesselin held. [There were] then 2 ploughs; now none. [There were] then 3 bordars; now none. [There is] woodland for 3 pigs. [There are] 12 acres of meadow. It was then worth 20s.; now 10.

[Folio 96v: ESSEX]

HUNDRED OF ROCHFORD.

T[heodoric] holds Sutton in demesne, which a free man held TRE as a manor and as 2 hides and 30 acres. Then as now [there were] 2 ploughs in demesne and 6 slaves. [There was] then 1 bordar; now 9. [There is] woodland for 50 pigs, pasture for 100 sheep. [There are] 4 acres of meadow. To this manor belonged 3 free men. One held half a hide and could leave without licence of the same lord of the manor. Another held 30 acres, which Grimbald holds of T[heodoric]

And the third [held] 30 acres, which Hunald holds

And they could leave [without licence]. In demesne, T[heodoric] received 2 horses and 7 head of cattle, 6 pigs, 100 sheep, 6 hives of bees. [There are] now 2 horses, 7 head of cattle, 21 pigs, 106 sheep. The whole was then worth £4; now 7. Of this manor Robert holds of T[heodoric] half a hide and 2 bordars and 2 ploughs and [this] is worth 10s. in the above

valuation. And to this manor belonged 1 sokeman who could not withdraw.

LXXII. Land of Roger God-save-the-ladies.

HUNDRED OF WITHAM.

Wulfsige, a free man, held Rivenhall as a manor and as 30 acres TRE. Then as now [there was] 1 plough. It is worth 20s.

HUNDRED OF HINCKFORD.

Wulfsige held Felsted under Earl Ælfgar as a manor and as half a hide and 30 acres. Then as now [there were] 2 ploughs in demesne and 3 slaves. [There is] woodland for 20 pigs. [There are] 10 acres of meadow. It was then worth 30s.; now 40.

Wulfsige, a free man, held [Great and Little] Baddow as a manor and as 1½ hides. Then as now [there was] 1 bordar; later and now 3. Then as now [there were] 4 slaves and 2 ploughs in demesne. [There is] woodland for 40 pigs. [There are] 8 acres of meadow. Then as now it was worth 40s.

LXXIII. Land of Gilbert fitzSalomon.

HUNDRED OF HINCKFORD.

In

[Folio 97: ESSEX]

Felstead a free man held 30 acres, which G[ilbert] holds. Then as now [there was] 1 plough. It is worth 20s.

LXXIIII. land of William fitzConstantine.

Swein held Theydon, as a manor and as 2 hides TRE and 40 acres. Now W[illiam] holds [it] as the same. [There were] then 5 villans; later and now 4. Then and later [there were] 7 bordars; now 10. [There were] then 4 slaves; now none. Then as now [there were] 2 ploughs in demesne. Among the men [there were] then 4 ploughs; later and now 3. [There is] woodland for 500 pigs. [There are] 20 acres of meadow. Then as now [there was] 1 mill. Then and later it was worth 60s.; now 100.

LXXV. Land of Esger the cook.

Godmann held Aveley freely as 50 acres. Then as now [there was] half a plough. And in Stifford a free man held 25 acres and now as then among [the men] in this and the abovesaid land [there] is half a plough and [this] is worth 10s.

LXXVI. Land of Robert fitzRoscelin.

HUNDRED OF UTTLESFORD.

Alwine, a free man, held Heydon TRE as a manor and as 5 hides and 15 acres. Then as now [there were] 18 villans. [There were] then 3 bordars; later and now 7. Then as now [there were] 5 slaves and 3 ploughs in demesne and the men [had] 8 ploughs and [there were] 8 acres of meadow. [There is] woodland for 8 pigs. [There were then] 2 horses, 206 sheep, 40 pigs, 13 hives of bees. [There is] now 1 horse, 206 sheep, 20 pigs, 10 hives of bees. Then and later it was worth £10; now 12. And a certain Englishman, Godwine, holds now as then 12 acres. Then as now [there was] 1 bordar. And Leofwine similarly [holds] 5 acres and [this] is worth 12d.

LXXVII. Land of Ralph Pinel.

HUNDRED OF TENDRING.

Beorhtmær held [Great and Little] Bromley and "Westnanetuna" as a manor and as 4½ hides, and 2 halls were there. Now R[alph] holds [it]. Then as now [there were] 5 villans. Then and later [there were] 25 bordars;

[Folio 97v: ESSEX]

now 23. [There were] then 6 slaves; now 9. [There were] then 3 ploughs in demesne; now 2. Then and later the men [had] 10 ploughs; now 6. [There is] woodland for 600 pigs. [There are] 16 acres of meadow. Then as now it was worth £7. R[alph] gave service for this land to G[eoffrey] de Mandeville because the same G[eoffrey] told him how the king had given him the service of that land, but he twice gave his rent to the king's servants when the king sent his officers to this land.

LXXVIII. Land of Robert fitzGosbert.

3 free men held Belstead as a manor and as 1½ hides and 40 acres. Then as now [there were] 3 bordars and 1 slave and 2 ploughs in demesne. [There is] woodland for 10 pigs. [There are] 15 acres of meadow. It was then worth 30s.; now 50.

LXXIX. Land of Reginald the crossbowman.

R[eginald] holds [South] Fambridge of the king as a manor and as 3½ hides. Then as now [there was] 1 villan and 7 bordars and 2 ploughs in demesne and the men [had] 2 ploughs. [There is] pasture for 100 sheep. Then as now it was worth 100s., but the monks of Ely claim [it] and the Hundred testifies for them. And he was seised of half a hide next to that land after the arrival of King William, which is worth 30s. a year.

LXXX. Land of Gundwin.

HUNDRED OF THURSTABLE.

Alric held Tolleshunt as a manor and as 1 hide. Now G[undwin] holds [it]. Then as now [there were] 2 bordars. [There were] then 4 slaves; now 5. [There was] then 1 plough; now half a plough. It was then worth 30s., and when received it was worth 20s. Now it is worth 10s.

LXXXI. Land of Otto the goldsmith.

HUNDRED OF HINCKFORD.

Otto the Goldsmith

[Folio 98: ESSEX]

Earl Ælfgar held Gestingthorpe as half a hide. Now Otto holds [it] as the same. Then as now [there were] 3 ploughs in demesne and the men [had] 3 ploughs. [There were] then 13 bordars; now 16. Then as now [there were] 6 slaves. [There is] woodland for 60 pigs. [There are] 25 acres of meadow, 80 sheep, 32 head of cattle, 88 pigs and 3 horses. And [there] were 12 sokemen TRE; now [there] are 11 dwelling on this manor and they hold half a hide and 30 acres. Then as now [there were] 4 bordars and 1 plough and 1 slave. It was then worth £10; now 12 and when the king gave [it to Otto] 15.

LXXXII. Land of Gilbert the priest.

HUNDRED OF HINCKFORD.

9 sokemen held Middleton of Earl Ælfgar as 1½ hides and 28 acres. Then as now [there were] 1½ ploughs in demesne, 4½ acres of meadow. It is worth 20s. He claims [to hold] this land of the queen's gift.

HUNDRED OF BARSTABLE.

LXXXIII. Land of Grim the reeve.

In Bowers [Gifford] Grim has 2 hides in which [there] was 1 plough and 2 slaves TRE, now [there] are 2 ploughs in demesne and the men [have] half a plough and [there are] 3 villans, 6 bordars, 3 slaves. [There is] pasture for 100 sheep . And of these 2 hides, 1 is from men [who] forfeited [it] to the king, which G[rim] added to his other land after the arrival of the king, through R[obert] fitzWymarc, the sheriff, as G[rim] says. And all this was worth 40s. TRE; now 50. In Chadwell Godmann, a free man, held 20 acres and [he] forfeited [them because] he could not pay the fine [for this land], but Grim gave 30s. to the king for it and holds the land by licence of Hubert de Port. And it is worth 20d.

LXXXIIII. Land of Wulfgifu, wife of Fin.

HUNDRED OF BARSTABLE.

In Pitsea [there] were 3 hides TRE, which Wulfgifu holds. [There were] then 2 ploughs in demesne and

[Folio 98v: ESSEX]

and 1 villan with half a plough and 4 slaves and 1 mill. [There is] pasture for 60 sheep, half a hide of woodland. [There are] now 2 ploughs in [sic] demesne, 3 bordars, 5 slaves. It is worth 60s. To these hides have now been added 3 other hides and 30 acres of woodland on which 8 free men with 2 ploughs dwell.

[There is] pasture for 130 sheep. The whole is worth 60s. and these 3 hides still belong to the king.

HUNDRED OF DENGIE.

Fin, a free man, held Latchingdon TRE as a manor and as 5 hides and 15 acres. Now W[ulfgifu] holds [it]. [There were] then 6 villans. [There are] now 3 bordars. [There were] then 4 slaves; now 5. Then as now [there were] 3 ploughs in demesne, 7 horses, 13 head of cattle, 31 pigs, 245 sheep. Then as now it was worth £4.

LXXXV.

In the Hundred Of Chafford Edward, son of Swein, held half a hide. Now Eadgifu his wife holds [it]. [There was] then 1 plough; now half a plough. [There is] pasture for 30 sheep. It is worth 10s.

LXXXVI. Land of Thorkil the Reeve.

HUNDRED OF CHELMSFORD.

In Walter T[horkil] holds 1 hide less 10 acres. Then as now [there were] 3 bordars and 1 slave and 1 plough in demesne. Among the men [there was] then half a plough. [There is] woodland for 40 pigs. [There are] 6 acres of meadow. It was then worth 20s.; now 30.

And a certain servant of the king holds 8 acres and [this] is worth 2s.

LXXXVII.

And a certain free man named Stanheard held and holds 30 acres of the king and they belong to Wethersfield. Then as now [there were] 3 bordars. [There was] then 1 plough; now half a plough. [There is] woodland for 8 pigs. [There are] 7 acres of meadow. Then as now [there was] 1 mill. It is worth 8s.

LXXXVIII.

And Godwine the deacon held and holds 9 acres and they are worth 16d. And 1 man of William fitzGross holds 2 acres of the king's soke and he renders customary dues to the king.

[Folio 99: ESSEX]

LXXXIX. Free Men of the King.

In the Hundred Of Lexden the king has 7 free men and the Hundred-reeve has them, holding half a hide. And [this] is worth 8s. And 1 free man held 3½ acres, and in these is pasture for 100 sheep and land for 2 oxen. It was then worth 10s. and when Robert de Montbegon appropriated [it] it was worth 10s.; now nothing. And 1 free man held 13 acres. Now as then there is 1 plough and woodland for 20 pigs and 1 acre of meadow. It was then worth 10s.; now it renders 20s. And Richard, a man of Hamon, appropriated this land and he has still the spoils from it.

XC. Appropriations of the King['s land] in Essex.

In Horndon [on the Hill] Godwine [Woodhen] appropriated 2 places, which are [part] of the land which Hugh de Saint-Quentin holds of the king and he gave a pledge for them. In this same vill the same Godwine appropriated 3 virgates of land of the king from the land of a certain free man, which still belongs to the king by judgement of the Hundred, and he again gave a pledge [for them]. In Dunton [are] 15 acres of land, which Wulfwine held and they belong to the king undisputed. Appropriation[s] of Theodoric Pointel.

In [Little] Thurrock, which 11 free men held TRE [and hold] now, [there are] 1½ hides and 42 acres of land. And [there were] then 3 ploughs in demesne; now 2. [There is] pasture for 30 sheep. It was then worth 41s.; now 20. T[heodoric] Pointel appropriated this land and it is in the king's hands.

[Folio 99v: ESSEX]

HUNDRED OF WINSTREE.

Wulfric, a free man, held Layer TRE as a manor and as 2 hides. And the same T[heodoric] appropriated this. [There were] then 2 ploughs; now none, nor when received. [There are] now 2 bordars. [There was] then woodland for 40 pigs; now 30. It was then worth 60s., and when received 40; now 20. And in Burnham T[heodoric] appropriated 15½ acres and they were still in the king's hands after this plea was made.

HUNDRED OF ROCHFORD.

T[heodoric] appropriated [Great and Little] Stambridge, which a free man held TRE as a manor and as 1½ hides and 20 acres. And 3 knights hold this manor of T[heodoric]. [There were] then 3 villans; now 2. [There was] then 1 slave; now none. [There were] then 2 bordars; now 5. Then as now [there was] 1 plough in demesne. The men [had] then 2 ploughs; now 1. It was then worth 40s.; now 100. T[heodoric] appropriated Paglesham, which 2 free men held as half a hide and 15 acres. Then as now [there was] 1 plough. It is worth 20s. T[heodoric] Pointel held these 2 manors by exchange for [Great and Little] Coggeshall and now they are in the king's hands. In "Midebroc" he appropriated 20 acres. Then as now [there was] 1 villan and [this] is worth 4s. And the soke belongs to the church of Holy Trinity of Canterbury, as the Hundred testifies. T[heodoric] Pointel also held this by exchange and [now] it is in the king's hands.

Appropriation of Ranulf Peverel. In Terling R[anulf] appropriated 5 free men, holding 3 hides less 15 acres TRE. Of this manor, Roger holds 2 hides and 80 acres of R[anulf] and Ranulf [holds] 30 acres. [There were] then 3½ ploughs; now 6. [There were] then 2 villans; now 5. [There are] now 5 bordars. [There is] woodland for 20 pigs. [There are] 22 acres of meadow. It was then worth 75s.; now £4 and 15s.

And in Widdington R[anulf] appropriated 30 acres, which he holds in demesne. And they are worth 5s.

In Stansgate R[anulf] appropriated 1 hide and 30 acres, which Ralph fitzBrian holds of him [and] which 2 free men held TRE. Then as now [there were] 2 bordars and 1 plough. [There is] pasture for 20 sheep. It was then worth 15s.; now 10. And in [Great and Little] Henny [there are] 20½ acres, which 12 free men held TRE. Now Turold holds [them] and they are worth 3s. And in Lamarsh [there are] 2 acres of land [held] freely and they are worth 4d.

[Folio 100: ESSEX]

Appropriation[s] of Hugh de Montfort in Essex.

Hugh de Montfort appropriated 1 free man of the king and William fitzGross [appropriated] 10 free men. All these [men] held 3 hides and 9 acres TRE, in which were then 8½ ploughs; now 7½. Then as now [there were] 13 bordars and 5 slaves. [There were] then 2 mills; now 1. [There is] woodland for 157 pigs. [There are] 30 acres of meadow. Then as now it was worth £6. 2s. And he appropriated a further 4 free men with 2 hides and 20 acres, which are worth 30s. And there were then 2½ ploughs; now none. And in the Hundred of Lexdenhe appropriated 3 free men holding 1 hide and 30 acres in which [there] were 3 ploughs; now 2½. [There was] then 1 bordar; now 6. [There is] woodland for 100 pigs. [There are] 12 acres of meadow. It was then worth 30s.; now 50. And one of these 3 [free men] belongs to the fief of St Peter of Westminster at Feering. And this is the testimony of the Hundred, but he was delivered to Hugh in the numeration of his manors, as his men say. And in Bockingham [there are] 15 acres of land which a free man held and now William fitzGross holds [them] and they are worth 32d.

In the Hundred of Chaffordis 1 free man with 40 acres, who belonged to Havering[-atte-Bower] TRE, whom St Peter of Westminster now has [and] because he came to the abbey of his own will, and he does not pay customary dues to Havering[-atte-Bower]. Appropriation[s] of G[eoffrey] de Mandeville. Ælfgifu, a free woman, held Mashbury TRE, which now Wulfric holds of the king's gift. And G[eoffrey] appropriated it from the king, in which land [there] is 1 hide. And then as now [there was] 1 plough and 1 slave and 8 acres of meadow. It was then worth 10s.; now 30. And in [Great and Little] Canfield [there are] 8 acres of land which G[eoffrey] appropriated from the king and Richard holds [them] of him.

Bosi, a free man, held Rockells TRE as a manor and as 2½ hides. Then and later [there were] 2 ploughs in demesne; now 1½. The men [had] then 4 ploughs; later and now 6. Then and later [there were] 7 villans; now 8. [There were] then 5 slaves; later and now 7. [There is] woodland for 30 pigs. [There are] 24 acres of meadow. Then as now [there was] 1 mill. Then and later it was worth 100s.; now £6.

[Folio 100v: ESSEX]

A free man held Rockells TRE as a manor and as 3 hides. Then and later [there were] 2 ploughs in demesne; now 1½. The men [have] now 1 plough and [there is] 1 villan. Then as now [there were] 5 bordars. [There was] then 1 slave; now none. Then as now it was worth 40s. And in Wendens [Ambo and Lofts] a free man holds 6½ acres and it is worth 2s.

In Farnham 4 free men held 3 hides and 3 virgates TRE. And now 4 knights hold [them] of G[eoffrey]. Then and later [there were] 8 ploughs; now 5. Then and later [there were] 6 villans; now 3. Then and later [there were] 4 bordars; now 15.

Then and later [there were] 7 slaves; now 3. Then and later [there was] woodland for 60 pigs; now 50. [There are] 14 acres of meadow. Then as now it was worth £6.

In Stambourne a free man held half a hide TRE. Then and later [there were] 2 ploughs in demesne; now none. Then as now the men [had] half a plough and [there were] 3 bordars and 1 slave. [There are] 12 acres of meadow. Then and later it was worth 40s.; now 50.

In "Wesuunic" [there were] 6 free men TRE with 1 hide and 46 acres. [There was] then 1 plough; now none. Then and later it was worth 15s.; now 10.

In Arkesden Godwine Sack held 1 hide less 8 acres. Now it is in the king's hands. [There was] then 1 bordar and 1 plough; now nothing. [There are] 2 acres of meadow. It was then worth 20s.; now 10. And G[eoffrey] de Mandeville held this land and Wulfmær held 15 acres of the fief of Esger under G[eoffrey], and the Shire does not testify [to this].

Hugh de BerniÒres held 37 acres of the king, which he denied, and later it was adjudged to [be] to the use of the king and he gave a pledge. Then as now [there was] 1 plough in demesne and 1 bordar. [There is] woodland for 40 pigs. [There are] 4 acres of meadow. It was then worth 10s.; now 20.

In "Plesingho" a free man held 1 hide of land, which Humphrey Goldenbollocks appropriated from the king. Then as now [there was] 1 plough in demesne and 7 bordars and 2 slaves. [There is] woodland for 30 pigs. [There are] 7 acres of meadow. [There was] then 1 mill. It was then worth 16d.; now 23.

In [Great and Little] Wigborough Hamo the steward added 2 sokemen of the king, whom he appropriated from the king, with 30 acres and it is worth 4s. In 'Carseia' [Northey Island] [there are] 8 acres and they are worth 8d. And in Stambourn [there are] 40 acres, which Æthelstan, a free man, and 12 free men held TRE and hold still. Then as now [there were] 2 ploughs and 3 bordars and it is worth 40s.

In the Hundred of Odsey W[illiam] Cardon appropriated 1 sokeman with 8 acres and he belongs to Chishall of the fief of G[eoffrey] de Mandeville and it is worth 2s.

[Folio 101: ESSEX]

HALF-HUNDRED OF CLAVERING.

Appropriation[s] of Swein. Godwine, a free man, held Bollington and "Bertuna" of Harold TRE as a manor and as 4½ hides. Now Alvred holds [it] of him. Then as now [there were] 2 ploughs in demesne and the men [had] 5 ploughs and [there were] 7 villans and 13 bordars and 5 slaves. [There is] woodland for 20 pigs. [There are] 2 acres of meadow. Then and later it was worth £4; now 6. Robert fitzWymarc appropriated this land TRW and Swein holds [it] still.

In Manuden Aubrey de Vere appropriated 1½ hides and 15 acres, which 3 free men held TRE. [There were] then 5 ploughs; later and now 4. Then as now [there were] 6 villans and 6 bordars and 3 slaves. [There is] woodland for 30 pigs and [there are] 9 acres of meadow. Then and later it was worth 60s.; now £4.

And in Smalton [there are] 15 acres of land, which a free man held TRE. There was] then 1 plough; later half a plough [and] now none. And it is worth 3s. In [Great and Little]

Maplestead and in Pebmarsh the wife of Aubrey de Vere appropriated 5 free men with 1 acre and the fourth part of another, which Tidbald held under her. And it is worth 3s.

Ralph Baynard appropriated half a hide and 10 acres in Henham, which 2 free men held TRE. Then as now [there was] 1 plough. It is worth 12s. And in Coupals [there is] 1 hide and 43 acres, which 6 free men held TRE. Then and later [there were] 4 ploughs; now 3. [There are] 15 acres of meadow. It is worth 40s.

In Bollington 1 free man held 20 acres TRE and still hold [them], but he concealed [them] and [so] he gave a pledge. And it is worth 10s. In Farnham a free man held 30 acres. Now Ralph Latimer holds [them], but he concealed [them] and he gave a pledge. And it is worth 10s.

In "Liffildewella" 1 free man held and holds now as then 30 acres, and it is worth 6s. 8d.

Appropriation[s] of Turold. In [Great and Little] Henny 4 free men held 18 acres TRE and still hold [them]. Then as now [there was] half a plough among them, and it is worth 3s.

[Folio 101v: ESSEX]

In Lamarsh Turold appropriated 47 acres, which 8 free men held TRE and they hold [them] still. Then as now [there was] half a plough and it is worth 5s.

Appropriation[s] of Waleran. In [Great and Little] Henny [there is] half a hide and 10½ acres, which 7 free men held TRE and they have now as then 1 plough and 4 acres of meadow. And it is worth 10s. Roger holds this of John [fitzWaleran]. In Halstead Wulfwine held 10 acres, which Waleran appropriated. Then as now [there was] 1 plough. [There was] then 1 bordar; now 40. [There were] then 3 slaves; now none. [There is] woodland for 16 pigs. [There are] 5 acres of meadow. It was then worth 20s.; now 30.

In Braintree 3 free men held 30 acres of land and they are worth 3s. Leodmær of Hempstead appropriated this land and he held [it] of the fief of Richard [fitzGilbert]. And R[ichard] is not protector to him for it.

Appropriation[s] of Richard, son of Count Gilbert. Almær of Borley, Goldstan, Ælfric of Alderford [and] Wulfric of Brundon hold half a hide and 6 acres and they held [them] TRE. Now Goismer holds them of R[ichard]. Then as now [there was] 1 plough and 1 bordar and 5 acres. Then as now it was worth 28s.

In Finchingfield Arnold holds 80 acres of R[ichard], which Beorhtric, a free man, held TRE. Then as now [there were] 2 ploughs in demesne. Then and later [there was] 1 villan; now none. Then and later [there were] 3 bordars; now 8. Then as now [there were] 3 slaves. [There was] then woodland for 40 pigs; now 30. Then and later it was worth 40s.; now 60.

At Lashley Grim, , held half a hide, which Arnold holds. Then as now [there were] 2 ploughs. Then and later [there were] 4 bordars; now 8. [There were] then 2 slaves; now none. Then and later [there was] woodland for 80 pigs; now 60. [There are] 10 acres of meadow. Then and later it was worth 40s.; now 60.

At Horseham Beorhtmær, a free man, held 1 hide TRE. Now Widelard holds [it]. Then and later [there was] 1 plough; now 1½. [There were] then 2 bordars; later and now 7. [There are] 9 acres of meadow. It was then worth 30s.;

later and now 40.

In Howe Germund holds 37½ acres,

Richard

[Folio 102: ESSEX]

which Colman, a free man, held TRE. Then as now [there were] 3 ploughs in demesne. Then and later the men [had] 2 ploughs; now 3. [There is] 1 slave, woodland for 4 pigs. [There are] 10 acres of meadow. It was then worth 60s.; now £4. 10s.

In [Great and Little] Yeldham Bernard holds 40 acres, which Godwine, a free man, held TRE. Then as now [there was] 1 plough and 2 bordars. [There is] woodland for 10 pigs. [There are] 5 acres of meadow. It was then worth 20s.; later and now 30.

In Borley Ansketil holds half a hide and 23 acres, which Grim and Godgifu, free men, held TRE. [There was] then 1 plough; now 1½. Then and later [there were] 3 bordars; now 5. [There are] 9 acres of meadow. It was then worth 20s.; later 30 [and] now 40.

In Toppesfield Ralph holds 15 acres, which Æthelstan, a free man, held TRE. Then as now [there was] 1 plough. Then and later [there were] 4 bordars; now 7. Then and later [there were] 4 slaves; now none. [There is] woodland for 20 pigs. [There are] 6 acres of meadow. Then and later it was worth 20s.; now 30.

In Toppesfield G. holds 15 acres, which Dufa held. Then as now [there was] 1 plough in demesne and the men [had] 1 plough and [there were] 3 villans and 2 bordars and 2 slaves. [There is] woodland for 30 pigs. [There are] 8 acres of meadow. Then and later it was worth 50s.; now 60.

In 'Nortuna' [Cornish Hall] Mascerel holds 55 acres, which Beorhtric, a free man, held TRE. [There was] then 1 plough in demesne; later and now 2. Then as now the men [had] 1 plough and [there were] 5 villans. Then and later [there were] 5 bordars; now 8. Then and later [there were] 3 slaves; now 2. [There is] woodland for 40 pigs. [There are] 10 acres of meadow. It was then worth 40s.; later and now 60.

In Pebmarsh Leofcild, a free man, held 3 acres and holds [them] still. And in Alphamstone Deorwulf [holds] 4 acres and Hold, a free man, [holds] 1 acre. And in [Steeple] Bumpstead Leofwine and Leofmær [hold] 5 acres. And in [Great] Saling Algar [holds] 20 acres. And in Ovington Beorhtwulf [holds] 30 acres. All these [men] had TRE 3 ploughs. Then and later [there were] 3 bordars; now 8. Then and later [there were] 2 slaves; now none. [There is] woodland for 12 pigs. [There are] 8½ acres of meadow. Then and later it was worth 30s.; now 45[s.] 2d. Of these abovesaid men, Wihtgar had only commendation.

[Folio 102v: ESSEX]

In Bendysh Wihtgar, predecessor of R[ichard], appropriated 30 acres after the king came into this land, and later Engelric had it. And the Hundred testifies that it belonged to the fief of Engelric, but R[ichard] held it up to now.

In [Great and Little] Bardfield Felagi held 1 hide and 30 acres of Earl Ælfgar and after the king came into this country R[ichard] appropriated this land, which his predecessor did not hold, as the Hundred testifies. Then as now [there were] 3 villans. [There are] now 7 bordars. [There were] then 3 slaves; now 1. [There was] then 1½ ploughs in demesne; now 1. Then as now the men [had] 1 plough. [There is] woodland for 100 pigs. [There are] 27 acres of meadow. [There is] now 1 mill. It was then worth £4; now 60s.

In "Hocsenga" Felagi held half a hide. Now Richard holds [it], as he [holds] the abovesaid [land], and Walter [holds it] of him. Then as now [there were] 2 villans and 1 plough. [There is] woodland for 2 pigs. [There are] 4 acres of meadow. It is worth 12s.

In "Hasingham" a free man held 2½ acres in the Hundred of Lexden.

Now R[ichard] holds [them]. And there is now 1 mill, rendering 15s., and yet he was commended to Richard's predecessor.

In the Hundred of LexdenLuttin held 40 acres in Colne. Now R[ichard] holds [them]. And in this land his predecessor had neither customary dues nor commendation. [There were] then 4 bordars; now 6. Then as now [there was] 1 plough. [There is] woodland for 20 pigs. [There are] 4 acres of meadow. [There is] now 1 mill. It is worth 20s.

In Crepping Alweard holds 60 acres and 4 acres and 4½ acres freely, which R[ichard] now holds as [he holds] the others. [There were] then under him 4 bordars; now 6. Then as now [there was] 1 plough. [There is] woodland for 20 pigs. [There are] 2 acres of meadow. It is worth 20s. And Alwig the huntsman held freely half a hide and 26½ acres. Now R[ichard] holds [them] in [West] Bergholt, as [he holds] the others. [There were] then 2 bordars; now 6. Then as now [there was] 1 plough. [There is] woodland for 15 pigs. [There are] 2 acres of meadow. [There was] then half a mill; now none. It was then worth 20s.; now 36.

In Colne, Wulfric held freely 5 acres. Now R[ichard holds them] as [he holds] the others. It is worth 2s.

In Fordham Tofa-Hildr held 3 acres. Now R[ichard holds them] as [he holds] the others, and it is worth 7d.

In [West] Bergholt Goding held 6 acres. Now R[ichard holds them]. [There was] then half a plough. [There are] now 2 oxen. [There is] 1 acre of meadow. It was then worth 32d. now 5s.

Richard

[Folio 103: ESSEX]

In Halstead a free man held TRE 2½ acres and [this] is worth 30d. Alvred, reeve of R[ichard], received those pence and gave a pledge for them.

In Horseham a free woman held 30 acres. Now Widelard holds [them] of the king, as he says, but the Hundred does not testify [to it]. And R[ichard], son of Count Gilbert had the service. [There was] then half a plough; now none. [There are] now 2 bordars. It is worth 10s.

In Braintree 3 free men [held] 30 acres TRE, which Leodmær the reeve claimed [to belong to] the fief of Richard, but these men do not testify [to it] and he gave a pledge for them. And it is worth 3s.

In Chaureth [there are] 30 acres, which Wulfric, a free

man, held TRE. Now Warner, Richard's man, holds [them] and he called Ilbod as protector. And later he did not produce a protector. And it is worth 8s.

In the same vill 2 free men held half a hide TRE. Æthelmær, reeve of Richard, appropriated this land and called him as protector, but he failed him. And because of this, he gave a pledge. And it is worth 16s.

The monks of Canterbury hold 1 hide in Lawling, which 3 free men held TRE. Then as now [there was] 1 plough. It is worth 20s. This land was added to that manor TRW.

In Colne, Turbern holds 22 acres without the king's gift and he renders no customary dues.

Henry de Ferrers appropriated 1 free man with 16 acres in Steeple and it is worth 2s.

W[illiam] Leofric appropriated 1 free man with 6 acres in "Sciddeham". It is worth 2s 12d.

In [Helions] Bumpstead Robert Blunt appropriated 10 acres, which Eadwig, a free man, held. Then as now [there was] 1 plough. It is worth 20s.

[Folio 103v: ESSEX]

In Middleton R[obert] Malet appropriated 15 acres, which a free man held TRE. Then as now [there was] half a plough. It is worth 5s.

Frodo, the abbot's brother held 2 free men up to now in Stevington [End], whom Ordgar, his predecessor, appropriated, dwelling in the king's soke. And they have 20 acres. Then as now [there was] half a plough and it is worth 4s.

In [Great and Little] Chishall Leofwine held 5 acres and now Roger d'Auberville holds [them], because his predecessor was seised [of them].

In the Hundred Of Rochfordlie 15 acres at Ongar [Chipping and High], which Berengar, a man of Count E[ustace], holds. They were then worth 15d.; now 20.

[Folio 104: ESSEX]

HUNDRED OF COLCHESTER.

In the same Colchester Godric, a free man, held TRE 4 pieces of land and 1 church and 4 hides in Greenstead. At his death his son demised the land in 4 parts, of which the king has 2, in which belong 2 houses in the borough [and] which then as now rendered a customary due to the king and still render [it]. In 2 hides [there were] 2 ploughs in demesne then and now. [There were] 3 villans then and now. Then and now [there were] 2 slaves. [There were] 24 acres of meadow and marsh then and now. [There was] then 1 mill; now half. It was worth 40s. then and now. And of the 2 other parts, Count Eustace has 1 hide, and John fitzWaleran [has] the other hide. And in the quarter of Count Eustace [there] is a whole church and the fourth part of a mill and the fourth part of a meadow. [There was] then 1 plough; now none. And it is worth in total 30s. And in John's quarter [there] was 1 plough TRE; now none. And [there is] the fourth part of a mill, the fourth part of a meadow, and it is worth in total 30s. And the king has no customary dues from these 2 parts.

And the burgesses claim 5 hides of Lexden, which belonged to the aforesaid land which Godric held, [to be liable] for the customary dues and levy of the city.

These are the burgesses of the king who render customary dues. Colman has 1 house in Colchester and holds 5 acres of land and now as then renders customary dues to the king. Leofwine [has] 2 houses and 25 acres of land. Wulfric [has] 1 house. Edwin the priest [has] 1 house and 20 acres. Thorkil [has] 1 house and 9 acres. Wulfstan Eadlac [has] 4 houses and 20 acres. Leofwine [has] 1 house and 10 acres. Manwine [has] 4 houses and 30 acres.

[Folio 104V: ESSEX]

Ælfric [has] 1 house and 5 acres. Hardekin [has] 10½ houses and 20 acres. Ælfheah the priest [has] 1 house and 25 acres. Leofweald [has] 1 house and 15 acres. Wulfric [has] 1 house and 7 acres. Svartlingr [has] 1 house and 10 acres. Alweard [has] 1 house and 2 acres. Edwin [has] 1 house. Goda [has] 13 houses and 20 acres. Sprot [has] 2 houses and 3 acres. Eadric [has] 4 houses and 15 acres. Godwine [has] 1 house and 15 acres. Godwine Weakfeet and his sons [have] 5 houses and 12 acres. Blanc [has] 6 houses and 20 acres. Ælfric [has] 2 houses and 14 acres. Stanheard [has] 2½ houses and 10 acres. Godwine [has] 1 house and 9 acres. Wulfric [has] 2 houses and 1 acre. Alsige [has] 1 house and 3½ acres. Alweard [has] 2 houses and 23 acres. Manwine [has] 2 houses and 7 acres. Leofsexe [has] 1 house and 2½ acres. Leofwine [has] 10 acres. Wulfwine [has] 1 house and 2½ acres. Goding [has] 2 houses and 10 acres. Goda [has] 1 house and 7 acres. Wulfwine the summoner [has] 1 house and 7 acres. Ælfgar [has] 1 house. Wulfweard [has] 2 houses and 1 acre. Alwine [has] 1 house and 10 acres. Ælfgar the priest [has] 1 house and 1 acre. Freond [has] 1 house and 2 acres. Asgot [has] 2 houses and 1 acre. Wulfric [has] 2 houses. Arthur [has] 1 house and 4 acres. Edwin [has] 1 house and 4 acres. Sæwaru [has] 1 house and 7 acres. Leofflæd [has] 3 houses and 25 acres and 1 mill. Ælfric [has] 1 house. Godwine [has] 1 house. Sprot [has] 1 house and 3 acres. Grimulf [has] 2 houses and 9 acres. Sægar [has] 1 house and 10 acres. Ælfric [has] 1 house. Alwine [has] 3 houses and 9 acres. Wulfric [has] 1 house and 6 acres. Sprot [has] 1 house and 3 acres. Wulfweard [has] 1 house and 8 acres. Leofwine [has] 1 house and 10 acres by agreement. Godwine [has] 1 house. Goldstan [has] 1 house and 5 acres. Wulfwine [has] 1 house and 4 acres. Wulfweard [has] 1 house and 3 acres. Wulfwine [has] 2 houses and 7 acres. Godwine [has] 2 houses and 6 acres by agreement. Alfsige [has] 2 houses. Leofstan [has] 1 house and 1 acre. Godric [has] 1 house.

[Folio 105: ESSEX]

Alric [has] 1 house. Hnott [has] 1 house. Beorhtwine [has] 1 house and 5 acres. Leofflæd [has] 1 house. Alric [has] 1 house and 4½ acres. Edwin [has] 1 house and 2½ acres. Scadebutre [has] 1 house. Manwine [has] 4 acres. Goldwine [has] 1 house. Wulfric [has] 1 house and 2 acres. Osgeat [has] 1 house. Edwin [has] 1 house and 10 acres. Wulfric [has] 2 houses and 5 acres. Alwine [has] 2 houses. Edwin [has] 1 house and 3 acres. Wulfwine [has] 1 house and 5 acres. Alwine [has] 2 houses. Edwin [has] 1 house and 3 acres. Wulfwine [has] 1 house. Blæcstan [has] 2 houses. Manstan [has] 2 houses and 10 acres. Ælfric [has] 1 house and 1 acre. Leofwine [has] 1 house. Alwine [has] 2 houses and 22 acres.

Leofwine [has] 2 houses. Eadric [has] 1 house. Leofwine [has] 1 house. Wulfgyth [has] 1 house. Wulfsige [has] 1 house. Goldric [has] 2 houses and 22 acres. Goda [has] 22 acres. Calebot [has] 7 acres. Manstan [has] 2 houses and 1 acre. Wulfheah [has] 1 house. Manwine [has] 1 house. Winemar [has] 1 house. Segrim [has] 3 houses and 4 acres. Leofric [has] 1 house. Wulfweard [has] 1 house and 4 acres. Wulfwine [has] 1 house and 10 acres. Leofflæd [has] 1 house and 25 acres. Godric [has] 1 house. Deormann [has] 1 house. Thorsten [has] 1 house. Dublel [has] 1 house and half an acre. Goddæg [has] 2 houses. Goti Chill [has] 1 house and 1 acre. Stane [has] 1 house. Ordgeat [has] 1 house. Ælfstan [has] 1 house. Tovi [has] 1 house. Golding [has] 1 house. Leofgeat [has] 1 house and 2 acres. Blæcstan [has] 1 house. Manwine [has] 1 house. Alwine [has] 1 house. Leofsunu [has] 2 houses. Ælfric [has] 1 house and 2 acres. Brunmann [has] 1 house. Alwine [has] 1 house. Sæwulf [has] 2½ houses and 10 acres. Leofwine [has] 3 acres. Wulfric [has] 1 house. Ælfstan [has] 1 house. Godwine [has] 3 acres. Goldwine [has] 1 house. Godwine [has] 1 house and 1 acre. Wicga [has] 1 house. Leodmær [has] 1 house. Wulfstan [has] 2 houses. Godsunu [has] 1 house and 3 acres. Æthelbald [has] 2 houses and 1 acre. Godwine [has] 1 house. Godgifu [has] 1 house. Leofstan [has] 1 house. Edward the priest [has] 1 house. Hakon [has] 1 house. Æthelbert [has] 1 house. Tæte [has] 1 house. Sæweard [has] 1 house. Bearda [has] 1 house and 5 acres. Wulfweard the priest [has] 1 house and 1 acre. Colling [has] 2 houses and 7 acres. Alweald [has] 1 house. Filiman [has] 1 house and 5 acres. Godgifu [has] 1 house.

[Folio 105V: ESSEX]

Siward the priest [has] 1 house and 4 acres. Pic [has] 1 house. Wulfwine [has] 3 houses and 4 acres. Leofgifu [has] 1 house and 4½ acres. Ælfric [has] 15 acres. Alwynn [has] 2 houses. Wulfric [has] 1 house and 1½ acres. William Pecche [has] 1 house. Best [has] 1 house. Rosell [has] 1 house and 4 acres. Leofwine [has] 1 house and 2 acres. Goda [has] 1 house. Wulfwine [has] 1 house. Leofsunu [has] 1 house. Goldmann [has] 1 house. Pote [has] 4 acres. Godric [has] 1 house. Sigeric [has] 1 house and 2 acres. Alric [has] 1 house and 2 acres. Lundi [has] 1 house. Beorhtric [has] 1 house and 9½ acres. Leofstan [has] 1 house. Wudubill [has] 1 house. Blæcstan [has] 1 house. Ælfflæd [has] 1 house. Wulfgifu [has] 1 house and 20 acres. Goda [has] 1 house and 20 acres. Æschere [has] 1 house and 19 acres. Godric [has] 1 house. Brunlocc [has] 1 house. Alnoth [has] 2 houses and 4 acres. Godwine [has] 1 house and 10 acres. Leofwine [has] 1 house and 10 acres. Ælfric the priest [has] 3 houses and 2 acres. Roger [has] 1 house and 4 acres. Godric [has] 1 house. Ælfric [has] 1 house and 2 acres. Swærting [has] 1 house and 10 acres. Godgyth [has] 2 houses and 14 acres. Brunwine [has] 1 house and 3 acres. Wulfwine [has] 1 house. Brungar [has] 2 houses and 18 acres. Sunegod [has] 1 house. Siward [has] 1 house and 6½ acres. Wulfstan [has] 11 acres. Leofswith [has] 2 houses and 8 acres. Segrim [has] 1 house. Wulfwine [has] 1 house. Leofwine [has] 1 house. Leofric [has] 1 house. Goding [has] 1 house and 1 acre. Wigstan [has] 2 houses and 30 acres. Ainulf [has] 1 house and 15 acres. Tunric [has] 1 house. Alstan [has] 5 acres. Ælfsige [has] 1 house. Goldhere [has]

1 acre. Godsunu [has] 1½ acres. Wulfwine [has] 1 house. Ælfric [has] 1 house. Godwine [has] 1 house. Pecoc [has] 1 house. Alwine [has] 1 house. Beorhtric [has] 1 house. Manwine [has] 1 house. Wulfric [has] 1 house. Godsunu [has] 6½ acres. Brunwine [has] 1 house. Manwine [has] 1 house. Eadric [has] 1 house. Leofgifu [has] 1 house. Owine [has] 1 house. Alstan [has] 2 houses. Alweald [has] 6½ acres. Manwine [has] 1 house and 5 acres. Alweard [has] 1 house and 15 acres. Leofmær [has] 10 acres. The abbot of St Edmund [has] 2 houses and 30 acres. Stanheard [has] 1 house.

[Folio 106: ESSEX]

Wulfwine [has] 1 house. Sæfugel [has] 1 house. Leofræd [has] 1 house and 6 acres. Ælfgifu [has] 10 acres. Wulfstan [has] 1 house and 13 acres. Leofwine [has] 2 houses. Leofgifu [has] 1 house. Ælfric [has] 1 house. Godric [has] 1 house and 9 acres. Wulfric [has] 1 house and 4 acres. Wulfwine [has] 1 house. Alwynn [has] 1 house. Tesco [has] 2 houses and 20 acres of land and owes customary dues to the king and never renders [it]. Wulfric [has] 3 acres. Stoting [has] 1 house. Herestan [has] 1 house. Leofric [has] 1 house and 42 acres. Eadric [has] 1 house. Dela [has] 1 house. Hunning [has] 2 houses. Manwine [has] 2 houses. Ælfric [has] 2 houses. Goti Hugh [has] 6 acres. Leofwine [has] 1 house and 25 acres. Demiblanc [has] 4 houses. Leofsunu [has] 1 acre. Ælfgifu [has] 1 house. Leofgifu [has] 3 acres. Swein [has] 1 house. Wulfsige [has] 1 house. Ælfflæd [has] 1 house. Ralph Pinel [has] 4 houses within the walls and 5 acres and he does not render customary dues and gave a pledge [for them]. Ordlaf [has] 3½ acres. Walter [has] 2 houses. Horrap [has] 1 house. Alwine [has] 1 house. Stanburh [has] 1 house. Wulfstan [has] 2 houses and 5 acres. Cyneting [has] 1 house. Sprot [has] 1 house and 5 acres. Edwin [has] 1 house and 3 acres. Goti Fleet [has] 20 acres. Mansunu [has] 10 acres. Goding [has] 1 house and 5 acres. Wulfgifu [has] 5 acres. Wulfric [has] 1 house and 1½ acres. Lorce the Breton [has] 1 house and 10 acres. Goldhere [has] 1 house. In addition to their land, these burgesses have 51 acres of meadow.

Hamo the steward [has] 1 house and 1 court and 1 hide of land and 15 burgesses and his predecessor Thorbiorn held this TRE. And for all this, apart for his hall, he rendered customary dues TRE. And the burgesses still render their personal amercements, but for their land and the hide which they hold of Hamo, they have not paid customary dues. In the hide, [there was] then 1 plough; now none. [There were] 6 acres of meadow then and now. And this whole was worth £4 TRE, and when received the same, and now 40s. Mansunu [has] 2 houses and 4 acres. Goda [has] 1 house. Eudo the steward [has] 5 houses and 40 acres of land which the burgesses held

[Folio 106v: ESSEX]

TRE and they rendered all the customary dues of burgesses, but now they do not render customary dues, only their personal amercements. All this with the fourth part of the church of St Peter renders 30s. Hugh de Montfort [has] 1 house, which Godric, his predecessor, held TRE and he rendered then the customary dues of the king. Now she

does not render [it], nor did she render [it] later, since Hugh has had [it].

Roger de Poitou [has] 1 house, which Ælfflæd, his predecessor, held TRE and she rendered the customary dues of the king. Now he does not render [it], nor [has] he render[ed it] since Roger has had [it]. Count Eustace [has] 12 houses and 1 which Engelric appropriated and they rendered the customary dues of the king TRE. Now they do not render [it], nor have they rendered [it] since Eustace has had [them], and [these] are worth 12s. William, the nephew of the bishop [has] 2 houses, which Thorkil held and he renders the customary dues. Otto the goldsmith [has] 3 houses which belong to Shalford, which Countess Ælfgifu held, and they rendered a customary due of the king and now they do not render [it], and this [belongs] to the land of the queen. The abbot of Westminster [has] 4 houses, which Earl Harold held TRE [and which belong] to Feering. And they rendered the customary dues then; now they do not render [it]. Geoffrey de Mandeville [has] 2 houses, which Ginni held TRE [belonging] to Ardleigh, and they rendered a customary due; now they do not render [it]. Swein [has] 1 house, which Goda held TRE [belonging] to Elmstead, and they rendered then a customary due of the king. Now they do not render [it], only the man's personal amercements.

William de Vatteville [has] 1 house of Swein, which Robert fitzWymarc held TRE and he rendered a customary due; now he does not render [it]. Turstin Guiscard [has] 3 houses of John fitzWaleran and half a hide of land, which 2 burgesses held TRE and they rendered the customary dues of the king. Now they do not render the customary dues. That half hide was then worth 10s., and when

[Folio 107: ESSEX]

received 6s.; now 5s. Ranulf Peverel [has] 5 houses, which Æthelmær held TRE [belonging] to Terling, and they rendered the customary dues; now they do not render [it]. One of these is outside the walls. Ralph Baynard [has] 1 house, which Æthelmær Milk held TRE [belonging] then to Tolleshunt, and they rendered the customary dues; now [they do] not.

The abbess of Barking [had] 3 houses TRE and she rendered then the customary dues; now [she does] not. Aubrey de Vere [has] 2 houses and 3 acres of land, which Wulfwine, his predecessor, held TRE. They rendered the customary dues then.

The king's demesne in Colchester [is] 102 acres of land, of which 10 are meadow [and] in which [there] are 10 bordars. And 240 acres of pasture and scrubland, and all this belongs to the farm of the king. In the common [property] of the burgesses [there are] 80 acres of land and around the wall [there are] 8 perches, from the whole of which the burgesses have 60s. a year for the king's service, if it were needed, but if not, it is divided in common.

[There] is, moreover, a custom that every year, on the fifteenth day after Easter, the burgesses render to the king 2 marks of silver, and this belongs to the farm of the king. In addition to this, from each house every year that can render [them, there are] 6d. for the victuals of the king's soldiers or for a [military] expedition on land or at sea, and this is not [included] in the farm of the king. And this is [to be], whether the king has soldiers or makes [an] expedition. And on account of these 6d., the whole city rendered TRE £15. 5s. 3d. a year, in addition to all dues. Of these, the moneyers rendered £4 TRE. Now it [the city] renders £80 and 4 sesters of honey or 40s. 4[d.]. And in addition to this, [they render] 100s. to the sheriff for exactions. And [they render] 10s. 8d. for feeding the prebendaries.

[Folio 107V: ESSEX]

And in addition to this, the burgesses of Colchester and Maldon render £20 for the mint and Waleran arranged this. And they summon the king as guarantor [to the fact] that he

pardoned them £10. And Walkeline the bishop holds [it]; he demands £40 from them.

In Colchester [there] is a certain church of St Peter, which 2 priests held TRE of the king's alms, to which belong 2 hides of land in which [there] were and [are] now 2 ploughs. [There were] then 3 bordars; now 4. [There were] then 3 slaves; now 2. [There were] then and [are] now 12 acres of meadow. [There was] then and [is] now 1 mill. [There were] then and [are] now 2 houses in the borough. The whole was then worth 30s.; now 48s. Of these alms, Robert fitzRalph of Hastings claims 3 parts and Eudo the steward holds the fourth. And they rendered the customary dues TRE and now it does not render [them].

NORFOLK

[Holders of Lands]

I King William
II The Bishop of Bayeux
III The Count of Mortain
IV Count Alan
V Count Eustace
VI Earl Hugh
VII Robert Malet
VIII William de Warenne
IX Roger Bigod
X Bishop William
XI Bishop Osbern
XII Godric the steward
XIII Hermer of Ferrers
XIV The Abbot of St Edmund
XV The Abbey of Ely
XVI The Abbey of St Benedict of Ramsey
XVII The Abbey of Hulme
XVIII Saint-Étienne of Caen
XIX William d'Écouis
XX Ralph de Beaufour
XXI Reginald fitzIvo
XXII Ralph de Tosny
XXIII Hugh de Montfort
XXIV Eudo the steward
XXV Walter Giffard
XXVI Roger of Poitou
XXVII Ivo Taillebois
XXVIII Ralph de Limésey
XXIX Eudo fitzSpirewic
XXX Drogo de la BeuvriÒre
XXXI Ralph Baynard
XXXII Ranulf Peverel
XXXIII Robert Gernon
XXXIV Peter de Valognes
XXXV Robert fitzCorbucion
XXXVI Ranulf, brother of Ilger
XXXVII Tihel the Breton
XXXVIII Robert de Verly
XXXIX Humphrey fitzAubrey
XL Humphrey de Bohun
XLI Ralph de FougÒres
XLII Gilbert fitzRicher
XLIII Roger de Rames
XLIV Judicael the priest

XLV Colebern the Priest
XLVI Edmund, son of Pain
XLVII Isaac
XLVIII Tovi
LIX John, nephew of Waleran
L Roger fitzReinhard
LI Berner the crossbowman
LII Gilbert the crossbowman
LIII Ralph the crossbowman
LIV Robert the crossbowman
LV Rabel the artificer
LVI Hagni
LVII Ralph son of Hagni
LVIII Ulfkil
LIX Alfred
LX Ealdgyth
LXI Godwine Halfdan
LXII Starkulf
LXIII Eadric the falconer
LXIV King's free men belonging to no estate
LXV The King's men in demesne
LXVI Annexations

[Land of the King]

I.

FREEBRIDGE HUNDRED

and a half. [Great or Little] Massingham was held by Harold TRE [as] 3 carucates of land. Then [there were] 4 villans. When Roger acquired it [there were] 3 and now the same; there has always been 1 bordar. Then [there were] 4 slaves. Afterwards and now [there was] 1, and 7 acres of meadow. Then [there were] 2 ploughs in demesne; afterwards and now 1 [and] woodland for 10 pigs. 25 sokemen belong here with 3 carucates of land and 20 acres. Then and afterwards [there were] 6½ ploughs, now [there are] 3½; there have always been 7 pigs and 64 sheep. Then and afterwards it was worth 40s.; now [it is worth] £10. 25 sokemen who were on this manor TRE, paying all customary dues, are now missing; Guy d'Anjou holds 20 of them and they have 2 carucates of land, 58 acres and the fourth part of an acre. And William de Warenne holds 3 who have 120½ acres. And Roger Bigod holds 1 who has 15 acres. And William d'Écouis holds 1 who has 10 acres. 14 free men and 12 villans, whom Ralph Baynard holds, have also been taken from this manor. The whole [manor] is 1 mile in length and half in breadth, and pays 16d. of a 20s. geld

DOCKING HUNDRED.

Southmere was held by Harold TRE. Then [there were] 3 ploughs in demesne; afterwards and now [there were] 2. Then [there were] 21 villans, afterwards and now 19. Then and now [there were] 2 bordars and 6 slaves, 1 plough belonging to the men, 3 horses, 1 ox, 3 pigs and 87 sheep. 31 sokemen belong here with 16 acres and 1 plough; and 15 sokemen, each with 60 acres and 8 ploughs; and 1½ ploughs could be restored. And there is 1 sokeman with 14 acres; and 1 sokeman with 60 acres; and [there was] then 1 plough. And 1 berewick, Titchwell, always had 1½ ploughs in demesne and 14 villans, 6 bordars and 4 slaves. [There is] meadow of 16 acres and woodland for 60 pigs. Now [there is] 1 mill and there has always been 1 plough belonging to the men. And [there are] 4 sokemen with 2 carucates of land and 2 ploughs; and 2 sokemen with 5 acres, and 1 sokeman with 60 acres and 2 oxen and 1 sokeman with the fourth part of an acre. In the berewick are 260 sheep, 11 pigs, 2 head of cattle and 5 horses. And [there is] 1 carucate of land which was held by 1 free man TRE.

The King

[Folio 110: NORFOLK]

The whole was then worth £7, afterwards £20 and now £30. And [there were] 4 sokemen with 4 acres of land TRE, which Brun, Roger Bigod's reeve, took from this manor after the came and after Roger acquired the manor, and which Roger now holds. And [there is] 1 sokeman with 60 acres and half a plough. Ælfric, a free man, held Stanhoe under Stigand TRE as 1 carucate. Then [there was] 1 plough; afterwards and now [there were] 2 oxen and 1 bordar. It is worth 16s. and belongs to Fakenham.

WAYLAND HUNDRED.

King Edward held Saham [Toney] as 3 carucates of land and 45 acres. Then [there were] 43 villans, afterwards 9 and now 4. Now [there are] 11 bordars [and] there has always been 1 slave. Then and afterwards [there was] 1 plough in demesne; now [there are] 2. Then [there were] 12 ploughs belonging to the men; afterwards and now 3. [There are] 40 acres of meadow and woodland for 730 pigs; there has always been 1 mill; then [there were] 3 horses, now 2. Then [there were] 3 head of cattle, now 8; then 28 pigs, now 20 and now [there are] 60 sheep and 40 goats. 46 sokemen belonged to this manor TRE with all customary dues; afterwards and now 31 with 3 carucates of land, 27 acres, and 40 acres of meadow. Then and afterwards [there were] 12 ploughs, now 8. There is woodland for 100 pigs. Reginald fitzIvo has 15 of these men and Berner the crossbowman 2. And in Griston [there were] 19 sokemen with 1 carucate of land TRE. Then [there were] 4 ploughs; afterwards and now 3, and 2 acres of meadow. And in Caston [there are] 4 of Harold's free men with 204 acres of land, added to this manor after the king came, by his command. Then [there were] 3½ ploughs[...]; now [there are] the same

and 6 acres of meadow. And in Breckles [there are] 8 of Harold's free men in with 2 carucates of land. Then [there were] 5 ploughs, afterwards and now 3. These were added TRW. [There are also] 2 bordars and 20 acres of meadow, and in Griston 2 of Harold's free men and 7 acres. The whole was worth £12 TRE and paid half a day's [provision of] honey, and the customary dues of honey; now it pays £20 by weight. And Harold's free men were worth 53s. TRE; now they are at farm for £20. The whole is 1½ leagues in length

[Folio 110V: NORFOLK]

and 1 league in breadth, and pays 2s. 6d. of a 20s. geld.

In Breckles [there are] 25 acres. There has always been half a plough. 5 sokemen [were] in Saham [Toney] and the reeve of Saham [Toney] sold them TRW for 1 bridle to Eudo, a man of Earl Ralph's, and they belonged to [Little] Ellingham, in the farm of Ralph, and he was holding them on the day of his forfeiture. And Robert Blund had 10s. 8d. from them as long as he held office; now [they belong] again to Saham [Toney] and do not pay rent to Godric. And in Caston [there is] 1 sokeman with 10 acres of land and half a plough and he likewise used to pay 5s. 4d. The whole of Breckles is 1 league in length and a half in breadth and pays geld of 11d. In the same place there is 1 free man in Saham [Toney] with 26 acres and 2 acres of meadow and half a plough, and it is worth 2s. The king and the earl [had] the soke. In Breckles [there is also] the fourth part of an acre, and a certain customary due in pasture; this belonged to Saham [Toney] TRE, and still does; but Godric claims it back as the fief of Earl Ralph in Stow [Bedon], saying that he had held it for 2 years before he forfeited, and for 2 years afterwards. A member of the king's household at Stow [Bedon] offers to undergo the judicial ordeal over this.

FORHOE HUNDRED and a half.

Hingham was held by King Edward as 2 carucates of land and 25 acres. There have always been 60 villans. Then [there were] 18 bordars and a half, now [there are] 29. There has always been 1 plough in demesne; then [there were] 15 ploughs belonging to the men, now [there are] 20. [Then there were] 43 sokemen, now [there are] 20. William de Warenne has 12 of the rest, Count Alan 3, and Eudo fitzClamahoc took 8 of them now belonging to Ralph de Beaufour. These 20 have

The King

[Folio 111: NORFOLK]

1 carucate of land, and one of them has 3 bordars. There have always been 2 ploughs and 8 acres of meadow. The whole was then worth £7 and a half blanched and with a customary payment of 30s. and 3 sesters of honey; now [it is worth] £12 by weight, 30s. in exactions and 3 sesters of honey, with the same customary payment. It is half [a league] in length and half in breadth and pays geld of 13½d.

MITFORD HUNDRED AND A HALF.

In Flockthorpe [there are] 40 acres and 3 bordars and 1 acre of meadow and it is in the valuation of Hingham.

In Flockthorpe [there are] 30 acres of land, 1 free man and 1½ acres of meadow. Then [there was] half a plough and 2 bordars.

In [Wood] Rising and in "Ocselea" [there are] 3 bordars [and] 12 acres of land and it is in the valuation of Hingham.

GALLOW HUNDRED.

In Fakenham Harold held 2 carucates of land TRE. There have always been 5 villans, 20 bordars and 4 slaves. There have always been 2 ploughs in demesne and 4 ploughs belonging to the men. [There is] woodland for 12 pigs, 5 acres of meadow, 3 mills and half a salt-pan. There have always been 3 horses, 20 pigs and 200 sheep. To this manor belongs 1 berewick, Alethorpe, consisting of 1 carucate of land. There have always been 3 bordars and 1 slave and 1 plough in demesne and 2 oxen belonging to the men and 2 acres of meadow. And there is another berewick, Thorpland, consisting of 1 carucate of land with 1 plough and 1 slave. There is also 1 berewick consisting of 2 carucates of land in [North or South] Creake. There have always been 10 villans. Then [there were] 11 bordars, now [there are] 4. There has always been 1 plough in demesne. Then [there were] 3 ploughs belonging to the men, now 1; and half an acre of meadow. There has always been 1 horse, 30 pigs and 80 sheep and 4 sokemen with 6 acres and 1 plough. And [there is] another berewick, Stanhoe, comprising 1 carucate of land. There have always been 3 villans. Then [there was] 1 plough in demesne and now [there are] 2 [ploughs belonging to the] men. In Stibbard [there are] 3 free men and in Barsham 1 [free man] and in [Little] Snoring 3 free men and among these men 3 acres of land. There has always been 1 plough. All this was worth

[Folio 111V: NORFOLK]

£8 TRE; now [it is worth] [£]43. Fakenham is 7 furlongs in length and half in breadth and [pays] 12d. in geld; Stibbard is 3 furlongs in length and 2 in breadth and [pays] 12d. in geld. There is also 1 berewick, Caston, comprising 1 carucate of land. There have always been 3 bordars and 1 plough and 2 acres of meadow and 8 sheep. It is assessed above. In [Pudding] Norton [there is] a church [with] 8 acres and [it is worth] 6d.

BROTHERCROSS HUNDRED.

In Dunton [there is] 1 berewick comprising 1 carucate of land. Then [there were] 6 bordars, now [there are] 4. Then [there were] 2 slaves. There has always been 1 plough in demesne. Then [there was] 1 plough belonging to the men, now half, and 4 acres of meadow and 1 mill. There has always been 1 horse and 60 sheep and 16 sokemen with 1 carucate of land. There have always been 5 bordars. Then [there were] 8 ploughs, afterwards 3, now 1. It is assessed with Fakenham and is 1 league in length and half in breadth and [pays] 13d. in geld.

In [Pudding] Norton 1 berewick of half a carucate belongs to Fakenham. There has always been 1 bordar and half a plough and half an acre of meadow. There has always been 1 horse and 1 pig and 7 sokemen with 20 acres and 1 plough and it is 3 furlongs in length and 2½ in breadth and pays 6½d. in geld.

HOLT HUNDRED.

Holt was held by King Edward [as] 2 carucates of land. There have always been 24 villans and 24 bordars and 2 slaves. There have always been 1 plough in demesne [and another] could be restored. There have always been 11 ploughs belonging to the men. [There is] woodland for 60 pigs, 6 acres of meadow and 5 mills. There has always been 1 horse, 1 market, 1 park and 20 pigs [and] now 90 sheep. There is also 1 berewick, Cley [next the Sea], comprising 2 carucates of land. There have always been 24 villans and 21 bordars. Then [there were] 2 slaves, now [there are] 4. There has always been 1 plough in demesne and another could be restored, and 12 ploughs belonging to the men; and 1 acre of meadow. There have always been 7 pigs [and] now [there are] 140 sheep. There is also 1 berewick, in 'Snitterley' [in Blakeney], comprising 1 carucate of land. There have always been 7 villans and 1 bordar. There has always been 1 plough belonging to the men. Then it was worth £20, 1 night's [provision of] honey and 100s. in customary dues; now [it is worth] £50

The King

[Folio 112: NORFOLK]

by tale and Holt and Cley [Next the Sea] are 2 leagues in length and 1 in breadth and [pay] 2s. 4[d.] in geld. 8 freemen with 3½ carucates of land belonged to this manor TRE; now Walter Giffard holds them by livery of the king, so his men say. And there also belonged to this manor 1 free man and 23 acres; now Earl Hugh holds them. 1 berewick in Hemstead [near Holt], of 30 acres, belongs to this manor. There have always been 5 bordars and 1 plough and half a plough belonging to the men. [There is] woodland for 6 pigs. There have always been 8 pigs. Then [it was worth] 5s. 4d.; now [it is worth] 33s. 4d. and it is 1 league in length and 1 in breadth and [pays] 7d. in geld.

In Bale [there is] 1 free man with 2 carucates of land. There have always been 10 bordars. Then [there were] 2 slaves, now [there are] none. Then [there were] 2 ploughs in demesne, now 1. There has always been 1 plough belonging to the men. [There is] woodland for 30 pigs, 4 acres of meadow and 2 sokemen with 20 acres of land and half a plough and 1 acre of meadow. It has always been worth 20s. and is 1 league in length and half in breadth and [pays] 6½d. in geld.

In Briston 5 sokemen belong to Holt with 20 acres of land and 1 plough. [There is] woodland for 10 pigs and it is worth 12s. and is 1 league in length and half in breadth and pays 13d. in geld, whoever holds it.

In Hunworth [there are] 3 sokemen with 16 acres and 1 acre of meadow, 1 plough [and] 1 mill. Then it was worth 40d., now [it is worth] 11s. and it is 1 league and 2 furlongs in length and half in breadth and [pays] 12d. in geld, whoever holds it.

In Stody [there is] 1 sokeman with 2½ acres and it pays 2

oras. In Bayfield [there are] 9 sokemen with 20 acres and they had, and still have, 2 carucates of land; and [there is] the fourth part of 1 mill and it is worth 10s. 8d. and is 1 league in length and half in breadth and [pays] 8d. in geld. In Glandford [there are] 3 sokemen with 20 acres and 1 plough and 1 acre of meadow and it is worth 4s. and is

[Folio 112v: NORFOLK]

8 furlongs in length and 3 in breadth and [pays] 6½d. in geld.

In Newton [there are] 3 sokemen and a half with 12 acres of land and it is worth 16d.

In Gunthorpe [there is] half a carucate of land, which Alwine held TRE, and 4 bordars. [There is] woodland for 4 pigs and 1 acre of meadow. There have always been 1½ ploughs. Then it was worth 20s., now 40[s.]. This was added to this manor from the land of Bishop Æthelmær. It is 1 league in length and 4 furlongs in breadth and [pays] 6½d. in geld. The whole of Holt pays £66 by tale. There is 1 berewick in Sharrington and it belongs to Fakenham and comprises 1 carucate of land and 9 bordars. There has always been 1 plough in demesne. Then [there was] 1 plough belonging to the men. Then [there were] 30 sheep, now 60 and 3 sokemen with 6 acres and it is 7 furlongs in length and 6 in breadth and pays 10d. in geld. 1 free man, Ketil, was added to Holt after the death of King Edward, [belonging] in Morston, [the manor of] Gyrth, with 30 acres, 1 bordar and half a plough and it is worth 2 oras.

HOLT HUNDRED.

Gunthorpe, [consisting of] 1 carucate of land, belongs to Cawston. Then [there were] 11 bordars, now 6. There has always been 1 plough in demesne and 1 plough belonging to the men. [There is] woodland for 4 pigs, 2 acres of meadow, 2 pigs and 24 sheep. This all belongs to Cawston.

In Sharrington [there are] 8 sokemen and 6 bordars which belong to Holt and these plough 2 carucates. It was worth 20s. TRE, now 40s.

[NORTH] GREENHOE HUNDRED.

Wighton was held by King Edward [as] 12 carucates of land. Then and now [there were] 26 villans; then [there were] 24 bordars, now [there are] 17; then and now [there was] 1 plough in demesne; then [there were] 10 ploughs belonging to the men, and afterwards and now 7. There is woodland for 20 pigs, 8 acres of meadow and 1 mill. There has always been 1 horse, now [there are] 20 pigs; when [it was] acquired [there were] none. [There are] now 180 sheep. Then [there were] 19 sokemen; there have always been 45 acres of land. There have always been 4 ploughs, 1 mill and 3 bordars.

The King

[Folio 113: NORFOLK]

Then it was worth £10, 6½ sesters of honey and 41s. in customary dues; now [it is worth] £23 by weight and it is 1 league in length and 1 in breadth and it pays geld of 7d.

1 berewick, Houghton [St Giles], belongs to this manor, comprising 4 carucates of land; there have always been 5

villans and 5 bordars; always 1 plough in demesne; then [there were] 3 ploughs belonging to the men, afterwards and now [there are] 2. [There is] pasture for 1,000 sheep, 3 acres of meadow and 2 mills. It is half a league in length and half in breadth and pays 4d. in geld. A berewick, Holkham, belongs to this manor, [and consists of] 3 carucates of land, but it is waste and 3 ploughs could be [employed] there. Quarles [is] another berewick which belongs to this manor, of half a carucate of land, but nothing is there; but 1 plough could be [employed] there. It is 4 furlongs in length and 4 in breadth and [pays] 6d. in geld

And Egmere [is] another berewick, [comprising] half a carucate of land. Nothing else is there but 1 plough could be [employed]. It is half a league in length and half in breadth and [pays] geld of 6d. In Wells [-next-the-Sea] and in Warham [All Saints or St Mary] [there is] 1 carucate of land but 1 plough could be [employed]. And in Stiffkey [there is] half a carucate of land. And in Hindringham [there is] half a carucate of land but 1 plough could be [employed]. Harold held [Great or Little] Walsingham TRE as a berewick of Fakenham [comprising] 3 carucates of land. Then and afterwards [there were] 13 villans, now 6; then and afterwards 7 bordars, now 5; there has always been 1 plough in demesne and 2 ploughs belonging to the men. [There is] woodland for 10 pigs, 1½ acres of meadow and 2 mills. There have always been 2 horses and 5 head of cattle. Then [there were] 12 pigs, now [there are] 14. Then [there were] 24 sheep, now 40 and 9 sokemen [with] 1 carucate of land belong to this manor [and] 2 bordars, half an acre of meadow and half a mill. Then [there were] 3 ploughs; afterwards and now [there are] 2. All this is assessed in Fakenham.

In Holkham [there is] 1 carucate of land which Alwine, a free man, held TRE

[Folio 113v: NORFOLK]

and it belongs to Wighton [with] 3 bordars and 7 sokemen. There have always been 2 ploughs among all [the men] and the man who has the land. In [Field] Dalling Ospakr held 1 carucate of land TRE. It is a berewick in Holt [with] 11 bordars; there have always been 2 slaves and 6 acres of meadow; there has always been 1 plough in demesne and always 2 ploughs belonging to the men. [There are] 8 sokemen with 24 acres of land and 4 acres of meadow; there has always been 1 plough; then and afterwards [there was] 1 horse; there have always been 3 head of cattle, 8 pigs and 20 sheep. Then it was worth 10s., now £4. It is half a league in length and half in breadth and [pays] 2s. in geld. And in Warham [All Saints or St Mary] [there is] half a carucate of land and 1 acre of meadow and it is worth 2½s. All this belongs to Holt. The sake and soke of [North] Greenhoe Hundred belongs to Wighton, the king's manor, whoever holds there, and the king and the earl have it.

WALSHAM HUNDRED.

In Moulton [St Mary] [there are] 3 free men [and] 37 acres of land, 4½ acres of meadow and half a plough and it is worth 2s. 8d. In [Wood] Bastwick [there is] 1 free man [and] 30 acres of land, 2 acres of meadow and half a plough and it is worth 16d. And Walsham Hundred pays 40s. to the king and 20s. to the earl.

WEST FLEGG HUNDRED.

In Martham [there are] 2 free men, 1 [commended to] Gyrth, the other commended to Harold with 60 acres of land and 6 acres of meadow. Then [there was] 1 plough, afterwards and now half. Then and afterwards [they were worth] 4s., now 6s. 8d., and they are paying rent to Ormesby [St Margaret or St Michael].

In Clippesby [there was]1 free man commended to Gyrth TRE with 20 acres of land and 4 acres of meadow, and 3 free men under him [with] 17 acres of land and 3 acres of meadow. There has always been 1 plough. It has always been worth 2s. 6d. and it is paying rent to Ormesby [St Margaret or St Michael].

In Clippesby [there is] 1 free man of the king's with 20 acres of land. There has always been half a plough and 3 acres of meadow. It has always been worth 2s. In Winterton [there is] 1 free man with 7 acres of land and 5 bordars. There has always been half a plough. It has always been worth 8d. And it is

The King

[Folio 114: NORFOLK].

HENSTEAD HUNDRED.

In [Earl or Pigot] Framingham and in Trowse 2 burgesses of Norwich hold 12 acres of land. It has always been worth 2s.

HUNDRED of the half-Hundred OF DISS.

King Edward held "Watlingeseta" [in Diss] as a manor [of] 5 carucates of land. Then [there were] 20 villans, afterwards and now 24, and there have always been 25 bordars [and] always 19 ploughs belonging to the men. Then [there was] woodland for 20 pigs, now [there is] none, and 9 acres of meadow and 1 free man with 20 acres of land and 1 bordar under him. There has always been 1 plough and 3 acres of meadow. In Burston [there are] 6 sokemen with 40 acres of land and there has always been 1 bordar. Then [there were] 1½ ploughs, afterwards and now 1, and 2 acres of meadow. It is 1 league in length and half in breadth and [pays] geld of 7d. This belongs to Diss in Suffolk and is assessed there [as is] the whole sake and soke of this half-Hundred, except St Edmund's land, and of that the Saint [holds] half and the king the other half, [and] except Wulfgeat's land and except the land of Stigand and of all other [lands] the soke was in the Hundred TRE.

EYNSFORD HUNDRED.

Foulsham was held by King Edward [as] 12 carucates of land and 3 acres. Then [there were] 30 villans, later and now 33. Then and afterwards [there were] 38 bordars, now [there are] 44, and 40 acres of meadow. Then and afterwards [there were] 2 ploughs in demesne, now [there are] 3. Then and afterwards [there were] 18 ploughs belonging to the men, now 20. There is woodland for 400 pigs; then and afterwards [there was] 1 mill, now 2 [and] 1 church [with] 16 acres. When [King William] acquired [it] [there was] 1 horse, now [there are] 2;

then [there were] 3 head of cattle, now [there are] 12; then 47 pigs, now 50 and now 60 sheep; there have always been 50 goats. [There were] 30 sokemen TRE; now [there are] 24, and 1 acre of land and 10 acres [sic]; there have always been 5 ploughs and 5½ acres of meadow. And 6 of these [sokemen] Walter Giffard now holds. Then it was worth £13

[Folio 114v: NORFOLK]

by tale and 13 sesters of honey with customary dues; and [it is worth] £23 by weight now and £11 10s. blanched for the honey. It is 1 league in length and 1 in breadth and pays 8½d. in the king's geld. [There is] 1 church [with] 22 acres. TRW 2 free men were annexed to this manor by Ralph Taillebois; to this the Hundred testifies. [There are] 14 acres of land [and] there have always been half a plough and 1 acre of meadow. It has always been worth 4s.

In Whitwell 1 berewick which belongs to Cawston was held by Harold TRE [as] 1 carucate of land. Then [there were] 10 bordars, now [there are] 7. There has always been 1 plough in demesne; then [there was] 1 plough belonging to the men, now none. [There is] woodland for 20 pigs and 5 acres of meadow. It is in the valuation of Cawston.

In Brandiston [there are] 4 free men, 52 acres of land, 1½ ploughs, 7 acres of meadow and woodland for 6 pigs. They are in the valuation of Cawston.

TAVERHAM HUNDRED.

In Taverham Harold held 1 carucate of land and 2½ acres TRE. [This is] a berewick in Cawston. There have always been 2 villans and 4 bordars, 1 plough in demesne and half a plough belonging to the men. [There are] 10 acres of meadow and woodland for 10 pigs. There have always been 1½ mills [and] 2 horses. This is in the valuation of Cawston. 13 sokemen belonged to this manor TRE [with] 2 carucates of land and 21 acres; these Walter Giffard holds. In Felthorpe [there are] 4 free men and 100 acres of land. There have always been 7 bordars, 2 ploughs, 5 acres of meadow and woodland for 4 pigs, and it is worth 10s. The king and the earl [have] the soke.

SOUTH ERPINGHAM HUNDRED.

Cawston was held by Harold TRE [as] 11 carucates of land and 40 acres. Then and afterwards [there were] 36 villans, now [there are] 35; [there were] 26 bordars, now 34; [there were] 6 slaves,

The King

[Folio 115: NORFOLK]

now 4; [there were] 4 ploughs in demesne, now 3, and 2 could be restored; [there were] 26 ploughs belonging to the men, now 16, and the others could be restored, and 20 acres of meadow. Then [there was] woodland for 1,500 pigs, now 1,000. There have always been 2 mills. Then [there were] 4 horses, now [there are] the same. Then and now [there were] 20 head of cattle. There have always been 40 pigs, 60 sheep, 50 goats and 5 beehives. And [there were] 10 freemen TRE of which Reginald fitzIvo has 2, Bishop William 2, Count Alan 1 and Godric 2 - as part of the king's fief which Earl Ralph held when he forfeited - and William de Warenne 2, and Roger Bigod 1. In addition Harold held Marsham and Blickling [as appurtenant] to Cawston TRE and 23 sokemen, and these two manors Bishop William holds and Herfast held; and Walter Giffard also holds 26 sokemen whom his predecessor Bodin held. Harold also held in this manor 5 sokemen whom Earl Ralph held; now Godric [holds them] as part of the king's fief. Then it was worth £30; now 40 by tale; and it is 2 leagues in length and 2 in breadth, whoever holds it, and [pays] 7d. in geld. To this manor also 1 berewick, Oulton, has always belonged, [comprising] 1 carucate of land; there have always been 9 bordars; there has always been 1 plough in demesne and 1 plough belonging to the men and 3 acres of meadow and woodland for 60 pigs. Now [there is] 1 horse, and 8 pigs and 4 sokemen and a half - R[alph] held a moiety of this half when he forfeited, [with] 110 acres and it is worth 15d. - [with] 1 carucate of land and 40 acres; there has always been 1 villan and 2 ploughs and 1 acre of meadow, and it is in the valuation of Cawston. One of those 4 sokemen the reeve of Cawston sold [for] 10s. and Ralph was holding him when he forfeited, and he has 13 acres and is worth 16d. And of the same sokemen R[alph] was seised of one when he forfeited;

[Folio 115v: NORFOLK]

he has 5 acres and is worth 8d. To this manor was added 1 free man of St Benet [of Hulme] [with] 84 acres of land TRW; there have always been 3 villans; then and afterwards [there was] 1 plough, now 2 oxen. And it is worth 5s. In Matlask Harold held 30 acres of land and they are worth 5s. In Stratton [Strawless], 60 acres of land [make up] a berewick in Cawston; there have always been 6 bordars and 1 plough in demesne. Then and afterwards [there was] 1 plough [belonging to the men], now [there is] half. This is in the valuation of Cawston. In Colby [there are] 2 free men [with] 2 carucates of land; there have always been 8 bordars. Then [there were] 6 ploughs, now 2, and 8 acres of meadow. Then [there was] woodland for 12 [pigs], now 8; now [there is] 1 mill and 1 sokeman [with] 1 acre. In Wickmere 1 free man of Harold's [has] 30 acres. Then [there was] 1 plough, now half and half an acre of meadow. Then it was worth 25s., now 20. This land Drogo de la BeuvriÒre claims for his fief because Humphrey held it, and it is 7 furlongs in length and 5½ in breadth and [it pays] 2¥d. in geld.

TUNSTEAD HUNDRED.

In Felmingham [there is] 1 free man, Asfrothr, [and] 6 acres of land and it is worth 6d.

EAST FLEGG HUNDRED.

Gyrth held Ormesby [St Margaret or St Michael] TRE as 3 carucates of land; and 30 acres which he held from St Benet [of Hulme]; there have always been 4 villans and 3 bordars and 2 ploughs in demesne and half a plough belonging to the men, 16 acres of meadow and 3 horses, 4 head of cattle and 6 pigs and then [and] now 381 sheep. And [there are] 80 sokemen [with] 4 carucates of land and 46 acres and 3 bordars. Then [there were] 33 ploughs, afterwards and now 23 and 16 acres of meadow. Of these sokemen Richard holds 3 by the gift of Bishop Herfast and has half a carucate of land. Then the

whole was worth £10; now 21 by tale, and it is 1½ leagues in length and 1 league in breadth and [pays] 3s. 8d. in geld,

The King

[Folio 116: NORFOLK]

whoever holds there. In Runham [there are] 4 free men of Gyrth's [with] 28 acres and half a plough, and 2 acres of meadow and [it is worth] 3s. and has always paid 3s. in Ormesby [St Margaret or St Michael]. The king and the earl [have] the soke.

CLAVERING HUNDRED.

[In] Gillingham [there are] 2 free men of Gyrth's [with] 35 acres and half a plough and 1 acre of meadow. This is in the valuation of Gorleston. Stigand [had] the soke. All the churches [are] in the valuation with the manors.

NORWICH HUNDRED.

There were 1,320 burgesses in Norwich TRE of whom one was [subject to the] lordship of the king to the extent that he could not withdraw nor do homage without his licence, and his name was Eadstan [and] he had 18 acres of land and 12 [acres] of meadow and 2 churches in the borough and a sixth part of a third; and to one church belonged a messuage in the borough and 6 acres of meadow. Roger Bigod holds this of the king's gift. And of 1,238 [burgesses] the king and the earl had sake and soke and customary dues; and over 50 Stigand had sake and soke and commendation; and over 32 Harold had soke and sake and commendation, of whom 1 was subject to his lordship to the extent that he could neither withdraw nor do homage without his licence. Altogether they had 80 acres of land and 20½ acres of pasture. And of these 1 was a woman, Stigand's sister, [with] 32 acres of land. And between them all they had half a mill and the fourth part of one mill and still have [them]. And in addition [they had] 12½ acres of meadow

[Folio 116v: NORFOLK]

which Wihenoc took from them; now Reginald fitzIvo has them. And in addition [they had] 2 acres of meadow which belonged to the Church of All Saints; those also Wihenoc took and now Reginald has them. There is also in the borough a certain Church of St Martin which Stigand held TRE with 12 acres of land; this William de Noyers now has as part of Stigand's fief. Stigand also held a Church of St Michael to which are attached 112 acres of land and 6 of meadow and 1 plough. Bishop William holds this, but not of his bishopric. And the burgesses held 15 churches to which belonged 181 acres of land and meadow in alms. And 12 burgesses held the Church of Holy Trinity TRE; now the bishop [holds it] by the gift of King William. The king and the earl had 180 acres of land. The Abbot has a moiety of the church of St Laurence and 1 house belonging to St Edmund. This was all TRE. Now there are 665 English burgesses in the borough and they pay customary dues; and 480 bordars who, because of their poverty, pay no customary dues. And on that land which Stigand held TRE, 39 of the above-mentioned burgesses now dwell and on the same [land] there are 9 empty messuages. And on the land of which Harold had the soke there are 15 burgesses and 17 empty messuages which are in the occupation of the castle. And in the borough [there are] 190 empty messuages in this [quarter] which was in the soke of the king and the earl, and 81 in the occupation of the castle. In addition there are in the borough 50 houses from which the king does not [....] have his customary dues. Of these, Reginald, Roger Bigod's man, [has] 2

The King

[Folio 117: NORFOLK]

houses and 2 messuages and Robert Baron 2 houses, and Abba 1 house, and Rabel the artificer 2 houses and 2 messuages; and 2 messuages which 2 women hold, and Ansculf Unlike 1 house, and Theobald, the Abbot of St E[dmund]'s man, 1 house and Burgheard 1 house, and Wala 1 house, and William, Hervey de Vere's man, 1 house, and Mainard the watchman 1 house, and the lesser burgesses 1 house, and Hervey de Vere 1 house, and Ralph the crossbowman 2 houses and 1 messuage, and Hereberd the ditcher 3 houses, and Roger de Poitou 2 houses, and Mainard, the Abbot of St Benet [of Hulme]'s man, 1 house, and Peter, the Abbot of St E[dmund]'s man, 1 messuage, and Eburwin a burgess 1 house, and Baldwin 1 house, and William the Englishman 1 house, and Gerard the watchman 1 house, and Robert the lorimer 1 messuage, and Hildebrand the lorimer 1 house, and Godwine the burgess 1 house, and William, Hermer [de Ferrer]'s man, 1 house, and Gilbert the watchman 1 house, and Fulbert, a certain priest of Hermer's, 1 house, and Walter 1 house, and Reginald fitzIvo 1 house, and Richard de Saint-Clair 1 house, and Hugh, William d'Écouis's man, 1 house.

And the bishop's men 10 houses, and in the bishop's own court 14 messuages which King William gave to Herfast for the principal seat of the bishopric, and Gilbert the crossbowman 1 house and 2 messuages, and William d'Écouis 1 house, and Mainard 1 house [and] the Abbot of Ely 1 messuage. And in the borough the burgesses hold 43 chapels. And the whole of this town paid £20 to the king and £10 to the earl TRE, and besides this 21s. 4d. [to certain] prebendaries, 6 sesters of honey, 1 bear and 6 dogs for the bear.

[Folio 117v: NORFOLK]

And now [it pays] £70 king's weight and 100s. by tale in exactions to the queen and 1 goshawk and £20 blanched to the earl and 20s. in exactions by tale to G[odric].

And Bishop Æthelmær held the Church of SS Simon and Jude TRE; afterwards Herfast, now William [holds]. To this belong three parts of a mill, half an acre of meadow and 1 messuage, and it is not of the bishopric but of Bishop Æthelmær's patrimony. In the borough he [William] has 2 acres of meadow belonging to the bishopric, and they are worth 20s.

Ewicmann held carucates of land TRE, 16 acres of pasture and 7 acres of meadow under Stigand; now Reginald fitzIvo [holds it]. Then and afterwards [there was] 1 plough, now 2. It has always been worth 30s. Of the burgesses who dwelt in the

borough of Norwich 22 left and dwell in Beccles, a vill of the Abbot of St Edmund, and 6 [dwell] in Humbleyard Hundred and have quitted the borough, and in Thorpe [St Andrew], the king's [manor] 1, and on the land of Roger Bigod 1, and under W[illiam] de Noyers 1, and [under] Richard de Saint-Clair 1. Those fleeing and the others remaining have been entirely ruined, partly by reason of Earl R[alph]'s forfeitures, partly by reason of fire, partly by reason of the king's geld, partly by Waleran.

In this borough the bishop can if he wishes have 1 moneyer. In the borough was a certain ruined house; this Ranulf fitzWalter received of the king's gift. And Walter the deacon has 1 house in the borough but it did not [exist] TRE. And 2 acres of meadow belonging to St Sepulchre were taken by two of Earl R[alph]'s men; afterwards the priest regained it by grant of the sheriff. Earl Ralph held 14 acres of land and 1½ acres of meadow; afterwards Alweard of Newton held [it].

The King

[Folio 118: NORFOLK]

LAND of the Burgesses. In Humbleyard Hundred there have always been 80 acres and 14 bordars and 1 plough and 3 acres of meadow, and they are worth 13s. 4d.

The Frenchmen of NORWICH. In the New Borough [were] 36 burgesses and 6 Englishmen and of his annual customary due each paid 1d. besides forfeitures. Of all this the king had 2 parts and the earl the third. Now [there are] 41 French burgesses in the demesne of the king and the earl, and Roger Bigod has 50, Ralph de Beaufour 14, Hermer 8, Robert the crossbowman 5, Fulcher the abbot's man 1, Isaac 1, Ralph Visdeloup 1, and in the earl's bakehouse Robert Blund has 3 and Wymer 1 ruined messuage.

All this land of the burgesses was in the demesne of Earl Ralph and he granted it to the king in common for the founding of the borough between himself and the king, as the sheriff testifies. And all these lands both of the knights and of the burgesses pay the king his customary dues. There is also in the new borough a certain church which Earl Ralph built and he gave to his chaplains. Now a certain priest of the sheriff's, Wala by name, holds it of the king's gift and it is worth 60s. and as long as Robert Blund held the county he had 1 ounce of gold from it every year.

EAST FLEGG HUNDRED.

YARMOUTH was held by King Edward. There have always been 70 burgesses. Then it was worth - with 2 parts of the soke of 3 Hundreds - £18 by tale, and the earl's part was £9 by tale. Now the king's 2 parts [are worth] £17 16s. 4d.

[Folio 118v: NORFOLK]

blanched, and the earl's part £10 blanched, and the sheriff has £4 and 1 hawk of the land in exactions; these £4 the burgesses give freely and in goodwill. In the same Bishop Æthelmær had a certain Church of St Benedict; now Bishop William has it of the bishopric and it is worth 20s. The whole pays 12d. in geld.

THETFORD HUNDRED.

In Thetford there is a Church of St Mary which Archbishop Stigand held. Now the sons of Bishop Herfast hold it. Now as then attached to this church are 4 churches; St Peter's, St John's, St Martin's and St Margaret's and 6 carucates of land less half a bovate. Then [there were] 2 ploughs, now 1. There have always been 5 burgesses and 2 empty messuages and 12 acres of meadow. And 3 ploughs could be restored and 2 carucates remain in pasture; there have always been 35 sheep and it is worth 40s.

Of the King's land in Thetford on the NORFOLK side of the river there is 1 league of land in length and half [a league] in breadth of which the king has 2 parts but a third part of these two parts belongs to the earldom. Of the above league Roger Bigod [has] the third part. All this land is one half arable, the other [half] in pasture. On this land the king has 1 plough and 3 bordars and 1 slave and 1 horse. And of 2 mills the king has 2 parts and the earl the third. The king also has 2 parts of a third mill and of these 2 parts the earl has a third. On the other, Suffolk, side [of the river] there is half a league of land in length and half [a league] in breadth; of this land a third part belongs to the earldom [with] 4 acres of meadow. All this land is arable and 4 ploughs can till it. In the borough, moreover, there were 943 burgesses TRE; of all these the king has customary dues. Of those

The King

[Folio 119: NORFOLK]

men 36 [belonged to] the lordship of King Edward to the extent that they could not be anyone else's men without the king's permission. All the others could be anyone else's men but nevertheless the customary dues remained the king's, except heriot. Now there are 720 burgesses and 224 empty messuages. Of these burgesses 21 have 6 carucates and 60 acres which they hold of the king and it is in the soke of St Edmund. Besides this, 2 burgesses have 1 mill. All this above was worth £20 by tale TRE and £10 to the use of the earl. Now it renders to the king £50 by weight and to the earl £20 blanched and £6 by tale. Now it also renders to the king £40 from the mint and always 16s. to 2 prebendaries. It also used to render 4 sesters of honey and 40d. and 10 goatskins and 4 ox-hides TRE. In the borough the Abbot of St Edmund has 1 church and 1 house [which are] free. The Abbot of Ely [has] 3 churches and 1 house [which are] free and 2 messuages by custom, on one [of which] is a house. And the bishop [has] 20 houses [which are] free and 1 mill and half a church; Roger Bigod [has] 1 house [which is] free and 1 minster and 2 bordars [belonging] to the minster.

[Folio 119v: NORFOLK]

LAND OF THE KING OF WHICH GODRIC HAS CUSTODY.

[SOUTH] GREENHOE HUNDRED.

OF 14 leets. Sporle was held by King Edward, and this manor was of the royal demesne but King Edward gave it to Earl Ralph. Then and afterwards [there were] 32 villans, now 20;

now [there are] 3 bordars. Then and afterwards [there were] 2 slaves, now 6. Then and afterwards [there was] 1 plough in demesne, now 4. Then and afterwards [there were] 10 ploughs between the men, now 3. Then [there was] 1 mill, now the same. [There is] woodland for 60 pigs. Then [there were] 6 head of cattle and 2 horses and 60 pigs and 180 sheep and 1 free man [with] half a carucate [of land]. And this land is 1 league in length and half [a league] in breadth. To this manor belongs 1 berewick which is called Palgrave. Then and afterwards [there were] 13 villans, now 11; there have always been 2 bordars. There have always been 2 slaves. Then [there was] 1 plough, and 1 when Godric received it, and now [the same] Then [there were] 2 [ploughs] and there has always been 1 plough belonging to the men. There has always been 1 mill. Then [there were] 2 head of cattle and 12 pigs and 36 sheep. This land [is] half a league in length and 5 furlongs in breadth. In addition there is also another berewick which is called [South] Acre. There have always been 6 villans. Then and afterwards [there were] 2 men, now 4; now [there is] 1 plough. Then and afterwards the villans [had] 3 ploughs, now 2. There have always been 2 mills and this [land is] 1 league in length and half [a league] in breadth.

Another berewick [is called] [North or South] Pickenham. Then [there were] 14 villans, and when he received it 1; now [there are] 4 bordars. Then [there were] 3 slaves, now 2. Then [there were] 2 ploughs in demesne and afterwards 1; now [there are] 2. Then [there were] 4 ploughs between the men. [There is] woodland for 6 pigs. There has always been 1 mill, 8 acres of meadow and 8 sokemen on this land and between them then [they had] 5 ploughs and afterwards 3 and 24 [acres] of land; now [there are] 5 ploughs. There has always been 1 mill [and] 4 acres of meadow. Then [there were] 2 head of cattle and 12 pigs and 1 horse, 20 sheep [and] 20 goats. And this [land is] half a league in length and 5 furlongs in breadth. In Sporle and in Palgrave 18d. [was rendered] when the Hundred was taxed at 20s. and in [South] Acre 6d., and in [North or South] Pickenham 12d., whoever holds there. This whole manor together TRE was worth £10, and when G[odric] received it [£]22,

The King

[Folio 120: NORFOLK]

now £24 2s., and besides these it renders exactions of 60s.

Newton [near Castle Acre] was held by Osmund TRE and afterwards by R[alph]; now it is in the king's hand. Then [there were] 8 villans, and afterwards when G[odric] received it 8, now [there are] 2. Then and afterwards [there were] 7 bordars, now 11. Always [there were] 4 slaves. There have always been 2 ploughs in demesne. Then and afterwards [there were] 6 ploughs belonging to the men, now 2½. There have always been 2 mills. There has always been half a salt-pan, and 6 free men dwelt there and when G[odric] received it he found 9 head of cattle and 1 horse, 30 pigs [and] 30 sheep and [it is] 5 furlongs in length and 5 in breadth and pays 9d. in geld. Then it was worth £4; now 8.

[Cockley] Cley was held by 2 free men [TRE] and afterwards by R[alph]; now it is in the king's hand. Then and afterwards [there were] 10 villans, now 8. There have always been 7 bordars. There have always been 4 slaves. Then [there were] 4 ploughs in demesne, afterwards 3 head of cattle, now 2 ploughs. Then [there were] 5 ploughs belonging to the men and afterwards 4, now 3; and always 6 free men have dwelt there. They are accounted for above. There have always been 2 mills. [There is] woodland for 20 pigs [and] 8 acres of meadow; and G[odric] found 60 sheep. And it pays 14d. in geld and is 1 league in length and another in breadth. Then it was worth £6 and afterwards 4; now [it is worth] 100s.

Holme [Hale] was held by Godric, now by the king. Then [there was] half a carucate of land. Then [there were] 5 bordars, now 4. Then [there was] 1 plough, now half. [There is] woodland for 20 pigs. There have always been 2 parts of a mill [and] 2 acres of meadow. Then it was worth 10s.; now 15s. And in [North or South] Pickenham 1 free man held 60 acres TRE and after the king came into that country Earl Ralph gave it to the reeve of the Hundred and he still holds that land from the king's sheriffs, and it is worth 16d. And in the same vill a certain free man [holds] 12 acres and another free man holds 3 acres of the king's soke. They are assessed above. In [South] Acre a villan [has] half a carucate of land and 1 plough and it pays rent to the Hundred.

GUILTCROSS HUNDRED.

In Knettishall [there is] 1 free man with 30 acres of land

and it belongs to Kenninghall, and there are 2 villans, and 1 acre of meadow; there has always been half a mill and half a plough and 24 acres of land. The whole is in the valuation of Kenninghall.

LAUNDITCH HUNDRED.

Horningtoft was held by Ælfric, a free man TRE, as 3 carucates of land. Then [there were] 7 villans, afterwards and now 5; there have always been 3 bordars and 2 slaves and 4 acres of meadow. Then [there were] 2 ploughs in demesne, afterwards and now [there were] 1½ ploughs, and a half could be restored. Then [there was] 1 plough belonging to the men, afterwards and now half, and a half could be restored; [there is] woodland for 300 pigs, and half a fishery; there has always been 1 ox and 20 pigs and 160 sheep and 20 goats. And [there are] 9 sokemen and 2 bordars [with] 1 carucate of land and half an acre of meadow; woodland for 40 pigs; then 2 ploughs, afterwards and now, 1, and another could be restored. Of these 9 sokemen Stigand had the soke TRE but Ralph appropriated it and therefore Godric has it.

And Kipton was held by Ælfric and Ælfhere as 3 carucates of land; there have always been 2 bordars and 3 acres of meadow. Then [there were] 2 ploughs in demesne, afterwards and now none, but 4 could be restored. And [there were] 9 sokemen [with] half a carucate of land and 1 acre of meadow [and] always 1 plough. The whole was then worth £4, afterwards £6, now [£]7 by tale. Of these 9 sokemen Stigand had the soke TRE and before he forfeited it Ralph appropriated it and held it, therefore Godric holds it. The whole of Horningtoft is 8 furlongs in length and 5 in breadth and [pays] 4d. in geld.

Rougham, 1½ carucates of land, was held by Alwine, a free man, TRE; then [there were] 7 villans, afterwards and now 3; there have always been 3 slaves. Then [there were] 3 ploughs in demesne, afterwards and now none, and 4 could be restored. Then [there was] 1 plough belonging to the men, afterwards and now none, but it could be restored; there have always been 12 pigs and 30 sheep. 14 sokemen belonged here now as then [with] 1½ carucates of land and 2 villans

The King

and 4 bordars. Then [there were] 2½ ploughs, afterwards and now 2, and the half could be restored. The whole belonged to Stigand's soke and to his manors TRE; afterwards Ralph had the whole, now Godric has it. Then and afterwards it was worth 40s.; now 60 and it is 7 furlongs in length and 6 in breadth and [pays] 20d. in geld.

In Weasenham [All Saints or St Peter] [there are] 4 free men, 1 carucate of land and 1 acre of meadow; there have always been 2 bordars and 2 ploughs. Stigand [had] the soke TRE; now W[illiam] de Noyers [has it] in Mileham. This is in the valuation of Sporle. In Mileham and Bittering [there is] 1 carucate of land and 12 acres which Alwine, a free man, held; now a certain widow holds it. Then [there were] 2 ploughs, now none. And [there is] 1 sokeman [with] 24 acres of land. There has always been half a plough, and 3 sokemen [with] 15 acres and half a plough TRE. All this was then worth 20s. Now [she] pays nothing because [she] has nothing. Then [sic] Godric pays the rent for it.

FORHOE HUNDRED.

Kimberley was held by Hagni TRE as 2 carucates of land. Then [there were] 10 villans, now 14. Then [there were] 8 bordars, now 12; always 4 slaves and always 2 ploughs, but Godric received nothing except 5 oxen. There have always been 8 ploughs belonging to the men. [There is] woodland for 10 pigs. There has always been 1 mill and 12 acres of meadow; always 8 pigs and 20 sheep. Then [there were] 10 sokemen, now 17. Then [there were] 30 acres of land, now 40; there have always been 2 ploughs. Then the whole was worth 60s.; now £7 blanched and it is 5 furlongs in length and 3 in breadth, and pays 13½d. in geld. Besides this there belong to this manor in Carleton [Forehoe] 16 free men [with] 60 acres of land [and] there have always been 2 ploughs, and they are in the valuation above; and of these, 9 were Stigand's sokemen TRE but Earl Ralph had them all before he forfeited.

Bowthorpe was held by Hagni TRE as 2 carucates of land; then [there were] 10 villans,

now 14; there have always been 3 slaves and 2 ploughs in demesne and 2 ploughs belonging to the men; [there is] woodland for 16 pigs and 10 acres of meadow; there has always been 1 mill and 7 pigs and 16 sheep. To this manor belong 2 sokemen [with] 4 acres of land. The whole was worth 40s.; now £6 blanched and it is 3 furlongs in breadth and 3 in length and [pays] 6½d. in geld.

In Crownthorpe Bondi, a free man, held 20 acres of land TRE; there has always been 1 bordar, and it is in the above valuation. In Runhall 1 carucate of land was held by Hagni, and 2 bordars and 1 sokeman and 1 mill. This berewick is in Swathing and is in [its] valuation. And to this berewick belong 7 free men, 24 acres of land and half a plough and it is in the same valuation.

MITFORD HUNDRED.

Cranworth was held by Ulf TRE [as] 2 carucates of land. There have always been 13 villans and 3 bordars. Then [there were] 2 slaves, now none. There have always been 2 ploughs in demesne and 2 ploughs belonging to the men. [There is] woodland for 200 pigs [and] 8 acres of meadow. There has always been 1 mill, 2 head of cattle, 15 pigs, 20 sheep and 20 goats, and 14 sokemen with 40 acres of land. There have always been 2 ploughs. Then it was worth 100s.; now £10 and 10s. in exactions and it is 1 league in length and half [a league] in breadth and pays 15d. in geld. In Swathing Hagni, a free man, held 2 carucates of land TRE. There have always been 9 villans and 11 bordars and 4 slaves. Then [there were] 2 ploughs in demesne; afterwards and now half, and all could be restored. Then [there were] 2 ploughs belonging to the men, now 1, and the other could be restored. Then [there was] woodland for 60 pigs, now 40 [and] 5 acres of meadow [and] 2 mills. Then and now [there were] 30 sheep and 6 goats. To this manor belong 13 sokemen; 5 dwell in the same vill, 4 in "Thurstuna", and 4 in Thuxton. Between them all they have 1 carucate of land. Then [there were] 5 ploughs, now 3. Then it was worth 100s., now £6 13s. 4d., and it is 7 furlongs in length and 6 in breadth, whoever holds there, and [pays] 12d. in geld.

The King

Flockthorpe was held by Hagni, a free man, as 2 carucates of land TRE. There have always been 12 villans; then [there were] 6 slaves, now 3, and 12 bordars. Then [there was] woodland for 60 pigs, now 40, and 10 acres of meadow; there has always been 1 mill. Then [there were] 3 ploughs in demesne, afterwards and now 2, and 1 could be restored. Then [there were] 4 ploughs belonging to the men, now 5 and 12 pigs, 26 sheep and 80 goats. To this manor belongs 1 berewick, Manson, of 30 acres of land [and] then [there was] 1 plough; and another berewick of 30 acres of land; then [there was] 1 plough and 22 sokemen [with] 1 carucate of land and 6 acres of meadow. Then [there were] 5 ploughs, now 3½. The whole was then worth 100s., now £10 blanched, and it is 1 league in length and half [a league] in breadth and [pays] 28d. in geld. In Cranworth and in Shipdham 30 acres of land were held by 1 sokeman of Stow [Bedon], and 8 acres of meadow [and] woodland for 3 pigs, and it was worth 2s. and Robert Blund had them but Godric never had [them].

BROTHERCROSS HUNDRED.

[East or West] Raynham, which Wulfgeat held TRE, [is] 2 carucates of land. There have always been 11 bordars and 2 slaves. Then [there were] 2 ploughs, afterwards half [and] now 1. Then [there was] 1 plough belonging to the men, afterwards half [and] now the same. [There is] woodland for 10 pigs, 4 acres of meadow [and] 1 mill. There has always been 1 horse and 3 head of cattle and 14 pigs and 63 sheep; and 1 berewick, Helhoughton, of half a carucate of land. There have always been 2 bordars and half a plough and 1 slave and 1 mill [and] 1 acre of meadow, 1 fishery and 1 salt-pan, and 1 horse and 2 head of cattle and 42 sheep. There belong to this manor 16 sokemen [with] 1 carucate of land. Then [there were] 2½ ploughs, afterwards 2 [and] now 2, and 6 bordars. [There is] woodland for 4 pigs, and 2 acres of meadow. And in Helhoughton [there are] 6 sokemen with half a carucate of land. There have always been 2 bordars. Then [there were] 2 ploughs, afterwards half [a plough], now 1 [and] 2 acres of meadow. Then it was worth 40s., now £6; and [East or West] Raynham is 1 league in length and 3 furlongs in breadth and [pays] 20d. in geld. And Helhoughton is 4 furlongs in length and 3 [furlongs] in breadth and [pays] 10d. in geld.

[NORTH] GREENHOE HUNDRED.

Stiffkey was held by Toki in [North] Greenhoe.

It has 1½ carucates of land. There have always been 11 bordars; then [there were] 6 slaves, and afterwards and now 3; there have always been 1½ ploughs in demesne. Then [there was] 1 plough belonging to the men, afterwards 1 plough belonging to the men, now half [and] 5 head of cattle, 12 pigs, 200 sheep, woodland for 8 pigs, 2 acres of meadow, and half a mill.

And to this vill belongs 1 berewick, Wells [-next-the-Sea], [which was] 1 carucate of land TRE, but Godric found nothing. [There were] 4 bordars [who had] then half a plough, afterwards and now 1 ox, and 4 sokemen [with] 8 acres of land [and] there has always been half a plough. And to this manor belong 13 sokemen [with] 40 acres of land TRE [and] half a plough and now [the same]. Then it was worth £4, now it pays £6. And [in] Stiffkey 1 berewick which belongs to Aylsham [with] 4 bordars [and] 1 plough TRE, and when Godric received it, and now half a plough [and] half an acre of meadow. This all belongs to Aylsham and is assessed [there].

[Great] Snoring was held by Ketel TRE, now [by] the king [as] 3 carucates of land; then and now [there was] 1 villan and 22 bordars; then [there were] 9 slaves, now 8; then [there were] 3 ploughs in demesne, afterwards and now 2; then and now [there were] 3 ploughs belonging to the men; then and now [there was] woodland for 8 pigs, 8 acres of meadow [and] 2 mills; there have always been 30 pigs [and] afterwards and now [there were] 180 sheep.

Thursford, 1 berewick, belongs to this vill [and consists of] 40 acres of land, and afterwards and now [there was] 1 plough, 1 bordar, 2 acres of meadow [and] 1 mill; 27 sokemen belong to this manor [with] 1 carucate of land [and] there have always been 4 ploughs. And in Thursford [there are] 5 sokemen [with] 60 acres of land [and] always half a plough; and 3 free men [with] 3 carucates of land [and] always 1 plough. Then it was worth £8, now it pays £11 10s. and 8d. in exactions and it is 1 league in length and half in breadth and [pays] 24d. in geld.

BLOFIELD HUNDRED.

Cantley was held by R[alph] the staller TRE [as] 4 carucates of land and 3 acres, and Alsige [held] from him. There have always been 4 villans; then [there were] 33 bordars and afterwards the same; now 42. Then [there were] 4 slaves, afterwards 3, and now 2. Then [there were] 3 ploughs in demesne, afterwards and now 2. There have always been 8 ploughs belonging to the men. [There is] woodland for 60 pigs,

The King

[Folio 123: NORFOLK]

and 40 acres of meadow; now [there is] 1 salt-pan. There has always been 1 horse and 3 head of cattle. There have always been 6 pigs. There have always been 400 sheep; and there are 10 sokemen with 60 acres of land and 4 acres of meadow. There have always been 2 ploughs. Then it was worth £7, afterwards [£]8; now [it is worth] £10 blanched and 10s. in exactions. And it is 1 league in length and 1 in breadth and [pays] 20d. in geld.

And in Limpenhoe TRE [there were] 16 free men of Alsige under Earl R[alph] [with] 1 carucate of land and 13 acres of meadow and 1 bordar. There have always been 3½ ploughs; and it is 1 league in length and 10 furlongs in breadth, and [pays] 20d. in geld.

In Hasingham [there were] 6 free men of R[alph] the staller, and of one he had the soke TRE; [they have] 70 acres of land [and] 1 has 5 bordars. Among them all [are] 5½ acres of meadow; then [there were] 3 ploughs, now [there are] 1½ ploughs. It is 1 league in length and 4 furlongs in breadth. And [it pays] geld of 6d. and 3s. And of those 2 vills the soke was the king's TRE, as the Hundred testifies. But R[alph] held it from the time he was earl; now Godric holds it in the king's hand.

In Freethorpe [there are] 9 free men; over 5 R[alph] had the soke TRE and over 4, the king. But from the time R[alph] was earl he had it; [they have] 60 acres of land. All these are assessed in the £13. There have always been 1½ ploughs.

In Strumpshaw [are] 2 free men of R[alph] the staller with sake and soke with 82 acres of land. [There is] woodland for 4 pigs [and] there have always been 4 bordars. There have always been 1 plough between him and the men; and in the same [place there is] another free man of R[alph] the staller in the king's soke [with] 30 acres of land and 8 acres of meadow. It has always been worth 8s.

In [North or South] Burlingham [there is] 1 free man of R[alph] the staller with soke of 30 acres of land, and 10 acres of free land belonging to the church and 5½ acres of meadow. In addition, in [North or South] Burlingham [there are] 3 free men and a half; over 1 R[alph] [had] soke. Over 2½ the king

[has the soke]; [there are] 42 acres of land and 4 acres of meadow.

[Folio 123v: NORFOLK]

There has always been 1 plough. In [Great or Little] Plumstead [there were] 2 free men TRE [with] 1 carucate of land and 30½ acres and always 1 bordar, and under them 18 sokemen and 7 acres of meadow. Then and afterwards [there were] 2 ploughs, now 4. [There is] woodland for 6 pigs.

In Witton [near Norwich] [there are] 4 free men [...] 60 acres of land and 11 acres of meadow. There has always been 1 plough. Of these the soke is in the Hundred to the third penny; and it pays 8s. [in geld].

In [Great or Little] Plumstead [there is] 1 free man [with] 10 acres of land. In Buckenham [near Acle] [there is] 1 free man with 8 acres of land. And all these free men are assessed in the £13 of the out-soke of [South] Walsham. In [Great or Little] Plumstead [there is] 1 berewick and it was held by Eadric TRE [as] half a carucate of land and it belongs to Eaton. There have always been 3 bordars. There has always been 1 plough among the whole, and 3 acres of meadow. And it is in the valuation of Eaton.

In [Great or Little] Plumstead [there is] 1 free man [with] 5 acres of land. The king has the soke.

HENSTEAD HUNDRED.

Howe was held by Alnoth, 1 free man of Archbishop Stigand TRE, for 1 carucate of land. Then [there were] 12 villans and afterwards 11, and now the same. There has always been one bordar. Then [there were] 6 slaves, afterwards and now [there were] 3. Then [there were] 2 ploughs in demesne, afterwards and now [there were] 1. There have always been 3 ploughs belonging to the men. [There is] woodland for 40 pigs, and 2 acres of meadow. There have always been 4 head of cattle and 41 pigs and 80 sheep. Then it was worth 40s., afterwards and now [it was worth] 60. Howe is 6 furlongs in length and 4 in breadth. And [it pays] 12d. in geld. Shotesham [All Saints or St Mary] was held by the same Alnoth TRE for 1 carucate of land; afterwards [there were] 2 bordars, now [there are] 3. Then [there was] 1 plough on the demesne; afterwards and now [there were] 2 oxen. And in the same [vill] the same Alnoth held 2 free men and the moiety of another 4 in commendation; and between them they hold 32 acres of land and 1 plough. Of these Earl Ralph held 3 whole [free men] with their land,

The King

[Folio 124: NORFOLK]

12½ acres, when he forfeited. Now Aitard, a man of R[oger] Bigod's, holds them, and claims them from the fief of the Bishop of Bayeux. But this Aitard has nothing from his predecessor except in one half commended [freeman], as the Hundred testifies.

In Stoke [Holy Cross] [there is] 1 free man in commendation to Alnoth with 5 acres of land. In Surlingham [are] 3 free men and a half in commendation to Alnoth with 45 acres of land; there has always been 1 plough and 5 acres of meadow, and under them 5 bordars. In Rockland [St Mary] [are] 2 free men in commendation to Alnoth [with] 24 acres of land, and there have always been 2 oxen and 2 acres of meadow.

In the other Shotesham [All Saints or St Mary] [are] 1 free man and 2 halves in commendation to Alnoth with 40 acres and 2 bordars and 4 acres of meadow. Between them all [is] 1 plough.

In Yelverton [there were] 2 free men TRE, and half belonged to Alnoth and half to Alfred by commendation; these Earl Ralph held when he forfeited; afterwards Godric [held them] in the king's hand; now Aitard [de Vaux], a man of R[oger] Bigod, has a moiety of one, and 15 acres, and claims it for the fief of the Bishop of Bayeux. Between the men [there are] 33 acres of land, and there have always been 2 bordars. There has always been 1 plough and 3 acres of meadow.

In Poringland [there are] 2 free men of Alnoth's in commendation with 13 acres of land. There has always been 1 plough and 1 acre of meadow.

In Shotesham [All Saints or St Mary] [there is] 1 free man with 10 acres of land; then [there was] half a plough, afterwards and now nothing. Shotesham [All Saints or St Mary] was worth 30s., afterwards and now 20s., and all these free men are worth 40s., but TRE Shotesham [All Saints or St Mary] was not paying rent. R[obert] Blund put it to rent.

In Eaton 1 berewick, Whitlingham, was held by Eadric TRE as 80 acres of land. There have always been 2 bordars. Then [there was] 1 plough in demesne; afterwards and now [there was] half, and 4 acres of meadow.

In Kirby [Bedon] [there are] 12 men following the fold of Eadric [with] 80 acres of land and 3 acres of meadow. There have always been 1½ ploughs in demesne. In Rockland [St Mary] [there was]

[Folio 124V: NORFOLK]

1 free man of Eadric's TRE in commendation with 15 acres of land, and under him 5 free men with 23 acres of land, 3 acres of meadow, and now as then half a plough.

In Stoke [Holy Cross] [there were] 2 sokemen of Eadric's with 30 acres of land and 1 acre of meadow; there has always been 1 plough. In Saxlingham [Nethergate or Thorpe] [there was] 1 sokeman of Eadric's in commendation TRE with 30 acres of land [and] 1 acre of meadow. There has always been half a plough.

In Kirby [Bedon] [there was] 1 free man of Eadric's TRE [with] 30 acres of land and 2 bordars and 4 acres of meadow. There has always been half a plough. In Kirby [Bedon] [there was] 1 free man of Eadric's TRE with 6 acres and there have always been 2 oxen.

In Whitlingham [there is] 1 free man of Eadric's in commendation, and in Bramerton 3, and in Rockland [St Mary] 1; of 4½ Eadric had commendation TRE, and Ulfkil of 1½ and Alfred [had] only commendation of half [one free man] after King William conquered England, and R[alph] held them all when he forfeited; and afterwards Godric, as the king's steward. This the Hundred testifies. Now Aitard de Vaux [holds them] and claims them for the fief of the Bishop of Bayeux as of the tenure of Alfred, his predecessor; and the Hundred does not support him because they did not belong to

his predecessor. All these [free men] hold 40 acres of land and 3 acres of meadow. Then [there were] 2 ploughs and afterwards 2, now 1½.

In Trowse [with Newton] [there was] 1 sokeman of Archbishop Stigand's TRE with 10½ acres of land. When R[aph] forfeited he held him; now Aitard de Vaux claims him for the fief of the Bishop of Bayeux from Alfred, his predecessor, to whom he belonged in commendation only after King W[illiam] came into the land of England. [He] is in the valuation of those [men].

In Holverston Aitard holds half of a free man in the same way, with

The King

[Folio 125: NORFOLK]

8 acres of land and half an acre of meadow, and with 6 whole men with 6 halves, whom Aitard claims for the fief of the Bishop of Bayeux; they were worth 10s. TRE [and] when Godric received the stewardship 36s.; now Aitard has 13s. 8d.

Newton [near Norwich] [with Trowse] was held by 1 free woman under Stigand for 1 carucate of land. There have always been 8 villans and 8 bordars. There has always been 1 plough in demesne. Then [there were] there were 4 ploughs belonging to the men, afterwards 1½, now 2 ploughs belonging to the men, and 40 acres of meadow [and] now [there are] 10 cattle. Then [there were] 2 pigs, now 3, and 5 sheep.

In Trowse [there are] 6 sokemen belonging to this manor with 56 acres and 2 bordars and 5 acres of meadow and 1 mill. Then as now [there were] 1½ ploughs. Then the whole was worth 20s., afterwards and now 30. This manor was paying rent under G[odric's] stewardship for 30s.; but G[odric] did not have them because she [the free woman] vouches the king to warranty. It is 3 furlongs in length and 4 in breadth and [pays] 8d. in geld.

In Stoke [Holy Cross] 12 acres of land are held by 1 free man. In Kirby [Bedon] [there are] 4 acres of land; this belongs to Eaton. In Saxlingham [Nethergate or Thorpe] 1 free man of Harold's [held] in commendation TRE with 30 acres of land. There have always been 3 bordars. Then [there was] 1 plough in demesne, now half, and 1 sokeman [with] 1 acre of land. This land Godric the steward has kept in the king's hand, but the land does not pay rent to him.

EARSHAM HALF HUNDRED.

Redenhall was held by Rada, a free man of Eadric's, in commendation TRE as 2 carucates of land. Then [there were] 30 villans, afterwards and now [there were] 10. There have always been 6 bordars. Then [there were] 4 slaves, afterwards 2, and now 1. There have always been 2 ploughs in demesne. Then [there were] 6 ploughs belonging to the men [and] afterwards and now 2½. Then [there was] wood[land] for 60 pigs, now 20, and 8 acres of meadow.

[Folio 125V: NORFOLK]

There has always been 1 mill. Then as now [there were] 6 head of cattle and 30 pigs [and] 12 goats. Then it was worth 60s., afterwards and now £8 blanched, and it is 1½ leagues in length and half [a league] and 3 perches in breadth. And [it pays] 10d. in geld.

In Redenhall [there are] 2 free men with 100 acres. There has always been 1 plough; Bishop William claims 20 acres; [as to] 10 of these the Hundred also testifies and Agnelli holds 80 acres.

In Alburgh [there were] 15 free men of Rada's and Wulfmær's TRE in commendation with 60 acres of land. There have always been 3 ploughs and 3 acres of meadow. In Starston [there are] 12 free men, 9 belonging to Rada in commendation TRE and 1 to Wastret, and 1 to Wulfmær, and 1 [in] common to the Abbot[s] of St Edmund and Ely; between them all [is] 60 acres of land. There have always been 3 ploughs and 13 acres of meadow.

In Redenhall [there are] 20 free men of Rada's in commendation with 80 acres of land. These men were then worth £4, now 8; Earl R[alph] put them to farm [and] afterwards Ivo Taillebois. There have always been 5 ploughs and 4 acres of meadow.

In the same place [there is] 1 free man of Eadric's in commendation [with] 1 carucate of land. There have always been 2 villans and 8 bordars. Then and afterwards [there were] 2 ploughs in demesne, now 1. There have always been 2 ploughs belonging to the men. [There is] wood[land] for 20 pigs, and 3 acres of meadow. And under him [there are] 5½ free men with 20 acres of land. There have always been 2 ploughs. Then it was worth 20s.; in the time of Earl R[alph] his men and Judicæl paid 30s., but he was quit of the hall because he was the earl's falconer; after R[alph] forfeited and he was in the king's hand under G[odric], however, he paid nothing and vouches the king to warranty.

FREEBRIDGE HUNDRED AND A HALF.

In East Winch [there are] 2 carucates of land, a berewick of Sporle [with Palgrave] TRE; there have always been 11 villans and 24 acres of meadow. Then [there were] 2 ploughs in demesne;

The King

[Folio 126: NORFOLK]

afterwards and now 1; there has always been 1 plough belonging to the men. When Godric received this manor he found 24 sheep and 9 pigs and now the same, and 1 fishery. To this land 13 sokemen have always belonged, 54 acres of land, and 8 acres of meadow; there have always been 1½ ploughs, and 1½ salt-pans, and 10 acres of meadow. The whole of this is valued in Sporle. The whole is half a league in length and 4 furlongs in breadth, and pays 8d. for 20s. of geld.

[North and South] Wootton was held by Godwine, a free man, TRE. Then [there were] 2 ploughs in demesne, afterwards and now [there was] 1. Then [there were] 24 villans; afterwards and now [there were] 15. There has always been half a plough and 2 sokemen. [There are] 24 acres of meadow. Then [there were] 20 salt-pans [and] afterwards and now 14. Here belong 22 sokemen, 12 acres of land [and] half a plough; when it was acquired [there was] 1 horse and 4 cows and 10 pigs and 120 sheep [and] now [there are] the same. Then it

was worth £4; afterwards and now [it is worth] £9, and 20s. in exactions. The whole is half a league in length and [the same] in breadth, whoever holds there, and pays 12d. in a geld of 20s.

SMETHDEN HUNDRED.

In Holme [-next-the-Sea] 1 free man held 40 acres and 3 bordars and 1 plough TRE and it was worth 10s. St Benedict [of Ramsey] [has] the soke.

WAYLAND HUNDRED.

Stow [Bedon] was held by Ælfhere TRE; [there were] 5 ploughs in demesne, afterwards and now 2. Then and afterwards [there were] 17 villans, now 16. There have always been 2 bordars. Then and afterwards [there were] 10 slaves, now 7 [and] 30 acres of meadow; there have always been 5 ploughs belonging to the men [and there is] woodland for 10 pigs; there has always been 1 mill; there have always been 2 head of cattle and 28 pigs [and] 40 sheep. In Caston [there is] 1 sokeman [with] 40 acres. The soke is in Saham [Toney] and the land lies in Stow [Bedon] and [is] in [its] rental. To this manor belong 29 sokemen, 3 carucate of lands and 36 acres. Then it was worth £10; when it was acquired [it was worth] 13s. 4d., and Godric gave it for £13 13s. 4d. and 20s. in exactions as long as he had the soke; now since he lost the soke it pays £7, and upon the sokemen whom he lost are £7.

[Little] Ellingham was held TRE

[Folio 126v: NORFOLK]

by Ælfric, a free man, as 2 carucates of land. There have always been 4 villans and 2 bordars. Then [there were] 4 slaves [and] 20 acres of meadow; there have always been 2 ploughs in demesne and 2½ ploughs belonging to the men; [there is] woodland for 100 pigs, and 1 plough could be in demesne; there have always been 12 cattle and 24 pigs and 37 sheep, 34 goats and 5 sokemen with 2½ acres. Then and afterwards it was worth £4, now £4 blanched and 4s. To this manor 6 sokemen used to belong on the day that Ralph forfeited, who used to pay 15s. to Robert Blund, and now they are in Saham [Toney] as the Hundred testifies. The whole is 1 ½ leagues in length and [the same] in breadth and [pays] 10 ƒd. in geld.

In Breckles 1 free man held 1 carucate of land TRE. Then [there were] 3 villans, afterwards and now 2; there has always been 1 slave [and] 4 acres of meadow. Then [there were] 2 ploughs in demesne, afterwards and now half; there has always been 1 plough belonging to the men, and 1½ ploughs could be [employed]. This is a berewick of Sporle and is in the valuation of Sporle.

In Griston 80 acres of land were held by 1 free woman TRE; there has always been 1 villan. Then [there were] 5 bordars; there has always been 1 slave [and] 6 acres of meadow; there has always been 1 plough in demesne [and] woodland for 24 pigs; there have always been 12 pigs and 11 sheep. And this is a berewick and is assessed in Sporle.

SHROPHAM HUNDRED.

Buckenham [near Attleborough] was held by Earl Ralph as 3 carucates of land TRE and now [is] 4½. Then and afterwards [there were] 9 villans, then 24, now 15 [sic], now 28 bordars, and then 12 acres of meadow, now 20; then [there was] 1 plough in demesne [and] afterwards and now 2; there have always been 3 ploughs belonging to the men. Then [there was] woodland for 120 pigs, now [for] 60. Here belong 21 sokemen [with] 2 carucate of lands, and 10 acres of meadow and 1 bordar; there have always been 3 ploughs [and] woodland for 10 pigs; there have always been 4 head of cattle, 12 pigs and 68 sheep. And [there are] 43 sokemen with 10 carucates of land and 60 acres of meadow [and] woodland for 40 pigs;

The King

there have always been 12 villans and 46 bordars. Then [there were] 24 ploughs, afterwards and now 16 and 2 mills; and of the aforesaid 43 sokemen other men had commendation, but Ralph added them all to this manor TRW. The whole was then worth £6 13s. 4d. and 2 sesters of honey [and] afterwards and now £32 blanched and 13s. 4d. and 20s. in exactions by tale. The whole is 1 league in length and 1 league in breadth and [pays] 19d. in geld.

Ashby [in Snetterton] was held by Ralph TRE as 1 carucate of land; there have always been 2 villans and 1 bordar. Then [there were] 4 slaves and now [there are] 2 and 3 acres of meadow; there has always been 1 plough in demesne, and 2 ploughs belonging to the men; then as now [there were] 6 sheep. It has always been worth 20s. blanched. Roudham was held by 1 free man under Harold TRE as 1 carucate of land; [there is] 1 carucate of land and 4 villans and 2 acres of meadow; there has always been 1 plough in demesne; there has always been half a plough belonging to the men, and 14 sheep; and then it was worth 20s., afterwards and now 10s. blanched.

Kilverstone was held by a free man under Stigand TRE as 1½ carucates of land; there have always been 5 villans and 1 slave and 5 acres of meadow; then [there were] 2 ploughs in demesne, afterwards and now [there was] 1 ox. Then [there was] 1 plough belonging to the men, afterwards nothing, now half a plough. There has always been 1 mill and 1 fishery [and] it has always been worth 40s. The whole is 2 leagues in length and in breadth whoever holds there and [pays] 7d. in geld. The whole Hundred pays 40[s.] and belongs to the office of Godric.

GUILTCROSS HUNDRED.

Kenninghall was held by King Edward [as] 5 carucates of land; there have always been 24 villans and 24 bordars and 12 acres of meadow and 1 mill [and] woodland for 300 pigs. Then [there was] 1 plough in demesne, afterwards and now 2; then 12 ploughs belonging to the men; afterwards and now 11, and 1 could be restored; there has always been 1 horse and 12 sokemen, 100 acres of land and 18 acres of meadow and 2 mills; there have always been 3 ploughs and 1

free man [with] 1 carucate of land and 2 villans and 3 bordars; [there is] woodland for 24 pigs; there has always been 1 plough and half a plough belonging to the men. And [West] Harling, 1 berewick, always belonged to this manor [comprising] 1 carucate of land and 3 villans and 4 bordars and 5 acres of meadow. Then [there was] 1 plough in demesne and it could be restored; afterwards [there was] half [a plough] and 3 ploughs belonging to the men; now [there are] 2, and the third could be restored. The whole was worth £10 and 5 sesters of honey TRE; afterwards [it was worth] £26, now £24 blanched and £6 by tale and in exactions. The whole of Kenninghall is 1½ leagues in length and half in breadth and [pays] 25d. in geld.

Quidenham was held by Goding, a free man, of whom the Abbot of St Edmund had commendation only TRE, as 1 carucate of land; there have always been 2 villans and 2 bordars and 3 acres of meadow and 1 mill. Then [there was] half a plough in demesne; afterwards and now [there was] 1; there have always been 2 oxen belonging to the men; there has always been 1 horse and 6 pigs [and] 16 sheep. Then it was worth 15s., afterwards and now 30. This land the same Godric held of the abbot for 3 years after King W[illiam] came. This same [land] Godwine, the uncle of Earl Ralph, took away from him wrongfully. The soke was in Kenninghall TRE, [a manor of] the king. The whole is 5 furlongs in length and 4 furlongs in breadth and [pays] 17¥d. in geld.

Garboldisham was held by 1 free man, Ælfric, TRE for a manor [of] 2 carucates of land; there have always been 3 bordars and 1 slave and 4 acres of meadow; then [there were] 2 ploughs in demesne, afterwards and now 1½ ploughs, and a half could be restored. Then [there was] half [a plough belonging to the men] and afterwards and now the same, and 8 pigs, and 3 sokemen with 16 acres of land. There has always been half a plough. Then it was worth 30s., afterwards and now 40.

In Gasthorpe 1 freeman [held] 1 carucate of land TRE; then [there were] 6 villans,

The King

now [there are] 8; then as now [there were] 5 bordars and 2 slaves and 8 acres of meadow; there has always been 1 plough in demesne, and 2 ploughs belonging to the men, and 5 sokemen [with] 20 acres of meadow; there has always been 1 plough; [there is] woodland for 12 pigs. Then it was worth 20s., now 40. The whole Hundred pays 20[s.], and the whole soke [is] in Kenninghall; the whole of Gasthorpe is half a league in length and half in breadth and [pays] 7d. in geld.

GALLOW HUNDRED.

In Burnham [Overy] Ulf held 3 carucates of land TRE. Then [there were] 20 bordars, now [there are] 16. Then [there were] 12 slaves, now 8. Then [there were] 3 ploughs in demesne, afterwards and now 2. Then [there was] 1 plough belonging to the men, afterwards and now nothing. [There is] woodland for 4 pigs [and there are] 2½ mills. Then [there were] 7 horses and now [the same] and 40 pigs and 600 sheep [and] 1 salt-pan. There is 1 berewick [belonging] to this manor of 1 carucate of land. Then [there was] 1 plough, afterwards none [and] now 1. And [there is] another berewick of 1 carucate of land. Then [there was] 1 plough, and afterwards none; now [there is] 1. To this manor belong 30 sokemen with 1 carucate of land; then [there were] 2 ploughs, afterwards none, now 1. All this was worth £8 TRE, and afterwards when Earl Ralph held it £23 13s. 4d, now £20 by tale; and in the same vill [is] 1 free man, Ketel, with 20 acres, and another free man, Oia, with 30 acres.

HOLT HUNDRED.

In Morsto n [there is] 1 free man with 30 acres of land and 1 bordar and half a plough, and he is worth 2 oras. He was Gyrth's man TRE and belongs in Stiffkey.

NORTH ERPINGHAM HUNDRED.

In [East] Beckham Siward Barn held 1 free man TRE; R[alph] annexed him to Aylsham [with] 30 acres of land. There has always been 1 villan belonging in Aylsham, 1 bordar of 1 acre, and 1 sokeman [with] 1 acre. There has always been 1 plough. They are valued in Aylsham. The king has sake and soke of the Hundred of NORTH ERPINGHAM except over the land of Siward Barn. H

WALSHAM HUNDRED.

[South] Walsham was held by Ælfflæd, a free woman, TRE

[for] 4 carucates of land. There have always been 4 villans; then [there were] 18 bordars, afterwards and now 23. There have always been 2 slaves in demesne; then [there were] 4 ploughs belonging to the men, afterwards and now 2; [there are] 40 acres of meadow. [There is] woodland for 15 pigs. There have always been 2 head of cattle and 18 pigs and 20 sheep. And [there are] 22 sokemen with 80 acres of land and 10 acres of meadow; then [there were] 5 ploughs, afterwards and now 4. To this belongs 1 berewick, Moulton [St Mary], [of] 1 carucate of land. There have always been 2 bordars and 1 plough and 1 acre of meadow, and 3 sokemen with 18 acres of land and half a plough. The whole of this was then worth 100s. and afterwards £11, and now £12 13s. 4d. blanched, and 20s. by tale in exactions. And it is 1 league in length and 1 in breadth and [pays] 4s. in geld. Acle was held by Earl R[alph] the elder [as] 5 carucates of land TRE. There have always been 23 villans; then [there were] 38 bordars, afterwards 30 [and] now 38 [and] then [there were] 3 slaves. There have always been 3 ploughs in demesne; then and afterwards [there were] 10 ploughs belonging to the men, now [there are] 12 [and] 50½ acres of meadow. [There is] woodland for 40 pigs; afterwards and now [there was] 1 mill. There have always been 3 horses and 2 head of cattle and 20 pigs [and] 120 sheep; afterwards [there were] 11 hives of bees, now [there are] 15; and [there are] 4 sokemen with half a carucate of land. There has always been 1 plough [and] 4 acres of meadow. Then it was worth £8, and afterwards 12; now [it is worth] £14 13s. 4d.; and of this 53s. are by tale and it pays the

rest blanched. And it is 1 league in length and 1 in breadth and [pays] 2s. in geld.

Halvergate was held by Earl R[alph] TRE as 6 carucates of land. There have always been 6 villans; then and afterwards [there were] 46 bordars [and] now [there are] 50; then [there were] 3 serfs; then [there were] 4 ploughs in demesne,afterwards and now [there were] 3; then [there were] 7 ploughs belonging to the men, afterwards and now [there were] 9; [there are] 30 acres of meadow and 1 salt-pan. There have always been 2 horses and 7 head of cattle and 13 pigs [and] 260 sheep; and 13 sokemen with half a carucate and 15 acres of land. There have always been 2½ ploughs [and] 6 acres of meadow. Then it was worth £8, afterwards [£]9, and now £10 blanched and 40s. of customary dues by tale, and 20s. in exactions; and it is 1 league in length and 1 in breadth, and [pays] 2s. in geld. And besides the aforesaid sheep, there belong to this manor 700

The King

sheep and they render 100s.

In Fishley Earl R[alph] the elder held 25 sokemen, 1 carucate of land and 30 acres of meadow. One of them, called Wulfweard, is of the king's soke. There have always been 3½ ploughs, and it is 8 furlongs in length and 5 in breadth and [pays] 10d. in geld.

In Upton [with Fishley] [there are] 27 sokemen, 1½ carucates of land and 35 acres of meadow. There have always been 3 ploughs. It is 1 league in length and 1 in breadth and [pays] 2s. in geld. Over all these the king and the earl had sake and soke except 7 whom [the earl] had in commendation in the soke. And between these two, Fishley and Upton, [there are] 25 sokemen, 60 acres of land, and 13 acres of meadow. There has always been half a plough. In Upton, 1 sokeman [with] 12 acres is worth 2s. Of these the soke is in the Hundred.

In [South] Walsham [there was] 1 free man of Gyrth's TRE with 1 carucate of land. There have always been 3 bordars and half a plough [and] 20 acres of meadow. [There is] woodland for 7 pigs [and there is] half a salt-pan; and [there are] 17 sokemen, 1 carucate of land, and 1½ ploughs [and] 12 acres of meadow. And in the same [place there is] 1 free man with 30 acres of land and 2 bordars; and he and the men have always had 1½ ploughs and 8 acres of meadow. And under him are 6 sokemen with 6 acres of land [and] 3 acres of meadow; then [there was] 1 plough, afterwards and now [there was] half a plough. And in the same [place are] 11 sokemen with 16 acres of land, 2 acres of meadow [and] always 1 plough.

In Panxworth [there are] 3 sokemen, 1 carucate [and] 19 acres [of land] and 12 acres of meadow, and 9 bordars; then [there was] 1 plough, afterwards and now [there were] 2. In Ranworth [there are] 7 sokemen, 50 acres of land and 8 acres of meadow, and there has always been 1 plough. Of these the soke is in the Hundred; and Panxworth and Ranworth are 1 league in length and half in breadth and [pay] 16d. in geld.

In [Wood] Bastwick [there is] 1 sokeman with 27 acres of land and 3 acres of meadow. There has always been 1 plough.

In Hemblington [there are] 6 sokemen with 30 acres of land [and] 2 acres of meadow. There have always been 2 ploughs. In the same [place are] 2 sokemen, and 1 of these is in the soke of the Hundred [with] half a carucate of land and 1 bordar [and] 6 acres of meadow; and they have under them 7 sokemen with 20 acres of land [and] 1 acre of meadow. There have always been

1½ ploughs among them all. And it is 1 league in length and a half in breadth and [pays] 16d. in geld. In Moulton [St Mary] [there are] 10 sokemen, 2 carucates of land, and 5 bordars [and] 20 acres of meadow; and there have always been 4 ploughs; and it is 8 furlongs in length and 5 in breadth, and [pays] 15½d. in geld.

In Wickhampton [there is] 1 sokeman, 1 carucate of land, and 5 bordars and 4 acres of meadow; there has always been 1 plough. And it is 6 furlongs in length and 5 in breadth, and [pays] 10½d. in geld. King Edward had the soke and R[alph] [had it] when he forfeited.

In Reedham [there are] 3 sokemen with 40 acres of land and 7 bordars and 6 acres of meadow; and under them [there are] 6 sokemen with 20 acres of land, and among them all there has always been 1 plough.

In Moulton [there are] 7 free men. In Wickhampton [there is] 1 sokeman with 56 acres of land; and they have 2 ploughs [and] 4 acres of meadow and are in the soke of the Hundred. And all of these, with others who are in another Hundred, pay £8 blanched and 100s. of customary dues by tale and 20s. in exactions. Over all those who used to resort to the fold of the earl the earl, had the sake and soke; over all the others the king and earl [had it].

WEST FLEGG HUNDRED.

And in Burgh [St Margaret] [there are] 20 acres; the whole is assessed in Caister. In Clippesby [there is] 1 free man with 4½ acres of land. In Rollesby [there is] 1 free man [with] 15 acres of land. In Winterton [there is] 1 free man [with] 10 acres of land; he is assessed with the free men in [South] Walsham.

DISS HALF HUNDRED.

Winfarthing was held by Algar, a free man of Harold's, TRE for a manor [as] 6 carucates of land. There have always been 8 villans, and there have always been 20 bordars. Then and afterwards [there were] 4 slaves [and] now [there are] 2. There have always been 2 ploughs in demesne and 4 ploughs belonging to the men. Then [there was] woodland for 250 pigs, afterwards and now 200 [and] 9 acres of meadow.

The King

There have always been 2 horses at the hall and 6 head of cattle. There have always been 14 pigs and 14 goats; and in the same [place there were] 5 free men of Algar's in commendation only TRE with 40 acres. There has always been 1 plough and 1 acre of meadow.

In Burston [there were] 4 free men of Algar's TRE in commendation only with 40 acres of land and 1 bordar. There has always been 1 plough and 3 acres of meadow.

In Gissing [there were] 8 free men of Algar's in commendation only TRE, with 60 acres of land, and there have always been 4 bordars. Then [there were] 3 ploughs among them all; afterwards and now [there were] 1½ and 2 acres of meadow. In Shimpling [there was] 1 free man of Eadric's TRE with 12 acres of land. There has always been 1 plough. In the same place [there are] 2 sokemen with 16 acres of land; there has always been half a plough. This St E[dmund] claims, and the Hundred testifies [in the abbey's favour] but Earl R[alph] was holding it when he forfeited. Of these St E[dmund] claims 14 acres. In Tivetshall [St Margaret or St Mary] [there are] 2 free men of Algar's in commendation with their land, 35 acres of land and 1 acre of meadow. [There is] woodland for 4 pigs. There has always been 1 plough.

In Shelfanger [there is] 1 villan [and] 15 acres of land. There has always been half a plough and 2 bordars. [There is] woodland for 5 pigs and 2 acres of meadow. Then Winfarthing was worth 40s., afterwards and now £8 3s. 4d. blanched; and all these [were] free with soke when G[odric] acquired them and now they render £7 but they are not able any longer to pay so much. Winfarthing is 1 league in length and a half in breadth and [pays] 9d. in geld.

Fersfield was held by Alsige, a thegn of King Edward's, for 2 carucates of land. There have always been 5 bordars. Then and afterwards [there were] 3 slaves, now 1. There have always been 2 ploughs in demesne. Then [there were] 1½ ploughs belonging to the men; afterwards and now [there was] 1. In Burston [there is] 1 berewick of 1 carucate of land belonging to Fersfield. There have always been 2 villans and 1 bordar.

Then [there was] half a plough in demesne, afterwards nothing; now [there is] half a plough.

In Fersfield [there are] 13 sokemen [with] 60 acres of land. There have always been 3 ploughs. In the same place [there were] 3 free men of Alsige TRE [with] 80 acres of land and 3 bordars. Then and afterwards [there were] 3 ploughs, now 1½.

In Burston [there were] 11 free men of Alsige TRE with 30 acres of land. There has always been 1 plough and 1 acre of meadow. In Bressingham [there are] 7 free men of Alsige in commendation with 30 acres of land. Then [there were] 3 ploughs, afterwards and now 2. [There is] woodland for 6 pigs, and 2 acres of meadow. Fersfield, with the berewick of Burston, was then worth 60s., afterwards £7 6s. 8d. between rent and customary dues; now it is worth £12 6s. 8[d.] blanched; and of these £12 the free men contribute 100s. and 6[s.] 7d. Fersfield is 8 furlongs in length and 4 in breadth and [pays] 7d. in geld. Burston is 8 furlongs in length and 4 in breadth and [pays] 12d. in geld.

In Shimpling [there is] 1 half free man with 4 acres of land. In Fersfield TRE belonged the sake and soke of all those who had less than 30 acres. Of all those who have 30 acres the sake and soke belongs to the Hundred and in Winfarthing; when R[alph] forfeited he had it.

LODDON HUNDRED.

Bedingham was held by Hagni, a thegn of the king and Stigand's [man] by commendation, TRE for 2 carucates of land. Then [there were] 4 villans, afterwards and now 2. then [there were] 4 bordars, afterwards and now 5. There have always been 3 slaves. Then [there were] 5 ploughs in demesne, afterwards and now 1½. Then [there were] 2½ ploughs belonging to the men, afterwards and now 1. [There is] woodland for 20 pigs.

The King

[Folio 131: NORFOLK]

and 8 acres of meadow. There has always been 1 horse at the hall and 1 ox, and always 14 pigs. There belonged to this manor 6 sokemen with all customary dues TRE; afterwards and now [there were] 26 of whom Earl R[alph] added 20 with soke of the fold. Between [them] all 80 [?acres]. Then [there were] 5 ploughs, afterwards and now [there were] 4. In the same [place] [there were] 5 free men; of 3 Hagni had commendation and Algar of 2, and in Woodton 1 free man of Godwine's in commendation. Among them all [there were] 1½ carucates of land and 12 bordars. There have always been 5 ploughs among them all and 4 acres of meadow. Then the whole was worth £4; afterwards and now 8 blanched, and 20s. by tale in exactions. Of this £8 these 6 free men contribute 27s. 4d. It is 1 league in length and a half in breadth and [pays] 11d. in geld whoever holds there. Over these free men King Edward used to have the soke, but Earl R[alph] held it wrongfully when he forfeited.

Sisland was held by Ketil, a free man of Edwin's by commendation only, for a manor [and] 2 carucates of land. There have always been 3 bordars and 1 slave. Then [there were] 2 ploughs in demesne; afterwards and now [there were] none. There has always been half a plough belonging to the men. [There is] woodland for 4 pigs, and 5 acres of meadow. Then [there was] 1 mill; afterwards [there was] none. Then [there were] 13 sokemen, afterwards and now 9½, and King Edward [had] the soke [of] 26 acres of land. There have always been 2 ploughs. Then it was worth 20s., afterwards and now 40[s.] blanched; and it is 8 furlongs in length and 7 in breadth and 11 perches, and [pays] 8d. in geld. In Mundham [there is] half a church with 10 acres.

In Woodton [there are] 2 free men [with] 12 acres of land, and they belong to Eaton and are assessed there. In Shotesham [All Saints or St Mary] [there are] 10 acres, and it belongs to Bedingham.

EYNESFORD HUNDRED.

Sall was held by Godwine, uncle of Earl R[alph], TRE [for] 3 carucates of land; there have always been 7 villans, then [there were] 6 bordars, afterwards and now 8; there have always been 2 slaves; then [there were] 3 ploughs in demesne,

[Folio 131v: NORFOLK]

afterwards and now [there were] 2; there have always been 3 ploughs belonging to the men, and 6 acres of meadow; [there is] woodland for 100 pigs. There have always been 2 horses

and 10 head of cattle and 30 pigs and 30 sheep. And [there are] 9½ sokemen [with] 46 acres of land and half an acre of meadow; there have always been 1½ ploughs. And [there are] 6 free men, 1½ carucates of land and 6 bordars, and 6 acres of meadow; [there is] woodland for 16 pigs. Then [there were] 6 ploughs, afterwards and now 4; then it was worth £4, afterwards 100s., now £10 blanched and 20s. in exactions by tale; and it is 1 league in length and half in breadth and pays 6½d. towards the king's geld whoever holds there. The soke of those sokemen is in the king's manor of Foulsham.

Thurning was held by Ulf, a free man, TRE [as] 1 carucate of land; there have always been 6 villans and 9 bordars and 1 serf; there have always been 2 ploughs in demesne and 1½ ploughs belonging to the men, and 10 acres of meadow; [there is] woodland for 60 pigs, and half a mill, and 4 horses and 20 cattle and 16 pigs and 50 sheep. And [there are] 6 sokemen [with] 16 acres of land; there have always been 1½ ploughs upon the soke. The soke is in the king's [manor of] Foulsham; then and afterwards it was worth 60s., now 100s. blanched and 10s. in exactions by tale; and it is 5 furlongs in length and 6 in breadth, and pays 5d. to the king's geld.

In [Great or Little] Witchingham [there are] 3 free men [with] 1½ carucates of land; there have always been 2 villans and 9 bordars; there have always been 4 ploughs and 9 acres of meadow. Then it was worth 20s., now 30s. blanched.

TAVERSHAM HUNDRED.

Sprowston was held by Eadric TRE [as] 3 carucates of land. Then [there was] 1 villan. Then [there were] 6 bordars, now 5. Then [there was] 1 plough in demesne; afterwards and now half. Then [there were] 2 ploughs belonging to the men, afterwards and now 1, and the others [sic] could be restored. [There is] woodland for 6 pigs. Here belong 2 free men in Catton [near Norwich] [with] 60 acres. Then [there were] 2 ploughs; afterwards and now 1.

The King

[Folio 132: NORFOLK]

And in Beeston [St Andrew] [there are] 6 free men [with] 30 acres of land. Then [there were] 2 ploughs, afterwards and now 1, and 2 acres of meadow. And in Wroxham [there are] 2 free men, 60 acres of land and 2 bordars. Then [there were] 2 ploughs; afterwards and now 1. This is all in the valuation of Eaton. In Rackheath [there are] 3 free men, 3 carucates of land and 3 villans and 12 bordars; then [there were] 4 slaves. Then [there were] 5 ploughs, afterwards and now 4, and 7 acres of meadow. Then it was worth 20s., now 60, and it is 1 league in length and 8 furlongs in breadth and [pays] 15d. in geld. Here belong 9 free men in Beeston [St Andrew] with 40 acres [and] there has always been 1 plough; and they are in the same valuation. The king and the earl [have] the soke. And Beeston [St Andrew] is half a league in length and 5 furlongs in breadth and pays 10d. towards the king's geld.

SOUTH ERPINGHAM Hundred.

Aylsham was held by Gyrth as 10 carucates of land TRE. Then [there were] 2 villans; afterwards and now 11. Then and afterwards [there were] 88 bordars, now 65. Then and afterwards [there were] 2 slaves, now 3. Then [there were] 6 ploughs in demesne, afterwards and now 1, and 6 can be employed [and there are] 12 acres of meadow. Then [there was] woodland for 400 pigs, afterwards and now 300. Then as now [there were] 2 mills; there have always been 7 pigs, 6 sheep and 7 goats. Then and afterwards [there were] 60 sokemen, now [there are] 46, and they have 1½ carucates and 14 bordars. Then [there were] 30 ploughs, afterwards and now 24, and 9 acres of meadow [and] woodland for 12 pigs; there have always been 2 mills and 6 ploughs.

To this manor belongs 1 berewick, Shipdham, [comprising] 1 carucate of land, and there have always been 4 villans. Then [there were] 4 bordars, afterwards and now 2; there has always been 1 plough in demesne and 1 plough belonging to the men, and half an acre of meadow [and] woodland for 8 pigs.

And Brundall belongs to this manor [and comprises] 30 acres of land. Then [there was] 1 plough and 2 acres of meadow. Then it was worth £12, afterwards £25 blanched, now £29 blanched and 20s. in exactions; and it is 2 leagues in length and 2 in breadth and [pays] 20d. in geld. Here [there is] 1 free man [with]

[Folio 132v: NORFOLK]

5 acres and he is worth 16d. Humphrey, nephew of Ranulf, brother of Ilger, held, but the Hundred awarded it to the king, and thereupon he gave pledge and yet his predecessor held it.

Saxthorpe was held by Godwine [for] 2 carucates of land TRE; then as now [there were] 10 villans and 10 bordars and 2 slaves; there have always been 2 ploughs in demesne. Then and afterwards [there were] 3 ploughs belonging to the men, now 2, and 4 acres of meadow. [There is] woodland for 60 pigs. Then [there was] 1 mill, afterwards and now 2; there have always been 4 horses and 20 head of cattle and 50 pigs, and 1½ sokemen, 40 acres of land and 3 ploughs, and 2 acres of meadow [and] woodland for 12 pigs; and 1 free man, 30 acres of land, always 1 plough, woodland for 4 pigs, and 1 acre of meadow. And [there is] 1 berewick, Matlask, [of] 1½ carucates [...] of land; there have always been 7 villans, and 1 plough on the demesne and 1 plough belonging to the men, woodland for 20 pigs, and 15 sokemen with 1½ carucates of land, and 2 acres of meadow [and] woodland for 20 pigs; there have always been 4 ploughs. Then it was worth £4, afterwards 6, now £10 blanched, and 20s. in exactions. And it is 1 league in length and another in breadth, and [pays] 12d. in geld. And Matlask is 3 furlongs in length and 2 in breadth, and [pays] 3d. in geld.

Mannington was held by Godwine [as] 2 carucates of land TRE; then [there were] 6 villans, afterwards 5, now 4; there have always been 10 bordars; then [there were] 2 slaves, afterwards and now 1. Then [there were] 2 ploughs in demesne, afterwards and now 1. Then [there were] 3 ploughs belonging to the men, afterwards and now 2, and 2 acres of meadow. Then [there was] woodland for 60 pigs, afterwards

and now 30; there have always been 2 mills and 2 horses and 14 pigs and 8 sheep and 40 goats; and 5 sokemen [with] 24 acres of land [and] there has always been 1 plough [and] woodland for 4 pigs. Then it was worth 60s., afterwards 80, now 100 blanched and 16d. and 20s. in exactions

The King

[Folio 133: NORFOLK]

and it is 1 league in length and 4 furlongs in breadth and [pays] 3ƒd. in geld. In Belaugh [there are] 2 sokemen belonging to St Benet [of Hulme] [with] 34 acres of land, and in [Little] Barningham [there is] 1 sokeman belonging to the same [with] 16 acres; there have always been 3 bordars and 1½ ploughs and 3 acres of meadow. These sokemen Ralph held when he forfeited. Now Godric [holds them] as part of the king's fief; and it is the valuation of Aylsham. In Scottow [there is] 1 sokeman belonging to St Benet [with] 43 acres [of land]; there have always been 2 bordars. He is held in the same way as the others.

In 'Crackford' [in Colby] [there is] 1 free man of Gyrth's [with] 1 carucate of land; there have always been 3 bordars; then [there were] 1½ ploughs, now 1, and 2 acres of meadow [and] now 1 mill; and this is in the valuation of Aylsham and is 4½ furlongs in length and 4 furlongs in breadth and [pays] 4d. in geld. In Itteringham [there is] 1 free man of Gyrth's [with] 1 carucate of land; there have always been 5 bordars and 2 ploughs and 1 acre of meadow [and] woodland for 5 pigs; [it is] in the same valuation and the whole is 1 league in length and a half in breadth and [pays] 5½d. in geld. In Hevingham [there is] 1 free man, a priest, [with] 40 acres of land in alms, and he sings 3 masses every week; there has always been 1 plough and 1 acre of meadow [and] woodland for 10 pigs; and he is worth 5s. And [there is] 1 sokeman [with] 8 acres, and he is worth 20d. Leofstan, the predecessor of Tihel, held him TRE and Ralph held him when he forfeited, and he is of the soke of Cawston. Now Godric holds him. But Turold, a man of William de Warenne's, was seised of him against the king and held him for 3 years. Now he has been deraigned against him, and Turold pays 5s. for [him as] the king's chattel and has given pledge to do justice.

TUNSTEAD HUNDRED.

In Witton [near North Walsham] [there is] 1 priest [with] 30 acres of land in alms; there have always been 9 sokemen with 12 acres of land; there have always been 2 ploughs and 2 acres of meadow.

[Folio 133v: NORFOLK]

For this he sings 3 masses for the king and queen, and in addition pays 2s. And the whole is 1 league in length and a half in breadth and [pays] 10d. in geld whoever holds there.

HAPPING HUNDRED.

Happisburgh was held by Eadric [as] 13 carucates of land TRE; there have always been 21 villans and 20 bordars. There have always been 3 slaves, and 3 ploughs on the demesne. Then [there were] 9 ploughs belonging to the men, afterwards and now 7, 10 acres of meadow, woodland for 16 pigs, and 4 head of cattle and 18 pigs and 200 sheep. And [there are] 21 sokemen [with] 86 acres. Then [there were] 5 ploughs [and] afterwards and now 4; and 12 free men of whom Eadric had the commendation only, 4 carucates of land and 8 villans, and 9½ bordars, and 1 slave; half a carucate of land Eadric, a man of Count Alan's, appropriated from them and he has given pledge. Then [there were] 10 ploughs, afterwards and now 9. Those free men Earl Ralph added to this manor, and they are now at rent in the same [place]; and he held them when he forfeited.

Then the whole was worth £7, and the free men 40s.; and in the time of Ralph the whole was worth £10, now [£]16 blanched and 20s. in exactions; and it is 1½ leagues in length and the same in breadth whoever holds there and [pays] 30d. in exactions. This land Robert Malet claims and says that his father held it when he went into the marsh, and this the Hundred testifies; and yet he was not holding it on the day that he died.

HAPPING HUNDRED.

Lessingham was held by a thegn, Godwine, TRE [as] 3 carucates of land and 30 acres; there have always been 15 villans and 16 bordars and 6 slaves. Then [there were] 2 ploughs in demesne, afterwards and now 1; there have always been 3 ploughs belonging to the men

The King

[Folio 134: NORFOLK]

and 12 acres of meadow. [There is] woodland for 10 pigs, and 2 horses

and 3 head of cattle and 7 pigs and 20 sheep. And [there are] 8 free men [with] 100 acres; there have always been 2 ploughs and 2 acres of meadow. Then it was worth 60s. and the free men 10s.; afterwards the whole [paid] £4 now £6 blanched and 20s. in exactions by tale; and it is 1½ leagues in length [sic] and [pays] 10½d. in geld. The king and earl [have] the soke. Hempstead [near Stalham] [is] 2½ carucates of land [and] there have always been 10 bordars. Then [there was] 1 plough in demesne, afterwards and now 2; there has always been 1 plough belonging to the men, and 15 acres of meadow, and 2 head of cattle and 13 pigs and 160 sheep; and 36 sokemen [with] 108 acres [and] there have always been 6 ploughs; and 16 free men [and] 2 carucates of land; there have always been 3 bordars and 6 ploughs and 14 acres of meadow. Then it was worth 50s. and the free men 40s.; afterwards and now £8 blanched and 20s. in exactions by tale; and it is 1 league in length and another in breadth and [pays] 18d. in geld.

Palling was held by Godwine TRE [as] 3 carucates of land; there have always been 9 villans and 14 bordars; there has always been 1 plough in demesne and 1 plough belonging to the men, 20 acres of meadow and 14 wild mares and 2 horses and 23 pigs and 71 sheep. Then it was worth £4, afterwards and now £6 blanched; and it is 8 furlongs and 12 perches [in length] and 8 furlongs in breadth and [pays] 7½d. in geld.

EAST FLEGG HUNDRED.

Caister was held by 80 free men TRE and likewise now [as] 4 carucates of land. Then [there were] 22 ploughs, and of the whole of this Earl R[alph] made a manor; now there is 1 plough in demesne and 21 belonging to the men; there has always been half a mill, and 39 salt-pans, and 3 horses and 8 head of cattle and 12 pigs and 360 sheep. Then it was worth £8, afterwards and now 14; and yet the Abbot of St Benet

[Folio 134v: NORFOLK]

has out of this manor £6. And it is 1 league and 100 perches in length and 1 league in breadth and [pays] 44d. in geld whoever holds there. This was given in exchange for land in Cornwall with all customary dues, as Godric says.

Mautby was held by Wistan, a free man of Ralph the staller [as] 1½ carucates of land. There have always been 7 villans and 2 bordars and 2 slaves and 1½ ploughs in demesne and 1 plough belonging to the men [and] 4 acres of meadow; now [there is] half a mill, and then as now 7 salt-pans and 7 head of cattle and 2 pigs and 122 sheep; and 16 free men and a half in commendation only [with] 80 acres of land. There have always been 4 ploughs and 2½ acres of meadow, and 4 salt-pans, and 14 free men whom Earl R[alph] added, and they have 2 carucates of land and 50 acres and 7½ bordars; there have always been 9 ploughs, 10 acres of meadow, and 6 salt-pans and a half and the fourth part of one. The king and earl always [had] the soke of the whole. And all these free men were worth 30s. then; now [they are worth] 53s. 7d. And the manor was then worth 40s. and afterwards 50, now 66[s.] 6d. and is 1 league in length and 8 furlongs in breadth and [pays] 2s. in geld.

Runham was held by 2 free men TRE; 1 was a man of Eadric Laxfield and the other of Ralph the staller, and there have always been 1½ carucates of land and 10 villans and 1 plough in demesne and 1 plough belonging to the men, 16 acres of meadow and 10 salt-pans in demesne, 1 horse and 1 ox and 101 sheep and 9 pigs; and 11 sokemen and a half with half a carucate of land; there have always been 3 ploughs and 2 acres of meadow and 2½ salt-pans; and 11 free men and a half with half a carucate of land and 5 acres. Then [there were] 4 ploughs, afterwards and now 3, and 3 acres of meadow and 2 salt-pans; they have always been worth 10s. The king and earl [had] the soke [then] and now. It was

The King

[Folio 135: NORFOLK]

then worth 30s., afterwards 50, now 90s. blanched and 20s. in exactions. And it is 10 furlongs in length and 7 in breadth and [pays] 2s. in geld, whoever holds there. In Thrigby [there are] 6 free men of Ralph the staller's [with] 40 acres [of land]; there has always been 1 plough and half a salt-pan and 4 acres of meadow, and it is worth 9s. in the outsoke of Walsham. The king and earl [have] the soke.

HUMBLEYARD HUNDRED.

Eaton was held by Eadric of Laxfield, the predecessor of Robert Malet, [as] 1 carucate of land TRE; there have always been 2 bordars. Then [there were] 2 ploughs in demesne, afterwards nothing, now 1, and 12 acres of meadow; [there is] woodland for 6 pigs, and 1 mill; and now [there are] 6 head of cattle and 6 pigs and 6 sheep; and 10 sokemen [with] 80 acres; there have always been 2 ploughs and 4 acres of meadow; [there is] 1 church [with] 14 acres and it is worth 14d. And [there are] 4 free men in Stoke [Holy Cross] under Eadric in commendation only [with] 45 acres; there has always been 1 plough and 3 acres of meadow and the fourth part of a mill.

And in Earlham [there is] 1 free man, Wulfgeat by name, [with] 1½ carucates of land; there has always been 1 villan and 4 bordars; there has always been 1 plough in demesne and 1 plough belonging to the men, 16 acres of meadow [and] now 1 villan. The same Wulfgeat also has under him 10 free men with 80 acres of land; there have always been 2 ploughs. Then the whole was worth £4, and when Robert Blund held it, the same; now [it is worth] £7, and the free men now 60s. And it is 1 league in length and 1 in breadth and [pays] 7¼d. in geld. And Earlham is 1 league in length and 1 furlong and 1 league in breadth and [pays] 8¼d. in geld.

In Earlham [there are] 3 free men [with] 42 acres; there has always been 1 bordar and 1 plough and 1 acre of meadow; then they were worth 4s., now 5, and they belong to Bowthorpe [St Michael] [and there is]

[Folio 135v: NORFOLK]

1 church [with] 14 acres and 1½ acres of meadow; and it is worth 15d.

DEPWADE Hundred.

In Carleton [Rode] [there are] 4½ acres [of land] and it is in the valuation of Howe.

CLAVERING HUNDRED.

Raveningham was held by Ulf, a man of the predecessor of Robert Malet, [as] 3 carucates of land; there has always been 1 villan and 2 bordars. Then [there were] 2 ploughs in demesne, afterwards and now 1 [and] 6 acres of meadow, 13 pigs and 200 sheep. And [there are] 10 free men in the soke of the fold and commendation [with] 64½ acres [of land]; then [there were] 4 ploughs, afterwards 2, now 2½ ploughs, and 3 acres of meadow. And [there are] 3 sokemen [with] 4 acres [of land]. Then it was worth 30s., now 60s. blanched. In the same [place] [there is] 1 free man, Ketil Friday, [with] 7 acres and 1 marsh, and he is worth 12d.

LANDS of Bishop Stigand which W[illiam] de Noyers keeps in the king's hand. Smethden Hundred.

Hunstanton was held by Stigand TRE; then [there were] 2 ploughs in demesne, when W[illiam] received it 1½, now the same; then as now [there were] 16 villans and 4 bordars. Then [there were] 3 slaves, afterwards and now 1, and 8 acres of meadow. Then [there were] 2 ploughs belonging to the men, afterwards and now 1½; then [there was] 1 mill [and] half a fishery. Then [there was] 1 horse and now the same and 2 oxen.

The King

[Folio 136: NORFOLK]

And [there are] 14 pigs and 44 sheep and 4 sokemen [with] 60 acres. Then it was worth 70s., afterwards and now 110. Here [there] used to belong 1 free woman [with] 30 acres of land TRE; afterwards Earl Ralph had [this] for 3 years before he forfeited and [at the time] when he forfeited. Afterwards Robert Blund held [this] and Godric [held it] at farm for 30s. with other land. She [and] Siward were once more joined this to this manor and does [sic] not pay farm to Godric; and W[illiam] de Noyers has added 3 sokemen of St Benet [of Hulme]'s with 4 acres of land. The whole is 1 league in length and a half in breadth and pays 6d. [of a geld] of 20s. whoever holds there.

GRIMSHOE HUNDRED.

Methwold was held by Stigand [as] 20 carucates of land TRE. Then [there were] 28 villans, afterwards 24, now 18. Then [there were] 4 bordars, afterwards 8, now 13; there have always been 24 slaves [and] 30 acres of meadow; then [there were] 6 ploughs in demesne, afterwards and now 5. Then [there were] 23 ploughs belonging to the men, afterwards 13, now 7; there have always been 2½ mills, 7 fisheries in demesne, 4 horses, 12 head of cattle, 84 pigs, 800 sheep [and] 27 beehives. To this a berewick, Weeting, has always belonged; there have always been 3 villans and 1 bordar and 3 slaves and 1 acre of meadow. Then [there were] 2 ploughs in demesne, afterwards and now 1; then [there was] 1 plough belonging to the men; then as now [there were] 2 horses. In Feltwell [there are] 60 acres of land. And in Thetford [there was] half a carucate of land, and 5 bordars TRE, now [there are] 3, and 2 messuages are vacant [and there is] 1 church; and 1 church of St Helen with 1 carucate and 1 villan, and there could be 1 plough.

And in Hilgay [there is] 1 free man [with] 30 acres of land [and] 1 plough, and in Upwell [there are] 3 bordars; and in the whole manor there could be 8 ploughs [employed]. Then it was worth £20, now 30; and it is 2 leagues in length and half a league in breadth,

[Folio 136v: NORFOLK]

and pays 2s. ½d. in a geld of 20s. And 4 free men belonged to this manor TRE; now W[illiam] de War[enne] has them].

Croxton [near Thetford] was held by Stigand TRE; there have always been 5 carucates of land. Then there were 8 villans, afterwards 4, now none; now [there are] 4 bordars. Then [there were] 5 slaves, afterwards 4, now none. Then [there were] 3 ploughs in demesne, afterwards and now [there were] 2. Then [there were] 2 ploughs belonging to the men; then [there was] 1 mill which afterwards Earl Ralph took TRW and 3 acres of meadow; then as now [there was] 1 horse, 6 head of cattle, 19 pigs [and] 215 sheep. Here [there] used to belong 17 sokemen TRE. Of these W[illiam] de War[enne] has 16 and Ralph de Tosny [one]. Then it was worth £10, now it is worth 40s., but it pays 100s.; and 3 ploughs could be [employed]. The whole is 1½ leagues in breadth [sic] and 1 in breadth and pays 12d. in a geld of 20s.

LAUNDITCH HUNDRED.

Mileham was held by Stigand as 10 carucates TRE; there have always been 20 villans and 44 bordars. Then [there were] 6 slaves, afterwards and now 1, and 10 acres of meadow; then as now [there were] 2 ploughs in demesne, and 1 plough could be restored. Then [there were] 24 ploughs belonging to the men, afterwards and now 19, and 5 could be restored; [there is] woodland for 1,000 pigs; there has always been 1 mill and 1 salt-pan and 3 sokemen [with] 1 carucate and 1 acre. Then and afterwards [there were] 12 villans, now 4; there have always been 10 bordars and 4 acres of meadow. Then [there was] 1 plough in demesne, afterwards and now half, and a half could be restored. Then [there were] 4 ploughs belonging to the men, afterwards and now 2, and the others could be restored; then [there was] woodland for 100 pigs, now for 50. And [there are] 4 sokemen [with] 30 acres of land and 1 bordar; then as now [there was] 1 plough and 4 acres of meadow. And [there is] 1 sokeman [with] 1 carucate of land, and 1 sokeman [with] 8 acres; between the whole [are] 10 bordars and 5 acres of meadow. Then [there were] 2 ploughs in demesne, afterwards and now 3; now [there is] 1 plough belonging to the men [and] woodland for 10 pigs. And [there are] 7 sokemen [with] 40

The King

[Folio 137: NORFOLK]

acres of land and 1 bordar and 4 acres of meadow; there have always been 2 ploughs in the demesne, always 1 horse, and 13 head of cattle and 24 pigs and 30 sheep and 50 goats. To this manor there has always belonged a berewick, Litcham [of] 4 carucates of land; there have always been 9 villans and 11 bordars and 5 slaves and 4 acres of meadow; there have always been 2 ploughs in demesne. Then and afterwards [there were] 9 ploughs belonging to the men, now 5, and the other could be restored; and 2 sokemen [and] 4½ acres of land; then as now 1 horse and 1 ox and 16 pigs and 104 sheep and 20 goats. Another berewick, [Great or Little] Dunham, also belongs there [of] 4 carucates of land. Then [there were] 19 villans, afterwards and now 10, then as now 8 bordars, then and afterwards 2 slaves [and] now none; [there is] woodland for 20 pigs, and 1 acre of meadow. And [there are] 8 sokemen [with] 34 acres of land and 1 bordar and 1 acre of meadow; then [there were] 1½ ploughs, afterwards and now 1. There has always been 1 plough in demesne, and a half could be restored; and then [there were] 1½ ploughs belonging to the men, afterwards 1, now a half, and 1 could be restored; there have always been 2 head of cattle and 8 pigs and 6 sheep. In this berewick there has always been half a market. And in Thetford [there is] half an acre of land, and 2 sokemen [with] 40 acres of land, and 2 bordars; then as now [there was] 1 plough. All this was worth £30 TRE, and afterwards and now £60 blanched; and it is 3 leagues in length and 1 in breadth and [pays] 27d. of a geld of 20s. whoever holds the land there.

In Bittering [there are] 7 acres of woodland and 1 acre of land on which there are 4 bordars. This Godric claims as of the fief of Earl Ralph, and a certain woman who held it TRE is willing to undergo judicial ordeal that it has been released

from pledge. This is held by Siward in pledge. In Kirtling [there are] 2 sokemen [with] 17 acres of land and 1 acre of meadow; TRE [there was] half a plough, now nothing; and this is in the valuation of Mileham.

[Folio 137v: NORFOLK]

FOREHOE HUNDRED.

Wymondham was held by Stigand [as] 4 carucates of land TRE. There have always been 60 villans and 50 bordars and 8 slaves; there have always been 4 ploughs in demesne. Then [there were] 60 ploughs belonging to the men, now 24; this derangement Ralph Wader caused before he forfeited and they could all be restored. Then [there was] woodland for 100 pigs, now 60, and 60 acres of meadow; there have always been 2 mills and 1 fishery; there have always been 2 horses and 16 cattle and 50 pigs and 24 sheep. To this manor belonged 87 sokemen TRE, now [there are] only 18, and they have 30 acres of land; there has always been 1 plough; and in addition [there is] 1 sokeman [with] 1 carucate of land; there have always been 4 villans and 10 bordars and 1 mill [and] woodland for 16 pigs, and 4 acres of meadow. This manor with all the soke was worth TRE with the soke [sic] £20, now 60; and it is 2 leagues in length and 1 in breadth and [pays] 6s. 8d. in geld. Of those sokemen who have been removed, William de War[enne] has 55, and they have under them 57 bordars; among them all they have 5 carucates of land and 12 acres of meadow, and TRE they had 20 ploughs, now 13, and half a mill; they have always been worth £10. And Ralph de Beaufour has 10 sokemen [with] 2 carucates of land and 32 bordars; there have always been 7 ploughs and 12 acres of meadow and 1½ mills. And Count Alan [has] 1 sokeman [with] 1½ carucates of land and 13 bordars and 3 ploughs and 9 acres of meadow and 1 mill, and they are worth 30s. And Roger Bigod [has] 2 sokemen [with] 45 acres of land and 6 bordars and 2 ploughs and 2 acres of meadow; then [there was] woodland for 60 pigs, now 16; and they are worth 7s. 6d.

BLOFIELD HUNDRED.

Thorpe [St Andrew] was held by Archbishop Stigand [as] 3 carucates of land TRE. Then [there were] 24 villans, afterwards 23, now 22,

The King

[Folio 138: NORFOLK]

and 5 bordars then as now; there have always been 2 slaves, now [there is] 1. Then [there were] 2 ploughs in demesne, afterwards and now 1. There have always been 4 ploughs belonging to the men. [There is] woodland for 1,200 pigs, and 40 acres of meadow; there has always been 1 horse, always 2 head of cattle and 13 pigs [and] always 36 goats. There have always been 26 sokemen with 2 acres of land; one has 3 bordars. There have always been 4½ ploughs, and one of them Earl R[alph] had a half with 30 acres of land, and the soke of Stigand; and when R[alph] forfeited he had the man and the soke, and afterwards R[obert] Blund [had it] at farm; now W[illiam] de Noyers [has it included] in the rent of Thorpe [St Andrew]. Then it was worth £12 and 1 sester of honey and

2,000 herrings, afterwards and now £30 blanched; and it is 3 leagues in length and 1 league and 3 furlongs in breadth and [pays] 8d. in geld. And in the same [place] [there are] 3 sokemen and a half, with sake and soke of 32 acres of land and 4 acres of meadow. There has always been 1 plough among the men; now Godwine Halfdan holds them by gift of Earl R[alph] and the Hundred testifies to it, but they belong to Thorpe [St Andrew] with the customary dues. In addition [there are] 140 sheep. They have always been worth 24d.

WEST FLEGG HUNDRED.

[East or West] Somerton was held by Archbishop Stigand [with] 1 free man and 1 carucate of land. There have always been 12 villans and 11 bordars and 6½ acres of meadow and 1½ salt-pans. There has always been 1 plough in demesne and 1½ ploughs belonging to the men, and there have always been 3 horses; then, and since, [there were] 8 head of cattle and 145 sheep and 2 beehives. In addition there are 19 sokemen and 1 carucate of land and 3 ploughs. It has always been worth 20s. And this land W[illiam] de Noyers holds in the farm of Mileham and the soke is in the Hundred and he could sell it without licence of Stigand. Richard Poignant put it to rent.

HENSTEAD HUNDRED.

Arminghall [is] 1 berewick of 1 carucate of land belonging to Thorpe [St Andrew]. Then [there were] 16 villans; afterwards and now 8.

[Folio 138v: NORFOLK]

Then [there were] 2 slaves, now none. There have always been 3 bordars. Then [there were] 1½ ploughs in demesne, afterwards and now 1. Then [there were] 4 ploughs belonging to the men, afterwards and now 2. [There is] woodland for 8 pigs and 12 acres of meadow. Then [there was 1 mill, afterwards and now none, because Eudo fitzClamahoc withdrew it TRW; now R[alph] de Beaufour, his successor, holds it, as the Hundred testifies; and it pays 24s. In the berewick are 4 sokemen with 20 acres of land. There has always been 1 plough. It is 5 furlongs in length and 3 in breadth and [pays] 8d. in geld.

EARSHAM HALF HUNDRED.

Earsham was held by Stigand as 3 carucates of land TRE. Then and afterwards [there were] 21 villans, now [there are] 25. There have always been 24 bordars [and] always 5 slaves. Then [there were] 3 ploughs in demesne, afterwards and now 2. Then [there were] 16 ploughs belonging to the men, afterwards and now 12. Then [there was] woodland for 300 pigs, afterwards and now 200 [and] 20 acres of meadow. There have always been 2 mills and always 3 horses at the hall and 1 ox. Then [there were] 40 pigs, and now the same. There have always been 30 goats and 11 sokemen with 1 carucate of land and 4 bordars. Then [there were] 4 ploughs, afterwards and now 3. [There is] woodland for 40 pigs, and 12 acres of meadow. Then it was worth £11, afterwards and now £40 blanched; with everything that belongs to it, it is 1½ leagues in length and 1 league in breadth and [pays] 6d. in geld.

In Denton [there are] 12 sokemen. Of these Stigand had the soke in Earsham and they had 60 acres, and of 4 [sic] St

Edmund had the soke and they had 40 acres, so that they could neither give nor sell their land away from the church, but Roger Bigod added them to Earsham on account of the customary dues because the soke was in the Hundred. There have always been 5 ploughs among them all. In Alburgh [there are]

The King

[Folio 139: NORFOLK]

15 free men; of 13 the predecessor of Eudo fitzSpirewic had commendation, of 2, St Edmund. Among them all [there are] 80 acres of land and 4 acres of meadow. There have always been 5 ploughs; and it is 1 league in length and 5 furlongs in breadth and [pays] 10d. in geld. But more [tenants] hold there. In Redenhall [there were] 7 free men of Stigand's by commendation TRE with 60 acres of land and 2 bordars; then [there were] 3 ploughs, afterwards and now 2. [There is] woodland for 4 pigs, and 2 acres of meadow.

In Starston 15 sokemen of Stigand's belonging to Earsham with the soke hold 80 acres of land and 2 acres of meadow and 6 bordars. There have always been 8 ploughs among them all. In the same [place were] 15 sokemen, of whom St Edmund had commendation TRE; but their land was entirely in the church, but the sake and soke [were] in Earsham, and R[oger] Bigod therefore annexed them when he held the manor of Earsham in Stigand's time. Among them all [there are] 60 acres of land and 1 acre of meadow. There have always been 3 ploughs.

In Rushall [there were] 10 free men of Stigand's TRE with 60 acres of land and 3 bordars. There have always been 3 ploughs. [There is] woodland for 6 pigs, and 2 acres of meadow. In Thorp [Abbots] [there are] 20 free men: 2 were Stigand's by commendation, and they had 100 acres of land TRE, and 18 were St Edmund's by commendation, and they could not give [their land] without licence of St [Edmund], but sake and soke were in Earsham. There have always been 6 ploughs among them all. [There is] woodland for 4 pigs and 4 acres of meadow. It is half a league in length and 5 furlongs in breadth and [pays] 6d. in geld. In Brockdish [there are] 28 free men, 5 of Stigand's with half a carucate of land TRE, and 23 of St Edmund's with 140 acres, but they could neither give nor sell [their land]

[Folio 139v: NORFOLK]

without licence of Stigand, for he had the soke. Then [there were] among them all 8 ploughs, now 7. [...] [There is] woodland for 12 pigs [and] 6 acres of meadow. It is 7 furlongs in length and 5 furlongs in breadth and 4 perches and [pays] 6d. in geld. The sake and soke of all these belonged to Stigand TRE. All these free men used to pay 40s. to Stigand TRE but if they did not pay they forfeited £4; now they pay £16 by tale in Earsham under which Richard Poignant put them at rent. Stigand had the sake and soke of this half Hundred TRE except Thorpe [Abbots] [which belonged to] St Edmund, and except Pulham [St Mary Magdalene and St Mary the Virgin] [which belonged to] St Æthelthryth in Earsham. When

R[alph] forfeited he had the sake and soke of Redenhall and of his commended men. When Raymond Gerald

departed he had the sake and soke of his land; [as had] afterwards R[oger] de Poitou, his successor. But of the land which St Edmund has in this half Hundred [St Edmund] held the soke. In 'Pyrleston' [in Scole] Warengar retained [the estate] as part of the fief of Roger de Rames.

In Redenhall and in Denton [there are] 2 freemen of Stigand's with the soke [of] 23 acres of land. There has always been half a plough and half an acre of meadow. It is assessed with the others.

LODDON HUNDRED.

Ditchingham [is] 1 berewick in Earsham of 3 carucates of land which Stigand [held] TRE. Then [there were] 9 villans, afterwards and now 8. Then [there were] 5 bordars, afterwards and now 4. Then [there were] 4 slaves, afterwards and now 2. Then [there were] 2 ploughs in demesne, afterwards 1, now 2. There have always been 4 ploughs belonging to the men. [There is] woodland for 100 pigs, and 18 acres of meadow. Then [there were] 2 mills, afterwards and now 1. There have always been 48 pigs and 64 sheep and 55 goats. And 22 sokemen are there with 1½ carucates of land. There have always been

The King

[Folio 140: NORFOLK]

8 ploughs among them all. [There is] woodland for 4 pigs, and 9 acres of meadow, and 1 mill; it is assessed in Earsham and it is 1 league and 4 furlongs in length and 9 [furlongs] in breadth and pays 8d. in geld whoever holds there.

In Mundham [there are] 7 free men belonging to this berewick. Of these 7, 3 were Stigand's and 2 Edwin's by commendation and 1 Algar's and 1 Toli the sheriff's. Between them all [there are] 60 acres of land. There have always been 3 ploughs. Four of these Robert fitzCorbucion claims by livery of the king [with] 24 acres of land as the Hundred testifies. But afterwards R[oger] Bigod annexed them to Earsham and [he] has 52 acres. The king and the earl [have] the soke. They are valued in Earsham.

In Seething 1 free man under Stigand held 1 carucate of land; after King William came into England Stigand himself annexed [this] as a berewick in Toft [Monks]. Then as now [there was] 1 villan. Then [there were] 2 bordars, afterwards and now 3 bordars. Then and afterwards [there was] 1 plough in demesne, now 1½. There has always been half a plough belonging to the men and 1½ acres of meadow. There has always been 1 horse at the hall [and] now [there are] 3 pigs. And [there were] 21 sokemen TRE, afterwards and now 12, and they have 24 acres of land. There has always been 1 plough [and] half an acre of meadow, and it is in the valuation of Toft [Monks]. Then it was worth 40s., now it pays £4 10s. in Toft [Monks] and is 1 league in length and 1 in breadth and [pays] 16d. in geld.

TAVERHAM HUNDRED.

Horstead was held by Stigand [as] 4 carucates of land TRE. Then [there were] 19 villans, afterwards and now 16 [and] 9 bordars; then [there were] 8 slaves, afterwards and now 4. There have always been 2 ploughs in demesne; then [there were] 10 ploughs belonging to the men, afterwards and now 6, and 12 acres of meadow; [there is] woodland for 60 pigs; there have always been 3 mills and 1 horse and 2 head of cattle and 7 pigs and 20 sheep. Then [there were] 30 goats,

[Folio 140v: NORFOLK]

now 40 and there has always been 1 beehive. Then there used to belong to this manor 18 sokemen with 3 carucates of land which were delivered to Robert Blanchard; now they are part of the fief of Roger of Poitou.

In Stanninghall [there is] 1 free man [with] 1 carucate of land and 4 villans and 4 bordars and 2 ploughs, 2 mills [and] woodland for 20 pigs. This belongs to Horstead and the whole is in the valuation of Mileham. And Horstead is 1 league in length and another in breadth and [pays] 15d. in geld.

In Catton [near Norwich] [there are] 13 sokemen [with] 1 carucate of land [and] there have always been 3 bordars. Then [there were] 3 ploughs, afterwards and now 2 [and] woodland for 12 pigs and it is 1 league in length and 5 furlongs in breadth and [pays] 8ƒd. in geld. This is in the valuation of Thorpe [St Andrew].

In Sprowston [there are] 140 acres of land. Then [there were] 3 ploughs, afterwards and now 2 and 4 acres of meadow. [There is] woodland for 4 pigs and it is 1 league in length and 8 furlongs in breadth and [pays] 15d. in geld whoever holds there. This also is in the valuation of Thorpe [St Andrew]. In Belaugh [there is] 1 carucate and 24 acres which Stigand held; there have always been 2 bordars and 8 acres of meadow. Then [there was] 1 plough; and it is in the valuation of Horstead.

HUMBLEYARD HUNDRED.

Lakenham was held by Stigand as a berewick in Thorpe [St Andrew] [as] 2 carucates of land TRE; there have always been 11 villans and 2 sokemen [with] 4 acres [of land]. Then [there were] 2 ploughs in demesne, afterwards and now 1, and 1 church with 13 acres in alms. Then [there were] 3 ploughs belonging to the men, afterwards and now 2, and 3 ploughs could be restored; [there are] 7 acres of meadow; there has always been 1 mill. This is in the valuation of Thorpe [St Andrew]; and it is 2 leagues in length and 7 furlongs in breadth and [pays] 3ƒd. in geld.

The King

[Folio 141: NORFOLK]

DEPWADE HUNDRED.

Talconeston was held by Stigand for a berewick in Wymondham [as] 5 carucates of land; there have always been 16 villans and 21 bordars and 6 slaves and 4 ploughs in demesne. Then [there were] 14 ploughs belonging to the men, afterwards and now 5 [and] 12 acres of meadow. [There is] woodland for 20 pigs and there has always been 1 mill and 4 horses and 16 head of cattle and 50 pigs, 80 sheep and 15 goats. And [there are] 5 sokemen [and] 12 acres [of land] [and] there has always been half a plough. And [there are] 8 free men [with] 1 carucate of land, and 2 villans and 8 bordars. Then [there were] 3 ploughs, afterwards and now 2 [and] 8 acres of meadow. Then it was worth £10, now £20 blanched, and it is 1½ leagues in length and half in breadth and [pays] 10½d. in geld.

CLAVERING HUNDRED.

Toft [Monks] was held by Stigand for a manor TRE [as] 4 carucates and 20 acres of land; there have always been 14 villans and 18 bordars and 8 slaves and 3 ploughs in demesne and 8 ploughs [belonging to the men] and 20 acres of meadow. [There is] woodland for 80 pigs, and 1 horse and 4 head of cattle and 20 pigs and 100 sheep; and 5 sokemen with 1½ carucates of land; there have always been 5 ploughs and 8 acres of meadow. And Haddiscoe [is] 1 berewick of 220 acres of land; there have always been 7 villans and 4 bordars and then [there were] 2 ploughs in demesne, afterwards and now 2, and 4 acres of meadow. Then [there was] 1 plough, now half, and 100 sheep. And [there are] 4 sokemen [with] 80 acres. Then [there were] 3 ploughs, afterwards and now 2, and 4 acres of meadow. Then it was worth £10, now [£]24 blanched. And it is 1 league in length and 2 furlongs and 10 perches, and 1 league in breadth, and [pays] 10¾d. in geld.

Stockton was held by S[tigand] for a berewick TRE in Earsham [with] 2 carucates of land and 3 bordars. Then [there were] 2 ploughs in demesne, afterwards and now 1; there has always been half a plough belonging to the men, 12 acres of meadow, woodland for 4 pigs and 1 mill and 2 horses and 4 head of cattle and 4 pigs. And [there are] 30 sokemen [with] 3 carucates of land; there have always been 8 ploughs and 16 acres of meadow. And in

[Folio 141v: NORFOLK]

the same [place] [there is] 1 church [with] 65 acres [of land], and 3 bordars and 12 sokemen [with] 25 acres; there have always been 3 ploughs and 6 acres of meadow. There belong also to Stockton 10 sokemen [with] 2½ carucates of land; there have always been 6 bordars and 7½ ploughs and 8 acres of meadow. [There is] woodland for 16 pigs. And [there are] 21 sokemen in "Iarpestuna" [with] 120 acres. Then [there were] 8 ploughs, now 5, and 5 acres of meadow. And 8 free men were added to this manor and they have 12 acres [of land] and half a plough.

In Ellingham [there are] 5 sokemen [with] 15 acres [of land] and half a plough, and 1 church with 24 acres.

In Gillingham [there are] 12 free men, 3 carucates of land and 9 bordars. Then [there were] 8 ploughs, now 5, 12 acres of meadow, woodland for 8 pigs and 1 church [with] 30 acres of free land. Of these, 9 belonged to the predecessor of Ralph de Beaufour in commendation TRE and 1 to Æthelwig of Thetford and 1½ to the Abbot of St Edmund and a half to Stigand. In the same [place] [there are] 4 free men [with] 15 acres and half a plough. Stigand had the soke TRE and they have been added to the farm of Earsham; and all this is in the rental of Earsham. The whole of Stockton is 2 leagues in length and 1 league in breadth and [pays] 5s. 4d. in geld whoever holds there.

In Raveningham [there are] 3 free men [with] 30 acres of land and 1 plough and half an acre of meadow, and it is in the valuation of Toft [Monks]. In the same [place] is 1 free man [with] 60 acres of land which he held in pledge from many men; there has always been 1 plough and 27 bordars [and] 1 acre of meadow and it is worth 20s.

In Thurlton [there is] 1 free man [with] 20 acres and half a plough and 1 acre of meadow and he is worth 2s. In the same [place] [there are] 2 free men, 10 acres and 2 bordars, and half a plough and 1 acre of meadow and they are worth 16d. In Thurlton [there is] 1 free man belonging to the predecessor of Ralph de Beaufour and he has 8 acres and is worth 12d.

[Folio 142: NORFOLK]

Lands of the Bishop of Bayeux.

Freebridge Hundred
and a half.

In [Gayton] Thorpe [there were] 2 free men TRE with 60 acres of land. There has always been 1 villan and 1 bordar and 1 acre of meadow; there has always been 1 plough; and it is worth 6s. 8d.; one of these men was in commendation only to the predecessor of Roger Bigod. This all belongs to Snettisham. All [Gayton] Thorpe is 8 furlongs in length and 4 in breadth and pays 8d. in a 20s. geld.

Grimston was held by Stigand TRE [as] 3 carucates of land. Then [there were] 16 villans, afterwards and now 8; there have always been 13 bordars; then [there was] 1 slave [and] 28 acres of meadow. Then [there were] 2 ploughs in demesne, afterwards and now 1. Then [there was] 1 plough belonging to the men, afterwards and now half, and 3 mills; there has always been 1 horse. Then there were 3 head of cattle, now 4; there have always been 60 sheep. Here belong 14 sokemen with 1 carucate of land [and] there has always been 1 plough. then and afterwards it was worth 100s., now £7. All Grimston is 1½ leagues in length and in breadth and pays 2s. in a 20s. geld.

Harpley was held by Stigand TRE for 1 berewick in Snettisham [as] 2 carucates of land; there have always been 2 villans and 9 bordars. Then [there were] 2 ploughs in demesne, now 1; and [there are] 5 sokemen [with] 12 acres of land. Then [there were] 2 ploughs belonging to the men, now 1½. Then it was worth 40s., now 80. This Hugh de Port holds.

Snettisham was held by Stigand TRE [for] 8 carucates of land; there have always been

[Folio 142v: NORFOLK]

20 villans and 12 bordars. Then [there were] 6 slaves, afterwards and now 3, and 30 acres of meadow. Then [there were] 4 ploughs in demesne, afterwards and now 2. Then [there were] 6 ploughs belonging to the men, afterwards and now 4, and 5 mills and 1 salt-pan and 1 fishery [and] woodland for 100 pigs; there have always been 4 horses and 38 pigs and 440 sheep. And [there are] 6 sokemen [with] 2 carucates of land and 10 villans, and 6 bordars and 1 slave and 10 acres of

meadow, and half a mill and 1 fishery. And in Shernborne [there is] 1 sokeman [with] 5 acres. To this manor belongs 1 berewick, Flitcham, [of] 7½ carucates of land; there have always been 18 villans and 14 bordars and 3 slaves and 8 sokemen and 4 mills. Then [there were] 3 ploughs on the demesne, afterwards and now there have always been 5 ploughs belonging to the men. [...] There belongs also 1 berewick, [West] Newton, [of] 1½ carucates of land and 6 villans and 3 bordars and 2 slaves and 2 ploughs in demesne. There have always been 2 ploughs belonging to the men, and 20 acres of meadow, and 2 sokemen [with] 16 acres of land and half a plough; there has always been 1 horse and 7 sheep. And in addition [there is] 1 berewick, [Castle] Rising, [of] 3 carucates of land; there have always been 12 villans and 38 bordars; then [there were] 4 slaves, now 3, [and] 14 acres of meadow; there have always been 2 ploughs in demesne, and 2 ploughs belonging to the men, and 7 sokemen [with] 24 acres of land; there has always been 1 plough and 3 mills and 12 salt-pans, and 1 fishery. And [there are] 3 sokemen [with] 60 acres of land; there has always been 1 plough and 1 sokeman [with] 60 acres and 1 plough, and 26 bordars and 1 plough and 8 acres of meadow and 1 mill and 1 salt-pan. And in Roydon [there is] 1 sokeman [with] 1 carucate of land; there have always been 25 bordars and 2 slaves and 6 acres of meadow and 1 plough in demesne and half a plough belonging to the men, and 2 salt-pans. And [there are] 8 sokemen [with] 2 carucates of land and 16 acres and 5 bordars and 2 ploughs and 1½ salt-pans. The whole was worth £50 TRE, afterwards and now £80 and 100s. The whole is 2½ leagues in length and half a league in breadth, whoever holds there, and pays 4s. in 20s. of the king's geld.

The Bishop of Bayeux

[Folio 143: NORFOLK]

DOCKING HUNDRED.

Docking was held [as] 1 carucate of land by 1 free man under Stigand; there has always been half a plough [and] 3 bordars. This is in the valuation of Snettisham. In Stanhoe [there were] 12 free men under Stigand TRE; then [there were] 4 carucates of land and 4 ploughs, afterwards and now 3. In [Bircham] Tofts 4 carucates of land were held by 1 free man under Stigand TRE; then [there were] 2 ploughs in demesne, afterwards and now [there was] 1; there have always been 8 villans and 5 bordars. This is in the valuation of Snettisham. All this is 1 league in length and 4 furlongs in breadth and pays 10d. in a 20s. geld. And the whole of Stanhoe is 1 league in length and 4 furlongs in breadth and pays 14½d. in a 20s. geld.

NORTH GREENHOE HUNDRED.

In [All Saints or St Mary] Warham Stigand held 2 sokemen with half a carucate of land; there has always been half a plough, and it has always been worth 30d.

HENSTEAD HUNDRED.

In [Earl or Pigot] Framingham Roger Bigod holds 60 acres of land which Godwine held under Stigand TRE. Then [there were] 4 bordars and now 7. Then [there were] 2 ploughs,

afterwards 1½, now 2 in demesne. There have always been 3 oxen belonging to the men and 4 sokemen and a half with 16 acres of land and 4 acres of meadow. They have always ploughed with 3 oxen. And in Yelverton [there is] 1 sokeman and a half with 16 acres. They have always ploughed with 3 oxen. And in Holverston [there are] 3 sokemen and 2 halves with 16 acres of land [and] there has always been half a plough. And in Kirby [Bedon] [there are] 2 sokemen and a half with 12 acres [of land]. They have always ploughed with 3 oxen; there has always been 1 horse at the hall. Then [there were] 8 pigs, now 28, and 6 beehives. Then and afterwards it was worth 20s., now 40. In Shotesham [All Saints or St Mary] Alfred, a free man, held under Stigand TRE 12 acres and 3 sokemen with 12 acres of land and 1 acre of meadow. There has always been 1 plough. And in Poringland [there is] 1 free man and 1 sokeman with 21 acres

[Folio 143v: NORFOLK]

[of land]. There has always been half a plough. In Bramerton [there are] 2½ acres of land; they are assessed in Cringleford. Holverston is 4 furlongs in length and 3 in breadth and [pays] 8d. in geld.

EYNESFORD HUNDRED.

In Weston [Longville] Stigand held 1 berewick TRE [of] 50 acres of land and 20 acres [of meadow]; there have always been 6 bordars, always half a plough, and it is in the valuation of Snettisham.

SOUTH ERPINGHAM HUNDRED.

In Wickmere [there are] 2 free men [with] 30 acres of land; there have always been 3 bordars and half a plough and 1 acre of meadow, and it is worth 4s. This is held by Tihel de Helléan.

HUMBLEYARD HUNDRED.

In Cringleford 1 carucate was held by Alfred the priest, a free man of Stigand's; there have always been 3 villans and 1 plough in demesne and half a plough belonging to the men [and] 8 acres of meadow; there has always been 1 mill and 17 sokemen [with] 1 carucate of land; there have always been 3 ploughs [and] 4 acres of meadow; and 3 free men and a half in commendation only TRE [with] 51 acres; there has always been 1 plough and 2 acres of meadow and 3 parts of a mill and 4 sokemen with 7½ acres under them. Then it was worth 20s., now 40. This Roger Bigod holds, and it is half a league and 2 furlongs in length and 6 furlongs in breadth and pays 11d. in geld, whoever holds there.

In Flordon [there are] 2 free men and a half of Stigand's [with] 25 acres. Then [there was] half a plough and 1 acre of meadow, and it is worth 2s. This Roger Bigod holds.

III. Lands of the Count of Mortain.

NORTH ERPINGHAM HUNDRED.

In Roughton TRE Wulfnoth held 1 carucate

The Count of Mortain

of land; there have always been 2½ villans and 5 bordars and 1 plough in demesne, and 1½ ploughs belonging to the men [and] woodland for 8 pigs, and 2 acres of meadow [and] there has always been 1 mill. Then [there was] 1 horse and now [the same] and 3 head of cattle; then [there were] 5 pigs and now 20 sheep and 12 goats. It has always been worth 20s. and is 9 furlongs in length and 5 in breadth and [pays] 10½d. in geld.

TUNSTEAD HUNDRED.

"Clareia" was held by Earl Harold TRE [as] half a carucate of land; there have always been 3 bordars and 1 plough and 1 acre of meadow, and it is worth 6s.

SOUTH GREENHOE HUNDRED.

Lands of Count Alan.

Swaffham belonged to the royal demesne and King E[dward] gave it to Earl R[alph]. Then [there were] 12 villans and afterwards 8, and now [the same]. Then [there were 26 bordars and ever since; when he acquired it [there were] 3 slaves, and now [the same]. Then [there was] 1 plough in demesne, and when he acquired it 2 [and] now 4, and 12 free men used to dwell there. There have always been 8 ploughs among the men. [There is] woodland for 13 pigs, and 1½ mills, and 1 fishery [and] 1 horse was found then, now [there are] 2. There have always been 4 head of cattle. There have always been 12 pigs. There have always been 200 sheep; and it is 1 league in length and another in breadth and pays 16d. in geld. Then it was worth £8 and afterwards £16 and now [the same]; and besides that 20s. This land was acquired as 2 manors.

Narford, which Ælfheah held TRE, is held by Phanceon. [...] Then [there were] 8 villans and always have been. There have always been 12 bordars. Then [there were] 3 slaves; when he received it and now 1. Then [there were] 3 ploughs in demesne, afterwards 2 and now 3. Then [there were] 6 ploughs belonging to the men, and when he acquired it, and now 5; and 4 free men there held 1 carucate of land and a plough and 1½ mills and 1 fishery [and] 8 acres of meadow; and when he acquired it he found 3 horses, now [there are] 2. Then [there were] no cattle, now [there are] 7 head; then [there were] 16 pigs, now 35.

NORFOLK FOLIO 144V

Then [there were] 100 sheep less 6, now 86, and 5 beehives and it is 1 mile in length and 8 furlongs in breadth and pays 18d. in geld. Then and afterwards it was worth £4, and now 100s.

In Foulden Ribald holds [the land] which Alstan held, half a carucate. There has always been 1 plough [and] always 1 mill [and] 1 acre of meadow. It is valued with Swaffham. In the same vill 2 free men hold 1 carucate of land and under them 5 bordars and 1 slave and 2 ploughs [and] 4 acres of meadow. Then it was worth 20s., now 40s. It is measured with the land of W[illiam] de Wa[renne].

In Sculthorpe [there is] 15 acres and it renders 20d. In Palgrave Eadric held half a carucate of land. Then [there were] 6 bordars and now [the same]; then [there were] 1½ ploughs and now [the same]. It has always been worth 10s. In [North or South] Pickenham Ribald holds what Godwine held: 2 carucates of land. There have always been 6 villans and 3 bordars and 2 slaves and 2 ploughs, and the villans [have] 3 ploughs. [There is] woodland for 10 pigs, 8 acres of meadow, 1 mill [and] 1 fishery; and 6 free men have always dwelt there and have 1 plough. Then it was worth 30s., now 60s.

In the other [North or South] Pickenham the same Ribald holds. [There were] 9 free men TRE [with] 3 ploughs; now [there are] 7 free men and they have 5 ploughs and 2 bordars [and] 10 acres of meadow and it is 10 furlongs in length and 6 in breadth and pays 12d. in geld. Then it was worth 40s., now 50s.; and in [Great or Little] Cressingham he holds 1 villan [with] 10 acres. He is assessed above.

LAUNDITCH Hundred. In Mileham [there is] half a carucate of land and 6 acres in Stanfield which the son of Almær holds, which 2 sokemen of Stigand's held TRE; there have always been 3 bordars and 2 acres of meadow; there have always been 2 ploughs [and] woodland for 20 pigs and it is worth 10s.

FOREHOE Hundred. Costessey was held by Gyrth TRE [as] 4 carucates of land; there have always been 8 villans and 8 bordars. Then [there were] 4 slaves, now 1; there have always been 2

Count Alan

ploughs in demesne and 5 belonging to the men. [There is] woodland for 10 pigs, and 6 acres of meadow; there have always been 2 mills; there have always been 14 head of cattle and 1 deer-park and 27 pigs and 13 goats. To this manor belongs 1 berewick, Bawburgh, [of] 2 carucates of land; there have always been 6 villans and 6 bordars and 2 slaves; then [there was] 1 plough in demesne, now 2; there has always been 1 plough belonging to the men, and 4 acres of meadow; there has always been 1 mill. In [Honingham] Thorpe [there is] 1 carucate, a berewick of this manor; there have always been 4 villans and 3 bordars and 1 plough in demesne, and half a plough belonging to the men, and 4 acres of meadow; there has always been 1 mill.

To this manor belong 44 sokemen [with] 3 carucates of land. Then [there were] 12 ploughs, now 8, and 4 could be restored. In Barford [there are] 7 sokemen and a half [with] acres of land and 2 ploughs and 6 free villans and 5 bordars and half a mill and 2 acres of meadow. Then it was worth £20, now 45. And it is 7 furlongs in length and 6 in breadth and [pays] 13½d. in geld.

And Bawburgh is 5 furlongs in length and 4 in breadth and [pays] 8½d. in geld; [...] and [Honingham] Thorpe is 5 furlongs in length and 4 in breadth and [pays] 6½d. in geld. And the land of the sokemen is 6 furlongs in length and 5 in breadth and [pays] 13½d. in geld. And this is Easton [near Norwich];

and Honingham, which a certain one of these sokemen holds, is 6 furlongs in length and 5 in breadth.

In Wramplingham 15 acres of land are held by 1 sokeman of Gyrth's; there has always been 1 plough and 1 villan and half a mill, and it is worth 20s. Of this, Godric claims half a house for the king's fief; and to this the Hundred testifies.

In Brandon [Parva] [there are] 6 sokemen [with] 12 acres of land and 1 plough. This is in the valuation of Costessey. In Runhall [there are] 4 sokemen [with] 10 acres [and] half a plough.

In Carleton [Forehoe] [there are] 3 sokemen [with] 10 acres and half a plough. In Honingham [there is] 1 sokeman [with] 30 acres and 1 plough and 4 villans and 3 bordars. All this is in the valuation of Costessey. In Wramplingham [there are] 2 sokemen [with] 4 acres of land.

In Marlingford [there are] 2 sokemen [with] 16 acres [of land] [and] half a plough. In "Toketorp" Enisant Musard holds 30 acres which belong to the same manor; there has always been 1 plough and 4 villans and the fourth part of a mill, and it is worth 20s.

In the same [place] [there are] $1\frac{1}{2}$ carucates of land which [...] Toki held under Stigand [and] now Ribald [holds it] for a manor; there have always been 7 villans and 3 bordars and 2 ploughs in demesne and 1 plough belonging to the men; now [there is] 1 mill [and] 10 acres of meadow; there have always been 5 head of cattle and 2 pigs. Then it was worth 20s., now 30.

MIDFORD HUNDRED.

In [East] Tuddenham [there were] 10 sokemen of Gyrth's in Costessey TRE [with] 42 acres of land and 3 acres of meadow; there have always been $1\frac{1}{2}$ ploughs and they are in the valuation of Costessey. In "Appetorp" [there is] 1 sokeman of Gyrth's [with] 30 acres of land; there have always been 2 bordars and 1 plough and 3 acres of meadow [and there is] woodland for 15 pigs. [This is included] in the same valuation. In Yaxham [there are] 2 sokemen of the same [Gyrth] [with] 24 acres of land; there has always been half a plough. [This is included] in the same valuation. In "Baskenea" [there are] 12 acres of land; [there is] 1 sokeman of the same [who] is in the same valuation. In Flockthorpe [there is] 1 sokeman of Harold's belonging in Costessey [with] 30 acres of land, and 2 slaves, and 1 plough, and 2 acres of meadow; and he is worth 5s.

Phanceon holds Westfield which St Æthelthryth held TRE [as] 1 carucate of land. There were always 8 villans and 8 bordars. There has always been 1 plough in demesne and 2 ploughs belonging to the men, 3 acres of meadow [and] 1 mill. Then it was worth 60s., now 40s., and it is 6 furlongs in length and 6 in breadth, and [pays] 6d. in geld.

BROTHERCROSS HUNDRED.

In Syderstone TRE Ælfheah held 3 carucates of land. There have always been 14 bordars, always 3 ploughs in demesne and 2 ploughs belonging to the men [and]

Count Alan

4 acres of meadow. There has always been 1 horse. Then [there were] 4 pigs, now [there are] 16. Then [there were] 40 sheep, now [there are] 100. Then it was worth 60s., now the same; and it is 10 furlongs in length and 8 in breadth and [pays] 13d. in geld. The same [Phanceon] holds [it].

In [East or West] Rudham there is a berewick [belonging] to this manor of half a carucate of land and half a plough, and it is in the valuation of Syderstone. And the same [Phanceon] holds it.

HOLT HUNDRED.

In Briningham Geoffrey holds what Thorbiorn, a freeman who was commended to Harold, held TRE: 30 acres. There has always been 1 villan and 1 bordar and 1 plough. [There is] woodland for 3 pigs, [and] 2 acres of meadow. Then it was worth 10s., now 5s.

In Bale [there is] 1 freeman of Harold's with half a carucate of land, and 1 bordar. There has always been half a plough. He has always been worth 3s., and the same [Geoffrey] holds [him].

NORTH GREENHOE HUNDRED.

In [Field] Dalling Count Alan holds 1 sokeman with half a carucate of land, and he was a man of Harold's TRE; there have always been 6 bordars [and] 2 acres of meadow; there has always been half a plough; it has always been worth 7s. The same [count] holds [it]. And in Warham [All Saints or St Mary] and in Holkham and in Wells [-next-the-Sea] Count Alan holds 11 sokemen with 2 carucates of land and 6 bordars [and] 1 acre of meadow; then it was worth 40s., and now [the same]. And there Eadwig, the king's reeve, claims 1 man with 30 acres, and to this the Hundred testifies.

HOLT HUNDRED.

Hunworth was held by Æthelstan TRE and now [he holds it] of Count Alan [as] 30 carucates of land, 8 villans, woodland for 3 pigs, half an acre of meadow [and] 2 mills; then they used to have 2 ploughs, now $1\frac{1}{2}$ ploughs. The whole of this is assessed in Saxthorpe. It is held by the same Ri[bald].

NORTH ERPINGHAM HUNDRED.

In Matlask Estan, a free man of Earl [Harold] held 16 acres of land TRE. There have always been 2 bordars, and with 2 oxen;

it is assessed in Saxthorpe. The same [Ribald] holds it. In Suffield Gunni held 1 free man of Ralph the staller TRE [with] half a carucate of land. There have always been 4 bordars and half a plough in demesne and half belonging to the men, and half an acre of meadow. In Gunton [there is] 1 sokeman with 12 acres of land and $1\frac{1}{2}$ [acres] of meadow. It has always been worth 6s.

In Matlask, where Count Alan holds [an estate], 1 man of the king's claims 16 acres of land by offering judicial ordeal or battle against the Hundred which testifies that they belong to the count; but a certain man of the count's is willing to prove that the Hundred testifies the truth, either by judicial ordeal or by battle. Ribald holds [it].

WEST FLEGG HUNDRED.

Wymarc holds [East or West] Somerton which Ælfric, a man of Harold's, held [as] 3 carucates of land TRE. Then [there were] 4 villans, afterwards and now 2. There have always been 11 bordars. Then [there were] 6 serfs and now 2. There have always been 3 ploughs in demesne [and] always 1½ ploughs belonging to the men, and 30 acres of meadow and 1½ salt-pans, and 9 free men [with] 2 carucates of land. There have always been 3 horses at the hall and 2 head of cattle; then [there were] 12 pigs, now 24; then there were 100 sheep, now 200. There have always been 10 pigs and 20 acres of meadow. And 2 halves of those [free men] belonged to St Benet of Hulme and Godram

appropriated them in the time of Earl Ralph. There have always been 3 ploughs; and in addition there are 7 sokemen [with] 67 acres of land. There have always been 1½ ploughs. Then and afterwards the whole of this was worth £5, now £9 with the sokemen who are in the Hundred; and it is 1 league in length and 8 furlongs and 10 [perches] in breadth and [pays] 30d. in geld. In Martham [there are] 2 free men and a half with 6 acres of land and 20 acres in demesne. There has always been half a plough. In Repps with Bastwick [there are] 1½ free men [with] 10 acres of land. There has always been half a plough. They are valued in [East or West] Somerton. In Bastwick [there are] 2 free men belonging in [East or West] Somerton [with] 12 acres [of land] [and] 1 acre of meadow.

Count Alan

[Folio 147: NORFOLK]

EYNESFORD HUNDRED.

[In] Weston [there are] 20 sokemen, 1 carucate of land and 16 bordars. Among them all [there were] 8 ploughs TRE, afterwards and now 5, and 4 acres of meadow; and these sokemen are in the valuation of Costessey. The soke was in the king's [manor of] Foulsham TRE; now A[lan] holds it because [Earl] Ralph held it.

Lyng was held by Ælfheah, a free man, TRE [as] 3 carucates of land; there have always been 15 villans and 2 slaves; there have always been 2 ploughs in demesne; then [there were] 3 ploughs belonging to the men, afterwards and now 2, and 9 acres of meadow. [There is] woodland for 300 pigs, and 1 mill, and 5 sokemen [and] 24 acres of land; there has always been 1 plough [and] 2 acres of meadow. And in [East] Tuddenham half a sokeman, 12 acres of land and 2 acres of meadow. There has always been half a plough. And in Bawdeswell [there is] 1 sokeman [with] 30 acres of land; then and afterwards [there was] 1 plough, now [there is] none. And [there is] 1 acre of meadow. Then it was worth £4, afterwards £10, now 100s.; and it is 1 league in length and in breadth and pays 4½d. in king's geld.

Wigwin holds Bylaugh which Earl Ralph held as 4 carucates of land TRE; there have always been 9 villans and 7

bordars; there have always been 2 ploughs in demesne, then [there were] 4 ploughs belonging to the men, afterwards and now 2, and 6 acres of meadow; [there is] woodland for 30 pigs, and 1 mill; now [there is] 1 horse, then [there were] 8 head of cattle, now 12; then [there were] 35 pigs, now 40; there have always been 100 sheep, now there are 3 beehives and 12 sokemen [with] 2 carucates of land; then [there were] 6 ploughs, afterwards 3, now 2; [there is] woodland for 30 pigs. And [there is] 1 free man [with] 30 acres of land; there has always been 1 plough and 1 acre of meadow. Here belongs 1 berewick which is called Beck [of] 1 carucate of land; there has always been 1 plough and 1 acre of meadow. Then and afterwards it was worth £3, now 100s., and it is 1 league in length and half in breadth and pays 4½d. in geld.

Godric holds Foxley which Lord, a free man, held TRE; now Alan +

[holds it] and Godric of him; [there are] 3 carucates of land [and] there have always been 10 villans,

[Folio 147v: NORFOLK]

and 3 of these dwell in Beck; and 21 bordars, and 2 of these dwell in Billingford [near East Dereham]. Then [there were] 2 slaves. There have always been 3 ploughs in demesne, and then [there were] 5 ploughs belonging to the men, afterwards and now 3, and 3 acres of meadow; [there is] woodland for 300 pigs. When he acquired it [there were] 2 horses, now [there is] 1 [and] now 14 head of cattle; then [there were] 30 pigs, now 22; then [there were] 40 sheep, now 100; then [there were] 60 goats, now none; then [there were] 5 beehives, now 7. And [there are] 2 sokemen in the same vill and 12 in Bawdeswell and they have 48 acres of land; there have always been 2½ ploughs; [there is] woodland for 10 pigs. Then it was worth 100s., afterwards £8, now £10; and it is 1 league in length and half in breadth and pays 8½d. towards the king's geld. Bawdeswell is 6 furlongs in length and 6 in breadth and [pays] 8½d. in geld, whoever holds there [and it is] separate from the measurement of Foxley.

In Swannington Ansketil holds what Thorbiorn, a free man, held TRE: half a carucate of land; then [there were] 8 sokemen, afterwards and now 5; there has always been 1 plough in demesne. Then [there were] 2 ploughs belonging to the men, afterwards and now 1, and 4 acres of meadow [and] woodland for 5 pigs; and it is worth 20s.

TAVERHAM HUNDRED.

In Taverham Thurbert, a free man TRE, held 1 carucate of land; there have always been 3 villans and 3 bordars, always 1 plough in demesne and half a plough belonging to the men, and 5 acres of meadow; [there is] woodland for 5 pigs. Then it was worth 20s., and now Haimer holds it. In Felthorpe [there are] 80 acres and 8 acres [sic] of land and 20 free men; there have always been 2 ploughs and 3 acres of meadow [and] woodland for 12 pigs; and it is in the valuation of Costessey. The soke belongs to the king and earl; and it is 10 furlongs in length and 5 in breadth and pays 8½d. in geld.

In Attlebridge [there were] 3 free men under Gyrth [with] 30 acres [of land]; then [there was] 1 plough, now a half, and 2 acres of meadow, and it is worth 4s.

Count Alan

[Folio 148: NORFOLK]

SOUTH ERPINGHAM HUNDRED.

Saxthorpe was held by Æthelstan under Harold TRE; now Ribald holds it [as] 1 carucate of land. Then and afterwards [there were] 20 villans, now 8. There have always been 8 bordars and 1 plough in demesne. Then [there were] 3 ploughs belonging to the men, afterwards and now 2, and 1 acre of meadow. [There is] woodland for 30 pigs [and] there have always been 1½ mills. There have always been 4 sokemen [with] 28 acres of land and half a plough. Then it was worth 20s., now 30. In Scottow [there is] 1 free man [with] 12 acres of land, and the same is worth 12d. The same [Ribald holds him].

TUNSTEAD HUNDRED.

Worstead was held by St Benet [of Hulme] TRE [as] 2 carucates of land [and] there have always been 4 villans. Then and afterwards [there were] 5 bordars, now 10. There has always been 1 plough in demesne and 1 plough belonging to the men and 2 acres of meadow; [there is] woodland for 6 pigs [and] it has always been worth 20s.

In Dilham and Panxworth [there are] 50 acres of land [held by] 1 sokeman of Ralph the staller's. Then [there were] 3 villans and now 3. Then [there were] 3 bordars, now 2½; there has always been 1 plough and 1 acre of meadow. Then it was worth 8s., now 5.

HAPPING HUNDRED.

Hickling was held by Godwine, a free man of Eadric of Laxfield TRE, and now Wymarc holds [it as] 3½ carucates of land; there have always been 9 villans and 11 bordars; then [there were] 3 slaves, now 1; there have always been 2 ploughs in demesne, then [there were] 2½ ploughs belonging to the men, now 3; [there is] 1 church [with] 20 acres and it is worth 20d. [There is] woodland for 60 pigs, 24 acres of meadow, and 1 horse and 5 wild mares and 4 head of cattle; then [there were] 12 pigs, now 24; then [there were] 100 sheep, now 200, and 2 beehives. And [there are] 9 sokemen [with] 1 carucate of land. Then [there were] 1½ ploughs, now 2 and 1½ acres of meadow. And in Stalham [there are] 11 free men [with] 100 acres of land in commendation only and half the soke; and the king has the other moiety of the soke. Then [there were] 2 ploughs, now 1, and 2 acres of meadow. And in Ludham [there are] 7 free men [with] half a carucate of land. The king and earl [have] the soke; there has always been 1 plough and 1 bordar.

In Ingham [there are] 4 free men with 12 acres [of land]. The king and earl have the soke. There has always been half a plough.

[Folio 148v: NORFOLK]

The whole of this was worth 40s. TRE and afterwards the same, now £9.

In the same [place] Eadric, a man of Eadric of Laxfield, held 3 carucates of land TRE; there have always been 9 villans and 14 bordars. Then [there were] 4 slaves, now 2 [and] there have always been 2 ploughs in demesne. Then [there were] 2½ ploughs belonging to the men, now 2; [there is] woodland for 60 pigs, [and] 24 acres of meadow; then [there were] 2 horses, now 1, and 6 head of cattle and 7 pigs and 350 sheep and 44 goats and 7 sokemen [with] 35 acres; there has always been 1 plough and half an acre of meadow. The same [holds it].

In Stalham [there are] 3 free men [with] 15 acres of land, of which Eadric had the commendation and half the soke and the king and earl the other moiety. Then and afterwards they were worth 100s., now £6, and the same holds [them]. These two manors Robert Malet claims because Eadric, his predecessor, had commendation only TRE of those who were holding [there] and he says his father was seised of them, and to this Roger Bigod testifies. And this manor is 2½ leagues and 12 perches in length and 1 league and 10 perches in breadth and pays 15d. in geld, whoever holds there.

In Waxham [there are] 2 free men; 1 was a man of Eadric's and the other a man of Eadric's and St Benet [of Hulme]'s with 161 acres of land; then as now [there were] 13 bordars and 2½ ploughs and 18 acres of meadow; and 4 free men [with] 10 acres of land and half a plough. Then it was worth 20s., now 35 [and there is] 1 church [with] 20 acres and it is worth 16d.

Ingham was held by Eadric, a man of E[adric] of Laxfield's, [as] 1 carucate of land. Then [there were] 3 villans, afterwards and now 2; there have always been 6 bordars and 1 plough in demesne, woodland for 6 pigs, and 4 acres of meadow, and 7 wild mares and 6 head of cattle and 12 pigs and 60 goats, and 16 free men in commendation only [with] 1 carucate of land and 20 acres; there have always been 2 bordars and 3 ploughs. Then the manor was worth 12s. and the free men 12s., and now the same; and it is 11 furlongs

Count Alan

[Folio 149: NORFOLK]

in length and 7 in breadth, whoever holds there, and [pays] 11¼d. in geld.

In Waxham 80 acres of land were held by the same Eadric, a free man; there have always been 12 bordars and 1 plough in demesne; then and afterwards [there was] 1 plough belonging to the men, now [there is] half and 6 acres of meadow and 6 pigs and 2 head of cattle and 100 sheep; it has always been worth 10s.; [there is] 1 church [with] 18 acres [of land] and it is worth 18d. To this Eadric added 2 sokemen of St Benet [of Hulme] in the time of Earl R[alph], and they have 3½ acres and are worth 6d.; and [there are] 8 free men in commendation only [with] 80 acres of land; then and afterwards [there were] 2 ploughs, now 1½ ploughs, and 3 acres of meadow and they are worth 5s. All this was held by Eadric when Ralph made forfeiture. The king and earl [have] the soke.

CLACKCLOSE HUNDRED AND A HALF.

In Beechamwell Ribald holds [an estate]; [there were] 60 acres of land TRE; then [there was] 1 plough, now half; then as now it was worth 5s. In Stoke [Ferry] the same holds 3 free men with 7 acres TRE and it is worth 12d.

FREEBRIDGE HUNDRED AND A HALF.

In Islington 1 carucate of land was held by Hrolf, a free man TRE; there have always been 6 bordars and 2 free men [with] 2½ acres [of land]; there has always been 1 plough and 3½ salt-pans and 16 acres of meadow and it is worth 20s. This land the Bishop of Bayeux had on the day that Earl Ralph forfeited; now Count Alan has half in his share and Ivo Taillebois delivered it [to him].

In the same [place] Geoffrey holds 1 free man [with] 1 carucate of land [and] 7 bordars; there has always been 1 plough. [There is] also 1 free man and a half [with] 10 acres of land and 1 salt-pan [and] 12 acres of meadow. The whole is worth 20s.

In Middleton [near Kings Lynn] Ribald holds 2 carucates [of land which] Earl Ralph had; there have always been 3 villans and 1 priest and 3 bordars; there have always been 2 ploughs and 18 acres of meadow. Then [there was] 1 fishery and it is worth 20s. In [East] Walton TRE Thorkil held 1 carucate of land; there have always been 6 villans and 1 bordar and 1 plough in demesne, half a plough belonging to the men and 1 mill and it is worth 20s. The same [Ribald] [holds] in Wicken [Ash] and Bawsey half a carucate of land held by Wulfgeat,

[Folio 149v: NORFOLK]

a free man, TRE; [there are] 7 bordars, 9 acres of meadow, half a plough, half a mill [and] half a salt-pan and it is worth 5s. The same [Ribald] holds it. All [East] Walton [is] one league in length and half in breadth and pays 18d. in a 20s. geld.

SHROPHAM HUNDRED.

In 'Baconsthorpe' [in Attleborough] Turstin holds half a carucate of land which Ketilbiorn, a free man, held TRE; there have always been 3 bordars and 2 acres of meadow [and] woodland for 4 pigs. There has always been 1 plough and it is worth 10s. The soke TRE was in Buckenham [near Attleborough].

Guiltcross Hundred. In [East or West] Harling Ansketil holds 4 carucates of land which Ulfkil, a free man, held TRE. Then [there were] 15 villans, afterwards and now 13; there have always been 4 bordars. Then [there were] 2 slaves, afterwards and now 1 [and] 8 acres of meadow; then as now [there were] 2 ploughs in demesne; then [there were] 7 ploughs belonging to the men, afterwards now 4; there as always been 1 mill; then [there were] 5 fisheries, now 1½ fisheries, and 4 sokemen [with half a carucate of land]. The soke [is] in Kenninghall; there have always been 1 bordar and 4 acres of meadow. Then and afterwards [there were] 2 ploughs, now 1 [and] there has always been 1 horse; now there are 4 head of cattle and 20 pigs; there have always been 70 sheep. Then it was worth £6, afterwards £7, now 100s. the whole is 1½ leagues in length and 1 league in breadth, who-ever holds there, and pays 27d. in geld.

EARSHAM HALF HUNDRED.

In Aldburgh [there are] 12 acres of land and half an acre of meadow and it belongs to Rumburgh [Suffolk].

DISS HALF HUNDRED.

Shelfanger was held by Cola, a free man of Esger the staller TRE, for a manor; now Hervey holds [it as] 2 carucates of land. There have always been 2 villans and 15 bordars. Then and afterwards [there were] 2 slaves, now 1. There have always been 2 ploughs in demesne and 2 ploughs belonging to the men. [There is] woodland for 40 pigs, and 3 acres of meadow, and 1 sokeman with 4 acres [of land]. It has always been worth 20s.

In Shelfanger Modgifu, a free woman of Algar's, holds 2 carucates of land. There have always been 3 villans and 15 bordars. There have always been 2 ploughs in demesne and 2 ploughs belonging to the men, and 1 sokeman with 4 acres [of land]. [There is] woodland for 40 pigs, and 3 acres of meadow. It has always been worth 40s.

Count Alan

[Folio 150: NORFOLK]

Shelfanger is 1 league in length and a half in breadth and [pays] 9d. in geld.

HAPPING HUNDRED.

In Happisburgh [there were] 2 free men [with] 100 acres of land TRE. Of these 100 acres, 60 were in demesne of Happisburgh when R[alph] forfeited, but Eadric seized them and vouches to warranty Ivo Taillebois and his associ-ates and gave pledge of this; and he has 5 bordars and 1 plough and 60 acres, and they are worth 6s.; and [the other] 40 acres are worth 4s. In Ludham Eadric, a free man of Eadric of Laxfield, held TRE 60 acres of land and 4 bordars and half a plough and 2½ acres of meadow and 11 free men and 80 acres of land.

In Catfield [there is] 1 free man [with] 5 acres and he is worth 6d. In Ludham [there is] 1 carucate of land [held by] 19 sokemen of St Benet [of Hulme]'s TRE, and this Eadric, a man of Count Alan's, seized in the time of Earl R[alph], and was seised of it when the division of land was made between the king and the earl; and it has 1½ ploughs [and] 4 acres of meadow and is worth 10s. In Palling the same Eadric seized 1 free man with 30 acres of land in the time of Earl R[alph] and he has half a plough and is worth 2s.

HUMBLEYARD HUNDRED.

Hethersett was held by Ulf, a thegn, TRE; now Ribald holds [it as] 3 carucates of land; there have always been 8 villans and 7 bordars. Then [there were] 3 slaves, afterwards and now 2, always 2 ploughs in demesne and half a plough belonging to the men. [There is] woodland for 40 pigs, [and] 12 acres of meadow. Then [there were] 7 horses, now 1; there have always been 5 head of cattle and 5 pigs and sheep and 7 beehives [and there is] 1 church with 60 acres and it is worth 5s.; and another church [with] 8 acres [of land] and it is worth 8d.; and 80 sokemen less 3 [with] 4 carucates of land. Then [there were] 10 ploughs and afterwards and now 7; 10 acres of meadow [and] 1 mill; and 2 free men in commendation only with 60 acres of land and Earl R[alph] [had] the soke. There has always been 1 villan and 5 bordars and 2 ploughs and 5 acres of meadow. Then and afterwards it was worth £8, now 10, and it is 1 league in length and a half in breadth and [pays] 26¾d. in geld.

In Dunston [there is] 1 free

man of Harold's [with] 30 acres [of land] and 4 bordars; there has always been half a plough and 3 acres of meadow and the third part of 1 mill and 2 free men and a half in commendation only; the king and earl have the soke; and they have 14 acres, always 1 plough and they are worth 5s. In Earlham [there is] 1 free man of Eadric, the predecessor of R[obert] Malet, with 30 acres and 5 bordars; there has always been 1 plough and 4 sokemen with 15 acres of land; there has always been half a plough and 1 mill and 8 acres of meadow. Then it was worth 8s., now 12. In Flordon [there is] 1 free man [of] Gyrth's [with] 7 acres of land, and 1 villan with 5 acres and 2 oxen, and he is in the valuation of Costessey.

In Cringleford R[oger] Bigod holds 1 free man of Stigand's [with] 15 acres of land and 2 bordars; and [there are] 2 free men [with] 7½ acres [of land]; there has always been half a plough and 1½ acres of meadow and the eighth part of a mill and it is worth 3s.

DEPWADE HUNDRED.

In Carleton [Rode] [there are] 14 free men with 95 acres [of land]. Then [there were] 1½ ploughs, now 2, and 2 acres of meadow. In Kettleton [there are] 3 free men [with] 73 acres and 3 bordars. Then [there were] 2 ploughs, afterwards and now 1½ ploughs, and 4 acres of meadow. In Wacton [there were] 2 free men [with] 28 acres of land, then half a plough, and 2 free men with 20 acres and half a plough [and] 2½ acres of meadow. In Tibenham [there is] 1 free man [with] 30 acres [of land] and 1 acres of meadow. In Aslacton [there is] 1 sokeman [with] 6 acres. In Moulton [St Michael] [there are] 6 free men [with] 57 acres [of land] and half a plough and 3 acres of meadow. In Stratton [there are] 8 free men [with] 100 acres and 1 plough and 1 acres of meadow. In Tasburgh [there are] 6 sokemen [with] 21 acres and 1 acres of meadow and half a plough. One of these was the man of the predecessor of Roger Bigod, and Earl R[alph] held him when he forfeited. In Swanton [there are] 2 sokemen [with] 7 acres [of land] and half a plough. In Middleton [in Forncett] [there is] 1 free man and a half [with] 12½ acres and half a plough and 2 acres of meadow. This all is in the valuation of Costessey.

In Morningthorpe [there is] 1 free man [with] 33 acres [of land] and 7 bordars and 1 plough

Count Alan

and 2 acres of meadow and he is worth 4s. In Stratton [St Mary or St Michael] [there is] 1 free man [with] 25 acres and half a plough and 1 acre of meadow and he is worth 2s. In the same [place there is] 1 free man [with] 91 acres and 3 villans and 5 bordars; then [there were] 1½ ploughs, now 1, and 4 acres of meadow. In the same [place there are] 7 sokemen [with] 27 acres. In the same [place there are] 15 free men [with]

17 acres and half a plough and they are worth 8s.; and the fifth part of a mill. All Stratton [St Mary or St Michael] is 2 leagues and 6 furlongs in length [and] 1 league and 4 furlongs in breadth and [pays] 25d. in geld. In Tasburgh [there is] 1 free man [with] 30 acres [of land] and half a plough and 2 acres of meadow; he is worth 2s.

CLAVERING HUNDRED.

In Thurlton [there is] 1 free man [with] 10 acres and 2 sokemen [with] 4 acres and it is worth 16d.

Lands of Count Eustace.

FREEBRIDGE HUNDRED AND A HALF.

[Great or Little] Massingham was held by Ordgar, a freeman, TRE [as] 4 carucates of land; always [there were] 5 villans and 5 bordars and 2 acres of meadow. Then and afterwards 2 ploughs on the demesne, now 3; then and now 1 plough belonging to the men, and the fourth part of a salt-pan. Here belongs 1 sokeman [with] 12 acres of land. Then 24 sheep, now 260, and 23 pigs. Then and afterwards it was worth 20s., now 50. And 20 sokemen of Harold's [are] in [Great or Little] Massingham with 2½ carucates of land; always 5 bordars. Then and afterwards 6 ploughs, now 3, and they are worth 50s. These men were delivered as Harold held them. Now the whole of this is held by Guy d'Anjou. The whole is 1 league in length and a half in breadth and pays 8d. for a geld of 20s.

Anmer was held by Ordgar a freeman TRE [as] 2 carucates of land; always [there were] 1 villan and 6 bordars, then 4 slaves and 3 parts of one acre [of meadow]; always 4 ploughs in demesne and half a plough belonging to the men, and 1 fishery and half a salt-pan. Then 11 pigs,

now 8. Then 100 sheep, now 80. Then and afterwards it was worth 40s., and now [the same]. And 6 free men with 1 carucate and 2 bordars; always 1 plough and 1 salt-pan, and they are worth 15s. 4d. These free men he claims of the king's gift. The whole is half a league in length and 5 furlongs in breadth and pays 4½d. of 20s. geld. And 3 sokemen with 30 acres which Osmund holds by livery and 1 sokeman with 8 acres and they are worth 5s.

DOCKING HUNDRED.

Fring, 1 carucate of land, was held by Ordgar, a freeman, TRE and 1 plough in demesne; always 3 ploughs belonging to the men and 4 villans and 6 bordars and 1 acre of meadow; now 16 pigs, then 100 sheep, now 106. Then and afterwards it was worth 40s., now 60. And 1 free man [with] 1½ carucates of land TRE. Then 1½ ploughs, afterwards and now 1 plough and 7 bordars. And 1 sokeman [with] 30 acres; and it is worth 20s. And 1 sokeman [with] 15 acres. The whole is half a league in length and a half in breadth, whoever holds there, and pays 27d. of a 20s. geld.

EYNESFORD HUNDRED.

[Great or Little] Witchingham was held by Godwine, a free-man, TRE [as] 2 carucates of land; always [there were] 2 villans and 18 bordars and 3 serfs; always 2 ploughs in demesne, and 3 ploughs belonging to the men and 3 acres of meadow and 2 mills and 2 horses and 12 head of cattle and 24 pigs and 80 sheep and 4 beehives; and 8 sokemen with 20 acres of land, the soke of whom is in Foulsham, but the count holds [it]; always 2 ploughs and 1 acre of meadow. Then and afterwards it was worth 100s., now £7.

HUMBLEYARD HUNDRED.

In Nayland [are] 11 freemen of Stigand's [with] 50 acres; always 1½ ploughs and 5 acres of meadow; and they are worth 10s.

DEPWADE HUNDRED.

Ashwellthorpe was held by a thegn of Stigand's [as] 3 carucates of land; always 12 villans. Then 10 bordars, now 15. Then 4 serfs, now 3; always 3 ploughs in demesne; then 7 ploughs [belonging to the men], now 5; 30 acres of meadow, woodland for 30 pigs.

Count Eustace

[Folio 152: NORFOLK]

then 1 horse, then 16 head of cattle. Then 40 pigs, now 17. Then 24 sheep; then 34 goats, now 40, and 8 beehives. Then it was worth 100s., now £6, and is 1½ leagues in length and 5 furlongs in breadth, and [pays] 6ƒd. in geld.

the Lands of Earl Hugh.

SHROPHAM HUNDRED.

Richard holds SHROPHAM which was held by Anund, a free man, TRE [as] 2 carucates of land; always [there were] 4 villans and 13 bordars and 2 serfs and 20 acres of meadow; always 2 ploughs in demesne and 1 plough belonging to the men, and 2 mills and the fourth part of 2 mills. Then 1 ox, now 2. Then 10 pigs, now 6. Then 30 sheep, now 29, and 2 sokemen [with] 1 acre of land and the fourth part of 1 acre. Then it was worth 60s. and now the same but it renders 80. The whole is 1 league in length and half in breadth and [pays] 18d. in geld. The soke [was] the king's in Buckenham [near Attleborough] TRE and always until Walter de Dol had [it] of the gift of Ralph, as Godric says. In Snetterton 40 acres of land were held by the same, and 1 bordar and half an acre of meadow; then half a plough.

HOLT HUNDRED.

Weybourne was held by Hagni TRE, now Ranulf holds [it as] 2 carucates of land. Always [there were] 9 villans and 30 bordars and 5 slaves, always 2 ploughs in demesne, and 4 belonging to the men. Woodland for 10 pigs, 3 acres of meadow, 2 mills. Then 8 head of cattle, now 10; then 26 pigs, now 28. Then 60 sheep, now 48. Then 47 goats, now 36.

Then it was worth £4, now 7, and it is 1 league and 3 furlongs in length and 1 league in breadth, and [pays] 18d. in geld.

In S Asgot held 3 carucates of land TRE. Then [there were] 2 villans, now 1. Then

[Folio 152v: NORFOLK]

13 bordars, now 22. Then 4 slaves, now 6. Then and after-wards 3 ploughs in demesne, now 2. Then and afterwards 4 ploughs belonging to the men; 1 acre of meadow, always 1 horse. Then 3 head of cattle, now 4. Then 11 pigs, now 5. Then 40 sheep, now 18. Then it was worth 40s., now 60s. and it is 1½ leagues in length and 1 in breadth, and [pays] 18d. in geld. The same [Ranulf] holds [this].

LODDON HUNDRED.

Waring held Hedenham which Algar, a thegn of Stigand's, held TRE for a manor [of] 2 carucates of land. Always [there were] 5 villans and 9 bordars. Then 6 slaves, afterwards and now none. Then 3 ploughs in demesne, afterwards none, now 2. Then and afterwards 1½ ploughs belonging to the men, now 2, and 12 acres of meadow. Then 1 mill, and now 2 head of cattle, now 12 pigs, now 40 goats. And under him [are] 20 freemen in commendation [with] half a carucate of land. Then 3 ploughs, afterwards none, now 4; and 4 acres of meadow. In Seething [were] 9 freemen and 4 halves belonging to Stigand TRE and Walter de Dol removed them and added them to Hedenham and they have half a carucate of land. Then 1 plough, afterwards none, now 1.

In Woodton 2 free men and a half of whom Algar had commendation, [with] half a carucate. Always [there were] 2 villans and 1 bordar. Then 1 plough, afterwards nothing, now a half, and 1 acre of meadow. Then and afterwards the whole was worth 40s., now £4. The soke [belonged] to Stigand; it is 1 league in length and 1 in breadth, and [pays] 8d. in geld.

DEPWADE HUNDRED.

Fundenhall is held by Roger Bigod which Burgheard a thegn held TRE [as] 2 carucates of land; always [there were] 11 villans and 11 bordars. Then 4 slaves, now 3. Always 2 ploughs in demesne and 4 ploughs belonging to the men; 20 acres of meadow; . Woodland for 13 pigs, now 1 horse and 9 head of cattle and 30 pigs and 48 sheep and 48 goats; and 1 sokeman [with] 1 acre. Then it was worth 40s.

Earl Hugh

[Folio 153: NORFOLK]

In the same [place] 2 carucates of land are held by Ælfric, a free man of Stigand's. Always [there were] 5 villans and 16 bordars; then 6 slaves, now 4; always 2 ploughs in demesne. Then 4 ploughs belonging to the men, afterwards and now 3, and 20 acres of meadow. Woodland for 30 pigs. Then and now 1 mill and 3 sokemen [with] 12 acres. Then it was worth 60s. And here belongs 1 berewick called Nayland [of] 30 acres; then [there was] 1 villan; always 4 bordars and 1 plough in demesne, and half a plough belonging to the men [and] 1 acre of meadow.

Woodland for 12 pigs. To this manor Walter de Dol added

2 free men who are in Hapton, 1 Stigand's, the other Gyrth's, and they have 90 acres; always 5 villans and 7 bordars. Then 3 slaves. Then 3½ ploughs, now 2, and 17 acres of meadow. He added also 3 free men [with] 8 acres. Then they were worth 12s. In Hapton [there is] 1 church [with] 15 acres. Of the whole of this Walter de Dol made 1 manor, and the whole together is worth £9. And it is 1½ leagues in length and a half in breadth and [pays] 4½d. in geld. Roger Bigod holds of the earl. And Hapton [is] 1 league in length and 5 furlongs in breadth and [pays] 6fd. in geld.

CLAVERING HUNDRED.

Kirby [Cane] was held by 1 thegn of Stigand's, Osmund the predecessor of Ralph de Beaufour, TRE as 1 carucate; now Waring holds it; [there is] 1 bordar; then and afterwards 1 plough and 3 acres of meadow; woodland for 3 pigs. And 4 free men in commendation [with] 15 acres and half a plough, and they are worth 15s. In Raveningham 1 free man of King Edward's [with] 30 acres and 1 bordar, and he is worth 5s.

[Folio 153v: NORFOLK]

VII. Lands of Robert Malet

FREEBRIDGE HUNDRED AND HALF.

Glosthorpe was held by Godwine, a free man, [as] 2 carucates of land TRE. Then and afterwards [there were] 8 villans, now 3. Then and afterwards 3 bordars, now 5; always 3 slaves and 30 acres of meadow. always 2 ploughs in demesne. Then half a plough belonging to the men and [the same] now; woodland for 8 pigs, and 2 mills. Here belong 13 sokemen with 40 acres of land; when he received it [there were] 2 horses, now 1; always 8 pigs; then 20 sheep, and it is worth 60s.

There belongs also 1 berewick [held] for a manor [called] Bawsey TRE [as] 1 carucate; then and afterwards [there were] 7 villans, now 5; always 12 bordars and 3 slaves and 40 acres of meadow, and 1 plough in demesne, and 2 oxen belonging to the men, and 1 mill. Woodland for 16 pigs and 1½ salt-pans; then 1 horse and now; and 14 pigs, 30 sheep and 50 goats. To this berewick belong 3 sokemen [with] 10 acres of land, and they are worth 30s. These 2 manors are 2 leagues in length and 4 furlongs in breadth whoever holds these, and they pay 12d. of a 20s. geld.

SHROPHAM HUNDRED.

Kilverstone was held by Eadric TRE [as] 2 carucates of land. Always [there were] 4 villans and 1 bordar and 4 slaves, 5 acres of meadow and 2 ploughs in demesne. Then and afterwards 1 plough, now half. Always 1 mill and 1 fishery. Here belongs 1 sokeman of the king's [with] 60 acres of land of whom his predecessor had commendation only and he claims the land of the king's gift. Then and afterwards 1 plough, now 2 oxen, and 2 acres of meadow. Always 2 horses and 4 cattle; then 300 sheep, now 300 less 12;

Robert Malet

[Folio 154: NORFOLK]

then 16 pigs, now 3. Then and afterwards it was worth 60s., now 80 and 1 plough could be [employed]. Walter de Caen holds [it] of R[obert].

HENSTEAD HUNDRED.

In [Nethergate or Thorpe> Saxlingham Eadric the predecessor of Robert Malet held 2 sokemen and a half with 66 acres of land; now Walter holds [them]. Then [there were] 9 bordars, now 13. Always 3½ ploughs among them all and 3 acres of meadow, and the eighth part of a mill. And under them 1 sokeman with 6 acres of land, always half a plough. Then it was worth 30s., now it renders 50s.

In Shotesham [All Saints or St Mary] Ulfkil, a free man of Eadric's in commendation, held TRE, with 30 acres of land. Then [there was] 1 bordar, afterwards and now 2. Then half a plough, but not afterwards or now. Always it was worth 5s. 4d. The same [holds it].

EARSHAM HALF HUNDRED.

In Shotford Humphrey holds [the land] that 1 free man of Eadric's held in commendation, with 43 acres of land. And always [there were] 2 villans and 2 bordars, always 1 plough among the men. Woodland for 15 pigs, and 3 acres of meadow. Always it was worth 10s.

DISS HALF HUNDRED.

Gissing was held by Alstan, a free man of Eadric's, by commendation only, [as] 60 acres of land; now William holds it. Always [there were] 4 bordars, always 1 plough in demesne, and half a plough belonging to the men, and 2 acres of meadow. Then and afterwards it was worth 8s., now 15.

In Burston Walter holds what Acwulf, a free man of Eadric's by commendation only, held, 26 acres and 2 bordars. Always [there was] 1 plough and 2 acres of meadow and 1 sokeman

[Folio 154v: NORFOLK]

with 2 acres of land. Always it was worth 8s.

In Thorpe [Parva] 80 acres were held by Eadric, a sokeman under Eadric the predecessor of Malet; now Hubert holds them. Always [there were] 3 villans and 3 bordars, always 1 plough in demesne, always 2 ploughs belonging to the men and 6 acres of meadow. And in Thelveton 2 free men of the same [with] 14 acres of land. Always half a plough. Then the whole was worth 10s., afterwards and now 20. The soke belongs to the king. Thorpe [Parva] is 4 furlongs in length and 3 in breadth and [pays] 3d. in geld.

In Burston Morcar, a free man of Eadric's, held 30 acres of land [and] 4 bordars. Then [there was] 1 plough in demesne, now half [a plough]. In the same [place are] 4 free men under the same [Morcar] with 26 acres of land. Always [there was] half a plough and 2 acres of meadow. Then and afterwards it was worth 8s., now 15.

Frenze was held by Eadric under Eadric for 1 carucate of land; now Hubert holds it. Then and afterwards [there was] 1 villan, now 2; then and afterwards 1 bordar, now 2. There has always been 1 plough in demesne. The men have always ploughed with 2 oxen; and 4 acres of meadow, now 1 mill. Then and afterwards it was worth 10s., now 15. It is 5 furlongs in length and 4 in breadth and pays 3d. in geld.

In Roydon [near Diss] 1 free man of Eadric's by commendation held 20 acres; now Walter holds them. There has always been half a plough and 1 acre of meadow. Then and afterwards it was worth 2s. 6d., now 3s.

In Shimpling [there are] 2 free men of the same by commendation only [with] 15 acres of land. Then [there was] half a plough, now 1 ox. It has always been worth 16d.

In Thelveton [there are] 2 free men of the same by commendation [with] 8 acres of land; and Walter holds them. Then and afterwards [there was] half a plough, now nothing. It has always been

Robert Malet

[Folio 155: NORFOLK]

worth 16d. In Semere [there is] 1 free man under Eadric by commendation only [with] 40 acres and under him 3 bordars. There has always been 1 plough among the men. Woodland for 4 pigs, and 2 acres of meadow. He was always worth 8s. The same [holds him].

In Gissing [there is] half a free man of Eadric's in commendation only with 11 acres, and under him 1 bordar; and he is worth 12d., and William holds [him].

In Burston [there is] 1 free man of Leofric of Thorndon in commendation [with] 20 acres; now R[obert] Malet holds him of the queen's gift; there have always been 2 bordars; and under him 1 free man [with] 6 acres; always half a plough; it was always worth 3s., and now the mother of Robert Malet holds [him].

LODDON HUNDRED.

Woodton was held by Ulfkil, a free man of Eadric's by commendation, for 30 acres and Walter holds it. There have always been 5 bordars. Then [there were] 2 ploughs, afterwards 1, and now 2. There has always been half a plough belonging to the men. Woodland for 4 pigs, and 1 acre of meadow; now 7 pigs; now 40 sheep. And there were 8 free men of Ulfkil's in commendation TRE [with] 30 acres of land. There has always been 1 plough among the men. Then and afterwards it was worth 20s. and now 30. It is 1 league in length and half [a league] in breadth and [pays] 15d. in geld. The soke is in the Hundred.

TAVERHAM HUNDRED.

HORSFORD was held by Eadric, a free man, TRE [as] 2½ carucates of land. Then and afterwards [there were] 5 villans, now 7; there have always been 5 bordars; then and afterwards [there were] 2 ploughs in demesne, now 1; then and afterwards 1 plough belonging to the men, now half [a plough] and 4 acres of meadow. Then and afterwards woodland for 160 ; now 60, and 1 mill; always 1 horse. Then 3 head of cattle, now 4, and now 17 pigs; then 30 sheep, now 92; and now 15 beehives. And then and afterwards 22 sokemen, now 21

[Folio 155v: NORFOLK]

carucates of land and 2 acres of meadow. Then and afterwards 1½ ploughs, now 1. Of 2 sokemen the king and earl have the soke, and over the others the 6 forfeitures. Then and afterwards it was worth £3, now 110s.; and it is 1½ leagues in length and 1 in breadth and pays 17¥d. [in] the king's geld.

Horsham [St Faith] was held by the same Eadric, a free man, TRE [as] 3 carucates of land; then and afterwards [there were] 12 villans, now 16; always 9 bordars. Then and afterwards 2 ploughs in demesne, now 1. There has always been 1 plough belonging to the men, and half an acre of meadow. Then and afterwards [there was] woodland for 160 pigs, now 60 and 2 mills. There has always been 1 horse; then 2 head of cattle, now 4; then 6 pigs, now 18; then 10 goats, now 35. And 19 sokemen [with] 1 carucate, always 1 plough. Of 3 the king and earl have the soke, and over the others the 6 forfeitures. Then and afterwards it was worth £3, now £4 10s.; and it is 1½ leagues in length and 1 in breadth, and pays 17¥d. [in geld], And in Beeston [St Andrew] [there are] 2 free men and in Sprowston 3, and they have 64 acres of land, and 1 bordar; there has always been 1 plough and 1 acre of meadow, and they are worth 6s. The king and earl [have] the soke.

TUNSTEAD HUNDRED.

Robert [Malet] holds Bacton which Eadric held TRE [as] 3 carucates of land. Then [there were] 14 villans, now 10, and 3 bordars. Then 4 slaves, now 3; always 3 ploughs in demesne. Then [there were] 5 ploughs belonging to the men, afterwards and now 1; 14 acres of meadow, woodland for 60 pigs, always 2 mills, now 2 horses and 1 ox. Then 8

Robert Malet

[Folio 156: NORFOLK]

[...] pigs, now 13. Then 180 sheep, now 50, and 16 goats; and 28 sokemen with 178 acres. Then and afterwards 10 ploughs, now 9½. And 14 free men and a half [with] 2 carucates of land and 33 acres; always 11 bordars. There have always been 10½ ploughs and 5 acres of meadow. It has always been worth 110s., and the free men are worth 40s., and it is 1 league in length and 1 league in breadth, and [pays] 15d. in geld.

In Dilham 1 carucate was held by Eadric TRE. Then [there were] 9 bordars, now 4. There has always been 1 plough in demesne and 6 acres of meadow and 1 horse; now [there are] 7 pigs, and 2 sokemen and a half [with] 50 acres. There have always been 2 bordars and 2 acres of meadow. Then it was worth 30s., now 35; and it is 11 furlongs in length and 6 in breadth, and pays 9d. in geld.

DEPWADE HUNDRED.

[At] Fritton [there is] 1 free man of whom his predecessor had commendation TRE [with] 30 acres and 2 bordars; now half a plough and half an acre of meadow; and he is worth 7s. and Warin the Cook holds him.

In Hardwick [there is] 1 villan with 5 acres and he is in the valuation of Eye [Suffolk]. In Fritton [there is] 1 free man of whom his predecessor had the commendation only TRE and he has 15 acres and 2 bordars and half a plough, and is worth 4s. 3d.

[Folio 156v: NORFOLK]

[BLANK IN MS]

[Folio 157: NORFOLK]

Lands of William de Warenne.

EYNESFORD HUNDRED.

Randolf holds Stinton which Withar, 1 free man, held TRE [as] 3 carucates of land; there have always been 9 villans, 39 bordars and 3 slaves. There have always been 3 ploughs in demesne and 8 ploughs belonging to the men, and 4 acres of meadow; woodland for 100 pigs, and 1 mill. There have always been 2 horses and 20 head of cattle and 40 pigs and 120 sheep and 27 goats and 3 beehives; 1 church [with] 14 acres. And 14 sokemen [with] 80 acres, always 4 ploughs, woodland for 10 pigs, and 1 acre and 1 bordar. Two of these sokemen R[alph] held when he made forfeiture and they had 12 acres and were worth 20d. In the whole it was then worth 100s., now £7, and it is 1 league in length and a half in breadth and pays 11d. towards the king's geld. Kerdiston was held by Godwine, 1 free man, TRE, now the same R[andolf] [holds] 2 carucates of land. There have always been 16 villans and 20 bordars; then [there were] 2 slaves; always 2 ploughs in demesne and 3 ploughs belonging to the men, and 8 acres of meadow; woodland for 40 pigs. Then [there were] 2 horses; now none; then 4 head of cattle, now 6; then 40 pigs, now 7, and now 60 sheep and 24 goats, and half a church [with] 7 . And 1 sokeman [with] 5 acres of land. And 1 free man [with] 30 acres of land. And half of 1 priest [with] 7 acres of land. Among them all there has always been 1 plough. It has always been worth 100s. And 1 free man was added to this manor TRW [with] 45 acres of land and 6 bordars; there have always been 1½ ploughs between himself and the men, and 1½ acres of meadow; woodland for 10 pigs, and the fourth part of 1 mill; and he is worth 20s. And all this is by way of exchange with 2 manors of Lewes [Sussex]; and it is 1 league in length and a half in breadth, and pays 15d. towards the king's geld, whosoever holds there.

[Folio 157v: NORFOLK]

Turold held Hackford [near Reepman] which Withar, 1 free man, [as] 1½ carucates of land; there have always been 6 villans and 10 bordars and 1 slave; always 2 ploughs in demesne and 3 ploughs belonging to the men, and 4 acres of meadow; woodland for 60 pigs. And 1 sokeman [with] 11 acres of land, and half a plough; 1 mill; when it was taken over 4 horses, now 3, and 10 head of cattle and 50 pigs and 60 sheep; now 5 beehives; and 1 church [with] 9 acres [of land] and 2 acres of meadow; it has always been worth 50s., and it is 5 furlongs in length and 3 in breadth, and pays 4d. [in geld] whosoever holds there. This is by exchange of Lewes [Sussex]. In [Wood] Dalling [there are] 5 free men. In Thurning [holds] 1 free man and 1 carucate of land; among them all there have always been 3½ ploughs and 2 acres of meadow [and] woodland for 8 pigs. Then it was worth 20s.,

now 30. It is by exchange of Lewes [Sussex]. The man of Thurning was paying rent to the king's [manor of] Sall, in the time of Earl Ralph and under R[obert] Blund, and [for] 1 year under Godric; now he is held by W[illiam] de Warenne; and to this the Hundred testifies, that he was a free man TRE.

Elsing is held by Wimer. Lokki the same for a manor [as] 1 free man TRE [with] 2 carucates of land; There have always been 6 villans; then [there were] 12 bordars, now 10; then 4 slaves. Then and afterwards [there were] 3 ploughs in demesne, now 2; then 4 ploughs belonging to the men, afterwards and now 3, and 7 acres; woodland for 300 pigs and 2 mills. There have always been 2 horses and 10 head of cattle, and then 40 pigs, now 14. There have always been 40 sheep and 12 beehives and 1 church [with] 18 acres of land and 1 acre of meadow. It has always been worth £4. This is of the fief of Frederick, and is 1 league in length and half in breadth and 1 rod and pays 8½d. towards the king's geld.

TAVERHAM HUNDRED.

In Taverham the same Toki, 1 free man TRE, held 1 carucate of land for a manor; there have always been 6 villans

William de Warenne

[Folio 158: NORFOLK]

and 6 bordars and 1 slave; then and afterwards [there was] 1 plough in demesne, now 2; then and afterwards 1½ ploughs belonging to the men, now 2, and 10 acres of meadow; woodland for 5 pigs, and the fourth part of 1 mill; the fourth part of a church [with] 3 acres, and 2 horses; then 4 cattle, now 7; then 8 pigs, now 40; then 40 sheep, now 300. Then and afterwards it was worth 30s., now 40s. This is of the fief of Frederick and is 1½ leagues in length and 1 league in breadth, and pays 17¥d. towards the king's geld, whoever holds there.

SOUTH ERPINGHAM HUNDRED.

In Coltishall Turold holds what 16 sokemen of Stigand's and Ralph the staller's held, 110 acres of land; there have always been 3 bordars, 1 church [with] 10 acres, and 5 ploughs, and 8 acres of meadow. Then it was worth 30s., now 40. Ralph gave to St Benet [of Hulme] his part of the soke with his wife, as the abbot says. [...] And the whole is 1 league in length and a half in breadth and [pays] 12d. in geld. In Mortoft there are in demesne 2 free men [with] half a carucate; there have always been 8 bordars and 3 ploughs and 4 acres of meadow and 1 mill. Then they were worth 20s., now 20. The king and the earl [have] the soke. In Itteringham [there is] 1 free man of Harold's [with] 15 acres; there have always been 3 bordars and 1 plough and 1 acre of meadow; woodland for 4 pigs, and half a mill, and [this] is worth 3s. In Wickmere [there is] 1 free woman of Harold's [with] 24 acres of land and 3 bordars; always 1 plough, and 1½ acres of meadow, and she is worth 5s. In [Little] Barningham [there are] 2 free men of Harold's [with] 30 acres of land; there have always been 5 bordars and 2 ploughs and the third part of a mill, and 2 acres of meadow; woodland for 20 pigs, and they are worth 13s. 4d., and 1 church [with] 9 acres. In Mannington [there are] 2

[Folio 158v: NORFOLK]

free men of Ralph the staller's [with] 17 acres of land; always 1 plough, woodland for 3 pigs; and they are worth 5s. In Irmingland Turold holds 1 free man, 8 acres of land [and] 1 plough, and he is worth 11d. In Corpusty [there are] 2 free men, 14 acres of land [and] there has always been 1 plough; and they are worth 11d.

In Tuttington [there are] 2 free men of Gyrth [with] 16 acres; there has always been 1 plough and 1 acre of meadow, and they are worth 16d. The soke was in Aylsham TRE.

In 'Crackford' [in Colby] Turold holds 10 acres which a free man [of] Gyrth held as of Aylsham; there has always been half a plough, and it is worth 3s. In Brampton the same [holds] 3 sokemen [...] of Harold's; the soke is in Cawston [and there are] 6 acres. There has always been 1 plough and 1 acre of meadow, and they are worth 3s. These sokemen Humphrey de Saint-Omer held as of the fief of his predecessor, and to this the Hundred testifies, and Drogo claims them. This land Humphrey held when he made forfeiture, and Drogo afterwards, but William de Warenne had it after him, and now has it in like manner.

In Irmingland the same holds 1 sokeman of Harold's; [the soke is] in Cawston, [with] 1 carucate of land; there have always been 5 villans and 1½ ploughs and 4 acres of meadow; woodland for 60 pigs, the third part of a mill; and it is worth 10s.

In [Great or Little] Hautbois [there is] 1 sokeman of Ralph the staller [with] 160 acres and he belongs to Hoveton [St John or St Peter] which Earl Ralph gave to St Benet [of Hulme] with his wife by the king's permission as the abbot says; there have always been 2 bordars and 1 sokeman and a half [and] 13 acres of land; then [there were]1 ½ ploughs, now 1; always half a mill [and] 4 acres of meadow; it is worth 5s. 4d. In the same place [there are] 2 sokemen of St Benet's [with] 175 acres of land; there has always been 1 villan and 2 bordars. Then [there were] 2 ploughs, now 1½ ploughs. It is worth 10s. This was delivered for 1 carucate of land. The whole is by exchange of Lewes [Sussex].

TUNSTEAD HUNDRED.

In Paston Turold 5 free men, 1 carucate of land and 30 acres; there has always been 1 villan and 19

William de Warenne

[Folio 159: NORFOLK]

bordars, always 5 ploughs and 2 oxen; [there is] woodland for 6 pigs and 2 acres of meadow; then [there was] 1 mill [and] 1 church [with] 1 acre, and it is worth 40s. The soke [belongs to] St Benet [of Hulme].

In Witton [near North Walsham] [there is] 1 free man [with] 30 acres; there have always been 10 bordars and 2 ploughs, and 4 sokemen [with] 20 acres, always 1 plough and 2 acres of meadow and 1 church [with] 10 acres. Then it was worth 15s., now 20. Of this Bishop Æthelmær had a moiety TRE and TRW and W[illiam] Malet likewise the other moiety.

In [North] Walsham [there are] 2 free men [with] 105 acres;

there has always been 1 villan and 4 bordars and 2 sokemen; always 4½ ploughs and 3½ acres of meadow; woodland for 4 pigs [and] always 1 mill. Then it was worth 30s., now 40. St Benet [of Hulme] had the soke and commendation TRE.

In [Sco] Ruston [there are] 4 sokemen of Stigand's [with] 10 acres; there has always been half a plough, and it is in the valuation of Coltishall. This is of the exchange of Lewes [Sussex].

In Barton [Turf] [there is] 1 free man [with] 16 acres, and it is worth 2s. St Benet [of Hulme] had the soke TRE and [it was] by the same exchange. Of all this the soke was St Benet [of Hulme]'s. Now W[illiam de Warenne] holds it with the land.

EAST FLEGG HUNDRED.

In Filby Turold holds 1 free man of Eastgar's: TRE [there was] 1 carucate of land and 9 acres, then 1 villan; there have always been 3 bordars and 1 plough in demesne and half a plough belonging to the men and 2 acres of meadow; then [there were] 3 salt-pans, now 2. Then it was worth 8s., now 16. This is of the exchange of Lewes [Sussex].

[Folio 159v: NORFOLK]

DEPWADE HUNDRED.

In Carleton [Rode] Almær, a free man TRE, held 30 acres of land under Stigand, and always 1½ bordars and 1 slave and 1 acre of meadow and 1 plough, and it is worth 5s. This is of the king's gift. All the churches are valued with the manors.

CLACKCLOSE HUNDRED.

In Marham Ralph holds half a carucate which St Æthelthryth held TRE. There have always been 3 bordars and 1 plough and 4 acres of meadow. Then it was worth 20s., and afterwards; now 26s. 8d.

In Fincham a free man held of the soke of the abbot of Ramsey 2 carucates of land TRE; now Hugh [de Wanchy] holds [them]. Then [there were] 24 free men and now, and 6 bordars and 4 slaves and 10 acres of meadow. There have always been 2 ploughs in demesne. Then [there was] half a plough belonging to the men, now 1. It has always been worth 60s. In the same vill there have always been 8 free men and 11 bordars and 5 slaves; there have always been 2 ploughs in demesne and half a plough belonging to the men [and] 16 acres of meadow. When he received it [there were] 200 sheep less 20, and now 100. There have always been 6 head of cattle, 24 pigs and 4 horses. Then it was worth 40s.; afterwards and now 60. In the same vill William Brand holds 2 carucates of land, which 1 free woman held TRE. There have always been 2 free men and 4 bordars and 4 slaves and 16 acres of meadow. There have always been 2 ploughs in demesne and 20 sheep and 3 pigs, and they are worth 30s. In the same vill [there are] 12 acres, and they are worth 12d. All this manor of Fincham is 1 league in length and a half in breadth, whoever holds there; when the Hundred and half pays 20s. in geld, this vill also [pays] 16d.

In Hilgay [there are] 22 acres of land which were held by 8 men TRE and they are worth 7s. 8d. But the Hundred testifies that it was for the sustenance of the monks of St Benedict [of Ramsey].

William de Warenne

[Folio 160: NORFOLK]

In Wimbotsham [there are] 1½ carucates of land and 1½ ploughs and 10 acres of meadow, and it is worth 40s.; and this land was held by 23 free men at the soke of St Benedict [of Ramsey].

In Denver Hugh [de Wanchy] holds 2 carucates of land and 3 acres which Ælfric a free man held TRE. There have always been 2 ploughs in demesne and 12 bordars; and 8 free men [with] 40 acres of land. Then and afterwards [there was] 1 plough, now 1, and 12 acres of meadow; he has always had 1 fishery. Then it was worth 60s., now 40. This he claims as of the exchange. The whole is 1 league in length and a half in breadth, and pays 8d. in geld.

In the same place Will[iam de Warenne] holds 2 carucates of land and 2 ploughs which 1 free man, Osmund, held TRE. There have always been 8 villans and 1 slave and 8 acres of meadow and 1 fishery. In Denver the same holds 4 free men [with] 71 acres which Osmund held. Of these the predecessor of Hermer [de Ferrers] had commendation only; and always he has had half a plough. In the same vill [there are] 5 free men and a half [with] 36 acres [and] there has always been half a plough. These Osmund held in commendation only, and St Benet [of Hulme] has the soke of 2 men. In the same place [there are] 3 free men which the same Osmund held [with] 2 acres of land and 2 bordars. The whole of this is worth 40s.

In [West] Dereham [there is] 1 free man [with] 30 acres; there has always been half a plough. In Fincham [there are] 2 free men [with] 3 acres of land. In Downham [Market] [there are] 30 acres that 9 free men hold [and] there has always been half a plough, and they are worth 12s. 4d. Of these 9 men St Benet [of Hulme] has the commendation and the soke, and William de War[enne] claims them in exchange.

In Outwell [there are] 6 bordars, and they have been valued.

FREEBRIDGE HUNDRED AND A HALF.

[West] Walton was held by Toki, a free man, TRE. Now Saint-Pierre [of Cluny] holds [it as] 4 carucates of land; there have always been 9 villans. Then [there were] 63 bordars, now 66. Then [there were] 14 slaves, now 8, and 100 acres of meadow. Then [there were] 6 ploughs in demesne, afterwards none, now 5; there have always been 6 ploughs belonging to the men. Then

[Folio 160v: NORFOLK]

[there were] 1½ salt-pans, now 7. Then [there were] 14 horses, now 8. Then [there were] 36 mares, now none. Then [there were] 24 head of cattle, now 23. Then [there were] 100 pigs, now 114. Then [there were] 700 sheep, now 800. To this manor belong 6 sokemen, 1 carucate of land and 10 acres [of land] and 30 acres of meadow; there have always been 17 bordars, and 3½ ploughs and 7 salt-pans. The whole is worth £17 10s. The whole is 4 leagues in length and 2 furlongs in breadth, whoever holds there, and pays 2s. of a 20s. geld. This is of the fief of Frederick.

[Castle and West] ACRE was held by Toki, a free man

TRE; [there are] 3 ploughs in demesne and 8 ploughs belonging to the men; there have always been 2 villans. Then [there were] 42 bordars, now 48. Then [there were] 8 slaves, now 3, and 8 acres of meadow, and 2 mills and half a salt-pan and 1 fishery. Then [there were] 6 horses, now 1. Then [there were] 8 head of cattle, now 11. Then [there were] 45 pigs, now 70. Then [there were] 160 sheep, now 540. To this land belong 2 free men [with] 1 carucate of land and 8 bordars. Then [there were] 2 ploughs, now 1, and 8 acres of meadow. Then it was worth 100s., now £9, and those 2 free men [are worth] 20s. The whole is 1 league and 10 perches and 1 league in breadth and 4½ feet and pays 8d. of a 20s. geld. To the church [belong] 30 acres.

In Gayton [there are] 16 free men [with] 2 carucates of land and 11 bordars; there have always been 3 ploughs, and it is worth 40s. This he has for the exchange.

In Gayton Ralph holds 1 carucate of land which Ælfgifu, a free woman, held TRE. There have always been 4 villans and 2 bordars and 1 slave. There has always been 1 plough in demesne and 8 acres of meadow, and 1½ salt-pans and 3 free men and a half [with] 60 acres, and 1 plough and 3 acres of meadow. And it is worth 30s. This [is held] for a manor.

In Grimston 1 carucate of land was held by Ælfgifu, a free woman.

William de Warenne

[Folio 161: NORFOLK]

TRE [and there are] 11 bordars and 7 free men with 4 acres of land, 12 acres of meadow; there has always been 1 plough in demesne, and the 7 free men [have] half a plough. The whole is worth 20s.

In the same place [there are] 2 free men with 1 carucate of land and 1 plough and 14 bordars. And [there are] 12 free men [with] 12 acres of land; there has always been 1 plough and 10 acres of meadow. The whole is worth 20s.

In the same place [there is] 1 free man [with] 1 carucate of land [and] there have always been 13 bordars and 1 mill. And [there are] 6 free men [with] 9 acres and 10 acres of meadow. Then and afterwards [there was] 1 plough in demesne, now half [a plough] and those 6 free men [have] half a plough. The whole is worth 30s.

In Congham [there is] 1 carucate of land, a free man [and] 14 bordars; there has always been 1 plough in demesne and half [a plough] belonging to the men, and ; and 12 free men, 15 acres of land and half a plough and half a salt-pan, and 8 acres of meadow; and it is worth 20s. The whole of this is for the exchange of Lewes [Sussex].

In Congham [there is] , 1 free man holds 1 carucate of land, 11 bordars and 1 slave and 10 acres of meadow; there has always been 1 plough in demesne; and 5 free men [with] 8 acres of land, half a plough, and 1 mill, and it is worth 20s. In the same place [there is] 1 free man and in Grimston 2 free men; all [hold] among them 1 carucate of land [and] 14 bordars; 1½ ploughs and 15 acres, and 11 acres of meadow; and 8 free men [with] 11 acres of land and half a plough and half a salt-pan. And it is worth 22s.

[In] Hillington 2 carucates of land were held by 2 free men

TRE; there have always been 5 villans and 6 bordars and 2 slaves, and 8 acres of meadow, and 2 ploughs in demesne and half a plough belonging to the men, and 1 mill. And William holds 1 carucate of this land. 1 free man always [held] 15 acres [and] half a plough. The whole is worth 60s. This is by exchange.

In Massingham William holds 1 carucate of land which Alflæd, a free woman, held TRE. [There were] always 3 bordars and 1 slave and 1 plough and it is worth 15s.

Of this his predecessor had commendation only and Harold the soke, and Reginald fitzIvo claims it for his fief, and Wihenoc was seised of it, and the father of Reginald, and Reginald himself, and to this the Hundred witnesses.

In Harpley Walter holds 2 ploughs in demesne which Toki held TRE and 2 ploughs belonging to the men, and 2 villans and 10 bordars. Then [there were] 6 slaves, now 3 and half a salt-pan; there has always been 1 horse and 4 head of cattle. Then [there were] 10 pigs, now 30. Then [there were] 180 , now 308. 12 sokemen belong here with 60 acres of land; there has always been half a plough. The whole was then worth 60s., now 70.

The whole is 1 in length and 5 furlongs in breadth and pays 8d. of a 20s. [geld] whoever holds there.

In Anmer [there is] half a carucate of land and 1 plough and 4 bordars which 1 free man held TRE; of this his predecessor had the commendation only. The whole is worth 5s. This land Guy [d'Anjou] demands [on the grounds] that it was delivered to his uncle, Osmund, and to Count Eustace, and the men of William de Warenne disseised them.

In Flitcham 4 free men held 1 carucate of land TRE; there have always been 5 bordars and 6 acres of meadow [and] always 2 ploughs, and it is worth 20s. This he claims for the exchange.

DOCKING HUNDRED.

Barwick; [there are] 2 free men, 1 was a man of Harold's, and the other [belonged to] the predecessor of Frederick in commendation only; and they have 1 carucate of land; there have always been 12 bordars, always 1 plough, and half a plough belonging to the men [and] always 1 horse. Then [there were] 30 sheep, now 160; [there is] [with] 10 acres. And [there is] 1 free man in commendation only [with] 60 acres of land and 2 bordars; there has always been half a plough. Then it was worth 15s., now 20.

GRIMSHOE HUNDRED.

Wilton was held by Ælfgifu TRE; there have always been 5 ploughs in demesne, and 16 villans [and] 24 bordars. Then [there were] 10 slaves, now 8; [there are] 12 acres of meadow, and 3 ploughs belonging to the men, and 6 fishponds. In demesne

William de Warenne

[there are] 7 head of cattle and 30 pigs [and] [...] 200 sheep. 8 sokemen belong here [with] 20 acres of land; there has always

been [...] half a plough. Then and afterwards it was worth £6, now 10. The whole is 1 league [...] in length and half in breadth, and pays 17d. [...] of a geld of 20s.

Feltwell was held by Ælfgifu TRE; [there are] 2 ploughs in demesne, and in Hockwold 1 plough in demesne, and in 'Rising' [in Feltwell] 1 plough in demesne. Between them all there have always been 16 villans and 18 bordars and 4 slaves and 4 ploughs belonging to the men, and 16 acres of meadow, woodland for 200 pigs [and] 30 goats; there have always been 2 horses and 6 head of cattle and 40 pigs and 100 sheep and 17 beehives.

In Rising [in Feltwell] [there are] 2 sokemen [with] 20 acres. Then [there was] half a plough, now 1. Then and afterwards it was worth £6, now £10.

In Feltwell [there are] 40 sokemen [with] 3 carucates of land, and 40 acres, 5 ploughs and 8 acres of meadow, and [this] is worth 70s. And Simon 1 sokeman [with] 1 carucate of land and 7 villans and 5 bordars and 4 slaves and 1 plough in demesne, and 3 acres of meadow and 1 plough belonging to the men, and it is worth 20s., and 1 church; this Godric claims as of the fief of Ralph which belonged to Stow [Bedon], and in respect of this 1 man of Godric is willing to undergo judicial ordeal. Over all these St Æthelthryth had the soke and all customary dues and commendation. And of these 7 were free with their lands, but the soke and commendation remained with St Æthelthryth. The whole was delivered to W[illiam de Warenne] for the exchange.

In Methwold [there are] [with] 3 carucates of land [and] there have always been 4 villans and 1 bordar and 4 acres of meadow. Then [there were] 4 ploughs, afterwards and now 3. Then it was worth 20s., now 45. Stigand [had] the soke; and they were made over for the exchange. Simon and Walter [hold] 2 carucates of land [with] 2 ploughs, and they are worth 40s.

[In] Northwold [are] 34 sokemen of St Æthelthryth [with] 5 carucates of land; there have always been 7 ploughs, and 8 acres of meadow. Then they were worth 60s., now 100. St Æthelthryth has the soke and commendation,

and all customary dues of 30 of the men only, and 4 were free. Their soke and commendation [belonged] [...] to St Æthelthryth.

In Mundford [there are] 7 sokemen [...] belonging to St Æthelthryth with all customary dues; [and] half a carucate of land and 1 plough, [...] and they are worth 10s. This also is by the exchange. In the same place [is] 1 free man of Harold's [with] half a carucate of land, 2 bordars [and] 2 acres of meadow; there has always been half a plough; and it is worth 10s. [This also is] for the exchange.

In Colveston [there is] 1 carucate of land, 1 free man of Harold's, 4 villans [and] 4 bordars. Then [there were] 2 slaves, 12 acres of meadow. Then and after [there were] 2 ploughs in demesne. A third could be [employed]; now there is 1, and there always has been 1 plough belonging to the men, and 2 mills and 1 fishery [and] woodland for 15 pigs; and it is worth 8s. This is for the castellany of Lewes [Sussex]. The whole is 5 furlongs in length and 4 in breadth and pays 5½d. in a geld of 20s.

In Ickburgh Roger holds 2 free men, [with] half a carucate of land, and 6 acres and 1 bordar and 1 acre of meadow. There has always been 1 plough, and it is worth 3s.

In Santon [there are] 5 free men [with] 2 carucates of land. Walter holds a moiety [with] 1 villan [and] 3 bordars. There have always been 3 ploughs, and it is worth 10s.

[In] 'Otringhithe' [in Weeting] [there is] 1 carucate of land, 3 free men [and] 3 bordars; there have always been 2 ploughs, and it is worth 5s. The same Walter [holds] the moiety.

[In] Weeting [there are] 9 free men [and] 5½ carucates of land; ; [there are] 15 villans and 2 bordars and 6 slaves, 13 acres of meadow [and] there always have been 6 ploughs. There is woodland for 5 pigs, half a Wshery, and 2 ploughs belonging to the men; they have always been worth 60s. Of 7 of these the commendation and soke belonged to St Æthelthryth, and of 2, the soke only. The whole is 1½ leagues in breadth and pays 14d. in geld.

'Otringhithe' [in Weeting] [is] 4 furlongs in length and 3 in breadth and pays

William de Warenne

4d. in geld. All this is of the castellany of Lewes [Sussex].

[In] Cranwich 1 free man of Harold's [held]; there have always been 2 ploughs in demesne, and 10 villans and 5 bordars and 3 slaves, and 4 acres of meadow. Then and afterwards [there were] 4½ ploughs belonging to the men, now 3; [there is] half a mill and half a fishery; woodland for 10 pigs, always 4 horses. Then [there were] 7 head of cattle; always 13 pigs, then 100 sheep, now 120, and 7 beehives; and it is worth 60s. In the same place the same William [de Warenne] [holds] 1 free man; St Æthelthryth [has] the soke and commendation; [with] 2 carucates of land; there have always been 2 ploughs in demesne, and 9 villans and 5 bordars and 2 slaves and 4 acres of meadow. Then and afterwards [there were] 4½ ploughs belonging to the men, now , and 2 ploughs in demesne, and half a mill and half a fishery; woodland for 10 pigs and 4 horses and 6 cattle and 14 pigs. Then [there were] 100 sheep, now 120, and 7 beehives; and it is worth 60s. The whole is 7 furlongs in length and 4 in breadth, and pays 9½d. of a geld of 20s. This [is] of the castellany of Lewes [Sussex].

SMETHDEN HUNDRED.

Heacham was held by Toki, a free man, TRE. There have always been 7 ploughs in demesne and 70 bordars and 6 slaves, and 12 acres of meadow and 7 ploughs belonging to the men; woodland for 100 pigs, and 3½ mills; 1 fishery; always 1 horse, 30 head of cattle, 60 pigs, 600 sheep. Here belong 35 sokemen, 1½ carucates of land; always 6 ploughs, 4 acres of meadow. Then it was worth £12, now 15. In the same place W[illiam de Warenne] holds 2 carucates of land which Alnoth, a free man, held TRE. There have always been 26 bordars and 2 slaves and 6 acres of meadow, and 2 ploughs in demesne, and 1½ ploughs belonging to the men, and half a

mill, and 1 salt-pan and 1 fishery, and 4 sokemen [with] 2 acres. Then [there were] 12 head of cattle, now 16. Then [there were] 30 pigs, now 40. Then [there were] 80 sheep, now 60;

and it is worth 60s. The whole is 1 league in length and half in breadth, and pays 4s. of a geld of 20s.

In Snettisham [there are] 7 sokemen of Stigand's [with] 2 carucates of land, and 11 sokemen of Stigand's [with] 20 acres, 4 villans, 15 bordars, 4 ploughs and 8 acres of meadow, and 1 mill, and half a fishery and 2 parts of a salt-pan. Then and afterwards they were worth 30s., now 50. This is by the exchange.

DOCKING HUNDRED.

In Fring [there is] 1 free man [with] 20 acres of land, and he is worth 16d. Of this his predecessor had commendation only. Stigand [had] the soke.

WAYLAND HUNDRED.

In Threxton Hugh [fitzGolde] holds 1 carucate of land and 4 villans and 4 bordars and a slave and 10 acres of meadow; there have always been 1½ ploughs in demesne and half a plough belonging to the men and 1 free man [has] 12 acres; and it is worth 30s.; and this belongs to Lewes [Sussex], and is 10 furlongs in length and half a league in breadth, and pays 15d. in geld, whoever holds there.

In Caston [there are] 3 free men [with] 1 carucate of land. Then [there were] 2 bordars, now 10, and 12 acres of meadow; there have always been 2 ploughs, and they are worth 17s. 4d. Over 2 the king and the earl have the soke, and the predecessor of John, nephew of Waleran, of the third. This belongs to the castle of Lewes [Sussex]. The whole is 1 league in length and a half in breadth and [pays] 11d. in geld.

In Rockland [St Peter] [there are] 4 free men [with] 1½ carucates of land. Then [there were] 7 bordars, now 17; 20 acres of meadow. There have always been 5 ploughs, always 1 mill, [and] woodland for 8 pigs, and they are worth 40s.; and it is 6 furlongs in length and 4 in breadth and [pays] 5d. in geld. This is for the exchange [of Lewes]

William de Warenne

[Little] Ellingham [there are] 6 free men [with] 80 acres of land. Then [there was] 1 plough, now 1½. Then[there were] 2 bordars, now 3. And in Scoulton [there are] 6 free men [with] 30 acres of land. Then [there was] 1 plough, now 1½ ploughs. And in Thompson [there are] 6 free men [with] 1 carucate of land. Then and afterwards [there was] 1 bordar, now 3; [there are] 12 acres of meadow. Then and afterwards [there were] 2 ploughs, now 2½ ploughs. The whole is worth 49s. This is by the exchange.

SHROPHAM HUNDRED.

LARLING is held by Hugh [as] 1½ carucates of land, but it was delivered for 1 carucate of land which a free man held TRE; there have always been 9 bordars and 3 free men, and

15 acres of land and 2 oxen and 1 bordar; always 2 ploughs in demesne, and 1 plough belonging to the men, and 8 acres of meadow. It has always been worth 30s.

In [All Saints or St Andrew] Rockland Simon holds 3 carucates of land which 1 free man, Broddi, held TRE; there have always been 2 villans and 12 bordars. Then [there were] 4 slaves, now 1, and 8 acres of meadow; always 2 ploughs in demesne and 1 plough belonging to the men; [there is] woodland for 6 pigs. Then [there were] 4 horses, now none. Then [there were] 8 head of cattle, now 5. Then [there were] 30 pigs, now 15. Then [there were] 100 sheep, and now the same. And in the same place the same Simon holds 6 free men and a half, the soke [was] in the king's [manor of] Buckenham [near Attleborough] TRE and afterwards, until William de War[enne] had it. They have always been worth £3 10s.

Besides this there were added to this land 9 free men and a half, 1 carucate of land, 54 acres. . There have always been 9 bordars and 8 acres of meadow; always 6 ploughs and 2 half mills. The whole of this is for 1 manor of Lewes [Sussex] and is worth £3 11s. Of 4½ of the 9 [free men] the soke and commendation was in the king's [manor of] Buckenham [near Attleborough] TRE and afterwards, until W[illiam de Warenne] had it; and the whole was delivered in the time of Earl Ralph. The whole is 1 league in length and a half in breadth, and [pays] 15d. in geld.

[Folio 164v: NORFOLK]

In Roudham [there are] 2 free men [with] 1 carucate of land and 3 sokemen and 5 bordars and half an acre of meadow. Then [there was] 1 plough, now 2, and it is worth 10s. The soke TRE was in the king's [manor of] Buckenham [near Attleborough], and [the land] was delivered in the time of Earl Ralph. Afterwards he retained the soke.

In Illington William [de Warenne] holds 1 free man [with] 1½ carucates of land; there have always been 7 villans and 10 bordars and 4 acres of meadow. And [there are] 6 free men [with] 22 acres of land; there has always been 1 plough in demesne and 3 ploughs belonging to the men. Then it was worth 20s., afterwards and now 30. The soke [is] in Buckenham [near Attleborough]. The whole is half [a league] in length and 4 furlongs in breadth, and [pays] 7d. in geld. And this is of the castle of Lewes [Sussex].

GUILTCROSS HUNDRED.

In [Blo] Norton Fulcher holds 1 carucate of land which 1 free man held TRE; there have always been 6 villans and 2 bordars and 1 acre of meadow. Then and afterwards [there was] 1 plough in demesne, now 1½ ploughs, and half a plough belonging to the men; half a mill, and 1 sokeman [with] 1 acre of land. Then and afterwards it was worth 20s., now 30. This is of the castle of Lewes [Sussex]. The soke [was] always in the king's [manor of] Kenninghall until William [de Warenne] had it.

In 'Wick' [in Garboldisham] William [de Warenne] holds 1 carucate of land which 1 free man held TRE; there have always been 5 villans and 10 bordars and 4 acres of meadow. Then and afterwards [there was]1 plough in demesne, now 2, always 1 plough belonging to the men; now 1 mill. Then it was

worth 20s., now 30; and [there are] 8 sokemen [with] 32 acres, there have always been 1½ ploughs, and they are worth 10s. This all was delivered for 1 carucate of land and is of the castle of Lewes [Sussex]. The soke [was] always in Kenninghall always until W[illiam] had it.

In Banham 1 free man, Leofsige, held 1 carucate of land TRE; there have always been 9 villans and 6 bordars. Then [there was]1 slave and 12 acres of meadow. Then and afterwards [there was] 1 plough in demesne, now 2; there have always been 1½ ploughs belonging to the men; [there is] woodland for 100 pigs; and it is worth 40s. And the same held 5 sokemen [with] 31 acres of land and 2 acres of meadow. Then

William de Warenne

[Folio 165: NORFOLK]

[there were] 1½ ploughs; afterwards and now 1 and it is worth 5s. The whole is 1½ leagues in length and 1 league in breadth, and [pays] 24½d. in geld whoever holds there. The whole is of the castle of Lewes [Sussex].

LAUNDITCH HUNDRED.

In Gressenhall Toki, a free man, held TRE [and] afterwards Frederick [held] 1½ carucates of land; there have always [been] 10 villans and 18 bordars. Then [there were] 4 slaves, now 1, and 4 acres of meadow; there have always been 2 ploughs in demesne, and 2 belonging to the men; [there is] woodland for 100 pigs. Then [there was] 1 mill, now 2. And there have always been 18 sokemen with all customary dues, [with] 1 carucate of land, always 3 bordars, and 4 acres of meadow. Then and afterwards [there were] 3 ploughs, now 2; always 2 mills, and 1 horse. Then [there were] 10 head of cattle, now 11, always 30 pigs; now 30 sheep and 30 goats. 1 berewick, Scarning, has always belonged here [comprising] half a carucate of land and 5 bordars and 1 acre of meadow; there has always been 1 plough in demesne and 1 plough belonging to the men, and 20 pigs and 4 cattle. Then the whole was worth 40s., now £4. The whole is 7 furlongs in length and 4 in breadth, and [pays] 7½d. in geld. Wimer holds it.

In [East or West] Lexham the same [holds] Ulfkil, a free man, held TRE [and] afterwards Frederick held for a manor; 2 carucates of land. Then [there were] 8 bordars, now 12; then 4 slaves [and] 2 acres of meadow; there have always been 2 ploughs in demesne. Then [there was] 1 plough belonging to the men, now 2; [there is] woodland for 30 pigs; there has always been 1 mill, and 12 sokemen [with] 1 carucate of land. Then [there were] 3 ploughs, now 2. In demesne [there were] 4 horses, now 3; 8 head of cattle, now 9, always 24 pigs and 200 sheep; it has always been worth 40s.

In Weasenham [All Saints or St Peter] 12 sokemen of Stigand's held 2 carucates of land TRE; now [there are] 6 sokemen more; now as then [there are] 4 bordars. Then [there were] 4 ploughs among the whole, of which 2 are in demesne, and 1 acre of meadow; there have always been 3 ploughs belonging to the men, now [there are] 6 head of cattle and 8 pigs and 60 sheep and 2 horses. Then it was worth 40s., now 60. This is of the exchange of the new land. The whole is 1 league in length and half in breadth, and pays 20d. in geld, whoever holds there. Wimer holds it.

In Kempstone [there were] 4 sokemen [with] 1 carucate of land under Stigand; there have always been 4 villans and 1 slave and 1 acre of meadow. Then [there were] 3 ploughs, afterwards and now 2½ [and there is] woodland for 10 pigs; it has always been worth 20s.

In [Great or Little] Fransham 2 free men held [land] TRE, of whom the predecessor of Frederick had commendation only. Afterwards Frederick [held], now W[illiam de Warenne] has it, and Gilbert of him; [it comprises] 1½ carucates of land; there have always been 4 villans and 8 bordars. Then [there were] 2 slaves and 4 acres of meadow; there have always been 3 ploughs [and] woodland for 60 pigs. Then [there was] 1 mill, now 1½: it has always been worth 30s.

[holds] Scarning; it was held by Fredegis, a free man, TRE [for] 1½ carucates of land; there have always been 4 villans and 6 bordars, 3 acres of meadow, always 1 plough in demesne and 1 plough belonging to the men, woodland for 20 pigs; always 1 mill. Then it was worth 20s., now 30; [it is] of the fief of Frederick, and his predecessor had commendation only, and his predecessors had the soke themselves.

In Rougham and in [Great or Little] Fransham 2 carucates of land were held by Toki, a free man, TRE; there has always been 1 villan. Then [there were] 12 bordars, now 10. Then [there were] 3 slaves, now 1, and 1 acre of meadow: there have always been 3 ploughs in demesne and 1½ ploughs belonging to the men; [there is] woodland for 10 pigs and now half a mill. And [there are] 16 free men [with] half a carucate of land and 8 acres of land; there have always been 1½ ploughs. Then it was worth 50s., now 60, This is by exchange of Lewes [Sussex]. The whole of [Great or Little] Fransham is 9 furlongs in length and 8 in breadth, and pays 10d. in geld, whoever may hold there holds it. [William holds[it]

In Tittleshall 5 free men held 1 carucate of land TRE; now Wimer [holds it]

William de Warenne

of William [de Warenne]. There have always been 7 bordars [and] 6 acres of meadow; there have always been 3½ ploughs, and woodland for 40 pigs and 1 fishery. Then it was worth 20s., now 30. This is by exchange of Lewes [Sussex]. The soke is in the king's [manor of] Mileham.

In Stanfield 2 carucates of land were held by 33 free men under Stigand by soke and commendation; there have always been 5 bordars and 6 acres of meadow. Among the whole there were always 10 ploughs; [there is] woodland for 60 pigs. Then it was worth 40s., now 60. This is of the exchange of Lewes [Sussex] The soke is in the king's [manor of] Mileham.

WAYLAND HUNDRED.

In Griston [there is] 1 church and 10 acres of land; this Godric claims to have belonged in the time of Earl Ralph to Stow [Bedon], and the men of the Hundred testify that it is of the fief of William de Warenne, and a certain king's man is willing to undergo the judicial ordeal [to confirm] that it belonged to Stow [Bedon] when Ralph made forfeiture and 1 year before, and 1 year after [his forfeiture].

FOREHOE HUNDRED AND A HALF.

In Barnham [Broom] 2 carucates of land and 6 acres were held by 47 free men when he received it, and now by 57; there have always been 7 bordars and 8 ploughs and 10 acres of meadow; there have always been 1½ mills. Then they were worth 100s., now £9. The soke is in the king's [manor of] Wymondham. The whole is 6 furlongs in length and 4 in breadth, and [pays] for the king's geld 8s. 5d., whoever holds there.

In Colton [there are] 2 free men [with] 30 acres of land, and they are in the same valuation.

In "Toketorp" [there are] 24 acres of land, and they are in the same valuation.

In Welborne, 10 free men TRE held 1 carucate of land and 40 acres. Now there are 20 free men. There have always been 4 ploughs and 3 acres of meadow.

In "Toketorp" [there are] 3 free men [with] 20 acres of land. The whole is worth 60s.

In Wicklewood [there is] 1 free man [with] 1 carucate of land; there have always been 17 bordars and 3 ploughs and 6 acres of meadow. Then it was worth 20s., now 40.

In Morely [St Botolph or St Peter] [there are] 2 carucates of land; 1 was held by a priest and the other by 5 free men, and the priest had 19 bordars, and TRE 5 ploughs, now 3, and 5 acres of meadow. Then it was worth 60s., now 40. And the 5 free men had under them 10 bordars, there have always been 2 ploughs and 4 acres of meadow, and it is worth 40s.

In Deopham [there are] 30 acres of land [and] 1 free man on the same carucate of land. There have always been 5 bordars and 1 plough, and it is in the same valuation. All the soke is in the king's [manor of] Hingham.

In Wymondham [there were] 30 free men when he received it, now [there are] 43; there has always been 1 carucate of land. Then and afterwards [there were] 5 ploughs, now 2; there have always been 6 bordars and 6 acres of meadow. The whole is worth 40s. The whole is of the exchange of Lewes [Sussex] of the land of the saints.

MIDFORD HUNDRED.

In Thuxton [there are] 10 free men, for half a carucate of land TRE; there have always been 2 bordars and 5 acres of meadow; always 2 ploughs. Then it was worth 10s., now 20. And in Mattishall [there are] 14 acres of land, 1 free man, and [it] is in the same valuation.

In Southburgh [there are] 7 free men, for half a carucate of land, and 3 bordars and 5 acres of meadow. Then [there were]

2 mills, now 3. Then [there was] woodland for 8 pigs, now for 4. Then and afterwards [there were] 2 ploughs, now 1½ ploughs; ; and it is worth 20s.

In Letton [there were] 9 free men TRE, for half a carucate of land, and 2 bordars and 8 acres of meadow; [there is] woodland for 8 pigs; there have always been 3 ploughs. Then it was worth 10s., now 20; [there is] 1 church [with] 12 acres.

In Shipdham [there are] 11 free men, for 1 carucate of land, and 3 bordars and 10 acres of meadow. Then [there was] woodland for 60 pigs, now for 40. Then [there were] 5 ploughs, afterwards and now 4. Then it was worth 30s., now 40s.; ; and [it is] 1 league in length and 5 furlongs in breadth and [pays] 15d. in geld. And Southburgh is 6 furlongs in length

William de Warenne

[Folio 167: NORFOLK]

and 5 in breadth, and pays 15d. in geld. And Letton pays the same. All this is by exchange of Lewes [Sussex]. In "Thurstuna" [there are] 9 acres, 1 free man, and it is worth 2s. [and is] of the same exchange.

DOCKING HUNDRED.

Stanhoe, 1 free man, Ulfkil, [holds] in commendation only [with] 1 carucate of land and 3 bordars. There has always been 1 plough, and it is worth 20s.

In Shernborne [there are] 4 free men [with] 2 carucates of land, and 1 free man with 40 acres. There have always been 5 villans, and always 3 ploughs, and they are worth 60s.

MIDFORD HUNDRED.

[Wood] Rising was held by Ælfgifu TRE [as] 1 carucate of land; there has always been 1 plough in demesne, and 16 villans and 6 bordars, and 5 ploughs belonging to the men, and 15 acres of meadow. Then [there was] woodland for 200 pigs, now 160; and there are 8 free men [with] 3 carucates of land. There have always been 3 ploughs. [There is] woodland for 6 pigs, and 7 head of cattle and 1 horse, and 20 pigs [and] 30 goats. Then it was worth 40s., now 60. And it is 8 furlongs in length and 6 in breadth, and [pays] 15d. in geld.

HENSTEAD HUNDRED.

In Yelverton [there is] 1 free man of Harold's by commendation [with] 30 acres of land and 3 bordars [and] 1 acre of meadow. There has always been 1 plough. It is assessed in [Castle] Acre. By exchange.

[SOUTH] GREENHOE HUNDRED.

In Didlington 32 free men held 4 carucates of land, and still hold [them]. There have always been 15 bordars under them. There have always been 5 ploughs between them; and it is 8 furlongs in length and 4 in breadth, and pays 13d. in geld. Of these Oger holds 1 carucate of land [with] 1 plough upon it. [It pays] 20s. when the Hundred pays 20s. Then it was worth 100s., now £4 5s.

In Foulden 24 free men held 6 carucates of land, and still hold [them] under

[Folio 167v: NORFOLK]

William [de Warenne], and William [fitzReginald] holds 1 carucate of land and 1 plough upon it, and it is worth 20s. Then under them [were] 16 villans and 16 bordars, and now [the same]. There were then 7 ploughs and always have been. There has always been 1 mill, 10 acres of meadow and 2 fisheries, and it is 1 mile in length and a half in breadth, and pays 16d. in geld. Then it was worth 60s., now 120s.; and this land he says he has for the exchanges of Lewes [Sussex].

Osmund held Hilborough TRE, now W[illiam] [holds it] for a manor, of the king's gift . Then [there were] 22 villans and always have been. Then [there were] 10 bordars and always have been. Then [there were] 6 slaves, and now [there are the same]. There have always been 4 ploughs in demesne. Then [there were] 10 ploughs among all [the men] and afterwards 7, and now 8 acres of meadow. When he received it 5 head of cattle were found, now the same and then 15 pigs and now [the same]. Then [there were] 100 sheep, and now 120, now 17 goats, and 5 beehives, and 3 mills; [there is] woodland for 20 pigs; and it is half a mile and 2 furlongs in length and 7 [furlongs] in breadth, and pays 8d. in geld Then it was worth £6, now 7.

And in [Cockley] Cley Osmund held half a carucate of land. Then [there were] 5 bordars, and now [the same]. There has always been 1 plough [and] 1 acre of meadow. Then it was worth 10s., now 15s.; and in [Cockley] Cley were found 3 horses, and now [also], and 6 head of cattle and 20 pigs and 102 sheep and 1 beehive. The same W[illiam] holds it.

In [East and West] Bradenham a certain free man holds 30 acres; there have always been 3 bordars, but Osmund had sake and soke; [there is] woodland for 10 pigs [and] 2 acres of meadow. Then it was worth 5s., now 5s.

In Palgrave Saint-Riquier holds 1 carucate of land which a certain free man held TRE. Then [there were] 4 villans and always have been. Now [there are] 2 bordars. There has always been 1 plough in demesne, and always half a plough among all [the men]. Then it was worth 20s., now 25s.

In [South] Acre a certain free man held 1 carucate of land; there have always been 6 villans and 1 bordar and 3 slaves,

William de Warenne

[Folio 168: NORFOLK]

and 1 plough on the demesne.Then [there were] 3 ploughs among all [the men], now 1. [There is] woodland for 15 pigs. There has always been half a mill. Then it was worth 20s. and always has been. This is of the fief of Frederick. Wimer holds it.

In Bodney 3 free men held 1 carucate of land, now W[illiam de Warenne] holds it in exchange. There has always been 1 villan. There has always been 1 plough. [There is] woodland for 12 pigs, 2 acres of meadow, and the fourth part of 1 mill. Then it was worth 20s., now the same.

In [North or South] Pickenham William [de Warenne] holds half a carucate of land which Asfrothr held TRE. Then [there were] 2 villans, and now. There has always been 1 plough; [there is] woodland for 4 pigs [and] 2 acres of meadow. There has always been 1 mill. It has always been worth 10s.

GALLOW HUNDRED.

Sculthorpe was held by Toki, of the fief of Frederick, TRE [as] 3 carucates of land. There have always been 12 villans and 34 bordars. Then [there were] 6 slaves, now 3. Then and afterwards [there were] 3 ploughs, now 4. There have always been 5 ploughs belonging to the men. [There is] woodland for 20 pigs [and] 4 acres of meadow [and] 3 mills. When he received it [there were] 4 horses, now 6. Then [there were] 6 head of cattle, now 20. Then [there were] 40 pigs, now 20. Then [there were] 100 sheep, now 400. And 30 sokemen belong to this manor with all customary dues, dwelling on 1½ carucates of land. There have always been 4 ploughs; and 2 other sokemen with 40 acres dwell in Toftrees; and under them 12 bordars [with] 1 acre [and there are] 1½ acres of meadow. There have always been 2 ploughs [and there is] 1 church [with] 60 acres. Then it was worth £6, and afterwards; now [it is worth] £10, but it was at farm for £15, but could not pay it. And it is half a league in length and half in breadth, and [pays] 6d. in geld. And [there are] 12 wild mares, and they are worth 12s. To the church [belong] 60 acres.

[fitzGolde] [holds] [East or West] Barsham which was held by TRE [as] 4 carucates of land. There have always been 10 villans and 26 bordars. Then [there were] 4 slaves, now none. Then [there were] 4 ploughs in demesne, and afterwards none; now [there are] 2 but [the others] could be restored. Then [there were] 5 ploughs belonging to the men, and afterwards none, now 3, and [the rest] could be restored. There is woodland for 20 pigs, 3 acres of meadow [and] 4 mills. Then [there was] nothing, now [there are] 2 horses; now 4 head of cattle and 30 pigs and 200 sheep and a half [sic]; and 6 sokemen [with] half a carucate of land [and]

[Folio 168v: NORFOLK]

3 bordars. Then as now [there were] 2 ploughs [and there is] 1 church with 100 acres. Then it was worth £4, now £6; and it is half a league in length and half in breadth, and [pays] 6d. in geld. In the same vill there is 1 free man with 1 carucate of land as a manor, and he was delivered instead of land. There have always been 21 bordars and 1 slave; and he used to live in 2 halls. Then [there were] 2 ploughs and afterwards nothing, now [there is] half [a plough]; and among the men [there are] 2 ploughs and 2 acres of meadow [and] 2 half mills. [There is] woodland for 10 pigs; and [there are] 6 sokemen with 6 acres of land; now [there are] 80 sheep and 30 pigs; [there is] . Then and afterwards it was worth 40s., now 50s., and this land pays 12d. in geld. [It is all] in the same measurement.

In the same vill Toki held 1 carucate of land for a manor TRE; [now]. There have always been 3 villans and 7 bordars. Then [there were] 2 slaves; then [there was] 1 plough in demesne and afterwards nothing; now [there is] 1; and there has always been 1 plough belonging to the men [and there are] 2 acres of meadow, 3½ mills; and 2 horses and 4 head of cattle and 8 pigs [and] 86 sheep; and 15 sokemen with half a carucate of land, and 2 bordars. Then as now [there was] 1 plough; [there is] 1 acre of meadow [and] 1 church [with] 8 acres, and half an acre of meadow.

In [Little] Snoring [there are] 2 sokemen and in Clipstone 4, and in Kettlestone 8, and they have half a carucate of land. Then [there were] 3 ploughs and afterwards none; now [there are] 3 [and] 2 acres of meadow [and] 1 church [with] 8 acres. Then it was worth 40s., now £3, and this land pays 12d. in geld. It has been measured above. The same [man] holds it.

In Waterden Lambert [de Rosay] holds 1 carucate of land which was held by 2 free men TRE. There have always been 17 bordars. Then [there were] 2 slaves. There have always been 2 ploughs in demesne and among them all. And in [North or South] Creake 1 of them used to hold 1 other free man with half a carucate of land; and under them [there were] 6 bordars and among them [there was] 1 plough, one of which is in demesne; now [there is] 1 horse and 5 pigs and 60 sheep [and there is] . Then it was worth 20s., now 17s. 4d., and it is 3 furlongs in length and 2 in breadth, and [pays] 12d. in geld.

In Fulmodeston Toki held 2 carucates of land for a manor TRE. There have always been 29 bordars. Then [there were] 2 slaves [and] there have always been 2 ploughs in demesne and 4 ploughs belonging to the men [and] woodland

William de Warenne

[Folio 169: NORFOLK]

for 30 pigs [and] 16 acres of meadow. Then [there was] 1 mill. There has always been 1 horse and 6 head of cattle and 23 pigs. When he received it [there were] 180 sheep, now none. Then [there were] 40 goats, now none; now [there is] 1 beehive [and] 1 church without land. Walter holds it. Then it was worth 40s., now 60s., and the whole is 4 furlongs in length and 3 in breadth, and pays 12d. in geld.

In Croxton [near Fakenham] Toki held 1 carucate of land TRE. Then [there were] 4 free men. Then [there was] 1 plough and 4 acres of meadow, and it is in the valuation above; ; and it is 2 furlongs in length and 1 in breadth, and [pays] 12d. in geld. The same [Walter] holds it.

In Burnham [Thorpe] Walter holds 2 carucates of land which Toki held TRE [as] 2 carucates of land. There have always been 10 villans and 29 bordars. Then [there were] 3 slaves. [...] There have always been 2 ploughs in demesne and then [there were] 5 ploughs belonging to the men, [...] now 2; [the rest] could be restored. [There is] woodland for 8 pigs [and] 1 acre of meadow. [...] [There is] the third part of 1 mill. Then [there were] 2 horses, now 6, and 1 ass. Then [there were] 4 head of cattle and now [the same]; and [there are] 28 pigs and 345 sheep; and 9 sokemen belong to this manor with 1 carucate of land and they have 2 ploughs [and there is] . Then it was worth 60s., and afterwards; now £4; and it is 1½ leagues in length and 1 league in breadth, and for 20s. pays 3s. in geld whoever holds there.

In [Little] Ryburgh [there is] 1 sokeman and in Stibbard [has] another with 30 acres of land and 1 plough, 1 acre of meadow [and] half a church [with] 3 acres; and it is worth 5s. 4d.

BROTHERCROSS HUNDRED.

In [East or West] Rudham Ralph holds 3 carucates of land which Toki held TRE. There have always been 6 villans and 16 bordars. Then [there were] 3 slaves, now 1. Then [there were] 3 ploughs, now 1. There has always been 1 plough belonging to the men, 4 acres of meadow, 2 mills [and] 1 salt-pan; there have always been 11 cattle, and then 30 pigs, now 28. Then [there were] 400 sheep, now 180; [there are] . Then [there were] 14 horses, now 22 wild mares.

[Folio 169v: NORFOLK]

To this manor belongs 1 berewick, Bagthorpe, 1 carucate of land. There have always been 3 bordars and 1 plough. There have always been 2 horses and 3 cattle and 4 pigs. Then [there were] 80 sheep, now 100. And [there is] another berewick, Houghton, of 1 carucate of land. . There have always been 13 sokemen with all customary dues. There has always been 1 plough in demesne and 1 plough belonging to the men. Then [there were] 4 pigs. Then [there were] 60 sheep, now 40. And 25 sokemen in [East or West] Rudham belong to this manor with 1½ carucates of land; and there have always been 4 ploughs among them; and in Houghton [there is] 1 sokeman with 30 acres; and under them [there are] 3 villans and 3 bordars. There has always been 1 plough; [there is] 1 church without land. Ralph holds it. And in Barmer Ralph holds 4 sokemen with 60 acres of land and 3 bordars. There has always been 1 plough, and half a church. And in Syderstone the same Ralph holds 4 sokemen with 40 acres. Then and afterwards [there was] 1 plough, now half. And in Helhoughton the same holds 1 sokeman with 12 acres and half a plough. All this [...] was worth TRE £8, now £10; in demesne [there] are 20s. And the whole [...] of [East or West] Rudham is 1 league in length and 1 in breadth and [pays] 4s. 3d. in geld.

The whole of Barmer is 3 furlongs in length and 2 in breadth, and [pays] 6½d. in geld.

In [East or West] Rudham Lambert [de Rosay] holds 1 carucate of land which 1 free man held TRE. There has always been 1 villan and 14 bordars. Then [there were] 3 slaves, now 2. Then [there were] 2 ploughs in demesne, now 1. There has always been 1 plough belonging to the men [and there is] half an acre of meadow. Then [there were] 4 horses, now 5 and 1 mule. Then [there were] 6 head of cattle, now 11. Then [there were] 16 pigs, now 20. Then [there were] 450 sheep, now 300. To this manor belong 18 sokemen on the same carucate of land. There have always been 2 ploughs. Then it was worth 20s., now 30s. This was delivered to him for land. To this manor belongs 1 berewick, Syderstone, of 30 acres, half a plough, and 3 bordars. Then it was worth 5s. 4d., now it pays 12s.

In Tattersett Rainier holds 1 carucate of land which Toki held TRE. There have always been 15 bordars and 1 slave and always 1 plough in demesne, and 1 plough belonging to the men, 1 acre of meadow [and]

William de Warenne

[Folio 170: NORFOLK]

2 mills Then [there was] 1 horse, now 2 and 5 head of cattle and 6 pigs. Then [there were] 40 sheep, now 80; [there are] 2 churches [with] 40 acres; and 14 sokemen belonging to this manor with 69 acres. There have always been 6 bordars and 2 ploughs [and] 1 acre of meadow. Then it was worth 10s., now 60s.; and it is half a league in length and 4 furlongs in breadth, and [pays] 13d. in geld.

In Helhoughton [there is] 1 sokeman with 60 acres. There have always been 8 bordars and 1 plough [and] 1½ acres of meadow. Then [there was] half a mill. [There is] woodland for 8 pigs. It has always been worth 5s. This land is entered above, of the fief of Frederick.

In Shereford 1 carucate of land was held by 6 free men TRE. There have always been 6 bordars. There have always been 2 ploughs [and] 2½ acres of meadow; . Then it was worth 10s., now it pays 20; and it is 3 furlongs in length and 3 in breadth, and [pays] 9½d. in geld. This is for the exchange of Lewes [Sussex].

In [Great] Ryburgh Peter [de Valognes] holds 8 sokemen with 1 carucate of land. There has always been 1 villan and 6 bordars and 2 ploughs. [There is] woodland for 20 pigs, 2 acres of meadow [and] 1 mill. It has always been worth 20s. This is of the fief of Frederick.

In Hempton [there are] 4 free men with half a carucate of land, and 4 bordars, and 1 plough [and there is] 1 church with 1 acre. Then it was worth 5s., now 3s., and it is 2 furlongs in length and in breadth, and [pays] 4½d. in geld.

HOLT HUNDRED.

In Wiveton William [de Warenne] holds 2 carucates of land which Thorgrim held TRE for a manor. There have always been 2 villans and 22 bordars and 1 sokeman with 12 acres of land, and 2 slaves, and 2 ploughs in demesne, and 2 ploughs belonging to the men, 2 acres of meadow [and] half a mill. Then [there were] 6 pigs, now 6. Then [there were] 60 sheep, now 30, and half a sokeman with 2 acres. Then it was worth 40s., now 60s.

In Briston, 14 sokemen are held, whom Toki held TRE [with] half a carucate of land, and 3 bordars. There have always been 4 ploughs. [There is] woodland for 20 pigs; and it is worth 16s.

[Folio 170v: NORFOLK]

[NORTH] GREENHOE HUNDRED.

Egmere was held by Alweald, a free man, TRE and was delivered to Frederick for land to complete his manors [as] half a carucate of land; there have always been 3 bordars, and 1 sokeman with 12 acres, and it is assessed in Barsham.

In Holkham Walter holds half a carucate of land; there has always been 1 bordar; and it belongs to Burnham and is of the fief of Frederick, and is assessed there.

NORTH ERPINGHAM HUNDRED.

In Gimingham 1 free man, Rathi, holds 2 carucates of land. There have always been 12 villans and 40 bordars. Then [there were] 2 slaves, now 1. Then and afterwards [there were] 2 ploughs on the demesne, and now 3. There have always been 4 ploughs belonging to the men. [There is] woodland for 80 pigs [and] 12 acres of meadow. Then and afterwards [there were] 2 mills, and now 4. Then [there were] 2 horses. Then [there were] 11 wild mares, now 7; now 8 head of cattle. Then [there were] 30 pigs, now 40. Then [there were] 30 sheep, now 160. There have always been 30 goats; and 23 sokemen with 48 acres of land. There have always been 3½ ploughs [and there is] 1 church [with] 28 acres.

Sidestrand was held of Archbishop Stigand by 1 free man for a manor of 1 carucate of land. There have always been 8 villans and 1 slave. Then and afterwards [there was] 1 plough in demesne, and now 2, and 1 plough belonging to the men; and 5 sokemen with 21 acres of land. There has always been 1 plough [and] 1½ acres of meadow. There have always been 2 horses. Then [there were] 3 head of cattle and 3 pigs. This Waleran delivered to complete the manor of Gimingham.

Knapton is held by 1 free man [as] 1 carucate of land. There have always been 10 villans and 5 bordars. Then [there was] 1 slave, now 2. Then and afterwards [there was] 1 plough in demesne, and now 2. There has always been 1 plough belonging to the men, 2 acres of meadow, and 13 sokemen with 3 carucates of land and 1 bordar. There have always been 3½ ploughs and 4 head of cattle and 4 pigs; and it was delivered to complete [the manor of] Gimingham. And Gimingham then was worth 40s., and afterwards £4; now £8.

William de Warenne

Sidestrand was worth then and afterwards 20s., now 60. Then and afterwards Knapton was worth 20s., now 60; and the whole of this was delivered for 1 manor and 4 carucates of land. And the whole of this is 2 leagues and 8 perches and 5 feet in length, and in breadth 1 league and 12 perches and 4 feet, and [pays] in geld 5s. 1d., whoever holds there.

In Thorpe [Market] Ralph holds 2 carucates of land which were held by 1 free man of Stigand TRE. There have always been 4 villans and 24 bordars and 1 slave. There have always been 2 ploughs in demesne, and 3 ploughs belonging to the men. [There is] woodland for 40 pigs, 2 acres of meadow and 2 mills; 1 beehive. There have always been 2 horses and 3 head of cattle. Then [there were] 6 pigs, now 11, and now 50 sheep. There have always been 20 goats. And [there are] 5 sokemen with 32 acres of land, and they have 1 plough; . Then and afterwards it was worth 40s., and now £8.

In Mundesley Grimkel, a free man, holds 30 acres of land and 2 bordars. There has always been 1 plough. And in addition to this William [de Warenne] holds in the same place 3 free men [who were] Eadric's TRE with 10 acres of land and 1 plough. It always paid 4s. [There is] 1 church with 12 acres.

In Trunch 3 free men the first Harold's, the second Ralph the staller's, the third Ketil's - hold 90 acres of land and 14 bordars. There have always been 5 ploughs among them [and there is] 1 church [with] 10 acres. [There is] woodland for 3 pigs [and] 3 acres of meadow. It was always worth 30s. And in addition there are 6 free men [who were] Eadric's TRE with 34 acres of land and 2 ploughs and 2½ acres of meadow. It was always worth 7s. 4d.

In Northrepps or Southrepps 2 free men of Eadric's hold 30 acres of land. There have always been 2 villans, 2 ploughs, and 4 bordars. It was always worth 6s.

In Northrepps [there is] 1 free man of Ketil's with 30 acres of land. There were always 2 villans and 5 bordars. [There is] woodland for 5 pigs. There have always been 1 plough, 2 acres of meadow, 2 mills [and] 1 church with 18 acres. It has always been worth 10s.

In Sidestrand [there are] 2 free men, 1 Eadric's, the other Almær's, with 60 acres of land. There have always been 5 villans and 5 bordars and 3 ploughs; 1 acre of meadow. [There is] woodland for 3 pigs. It has always been worth 10s.

In Southrepps and Northrepps [there are] 8 free men, 2 Abbot Ælfweald's, 5 Rathi of Gimingham's, 1 Osbert's, with 16 acres, and they have 2 ploughs. It has always been worth 4s. [and there is] 1 church [with] 12 acres. And the whole is half a league and 2 perches in length, and 4 furlongs and 4 feet in breadth, and [pays] 6½d. and a farthing in geld. And this whole land was delivered to W[illiam de Warenne] for 1 manor [as] 5 carucates of land belonging to Thorpe Market.

In Mundsley and in Trunch R[obert] Malet claims 19 free men, 3 in commendation, and the others with all their customary dues.

William [de Warenne] holds Gresham [as] 2 carucates of land, which Wulfstan, a free man, held. There have always been 4 villans and 6 bordars and 1 slave. There have always been 2 ploughs in demesne, and 4 ploughs belonging to the men; [there are] 11 sokemen, [with] 35 acres and 1 plough, 2 acres of meadow [and] 1 mill. To this belongs 1 berewick, Aldborough, of 60 acres of land. There have always been 3 villans and 4 bordars, and 1½ ploughs among them. And in Salthouse [there are] 30 acres, 1 villan and 1 bordar, 40 goats, and 3 sokemen, 15 acres [and] half a plough. It has always been worth £4, and it is 9 furlongs in length and 6 in breadth, and [pays] 7d. in geld. And it is of the fief of Frederick. And Aldborough is 8 furlongs in length and 3 in breadth, and [pays] 5½d. in geld.

In Sustead [there is] 1 half free man with 15 acres of land and 1 bordar, 1 rod of meadow and half a mill. There has always been half a plough. Then and afterwards [it was worth] 2s. 6d., and now 3s.

In Aylmerton William holds 2 carucates of land which Wighulf, 1 free man of Eadric's, held. There have always been 3 villans and 13 bordars. Then [there were] 2 slaves.

William de Warenne

Then and afterwards [there were] 2 ploughs in demesne, now 1. There have always been 2 ploughs belonging to the men.

[There is] woodland for 4 pigs [and] 2½ acres of meadow. Then [there was] 1 horse. Then [there were] 3 head of cattle. Then [there were] 9 pigs, now 3. Then [there were] 40 sheep, now 15. Then [there were] 60 goats, [and] half a church [with] 10 acres; and 2 sokemen with 20 acres of land, half a plough [and] 1 acre of meadow. Then it was worth 20s., and afterwards and now 40. And it is 9 furlongs in length and 6 in breadth, and [pays] 8 ƒ d. in geld. And this is a manor of the fief of Frederick.

OF THE EXCHANGE OF LEWES. In [North] Barningham Turold holds 30 acres of and which 1 free man of Ketil's held TRE. There have always been 3 bordars and 1 plough and half an acre of meadow. And there are 10 free men of Alwine Cild TRE with 28 acres of land. There have always been 2 ploughs.

In Plumstea d the same Turold holds 1 free man with 12 acres of land. There has always been 1 plough. [There is] woodland for 10 pigs. Then and afterwards [it was worth] 10s., now 20. These Drogo de la Beuvrière claims, for homage only.

In Wolterton the same holds 4 bordars. There has always been half a plough, with 16 acres.

In Banningham the same holds 3 bordars with 16 acres and half a plough, and 1 sokeman with 3 acres: and they have been assessed. [...] All the churches of the land of William de Warenne have been assessed with the manors.

BROTHERCROSS HUNDRED.

Helhoughton is held by William de Warenne of the fief of Frederick; [there is] 1 free man [whom he has] because his predecessor so held that he could not

[Folio 172v: NORFOLK]

withdraw from the land without his leave, and the Hundred testifies to this. And a certain man of Drogo de la Beuvrière, Franco by name, claims it for the fief of his lord, of the king's gift, by livery, saying that his predecessor, Humphrey [de Saint-Omer], held it, that is, in the time of Frederick, and after him Drogo held it; and the Hundred testifies to this, that they held it, but it has not seen this in a writ, nor the delivery.

GALLOW HUNDRED.

In North Barsham, which W[illiam] de Warenne holds, Harold held 2 free men with 1 carucate of land belonging to Fakenham, and now William holds them but his men do not know how; and the Hundred testifies them [to be] William's, that he is seised of them. But a man of the king offers judicial ordeal that they used to belong TRE to Fakenham, a manor of the king's.

[Folio 173: NORFOLK]

LAND of Roger Bigod. In Thetford Roger has [land] in demesne quit of all customary dues; to which used to belong 2 carucates of land TRE, and now the same. There have always been 2 ploughs in demesne, 20 bordars, 2 slaves, 1 mill, 13 acres of meadow, and 30 acres of land; there is there 1 mill and 5 acres of meadow. There have always been 128 sheep. Then it was worth £7; afterwards and now £8. Of the abovesaid bordars the king has their personal dues only. In the borough

Roger has 33 men commended to him whom his predecessor held, in whom he had nothing except commendation. He also has 1 mill, which Turstin, a burgess, holds. He lays claim to this by the king's gift, but the Hundred does not know how. This mill is worth 32s. [There is] 1 church.

FREEBRIDGE HUNDRED AND A HALF.

Pentney was held by Hagni TRE for a manor [and] 3 carucates of land; now it is held by Robert de Vaux. There have always been 11 villans, 14 bordars [and] 6 slaves; [there are] 3 ploughs in demesne, 3 ploughs belonging to the men, 20 acres of meadow, 3 mills [and] the third part of a salt-pan. To this land belongs 1 berewick, [East] Walton, 1 carucate of land. There have always been 6 bordars, 2 slaves, 1 plough in demesne, 16 acres of meadow [and] 3 horses. Then [there were] 20 mares, now 7. There have always been 21 head of cattle [and] 30 pigs; then [there were] 40 sheep, now 92 [and] 7 beehives. In the same place [there are] 10 sokemen [with] 72 acres. There has always been 1 plough. The whole was worth 100s. TRE and when he received it; now [it is worth] £7. The whole of this is held by Robert [de Vaux]. [It is] 5 furlongs in length and 4 in breadth, and [pays] 8d. in geld. To the church [belong] 30 acres. It is worth 2s. 8d.

In [Gayton] Thorpe 80 acres were held by a free man TRE; now the same R[obert] holds them. There have always been 6 villans, 6 bordars, 3 acres of meadow, 1 plough in demesne [and] half a plough belonging to the men. In the same [vill] is a free man [with] 20 acres; it is worth 12d.

East Winch a free man of Gyrth's held TRE 60 acres; now the same R[obert] also [holds]. There have always been 6 villans, 3 bordars, 2 ploughs [and] 11 acres of meadow. Then the whole was worth 40s., now 60. In Flitcham [there is] 1 sokeman with 30 acres. The same R[obert] holds it; [there is] 1 bordar and 1 acre of meadow; then [there were] 2 oxen, now 3. It is worth 3s. To the church 8 [acres belong]. It is worth 8d.

In [Great or Little] Massingham [there is] 1 free man [with] 30 [acres] which Humphrey de Culey holds [and] 2 bordars; it is worth 18d. This land Æthelwig [of Thetford] seized after the king came into this country. The soke lies in [Great or Little] Massingham, [a manor] of the king. In Flitcham Algar held of Archbishop Stigand

[Folio 173v: NORFOLK]

for a manor 2 carucates of land; now Ranulf fitzWalter [holds them]. Then [there were] 20 bordars, now 23; then 3 slaves, now 2; then 2 ploughs on the demesne, and afterwards 1, now 2; there has always been 1 plough belonging to the men, 5 acres of meadow, and 1 mill; then [there was] 1 horse, and now [the same]; then 3 head of cattle, then 27 pigs, now 32; then 180 sheep, now 1. Then and afterwards [it was worth] 40s., now 1s. The whole is 1½ miles in length and 5 furlongs in breadth, and pays 16d. for a geld of 20s., whoever holds there. Here belongs 1 sokeman [with] 5 acres of land, and it is worth 2 shillings. Over this manor and over all the men who were in it Stigand used to have the soke; and it was delivered to Roger during his lifetime. The same R[obert de Vaux] holds it.

Appleton was held by Abba, 2 carucates of land, for a manor, of Stigand; always 20 bordars and 2 slaves, 10 acres of meadow, and 2 ploughs in demesne, and 4 ploughs belonging to the men. Then 1 horse; then 6 pigs, now 35; then 63 sheep, now 14; and it was worth then 40s., now 50, and the same [Robert] holds it. [There is] 1 church [with] 12 acres, and it is worth 12d.

SMETHDEN HUNDRED.

In Ringstead Tovi, a free man, held TRE; there has always been 1 plough in demesne and 2 slaves and 5 villans; there has always been half a plough belonging to the men, and 2 acres of meadow, and the eighth part of a mill, and 1 horse; then [there were] 82 sheep, and now the same. And [there are] 4 sokemen [with] 10 acres of land, and 1 sokeman of St Benedict [of Ramsey] [with] 2 acres, who has been added TRW. The whole was then worth 10s., now 2 0. St Benedict [has] the soke, and Ralph fitzHerluin holds it.

In the same place 1 carucate of land was held by Alstan under Stigand TRE; now Ralph de Tourleville holds it. Then and afterwards [there was] 1 plough, now 2 oxen, and 2 acres of meadow; and it is worth 5s.

In the same place [there is] 1 sokeman [with] 6 acres; and it is worth 6d., and the same [Ralph] holds it. And [there are] 2 sokemen of St Benedict [with] 16 acres of land [and] then [there was] 1 plough; and it is worth 4s. The same [holds it] And [there is] 1 free man [with] 24 acres of land; then and afterwards [there was] 1 plough, now 1 ox, and it is worth 2s. This was delivered to him to complete the manors. The same [holds it].

Hunstanton is held by Ralph fitzHerluin; [there are] 2 ploughs in demesne, and it was held by 1 free man, TRE. Then and afterwards [there were] 12 villans, now 6; there have always been 6 bordars; then and afterwards [there were] 3 slaves, now 2. Then and afterwards [there were] 6 ploughs belonging to the men, and 5 acres of meadow; now 5½; then 1 mill, now 2, and 1 fishery. There has always been 1 horse, then 1 ox; [there is] woodland for 40 pigs. Then [there were] 16 pigs, now 51. Then [there were] 80 sheep, now 50; [there are] 5 beehives. Here belong 2 sokemen [with] 10 acres. The same [holds it].

Roger Bigod

[Folio 174: NORFOLK]

Then and afterwards it was worth £3, now £4. In the same place Thorn, a free man, held TRE; [there is] 1 plough in demesne; then [there were] 3 villans, now 2. Then [there were] 4 bordars, now 5. Then and afterwards [there were] 3 slaves, and 2½ acres of meadow; there has always been half a plough belonging to the men [and] 1 fishery. Then [there was] 1 cow. Then [there were] 30 sheep. And [there are] 3 sokemen [with] 5 acres of land. It has always been worth 20s. The whole is 1 league in length and 1 league in breadth, and pays 16d. in 20s. of geld.

GRIMSHOE HUNDRED.

In Lynford Æ[thelwig] held 1 sokeman [with] 60 acres of land. There has always been half a plough and 1 slave [and] 3 acres of meadow, and it is worth 20d. This is held by Stanheard.

WAYLAND HUNDRED.

Watton was held by Ealdthryth, a free woman, TRE [as] 5 carucates of land; now Ranulf fitzWalter holds it. Then and afterwards [there were] 9 villans, now none. Then and afterwards [there were] 11 bordars, now 12; there have always been 3 slaves [and] 30 acres of meadow; there have always been 4 ploughs in demesne. Then and afterwards [there were] 4 ploughs belonging to the men, now 3 ; [there is] woodland for 400 pigs; now [there is] 1 mill; there have always been 3 horses; and 13 head of cattle, now 5; and 35 pigs, now 30; and 17 sheep, now 62. Here belonged 15 sokemen TRE, now 23 [with] 82 acres; [there have] always 4 ploughs. The same holds 1 church [with] 20 acres and it is worth 20d. This vill was in 2 manors TRE, each one was worth £4; now the whole is worth £7. And it is 1 league in length and half [a league] in breadth whoever holds there; and of 20s. of geld [it pays] 13½d.

In Tottington Ralph fitzHerluin holds 4 carucates of land which Æthelwig held TRE; then and afterwards [there were] 15 villans, now 4; then and afterwards 10 bordars, now 17. Then and afterwards [there were] 8 slaves, now 4; [there are] 24 acres of meadow [and] there have always been 3 ploughs in demesne. Then and afterwards [there were] 5 ploughs belonging to the men, now 3. [There is] woodland for 30 pigs [and] now [there is] 1 mill. And there have always been 3 sokemen [with] 95 acres. Then and afterwards [there were] 2 ploughs, now nothing, but they could be [restored]; there has always been 1 horse; then [there were] 17 head of cattle, now 19. Then [there were] 32 pigs, now 12. Then [there were] 140 sheep, now 140 less 3 [and] 24 goats. Then [there were] 63 mares, now 15. Then and afterwards it was worth 80s., and now 60. The whole is 2 leagues in breadth [sic: recte length] and 1 in breadth. Whoever holds there, [it pays] 15d. in geld.

WEST FLEGG HUNDRED.

In Sutton [there] belong 7 free men, and they are in Repps and Rollesby [with] 1 carucate of land and 9 acres of meadow, and [there are] 3 free men under them [with] 7 acres of land. There have always been 2 ploughs. And 1 half [free man] of these 7 free men the Hundred testifies [belongs] to

[Folio 174v: NORFOLK]

St Benet of Hulme; and a man of Earl R[alph] seized [him], and this half [free man] has 6 acres of land. They are assessed in the £10 of Sutton [near Stalham]. But upon them 14s. [are charged], and he [Roger Bigod] holds in demesne.

In Oby Stanheard holds 30 acres of land which Hringwulf, 1 free man, held TRE. [...] There has always been half a plough; [there are] 6 acres of meadow. And there are under him 6 free men [with] 30 acres of land and 1 acre of meadow. There has always been half a plough. These men R[oger] Bigod claims by gift of the king, and they are of the fief of Æthelwig of Thetford, his predecessor. It has always been worth 4s. In the same place 1 free man, Godwine, held 30 acres of land, now 5 bordars; the same Stanheard [holds]. There has always been 1 plough and 3 free men under him with 15 acres of land [and] 1 acre of meadow. There has always been half a plough. It has always been worth 4s. These R[oger] Bigod has of the fief of Æthelwig his predecessor. In Clippesby [there is] 1 free man of St Benet [of Hulme] and in Ormsby [St Margaret or St Michael] 2 of St Benet [of Hulme] in commendation; and afterwards Æthelwig held them, now R[oger] Bigod by the king's gift, with 33 acres of land, and 5 acres of meadow and 1 bordar. There has always been half a plough. It has always been worth 2s. The same Stanheard [holds it]. In Thurne [there is] a half free man [with] 21 acres [and] 4 acres of meadow. There has always been half a plough. And under him [there is] 1 free man [with] 4 acres. It has always been worth 4s. The same [Stanheard holds it]. In Burgh [St Margaret] Ulfkil, a free man of Eadric's by commendation, held 30 acres of land TRE, and 3 free men of Æthelwig's in commendation [held] 45 acres and 3 acres of meadow. There has always been 1 plough. Then it was worth 3s., afterwards and now 6. In Billockby [there is] 1 free man of Æthelwig TRE in commendation [with] 20 acres of land, 2 acres of meadow, and 1 bordar. There has always been half a plough. It has always been worth 20d. The same holds it.

In Repps 7 free men - 4 belonging to St Benet [of Hulme], 2 to Æthelwig, 1 to Bishop Æthelmær in commendation - TRE [with] 80 acres of land, 10 acres of meadow. There have always been 1½ ploughs. They have always been worth 8s. The same [holds it].

In Bastwick [there are] 2 free women of Eadric and Hringwulf [with] 13 acres of land in commendation TRE [and] 1 acre of meadow, and they plough now as then with 2 oxen. They have always been worth 18d. The same holds [them].

In Oby [there is] 1 free man [with] 6 acres of land and 1 acre of meadow with 2 oxen. It has always been worth 8d.

In [East or West] Somerton [there is] 1 free man [with] 21 acres of land [and] 3 acres of meadow. There has always been half a plough. Then it was worth 16d.; afterwards and now it renders 24d. These free men the king gave to Æthelwig of Thetford with their lands as R[oger] Bigod claims. Repps is 7 furlongs in length and 5 in breadth, and [pays] 15d. in geld.

[...] HENSTEAD HUNDRED.

In Shotesham [All Saints or St Mary] 1 free man of Stigand's held

Roger Bigod

by commendation TRE 2 carucates of land for a manor; now Ranulf fitzWalter holds [them]. There have always been 5 villans and 17 bordars. There have always been 2 slaves. Then and afterwards [there were] 2 ploughs in demesne; now 3. There have always been 4 ploughs belonging to the men. [There is] woodland for 20 pigs, and 6 acres of meadow, and half a mill. Then [there was] 1 horse, now 2; then [there were] 24 pigs, now 20; then 24 goats, now none. And 6 sokemen are there with 36 acres of land. There has always been 1 plough. Then and afterwards it was worth 40s., now £4. It is 1½ leagues in length and half in breadth; and pays 16d. in geld; half a church [with] 15 acres is worth 15d. In Stoke [Holy Cross] Æthelwig of Thetford held 80 acres of land TRE; now W[illiam] Pecche holds it. There have always been 3 bordars,

and always 1 plough in demesne, and 2 acres of meadow. And in Seething [there is] 1 villan with 12 acres belonging to this Stoke Holy Cross. It has always been worth 26s. 6d.; [and there is] 1 church [with] 18 acres, and it is worth 2s.

OF THE EXCHANGE OF THE LAND OF ISAAC. In Surlingham Esger, a free man of Godwine's, held TRE 8 acres of land and 2 acres of meadow. Aitard [de Vaux] holds it.

Also in the same [vill there are] 30 free men of Ulfkil [with] 150 acres of land, and 10 free men of Stigand's [with] 50 acres of land; under these 30, [there is] 1 bordar, and under the 10 free men, 2 bordars. Among them all [there are] 32 acres of meadow. Then the 30 had 4 ploughs, afterwards 2½, now 4. Then they used to have among the 10 1½ ploughs, afterwards and now 1. Then these 30 were worth 15s., afterwards and now 22s. 6d. Then these 10 were worth 5s., afterwards and now 18s. 6d.; and it is 1 league in length and a half in breadth; and [pays] 19d. in geld but many others hold there. .

In Rockland [St Mary] [there were] 14 whole free men of Ulfkil's in commendation TRE and 6 half [free men]. Among the men [there were] 90 acres of land and 10 acres of meadow. There have always been 2½ ploughs. Then and afterwards they were worth 10s., now they render 20s. Rockland [St Mary] is 1 league in length and a half in breadth, and [pays] 16d. in geld; [and there is] 1 church [with] 12 acres, and it is worth 8d.; and the same holds it. In Bramerton [there are] 12 free men - 9 Ulfkil's by commendation, 1 of St Edmund's, the other 2 of the fief

of Stigand. The 10 hold 40 acres of land among them. Between the 2 [free men] of Stigand's fief, 33 acres of land were held TRE, now 15 acres. Among the 10 [free men], there have always been 2½ ploughs. Between the 2 then half a plough, afterwards nothing, now 1 ox. Then and afterwards they all were worth 5s., now 6s. 4d. It is 4 furlongs in length and 2½ in breadth, and [pays] 10½d. in geld; [and there is] 1 church [with] 24 acres [and] it is worth 24d. The same holds it.

In Kirby [Bedon there were] 6 whole free men - 3 of Ulfkil's, the third [sic] of Æthelwig of Thetford, the fourth [sic] of Genred's, the fifth [sic] of Alfred's, by commendation TRE - with 41 acres of land and 2 acres of meadow. There has always been 1 plough. Then and afterwards they were worth 5s., now 3s. 4d.; [and there is] 1 church [with] 10 acres [and] it is worth 12d.; and Robert de Courson holds [it]. In the same place are 3 free men - 1 whole, 2 halves belonging to Stigand by commendation [with] 46 acres of land - and under them 1 bordar and 3 acres of meadow. There has always been 1 plough. It has always been worth 5s. It is half a league in length and half in breadth; and [pays] 20d. in geld whoever holds there; [and there is] 1 church [with] 10 acres [and] it is worth 12d. Robert de Courson holds it. In [Earl or Pigot] Framlingham [there was] 1 free man belonging to Edwin by commendation, and afterwards to Godric the steward, his successor, under Earl R[alph]; when Earl R[alph] forfeited, Bishop Æthelmær held him; now Roger B[igod]. Turold [holds] 20 acres on which dwell 2 bordars. There has always been half a plough and half an acre of meadow. It has always been worth 2s.; [and there is] 1 church with 30 acres [and] it is worth 3s.

In Whitlingham 1 free woman, Wulfflæd, held under Bishop [sic] Stigand 160 acres of land TRE. There have always been 9 bordars; then [there were] 1½ ploughs in demesne, afterwards and now 1, and half a plough belonging to the men [and] 8 acres of meadow, and 13 whole sokemen and 3 halves, 43 acres of land and 3 acres of meadow. There have always been 1½ ploughs. Then it was worth 20s., afterwards and now 30. It is half a league in length and 4 furlongs in breadth; and [pays] 7d. in geld, whoever holds there; [there is] 1 church [with] 10 acres, and it is worth 12d. The whole of this land is of the fief of Bishop Æthelmær, and the same Robert [de Courson] holds it.

Roger Bigod

[Folio 176: NORFOLK]

OF THE EXCHANGE OF THE LAND OF ISAAC. Bixley was held by Genred, a free man, under Stigand TRE for 1½ carucates of land, and Ranulf fitzWalter holds it. There have always been 2 villans. There have always been 4 bordars. Then and afterwards [there was] 1 plough in demesne, now 2. There has always been 1 plough belonging to the men, and 5 acres of meadow. There has always been 1 horse in demesne. Then [there were] 2 head of cattle, now 10 pigs. And 13 sokemen dwell on the half carucate of land aforesaid; and 1 free man with 2 acres of free land. Among them all there have always been 4 ploughs. Then and afterwards it was worth 20s., now 50s. It is half a league in length and 4 furlongs in breadth, and in geld [pays] 10½d.; [and] 1 church [with] 24 acres is worth 2s. This he received as 1½ carucates of land. In [Earl or Pigot] Framingham Ulfkil, 1 free man of Earl Ælfgar by commendation, held 1 carucate of land; now Ulfkil holds it. There have always been 24 bordars. There has always been 1 plough in demesne, and 3 ploughs belonging to the men, and 3 acres of meadow. There have always been 2 horses; then 2 head of cattle, now 3. Then [there were] 12 pigs, now 16, and 4 beehives. And in the same [vill are] 10 free men under him, 50 acres of land, and 2 acres of meadow. There have always been 2 ploughs. Then and afterwards it was worth 20s., now 60s., and it is half a league in length and half in breadth. And [it pays] 13½d. in geld.

In Kirby [Bedon] [there are] 4 free men of Ulfkil's [with] 10 acres of land and half an acre of meadow. There has always been half a plough, and .

In Holverston [there are] 3 free men of the same [Ulfkil], [with] 10 acres of land. They have always ploughed with 2 oxen. In Yelverton [there are] 3 free men of the same with 20 acres of land. There has always been half a plough; [and there is] 1 church [with] 20 acres, it is worth 20d. And the same [Ulfkil] holds it. In Poringland [there are] 7 whole free men of the same [with] 30 acres. There has always been half a plough; [and there is] 1 church [with] 12 acres [and] it is worth 12d. The same [holds it]. In Shotesham [All Saints or St Mary] [there are] 3 free men belonging to the same [with] 16 acres of land [and] 1½ acres of meadow. They have always ploughed with 2 oxen. The same [holds it].

In Stoke [Holy Cross there is] 1 free man belonging to the same; [he is] a half [free man], [with] 24 acres of land. There

has always been half a plough. The same [holds it]. In Surlingham [there are] 2 free men belonging to the same [with] 12 acres of land. They have always ploughed with 2 oxen. The same [holds it]. In Rockland [St Mary there is] 1 free man of Ulfkil's with 6 acres of land. All these are assessed in [Earl or Pigot] Framingham. The same holds them.

In Bixley [there is] 1 free man of Ulfkil's in commendation and half a free man under him with 17 acres of land, and 1 villan and 1 bordar and 1 acre of meadow. There has always been half a plough. Then it was worth 30d., now 4s. The same holds it. This land Godric the steward claims by his man, that is, Ralph, by judicial ordeal or battle, that he held it as of

[Folio 176v: NORFOLK]

the fief of Earl R[alph], and the Hundred testifies [that it is] of the fief of R[oger] Bigod. But Godric claims this with the moiety which is [mentioned] in the king's writ. This Godric received for half a carucate of land. In Surlingham [there are] 2 whole free men and a half of Godwine's under Stigand with 20 acres of land. The same holds it. In Rockland [St Mary] [there are] 1 whole free man and 2 halves of [free] men of Godwine's under Stigand with 20 acres. The same holds [them].

In Bramerton Ranulf fitzWalter holds 3 free men and 2 half men belonging to the same, with 20 acres. Among them all [there are] 5 acres, and half an acre of meadow. There have always been 2 ploughs. Then they were worth 8s., now 10. These were delivered to complete the manor of Bixley.

DISS HALF HUNDRED.

Shimpling is held by Robert de Vaux for a manor and for 40 acres of land, which Thurbert, a free man of Stigand's, held TRE. Then [there were] 9 bordars, afterwards and now 7. There has always been 1 plough in demesne. Then [there was] 1 plough belonging to the men, afterwards and now half [a plough]. [There is] woodland for 7 pigs and 6 acres of meadow. There has always been 1 horse, and 3 head of cattle. Then [there were] 5 pigs, now 23. There have always been 9 sheep, and 4 free men [were] delivered to complete this manor, [with] 16 acres of land. Then [there was] 1 plough, afterwards and now a half. It has always been worth 20s. It is 5 furlongs in length and 4 in breadth, and [pays] 5d. in geld, whoever holds there; [and] 1 church [with] 10 acres is worth 12d. Gissing was held by 1 free man under Stigand TRE; [there are] 42 acres, and there have always been 6 bordars. There has always been 1 plough in demesne. The men always ploughed with 2 oxen. [There is] woodland for 8 pigs and 4 acres of meadow. Then and afterwards it was worth 5s., now 10; and the same holds it.

'Osmondiston' [in Scole] was held by Algar Trec under Eadric TRE [as] half a carucate of land, and Hugh de Corbon holds it. There have always been 2 villans and 6 bordars. There has always been 1 plough in demesne, but 2 could be employed. Then and afterwards [there were] 2 ploughs belonging to the men, now 2½. [There is] woodland for 15 pigs, and 6 acres of meadow; and 1 free man and a half with 16 acres was delivered to make up this manor. Then [there was] half a plough, now nothing. It has always been worth 50s.

LODDON HUNDRED.

In Mundham Ælfric, a free man under Stigand, held 30 acres of land TRE, and there is half a bordar [and] now 1 plough. [There is] woodland for 4 pigs, and half an acre of meadow. It has always been worth 5s. This Ælfric was outlawed and Ulfkil, the king's reeve, seised the land into the king's hand, and Roger Bigod asked the king for it, and he granted it to him.

Roger Bigod

[Folio 177: NORFOLK]

This Count Alan claims because Earl R[alph] held it as of Rumburgh [Suffolk], his manor. And the men of the Hundred heard this Ulfkil acknowledge on one occasion during 1 year before R[alph] forfeited, and similarly after he had forfeited on one occasion, that he, Ulfkil, was doing service in Rumburgh [Suffolk]; and finally this Hundred heard the same [Ulfkil] say that he was doing service to Roger Bigod. The men of Count Alan each year had 10s. from it, except for the last 4 years, and this they are willing to prove by any means. And Ulfkil holds [it].

In Mundham [there are] 8 free men of Ulfkil's [with] 60 acres of land and 3 bordars, and Ulfkil holds them. There have always been 3 ploughs among them all. Then it was worth 8s., now 10. This Roger has as part of 5 carucates of land which the king gave him. The same Ulfkil [holds] it. In Seething [there are] 5 bordars with 10 acres, and they belong in [Earl or Pigot] Framingham [and] 2 churches [with] 16 acres are worth 2s.; and [there are] 3 oxen. In "Algamundestuna" [there are] 13 free men of Ulfkil's with 50 acres of land, and 7 bordars with 12 acres of land. There have always been 4 ploughs among them all and 2 acres of meadow. Then it was worth 8s., now 10. The same [holds it]. In Claxton 4 free men belonging to the same and 3 bordars with 14 acres. There has always been half a plough. It has always been worth 2s. This is held by Robert de Vaux. In Woodton [there is] 1 free man belonging to the same with 20 acres, and under him 1 free man and 1 bordar with 4 acres, and there has always been half a plough. It has always been worth 32d. [and there is] 1 church [with] 12 acres, it is worth 12d. In Norton [Subcourse] Ulfkil holds 1 free woman with 8 acres, and she is worth 8d. The sake and soke of Mundham is in the Hundred.

Claxton was held by Swetmann, a free man under Stigand, TRE for 30 acres of land. Robert de Vaux [now holds it]. There have always been 7 bordars. There has always been 1 plough in demesne. The men always ploughed with 2 oxen; and [there are] 5 acres of meadow [and] 1 church [with] 30 acres; it is worth 3s. And in the same place [there are] 15 free men of Swetmann's with 30 acres. There has always been 1 plough and 2 acres of meadow among them all. In the same place [there are] 13 half free men belonging to the same [with] 50 acres. There has always been 1 plough and 1 acre of meadow. In Ashby [St Mary] [there are] 10 free men belonging to the same with 30 acres; there has always been 1 plough and 2 acres of meadow. In the same place [there are] 7 half free men with 27 acres. There has always been 1 plough. The same

[holds them]. In Hellington [there is] half a free man with 8 acres. [He] always [ploughed] with 2 oxen. In Carleton [St Peter there is] 1 free man of the same [man's] [with] 5 acres. There has always been 1 horse at the hall, and 3 head of cattle, and 90 sheep, and 14 pigs.

[Folio 177v: NORFOLK]

This Roger Bigod holds of the king's livery. The whole of this has always been worth 60s. There they hold. Claxton is 6 furlongs in length and 5 in breadth, and [pays] 9½d. in geld But many others hold there. In Mundham [there is] 1 free man in commendation of Æthelwig of Thetford [with] 30 acres of land which Turold holds, but he could neither give nor sell it without licence. There has always been 1 villan and 1 bordar. Then [there was] 1 plough, now half; and under him 2 free men and a half with 8 acres and 2 slaves and 2 acres of meadow. There has always been 1 plough among them all. Then it was worth 5s., now 8.

In Ashby [St Mary] [there is] 1 sokeman with 4 acres of land and 2 oxen, and it is worth 6d. Robert [de Vaux holds it]. In Seething [there is] 1 free man of Æthelwig's by commendation with 16 acres, and it is worth 24d., and Turold holds it.

Pirnhow was held by Algar, a free man, under Stigand TRE for half a carucate of land. This Godwine holds. There have always been 6 bordars. Then [there was] half a plough in demesne, and now 2, and half a plough belonging to the men; now 1 mill, now 2 horses at the hall, and 5 head of cattle; now 60 sheep. And [there is] 1 sokeman with 4 acres. Then it was worth 10s., now 20. It is 8 furlongs in length and 3 in breadth, and [pays] 8d. in geld, whoever holds there. The soke is in Earsham. In Thurton [near Loddon] Almær, a free man under Stigand TRE, held 30 acres. This Robert de Vaux holds. There have always been 2 bordars. There has always been 1 plough in demesne and 4 acres of meadow and 17 free men and a half of Algar] Almær's by commendation, with 80 acres. Then and afterwards [there were] 2 ploughs, now 1½. In the same place [there is] half a free man with 15 acres. There has always been half a plough [and] 1 acre of meadow. In Ashby [St Mary] [there are] 2 free men of the same [Almær] [with] 9 acres. They have always ploughed with 2 oxen. The same [holds it]. In Carleton [St Peter] [there are] 2 free men with 5 acres of land. In Mundham [there are] 9 acres in demesne. And [there are] 5 free men of the same with 19 acres. There has always been half a plough. The same [holds it]. In Alpington [there are] 30 acres of land in demesne, and 1 bordar. The whole has always been worth 30s. The soke is in the Hundred. Thurton [near Loddon] is 10 furlongs in length and 5 in breadth and [pays] 7½d. in geld. In Seething [there is] 1 free man of Ulfkil's with 6 acres, and it is worth 6d. Ashby [St Mary] is 9 furlongs in length and 5 in breadth and [pays] 9d. in geld.

[SOUTH] GREENHOE HUNDRED.

Narborough was held by Æthelwig TRE, now R[oger] [holds] 6 carucates of land for a manor. Then [there were] 33 villans, and afterwards 28, now the same. Then and always [there were] 10 bordars. Then [there were] 4 slaves, now 3. Then and afterwards [there were] in demesne 3 ploughs, now 2. Then and afterwards [there were] among the men

Roger Bigod

[Folio 178: NORFOLK]

11 ploughs, now 7 [and] 16 acres of meadow [and] 3 mills. When he received it [there were] 2 horses, and now [the same]. There have always been 13 head of cattle and 25 pigs and 200 sheep and 3 beehives. And it is in length 1 mile, and 10 furlongs in breadth; and when this [Hundred] pays 20s., then it pays 12d. Then it was worth £8, and always [has been].

SHROPHAM HUNDRED.

Hockham was held by Eadric, a thegn, TRE [as] 5 carucates of land. Then and afterwards [there were] 13 villans, now [there are] 7. When he received it [there were] 11 bordars, and now the same. Then and afterwards [there were] 7 slaves now 3; [there are] 37 acres of meadow [and] woodland for 100 pigs. Then and afterwards [there were] 3 ploughs in demesne, now 2; then [there were] 3 ploughs belonging to the men, afterwards and now 2, and 2 ploughs could be restored; and [there are] 4 sokemen [with] 3½ acres. Then [there were] 220 wild mares, now none; then 5 horses, now 2. Then [there were] 12 head of cattle, now 2; then 12 pigs, now 8. There have always been 220 sheep; now [there are] 2 beehives. Then and afterwards it was worth £4, and now the same. The whole is 1½ leagues in length, and half a league in breadth, whoever holds there, and [pays] 15d. in geld. In Little Hockham Æthelwig held half a carucate of land; there have always been 3 villans and 3 bordars and 2 slaves, and 3 acres of meadow; there has always been 1 plough in demesne and half a plough belonging to the men; and 1 sokeman [with] 3½ acres. It has always been worth 13s. 4d., and Turold holds it. In Snetterton the same held [an estate] for 1 carucate of land, and for a manor. And Ralph fitzHerluin holds [the same]. There have always been 2 villans and 3 bordars and 1 slave [and] 8 acres of meadow; there has always been 1 plough in demesne and half a plough belonging to the men. Then [there were] 3 head of cattle, now 7, and 9 pigs; then 60 sheep, now 160, and 14 goats and 2 beehives. It has always been worth 20s.; and it is 1 league in length and a half in breadth, whosoever holds there, and [pays] 17¼d. in geld.

GUILTCROSS HUNDRED.

In [Great or Little] Snarehill Thorsten, a free man, held 2 carucates of land TRE; there have always been 6 bordars and 1 slave and 3 acres of meadow. Then and afterwards [there were] 2 ploughs in demesne, now 1, and another could be restored; there has always been half a plough belonging to the men, and half a fishery. Then [there were] 4 horses, now 1; then 3 head of cattle, now 2; then 12 pigs. Then [there were] 80 sheep, now 60. Then it was worth 16s., now 20. In the other [Great or Little] SNAREHILL Æthelwig held 1 carucate of land and 60 acres. This Æthelstan the Englishman holds. Then [there were] 2 slaves, now 1, and 6 sokemen with all customary dues; but each one always paid 4d. in the king's [manor of] Kenninghall for average [carting-service], and the

king has the 6 forfeitures from them. In demesne there has always been 1 plough, and half a plough could be added; [and there is] half a plough belonging to the men. Then [there was] 1 horse; there have always been 4 head of cattle, then [there were] 7 pigs, now 5; then 100 sheep, now 300, and 5 beehives, and it is worth 20s.

[Folio 178v: NORFOLK]

The whole is 1 league in length and a half in breadth and [pays] 11½d. in geld. [North or South] Lopham was held by Ulf, a free man TRE, 3 carucates of land, as a manor; there have always been 2 villans and 13 bordars and 4 slaves and 12 acres of meadow. Then and afterwards [there were] 2 ploughs in demesne, now 3; there have always been 2 ploughs belonging to the men, and woodland for 100 pigs. And [there are] 18 sokemen [with] 1 carucate of land with all customary dues, and 12 acres and 2 ploughs. Then [there was] 1 horse, now 1 horse [sic], now 2; then [there was] 1 ox, now 13; now 40 pigs; then 100 sheep, now 60. Then and afterwards it was worth 60s., now 112s. In the other [North or South] Lopham Alsige, a free man, held 2 carucates of land TRE; there have always been 2 villans and 7 bordars and 4 slaves, and 11 acres of meadow; always 2 ploughs in demesne, and half a plough belonging to the men and 1 plough could be restored; [and] woodland for 80 pigs. And [there are] 4 sokemen [with] 13 acres of land, and 2 oxen, and 1 free man [with] 40 acres of land, 1 bordar, and 1½ acres of meadow. There has always been half a plough. There has always been 1 horse. Then [there was] 1 ox, now 3; there have always been 40 pigs; then [there were] 100 sheep, now 60, and 10 beehives. The soke of the free man [is] in Kenninghall. In [Blo] Norton 1 carucate of land was held by the same for a manor TRE, now Alfred the Englishman holds it. Then as now [there were] 4 villans and 4 bordars and 1 acre of meadow. Then [there were] 2 ploughs in demesne, afterwards and now 1, and the other could be restored; there has always been half a plough belonging to the men. And [there are] 7 sokemen [with] 60 acres of land and 2 bordars and 1 acre of meadow; there has always been 1 plough. This land Alsige added to [North or South] Lopham for a berewick TRW, and [...] had it for a manor TRE. On it [there are] 20 sheep. [North or South] Lopham TRE was worth 60s. and [Blo] Norton 20s. Now the whole [North or South] Lopham is worth 70s. and [Blo] Norton 30s. The whole of [North or South] Lopham is 1 league in length and 1 league in breadth, and [pays] 34½d. in geld. In Banham [there is] 1 sokeman with all his customary dues belonging to St Æthelthryth TRE, whom after King W[illiam] came into England the predecessor of R[oger] Bigod had in commendation only; and he has 10 acres of land, and is worth 2s. Now Berard holds [him].

LAUNDITCH HUNDRED.

In Whissonsett Ranulf fitzWalter holds for a manor 3 carucates of land, . Then and afterwards [there were] 8 villans, now 5. Then and afterwards [there were] 6 bordars, now 10. Then [there were] 4 slaves, and there have always been 15 acres of meadow. Then [there were] 4 ploughs among the whole, of which 2 are now in demesne and 2 belong to the men; [and there is] woodland for 100 pigs. [There is] the fourth part of a fishpond. There have always been 2 horses, now 12 head of cattle.

Roger Bigod

[Folio 179: NORFOLK]

Then [there were] 9 pigs, now 25. Then [there were] 60 sheep, now 67; now [there are] 36 goats, and 7 beehives. Then it was worth 40s., now 60. Of 3 free men the soke is in the king's [manor of] Mileham. The whole is half a league in length and half in breadth and [pays] 10d. of geld whoever holds there.

FOREHOE HUNDRED.

Stanheard the Englishman holds Hingham, half a carucate of land for a manor, which Æthelwig held TRE. Then [there were] 5 bordars, now 6; there have always been 2 slaves, woodland for 12 pigs and 4 acres of meadow; there has always been 1 plough in demesne, and half a plough belonging to the men; there have always been 2 horses and 8 head of cattle and 6 pigs and 20 sheep and 16 goats and 2 beehives. And [there is] 1 sokeman and a half [with] 27 acres. Then it was worth 20s., now 25.

MIDFORD HUNDRED

. In Yaxham Ranulf fitzWalter holds 3 acres of land which Ealdwig the priest, a free man, held TRE and 8 bordars [and] there has always been 1 plough, woodland for 5 pigs, and 4 acres of meadow, and it is worth 10s.; and it is 7 furlongs in length and 5 in breadth and [pays] 20d. in geld.

GALLOW HUNDRED.

[North or South] Creake is held by Turstin fitzGuy [as] 4 carucates of land which Cock-Hagni held TRE. There have always been 6 villans and 14 bordars and 10 slaves. Then [there were] 4 ploughs in demesne, and afterwards; now [there are] 3. Then [there were] 3 ploughs belonging to the men, now 2, and they could be restored. [There is] woodland for 20 pigs [and] 6 acres of meadow. There has always been 1 horse. Then [there were] 18 pigs, now 13. Then [there were] 320 sheep, now 264; and 25 sokemen with 1 carucate of land. Then [there were] 7 ploughs, now 5. Then it was worth £4, now 6.

BROTHERCROSS HUNDRED.

In Burnham Humphrey de Culey holds 1 carucate of land which Cock-Hagni held TRE. Then [there were] 2 villans and now [the same]. There have always been 10 bordars. Then [there were] 2 slaves, now 1. There has always been 1 plough in demesne. Then [there were] 2 ploughs belonging to the men, now 1, but [the other] can be restored. Now [there are] 40 sheep. Then it was worth 20s., now 16s.

[NORTH] GREENHOE HUNDRED.

In Quarles Turstin fitzGuy holds 1 berewick which belongs to 1 carucate of land at [North or South] Creake: [there are] 5 bordars [and] there has always been 1 plough; and it is in the valuation of [North or South] Creake. [Field] Dalling was held by Alsige and Leofstan, a free man, TRE, now by

R[oger] the sheriff; [there are] 2 carucates of land; and this the same Roger claims in exchange for that land which the king gave to Isaac; [there are] 1 villan and 3 bordars; [and] 6 sokemen [with] 18 acres of land [and] 7 acres of meadow. On the whole

[Folio 179v: NORFOLK]

there have always been 3 ploughs, and then it was worth 30s., now 40s.

NORTH ERPINGHAM HUNDRED.

Hanworth was held by 1 free man, Withri, TRE; now R[oger] Bigod holds it; [there are] 4 carucates of land [and] there have always been 11 villans and 30 bordars. Then and afterwards [there were] 2 slaves, and now 1. Then [there were] 4 ploughs in demesne, and afterwards 2, and now 3, and always 5 ploughs belonging to the men. [There is] woodland for 60 pigs [and] 6 acres of meadow. Then and afterwards [there was] 1 mill, now 2. Then [there was] 1 horse and now 5. Then [there were] 14 head of cattle and now 24. Then [there were] 7 pigs, then 7 pigs, and now 40. Then [there were] 11 sheep, now 105. Then [there were] 30 goats, now 26. Then [there were] 7 beehives, and now 8. To this belongs 1 berewick, Roughton, 1 carucate of land; there have always been 2 villans and 8 bordars and 1 slave; always 1 plough in demesne, and 1½ ploughs belonging to the men [and] 3 acres of meadow.

In Alby [there is] 1 villan, and 3 in Sustead and 1 bordar belonging to the manor aforesaid. In Ingworth [there is] 1 villan whom Toki of Winterton held; and this the predecessor of R[oger] added to this manor. In Aldborough 1 bordar whom Wulfstan held TRE was added in the same way. In Thurgarton [there are] 2 bordars belonging to the manor. In Calthorpe 1 villan whom Godwine of Scottow held was added in the same way; and these three that were added hold 36 acres of land. The whole of this was worth TRE £4, and afterwards 60s., and now £6: and the manor is 8 furlongs in length and 5½ in breadth, and [pays] 9½d. in geld. And that Withri had sake and soke upon his land, and the king and earl had the 6 forfeitures.

HAPPING HUNDRED.

Sutton [near Stalham] was held by Eadric of Laxfield TRE [as] 3½ carucates of land; there have always been 6 villans and 17 bordars, and 2 ploughs in demesne and 3 ploughs belonging to the men, woodland for 60 pigs, 39 acres of meadow, half a salt-pan, and 2 horses. Then [there were] 23 wild mares, now 7. Then [there were] 13 head of cattle, now 22; then 9 pigs, now 23. Then [there were] 180 sheep, now 200; and 4 beehives. And [there are] 2 sokemen with 12½ acres . To this manor belongs 1 berewick, Catfield [of] 1 carucate of land [and] there have always been 2 bordars, and 1 plough in demesne, and half a plough belonging to the men, and 18 acres of meadow [and] woodland for 10 pigs. And [there are] 14 sokemen [with] 75 acres; there have always been 2½ ploughs, and half an acre of meadow; [there is] 1 church [with] 20 acres. And [there are] 24 free men in commendation only [with] 2 carucates of land; there have always been 4 ploughs, and 14 acres of meadow. The king and earl [have] the soke. To this manor also belongs Brumstead. Robert holds what Eadric held [as] 2 carucates of land; there have always been 2 villans, and 4 bordars;

Roger Bigod

then and afterwards [there was] 1 plough in demesne, now 2; there has always been 1 plough belonging to the men; [there is] 1 church [with] 9 acres. [There is] woodland for 16 pigs, and 8 acres of meadow; now [there is] 1 mill, and 1 ox, now 10 pigs, and 40 sheep, and 30 goats. And [there are] 17 free men [with] 110 acres in commendation only, and St Benet [of Hulme] has the commendation of 1; there have always been 2 bordars, and 2 ploughs and 2 acres of meadow. And the same holds it. In Stalham of 9 free men the commendation only [belonged to] Eadric, and half the soke; the king and earl [have] the other moiety: and they have 60 acres of land and 1½ ploughs and 3 acres of meadow. In Horsey [there are] 4 free men in commendation only, the king and earl [have] the soke; and they have 50 acres and 1 plough and 6 acres of meadow. All these free men were then worth 40s., now 68s. 8d. And the whole manor with the berewick was then worth 90s., now [it is worth] £6 11s. 4d. Now the whole together, with the free men, is worth £10. This was of the manors of Earl Ralph, and was at rent for £10, and as such the king gave it to Roger Bigod, as he himself says, when his brother William came from Apulia with Geoffrey Ridel.

EAST FLEGG HUNDRED.

In Thrigby [there are] 3 half free men of Æthelwig [with] 31 acres; Æthelwig had commendation of 2 only, and of the other Gyrth; and there has always been 1 plough and 2 acres of meadow, and they are worth 4s. In Runham [there are] 3 half free men of Æthelwig's by commendation only [with] 13½ acres, and half an acre of meadow; there has always been half a plough and 2½ salt-pans, and it is worth 18d. In Filby [there are] 4 free men of the same, together with 118 acres of land and 1 bordar; there have always been 2 ploughs and 4 acres of meadow and 2½ salt-pans; and it is worth 5s. This Stanheard holds. In 'Ness' [in Mautby] [there is] 1 free man [with] 15 acres which Æthelwig seized in the time of King William, and R[oger] Bigod claims it for his fief of the king's gift; there have always been 2 oxen and 1 acre of meadow and 3 parts of a salt-pan, and it is worth 16d.; and the same holds it. In Mautby [there is] 1 free man under Æthelwig by commendation only [with] 20½ acres of land; there have always been 3½ bordars and 2 oxen and 1 acre of meadow and 1 salt-pan, and it is worth 8d.

HUMBLEYARD HUNDRED.

Hethel was held by Ulf, a thegn, [for] 2 carucates of land and 35 acres TRE. Then [there were] 12 villans, afterwards 10, now 12. Then and afterwards [there were] 7 bordars, now 11 [and] there have always been 2 slaves. Then [there were] 2 ploughs in demesne, afterwards 1, now 2, and 1 church [with] 30 acres. Then [there were] 5 ploughs, afterwards and now 3

[and] 12 acres of meadow; [there is] woodland for 60 pigs [and] now [there is] 1 mill. Then [there were] 2 horses, now 5. Then [there were] 5 head of cattle, now 8, and 3 wild mares. Then [there were] 18 pigs, now 25; then 1 sheep, now

80; then 2 beehives. And [there are] 8 sokemen [with] 30 acres of land; then and afterwards [there was] 1 plough, now a half, and 1 acre of meadow. And there has always been 1 berewick, Keswick, of 1 carucate of land and 20 acres. Then [there were] 2 villans, afterwards and now 1; there has always been 1 slave. Then and afterwards [there was] 1 plough in demesne, now 2, and 3 acres of meadow. There has always been 1 mill. Then it was worth 106s. 6d.; afterwards £6, now [it is worth] 8. And it is 1 league in length and 6 furlongs in breadth, and [pays] 6¾d. in geld. And Keswick is 6 furlongs in length and 5 furlongs in breadth, and [pays] 6½d. in geld. And Aitard [de Vaux] holds it. The same Ulf held KETTERINGHAM TRE [as] 2 carucates of land; now Ranulf fitzWalter [holds]; there have always been 4 villans and 7 bordars. Then [there were] 3 slaves, now 1; there have always been 2 ploughs in demesne, and 1½ ploughs belonging to the men [and] 8 acres of meadow; there have always been 2 horses; [there is] 1 church [with] 40 acres. Then [there was] 1 mill, now none, but it is in Hethel; then 1 ox, now 3; now 20 pigs and 80 sheep. And [there are] 8 sokemen with 60 acres; there have always been 1½ ploughs. Then and afterwards it was worth 50s., now 60. And it is 1 league in length and a half in breadth, and [pays] 16½d. in geld whoever holds there. [East] Carleton is held by Walter, which Ulf held [as] 1 carucate of land for a manor; there have always been 2 bordars, and 1 plough in demesne [and] 4 acres of meadow; there is woodland for 2 pigs, then [there was] 1 horse, and it is worth 10s. [There are] two churches [with] 38 acres. In Flordon [there are] 10 acres, and in Newton [Fotman] 15 acres of the demesne of Hethel; there has always been 1 plough and 1 mill, and it is worth 5s. And Flordon is 8 furlongs in length and 5 in breadth, and [pays] 9¾d. in geld.

DEPWADE HUNDRED.

Forncett [St Mary or St Peter] was held by Colman, a free man under Stigand, [as] 1 carucate of land. Then [there was] 1 villan, afterwards and now 2, and 1 church [with] 15 acres. Then [there were] 8 bordars, afterwards 10, and now 14; there have always been 2 ploughs in demesne, and 2 ploughs belonging to the men [and] 12 acres of meadow. Then [there were] 2 horses, now 5; then 10 head of cattle, now 12; then 1 sheep, now 80. Then [there was] 1 pig, now 18; and 3 sokemen [with] 27 acres; then 1 plough, now half [a plough]. And [there is] 1 berewick, Aslacton, [of] 80 acres; there have always been 6 bordars, then 2 ploughs in demesne, and now the same. Then [there was] 1 plough belonging to the men, 6 acres of meadow, woodland for 4 pigs [and] then [there was] 1 horse. Then [there were] 5 head of cattle, now 1 [and] now 1 pig. And [there are] 3 sokemen [with] 6 acres; then [there was] half a plough. And William holds another berewick, Swanton, of 40 acres; there have always been 3 bordars, always 1 plough in demesne and [there is] half a plough belonging to the men, and 4 acres of meadow and 3 cattle. And [there is] 1 sokeman [with] 3 acres. In Kettleton [there are] 2 sokemen [with] 7 acres; then [there was] half a plough, now [there are] 2 oxen. In "Halas" [there are] 3 sokemen [with] 12 acres; then [there was] 1 plough, now half . Then the whole

Roger Bigod

[Folio 181: NORFOLK]

was worth 60s., now £6. The whole of "Halas" is half a league in length and 4 furlongs in breadth, and [pays] 4d. in geld. Forncett [St Mary or St Peter] is 1 league in length and a half in breadth, and [pays] 6½d. in geld. And Aslacton [is] 1 league in length and a half in breadth, and [pays] 9d. in geld. And Swanton [is] 11 furlongs in length and 6 [furlongs] and 10 perches in breadth, and pays 11¼d. in geld. In Forncett [St Mary or St Peter] Ulf held 30 acres TRE; there have always been 1 villan, 3 bordars, and 1 slave. Then and afterwards [there was] 1 plough in demesne, now none; there has always been half a plough belonging to the men [and] 6 acres of meadow. [There is] woodland for 8 pigs; then [there was] 1 horse, then 3 head of cattle. In Kettleton [there are] 2 sokemen, 6 acres. And in Swanton [there are] 2 sokemen, 6 acres. In Wacton [there is] 1 sokeman [with] 4 acres. In Moulton [St Michael] [there is] 1 sokeman [with] 10 acres. In Aslacton [there is] 1 sokeman [with] 30 acres; there has always been 1 plough and 2 bordars and 3 acres of meadow. In Tibenham [there are] 2 sokemen [with] 66 acres, and 8 bordars. Then [there were] 2 ploughs, now 1½ ploughs [and] 3 acres of meadow. In Tharston [there are] 2 sokemen [with] 45 acres. Then [there was] 1 plough, now half , and 1 acre of meadow. In [Long] Stratton [there is] 1 sokeman [with] 12 acres. In Shelton [there is] 1 sokeman [with] 60 acres, and 14 bordars and 6 villans and 1 slave, and 1½ ploughs in demesne, and 2 ploughs belonging to the men and 3 acres of meadow; [there is] woodland for 8 pigs. In Hardwick [there are] 2 sokemen [with] 35 acres, and 5 bordars; there have always been 2 ploughs and 2 acres of meadow; [there is] woodland for 2 pigs. In Fritton [there is] 1 sokeman [with] 8 acres and 2 oxen. Then the whole was worth 80s., now 100[s.] and 10d. The king and the earl [have] the soke. Tharston is held by Robert de Vaux, which Wulfric held under Stigand [as] 2 carucates of land; there has always been 1 villan; then and afterwards [there were] 26 bordars; now 24; there have always been 2 ploughs in demesne; [and there is] 1 church [with] 40 acres, and it is worth 3s. Then [there were] 2 ploughs belonging to the men, now [there is] 1, and 1 plough could be restored; [there are] 12 acres of meadow [and] woodland for 10 pigs, and 2 mills. Then [there were] 4 horses, now 4 head of cattle. Then [there were] 40 pigs, now 20. Then [there were] 40 sheep, now 80, and 1 beehive. And [there are] 33 sokemen [with] 1 carucate of land. Then [there were] 8 ploughs, afterwards and now 4, and 2 acres of meadow. Then it was worth £5 6s., and now the same: and it is 1½ leagues in length and 1½ furlongs in breadth, and [pays] 15¼d. in geld. To this manor Robert de Vaux added 7 free men and a half; of all [these] his predecessor had commendation

[Folio 181v: NORFOLK]

only, except of one who was a sokeman of Stigand's; and they have 82 acres. Then and afterwards [there were] 3 ploughs, now 2, and 3 acres of meadow, and they are worth 14s. Hudeston was held by Æthelwig of Thetford [as] 2 carucates of land; now Robert de Courson holds it; there have always been 1 villan and 21 bordars and 2 slaves; then [there was] 1 plough in demesne, now [there are] 2. Then and afterwards [there were] 3 ploughs belonging to the men, now 2 [and there are] 6 acres of meadow. [There is] woodland for 6 pigs. There has always been 1 mill, and 1 horse, and 3 head of cattle, and 46 pigs. And [there were] 11 men in the soke of the fold and commendation TRE, and they could sell the land, but the dues remained in the manor; and they have 26 acres; then [there were] 1½ ploughs, now 1, and [there is] 1 church [with] 30 acres, and 2 acres of meadow and half a plough. The king and earl [have] the soke. Then it was worth 40s., now 70s. And [there are] 5 free men, of 2 [of which] and 1 bordar Æthelwig had commendation only; and of the third the predecessor of [Robert] Malet, and of the fourth the predecessor of Ralph Baynard, and of the fifth the predecessor of Eudo fitzSpirewic; and they have 42 acres. There has always been 1 plough, and 3 acres of meadow: and they are worth 6s. The king and earl [have the soke]. And in Hempnall [there is] 1 free man of Æthelwig by commendation only [with] 30 acres, and 1 plough and 1 acre of meadow [and] woodland for 8 pigs; and it is worth 10s., and Turold holds it.

In Swanton 30 acres were held by Hardekin, a free man, TRE; there have always been 4 bordars; then [there were] 3 slaves, now 2; there has always been 1 plough in demesne, and half a plough belonging to the men, and 1 mill and 3 acres of meadow. And [there were] 11 free men under him TRE in commendation [with] 20 acres. Then [there were] 1½ ploughs, now 1. Then it was worth 15s., now 23[s.] 7d. This he [Roger Bigod] claims of the king's gift. This Walter holds.

CLAVERING HUNDRED.

Haddiscoe [was held by] 9 free men of Stigand's, 120 acres and 1 bordar; there have always been 2 ploughs; [there is] pasture for 80 sheep [and] 9 acres of meadow, and it is worth 15s. And it is 1 league in length and 8 furlongs in breadth [...] and [pays] 9¼d. in geld. Robert holds it. Hales was held by Æthelstan, a thegn of Harold's, TRE; [there is] 1 carucate of land and 40 acres; there have always been 9 bordars and 2 ploughs in demesne and 1 plough belonging to the men, and 5 acres of meadow; [there is] woodland for 3 pigs. Then [there was] 1 horse, now 2. Then [there was] 1 ox, now 2. Then [there were] 14 pigs, now 27. Then [there were] 10 sheep. And [there are] 13 free men in soke, right of fold and commendation [with] 40 acres. Then it was worth 20s., now 40. This Æthelstan commended himself to Æthelwig of Thetford TRW, and he [Æthelwig] was seised of him when King William gave his [Æthelwig's] land to Roger; but the Hundred has not seen [any] writ or [the] livery officer that gave [him] to Æthelwig. The whole

Roger Bigod

[Folio 182: NORFOLK]

of Hales is 15 furlongs and 13 perches [in length] and 6 furlongs in breadth, and pays 8d. in geld.

In Haddiscoe 1 sokeman of Eadric of Laxfield [has] 30 acres and 3 bordars, and 1½ ploughs, 6 acres of meadow, and 4 free men under him [with] 19 acres. Then it was worth 10s., now 13[s.] 4d. There is also pasture for 50 sheep.

This sokeman commended himself to Æthelwig TRW and he was seised of him when the king gave the land to Roger Bigod.

Heckingham, which a free man held T[R]E, is held by Turold of Roger; [there are] 26 acres and 1 bordar and 1 acre of meadow. Then [there was] half a plough, now [there is] none, but it could be restored. And it is worth 16d.

IN Haddiscoe 1 free man held 1½ acres and 1 bordar, and is worth 3d. Robert holds him of Roger [Bigod].

IN Raveningham 1 free man held 12 acres TRE, of whom Æthelwig was seised when Roger received his land. This is in the valuation of Haddiscoe. The same R[obert] holds it.

[Folio 182v: NORFOLK]

In Norton [Subcourse] Ulfkil, a free man, held 30 acres, now 2 men hold them of the fief of Ulfkil. There has always been 1 bordar and half a plough and 1 acre of meadow; and 1 free man under him [with] 1 acre. The whole is 1 league in length and half in breadth, and [pays] 12d. in geld.

In Thurlton [there are] 2 free men [with] 22 acres and 1 acre of meadow, and half a plough. This Robert holds of Roger [Bigod].

In Heckingham [there is] 1 free man, Bondi, [with] 30 acres of land, whom Roger holds as part of the fief of Ulfkil: but Ulfkil himself had half the commendation of him TRE, and of his wife, the whole commendation. And Godric the steward claims him because he held him when Earl Ralph forfeited. And the Hundred testifies that he used to do service to Godric, but they do not know on what terms. And he always had 1 plough and 2 acres of meadow. He is worth 4s.

IN the Hundred of North ERPINGHAM

Roger [Bigod] has 2 bordars with 15 acres.

In [Earl or Pigot] Framingham [there are] 8 bordars [with] 16 acres of land. In Bixley [there is] Alvric, a free man [with] 24 acres. In Poringland [there is] 1 free man, 24 acres and 2 bordars. And it is worth 8s. The whole is of the HUNDRED of Henstead.

Roger Bigod

[Folio 183: NORFOLK]

These are the free men belonging to Roger Bigod in Freebridge Hundred and half.

In Grimston 1 free man [with] 60 acres of land whom Robert de Vaux holds, 3 bordars, and 8 acres of meadow; there has always been half a plough, and it is worth 5s. In the same place the same holds 4 free men [with] 40 acres and 2

acres of meadow; TRE [there was] 1 plough, now a half, and it is worth 5s.

DOCKING HUNDRED.

In Titchwell Tovi, a free man under Harold TRE, held 1 carucate of land; now Ralph holds it. Then [there was] 1 plough in demesne, and now [the same]; there has always been 1 plough belonging to the men, and 6 villans and 1 bordar, and 2½ acres of meadow. Then it was worth 13s. 4d., now 12[s.].

SMETHDON HUNDRED.

In Hunstanton [there were] 4 free men TRE [with] 65 acres whom Ralph fitzHerluin holds. Then [there was] 1 plough, now 2 oxen. Then they were worth 16s., now 4[s.].

GRIMSHOE HUNDRED.

In Mundford [there are] 60 acres of land which 1 free man holds; there has always been 1 plough and 2 bordars and 2 acres of meadow; [there is] woodland for 5 pigs. Then it was worth, and now 2s. In Sturston [there is] 1 free man with 60 acres whom R[alph] fitzH[erluin] holds. Then [there was] half a plough. Then he was worth 30d., now 8d.

In Stanford [there is] 1 free man [with] 60 acres of land. Now Stanheard holds him. Then and afterwards [there was] half a plough and 2 acres of meadow, and he is worth 2s. 8d.

WAYLAND HUNDRED.

In Griston [there is] 1 free man [with] 28 acres of land, half a plough and 3 acres of meadow, and he is worth 4s.

In Breckles [there are] 9 free men with 110 acres, 1 villan and 1 bordar and 10 acres of meadow; there have always been 2 ploughs; and they are worth 10s.

In Saham [Toney] [there is] 1 free man [with] 60 acres of lands, whom Robert holds; [there is] 1 plough and 5 bordars and 8 acres of meadow [and] woodland for 15 pigs; and it is worth 30s.

In Thompson [there are] 40 acres of land and half a plough, and it is worth 3s.

SHROPHAM HUNDRED.

In Hockham [there are] 4 free men and in Shropham 5, and in Wilby 1, and in Besthorpe 1; among them all [there are] 3 carucates of land

[Folio 183v: NORFOLK]

and 2½ acres, and 6 bordars, and 17 acres of meadow; woodland for 8 pigs [and] there have always been 5 ploughs. The whole is worth 68s. The soke is in the king's [manor of] Buckenham [near Attleborough]. In Shopham [there is] 1 free man [with] 30 acres of land; there has always been 1 bordar, and 3 acres of meadow, and half a plough, and it is worth 4s. The soke is in the same Buckenham [near Attleborough]. In Shropham [there is] 1 free man, 8 acres of land and 1½ acres of meadow, and 2 oxen; and it is worth 16d.

In Besthorpe [there is] 1 free man [with] 1 half carucate of land, 1 villan and 7 bordars and 6 acres of meadow; there has always been 1 plough in demesne. Then and afterwards [there was] 1 plough belonging to the men, now [there are] 2 oxen;

[there is] woodland for 8 [pigs]. Then it was worth 10s., now 20. The soke is Buckenham [near Attleborough]. In [All Saints or St Andrew] Rockland [there is] half a carucate of land, 1 free man whom Pain holds, 2 bordars, and 3 acres of meadow; there has always been half a plough, and it is worth 5s. The soke [is] in Buckenham [near Attleborough]. In Brettenham [there are] 3 free men [with] 1 carucate of land whom William de Bournville holds, and 3 bordars and 4 acres of meadow. Then and afterwards [there were] 1½ ploughs, now 1, and it is worth 23s. 8d. The soke [is] Buckenham [near Attleborough].

GUILTCROSS HUNDRED.

In [North or South] Lopham [there are] 5 free men, 1 carucate of land and 20 acres, and 5 bordars and 5 acres of meadow; there have always been 2½ ploughs; [there is] woodland for 40 pigs. The whole is worth 48s . The soke [is] in Kenninghall. In Quidenham [there was] 1 free man [with] 24 [acres] TRE, now [there are] 3 free men [and] 2 acres of meadow. Then [there was] half a plough, and it is worth 2s. The soke [is] in Kenninghall. Mid [sic].

MIDFORD HUNDRED AND HALF.

In "Thurstuna" [there are] 20 acres of land, 1 free man whom Robert holds, 1 plough, and 4 acres of meadow, and 4 sokemen and a half [and] 10 acres, and it is worth 4s.; [there is] 1 church [with] 16 acres, and it is worth 16d.

GALLOW HUNDRED.

In [North or South] Creake [there are] 4 free men with half a carucate of land whom Turstin fitzGuy holds. Then [there were] 1½ ploughs, now [there are] 2 oxen, and it is worth 3s.

BROTHECROSS HUNDRED.

In Burnham the same holds 2 free men with 1 carucate of land. Then and now [there were] 10 bordars [and] then and now 1 plough in demesne. Then [there was] 1 plough belonging to the men, now a half, and 2 parts of a mill [and] half an acre of meadow. Then it was worth 8s., now

Roger Bigod

[Folio 184: NORFOLK]

18s. In the same place the same holds 2 free men with half a carucate of land. There have always been 2 bordars. There has always been half a plough. Then it was worth 2s., now 12d.

In [Burnham] Deepdale 1 free man with half a carucate of land is held by the same. There have always been 3 bordars. There has always been 1 plough. Then it was worth 20s., now 10.

In [East or West] Raynham of the fief of Bishop [sic] Stigand 1 free man holds half a carucate of land. Now Edwin holds him. There have always been 4 slaves. Then [there was] 1 plough, now a half, [and there are] 2 acres of meadow. Then it was worth 10s., now 5s. In [South] Raynham [there is] 1 free man with 20 acres of land, whom Aitard holds, and 1 bordar. There has always been half a

plough, [and there is] 1 acre of meadow. Then it was worth 5s., now 3s.

HOLT HUNDRED.

In Morston [there is] 1 free man with half a carucate of land whom Turold holds, and 4 bordars, and 1 plough, and it is worth 20s.

NORTH ERPINGHAM HUNDRED.

In Hanworth Withri held 3 free men, now R[oger] Bigod [holds them]. Now they have 1 bordar and 60 acres of land. Then [there were] 1½ ploughs, and always have been, and[there are] 3 roods of meadow. Then and afterwards they were worth 10s., now 18. In Metton Withri held 3 free men TRE, and Harold, 1; now R[oger] Bigod [holds them]. There has always been 1 carucate of land and 1 villan and 3 bordars and a half, and 2 ploughs, 3 acres of meadow, and 1 mill. Then and afterwards they were worth 20s., now 30[s.] 8d.

In Sustead Withri held 1 free man and Wulfstan 1 TRE; now R[oger] [holds them]. And they have 30 acres of land and 1 bordar and a half, then as now, and 1 plough [and] 1½ acres of meadow; and now [there is] 1 mill. Then and afterwards they were worth 8s., and now 12[s.]. In Aylmerton [there is] 1 free man of Æthelwig's, now Roger's; and he has 1 carucate of land; there have always been 7 villans and 7 bordars, and 1 plough in demesne, and 1 plough belonging to the men. And under him [there are] 2 sokemen [with] 16 acres of land; and there has always been half a plough and woodland for 4 pigs [and] 1½ acres of meadow. Then and afterwards it was worth 20s., and now 40. In Felbrigg [there are] 2 free men of Gyrth's, and they have 2 carucates of land; there has always been 1 villan and 7 bordars and 2 ploughs in demesne, and 1 plough belonging to the men. [There is] woodland for 60 pigs [and] 4 acres of meadow. And he has 8 sokemen with 63 acres of land, and there have always been 1½ ploughs belonging to the men. [There is] wood[land] for 6 pigs. Then and afterwards it was worth 40s., and now £4. It is half a league in length and 4 furlongs and 3 perches

[Folio 184v: NORFOLK]

in breadth and [pays] 3½d. in geld. And Metton is 5 furlongs in length and 4 [furlongs] and 6 perches in breadth, and [pays] 5d. in geld.

In Gresham Alweard holds 4 sokemen with 13 acres of land. There has always been half a plough [and] 1 acre of meadow; they are assessed with the 4 free men. In the same vill [there is] 1 free man with 30 acres of land; and there have always been 2 bordars, and half a plough. In Sustead Alweard holds 3 bordars, and they have half a plough. In [North] Barningham [there is] 1 sokemen with 12 acres of land. Then he used to plough with 2 oxen, now with half a plough. In Aldborough [there is] 1 free man with 30 acres of land whom Ketil held TRE, [and] half an acre of meadow. In Aylmerton [there are] 2 sokemen whom Alweard holds, with 12 acres of land and 3 bordars. They have always ploughed with half a team; and the whole of this is in the valuation of Felbrigg.

In Runton Bondi held 1 free man TRE with 30 acres of land; he was delivered for 1 free man, but now 2 free men hold it; [there are] 5 villans and 2 bordars; there has always been 1 plough. [There is] woodland for 4 pigs [and] 1 acre of meadow. Then and afterwards it was worth 8s.; it stood at 20s., but could not pay it; and therefore it now stands for 15[s.].

In Roughton Withri held 2 free men with 30 acres of land TRE. [There is] woodland for 2 pigs [and] half an acre of meadow. Then and afterwards it was worth 5s., now 10s. 4d. Here Eadric held 1 free man [with] 3 acres who could not withdraw without Eadric's licence; but Robert Malet claims the men.

In Suffield [there are] 4 free men, and Withri held 1 of them and the king another, and Harold the 2 others; [there are] 2 carucates of land. There have always been 10 villans and 11 bordars. Then and always there have been 4 ploughs in demesne and 3 ploughs belonging to the men. [There is] woodland for 12 pigs [and] 4 acres of meadow. Then and afterwards [there were] 2 mills, now 4. Then and afterwards it was worth £4, and now £6 15s. And it is 8 furlongs in length and 5½ in breadth, and [pays] 13½d. in geld..

In [North] Barningham [there are] 16 acres of land of the demesne aforesaid. [There is] woodland for 4 pigs.

In Antingham 2 bordars have half a plough. They are assessed in Suffield.

In this Antingham 3 free men the first was Almær's, another Alweald's,

Roger Bigod

the third Ospakr's - hold 1½ carucates of land, and Turstin fitzGuy holds them; there have always been 4 villans and 4 bordars. Then and afterwards [there were] 1½ ploughs, and now 2½ ploughs, 3 acres of meadow and 2 ploughs that have always belonged to the men. Then and afterwards it was worth 25s., now 36[...]s.

In Aldborough [there are] 4 free men whom Harold held TRE, with half a carucate of land. There have always been 6 bordars. There have always been 3 ploughs [and there is] 1 acre of meadow [and] 1½ mills. Then and afterwards [they were worth] 15s., now 30, but they were [valued] at 40s., but could not pay it. In Thurgarton [there is] 1 free man whom Ylfing holds, with 12 acres of land; he always ploughed with half a plough [team]. Then and afterwards he was worth 2s., now 5.

In 'Shipden' [there is] 1 free man [whom] Esbiorn held TRE, with 40 acres of land; now Turstin holds him. Then [there were] 3 bordars, now 5; there has always been 1 plough in demesne, and half a plough belonging to the men; [there is] 1 acre of meadow. [There is] woodland for 30 pigs, and 1 sokeman with 3 acres of land. Then and afterwards he was worth 8s., now 10.

In [North] Barningham Osfrith holds 3 free men with half a carucate of land. There have always been 5 bordars. Then and afterwards [there were] 1½ ploughs, now 2½ ploughs; [there is] 1 acre of meadow. Then and afterwards it was worth 10s., now 50. And it is 10 furlongs in length and 6 in breadth, and [pays] 16d. in geld.

In [East] Beckham [there is] 1 free man with 60 acres of land. There has always been 1 villan, and 3 bordars; and 1 plough in demesne, and half [a plough] belonging to the men. [There is] woodland for 5 pigs, 1 acre of meadow, and 1 sokeman with 4 acres of land. Then and afterwards it was worth 5s. 4d., now 10s.

In [North] Barningham [there is] 1 free man with 3 acres of land, with 2 oxen for ploughing. Then and afterwards he was worth 16d., now 3s. Over all the free men of this Hundred the king has sake and soke.

WEST FLEGG HUNDRED.

In Burgh [St Margaret] Æthelwig held 1 free man by commendation only TRE with 106 acres of land; now Stanheard holds [him]; [there are] 12 acres of meadow. There has always been 1 villan [and] 8 bordars. There has always been 1 plough in demesne, and half a plough belonging to the men. And under them [sic] [there are] 17 free men [with] 89 acres of land [and] 12 acres of meadow. There have always been 3 ploughs.

It has always been worth 20s. This the same holds.

In Winterton [there is] 1 free man with 21 acres of land and half an acre of meadow. There has always been half a plough, and he is in the valuation of Æthelweard of Felbrigg. This the same [Stanheard] holds.

HENSTEAD HUNDRED.

In Shotesham [All Saints or St Mary] [there are] 4 free men belonging to St Benet [of Hulme], 1 belonging to Ulf, the fourth to Gyrth by commendation TRE [with] 60 acres of land and 1 acre of meadow and 3 bordars. There have always been 1½ ploughs. Then it was worth 2 oras, afterwards and now 10s. This the same [Stanheard] holds.

In Stoke [Holy Cross] [there was] 1 free man of Gyrth's by commendation TRE with 24 acres of land, whom Earl R[alph] held when he forfeited with half the land and Ra[lph] Bay[nard] the other [half] as the Hundred testifies. Now R[oger] Bigod holds it, and claims it as part of the fief of his free men by the king's gift; and Aitard contradicts the Hundred which testifies this, but Mainard affirms it with the Hundred. Under him there have always been 3 bordars, and always 1 plough; and in addition under him [there are] 3 sokemen with 9 acres of land, and 3 parts of 1 mill and 3 acres of meadow. Then it was worth 5s., and always [has been]. And this R[oger] Bigod acknowledges to have received, after R[alph] forfeited, to be kept in the king's hand, and he still keeps it. In Fritton [there is] 1 free man of Ulf's by commendation. [...] This Ranulf holds. In [Earl or Pigot] Framingham [there is] 1 free man of Ulf's by commendation. In Yelverton [there is] 1 free man of Stigand's. This the same holds. In Rockland [St Mary] [there are] 3 free men of Ulf's. This the same holds. In Surlingham [there are] 2 half free men of Ulf's. This the same holds. In Bramerton [there is] 1 free man of Ulf's by commendation. This the same holds. Among them all [there are] 68 acres of land and 4 bordars and 3 acres of meadow. There have always been 1½ ploughs. Then it was worth 16s., now 20s. In Trowse [there is] 1 free man, Asgot's, by commendation TRE [with] 40 acres of land and 4 bordars;

this the same holds; and 1 free man and a half under him [with] 4 acres of meadow. Then and afterwards [there was] 1 plough among them all, now 2. Then and afterwards [it was worth] 5s., now 7s. It is 3 furlongs in length and 3 furlongs in breadth, and [pays] 9½d. in geld. In Shotesham [All Saints or St Mary] [there is] 1 free man of Ulf's by commendation [with] 10 acres of land, and half an acre of meadow. Then [there were] 2 oxen, now [there is] half a plough [team]. It has always been worth 16d. The same holds [it]. In Saxlingham [Nethergate or Thorpe] [there is] 1 free man of Ulf's

Roger Bigod

[Folio 186: NORFOLK]

by commendation TRE [with] 24 acres of land, and 1 acre of meadow. There has always been half a plough. Then as now it was worth 3s. This the same holds. In Yelverton [there was] 1 free man of Stigand's with the soke by commendation TRE with 20 acres of land. Now Aitard holds [him]; [there are] 3 bordars [and] 1½ acres of meadow. There have always been 1½ ploughs, and under him 3 sokemen and a half with 10 acres of land. Then and afterwards it was worth 5s., now 20. In Poringland [there is] 1 free man of Eadric's with 12 acres of land and half an acre of meadow. They always plough with 3 oxen. Then and always it was worth 12d. Yelverton is 4 furlongs in length and 3 furlongs in breadth, and [pays] 1¼d. in geld. This the same holds. Poringland is 5 furlongs in length and 4½ in breadth, and [pays] 12d. in geld.

EARSHAM HALF HUNDRED.

In Starston 1 free man belonging to St Æthelthryth and to Stigand TRE held half a carucate of land; the sake and soke was in Earsham, but he could neither give nor sell his land without licence of St Æthelthryth and Stigand. Now Godwine holds it, and under him 3 bordars. There has always been 1 plough in demesne. And [there are] 8 free men under him with 20 acres. There have always been 3 ploughs. It has always been worth 10s. Now R[oger] Bigod claims it as part of the fief of his free men by gift of the king. But the Hundred testifies that when Richard Poignant was reeve in Earsham it used to belong in Earsham, but he who now holds it, then Richard's under-reeve in Earsham, has withdrawn it, and by the testimony of the Hundred he paid rent in Earsham of 20s. 6d. each year, expressly for this and other land; but this year he has not paid. And W[illiam] de Noyers has had the rent up to now.

LODDON HUNDRED.

In Bedingham Offa, a thegn of Stigand's, held for a manor 1 carucate of land TRE; now the same holds it. There have always been 12 bordars and 2 slaves. There have always been 2 ploughs in demesne, and 3 ploughs belonging to the men, and 3 acres of meadow. There have always been 2 horses in demesne and 9 pigs. There have always been 20 goats. Then it was worth 10s., now 30.

In Seething 1 free man under Gyrth held 30 acres of land and 2 slaves TRE. Then [there was] half a plough, now 1, in demesne; the same holds [this] and under him the same holds

6 free men [with] 30 acres of land; [they are] in Stigand's soke. There have always been 2 ploughs among them.

[Folio 186v: NORFOLK]

In the same place [there was] 1 free man of Stigand's in commendation TRE [with] 1 carucate of land. Now the same holds it. There has always been 1 villan and 7 bordars. [There is] woodland for 12 pigs. Then [there was] half a plough in demesne, now 1 plough. There has always been half a plough belonging to the men and 3 acres of meadow and 1 mill. And under him, 8 free men in commendation in the soke of Stigand, [with] 20 acres of land and 2 slaves. There has always been 1 plough. Then the whole was worth 20s., now 40. In Mundham [there is] 1 free man of Godwine's under Gyrth TRE [with] 30 acres of land. Now the same holds it. There have always been 5 bordars. There has always been half a plough. It is assessed in the 40s. In the same place are 3 free men of the same under Gyrth [with] 16 acres of land. There have always been 1 plough. It has always been worth 5s. The same holds this.

In Seething [there was] 1 free man of Stigand's in commendation [with] 16 acres. Then [there was] half a plough, now 1. It has always been worth 32d. This the same holds. In Broome Toki, 1 free man of Harold's by commendation, held 30 acres [of land] and 6 acres of meadow TRE. Then [there was] 1 plough, now a half. The soke is in the Hundred. It has always been worth 10s.

In Carleton [St Peter] [there is] 1 free man of Godwine's [with] 20 acres and 2 bordars. There has always been half a plough. It has always been worth 20d.

HUNDRED OF SOUTH ERPINGHAM.

[In] Alby one carucate of land was held by a free man, Asfrothr, for a manor under Harold; now his 4 sons hold it. There have always been 3 villans and 5 bordars. Then and afterwards [there was] 1 plough in demesne. Then and afterwards [there were] 2 [ploughs] belonging to the men; now among the whole [there are] 4 [ploughs] and 1 mill. Then and afterwards it was worth 20s., now 40; and it is 6 furlongs in length and 5 in breadth, whoever holds there, and [pays] 3½d. in geld. In Burgh [next Aylsham] [there are] 2 free men [with] 90 acres of land; there have always been 2 bordars and 1½ ploughs, and half an acre of meadow; now [there is] half a mill. Then and afterwards it was worth 15s., now 25s. 4d. And it is 3 furlongs in length and 2 in breadth, and [pays] 2d. in geld. In Erpingham [there is] 1 free man of Harold's [with] 30 acres of land. There has always been 1 bordar and half a plough and half an acre of meadow. Then and afterwards it was worth 40s., now 5[s.] 4d. In Baconsthorpe [near Holt] [there is] 1 free man of the same [Harold's] [with] 60 acres of land; now Turold holds him. Then and afterwards [there were] 5 bordars, now 2;

Roger Bigod

[Folio 187: NORFOLK]

then as now [there was] 1 plough in demesne, and half a plough belonging to the men. [There is] woodland for 5 pigs, and 1 sokeman [with] 1 acre. Then it was worth 10s., now 20.

In Wickmere [there are] 9 free men of the same [Harold's] [with] 1 carucate of land; now Robert de Courson holds [them]; there have always been 5 bordars and 2 slaves and 2 ploughs and 1 acre of meadow [and] woodland for 10 pigs. Then it was worth 20s., now 30.; and [it is] 6 furlongs in length and 4 in breadth and [pays] 8d. in geld. In the same place [there are] 2 free men of Harold's and Bishop Æthelmær's [with] 30 acres; there have always been 2 bordars, and half a plough, and half an acre of meadow. Then [there were] 3 parts of 1 mill. Then it was worth 8s., now 12.

TUNSTEAD HUNDRED.

In Felmingham [there is] 1 carucate of land which belongs to the 4 men in Suffield; there have always been 7 bordars and 4 sokemen on the same land, always 2 ploughs and 1½ acres of meadow. And this is in the valuation of Suffield. In the same place [there are] 4 free men [with] 80 acres, then as now 4 bordars, and 2 ploughs, and 2 acres of meadow, and 1 mill. Then it was worth 10s., 16[s.] 4d. And it is 1 league in length and 5 furlongs in breadth, and [pays] 18d. in geld. One of those 4 was the man of the predecessor of R[obert] Malet.

In Smallburgh [there are] 3 free men [with] 1 carucate of land; there have always been 12 bordars and 3 sokemen. Then and afterwards [there were] 3 ploughs, now 4, and 2 acres of meadow [and] woodland for 6 pigs. Two of these are in the valuation of Antingham and the third is worth 10s. One of them was the man of the predecessor of Robert Malet, and the others belonged to St Benet [of Hulme]; St Benet itself [has] the soke. In Dilham [there is] 1 free man of Eadric [with] 60 acres of land; there have always been 5 bordars and 1 plough and 1 acre of meadow. This is in the valuation of Suffield.

HAPPING HUNDRED.

In Palling [there is] 1 free man of Gyrth [with] 1 carucate of land; there have always been 5 bordars, and 1 plough in demesne, and 24 acres of meadow and 1 plough belonging to the men. In the same place [there are] 5 men [with] 23 acres whom Hugh de Houdain holds; there has always been 1 plough. Then it was worth 20s., now 40. Of those, 4 were free, but they could not withdraw except on giving 2s.

In Waxham [there is]a half free man [with] 7 acres of land; and he is in the same valuation.

In Stalham [there is] 1 free man [with] 15 acres. This the same holds.

In Brumstead [there is] 1 free man [with] 15 acres, and in Horsey 1 free man [with] 12 acres. Of these Æthelwig, his predecessor, did not even have the commendation TRE and yet he claims them as part of his fief by the king's gift, because the said Æthelwig had commendation of them TRW. There has always been 1 plough and 4 acres of meadow, and it is worth 4s. The king and the earl [have] the soke.

HUMBLEYARD HUNDRED.

In [East] Carleton [there are] 27 free men and a half under Ulf by commendation only and soke of the fold TRE, and they have 1½ carucates of land, and 10 acres; and 4 free men, and of

2, the predecessor of Ranulf Peverel had commendation and of a moiety of a third; and the predecessor of Eudo the steward in like manner of 1 and of the moiety of the other, and of these his predecessor had nothing: and they have 50 acres. Between them all they have 4 ploughs and 5 acres of meadow. In Swardeston [there is] 1 free man [with] 8 acres. In Swardeston is 6 furlongs in length and 5 in breadth, and [paid] 13d. in TRE.

[In] Flordon [there are] 15 free men under Ulf by soke of the fold and commendation only. In Bracon [Ash] [there is] 1 free man in the same way. Among them all they have 100 acres less 2, and 5 bordars, and 1 acre of meadow; there have always been 2 ploughs. In Nayland and in Wreningham 9 free men; of 8 and a half of these the predecessor of R[oger] had the commendation only and soke of the fold, and the predecessor of Hermer de Ferrers the moiety of 1 by soke of the fold and commendation only. In 'Walsingham' [in East Carleton] [there are] 6 free men under the predecessor of Roger by soke of the fold and commendation only. Among them all they have 130 acres; there have always been 3 ploughs and 1 mill and 1 bordar. In Bracon [Ash] [there are] 5 free men; of 4 the predecessor of Roger Bigod had half commendation and of the fifth the whole, and the predecessor of Ranulf Peverel of the four likewise; and they have 150 acres of land. There have always been 2½ ploughs and 6 acres of meadow. In Flordon [there are] 5 free men; of these R[oger]'s predecessor had half commendation only, and the predecessor of

Roger Bigod

Godric the steward the same, and they had 1 carucate of land and 30 acres and 2 bordars and 2 acres of meadow; there have always been 2 ploughs. In Nayland [there were] 4 free men [with] 1 carucate of land and 4 bordars; there have always been 2 ploughs, and 4 acres of meadow. Of 2 free men and a half Roger's predecessor had commendation TRE and Stigand of 1 and the predecessor of Hermer [de Ferrers] of a half.

In Dunston [there were] 3 free men and a half [with] 49 acres in commendation only TRE; there have always been 3 bordars and 1 plough and 2 acres of meadow. In Mangreen [there is] 1 free man and a half. Of this the predecessor of Roger had half the commendation and the predecessor of Godric [half] the same; and he has 33 acres.

In Swardeston [there are] 8 free men; of 3 and a half his predecessor had commendation only TRE and of 4 the predecessor of Godric the same, and of the [other] half the predecessor of R[anulf] Peverel in like manner. Among the whole they have 45 acres of land and 2 bordars; there have always been 1½ ploughs [and] 2 acres of meadow.

In Swainsthorpe [there is] 1 free man in commendation only with 15 acres and 2 free men with 4 acres, half an acre of meadow, and half a plough. In Mulbarton [there is] 1 free man with 30 acres under the predecessor of Godric by commendation only TRE; there have always been 2 bordars, then half a plough, now 1. In the same place [there was] 1 free woman under the predecessor of Godric in commendation only TRE [with] 30 acres of land and of this Godric was seised when R[alph] forfeited, and as was due [...]she used to pay him [Godric] 5s.; and a certain man of Roger's by commendation only, [...]son of the same woman, used to live on the same land with [...] his mother and therefore R[oger] claims half the land; and the father of the same man had in another place other free land under the predecessor of R[oger] by commendation only, and all that land Roger holds. On those former 30 acres then [there were] 1½ ploughs, now 1, and 4 bordars and 2 acres of meadow; and under those 2 free men and a half in commendation only, and 17½ acres [and]

[Folio 188v: NORFOLK]

there has always been half a plough. All these free men were worth £8 TRE, afterwards 10, now £15 5s. 5½d.

In Ketteringham [there are] 5 free men by half commendation only under the predecessor of Roger and by half commendation under the predecessor of Godric and they have 1 carucate of land and 16 acres; now Ranulf fitzW[alter] holds them. There has always been 1 bordar. Then and afterwards [there were] 2 ploughs, now 1½ ploughs and 4 acres of meadow; and they are worth 10s. In Keswick [there are] 14 free men whom Aitard holds; 4 under the predecessor of Roger by commendation only, and 5 by soke of the fold and commendation and 5 under the predecessor of Godric by commendation only; and they have 60 acres. Then [there were] 1½ ploughs, afterwards and now 1, and half an acre of meadow.

In the same place [there are] 4 free men; 2 in commendation only, and 1 under Godric's predecessor in like manner, and the fourth belonged to Stigand in the same way. And they have 1 carucate of land. Godric was seised of 30 acres of land when R[alph] forfeited and 2 women of his used to live there; now Aitard holds it of Roger. [There are] two bordars [and] there have always been 2 ploughs and 6 acres of meadow. Then it was worth as a whole 15s., now 25. The king and the earl have the soke of all these free men.

In Colney [there is] 1 free man of Stigand's by commendation only [with] 1 carucate of land whom Warengar holds; there have always been 2 villans; and 9 free men under him by commendation only, [with] 24 acres [of land]. Then [there were] 3 ploughs, afterwards 3½ ploughs, now 1 plough and 2 oxen and 6[...] acres of meadow and 1 mill. Then it was worth 20s., now 30.

In Flordon [there are] 5 free men; of 4 Roger's predecessor had [...] commendation only, and the predecessor of Roger de Rames [had commendation] of the fifth; and they have 15 acres and half a plough, and are worth 16d.

In the same place [there are] 2 free men; of 1 and of a moiety of the other Stigand had commendation TRE and of the other moiety

Roger Bigod

[Folio 189: NORFOLK]

the predecessor of Roger Bigod had commendation only TRE. And they have 30 acres and 2 bordars and half a plough

and 1 acre of meadow and are worth 4s. Of half this land Godric was seised as of his fief when R[alph] forfeited. In Cringleford [there is] 1 free man of Stigand's, 15 acres and 2 bordars; and 2 free men [with] 7½ acres; there has always been half a plough and 1½ acres of meadow, and the eighth part of a mill; and they are worth 3s.

In Rainthorpe [there is] half a free man in commendation TRE [with] 30 acres of land; now Warengar holds [it]. Then [there were] 2 villans, now 1; there has always been half a plough and 1 acre of meadow; and it is worth 5s. In Newton [Flotman] [there is] 1 free man [with] 15 acres and 2 bordars, and it is worth 16d. In Flordon [there is] 1 free man [with] 30 acres; then [there was] half a plough. Of him Godric's predecessor had commendation, and he is worth 3s.

DEPWADE HUNDRED.

In Forncett [St Mary or St Peter] [there are] 6 free men in commendation [with] 85 acres; then [there were] 3 ploughs, now 2. [There are] 5 acres of meadow. And in "Halas" [there are] 4 free men [with] 36 acres [and] there have always been 2 ploughs and 3 acres of meadow. In Carleton [Rode] [there are] 3 free men, 12 acres and half a plough and 1 acre of meadow. In Fritton [there are] 3 free men and a half, 80 acres and 13 bordars, there have always been 2 ploughs and half a plough belonging to the men and [there are] 3 acres of meadow and 1 church [with] 40 acres and 1 sokeman and a half under it [with] 5 acres.

In Carleton [Rode] [there are] 16 free men and a half and 1 carucate of land, and 6 acres and 10 bordars. Then [there were] 3 ploughs, now 2, and 5 acres of meadow and 2 churches [with] 30 acres.

In Kettleton [there are] 3 free men, 48 acres, and 1 plough and 3 acres of meadow.

In Aslacton [there are] 11 free men [with] 54 acres. Then [there were] 2 ploughs, now 1 [and] 4 acres of meadow. Of 3 of these 11 the predecessor of Robert Malet had commendation TRE; and on the day on which William Malet died he was seised of 2. This Hugh holds. In Moulton [St Michael] [there are] 9 free men and a half [with] 140 acres and 15 bordars. Now Mauger holds them. Then and afterwards [there were] 4 ploughs, now 3; and 2 free men and a half under them [with] 15 acres and 8 acres of meadow. [There is] woodland for 5 pigs. In Moulton [St Michael] [there is] 1 free man [with] 60 acres. The same holds him and [there are] 7 bordars

[Folio 189v: NORFOLK]

and 2 ploughs and 6 acres of meadow; and 1 church with 15 acres. [There is] woodland for 8 pigs. Then [there was] 1 mill. And under him [there are] 14 free men with 20 acres [and] there has always been 1 plough and 2 acres of meadow.

In the same place [there are] 4 free men [with] 6 acres. The whole of Moulton [St Michael] is 1½ leagues in length and half in breadth and [pays] 13½d. in geld.

In Swanton [there are] 12 free men [with] 140 acres, and 3 bordars. Now William holds them. Then [there were] 5 ploughs, afterwards 4, now 3, and 8 acres of meadow. In the same place under them [there are] 4 free men and a half [with] 6 acres and half a plough. In Wacton [there are] 6 free men and a half [with] 86 acres and 5 bordars. Then [there were] 3 ploughs and afterwards [the same]; now [there are] 2, and 4 acres of meadow. In the same place under these [are] 4 free men [with] 15 acres. In Stratton [St Mary or St Michael] [there are] 7 free men [with] 60 acres. Then and afterwards [there were] 3 ploughs and half a mill. In Shelton [there are] 9 free men and a half and 3 bordars and 1 church [with] 16 acres; and under these [there are] 4 free men; between them all [there are] 59 acres; there have always been 2 ploughs and 2 acres of meadow. And the whole of Shelton is 1 league in length and a half in breadth and [pays] 9d. in geld. This Durand holds, and Wacton also.

In Tibenham [there are] 3 free men [with] 69 acres and 7 bordars. Then and afterwards [there were] 2 ploughs, now [there are] 1½ and 2 acres of meadow. In Hapton [there is] 1 free man of Stigand's TRE [with] 30 acres. Then [there was] 1 villan, there have always been 2 bordars, and 1 plough in demesne. Then [there was] half a plough. In the same place [there are] 4 free men [with] 36 acres and half a plough and 3 acres of meadow. In Tasburgh [there are] 7 free men [with] 110 acres. Now Berard and Azelin hold them; then as now [there were] 2 ploughs, and [there are] 7 acres of meadow; and they are worth 24s.

In Fundenhall [there is] 1 free man [with] 8 acres [and] half a plough. In Swanton [there is] 1 free man, Aslak, [with] 30 acres. Then [there were] 5 bordars, now 10. Then [there were] 3 slaves, now 1. Then as now [there was] 1 plough in demesne and 1 plough belonging to the men; [there are] 4 acres of meadow and 4 sokemen [with] 6 acres and half a plough. And [there is] 1 church with 60 acres of free land, the alms of a number of men. In Carleton [Rode] [there are] 2 free men commended to Aslak only, and they have 7 acres. In Kettleton [there are] 2 free men [with] 2 acres. In Forncett [St Mary or St Peter] [there is] 1 free man [with] 2 acres. In Swanton [there are] 3 free men [with] 4 acres. In Wacton [there are] 2 free men [with] 1½ acres. In Stratton [St Mary or St Michael] [there is]

Roger Bigod

[Folio 190: NORFOLK]

1 free man [with] 4 acres. In Moulton [St Michael] [there are] 3 free men [with] 5 acres. In Tibenham [there are] 2 free men [with] 7 acres. In Aslacton [there is] 1 free man [with] 1 acre. Among the whole [there are] 2 ploughs and 2 acres of meadow.

In Tacolneston [there is] 1 free man of Stigand's [with] 25 acres and 3 bordars, 1 plough and 2 acres of meadow. In Fundenhall [there are] 2 free men [with] 60 acres whom Osbert holds, and 2 bordars. Then [there were] 2 ploughs, now 1½. In Tibenham [there are] 3 free men with 28 acres and 1 plough and 1 acre of meadow. The whole together was worth £10 TRE, now £22 2s. 9d. One of those 7 [free men] of Tasburgh, Herme[r de Ferrers] claims; and a certain Englishman, his man, hereupon offers [to undergo] judicial ordeal [to the effect] that his predecessor was seised of him on the day that King Edward was alive and dead; and this the whole Hundred disputes either by battle or judicial ordeal; hereupon that Englishman gives [his] pledge.

CLAVERING HUNDRED.

[In] HADDISCOE [there is] 1 free man of King Edward's whom Æthelwig his [Roger Bigod's] predecessor had in commendation after [King] William came, and he has 40 acres. Now Turold holds him and [there are] 6 bordars [and there is] pasture for 40 sheep. Then [there was] half a plough, now 1, and 6 acres of meadow; and 6 free men under him by commendation. Then [there was] 1 plough, now 1 plough and 4 acres of meadow. Then it was worth 10s., and now the same. Stigand had the soke. In Heckingham [there is] 1 free man of Stigand's [with] 30 acres; now Robert de Vaux holds him; and [there are] 2 bordars; and 2 free men under him [with] 3½ acres; then as now [there was] half a plough, and it is worth 4s.

CLACKCLOSE HUNDRED.

In Wallington 30 acres of land were held by Huscarl, a free man, TRE; now Hugh holds it. It has always been worth 3s.

In Hilgay 1½ acres were held by a free man TRE and it was worth 3d. This the same holds. In Bexwell [there was] 1 free man under Harold [with] 20 acres of land, now R[alph] fitzHerluin holds him, and he is worth 2s. 8d. In Downham [Market] [there is] 1 free man [with] 12 acres, and he is worth 16d. This the same holds. In [West] Dereham [there are] 6 free men, 9 acres of land and 2 bordars, and they are worth 10s. This Hugh holds. In the same place [there is] 1 free man [with] 16 acres, and it is worth 12d. This the same holds. Of him his [Roger Bigod's] predecessor had commendation only. In the same place [there are] 60 acres of land which Godric, a free man, held TRE;

[Folio 190v: NORFOLK]

now the same holds it. Of this the predecessor of Roger and the predecessor of Baynard had commendation only, and it is assessed after. In Stradsett [there is] 1 free man [with] 6 acres of land, and it is worth 6d. This the same holds. In Beechamwell Ælfheah, a free man, held TRE 2 carucates of land and 2 acres of land [and] 14 bordars; now R[obert] de Vaux holds it. Then [there were] 4 slaves, now 1; then as now [there was] 1 plough belonging to the men, [and there are] 6 acres of meadow. Then [there were] 4 pigs, now 12. Then [there were] 80 sheep less 1, now 100 [and there is] 1 ass. To this manor, then as now, belonged 3 free men in commendation only [with] 60 acres. Of these Harold had the soke and they are worth 40s. Of the demesne of this land Wihenoc took 30 acres. He claims them by gift of the king and 1 church [with] 30 acres is worth 2s. 6d.

FREEBRIDGE HUNDRED AND A HALF.

[In] East Winch [there is] 1 free man [of] Gyrth TRE [with] 60 acres of land and 11 acres of meadow; then as now [there were] 6 villans and 3 bordars; then and now [there were] 2 ploughs. Then it was worth 40s., now 60. This R[obert] de Vaux holds.

Land of the Bishop of Thetford

belonging to the bishopric TRE.

land of Bishop William.

[SOUTH] GREENHOE HUNDRED.

[Great] Cressingham was held by the bishop in demesne for a manor and for 2 carucates of land. Then [there were] 7 villans, now 4; now [there are] 3 bordars. Then [there were] 4 slaves, now 1. Then [there were] 2 ploughs in demesne, now 3. Then amongst the men [there was] 1 plough, now half. [There is] woodland for 60 pigs, 8 acres of meadow, 2 mills [and] 2 fisheries. There have always been 22 head of cattle, and 5 horses and 17 pigs and 80 sheep. And [there is] 1 church [with] 20 acres, and it is worth 20d.; and [there are] 17 sokemen with 60 acres and 3 acres of meadow and 3 ploughs. Then it was worth £6, now 9, and it is 1 league in length and half in breadth; and the whole together with the tenants on it pays 14d. [in geld] when the Hundred pays 20s.

Gaywood was held by Bishop Æthelmær TRE for a manor and for 3 carucates of land; now the bishop [William] holds it in demesne. There have always been 2 ploughs in demesne, and 1 plough belonging to the men and 16 villans. Then [there were] 28 bordars, now 24. There has always been 1 slave [and there are] 40 acres of meadow; [there is] woodland for 160 pigs, 1 mill and 32 acres of land. Then [there were] 30 salt-pans, now 21. And [there are] 3 sokemen with 29 acres, and 4 acres of meadow. There has always been 1 horse and 3 and 25 pigs [and] 190 sheep. Then it was worth £13, now £18 10s. The whole is 1 league in length and half [a league] in breadth, and pays 12d. in geld.

SMETHDEN HUNDRED.

Thornham was held by Bishop Æthelmær TRE for a manor. Now the bishop [holds it] in demesne for a manor and for 3 carucates of land; and there have always been 3 ploughs in demesne, and 3 ploughs belonging to the men, and 21 villans, [and] 14 acres of meadow; now [there is] 1 mill and 16 sokemen with 1½ ploughs and 5 bordars. In demesne [there are] 2 horses, 2 head of cattle, 30 pigs and 500 sheep. Then it was worth £14, now £16. The whole is 1 league in length and a half in breadth, and pays 2s. in geld.

GRIMSHOE HUNDRED.

[West] Tofts was held by Bishop Æthelmær

TRE [for a manor] and for 6 carucates of land. Now Richard and Eli hold it of the bishop [William]. There have always been 3 villans. Then [there were] 19 bordars, now 15. Then [there were] 4 slaves, now 1 [and there are] 8 acres of meadow. Then [there was] 1 plough in demesne, now 3. Then [there were] 2 ploughs belonging to the men, now 1. There have always been 22 pigs [and] 280 sheep. Then it was worth

40s., now 60. The whole is 1 league in length and a half in breadth, and pays 17d. in geld.

LAUNDITCH HUNDRED.

[North] Elmham was held by Bishop Æthelmær TRE for a manor and for 8 carucates of land; now the bishop [William] holds it in demesne. There have always been 41 villans and 63 bordars. Then [there were] 6 slaves, now 4; [there are] 24 acres of meadow; there have always been 4 ploughs in demesne, and 16 ploughs belonging to the men. Then [there was] woodland for 1,000 pigs, now for 500. There have always been 4 mills and 3 horses and 32 pigs and 300 sheep [and] 35 goats. And [there are] 24 sokemen with 1 carucate of land. Stigand [had] their soke TRE and now [it is] in Mileham. There have always been 4 ploughs [and] 4 acres of meadow; [there is] woodland for 30 pigs [and] 1 mill. Here there has always belonged 1 berewick, which is called Beetley, of 1 carucate of land, and 7 villans [and] 10 acres of meadow, 1 plough in demesne, and 2 could be employed [and] 2 ploughs have always belonged to the men. And here belongs 1 sokeman with 26 acres, always 1 plough, and 1½ acres of meadow. [There is] woodland for 5 pigs and 1 church is on the manor with 60 acres and 1 plough, and it is worth 5s. Then the whole was worth £10; afterwards and now £32. It is 1 league in length and a half in breadth, and pays 20d. in geld. And the berewick is 8 furlongs in length and 4 in breadth.

BROTHERCROSS HUNDRED.

Colkirk was held by Æ[thelmær] TRE for a manor and 2 carucates of land. Now the bishop holds it in demesne. Then [there was] 1 villan, now none. There have always been 12 bordars. Then [there were] 4 slaves, now 2. There have always been 2 ploughs in demesne. [There is] woodland for 60 pigs, 4 acres of meadow, 7 head of cattle [and] 27 pigs. Then [there were] 10 sheep, now 100 [and] 60 goats. The church [has] 40 acres; it is worth 2s.; and [there are] 14 sokemen with 66 acres. Then [there were] 3 ploughs, now 2½. Then it was worth £6, now 9. It is 5 furlongs in length and 4 in breadth, and [pays] 11d. in geld.

GALLOW HUNDRED.

Saxlingham was held by Æ[thelmær] TRE for a manor

Bishop William

and for 1 carucate of land; now the bishop holds it. There have always been 7 bordars, 1 slave and 1 plough in demesne, and half a plough belonging to the men [and] 2 acres of meadow. It is assessed in Thornage [and there is] 1 church with 12 acres. Of this manor W[illiam] holds half a carucate of land and 1 plough, and it is worth 20s. It is 7 furlongs in length and 5 in breadth and [pays] 2s. in geld.

HOLT HUNDRED

Thornage was held by Bishop Æthelmær for a manor and for 8 carucates of land TRE and now the bishop [holds it] in demesne. There have always been 40 bordars and 8 slaves and 8 ploughs in demesne and 10 ploughs belonging to the men. [There is] woodland for 50 pigs [and] 9 acres of meadow, 3 mills, 4 horses, 12 pigs [and] 100 sheep. To this manor belong 4 berewicks, that is, Brinton and Saxlingham and [East] Beckham and Hempstead [near Holt], and they are reckoned in Thornage. And [there are] 16 sokemen with 36 acres. There have always been 4 ploughs between them. The whole was worth TRE £13; now it renders £30. It is 1 league in length and 4 furlongs in breadth, and [pays] 12d. in geld. 1 church [with] 32 acres is worth 32d.

Swanton [Novers] was held by Æ[thelmær] TRE for 2 carucates of land, and it belongs to Hindolveston. There have always been 8 bordars and 2 ploughs in demesne. Then [there were] 3 ploughs belonging to the men, now 1, and 2 could be restored. [There is] woodland for 100 pigs. Then [there were] 12 pigs, now 6; now [there are] 200 sheep. Then it was worth £6, now £8; and it is half a league in length and a half in breadth, and [pays] 3d. in geld.

[NORTH] GREENHOE HUNDRED.

The bishop holds Hindringham in demesne, which Æthelmær held for a manor and for 4 carucates of land TRE. There have always been 11 villans. Then [there were] 20 bordars, now [there are] 15. Then [there were] 8 slaves, now 7. There have always been 4 ploughs in demesne. Then [there were] 5 ploughs belonging to the men, now [there are] 3. Then [there was] woodland for 10 pigs; there has always been 1 mill, 5 acres of meadow, 17 pigs, 160 sheep [and] 6 hives of bees. There [are] 7 sokemen [with] half a carucate of land, and TRE they ploughed with 2 ploughs, now 1. Then it was worth £10, now it renders £15. It is 1 league in length and 1 in breadth, and [pays] 2s. in geld. And in Warham [All Saints or St Mary] [there] is 1 man belonging to this manor with 12 acres. In Wells [-next the Sea] [there are] 2 men who belong to this manor with 12 acres. [There is] pasture for 100 sheep.

[Folio 192v: NORFOLK]

Egmere was held by Bishop Æthelmær for a manor and for 3 carucates of land TRE; now Morel holds it of the bishop. Then [there were] 14 villans, now 8. Then [there were] 2 slaves, now none. Then [there were] 2 ploughs in demesne, now 1. Then [there were] 2 ploughs belonging to the men, now 2 oxen, and 2 ploughs could be restored; There has always been 1 horse, 1 acre of meadow [and] 8 pigs. Then [there were] 180 sheep, now 90. And 7 sokemen belong to the vill with 45 acres; then [there were] 2 ploughs, now 1. Then it was worth 70s., now 45s. 4d.; and [there is] 1 sokeman, a man of Bishop William's, who is in "Murlai". Then he used to plough with 1 [full] plough team, now with 2 oxen.

In Cockthorpe Æ[thelmær] held 1 sokeman with 2 bordars and it belongs to Langham.

In Holkham William de Noyers holds of the bishop O., a free man, whom Bishop Æ[thelmær] held TRE, with 23 acres of land; and he could not give or sell his land; and he was in the king's soke. Then he was worth 5s., now 17s. 4d. And in Holkham he holds 1 sokeman with 10 acres, and he belongs in Hindringham.

WALSHAM HUNDRED.

In Hemblington [there are] 21 sokemen with 140 acres of land and 8 acres of meadow; then [there were] 3½ ploughs, now 2. This is assessed in Blofield. In the same vill [there are] 60 acres of land in demesne.

EYNESFORD Hundred.

The bishop holds Hindolveston in demesne for a manor and for 200 acres. There have always been 12 villans and 22 bordars and 3 slaves, and 2 ploughs in demesne and 5 ploughs belonging to the men; then [there was] woodland for 600 pigs, now 300 [and there are] 12 acres of meadow [and] 1 mill. There have always been 2 horses and 20 head of cattle and 40 pigs, 40 goats [and] 2 beehives. Here belongs 1 berewick which is called [Wood] Norton, of 200 acres. There have always been 9 villans and 6 bordars [and] then [there were] 2 slaves, now 1; there has always been 1 plough in demesne, and 2 ploughs belonging to the men [and] 8 acres of meadow. [There is] woodland for 30 pigs. And [there is] 1 church on the manor with 26 acres, and it is worth 20d. And a third part of a church is in the berewick with 2½ acres, and it is worth 4d. And [there are] 8 sokemen with 51 acres of land, which Hugh holds of the bishop; [there are] 3 bordars [and] there have always been 2 ploughs, and 4 acres of meadow. [There is] woodland for 10 pigs.

[...]And in Guestwick [there is] 1 sokeman with 24

Bishop William

[Folio 193: NORFOLK]

acres of land and 2 bordars. Then [there was] half a plough, now 1. And in Guist [there are] 2 sokemen with 2 acres which the same Hugh holds. Then the whole was worth £10, now [it is worth] £13 8s. And Hindolveston is 1 league in length and 1 in breadth, and pays 8½d. in geld.

Helmingham was held by Æthelmær the bishop for a manor TRE, and for 3 carucates of land; now Gunfrid the archdeacon [holds it] of the bishop. Then [there were] 8 villans, now [there are] 4. There have always been 9 bordars. Then [there was] 1 slave, now none; there have always been 2 ploughs in demesne [and] always 1½ ploughs belonging to the men and 8 acres of meadow and 1 mill; now [there are] 11 pigs and 19 sheep. And 13 sokemen are held by the same with 40 acres of land. There have always been 5 ploughs and 2 acres of meadow. It has always been worth £4.

In Corpusty 30 acres of land were held by Æthelmær the bishop TRE; there has always been half a plough and 1 acre of meadow [and there is] woodland for 4 pigs; and it is worth 2s. The sois in Cawston. Tunstead HUNDRED.

In Swafield Gunfrid holds 1 sokeman, 24 acres of land, and 2 bordars and a half, and a plough, and it is worth 5s. 4d.

In the same place 28 acres [belong] to the church; there has always been 1 bordar, and 2 acres of meadow, and it is worth 2s. And the whole is 1 league in length and 4 furlongs and 1 perch in breadth, whoever holds there, and [pays] 18d. in geld.

DEPWADE HUNDRED.

Stratton [St Mary or St Michael] is held by Walter the deacon [as] 2 carucates of land [and] 30 acres, which Æ[thelmær] the bishop held TRE. There have always been 7 villans, and 6 bordars and a half. Then [there were] 2 ploughs in demesne, now [there is] 1. Then [there were] 2 ploughs belonging to the men, now 1 [and] 6 acres of meadow. [There is] woodland for 6 pigs [and] there has always been 1 mill and 1 ox and 11 pigs. And 26 sokemen are held by Ranulf and Walter the deacon; the king and earl [have] half the soke and they have 83 acres [and] there have always been 2 ploughs. It has always been worth £4 2s. [The same] A certain man of Count Alan's claims half [of] one of these and he says that R[alph] held him after he forfeited. Upon this [matter] he offers judicial ordeal.

[Folio 193v: NORFOLK]

LAND OF THE FIEF OF THE SAME BISHOP.

SMETHDEN HUNDRED.

Sedgeford was held by Gyrth TRE. In demesne [there are] 3 carucates of land and 15 acres. Then [there were] 15 villans, afterwards and now 5. There have always been 39 bordars and 5 slaves [and] 8 acres of meadow. There have always been 5 ploughs belonging to the men, woodland for 60 pigs [and] 4 mills. There has always been 1 horse and 45 pigs and 300 sheep. To this manor belongs a berewick called Fring. There has always been 1 plough in demesne, and 7 villans and 2 sokemen holding 1½ carucates of land, and of [the holding of] 1 sokeman Bishop Æthelmær made a berewick and [he has] 7 bordars. And the other sokeman has 4 bordars, and 1 free man [had] 1 plough in demesne [and] of this he also made a bewick; there have always been 6 bordars and 2 slaves. And another free man [had] always 1 plough in demesne, and of this he made a berewick; there have always been 4 bordars and 2 slaves. And [there are] 2 free men [holding] 2 carucates of land [and] of this also [he made] a berewick; [there are] 2 ploughs in demesne and 5 bordars and 2 slaves and 2 acres of meadow and TRE [there was] 1 mill. This, Anund the predecessor of Peter de Valognes took away. All this was worth £16 TRE, afterwards and now £24.

In the same place Ingulf holds 1 carucate of land which Gyrth held TRE: there has always been 1 plough in demesne, and it is worth 10s. The whole is 1 league in length and 1 league in breadth and renders 4s. of a 20s. geld.

Here 8 free men have always belonged by soke and commendation only [with] 4 carucates of land. There have always been 5 villans [and] 4 acres of meadow. Then [there were] 4 ploughs, now 3. It was worth then 40s., now 80s. The whole is 1 league in length and a half in breadth, and renders 17½d. a 20s. geld.

Bishop William

[Folio 194: NORFOLK]

SHROPHAM HUNDRED.

In Eccles Earl Ralph held 4 carucates of land TRE; afterwards Earl Ralph, his son, held them. Afterwards Bishop Æthelmær held of both [of them]. Afterwards Bishop Herfast [held it]. Now Bishop William holds [it]. There have always been 12 villans and 11 bordars. Then [there were] 5 slaves, now [there are] 2. [There are] 20 acres of meadow [and there is] woodland for 100 pigs. There have always been 2 ploughs in demesne. Then [there were] 5 ploughs belonging to the men, now 4. There has always been 1 mill. Now [there are] 3 head of cattle and 7 pigs [and] 180 sheep. It was then worth 100s., now 60. The whole is 1 league in length and 4 furlongs in breadth, and [renders] 7d. in geld. Bishop Æ[thelmær] had this land in the time of both [earls], and the Hundred does not know by what [title]. And it was never of the bishopric, as the Hundred witnesses.

HOLT HUNDRED.

In Langham Gyrth held 4 carucates of land TRE. There have always been 31 villans and 4 bordars and 5 slaves. There have always been 4 ploughs in demesne and 8 ploughs belonging to the men, 6 acres of meadow [and] 1 mill. There has always been 1 horse and 1 ox and 16 pigs and 60 sheep and 17 sokemen and 80 acres of land and 4 ploughs; It was then worth £8, it now renders £20, and is 1 league in length and 1 league in breadth, and [pays] 2s. in geld. 60 acres have been taken from this manor; Peter de Valognes holds them now.

NORTH ERPINGHAM HUNDRED.

In Gunton, which Æthelmær bought TRE for the bishopric, he held at the day of his death 2 carucates of land, 8 villans [and] there have always been 6 bordars. There has always been 1 plough in demesne, 2 ploughs belonging to the men [and] 4½ acres of meadow. Then [there was] 1 mill and now 1. There have always been 1 horse and 1 ox and 2 pigs; and [there are] 7 sokemen with half a carucate of land and 1 bordar; [there is] 1 mill [and] half an acre of meadow [and] there have always been 2 ploughs. It was then worth 20s., now £4. It is half a league in length and 6 furlongs in breadth, and [pays] 6d. in geld. Of this William de Noyers [holds] 1 carucate of land and 1 plough upon it, and it is worth 12s. in the same valuation.

[Folio 194v: NORFOLK]

In 'Shipden', a berewick of Gunton, [there is] 1 carucate of land. There have always been 3 villans. Then [there was] 1 plough in demesne, now [there is] half [a plough]. There has always been 1 plough belonging to the men. [There is] woodland for 6 pigs. It was then worth 10s., now 5s. 4d., and it is half a league in length and 4 furlongs in breadth. And it [pays] 6d. in geld.

WALSHAM HUNDRED.

In Beighton Bishop Æthelmær held by purchase from Earl Ælfgar TRE 3 carucates of land, with sake and soke over the bordars and those who owe suit to the fold. Then [there were] 40 bordars, now 29. There have always been 2 ploughs in demesne. Then [there were] 5½ ploughs belonging to the men, now [there are] 5 [and there are] 16 acres of meadow. Now [there is] 1 horse [and] now 16 pigs [and] now 140 sheep; and [there are] 5 sokemen with 32 acres of land, and 9 sokemen with 50 acres of land and 8 acres of land. There has always been 1 plough. The whole was then worth £6, now £7 13s. 4d. and it is half a league in length and half in breadth. And it [pays] 12d. in geld. [There is] 1 church [holding] 7 acres, worth 7d.

[NORTH] GREENHOE HUNDRED.

In Holkham William de Noyers holds of Bishop William 1 free man whom Bishop Æthelmær held TRE with 23 acres of land; but he could not give or sell his land, and he was in the king's soke. It was then worth 5s., it now pays 22s. 4d. And in Holkham [the bishop] holds 1 sokeman, of 10 acres of land, and he belongs to Hindringham.

WALSHAM HUNDRED.

In [South] Walsham [there is] 1 free man with 18 acres which that free man gave to St Benet of Hulme, but Bishop Herfast took them away. Now Bishop William holds him and he is worth 4s.

BLOFIELD HUNDRED.

In Blofield Bishop Æthelmær held 2 carucates of land TRE. There have always been 9 villans and 2 slaves. There have always been 2 ploughs in demesne and half a plough belonging to the men. [There is] woodland for 8 pigs and 4 acres of meadow.

Bishop William

[Folio 195: NORFOLK]

There have always been 2 horses and 2 head of cattle; now [there are] 11 pigs and 3 goats. And to this manor belonged 43 sokemen, TRE and always, who could neither sell nor grant their lands, [holding] 3 carucates of land and 4 acres of meadow. Then [there were] 10 ploughs, now 9. William holds 5 sokemen, Reginald, Baldwin, and Eli [hold the others]. Over these the bishop had the six forfeitures TRE, but the Hundred has seen neither the king's writ, nor seal, nor grant. [...] Then the whole was worth £7, now £8, and it is 1 league and 3 furlongs in length, and 1 league and 1 furlong in breadth; and [it renders] 30d. in geld. This manor Æthelmær got with his wife before he was bishop, and afterwards held it in his bishopric. Now Bishop William holds it.

In [Great or Little] Plumstead 1 sokeman was added by Herfast but he belonged to Stigand; [he has] 3 acres of land. He has always ploughed with 2 oxen and pays 5d.

WEST FLEGG HUNDRED.

Hemsby was held by Earl Ælfgar TRE and Alwig bought it. Stigand took it from him and gave it to his brother, Æthelmær, but the Hundred does not know by what right. Thenceforth it was in the bishopric. In demesne [there are] 3 carucates of land and there have always been 33 villans and 13 bordars. Then [there were] 6 slaves, now 3. There have always been 3 ploughs in demesne, and 11 ploughs belonging to the men, and 40 acres of meadow and 2 salt-pans. Now [there are] 12 pigs and 160 sheep and 4 sokemen with 60 acres of land, 3 acres of meadow, and always 1 plough. To this manor belongs 1 berewick, Martham, [of] 2 carucates of land. There have always
been 7 villans and 3 bordars and 1 slave. There have always been 2 ploughs in demesne and 1 plough belonging to the men, and 50 acres of meadow.

[Folio 195v: NORFOLK]

To this manor belong also 27 sokemen with 30 acres of land and 5 acres of meadow. There have always been 3 ploughs. And in Winterton [there are] 2 sokemen of 10 acres and there has always been half a plough. It was then worth £26, now £29. All this is 1½ leagues in length and 10 furlongs in breadth, and [pays] 30d. in geld. And Martham is 1½ leagues [in length] and 1 league in breadth, and [pays] 30d. in geld, but several [...] hold there. In Sco [there are] 2 bordars with 6 acres of land, and they belong to Hemsby.

HENSTEAD HUNDRED.

In Rockland [St Mary] and Surlingham W[illiam] de Noyers [holds] 2 villans with 16 acres and 2 acres of meadow. Then and afterwards they held half a plough and now they plough with 2 oxen. This belongs in Langley.

EARSHAM HALF HUNDRED.

In Mendham [now Suffolk] W[illiam] de Noyers holds 1 priest, Algar, [with] 43 acres of church land; now [he is] under William de Noyers. There have always been 3 bordars. There has always been 1 plough between himself and the men. [There is] woodland for 15 pigs and 3 acres of meadow. It has always been worth 10s.

LODDON HUNDRED.

Langley was held by Anund, a free man, under King Edward for 3 carucates of land. Then and afterwards [there were] 2 villans, now 1. There have always been 8 bordars. Then [there were] 2½ ploughs, afterwards 1½, now [there is] 1 plough in demesne. There has always been 1 plough belonging to the men. [There is] woodland for 20 pigs, and 8 acres of meadow and 1 mill. Then [there were] 7 horses, now [there are] 6. Then [there were] 4
head of cattle, now 1. Then [there were] 20 pigs, now 14. Now [there are] 95 sheep and 25 sokemen of Anund with 1 carucate of land. Then and afterwards [there were] 4 ploughs, now 3.

Bishop William

[Folio 196: NORFOLK]

And [there are] 3 free men of the same by commendation [with] 40 acres, and their soke is the king's. Then [there were] 1½ ploughs, afterwards and now [there was] 1. In the same place 1 whole priest and 2 halves hold 100 acres of free land and they belong to the church of St Andrew. Then and always it was worth £4. It is 1 league in length and 1 in breadth, and [pays] 11d. in geld. Æthelmær had the land of this Anund TRE, and they were partners and [Anund] died suddenly.

EYNESFORD HUNDRED.

And in Thurning [there is] 1 free man with 15 acres of land and half a plough and 1 acre of meadow. Then [there was] woodland for 5 pigs. And in Guist 2 sokemen with 2 acres. And the whole was worth then £10, and now £13 and 8s. and[sic]

In Helmingham Reginald, 1 free man, holds 30 acres of land, of whom Bishop Æthelmær had the commendation only. There have always been 2 villans and 3 bordars. Then [there were] 2 ploughs between himself and his men, now [there is] 1. It has always been worth 10s., and it is 1½ leagues in length and 1 in breadth, and renders 40d. of the king's geld whosoever holds there.

TAVERHAM HUNDRED.

In Taverham 1 free woman held half a carucate TRE. Then [there were] 3 villans and 2 bordars [and] there has always been 1 plough in demesne. Then and afterwards [there was] half a plough belonging to the men, and 5 acres of meadow. [There is] woodland for 2 pigs. Then [there were] 3 sokemen with 13 acres of land; now [there is] 1 sokeman. Then [there was] half a plough. It was then worth 12s., now [it is worth] 20s.

In Attlebridge 1 free man, Geoffrey, holds 16 acres of land and 1 bordar. There has always been half a plough [...] and 2 acres of meadow, and it is worth 6s. 8d. [There is] 1 church [with] 6 acres and worth 6d.

SOUTH ERPINGHAM HUNDRED.

Blickling

[Folio 196v: NORFOLK]

was held by Harold TRE as 3½ carucates of land. There have always been 12 villans and 16 bordars and 1 slave. There have always been 2 ploughs in demesne, and 6 ploughs belonging to the men [and] 10 acres of meadow. Then [there was] woodland for 200 pigs; now 100. There has always been 1 mill and 1 horse and 16 pigs. It was then worth £6, now £8, and is 1 [league in] length and 1 in breadth, and [pays] 4½d. in geld. To this manor belong 2 sokemen in Heringham. There have always been 60 acres of land and 14 bordars. There have always been 1½ ploughs and 2½ acres of meadow. [There is] woodland for 18 pigs and 2 thirds of another and 7 eighths of a mill. It was then worth 15s., now [it is worth] 25.

In [Little] Barningham 1 carucate of land and 50 acres and 3 villans and 11 bordars. There have always been 2½ ploughs and 5 acres of meadow. [There is] woodland for 28 pigs. Then

[there was] 1 mill which Godric now holds as of the king's fief. It was then worth 12s., now 22. This belongs in Blickling.

Marsham was held by Harold as 4 carucates of land. There have always been 6 villans and 29 bordars; and always 2 ploughs in demesne and 4 ploughs belonging to the men [and] 6 acres of meadow. [There is] woodland for 100 pigs, and 4 sokemen [whom] Roger holds [with] 1 carucate of land and 3 bordars and 2 ploughs and 1 horse and 2 head of cattle and 12 pigs and 26 goats and 6 beehives. It was then worth £6, now £9. And it is 1 league and 3 furlongs in length and 7 furlongs in length [sic] and [pays] 11d. in geld.

In Stratton [Strawless] [there is] 1 sokeman [holding] 30 acres [belonging] to Marsham and half a plough. And it is worth 2s.

HAPPING [...] HUNDRED.

In Horsey William de Noyers holds [what was held by] 1 free man of Bishop Æthelmær's by commendation only, [that is] 25 acres and 3 bordars and half a plough and 10 acres of meadow. And it is worth

Bishop William

[Folio 197: NORFOLK]

2s. The king and the earl have the soke.

In the same place [there are] 2 free men, commended to Bishop Æthelmær, of 17 acres and 5 acres of meadow; and it is worth 30d. [...][East] FLEGG HUNDRED.

In Scratby [there are] 7 sokemen [holding] 20 acres. There has always been 1 plough. And it is worth 32d. And these sokemen belong to Hemsby. [There is] 1 church [with] 36 acres and worth 3s. In the same place [there are] 10 free men; of these Bishop Æthelmær had the commendation TRE. And they have 2 carucates of land and 5 acres. There have always been 5 ploughs and 3 acres of meadow. It was then worth 20s., now 30. All these were held TRE by Bishop Æthelmær and [afterwards by] Herfast, now by Bishop William. And yet of one the Abbot of St Benet of Hulme had the commendation only TRE. And 6 of these free men are held by Richard fitzAlan, of the bishop, and the bishop has the others.

In Ormesby [St Margaret or St Michael] [there are] 2 free men [of] Gyrth [holding] 40 acres. There has always been 1 plough and 2 acres of meadow. And it is worth 8s. This, too, is held by the same Richard.

In Thrigby [there was] 1 free man [holding] 12 acres of land under Bishop Æthelmær by commendation only. There has always been half a plough. And it is worth 12d., and is half a league in length and half in breadth, and [pays] 14½d. in geld.

DEPWADE HUNDRED.

In Stratton [St Mary or St Michael] [there are] 12 free men of whom Bishop Æthelmær had the commendation only TRE. [They hold] 203 acres and [have] 10½ bordars and 3 ploughs and 6 acres of meadow. It was then worth 20s., now 40.

CLAVERING HUNDRED.

In Raveningham [there is] 1 free man of Bishop Æthelmær by commendation [holding] 30 acres and 2 bordars and half a plough. And it is worth 3s.

[SOUTH] GREENHOE HUNDRED.

Of the ENCROACHMENTS OF THE SAME FIEF. In [Great] Cressingham Ralph, the Bishop of Thetford's man, has appropriated a certain free man with 1 carucate of land who was in the soke of the king's [manor] of [Little] Cressingham and he detains the soke of 2 free men, and it is worth 20s.

In [Great] Cressingham [there are] 6 free men of Edwin [with] 3 carucates of land. Then [there were] 6 ploughs, now [there are] 2 and 4 acres of meadow [and] 1 mill. It was then worth 60s., now 30s.

FREEBRIDGE HUNDRED.

In Mintlyn [there are] 15 free men [with] 40 acres of land; there has always been half a plough and 6 bordars, and it is worth 30s. His predecessors had the commendation only of these. Stigand had the soke.

IN SMETHDEN HUNDRED.

Hunstanton was held by 1 sokeman of Stigand TRE [as] 1 carucate of land, and [there was] 1 plough. Then [there were] 3 bordars, now 2 and 2½ acres of meadow; [there is] half a mill [and] woodland for 24 pigs. Then [there was] 1 fishery. The whole is worth 10s.

GRIMSHOE HUNDRED.

In Stanford [there is] 1 free man of 60 acres. Then and afterwards [there was] 1 plough; now nothing. There has always been 1 villan [and] 2 acres of meadow. It has always been worth 6s. 8d. Of this man the predecessor of the same W[illiam] had the commendation only, and the king the soke, and [now] Bishop William has him.

LAUNDITCH HUNDRED.

In Gateley [there is] 1 free man [holding] 6 acres of land, and it is worth 6d. And Bondi, a free man, the predecessor of Hugh de Montfort held him TRE. Afterwards he became Bishop Herfast's man, and therefore William has him. The soke is in Mileham.

BROTHERCROSS HUNDRED.

To Colkirk Herfast appropriated the wood of Fakenham and it is 60 acres in length.

GALLOW HUNDRED.

In Saxlingham Harold held 2 free men of 1½ carucates of land; now Bishop William holds them,

Bishop William

and there have always been 7 bordars. Then [there were] 2 ploughs, now 2½; [and there are] 5 acres of meadow and half a mill. It was then worth 20s., now 30. Besides this H[arold] held in the same vill [with] 30 acres and 1 bordar. There has always been 1 plough [and] 2 acres of meadow. It was then worth 5s., now 7s.

HOLT HUNDRED.

In 'Snitterley' [in Blakeney] Eadric held under King Edward freely [from] Harold 2 carucates of land. There have always been 2 villans and 25 bordars and 1 slave. There have always been 2 ploughs in demesne and 2 ploughs belonging to the men, 3 acres of meadow, 1 mill, and 4 sokemen with 24 acres and half a plough. The whole was worth TRE 40s., now £4. [There is] 1 church [holding] 30 acres, worth 16d.

In Briningham [there were] 4 free men of Harold's, of 2½ carucates of land, whom Roger Longsword holds of Bishop W[illiam]. There have always been 9 villans. Then [there were] 13 bordars, now 17. Then [there were] 3 ploughs in demesne, now 2½, and half a plough might be added. Then [there were] 2½ ploughs belonging to the men, now 4. [There is] woodland for 30 pigs, 6 acres of meadow [and] 1 mill. Then [there were] 2 horses, now the same. Then [there were] 4 pigs, now 8. Then [there were] 9 sheep, now 104. Now [there are] 5 beehives and 3 sokemen with 12 acres and half a plough. It was then worth 50s., now £4, and is 1 league in length and 8 furlongs in breadth, and [pays] 13d. in geld. [There is] 1 church [with] 12 acres and [it is] worth 12d.

In Melton [Constable] [there were] 4 free men of Harold's; now Bishop W[illiam] [holds them] and Roger Longsword of him, and [so do] Ansketil the reeve and Roger. And [there are] 3 carucates of land. There have always been 2 villans and 32 bordars, and among them 7½ ploughs. [There is] woodland for 60 pigs [and] 6 acres of meadow. There have always been 2 horses. Then and now [there were] 8 head of cattle. Then [there were] 5 pigs, now 10. [There is] 1 church of 6 acres, and it is worth 5d. [The whole] was then worth 30s., now 40s. And it is

1 league in length and a half in breadth, and [pays] 10d. in geld. In Briningham Roger Longsword holds 6 acres which Earl R[alph] held and afterwards Count A[lan] and to this the Hundred testifies.

[NORTH] GREENHOE HUNDRED.

Hindringham was held by Bishop Æ[thelmær] TRE. Now Bishop W[illiam] [has it]. [There are] 8 free men [holding] 3 carucates of land [and] 14 bordars. There has always been woodland for 10 pigs [and] 5 acres of meadow. Then [there were] 5 ploughs, now 3. Then it was worth 40s., now it pays 50s., and of this land William de Noyers holds the half.

In Hindringham Drogo de la Beuvrière held 1 [free] man with 1 acre of land, and his predecessor [also] and afterwards a certain reeve of Bishop William who is called Sæwulf was seised of him and holds him.

In [Cock]thorpe [there were] 2 free men. Now William de Noyers holds them of Bishop W[illiam]. [They have] 100 acres of land, half an acre of meadow [and] there have always been 1½ ploughs. TRE it was worth 20s., now [it is worth] 30.

NORTH ERPINGHAM HUNDRED.

In "Hottune" Bishop Æthelmær held 1 free man by commendation with 15 acres of land, and William de Noyers holds him [of] Bishop William, and he has half a bordar. [There is] woodland for 2 pigs [and there is] half a plough. It was then worth 2s., now 16d.

In [North] Barningham [there is] 1 free man with 15 acres of land, whom Wighulf held TRE. Now W[illiam] de Noyers holds him of Bishop W[illiam]. There has always been half a plough. It has always been worth 16d.

In [East] Beckham 1 free man of Bishop Æthelmær held by commendation 80 acres of land. There have always been 2 villans and 5 bordars. [There is] woodland for 5 pigs; and 1 sokeman with 2½ acres of land. There have always been 2 ploughs [and there is] 1 church with 2½ acres. And it was added as a berewick to Blickling. It was then worth 7s., and now 12, and it is half a league in length and 4 furlongs in breadth, and [pays] 4½d. [in geld].

Bishop William

[Folio 199: NORFOLK]

WALSHAM HUNDRED.

In Hemblington [there were] 2 free men with 60 acres of land [belonging to] Ralph the staller with sake and soke, but of one Bishop Æthelmær had the commendation only. Bishop W[illiam] has one, and Earl R[alph] [held] the other, and they are worth 2s.

BLOFIELD HUNDRED.

In [Great or Little] Plumstead Godwine had 1 free man of Gyrth [with] 1 carucate of land, now Bishop W[illiam] has him. There have always been 5 bordars. There has always been 1 plough in demesne. There has always been half a plough belonging to the men. [There is] woodland for 8 pigs [and] 1 acre of meadow. There have always been 2 head of cattle; and [there are] there 10 free men with 30 acres of land [who were] in commendation only to Godwine. There has always been 1 plough and 1 acre of meadow. It was then worth 10s., now 40. And after King William came into this land Bishop Æthelmær seized it for a forfeiture, because a woman who held it married within a year of her husband's death.

In [North or South] Burlingham 2 carucates of land were held by 15 free men, Bishop Æthelmær's by commendation only. There have always been 9 bordars [and] 8 acres of meadow. There have always been 8 ploughs. It was then worth 20s., and now 26s. [There is] 1 church [holding] 30 acres and worth 2s. 8d. W[illiam] de Noyers holds it now.

[There were] also in [Great or Little] Plumstead 2 free men of Gyrth and of Stigand whom Bishop Herfast seized. [They

had] 50 acres of land and 2 acres of meadow. There have always been 2 bordars. There has always been 1 plough. Earl R[alph] had them when he forfeited [his lands] and R[obert] Blund [has them] at a rent. It was then worth 5s., now 3.

In [Great or Little] Plumstead 1 free man, Æthelmær's by commendation only, held 16 acres of land. Then [there was] half a plough, now [there are] 2 head of cattle. It was then worth 2s., now 16d.

In Freethorpe, 1 free man, Alsige, [held] under Earl R[alph] 16 acres of land. There has always been half a plough [and] 1 acre of meadow. It has always been worth 2s. Baldwin, the bishop's reeve, held this [...] by commendation only, but now he is commended to

[Folio 199v: NORFOLK]

Godric [and] in the king's hand.

In 'Letha' [there were] 7 free men, Æthelmær's by commendation only TRE; now Reginald has 1½ carucates of land. There have always been 3 ploughs and always 4 bordars. [There is] woodland for 4 pigs and 12 acres of meadow. It was then worth 10s. 4d.; [there is] 1 church [with] 5 acres and worth 5d. And it is 1 league in length and 5 furlongs in breadth, whoever holds there, and [pays] 6½d. in geld.

In [North] Burlingham [there were] TRE 3 free men of Æthelmær by commendation only; now Eli holds 46 acres of land and 4 acres of meadow. There has always been 1 plough and it has always been worth 4s.

In the same place [there was] 1 free man of Bishop Æthelmær by commendation only TRE; now the same Eli has [him] with 60 acres of free land and 40 which belong to a certain church [and there are] 7 acres of meadow. Then [there were] 4 bordars in the free [land], now 5, and 2 bordars in the land which belongs to the church. Then [there were] 1½ ploughs, afterwards and now 2 ploughs. And under him [there is] 1 church with 10 acres and [it is] worth 10d. And under him there are 7 free men by commendation only, holding 40 acres of land and 3 acres of meadow. There has always been 1 plough. It has always been worth 13s.

In the same place [were] 2 free men of Æthelmær's by commendation only TRE; now W[illiam] de Noyers has [them] with 50 acres of land. There have always been 1 villan and 4 bordars and 12 acres of meadow. There have always been 1½ ploughs and half a salt-pan. It was then worth 50d., now it pays 10s. And the said vill is 10 furlongs in length and 6 in breadth and [pays] 20d. [in] geld.

In [South] Burlingham [there were] 8 free men of Bishop Æthelmær's by commendation only, now W[illiam] the Bishop de Noyers has [them] with 140 acres of land. There have always been 11 bordars and 8 acres of meadow. Then [there were] 3 ploughs, afterwards and now 2½. It has always been worth 20s. [There is] half a church [with] 15 acres, worth 15d. In the same place [there were] 2 free men of Bishop Æthelmær's by commendation. Now the same W[illiam] holds [them as] 1 carucate of land. There have always been 6 bordars. There have always been 1½ ploughs, and 3 acres of meadow, and 4 free men under them [with] 8 acres of land

Bishop William

and 1 acre of meadow. Always $\frac{1}{2}$ a plough and it has always been worth 10s. And [South] Burlingham is 1 league in length and a half in breadth, but several hold there, and it [pays] 20d. [in] geld.

In "Letha" [there was] 1 free man of Bishop Æthelmær's by commendation. And he holds 16 acres of land and $1\frac{1}{2}$ acres of meadow. It has always been worth 5d.

In Bradeston there was 1 free man, Eadric, King Edward's steersman [with] 1 acre carucate of land. There have always been 4 villans and 1 bordar, and 2 slaves, and 3 acres of meadow. There has always been 1 plough in demesne and half a plough belonging to the men. [There is] woodland for 2 pigs, and always 1 horse and 6 head of cattle and 60 sheep now and 16 pigs and 16 goats. [There is] 1 church with 10 acres and [it is] worth 10d. And to this belong 10 free men and a half, in commendation only to his [the bishop's] predecessor with 80 acres of land [and] 3 acres of meadow. There have always been 2 ploughs. And in [North or South] Burlingham [holds] $4\frac{1}{2}$ acres of land belonging to Bradeston. It was then worth 10s. and the same afterwards [and] now 30s. And after King William came into England this Eadric was an outlaw in Denmark and Bishop Æthelmær seized his land. Now W[illiam] de Noyers has it.

In Catton [in Postwick] [there was] 1 free man of Gyrth by commendation only TRE with 60 acres of land. When Herfast came to the bishopric he gave it to a certain man of his [called] Reginald. Then [there were] 5 bordars, now 4. Then [there was] 1 plough in demesne and [there has been] always and half a plough belonging to the men. [There is] woodland for 5 pigs, and 1 horse, and 12 pigs [and] 7 acres of meadow. It has always been worth 15d.

In Buckenham [near Acle] [holds] 2 free men and in Catton [in Postwick] [holds] 1 and Æthelmær had the commendation; [it is] 50 acres of land and 6 acres of meadow. Then [there was] 1 plough, and now half. Then it was worth 6s. 8d., now 5. And of all these above-mentioned [holdings] the king and the earl have sake and soke.

BLOFIELD HUNDRED.

In Brundall [there was] 1 free man of Bishop Æthelmær by commendation only, but the soke belonged to R[alph] the staller. Now Bishop W[illiam] has [him] with 30 acres of land and 6 acres of meadow. There has always been 1 villan and 2 bordars. Then [there was] half a plough.

Now he ploughs with 2 head of cattle. It was then worth 3s., now 2s.

In addition in Brundall [there was] 1 free man, Æthelmær's by commendation only, [with] $11\frac{1}{2}$ acres of land. Then [there was] half a plough, now nothing. It was then worth 12d., afterwards and now 6. Bishop W[illiam] has it now.

In Witton [near Norwich] [there were] 18 free men in commendation to Æthelmær [with] 200 acres of land, and 5 bordars, and 11 acres of meadow. There have always been 3 ploughs. Eli has 2 men [with] 1 carucate of land, and 5 bordars, and 11 acres of meadow. It was then worth 10s. [and] now it pays 30. And Witton [near Norwich] is 11 furlongs in length and 5 furlongs in breadth and [pays] 7d. in geld. The king has the soke.

In the same place [there was] 1 free man of Gyrth's TRE by commendation only [and] half [with] 26 acres of land. And Godric held under Earl Ralph. And Heloise the niece of Bishop Herfast held from Herfast, and now from Bishop W[illiam]. He has always ploughed with 2 oxen. It has always been worth 16d.

WEST FLEGG HUNDRED.

In Winterton [there was] 1 free man of St Benet of Hulme by commendation only [holding] 60 acres of land [and] 3 acres of meadow. There have always been 5 bordars and half a salt-pan. There has always been 1 plough. And under him [there was] 1 free man with 4 acres of land. It was then worth 2s., now 4.

In [East or West] Somerton [there were] 3 free men TRE, but after [Earl] Tosti went out of England [had them]. There was 1 church of St Be of Hulme. They hold 106 acres of land [and] 9 acres of meadow. There have always been 9 bordars. There have always been $1\frac{1}{2}$ ploughs. It has always been worth 4s. 8d.

In Ashby [near Acle] [there were] 2 free men of St Benet of Hulme [with] 16 acres of land and 2 acres of meadow. There has always been half a plough. It was then worth 12d. and now 16d.

In Winterton [there were] 8 free men of Æthelmær's by commendation only [holding] 14 acres of land. There has always been half a plough. It was then worth 8d., now 24.

In Martham [there were] 36 free men of Æthelmær's by commendation only [with] 5 carucates

Bishop William

of land and 10 acres and 50 acres of meadow. Bishop W[illiam] has them now. There have always been 16 ploughs. It was then worth £6, now £8 10s. [There is] 1 church [with] 50 acres and [it is] worth 50d.

In Rollesby 1 free man was commended to Bishop Æthelmær [with] 80 acres of land, 2 acres of meadow, and 5 bordars and 10 free men. There have always been 2 ploughs. And in Burgh [St Margaret] [there were] 2 free men with 50 acres of land. It has always been worth 10s.

In addition in this Rollesby [there was] 1 free man with 80 acres of land [belonging to] Bishop Æthelmær and Abbot Ælfweald by commendation only. And this man was the man of the monastery [St Benet of Hulme] to the extent that he could not grant nor sell his land. There has always been 1 bordar [and] 2 acres of meadow. And under him [there were] 12 free men with 40 acres of land and $3\frac{1}{2}$ acres of meadow. They always had $2\frac{1}{2}$ ploughs among them. It was worth 10s. [and] now it pays 30s.

In Bastwick [there was] 1 free man of Bishop Æthelmær's by commendation only, and under them another free man, and they have 30 acres of land and 2 acres of meadow. Then [there was] half a plough and now [the same]. It was then worth 2s., now 22d.

In Sco [there was] 1 free man of Bishop Æthelmær's by commendation only, with 15 acres of land and half a plough [and] half an acre of meadow. And it is worth 16d.

In Billockby, Ketil, a free man held. He was half Bishop Æthelmær's by commendation, but all his land was in the monastery of St Benet of Hulme for the sustenance [of the monks] to the extent that he could neither grant nor sell it. [He had] 57 acres of land [and] 10 acres of meadow. Herfast appropriated it. Now Bishop W[illiam] holds and Bernard under him. There has always been 1 plough in demesne. And under him [there are] 8 free men [with] 45 acres of land [and] 7 acres of meadow. There have always been 1½ ploughs. It was then worth 10s., afterwards and now [it is worth] 20s. [There are] two thirds of a church [with] 7 acres and [it is] worth 5d. [Billockby] is 5 furlongs in length and 3½ in breadth and [pays] 20½d. in geld.

[Folio 201v: NORFOLK]

In Clippesby [there were] 4 free men, 2 of them Bishop Æthelmær's by commendation, and 1 Alsige's, and 1 St Benet's [of Hulme], with 100 acres of land [and] 10 acres of meadow. Bishop W[illiam] holds it now. And under them [there are] 6 bordars. There has always been half a plough and 1 plough. It was then worth 5s., afterwards and now [it is worth] 20s. It is 7 furlongs in length and 5 in breadth and [pays] 12d. in geld.

HENSTEAD HUNDRED.

In Surlingham [there was] 1 free man, Æthelmær's by commendation TRE, holding 10 acres of land and 2 acres of meadow and 2 bordars. Now as then he ploughs with 2 oxen. It has always been worth 16d. Now Bishop W[illiam] holds it.

In Tivetshall [St Margaret or St Mary] [there was] 1 free man of 40 acres of land TRE as the Hundred testifies. And the man's part, , belonged to St Æthelthryth and [his] wife's part, 20 acres, to St Edmund [of Bury]. There has always been half a plough and 2 bordars. Herfast appropriated it. Now Bishop W[illiam] holds it from his predecessor, and Reginald de Pierrepoint under him. It was then worth 5s., now 20.

LANDS OF ST MICHAEL OF NORWICH.

TAVERHAM HUNDRED.

In Taverham 1 carucate of land was held by St Michael TRE and by Stigand under him. There have always been 4 villans and 2 bordars. There have always been 1 plough on the demesne, and 1 plough belonging to the men; and 4 sokemen [with] 12 acres of land. There have always been 8 acres of meadow. [There is] woodland for 12 pigs. And it is worth 20s.

XI. Lands of Bishop Osbern.

GUILTCROSS HUNDRED.

In Banham Ælfric, a free man, held 1 carucate of land TRE. There have always been 3 villans and 5 bordars. Then [there was] 1 slave and 10 acres of meadow. There has always been 1 plough in demesne,

Bishop Osbern

[Folio 202: NORFOLK]

and half a plough belonging to the men. [There is] woodland for 100 pigs, and 3 sokemen [with] 5 acres. Now [there is] 1 horse [and] there have always been 3 head of cattle. Then [there were] 6 pigs, now 27. Then [there were] 6 sheep, now 30. Then [there were] 5 goats, now 30. Then it was worth 20s., now 40.

In 'Wick' [in Garboldisham] 1 free man held 1 carucate of land TRE. Then and afterwards [there were] 7 villans, now 8. There have always been 5 bordars and 1 slave, and 4 acres of meadow. Then and afterwards [there was] 1 plough in demesne, now 2. There have always been 3 ploughs belonging to the men. It was then worth 20s., now 4 0. And 10 free men and a half [have] 1 plough and half an acre of meadow. There have always been 2 ploughs, and it is worth 10s. The whole soke is in Kenninghall.

[NORTH] GREENHOE HUNDRED.

Hindringham was held by 3 free men TRE [as] 32 acres of land. There has always been 1 plough. It has always been 10s. TRE, and the king and the earl have always had the whole soke, and these 3 men whom Berard holds are claimed by the men of Drogo [de la Beuvrière] as of the fief of their lord.

DEPWADE HUNDRED.

Tasburgh was held by Thorolf, a free man of Stigand's, [with] 30 acres. There has always been 1 bordar and 1 plough in demesne, and 4 acres of meadow, the eighth part of a mill; and 6 free men [with] 10 acres by commendation only. TRE and always there has been half a plough.

In Forncett [St Mary or St Peter] [there is] 1 free man of Stigand's [with] 30 acres. There have always been 2 bordars. Then and afterwards [there was] 1 plough, now a half [and] 4 acres of meadow. Then [there were] 2 mills, afterwards 1 [and] now nothing; and [there were] 2 free men [with] 2 acres. Then it was worth 20s., afterwards and now 30. All Tasburgh is 10 furlongs in length and 7 in breadth and [pays] 9d. in geld.

HUNDRED OF GREENHOE.

the Lands of Godric the steward.

Gooderstone Asgot held freely. [There have] always [been] 12 villans and 16 bordars. Then [there were] 4 slaves; afterwards and now 1. [There have] always [been] in demesne 2 ploughs and 5 [ploughs] belonging to the men. And 10 free men used to live there whom King W[illiam] gave to Earl R[alph] and afterwards to G[odric], 2 of whom Archbishop Stigand used to have in commendation. [There have] always [been shared] between them 3 ploughs. [There is] woodland for 20 pigs. Then [there were] 3 mills; now 5. And [there is] 1 fishery and 4 acres of meadow. G[odric] found 7 head of head of cattle; now likewise. Now [there are] 3 horses. Then [there were] 51 sheep; now 100. And it is 1 league in length and half [a league] in breadth. And in geld it renders 13d. Then it was worth 50s. and afterwards 100s.; now £6.

In [South] Acre a certain free man, Osweard, held land for 2 oxen. Now Godric [holds it]. And it is worth 15d.

In Oxborough belong 60 acres, which 1 free man holds and 1 villan and it belongs to Gooderstone. They have been valued.

FOREHOE HUNDRED.

WRAMPLINGHAM [holds]: 45 acres of land. Edwin, a free man, held TRE. [There have] always [been] 2 villans and 6 bordars and 4 acres of meadow and half a mill and 3 ploughs. Then it was worth 20s.; now 40[s.]

In "Toketorp" Walter, 1 sokeman of Eadric's, holds 20 acres of land. And [there is] half a plough and half a mill. And it is worth 5s. And the whole of Wramplingham is half a league in length and half [a league] in breadth. And [it renders] 9d. in geld.

WALSHAM HUNDRED.

In Upton Ralph holds. [There are] 3 free men and 1 in [South] Walsham at 50 acres of land, 10 acres of meadow. [There has] always [been] 1 plough. Then it was worth 10s.; now 21s. And they are in the king's soke. In addition in [South] Walsham Gyrth holds 1 free man, the woman Tove, at 1 carucate. [There have] always [been] 3 bordars and half a plough and 20 acres of meadow. [There is] woodland for 7 pigs. [There is] half a salt-pan. And [there are] in addition 17 sokemen there at 1 carucate. [There have] always [been] 1½ ploughs, 12 acres of meadow. Then it was worth 10s.; now 20[s.]. The earl has the soke. Of these [there are] 3 in Upton and 1 free man in [South] Walsham. [There was] one in the commendation of Tove, a second of the Abbot of [St Benet of] Hulme, a third of Redger.

Godric

HENSTEAD HUNDRED.

In Stoke [Holy Cross] the same man holds 1 free man and 1 sokeman of Edwin's at 54 acres of land. And [there are] 3 acres of meadow. And under them [there is] 1 villan. [There have] always [been] 1½ ploughs.

In Poringland [there was] one free man of Edwin's TRE at 12 acres. And [there is] 1 bordar and half an acre of meadow. [There has] always [been] half a plough.

In [Earl or Pigot] Framingham [there is] 1 free man in the commendation of Edwin at 20 acres of land. And [there have] always [been] 2 bordars. And [there are] 1½ acres of meadow.

[There has] always [been] half a plough. And under him [there are] 3 whole free men and 3 half [free men]. Between them all [there are] 10 acres of land. [There has] always [been shared] between them all half a plough.

In Yelverton [there are] 2 free men of Edwin's at 13½ acres. Then [there was] half a plough; now nothing.

In Holverston [there are] 4 whole free men and 4 half [free men] of Edwin's at 40 acres of land. And [there are] 3 acres of meadow and 1 bordar. [There have] always [been] 1½ ploughs. In the same [vill there are] 2 sokemen, 2 acres of land. In Rockland [St Mary] [there are] 6 whole free men of Edwin's and 2 half [free men], 60 acres. [There have] always been 1½ ploughs.

In Bramerton [there are] 2 free men of Edwin's at 11 acres. [There has] always [been] half a plough and 1½ acres of meadow.

In Surlingham [there are] 2 full free men of Edwin's and 4 half [free men], 40 acres of land. And [there are] 3 acres of meadow and 4 bordars. [There has] always [been] 1 plough.

In Kirby [Bedon] [there is] 1 free man of Edwin's at 6 acres of land and under him 3 free [men] at 11 acres of land. Between them all half a plough [is shared].

In Rockland [St Mary] [there are] 4 free men of Aslak's, 8 acres of land. And [there is] half an acre of meadow and 3 bordars. And that same Edwin was a household thegn of King E[dward's]. Then all were worth 40s.; now 60[s.] And the soke of all these free men [is] in the Hundred.

Alpington Edwin held TRE for 2 carucates. [There have] always [been] 8 bordars and 1 slave. [There have] always [been] in demesne 1 plough and half a plough belonging to the men. And [there are] 6

acres of meadow. [There is] woodland for 12 pigs. And [there are] 4 hives of bees. [There has] always [been] 1 horse and 5 head of cattle and 60 sheep and 8 pigs. And [there are] 8½ sokemen at 40 acres of land. And [there are] 1½ ploughs. And [there are] 2 free men of Edwin's, the predecessor of Godric, at 40 acres. And [there is] 1 acre of meadow. [There has] always [been] 1 plough. Then it was worth 40s.; now £3 and 10s.

LODDON HUNDRED.

Hellington Ralph held, which 3 free men (2 in the commendation of Edwin, 1 of Gyrth) held TRE: 2 carucates. Under them [there have] always [been] 12 bordars. [There have] always [been] 3½ ploughs between them all. In the same vill [there are] 12 men, of whom 6 were in the soke of the fold and the other 6 were free. Between them all [there are] 40 acres of land. [There have] always [been] 2 ploughs.

In half of Ashby [St Mary] [there are] 6 full free men and 6 half [free men] in the commendation of Aslak and Leofric at 20 acres of land. [There have] always [been] 1½ ploughs.

In Claxton [there are] two free men in the commendation of Aslak and Leofric and 6 half [free] men. Between them all [there are] 16 acres of land. [There has] always [been] half a plough. Between them all [there are] 16 acres of meadow. And this was delivered to Godric for 1 manor. Then [there was] 1 horse; now 2. And [there are] 2 head of cattle. Now [there are] 200 sheep. Then [there were] 5 pigs; now 40. Then the whole thing was worth 40s.; now £4. The king and the earl [have] the soke and the sake. Hellington is 4 furlongs in length and 3 in breadth. And of the geld [it renders] 4d.

In Norton [Subcourse] [there is] 1 free woman, 16 acres of land, and she belongs to Hellington.

In Claxton [there are] $5\frac{1}{2}$ free men in the commendation of Edwin, 34 acres of land. [There has] always [been] half a plough between them all. [There is] 1 acre of meadow. The soke [is] in the Hundred. In Ashby [St Mary] [there are] $1\frac{1}{2}$ free men, 5 acres.

In Carleton [St Peter] [there are] 4 free men of the same Edwin, 30 acres. [There has] always [been] half a plough and 2 acres of meadow. The soke [is] in the Hundred. In Loddo n [there are] 2 free men of the same man at 24 acres. Then and afterwards [there was] 1 plough; now half [a plough].

In Washingford [there is] 1 free man of the same man, half of 30 acres and 2 bordars. The soke [is] in the Hundred. And under that man [there are] 6 free men of the same man, 16 acres. [There have] always [been] 2 ploughs, 4 acres of meadow and 1 mill.

Godric

[Folio 204: NORFOLK]

In Sisland [there is] 1 free man of the same man at 3 acres. In "Alcmuntona" [there are] 3 free men of the same man at 8 acres of land. They always plough with 3 oxen. The soke [is] in the Hundred. And all of those free men render 20s. "Alcmuntona" is 6 furlongs in length and 3 in breadth. Whoever holds there, [it renders] 6d. of the geld. "Torp" is 1 league in length and half [a league] in breadth. And of the geld [it renders] $4\frac{1}{2}$d., whoever may hold there.

HUNDRED OF EYNSFORD.

Sparham Edwin, 1 free man, held TRE; now G[odric] [holds it] of the king: 2 carucates. [There have] always [been] 2 villans and 16 bordars. Then and afterwards [there were] 2 slaves; now 1. Then and afterwards [there were] 2 ploughs in demesne; now 3. Then [there were] 4 ploughs belonging to the men; afterwards and now 2. And [there are] 6 acres of meadow and half a mill. [There is] woodland for 100 pigs. When he received [it, there were] 2 horses; now 3. [There have] always [been] 7 head of cattle and 23 pigs. Then [there were] 60 sheep; now 80. Now [there are] 10 hives of bees. And [there is] a free man, 30 acres of land, 1 acre of meadow. [There has] always [been] half a plough. [There is] 1 church, 40 acres and 6 acres of woodland. Then and afterwards it was worth 60s.; now 100s. And it is 1 league in length and 10 furlongs in breadth. And it renders $8\frac{1}{2}$d. of the geld.

In Bintree [there are] 2 free men, 20 acres of land and 2 acres of meadow. [There has] always [been] 1 plough. And it is worth 3s.

HUNDRED OF TAVERHAM.

In Beeston [St Andrew] [there is] 1 free man, 30 acres, half a plough and 2 acres of meadow. And it is worth 2s. The king and the earl [have] the soke.

HUNDRED OF HUMBLEYARD.

[Great] Melton Edwin, a thegn, [held] TRE: 2 carucates. [There have] always [been] 9 villans and 5 bordars and 4 slaves. Then [there were] 2 ploughs in demesne; afterwards 1; now 2. Then [there were] 3 ploughs belonging to the men; afterwards and now 2. [There is] woodland for 60 pigs, 20 acres of meadow. [There has] always [been] 1 mill. Then there was 1 horse; now 2. [There have] always [been] 10 head of cattle and 13 pigs. Now [there are] 40 sheep, 3 hives of bees. And [there are] 9 free men in soke of the fold and commendation only.

[Folio 204v: NORFOLK]

[There are] 50 acres. [There have] always [been] 2 ploughs and 3 acres of meadow. The king and the earl [have] the soke. And it is worth 8s. And the manor was then worth £6; afterwards 100s.; now £7. And [there are] 4 free men in commendation only, 30 acres of land. [There has] always [been] 1 plough. And [there are] $1\frac{1}{2}$ acres of meadow. And it is worth 5s.

In Hethersett [there are] 9 free men, 43 acres, in commendation only and soke of the fold. [There has] always [been] 1 plough and 2 acres of meadow. And it is worth 5s.

Little Melton Edwin held TRE of St Benet [of Hulme]. And it was such that he had granted it to the abbot after his death. [There have] always [been] 2 carucates and 3 bordars and 1 slave and 2 ploughs in demesne. [There are] 3 acres of meadow. [There has] always [been] 1 horse and 5 head of cattle. Now [there are] 15 pigs and 90 sheep. Then it was worth 40s.; afterwards 60[s.]; now £4. To this manor have always attached 12 free men in commendation only and soke of the fold. [There is] half a carucate and 3 acres. [There have] always [been] 3 ploughs. And [there are] 3 acres of meadow. And it is worth 20s. In these two [Great and Little] Meltons 1 carucate [which] a certain free man, a thegn, also held TRE for a manor. Then [there were] 3 villans and 1 plough in demesne and half a plough belonging to the men. This Godric holds and was holding when R[alph] forfeited and it is in the value of the two manors.

In [Great or Little] Melton [there are] 9 free men in commendation only, 110 acres. [There have] always [been] 2 bordars. Then [there were] $3\frac{1}{2}$ ploughs; now 4. [There are] $5\frac{1}{2}$ acres of meadow. [There is] woodland for 4 pigs. Then it was worth 23s.; now 30[s.] and 8d. And Little Melton is 10 furlongs in length and 5 in breadth. And [it renders] $8\frac{1}{4}$d. of the geld.

In Colney Walter holds. [There are] 18 free men in commendation only and 30 acres, $1\frac{1}{2}$ carucates and 2 bordars. Then [there were] 5 ploughs; now 4. And [there are] 7 acres of meadow and 1 mill. And [there was] 1 free man in commendation only under the predecessor of Roger Bigod and he holds half an acre of land which he bought after Ralph forfeited from Roger's land. Then it was worth 30s.; now 40[s.] And it is 8 furlongs in length and 8 in breadth.

Godric

And [it renders] 8¼d. of the geld.

In Hethersett the same man holds. [There are] 4 free men in commendation only, 60 acres. [There have] always [been] 1½ ploughs. And [there are] 5 acres of meadow. And it is worth 10s. 8d. The king and the earl [have] the soke. In the same [vill] the same man holds. [There are] 16 free men in commendation only, 33 acres. [There have] always [been] 1½ ploughs. And it is worth 3s. 4d. Count Alan [has] the soke.

In Dunston [there are] 7½ free men in commendation only, 111 acres and 1 bordar. [There have] always [been] 1½ ploughs and 1 mill and 2 acres of meadow. And it is worth 13s. And it is half a league in length and 3 furlongs in breadth. And [it renders] 6½d. of the geld.

In Swardeston [there are] 7 [free men], 42 acres. [There are] 2½ free men in commendation only and 1 bordar. [There has] always [been] 1 plough. And [there is] 1 acre of meadow. And it is worth 6s.

In Flordon [there were] 3 free men, 19 acres of land, TRE. [There has] always [been] half a plough. And it is worth 2s. and 8d. Two of these the predecessor of Roger Bigod held in commendation only and the third the predecessor of Godric [held] likewise. Now Godric holds the whole. In Kenningham Ansculf, 1 sokeman, holds 30 acres. [There has] always [been] half a plough. And it is worth 5s.

In Swainsthorpe [there are] 2 sokemen, 35 acres. [There has] always [been] half a plough and 1 bordar. And [there is] 1 acre of meadow. And it is worth 2s. 8d.

In Keswick [there is] 1 man, 10 acres. And it is worth 16d. The king and the earl [have] the soke over all.

CLAVERING HUNDRED.

Heckingham Hagni held of Stigand TRE: 4 carucates. [There have] always [been] 6 villans and 6 bordars and 1 slave. Then [there was] one plough in demesne; now 2. Then [there were] 2 ploughs belonging to the men; now 1 and there could be 2 assembled. [There are] 10 acres of meadow. [There is] woodland for 4 pigs. [There has] always [been] 1 mill, a marsh, 60 sheep. Then [there was] 1 horse; now 2. Now [there are] 4 head of cattle and 20 pigs. And [there is] 1 church, 8 acres. Of these Roger Bigod claims 30 acres of land as part of the fief of Æthelstan.

And [there are] 17 free men, [holding] 1 carucate, in commendation only. Then [there were] 4 ploughs; now 3. And [there are] 3 acres of meadow. To this manor Earl R[alph] added 8 free men TRW. And they have 1 carucate and 2 bordars. And [there are] 6 free men under them, 12 acres. Then and afterwards [there were] 4 ploughs; now 3. [There are] 7 acres of meadow. The manor was then worth 20s.; now 60[s.] And the free men, 30s. The whole is 1 league in length and 8 furlongs in breadth. And [it renders] 12d. of the geld.

In Hales [there is] a half free man, 1½ acres. And it is worth 3d.

In Norton [Subcourse] [there are] 3 free men of St Benet [of

Hulme's], 37½ acres. [There has] always [been] 1 plough. And it is worth 5s. In Southwood [there is] 1 free man, [holding] 1 acre of land, of whom the predecessor of Roger fitzReinhard had the commendation TRE. And it is worth 2d.

This Godric was holding when R[alph] forfeited.

XIII. Lands of Hermer.

HUNDRED OF CLACKCLOSE.

In Marham Thorkil held 20 acres in the soke of St Æthelth[ryth]. [There have] always [been] 2 villans who were then holding 3 oxen; now 2. And [there is] 1 acre of meadow. It has always been worth 3s. less 4d. This land has been measured in the return of St Æthel[thryth].

In Fincham [there are] 3 villans and 15 bordars and 7 slaves and 3 ploughs in demesne and 13 acres of meadow. Then [there were] 4 horses; now 1. Then [there were] 12 head of cattle; now 9. Then [there were] 30 pigs; now 26. Then [there were] 260 sheep; now 175. . It has always been worth £8. To this manor is attached half a league of woodland. And [it is] 1 furlong in length and 1 furlong in breadth.

In Barton [Bendish] William holds 2 carucates which Thorkil, a free man, held. [There have] always [been] 5 villans and 3 bordars. Then [there were] 3 slaves; now 1. [There have] always [been] 4 acres of woodland and 20 acres of meadow. [There have] always [been] 2 ploughs in demesne. Then [there were] 2 ploughs belonging to the men; now 1. [There have] always [been] 3 head of cattle. Now [there are] 4 horses. Then [there were] 30 sheep; now 61. [There is] 1 church,

Hermer

12 acres. Then [there were] 5 pigs; now 15. It has always been worth 60s. To this manor have always belonged 7 free men in soke of the fold and commendation only who have 30 acres of land. [There have] always [been] 1½ ploughs.

Wormegay Thorkil held for a manor: 1 carucate. [There have] always [been] 8 villans and 2 slaves. And [there are] 8 acres of meadow. And [there is] 1 plough in demesne, 1 plough belonging to the men, a quarter part of a mill and 3 fish ponds. [There have] always [been] 3 cows and 18 pigs. Now [there are] 60 sheep. Then [there were] 4 hives of bees; now 2. [It has] always [been worth] 60s. And it is 5 furlongs in length and 2 in breadth. And it renders 2d. of the king's geld of 20s.

West Briggs the same Thorkil held TRE: 2 carucates. [There have] always [been] 9 villans and 7 bordars and 4 slaves. And [there are] 2 ploughs in demesne. [There is] half a plough belonging to the men and 6 acres of meadow and half an acre of woodland and 1 mill. Then [there were] 2 horses; now 1. Then [there were] 10 head of cattle; now 13. [There have] always [been] 6 pigs. .

Then [there were] 120 sheep; now 60. It has always been worth 60s. This vill is in length 5 furlongs and in breadth 3. And it renders 2d. of a geld of 20s.

Thorpland [near Downham Market] Bordin holds: 1 carucate which Thorkil held TRE. [There have] always [been] 5 villans, 2 bordars, 20 acres of meadow. [There has] always [been] 1 plough in demesne. Then [there was] 1 plough belonging to the men; now 2 oxen. [There have] always [been] 4 head of cattle. Then [there were] 24 sheep; now 80. Then [there were] 9 pigs; now 10. [There is] 1 church, 6 acres. Then it was worth 30s.; now 20[s.] This land is 1 league in length and 4 furlongs in breadth. And it renders 8d. of the king's geld of 20s. Stow [Bardolph] the same man held TRE: 3 carucates. Then and afterwards [there were] 7 villans; now 2. [There have] always [been] 15 bordars and 8 slaves. And [there are] 40 acres of meadow and 1 [acre] of woodland. [There have] always [been] 3 ploughs in demesne and 1 fishpond. Then [there were] 5 horses; now 2. And [there are] 26 wild mares. Then [there were] 7 cows; now 1. [There are] 44 pigs. Then [there were] 240 sheep; now 160. Then [there were] 2 hives of bees; now 4. 5 free men are attached to this manor with every customary due and [are] part of the soke. There are also 17 free men attached to the custom of the fold and they [are] commended,

at 24 acres. And their soke is St Benet [of Hulme's] and Herm[er de Ferrers']. The whole of this was then and afterwards worth £8; now [£] 7. [There is] 1 church, 53 acres of land, and it is worth 3s.

Wimbotsham and Stow [Bardolph]: these vills are 1 league in length and half [a league] in breadth. And they render 16d. of the king's geld of 20s.

Ryston Helmer holds: 1 carucate which Ketil, 1 free man, held TRE. [There have] always [been] 7 villans and 1 bordar and 2 slaves. And [there is] a plough in demesne. Then [there was] half a plough belonging to the men and [there is] now. And [there are] 8 acres of meadow. [There is] half a fishpond. [There has] always [been] 1 horse. Then [there were] 5 cows; now 4. Then [there were] 6 pigs; now 19. And [there are] 108 sheep. Then it was worth 20s.; afterwards and now 20[s.] In the same [vill there are] 7 sokemen at 21 acres of land. And [there are] 3 acres of meadow. [There has] always [been] 1 plough. And it is worth 5s.. The whole is 4 furlongs in length and 3 in breadth. And it renders 4d. of a geld of 20s.

Stradsett Fulbert holds: 2 carucates which Swærting, a free man, held TRE. [There have] always [been] 6 villans and 2 bordars and 1 slave. And [there are] 8 acres of meadow and half a fishery. And [there are] 2 ploughs in demesne, 2 oxen belonging to the villans. [There has] always [been] 1 horse and 2 head of cattle and 8 pigs. Then [there were] 140 sheep; now 80. . In the same [vill there are] 13 free men, 210 acres. And [there is] 1 church at 30 acres. [There have] always [been] 2 ploughs. And [there are] 7 acres of meadow. This was delivered for 1 carucate to complete 1 manor. The whole of this is worth £4 and 15s. The commendation of those two men was with the predecessor of [Ralph] Baynard. This vill is 7 furlongs in length and 4 in breadth. And it renders 8d. of a geld of 20s.

In Upwell [there are] 6 bordars and they have been valued in the Hundred and a half of Freebridge.

Terrington [St Clement or St John]: 1 carucate, Thorkil, a free man, held TRE. [There have] always [been] 7 villans and 7 bordars. Then [there were] 2 slaves; now 1. And [there are] 24

acres of meadow. [There has] always [been] 1 plough in demesne and 1 plough belonging to the men. And [there are] 7 salt-pans. Then [there was] 1 horse; now none. [There have] always [been] 6 head of cattle. Then [there were] 16 pigs; now 7. Then [there were] 310 sheep; now 315. It has always

Hermer

been worth 60s. To this 1 sokeman belongs, 6 acres of land. And it is worth 12d.

In Islington Thorkil has always held [with] 1½ carucates. [There have] always [been] 4 villans and 11 bordars. Then [there were] 2 ploughs in demesne; now 1. [There has] always [been] half a plough belonging to the men. And [there are] 10 acres of meadow. [There is] 1 church, 2 acres. And [there is] half a salt-pan. [There have] always [been] 4 head of cattle. Then [there were] 20 pigs; now 3. Then [there were] 120 sheep; now 100. It has always been worth 60s. To this manor belonged TRE and now 15 free men at 30 acres. [There has] always [been] 1 plough. And [there are] 4 acres of meadow. Then it was worth 15s.; now 10[s.] Over these his predecessor had the commendation and they can withdraw if they give 2s. Stigand had the soke.

In [North] Runcton Thorkil, a free man, held TRE: 2 carucates. [There have] always [been] 11 villans and 7 bordars and 2 slaves. [There are] 30 acres of meadow. [There have] always [been] 2 ploughs in demesne and 1 plough belonging to the men. And [there is] 1 mill and half a wood at 20 pigs and 4 salt-pans and one-third of a Wfth one. [There has] always [been] 1 horse and 4 head of cattle and 27 pigs. [There are] 400 sheep. To this manor belong 13 sokemen, 37 acres. [There has] always [been] 1 plough. It has always been worth £6 and 4s. The whole is 1 league in length and in breadth. And it renders 12d. of the 20s. of the king's geld. And West Winch is within this same measurement.

SHROPHAM HUNDRED.

[Great] Ellingham Warenbold holds, which Thorkil, a free man, held TRE: 3 carucates. [There have] always [been] 3 villans and 2 bordars and 5 slaves. [There is] woodland at 100 pigs. [There are] 30 acres of meadow. [There have] always [been] 3 ploughs in demesne. [There have] always [been] 4 horses and 8 head of cattle and 6 mares with foals. Then [there were] 20 pigs; now 27. Then [there were] 120 sheep; now 100. [There is] 1 church, 20 acres. And [there are] 28 sokemen, 60 acres. And [there are] 6 acres of meadow. [There have] always [been] 3 ploughs. Then and afterwards it was worth £4; now 100s. And the whole is 1 league in length and half [a league] in breadth. And whoever may have it there, [it renders] 19d. of the geld.

LAUNDITCH HUNDRED.

Litcham Thorkil, a free man, held

TRE: 3 carucates, for a manor. Then and afterwards [there

were] 4 villans; now 3. Then and afterwards [there were] 4 bordars; now 3. Then [and] afterwards [there were] 4 slaves; now [...]. [There are] 8 acres of meadow. [There have] always [been] 2 ploughs in demesne and 1 plough belonging to the men. [There is] woodland for 7 pigs. [There has] always [been] 1 mill. And [there are] 3 sokemen, 4 acres of land and 1 virgate. Then [there were] 2 horses. Then [there were] 9 head of cattle; now 3. [There have] always [been] 27 pigs. Then [there were] 200 sheep; now 220. [There is] half a church, 4 acres. To this manor belongs half a carucate. [There have] always [been] 2 bordars and a quarter part of one market. Now William holds it. Then [there was] 1 plough; now half a plough. And [there are] 2 acres of meadow. [There have] always [been] 25 sheep and 2 pigs. This is in [Gayton] Thorpe. Then and afterwards it was worth 40s. and now 50[s.] and above that 10s.

In Roughham Fulbert holds 1 carucate. The same man held it TRE. Then [there was] 1 bordar. Then [there was] 1 plough; now half [a plough] and half can be restored. And it is worth 10s. The soke [is] in Mileham, [a manor] belonging to the king. The whole of Litcham above is 8 furlongs in length and 6 in breadth. Whoever may hold it there, [it renders] 7½d. of the geld.

HUNDRED OF MITFORD.

Whinburgh Thorkil, a free man, held TRE: 3 carucates and 1½ acres. Then [there were] 9 villans; now 13. Then [there were] 8 bordars; now 12. [There have] always [been] 8 slaves. And [there are] 4 ploughs in demesne. Then and afterwards [there were] 3 ploughs belonging to the men; now 4. Then [there was] woodland for 150 pigs; now for 110. And [there are] 16 acres of meadow. Then [there was] 1 mill; now 2. [There have] always [been] 2 horses and 8 head of cattle and 47 pigs. Now [there are] 100 sheep less 2. Then [there were] 60 goats. [There is] 1 church, 6 acres. And [there is] 1 berewick [at] Garveston, 1 carucate. [There has] always [been] 1 villan and 1 bordar and 1 plough and 4 acres of meadow and 1 horse and 3 head of cattle and 44 sheep. Then it was worth £6; now [£]7. [There is] 1 church, 7 acres.

In the same Garveston [there are] 19 free men, 100 acres of land. [There are] 4 ploughs and 9 acres of meadow. Then it was worth 20s.; now 55[s.] 4d. Of these Bordin holds

Hermer

24 acres. And it is worth in the same value 4s. Over these the Hundred testifies that his predecessor had no rights of custom except for commendation and it oVers the judicial ordeal in support of this. And a certain man of Hermer [de Ferrers] oVers the judicial ordeal that his predecessor had every customary right TRE except for the soke of St Æthelthryth and that he could sell his land. They gave pledges of this. The whole is 1 league in length and 1 league in breadth. And [it renders] 3½d. of the geld. And Garveston [is] 5 furlongs in length and 4 in breadth. And [it renders] 13d. of the geld.

In Shipdham Adelelm holds. [There is] 1 sokeman, 16 acres of land. And it is worth 4s.

In Whinburgh [there is] 1 sokeman, 30 acres. And [there are] 2 acres of meadow. Then [there was] 1 plough; now half [a plough]. Then it was worth 16s.; now 8[s.] The Hundred testifies that he could not sell his land but the sheriff asserts in opposition that he could sell without [securing] his lord's permission.

In Yaxham [there were] 4 sokemen of his predecessor's, 20 acres of land, TRE. Then [there was] 1 plough; now half [a plough]. And [there is] 1 acre of meadow. Then it was worth 4s.; now 2[s.] [East] Tuddenham Thorkil held TRE: 66 acres of land, for a manor. [There have] always [been] 3 slaves and 2 villans. And [there is] 1 plough in demesne and 1 acre of meadow and half a mill and 1 ox. Then [there were] 140 sheep; now 160. And [there are] 38 pigs. .

Then it was worth 16s.; now 20[s.]. And it is 7 furlongs in length and 6 in breadth. Whoever may hold it there, [it renders] 22½d. of the geld. All the churches of the whole of Hermer [de Ferrers'] land have been valued with the manors.

HUMBLEYARD HUNDRED.

Wreningham Vagn holds: 3 carucates and 12 acres which Leofweald, a thegn, held

TRE: 3 carucates and 12 acres. Then [there were] 4 villans; afterwards 2; now none. [There have] always [been] 14 bordars. Then [there were] 3 slaves; now 1. [There have] always [been] 3 ploughs in demesne. Then [there were] 1½ ploughs belonging to the men; now 1. [There are] 16 acres of meadow. [There is] woodland for 6 pigs. [There have] always [been] 2 horses. Then [there were] 2 head of cattle; now 9. Then [there were] 2 pigs; now 13. Then [there were] 60 sheep; now 50. Then and afterwards it was worth 60s.; now 80[s.] And it is 1 league in length and half [a league] in breadth. And [it renders] 10d. of the geld. And to this land belong 8 free men in soke of the fold and commendation only, 28 acres. [There has] always [been] 1 plough. And it is worth 4s. The king and the earl [have] the soke over this and over the manor.

THE LAND of the Abbot of St Edmund.

HUNDRED OF CLACKCLOSE.

In Fincham [there are] 16 acres of land and 4 acres of meadow. And it is worth 2s. 8d. In Runcton [Holme or South Runcton] St E[dmund] held TRE 2 carucates. [There have] always [been] 5 villans and 4 bordars and 2 slaves. [There are] 12 acres of meadow, 16 acres of woodland, 1 mill, 1 fishpond. And [there are] 2 ploughs in demesne. Then [there was] 1 plough belonging to the men; now 2 oxen. [There has] always [been] 1 horse, 8 head of cattle, 30 pigs, 15 sheep. To this manor belong 27 free men (but the soke remained with St E[dmund]) having 1 carucate. [There have] always [been] 3 ploughs, 2 bordars. Also half a carucate belongs to this manor. [There have] always [been] 4 bordars and 1 slave. And [there is] 1 plough in demesne. And in addition belong 30 acres and 1 villan and 2 bordars. It has always been worth £7 4s. To this manor belongs 1 berewick which is called Islington and it is in another Hundred. The whole of this manor is 1 league in length and 5 furlongs in breadth. And it renders 8d. when the whole Hundred renders 20s. of the geld.

Southery: 2 carucates. [There have] always [been] 13 villans and 7 bordars and 5 slaves. [There are] 24 acres of meadow. Then [there were] 2 ploughs in demesne; now 3. Then [there were] 2 ploughs belonging to the men; now 3. [There is] 1 fishery, 4 horses, 31 head of cattle, 11 pigs, 80 sheep, 11 wild mares. Then it was worth 32s.; now £4. It is half a league in length and 4 furlongs in breadth. And [it renders] 3d. of the geld.

In Hilgay: 58 acres of land. [There are] 3 villans, 1 plough, 4 acres of meadow. It has been valued above. In the same [vill there are] 2 bordars, 1 acre, and they belong to Runcton [Holme or South Runcton]. In [West] Dereham [there is] 1 sokeman, 6 acres. It is worth 6d. In Thorpland [near Downham Market] [there is] 1 free man, 4 acres, in commendation only. And St Benet [of Hulme has] the soke. It is worth 8d.

FREEBRIDGE HUNDRED AND A HALF.

In Islington St E[dmund] holds 1 carucate. [There have] always [been] 25 villans. [There is] 1 plough in demesne, 1 plough belonging to the men. [There are] 20 acres of meadow, 4 head of cattle, 80 sheep. To this manor belong 6 sokemen in [North] Lynn, 26 acres of land. [There has] always [been] 1 plough and 1 salt-pan. It is worth 40s.

In Middleton [near Kings Lynn] Richard holds of the abbot 1 carucate, which St E[dmund] held TRE. [There are] 3 villans and 2 bordars, 1 slave. [There is] 1 plough in demesne. [There are] 20 acres of meadow, 2 salt-pans, 3 cows, 24 sheep, 4 pigs. [There is] 1 sokeman at 5 acres. It is worth 20s.

SHROPHAM HUNDRED.

In Buckenham [near Attleborough] St E[dmund] held 1 carucate TRE. Then [there were] 4 villans; now 5. [There have] always [been] 8 bordars. Then [there were] 4 slaves; now 2. [There are] 10 acres of meadow. Then [there was] 1 mill; now none.

[There has] always [been] 1 plough in demesne and 1 plough belonging to the men. [There is] 1 horse, 7 head of cattle, 6 pigs, 28 sheep. [There are] 7 sokemen, half a carucate. [There have] always [been] 2 ploughs. [There are] 3 acres of meadow. [There are] 3 bordars. [There is] woodland for 5 pigs. It is worth 40s.

GUILTCROSS HUNDRED.

Quidenham Goscelin holds of the abbot, which St E[dmund] held for half a carucate with the soke. [There have] always [been] 2 villans, 1 bordar. [There are] 3 acres of meadow. [There is] half a plough in demesne and 2 oxen belonging to the men. Then [there was] 1 mill. It is worth 10s.

In [Blo] Norton the same man holds 1 carucate which 1 sokeman of St E[dmund's] held. [There have] always [been] 5 villans. And [there were] 3 bordars; now 5. [There is] 1 acre of meadow. [There have] always [been] 2 ploughs in demesne and half a plough belonging to the men. [There is] woodland for 10 pigs. [There is] 1 mill. And [there is] 1 sokeman, half an

acre. Now [there are] 3 horses, 12 head of cattle, 10 pigs, 45 sheep, 6 hives of bees. It is worth 30s. It is 1 league in length and a half [a league] in breadth. Whoever may hold it there, [it renders] 8fd. of the geld. 5 acres belonging to the church are worth

In Gasthorpe a free man held TRE 30 acres. Now a certain Englishman [holds it] of the abbot. Now [there is] 1 bordar. [There are] 3 acres of meadow. Then [there was] half a plough; now 1. Then it was worth 5s.; now 10[s.] Of this the abbot had the commendation TRE. The soke is in Kenninghall, [a manor] belonging to the king.

In [Great or Little] Snarehill Fulcher holds of the abbot 30 acres which 1 sokeman held. [There has] always [been] 1 bordar, half a plough. It is worth 2s.

In [East or West] Harling Richard [holds] 1 carucate of the abbot which St E[dmund] held TRE. [There have] always [been] 4 villans, 3 bordars, 1 slave. [There are] 3 acres of meadow. Then [there was] 1 plough in demesne; now 2. [There have] always [been] 2 ploughs belonging to the men. [There is] 1 horse, 8 head of cattle, 3 pigs. [there were] 120 sheep; now 180. Then it was worth 20s.; now 40[s.]

LAUNDITCH HUNDRED.

In Wendling the same R[ichard] holds of the abbot which St E[dmund] held for 1 carucate. [There are] 2 villans, 6 bordars, 6 acres of meadow, 1 plough in demesne and 1½ ploughs belonging to the men. [There is] woodland for 100 pigs. And [there is] 1 sokeman, 12 acres. [There has] always [been] 1 bordar. Then [there was] 1 plough; now half [a plough]. [There has] always [been] 1 mill, 19 pigs. Then it was worth 20s.; now 30[s.] It is 9 furlongs in length and 6 in breadth. And [it renders] 2½d. of the geld.

FOREHOE HUNDRED.

Marlingford St E[dmund] held TRE. [There have] always [been] 4 villans and 1 slave. Then [there was] 1 plough; now 2. And [there are] 1½ ploughs belonging to the men. [There is] woodland for 8 pigs. [There are] 6 acres of meadow. [There have] always [been] 2 mills, 2 horses, 22 head of cattle, 8 pigs, 130 sheep, 9 goats and 3 sokemen. It has always been worth 40s. It is 1 league in length and 3½ furlongs in breadth. And [it renders] 6½d. of the geld. Others hold there.

BLOFIELD HUNDRED.

Buckenham [near Acle] Roger holds of the abbot, which St E[dmund] held

Abbot of Bury

as sustenance TRE. Now Roger Bigod holds it of St E[dmund] for 1 carucate. [There have] always [been] 8 bordars. And [there is] 1 plough in demesne. Then and afterwards [there were] 2 ploughs belonging to the men; now half [a plough]. [There are] 9 acres of meadow. Then [there were] 2 horses; now 1. Then [there were] 2 head of cattle; now nothing. Now [there are] 6 pigs, 21 sheep. Then and afterwards it was worth 30s.; now 20[s.] And [it is] 11 furlongs in length and 6 in breadth. And [it renders] 20d. of the geld, whoever may hold there. And to this manor are attached 10 free men in commendation at 60 acres. [There are] 6 acres of meadow. Then and afterwards [there were] 5 ploughs; now 2½. Then and afterwards it was worth 10s.; now 20[s.]

HENSTEAD HUNDRED.

Caistor [St Edmund] St E[dmund] has always held for a manor and for 3 carucates. [There have] always [been] 10 villans and 7 bordars and 2 ploughs in demesne and 4 ploughs belonging to the men, 6 acres of meadow, half a mill. Now [there are] 3 horses, 5 head of cattle, 30 pigs, 40 sheep. And [there are] 4 sokemen at 25 acres of land by grant of the king with every customary due. And they belong in the same manor according to the testimony of the Hundred. Then it was worth 40s.; now 100[s.] It is 6 furlongs in length and 4 in breadth. And [it renders] 16d. of the geld. And more hold there. [There are] 11 acres belonging to the church: it is worth 16d.

Brooke Earl Gyrth held TRE and King William gave it to St E[dmund] when he first came to St E[dmund]: 4 carucates. Then [there were] 33 villans; now 38. [There have] always [been] 3 slaves. Now [there are] 3 ploughs in demesne and 6 [ploughs] belonging to the men. [There is] woodland for 30 pigs. [There are] 9 acres of meadow. Now [there are] 5 horses, 14 head of cattle, 40 pigs. Now [there are] 65 sheep and 20 goats. And [there are] 47 sokemen, 1½ carucates. And [there have] always [been] 9 ploughs [shared] between the men. In Shotesham [All Saints or Saint Mary] 16 free men in the commendation of Gyrth at 1 carucate belong to Brooke and under them are 7 bordars. And [there are] 4 acres of meadow and 3 ploughs and a quarter part of a church. Of this Berengar holds 20 acres.

In Howe [there is] 1 free man of Gyrth's at 1 carucate, which Berengar holds. [There have] always [been] 5 villans and 6 bordars. And [there are] 2 ploughs in demesne. Then and afterwards [there were] 3 ploughs belonging to the men; now 2. [There is] woodland for 40 pigs. [There are] 15 acres belonging to the church: it is worth 2s.

In Poringland [there is] 1 free man in the commendation of Gyrth belonging to Brooke, 30 acres, and 1 bordar at half an acre. [There has] always [been] 1 plough. King E[dward] had the soke and sake over all those free men and afterwards Gyrth obtained it by force. But King William gave the soke and sake of the free men of Gyrth's with the manor just [as] he himself used to hold it. This the monks claim.

[Folio 210V: NORFOLK]

Then and afterwards it was worth £10; now [£]15. Brooke is 1 league and 4 furlongs in length and 1 league in breadth. And of the geld [it renders] 17½d. Others hold there.

EARSHAM HALF HUNDRED.

Thorpe [Abbots] St E[dmund] held TRE for a manor and for 2 carucates. Then [there were] 8 villans; now 9. And [there are] 8 bordars. [There have] always [been] 2 ploughs in demesne and 6 ploughs belonging to the men. Then [there was] woodland for 60 pigs; now 40. [There are] 12 acres of meadow. Then [there was] 1 mill; now none. [There have] always

[been] 4 horses, 10 head of cattle, 11 pigs, 10 sheep, 20 goats. And in Brockdish [there are] 2 sokemen belonging to the same manor at 1 carucate and 2 villans and 2 bordars. Then it was worth £4; now 100s. It is 7 furlongs in length and 6 in breadth. And of the geld [it renders] 4d. [There are] 12 acres belonging to a church: it is worth 2s.

In Mendham [now Suffolk] Frodo holds of the abbot 1 carucate and 30 acres which 2 sokemen held and under them 9 villans and 7 bordars. Then [shared] between them all [there were] 5 ploughs; now 7. [There is] woodland for 52 pigs. [There are] 12 acres of meadow. [It has been] valued in Mendham [Suffolk]. Then [there was] 1 mill; now none. It is 2 leagues and 5 furlongs in length and 7 in breadth. And of the geld [it renders] 7d.

In Harleston [there is] 1 free man in the commendation of St E[dmund] and the soke [was] Stigand's in Earsham. [There are] 12 acres of land. It has always been worth 20d.

In Starston [there is] 1 free man in the commendation of St E[dmund] but the soke [was] Stigand's in Earsham. [There are] 5 acres of land. It is worth 10d. This is in demesne.

Starston Roger Bigod holds of the abbot, which BeorhtXæd, a free woman in the commendation of St E[dmund], held for 2 carucates. Then [there were] 3 villans; now 2. [There have] always [been] 3 slaves. Then [there were] 2 ploughs in demesne; now none. [There are] 6 acres of meadow. Then and afterwards [it was worth] 40s.; now 20[s.] It is 1 league and 5 furlongs in length and 5 furlongs in breadth. And [it renders] 13d. of the geld, whoever may hold there.

In Harleston Frodo holds. [There are] 1½ villans at 13 acres. And it belongs to Mendham [now Suffolk].

DISS HALF-HUNDRED.

Tivetshall [St Margaret or St Mary] St E[dmund] has always held for 3 carucates. [There have] always [been] 18 villans and 15 bordars and 2 slaves. And [there are] 3 ploughs in demesne and 12 ploughs belonging to the men. [There is] woodland for 80 pigs. [There are] 10 acres of meadow. [There have] always [been] 5 horses, 24 head of cattle, 35 pigs, 40 sheep, 24 goats. And [there are] 5 sokemen in the same [vill] at 60 acres. [There have] always [been] 2 ploughs. In the same [vill there is] 1 free man of St E[dmund], half a carucate. [There are] 1½ villans, 2 bordars. [There has] always [been] 1 plough. [There is] woodland for 15 pigs. [There are] 2 churches

Abbot of Bury

[Folio 211: NORFOLK]

at 40 acres worth 7s. 6d. 1 berewick, Gissing, at 1 plough and 2 villans and 2 bordars, is attached to the same manor. [There has] always [been] 1 plough in demesne and 2 ploughs belonging to the men. [There is] woodland for 15 pigs. And [there are] 18 sokemen at 90 acres. Fulcher holds 22 acres. [There have] always [been] 3 bordars and 5 ploughs and 2 acres of meadow. Then it was worth £7; now [£]9 15s. Tivetshall [St Margaret or St Mary] is 1 league and 4 furlongs in length and half a league in breadth. And of the geld [it renders] 17d.

In Shimpling 6 sokemen belong to the same manor at 32 acres. And [there is] 1 bordar and 2 acres of meadow. [There has] always [been] between them all 1 plough. They have been valued above.

In the same [vill there is] a free man, 40 acres, which Fulc[her] holds. And [there are] 2 bordars. [There has] always [been] 1 plough. And [there are] 2 acres of meadow. [There is] woodland for 4 pigs. It is worth 10s.

Bressingham St E[dmund] has always held for a manor and for 2 carucates. [There have] always [been] 6 villans, 16 bordars. And [there are] 2 ploughs in demesne and 2 ploughs belonging to the men. [There is] woodland for 20 pigs. [There are] 12 acres of meadow. Now [there are] 2 head of cattle, 11 pigs. And [there are] 12 sokemen at 60 acres and they are not able to give or sell their land. [There have] always [been] 2½ ploughs. [There is] woodland for 6 pigs. [There are] 4 acres of meadow. Then it was worth 40[s.]; now 60[s.] [There are] 15 acres belonging to a church. It is worth 2s. It is 8 furlongs in length and 6 in breadth. And [it renders] 12d. of the geld.

In Bressingham Almær held from St Edm[und's] TRE: 1 carucate. Now Roger Bigod holds it from the saint. [There has] always [been] 1 villan and 4 bordars. Then [there were] 2 ploughs in demesne; afterwards and now 1½. Then and afterwards [there were] 2 ploughs belonging to the men; now 1. [There is] woodland for 6 pigs. [There are] 6 acres of meadow. Then [there were] 3 horses; now 1. Then [there were] 4 head of cattle; now 3. Then [there were] 20 pigs; now 8. Now [there are] 60 sheep. And [there is] 1 sokeman at 1½ acres. It has always been worth 20s.

In Roydon [near Diss] Fulcher holds 1 carucate of the demesne which St E[dmund] held. [There have] always [been] 2 villans and 7 bordars. And [there is] 1 plough in demesne and 2 ploughs belonging to the men. And [there are] 2 acres of meadow. And [there are] 5 sokemen at 21 acres of meadow. [There have] always [been] 2 ploughs and 1 horse and 2 head of cattle and 5 pigs and 12 sheep. It is worth 20s.

In Shelfanger [there are] 2 sokemen, half a carucate and 6 acres. And under him [there are] 7 bordars and 1 plough. [There is] woodland for 12 pigs. [There are] 2 acres of meadow. It is worth 11s. In Frenze [there are] 2 sokemen of St E[dmund's] at 16 acres. [There has] always [been] half a plough. It is worth 2s.

Dickleburgh St E[dmund] has always held for a manor and for 2 carucates. Now 2 priests hold [it] of the abbot. [There have] always [been] 4 villans and 12 bordars. And [there are] 2 ploughs in demesne and 4 ploughs belonging to the men.

[Folio 211V: NORFOLK]

[There is] woodland for 16 pigs. [There are] 6 acres of meadow and 4 sokemen, 20 acres. [There has] always [been] 1 plough. [There is] 1 acre of meadow. It is worth 40s. It is 5 furlongs in length and 4 in breadth. And [it renders] 6d. of the geld. [There are] 30 acres belonging to a church. It is worth 3s.

Semere St E[dmund] has always held for a manor at 2 carucates. [There have] always [been] 12 bordars And [there are] 2 ploughs in demesne and 2 ploughs belonging to the men. [There is] woodland for 12 pigs. [There are] 3 acres of

meadow and 1 sokeman at 10 acres. They have always ploughed with 2 oxen. It is worth 40s. It is 5 furlongs in length and 5 in breadth. And [it renders] 6d. of the geld.

In the same [vill] Fulcher holds 1 sokeman of St E[dmund] at 20 acres. And [there are] 2 bordars and half a plough and 1 acre of meadow. It is worth 5s.

In Gissing [there are] 1½ free men at 33 acres and 2 bordars. Then [there was] 1 plough; now half [a plough]. Then it was worth 4s.; now 10[s.] Roger, a man of R[obert] Malet, appropriated this.

In Shelfanger [there is] 1 free man of St E[dmund], 12 acres and 2 oxen. It is worth 16d. [There are] 16 acres belonging to a church. It is worth 2s. 6d. When Earl Ralph had power and his men and his lands, his sergeants exchanged with the sergeants of St E[dmund] 4 men from Burston for 4 others in Gissing, so that the earl had 4 and the abbot 4.

In Shimpling [there are] 1½ free men at 14 acres. [There has] always [been] half a plough. And [there is] 1 acre of meadow. It is worth 28d.

In Roydon [near Diss] [there are] 4 sokemen at 5 acres. These have been valued in Bressingham.

Loddon Hundred. Loddon Frodo holds of the abbot, which St E[dmund] held TRE for 3 carucates and 10 acres. [There have] always [been] 3 villans. Then [there were] 8 bordars; now 16. Then [there were] 2 ploughs in demesne; now 3. Then [there were] 2 ploughs belonging to the men; now 1. [There is] woodland for 60 pigs. [There are] 8 acres of meadow. Now [there is] 1 mill. [There has] always [been] 1 horse. Now [there are] 12 head of cattle and 30 pigs and 80 sheep, 2 hives of bees. And [there are] 11 sokemen there owing every customary due, 20 acres. [There have] always [been] 2 ploughs. Then it was worth 40s.; now 80[s.] It is 14 furlongs in length and 9 in breadth. And of the geld [it renders] 16d., whoever may hold there. St E[dmund has] the soke. In Broome the same man holds 1 carucate which Toli the sheriff held and gave to St Edm[und] TRE and afterwards he held it from him for a farm of two days. [There has] always [been] 1 plough in demesne. And [there are] 4 acres of meadow and 1 horse and 4 sokemen at 5 acres. [There has] always [been] half a plough. It is worth 20s. St Edmund has the soke.

In Mundham Goscelin holds 1 sokeman at 30 acres. [There has] always [been] 1 villan and 1 bordar and half a plough. It is worth 32d. In Topcroft Berengar holds of the abbot 2 carucates which 2 priests held TRE. [There have] always [been] 4 villans and 10 bordars. Then [there were] 2 slaves; now 1. [There have] always [been] 2 ploughs

Abbot of Bury

[Folio 212: NORFOLK]

in demesne and 3 ploughs belonging to the men. [There is] woodland for 3 pigs. [There are] 3 acres of meadow and 1 sokeman at 2 acres. Then it was worth 30s.; now 40[s.] St E[dmund has] the soke. In Langhale and in Kirstead [there are] 27 sokemen, 2½ carucates . And [there are] 2 villans and 11 bordars. [There have] always [been] 6 ploughs. [There are] 8 acres of meadow. They have been valued in Brooke. [There are] 12 acres [...] belonging to a church. It is worth 16d.

Langhale is 1 league in length and half [a league] in breadth. And of the geld [it renders] 16d., whoever may hold there.

DEPWADE HUNDRED.

Tibenham St E[dmund] held TRE for 2 carucates and 60 acres; now Richard holds [it]. [There have] always [been] 5 villans and 9 bordars and 1 slave. And [there are] 2 ploughs in demesne and 1 plough belonging to the men. [There are] 5 acres of meadow, 6 head of cattle, 40 goats. Then it was worth 40s.; now 60[s.] And it is 1½ leagues in length and 1 league in breadth. And [it renders] 18d. of the geld.

Morningthorpe Robert de Vaux holds, which St E[dmund] held for a manor and for 1 carucate. [There have] always [been] 7 villans and 3 bordars and 1 slave. And [there is] 1 plough in demesne and 1 plough belonging to the men. [There are] 2 acres of meadow and 1 mill and 2 head of cattle and 4 pigs, 16 sheep. And [there are] 3 sokemen, 30 acres. [There has] always [been] plough. [There are] 12 acres belonging to a church. Then it was worth 20s.; now 30[s.] And [there is] 1 free man over whom the abbot had half the commendation TRE at 1 carucate, which the same man holds. And [there are] 9½ free men under him in commendation only, 30 acres, and 1 villan and 1 bordar. Then [there were] 3½ ploughs between them; now 3. [There are] 2 acres of meadow. In Fritton the same man holds two free men at 23 acres and 1 villan and 3 bordars and 1 plough. In Stratton [St Mary or St Michael] [there is] 1 free man, 15 acres, and half a plough. In Morningthorpe [there are] 2 free men, 12 acres, and half a plough. Then it was worth 30s.; now 50[s.] This the same R[obert] holds. Morningthorpe is 1 league in length and 3 furlongs in breadth. And [it renders] 1ƒd. of the geld. In Fritton [there is] 1 free man of the king's at 15 acres and 2 bordars. And it is worth 5 s. The same R[obert] holds this.

CLAVERING HUNDRED.

Kirby [Cane] Radfrid holds of the abbot, which St E[dmund] held TRE for 2 carucates. [There has] always [been] 1 villan and 11 bordars. Then [there were] 2 ploughs in demesne; now 3. [There have] always [been] 5 ploughs belonging to the men. [There are] 14 acres of meadow. [There is] woodland for 6 pigs. Then [there was] half a mill; now 1½. [There are] 20 acres belonging to a church in alms and [there are] two parts of one church at 14 acres. In demesne [there are] 4 horses, 4 head of cattle, 15 pigs, 100 sheep. And [there are] 3 free men, 3 carucates, and 4½ ploughs and 3 acres of meadow. Then it was worth 40s.; now £6. [There are] 20 acres belonging to a church. It is worth 20d. It is 9 furlongs in length and 5 in breadth. And of the geld [it renders] 10½d.

Hales 9 men held at 60 acres. 2 were sokemen and 7 were in soke and commendation only.

[Folio 212v: NORFOLK]

[There have] always [been] 2 bordars and 5 free men, 6 acres. This is in the value of Loddon. And Frodo holds of the abbot in Norton [Subcourse] 1 free man in commendation, 30 acres. [There has] always [been] 1 plough. And [there is] 1 acre of meadow. And [there are] 9 free men under him at 20 acres, which Goscelin holds. [There has] always [been] half a plough. It is worth 5s. Over these 9 the king and the earl [have] the soke. [There are] 20 acres of free land belonging to a church. In the same [vill there was] a free man in commendation TRE, 8 acres and 2 oxen. It is worth 12d.

In Heckingham [there is] 1 free man likewise, 8 acres, which the abbot holds in demesne. And it is worth 8d.

In Hales [there are] 2 free men, 1 acre. It is worth 4d. This the same F[rodo] holds.

XV. The land of St Æthelthryth.

HUNDRED AND A HALF OF CLACKCLOSE OF 10 LEETS.

Marham St Æ[thelthryth] held TRE. Then [there were] 4 ploughs in demesne; now 3. Then [there were] 6 ploughs belonging to the men; now 3. [There have] always [been] 19 villans and 13 bordars. Then [there were] 7 slaves; now 5. [There are] 26 acres of meadow and 1 mill. Then [there were] 10 horses; now 4. Then [there was] 1 cow; now 6. Then [there were] 131 sheep; now 300. Then [there were] 24 pigs; now 23. This land is 1 league and 100 perches in length and half a league and 1 furlong in breadth. And the area of marshland is not known. It has always been worth £10. To this manor were attached TRE 27 sokemen with every customary due but after King William came, Hugh de Montfort had them except for one. And W[illiam] de War[enne holds] 1 sokeman at 6 acres of the church. The whole of this land renders 14d. of the geld when the Hundred and a half used to return a geld of [...] 20s.; now likewise.

In Bexwell [there is] 1 carucate. And [there is] 1 plough in demesne and 1 plough belonging to the men. [There are] 7 villans, 1 slave, 10 acres of meadow. It is worth 20s.

In Fincham St Æ[thelthryth] held TRE 30 acres of land. [There have] always [been] 3 bordars. And [there is] 1 plough, 10 acres of meadow.

St Æthelthryth

[Folio 213: NORFOLK]

It is worth 10s. In Hilgay [there are] 4 bordars, 2 acres. And it is worth 6d.

In Fodderstone [there is] 1 carucate and 3 villans and 2 bordars. [There has] always [been] 1 plough in demesne and half a plough belonging to the men. And [there are] 2 acres of meadow and 80 sheep, 8 pigs. It is worth 20s. It is 4 furlongs in length and 3 in breadth. And [it renders] 4d. of the geld. Ulfkil, a man of Hermer's, claims this land to be free by whatever method it may be judged, either by battle or by judicial ordeal. And another is ready to prove in that way that it belonged to the church on the day when King E[dward] died. But the whole Hundred testifies that it belonged TRE to St Æthelth[ryth].

In Fordham [there are] 3 bordars, 12 acres. It is worth 2s. In Downham [Market] [there are] 2 villans, 12 acres. And [there is] 1 acre of meadow. It is worth 12d. The whole of Downham

[Market] is 3 leagues in length and 2 in breadth. And [it renders] 4d. of the geld, whoever may hold there.

THE HUNDRED AND A HALF OF FREEBRIDGE.

[West] Walton St Æthelthryth held TRE for 4 carucates. [There have] always [been] 20 villans, 40 bordars. Then [there were] 17 slaves; now 13. [There are] 100 acres of meadow. [There is] 1 fishery. [There have] always [been] 5 ploughs in demesne and 3 ploughs belonging to the men. Then [there were] 22 salt-pans; now 24. [There have] always [been] 6 horses. Then [there were] 18 head of cattle; now 16. Then [there were] 22 pigs; now 23. [There have] always [been] 800 sheep. Here belong 47 acres of land in Islington, which 2 villans and 7 sokemen have always held at 1 carucate and 11 bordars and 3 slaves. [There have] always [been] 2 ploughs. It has always been worth £15. In [Castle or West] Acre St Æ[thelthryth] held half a carucate TRE. [There are] 2 bordars, 1 slave, 1 acre of meadow. [There has] always [been] half a plough. [There are] 300 sheep. It is worth 3s.

In Islington St Æ[thelthryth] held 1 carucate TRE. Then [there was] 1 plough; now half [a plough]. [There are] 2 villans, 3 bordars, 20 acres of meadow, 2 salt-pans. To this manor belong 18 sokemen at 17½ acres. The whole is worth 16s.

HUNDRED OF GRIMSHOE.

Feltwell St Æ[thelthryth] has always held for 6 carucates. Then [there were] 40 villans; now 28. Then [there were] 5 bordars; now 10. Then [there were] 14 slaves; now 12. Then [there were] 5 ploughs in demesne; now 4. Then [there were] 8 ploughs belonging to the men; now 7. [There are] 30 acres of meadow. [There have] always [been] 2 horses, 11 head of cattle, 140 sheep. Then [there were] 33 pigs; now 22. [There is] 1 mill and 2 fisheries. It has always been worth £12. It is 1½ leagues in length and 1 league in breadth. And [it renders] 30½d. of the geld.

[Folio 213V: NORFOLK]

To this manor used to belong 34 sokemen with every customary due TRE, whom W[illiam] de War[enne] now holds and 6 free men in soke and commendation only. The same William has the whole [of it].

Northwold St Æ[thelthryth] has always held for 6 carucates. [There have] always [been] 8 villans, 19 bordars, 4 slaves. Then [there were] 3 ploughs in demesne; now 4. Then [there were] 5 ploughs belonging to the men; now 3. [There are] 16 acres of meadow, 2 mills, 2 fisheries, 2 horses, 11 head of cattle, 130 sheep. Then [there were] 31 pigs; now 22. Then it was worth £8; now [£]9. Here used to belong TRE 3 sokemen with every customary due. And [there were] 4 free men in soke and commendation only. The whole [of it] W[illiam] de War[enne] holds. It is 1 league in length and a half [a league] in breadth. And [it renders] 30½d. of the geld. Others hold there.

Mundford St Æ[thelthryth] has always held: 3 carucates. Then [there were] 14 villans; now 10. Then [there were] 4 bordars; now 8. Then [there were] 4 slaves; now 2. [There have] always [been] 2 ploughs in demesne. Then [there were]

3 ploughs belonging to the men; now 2. [There are] 16 acres of meadow. [There has] always [been] half a mill, 5 head of cattle, 33 sheep. Then [there were] 2 slaves; now 3. It is worth 40s. To this manor belong 7 sokeman with every customary due, whom W[illiam] now holds. It is 1 league in length and half [a league] in breadth. And [it renders] 11d. of the geld.

SHROPHAM HUNDRED.

Bridgham St Æ[thelthryth] has always held: 4 carucates. [There have] always [been] 12 villans. Then [there were] 10 bordars; now 17. [There have] always [been] 4 slaves. [There are] 3 ploughs in demesne, 3 ploughs belonging to the men. [There are] 4 acres of meadow. [There is] woodland for 15 pigs. [There are] 2 mills, 2 horses, 5 head of cattle. Then [there were] 200 sheep; now 180. [There are] 25 pigs. To this manor belong 30 acres in demesne, which are in Brettenham and 30 acres in Roudham. Then it was worth £6; now [£]8. The whole of it is 1 league in length and 3 furlongs in breadth. And [it renders] 12d. of the geld. To this manor belongs 1 priest. And it is worth 2s. And he could not sell his land. And [there is] 1 sokeman, half a carucate, and half a plough. It is worth 2s. The same man was among the free men of Roger Bigod's but the abbot established title to him and holds him.

GUILTCROSS HUNDRED.

In Banham St Æ[thelthryth] held 1 sokeman, 2 carucates TRE. Then and afterwards [there were] 10 villans; now 4. [There have] always [been] 6 bordars. Then [there were] 4 slaves. [There are] 24 acres of meadow. [There is] woodland for 100 pigs. Then [there were] 2 ploughs in demesne; afterwards half [a plough]; now 1 and 1 plough can be restored. Then and afterwards [there were] 2 ploughs belonging to the men; now 1 and another can be restored. Then [there were] 4 head of cattle; now 2. Then [there were] 16 pigs; now 2. This manor W[illiam] d'Écouis holds of the abbot. And [there are] 3 sokemen, 20 acres of land. [There has] always [been] half a plough. [There are] 2 acres of meadow. Then it was worth 60s.; now 40[s.] In the same [vill there are] 3 free men, half a carucate and 5 acres, of whom he has nothing except the commendation. The soke [is] in Kenninghall, [a manor] belonging to the king.

St Æthelthryth

[Folio 214: NORFOLK]

[There are] 6 acres of meadow. Then [there were] 1½ ploughs; now 1. It is worth 10s. Radfrid held these free men; afterwards W[illiam] d'Écouis and the abbot were seised of them on account of their commendation.

In Rushford St Æ[thelthryth] holds 1½ carucates. [There have] always [been] 3 villans, 1 slave. [There are] 8 acres of meadow. Then [there were] 2 ploughs; now none but they can be restored. Then [there was] half a plough belonging to the men; now 1 ox. And [there is] 1 sokeman, 2 acres. Then it was worth 20s.; now 8[s.]. John, nephew of Waleran, holds this.

In Rushford Wulfric, a free man, held 60 acres TRE. [There are] 4 acres of meadow. Then [there was] 1 plough. Kenninghall [has] the soke. Then it was worth 10s.; now 5[s.]

This Wulfric had forfeited to King W[illiam] because of £8 and therefore it has remained in the king's hand. The same man also holds this of the abbot.

In [Blo] Norton [there is] 1 sokeman, 80 acres. And [there is] 1 acre of meadow and 1 villan and 7 bordars and 1 plough. It is worth 15s. That man was one of Roger Bigod's free men but the abbot has established title to him.

[sic] Launditch Hundred.

Oxwick St Æ[thelthryth] has always held: 1 carucate. [There have] always [been] 4 bordars and 3 sokemen, 6 acres. [There has] always [been] 1 plough in demesne. Then [there were] 2 ploughs belonging to the men; now a half, and half a plough can be restored. [There are] 2 acres of meadow. [There is] woodland for 24 pigs. It is worth 20s. Reginald fitzIvo holds [it] of the abbot but earlier he held [it] of the king.

In Hoe [St Æthelthryth] has always held 1 carucate. [There have] always [been] 8 villans, 10 bordars. [There are] 8 acres of meadow, 3 ploughs. [There is] woodland for 100 pigs. [There is] 1 mill. This belongs to [East] Dereham with every customary due and [is] in [its] value. The soke [is] in Mileham, [a manor] belonging to the king, at 2 sokemen, who have 24 acres. And [there are] 4 acres of meadow, woodland for 4 pigs, half a plough. It is worth 4s. The abbot had the commendation and the soke of the fold.

MITFORD HUNDRED AND A HALF.

[East] Dereham St Æ[thelthryth] has always held: 5 carucates. Then [there were] 20 villans; now 16. Then [there were] 20 bordars; now 25. And [there are] 2 slaves. Then [there were] 2 ploughs in demesne; now 3. Then [there were] 8 ploughs belonging to the men; now 7. Then [there was] woodland for 600 pigs; now 300. [There have] always [been] 3 mills, 3 horses, 12 head of cattle, 20 pigs, 100 sheep. [There are] 7 sokemen, 30 acres. [There are] 2 acres of meadow, 3 acres of woodland. Then it was worth £10; now [£]13. It is 1 league in length and half [a league] in breadth. And [it renders] 15d. of the geld. The whole soke of that Hundred and a half used to belong to St Æ[thelthryth] TRE. And it is worth 60s.

Thorpe [in Shipdham] St Æ[thelthryth] has always held: 3 carucates. [There have] a1ways [been] 10 villans, 20 bordars. Now [there are] 4 slaves. Then [there was] 1 plough in demesne; now 2. [There have] always [been] 7½ ploughs belonging to the men. Then [there was] woodland for 800 pigs; now 600.

[There are] 8 acres of meadow. [There has] always [been] 1 mill, 2 horses, 11 head of cattle, 27 pigs, 97 sheep, 38 goats. And [there are] 12 sokemen, 40 acres. [There have] always [been] 5 ploughs, 12 acres of meadow, woodland for 12 pigs. Then it was worth 60s.; now £11. And it is 1 league in length and 1 length in breadth. And [it renders] 15d. of the geld. And over all the sokemen of these 2 manors [it renders] 15d.

Calvely Berner holds of the abbot, which St Æ[thelthryth] held TRE: 1 carucate. [There have] always [been] 4 villans, 11 bordars, 1 plough in demesne, half a plough belonging to the men and that is all that there can be. [There is] woodland for 20 pigs. [There are] 20 acres of meadow. Now [there is] 1

horse, 4 head of cattle, 5 pigs. [There are] 5 sokemen, 20 acres. It is worth 20s. It is 4 furlongs in length and 4 in breadth. And [it renders] 5d. of the geld. This land Godric claimed as part of the fief of Earl R[alph] that he held before he forfeited and the Hundred testifies to this.

In [North] Tuddenham [there is] 1 sokeman of St Æ[thelthryth's], 2 carucates. [There are] 7 bordars, 1 mill, [...] 3 acres of meadow. [There have] always [been] 1½ ploughs. Then it was worth 20s.; now 12[s.]. Ralph de Beaufour holds it of the abbot.

In Mattishall [there are] 8 sokemen, 30 acres. Then [there were] 2 ploughs; now 1. [There are] 8 acres of meadow. Then it was worth 20s.; now 13[s.] 8d.

In Thorpe [in Shipdham] and in "Thurstuna" and in Yaxham [there are] 5 sokemen of St Æ[thelthryth], 50 acres. [There has] always [been] 1 plough. It is worth 8s. In Yaxham [there are] 14 sokemen, 90 acres. [There have] always [been] 2 ploughs. [There are] 4 acres of meadow. It is worth 20s. Roger Bigod holds it of the abbot but earlier he held it of the king.

HUNDRED OF BROTHERCROSS.

In Broomsthorpe [there is] 1 sokeman and [...] carucates of land. [There have] always [been] 8 bordars. And [there is] 1 plough in demesne and 1 plough belonging to the men. [There are] 3 acres of meadow. [There is] 1 mill. It is worth 10s.

HENSTEAD HUNDRED AND A HALF.

Pulham [St Mary Magdalene and St Mary the Virgin] St Æ[thelthryth] held TRE for 15 carucates. [There have] always [been] 60 villans, 25 bordars, 7 slaves. [There are] 3 ploughs in demesne. Then [there were] 20 ploughs belonging to the men; now 16. [There are] 16 acres of meadow. Then [there was] woodland for 600 pigs; now 300. And [there is] 1 mill, 3 horses, 11 head of cattle, 40 pigs, 50 sheep, 40 goats, 4 hives of bees. Then it was worth £8; now [£]15. It is 2 leagues in length and 1 league in breadth. And of the geld [it renders] 30d.

In 'Pyrleston' [in Scole] a free man held under St Æ[thelthryth] TRE: 1 carucate. Now Roger de Rames holds it of the abbot. [There have] always [been] 5 bordars and 1 slave. Then and afterwards [there were] 2 ploughs in demesne; now 3. [There has] always [been] half a plough belonging to the men. [There is] woodland for 16 pigs. [There are] 8 acres of meadow. Then and afterwards

St Æthelthryth

it was worth 20s.; now 10[s.] It is 5 furlongs in length and 5 in breadth. And of the geld [it renders] 4d. More hold there.

DISS HALF-HUNDRED.

Thelveton St Æ[thelthryth] has always held for 2 carucates. [There have] always [been] 6 villans and 1 bordar. Then [there were] 2 ploughs in demesne; now none. [There has] always [been] 1 plough belonging to the men. [There are] 4 acres of meadow. Then [there was] woodland for 60 pigs; now

30. It is worth 20s. It is 1 league in length and half [a league] in breadth. And of the geld [it renders] 7d.

In Tivetshall [St Margaret or St Mary] [there are] 2 sokemen, half a carucate and 2 acres. And [there are] 2½ villans and 2 bordars and 1 plough. [There is] woodland for 15 pigs. [There are] 1½ acres of meadow. It is worth 10s.

LODDON HUNDRED.

In Thurton [near Loddon] [there are] 6 sokemen whom Godric the steward holds at 20 acres. [There has] always [been] 1 plough. And in "Torp" [there are] 6 sokemen at 13 acres. And they have 1 plough and 8 bordars. And it belongs to Bergh [Apton] with every customary due and it has been valued there.

DEPWADE HUNDRED.

In Stratton [St Mary or St Michael] 1 sokeman held 12 acres TRE. It is worth 12d. In Hardwick [there is] 1 sokeman, 15 acres. And [there is] half a plough. It is worth 2s. The king and the earl [have] the soke.

The land of St Benedict of Ramsey.

HUNDRED OF CLACKCLOSE.

Hilgay St Benedict holds: 2 caucates. [There have] always [been] 8 villans and 11 bordars. [There are] 5 slaves, 8 acres of meadow. [There are] 2 ploughs in demesne and 2 oxen belonging to the men. [There are] 3 horses, 5 head of cattle, 10 pigs, 70 sheep. Then it was worth 80s.; now 70[s.] From this manor William de Warenne took 8 men, customary tenants of this manor, at 44 acres of land as the Hundred testifies. This manor is 5 furlongs in length and 4½ [furlongs] in breadth. And it renders 8d. of a geld of 20s.

[Folio 215v: NORFOLK]

Wimbotsham St B[enedict] holds: 2 carucates. [There have] always [been] 13 bordars and 2 ploughs in demesne. And [there are] 12 acres of meadow. [There is] pasture at 18d. [There are] 4 pigs, 16 sheep. Then it was worth £4; now [£]3.

In Snore [there is] half a carucate. It is worth 10s.

In West] Dereham [there were] 3 sokemen TRE, 6 acres of land and half a plough. It is worth 12d. In Fordham [there are] 24 acres. And it is worth 2s. 8d. In the same [vill there is] a free man, 24 acres. It is worth 3s. In Outwell [there are] 16 bordars. It is worth 5s. From the soke of the Hundred and a half St B[enedict]
has 70s.

HUNDRED AND A HALF OF FREEBRIDGE.

Walsoken St B[enedict] has always held: 1 carucate. [There have] always [been] 11 villans and 6 bordars. [There are] 12 acres of meadow. [There is] 1 plough in demesne, half a plough belonging to the men. [There is] 1 fishery. [There are] 7 head of cattle. To this manor have always belonged 7 sokemen at 13 acres. It is worth 20s.

HUNDRED OF DOCKING.

Brancaster St B[enedict] has always held. [There are] 3 ploughs in demesne and 7 ploughs belonging to the men. [There are] 25 villans, 16 bordars, 5 slaves. [There are] 2 acres of meadow, 1 mill, 5 bordars, 6 acres. And [there are] 60 acres of land which have always been in demesne. [There are] 2 horses, 6 head of cattle, 24 pigs, 600 sheep. The whole is worth £10. The whole is 1 league in length and half [a league] in breadth. And [it renders] 28d. of the geld.

HUNDRED OF SMETHDON.

Ringstead St B[enedict] has always held. [There are] 2 ploughs in demesne. [There are] 21 villans, 5 bordars, 3 slaves having 3 ploughs. [There are] 5 acres of meadow, 1 horse, 24 pigs, 100 sheep. And [there are] 22 sokemen, 1 carucate. And [there are] 3 ploughs. And in this manor 2 ploughs can be restored. Then it was worth £6; now [£]5 and 10s. It is 1 league and a half in length and 1 league in breadth. And [it renders] 42d. of the geld. St B[enedict has] the soke. 31 sokemen have been taken away from this manor who used to belong there TRE. Of these Radfrid had 9 and now W[illiam] d' Écouis has them and W[illiam] de War[enne] 7 and 3 [are] in Titchwell, a manor belonging to the king, and W[illiam] de Noyers [has] 4, Roger Bigod 5 and in Hunstanton, [a manor] belonging to the king, [there is] 1 at 2 acres.

HUNDRED OF BROTHERCROSS.

In Burnham St B[enedict] held TRE 1 free man at half a carucate. [There have] always [been] 18 bordars. Then [there was] half a plough; now nothing. [There have] always [been] 2 ploughs belonging to the men. It has always been worth 10s. This Roger Bigod holds of the abbot.

[Folio 216: NORFOLK]

The land of St Benet of Hulme for the sustenance of the monks.

WALSHAM HUNDRED.

[South] Walsham St B[enet] held for 2 carucates TRE. TRE. There have always been 8 bordars. Then [there was] 1 plough in demesne; now 2. And [there are] 1½ ploughs belonging to the men. [There are] 22 acres of meadow. [There are] 2 salt-pans, 1 horse, 7 pigs, 200 sheep. And [there are] 4 sokemen at 32 acres. And [there is] 1 acre of meadow. [There has] always [been] half a plough. In Fishley [there are] 24 acres of land and 2 bordars. The whole has always been worth 40s. [There is] also in [South] Walsham half a plough and 6 bordars and 6 acres of meadow and 5 sokemen. [There has] always [been] 1 plough. It is worth 10s.

In Upton [there are] 5 acres of land in the same value. In Woodbastwick TRE [there was] 1 carucate and 20 acres. [There have] always [been] 9 villans and 1 slave. And [there is] 1 plough in demesne and 1 plough belonging to the men. [There are] 14 acres of meadow. [There has] always [been] 1 horse, 20 sheep. And [there are] 9 sokemen at 46 acres. And [there are] 3 acres of meadow and 1 plough. It was worth 20s. then; now 40.

In Reedham St B[enet] held TRE 1 carucate. [There have] always [been] 2 villans, 5 bordars. [There is] 1 plough in demesne and 1 plough belonging to the men. [There are] 20 acres of meadow, 6 head of cattle. Now [there are] 6 pigs, 20 sheep. And [there is] 1 sokeman, 3 acres. Then it was worth 10s.; now 20[s.] And Woodbastwick is half a league in length and half in breadth. And of the geld [it renders] 16d. The abbot used to have the soke of Reedham over those who followed the fold and the soke of the others [belonged] to the Hundred.

FOREHOE HUNDRED.

In Carleton [Forehoe] St B[enet] held 60 acres TRE. [There have] always [been] 5 villans and 2 bordars. And [there is] 1 plough belonging to the men. [There are] 3 acres of meadow. It is worth 5s. In Barford St B[enet] holds 30 acres.

NORTH ERPINGHAM HUNDRED.

Thurgarton St B[enet] has always held: 2 carucates. [There have] always [been] 4 villans and 4 bordars. And [there are] 2 ploughs in demesne and 1 plough belonging to the men. [There are] 4 acres of meadow. [There is] woodland for 20 pigs. [There is] 1 mill. Then [there was] 1 horse and 2 head of cattle; now 3. Then [there were] 9 pigs; now 11. Then [there were] 30 goats; now 18. And [there are] 49 sokemen at 1 carucate. [There have] always [been] 5 ploughs. [There are] 2½ acres of meadow. Then it was worth £4; now [£]6. It is 13 furlongs in length and 6 in breadth. And of the geld [it renders] 16½d. And St Benet has the soke.

In 'Shipden' [there is] half a carucate for the sustenance of the monks. [There is] 1 villan, 3 bordars. [There has] always [been] 1 plough in demesne and half a plough belonging to the men. And [there is] 1 acre of meadow. It is worth 10s.8d.

In Northrepps or Southrepps [there is] half a carucate. [There is] 1 villan, 5 bordars. [There is] 1 plough in demesne. Then [there was] 1 plough belonging to the men; now half [a plough]. It is worth 10s.

In Antingham [there are] 2 carucates. [There have] always [been] 2 villans and 8 bordars. [There are] 2 ploughs in demesne, 2 ploughs belonging to the men. [There is] woodland for 4 pigs. [There are] 2 acres of meadow. [There are] 2 horses, 3 head of cattle, 5 pigs, 60 sheep. And [there are] 3 free men who can

give and sell their land. [There is] half a carucate and 1 acre of meadow. [There has] always [been] 1 plough. Then it was worth 30s.; now 40[s.] It is 8 furlongs in length and 5½ in breadth. And [it renders] 13½d. of the geld.

WEST FLEGG HUNDRED.

Winterton St B[enet] has always held for 1 carucate. [There are] 5 bordars. And [there is] 1 plough in demesne, half a plough belonging to the men. [There are] 6 pigs. And [there are] 5 free men there in the commendation only of St B[enet] at 45 acres. [There is] half an acre of meadow. [There has] always [been] 1 plough. And [there is] 1 sokeman at 100 acres and he is so tied to the monastery that he can neither sell nor forfeit outside the church, but the soke is in the Hundred. [There are] 6 acres of meadow. [There have] always [been] 9

bordars. [There is] 1 plough in demesne and 1 plough belonging to the men. And under him [there are] 4 free men in commendation only, 9 acres. It is worth 24s. And [there are] 5 free men, 24d. It is 9 furlongs in length and 8 in breadth. And [it renders] 30d. of the geld.

In Rollesby St Benet held TRE 1 carucate. [There have] always [been] 6 villans. And [there is] 1 plough in demesne and half a plough belonging to the men, 7 pigs, 8 acres of meadow. And [there are] 11 free men in the commendation only of St Benet at 44 acres of land. And [there is] 1 acre of meadow and half a salt-pan. [There have] always [been] 2 ploughs. [There is] woodland for 3 pigs. Then it was worth 20s.; now 26[s.] 8d. Also to this same manor pertains 20 acres of land. It is 10 furlongs in length and 9 in breadth. And [it renders] 25 f d. of the geld.

Ashby [near Acle] St B[enet] has always held: 2 carucates. [There have] always [been] 7 bordars. [There is] 1 plough in demesne and half a plough belonging to the men. [There are] 10 acres of meadow. [There is] woodland for 6 pigs. And [there are] 13 sokemen with soke and sake, 62 acres. [There are] 5 acres of meadow. [There have] always [been] 2 ploughs. Then it was worth 20s.; now it renders 26s. 8d. And it is 8 furlongs in length and 4½ in breadth. And [it renders] 15d. of the geld, whoever may hold there.

Thurne St B[enet] has always held: 1 carucate. [There have] always [been] 6 bordars. [There are] 8 acres of meadow. [There is] 1 plough in demesne and half a plough belonging to the men. [There are] 2 horses, 6 pigs. [There are] 10 sokemen, 45 acres. [There are] 6½ acres of meadow. [There are] 2 ploughs. Then it was worth 20s.; now 26[s.] 8d. It is 5 furlongs in length and 4 in breadth. And [it renders] 9d. of the geld. Others hold there.

Oby St B[enet] has always held [with] 1½ carucates. [There have] always [been] 2 villans. [There are] 10 acres of meadow. [There are] 2 ploughs in demesne and 2 oxen belonging to the men. [There are] 3 horses, 2 head of cattle, 6 pigs. Then it was worth 20s.; now 30[s.] It is 6 furlongs in length and 3 in breadth. And of the geld [it renders] 9d., whoever may hold there. 10 free men of St Benet's pertain to the same manor in commendation at 84 acres. And [there are] 14 acres of meadow. [There have] always [been] 2 bordars, 2 ploughs. It is worth 6s.

St Benet of Hulme

Burgh [St Margaret] and Billockby St B[enet] has always held: 1 carucate. Then [there was] 1 plough in demesne; now half [a plough]. [There are] 5 acres of meadow. And [there are] 6 free men in the commendation only of St B[enet], 44 acres. [There are] 7 acres of meadow. [There have] always [been] 2 bordars. It is worth 18s. And these free men were then worth 16d.; now 2s. In Burgh [St Margaret] St B[enet] holds 30 acres. And [there are] 4 acres of meadow. [There are] 3 bordars. [There is] 1 plough in demesne. It is worth 3s.

In Martham [there are] 3 sokemen, 10 acres. It is worth 12d. In Bastwick [there is] 1 free man in the commendation of St B[enet], 2½ acres. It is worth 4d. In Repps [there are] 6 free men, 36 acres. [There are] $2\frac{1}{2}$ acres [of meadow] and half a plough. Then it was worth 2s.; now 3[s.] In Martham [there is] a free man of St B[enet]'s, 6 acres. And [there are] 3 acres which a blind man holds. And [there is] half an acre of meadow. It is worth 12d. In Clippesby [there is] 1 free man. In Oby [there is] 1 free man at 23 acres. [There has] always [been] 1 plough. [There are] 6 acres of meadow. It is worth 30d. In Rollesby [there is] 1 free man, 5 acres. It is worth 4d. Bastwick is 6 furlongs in length and 3 in breadth. And of the geld [it renders] 3d.

HENSTEAD HUNDRED.

In Shotesham [All Saints or St Mary] St B[enet] holds: [there have] always [been] 3 carucates. Then [there were] 11 villans; now 5. Then [there were] 12 bordars; now 10. [There has] always [been] 1 slave. And [there are] 2 ploughs in demesne. Then [there were] 5 ploughs belonging to the men; now 3. [There is] woodland for 20 pigs. [There are] 8 acres of meadow, 1 mill, 1 horse, 1 ox. Now [there are] 8 pigs; 22 sheep. And [there are] 5 sokemen in the same [vill], 58 acres. And [there are] $1\frac{1}{2}$ acres of meadow. And [there are] $1\frac{1}{2}$ ploughs between them all. Then it was worth £3; now [£]3. It is $1\frac{1}{2}$ leagues in length. And of the geld [it renders] 2s. 16d. Others hold there.

In Grensvill St B[enet] has always held 1 carucate. Then [there were] 2 villans; now 1. [There have] always [been] 6 bordars. Then [there were] 2 slaves. Then [there were] $1\frac{1}{2}$ ploughs in demesne; now 2. Then [there was] 1 plough belonging to the men; now half [a plough]. [There is] 1 mill, 1 horse. [There have] always [been] 12 pigs, 12 sheep, 1 hive of bees. Then it was worth 20s.; now 30[s.] It is 1 league in length and half [a league] in breadth. And [it renders] 2s. of the geld but more hold there.

In Saxlingham [Nethergate or Thorpe] Eadric, a free man of Stigand's, held $1\frac{1}{2}$ carucates under him TRE with soke and sake. After the king came to England that same Eadric mortgaged it for 1 mark of gold and for £7 to St Benet in order that he might, however, redeem himself from capture by Waleran. Now John, the nephew of the aforementioned Waleran, holds it of St Benet as a fief. Then [there were] 11 bordars; now $9\frac{1}{2}$. [There has] always [been] 1 slave.

Then [there were] 2 ploughs in demesne; afterwards none; now 1. Then [there were] 2 ploughs belonging to the men; now 1. Now [there is] 1 horse in demesne. And TRE [there were] 9 sokemen; now 5 at 30 acres. And [there are] 4 acres of meadow. Then [there were] 2 ploughs; now half [a plough]. And [there is] 1 mill. Then it was worth 40s.; afterwards and now 30[s.] It is 2 leagues in length and half [a league] in breadth. And [it renders] 16d. of the geld but more hold there.

In the same [vill] 10 acres of land belong to St B[enet]'s demesne and it was leased to Eadric according to the testimony of the Hundred.

LODDON HUNDRED.

Hardley St B[enet] has always held for 2 carucates. [There have] always [been] 5 bordars. Then [there were] 2 ploughs in demesne; now 1. Now [there are] 2 oxen belonging to the men.

[There is] woodland for 3 pigs. [There are] 8 acres of meadow. And [there is] 1 horse, 4 head of cattle, 24 pigs. Now [there are] 150 sheep. And [there are] 4 sokemen at 7 acres. [There has] always [been] half a plough. Then it was worth [...]; now 30 [...]. It is 8 furlongs in length and 7 in breadth. And of the geld [it renders] 11d. Others hold there.

HUNDRED OF EYNSFORD.

In [Great or Little] Witchingham [there is] half a carucate, 1 bordar, 1 plough, 2 acres of meadow. It is worth 10s. The soke [is] in Foulsham, [a manor] belonging to the king.

HUNDRED OF TAVERHAM.

In Wroxham Ralph the staller held 4 sokemen at 1 carucate and they belong to Hoveton [St John or St Peter], which the same R[alph] gave to St B[enet] TRW. [There has] always [been] 1 plough. [There are] 8 acres of meadow. It is worth 6s.

In Rackheath [there was] a free man, 30 acres, TRE. Then [there was] 1 plough; now half [a plough]. [There are] 2 acres of meadow. It is worth 16d. This land was forfeited TRW but a certain monk gave half a mark of gold for the forfeiture to the reeves, namely Alwig of Colchester, and so he had the land without the permission of the king.

NORTH ERPINGHAM HUNDRED.

Scottow St B[enet] always held for 3 carucates. Then [there were] 14 villans; now 9. [There have] always [been] 3 bordars. [There are] 2 ploughs in demesne. Then [there were] 6 ploughs belonging to the men; now $1\frac{1}{2}$. [There are] 10 acres of meadow. [There is] woodland for 20 pigs. Then [there was] 1 mill. [There have] always [been] 2 horses, 3 head of cattle, 11 pigs. And [there are] 9 sokemen, half a carucate. [There have] always [been] $3\frac{1}{2}$ ploughs. Then it was worth 40s.; now 60[s.] [There are] 14 acres belonging to a church. pigs perches in breadth. And [it renders] 16d. of the geld. In Easton [in Scotton] Ralph the staller held TRE 1 carucate. And he together with his wife gave it

St Benet of Hulme

TRW to the abbey by grant of the king. [There have] always [been] 2 bordars and 1 plough and $1\frac{1}{2}$ acres of meadow. In the same [vill] St B[enet] held half a carucate and 2 bordars. And it is in the value of Hoveton [St John or St Peter].

Swanton [Abbot] St B[enet] has always held for 3 carucates. [There have] always [been] 15 villans and 5 bordars. Then [there were] 2 slaves. [There have] always [been] 2 ploughs in demesne, 4 ploughs belonging to the men, 12 acres of meadow, woodland for 100 pigs, 2 horses, 11 pigs, 25 goats. And [there is] 1 sokeman, 30 acres. Then [there was] half a plough. It has always been worth 60s. It is 1 league in length and 1 league in breadth. And [it renders] 4d. of the geld. [There are] 7 acres belonging to a church.

Calthorpe St B[enet] has always held: $1\frac{1}{2}$ carucates. Then [there were] 6 villans; now 7. [There have] always [been] 3 bordars. [There is] 1 plough in demesne and 3 ploughs belonging to the men. [There are] 4 acres of meadow. [There is] woodland for 15 pigs. [There is] 1 mill and a third part of another. [There have] always [been] 10 head of cattle, 5 pigs. And [there are] 3 sokemen, 20 acres. And [there is] 1 plough and 1 acre of meadow. Then it was worth 20s.; now 30[s.] In the same [vill] St B[enet] held 1 carucate TRE. [There have] always [been] 3 villans and 4 bordars. And [there are] 1½ ploughs. [There is] 1 acre of meadow, woodland for 15 pigs, a third part of a mill. It is worth 15s. [There is] a church without land. The whole is 9 furlongs in length and 6 in breadth. And [it renders] 5d. of the geld.

In Thwaite St B[enet] has always held 2 carucates. [There have] always [been] 3 villans, 12 bordars. Then [there was] 1 plough in demesne; now 1½. Then [there were] 3 ploughs belonging to the men; now 2½. [There is] 1 acre of meadow. [There is] woodland for 50 pigs. [there was] 1 mill; now 1½. [There are] 3 head of cattle, 13 pigs. Then it was worth 30s.; now 40[s.] It is half a league in length and half in breadth. And it renders 5d. less ½d. of the geld. [There are] 6 acres belonging to a church.

In [Great or Little] Hautbois St B[enet] holds 1 carucate. [There have] always [been] 2 bordars and 1 plough. [There are] 2 acres of meadow. [There is] woodland for 20 pigs. [There is] half a mill. Then it was worth 20s.; now 16[s.]

In Erpingham the same held 1 carucate. [There have] always [been] 4 villans, 3 bordars, 2 ploughs, 1 acre of meadow. It is worth 10s.

In Tuttington St B[enet] held 1 carucate TRE. [There have] always [been] 1 villan and 2 bordars and 1 plough. [There are] 2 acres of meadow, 1 mill. It is worth 10s. Earl R[alph] had been seised of half of this land when he forfeited and of the commendation of one woman who was holding it.

In Banningham St B[enet] has always held 30 acres of land. [There has] always [been] half a plough. It is worth 5s.

In Wolterton St Ben[et] held 1 carucate TRE. [There have] always [been] 4 bordars and 1½ ploughs. [There is] 1 acre of meadow. Then it was worth 16s.; now 20[s.] It is 6 furlongs in length and 5 in breadth. And [it renders] 2½d. of the geld. [There are] 4 acres belonging to half a church.

In Belaugh [there is] 1 sokeman, 3 acres. It is worth 6d. [There are] 3 acres belonging to half a church. In the same [vill] Ralph the staller held 10½ sokemen TRE, 63 acres. [There are] 2 acres of meadow. [There have] always [been] 2 ploughs. In the same [vill there is] 1 sokeman of St Benet's, 30 [acres]. [There have] always [been] 2 villans and 1 bordar and 1 plough. This is in the value of Hoveton [St John or St Peter].

In Wickmere St B[enet] held 12 acres of land TRE. It is worth 16d.

THIS [IS] THE SITE OF THE ABBEY.

TUNSTEAD HUNDRED.

HORNING St B[enet] has always held for 3 carucates. [There have] always [been] 18 villans, 11 bordars. Then [there were] 2 slaves; now none. [There have] always [been] 2 ploughs in demesne and 6 ploughs belonging to the men. And [there are] 100 acres of meadow. [There is] woodland for 100 pigs. [There has] always [been] 1 mill, 1 horse, 4 head of

cattle, 10 pigs, 360 sheep. It has always been worth £4. It is 1½ leagues in length and 1 league in breadth. And [it renders] 6d. of the geld.

Neatishead the same has always held, 5 carucates of land. [There are] 5 carucates. [There have] always [been] 5 villans, 16 bordars. [There is] 1 plough in demesne, 6 ploughs belonging to the men. [There are] 4 head of cattle, 5 pigs. And [there are] 27 sokemen on the same land. [There have] always [been] 8 ploughs. It is worth £4. It is 1½ leagues in length and 1 league in breadth. And [it renders] 28d. of the g[eld]. [There are] 10 acres belonging to a church.

Hoveton [St John or St Peter] Ralph the staller held TRE, 6 carucates. [There have] always [been] 4 villans, 6 bordars. And [there are] 2 ploughs in demesne and 3 ploughs belonging to the men. [There is] woodland for 16 pigs. [There are] 10 acres of meadow. And [there are] 4 sokemen, 1½ carucates and 30 acres. [There have] always [been] 5 villans, 11 bordars, 5½ ploughs, 10 acres of meadow. And [there is] 1 sokeman, 28 acres, and 7 sokemen, 110 acres. [There have] always [been] 5½ ploughs. Then it was worth £7; now 100s. It is 1 league and 2 furlongs in length and 1 league in breadth. And [it renders] 18d. of the geld. 2 churches [have] 16 acres.

[North] Walsham St B[enet] has always held: 3½ carucates. [There have] always [been] 12 villans and

St Benet of Hulme

5 bordars. [There are] 2 ploughs in demesne and 2½ [ploughs] belonging to the men. [There are] 8 acres of meadow. [There is] woodland for 100 pigs, 1 mill, 1 horse, 1 ox, 8 pigs. [There are] 31 sokemen, 3 carucates and 50 acres. And [there is] 1 villan and 1 villan [sic] and 1 bordar. [There have] always [been] 15 ploughs. [There is] woodland for 16 pigs. [There are] 4 acres of meadow. It is worth 100s. It is 1½ leagues in length and 1 league and 6 perches in breadth. And [it renders] 18d. of the geld. [There are] 30 acres belonging to a church.

Felmingham St B[enet] has always held: 77 acres. [There have] always [been] 5 bordars. [There is] 1 plough in demesne and half a plough belonging to the men. [There is] 1 acre of meadow. And [there are] 4 sokemen, 50 acres. [There is] 1 plough, 1 acre of meadow. . It is worth 21s.

Paston the same held TRE: 1 carucate. [There are] 2 villans, 2 bordars, 1 plough in demesne, half a plough belonging to the men. Now [there is] 1 mill. It is worth 10s. It is 1 league in length and 4 in breadth. And [it renders] 15d. Others hold there.

In Witton [near North Walsham] St B[enet] holds 1 carucate. [There have] always [been] 2 villans and 2 bordars. And [there is] 1 plough in demesne and half a plough belonging to the men. It is worth 8s.

In Barton [Turf] St B[enet] has always held half a carucate. [There has] always [been] 1 bordar and 1 plough and 1 acre of meadow. It is worth 5s. 4d. In the same [vill there is] 1 sokeman, 30 acres. [There are] 5 bordars, 1 plough, 1 acre of meadow. It is worth 10s.

Worstead St B[enet] has always held TRE: 2½ carucates. [There have] always [been] 8 villans, 30 bordars. [There are] 2 ploughs in demesne and 3 ploughs belonging to the men. [There are] 8 acres of meadow. [There is] woodland for 16 pigs. [There has] always [been] 1 mill. And [there are] 3 sokemen on the same land. Then it was worth 60s.; now £4. 2 churches [have] 28 acres in the same value. This land was for the sustenance of the monks TRE; now Robert the cross-bowman has it of the abbot. It is 1 league in length and half [a league] in breadth. And of the geld [sic]. And [it renders] 18d. of the geld. In the same [vill] St B[enet] has always held 1 carucate TRE. [There have] always [been] 2 villans, 10 bordars. And [there is] 1 plough in demesne and 2 ploughs belonging to the men. [There are] 2 acres of meadow. [There is] woodland for 6 pigs. It is worth 40s.

[Folio 219v: NORFOLK]

In Beeston [St Lawrence] [there is] 1 sokeman of St B[enet]'s, 30 acres. [There are] 4 bordars, 2 acres of meadow. It is worth 5s. 4d. All the churches are included in the value with the manors.

In [Sco] Ruston [there are] 3 sokemen of St B[enet]'s, 60 acres. [There has] always [been] half a plough. [It is] in the value of Scottow.

In Barton [Turf] [there are] 3 sokemen, 33 acres. [There have] always [been] 3 bordars, 1 plough. It is worth 7s.

In Dilham [there is] 1 sokeman, 30 acres. [There is] 1 bordar, 1 plough. It is worth 6s. 8d.

In Sloley [there is] 1 sokeman, 16 acres. It is worth 16d. In the same [vill there are] 20 acres and they belong to Easton [in Scotton] and [are included] in [its] value.

In Smallburgh [there is] 1 sokeman of St B[enet]'s who used to hold 1 free carucate and he gave it to St B[enet] TRE and he still holds it of the abbot. [There have] always [been] 2 villans. And [there are] 1½ ploughs and 2 acres of meadow. It is worth 20s. In the same [vill there are] 28 sokemen, 1 carucate. [There have] always [been] 4 ploughs. [There is] 1 acre of meadow. It is worth 20s. The whole is 10 furlongs and 12 perches in length and 6 furlongs in breadth. And [it renders] 8d. of the geld.

In Barton [Turf] [there was] 1 sokeman of St B[enet]'s and Earl Ralph's TRE, 16 acres. It is worth 16d. And [there are] 33 acres belonging to 2 churches. It is worth 15d.

In Honing St B[enet] held 2 carucates TRE and Eadric [held it] of it, so that the abbot gave to him half of its demesne and he had granted to the abbot the other half of his fief and he was thus holding it of the abbot and giving service. On this land [there were] always 13 bordars. And [there are] 2 ploughs in demesne and 3 ploughs belonging to the men. [There are] 25 acres of meadow. [There is] woodland for 8 pigs. [There is] 1 mill, 2 horses, 4 head of cattle, 12 pigs, 40 sheep, 30 goats. And [there are] 8 sokemen, 41 acres. [There have] always [been] 2 ploughs. [There are] 5 acres of meadow. The whole is worth 40s. It is 1 league in length and 40 furlongs in breadth. And [it renders] 10d. of the geld, whoever may hold there. Robert Malet holds this and Robert de Gla[n]ville [holds it] of him.

In [North] Walsham [there are] 4 sokemen, 57 acres. [There has] always [been] 1 plough. [There is] 1 acre of meadow. It is worth 5s.

St Benet of Hulme

[Folio 220: NORFOLK]

and 8d. Of the two of these, W[illiam] Malet had the commendation only. In the same [vill there are] 10 bordars, 7 acres. And it is worth 10d.

HUNDRED OF HAPPING.

Ludham St B[enet] has always held for 5 carucates. [There have] always [been] 15 villans and 13 bordars. [There are] 2 slaves. [There are] 3 ploughs in demesne, 2½ ploughs belonging to the men. [There is] woodland for 16 pigs. [There are] 100 acres of meadow, 3 horses, 16 pigs, 3 hives of bees. And [there are] 115½ sokemen, 3 carucates and 15 acres. [There have] always [been] 10 ploughs. [There are] 15 acres of meadow. And [there are] 4½ free men, 1 carucate and 15 acres. [There have] always [been] 3 bordars, 2 ploughs, 5 acres of meadow. Of these the abbot has the commendation only. The king and the earl [have] the soke. Then the whole was worth 100s.; now £6. And it is 2½ leagues and 15 perches in length and 1½ leagues and 70 perches in breadth. And [it renders] 5s. of the geld, whoever may hold there.

Waxham St B[enet] has always held for 2 carucates and 8 acres. [There have] always [been] 3 bordars. And [there is] 1 plough in demesne and half a plough belonging to the men. [There are] 60 acres of meadow, 2 horses, 6 pigs, 8 sheep. And [there are] 25½ sokemen, 160 acres. Then [there were] 3½ ploughs; now 3. [There are] 12 acres of meadow. And [there are] 2 free men in commendation only, 20 acres. And [there is] 1 plough. The king and the earl have the soke over these 2 and St Ben[et] over the whole of the others. The whole has always been worth £4 and the free men 34d. And it is 1½ leagues and 1 furlong in length and 1 league in breadth. And [it renders] 30d., whoever may hold there.

WHIMPWELL H[UNDRED]. ST B[ENET] HAS ALWAYS HELD FOR 1½

carucates. [There have] always [been] 5 villans and 2 bordars. And [there is] 1 plough in demesne and 1 plough belonging to the men. [There are] 4 acres of meadow and 1[...] horse, 4 pigs. And [there is] 1 free man in commendation only, 9 acres. And [there is] half a plough. It is worth 12d. The king and the earl [have] the soke. The whole manor is worth 30s. but Godric used to render £4 when he was holding it in the earl's fief.

[Folio 220v: NORFOLK]

Stalham St B[enet] holds: 1 carucate. [There have] always [been] 2 villans and 1 bordar. And [there is] 1 plough in demesne and 1 plough belonging to the men. [There is] woodland for 3 pigs. [There are] 4 acres of meadow, 1 horse, 6 pigs. And [there was] 1 man, 29 acres, holding his land of St Ben[et] TRE. [There has] always [been] half a plough. [There are] 2 acres of meadow. The king and the earl [have] the soke. And [there are] 9 free men, 75 acres. Then [there were] 2 ploughs; now 1½. Of these the abbot has the commendation only and the king and the earl [have] the soke. The whole manor has always been worth 20s. and the free men 2s. And it is 1 league and 3 furlongs in length and 5 furlongs in breadth. And [it renders] 17½d. of the geld.

In Ingham St B[enet] has always held 30 acres of land. [There has] always [been] half a plough. And [there is] 1 acre of meadow. It is worth 6s. 8d.

In Eccles [on Sea] [there is] 1 free man, 15 acres, which St B[enet] holds with every customary right but the king and the earl [have] the soke. And it is worth 15d.

In Ludham [there is] 1 sokeman of St B[enet]'s, 30 acres. [There are] 4 bordars, 3 acres of meadow, half a plough. It is worth 2s.

In Whimpwell H[UNDRED].

[There is] 1 free man, 12 acres. It is worth 32d.

EAST FLEGG HUNDRED.

In Filby St B[enet] has always held 1 carucate and 20 acres. [There have] always [been] 4 bordars. And [there is] 1 plough in demesne and 3 acres of meadow and 1 salt-pan. Now [there is] 1 horse. And [there are] 3 free men in commendation only, 42 acres. [There has] always [been] 1 villan and 1½ ploughs and 1½ acres of meadow. It is worth 3s.

In Scratby St B[enet] has always held 109 acres.

[There have] always [been] 3 bordars. Then [there was] 1 plough in demesne. [There has] always [been] half a plough belonging to the men.

[There are] 2 acres of meadow. It is worth 10s.

St Benet of Hulme

[Folio 221: NORFOLK]

And it is 1 league in length and 5 furlongs in breadth. And [it renders] 20d. of the geld.

In Caister St B[enet] has always held 1 carucate. [There have] always [been] 4 bordars. And [there is] 1 plough in demesne and half a plough belonging to the men. [There are] 7½ acres of meadow, 6 salt-pans. And [there are] 14 free men under the abbot in commendation only, 1 carucate. And [there is] 1 bordar. Then [there were] 2 ploughs belonging to the men; now 4. Then it was worth 20s.; now 5[s.] And [there are] 14 free men in commendation only under the abbot to whom the abbot established title against Godric. It is worth 40s.

HUMBLEYARD HUNDRED.

Heigham St B[enet] has always held: 3 carucates. [There have] always [been] 3 villans, 5 bordars. [There are] 2 ploughs in demesne. Then [there was] 1 plough belonging to the men; now half [a plough], and 1½ could be restored. [There are] 20 acres of meadow, 2 mills, 1 horse, 7 pigs, 12 sheep. And [there are] 6 sokemen at half a carucate. [There have] always [been] 2 ploughs. Then it was worth £4; now 100s. [Belonging to] this manor is 1 free man in commendation only under the abbot and he has 30 acres and half a plough. [There are] 3 acres of meadow. It is worth 2s. It is 10 furlongs in length and 7 in breadth. And [it renders] 2ƒd. of the geld.

DEPWADE HUNDRED.

Tibenham St B[enet] has always held: 1½ carucates and 15 acres. [There have] always [been] 4 villans, 5 bordars. [There is] 1 plough in demesne. Then [there were] 1½ ploughs belonging to the men; now 1. And [there are] 3 acres of meadow. [There is] woodland for 10 pigs. [There are] 6 pigs. It is worth 25s.

[Folio 221V: NORFOLK]

XVIII. The land of Saint-Étienne of Caen.

HUNDRED AND A HALF OF FREEBRIDGE.

[...] Well Stigand held TRE. [There have] always [been] 10 villans. And [there are] 2 carucates and 6 bordars and 1 slave. [There are] 30 acres of meadow. Then [there were] 2 ploughs in demesne; afterwards 5 oxen; now 2 ploughs. [There is] 1 plough belonging to the men. [There are] 2 mills. 14 sokemen belong to this manor at 28 acres of land. Then [there was] 1 plough; now 5 oxen. [There have] always [been] 7 pigs. Then [there were] 15 sheep; now 60. Then and afterwards it was worth £9; now [£]10. Well and Gayton are 1½ leagues in length and half [a league] in breadth. And it renders 16d. of the geld, whoever may hold there. Pasture 5 furlongs in length and 4 in breadth still belongs to Well and is in the same value.

XIX. The land of William d'Écouis.

HUNDRED AND A HALF OF FREEBRIDGE.

Islington Skuli, a free man, held TRE for a manor and for 2 carucates. Now W[illiam] holds [it] in demesne. [There have] always [been] 3 villans, 7 bordars. Then [there were] 2 ploughs in demesne; afterwards and now 1. [There are] 10 acres of meadow, 100 sheep. Then [there were] 30 pigs; now 16. 7 sokemen, 12 acres, belong here. Then it was worth 40s.; now 60[s.]

In Clenchwarton Richard holds of W[illiam] 40 acres. And it is worth 6s. This land Radfrid held and Earl Ralph established title to half and held [it] on that day when he forfeited. Now Wulfwig, a man of Radfrid's, holds it in the fief of William d'Écouis and claims the king as warrantor.

William d'Écouis

[Folio 222: NORFOLK]

In Islington Th[or]kil, a free man, held half a carucate TRE; now W[illiam holds it] in demesne. [There have] always [been] 3 bordars. Then [there was] half a plough; now 2 oxen. [There are] 40 acres of meadow and half a salt-pan. Then it was worth 10s.; now 20[s.] The whole of Islington is 1½ leagues in length and half a league in breadth. And it renders 12d. of a 20s. geld.

Middleton [near Kings Lynn] Thorkil held for a manor and for 2 carucates. Now W[illiam holds it] in demesne. [There have] always [been] 4 villans and 6 bordars and 4 slaves. [There are] 30 acres of meadow. [There are] 2 ploughs in demesne. Then [there was] 1 plough belonging to the men; now half [a plough]. [There is] 1 mill, 1 fishery, 8 salt-pans. [There has] always [been] 1 horse. Then [there were] 2 cows. Then [there were] 16 pigs; now 10. Then [there were] 80 sheep; now 70. Then it was worth 100s.; now £7.

[North] Runcton the same man held TRE for a manor and for 1 carucate. Now W[illiam holds it] in demesne. [There have] always [been] 2 bordars. [There are] 20 acres of meadow. [There is] 1 plough in demesne, half a plough belonging to the men. 7 sokemen belonged to this manor TRE at 60 acres. Then [there were] 2 ploughs; now 1. [There are] 8 acres of meadow. The whole is worth 60s. In Middleton [near Kings Lynn] W[illiam] holds in demesne 6 free men at 1 carucate. [There has] always [been] 1 plough. [There is] woodland for 100 pigs. It is worth 24s. 8d. Stigand held the soke over 2 men and it was delivered to Radfrid for 1 carucate.

Gayton Wulfwig holds: 1 carucate, which Th[or]kil held TRE. Then [there were] 8 bordars; now 6. [There are] 12 acres of meadow. [There has] always [been] 1 plough in demesne. Then and afterwards [there was] half a plough belonging to the men; now 2. And it is worth 20s.

[Great or Little] Massingham Ralph fitzHerluin holds, which Godwine, a free man, held TRE: . [There have] always [been] 6 villans. Then [there was] 1 plough in demesne. Then it was worth 10s.; now 5[s.]

Of this the predecessor of William de Warenne held the commendation only and the soke [was] in [Great or Little] Massingham, [a manor] belonging to the king.

DOCKING HUNDRED.

[Great] BIRCHAM

[Folio 222v: NORFOLK]

Beorn held under King Edward: 1 carucate; now R[oger] d'Évreux holds [it]. Then [there was] 1 plough; afterwards none; now 1. [There have] always [been] 1 villan and 2 bordars. [There is] half a plough belonging to the men. And it is worth 10s. [There is] 1 church, 4 acres. In the same [vill] a free man, Thor, held TRE under Stigand 4 carucates. Then [there were] 2 ploughs in demesne and now [ ]. Then and afterwards [there were] 2 ploughs belonging to the men; now 1. Then and afterwards [there were] 14 villans; now 2. [There has] always [been] 1 bordar. Then it was worth 40[s.]; now £4. Stigand had the soke. And there are 3 free men. : 85 acres of land TRE. Then [there were] 2 ploughs and afterwards and now 1. Then [there were] 2 bordars. And 1 free man, Brunard, holds 30 acres of land. [There have] always [been] 2 oxen. The whole was worth 12s. Radfrid held these men and now they are in the king's hand because there was no one who proved title. The whole is 1 league in length and 1 league in breadth. Whoever may hold there, it renders 27d. of 20s. of a geld.

H[UNDRED] OF SMETHDON.

In Ringstead Roger holds 2 free men: 1 carucate. And in Holme [next the Sea] [there are] 2 free men, 40 acres, and 3 bordars. [There have] always [been] 1½ ploughs and they are in [Great] Bircham's valuation. In the same [vill] the same man holds 1 free [man]: half a carucate. Then [there was] 1

plough; afterwards half [a plough]; now 2 oxen. It has always been worth 5s.

H[UNDRED] OF SHROPHAM.

In Wilby Fathir held 2 carucates TRE. Then [there were] 10 villans; afterwards and now 6. [There have] always [been] 9 bordars. Then [there were] 4 slaves; now 1. And [there are] 14 acres of meadow. Then [there were] 1½ ploughs in demesne; afterwards 1; now 2. Then [there were] 1½ ploughs belonging to the men; afterwards and now 1.

[There is] woodland for 10 pigs. Then [there was] 1 horse; now 3. [There have] always [been] 5 head of cattle and 9 pigs. Then [there were] 40 sheep; now 52. And [there are] 12

William d'Écouis

[Folio 223: NORFOLK]

sokemen, 40 acres. Then [there was] 1½ ploughs; afterwards and now 1. Then and now it was worth 40s.; now 60[s.] And it is half a league in length and half in breadth. Whoever may hold there, [it renders] 15d. of the geld. [There is] 1 church, 10 acres. And it is worth 3s.

In Buckenham [near Attleborough] Roger holds 1 carucate. [There have] always [been] 4 bordars. And [there are] 4 acres of meadow and 1 plough in demesne. [There is] woodland for 60 pigs. Then [there were] 24 sheep; now 30. Then and afterwards it was worth 12[s]; now 20[s.] Then [there were] 6 pigs; now 11.

GUILTCROSS H[UNDRED].

In Banham Fathir, a free man, held 2 carucates for a manor TRE. [There have] always [been] 5 villans and 6 bordars and 1 slave. And [there are] 20 acres of meadow. [There is] woodland for 100 pigs. [There has] always [been] 1 plough in demesne and 1 plough belonging to the men. [There was] always 1 horse and 2 head of cattle. And then [there were] 8 pigs. Then [there were] 30 sheep. And [there are] 16 sokemen, 24 acres of land. Then and afterwards [there were] 2 ploughs; now 1½ ploughs and 1 plough could be restored. [There is] 1 church, 30 acres. And it is worth 22s. Then and afterwards it was worth 40[?s.]; now 50[?s.] Othar holds 1 carucate of this manor. And [there are] 2 bordars and 1 plough. It has always been worth 20s.

In Kenninghall [there is] soke of the 6 forefeitures.

In [East or West] Harling Ketil, a free man, held TRE 2 carucates for a manor. Now Ingulf holds [it]. [There have] always [been] 5 villans and 4 bordars. Then [there was] 1 slave. And [there are] 4 acres of meadow. [There is] 1 plough in demesne and 1 plough belonging to the men. [There is] woodland for 16 pigs. And 1 plough could be restored. [There has] always [been] 1 mill. And [there are] 2 sokemen, 20 acres of land. And [there are] 3 acres of meadow. [There has] always [been] half a plough. Now [there is] 1 horse. [There have] always [been] 3 head of cattle. Now [there are] 8 pigs and 20 sheep and 1 hive of bees. [There is] 1 church, 4 acres. Then it was worth 30s.; now 40[s.] The whole is 1 league in length and 1 league in breadth. And [it renders] 17¥d., whoever may hold there. And 7½ acres of land belong to this land. And [there is] woodland for 12 pigs.

[Folio 223v: NORFOLK]

MITFORD H[UNDRED].

In Letton [there is] 1 free man, 27 acres. And [there are] 1½ acres of meadow. And [there is] 1 bordar and half a plough. And it is worth 32d.

GALLOW H[UNDRED].

In [North or South] Creake Thorkil held TRE 1 carucate; now Turstin [holds]. [There have] always [been] 1 villan and 12 bordars. Then [there was] 1 slave. [There have] always [been] 2 ploughs in demesne and 1 plough belonging to the men. [There are] 3 acres of meadow. [There is] 1 mill. Then [there were] 60 sheep; now none. And [there are] 2 sokemen at 2 acres. Then and afterwards it was worth 40s.; now 30[s.]

NORTH ERPINGAM H[UNDRED].

Sheringham Siward Barn held TRE: 3 carucates. [There have] always [been] 10 villans and 12 bordars. Then [there were] 6; afterwards and now 5. Then [there were] 3 ploughs in demesne; afterwards and now 2. Then [there were] 4 ploughs belonging to the men; afterwards and now [...]2. Then [there was] woodland for 160 pigs, now 100. 4 acres of meadow. [There has] always [been] one horse and 2 head of cattle. Then [there were] 5 pigs; now 15. Then [there were] 60 goats; now 50. And [there is] 1 sokeman at 12 acres of land. It has always been worth £4. And it is 1 league in length and 1 in breadth. And of the geld [it renders] 11½d.

Salthouse Siward Barn held TRE: 3 carucates. [There have] always [been] 4 villans, 10 bordars. Then [there were] 3 [ploughs] in demesne and afterwards half [a plough]; now 1. [There have] always [been] 2 ploughs belonging to the men. [There is] woodland for 100 pigs. Then and always it has been worth 40s. And he has the soke and sake. And it is measured in Sheringham.

In Northrepps or Southrepps Gyrth held 1 free man TRE and Hardwin held when Ralph forfeited; now Quentin holds it of William and vouches Robert Blund as livery officer, 30 acres of land. [There has] always [been] 1 villan and 1 bordar. And [there is] 1 acre of meadow and 1 plough. Then it was worth 2s. and now 10[s.]

In Beeston [Regis] Thorkil Haki held 1 carucate TRE.

William d'Écouis

[Folio 224: NORFOLK]

Now Ingulf holds [it]. [There have] always [been] 3 villans and 15 bordars. Then and afterwards [there was] 1 plough in demesne; now 1½. [There have] always [been] 1½ ploughs belonging to the men. [There is] woodland for 20 pigs. [There is] 1 acre of meadow. [There has] always [been] 1 horse and 2 head of cattle. Then 7 pigs; now 2. Then [there were] 22 goats. Then and afterwards it was worth 20s. and now 40[s.] And it is 1 league in length and 5 furlongs in breadth. And of the geld [it renders] 11½d.

In Runton the same man holds 1 carucate. [There have] always [been] 10 bordars. And [there is] 1 plough in demesne and 1 plough belonging to the men. [There is] woodland for 10 pigs. Now [there are] 7 pigs. Now [there are] 60 sheep. And [there are] 5 sokemen at 15 acres of land. [There has] always [been] half a plough. Then it was worth 20s.; now 40[s.] [There is] 1 church, 6 acres. And it is measured in Beeston [Regis].

WALSHAM H[UNDRED].

In [North or South] Burlingham Edwin, 1 free man, held a berewick TRE: 40 acres of land. [There are] 3 bordars. Then [there was] 1 plough; afterwards half [a plough]; now 1. And [there are] 2 acres of meadow. [There are] 30 sheep. It has been valued in Stokesby.

In Reedham Beorhric held TRE 2 carucates. Now Richard holds [it] for a manor. [There have] always [been] 11 bordars. Then [there were] 3 slaves; afterwards and now 1. Then [there were] 1½ ploughs in demesne; now 1. [There have] always [been] 1½ ploughs belonging to the men. [There are] 20 acres of meadow. Then it was worth 40[s.]; now 60s. It is 1 league and 3½ furlongs in length; 1 league in breadth. And of the geld [it renders] 16d., whoever may hold there. [There is] 1 church, 40 acres. And it is worth 6s. 8d. Here the Abbot of [St Benet of] Hulme claims 1 sokeman, 40 acres of land and the Hundred testifies [to this]. And also he claims 1 bordar and 1 acre of land according to the testimony of the Hundred.

In Panxworth Godwine, 1 free man, held TRE 30 acres of land; now Hugh holds 4 bordars. Then [there was] 1 plough. [There are] 6 acres of meadow. [There has] always [been] half a plough belonging to the men. [There is] 1 church, 8 acres, and it is worth 12d. Then it was worth 10s.; now 20[s.] But Earl R[alph] had the soke.

[Folio 224v: NORFOLK]

In Fishley the same man holds 1 half of a man, 2 acres at 12d.

BLOFIELD H[UNDRED].

In Limpenhoe Hardwin held 2 in commendation only; now Othar [holds]. [There were] 34 acres of land and 1 bordar. [There are] 5 acres of meadow. [There has] always [been] 1 plough. Then it was worth 10s.; now 23s.

And in [Great or Little] Plumstead [there were] 2 free men of Hardwin's TRE, 8 acres of land. This Hugh holds. He has always ploughed with 2 oxen. It has always been worth 2s.

In [North or South] Burlingham the same man holds 20 acres of land in demesne and it belongs to Stokesby.

In Southwood the same man holds 29 [...] acres of land and in it [there have] always [been] 1½ bordars and 3 acres of meadow and half a plough. Always it was worth 32d.

WEST FLEGG H[UNDRED].

In Winterton the same man holds 1 free man and in Repps 1. In Ashby [near Acle] 1 but also 2½ in the commendation only of St Ben[et] of Hulme at 46 acres of land. [There has] always [been] 1 plough. And they are in the value of Stokesby.

LODDON H[UNDRED].

In "Brant" Alwine, a free man, held under Stigand TRE; now Othar holds 50 acres of land and 1 bordar. Then [there was] 1 plough; afterwards and now nothing. And it is worth 10s. The soke [is] in the Hundred.

H[UNDRED] OF EYNSFORD.

[Great or Little] Witchingham Hardwin, 1 free man, held TRE: 3 carucates. Then [there were] 16 bordars and afterwards and now 13. [There have] always [been] 4 slaves. [There have] always [been] 2 ploughs in demesne and 1 plough belonging to the men. And [there are] 8 acres of meadow. [There is] woodland for 5 pigs. [There have] always [been] 2 mills. Now [there is] 1 horse and 4 head of cattle. Then [there were] 12 pigs; now 16. Then [there were] 80 sheep; now 100. Then [there were] 30 goats; now 10. And [there are] 12 sokemen, 70 acres of land. [There have] always [been] 5 ploughs. And [there are] 2 acres of meadow. [There is] 1 church without land.

William d'Écouis

In Weston [Longville] [there is] 1 berewick, 1 carucate. And [there has] always [been] 1 villan and 12 bordars and 1 slave. [There has] always [been] 1 plough in demesne and 1 plough belonging to the men. And [there are] 2 acres of meadow. And [there are] 10 sokemen, 80 acres of land. Then and afterwards [there were] 8 ploughs; now 7, and 1 can be there. And [there are] 2 acres of meadow. [There is] 1 church, 2 acres, and it is worth 4d. The whole was then worth £7; afterwards £8 10s.; now the same. And [there are] 2 free men of Quentin's, half a carucate, and 2 bordars. [There have] always [been] 1½ ploughs. And it is worth 30s. from these two. The soke [is] in Foulsham, [a manor] belonging to the king. W[illiam] holds [it]. And it is 1 league in length and in breadth. And it renders 20d. to the geld, whoever may hold there.

H[UNDRED] OF TAVERHAM.

In Attlebridge [there are] 35 acres of land, 2 free men. [There have] always [been] 2 bordars and half a plough and 2 acres of meadow. And they are in the value of [Great or Little] Witchingham. The king and the earl [have] the soke.

H[UNDRED] OF SOUTH ERPINGHAM.

In Corpusty 1 villan pertains to [Great or Little] Witchingham, 40 acres of land. And [there are] 2 bordars. [There has] always [been] 1 plough. And it is worth 6s. [There are] three parts of 1 church, 9 acres, and it is worth 6d. And [there is] 1 sokeman, 4 acres, in Thurton [in Witchingham] and it is worth 8d.

TUNSTEAD H[UNDRED].

In Paston [there is] 1 free man in the commendation only of Eadric, 20 acres of land. [There has] always [been] 1 bordar. And it is worth 12d. In Swafield [there are] 6 acres, a free man. And it is worth 6d. St Benet [of Hulme has] the soke.

EAST FLEGG H[UNDRED].

Edwin, a free man of Gyrth's, held Stokesby: 3 carucates. [There have] always [been] 15 villans and 6 bordars and 4 slaves. Then [there were] 2½ ploughs in demesne; afterwards and now 3. And [there has] always [been] 1 plough belonging to the men. [There are] 20 acres of meadow and 2 salt-pans and 2 horses. Then [there were] 4 head of cattle; now 6. [There have] always [been] 10 pigs. Then [there were] 120 sheep; now 180. And [there is] 1 church, 23 acres of land. And [there are] 3 [acres] of meadow. And it is worth 16d. And 21 men, 80 acres of land, have

always belonged to this manor. The king and the earl [have] the soke of the whole. [There have] always [been] 5 ploughs. [...] And [there are] 8 acres of meadow. And [there are] 3 free men whom Hardwin added TRE belonging to William and they have 100 acres of land. Of these his predecessor had the commendation TRE. [There have] always [been] 9 bordars and 3 ploughs. And [there are] 8 acres of meadow and 1 salt-pan. Then it was worth 10s.; now 16[s.] And the manor was worth then 100s.; now £10. And yet it returned over two years £15 4s. each year. And it is 1 league in length and 1 league in breadth. And [it renders] 2s. of the geld. [...] In Thrigby Hugh holds 10 free men and in Mautby 2½. And in Filb [there are] 2½ carucates and 13 acres. [There have] always [been] 2½ bordars and 2½ ploughs. And [there are] 13 acres of meadow, 5 salt-pans. [There is] 1 church, 5 acres, and it is worth 6d. Then it was worth 40s.; now 80[s.] The king and the earl [have] the soke.

H[UNDRED] OF MBLEYARD.

In Colney Robert de Vaux holds 1 free man, 30 acres of land. And [there are] 3 acres of meadow. Then [there was] half a plough. And it is worth 2s.

H[UNDRED] OF DEPWADE.

In Tasburgh Almær held of Stigand 30 acres of land. Now Roger d'Évreux holds it. [There are] 4 acres of meadow. Then [there was] 1 plough; now half [a plough]. And [there is] a third part of a mill. And it is worth 15s.

CLAVERING H[UNDRED].

In Thurlton Othar holds. [There are] 7½ free men of whom the predecessor of Ralph de Beaufour had the commendation only TRE, 45 acres. Then [there were] 1½ ploughs; now half [a plough]. And it is worth 10s.

XX. Land of R[alph] de Beaufour.

H[UNDRED] OF DOCKING.

[Bircham] Newton Tovi, a free man, held TRE: 2 carucates. [There were] always 4 villans and 3 bordars. Then [there were] 3 slaves; afterwards and now 1. Then [there was] 1 plough in demesne; afterwards 2; now 3. Then and afterwards [there were] 4 ploughs belonging to the men; now 2½. [There have] always [been] 2 horses and 10 pigs. Then [there were] 220 sheep; now 540. Here belong 11 free men, 1½ carucates and 11½ acres. Then [there were] 4 ploughs belonging to the men;

Ralph de Beaufour

now 2½. [There is] 1 church, 20 acres; it is worth 16d. Eudo, his predecessor, had these free men. Stigand [had] the soke. Then it was worth 60s.; afterwards and now 100[s.] The whole is half a league in length and half in breadth. And it renders 15d. of a 20s. geld.

In [Great] Bircham Fathir, a thegn of King E[dward's], held 3 carucates. [There have] always [been] 5 villans and 4 bordars. Then [there were] 2 ploughs in demesne; afterwards and now, nothing. [There have] always [been] 2½ ploughs belonging to the men. And [there are] 2 free men, 2 acres. Then it was worth 50s.; now 20[s.] And it is 1 league in length and 1 league in breadth. Whoever may hold there renders 27d. of the geld.

SMETHDON H[UNDRED].

Ringstead 1 free man held [...] TRE: half a carucate; . [There have] always [been] 2 villans and half a plough. And it is worth 3s. St Benedict [of Ramsey has] the soke.

H[UNDRED] OF FREEBRIDGE.

In [West] Walton Bondi, a free man, held TRE 1 carucate; now Othar holds [it]. And [there are] 4 villans and 8 bordars and 4 acres of meadow. [There has] always [been] 1 plough in demesne and 1 plough belonging to the men. And [there is] 1 free man, 8 acres of land. And it is worth 20s.

SHROPHAM H[UNDRED].

In [Great] Ellingham [there are] 2 free men, 49 acres. [There are] 2 bordars and 2 free men, 22 acres of land. And [there are] 6½ acres of meadow. [There is] woodland for 8 pigs. [There has] always [been] half a plough and 2 oxen. Then it was worth 10s.; now 20[s.] The soke [is] in Buckenham [near Attleborough]. In Hargham Waring holds 3 carucates where Ulf, 1 free man, held TRE. Then and afterwards [there were] 2 villans; now 1. [There have] always [been] 2 bordars. Then and afterwards [there were] 2 slaves. [There are] 12 acres of meadow. Then [there was] 1 plough; afterwards 2 oxen; now 1½ ploughs. Then [there were] 2 ploughs belonging to the men; afterwards 1; now 1½. And [there are] 10 sokemen, 8 acres of land. [There have] always [been] 2 horses. Now [there are] 2 cows. Then [there were] 6 pigs; now 3. Then [there were] 44 sheep; now 28. Then it was worth 20s.; now 30[s.] The whole is half a league in length and half [a league]

in breadth. And [it renders] 6¾d. of the geld.

LAUNDITCH H[UNDRED].

Swanton [Morley] Godwine, a free man, held TRE: 8 carucates. [There have] always [been] 24 villans. Then and afterwards [there were] 39 bordars; now 54. [...] Then and afterwards [there were] 6 . [There are] 10 acres of meadow. Then

[there were] 4 ploughs in demesne; afterwards 3; now 5. Then and afterwards [there were] 13 ploughs belonging to the men; now 18. [There is] woodland for 500 pigs. [There have] always [been] 3 mills and 1 fishery. [There has] always [been] 1 horse. Then [there were] 2 head of cattle. Then [there were] 39 pigs; now 48. Then [there were] 60 sheep; now 85. To this manor belong 7 sokemen with every customary due. And it has 11 bordars. And [there are] 2 acres of meadow. [There have] always [been] 2 ploughs. And [there is] 1 free man, 12 acres of land. And [there are] 2 acres of meadow. Then [there was] half a plough; now nothing. Of this [man] his predecessor had the commendation only TRE. The soke [is] in Mileham and Eudo held it and Ralph holds it as a gift of the king. [There is] 1 church, 1½ acres: it is worth 2d. Then and afterwards it was worth £8; now [£]12 but after he had it, he gave it for a farm of £25. And it is 1½ leagues in length and 1 league in breadth. And [it renders] 10d. of the geld.

In [East or West] Lexham Fathir held TRE 3½ carucates; now Richard holds [it]. Then [there were] 9 villans; afterwards 8; now 5. [There have] always [been] 7 bordars. Then [there were] 3 slaves. [There are] 6 acres of meadow. Then and afterwards [there were] 2 ploughs in demesne; now 1, and another could be restored. [There have] always [been] 1½ ploughs belonging to the men. [There is] woodland for 30 pigs. [There has] always [been] 1 mill. Then [there was] 1 fishery and a quarter part of a salt-pan. [There has] always [been] 1 horse. Then [there were] 7 head of cattle. Then [there were] 24 pigs; now 5. Then [there were] 80 sheep; now 210. [There are] 4 hives of bees. And [there are] 6 sokemen, half a carucate. And [there are] 2 acres of meadow. [There has] always [been] 1 plough. Then it was worth 40s.; afterwards and now 60[s.] And [there was] 1 free man, 60 acres of land, under Harold and 2 bordars. And [there are] 1½ acres of meadow. Then [there was] half a plough but there could be [more]. Then it was worth 5s.; now 4[s.] The soke [is] in Mileham.

Ralph de Beaufour

[There is] 1 church, 30 acres, and it is worth 16d. The whole is 1 league in length and half [a league] in breadth. And [it renders] 7½d. of the geld.

In [East] Derham Harold held 2 carucates under Stigand. Now Othar holds [them]. [There have] always [been] 4 villans and 15 bordars. Then [there were] 2 slaves. [There are] 6 acres of meadow. Then [there were] 2 ploughs in demesne; afterwards and now 1 and another could be restored. [There have] always [been] 2 ploughs belonging to the men. [There is] woodland for 30 pigs. [There has] always [been] 1 mill and 5 sokemen, 43 acres of land. And [there are] 2 acres of meadow. Then and afterwards [there was] 1 plough; now half [a plough] and the whole could be restored. Then [there was] 1 horse. Then [there were] 4 head of cattle. Then [there were] 7 pigs; now 2. Then [there were] 7 goats; now 8. Then it was worth 20s.; now 40[s.] The whole is 1 league and 5 furlongs in length and half [a league] and 3 furlongs in breadth. And of the geld [it renders] 10d., whoever may hold there. The whole soke [is] in Mileham.

FOREHOE H[UNDRED]

and a half. Deopham Leofwine, a free man, held TRE: 1 carucate . Now the same man holds [it]. [There have] always [been] 9 villans. Then [there were] 10 bordars; now 9. Then and afterwards [there were] 2 slaves; now none. [There have] always [been] 3 ploughs in demesne and 1½ [ploughs] belonging to the men. [There is] woodland for 12 pigs. And [there are] 10 acres of meadow. [There has] always [been] 1 horse and 10 head of cattle and 17 pigs, 32 goats. To this manor have always belonged 25 sokemen and 1 carucate and 26 acres. [There have] always [been] 6½ ploughs. And after this 6 free men were added to this manor TRW whom Eudo held. And it has 120 acres of land and 20 bordars and 5 ploughs and 6 acres of meadow. Then the head manor was worth £4. And Ralph gave the whole to farm for £12 but now, however, it has not rendered anything except for £6. And 6 free men are worth 55s. The Hundred testifies to this. Of these, 3 were sokemen

of Stigand's and the soke is in Hingham, [a manor] belonging to the king. And it is 10 furlongs in length and 6 in breadth. And [it renders] 17¾d.

Morley [St Botolph or St Peter] Leofwine, a free man, held TRE: 1 carucate for a manor. Now Hugh holds [it]. [There have] always [been] 9 villans. Then [there were] 1½ ploughs; now 2, and half [a plough] belonging to the men. And [there are] 3 acres of meadow. [There has] always [been] 1 horse. Then [there was] 1 ox; now 2. Then [there were] 8 pigs; now 47. And [there were] 5 free men TRE. Their soke [is] in Hingham, [a manor] belonging to the king. It has always been worth 40s. To this manor have been added 14 free men, 60 acres of land and 2 ploughs and 3 acres of meadow. And it is worth 40s. Those same were Stigand's men. The soke [is] in Hingham. And after this were added 2 free men of William's TREW, 30 acres. And it is worth 22s. One was a man of Stigand's and another the king's. Their soke [is] in Hingham. And it is half a league in length and half in breadth. And [it renders] 14¾d. in geld. [...] Barford Stigand held in soke TRE: 30 acres of land. Now Richard holds [it]. [There have] always [been] 8 villans. And [there is] 1 plough in demesne and 1 plough belonging to the men. [There are] 3 acres of meadow. And it is worth 20s. In the same [vill] a free man held 30 acres TRE under Stigand. The soke [is] in Hingham, [a manor] belonging to the king. And it is worth 5s.

In Crownthorpe the same man holds 30 acres of land where Colman, a free man held in soke and commendation under Stigand. [There have] always [been] 6 bordars and half a plough and 1 mill and 5 acres of meadow. And it is worth 30s. Ralph Bay[nard] claims from this one half a man at 3 acres. And it is 3 furlongs in length and 2 in breadth. And [it renders] 7¼d. of the geld.

MITFORD H[UNDRED] AND A HALF.

Hockering Sigar, a free man, held TRE: 4 carucates. And [there have] always [been] 3 villans and 23

Ralph de Beaufour

bordars and 4 slaves. Then [there were] 4 ploughs in demesne; now 5. Then [there were] 7 ploughs belonging to the men; now 5. [There is] woodland for 200 pigs. And [there are] 15 acres of meadow and 1½ mills. [There have] always [been] 9 head of cattle and 33 pigs. Then [there were] 80 sheep; now 113. And then [there were] 3 sokemen; now 7. [There are] 60 acres of land. Then it was worth £4; now 100s. To this manor belong 10½ free men, 2 carucates.

In [North] Tuddenham Richard holds 11 bordars. [There have] always [been] 5 ploughs and 10 acres of meadow. [There have] always [been] 2 mills. It has always been worth £4. The whole of this Hockering is half a league in length and half in breadth. And [it renders] 5½d. of the geld.

And [North] Tuddenham is 5 furlongs in length and 4 in breadth. And of the geld [it renders] 21¼d., whoever may hold there. In Mattishall [there are] 14 free men, 2½ carucates and 20 acres and 12 villans and 5 ploughs and 6 acres of meadow. [There is] 1 church, 20 acres, and it is worth 16d. Then it was worth 60s.; now 43[s.]. And it is 7 furlongs in length and 6 in breadth. And [it renders] 36½d. of the geld.

In East Tuddenham [there are] 6 free men, half a carucate and 3 acres. One man has 4 bordars. [There have] always [been] 1½ ploughs and 2 acres of meadow. And it is worth 14s. 8d. The whole of this was delivered to him and his predecessor for land.

In Mattishall [there were] 5 free men TRE, 2 carucates. [There have] always [been] 4 bordars. Then [there were] 4 ploughs; now 2. [There are] 10 acres of meadow. And it was then worth 20s.; now 32[s.] 4d. They have their soke from the abbot.

WALSHAM H[UNDRED].

In Woodbastwick Godric, 1 free man, TRE held 4 sokemen belonging to Wroxham, 7 acres of land and 1 villan at 15 acres of land.

The same Godric held Tunstall TRE for a manor. Now Turold holds: 60 [acres]. Then [there were] 3 bordars; now 5. And [there are] 8 acres of meadow.

[There has] always [been] 1 plough between himself and the men. It has always been worth 10s. And the soke is the king's.

In Woodbastwick Ulfkil and Withri, men of Harold's, held 4½ sokemen and 6 bordars, 11 acres of land, 1 acre of meadow. [There has] always [been] half a plough. And they are in the value of Wroxham.

In the same vill Ulfkil holds held 40 acres of land, 4 acres of meadow. It has been valued.

BLOFIELD H[UNDRED].

In [Great or Little] Plumstead [there is] 1 bordar, at 9 acres of land. He always ploughs with 2 oxen. They have been valued in Wroxam.

In Blofield [there are] 2 bordars at 12 acres of land. [There is] 1 acre of meadow. They have been assessed in Wroxham.

HENSTEAD H[UNDRED].

In Caistor [St Edmund] [there are] 5½ free men of Godwine's at 42½ acres of land. And [there are] 2 acres of meadow. [There has] always [been] half a plough. And it belongs to Markshall. In Caistor St Edmund there is also 1 carucate. In demesne [there is] half a mill and it is in the value of Markshall.

DISS HALF-H[UNDRED].

Roydon [near Diss] Leofric son of Bosi, a thegn of the king's, held for a manor. Now Hugh holds [it]. Then and afterwards [there were] 9 villans; now 5. Then and afterwards [there were] 12 bordars; now 11. [There has] always [been] 1 slave. [There have] always [been] 2 ploughs in demesne and 2 ploughs belonging to the men. [There is] woodland for 30 pigs. And [there are] 4 acres of meadow. [There have] always [been] 2 horses at the hall. [There have] always [been] 6 head of cattle. Then [there were] 40 pigs; now 30. Then [there were] 60 sheep. Now [there are] 22 goats. And [there are] 6 sokemen at 24 acres of land. Then and afterwards [there was] 1 plough; now half [a plough]. It has always been worth 40s. It [is] 10 furlongs in length and 8 in breadth. And of the geld [it renders] 9d.

H[UNDRED] OF TAVERSHAM.

Wroxham Stigand held TRE: 2 carucates. Then [there were] 9 villans, afterwards and now 5 bordars. And [there are] 2 ploughs in demesne. Then [there were] 1½ ploughs belonging to the men; now 1. And [there are] 20 acres of meadow and 4 head of cattle and 20 pigs, [There is] woodland for 100 pigs. [There are] 100 sheep. And [there are] 13 sokemen,

Ralph de Beaufour

[Folio 229: NORFOLK]

40 acres of land and 2 acres of meadow Then [there were] 2 ploughs; now 1½. The king and the earl [have] the soke. And [there are] 7 free men, 210 acres. Then [there were] 3½ ploughs; afterwards and now 2. And [there are] 15 acres of meadow. [There is] woodland for 12 pigs. And 1½ ploughs could be restored. Then the manor was worth £3; now [£]4. And [there are] 7 free men, 38s.

In the same [vill there are] 3 free men , 1 carucate and 30 acres. [There have] always [been] 2 villans and 6 bordars. Then [there were] 3 ploughs; afterwards and now 2, and a third could be restored. And [there are] 10 acres of meadow. [There is] woodland for 20 pigs. And in the same [vill there are] 3 free men, 20 acres, 1 plough.

[...] 2 churches, 33 acres of land, and it is worth 3s. In Rackheath [there are] 3 free men, 20 acres and 3 bordars. Then [there was] 1 plough; afterwards and now half [a plough]. In Beeston [St Andrew] [there is] 1 free man, 30 acres of land. Then [there was] 1 plough; afterwards and now half [a plough]. And [there are] 2 acres of meadow [There is] half a church and it is worth 12d.

In Crostwick [there are] 6 free men, half a carucate and 3 bordars. Then [there were] 2 ploughs; afterwards and now 1. Then the whole was worth 30s.; now 45[s.] 4d. The king and the earl [have] the soke but Ralph used to hold it. The whole [of] Wroxham [is] 1½ leagues in length and 1 league in breadth. And [it renders] 30d. of the geld, whoever may hold there.

Drayton Ealdwulf, a free man, held TRE: 2 carucates. Now Othar holds [it]. [There have] always [been] 7 villans and 8 bordars. Then [there were] 3 slaves. [There has] always [been] 1 plough in demesne and 3 ploughs belonging to the men and 1 plough could be restored. And [there are] 10 acres of meadow. [There is] woodland for 3 pigs. And [there is] 1 horse and 2 head of cattle, 14 pigs. Then [there were] 180 sheep; now 60. Then [there were] 60 goats. And [there are] 2 sokemen, 22 acres of land. Then [there was] half a plough. [There is] 1 church, 8 acres, and it is worth 16d. Then it was worth 40s.; now 50[s.] And it is 1 league in length and half [a league] in breadth. And [it renders] 8ƒd. of the geld. The king and the earl [have] the soke. In Felthorpe Richard holds 3 free men, 43 acres of land, and it is worth 2s. The king and the earl [have] the soke.

In Taverham the same man holds 1 carucate, which Ulf held TRE. [There have] always [been] 4 villans and 3 bordars. [There has] always [been] 1 plough in demesne and 1 plough belonging to the men. And [there are] 10 acres of meadow. [There is] woodland for 5 pigs, and a quarter part of a mill. And [there are] 5 sokemen, 13 acres of land. [There has] always [been] 1 plough in demesne. [There are] 2 horses and 1 ox. Now [there are] 12 pigs and 60 sheep. Then and afterwards it was worth 20s.; now 30[s.] [There is] a quarter part [of] 1 church, 15 acres, and it is worth 16d.

H[UNDRED] OF EYNSFORD.

In Sall Othar holds 1 free man TRE. [There are] 30 acres of land. [There have] always [been] 8 bordars and 1½ ploughs and 1 acre of meadow. [There is] woodland for 5 pigs, and a quarter part of a mill. And it is worth 10s.

SOUTH ERPINGHAM H[UNDRED].

In Buxton [there are] 5 free men, 7 carucates. One of these brothers was in the commendation of the predecessor of [Robert] Malet and he was not seised of him. Then [there were] 20 villans; afterwards and now 12. Now [there are] 17 bordars. Then [there were] 8 ploughs in demesne; afterwards 4; now 4. Then [there were] 8 ploughs belonging to the men; afterwards 3; now 3½. [There are] 12 [acres] of meadow. Then [there was] woodland for 1000 pigs; now 200. [There has] always [been] 1 mill and 3 horses. Then [there were] 3 head of cattle. Then [there were] 32 pigs; now 18. And [there is] 1 church at 30 acres in alms and it is worth 3s. And it is worth 100[s.] And it is 1 league in length,

6½ furlongs in breadth. And [it renders] 10d. of the geld. In Brampton [there are] 25½ sokemen, 1 carucate and 30 acres. Then [there were] 7 ploughs; afterwards 5; now 3. Then it was worth 20s.; now 40s. The soke [is] in Marsham.

In Scottow 1 sokeman of St Benet of Hulme holds 1

carucate and 8 acres. [There have] always [been] 2 villans and 4 bordars. Then [there were] 2 ploughs; now 1½. And [there are] 3 acres of meadow. And [there is] 1 sokeman, 3 acres of land. Then it was worth 10[s.]; now 8[s.] And Brampton is 6 furlongs in length and 5 in breadth. And [it renders] 5½d. of the geld. In Belaugh [there is] 1 free man of Harold's, 1 carucate and 11 acres. Then [there was] 1 plough; now half [a plough]. And [there are] 3 acres of meadow. In the same [vill] [there was] 1 sokeman of Ralph the staller's TRE, 15 acres, and it was worth 2s. in Hoveton [St John or St Peter]. The same Ralph gave this to St Benet [of Hulme] and Eudo took him; now Ralph de Beaufour has [him]. In Belaugh [there are] 22 acres of land, 7 sokemen. Then [there were] 2 ploughs; afterwards and now 1. And it is worth 8s. Ralph the staller and Stigand [had] the soke and Ralph gave his portion to St Benet [of Hulme]. The whole of Belaugh is 9 furlongs in length and 3½ in breadth. And [it renders] 6d. of the geld. In Skeyton [there are] 11½ acres, 1 sokeman of St Benet [of Hulme's] and it is worth 17d. Radbod, Ralph's reeve, took this [man] from the abbey under Eudo, Ralph [de Beaufour]'s predecessor. In [Great or Little] Hautbois [there is] half a carucate, 1 sokeman of St Bene[t of Hulme's]. [There have] always [been] 4 bordars. And [there is] 1 plough. And [there are] 2 acres of meadow. [There is] woodland for 20 pigs and half a mill. Then it was worth 10s.; now 12[s.] Eudo had this land by livery as Ralph says.

[Great or Little] Hautbois is 6 furlongs in length and 4 in breadth. And [it renders] 2d. of the geld.

In Lamas [there are] 20 acres of land, 1 free woman. [There has] always [been] 1 bordar. And it is in the value of Buxton. In Wolterton Thorvald, 1 free man, held 30 acres of land TRE. [There have] always [been] 3 bordars and 1 plough. And it is worth 10s. The king and the earl [have] the soke. In Scottow [there are] 3 free men of St Ben[et of Hulme's], 30 acres. [There has] always [been] half a plough. And it is worth 3s.

TUNSTEAD H[UNDRED].

In Sloley [there is] 1 sokeman of St Benet [of Hulme's], 1 carucate. [There have] always [been] 12 villans and 8 bordars and 2½ ploughs and 6 acres of meadow. [There is] woodland for 26 pigs. And [there are] 3 sokemen, 16 acres. [There has] always [been] half a plough. And it is worth 40s. And it is 6 furlongs in length and 5 furlongs in breadth. And [it renders] 4½d. of the geld. [There is] 1 church, 1 acre, and it is worth 2d.

HUMBLEYARD H[UNDRED].

Mulbarton Richard holds, which Ording, a thegn, held TRE: 2 carucates. Then and afterwards [there were] 10 villans; now 7. Then [there were] 7 bordars; now 16. Then [there were] 2 slaves; now 1. [There have] always [been] 2 ploughs in demesne and 2 ploughs belonging to the men. [There are] 10 acres of meadow. [There is] woodland for 16 pigs. [There has] always [been] 1 mill. Now [there is] 1 horse. Then [there was] 1 ox. Now [there are] 6 pigs. And [there are] 6 sokemen, 60 acres. [There have] always [been] 1½ ploughs. And in [East] Carleton the same man holds. [There are] 4 free men. And in Swardeston the same man holds. [There are] 7 [free men]. Between the whole [of them there are] 56 acres. [There have]

always [been] 1½ ploughs and 2 acres of meadow. Then and afterwards it was worth 60s.; now 100[s.] And the free men men [sic] are worth 6s. And it is 6 furlongs in length and 5 in breadth. And [it renders] 6d. of the geld. [There is] 1 church, 15 [acres], and it is worth 2s. In Mulbarton the same holds. [There was] 1 free man in commendation only under Stigand, 30 acres. Then [there were] 2 ploughs. And [there is] 1 acre of meadow. It has always been worth 20s.

Ralph de Beaufour

Markshall Godwine, a free man of Stigand's, held: 2 carucates. Then [there were] 12 villans; afterwards and now 11. Then [there were] 8 bordars; afterwards and now 7. Then and afterwards [there were] 2 slaves; now 1. Then [there were] 2 ploughs in demesne; afterwards 1; now 2. [There have] always [been] 5 ploughs belonging to the men. [There are] 16 acres of meadow. And [there have] always [been] 2½ mills. Now [there are] 2 horses and 4 head of cattle and 20 pigs. Then [there were] 4 sheep; now 24. And [there is] 1 free man, 8½ acres of land. [There has] always [been] half a plough. Then it was worth 100s.; afterwards £8; now £11. [There is] 1 church, 6 acres, and it is worth 12d.. And it is 6 furlongs in length and 5 in breadth. And it renders 6½d. of the geld. The king and the earl [have] the soke of the free men. In Dunston [there is] 1 free man, 6 acres, and it is in the value of Markshll

CLAVERING H[UNDRED].

"Thurketelliart" [in Aldeby] 1 free man of Stigand's held: 2 carucates. [There have] always [been] 3 villans and 12 bordars and 3 slaves. And [there are] 2 ploughs in demesne. Then [there were] 2 ploughs belonging to the men; now 1. 10. 1. [sic] [There are] 15 acres of meadow. Now [there is] 1 mill. [There has] always [been] 1 horse. Now [there are] 8 head of cattle. Then [there were] 7 pigs; now 36. Then [there were] 120 sheep; now 200. [There are] 5 hives of bees. And [there is][...] 1 church, 20 acres, and it is worth 40d. And [there are] 15 free men in fold and commendation, 40 acres. [There have] always [been] 6 ploughs and 6 acres of meadow. Then it was worth £4 and now likewise. Aldeby 1 free man of Stigand's held: 2 carucates. [There has] always [been] 1 villan and 5 bordars. Then [there were] 3 slaves; now 2. And [there have] always [been] 2 ploughs in demesne. Then [there was] 1 plough belonging to the men. [There are] 15 acres of meadow. [There is] woodland for 20 pigs. And [there has] always [been] 1 horse. And [there are] 15 free men in soke of the fold and commendation, 40 acres. Then [there were] 3 ploughs; now 2. And [there are] 2 acres of meadow. And it is worth 40s. [There is] 1 church, 12 acres, and it is worth 2s. To this manor belong 11 free men, 2½ carucates and 30 acres. Of 7 of these his [i.e., Ralph's] predecessor had the commendation TRE and Stigand 4. And it was delivered to his predecessor for land. [There have] always [been] 12 bordars and 5½ ploughs and 24 acres of meadow. [There is] woodland for 6 pigs. Then it was worth 33s.; now £6 and 10s. The whole is 1 league in length and half [a league] in breadth. And [it renders] 2s. 1½d. of the geld, whoever may[...]hold [there]. In

Norton [Subcourse] [there were] 2 free men in commendation TRE, 23 acres. Then [there was] 1 plough and 1 acre of meadow. And it is worth 2s. In Raveningham [there is] 1 sokeman, 1 acre, and it is worth 2d.

In Toft [Monks] [there is] 1 sokeman, 10½ acres, and it is worth 12d.

The Lands of Reginald fitzIvo.

H[UNDRED] OF CLACKCLOSE.

In Fincham 1 free man [held] TRE 16 acres of land. And [there is] 1 acre of meadow. [There have] always [been] 2 bordars. And it is worth 2s. This land Wihenoc appropriated. In Barton [Bendish] Toli, 1 free man, [held] 6 carucates of land TRE. Then [there were] 6 villans and afterwards [and] now 7. [There have] always [been] 5 bordars. Then [there were] 5 slaves; now 2. [There are] 12 acres of meadow. [There have] always [been] 2 ploughs in demesne. Then and afterwards [there was] 1 plough belonging to the men; now half [a plough]. 5 free men belong to this manor in soke [and] in commendation only and 2 with every customary due. Those 5 have 1 plough. And [there are] 12 acres of meadow. And those 2 [held] 6 acres of land in demesne when he received it. [There were] 60 sheep [then] and now. Then [there were] 11 pigs;

[Folio 230v: NORFOLK]

now 15. Then the whole was worth 80s.; afterwards and now 60. And 5 men were worth 10s. In the same vill Thorkil, 1 free man, [held] 3 carucates TRE. [There have] always [been] 6 villans and 5 bordars. Then and afterwards [there were] 5 slaves; now 2. [There are] 20 acres of meadow. Then [there were] 3 ploughs in demesne; afterwards none; now 2. [There has] always [been] 1 plough belonging to the men. And [there are] 60 sheep and 7 pigs. 5 free men belong to this manor in soke only and they have 30 acres of land. Then [there was] 1 plough; now a half. And [there are] 8 acres of meadow and 4 acres of woodland. Then the whole was worth £10; afterwards 60s.; now 85[s.] And [there are] 5 free men. [They are worth] 42s. 8d. In Barton [Bendish] Ketil, a free man, held TRE 1 carucate. Then [there were] 2 ploughs in demesne [There have] always [been] 4 villans and 2 bordars and 20 acres of meadow. Then [there were] 2 ploughs in demesne; afterwards none; now 1. [There has] always [been] [1] plough belonging to the men. Then it was worth 40s.; afterwards and now 30[s.] The whole of this manor is 1 league in length; in breadth half a league and 3 furlongs . When the whole of this Hundred renders 20s. of the geld, the whole of this vill [renders] 16d.

In Crimplesham Æthelgyth, a free woman, held TRE 2 carucates. [There have] always [been] 8 villans and 4 bordars and 7 slaves. And [there are] 8 acres of meadow. Then in demesne [there were] 3 ploughs; afterwards 3; now 4. [There has] always [been] 1 fishery and 1 horse. [There are] 2 head of cattle. Then [there were] 2 pigs. Then [there were] 240 sheep; now 300. To this manor belong 20 free men in soke and commendation at 60 acres. Then [there were] 1½ ploughs; now 1. In the same vill Thorkil holds 1 carucate. [There has] always [been] 1 bordar and 1 slave. And [there are] 8 acres of

meadow and half a fishery. [There was] 1 plough. 5 free men also belong at 4 acres in soke and commendation only. The whole of this was always worth £8. In Crimplesham [there were] 3 free men at 1 carucate. [There have] always [been] 4 bordars and 12 acres of meadow. From these he has commendation and the customary due[s]. Then it was worth 16s.; now 8[s.] In Toombers [there are] 3 free men in soke of the fold and commendation. Others [are in] the soke of St Benedict [of Ramsey]. It has always been worth 14d. [There is] 1 free man, 40 acres, and it is worth 2s. The whole of Crimplesham is 1 league in length and a half [a league] in breadth. And it renders 8d. of 20s. of the king's geld, whoever may hold there. Wereham: 2 carucates Toli, a free man, held TRE. Then [there were] 15 villans; afterwards and now 11. [There have] always [been] 8 bordars. Then [there were] 6 slaves; now 4. And [there are] 20 acres of meadow. [There is] woodland for 12 pigs. [There have] always [been] 2 ploughs in demesne. Then [there were] 1½ ploughs belonging to the men; now 1. [There has] always [been] half a mill and 1 fishery. [There has] always [been] 1 horse and 28 mares and 25 hens and 2 head of cattle. Then [there were] 15 pigs; now 7. Then [there were] 90 sheep; now 260. And it is worth 100s. but it used to render £8 with every customary due. To this manor belong 4 free men at 12 acres. In Stoke [Ferry] [there are] 4 free men in commendation and every customary due at 12 acres. And [there is] 1 free man at 2 acres. In the same [vill] Roger and Hugh hold 2 sokemen at 74 acres. [There have] always [been] 1½ [?ploughs]. And [there are] 10 acres of meadow. The whole of this is worth 20s. The whole of Wereham is half a league in length and in breadth. And it renders 6½d. of 20s. of the king's geld. Upwell Toli, a free man, held TRE: a carucate.

Reginald fitzIvo

[Folio 231: NORFOLK]

[There have] always [been] 9 villans and 5 bordars. Then [there were] 6 slaves; afterwards and now 2. And [there are] 8 acres of meadow. [There have] always [been] 2 ploughs in demesne. Then [there were] 2 ploughs belonging to the men; afterwards and now 1. And [there is] 1 fishery. [There has] always [been] 1 horse and 2 head of cattle. Then [there were] 12 pigs; now 7. Then [there were] 80 sheep; now 160. It has always been worth £6 but it used to render £8. To this manor belong 17 free men at 64 acres of land. Then [there were] 1½ ploughs; now 1. And it is worth 13s. 4d. Those Wihenoc appropriated. The whole of Upwell is 1 league in length and in breadth. And it renders 2s. of 20s. of the king's geld.

Boughton Thorkil held TRE. Now Ranulf holds [it]. [There has] always [been] carucate and 24 acres. And [there are] 5 villans. Then [there were] 2 slaves. [There have] always [been] 10 acres of meadow. And [there is] 1 plough in demesne. [There has] always [been] 1 horse and 4 head of cattle and 8 pigs. [There are] 126 sheep. To this manor belong 5 sokemen at 12 acres and the same man holds [them]. Then it was worth 40s.; now 62[s.] 6d. The whole of Boughton is 5 furlongs in length and 4 in breadth. And it renders 8d. of 20s. of the king's geld. Shouldham [All Saints and St Margaret] the same Thorkil held TRE: 1 carucate and 6 acres. Now Ranulf holds [it]. Then [there were] 3 villans; now 5. Then [there were] 7 bordars; now 7. [There have] always [been] 3 slaves. Then and afterwards [there were] 2 ploughs in demesne; now 1. Now [there is] half a plough belonging to the men. [There is] woodland for 20 pigs. [There are] 6 acres of meadow. Then [there was] 1 horse. Then [there were] 4 head of cattle; now 6. Then [there were] 16 pigs; now 3. Then [there were] 120 sheep; now 126. And [there are] 3 hives of bees and half a fishery. To this manor belong 2 sokemen at 10. Then it was worth 60s.; now 40[s.] 6d. To this also belonged 10 free men at 30 acres TRE in commendation only and the same man holds [them]. [There has] always [been] half a plough and 2 acres of meadow. Then it was worth 6s.; now 16[s.] These Wihenoc appropriated. In Beechamwell 1 free man held TRE 24 acres. This [man] Wihenoc appropriated. And his predecessor

[Folio 231v: NORFOLK]

Heremann had the commendation only. And it renders 5s. In Fodderstone [there was] half a carucate TRE. Now Ranulf holds [it]. [There has] always [been] half a plough and 1 bordar. And it is worth 10s. This Wihenoc appropriated. In Upwell [there is] 1 bordar. In [Shouldham] Thorpe [there is] 1 sokeman, 2 acres, and it is worth 3d.

H[UNDRED] AND A HALF OF FREEBRIDGE.

In West Winch Godwine, a free man, held 2 carucates TRE. Now the same man holds [it]. [There have] always [been] 14 villans and 6 bordars. Then [there were] 4 slaves; now 1. And [there are] 20 acres of meadow. [There have] always [been] 2 ploughs in demesne and half [a plough] belonging to the men. And [there are] 2 salt-pans. [There have] always [been] 10 head of cattle and 19 pigs. [There are] 80 sheep. To this manor belong 23 sokemen, 36 acres of land and the same man holds [them]. [There has] always [been] half a plough and 4 acres of meadow. Then it was worth £3, afterwards 100s.; now £10. Ashwicken Leofric, a free man, held: 2 carucates TRE. Now Roger holds [it]. Then [there were] 12 villans; now 7. [There have] always [been] 3 bordars and 2 slaves. And [there are] 20 acres of meadow. Then [there were] 2 ploughs in demesne; now 1. Then [there was] 1 plough belonging to the men; now half [a plough]. Here belong 7 sokemen, 12 acres of land, and the same man holds [them]. And [there are] 2 acres of meadow. [There has] always [been] half a plough. Then [there were] 5 head of cattle. Then [there were] 7 pigs.; now 5. Then [there were] 200 sheep; now 300. Then [there was] half a salt-pan. Then it was worth £4; now 40s. And 1 plough can be restored. The whole is 6 furlongs in length and 3 in breadth. And it renders 6d. of a 20s. geld, whoever may hold there.

In [Great or Little] Massingham Wulfmær, a free man, held 60 acres of land TRE. Now Ralph holds [them]. [There have] always [been] 4 villans. Then [there was] 1 plough; now half [a plough]. And it is worth 13s. 4d.

H[UNDRED] OF GRIMSHOE.

In Stanford 2 free men held 14 acres of land and they were delivered to Wihenoc. Now Ralph holds [them]. [There has] always [been] half a plough. And it is worth 2s. 8d.

H[UNDRED] OF GREENOE.

In Caldecote a certain free man held

Reginald fitzIvo

[Folio 232: NORFOLK]

half a carucate TRE. Then [there were] 2 villans and 1 free man at 5 acres under him. Then and always [there has been] half a plough and 1½ acres of meadow and 1 mill. Then it was worth 3s.; now 5s. And this land a certain free man held but after the king came to this land, Wihenoc occupied it. Thus R[eginald] holds it and the king has the soke and sake. In the same vill [there were] 3 free men holding 50 acres and they have half a plough. And it is worth 3s. And he holds them in the same manner. Cleythorpe Toli held TRE. Now Arnold holds. Then and afterwards [there were] 6 villans; now 1. And [there are] 2 bordars. [There have] always [been] 3 slaves. Then and afterwards [there were] 2 ploughs; now 1. Then [there was] 1 plough belonging to the men and afterwards [and] now half [a plough]. [There is] woodland for 16 pigs. [There are] 2 [acres] of meadow. When it was received, [there was] 1 horse. Now [there are] 15 wild mares. Then [there were] 20 pigs; now 11. Then [there were] 100 sheep; now 300. And the same man holds 3 sokemen, 20 acres. And [there has] always [been] half a plough. And of these 3 the king has the soke. Then it was worth 60s.; now 40[s.] A certain free man [...]. In [North or South] Pickenham the same man [i.e., Reginald] holds 30 acres of land. And after the king came to the country Earl R[alph] held that land. But a man of Wihenoc's loved a certain woman on that land and he took her [in marriage] and afterwards he held that land in W[ihenoc's] fief without the king's grant and without livery [to him] and his successors [also]. [There has] always [been] half a plough and 1 bordar and 1 acre of woodland and 2½ acres of meadow. It has always been worth 3s. In Houghton [on the Hill] 1 free man, at 16 acres and it is worth 16d. This man Wihenoc appropriated. In [North or South] Pickenham Wihenoc has appropriated 15 acres and it is worth 16d. This Ralph de Tosny has claimed; the Hundred testifies [to it].

WAYLAND H[UNDRED].

Panworth Harold held TRE: 1½ ploughs. Now the same man [i.e., Reginald] holds [it]. Then and afterwards [there were] 6 villans; now 8 bordars. Then and afterwards [there were] 4 slaves; now 2. [There are] 10 acres of meadow. [There have] always [been] 2 ploughs in demesne and half a plough belonging to the men. [There is] woodland for 100 pigs. And [then there was] 1 horse; now 2.

[There have] always [been] 6 head of cattle. Then [there were] 35 pigs; now 22. Then [there were] 27 sheep; now 60. And [there are] 3 hives of bees, and 7 sokemen, half a carucate and 16 acres.

[There have] always [been] 1½ ploughs.

It has always been worth 40s.

[Folio 232v: NORFOLK]

In Ashill the same man holds 15 [sokemen], 1 carucate and 8 acres. The soke is the king's in Saham [Toney]. [There have] always [been] 3 villans and 3 bordars. Then [there was] 1 slave. And [there are] 6 acres of meadow. [There have] always [been] 6½ ploughs. [There is] woodland for 100 pigs. It has always been worth 30s. The whole is half a league in length and half in breadth. And of the geld [it renders] 15d. In Threxton [there were] 8 free men, 3 carucates and 28 acres TRE. Now Ranulf holds [it]. And [there are] 2 bordars, 20 acres of meadow. Then [there were] 6 ploughs; afterwards 4; now 2½. And there could be 3 ploughs. This has been handed over for one carucate. Then it was worth £4 10s. Now it is worth 60s.

LAUNDITCH H[UNDRED].

Sutton [near Mileham] Olof, a certain woman, held TRE for a manor: two carucates. Now Boteric holds [it]. Then and afterwards [there were] 16 villans; now 10. [There have] always [been] 2 slaves and 10 acres of meadow. Then [there was] woodland for 200 pigs; now 100. Then [there was] 1 plough in demesne; afterwards half [a plough]; [now] 1½ ploughs. Then [there were] 3 ploughs belonging to the men; afterwards and now 1; and half a plough could be restored. Then [there were] 5 pigs; now likewise. Then [there were] 120 [sheep]; now 100. Stigand held this in Mileham. Then it was worth 40s.; now 80[s.] And it is half a league in length and 5 furlongs in breadth. And [it renders] 5d. of the geld.

MITFORD H[UNDRED].

In Yaxham Æthelgyth held TRE 4 acres of woodland. And [there is] 1 acre of meadow. And it is worth 12d.

H[UNDRED] OF GALLOW.

Pensthorpe Skuli held TRE: 2 carucates.

Now Ranulf holds [it]. [There have] always [been] 13 bordars and 2 slaves. [There has] always [been] in demesne 2 ploughs.; now 1. [There is] woodland for 12 pigs. [There are] 3 acres of meadow, 1 mill. Then [there was] 1 horse; now likewise. [There have] always [been] 4 head of cattle. Then [there were] 20 pigs; now 60. [There have] always [been] 240 sheep. Now [there are] 4 hives of bees. Then it was worth 40s.; now likewise. And it is 4 furlongs in length and 3 in breadth. And [it renders] 6d. in geld.

Reginald fitzIvo

[Folio 233: NORFOLK]

H[UNDRED] OF BROTHERCROSS.

In [East or West] Raynham TRE Bondi held. [There were] 4 free men. Now Boteric holds [them]. And Harold [held] 1. Now Rainald [holds it] at half a carucate. [There has] always [been] 1 plough [There are] 3 acres of meadow. Then it was worth 10s.; now 5[s.] And the sheriff claims Harold's man to be in Fakenham and the Hundred testifies [to this].

H[UNDRED] OF HOLT.

In Wiveton Thorkil held 2 carucates TRE; now the same man [i.e., Reginald] [holds them]. [There have] always [been] 7 villans and 27 bordars. [There have] always [been] in demesne 2 ploughs. Then belonging to the men [there were] 5 ploughs; now 3½. [There are] 4 acres of meadow, 1½ mills. Now [there are] 3 head of cattle. Then [there were] 15 pigs; now 28. Then [there were] 107 sheep; now 80. Then and afterwards [it was worth] 40s.; now £6. And it is in length 1 league and [1 league] in breadth. And [it renders] 17½d. in geld.

GREENHOE H[UNDRED].

[Great or Little] Walsingham Ketil, 1 free man, held TRE. [There have] always [been] 19 bordars, 1 plough, 2 carucates. Then [there were] 2 slaves; now 1. [There are] 2 acres of meadow. Then and afterwards [there were] 2 ploughs in demesne; now 3. [There is] woodland for 8 pigs. [There were] 3 horses when he received [it]. [Then there were] 2 head of cattle; now 1. Then [there were] 15 [pigs]; afterwards [and] now 19. [There have] always [been] 120 sheep. 24 sokemen belong to this vill, 60 and 10 acres of land, 2 bordars and half a mill. Then [there were] 3 ploughs and when he received it and now 1½ ploughs. Then it was worth £6; now likewise. And it is half a league in length and half [a league] in breadth. And [it renders] 18d. of the geld. And the other [Great or Little] Walsingham Ketil held TRE: 2 carucates. [There have] always [been] 4 villans. Then [there were] 21 bordars; [now] 18. [There have] always [been] 2 slaves. Then [there were] 2 ploughs in demesne and when he received [it] 1; now 2. [Then there were 2] ploughs belonging to the men and afterwards 1; now 1. [There is] woodland for 6 pigs, 1 acre of meadow, 1 mill. [There are] 5 sokemen, 14 acres of land, 1 mill. Then [there was] half a plough and now. When he received [it], [there were] 5 horses ; now 4. [There have] always [been] 5 [...]. Then [there were] 12 pigs; now 14. [There have] always [been] 80 sheep. Then [there were] 6 hives of bees; now 2. Then [it was worth] £4; now 100s. And it is 1 league in length and half [a league] in breadth. [It renders] 24d. of the geld, whoever may hold there. StiVkey Ketil held TRE: 2 carucates; now Ran[ulf] holds [it]. [There have] always [been] 16 bordars. Then [there were] 3 [slaves], [afterwards] 1 slave; now 3. [There are] 3 acres of meadow. Then [there were] 2 ploughs in demesne and [there has] always [been] 1 plough belonging to the men. [There were] 2 mills then; now 1

[Folio 233v: NORFOLK]

When he received it, [there were] 3 horses; now 4. And now [there are] 5 head of cattle. When he received [it, there were] 30 pigs and now 12. And when he received [it, there were] 180 sheep and now 240. [holds] 6 sokemen belonging to this vill, 5 acres of land. [There has] always [been] half a carucate. To this manor have been added 4 sokemen. The same man holds through livery of the king 1½ carucates. [There are] 7 bordars. [There have] always [been] 3 ploughs. [There are] 2 acres of meadow and 1½ mills. Then the same vill was worth £4 and these 4 men rendered 40s. and now likewise. And it is half a league in length and half [a league] in breadth. And [it renders] 24d. of the geld. [There is] 1 church, 30 acres, and it is worth 2s.

LODDON H[UNDRED].

Carleton [St Peter] Ælfric, a free man under King E[dward], held for 30 acres of land. Then [there were] 7 bordars; afterwards 6; now 4. [There have] always [been] 1½ ploughs. Then [there were] 2 ploughs belonging to the men; afterwards 1½; now 1. Then [there were] 14 pigs; now 3. Now [there are] 60 sheep. And 14 free men in the commendation of Wulfsige have been handed over to complete this manor at 60 acres. Then [there were] 2 ploughs; afterwards and now 1. And [there are] 5 acres of meadow. And here there is free land of the church, 80 acres. Then it was worth 20s.; now 40[s.] It is 1 league in length, 4 furlongs in breadth. And of the geld [it renders] 8d.

H[UNDRED] OF EYNSFORD.

Whitwell Ketil, 1 free man, held TRE: 2 carucates and 15 acres for a manor. Then and afterwards [there were] 8 villans; now 7. [There have] always [been] 17 bordars. Then and afterwards [there were] 4 slaves; now 2. [There have] always [been] 2 ploughs in demesne. Then [and] afterwards [there were] 6 ploughs belonging to the men; afterwards and now 4. And [there are] 14 acres of meadow. [There is] woodland for 80 pigs. [Then there were] 3 mills; now 2. And [there is] half a fishery. When he received [it there were] 2 horses; now 1. [There have] always [been] 6 head of cattle. Then [there were] 80 pigs; now 34. Then [there were] 50 sheep; now 60. [There have] always [been] 20 goats. Then [there were] 6 hives of bees; now 12. And [there are] 2 free men, half a carucate. Then and afterwards [there were] 1½ ploughs; now 1. And [there are] 3 acres of meadow. And [there are] 2 free men, half a carucate. [There has] always [been] 1 plough. And [there are] 2 acres of meadow. [There is] woodland for 5 pigs. Then it was worth £4; now £6 16d. Those 2 free men are worth 6s. And it is 1 league in length and half [a league] in breadth. And it renders 5d. in a geld of the Hundred's of 20s. In [Great or Little] Witchingham

Reginald fitzIvo

[Folio 234: NORFOLK]

Ketil, 1 free man, held TRE half a carucate and [...] 3 acres. Now Boteric holds [it]. [There has] always [been] 1 villan and 10 bordars. [There has] always [been] 1 plough [...] in demesne and 1 plough belonging to the men. And [there are] 3 acres of meadow. [There has] always [been] 1 mill. [There have] always [been] 4 head of cattle and 6 pigs. [...] Then and afterwards it was worth 20s. and now 30s. Haveringland Godwine, 1 free man, held TRE: 1 carucate. Then [and] afterwards [there were] 3 villans; now 2. [There have] always [been] 3 bordars. Now [there are] 3 slaves. [There have] always [been] 2 ploughs in demesne. Then [there was] 1 plough belonging to the men and afterwards and now half [a plough]. And [there are] 8 acres of meadow. [There is] woodland for 30 pigs and half a fishery. [There have] always [been] 2 horses and 5 head of cattle. Then [there were] 30 pigs;

now 20. Then [there were] 40 sheep; now 80. [There have] always [been] [...] goats and 20 hives of bees. And [there are] 3 sokemen, 5 acres of land. It has always been worth 60s. [There is] a church, 10 acres.

In the same [vill] Godwine held TRE 100 acres of land. [There have] always [been] 2 villans. Then and afterwards [there were] 3 bordars; now none. Then [there was] 1 plough in demesne; afterwards and now none. [There has] always [been] 1 plough belonging to the men. And [there are] 8 acres of meadow. [There is] woodland for 20 pigs. And [there is] 1 sokeman, 11 acres of land. It has always been worth 20s. In the same [vill] Eadric, 1 free man, held TRE 100 acres of land. Now Herluin holds [them]. [There have] always [been] 3 bordars. Then [there was] 1 slave. Then [there was] 1 plough in demesne; afterwards none; now 1. And [there are] 2 sokemen, 16 acres of land. And [there are] 16 acres of meadow. [There has] always [been] half a plough. [There is] woodland for 20 pigs. Now [there are] 4 horses and 7 head of cattle and 8 pigs and 85 sheep. It has always been worth 20s. In the same [vill] Ulfkil held TRE half a carucate; now Ran[ulf] holds [it]. Then [there were] 4 bordars; afterwards and now 3. Then [there was] 1 plough in demesne; afterwards and now half [a plough]. And [there are] 6 acres of meadow. [There is] woodland for 40 pigs. And it is worth 20s. And it is 1 league in length and in breadth. And it renders 7d. to the king's geld. In [Wood] Norton St Edmund held TRE 2 carucates. [There have] always [been] 8 villans. Then [there were] 8 bordars; now 16. [There has] always [been] 1 plough in demesne. Then and afterwards [there were] 3 ploughs belonging to the men; now 2. And [there are] 8 acres of meadow. [There is] woodland for 30 pigs. [There have] always [been] 6 head of cattle and 6 pigs and 12 goats. Then and afterwards it was worth 20s.; now 30[s.] [...]

H[UNDRED] OF TAVERHAM.

In Felthorpe Godwine held 20 acres. [There has] always [been] 1 villan and 8 bordars. [There has] always [been] half a plough. And [there are] 2 acres of meadow. And it is worth 10s. This belongs to Haveringland.

H[UNDRED] OF SOUTH ERPINGHAM.

Scottow Ketil held TRE: 2 carucates

[Folio 234v: NORFOLK]

and ½ of land. Now [...] Roger holds [it]. [There have] always [been] 8 bordars and 2 ploughs in demesne. [...] Then [there was] 1 plough belonging to the men and now likewise. And [there are] 6 acres of meadow. [There is] woodland for 5 pigs [...] and a third part of a mill. Then [there were] 3 pigs; now 4. And [there are] 20 sheep and 3 hives of bees. And [there are] 6 sokemen, 42 acres of land. [There have] always [been] 3 ploughs. Then it was worth 20s.; now 40[s.] To this manor Wihenoc added 2 sokemen of St Benet [of Hulme's] at 18 acres of land, whom the same man [i.e., Roger] holds. Then [there was] 1 plough; now half [a plough]. And they are in the same value. In Ingworth 1 free man of Harold's [held] half a carucate, which the same man holds. [There have] always [been] 6 bordars and 1 plough in demesne and 1 plough belonging to the men. And [there are] 2 sokemen, 4 acres. And [there are] 2 acres of meadow. [There are] 5 pigs and half a mill and 30 sheep. And it is worth 15s. And it is 10 furlongs in length and 8 in breadth. And [it renders] 13d. of the geld.

In Thurton [in Witchingham] Herluin holds half a carucate. [There have] always [been] 5 bordars and 1 slave. And [there is] 1 plough in demesne and half [a plough] belonging to the men. [There are] 4 acres of meadow. And it is worth 10s. In the same [vill] the same man held 2 sokemen of Harold's from Cawston, 60 acres of land and 2 bordars. [There has] always [been] 1 plough. And [there are] 3 acres of meadow. And it is worth 12s. And it is half a league and half in breadth. And [it renders] 7d. of the geld. In BANNINGHAM Roger holds 1 villan from Cawston, 16 acres. It is worth 2s. Wihenoc appropriated this. And the same villan used to render 5s. to Cawston.

TUNSTEAD H[UNDRED].

In Sloley the same man holds 20 acres, which Skiotr held in the demesne of Scottow. [There has] always [been] 1 villan. And it is in the value of Scottow. In Worstead the same man holds 3 acres and [it is] in the same value. All the churches are in the value with the manors.

H[UNDRED] OF NORWICH.

Ewicmann held TRE 1½ carucates under Stigand. And [there are] 16 acres of pasture and 7 acres of meadow. Now Reginald fitzIvo [holds it]. Then and afterwards [there was] 1 plough; now 2. And [there are] 100 sheep. It has always been worth 30s.

[Folio 235: NORFOLK]

The land of Ralph de Tosny.

H[UNDRED] OF GREENHOE.

Necton Ralph holds, which Harold held TRE. Then and always [there were] 32 villans and 11 bordars and 6 slaves. And [there are] 4 ploughs in demesne and 10 belonging to the men. [There is] woodland for 1000 pigs. [There are] 20 acres of meadow and 1 mill and 1 salt-pan. When he received [it, there were] 4 horses. And now [there are] 19 head of cattle and 100 pigs and 100 sheep and 85 goats. [There is] 1 church at 36 acres and it is worth 36d. And 4 sokemen dwell there. They have 5 ploughs. And it is in length 1 mile and half [a mile] in breadth. And it renders in geld 9d. when the Hundred pays 20s. And [there is] 1 sokeman in [East or West] Bradenham. [There have] always [been] half a carucate and 1 plough. And under him [there are] 8 sokemen holding half a carucate. And [there has] always [been] 1 plough. [There is] woodland for 20 pigs. [There are] 4 acres of meadow. And in [North or South] Pickenham [there is] 1 berewick, 2 ploughs in demesne. Then and afterwards [there were] 8 villans; now 5. Now [there are] 2 bordars. Then and afterwards belonging to the men [there was] 1 plough; now half [a plough]. And 6 sokemen on 20 acres have 1 plough. [There is] woodland for 20 pigs. [There are] 4 acres of meadow. When he received [it], he found 2 horses and 18 pigs and 36 sheep and now [likewise].

And [there is] another berewick which they call [Great]

Cressingham. Then and always [there were] 5 villans and 1 bordar and 2 slaves. [There is] 1 plough in demesne. And [there are] 2 sokemen. Between [them] all [there are] 2 ploughs. [There is] woodland for 8 pigs. [There are] 3 acres of meadow, 1 mill, 1 fishery. [There have] always [been] 1 horse and 2 head of cattle. [There are] 60 sheep less 2. In Little Cressingham [there is] another berewick. [There have] always [been] 20 villans and 7 bordars, 4 slaves. [There have been] 2 ploughs in demesne always and belonging to the men 6 ploughs. And 6 sokemen held 2 ploughs and hold [them now]. [There are] 10 acres of meadow, 1 mill. When he received [it, there were] 2 horses. And now [there are] 31 pigs, 32 sheep, 6 head of cattle. And it is in length 1 mile and half [a mile] in breadth. And it renders in geld 3d.

In Caldecote [there is] another berewick where the king has soke and sake, 1 carucate. [There have] always [been] 2 villans, 2 bordars, 1 slave and 3 sokemen. Then in demesne [there was] 1 plough; now half [a plough]. [There is] 1 plough belonging to the men. When he received [it], [there was] 1 horse and 60 sheep,

[Folio 235v: NORFOLK]

now 24 sheep. And it is in length half a league and 4 furlongs in breadth. And it renders in geld with those holding in the same [vill] 5d.

In Custthorpe [there are] 3 sokemen over whom the king used to hold soke and sake. And it has 1 carucate and 1 plough and 1 bordar.

In Bodney [there are] 4 sokemen, 1 carucate, and 1 plough and 1 villan, 2 acres of meadow. And over them the king has soke and sake. And from 1 mill [it renders] 8d. The whole of this together used to render to H[arold] 6 nights' farm. Now it renders £60 pounds in weight. H[undred] of Grimshoe.

In Sturston 1 free man holds 30 acres of land. Then [there was] half a plough. Then it was worth 2s.; now 12d.

WAYLAND H[UNDRED].

In Carbrooke Harold held TRE 3 carucates. [There is] a berewick in Necton. [There has] always [been] 1 plough in demesne. Then [there was] 1 villan. [There have] always [been] 13 sokemen and 1 slave. [There are] 16 acres of meadow. And [there are] 2 ploughs belonging to the men. [There is] woodland for 300 pigs. Then [there was] 1 horse and 3 cows and 9 pigs. And it is in the value of Necton.

LAUNDITCH H[UNDRED].

In [Great or Little] Fransham [there were] 16 sokemen of Harold's TRE, 3 carucates. [There have] always [been] 12 bordars. And [there are] 6 acres of meadow. Then [there were] 3 ploughs; now 4. [There is] woodland for 60 pigs. [There has] always [been] 1 mill. And it is in the value of Necton. Eudo fitzClamahoc had 1 carucate from these 3 by livery as long as he lived and Ralph de Beaufour held the same [vill]. Now Ralph de Tosny has it in Necton where it belonged TRE.

In [Great or Little] Dunham [there was] 1 sokeman of Harold's, 30 acres of land TRE. [There have] always [been] 4 bordars. [There has] always [been] 1 plough. And this is in the value of Necton.

In Godwick 1 free [man] of King E[dward's] held TRE 1

carucate. [There have] always [been] 6 villans and 7 bordars and 9 acres of meadow. [There have] always [been] 2 ploughs. [There is] woodland for 200 pigs. And [there is] 1 sokeman, 4 acres of land. And it is in the value of Necton. And it is 6 furlongs

Ralph de Tosny

in length and 4 in breadth. And [it renders] 6½d. of the geld. This land Ralph held in Necton but it did not belong to Necton TRE nor in the time of Harold. And Roger Bigod claims it by gift of the king and vouches the livery officer.

H[UNDRED] OF CLACKCLOSE.

In Shingham [there were] 2 free men of H[arold's], 80 acres of land TRE. Then [there was] 1 plough; now half [a plough]. And they belong to Necton.

H[UNDRED] AND A HALF OF FREEBRIDGE.

In [East] Walton [there are] 2 sokemen in [Castle or West] Acre, 30 acres and 5 bordars. And it is in the value of Necton. [Castle or West] Acre Harold held TRE, a berewick in Necton, 3 carucates. [There have] always [been] 6 villans and 8 bordars and 2 slaves. And [there are] 4 acres of meadow. [There have] always [been] 2 ploughs in demesne and 1[...] plough belonging to the men. [There is] woodland for 40 pigs and 3½ mills and 1 fishery [...] and 5 salt-pans. [There have] always [been] 5 head of cattle and 18 pigs. Then [there were] 100 sheep; now 165. To this land has always belonged 17 sokemen, 405 acres of land and 14 bordars. And [there are] 2 acres of meadow. [There have] always [been] 5 ploughs. In the same [vill] Thorbiorn held under Harold 2 carucates TRE. Then [there were] 13 bordars and now [likewise]. And [there are] 4 acres of meadow. Then [there were] 2 ploughs in demesne; now 1½. Then [and] afterwards [there was] 1 plough belonging to the men; now [there are] 2 oxen. [There has] always [been] 1 mill. To this land belong 4 sokemen, 30 acres. [There has] always [been] half a plough. Also [there is] 1 free man in [Gayton] Thorpe, 60 acres and 3 bordars and half a plough. And in Necton [there are] 3 sokemen, 60 acres of land and 1 bordar. And [there are] 3 acres of meadow. And [there is] 1 plough. And in [South] Lynn [there are] 5 sokemen, 80 acres of land, and 3 bordars and 5 salt-pans and 2 ploughs. And in East Winch [there are] 2 sokemen, 8 acres of land. [...] The whole of [CASTLE or WEST] ACRE is 1 league in length and breadth.]. And it renders 16d. of a 20s. geld. The whole of this above is in the value of Necton.

H[UNDRED] OF GRIMHOE.

In Icburgh [there was] 1 sokeman of Harold's, 30

acres of land. And it has been valued in Necton.

WAYLAND H[UNDRED].

In Breckles [there was] 1 [man] of Harold's, 40 acres of land and half a plough and 1 villan. And it is in the value of Necton.

H[UNDRED] OF SHROPHAM

Harold held [East or West] Wretham TRE: 2 carucates. [There have] always [been] 12 villans. [There are] 8 bordars and 3 slaves and 8 acres of meadow. [There have] always [been] 2 ploughs in demesne and 4 ploughs belonging to the men. [There is] woodland for 30 pigs. And [there is] 1 horse and 12 pigs. [There are] 80 sheep. In the other [East or West] Wretham the same man held 3 carucates. [There have] always [been] 11 villans and 9 bordars and 4 slaves. And [there are] 6 acres of meadow. Then [there were] 3 ploughs in demesne; afterwards and now 2 and there could be a third. [There have] always [been] 4 ploughs belonging to the men. And [there is] 1 mill and 1 horse and 21 pigs and 81 sheep. In the other [East or West] Wretham the same man held 4 carucates [...] TRE. Then and afterwards [there were] 8 villans; afterwards and now and 3 [...]. [There have] always [been] 4 bordars and 2 slaves. And [there are] 2 acres of meadow. [There have] always [been] 2 ploughs in demesne. Then and afterwards [there were] 3 ploughs belonging to the men; and now 1. And they can be 3. And [there are] 2 acres of meadow. And 2 sokemen [hold] 1 carucate and 12 acres. [There are] 8 acres of meadow and 5 bordars and 56 acres of land and 1½ ploughs. These three are berewicks in Necton and [are] in the value. The whole is 2 leagues in length and 2 in breadth. And [it renders] 20d. of the geld.

[erasure]

H[UNDRED] OF GREENHOE.

The Lands of Hugh de Montfort.

Bondi held Bodney. Then [there were] 8 villans and afterwards 4; now [there are] 7 bordars. Then [there were] 6 slaves; now 3. Then [there were] 3 ploughs in demesne and afterwards 2; now 1. Then between the men [there were] 3 ploughs; now half [a plough]. [There is] woodland for 100 pigs. [There are] 5 acres of meadow. [There is] 1 mill and a quarter part of another. When he received [it there was] 1 horse; now 2. Then [there were] 13 head of cattle; now 3. Then [there were] 41 pigs; now 9. Then [there were] 51 sheep; now 11. Then [there were] 16 goats; now 5. And it is 1 league less 2 furlongs in length and 4 furlongs in breadth. And it renders in geld 8d. with those holding in it. Then it was worth 100s.; now 60s. Langford Bondi held TRE. Then and afterwards [there were] 21 villans; now 17. Then [there were] 9 bordars and 6 slaves and now [likewise]. [There have] always [been] 2 ploughs in demesne. Then and afterwards [there were] 4 [ploughs] belonging to the men; now 2. [There is] woodland for 100 pigs. [There are] 25 acres of meadow. [There are] 2 mills, 1 fishery. When he received it, [there were] 2 [?horses]; now none. Then [there were] 4 head of cattle; now 1. Then [there were] 17 pigs; now 9. Then [there were] 71 sheep; now 41. Now [there are] 2 hives of bees. And it is 1 mile in length and half [a mile] in breadth. And it renders in geld 4d. when the Hundred renders 20s. Then it was worth £6; now it renders 105s.

H[UNDRED] OF GALLOW.

[South] Creake Hugh holds, Bondi held: 2 carucates. [There have] always [been] 4 villans and 6 bordars. Then [there were] 4 slaves; now 2. [There have] always [been] 2 ploughs in demesne. Then [there were] 3 ploughs belonging to the men; now 2, but there can be [more] there. Then [there were] 4 horses. Then [there were] 20 pigs; now 7. Then [there were] 200 sheep; now 80. Then it was worth 60s.; £4. And it is 1 [?league] in length and another in breadth. And it renders in geld 4s.

H[UNDRED] OF BROTHERCROSS.

In Burnham the same man

holds what Bondi, a free man, held TRE: 2 carucates. [There have] always [been] 14 bordars. [There have] always [been] 2 ploughs in demesne. Then [there was] 1 plough belonging to the men

now half [a plough]. [There is] woodland for 8 pigs. . [There is] 1 mill. Then [there was] 1 salt-pan. [There have] always [been] 2 horses. Then [there were] 7 pigs; now 3. Then [there were] 100 sheep; now 20. And [there were] 7 sokemen at 60 acres of land. Then [there were] 1½ ploughs; now 1. Then it was worth £4; now likewise. In this Hundred it renders 3s. of the geld and it is measured in another [place].

In [East or West] Raynham Bondi held TRE 2 carucates. [There have] always [been] 4 villans and 14 bordars and 4 slaves. And [there are] 2 ploughs in demesne and 1 plough belonging to the men. [There is] woodland for 120 pigs. [There are] 6 acres of meadow, 2 mills, 1 salt-pan. [There have] always [been] 3 horses and 4 head of cattle and 6 pigs and 100 sheep. Then [there were] 2 hives of bees. And [there are] 14 sokemen, half a carucate, and 15 bordars. [There have] always [been] 1½ ploughs. [There are] 7 acres of meadow. [There is] 1 berewick, South Raynham, [attached] to this manor at 1 carucate. Then [there were] 5 bordars; now 4. And [there are] 2 slaves. [There has] always [been] 1 plough in demesne. Then [there was] 1 plough belonging to the men; now a half. [There are] 5 acres of meadow. [There is] 1 mill. Then [there were] 3 horses. [There have] always [been] 6 pigs.

In Helhoughton [there is] 1 sokeman at half a carucate. Then [there were] 8 bordars; now 12. [There has] always [been] 1 plough. [There are] 2 acres of meadow. Then it was worth £8 and afterwards 60s.; now £8 10s. with great diViculty. And the whole of South Raynham is 6 furlongs in length and 3 in breadth. And [it renders] 10[?d.] in geld.

NORTH ERPINGHAM H[UNDRED].

In Runton Hugh holds 1 carucate which Bondi, 1 free man, held TRE. [There have] always [been] 12 bordars. [There has] always [been] 1 plough in demesne and half a plough belonging to the men. [There is] woodland for 12 pigs. [There are] 1½ acres of meadow. [There has] always [been] 1 horse. Then [there were] 5 head of cattle and now 3. Then [there were] 5 pigs; now 7. Then [there were] 20 sheep; now 15. And [there are] 8

sokemen at 24 acres of land. [There has] always [been] 1 plough. Then
and afterwards it was worth 20s.; now 30s.

In Beeston [Regis] the same Hugh holds 1 carucate which Bondi, 1 free man, held TRE. [There have] always [been] 8 bordars.

Hugh de Montfort

[There has] always [been] 1 plough in demesne and half a plough belonging to the men. [There is] woodland for 5 pigs. [There is] 1 acre of meadow. [There has] always [been] 1 horse. Then [there were] 2 head of cattle; now [likewise]. Then [there were] 5 pigs and now 11. Then [there were] 20 goats; now 30. And [there are] 3 sokemen, 12 acres of land, and half a bordar. [There has] always [been] half a plough. Then and afterwards it was worth 20s.; now 30s.

H[UNDRED] AND A HALF OF CLACKCLOSE.

In Marham [there are] 26 sokemen whom Walter holds; St Æthelthryth [held them] TRE in soke. Then [there were] 8 bordars; now 9. Then [there were] 5 ploughs; now 4. And [there are] 6 acres of meadow. Then it was worth 80s.; afterwards 60[s.]; now 40[s.] He received this land in exchange and it has been measured in the return of St Æthelthryth.

FREEBRIDGE H[UNDRED]

and a half. In Islington Bondi held 2 carucates TRE. [There have] always [been] 8 bordars. And [there are] 15 acres of meadow. Then [there were] 2 ploughs in demesne. [There has] always [been] half a plough belonging to the men. To this manor belonged 11 sokemen. [There has] always [been] 1 carucate and 30 acres. Stigand had the soke of 5 [of these]. The whole is worth 100s. In the same [vill] the same men hold half a carucate. [There have] always [been] 4 bordars. Then [there was] 1 plough. [There have] always [been] 40 acres of meadow. And it has been assessed in the 100s. above.

Middleton [near Kings Lynn] Adelold holds, which Bondi held TRE: 2 carucates. [There have] always [been] 12 villans and 17 bordars. [There is] woodland for 4 pigs. Then [there were] 4 slaves; now 1. And [there are] 32 acres of meadow. Then [there were] 2 ploughs in demesne; now 1. [There have] always [been] 3 ploughs belonging to the men. And [there is] 1 mill and 1 fishery. Then [there were] 10 salt-pans; now 8. Then [there were] 3 head of cattle; now 5. Now [there is] 1 horse. Then [there were] 10 pigs; now 6. Then [there were] 40 sheep; now 35. Then it was worth 100s.; now £6. Here 2 sokemen belong whom the same man holds, 84 acres. Then [there was] 1 plough; now half [a plough]. And it is worth 5s. And they were able to sell their land. [West] Bilney L. [sic] Bondi held for a manor TRE: 5 carucates. [There have] always [been] 20 villans and 14 bordars

and 5 slaves. [There are] 20 acres of meadow. [There have] always [been] 2 ploughs in demesne and 3 ploughs belonging to the men. And [there are] 3 mills. [There is] woodland for 200 pigs and half a salt-pan. [There has] always [been] 1 horse and 3 head of cattle and 10 pigs and 81 sheep. Then it was worth £8; afterwards 60s.; now £6. The whole is 8 furlongs in length and 4 in breadth. And it renders 6d. of a 20s. geld.

In Gayton Roger holds 1 carucate which Bondi, a free man, held TRE. Then [there were] 6 bordars and now [there are] 3 bordars and 1 slave. And [there are] 12 acres of meadow. [There has] always [been] 1 [...] plough in demesne and half a plough belonging to the men. And [there is] half a mill. Then [there were] 3 pigs and now [likewise]. [There have] always [been] 60 sheep. And it is worth 45[s.] This is 1 berewick in [West] Bilney.

H[UNDRED] OF GRIMSHOE.

In Stanford 1 free man holds 1 carucate. [There has] always [been] 1 plough in demesne. And [there are] 7 villans and 1 bordar. [There are] 2 acres of meadow. [There has] always [been] half a plough belonging to the men. And it is worth 10s. but he himself renders 15[s.] And his [Hugh's] predecessor had no [power] over this man except for commendation only. And the king [has] the soke.

In Buckenham [Tofts] [there was] 1 free man TRE, 1 carucate. [There have] always [been] 4 villans and 1 bordar. And [there are] 4 acres of meadow. And [there is] 1 plough in demesne and half a plough belonging to the men. [There is] half a mill. And [it is worth] 8s. It is 1 league in length and half [a league] in breadth. And it renders 8d. of a 20s. geld. The king and the earl have the soke.

H[UNDRED] OF GUILTCROSS.

In 'Wick' [in Garboldisham] Guthmund held 2 carucates TRE for a manor. Then [there were] 7 villans; afterwards and now 4. [There have] always [been] 4 bordars. Then [there were] 3 slaves; afterwards and now 2. And [there are] 3 acres of meadow. [There have] always [been] 2 ploughs in demesne and 1 plough belonging to the men. [There is] woodland for 12 pigs.

And [there are] 7 sokemen, 90 acres of land, 5 bordars and 1 acre of meadow. Then and afterwards

Hugh de Montfort

[Folio 239: NORFOLK]

[there were] 2½ ploughs; now 3. [There has] always [been] 1 horse. Then [there were] 3 head of cattle. Now [there are] 2 pigs. [There have] always [been] 70 sheep. Then and afterwards [it was worth] 60s.; now £6. The whole is 1 league in length and 1 league in breadth. And [it renders] 34½d. of the geld.

LAUNDITCH H[UNDRED].

Ralph holds Gateley, which Bondi, a free man, held TRE for a manor: 4 carucates. [There have] always [been] 23 villans. Then [there was] 1 slave. [There are] 30 acres of meadow. [There have] always [been] 2 ploughs in demesne. Then and afterwards [there were] 6 ploughs belonging to the men; now

4. Then [there was] woodland for 300 pigs; now 80. [There have] always [been] 2 horses. Then [there were] 7 head of cattle; now 5. Then [there were] 23 pigs; now 7. Now [there are] 29 sheep. Then [there were] 60 goats; now 17. And [there are] 5 sokemen, 30 acres of land. And [there are] 4 acres of meadow. [There has] always [been] 1 plough. Then and afterwards it was worth 110s.; now £4. The whole is half a league in length and half in breadth. And [it renders] 10d. of the geld.

H[UNDRED] OF HOLT.

In Bodham RALPH holds 2 carucates which Bondi, a free man, held TRE for a manor. Then [there were] 17 villans; now 4 and 4 bordars. Then [there were] 2 ploughs in demesne and afterwards 1; now 1. Then [there were] 2 [ploughs] belonging to the men; now none. [There are] 2 acres of meadow. [There has] always [been] 1 horse and 3 head of cattle. Then [there were] 5 pigs. [There have] always [been] 17 goats. And [there are] 2 sokemen at 30 acres of land. [There has] always [been] half a plough. Then it was worth 20s.; now 10s. And it is 10 furlongs in length and 5 in breadth. And [it renders] 12d. in geld.

[Folio 239v: NORFOLK]

XXIIII. The Lands of Eudo the Steward.

SHROPHAM H[UNDRED].

In [All Saints or St Andrew] Rockland Richard holds 10 free men, 1 carucate. [There has] always [been] 1 bordar. And [there are] 3 acres of meadow. [There is] woodland for 4 pigs. Then [there were] 4 ploughs; afterwards 2; now 3. [There is] an eighth part of a mill. Then it was worth 100s.; afterwards and now 40[s.] The soke belonged TRE to Buckenham [near Attleborough], the king's [manor] and afterwards while Lisois [de Moutiers] had the land. And the Hundred testifies to this.

In Shropham [there are] 8 free men, 1½ carucates. Roland holds [it]. And [there is] 6 [acres] of meadow. [There is] woodland for 6 pigs. Then [there were] 3 ploughs; afterwards and now 2. Then it was worth 60s.; now 37[s.] The soke [is] in Buckenham [near Attleborough], the king's [manor], but Lisois kept it and Eudo likewise.

In Roudham Ralph holds. [There are] 8 free men, 1 carucate and 10 acres. And [there are] 1 acre and 1 virgate of meadow. [There have] always [been] 2 ploughs. Then it was worth 40s.; afterwards and now 30[s.] The soke [is] in Buckenham [near Attleborough] but Lisois kept it and E[udo] likewise.

In Brettenham Thorgisl held. [There were] 7 free men TRE, 1½ carucates. [There are] 2 acres of meadow. Then and afterwards [there were] 1½ ploughs; now 1 plough and there could be [another] half. Then it was worth 30s.; afterwards [and] now 20[s.] The soke of 6 of these [is] in Buckenham [near Attleborough], the king's [manor]. St Æthelthryth [has] the soke and commendation of the seventh. But Lisois kept the whole and E[udo] keeps the whole. It is 1 league in length and 5 furlongs in breadth. And [it renders] 13½d. of the geld.

WALSHAM HUNDRED.

In Tunstall Skuli, a man of Harold's, held TRE 1 carucate. Then [there were] 6 bordars; afterwards and now 5. And [there are] 8 acres of meadow. [There has] always [been] half a plough in demesne and half [a plough] belonging to the men. Then [there were] [...] 200 sheep; now 240. [There is] 1 church, 8 acres, and it is worth 8d. Then it was worth 40s.; afterwards and now £3. And it is

Eudo the Steward

[Folio 240: NORFOLK]

7 furlongs in length and 6 in breadth. And of the geld [it renders] 8d.

BLOFIELD H[UNDRED].

In Postwick Skuli, 1 free man, held TRE 2 carucates. Then [there were] 6 villans; afterwards and now 5. [There have] always [been] 9 bordars and 2 slaves. Then [there were] $1\frac{1}{2}$ ploughs in demesne; afterwards and now 1. [There have] always [been] 3 ploughs belonging to the men. [There is] woodland for 40 pigs. And [there are] 15 acres of meadow. Now [there is] 1 mill. [There have] always [been] 3 horses and 15 head of cattle. Then [there were] 40 pigs; now 16. [There is] 1 church, 20 acres, and it is worth 2s. To this is attached 1 berewick, Catton [in Postwick], at 30 acres of land and 3 bordars. Then [there was] half a plough between the whole [of them] and now 5 oxen. [There are] 5 acres of meadow. Then it was worth 40s.; afterwards and now £4.

In the same [vill] Rathi, 1 free man, held TRE 1 carucate. [There have] always [been] 3 villans and 5 bordars and 1 slave. [There has] always [been] 1 plough in demesne and half [a plough] belonging to the men. [There is] woodland for 20 pigs and 8 [acres] of meadow. [There have] always [been] 3 pigs. And [there are] 2 sokemen at 4 acres of land. Then it was worth 20[s.] and afterwards and now 40[s.]

In addition in the same [vill] Skalpi, a free man, held TRE 1 carucate. [There have] always [been] 3 villans. Then [there was] 1 plough in demesne. And [there has] always [been] half a plough belonging to the men. [There is] woodland for 15 pigs. [There are] 8 acres of meadow. Then it was worth 15s. and now 40[s.] The whole is 1 league in length and half [a league] in breadth. And of the geld [it renders] $13\frac{1}{2}$d. The whole of this Lisois held for 1 manor. Now Eudo, his successor, holds [it]. And TRE the soke and sake was in the Hundred but now Eudo holds [it].

H[UNDRED] OF HUMBLEYARD.

In Intwood Ralph holds $1\frac{1}{2}$ carucates which Colman, a free man of Stigand's, held. [There have] always [been] 3 villans and 3 bordars. Then [there were] 2 slaves; now 3. [There have] always [been] 2 ploughs in demesne and $1\frac{1}{2}$ ploughs belonging to the men. [There are] 3 acres of meadow. [There is] woodland for 8

[Folio 240v: NORFOLK]

pigs and a quarter part of a mill. Then [there were] 4 horses; now 3. [There have] always [been] 4 head of cattle. Then

[there were] 40 pigs; now 30. Then [there were] 60 sheep; now 50. [There is] 1 church 14 acres of land and $1\frac{1}{2}$ acres of meadow. And [there is] a berewick, Swainsthorpe, 60 acres, and a plough in demesne and $1\frac{1}{2}$ acres of meadow. And [there are] 15 sokemen, 40 acres of land. [There have] always [been] 2 ploughs. And [there are] 4 acres of meadow. And [there are] 5 free men, 20 acres, and 1 plough. Of these his predecessor had the commendation TRE. And [there were] $2\frac{1}{2}$ free men, 75 acres, in commendation only TRE and $1\frac{1}{2}$ bordars. [There have] always [been] $2\frac{1}{2}$ ploughs. And [there are] 2 slaves. And [there is] 1 free man at half an acre. Then it was worth 10s.; now 17[s.] And Intwood is 1 league in length and half [a league] in breadth. And [it renders] $9\frac{3}{4}$d. of the geld. And this manor was worth TRE 60s.; now 80[s.]

XXV. The Lands of Walter Giffard. H[undred] of Eynsford.

Bintree Eadric, a free man, held TRE: 1 carucate. [There have] always [been] 3 villans and 9 bordars. Then [there was] 1 slave. [There have] always [been] 2 ploughs in demesne and 2 ploughs belonging to the men. And [there are] 8 acres of meadow. Now [there are] 9 pigs and 60 sheep. Then it was worth 20s.; afterwards [and] now 60[s.] And [there are] 4 free men, 1 carucate. [There have] always [been] 2 ploughs and 1 bordar. And [there are] 3 acres of meadow. Then it was worth 20s.; now 12[s.] The soke of that land TRE belonged to Foulsham, [a manor] belonging to the king; now Walter has [it]. And it is 5 furlongs in length and 3 in breadth. And it renders $12\frac{1}{2}$d. of the king's geld.

Walter Giffard

[Folio 241: NORFOLK]

In Guist [there are] 5 free men, $1\frac{1}{2}$ carucates and 5 bordars. [There have] always [been] 4 ploughs. And [there are] 6 acres of meadow. [There is] woodland for 8 pigs. Then it was worth 20s.; now 40[s.] And the soke [was] in Foulsham, [a manor] belonging to the king TRE. Now Walter has [it]. And it is half a league in length and in breadth. And it renders $8\frac{1}{2}$d. of the king's geld, whoever may hold there.

In [Wood] Norton [there are] 3 free men, 72 acres of land. [There have] always [been] 6 bordars. [There have] always [been] 2 ploughs. And [there are] 4 acres of meadow. [There is] woodland for 8 pigs. Then it was worth 13s.; now 20[s.]. And 1 of these men was in the commendation of Bishop Æthelmær.

In [Wood] Dalling [there are] 5 free men, 70 acres of land. Then and afterwards [there were] $2\frac{1}{2}$ ploughs; now $1\frac{1}{2}$. And [there is] half an acre of meadow. It has always been worth 10s. The soke [is] in Foulsham, [a manor belonging] to the king.

In [Great or Little] Witchingham 1 free man held half a carucate TRE. [There has] always [been] 1 villan and 3 bordars. And [there are] 2 sokemen, 3 acres of land. And [there are] 3 acres of meadow. [There is] woodland for 10 pigs. Then it was worth 10s.; now 20s.

In Swannington [there are] 7 free men, $1\frac{1}{2}$ carucates and 16 acres of land. And [there are] 3 acres of meadow and 1 bordar. Then and afterwards [there were] 5 ploughs; now [?3] . And [there are] 12 sokemen, 40 acres of land. [There have] always [been] 2 ploughs. And [there are] 3 acres of meadow. [There is] woodland for 6 pigs. It has always been worth 40s. The soke [was] in Foulsham, [a manor] belonging to the king TRE; now W[alter] holds [it]. And it is half a league in length and in breadth. And it renders 12d. of the king's geld.

In Helmingham 1 free man held TRE 2 carucates. [There has] always [been] 1 villan and 3 bordars and 3 slaves. Then [there were] 2 ploughs in demesne; afterwards and now 1, and 1 could be restored. [There has] always [been] half a plough belonging to the men. And [there are] 4 acres of meadow and 1 mill. And [there are] 12 sokemen, 30 acres of land

[Folio 241v: NORFOLK]

[There have] always [been] 3 ploughs. And [there are] 2 acres of meadow. It has always been worth 40s.

In Ringland [there are] 3 free men, 60 acres of land. [There has] always [been] 1 plough. And [there are] 2 acres of meadow. It is worth 10s. The soke [was] in Foulsham, [a manor] belonging to the king TRE; now W[alter] holds [it].

H[UNDRED] OF TAVERHAM.

In Attlebridge [there are] 3½ free men and 5 acres of land. [There have] always [been] 2 bordars. Then [there were] 2 ploughs; afterwards and now 1. And [there are] 2 acres of meadow. And it is worth 10s. In Felthorpe [there is] 1 free man, 30 acres. Then [there was] 1 plough; afterwards and now half [a plough]. [There are] 2 acres of meadow. And it is worth 8s. The king and the earl [had] the soke of the whole TRE and now Walt[er] has it. The whole of Attlebridge is 1 league in length and 3 furlongs in breadth. And [it renders] 8¾d. of the geld.

SOUTH ERPINGHAM H[UNDRED].

In Stratton [Strawless] [there were] 19 sokemen of Harold's in Marsham. [There have] always [been] 2 bordars. Then [there were] 4 ploughs; afterwards and now 3. [There are] 6 acres of meadow. [There is] woodland for 30 pigs. Then it was worth 20s.; now 40[s.] And it is 1 league in length and half [a league] in breadth. And [it renders] 11d. of the geld.

In Hevingham 22 sokemen of Harold's [held] 2 carucates and 2 bordars. [There have] always [been] 6 ploughs. And [there are] 4 acres of meadow. [There is] woodland for 10 pigs. Then it was worth 30s.; now 50[s.] And it is 9 furlongs and 1 perch in length and 5 furlongs and 2 perches in breadth. And [it renders] 5½d. of the geld. And Rippon is in the same measure and renders likewise 5½d.

In Irmingland Eadric, a free man, held 1 carucate TRE. [There has] always [been] 1 villan and 4 bordars. And [there are] 3 sokemen, 8 acres of land. [There has] always [been] 1 plough in demesne and 1 plough belonging to the men. And [there are] 3 acres of meadow. [There is] woodland for 30 pigs

Walter Giffard

[Folio 242: NORFOLK]

and 2 parts of a mill. Then [there were] 5 head of cattle; now 8 and 1 horse and 9 pigs. Then it was worth 20s.; now 30[s.] And it is 6 furlongs in length and 6 in breadth. And [it renders] 3d. of the geld. In [West] Beckham [there are] 3 free men, 30 acres . [There has] always [been] 1 plough. Then it was worth 6s.; now 12[s.]

H[UNDRED] OF GREENHOE.

In Foulden [there was] 1 carucate TRE. Then [there was] 1 plough; afterwards half [a plough]; now none. And it is worth 8s.

H[UNDRED] OF GRIMSHOE.

In Lynford and Ickburgh [there are] 14 free men, 4 carucates, and 35 acres. Then [there were] 6 ploughs; afterwards 3; now [?likewise]. And [there are] 3 bordars. [There are] 9 acres of meadow. Then it was worth 20s.; now 10[s.] They were commended to a predecessor, Ralph Wader; afterwards they were handed over to Bodin de Vere on behalf of the king. Afterwards he established his claim that they [were] in his Wef. Ralph when he forfeited was holding them. Hervey de Vere [held] of him. The Hundred testifies to this. And the whole is half a league in length and 4 furlongs in breadth. And it renders 4d. of a 20s. [geld].

In Ickburgh [there were] 4 free men TRE, 1½ carucates and 8 acres. Then [and] afterwards [there were] 3 ploughs; now 2. [There are] 3 acres of meadow. Then [there were] 4 pigs; now 1. Then [there were] 100 sheep; [now] 200. Then and afterwards it was worth 20s.; now 30s. The whole is half a league in length and half in breadth. And it renders 8d. in the king's geld of 20s.

H[UNDRED] OF HOLT.

In Letheringsett Aslak, a free man, held TRE 1 carucate. [There have] always [been] 7 borders. And [there are] 1½ ploughs in demesne and 1 plough belonging to the men. [There are] 2 acres of meadow. [There is] 1 mill. Then [there were] 2 horses. [There have] always [been] 2 head of cattle and 20 pigs and 80 sheep. Now [there are] 2 hives of bees. And [there is] 1 sokeman

[Folio 242v: NORFOLK]

at 1 acre. Then it was worth 20s.; now 25[s.] And it is 8 furlongs in length and 5 in breadth. And [it renders] 12d. of the geld, whoever may hold there.

In BayWeld Godric, a free man, held TRE 40 acres of land. [There have] always [been] 3 bordars. And [there is] 1 plough and 3 parts of 1 mill. And [there is] 1 sokeman at 10 acres. Then it was worth 10s.; now 20s.

In Glandford a certain free man held 30 acres TRE. [There have] always [been] 3 bordars. And [there is] 1 plough, 1 acre of meadow. Then it was worth 8s.; now 5s.

And in 'Snitterley' [in Blakeney] Toki held under Harold 30 acres. Then [there was] 1 plough; now half [a plough]. Then it was worth 5s.; now 10s.

In Bodham [there was] 1 carucate TRE. And it belongs to Letheringsett. [There have] always [been] 9 bordars and 2 slaves. And [there is] 1 plough in demesne and 1 plough belonging to the men. [There is] woodland for 5 pigs. [There are] 2 acres of meadow. Then it was worth 10s.; now 30s.

In Hunworth [there are] 60 acres and they belong to Letheringsett. Then [there were] 2 ploughs; now 1. [There is] 1 acre of meadow. [There are] 1½ mills. Then and always it has been worth 10s.

GREENHOE H[UNDRED].

In Warham [All Saints or St Mary] Gyrth held 2 free men. Now Walter GiVard holds for half a carucate. [There has] always [been] 1 bordar. Then and afterwards [there were] 2 ploughs; now 1½ ploughs . Then it was worth 16s.; afterwards and now [likewise].

NORTH ERPINGHAM H[UNDRED].

In [North] Barningham 1 free man, Kene, held 20 acres TRE. And [there is] 1 bordar. Then it was worth 5s.; now 2[s.] And it was delivered to complete Letheringsett.

HENSTEAD H[UNDRED].

In Shotesham [All Saints or St Mary] [there are] 3 free men of St B[enet] of Hulme's in commendation

Walter Giffard

[Folio 243: NORFOLK]

and 5 sokemen with every customary due. Now Walter holds it from Bodin, his predecessor. And it has between [them] all 90 acres of land and under them [are] 3 bordars. And [there is] 1½ acres of meadow. [There have] always [been] 2 ploughs. Then it was worth 10s.; afterwards and now 15s.

In Saxlingham [Nethergate or Thorpe] [there are] 2 free men of St B[enet] of Hulme's in commendation at 50 acres of land. And [there are] 2 acres of meadow and 2 bordars. [There has] always [been] 1 plough. Then it was worth 5s.; now it renders 10[s.]

In Stoke [Holy Cross] [there were] 5 sokemen of St B[enet] of Hulme's TRE at 50 acres of land. And [there are] 2 acres of meadow and 1 bordar. [There has] always [been] 1 plough. Then it was worth 5s. and 4d.; afterwards and now 10s.

In Shotesham [All Saints or St Mary] [there is] 1 sokeman of St B[enet of Hulme's] at 13 acres of land. And [there is] 1 acre of meadow. [There has] always [been] half a plough. Then it was worth 2 oras; afterwards and now 5s.

The Lands which were Roger de Poitou's.

H[UNDRED] OF TAVERHAM.

Frettenham Eadric, a free man, held TRE for 4 carucates. [There have] always [been] 18 villans and 12 bordars. Then and afterwards [there were] 2 ploughs; now 1. Then [there were] 8 ploughs belonging to the men; afterwards 6; now 5. And [there are] 6 acres of meadow. [There is] woodland for 60 pigs. And [there are] 4 men, half a carucate. [There has] always [been] 1 plough. [There is] 1 [acre] of meadow. Then

[there was] 1 ox. Then [there were] 26 pigs; now 24. Then 200 sheep; now 2 sheep. Then it was worth £4;

[Folio 243v: NORFOLK]

now [£]8. And it is 1 league in length and a half [a league] in breadth. And [it renders] 15d. of the geld.

Hainford Ketil held under Stigand TRE: 1 carucate. Then [there were] 7 villans; afterwards and now 5. [There have] always [been] 4 bordars. Then and afterwards [there were] 2 ploughs in demesne; now 1. [There has] always [been] 1 plough belonging to the men. And [there are] 2 acres of meadow. [There is] woodland for 100 pigs. And [there are] 14 men, 1 carucate. [There have] always [been] 3 ploughs. [There is] woodland for 60 pigs. And [there are] 5 men, 30 acres of land in Stratton [Strawless]. Then [there were] 2 ploughs; afterwards and now 1½ ploughs. [There is] woodland for 12 pigs. In Mayton Albert holds 1 carucate. [It is] a berewick of this manor. [There have] always [been] 2 villans and 1 mill. And afterwards [there was] 1 plough. And [then] it was worth 30s.; now nothing.

In Crostwick [there are] 6 men, 1 carucate. Then and afterwards [there were] 2 ploughs; now half [a plough]. Stigand had the soke of these men. In the demesne of this manor [there were] then 20 pigs and 60 sheep and 4 head of cattle and now nothing. [There have] always [been] 20 goats. Then and afterwards it was worth 100s.; now £7. And the whole of Hainford is 1 league in length and half [a league] in breadth. And [it renders] 23½d. of the geld. And Mayton is 3 furlongs in length and 3 in breadth and Crostwick [is] half a league in length and 4 furlongs in breadth. And [it renders] 10d. of the geld.

Spixworth Albert holds, which Swart, a free man under Harold, held TRE: 2 carucates. Then [there were] 10 villans; afterwards and now 4. [There have] always [been] 3 bordars. Then and afterwards [there were] 2 ploughs in demesne; now none. Then [there was] 1 plough belonging to the men; afterwards and now half [a plough]. And [there are] 6 acres of meadow. [There has] always [been] 1 mill. Then [there were] 10 pigs. Then [there were] 193 sheep; now 13 sheep. In Spixworth the same man [holds]. [There are] 6 free men of Stigand's, 1 plough, who were added by Robert Blanchard in the time of King W[illiam]. [There have] always [been] 4 villans.

Roger de Poitou

[Folio 244: NORFOLK]

Then [there were] 2 ploughs; afterwards and now 1. And [there are] 4 acres of meadow. And the whole has always [been] worth £4. And it is 1½ leagues in length and 1 league in breadth. And [it renders] 10d. of the geld. Stigand had the soke and Roger held it with the land.

SOUTH ERPINGHAM H[UNDRED].

In Coltishall the same man held 4 sokemen of Stigand's from Frettenham, 30 acres of land and 180 acres of the demesne of Frettenham. [There have] always [been] 4 bordars. And [there are] 5 acres of land and 4 villans. Then [there were] 2 ploughs; now 1½. This is in the value of Frettenham.

TUNSTEAD H[UNDRED].

Tunstead the same man holds. Ælfhere, a thegn of Harold's, [held it] TRE: 5½ carucates. [There have] always [been] 23 villans and 16 bordars. Then and afterwards [there were] 2 ploughs; now half [a plough]. Then [there were] 12 ploughs belonging to the men; afterwards and now 7. [There are] 8 acres of meadow. [There is] woodland for 12 pigs. Then [there were] 3 head of cattle. Then [there were] 4 pigs; now 1. Then [there were] 140 sheep; now 100. And [there are] 24 sokemen, 1 carucate. Then [there were] 12 ploughs; afterwards and now 5. And [there are] 2 acres of meadow. And the same were added TRW. And Earl R[alph] added 6 free men, 1½ carucates. Of these St Benet [of Hulme] has the soke and the commendation of one [of them]. And of the 24 [there are] 3 forfeitures. And the 6 free men have 4 bordars under them. Then [there were] 4 ploughs; afterwards and now 3. And [there are] 2 acres of meadow. To this manor Robert the crossbowman added after Earl Ralph forfeited (as he says by Godric's command but the latter denies [it]) 1 carucate which used to belong to Hoveton [St John or St Peter] TRE which Earl Ralph together with his wife gave to St Benet [of Hulme]. Then [there were] 7 villans and when Robert took [it], [there were] 7; now 6. And it is worth 10s. Then [there were] 1½ ploughs and when Robert took [it], likewise; now 1 plough. And [there are] 4 acres of meadow. Then it was worth 100s. and when Robert the crossbowman held it in the king's hand of Godric £10; now [£]11. It is 1 league and 1 furlong in length and 1 league in breadth.

[Folio 244V: NORFOLK]

And [it renders] 18d. of the geld. In [Sco] Ruston [there is] 1 free man, 6 acres of land. And [there is] 1 acre of meadow in the same value. In Westwick [there are] 1½ free men, 12 acres of meadow in the same value.

EARSHAM HALF H[UNDRED].

In Shotford Wulfric, 1 free man, held TRE 1 carucate and 15 acres. [There have] always [been] 10 villans and 4 bordars. [There has] always [been] 1 plough in demesne and 2 ploughs belonging to the men. [There is] woodland for 40 pigs. And [there are] 7 acres of meadow. Then it was worth 10s.; now 20[s.]

XXVII. The Lands of Ivo Taillebois.

H[UNDRED] OF GREENHOE.

Newton [near Castle Acre] Odo holds, where Ælfhere, a free man, held. Then [there were] 6 villans and now 8. Then [there were] 3 bordars; now 5. And [there is] 1 slave. Then and now [there has been] 1 plough in demesne. Then [there were] 2 ploughs belonging to the men; now 1. When he received [it, there were] 4 [?horses]; afterwards [and] now 6. Then and now [there have been] 5 head of cattle. Then [there were] 12 sheep; now 16. And 2 free men live there whom his predecessor held. They hold 1 carucate and 1½ ploughs. It is 4 furlongs

in length and 3 in breadth. And it renders in geld 6d. Then it was worth 40s.; now £4.

H[UNDRED] OF DOCKING.

In Shernborne [there were] 16 free men TRE whom Harold held, holding 5 ploughs; and when he received [it], likewise; now 3. And the same men now hold of Ivo. [There have] always [been] 2 villans. And [there are] 1½ acres of meadow and 1 mill. Then and afterwards it was worth 40s.; now £4. Ralph was holding this land when he forfeited. The whole is 1 league in length

Ivo Taillebois

[Folio 245: NORFOLK]

and half [a league] in breadth. Whoever may hold there, it renders 27d. of [a] 20s. [geld]. Of this land Earl Ralph took 1 carucate one year before he forfeited for Roger fitzReinhard according to the testimony of the Hundred.

H[UNDRED] OF GREENHOE.

The Lands of Ralph de Limésy.

Oxborough Thorkil held. Then [there were] 15 villans; now 7. [There have] always [been] 9 bordars and 3 slaves. Then and afterwards [there were] 3 ploughs in demesne; now 3. Then [there were] 2 [ploughs] between the men; now 1. [There is] woodland for 20 pigs. [There are] 12 acres of meadow, 2 mills, 1 fishery. When he received [it there was] 1 horse and now [likewise]. Then [there were] 31 pigs; now 15. Then [there were] 220 sheep; now 180. And 8 free men hold 100 acres. And [then there were] 6 ploughs; now 3 ploughs. [There are] 12 acres of meadow. [There have] always [been] 2 villans and 4 bordars. And it is in length 1 mile and half [a mile] in breadth. And it renders 11d. in geld when the Hundred renders 20s. It has always been worth 100s. And 1 of those free men is claimed [to be] Ralph de Tosny's because his predecessor held [him] with soke and sake as the Hundred testifies.

Didlington Hardwin held. Then and now [there have been] 3 bordars and 1 slave and 1 plough. [There is] woodland for 16 pigs. [There are] 2 acres of meadow, 1 mill, 1 fishery. When he received [it] and now [there has been] 1 horse. Then [there were] 11 pigs; now 5. Then [there were] 60 sheep; now 6. Then it was worth 20[s.]; now likewise.

[Folio 245V: NORFOLK]

XXIX. The Lands of Eudo fitzSpirewic.

FREEBRIDGE HUNDRED AND A HALF.

In Hillington Geoffrey holds 2 carucates and 15 acres of land which Godric, a free man under Harold, held TRE. [There have] always [been] 8 villans and 4 bordars. And [there are] 8 acres of meadow. And [there are] 2 ploughs in demesne and 1 plough belonging to the men. And [there is] 1 mill and half a salt-pan. And 1 free man [holds] 2½ acres. Now [there are] 17 pigs and 60 sheep. The whole is worth £4.

[Great or Little] Massingham Berold holds, which Skuli, a free man, held TRE. [There have] always [been] 3 carucates. Then [there were] 8 villans; now 7. And [there is] 1 slave. Then [there were] 2 ploughs in demesne and now [likewise]. And [there is] 1 plough belonging to the men. And 3 ploughs can be restored. [There have] always [been] 5 pigs and 40 sheep. And it is worth 20s.

Babingley Geoffrey holds, which Skuli held TRE: 2 carucates. [There have] always [been] 4 villans and 25 bordars and 1 slave. And [there are] 16 acres of meadow. Then [there were] 2 ploughs in demesne; afterwards [and] now 1. [There has] always [been] 1 plough belonging to the men. [There is] woodland for 60 pigs. And [there has] always [been] 1 pig and 60 sheep. Here belong 62 acres which 7 free men held. And [there are] 2 acres of meadow. [There has] always [been] 1 plough and 1 mill. Then [there were] 9 salt-pans. It has always been worth 60s.

Dersingham Ricwald holds, which Skiotr, a free man, held TRE for a manor. [There has] always [been] 1 plough in demesne and 1 plough belonging to the men. [There has] always [been] 1 villan and 4 bordars and 1 slave. And [there are] $7\frac{1}{2}$ acres of meadow. Then [there was] 1 salt-pan. And [there are] 4 free men, 44 acres. These he received for completing his manor and 1 free man at 20 [acres]. [There has] always [been] half a plough and 4 bordars. The whole is worth 20s.

H[UNDRED] OF DOCKING.

Docking the same man holds, where Ælfric held TRE under Stigand. [There has] always [been] 1 plough in demesne. And [there are] 5 villans and 5 bordars. Then [there were] 2 slaves. Then [there was] 1 plough belonging to the men; now $1\frac{1}{2}$ ploughs. [There has] always [been] 1 horse and 1 cow and 17 pigs. [There are] 80 sheep. And 1 plough could be restored. And it is worth 20s.

Eudo fitzSpirewic

[Folio 246: NORFOLK]

The whole is 1 league in length and half [a league] in breadth. And it renders 5s. $2\frac{1}{2}$d. of the geld, whoever may hold there.

EARSHAM HALF-H[UNDRED].

In Denton Thormoth, 1 free man of King E[dward's], held 2 carucates. Then [there were] 10 villans. And [there were] 6 bordars then; 8 now. [There have] always [been] 3 slaves. Then [there were] 2 ploughs in demesne; now half [a plough]. Then [there were] 6 ploughs belonging to the men; now 4. Now [there is] woodland for 30 pigs. [There are] 5 acres of meadow and half a mill. And [there are] 4 [?free men] at 20 acres of land. Then it was worth 60s.; now £4.

In the same [vill] Ælfric, 1 free man of Stigand's, held TRE 2 carucates. Then [there were] 10 villans; now 8. Then [there were] 8 bordars; now 6. [There have] always [been] 3 slaves. Then [there were] 2 ploughs in demesne; now a half [a plough]. Then [there were] 6 ploughs belonging to the men; now 4. Now [there is] woodland for 30 pigs. [There are] 6 acres of meadow and half a mill. And [there are] 4 sokemen at

20 acres of land. Then it was worth 60s.; now £4. It is 1 league in length and 4 furlongs in breadth. And of the geld [it renders] 18d., whoever may hold there. The soke [is] in Earsham.

In Alburgh Morvan holds where Ælfric held TRE 1 berewick in Tibenham containing 1 carucate. Then [there was] half a plough; now nothing. It has been valued.

In the same [vill] the same man held 1 free man in the commendation of St Æthelthryth who could neither give nor sell the land outside the church. Heinfrid had [him] by livery in order to complete his manors. Now Eudo, his successor, holds [him]. He has half a carucate. [There has] always [been] 1 bordar and 1 slave. [There has] always [been] half a plough. And [there are] 2 acres of meadow. It has always been worth 10s.

LODDON H[UNDRED].

Topcroft Godwine, a free man in the commendation only of Gyrth, held TRE for a manor: 3 carucates. Then [there were] 12 villans; afterwards and now 2. Then [there were] 30 bordars; afterwards and now 36. Then [there were] 7 slaves; now 4. Then [there were] 4 ploughs in demesne; now 2. Then [there were] 7 ploughs belonging to the men

[Folio 246v: NORFOLK]

now 5. [There is] woodland for 20 pigs. And [there are] 4 acres of meadow. And under him [there were] 4 free men, 1 carucate, delivered to Heinfrid, his predecessor, for land, and under them 5 villans and 12 bordars. Then [there were] 4 ploughs between [them] all; now 4. And [there is] 1 horse at the hall. Now [there are] 40 pigs and 20 goats. Then the whole was worth £6; now [£] 8.

In the same [vill] Godwine, a free man half in the commendation only of Eadric and half of St Edmund, held TRE $1\frac{1}{2}$ ploughs where Godwine held. [There have] always [been] 8 villans and 11 bordars. [There have] always [been] 4 slaves. Then [there were] 2 ploughs; now none. Then [there were] $8\frac{1}{2}$ ploughs belonging to the men; now $5\frac{1}{2}$. And [there are] 3 acres of meadow. Then the whole was worth 30s.; now 40[s.] It is 1 league and 1 furlong in length and 9 furlongs in breadth. And of the geld [it renders] 20d., whoever may hold there.

In Woodton the same man holds. [There are] 11 free men of Godwine son of Toki and of another Godwine under King E[dward] and Gyrth, half a carucate and 4 bordars. Then [there were] 3 ploughs; now 2. And [there are] $1\frac{1}{2}$ acres of meadow. It has been valued. The soke [is] in the Hundred.

H[UNDRED] OF DEPWADE.

Tibenham Alric, a thegn, held TRE: 3 carucates. [There have] always [been] 2 villans and 21 bordars. Then [there were] 4 slaves; now 2. [There have] always [been] 2 ploughs in demesne. Then [there were] 6 ploughs belonging to the men; now 3. And [there are] 12 acres of meadow. [There is] woodland for 12 pigs. Then [there was] 1 mill. Now [there are] 40 pigs and 17 sheep and 9 goats. And [there are] 26 men in soke of the fold and commendation and they would be able to sell their land but after they had oVered it to their lord. The king and the earl [have] the soke. And he has 50 acres. Then [there were] 4 ploughs; now 2. And [there is] 1 acre of meadow.

In Carleton [Rode] [there is] 1 free man, 8 acres. Then it was worth £7; now [£]8 Heinfrid received those free men for land. The whole of Carleton [Rode] is 1 league and 4 furlongs in length and 10 furlongs in breadth. And [there are] 4 pigs. And [it renders] 22½d. of the geld.

[Folio 247: NORFOLK]

The land of Drogo de La Beuvrière.

H[UNDRED] OF GREENHOE.

Hindringham Ulf and Osweard held, 2 carucates, and now Drogo de la Beuvrière holds [it] for 1 manor. Then TRE [there were] 8 villans and 8 bordars; now 2 villans and always 8 bordars. Then [there were] 2 ploughs in demesne; now 1 between him and those men. [There are] 3 acres of meadow. Then it was worth £4; now 30s.

ERPINGHAM NORTH H[UNDRED].

Bessingham 1 free man held TRE in the commendation of Eadric: 1 carucate. And on the day when the father of R[obert] Malet went [away] on the king's service he was holding him and Drogo's man retains [him]. [There have] always [been] 8 villans and 7 bordars. [There has] always [been] 1 plough in demesne and 2 [ploughs] belonging to the men. [There is] 1 acre of meadow. Now [there are] 2 pigs. Then it was worth 20[s.]; now 60[s.]

In [North] Barningham Alwine [Cild], 1 free man, holds 1 carucate. Then [there were] 5 bordars; now 3. [There is] woodland for 100 pigs. [There is] 1 acre of meadow. Now [there are] 4 [horses]. Afterwards and now [there are] 8 sheep. Then it was worth 20s. and now likewise.

HENSTEAD H[UNDRED].

In Saxlingham [Nethergate or Thorpe] Æthelweard, 1 free man of King E[dward's], held 2 carucates. Then [there were] 12 bordars; afterwards 12; now 9. Then and afterwards [there were] 2 ploughs in demesne; now none. [There has] always [been] 1 plough belonging to the men. And [there are] 1½ acres of meadow. And [there are] 5 sokemen at 17 acres of land. [There has] always [been] 1 plough. Then it was worth 20s.; afterwards and now likewise.

In the same [vill] Wulfnoth, 1 free man in the commendation of Stigand held at 30 acres of land. [There have] always [been] 5 bordars. Then [there was] 1 plough in demesne; now none. Then and afterwards [there was] 1 plough belonging to the men;

[Folio 247v: NORFOLK]

now 1½. And [there are] 3 acres of meadow. And [there are] 5 sokemen at 17 acres of land. Then [there was] 1 plough; afterwards likewise; now half [a plough]. And [there is] 1 free [man] at 6 acres of land. Then it was worth 20s.; afterwards and now 20s.

SOUTH ERPINGHAM H[UNDRED].

Burgh [next Aylsham] Mærwynn, a certain free woman, held TRE: 3 carucates. [There have] always [been] 8 villans and 9 bordars. And [there are] 2 ploughs in demesne. Then and afterwards [there were] 3 ploughs belonging to the men; now 4. And [there are] 7 acres of meadow. [There is] woodland for 60 pigs. [There has] always [been] 1 mill. Then [there were] 24 pigs; now 12. Now [there are] 3 head of cattle and 16 sheep and 20 goats. Then it was worth 40s.; now 60[s.] And it is 1 league in length and 5 furlongs in breadth. And [it renders] 5d. of the geld. The king and the earl [have] the soke. In Erpingham 1 free man [held] 1 carucate TRE. [There have] always [been] 2 bordars. And [there is] 1 plough and 1 acre of meadow. And [there are] 2 sokemen, 4 acres of land. And [there is] 1 church at 6 acres and it is worth 6d. And it is worth 10s. [sic]. The king and the earl [have] the soke.

XXXI. Lands of Ralph Baynard.

H[UNDRED] OF EYNSFORD.

In Kerdiston Thorth, 1 free man, held 2 carucates for a manor TRE; now Geoffrey Baynard holds [it]. Then and afterwards [there were] 30 villans and now 16. And now [there are] 14 bordars. Then and afterwards [there were] 2 slaves; now 1. [There have] always [been] 2 ploughs in demesne. Then and afterwards [there were] 4 ploughs belonging to the men; now 3. And [there are] 5 acres of meadow. [There is] woodland for 20 pigs. When [he received it, there were] 2 horses; now 4. Then [there were] 4 head of cattle; now 10. [There have] always [been] 40 pigs. Now [there are] 50 sheep. Then [there were] 60 goats; now 28. And [there are] 2 hives of bees. And [there are] 3½ sokemen, 25 acres of land. [There has] always [been] half a plough. It has always been worth £4 5s. The men in Reepham belong to this land and they have been valued with this land. And Reepham, whoever may hold there, is half a league in length and 4 furlongs in breadth. And [it renders] 3d. of the geld.

Ralph Baynard

[Folio 248: NORFOLK]

H[UNDRED] OF SOUTH ERPINGHAM.

Skeyton Esger, 1 free man, TRE held: 2 carucates and 27 acres. Now Geoffrey Baynard holds [it]. Then and afterwards [there were] 7 villans; now 6. [There has] always [been] 1 plough in demesne; then and afterwards [there was] 1 plough belonging to the men; now half [a plough]. [There is] woodland for 60 pigs. [There are] 20 acres of meadow and 1 mill. When he received [it, there were] 2 horses; now 4. And now [there are] 17 head of cattle. Then [there were] 12 pigs; now 20. Then [there were] 24 sheep; now 15. Then [there were] 24 goats; now 37. Then and afterwards it was worth 20s.; now 30[s.] And [there were] 3 sokemen, 78 acres, TRE. And [there were] 2 bordars. Then [there was] 1 plough; now half [a plough]. And [there are] 8 acres of meadow. [There is] woodland for 15 pigs. And it is worth 6s. The whole of this St B[enet of Hulme] held TRE except for 4 acres. And it is 1 league in length and half [a league] in breadth. And it renders 8d. to the king's geld.

TUNSTEAD H[UNDRED].

In Crostwight Geoffrey holds. [There are] 12 free men, 150 acres. [There have] always [been] 12 bordars. And [there are] 16 acres of meadow and 3½ ploughs. Then it was worth 27s.; now 22[s.] and 4d. And the whole is 1 league in length and 7 furlongs in breadth. Whoever may hold there, renders 10d. of the geld. St Benet [of Hulme] has the commendation of one half a man and the soke over all.

In Barton [Turf] Geoffrey holds. [There are] 3 free men, 90 acres. [There have] always [been] 12 bordars. And [there are] 2½ ploughs and 1½ acres of meadow. And it is worth 24s. 8d. St B[enet of Hulme has] the soke. And the whole is 10 furlongs in length and 6 in breadth. And [it renders] 18d. of the geld, whoever may hold there. One those 3 with 30 acres was a sokeman of St Benet [of Hulme's] such that in no way could he withdraw.

HAPPING H[UNDRED].

In [East] Ruston Geoffrey holds 1 free man whom Esger held under Esger the staller, 2 carucates. Then [there were] 15 villans; now 10. Then [there were] 5 slaves; now 1. [There have] always [been] 2 ploughs in demesne. Then [there were] 2 ploughs belonging to the men; now 1. [There is] woodland for 4 pigs. And [there are] 5 acres of meadow.

Then [there were] 5 horses and 10 head of cattle; now 2. Then [there were] 40 pigs; now 14. Then there were 12 sheep; now 26. Then [there were] 40 goats; now 51. It has always been worth 60s. And [there are] 41 free men, 1 carucate. Then and afterwards [there were] 8 ploughs; now 4. And [there are] 2 acres of meadow. It has always been worth £4.

In the same [vill there is] 1 free man, 30 acres of land. [There have] always [been] 2 bordars. Then and afterwards [there was] 1 plough; now half [a plough]. It is worth 6s. In the same [vill] [there was] 1 free man, 2 carucates, under Stigand. Then [there were] 15 villans; now 11. Then [there were] 3 slaves; now 1. Then and afterwards [there were] 1½ ploughs in demesne; now 1. [There has] always [been] 1 plough belonging to the men. And [there are] 5 acres of meadow. [There is] woodland for 4 pigs. It has always been worth 40s. And [there are] 3 free men, 12 acres. [There has] always [been] half a plough. And it is worth 4s. In the same [vill] [there is] 1 free man of Bishop Æthelmær's, 2 carucates. Then [there were] 15 villans; now 11. Then [there were] 3 slaves. Then and afterwards [there was] 1 plough; now none. [There has] always [been] 1 plough belonging to the men. And [there are] 5 acres of meadow. [There is] woodland for 4 pigs. And it is worth 20s. And [there are] 3 sokemen , 5 acres. Then [there was] 1 mill. And it is worth 2s. Amongst the whole there were £10 12s.; now the whole renders £20. The whole is 1½ leagues in length and 1 league and 4 furlongs in breadth. And [it renders] 19½d. of the geld.

DEPWADE H[UNDRED].

Hempnall Thorn held TRE for a manor: 8 carucates . Then [there were] 54 villans; now 34. Then [there were] 41 bordars; now 58 and a priest. [There are] 2 churches, 1 carucate and 4 villans and 4 bordars and 2 ploughs. And it is worth 15s. Then and afterwards [there were] 7 [?slaves]; now none. Then and afterwards [there were] 3 ploughs in demesne; now 4. Then and afterwards [there were] 35 ploughs belonging to the men; now 24. [There are] 12 acres of meadow. [There is] woodland for 200 pigs. St B[enet of Hulme] claims part of that woodland which it held

TRE and it is called "Schieteshaga" [in Hempnall]. Then [there was] 1 mill; now 2. [There have] always [been] 5 horses. Then [there were] 9 head of cattle; now 12. Then [there were] 100 pigs; now 60. Then [there were] 5 sheep; now 186. Then and afterwards it was worth £15; now £24 5s. And [there are] 3 free men and a quarter part

Ralph Baynard

of one. [There are] 53 acres. And [there are] 2 acres of meadow and 8 bordars. Then [there were] 1½ ploughs; now 1. And it is worth 15s. Apart from this the whole of this manor renders 6 cows and 20 pigs and 20 rams. And it is 2 leagues in length and 1½ leagues in breadth. And [it renders] 18d. of the geld. Baynard [has] the soke and sake.

Boyland Randolf holds, where Thorn held TRE: 1 carucate. [There have] always [been] 2 villans and 5 bordars. Then [there were] 2 slaves. [There has] always [been] 1 plough in demesne and 2 ploughs belonging to the men. Then and afterwards [there were] 2 acres of meadow; now 1. [There is] woodland for 3 pigs. Now [there is] 1 mill and [there are] 20 sheep and 3 hives of bees. And [there are] 1½ sokemen and 1½ acres. Then it was worth 20s.; now 40[s.] Baynard [has] the soke and sake.

Hudeston Geoffrey holds, where Thorn held TRE: 4 carucates and 1 acre. Then [there were] 2 villans; now 1. Then [there were] 34 bordars; now 28. Then [there were] 4 slaves; now 1. Then [there were] 2 ploughs in demesne; now 4. Then [there were] 5 ploughs belonging to the men; now 2. [There is] woodland for 20 pigs. [There are] 15 acres of meadow. Then [there were] 4 horses; now 1. Then [there were] 8 head of cattle; now 11. Then [there were] 40 pigs; now 33. Then [there was] 1 sheep; now 190. And [there is] 1 hive of bees. Then and afterwards it was worth 100s.; now £10 and 12s. And 18 free men used to belong to this manor in commendation only; now 12. [There is] 1 carucate and 20 acres. And [there are] 5 acres of meadow. Then and afterwards [there were] 4 ploughs; now 2. Then it was worth 20s.; now 28[s.] Those free men are by exchange. The whole is 2 leagues and 1 furlong in length and 1 league and 15 perches in breadth. And [it renders] 9d. of the geld.

In Fritton and in Hardwick a free man held 10 acres TRE.

And it was worth 20d. This has been added to this manor. This is in Hempnall.

CLAVERING H[UNDRED].

Raveningham Einbald holds, where [...] Thorn held TRE: 2 carucates. [There have] always [been] 3 villans and 6 bordars.

Then [there were] 2 slaves. Then and afterwards [there was] 1 plough in demesne; now 1½ ploughs. [There has] always [been] half a plough belonging to the men. [There is] woodland for 5 pigs. [There are] 8 acres of meadow. Now [there is] 1 horse and 8 pigs. And [there are] 15 sokemen, 56 acres. [There have] always [been] 3 ploughs. And [there is] 1 acre of meadow. Then it is worth 30s.; now 50[s.] And it is 1 league in length and 9½ furlongs in breadth. And [it renders] 12d. of the geld.

In Southwood Wimund, 1 free man, holds 50 acres, of whom the predecessor of Godric had the commendation TRE. [There have] always [been] 2 bordars. Then and afterwards [there was] 1 plough. And [there are] 3 acres of meadow. And [there were] 26 free men in commendation under him, 83½ acres. Then and afterwards [there were] 6 ploughs; now 2. Then it was worth 20s.; now 40[s.] This is by exchange. Robert fitzCorbucion claims this land by gift of the king and vouches the livery offices but but [sic] the Hundred testifies that Baynard had earlier been seised of that. The whole of Southwood is 1 league in length and half [a league] in breadth. And [it renders] 8d. of the geld.

In Kirby [Cane] [there is] 1 free man of the king, Wulfmær by name, 30 acres. Robert fitzCorbucion claims this man and has a livery officer. [There have] always [been] 2 bordars. Then [there was] 1 slave. Then [there were] 2 ploughs; afterwards and now 1. Then [there was] half a plough belonging to the men; now 2 oxen. [There is] woodland for 2 pigs. [There are] 3 acres of meadow. And [there are] 8 free men in soke of the fold and commendation, 20 acres. [There have] always [been] 2 ploughs. And [there is] half an acre of meadow. Then it was worth 20s.; now 40[s.] This is in exchange.

In Norton [Subcourse] [there is] 1 free man, 30 acres, and 2 free men, 2½ acres. [There has] always [been] 1 plough. And [there are] 2 acres of meadow. It is worth 10s.

In "Iarpestuna" [there is] 1 free man, 30 acres. A half of that man was in the commendation only of the predecessor of Baynard and the other half [in the commendation] of St Edmund with half of the land. Then and afterwards [there was] 1 plough; now none. [There is] half an acre of meadow. And it is worth 5s.

In Raveningham [there is] 1 free man, 30 acres and 3 bordars. Then and afterwards [there was] 1 plough; now a half. Another plough could be restored. [There are] 3 acres of meadow. This also

Ralph Baynard

Robert claims and has a livery officer.

In the same [vill there are] 4 free men, 30 acres, and 1 plough. Then it was worth 20s.; now 30[s.] In Hales [there was] 1 free man of Stigand's, Toki; Frenchmen [now hold him], 30 acres of land. Then [there were] 3 villans; now 2. [There has] always [been] 1 plough. And [there are] 3 acres of meadow. Now [there are] 12 pigs and 60 sheep. And [there are] 12 free men under him in soke of the fold and commendation. And now [there are] 10 and they have 41 acres of land. [There have] always [been] 1½ ploughs. And [there are] 3 acres of meadow. And [there are] 2 free men in commendation only, 18½ acres and half a plough. And [there is] 1 free man in commendation only, 30 acres of land and 1 bordar and 1 plough and 1 acre of meadow. The whole was then and afterwards worth 17s.; now 30s.

In Wheatacre [there was] 1 free man of Harold's, 2 carucates, where a Frenchman holds. [There have] always [been] 10 villans and 5 bordars. Then [there were] 4 slaves; now 2. [There have] always [been] 2 ploughs in demesne and 2 ploughs belonging to the men. [There is] woodland for 8 pigs. And [there are] 30 acres of meadow. [...] This man R[obert] fitzCorbucion, claims and he has a livery officer. [There is] pasture for 200 sheep. [There have] always [been] 2 horses. Then [there were] 7 head of cattle. Then [there were] 12 pigs; now 17. Then [there were] 200 sheep; now 100. Then [there were] 6 hives of bees. And [there are] 7 free men in soke of the fold [and] commendation, 18 acres. [There have] always [been] 2 ploughs. And [there is] 1 acre of meadow. Then it was worth 30s.; now 45[s.] The whole [was] in exchange.

Wheatacre Geoffrey holds, where Thorth, a thegn, held TRE: 2 carucates. [There have] always [been] 6 villans and 12 bordars. Then [there were] 2 slaves. [There have] always [been] 2 ploughs in demesne and 2 ploughs belonging to the men. [There is] woodland for 8 pigs. [There are] 30 acres of meadow. [There have] always [been] 2 horses and 11 head of cattle. Then [there were] 15 pigs; now 30. Then [there were] 160 sheep; now 176. And [there were] 6 free men in soke of the fold and commendation TRE, 18 acres. [There have] always [been] 1½ ploughs. And [there is] 1 acre of meadow. And [there are] 2 churches, 60 acres in alms, and they are worth 5s. Then the manor was worth 30s.

now 50[s.] And it is 1 league in length and half [a league] in breadth. And [it renders] 16d. of the geld.

In Haddiscoe [there was] 1 free man of Stigand's, 15 acres. [There has] always [been] half a plough. And [there is] 1 acre of meadow. And it is worth 2s. This is [Ralph's] as an exchange. Stigand [had] the soke.

In Thurlton [there is] 1 free man in commendation, 12 acres. And it is worth 12d.

H[UNDRED] OF CLACKCLOSE.

In Fincham Æthelgyth, a free woman, held 1 carucate. [There have] always [been] 4 bordars. Then [there were] 3 slaves. [There has] always [been] 1 plough. [There are] 12 acres of meadow. When he received [it, there were] 2 horses; now 1. Then [there were] 8 pigs. Then [there were] 40 sheep; now 18. Then it was worth 50s.; afterwards 60[s.]; now 40[s.] This land St Æthelthryth claims and the Hundred testifies [to this].

In the same vill [there were] 6½ free men TRE; now 7½, who hold 1 carucate. [There have] always [been] 2 bordars and 1 plough. [There are] 9 acres of meadow.

In Barton [Bendish] Æthelgyth, 1 free woman, held TRE 2 carucates and 2 ploughs. [There have] always [been] 4 villans and 7 bordars. Then [there were] 4 slaves. [There are] 20 acres of meadow. When Ralph [received it], [there were] 2 horses; now 3. Then [there were] 2 head of cattle. Then [there were] 60 pigs; now 15. Then [there were] 140 [sheep] ; now 40. Then and afterwards it was worth 80s.; now 60s. [There is] 1 church, 34 acres, and [it is worth] 2s. They are attached to this manor. [There have] always [been] 4 men with every customary due and another 4 in soke only. And they have 1 plough. And [there are] 6 acres of meadow. Then it was worth 20s.; now 30s.

Shouldham [All Saints and St Margaret] Æthelgyth held TRE. [There have] always [been] 2 ploughs in demesne. Then [there were] 2 ploughs belonging to the men; now 1½. Then [there were] 14 villans; now 15. [Then there were] 2 bordars; now 12. Then [there were] 4 slaves [and] always [have been]. And [there are] 10 acres of meadow and three-quarters of a mill and 1 fishery. Then [there were] 2 horses; now 1. Then [there were] 6 head of cattle. Then [there were] 16 pigs; now 9. Then [there were] 60 sheep; now 50. [There are] 2 churches, 73 acres, and [they are worth] 6s. and 1d. Then it was worth £7 and now [likewise]. In the other Shouldham [All Saints and St Margaret] Æthelgyth held 2 ploughs in demesne. Then [there were] 8

Ralph Baynard

[Folio 251: NORFOLK]

villans; now 6. Then [there were] 7 bordars; now 6. Then [there were] 4 slaves. [There are] 10 acres of meadow and 1 salt-pan. [There has] always [been] 1 plough belonging to the men. Then [there were] 2 horses and 15 pigs and 60 sheep; now nothing. Then it was worth 100s.; now £8. To this manor belong 15 sokemen at 23 acres. [There has] always [been] half a plough. And they are in the rent above. The whole of Shouldham [All Saints and St Margaret] is 1 league in length and half [a league] in breadth. And it renders 12d. of the 20s. of the king's geld. In Shouldham Thorpe and in Tottenhill 22½ free men hold at 110 acres. Æthelgyth [held] TRE. [There has] always [been] 1 plough. The whole is 4 furlongs in length and 3 in breadth. And it renders 6d. of the geld. This he [i.e., Ralph] claims by exchange.

Wiggenhall Æthelgyth held, 2 carucates. [There have] always [been] 13 villans and 11 bordars. Then [there were] 5 slaves. [There have] always [been] 2 ploughs in demesne and 1½ ploughs belonging to the men. And [there is] half a mill and 1 fishery and 20 acres of meadow. Then [there were] 2 horses and now [likewise]. Then [there were] 5 head of cattle; now 4. [There have] always [been] 20 pigs. Then [there were] 400 sheep; now 160. Then it was worth £6; now [£]12.

Boughton Æthelgyth held: 1 carucate. Then [there were] 5 bordars; now 7. Then [there was] 1 slave. [There has] always [been] 1 plough in demesne. Then [there was] 1 plough belonging to the men; now half [a plough]. And [there are] 6

acres of meadow. [There has] always [been] 1 horse and 1 cow. Then [there were] 11 pigs. [There have] always [been] 100 sheep. And [there is] 1 church, 20 acres, and [it is worth] 20d. And it is worth 40s. To this manor belong in soke 7 sokemen at 30 acres of land. And [there are] 4 acres of meadow and 1 plough. And it is worth 10s.

In Stoke [Ferry] [there are] 13 free men in soke. [There have] always [been] 6 bordars. And [there is] 1 fishery and 2 ploughs. And it is worth 60s. [There is] a quarter part of a church, 5 acres, and it is worth 5d. and another church, 27 acres, [and it is worth] 27d.. This he [i.e., Ralph] claims by exchange.

In Fordham 3 free men hold 30 acres [and] 1 bordar. [They have] been valued above.

In [West] Dereham Lovell holds 1 carucate and 1 plough. [There has] always [been] 1 villan. St B[enet of Hulme] had 20s. from this TRE according to the testimony of the Hundred. They are attached

[Folio 251v: NORFOLK]

to this manor. [There are] 50 acres which free men held TRE. Then [there were] 1½ ploughs; now 1 plough. And it is worth 10s. St B[enet of Hulme] has the soke of these. The whole of Stoke [Ferry] is 6 furlongs in length and 4 in breadth. And it renders 6½d. [of the geld], whoever may hold there.

In Beechamwell [there are] 12 free men at 1 carucate. And [there are] 4 villans. Then [there were] 3 ploughs, afterwards [and] now 2. [There are] 10 acres of meadow. [There is] woodland for 20 pigs. It has always been worth 40s. W[illiam] de Warenne claims one of these at 30 acres and vouches the livery officer. This he claims by exchange. The whole of Beechamwell is half a league in length and breadth. And it renders 8d. of the 20s. of geld. In [West] Dereham [there are] 2 free men, 6 acres, and they have been appraised.

H[UNDRED] AND A HALF OF FREEBRIDGE.

[There is] 1 carucate. Terrington [St Clement or St John] Geoffrey holds: 1 carucate, where Thorth held TRE. [There have] always [been] 5 villans and 4 bordars. And [there are] 24 acres of meadow. [There has] always [been] 1 plough in demesne and 1 plough belonging to the men. And [there are] 5½ salt-pans. Now [there is] 1 horse and 5 head of cattle and 7 pigs. Then [there were] 15 sheep; now 200. Then it was worth 40s.; afterwards 10[s.]; now 60[s.]

In [West] Lynn [there are] 58 acres of meadow and 3 acres of land and 2 salt-pans. And [he holds] 1 free man at 3 acres. And [there are] 8 acres of meadow. And [there is] half a salt-pan by exchange.and over this Stigand had the soke.

H[UNDRED] OF GRIMSHOE.

In Sturston Lovell holds 6 carucates where Thorp held. Then [there were] 9 villans and afterwards [and] now 2. [There have] always [been] 2 bordars. [There are] 10 acres of meadow. [There have] always [been] 2 ploughs in demesne and there can be a third. Then [there were] 3 ploughs belonging to the men; now 2 oxen. Then [there were] 2 horses; now 3. Then [there were] 8 head of cattle; now 11. Then [there were] 20 pigs; now 11. Then [there were] 3 sheep; now 200. Then [there were] 11 mares; now none. It has always been worth 60s.

And in the same [vill] 16 free men hold 2 carucates and 1 acre. Then [there were] 6 ploughs between them and afterwards [and] now 3. Then it was worth 20s. He has these by exchange. The whole is 1 league in length and half [a league] in breadth. And [it renders] 11d. of the geld.

Ralph Baynard

[Folio 252: NORFOLK]

H[UNDRED] OF GREENHOE.

[EAST OR WEST] BRADENHAM Æthelgyth, a certain free woman, held TRE. Now B[aynard has it] for a manor. Then and afterwards [there were] 12 villans; now 15. Then and afterwards [there were] 6 bordars; now 8. Then [there were] 4 slaves; now none. Then [there were] 2 ploughs in demesne; now likewise. [There have] always [been] 3 ploughs belonging to the men. [There are] 8 acres of meadow. [There is] woodland for 250 pigs. When he received [it, there were] 2 horses; now 1. Then and now 1 [sic]. Then and now 8 head of cattle and 18 pigs and 75 sheep. Then [there were] 80 goats; now 26. And it is half a league and 2 furlongs in length and 3 furlongs in breadth. And it renders in geld 18d. And 8 sokemen belong to this manor and have $1\frac{1}{2}$ ploughs and always [have done]. Then it was worth £6 and afterwards [and] now [£]12. [There is] 1 church, 15 acres, and it is worth 15d.

WAYLAND H[UNDRED].

Merton Æthelgyth held TRE: 3 carucates and 1 virgate. Then and afterwards [there were] 17 villans; now 6. Then and afterwards [there were] 3 bordars; now 1. Then and afterwards [there were] 6 slaves; now none. [There is] woodland for 240 pigs. [There are] 36 acres of meadow. [There have] always [been] 3 ploughs in demesne. Then [there were] 4 ploughs belonging to the men; afterwards 2; now none. Then [there were] 5 horses; 4. Then [there were] 18 head of cattle; now 22. [There have] always [been] 24 pigs. Then [there were] 150 sheep; now 90. [There have] always [been] 29 sokemen, 2 carucates with every customary due except for 6 [of them]. Then [there were] 7 ploughs; afterwards [and] now 6.

In Griston [there is] 1 sokeman, 20 acres. Then it was worth 100s.; now £6 but it used to render £8. The whole is 1 league in length and half [a league] in breadth. And [it renders] 15d. of the geld.

SHROPHAM H[UNDRED].

Wilby Æthelgyth held: 1 carucate TRE. Now a [stipendiary] soldier holds [it]. [There have] always [been] 2 villans and 2 bordars. Then [there was] 1 slave. And [there are] 6 acres of meadow. [There is] woodland for 5 pigs. [There has] always [been] 1 plough in demesne and half a plough belonging to the men. [There has] always [been] 1 horse. Then [there were] 3 head of cattle; now 5. Now [there are] [...] pigs. Then [there were] 120 sheep; now 109. Then and afterwards it was worth 40s.; now 60s.

[Folio 252v: NORFOLK]

LAUNDITCH H[UNDRED].

Tittleshall Northmann, a free man, held TRE. Now Ralph Sturmy holds [it]: 4 carucates. Then and afterwards [there were] 12 villans; now 8. Then and afterwards [there were] 4 bordars; now 14. Then and afterwards [there were] 6 slaves; now 2. [There are] 10 acres of meadow. [There have] always [been] 2 ploughs in demesne. Then and afterwards [there were] 4 ploughs belonging to the men; now 2. And [there is] woodland for 100 pigs. [There has] always [been] 1 mill. Then [there were] 6 head of cattle. Then [there were] 30 pigs; now 19. Then [there were] 100 sheep; now 80. Then [there were] 40 goats; now 73. And [there are] 4 hives of bees. And [there is] 1 sokeman, 6 acres. Then it was worth 70s. and now likewise. And [there is] 1 church, 6 acres, and it is worth 5d. The whole is 9 furlongs in length and half a league in breadth. And [it renders] 5d. of the geld.

Wellingham the same Ralph holds, where Harold held TRE for a manor: 2 carucates. [There have] always [been] 9 villans. Then [there were] 3 bordars; afterwards and now 2. [There are] 14 acres of meadow. Then [there was] 1 plough in demesne and [another] could be restored. [There have] always [been] 2 ploughs belonging to the men. [There is] woodland for 60 pigs. And [there are] 7 sokemen, 20 acres of land. Then and afterwards [there was] half a plough; now nothing. And [there were] 3 sokemen of Stigand's who then belonged to Mileham, [a manor] belonging to the king, with every customary due but while Stigand was alive it was delivered to Baynard by exchange as his men declare. And it has 40 acres of land. Then and afterwards [there was] 1 plough; now none. The manor was worth TRE 20s. and now 10[s.] And the 3 sokemen were worth TRE 4s.; now 40d. The whole is 1 league in length and 9 furlongs in breadth. And [it renders] 10d. of the geld, whoever may have land there.

IN Scarning [there are] 80 acres of land. This belongs to [East or West] Bradenham and [is] in the value. And [there are] 2 sokemen, 12 acres of land. The soke has always rightly been in Mileham.

FOREHOE H[UNDRED].

Wicklewood Ulf, a free man, held

Ralph Baynard

[Folio 253: NORFOLK]

TRE: 1 carucate. Now Ralph Sturmy holds [it]. [There are] 11 villans and 8 bordars. Then [there were] 3 slaves; now 1. [There have] always [been] 2 ploughs in demesne and 1 plough belonging to the men. [There are] 6 acres of meadow. [There has] always [been] 1 mill. And [there are] 8 sokemen, 24 acres of land. The soke [is] in Hingham. And they have 1 plough. Then [there was] 1 horse. Then [there were] 7 pigs; now 30. Then [there were] 6 sheep. Now [there are] 4 hives of bees. Then and afterwards it was worth 40.; now 60[s.] And it is 1 league in length and 7 furlongs and 1 perch in breadth. Whoever may have [it] there, [renders] 17fd. of the geld.

I[n] Dykebeck Northmann, a free man, held TRE 1 [carucate]. [There has] always [been] 1 villan. And then [there was] 1 bordar; now 4. Then [there were] 3 slaves. [There have] always [been] 2 ploughs in demesne. And [there are] 4 acres of meadow. Now [there is] 1 horse. [There have] always [been] 4 head of cattle. Now [there are] 22 pigs. Then [there were] 5 sheep; now 40. Then it was worth 40s.; now 80[s.] [There is] a quarter part of [?a church], 5 acres, and it is worth 5d. And it is 4 furlongs in length and 4 in breadth. And [it renders] 11d. of the geld.

LODDON H[UNDRED].

In Chedgrave Thorth held 2 carucates; now Einbald holds [them] for a manor. [There have] always [been] 2 villans and 19 bordars and 4 slaves. [There have] always [been] 2 ploughs in demesne and 1½ [ploughs] belonging to the men. [There is] woodland for 15 pigs. And [there are] 12 acres of meadow and 1 mill. Then [there were] 2 horses. Then [there were] 4 head of cattle; now 3. Then [there were] 7 pigs. Then [there were] 200 sheep; now 160. It has always been worth 40s. And it is 9 furlongs in length and 8 in breadth. And of the geld [it renders] 2d. And [there were] 13½ sokemen, free men of Thorth's, 99 acres. [There have] always [been] 4½ ploughs between the men. And [there are] 5 acres of meadow. And it is worth 10s. And he claims these by exchange.

In Chedgrave Leofric, 1 free man in the commendation of Harold, held 2 carucates; now Geoffrey holds [it] for a manor. [There have] always [been] 4

[Folio 253v: NORFOLK]

villans and 6 bordars. Then [there was] 1 slave; now none. Then [there were] 2 ploughs in demesne; afterwards half [a plough]; now 1. Then [there were] 2 ploughs belonging to the men; afterwards and now 1½. [There is] woodland for 15 pigs. And [there are] 12 acres of meadow and 1 mill. Then [there were] 2 head of cattle; now 1. Then [there were] 5 pigs; now none. [There is] 1 church, 50 acres, 1 [acre] of meadow; it is worth 2 oras. And [there are] 6½ sokemen at 23 acres and 1 free man in the commendation of Leofric with 17½ sokemen. Then [there was] 1 plough; now 1½. [There has] always [been] half a plough [belonging to the men]. And [there is] half an acre of land. Then and afterwards it was worth 30s.; now 40[s.]. . Robert fitzCorbucion claims this land by livery but Baynard was seised Wrst and afterwards Robert. And the Hundred does not know how. The soke [is] in the Hundred.

In Carleton [St Peter] 1 free man held under Thorth 30 acres of land TRE. Now Nigel holds [it]. [There have] always [been] 3 villans. Then [there were] 2 bordars; now 4. [There has] always [been] between the men 1 plough. And [there are] 3 acres of meadow. And [there are] 3 sokemen at 24 acres. [There has] always [been] 1 plough. Then it was worth 10s.; now 20[s.] The soke [is] in the Hundred. This is [Ralph's] by exchange.

[Folio 254: NORFOLK]

The Lands of Ranulf Peverel.

H[UNDRED] OF EYNSFORD.

Billingford [near East Dereham] Thorth, 1 free man, held TRE: 3 carucates. Now Humphrey holds [it]. [There have] always [been] 7 villans and 8 bordars and 2 slaves. Then [there were] 3 ploughs in demesne; afterwards 1½; now 2. Then and afterwards [there were] 8 ploughs belonging to the men; now 5 and there could be 3 ploughs [in addition]. [There is] woodland for 12 pigs. And [there is] 1 mill and 6 acres of meadow. Here used to belong TRE 6 sokemen, 48 acres, and Earl Ralph took them away and now Count Alan holds [them]. [There has] always [been] 1 horse and 10 head of cattle and 16 pigs. [There are] 70 sheep. Now [there are] 4 hives of bees. It has always been worth £4. And it is 1 league in length and half [a league] in breadth. And it renders 8½d., whoever may hold there. The soke [is] in Foulsham, [a manor] belonging to the king.

HUMBLEYARD H[UNDRED].

'WALSINGHAM' [in East Carleton] Warin holds, where Ketil, a thegn of Stigand's, held TRE for 1½ carucates. [There have] always [been] 2 villans and 3 slaves. And [there are] 2 ploughs in demesne and half a plough belonging to the men. [There are] 4 acres of meadow. [There is] woodland for 12 pigs. Then [there were] 4 horses. Then [there were] 4 head of cattle. Then [there were] 35 pigs; now 20. Then [there were] 25 sheep; now 60. [There are] 2 hives of bees. And [there were] 13 free men in soke of the fold and commendation only TRE, 30 acres. Then [there was] 1 plough; afterwards [and] now half [a plough]. [There are] 2 acres of meadow. [There is] 1 church, 60 acres; [it is] in the value of the manor.

In [East] Carleton the same Warin holds where Godric, a free man of Ketel's, held 75 acres. Then [there was] 1 plough; afterwards 1; now nothing. [There are] 2½ bordars and 9 free men in soke of the fold and commendation only. The king and the earl [have] the soke. And they have 33 acres. Then and afterwards [there were] 2 ploughs; now 1. And [there are] 2 acres of meadow. And [there is] 1 free man in commendation only, 24 acres. [There has] always [been] half a plough. And [there are] 2 acres of meadow. Then and afterwards it was worth 60s.; now 110[s.]. And [East] Carleton is worth 20s. And the free man

[Folio 254v: NORFOLK]

is worth 2s. but he is in the number of 110s. And 'Walsingham' [in East Carleton] is 6 furlongs in length and 5 in breadth. And [it renders] 6fd. of the geld.

[Great] Melton Warin holds, where Ketil held TRE: 2 carucates. [There have] always [been] 2 villans and 17 bordars and 2 slaves. And [there are] 2 ploughs in demesne. Then [there were] 5 ploughs belonging to the men; afterwards and now 4. [There are] 20 acres of meadow. [There is] woodland for 100 pigs. [There has] always [been] 1 mill and 2 horses. Then [there were] 4 head of cattle; now 6. Then [there were] 30 pigs; now 45. Then [there were] 60 sheep; now 114. [There are] 2 hives of bees. And [there are] 6 free men at 17 acres in soke of the fold TRE and commendation only. [There have] always [been] 77 acres. [There is] 1 church, 3 acres, within the value of the manor and it is worth 2s. And they are in the value of £7. Then and afterwards it was worth £6; now [£]7. And it is 1 league and 3 furlongs in length and half a league in breadth. And of the geld [it renders] 16½d., whoever may have [it] there.

Ketteringham the same Warin holds, where Ketil held TRE: 1½ carucates. [There have] always [been] 3 bordars. And [there are] 1½ ploughs in demesne and half a plough belonging to the men. [There are] 4 acres of meadow. [There has] always [been] 1 horse and 7 pigs. Now [there are] 40 sheep. And [there are] 4 free men in soke of the fold and commendation only. [There are] 15 acres and half a plough and 1 acre of meadow. Then it was worth 30s.; afterwards 40[s.]; now 60[s.] And the free men are worth 2s. and they are in the same valuation. I [sic].

In [Great or Little] Melton the same Warin holds 1 free man, 6 acres of meadow. And it is worth 6d. This Ranulf Peverel appropriated.

EARSHAM H[UNDRED] AND A HALF.

Rushall Warin holds, where Heanric held from St Edmund wholly within the church TRE for 1½ carucates. [There have] always [been] 7 villans and 3 bordars. [There have] always [been] 2 ploughs in demesne and 1 plough belonging to the men. [There is] woodland for 40 pigs. And [there are] 5 acres of meadow. Now [there is] 1 horse and 3 head of cattle. Then [there were] 50 pigs; now 17. Then [there were] 19 sheep; now 18. Now [there are] 12 goats.

Ranulf Peverel

[Folio 255: NORFOLK]

Then [there were] 3 hives of bees; now 1. Then and afterwards it was worth 40s.; now 60[s.] It is half a league in length and 5 in breadth. And of the geld [it renders] 8d. But more hold there. Now Ranulf holds this land in the king's fief.

The land of Robert [...] Gernon.

H[UNDRED] OF EYNSFORD.

Sparham Osbert holds, where Wulfric, 1 free man, held TRE for a manor: 3 carucates. [There have] always [been] 6 villans and 5 bordars. Then [there were] 2 slaves; now none. [There have] always [been] 2 ploughs in demesne and 2 ploughs belonging to the men. And [there are] 6 acres of meadow and half a mill. [There is] woodland for 100 pigs. When he received [it], [there were] 9 pigs. Now [there are] 6 sheep and 25 goats. And [there are] 3 sokemen, 20 acres of land. [There has] always [been] half a plough. Then and afterwards it was worth 60s. and now £4.

SOUTH ERPINGHAM H[UNDRED].

Baconsthorpe [near Holt] Osbert holds, where Wulfric, a free man of Gyrth's, held 2 carucates TRE. [There have] always [been] 3 villans and 10 bordars. Then [there were] 2 slaves;

now 1. Then [there were] 3 ploughs in demesne; now 2. [There have] always [been] [...] 1½ ploughs belonging to the men. And [there is] 1 church

[Folio 255v: NORFOLK]

at 30 acres in alms. Then [there was] woodland for 40 pigs; now 30. [There have] always [been] 2 horses and 17 pigs. Then [there were] 100 sheep; now 80. And [there are] 40 goats. And [there is] 1 sokeman, 8 acres of land. There [has] always [been] half a plough. It has always been worth 30s. And it is 6 furlongs in length and 5 in breadth. And [it renders] 6¾d. of the geld

CLAVERING H[UNDRED].

In Norton [Subcourse] the same man holds 12 acres of the demesne of Loddon. And it is worth 12d.

In "Naruestuna" [there were] 4 acres of land and 1 free man, Wulfric by name, TRE. And it is worth 4d.

NORTH ERPINGHAM H[UNDRED].

In Thorpe [Market] Osbert holds. [There are] 7 free men at 40 acres of land. [There is] 1 acre of meadow. [There has] always [been] 1 plough. And it is worth 12s.

LODDON H[UNDRED].

In Loddon Osbert holds 1½ carucates where Wulfric, a free man under Gyrth, held TRE. [There have] always [been] 2 villans and 12 bordars. Then [there was] 1 slave. [There have] always [been] 2 ploughs in demesne. Then and afterwards [there were] 2 ploughs belonging to the men; now 1½. [There is] woodland for 20 pigs. And [there are] 4 acres of meadow and half a mill. Now [there are] 4 horses at the hall. And [there are] 4 head of cattle. Then [there were] 100 sheep; now 60. Then [there were] 10 pigs; now 21. And [there is] 1 sokeman at 10 acres. [There has] always [been] 1 plough between them all. Then and afterwards it was worth 20s.; now 40[s.] Earl R[alph had] the soke.

In Loddon [there are] 4 acres of land. It is in the value of 40s.

[Folio 256: NORFOLK]

The lands of Peter de Valognes.

H[UNDRED] AND A HALF OF FREEBRIDGE.

Babingley William holds, which Thorth, a free man, held TRE for a manor: 1 carucate. [There are] 4 villans and 15 bordars and 5 slaves. And [there are] 16 acres of meadow. [There is] woodland for 60 pigs. Then [there were] 2 ploughs in demesne; afterwards and now 1. Then [there were] 3 ploughs belonging to the men; afterwards and now 2. And [there is] a moiety of two mills and 5 salt-pans. When he received [it], [there was] 1 horse. Then [there were] 10 head of cattle; now 8. Then [there were] 12 pigs; now 13. Then [there were] 160 sheep; now 177. Here belong 7 sokeman, 6 acres of land. [There has] always [been] 1 plough. Yet of these Stigand then had the soke. The whole is worth 40s. The whole is 2 leagues in length and 1 league in breadth. Whoever may hold there, it renders 2s. of a 20s. geld.

Dersingham 1 free man held TRE for a manor. [There

have] always [been] 2 ploughs in demesne. And [there are] 7 villans and 4 bordars. Then and afterwards [there were] 4 slaves; now 2. And [there are] 7½ acres of meadow. And [there is] 1 plough belonging to the men. And [there is] 1 salt-pan. Then [there were] 5 horses; now 1. Then [there were] 3 head of cattle and 18 pigs and 300 sheep; now nothing.

In the same [vill] Anund, a free man, holds 2 carucates in demesne for a manor. [There have] always [been] 1½ ploughs. And [there are] 30 villans and 6 bordars and 7 slaves. And [there are] 18 acres of meadow and 1 mill and 1 fishery and 1 salt-pan. Then [there were] 6 horses; now 5. Then [there were] 4 head of cattle and now [likewise]. Then [there were] 40 pigs; now 21. Then [there were] 560 sheep; now 646.

In Appleton Turgis holds [in] 1 berewick 1 carucate which has always belonged to this manor. And [there is] 1 plough in demesne. Then and afterwards [there were] 3 bordars; now 5. And [there are] 7½ acres
of meadow. Then and afterwards [there was] 1 slave. Then [there were] 100 sheep; now 2 sheep. The whole is worth £15 but yet it renders £17 13s.

[Folio 256v: NORFOLK]

The whole of Dersingham is 1 league in length and half [a league] in breadth. Whoever may hold there, it renders 16d. of a 20[s.] geld.

H[UNDRED] OF SMETHDON.

In Ingoldisthorpe Thurbert, a free man, held TRE 3 ploughs in demesne. Then and afterwards [there were] 10 villans; now 7. [There have] always [been] 15 bordars. Then and afterwards [there were] 2 slaves; now 5. And [there are] 50 acres of meadow. Then [there were] 3 ploughs belonging to the men; afterwards and now 2. [There have] always [been] 2 mills and 1 salt-pan. Then [there was] 1 fishery. Then [there were] 8 horses; now 4. Then [there were] 14 mares. Then [there were] 5 head of cattle. Then [there were] 60 pigs; now 15. Then [there were] 340 sheep; now 420. And [there are] 3 free men, 38 acres of land. [There is] 1 plough. His predecessor had soke of the fold and commendation of these men. Stigand [had] the other soke. Then and afterwards it was worth £9 and now [£]10 but it renders £12. The whole is half a league in length and 5 furlongs in breadth. Whoever may hold there renders 12d. of a 20s. geld.

LAUNDITCH H[UNDRED.

Pattesley Roger holds, which Æthelstan, a free man, held TRE for a manor: 2 carucates in demesne. Then and afterwards [there was] 1 plough belonging to the men; now none, but there could be. [There is] woodland for 10 pigs and half a fishery. Now [there is] 1 horse and 15 head of cattle. Then [there were] 4 pigs. Now [there are] 13 head of cattle. Now [there are] 59 sheep. It has always been worth 20s. And it is 4 furlongs in length and 2 in breadth. And [it renders] 3d. of the geld. The soke [is] in Mileham, [a manor] belonging to the king.

And in Gateley Ralph holds 2 sokemen, 34 acres of land of which the predecessor of Hugh de Montfort had soke of the fold and commendation.

And the other soke [is] in Mileham, [a manor] belonging to the king.

Peter de Valognes

[Folio 257: NORFOLK]

Now [...] Peter holds them by livery. [There has] always [been] 1 [?plough] and 1½ acres of meadow. It has always been worth 20s.

H[UNDRED] OF GALLOW.

In [Little] Snoring Ralph holds 1 carucate, which Manni, 1 free man, held TRE. [There have] always [been] 24 bordars. [There has] always [been] 1 slave. Then [there was] 1 plough in demesne and afterwards [and] now 2. [There has] always [been] 1 plough belonging to the men. [There are] 4 acres of meadow. Then [there was] 1 mill. [There have] always [been] 6 head of cattle. And now [there are] 60 pigs. Then [there were] 80 sheep; now 50. And [there are] 6 sokemen at 40 acres of land and 2 bordars and 1 plough. [There are] 5 acres of meadow. To this manor belongs 1 sokeman at 3 acres in Helhoughton. Then it was worth 40s.; now likewise. And it is half a league in length and 3 furlongs in breadth. And [it renders] 12d. of the geld.

In LITTLE RYBURGH Thyri holds 1 carucate which a free man held TRE. Then [there were] 9 bordars; now 6. Then [there were] 2 slaves. [There has] always [been] 1 plough in demesne. Then [there was] 1 plough belonging to the men; now half [a plough]. [There is] woodland for 6 pigs. [There are] 4 acres of meadow. [There is] 1 mill. Then [there were] 2 horses; now 1. [There have] always [been] 8 head of cattle. Then [there were] 4 pigs; now 11. Then [there were] 30 sheep. It has always been worth 40s. And it is 3 furlongs in length and 2 in breadth. And [it renders] 12d. in geld.

H[UNDRED] OF BROTHERCROSS.

In [Great] Ryburgh Ralph the fat holds 2 carucates which Gyrth held TRE. [There has] always [been] 1 villan and 11 bordars and 4 slaves. [There are] 2 ploughs in demesne and 1 plough belonging to the men. [There is] woodland for 40 pigs. [There are] 6 acres of meadow. [There is] 1 mill. [There have] always [been] 2 horses. Now [there are] 11 head of cattle. [There have] always [been] 40 pigs. Then [there were] 7 sheep; now 60. To this manor belongs 1 berewick of Toftrees at 30 acres of land. [There have] always [been] 4 bordars. [There has] always [been] 1 plough in demesne. Then and always [there has been] half a plough belonging to the men. Then it was worth £4 and now £5. [Great] Ryburgh is 7 furlongs in length and 5

[Folio 257v: NORFOLK]

in breadth. And [it renders] 9¼d. in geld. And Toftrees is 4 furlongs in length and 3 in breadth. And [it renders] 15d. in geld.

In Testerton Richard holds half a carucate which Toki, a free man, held TRE. [There have] always [been] 7 bordars and 1 slave. [There has] always [been] 1 plough in demesne. Then [there was] 1 [plough]
belonging to the men, and afterwards [and] now half a

plough. [There is] half an acre of meadow. Then it was worth 10s.; now likewise.

In [East or West] Rudham Turgis, 1 free man, holds at half a carucate. [There have] always [been] 3 bordars and 1 slave. Then [there was] 1 plough; afterwards a half and now 1. And [there is] 1 acre of meadow. And [there are] 4 sokemen at 6 acres. [There has] always [been] half a plough. It has always been worth 10s.

H[UNDRED] OF GALLOW.

In Saxlingham Theodoric, 1 free man, holds at half a carucate. Then [there was] 1 plough; now likewise. [There have] always [been] 2 bordars. [There are] 2 acres of meadow. Then it was worth 2s.; now 5s.

H[UNDRED] OF HOLT.

In Gunthorpe 1 free man of Harold's [held] at half a carucate. [There have] always [been] 6 bordars and 1 slave. [There have] always [been] 2 ploughs. [There is] woodland for 4 pigs. [There is] 1 acre of meadow. And it is worth 10s. This was handed over to him to make up 1 manor [at] Barney.

In Edgefield Skiotr, a free man, held TRE 60 and 20 acres. [There have] always [been] 5 villans and 1 bordar. And [there is] 1 plough. [There is] woodland for 100 pigs. [There are] 2 acres of meadow. And [there are] 2 sokemen at 12 acres of land. And it belongs to Binham.

H[UNDRED] OF GREENHOE.

Binham Skiotr held TRE: 3 carucates. [There are] 3 villans. [There have] always [been] 13 bordars, 2 slaves. And then [there were] 2 ploughs and afterwards and now 6 in demesne. Then and afterwards [there were] 2 ploughs belonging to the men and now 1½. [There are] 11 acres of meadow. Then [there was] 1 mill. And [there are] 16 sokemen pertaining to this vill, 30 acres of land. Then [there were] 2 ploughs; now 1½ ploughs. [There are] 2 acres of meadow. In the lord's hall [there were] then 8 horses; now 5. Then [there were] 3 head of cattle; now 1. Then [there were] 16 [?pigs];

Peter de Valognes

[Folio 258: NORFOLK]

afterwards [and] now 10. Then [there were] 120 [sheep]; now half a 100 sheep.

Wells [-next-the-Sea] belongs to this manor, half a carucate. [There is] 1 bordar. Then it was worth £4 and afterwards; now it is worth £20. And it is 1 league in length and half [a league] in breadth. And it renders 2s. of the geld.

Barney William holds: which Thorkil held TRE 2 carucates. Then and afterwards [there were] 14 bordars; now 13. [There have] always [been] 2 ploughs in demesne and 1 plough belonging to the men. Then and afterwards [there were] 2 slaves; now 1. [There is] woodland for 60 pigs. [There are] 14 acres of meadow. [There has] always [been] 1 horse. Then [there were] 14 wild mares. Then and afterwards [there were] 10 head of cattle; now 14. Then [there were] 20 pigs; now 28. Then [there were] 60 sheep; now 100. Then 40 goats; now 38. [There are] now 2 hives of bees. And 17 free men, 80

acres of land: these he claims by livery to make up this manor. [There have] always [been] 2 ploughs. [There are] 6 acres of meadow. Then and afterwards it was worth £4. And it is half a league in length and half in breadth. And of the geld [it renders] 6d. And of these [free men], 1 royal sergeant claims by whatever judicial ordeal he is judged [that] 13½ [were] in the fief of Earl Ralph, whom he was holding when he forfeited, and the Hundred testifies to this. And they hold 80 acres of land. And [there are] 2 acres of meadow. And they render in [Great] Snoring 17s. 4d.

In Great Walsingham Humphrey holds 1½ carucates, which Bondi, 1 thegn, held. [There have] always [been] 3 villans and 7 bordars. And [there are] 2 ploughs in demesne. [There are] 4 acres of meadow. Then and afterwards [there were] 1½ ploughs belonging to the men and now 1. Afterwards [there were] 3 slaves; now 4. Then [there were] 5 animals; now 1. Then [there were] 20 pigs; now 25. [There have] always [been] 180 sheep. Then [there were] 9 hives of bees; now 5. And [there is] 1 sokeman, 4 acres of land. Then and afterwards it was worth 30s. and now 40[s.] This land was delivered to make up a manor: his [i.e., Peter's] men do not know which one.

In Holkham Toki, 1 free man, held 33 acres of land. [There have] always [been] 2 bordars. It has always been worth 2 oras. And he [i.e., Peter] holds that [vill] just as has been declared above.

[Folio 258v: NORFOLK]

H[UNDRED] OF EYNSFORD.

In [Wood] Dalling 1 free man, Fisc, held TRE 1 carucate. [There have] always [been] 9 villans and 16 bordars and 2 slaves. [There has] always [been] 1 plough in demesne and 3 ploughs belonging to the men. And [there are] 2 acres of meadow. [There is] woodland for 6 pigs. When he received [it], [there was] 1 horse; now 2. Then [there were] 6 head of cattle; now 20. Then [there were] 6 pigs; now 30. Then [there were] 16 sheep; now 80. And [there are] 30 goats. And [there are] 5 sokemen, 20 acres of land. [There has] always [been] 1 plough. The soke [is] in Foulsham, [a manor] belonging to the king. And it is worth 40s. And it is 1 league in length and half [a league] in breadth. And it renders 19d. to the king's geld, whoever holds there.

XXXV. The lands of Robert fitzCorbucion.

S [sic]. H[undred] and a half of Freebridge.
Sandringham Ranulf holds, which 1 free man under Harold held TRE. Then and afterwards [there was] 1 plough; now none. Then and afterwards [there were] 5 bordars; now none. Then and afterwards [there were] 3 slaves; now 1. And [there are] 3½ acres of meadow. Then and afterwards [there was] plough belonging to the men. Then and afterwards [there was] 1 salt-pan. It has always been worth 20s.

HENSTEAD H[UNDRED].

In Saxlingham [Nethergate or Thorpe] Gunfrid holds what Leofweald, 1 free man in the commendation of Harold, held at 30 acres of land. [There have] always [been] 5 bordars. Then [there were] 2 slaves. Then and afterwards [there was] 1 plough in demesne and 1 plough belonging to the men. And [there are] 2 free men at 3 acres of land. And [there are] 2 acres of meadow. Then it was worth 16s.; now 22s.

In Stoke [Holy Cross] Giffard holds 1 carucate [which] 3 free men in the commendation of Stigand [held]. [There have] always [been] 10 bordars and 2 slaves. [There have] always [been] 1½ ploughs in demesne

ROBERT FITZCORBUCION

and half [a plough] belonging to the men. And [there are] 3 acres of meadow. Then [there was] 1 horse. It has always been worth 30s.

EARSHAM HALF H[UNDRED].

In Rushall Gunfrid holds 1½ carucates which Beorhtric, 1 free man in the commendation of Stigand, held but he could neither give nor sell his land without his permission. Then [there were] 6 villans; afterwards and now 3. Then [there were] 1½ ploughs; now half a plough]. [There has] always [been] half a plough belonging to the men. [There is] woodland for 40 pigs. And [there are] 6 acres of meadow. Then and afterwards it was worth 20s.; now 10[s.]

In Starston the same man holds 1 carucate which Leofstan, 1 free man in the commendation only of Ulf, held TRE. [There has] always [been] 1 plough in demesne. And [there are] 3 acres of meadow. Then and afterwards it was worth 20s.; now 15[s.]

LODDON H[UNDRED].

In Loddon Humphrey holds 1½ carucates which Ælfric, 1 free man, held TRE under Stigand. And [there has] always [been] 1 villan and 3 bordars and 1 slave. Then [there were] 1½ ploughs; afterwards 1; now 1½ in demesne. Then [there were] 1½ ploughs belonging to the men; afterwards and now 1. [There is] woodland for 12 pigs and half a mill and 4 acres of meadow. Then [there were] 50 sheep; now 55. Then [there were] 13 [pigs]; now 14 pigs. And [there are] 4 sokemen at 12 acres of land. Then [there were] 1½ ploughs between them all; afterwards and now 1. Then it was worth 20s.; afterwards and now 30[s.]

In Ingloss the same man holds 1 carucate which Wulfric held under Stigand. [There have] always [been] 3 villans and 7 bordars. [There has] always [been] 1 plough in demesne. Then [there was] 1 plough belonging to the men; afterwards and now 1½. [There is] woodland for 4 pigs. [There has] always [been] 1 horse. It has always been worth 20s. And [there are] 9 sokemen under him at 20 acres. Then [there were] 3 ploughs; afterwards and now 2. Then it was worth 7s.; now 10s. The king and the earl [have] the soke.

LODDON H[UNDRED].

In Mundham Nigel holds 30 acres of land which Godwine, 1 free man in the commendation of Edwin, the predecessor of Godric the steward, held TRE. [There has] always [been] 1 plough in demesne. [There is] woodland for 2 pigs. And [there are] 4 acres of meadow.

And [there are] 11 free men of Edgar's, 30 acres. [There have] always [been] 1½ ploughs. Then it was worth 10[s.]; now 20[s.] The king and the earl [have] the soke.

In Mundham Ansgar holds 1 carucate which Algar, a free man under Stigand, held for a manor TRE. [There have] always [been] 4 villans. Then and afterwards [there were] 2 ploughs in demesne; now half a plough. [There has] always [been] half a plough belonging to the men. And [there is] half an acre of meadow. [There has] always [been] 1 horse at the hall. Then [there were] 2 head of cattle; now none. Then [there were] 8 pigs; now 4. Then [there were] 20 sheep; now 5. And [there are] 4½ sokemen at 4½ acres of land and 1 free man in the commendation only of Algar, 6 acres of land. Between them all [there is] 1 plough. It has always been worth 10s.

In Broome Humphrey holds 2 carucates which Anund, a thegn, held TRE. Then and afterwards [there were] 2 bordars; now none. [There has] always [been] 1 slave. [There have] always [been] 2 ploughs in demesne. Then [there were] 2 oxen; now 1. [There is] woodland for 20 pigs. And [there are] 20 acres of meadow and 1 mill and half a fishery and 3 head of cattle. Now [there are] 50 sheep. Then [there were] 40 pigs; now 20. And [there are] 2 hives of bees. And [there are] 5 men in commendation under him, 10 acres of land. All [of them have] always [had] half a plough. Then and afterwards it was worth 40s.; now 50[s.] And it is 1 league in length and 5 furlongs in breadth. And [it renders] in geld 8d. Mundham is 20 furlongs in length and 10 [furlongs] in breadth. And of the geld [it renders] 2s.

In Loddon Humphrey holds under R[obert] half an acre of land which St Be[net] of Hulme claims and the Hundred testifies that it was in the demesne of St Be[net].

H[UNDRED] OF SOUTH ERPINGHAM.

In [Little] Barningham , 1 free man, 82 acres of land. [There have] always [been] 5 bordars. And [there is] 1 plough in demesne and half [a plough] belonging to the men. And [there are] 2 acres of meadow. [There is] woodland for 15 pigs. And it is worth 10s. And it is 7 furlongs in length and 4 in breadth. And [it renders] 3¾d. of the geld.

DEPWADE H[UNDRED].

Shelton Nigel holds: 30 acres which Ealdwine, a free man of Stigand's, held. [There has] always [been] 1 villan and 9½ bordars.

Robert fitzCorbucion

And [there is] 1 plough in demesne and 1 plough belonging to the men. And [there are] 2½ acres of meadow. Then it was worth 10s.; now 20[s.]

In Tharston the same man holds 1 carucate [which] 1 free man held. [There has] always [been] 1 villan and 5 bordars. And [there is] 1 plough in demesne and ½ a plough belonging to the men. [There are] 3 acres of meadow. [There is] woodland for 4 pigs. And [there is] 1 mill. And [there is] 1 free man,

2 acres. And [there is] 1 horse and 3 head of cattle. Then it was worth 10s.; now 20[s.]

Stratton [St Mary or St Michael] Humphrey holds: 2 carucates which 1 thegn held TRE. [There have] always [been] 17 bordars. And [there are] 2 ploughs in demesne. And then [there were] 3 ploughs belonging to the men; afterwards 2; now 1. [There are] 6 acres of meadow. [There is] woodland for 6 pigs. [There has] always [been] 1 horse. And then [there were] 5 pigs; now 11. Then [there were] 10 sheep; now 26. And [there are] 6 goats. And [there are] 7 free men, 17 acres, over whom his predecessor had the commendation TRE and he has them for land. Then [there was] 1 plough. [There is] 1 acre of meadow. Then it was worth 30s.; now 40[s.]

Fritton Giffard holds: 30 acres and 3 bordars which Ulfkil, a free man of Eadric of Laxfield's, the predecessor of Robert Malet, held. Then and afterwards [there were] 2 ploughs. Then [there were] 16 pigs; now 8. Then [there were] 6 head of cattle and 60 sheep; now nothing. [There has] always [been] half a plough belonging to the men. [There are] 1½ acres of meadow. [There is] soke of the fold. And [there are] 7 men who could sell their land if they had first offered it to their lord. And they have 14 acres. And [there is] 1 free man, 4 acres. [There has] always [been] half a plough. It was always worth 25s. And it is 1 league in length and half [a league] in breadth. And [it renders] 9d. of the geld. William Malet was seised of this land when he went into the marsh.

CLAVERING H[UNDRED].

In Haddiscoe the same man holds 30 acres and 3 bordars [which] 1 sokeman of Stigand's [held]. And then [there was] 1 plough. And [there are] 4 acres of meadow. And under that man [there are] 2 sokemen, 4 acres and half a plough. Then it was worth 5s.; now 11[s.]

In "Iarpestuna" [there is] 1 sokeman of St Edmund's, 46 acres and 2 bordars.

[Folio 260v: NORFOLK]

Then [there was] 1 plough; now 2 oxen. Then it was worth 20s.; now 10[s.]

XXXVI. The lands of Ranulf, brother of Ilger.

H[UNDRED OF SOUTH ERPINGHAM.

In Erpingham Humphrey holds 1 carucate which Bondi, a free man of Harold's, held. [There have] always [been] 3 villans and 9 bordars. And [there is] 1 plough in demesne and 1 belonging to the men. And [there are] 2 acres of meadow. And then [there was] 1 horse and 3 head of cattle. Then it was worth 10s.; now 20[s.]

TUNSTEAD HUNDRED.

In Honing the same man holds 1 carucate [which] 1 free man [held] TRE. [There have] always [been] 8 villans and 1 bordar. And [there is] 1 plough in demesne and 1 plough belonging to the men. And [there are] 9 acres of meadow. [There is] woodland for 4 pigs. [There has] always [been] 1

mill. And [there are] 3 head of cattle and 3 pigs. And [there are] 2 sokemen, 15 acres of land. And [there is] 1 plough and 2 acres of meadow. It has always been worth 20s. St B[enet of Hulme has] the soke. Swafield 2 free men [hold:] 18 acres. [There has] always [been] half a plough. And [there is] half an acre of meadow. And it is worth 16d.

In Ridlington [there are] 16 sokemen, 120 acres of land. [There have] always [been] 5 ploughs. And [there is] 1 acre of meadow. And it is worth 20s.

H[UNDRED] OF HAPPING.

Walcott the same man holds: 4 carucates and 6 acres which Eadric, a thegn, held TRE. [There have] always [been] 8 villans and 16 bordars. Then and afterwards [there were] 2 ploughs in demesne; now 3. [There have] always [been] 2 ploughs belonging to the men. [There are] 8 acres of meadow and 1 mill. Now [there are] 2 horses. Then [there were] 3 head of cattle; now 16. Then [there were] 3 pigs; now 24. Then [there were] 80 sheep; now 70. And [there are] 4 hives of bees. [There is] 1 church, 20 acres, and it is worth 20d.. And the same man holds 7½

Ranulf, brother of Ilger

[Folio 261: NORFOLK]

free men in commendation only, 70 acres. Then and afterwards [there were] 2 ploughs; now 2½. And the same man holds 4 free men who were added to this manor TRW. [There are] 90 acres which Ranulf, brother of Ilger, added, and Humphrey holds them. Then [there were] 3 ploughs; now 2½. And it is worth 15s. His predecessor had the commendation only of two [of them] and the predecessor of Robert Malet of one likewise. The king and the earl [have] the soke. And the manor was then worth 40s.; now 60[s.] And it is 1 league in length and half [a league] in breadth. And [it renders] 15d. of the geld, whoever may hold there.

H[UNDRED] OF HOLT.

In Edgefield Humphrey holds 2 carucates which Bondi, a free man of Harold's, held TRE. [There have] always [been] 2 villans and 7 bordars and 2 slaves. [There have] always [been] 2 ploughs in demesne and 2 ploughs belonging to the men. [There is] woodland for 100 pigs. [There are] 5 acres of meadow. [There is] 1 mill. Now [there are] 2 horses. Then [there were] 7 pigs; now 23. Then [there were] 7 sheep; now 80. Then [there were] 13 goats; now 21. Then [there was] a hive of bees; now 2. And [there are] 17 sokemen at 24 acres of land. Their ploughs are [enumerated] above. Then it was worth 30s.; now 40[s.] It is 1 league in length and half [a league] in breadth. And [it renders] 9d. in geld.

In Stody the same man holds 1 free man of Harold's, now Ro[bert]'s, at 2 carucates for a manor. [There have] always [been] 8 villans and 7 bordars and 1 slave. And in demesne [there are] 2 ploughs and 1½ ploughs belonging to the men. [There is] woodland for 40 pigs. [There are] 6 acres of meadow. [There are] 3 mills. Then [there were] 2 horses; now 1. Now [there are] 9 head of cattle. Then [there were] 5 pigs; now 12. Now [there are] 40 sheep. Then [there were] 60 goats; now 25. And [there are] 3 hives of bees. And [there are] 4 sokemen at 16 acres and half a plough. Then it was worth 30s.; now 40[s.] To this manor belong 25 acres. And half a plough in Letheringsett has been valued with the manor.

65. 120. 90

[Folio 261V: NORFOLK]

XXXVII. The lands of Tihel. H[undred] of Eynsford.

GUTON Osbert holds: 4 carucates which Leofstan, a free man, held TRE. Then and afterwards [there were] 9 villans; now 4. Then and afterwards [there were] 17 bordars; now 15. And [there are] 2 slaves. Then and afterwards [there were] 2 ploughs in demesne; now 3. [There have] always [been] 4 ploughs belonging to the men. And [there are] 30 acres of meadow. [There is] woodland for 60 pigs. And [there is] 1 mill. [There have] always [been] 4 horses. Then [there were] 8 head of cattle; now 14. Then [there were] 14 hives of bees. And the same man holds 18 sokemen, 113 acres of land. And [there is] 1 bordar. Then and afterwards [there were] 4 ploughs; now 3. And [there are] 3½ acres of meadow. The king and the earl [have] the soke over the whole. Then and afterwards it was worth £4; now £6. And it is 1 league in length and half [a league] in breadth. And it renders 7d. to the king's geld.

H[UNDRED] OF SOUTH ERPINGHAM.

In Calthorpe Guerri and Osbert hold 1 carucate which 1 free man, Leofstan, held. [There have] always [been] 3 villans and 8 bordars. And [there is] 1 plough in demesne and [there are] 1½ ploughs belonging to the men. [There are] 6 acres of meadow. [There is] woodland for 15 pigs. [There is] a third part of a mill. Then [there were] 3 horses. Then there were 3 horses [sic]. Then [there were] 13 head of cattle; now 1. Then [there were] 30 pigs; now 10. Then [there were] 7 hives of bees; now 2. Then it was worth 20s. 20s. [sic]; now 30[s.]

Booton the same men hold: 1 carucate [which] 1 sokeman of Harold's [held] TRE. [There has] always [been] 1 villan and 4 bordars and 1 slave. And [there is] 1 plough in demesne and half [a plough] belonging to the men. And [there are] 2 acres of meadow. [There is] woodland for 16 pigs. Then it was worth 10s. and now [likewise]. The soke [is] in Cawston. The whole of this was delivered for one manor.

[Folio 262: NORFOLK]

The lands of Robert de Verly.

H[UNDRED] OF GUILTCROSS.

[East or West] Harling Outi held TRE: 1 carucate. [There have] always [been] 3 villans and 3 bordars and 2 slaves. [There are] 4 acres of meadow. Then [there was] in demesne 1 plough and afterwards 2 oxen; now 1 plough. Then [there was] 1 plough belonging to the men and afterwards half [a plough]; now 1 plough. [There is] woodland for 12 pigs. Then [there were] 8 head of cattle; now 3. And [there are] 8 pigs. Then [there were] 14 sheep; now 120. And [there are] 5 sokemen, 30 acres of land. And [there are] 3 acres of meadow.

[There has] always [been] 1 plough. And it is worth 30s. And [there are] 7½ acres of land.

H[UNDRED] OF GALLOW.

In Burnham Thorpe Godwine held 1 carucate TRE and afterwards Ralph when he forfeited. [There have] always [been] 8 bordars. Then [there was] 1 slave. Then [there was] 1 plough in demesne; now half [a plough]. Then [there was] 1 plough belonging to the men; now half [a plough]. Then [there were] 2 horses; now 1. Then [there were] 180 sheep; now 21. And 2 free men dwell on this carucate. Then it was worth 40s.; now 30[s.]

H[UNDRED] OF GREENHOE.

In [Field] Dalling G[odwine], uncle of Ralph, held TRE. [There are] 11 free men, 1 carucate. Now R[obert] de Verly holds, saying that he holds it in exchange for Roding in another county [Essex]. Then [there were] 2 ploughs; now 1. And [there are] 3 acres of meadow. It has always been worth 20s. And of that he vouches Robert Blund as livery officer.

WALSHAM H[UNDRED].

In Tunstall Skalpi held TRE 80 acres of land. [There have] always [been] 6 bordars. [There has] always [been] 1 plough in demesne, 1 plough belonging to the men. [There are] 10 acres of meadow. Then [there were] 60 [sheep]; now 50 sheep. [There is] 1 salt-pan. It has always been worth 20s.

The lands of Humphrey fitzAubrey.

GUILTCROSS H[UNDRED].

[In] Riddlesworth Ordgar, a free man, held 1 carucate TRE.

[Folio 262V: NORFOLK]

Then and afterwards [there were] 2 bordars; now none. [There has] always [been] 1 slave. And [there are] 9 acres of meadow. Then and afterwards [there were] 2 ploughs in demesne; now 1½ ploughs. And [there are] 4 free men, 27 acres of land, and 3 bordars. And [there are] 2 acres of meadow. [There has] always [been] 1 plough. [There has] always [been] 1 horse. Then [there were] 9 pigs; now 13. Then [there were] 26 sheep; now 21. It has always been worth 30s. The soke of 4 men [is] in Kenninghall. The whole is half a league in length and half in breadth. And [it renders] 12½d. of the geld.

H[UNDRED] OF EYNSFORD.

In Billingford [near East Dereham] 1 free woman held 1 carucate for a manor TRE. [There has] always [been] 1 villan and 7 bordars. [There has] always [been] 1 plough in demesne and 1 plough belonging to the men. And [there are] 2 acres of meadow and 1 mill. When he received [it, there was] 1 horse; now none. [There have] always [been] 5 head of cattle and 60 sheep. It has always been worth 20s. The soke [was] in Foulsham, [a manor] belonging to the king TRE; now Humphrey holds [it].

XL. The land of Humphrey de Bohun.

H[UNDRED] OF BROTHERCROSS.

In Tatterford Wulfnoth held TRE of Bishop Stigand 1 carucate TRE. [There have] always [been] 3 villans and 11 bordars and 2 slaves. [There has] always [been] 1 plough in demesne. Then [there were] 2 ploughs belonging to the men; now 1½. [There are] 3 acres of meadow. [There is] 1 mill. [There have] always [been] 2 head of cattle. Then [there were] 10 pigs; now 14. And [there are] 100 sheep. And 1 berewick of half a carucate [belongs] to this manor. [There have] always [been] 3 bordars and 1 plough. [There are] 2 acres of meadow. [There is] 1 mill. Then and always it has been worth 40s. And it is half a league in length and 3 furlongs in breadth. And [it renders] 3d. in geld. And [there are] 3 slaves. 4 sokemen, 40 acres, have been taken from this manor and W[illiam] de War[enne] holds [them].

[Folio 263: NORFOLK]

The lands of Ralph de Fougàres.

DISS HALF HUNDRED.

'Osmondiston' [in Scole] Algar held under Harold TRE for half a carucate. [There have] always [been] 2 villans. [There have] always [been] 6 bordars. Then [there were] 2 slaves; now 1. [There has] always [been] 1 plough in demesne, but there could be two. [There have] always [been] 2 ploughs belonging to the men. [There is] woodland for 10 pigs. [There are] 6 acres of meadow. [There has] always [been] 1 horse at the hall. And [there are] 2 head of cattle and 10 pigs. And [there are] 4 free men at 40 acres of land. Then [there were] 1½ ploughs; afterwards and now 1. And [there are] 4 acres of meadow. Then it was worth 40s.; afterwards 50[s.] and now [likewise]. It is 5 furlongs in length and 4 in breadth. And of the geld [it renders] 2d.

The lands of Gilbert fitzRicher.

H[UNDRED] OF CLACKCLOSE.

Mildenhall [Suffolk] Æthelgyth held TRE. Then [there were] 2 ploughs; now 1. [There have] always [been] 15 villans and 5 bordars. Then [there were] 4 slaves; now 2. Then [there were] 2 ploughs belonging to the men; now 1. Then [there was] 1 horse. Then [there were] 16 pigs; now 8. And [there are] 2 head of cattle. [There have] always [been] 29 sheep. And [there are] 10 acres of meadow. Then it was worth £5; now [£]4.

The lands of Roger de Rames.

WAYLAND H[UNDRED].

Tottington Warengar holds: 3 carucates which Alwine, a free man, held TRE. Then and afterwards [there were] 9 villans; now 7. Then [there was] 1 bordar. Then and afterwards [there were] 2 slaves; now none. [There are] 12 acres of meadow. Then and afterwards [there was] 1 plough in demesne; now 1½. Then and afterwards [there were] 2 ploughs belonging to the men; now half [a plough]. [There have] always [been] 2 horses and 15 head of cattle. Then [there were] 20 pigs; now 5. Then [there were] 80 [?sheep]; now 14. [There are] 6 goats. Then and afterwards it was worth 40s.; now 20[s.]

EARSHAM HALF-H[UNDRED].

In 'Pyrleston' [in Scole] the same man holds 24 actres of land but they were

[Folio 263v: NORFOLK]

in the hall of St Edmund and [there were] 12 free men of St Edmund's who could neither give nor sell their land without the permission of the saint and of Stigand who had the soke and sake in Earsham. The men had 60 acres and 2 bordars. Then and afterwards [there were] 2 ploughs; now 1½. Then and afterwards it was worth 10s.; now 5[s.].

In the same [vill] also holds 40 acres of land which St Ed[mund] held TRE according to the testimony of the Hundred; now Warengar [holds it] but the Hundred does not know by what means.

In Starston the same man holds. [There were] 2 free men of Stigand's TRE belonging to Earsham whom Warengar holds under R[oger] de Rames at 16 acres of land. [There has] always [been] 1 plough. Then and afterwards it was worth 4s.; now 32d.

H[UNDRED] OF HUMBLEYARD.

Rainthorpe Alwine, 1 free man, held: 60 acres of land; now William holds [them]. [There has] always [been] 1 plough. And [there are] 7 acres of land and 2 mills and a fifth part of a mill. And [there are] 6 free men, 7 acres. [There has] always [been] half a plough. And [there is] 1 free man in commendation, 30 acres. Then [there were] 2 villans; now 1. [There has] always [been] half a plough. And [there is] 1 acre of meadow. Then it was worth 30s.; now 43[s.].

XLIV. The land of Judicael the Priest.

H[UNDRED] OF HUMBLEYARD.

In Hethel Algar held half a carucate in commendation only under Eadric, the predecessor of Rober Malet, TRE. [There have] always [been] 2 villans and 2 bordars. And [there is] 1 plough in demesne and half a plough belonging to the men. [There are] 3 acres of meadow. [There is] woodland for 4 pigs. Then it was worth 20s.; now 30s.

XLV. The land of Colebern the Priest.

In the H[undred] of Humbleyard, Coleb[er]n built a certain church of St Nicholas by permission of the king. And if the king agrees, he will give 20 acres. And therefore he sings the mass and the psalter each week for the king. And it is worth 2s.

The lands of Edmund, son of Pain.

IN [Great or Little] Dunham Pain held TRE 4 carucates. [There have] always [been] 12 villans. Then and afterwards [there were] 4 bordars; now 13. Then [there were] 4 slaves; afterwards and now 2. [There are] 14 acres of meadow. [There has] always [been] 1 plough in demesne. Then and afterwards [there were] 5 ploughs belonging to the men; now 4 and 1 plough can be restored. [There is] woodland for 100 pigs. [There has] always [been] 1 mill. Then [there was] 1 horse; now 2. Then [there were] 4 head of cattle; now 9. Then [there were] 4 pigs; now 17. Now [there are] 100 sheep. And [there are] 4 hives of bees. And [there are] 3 sokemen, 43 acres of land. [There has] always [been] 1 plough. Then and afterwards it was worth 100s.; now £8. This Reginald the priest holds with the daughter of Pain. And it is 1 league and 3 furlongs in length and 1 league in breadth. And [it renders] 5d. of the geld.

The lands of Isaac.

WAYLAND H[undred].

In Thompson [there is] 1 free man, 1 carucate. [There has] always [been] 1 plough. And it is worth 20s. This is from the Wef of Earl Ralph of Stow [Bedon]. Robert Blund delivered [it].

WALSHAM H[UNDRED].

Beighton 1 free man, Hofweard, held TRE: 1 carucate. [There have] always [been] 3 villans and 7 bordars. Between them all [there is] 1 plough. [There are] 7 acres of meadow. It has always been worth 40s. And it is of the soke of Earl R[alph].

LODDON H[UNDRED].

In Woodton 2 free men in the commendation only of Godwine TRE were delivered for 60 acres. Then [there were] 2 ploughs and afterwards [and] now 1. And [there is] half an acre of meadow. Then and afterwards it was worth 10s.; now 5[s.] The king and the earl [have] the soke.

In Langhale 1 free man in commendation to Toli the sheriff TRE [held] 1 carucate. [There has] always [been] 1 plough in demesne, but another could be restored. And [there were] 5 free men under him, 8 acres of land and 3 bordars and half a plough. Then it was worth 7s.; now 10[s.]

In Seething TRE 3 free men in the commendation of Godwine [held] 80 acres of land and under them [there were] 2 villans. Then [there were] 3 ploughs; afterwards 1½ ploughs; now none. Then it was worth 20s.; now 30s. In Mundham [there is] 1 free man in the commendation of Godwine at 10 acres of land.

And [there is] 1 bordar. It is valued above.

In Seething a certain poor nun claims 4 acres of land which she held under Ralph both before and after he forfeited and so

the Hundred testifies. And Isaac claims it as part of his fief by gift of the king.

XLVIII. The land of Tovi.

FOREHOE H[UNDRED].

Hackford [Hinghan] Ketil, a free man, held TRE: 60 acres of land and 6 bordars. And [there is] 1 acre of woodland for 10 pigs. And it is worth 10s. And it is 3 furlongs in length and 2 in breadth. And [it renders] 7¼d. of the geld.

GREENHOE H[UNDRED].

Holkham Ketil, 1 free man, held: 3 carucates. [There have] always [been] 2 villans and 8 bordars. Then [there were] 5 slaves. [There have] always [been] 2 ploughs in demesne. Then [there were] 1½ ploughs belonging to the men; afterwards and now 1. And [there is] 1 virgate of meadow. There [has] always [been] 1 mill. Then [there were] 4 head of cattle; now 1. Then [there were] 21 pigs; now 5. [There have] always [been] 300 sheep. And [there are] 18 sokemen with every customary due but he has the soke. [There are] 56 acres of land. [There have] always [been] 2 ploughs. To this manor were added 3 free men, two in the commendation of Harold and 1 of Gyrth, 1½ carucates. These his predecessor held. Under them [are] 9 bordars. [There have] always [been] 7 sokemen, 16 acres of land. Then [there were] 4 ploughs between them and afterwards and now 1. Then it was worth £6; afterwards and now [£]8. It is 1 league in length and in breadth. And of the geld [it renders] 2s.

H[UNDRED] OF HUMBLEYARD.

Stoke [Holy Cross] Ingeld, a thegn, held TRE: 60 acres of land. Then [there were] 7 villans; now 1. [There have] always [been] 8 bordars. And [there are] 2 ploughs [in demesne] and 2 ploughs belonging to the men. And [there are] 6 acres of meadow. Of this meadow St Benet [of Hulme] claims 4 acres which it held TRE. [There is] woodland for 5 pigs. And [there has] always [been] 1 mill.

In the same [vill] Ketil, a free man of Stigand's, held 30 acres. [There has] always [been] 1 villan and

Tovi

5 bordars. Then [there was] 1 plough. Then [there was] half a plough belonging to the men. [There are] 4 acres of meadow.

In the same [vill] 1 free man of Stigand's [held] 30 [acres]. Then [there was] 1 plough. These three manors Tovi holds for one [manor]. [There has] always [been] 1 horse. Then [there was] 1 ox; now 3. Then [there were] 3 pigs; now 20. Then [there were] 40 sheep; now 25. And [there is] 1 hive of bees. And [there were] 5 men in commendation and soke of the fold TRE, 25 acres. [There has] always [been] 1 plough. It has always been worth £4 17d. And [there are] 1½ churches, 23 acres.

In Swainsthorpe [there are] 15 free men, 155 acres. And Ralph the staller had the commendation of 11½ [of them] TRE and Stigand of three likewise; and of half [a free man] the predecessor of Godric the steward likewise. Then [there were] 6 ploughs; now 7½. And [there are] 11 acres of meadow and half a mill and 12 bordars. And it is worth 29s. [There is] 1 church, 23 acres and 1½ bordars. And Stoke [Holy Cross] is 1 league in length and 4 furlongs in breadth. And [it renders] 11[d.] of the geld. And Swainsthorpe is half a league in length and half a league in breadth. And [it renders] 11d. of the geld.

In Newton [Flotman] [there are] 2 free men, 30 acres. The predecessor of Roger Bigod had 1½ TRE and the predecessor of Ralph de Beaufour half [a free man]. [There have] always [been] 5 bordars. And [there is] 1 plough and 3 acres of meadow. And [there are] 4 free men at 12½ acres. Then it was worth 10s.; now 13s. 4d.

In KENNINGHAM [there are] 3 free men. Of two of these the predecessor of Roger Bigod had the commendation TRE.; of one the predecessor of R[alph] de Beaufour [had the commendation]. And they have 75 acres. And [there are] 5 free men under them at 18½ acres. And [there are] 2 bordars and 2 ploughs. Then [it was worth] 10s.; now 13[s.] and 3d. And in the same [vill there is] half a free man, 7½ acres and 2 oxen. And it is worth 16d. And it is half a league in length and 5 furlongs in breadth. And [it renders] 11d. of the geld.

In Kenningham [there is] 1 free man, 2 acres. And it is worth 16d.

H[UNDRED] OF HENSTEAD.

[There was] 1 free man of St Ben[et of Hulme's] TRE, 5 acres. And [there are] 2½ bordars and half a plough. And it is worth 8s. All the churches are in the value with the manors.

5 . 75 . 30 . 3½ . 155 . 30 . 30 . 60 . 60 . 25 . And 18.

[Folio 265v: NORFOLK]

XLIX. The lands of John, nephew of W[aleran].

H[UNDRED] OF SMETHDON.

Ringstead Bovi, a free man, held TRE. Then [there were] 4 ploughs in demesne; afterwards 1; now 3. Then and afterwards [there were] 8 bordars; now 16. Then [there were] 6 slaves; afterwards 4; now 5. [There are] 10 acres of meadow. [There has] always [been] 1 plough belonging to the men. And [there is] 1 mill. [There has] always [been] 1 horse. Then [there was] 1 pig; now 20. Then [there were] 3 sheep; now 100. Then it was worth £4; afterwards 40s.; now £6.

Hunstanton John holds; the same man [i.e., Bovi] [held it] TRE. Then [there were] 2 ploughs; afterwards 1; now 2. [There have] always been 4 [?villans]. Then and afterwards [there were] 5 bordars; now 7. Then and afterwards [there were] 3 slaves; now 4. And [there are] 2 acres of meadow always belonging to the men. Then [there was] 1 cow; now [there are] 8 head of cattle. Now [there are] 40 pigs. Then [there was] 1 sheep; now 40. And [there are] 3 hives of bees. And [there is] 1 sokeman, 5 acres. Then and afterwards it was worth 20s.; now 40[s.] There is 1 church without land. The whole of Ringstead is 1 league in length and half [a league] in breadth. And it renders 8d. of a 20s. [geld].

WAYLAND H[UNDRED].

WAYLAND H[UNDRED].

Carbrooke Ælfhere, a free man, held TRE: 4½ carucates. Then and afterwards [there were] 10 villans; now 6. [There have] always [been] 18 bordars. [There are] 24 acres of meadow. Then [there were] 3 ploughs in demesne; afterwards 1; now 3. [There have] always [been] 6 ploughs belonging to the men. [There is] woodland for 400 pigs. Now [there is] 1 mill, half a fishery. Here have always belonged 24 sokemen, 1 carucate, owing every customary due.

In Griston Osbert holds 1 berewick, 1 carucate, which has always belonged to this manor. And [there are] 2 villans and 2 slaves. And [there are] 2 acres of meadow. Then [there was] 1 plough; afterwards [and] now 1½ ploughs. In demesne [there were] 4 horses and now [likewise]. And now [there are] 10 head of cattle. Then [there were] 20 pigs; now 30. Then [there were] 40 sheep; now 44. Now [there are] 10 hives of bees. The whole is worth £7. [There is] 1 church, 24 acres, and it is worth 2s.

In 'West Carbrooke' [in Carbrooke] the same man holds 1 free man, 40 acres of land. [There has] always [been] 1 bordar and 1 slave.

John, Nephew of Waleran

[Folio 266: NORFOLK]

Then and afterwards [there was] 1 plough. And it is worth 10s. The soke [is] in Saham [Toney], [a manor] belonging to the king. The predecessor of Roger Bigod [had] the commendation only. The whole of Carbrooke is 8 furlongs in length and half a league in breadth. And [it renders] 15d. of the geld. [There is] 1 church, 20 acres; it is worth 12d.

SHROPHAM HUNDRED.

BRETTENHAM William holds: 2 carucates which a free man held TRE. [There have] always [been] 4 villans and 1 bordar and 1 slave. [There are] 12 acres of meadow. Then [there were] 2 ploughs in demesne; afterwards and now 1. [There has] always [been] 1 plough belonging to the men. And [there is] 1 mill. [There have] always [been] 60 sheep. And [there are] 2 free men, 19 acres of land, whom he had in commendation only. The soke [is] in Buckenham [near Attleborough]. And [there is] 1 free man, 30 acres of land. The soke [is] St Æthel[thryth]'s. The whole is worth 60s.

In the same [vill] 1 free man [held] 2 carucates TRE. Then [there were] 12 villans; afterwards and now 3. [There have] always [been] 3 bordars. And [there are] 8 acres of meadow. [There have] always [been] 2 ploughs in demesne. Then [there were] 3 ploughs belonging to the men; afterwards and now 2. [There has] always [been] 1 mill. [There have] always [been] 2 head of cattle. Now [there are] 14 pigs and 70 sheep and 5 hives of bees. Then it was worth 60s.; now 40[s.] The soke [is] in Buckenham [near Attleborough].

Henstead H[undred]. In Saxlingham [Nethergate or Thorpe] Styrger, a housecarl of King E[dward's], held 30 acres of land. [There has] always [been] half a bordar. Then [there were] 2 slaves; now 1. And [there is] 1 mill. [There are] 1½ acres of meadow. Then [there was] 1 plough; now none [...]. Then and afterwards it was worth 20s.; now 13[s.] [There is] 1 church, 10 acres, and it is worth 16d.

In Thurton [near Loddon] 1 free man, Ketil, held TRE under Stigand 8 acres. And [there is] half an acre of meadow. Then [there were] 2 oxen. Then it was worth 2s.; now 12d.

H[UNDRED] AND A HALF OF FREEBRIDGE.

Walpole a free man held TRE: half a carucate. [There have] always [been] 6 bordars. And [there is] half a plough. And it is worth 5s.

[Folio 266v: NORFOLK]

L. The lands of Roger fitzReinhard.

H[UNDRED] OF GRIMSHOE.

Stanford Alstan held TRE: 2 carucates. [There have] always [been] 5 villans and 2 bordars. Then [there were] 5 slaves and afterwards [and] now 2. [There are] 8 acres of meadow. [There have] always [been] 2 ploughs in demesne. Then and afterwards [there was] 1 plough belonging to the men; now 2 oxen. [There have] always [been] $1\frac{1}{2}$ mills. Then and now [there have been] 2 horses. Then [there were] head of 8 head of cattle; now 12. Then [there were] 8 pigs; now 10. Then [there were] 200 sheep; now 80. Then it was worth, and now, 40s. In the same vill there are 8 free men at 2 carucates and 36 acres and 1 bordar and 1 slave. [There are] 4 acres of meadow. Then [there were] 3 ploughs; now 2. It has always been worth 20s. These he claims as a gift of the king. The whole is 1 league in length and half [a league] in breadth. And it renders 15d. of a 20s. geld. And over these the king and the earl have the soke.

In Buckenham [Tofts] [there are] 7 free men, 1 carucate and 20 acres. And [there are] 6 villans. [There have] always [been] 2 ploughs. And it is worth 11s. The king and the earl [have] the soke.

In Ickburgh [there is] 1 free man, 40 acres. [There has] always [been] half a plough. And [there are] 2 acres of meadow. And it is worth 16d.

SMETHDON H[UNDRED].

Ingoldisthorpe Thorkil, a free man, held TRE: $1\frac{1}{2}$ carucates. And [there are] 5 bordars. Then [there were] 2 slaves; now 1. And [there are] 3 acres of meadow. Then [there were] 2 ploughs in demesne; afterwards 6 oxen; now $1\frac{1}{2}$ ploughs. [There has] always [been] half a plough belonging to the men. And [there is] half a mill and 1 fishery. [There has] always [been] 1 horse. Now [there are] 12 pigs. Then [there were] 16 sheep; now 100. Then it was worth 20s.; now 30[s.] [It was] Stigand's soke.

WAYLAND [HUNDRED].

Scoulton 1 free man held TRE: 2 carucates. Then and afterwards [there were] 5 villans; now 6. Then and afterwards [there was] 1 bordar; now 3. Then and afterwards [there were] 2 slaves; now 1. [There are] 16 acres of meadow. [There have] always [been] 2 ploughs in demesne. Then [there were] $2\frac{1}{2}$ ploughs belonging to the men; now 2. [There is] woodland for 300 pigs. Then [there were] 10 head of cattle. Then [there were] 30 pigs; now 15. Then [there were] 65 sheep; now 18.

And [there are] 4 sokemen, 12 acres of land. And it is worth 40s.

Roger fitzReinhard

[Folio 267: NORFOLK]

H[UNDRED] OF SHROPHAM.

Attleborough [or Attleborough Minor] Thoroddr held TRE: 2 carucates and 3 acres.

[There have] always [been] 6 villans and 5 bordars. Then [there was] 1 slave; now 3. [There are] 24 acres of meadow. [There has] always [been] 1 plough in demesne and 2 ploughs belonging to the men. [There is] woodland for 60 pigs. And [there are] 2 parts of a mill. [There is] half a fishery. Then [there were] 2 horses; now 1. [There has] always [been] 1 cow. Then [there were] 6 pigs; now 5. And [there are] 8 sheep. And [there are] 21 sokemen, 80 acres of land. And [there are] 12 acres of meadow. [There is] woodland for 8 pigs. Then and afterwards [there were] 2 ploughs; now 3. Then and afterwards it was worth 40s.; now 60[s.]

In the other Attleborough [or Attleborough Minor] Thorkil held TRE 2 carucates. [There have] always [been] 6 villans and 5 bordars. [There are] 24 acres of meadow. [There is] woodland for 60 pigs. [There has] always [been] 1 plough in demesne and 2 ploughs belonging to the men and there could be 1 plough [in addition]. Now [there is] half a mill and half a fishery. And [there are] 17 sokemen, 47 acres of land. [There are] 8 acres of meadow. [There is] woodland for 12 pigs. [There have] always [been] 3 ploughs. Then [there was] 1 horse. [There have] always [been] 2 head of cattle. Then [there were] 6 pigs; now 4. Then and afterwards it was worth 40s.; now 60[s.] The whole is 2 leagues in length and 1 league in breadth. Whoever may hold there, [it renders] $34\frac{1}{2}$d. of the geld.

In Rockland [All Saints or St Andrew] Hringwulf, a free man, held 1 carucate TRE. [There has] always [been] 1 villan and 8 bordars. Then [there were] 2 slaves; now 1. And [there are] 8 acres of meadow. [There is] woodland for 8 pigs. Then [there were] 2 ploughs in demesne; afterwards and now 1. Then and afterwards [there was] 1 plough belonging to the men; now half [a plough], and there could be 1 plough [in addition]. Now [there is] 1 ox and 5 pigs and 24 sheep. It has always been worth 20s.

H[UNDRED] OF HOLT. In Kelling Wester, a free man of Gyrth's, held TRE 2 carucates; now Ralph son of Hagni [holds them]. [There have] always [been] 6 villans and 20 bordars. Then [there were] 2 ploughs in demesne and afterwards 1; now 2. [There have] always [been] 2 [ploughs] belonging to the men. [There is] 1 acre of meadow. [There has] always [been] 1 horse. Then [there were] 16 [?pigs] ; now 20. [There have] always [been] 40 sheep and 24 goats. Then it was worth 20s.; now 40s.

LODDON H[UNDRED]. In Mundham St Æthelthryth held TRE

[Folio 267v: NORFOLK]

in demesne 20 acres ; now Ro[ger] holds [them]. [There have] always [been] 2 bordars. And it is worth 3s

DEPWADE H[UNDRED].

Hudeston Esbiorn, a thegn, held TRE: 1 carucate. [There have] always [been] 3 villans and 20 bordars. Then [there was] 1 plough in demesne; now 1½. [There have] always [been] 3 ploughs belonging to the men. [There are] 6 acres of meadow. Then [there were] 24 pigs; now 12. And [there are] 20 sheep. Then it was worth 20s.; now 40s.

CLAVERING H[UNDRED].

Raveningham Esbiorn, a thegn, held TRE: 2 carucates and 2½ acres. Then [there were] 2 villans; now 3. Then [there were] 2 slaves. [There has] always [been] 1 plough in demesne, and there could be 1 plough [in addition]. And [there is] 1 plough belonging to the men. [There are] 8 acres of meadow. [There is] woodland for 5 pigs. Then [there were] 4 head of cattle. Now [there are] 12 pigs. And [there are] 5 sokemen, 13 acres. And [there is] 1 church, 60 acres. Then it was worth 20s.; now 40[s.]

In Thurlton [there was] 1 free man, 20 acres, under the predecessor of R[alph] de Beaufour in commendation only. And [there are] 2 acres of meadow and half a plough. And it is worth 8s.

LI. The lands of Berner the Crossbowman.

FREEBRIDGE H[UNDRED] AND A HALF.

In Grimston Wulfrun, a free woman, held 1 carucate TRE. [There have] always [been] 6 bordars and 1 slave. And [there are] 10 acres of meadow. Then [there was] 1 plough; afterwards nothing; now 1. [There has] always [been] 1 mill. Here belong 2 sokemen, 3 acres. And [there are] 3 free men, 4 acres. The whole is worth 20s.

In Congham [there is] 1 free man, 60 acres of land and 1 bordar. And [there are] 3 acres of meadow. Then [there was] half a plough. In the same [vill there are] 4 free men, 3 acres. The whole is worth 10s. He claims all those free men by gift of the king.

In Hillington the same Wulfrun held 2 carucates and 15 acres TRE. [There have] always [been] 7 villans and 8 bordars and 2 slaves. [There are] 10 acres of meadow. Then [there were] 2 ploughs in demesne; afterwards 1; now 2. [There has] always [been] 1 plough belonging to the men. [There is] 1 mill and 1 salt-pan. Then [there were] 100 sheep; now 80. Then

Berner the Crossbowman

[...] [there were] 12 pigs; now 7. Then and afterwards it was worth £4; now 100s. The whole is 1½ leagues in length and half a league in breadth. Whoever may hold there, it renders 8d. of a geld of 20s.

DOCKING [HUNDRED].

SHERNBORNE 1 free man held TRE: 1 carucate. Then [there was] 1 [plough] in demesne; afterwards none; now 1. [There are] 5 bordars, 1 mill, a twelfth part of 1 salt-pan and a

twelfth part of 1 mill. [There are] 2½ acres of meadow. Then and afterwards [it was worth] 16s.; now 20[s.]

WAYLAND H[UNDRED].

Ashill Ælfric, a thegn of Harold's, held TRE: 2 carucates. Then [there were] 10 villans; afterwards and now 7. [There have] always [been] 11 bordars. [There are] 13 acres of meadow. Then [there was] 1 plough in demesne; afterwards 1; now 2. Then [there were] 5 ploughs belonging to the men; afterwards 3; now 2. [There is] woodland for 120 pigs. And [there is] 1 fishery. Now [there is] 1 ox. Then [there were] 10 pigs; now 8. And [there are] 24 goats. And [then there were] 60 sheep; now 67. It has always been worth 50s. In the same [vill] [there are] 6 free men, half a carucate and 7 acres of land. Then [there were] 4 ploughs; afterwards and now 2. [There are] [...] acres of meadow. And it is worth 10s. This is in exchange and was [one] of the manors of Earl Ralph.

In Scoulton 1 free man held under Harold TRE 3 carucates. Then and afterwards [there were] 6 villans; now 5. [There have] always [been] 5 bordars. [There are] 26 acres of meadow. And [there are] 2 ploughs in demesne. There [has] always [been] 1 plough belonging to the men. [There is] woodland for 300 pigs. [There have] always [been] 2 horses. And [?then there were] 4 head of cattle; now 10. And [?then there were] 24 pigs; now 10. And [?then there were] 15 sheep; now 110. And [there] always [have been] 30 goats. It has always been worth 50s. The whole is 1½ leagues in length and 1 league in breadth. Whoever may hold there, of the geld [it renders] 15d. This is [one] of the manors of Ralph.

In Thompson [...] held 1 carucate TRE. Then [there was] 1 plough; afterwards and now half [a plough]. [There is] 1 bordar. And it is worth 16s. This is also from the fief of Ralph.

NORTH ERPINGHAM H[UNDRED].

In Overstrand Skiotr held TRE for two carucates. [There have] always [been] 6 villans and 18 bordars and 2 slaves. Then [there were] 2 ploughs in demesne; afterwards and now 1. And [there are] 2 ploughs belonging to the men. [There is] 1 mill. [There is] woodland for 3 pigs. Then [there was] 1 horse;

now 2. Then [there were] 2 head of cattle; now 6. Then [there were] 4 [pigs]; now 5 pigs. Now [there are] 19 sheep. Then [there were] 1[...]8 goats. And [there are] 5 sokemen at 32 acres of land. And the king has the soke. [There is] 1 acre of meadow. [There has] always [been] 1 plough. Then it was worth 40s. and always [has been]. And it is 7 furlongs in length and 4 in breadth. And of the geld [it renders] 6¼d.

H[UNDRED] OF GREENHOE.

In [North or South] Pickenham 1 free man holds 12 acres and 1 house from the fief of Earl R[alph] and it is in the soke of the Hundred . [There has] always [been] 1 mill. And it is worth 7s. This R[obert] Blund delivered.

H[UNDRED] OF EYNSFORD.

In Hackford [near Reepman] 1 free man held TRE 1 carucate. [There have] always [been] 3 villans and 3 bordars. [There has] always [been] 1 plough in demesne and half a plough belonging to the men. And [there are] 2 acres of meadow. [There is] woodland for 30 pigs. [There have] always [been] 1 horse and 5 pigs and 12 sheep. And it is worth 20s.

LII. The lands of Gilbert the crossbowman.

SHROPHAM H[UNDRED].

TRE Ælfric held 1 carucate for 1 manor. [There have] always [been] 3 bordars. Then and afterwards [there were] 2 slaves; now 1. And [there are] 10 acres of meadow. Then [there were] 2 ploughs; afterwards and now 1. [There has] always [been] 1 mill. And 1 free man has been added here in exchange for 30 acres. [There are] 4 acres of meadow and 1 bordar. And [there has] always [been] half a plough. Now [there is] 1 horse and 2 head of cattle. Then [there were] 3 pigs; now 8. Then [there were] 80 [?sheep]; now 40. And [there are] 3 hives of bees. The whole is worth 30s. The soke of the free man [is] in Buckenham [near Attleborough].

WALSHAM H[UNDRED].

In Tunstall 1 free man, Rathi, held half a carucate. [There have] always [been] 6 bordars. [There are] 8 acres of meadow. Then [there was] half a plough; now [there is] 1 plough in demesne. [There has] always [been] half a plough belonging to the men. [There are] 3 head of cattle. Then [there were] 52 sheep; now 28. Then it was worth 10s.; now 22s.

BLOFIELD H[UNDRED].

In Brundall 1 free man, Godwine, held for 1 carucate

Gilbert the Crossbowman

[Folio 269: NORFOLK]

in the commendation of Gyrth. After the king came, Earl R[alph] received [it]. Now Gilbert the crossbowman holds [it] for 2 carucates. Then [there were] 5 [bordars] and now 4 bordars. Then and afterwards [there was] 1 plough in demesne; now 2. The men have always ploughed with 2 oxen. [There is] woodland for 5 pigs. And [there are] 25 acres of meadow. And there [there are] 12½ free men at 90 acres of land. [There have] always [been] 1½ ploughs. Then it was worth 25s.; now 40[s.] It is 1 league in length and half [a league] in breadth. And [it renders] 7d. of the geld.

DISS HALF-H[UNDRED].

In Thelveton Alsige held under King E[dward] for 2 carucates. [There have] always [been] 4 villans and 2 bordars. Then and afterwards [there were] 2 ploughs in demesne; now 1. [There has] always [been] 1 plough belonging to the men. [There is] woodland for 30 pigs. And [there are] 4 acres of meadow. Now [there is] 1 horse at the hall. Then [there were] 9 head of cattle; now 8. Then [there were] 8 pigs; now 11. Now [there are] 20 sheep and 1 hive of bees. And [there are] 6 free men in the commendation of the same man at 60 acres of land. [There have] always [been] 2 ploughs between them all. And [there are] 2 acres of meadow. Then and afterwards it was worth 40s.; now 20[s.]

The lands of Ralph the Crossbowman.

BLOFIELD H[UNDRED].

In [Great or Little] Plumstead Tovi, 1 free man of Gyrth's, held TRE 1 carucate. [There has] always [been] 1 villan. Then [there was] half a plough; afterwards nothing; now half. And [there are] 2 acres of meadow. Then [there were] 11 sheep. In the same manor 6½ free men used to live, 20 acres of land. [There are] 2 acres of meadow. [There has] always [been] 1 plough. He claims these men by livery. What is in demesne was then worth 5s.; now 10s. And the free men [are worth] 5s. And it is 1 league in length and half [a league] in breadth. And of the geld [it renders] 14d., whoever may hold there.

The lands of Robert the crossbowman.

FOREHOE H[UNDRED].

In "Appethorp" Ælfhere, a free man, held 1 carucate [and] 30 acres of land TRE for a manor.

[Folio 269v: NORFOLK]

Then [there were] 2 villans; now 4. And [there are] 15 sokemen. [There have] always [been] 3 ploughs. [There is] woodland for 15 pigs. And [there are] 4 acres of meadow. Now [there are] 6 pigs, 20 sheep, 20 goats. Then it was worth 20s.; now 32. And it is 4 furlongs in length and 2 in breadth. And [it renders] 5d. of the geld.

LV. The lands of Rabel the Artificer.

BLOFIELD H[UNDRED].

In Moor Sigeric, 1 free man, held TRE 2 carucates. Then [there were] 8 villans; afterwards and now 5. Then [there were] 4 slaves; afterwards and now 2. Then [there were] 1½ ploughs; afterwards 1; and now 2 in demesne. [There has] always [been] half a plough belonging to the men. And [there are] 10 acres of meadow. Now [there is] 1 horse. [There have] always [been] 3 head of cattle. Then [there were 3 [?pigs]; afterwards and now 12. Now [there are] 100 sheep. And [there is] 1 salt-pan. Then it was worth 40[s.]; afterwards 30[s.]; now 40[s.] And it is 8 furlongs in length and 5 in breadth. And of the geld [it renders] 20s. And the soke and sake are the king's and the earl's.

H[UNDRED] OF EAST FLEGG.

In Filby R[alph] the staller held 2 carucates and 47 acres TRE for a manor. Then [there were] 8 villans; afterwards and now 6. And there are 2 bordars. [There has] always [been] 1 plough in demesne and 1 plough belonging to the men. And [there are] 14 acres of meadow. [There have] always [been] 2 horses and 1 ox. Then [there were] 7 pigs; now 10. And there are 3 sokemen, 15 acres. [There have] always [been] 1½ ploughs. And [there is] 1 acre of meadow. And [there are] 14 free men, half a carucate and 6 acres. [There have] always [been] 2½ ploughs. And [there is] 1 acre of meadow. Then it was worth 40s.; afterwards and now 50[s.] The king and the earl [have] the soke of the free men. And it is 1 league and 3½ furlongs in length and half a league and 25 perches in breadth. And [it renders] 2s. of the geld, whoever may hold there.

LVI. Lands of Hagni.

H[UNDRED] OF EYNSFORD.

In Bintree Hagni, a reeve of the king, held 100 acres of land. [There have] always [been] 10 sokemen. [There have] always [been] 4 ploughs between the men themselves. And [there are] 7 acres of meadow. It has always been worth 20s.

In Guist [there are] 100 acres of land. [There have] always [been] 2 villans and 5 bordars. [There have] always [been] 2 ploughs between the men themselves. And [there are] 4 acres of meadow. [There is] woodland for 8 pigs. It has always been worth 20s.

Hagni

[Folio 270: NORFOLK]

In [Wood] Norton [there are] 50 acres of land. And [there are] 5 sokeman dwelling on that land. [There have] always [been] 2 ploughs between the men themselves. And [there are] 2 acres of meadow. [There is] woodland for 5 pigs. It has always been worth 10s.

In Guestwick [there are] 50 acres of land. [There have] always [been] 2 sokemen and 1 bordar on the land itself. [There have] always [been] $1\frac{1}{2}$ ploughs between the men themselves. And [there are] 5 acres of meadow. [There is] woodland for 10 pigs. It has always been worth 10s. And in Weston [Longville] [there is] 1 sokeman, 16 acres of land. [There has] always [been] half a plough. And it is worth 2s.

And in Sparham [there is] 1 free man, 30 acres of land and 1 bordar; over [the former] his predecessor had the commendation only. [There has] always [been] half a plough. And [there are] 2 acres of meadow. And it is worth 4s. And in Tyby [there is] 1 free man, 15 acres and 2 bordars. [There has] always [been] half a plough. And [there is] half an acre of meadow. [There is] woodland for 3 pigs. It has always been worth 3s. And in Sall [there is] 1 sokeman. And in Thurning [there is] 1 [sokeman], 20 acres of land. [There has] always [been] 1 plough. And it is worth 4s.

The lands of Ralph son of Hagni.

H[UNDRED] OF HOLT.

In Kelling Wester, a free man of Gyrth's, held TRE 2 carucates. Now Ralph son of Hagni . [There have] always [been] 6 villans and 20 bordars. And afterwards [there was] 1 [?plough in demesne]; now 2. [There have] always [been] 2 ploughs belonging to the men. [There is] 1 acre of meadow. [There has] always [been] 1 horse. Then [there were] 16 pigs; now 20. [There have] always [been] 40 sheep and 24 goats. Then it was worth 20s.; now 40[s.]

LODDON H[UNDRED].

In Mundham St Æthelthryth held in demesne TRE 20 acres. Now R[alph] holds [them. There have] always [been] 2 bordars. And it is worth 3s.

H[UNDRED] OF EYNSFORD.

In Sall Wester, 1 free man, held TRE 1 carucate. [There has] always [been] 1 villan and 10 bordars. [There has] always [been] 1 plough in demesne and 2 ploughs belonging to the men. And [there is] 1 acre of meadow. [There is] woodland for 6 pigs and half a mill, and 4 head of cattle and 6 pigs. And it is worth 20s.

[Folio 270v: NORFOLK]

LVIII. The lands of Ulfkil.

H[UNDRED] OF SHROPHAM.

In LARLING the same Ulfkil held 2 carucates TRE. Then and afterwards [there were] 6 villans; now 4. [There has] always [been] 1 bordar. Then and always [there have been] 8 acres. [There have] always [been] 2 ploughs in demesne. Then [there were] 2 ploughs belonging to the men; now 1. Now [there is] 1 mill. And [there have] always [been] 2 free men, 26 acres of land, in commendation only. And the soke [is] in Buckenham [near Attleborough], [a manor] belonging to the king. [There has] always [been] 1 plough. And [there are] 2 acres of meadow. It has always been worth 40s. The whole is half a league in length and half [a league] in breadth. Whoever may hold there, [it renders] $8\frac{1}{2}$d. of the geld.

GUILTCROSS H[UNDRED].

IN Rushford Bondi, a free man, held 2 carucates TRE. [There have] always [been] 6 villans and 1 bordar and 1 slave. And [there are] 12 acres of meadow. And [there are] 2 ploughs in demesne. Then [there were] 2 ploughs belonging to the men; now 1, and another could be restored. And [there is] 1 free man, 14 acres of land, whom he claims by gift of the king. [There has] always [been] 1 plough. Now there are 100 sheep and 52 goats and 7 pigs. And the whole is worth 40s. And it is $1\frac{1}{2}$ leagues in length and 4 furlongs in breadth. Whoever may hold there, [it renders] $11\frac{1}{2}$d. of the geld. The soke of the free man [is] in Kenninghall.

WALSHAM H[UNDRED].

In Witton [near Norwich] 2 free men of Gyrth's held TRE at 140 acres of land. [There have] always [been] 6 bordars. And [there are] 10 acres of meadow. Then [there was] 1 plough in demesne; now $1\frac{1}{2}$. [There has] always [been] 1 plough belonging to the men. It has always been worth 15s. When Ralph forfeited, he held [it] in his own hand and afterwards [Robert] Blund [held it] and afterwards by writ of the king it was seised again into the hand of the king.

LIX. The land of Alfred.

SHROPHAM H[UNDRED].

IN ATTLEBOROUGH [or ATTLEBOROUGH MINOR] [there are] 2 carucates [held] for a manor. [There have] always [been] 8 villans. And [there are] 16 acres of meadow. And [there have] always [been] 2 ploughs in demesne and 1 plough belonging to the men. [There is] woodland for 40 pigs. And [there are] 20 sokemen, half a carucate. [There are] 6 acres of meadow. [There have] always [been] 4 ploughs. And [there are] 5 free men, 1½ carucates

Alfred

[Folio 271: NORFOLK]

and 3 bordars. And [there are] 12 acres of meadow. [There have] always [been] 3 ploughs. [There is] woodland for 8 pigs. [There have] always [been] 2 horses. And then [there were] 6 head of cattle; now 8. Then [there were] 20 pigs; now 28. Then [there were] 20 sheep; now 38. [There have] always [been] 26 goats. Then it was worth 60s.; afterwards and now £4. The soke of those Wve [is] in Buckenham [near Attleborough].

The land of Ealdgyth.

H[UNDRED] OF GREENHOE.

Wells[-next-the-Sea] Ketil, 1 free man, held TRE: 2 carucates; now Ealdgyth holds [it]. [There have] always [been] 5 villans, always 7 bordars, always 2 ploughs in demesne, always 1 plough belonging to the men. [There is] pasture for 200 sheep. [There are] 4 head of cattle. Then [there were] 4 pigs;now 16. When she received it, [there were] 60 sheep; now 200. [There is] 1 mill. [There are] 19 sokemen, 2 carucates. [There is] half a mill. And these men live in Warham [All Saints or St Mary] and belong to Wells [-next-the-Sea]. Then it was worth 100s.; now £4. And it is [1] league in length and another [in] breadth but more have land there. And [it renders] 24d. of the geld between Wells [-next-the-Sea] and Warham [All Saints or St Mary].

The lands of Godwine Halfdan.

H[UNDRED] OF TAVERHAM.

In Hellesdon Stigand held 2 carucates TRE. [There have] always [been] 12 villans and 11 bordars. Then [there was] 1 plough in demesne; now 2. Then [there was] 1 plough belonging to the men; now 1½ ploughs. [There is] woodland for 60 pigs. [There are] 12 acres of meadow. [There have] always [been] 2 mills and 1 fishery. [There has] always [been] 1 ox and 10 pigs. Then [there were] 10 sheep; now 29. Now [there are] 60 goats.

[Folio 271v: NORFOLK]

And [there are] 6 sokemen, 1 acre of land. [There have] always [been] 1½ ploughs. And [there are] 4 acres of meadow. It has always been worth £4 12s. 8d. [There is] one church

without land. And it is 1½ leagues and 20 perches in length and 1 league and 3 furlongs in breadth. And [it renders] 8ƒd. of the geld.

H[UNDRED] OF SOUTH ERPINGHAM.

Oxnead Aildag, a free man under Gyrth, held TRE: 1 carucate. [There have] always [been] 5 villans and 7 bordars. Then [there was] 1 plough in demesne; afterwards 1 ox; now 2. [There has] always [been] 1 plough belonging to the men. And [there are] 12 acres of meadow. [There is] woodland for 30 pigs and 1 mill. Now [there are] 20 pigs and 6 hives of bees. And [there are] 3 sokemen, 60 acres. [There has] always [been] half a plough and 4 acres of meadow. [There is] 1 church, 24 acres, and it is worth 2s. Then it was worth 20s.; afterwards 10s.; now 30s. And it is 7 furlongs in length and 6 in breadth. And it renders 5d. to the king's geld. The king and the earl [has] the soke.

SMETHDON H[UNDRED].

Gnatingdon the same Godwine, a free man, held TRE. [There was] 1 carucate under Gyrth and under Ralph and now of the king. [There have] always [been] 2 bordars and 1 sokeman, 1 acre. Then it was worth 10s.; now 20[s.]

FORHOE H[UNDRED].

Barnham [Broom] 1 free man held TRE, 1 carucate. [There have] always [been] 2 villans and 3 bordars. [There has] always [been] 1 plough and 3 acres of meadow. [There has] always [been] 1 mill. And it is worth 20s.

The lands of Starkulf.

FOREHOE H[UNDRED].

Barnham [Broom] the same man held TRE: 60 acres of land. And [there are] 3 bordars and 1 plough and 2 acres . And it is worth 10s.

H[UNDRED] AND A HALF OF MITFORD.

In [North] Tuddenham [there are] 40 acres of land. [There have] always [been] 3 bordars. And [there is] 1 plough.

[Folio 272: NORFOLK]

And [there are] 3 acres of meadow. And it is worth 10s.

The lands of Eadric the Falconer.

HALF-H[UNDRED] OF DISS.

In Shelfanger Eadric holds 15 acres. There have always been 2 bordars and half a plough. [There is] woodland for 3 pigs and 1 acre of meadow. It has always been worth 2s.

These are the free men TRE not belonging to any farm whom Almær keeps, who have been added to a farm TRW.

WEST FLEGG H[UNDRED].

In Burgh [St Margaret] the same Gyrth held freely TRE 60 acres of land and 8 acres of meadow and 1 villan and 8 free men under him at 27 acres of land and 6 acres of meadow. And [there have always] always [been] 2 ploughs between them all and 2 salt-pans. Then it was worth 10s.; now 20s. in the farm of Cawston, to which they do not belong. And Roger [Bigod] appointed the reeve. And Burgh [St Margaret] is 10 furlongs in length and 8½ in breadth. And of the geld [it renders] 2s. 1¼d. But more hold there.

And in Rollesby the same Almær holds 8½ free men held under Gyrth, 55 acres of land in the soke and 6 acres of meadow. [There have always] always [been] 1½ ploughs. Then it was worth 4s.; now 8[s.] in the above-mentioned farm. But they did not belong TRE and they have been added there.

In Repps the same man holds 20 acres of land and 7½ free men at 30 acres of land and 3 acres of meadow. [There has] always [been] 1 plough. Then it was worth 3s.; now 4[s.]

In Clippesby the same man holds 5 free men at 46 acres of land and 5 acres of meadow and a quarter part of 1 salt-pan. [There has] always [been] 1 plough. Then it was worth 3s.; now 4[s.]

[Folio 272v: NORFOLK]

In Bastwick the same man holds 2 free men at 25 acres of land and 3 acres of meadow. [There has] always [been] half a plough. Then it was worth 12d.; now 16[d.]

In Billockby the same man holds 4 free men at 30 acres of land. And [there has] always [been] half a plough. Then it was worth 16d.; now 20[d.]

In [East or West] Somerton the same man holds 20 acres of land in demesne and 5 free men at 15 acres. And [there has] always [been] half a plough. It has always been worth 2s.

In Winterton the same man holds 8 free [men] at 54 acres of land and 1 acre of meadow. And [there have] always [been] 1½ ploughs. Then it was worth 4s.; now 6[s.]

In Martham he also holds 1 free [man] at 10 acres of land. He has always ploughed with two oxen. And it has always been worth 8d. And the whole of this is in the above-mentioned farm.

LXV.

[These] are the free men of the king.

H[UNDRED] OF HAPPING.

In Horsey Ralph [holds] 31½ acres. [There have] always [been] 3 bordars and half a plough and 4½ acres of meadow.

In Stalham Æthelmær son of Godwine has 7 free men at 50 acres and 1 bordar and half a plough and 1 acre of meadow. And it is worth 2s.

In Ludham the same man holds 4 free men, 12 acres and half a plough. And it is worth 16d. And in Eccles [on Sea] [he holds] 4 free men, 20 acres and half a plough. And it is worth 3s. [...] In Waxham [he holds] 3 free men, 10 acres and half a plough. And it is worth 16d. In Horsey [he holds] 4 [free men], 20 acres and half a plough. And it is worth 2s.

In [Potter] Heigham [there are] 2 free [men], 2 acres. And it is worth 2d. Godric of Heigham holds these [men].

[Folio 273: NORFOLK]

H[UNDRED] OF EAST FLEGG.

In Herringby [there are] 100 acres, 1 free man of Bishop Æthelmær's TRE. [There have] always [been] 12 villans and 2 bordars and 1 plough in demesne. And [there are] 1½ ploughs belonging to the men. [There are] 4 acres of meadow and 4½ salt-pans. To this land belong 8 free men, 43½ acres and 1½ ploughs and 3 acres of meadow and 1 salt-pan. [There is] pasture for 100 sheep. It has always been worth 20s. Reinbald the goldsmith holds this and it was in the Wef of Earl R[alph].

In Runham [there are] 4 free men, 17 acres. [There has] always [been] 1 plough and 2 acres of meadow and half a salt-pan. In the same [vill there is] 1 free man, 30 acres, and he ploughs with two oxen. And [there are] 2 acres of meadow and 1 salt-pan. And it is worth 2s. 4d. Æthelmær son of Godwine holds them.

In Scratby [there is] 1 free man, 10 acres. [There has] always [been] half a plough and 1 acre of meadow. And it is worth 10d. This Æthelwig of Thetford added to the rent of Ormesby [St Margaret or St Michael] TRW.

H[UNDRED] OF HUMBLEYARD.

In [East] Carleton [there is] 1 free man, 32 acres. [There has] always [been] half a plough and 1 acre of meadow. And it is worth 3s. In Dunston [there is] 1 free man, 13 acres. And it is worth 12d.

DEPWADE H[UNDRED].

In Moulton [St Michael] [there are] Goti and Eskil, 2 free men, 2½ acres. And it is worth 2½d. Aski the priest, a man of the Abbot of Hulme, held them and gave the pledge. In Hardwick [there is] 1 free man, Wihtræd by name, 30 acres. [There have] always [been] 4 villans and 5 bordars and 2 ploughs and 2 acres of meadow. And it is worth 10s. The whole of Harwick is 1 league in length and half [a league] in breadth. And [it renders] 9d. of the geld.

CLAVERING H[UNDRED].

In Norton [Subcourse] [there is] 1 free man of St Benet [of Hulme's], 30 acres. And [there are] 2 bordars and half a plough and half an acre of meadow. And [it is worth] 4s. This Goscelin of Norwich holds.

In Thurlton [there are] 8 acres, 1 free man belonging to the predecessor of Ralph

[Folio 273v: NORFOLK]

de Beaufour. And it is worth 12d. This H. Malesmains held according to the testimony of the Hundred but he conceals it.

In Raveningham [there is] 1 free man, Ketil Friday, 7 acres. And [there is] 1 bordar and 1 marsh. And it is worth 12d. This is of the fief of Earl R[alph] and was mensal land of the same manor when R[alph] forfeited. Afterwards he held his land so that he returned no service to the king. And he gave pledge of this.

LXVI. Appropriations In Norfolk.
Appropriation of Hermer de Ferrers.

HUNDRED OF CLACKCLOSE.

In Fincham [there were] 20 free men holding TRE 2 carucates. But yet 8 of them were customary tenants at the fold of his predecessor. Others were free except for commendation. On their land there have always been 2 ploughs, 10 acres of meadow. Then it was worth 40s.; now 58[s.] 4d. In the same [vill there are] 16 acres of land. It is worth 16d. In Barton [Bendish] [there is] 1 free man, 12 acres, which W. holds of Hermer. [There has] always [been] half a plough. It is worth 3s. Of this his predecessor did not have anything except for the commendation. In the same [vill there was] 1 free man in the commendation only of his predecessor, 60 acres. [There has] always [been] 1 bordar, half a plough, 8 acres of meadow. It is worth 2s. 8d.

In Wormegay [there are] 2 free men holding 4 acres but his predecessor had every customary due.

In [West] Briggs [there are] 3 free men. [There is] half a plough. It is worth 5s. Of these his predecessor had only the customary right[s] and St Benedict [of Ramsey] the soke. In the same [vill there are] 8 free men with customary due[s] and soke of the fold at 10 acres. It is worth 9s.

In Thorpland [near Downham Market] [there are] 8½ [free men] at 20 acres [of land]. And [there are] 2 acres of meadow. It is worth 12s. In the same [vill there were] 8 customary tenants at the fold of his predecessor. It is worth 10s.

Hermer de Ferrers

[Folio 274: NORFOLK]

And there are also 3 at 28 acres. And it is worth 2s. 8d. And also [there are] 30 acres of land which Godwine, a free man, held who was afterwards outlawed and he has 3 acres of meadow and 1 plough and 2 horses, 6 pigs, 40 sheep and 4 carucates of wheat. And he has given a pledge about that and other matters.

In Stow [Bardolph] [there are] 34 acres of land which a free man held TRE. Then [there was] 1 plough; now none. In Hilgay [there are] 6 acres of land which St Edmund held in commendation only. And it is worth 8d. In the same vill there are] 2 free (men) with 2 acres. It is worth 8d. The predecessor of Hermer had them in commendation only and now Hermer was holding them.

In Wimbotsham 3 free men held 40 acres of land TRE. And [there are] 4 free men in Stow [Bardolph] at 40 acres. All of these have 2 ploughs. The predecessor of Hermer had nothing in these except for commendation and half the soke with St Benedict [of Ramsey]. And it is worth 20s. In Bexwell [there are] 7 free men at 1 carucate of land. [There have] always [been] 3 bordars. Then [there were] 3 ploughs; afterwards and now 2. [There are] 5 acres of meadow. [There is] half a fishery. It is worth 12s. Of these his predecessor had the commendation only. In Ryston [there are] 3 free men in commendation only, 90 acres. [There have] always [been] 2 ploughs. It is worth 5s. In Fordham [there are] 3 free men, 24 acres, in

commendation only. [There has] always [been] half a plough. It is worth 2s. His predecessor had no interest in these except for the commendation. In [West] Dereham [there were] 32 free men at 120 acres TRE. The predecessor of Hermer had the commendation of 25 of these. [There have] always [been] 2 ploughs. It is worth 35s. Bordin holds from Hermer 3 with a complete moiety and 7 were in the commendation of his predecessor, Roger Bigod. And the predecessor of Hermer had no interest in these. And they are worth 5s. Hermer appropriated these 7.

In Downham [Market] [there are] 13 free men, 40 acres. [There has] always [been] 1 plough. It is worth 10s. His predecessor had no interest in these except for the commendation. In Shouldham Thorpe [there are] 11½ free men, 80 acres [of land] and 5 acres of meadow, 1 bordar. Then [there were] 3 ploughs; now 2. It is worth 17s. And [his predecessor had no interest] in these except for the commendation. [There is] half a church, 16 acres; it is worth 12d.

In Fodderstone [there are] 6 free men, 40 acres. [There is] 1 plough, 3 acres of meadow. It is worth 5s. [His predecessor had no interest] in these except for the commendation. And because they are not able to be without their pasture, they render customary due[s] to him.

In Wallington Thorsten, a free man, held 100 acres TRE. [There have] always [been] 11 bordars, 15 acres of meadow,

[Folio 274v: NORFOLK]

1 plough. It was worth 12s. [His predecessor had no interest] in this except for the commendation. [There are] 26 acres belonging to the church; it is worth 16d. In the same vill [there were] 7 free men TRE, 60 acres. Then [there were] 1½ ploughs; afterwards and now 1. It is worth 14s. His predecessor had the commendation of 6 [of these] and Earl Gyrth of the seventh. And it is worth 20d. Hermer appropriated this. The whole [of it] is 4 furlongs in length and 3 in breadth. And [it renders] 6d. of the geld. Over all of these St Benedict [of Ramsey] [has] the soke.

AND THE HUNDRED AND A HALF OF FREEBRIDGE.

In Lynn Hermer holds 2 free men of whom his predecessor held the commendation only at 25 acres. And [there is] 1 salt-pan. It is worth 4s. 6d. In West Winch [there is] 1 free man, one carucate. And [there are] 12 bordars. It is worth 6s. 8d. And [his predecessor had no interest] in this except for the commendation. In Wiggenhall a free man held half a carucate TRE. And it is worth 3s. And [his predecessor had no interest] in this except for the commendation. In East Winch [there are] 2 free men, 30 acres, which Bordin holds. [There has] always [been] half a plough, 2 acres of meadow. It is worth 15d. And [his predecessor had no interest] in these except for the commendation. Stigand [had] the soke. In [West] Walton [there are] 3 free men, 91 acres, which Bordin holds. [There have] always [been] 9 bordars, 12 acres of meadow. Then [there were] 1½ ploughs; now 1. It is worth 9s. 4d. And [his predecessor had no interest] in this except for the commendation. [There is] half a church, 15 acres; it is worth 2s.

In [Gayton] Thorpe [there is] one carucate, which Thorkil,

a free man, held. [There have] always [been] 9 villans, 8 bordars. [There is] 1 plough in demesne, 1 plough belonging to the men, 6 acres of meadow and a quarter part of a fishery. It is worth 20s. and [his predecessor had] the commendation of this only. And Stigand [had] the soke. [There is] half a church, 30 acres; it is worth 12s. In Gayton [there is] a free man, 60 acres, which Bordin holds. [There are] 2 bordars, 6 acres of meadow, half a plough. It is worth 3s. And [his predecessor had no interest] in this except for the commendation. Stigand [had] the soke.

SHROPHAM HUNDRED.

In [Great] Ellingham [there are] 3 free men, 110 acres, which Warenbold holds. And [there are] 5 acres of meadow. [There have] always [been] 2 ploughs. [There is] woodland for 12 pigs. It is worth 15s. And [his predecessor had] the commendation of these only. The soke [is] in Buckenham [near Attleborough], [a manor] belonging to the king.

LAUNDITCH HUNDRED.

In Longham [there is] 1 free man, half a carucate. [There has] always [been] 1 villan and 1 bordar. And [there is] half a plough, 2 acres of meadow, woodland for 10 pigs. It is worth 5s. And [his predecessor had no interest] in this except for the commendation. The soke [is] in Mileham, [a manor] belonging to the king.

MITFORD HUNDRED.

In "Thurstuna" [there are] 7 free men, 100 acres. Then [there were] 4 ploughs; now 3. [There are] 5 acres of meadow. Then it was worth 20s.; now 26[s.] 8d. And [his predecessor had no interest] in this except for the commendation.

Hermer de Ferrers

[Folio 275: NORFOLK]

In Reymerston [there were] 5 free men, 30 acres, TRE. Then [there was] 1 plough; now half a plough. [There are] 2 acres of meadow. Then it was worth 10s.; now 6[s.] And [his predecessor had no interest] in this except for the commendation.

In Yaxham [there are] 10 free men, 53 acres of land, which Adelelm holds of Hermer. [There are] 4 acres of meadow. Then [there were] 1½ ploughs; now 1. Then it was worth 20s.; now 10[s.] And [his predecessor had no interest] in this except for the commendation. In Mattishall [there are] 20 free men in commendation only, 1 carucate, 39 acres. [There have] always [been] 3 villans, 2 bordars. [There are] 12 acres of meadow and half a mill. Then [there were] 4 ploughs; now 3. Then it was worth 30s.; now 42[s.]. And [his predecessor had no interest] in this except for the commendation. In [North] Tuddenham [there are] 6 free men in the commendation only, 100 acres, 15 bordars, 2 slaves. [There is] woodland for 6 pigs. [There are] 3 acres of meadow. [There have] always [been] 3 ploughs. Then it was worth 26s. 8d.; now 24s. In Bickerston [there is] 1 free [man], 8 acres, in commendation only. It is worth 6d. In North Tuddenham [there are] 3 free men in commendation only, 32 acres. [There has] always [been] 1

plough. [There is] 1 acre of meadow. It is worth 5s. In Letton [there are] 2 free men in commendation only. [There were] 21 acres TRE; now 1 free man holds [them]. And [there are] 4 acres of meadow. [There is] woodland for 4 pigs. It is worth 5 s. 4d. In [South]burgh [there is] half a free man in commendation only, 2 acres. It is worth 6d.

The appropriation of Baynard. In Fincham Baynard appropriated 1 carucate, which free men held TRE; now 7½. [There have] always [been] 2 bordars and 1 plough. [There are] 8 acres of meadow. Then it was worth 20s.; now 40[s.] His men claimed [he holds] this land through exchange but they do not have a livery officer. In Barton [Bendish] [there are] 30 acres which a free man held TRE. Of those he gave 4 acres in pledge and 8 Wihenoc of Burley took. In Stoke [Ferry] Ulfkil held 100 acres TRE. [There have] always [been] 4 villans and 4 bordars. [There is] 1 plough, 10 acres of meadow. It is worth 40s. He claims this through exchange. In Scarning [there is] 1 free man, 24 acres, in commendation only. [There are] 2 bordars, 2 acres of meadow, half a plough. It is worth 5s. The soke [is] in Mileham, [a manor] belonging to the king.

FOREHOE HUNDRED.

In Dykebeck [there are] 24 free men, 120 acres, which Baynard holds, of which his predecessor did not have the commendation. Of these 3 were in Wymondham and one in the bishopric and 3 in Kimberley and 17 in Hingham. Between the whole [of them] they have 4 ploughs. [There are] 5 acres of meadow. It is worth 30s.

[Folio 275v: NORFOLK]

The Abbot of St Edmund holds in Runcton [Holme or South Runcton] 150 acres which 5 free men held TRE. Then [there were] 2½ ploughs; now 2. [There are] 4 bordars. It is worth 20s. He claims this land as a gift of the king. In the same vill [there is] a free man, half a carucate, 4 bordars, 2 free men at 6 acres. It is worth 10s. In the same [vill there are] 46 acres which 3½ free men hold. [There has] always [been] 1 bordar, 3 ploughs, 6 acres of meadow. It is worth 10s.

In Shelfanger 1 free man in the commendation only of Algar TRE, who was killed at the battle of Hastings, [held] 12 acres of Winfarthing. Afterwards the Abbot held it in his manor of Bressingham. It has always been worth 16d. but his steward claims that he did not know, [and offers proof] just as the judicial ordeal demands. In Winfarthing [there is] 1 free man at 2 acres, whom Earl R[alph] held when he forfeited. And afterwards Godric [held] in the king's hand. After Godric, Herewulf held [him] in the land of St Edmund by permission of the abbot's reeve according to the testimony of the Hundred.

In Shropham [there is] 1 free man, 30 acres. And [there are] 3 acres of meadow, 1 bordar, half a plough. It is worth 4s.

In [West] Dereham Reginald fitzIvo holds 6 free men at 32 acres, whom Wihenoc appropriated, they being commended to his predecessor only. In Roxham [there is] 1 free man in commendation only at 9 acres. It is worth 8s. 1d. In Fordham [there are] 3 free men in commendation and St Ben[edict of Ramsey has] the soke at 25 acres. And [there is] 1 free man at 5 acres. St Edmund held the commendation of the same man

TRE. Reginald holds this. It is worth 5s. In Downham [Market] [there are] 3 free men

Reginald fitzIvo

[Folio 276: NORFOLK]

at 2½ acres in commendation only. It is worth 10d. In the same [vill there was] 1 free man at 7 acres commended to the predecessor of William de Warenne; now Reginald holds [him]. And it is worth 12d. In Bexwell [there are] 2 free men, 1 at 15 acres of whom the predecessor of Hermer had the commendation. And it is worth 2s. 8d. And the other had 3 acres and it is worth 6d. These Reginald now holds.

In Upwell 6 free men held 2 carucates and 15 acres. [There have] always [been] 2 ploughs and 9 bordars. It is worth 26s. 8d. And three of these were commended to the predecessor of Hermer. And Wihenoc seized all of these.

In West Winch Wihenoc added 1 free man at 3 acres. [There have] always [been] 4 villans. [There are] 6 acres of meadow. It is worth 5s.

Herluin, a man of Ivo's, appropriated in Fincham 1 free man at 15 acres. And it is worth 16d. And [there are] 1½ acres which Mainard appropriated. And it is worth 9d.

In [North or South] Pickenham [there is] 1 free man, 10 acres. This Wihenoc appropriated. And it is worth 20d.

In Fordham the Abbot of Ely holds of St Æ[thelthryth] 30 acres, which a free man held. [There have] always [been] 3 bordars and half a plough. It is worth 4s. In this he does not have any interest except for the commendation. In Ryston [there are] 3 free men, 6 acres. It is worth 16d. He did not have any interest in this except for the commendation. And St Bened[ict of Ramsey has] the soke.

HUNDRED AND A HALF OF FREEBRIDGE.

In Lynn [there is] 1 free man, 13 acres. And [there is] 1 salt-pan. It is worth 4s. The Abbot of Ely held this and it was in Stigand's soke.

In Islington William d'Écouis held 2 free men at 6 acres. It is worth 12d.

[Folio 276v: NORFOLK]

SHROPHAM HUNDRED.

In Kilverstone [there is] 1 free man in commendation only, 11 acres. It is worth 8d.

In Leziate Robert Malet held 2 free men at 60 acres. . [There are] 4 acres of meadow. Then [there was] 1 plough, 1 bordar, 1 mill. It is worth 5s. Of this the predecessor of Robert Bigod had the commendation only.

In Gissing Drogo, a man of Robert Malet's, appropriated 10 acres from the demesne of St Edmund. And it is worth 20d. In Fritton [there was] 1 free man of King E[dward's] at 15 acres whom William Malet held. Now R[obert Malet] was holding [him]. And because now at last he has acknowledged that he is not from the fief of his father, he has demised him into the hand of the king. And he has half a plough and 2 bordars. It is worth 40d. William the fat was holding of Robert in Fersfield 1 free man in the commendation of Alsige, 104 acres, whom W[illiam] Malet held on the day

when he was alive and dead. And Walter now [holds him] of R[obert Malet] but Robert Malet asserts in opposition that he did not know about it until the day when it was recorded in writing. Then he ploughed with 2 oxen; now with 1. It is worth 8d. In Diss [there is] 5 free man, [...] 5 acres in the demesne of the manor, whom W[illiam] Malet held but it did not belong to his fief. In like manner he [i.e., Robert] declares that he did not know. There have always been 10x . It is worth 10d.

Germund, a man of Walter Giffard's, appropriated 4 acres of Swaffham from the manor belonging to Count Alan.

William de Warenne holds half a carucate in [East or West] Bradenham, which Godric held. [There have] always [been] 5 villans and 2 bordars and 1 slave. [There is] 1 plough in demesne, 1 plough belonging to the men and 2 free men holding land for 2 oxen. [There is] woodland for 20 pigs. [There are] 4 acres of meadow. Then it was worth 10s. and now the same, but William's men say that he had nothing from it. W[illiam] was holding this land before he [i.e., Ralph] forfeited but as the Hundred testify R[alph] was holding it when he forfeited and afterwards Rob[ert] Blund [held it] at farm from the king and Godric [answered for it] in the king's treasury in his return for 20s. and afterwards it was in the king's hand. The men of the Hundred have not seen the writ nor the officer who delivered it to W[illiam].

In [Cockley] Cley [there are] 2 free men, 14 acres. It is worth 7d.

In Wilton [there was] 1 free man TRE, 40 acres, 2 bordars, 1 acre of meadow. Then and afterwards [there was] half a plough.

William de Warenne

[Folio 277: NORFOLK]

It is worth 20d. His predecessor did not have any interest in this except for the commendation.

In Shipdham of William de Warenne hold 44 acres which Broddi and Alwine held of the king TRE. [There is] 1 bordar, half a plough. Then [there was] woodland for 40 pigs; now 20. [There are] 4 acres of meadow. It was worth 8s. 1½d.. This has always [belonged] to the king's manor of Saham [Toney]. And it did not have a livery officer as the Hundred testifies. In [East] Tuddenham [there are] 4 free men, half a carucate of the fief of Frederick, commended to his predecessor. [There has] always [been] 1 bordar, 2 ploughs, 1 acre of meadow. It is worth 2s. Winemar holds it of W[illiam].

In Little Cressingham the king has in demesne 2 free men at 1 carucate. And [1] has 2 ploughs and 2 villans and 1 bordar and the other 3 villans and 1 bordar. [There are] 4 acres of meadow. And it renders 12s. which Ralph de Tosny has had up to now. In Holme [Hale] 1 free man held half a carucate. [There has] always [been] half a plough and a fourth part of a mill. [There are] 2 acres of meadow. It is worth 5s. This R[alph] also had likewise.

HUNDRED AND A HALF OF FREEBRIDGE.

In Flitcham Roger Bigod holds 10 free men at 80 acres, which Ranulf fitzWalter holds. [There are] 6½ acres of meadow, two ploughs. It is worth 12s. His predecessor had the commendation only over this and Stigand the soke and commendation over one and the soke over the others.

H[UNDRED] OF WAYLAND.

In Griston [there are] 4 free men, 26 acres, which the same R[anulf] holds from R[oger]. And it is worth 4s. And Roger's predecessor did not have an interest in this except for the commendation. The king and the earl [have] the soke. In Thompson [there is] 1 free man, 15 acres and 1 acre of meadow. Then [there was] half a plough;

now 2 oxen. It is worth 2s. The same R[anulf] holds [it]. The king and the earl [have] the soke.

In Hockham [there is] 1 free man in commendation only, 8 acres. It is worth 8d. The soke [is] in Buckenham [near Attleborough].

In Snetterton [there is]a free man, 5 acres and 3 virgates, and 2 oxen. And it is worth 16d. [There is] commendation of this only. The soke [is] in Buckenham [near Attleborough]. Ralph fitzHerluin holds of Roger.

HUNDRED OF GUILTCROSS.

In [Great or Little] Snarehill [there is] 1 free man, 15 acres, in the Wef of Turstin of Thetford. And from that his predecessor had the commendation only. The soke [is] in Kenninghall, [a manor] belonging to the king. It is worth 15d. In [Great or Little] Snarehill [there are] 3 free men in commendation and soke of the fold. The whole of the other soke [is] in Kenninghall. And they have 20 acres. [There has] always [been] half a plough. It is worth 20d. Turstin holds this.

In Thurne [there is] 1 free man in the commendation only of St Benet [of Hulme], 43 acres. And he was an outlaw. And because Æthelwig made him an outlaw, he has half of the land in the Wef of Roger Bigod. [There are] 9 acres of meadow. [There has] always [been] 1 plough. Then it was worth 3s.; now 4[s.] In [East or West] Somerton [there was] 1 free man of Harold's, 30 acres and 1 bordar and 1½ ploughs and half a plough. Roger's reeve holds [it] and renders 2 oras every year to the king's reeve under Roger Bigod but it did not belong [to him] and Roger did not know.

HENSTEAD HUNDRED.

In Bramerton Aitard holds of Roger 16 acres which a free woman held in the commendation of Eadric. And Earl R[alph] was holding [it] when he forfeited according to the testimony of the Hundred. And Robert Blund afterwards [had it] in the king's hand and now Aitard, a man of Roger Bigod's, has [it] in commendation after R[alph] forfeited. The Hundred witnesses that it is so. And that woman offered judicial ordeal that the witness of the Hundred is true. And Aitard disputes [that]. And under her [there were] 2½ whole free men at 6 acres. And [there are] 1½ acres of meadow. Between all of them [there has] always [been] half a plough. Then it was worth 2s.; now 4[s.]

In Bixley [there is] 1 free man in the commendation of Aslak with half a free [man] TRE at 17 acres. [There has] always [been] half a plough, 1 villan, 1 bordar. Roger Bigod kept that man in the king's hand according to what he says

and returns the customary payment to the Hundred but the Hundred testifies that Godric the steward held under the king for 1 year in the fief of Earl R[alph] before he forfeited and afterwards for 2 years as a gift from the king. And this Roger Bigod disputes, overing judicial ordeal or trial by battle. Godric claims that with half of the land which is in the return of Roger Bigod. This

Roger Bigod

Godric the steward received in return for half a carucate.

In Poringland [there was] one free man in the commendation of Edwin TRE; afterwards Godric and after [that] Alfred because of forfeiture. And he had discharged himself from that forfeiture according to the testimony of the Hundred but by instruction of the Bishop of Bayeux Roger Bigod kept [it] in the king's hand and still keeps it and holds 15 acres. Then [there was] half a plough; now 2 oxen. It has always been worth 16 pence.

DISS HALF-HUNDRED.

In 'Osmondiston' [in Scole] Hugh de Corbon appropriated under Roger Bigod half of one man with 10 acres of land and part of an enclosure. This Earl R[alph] held when he forfeited and afterwards, when it was in the king's hand, Hugh de Corbon, who now holds [it], appropriated it. Ralph de Fougères holds the manor but does not have this part. It has always been worth 2s.

HUNDRED OF EAST FLEGG.

In Filby 1 free man had 61 acres through his wife TRE. Then Æthelwig [had] the commendation only and the same woman had nothing from this land. And Earl R[alph] was seised of this land when he forfeited. And Robert Blund held it for customary payment in the king's hand. Afterwards the same Æthelwig, the predecessor of R[oger] Bigod, appropriated it under Godric and Stanheard, his son, was holding it and from this Roger Bigod has given a pledge [that] he does not claim this land as part of his Wef. Now Godric keeps [it] in the king's hand. And there is on that land 1 plough and 1½ acres of meadow. It is worth 5s.

HUNDRED OF HUMBLEYARD.

In Swardeston [there is] half a free man of whom the predecessor of Godric had the commendation only TRE and the same Godric was seised of it when Earl R[alph] forfeited. Now Ralph de Noron is holding it. And [it has] 15 acres and half a bordar and half a plough and half an acre of meadow. And Godric was rendering 10s.; now Ralph is rendering 12s. And he has withheld this man from Godric and another half a man likewise at 5 acres. It is worth 12d.

DEPWADE HUNDRED.

In Hapton [there is] 1 free [man], 15 acres. It is worth 32d. Herbert, the chamberlain of Roger Bigod, used to hold this man and the men of Count Eustace claim him as belonging to his Wef and he is from his Wef; now it is in the king's hand.

Herbert gave a pledge about this of 16d. which he had.

HUNDRED AND A HALF OF FREEBRIDGE.

In Dersingham [there is] 1 free man, 12 acres. It is worth 12d. This Peter de Valognes holds. His predecessor had the commendation only of this and Stigand the soke. In the same [vill] 21 free men hold 2 carucates and 35 acres. [There are] 5 bordars. [There have] always [been] 3 ploughs. [There are] 7 acres of meadow. The whole is worth 40s. His predecessor had the commendation only of all of these. And 18 of them, if they should want to withdraw, should each give 2s. Stigand [had] the soke over all of them. In the same [vill there are] 2 free men, [...] 2 carucates. Then and afterwards [there were] 2 ploughs in demesne; now 1. One of them had 6 free men and 5 bordars and the other 4 bordars. [There has] always [been] 1 plough belonging to the men. [There are] 11½ acres of meadow. Then and afterwards it was worth 40s.; now 25[s.]

HUNDRED OF DOCKING.

In Shernborne [there was] 1 sokeman of Harold's, 60 acres, who belonged to Sedgeford TRE. Now W[illiam] de Parthenay holds of him and claims [to have had] a livery officer. It is worth 6s. 8d. In the same [vill there is] 1 free man in commendation only, 6 acres. It is worth 6d.

GREENHOE HUNDRED.

In Binham Peter holds 9 free men commended to Gyrth who were men of the king and Gyrth. [There are] 5 carucates and 22 bordars. Then [there were] 9 ploughs between them all; now 6½. [There are] 8 acres of meadow. Then [there was] 1 mill. Then it was worth £4; now [£]7 of the £20 which are in Binham.

SHROPHAM HUNDRED.

In Hargham Ralph de Beaufour has 2 free men at 20 acres whom Warin holds of him. [There are] 2 acres of meadow. Then [there was] 1 plough; afterwards half [a plough]; now 2 oxen. It is worth 20d. His predecessor had the commendation only of this TRE. And Eudo held them. The soke [is] in Buckenham [near Attleborough].

WALSHAM HUNDRED.

In Woodbastwick Godric, a free man in commendation, held TRE 30 acres.

Ralph de Beaufour

And he [was] a man of Godric of Ross. Now Ralph de Beaufour holds [him]. [There are] 4 acres of meadow. [There has] always [been] 1 plough between himself and the men. It has always been worth 4s., less 4d.

In Upton [he has] 4 free men of Godric's TRE in commendation only at 26 acres of land. [There are] 6 acres of meadow. [There has] always [been] half a plough. And it is worth 3s. 8d. And in addition in Woodbastwick Ulfkil holds 4 free men [who were] in the commendation of Harold at 30 acres of land.

[There has] always [been] half a plough. [There are] 4 acres of meadow. Then it was worth 2s.; now 3s 6d. And furthermore the same Ulfkil holds 4 free men at 4 acres of land. [There is] half an acre of meadow. They have always ploughed with two oxen. And it is worth 12d.

BLOFIELD H[UNDRED].

In Thorpe [St Andrew] [there is] 1 sokeman, 8 acres of land, with every customary due by his predecessor Eudo fitzClamahoc. And it is worth 17d.

H[UNDRED] OF GUILTCROSS.

In 'Wick' [in Garboldisham] Hugh de Montfort holds 1 free man at 30 acres of land in commendation only. [There is] 1 villan, 3 bordars. [There has] always [been] 1 plough in demesne and half a plough belonging to the men. And it is worth 3s. 4d. The soke [is] in Kenninghall. In [West] Bilney Hugh holds 8 free men in commendation only. [There is] 1 carucate, 1 plough, 8 acres of meadow, 3 bordars. It is worth 10s.

H[UNDRED] OF HOLT.

In Weybourne Ranulf holds Earl Hugh 12½ free men [who were] in the commendation of Harold, living in Weybourne, in Salthouse and in Kelling and in Bodham. He holds 3 carucates 15 acres. [There has] always [been] 1 villan, 25 bordars. Then [there were] 7½ ploughs and now 6. [There is] woodland for 30 pigs, 4 acres of meadow, 7 mills. Then it was worth £7; now [£]6.

CLAVERING H[UNDRED].

In Raveningham [he has] 1 free man at 3 acres and it was in the value of Raveningham when Ralph forfeited. Nicholas, the goldsmith of Earl Hugh, withheld him. And it was worth 6d. Now it is in the king's hand.

NORTH ERPINGHAM H[UNDRED].

In [North] Barningham [there were] 7 free men of Wulfric's TRE. Now Robert Gern[on] holds at 40 acres of land. And [there is] 1 acre of meadow. Then [there were] 1½ ploughs;

afterwards and now 1. Then it was worth 5s. 4d.; now 8s.

In the same vill [there were] 2 men commended TRE and now Ansketil fitzUnspac holds at 28 acres. Then [there was] half a plough; now 2 oxen. [There is] half an acre of meadow. It is worth 3s. These same men are in the king's hand because there was no one who could render the account.

BLOFIELD HUNDRED.

In Postwick [there are] 2 free men in the commendation of Skuli at 60 acres. Now Eudo the steward holds [them] from his predecessor, Lisois. [There are] 8 acres of meadow. [There has] always [been] 1 plough. Then it was worth 5s.; now it renders 2s. with service.

In Freethorpe and Limpenhoe Rabel the carpenter holds 20 free men in the commendation of Finch at 1 carucate and 20 acres. And [there are] 7 acres of meadow. Then and afterwards [there were] 2 ploughs; now 3. Then it was worth 10s.;

now 11[s.] 6d. In Southwood he held 1 free man in the commendation of Alsige TRE. When R[alph] forfeited he was in
the rent [paid] to the king's manor; now Rabel the carpenter
holds: 4 acres of land. It is worth 8d.

SOUTH ERPINGHAM HUNDRED.

In Erpingham [there is] 1 free man, 4 acres. And it is worth
16d. Humphrey holds this under Ranulf, brother of Ilger.

HUNDRED OF HAPPING.

In Walcott [there are] 3 free men, 90 acres. Then [there were] 3
ploughs; now 2½. It is worth 20s.

In [Great or Little] Melton [there is] 1 free man whom
Ranulf Peverel appropriated. And it has 6 acres [of land]. And
[there is] half an acre of meadow. It is worth 6d.

In Forncett [St Mary or St Peter] Skuli, a free man, held 13
acres of whom the predecessor of Hermer had the commendation TRE. Now it is in the king's hand. It is worth 10d. On
this land there was a house TRE which Ulfkil, the king's
reeve, took away and he has given a pledge of this.

In Tibenham [there is] 1 free man, 15 acres, of whom the
predecessor of Robert Malet had the commendation TRE.
[There has] always [been] 1 bordar. It is worth 2s. Walter
Canute held this land because his predecessor had it in pledge
for 16s. TRE.

In East Winch Rainier held TRE 1 free man at 1 acre.

Folio 280v

[blank in MS]

SUFFOLK

[HOLDERS OF LANDS]

[Folio 281v: SUFFOLK]

I. Land of the King Belonging To the Realm, which Roger Bigod keeps in Suffolk.

HUNDRED OF STOW.

King William holds Thorney which King Edward held as one manor and as 5 carucates of land. Then as now 36 villans and 18 bordars. Then 6 slaves, afterwards 1, now none. Then and afterwards 1 plough in demesne, now none; but TRE there could have been two besides that one. Then and afterwards 45 ploughs belonging to the men, now 19. Then woodland for 30 pigs, now for 6. Then 14 acres of meadow, afterwards and now 12. Then 2 mills, afterwards and now 1. There is also a market there. There was a church TRE with 1 carucate of free land, but Hugh de Montfort has 23 acres of this carucate and claims it as belonging to a certain chapel which 4 brothers, free men under Hugh, built on land of their own next to the cemetery of the mother church they were inhabitants of the parish of the mother church because it could not contain the whole parish. The mother church had by purchase half of the burial fees for all time and a fourth part of the other alms that were made. And whether this chapel was consecrated or not, the Hundred does not know. In this carucate of the church there were 5 bordars and 1 villan. Then as now 2 ploughs. In this manor there were TRE 40 sokemen with every customary due. After Roger acquired it they were all removed except for 7. Then as now these men had 58 acres and half a plough but TRE 1 plough between 4. And the reeve of this manor held 26 acres in the king's soke TRE. When this manor was undivided it was £15 by tale; when Roger acquired it, it was worth £35, now £40 blanched. Thorney is 1 league long and 1 broad and whoever is tenant there pays 15d. of geld. Of this manor Hugh de Montfort has 20 sokemen and Count Robert 6, Roger d'Auberville 4, Frodo has 2, Roger de Poitou 3. Hundred of Bosmere.

King Edward held Bramford as 12 carucates of land and as a manor. Then as now 40 villans and 8 bordars and 1 slave. Then and afterwards 1 plough in demesne, now a half. Then as now 18 ploughs belonging to the men. 30 acres of meadow. Then as now 1 mill. A church with 80 acres of free land and 1 plough. Then 10 pigs, now 12. Then as now 30 sheep. Then it was worth £[...], now £15 by weight. It is one league long and 1 league broad. In [Great] Blakenham are 9 sokemen with half

a carucate of land in the king's soke. Then as now 3 ploughs. Then it was worth 10s., now 20s. In Somersham 4 sokemen with 30 acres. Then as now 1 plough. Then it was worth 5s., now 10s. In Olden 1 sokeman and a half, with 10 acres

The King

[Folio 282: SUFFOLK]

and half a plough, worth 20d. In [Earl and Little] Stonham 1 sokeman with 12 acres TRE whom the Bishop of Bayeux now holds and Roger Bigod holds him from him. That sokeman could not withdraw. Hundred of Claydon.

In Hemingstone 1 free man, Alwine, commended to Gyrth with 30 acres. Then half a plough. It was worth 5s. Wulfmær the reeve added this free man to the king's farm at Bramford and Roger the sheriff is guarantor for him; and he pays 5s. each year. The king and the earl have the soke.

HUNDRED OF HARTISMERE.

King Edward held Diss [Norfolk] TRE; 4 carucates of land as a manor TRE. Then as now 14 villans and 24 bordars and 2 slaves. 1 plough in demesne and 18 ploughs belonging to the men. 10 acres of meadow. A church with 24 acres and half a plough. Then as now 7 head of cattle. Then 5 pigs; then 9 sheep, now 11. Then as now 5 goats. Then it was worth £15 with the soke over one and a half Hundreds and half a day's supply of honey with the customary dues; now £30 by weight. It is 1 league long and a half broad. 4d. in geld. Anund held Brome TRE with 60 acres as a manor. Then as now 4 bordars. Then 1 slave. Then as now in demesne half a plough and half a plough belonging to the men. 4 acres of meadow. It is worth 10s. And 3 free men and a half commended to Anund. 14 acres and 1 plough. It is worth 2s. 2d.

In Easton [Bavents] 2 villans; 1 carucate of land. Earl Ralph held them and afterwards Fulcred added them to the manor of Blythburgh in the time of Robert Malet. In Gislingham 1 free man, Leofric, with 3 acres, worth 6d. In the same place 7 acres which William de Bournville holds at Diss [Norfolk].

HUNDRED OF BLYTHING.

King Edward held Blythburgh as a manor with 5 carucates of land and 15 acres. Then as now 8 villans and 39 bordars and 1 slave. Then 1 plough in demesne. Land for 5 ploughs in demesne but Roger acquired 3 oxen and now there are the same number. Then as now 21 ploughs belonging to the men. Woodland for 40 pigs; 6 acres of meadow. 7 sokemen subject to every customary due [held] 3 carucates of land and 84 acres. Then as now 16 bordars and 9 ploughs and 1 market. Woodland for 30 pigs and 2 acres of meadow. To this manor belongs the fourth penny of the rent of the enclosure of "Riseburc", between the king and the earl. All this rendered TRE £30 and one day's supply of honey with every customary due; when Roger acquired it, £50 by weight, now £23 by weight. A church with 2 carucates of land. Then as now 9 villans and 4 bordars. Then 1 plough in demesne, now a half. Then four ploughs belonging to the men, now 1. Woodland for 20 pigs; half an acre of meadow. Then it rendered ten thousand herrings, now 50s. and three thousand herrings. Osbern Masculus holds this in alms of the king. To this church belong two others without land.

[Folio 282v: SUFFOLK]

In Darsham Alwine the priest held TRE 30 acres of land as a manor and 1 bordar and 1 free man with 2 acres. Half a church with 6 acres, worth 12d. Then as now 1 plough. 1 acre of meadow. It is worth 10s. And in Strickland the same Alwine held TRE 1 carucate of land and 40 acres as a manor. Then as now 2 villans. Then 4 bordars, now 11. Then as now in demesne 1 plough. Then 1 plough belonging to the men, now 2½ ploughs. 3 acres of meadow. 1 horse, 4 head of cattle, 1 pig and 16 sheep. Then it was worth 25s., now 30s. The predecessor of Robert Malet had commendation over this TRE.

HUNDRED OF CARLFORD.

In Rushmere [St Andrew] 9 free men with 31 acres. Then 1 plough, now a half. Then it was worth 5s., now 3s.

HUNDRED OF WANGFORD.

In Ringsfield 1 free man of King Edward [held] 1½ carucates of land as a manor. Then as now 1 villan and 5 bordars. 1 plough in demesne and 1 plough belonging to the men. 2 acres of meadow. Woodland for 20 pigs. Half a mill. 1 church with 15 acres, worth 2s. 8d. Then as now 2 ploughs, 2 head of cattle, 5 pigs, 30 sheep and 16 goats. Then it was worth 20s., now 16s. In the same place 11 free men commended to Wulfsige TRE [held] 1 carucate of land. Then 4 ploughs, now 1½. 2 acres of meadow. 83 free men were added from this Hundred to de Montfort's manor in the time of King William, among whom are the aforesaid 12 who did not pay any customary due to the above-mentioned manor TRE but now they pay £15. Ælfric the reeve arranged this customary due for them in the time of Roger Bigod. In Weston 1 free man, Hakon, a free man of King Edward, [held] 40 acres as a manor. Then as now 1 villan and 2 bordars; half a plough in demesne and his own men have half. Woodland for 10 pigs. In the same place 1 free man, Æthelric, commended to Gyrth [held] 40 acres as a manor. Then as now 1 bordar. Then as now half a plough. Woodland for 4 pigs. 1 acre of meadow. All these rendered TRE 6s. 8d. In the same place 1 free man, Sprotulf, under the same commendation [held] 30 acres as 1 manor. Then as now 2 bordars. Then 1 plough, now a half. 2 oxen belonging to the men. Half an acre of meadow. In Worlingham 1 free man, Ulf, commended to Gyrth [held] 40 acres as one manor. Then as now 2 bordars and 1 plough. 2

acres of meadow. In the same place 1 free man, Æthelstan, commended to Wulfsige, [held] 40 acres as one manor. Then as now 1 plough. 2 acres of meadow. In the same place 1 free man, Æthelsige, commended to Gyrth, [held] 30 acres as one manor. Then as now 1 plough. Half an acre of meadow. In the same place 1 free man, Godric, commended to Wulfsige [held] 30 acres and 1 bordar and 1 plough. 1 acre of meadow. Another 64 free men hold 5 carucates of land and then as now they ploughed with 7 ploughs. 4 acres of meadow. In Ringsfield the king has part of one church with 20 acres.

The King

[Folio 283: SUFFOLK]

Others have a share there. It is worth 3s. In Weston 1 church which the king's men hold with 20 acres, worth 3s. In Worlingham 2 churches with 40 acres, worth 6s. Others have a share there. Robert de Vaux holds a half part of one of these churches with 30 acres. 1 bordar.

HUNDRED OF LOTHING.

Earl Gyrth held Mutford and Wulfsige under him TRE with 3½ carucates of land as one manor. Then as now 18 villans and 6 bordars. Then 16 slaves, now 10. Then in demesne 4 ploughs, now 3. Then as now 3 ploughs belonging to the men. Woodland for 60 pigs. 6 acres of meadow. Then 3 horses, now 2. Then as now 7 head of cattle, 30 pigs, 160 sheep, 50 goats and 2 beehives. Then it was worth 60s., now the same. It is 2 leagues long and 9 furlongs broad. And in geld it pays 4s. In the same place 12 free men commended to Gyrth TRE held 3 carucates of land. Then as now 2 villans and 4 bordars. Then between them 9 ploughs, now 7; 8 acres of meadow. Woodland for 16 pigs. 2 churches with 43 acres. 4 of these 12 [free men] dwell in Mutford, 2 in Rushmere, 2 in Gisleham, in Pakefield 3 and in Kirkley 2. Another 26 free men dwell in Mutford with 2 carucates of land. Then as now 4 ploughs. In "Kislea" 20 free men with 1 carucate and 10 acres of land. Then as now 2 ploughs. In Rushmere 4 free men with 33 acres. Then 1 plough, now a half. In Pakefield 6 free men with 30 acres and 1 plough. In Kirkley 6 free men with 30 acres and 1 plough. In "Bechetuna" 5 free men with 1 carucate of land. Then 3 ploughs, now 2. In Barnby 8 free men with 80 acres. Then 3 ploughs, now 2. All these paid TRE 13s. 6d. but now they pay £30. Ælfric imposed this this custom upon them in the time of King William under Roger Bigod. In Kessingland 1 free man, Osfrith, commended to Eadric of Laxfield, held 15 acres and 1 bordar. Half an acre of meadow. It is worth 2s.

HALF-HUNDRED OF LOTHINGLAND.

Gyrth held Gorleston [Norfolk] TRE with 5 carucates of land as one manor. Then 20 villans, now 12. Then as now 5 bordars. Then 5 slaves, now 4. Then in demesne 2 ploughs, now 1. Then 5 ploughs belonging to the men, now 3. Woodland for 5 pigs. 10 acres of meadow. 3 salt-pans. Then 2 horses, now none; then 5 head of cattle, now none. Then as now 300 sheep. In Yarmouth [Norfolk] 24 fishermen belong to this manor. In Lowestoft 1 berewick with 4 carucates of land, less 30 acres. Then 5 villans, now 3. Then as now 10 bordars. Then 5 slaves, now 3. Then as now

10 bordars. Then 5 slaves, now 3. Then as now in demesne 2 ploughs. Then 5 ploughs belonging to the men, now 3. Woodland for 8 pigs. 5 acres of meadow. Then 14 head of cattle, now 8. Then as now 10 pigs and 160 sheep. Lound. 1 berewick Gyrth as 2 carucates of land. Then as now 4 bordars and 2 slaves. Then as now 1 plough. Then 1 plough belonging to the men, now a half. Woodland for 50 pigs. 1 [...] horse. In Belton 1 berewick with 1 carucate of land. Then as now 1 villan and 4 bordars and 1 slave. 1 plough in demesne. Then 1 plough, now a half. Then 1 horse; then as now 160 sheep. In Gapton [in Belton Bradwell] Wulfsige held 2 carucates of land as a manor. Then 3 villans, now 2. Then 3 bordars, now 2. Then in demesne 2 ploughs. Then belonging to the men 2 ploughs, now 1; 2 acres of meadow. Then as now it was worth 60s. Hundred of Wangford.

1 berewick in Ellough and in Willingham with 60 acres [...]. 3 villans and 1 plough. Woodland for 40 pigs. In Norfolk, in Gillingham 30 acres. 1 villan and half a plough. And in Beccles 82 acres and 5 villans and 1 plough. Of Beccles market the king has a fourth part and of every customary due. All this was worth TRE, apart from 2 carucates of land, £10; now it renders £27. This half-Hundred is 6 leagues long and 2½ leagues and 2 furlongs broad. 10s. in geld. Also in Somerleyton 90 acres; they belong to Gorleston. There are 20 free men with 90 acres belonging to the manor with regard to all customary dues and in the valuation of the manor. Then 7 ploughs, now 5. And at Beccles are 12 free men with 48 acres and 1 plough. And these [belong] in like manner. All this is in the valuation of the manor. In Lound Alric, a free man of Gyrth, held 1½ carucates of land as a manor. Then as now 2 villans and 3 bordars. Then and now 1 plough and 1 plough belonging to the men. Woodland for 30 pigs; 3 acres of meadow. 2 horses, 5 head of cattle, 12 pigs and 50 sheep. Then it was worth 10s., now 20s. Under him 4 free men with 1 carucate of land. Then 2 ploughs, now 1½.Woodland for 10 pigs. Then as now worth 10s. Also in Corton the same free man, Alric, commended to Gyrth [held] 2 carucates of land. Then as now 5 bordars. In demesne 2 ploughs and 1 plough belonging to the men. Then as now 2 horses, 5 head of cattle, 12 pigs and 50 sheep. Then and now worth 20s. and under the same, 15 free men with 80 acres. Then 4 ploughs; now 3. Woodland for 3 pigs. Then worth and [sic] now 10s. In Lound 1 free man, Wulfsige, under the same commendation [held] 1 carucate of land as a manor and 3 bordars. Then as now in demesne 1 plough and 1 plough belonging to the men. Woodland for 12 pigs. 2 horses, 5 head of cattle, 15 pigs, 60 sheep and 2 beehives. Then it was worth 10s., now the same. And under him 3 free men with 40 acres of land. Then 1 plough, now a half. It is worth 5s. In Flixton 1 free man, Hakon, commended to Gyrth TRE [held] 3 carucates of land as a manor. Then and now 2 villans and 14 bordars

The King

and 4 slaves. Then in demesne 3 ploughs, now 2. Then 3 ploughs belonging to the men, now 2. Woodland for 10 pigs. 3 acres of meadow. 2 horses, 6 head of cattle, 15 pigs, 160 sheep and 20 goats. Then as now worth 30s. Under him 21 free men with 3 carucates of land and 6 bordars. Then 10 ploughs, now 8. Woodland for 10 pigs. 4 acres of meadow. Then as now worth 40s. In Somerleyton 1 free man, Ulf, under the same commendation [held] 2 carucates of land as a manor. Then as now 4 villans and 4 bordars. Then and now 2 ploughs. Then as now half a plough belonging to the men. Woodland for 15 pigs. 1 acre of meadow. 2 horses, 6 pigs and 80 sheep. Then as now worth 20s. 5 free men under him with 40 acres. Then as now 1 plough. Woodland for 4 pigs. It is worth 3s. In Fritton 1 free man, Godwine, under the same commendation, [held] 2 carucates of land as a manor. Then as now 2 villans and 2 bordars and 3 slaves. In demesne 2 ploughs and 1 plough belonging to the men. Woodland for 20 pigs. 2 horses, 8 head of cattle, 16 pigs, 160 sheep, 3 goats and 3 beehives. Then as now worth 20s. Under him 2 free men with 60 acres. Then as now 1 plough. Then as now worth 5s.In Flixton 1 free man, Eadric, [held] 2 carucates of land as a manor. Then as now 2 villans and 6 bordars. Then as now in demesne 2 ploughs. Then 2 ploughs belonging to the men, now 1½. Woodland for 6 pigs. 2 acres of meadow. 6 pigs and 40 sheep. Then as now worth 30s. In the same place 2 free men of Eadric with 5 acres, worth 10d. In Hopton 1 free man, Thorger, commended to Gyrth [held] 80 acres as a manor TRE. Then as now 1 bordar. Then as now in demesne 1 plough. Woodland for 10 pigs. 3 acres of meadow. 1 horse, 5 head of cattle, 8 pigs, 60 sheep and 3 beehives. Then as now worth 5s. In the same place 1 free man, Sigeric, under the same commendation, [held] 60 acres as a manor. 1 bordar and 1 slave and 1 plough. Woodland for 10 pigs. 1½ acres of meadow. 1 horse, 4 head of cattle, 8 pigs and 69 sheep. Then as now it was worth 5s. Under Thorger and Sigeric 8 free men with 80 acres. Then 3 ploughs, now 2 ploughs. 2 acres of meadow. Then as now worth 10s. In Somerleyton 1 free man, Wihtræd the priest, [held] 40 acres as one manor. Then 1 bordar, now 2. Then as now 1 plough. Woodland for 5 pigs. 1 horse, 4 head of cattle, 5 pigs and 33 sheep. It is worth 5s. 1 church with 20 acres, worth 3s. In Browston 1 free man, Ulfkil, [held] 40 acres as a manor. Then as now half a plough. Woodland for 10 pigs. 1 horse, 2 head of cattle, 7 pigs, 30 sheep and 3 goats. It is worth 5s. Under him 1 free man with 30 acres. It is worth 2s. In the same place 1 free man, Brothir, [held] 60 acres as a manor. Then as now 2 bordars. Then as now in demesne 1 plough and half a plough belonging to the men. 1 horse, 2 head of cattle, 7 pigs and 40 sheep. Then as now it was worth 5s. Also in the same place 1 free man, Godwine, [held] 30 acres and half a plough, worth 3s. In the same place 2 free men [held] 80 acres TRE and 1 bordar.

Then as now 1½ ploughs. Then as now worth 6s. In Gorleston [Norfolk] 4 free men [held] 1 carucate of land.

Then 2½ ploughs, now 2. Then it was worth 20s., now 16s. In Gapton 1 free man, Ulf, [held] 60 acres as 1 manor and 1 bordar. Then as now 1 plough. Half an acre of meadow. 1 horse, 3 head of cattle, 6 pigs and 80 sheep. It is worth 5s. In the same place 1 free man, Æthelstan, [held] 60 acres and 1 manor. Then as now half a plough. 1 acre of meadow. 4 head of cattle, 3 pigs and 30 sheep. It is worth 4s. Also in the same place 1 free man, Sprotulf, [held] 40 acres and 1 bordar. Then as now 1 plough. Woodland for 3 pigs. 1 acre of meadow. It is worth 4s. In the same place 1 free man, Wulfnoth, [held] 30 acres, worth 2s. In Akethorpe 1 free man, Æthelmær the priest, [held] 80 acres as one manor. Then as now 3 bordars. In demesne 1 plough and half a plough belonging to the men. Woodland for 5 pigs. 1 acre of meadow. 3 pigs and 48 sheep. It is worth 10s. In 'Neutuna' [near Corton] 1 free man [held] 30 acres and half a plough, worth 3s. In Fritton 2 free men [held] 80 acres. Then 2 villans, now 1 bordar. Then 2 ploughs, now 1. Then 1 salt-pan. Then as now worth 10s. In the same place 1 free man, Leofric, [held] 30 acres. Then half a plough, now none. It is worth 3s. In Belton 3 free men [held] 90 acres. Then 3 ploughs, now 1. Then as now worth 10s. In Herringfleet 1 free man, Wulfsige, [held] 1 carucate of land as one manor. Then as now 2 villans and 1 bordar. Then in demesne 1 plough, now none. Then half a plough belonging to the men, now none. Woodland for 12 pigs. Then as now worth 4s. All these men rendered TRE 20s. at farm and afterwards in the time of Roger Bigod, Ælfric the reeve increased it to 100s. and in the time of Henry de Houdain to £50, as the men say.

Lands of Earl Ralph which Godric the steward has custody of in Suffolk in the king's hand.

HUNDRED OF THEDWESTRY.

In Tostock the king has 36 free men, under the commendation of Eadgifu the Rich TRE, belonging to Norton [near Bury St Edmunds]. Between the men carucate of land. And then as now 5 ploughs and 2 acres of meadow. Then as now worth 13s. 4d. In Thurston 14 free men. Of these St Edmund had the commendation with all customary dues over 4 full men and 4 half men belonging to Norton [near Bury St Edmunds]. Earl Ralph held them when he forfeited. Between them all half a carucate of land and under them 3 bordars. 1 acre of meadow. Then as now 2 ploughs. Then as now worth 6s. 8d.

The King

[Folio 285: SUFFOLK]

HUNDRED OF THINGOE.

In [Great and Little] Saxham were 6 free men commended to Eadgifu the Rich TRE, and the soke was in Norton [near Bury St Edmunds]. 1 carucate of land and 2 bordars and 2 ploughs. Woodland for 2 pigs. Then as now worth 10s.

HUNDRED OF STOW.

In [Great and Little] Finborough 2 free men commended to Eadgifu held 25 acres. They are in the soke of the Hundred and belong to Norton [near Bury St Edmunds]. Then as now half a plough. It is in the valuation of Norton [near Bury St Edmunds]. In Mendlesham 1 free man belonging to Thorney with 3 acres, worth 6d. The soke and sake are in the Hundred.

HUNDRED OF BOSMERE.

In [Earl and Little] Stonham 5 sokeman with 18 acres. The soke is in the Hundred of Bosmere belonging to Mendlesham. Then as now 1 plough and half an acre of meadow. It is worth 4s. In the same place have been added 3 free men with 12 acres now belonging to Mendlesham. 1 plough and half an acre of meadow. It is worth 3s. In [Great] Blakenham 5 free men in the soke and commendation of Eadgifu the Fair [held] 60 acres. And they have been added to Norton [near Bury St Edmunds]. Then as now 2 ploughs and 2 acres of meadow, less one virgate. Then it was worth 12s., now 16s. 4d. In "Langhedena" 3 free men with 72 acres and 1½ ploughs and 3 acres of meadow, worth 12s. 4d. In Offton 2 free men and 50 acres. Then as now 1 plough. Then it was worth 20s., now 11s. 4d. In the church, however, there are 16 acres. In Badley 1 free man with 30 acres. Then as now 1 plough and 2½ acres of meadow. It is worth 7s. 8d. And 1 sokeman with 20 acres, worth 4s.

In Darmsden 1 free man [held] 50 acres as 1 manor. Then 1 plough. 3½ acres of meadow. Then 1 mill, and now. Then it was worth 16s., now 9s. 4d. In 'Sharpstone' [in Barham] 1 free man with 2 acres, worth 2s. In Ashbocking 1 free man, Almær, with 93 acres and 20 acres of pasture as one manor. Then 3 bordars, now 6. Then as now 1 plough. 3 acres of meadow. Half a church with 16 acres. Then it was worth 30s., now 20s. 6d. A church with 3 acres, worth 6d. Over all these Eadgifu the Fair had soke and commendation TRE. They pay £4 to the farm of Norton [near Bury St Edmunds] and they were added in the time of Earl [...] Ralph.

HUNDRED OF CLAYDON.

In Coddenham Almær, a free man, held 8 acres, worth 16d. The soke is the king's and the earl's.

HALF-HUNDRED OF PARHAM.

Thormoth held Parham with 2 carucates of land as one manor. Then as now 4 bordars. Then 2 slaves, afterwards and now 1. Then as now 2 ploughs in demesne and 1 plough belonging to the men. 8 acres of meadow. Then woodland for 20 pigs, now 10. Then 50 pigs, now 30. Then as now 5 head of cattle. Then 24 [...] sheep,

[Folio 285v: SUFFOLK]

now 38. Then 50 goats, now 58. Then it was worth 100s., afterwards £7, now £10 blanched and 20s. of exactions by tale. In the same place 6 free men with 24 acres. Then as now half a plough. They are in the same valuation. Thormoth had the soke of the manor and of three free men and the Abbot of Ely had it of three. It is 11 furlongs long and 6 broad. 40d. in geld. Hundred of Hartismere.

Burgheard held Mendlesham with 7 carucates of land and 42 acres as one manor. Then 33 villans, afterwards 27, now 24. Then as now 19 bordars. Then 3 ploughs in demesne, afterwards and now 2. Then 15½ ploughs , afterwards and now 13; 12 acres of meadow. Then woodland for 1000 pigs, afterwards and now 800. 2 horses, 11 head of cattle, 90 pigs and 35 goats. 1 berewick with 26 acres and 1 bordar and 1 plough. A church with 40 acres and 1 plough. Then it was worth £25; when Godric acquired it £20, now it renders £25 blanched by tale and 40 as exactions. It is 1 league and 6 furlongs long and 1 league broad. 8d. in geld. Burgheard had the soke. In Cotton 18 free men over one, Alwine by name, with 10 acres, the abbot had half the commendation were added to this manor with 1 plough TRE and 15 acres of land. Then as now 3 ploughs and 1 acre of meadow. Then it was worth 10s., now 6s. 8d. They are in the same valuation. The king and earl have the soke. It is 6 furlongs and 8 perches long and 6 furlongs broad. 12d. in geld. The Hundred testifies that the king and earl truly had soke and sake TRE but the men of that vill testify that Burgheard likewise had soke over the free men, just as over his own villans. And they have no testimony apart from themselves but they are willing to prove it by every means.

In Wickham [Skeith] 8 bordars with 18 acres of the demesne of Mendlesham. 1 plough and 2 half free men and two full free men with 8 acres. It is in the valuation of Mendlesham. In the same place 37½ acres; 6 free men. Then as now 1½ ploughs. Then it was worth 20s., now 12s. They are in the above valuation. The king and earl have the soke. In Cotton half a free man with 10 acres and half a plough. Woodland for 2 pigs. [...] It is worth 20d. and is in the valuation of Mendlesham. In Wetheringsett 2 half free men with 12 acres and half a plough. It is worth 2s. and is in the same valuation. In the same place 4 free men with 33 acres; 1 plough and 5 bordars. They render 40d. in the same valuation. In Thornham [Magna] 1 free man with 2 acres, 4d. In Occold 1 free man [held] 33 acres as one manor; 1 plough and 2 bordars. 1 free man with 1 acre. Woodland for 4 pigs.

The King

[Folio 286: SUFFOLK]

Then it was worth 10s., now 15s. And it renders 5s. in the above valuation. In Wyverstone 1 free man commended to Burgheard with 8 acres, worth 16d. In Cotton 2 free women under the same commendation, with 5 acres, worth 12d. In the same place 1 bordar under the same commendation, with 1½ acres, worth 3d. In Wickham [Skeith] 1 berewick which belongs in the demesne of Mendlesham with 61 acres and 1 acre of meadow. In Stoke Ash 4 free men commended to Burgheard with 8 acres and half an acre of meadow. It is worth 2s. 4d. In Gislingham 1 free man with 1 acre, worth 2d. All this is in the valuation of Mendlesham.

HUNDRED OF BLACKBOURN.

Edith, a certain free woman, held Norton [near Bury St Edmunds] TRE as one manor with 4 carucates of land. Then as now 9 villans and 21 bordars and 6 slaves. 2 ploughs

in the demesne and 5 ploughs belonging to the men. Woodland for 150 pigs. 8 acres of meadow. Then as now 2 horses, 10 head of cattle, 50 pigs, 100 sheep and 30 goats. 34 sokemen with 2 carucates of land. Then as now 10 ploughs and 2 acres of meadow. Then it was worth £10, afterwards £15 10s., now £16 blanched. A church with 30 acres. It is 1 league long and 8 furlongs broad. 17¼d. in geld. This manor was in the demesne of the Abbot of St Edmund. Edith held it on a lease from the abbot on the agreement that after her death the abbot was to repossess it. Thus she held this manor on the day King Edward died. Hunston, 7 free men; of these Edith had the commendation TRE. Half a carucate of land. Then as now 1 plough. It is worth 6s.

HUNDRED OF RISBRIDGE.

The same woman held [Great and Little] Thurlow TRE with 7 carucates of land. Then as now 16 villans. Then 6 bordars, now 9; 2 slaves. Then as now 3 ploughs in demesne and 7 ploughs belonging to the men. 18 acres of meadow. Woodland for 80 pigs. Then as now 10 head of cattle, 36 pigs, 46 sheep and 33 goats. A church with 32 acres of free land and half a plough. 5 free men with 1 carucate of land and 2 bordars and 3 ploughs. 3 [...] acres of meadow. Then the manor was worth £9, now £16. And the free men 20s. and 20s. as exactions by tale. And it is 1 league long and 7 furlongs and 10 perches broad. 6d. in geld. In Chilbourne 1 sokeman with 30 acres and 1 bordar and 1 plough. 6 acres of meadow. Then it was worth 10s., now 20s.

HUNDRED OF BISHOP.

In Weybread 1½ bordars with 7½ acres of land and half an acre of meadow. Woodland for 6 pigs. Half a plough. It is in the valuation of Redenhall [Norfolk]. The soke is in Hoxne.

HUNDRED OF LOOSE.

In Marlesford 6 free men commended to Thormoth of Parham [held] 25 acres of land.

[Folio 286v: SUFFOLK]

Then as now half a plough. In Hacheston 3 free men under the same commendation [held] 19 acres and half a plough. 1½ acres of meadow. They are in the valuation of Parham. In Marlesford 35 acres in demesne. 1 church with 16 acres, worth 2 ores. It is 1 league long and 4 furlongs broad. 15d. in geld.

HUNDRED OF HARTISMERE.

In Cotton 3 free men commended to Burgheard TRE; 8 acres. Then as now half a plough. Woodland for 2 pigs. Half an acre of meadow. It is worth 2s. The king and the earl have the soke. 1 church with 11 acres, worth 2s.

Land of the King which Peter de Valognes has charge of.

HUNDRED AND A HALF OF SAMFORD.

Harold held Harkstead TRE with 5 carucates of land as a berewick in Brightlingsea in the county of Essex. Then there were 21 villans, afterwards and now 8. Then as now 13 bordars. Then 4 slaves. Then as now 2 ploughs in demesne. Then 8 ploughs belonging to the men, afterwards 2, now 1; 4 acres of meadow. A church. Then as now 1 horse, 3 head of cattle, 7 pigs and 12 sheep. Then and afterwards it was worth £6 by tale, now £6 by weight and 30s. by tale. It is 12½ furlongs long and 12 broad. 30d. in geld.

Land of Earl Morcar's Mother which William the chamberlain and Otto the goldsmith have custody of in the king's hand.

HUNDRED OF THINGOE.

Earl Morcar's mother held Sudbury TRE; now King William holds it in demesne with 3 carucates of land. Then there was 1 villan, now 2, and 63 burgesses in demesne dwelling at the hall. Then 6 slaves, now 2. Then as now 3 ploughs in demesne and 55 burgesses in demesne. 2 carucates of land. Between them all 4 ploughs. A CHURCH OF ST GREGORY with 50 acres of free land, as the Hundred testifies. 25 acres of meadow and 1 mill. 2 horses in the demesne of the hall. 17 head of cattle, 24 pigs and 100 sheep. 9 acres of meadow belonging to the burgesses. 1 market and there are moneyers there. Then it was worth £18, afterwards and now £28 by tale. It is 4 furlongs long and 3 broad. 5s. in geld. The soke is in the same town.

TWO HUNDREDS OF BABERGH.

The mother of Earl Morcar held [Great and Little] Cornard TRE as one manor with 3 carucates of land. Then there were 8 villans, now 10; then 9 bordars, now 25; then 8 slaves, now 9. Then and afterwards 3 ploughs in the demesne, now 1. Then 8 ploughs belonging to the men, afterwards and now 10. 1 mill and 14 acres of meadow. Woodland for 10 pigs. A church without land. Then as now 4 horses at the hall, 18 head of cattle and 80 pigs.

The King

Folio 287: SUFFOLK]

Then as now 363 sheep. In Groton 4 sokemen belonging to that manor. 100 acres of land and 3 bordars. Between them all 1 plough. Then the whole was worth £10, afterwards and now 26s. 8d. by tale. It is 6 furlongs and 3 perches and 4½ furlongs and 4 perches broad. 10½d. in geld. The soke is in the same vill.

Lands of the King which Ælfric Wand has charge of.

HUNDRED AND A HALF OF SAMFORD.

Harold held [East] Bergholt TRE; 13 carucates of land as a manor. Then 42 villans, now 43. Then 5 bordars, now 22. Then 6 slaves, now 4. Then and afterwards 3 ploughs in demesne, now 2. Then 20 ploughs belonging to the men, afterwards and now 10; 12 acres of meadow. Woodland for 1000 pigs. Then as now 1 mill. Then as now 1 horse, 10 head of cattle, 29 pigs, 85 sheep and 26 goats. To this manor belongs 1 berewick, Shelley, with 2 carucates of land TRE. Then 10 villans, afterwards and now 6. Then as now 7 bordars. Then 4 slaves, now 2. Then 2 ploughs in demesne, afterwards and now 1. Then 8 ploughs for the men, afterwards and now 4; 16 acres of meadow. 1 mill. Then as now 1 horse, 4 head of cattle, 7 pigs and 23 sheep. Earl Gyrth held Bentley TRE. Afterwards Earl Ralph the staller joined it to this manor as a berewick, in the time of King Edward William, as 2 carucates of land. Then 19 villans, now 13. Then as now 3 bordars. Then 4 slaves. Then 2 ploughs in demesne, afterwards and now 1. Then 8 ploughs belonging to the men, afterwards and now 1; 8 ploughs could be restored between the demesne and the villans. 8 acres of meadow. Woodland for 12 pigs. 8 head of cattle, 7 pigs, 42 sheep and half a park. It is worth 6d. Earl Gyrth held Shotley with 2½ carucates of land and 1 acre, worth 2d., as 1 manor TRE. Then 12 villans, now 6. Then as now 2 bordars; then 4 slaves, now 1. Then 2 ploughs in demesne, afterwards and now 1. Then 4 ploughs belonging to the men, afterwards and now 1; 4 ploughs could be restored. 4 acres of meadow. 1 horse and 40 sheep. To this manor there belonged TRE 210 sokemen, now there are only 119 and they have 22½ carucates less 30 acres, and 42 bordars. Then 29 ploughs, now 27; 24½ acres of meadow. 2 churches with 52 acres. Of these men who still dwell at the manor Harold did not even have commendation TRE, except over 4; Wulfnoth, Eastmund, Ælfric, Wihtric; and Gyrth, the brother of Harold, had commendation of 2: Mann and Ælfgeat. All the others were commended to other barons TRE.

[Folio 287v: SUFFOLK]

Malet's predecessor had commendation over 1 and Robert fitzWymarc over 4. But then as now Harold had the soke. The aforesaid manor, namely [East] Bergholt, with that which belonged to it and with the soke of the Hundred and a half rendered TRE £24. And the two aforesaid manors [Bentley and Shotley] of Gyrth's which were added to this farm rendered £9 at that time. And when Robert Malet had it the whole of it paid £60 by weight and £8 by tale as an exaction and it paid the same amount to Roger Bigod, as the reeve himself says. But Roger says that it rendered 40s. more by tale and 1 mark of gold, but Ælfric the reeve denies this. Roger is willing to prove it through those men who were present at his agreements. Now this Ælfric renders £50 £60 by weight and he holds it from the king according to an agreement by which he must make a payment to the king of £60 from the profit and for this he calls the king as guarantor, as he himself says. And he says too that there does not remain in it enough to make that profit. The whole of [East] Bergholt is 1 league and 2 furlongs long and 1 league broad. 8d. in geld. And Shelley is 8 furlongs long and 3 broad; 4d. in geld. And Bentley is 1 league long and 3 furlongs broad; 5d. in geld. And Shotley is 12½ furlongs long and 12 broad; 30d. in geld. Aubrey de Vere holds 1 sokeman of [East] Bergholt with 4 acres, worth 12d. And he holds him as of Aldham. These free men who TRE belonged in the soke of [East] Bergholt each gave freely to the reeve only 4d. a year and rendered soke as the law required. When Roger Bigod first had the shrievalty his officials decided that they should render £15 a year which they did not do TRE. And when Robert Malet had the shrievalty his officials increased them to £20. And when Roger Bigod had them again they likewise gave £20 and now Ælfric Wand holds them with such customary dues as there were TRE. "Canappetunam" is 5 furlongs long and 2 broad; 6½d. in geld. And Chattisham is 8 furlongs long and 6 broad; 6½d. in geld.

The King

Lands of Stigand which William de Noyers has custody of in the king's hand.

HUNDRED OF BLYTHING.

In Bampton a free man, Thorsten, held 20 acres TRE, commended to Stigand. Then as now 2 bordars. Then 1 plough, now a half. Half an acre of meadow. Woodland for 3 pigs. 1 horse, 2 pigs and 12 sheep. Then as now worth 4s. Also 1 free man under him, with 2 acres of land, worth 6d. In Covehithe 2 free men of Stigand with 32 acres. Then as now 1 plough. It is worth 4s. All this belongs to Bungay, [and] the soke to Stigand.

HUNDRED OF COSFORD.

In Layham 1 sokeman with 4 acres, worth 12d.

HUNDRED OF WANGFORD.

At Bungay Stigand held TRE 9 carucates of land as a manor. Then as now 20 villans and 16 bordars. Then 6 slaves, now 3. Then in demesne 3 ploughs, now 2. Then as now belonging to the men 12½ ploughs. 29 acres of meadow. 2½ mills. Woodland for 100 pigs. Then as now 2 horses, 4 head of cattle, 3 pigs, 9 sheep and 60 goats. 1 church with 5 acres. Then it was worth 100s., now it renders £12. In the same vill 1 free man, Wulfmær, commended to Stigand, holds a carucate of land as one manor. Then as now 3 villans and 6 bordars. Then as now in demesne 1 plough and belonging to the men 1 plough. Woodland for 20 pigs. 2 acres of meadow. 4 horses, 3 head of cattle, 6 pigs, 20 sheep and 16 goats. Under him 1 free man with 1 acre. Then as now worth 20s. but it pays 13s. at farm. Also in the same vill 1 free man, Alwine, under the same commendation, [held] 1 carucate of land as 1 manor TRE. 6 villans and 8 bordars. 1 plough in demesne and 2 ploughs

belonging to the men. Woodland for 10 pigs. 4 acres of meadow. 4 horses, 15 pigs and 13 sheep.

[...] Then it was worth 20s. 6 free men with 14 acres and 1 plough. Then it was worth 4s. and after King William came into this country 2 brothers have shared it. One of these, Wulfsige, is in the king's hand; Wulfric is in the hand of Earl Hugh. This Wulfsige has 60 acres. 3 villans and 4 bordars. 4½ free men and 10 acres. 1 plough in demesne and 1 plough belonging to the men. 2 acres of meadow. Woodland for 6 pigs. Now this, the king's part, is worth 18s. 8d., but it renders 14s. 4d.

In Bungay a free man, Godric, [held] 30 acres as one manor. 1 bordar and 1 plough. 2 acres of meadow. Then it was worth 8s., now 10s. and it pays 8s. at farm. In the same place a free man, Pat,

held TRE 60 acres as one manor. Now 2 free men hold it, Howard and Wulfsige. Then as now 8 villans, then 8 bordars, now 4. Then 4 slaves, now 2. Then as now 2 ploughs in the demesne and 2 ploughs belonging to the men, woodland for 12 pigs. 2 acres of meadow. Then as now 4 horses. Then 6 head of cattle, now 8, and 12 pigs. Then 30 sheep, now 100. Then it was worth 20s., now 30s. and they render at farm 16s. 1 church with 12 acres, worth 2s. To this manor belong 2 half free men and one whole one, with 16 acres. Then as now 1 plough. It is worth 3s. In the same place Ælfgar, a free man, held 30 acres as one manor TRE; now Eadric holds it. Then as now 2 villans and 2 bordars and 2 slaves. 1 plough in demesne and 1 plough belonging to the men. Woodland for 16 pigs and 2 acres of meadow. It is worth 8s. and renders as much at farm. Also in the same place 2 free men with 7 acres, worth 12d. 1 church with 8 acres, worth 12d. In the same place 15 free men commended to Stigand with 80 acres and 3 bordars. Then and now 4 ploughs. 3 acres of meadow. Then it was worth 13s., now it renders 20s. 1 church with 30 acres, worth 3s. It is 2 leagues long and 1 [league] and 8 furlongs broad. 5s. in geld. In Shadingfield 1 free man under the same commendation [held] 30 acres as one manor. 4 bordars. Then as now 1 plough and half a plough belonging to the bordars. Woodland for 6 pigs. 1 acre of meadow. Then it was worth 10s., now the same. In Weston 2 free men and a half commended to Stigand [held] 12 acres and 1 plough, worth 2s. 1 church with 20 acres, worth 3s.

HUNDRED OF BISHOP.

In Denham 1 free man by commendation [held] 30 acres and 1 bordar. Then as now 1 plough and half an acre of meadow. Woodland for 3 pigs. It is worth 6s. The soke is in Hoxne.

HUNDRED OF LACKFORD.

King Edward gave Mildenhall to St Edmund and afterwards Stigand held it under St Edmund as a manor in the lifetime of King Edward with 12 carucates of land. Then and 30 villans, now 33. Then 8 bordars, afterwards and now 15. Then as now 16 slaves. Then as now 6 ploughs in demesne and 8 ploughs belonging to the men. 20 acres of meadow. A church with 40 acres. 1 mill and 3½ fisheries. 31 wild mares, 37 head of cattle, 60 pigs and 1000 sheep. 8 sokemen with 30 acres. Then as now half a plough. To this belongs 1 berewick, Icklingham, with 6 carucates of land. Then 6 villans, now 4. Then 7 bordars, now 5. Then as now 8 slaves. Then as now 3 ploughs in demesne. Then 4 ploughs belonging to the men, afterwards and now 2.

The King

1 mill. A church with 24 acres. 2 horses, 3 head of cattle, 4 pigs, 500 sheep. There is 1 sokeman there with 30 acres. Then as now 1 plough. Then and afterwards the whole was worth £40, now £70 by tale. This vill is 1 league long and 1 league broad. 11¼d. in geld. Several persons hold land there. The aforesaid berewick is 2½ leagues long and the same in breadth. 11¼d. in geld.

HALF-HUNDRED OF IPSWICH.

In the borough of Ipswich Stigand had 2 burgesses TRE with soke and sake and the king had the customary dues. Now they are dead and the king has the customary dues and the soke and sake.

HUNDRED OF CLAYDON.

In Akenham 1 sokeman belonging to Stigand with 30 acres. Then 1 plough, now a half. 1 bordar. 1 acre of meadow. It is worth 5s.

HUNDRED OF SAMFORD.

Stigand held Hintlesham TRE as a manor and as 10 carucates of land and 40 acres. Then as now 25 villans and 17 bordars. 2 ploughs in demesne. Then 16 ploughs belonging to the men, afterwards and now 12; 10 acres of meadow. Woodland for 30 pigs. Then as now 1 mill. 1½ churches with 35 acres of free land. Then 2 horses, now 1; 8 head of cattle, 30 pigs, 200 sheep. Then it was worth £10, now £22 by weight. It is 1 league and 2 furlongs long and 1 league broad. 13½d. in geld.

In the same place 8 sokemen with 1 carucate of land and 70 acres. Then as now 1 villan and 3 bordars and 4 ploughs. 3 acres of meadow and 1 salt-pan. The whole is in the above valuation. Stigand had the soke and sake.

Stigand held Bramford TRE as one manor and as 10 carucates of land. Then as now 28 villans and 7 bordars. Then 4 slaves, now 2. Then as now 3 ploughs

in demesne. Then 13 ploughs belonging to the men, afterwards and now 10; 22 acres of meadow. 1 mill. A church with 30 acres of free land. 6 horses, 24 head of cattle, 20 pigs, 90 sheep. Then it was worth £10, now £22 by weight. It is 1 league long and 10 furlongs broad. 13½d. in geld.

In the same place 3 sokemen with 9½ acres. Then 1 plough, now 2 oxen. This is in the same valuation. Stigand had the soke and sake.

In the same place a free man, Brun, [held] by commendation 30 acres as a manor. Now 2 villans and 2 bordars. Then 1 plough, now a half. It is worth 5s. in the same valuation. Harold had the soke in [East] Bergholt and this was added in the time of Bishop Herfast.

Lands of the king belonging to the realm of which Picot has charge. Hundred of Thingoe.

King Edward held Barrow as a manor and as 7 carucates of land. Then 6 villans, now 15. Then 4 bordars, now 10. Then 2 slaves, now 1. Then 2 ploughs in demesne, now 3. Then 5 ploughs belonging to the men, now 14. Woodland for 8 pigs. 3 acres of meadow. 1 mill. A church with 17 acres of free land. Then 16 pigs, now 40; now 100 sheep and 60 goats. 1 sokeman with 30 acres. Then as now 1 plough. Then the whole was worth £10, now £20 by weight. It is 1 league long and 8 furlongs wide. 7d. in geld.

HUNDRED OF RISBRIDGE.

Ælfgar held Badmondisfield TRE as one manor and as 10 carucates of land. Then and afterwards 18 villans, now 14. Then as now 14 bordars and 4 slaves. 5 ploughs in demesne and 10 ploughs belonging to the men. 7 acres of meadow. Woodland for 60 pigs. 2 horses, 7 head of cattle, 88 pigs, 24 sheep, 25 goats. A church with 10 acres of free land. 12 free men with 2½ carucates of land. Ælfgar had the soke and commendation. They did not pay rent TRE. Then and afterwards 3½ ploughs, now 2½; 9 acres of meadow. Then the manor was worth £7, now £10. The free men render 40s. It is 12 furlongs long and 8 broad. It renders

The King

13½d. in geld.

Roger Bigod has CUSTODY OF THIS in the king's hand.

OF THE HALF-HUNDRED OF IPSWICH and of the borough [Ipswich] Queen Edith had TRE 2 parts and Earl Gyrth had the third part. The queen also had in her demesne a grange to which belonged TRE 4 carucates of land and now the same. Of this land 12 free men dwelling on other land of their own held then as now 80 acres for the king's service and customary dues. And there are another 10 men, bordars, who do not have their own land but live on 86 acres of the aforesaid land. 2 burgesses also belong to the demesne of the aforesaid grange, who render to the king 6d. of customary dues. And then there were 2 ploughs in demesne and afterwards the same, now 1. Then 3 head of cattle, now 8. Then 2 horses, now 1. Then 14 goats, now 7. Then 40 sheep, now 13. The villans then as now have 6 ploughs. This land is 8 furlongs long and the same broad. It pays nothing of the king's geld. In the borough [Ipswich] there were TRE 538 burgesses rendering customary dues to the king. They had 40 acres of land. But now there are 110 burgesses who render customary dues and 100 poor burgesses who cannot render anything to the king's geld apart from one penny a head. And amongst them all they likewise have 40 acres of land. And 328 dwellings have been laid waste in the borough [Ipswich] which TRE used to pay scot to the king's geld. In the same borough Alwulf the priest has one church, Holy Trinity, to which belong 26 acres in alms. And Colling, a burgess, has one church, St Mary's, with 26 acres. Tumbi [has] one church, St Mary's, with 2 acres. Leofstan the priest has 1 church, St Augustine's, with 11 acres. Wulfwine the priest has 1 church, St Michael's, with 8 acres. In Thurlston in Claydon HundredGodric has one church, St Botulf's, with 1 acre. Thorkil and Eadric hold one church, St Lawrence's, with 12 acres, half a year at the feast of St John. Leofflæd, a free woman, held this church TRE which Count Alan claims for the fief of Earl Ralph and vouches Ivo Taillebois as deliverer. However Thorkil and Eadric vouch Roger the sheriff as guarantor, saying that they had this church through him and Roger was such a guarantor for it as any sheriff could have been TRE. All this rendered TRE £15 and 6 sesters of honey and 4s. towards the customary dues of honey and 8s. to the prebendaries. And Roger the sheriff gave the whole at farm for £40 at the feast of St Michael. Afterwards he was not able to have the rent and because of this he waived payment of 60s. Now it renders £37. And the moneyers rendered TRE £4 a year for the mint. Now they ought to pay £20 but in four years they have only paid £27. And then as now the earl had a third part.

II. Lands of Robert, Count of Mortain, In Suffolk.

Hundred of Thedwestry.

In Drinkstone 1 free man commended to St Æthelthryth in the soke of St Edmund [held] 1 carucate of land and 8 bordars. Then 2 slaves, now 1. Then as now 1½ ploughs. 4 acres of meadow. It is worth 16s.

In Rattlesden 1 free man commended to St Æthelthryth together with the soke [held] 1 carucate of land and 1 bordar. Then as now 1 plough. It is worth 10s. In Bradfield 1 free man commended to Bishop Æthelmær in the soke of St Edmund [held] 20 acres of land. Then half a plough, now 1 ox. It is worth 2s. In [Great and Little] Welnetham 1 free man commended to Bishop Æthelmær in the soke of St Edmund [held] 40 acres. Then 1 plough, now 2 ox. Then it was worth 10s., now 20s. In Stanningfield 1 free man commended to Bishop Æthelmær in the soke of St Edmund [held] 60 acres of land. Then 1 plough, now a half. Then it was worth 10s., now 30s., but it renders it with difficulty. All this was delivered to Count Brian, Count Robert's predecessor as 2 carucates and 40 acres of land.

HUNDRED OF STOW.

Wulfnoth, a free man, held Combs under King Edward as 2 carucates of land. Then and always 12 villans and 8 bordars. Then and afterwards 6 slaves, now 2. Then as now 3 ploughs in demesne. Then 5, afterwards 3 ploughs belonging to the men, now 1. Then as now 2 mills. Woodland for 16 pigs. 12 acres of meadow. Then as now 2 horses. Then as now 24 head

of cattle and 16 pigs. Then as now 121 sheep and 60 goats. There are there 50 free men belonging to the same Wulfnoth. They have 1 mill. Afterwards [they were] under Brian, Count Robert's predecessor, by commendation only, in the king's soke. And under them 7 bordars. They have between them all 8 carucates of land. Then 16 ploughs and afterwards, now 8, but TRE there were 62 free men. Then and afterwards the manor of Combs was worth £10, now it renders £16 but it can scarcely render this. These 50 free men were worth then and afterwards £16, now £31 but they cannot bear it without ruin. After Count Brian, Robert's predecessor, had this manor it paid no customary dues in the Hundred. Combs is 2 leagues long and 1 broad. 37½d. in geld. Hugh de Montfort holds half a mill; it belonged to one free man of that manor in the time of Brian. He claims a deliverer for the fief of his predecessor but it never belonged [there], as the Hundred testifies. Wihtmær held Onehouse under King Edward as 1 carucate of land. Then 3 bordars, afterwards and now 6. Then and afterwards 2 slaves, now none. Then as now 1 plough in demesne. 4 acres of meadow. 2 sokemen with 3 acres of land but they could sell without permission. In the same place 1 free man with 9 acres which Nigel held under Count Robert but Frodo was seised of it before and claims a livery officer but the Hundred knows nothing. Then as now the whole was worth 20s. It was in the soke of the king. After Brian had it, it rendered no customary due in the Hundred.

Nigel, Count Robert's sergeant, appropriated 11 acres of land of the church of Stow and added it to the manor of Combs, but he died and there is no one to answer for it. The Hundred testifies that they were in the alms of the Church. 12 sokemen in Combs used to be parishioners in the church of Stow but now they are in the church of Combs. This same Nigel took them away. In Creeting [St Peter] Wulfnoth, a free man of King Edward's, Count Brian's predecessor, held 1 carucate of land. Then as now 2 villans. Then as now 1 plough in demesne and half a plough belonging to the men. 4 acres of meadow. 7 head of cattle and 12 pigs. Then as now worth 20s. Sainte-MARIE of Grestain holds this land from Count Robert with soke and sake.

HUNDRED OF BOSMERE.

Wulfnoth, a free man, held Creeting TRE with 2 carucates of land as a manor TRE. The Count gave it to Sainte-MARIE of [Grestain]. Then as now 6 villans and 5 bordars and 4 slaves and 1 plough in demesne. Then 3 ploughs belonging to the men, now 1½; 7 acres of meadow. Woodland for 24 pigs. 5 head of cattle and 16 pigs. Then as now worth 60s. 12 free men and a half were added at the time of King William with 58 acres. Then 4 ploughs, now 2½. It is worth 11s. 4d. 1 league in length and half a league broad. 10d. in geld. Others hold [land] there. The king and the earl have the soke. To this manor belongs half a mill which Hardwin, the earl's brother, took away at the time of King William.

In Ringshall the Count holds in demesne 1 manor with 30 acres which Wulfmær, a free man, held. Then 2 bordars. 2 acres of meadow. The twelfth part of a church in Battisford. Then 1 plough and now the same. It is worth 10s. In the same place 1 free man, Boti, with 4 acres. It is worth 10d. The king and the earl have the soke. Hundred of Claydon.

In Helmingham the Count holds in demesne one manor of 30 acres. [held it]. It is worth 12s. In the same place 3 free men with 3 acres. 1 acre belonging to the church. It is in the same valuation. Anund, a free man, held this manor. The king and the earl have the soke.

HALF-HUNDRED OF COSFORD.

The Count holds Brettenham in demesne as one manor and as 4 carucates of land which Wulfnoth held TRE. Then as now 4 villans and 9 bordars. Then 4 slaves, now 2. Then as now 2 ploughs in demesne and 2 ploughs belonging to the men. 5 acres of meadow. Woodland for 4 pigs. A church with 24 acres. Then as now 1 horse, and 3 head of cattle and now 4 pigs. Then it was worth 60s., now 100s. In the same place 5 free men with 32 acres which Brian added. Then as now half a plough. Half an acre of meadow. It is worth 5s. 4d. It is 12 furlongs long and 6 broad. 10d. in geld.

Count Robert

The Count holds Ash [Street] in demesne as one manor and as 1½ carucates of land which 1 free woman held TRE. 5 bordars. Then 2 ploughs. 6 acres of meadow. 1 mill. It is worth 40s. It is half a league long and 3 furlongs broad. 1½d. in geld. In Whatfield 1 free man with 15 acres. It is worth 40d. St Edmund has the soke.

HUNDRED OF COLNEIS.

In Bucklesham 30 free men commended to Harold TRE with 2 carucates of land. Then as now 2 bordars. Then between them 5 ploughs, now 4; 2 acres of meadow. 1 church with 8 acres; 2 bordars. Also 2 free men, Eadric and Wulfric, commended to St Æthelthryth TRE, with 18 acres and half a plough. Then it was worth 60s., now £4. Eudo fitzNigel holds this from the Count. It is 8 furlongs long and 4 broad. 12d. in geld. Others hold [land] there. In Morston 5 free men, Godwine the man of Ælfric the priest, and Wulfhere and Beorhtric, the men of Roger Bigod's predecessor, and Wulfwine, the man of Robert Malet's predecessor, and Godric, the man of Godmann, Roger Bigod's predecessor, with 50 acres. Then 1½ ploughs, now 1. Half an acre of meadow. Then it was worth 10s., now 17s. In Thorpe 1 free man, Brunmær, [of whom] Robert Malet's predecessor had commendation, had 10 acres. Then as now half a plough. Then it was worth 2s. 8d., now 40d. In 'Alteston' [in Trimley] 1 free man commended to Harold TRE. Also 2 free men in the same place, Leofstan and Godwine, commended to Northmann TRE with 48 acres of land. Then 1½ ploughs, now 1. Then it was worth 8s., now 15s. In Grimston 2 free men, Ælfric commended to Harold, and Beorhtnoth, commended to Robert Malet's predecessor, [held] 14 acres of land. Then as now half a plough. Then it was worth 40d., now 5s., less 4d. St Æthelthryth has the soke. The same Eudo holds all this.
    Count Alan.
    Earl Hugh.

III. Lands of Count Alan.

HUNDRED OF RISBRIDGE.

The thegn Manni Swart held Cowlinge TRE as one manor and as 9 carucates of land. Now the count holds it in demesne. Then as now 19 villans and 16 bordars. Then 6 slaves, now 3. Then 2½ ploughs in demesne, now 3. Then 9 ploughs belonging to the men, afterwards and now 6; 60 acres of meadow. Woodland for 60 pigs. A church with 50 acres and half a plough. Then as now 7 head of cattle, 40 pigs, 40 sheep, 40 goats. Then it was worth £9, now £20. It is 1 league long and 8 furlongs broad. 12½d. in geld. In the same place 1 free man under King Edward held 40 acres; 1 bordar and 1 plough; it is worth 10s. All this Earl Ralph held. In this same Hundred 9 acres and 1 villan. It is in the valuation of Weston [Colville] in Cambridgeshire.

HUNDRED OF BRADMERE.

In Stone [Street] 60 acres and 3 bordars. Then 1 plough, now a half. It is in the valuation of Rumburgh. St Edmund has the soke.

HUNDRED OF BLYTHING.

Manni Swart held Bramfield TRE as one manor and as 7 carucates of land. Now the count holds it in demesne. Then 24 villans, afterwards and now 35. Then 5 bordars, afterwards and now 7. Then 4 slaves, afterwards and now none. Then 4 ploughs, afterwards 3, now 4. Then as now 10 ploughs belonging to the men. Woodland for 300 pigs. 7 acres of meadow. Then 1 horse. Then as now 8 head of cattle, 24 pigs and 30 goats. Then it was worth £8. The king and the earl have the soke. Later £16, now £15 13s. 4d. It is 1 league long and another broad. 3¾d. in geld. A church with 28 acres of free land and half a plough, worth 3s.

In Walpole 7 free men TRE by commendation and soke and sake, now 17. They have 4 carucates of land and 90 acres. Then 11 villans, afterwards and now 6. Then 6 bordars, afterwards and now 5. Then 10 ploughs belonging to the men, afterwards and now 6; 6 acres of meadow. Woodland for 30 pigs. 12 furlongs long and 11 broad. 7½d. in geld. Others hold [land] there. This is in the valuation of Bramfield. The king and the earl have the soke. A church with 16 acres and half an acre of meadow. In Thorington and in Wenhaston 6 free men with 2½ carucates of land. Then as now 3 villans and 16 bordars and 5 ploughs. 4 acres of meadow. Woodland for 16 pigs. Then as now 1 mill. A church with 10 acres of free land and half an acre of meadow. In Middleton 1 free man with 12 acres and 2 oxen. In Darsham 1 free man with 8 acres and 2 oxen. [It is] in the same valuation. The king and the earl have the soke.

In Thorpe livery was made of 1 free man for an estate of 69 acres; 3 bordars. 2 acres of meadow. Woodland for 20 pigs. Then it was worth 5s., now 10s. The king and the earl have the soke. In Sibton 1 free man, Alwine, [held] 1 carucate of land and 20 acres as one manor. Then as now 4 villans and 10 bordars and 2 slaves. Then and afterwards 1 plough

Count Alan

in demesne, now 2. Then as now 2 ploughs belonging to the men. 6 acres of meadow. Woodland for 60 pigs. Then as now worth 40s. 1 horse in demesne and 8 head of cattle. Then 1 pig, now 30; 2 sheep, now 30, and 5 beehives. Mainard holds this. The king and the earl have the soke.

Ralph the staller held Wissett TRE as one manor and as 4 carucates of land. Now the count holds it in demesne. Then as now 10 villans and 10 bordars. Then 2 slaves. Then as now 2 ploughs in demesne and 5 ploughs belonging to the men. Woodland for 300 pigs. 4 acres of meadow. 4 horses, 20 head of cattle, 60 pigs, 63 sheep and 51 goats. Then it was worth £8, afterwards £15, now £20. In the same 14 free men by commendation with 4 carucates of land and 15 bordars. Then as now 8 ploughs and 2 acres of meadow. Woodland then for 300 pigs, now for 60. In Halesworth 5 free men with 1 carucate of land and 2 bordars. Then as now 3 ploughs and 1 acre of meadow. Then woodland for 60 pigs, now 20. In [South] Cove 6 free men with half a carucate of land and 4 bordars and 2 ploughs. In Chediston 2 free men TRE, now 3. They have 80 acres and 3 bordars and 2½ ploughs; 2 acres of meadow. Woodland for 60 pigs. The whole is in the valuation of the manor. The count has the soke and sake. 10 furlongs long and 10 broad. 7½d. in geld. In the same Wissett 1 church with 2 carucates of free land. Then as now 12 villans and 16 bordars and 6 ploughs. Woodland for 130 pigs. 3 acres of meadow. 5 villans are attached to this church with 52 acres and 4½ ploughs. 1 acre of meadow. In this church are 12 monks and under it 1 chapel. The whole is in the above assessment of £20. In ''Wrabetuna'' which Ralph the staller held TRE, 1 villan with 15 acres, worth 15d. Then Hamo de Valognes holds. In Covehithe 4 free men with 16 acres. Then as now half a plough. They are in the valuation of Whitfield and in the earl's demesne.

HUNDRED OF CARLFORD.

In Bixley 1 sokeman with 5 acres, worth 12d. In the same place 1 free man commended to Ralph the staller TRE with 20 acres and 1 plough. 1 acre of meadow. Then as now worth [...] 4s. The same free man also holds 20 acres in Rushmere [St Andrew] and they are in the same valuation. In Tuddenham 1 free man of Ralph the staller with 4 acres, worth 8d. In Rushmere [St Andrew] 11 free men commended to Gyrth TRE with 31 acres of land. Then as now 1 plough. It is worth 5s. Also in the same place 6 acres, worth 12d. 1 church with 20 acres, worth 40d. In Burgh 1 villan with 11 acres; it is in the valuation of [Earl] Soham.

HUNDRED OF WILFORD.

In Capel [St Andrew] 6 free men commended to Eadric Grim TRE with 41 acres and 1 bordar. Then as now 1 plough. In Sutton 3 free men under the same commendation with 34 acres. Then as now 2 ploughs. In Bromeswell 1 free man and a half commended to Eadric Grim with 4 acres. In Melton 6 free men

commended to Eadric with 43 acres. Then 2 ploughs, now 1; 2 acres of meadow. In Loudham 1 free man of Eadric [held] 9 acres. In Charsfield 9 acres. Then as now half a plough. 1 acre of meadow. In the same place 1 free man commended to Eadric with 18 acres. Then as now half a plough and half an acre of meadow. In Bredfield 5 free men commended to Eadric, apart from 1 who was commended to St Æthelthryth with 26 acres. Then as now half a plough. In [Little] Charsfield 9 free men commended to Eadric Grim, apart from 1 who was commended to Robert Malet's predecessor, [held] 16 acres. Then half a plough. In Wickham [Market] 1 free man commended to Eadric [held] 12 acres. In Debach 7½ acres. Æthelweald the priest held Bredfield by commendation to St Æthelthryth TRE as one manor with 50 acres. Then 1 plough. Under him 9 free men with 41 acres. Then 1 plough, now a half. All this is in the valuation of Kettleburgh. In Harpole 1 free man commended to Anund with 12 acres. In Boulge 2 free men under commendation of the same man with 29 acres. Then as now half a plough. They are in the valuation of [Earl] Soham.

HUNDRED OF LOOSE.

Eadric Grim held Kettleburgh as one manor and as 4 carucates of land under commendation half to St Æthelthryth TRE and half to Eadric of Laxfield. Now the count holds it in demesne. Then as now 10 villans and 5 bordars. Then 4 slaves, now 2. Then 4 ploughs in demesne, now 3 but it can be restored. Then as now 5 ploughs belonging to the men. Woodland for 8 pigs. 10 acres of meadow. Then and now 2 horses, 6 head of cattle, 30 pigs and 32 sheep. Then the head of the manor was worth 100s. 1 church with 16 acres, worth 3s. It is 1 league long and a half broad. 11d. in geld. In the same place 6 sokemen with 36 acres. Then as now 2 ploughs. In the same vill 2 free men and a half under commendation to St [...] Æthelthryth with 1 carucate of land. Then as now 1 plough. Then 2 villans, now 1. In Martley 12 free men and a half under commendation to Eadric Grim TRE [held] 1 carucate of land and 2 bordars. Then as now 4 ploughs. In Charsfield 16 free men 12 of these were commended to Eadric Grim and 1 to St Æthelthryth and of the three others St Æthelthryth had half the commendation [held] 1 carucate of land. Then 5 ploughs, now 4; 1 acre of meadow. In Hacheston 10 free men and 2 half free men commended to Eadric Grim with 80 acres of land. Then 3 ploughs, now 2; 3 acres of meadow. In Campsey Ash 3 whole and 3 half free men commended to Eadric Grim with 32 acres of land. 1½ acres of meadow. Then as now 1 plough. In Rendlesham 5 whole and 7 half free men commended to Eadric Grim with 50 acres and 1 bordar. Then 2 ploughs, now 1; 2 acres of meadow. In the same vill 1 free man commended half

Count Alan

to Eadric of Laxfield William Malet was seised of him on the day he died and half to Eadric Grim. 34 acres as one manor; 2 bordars. 1 acre of meadow. Then as now 1 plough. In Butley 7 free men and a half commended to Eadric Grim [held] 34 acres. Then 1 plough, now a half. Of these William Malet was seised when he died and Earl Ralph when he forfeited. In "Brodertuna" 7 free men commended half to Eadric Grim and half to Eadric of Laxfield [held] 56 acres. Then 2 ploughs, now 1½; 2 acres of meadow. And Robert Malet was seised of half of this land on the day when Earl Ralph forfeited but Count Alan had it by livery. In Dallinghoo 1 free man commended to Eadric Grim [held] 4½ acres. In Marlesford half a free man with 13 acres and half a plough. In Harpole 8 acres in demesne. Now this whole manor is worth £23 11s. with the whole soke. In Woodbridge 3 free men commended to Eadric [held] 11 acres. They are in the above valuation.

Anund, a free man commended to St Edmund, held [Earl] Soham TRE with 4 carucates of land as one manor. Now the count holds it in demesne. Then as now 15 villans. Then 8 bordars, now 21. Then 2 slaves, now 1. Then as now in demesne 2 ploughs. Then 6 ploughs belonging to the men, now 5. Woodland for 100 pigs. 12 acres of meadow. Then as now 2 horses, 4 head of cattle, 30 pigs, 42 sheep and 60 goats. Then it was worth £10, afterwards £16, now £18 13s. 4d. It is 1 league long and half a league broad. 7½d. in geld. In Cretingham 5 free men commended to Anund held 24 acres. Then as now 1 plough. 2 acres of meadow. In Dallinghoo half a free man under the same commendation with 1 acre. They are all in the valuation of [Earl] Soham. 1 church with 29 acres and 2 acres of meadow. In Gedgrave 2 villans and 8 bordars with 50 acres and 1½ ploughs. They are in the valuation of Carlton. In Butley 2 free men commended to Eadric Grim with 8 acres. They are in the same valuation. In Gedgrave 3 free men commended to Eadric Grim with 15 acres and half a plough. In Martley 1 church with 12 acres, worth 2s. In the same place 2 free men commended to Eadric Grim with 2 acres. Also 5 free men under the same commendation with 45 acres. Then as now 1 plough. All this is in the valuation of Kettleburgh.

In Bromeswell 1 free man commended to Wulfric with 2 acres in the same valuation. Half-Hundred of Lothingland.

In Blundeston 1 free man, Thorth, with 15 acres, worth 30d.

HALF-HUNDRED OF IPSWICH.

In the town of Ipswich Earl Gyrth held TRE one grange to which belong 2 carucates of land. Then as now 7 bordars. Then and afterwards 1 plough, now none.

[Folio 294v: SUFFOLK]

Then as now 3 ploughs belonging to the men. 4 acres of meadow. The third part of a mill. This land is 4 furlongs long and 4 broad. Then it was worth 100s., with the third penny from the borough; it was delivered as worth £20 with the third penny from the borough and with the third penny from the two Hundreds. Now however it renders only £15.

HUNDRED OF BOSMERE.

Goti, a free man, held Nettlestead TRE with 5 carucates of land as one manor. Now Erland holds it from the count. Then as now 7 villans and 6 bordars and 4 slaves. Then 5 ploughs in demesne, afterwards a half, now 1. Then as now 2 ploughs

belonging to the men. 8 acres of meadow and 1 mill. Now 1 horse, 27 pigs and 36 sheep. A church with 8 acres. And Earl Ralph added 34 free men over 26 only did his predecessor have commendation only TRE. They have 2½ carucates of land. Then 8 ploughs, now 6; 3 acres of meadow. A church with 70½ acres. The manor was worth, then as now, £7 10s., and the free men 50s. It is 1 league long and a half broad. 5d. in geld. In the same place 1 free man with 60 acres as a manor which Humphrey holds from the count. Then as now 1 bordar and 1 plough. 5 acres of meadow. Then it was worth 10s., now 20s. In Darmsden Cyneric, a free man, held 30 acres as a manor. Now Nardred holds it from the count. Then 1 bordar, now 3. Then as now 1 plough. 3 acres of meadow. It is worth 10s. The Abbot of Ely has the soke. From this land Roger Bigod took 5 acres from the demesne which William holds from him; but he was seised thereof when Ralph forfeited.

In Hemingstone the count has in demesne 1 sokeman with 15 acres. Then as now 1 plough. It is worth 2s. 6d. In [Earl and Little] Stonham Wulfmær holds from the count 5 free men with 48 acres and they hold 12 acres from the demesne of the count. Then as now 2 ploughs. Woodland for 6 pigs. 1 acre of meadow. It is worth 12s. To the above land which Humphrey holds belonged in demesne 28 acres, in woodland and in open land which Godmær held; now Roger Bigod holds it and Warenger from him. And he held it likewise when Ralph forfeited. In the same place 2 acres of land, 1 free man and 1½ acres of woodland, worth 7d. In Coddenham 3 free men with 4 acres, worth 8d. The king and the earl have the soke.

HUNDRED OF CLAYDON.

Beorn, a free man commended to Ralph the staller, held Westerfield with 1 carucate of land as one manor; now Norman holds it from the count. Then as now 2 villans; now 2 bordars. Then in demesne 1 plough, now 2. Then as now 1 plough belonging to the men. 2 acres of meadow. Now 1 horse, 4 head of cattle, 20 pigs and 100 sheep. Then it was worth 10s., now 20s. The earl has the soke.

Count Alan

[Folio 295: SUFFOLK]

In the same place the same man holds 6 free men commended to Ralph the staller TRE, with 24 acres. Then as now 1 plough. It is worth 4s. The soke is the earl's. In the same place Stanwine, a free man, held 14 acres, now Osbern holds them. It is worth 2s. 4d. It is 8 furlongs long and 4 broad. 20d. in geld. The soke is the earl's. In 'Sharpstone' [in Barham] 3 free men commended to the Abbot of Ely with 12 acres. Then as now 2 oxen. Erland holds two of these men and it is in the valuation of Nettlestead; the third is in the demesne of the count and it is in the valuation of Hemingstone. The soke is the abbot's. In Westerfield 6 free men TRE [held] 20 acres. Then as now 1 plough. They are in the valuation of Ipswich. The count holds it in demesne. The king and the earl have the soke. In Thurlston 1 free man with 2 acres and in Westerfield 2 free men with 3 acres, worth 10d. Ælfric the priest holds it from the count. In the same place Wulfric, a free man, held 6 acres, worth 12d. The king and the earl have the soke. In

Ashfield 4 free men with 27 acres. Then 1 plough, now a half. It is worth 3s. In the same place Beorhtmær, a free man, [held] 24 acres as a manor TRE. Then 1 plough. It is worth 5s. In Thurlston Ælfric, a free man, held 16 acres of land TRE, worth 32d. In the same place a free man with 7 acres, worth 14d. In the same place a free man with 12 acres, worth 2s. The king and the earl have the soke.

HUNDRED OF SAMFORD.

Asgot commended to Eadgifu the Fair held [Great and Little] Welnetham with 1 carucate of land as one manor. Now Ermengot holds it from the count. Then as now 3 villans and 3 bordars and 2 slaves. 2 ploughs in demesne and 2 ploughs belonging to the men. 4 acres of meadow. Part of a church. 8 head of cattle, 35 pigs and 71 sheep. Then it was worth 60s., now 40s. Eadgifu had the soke. It is 6 furlongs long and 3 broad. 4d. in geld. Godmann, commended to Eadgifu, held Holbrook with 1 carucate of land as one manor. Now Odo holds it from the count. Then as now 2 villans and 2 bordars. Then 1 plough in demesne, afterwards none, now 1. Then as now 1 plough belonging to the men. Then it was worth 20s., now 15s. The soke is in [East] Bergholt.

Eadgifu held "Beria" TRE with 2 carucates of land as one manor. Now Humphrey holds it from the count. 1 bordar. Then 2 ploughs in demesne, now 1; 1 acre of meadow. Then 1 mill. Then 2 horses, now 1. Then 4 head of cattle, now 1. Then 20 pigs, now 40. Then as now 100 sheep and 12 goats. It is worth 40s. It is 8 furlongs long and 6 broad. 5d. in geld. Others hold [land] there. Eadgifu had the soke.

[Folio 295v: SUFFOLK]

Edmund, a free man of Robert fitzWymarc, held Wherstead TRE as one manor with 1 carucate of land. Now Fulcric holds it from the count. Then as now 2 villans and 2 bordars. Then 1 plough in demesne, afterwards none, now a half. Then as now 1 plough belonging to the men. 3 acres of meadow. It is worth 20s. The soke is in [East] Bergholt. In Bentley the same Edmund held 40 acres as one manor TRE, worth 10s. Eadgifu had the soke. The same Fulcric holds of the count. Edwin held Dodnash by commendation to Eadgifu and in her soke with 1 carucate of land as one manor TRE. Then as now 1 villan and 6 bordars. Then 3 slaves. Then as now 1½ ploughs in demesne and 1 plough belonging to the men. 4 acres of meadow. Woodland for 30 pigs. 1 mill. A church with 30 acres of free land. Then it was worth 15s., now 20s. It is 8 furlongs long and 6 broad. 10d. in geld. Others hold [land] there. The same Edwin holds Brantham in Eadgifu's soke with 1 carucate of land as one manor TRE. Then as now 4 villans and 5 bordars. 1 plough in demesne and 2 belonging to the men. 1 acre of meadow. Then it was worth 13s., now 16s. Goding holds these two from the count. Thorsten held Woolverstone in Eadgifu's soke and commendation with 1 carucate of land as one manor. Then as now 5 villans and 2 bordars. Then 1½ ploughs in demesne, now 2, and half a plough belonging to the men. 2 acres of meadow. Woodland for 15 pigs. A church with 10 acres. Then 5 horses, now 7. Then 8 head of cattle, now 12. Then 20 pigs, now 30. Then 60 sheep, now 100; 36 goats. Then it was worth 20s., now 30s. It

is 8 furlongs long and three broad. 2½d. in geld. [...] Ælfric the priest [holds it] from the count. In Bentley the same Thorsten held 40 acres as one manor TRE in the same way. Then 1 bordar, now 2. Then half a plough, now 1. Then it was worth 5s. 4d., now 6s. The same Ælfric holds this from the same count. The same Thorsten [...] held Pannington TRE with 60 acres as one manor. Then as now 2 villans and 1 plough. Two acres of meadow. It is worth 8s. Eadgifu had the soke. The same Ælfric [holds this]. In Wherstead the same person held TRE as one manor 40 acres. Then 1 plough, now a half. 1 salt-pan. It is worth 5s. Eadgifu had the soke. The same Ælfric [holds this]. The same person held Kaleweton TRE as a manor with 40 acres. Then as now 1 bordar and half a plough. It is worth 5s. 4d. The soke [is held] in the same way. Ælfric [holds it] from the count.

Siward, a sokeman of

Count Alan

[Folio 296: SUFFOLK]

Stigand, held Hintlesham with 1 carucate of land as one manor TRE. Now Ralph holds it from the count. Then as now 3 villans and 3 bordars. 2 ploughs in demesne and 1 plough belonging to the men. 4 acres of meadow. It is worth 40s. Stigand had the soke.

In "Canapetuna" the same Siward, a free man, held 30 acres as one manor TRE. It is in the soke of [East] Bergholt. This is in the above valuation.

Wulfstan, a free man of Eadgifu, held Boynton with 50 acres as a manor TRE. The soke is in [East] Bergholt. Now Wulfstan holds it from the count. Then as now 2 bordars. Then half a plough, now 1; 2 acres of meadow. It is worth 8s.

In Brantham Godwine, a free man, [held] 35 acres as one manor TRE. Godwine holds it from the count. Then as now 2 bordars and half a plough. 1 acre of meadow. It is worth 4s. In the same place 8 free men [held] 1 carucate of land and 11 acres. Then as now 2 ploughs. 4 acres of meadow. 1 salt-pan. It is worth 22s. 8d. Now the count holds it in demesne. The soke is in [East] Bergholt.

Edwin, a free man, held Stutton with 60 acres as one manor. Then as now half a plough and 3 bordars. 1 acre of meadow. It is in the same valuation.

In [Great and Little] Welnetham Asgot held 15 acres and 1 acre of meadow, worth 2s. 6d. Eadgifu had the soke. The whole of Brantham is 1 league long and half a league broad. 18d. in geld.

HALF-HUNDRED OF PARHAM.

In the soke of the Abbot of Ely. In Wantisden 16 free men, half by commendation to Malet's predecessor, half by commendation to the Abbot of Ely they are all in his soke [held] 60 acres. Then as now 2 ploughs. It is worth 10s. Now the count [holds this] in demesne. In the same place Edwin, a free man, held 14 acres. Then as now half a plough. It is worth 2s. 8d. The count [holds it] in demesne.

In Blaxhall 1 free man with 2 acres, worth 4d. Hamo de Valognes [holds it]. Ælfric, a thegn of the king, held Parham

TRE with 1 carucate of land as one manor. Now Hamo holds it from the count.

[Folio 296v: SUFFOLK]

Then as now 8 bordars and 1 slave. 2 ploughs in demesne. Then half a plough and 4 acres of meadow. Now 8 pigs and 20 sheep. Then it was worth 20s., now 40s.

In Blaxhall Brothir, a free man, held 12 acres, worth 2s. The count holds this in demesne. The soke is the abbot's. In the same place Eadric Grim, a free man, half by commendation to Malet's predecessor and half to the Abbot of Ely, [held] 20 acres. It is worth 40d. Hamo holds it from the count. In Parham 3 free men with 16 acres, worth 32d. In Wantisden Aslak, a free man, [held] 3 acres, worth 6d. In the same place Eadhild, a free [wo]man, held 8 acres, worth 16d. Now the count [holds it] in demesne.

In Blaxhall Wulfric, a free man, [held] 4 acres, worth 8d. [Now the count holds it] in demesne. The soke is the abbot's.

HUNDRED OF PLUMESGATE.

The count holds Chillesford in demesne. Ulf, a free man in the soke and commendation of the Abbot of Ely, held TRE 80 acres as one manor. Then as now 1 villan and 4 bordars. Then and afterwards 1½ ploughs in demesne, now 1. Then and afterwards 1½ ploughs belonging to the men, now 1. A church with 5 acres of free land. It is worth 13s. 4d. And 3 free men with 20 acres. Then as now 1 plough. It is worth 40d.

Hamo holds Carlton from the count with 1 carucate of land as one manor. Eadric Grim, by commendation half to the Abbot of Ely and half to Robert Malet's predecessor, [held it] and William Malet was seised thereof. Then as now 1 villan and 3 bordars and 1 slave. 2 ploughs in demesne and half a plough belonging to the men. Half a fishery. 2 acres of meadow. It is worth 40 60s. In demesne then as now 1 horse. Then 100 sheep, now 170 180. 1 free man by commendation with 2 acres. It is in the same valuation. It is 9 furlongs long and 4 broad. [...] 20d. in geld. And in demesne 8 in demesne free men with 60 acres. Sten and Ælfric were commended to Malet's predecessor and William Malet was seised thereof. The others were commended to the Abbot. Then as now 2 ploughs.

Count Alan

[Folio 297: SUFFOLK]

It is worth 12s. 4d. The soke over the whole belongs to the Abbot of Ely.

The aforesaid Eadric held [Great] Glemham in demesne with 20 acres. It belongs in Kettleburgh. It is worth 40d. The soke is the abbot's.

In the same place Spearhavoc, a free man, held 60 acres as one manor, by commendation to Eadric, Robert Malet's predecessor and William Malet was seised thereof. Then as now 1 bordar and 1 plough. Half a church with 10 acres and half a plough, worth 10s. In the same place 8 free men with 60 acres: Leofric, Eadric, Wulfmær, Hunepot, half a [free man], Godric, Almær, Leofric, Wulfmær. All these were commended to

Malet's predecessor. Then 4 ploughs, afterwards and now 3. It is worth 10s.

In the same place a free man [held] 10 acres, worth 8d. It is 1 league long and half a league broad. It renders 20d. in geld.

In Little Glemham Uhtred a free man commended to Bishop Æthelmær TRE [held] 20 acres. Then half a plough, now 1; 1½ acres of meadow. 2 free men by commendation with 5 acres. Then it was worth 6s., now 5s.

In Sternfield Osbern, a free man, [held] 24 acres TRE. Then as now half a plough. It is worth 4s. Now the count [holds it] in demesne. In the same place 2 free men have been added with 8½ acres, worth 18d. The soke is the abbot's.

In Bruisyard Ulf held 85 acres [...] as one manor. Then as now 3 villans and 7 bordars. Then 2 ploughs in demesne, afterwards and now 1. Then as now 2 ploughs belonging to the men. [...] 2 acres of meadow. Woodland for 10 pigs; 2 horses and 17 head of cattle. Then 9 pigs, now 15. Then 40 sheep, now 6 and 15 goats. In the same place Eadric, a free man, [held] 91 acres [...] as one manor. Then and afterwards 2 ploughs, now 1 and 1 bordar. 2 acres of meadow. Woodland for 10 pigs. Then and afterwards it was worth 60s. and now 60s. Hamo holds it from the count. Ralph the staller had the soke TRE. In the same place Stærling, a free man by commendation half to Malet's predecessor his father was seised thereof and half by commendation to the abbot, [held] 60 acres

[Folio 297v: SUFFOLK]

as one manor. Then as now 7 bordars. Then and afterwards 1 plough in demesne, now a half. Then as now 1 plough belonging to the men. 3 acres of meadow. It is worth 10s. Hamo holds it. It is 8 furlongs long and 6 broad. 10d. in geld. The soke is the abbot's.

In Rendham Ostula, a free man commended to Malet's predecessor, [held] 40 acres as one manor. William his father was seised of it. Then as now 1 villan, 2 bordars and 1 plough in demesne. Half a plough belonging to the men. It is worth 7s. The soke is the abbot's.

In the same place Hune, a free man, by commendation to Ralph the staller, [held] 30 acres as one manor. Then as now half a plough and 1 acre of meadow. It is worth 5s. In the same place 9 free men [held] 91 acres as one manor. Then as now 2 bordars and 4½ ploughs. 4 acres of meadow. Then it was worth 20s., now 27s. These men were commended to Malet's predecessor. William his father was seised thereof. The soke is the abbot's.

In Swefling Osmund, a free man commended to Malet's predecessor, [held] 30 acres as a manor in the soke of the abbot. Then as now 3 bordars. And 1 plough and 2 acres of meadow. It is worth 5s. William Malet was seised thereof. The soke is the abbot's. In the same place 5 free men with 54 acres. Two of these, Ælfric and Dot, were commended to Malet's predecessor with 10 acres and one, Burgric by name, was in the commendation and in the soke of Ralph the staller, with 24 acres. Then as now 2 ploughs and 4 acres of meadow. It is worth 10s. The soke is the abbot's.

In the same place 14 free men with 94 acres and 3 bordars. 3½ Malet's predecessor had commendation and over a half the sub-commendation. William Malet was seised thereof. Then as now 4 ploughs and 6 acres of meadow. Then it was worth 30s., now 25s. 4d. The soke is the abbot's. It is 1 league long and 6½ furlongs broad. 20d. in geld. Others hold [land] there. In Benhall 7 free men with 44 acres. 4 of these were commended . His father was seised thereof. [...] Eadric,

Count Alan

[Folio 298: SUFFOLK]

Beorhtmær, Tutflæd, Magni. Then 1½ ploughs, now 1. Then it was worth 8s., now 6s. 8d. The soke is the abbot's.

In [Great] Glemham 2 free men. Wacra, commended to Malet's predecessor, and Wulfgifu, commended to Malet's predecessor, [held] 20 acres. Then as now 1 plough. It is worth 7s. All this Hamo holds from the count. The soke is the abbot's.

In Cransford Ulf, a free man, held 30 acres as one manor. Now the count holds it in demesne. Then as now 1 plough. It is worth 5s. The soke is the abbot's.

In the same place 2 free men with 4 acres, worth 8d. In Swefling 3 free men with 41 acres and 1 bordar and 1 plough and 1 acre of meadow. Then it was worth 6s. 8d., now 5s. 10d.

HUNDRED OF WANGFORD.

In [South] Elmham 40 acres. They belong to the church of Rumburgh. 6 bordars and 1 plough. Woodland for 6 pigs. It is in the valuation of the same.

[Folio 298v: SUFFOLK]

IIII. Land of Earl Hugh.

HUNDRED OF CLAYDON.

Æthelstan, a thegn, held Framsden TRE with 6 carucates of land and 40 acres as a manor. Then 25 villans, now 29. Then as now 23 bordars. Then 4 ploughs in demesne, now 3. Then 20 ploughs belonging to the men, now 16; 16 acres of meadow. Then woodland for 80 pigs, now for 40. Then as now 1 mill. Then 2 horses, now 3. Then 6 head of cattle, now 13. Then 20 pigs, now 31. Then 50 sheep, now 100. Then 7 goats, now 31. A church with 30 acres of free land TRE with 1 plough. Then it was worth £16, now £20, and it was at farm for £25. It is 1 league long and 8 furlongs broad. It renders 10d. in geld.

In "Manuuic" Godric, a free man commended to the predecessor of the earl held 42 acres as a manor. Then as now 1 bordar. Then 1 plough, afterwards a half, now none. 1 acre of meadow. Then it was worth 20s., now 13s. 4d.

In the same place 1 free man likewise commended held 27 acres with 7 bordars, 1 plough and 1 acre of meadow, worth 10s.

In "Manuuic" Wailolf, a free man commended to the Abbot of Ely, [held] 60 acres and 2 bordars. Then 1½ ploughs, now 2; 1 free man with 1 acre and 2 acres of meadow. Woodland for 6 pigs. It is worth 20s. Half the soke is the abbot's and half the earl's.

In the same place a free man by commendation [held] 13½ acres. Then 2 oxen. It is worth 4s. 8d. The soke [belongs] in the same way.

In Winston 1 free man, Erik, by commendation [held] 30 acres. 4 bordars. Then 2 ploughs, now 1; 3 acres of meadow. Then it was worth 20s., now 15s. Over two of these the abbot has half the soke and over the third, the whole. The earl has the rest of the soke.

In Winston half a free man by commendation [held] 7½ acres. It is worth 18d. In Thorpe and in Ashfield 21 free men with 1 carucate of land and 14 acres, commended to his predecessor TRE. A church with 12 acres. Then 3 ploughs, now 2, and 3 acres of meadow. Woodland for 12 pigs. Then it was worth 40s., now 30s.

Earl Hugh

[Folio 299: SUFFOLK]

Half the soke is the abbot's and half the earl's. Ashfield is 1 league long and 7 furlongs broad. 20d. in geld. Others hold [land] there. Hugh fitzNorman holds all this from the earl. In Thorpe Aslak, a free man by commendation, held 10 acres, worth 2s.

In Helmingham a free man with 8 acres, worth 16d. The soke belongs in the aforesaid way.

HALF-HUNDRED OF PARHAM.

In Parham 4 free men commended to his predecessor with 20 acres, worth 4s. Roger Bigod [holds this] from the earl.

HUNDRED OF BRADMERE.

Skuli, a thegn of King Edward, held Barnham as a manor with 2 carucates of land. Then as now 1 bordar and 2 slaves. And 2 ploughs in demesne. 1 acre of meadow and 1 mill. Now 3 head of cattle. Then 25 pigs, now 14. Then 10 sheep, now 120. Then as now worth 30s. St Edmund has the soke.

Ælfric the thegn held Wattisfield TRE as one manor with a carucate of land. Then as now 1 villan. Then 2 ploughs. Then it was worth 25s., now 17s.

HUNDRED OF BISHOP.

Burgheard held Saxtead TRE as a berewick in Framlingham with 60 acres. Then as now 11 villans and 5 bordars. Then as now 9 ploughs and 4 acres of meadow. Woodland for 200 pigs. This is in the valuation of Framlingham.

HUNDRED OF BLYTHING.

Ælfric held Halesworth TRE as a manor with 2 carucates of land. Then 4 villans, now 5. Then 7 bordars, now 10. Then as now 2 slaves. Then as now 2 ploughs in demesne. Then 3 ploughs belonging to the men, now 2. Then woodland for 300 pigs, now for 100. Then as now 4 acres of meadow. 1 mill. 1 horse. Then as now 6 head of cattle. Now 10 pigs. 18 sheep. Then it was worth 30[s.], now 40[s.] In the same vill Ulf the priest held 40 acres of land as one manor. 2 bordars. 1 plough in demesne. Woodland for 6 pigs. 4 acres of meadow. 14 sheep and 2 goats. It is worth 5s. To this manor have been joined 4 free men with 60 acres of land. 2 bordars. 2 ploughs in demesne. It is worth 10s. And Bigod de Loges holds these 3 estates from Earl Hugh.

[Folio 299v: SUFFOLK]

It is 1 league long and another broad. It renders 7½d. in geld. Count Alan claims the land of the aforesaid priest and those 4 men through his predecessor and his own seisin, and the Hundred testifies [for him].

Eskil, a free man, held Uggeshall TRE as a manor with 2 carucates of land. Then as now 5 bordars; 1 slave. Then 3 ploughs, now 2. Then as now 1 plough belonging to the men. 2½ acres of meadow. Then 1 mill, now none. 1 salt-pan. 24 pigs. 1 church. Then it was worth 40s., now 30s. Robert de Courson holds this from Earl Hugh. To this manor is attached 1 man in the same land and in the same valuation. It is 1½ leagues long and 1 broad. It renders 6d. in geld. Over this land and over all other lands which Eskil the priest had, Ralph the staller had soke and sake.

Munulf held Middelton TRE, now R[oger] Bigod holds it from Earl Hugh. Over this the predecessor of Earl Hugh had half the commendation TRE and Robert Malet's predecessor [had] the other half of the commendation. And he had 80 acres as one manor. Then as now 2 villans and 2 bordars. 1 plough in demesne and 1 plough belonging to the men. 2 acres of meadow. Then it was worth 10s., now 20s.

In the same place 6 free men. Brunwine was wholly Munulf's man TRE; Ælfheah was half [Munulf's man] and Leofric half. Asmoth was wholly the woman of Toli the sheriff and Beorhtmær her son was the man of Beorhtmær the reeve of Robert Malet, with a sixth part of the land. Cyneric was the man of Eadric, son of Ingeld and Grim was his man also. They have 50 acres of land and 1½ ploughs. 1 acre of meadow. It is worth 8s. The king and the earl have the soke. Grim and Cyneric were commended to Eadric, Robert Malet's predecessor. And he himself commended them to Walter de Caen after Walter de Dol forfeited. Now Roger Bigod holds this from Earl Hugh's fief.

Earl Hugh

[Folio 300: SUFFOLK]

HUNDRED OF CARLFORD.

In Grundisburgh 1 free man, commended to Harold, TRE and his wife, commended to Halfdan, [held] 60 acres of land as one manor. Now 4 free men hold it. Then as now 1 villan and 2 bordars and 1 plough. 2 acres of meadow. Then it was worth 10s., now the same.

In Burgh 1 free man commended to Countess Eadgifu with 5 acres. Half an acre of meadow. It is worth 12d.

HUNDRED OF LOOSE.

In Cretingham Eadric, a free man by commendation [half] to Eadric and half to Æthelstan, held 1 carucate of land. Then as now 7 bordars and 1 slave. Then as now 1½ ploughs belonging to the men and in demesne the same. Woodland for 12 pigs. 8 acres of meadow. 1 horse, 4 head of cattle, 16 pigs, 24 sheep and 7 goats. 1 church with 18 acres, worth 3s. Then it was worth 40s., now the same. In the same place 3 free men under the same commendation with 6½ acres and half a plough. It is in the same valuation. Also in the same place 4 free men

commended to Æthelstan TRE with 58 acres of land and 4 bordars. Then 1 plough, now 2; 4 acres of meadow. Then it was worth 15s., now 20s. And 8 acres of land laid waste. It is worth 16d.

HUNDRED OF WANGFORD.

Ælfric, a free man, held Bungay TRE with 5 carucates of land as one manor TRE. Now William holds it from the earl. Then as now 22 villans and 12 bordars and 3 slaves. 2 ploughs in demesne. Then 6 ploughs belonging to the men, afterwards 2, now 3 and the others could be restored. 1 church with 20 acres and 2 acres of meadow, worth 40d. Woodland for 30 pigs. 14 acres of meadow. Then as now 1 mill and three parts of another. Then as now 3 head of cattle. [...] Then 22 pigs, now 12; then 32 sheep, now 100.

[Folio 300v: SUFFOLK]

Then it was worth 60s., now 100s.

In the same place a free man, Ulfkil, [held] 40 acres as one manor [...] TRE; now the said William [holds it]. Now 4 bordars. Then as now 1 plough in demesne and 1 plough belonging to the men. 1 acre of meadow. 1 mill. Then as now 2 horses and 2 head of cattle. Now 5 pigs. Then 20 sheep, now 80. It is worth 13s. 4d.

In the same place Sumarlithr, a free man, held 40 acres TRE; now the said William [holds them] as a manor. Then as now 1 villan and 3 bordars and 1 slave. Then as now in demesne 1 plough and 1 plough belonging to the men. Woodland for 6 pigs. 2½ acres of meadow. The fourth part of a mill. Then Then and now worth 13s. 4d.

In the same place 27 free men commended to Ælfric TRE [held] 1 carucate of land and 10 acres and 1 bordar. Then 3 ploughs, now 2; 4 acres of meadow. Woodland for 3 pigs. Then as now worth 40s.

In Ilketshall Warin . A free man, Wufsige, commended to Gyrth, [held] 2 carucates of land as a manor. Then as now 5 villans and 13 bordars. Then 6 slaves. Then in demesne 3 ploughs, now 1. Then 2 ploughs belonging to the men, now 1½; 4 acres of meadow. Woodland for 10 pigs. Half a mill. Now 5 pigs. Then 30 sheep, now 40. Now 16 goats. Then as now worth 40s. Warin fitzBurnin holds this from him.

In Mettingham 1 free man, Ælfric, commended to Wulsige, [held] 60 acres as a manor. Then as now 3 bordars. Then as now in demesne 1 plough. Then 1 plough belonging to the men, now a half. Woodland for 2 pigs. 3 acres of meadow. Then it was worth 8s., now 10s. Under him 8 free men under the same commendation [held] 20 acres. Then 1 plough, now a half. It is worth 5s. 1 church with 20 acres, worth 3s. The said Warin [holds this].

In Ilketshall 1 free man Alwine commended to Wulfsige [held] 60 acres as one manor.

Earl Hugh

[Folio 301: SUFFOLK]

Then as now 10 bordars and 1 slave. In demesne 1 plough and 1 plough belonging to the men. 2 acres of meadow. Woodland for 10 pigs. Then it was worth 10s., now the same.

Also in Ilketshall and in Mettingham and in Shipmeadow dwell 7 free men under the same commendation with 80 acres and 1 bordar. Then 3 ploughs, now 2; 2 acres of meadow. Then as now worth 10s.

In Ilketshall 1 free man, Burgheard, held 2 carucates of land as a manor. Then as now villans and 7 bordars. Then 5 slaves. Then in demesne 3 ploughs, now 1, but there could be [more]. Then 3 ploughs belonging to the men, now 2 but they could be restored. Woodland for 30 pigs. 4 acres of meadow. Then 2 horses, now 1; now 2 head of cattle and 60 sheep. Then it was worth 30s., now 40s.

In Bungay 60 acres and they belong to the one manor which the king holds. It is worth 10s. To this land belongs 1 free man and a half with $5\frac{1}{2}$ acres, worth 2s.

In Ilketshall 1 free woman commended to Burgheard [held] 20 acres. Then as now 5 bordars. In demesne 1 plough and 1 plough belonging to the men. Woodland for 10 pigs. $1\frac{1}{2}$ acres of meadow. Then as now worth 5s. 1 church with 20 acres, worth 2s.

In Shipmeadow 3 free men with 15 acres. Then 1 now a half. It is worth 3s. In Ilketshall 3 free men commended to Burgheard with 30 acres. Then as now 1 plough. It is worth 5s.

In Ringsfield 2 free men commended to Burgheard with 12 acres and 1 bordar. Half a plough. Woodland for 2 pigs. It is worth 3s. 6d. All this Warin fitzBurnin holds from him.

Mundred Sotterley which Burgheard held TRE with $1\frac{1}{2}$ carucates of land as one manor. Then 4 villans, now 3; 1 church with 7 acres. Then 3 bordars,

now 16, and 2 slaves. Then 2 ploughs in demesne, now 3, and 3 belonging to the men. Woodland for 100 pigs. 4 acres of meadow. Then as now 1 horse, 14 head of cattle, 31 pigs, 120 sheep and 30 goats. Then as now worth 53s. 4d.

In "Croscroft" 1 free man, Burgheard, held $1\frac{1}{2}$ carucates of land. Then as now 3 villans and 5 bordars. Then 2 ploughs, now one but 2 could be made. 2 ploughs belonging to the men. Then 1 horse and 5 head of cattle, now none. 3 acres of meadow. Woodland for 10 pigs. It is worth 26s. 5d. Sotterley is 1 league long and 9 furlongs broad. 3d. in geld. Mundred holds this from Earl Hugh. In Ilketshall 1 free man with 12 acres whom Ralph, a man of W. the constable, appropriated. And Earl Ralph was seised of him on the day when he forfeited. Also in the same place 1 free man with 10 acres which Roger Bigod held but Burnin appropriated this against his right.

In "Hetheburgafella" 3 free men commended to Burgheard with 22 acres and 1 plough, worth 4s.

In Worlingham 1 free man commended to Gyrth [held] 6 acres, worth 12d.

HUNDRED OF LOTHING.

Burgheard held Kessingland TRE with 2 carucates of land as one manor. Now fitzNorman, holds it. Then as now 2 villans and 6 bordars and 2 slaves. Then as now in demesne 2 ploughs and 1 plough belonging to the men. 1 acre of meadow. 1 mill. Then as now 1 ox, 23 pigs and 40 sheep. Then it was worth 30s., now 40s. It is 1 league long and 1 broad. 32d. in

geld. In the same place 40 free men. 11 of them were commended to Gyrth and the others were commended to Burgheard. Between them [were]

Earl Hugh

3 carucates of land. Then 8 ploughs, now 5; 1 acre of meadow. Then it was worth £4, now 100s.

In "Rodenhala" 1 free man commended to Thorth the predecessor of R[alph] Baynard [held] 30 acres as one manor. 5 bordars. Then as now 1 plough and half a plough belonging to the men. Woodland for 4 pigs. $1\frac{1}{2}$ acres of meadow. Then it was worth 8s., now it renders 12s.

In Gisleham 1 free man commended to Gyrth [held] 15 acres. Then 1 plough, now a half. 2 villans and half an acre of meadow. Then it was worth 8s., now the same.

Burgheard held Carlton [Colville] TRE with 2 carucates of land as a manor. Then 8 villans, now 4. Then 6 bordars, now 4. Then as now 4 slaves and in demesne 2 ploughs. Then 2 ploughs belonging to the men, now 1. Woodland for 30 pigs. 4 acres of meadow. Then as now 1 horse, 8 head of cattle, 23 pigs and 100 sheep. Then it was worth 30s., now 40s. It is 1 league and 8 furlongs long and 10 furlongs broad. 4s. in geld. In the same place 30 free men commended to Burgheard with 2 carucates of land. Then 8 ploughs, now 4; 6 acres of meadow. Then it was worth £4, now 60s.

In Barnby 5 free men commended to Burgheard with 44 acres. Then as now 1 plough; half an acre of meadow. Then and now worth 6s. The king and the earl have the soke over the free men. A church with 80 acres, worth 2s. Hugh fitzNorman holds all this from [Earl] Hugh.

Ælfric, a free man of Gyrth, held Rushmere TRE with 1 carucate of land as one manor. Then as now 3 bordars. In demesne 1 plough and half a plough belonging to the men. Woodland for 10 pigs. Then it was worth 5s., now 10s.

In Pakefield 1 free man under the same commendation with 15 acres. Half a plough. Half a church with $16\frac{1}{2}$ acres. It is worth 5s.

HUNDRED OF LOOSE.

Æthelmær, a thegn, held Framlingham; now Roger Bigod holds it with 9 carucates of land as a manor. Then 24 villans, now 32. Then 16 bordars, now 28. Then 5 ploughs in demesne, now 3. Then 20 ploughs belonging to the men, now 16. Woodland for 100 pigs. 16 acres of meadow. Then 2 horses, now 3. Then 4 head of cattle, now 7. Then 40 pigs, now 10. Then 20 sheep, now 40. Then as now 60 goats. Now 3 beehives. Then it was worth £16, now £36.

In the same place Munulf, half commended to Æthelmær and [...] half to Malet's predecessor, held 1 carucate of land and 40 acres as a manor. Then as now 4 villans and 12 bordars and 2 ploughs in demesne and $2\frac{1}{2}$ ploughs belonging to the men. Woodland for 100 pigs. 6 acres of meadow. 8 head of cattle and 20 pigs and 60 sheep and 40 goats and 4 beehives. Then as now worth 40s. William Malet was seised. Under him 6 whole free men and 4 half free men with 30 acres of land. Then as now 1 plough and 1 acre of meadow. They are in the valuation of 40s.

In the same place 1 free man by commendation [held] 40 acres. 1 villan dwelling in "Ethereg". 3 bordars. 1 acre of meadow and 1 plough. Woodland for 4 pigs. It is worth 8s. In the same place 3 free men by commendation [held] 56 acres. Then as now 3 ploughs and 2 acres of meadow. Woodland for 4 pigs. It is worth 17s. 1 church with 60 acres. 1 villan and 4 bordars and 2 ploughs. It is worth 15s. It is 14 furlongs long and 12 broad. 20d. in geld. St Æthelthryth had the soke but [Earl] Hugh's predecessor had it from her.

V. Lands of Count Eustace.

HUNDRED OF RISBRIDGE.

Leofric, a thegn, held Ousden with 6 carucates as one manor TRE. Then 22 villans, afterwards and now 15. Then and afterwards 2 bordars, now 9. Then 8 slaves, now 2. Then and afterwards 4 ploughs in demesne, now 2. Then 10 ploughs belonging to the men, afterwards 8, now 6; 6½ acres of meadow. Woodland for 20 pigs. Then 4 horses. Then 15 head of cattle, now 5. Then 22 pigs, 30. Then 164 sheep, now 88. A church with 30 acres of free land and half a plough. Then it was worth £6, now £7 but it was given at farm for £14. It is 8 furlongs long and 5 broad. 3½d. in geld. Others hold [land] there. HUNDRED OF THEDWESTRY.

In Rattlesden 1 free man in the commendation and soke of St Æthelthryth held TRE 60 acres of land which he could not sell. Now Ealdræd holds it under Count Eustace, who appropriated 7 acres from the demesne of St Æthelthryth in the same vill to the fief of Count Eustace. Then as now 1 plough and 4 acres of meadow. It is worth 10s.

HUNDRED OF LACKFORD.

In Elveden Ælfsige, and later Engelric, held 2 carucates of land as a manor; now Eustace holds it. Then as now 3 villans and 3 bordars and 2 slaves. Then and afterwards 2 ploughs in demesne, now 1; 1 plough belonging to the men. The fourth part of a fishery. A church with 15 acres of land. 4 pigs and 150 sheep. Then it was worth 30s., now 40s.

HUNDRED OF STOW.

In [Little] Finborough Engelric, Count Eustace's predecessor, held TRE 2½ carucates of land in the soke of the king and the earl. 9 bordars then as now. Then and afterwards 6 slaves, now none. Then and afterwards 3 ploughs in demesne,

now 2, and 18 acres of meadow. Then 1 ox, now 2, and 8 pigs. Then and afterwards [worth] 50s., now 100s. In the same place 7 free men commended to the said Engelric with 30 acres of land in the soke of the king. Then and afterwards 1 plough. They have been assessed in the 100s. above.

In Buxhall Engelric held 1½ carucates of land. Then as now

7 bordars. Then as now 2 ploughs in demesne. 2 sokemen and 3 acres. 8 acres of meadow. 1 ox. Then 30 sheep, now 40. Now 11 goats. Then and afterwards it was worth 40s., now £4.

HUNDRED OF SAMFORD.

Leodmær, a free man, held Highham with 1 carucate of land as a manor TRE. Then as now 2 bordars and 1 plough in demesne. 6 acres of meadow. The fifth part of a church with 4 acres and 24 [....] Then it was worth 10s., now 20s. Ralph de Marcy holds it from the Count. The soke is in [East] Bergholt.

Ælfric, a free man, held "Stanfelda" with 1 carucate of land and 15 acres as one manor. Now Hato holds it from the count. Now 4 bordars and 1 villan. Then as now 1 plough in demesne and 1 plough belonging to the men. 1½ acres of meadow. Then it was worth 20s., now 40s. The soke is in [East] Bergholt.

In Raydon Wulfrun, a free woman, held 12 acres TRE. Then half a plough. It is in the same valuation. The soke is in [East] Bergholt.

VI. Lands of Robert Malet In Suffolk.

HUNDRED OF BABERGH.

Hubert holds Edwardstone from Robert Malet which Godwine son of Ælfhere held TRE under the king with the soke as a manor. 4 carucates of land. A church with 30 acres of free land. Then 10 villans, afterwards 9, now 6. Then and afterwards 7 bordars, now 13. Then and afterwards 6 slaves, now 4. Then and afterwards 3 ploughs in demesne, now 2. Then and afterwards 6 ploughs belonging to the men, now 3; 8 acres of meadow. Woodland for 10 pigs. A winter mill. Then 2 horses at the hall, now 1. Then 17 head of cattle, now 11. Then 60 pigs, now 37. Then 80 sheep, now 22. Then and afterwards it was worth 100s., now £7.

In the same place 9 sokemen with half a carucate of land. Then and afterwards 1 plough, now a half. It is [included] in the valuation. This manor is 6 furlongs long and 6 broad. Whoever holds land there [pays] 10d. in geld. Walter fitzAubrey holds Chilton from the Count. The same Godwine held it with the soke TRE with 2 carucates of land as a manor. A church with 5 acres of free land. Then as now 1 villan and 5 bordars. Then 4 slaves, now 1. Then as now 2 ploughs in demesne and between the men. 5 acres of meadow. Now 3 pigs. Then 80 sheep, now 40. And the same 3 free men in the commendation and soke of the same Godwine, Robert's predecessor, [held] 40 acres of land. Then as now 1 plough among the men. 1 acre of meadow. Then the free men were worth 12s., now 7s. The manor was then worth 20s., now 40s. It is 4 furlongs long and 3 broad. Whoever holds land there [pays] 5d. in geld.

HUNDRED OF STOW.

Robert de Glanville holds Creeting [St Peter] from Robert Malet. Leofwine, a free man of Eadric,

Robert Malet's predecessor, held it by commendation only

as 1 carucate of land in the soke of the king and the earl. Then as now 6 bordars. Then 1½ ploughs, afterwards half a plough, now 2 in demesne. Then half a plough belonging to the men. 3 acres of meadow. The fourth part of a mill. Then 2 horses, now none. Now 4 head of cattle. Now 14 pigs. Now 43 sheep. 6 free men by commendation only to the said Leofwine, with 12½ acres. Then as now half a plough between them all. In the same place 1 sokeman of Eadric with 20 acres. Then as now half a plough. Then and afterwards the whole was worth 20s., now 30s.

HALF-HUNDRED OF IPSWICH.

In the borough [Ipswich] Robert has 1 burgess whom his predecessor had by commendation TRE. The king has the customary dues.

HUNDRED OF BOSMERE.

In Creeting 1 free man of Eadric by commendation TRE held 20 acres. 2 bordars. Then half a plough, now 1 oxen. 1 acre of meadow. It is worth 3s. 4d. Walter de Caen holds this. In the same place 1 free man with 1½ acres who was the man of someone commended to Eadric. It is worth 2s. Robert de Glanville holds it.

In the same place 1 free man of Eadric [held] 8 acres. One part of one dam. It is worth 2s. Now Robert Malet holds it in demesne.

In Coddenham 1 free man of Eadric by commendation TRE [held] 10 acres. It is worth 20d. The same man [holds it] in demesne.

Walter de Caen holds Olden from Robert. 1 free man by commendation [held] 6 acres, worth 32d. In the same place 1 free man by commendation [held] 5 acres, worth 10d. Robert holds this in demesne. The king and the earl have the soke over the whole.

In Hemingstone 1 free man, Eadmær. Leofric, the predecessor

Robert Malet

[Folio 305: SUFFOLK]

of Robert Malet's mother, had the commendation TRE with 4 acres, worth 8d. The king and the earl have the soke. Robert's mother holds it. In [Earl and Little] Stonham 1 free man, Æthelmær, TRE [held] 3 acres, worth 6d.

HUNDRED OF CLAYDON.

In Barham 1 free man, Beorhtweald commended to Eadric, [held] 40 acres as a manor TRE. It is worth 6s. 8d. William Goulafre holds it. The king and the earl have the soke. Eadric, a free man commended to Robert Malet's predecessor, held Debenham with 1 carucate of land as a manor in the soke of the abbot. Then as now 16 bordars and 2 ploughs in demesne. Then 3 ploughs belonging to the men, now 1½ ploughs. 4 acres of meadow. Then woodland for 60 pigs, now 40. Then as now 1 horse. Then 4 head of cattle, now 6. Then 40 pigs, now 20. Then 30 sheep, now 45. Then 40 goats, now 28. There are 30 acres of the demesne which are in another Hundred. Then it

was worth 60s., now 50s. William Goulafre holds this. The soke is the abbot's.

In the same place 6 free men commended to the aforesaid Eadric with 36 acres. Then 2 ploughs, now 1½ ploughs. 1 acre of meadow. Then it was worth 10s., now 6s. The soke is the abbot's. The said William holds this. In the same place 1 carucate of land which Robert's mother holds from Robert Malet. Beorhtmær, a free man, held it as a berewick in Kenton TRE. Then as now 1 villan and 9 bordars and 2 ploughs in demesne. Then 3 ploughs belonging to the men, now 2; 4 acres of meadow. Then woodland for 100 pigs, now 40. This is in the valuation of Kenton. In the same place 11 free men and a half, commended to Beorhtmær, [held] 60 acres less 1. Then 3 ploughs, now 2; 2 acres of meadow. Then it was worth 30s., now 20s. The soke is the abbot's.

In the same place Saxi, Ranulf Peverel's predecessor, held 6 acres TRE. Now the mother of Robert [holds it]. William Malet and his predecessor were seised of this

[Folio 305v: SUFFOLK]

in the time of King William. It is worth 12d. In the same place 2 acres. The whole [is held] in the same manner. It is worth 4d. The soke is the abbot's. In Thorpe Godwine, a free man by commendation, held 16 acres TRE; now Walter holds them from Robert Malet. Then it was worth 32d., now 3s. This land is in the manor of Bedingfield. The soke is the abbot's.

In Westerfield Wulfgeat, a free man commended to Gyrth, held 60 acres of land; they belong in Rushmere [St Andrew]. Now Humphrey holds them from Robert Malet. Then 1 bordar. It is worth 10s. In the same place 2 free men commended to Wulfgeat [held] 6½ acres, worth 2s. The said Humphrey [holds this]. The soke is the king's and the earl's.

In Winston 2 free men commended to someone who is commended to Eadric [held] 19 acres TRE. Then 1 plough, now a half. 1 acre of meadow. 2 bordars. It is worth 4s. William Goulafre [holds it] The soke is the abbot's.

In Debenham Wulfgeat, a free man commended to Eadric, held 10 acres. Then as now half a plough. It is worth 2s. The said William [holds it]. The soke is the abbot's.

In Debenham half a free man commended to someone who was commended to Eadric [held] 2 acres, worth 4d. In Henley a free man commended to Stanwine held 3 acres under Harold, worth 8d. Humphrey holds this. The soke is the abbot's.

In Debenham Robert has two parts of the church of St Mary with 20 acres to answer for, and a fourth part of the church of St Andrew and a fourth part of [its] land. In "Manuuic" Sigtrygg held 27 acres. He could not sell his land. Then as now 1 plough. It is worth 26s. 8d. Now Goscelin holds it from Robert Malet. The abbot has half the soke and Earl Hugh has the other half. In the same place 1 free man [held] 13½ acres by commendation, worth 5s. Gilbert holds this.

Robert Malet

In Ashfield 3 free men by commendation [held] 15 acres.Then as now half a plough. It is worth 5s. The said Gilbert [holds this]. The abbot and Earl Hugh have the soke.

In Thorpe 1 free man by commendation [held] 3 acres, worth 10d. The soke [is held] in the same manner. The said Gilbert [holds this].

In Ashfield Thorbiorn held 20 acres and he could not sell them. It is in the valuation of [Earl] Soham. The soke [is held] in the same way. In Thorpe 1 free man under commendation [held] 5 acres. Then half a plough, now 2 oxen. It is worth 16d. The Abbot of Ely has the soke. Tigier holds this. In Westerfield 1 free man by commendation [held] 10 acres, worth 2s. The king and the earl have the soke. In Thorpe 1 free man under commendation [held] 10 acres, worth 20d. William Goulafre holds it. The abbot has the soke.

HUNDRED AND A HALF OF SAMFORD.

Godwine, son of Alsige, a thegn of Queen Edith, held Belstead with 2 carucates of land as a manor. Then as now 8 villans and 3 bordars. Then 2 ploughs in demesne, now 1. Then as now 4 ploughs belonging to the men. 10 acres of meadow. Then 1 mill. Then 2 horses, now 1; 11 pigs. Then 100 sheep, now 30. Then it was worth £4, now 100s. The said Godwine has the soke. It is half a league long and 4 furlongs broad. 4½d. in geld.

The said Godwine held Brantham with 1 carucate of land and 20 acres as a manor. 3 bordars. Then 2 ploughs in demesne, afterwards and now 1; 2 acres of meadow. It is worth 20s. Godwine had the soke. Hubert holds this from Malet.

HALF-HUNDRED OF PARHAM.

Eadric of Laxfield held "Brutge" with 40 acres as a manor TRE. Then as now 1 plough and 3 acres of meadow. The fourth part of a church with 6 acres. Now 6 head of cattle, 14 pigs, 20 sheep and 8 goats. Then it was worth 14s. 8d., now the same. Walter de Risboil holds this from Robert. The soke is the Abbot of Ely's. In the same place 5 free men were

added by commendation, in the soke of the abbot, with 20 acres. The wife of one of them was commended to Northmann. It is worth 4s. The said Walter [holds it]. In Blaxhall 6 free men by commendation with 61 acres in the soke of the abbot. Then as now 2 ploughs. It is worth 10s. Gilbert holds it. In the same place 3 free men by commendation with 30 acres. Then 1 plough. 2 acres of meadow. It is worth 5s. The soke is the abbot's.

In Wantisden 22 free men by commendation in the soke of the abbot. Half a church with 20 acres of free land. 121 acres. Then and afterwards 10 ploughs, now 5, and 1 slave. Then as now worth 30s. Of these men Hubert holds 5 and a half, Gilbert 4 and a half, Gilbert de Wissant 7 and William d'Émalleville 5. It is 8 furlongs long and 6 broad. 40d. in geld. In the same place 16 acres of the demesne of Staverton and in the same valuation. In Parham 40 acres of the demesne

of "Nivetuna". It is worth 6s. 8d. In the same place 2 free men by commendation in the soke of the abbot [held] 12 acres. It is worth 2s. In the same place Alnoth, a free man commended to Eadric, [held] 1 carucate of land as one manor TRE. Then 4 villans, now 2. Then and afterwards 1 plough in demesne, now none. Then and afterwards 1 plough belonging to the men, now a half. 3 acres of meadow. To the church [belong] 24 acres of free land. Then as now worth 30s. Walter fitzAubrey [holds it] from Robert. In the same place Blæcesunu, a free man by commendation, [held] 40 acres as one manor TRE. Then as now half a plough. Then it was worth 6s. 8d., now 7s. The said Walter [holds it]. In the same place Earnwulf, a free man by commendation, held 40 [acres] as one manor. Then as now half a plough and 1 acre of meadow. It is worth 7s. In the same place Alnoth, a free man, held by commendation 30 acres. Then as now half a plough and 1 acre of meadow. It is worth 5s.

In the same place 2 free men by commendation [held] 40 acres. Then as now 1 plough and 1 acre of meadow. It is worth 7s. The said Walter [holds it] from Robert. The soke is the Abbot of Ely's.

Robert Malet

In Blaxhall 2 free men [held] 14 acres. One and a half were commended to the Abbot of Ely and half was commended to Malet's predecessor. Then as now half a plough. It is worth 28d. William d'Émalleville holds it from Robert. In the same place a free man [held] 3 acres by commendation to Eadric. It is worth 6d. The said William [holds it]. The soke is the abbot's. In Blaxhall 1 free man, by commendation to Eadric [held] 10 acres, worth 3s. Gilbert [holds it] from Malet. The soke is the abbot's. In the same place 1 free man, half by commendation to his predecessor and half to the abbot. As a result of this half he came to an agreement with the abbot and he has 12 acres. Then as now half a plough. It is worth 2s. The said Gilbert [holds it]. In the same place 1 free man by commendation [holds] 1 acre, worth 2d. In the same place 2 free men: one and a half commended to Eadric, and one half to the abbot [held] 8 acres, worth 16d. The said Gilbert [holds it]. In Parham 1 free man by commendation [held] 12 acres, worth 2s. The said Gilbert [holds it]. The soke is the abbot's. In Tunstall Godric, a free man half commended to Eadric and half to the abbot, held 4 acres. It is worth 8d. The said Gilbert [holds it].

In Blaxhall Gilbert holds from Robert Malet 3 free men commended to Eadric with 6 acres, worth 12d. The soke is the abbot's.

In Wantisden 2 free men, Alwine and Alflæd commended to Malet's predecessor, [held] 7 acres, worth 14d. The fourth part of a church with 10 acres. In Blaxhall Huna a free man commended to Malet's predecessor held 12 acres, worth 2s. Ranulf holds it from Malet. The soke is the Abbot of Ely's. In Wantisden Ælfric, a free man, held 4 acres, worth 8d. Gilbert holds it.

[Folio 307v: SUFFOLK]

In Blaxhall 16 acres of the demesne of 'Kelton', worth 25d. The soke is the abbot's.

HUNDRED OF PLUMESGATE.

Eadric held 'Kelton' TRE with 4 carucates of land and 20 acres as one manor. Then as now 10 villans and 10 bordars. Then 3 slaves. Then and afterwards 3 ploughs in demesne, now 2. Then and afterwards 5 ploughs belonging to the men, now 4. 10 acres of meadow. Then as now 1 mill. Then 12 head of cattle, now 2. Then 30 pigs, now 14. Then 100 sheep, now 50. 1 sokeman with 80 acres and 2 bordars. Then and afterwards 2 ploughs, now 1½ ploughs. Then it was worth £8, now £9 10s. In the same place 16 free men and a half, by commendation only, have been added to this manor with 153 acres. Then and afterwards 8 ploughs, now 3½. Then it was worth 30s., now 20s. It is 9 furlongs long and 4 broad. 2¼d. in geld. Robert [holds this] in demesne.

In Rendham 1 carucate of land and 69 acres as a berewick to this manor. Then as now 3 villans and 2 bordars. Then and afterwards 2 slaves, now 1. Then as now 2 ploughs in demesne. Then 1½ ploughs belonging to the men, now 1; 6 acres of meadow. Then woodland for 40 pigs, now 30; 1 horse, 24 pigs, 18 sheep and 30 goats. It is worth £3 10s. A church with 24 acres and 1 plough. To this manor have been added 13 free men with 80 acres. Then 2 ploughs, now 1 and 3 acres of meadow. It is worth 20s. Robert Malet holds this. It is 1 league long and 7 furlongs broad. 20d. in geld. The soke is the abbot's.

In Cransford Cus, a free man commended to Eadric TRE, [held]

Robert Malet

[Folio 308: SUFFOLK]

90 [...] acres as one manor. Then as now 9 bordars. Then and afterwards 2 ploughs in demesne, now 1. Then as now 1 plough belonging to the men. 4 acres of meadow. Now 16 pigs. Then 13 sheep, now 30. Then 16 goats. Then it was worth 20s., now 25s. Walter holds it from Malet. To this manor have been added 2 free men with 14 acres and half a plough. It is worth 3s. The same Walter [holds this]. The soke is the abbot's.

In [Great] Glemham 1 free man, Huna, half commended to the Abbot of Ely and half to his predecessor, [held] 30 acres as one manor. Then 1 plough, afterwards and now a half. It is worth 7s. The same Walter [holds this]. The soke is the abbot's. In the same place Spearhafoc, a free man commended to Eadric, held 60 acres as a manor TRE. 2 bordars. Then and afterwards 1½ ploughs, now 1. It is worth 10s. The same Walter [holds this]. The soke is the abbot's.

In the same place 2 free men [hold] 3 acres, worth 8d. The same Walter [holds this].

In Swefling 1 free man, Osbern, commended to Eadric [held] 60 acres as a manor TRE. Then 2 ploughs, afterwards and now 1½. Then it was worth 20s., now 20s. Robert de Claville holds it from Robert. In the same place a free man, Beorhtnoth, by commendation 5 acres, worth 10d. Robert

fitzFulcred holds [this]. In the same place Æthelwig, commended to his predecessor, held 60 acres as a manor TRE. Then 1 plough and 4 acres of meadow. Then it was worth 10s., now 5s. The same Robert [holds it]. The soke is the abbot's. In the same place 11 free men [held] 90 acres; they were commended to Malet's predecessor, apart from one, Hardwin by name, who was commended to the predecessor of Roger Bigod. Then and afterwards 3 ploughs,

[Folio 308v: SUFFOLK]

now 1½, and 4 acres of meadow. A church with 15 acres. Then it was worth [...] 10s., now 6s. The same Robert [holds this]. The soke is the abbot's. In Benhall 6 free men, commended to Malet's predecessor, [held] 80 acres. Then and afterwards 3 ploughs, now 2. The same Robert [holds this]. The soke is the abbot's. Then it was worth 20s., now 30s. It is 8 furlongs long and 6 broad. 9¼d. in geld. In Stratford [St Andrew] Huna, a free man commended to Eadric, held 80 acres as a manor. Then as now 1 plough and 5 bordars and half a plough belonging to the men and 4 acres of meadow. Then 1 horse, now 2 head of cattle. Then 12 pigs, now 15. Then 16 sheep, now 30, and 27 goats. Then it was worth 20s., now 25s. The same Robert [holds it]. In the same place 1 free man and a half , Alwine [held] 14 acres. Then as now half a plough. It is worth 3s. 4d. The same Robert [holds it]. The soke is the abbot's.

In [Great] Glemham Wulfmær, a free man commended to Malet's predecessor, [held] 100 acres; 5 bordars. Then as now 1 plough in demesne and 1 plough belonging to the men. A church with 10 acres and 1 acre of meadow. Then 1 horse. Then it was worth 20s., and now. The same Robert [holds it] likewise. In the same place 2 free men commended to Leofric [held] 41 acres as a manor TRE. Then and afterwards 1 plough, now 1 ox and 1 acre of meadow. It is worth 10s. The same Robert [holds this]. In the same place 2 free men [held] 1½ acres. It is worth 26d. The soke is the abbot's. The same Robert [holds this]. In the same place 1 free man [held] 5 acres. It is worth 10d. The soke is the abbot's. The same Robert [holds this]. In Farnham 2 free men by commendation [held] 40 acres. In [Great] Glemham 2 free men [held] 26 acres and 1½ ploughs and 6 acres of meadow. 2 bordars. It is worth 21s. Robert holds it from Malet. In [Great] Glemham Alwynn, a free [wo]man, [held] 15 acres, worth 2s. Robert de Glanville holds it. The soke is the abbot's. In Cransford

Robert Malet

[Folio 309: SUFFOLK]

1 free man by commendation [held] 15 acres and half a plough. It is worth 2s. Gilbert holds [this]. The soke is the abbot's. In Benhall 2 free men with 20 acres and 1 plough. It is worth 5s. Hubert holds it from Malet. The soke is the abbot's. In Benhall 4 free men by commendation [held] 8 acres. It is worth 16d. [This is] in demesne. The soke is the abbot's.

In the same place 1 free man by commendation [...] with 1 acre and it is worth and a half. And it is worth 6d. Robert de Glanville [holds this]. The soke is the abbot's. In the same place 3 free men by commendation with 17 acres and half a plough. It is worth 36d. [This is] in demesne.

In Cransford 30 acres of demesne land of Badingham, worth 5s. Robert [holds this] from Malet. The soke is the abbot's. In [Great] Glemham a free man by commendation with 6 acres, worth 12d. [This is] in demesne. The soke is the abbot's.

HUNDRED HARTISMERE.

Alwine, a free man commended to Eadric, and his wife commended to the abbot of Edmund held Wyverstone TRE with 100 acres as one manor. Now Hubert holds it from Robert. Then as now 2 bordars. Then 1 slave. Then 2 ploughs, afterwards 1, now 1½; 3 acres of meadow. Then as now; for 20 pigs. Now 1 horse. Then 2 head of cattle, now 3. Then 15 pigs, now 10, and 24 goats. It is worth 20s. The king and the earl have the soke. In the same place some free men, namely 3 brothers and their mother, held 30 acres as a manor. One of them, Ælfric, for the six part of him was commended to Malet's predecessor. Aki, Robert Blunt's predecessor, had five parts of the commendation over him. On this land there was then and afterwards half a plough, now none. It is worth 5s. The king and the earl have the soke. Hubert holds it from Malet.

[Folio 309v: SUFFOLK]

In the same place 1 free man, half by commendation to the abbot and half by commendation to Malet's predecessor, [held] 16 acres of land. Then as now half a plough. It is worth 3s. The same Hubert [holds this]. The king and the earl have the soke. In the same place 1 free woman, Alflæd, commended to Malet's predecessor, [held] 3 acres, worth 6d. The same Hubert [holds this]. In the same place 1 free man by commendation [held] 3 acres, worth 6d. Hubert holds Westhorpe from Robert Malet. 1 free man, Leofric, commended to Eadric of Laxfield, [held] 42 acres TRE. Then as now 3 bordars and 1 plough. Woodland for 8 pigs. 1½ acres of meadow. Then it was worth 10s., now 30s. Under him 4 free men with 12 acres. Then as now half a plough. They are in the same valuation.

In Finningham 1 free man [held] 3 acres and he could not sell his land. And [there was] another half a free man with 5 acres and 1 bordar. They are in the same valuation. The king and the earl have the soke. Also in Westhorpe 4 free men commended to Eadric with 28 acres. Then as now 1 plough. 1 acre of meadow. Then it was worth 4s., now 5s. In the same place 1 free man under the same commendation [held] 7 acres, worth 14d., and he could not sell his own land.

In Cotton 1 free man commended to Eadric [held] 20 acres. Then as now half a plough. Woodland for 4 pigs. Half an acre of meadow. Then it was worth 40d., now 5s. Under him 3 free men with 5 acres, worth 10 pennies. In the same place 1 free man under the same commendation [held] 7 acres and half a plough. Woodland for 2 pigs. It is worth 14d. All of this is worth 21s. In Rickinghall Superior Beorhtflæd, a free woman of Eadric of Laxfield, held 1 carucate of land and 30 acres TRE. Then as now 1 villan and 4 bordars and 1 slave. In demesne 2 ploughs, and half a plough belonging to the men. Woodland for 8 pigs. 2 acres of meadow. 4 horses, 6 head of cattle, 20 pigs, 60 sheep and 16 goats. Then it was worth 20s.,

now 60s. The king and the earl have the soke. In the same place 2 free men commended to St Edmund with 5 acres

Robert Malet

[Folio 310: SUFFOLK]

and a half, worth 12d. Hubert holds this from Robert Malet. In Brome 6 acres, worth 12d. In the same place 3 half free men with 7 acres, worth 14d. William Scudet holds this from Robert Malet. In Brome Warin holds from Robert Malet; 1 free man, Wulfmær, commended to Eadric with 30 acres. Then as now 1 plough. 1½ acres of meadow. Then as now worth 5s. 5 free men commended to Eadric with 14 acres, worth 2s. The same Warin holds this from Robert.

In Oakley William Goulafre holds from Robert Malet 30 acres which 1 free man, Godmann, commended to the same Eadric [held]. 2 free men with half an acre. Then as now half a plough. 1½ acres of meadow. 1 mill. Then as now worth 10s.

In Thrandeston the same Godmann holds 16 acres, worth 2s. William Goulafre holds this from Robert Malet. 1 church with 6 acres, worth 12d. In Thrandeston William de Caen holds from Robert Malet 5 acres which 1 free man commended to Eadric [held] TRE, worth 12d. The king and the earl have the soke. In the same place Hugh holds from Robert Malet 9 acres, worth 12d.

HUNDRED OF BISHOP.

In Bedingfield 1 free man commended to Eadric [held] 20 acres and 3 bordars and half a plough. Woodland for 10 pigs. It is worth 5s.

In Carlton Eadric held 80 acres as one manor. 1 villan and 5 bordars. 1 plough and 1 acre of meadow. In the same place 10 free men with 160 acres of land less 2, and 3 ploughs. The whole is the valuation of Leiston. The soke is in Kelsale, Roger Bigod's manor. In Aldringham 7 villans and 1 bordar in the valuation of Leiston. They have 90 acres. The soke is the bishop's in Hoxne. In Denham 1 sokeman with all customary dues with 50 acres of demesne land. It is in the valuation of Eye. Then as now 1 bordar

[Folio 310v: SUFFOLK]

and 1 plough. 1 acre of meadow. In the same place 4 free men by commendation [held] 30 acres and half a plough, worth 5s. The soke is the bishop's. In Mendham 1 sokeman with 10 acres and half an acre of meadow, worth 24d. The soke is the bishop's. In Kelsale 1 free man by commendation. He has 30 acres and 1 bordar. Then 1 plough, now a half. It is worth 5s. Roger Bigod has the soke.

In Aldringham 1 free man by commendation and by foldsoke and other services with 20 acres and half a plough. It is worth 40d. In Bedingfield 6 free men by commendation [held] 80 acres. Then as now 2 ploughs. Then it was worth 10s., now 15s. The fourth part of a church with 6 acres. The land of Robert Malet's mother of the queen's fief. In Bedingfield 3 free men commended to Stigand [held] 44 acres and 1 bordar. Woodland for 20 pigs. 1 acre of meadow. It is worth 5s. The bishop has the soke. In the same place in Bedingfield 2 free men commended to Stigand [held] 26 acres of land. Woodland for 6 pigs. Then as now 1 plough. It is worth 4s. The soke is the bishop's.

OF BLYTHING.

In Darsham Hundred 1 free man, Eadric, held TRE 94 acres as a manor. Then as now 4 bordars. Then 2 ploughs, now 1½; 2 acres of meadow. It is worth 12s. 8d. Under him 6 free men by commendation [held] 36 acres. Then as now 1 plough. Worth 6s. In Fordley the same Eadric held 60 acres and 3 bordars and 1½ ploughs. 4 acres of meadow. 1 mill. It is worth 10s. And under him 6 free men by commendation [held] 26 acres and 1 plough, worth 4s.

This Eadric was commended to Eadric of Laxfield, Robert Malet's predecessor, before King Edward died. After Eadric was outlawed, King Edward took seisin of all his land. Afterwards he was reconciled to King Edward and he granted to him his own land. [King Edward] also gave him a sealed charter so that whichever of his free men by commendation wished to return to him, could return by his permission. King Edward took seisin

Robert Malet

of this Eadric in his own hand. Afterwards the Hundred did not see that he returned to Eadric his lord but then he himself says, and proof by ordeal, that he did return. He holds the free men whom he has commended under him and of these he claims Robert as guarantor.

[...] Eadric of Laxfield held [...] Huntingfield TRE and now Walter fitzAubrey holds it under Robert Malet. Then as now 6 carucates of land. Then and afterwards 18 villans, now 12. Then as now 28 bordars. Then 1 slave. Then as now 4 ploughs in demesne. Then as now 18 ploughs belonging to the men. Then woodland for 150 pigs, now for 100; 15 acres of meadow. Then as now 2 horses, 10 non-working cattle, 30 pigs and 100 sheep. 60 goats and 6 beehives. Then it was worth £8, now £7. 1 church with 14 acres, worth 2s. In Linstead [Magna and Parva] Wulfric, a free man, held 1 manor TRE; now Walter holds it under Robert Malet with 60 acres of land, 6 bordars, 2 ploughs in demesne and 1 plough belonging to the men. Then woodland for 30 pigs, now for 20; 2 acres of meadow. 1 horse, 4 head of cattle and 20 pigs. 30 sheep and 20 goats. TRE it was worth 20s., now 30s. And there also belong to this manor in Huntingfield 200 acres of land which 21 free men held TRE. Then as now 10 ploughs. Under them 2 bordars. Woodland for 20 pigs. 2 acres of meadow. Then as now worth 40s. And this land is 1 league long and 9 furlongs broad. It renders 7½d. to the king's geld. And there also belong to this manor in Huntingfield 40 acres of land which 4 free men held. Then 2 ploughs, now 1. They have 1 bordar. It is worth 8s. The soke and sake over all this land of the free men belongs in Blythburgh for the use of the king and earl. And over all these men Eadric, Robert Malet's predecessor, had the commendation. Eadric of Laxfield held Leiston as one manor and

carucates of land. Then as now 25 villans and 27 bordars. Then 3 slaves, now 7. Then in demesne 11 ploughs, now 7. Then 6 ploughs belonging to the men, now 3½. Then woodland for 500 pigs, afterwards and now for 200. Then as now 1 mill. 5 acres of meadow. 4 horses, 5 head of cattle, 72 pigs, 112 sheep, 7 beehives and 1 park. And 3 churches with 100 acres of free land, TRE worth £16, afterwards £28 and now the same. 3 leagues long and 2 leagues and 1 furlong broad. It renders 3s. 3½d. in the king's geld. And in the same vill is 1 free man with 40 acres and he holds it as a manor. It is worth 6s. but they are part of the £28 mentioned above. Also to this manor belong 47 free men with 7 carucates of land. Then 8 ploughs, now 6½. Then as now worth £4. In the same vill Gilbert holds 27 acres under Robert Malet which Eadric held as a manor. Then 4 bordars and 2 villans. Then as now 2 ploughs in demesne and half a plough belonging to the men. Now 1 horse and 2 head of cattle. Then as now worth 20s. In the same vill 8 free men with 1½ carucates of land. Then 3 ploughs in demesne, now 2; 1 acre of meadow. Then as now worth 30s. Fulcred holds this land from Robert Malet.

Eadric of Laxfield held Dunwich TRE as one manor. Now Robert Malet holds it. Then 2 carucates of land, now 1: the sea carried off the other one. Then as now 1 plough in demesne. Then 12 bordars, now 2, and 24 Frenchmen with 40 acres of land. They render every customary due to this manor. Then 120 burgesses, now 236. Poor men, 180 less 2. Then 1 church, now 3. They render £4 10s. Altogether it is worth £50 and 60,000 herrings

Robert Malet

by way of gift. And TRE it rendered £10. Also Robert de Vaux holds 1 acre of land, worth 8d. And Norman holds 1 acre, worth 2s. 8d. and Godric 1 acre, worth 8d. They hold this from Robert Malet. Gilbert Blund holds 80 men from the same Robert and they pay £4 and 8000 herrings. Aki, one free man, held Westleton as a manor with 4 carucates of land. Then as now 13 villans and 14 bordars. Then 4 slaves, now none. Then 3 ploughs in demesne, now none. Then 10 ploughs belonging to the men, now 5. Woodland for 7 pigs. 3 acres of meadow. 3 head of cattle, 20 pigs, 60 sheep. Then as now 24 goats, 2 beehives. Then it was worth 100s., now the same. 1 church with 20 acres, worth 40d. To this manor belong 14 free men and a half with 103½ acres. Then 6 ploughs, now 3. Then as now worth 20s. It is 2 leagues and 2 furlongs long and 2 leagues broad. 7½d. in geld. Gilbert Blund holds this from Robert Malet. In Middelton 2 free men held 80 acres. Now Gilbert Blund holds them from Robert Malet. Then as now 1 bordar. Now half a plough. 2 acres of meadow. Then as now worth 16s. In Strickland Eadric, a free man, held 40 acres. Then as now 1 bordar. Then 1 plough, now none. It is worth 6s. 8d. Gilbert Blund holds this from Robert Malet.

In Fordley 2 free men held 24 acres TRE. Now the same. Gilbert [holds this] from Robert Malet. Then in demesne 1 ploughs, now none. Then it was worth 10s., now 4s. The king has in Dunwich this customary due, that two or three will go to the Hundred if they have been duly notified. If they do not do this they are fined 2 ora. If a thief is caught there he will be judged there and he will suffer corporal punishment in Blythburgh; his goods will remain

with the lord of Dunwich. TRE there was no money-changer there but in Blythburgh.

In Sibton 1 free man held 25 acres TRE as a manor. Now Walter de Caen holds it from Robert Malet. Then as now 1 bordar. Then as now half a plough in demesne. 1 acre of meadow. Then as now worth 4s. 1 church. In the same vill 1 free man held 1 carucate of land and 20 acres as a manor. Then as now 4 villans and 10 bordars. Then as now 2 ploughs in demesne and 2 ploughs belonging to the men. Woodland for 60 pigs. 4 acres of meadow. Then as now 2 horses and 7 head of cattle. Then 30 pigs, now 26. Then 50 goats, now 50 sheep. Then it was worth 20s., now 40s. Walter de Caen holds this from Robert Malet. In the same vill 1 free man held 25 acres TRE as a manor. Then as now 3 bordars. Then as now half a plough. 1 acre of meadow. Then as now 1 horse. Then 6 pigs, now none. Then as now worth 4s. Walter holds this from Malet. In the same vill Eadric held 16 acres of land. Then as now 1 bordar. Woodland for 12 pigs. 2 acres of meadow. It is worth 3s. In the same vill Ælfric held 60 acres TRE as a manor. Then as now 2 bordars. Then as now 2 ploughs in demesne. 1 acre of meadow. Then 1 horse, now none. 60 and 13 sheep and 6 goats. Then it was worth 10s., now 16s. Walter holds this from Malet. In the same vill 3 free men and a half held 72 acres. 1 bordar. Then as now 1 plough in demesne. 1 acre of meadow. Then as now worth 10s. It is 1 leagues long and 1 broad. It renders in geld 7½d. 2 churches with 18 acres and 3 acres of meadow.

In "Uurabretuna" a free woman, Asmoth, held TRE 30 acres of land, over whom Northmann the sheriff had commendation. 2 bordars. 2 acres of meadow. It is worth 4s. Now Robert Malet holds it. Roger Bigod claims it back.

In Peasenhall Leofsige, a free man, held TRE 40 acres of land as one manor. Now Fulcred holds it from Malet. Then as now 4 bordars. Woodland for 10 pigs. 1 plough and 1 acre of meadow.

Robert Malet

It is worth 8s. The king and the earl have the soke. In the same place 1 free man, Stanwine, [held] TRE 1 carucate of land as a manor. Now Fulcred holds it. This Stanwine was commended to Eadric, Robert's predecessor before he was outlawed. Later he was Harold's man on the day on which King Edward was alive and dead, so the Hundred says. Stanwine says that he was Eadric's man, with Harold's permission, on the day on which King Edward died and he offers proof by ordeal. There are 2 bordars. Then as now 1 plough in demesne and 1 plough belonging to the men. 1 acre of meadow. Woodland for 20 pigs. 2 head of cattle. Then 6 pigs, now 12. Now 26 sheep. Then it was worth 12s., now 22s. Harold had the soke and Stanwine [had it] from him. And Stanwine added 2 free men

by commendation in the time of King William with 8 acres, worth 16d. The same Stanwine had the soke from Harold. In the same place 1 free man, Æthelmær, commended to Eadric with 12 acres and half a plough, worth 2s. The king and the earl have the soke. Gilbert holds it from Malet.

In Sibton Blæcmann, a free man, held 50 acres as one manor. Then as now 2 bordars. Then as now 1 plough in demesne. 1 acre of meadow. 1 horse, 16 sheep. Then as now worth 10s. Blæcmann was Eadric's man and he had commendation over him and the king had the soke. But that man's wife was Bishop Stigand's man and he had commendation over the woman. William Malet held this land. In the same vill 2 free men held 32 acres of land. Then as now 1 bordar. Then as now 1 plough in demesne. Half an acre of meadow. It is worth 4s. Walter de Caen holds this from Robert Malet.

In Darsham 1 free man, Blæcmann, commended to Eadric, [held] TRE 30 acres as one meadow. Now Walter fitzRichere [holds it]. Then as now 1 bordar. Then 1 [...] plough,

now half a plough. 2 acres of meadow. It is worth 10s. To this manor was added 1 free man with 22 acres over whom that Blæcmann had commendation TRE. Then as now half a plough. It is worth 4s. 4d. The king and the earl have the soke.

In Darsham Eadric [held] 60 acres as one manor TRE, now Fulcred [holds it]. Then 1 plough and 2 acres of meadow. It was worth then 8s., now 10s. The king and the earl have the soke. I [sic]

In Westleton 1 free man by commendation [held] 30 acres as one manor. Now the same Fulcred [holds it]. A church with 3 acres. Then and afterwards 1 plough, now none. 1 acre of meadow. Then it was worth 8s. and when Robert received it, it was at farm for 20s. Now it renders 8s. The king and the earl have the soke. In [South] Cove Eadric holds from Robert Malet 2 free men by commendation to Eadric who was commended to Eadric, Robert Malet's predecessor. He has 16 acres. Then as now half a plough. It is worth 3s. The same Stanwine, mentioned above, held Strickland with 80 acres as one manor TRE; now Walter de [...] Caen [holds it]. Then as now 2 bordars. Then 1 plough, now a half. 1 acre of meadow. Then it was worth 10s., now 8s. The king and the earl have the soke. In the same place half a free man by commendation with 8 acres, worth 12d. In the same place Talcha, a free man, held by commendation TRE 10 acres, worth 20d.

In "Warabetuna" 2 free men by commendation [held] 9 acres, worth 18d. Walter de Caen holds it all. The king and the earl have the soke.

In "Hoppetuna" a free man, Alnoth, by commendation [held] 42 acres as one manor TRE; now Gilbert holds it. Then as now 2 bordars. Then 1 plough, now the same. 2 [...] acres of meadow. Then it was worth 10s., and now [the same]. In the same place 2 free men by commendation [held] 18 [...] acres, worth 3s. The king and the earl have the soke.

Robert Malet

[Folio 314: SUFFOLK]

In Darsham 1 free man by commendation [held] 4 acres, worth 8d. This is in demesne.

In Holton Eadric held 20 acres as a manor; now Robert [holds it] in demesne. It is worth 3s. 4d. The king and the earl have the soke.

In Peasenhall a free man by commendation [held] 6 acres, worth 8d. Walter de Caen [holds it].

In Linstead [Magna and Parva] 8 acres which belong in Withersdale and [are] in the valuation.

In Westleton 1 villan with 6 acres. Gilbert Blund holds this. It has been assessed.

In Fordley 3 free men and a half, Swærting, Algar, Hereweald and Osfrith the half, by commendation to Eadric. Osfrith was wholly Toli's man [...]. They have 27 acres of land. Then as now 1 plough. 2 acres of meadow. [It is] in the valuation [...] of Leiston. The king and the earl have the soke.

In Minsmere 12 acres of free land, worth 12d. The king and the earl have the soke. In the same place 2 free men with 8 acres, worth 12d. In the same place also 12 acres which Leofric Cocc holds, worth 12d. The king and the earl have the soke over everything.

In "Wrabbatuna" Godric, son of Herebeald holds 8 acres, worth 12d. The king and the earl have the soke.

In Theberton 1 free man, Swart Hoga, held TRE from Ulf, son of Manni Swart 60 acres as one manor. Then 1 plough, now none. 2 acres of meadow. It was worth TRE 20s., now 10s. Hubert holds this from Robert Malet.

HUNDRED OF COLNEIS.

In Stratton Wulfmær, a free man of Eadric of Laxfield, held TRE 1 carucate of land as a manor. Then 4 villans, now 2. Then as now 3 bordars. Then as now in demesne 1 plough. Then 1 plough belonging to the men, now a half. Woodland for 6 pigs. 10 acres of meadow. 12 pigs and 80 sheep.

[Folio 314v: SUFFOLK]

Then it was worth 20s., now 30s. To this manor were added 12 free men in the time of King William: Leofric of Helmley, Brunman of Burgh, Goda of Struostuna, Leofstan of Falkenham, Gliwman of Levington, Wihtric of Carlewuda, Edwin the smith in the same place, Ælfric of Hopewella, Thorir of Kylvertestuna, Ælfric, son of the smith in Carlewuda, Ordgar of Kylvertestuna and Modgifu of Colcar, all under the same commendation TRE with 87½ acres. 2 bordars. 2½ ploughs. 2 acres of meadow. 1 mill. Then it was worth 60s., now it renders 50s. All this [...] Bernard of London holds from Robert Malet. In the same Stratton 1 free [...] man, Leofwin, son of Brun commended to Eadric, [held] 24 acres of land. [...] Then as now half a plough. Half an acre of meadow. It is worth 4s. Half a free man, Ælfric under the same commendation with 1 acre, worth 5d. R[obert] de Claville holds this from Robert Malet. In "Mycelegata" 1 free man, Leofstan commended to Eadric, [held] 4 acres of land, worth 12d.

HUNDRED OF CARLFORD.

Humphrey fitzRobert holds Playford from Robert Malet. Godwine, son of Ælfhere, held under the queen TRE 3 carucates of land as one manor. Then 8 villans, now 4. Then 3 bordars, now 23 and 1 burgess of Ipswich. Then 6 slaves, now 1. Then in demesne 3 ploughs, now 2. Then 8 ploughs belonging to the men, now 4. Woodland for 20 pigs. 20 acres of meadow and 1 mill. Then 3 horses. Then 15 head of cattle, now 1. Then 69 pigs, now 25. Then 160 sheep, now 26. Then 6 beehives, now 1. Then it was worth £8, now 100s. 1 church with 10 acres, worth 20d. In the same place 12 free men under commendation the same Godwine apart from 2, Æthelric

Robert Malet

[Folio 315: SUFFOLK]

and Blæcmann over whom Halfdan the predecessor of Geoffrey de Mandeville had commendation [held] 100 acres of land. Then 3 ploughs, now 2; 2½ acres of meadow. It is worth 20s. The soke and sake and the customary dues are Robert's. It is 1 league long and a half broad. 9d. in geld.

In "Necchemara" 4 free men commended to the same Godwine TRE with 28 acres. Then 2 ploughs, now none. It is worth 2s. Robert Malet has the soke and sake as over the aforementioned men. It is 3 furlongs long and 2½ broad. 4½d. in geld. Others hold [land] there.

In Kesgrave 3 free men, 3 commended to Godwine, [held] 20 acres of land and 1 plough, worth 3s. 4d. Robert has the soke and sake. Also in the same place 1 free man, Aslak, commended to Eadric of Laxfield TRE, [held] 10 acres. Then 1 plough, now none. It is worth 16d. Half a church with 2 acres. Æthelthryth has the soke and sake. It is half a league long and 4 furlongs broad. 4½d. in geld. In Lesser Waldringfield 1 sokeman of Eadric [held] 22 acres of land, 1 bordar and 1 plough, worth 2s.

In Rushmere [St Andrew] 2 sokemen of Godwine with 30 acres. Then 1 plough, now a half. 1 acre of meadow. It is worth 5s. In the same place 3 free men, Leofric, Thorkil and Ælfric, commended to Eadric [held] 44 acres and 1 bordar. Then 2 ploughs, now 1; 2 acres of meadow. It is worth 10s. St Æthelthryth has soke and sake.

In "Hopestuna" 1 free man of Eadric [held] 25 acres of land. Then 1 plough, now none. 1 bordar. Then it was worth 2s. 8d., now 4s. St Æthelthryth has the soke.

In Hasketon 1 free man by the name of Lustwine commended to Eadric, and his wife commended to Halfdan TRE [held] 40 acres and half a plough. Worth 8s.

[Folio 315v: SUFFOLK]

St Æthelthryth has the soke. Also in the same place 2 free men, commended to Eadric, held 17 acres but they dwell in another Hundred. It is worth 3s.

In Burgh 2 free men commended to Eadric [held] 16 acres and half a plough. 1 acre of meadow. Then it was worth 4s., now 3s. In Tuddenham 1 free man commended to Eadric TRE [held] 12 acres. Then 1 plough, now none. Half an acre of meadow. It is worth 2s. 1 church with 15 acres in that Hundred. Another free man commended to Godwine with 4 acres, worth 8d. In [Great] Bealings 1 sokeman, Wulfnoth by name, with 14 acres. Then 1 plough, now none. Half an acre of meadow. Then it was worth 2s., now 28d.

In Grundisburgh 2 sokemen commended to Eadric [held] 5 acres and half a plough, worth 12d. All this Humphrey fitzRobert holds from Robert Malet.

In Burgh 1 free man, Æthelweald, commended to Eadric TRE with 16 acres of land. Then half a plough, now 2 oxen. It is worth 2s. Robert Malet holds this in demesne.

In Burgh R[obert] de Glanville holds 1 free man, Wulfwine the priest, commended to Eadric TRE with 6 acres, worth 12d., and 11 acres of free land, worth 11d. In Rushmere [St Andrew] Wulfgeat, a free man of Gyrth, held TRE 60 acres as one manor. Humphrey holds it in demesne. [...] Then 1 plough and now 5 acres of meadow. It is worth 20s. In the same place 2 free men under him with 4 acres, worth 16d. Humphrey holds this from Robert Malet.

In Hasketon 1 free man of Eadric with 5 acres, worth 12d.

In Clopton 2 free men commended to Eadric with 40 acres of land and half a plough, worth 7s. 4d. Tigier holds one of these and Gilbert de Coleville the other from Robert Malet.

Robert Malet

HUNDRED OF PLUMESGATE.

Godric the priest commended to Eadric of Laxfield held Cransford with 40 acres. Then and now 1 plough. 1 acre of meadow. Then as now worth 10s. Durand holds this from Robert Malet. Walter holds Snape from Robert Malet which Eadric of Laxfield held as a manor with 4 carucates of land TRE. Then as now 8 villans and 16 bordars. Then in demesne 5 ploughs, now none but there could be. Then 8 ploughs belonging to the men, now 4. Woodland for 6 pigs. 6 acres of meadow. 1 mill. Then 2 horses. Then 6 head of cattle, now 2. Then 24 pigs. Then 160 sheep. Then as now £6. It is 3 leagues long and 4 furlongs broad. 4od. in geld. Robert Malet has the soke. Also in the same vill 25 free men commended to Eadric of Laxfield with 108 acres. Then between them 6 ploughs, now 4. Then it was worth 23s., now 20s.

In Aldeburgh Wulfric, a sokeman of Eadric, held TRE 80 acres as a manor and 3 bordars. Then 2 ploughs, now 1; 2 acres of meadow. 5 pigs and 20 sheep. Then as now worth 20s. 2 churches with 60 acres, worth 10s. In the same place 12 acres of free land, worth 2s. In the same place 1 free man, Arnketil, commended to Eadric with 30 acres. Then as now 1 plough. 1 acre of meadow. It is worth 5s. In Sternfield 1 sokeman with 30 acres and 1 acre of meadow, worth 5s. In Boyton 1 free man commended to Eadric with 24 acres and 1 plough, worth 5s. In the same place 30 acres of demesne and half a plough, worth 5s. Walter fitzGrip held all this. In Snape Gilbert Bl holds from Robert Malet 21 free men commended to Eadric with 1 carucate of land and 30 acres. Then 6 ploughs, now 3. Then it was worth 20s., now 40s. 1 church with 8 acres, worth 16d.

In Boyton 8 free men commended to Eadric with 20 acres. Then 2 ploughs, now 1. It is worth 5s. Gilbert holds this from Robert Malet.

Norman holds Farnham from Robert Malet which Eadric of Laxfield [held] as a berewick with half a carucate of land and 10 acres of meadow. 3 bordars and 1 plough in demesne and 1 mill. Then it was worth 20s. and now the same. In the same place 9 free men commended to Eadric with 28 acres and 1 plough and 1 acre of meadow. Then it was worth 5s. and now the same. It is 8 furlongs long and 5 broad. 7½d. in geld. Norman holds this.

In Thorpe 4 free men commended to Eadric with 24 acres. 1 plough. 3 bordars with 6 acres. They are all in the valuation of Leiston.

In Cransford 5 free men commended to Eadric with 35 acres. Then 1 plough, now a half. Their valuation is in Dennington. He holds this in demesne.

In Boyton William Goulafre holds from Robert Malet 12 free men commended to Eadric with 60 acres. Then 4 ploughs, now 3. Half an acre of meadow. It is worth 16s. 2 churches with 30 acres, worth 5s.

In Rushmere 8 free men commended to Eadric with 52 acres of land. Then 3 ploughs, now 2. It is worth 7s. but it renders 17s. The same William holds it. In Boyton 1 free man commended to Eadric with 24 acres, worth 4s. The same William [holds it]. In Sternfield 15 free men commended to Eadric with 100 acres. 1 acre of meadow. Then 5 ploughs, now 4. 1 acre of meadow. Then it was worth 20s. now 44s. The same William [holds it]. In "Clepham" 10 acres in demesne, worth 2s. In Sudbourne Gilbert de Wissant holds from Robert Malet 12 free men commended to the same Eadric, with 60 acres. Then 3 ploughs, now 2. It is worth 20s. To one of these free [men] belonged a manor of 20 acres. 1 ox, 30 pigs, 40 sheep. 1 plough could be there. 1 mill. It is worth 10s. A church with 16 acres, worth 2s. In the same place

Robert Malet

Walter de Caen holds from Robert Malet 1 free man commended to Eadric with 30 acres and 1 bordar. Then as now 1 plough. 1 fishery. 1 acre of meadow. 1 salt-pan. It is worth 12s. In "Burgesgata" 1 acres, worth 3d.

In "Burch" 1 free man commended to Eadric TRE [held] 6 acres, worth 12d. In "Ingoluestuna" 6 acres, worth 12d. In "Prestetuna" 1 bordar with 3 acres and half an acre of meadow, worth 6d.

HUNDRED OF WILFORD.

In Hollesley Eadric of Laxfield held TRE 6 carucates of land as a manor. Then 18 villans, now 13. Then 4 bordars, now 12. Then in demesne 4 ploughs, now 2 and there could be 2 others. Then 8 ploughs belonging to the men, now 5; 30 acres of meadow. 1 fishery. 2 horses, 8 head of cattle, 30 pigs and 100 sheep. Robert has the soke and sake from the king. To this manor belong 5 men with 56 acres. Then 2 ploughs, now 1; 4 acres of meadow. These 5 could not sell their land nor give it to anyone. Then it was worth 100s., now £13. It is 1 league long and half a league and 1 furlong broad. 7d. in geld throughout the whole Hundred. 1 church with 14 acres, worth 2s. St Æthelthryth has the soke throughout the whole Hundred.

In Sutton 22 free men, 20 commended to Eadric and 2 to St Æthelthryth with 80 acres of land. Then 6 ploughs, now 5; 4 acres of meadow. They are in the valuation of Hollesley. It is 1 league long and 8 furlongs broad. 27d. in geld. In Capel [St Andrew] 2 free men commended to Eadric TRE with 3 acres of land. In "Laneburh" 1 free man commended to Eadric with 1 acre of land.

In Alderton 1 free man of Eadric with 1 acre of land. In 'Turstanestuna' [in Bromeswell] 3 free men commended to Eadric with 4½ acres. In Bawdsey 2 free men commended to Eadric with 13 acres. They are all in the valuation of Hollesley.

[Folio 317V: SUFFOLK]

In Sutton Leofstan, a free man of Eadric, held TRE 60 acres of land as one manor. Then 1 plough, now a half. 2 acres of meadow. Then as now worth 3s. 2 half free men under him with 4 acres in the same valuation. The mother of Robert Malet holds from him "Culeslea", 1 berewick of Hollesley, with 1 carucate of land and 80 acres. Then as now 1 villan and 13 bordars. Then in demesne 4 ploughs, now 2. Then as now 3 ploughs belonging to the men. 6 acres of meadow. Then it was worth 60s., now the same. It is 1 league long and 6 furlongs broad. 27d. in geld. In the same place 2 free men commended to Eadric TRE [held] 8 acres, worth 16d. Bawdsey. 1 berewick of Hollesley which Robert de Glanville holds from Robert Malet with 1 carucate of land. Then as now 3 bordars. Then 1½ ploughs, now 2. Then it was worth 25s., now 40s. It is 1 league long and 5 furlongs broad. 27d. in geld. In the same vill 17 free men commended to Eadric TRE [held] 60 acres of land. Then 3 ploughs, now 1 and a half. 4 acres of meadow. Then it was worth 10s., now 12s.

In Hoo [in Sutton] 1 free man with the fourth part worth 2d. In Alderton 31 free men TRE, now 34, commended to Eadric. Of these Godric the predecessor of Swein had commendation over two and a half but William Malet was seised. 1 carucate of land and 80 acres and 1½ bordars. Then 6 ploughs, now 5; 20 acres of meadow. Then it was worth 40s. now 100s. 1 church with 24 acres and 1 acre of meadow, worth 3s.

In Hollesley 1 mill, worth 12s. All this Robert de Glanville holds from Robert Malet. In Bawdsey 12 free men and a half commended to Eadric TRE [held] 72 acres. Then as now 2 ploughs. 1 acre of meadow. Then it was worth 12s., now 30s. 1 church with 20 acres, worth 3s. The mother of Robert Malet holds this from him. In Alderton 2 free men

Robert Malet

[Folio 318: SUFFOLK]

commended to Eadric [held] 32 acres. Then as now 1 plough. Half an acre of meadow. Then it was worth 4s., now 10s. Walter de Caen holds this from Robert Malet.

In "Littlecros" 7 villans with 40 acres. Then 2 ploughs, now 1; 3 acres of meadow. Then it was worth 5s., now 10s. In Alderton 1 free man with 12 acres commended to Eadric; worth 2s. In Sutton Walter de Caen holds from Robert Malet half a free man by the name of Godwine, commended to Eadric, with 12 acres as one manor. [...] Half a bordar. Then half a plough, now the same. 1 acre of meadow. 3 head of cattle, 60 sheep. Then it was worth 2s., now 5s. In the same place 9 free men under him and 1 free man commended to Halfdan TRE [held] 40 acres of land. Then 1 plough, now 1. Half an acre of meadow. Then it was worth 4s., now 7s. In Capel [St Andrew] 3 free men and a half commended to Godwine with 15 acres of land. Then 1 plough, now a half. Then it was worth 2s., now 4s. It is 1 league long and a half broad. 27d. in geld. Others hold [land] there.

In Shottisham 1 free man and a half under the same commendation with 7 acres, worth 12d.

In Bromeswell 1 free man and a half commended to Godwine [held] 8 acres. Half a plough. It is worth 16d. The same Walter holds this from Robert Malet.

In Bredfield the same W[alter] holds from Robert Malet 3 whole free men and 3 half free men and a fourth part of 1 free man, with 24 acres. Then 2 ploughs, now a half. It is worth 6s. 2d. Mainard claims of this Godwine of Sutton that Earl Ralph was seised of him one year before he forfeited and the Hundred testifies that Robert Malet was seised of him.

In Sutton the same Walter holds from Robert Malet 2 free men commended to Eadric with 61 acres and under one of them 5 free men. Then as now 2 ploughs. 1½ acres of meadow. Then it was worth 7s., now 15s. 1 church with 20 acres. [It is] in the above valuation.

[Folio 318v: SUFFOLK]

In Wilford Robert Malet holds in demesne 1 sokeman, Ædi, commended to Eadric with 60 acres. Then as now 2 bordars. Then 1 plough, now none. 4 acres of meadow. Then it was worth 16s., now 10s. It is 1 league long and a half broad. 13½d. in geld.

Humphrey fitzRobert holds Boyton from Robert Malet which Stanwine, commended to Eadric, held TRE with 2 carucates of land as one manor. Then 3 villans, now none. Then 18 bordars, now 15. Then in demesne 2 ploughs, now 1. Then 4 ploughs belonging to the men, now 1 but there could be [3 more]. 10 acres of meadow. Then 2 horses, now none. Then 9 head of cattle, now 1. Then 24 pigs, now 17. Then 300 sheep, now 70. Then 1 mill. Then it was worth 60s. now 60s. 1 church with 8 acres, worth 12d.

In the same place 8 free men commended to Stanwine with 63 acres. Then 2 ploughs, now 1½. Then it was worth 24s., now 22s. In "Laneburc" Beorhtmær, commended to Eadric, with 5 acres, worth 12d. Walter holds it in demesne.

In "Laneburc" 3 free men commended to Eadric with 30 acres and 1 bordar. Then 1½ ploughs, now a half. Then it was worth 10s., now 12s. In Melton 2 free men commended to Eadric with 64 acres and 1 free man under him with 1 acre. Then as now 1½ ploughs. Then it was worth 15s., now 10s. Humphrey holds this from Robert Malet.

Malet's mother holds "Halgestou" which Godric, Eadric's sokeman, held. He could not sell or give it TRE. 1 carucate of land and 20 acres. 1 villan and 1 bordar. Then 2 ploughs, now 1; 2 acres of meadow. 1 mill. Then as now worth 17s. 4d. Ralph holds Ramsholt from Robert Malet 3 free men and a half, commended to Godric Swein's predecessor, TRE with 29 acres. Then 1 plough, now 2. Then it was worth 10s., now 5s. In the same place 5 free men commended to Eadric except that one was half commended to Roger Bigod's predecessor

Robert Malet

[Folio 319: SUFFOLK]

[held] 16 acres. Then 1 plough, now a half. It is worth 2s. Also in the same place 80 acres in Malet's demesne. Then it was worth 5s., now 7s.

In Sutton 1 free man commended to Eadric TRE; now his 3 sons dwell there with 25 acres. 1 free man under him with 1 acre. Then as now half a plough. Then it was worth 4s., now 5s. In the same place 1 free man under the same commendation with 10 acres and 1 plough. 1 acre of meadow. It is worth 2s. 8d. This Ralph holds from Robert Malet.

In Charsfield Robert de Glanville holds from Robert Malet 24 free men, commended to Eadric TRE, with 2 carucates of land and 5 bordars. Then 5 ploughs, now 4; 4 acres of meadow. Then it was worth 30s., now 40s. It is 1 league long and 5 furlongs broad. 13½d. in geld. To the church belong 36 acres, worth 3s.

In Bromeswell Gilbert de Coleville holds from Robert Malet 4 free men and a half, commended to Eadric with 26 acres of land and 1½ acres of meadow. Then as now half a plough. It is worth 4s. In Boulge Robert de Glanville holds from Robert Malet 1 priest, Wulfwine. 1 church with 25 acres and 3 bordars and 1 acre [of meadow], worth 3s. 2d. In Bredfield 1 church with 36 acres, worth 3s.

In Capel [St Andrew] Walter fitzAubrey holds from Robert Malet 20 free men commended to Eadric with 1 carucate of land and 61 acres and 4 acres of meadow. Then 6 ploughs, now 3. Then it was worth 60s., now the same. A church with 12 acres, worth 2s. In Sutton 1 free man commended to Eadric [held] 80 acres as a manor. Then as now 1 plough. 3 acres of meadow. Then it was worth 20s., now the same. In the same place 8 free men commended to Lustwine TRE [held] 40 acres. 2 acres of meadow. Then 2 ploughs, now 1. Then it was worth 4s., now 7s. In Bromeswell 6 acres, worth 12d. In Shottisham 1 free man, Sigeric, commended to King Edward [held] 12 acres and half an acre of meadow. Then it was worth 2s., now 4s. In the same place 4 free men, 2 commended to Godric and the other 2 commended to

[Folio 319v: SUFFOLK]

Osmund TRE, [held] 32½ acres. Then 1 plough, now a half. Then it was worth 4s., now 6s. In Bing, 1 berewick of Staverton; Eadric held 1½ carucates. Then 1 villan and now [the same]. Then 1 bordar, now 2. Then and now 1 slave. Then 1 plough, now none ; 2 acres of meadow. 1 horse, 4 head of cattle, 16 pigs and 80 sheep. Then it was worth 20s. now 40s. In the same place 20 free men and in Loudham 10 whole and two half [free men] with 1 carucate of land commended to Eadric TRE. Then 6 ploughs, now 3, and 4 acres of meadow. Then it was worth 30s., now 40s.

In Loudham 2 free men under the same commendation with 24 acres and 4½ acres of meadow. Then 1 plough and 1 mill;

now half a plough. Then it was worth 20s., now the same. Walter fitzAubrey holds this from Robert Malet.

In Bromeswell Hubert de Mont-Canisy holds from Robert Malet 16 free men commended to Eadric with 60 acres and 1 bordar. Then 2 ploughs, now 1½. 4 acres of meadow. Then it was worth 16s., now 20s.

HUNDRED OF HARTISMERE.

Eadric held Eye with 12 carucates of land TRE; now Robert holds it in demesne [...] and his mother holds 100 acres. 1 villan and 3 bordars and 9 sokemen with 16 acres. Then 2 ploughs, now 1. It is worth 20s. Then 39 villans, now 20. Then and afterwards 9 bordars, now 16. Then 12 slaves, now none. Then and afterwards 8 ploughs in demesne, now 5. Then and afterwards 15 ploughs belonging to the men, now 6, and other ploughs could be restored. 50 acres of meadow. Then woodland for 120 pigs, now 60. Then as now 1 mill and 1 fishery. Then 7 horses, now 1. Then 24 head of cattle, now none. Then 50 pigs, now 17. Then 80 sheep, now 90. Now 1 market and 1 park and in the market dwell 25 burgesses. To this manor belong 48 sokemen with 121 acres of land. Of these sokemen 37 are in demesne. Herbert holds 9

Robert Malet

[Folio 320: SUFFOLK]

with 20 acres and Walter 1 with 5 acres and Walter the crossbowman 1 with 16 acres. All this is worth 9s. Then 4 ploughs, now 3, and 1 acre of meadow. Then it was worth £15, now £21. Eadric had soke and sake of the bishopric . There belong also to this manor 9 free men with 110 acres of land in the soke and commendation of Eadric TRE. Then 4½ now 4, and 3 acres of meadow. Then woodland for 16 pigs, now 6. It is worth 20s. These nine are called Æthelstan, Wulfric, Godwine, Leofwine, Eadric, Ælfsige, Ælfric, Godric, Dynechaie.

In the same vill 1 free man, Wulfric commended to Eadric, [held] 30 acres as one manor TRE; now Walter de Caen holds it from Robert. Then as now 2 bordars. Then 1 plough, now a half. It is worth 20s. In the same place 1 church, St Peter's, to which belong 2 carucates of free land and 7 bordars. Then 1 plough in demesne, now 3. Then as now 1 plough belonging to the men and 3 acres of meadow and 1 mill. It is worth 40s. In the same place 1 free man, Svartrikr commended to Harold and in his soke, held 120 acres as one manor TRE; now Robert holds it in demesne. Then as now 4 bordars and 1 plough in demesne. 4 acres of meadow. Woodland for 3 pigs. It is worth 20s. It is 2½ leagues long and 1½ leagues broad. 2s. in geld.

In Redlingfield 1 free man, Ælfric commended to Eadric, [held] 3 carucates of land as a manor TRE. Then as now 11 villans and 4 bordars. Then 2 slaves. Then 2 ploughs in demesne, now 3. Then as now 2 ploughs belonging to the men. Then woodland for 100 pigs, now 50, and 6 acres of meadow. 1 church with 12 acres. Now 1 horse. Then as now 12 pigs and 24 sheep and 34 goats. Then it was worth 60s., now 100s. William d'Arques holds it from Robert Malet. The king and the earl have the soke. 7 furlongs broad and 7 long. 6d. in geld. In Occold 5 free men

[Folio 320V: SUFFOLK]

Smert, Rawn, Wynstan, Godric, Leofric, Ælfgifu commended to Eadric and in his soke [held] 46 acres. Then 2 ploughs, now 1½. Woodland for 6 pigs and 1 acre of meadow. It is worth 10s. The mother of Robert Malet holds it.

In Gislingham 2 free men, Stanheard and Stubart, commended to Eadric [held] 30 acres in the soke of the king and the earl. Then as now 2 bordars. Then [and] later 1½ ploughs, now 1; 1½ acres of meadow. Woodland for 5 pigs. Then it was worth 4s., now 5s. The mother of Robert Malet holds it.

In Mellis 1 free [man], Fulcard, half commended to Eadric with 27 acres and 1 bordar and 1 plough and 1 acre of meadow. Half a church with 8 acres, worth 10s. The king and the earl have the soke. The mother of Robert holds it.

In Yaxley Alnoth, a free man half commended to Eadric, [held] 8½ acres, worth 12d. The king and the earl have the soke. Hubert holds it.

In Wortham 1 free man, Algar commended to Eadric, [held] 4 acres, worth 8d. The king and the earl have the soke.

In Braiseworth 4 free men commended to Eadric [held] 38 acres of land. Then 1½ ploughs, now 1. It is worth 7s. 6d. The king and the earl have the soke.

In Thornham Parva 2 free men commended to Eadric [held] 7 acres, worth 16d. And the mother of Robert holds it.

In Thornham Magna 1 free man, Stanheard commended to Eadric, [held] 4 acres, worth 12d. The king and the earl have the soke. The mother of Robert holds it.

In Aspall Beorhtmær, a free man commended to Eadric, [held] 30 acres as one manor TRE. Then as now 1 plough and 1 acre of meadow and 24 sheep. It is worth 10s. The mother of Robert [holds it].

In Thrandeston Alweard, a free man commended to Eadric, [held] 36 acres as a manor TRE. Then and afterwards 1 plough, now 2 oxen. 1 acre of meadow. It is worth 5s.

Robert Malet

[Folio 321: SUFFOLK]

The same Alweard holds from Malet. The king and the earl have the soke. In the same place 2 free men, Godric and Leofstan, commended to Eadric [held] 15 acres in the king's and the earl's soke. And half a plough. It is worth 26d. Walter holds it from Robert. In Brome 2 free men commended to Edric [held] 4 acres in the king's soke, worth 8d. The same Walter [holds this]. In Thrandeston the same Walter holds 2 villans with 24 acres of the demesne of Eye, worth 4s.

In Braiseworth 3 free men commended to Eadric [held] 17 acres and half a plough, worth 6d. William Goulafre holds it. The king and the earl have the soke. In the same place Robert has two parts of a church. In Fressingfield Alwine, a sokeman, held 6 acres, worth 12d. In Knettishall 1 free man by commendation [held] 3 acres, worth 6d. The king and the earl have the soke.

HUNDRED OF HARTISMERE.

In Finningham the mother of Robert Malet holds from Robert Malet and from the queen's fief 18 free men with 1½ carucates of land. 1 of these had the name Almær over whose wife St Edmund had commendation and 2 of these, Leofwine and Beorhtmær, were commended to Leofwine. All the others were commended to Leofric and Wulfgifu TRE and under them [were] 3 free men with 5 acres and 1 bordar. Then 3½ ploughs, now the same. Woodland for 16 pigs. 5 acres of meadow. Then it was worth 30s., now 50s. It is half a league long and a half broad. 8d. in geld. The king and the earl [have] the soke.

In Westhorpe 3 free men and a half [held] 30 acres. Then as now 1 plough. 1 acre of meadow. Then it was worth 50d., now 5s. The king and the earl [have] the soke. Of these three the Abbot of St Edmund claims 1, Ordric, with 10 acres and the others are commended to Wulfric, the predecessor of Eudo fitzSpirewic.

[Folio 321V: SUFFOLK]

In Wyverstone 4 free men, Wulfmær, Alflæd, Wulfwine and Alwine. Alflæd and Alwine were commended to Malet's predecessor. The Abbot of St Edmund had three parts of the commendation over Wulfwine. Altogether they have 67 acres. Then 1 plough, now a half. Woodland for 4 pigs. Then it was worth 6s. 8d. and now the same. The king and the earl [have] the soke apart from over him who was commended to the abbot so far as relates to three parts of the commendation.

In "Caldecota" 6 free men commended to Leofwine of Bacton [held] 74 acres. Under them 7 free men by commendation with 6½ acres. Then as now 1 bordar and 1½ ploughs. 1 acre of meadow. It is worth 11s. 10d. The king and the earl [have] the soke. Afterwards Walter de Dol was seised of one, namely Wulfgifu, and her son, on the day when he forfeited.

Wulfgifu, commended to Stigand, held Stoke [Ash] with 1 carucate of land and 40 acres as a manor. Then 4 bordars, now 8. Then as now 2 slaves and 3 ploughs in demesne. 4 acres of meadow. Woodland for 8 pigs. A church with 15 acre. Then 1 plough, now a half. Then 1 horse, now 2 and 6 head of cattle. Then 12 pigs, now 6, and 20 goats. Then as now worth 100s. 5 free men by commendation with 32 acres. Then 1 plough, now a half. 1 acre of meadow. It is worth 5s. 4d. It is 10 furlongs long and 6 broad. 6d. in geld. Wulfgifu has the soke. The king and the earl [have] the soke over the free men.

In Thornham Magna 24 free men with 1 carucate of land and 12 acres. Then and afterwards 6 ploughs, now 4. And 2 head of cattle. 4 acres of meadow. Then as now worth 23s. Over all these Wulfgifu had the commendation except over one by the name of Wulfric who was half under commendation to the Abbot of St Edmund. The king and the earl [have] the soke.

Robert Malet

[Folio 322: SUFFOLK]

In Thornham [Magna] Beorhtmær, commended to Wulfgifu, held 26 acres and half a plough. Then [it was worth] 5s., now 7s. The king and the earl [have] the soke. In the same place 4 free men. Walter de Dol was seised of half one [free man], by the name of Brungar, when he made made 108 acres. Over 2 and a half Wulfgifu had commendation and over half a [free man] the Abbot of St Edmund had commendation and over a fourth Burgheard had commendation. Then 4 ploughs, now 2; 1½ acres of meadow. 1 horse, 1 ox, 25 pigs, 16 sheep and 27 goats. Then as now worth 20s. The king and the earl [have] the soke.

In Gislingham 3 free men. Over two Wulfgifu had commendation. 7 acres and half a plough, worth 16d. In the same place 2 free men with 26 acres, one by the name of Coleman commended to Wulfgifu with 6 acres. Then half a plough, now none. It is worth 4s. In the same place Ælfgeat, a free man commended to Alsige, nephew of Earl Ralph, held 30 acres as a manor TRE. Then 1 plough, now none. 1 acre of meadow. In the same place 6 free men commended to Ælfgeat [held] 13 acres. Then as now half a plough. Then it was worth 20s., now 12s. In the same place Hringwulf, a free man commended to Alsige, nephew of Earl Ralph, held 30 acres as one manor. Then 1 plough, now none. Of this land Leofwine, son of Hringwulf, holds 3 acres [and] a fourth part of the woodland. In the same place 4 free men commended to Hringwulf [held] 10 acres. Half a plough and 4 acres of meadow. Woodland for 10 pigs. Then it was worth 20s. now 10s.

In the same place Bosi, a free man commended to Alsige, [held] 16 acres. Then and afterwards 1 plough, now none. It is worth 6s. 8d. Of this land the predecessor of Aubrey de Vere held 5 acres. The king and the earl [have] soke over the whole.

In the same place 1 free man, Sorcbes commended to Wulfgifu, [held] 6 acres,

[Folio 322v: SUFFOLK]

worth 12d. In the same place Cypping, a free man commended to Wulfwine the predecessor of Aubrey de Vere and in his soke, [held] 12 acres and he also held 1 acre of land from the demesne of Wulfwine and a fourth part of another. Now the mother of Robert holds it all. It is worth 2s. The king and the earl [have] the soke over all the rest. In Cotton Esger, a free man commended to Leofwine of Bacton, held 30 acres as a manor TRE. Then 1 plough, now a half. 1 acre of meadow. Woodland for 6 pigs. And 3 free men by commendation [held] 60 acres and half a plough, worth 10s. The king and the earl [have] the soke.

In the same place Tet, half under commendation to Eadric the king's reeve and half under commendation to Malet's predecessor, held 8 acres. Then as now half a plough. It is worth 4s. The soke is the king's and the earl's.

In Thornham Parva 8 free men commended to Wulfgifu [held] 28 acres. Then 2 ploughs, now 1½. It is worth 5s. In the same place 2 free men one of them commended to Wulfgifu and the other half commended to Malet's predecessor [held] 15 acres. Then as now 1 plough. Then it was worth 40d., now 5s. In the same place a free man, Sigeric commended to Wulfgifu, [held] 14 acres. Then 1 plough, now a half. Then it was worth 3s., now 4s. In the same place 3 parts of a church with 10 acres and half a plough. The king and the earl have the soke over the whole.

In Wortham Sigeric, a free man commended to Stigand, [held] 20 acres. Then as now 2 bordars and half a plough. 1

acre of meadow. Woodland then for 6 pigs, now for 2; 3 free men under him with 6 acres. It is worth 5s. Stigand had the soke. In Stoke [Ash] the same Sigeric held 20 acres and 2 bordars. Then 1 plough in demesne, now a half. 2 acres of meadow. It is worth 5s. Stigand had the soke. In Aspall the same Sigeric

Robert Malet

[Folio 323: SUFFOLK]

held 30 acres as a manor. Then as now 3 bordars and 1 plough and 4 acres of meadow. Woodland for 60 pigs. 13 head of cattle. Then it was worth 10s., now 15s. Stigand had the soke.

In Rishangles Wulfgifu, commended to Stigand, held 220 acres as a manor TRE. Then as now 3 villans and 7 bordars. Then 3 slaves, now 2. Then as now 3 ploughs in demesne and 2 ploughs belonging to the men. 4 acres of meadow. Then woodland for 240 pigs, now for 120. A church with 20 acres and 1 plough. Then as now 2 horses and 7 head of cattle, now 7 pigs and 30 goats. Then it was worth 50s., now 60s. Wulfgifu had the soke from Stigand. In the same place 4 free men commended to Wulfgifu [held] 40 acres. Then as now 2 ploughs and 1 acre of meadow. Woodland for 6 pigs. It is worth 6s. 8d. The king and the earl [have] the soke. It is 14 furlongs long and 10 broad. 9d. [...] in geld.

Wulfgifu held Thorndon under Stigand with 3 carucates of land and 40 acres as one manor TRE. Then as now 4 villans and 16 bordars. Then 4 slaves, now 2. Then as now 4 ploughs in demesne and 3 ploughs belonging to the men. 6 acres of meadow. Then woodland for 200 pigs, now 120. Now 1 mill. A church with 50 acres of free land and 1 plough and 1 acre of meadow. Then as now 2 horses and 15 head of cattle. Then 40 pigs, now 31. Then 60 sheep, now 24. Then it was worth £5, now £8. Wulfgifu had the soke from Stigand.

In the same place Thorkil, a free man commended to Wulfgifu, [held] 30 acres as a manor. Then as now 2 bordars and 1½ ploughs. 1 acre of meadow. It is worth 10s. The king and the earl [have] the soke. In the same place 7 free men with 88 acres. Then as now 2 ploughs and 2 acres of meadow. It is worth 20s. The king and the earl [have] the soke. In Occold 7 free men commended to Wulfgifu [held] 50 acres. Then

[Folio 323v: SUFFOLK]

2 ploughs, now 1½; 1 acre of meadow. It is worth 9s. The soke is the king's and the earl's. Wulfgifu held Braiseworth as a manor with 60 acres and 1 villan and 1 plough and 4 acres of meadow and 1 mill. Half a church with 17 acres and half a plough. 4 head of cattle and 8 pigs. It is worth 15s. Wulfgifu [had] the soke from Stigand. In the same place 1 free man with 3 acres in the same valuation. In the same place 15 free men with 140 acres and 1 bordar. Then 4 ploughs, now 3; 1 acre of meadow. Half a church with 15 acres and half a plough, worth 30s. The king and the earl [have] the soke. It is 6 furlongs long and 5 broad. 9d. in geld.

In Braiseworth 8 free men [held] 5 acres, worth 12d. The king and the earl [have] the soke. In the same place Beorhtmær Bubba, a free man of Harold, held 20 acres.

Then half a plough, now none. It is worth 5s. The king and the earl [have] the soke.

In Mellis Leofric held 60 acres as a manor. Then and afterwards 1 plough, now none. 3 free men by commendation [held] 15 acres. Then and afterwards half a plough, now 2 oxen. Then it was worth 20s., now 10s. Wulfwine, the predecessor of Aubrey de Vere, [had] half the commendation and half the soke and Wulfgifu [had] half the commendation and the king [had] half the soke.

In Braiseworth Æthelstan, a free man commended to Wulfgifu, [held] 30 acres as a manor. Then as now 1 plough and 1 acre of meadow. It is worth 5s. The king and the earl [have] the soke.

In Yaxley Hagris, commended to Wulfgifu, held 15 acres. Then as now half a plough. It is worth 4s. The king and the earl [have] the soke. The mother of Robert Malet holds all this from him from the queen's fief.

In Wickham [Skeith] 2 free men commended to Wulfgifu [held] 16 acres and half a plough. It is worth 3s. The king and the earl [have] the soke. The mother of Robert holds it from the same fief. In Finningham 1 free man by commendation [held] 2 acres, worth 4d.

In Bedingfield 1 free man commended to Wulfgifu [held] half an acre,

Robert Malet

[Folio 324: SUFFOLK]

worth 2d. The mother of Robert holds it. The king and the earl [have] the soke.

In Gislingham 1 free man commended to Alsige, the nephew of Earl Ralph, [held] 3 acres, worth 12d. The king and the earl [have] the soke. In Wetheringsett 1 free man, Godric, [held] 7 acres, worth 4s.

HUNDRED OF WILFORD.

In Bromeswell Hubert holds from Robert Malet 44 acres of land and 6 acres of meadow. It is in the demesne of Staverton.

In Stokerland Gilbert holds from Robert Malet 2 free men commended to Eadric with 30 acres. Then as now half a plough. Half an acre of meadow. Then it was worth 20d., now 5s. In the same place 1 sokeman with 30 acres and he was not able to sell nor to give it. Then as now 1 plough. 2 acres of meadow. Then it was worth 5s., now 8s. In Loudham 1 free man under the same commendation, Eadric, with 8 acres, worth 16d. Walter the crossbowman holds Shottisham from Robert Malet, which Osmund, a free man commended to Eadric, held TRE with 44 acres as a manor and 1 bordar. Then 1 plough, now a half. 2 acres of meadow. Then it was worth 20s., now 10s. It is 7 furlongs long and 4 broad. 13½d. in geld. 1 church with 13 acres, worth 32d.

In the same place 12 free men commended to Eadric and 3 commended to Godric of Peyton [held] 80 acres. Then 3 ploughs, now 1½; 1 acre of meadow. Then it was worth 16s., now 20s. Walter the crossbowman holds this from Robert Malet.

Gilbert de Wissant holds Ufford from Robert Malet which Almær, a free man, commended half to Eadric and half to St

Æthelthryth, held as one manor TRE with 60 acres. Then 4 bordars, now 2. Then 1½ ploughs, now a half. 3 acres of meadow and 1 mill. Then as now worth 10s. In the same place 9 free men under the same commendation except 2 who were commended to St Æthelthryth [held] 25 acres and 2 acres of meadow. Then as now

[Folio 324V: SUFFOLK]

1 plough. Then and always it was worth 4s. In Alderton 1 free man commended to Eadric [held] 8 acres, worth 16d. In Wickham [Market] 4 free men under the same commendation TRE [held] 16 acres, worth 12d. In Sogenhoe 1 free man commended to Eadric [held] 20 acres. Half an acre of meadow. It is worth 16d. In Ufford 1 free man commended to Eadric [held] 6 acres, worth 12d. In Boulge 1 free man and a half commended to Eadric [held] 3½ acres, worth 6d. Gilbert holds this from Robert Malet.

In Bing Walter de Caen holds from Robert Malet one free man, Godric, commended to Eadric with 40 acres and 1 bordar. Then as now 1 plough. Then as now worth 7s. 2 free men under him with 12 acres and half a plough, worth 2s.

In Bredfield 2 free men commended to Eadric [held] 27 acres. Then half a plough, now none. It is worth 3s. 4d. In Loudham 1 free man, Morewine, commended half to St Æthelthryth and half to Eadric held as a manor 40 acres and 1 bordar. Then as now 1 plough. And under him [were] 14 free men with 40 acres and 5 acres of meadow. Then 2 ploughs, now 1. Then as now 20s. Walter de Caen holds this from Robert Malet. It is 1 league long and 7 furlongs broad. In geld 27d. In Sutton 1 free man commended to Eadric [held] 13 acres of land. Then half a plough, now 2 oxen. It is worth 16d. Hubert holds this from Robert Malet.

In Bromeswell 1 free man commended to Eadric [held] 16 acres, worth 16d. 1 church with 6 acres, worth 6d. Hubert holds this from Robert Malet.

In "Hundesthoft" William holds from Robert Malet 2 free men commended with 22 acres, worth 2s. 4d. The mother of Robert Malet holds Harpole which Huna, a free man of Eadric, held TRE as a manor with 100 acres and 4 bordars. Then 1½ ploughs, now 1; 5 acres of meadow. 8 pigs, 30 sheep. Then and always worth 20s. In the same place 10 free men commended to Eadric and 4 in Wickham [Market] over 2 St Æthelthryth had half the commendation

Robert Malet

[Folio 325: SUFFOLK]

and Robert Malet's predecessor had half [held] 29 acres. Then 1 plough, now a half. Then as now worth 40d. In Sutton Robert Malet holds in demesne 1 free man commended to Eadric with 16 acres and half a plough, worth 4s. In Harpole 1 free man, Bondi, commended half to Eadric with 15 acres and half a plough. 1½ acres of meadow. It is worth 5s. The mother of Robert Malet holds this.

In Sutton 3 free men commended to Eadric [held] 44 acres. Then 2 ploughs, now a half. 1 acre of meadow. Then it was worth 5s., now 4s. Gilbert Blond holds this from Robert Malet.

In Ufford 1 free man commended to Eadric [held] 8 acres and 1 acre of meadow. It is in the valuation of Dennington. In Wilford 1 free man commended to Eadric [held] 8 2 acres, worth 4d. I [sic]

In the same place 30 acres and they belong to Hollesley and [are] in the valuation. In Loudham 1 free man of Eadric with 8 acres. It is in the valuation of Dennington. In Bredfield 1 free man commended to St Æthelthryth [held] 6 acres, worth 12d. Norman holds it from Robert Malet. In Harpole 1 free man [held] 3 acres, worth 7d.

HUNDRED OF LOOSE.

Hubert holds Staverton from Robert Malet which Eadric of Laxfield [held] as a manor with 4 carucates of land TRE. Then 14 villans, now 9. Then 6 bordars, now 15. Then 4 slaves. Then in demesne 4 ploughs, now 2, and 2 could be remade. Then as now 2 ploughs belonging to the men. 8 acres of meadow. Woodland for 30 pigs. 1 mill. 2 head of cattle, 12 pigs, 80 sheep, 20 goats and 4 beehives. Then it was worth £6, now £4. 1 church with 10 acres, worth 20d. It is 1½ leagues long and a half broad. In geld 22d. In the same vill 13 free men commended to Eadric of Laxfield with 57 acres and 3 acres of meadow. Then 2 ploughs, now 1½. Then it was worth 10s., now the same. Hubert de Mont-Canisy holds this from Robert Malet.

In Kettleburgh Humphrey holds from Robert Malet 1 free man commended to Eadric TRE with 100 acres of land as a manor and 3 bordars. Then and now 1 plough. 3½ acres of meadow. 4 head of cattle and 7 pigs and 30 sheep. Then it was worth 10s., now 15s.

[Folio 325v: SUFFOLK]

1 free man, commended to the same Eadric, held Monewden as a manor with 1 carucate of land TRE. Then 2 bordars, now 3. Then 2 ploughs, now 1 and half a plough belonging to the men. 3 acres of meadow. Then 3 head of cattle, now none. Now 3 goats. Then it was worth 40s., now 30s. The same Humphrey holds [this]. 1 free man under him [holds] 5 acres, worth 10d. It is 1 league long and 4 [furlongs] broad. In geld 9d. In Woodbridge 1 free man commended to Robert Malet's predecessor [held] 20½ acres and half a plough, worth 5s. 8d. The same Humphrey holds this.

Eadric of Laxfield held Framlingham TRE with 80 acres and 14 as a berewick. Then as now 2 villans and 4 bordars. Then as now in demesne 2 ploughs and 1 belonging to the men. Woodland for 4 pigs. 2 acres of meadow. Then as now horse, 4 head of cattle, 4 pigs and 5 beehives. It is in the valuation of Dennington. A half free man commended to Eadric [held] 4 acres in the above valuation. In the same place a half free man, Beorhtnoth, under the same commendation with 2 acres. Robert Malet holds [this] in demesne. In the same place Walter de Caen holds from Robert Malet that which 1 sokewoman, Gifu, commended to Eadric, held TRE with 80 acres as one manor. Then as now 1 villan and 4 bordars. 1 plough in demesne and 1 plough belonging to the men. Woodland for 4 pigs. 4 acres of meadow. Then it was worth 13s. 4d., now the same. 1 free man, Thorkil, under the same commendation [held] 4 acres, worth 2s. The same Walter holds this. In Dallinghoo 1 free man half commended

to Eadric and half to St Æthelthryth [held] 13 acres and half a bordar and half an acre of meadow, worth 2s. 8d. The same Walter holds it.

In Framlingham 1 free man commended to Eadric [held] 2 acres, worth 8d. They are in the valuation of Dennington. In Hacheston 12 whole

Robert Malet

[Folio 326: SUFFOLK]

free men and 9 half free men commended to Eadric TRE [held] 60 acres and 28 and 6 bordars. Then 2 ploughs, now 1½; 2 acres of meadow. They are in the valuation of Dennington and he holds it in demesne. In Rendlesham 4 half free men commended to Eadric [held] 33 acres and 1 bordar. Then 1 plough, now a half. Half an acre of meadow. 2 free men under them with 2 acres. They are in the valuation of Dennington.

In Kettleburgh 1 sokeman commended to Eadric [held] 9 acres in the valuation of Dennington. In Rendlesham 1 free man and in Easton another one commended to Eadric with 15 acres. They are in the same valuation.

The mother of Robert Malet holds Kenton from Robert Malet which Beorhtmær, commended to Eadric, held TRE with 82 acres as a manor. Then as now 1 villan and 5 bordars and 1 slave. Then as now 1 plough in demesne and 2 ploughs belonging to the men. Woodland for 12 pigs. 2 acres of meadow. 1 horse, 16 head of cattle, 40 pigs and 3 beehives. Then as now worth 20s. 2 free men, 1 commended to Beorhtweald, the other commended to Beorhtmær, [held] 30 acres and 3 free men with 4 acres commended to Eadric. Then as now 1 plough. It is worth 7[s.] The mother of Robert Malet [holds this] from him. In the same place 1 free man, Huna, commended to Eadric [held] 30 acres Then as now half a plough and 1 bordar. It is worth 7s. In the same place William Goulafre holds 1 free man, Wudu-Brun, commended to Eadric, with 30 acres as a manor. Then 1 plough. Half an acre of meadow. It is worth 10s. It is 1 league long and a half broad. In geld 9d. 1 church with 30 acres, worth 5s. Several persons have a share there.

Gilbert de Coleville holds Rendlesham from Robert Malet which Ulfkil held TRE by commendation to Eadric of Laxfield with 1 carucate of land as a manor. Then as now 7 villans and 3 bordars. Then as now in demesne 2 ploughs. Then 1 plough belonging to the men, now a half. 4 acres of meadow. 1 mill. Then 2 horses, now none. Now 2 head of cattle. Then 26 pigs, now 8. Then 36 sheep, now 10. Then and now worth 40s. In the same place 9 free men [...]

[Folio 326v: SUFFOLK]

under the same commendation with 30 acres of land. Then 2 ploughs, now 1; 1 acre of meadow. It is worth 5s. In Staverton 1 free man commended to Eadric of Laxfield [held] 30 acres. Then 1 bordar. Then as now 1 plough. 1½ acres of meadow. It is worth 10s.

In "Clachestorp" 6 whole free men half free men commended to Ulfkil [held] 42 acres. Then 2 ploughs, now 1. It is worth 7s. In Gedgrave 5 bordars under the same commendation with 30 acres. Then 1 plough. It is worth 5s. It is 1 league long and 2 furlongs broad. 7½d. in geld.

In Marlesford 1 free man commended to Eadric [held] 36 acres as one manor. Then 1 plough, now a half. 1 acre of meadow. Then [worth] 10s., now 5s. And 6 free men under the same commendation with 21 acres. Then half a plough. Worth 2s. 8d.

In "Possefelda" 2 free men commended to Eadric [held] 30 acres and 1 bordar. Then 1 plough, now a half. 3 acres of meadow. Then as now worth 10s.

In "Brodertuna" 1 free woman under the same commendation [held] 4 acres, worth 8d. In Campsey [Ash] 4 acres, worth 8d. Gilbert holds this from Robert Malet. In Staverton Hubert holds from Robert Malet 2 free men commended to Eadric with 14 acres. Then as now half a plough. Worth 2s. 4d. In Rendlesham 1 free man commended to Eadric [held] 30 acres and 1 villan and 1 bordar and 1 plough. Worth 5s. 1 church with 20 acres, worth 40d. Gilbert de Wissant holds it from Robert Malet.

In the same place 1 free man under the same commendation [held] 12 acres. Half a plough. Worth 2s.

In Ash 12 free men commended to Eadric TRE [held] 1 carucate of land. Then 2½ ploughs, now 1½. Then as now worth 20s.

In Hacheston 1 sokeman with 30 acres, commended to Eadric, and 1 bordar. Then and now [...] 1 plough. 2 acres of meadow. Then it was worth 5s., now 8s.

Robert Malet

[Folio 327: SUFFOLK]

In the same place 1 free man commended to Eadric [held] 6 acres, worth 12d. In the same place 4 free men commended to Eadric [held] 40 acres. Then 1 plough, now 1; 2 acres of meadow. Then it was worth 7s., now 6s. Also in the same place 7 free men commended to Eadric with 24 acres. Then 1½ ploughs, now a half. 1 acre of meadow. It is worth 4s. Gilbert holds this from Robert Malet.

In "Clachestorp" Walter de Risbou holds from Robert Malet 3½ free men commended to Eadric with 22 acres. Then as now half a plough. Half an acre of meadow. It is worth 3s. In [Earl] Soham 1 sokeman commended to Eadric [held] 8 acres, worth 2s. The same Walter de Risbou [holds it] from Robert Malet.

In Gedgrave Gilbert de Wissant holds 1 free man commended to Eadric with 30 acres and 4 bordars and 1 plough, worth 5s.

In Woodbridge 2 free men with 43 acres and 1 sokeman with 8 acres. They were all commended to Eadric. Then as now 1 plough and 1 acre of meadow. It is worth 8s. It is 10 furlongs long and 5 long broad. In geld 11d. 1 church with 19 acres, worth 2s. The same Gilbert holds it.

In Campsey [Ash] 1 free man commended to Eadric [held] 10 acres and they are in the valuation of 'Kelton'. And in Framlingham 1 free man, Hereweald, commended to Eadric [held] 2 acres and they are in the valuation of Dennington.

In the same place Fulcred holds from Robert Malet 1 free man commended to Eadric with 10 acres, worth 2s.

In Ash 1 free man commended to Eadric [held] 17 acres and 3 bordars and half a plough, worth 3s. Northmann the sheriff holds this from Robert Malet. In Dallinghoo Robert de Glanville holds from Robert Malet 4 free men commended to Eadric with 80 acres and 17

[Folio 327v: SUFFOLK]

and 1 bordar. Then as now 2 ploughs. 2 acres of meadow. Woodland for 4 pigs. Then as now worth 21s. In Butley Walter fitzAubrey holds from Robert Malet 3 free men and a half commended to Eadric with 38 acres. Then 1½ ploughs, now 1. Then as now worth 5s. It is 6 furlongs long and 4 broad. In geld 7½d.

In Martley 1 free man commended to Eadric with 20 acres and half an acre of meadow. 5 bordars and half a plough. It is worth 8s. William Goulafre holds it from Robert Malet.

In Woodbridge 2 acres in the demesne of Hollesley.

HUNDRED OF WANGFORD.

In "Thicchebrom" Humphrey holds from Robert Malet 1 free man commended to Eadric of Laxfield with 16 acres of land, worth 2s. In the same place 1 free man under the same commendation [held] 16 acres and 1 bordar with half an acre. They are assessed in another Hundred.

In Barsham Warin fitzBurnin holds from Robert Malet 1 free man, Alwine, commended to Eadric with 10 acres. Then as now half a plough. It is worth 3s. In "Icheburna" 1 free man [held] 8 acres, worth 16d. In [South] Elmham 15 acres, worth 30d.

HUNDRED OF BLACKBOURN.

In Walsham [Le Willows] Hubert holds from Robert Malet 1 free man with 60 acres over whom his predecessor had commendation TRE. Then as now 1 plough and 2 acres of meadow. Woodland for 4 pigs. Then as now worth 10s. St Edmund has the soke and sake.

In Thelnetham 2 men with all customary dues but St Edmund [has] the soke. It has 20 acres and half a plough and 1 acre of meadow. It is worth 5s. 4d. and he holds it in demesne. In Stanton Walter de Caen holds from Robert Malet 1 free man over whom his predecessor had

Robert Malet

[Folio 328: SUFFOLK]

half the commendation and St Edmund half the commendation and the soke and sake. He has 90 acres and 3 bordars. 4 acres of meadow. Then as now 1 plough. Under him 1 free man who holds 10 acres which the same Walter holds. A church with 4 acres. The whole is worth 16s.

In Rickinghall [Inferior] Hubert holds from Robert Malet 1 free man with 30 acres. His predecessor [had] the commendation and St Edmund the soke. It is worth 5s.

HUNDRED OF BISHOP.

Eadric of Laxfield held Dennington TRE as a manor with 6 carucates of land and 20 acres. Then and afterwards 12 villans, now 16. Then and afterwards 16 bordars, now 15.

Then as now 2 slaves. 4 ploughs in demesne. Then and afterwards 12 ploughs belonging to the men, now 9. Woodland for 160 pigs. 1 park. 20 acres of meadow. Then 2 horses, now 1 and 20 head of cattle. Then 60 pigs, now 40. Then 40 goats, now 30; now 30 sheep. Then as now 5 beehives. A church with 40 acres of free land and half a plough. Then it was worth £14, and now the same. It is 1 league and 2 furlongs long and 6 furlongs broad. 10d. in geld.

The same Eadric held Tannington with 8 carucates of land. Then and afterwards 13 villans, now 15. Then and afterwards 17 bordars, now 19. Then as now 3 ploughs in demesne. Then and afterwards 12 ploughs belonging to the men, now 8. Woodland for 200 pigs. 20 acres of meadow. 11 head of cattle. Then 16 pigs, now 60. Then 16 sheep, now 20; 20 goats and 3 beehives. A church with 30 acres and half a plough. Then as now worth £14. It is 1 league and 3 furlongs long and 1 league broad. 10d. in geld. Richard holds of this manor 30 acres. It is worth 10s. in the same valuation. Warin [holds] 24 acres, worth 5s. in the same valuation. [...]

[Folio 328v: SUFFOLK]

Eadric held Laxfield with 6 carucates of land and 80 acres. Then 14 villans, afterwards 8, now 6. Then and afterwards 14 bordars, now 37. Then then as now 4 ploughs in demesne, afterwards 3, now 2. Then and afterwards 14 ploughs now 11. Woodland for 260 pigs. 27 acres of meadow. 5 head of cattle. Then 40 pigs, now 30. 6 sheep and 24 goats. A church with 43 acres and half a plough. Then it was worth £15, now £8. It is 1½ leagues long and 1 league broad. 6½d. in geld. Walter holds of this manor 3 villans with 50 acres. It is worth 20s. in the same valuation. Loernic holds 40 acres, worth 10s. in the same valuation.

The same Eadric held Badingham with 9 carucates of land. Then 4 villans, Then as now 26 bordars. Then and afterwards 10 ploughs in demesne, now 5. Then 7 ploughs belonging to the men, now 5. Woodland for 100 pigs. 20 acres of meadow. Then 1 horse. Then as now 15 head of cattle. Then 40 pigs, now 32; 20 sheep and 60 goats and 1 beehive. A church with 60 acres and 1 plough and 1 bordar and 1 acre of meadow. Then it was worth £15, now £10. It is 1 league and 6 furlongs long and 1 league broad. 10d. in geld. Walter holds of this manor 100 acres and 2 villans and 6 bordars, worth 30s. It is in the same valuation of £10. Loernic [holds] 40 acres in the same valuation. Robert [holds] 40 acres in the same valuation of 10s [sic, recte £10]. Eadric had the soke and sake. Godwine held Bedfield TRE as a manor with 4 carucates of land. Then 18 bordars, now 23. Then as now 2 ploughs in demesne. Then 8 ploughs belonging to the men, now 9. Woodland for 200 pigs. 9 acres of meadow. Then 2 horses, now 1. Then 9 head of cattle, now 20. Then 40 pigs, now 60, and 83 sheep. Then it was worth £6, now £7. It is 6 furlongs long and 5 broad. 3½d. in geld. Eadric held Stradbroke TRE with 5½ carucates of land. Then and afterwards 16 villans, now 11. Then 11 bordars, now 30. Then 11 ploughs in demesne, afterwards 6, now 5. Then and afterwards 12 ploughs belonging to the men, now 5. 12 ploughs could be restored.

Robert Malet

[Folio 329: SUFFOLK]

Altogether 20 acres of meadow. Woodland for 400 pigs. Then 3 horses. Then 16 pigs, now 30 and 30 sheep. 2 churches with 40 acres and half a plough. 17 sokemen with 1 carucate of land and 3 ploughs. Woodland for 40 pigs. 5 acres of meadow. Of these the soke and sake is in Hoxne, the bishop's manor and Eadric held half from the bishop. Then it was worth £14, now £16. Walter holds from this manor 2 sokeman with 40 acres, worth 8s. in the same valuation. Robert de Glanville [holds] 4 [sokemen] with 20 acres, [worth] 5s. in the same valuation. Walter fitzGrip [holds] 1 with 15 acres, [worth] 30d. in the same valuation, Loernic 1 with 20 acres, worth 3s. in the same valuation. Eadric had the soke and sake. It is 2 leagues long and 1 league broad. 14½d. in geld. Others hold [land] there.

In Horham 1 free man, Ælfric, by commendation [held] 1 carucate of land. Then as now 3 villans and 4 bordars and 1 slave. 2 ploughs in demesne and 1 plough belonging to the men. 4 acres of meadow. Woodland for 30 pigs. And 1 horse, 9 head of cattle, 9 pigs, 40 sheep, 30 goats and 2 beehives. 2 free men with 17 acres by commendation and half a plough. Then it was worth 40s. and now the same. Robert de Glanville holds it from Robert Malet. In Wilby Loernic holds 20 acres which the same Ælfric held. 1 bordar. It is in the same valuation. It is 12 furlongs long and 4 furlongs broad. 10½d. in geld. In Chippenhall 9 free men by commendation [held] 2½ carucates of land. Then as now 17 bordars. And 10 ploughs and 12 acres of meadow. Woodland for 300 pigs. Then it was worth 100s., now £6. Half a church with 20 acres and 1 plough. It is 2 leagues long and 1 broad. 15d. in geld. The soke is in Hoxne, [manor] but Eadric held half from Bishop Æthelmær. Of this manor Walter holds 4 with 1 carucate of land. [It is worth] 30s. and it is in the same valuation of £6. The mother of Robert [holds] 3 [sokemen] with 80 acres [worth] 45s. in the same valuation. Humphrey [holds] 1 [sokeman] with 20 acres.

[Folio 329v: SUFFOLK]

It is worth 5s. in the same valuation. Walter fitzGrip [holds] 1 free man, 120 acres and it is worth 40s. in the same valuation.

In Weybread 1 free man by commendation held 2 carucates of land which Humphrey holds as a manor with 10 bordars. Then as now 2 ploughs in demesne. Then 2 ploughs belonging to the men, now 1½; 10 acres of meadow. Woodland for 60 pigs. 1 mill. 1 horse, 4 head of cattle, 30 pigs, 30 sheep and 4 beehives. 1 free man holds 20 acres and half a plough. Then it was worth 30s., now 50s. The same Humphrey holds this. The soke is in Hoxne. In the same vill Humphrey holds 3 free men by commendation with 91½ acres and 17 bordars. Then 3 ploughs, afterwards and now 2; 6 acres of meadow. Then as now 1 mill and three parts of another. It is worth 40s. The soke is in Hoxne. In Menham 1 free man by commendation [held] 1 carucate of land and 5 bordars. 1 free man under him with 3 acres. Then as now 1 plough in demesne. Then 2 ploughs, now 2 oxen. 5 acres of meadow. Woodland for 100 pigs. A church with 8 acres and an eighth part of another with 5 acres. In the same place 1 sokeman with 12 acres. Then it was worth 25s., now 30s. The same Humphrey holds this. The soke is in Hoxne.

In Weybread 6 free men, and the same Humphrey holds 5 and Walter 1. It is worth 10s. 72 acres and 5 bordars. Then 2 ploughs, now 1 and 4½ acres of meadow. Woodland for 14 pigs. Then as now 1 mill. It is worth 17s.

In Weybread the same Humphrey holds 3 sokemen with 90 acres and 2 bordars. Then 2½ ploughs, now 1 ox. 4 acres of meadow. Woodland for 20 pigs. 1 mill. Then it was worth 15s., now 25s. 6d.

In Horham Walter de Caen holds from Robert Malet 3 free men by commendation with 60 acres and 2 bordars. Then as now 1 plough and 2 acres of meadow. Woodland for 6 pigs. It is worth 12s. In Horham Walter fitzGrip holds from Robert Malet 2 free men with 1 carucate of land and 30 acres and 5 bordars.

Robert Malet

[Folio 330: SUFFOLK]

Then as now 2½ ploughs and 3 acres of meadow. Woodland for 28 pigs. Then as now worth 25s. 4d. In Chickering [holds] 3 free men by commendation with 36 acres. Then 1 plough, now a half. 1½ acres of meadow. It is worth 6s. In the same place holds 1 free man by commendation with 60 acres. Then 1 plough, now a half and 2 acres of meadow. Woodland for 6 pigs. Then worth 10s. and now [the same]. Over this his predecessor had commendation and he had the land in pledge for 60s.

In Badingfield the same Humphrey holds from Robert Malet 1 free man by commendation with 84 acres and 8 bordars and 1 priest by commendation with 6 acres. 2 ploughs and 1 acre of meadow. Woodland for 10 pigs. Under him 6 free men with 25 acres and 1 plough. It is worth 22s. 8d. [...]

[Folio 330v: SUFFOLK]

VII. Lands of Roger Bigod. Hundred of Bradmere.

Stanheard holds Barnham of Roger Bigod which Æthelwig of Thetford held as a manor TRE with 1 carucate of land. Then as now 6 bordars and 1 slave. 2 ploughs in demesne and half a plough belonging to the men. 2 acres of meadow. Then as now 1 mill. Then 2 horses, now 1. Then 3 head of cattle, now 6. Then as now 14 pigs and 12 wild mares. Then 160 sheep, now 300; 5 free men with 40 acres. Over these Roger's predecessor had the commendation TRE. This the same Stanheard holds. St Edmund has the soke and sake. Then the manor was worth 30s., now 40s. and the free men 3s. It is 12 furlongs long and 10 broad. 11¾d. in geld.

HALF-HUNDRED OF COSFORD.

In Whatfield 1 free man over whom St Edmund had commendation and full soke TRE. He has 15 acres, worth 2s. 6d. [Hugh] de Houdain holds this.

HUNDRED OF BISHOP.

Roger Bigod holds Kelsale in demesne which Northmann held TRE with 4 carucates of land. Then and afterwards 10 villans, now 15. Then and afterwards 7 bordars, now 17. Then as now 3 ploughs in demesne and 10 ploughs belonging to the men. 5 acres of meadow. Woodland for 60 pigs. Now 3 horses, 2 head of cattle and 30 pigs. Then 25 sheep, now 100. A church with 30 acres and 1 plough. Then it was worth 100s.

In the same place Wulfgifu held 2 carucates of land as a manor which Roger holds in demesne. Then 5 villans, now 7. Then 4 bordars, now 9. Then as now 2 ploughs in demesne and 5 ploughs belonging to the men. 3 acres of meadow. Then it was worth 60s.

In that manor which Northmann held there are 35 free men able to sell and give their lands. Roger holds these men in demesne with the soke and sake and every customary due. They have 3 carucates of land. Then as now 12 ploughs and 1 acre of meadow. Now one market by the king's gift. Then

Roger Bigod

[Folio 331: SUFFOLK]

the free men were worth £4. The manor with the free men is now worth £24 and the other manor £8. All this is 1½ leagues long and 1 league broad. 42d. in geld. Roger Bigod [has] the soke and sake. Aitard holds Denham from Roger Bigod which Stigand held with 1½ carucates of land. Then as now 3 villans and 11 bordars and 2 ploughs in demesne and 2 ploughs belonging to the men. 2 acres of meadow. Woodland for 30 pigs. 2 head of cattle, 10 pigs and 30 sheep and 20 goats. A church with 12 acres. 1 sokeman belongs to this land which the same Aitard holds and who belongs in Horham, with 40 acres. 1 bordar and 1 plough and 2 acres of meadow. Woodland for 6 pigs. Then it was worth 40s., now 50s. In the same place 1 free man of Stigand which the same Aitard holds with 30 acres. 2 bordars and 1 plough and 1 acre of meadow. Woodland for 4 pigs. It is worth s. This is by exchange with Isaac's land. It is half a league long and 3 furlongs broad. 7½d. in geld. In the same place 1 free man commended to Stigand with 10 acres, worth 2s. This is by the same exchange and the same Aitard holds it. All this Bishop Æthelmær had after the king arrived.

HUNDRED OF BLYTHING.

Æthelweard, a free man, held Hinton as one manor TRE; now Robert of Blythburgh holds it under Roger Bigod with 50 acres and 2 bordars. Then as now 1 plough in demesne. 1 horse and 4 head of cattle. 4 pigs. 50 sheep. It is worth 8s. Of this land Robert of Blythburgh holds 12 acres of the king's alms, in other words of the church of Blythburgh, and to this the Hundred testifies. To this manor have been added 6 free men over whom Roger's predecessor had the commendation and they have 50 acres of land. Then as now 1 plough. 1 acre of meadow. It is worth 4s.

Wulfsige held Bridge as one manor TRE with 1½ carucates of land. Then 2 villans and 8 bordars, now 10 bordars. Then 4 slaves, now 1. Then 4 ploughs in demesne and now 2, and a third could be there. The 2 ploughs belonging to the men, now 1½ ploughs. Woodland for 8 pigs. 18 acres of meadow. 2 mills. 1 salt-pan. 11 pigs and 20 goats. Then it was worth 30[s.], now 40[s.]. 3 acres of land in Dunwich belong to this manor. The soke is Robert Malet's. It is worth 22d. To this manor have been added 4 free men with 60 acres of land. Then 2 ploughs, now 1. It is worth 8s. And Robert de Courson holds this from Roger Bigod. And it is 9 furlongs long and 7 broad. It renders 1¾d. to the king's geld. The soke is the king's and the earl's.

Padda held Brampton TRE as one manor, now Robert de Courson holds it with 2 carucates of land. Then 4 villans, now 2. Then 4 bordars, now 6. Then as now 1 slave. Then as now 2 ploughs in demesne and 2 ploughs belonging to the men. Woodland for 6 pigs. 1 acre of meadow. 14 pigs, four score sheep. Then as now worth 40s. To this manor have been joined 9 free men and a half with 100 acres. Then 5 ploughs in demesne, now 3. It is worth 12s. The soke is the king's and the earl's.

In Uggeshall Godric [held] one manor with 2 carucates of land. Then as now 5 villans. Then as now 5 bordars. 3 ploughs belonging to the men. 1 acre of meadow. Then as now worth 20s. And now [Robert] de Courson holds this under Roger Bigod. And of this land William Malet was seised. In Holton Godric, a free man, held 30 acres and 2 bordars, worth 4s. Godric the steward hold this from Roger Bigod. Northmann held Peasenhall as 2 manors with 2 carucates of land TRE. Now the same Northmann holds it. Then as now 8 villans and 10 bordars

Roger Bigod

and 2 slaves. 2 ploughs in demesne and 5 ploughs belonging to the men. 4 acres of meadow. Woodland for 200 pigs. Then it was worth 60s., now 80s. In the same place 4 free men by commendation [held] 40 acres. Then as now 1½ ploughs. Woodland for 8 pigs. It is worth 6s. The same Northmann [has] the soke of the manor and of two of the free [men] and the king and the earl [have it] of the other two.

In "Warabetuna" a free woman TRE over whom Northmann had commendation, and she had 100 acres. Of these Robert Malet holds 30 acres and Northmann holds the rest from Roger Bigod as a manor. Then as now 2 villans and 2 bordars and 1 acre and 2 acres of meadow. Then it was worth 8s., now 12s. The king and the earl have the soke. In Covehithe Northmann holds then as now 6 acres. It is assessed in Peasenhall.

In Heveningham Stanwine, a free man commended to Harold, held 1 carucate of land as a manor TRE, as the Hundred testifies, but he himself alone offers to undergo the judicial ordeal, saying that he was the man of Eadric, Robert Malet's predecessor. Now Ansketil holds it from Roger. Then as now 6 villans and 4 bordars and 2 slaves. Then 2 ploughs in demesne, now 1. Then as now 1½ ploughs belonging to the men. 3 acres of meadow. Woodland for 40 pigs. 1 horse and 4

head of cattle and 10 pigs. Then 16 sheep, now 22. Then it was worth 40s., now 20s. It is half a league long and 4 furlongs broad. 4½d. in geld.

In Chediston Godwine, a free man of the queen, held 55 acres TRE as a manor. Now Robert de Vaux [holds it]. Then as now 2 villans and 2 bordars. And 1 plough in demesne and 1 plough belonging to the men. 1½ acres of meadow. Woodland for 30 pigs. 2 head of cattle, 12 pigs and 20 sheep. It is worth 10s.

In Chediston 1 free man, Wulfsige, with 13 acres over whom someone commended

to Robert Malet's predecessor had half the commendation and the queen had the other half TRE.

In the same place 1 free man by name Anund with 13 acres in like manner and another free man, Ulf, with 13 acres by commendation to the queen TRE. Between them they had then 1 plough, now a half. 1 acre of meadow. It is worth 4s. The king and the earl have the soke.

In the same place 1 free man, Eadric, over whom Robert Malet's predecessor had half the commendation and the Abbot of Ely the other half TRE. He has 100 acres as a manor. Then as now 2 villans and 5 bordars. Then as now 1 plough in demesne. Then 2 ploughs belonging to the men, now 1. And 3 acres of meadow. Woodland for 60 pigs. 1 ox, 4 pigs, 22 sheep and 7 goats. Five parts of a church with 16 acres. Then as now worth 30s. Of this William Malet was seised when he went in the king's service where he died.

In the same place 2 free men, Ledman and Stanheard these were in the commendation of the king and the queen TRE with 30 acres as a manor and 1 bordar. Then 1 plough. Woodland for 20 pigs. 1 acre of meadow. It is worth 5s. In the same place 1 free man, Leofric, [held] 26 acres as a manor TRE, over whom the predecessor of Baynard had commendation. Then as now 1 villan and 2 bordars and 1 plough. 3 acres of meadow. Woodland for 12 pigs. 2 head of cattle, 4 pigs and 20 sheep. It is worth 10s.

In the same place 1 free man, Goti, with 15 acres, over whom Robert Malet's predecessor had commendation. Then half a plough. It is worth 2s. William Malet was seised of it. In the same place 1 free man by name Leofwine with 14 acres, over whom Robert Malet's predecessor had commendation. William his father was seised of it. Then half a plough. It is worth 2s. 4d. Robert de Vaux holds the whole. The king and the earl have the soke over the whole. It is 1 league long and 5 furlongs broad. 5½d. in geld.

Roger Bigod

In "Torp" 1 free man, Wulfmær of Robert Malet's predecessor, with 20 acres as one manor. Then 1 plough. Woodland for 6 pigs. It is worth 40d. William Malet his father was seised [of it]. 15 acres as a manor and 2 bordars. Then as now half a plough and half an acre of meadow. It is worth 3s. Robert de Vaux holds all this. The king and the earl have the soke.

Northmann, a thegn, held Yoxford TRE as a manor with

100 acres; now Hugh de Corbon holds it. Then as now 4 villans and 7 bordars and 1 slave. Then 3 ploughs in demesne, now 2. Then 3 ploughs belonging to the men, now 2; 5 acres of meadow. Then 3 horses, now 2. Now 7 head of cattle and 5 pigs and 12 sheep. Then as now worth 40s. In the same place 5 free men were added over whom the same Northmann had the commendation TRE with 14 acres and half a plough, worth 2s. The same Northmann [had] soke over the whole. There were also added 2 free men from the king's soke, namely Algar and Edwin, by commendation to Æthelweard the king's reeve TRE with 7 acres and 2 oxen, worth 15d.

In Bulcamp Ali, a free man commended to Manni, the predecessor of Robert Malet de Tosny, held TRE four score acres and 10 as a manor. Then as now 2 villans and 3½ bordars. 1 plough in demesne and 1 plough belonging to the men. 3 acres of meadow. Woodland for 100 pigs. 12 pigs, 12 sheep and 40 goats. It is worth 15s. Robert de Vaux holds this from Roger Bigod. It is 1 league long and half a league broad. 1¼d. in geld. This land Earl Ralph held on the day on which he forfeited. Now Roger Bigod holds it by the king's gift, so he says; and Robert de Vaux [holds it] from him.

In Peasenhall Ranulf fitzWalter has 3 villans and 1 bordar with

60 acres of land from Roger Bigod. Then as now 2 ploughs belonging to the men. Woodland for 40 pigs. This land belongs in Saxmundham. The king and the earl have the soke.

In Knodishall Ranulf fitzWalter holds from Roger Bigod four score acres of land. It is a berewick of Saxmundham. Then as now 3 bordars and 1 villan. They have between them 2 ploughs and Robert Malet has the soke.

In Stoven 2 free men, Langabein and Goda, commended to Godwine son of Toki TRE, with 14 acres of land and 2 bordars and half a plough, worth 2s. The king and the earl have the soke. Free men Free men of Roger Bigod. Hundred of Blything.

In Holton Alwine, a free man, [held] 1 carucate of land, over whom Eadric of Laxfield had commendation. Then as now 1 villan and 3 bordars. Then as now 1 plough. Woodland for 3 pigs. It is worth 12s. The king and the earl have the soke. Robert of Courson holds this [from] Roger Bigod. In Cookley Godric, 1 free man, held 30 acres and Wulfsige, the predecessor of Roger Bigod, had a third part of the commendation and Wulfsige's 2 brothers had 2 parts of the commendation. Then as now 2 bordars and 1 plough. 2 acres of meadow. Woodland for 7 pigs. It is worth 4s. The king and the earl have the soke. Robert de Vaux holds this from Roger Bigod.

In Covehithe 1 free man, Hearding by name, commended to Ulfkil the predecessor of William de Warenne, held 20 acres. Then as now half a plough and 1 bordar, worth 3s. The king and the earl have the soke.

In "Thorpe" Wulfmær, 1 free man, held 50 acres as a manor over which the predecessor of William Malet had the commendation and the same William himself was seised. Then as now 1 plough in demesne and 4 bordars and half a plough belonging to the men. Woodland for 12 pigs. Half an acre of meadow. It is worth 16s. Roger Bigod has the soke. To this manor belong

Roger Bigod

2 acres in Dunwich in the same valuation. Robert Malet has soke over these 2 acres.

In Heveningham Ulfkil, 1 free man, held 24 acres, over whom Ulf had commendation. Then as now 2 bordars and 1 plough. Woodland for 8 pigs. Half an acre of meadow. A fourth part of a church with an acre and a half. It is worth 8s. The king and the earl have the soke. In "Uurabetuna" Mansunu, 1 free man, held 12 acres, over whom Northmann had the commendation. Then as now half a plough and 1 bordar and 1 acre of meadow. 1 church with 6 acres, worth 40d. The king and the earl have the soke.

In the same vill 4 free men and a half held 40 acres. Then as now 1 plough. 2 acres of meadow. Woodland for 6 pigs. It is worth 12s. The king and the earl have the soke.

In "Opituna" Bondi, 1 free man, held 60 acres as a manor, over whom Toli had the commendation. Then 3 bordars, now none; 1 plough in demesne and half a plough belonging to the men, now 1; 2 acres of meadow. Woodland for 2 pigs. Then as now worth 16s. The king and the earl have the soke. Half a church with 4 acres and half an acre, worth 3d.

In Fordley 15 free men held 100 acres of land and 15 acres. Of these 15 Northmann had the commendation over 13 and over 2 Robert Malet's predecessor had half the commendation and Northmann half. Half a bordar. Then as now 4½ ploughs. 2 acres of meadow. Then as now worth 24s. The king and the earl have the soke.

In Middelton Leofric the deacon, half a free man, held 3 acres, over whom Toli the sheriff had half the commendation. It is worth 12d. The king and the earl have the soke. In Minsmere 4 free men with 45 acres but 3 were under commendation to Northmann and the fourth was commended to someone commended to Northmann. Then as now 1 plough. It is worth 13s. 4d. The king and the earl have the soke. In Knodishall 1 free man, Boti by name, with 30 acres; he was King Edward's man. Then as now 1 plough. It is worth 8s. Robert Malet has the soke and William Malet was

seised of it on the day of his death. In Fordley 20 acres which belong in Kelsale and are in the same valuation. And in Strickland 9 acres which belong in the same place.

In Darsham Ansketil the priest holds 1 carucate of land which belonged to 7 free men. Of these 7 men 1 was Toli's man. Then 2 bordars, now 11. Then half a plough in demesne, now 1 plough. Then as now 2 ploughs belonging to the men. Leofric Cobba, over whom Æthelweard the king's reeve had half the commendation, and Thorkil, over whom the same Æthelweard had half the commendation. And Alnoth, Northmann the sheriff's man. And Brunmann Beard, half Northmann's man and half Brunmær's man. Wulfric the deacon, Godwine the son of Algar's man, Osmund, Eadric of Laxfield's man. 16 acres and 1 virgate which Ælfgifu, a free woman, over whom Northmann had the commendation, held TRE. 24 acres less 1 virgate which Blæcmann held TRE. The same Blæcmann was Eadric of Laxfield's man. William Malet was seised of it on the day of his death. And all this Ansketil, the chaplain of Roger Bigod, holds. It is worth 25s. Of this land Robert Malet claims 6 acres which one of his men gave with his daughter whom 1 of Roger Bigod's married in the time of King [...] William. Alnoth holds 24 acres in the [...] manor of Kelsale, worth 5s. They are in the same valuation. The king and the earl have the soke.

Svartlingr, 1 free man, held Strickland TRE; now Cus and Akile Soufrant, 2 free men, hold it from Roger Bigod with 80 acres as a manor. Then as now 1 plough in demesne and 6 bordars and 1 plough belonging to the men. 2 acres of meadow. 4 head of cattle, 8 pigs, 24 goats. Then as now worth 16s. This land is 1 league long and 5 furlongs broad whoever holds [...] land there. 7½d. in geld. The king and the earl have the soke.

In the same vill 5 free men who were Ulf's men: Goda, Ælfwine his brother, Ælfric the son of Bondi, Eskil, Bondi the smith. These 5 held 60 acres. Then as now

Roger Bigod

[Folio 335: SUFFOLK]

1 bordar. Then as now 2 ploughs. 2 acres of meadow. 1 free woman in the same vill over whom Northmann had the commendation and she held 20 acres. Then as now 1 bordar. Then as now half a plough. 1 acre of meadow and half 1 free man who holds 8 acres of land. And one church which has 24 acres and 1 acre of meadow. This is worth 19s. The king and the earl have the soke.

Hugh de Corbon holds it from Roger Bigod.

In Thorington Northmann holds 30 acres from Roger Bigod and under him 1 free woman, Ælfgifu, half under commendation to Northmann held [land]. Then as now 1 villan and half a plough in demesne. It is worth 4s. The king and the earl have the soke. In Middleton the same woman held from him 16 acres under the same commendation. Then as now 1 plough. It is worth 4s. The king and the earl have the soke.

HUNDRED OF WANGFORD.

Robert de Vaux holds Barsham from Roger Bigod which Leofstan the priest, by commendation to Gyrth, held TRE with 35 acres as one manor. Then 2 bordars, now 1. Then as now 1 plough. Woodland for 20 pigs. 2 acres of meadow. Then it was worth 5s., now 10s. It is 1½ leagues long and a half broad. 30d. in geld. Half a church with 20 acres, worth 3s. In the same vill 12 free men under the same commendation apart from 2, 1 of whom was commended to Halfdan and the other commended to Ælfric [held] 80 acres of land and 3 bordars. Then as now 2 ploughs. 1 acre of meadow. Woodland for 4 pigs. Then it was worth 10s., now 20s. In Ringsfield 8 free men commended to Leofstan apart from 2, one of whom was commended to Ulfkil and the other commended to Wulfsige of Mutford [held] 76 acres. Then 2 ploughs, now 1. Woodland for 6 pigs. 1 acre of meadow. Then it was worth 10s., now 17s. Gunnulf, commended to Burgheard, held Willingham TRE with 30 acres as a manor. Then 1 villan and 3 bordars, now the same. Then 1 plough, and now [the same] and 1 plough

belonging to the men. Woodland for 10 pigs. 1½ acres of meadow. Then as now 2 head of cattle,

[Folio 335v: SUFFOLK]

8 pigs, 20 sheep and 20 goats. Then it was worth 10s., now 20s. It is 1 league long and 1 broad. 5d. in geld. In the same place 5 free men under the same commendation [held] 80 acres of land. Then as now 1 villan and 1 bordar. Then as now 2 ploughs. Woodland for 10 pigs. 1 acre of meadow. Then worth 10s., now 20s.

In Weston 5 free men commended to Burgheard [held] TRE 18 acres of land. Then as now 1 plough. They are in the above valuation of 20s.

In Ellough 2 free men under the same commendation [held] 7 acres and half a plough, worth 36d. Of all this Earl Ralph was seised when he forfeited but Roger Bigod held it by the king's gift. Now Robert de Vaux holds it from him.

In Barsham 3 free men commended to the king [held] 32½ acres. Then 1 plough, now 1½. 4 acres of meadow. Half a mill. 1 villan and 5 bordars. Then as now 1 plough. Then it was worth 5s., now 10s. The same Robert holds this. In Ellough 1 villan with 10 acres. It belongs to Mutford.

Godwine son of Toki, commended to Gyrth, TRE held and holds Shadingfield with 1 carucate of land as a manor. Then as now 5 bordars and 3 slaves. Then 1 plough in demesne, now 1½. And belonging to the men then as now 1 plough. Woodland for 12 pigs. 1 acre of meadow. 1 horse and 20 sheep. Then it was worth 10s., now 20s. It is 1 league long and a half broad. 5d. in geld.

In Shipmeadow 1 free man commended to Ælfric TRE [held] 10 acres. Half a plough. 1 acre of meadow. Then it was worth 3s., now 4s. Godwine holds this from Roger Bigod. In Weston 3 free men, of whom 1, Ketil, was commended to Ælfric [held] 30 acres, and the other 2 [held] 6 acres under him. Then as now 1 villan and 5 bordars. Then as now 1 plough. Woodland for 6 pigs. 1 acre of meadow. Then it was worth 10s. Afterwards it was at farm for 40s.; now it renders 30s.

Roger Bigod

[Folio 336: SUFFOLK]

Robert de Vaux holds it. In Darsham 1 free man commended to Wulfsige [held] 15 acres, worth 3s. In the same place 1 free man commended to Halfdan with 5 acres, worth 12d. Robert de Vaux holds this from Roger Bigod. In Redisham Robert de Courson holds from Roger Bigod 1 free man, Godwine, commended to Stigand, with 60 acres as a manor. Then as now 2 villans and 2 bordars. Then as now in demesne 1 plough and belonging to the men half a plough. Woodland for 4 pigs. Then it was worth 10s. and afterwards 40s., now it renders 30s. 1 free man under him with 4 acres, worth 8d. In Shadingfield 1 free man commended to Wulfsige with 8 acres. They are assessed with Bridge.

HUNDRED OF LOTHING.

In 'Wimundahala' [are] 24 acres and they belong to Weston.

HALF-HUNDRED OF LOTHINGLAND.

Ali, commended to Manni, held Blundeston with 45 acres as a meadow and half a bordar. Then as now half a plough. Woodland for 4 pigs. Half an acre of meadow. Then it was worth 10s. now 3s. Robert de Vaux holds this from Roger Bigod. Of the fief.

HUNDRED OF STOW.

In Buxhall 1 free man by commendation only to St Æthelthryth TRE held 40 acres of land in the soke of the Hundred. Then and afterwards 1 plough, now none. 5 acres of meadow. Then and afterwards worth 20s., now 10s. Roger acquired this to make up for [the value of] Baylham in another Hundred but the Hundred has seen neither writ nor livery officer.

HUNDRED OF BOSMERE.

Leofwine, a free man commended to the Abbot of Ely, held Ringshall with 1 carucate of land and 80 acres as a manor TRE. Then and afterwards 2 villans, now 4 bordars. Then and afterwards 1 . Then 2 ploughs in demesne, afterwards 1, now 2. Then 1 plough belonging to the men, afterwards and now a half. 4 acres of meadow. Half a church with 15 acres. Then 3 horses, now 4. Then 4 head of cattle, now 18. Then 20 pigs, now 40. Then 40 sheep, now 100 and now 30 goats. Then it was worth 30s., now 50s.

In the same place Grim, a free man commended to the Abbot of Ely TRE, held 100 acres as a manor. Then and afterwards 1½ ploughs, now none. 4 acres of meadow. Then as now 1 horse and 3 head of cattle. Then it was worth 20s., afterwards and now 30s. William de Bournville holds these two manors from Roger. The king and the earl have the soke. In the same place 4 free men. Leofwine, Roger Bigod's predecessor, had the commendation of two who were called Frothi and Leofric and the other two were called Lustwine and Eadric he did not have commendation over these. And they had 50 acres and 1 plough and 1 acre of meadow, worth 12s. The king and the earl have the soke. The same William holds [this]. It is 1 league long and a half broad. 15d. in geld. Others hold [land] there.

In Battisford 1 free man, Godric, commended to Harold, held 10 acres. Then as now 2 oxen. Now 1 bordar. [Then] worth 20d., now 3s. The same William holds [this]. The king and the earl have the soke.

Munding, a free man commended to the Abbot of Ely, held Baylham. He held 1 carucate of land as a manor TRE. Now the same William holds it from Roger. Then as now 1 plough and 2 acres of meadow. A third part of a mill and a third part of another mill. Half a church with 12 acres. Then 1 horse, now 2. Then 2 head of cattle, now 8. Then 20 pigs, now 40. Then 20 sheep, now 105. Then it was worth 30s., now 60s. In the same place Manstan, a free man commended to the Abbot of Ely, held 60 acres of land as a manor TRE. Now the same William [holds it]. Then as now half a plough and 1 acre of meadow and the six part of a mill. Then and afterwards it was worth 20s., now 10s. In the same place Wulfric, a free man com-

mended to Robert Malet's predecessor, namely Eadric, held 60 acres as a manor TRE. Now the same William [holds this].

Then and afterwards half a plough, now none. 1 acre of meadow and a sixth part of a mill. Then and afterwards worth 20s., now 10s. The king and the earl have the soke. In the same place 20 free men with 92 acres. None of these were commended to Roger's predecessor. Then and afterwards 4 ploughs, now 2. Then it was worth 40s., now 20s. It is 1 league long and 8 furlongs broad. 15d. in geld. William

Roger Bigod

de Bournville holds it all. The king and the earl have the soke.

In Somersham 1 free man, Leofsunu, commended to Leofric Hobbesune, Bigod's predecessor, held 30 acres as a manor TRE. Now the same William [holds it] from Bigod as a manor. Then as now 1 villan. Then and afterwards half a plough, now 2 oxen. A fourth part of a church with 7½ acres. It is worth 8s. The king and the earl have the soke. Leofcild, a free man commended to Stigand, held Offton with 2 carucates of land as a manor. Now Hugh de Houdain [holds it] from Bigod. Then and afterwards 2 villans, now 1. Then as now 7 bordars and 2 slaves. Then 2 ploughs, afterwards and now none. 1 acre of meadow. Then half a plough, now 1. Then 1 horse, 2 head of cattle, 12 pigs and 40 sheep, now none. Then as now 60s. A church with 16 acres, worth 33d. Stigand had the soke.

In the same place the same Hugh holds from Roger Bigod 10 free men. Of these one and a half Blæcsunu the whole and Ealdwine the half were commended to Bigod's predecessor. Over the others he had nothing. They had 1½ acres of land and the others had 1 carucate of land and 4 acres. Then 3 ploughs, afterwards and now 2. One of these, Blæcwine by name, had 40 acres of the same land. Then it was worth 30s., now 20s. The king and the earl have the soke. It is 1 league long and 5 furlongs broad. 6½d. in geld.

In Baylham Wihtric, a free man commended to the Abbot of Ely, held 120 acres of land as a manor TRE. Now Wulfmær [holds it] from Bigod. Then as now 7 bordars and 1 plough in demesne and 1 plough belonging to the men. 4 acres of meadow. Now 1 mill. Then as now 1 horse. Then 2 head of cattle, now 5. Then 7 sheep, now 30. Then it was worth 20s., now 35s. The king and the earl have the soke. In the same place 6 free men with 20 acres, less half an acre. Over these Wihtric had only the commendation. It is worth 5s.

The same Wulfmær holds it. The king and the earl have the soke. Hugh de Houdain holds it. In Flowton 1 free man, Brungar by name. Leofcild had the commendation TRE, with 10 acres. It is worth 2s. Hugh de Houdain holds it.

In Baylham Warenger holds from Roger Bigod 1 free man, Brun by name, the reeve of Ipswich, and commended to the queen. He has 17 acres. This belongs to [Earl and Little] Stonham and is in its valuation. The king and the earl have the soke.

The same Brun held [Earl and Little] Stonham as a manor

with 60 acres TRE. Now Warenger [holds it] from Roger. Then 2 ploughs, afterwards 1, now 2; 2 acres of meadow. Woodland then for 80 pigs, now for 40. Now 8 head of cattle. Then 10 pigs, now 35; 80 sheep and 23 goats. Some part of a mill. Then it was worth 20s., now 40s. In the same place 5 free men with 16 acres over whom the aforesaid Brun had the commendation. Then 1 plough, now a half. It is worth 3s. The king and the earl have the soke. In the same place 17 free men have been added to this manor in the time of [King] William over whom Roger Bigod's predecessor had nothing. Roger de Rames claims to have held these free men in his fief before Roger Bigod acquired land in Suffolk. But the Hundred testifies that Roger Bigod acquired them earlier for his fief and Roger de Rames opposes this by every legal procedure. They have 69 acres. Of these [men] 5 were commended to the predecessor of Ranulf Peverel, namely to Saxi. Then and afterwards 6 ploughs, now 3; 1½ acres of meadow. It is worth 16s. The king and the earl have the soke.

In Baylham 3 free men over one of whom who is called Wulfbeald Roger Bigod's predecessor, namely Brun, had the commendation. And over two, namely Leofstan [sic], he had nothing, but the predecessor of Ranulf Peverel had

Roger Bigod

[Folio 338: SUFFOLK]

the commendation. Altogether they have 12 acres, worth 2s. Warenger holds it from Roger. The king and the earl have the soke.

In "Langhedena" 1 free man, Ælfric by name, commended to Brun, the predecessor of Bigod, having 10 acres and 2 oxen, worth 2s. The same man holds it from Roger. The king and the earl have the soke. The same Warenger holds Coddenham from Roger Bigod, which the free man Wighulf by commendation to Toli the sheriff TRE held with 76 acres as a manor. Then as now 1½ villans and 3 bordars. Then 2 slaves. Then and afterwards 2 ploughs in demesne, now 1. Then and afterwards 2 oxen belonging to the men, now none. 4 acres of meadow. Then woodland for 30 pigs, now for 10. Then half a mill, but Hardwin, the brother of Earl Ralph, took it away in the time of King William. Half a church with 2½ acres of land. Then as now worth 36s. A church with 12½ acres, worth 25d. Another church with 8 acres, worth 16d. The king and the earl have the soke.

In the same place 1 free man, Wailolf, commended to the Abbot of Ely, having 36 acres as a manor TRE. The same Warenger holds it. Then half a villan. Then and afterwards 1 plough, now none. 4 acres of meadow. Then woodland for 30 pigs, now for 10. Then as now worth 15s. The king and the earl have the soke.

In the same place 27 free men with 75 acres. Of these 12 were commended to Wighulf, Roger Bigod's predecessor, TRE; over the others he had nothing. The same Warenger holds this. Then and afterwards 3 ploughs, now 2; 1 acre of meadow. Then it was worth 16s., now 20s. 6d.

In Hemingstone 1 free man, Farman by name, commended to Wighulf, with 5 acres which the same Warenger holds. It is worth 10d. The king and the earl have the soke. Roger de

Rames claims all the land of Wighulf and all those men which Warenger holds from Roger Bigod. And he says that it was

[Folio 338v: SUFFOLK]

delivered to him before [it was delivered] to Roger Bigod. And the Hundred does not know how to tell the truth of this because that Warenger held from both of them but nevertheless that Warenger vouches [it] to Roger Bigod's fief. Roger de Rames opposes this with all legal procedures.

Coddenham is 1 league long and 8 furlongs broad. 20d. in geld.

HUNDRED OF PLUMESGATE.

Northmann held Saxmundham TRE with 140 acres as a manor. Then as now 2 villans and 3 bordars. 2 ploughs in demesne and 2 ploughs belonging to the men. 3 acres of meadow. A church with 15 acres. It is worth 30s. The same Northmann has the soke and he holds this from Roger. This [is] one of three manors which the king gave back to Northmann and now he holds it from Roger.

Algar, a thegn of King Edward, held Saxmundham as a manor TRE with 2 carucates of land and 40 acres. Then as now 5 villans and 10 bordars. Then 3 slaves, now 1. Then as now 3 ploughs in demesne. Then 3 ploughs belonging to the men, afterwards and now 2½; 5 acres of meadow. churches with 24 acres and half a plough. Then as now 2 horses. Then 3 head of cattle. Then 16 pigs, now 30. Then as now 80 sheep. And 1 berewick, Knodishall, with 80 acres; it is in another Hundred. And another berewick, Peasenhall, with 60 acres in another Hundred. Then the whole was worth £7 and afterwards it was at farm for £9 10s.; now it is assessed for £7. Ralph holds it from Roger. The soke is the abbot's. In the same place 7 free men, commended to Algar, have been added to this manor with 48 acres. One, Wulfnoth by name, was commended to Malet's predecessor. Now the same Ranulf holds it. Then and afterwards 3 [...], now 2; 4 acres of meadow. Then it was worth 10s. 4d., now 10s. The soke is the abbot's.

In "Becclinga" [near Friston] 1 sokeman with 20 acres. It belongs in Kelsale. It is worth

Roger Bigod

[Folio 339: SUFFOLK]

2s. Ranulf holds it in demesne. The soke is the abbot's.

Wulfric, commended to Harold, held Bruisyard with 80 acres as a manor TRE . 4 bordars. Then and afterwards 1½ ploughs in demesne, now 1; half a plough belonging to the men. 4 acres of meadow. Woodland for 40 pigs. Then 1 horse. Then 3 head of cattle. Then 4 pigs, now 20, and 24 sheep. Then 6 goats, now 12. Then it was worth 20s., now 30s. Ralph de Tourleville holds it from Roger. In Saxmundham 30 acres and they belong in the demesne of Kelsale. Har [sic].

HUNDRED OF HARTISMERE.

Gode, a free woman commended to Stigand, held Brome TRE with 2 carucates of land as a manor, 1 in Brome and the other in Oakely. Then as now 1 villan and 7 bordars. Then 1 slave.

Then as now in demesne 2 ploughs and half a plough belonging to the men. 8 acres of meadow. 1 horse, 10 pigs and 40 pigs. Then it was worth 30s., now 61s. And half a church with 14 acres, worth 2s.

In the same place 25 free men and 3 half [free men] under the same commendation with 80 acres and 16; 2 acres of meadow. Then 3 ploughs, now 1½. Then it was worth 30s., now 20s. William Scudet holds this from Roger Bigod. It is 5 furlongs long and 4 broad. In geld 3½d.

In the same place Hugh holds of Roger Bigod 1 free man, Ælfric, commended to Gyrth TRE with 60 acres as a manor. Then as now 3 bordars. Then as now in demesne 1 plough. Then and now half a plough belonging to the men. 3 acres of meadow. Then as now worth 10s. And 1 free man commended to Ælfric with 8 acres, worth 16d. The wife of this free man was commended to Robert Malet's predecessor. Hugh de Corbon holds this from Roger Bigod.

[Folio 339v: SUFFOLK]

HUNDRED OF COLNEIS.

Northmann held Walton TRE and now he holds it under Roger with 2 carucates of land as a manor. Then 14 villans, now 6. Then 6 bordars, now the same. Then in demesne 2 ploughs, now 2½. Then as now 2 ploughs belonging to the men. 4 acres of meadow. Now 1 mill. 1 church with 8 acres, worth 16d. Then 1 fishery, now none. 6 horses, 26 pigs and 140 sheep. To this manor [belongs] 1 berewick, Falkenham, with 1 carucate of land. Then as now 3 bordars. 1 plough in demesne and half a plough belonging to the men. 2 acres of meadow. 1 horse and 80 sheep. Then as now the whole together worth £6. It is half a league long and 4 furlongs broad. In geld 12d.

In the same vill 18 15 free men under commendation Godric the smith, Eadric, Wulfnoth, Oswulf, Wulfric, Stanmær, Leofgeat, Wihtric, Blæcmann, Mansunu, Leofwine, Wulfmær, Wulfheah and another Wulfheah, and Leofstan with 40 acres. They have 2 ploughs. It is worth 10s. Free men In "Buregata" the same Northmann held TRE 13 [sic] free men. These are free men of Roger Bigod: Godric, Scearmann, Swein, Leofric, Morcar, Swetmann, Sprot, Godric and another Godric, and Wulfmær and Ælfric Stikestac, Colman and Godric Long and Sigefrith, with 80 acres of land and under them 6 bordars. Then as now between them 3 ploughs. 1 acre of meadow. It is worth 30s. It is half a league long and 4 furlongs broad. In geld 20d. Of these men one who is called Ælfric Stickestac was half Eadric's man.

In the Hundred of Colneisthere is a pasture common to all the men of the Hundred. In 'Morston' [in Trimley] the same Northmann held TRE 6 free men Eadric, Burgric, Wulfbeald, Ælfric, Almær and Wulfric by commendation, with 100 acres of land.

Roger Bigod

[Folio 340: SUFFOLK]

1 villan with 4 acres and 4 bordars. Then as now between them 3 ploughs. 2 acres of meadow. It is worth 20s. Of these Wulfheah, the father of Wulfbeald, was half the man of Eadric, Robert Malet's predecessor. It is half a league long and 2 furlongs broad. 4d. in geld.

In 'Burch' the same Northmann held TRE 16 free men by commendation Leofric, Swetmann, Godric, Beorhtric, Almær and another Almær, Beorhtnoth, Leofric, Toki, Godric and another Godric, Northmann, Gode, Lunden, Ealdwulf and Colman with 1 carucate of land and 6 bordars. They belong to Walton. 4 ploughs between them. 2 acres of meadow. It is worth 40s. It is half a league long and 2 furlongs broad. In geld 22d. A church with 12 acres, worth 2s.

In Gulpher 5 free men commended to Northmann TRE, with 40 acres of land and 2 ploughs. 1 acre of meadow. It is worth 5s. It is 2 furlongs long and 2 broad. In geld 3d. In Wadgate 5 free men commended to Northmann Leofric, Mor-Grimr, Aldulf, Gode and Godwine with 20 acres. Then as now 1 plough. Half an acre of meadow. It is worth 4s. It is 2 furlongs long and 2 broad. 2d. in geld.

In 'Turstanestuna' [in Bromeswell] 3 free men commended to Northmann Earngeat, Wihtric and Almær with 15 acres and 1 plough. Half an acre of meadow. It is worth 3s. It is 2 furlongs long and 2 broad. In geld 4d.

In "Nortuna" 4 free men commended to Norman Mansunu, Wihtmær, Durand, and Otti with 31 acres and 1 bordar and 1 plough. 1 acre of meadow. It is worth 10s. It is 6 furlongs long and 2 broad. 12d. in geld

In "Plumgeard" 6 free men commended to Northmann with 30 acres Osfrith, Alwine, Wulfmær, Eadnoth, Godric and Harthacnut. And under them 4 bordars.

[Folio 340v: SUFFOLK]

TRE 2 ploughs, now 1. Half an acre of meadow. It is worth 4s. It is 2 furlongs long and 2 broad. In geld 4d.

In Falkenham 4 free men Leofric, Suneman, Mansunu, Leofstan commended half to Northmann and the other half to Ralph de Tourleville, with 30 acres and 1 bordar and 2 ploughs. 1 acre of meadow. It is worth 5s. It is half a league long and 4 furlongs broad. In geld 22½d.

In Kirton 3 free men Grim, Beorhtric and Stanmær commended to Northmann, with 20 acres and 1 bordar and 1 plough. It is worth 3s. It is 2 furlongs long and 2 broad. 2d. in geld.

In "Struustuna" 1 free man of Northmann, Wulfric by name, with 16 acres and 1 bordar and half a plough. Half an acre of meadow. It is worth 2s. It is 5 furlongs long and 2 broad. In geld 6½d.

In "Guthestuna" 6 free men Grim, Mor-Grimr, Goding, Leofstan, Wulfmær and Goding commended to Northmann, and 7 bordars with 40 acres. 2 ploughs. 1 acre of meadow. It is worth 5s. It is 2 furlongs long and 2 broad. 3d. in geld. In 'Morston' [in Trimley] 3 free men Godmann, Leofsunu, Godgifu commended to Northmann with 50 acres and 1 villan and 3 bordars. 1½ ploughs. 1 acre of meadow. It is worth 8s. It is 5 furlongs long and 2 broad. 4d. in geld. Two were men belonging half to Eadric.

In Hemley 2 free men Osfrith and Godric by commendation, with 20 acres and 2 bordars and half a plough. 1 acre of meadow. It is worth 3s. 4d. It is 4 furlongs long and 3 broad. 4d. in geld.

In Kembroke 5 free men belonging to Northmann

Sigeweald, Wulfwine, Ordric, Godwine and Spreotmann with 30 acres and 4 bordars and 1½ ploughs.

Roger Bigod

[Folio 341: SUFFOLK]

1 acre of meadow. It is worth 3s. It is half a league long and 3 furlongs broad. 10d. in geld. Others hold [land] there.

In Lestaneston 2 free men belonging to Northmann Leofstan and Stanflæd with 6 acres, worth 12d. It is 3 furlongs long and 3 broad. 6d. in geld. In Levington 1 free man, Leofric, belonging to Northmann, with 4 acres, worth 8d. It is 4 furlongs long and 2 broad. 4d. in geld.

In Candlet 1 free man, Beorhtric, with 3 acres, worth 6d. It is 1 furlong long and 1 broad. 2d. in geld.

In Alteston [in Trimley] 2 free men, Thorbiorn and Wulfwine, with 11 acres, worth 22d. 1 church with 5 acres of free land, worth 16d. It is 6 furlongs long and 2 broad. 7d. in geld. Others hold [land] in these manors. All these are free men of Roger Bigod and Northmann holds them from him.

Godric, commended to Northmann, held Trimley [St Martin and St Mary] TRE with 50 acres of land as a manor. Now Turold [holds it] from Roger Bigod. 3 bordars and 1 plough. 2 acres of meadow. And 1 free man, Leofric, under him, with 4 acres. It renders 35s. 1 church with 20 acres, worth 40d. It is 4 furlongs long and 3 broad. 4d. in geld. 1 church with 8 acres, worth 8d. Others hold [land] there.

In Falkenham Eadric, commended to Northmann, held TRE 1 carucate of land as a manor. Now Ralph de Tourleville [holds] from Roger Bigod. Then as now 6 bordars and 1 slave. Then as now in demesne 2 ploughs. 2 acres of meadow. Then 4 horses, now 3; 10 pigs and 60 sheep. It is worth 30s. 7 free men and a half Beorhtmær, Wulfmær, Godwine, Wulfweard, Godric, Sweting of this man Sweting Roger was seised Leofric, Leofstan commended to Northmann, with 57 acres. Then as now 3 ploughs. It has half an acre of meadow.

[Folio 341v: SUFFOLK]

It is worth 10s. In Grimston the same Roger holds 1 free man, called Blæcmann, belonging to Northmann, with 40 acres. Under him 7 bordars. 1 plough. 2 acres of meadow. It is worth 10s. 3 free men in the same place commended to B[læcmann] 30 acres Herman, Cyneric and Wulfheah. They have 1½ ploughs. Half an acre of meadow. It is worth 5s. It is 3 furlongs long and 3 broad. In geld 7d. Others hold [land] there.

In Langer 2 free men and a half Wulfheah, Thorbiorn and Rawn half under commendation to Northmann TRE with 30 acres and 1½ ploughs. Half an acre of meadow. It is worth 10s. It is 4 furlongs long and 2 broad. 4d. in geld. The same Ralph holds it.

In Alteston [in Trimley] the same Ralph holds 3 free men Leofric, Almær and Rawn with 30 acres by commendation to Northmann. 1 bordar and 1 plough. Half an acre of meadow. It is worth 5s. In Langer Alnoth, 1 free man of Harold, TRE [held] 40 acres and 1 villan and 3 bordars. Now Bernard [holds it] from Roger Bigod. Then 1 plough and now [the

same]. 1 acre of meadow. It is worth 10s. 1 free man, called Sæwine, commended to Alnoth, with 4 acres, worth 8d.

In "Struestuna" 1 free woman, Thorild, commended to Northmann TRE [held] 55 acres of land. Now Hugh de Houdain [holds it] from Roger Bigod. 7 bordars and 1 plough. 2 acres of meadow. It is worth 40s.

In Thorpe the same Hugh holds 5 free men Wulfric, Almær and another Wulfric, Ælfric and Ketil Uva commended to Northmann with 72 acres and 2 ploughs. 1 acre of meadow. It is worth 20s. It is 4 furlongs long and 2 broad. 5d. in geld.

In "Struestuna" the same Hugh holds 3 free men belonging to Northmann Husteman,

Roger Bigod

[Folio 342: SUFFOLK]

Eadric and Goda with 6 acres, worth 12d. In Lestaneston 2 free men, Burgric and Beorhtric, commended to Northmann, with 20 acres and 1 bordar and 1 plough. 2 acres of meadow. 1 mill and 1 salt-pan. It is worth 10s. Wihtmær holds this from Roger Bigod.

In "Nortuna" the same Wihtmær holds 1 free man, Ealdwulf, commended to Northmann, with 20 acres and 3 bordars and 1 plough. 2 acres of meadow. It is worth 5s. In "Buregata" 1 free man, Wihtmær, commended to Godric [held] 20 acres and 4 bordars. 1 acre of meadow. It is worth 5s. The same Wihtmær [now holds].

In the same place 9 free men Ealdwulf, Ælfric, Beorhtric, Asgot, Goda, Wihtmær, Brunmann, Viking, Leofric commended to Northmann with 15 acres and 1 plough, worth 3s.

In Wadgate the same Wihtmær holds 8 free men Langfer, Sægar, Brunmær, Goda, Edward, Godric, Ealdwulf, Eskil commended to Wihtmær, and Langfer and Ealdwulf commended to Northmann TRE, with 15 acres. Then as now 1 plough. It is worth 3s.

In "Mycelegata" 4 free men TRE: Regifer and Goda, commended to Northmann, with 12 acres and Leofstan and another Goda, commended to Wihtmær with 4 acres. Then as now 1 plough between them. 1 virgate of meadow. It is worth 3s. It is 3 furlongs long and 2 broad. 2d. in geld. The same Wihtmær holds it.

In Lestaneston 4 free men commended to Northmann TRE Blæcmann, Durand, Sæwine and Wulfric with 14 acres. Then as now half a plough. It is worth 2s. In the same place 8 free men Blæcmann, Brunmær, Eadric,

[Folio 342v: SUFFOLK]

Leofric, Alwine, Wulfbeald, Theodric, Leofflæd commended to a certain man of Northmann with 12 acres. Half a plough. It is worth 2s.

In Trimley [St Martin and St Mary] 3 free men Goda, Hildefrith, Deorstan commended to Northmann and Deorstan, commended to Wihtmær, with 6 acres. Half a plough. It is worth 12d. In Alteston [in Trimley] the same Wihtmær holds 1 free man, Wulfric by name, belonging to Northmann with 12 acres, worth 2s.

In Kirton 1 free man, Godric the priest commended to Eadric TRE before he made himself an outlaw and after he made himself an outlaw he was Northmann's man [held] 7 acres and 1 plough.

1 acre of meadow. It is worth 3s. In the same place a church with 6 acres, worth 12d. All this Wihtmær holds from Roger Bigod. In Morston [in Trimley] 1 free man, Beorhtmær, commended to Northmann TRE with 20 acres and 1 bordar and 1 plough. Half an acre of meadow. It is worth 6s. William de Bosc holds this from Roger Bigod.

In Thorpe [in Trimley] the same William holds 1 bordar with 8 acres, worth 2s.

In Levington William de Bournville holds from Roger Bigod 10 [sic] free men commended to Northmann Godmann, Leofric, Beorhtric, Gunnar, Wulfric, Sigeweald, Huna, Hwita, Godric with 32 acres. Then as now 2 ploughs. 2 acres of meadow. It is worth 10s. 1 church with 8 acres, worth 12d.

In "Kuluertestuna" 7 free men commended to Northmann TRE Dyring, Godric, Leofric, Algar, Wulfweard, Durand, Ælfric with 25 acres. Then as now 1 plough. 1 acre of meadow. 2 mills. It is worth 5s. It is 3 furlongs long and 2 broad. 4d. in geld. In Stratton 1 free man, Wihtric, Harold's man

Roger Bigod

[Folio 343: SUFFOLK]

TRE [held] 32 acres as a manor. 3 bordars and 1 plough. 1 acre of meadow. It is worth 5s. Also in the same place 1 free man commended to Northmann, Ulfkil, and 38 acres as a manor. 2 bordars. Then as now 1 plough. 1 acre of meadow. It is worth 6s. In the same place 1 free man commended to Northmann, Godmann, with 10 acres and 1 bordar. Half a plough. It is worth 2s. 1 church with 10 acres, worth 2s. It is 6 furlongs long and 4 broad. In geld 7d. Others hold [land] there. All this William de Bournville holds.

In "Oxlanda" 5 free men commended to Northmann Blæcmann, Osbert, Wihtric, Godric, Beorhtnoth with 42 acres and 4 bordars and 2 ploughs. Half an acre of meadow. It is worth 5s. It is 3 furlongs long and 2 broad. In geld 4d.

In Kembroke 14 [sic] free men [over whom] Northmann had the commendation Wihtgar, Osbert, Leofstan, Eadric, Freowine, Beorhtmær, Blæcmann, Wulfweard, Durand, Godric, Sigeric, Wulfwig, Ælfric, Almær, Bondi with 73 acres and 3 ploughs. 3 acres of meadow and 1½ mills. It is worth 15s. All this William de Bournville holds under Roger Bigod. The men of the Hundred have assessed this land at 48s. but formerly it rendered, and they render, £6.

In "Nortuna" 1 free man, Godwine the priest, Harold's man, TRE [held] 50 acres as a manor. Then as now 3 bordars. Then as now in demesne 1 plough and half a plough belonging to the men. Half an acre of meadow. It is worth 34s. And 3 free men under him with 3 acres and half a plough, worth 12d.

[Folio 343v: SUFFOLK]

Turstin fitzGuy holds this from Roger Bigod. Over all this land St Æthelthryth has the soke, apart from over the hall of Walton and the vill.

HUNDRED OF WILFORD.

In Loudham 1 free man, Thorvald, commended to Eadric with 7 acres and 1 acre of meadow, worth 16d.

In Harpole 1 free man of Stigand's, commended to Algar, held 10 acres, worth 2s. Ranulf fitzWalter holds it.

In Debach Turstin fitzGu[...]y holds 1 free man and a half commended to Eadric with 8 acres, worth 16d.

In Capel [St Andrew] 1 free man commended to Northmann with 20 acres. Then 1 plough, now a half. Half an acre of meadow. It is worth 4s. Northmann holds it.

In Ufford 1 free man under the same commendation with 3 acres and in Loudham 2 acres, worth 12d. In Wilford 1 free man commended to Northmann with 7 acres and half an acre of meadow, worth 14d. Northmann holds this from Roger Bigod. In Bredfield 1 free man commended to Northmann with 4½ acres, worth 12d. In Wickham [Market] 1 free man with 2½ acres, worth 4d. The same Northmann holds this.

HUNDRED OF LOOSE.

In Rendlesham 1 free man commended to Eadric with 18 acres of land and 1 bordar, worth 2s. 8d. William Malet was seised of it on the day on which he died. In Gedgrave 1 free man commended to Northmann with 10 acres. It is in the valuation of Kelsale.

In Charsfield Turstin fitzGuy holds 1 free man, Beorhtmær, commended to St Æthelthryth TRE with 30 acres. Then as now 1 plough. 1 acre of meadow. Then it rendered 30s. And 5 free men

Roger Bigod

[Folio 344: SUFFOLK]

under the same commendation apart from 1 who was commended to Earl Ralph [...] and he was seised of it, with 16 acres. They are in the same valuation but they could not [...] pay. One of these was commended to Eadric and William Malet [...] was seised thereof. Now it is worth 20s. Turstin holds this from Roger Bigod.

In Woodbridge 1 free man commended to Ælfric with 4 acres, worth 8d. William de Bosc holds it.

HUNDRED OF PLUMESGATE.

In Rendham 1 bordar with 10 acres, worth 20d.

Free men

Free men of Roger Bigod. Half-Hundred of Parham.

In Blaxhall 8 free men with 66 acres. Of these 5 were commended to Northmann and 2 to the Abbot of Ely and 1 to the predecessor of Malet, Alwine by name. Then as now 2½ ploughs and 4 acres of meadow. Then it was worth 20s., now 25s. In the same place half a free man with 3 acres, worth 6d. The soke is the Abbot of Ely's. In the same place 2 acres and 1 slave, worth 8d. Northmann holds it. In the same place 1 free man, Ulf, commended to Northmann with 10 acres and half a plough. It is worth 2s. Northmann [holds it] from Roger. The soke is the abbot's.

In Wantisden Ælfric, Beorhtric, Eadhild, free men commended to Bigod's predecessor, with 11 acres, worth 2s. The same Northmann [holds it]. The soke is the abbot's. In the same place the same Northmann holds the fourth part of a church with 10 acres which one of his men held by commendation TRE.

HUNDRED OF PLUMESGATE.

Leofric, commended to Northmann, held Sternfield TRE with 50 acres as a manor. Then as now 3 bordars and 1½ acres and 1 acre of meadow. In the same place 2 free men commended to Northmann with 3 acres, worth 20s. Northmann [holds it] from Roger. The soke is the abbot's.

[Folio 344v: SUFFOLK]

William Malet held this manor on the day of his death, and Robert his son [likewise] [...]. In Farnham the same Leofric [held] TRE 20 acres [...] and 3 bordars and half a plough and 4 acres of meadow and 1 mill, [...] worth 5s. William Malet also held this and Robert Malet. Now Northmann [holds it] from Roger. The soke is the abbot's.

Wulfnoth, a free man commended to Malet's predecessor, held Benhall with 40 acres as a manor TRE. Then as now 2 bordars and 1 plough and 1 acre of meadow, worth 10s. The same Northmann holds it. William Malet held it and was seised of it and Robert his son [likewise]. The soke is the abbot's. In the same place 1 free man, Beorhtmær, commended to Malet's predecessor and William was seised of it and Robert likewise. 16 acres and 1 bordar. 1 acre of meadow. It is worth 32d. Northmann holds it.

In Rendham Ulf, a free man commended to Northmann, [held] 30 acres as a manor. 1 bordar and half a plough. 1 acre of meadow. It is worth 5s. Northmann holds it from Roger. The soke is the abbot's.

In Cransford Eadric, a free man commended to Eadric, held 14 acres TRE. Then as now half a plough. It is worth 26d. The same Northmann [holds it]. The soke is the abbot's.

In Sternfield Eadric, a free man commended to Northmann, [held] 34 acres and William Malet was seised thereof and Robert likewise. Then as now half a plough and 2 acres of meadow. It is worth 10s. 8d. The soke is the abbot's. Roger [holds this] in demesne. In the same place 16 free men and a half with 130 acres. Then as now 5 ploughs. It is worth 30s. Northmann had the commendation of 7 and a half TRE. The same Roger [holds this] in demesne.

Roger Bigod

[Folio 345: SUFFOLK]

Robert Malet's predecessor [had commendation over] 3 and a half Eskil, Leofric, Osgeat; Leofric Snipe [was] the half. Of these William Malet was seised and Robert likewise. The soke is the abbot's.

In [Great] Glemham 5 free men with 54 acres. Then as now 1½ ploughs. It is worth 10s. 4 of these were commended to Malet's predecessor and he was seised thereof, and William his father [likewise]. The same Roger [holds this] in demesne. The soke is the abbot's. In Bruisyard Beorhtmær, a free man commended to Eadric, Malet's predecessor, [held] 30 acres as a manor TRE. Then 1 plough, afterwards and now half. 1½ acres of meadow. 1 free man and a half commended with 2

acres. It is worth 5½s. Ralph holds this of Roger. The soke is the abbot's.

In Rendham Blæcsunu, a free man commended to Eadric, Malet's predecessor, held 66 acres as a manor TRE. and William was seised thereof. Then as now 1 villan and 3 bordars. 1½ ploughs and 2 acres of meadow. Woodland for 4 pigs. It is worth 12s. The same Ralph [holds this]. The soke is the abbot's.

In Swefling Wulfric, a free man belonging to Harold, [held] 60 [acres] as a manor TRE. Then as now 3 bordars and 1 plough in demesne. 3 free men added by commendation with 9 acres and 1 plough and 2 acres of meadow. Then 1 horse, now 2 head of cattle, 10 pigs and 15 sheep. It is worth 15s. The same Ralph [holds this].

In Rendham 4 free men and a half with 35 acres. Then as now 1 plough. It is worth 5s. 10d. Of these 3 Godric, Godric and Tholf were commended to Malet's predecessor and William Malet was seised thereof. The same Ralph [holds this]. The soke is the abbot's.

[Folio 345v: SUFFOLK]

In Dunningworth 1 free man with 8 acres and in Benhall 3 free men with 3 acres, worth 24d. Roger [holds this] in demesne. In Benhall Eadric, a free man, held 8 acres, worth 2s. This is in demesne. In [Great] Glemham 1 free man by commendation [held] 5 acres, worth 12d. And Northmann holds it from Roger. The soke is the abbot's.

HUNDRED OF CARLFORD.

[Folio 346: SUFFOLK]

HUNDRED OF CARLFORD.

Lands of Roger of Poitou.

In Culpho Beorhtric, a free man of St Æthelthryth held TRE 80 acres of land as a manor. Then as now 10 bordars. Then 4 slaves. Then in demesne 2 ploughs, now 3. Then 2 ploughs belonging to the men, now 1; 4 acres of meadow. Then 2 horses, now 1. Then 36 pigs, now 15. Then 100 sheep, now 60. Then it was worth 20s., now 30s. In Grundisburgh 1 free man of St Æthelthryth, Beorhtnoth, [held] 60 acres as a manor. Then as now 3 bordars. Then 1 plough, now none, and half a plough belonging to the men. 1 acre of meadow. Then and now worth 15s. Also in Culpho Godric, a free man of Harold, held TRE 40 acres of land as a manor and 3 bordars. Then 1 plough, now none. 2 acres of meadow. Then as now worth 10s.

In Tuddenham Leohtwine, a free man of Halfdan the predecessor of Geoffrey de Mandeville, held 30 acres and 2 bordars. Then 1 plough, now none. 3 acres of meadow. It is worth 10s. In the same place Godhere, a free man of St Æthelthryth, held TRE 68 acres of land as a manor. Then 3 bordars, now none. Then 2 ploughs, now a half. 4 acres of meadow. Then as now worth 25s. Also in the same place 12 free men commended to St Æthelthryth TRE [held] 50 acres of land and 2 bordars. Then 3 ploughs, now 2; 4 acres of meadow. Then it was worth 20s., now 15s.

In Culpho 5 free men commended to St Æthelthryth TRE

[held] 21 carucates. Then 1 plough, now a half. Half an acre of meadow. Then it was worth 7s., now 5s. 1 church with 10 acres, worth 20d.

In Grundisburgh 7 free men commended to St Æthelthryth TRE [held] 20 acres of land. Then 1 plough, now a half. Then it was worth 4s., now 5s. In the same place 1 free man, Sigeric, a man of King Edward, with 1½ acres.

[Folio 346v: SUFFOLK]

1½ acres [sic]. 1 free man commended to Beorhtric with 4 acres of land and 2 free men, Ælfric and Beorhtmann, commended to Æthelric of Burgh with 14 acres. Then between them 1 plough, now none. It is worth 10s. In the same place 2 free men, 1 commended to St Æthelthryth, the other commended to Halfdan, with 60 acres and 6 bordars. Then as now 2 ploughs. 2 acres of meadow. Then it was worth 12s., now 10s. In the same place Roger holds from Roger de Poitou 1 free man of St Æthelthryth TRE, with 40 acres and 1 bordar. Then 1 plough. 2 acres of meadow. Then it was worth 10s., now 8s.

In Clopton 1 free man, Wulfric, TRE commended to Harold held 1 carucate of land and 22 acres as a manor. Then as now 1 villan, 6 bordars and 1 slave. In demesne 2 ploughs. 4 acres of meadow. Then 1 plough belonging to the men, now none. Then 1 horse and now 4 head of cattle and 80 sheep. Then it was worth 40s., now 21s. It is 1 league long and a half broad. 13d. in geld. Roger holds it in demesne. In the same place 1 free man commended to the same Wulfric TRE with 1½ acres, worth 3d. Roger fitzArnold holds it.

In Hasketon Alwine, a free man of St Æthelthryth TRE, held 40 acres as a manor. Then and now 1 plough. 1 acre of meadow. Then it was worth 10s., now 6s. This Alwine could not sell his land nor give it away from the church of Ely.

In the same place 7 free men commended to St Æthelthryth [held] 16 acres. Then as now half a plough. It is worth 3s. Also in the same place 2 free men, half under commendation to Eadric, Robert Malet's predecessor, and 1 free [man] commended to someone commended to Eadric and 1 commended to Brun with 12 acres, worth 2s. In the same place 1 free man given to St Æthelthryth TRE with 9½ acres. Half an acre of meadow. It is worth 2s. And it is 6 furlongs long and 4 broad. In geld 4d. Roger fitzArnold holds this. In Thistleton 8 and a half

Roger de Poitou

[Folio 347: SUFFOLK]

free men commended to St Æthelthryth TRE with 30 acres. Then 2 ploughs, now 1. Then it was worth 20s., now 8s. In the same place 1 free man and a half commended to Æthelric of Burgh [held] 10 acres and half a plough, worth 2s. Also in the same place Arnold holds from Roger de Poitou 1 free man commended to St Æthelthryth TRE with 50 acres as a manor and 2 bordars. Then 1 plough. 1 acre of meadow. Then it was worth 20s., now 11s. In Burgh 1 free man of St Æthelthryth with 16 acres and 2 bordars. 1 acre of meadow. Then half a plough, now none. Then it was worth 5s., now 7s. Arnold holds this from Roger.

In Otley Andrew holds from Roger de Poitou [land] which

Eadweald, a free man of Harold, and his wife, commended to Eadric, held TRE with 2 carucates of land as a manor. Then as now 3 villans and 10 bordars. Then 3 slaves, now 1. Then in demesne 3 ploughs, now 1 but [more] could be there. Then 5 ploughs belonging to the men, now 3. Woodland for 4 pigs. 3 acres of meadow. Then 3 horses, now none. Then 12 head of cattle, now 1. Then 30 pigs, now 10. Then 60 sheep, now none. Then it was worth 100s., now 40s. It is 10 furlongs long and 6 broad. In geld 15d.

In Hasketon 2 free men, 1 commended to St Æthelthryth and the other commended to Lustwine TRE, [held] 13 acres, worth 2s. In the same place 7 free men and a half commended to Eadweald TRE. 1 and a half of these were commended to Grimulf, with 25 acres and 1 bordar. Then as now 1 plough. Half an acre of meadow. Then it was worth 5s., now 4s.

In Alnesbourn Albert holds of Roger de Poitou [land] which St Andrew held TRE with 1 carucate of land as a manor. Then as now 4 bordars. Then as now 1 plough in demesne. 6 acres of meadow and 60 sheep. Then it was worth 30s., now 10s. It is 6 furlongs long and 2 broad. In geld 5d.

In "Grenewic" 2 free men, 1 commended to King Edward and the other to Gyrth, with 2 carucates of land as 2 manors. Then as now 3 villans and 7 bordars. Then 4 ploughs

[Folio 347v: SUFFOLK]

in demesne, now none. Then 6 ploughs belonging to the men, now none. 3 acres of meadow. Then it was worth 40s., now 10s. It is 6 furlongs long and 4 broad. In geld 5d. In Newbourn 1 free man of Gyrth's with 15 acres, worth 16d. Albert Crematus holds this from Roger de Poitou.

In Rushmere [St Andrew] 6 acres, worth 12d. Hunebot holds these from Roger de Poitou.

HUNDRED OF WILFORD.

In Melton Roger fitzArnold holds from Roger de Poitou 7 free men commended to St Æthelthryth with 60 acres. Then as now 1 plough. Then it was worth 8s., now the same. In the same place 1 free man of St Æthelthryth with 26 acres, worth 50d. In Boulge 6 acres, worth 12d. In Debach 2 free [men] and a half commended to Wulfric with 15 acres and 1 acre of meadow, worth 3s.

HUNDRED OF LOOSE.

Wulfmær, a free man of St Æthelthryth, held Monewden TRE as a manor 1 carucate of land and 40 acres. Then 2 villans, now none. Now 9 bordars. Then 2 ploughs in demesne, now 1. And belonging to the men then as now 1 plough. 3 acres of meadow. Now 2 head of cattle. Then it was worth 40s., now 30s.

The same Wulfmær held Kettleburgh with 80 acres as a manor. Then as now 2 villans and 2 bordars. Then as now in demesne 1 plough and 1 belonging to the men. 3 acres of meadow. Then as now worth 20s. To this manor [belongs] 1 free woman under the same commendation with 14 acres. 1½ acres of meadow. It is worth 2s. 4d.

In Monewden TRE 14 free men and a half, now 10 under the same commendation with 80 acres and 4 acres. Then 4 ploughs, now 2. Then it was worth 20s., now 16s. Humphrey the chamberlain held the half of one of these but Ertald took it from him. 1 church with 30 acres and 1½ acres of meadow, worth 5s. In Easton 1 free man, commended to Wulfmær, held 10 acres

Roger de Poitou

[Folio 348: SUFFOLK]

worth 2s. In Letheringham 1 free man under the same commendation [held] 1½ acres, worth 4d. In Butley 5 free men and a half St Æthelthryth had the commendation over 4 and Eadric over 2 with 32 acres. Then 1½ ploughs, now 1. They are assessed with Sudbourne.

In Dallinghoo half a free man commended to Eadric Grim [held] 6 acres of land, worth 30d. In Woodbridge 16 free men commended to St Æthelthryth [held] 1 carucate of land and 2 acres and 2 bordars. Then 3 ploughs, now 2. Half an acre of meadow. Then it was worth 24s., now 20s. In the same place 10 acres in demesne.

In Monewden 1 free man with half an acre and in Martley 1 with half an acre, worth 2d.

HUNDRED OF WANGFORD.

In "Catesfella" 5 free men 2 were commended to Eadric of Laxfield and 3 commended to Wulfric [held] 30 acres. Then 2 ploughs, now 1. It is worth 5s. In Thrandeston 3 half free men commended to Eadric [held] 20 acres, worth 40d.

HUNDRED OF HARTISMERE.

Alflæd, a free woman commended to Harold, held Wickham [Skeith] with 2 carucates of land as a manor. Then as now 21 bordars. Then 6 slaves. Then in demesne 3 ploughs, now 1. Then 6 ploughs belonging to the men, now 2. Woodland for 40 pigs. 4 acres of meadow. Then 2 horses. Then 18 head of cattle, now 1. Then 40 pigs, now 14. Then 260 sheep, now 33. Then 60 goats. Then it was worth 100s., now 40s. In the same Wickham [Skeith] 1 free man and three half [free men] under the same commendation [held] 16 acres and half a plough and 1 bordar. Half an acre of meadow. It is worth 3s. 1 church with 12 acres, worth 2s.

HUNDRED OF BRADMERE.

Leofwine, a thegn of King Edward, held Ingham with 1 carucate of land as a manor. Then as now 2 bordars. Then 2 ploughs in demesne, afterwards [and] now a half. 4 acres of meadow. Then 1 horse. Then it was worth £4, now 20s.

[Folio 348v: SUFFOLK]

In the same place 10 free men over whom his predecessor had commendation TRE; they have 40 acres. Then 1 plough, now a half. Then it was worth 5s., now 3s. St Edmund has the soke.

HUNDRED OF RISBRIDGE.

Eadmær, a thegn of Earl Ælfgar, held Thurston [in Hawkendon] TRE as a manor with 2 carucates of land. Then as now 2 villans and 6 bordars and 2 ploughs in demesne. Then half a plough belonging to the men. 3 acres of meadow. Woodland for 6 pigs. Then 2 head of cattle, now 5.

Then 13 pigs, now 20. Then 40 sheep, now 50 and 6 beehives. Half a church with 15 acres of free land. Then as now worth 40s. Ulf held Hawkendon as a manor TRE with 2 carucates of land. Then as now 2 bordars and 3 slaves and 2 ploughs in demesne. 3 acres of meadow. Woodland for 4 pigs. Then as now 1 horse, 2 head of cattle, 16 pigs, 40 sheep and 12 goats. Half a church with 15 acres of free land. Then it was worth 30s., now 40s. It is 1 league long and a half broad. 13½d. in geld. Others have land there.

HALF-HUNDRED OF COSFORD.

In Thorpe [Morieux] 1 free man [held] 4 acres of land as a manor. Then 7 villans, now 3. Then as now 1 bordar and 2 slaves. Then 3 ploughs, now 2. Then 1 plough belonging to the men, now 2 oxen and 7 acres of meadow. Then 2 horses. Then 7 head of cattle, now 1. Then 60 pigs, now 9. Then 140 sheep. Then it was worth £6 [...], now £4. To this manor Norman fitzTancred added 7 free men with 25 acres. St Edmund has the soke and commendation over this. Then 1 plough. It is worth 3s. A church with 50 acres and 2 acres of meadow. Then 1 plough, now 2 oxen. 2 villans. It is worth 6s. It is 1 league long and 8 furlongs broad. 5d. in geld. In the same place 1 free man [held] 1½ carucates of land as a manor. Then 6 villans, now 7. And 2 bordars. Then

Roger de Poitou

[Folio 349: SUFFOLK]

2 slaves, now 1. Then 2 ploughs in demesne, now 1. Then 1 plough belonging to the men, now a half. 5 acres of meadow. Woodland for 4 pigs. 2 head of cattle. Then 26 pigs, now 14. Then 30 sheep, now 13 and 13 goats. Then it was worth 60s., now 40s. Over this Richard's predecessor, namely Wihtgar, had the commendation and the soke. St Edmund [holds] the 6 forfeitures.

HUNDRED OF BISHOP.

Wulfric, a thegn, held Whittingham TRE with 1½ carucates of land as a manor. Then 9 bordars, afterwards and now 14. Then as now 2 ploughs in demesne. Then 2 ploughs belonging to the men, afterwards and now 1. Woodland for 100 pigs. 16 acres of meadow and 4 acres of free land. Then as now 5 head of cattle. Then 20 pigs, now 18. Then 30 goats, now 40 and 1 beehive. Then as now worth 60s. The soke is in Hoxne. The same man held Mendham TRE as a manor with 1 carucate of land and 40 acres. Then as now 1 villan. Then 6 bordars, afterwards and now 10. Then as now 1 plough in demesne. Then 3 ploughs belonging to the men, afterwards and now 1½. Woodland for 100 pigs. 10 acres of meadow. Then as now 1 mill. 3 men with 20 acres of land. Then 1 plough, now a half. The fourth part of a church with 10 acres. Those men could not give or sell the land but the soke is in Hoxne. Here belong 60 acres and they lie in Weybread. Then as now 2 villans and 2 bordars. Woodland for 6 pigs. 3 acres of meadow. Then as now worth £4. In Weybread 4 free men and a half by commendation [held] 35½ acres. Then 2 ploughs, afterwards 1, now a half. It is worth 10s.

In Stradbroke 2 free men by commendation [held] 30 acres.

Woodland for 8 pigs. Then 1 plough, afterwards and now a half. It is worth 10s.

In Chickering 1 free man by commendation [held] 24 acres. Woodland for 4 pigs. Half an acre of meadow. Then and [afterwards] half a plough, now none. It is worth 4s. In Weybread 4 acres in demesne. In Mendham 3 free men

with 1 carucate of land. Of these William Malet was seised of two who were commended to Robert Malet's predecessor and the third to Bishop Æthelmær with a fourth part of the land. Then as now 1 villan. Then 6 bordars, now 9. Woodland for 60 pigs. 5 acres of meadow. In the same place 2 men with 3 acres. Then half a plough, now 2 oxen. In the same place 1 free man with 15 acres. Ulf, his predecessor, [had] the commendation TRE. Then half a plough. The whole is worth 56s. The soke over the whole is in Hoxne, the Bishop's [manor].

HUNDRED OF COLNEIS.

In Hemley 10 acres which belong to Clopton. 2 bordars have 2 oxen. It is in the valuation of Clopton

HUNDRED OF THINGOE.

Wulfmær, a thegn under Stigand, held Risby with 2 carucates of land. Then 6 bordars, now 3. Then 4 slaves, now none. Then 2 ploughs, now 1; 2 acres of meadow and half a mill. Then it was worth 60s., now 20s.

In Brockley 3 free men. Of these St Edmund had commendation with the soke over one and he could not sell. Over the other 2 the king had commendation but they could not sell in St Edmund's soke. Between them all [they had] 60 acres of land and 1 villan and 1 slave. Then as now 1 plough and 1½ acres of meadow. Then as now worth 10s.

TWO HUNDREDS OF BABERGH.

Wulfric, a thegn of King Edward's, held Boxted as 2 carucates of land. Then and afterwards 2 villans, now 1. Then as now 11 bordars. Then 4 slaves, afterwards and now 3. Then 3 ploughs in demesne, afterwards and now 2, and half a plough belonging to the men. 15 acres of meadow. Woodland for 5 pigs. Then 3 horses; when Roger left, 2; now none. Then 5 head of cattle, now 4. Then 24 pigs, now 15. Then 30 sheep, now 71. In the same place 5 free men in the commendation and soke of Wihtgar with 2 carucates of land and they could sell but the king gave them to Norman fitzTancred. And in the same place 1 free man with 45 acres commended to the same Wulfric. Of this land 30 acres are in the soke of St Æthelthryth

Roger de Poitou

and 15 in the soke of Northmann, the predecessor of Ralph de Limésy, in Cavendish. And under them [are] 3 bordars. Then between them all 4 ploughs, afterwards and now 2. And in the same manor half a carucate of land under St Edmund which they could not sell without the abbot's permission, but the king gave it to Norman fitzTancred. And 1 slave. Then 1 plough, now none. Boxted then was worth £8, afterwards £7,

now 100s. The free men were at farm for 52s.; now the manor and free [men] together are worth £6. It is 1 league long and 5 furlongs broad. In geld 7d.

Wulfweard, a free man under Stigand, held Preston [near Lavenham] TRE as a manor with 2 carucates of land together with the soke. Then as now 4 villans and 4 bordars and 1 slave. Then 3 ploughs in demesne, afterwards and now 2. Then as now 1 plough belonging to the men. 9 acres of meadow. Then 5 head of cattle, now 4. Then 24 pigs, now 3. Then 40 sheep, now 36. In the same place 3 free men commended to Wulfweard. Over 2 St Edmund had the soke and sake and over the third Wihtgar, Richard's predecessor. But earlier Norman fitzTancred [had it]; now Roger de Poitou [has it]. They have 23 acres between them and half a plough. Then and afterwards the whole was worth £4, now £3. In [Great and Little] Waldingfield Wulfmær, a thegn under Harold TRE, held 1 carucate of land together with the soke. Then as now 1 villan and 5 bordars. Then 1 slave, now none. Then as now 2 ploughs in demesne. Woodland for 3 pigs and 4 acres of meadow. Then as now 1 horse. Then as now 2 head of cattle. Then 12 pigs, now none. Then it was worth 30s., afterwards and now it renders 40s. It is half a league long and half a broad. In geld 7½d., whoever holds [land] there. A church with 30 acres.

HUNDRED OF STOW.

Leofwine Croc held Buxhall TRE with 2 carucates of land. Then as now 4 bordars. Then 3 slaves, afterwards and now none. Then as now 2 ploughs

in demesne and 16 acres of meadow. Then half a mill. Then 2 horses, 1 ox. Then 53 pigs, now 16. Then 28 sheep, now 30. A church with 30 acres and half an acre of meadow. Then as now worth 60s. He had soke and sake over the hall and the bordars. And 7 free men and a half under the same by commendation only TRE. The soke is in the Hundred. It has 37 acres. Then 2 ploughs, afterwards and now a half. 1 acre of meadow. Then as now worth 10s. And to this manor Norman fitzTancred added 3 free men in the king's commendation and soke with 24 acres. Then and afterwards 1 plough, now 2 oxen. It is worth 40d.

In [Old] Newton 2 free men of Alsige TRE, the nephew of Ralph [the staller], by commendation only, with 70 acres of land in the soke and sake of the king and the earl, and 2 bordars. Then 1½ ploughs, afterwards and now none. Then it was worth 30s., afterwards and now 20s.

In Thorney 1 free man of King Edward's with the soke and sake and after King William came, likewise. And Norman received him from this manor without livery and afterwards Gerald held him; after Gerald, Roger de Poitou. He has 60 acres. Then 1 plough and afterwards a half. Now 1 ox. Then it was worth 10s., now it hardly renders 5s.

In [Earl and Little] Stonham there are 50 acres of demesne land of the hall in Creeting [St Peter].

In Creeting [St Peter] 7 free men. 5 were under Alflæd TRE by commendation only; 2 were commended to the king, with soke and sake over all in the Hundred. 30 acres. Then as now 2 ploughs. It is worth 20s. In the same place 1 sokeman with 3 acres of forfeited land.

In Thorney 24 and 1 bordar and they belong to the hall of [Earl and Little] Stonham.

HUNDRED OF BOSMERE.

Wulfric, a thegn, held [Earl and Little] Stonham TRE with 2 carucates of land. Now Roger [holds it] in demesne. Then as now 8 villans and 3 bordars and 4 slaves and 2 ploughs in demesne. Then and afterwards 3 ploughs belonging to the men, now 2½; 5 acres of meadow. Woodland for 60 pigs. A third part of this woodland belonged to Tunstall to the manor of William de Warenne TRE. Now Roger de Poitou holds it.

Roger de Poitou

[Folio 351: SUFFOLK]

Raymond Gerald held it formerly. The third part of a church with 5 acres. Then as now 2 horses and 30 pigs. Then 5 head of cattle, now 9. Now 60 sheep. Then 30 goats, now 50. Then it was worth 100s., now £6. The king and the earl have the soke.

In the same place Wulfmær, a thegn commended to Harold, held 2 carucates of land as a manor TRE. Then as now 8 villans and 3 bordars and 4 slaves and 2 ploughs in demesne. 1 mill in Claydon. Then and afterwards 3 ploughs belonging to the men, now 2½; 5 acres of meadow. Woodland for 60 pigs The third part of a church with 4 acres. Then as now 2 horses; now 60 sheep. Then it was worth 100s., now £6. The king and the earl have the soke.

In the same place Alflæd, commended to Harold, held 2 carucates of land as a manor TRE. Then as now 8 villans and 3 bordars and 4 slaves and 2 ploughs in demesne. Then and afterwards 3 ploughs belonging to the men, now 2½. 5 acres of meadow. Woodland for 60 pigs. The third part of a church with 4 acres. Then as now 1 horse; now 60 sheep. Then it was worth 100s., now it is worth £6. The king and the earl have the soke over the whole. In the same place Wulfwine, a free man commended to Wulfmær, Roger de Poitou's predecessor, held 40 acres as a manor; now Roger [holds it] in demesne. Then as now 3 bordars. Then 1 plough, now a half. 2 acres of meadow. [It is] in the above valuation of [Earl and Little] Stonham. In the same place a free man, Wulfræd, commended to Alflæd, Roger's predecessor, held 20 acres. And they are in the same valuation. It is 1 league long and a half broad. 7½d. in geld.

In the same place 1 free man, Ælfric, held 12 acres over whom the Abbot of St Edmund had half the commendation and the other half of the commendation was in the king's manor of Mendlesham. The abbot held this half of the commendation and of the land until Artald was seised of it. And it is in the above valuation.

Alflæd, a free woman commended to Harold, held Willisham

[Folio 351v: SUFFOLK]

TRE with 2 carucates of land as a manor; now Albert [holds it] from Roger. Then as now 3 villans and 10 bordars. Then 3 slaves, now 1; 2 ploughs in demesne. Then 5 ploughs belonging to the men, now 3; 5 acres of meadow. A church

with 32 acres. Then it was worth £4, now £3. In the same place 1 free man, Leofric by name, with 20 acres. It is worth 4s. In the same place 1 free man, Wighulf, [held] 40 acres as a manor TRE; now the same Albert [holds it]. Then half a plough. It is worth 8s. The king and the earl have the soke. In the same place a free man, Theodric, held 80 acres as a manor TRE. Then as now 2 bordars and 1 plough in demesne and half a plough belonging to the men. 2 acres of meadow. It is worth 16s. The king and the earl have the soke. And 2 free men, Leofric and Godmann, [held] 9 acres. This Godmann was commended to the Abbot of Ely and he had the soke TRE. It is worth 3s. Albert holds the whole. It is 1 league long and 4 furlongs and 20 perches broad. 6½d. in geld.

Leofstan, commended to the Abbot of Ely, held [Great] Blakenham with 1½ carucates of land as a manor. Now the same Albert [holds it]. Then as now 4 bordars. Then 1½ ploughs in demesne, now none. 5 acres of meadow. Then it was worth 40s., now 30s. The king and the earl have the soke. In the same place 3 free men [held] 6½ acres, worth 12d. The king and the earl have the soke. Eadred, a free man commended to Wihtgar, held Tunstall with 60 acres and 2 acres of meadow. Then as now 2 bordars. And 1 free man, Eadwig, with 3 acres. It is worth 10s. The same Albert [now] holds. It is 1 league long and 5 furlongs broad. 5d. in geld. In Hemingstone 20 free men [held] 142 acres. One of these was commended to the Abbot of Ely with 13 acres, and he had the soke. 6 bordars. Then as now 5 ploughs and 2 acres of meadow. Half a church with 15 acres, worth 30d. 8 acres belonged [to this]

Roger de Poitou

[Folio 352: SUFFOLK]

which Hervey de Bourges took. To the aforementioned church belong also 6 acres which Fin, Richard's predecessor, took. Then it was worth 40s., now 30s. Roger holds these men in demesne. The king and the earl have the soke. It is 6 furlongs long and 6 broad. 8d. in geld. A church with 3 acres, worth 6d.

In Hemingstone 1 free man, Leofwine, held 1 acre of land and 1 bordar TRE; now Almær, the king's reeve, holds it. It is worth 2s. The king and the earl have the soke.

In Olden [in Coddenham] 1 free man, Almær, [held] 4 acres and half a and 1 bordar, worth 8d. The king and the earl have the soke. In "Langhedena" Algar, a free man, [held] 3 acres, worth 6d. In [Earl and Little] Stonham 1 free man, Leofric, commended to the Abbot of Ely, [held] 6 acres, and in Coddenham 3 acres, worth 18d. In the same place Godwine, a free man, [held] 10 acres and 2 oxen by commendation to Wihtgar, the predecessor of Richard fitzGilbert. It is worth 4s. Raymond Gerald was seised of this and Roger de Poitou holds him. Roger de Rames [held it] by right of the first livery. The Hundred testifies that it was first delivered to him.

In "Langedana" Ginni, a free man, [held] 1½ acres, worth 3d. The king and the earl have the soke. In Hemingstone 1 free [man], Æthelwine, [held] 1½ acres, worth 3d. In the same place 1 free man, Beorhtmær, [held] 1½ acres, worth 4d.

HUNDRED OF CLAYDON.

In Barham Lustwine held 60 acres as a manor. Wihtgar had half the commendation and soke and the Abbot of Ely the other half and soke. Then 1 plough. Then as now 5 bordars. 3 acres of meadow. It is worth 10s. Gosbert holds it from Roger.

[Folio 352v: SUFFOLK]

In the same place 7 free men [held] 47 acres. Then 2 ploughs, now 1; 2 bordars. It is worth 10s. The same Gosbert [holds it]. In the same place 4 free men [held] 40 acres. Then as now 1 plough. Then it was worth 8s., now 6s. 8d. Over three of these the abbot had half the soke and the whole commendation and over the fourth the king had the soke and commendation.

In Hemingstone 1 free man [held] 1½ acres. Then it was worth 4d., now 3d. Isaac [holds this] from Roger. The king and the earl have the soke. In Akenham 1 free man, Leofweald, [held] 20 acres in the soke and commendation of the king. It is worth 4s.

In the same place Alweald, a free man, with 6 acres in the soke and commendation of the abbot. It is worth 12d. In Thurlston 5 free men [held] 26 acres in the soke of the king. Then half a plough. It is worth 4s. Gosbert holds it. The soke is the king's and the earl's.

In Thurlston the same Gosbert holds 18 free men with 80 , less 2 acres. Then 3 ploughs, now 2; 1 acre of meadow. Half a church with 5 acres. Then it was worth 20s., now 13s. 4d. The soke is the king's and the earl's.

In Akenham 3 free men [held] 16 acres and half a plough and half a church with 5 acres, worth 32d. The soke is the king's and the earl's. In Henley 1 free man [held] 6 acres, worth 12d. The soke is the king's.

In Westerfield half a church with 7½ acres. In Helmingham 3 free men [held] 9 acres, worth 2s. The king and the earl have the soke. In Thurlston 1 free man, Algar the priest, with 3 acres, worth 6d.

In Westerfield 2 free men with 9 acres, worth 18d. The soke is the king's and the earl's. In Coddenham 2 free men [held] 18 acres TRE. 1 plough, now none. It is worth 4s. In Barham 1 free man with 1 acre,

Roger de Poitou

[Folio 353: SUFFOLK]

worth 3d. In Henley 1 free woman with half an acre, worth 1d. The soke is the king's and the earl's.

HALF-HUNDRED OF PARHAM.

In the soke of the Abbot of Ely. In Wantisden 14 free men [held] 40 acres in the soke and commendation of the Abbot of Ely. In Blaxhall 1 free man [held] 10 acres in the soke and commendation of the Abbot of Ely. Then and afterwards 2 ploughs, now 1½; 2 acres of meadow. It is worth 8s. Roger [holds it] in demesne.

HUNDRED OF PLUMESGATE.

Edwin the priest, a sokeman of the abbot, held "Nordberia" with 30 acres as a manor TRE. Then as now 1 plough and 4 head of cattle and 8 pigs. Then 60 sheep, now 40. Then and afterwards worth 20s. and now the same. In the same place 48 free men have been added to his manor with 260½ acres. Then as now 10 ploughs and 2 acres of meadow. Woodland for 8 pigs. Then and afterwards worth £10, now £11. All these were in the soke and commendation of the abbot and one [was] a sokeman, Godric by name. In [Great] Glemham 1 free man [held] 5 acres, worth 12d. [This is] in demesne. The soke is the abbot's.

IX land of William d'Écouis.

Hundred of Bosmere.

Ælfric, a thegn, held [Great] Blakenham TRE with 1 carucate of land as a manor. Then as now 6 bordars. Then 1 plough in demesne, now 2. Half a plough belonging to the men. 5 acres of meadow. Then as now

[Folio 353v: SUFFOLK]

2 mills and 1 horse. Then 2 head of cattle, now 4. Then 7 pigs, now 11. Then 12 sheep, now 14. A church with 1 acre and [worth] 2d. To this manor Hardwin added 28 free men with 171 acres and 1 bordar. Brunard holds 60 acres of this land and 1 plough, worth 15s. Then 6 ploughs, afterwards and now 2; 10 acres of meadow. 2 parts of a mill. Then as now the manor is worth £3 and the free men 45s. The king and the earl have the soke over the whole. It is 5 furlongs long and 5 broad. 7d. in geld. This manor was at farm for three years at £12 and also 1 ounce of gold in three years as exactions. But the men who received it thus at farm have all been ruined.

HUNDRED OF BLACKBOURN.

Howard de Vernon holds [Market] Weston from William which Ælfric, a free man, held TRE as a manor with 1 carucate of land and 8 acres in [Ixworth] Thorpe. Then 4 villans, now 2. Then as now 1 plough in demesne and 1 plough belonging to the men. 2 acres of meadow. Woodland for 10 pigs. Now 2 horses. Then as now 10 pigs. Then 15 sheep, now 80. A church with 4 acres. It is worth 20s. 3 free men with 1 carucate of land and 20 acres. Then 3 ploughs. 3 acres of meadow. It is worth 20s. Of this land Hugh, William's man, annexed 25 acres against the abbot. These men could not give or sell their land TRE but the commendation and soke and sake remained with St Edmund. In the same place 10 sokemen of St Edmund with every customary due TRE but Hardwin held them in the time of King William. They have 60 acres of land. Then 2 ploughs, now a half. It is worth 4s. It is 7 furlongs and 5 broad. 9d. in geld. Others hold [land] there.

HUNDRED OF BLYTHING.

William d'Écouis has the manor of Cookley.

William d'Écouis

[Folio 354: SUFFOLK]

Wulfric, a free man, held it TRE. Then as now 6 carucates of land. Then 6 villans, now 2. Then 6 bordars, now 11. Then as now 1 slave. Then as now 2 ploughs in demesne. Then as now 2 ploughs belonging to the men. Then as now woodland for four score pigs. 6 acres of meadow. 1 mill. Then 2 horses and then as now 1 cow, 8 pigs, 7 sheep and 30 goats and 2 beehives. Half a church with 1 acre. Of this manor Howard de Vernon and Robert de Vaux are enfeoffed and Howard's part is worth 50s. and Robert's part 8s. It is 14 furlongs long and 7 broad. It renders 7½d. to the king's geld.

HUNDRED OF CLAYDON.

In Thurlston 2 free men [with] 5 [acres] and 1 bordar. Then half a plough. It is worth 15d.

X. Lands of Hermer de Ferrers.

HUNDRED OF BLACKBOURN.

Osmund, a free man over whom St Edmund had the commendation TRE and the soke and sake, held Barningham as a manor with half a carucate of land. Then as now 1 villan and 2 bordars and 1 plough in demesne. Half a plough [belonging to the men]. 2 acres of meadow. It is worth 10s. St Edmund has the soke.

HUNDRED OF WILFORD.

XI. Lands of R[alph de] Beaufour.

In Bawdsey 14 free men commended to Godric TRE [held] 62 acres as a manor with 1 bordar. Then 3 ploughs, now 2; 2 acres of meadow. It is worth 30s. In 'Thurstanestuna' [in Bromeswell] 6 free men under the same commendation with 40 acres as a manor.

[Folio 354V: SUFFOLK]

Then 2 ploughs, now 1. It is worth 20s. In Ramsholt 6 free men under the same commendation with 20 acres. Then 1 plough, now a half. It is worth 10s.

Hundred of Hartismere. Richard de Saint-Clair holds Wortham from Ralph which Modgifu, a free woman commended to St Edmund, held TRE with 1½ carucates of land as a manor. Then as now 18 bordars and 2 slaves. In demesne 2 ploughs and belonging to the men 2 ploughs. Woodland for 10 pigs. 2 acres of meadow. 1 horse and 3 head of cattle and 20 pigs; now 20 goats. Then it was worth 40s., now 100s. He could not sell or give this land away from the church. St Edmund has the soke. In the same place 1 free woman, Godgifu, under commendation and in the soke and sake of St Edmund TRE, [held] 80 [acres] as a manor. Then as now 6 bordars. Then 1 plough, now none. Then and now belonging to the men 1 plough. 4 acres of meadow. Then it was worth 20s., now the same. 2 churches with 40 acres, worth 7s. In the same place 14 free men under the same commendation with 90

acres. Then as now 3 ploughs. 1 acre of meadow. Then as now worth 13s. Richard holds this from Ralph. In Brome 1 bordar with 8 acres. It belongs to Wortham and is worth 12d.

XII. Lands of Frodo, the Abbot's Brother.

HUNDRED OF BLACKBOURN.

Acwulf, a thegn, held Thelnetham as a manor TRE with 2 carucates of land. Then as now 8 bordars. Then 6 slaves, now 2. Then as now 3 ploughs in demesne and 1 plough belonging to the men. 4 acres of meadow. Woodland for 30 pigs. Then as now 1 mill. Then 1 horse. Then as now 3 head of cattle. Then 50 pigs, now 25. Then 2 sheep, now 35. And now 3 beehives.

Frodo

[Folio 355: SUFFOLK]

15 free men by commendation [held] 40 acres. Then as now 2 ploughs. Then it was worth £3 and now 50s. and the free men 60s. A church with 20 acres. St Edmund has the soke and sake. It is 10 furlongs long and 4 broad. 9¼d. in geld.

HUNDRED OF THEDWESTRY.

In Hessett 6 free men commended to St Æthelthryth in the soke of St Edmund [held] 1 carucate of land and 1 bordar. Then and afterwards 3 ploughs, now 1 and 1 acre of meadow. Then it was worth 60s., now 20s.

HUNDRED OF LACKFORD.

Ordmær held Worlington TRE with 6 carucates of land. Then as now 16 villans and 6 bordars and 2 slaves. 2 ploughs in demesne and 4 ploughs belonging to the men. 12 acres of meadow. 2 fisheries and 1 mill. 1 church without land. Then as now 1 horse. Then 20 head of cattle, now 8. Then 80 sheep, now 100. Then and afterwards [worth] £6, now £7. It is 10 furlongs long and 8 broad. In geld 20d.

In Tuddenham Leofric, 1 free man of Earl Ælfgar, held 1½ carucates of land. Then as now 2 villans and 2 bordars and 2 slaves. Then as now 1 plough in demesne and half a plough belonging to the men. 1½ acres of meadow. 1 mill. Now 6 pigs. Then 160 sheep, now 80 sheep. Then it was worth 40s., now 60s. The soke and sake are St Edmund's.

TWO HUNDREDS OF BABERGH.

Ælfgar held Kentwell freely under Siward of Maldon TRE as a manor with 2 carucates of land with the soke. Then 7 villans, afterwards and now 4. Then and afterwards 1 bordar, now 3. Then as now 2 ploughs in demesne. Then and afterwards 2 ploughs belonging to the men, now 1; 8 acres of meadow. Then as now 1 horse at the hall. Then 5 head of cattle, now 8. Then 30 pigs, now 40. Then 80 sheep, now 50. Then and afterwards it was worth 40s., now £4.

Alwig held Lavenham under St Edmund with the soke TRE as a manor with 2 carucates of land which he could not sell without the abbot's permission. Now Frodo holds it from King William and claims it for his fief saying that it was delivered to him.

Then as now 5 bordars and 1 slave. Then as now 2 ploughs in demesne and 2 ploughs belonging to the men. 3 acres of meadow. Now 2 horses at the hall. Now 12 head of cattle. Then 12 pigs, now 4. Then 40 sheep, now 102. Then it was worth 40s., now £4. It is half a league long and 4 furlongs broad. In geld 1½d.

HUNDRED OF STOW.

In Buxhall 25 free men in the king's soke who were delivered to Frodo held 3½ carucates of land as a manor; 3½ carucates of land. Then as now 5½ bordars. And TRE and afterwards 7 ploughs between them all, now 2 in demesne and 3 belonging to the men. 10 acres of land. Then 2 horses, now 1. Then as now 6 head of cattle. Now 22 pigs. Now 36 sheep. Then and afterwards worth 60s., now 100s. It is 1 league long and 8 furlongs broad whoever holds [land] there. In geld 25d. The king and the earl have the soke.

XIII. Land of Godric the Steward. Hundred of Bishop.

In Mendham 1 bordar with 4 acres, worth 12d.

HUNDRED OF BLYTHING.

Edwin, a free man, held Blyford TRE with 2 carucates of land as a manor. Now Godric [holds it] in demesne. Then as now 5 villans and 3 bordars and 2 slaves. 2 ploughs in demesne and 3 ploughs belonging to the men. 1 acre of meadow. Woodland for 160 pigs. Now 1 mill. Then as now 1 horse. Then 4 head of cattle, now 9, and 17 pigs and 3 sheep. A church with 12 acres. Then as now worth 40s. It is 1 league long and 1 league broad. 3½d. in geld. The same Godric has the soke. In Holton 3 free men,

Godric

Wulfmær, Æthelmær, Othulf, [held] 33 acres. Half an acre of meadow. Then as now 1 plough in demesne. It is worth 5s. Count Alan has the soke over the whole of Holton apart from Osbert's land. In the same vill 6 free men with 27 acres. 1 plough. It is worth 10s. 1 free man held "Uuarle" with 50 acres as a manor. 4 bordars. Then as now 1 plough. 4 acres of meadow. Woodland for 12 pigs. It is worth 7s. The soke is in the Hundred. In Bulcamp Thorth, 1 free man, held 30 acres of land as a manor. Then as now 2 villans and half a bordar. 1 plough. 1 acre of meadow. Woodland for 40 pigs. It is worth 5s.

HUNDRED OF WANGFORD.

Godric, a free man commended to Ralph the staller, held [South] Elmham with 40 acres as a manor. Then as now 2 villans and 1 bordar and 1 slave. 1 plough in demesne and half a plough belonging to the men. Woodland for 4 pigs. 2 acres of meadow. The fifth part of 1 mill. 1 church with 8 acres and the fifth part of 1 church with 6 acres, worth 12d. Then it was

worth 7s., now it renders 20s. And under him 2 free men with 5 acres and half a plough, in the same valuation. In Ilketshall 1 free man, Anund, commended to Edwin, [held] 30 acres and 5 bordars. Then as now 1 plough and half a plough belonging to the men. 1 acre of land. Then it was worth 8s. 4d., now 10s.

XIIII. Land of St Edmund In Suffolk.

HUNDRED OF THINGOE.

St Edmund held Risby TRE as a manor with 2 carucates of land. Then as now 4 villans and 2 bordars. Then 2 ploughs in demesne, now 4. Then as now 1 plough belonging to the men. Then 3 slaves, now 1 and 1 acre of meadow. Now 3 horses, 12 head of cattle, 30 pigs, 90 sheep and 32 goats. 7 sokemen with 1½ carucates of land. 1 bordar and 1 slave. Then as now 3 ploughs. Over these men St Edmund had the sake and soke and the commendation and all customary dues. And they could not give or sell the land without the abbot's consent. All also [belong] to the fold except one who had a fold for himself. In the same place 1 free man gave a carucate of land which Norman holds from the abbot. 4 bordars and 1 slave. Then 1 plough and now, and 1 acre of meadow. He could give and sell the land but the sake and soke and commendation continued to belong to St [Edmund]. Then as now worth 10s. A church with 24 acres of free land. This manor, not including the free man, was then worth £4, now £6. It is 9 furlongs long and 8 broad. In geld 20d. Others hold [land] there.

St Edmund held [Little] Horringer TRE as a manor with 4 carucates of land. Then as now 3 villans and 15 bordars. Then as now 4 ploughs in demesne and then as now 5 ploughs belonging to the men. Then as now 7 slaves and 3 acres of meadow. Woodland for 5 pigs. Now 5 horses. Now 4 head of cattle, 30 pigs and 45 sheep. 15 sokeman with 1 carucate of land and 1 bordar. Then as now 4 ploughs. These men belong to St Edmund with the sake and soke and every customary due. They cannot give or sell the land without the abbot's permission. A church with 6 acres of free land. Then this manor was worth £6, now £8. It is 9 furlongs long and 8 broad. In geld 20d. Others hold [land] there.

St Edmund held Whepstead TRE as a manor with 5 carucates of land. Then as now 10 villans and 18 bordars. Then as now 4 ploughs in demesne. Then as now 6 ploughs belonging to the men. Then as now 9 slaves and 10 acres of meadow. Woodland for 40 pigs. Now 5 horses and 18 head of cattle and 30 pigs and 100 sheep. 1 sokeman with 30 acres of land. 4 bordars and 1 slave. Then as now 1 plough and 2 acres of meadow. Woodland for 5 pigs. Over this man St [Edmund] has the sake and soke and the commendation with every customary due. And he cannot give or sell the land without the abbot's permission. In the same place 6 free men with 1½ carucates of land which Ralph holds apart from 30 acres and 4 bordars. Then as now 3 ploughs and 3 acres of meadow. Woodland for 3 pigs. It is worth 50s. These men could give and sell the land but the sake, soke, commendation and service continued to belong

St Edmund

to St [Edmund]. Then as now worth 60s. A church with 30 acres of free land. This manor, not including the free men, was then worth £7, now £10. It is 9 furlongs long and 8 broad. In geld 20d.

St Edmund held Nowton TRE as a manor with 4 carucates of land. Then as now 10 villans and 10 bordars. Then as now 4 ploughs in demesne and then as now 4 ploughs belonging to the men. Then as now 4 slaves. 4 acres of meadow. Woodland for 5 pigs. 1 mill. Now 4 horses, 18 head of cattle, 23 pigs, 80 sheep and 3 beehives. 10 sokemen with half a carucate of land. Then as now 2 ploughs. 4 acres of meadow. Over these he had then, and now has, sake and soke and commendation with all the customary dues. And they could not give or sell the land without the abbot's permission. A church with 8 acres of free land. Then this manor was worth £5, now £10. It is 10 furlongs long and 6 broad. In geld 6½d.

St Edmund held Chevington as a manor with 6 carucates of land. Then as now 13 villans and 9 bordars. Then as now 4 ploughs in demesne and then as now 4 ploughs belonging to the men. Then 6 slaves, now 7; 10 acres of meadow. Woodland for 100 pigs. Now 7 horses, 22 head of cattle and 30 pigs. Now 140 sheep and 40 goats and 3 beehives. 1 sokeman with 30 acres of land. 2 bordars. Then as now 1 plough. 1 acre of meadow. Woodland for 4 pigs. Over this man St [Edmund] has sake and soke and commendation with all customary dues. And he could not give or sell the land without permission. A church with 30 acres of free land. This manor was then worth £6, now £10. It is 10 furlongs long and 8 broad. In geld 6½d.

St Edmund held [Great and Little] Saxham as a manor with 5 carucates of land. Then as now 12 villans and 6 bordars. Then as now 3 ploughs in demesne. Then as now 6 ploughs belonging to the men. Then as now 4 slaves. 5 acres of meadow. Woodland for 80 pigs. Now 4 horses, 15 head of cattle, 36 pigs and 100 sheep. Then it was worth £6, now £10. It is 1 league long and 5 furlongs broad. In geld 7d.

St Edmund held Lackford TRE as a manor with 5 carucates of land. Then as now 14 villans and 7 bordars. Then as now 3 ploughs in demesne and then as now 4 ploughs belonging to the men. Then as now 4 slaves. 30 acres of meadow. 2 mills. Now 2 horses, 9 head of cattle, 13 pigs and 160 sheep. 1 sokeman with 8 acres of land. Then as now 2 oxen. Over this man St [Edmund] has sake and soke and commendation. He could not give or sell the land without permission. A church with 20 acres of free land. Then this manor was worth £6, now £8. It is 1 league long and 10 furlongs broad. In geld 6d.

St Edmund held Hengrave TRE as a manor with 3 carucates of land. Then as now 2 villans. Then 2 bordars, now 6. Then as now 2 ploughs in demesne and then as now 3 ploughs belonging to the men. Then as now 3 slaves. 1 acre of meadow. 1 mill. Now 2 horses, 12 head of cattle, 20 pigs and 60 sheep. 8 sokemen with 60 acres of land. Then as now 1 plough. Over these men [St Edmund] has sake and soke and commendation with regard to all customs. They could not give or sell the land without the abbot's permission. A church with 30 acres of free land. Then this manor was worth 50s. now 60s. It is 6 furlongs long and similarly 6 broad. In geld 10d.

St Edmund held Fornham [All Saints] TRE as a manor with 1 carucate of land. Then as now 4 bordars. Then as now 1 plough in demesne and then as now 1 plough belonging to the men. Then as now 1 slave. 4 acres of meadow. 1 mill. Then as now 2 horses, 14 head of cattle, 30 pigs and 60 sheep. 3 sokemen with 30 acres of land. Then as now half a plough. These men belong to St Edmund with sake and soke and commendation and all customary dues. And they could not give or sell the land without permission. In the same place 2 free men with 1½ carucates of land. 1 villan. 3 bordars. Then as now 2 ploughs. They could give and sell the land but the sake and soke and commendation continued to belong to St Edmund. Then as now worth 40s. A church with 12 acres of free land. This manor, not including the free [men], was worth then as now 40s. It is 8 furlongs long and 5 broad. In geld 10d.

St Edmund held Ickworth TRE as 3 carucates of land. Then as now 9 villans and 4 bordars. Then as now 2 ploughs in demesne. Then as now 4 ploughs belonging to the men. Then as now 4 slaves. 6 acres of meadow. Woodland for 24 pigs. Mill, 1; 2 horses, 16 head of cattle, 30 pigs and 80 sheep. A church with half an acre of land. Then this manor was worth £3, now £4. It is 8 furlongs long and 5 broad. In geld 7½d. In [Great and Little] Saxham Albert and Fulcher hold from the abbot 3 free men with 2½ carucates of land. 8 bordars. Then as now 4 ploughs. 3 acres of meadow. Woodland for 5 pigs. Half a mill. Two of these could give and sell the land but the sake and soke and commendation continued to belong to St Edmund. The third could not [give or sell] without the abbot's [permission]. Then as now worth 80s. Two parts of a church with 6 acres of land. It is 8 furlongs long and 5 broad. In geld 7d. Others hold [land] there.

[...] In Flempton Wulfweard holds from the abbot 10 sokemen with 1 carucate

St Edmund

of land. 6 bordars. Between them all then as now 3 ploughs. 1 acre of meadow. 1 mill. These men belong to St Edmund with sake and soke and commendation and they owe service in Risby and in Lackford and in Hengrave. And they could not give or sell the land without the abbot's permission. Then as now worth 40s. A church with 8 acres of free land. It is 6 furlongs long and 4 broad. In geld 6d.

In Hawstead 28 free men with 4 carucates of land. Odo holds 1 carucate and two clerics; Albold and Peter [hold] 2 carucates and Agenet [holds] 20 acres. Then as now 3 villans and 21 bordars. Then as now 13 ploughs and 2 slaves. 16 acres of meadow. Woodland for 3 pigs. These men could give and sell the land but the sake and soke and commendation continued to belong to St [Edmund]. Then as now worth £4. A church with 30 acres of free land. It is 8 furlongs long and 6 broad. In geld 13½d. In Brockley Theobald and Robert hold from the abbot 3 free men with 2 carucates of land. 3 villans and 6 bordars and 6 slaves. Then as now between them 4 ploughs. 5 acres of meadow. Woodland for 24 pigs. Of these men two could give and sell the land but the sake and soke and commendation continued to belong to St [Edmund]. The third cannot give or sell the land without the abbot's permission. Then as now worth £4. A church with 6 acres of free land. It is 8 furlongs long and 5 broad. In geld 7d. Others hold [land] there.

In Manston Warin has from the abbot 1 sokeman with 20 acres of land. 1 bordar. Then as now half a plough and 1 acre of meadow. Woodland for 2 pigs. Over him St [Edmund] has sake and soke and commendation and he owes service to him. He could not give or sell the land without the abbot's permission. Then as now worth 4s. It is 3 furlongs long and 2½ furlongs broad. In geld 6d. Others hold [land] there.

In Rede Henry has from the abbot 1 sokeman with half a carucate of land. 4 bordars and 1 slave. Then as now 1 plough and 3 acres of meadow. Woodland for 3 pigs. Over this man St [Edmund] has the sake and soke and commendation. He could not give or sell the land without the abbot's permission. Then worth 20s., now 40s. In the same place Berard holds from the abbot 7 free men with half a carucate of land and Then as now 2 ploughs. 3 acres of meadow. Woodland for 6 pigs. These men could give or sell the land but the sake and soke and commendation and service continued to belong to St [Edmund].Then as now worth 30s. It is 8 furlongs long

and 4 broad. In geld 7d. Others hold [land] there.

In Westley 11 free men with 2 carucates of land. Peter holds 1 from the abbot. 5 bordars. Then as now 3 ploughs. 1½ acres of meadow. Woodland for 3 pigs. These men could give and sell the land but the sake and soke and commendation and service continued to belong to St Edmund. Then worth 30s., now 40s. The third part of a church with 4 acres of land. It is 7 furlongs long and 5 broad. In geld 6½d. Others hold [land] there.

HUNDRED OF LACKFORD.

St Edmund held Herringswell TRE as a manor with 4 carucates of land. Then as now 7 villans and 6 bordars and 1 slave. Then as now 3 ploughs in demesne. Then as now 3 ploughs belonging to the men. 4 acres of meadow. Then 1 mill, now 2; 1 horse. 5 head of cattle, 12 pigs and 80 sheep. 2 sokemen with 54 acres of land. Then as now 1½ ploughs. 1 acre of meadow. Over these men St [Edmund] has the sake and soke and commendation then as now, together with all customary dues. But they could give and sell the land without the abbot's permission. A church with 30 acres of free land. This manor was then worth £6, now £7. It is 1 league long and 6 furlongs broad. In geld 20d. Several hold [land] there.

St Edmund held Wangford as a manor with 2 carucates of land; now Wulfweard holds it from the abbot. Then as now 4 villans and 4 bordars and 5 slaves. Then as now 2 ploughs in demesne and then as now 1 plough belonging to the men. 8 acres of meadow. Now 5 horses, 18 head of cattle, 26 pigs and 413 sheep. Now 2 beehives. A church with 15 acres of free

land. Then it was worth 40s., now 60s. It is 1 league long and 5 furlongs broad. In geld 6d. Others hold [land] there.

St Edmund held Elveden TRE as a manor with 2 carucates of land . Then as now 4 villans and 4 bordars and 1 slave. Then 2 ploughs in demesne, now 1. Then as now 1½ ploughs belonging to the men. Now 2 horses and 4 head of cattle. 12 pigs and 260 sheep. 13 goats. The fourth part of one fishery. A church with 15 acres of free land. 4 free men and a half with 1 carucate of land. 3 bordars. Then 3 ploughs, now These could give and sell the land but the sake and soke and commendation and service continued to belong to St [Edmund]. Then it was worth 10s., now 15s. This manor, not including the free men, was then worth 30s., now 40s. It is 1 league long and similarly 1 league broad. In geld 20d. Several hold [land] there.

St Edmund

St Edmund held [Santon] Downham as a manor with 3 carucates of land. Now Frodo holds it. Then as now 1 bordar. Then 5 slaves , now 3. Then as now 3 ploughs in demesne. 5 acres of meadow. 1 fishery and 1 ox, 21 pigs and 900 sheep. 9 free men with 2½ carucates of land and 60 acres. 3 bordars. Then 8 ploughs, now 4½ between them all. 4 acres of meadow. These men could give and sell but the sake and soke and commendation and all the customary dues continued to belong to St Edmund. Then it was worth 35s. and now the same. A church with 20 acres of land. This manor, not including the free men, was then worth £8, now £11. It is 1 league long and 8 furlongs broad. In geld 20d. Others hold [land] there.

In [Great] Livermere Fulcher holds from the abbot 2 free men with 20 acres of land. 1 bordar. Then as now half a plough and half an acre of meadow. These men could give and sell the land but the sake and soke and commendation continued to belong to St [Edmund]. Then as now worth 3s.

TWO HUNDREDS OF BABERGH.

St Edmund held [Long] Melford TRE as a manor with 12 carucates of land. Of this land Walter holds 40 acres from the abbot. Then as now 37 villans. Then 25 bordars and now 10. Then 8 ploughs in demesne, now 6. Then 20 ploughs belonging to the men, now 13. Then as now 16 slaves. 50 acres of meadow. Woodland for 60 pigs. 2 mills. Now 3 horses. Then as now 30 head of cattle. Now 300 sheep. Then as now 140 pigs. Now 12 [bee]hives. 40 wild horses now. 2 sokemen with 80 acres of land. The same Walter held one from the abbot with 40 acres. Then as now 2 ploughs. Over these men St [Edmund] has commendation and sake and soke and every customary due and they could never give and sell their lands without the abbot's full consent. A church with 2 carucates of land. 4 villans. 9 bordars. Then as now 2 ploughs belonging to the church. Then as now 2 ploughs belonging to the men. Then this manor was worth £20, now £30. It is 18 furlongs long and 1 league broad. In geld 20½d. whoever holds [land] there.

St Edmund held Cockfield TRE as a manor with 4½

carucates of land. Then as now 14 villans. Then 16 bordars, now 22. Then 2 ploughs in demesne, now 3. Then 12 ploughs belonging to the men, now 6. Then as now 4 slaves. 8 acres of meadow. A winter mill. Now 3 horses, 12 head of cattle, 37 pigs and 80 and 18 sheep. Now 12 beehives. This manor was then worth £6, now £8. In the same place 21 free men with 5 carucates of land which 4[sic] men hold from the abbot: Berard [holds] 3 carucates and James 1 and Colman 1.

[Folio 359v: SUFFOLK]

13 bordars and 3 slaves. Then between them all 8 ploughs, now 7; 16 acres of meadow. Woodland for 6 pigs. All these could give and sell their land but the soke and commendation belonged to St Edmund, except in the case of one over whom he had the soke only. Then it was worth £3, now £4. This vill is 13 furlongs long and 1 league broad. In geld 23½d. But others hold [land] there.

St Edmund held Groton TRE as a manor with 1½ carucates of land. Then as now 8 villans and 5 bordars. Then as now 1 plough in demesne. Then as now 2 ploughs belonging to the men. 1 acre of meadow. Woodland for 10 pigs. A winter mill. Then as now 1 horse, 6 head of cattle, 16 pigs and 30 sheep. 2 free men with half a carucate of land. They could give and sell their land. 6 bordars. Then as now 1 plough and 1 acre of meadow. Then it was worth 30s., now 40s. It is 7 furlongs long and 4 broad. In the same place 12 free men. They have 1 carucate and it is worth 20s. All these could give and sell their land TRE. St Edmund has soke, commendation and service. 7d. in geld. But others hold [land] there.

In Preston [near Lavenham] St Edmund TRE held 1 free man; [now] [holds him]. He could give and sell his land. He has 3 carucates of land in demesne. And then he ploughed with 3 ploughs, now with 2. Then as now 2 villans, 4 bordars. And they plough with half a plough. 1 slave. 3 acres of meadow. 3 sokemen dwell. These men have 26½ acres of land and half an acre of meadow. They could give and sell their land. Then it was worth £4, now £3. It is 12 furlongs long and 6 broad. A church with 7 acres. King William gave this man and his land to St Edmund and to Abbot B[aldwin], and the soke and all customary dues. 2d. in geld but others hold [land] there.

In Eleigh [Brent and Monks] St Edmund held 5 free men whom the same Arnulf holds from the abbot. Then as now they have 3½ ploughs. 5 bordars. 3 acres of meadow. Woodland for 2 pigs. 1 slave. Then they ploughed with 4 ploughs, and [also] now. They could give and sell their land but the soke and the commendation and customary dues belonged to St Edmund. Then it was worth £3, now £4. It is 12 furlongs long and 6 broad. 3½d. in geld but others hold [land] there.

St Edmund held Somerton. In the same place Frodo holds 1 carucate of land. 1 villan, 5 bordars. Then they ploughed with 3 ploughs, now the same. And then it was worth 43s. less 4d. and now [the same]. King William gave this land to St Edmund with the soke and commendation and all customary dues. It is

St Edmund

[Folio 360: SUFFOLK]

6 furlongs long and 4 broad. 3d. in geld but others hold [land] there.

St Edmund held [Great and Little] Cornard with 2 free men. They had 50 acres of land. 1 acre of meadow. TRE it was worth 6s. and [also] now. They could give and sell their land but St Edmund had the soke and all customary dues.

St Edmund held Bures with 3 sokemen. They have 8 acres of land and 1 [acre of] meadow. Those 8 acres are worth 16d. And these men could give [and] sell their land . The soke and all the customary dues belonged to St Edmund.

St Edmund held [Great and Little] Waldingfield with 11 free men. Under them, half a carucate of land. 3 bordars. 2 acres of meadow. They could give and sell their land but the soke and commendation and service belonged to St [Edmund]. Then it was worth 10s., and [also] now. 1d. in geld.

St Edmund held Newton as a manor TRE. Now Adelund [holds it] from the abbot. Then as now there are 2 carucates of land there. Then as now 2 ploughs in demesne and 1½ ploughs belonging to the men. Then 2 slaves, now none. Then 3 head of cattle, now 7. Then 40 pigs, now 29. Then 97 sheep, now 102. Then as now 3 villans. Then 4 bordars, now 10. Now 14 goats, then none. Then 16 beehives, now 9. Woodland for 8 pigs then, now 6. Then as now 2 acres of meadow. This manor is 6 furlongs long and 3 broad. Then it was worth £2, now £2½. In geld 4d. less ¼d.

In Somerton 1 free man belonging to St Edmund [held] 30½ acres of land. Now Frodo [holds it] from the abbot. It is worth 2s. In Milden 1 free man [held] 15 acres of land and 3 bordars, worth 2s.

HUNDRED OF STOW.

In Wetherden 20 free men belonging to St Edmund TRE [held] 2 carucates of land. Ralph holds half a carucate and Arnulf 40 acres. 13 bordars. Then 5 ploughs, now 7; 8 acres of meadow. Half a church with 15 acres and 1 acre of meadow. Then it was worth 30s., now 40s.

In Harleston 2 free men belonging to St Edmund TRE with 1 carucate of land and 20 acres. Now Adelund [holds it] from the abbot. Peter holds 20 acres. Then as now 2 villans and 11 bordars and 2 slaves. Between them 1½ ploughs. 8½ acres of meadow. Under them there are 11 free men with 23 acres. Then 2 ploughs between them, now a half. A church with 25 acres of free land.

[Folio 360v: SUFFOLK]

Then as now the whole is worth 26s.

In Onehouse 1 free man belonging to St Edmund with half a carucate of land. 3 bordars. Then as now 1 plough. 4 acres of meadow. Then as now worth 20s. TRE the sake and soke and commendation over all these men belonged to St Edmund by the gift of King Edward as the writs and seal, which the abbot has, show. Afterwards King William granted [it] but the king's reeve had 4s. on account of the soke over 1 of them, whether justly or unjustly, without the knowledge of the abbot or his servants. The Hundred testifies that it did not know that St Edmund had later been dispossessed after King Edward gave it.

HUNDRED OF BOSMERE.

St Edmund held Mickfield TRE with 60 acres as a manor. Then as now 2 villans and 3 bordars and 1 slave. 1 plough in demesne and 1 plough belonging to the men. 3 acres of meadow. 5 head of cattle and 10 pigs and 27 sheep and 21 goats. Then it was worth 10s., now 15s. The king and the earl have the soke. In the same place Æthelric, a free man, [had] 60 acres of land. St Edmund [had] the commendation. 1 villan and 1 bordar. 1 plough. 2 acres of meadow. A church with 8 acres and half a plough. Then it was worth 10s., now 15s. The abbot holds this land because that man Æthelric took a wife TRE who held this land freely in the king's soke but the abbot claims the soke by the king's gift. Berengar holds from the abbot. It is 1 league long and 8 furlongs broad. 2d. in geld.

Wulfweard, a free man, held [Earl and Little] Stonham in the soke of the king and the earl with 60 acres as a manor. Then as now 4 bordars and 1 plough in demesne and 1 acre of meadow. Woodland for 5 pigs. 1 horse and 2 head of cattle and 16 sheep. It is worth 10s. Ailbald the priest holds [this]. The abbot has this land in pledge for two marks of gold with the consent of Engelric since the English redeemed their lands.

HUNDRED OF CLAYDON.

In Thorpe 2 free men with 6 acres of land, worth 16d. St Edmund has the soke over 1 and St Æthelthryth over the other.

HUNDRED OF PLUMESGATE.

In [Great] Glemham 1 free man, Ælfric, and 6 free men and a half with 21 acres and 2 acres of meadow. Then as now 1 plough. It is worth 5s. The soke belongs to the abbot. Norman [holds it] from the abbot.

HUNDRED OF HARTISMERE.

St Edmund held Redgrave TRE with 6 carucates of land as a manor. Then as now 10 villans and 19 bordars. Then 8 slaves, now 6. Then as now 4 ploughs in demesne and 6 ploughs belonging to the men. 8 acres of meadow. Woodland for 120 pigs. A church with 30 acres of free land.

St Edmund

[Folio 361: SUFFOLK]

Half a plough. 2 horses, 12 head of cattle, 30 pigs, 60 sheep and 30 goats. Then as now worth £10.

In the same place 24 free men with 80 acres in the soke and commendation of the abbot. Then as now 8 ploughs. Then as now worth 30s. It is 1 league long and a half broad. 8d. in geld. The abbot [holds it] in demesne. In Wortham 2 sokemen [held] 60 acres as two manors TRE. Then as now 8 bordars and 2½ ploughs. 4 acres of meadow. Woodland for 14 pigs. It is worth 20s. In the same place 1 sokeman with 14 acres and half a plough, worth 32d.

In the same place Ælfheah, a free man in the soke and

commendation of the abbot, [held] 30 acres as a manor TRE and 4 bordars and 1 plough. 1 acre of meadow. It is worth 10s.

In the same place Wulfric, a free man, [held] 30 acres in the soke and commendation of the abbot. 6 bordars and a half. 1 plough in demesne and half a plough belonging to the men. 1 acre of meadow. It is worth 10s.

In the same place 25 free men [held] 3 carucates of land. Then as now 6 ploughs. It is worth 30s. The soke and the commendation belong to the abbot. It is 1 league long and 10 furlongs broad. 12d. in geld.

In Gislingham a sokeman, with 30 acres. Then as now 1 plough and 1 bordar. 1 acre of meadow. It is worth 10s. In the same place 12 free men and 1 sokeman with 8 acres out of the 30 acres. The same land is in the soke and commendation of the abbot. Then 3 ploughs, now 2; 1 acre of meadow. It is worth 10s.

St Edmund held Palgrave TRE with 4 carucates of land as a manor. Then as now 11 villans and 17 bordars. Then 3 slaves, now 1. Then as now 1 plough in demesne and 4 ploughs belonging to the men. 6 acres of meadow. 2 churches with 30 acres and half a plough. 2 horses, 12 head of cattle, 6 pigs and 8 sheep. Then it was worth £6, now £8. The soke is the abbot's. In the same place 28 29 free men with 2 carucates of land, less 12 acres. Then as now 8 ploughs. 2 acres of meadow. It is worth 40s. The soke and the commendation are the abbot's. It is 1 league long and a half broad. 12d. in geld.

In Rickinghall [Superior] 14 free men in the soke and commendation of the abbot [held] 80 acres. Then as now 3 ploughs and 2 acres of meadow. The fifth of a church with 5 acres. It is worth 20s.

St [...] Edmund held Brockford TRE with 3 carucates of land and 43 acres. Then as now 14 bordars and 3 slaves. 2 ploughs in demesne. 2 ploughs belonging to the men. 4 acres of meadow. Woodland for 40 pigs. 8 head of cattle, 6 pigs, 20 sheep and 20 goats. Then as now worth 100s.

[Folio 361v: SUFFOLK]

[...] Hundred of Thedwestry.

St Edmund held [Great] Barton TRE as a manor with 5 carucates of land. Then as now 22 villans and 5 bordars. Then 4 ploughs in demesne, now 3. Then 6 ploughs belonging to the men. Then 11 slaves, now 4; 3 acres of meadow. Woodland for 4 pigs. 3 horses, 18 head of cattle, 44 pigs and 402 sheep. Now 2 beehives. 70 free [men] with 5 carucates of land. Then as now between them all 18 ploughs 1 acre of meadow. Over these men [St Edmund] has and has always had sake and soke and every customary due. They all belong to the fold apart from 3; 50 acres of free land belong to the church of this vill as alms. Then it was worth £16, now £20. It is 1 league and 2 furlongs long and 1 league broad. 27d. in geld.

St Edmund held Pakenham TRE as a manor with 7 carucates. Then as now 44 villans and 23 bordars. Then 3 ploughs in demesne, now 4. Then as now 23 ploughs belonging to the men. Then 6 slaves, now 9; 26 acres of meadow. Woodland for 100 pigs. Then 2 mills, now 1; 3 horses, 48 head of cattle, 65 pigs and 190 sheep. Now 8 beehives. 31 free men and 1 bordar with 2 carucates of land. Then as now between them 11 ploughs. 3 acres of meadow. All these men belong then as now to St [Edmund] with sake and soke and every customary due. They belong to the fold.

In the same place 3 free men with 30 acres of land. Then as now 1 plough. Woodland for 4 pigs. These could give and sell the land but the sake and soke and commendation continued to belong to St [Edmund].

In the same place TRE one free man with 1 carucate of land petitioned the abbot to lease to him half a carucate of land by such an agreement that all his land, wherever it was, would continue to belong to St [Edmund] after his death. Now of this land 1 carucate belongs to Pakenham in demesne. 1 plough. 5 bordars and 2 slaves. A winter mill. St [Edmund] has always had commendation and sake and soke over him. 30 acres belong to the church of this vill as alms of free land. Then Pakenham with these things which belong to it was worth £10, now £25. It is 16 furlongs long and 1 league broad. 13½d. in geld.

St Edmund held Fornham [St Martin] TRE as a manor with 1 carucate of land. Then as now 3 villans and 4 bordars. Then 1 plough in demesne, now 2. Then as now 2 ploughs belonging to the men. Then 4 slaves, now 3; 2 horses.

St Edmund

[Folio 362: SUFFOLK]

Then as now 4 head of cattle. Now 12 pigs and 80 sheep. 10 free men and 6 bordars with 30 acres of land. Then as now 1 plough. These men also belong entirely to St [Edmund] with regard to every customary due and to the right of fold. In the same place 1 free man with 12 acres of land. This man could give and sell the land; the sake and soke and commendation, however, continued to belong to St [Edmund]. To the church of this vill belong 16 acres of free land as alms. This manor TRE was worth £3, now £4. It is 9 furlongs long and 7 broad. In geld 6½d.

St Edmund held Rougham TRE as a manor with 5 carucates of land. Then as now 15 villans and 4 bordars. Then as now 3 ploughs in demesne. 2 ploughs belonging to the men. Then as now 6 slaves. 4 acres of meadow. 3 horses, 22 head of cattle, 25 pigs and 55 sheep. 90 free men and 11 bordars and 1 slave. 5 carucates of land. Then as now 18 ploughs. 3 acres of meadow. These men also belonged then and belong now to St [Edmund] with the commendation and every customary due [and] with regard to the right of fold. To the church of this vill belong 40 acres of free land as alms. Then it was worth £14, now £16. It is 16 furlongs long and 1 league broad. 20d. in geld.

St Edmund held Bradfield TRE as a manor with 3 carucates of land. Then as now 15 villans and 18 bordars. Then 2 ploughs in demesne, now 3. Then as now 4 ploughs belonging to the men. Then 1 slave, now 6; 7 acres of meadow. 3 horses, 10 head of cattle, 28 pigs and 99 sheep; now 80 goats. 3 free men with 24 acres of land. Then as now 1 plough. 1 acre of meadow. Over these men St [Edmund] has commendation and sake and soke with regard to every customary due. And they could not give or sell their lands without the abbot's permission. In the same place free men with 1 carucate of land. 2 bordars. Then as now between them 3 ploughs. 2 acres

of meadow. It is worth 6s. These men could give and sell their lands but the soke and the service continued to belong to St [Edmund], whoever bought the land. To the church of this vill belong 10½ acres of free land as alms. This manor TRE was worth £6, now £8. It is 1 league long and 4 furlongs In geld 5d.

St Edmund held Fornham St Genevieve TRE as a berewick with 2 carucates of land. Of these 2 carucates Peter has 40 acres; he holds them from the abbot. 2 villans [and] 2 bordars have 1 of these carucates. The hall to which it belongs is in another Hundred. Ralph holds from the abbot 12 acres of these 2 carucates. Then as now 8 villans and 3 bordars. Then as now 2 ploughs and 3 ploughs belonging to the men. Then as now 3 slaves. 4 acres of meadow. Then as now 3 mills. 1 horse and 100 sheep. 6 free men and

[Folio 362v: SUFFOLK]

1 villan and 5 bordars with 1 carucate of land. Then as now 3 ploughs. These could give and sell their lands but the soke over the land and the service continued to belong to St Edmund. They are worth 10s. A church with 14 acres of free land as alms. Then as now this berewick is worth £4. It is 9 furlongs long and 4 broad. 8d. in geld.

St Edmund held Thurston TRE as a manor with 1½ carucates of land. Then 6 bordars, now 8. Then as now 2 ploughs and 1 plough belonging to the men. Now 1 slave. 5 acres of meadow. Woodland for 8 pigs. Now 1 horse. Then as now 5 head of cattle, 32 pigs and 52 sheep. 28 free men with 2½ carucates of land. Richard holds from the abbot 1 carucate of land. He has 8 free men and 12 bordars. Then as now 8 ploughs. 5 acres of meadow. Woodland for 3 pigs. Value of the whole mesne[-tenure], 40s. The other men belonging to the abbot [are worth] 12s. These could give and sell their lands but the soke and the service over these lands continued to belong to St [Edmund]. They are worth £2. A church with 30 acres of free land as alms. This manor, not including those free [men], has always been worth £1½. It is 10 furlongs long and 6 broad. In geld 16d. But several hold [land] there.

St Edmund held Woolpit TRE as a berewick with 3 carucates of land. The hall to which it belongs is in another Hundred. Then as now 17 villans and 3 bordars. Then as now 3 ploughs belonging to the men. In demesne [the same number]. 4 acres of meadow. Woodland for 20 pigs. 40 free men with 1 carucate of land. Then as now 6 ploughs. 3 acres of land. All these could give and sell their [their] lands TRE but the soke always belonged to St [Edmund] over the land and every service with regard to the right of fold. They also all belong to the right of fold. It is worth 10s. 8d. To the church [belong] 15 acres as alms. This berewick has always been worth £3. It is 9 furlongs long and 6 broad. 11d. in geld but several hold [land] there. In Drinkstone 11 free men with 1 carucate of land. They have 6 bordars and 3 ploughs. 8 acres of meadow. These men could give and sell their lands TRE; however the soke over the lands continued to belong to St Edmund. It is worth 10s. 8d. In Hessett 60 free men with 5½ carucates of land and 6 bordars. Berard holds half a carucate of land and 2 bordars and 1 plough. He is charged 20s. Between them all then as now 6 ploughs. 5 acres of meadow. These men could sell and give their lands TRE but the soke continued to belong to St [Edmund] and they owe every service in Rougham. They all belong also to the right of fold, apart from 6. It is worth 40s. To the church [belong] 12 acres. It is 8 furlongs long and 7 broad. In geld 18d. whoever has [land] there.

In Felsham 25 free men with 3 carucates of land. 1 villan and 5 bordars. Adelund [holds] 1½ carucates of land. 8 free men hold 4 carucates, worth 50s. Then as now between them 8 ploughs. 5 acres of meadow. These [could] give and sell their lands. [The soke] continued to belong to St [Edmund]. It was then worth 30s., now 60s. A church with 10 acres of free land as alms. It is 8 furlongs long and 6 broad. In geld 5d.

In Bradfield 10 free men with 2½ carucates of land. Roric holds

St Edmund

[Folio 363: SUFFOLK]

from the abbot 1½ carucates of land. Falc [holds] half a carucate. 4½ ploughs under them. [It is worth] 54s. They have 12 bordars. Then as now 6 ploughs. 8 acres of meadow. These could give and sell their lands but the soke to belong to St [Edmund] It was worth TRE £2, now £3. This vill is 10 furlongs long and 3 broad. 5d. in geld.

In Gedding 13 free men with 55 acres of land. Between them all half a plough. These could also give and sell their land but the soke continued to belong to St [Edmund]. Then it was worth 16d., now 2s. A church with 6 acres of free land in alms. It is 3 furlongs long and 2 broad. In geld 5d. Others hold [land] there.

In Rattlesden 1 free man with half a carucate of land. 4 bordars have then as now 1 plough. 2 acres of meadow. Woodland for 4 pigs. Then it was worth 10s., [...] now 20s. Peter holds from the abbot. He could give and sell his land but the soke continued to belong to St [Edmund].

In [Great and Little] Welnetham 41 free men with 6 carucates of land. Of these 6 carucates Arnulf holds 1 carucate from the abbot. 1 plough. He is charged 20s. And Robert [holds] 20 acres. 12 bordars. Then as now 16 ploughs between them all. 13 acres of meadow. Woodland for 10 pigs. All these could give and sell their land but the soke continued to belong to St [Edmund]. TRE [it was worth] £2, now £3 10s. Two churches with 40 acres of free land as alms. This vill is 1 league long and 6 broad. In geld 10d.

In Timworth 29 free men with 3½ carucates of land. John holds from the abbot 6 free men with 1 carucate of land worth 20s. In the demesne of the abbot 8 bordars and 5 ploughs. 6 acres of meadow. these could give and sell their land but the soke continued to belong to St [Edmund], and the service. Then it was worth £1 10s., now 20s. A church with 30 acres of free land in alms. It is 8 furlongs long and 6 broad. In geld 14d.

In Ampton 22 free men with 2 carucates of land. Robert holds from the abbot half a carucate of land and 1 plough. [...] It is worth 20s. then as now 5 ploughs. 2 acres of meadow. Those men could give and sell their land but the soke continued to belong to St [Edmund], and the service in Ingham.

[Folio 363v: SUFFOLK]

Then it was worth 20s., now 30s. A church with 8 acres of

free land as alms. It is 6 furlongs long and 4 broad. In geld [...] 7d.

In Tostock TRE St [Edmund] held 1 carucate of land as a manor, now Frodo holds it from St Edmund. Then 2 bordars, now 1. Then as now 1 plough in demesne. 4 acres of meadow. Woodland for 8 pigs. 1 horse. 17 free men and a half with 1 carucate. They have 3 bordars. Then 3 ploughs between them, now 2; 2 acres of meadow. And these men could give and sell their land but the soke continued to belong to St [Edmund], and the service. Then it was worth 10s., now 10s. 8d. A church with 12 acres of free land in alms. It is 7 furlongs long and 6 broad. In geld 10½d. Others hold [land] there.

In Stanningfield 11 free free [sic] men with 1½ carucates and 12 acres of land. Warin holds from the abbot 80 acres and 1½ ploughs. It is worth 20s. In the abbot's demesne 5 bordars. Then as now 4 ploughs between them. 9 acres of meadow. These men could give and sell their land but the soke continued to belong to St [Edmund], and the service. Then as now worth 12s. A church with 16 acres of free land in alms. It is 8 furlongs long and 4 broad. In geld 10d. But others hold [land] there.

In Rushbrooke 22 free men with 2 carucates of land. 4 bordars. Then as now 4 ploughs between the men. 2 acres of meadow. These men could give and sell their land but the soke continued to belong to St [Edmund], and the service in Rougham. They all belong to the right of fold also, apart from 3. Then it was worth 16s., now 20s. 23d. It is 7 furlongs long and 4 broad. In geld 7d.

In [Great] Livermere 10 free men with 1 carucate of land. Then as now 3 ploughs between them. 2 acres of meadow. These men could give and sell their land but the soke continued to belong to St [Edmund]. Then as now worth 10s. 8d. In the same place Frodo holds 12 free men with 2 carucates of land and 5 ploughs, worth 60s. In the same place Frodo holds 1 free man belonging to Eadric of Laxfield with 2 carucates of land 2 villans. 8 bordars. 2 slaves. Then as now 2 ploughs in demesne and 2 ploughs belonging to them. 4 acres of meadow. These men could give and sell the land but the sake and soke and commendation over the woman only continued to belong to St [Edmund]. This man's land the king received from the abbot and he gave it to Werno de Poix. Afterwards when he became a monk with the king's permission he gave back the land. Then as now worth 40s. A church with 12 acres of land. It is 10 furlongs long and 8 broad. 12d. in geld.

St Edmund

[Folio 364: SUFFOLK]

HUNDRED OF BRADMERE.

A certain man-at-arms of St Edmund, Wulfwig, held Ingham TRE from him as a manor. Now St [Edmund] himself holds 3 carucates of land and the fourth carucate of land belongs in another Hundred. Then as now 1 villan and 2 bordars. Then 3 ploughs in demesne, now 4. Then as now 1 plough belonging to the men. Then 3 slaves, now 9; 27 acres of meadow. 1 mill. Now 4 horses. Now 19 head of cattle. Now 30 pigs and 520 sheep. 21 sokemen with 1 carucate of land. Then as now 7 ploughs. 2 acres of meadow. All these men belong to St [Edmund] with the sake and soke and all customary dues, also as to the right of fold. Neither could they give or sell without the abbot's consent. A church with 24 acres of free land in alms. Then this manor was worth £4, now £8. It is 16 furlongs long and 8 broad. In geld 16d. But the king holds [land] there.

St Edmund held Culford TRE as a manor with 1 carucate of land. Then as now 2 villans. 2 bordars. Then as now 1 plough in demesne. Then 1 plough belonging to the men, now a half. 8 acres of meadow. 1 ox. 2 pigs. 85 sheep. 18 sokemen with half a carucate of land. Then as now 2 ploughs. These also belonged to St [Edmund] with sake and soke and every customary due. And they could not give or sell without the abbot's permission. Then it was worth £4, now £3. In the same place 1 free man with 1 carucate of land which Peter holds from the abbot. 7 bordars and 2 slaves. Then as now 2 ploughs and 2 oxen belonging to the men. 6 acres of meadow. Then it was worth 10s., now 30s. It is 1 league long and 5 furlongs broad. In geld 7¼d.

In [West] Stow 21 free men with 2 carucates of land. Then as now 6 ploughs between them all. 2 acres of meadow. These belong to St [Edmund] with sake and soke and every customary due and they do service in Lackford. Then as now worth 20s. In the same place 1 free man with half a carucate of land. Then as now 1 plough. Then as now worth 4s. A church with 12 acres of free land in alms. It belongs in another Hundred. It is 9 furlongs long and 7 broad. In geld 17d.

HUNDRED OF BLACKBOURN.

St Edmund held Stanton TRE as a manor with 1 carucate of land.

[Folio 364v: SUFFOLK]

Then 1 plough in demesne, now 2. Then 4 slaves, now 3; 2 acres of meadow. Woodland for 8 pigs. Now 2 horses and 3 head of cattle. 28 pigs and 52 sheep. 30 goats. 60 sokemen with 2 carucates of land. Then as now 5 ploughs. 4 acres of meadow. These belong to St [Edmund] and they were commended with sake and soke and every customary due and with regard to the right of fold. Nor could they ever give or sell their land without the abbot's permission. Then this manor was worth £6 and now £6. In the same place 7 free men with 1 carucate and 30 acres of land. Then as now 4 ploughs and 4 acres of meadow. Woodland for 10 pigs. These men could give and sell their land but the commendation and the soke continued to belong to St [Edmund], and the service. A church with 28 acres and the fourth part of one church with 7 acres of land. Then it was worth 10s., now 13s. It is 1 league long and 6 broad. In geld 2s. 10½d.

St Edmund held Elmswell TRE as a manor with 2 carucates of land. Then as now 16 villans. 14 bordars. Then and now 2 ploughs in demesne. Then as now 4 ploughs belonging to the men. Then 4 slaves, now 5 and 8 acres of meadow. Woodland for 80 pigs. Now 3 horses, 5 head of cattle, 15 pigs, 18 sheep and 48 goats. 5 sokemen with 40 acres of land. Then as now 2 ploughs. 1 acre of meadow. These men belong entirely to St [Edmund] and they cannot give or sell without the abbot's permission. A church with 20 acres of free land in

alms. Then this manor was worth £5, now £6. It is 1 league long and 10 furlongs broad. In geld 11¼d. Others hold there.

St Edmund held Hinderclay TRE as a manor with 4 carucates of land. Then 6 villans, now 8. Then 8 bordars, now 12. Then 6 ploughs in demesne, now 5. Then 10 slaves, now 8. Then as now 2 ploughs belonging to the men. 8 acres of meadow. Woodland for 60 pigs. Now 3 horses, 8 head of cattle, 20 pigs and 60 sheep. And 7 sokemen with 40 acres of land. Then as now 2 ploughs. A church with 1 acre of free land in alms. This manor then as now worth £8. It is 1 league long and 6 furlongs broad. In geld 5½d. Others hold [land] there.

St Edmund held Rickinghall [Inferior] TRE as a manor with 2 carucates of land. Then 4 villans, now 2. Then as now 6 bordars. Then as now 2 ploughs in demesne. Then 1 plough

St Edmund

[Folio 365: SUFFOLK]

belonging to the men, now half a plough. A winter mill. Then 4 slaves, now 2; 8 acres of meadow. Woodland for 60 pigs. Now 2 horses, 8 head of cattle, 16 pigs, 24 sheep and 30 goats. 22 sokemen with half a carucate of land. Then as now between them 6 ploughs. 6 acres of meadow. These men are commended to St [Edmund] by sake and commendation and every customary due. Nor could they ever give or sell their land without permission. All [belong] to the fold. This manor, with those things which belong to it, was then worth £5, now £7. In the same place 2 free men with half a carucate of land. 1 bordar. Then as now 2 ploughs. 2 acres of meadow. Woodland for 8 pigs. These could give and sell their land but the sake and commendation and service continued to belong to St [Edmund]. Then as now worth 10s. A church with 24 acres of free land in alms. It is 1 league long and 3 furlongs broad. In geld 12d. Others hold [land] there.

St Edmund held Coney Weston TRE as a manor with 2 carucates. Then 2 villans, now and always 3 bordars. Then as now 2 ploughs in demesne. Then as now half a plough belonging to the men. Then as now 1 slave and 2 acres of meadow. Woodland for 4 pigs. Now 1 horse, 10 head of cattle, 12 pigs, 80 sheep and 24 goats. 12 sokemen with half a carucate and 30 acres of land. Then 6 ploughs, now 4; 2 acres of meadow. A church with 8 acres of free land in alms. Then this manor was worth £5, now £6. It is 1 league long and 6 furlongs broad. In geld 17¼d.

In Stowlangtoft Durand holds from the abbot 4 carucates of land which 2 free men held TRE. Then as now 8 bordars. Then 4 ploughs in demesne, now 2; 1 mill. Woodland for 20 pigs. 30 sheep. 8 acres of meadow. Then it was worth £6, now £6. In the same place 14 free men with half a carucate of land. Then as now 4 ploughs. 2 acres of meadow. These men could give and sell their land. However the soke and commendation continued to belong to St [Edmund], and the service. All also [belong] to the fold, except one. Worth then as now 6s. 8d. A church with 40 acres of free land. This vill is 1 league long and 8 furlongs broad. In geld 10d. Several hold [land] there.

[Folio 365v: SUFFOLK]

In Hepworth 20 free men with 2½ carucates of land. They

have 3 villans and 4 slaves. Then as now 8 ploughs. 4 acres of meadow. Woodland for 6 pigs. A church with 15 acres of free land in alms. All these men could give and sell their land but the sake and soke and commendation and every customary due continued to belong to St [Edmund], and the service in Stanton and Coney Weston. Then it was worth 20s., now 40s. Of this land Fulcher holds from the abbot 1 carucate as a whole mesne[-tenure], and Peter de Valognes 30 acres and 3 bordars. It is worth 30 s. in the same valuation. It is 7 furlongs long and 5 broad. In geld 17¼d. Others hold [land] there.

In Wattisfield 20 free men with 1½ carucates of land. 1 bordar. 1 slave. Then 8 ploughs, now 6; 1 acre of meadow. Woodland for 12 pigs. A church with 12 acres of free land in alms. These men could give and sell their land but the sake and soke and commendation continued to belong to St [Edmund], and the service in Rickinghall [Inferior]. Then it was worth 30s., now 40s. Of this land Roric holds 1 carucate and 3 ploughs. It is worth 30s. in the same valuation. It is 7 furlongs long and 5 broad. In geld 17¼d. Others hold [land] there.

In Hopton 23 free men with 2 carucates of land. 4 bordars. Then as now 6 ploughs. And 4 acres of meadow. Woodland for 2 pigs. And 1 mill. A church with 13 acres of free land in alms. These men could give and sell their land but the sake and soke and commendation continued to belong to St [Edmund], and the service in Coney Weston. Then it was worth 20s., now 30s. Of this land Fulcher holds half a carucate of land. It is worth 20s. in the same valuation. It is 6 furlongs long and 4 broad. In geld 16d. Others hold [land] there.

In Barningham 19 free men 2 villans and 2 bordars. Then 9 ploughs, now 6; 4 acres of meadow. A church with 15 acres of free land in alms. These men could give and sell their land

St Edmund

[Folio 366: SUFFOLK]

but the sake and and commendation continued to belong to St [Edmund], and the service in Coney Weston. Then it was worth 20s., now 40s. Of these free men Burcard holds 3 free men with 1 carucate of land and 2 ploughs, worth 15s. in the same valuation. And Peter de Valognes [holds] 6 free men with 3 and a half carucates, worth 20s. in the same valuation. It is 1 league long and 6 furlongs broad. In geld 17d. Others hold [land] there.

In Bardwell 8 free men with 2 carucates and 30 acres of land. Burcard holds these men. 4 bordars and 2 slaves. Then as now 4 ploughs. 2 parts of one mill. 11 acres of meadow. Woodland for 8 pigs. A church with 8 acres of free land. These men could give and sell their land but the sake and soke and commendation continued to belong to St [Edmund]. Then worth 20s., now 60s. Under them 20 sokemen of whom the abbot holds 10 with 30 acres and 1 plough, worth 5s. Peter de Valognes holds 10 with half a carucate of land and 1 plough, worth 10s. It is 1 league long and 5 furlongs broad. In geld 34¼d. But several hold [land] there.

In Sapiston 11 free men with 1½ carucates of land. Then as now 2 ploughs. 2 mills. 6 acres of meadow. These men could give and sell their land but the soke and sake and commendation continued to belong to St [Edmund]. Two parts of a church with 6 acres of free land in alms. Then as now worth 25s. Of these free men Peter de Valognes holds 4 free men with 80 acres and 1 slave and 1 plough, worth 10 s. It is 10 furlongs long and 5 broad. In geld 17¼d. Several hold [land] there.

In [Market] Weston 3 free men and a half with 1 carucate of land. 6 bordars. Then as now 2 ploughs. 1 acre of meadow. Woodland for 4 pigs. All these, apart from one with 40 acres could give and sell their land but the soke and sake and commendation continued to belong to St [Edmund], and the service in Coney Weston. Then as now worth 10s.

In Honington 16 free men with 2 carucates of land. 2 bordars. Then as now 5 ploughs.

[Folio 366v: SUFFOLK]

8 acres of meadow. Woodland for 2 pigs. These men could give and sell their land but the sake and soke and commendation continued to belong to St [Edmund]. Then as now worth 20s. A church with 20 acres of free land. Of this land Peter holds 1 carucate. It is 6 furlongs long and 4 broad. In geld 12½d. Others hold [land] there.

In Troston 24 free men with 2½ carucates of land. Then as now 5 ploughs. These men could give and sell their land but the sake and soke and commendation continued to belong to St [Edmund]. Then it was worth 20s., now 30s. Of these [men] Frodo holds 12 free men with 1 carucate of land and 2 ploughs, worth 20s. in the same valuation. It is 10 furlongs long and 5 broad. In geld 11½d. Others hold [land] there.

In Little Livermere 7 free men with 2 carucates of land. 3 bordars. Then as now 4 ploughs. Half an acre of land. These men could give and sell their land but the sake and soke and commendation continued to belong to St [Edmund]. A church with 12 acres of free land. Then as now worth 30s. Of these [men] Walter holds 3 free men with 1 carucate of land and 1 plough, worth 15s. in the same valuation. It is 1 league long and 4 broad. In geld 3¼d.

In Wordwell 11 free men with 2 carucates of land. 4 bordars and 2 slaves. Then as now 5 ploughs. 3 acres of meadow, now 1 mill. These men could give and sell their land but the sake and soke and commendation continued to belong to St [Edmund], and the service in Culford. Then as now worth 30[s.] A church with 1 acre of free land. It is 1 league long and 4 furlongs broad. In geld 7½d.

In Barham 3 free men with 1 carucate of land. Then as now 2 ploughs. 1 mill. These men could give and sell their land but the sake and soke and commendation continued to belong to St [Edmund]. Half a church with 8 acres of land. Then as now worth 25s. Of this land Fulcher holds 80 acres and 1 plough, worth 20s.

In Thelnetham Fulcher holds from the abbot 8 free men with 1 carucate of land. 6 bordars and 1 slave. Then as now 2½ ploughs. 3 acres of meadow. Woodland for 30 pigs. These men could give and

St Edmund

[Folio 367: SUFFOLK]

sell their land but the sake and soke and commendation continued to belong to St [Edmund]. Then it was worth 20s., now 30s.

In [Ixworth] Thorpe 2 free men with 16 acres of land. Then as now half a plough and half an acre of meadow. These men could give and sell their land but the sake and soke and commendation continued to belong to St [Edmund]. Then as now worth 12d.

In Walsham [Le Willows] 30 free men with 3 carucates [...] of land. 2 bordars. Then 9 ploughs, now 6; 8 acres of meadow. Woodland for 30 pigs. These men could give and sell their land but the sake and soke and commendation continued to belong to St [Edmund]. Then it was worth 30s., now 45s. Of these free men and of this land Robert Blund holds 10 free men with 2 carucates of land and 2 ploughs, worth 40s. in the same valuation.

In [Great] Ashfield 21 free men with 1½ carucates of land. 1 villan and 4 bordars. Then as now 5 ploughs. 12 acres of meadow. Woodland for 20 pigs. These men could give and sell their land but the sake and soke and commendation continued to belong to St [Edmund]. Then as now worth 33s. Of these free men and of this land Odard holds 17 free men with 1 carucate of land and 30 acres and 4 ploughs, worth 30s. in the same valuation.

In the same place 1 sokeman with half a carucate of land and 2 bordars. Then as now 1 plough. 4 acres of meadow. Woodland for 4 pigs. Then as now St [Edmund] had sake and soke and commendation over this and he could not give or sell his land without permission. Then as now worth 10s. A church with 12 acres of free land. It is 10 furlongs long and 5 broad. In geld 11½d. Others hold [land] there.

In Langham 7 free men with 1 carucate of land and 1 bordar. Then as now 3 ploughs. 6 acres of meadow. Woodland for 6 pigs. These men could give and sell their land but the sake and soke and commendation continued to belong to St [Edmund]. Then as now worth 10s. A church with 20 acres of free land.

In Hunston 9 free men with 2 carucates of land. 4 bordars. Then as now 4 ploughs. 10 acres of meadow. Woodland for 12 pigs. These men could give and sell their land but the sake and soke and commendation continued to belong to St [Edmund]. Half a church with 15 acres of free land. Of this land and of these free men Burcard holds 6 free men with 1½ carucates of land and 3 ploughs, worth 35s. in the same valuation. It is 8 furlongs long and 7 broad. In geld 9½d. and ¼[d].

[Folio 367v: SUFFOLK]

In [Great] Fakenham Peter holds from the abbot 2 free men with 1 carucate of land. 3 villans and 4 bordars. Then as now 1 plough in demesne and half a plough belonging to the men. 4 acres of meadow. Woodland for 4 pigs. These men could give and sell their land but the sake and soke and commendation continued to belong to St [Edmund]. Then as now worth 20s.

In Little Fakenham the same Peter holds 1 free man with 60

acres of land. Then as now 1 plough. This man belongs to St Edmund with sake and soke and commendation. And he could not give and sell the land without the abbot's permission. Then as now worth 5s.

In Euston Adelund holds from the abbot 2 free men with 1 carucate of land. 4 villans. Then as now 2 ploughs in demesne and half a plough belonging to the men. 3 acres of meadow. 2 mills. These men could give and sell their land but the sake and soke and commendation continued to belong to St [Edmund]. Then as now worth 30s. It is 1 league long and 5 furlongs broad. In geld 11½d. Others hold [land] there.

In Knettishall Fulcher holds from the abbot 4 free men with 1 carucate of land and 30 acres. 6 bordars. Then as now 3 ploughs between them. 1 mill. 2 acres of meadow. These men could give and sell their land but the sake and soke and commendation continued to belong to St [Edmund]. Then as now worth 20s. A church with 12 acres of land. It is 8 furlongs long and 3 broad. In geld 11½d. Others hold [land] there.

At Ixworth Robert Blund holds from the abbot 1 carucate of land and 5 men. 3 acres of meadow. Then as now 2 ploughs. Then as now worth 10s. All these men could give their land TRE. St Edmund has the soke and sake and commendation.

In [Ixworth] Thorpe 9 free men with 1 carucate of land. Then as now 2 bordars and 2 ploughs. 1 acre of meadow. 1 mill. It is worth 20s. These could give and sell their land but the sake and soke continued to belong to St [Edmund]. It is 1 league long and a half broad. 9d. in geld.

In the same place Robert holds from the abbot 1 free man with 60 acres and 1 bordar. Then as now 1 plough. 4 acres of meadow. It is worth 10s. The abbot put this land in pledge to the king's barons, namely Bishop W[illiam], Engelric and Ralph the staller, for 100s. This man could sell and give his land but the soke and sake continued to belong to St [Edmund].

St Edmund

[Folio 368: SUFFOLK]

HUNDRED OF BISHOP.

St Edmund held [Monk] Soham TRE as a manor with 4 carucates of land together with the soke. Then as now 8 villans and 11 bordars. Then 2 slaves, now 1. Then as now 2 ploughs in demesne. Then as now 6 ploughs belonging to the men. 6 acres of meadow. Woodland for 40 pigs. Now 1 horse, 5 head of cattle, 31 pigs, 31 sheep and 21 goats. A church with 50 acres of land. Then this manor was worth £4, now £5. It is 7 furlongs long and 6 broad. In geld [...] 10d. Others hold [land] there.

St Edmund held Worlingworth TRE as a manor with 6 carucates of land together with the soke. Then as now 16 villans and 14 bordars and 1 slave. Then as now 2 ploughs in demesne. Then as now 12 ploughs belonging to the men. 16 acres of meadow. Woodland for 100 pigs. Then as now 2 horses, 8 head of cattle, 24 pigs, 25 sheep and 33 goats. Now 6 beehives. 1 sokeman with 20 acres. A church with 10 acres of free land. Then this manor was worth £6, now £8. It is 1 league long and 5 furlongs broad. In geld 10d.

In Bedingfield 10 free men with half a carucate of land.

Then as now 2 bordars. Then as now 2 ploughs between them all. Woodland for 8 pigs. One of these [free men] with 30 acres of land could never give and sell the land without the full consent of the abbot. The Hundred testifies to this. Nine could give and sell the land. Then the whole was worth 5s., now 8s. It is 1 league long and 6 furlongs broad. In geld 15d. Others hold [land] there.

St Edmund held Chippenhall TRE as a manor with 1½ carucates of land together with the soke. Then as now 6 villans and 12 bordars. Then 1½ ploughs in demesne, now 2 ploughs. Then 3 ploughs belonging to the men, now 5; 10 acres of meadow. Woodland then for 160 pigs, now 100. Then as now 1 horse. Now 16 head of cattle, 16 pigs and 30 goats. Half a church with 20 acres. Then this manor was worth 40s., now 60s. It is 1½ leagues long and 1 league broad. In geld 15d. Others hold [land] there.

Frodo holds Mendham from the abbot which St Edmund held TRE as a manor with 2 carucates and 19 acres of land. Then as now 2 villans. Then 18 bordars, now 26, and 1 slave.

Then as now 2 ploughs in demesne. Then 6 ploughs belonging to the men, now 8; 18 acres of meadow. 1 mill. Woodland then for 360 pigs, now 300. Then as now 1 horse. Now 10 head of cattle, 41 pigs, 40 sheep and 36 goats. 6 sokemen with half a carucate of land. Then as now 3 ploughs and 2 acres of meadow. Woodland for 3 pigs. And 1 free man holds 3 acres, worth 6d. These men belong to St [Edmund] with sake and soke and commendation. They could never give or sell the land without the abbot's permission. A church with 20 acres. Then this manor was worth £4 10s., now £12 4s. It is 1 league and 9 furlongs long and 1 league broad. In geld 15d. Others hold [land] there.

In Weybread St Edmund [holds] 30 acres and 2 villans and 1 plough. 3 acres of meadow. Woodland for 10 pigs. It is worth 10s.

HALF-HUNDRED OF COSFORD.

St held Semer TRE as a manor. Then as now there are 3¼ carucates of land and 11 acres of meadow there. 6 villans and 13 bordars. 1 slave. Then as now 3 ploughs in demesne and 2 belonging to the men. 1 mill. 2 horses, 16 head of cattle and 24 pigs. 97 sheep. Then it was worth £5, now £6. In the same place there is a church with 30 acres of land and 1 acre of meadow. Then as now 1 plough belonging to the church. This vill is 9 furlongs long and 7 broad. 2½d. in geld. But others hold there.

St Edmund held Chelsworth TRE as a manor. Then as now 3½ carucates of land. 8 villans. 10 bordars. 4 slaves. Then 2 ploughs in demesne and 4 belonging to the men, and now the same number. 12 acres of meadow. Then and now always mill. Then as now 2 horses. Then 10 head of cattle, now 9. Then 16 pigs, now 20. Then 30 sheep, now 60. This manor was then worth £4, now £5. It is 7 furlongs long and 6 broad. A church with 30 acres of land. 1 acre of meadow. 3½d. and ¼[d.] in geld.

In Layham St Edmund held TRE 26 free men. They had 2 carucates of land. 6 acres of meadow. 2 bordars. Then they ploughed with 6 carucates, now with 4. They could give and sell their land but St Edmund had the soke and sake and commendation and every customary due. Then their land was worth 30s., now 40s. Berard holds half a carucate of land and 1 plough. It is worth 22s. in the same valuation. It is 6 furlongs long and 4 broad. 3½d. in geld. But others hold there.

St Edmund

In Whatfield St Edmund held TRE 18 free men. They had 2½ carucates of land. 7 acres of meadow. 6 bordars. Then they ploughed with 4 ploughs, and now [also]. Then it was worth 40s., now 50s. [...] Of this land the same Berard holds 1 carucate of land and 3 free men and 1 plough. It is worth 20s. in the same valuation. St Edmund [has] the commendation and the soke and sake. It is 6 furlongs long and 5 broad. In geld 5d. But others hold [land] there.

In the ferling of Aldham St Edmund held TRE 6 free men and 10 in the other Whatfield. They 6 had 1½ carucates . Then as now they plough with 6 ploughs. 4 bordars. 6 acres of meadow. They could give and sell their land but the soke and commendation and every customary due [belonged] to St [Edmund]. Their land was worth 30s. then, now 40s. . Of this land Berard holds 40 acres; 1 plough. It is worth 10s. in the same valuation. These two vills are 6 furlongs long and 3 broad. 6d. in geld. But others hold [land] there. In the same place there is a church with 2 acres of land.

In Lindsey St Edmund held TRE 20 free men. They had 1½ carucates of land. 16 bordars and 2 slaves. Then as now they plough with 5 ploughs. TRE they could give and sell their land but St Edmund has the soke and commendation and every customary due. Then it was worth 20s., now 30s. It is 6 furlongs long and 5 broad, whoever holds there. A church with 10 acres of land. In geld 6d.

In Manton and in Kettlebaston St Edmund held TRE 4 free men. They had 2 carucates of land. 6 acres of meadow. 8 bordars. 3 slaves. Then as now they plough with 3 ploughs. They could give and sell their land. St Edmund had the soke and commendation and every customary due. Then as now worth 60s. Of this land Gamas holds 1 carucate of land and 2 ploughs in demesne. And Humphrey [holds] 1 carucate. It is worth 40s. in the same valuation. Their land is 6 furlongs long and 4 broad. 3d. in geld. But others hold [land] there.

In Brettenham and Rushbrooke and in Thorpe [Morieux], St Edmund held TRE 14 free men and they had then as now 2½ carucates. 8 acres of meadow. 7 bordars. Then they ploughed with 5 ploughs, now 2. Over them St Edmund has soke and sake and every customary due. Then it was worth 50s., now 30s.

Of this land Arnulf holds 7 free men and 1 carucate and 30 acres of land. It is worth 15s. in the same valuation.

In Thorpe [Morieux] [St Edmund held] 20 acres and 1 free man, worth 3s. 4d. St Edmund has the commendation and soke.

HUNDRED OF CARLFORD.

In Lesser Waldringfield Cwengifu held TRE under St [Edmund] 1½ carucates of land. Now 8 bordars. Then as now in demesne 2 ploughs and belonging to the men 1 plough. 2 acres of meadow. 1 horse and 10 pigs and 100 sheep. Then as now worth 20s. It is 3 furlongs long and 6 broad. 5d. in geld. In Newbourn 3 free men and in Haspley 1, by commendation to the same Cwengifu, with 6 acres, worth 12d. Roger Bigod holds this from the abbot.

HUNDRED OF LOOSE.

St Edmund held Marlesford TRE with 1 carucate of land and 12 acres as a manor. Then as now 5 bordars. 2 ploughs in demesne and half a plough belonging to the men. 6 acres of meadow. 1 mill. 5 horses, 4 head of cattle, 14 pigs, 50 sheep and 3 beehives. Then it was worth 30s., now 40s. And [it held] 9 whole [free] men and 2 half free men with 83 acres. Then 3 ploughs, now 2; 1 acre of meadow.

In Hacheston 4 half free men commended to St [Edmund] and a half with 21 acres. Then as now half a plough. It is worth 8s.

In Kenton Durand held 2 free men from the abbot with 80 acres. Then 2 villans, now 1. Now 3 bordars. Then as now 2 ploughs and half a plough belonging to the men. Woodland for 10 pigs. 1 acre of meadow. 1 horse, 3 head of cattle, 16 pigs, 80 sheep, 25 goats and 3 beehives. Then it was worth 20s., now 30s. Durand holds this from the abbot. St Æthelthryth has the soke and sake.

HUNDRED OF WANGFORD.

St Edmund held Beccles TRE with 2 carucates of land as a manor. Then as now 2 villans and 26 bordars. Then 2 slaves. Then as now 1 plough in demesne and [1] belonging to the men. acres of meadow. Woodland for 8 pigs. 1 market

St Edmund

[Folio 370: SUFFOLK]

and 26 burgesses. And the abbot has 3 parts of the market and the king the fourth. 2 horses.

In the same place 30 sokemen with every customary due. 1½ carucates of land. Under them 20 bordars. Then 7 ploughs, now 8. But they could sell their land TRE. 1 church with 24 acres. Then this manor rendered 30,000 herrings, now 60,000. It is 1 league long and 8 furlongs broad. In geld 16d.

In Linburne St Edmund held 30 acres of land. Then as now 5 bordars. Then as now 1 plough. 2 acres of meadow. The fifth part of 1 mill. Then and always worth 10s. Bishop W[illiam] [has] the soke and sake. In Worlingham half a church with 5 acres, worth 12d.

HUNDRED OF HARTISMERE.

In Stoke Ash 7 free men in the soke and commendation of the abbot [held] 10 acres. Half a plough. Woodland for 2 pigs. Half an acre of meadow. It is worth 3s.

In Wyverstone Robert Blund holds 19 acres from the abbot which 1 free man, Grim, held by commendation and in the soke of the abbot. . It is worth 40d. OF ST EDMUND.

In Wetheringsett 10 free men with 40 acres and 2 bordars and 2 ploughs and 1 acre of meadow. Woodland for 3 pigs. It is worth 6s. 8d.

In Stoke Ash 14 free men with 33½ acres. Then as now 2 ploughs. 1 acre of meadow. It is worth 6s. The soke and commendation belong to the abbot, except over one.

In Wickham [Skeith] 14 free men with 60 acres in the soke and commendation of the abbot. Then as now 2 ploughs. 1 acre of meadow. Woodland for 4 pigs. It is worth 10s.

In Thorham [Magna] 9 free men with 35 acres in the soke and commendation of the abbot. 1½ ploughs. Half an acre of meadow. It is worth 6s.

In Thorndon Leofric, a free man commended to the abbot, held 1 carucate of land. 6 bordars. 2 ploughs in demesne and half a plough belonging to the men. 1 acre of meadow. Woodland for 8 pigs. It is worth 20s.

[Folio 370v: SUFFOLK]

In OAKLEY IN THE HUNDRED OF HARTISMERE.

In Oakley 1 free man, Goding the reeve, commended to St Edmund TRE [held] 90 acres of land. He could not sell or give [the land]. Then as now 5 bordars. 1 plough and 1½ ploughs belonging to the men. Woodland for 5 pigs. 2 acres of meadow. 1 mill. 1 horse, 2 head of cattle and 5 sheep. Then as now worth 20s. Under him 10 free men with 30 acres. Then as now 1½ ploughs. 2 acres of meadow. It is worth 10s. St Edmund has the soke and sake and commendation. 2 parts of church with 12 acres, worth 16d. In Thornham [Magna] 5 free men in the soke and commendation of the abbot with 44½ acres. Then as now 1½ ploughs. 2 acres of meadow. Woodland for 4 pigs. Then as now worth 8s.

In Finningham 11 free men in the soke and commendation of St Edmund with 68 acres. Then as now 1½ ploughs and 2 bordars. 4 acres of meadow. Woodland for 8 pigs. 1 church with 26 acres, worth 4s. In Westhorpe 8 free men in the soke and commendation of the abbot with 60 acres. Then as now 1½ ploughs. 2 acres of meadow. Woodland for 4 pigs. Then as now worth 10s. In the same place 1 man with 7 acres, worth 14d. And he could not sell. And in Finningham 1 likewise with 8 acres, worth 16d.

In Wyverstone 6 free men in the soke and commendation of the abbot with 75 acres and 1 villan and 2 bordars. Then as now 1½ ploughs. Woodland for 4 pigs. 1 acre of meadow. Then as now worth 13s.

In Cotton 1 villan with 8 acres, worth 16d. It belongs to [Great] Ashfield.

In "Caldecota" 1 free man with 6 acres in the soke and commendation of the abbot. It is worth 12d. All those men perform their customary dues at Rickinghall [Superior]. Also the abbot has in Oakley and in Stuston 15 free men in soke and commendation with 1 carucate of land and 10 acres. Then as now 11 bordars and 3 ploughs. Woodland for 2 pigs. 6 acres of meadow. 1 church with 24 acres. It is worth 4s. Half an acre of meadow. Then as now worth 20s.

In Oakley Goscelin holds 1 free woman, Leofsidu by name, with 30 acres. But she could not

St Edmund

sell or give [the land]. 3 bordars. Then as now half a plough. Woodland for 4 pigs. 2 acres of meadow. It is worth 32d

In Thrandeston Anselm holds from the abbot 2 carucates of land as a manor. Then as now 6 bordars. In demesne 2 ploughs and 1 plough belonging to the men. 8 acres of meadow. 2 horses, 2 head of cattle, 12 pigs and 55 sheep. 12 free men and a half with 42 acres but they could sell. 1 church with 8 acres, worth 16d. Then as now 3 ploughs. Woodland for 4 pigs. 1 acre of meadow. Then it was worth 40s., now 60s. The soke and the commendation belong to St [Edmund]. It is 8 furlongs long and 7 broad. In geld 8d.

In Mellis 1 free man under the commendation and in the soke of St Edmund with 1½ acres. It is worth 6d. In Brome 1 free man belonging to [St] Edmund with 1 acre, worth 4d. In Westhorpe 1 free man belonging to [St] Edmund with 1 acre, worth 2d. In Thorndon 6 free men in the soke and commendation of the abbot with 16 acres, worth 3s. In Occold 3 acres in demesne. In Chippenhall 12 acres, worth 2s. In Stoke [Ash] Burgheard, a sokeman of the abbot, held TRE 14 acres, worth 3s. Robert Fardenc, Godric the steward's man, claims this land as belonging to the king's manor of Mendlesham and says that Walter de Dol held it when he forfeited and he wants to prove this against the whole Hundred by all lawful procedures.

In the same place 8 free men by commendation and soke [held] 24 acres. Then as now 1 plough and 2 acres of meadow, worth 5s. In Thornham [Magna] 1 free man by soke and commendation [held] 2 acres, worth 4d.

In Cotton 3 free men in the soke and commendation of the abbot [held] 3 acres.

In "Caldecota" 1 free man, Ælfric, by commendation [held] 4½ acres, worth 12d.

In Thrandeston Wulfric by commendation [held] 3 acres, worth 6d.

In Wyverstone 4 men by commendation [held] 16½ acres, worth 3s. Richard .

In Wickham [Skeith] 2 free men, Brunlocc and Hereweard, by commendation to Burgheard of Mendlesham [held] 5½ acres, worth 10d. The king and the earl have the soke. Ordgar the abbot's reeve holds these men. Ælfric who was reeve before him appropriated them. In Wetheringsett 3 acres in the demesne of the abbot, worth 6d. Godwine holds it.

HUNDRED OF RISBRIDGE.

In Poslingford 12 free men belonging to St Edmund by commendaton and soke and sake TRE. They had 60 acres and 1 bordar and 2 ploughs, worth 10s.

In Stansfield 7 free men [held] 75 carucates. Then as now 2 ploughs. St Edmund has the commendation and soke. It is worth 11s. 3d.

In [Great and Little] Thurlow 9 free men with 95 acres. 5 bordars. 4 ploughs. 4 acres of meadow. Woodland for 6 pigs. It is worth 15s. St Edmund has the soke and commendation. In

[Great and Little] Bradley 8 free men [held] 60 acres and 1 bordar. 2 ploughs. 1 acre of meadow. It is worth 11s. 3d. In the same place 4 free men [held] 60 acres. 1 bordar. 2 ploughs. 1 acre of meadow. It is worth 10s. St Edmund holds the commendation and the soke and sake.

In Kedington 1 free man [held] 5 acres, worth 12d. St Edmund has the commendation and the soke and sake. In [Great and Little] Wratting 1 free man [held] 7 acres, worth 12d. In Haverhill 2 free men [held] 5 acres, worth 7d. St Edmund has the soke and commendation.

HUNDRED OF BISHOP.

In Horham 4 free men [held] 30 acres and 1 plough, worth 5s. St Edmund has the commendation. The soke is in Hoxne. Southwold is 9 furlongs long and 5 broad. This division [extends] from the sea to Yarmouth [Norfolk]. 2½d. in geld.

HUNDRED OF BLYTHING.

St Edmund held Southwold for the supplies of the monks as a manor with 1 carucate of land. 5 villans and 4 bordars. 1 plough in demesne and 4 ploughs belonging to the men. 4 acres of meadow. 1 horse, 4 head of cattle and 3 pigs. 30 sheep. Half of one sea-weir and the fourth part of another half. Then it rendered 20,000 herrings, now 25,000. St Edmund [has] the soke and sake. Godwine held Uggeshall. St [Edmund] has the soke. 1 carucate of land. Then as now 3 villans and 12 bordars. 1 plough in demesne and 3 ploughs belonging to the men. Woodland for 3 pigs. 2 acres of meadow. 4 head of cattle and 1 pig and 80 sheep. 1 free man and a half with 22½ acres of land by commendation. Then as now 1 bordar and 1 plough. Half an acre of meadow. St Edmund has the soke. The manor is worth then as now 60s. and the free men 4s. 8d. In Benacre 1 sokeman with 10 acres, worth 16d.

HUNDRED OF WILFORD.

In Ufford 1 free man commended to St Edmund TRE with 24 acres of land and 2 acres of meadow. Then as now 1 plough. Then and now worth 5s.

St Edmund

IN the town [Bury St Edmunds] where St Edmund, king and glorious martyr lies buried, TRE Abbot B[aldwin] held for the supplies of the monks 118 men and they could give and sell their land and under them 52 bordars from whom the abbot can have some help. 54 free [men], somewhat poor, 43 almsmen, each of whom has 1 bordar. Now 2 mills and 2 ponds or fish ponds. This vill was then worth £10, now £20. It is 1½ leagues long and as much broad. And when in the Hundred pays £1 in geld, then 60d. goes from this for the supplies of the monks. But this refers to the town as it was TRE as if it were the same now. Now it is enclosed in a larger circuit of land which then used to be ploughed and sown where [now] there are 30 priests, deacons and clerics together, and 28 nuns together and poor people who daily pray for the king and all Christian people; 80 less five bakers, brewers, tailors, washerwomen, shoemakers, robemakers, cooks, porters, bursars together. And all these daily serve St [Edmund] and the abbot and the brothers. Besides these there are 13 reeves in charge of the land who have their houses in the same town and under them 5 bordars. Now there are 34 knights, French and English together, and under them 22 bordars. Now altogether [there are] 342 houses in demesne on land of St Edmund which was arable TRE.

    ARCHBISHOP LANFRANC
    BISHOP of Bayeux
    BISHOP of Thetford
    THE FIEF OF THE BISHOP of Thetford

[Folio 372v: SUFFOLK]

XV. Lands of Archbishop Lanfranc

for the monks' supplies. HUNDRED OF RISBRIDGE.

Stigand held Moulton TRE as a manor with 7 carucates of land. Then 32 villans, now 22. Then 7 bordars, now 16. Then 6 slaves, now 2. Then as now 3 ploughs in demesne and 6 ploughs belonging to the men. 8 acres of meadow. Woodland for 20 pigs. 2 horses, 2 head of cattle and 40 pigs. 270 sheep and 4 beehives. Then it was worth £15, now £12. It is 1 league long and 7 furlongs broad. 13½d. in geld. Stigand had the soke and sake and every customary due. HALF-HUNDRED OF COSFORD.

Holy Trinity held Hadleigh TRE with 5 carucates of land as a manor. Then as now 22 villans. Then 26 bordars, now 19. Then as now 2 slaves. 2 ploughs in demesne. Then 15 ploughs belonging to the men, now 10. Then as now 2 mills. 16 acres of meadow. Now 2 horses, 12 head of cattle, 120 sheep and 20 pigs. Then it was worth £12, now £15. A church with 1 carucate of free land and 1 plough and 1 mill, worth 12s. 1 sokeman with 60 acres TRE. Now on the same land dwell 3 sokemen. Then as now they have 1 plough and 1 acre of meadow. And 1 free man by commendation and soke [held] 60 acres TRE. On the same land dwell now 3 free men. They have 1 plough. 2½ acres of meadow. Then it was worth 8s., now 10s. The whole is 1 league long and 7 furlongs broad. 11½d. in geld.

In Toppesfield a certain free woman, Leofgifu by name, held 2 carucates of land as a manor. Then 2 bordars, now 5 and 1 slave. 2 ploughs. 5 acres of meadow. 1 mill. Then 7 sheep, now 34; 2 head of cattle and 1 horse. Then it was worth 40s., now 60s. Leofgifu gave half a carucate of this land to Holy Trinity after her death in return for another half carucate which she held from the archbishop during her lifetime. This agreement was made TRE and Leofgifu was lng in the time of King William and she was seised thereof. John, nephew of Waleran, claims this land. St Edmund held it with the whole soke and sake. In Toppesfield 1 free man with 20 acres over whom Wulfric the predecessor of the Abbot of St Edmund had the commendation and the soke TRE. Then as now half a plough. It is worth 3s. 4d.

The Archbishop

[Folio 373: SUFFOLK]

Two HUNDREDS OF BABERGH.

Holy Trinity held Eleigh [Brent and Monks] TRE as a manor with 5 carucates of land with the soke and sake. Then 21 villans, now 13. Then 13 bordars, now 12. Then 4 slaves, now 3. Then as now 2 ploughs in demesne. Then 21 ploughs belonging to the men, now 13; 12 acres of meadow. Then as now 1 mill. Now 2 horses. Now 19 head of cattle. Now 20 pigs. Now 160 sheep. A church with 22½ acres. Then it was worth £15, now £20. It is 1 league long and 5 furlongs broad. geld 14d.

XV. Lands of the Bishop of Bayeux.

HUNDRED OF RISBRIDGE.

In Haverhill 1 free man [holds] 24 acres and half a plough, worth 3s. Tihel holds this from the Bishop. His predecessor TRE [had] the commendation. St Edmund [had] the 6 forfeitures.

HUNDRED OF CARLFORD. In Seckford Ælfric, son of Wulfgeat, commended to Harold, held TRE 2 carucates of land as a manor. Then as now 4 villans. Then 13 bordars, now 15. Then in demesne 2 ploughs; a third could be made. 3 ploughs belonging to the men. 10 acres of meadow. 1 mill. Then 1 horse, now none. And 4 head of cattle. Then 30 pigs, now none. Then 100 sheep, now 36. Then it was worth £4, now 40s. It is 6 furlongs long and 6 broad. In geld 7½d. In the same place 4 free men under commendation to the same Ælfric with 8 acres, 1 acre of meadow, half a plough, worth 16d. Roger Bigod holds this from the bishop.

In Little Bealings the same Ælfric held TRE 50 acres as a manor. And 2 bordars. Then 1 plough, now ½. 3 acres of meadow. Then 1 mill, now none. Then it was worth 20s., now 10s.

In the same place Beorn, a free man, held TRE 50 acres as a manor and 3 acres of meadow. Then and always worth 8s. Beorn himself, a free man, bought this [land] from the abbot with an agreement that after his death it should revert to the church of St Æthelthryth, as the Hundred testifies. Roger Bigod holds this from the bishop and William de More from him. Earl Ralph held these three manors on the day he forfeited, and Hilary from him.

[Folio 373v: SUFFOLK]

HUNDRED OF WILFORD.

In Wickham [Market] Roger Bigod [holds] 1 free man commended to St Æthelthryth with 25 acres and under him 4 free men with 7 acres. Then 1 plough, now half an acre. 2 acres of meadow. It is worth 5s. Ralph de Savenay holds this from Roger Bigod from the fief of the bishop In Debach [are] 15 acres and they belong to Charsfield. In the same place [he holds] a free man with half an acre.

HUNDRED OF LOOSE.

In Charsfield 14 free men with 1 carucate of land. Roger Bigod it and Ralph de Savenay holds it from him. And 13 acres. Then 5 ploughs, now 3; 1 acre of meadow. Three of these men and 1 half [free man] were commended to St Æthelthryth and to Eadric of Laxfield. William Malet was seised [thereof] on the day of his death. And the others were commended to the abbot only. Then it was worth 60s., now the same. In the same place 2 sokemen belonging to St Æthelthryth with 7 acres. They are in the same valuation. In the same place 1 free man, Markulf, commended to Eadric of Laxfield. William Malet was seised [thereof] on the day he died. 1 bordar. Then 1 plough. 1 acre of meadow. And under him 4 free men with 4 acres. Then it was worth 10s., now 5s. It is 8 furlongs long and 6 broad. 11d. in geld.

Others hold [land] there.

In Cretingham the same Ralph holds 1 free man, Balki, commended to Æthelstan, with 24 acres of land. 1 acre of meadow. Then half a plough, now the same. Worth 4s. In the same place 1 free man under the same commendation with 38½ acres. 1 bordar. 2 acres of meadow. 1 plough. Then worth 12s., now the same.

In Kenton 5 free men 4 were commended to St Æthelthryth and Saxi the predecessor of Ralph de Savenay [had commendation] over one with 30 acres of land. Then as now 1 plough. Then worth 10s., now 6s. Now Ralph de Savenay holds it from Roger Bigod.

TWO HUNDREDS OF BABERGH.

In Eleigh [Brent and Monks] 3 free men under soke and commendation to Earl Ælfgar. Now Tihel de Helléan holds them from the bishop And they have 30 acres. Then 1 plough, now a half. Half an acre of meadow. It is worth 5s.

Ælfgifu, mother of Earl Morcar, held Brandeston TRE as a manor

The Bishop of Bayeux

[Folio 374: SUFFOLK]

with 3 carucates of land and 5 villans and 6 bordars and 5 slaves. Then as now 2 ploughs in demesne. Then and afterwards 2 ploughs belonging to the men, now 1; 4 acres of meadow. Woodland for 10 pigs. Then as now 2 horses at the hall. Then 5 head of cattle, now 3. Then 20 pigs, now 23. Then 100 sheep, now 120. In the same place 3 free men under Ælfgifu by commendation and soke and sake but they could sell without permission. 24 acres of land. Then as now worth £5. It is 1 league long and 3 furlongs broad. In geld 6d. Ralph de Courbépine holds this manor from the bishop.

HUNDRED OF STOW.

In Creeting [St Peter] Ælfric, son of Brune, 1 free man under Wihtgar by commendation only held TRE 1 carucate of land in the king's soke. Now William de Bouville holds it from the bishop.Then as now 5 bordars and 1 slave. Then as now 1 plough in demesne and half a plough belonging to the men. And the third part of the mill. 4 acres of meadow. 4 head of cattle and 8 pigs. Then 8 sheep, now 20. Then as now worth 20s. It is 1 league long and a half broad. In geld 30d. But several [others] hold [land] there. There [are] 5 free men under commendation only to the same Ælfric, with 18 acres and half a plough. And they were delivered with the manor. It is worth 2s. The king and the earl have the soke and sake.

In [Old] Newton 2 free men of Alsige by commendation only held 80 acres of land in the soke of the king and earl. Now Roger Bigod holds it from the bishop; Warenger holds under Roger. Then 2 bordars, afterwards and now 1. Then 1½ ploughs in demesne, afterwards none, now 1. And 3 acres of meadow. Now 2 head of cattle, 6 pigs and 40 sheep. The sixth part of a church with 10 acres of free land. Then it was worth 30s., afterwards 20s., now 40s.

In "Rodeham" 1 free man belonging to Saxi under commendation to St Æthelthryth TRE [held] 10 acres in the soke of the Hundred. Then as now half a plough. Roger Bigod holds it from the bishop and under him Ralph de Savenay. It is worth 2s.

HUNDRED OF BOSMER

e. In Crowfield Wudu-Brun, a free man commended to Eadric the predecessor of Robert Malet, held 20 acres as a manor. Then and afterwards 1 plough, now none. 1 acre of meadow. Then and afterwards 5s., now 3s. Roger Bigod holds it from the bishop.

[Folio 374v: SUFFOLK]

In the same place 5 free men [held] 40 acres. Then and afterwards 2 ploughs, now none. 1 acre of meadow. Roger Bigod holds this. Then it was worth 16s., now 20s.

In [Earl and Little] Stonham 1 free man, Leofwine, commended to Eadric of Laxfield, [held] 20 acres as a manor TRE. 2 bordars. Then as now 1 plough. 2 acres of meadow. 2 churches with 3 acres. Then it was worth 5s. 4d., now 10s. 8d. Roger Bigod holds it from the bishop. The king and the earl have the soke. In the same place 1 free man, Ælfric, with 20 acres. 2 bordars. 1 acre of meadow. Then it was worth 4s., now 8s. This man was commended to the predecessor of Richard, son of Count Gilbert. The king and the earl have the soke. In the same place 2 free men with 2 acres, worth 6d. In the same place Leofric, a free man commended to Leofwine, [held] 10 acres. Then half a plough. Then it was worth 3s. now 2s. In the same place 11 free men [held] 52 acres. 10 of these were commended to Leofwine who was commended to Robert Malet's predecessor. The eleventh [...], Sperun by name, was commended to Burgheard TRE; he had of this land. Then 4 ploughs, afterwards and now 2; 2 acres of meadow. Then it was worth 20s., now 30s. It is 1 league long and 6½ furlongs broad. 20d. in geld. Others hold [land] there. The king and the earl have the soke. In 'Olden' [in Coddenham] 1 free man, Ælfric, commended to Saxi, [held] 16 acres. Then as now 1 plough. Then 1 bordar, now none. Roger de Rames claims that he held this Ælfric in his fief after [the men] were delivered to the bishop. Then woodland for 24 pigs. 8 pigs and 22 sheep and 3 goats. Then it was worth 10s., now 8s. In the same place 6 free men with 52 acres. The Abbot of St Edmund had commendation TRE over one and a half of these, namely Leofwine and Thormær, and one by the name of Beorhtweald was commended to Eadric, the predecessor of

Malet. Then altogether 2½ ploughs, now 2. Then it was worth 20s. and now Roger Bigod holds it from the bishop and Warenger from him. In Creeting Asgot, a free man, held thirty acres TRE as a manor. Then as now 1 bordar and 1 plough. 8 pigs and 9 sheep. 1 acre of meadow. Then as now worth 12s.

The Bishop of Bayeux

[Folio 375: SUFFOLK]

Roger Bigod holds this from the bishop and Warenger from him. The king and the earl have the soke.

In Burstall 1 free man, Ailbern, held TRE 14 acres. A church with 26 acres. Then as now half a plough. 1 acre of meadow. Then it was worth 10s., now 8s. 4d.

In the same place a free man under King Edward, Æthelric, [held] 14 acres and half a plough. 1 acre of meadow. Then it was worth 5s. 4d., now 4s. In the same place Wulfwig, a free man under the king, [held] 2 acres. Then it was worth 5d., now 6d. It is 8 furlongs long and 1½ furlongs broad. 6½d. in geld. The king and the earl have the soke.

In "Pachetuna" 3 free men under King Edward [held] 24 acres. Then as now 1 plough. 1 acre of meadow. Then it was worth 8s. and now the same. In the same place 1 free man and a half under King Edward [held] 5½ acres, worth 12d. In Coddenham 1 free man, Almær by name, commended to the Abbot of Ely, [held] 60 acres of land as a manor. Then 2 ploughs, now 1½; 1 bordar. Then woodland for 10 pigs, now 2. Then as now worth 30s. A church with 3 acres, worth 6d.

In the same place 2 free men, Ælfric and Wulfric, [held] 60 acres as 2 manors. 1 villan and 2 bordars. 2 ploughs. 40 sheep and 2 head of cattle. 4 acres of meadow. Then woodland for 30 pigs, now 11. Then worth 30s., now 40s. The Abbot of Ely had the commendation. In the same place 2 free men, Ælfric and Wihtric, [held] 2 acres, worth 12d. A church with 1 acre, worth 2d. The king and the earl have the soke over the whole. In the same place Harold, a free man under soke and commendation of the Abbot of Ely, [held] 30 acres as a manor TRE. Then as now 2 bordars. 1 plough. 2 acres of meadow. Woodland for 10 pigs. It is worth In the same place 3 free men [held] 7½ acres and half a plough, worth 2s. The king and the earl have the soke. In the same place Leofgifu, a free woman, [held] TRE 10 acres and half a plough. 3 bordars and 1 acre of meadow, worth 4s. In the same place 15 free men with 80 acres, less 1. Of these, 6 were commended to Saxi, the predecessor of Ranulf Peverel. Then and afterwards 5 ploughs, now 1. Woodland for 10 pigs. 2 acres of meadow. Then and afterwards worth 30s., now 20s. The king and the earl have the soke.

[Folio 375v: SUFFOLK]

In Olden [in Coddenham] 8 free men [held] 40 acres. Of these, 4 were commended to Saxi, the predecessor of Ranulf Peverel, with 25 acres. Then between them all 2 ploughs, now 1 and 1½ acres of meadow. 1 horse. Then 6 head of cattle, now 7. Then 28 sheep and now 17 sheep. Now 20 goats. Then 5 pigs, now 19. Then it was worth 20s., now 21s. Then the king and the earl have the soke.

In [Earl and Little] Stonham Wulfric, a free man, held 60 acres as a manor in the Abbot of Ely's commendation. Then 4 bordars, now 3. Then 2 ploughs in demesne, now 1. Then 1 plough belonging to the men, now a half. 3 acres of meadow. A church with 7½ acres, worth 15d. Then it was worth 40s., now 20s.

In the same place Alweald the priest and Godwig, free men commended to Saxi, the predecessor of Ranulf Peverel, [held] 40 acres as 2 manors TRE. Then as now 3 bordars. Then and afterwards 2 ploughs in demesne. Then as now half a plough belonging to the men. 1½ acres of meadow. A church with 2 acres, worth 4d. Then it was worth 30s., now 12s. In the same place 26 free men commended to Saxi, apart from one by the name of Viking, [held] 142 acres. Then 7 ploughs, now 5. And 1½ acres of meadow. Then it was worth £4, now 40s. 4d.

In the same place 1 free man with 3 acres, worth 10d.

In Hemingstone 2 free men commended to Saxi, Peverel's predecessor, [held] 10 acres, worth 28d. Ralph de Savenay holds all this from Roger Bigod and Roger from the bishop. The king and the earl have the soke over the whole.

In the same place 2 free men, Brunwine and Godric, [held] 3 acres, worth 6d. The same Roger holds this. The king and the earl have the soke.

In Sharpstone 3 free men, Leofwine, Leofric, Eadric, [held] 4 acres and 2 oxen, worth 10d. Ralph de Savenay holds it from Roger. HUNDRED OF CLAYDON.

In Helmingham Durand, a free man commended to Eadric of Laxfield, the predecessor, held 80 acres as a manor TRE. Then as now 1 villan and 2 bordars. Then 2 ploughs in demesne, afterwards 1, now none.

The Bishop of Bayeux

[Folio 376: SUFFOLK]

Then as now 1 plough belonging to the men. 2 acres of meadow. Then it was worth 30s., now 20s.

In Helmingham Balki, commended to Æthelstan, held 40 acres as a manor. Then as now 4 bordars. 1 plough in demesne. 1 acre of meadow. 1 horse. Then 4 head of cattle, now 2. Then 30 pigs, now 27. Then 40 sheep, now 24. It is worth 10s.

In the same place a free man, Viking, commended to Burgheard, [held] 30 acres as a manor TRE. Then as now 1 plough. 1 acre of meadow. Woodland for 4 pigs. Then it was worth 6s., now 13s. 4d.

In the same place 1 free man under King Edward, Æthelric, [held] 25 acres and 1 bordar. Then and afterwards 1 plough, now a half. Then it was worth 50d. and was at farm for 10s. Now it is worth 4s. In the same place a free man, Blæcmann, half commended to someone commended to Eadric, Malet's predecessor and half commended to Saxi, [held] 24 acres as a manor. Then as now 1 plough. Then it was worth 5s. and was at farm for 15s. Now it is worth 8s.

In the same place Godric, a free man half commended to someone commended to Eadric, Malet's predecessor and half to Saxi, [held] 20 acres as a manor. 1 bordar. 1 plough. The fourth part of a church with 1½ acres of free land. Then it was worth 6s. 4d. and was at farm for 14s. Now it is worth 10s. In the same place a free man, Leofstan, commended to someone commended to Eadric [held] 20 acres as a manor. Then as now 1 plough. The fourth part of a church with 1½ acres of free land. Then it was worth 6s. and was at farm for 14s. Now it is worth 10s. In the same place 11 free men with 71 acres. Over two and a half of these men the aforementioned Saxi, the predecessor of Ranulf Peverel, had the commendation and 1 half [free man] was commended to someone commended to Eadric, Robert Malet's predecessor. Between them they had then 2 ploughs, now 3; 2 acres of meadow. And half a church with 3 acres. Then it was worth 20s., now 20s. The king and the earl have the whole soke.

In Sharpstone 27 free men under soke and commendation of the Abbot of Ely [held] 1 carucate of land. Then and afterwards 4 ploughs, now 3 and 2 acres of meadow. [...] Then as now worth 40s.

[Folio 376V: SUFFOLK]

In Debenham Godwig, 1 free man commended to Saxi, [held] 40 acres as a manor. Then as now 2 bordars and 1 plough. 1 acre of meadow. The fourth part of a church of St Mary with 10 acres, worth 20s. St Æthelthryth has the soke. And 3 parts of a church of St Andrew with 1½ acres. The four part

In Ulverston the same Godwig [held] 15 acres TRE and in Ashfield 8 acres. Then as now 3 bordars and 1 plough. In the same place 1 free man, Goda, commended to someone commended to Eadric, Robert Malet's predecessor, [held] 15 acres. Then 1 plough, now a half. 1 acre of meadow. These three make one manor. Now 4 head of cattle in demesne and 10 pigs, 30 sheep and 12 goats. Then as now worth 22s. The soke is the abbot's.

In Ulverston Alwine the priest, a free man the sixth part of whose commendation belonged to someone commended to Malet's predecessor and five parts belonged to Saxi, Peverel's predecessor, [held] 40 acres as a manor. Then as now 1 villan and 1 priest and 2 bordars. 2 acres of meadow. 1 plough in demesne. Then and afterwards worth 20s., now 10s. The soke belongs to the abbot. William Malet [...] was seised of the fourth part of this land and of the priest who lived in it. In the same place Ælfric the priest, a free man, [held] 30 acres as a manor in the soke and commendation of the abbot. Then 1 plough. Then it was worth 10s., now 5s.

In the same place 2 free men, Eadric and Alnoth, commended to Saxi, [held] 40 acres and 1 bordar. Then as now 1 plough. Now 2 cows, 12 pigs and 20 sheep. It is worth 20s.

In the same place Thorir, a free man, [held] 40 acres as a manor. 2 bordars and 1 plough. Then woodland for 8 pigs, now 4. It is worth 20s. The soke and the commendation belong to the abbot.

In the same place Leofwine Cild, a free man in the soke and commendation of the abbot, [held] TRE 40 acres as a manor. 2 villans in another Hundred. Then 1 plough and 1 acre of meadow. Woodland for 12 pigs. Then it was worth 20s., now 15s. Roger Bigod holds all this from the bishop and Ralph de Savenay from him.

In Debenham 1 free man, Æthelric, commended to Saxi in the soke of the abbot [held] half an acre, worth 4d.

The Bishop of Bayeux

[Folio 377: SUFFOLK]

In "Manewic" Wudu-Brun, a free man in the soke and commendation of the abbot, [held] 27 acres. Then as now 1 plough and 3 bordars. Half an acre of meadow. Then it was worth 10s., now 6s.

In Winston 21 free men with 1 carucate of land. And 2 acres of this land were TRE in the demesne of Saxi, the predecessor of Ranulf Peverel in Debenham. One of these was commended to St Edmund with 12 acres and he was seised thereof until Ralph forfeited. Then as now 5 ploughs. 4½ acres of meadow. Then it was worth 40s., now 45s. Saxi had the commendation over 8 and the Abbot of Ely had the soke and commendation over the others, apart from two, namely Alwine and Leofwine, who were commended to someone commended to Eadric, Malet's predecessor.

In Ashfield Snaring the priest, a free man in the soke and commendation of the abbot, [held] 30 acres. Then as now 2 bordars and 1 plough, worth 10s. Walter de Dol was seised of this priest when he forfeited his land and afterwards Earl Hugh [was seised], as the Hundred testifies. And Northmann says that the king sent him a writ that he should give to Ralph de Savenay seisin of all the free men over whom Hubert de Port had given seisin to the bishop. And so Northmann gave seisin of that priest to Ralph but still he does not know whether Hubert had given seisin of him to the bishop. And the king's barons when they came into the county found him in peace between Roger Bigod and Earl Hugh. And thus it will be in peace until this case be decided.

HUNDRED AND A HALF OF SAMFORD.

In Burstall 3 free men, Goding, Wulfmær, Ælfgeat, [held] 37 acres. One was commended to Gyrth and the second to Ælfric and the third to Skalpi. Then 1 plough, now a half. 4 acres of meadow. It is worth 8s. The soke is in [East] Bergholt. In the same place Godwine, a free man of Stigand, [held] 30 acres as a manor. Then and afterwards 1 plough and 1 mill, now a half. It is worth 7s. The sake is in [East] Bergholt, except over his house and over 3 acres. In the same place 3 free men, Wulfgeat, Brungar, Blæcsunu, with 18 acres. Then as now half a plough. It is worth 4s. Roger Bigod holds this from the bishop and Ralph de Savenay from him.

[Folio 377V: SUFFOLK]

HUNDRED AND A HALF OF SAMFORD.

In [Great and Little] Wenham Algar, a free man, [held] 24 acres as a manor TRE, worth 4s. The soke is in [East] Bergholt. In the same place 4 free men, Beorhtweald, Asgot, Leodmær, Godric, having 50 acres and 6 bordars, worth 10s. The soke is in [East] Bergholt.

In Raydon Eadnoth, a free man, held 1 carucate of land and 100 acres as a manor. Then as now 3 villans and 6 bordars. 1½ ploughs in demesne. Then as now 1 plough belonging to the men. 4 acres of meadow. Woodland for 10 pigs. The fifth part of a church with 5 acres. Then it was worth £3, now £4 but it was at farm for £6. The soke is in [East] Bergholt. Roger Bigod holds this from the bishop.

HUNDRED OF CLAYDON.

In Ulverston 2 free men, Ælfric and Leofwine the latter was commended to someone commended to Eadric, Malet's predecessor and Ælfric was commended to Wihtgar [held] 30 acres and 2 bordars. Then 2 ploughs, afterwards none, now a half. 2 acres of meadow. Then it was worth 10s., now 8s. Roger holds it from the bishop and Warenger from him. The soke is the abbot's. In the same place a half free man with 2 acres and they are in the same valuation.

In Pettaugh Siward, a free man, TRE [held] 5 acres, worth 2s. The soke is the abbot's. The same Warenger [holds this]. [...]

HUNDRED AND A HALF OF SAMFORD.

Tunmann, of King Edward's commended to Harold, held [Great and Little] Wenham TRE with 1 carucate of land as a manor. Then 7 villans, now 2. Then 3 bordars, now 17. Then 2 slaves, now 1. Then as now 2 ploughs in demesne. Then 5 ploughs belonging to the men, afterwards and now 2; 6 acres of meadow. Woodland for 8 pigs. A church with 6 acres. Then 1 horse, now 2. Then 4 head of cattle. Then 24 pigs, now 40. Then 60 sheep, now 70. Then it was worth 60s. and now the same. Roger Bigod [holds this] from the bishop. It is 6 furlongs long and 2½ furlongs broad. 4d. [in geld]. In the same place Wulfric, a free man, [held] 40 acres as a manor TRE.

The Bishop of Bayeux

[Folio 378: SUFFOLK]

Then 1 plough. Then it was worth 5s., now 6s. Harold [had] the soke. The same Roger [holds this] from the bishop.

Eadwig, a free man, held Raydon TRE with 1 carucate of land as a manor. Then as now 4 bordars. 1 plough. 5 acres of meadow. 1 mill. The fifth part of a church with 5 acres. Then it was worth 30s. and now the same. But it was at farm for 60s. It is 1 league long long and 8 furlongs broad. 30d. in geld. Others hold [land] there.

In the same place a free man, Alwine, held 60 acres as a manor. Then 1 bordar. Then as now 1 plough. 4 acres of meadow. The fifth part of a church with 5 acres. Now 4 head of cattle, 13 pigs and 36 sheep. Then it was worth 20s., now 15s. In the same place a free man, Smeri, commended to Ælfric Cempa the predecessor of Eudo the steward, [held] 30 acres as a manor TRE. Then as now 1 bordar. Then half a plough. 2 acres of meadow. It is worth 5s. In the same place 1 free man, Wulfwine, [held] 30 acres. Then as now 1 bordar and then half a plough. Now 2 oxen and 2 acres of meadow. And it is worth 5s. In the same place a free man, Ælfric, [held] 30 acres as a manor. Then as now half a plough. 2 acres of meadow. And then it was worth 5s., now 10s. The soke is in [East] Bergholt.

In Raydon 1 free man, Ælfric, [held] 5 acres. It is in the valuation of Raydon.

In Belstead Ælfric, a free man, held 30 acres as a manor and 2 bordars. Then 1 plough. It is worth 5s.

In Brantham 3 free men, Brun, Sigeric, Godstan, and in "Belenei" 1 free man, Burgric, and in Higham 1 free man, Eadric, having 60 acres. Then 2 ploughs, now 1. Then it was worth 10s., now 14s.

In Boynton Godwine, a free man, held TRE 60 acres as a manor. 3 villans. 1 plough in demesne and 1 plough belonging to the men. Woodland for 10 pigs. The fourth part of a church with 6 acres. It is worth 20s.

Alweald, a free man, held "Alfildestuna" TRE with 2 carucates of land as a manor. Then 1 bordar, now 5. Then 2 ploughs in demesne, now 1. And 1½ acres of meadow. Then as now 1 mill.

[Folio 378v: SUFFOLK]

It is worth 25s. It is 6 furlongs [...] long and 3 broad. 2½d. in geld.

In Tattingstone Thorgot, a free man, held 60 acres as a manor. Then 1 plough and 1½ acres of meadow. Then it was worth 10s., now 4s. Roger Bigod holds the whole from the bishop and the soke over the whole is in [East] Bergholt.

In Ipswich 1 house with half an acre. And in "Toft" Eadwig, a free man, with 2½ acres, worth 6d. Roger Bigod [holds this]. The soke is in [East] Bergholt.

HUNDRED OF HARTISMERE.

In Aspall Leofgifu, commended to the Abbot of Ely and in his soke, held 20 acres. It is worth 4s. Roger Bigod holds this and Ralph de Savenay holds it from Roger. In the same place 12 acres in the demesne of Debenham. 5 bordars. [It is] in the same valuation.

XVII. Lands of St Benedict of Ramsey.

TWO HUNDREDS OF BABERGH.

St Benedict held Lawshall TRE as a manor with 8 carucates of land together with the soke. Then 14 villans, now 16. Then 12 bordars, now 10. Then 4 slaves, now 5. Then 2 ploughs in demesne, now 3. Then as now 10 ploughs belonging to the men. 8 acres of meadow. Then as now 1 horse. Now 10 head of cattle and 30 pigs, 100 sheep and 12 goats. A church with 30 acres of free land. Then worth £8, now £12. It is 1 league long and a half broad. In geld 15d.

[Folio 379: SUFFOLK]

XVIII

Lands of William, Bishop of Thetford.

HUNDRED OF BISHOP. Bishop Æthelmær held Hoxne TRE as a manor with 9 carucates of land. Then 40 villans, now 20. Then 15 bordars, now 51. Then 4 slaves. Then as now 3 ploughs in demesne. Then 40 ploughs belonging to the men, now 22½. And 40 acres of meadow. Woodland for 250 pigs. Then as now 2 mills. 2 horses, 12 head of cattle, 80 pigs, 17 sheep and 40 goats. In this manor there was one market TRE and after King William came. And it took place on Saturdays. William Malet made his castle at Eye and on the same day when there was a market in the bishop's manor William Malet held another market in his castle. As a result of this the bishop's market has declined so much that it is worth little. Now it takes place on Fridays. But the Market at Eye takes place on Saturdays. Now Robert Malet holds it by the king's gift.

In this manor there is a church [which was] the episcopal see of Suffolk TRE. This manor was then worth £28, now £20 but it paid £30 to Herfast. It is 1 league long and 8 furlongs broad. 22½d. in geld. In Weybread 1 sokeman with 2 acres, worth 10d.

In Wilby 1 sokeman with 40 acres and 1 bordar and 1 plough and 2 acres of meadow. Woodland for 20 pigs. Then it was worth 10s., now 8s. [...]

HUNDRED OF WANGFORD.

Bishop Æthelmær held Homersfield TRE [as] 1 manor with 5 carucates of land. Now Bishop William holds it. Then as now 16 villans and then as now 12 bordars. Then as now 4 slaves. Then 2 ploughs in demesne, now 3. Then 10 ploughs belonging to all the men, now 5, and 5 could be restored there. 12 acres of meadow. Then woodland for 600 pigs, now 200. 1 mill. 1 church with 12 acres. 3 horses when he acquired it, and now. Then as now 6 head of cattle. Then as now 26 pigs. 200 sheep. Then it was worth £12 with the soke, now it renders £16. Over the ferling of [South] Elmham Bishop William has soke and sake apart from over the men belonging to Bishop Stigand. And Abbot B[aldwin] according to the testimony of the Hundred had a writ from King Edward [stating] that he ought to have had soke and sake over St Edmund's land and over his men.

In Barsham 16 acres, 2 bordars and half a plough, worth 2s.

[Folio 379v: SUFFOLK]

HUNDRED OF HARTISMERE.

In Yaxley and in Thrandeston BISHOP Æthelmaer held TRE 1 carucate of land as a manor. Then as now 5 bordars and 1 plough. 2 acres of meadow. It is worth 20s. It belongs to the church of Hoxne.

XVIIII.

The Fief of the Bishop of Thetford.

In Syleham 1 free man of Stigand [held] 2 carucates of land. 12 bordars. 2 ploughs in demesne. Then 4 ploughs belonging to the men, now 2; 5 acres of meadow. Woodland for 60 pigs. 1 mill. Then as now worth 60s. Æthelmær [and] Herfast held this.

Ulf, a thegn, held Mendham TRE with 1 carucate of land; afterwards Æthelmær and Herfast [held it]. Then as now 1 villan and 10 bordars. 1 plough in demesne. Then 3 ploughs, now 1½; 6 acres of meadow. Woodland for 60 pigs. 1 mill. 2 free men under commendation [held] 11 acres and half a

plough. The eighth part of a church with 40 acres and half a plough. More land belongs to it but it is listed in the returns of Norfolk. Then it was worth 30s., now 60s.

In Denham 5 free men commended to Æthelmær [held] 60 acres and 1 plough, worth 10s.

In Horham 7 free men by commendation [held] 42 acres. And then as now 1½ ploughs. Woodland for 16 pigs.

In Wilby 1 free man with 10 acres. In Chickering 1 free man with 16 acres and 2 bordars. Then as now half a plough. A church with 8 acres. The whole is worth 20s.

In Horham 2 free men by commendation and soke [held] 19 acres and half a plough, worth 3s. 10d.

In Wilby 1 free man by commendation and soke [held] 40 acres. Then as now 1 bordar. Then 1 plough. 2 acres of meadow. Woodland for 20 pigs. Then it was worth 10s., now 8s.

In Wingfield 1 free man by commendation and soke [held] 10 acres, worth 20d.

In Chickering 1 free man by commendation [held] 28 acres and 3 bordars. Then as now half a plough. It is worth 5s. In the same place a free man with 40 acres and half a plough. Woodland for 12 pigs. Half an acre of meadow. It is worth 6s. 8d. In the same place 1 free woman with 8 acres. Robert Malet's predecessor had commendation TRE. It is worth 16d. Æthelmær had the soke and sake.

In Bedingfield 2 free men by commendation [held] 30 acres and 1 plough. Then it was worth 6s., now 10s.

Bishop William

[Folio 380: SUFFOLK]

HUNDRED OF LOOSE.

In Framlingham 1 free man commended to Bishop Æthelmær [held] 20 acres of land and half a plough. It is worth 4s.

HUNDRED OF HARTISMERE.

In Oakley 1 free man, Algar, commended to St Edmund [held] TRE 14 acres and half a plough. Half an acre of meadow. It is worth 2s. Drogo holds it from the bishop.

HUNDRED OF WANGFORD.

1 free man commended to Æthelmær held Homersfield with 40 acres as a manor. Then as now 2 bordars. Then 2 ploughs, now 1; 2 acres of meadow. 1 church with 30 acres. Then it was worth 6s. 8d., now 9s. 4d. Also in the same vill 23 free men with 80 acres. Then 6 ploughs, now 5. Then it was worth 40s., now 30s. It is 1 league long and a half broad. In geld 20d.

In [South] Elmham 1 free man under the commendation and soke of Bishop Æthelmær [held] 40 acres as a manor and 4 bordars. Then as now 1 plough. 2 acres of meadow. Woodland for 8 pigs. 1 church with 6 acres. And under him 3 free men under the same commendation with 6 acres and half a plough. Then it was worth 10s., now it renders 12s.

In the same vill 1 free man, Alwine, under the commendation and soke of Æthelmær [held] 40 acres as a manor. 2 bordars. Then 1 plough, now a half. 2 acres of meadow. Then it was worth 6s., now 10s. 8d. Also in the same place 10 free men under the commendation and soke of the same person

[held] 60 acres. Then as now 1 plough. 2 acres of meadow. Then it was worth 10s., now it renders 14s. In the same place 10 free men under the same commendation [held] 34 acres. Then 3 ploughs, now 2. Then it was worth 10s., now it renders 20s. It is 1 league long and a half broad. In geld 20d. Others hold [land] there.

In Flixton 1 free man, Eskil, under the commendation and soke of Bishop Stigand, [held] 30 acres as a manor. 1 bordar. Then as now 1 plough. 2 acres of meadow. The fifth part of one mill. Then it was worth 8s., now it renders 10s. 8d. In the same place 8 free men under the commendation and soke and sake of Bishop Æthelmær [held] 107 acres. Then 2 ploughs, now 1½. Half a church with 12 acres. Then it was worth 10s., now it renders 31s. 4d.

William holds [South] Elmam from the bishop, which Alwine, a free man under commendation

to Ingvar, a thegn, held TRE with 2 carucates of land and 20 acres. Then villans, now 4. Then 11 bordars, now 20. Then 4 slaves. Then in demesne 3 ploughs, now a half . 1 horse, 7 head of cattle, 30 pigs, 13 sheep and 30 goats. Then 6 ploughs belonging to the men, now 3½. 11 acres of meadow. Woodland for 30 pigs. 1 church with 40 acres of free land and half a plough. Then it was worth [...]s., now £4. In the same place 1 free man, Bondi, commended to Bishop Æthelmær, [held] 60 acres as a manor. And 2 villans and 2 bordars and 1 plough in demesne. Then 1 plough belonging to the men, now a half. 2 acres of meadow. And under him 2 free men with 7 acres. Then 1 plough, now a half. Then it was worth 10s., now 13s. Also in the same place 1 free man under the commendation and soke and sake of Stigand [held] 30 acres as a manor. Then as now 2 villans and 1 plough. 1 plough belonging to the men. 2 acres of meadow. Woodland for 8 pigs. Then it was worth 8s., now 10s. 8d. In the same place 1 free man, Alwine, commended to Eadric of Laxfield [held] TRE 30 acres as a manor. Then 2 bordars, now 3. Then as now half a plough. 1 acre of meadow. Woodland for 8 pigs. And under him 2 free men with 4 acres and half a plough. Then it was worth 10s., now the same. William Malet was seised [thereof] on the day when he died. In the same place 25 free men commended to Bishop Æthelmær [held] 1½ carucates of land. Then 8 ploughs, now 6. And 6 acres of meadow. Woodland for 16 pigs. Then it was worth 30s., now 40s. 3 churches with 30 acres, worth 5s.

In Flixton 1 free man, Beorhtnoth, commended to Æthelmær [held] 30 acres as a manor. And 4 bordars. Then as now 1 plough and half a [plough] belonging to the men. 2 acres of meadow. Woodland for 4 pigs. Then it was worth 5s. 4d., now 20s. Also 3 free men under commendation and soke and sake to Æthelmær [held] 38 acres. Then as now 1½ ploughs. Woodland for 4 pigs. 3 acres of meadow. Then it was worth 6s., now 11s. 8d. William de Noyers holds all this from the bishop. Also in the same vill 1 free man under the commendation and soke of Stigand [held] 30 acres as a manor. Then 2 bordars, now 8. Then 1 plough, now 2; 2 acres of meadow. Woodland for 4 pigs. And under him 1 free man with 16 acres. Then half a plough, now 2 oxen. Then it

was worth 10s. and now the same. The same William [holds this].

In Barsham 10 free men of these Ælfric and Gyrth had commendation over 8 and a half

Bishop William

and Bishop Æthelmær over the others [held] 60 acres. Then 2 ploughs, now 1½. 2 acres of meadow. Then it was worth 8s., now 10s.

HUNDRED OF HARTISMERE.

In Yaxley and in Thrandeston 40 free men [held] 1 carucate of land and 19 acres. Then 3 ploughs, now 3½; 2 acres of meadow. Then as now worth 40s. The bishop has the soke and sake. Otheri holds this from the bishop.

In Brome 1 free man commended to someone commended to Bishop Æthelmær [held] 6 acres, worth 12d.

HALF HUNDRED.

In Flixton St Michael held in alms TRE 1 carucate of land. Then 13 bordars, now 8. Then as now in demesne 1 plough. Then 4 ploughs belonging to the men, now 1. Woodland for 8 pigs. 4 acres of meadow. Half a mill. Then as now worth 20s. The soke [belonged to] Stigand.

XX

Lands of the Bishop of Rochester.

HUNDRED OF LACKFORD.

Orthi, a thegn of Harold, held Freckenham TRE as a manor with 10 carucates of land. And afterwards Lanfranc by the king's command adjudged it to be in the bishopric of Rochester. Then as now 16 villans and 8 bordars and 6 slaves. Then as now 5 ploughs in demesne and 6 ploughs belonging to the men but 8 could be restored. And 20 acres of meadow. And 1 mill and 2 fisheries. A church with 20 acres. 3 horses, 13 head of cattle, 40 pigs, 230 sheep and 6 beehives. Then it was worth £12, now £14. It is 1 league long and a half broad. In geld 20d. Earl Ralph added to this manor 4 free men whom he annexed with 8 acres of land. Then as now half a plough. It is worth 8d. The same bishop had the soke of this manor and St Edmund had [the soke] over the free men.

XXI. Suffolk Lands of St Æthelthryth.

HUNDRED OF THEDWESTRY.

St Æthelthryth held Rattlesden TRE as a manor with 6 carucates of land. Then as now 18 villans. Then 20 bordars, now 27. Then 6 slaves, now 4. Then as now 3 ploughs in demesne. Then 12 ploughs belonging to the men, now 3. Woodland for 24 pigs. And 16 acres of meadow. Then as now 5 horses. Then [and] now 12 head of cattle and 80 and 10 sheep. 40 pigs. Now 11 goats. Then as now worth £10. 1

church with 24 acres. Humphrey, William de Warenne's man, holds 15 acres and Goscelin, a man belonging to the Count of Mortain, [holds] 2. It is 16 furlongs long and 10 broad. In geld 20d. The soke belongs to St Æthelthryth.

In the same place 1 free man under the commendation and soke of St Æthelthryth TRE [held] 3 acres, worth 6d. In Rattlesden 1 free man under the soke and sake of St Æthelthryth [held] 8 acres of land, worth 2s. Falc, a man belonging to St Edmund, had these 8 acres while the Abbey of St Æthelthryth was in the king's hand and he has held them up till now but he denies that he has withheld the service.

St Æthelthryth held Drinkstone TRE with 2 carucates of land and 1 church with 12 acres. Then 15 bordars, now 7. Then 6 slaves, now 4. Then as now 2 ploughs in demesne. Then 3 ploughs belonging to the men, now 1. Woodland for 100 pigs. And 6 acres of meadow. Then as now 2 horses at the hall. 10 head of cattle, 32 pigs, 30 sheep, 8 goats. Then it was worth 40s., now 60s. but it was at farm for 100s. and could not pay. It is 8 furlongs long and 7 broad. And in geld 11d.

HUNDRED OF THINGOE.

In Rede 20 acres in demesne. 4 bordars. 2 acres of meadow. Half a plough. The soke and sake belong to St Æthelthryth. It is worth 4s.

HUNDRED OF LACKFORD.

St Æthelthryth held Brandon TRE and now as a manor with 5 carucates of land. Then as now 8 villans and 4 bordars. 7 slaves. Then as now 3 ploughs in demesne. Then 4 ploughs belonging to the men, now 3 acres of meadow and 1 fishery.

St Æthelthryth

[Folio 382: SUFFOLK]

2 asses and 11 head of cattle and 200 sheep and 20 pigs. A church with 30 acres. Then it was worth £6, now £8. It is 1 league long and half a league broad. In geld 20d.

St Æthelthryth held Lakenheath TRE as a manor with 3 carucates of land. Then as now 6 villans and 5 bordars and 4 slaves. Then 3 ploughs in demesne, now 2. Then as now 2 ploughs belonging to the men and 5 acres of meadow. And half a mill and 2 fisheries. And 2 horses at the hall, 5 head of cattle, 100 sheep and 17 pigs. A church with 60 acres. Then it was worth £4, now £6. It is 1 league long and a half broad. And in geld 20d. St Æthelthryth held Undley with 1 carucate of land and 3 bordars and 4 slaves. Then as now 2 ploughs in demesne and 13 acres of meadow. 2 fisheries. 1 horse, 24 head of cattle and 62 sheep. Then as now worth 20s. A church without land. It is 2 furlongs long and 2 broad. The geld is in Lakenheath.

In [Santon] Downham a half free man under soke to St Æthelthryth [held] half a carucate of land. 3 bordars and 1 acre of meadow. Then as now half a plough. It is worth 5s.

In [Great] Livermere 3 free men by commendation only to St Æthelthryth TRE in the soke of St Edmund [held] 29 acres of land. Then as now half a plough. It is worth 5s.

TWO HUNDREDS OF BABERGH.

St Æthelthryth held Glemsford TRE and now as a manor with 8 carucates of land. Then as now 16 villans and 18 bordars. 5 slaves. Then as now 3 ploughs in demesne and 7 ploughs belonging to the men and 12 acres of meadow. Woodland for 5 pigs. 1 mill. Then as now 3 horses at the hall. 8 head of cattle and now 200 sheep and 32 pigs. A church with 30 acres of free land and 1 sokeman with 8 acres. Then it was worth £10, now £16. It is 1 league long and 8 furlongs broad. In geld 15d.

St Æthelthryth held Hartest TRE as a manor with 5 . Then as now 12 villans and 14 bordars and 4 slaves. Then as now 2 ploughs in demesne. Then 5 ploughs belonging to the men, now 6. And 10 acres of meadow. Woodland for 6 pigs. Then as now 4 horses at the hall. And 20 head of cattle,

[Folio 382v: SUFFOLK]

25 pigs and 60 sheep. A church with 80 acres of free land. Then it was worth £6, now £11. It is 1 league long and a half broad. In geld 10d.

In the same place 4 sokemen with 30 acres of land and half a plough, worth 5s. Also there is 1 sokeman with 1 carucate of land. Then as now 1 plough. It is worth 20s. Berner the crossbowman holds this from St Æthelthryth.

HUNDRED OF STOW.

In Chilton St Æthelthryth held 2 sokemen with 36 acres but they could not sell without the abbot's permission and 1 bordar. Then 1 plough, now none. Half an acre of meadow. It is worth 5s.

In Buxhall 1 sokeman with 10 acres of forfeited land and 1 bordar with 5 acres, worth 10d. In [Great and Little] Finborough Roger d'Auberville holds from St Æthelthryth 3 sokemen with 34 acres of land, worth 4s. In the same vill 7 acres of the demesne in Barking. The sake and soke are St Æthelthryth.

HALF HUNDRED OF IPSWICH.

St Æthelthryth held Stoke with 3 carucates of land as a manor TRE. Then as now 9 villans and then 5 bordars, now 15. Then 1 slave. Then as now 2 ploughs in demesne and 6 ploughs belonging to the men. 1 church with 40 acres of free land. 1 mill. 20 acres of meadow. 12 head of cattle and 20 pigs and 24 sheep and 14 goats. Also St Æthelthryth has half the soke which is beyond the bridge. Then it was worth £4, now 100s. It is 6 furlongs long and 6 broad. 4d. in a geld of 20s.

HUNDRED OF BOSMERE.

St Æthelthryth held Barking with the soke and sake TRE as a manor with 7 carucates of land. Then 27 villans, now 25. Then 24 bordars, now 30. Then 5 slaves, now 4. Then as now 3 ploughs in demesne. Then 24 ploughs belonging to the men, now 15. A church with 83 acres of free land and 2 ploughs. 52 acres of meadow. Woodland for 50 pigs. Then as now 1 mill and one dam of another mill. And in the dam of the other mill Robert Malet has a part. And 2 arpents of vineyard. In the demesne are 11 horses, 23 head of cattle, 30 pigs, 100 sheep and 48 goats. 4 free

St Æthelthryth

[Folio 383: SUFFOLK]

men with 6 acres and they have 1 plough. These men were added to this manor in the time of King William. It is worth 2s. The king and the earl have the soke. Hardwin had one and a half of these men when he forfeited. Now the abbot holds them. Then the manor was worth £16. The abbot gave it at farm for £20. It is 1 league and 4 furlongs long and 8 furlongs broad. 20d. in geld.

In Darmsden 25 free men held 1 carucate of land. St Æthelthryth had the commendation and soke over them TRE. Then 6 ploughs, now 2; 3 acres of meadow. It is worth 20s. Roger Bigod holds it from the abbot because the abbot established a claim against him before the Bishop of St. L but before that he held it from the king.

In Barking Roger holds 118 acres from the abbot of his demesne. 1 church with 6 acres. It is worth 10s.

In Horswold 1 free man under commendation and soke TRE with 22½ acres and half a plough. Half . It is worth 3s. [...] Roger d'Auberville held this from the . And the abbot proved his claim over him. Now he holds it from the abbot.

In Badley St Æthelthryth held 30 acres in demesne TRE. This is in the valuation of Barking.

In Hemingstone 1 sokeman of St Æthelthryth with 12 acres. William d'Écouis holds it from the abbot. It is in the valuation of [Little] Blakenham.

In Hemingstone 1 free man, Erik, commended to the abbot and in his soke, [held] 15 acres and 2 bordars. It is worth 2s. 6d.

In Olden [in Coddenham] 1 free man, Ælfric, by commendation only [held] 1½ acres, worth 3d. The king and the earl have the soke. This is in demesne.

In Coddenham 16 acres of demesne land. It is in the valuation of Barham.

In Ashbocking 1 free woman, Leohtgifu, commended to the abbot with 1 acre,

[Folio 383v: SUFFOLK]

worth 2d. The king and the earl have the soke.

In the same place 1 free man by commendation only [held] half an acre, worth 1d. The king and the earl have the soke.

HUNDRED OF CLAYDON.

St Æthelthryth held Barham TRE with 4 carucates of land as a manor. Then as now 24 villans. Now 9 bordars. Then 6 slaves, now 2. Then 3 ploughs in demesne, now 1. Then 8 ploughs belonging to the men, now 6. A church with 16 acres. Then as now 1 mill. 12 acres of meadow. Then woodland for 100 pigs, now 16. Now 9 pigs and 17 sheep. And 1 sokeman with 30 acres. Then as now 1 plough. Then worth £12, now 100s. It is 1 league long and 7½ furlongs broad. 20d. in geld.

In the same place 1 free man [held] 35 acres in the soke and commendation of the abbot. Then 1 plough, now a half. Then 1 bordar, now 2. And 3 acres of meadow. And 1 mill. Then worth 10s., now 20s. Roger d'Auberville held it from the king; now [he holds it] from the abbot.

In Sharpstone 3 free men in the soke and commendation of

the abbot [held] 8 acres and 2 oxen. Then worth 20d., now 2s. William d'Écouis [...] held this from the king; now [he holds it] from the abbot.

St Æthelthryth held Winston TRE with 1 carucate of land in demesne and 40 acres as a manor. Then as now 6 villans and 4 bordars. Then 2 ploughs now 1. Then as now 3 ploughs belonging to the men. 6 acres of meadow. Then woodland for 100 pigs, now 60. A church with 8 acres. 2 horses, 4 head of cattle, 20 pigs and 50 sheep. Then it was worth £4, now £4 10s. And 1 free man, Alsige, added to this manor, [held] 30 acres as a manor in the soke and commendation of the abbot. Then as now 2 bordars and 1 plough. It is worth 10s. It is 1 league long and 3 furlongs broad. 13½d. in geld.

In Westerfield Asrothr, 1 sokeman of the abbot, held 25 acres. Then as now 1 plough. 1 acre of meadow. It is worth 5s. Hervey holds it from the abbot by order of the king. In the same place Thorkil, a free man by commendation, [held] 8 acres, worth 16d. Hervey held this from the king. Now [he holds it] from the abbot by order of the king, as he says.

St Æthelthryth

[Folio 384: SUFFOLK]

The soke is the king's. In Pettaugh the same Thorkil, half commended to the abbot TRE and half to Gyrth, [held] 20 acres. 1 acre of meadow. 1 villan. Half a plough. It is worth 5s. Hervey also held this from the king. Now [he holds it] from the abbot by command of the king, as he says. Half of the soke belongs to the abbot and [half] to Hugh's predecessor.

In Debenham half a free man under soke and commendation [held] 4 acres, worth 8d. Robert Malet held this from the king; now [he holds it] from the abbot.

In Ashfield 1 free man under soke and commendation [held] 3 acres, worth 8d.

In Henley 1 free man under commendation and soke [held] half an acre, worth 1d.

In Thorpe Alsige, a free man, under soke and commendation [held] 10 acres, worth 20d.

In Sharpstone 1 free man under soke and commendation [held] 2 acres, worth 4d. Walter holds it.

HALF-HUNDRED OF PARHAM.

In Blaxhall 5 free men under soke and commendation of the abbot [held] 26 acres. Then as now half a plough. It is worth 4s.

In Wantisden 12 acres of demesne of Sudbourne, worth 24d. In the same place Morwine, a free man, held 2 acres, worth 4d. The same Morwine holds it from the abbot.

HUNDRED OF PLUMESGATE.

St Æthelthryth held Sudbourne TRE as a manor with 6 carucates of land. Then as now 14 villans. Then 15 bordars, now 21. Then 2 slaves, now 1. Then 3 ploughs in demesne, now 1. Then 12 ploughs belonging to the men, now 6 and 6 could be restored. 4 acres of meadow. Woodland for 12 pigs. Then 1 horse, . Then as now 7 head of cattle and 17 pigs. 120 sheep.

Then as now worth £7. . It is 1 league long and a half broad. 20d. in geld.

HUNDRED OF HARTISMERE.

St Æthelthryth held Wetheringsett TRE with 4 carucates of land as a manor. Now Ralph de Savenay holds a fourth part from Ranulf Peverel. Then as now 10 villans and 9 bordars. Then 4 slaves, . Then as now 2 ploughs in demesne. 3 ploughs belonging to the men. 4 acres of meadow. Then woodland for 500 pigs, now 400. A church with 16 acres. Half a plough. 2 horses, 8 head of cattle, 30 pigs, 107 sheep and 18 goats. Then it was worth £10 and now the same. In the same place 4 free men, Godwine, Beorhtmær, Oswulf, Deorwulf, under commendation [held] 40 acres. Then as now 2 ploughs. It is worth 10s. St Æthelthryth has the soke. It is 1½ leagues long and 1 league broad. 9d. in geld. Others hold [land] there.

HUNDRED OF RISBRIDGE.

2 free men held Chattisham TRE as 2 manors with 2 carucates of land. Then 2 bordars, now 5. Then as now 4 slaves. Then 2 ploughs in demesne, now 4. Half a plough belonging to the men. 8 acres of meadow. Woodland for 12 pigs. Frodo holds this from the abbot. When he acquired it, 4 horses, now none. Then 8 head of cattle, now 14. Then 20 sheep. All this land belonged in the demesne of the abbey TRE with all customary dues, apart from the six forfeitures of St Edmund. Then it was worth 40s., now 60s. It is half a league long and 3 furlongs broad. 1¼d. in geld. Others hold [land] there.

In Clopton 3 free men [held] 20 acres. St Æthelthryth had the soke and sake and commendation. It is worth 2s. St Edmund has the 6 forfeitures.

HALF-HUNDRED OF COSFORD.

St Æthelthryth held Hitcham TRE with 11 carucates of land. Then 30 villans, now 36. Then 18 bordars, now 26. Then as now 8 slaves. Then 4 ploughs in demesne, now 3. Then 20 ploughs belonging to the men, now 16. And 16 acres of meadow. Woodland for 20 pigs. Then as now 11 horses. 30 head of cattle, 175 sheep, 60 pigs and 42 goats.

St Æthelthryth

2 beehives. Then it was worth £20, now £40. It is 1 league and 4 furlongs long and 1 league broad. 15d. in geld. Others hold [land] there.

St Æthelthryth held Nedging TRE with 3 carucates of land. Then 8 villans, now 6. Then 6 bordars, now 9. Then 3 slaves, now 1. Then as now 3 ploughs in demesne. Then 2 ploughs belonging to the men, now 1; 8 acres of meadow. Woodland for 6 pigs. And 1 mill. 2 horses and 14 head of cattle. 100 sheep and 20 pigs. A church with 7 acres. And 2 sokemen with 14 acres. Then 1 plough, now 2 oxen. Then it was worth £4, now £8. It is 1 league long and 3 furlongs broad. 2½d. in geld.

In Hitcham 5 sokemen [held] 60 acres. Then 2½ ploughs, now 1. And 3 acres of meadow. It is worth 10s. Roger Bigod

holds it. In the same place [...] 120 acres of demesne land and 3 bordars. 1 plough. 1½ acres of meadow. It is worth 10s. In the same place 1 sokeman with 40 acres, worth 5s. Richard, son of Count Gilbert holds it.

HUNDRED OF BISHOP.

A free man over whom St Æthelthryth had commendation TRE held Wingfield with 2 carucates of land and 7 bordars. Then 2 ploughs in demesne, now 1. Then as now 2 ploughs belonging to the men. 11 acres of meadow. Woodland for 140 pigs. Then 2 horses, now 1. And 1 ox. Then 60 pigs, now 20. And 20 sheep and 2 hives. A church with 24 acres, worth 4s. 13 free men with 80 acres. Robert Malet's predecessor had commendation over one of them. Then 4 ploughs, now 3. Then it was worth £4 13s. 4d., now £4. Roger Bigod claims this of the king's gift but the Abbot of Ely has established his title against him. Now Roger holds it through a postponement. The soke is in Hoxne. 1 league and 2 furlongs long and 4 furlongs broad. 11½d. in geld. Others hold [land] there.

In [Monk] Soham 1 free man by commendation [held] 1 carucate of land. 2 villans and 3 bordars. Then as now 2 ploughs. 5 acres of meadow. Woodland for 10 pigs. Then it was worth 20s., now 25s.

The soke is in Hoxne. Robert Malet held this from the king. The abbot has established his title and Robert holds it from him.

HUNDRED OF BLYTHING.

St Æthelthryth held "Alneterne" as a manor TRE with 2 carucates of land. Then 9 villans, now 7. Then as now 13 bordars. Then as now 1 slave. Then as now 2 ploughs in demesne and 3 ploughs belonging to the men. Half a church with 2 acres. Woodland for 6 pigs. 2 acres of meadow. And 1 horse, 8 head of cattle, 28 sheep, 8 pigs and 16 goats. To this manor belong 80 burgesses in Dunwich and they dwell on 14 acres. Then as now worth 100s.

In the same place belong 3 free men who dwell in Bosmere with 14 acres. 1 plough. It is worth 3s. St Æthelthryth has the soke and sake.

HUNDRED OF COLNEIS.

In Morston 1 free man, Wulfgeat, with 5 acres commended to St Æthelthryth TRE. It is worth 16d. Robert Malet holds it from the saint.

In Trimley 1 free man, Leofric, commended to the abbot TRE, with 40 acres as a manor. Roger Bigod holds him from the king. The abbot has established his title and Roger holds it from him. 1 plough and 3 bordars. 1 acre of meadow. 1 free man under him with 4 acres. It is worth 20s.

In Walton 1 free woman, Ælfgifu, under commendation of the abbot [held] 16 acres. 2 bordars and half a plough. It is worth 3s. Hervey de Berry holds it from the abbot. He held it from the king but the abbot established title. And in "Plumgeard" 1 free man, Edwin, belonging to St Æthelthryth, with 2 acres, worth 4d. Now Hervey holds this from the abbot.

In Kembroke 1 free man, Godric, belonging to St

Æthelthryth [held] 7 acres and 2 oxen, worth 20d. Roger Bigod held this from the king but the abbot has established title and Roger Bigod holds him from him. St Æthelthryth has the soke of 5½ Hundreds and it renders to her £11.

St Æthelthryth

HUNDRED OF CARLFORD.

St Æthelthryth held Kingston TRE with 2 carucates of land as a manor. Then 8 villans, now 5. Now 8 bordars. Then 2 slaves, now 1. Then as now in demesne 2 ploughs and 3 ploughs belonging to the men. 8½ acres of meadow. Woodland for 5 pigs. Then as now 1 horse, 4 head of cattle, 30 sheep and 12 pigs. Then as now worth 40s. It is 4 furlongs long and 3 broad. 3d. in geld. Others hold [land] there.

St Æthelthryth held Brightwell TRE as a manor with 2 carucates of land. Then 6 villans, now 5. Then as now 3 bordars. Then 5 slaves, now 2. Then as now in demesne 2 ploughs. Then 4 ploughs belonging to the men, now 3. And 1 church without land. 6 acres of meadow. And 2 mills. Then as now 1 horse, 40 sheep and 8 pigs. 1 sokeman with 12 acres; and he dwells and he dwells in Newbourn. Then as now worth 40s. It is 10 furlongs long and 6 broad. In geld 4¼d. Others hold [land] there.

In Grundisburgh Algar, a free man of St Æthelthryth, held TRE 1 carucate of land and 30 acres as a manor. Then as now 2 villans and 5 bordars. Then as now in demesne 2 ploughs and 1 plough belonging to the men. 4 acres of meadow. Then as now 3 horses, 6 head of cattle, 16 pigs and 70 sheep. 3 beehives. Then it was worth 20s., now 40s. Hervey de Berry holds this from St Æthelthryth. It is 10 furlongs long and 6 broad. In geld 15d.

In Grundisburgh 3 half free men commended to Algar TRE [held] 7 acres, worth 12d.

In Haeton 22 acres, worth 4s.

In Thistleton 1 free man, Wulfmær, commended to St Æthelthryth, held 60 acres as a manor and 5 free men under him. Of these 2 were commended to the predecessor of Geoffrey de Mandeville.

Then 1½ ploughs, now 1; 3 acres of meadow. Then it was worth 10s., now 12s. When he acquired it and now 1 horse. Then and now 5 head of cattle. 15 pigs, 50 sheep and 12 goats. 5 beehives.

In Little Bealings 2 free men commended to St Æthelthryth with 20 acres and half a plough, worth 3s.

In Foxhall 15 acres, worth 2s. In Bucklesham 5 acres, worth 8d.

In Rushmere [St Andrew] Thorkil, a free man, commended half to St Æthelthryth and half to Gyrth, TRE held 80 acres of land as a manor. Then 1 plough, now a half. 5 acres of meadow. Then it was worth 20s., now 10s. In the same place 1 free man, Eadric, under the same commendation as the other, with 20 acres. Then 1 plough, now a half. And half an acre of meadow. Then it was worth 10s., now 6s. Also in the same place 5 free men commended to Thorkil [held] 15

acres. Then half a plough, now none. Then it was worth 30d., now 3s.

In Tuddenham 1 free man, Ælfric, commended to someone commended to St Æthelthryth, [held] 4 acres, worth 8d. Hervey de Berry holds all this from St Æthelthryth.

In "Kalletuna" Isaac held 8 free men commended to St Æthelthryth with 1 carucate of land and 2 bordars. Then 3 ploughs, now 1; 4 acres of meadow. It is worth 16s. It is 6 furlongs long and 2 broad. In geld 2½d. , Isaac, holds it from the abbot.

In "Ingoluestuna" 1 free man with 16 acres and half an acre of meadow and half a plough, worth 3s. Robert Malet holds this from the abbot.

In Isleton 1 free woman commended to St Æthelthryth [held] 30 acres. Then 1 plough, now a half. 2 bordars. 4 acres of meadow. And 1 free man with 10 acres, worth 4s.

In Burgh 6 acres, worth 12d. In Bixley 4 acres, worth 8d. In Rushmere [St Andrew] 1 free man, Leofric, commended to St Æthelthryth [held] 40 acres and 7 bordars.

St Æthelthryth

1½ ploughs. 1 acre of meadow. It is worth 10s.

In "Finesford" 1 free woman, Leofgifu, commended to St Æthelthryth [held] 40 acres and 1 plough and 4 bordars, worth 6s.

HUNDRED OF WILFORD.

In Sutton Robert Malet holds a half free man, Godwine, commended to St Æthelthryth with 12 acres as a manor and half a bordar. Then half a plough, and now. 1 acre of meadow. Then it was worth 2s., now 5s. In the same place 9 free men under him and 1 free man commended to St Æthelthryth with 40 acres. Then 1 plough, now the same. Half an acre of meadow. Then it was worth 4s., now 7s.

In Capel [St Andrew] 3 free men and a half [free man] commended to St Æthelthryth [held] 15 acres of land. Then 1 plough, now a half. Then it was worth 2s., now 4s. In Shottisham 1 free man and a half under the same commendation with 7 acres, worth 12d.

In Bromeswell 1 free man and a half commended to St Æthelthryth with 8 acres. Half a plough. It is worth 16d. Robert Malet holds this from St Æthelthryth.

In Bredfield 3 whole free men and 3 half [free men] and the fourth part of one free man with 24 acres. Then 2 ploughs, now a half. It is worth 6s. 2d. Robert Malet [holds it] from St Æthelthryth. And 1 free man, Farman, in the soke and commendation of the abbot [held] 12 acres, worth 2s.

In Bawdsey 2 free men commended to St Æthelthryth [held] 7 acres, worth 12d. In Alderton 12 acres, worth 2s. In Charsfield 2 free men commended to St Æthelthryth [held] 33 acres and 1 plough. 1 acre of meadow. It is worth 5s. In Capel [St Andrew] 1 free man and in Bredfield another with 32 acres of land. And the Abbot of Ely [had] commendation. Then 1 plough, now half a plough. Then as now worth 5s. Robert Malet holds this from the Abbot of Ely.

Melton belongs to the Abbot of Ely; 2 carucates of land as a manor. Then 18 villans, now 9. Then 6 bordars, now 13. Then 2 slaves, now none. Then as now 2 ploughs in demesne. Then 5 ploughs belonging to the men, now 3½. 17 acres of meadow. 1 horse and 1 mill.

[Folio 387V: SUFFOLK]

11 pigs. 37 sheep. To this manor belongs the berewick of Bawdsey and it is so reckoned. 4 sokemen with 32 acres of land. They could not give or sell the land. Then 2 ploughs, now 1½; 2 acres of meadow. Then as now worth 40s. It is 1 league long and 9½ furlongs broad. 27d. in geld.

In the same Bawdsey 5 free men with 19 acres. The Abbot of Ely [had] the commendation. Then as now worth 40d.

In Hoo [in Sutton] 1 free man with 19 acres of land. Then as now half a plough. 1 acre of meadow. Then as now worth 5.

In "Hundestuf" 1 free man with 6 acres of land. The Abbot of Ely [had] the commendation. It is worth 12d.

In Bromeswell 2 free men with 10 acres of land and the Abbot of Ely [had] the commendation. It is worth 12d.

In the same vill 1 church with 16 acres of land, worth 2s. This is the abbot's demesne. And in the same vill Hervey holds 70 free men over whom the abbot had the , soke and sake and every customary due. Of these Roger Bigod's predecessor had the commendation over 1 with 6 acres and now [there are] 45 with 2 carucates of land and 16 acres. Then 12 ploughs, now 6. And 3 acres of meadow. Then it was worth 40s. and now 60s. In the same place 4 free men commended to the abbot with 60 and 16 acres of land. Then 4 ploughs, now 3. And 4 acres of meadow. 2 horses, 6 pigs, 57 sheep. Then it was worth 20s. and now the same.

In Bredfield 3 free men commended to the abbot with 76 acres of land. Then 3 ploughs, now 2. And under them 3 free men with 5 acres. Half an acre of meadow. Then it was worth 15s., now 20s.

In Bredfield 6 acres which Robert Malet's predecessor [held]. Now Hervey de Berry holds it from the Abbot. Hervey holds all this from the abbot. Also in the same place 1 church with 31 acres of free land. 2 acres of meadow. It is worth 5s.

In Bromeswell Hervey [holds] 2 free men commended to St Æthelthryth with 22 acres. Then 2 ploughs, now a half. 1½ acres of meadow. Then it was worth 4s., now 5s.

St Æthelthryth

[Folio 388: SUFFOLK]

In Bredfield Hervey 2 free [men] commended to St Æthelthryth with 4 acres, worth 12d.

In Bromeswell Robert Malet holds 3 free men commended to St Æthelthryth with 4 acres, worth 2s. In Shottisham 1 acre, worth 2d.

In Ufford Almær, a free man, commended half to Eadric and half to St Æthelthryth, held 60 acres as a manor TRE. Then 4 bordars, now 2. Then 1½ ploughs, now a half. 4 acres of meadow. 1 mill. Then as now worth 10s.

In the same place 9 free men under the same commendation, apart from 2 who were commended to St Æthelthryth,

[held] 25 acres. 2 acres of meadow. Then as now 1 plough. Then as now worth 4s.

In Loudham half a free man, Morwine, commended to St Æthelthryth with 20 acres and half a bordar. Half a plough. And 7 free men under him with 20 acres. 2½ acres of meadow. Then 1 plough, now a half. Then as now worth 10s.

In Harpole 2 half free men with 13½ acres, worth 20d.

In Melton 1 free man of St Æthelthryth with 2 acres, worth 4d.

In Harpole a half free man of St Æthelthryth with 15 acres. Then half a plough, now none. It is worth 3s.

HUNDRED OF LOOSE.

St Æthelthryth held Hoo [near Kettleburgh] TRE as a manor with 3 carucates of land. Then 18 villans, now 10. Then 1 bordar, now 16. Then 6 slaves, now 2. Then in demesne 3 ploughs, now 2. Then 6 ploughs belonging to the men, now 5. Woodland for 20 pigs. 7 acres of meadow. 1 mill. 7 head of cattle, 24 pigs, 30 sheep and 40 goats. Then it was worth 100s., now £4. And W[illiam] de Bouville took one of these carucates. Afterwards it was adjudged through the king's command and seisin given to the church. But he vouches his lord Geoffrey de [...] Mandeville as guarantor and he has given a pledge thereof. Now the land is in the king's hand. To this manor belong 4 free men commended to St Æthelthryth with 6 acres of land, worth 12d. 1 church with 8½ acres, worth 16d.

[Folio 388V: SUFFOLK]

It is 8 furlongs long and 4 broad. In geld 3½d.

In Brandeston Hervey de Bourges holds 1 free man of St Æthelthryth with 8 acres, worth 4s. In Letheringham 3½ acres of demesne, worth 6d.

In Cretingham 1 villan with 16 acres and half a plough, worth 3s.

In Dallinghoo 4 free men commended to St Æthelthryth with half a carucate of land. Then 2 ploughs; now 1 acre of meadow. Then it was worth 8s., now the same.

In Woodbridge 7 free men TRE, now 2, commended to St Æthelthryth, with 40 acres. Then 1 plough. Then it was worth 6s., now 5s. In the same vill Robert Malet [holds] a free man with 16½ acres and half a plough. It is worth 5s.

In Dallinghoo half a free man with 16 acres, worth 2s. 8d. In Rendlesham half a free man with 6 acres, worth 12d. In Woodbridge 2 bordars with 10 acres, worth 2s.

In Monewden 1 free man and in Charsfield another with 18 acres, worth 3s.

HUNDRED OF PLUMESGATE.

In Aldeburgh 5 acres and it is in demesne. It is worth 10d. Norman [holds it].

XXII. The land of Gilbert, Bishop of Evreux.

HUNDRED OF WILFORD.

Thormod held "Udeham" as one manor with 2 carucates of land. Then 2 villans, now 7. Then as now 2 ploughs in demesne and 1 plough belonging to the men. 10 acres of meadow. 1 mill. 1 horse, 7 head of cattle, 56 pigs. Then it was worth 40s., now £12.

Beorhtmær, a sokeman of St Æthelthryth, held Campsey [Ash] with 50 acres as a manor and he could not sell nor give his land. Then as now 1 villan and 3 bordars. Then 1 plough. 2 acres of meadow. Then 1 mill. It renders 35s. in the above valuation. In Loudham 30 +4 [...] free men commended to Thormod. Of these 15 were commended to Eadric and one was commended to St Æthelthryth with 20 acres. Altogether they have 1½ carucates of land. Then 6 ploughs, now 3; 6 acres of meadow. It is worth £8. 1 church with 60 acres, worth 5s. Several [others] have a share there.

Folio 389: SUFFOLK]

XXIII.

The land of the Abbot of Bernay.

HUNDRED OF STOW.

In Creeting [St Peter] 1 free man with 20 acres. Half a church with 10 acres and 1 villan and 2 bordars. Then as now 1 plough between them all. 2 acres of meadow. It has been assessed in Creeting in another Hundred. In the same place 1 free man with 5 acres. It has been assessed. The king gave it from the fief of Hardwin.

HUNDRED OF BOSMERE.

Ælfric, a free man, held Creeting with 1½ carucates of land as a manor. Then as now 4 villans and 12 bordars and 2 slaves. Then 2 ploughs in demesne, now 1. Then 2 ploughs belonging to the men, now 1; 4 acres of meadow. And 6 head of cattle and 15 pigs. Then 100 sheep, now 36. Then it was worth 100s., now £6. Ælfric held [Old] Newton with 1 carucate of land as a manor TRE. Then as now 3 villans and 12 bordars and 1 slave. And 1 plough in demesne. Then 2 ploughs belonging to the men, now 1; 5 acres of meadow. Woodland for 6 pigs. And 2 mills. It is worth 60s.

In Creeting 24 free men with 1 carucate of land and 1 virgate. Then 3 ploughs, now 1½. It is worth 20s. A church with 12 acres. [Old] Newton is 6 furlongs long and 3 broad. 5d. in geld. The king and the earl have the soke over the whole. In Olden [in Coddenham] Alwine [held] 2 free men with 11 acres. Then half a plough, now none. [It is] in the same valuation.

XXIIII. Lands of the Abbey of Chatteris.

HALF-HUNDRED OF COSFORD.

St Mary held Kersey TRE with 3½ carucates of land. Then as now 6 villans and 18 bordars and 1 slave. 2 ploughs in demesne and 4 ploughs belonging to the men. 4 acres of meadow. Woodland for 60 pigs. And 1 mill. 1 horse, 10 head of cattle, 36 pigs, 140 sheep and 3 beehives. A church with 3 acres. 1 sokeman with 2 acres and 1 free man with 20 acres and 1 plough and 1 acre of meadow. Then this manor

was worth £4, now 100s. The free man [is worth] 4s. less 4d. It is 8 furlongs long and 6 broad. 7½d. in geld.

[Folio 389v: SUFFOLK]

XXV.

Lands of Richard, son of Count Gilbert.

HUNDRED OF RISBRIDGE.

Ælfric held Clare as a manor with 24 carucates of land TRE. Then 40 villans, afterwards 35, now 30. Then and afterwards 10 bordars, now 30. Then as now 20 slaves. Then 12 ploughs in demesne, afterwards 6, now 7. Then 36 ploughs belonging to the men, afterwards 30, now 24; 37 acres of meadow. Woodland for 12 pigs. Then as now 1 mill. Now 5 arpents of vineyard. Then as now 6 horses. Then 10 head of cattle, now 14. Then 12 pigs, now 60. Then 60 sheep, now 480; 12 beehives. Then as now 1 market. Now 43 burgesses. Ælfric, son of Wihtgar, gave this manor to St John TRE with the assent of his son and put in Leodmær the priest and others with him. When a charter had also been made he committed the church and the whole place to Abbot Leofstan to keep and into the protection of his son Wihtgar. The clerics could not give this land nor alienate it from St John. But after King William arrived he took possession of it in his own hand. To this manor then and now belonged 5 sokemen with every customary due and 1½ carucates of land. Then as now 1½ ploughs. 6 acres of meadow. Then it was worth £40 and now the same. And it is 2 leagues long and 1 broad. 15d. in geld.

Wihtgar [held] HUNDON TRE as a manor with 25 carucates of land and 20 acres. Then and afterwards 54 villans, now 41. Then as now 30 bordars and 14 slaves. Then 9 ploughs in demesne, afterwards 4, now 7. Then 31 ploughs belonging to the men, afterwards and now 23; 45 acres of meadow. Woodland for 160 pigs. Then as now 1 mill. A church with half a carucate of free land and another church with 4½ acres. Then as now 1 plough and 3 acres of meadow. Then 2 horses, now 6. Then 14 head of cattle, now 31. Then 130 pigs, now 160. Then 80 sheep, now 480. Now 17 beehives. Then it was worth £30, afterwards and now £40 4s. It is 2 leagues and 2 furlongs long and

Richard fitzGilbert

[Folio 390: SUFFOLK]

1 league broad. 15d. in geld. Others hold [land] there.

Wihtgar held Desning as a manor TRE with 20 carucates of land. Then as now 28 villans and 91 bordars and 20 slaves. 10 ploughs in demesne and 32 ploughs belonging to the men. 15 acres of meadow. Woodland for 80 pigs. Then 5 mills, now 4. Two churches with 1½ carucates of land and 1½ ploughs. Then 8 horses, now 5. Then 18 head of cattle, now 40. Then 100 pigs, now 80. Then 840 sheep, now 960; 9 beehives. Then it was worth £30, afterwards and now £40. But he gave it to a certain reeve at farm for £65, but the manor could not bear it.

And it is 2½ leagues long and 1 league broad. 37d. in geld in two Hundreds. .

In Denston 1 sokeman with 3 2 carucates of land and 10 acres as a manor; 3 bordars and 2 slaves. Then 3 ploughs, now 2; 2 acres of meadow. Woodland for 10 pigs. Now 2 horses, 13 head of cattle, 28 pigs, 32 sheep and 4 goats. Then and afterwards worth 40s., now 50s.

In Clopton 2 sokemen with 1 carucate of land and 81½ acres. 9 bordars and 2 slaves. [...] Then 2 ploughs in demesne, now 3½ ploughs belonging to the men. 3 acres of meadow. Woodland for 4 pigs. Then as now 2 horses. Then 6 head of cattle, now 12. Now 30 pigs. Then 40 sheep, now 80; 3 beehives. Then it was worth 20s., now 40s. Denston is 1 league long and 3 furlongs broad. 2½d. in geld. And Clopton is 1 league long and 3 furlongs broad. 6½d. in geld.

In Dalham 1 sokeman with 2 carucates of land. 1 villan and 5 bordars and 2 slaves. 2 ploughs in demesne. Then 2 ploughs belonging to the men, now 1½; 2 acres of meadow. Woodland for 60 pigs. Then as now 2 horses. 10 head of cattle, now 16. Then 24 pigs, now 30. Then 100 sheep, now 150. And 50 goats. Then it was worth 40s., now 60s. 1 church

[Folio 390v: SUFFOLK]

with 40 acres of free land. Half a plough. It is worth 5s. William Pecche holds this.

In Denham 2 sokemen with 3 carucates of land. Then as now 5 villans and 13 bordars and 1 slave. Then 4 ploughs in demesne, now 3. Then as now 4 ploughs belonging to the men. 6 acres of meadow. Woodland for 20 pigs. A church without land. W[illiam] Hurant holds this. Then 1 horse, now 2. Now 4 head of cattle. Then 15 pigs, now 33; 72 sheep and 38 goats. Then it was worth £3, now £4 10s.

In Hawkedon 1 sokeman with 1 carucate of land. Then as now 2 villans and 1 slave. Then as now 1 plough in demesne and half a plough belonging to the men. It is worth 20s. Gilbert holds this.

In Hawkedon 1 sokeman with 1 carucate of land. Now 3 bordars and 1 slave. Then as now 1 plough in demesne. 4 acres of meadow. Then as now worth 20s. Fulcred holds this.

In [Great and Little] Wratting 1 sokeman with 1 carucate of land. Then as now 1 villan and 3 bordars . 1 plough in demesne. Then half a plough belonging to the men, now 2 oxen. 4 acres of meadow. A church with 32 acres of free land. Then as now worth 20s. Wulfmær holds it then as now.

In Stansfield 1 sokeman with 1 carucate of land and 2 bordars. Then as now 1 plough and 3 acres of meadow. Roger holds it. When he acquired it there were 3 horses and now the same. Then 4 head of cattle, now 6. Then 7 pigs, now 30. Then 40 sheep, now 80. Then it was worth 20s., now 30s.

In Hundon 1 sokeman with 1 carucate of land. Then as now 2 bordars. 1 plough. Hamo holds it. Then 30 sheep, now 50. And it is worth 20s. In the same place 10 sokemen with 1 carucate of land. Then as now 1 plough. 2 acres of meadow. And it is worth 20s. In Farley 1 sokeman with 7 acres, worth 14d. In Brockley 1 sokeman with half a carucate of land. Then as now 1 plough. 2 acres of meadow. Then it was worth 8s., now 16s.

In Kedington 1 sokeman with 30 acres and half a plough, worth 5s. In Boyton 1 sokeman with 60 acres. 3 bordars. Then

as now 1 plough. 2 acres of meadow. It is worth 10s. In Stoke [by Clare] 1 sokeman

Richard fitzGilbert

[Folio 391: SUFFOLK]

with 37 acres. Then half a plough, now 2 oxen. And 3 acres of meadow. It is worth 6s. 2d. Wihtgar held these sokemen TRE with every customary due, apart from the 6 forfeitures of St Edmund.

HUNDRED OF RISBRIDGE.

In "Wimundestuna" 3 sokemen with 65 acres and half a plough, worth 10s. His predecessor had every customary due from them.

HALF-HUNDRED OF COSFORD.

In Wattisham Wulfric, a free man, held TRE 80 acres. This is part of Fin's fief. Then as now 3 bordars and 1 slave. 1 plough in demesne. 1½ acres of meadow. Then 3 horses, now 5. Then 8 head of cattle, now 11. Then 5 pigs, now 25. Now 80 sheep. It is worth 25s. St Edmund has the soke. In the same place 1 free man with 15 acres, worth 2s. 6d. Wihtgar had the soke. St Edmund has the 6 forfeitures.

In Hitcham 2 free men with 1 carucate of land. 4 bordars and 2 slaves. Then 2 ploughs, now 1; 4 acres of meadow. And it is worth 20s. Æthelweard son of Bell holds this.

HUNDRED OF BLACKBOURN.

In Bardwell 1 free man by commendation [held] 30 acres. 1 bordar. Then half a . It is worth 5s. In Stow[langtoft] 1 sokeman with 28 acres. Then half a plough. It is worth 3s. Robert Blund holds this. St Edmund has the soke.

HUNDRED OF WILFORD.

In Bredfield 12 acres of land and 1 villan, worth 2s. Norman holds this from Richard.

HUNDRED OF HARTISMERE.

In Cotton Fathir held 7 acres, worth 14d. Walter the deacon holds it.

HUNDRED OF THEDWESTRY.

In Timworth 1 free man under the commendation only of Wihtgar, Richard's predecessor TRE, [held] 60 acres. Then 1 plough. It is worth 10s. The soke is St Edmund's. In Rattlesden 2 sokemen with 7 acres, worth 12d.

HUNDRED OF THINGOE.

In Westley 3 free men commended to Wihtgar [held] 80 acres with the soke, apart from the 6 forfeitures of St Edmund. And 1 bordar. Then as now 2 ploughs.

[Folio 391v: SUFFOLK]

2 acres of meadow. A church with 8 acres. Woodland for 9 pigs. And 2 parts of a mill. It is worth 10s. In the same vill 1 free man under the commendation of St Edmund with the soke [held] half a carucate of land. 3 acres of meadow. Then as now

1 plough. Then as now worth 10s. In [Great and Little] Saxham 1 sokeman of Wihtgar's with 15 acres. Then as now half a plough. It is worth 3s. In Horringer 1 sokeman belonging to the same man with 20 acres and 2 bordars. Then as now 1 plough. It is worth 4s. In Hawstead 2 free men belonging to Wihtgar and in his sake but they could sell without permission [held] 15 acres. Then as now half a plough. It is worth 3s. In Manston 1 free man [held] half a carucate of land under Wihtgar and in his soke TRE. Then 3 bordars, now 1. Then and afterwards 1 plough, now a half. 2 acres of meadow. Then as now worth 10s. In Rede 7 free men belonging to Wihtgar and in his soke and sake but they could sell [held] 1 carucate of land and 6 bordars. Then and afterwards 3 ploughs, now 1½; 4 acres of meadow. Woodland for 3 pigs. Then and afterwards worth 30s., now 40s. A church with 12 acres of free land.

HUNDRED OF LACKFORD.

In Barton [Mills] Godgifu, 1 free woman under commendation only of Wihtgar and in the soke of St Edmund, held TRE 60 acres of land and 4 bordars and 1 slave. Then as now half a plough in demesne and 1 acre of meadow. It is worth 5s. In the same place 1 sokeman of Wihtgar's with 60 acres and 4 bordars. Then as now half a plough. 1 acre of meadow. It is worth 5s. Wihtgar has the soke. Leofgeat, a free man under Wihtgar under commendation only and in the soke of St Edmund, held Elveden TRE as a manor with 2 carucates of land. Then 4 villans, now 2. Then as now 3 bordars and 1 slave. Then 2 ploughs in demesne, afterwards and now 1. And half a plough belonging to the men. The fourth part of a fishery. Then as now 1 horse. 12 pigs and 150 sheep. Then it was worth 30s., afterwards and now the same. A church with 15 acres of free land. Wihtgar, Richard's predecessor, held Cavenham as a berewick in Desning as 5 carucates of land, with the soke. Then as now 25 villans and 5 ploughs. A church with 60 acres of free land. Then 5 mills, now 4;

Richard fitzGilbert

3 acres of meadow. It is 1 league long and 4 furlongs broad. In geld 20d.

In Lakenheath 1 carucate of land and 8 villans. Then 1 plough in demesne, now 1½; 4 fisheries in Ely [Cambs] and 1 boat for fishing. And 1 acre of meadow. These 2 lands are in the valuation of Desning. The same predecessor of Count Richard held Tuddenham with 1½ carucates of land and 9 villans. Then as now 2 ploughs and 1½ acres of meadow. It renders 50s. In Barton [Mills] 30 acres of land in the demesne of Wihtgar. 2 oxen. It is worth 3s. In Mildenhall 2 sokemen with 60 acres and 1 bordar. Then as now 2 ploughs. It is worth 5s. They belong in Desning. They could not sell. In Herringswell 3 sokemen of Wihtgar's with 60 acres. Then as now half a plough. It has been assessed in Desning. In the same place 1 sokeman, with half the land the soke belonging to Wihtgar, as the Hundred testifies, and half with the soke belonging to St Edmund. And he has 1 carucate of land and 5

bordars. Then as now 1 plough between them all. It is worth 15s.

In Wangford 4 sokemen under the same man and in his soke with 1 carucate of land and 1 bordar. Then as now 2 ploughs between them all. 3 acres of meadow. It is worth 10s. It belongs in Desning.

TWO HUNDREDS OF BABERGH.

In Bures Wihtgar held TRE 18 free men by commendation and soke and sake and they could sell the land TRE without his permission. And 4 sokemen who could not sell. The 18 [free men] had 1½ carucates of land. 3 sokemen with 1½ carucates of land. These three had under them 1 villan and 7 bordars. 3 ploughs. 4 acres of meadow. It is worth 30s. And these 18 free [men] had under them 10 bordars. Then as now 2 ploughs and 4 acres of meadow. Woodland for 6 pigs. And 1 mill. It is worth 30s. Bures is 1 league long and a half broad. In geld 24d. But others hold [land] there. A church with 18 acres of free land. In [Great and Little] Cornard 7 free men under the commendation and soke and sake of Wihtgar TRE [held] 2 carucates of land and 1 bordar. Then 3 ploughs, afterwards and now 2.

5 acres of meadow. It is worth 26s. 8d. In "Coresfella" 7 free [men] under the commendation and soke and sake of the same man [held] 3½ carucates of land [and] 25 acres and 10 bordars. Then as now 3 ploughs between them all. 13 acres of meadow. It is worth £3. In Eleigh [Brent and Monks] 7 free men under the commendation and soke and sake of the same man [held] 60 acres of land. Then as now 1 plough between them all. 1 mill. It is worth 10s. In [Great and Little] Waldingfield 3 free men under commendation and soke and sake of the same man [held] 1 carucate of land and 45 acres and 9 bordars. Then 3 ploughs, afterwards 2, now 1; 3 acres of meadow. 1 horse, 2 head of cattle and 93 sheep. Woodland for 3 pigs. It is worth 50s. Now Elinant holds it. The third part of a church with 10 acres of free land.

In Cavendish 9 free men under the commendation and soke and sake of the same man [held] 3 carucates of land and 5 bordars and 1 slave. 3 ploughs. 14 acres of meadow. 4 head of cattle and 1 horse. Now 15 pigs and 46 sheep. It is worth £3. Roger de Saint-Germain holds it.

In Hartest 2 free men under the commendation and soke and sake of the same man with 2 carucates of land and 3 bordars. Then as now 2 ploughs. 8 acres of meadow. It is worth £2.

In [Great and Little] Waldingfield 2 free men. One belonged to Robert fitzWymarc by commendation and both belonged to Wihtgar by soke and sake. They have 2 carucates of land. 9 acres of meadow. 2 ploughs. Now 9 head of cattle, 37 pigs, 69 sheep and 11 goats. It is worth 50s. It is 4 furlongs long and 4 broad. In geld 6d. whoever holds [land] there. In Groton 1 free man under commendation and sake and soke. He has 10 acres of land. It is worth 20d. [...]

HUNDRED OF STOW.

In Shelland Fin, [...] Richard's predecessor, held 23 acres and 4 bordars. Then as now half a plough and 2 oxen. It is worth 5s.

[...]

HALF HUNDRED OF IPSWICH.

In the borough of Ipswich Wihtgar held 1 church of St Peter, to which belonged, then and now, 6 carucates of land as a manor. Then and afterwards 6 villans, now 8. Then and afterwards 5 bordars, now 15. Then 4 slaves. Then as now

Richard fitzGilbert

[Folio 393: SUFFOLK]

2 ploughs in demesne. Then 3 ploughs, now 4. Then woodland for 8 pigs, now for 4. Then as now 1 mill. 3 acres of meadow. Now 1 horse, 1 ox, 9 pigs and 80 sheep. To this church also belong 5 burgesses and 15 acres of free land in the borough and 6 empty messuages. Of the above-mentioned 6 carucates of land Roger the sheriff claims 100 acres and 5 villans and 1 mill for the king's manor of Bramford. And 5 villans from the same manor testify for him and they offer to prove it by any law by which anyone might give judgment. But the half Hundred of Ipswich testifies that this belonged to the church TE and Wihtgar held it and it offers to prove the claim. Then it was worth 100s., now £15 with the other lands which belong to this church. In the same borough Richard has 13 burgesses whom Fin held TRE. Over 4 of these he had soke and sake and commendation. One of them is a slave. And over 12 [he had] commendation only but they dwelt on land of their own and they paid the whole of the customary due in the borough. And this is part of Fin's honour.

HUNDRED OF BOSMERE.

Eskil held Badley TRE; now Richard [holds it] in demesne as 2 carucates of land and 20 acres. Then as now 4 villans and 4 bordars and 5 slaves. And 2 ploughs in demesne and 2 ploughs belonging to the men. 8 acres of meadow. And half a mill. 2 horses, 26 head of cattle and 32 pigs. Then 60 sheep, now 100. A church with 14 acres. Then it was worth 60s., now £4. From this land the abbot claims half a carucate, as the Hundred testifies. The king and the earl have the soke. To this manor have been added in the time of King Edward 26 villans free men with 1 carucate of land and 45 acres. Richard holds all these men for this manor which Fin held and Fin himself held them on lease . Then and afterwards 5 ploughs, now 2. Then it was worth 40s., now 47s. The king and the earl have the soke and sake. It is 10 furlongs long and 5 broad. 10d. in geld.

In [Earl and Little] Stonham 5 acres of land and woodland for 4 pigs. It is in the valuation of £15.

[Folio 393v: SUFFOLK]

Godmann held Flowton TRE. Wihtgar had the commendation and the king and the earl had the soke. Germund holds this from Richard as a manor with 2 carucates of land. Then

as now 4 bordars. 1 slave. 2 ploughs in demesne and 9 acres of meadow. Then 1 horse. Then 4 head of cattle, now 8. Then 4 pigs. Then 15 sheep, now 60. Then it was worth £4, now 60s. It is half a league long and 4 furlongs broad. 2d. in geld. To this manor Germund added 15 acres in the time of King William which a priest held freely TRE in the soke of the king and the earl. It is worth 2s. 6d. Bondi, a free man, held [Great and Little] Bricett and Queen Edith had the commendation only but Richard claims it for the fief of Wihtgar. The king and the earl have the soke. Now Roger [holds it] as 1 carucate of land and as a manor. Then as now 1 villan. 1 bordar. 1 plough in demesne. Then 1 plough belonging to the men. Then it was worth 20s., now 30s. Roger de Rames claims this land from the king's gift and he was seised thereof.

In the same place the same Roger d'Orbec holds 2 free men with 15 acres, worth 30d. Roger de Rames also claims this as above but Richard claims it for the fief of Wihtgar. In the same place Ranulf Peverel holds 4 acres which belonged to the above-mentioned manor TRE. He claims this for the fief of Fin.

In "Rigneseta" Hardekin, a free man, held 100 acres as a manor TRE. Now Geoffrey holds it. Then as now 2 villans. 4 bordars. 1 plough in demesne. Then half a plough belonging to the men. 7 acres of meadow. Woodland then for 30 pigs, now for 16. And then it was worth 20s., now 35s. In the same place Godric, a free man, held 60 acres as a manor. Then as now 1 plough. Then it was worth 10s., now 20s. In the same place Godwig, a free man, held 60 acres as a manor. Then 1 plough. Then it was worth 10s., now 15s. Geoffrey holds the whole and gave it at farm for 70s. but he could only have 60s. To this manor Fin added in the time of King Edward William 3 free

Richard fitzGilbert

[Folio 394: SUFFOLK]

men with 20 acres. Then 1 plough. This is in the same valuation. It is

8 furlongs long and 3 broad. 5d. in geld. The king and the earl have the soke. In "Facheduna" 1 free man of Earl Ælfgar held 30 acres TRE. Now Wulfmær [holds it] from Richard. Then as now 1 plough. It is worth 5s. The king and the earl have the soke. Wulfric, a free man, held Ashbocking with 60 acres as a manor. Then as now 2 villans and 2 sokemen with 7 acres and 2 bordars. 1 plough in demesne and half a plough belonging to the men. 2 acres of meadow. Then it was worth 20s., now 30s. The king and the earl have the soke. In the same place Erik, a free man, held 60 acres as a manor. 2 bordars. Then as now 1 plough. 1 acre of meadow. It is worth 30s. The king and the earl have the soke. In the same place Eadric, a free man, held TRE 40 acres as a manor. Then 1 plough. 1 acre of meadow. The king and the earl have the soke. It is worth 20s. To this manor Fin added in the time of King William 8 free men with 35 acres and a sokeman with 12 acres who could not withdraw from St Æthelthryth. And between them they had then 3 ploughs, now 2. Then it was worth 15s., now 20s. Osbern de Wanchy holds the whole and Richard claims it for Fin's fief. The king and the earl have the soke. Roger de Rames claims

two of these free men for his own fief [...] and he was seised thereof. The whole is 6 furlongs long and 2 broad. 6d. [...] in geld. Fin had nothing of the whole of this TRE.

HUNDRED OF CLAYDON.

In Thurlston 18 free men . Of these 12 and a half were commended to Ælfric the priest, who was commended to Wihtgar. Altogether they have 64 acres. And of the others, namely five and a half, Richard's predecessor did not have commendation over Ælfric, Waldwin, Harold, Godwine, Wulfmær and Ælfric. These men had 24 acres TRE. Richard holds these men because Bishop Herfast held them

[Folio 394v: SUFFOLK]

when Richard established a claim to the church of St Peter in Ipswich against him. But now [he says that] he did not know that they did not belong to his fief. Altogether they have then as now 3 ploughs. 1 acre of meadow. The above 12 were then worth 6s. 8d and the others [were worth] 4s. 1d. The king and the earl have the soke over the whole.

In Helmingham from Fin's land Thorir, a thegn of the king, held 1 carucate of land as a manor. Then as now 1 plough and 2 ploughs belonging to the men. 3 villans and 5 bordars. 3 acres of meadow. Then woodland for 20 pigs, now for 10; 2 horses, 4 head of cattle, 24 pigs, 40 sheep and 2 beehives. Then it was worth 16s., now 20s. It is 1 league long and 7 broad. 20d. in geld. Others hold [land] there. The king and the earl have the soke. Walter de Caen [holds it].

IN THURLSTON 91 acres belonging to the church of St Peter of Ipswich, worth 15s. This is in the valuation of the above-mentioned £15. It is 10 furlongs long and 6 broad. 20d. in geld. Others hold [land] there.

HUNDRED AND A HALF OF SAMFORD.

Of Fin's land Thorir, a thegn of the king, held Erwarton as a manor with 1½ carucates of land. Then 8 villans, now 3. Then 4 bordars, now 7. Then as now 1½ ploughs in demesne. Then 4 ploughs in demesne, now 1; 3 acres of meadow. The third part of a fishery. Then 1 horse, [...] now 2. Then head of cattle, now 8. Then 20 pigs, now 26. [...] Then as now 80 sheep. Now 4 goats. Then it was worth 40s., now 30s. Roger [...] holds it from Richard. The same Thorir had the soke. In Shotley Ceolweald, commended to Ælfric, held TRE 60 acres as a manor. Then as now 1 villan. 1 bordar. Half a plough. It is worth 10s. The same Roger [holds it]. The soke is in [East] Bergholt. In "Torp" Osbern, a free man of Ælfric, held 100 acres as a manor TRE. Then as now 3 bordars. 1 plough and 3 acres of meadow. It is worth 20s. The soke is in [East] Bergholt. The same Osbern [holds it] from Richard. The same Osbern held "Purtepyt" TRE with 60 acres as a manor. Then as now 3 villans. 2 bordars. 2 slaves. Half a plough in demesne.

Richard fitzGilbert

[Folio 395: SUFFOLK]

2 ploughs belonging to the men. It is worth 10s. The same Osbern [holds it]. The soke is in [East] Bergholt.

In Kirkton Edmund, a free man, held 60 acres as a manor TRE. Then as now half a plough. 1 acre of meadow. Then it was worth 20s, now 23s. 2d. In the same place Strangwulf, a free man, held 60 acres as a manor TRE. Then as now half a plough. It is worth 4s. In the same place Thorir, a free man of Gyrth, [held] 60 acres as a manor TRE. Then as now 4 bordars. Half a plough. Then it was worth 10s., now 11s. 5d. In the same place 2 free men, Huna and Godric, [held] 15 acres TRE and 2 oxen. Then it was worth 5s., now 8s. The soke is in [East] Bergholt. It is 6 furlongs long and 5 broad. 4d. in geld.

In Erwarton Ailbern, a free man, held 60 acres as a manor. Then as now half a plough. It is worth 8s. In "Eduinestuna" Godric, a free man, held 30 acres as a manor. Then as now half a plough. Then it was worth 5s., now 3s. The soke is in [East] Bergholt. Also in the Hundred Richard has 3 free men, Godric, Edwin, Leofric, with 33 acres. Then as now half a plough. Then it was worth 5s., now 6s. 6d. The soke is in [East] Bergholt. In Burstall Ælfric Stari, commended to Gyrth, held 40 acres as a manor TRE. Then as now 2 bordars. Then 1 plough, now a half. 2 acres of meadow. It is worth 8s. In Boynton Leofstan, a free man commended to Fin, held TRE 50 acres. Then as now 3 bordars. Then 1 plough, now a half. 3 acres of meadow. Then it was worth 10s., now 11s. 5d. The soke is in [East] Bergholt. [...] In "Toft" Alwine, a free man commended to Esger the staller, [held] 20 acres. In the same place Ælfgeat, a free man, [held] 8 acres. Then as now half a plough. It was then worth 5s., now 20s. 4d. The soke is in [East] Bergholt.

In Raydon Leofric, a free man, held 30 acres as a manor. Then as now half a plough. 2 acres of meadow. Then it was worth 5s., now 11s. 5d. Richard holds all this

[Folio 395v: SUFFOLK]

in demesne. In igham Godric, a free man, held 1 carucate of land as a manor TRE. Then as now 1 villan. 2 bordars. 1 plough in demesne. 6 acres of meadow. A church with 4 acres. Then it was worth 20s., now 25s. Osbern holds it. Of all these free men Fin, Richard's predecessor, had nothing TRE apart from the commendation only over one alone. The soke over the whole is in [East] Bergholt. And Richard holds them as belonging to the honour of Fin.

Robert fitzWymarc held FRESTON TRE, [and] Roger d'Abernon holds it with 6 carucates of land as a manor. Then as now 24 villans. 4 bordars. 2 ploughs in demesne. Then 8 ploughs belonging to the men, now 6; 8 acres of meadow. 1 mill. A church. Then 11 head of cattle, now 3. Then 40 pigs, now 3. Then 140 sheep, now 101. Then it was worth £8, now £11 10s. It is 1 league long and a half broad. 10d. in geld. The same Robert has the soke.

In Burstall Leofric, commended to Earl Ælfgar, TRE [held] 17 acres, worth 3s. Richard claims this as Fin's land. Wulfmær holds it from Richard. The soke is in [East] Bergholt.

HUNDRED OF RISBRIDGE.

These are the free men who TRE could sell and grant their lands. Wihtgar, Richard's predecessor had the commendation and the soke and sake apart from the 6 forfeitures of St

Edmund. In Stansfield Eadric Spuda, a free man, [held] 2 carucates of land. 2 bordars. 3 slaves. Then as now 2 ploughs. 2 acres of meadow. Now 1 [...] 4 head of cattle. Then 4 sheep, now 80; 25 pigs. Then it was worth 40s., now 60s. Gilbert holds this.

In the same place Wulfflæd, 1 free [wo]man, [held] 1 carucate of land. Then as now 1 plough. 4 acres of meadow. Then it was worth 20s., now 30s. Robert holds it. In the same place Crawa, 1 free man, [held] 60 acres of land. 1 slave. Then as now 1 plough. 4½ acres of meadow.

Richard fitzGilbert

[Folio 396: SUFFOLK]

Then as now 1 mill. Then it was worth 10s., now 15s. Roger holds this. A church with 15 acres of free land. The whole of Stansfield is 12 furlongs long and 6 broad. 13½d. in geld. In Depden Beorhtric Black held 2 carucates of land. Then as now 7 bordars. 1 slave. 2 ploughs in demesne. Then half a plough belonging to the men. And 3 acres of meadow. Now 1 horse. Then 7 head of cattle, now 14. Then 15 pigs, now 30. Then 37 sheep, now 80. Now 10 goats. 3 beehives. Then as now worth 60s. Frodo, the abbot's brother, holds this. In the same place 2 free men, Blæcwine and Godwine, [held] 2 carucates of land. 3 bordars. Then 1½ ploughs, now 2; 3 acres of meadow. Then 1 horse. Then as now 6 head of cattle. Then 16 pigs, now 26. Then 40 sheep. Then it was worth 30s., now 50s. Osbern holds it.

In Clopton Leofgeat, 1 free man, held 1½ carucates of land. 1 villan. 1 bordar and 3 slaves. Then 1 plough, now 2; 4 acres of meadow. 1 horse and 10 head of cattle. Now 34 pigs and 83 sheep. Then it was worth 20s., now 30s. Roger holds it. In [Great and Little] Wratting Gode, 1 free woman, [held] 2 carucates of land and 30 acres. Then as now 9 bordars. And 2 ploughs in demesne. Half a plough belonging to the men. 7 acres of meadow. And 1 mill. Then 1 horse, now 2. Then 4 head of cattle, now 10. Then 1 pig, now [...] 52. Then 80 sheep, now 100. Then 4 goats, now 40. Then it was worth 30s., now 40s. Pain holds it. The whole is 1 league long and a half broad. 12d. in geld. In Haverhill Fridebern, 1 free man, holds 5 bordars. They had 80 acres and 1 plough in demesne. 2 oxen belonging to the men. 2 acres of meadow. Then it was worth 13s. 4d., now 15s. The same Pain holds it. In Hanchet Alwine, 1 free man, held 100 acres. 1 bordar. 1 plough. 2 acres of meadow. Then it was worth 10s., now 15s.

[Folio 396v: SUFFOLK]

In Withersfield Wulfmær, 1 free man, held 51 acres. 1 bordar. Half a plough. 1 acre of meadow. It is worth 8s. The same Pain holds it. In the same place 1 free [wo]man, Leofwaru, [held] 100 acres and 1 bordar and 1 plough, worth 20s. Godard holds it. In the same place 1 free man, Alwine, [held] 3 carucates of land. 2 villans. 11 bordars. 3 slaves. 3 ploughs in demesne. Then 1 plough belonging to the men, now a half. 2 acres of meadow. Woodland for 20 pigs. Then 2 horses, now 3. Then 22 head of cattle, now 20. Then 60 pigs, now 45. Then 60 sheep, now 123. Then 60 goats, now 57.

Then as now worth 60s. Willihard holds it. The whole is 1 league long and a half broad. 6d. in geld.

In [Great and Little] Wratting 1 free man, Ailbern, [held] 3 carucates of land. 5 villans and 10 bordars. Then 3 ploughs in demesne, now 2. Then as now 1 plough belonging to the men. 12 acres of meadow. Woodland for 8 pigs. And 1 mill. Then 2 horses, now 3. Then 9 head of cattle, now 13. Then 24 pigs, now 48. Then 60 sheep, now 700. And 6 beehives. Under him 9 free men with half a carucate of land. Then half a plough. 1 acre of meadow. A church with 13 acres. Then it was worth 50s., now 60s. In Chilbourne Godwine, 1 free man, held 2 carucates of land. 1 villan and 4 bordars. Then 2 ploughs, now 1; 6 acres of meadow. 1 mill. Then as now 1 horse. Then it was worth 40s., now 50s. Geoffrey fitzHamo holds it.

In Poslingford 1 free man, Eadric, [held] 35 acres. Half a plough. 2 acres of meadow. It is worth 8s. Lothar holds it. In Boyton [in Stoke-by-Clare] 1 free [...] man, Wulfgar, [held] 8 acres, worth 16d. Ralph holds it. In the other Boyton [in Stoke-by-Clare] Alnuar, 1 free man, held 24 acres, worth 4s. W[illiam] Perot holds it. In Hawkedon Alwine, 1 free man, held 40 acres and half a plough and 2 acres of meadow, worth 6s. 8d. Fulcred holds it. In Clopton 1 free man, Hroc, with 13 acres, worth 2s. William Pecche holds it. In [Great and Little] Bradley then as now 2 free men with 69 acres and 1 acre of meadow. Then as now 1 plough. It is worth 17s. 6d.

Richard fitzGilbert

[Folio 397: SUFFOLK]

In [Great and Little] Thurlow then as now 10 free men with 1 carucate of land. 1 plough and 1 acre of meadow. A church with 29 acres. It is worth 10s. The whole is 1 league long and 1 furlong broad. 12d. in geld. In Kedington then as now 10 free men with 1 carucate of land. 2 ploughs. It is worth 20s. In Haverhill then as now 13 free men with 1 carucate of land and 60 acres. 1½ ploughs. Woodland for 7 pigs. It is worth 30s.

In Withersfield 9 free men with 1½ carucates of land. Then as now 2½ ploughs. Then it was worth 20s., now 30s. In Stoke [by Clare] then as now 21 free men with 1 carucate of land and 68 acres. Then 1½ ploughs, now 2; 10 acres of meadow. Then it was worth 20s., now 31s. 4d. A church with 60 acres, worth 10s. In Poslingford then as now 6 free men with 85 acres. 3 bordars. 1 plough. It is worth 14s. 2d. In Wickhambrook then as now 1 free man with 60 acres and 2 bordars and 1 plough. 4 acres of meadow. It is worth 10s. In Stradishall then as now 16 free men with 1 carucate of land. Then as now 3 ploughs. 2 acres of meadow. It is worth 20s. A church with 30 acres, worth 5s. In Hawkedon then as now 8 free men with 30 acres. 2 bordars and 1 plough. It is worth 13s. 4d.

In Haverhill 2 free men [...] with 26 acres, worth 4½s. All these men could sell and give their lands but Wihtgar had TRE the soke and sake apart from the 6 forfeitures of St Edmund, as we said above.

In [Great and Little] Bradley [are] 4 free men. Wulfwine, Leofric and Leofwine have 15 acres; the fourth, Bondi, has 1 carucate of land. Then as now 2 ploughs and 2 acres of meadow. It is worth 22s. 6d. Over these men Richard's predecessor did not have the commendation TRE. St

Edmund had the whole soke. In [Great and Little] Thurlow 2 sokemen of Eadgifu with every customary due whom Ralph held when he forfeited. They have 25 acres. Then as now half a plough. It is worth 4s. 4d. Widard holds this.

In "Wimundestuna" 6 free men. Regarding the sixth who is called Beorhtric, the Hundred does not know if he could sell his land or not TRE but it testifies that they saw him swear that he could not give [nor] sell his land away from Richard's predecessor. They have 2 carucates of land and 11 acres. Then as now 2 ploughs. 7 acres of meadow. Now 2 horses. Then 2 cows, now 3. Then 6 pigs, now 30. Then 16 sheep, now 62. The whole is worth 40s. Gerald holds this.

HALF-HUNDRED OF COSFORD.

In Hitcham 14 free men with 60 acres. Then 2 ploughs, now 1; 2 acres of meadow. It is worth 10s.

In Lindsey 6 free men with 1 carucate of land. 6 bordars. 2 ploughs. 2 acres of meadow. It is worth 20s. In Kersey 1 free [man] with 5 acres, worth 10d. His predecessor had the soke and commendation.

In Brettenham 8 free men with 30 acres. 1 plough. It is worth 5s.

In Rushbrooke 2 free men with 10 acres, worth 20d.

In Whatfield 3 free men with 60 acres. 3 bordars. Then 1½ ploughs, now 2. It is worth 10s. Over these men his predecessor had the commendation TRE and the soke and sake. St Edmund had the 6 forfeitures. In Stone Street 1 free man with 24 acres, worth 4s. His predecessor had half the commendation and [...] the Abbot of Ely had the other half. Ralph Peverel claims half this land and it was delivered to him in Loose. St Edmund had the soke.

XXVI. Lands of William de Warenne.

HUNDRED OF THEDWESTRY.

In Rattlesden 2 free men of St Æthelthryth held with the soke and sake. One of them could sell the land and the other could not; the one who could sell had 40 acres and 5 bordars and the other who could not [had] 60 [acres]. Then as now 2 bordars. Then as now between them 2 ploughs. 2 acres of meadow. It is worth 20s. It is from the Lewes [Sussex] exchange. holds this. In Gedding 2 free men of St Edmund by commendation and [...] soke [held] 60 acres of land. 3 bordars. Then 1 plough, now none. 5 acres of meadow. It is worth 5s. From the Lewes [Sussex] exchange.

HUNDRED OF LACKFORD.

In Elveden 1 free man under commendation only to St Æthelthryth, in the soke of St Edmund, held 2 carucates of land in exchange for Lewes [Sussex] which Nicholas holds from William. Then and afterwards 4 villans, now 3. Then as now 2 bordars. 1 slave. Then and afterwards 2 ploughs in demesne, now 1. Then as now 1 plough belonging to the men. The fourth part of a fishery. 1 church with 15 acres of land.

Then 4 pigs, now 2. Then 200 sheep, now 300. Then 50 goats, now 100 less 6. Then and afterwards worth 30s., now 50s. In Herringswell 1 carucate of land; the reeve held and he was a free man of Toki but he could not sell. 2 bordars. Then as now 1 plough. 60 sheep. It is worth 16s. From the fief of Frederick in the soke of St Edmund. In the same place a free man of Frederick's predecessor, in the soke of St Edmund, held 40 acres which Nicholas holds from William. Then half a plough, now none. It is worth 40d.

HUNDRED OF STOW.

In Buxhall Humphrey holds. Munulf the priest, under commendation of St Æthelthryth in the soke of the king, held half a carucate of land and 30 20 acres. Now William holds it in exchange for Lewes [Sussex]. Then and afterwards 2 bordars, now 7. Then and always 1 plough in demesne. Then as now 2 oxen belonging to the men. 2 acres of meadow. In the same place 4 free men commended to the same Munulf with 2 acres, worth 12s.

HUNDRED OF BOSMERE.

Tunstall. Leofwine, a free man, held it with 1 carucate of land and 20 acres as a manor TRE. Then as now 1 villan. Then 2 ploughs in demesne; afterwards and now 1; 2 acres of meadow. Now 1 horse and 1 cow. Then 30 sheep, now 60. Then it was worth 24s., now 25s. The king and the earl have the soke. In Creeting Humphrey holds from William 1 free man with 38 acres. Then as now 1 plough. Then worth 8s., now 10s.

HUNDRED OF BRADMERE.

Hugh fitzGolde holds BARNHAM which Bosten held TRE. Half a carucate of land as a manor. Then as now 3 bordars. 2 slaves. 1 plough in demesne. Then half a plough belonging to the men, now 2 oxen. Then 2 horses, now 1. Then 13 pigs. Then 85 sheep, now 90; 3 free men with 4 acres and half a plough. Over these men his predecessor had commendation. Then it was worth 16s., now 20s.

HUNDRED OF RISBRIDGE.

OF FREDERICK'S FIEF.

Hugh de Wanchy holds Depden which Toki the thegn held TRE as a manor with 3 carucates of land. Then as now 16 villans and 7 bordars. Then 4 slaves. Then and afterwards 2 ploughs in demesne, now 4. Then as now 4 ploughs belonging to the men. 12 acres of meadow. Woodland for 100 pigs. Then as now 2 horses. Then 22 head of cattle, now 17. Then 40 pigs, now 72. Then 24 sheep, now 112. Now 13 beehives. A church with 24 acres of free land. Then it was worth £4, now £6. It is 1 league long and 8 furlongs broad. 5½d. in geld.

Wigmær holds Withersfield which the same person held TRE as a manor with 2 carucates of land. Then as now 5 villans, and 5 bordars. Then 3 slaves. Then 2 ploughs in demesne, now 3. Then as now 1 plough belonging to the men. 2 acres of meadow. Woodland for 20 pigs. Then 2 horses, now 3. Then 4 head of cattle, now 12. Then 20 pigs, now 30. Then 80 sheep, now 100. Then as now

William de Warenne

16 goats and 6 beehives. Then it was worth 70s., now £4. In the same place 1 free man with 24 acres. Then as now half a plough. It is worth 4s.

In Clopton Hugh holds [the land] which the same Toki held with 1 carucate of land. Then as now 1 plough. 2 acres of meadow. Then as now worth 20s.

HUNDRED OF BLYTHING.

Eadric, a free man, held Wrentham TRE with 2 carucates of land as a manor. Then as now 5 villans. Then as now 11 bordars. Then 6 slaves, now 3. Then 1½ ploughs in demesne, now 2. Then 3 ploughs belonging to the men, now 2. Then as now woodland for 20 pigs. Then as now 2 acres of meadow. Now 2 horses. Now 13 head of cattle. Now 12 pigs. Now 113 sheep. Now 20 goats and 5 beehives. And 1 church with 40 acres. Then as now worth 40s. And Robert de Pierrepoint holds this. In the same vill Thorkil, a free man, held TRE 2 carucates of land, then as now, as a manor. Then as now 5 villans and then as now 11 bordars. 2 ploughs could be made up in the demesne. And [there was] 1 when he acquired it. 2 acres of meadow. Woodland for 20 pigs. Then as now 40s. R[obert] himself holds this land.

In the same vill Wulfric, a free man, held 2 carucates of land as a manor. Then as now 5 villans and 11 bordars. 1 plough in demesne and another could be made up. 2 ploughs belonging to the men. 2 acres of meadow. Woodland for 20 pigs. Then as now worth 40s. And 1 church with 8 acres. The same Robert holds this.

In the same vill 20 free men dwelt with 360 acres. 2 bordars. Then as now 6 ploughs in demesne. Then as now worth 60s. Over 1 of these men Count Alan has half the commendation and half the land and the soke and sake. Robert holds all this from William de Warenne. The soke and sake over all this land belongs in Blythburgh Hundred.

Also William has in the same vill 1 manor which Halfdan, a free man, held. Then 6 villans and now 4. Then 11 bordars, now 13. Then 3 slaves, now 1. Then as now 3 ploughs in demesne. Then and now 2 ploughs belonging to the men. 2 acres of meadow. Woodland for 40 pigs. Now 7 head of cattle. Now 24 pigs. 80 sheep. Now 30 goats. TRE it was worth £4, now £3. William fitzReginald holds this from William de Warenne. In the same vill [...] 1 free man dwelt and he held half a carucate of land as a manor . Under him he had 2 free men with 10 acres. 1 bordar. Then as now 1 plough in demesne and half a plough belonging to the men. Woodland for 4 pigs. And half an acre of meadow. 2 horses, 6 head of cattle, 10 pigs, 30 sheep, 20 goats. Then it was worth 10s., and now the same. In the same vill Ælfric of Sandford held 50 acres as a manor. Then as now 2 bordars. Then as now 1 plough in demesne. 1 acre of meadow. 1 horse, 4 head of cattle, 8 pigs, 60 sheep, 7 goats. Then as now worth 10s. In the same vill dwell 8 free men and they hold 1½ carucates and 10 acres of land. And they hold 1 bordar. Then as now 2 ploughs in

demesne. Then as now worth 12s. William fitzReginald holds all this under William de Warenne.

Henstead, 1 berewick of Wrentham, 1 carucate of land. Then as now 4 villans and then as now 9 bordars. Then as now 1 plough in demesne and then as now 2 ploughs belonging to the men. 6 head of cattle, 40 sheep, 12 pigs, 20 goats. Then as now worth 20s. And now have been added 2 free men with 30 acres of land. They have 1 plough in demesne. It is worth 3s. Godfrey de point holds these 2 lands under William de Warenne. And all these lands are 3 leagues long and 2 broad. It renders 2s. in the king's geld.

William de Warenne

The king has the soke and sake throughout all this land apart from the demesne of Halfdan. And of this land 6 acres of land were taken away from Count Alan which William's men took away for themselves, as the Hundred testifies. And Thorkil of Wrentham was a man belonging to Eadric, the predecessor of Robert Malet.

Ranulf his nephew holds Middleton Ælfric, 1 free man, as 1 manor. Now William de Warenne holds it in demesne with 2 carucates of land. Then as now 2 villans. Then as now 8 bordars. Then 4 slaves and now 1. Then 2 ploughs in demesne. Now half a plough belonging to the men. 6 acres of meadow. Then 1 horse and now 2. Now 2 cows and 20 pigs and 50 sheep. Then and now it was worth 40s. 1 church with 15 acres, worth 2s. And to this manor were added 5 free men and half a priest. They hold 55½ acres. 1½ ploughs in demesne. 2 acres of meadow. It is worth 10s. It is 8 furlongs long and 7 broad, whoever holds land there. And it renders 7½d. And over these 6 free men the king and the earl have the soke and sake. Ælfric, who held this manor, was a man belonging to Eadric, the predecessor of Robert. And William Malet and Robert were seised of this land.

Ælfric, a free man, held Thorington as a manor TRE; now Godfrey de Pierrepoint holds it from William de Warenne. Then as now 2 carucates of land. Then as now 5 villans, 11 bordars. Then 3 slaves, now 2. Then 2 ploughs and now 3 in demesne. Then as now 4 ploughs belonging to the men. Woodland for 6 pigs. 2 acres of meadow. 6 non-working head of cattle, 40 pigs and 120 sheep. 4 beehives. It is worth 60s. And Robert Malet claims this land like the other. The Hundred testifies to this. The king and the earl have the soke and sake.

Eadric, a free man, held Covehithe TRE as 1 manor with 2 carucates of land.

Then 5 bordars, now 6. Then 1 slave. Then 2 ploughs in demesne, now 1½ ploughs and half a plough belonging to the men. 1 acre of meadow. Then 1 horse, now 1; 8 pigs and 105 sheep. Then it was worth 40s., now 20s. To this manor were added 100 acres of land which 14 free men held. Then 2 ploughs, now now 1; 1 acre of meadow. It is worth 10s. William fitzReginald holds all this land from William de

Warenne. Of these 14 men William's men have been seised of two half free men against Count Alan.

HUNDRED OF CARLFORD.

In Burgh Æthelric, a free man, held TRE 1 carucate of land and 20 acres as a manor. Then 2 bordars, now 7. Then 1 plough, now 2. Then half a plough belonging to the men, now 1; 4 acres of meadow. 1 horse and 7 head of cattle. Then 16 pigs, now 12, and 17 sheep. Then it was worth 20s., now 30s. In the same place 11 whole free men and 3 half [free men] commended to the same Æthelric with 50 acres and 2 bordars. Then 2 ploughs, now 1. Half an acre of meadow. Then it was worth 10s., now 8s. William acquired all this as 1 carucate of land and R[obert] de Glanville [holds it] from him. 1 church with 8 acres. Several [others] have a share.

HUNDRED OF WILFORD.

In Boulge Robert holds; 1 free man commended to Æthelric [held] TRE 13 acres and half a plough, worth 2s. In Debach 1 free man under the same commendation [held] 4 acres, worth 8d. In 'Torstanestuna' [in Bromeswell] 6 acres, worth 12d. R[obert] de Glanville holds this from William de Warenne.

In Bredfield Æthelric, a free man, holds 3 acres, worth 6d. The same Robert [holds].

[Folio 401: SUFFOLK]

XXVII.

Lands of Swein of Essex In Suffolk.

HUNDRED OF THINGOE.

In Rede 1 sokeman with 20 acres. 1 bordar. Half a plough. 1 acre of meadow. It is worth 5s. The soke is St Edmund's.

In Manston 1 sokeman with 20 acres. 1 bordar. Half a plough. 1 acre of meadow. It is worth 5s.

TWO HUNDREDS OF BABERGH.

Robert held Stoke [by Nayland] TRE as a manor with 4 carucates of land, together with the soke. Then 25 villans, now 15. Then 32 bordars, now 23. Then 8 slaves, now 6. Then 2 ploughs in demesne, now 3. Then 12 ploughs belonging to the men, now 7. Now 2 mills. 25 acres of meadow. Woodland for 60 pigs. Now 3 horses. Now 8 head of cattle. Now 20 pigs. Now 70 sheep. Now 4 goats. Then it was worth £10, now £12. A church with 60 acres of free land. In the same vill 11 free men under the commendation and soke of Robert. Between them all 1 carucate of land but they could sell. 1 free man with 12 acres commended to Robert but the sake and soke belonged to St Edmund. Between them all 1½ ploughs then, now 1. It is worth 30s. It is 8 furlongs long and 4 broad. In geld 20d.

Robert, Swein's father, held Withermarsh TRE as a manor with 4 carucates of land, together with the soke. Then 27 villans, now 24. Then 32 bordars, now 27. Then 2 slaves, now 1. Then 3 ploughs in demesne, now 2. Then 13 ploughs belonging to the men, now 8. Then as now 1 mill and 30 acres of meadow. Now 2 horses and 20 head of cattle. Now

24 pigs and 15 wild horses. Now 80 sheep. Then it was worth £10, now £12. It is 8 furlongs long and 4 broad. In geld 20d.

The same Robert, Swein's father, held Polstead TRE as a manor with 4 carucates

[Folio 401v: SUFFOLK]

carucates of land, together with the soke. Then 26 villans, now 21. Then 36 bordars, now 30. Then as now 1 slave. Then and always 2 ploughs in demesne. Then 15 ploughs belonging to the men, now 9. Then as now 1 mill. Woodland for 80 pigs. 1 acres of meadow. Now 8 horses at the hall. Now 28 head of cattle. Now 40 pigs. Now 150 sheep. Then it was worth £10, now £12. It is 8 furlongs long and 4 broad. In geld 20d., whoever holds [land] there.

The same Robert, Swein's father, held Nayland TRE as a manor with 2 carucates of land, together with the soke. Then as now 6 villans. Then 20 bordars, now 17. Then 6 slaves, now 2. Then as now 1 plough in demesne. Then 4 ploughs belonging to the men, now 3. Then as now 1 mill. 10 acres of meadow. Now 3 horses at the hall. Now 31 head of cattle. Now 45 pigs. Now 80 sheep. Now 35 goats. Then it was worth £6, now £8. It is half a league long and 2 furlongs broad. In geld 12d.

Brungar, a free man under the commendation only of Robert, held Aveley TRE as a manor with 1 carucate of land, together with the soke. Then as now 1 villan and 10 bordars. Then as now 2 ploughs in demesne and half a plough belonging to the men. Woodland for 6 pigs. 4 acres of meadow. 1 mill. 1 horse at the hall. Now 14 head of cattle. Now 49 pigs and 87 sheep. Then it was worth 20s., afterwards and now 30s. It is 6 furlongs long and 3 broad. In geld 3d. St Edmund had the soke and sake over this TRE and Robert fitzWymarc, the father of Swein, had the commendation only. At that time stolen horses were found at the house of that Brungar, so that the abbot who had the soke and sake, and Robert who had the commendation over him, came to the plea regarding this theft, and the Hundred testifies thus.

Swein of Essex

[Folio 402: SUFFOLK]

They went away amicably without a verdict that the Hundred had seen.

HALF-HUNDRED OF IPSWICH.

In the borough [Ipswich] Robert had TRE 41 burgesses together with the soke and sake and commendation. And the king had the other customary dues. He [Swein] lost the commendation over 15 of them who died but he has the soke and sake, and the same with the others. The king has the other customary dues.

HUNDRED OF SAMFORD.

Robert held Stratford [St Mary] TRE as a manor with 3 carucates of land. Then as now 20 villans. Then 8 bordars, now 10. Then 4 slaves. Then 2 ploughs in demesne, now 1. Then 10 ploughs belonging to the men, now 5, and 5 could be restored. 16 acres of meadow. Woodland for 16 pigs. Then as now 1 mill. A church with 20 acres of free land. Half a plough. 1 horse, 6 head of cattle, 36 pigs and 50 sheep. Then as now worth £6. Robert [hôlds] from him. Swein has the soke. It is 7 furlongs long and 5 broad. 9d. in geld. Robert held Pannington TRE with 2 carucates of land as a manor. Then 3 villans. Then as now 3 bordars. Then 2 ploughs in demesne, now 1. Then 3 ploughs belonging to the men. 10 acres of meadow. A church with 3 acres of free land. Now 1 salt-pan. 8 head of cattle, 20 pigs, 80 sheep and 28 goats. Then it was worth 40s., now 30s. It is 5 furlongs long and 4 broad. 4¼d. in geld. Robert has the soke. Algar [holds it] from Swein.

Toli, a free man commended to Robert, held Wherstead with 1 carucate of land. 1 bordar. 1 plough. 3 acres of meadow. 5 pigs. 30 sheep. 14 goats. Then it was worth 10s. and now the same. Swein [holds it] in demesne.

In Freston Robert held TRE 30 acres in demesne. Then as now 1 plough. 1 acre of meadow. It is worth 10s. Arnulf [holds it] from Swein. The same Robert had the soke.

[Folio 402v: SUFFOLK]

HUNDRED OF WILFORD.

Godric, commended to Harold, held Peyton TRE as a manor with 3 carucates of land. Then 10 villans, now 8. Then and now 4 bordars. Then 1 slave. Then as now in demesne 2 ploughs and belonging to the men 3 ploughs. 3 acres of meadow. And 1 mill. Then 2 horses. Then 4 head of cattle, now 2. Then 1 pig, now 6. And 27 sheep. Then it was worth 60s., now 40s. It is 1 league long and 4 furlongs broad. In geld 13½d.

In the same place belong 20 free men under commendation to the same person, with 80 acres of land. 2 acres of meadow. Then as now 2 ploughs. Then it was worth 13s., now 15s.

XXVIII.

Lands of Eudo the Steward In Suffolk.

HUNDRED OF LACKFORD.

Godwine, a thegn of King Edward, held Eriswell as a manor with 6 carucates of land. Then 11 villans, afterwards 10, now 11. Then as now 4 bordars. Then as now 11 slaves. Then and afterwards 5 ploughs in demesne, now 3. Then as now 5 belonging to the men. 14 acres of meadow. 2½ mills. A church with 60 acres of land. 2 fisheries. Then as now 2 horses at the hall. Then 20 head of cattle, now 13. Then 40 pigs, now 20. Then 900 sheep, now 800. Then and afterwards worth £10, now £16. It is 1 league long and 6 furlongs broad. In geld 10d. To this belongs 1 berewick, 'Coclesworda' [Chamberlain's Hall], with 8 acres of land. A church with 60 acres. Then and afterwards 15 villans, now 11 villans. Then as now 4 bordars. Then and afterwards 11 slaves, now 8; 22

Eudo the Steward

[Folio 403: SUFFOLK]

acres of meadow. Then and afterwards 5 ploughs. Then and afterwards 5 ploughs in demesne, now 4. Then and after-

wards 6 ploughs belonging to the men, [...] now 5. And 2 horses at the hall. Then 200 sheep, now 900 less 20. Then and afterwards worth £12, now £24. It is 1 league long and 8 furlongs broad. In geld 7d. The soke and sake are St Edmund's.

In Lakenheath and in Brandon 6 sokemen in the soke of St Æthelthryth and they could not sell. They were delivered to Lisois, Eudo's predecessor, for 2 carucates of land but afterwards he acknowledged that they belonged to St Æthelthryth. And Eudo held these men together with the soke and sake. 4 bordars. Then as now 3 ploughs and 3 acres of meadow. 2 fisheries. Then and afterwards worth 30s., now it renders 70s.

Cnut, a free man commended to Algar, held Tuddenham as a manor with 3 carucates of land. Then 6 villans, afterwards 4, now 6. Then 4 slaves, now 1. Then 3 ploughs in demesne, afterwards a half, now 2. And 1½ ploughs belonging to the men. 3 acres of meadow. 1 mill. There was one fishery but now there is not. A church with 30 acres. Now 10 horses at the hall and now 40 pigs and 11 head of cattle. Then 200 sheep, now 60. Then and afterwards it was worth £4, now 100s. And it is 1 league long and 6 furlongs broad. In geld 20d. In Cavenham 1 free man under the commendation only of Cnut, in the soke of St Edmund, [held] 60 acres. 1 bordar. Then as now 1 plough. Then as now worth 5s.

HUNDRED AND A HALF OF SAMFORD.

In Raydon Swærting, a free man, held 17 acres, worth 3s. Osbern holds it from Eudo. The soke is in [East] Bergholt.

HUNDRED OF PLUMESGATE.

Wulfric, half commended to the Abbot of Ely and half to Malet's predecessor held [Great] Glemham with 2 carucates of land as a manor TRE and William Malet was seised thereof. 7 bordars. 2 ploughs in demesne and half a plough belonging to the men. 8 acres of meadow.

[Folio 403v: SUFFOLK]

1 mill. And half a church with 10 acres. Then 9 pigs, now 16. Then 5 sheep, now 40. Then it was worth 40s., now [...] 50s. In the same place have been added 10 free men commended to Wulfric with 53 acres and 1 plough, worth 10s. 10d. Pirot holds from Eudo. The soke belongs to the Abbot of Ely. William Malet was seised of the whole. It is 12 furlongs long and 6½ broad. It renders 20d. in geld.

HALF-HUNDRED OF COSFORD.

Ælfric Cempa held Layham TRE with 4 carucates of land as a manor. Then as now 15 villans and 3 bordars and 1 slave. 2 ploughs in demesne. Then 6 ploughs belonging to the men, afterwards and now 3; 12 acres of meadow. Woodland for 10 pigs. And 1 mill. A church with 40 acres and 1 acre of meadow and 1 plough. Then as now 1 horse, 20 head of cattle, 36 pigs, 180 sheep and 23 goats. Then as now worth £6; 8 furlongs long and 6 broad. 7½d. in geld.

XXIX. Lands of Roger d'Auberville.

HUNDRED OF STOW.

In [Great and Little] Finborough Leofsunu, a free man under the commendation only of Guthmund Hugh de Montfort's predecessor, held 2 carucates of land. Then 4 bordars, afterwards and now 3. Then as now 2 ploughs in demesne. Woodland for 12 pigs. 16 acres of meadow. 1 mill. A church with 30 acres of free land and 1 acre of meadow. Then 1 horse,

Roger d'Auberville

[Folio 404: SUFFOLK]

now none. Then as now 8 head of cattle. Then 20 pigs, now 6. Then 30 sheep, now 100. Then it was worth £4, afterwards £2, and now 60s. It is 1 league long and 8 furlongs broad. In geld 22½d. In the same manor 18 free men under commendation only to the same Leofsunu [held] 1 carucate of land in the soke of the king and the earl. Then and afterwards 3 ploughs, now 1; 3½ acres of meadow. Roger holds these by exchange. In the same place 6 sokemen belonging in the king's manor of Thorney, together with the commendation and sake and soke and summage. They have 65½ acres of land. 1 bordar. Then and afterwards 3 ploughs between them all, now 1; 3 acres of meadow. He holds these by exchange. In the same place 2 free men under commendation only to Guthmund, Hugh's predecessor, [held] 80 acres in the soke of the king and the earl. Then 1½ ploughs, afterwards and now none. He holds these men in the same way. Also in the same place 1 free man commended to the predecessor of Eustace [held] 4 acres. In the same place Leofstan of Loose, 1 free man by commendation, [held] 4 acres. In the same place 1 free man also under commendation to the king the soke and sake being in the Hundred [held] 20 acres. Then half a plough and 1 acre of meadow. In the same place 1 free man commended to Wihtgar, Richard's predecessor but was in the Hundred [held] 30 acres and 1 villan. Then 1 plough, afterwards and now nothing. 2 acres of meadow.

In the same place 4 free men the soke being in the Hundred [held] 16 acres. Then 1½ ploughs, afterwards and now nothing. He holds these men by exchange. Then and afterwards all these free men were worth £4, now 40s.

HUNDRED OF BOSMERE.

Leofcild held Somersham in demesne with 1 carucate of land as a manor TRE. Then as now 1 plough. 1 acre of meadow. It is worth 30s. Dot, a free man, held "Pileberga" with 60 acres as a manor TRE. Now Roger [holds it] in demesne. 1 bordar. Then as now 1 plough. 1 acre of meadow. It is worth 20s. The king and the earl have the soke. In the same place 5 free men with 30 acres. [It is] in the same valuation. The king and the earl have the soke.

In Flowton Godmann, a free man, held 20 acres in demesne

[Folio 404v: SUFFOLK]

TRE. He still holds them from Roger. It is worth 40d. In the same place in demesne 2 free men, Vilgrip and Eadric, one

with 40 acres and the other with 10 acres. Then as now 1 plough. 1 acre of meadow. It is worth 16s. The king and the earl have the soke.

In [Little] Blakenham Wulfweard, 1 free man, held 30 acres in demesne. Then as now half a plough. 1 acre of meadow. It is worth 14s. In "Ella" 1 free man, Ælfgeat, held 12 acres and 2 oxen in demesne, worth 7s. In the same place 1 free man with 3 acres and it is in the valuation of Somersham. In Offton 1 free man, Waldwin, commended to Leofric, son of Hobba. He had 20 acres and 1 bordar. Then half a plough. Then it was worth 40d., now 4s. William holds it from Roger.

In [Great and Little] Bricett 1 free man, Leofric, commended to Godric of Ringshall, the predecessor of William d'Auberville. He had 10 acres. Then 2 oxen. It is worth 20d. Gilbert holds it from Roger. The king and the earl have the soke. In Horswold 2 free men, Hearding and Tovi commended to the king, held 22½ acres. Now William holds it from Roger. Then as now half a plough. Half an acre of meadow. It is worth 5s. 10d. The king and the earl have the soke. Roger holds this land from the Abbot of Ely by order of the Bishop of St. L, as Roger himself says. [...] In "Langhedana" 1 free man, Wulfbeald, [held] 24 acres as a manor. 1½ acres of meadow. And in [every] third year the fourth part of a mill. It is and was worth 5s. 8d.

HUNDRED OF CLAYDON.

Tepekin, a free man TRE commended to Harold, held Henley with 2 carucates of land as a manor and 16 bordars. Then 4 slaves. Then 3 ploughs in demesne, now 2. Then 4 ploughs belonging to the men, now 3; 8 acres of meadow. Woodland for 6 pigs. 7 head of cattle, 14 pigs and 30 sheep. A church with 2 acres. Then it was worth £4, now £3. Eudo the steward holds it in his demesne. In the same place 4 free men were added with 8 acres. 2 oxen. It is worth 2s. The king and the earl have the soke.

Roger d'Auberville

[Folio 405: SUFFOLK]

HALF-HUNDRED OF COSFORD.

Tovi, a thegn, held Elmsett as a manor TRE with 6 carucates of land and 40 acres. Then and afterwards 11 villans, now 2. Then as now 12 bordars. Then 4 slaves. Then as now 2 ploughs in demesne. Then and afterwards 12 ploughs belonging to the men, now 4. A church with 15 acres and half a plough. Then 2 horses. Then 16 head of cattle, now 4. Then 30 pigs, now 20. Then 240 sheep, now 200. Then it was worth £10, now £7. It is 10 furlongs long and 7 broad. 15d. d. in geld. St Edmund has half the soke.

In Whatfield 1 free man with 60 acres and 2 bordars. Then and afterwards 1 plough, now a half. 1 acre of meadow. It is worth 10s. St Edmund has the commendation and soke.

HUNDRED OF CARLFORD.

In "Finesford" Tepekin held 24 acres. 1 acre of meadow. Then half a plough and 1 free woman with half an acre. Then as now worth 4s.

XXX.

Lands of William, brother of Roger d'Auberville.

HUNDRED OF BOSMERE.

Godwig, a free man, held Ringshall with 1 carucate of land and 40 acres as a manor. Then 1 villan. Then 2 ploughs, now a half. 4 bordars. 6 acres of meadow. Woodland for 8 pigs. Half a church with 12 acres. Then 4 horses, now 1. And 13 pigs, 60 sheep and 32 goats. It is worth 47s. Of this land a man commended to the Abbot of St Edmund held 11 acres TRE. Of this manor Hugh holds 40 acres and they are worth 5s. in the same valuation. In the same place 1 free man, Wulfric, held 80 acres as a manor. Then 1 plough and 4 acres of meadow. Then it was worth 20s., now 8s. Fulk holds from William. The king and the earl have the soke.

[Folio 405v: SUFFOLK]

In the same place Trumwine, a free man of the king, held 18 acres TRE. Now William holds it in demesne. Then half a plough. Now it is worth 3s. In Ringshall Eadric, a free man commended to William's predecessor, held 5 acres. Now William holds it in demesne. It is worth 12d. [...] In [Great and Little] Bricett Fulk holds from William. Eskil, a free man commended to Leofric, son of Hobba held 60 acres TRE as a manor. Of these William has 40 acres but the whole was delivered to him altogether. On this land there is 1 bordar. Then as now 1 plough. It is worth 10s. The king and the earl have the soke. Of the above 60 acres Hugh de Houdain took 20 acres as William and the Hundred say, but Hugh himself is in the king's hands and therefore has been unable to give a reply.

XXXI.

Lands of Hugh de Montfort.

HUNDRED OF BRADMERE.

In Barnham in demesne 9 free men with 16 acres and half a plough.

In Wattisfield in demesne 9 free men with 16 acres and half a plough, worth 15s. St Edmund has the soke. Two of these belonged to St Edmund as regards the commendation TRE and 7 to the predecessor of Earl Hugh.

HUNDRED OF BISHOP.

Aslak, a thegn, held [MONK] SOHAM TRE as a manor with 1 carucate of land. [Now] Roger de Candos holds it. Then as now 1 villan. 3 bordars. 1 slave. 1 plough in demesne. Half a plough belonging to the men. 4 acres of meadow. Woodland for 10 pigs.

Hugh de Montfort

[Folio 406: SUFFOLK]

Then 10 pigs, now 12. And 5 head of cattle. Then 4 sheep, now 12. Then as now worth 20s. The soke is the bishop's. [...] In Horham the same person holds 1 free man under commendation with 14 acres and half a plough, worth 3s. [...] In Bedingfield [holds]. 5 free men under commendation with 60 acres and 2 bordars. $1\frac{1}{2}$ ploughs and 2 acres of meadow. It is worth 10s. The bishop has the soke.

In Bedingfield the same person [holds]. 7 villans with 60 acres. $1\frac{1}{2}$ ploughs. Woodland for 40 pigs. This belongs in Occold and in its valuation. The soke is the bishop's.

HUNDRED OF BLYTHING.

In Stoven Hugh de Montfort holds in demesne 50 acres which 4 free men held TRE and now 3 [free men hold it]. [...] Half an acre of meadow. 1 plough in demesne. Then as now worth $7\frac{1}{2}$s. and 100 herrings. The king and the earl had the soke and sake over these 4 men.

HUNDRED OF COLNEIS.

In Nacton Guthmund held in demesne 2 carucates of land as a manor TRE. Then as now 6 villans. Then as now in demesne 2 ploughs. Then 3 ploughs belonging to the men, now 2. Woodland for 8 pigs. 2 acres of meadow. Then 1 mill, now none. Then 4 horses, now 1; 1 ox. Then 8 pigs, now none. Then 23 sheep, now 123. Then 30 goats, now none. It is and was worth, then as now, 70s. It is $1\frac{1}{2}$ leagues long and 1 broad. In geld 2d.

In "Brihtoluestuna" 18 free men commended to Guthmund with 1 carucate of land and 20 acres. 4 bordars. Then 10 ploughs, now [...] ; 2 acres of meadow. Woodland for 2 pigs. A church with 6 acres. It is half a league long and 2 furlongs broad. 10d. in geld.

In Levington 3 free men with 20 acres under the same commendation. Then 2 ploughs, now 1.

In "Culuerdestuna" 5 free men under the same commendation with $21\frac{1}{2}$ acres. Then 2 ploughs, now 1. It is 3 furlongs long and 2 broad. 2d. in geld.

In "Isteuertona" 4 free men under the same commendation with 18 acres. Then 2 ploughs, now 1; 1 acre of meadow. It is worth £4 10s. Over all this land St Æthelthryth has the soke.

[Folio 406v: SUFFOLK]

In Walton 1 free man, Lurkr by name, commended to the same person N[orthmann], with 24 acres. It is worth 3s. Northmann holds it from Hugh. St Æthelthryth has the soke. And Guthmund held the afore-mentioned manor of Nacton from St Æthelthryth on the day when King Edward died in such a way that he could not sell or give it away from the church, on the agreement that after his death it must return to the church demesne. This the Hundred testifies.

HUNDRED OF CARLFORD.

In Bixley 3 free men commended to Guthmund held TRE 29 acres and 1 plough in demesne. 1 acre of meadow. It is in the valuation of "Brithtoluestuna". In Burgh 1 free man commended half to St Æthelthryth and half to the predecessor of Robert Malet TRE; now 3 men with 20 acres of land. Then 1 plough, now a half. 2 acres of meadow. Then it was worth 10s., now 5s. In the same place 1 free man commended half to St Æthelthryth and half to Eadric Grim with 19 acres of land and 1 bordar. Then 1 plough, now a half. 1 acre of meadow. It is worth 4s. 9d.

In Little Bealings 1 free man commended half to St Æthelthryth and half to Eadric with $4\frac{1}{2}$ acres, worth 8d. In Clopton 2 free men and a half commended in the same way as the others above, with 14 acres. Then half a plough, now none. It is worth 2s. 7d.

HUNDRED OF WILFORD.

In Charsfield in demesne 10 free men commended to Eadric and half to St Æthelthryth with 60 acres. 1 acre of meadow. Then 2 ploughs, now 1. Then it was worth 24s., now 22s. 8d.

HUNDRED OF LOOSE.

In Charsfield 2 free men commended to St Æthelthryth, and Hugh de Montfort's predecessor had half the commendation over one, with 7 acres, worth 16d.

In Cretingham . Ælfric, a free man of Harold, held it TRE with $2\frac{1}{2}$ carucates of land and 15 acres. Then as now 6 villans and 21 bordars. Then 2 slaves. In demesne 2 ploughs and 6 ploughs belonging to the men. 8 acres of meadow. Woodland for 8 pigs. 1 mill. Then 1 horse and 2 head of cattle,

Hugh de Montfort

[Folio 407: SUFFOLK]

20 sheep and 20 pigs. Then it was worth 100s., now £8 and 1 ounce of gold. It is 1 league long and 3 furlongs broad. In geld 11d. Others hold [land] there. In the same place 10 free men under the same commendation with 46 acres. William d'Arques claims $9\frac{1}{2}$ acres and 2 half [free] men. Then as now 1 plough. It is worth 20s. One of these was commended to Eadric of Laxfield and William Malet was seised thereof on the day he died. Roger holds this from Hugh.

HUNDRED OF WANGFORD.

In Willingham 15 free men commended to Burgheard [held] in demesne $1\frac{1}{2}$ carucates of land and 18 acres TRE. Then as now 2 villans. Then 7 ploughs, now 6. Woodland for 10 pigs. 1 acre of meadow. 1 church with 40 acres, worth 7s. Several [others] have a share there. Then it was worth 60s., now 30s. 30d. and 3000 herrings. The king and the earl have the soke.

In Weston 1 free man under the same commendation with 16 acres and half a plough, worth 5s. and 400 herrings. [...] In Willingham 1 free man commended to Burgheard [held] 3 acres of free land, and he could not sell the land nor give it. It is worth 18d. and 100 herrings. In "atheburgfelda" 6 free men commended to Burgheard [held] 60 acres. Then 2 ploughs, now $1\frac{1}{2}$. Then it was worth 10s., now 11s. 8d. and 900 herrings. [...] In Worlingham 5 free men and a half commended to Gyrth [held] 60 acres. Then as now 2 ploughs. 1 bordar. 2 acres of meadow. Then as now worth 10s. 6d. and 1000 herrings.

HUNDRED OF LOTHING.

In "Beketuna" 6 free men commended to Burgheard held 50 acres of land in demesne. Then 1 plough, now a half. Then it was worth 4s., now 21s. 4d. and 1500 herrings.

In Kessingland 1 free man commended to Eadric of Laxfield [held] 30 acres as a manor. Then as now 1 plough. 1 acre of meadow. Then it was worth 5s., now 8s. In the same place 4 free men,

[Folio 407v: SUFFOLK]

1 commended to Eadric and 3 commended to Burgheard TRE, [held] 90 acres. 2 bordars. Then as now 2 ploughs and 1 acre of meadow. Then it was worth 10s., now 22s. [and] 1000 herrings. In "Rodenhala" [in Pakefield] 1 free man, Aslak, commended to Burgheard [held] 40 acres as a manor. Then as now 4 bordars. Then as now 1 plough in demesne and half a plough belonging to the men. Woodland for 3 pigs. $1\frac{1}{2}$ acres of meadow. Then it was worth 5s., now 9s. and 600 herrings. The whole is [held] in demesne.

In "Wimundahala" 2 free men commended to Burgheard with 12 acres. Then as now half a plough. Then it was worth 2s., now 3s. and 500 herrings.

In Gisleham 2 free men under the same commendation with $1\frac{1}{2}$ acres, worth 2s. 6d. and 200 herrings. In the same place 1 free man under the same commendation with 6 acres and half a plough, worth 5s. and 300 herrings. [...] In "Hornes" 1 free man under commendation to Gyrth TR[E] [held] 5 acres, worth 3s. and 160 herrings.

In Carlton [Colville] 2 free men commended to Burgheard [held] 30 acres. Then as now 1 plough. It is worth 3s. [and] 400 herrings. In the same place 1 free man under the same commendation [held] 30 acres. Then 1 plough, now none. Half an acre of meadow. Then and now worth 5s. and 300 herrings.

In Kirkley 1 free man half under commendation to Burgheard and half to Wulfsige with 12 acres. Then half a plough, now none. Then worth 2s., now 3s. and 200 herrings.

In Rushmere 1 free man commended to Gyrth [held] 16 acres. Then 1 plough, now a half. It is worth 5s. and 300 herrings. Hugh holds the whole of this in his demesne. The fourth part of 1 church with 8 acres, worth 16d. The king and the earl have the soke. The Hundred testifies that Walter de Dol was seised of four of the above-mentioned men on the day when he forfeited. And afterwards Earl Hugh [held them]. Now Hugh de Montfort holds them but he does not hold them by livery, as the Hundred testifies. And Hugh de Montfort's men say that [W]alter himself held them from him.

Hugh de Montfort

[Folio 408: SUFFOLK]

HUNDRED OF HARTISMERE.

In Cotton 1 free man, Saxwine, commended to Burgheard [held] 20 acres TRE. Then 1 plough, now a half. Half an acre of meadow. Woodland for 2 pigs. It is in the valuation of the demesne of [Old] Newton.

In Wyverstone Hervey holds 2 free men commended to

Burgheard with 18 acres. Woodland for 2 pigs. It is worth 4s. 5[d.]

In "Caldecoten" he holds in demesne 1 free man with 2½ acres, worth 6d.

In Gislingham Gilbert holds 1 free woman commended to Guthmund with 15 acres and 1 acre of meadow, worth 2s. In "Caldecotan" 3½ acres in demesne, worth 6d.

HUNDRED OF LACKFORD.

Hugh de Beuerda holds [Great] Livermere holds from Hugh with 2 carucates of land as a manor. Guthmund held it TRE under St Æthelthryth and he could not sell it. Then as now 4 villans and 3 bordars. Then 3 slaves, now 1. Then 2 ploughs in demesne. Then and afterwards 2 ploughs belonging to the men, now 1; 4 acres of meadow. 1 fishery. Then as now 1 horse and 3 head of cattle. Then 10 pigs, now 3; 160 sheep, now 100. St Æthelthryth has the soke and sake. 3 free men commended to Guthmund, while the soke and sake belong to St Edmund, with 80 acres of land. St Edmund had half the commendation over one of them together with the land TRE. Between them all then as now 2 ploughs. 1 acre of meadow. The manor is worth 40s. and the free men 13s. It is 6 furlongs long and 4 broad. In geld 4d.

TWO HUNDREDS OF BABERGH.

holds Stanstead in demesne; Guthmund the thegn [held it] TRE as a manor with 5 carucates of land together with the soke. Then 4 villans, afterwards and now 3, and 10 bordars. Then and afterwards 10 slaves, now 6. Then 4 ploughs in demesne, afterwards and now 3. Then as now 2 ploughs belonging to the men. 16 acres of meadow. 1 mill. Woodland for 20 pigs. Then 3 horses, now 4. Then as now 16 head of cattle,

[Folio 408v: SUFFOLK]

60 pigs and 100 sheep. Then and afterwards worth £6, now it renders £12. It is 1 league long and 4 furlongs broad. In geld 7½d., whoever holds [land] there. A church with 25 acres of free land.

HUNDRED OF STOW.

Guthmund held Haughley under King Edward as a manor with 8 carucates of land together with the soke and sake over the hall demesne only. Then 32 villans, afterwards and now 30, and 8 bordars. Then 10 slaves, afterwards 6 and now 3. Then as now 4 ploughs in demesne. Then and afterwards 24 ploughs belonging to the men, now 8. Woodland for 200 pigs. 42 acres of meadow. A church with 31 acres of free land and half an acre of meadow. Then as now 6 horses at the hall. 18 head of cattle and 80 pigs; 96 sheep and 80 goats. In demesne 6 sokemen belonging to the same Guthmund, over whom the soke is in the Hundred and they could not sell the land. Then as now half a carucate of land and 20 acres. Then and afterwards 2 ploughs, now none. Then the whole was worth £16, afterwards £12, now £20. Of this manor Hervey holds 1 carucate and 30 acres, worth 63s. Ralph [holds] 1 carucate, worth 20s. Turold [holds] 1 carucate, worth 30s. Pesserera [holds] half a carucate, worth 10s. Robert [holds] 20 acres, worth 5s. Richard [holds] 30 acres, worth 5s. The whole is in

the valuation of the manor. It is 1 league long and a half broad. In geld 17d.

In Dagworth Hugh holds in demesne 7 free men which Guthmund, Hugh's predecessor, held by commendation only, with 2 carucates of land in the soke of the king and the earl and under them are 17 bordars. Then and afterwards 5 ploughs between them all, now 4. Woodland for 12 pigs. 8 acres of meadow. Then and afterwards worth 45s. and now 45s.

In the same Dagworth he holds in demesne 6 sokemen belonging to Thorney, the king's manor of the kingdom with every customary due. And they have between them all 1 carucate of land. 4 bordars. Then and afterwards 3 ploughs, now 2; 5 acres of meadow. Then and afterwards worth 30s., now 20s. . And these 6 sokemen Hugh claims by livery. Dagworth is 1 league [long] and a half

Hugh de Montfort

[Folio 409: SUFFOLK]

broad. In geld 30d., whoever holds [land] there.

In Wetherden [were] 17 free men by commendation only to Guthmund, the predecessor of Hugh. They had 2 carucates of land in the soke of the king and the earl. Then 10 bordars and always. Then 5 ploughs, afterwards 4, now 5 between them all. Woodland for 4 pigs and 6 acres of meadow. . Then and afterwards worth 50s., now 40s. It is 1 league long and a half broad. In geld 25d., whoever holds [land] there.

In "Eruestuna" 10 free men by commendation only to Guthmund, the predecessor [...] of Hugh, [held] half a carucate of land in the soke of the king and the earl. 2 bordars. Then and afterwards 3 ploughs between them. Now they have scarcely 1 plough. 4 acres of meadow. Then and afterwards it was worth 20s., now 10s. [...] A church with 10 acres of free land. It is 10 furlongs long and 6 broad. In geld 10d., whoever holds [land] there.

In "Torpe" 16 free men by commendation only to the predecessor [of Hugh], [held] 1 carucate of land in the sake of the king and the earl. 2 bordars under them. Then and afterwards 3 ploughs between them all, now 1; 3 acres of meadow. Then and afterwards it was worth 30s., now it is scarcely worth 10s. It is 5 furlongs long and 3 broad. In geld 8d., whoever holds [land] there.

In "Ultuna" 3 free men by commendation only to the same Guthmund [held] half a carucate of land and 13 acres in the soke of the king and the earl. Then and afterwards 3 bordars, now 1. Then as now 1 plough. 4 acres of meadow. 1 mill, but the count of Mortain claims half and the Hundred testifies to this. Then and afterwards worth 12s., and now the same.

In Chilton and in "Torstuna" Hugh holds in demesne by livery, so he says, 16 sokemen who belonged to King Edward's manor of Thorney with every customary due, as the Hundred testifies. They have 1 carucate of land and 7 bordars. Then and afterwards 4 ploughs between them all, now 3; 6 acres of meadow. Then and afterwards worth 50s., now 30s. The whole is 4 furlongs long and 3 broad. In geld 8d. And all these free men were delivered with the soke so all Hugh's men say as 2 manors with 5 carucates of land.

[Folio 409v: SUFFOLK]

In Dagworth Breme, a free man of King Edward's who was killed at the Battle of Hastings, held. He had 1½ carucates of land but it was delivered to Hugh as half a carucate by exchange. And the soke is the king's and the earl's. Then as now 11 bordars and 3 slaves. Then and always 2 ploughs in demesne. Then and afterwards 2 ploughs belonging to the men, now 1. Woodland for 60 pigs. 9 acres of meadow. 1 mill. 1 church without land and half a church with 30 acres of land and then 1½ acres of meadow. Then 13 head of cattle, now 10, and 12 pigs; 16 sheep and 40 goats. Then as now worth 60s. In the same manor 1 free man of Breme, by commendation only. He has 11½ acres. 1 bordar. Then and afterwards half a plough, now none. It is worth 3s. William fitzGross holds this manor from Hugh de Montfort.

In [Old] Newton Alwine of Mendlesham held 1 free man with half a carucate of land. Now Hugh holds it by exchange. Under him 2 bordars. Then as now 1 plough. 1½ acres of meadow. Now 40 sheep and 3 pigs. Then as now worth 40s. [...] In the same place Hugh holds in demesne by livery by exchange 2 free men over whom the soke was in the Hundred. They have 27 acres. Then as now half a plough. It is worth 5s. In Dagworth Hugh holds a half free man with 20 acres, worth 3s. [...] In Thorney Roger de Candos holds 1 carucate of land from Hugh which was in the demesne manor in the king's soke TRE but it was delivered as 1 carucate of land. Ralph the staller had this in pledge from the sheriff, Toli, as the Hundred heard say but it has not seen the writs nor the livery officer. He held it on the day on which King Edward died and afterwards Ralph his son [held it]. He has 4 villans and 3 bordars and 2 slaves. Then 2 ploughs in demesne, now 1. Then as now 2 ploughs belonging to the men. 4 acres of meadow. 1 mill.

Hugh de Montfort

[Folio 410: SUFFOLK]

Woodland for 4 pigs. Now 10 pigs and 30 sheep. Then as now worth 60s. And in the same place the same person holds 2 free men with 20 acres. Then and afterwards 1 plough, now a half. It is worth 40d. This is by exchange.

HUNDRED OF THEDWESTY.

In Beyton 1 free man of Eadgifu the Rich held 40 acres of land TRE. Now Hugh de Montfort holds it by exchange. Then as now half a plough. It is worth 5s.

HALF-HUNDRED OF IPSWICH.

In the borough [Ipswich] Hugh has in demesne 1 messuage and it belongs in Nacton. The king has all the customary dues.

HUNDRED OF BOSMERE.

Roger de Candos holds BATTISFORD from Hugh which Ælfric, a free man, held TRE as a manor with 1 carucate of land. Then as now 8 bordars. Then 2 ploughs in demesne, now 1. Half a plough belonging to the men. 6 acres of meadow. Woodland for 20 pigs. Half a church with 20

acres. Now 1 horse, 4 head of cattle, 12 pigs, 21 sheep and 4 goats. It is worth 30s. To this manor Hugh added 5 free men [...] with 1 carucate of land and 10 acres. 3 bordars. Then 3 ploughs, now 1[...]½ ploughs. 6 acres of meadow. Woodland for 5 pigs. It is worth 20s. This [...] is by exchange from the land of St Augustine. Roger de Candos [...] holds it. The king and the earl have the soke. It is 10 furlongs long and 5 [...] broad. Others hold [land] there. 10d. in geld. In Darms[...]den Wulfric, 1 free man by commendation, TRE [held] 18 acres and [...] half a plough, worth 2s. 7d.

HUNDRED OF CLAYDON.

In Westerfield Hugh holds in demesne a free man whom Ordric held with 8 acres, worth 16d. In [Earl] Soham 2 acres of land in demesne, worth 4d.

[Folio 410v: SUFFOLK]

HUNDRED OF HARTISMERE.

Guthmund held Occold from his brother Wulfric, Abbot of Ely, with 1 carucate of land and 40 acres as a manor. Now Roger de Candos holds it from Hugh. Then as now 5 villans and 8 bordars. Then 2 slaves. Then and afterwards 2 ploughs in demesne, now 1. Then 2 ploughs belonging to the men, afterwards and now 1½; 3 acres of meadow. Woodland for 40 pigs. A church with 8 acres and half a plough. Then as now 1 horse. Then 8 head of cattle. Then 60 pigs, now 13. Then 40 sheep, now 28; and 21 goats. Then it was worth 60s., afterwards £4, now 100s. And to this manor have been added 8 free men with 40 acres. Then and afterwards 2 ploughs, now 1½. A church with 12 acres, worth 10s. Guthmund had the soke over the whole. It is 10 furlongs long and 8 broad. 9d. in geld.

[Folio 411: SUFFOLK]

Lands of Geoffrey de Mandeville.

HUNDRED OF STOW.

In Creeting [St Peter] Wihtgar, a free man of the bishop of Ely by commendation only, held TRE 2 carucates of land in the soke of the king and the earl. Geoffrey has it as a manor by the king's gift and under him William de Bouville. But it did not belong to the fief of Esger, the predecessor of Geoffrey. Then as now 6 bordars. Then as now 2 ploughs in demesne. Then and afterwards half a plough belonging to the men, now none. 5 acres of meadow. The fourth part of a mill and half of another mill. Then as now 2 horses at the hall and 5 head of cattle and 8 pigs. Then 20 sheep, now 30. Then as now worth 35 . And in the same place 5 free men of the same Wihtgar, by commendation only, [held] 9 acres of land in the soke of the king and the earl. Half a plough. It is worth 2s. [...] In the same manor 1 free man of Eadric, the predecessor of Robert Malet, by commendation only. Now William de Bouville holds it under Geoffrey. He has 16 acres. 1 bordar and half a plough. 1 acre of meadow. It is worth 36d.

HUNDRED OF CLAYDON.

In Westerfield Langfer, a free man commended to Halfdan, held 14 acres, worth 2s. The same William [holds it]. The king and the earl have the soke. [...]

HUNDRED and a half of SAMFORD.

Esger held Holton [St Mary] TRE with 2 carucates of land as a manor. Then as now 13 villans and 2 bordars. Then 4 slaves, now 3. Then as now 2 ploughs in demesne. Then 5 ploughs belonging to the men, now 3; 24 acres of meadow. A church. Then 2 horses, now 1; 2 head of cattle. Then 12 pigs, now 6. Then 60 sheep, now 74. Then it was worth 60s., now 40s. It is 6 furlongs long and 4 broad. 7d. in geld. The same Esger has the soke.

Esger held Raydon with 2 carucates of land as a manor TRE. Then as now 8 villans and 3 bordars. 3 slaves. 2 ploughs in demesne. Then 7 ploughs belonging to the men, now 4; 6 acres of meadow. Woodland for 16 pigs. Then 2 horses,

[Folio 411v: SUFFOLK]

now 1. Then as now 5 head of cattle; 12 pigs. Then 30 sheep, now 50. Then as now worth £8. [It is held] in demesne. Of the same land Alvred holds 1 villan with 30 acres, worth 5s. Esger had the soke. Of the same land Gilbert the priest holds 1 villan with 30 acres and half a plough, worth 5s.

In Belstead Ulf, a free man commended to Esger, held TRE and still holds 80 acres. Then as now 1 villan and 2 bordars. Then 1 plough, now a half. 2 acres of meadow. Then 1 mill. The fourth part of a church. Then it was worth 10s., now 7s. The soke is in [East] Bergholt.

Rainalm holds Stutton from Geoffrey which Fridebern, a thegn of the king, held TRE with 2 [carucates] of land as a manor. Then as now 2 villans and 10 bordars. Then 2 slaves, now [...]. Then as now 1 plough in demesne and 1 plough belonging to the men. 4 acres of meadow. The third part of a church with 15 acres. Now 7 head of cattle. Then 2 pigs, now 13; 60 sheep. 1 salt-pan. 2 beehives. It is worth s. It is 6 furlongs long and 4 broad. 4d. in geld. The same Fridebern had the soke.

In Ipswich 1 messuage. It belongs in Moze [Essex].

In Raydon Edwin and Beorhtmær, free men commended to Esger TRE, [held] and half a plough. It is worth 5s. The soke is in [East] Bergholt.

HUNDRED OF WILFORD.

In Charsfield 1 free woman, Leofgifu, commended to Halfdan TRE, [held] 30 acres and 2 bordars. Then as now 1 plough. 2 acres of meadow. Then and always worth 10s. In the same place 1 free man commended to the same person [held] 11 acres, worth 2s.

In Debach 1 free man commended to someone commended to Ralph the staller [held] 6 acres, worth 12d. In Boulge 1 free man commended to Halfdan [held] 16 acres. Then 1 plough, now 2 oxen. It is worth 2s. In the same place 1 free man commended

Geoffrey de Mandeville

[Folio 412: SUFFOLK]

to Halfdan and Wulfric, with 6 acres, worth 12d.

In Wickam [Market] 1 free man commended to Halfdan with 3 acres, worth 6d.

In Melton 2 free men commended to Halfdan with 4 acres, worth 8d. William fitzSaxwalo holds this from Geoffrey de Mandeville.

HUNDRED OF LOOSE.

Halfdan, to Harold, held

Letheringham TRE with 80 acres as a manor. Then 5 bordars, now 10. Then 1 slave, now 2. Then as now in demesne 2 ploughs and 2 ploughs belonging to the men. Woodland for 4 pigs. 6 acres of meadow. 1 mill. Then as now 2 horses, 6 head of cattle, 30 pigs, 80 goats and 5 beehives. 1 church with 20 acres, worth 40d. Then it was worth 20s., now the same.

In the same place 13 free men and 2 half free men under the same commendation, apart from 6 who were commended to St Æthelthryth, [held] 60 acres. Then as now 4 ploughs. 2 acres of meadow. Then it was worth 17s., now the same. Also in the same place 1 free man commended half to St Æthelthryth and half to Halfdan [held] 60 acres as a manor and 2 bordars. 1 plough. 4 acres of meadow. Then as now worth 20s.

In Woodbridge 2 free men commended to the same Halfdan with 33 acres and half a plough and 1 bordar, worth 3s. The same William holds this from Geoffrey de Mandeville.

HUNDRED OF WANGFORD.

Halfdan, a free man commended to Harold, held Shadingfield with 1 carucate of land as a manor. Then as now 1 villan and 10 bordars. Then in demesne 2 ploughs, now 2. Then as now 1 plough belonging to the men. 4 acres of meadow. Woodland for 20 pigs. 1 horse, 11 pigs, 80 sheep and 2 beehives. Then it was worth 10s., now 20s. In the same place 1 free man commended to Bishop Stigand [held] 1 carucate of land as a manor. Then 1 villan, now the same. Then 5 bordars, now 4. Then in demesne 1 plough. Then 2 ploughs belonging to the men, now 1. Then it was worth 20s., now the same. This man was adjudged and seised to the king's use and afterwards Waleran was seised of him and gave a pledge thereon. Also in the same place 2 free men commended to Halfdan [held] 32½ acres as a manor. Then as now

[Folio 412v: SUFFOLK]

half a plough. It is worth 5s. 8d.

In Weston 1 free man with 5 acres, worth 16d. In "Wichedis" 1 free man with 1 acre, worth 4d.

HUNDRED OF BLYTHING.

Halfdan held Thorington TRE with 3 carucates of land as a manor. Then 8 bordars, now 13. Then 2 slaves. Then 2 ploughs in demesne, now 3. Then as now 3 ploughs belonging to the men. Woodland for 20 pigs. 7 acres of meadow. Then 1 horse, now 2. And now 14 pigs. Then 72 sheep, now 92. Now 4 beehives. 15 goats. 1 mill. 1 church with 8 acres. Then it was worth 40s., now 60s. William de Bouville holds it from Geoffrey de Mandeville and it does not belong to the honour of Esger.

To this manor belong 2 free men with 120 acres of land. 2 bordars. 4 acres of meadow. Then 2 ploughs in demesne, now none. Then it was worth 1 mark, now 8s. This land is 1½ leagues long and 1½ leagues broad. It renders 7½d. in geld.

In Covehithe 20 acres of land which 1 free man held TRE from Stigand. Now William de Bouville holds it from Geoffrey de Mandeville. Then as now half a plough. It is worth 4s.

HUNDRED OF CARLFORD.

In Thorpe Halfdan, a free man, held TRE 3 carucates of land as a manor. Then as now 4 villans and 11 bordars. Then 2 slaves, now 1. Then in demesne 2 ploughs. Then 2 ploughs belonging to the men, now 1; 7 acres of meadow. 2 horses and 7 head of cattle and 12 pigs and 100 sheep. Then it was worth 20s., now 40s. It is 8 furlongs long and 6 broad. 15d. in geld. Others hold [land] there.

In Burgh 8 free men commended to the same Halfdan [held] 54 acres. Then as now 2 ploughs. 2 acres of meadow. It is worth 10s.

In Grundisburgh 4 free men commended to Halfdan TRE with 26 acres

Geoffrey de Mandeville

[Folio 413: SUFFOLK]

of land and 1 plough. Half an acre of meadow. It is worth 4s. In the same place 1 free man, Almær commended to Æthelric of Burgh, with 8 acres and half an acre of meadow, worth 16d.

In Hasketon 3 half [free] men and 1 whole [free man] commended to Halfdan TRE with 22 acres of land and 1 plough and half an acre of meadow, worth 3s.

In "Neckemara" 2 free men commended to Halfdan with 20 acres and half a plough and half an acre of meadow, worth 2s. In "Ingoluestuna" 1 free man, Godric, commended half to Halfdan and half to St Æthelthryth, with 20 acres of land and 2 acres of meadow, worth 2s.

In Isleton 1 sokeman of Halfdan with 15 acres and 1 bordar. Then 1 plough, now 1 ox. 1 acre of meadow. It is worth 2s. In Burgh 3 free men TRE commended to Halfdan [held] 50 acres of land. Then 2 ploughs, now 1; 1½ acres of meadow. It is worth 10s. In the same place 1 free man, Beorhtric, commended to Æthelric of Burgh, [held] 10 acres, worth 20d. Also in the same place 1 free man, Beorhtweald Moufle, commended half to the predecessor of Hervey de Berry and half to the predecessor of Robert Malet, [held] 24 acres. Then 1 plough, now none. 1 acre of meadow. It is worth 5s. It is 9 furlongs long and 7 broad. 15d. in geld. Others hold [land] there. In Culpho 3 free men 2 commended to Halfdan and the third commended to St Æthelthryth [held] 30 acres of land. 1 bordar. Then 2 ploughs, now none. 2 acres of meadow. It is worth 5s.

In "Hobbestuna" 1 free man commended to St

Æthelthryth and his wife commended to Halfdan TRE [held] 30 acres. Then 1 plough, now none. 1 acre of meadow. Then as now worth 5s. In the same place 1 sokeman, Topi, commended to St Æthelthryth, with 15 acres, worth 3s. In "Finlesforda" Halfdan [] 2 acres TRE, worth 4d. William fitzSaxwalo de Bouville holds all this from Geoffrey de Mandeville. St Æthelthryth has the whole soke of this Hundred.

[Folio 413v: SUFFOLK]

XXXIII. Lands of Ralph Baynard.

HUNDRED OF RISBRIDGE.

Æthelgyth held Kedington TRE as a manor with 5 carucates of land. Then and afterwards 13 villans, now 11. Then and afterwards 1 bordar, now 2. Then and afterwards 9 slaves, now none. Then and afterwards 3 ploughs in demesne, now 2. Then and afterwards 8 ploughs belonging to the men, now 2½; 20 acres of meadow. Then 1 mill. Then 4 horses, now 3. Then 15 head of cattle, now 4. Then 27 pigs, now 18. Then 52 sheep, now 150. Now 6 beehives. Then it was worth £6, now £7 5s.

In the same place 25 free men [held] 2 carucates of land. 5 bordars and 2 slaves. Then as now 11 ploughs and 6 acres of meadow. It is worth 40s. His predecessor had the commendation and the soke and sake, apart from the 6 forfeitures of St Edmund. Over one of them the predecessor of Richard, son of Count Gilbert, had the commendation, but Baynard claims the whole by exchange. A church with 40 acres of free land and 1½ acres of meadow. It is worth 6s. It is 12 furlongs long and 6 broad. 12d. in geld. Others hold [land] there.

In Poslingford 3 free men. Over two of these his predecessor had the commendation TRE and the soke and sake apart from the 6 forfeitures of St Edmund. And the same St Edmund had the commendation over the third TRE. The king granted the land to him; we have seen the writ about this. They have 1 carucate of land and 20 acres and 7 bordars. 1½ ploughs. Woodland for 5 pigs. Then as now worth 31s. In the same place 1 free man with 1½ carucates of land. Then as now 6 bordars and 1 plough in demesne. Norigaud holds this. Then 2 horses and now the same. 6 head of cattle and 16 pigs. 20 sheep. Then it was worth 20s., now 25s. In the same place 1 free man with 1½ carucates of land. 3 bordars. 1½ ploughs. 4 acres of meadow. Now 2 horses and 4 head of cattle and 20 pigs and 29 sheep. Walter holds this. It is worth 30s. In the same place 2 free men with 160 acres and 8 bordars and 1 plough, worth 26s. 8d.

Ralph Baynard

[Folio 414: SUFFOLK]

Richer holds this. A church with 40 acres of free land, worth 6s. St Edmund has the 6 forfeitures. Baynard has the soke. It is 13 furlongs long and 12 broad. 15d. in geld. Others hold [land] there. This is by exchange.

Godwine, a thegn, held Wixoe TRE as a manor with 3 carucates of land and 15 acres. Then as now 6 villans. Then 4 bordars, now 5. Then 6 slaves, now 4. Then and afterwards 3 ploughs in demesne, now 2. Then as now 2½ ploughs belonging to the men. Woodland for 10 pigs. 12 acres of meadow. Then as now 1 mill. Then 2 horses. Then 24 head of cattle, now 12. Then 40 pigs, now 12. Then 60 sheep, now 40; 5 beehives. A church with 5 acres. 2 free men with 25 acres. 1 plough. 1 acre of meadow. His predecessor had the commendation and soke. St Edmund had the 6 forfeitures. Then and afterwards worth 83s., and now the same. It is half a league long and 3½ furlongs broad. 3d. in geld. Others hold [land] there.

HUNDRED OF BLYTHING.

Thorth held Reydon with 5 carucates of land. Then and afterwards 14 villans, now 5. Then and afterwards 16 bordars, now 20. Then 2 slaves, now 1. Then and afterwards 3 ploughs in demesne, now 2. Then and afterwards 11 ploughs belonging to the men, now 7. Woodland for 60 pigs. Then 2 horses, now 1. Then 12 head of cattle, now 5. Then 40 pigs, now 30. Then as now 110 sheep; now 15 goats. Then it was worth 100s., now £7 10s. In the same place 30 free men with 2 carucates of land and 5 acres. 2 bordars. Then and afterwards 8 ploughs, now 6. It is worth £12 10s. Over these his predecessor had the commendation and the soke and sake TRE. In the same place 2 free men by commendation [held] 16 acres and half a plough, worth 10s. The king and the earl have the soke. This is by exchange. It is 1 league and 3 furlongs long and 1 league and 3 perches broad. 6½d. in geld. 2 churches with 1 carucate of land. It is worth 10s.

In Brampton 11 free men by commendation TRE, now 10, with 2 carucates of land

[Folio 414V: SUFFOLK]

and 60 acres. Then 2 villans, now 1. Then 8 bordars, now 17. Then 9 ploughs, now 7. Woodland for 20 pigs. 2 acres of meadow. Then it was worth 30s., now 40s. The king and the earl have the soke by exchange. In the same place 1 sokeman with 2 carucates of land. 2 villans and 8 bordars. 3 ploughs. Woodland for 3 pigs. 2 acres of meadow. It is worth 30s. A church with 16 acres, worth 16d. The king and the earl have the soke.

Thorth held Frostenden as a manor with 3 carucates of land TRE. Then as now 10 villans. Then 14 bordars, now 20. Then 2 slaves. Then as now 2 ploughs in demesne. Then as now 1 seaport. Then and afterwards 9 ploughs belonging to the men, now 7. Woodland for 40 pigs. Then 1 none. 3 acres of meadow. Then 2 horses, now 1. Then 10 head of cattle, now 6. Then 60 pigs, now 13; 60 sheep and 24 goats. 2 beehives. Then as now worth £4. The king and the earl have the soke the 6 forfeitures. In the same place 8 free men TRE, now 3, with 113 acres. Then 3 ploughs, now 1. Half an acre of meadow. Then it was worth 10s., now 14s. [This is] by exchange. The king and the earl have the soke. 1 league and 24 perches long and 10 furlongs and 7 perches broad. 4d. in geld. Ralph holds it. 2 churches with 28 acres and , worth 3s.

Thorth held Wangford as a manor TRE with 2 carucates of land. Then as now 8 villans. Then and afterwards 13 bordars, now 21. Then 2 slaves. Then as now 2 ploughs in demesne. Then 8 ploughs belonging to the men, now 7. Woodland for 60 pigs. 2 acres of meadow. Then as now 1 mill. Then 1 salt-pan. Then 2 horses. Then 24 head of cattle, now 17. Then 35 pigs,

now 17. Then 100 sheep, now 80 and 8 goats. 5 beehives. Albold holds it. Then as now worth £4. 1 league and 1 furlong long and 9 furlongs broad. 7d. in geld. Others hold [land] there. The king and the earl have the 6 forfeitures.

In Henham 1 free man, Alwine by commendation [held] 1 carucate of land as a manor. Then as now 4 villans. Then 11 bordars, now 14. Then 2 ploughs in demesne, afterwards 1, now 2. Then and afterwards 5 ploughs belonging to the men, now 3. Woodland for 40 pigs. Half an acre of meadow.

Ralph Baynard

[Folio 415: SUFFOLK]

Then as now 1 mill. Now 1 horse and 8 head of cattle. Then 4 pigs, now 14. Then 20 sheep, now 40. Then as now 16 goats. Now 4 beehives. Then as now worth 40s. The king and the earl have the soke. Robert of Blythburgh holds this. This is by exchange.

HUNDRED OF BLYTHING.

Thorth held Ubbeston TRE as a manor with 3 carucates of land. Then 15 villans, afterwards 7, now 3. Then and afterwards 9 ploughs belonging to the men, now 10. Woodland for 160 pigs. 7 acres of meadow. Then 1 horse, now 2. Then 16 head of cattle, now 19. Then as now 30 pigs. Then 12 sheep, now 92. Then as now worth 100s. In this manor belong 3 free men with 42 acres and 1 bordar and 1 plough. Woodland for 16 pigs. 1 acre of meadow. TRE it was worth 6s. 8d., now 8s. 1 church with 3 acres, worth 3d. The whole of this land is 7 furlongs long and 4 broad. It renders 3d. of the king's geld.

In Cratfield Thorth held TRE 3½ carucates of land as a manor. Then as now 5 villans. Then and afterwards 9 bordars and now 31. Then as now 1 slave. Then as now in demesne 2 ploughs. Then 7 ploughs belonging to the men, now 10. Woodland for 250 pigs. 3½ acres of meadow. Then and now 1 horse. Then 8 head of cattle, now 14. Then 40 pigs, now 47. Then 26 goats, now 32. 1 church with 6 acres, worth 6d. Then as now worth £4. To this manor belong 5 free men with 26 acres. Then as now 2 ploughs. Woodland for 6 pigs. It is worth 6s. 8d. And these men render soke to this manor. In addition 2 men with 40 acres and 1 plough, worth 5s. The soke over these two men is in Blythburgh. And William Baynard holds these 2 manors from Ralph, his uncle. In the same vill a certain free man holds a manor with 40 acres and 3 bordars. Then as now 1 plough. Woodland for 6 pigs. 1½ acres of meadow. TRE it was worth 10s., now 20s. And this manor is in the demesne of Ralph. And the whole of this land is 8 furlongs long and 5 broad. It renders

[Folio 415V: SUFFOLK]

3½d. of the king's geld.

HUNDRED OF WANGFORD.

In Shadingfield 1 free man, Thorth, with 20 acres of land. Then 1 plough, now none. It is worth 3s.

HUNDRED OF THEDWESTRY.

In Stanningfield Alflæd, a free woman under St Edmund, held TRE 1 carucate of land. Now Baynard holds it by exchange. Then 1 bordar, now 3. Then 2 slaves, now 1. Then 2 ploughs in demesne, afterwards a half, now 1; 5 acres of meadow. Now 1 mill. Then it was worth 30s., now 40s. In the same place 3 free men commended to the same Alflæd [held] 30 acres of land in the soke of St Edmund. Then as now 1 plough. 1 acre of meadow. Then as now worth 5s.

TWO HUNDREDS OF BABERGH.

Æthelgyth, a free woman under the glorious King Edward, held Shimpling as a manor with 6½ carucates of land. Then 9 villans, now 12. Then 12 bordars, now 16. Then 3 slaves, now none. Then and afterwards 4 ploughs in demesne, now 3. Then 7 ploughs belonging to the men, now 6. Woodland for 100 pigs. 17 acres of meadow. Then 4 horses, now 5. Then 7 head of cattle, now 5. Then 60 pigs, now 33. Then 80 sheep, now 100. Then 16 goats, now 24. A church with 60 acres of free land. 1 bordar. 1 plough. Half an acre of meadow. Then it was worth £10, afterwards and now £12. It is 1 league long and a half broad. 15d. in geld. In the same vill 1 free man of Æthelgyth's by commendation and in the soke of St Edmund [held] 30 acres. 1 bordar. Then as now 1 plough. 1½ acres of meadow. Then as now worth 10s. Baynard holds this by exchange.

[Folio 416: SUFFOLK]

Lands of Ranulf Peverel.

HUNDRED OF LACKFORD.

In Icklingham Siward of Maldon held 3 carucates of land as a manor under King Edward but the soke and sake belonged to St Edmund. Then as now 6 villans. Then 2 bordars, now 1. Then and afterwards 4 slaves, now 3. Then as now 3 ploughs in demesne and 2 ploughs belonging to the men. 1 mill. Then 1 horse, now none. Then 3 head of cattle, now 2. Then 30 pigs, now 21. Then 250 sheep, now 350. Then and afterwards £4, now 100s. The soke is St Edmund's.

HUNDRED OF BABERGH.

Siward of Maldon, a thegn, held Acton TRE as a manor with 12 carucates of land, together with the soke and sake. Then as now 23 villans. Then as now 38 bordars. Then as now 17 slaves. Then 8 ploughs in demesne, afterwards and now 6. Then 20 ploughs belonging to the men, afterwards and now 14; 50 acres of meadow. Woodland for 40 pigs. Then and afterwards 2 mills, now 1. Then 8 horses at the hall, now 11. Then 34 head of cattle, now 31. Then 200 pigs, now 160. Then 300 sheep, now 423 sheep. Then 9 beehives, now 7. A church to which are attached 30 acres of free land. Then and afterwards worth £20, now £30. In Acton 4 free men whom Ralph acquired as an estate of 50 acres. In [Great and Little] Waldingfield 5 free men with 72 acres. In the other [Great and Little] Waldingfield 3 [free men] 50 acres. In "Honilega" 1 [free man] with 50 acres. In Manton 1 [free man] with 50

acres. Between them all they have 7 bordars. Then and afterwards 5 ploughs, now 4. These free [men] then and afterwards were worth £4, now 60s. Of all of these men, 11 could sell their lands and 4 could not but over all of them the predecessor of Ranulf had the commendation and sake, except over one who is in the soke of St Edmund. Ranulf acquired them all as an estate. Acton is 1 league long and 1 broad. In geld 13d.

The same Siward, Ranulf's predecessor, held Assington as a manor with 8 carucates of land together with

[Folio 416v: SUFFOLK]

the soke and sake TRE. Then and afterwards 14 villans, now 5. Then and afterwards 21 bordars, now 55. Then and afterwards 14 slaves, now 12. Then and afterwards 7 ploughs in demesne, now 6. Then and afterwards 13 ploughs belonging to the men, now 12. Woodland for 30 pigs. 15 acres of meadow. 1 mill. Then 6 horses at the hall, now 5. Then 24 head of cattle, now 23. Then 100 pigs, now 60. Then 210 sheep, now 90. Then 14 beehives, now 6. Now 12 goats. A church with 30 acres of free land. In the same place 5 free men under the commendation and soke of the same Siward. But they could not sell their land while remaining in the soke. They have between them all 30 acres of land. 1 acre of meadow. Then as now 1 plough. Also in the same place 1 free man delivered as an estate but he does not belong to the manor over which Ranulf's predecessor had commendation, together with the soke. He has 30 acres. Then as now 1 plough. Then it was worth £10 and afterwards £12, now £20. But it fell short of the render by 100s. Of these £20, 20s. are assessed upon these free men. It is 1 league long and 8 furlongs broad. In geld 7d.

In Glemsford Blæcwine, commended to Siward, held 30 acres as a manor TRE. It is worth 6s. Warin holds it. St Æthelthryth has the soke.

Leofstan holds and held LOOSE under the glorious King Edward with 1½ carucates of land as a manor. The soke over 1 carucate belongs to Trinity in Canterbury. Then as now 6 bordars. Then 2 slaves. Then as now 2 ploughs in demesne and none belonging to the men. 6 acres of meadow. Then 2 horses, now none. Then 10 head of cattle, now none. Then 30 pigs, now none. Then 64 sheep, now none. Then and afterwards worth 40s., and now [the same]. It is half a league long and 4 furlongs broad. In geld 1d.

HUNDRED OF STOW.

Ketil, a thegn of King Edward's, held Onehouse as 1½ carucates and 20 acres, together with the soke. Then as now 8 bordars and 4 slaves. Then and afterwards 3 ploughs in demesne, now 2. Then as now 1 plough belonging to the men. 12 acres of meadow. Woodland for 6 pigs. 1 horse and

Ranulf Peverel

[Folio 417: SUFFOLK]

6 head of cattle. Then 16 pigs, now 30. Then 40 sheep, now 87, and 22 goats. A church with 3 acres of free land. Then and

afterwards worth 40s., now 50s. It is 5 furlongs long and 3 broad. In geld 6½d.

In Onehouse belonged TRE 26 acres. Now Osbern Masculus holds them as belonging to the church of Stow. He held them before Ranulf had the manor of Onehouse.

HUNDRED OF BOSMERE.

Ralph de Savenay holds Burstall from Ranulf which Thorkil, a thegn, held TRE as a manor with 28 acres. Now 2 bordars. Then as now 1 plough in demesne. 2 acres of meadow. Then as now 1 horse. 1 ox. Now 9 pigs. Then 14 sheep, now 30. Then it was worth 5s. 4d., now 8s.

In [Great and Little] Bricett Ralph fitzBrian 1 free man who holds what Leofstan held TRE with 2 carucates of land and 4 acres as a manor. Then as now 1 villan and 10 bordars and 2 slaves. 3 ploughs in demesne and 6 acres of meadow. Woodland for 10 pigs. Then 2 ploughs belonging to the men, now 1. Of this land 54 acres belonging to a church; now Ralph fitzBrian holds them in his demesne. Then 2 horses, now 5. Then 10 head of cattle, now 15. Then 30 pigs, now 50. Then 80 sheep, now 140. In the same place 4 sokemen with 41 acres. Then 1½ ploughs, now 2 ploughs belonging to the men . The king and the earl have the soke. Then it was worth 60s., now 100s.

Humphrey fitzAubrey holds Coddenham he holds it from Ranulf which Leofric, a free man, held TRE with 60 acres as a manor. Then as now 3 bordars and 2 ploughs. 4 acres of meadow. Woodland for 60 pigs. A A part of three churches. 1 horse. Then 8 head of cattle, now 6. 14 pigs. 12 sheep. Then it was worth 20s., now 40s. A church with 3 acres, 6d.

In Mickfield Ralph de Savenay holds 12 acres. 3 bordars. Half a church with 2½ acres. It is in the valuation of Ulverston. The king and the earl have the soke over the whole. In [Earl and Little] Stonham the fourth part of a church with 7½ acres, worth 15d.

[Folio 417v: SUFFOLK]

HUNDRED OF CLAYDON.

Saxi held Debenham with 1 carucate of land as a manor and 22 acres. Of these 22 acres Robert Malet's predecessor had 8 acres TRE in the soke and commendation of the abbot. Then 4 villans, now 2. Then as now 19 bordars. Then 1 slave. Then as now 2 ploughs in demesne. The third part of the church of St Mary's with 10 acres. . Then and afterwards 3 ploughs belonging to the men, now 2; 4 acres of meadow. Then woodland for 100 pigs, now 40. Then 1 horse and 4 head of cattle. 40 pigs, now 28; 27 goats. Then 40 sheep, now 30; 30 acres of demesne land in Loose Hundred. Then it was worth 60s., now 50s. Ralph de Savenay holds it. The same Saxi held Ulverston in the same way as a manor with 1 carucate of land TRE. Then and afterwards 3 villans, now 1. Then and afterwards 9 bordars, now 14. Then and afterwards 2 ploughs in demesne, now 1. Then and afterwards 3 ploughs belonging to the men, now 2. Then 1 horse. Then 14 head of cattle. Then 60 pigs, now 22. Then 22 sheep, now 30. Then and afterwards worth 40s., now 30s. To this manor belonged 8 acres of demesne land TRE which the mother of Robert Malet now

holds. It is 1 league long and 7 furlongs broad. 26½d. in geld. Others hold [land] there.

HALF-HUNDRED OF COSFORD.

In Whatfield Leofstan held 20 acres, worth 20d. The soke is St Edmund's.

HUNDRED OF CARLFORD.

In Clopton [near Woodbridge] Eadric Grim, commended half to St Æthelthryth and half to Robert Malet's predecessor, held TRE 1 carucate of land and 42 acres. Then as now 2 villans and 13 bordars. Then in demesne 3 ploughs, now 2 but [another] can be there. Then 2 ploughs belonging to the men, now 1; 5 acres of meadow. Woodland for 10 pigs. 1 horse. Then 8 head of cattle, now 3. Now 30 pigs. Then 80 sheep, now 20. Then it was worth 60s., now 50s. Turold holds this from Ralph. 1 church with 15 acres from 4 demesnes, worth 2s.

HUNDRED OF WILFORD.

In Debach 15 acres. They belong to Clopton.

Ranulf Peverel

[Folio 418: SUFFOLK]

They are worth 3s.

HUNDRED OF HARTISMERE.

In "Tusemera" 1 carucate of land in the demesne of the Abbot of Ely which Saxi held TRE for his wages. Then and afterwards 1 plough, now none. Then it was worth 20s., now 10s. Ralph de Savenay holds it.

In Aspall 16 acres of demesne land and [they are] of Ulverston. 4 bordars. Half a plough. In the same place the third part of a church and the third part of a fair.

Lands of Aubrey de Vere.

TWO HUNDREDS OF BABERGH.

Wulfwine, a thegn of King Edward's, held Lavenham as a manor with 6 carucates of land, together with the sake and soke. Then and afterwards 11 villans, now 7. Then and afterwards 24 bordars, now 38. Then as now 6 slaves. Then as now 4 ploughs in demesne. Then and afterwards 9 ploughs belonging to the men, now 7; 10 acres of meadow. Woodland for 100 pigs. Then 5 horses at the hall, now 1. Then 24 head of cattle, now 25. Then 160 pigs, now 65. Then and always 200 sheep. Then 60 goats, now 80. Then 5 beehives, now 6; 1 arpent of vines. 1 sokeman who could not give or sell [his land], with 1 carucate of land. 5 bordars. Then as now 2 ploughs. Now 1 mill. 3 acres of meadow. Then and afterwards the whole was worth £10, now £15. It is 1 league long and a half broad. In geld 7½d.

[Folio 418v: SUFFOLK]

The same Wulfwine, Aubrey's predecessor, held [Great and Little] Waldingfield under King Edward as a manor with 2 carucates of land, together with the soke and sake. Then as now 4 villans. 10 bordars. 4 slaves. Then as now 2 ploughs in demesne. 2 ploughs belonging to the men. 4 acres of meadow. Woodland for 4 pigs. Then as now 1 horse at the hall. 3 head of cattle and 16 pigs. Then as now 100 sheep. Then as now worth £5. It is 12 furlongs long and 3 broad. In geld 6d.

HUNDRED OF SAMFORD.

Toki, a free man, by commendation only held Belstead with 80 acres as a manor. Then 2 villans; now 2 bordars. Then as now 1 plough. 2 acres of meadow. Then 1 mill. Then it was worth 16s., afterwards and now 15s. Fermeus holds it. The soke is in [East] Bergholt.

In the same place Thorgisl, a free man, by commendation only held 80 acres as a manor. Then as now 2 villans. 1 bordar. Then and afterwards 1 plough, now none. 2 acres of meadow. Then it was worth 16s., afterwards and now 15s. The soke is in [East] Bergholt. It is 5 furlongs long and 3 broad. 6½d. in geld. These two manors were adjudged from Ralph Taillebois and Fin into the king's hand. Later Aubrey received them without livery, as the reeve and the Hundred say.

In "Canapetuna" Brunwine, a sokeman from the king's manor of [East] Bergholt, held 4 acres, worth 12d.

HUNDRED OF HARTISMERE.

Wulfwine, a free man, held Burgate TRE as a manor with 5 carucates of land. Then as now 22 villans and 33 bordars. Then 4 slaves. Then as now 3 ploughs in demesne. Then and afterwards 15 ploughs [belonging to the men], now 10; 3½ acres of meadow. Then woodland for 100 pigs, now 40. Churches with 29 acres and half a plough. Then 7 head of cattle, now 12. Then 23 pigs, now 80. Then 63 sheep, now 176. Then 40 goats, now 57; 9 sokemen with 142 acres. 4 bordars. Then as now 5 ploughs. 3½ acres of meadow. Woodland for 6 pigs. The fourth part of a church with 1 acre. The whole was worth £16, now £19 4s. It is 1 league long

[Folio 419: SUFFOLK]

and 7 furlongs broad. 5d. in geld. Wulfwine had the soke. Adelelm holds the whole from Aubrey.

HALF-HUNDRED OF COSFORD.

Wulfwine held Aldham TRE as a manor with 5½ carucates of land. Then 7 villans, now 4. Then 6 slaves, now 2. Then 4 ploughs in demesne, now 3. Then 6 ploughs belonging to the men, now 4; 7 acres of meadow. Woodland for 8 pigs. Then as now 2 mills. 3 horses. Then 10 head of cattle, now 18. Then 80 pigs, now 60. Then 140 sheep, now 60. A church with 7 acres. Then it was worth £8, now £15. In the same place 1 free man by commendation only with 5 acres. The soke is St Edmund's. It is worth 10d. It is 8 furlongs long and 7 broad. 5d. in geld.

HUNDRED OF HARTISMERE.

In Burgate a free woman, Milde, and in Wortham 9 [sic] free men Bosi, Alwine, Godwine, Wulfgeat, Boti, Ordric, Stanheard, Godric, [...] In Thrandeston 2 free men, Fulcard, Alwine. In Mellis 4 free men and a half [free man] Leofric, Godric, Wulfweard, Leofwine Bynna, and Fulcard the half [free man]. In Thornham [Magna] 1 free man, Wulfmær. In

Ricckinghall [Superior] 1 free man, Beorhtmær. In Gislingham a free man, Eadric. In Wortham 1 free man, Colman. In Mellis, 1 free woman, Megenlioba. She had 14 acres of free land and TRE she had given that land to St Edmund. Altogether the others have 90 acres. Then as now 6½ ploughs. 1 acre of meadow. Then as now worth 60s. Adelelm holds the whole from Aubrey. Over these free men Aubrey's predecessor had the soke and commendation TRE.

In Gislingham 3 free men, Wulfmær, Leofstan, Leofcwen, [held] 23 acres and 1 plough, worth 4s. 8d. The same Adelelm holds it from Aubrey. [...]

[Folio 419v: SUFFOLK]

XXXVI. Lands of Robert Gernon.

HUNDRED AND A HALF OF SAMFORD.

Skalpi, a thegn of Harold's, held Churchford as a manor with 1 carucate of land TRE. Now William de Alno holds it from Robert. Then 6 villans, now 4. Then 4 bordars, now 3. Then 2 slaves, now 1. Then 2 ploughs in demesne, now 1. Then 1½ ploughs belonging to the men, now 1; 7 acres of meadow. Now 1 mill. Then 2 horses, 6 head of cattle, 140 sheep, now none. Then and afterwards worth 60s., now 40s. It is 6 furlongs long and 2 broad. 4d. in geld. Skalpi had the soke under Harold.

The same Skalpi held Stutton TRE with 2 carucates of land as a manor. Then 8 villans, now 5. Then 4 bordars, now 5. Then 6 slaves, now 3. Then and afterwards 2 ploughs in demesne, now 1. Then as now 2 ploughs belonging to the men. 5 acres of meadow. Woodland for 16 pigs. Then as now 1 mill. 2 salt-pans. Half a church with 15 acres. Then 2 horses. Then 16 head of cattle, now 2. Then 40 pigs, now 14. Then 190 sheep, now 35. Then and afterwards worth £6, now 60s. It is 6 furlongs long and 4 broad. 4d. in geld. The same William [holds it]. The soke [was held] in the same way.

In Brantham 1 free man, Mawa, by commendation only [held] 5½ acres, worth 12d. The same William [holds it]. Harold had the soke.

St Benedict of Ramsey held "Manesfort" in demesne TRE. Now the same William [holds it] as a manor with 1½ carucates of land. Then as now 2 villans. Then 4 bordars, now 5. Then and afterwards 2 ploughs in demesne, now 1. Then as now 1 plough belonging to the men. 3 acres of meadow. 1 mill. Then 2 horses. Then 5 head of cattle, now 3. Then 15 pigs, now 5. Then as now 30 sheep. Then and afterwards worth 40s., now 20s. It is 6 furlongs long and 3 broad. 3¼d. in geld. St Benedict had the soke.

Robert Gernon

[Folio 420: SUFFOLK]

In "Alfildestuna" Alwine, a free [man] commended to Ælfric, Robert's predecessor, held 30 acres of land as a manor TRE. Then as now half a plough. It is worth 4s. Harold had the soke. The same William [holds it].

Grim, a free man commended to Gyrth, held "Turchetlestuna" with 1 carucate of land as a manor TRE.

Then as now 2 villans and 2 bordars. Then and afterwards 1 plough, now none. 2 parts of a fishery. Then as now 1 plough belonging to the men. Then it was worth 40s., now 38s. The same William [holds it]. Robert claims this by exchange from the land of Hugh de Montfort. Harold had the soke.

The same Grim held Brantham with 60 acres as a manor TRE. Then as now 1 bordar. Then and afterwards half a plough, now 2 oxen. 1 acre of meadow. Then and afterwards worth 10s. 8d., now 5s. The same William [holds it]. Robert also claims this in the same way. Harold had the soke.

In Woolverstone Alfred, commended to Skalpi, held 80 acres as a manor TRE; now Robert [holds it] in demesne. Then as now 3 bordars. Then and afterwards 1 plough in demesne, now a half. 1 acre of meadow. Then it was worth 16s., now 10s.

In Tattingstone Trumwine and Wulfsige, free men by commendation, [held] 120 acres as 2 manors TRE. Then as now 1 bordar. Then and afterwards 2 ploughs, now 1; 2 acres of meadow. Then it was worth 10s., now 8s.

In Stutton Eadnoth, a free man, by commendation held 60 acres as a manor TRE. Then and afterwards 1 plough, now a half. 1 acre of meadow. Then it was worth 10s., now 8s.

In Brantham Tela, a free woman, by commendation [held] 30 acres as a manor TRE. Then and now 1 bordar and half a plough. 1 acre of meadow. Then and afterwards worth 5s., now 3s. 6½d. In Tattingstone Ælfric, a free man, by commendation held 30 acres as a manor and 2 bordars. Then and afterwards half a plough, now 2 oxen.

1 acre of meadow. Then it was worth 40d., now 42d.

In Harkstead Ælfric, a free man, by commendation [held] 30 acres as a manor TRE. Then and afterwards half a plough, now 2 oxen. Half an acre of meadow. Then it was worth 5s., now 42d.

In "Eduinestuna" Spieta, a free man, by commendation [held] 30 acres as a manor TRE. Then half a plough. Then it was worth 5s., now 42d. In this Hundred 7 free men have by commendation to Robert 120 acres in demesne. Then as now 3 ploughs. Then it was worth 20s., now 25s. Harold had the soke.

HUNDRED OF COSFORD.

In Layham 20 acres of the demesne of Churchford which Skalpi held, worth 3s. William de Alno holds it.

In Colneis Hundred 1 free man with 2 acres of free land, worth 4d. The same person holds it.

XXXVII. Land of Peter de Valognes.

HUNDRED OF BRADMERE.

Æthelstan, a thegn, held [Great] Fakenham as a manor with 5 carucates of land. Then as now 14 villans and 7 bordars and 10 slaves. Then as now 5 ploughs in demesne. 4 ploughs belonging to the men. 16 acres of meadow. Woodland for 8 pigs. Then as now 1 mill. Then 4 horses, now 3, and 16 wild horses. Then as now 12 head of cattle. Then 40 pigs, now 20. Then as now 300 sheep. 2 churches with 40 acres and 1 plough

and half an acre of meadow. To this manor belong 6 sokemen and a half with 30 acres. Then as now 1 plough. Then as now [worth] £13. It is 1 league long and 8

Peter de Valognes

furlongs broad. 2s. in geld. In the same place 20 free men over whom Æthelstan had commendation with 80 acres. Then as now 2 ploughs. 3 acres of meadow. It is worth 20s. He claims this by the king's gift.

In [Ixworth] Thorpe 1 free man, Spearhafoc, with 30 acres. This man belonged to Queen Edith and she gave him to Peter. After her death the king granted him to him, as his men say.

In Sapiston 3 free men with 13½ acres of land between them. Then as now 1 plough and 1 acre of meadow. This is by the king's gift. It is worth 5s.

In Barningham Æthelstan held 1 carucate of land as a manor. Then 5 villans, now 2, and 1 slave. Then as now 1 plough in demesne. Then half a plough belonging to the men, now 2 oxen. 2 acres of meadow. Then as now 1 horse. Then 30 sheep. It is worth 20s. 6 free men by fold-soke and commendation [held] 12 acres and half a plough, worth 5s.

In Wyken Æthelstan held TRE as a manor 1 carucate of land. Then as now 5 bordars. Then 2 slaves, now 1. Then 1 plough in demesne, now 2; 3 acres of meadow. Woodland for 8 pigs. 2 oxen belonging to the men. Now 1 horse. Then 3 head of cattle, now 11. Then 7 pigs, now 13. Then 40 sheep, now 100; 2 sokemen with 10 acres. Then as now 2 oxen. Then it was worth 20s., now 30s. In the same place 8 free men by commendation [held] 1 carucate of land and 11 bordars. Then as now 2 ploughs. 3 acres of meadow. Woodland for 2 pigs. Then it was worth 10s., now 20s. He has these men by livery and as an estate.

Auti [and] Ketil, free men and thegns, held Rushford TRE with 2 carucates of land. Then 2 ploughs in demesne and now. 4 acres of meadow. Now 1 horse. Then 1 ox, now 5. Then 11 sheep, now 80; 4 beehives. These men held this land TRE as two manors. Then as now worth 30s. In the same place 8 free men with 1 carucate of land and 9 acres by commendation. Over 7 they have fold-soke and commendation over one only. Then and afterwards 2 ploughs, now 1; 4 acres of meadow. It is worth 10s. It is 6 furlongs long and 3 broad. 11¼d. in geld. St Edmund has the soke over the whole Hundred.

HUNDRED OF HARTISMERE.

In Westhorpe 1 free man commended to Auti with 9 acres. Woodland for 2 pigs. It is worth 18d.

XXXVIII. Lands of Roger de Rames.

TWO HUNDREDS OF BABERGH.

In Bures Earl Ælfgar held 1 carucate of land. Now Roger [holds it]. 1 villan and 3 bordars and 1 slave. 1 plough in demesne. 1 plough belonging to the men. 2 acres of meadow.

Then half a mill, now none. Then as now 1 horse, 30 pigs, 100 sheep. It is worth 20s.

In "Linhou" Wulfric held 30 acres under Ælfric Cempa TRE and they could sell. 4 bordars and 3 oxen. It is worth 18s. St Edmund has the soke and sake.

HALF-HUNDRED OF IPSWICH.

In the town of Ipswich Roger has 1 church, St George's, and 4 burgesses and 6 messuages lying waste. One of these was claimed for the use of the Abbot of Ely and he was seised thereof, as the Hundred testifies. But Roger says that he holds it from the king. To the aforesaid church belongs 1 acre of land. The whole is worth 10s. The king has the customary dues.

HUNDRED OF BOSMERE.

In Crowfield Eadric, a free man, held TRE 20 acres. Then 1 plough, and now. Then 4 horses, now none. Then 2 head of cattle. Then 12 pigs and 5 sheep, now altogether nothing. Then as now worth 40d. In the same place Wighulf, a free man, held TRE 35 acres which that Eadric held with his land when it was delivered to Roger. Then as now 4 bordars. Woodland for 10 pigs. 2 acres of meadow. It is worth 8s.

Roger de Rames

[Folio 422: SUFFOLK]

In Coddenham 3 free men with 30 acres and 1 bordar. Then and afterwards 1 plough, now a half. $1\frac{1}{2}$ acres of meadow. Then it was worth 6s., now 5s. The fourth part of a church and the fourth part of what belongs to the church. Warenger held this land from Roger but he himself disseised him. The king and the earl have the soke over the whole.

1 free man, Æthelmær, held Stonham [Aspal] TRE by commendation only under Eadric, Robert Malet's predecessor, with 60 acres as a manor. Then as now 1 bordar. Then and afterwards 1 plough, now none. 2 acres of meadow. Woodland for 30 pigs. A church with 14 acres. Then it was worth 20s., now 15s.

In the same place 1 free man, Alwine, in the king's soke, [held] 90 acres as a manor. Then as now 1 villan and 1 bordar. Then 2 ploughs in demesne, now 1; 4 acres of meadow. Woodland for 20 pigs. Then it was worth 40s., now 25s. The king and the earl have the soke.

In the same place a free man with 60 acres. 1 bordar. 1 villan. Then and afterwards 1 plough, now a half. Then 1 plough belonging to the men, now a half. 1 acre of meadow. Woodland for 20 pigs. Then it was worth 20s., now 15s. The king and the earl have the soke. In the same place a free man with 30 acres and 1 bordar. Then and afterwards 1 plough, now a half. Woodland for 10 pigs. Then it was worth 10s., now 5s. The king and the earl have the soke. In the same place 8 free men with 30 acres. Two of these were commended to a certain man commended to Robert Malet's predecessor and William his father was seised thereof. Between them all they have 1 plough. It is worth 5s. Miles holds all this from Roger. He acquired 4 horses, now 1. Then 3 head of cattle, now 3. Then 14 pigs, now 36. Then 36 sheep, now none. It is half a

league long and a half broad. 6d. in geld. Others hold [land] there. The king and the earl have the soke.

In the same place Roger has Stonham [Aspal] in his demesne. 12 free men with 40 acres in the soke of the king and the earl. Then and afterwards 2 ploughs, now $1\frac{1}{2}$ ploughs. 1 acre of meadow.

[Folio 422v: SUFFOLK]

It is worth 15s.

In [Great and Little] Bricett Ansketil holds 1 carucate of land as a manor from Roger, in the soke of the king and the earl. Godwine, a free man, held it TRE. Then 2 bordars, now 5. A church with 15 acres. Then as now 1 plough in demesne. Now 2 oxen belonging to the men. 2 acres of meadow. 42 sheep and 15 pigs. Then it was worth 20s., now 25s. The whole is 1 league long and a half broad. $6\frac{1}{2}$d. in geld. Others hold [land] there.

In "Langhedana" Roger's daughter holds 1 free man with 9 acres, worth 18d. In Coddenham 1 free man, Alwine, with 1 acre, worth 2d. In the same place 4 acres of demesne land [...] and they have been assessed.

HUNDRED OF CLAYDON.

Godwine the priest, a free man, held Akenham TRE with 1 carucate of land and 20 acres as a manor. Now Roger's daughter [holds it]. Then in demesne 2 ploughs, now 3; 4 acres of meadow. 2 horses, 7 head of cattle, 6 pigs. .Then it was worth 24s. and now likewise. In the same place 1 free man, Godwine, [belonging to] , [held] 100 acres as a manor. Then 3 bordars and now 1. Then and now 1 plough. $2\frac{1}{2}$ acres of meadow. Then it was worth 16s., now 19s. 4d. In the same place 1 free man, Ælfric, commended to Saxi, the predecessor of Peverel, with 40 acres. Then as now 1 plough. 1 acre of meadow. Then it was worth 6s. 8d., now 10s. In the same place Sunwin, a free man commended to Gyrth, held 30 acres as a manor TRE. Then 1 plough. $1\frac{1}{2}$ acres of meadow. It is worth 6s.

In the same place Thorbiorn the priest, a free man, held 30 acres as a manor TRE. Then 1 plough. Then 1 bordar. Then worth 5s., now 10s. 10d. The king and the earl have the soke and commendation.

In the same place 35 free men with $203\frac{1}{2}$ acres. 2 acres of meadow. Then 7 ploughs, now a half. Then it was worth 40s., now £5 9s. The king and the earl have the soke. It is 1 league long and 7 furlongs broad. 20d. in geld.

In Westerfield 3 free men with 28 acres. Then and afterwards 1 plough, now

Roger de Rames

[Folio 423: SUFFOLK]

nothing. 1 acre of meadow. It is worth 10s. The king and the earl have the soke.

In Tuddenham 20 acres in the demesne of Tuddenham and it is in the valuation.

In Westerfield 5 free men with 23 acres and 1 virgate. Then and afterwards 1 plough, now none. It is worth 4s. Gerald holds it. In the same place 1 free man with 16 acres. Then and afterwards half a plough, now none. It is worth 32d. The king and the earl have the soke. Arnold holds it from him.

In this Hundred 20 acres which belong to the church of Tuddenham.

Arnold holds Newton from Roger which Beorhtmær, a free man, held TRE, with 102 acres as a manor TRE. Then and afterwards 2 villans and 2 bordars, now 4 bordars. Then as now 1 plough in demesne. Then and afterwards 2 ploughs belonging to the men, now none. 2 acres of meadow. 1 horse. Then 20 pigs, now 16. Then 20 sheep, now 12. It is worth 20s. In the same place Leofsunu, a free man commended to Stigand, held 40 acres as a manor TRE. Then 1 plough, now 2 oxen. 1 acre of meadow. Then it was worth 20s., now 10s. Ralph [holds it] from Roger. The king and the earl have the soke over the whole.

In Coddenham Roger holds in demesne 6 free men with 26 acres in the soke of the king and the earl. Then and afterwards 2 ploughs, now 1; 1 acre of meadow. It is worth 12s., less 2d.

In Helmingham 1 free man, Leofræd, [held] 20 acres. Then and afterwards 1 plough, now none. It is worth 3s. 1d. The king and the earl have the soke.

In Stonham [Aspal] 15 acres of demesne land and [it is] in the valuation. Miles holds it from Roger.

In Coddenham Ælfric and Boti, free men of Boti, held 9½ acres. Then half a plough, now 2 oxen. It is worth 3s. The same Miles [holds it].

HUNDRED AND A HALF OF SAMFORD.

In Higham Sigeric, a free man, held 30 acres as a manor TRE. Then as now half a plough. Then it was worth 5s., now 8s. Warenger holds it. Harold [had] the soke in [East] Bergholt.

[Folio 423V: SUFFOLK]

HUNDRED OF CARLFORD.

In Tuddenham Gerald holds 1 free man, Ælfric the deacon, under commendation to Saxi from the abbot TRE, with 12 acres as a manor. 3 bordars. Then as now 1 plough. 2 acres of meadow. Then 1 horse. Then as now 2 head of cattle. 11 pigs and 40 sheep. It is worth 3s. In the same place 2 free men, 1 commended to St Æthelthryth and the other commended to Harold, [held] 10 acres and half a plough. It is worth 2s. Gerald holds this from Roger.

In Grundisburgh Ralph [holds] 20 acres. They belong to Newton and they are in the valuation. In "Finlesford" 6 acres. 1 acre of meadow. They belong to Newton in another Hundred. Ralph holds this.

In Otley 4 acres. They belong to Stonham [Aspal] and are in the valuation. Miles de Belefol holds this.

HUNDRED OF COLNEIS.

In Kirton 2 acres, worth 4d.

HUNDRED OF LOOSE.

In Woodbridge 1 free man commended to Alwine [held] 11 acres. Half an acre of meadow. It is worth 27d.

XXXVIIII. Lands of Ranulf, brother of Ilger

HUNDRED OF COLNEIS.

In Burgh [near Woodbridge] 1 free man, Godric, commended to someone commended to Harold [held] 16 acres of land. 2 bordars. Half a plough. Half an acre of meadow. It is worth 3s. In Trimley 2 acres, worth 4d.

In 'Morston' [in Trimley] 1 free man commended to Beorhtmær [held] 4 acres, worth 12d.

In Falkenam the same Beorhtmær held 26 acres TRE as a manor. Then 1 plough and 1 horse. 4 head of cattle. 40 sheep. Now nothing at all. Then it was worth 10s., now 5s. This Beorhtmær held several estates and a

Ranulf, brother of Ilger

[Folio 424: SUFFOLK]

part was delivered to Engelric on the king's behalf. And other parts [were delivered] to Ranulf, brother of Ilger, and a third part to Ralph Pinel. And in that third part the above-mentioned estate was delivered to Ralph, ahe himself says and the same person offers the testimony of the Hundred that he himself was first seised of it. But whether he had been seised on behalf of the king or not, they do not know. They also say that Ranulf claimed that land against Ralph and Roger the sheriff named to them a set term so that they should both be present. But when Ranulf arrived, Ralph was not there and therefore the men of the Hundred judged that Ranulf was seised. Now he holds it but Ralph Pinel denies that he was summoned regarding that plea. In 'Morston' [in Trimley] 1 free woman, Wulfgifu, commended to Beorhtmær, [held] 10 acres. Then half a plough, now none. It is worth 2s.

In Hemley 1 free man, Beorhtmær, commended half to Beorht[mær] and the other half to St Æthelthryth TRE. Now Ranulf holds from the king by livery to his demesne. But the abbot says that he himself ought to hold a half from him. 22 acres. now none. 1 bordar. 1 acre of meadow. 1 slave. It is worth 4s. In the same place 1 free man, Wulfweard, commended to Godric, TRE [held] 20 acres of land. 2 bordars. 1 plough. Half an acre of meadow. It is worth 4s. Also in the same place 1 free man, Hardwin, [commended half] to someone commended to N[orthmann] and commended half to Eadric, TRE [held] 5 acres of land. Half a plough. Half an acre of meadow. It is worth 12d. In the same place 1 free man, Beorhtric, commended half to Beorhtmær and half to Stanmær [...], TRE [held] 9 acres and half a plough. Half an acre of meadow. It is worth 3s. A church with 8 acres, worth 2s.

The whole of this Ranulf, the brother of Ilger, holds by livery of the king and William de Bosc [holds it] from him. St Æthelthryth has the soke.

HUNDRED OF CARLFORD.

In Martlesham Eadweald held TRE

[Folio 424V: SUFFOLK]

2½ carucates of land as a manor. Then as now 10 villans and

10 bordars. Then 2 slaves. Then as now in demesne 2 ploughs and 5 ploughs belonging to the men, now 4; 12 a of meadow. Now 1 mill. Woodland for 16 pigs. Then 3 horses, now 5. Then 24 head of cattle, now 20. Then 40 pigs, now 27. Then 300 sheep, now 212. Then 16 goats. Then 6 beehives, now 12. Then it was worth 40s., now the same. It is 1 league long and 5 furlongs broad. In geld 6d. In the same place 1 church with 36 acres, worth 3s. 1 free man, Godric by name, [held] 16 acres and 1 bordar. Half a plough. 1 acre of meadow. It is worth 2s.

In Waldringfield Beorhtmær, a free man, held TRE 1 carucate of land as a manor and 1 bordar. Then 2 ploughs, now 1; 1 mill. Then 1 horse. Then 100 sheep, now 27. Then it was worth 20s., now 10s. It is 6 furlongs long and 3 broad. In geld 5d. In the same place 5 free men commended half to Beorhtmær and half to his mother with 40 acres and 1 plough, worth 4s.

In Preston [in Martlesham] 10 free men commended half to Beorhtmær and half to his mother Cwengifu. One of these was commended half to St Æthelthryth. 1 carucate of land. Now 9 bordars under them. Then 4 ploughs, now 2; 1 acre of meadow. Then it was worth 20s., now 10s. It is 6 furlongs long and 3 broad. In geld 6d.

In Haspley 5 free men, commended to the same Beorhtmær like the others, [held] 1 carucate of land and 5 bordars. 3 ploughs. 2 acres of meadow. Then it was worth 30s., now 20s. 1 of them was half Eadric's man and half Northmann's man. 2 of these were commended to Cwengifu TRE. It is 6 furlongs long and 3 broad. 5d. in geld.

In Newbourn 16 free men commended to Beorhtmær and Cwengifu TRE and 2 were half commended to St Æthelthryth with 1 carucate of land and 40 acres. Under them 14 bordars. Then 4 ploughs, now 3; 1½ acres of land. Then it was worth 40s., now 20s. And it is

Ranulf, brother of Ilger

[Folio 425: SUFFOLK]

1 church with 12 acres, worth 16d. It was Northmann's, as the Hundred testifies. And it is 6 furlongs long and 5 broad. In geld 7½d.

In "Kingsland" 1 carucate of land, waste land, worth 2s. It is 4 furlongs long and 3 broad. In geld 5d. William de Bosc holds all this from Ranulf, brother of Ilger. In "Aluredestuna" Durand, a free man of Robert Malet's predecessor, held TRE 1 carucate of land and 80 acres. Now Ivo holds it from Ranulf, brother of Ilger, as a manor. Then as now 7 villans and 3 bordars. Then in demesne 2 ploughs, now 1. Then as now 3 ploughs belonging to the men. 4 acres of meadow. 1 mill and 3 head of cattle. 50 sheep. 1 church with 12 acres, worth 12d. Then it was worth £4, now 60s. It is 6 furlongs long and 4 broad. 10d. in geld. In Ipswich 1 empty messuage and another inhabited. It renders 8d.

In Haspley 7 acres and they are in the valuation of Hemley. In "Eduluestuna" 9 acres, worth 2s. In Boulge 1 villan, Wulfric, with 4 acres, worth 8d.

TWO HUNDREDS OF BABERGH.

In [Great and Little] Waldingfield Wulfric, a thegn of King Edward, held 1 carucate of land. Now Ranulf holds it as a manor by the gift of King William, together with the soke and sake. Then as now 1 villan and 3 bordars. Then and afterwards 1 plough, now 2 between them all. 4 acres of meadow. Then as now 2 head of cattle. Then 12 pigs, now 16. Then 20 sheep, now 30. Then and afterwards 30s., now 40s.

HUNDRED OF SAMFORD.

Ælfric of Wenhou held Brantham with 2 carucates of land. Then and afterwards 4 villans, now 2. Then 1 bordar, now 8. Then 2 slaves, now 1. Then and afterwards 2 ploughs in demesne, now 1. Then as now 1 plough belonging to the men. Woodland for 12 pigs. 5 acres of meadow. 1 salt-pan. 1 mill. Then 1 horse. Then as now 12 head of cattle and 24 pigs and 60 sheep. It is worth 40s. Ælfric had the soke under arold.

Roger holds it from Ranulf[...].

[Folio 425v: SUFFOLK]

Xl. Lands of Robert fitzCorbucion.

THINGOE HUNDRED.

Richard holds Brockley which Sægeard, a free man, held under St Edmund TRE, in the soke of St Edmund, but he could not sell with half a carucate of land and 1 plough. 1½ acres of meadow. Then it was worth 10s., now 15s.

TWO HUNDREDS OF BAERGH.

Roger holds Somerton which Starcher held under the glorious King Edward as a manor with 1 carucate of land in the soke of St Edmund. Then as now 2 bordars. Then 4 slaves, now 1. Then and afterwards 2 ploughs in demesne, now 1; 3½ acres of meadow. Now 10 head of cattle. Then 15 pigs, now 8. Then 60 sheep, now 50. Now 5 goats. Then and afterwards worth 30s., now 40s.

HUNDRED AND A HALF OF SAMFORD.

Auti, a thegn, held [Great and Little] Wenham TRE as a manor with 3 carucates of land. Then 9 villans, afterwards and now 6. Then and afterwards 4 bordars, now 14. Then as now 1 slave. Then and afterwards 2 ploughs in demesne, now a half. Then 5 ploughs belonging to the men, afterwards 4, now 3; 11 acres of meadow. Then woodland for 10 pigs. Then as now 1 mill. A church with 20 acres of free land. Then as now half a plough. Then 2 horses and 4 head of cattle and 20 pigs, now nothing apart from 23 sheep. Then and afterwards worth £6, now 100s. Auti had the soke over his own demesne and the soke over the villans was in [East] Bergholt. Gerard holds 30 acres of this manor, worth 5s., and they are in the same valuation.

In [Great and Little] Wenham Godwine, a free man, held 10 acres and he was added to this manor. It is worth 2s. The soke is in [East] Bergholt. It is 12 furlongs long and 6 broad. 2s. in geld.

HUNDRED OF CARLFORD.

In Barkestone Tepekin, a free man commended to Harold, held 1 carucate of land as a manor. Then 6 bordars, now 4. Then in demesne 1 plough, now none. Then 7 ploughs belonging to the men, now none. 5 acres of meadow. 6 sheep.

Robert fitzCorbucion

Then it was worth 20s., now 12s. It is 6 furlongs long and 4 broad. In geld 3d.

HALF-HUNDRED OF COSFORD.

In Whatfield 1 sokeman of St Edmund with 100 acres. Then 1 plough, afterwards a half, now none. It is worth 10s. Berard, the abbot's man, holds it from the abbot.

HUNDRED OF SAMFORD.

Alwine, a free man of Stigand, held Thorington TRE with 2 carucates of land as a manor. Then and afterwards 6 villans, now 4. Then and afterwards 2 bordars, now 5. Then 2 slaves, afterwards and now 1. Then as now 2 ploughs in demesne. Then and afterwards 3 ploughs belonging to the men, now 2; 20 acres of meadow. Then as now 1 mill. A church with 50 acres of free land. Now 1 horse and 6 head of cattle. Then 4 pigs, now 30, and [...] 20 sheep and 30 goats. Then as now worth 50s. The same person had the soke under Stigand. It is 6 furlongs long and 4 broad. 5d. in geld. Gifard holds it from Robert.

XLI. Lands of Walter the Deacon.

HALF-HUNDRED OF COSFORD.

Queen Edith held Bildeston in demesne TRE as a manor with 6 carucates of land. Then as now 14 villans and 6 bordars and 8 slaves. 3 ploughs in demesne. 3 ploughs belonging to the men. 20 acres of meadow. Woodland for 10 pigs. 3 horses, 10 head of cattle, 40 pigs, 80 sheep. A church with 40 acres and 1 plough and 1 acre of meadow. Then it was worth £8, now £10, but it renders £12. It is 1 league long and a half broad. 5d. in geld.

HUNDRED OF CLAYDON.

Queen Edith held Swilland TRE with 2 carucates of land and 40 acres as a manor. Then as now 6 villans and 6 bordars and 1 slave. 2 ploughs in demesne. 3 ploughs belonging to the men. 4 acres of meadow. Woodland for 6 pigs. A church with 5 acres. 1 horse. 8 head of cattle and 19 pigs. Then 60 [...] sheep,

now 100. Then it was worth 50s., now 70s. It is 6 furlongs long and 4 broad. 20d. in geld. Walter [holds it] in demesne. The queen had the soke.

In Thurlston 1 free man with 16 acres and 4 bordars. Then as now half a plough. 1 acre of meadow. It is worth 2s. 8d. Half a church with 5 acres.

In Westerfield Almær, a free man, held 30 acres and 4

bordars. Then as now 1 plough. 2 acres of meadow. It is worth 8s. Turstin [holds it] from Walter, from Theodoric's fief. The king and the earl have the soke.

In Akenham 2 free men, Swein and Leofwine, [held] 50 acres, worth 5s. Turstin [holds it] from Walter, and Bernard from the same fief.

In Westerfield 3 free men [...] with 28 acres. Then half a plough. It is worth 36d. Bernard and Almær hold it. The king and the earl have the soke. In the same place 1 free man with 6 acres, worth 12d. [It is] from the same fief. Norman holds it. The soke is the king's and the earl's. [...]

HUNDRED OF HARTISMERE.

Leofwine, a free man of Harold's, held Bacton TRE with 3 carucates of land and 40 acres. Then 17 villans, now 8. Then 3 bordars, now 12. Then 2 slaves, now 1. Then as now in demesne 2 ploughs. Then 3 ploughs belonging to the men, now 2; 6 acres of meadow. Woodland for 100 pigs. Then 9 horses, now 8. Then as now 8 head of cattle. Then 60 pigs, now 40. Then 16 sheep, now 100. Then 40 goats, now 36. . Then it was worth £8, now £9 10s., and 40 free men under the commendation of Leofwine TRE have 80 acres of land and 1 bordar. Then 3 ploughs, now 2; 1 acre of meadow. Then it was worth 20s., now £4 10s. The king and the earl have the soke. It is 1 league long and 4 furlongs broad. In geld 6d.

In "Caldecota" 19 acres of the demesne of Bacton, worth 3s. 3d. It is 9 furlongs long and 2 [furlongs] and 5 perches broad. In geld 6d.

In Westhorpe Beorhtric, a free man, by commendation [held] 6 acres, worth 12d.

Walter the Deacon

TWO HUNDREDS OF BABERGH.

Walter holds Milden in demesne which Leofwine of Bacton, a thegn of King Edward, held as a manor with 2 carucates of land. Now Walter holds it and it belongs to the fief of Theodoric, his brother. Then as now 6 villans and 6 bordars and 4 slaves. Then as now 2 ploughs in demesne. Then and afterwards 3 ploughs belonging to the men, now 1; 6 acres of meadow. Woodland for 6 pigs. 1 mill. Then as now 2 horses. 6 head of cattle, now 7; 22 pigs. Then 40 sheep, now 50. Then 12 goats, now 16. Then and afterwards worth £4, now £6. It is 6 furlongs long and 4 broad. In geld 7d. A church with 15 acres of free land. Over 10 acres which 1 free man had and which he could sell, St Edmund has the soke and sake. It is worth 2s.

HUNDRED OF STOW.

In Dagworth William holds; 1 free man over whom Theodoric the predecessor of Barthetona [sic] had half the commendation and Guthmund the predecessor of Hugh [...] de Montfort had the other half. And he could sell his land without their permission. He had 60 acres and 1 bordar. Then and afterwards 1½ ploughs, now 2 oxen. Woodland for 10 pigs. 3 acres of meadow.

In "Weledana" 15 acres of land belonging to the same free man. 2 acres of meadow. Then and afterwards the whole was worth 20s., now 5s. Theodoric, the predecessor of Walter the Deacon, this land without a livery officer, as the Hundred testifies. The king and the earl have the soke and sake.

In Wetherden 1 free man in the soke of the Hundred with 5 acres, worth 12d.

HALF-HUNDRED OF IPSWICH.

In the borough Walter has 5 houses and 3 empty messuages which the queen held TRE. They pay the customary due. It is worth 20d.

HUNDRED OF CLAYDON.

Wulfric, a free man, held Henley with 1 carucate of land and 70 acres as a manor TRE. Then 2 bordars, now 6. Then and afterwards 2 ploughs in demesne, now 1. Then as now 1 plough belonging to the men. 4 acres of meadow.

[Folio 427v: SUFFOLK]

Then 3 horses. Then 2 head of cattle, now 3. Then 10 pigs, now 2. Then 40 sheep, now 44. A church with 8 acres. Then it was worth 40s., and now 48s. Roger [holds it] from Walter. The king and the earl have the soke. In the same place 6 free men by commendation [held] 36 acres. Then and afterwards 1½ ploughs, now 1 plough. Then it was worth 6s. 8d., now 7s. The same Roger [holds it]. The king and the earl have the soke. In the same place 1 free man by the name of Swein held 40 acres as a manor TRE. Then as now 1 plough and 1 bordar. Then it was worth 10s., now 18s. Walter holds it in demesne. It is 1 league long and a half broad. 20d. in geld. The king and the earl have the soke.

In "Bruntuna" Leofwine, a thegn, held TRE 1 carucate of land and 40 acres as a manor. Then as now 9 bordars and 2 slaves. Then and afterwards 2 ploughs, now 1. Then and afterwards 2 ploughs belonging to the men, now 1; 5 acres of meadow. Then 1 horse. Then 20 pigs, now 10. Then 20 sheep, now 16. Then it was worth 40s., now 30s. Robert [holds it] from Walter. The king and the earl have the soke.

In Akenham 4 free men with 32 acres of land. Then 1 plough. It is worth 5s. Roger [holds it] from Walter. The king and the earl have the soke.

HUNDRED OF CARLFORD.

In Witnesham Leofwine, a free man, held TRE 3 carucates of land. Then as now 10 villans and 4 bordars. [Then] 6 slaves, now 5. Then as now 3 ploughs in demesne and 4 ploughs belonging to the men. 10 acres of meadow. 3 horses, 8 head of cattle, 68 pigs, 180 sheep. 30 goats; 7 beehives. Then it was worth 60s., now £12. It is 8 furlongs long and 4 broad. 5d. in geld.

In "Finesforda" in demesne 26 free men commended to Walter's predecessor [held] 1 carucate of land. St Æthelthryth had the soke. Then between them 3 ploughs, now 2; 4 acres of meadow. It is worth 40s. It is 10 furlongs long and 3 broad. 10d. in geld. In Otley in demesne 6 acres, worth 12d.

XLII. Lands of Tihel de Helléan

TWO HUNDREDS OF BABERGH.

Wulfweard, a free man under Stigand, held Eleigh [Brent and Monks] TRE as a manor with 3 carucates of land. Then as now 5 bordars and 2 slaves. Then as now 2 ploughs in demesne and 3 acres of meadow. 1 mill. 2 horses at the hall. 6 head of cattle, 20 pigs and 100 sheep. Then it was worth 40s., afterwards and now 80s. It is half a league long and 4 furlongs broad. In geld 3½d.

Tihel de Helléan

[Folio 428: SUFFOLK]

HUNDRED OF RISBRIDGE.

Clarenbald held Haverhill TRE as a manor with 2½ carucates of land. Then and afterwards 6 villans, now 1. Then and afterwards 4 bordars, now 10. Then as now 10 slaves. Then and afterwards and always 2 ploughs in demesne. Then and afterwards 1 plough belonging to the men, now a half. Woodland for 20 pigs. 6 acres of meadow. The third part of a market: in it 10 bordars. 5 acres belonging to the church. The manor is worth 40s. and the market 13s. 4d. It is 1 league long and a half broad. 6d. in geld. Others hold [land] there.

XLIII. Lands of Ralph de Limésy.

TWO HUNDREDS OF BABERGH.

Uhtred under Harold held Houghton TRE as a manor with 2 carucates of land, together with the soke. Then as now 1 villan and 2 bordars and 5 slaves. Then 3 ploughs in demesne, afterwards and now 4. Then as now half a plough belonging to the men. Woodland for 20 pigs. 10 acres of meadow. Then as now 1 horse at the hall. Then 3 head of cattle, now none.

The same Uhtred held Fenstead TRE as 1 carucate of land. Now Ralph holds it as a berewick in Houghton from Edgar his predecessor. Then as now 1 plough in demesne. Houghton was then worth £4, now 100s. and Fenstead was then and afterwards worth 20s., now 30s., but it is [part] of the 100s. The whole is 8 furlongs long and 4 broad. In geld 4d.

Northmann held Cavendish with the soke and sake under King Edward as a manor with 2 carucates of land. A church with 30 acres of free land. Then as now 5 villans and 8 bordars and 7 slaves. Then 2 ploughs in demesne, afterwards and now 4. Then as now 3

[Folio 428v: SUFFOLK]

ploughs belonging to the men. 1 mill. 10 acres of meadow. Then 3 head of cattle, now 24. Then 40 sheep, now 110. Then 30 pigs, now 50. To this manor belongs 1 berewick, Coddenham, with 2 carucates of land. Then 5 villans and afterwards and now 3. Then 4 bordars, afterwards and now 13. Then and afterwards 2 slaves, now 1. Then 2 ploughs in demesne, afterwards and now 1 and 1½ ploughs belonging to the men. Then half a mill, afterwards and now none. A church with 20 acres of free land. Then and afterwards the whole was worth 100s., now £10. Cavendish is half a league long and 4 furlongs broad. In geld 10d. [...] Coddenham [in Boxford]

The same Uhtred under Harold held Newton together with the soke and sake as a manor with 2 carucates of land. Then as now 3 villans. Then 7 bordars, afterwards and now 20. Then 4 slaves, afterwards and now 1. Then as now 2 ploughs in demesne. Then and afterwards 2 ploughs belonging to the men, now 2½. Woodland for 6 pigs. 4 acres of meadow. A church with 30 acres of free land. Then 1 horse, now none. Then 3 head of cattle, now 8. Then 17 pigs, now 20. Then 60 sheep, now 103. Then 17 goats, now 35. Hal a church with 8 acres of free land. In the same place 1 free man, half under Uhtred and half under St Edmund by commendation, but wholly in the soke of St Edmund. And he could sell without permission. He had 20 acres. The whole was then worth 40s., afterwards and now 60s. It is half a league long and 4 furlongs broad. And in geld 6½d.

In [Great and Little] Cornard 1 free man of Wihtgar by commendation only and with the soke over 1 carucate of land. Then as now 5 bordars. Then as now 1 plough in demesne. 6 acres of meadow. Woodland for 4 pigs. Then as now 5 head of cattle. Then 10 pigs, now 20. Then 30 sheep, now 60. Then as now worth 20s. It is half a league long and a half broad. In geld 3½d.

HUNDRED OF BISHOP.

Ælfric, a free man of Harold, held Bedingfield as a manor TRE with 92 acres. Then 2 bordars, now 4. Then as now 1 plough in demesne.

Ralph de Limésey

[Folio 429: SUFFOLK]

1 plough belonging to the men. Woodland for 10 pigs. 1 acre of meadow. Then as now 12 pigs and 20 sheep. The fourth part of a church with 6 acres. Then it was worth 30s., now 16s. 8d. In the same place 6 free men; over all of them Ælfric had the commendation apart from a half [free man] who was under Robert Malet's predecessor by commendation only. They have 35 acres. 1 acre of meadow. Then as now 1 plough. It is worth 40d.

HUNDRED OF LOOSE.

Beorhtmær, a free man of Harold, held Framlingham TRE with 50 acres of land as a manor. Then as now 3 bordars and 1 slave. 1 plough in demesne and half a plough belonging to the men. Then and always worth 15s.

HUNDRED OF HARTISMERE.

Ælfric, a free man, held Cranley with 100 acres as a manor TRE. Then as now 10 bordars. 1 plough in demesne and 1 plough belonging to the men. Woodland for 6 pigs. It is worth 20s. Ælfric had half the soke and the king the other half.

In Hestley 2 free men by commendation [held] 10 acres, worth 20d.

In Occold 1 free man by commendation [held] 8 acres, worth 16d. Ralph holds the whole in demesne. The king and the earl have the soke. In the same place 1 free man com-

mended to the Abbot of St Edmund [held] 2 acres, worth 4d. The king and the earl have the soke.

XLIIII. Lands of Robert de Tosny.

HUNDRED OF RISBRIDGE.

Ulf, a thegn, held [Great and Little] Bradley as a manor TRE now Roger holds it in demesne with 7 carucates of land. Then as now 14 villans and 12 bordars and 6 slaves. 3 ploughs in demesne and 7 ploughs belonging to the men. 13 acres of meadow. Woodland for pigs. Then as now 1 horse. Then 12 head of cattle, now 18. Then 60 pigs, now 53. Then 20 sheep,

[Folio 429v: SUFFOLK]

now 63; 7 goats. 1 beehive. A church with 15 acres of free land. Then it was worth £6, now £8. It is 1 league long and 7 furlongs broad. 6d. in geld.

HUNDRED OF BISHOP.

Ulf held Syleham together with the soke TRE as a manor with 2½ carucates of land. Then 8 villans, now 3. Then 12 bordars, now 13. Now 1 slave. Then as now 3 ploughs in demesne. Then and afterwards 12 ploughs belonging to the men, now 4. Woodland for 150 pigs. 8 acres of meadow. Then as now 1 mill. Then 2 horses, now 1. Then 8 head of cattle, now 2. Then 80 pigs, now 44. Now 7 sheep, 3 goats and 1 beehive. Then it was worth 100s. and now likewise. In the same place 5 free men commended to his predecessor [held] 30 acres. Then 1 plough, now a half. 1 acre of meadow. It is worth 5s. A church with 16 acres, worth 2s. It is 1 league long and 8 furlongs broad. 7½d. in geld. The soke is in the bishop's manor of Hoxne.

HUNDRED OF BLYTHING.

Manni, a free man, held Mells as a manor and now Robert has it in demesne with 3 carucates of land. Then as now 8 villans. Then as now 12 bordars. Then as now 3 slaves. Then as now 2 ploughs in demesne. 3 ploughs belonging to the men. Woodland for 100 pigs. 5 acres of meadow. Then 1 mill, now none. Then as now 2 horses, 7 head of cattle, 30 pigs, 16 sheep. Then it was worth 50s., now 60s. It is 10 furlongs long and 7 broad. It renders 2d. in geld.

Manni held Yoxford as a manor now Robert holds it in demesne with 5 carucates of land. Then 12 villans, now 9. Then 2 bordars, now none. Then as now 1 slave. Then as now 2 ploughs in demesne and belonging to the men, 3. Woodland for 30 pigs. 20 acres of meadow. Then as now 1 horse, 7 head of cattle, 30 pigs. Then it was worth 40s., now 60s. It is 10 furlongs long and 7 broad. 3d. in geld.

XLV. Land of Walter Giffard.

HALF-HUNDRED OF PARHAM

In Blaxhall 1 free [man], Godric, half under commendation to Malet's predecessor and half to the Abbot of Ely, [held] 10 acres, worth 20d. Ralph de Lanquetot holds it. The soke is the abbot's.

HUNDRED OF PLUMESGATE.

Stærling, half commended to the Abbot of Ely and half to William Malet, held [Great] Glemham with 180 acres as a manor TRE and he was seised thereof. Then as now 11 bordars. 2 ploughs in demesne. 1 plough belonging to the men. 1 acre of meadow. Then as now 2 horses. Then 16 pigs, now 26. Then 30 sheep, now 50. Then it was worth 40s., now 60s. There were added 24 free men by commendation with 100 acres. Then as now 3 ploughs. It is worth 40s. It is 1 league long and a half broad. 20d. in geld.

In Stratford [St Andrew] the same person held 1 carucate of land as a manor TRE. Then as now 5 bordars. 1 plough in demesne and half a plough belonging to the men. 4 acres of meadow. Then it was worth 40s. In the same place 13 free men and a half by commendation [held] then as now 64 acres and 1½ ploughs, worth 7s. Ralph de Lanquetot holds the whole. The soke belongs to the Abbot of Ely.

XLVI. Lands of the Countess of Aumale.

TWO HUNDREDS OF BABERGH.

In Shimpling Wulfric, a thegn of King Edward, held as a manor 5 carucates of land. Now the Countess of Aumale holds it. Then 5 villans, now 3. Then and afterwards 4 bordars, now 10. Then as now 6 slaves. Then and afterwards 3 ploughs in demesne, now 2. Then as now 3 ploughs belonging to the men. Woodland for 8 pigs. 10 acres of meadow. Then as now 1 horse. Then 14 head of cattle, now 6. Then 40 pigs, now 24. Then 120 sheep, now 100. A church with 30 acres. In the same place 5 free men Wulfric had the commendation and St Edmund the soke and sake TRE [held] 1 carucate of land; now the countess holds it. 1 bordar and 1 slave. Then as now 2 ploughs. 2 acres of meadow. Then and always worth £9. It is 1 league long and a half broad. In geld 5d.

The same Wulfric held Chadacre TRE as a manor with 1 carucate of land. Then as now 1 villan and 3 bordars and 2 slaves. Then 2 ploughs in demesne, now none. Then as now 1 plough belonging to the men and 3 acres of meadow. Then as now worth 60s. It is 4 furlongs long and 2 broad. In geld 2½d.

HUNDRED AND A HALF OF SAMFORD.

Ælfric of Wenhou held Belstead with 3 carucates of land and 40 acres as a manor. Then as now 12 villans and 3 bordars. Then 5 slaves, now 1. Then 2 ploughs in demesne, now 1. Then 8 ploughs, afterwards and now 5; 6 acres of meadow.

Then woodland for 30 pigs, now 20. A church with 34 acres of free land. Now 27 pigs and 35 sheep. Then it was worth £8, now £6. The same Ælfric had the soke. It is 1 league long and 3 furlongs broad. In geld 7d. Eadgifu the Fair held Harkstead with 7 carucates of land as a manor TRE. Then as now 17 villans and 8 bordars. Then 1 slave. Then 3 ploughs in demesne, afterwards and now 2. Then as now 5 ploughs belonging to the men. 8 acres of meadow. Woodland for 30 pigs. 1 mill. A church with 24 acres. 4 head of cattle, 24 pigs, 40 sheep and 27 goats.

The Countess of Aumale

Then it was worth £10, now £14. It is 1 league long and a half broad. 14d. in geld.

Eadgifu held Gusford TRE with 2 carucates of land as a manor. Then as now 1 villan and 6 bordars. Then 2 ploughs belonging to the men, now 1, and 3 ploughs could be restored. 8 acres of meadow. Then woodland for 20 pigs. Then 1 mill. The third part of a church with 8 acres. It is worth £3. It is 8 furlongs long and 3 broad. 5d. in geld. Eadgifu had the soke.

HUNDRED OF COLNEIS.

In Hemley 1 villan with 9 acres, worth 20d. It belongs to Clopton.

HUNDRED OF CARLFORD.

In Clopton Burgric, a free man of Ralph the staller, held TRE 1 carucate of land and 20 acres as a manor. Then as now 11 bordars and in demesne 2 ploughs. Then 2 ploughs belonging to the men, now 1; 4 acres of meadow. 10 pigs and 35 sheep. Then as now worth 40s. In the same place 6 acres which Wulfwine the priest looks after and holds. It is worth 12d.

In Burgh 2 free men, 1 by commendation to St Edmund and the other by commendation to Earl Ralph, with 36 acres and 2 bordars. Then ploughs, now a half. 2 acres of meadow. It is worth 6s.

In Clopton 12 free men and a half commended to Burgric TRE [held] 92 acres. 2 bordars. Then 3 ploughs, now 2; 1 acre of meadow. It is worth 16s. 4d.

HUNDRED OF WILFORD.

In Debach 3 free men commended to Eadric Grim with 20 acres. 1 acre of meadow. Then 1 plough. It is worth 3s; 1 church with 8 acres, worth 16d. In Boulge 1 free man with half an acre, worth 2d.

HUNDRED OF LOOSE.

In Monewden 5 acres and in Charsfield 3 acres, worth 12d.

XLVII. Lands of William d'Arques.

HUNDRED OF COLNEIS

In Hemley 1 bordar with 5 acres and they belong to Clopton and are in [its] valuation.

HUNDRED OF CLAYFORD.

In Clopton Edmund the priest, a free man of St Æthelthryth, held TRE 1 carucate of land and 22 acres as a manor. 1 villan and 7 bordars. Then in demesne 3 ploughs, now 1. Then 1 plough belonging to the men, now a half. 4 acres of meadow. Now 1 horse. Then 4 head of cattle. Then 40 pigs. Then 30 sheep, now nothing at all. Then it was worth 30s., now 10s. Bernard de Saint-Ouen holds this from William.

HUNDRED OF LOOSE.

Edmund the priest, commended to St Æthelthryth, held Brandeston TRE and the land of Brandeston and Clopton which he received with his wife, he gave up to the church with his wife's consent by an agreement whereby he could not sell or give [it] away from the church. 60 acres as a manor. 5 bordars and 2 slaves and in demesne 1 plough and 1 plough belonging to the men. 5 acres of meadow. Woodland for 6 pigs. 80 acres of land as a manor were added to this manor TRE. Then 4 bordars, now 12 bordars. Now between them 1 plough. Woodland for 8 pigs. 4 acres of meadow. 1 mill. Now 1 horse, 20 pigs, 16 sheep, 30 goats and 3 beehives. Then it was all together worth 100s., now 60s. William has this as 1 manor but TRE there were two. 1 church with 12 acres, worth 2s. It is 1 league long and 3 furlongs broad. In geld 5½d.

[Folio 432: SUFFOLK]

XLVIII. Land of Drogo de La Beuvrière.

HUNDRED OF BLYTHING.

Rada, a free man of Harold, held Sotherton with 2 carucates of land as a manor. Now Franco holds it from Drogo. Then and afterwards 16 bordars, now 19. slaves. Then and afterwards 1 plough in demesne, now 2. Then as now 3 ploughs belonging to the men. 2 acres of meadow. Woodland for 100 pigs. A church with 5 acres. 1 horse and now 1 ox. Then 12 pigs, now 24, and 25 sheep. Then as now 40s. It is 1 league long and a half broad. 1¾d. in geld. Rada, Drogo's predecessor, had the soke and sake. To this manor Humphrey de Saint-Bertin added 1 free [man] with 12 acres over whom his predecessor had commendation TRE. Then as now 1 bordar and half a plough. It is worth 2s.

XLVIIII. Lands of Hugh de Grandmesnil

HALF-HUNDRED OF COSFORD.

Ælfnoth held Layham from Harold TRE as a manor with 3 carucates of land. Then as now 4 villans and 7 bordars. Then 5 slaves, now 6. Then as now 2 ploughs in demesne and 2 ploughs belonging to the men. 11 acres of meadow. 1 horse. 15 head of cattle, 15 pigs, 100 sheep and 19 goats. Then it was worth 70s., now 100s. It is half a league long and a half broad. 4½d. in geld. St Edmund had the soke.

L. Lands of Ralph de Fougères.

Wulfsige, a free man commended to Gyrth, held Stuston with 2 carucates of land as a manor TRE. Then as now 4 villans

[Folio 432v: SUFFOLK]

and 4 bordars. Then in demesne 2 ploughs, now 1. Then as now 1 plough belonging to the men. 6 acres of meadow. Then 2 head of cattle, now 1. Then 5 pigs. Then it was worth 60s., now 40s. 3 free men commended to Wulfsige with 12 acres, worth 2s. The king and the earl have the soke.

In Thrandeston 6 acres, worth 12d.

LI. Lands of Walter de Saint-Valéry.

HUNDRED OF STOW.

In Creeting [St Peter] Ælfric, a free man by commendation only to Eadric, Robert Malet's predecessor, held TRE and Robert held, but afterwards he was disseised 1½ carucates of land. 2 villans and 9 bordars. Then as now 2½ ploughs in demesne. Then 1 plough belonging to the men, afterwards and now a half. Then woodland for 40 pigs, now none. 1 mill. 6 acres of meadow. Half a church with 10 acres of free land. 5 head of cattle, 9 sheep, 12 pigs. It is worth 100s. In the same place Walter, 1 free man commended to Toli, held 10½ acres. Then and afterwards and now half a plough. It is worth 3s.

HUNDRED OF BOSMERE.

In Creeting 1 free man commended to Robert Malet's predecessor TRE [held] 60 acres, and his father was seised thereof. Then as now 4 villans and half a plough. This belongs to Creeting [St Peter] in the Hundred of Stow and in [its] valuation. In the same place 4 free men by commendation [held] 7 acres. In Olden 1 free man by commendation [held] 4 acres, worth 2s. The king and the earl have the soke. [...]

[Folio 433: SUFFOLK]

LII. Lands of Humphrey the Chamberlain.

HUNDRED OF CARLFORD.

In Otley Leofflæd, a free woman commended to Eadric, Robert Malet's predecessor, held 1½ carucates of land. Then as now 3 villans and 10 bordars. Then in demesne 2 ploughs, now 1½. Then 3 ploughs belonging to the men, now 2. Woodland for 20 pigs. 2 acres of meadow. Then as now 2 horses. Then 5 head of cattle. Then 40 pigs and now the same. Then as now 100 sheep, 25 goats and 6 beehives. Then it was worth 100s., now £6. William Malet was seied thereof on the day on which he died and afterwards Robert, as the Hundred testifies. In the same place Lustwine, commended to Eadric, held TRE half a carucate of land as a manor. Then as now 1 villan and 4 bordars. Then 1 plough, now 1½ in demesne. Then as now 1 plough belonging to the men. 2 acres of meadow. Woodland for 5 pigs. Then it was worth 20s., now 30s. In the same place 16 free men and a half commended to Leofflæd [held] 69 acres. Then 3 ploughs, and now. Then it was worth 20s., now 30s. 1

church with 20 acres, worth 4s. William Malet was seised of the whole of this on the day on which he died, and Robert afterwards. The king and the earl have the soke. In the same place Amund holds [what] Beorhtweald, a free man commended to Queen Edith, [held], 30 acres and 1 villan and 4 bordars. Then 1 plough, now 1½; 1 acre of meadow. Woodland for 10 pigs. Then it was worth 8s., now 10s.

In Clopton 20 acres and 1 bordar, worth 5s. Amund holds this from Humphrey.

In Otley 6 free men commended to Beorhtweald [held] 27 acres of land. Then 2 ploughs, now 1. Then it was worth 10s. and now the same. In Burgh 1 free man, commended half to the same person and half to St Æthelthryth, [held] 24 acres and half a plough. Half an acre of meadow. It is worth 10s.

HUNDRED OF LOOSE.

Cretingham. Beorhtweald, commended to the queen, held

[Folio 433v: SUFFOLK]

83 acres as a manor. Then and now 1 villan and 1 bordar and 1 slave. In demesne 1 plough and half a plough belonging to the men. 4 acres of meadow. 1 church with 8 acres. It is worth 16d. Then as now 3 horses, 3 head of cattle. 24 pigs, 40 sheep, 25 goats and 4 beehives. Then it was worth 20s., now 30s. In the same place 8 whole free men and 4 half free men commended to the same person with 66 acres of land. Then 2 ploughs, now 1½; 1 acre of meadow. Then it was worth 20s., now 31s.

HUNDRED BOSMERE.

In Ashbocking Alwine, a free man, held 4 acres. Then it was worth 16d., now 8d. In Otley Humphrey holds in demesne 1 free man with 3 virgates, worth 3d. In the same place 1 free woman, Leohtgifu, with 1 acre, worth 2d.

In "Bricticeshaga" there is woodland on which 16 pigs could feed TRE, now 4. Amund holds it from Humphrey and it belongs to Cretingham.

HUNDRED OF CLAYDON.

Grimulf, a free man commended to the queen, held Helmingham with 120 acres of land and it belongs in the demesne of Otley. Then as now 1 villan and 5 bordars. 1 plough belonging to the men. 3 acres of meadow. Woodland for 50 pigs and it is in the valuation of Otley. In the same place in demesne 11 free men under commendation to his predecessor, apart from two who were commended to Beorhtweald TRE, [held] 68 acres TRE. Then as now 2 ploughs. It is worth 20s. In the same place a free man,

Beorhtweald, held 40 acres TRE. Then as now 2 villans and 3

bordars. Then as now 2 ploughs. 3 acres . It is worth 20s. Amund holds it from Humphrey. The king and the earl have the soke.

Humphrey the Chamberlain

[Folio 434: SUFFOLK]

In Ashfield 2 free men with 4 acres, worth 8d. The soke is the abbot's. In "Bermounsden" Anund held 2 free men with 60 acres TRE. Then as now 1 bordar. Then 1 plough. 2 acres of meadow. Then it was worth 20s., now 30s. Humphrey [holds it] in demesne. The king and the earl have the soke. And 1 free man has been added with 4 acres, worth 2s.

LIII. Lands of Eudo fitzSpirewic.

HUNDRED OF LACKFORD.

In Icklingham Morvant holds from Eudo what Anund, a free man, held under St Æthelthryth TRE as a manor with 2 carucates of land but he could not sell. Now Eudo fitzSpirewic holds it from Heinfrid, his predecessor, but the soke and sake belong to St Edmund. Then and afterwards 7 villans, now 6 and 6 bordars and 1 slave. Then as now 2 ploughs in demesne and 1 plough belonging to the men. 5 acres of meadow. 1 mill. Now 84 sheep. Then it was worth £4, now 60s.

HUNDRED OF BOSMERE.

Sigeric, a free man, held Olden [in Coddenham] TRE as a manor now William holds it with 70 acres. Then as now 2 bordars. Then 2 ploughs, now 1½; 2 acres of meadow. Then 2 horses. Now 16 pigs and 28 sheep. It is worth 20s. In the same place 13 free men, over two of whom Roger's predecessor had commendation, with 40 acres and 1 plough, worth 10s. The king and the earl have the soke. It is 1 league long and 3 furlongs broad. 10d. in geld. Others hold [land] there.

[Folio 434v: SUFFOLK]

Iarnagot holds Battisford which Cyneric, a free man, held TRE with 1 carucate of land and 20 acres as a manor. Now Iarnagot holds it. Then as now 5 bordars and 1 slave. Then 2 ploughs in demesne, now 1. Half a plough belonging to the men. 6 acres of meadow. Then woodland for 60 pigs, now 10. Then 2 horses, now 20 pigs, 11 sheep and 12 goats. . It is worth 25s. In the same place 3 free men with 20 acres over two of whom his predecessor had commendation. Then as now half a plough. It is worth 5s. The king and the earl have the soke.

In Coddenham Sigeric, a free man, [held] in demesne 5 acres, worth 10d. The soke is the king's.

HUNDRED OF WANGFORD.

Geoffrey holds Flixton which Offa, a free man commended to Stigand, held TRE with 2 carucates of land as a manor. Then 16 villans, now 10. Then 11 bordars, now 14. Then as now 2 slaves. In demesne 2 ploughs. Then 13½ ploughs belonging to the men, now 9½. Then as now 1 horse, 2 head of cattle, 6 pigs and 26 sheep. 12 acres of meadow. Woodland for 20 pigs. Half a mill. Then it was worth 40s., now 60s. Half a church with 10 acres, worth 16d. In the same place 2 free men under the same commendation [held] 30 acres. Then as now 3½ bordars. 2¼ ploughs. Woodland for 2 pigs. 3½ acres of meadow. Then it was worth 7s., now 10s. 8d. It is 1 league long and a half broad. In geld 20d.

HUNDRED OF HARTISMERE.

Westhorpe; [...] Wulfric Hagni held it with 1 carucate of land as a manor TRE. Then as now 1 bordar and 1 slave. In demesne 1½ ploughs. Woodland for 12 pigs. 6 acres of meadow. 3 horses and 2 head of cattle. 31 pigs. 50 sheep. 15 goats and 5 beehives. Then it was worth 20s., now 30s. 15 free men commended to Wulfric with 33 acres. Then as now 1 plough. Woodland for 2 pigs. 2 acres of meadow. It is worth 10s. Over this manor

Eudo fitzSpirewic

[Folio 435: SUFFOLK]

St Edmund had TRE the soke and sake and commendation and he could not sell or give away from the church. Over these 15 free men and over Wulfnoth [sic], Robert Malet's predecessor had the commendation, as the Hundred testifies. He could not sell or give his land away from him.

HALF-HUNDRED OF COSFORD.

In Wattisham 1 free man, over whom the Abbot of Ely had the commendation and the soke TRE, [held] 1 carucate of land and 3 bordars and 1 plough. 3 acres of meadow. It is worth 20s. St Edmund [has] the 6 forfeitures. Iarnagot holds it.

LIIII. Lands of William de Vatteville.

HUNDRED OF RISBRIDGE.

Store held Lidgate as a manor TRE with 4 carucates of land and 60 acres. Then as now 9 villans and 12 bordars and 1 slave. 2 ploughs in demesne. Then 3 ploughs belonging to the men, now 2; 10 acres of meadow. Woodland for 15 pigs. Then as now 1 horse; now 5 head of cattle and 25 pigs. Then 33 sheep, now 140, and 13 goats. Then it was worth 80s. and now the same. It is 1 league long and 8 furlongs broad. 13½d. in geld. Others hold [land] there.

HUNDRED OF THINGOE.

Ælfgyth, 1 free woman, held Hargrave TRE under St Edmund and she could not sell, with 4 carucates of land. Then and afterwards 6 villans, now 8. Then and afterwards 4 bordars, now 7. Then 4 slaves, now 2. Then as now 2 ploughs in demesne. Then and afterwards 4 ploughs belonging to the men, now 3. Then 1 horse, now none. Then 2 head of cattle, now 8. Then 5 pigs, now 40. Now 100 sheep. 4 acres of meadow. Woodland for 16 pigs. A church with 12 acres of free land. Then and always worth £4.

[Folio 435V: SUFFOLK]

It is 8 furlongs long and 5 broad. In geld 7d.

HUNDRED OF LACKFORD.

Ælfgyth, 1 free [wo]man, held Barton [Mills] with 5 carucates of land. William held this land from the queen. Now Ælfgifu holds it from the king. Then 10 villans, now 7. Now 5 bordars. Then 9 slaves. Then 4 ploughs in demesne, now 1. Then as now 3 ploughs belonging to the men. 2 fisheries. 2 acres of meadow. Then 1 horse and now 2 horses. Then 10 head of cattle, now 5. Then 200 sheep, now 3. Then 40 pigs, now 3. Then it was worth £8 and afterwards £6, and now 30s. It is 1 league long and a half broad. In geld 20d. The soke and sake are St Edmund's.

LV. Land of John fitzWaleran.

TWO HUNDREDS OF BABERGH.

In Bures Wulfric, son of Brihtric, held TRE 2 carucates of land under King Edward. Then 7 slaves and 1 smith. Now 4 slaves. Now 2 bordars. Then as now 2 ploughs in demesne. Woodland for 40 pigs. 4 acres of meadow. Now 1 mill. Now 2 horses and 2 head of cattle. Then 60 sheep, now 140. Then 40 pigs, now 20. Now 35 goats. Then it was worth 60s., now 40s. In the same place Tostig, a free man, held under King Edward 1 carucate of land. Then 1 villan, now none. Now 2 bordars and 1 slave. Then as now 1 plough. Woodland for 10 pigs. 2 acres of meadow. Then 40 pigs, now 20, and 20 sheep. Now 15 goats. It is worth 20s. In the same place 2 free men of Harold. They could sell. They had 60 acres and 1 plough, worth 5s. They were delivered to make up the manor.

[Folio 436: SUFFOLK]

LVI. Land of Humphrey fitzAubrey.

HUNDRED OF STOW.

From the exchange of Normandy. In Onehouse 10 free men belonging to Ketil by commendation only [held] 60 acres of land and 1 bordar. Then 2 ploughs, afterwards and now 1; 3 acres of meadow. It is worth 10s. The king and the earl have the soke.

HUNDRED OF BOSMERE.

In Coddenham 11 free men with 80 acres, less 2. Then 2 ploughs, now 1½; 2 acres of meadow.

In Olden [in Coddenham] 5 free men with 20 acres. Then as now half a plough.

In Hemingstone 3 free men with 9 acres. The whole is worth 30s. The king and the earl have the soke. In Coddenham Ælfric, a free man, [held] 8 acres TRE in the same valuation.

HUNDRED OF CLAYDON.

In Coddenham 1 free man with 4 acres, worth 8d. The soke is the king's and the earl's. From the mill of Billingford [Norfolk] 7s. 4d.

In Eusfort Hundred in Norfolk.

LVII. Land of Hubert de Mont-Canisy.

HUNDRED OF HARTISMERE.

Leofwine the Bald held Wyverstone TRE with 1 carucate of land as a manor. Then 4 bordars, now 3. Then 2 ploughs in demesne, afterwards 1, now 1½. Half a plough belonging to the men. 3 acres of meadow. Then woodland for 40 pigs, now 20. A church with 16 acres and half a plough. Then as now 1 horse, 3 head of cattle, 12 goats and 10 pigs. Then as now worth 30s. In the same place 6 free men commended to Leofwine with 37 acres. Then as now 1 plough. It is worth 10s.

[Folio 436v: SUFFOLK]

Richard holds all this from Hubert. The king and the earl have the soke. It is 1 league long and 4½ furlongs broad. 8d. in geld.

LVIII. Land of Gundwin the chamberlain.

HUNDRED AND HALF OF SAMFORD.

Æscmann, a free man commended to Robert fitzWymarc, held Higham as a manor with 1 carucate of land. Then as now 1 villan. Then 3 bordars, afterwards and now 2. Then 2 ploughs in demesne, afterwards none, now 1 plough. Then 1 plough belonging to the men, afterwards and now a half. 7 acres of meadow. Woodland for 10 pigs. Then as now 1 mill. Part of a church with 2 acres. Now 3 head of cattle, 8 pigs, 6 sheep and 8 goats. Then it was worth 30s., now 20s. but it was at farm for 30s. It is 8 furlongs long and 6 broad. 12d. in geld. Others hold [land] there. The soke is in [East] Bergholt.

LIX. Lands of Sasselin.

HUNDRED OF BRADMERE.

Acwulf, a thegn, held [Ixworth] Thorpe TRE as a manor with 1 carucate of land. Then as now 2 bordars. Then and afterwards 2 ploughs in demesne, now 1 and half a plough belonging to the men. 6 acres of meadow. Then as now 1 mill. Then as now 2 head of cattle. Then 10 pigs, now 16. Then as now 30 sheep. 4 free men over whom his predecessor had commendation TRE and they have 13 acres and half a plough, worth 20s. Godmann, a thegn, held Sapiston

Sasselin

[Folio 437: SUFFOLK]

TRE with half a carucate of land. Then as now 2 bordars and 1 plough in demesne. 5 acres of meadow. Then as now 1 mill and 2 head of cattle. Then 3 pigs, now 5. Then 20 sheep, now 33. Then as now worth 15s. In the same place 8 free men by commendation [held] 24 acres, worth 3s. St Edmund has the soke and sake over them and over the whole Hundred.

LX. Land of Robert de Verly.

HUNDRED OF BLACKBOURN.

In [Market] Weston Alsige, a free man, held TRE as a manor 1 carucate of land and 1 bordar and 2 slaves. Then 2 ploughs in demesne, afterwards nothing, now 1. Then as now half a plough belonging to the men. 3 acres of meadow. Then as now 1 mill. Now 1 horse, 2 head of cattle, 8 pigs and 50 sheep. 6 free men by commendation [held] 103 acres. Then 2 ploughs, now 1; 1 acre of meadow. A church with 12 acres and half a plough. This manor is worth then as now 25s. and the free men 5s.

LXI. Land of Ralph Pinel.

In Raydon 2 free men, Earngeat and Alweard, held 40 acres. Then as now half a plough and 1 bordar. It is worth 10s. Ralph held this land as a gift of the king but Geoffrey de Mandeville received service from it. The soke is in [East] Bergholt.

HALF-HUNDRED OF COSFORD.

Beorhtmær held Layham TRE with 40 acres. Then as now 1 bordar and 1 slave. It is worth 10s. St Edmund has the soke.

[Folio 437v: SUFFOLK]

LXII. Land of Isaac.

HUNDRED OF BOSMERE.

Sigeric, a free man, held Offton TRE with 100 acres as a manor. Then as now 2 bordars. Then 1 plough, now a half. A church with 7½ acres. Then it was worth 20s., now 30s. The king and the earl have the soke.

In Somersham Wulfwine, a free man, held 60 acres of land as a manor TRE. Then 1 plough. Then it was worth 20s., now 20s. The king and the earl have the soke. In the same place Colman, a free man with 5 acres, worth 20d. The king and the earl have the soke.

In Hemingstone 4 acres of demesne, worth 8d. In the same place 1 free man with half an acre, worth 1d. The king and the earl have the soke.

HUNDRED OF CLAYDON.

Leofric, a free man, held Hemingstone TRE with 1 carucate of land as a manor. Then as now 2 bordars. Then 2 ploughs, now 1; 4 acres of meadow. Woodland for 2 pigs. Then as now 1 horse. Then 2 head of cattle, now 1. Then 11 sheep, now 20. Then 13 pigs, now 20. Then 7 goats. Then it was worth 20s., now 25s. less 8d. In the same place 3 free men with 24 acres. Then and afterwards 1 plough, now a half. It is worth 5s. The king and the earl have the soke.

HUNDRED OF HARTISMERE.

Leofric, commended to Beorhtric the reeve of St Edmund, held Thornham [Magna] TRE with 1 carucate of land as a manor. Then as now 2 bordars. Then 2 ploughs, afterwards a half, now 1; 2 acres of meadow. Woodland for 30 pigs, now 20. Then as now 2 horses. The fourth part of a church with 3½ acres. Then it was worth 30s., now 20s. Over this land the abbot had three parts of the soke and the king the fourth. In the same place 3 free men with 4½ acres, worth 8d. It is 8 furlongs long and 8 broad. 8½d. in geld.

HUNDRED OF CLAYDON.

In Henley 16 acres of free land

Isaac

[Folio 438: SUFFOLK]

belonging to Hemingstone and in [its] valuation.

HUN OF COSFORD.

In "Redles" 1 sokeman belonging to Stigand held half a carucate of land. Then and afterwards 1 plough, now none. 1 acre of meadow. It is worth 18s. To this estate belonged 14 acres of woodland which William de Bournville took away from there and holds now.

LXIII. Land of Northmann the Sheriff.

HALF-HUNDRED OF IPSWICH.

In the borough [Ipswich] Northmann has 2 burgesses, one in pledge to him, the other for a debt. But the king has his customary dues.

LXIIII. Land of Judicael the priest.

HUNDRED OF BOSMERE.

In [Earl and Little] Stonham Ælfric, a free man of Eadric, Robert Malet's predecessor, held 90 acres as a manor and Robert was seised thereof. Then as now 6 bordars and 1 slave. 1½ ploughs in demesne and half a plough belonging to the men. 2 acres of meadow. Woodland for 10 pigs. 7 head of cattle. Then 1 pig, now 5. Then 8 sheep, now 40. 5 free men with 24 acres and half a plough. . Then it was worth 20s., now 35s. In the same place 1 free man with 24 acres. Then 1 plough. It is worth 5s. The king and the earl have the soke. It is 1 league long and 3 furlongs broad. Others hold [land] there. 7½d. in geld.

In [Earl and Little] Stonham 1 church with 20 acres which 9 free men gave there for their souls.

HUNDRED OF BISHOP.

In Horham, Algar, a free man of Stigand, and 2 others, one a man of Bishop Æthelmær and the other a man of Eadric of Laxfield, held 1 carucate of land TRE.

Then as now 31 7 bordars and 1 slave and 1 plough in demesne. Woodland for 24 pigs. 2 acres of meadow. 1 plough belonging to the men. Then 2 horses. Then 8 head of cattle. Then as now 24 pigs. Then 24 sheep and 1 beehive. 4 free men with 24 acres whom he claims by livery. Then half a plough, now 2 oxen. A church with 22 acres, worth 22d. Then as now worth 20s. The soke is in the bishop's [manor of] Hoxne.

LXV. Lands of Gerald the marshal.

HUNDRED OF RISBRIDGE.

Earl Ælfgar held Denston as a berewick in Badmondisfield TRE with 2 carucates of land. Then as now 4 villans and 1 bordar and 3 slaves. 2 ploughs in demesne. Then it was worth 60s., now 70s. Then as now 1 horse. Then 2 head of cattle, now 15; 24 pigs and 44 sheep.

LXVI. Lands of Robert Blund.

HUNDRED OF BRADMERE.

Aki held Ixworth as a manor TRE with 3 carucates of land. Then as now 2 bordars. Then 5 slaves, now 2. Then as now 3 ploughs in demesne. 1 mill. 20 acres of meadow. Then 2 horses, now 1. Then as now 5 head of cattle. Then 40 pigs, now 22. Then 8 sheep, now 92; 3 arpents of vines. 1 park. Then it was worth 80s., now £6. In the same place 25 free men by commendation [held] 2½ carucates of land. Then 5 ploughs, now 4½; 4 acres of meadow. Then as now worth 20s. St Edmund had the sake and soke over the whole Hundred. In the same place 5 free men by commendation [held] 1 carucate of land and 80 acres. Then 5 ploughs, now 2; 3 acres of meadow. Then it was worth 30s., now 20s. A church with 80 acres of free land and 1 plough and 1 acre of meadow, worth 5s. The whole

Robert Blund

is 2 leagues long and 6 furlongs broad. 22¾d. in geld.

Aki held Walsham [Le Willows] TRE as a manor with 2 carucates of land. Then as now 4 bordars. Then 2 ploughs in demesne, now 3. And half a plough belonging to the men. 5 acres of meadow. Woodland for 20 pigs. Then as now 1 horse. Then 3 head of cattle, now 1. Then 40 pigs, now 29. Then 5 sheep, now 30. Then it was worth 40s., now 60s. In the same place 20 free men by commendation [held] 1 carucate of land. Then as now 2 ploughs. 2 acres of meadow. Woodland for 10 pigs. Then it was worth 10s., now 20s. In the same place 3 free men and a half with 1 carucate of land. Then and afterwards 3½ ploughs, now 2; 2½ acres of meadow. Woodland for 4 pigs. Then as now worth 20s. Half a church with 10 acres and 1 acre of meadow, worth 8d. It is 2 leagues long and 6 furlongs broad. 17d. in geld. Others hold [land] there.

Aki held [Great] Ashfield as a manor TRE with 3 carucates of land. Then as now 9 bordars. Then 4 ploughs in demesne, now 3; 12 acres of meadow. Woodland for 60 pigs. Then as now 2 horses and 2 head of cattle. Then 60 pigs, now 15. Then 25 sheep, now 10, and 10 beehives. Then as now worth 60s. In the same place 14 free men by commendation [held] 80 acres. Then as now 1 plough. 4 acres of meadow. Woodland for 4 pigs. It is worth 8s. In the same place 1 free man, Ketil, 1 free man, [held] 1 carucate of land as a manor. Then as now 2 bordars and 2 slaves. 2 ploughs in demesne. 4 acres of meadow. Woodland for 20 pigs. 4 3 free men under him with 22 acres and half a plough. Then as now 2 horses. Then 4 head of cattle. Then 24 pigs, now 23. Then 22 sheep, now 100. Then 40 goats, now 12. Then as now worth 30s. Over this man Robert's predecessor had the commendation. William holds it from Robert. In the same place 3 free men by commendation [held] 1 carucate of land and 60 acres and 1 bordar. Then as now 3 ploughs and 4 acres of meadow. Woodland for 4 pigs. Then as now worth 30s.; 2 knights hold this. A church with 9 acres.

It is 11 furlongs long and 11 broad. 5½d. in geld. Others hold [land] there.

Aki held Wyken TRE as a manor with 1 carucate of land. Then 3 bordars. Then 3 slaves, now 2. Then as now 2 ploughs in demesne. 3 acres of meadow. Woodland for 10 pigs. Then 1 horse, now 2. Then as now 1 ox. Then 12 pigs, now 23. Then 25 sheep, now 38. Then as now worth 30s.; 5 free men and a half by commendation [held] 1 carucate of land. Then as now 2 bordars. And under them 2 free men with 4 acres. Then as now 2 ploughs. 6 acres of meadow. The fourth part of a mill. Then it was worth 20s., now 13s.

In Sapiston 2 free men of King Edward [held] 18 acres, worth 3s. Haret, a free man over whom St Edmund [...] had the commendation TRE, held Langham as 3 carucates of land. Then 1 villan. Then as now 3 bordars and 3 slaves. Then and afterwards 3 ploughs in demesne, now 2. Then half a plough belonging to the men. 12 acres of meadow. Woodland for 6 pigs. Then 7 horses, now 1. Then 8 head of cattle, now 2. Then 30 pigs, now 16. Then 140 sheep, now 12. Then it was worth 80s., now 60s. In the same place 2 free men by commendation [held] 20 acres. Then half a plough, now 2 oxen. It is worth 3s. It is 7 furlongs long and 6 broad. 10d. in geld.

In Hepworth half a free man with 40 acres and 1 bordar. Then as now half a plough and half an acre of meadow. It is worth 10s.

In Wyken 1 free man by commendation [held] 60 acres and 1 bordar. Then as now 1 plough. It is worth 10s. In Ixworth 1 free man [held] 40 acres. Then as now 1 plough. It is worth 5s. Concerning all these free men the king as guarantor. St Edmund has the soke and sake over the whole.

Robert Blund

In Ixworth Ketil, a free man, held 200 acres as a manor. Then as now 2 bordars and 2 slaves. 2 ploughs in demesne. 6 acres of meadow. 1 mill. And under him 6 free men with 29 acres. Then 2 ploughs, now 1. Then as now worth 60s. Over these Esger the staller had the commendation TRE. Ralph, the brother of Robert, was seised [thereof] when he died and Robert acquired it from the king.

HALF-HUNDRED OF COSFORD.

In Whatfield 5 free men. Over one St Edmund had the commendation and the soke over all of them. Robert's predecessor did not have the commendation. They have 60 acres. Then 2 ploughs, now 1. Then as now worth 6s., now 20s. In the same place 4 free men with 63 acres. Then 2 ploughs, now a half. It is worth 10s. 8d. It is by exchange.

HUNDRED OF BLYTHING.

In Westleton 27½ acres were held by Brunmær the priest TRE. Then as now half a plough. It is worth 4s.

HUNDRED OF HARTISMERE.

In Gislingham 30 acres of the demesne of Walsham [Le Willows] which Aki held. 1 acre of meadow. It is worth 6s. 8d. In the same place 3 free men, Algar, Godric, Godwine, commended to Aki, [held] 53 acres and 1 free man under them with 1 acre. Then and afterwards 2 ploughs, now a half. 1 acre of meadow. Woodland for 24 pigs. It is worth 16s. The Abbot of St Edmund had half the commendation and half the soke over two of these men's wives.

HUNDRED OF HARTISMERE.

In Westhorpe 4 free men commended to Aki TRE [held] 4½ acres, worth 16d. In Finningham 2 acres of the demesne of Walsham [Le Willows].

In Wyverstone 2 free men commended to Aki TRE [held] 30 acres. Then half a plough. Woodland for 2 pigs. Half an acre of meadow. It is worth 5s. R. Oudkell holds this from Robert Blund. [...]

HUNDRED OF STOW.

In [Great] Ashfield belongs 1 bordar with 3 acres and he renders 12d.

LXVII. Land of Hervey de Bourges.

HUNDRED OF STOW.

In Thorney Euen holds from Hervey 1 carucate of land which Beorhtric Black held under Wihtgar, the predecessor of Richard of Clare. He could not sell without his permission. Now Hervey holds it by the king's gift. Then 6 bordars, afterwards and now 3. Then 2 ploughs, afterwards none and now 1 plough. 4 acres of meadow. Then 2 ploughs belonging to the men, afterwards and now none. Then it was worth 30s., now 47s. The king and the earl have the soke.

HUNDRED OF BOSMERE.

Reginald holds Hemingstone from Hervey which Wulfmær, a free man, commended only to Eadric, TRE the predecessor of Robert Malet, held with 100 acres of land as a manor. Then as now 6 bordars and 1 plough in demesne. Then 1 plough belonging to the men, now a half. 2 acres of meadow. 1 free man with 4 acres. The whole is worth 20s. The king and the earl have the soke. On the day on which he died William Malet was seised of this land and after him Robert Malet, his son.

HUNDRED OF CLAYDON.

Beorhtweald held Pettaugh in demesne with 1 carucate of land and 30 acres as a manor TRE. Robert Malet's predecessor had the commendation. Then as now 5 bordars. Then 2 ploughs in demesne, afterwards and now 2 1; 3 acres of meadow. Then as now 1 horse. Then 3 head of cattle, now 1. Then 14 pigs, now 8. Then 32 sheep, now 20. Then it was worth 60s., now 40s. In the same place 5 free men by commendation [held] 18 acres. Then 2 ploughs, now 1. A church with 2½ acres, worth 5s. This was at farm for £3 15s. but the men were thereby ruined and now it has been

Hervey de Bourges

[Folio 441: SUFFOLK]

assessed at 45s. It is 1 league long and 3 furlongs broad. 10d. in geld. The Abbot of Ely [had] half the soke and the predecessor of Earl Hugh [had] half.

In Ashfield Godmann, a free man commended TRE to Robert Malet, [held] 30 acres as a manor and 1 bordar. Then 1 plough, afterwards none, now half a plough. A church with 4 acres, worth 10s. Ranulf holds it. The soke belonged to the abbot and to the predecessor of Hugh. William Malet was seised of these two manors on the day of his death. In the same place 1 free man with 2 acres, worth 4d. The soke is the abbot's.

HALF-HUNDRED OF PARHAM.

Eadric, commended to Eadric, Robert Malet's predecessor, held "Brutge" with 120 acres as a manor. Then 2 ploughs, afterwards 1, now a half. 4 acres of meadow. Then as now 1 mill. The fourth part of a church with 6 acres. 8 pigs. Then it was worth 40s., now 20s. The Abbot of Ely has the soke. Warner holds it from Hervey. In the same place 8 free men were added with 20 acres. Then 1 plough, afterwards a half, now none. It is worth 40d. Concerning half of this land Hervey came to an agreement with the abbot and afterwards he held it from the king. It is 8 furlongs long and 8 6 broad. 40d. in geld.

In Beversham Ælfric, a free man under soke and commendation to the Abbot of Ely, held 60 acres as a manor. Then 1 plough. 3 acres of meadow. Then it was worth 20s., afterwards and now 5s.

In the same place 2 free men commended to the aforesaid Ælfric [held] 10 acres. Then half a plough, afterwards and now none. It is worth 2s. Warner holds it from Hervey and Hervey came to an agreement with the abbot about the aforesaid manor.

HUNDRED OF BISHOP.

In Chippenhall in demesne 1 free man of Harold [held] 60 acres TRE. Then as now 2 villans and 2 ploughs. 2 acres of meadow. Woodland for 30 pigs. Then it was worth 10s., now 20s. William fitzGorham holds this.

In Colston 1 free man commended to Eadric [held] 30 acres and 3 bordars. Half a plough.

[Folio 441v: SUFFOLK]

Then it was worth 10s., now 20s. It belongs to Cransford. Warner holds this from Hervey.

HUNDRED OF COLNEIS.

In Kembroke Cyneweald holds from Hervey 1 free man, Wulfric, commended to St Æthelthryth, with 14 acres. Half a plough. Half a mill. 1 acre of meadow. 2 bordars. Then it was worth 5s., now 9s.

HUNDRED OF CARLFORD.

In Grundisburgh Godric, a free man of Harold TRE, held 1 carucate of land as a manor. Then as now 1 villan and 4 bordars. Then as now 1 plough in demesne and 1 plough belonging to the men. 3 acres of meadow. Then it was worth 16s., now the same. In the same place 3 half free men, Godwine, Wulfric, Leofric, commended to the same person, [held] 7 acres of land. Then half a plough, now none. Then it was worth 2s., now 12d. Also in the same place in demesne 2 free men, Burgric and Æthelric, commended to Eskil the housecarl TRE, [held] 5 acres. Then half a plough, now none. It is worth 10d. In the same place in demesne 1 free man, Brun, commended to Eadric, Robert Malet's predecessor, [held] 20 acres and he held these 20 acres from Eadric. Then 1 plough, now a half. 2½ acres of meadow. Then it was worth 5s., now 4s.

In [Great] Bealings in demesne 10 free men Blæcmann, Alwine, Stanheard, Ani, Wulfric, Thorbern, Eadric, Godwine, Æthelstan, Anund the priest: Halfdan had the commendation over this man and St Æthelthryth [had it] over the others with 80 acres and 4 acres of land. Then 4 ploughs, now 2 ploughs. 8 acres of meadow. Then it was worth 20s., now the same.

In the same place 1 free man, Wulfmær, was a man of Halfdan's, the predecessor of Geoffrey de Mandeville, with 100 acres of land in demesne as a manor. Wulfmær himself had under him 3 villans. Then in demesne 2 ploughs, now 1; 1 plough belonging to the men. 3 acres of meadow. Then 2 horses, now 4. Then 4 head of cattle, now 3. Then 16 pigs,

Hervey de Bourges

[Folio 442: SUFFOLK]

now 12. Then 80 sheep, now 60. Then it was worth 20s., now 40s. 1 church with 20 acres, worth 40d. The soke is St Æthelthryth's.

In Little Bealings Geoffrey holds. [There were] 2 sokemen, Glædmann and Beorhtric Godwine had soke and sake and commendation over these men and 1 free man, Leofsige, over whom Eadric had the commendation. Those 2 sokemen had 28 acres. Then 1 plough, now none. 1 acre of meadow. It is worth 2s. Leofsige had in demesne 20 acres. Then 1 plough, now none. 3 acres of meadow. 1 mill. It is worth 3s. In the same place in demesne 2 free men, Leofric and Beorhtric, commended to St Æthelthryth TRE, [held] 10 acres. Then as now half a plough. Half an acre of meadow. It is worth 2s. Also in the same place in demesne 2 free men, Wulfmær and Bondi, commended to the same [St] Æthelthryth TRE, [held] 4 acres, worth 8d. In the same place [in] demesne Hardekin, a free man commended to Durand, who was half Eadric's man and half Harold's, [held] 3 acres, worth 6d. It is 6 furlongs long and 5 broad. In geld 7½d.

In "Nechemara" in demesne 1 free man, Wulfwine, commended to Ingulf the housecarl [held] 3 acres, worth 6d.

In Rushmere [St Andrew] 1 free man, Brunwine, commended to Gyrth, [held] 30 acres. Then as now 1 plough. 1 acre of meadow. Then as now worth 10s. It is 8 furlongs and 7 broad. 16d. in geld.

In Tuddenham in demesne are 4 acres and they belong in [Great] Bealings. It is worth 8d. In the same place 1 free woman, Ealdgyth, commended to Eadric of Laxfield, [held] 6 acres, worth 12d.

In the same place Bernard d'AlenÓon holds 80 acres which Beorhtmær, a free man TRE commended to Eadric of Laxfield, held as a manor. Then as now 6 bordars and 1 slave and 2 ploughs in demesne. 4 acres of meadow. Then 2 horses, now none. Then 3 pigs, now 5. Then 15 sheep, now 10. Then 6 goats,

now none. Then it was worth 20s., now the same. Eadric, Robert Malet's predecessor, was seised of this manor TRE and William Malet [was seised of it] when he died. He could not give or sell his land to anyone. 5 free men commended to the same Beorhtmær with 14 acres. Then half a plough, now none. Then it was worth 4s., now 3s. In the same place 2 free men, one commended to the predecessor of Ranulf, brother of Ilger, and the other commended to someone commended to St Æthelthryth, [held] 7 acres. Then half a plough, now none. It is worth 16d. It is 10 [...] furlongs long and 6 broad. 15d. in geld. Bernard d'AlenÓon holds the whole of this from Hevey.

1 free man, Frani, commended to Eadric, [held] Thistleton TRE with 30 acres of land. Then as now 2 bordars and 1 plough. 2 acres of meadow. It is worth 8s. Reginald holds this from Hervey but William Malet was seised thereof on the day on which he died.

In "Derneford" 11 free men, commended to Durand, who was half Eadric's man TRE and half Harold's, [held] 80 acres and 3 bordars. Then 4 ploughs, now 3; 2 acres of meadow. Then it was worth 40s., now 15s.

In "Ingoluestuna" 13 free men TRE, now 6, commended to the same Durand, [held] 1 carucate of land and 4 acres. Then 5 ploughs, now 1; 5 acres of meadow. It is worth 10s.

In the same place 1 free man commended to the same Durand [held] 12 acres. Half a plough. It is worth 40d. It is 6 furlongs long and 5 broad. 7½d. in geld. Peter de Palluel holds this from Hervey.

HUNDRED OF WILFORD.

Swærting, commended to Robert Malet's predecessor, held Bredfield TRE with 80 acres and 1 bordar. Then 1½ ploughs, now 1. Then 2 horses, now 2; 1 ox and 27 sheep. Then it was worth 20s., now 30s. It is 1 league and half a furlong long and 6 furlongs broad. In geld 13½d. In the same place 21 free men commended to Swærting TRE [held] 1 carucate

Hervey de Bourges

of land and 22 acres. Then 4 ploughs, now 3. Half an acre of meadow. Then it was worth 30s., now the same. Also in the same place 1 free man commended to someone commended to Robert Malet's predecessor, [held] 12 acres. Then as now half a plough. It is worth 2s. William Malet was seised of this on the day on which he died.

In Wickham [Market] holds; . a free man commended to

Eadric TRE, [held] 33 acres as a manor. 1 bordar. 3 acres of meadow. Then 1 plough, now none. 2 free men under him with 8 acres. Then half a plough. Then it was worth 10s., now 6s. Of this likewise [William Malet was seised].

In Sutton holds. The same Azur held 60 acres as a manor. Then as now 2 bordars. Then and afterwards 1 plough, now a half. Half an acre of meadow. Then it was worth 10s., now the same. In the same place the same Erchenbald holds 1 free man commended to Eadric [with] 6 acres. Then as now 2 oxen. Then it was worth 2s., now the same. Of this as many likewise [William Malet was seised].

In Harpole Odo holds 1 free man by commendation, [half] to St Æthelthryth and half to Eadric, with 16 acres, worth 3s.

In Bredfield Peter holds 1 free man by commendation to Durand of Offton, with 12 acres and 3 oxen and 23 sheep, worth 2s. In the same place 1 free man by commendation to Æthelric of Burgh with 4 acres, worth 8d.

In Loudham half a free man commended to Swærting TRE [held] 15 acres, worth 2s.

In Boulge 1 free man commended to Eadric Grim with 5 perches of land, worth 4d.

In Harpole 1 free man by commendation to Eadric with 5 acres and half an acre of meadow, worth 12d.

HUNDRED OF LOOSE.

Beorhtmær, commended to Harold, held Martley TRE as a manor with 80 acres. Then as now 5 bordars. In demesne 2 ploughs. 9 acres of meadow. 1 horse and 1 ox. 9 pigs, 17 sheep and 30 goats. Then it was worth 40s., now 30s. And 10 free men and 2 half [free men] commended to the same person with 60 acres. Then as now 2 ploughs. 1½ acres of meadow. It is worth 10s. Robert Malet

claims 1 of these men. It is 1 league long and a half broad. In geld 11d.

2 free men, Swærting and Eadric, commended to Eadric of Laxfield, held Campsey [Ash] with 60 acres of land as a manor. Then as now 3 villans. Then as now 2 ploughs and half a plough belonging to the men. 8 acres of meadow. 1 mill. 2 horses and 8 pigs. 20 sheep and 3 beehives. Then it was worth 20s., now 30s. 12 free men under the same commendation with 38 acres of land. Then 2 ploughs, now 1. Then it was worth 8s., now 10s. It is 6 furlongs long and 4 broad. In geld 7d. William Malet was seised [thereof] on the day on which he died.

Godgifu, a free woman commended half to St Æthelthryth and half to Eadric of Laxfield, held Rendlesham with 60 acres as a manor. Then 2 ploughs, now 1; 2 acres of meadow. 1 villan. Then as now worth 20s. 1 free man and half a [free man] under the same commendation [held] 10 acres and half a plough in the same valuation. Bernard d'AlenÓon holds this from Hervey. William was seised thereof on the day on which he died. It is 1 league long and a half broad. In geld 14d.

Odo holds Potsford as a manor with 80 acres as a manor which

Wynning, commended half to St Æthelthryth and half to Eadric, held. Then as now 2 villans and 2 bordars. 6 acres of meadow. Then 2 ploughs, now 1; 1 horse, 4 head of cattle and

10 goats. Then as now worth 20s. In the same place 8 free men [held] 30 acres. 3 of them forfeited their land to the abbot and the Hundred has not afterwards seen that they have redeemed it, and a fourth was the abbot's man and the other four were commended to Wynning. All these men [had] half a plough. 1½ acres of meadow. Then as now worth 10s. It is 1 league long

Hervey de Bourges

[Folio 444: SUFFOLK]

and a half broad. In geld 11d. William was seised [thereof] on the day on which he died.

Beorhtmær, commended to Eadric, held Glevering TRE with 40 acres as a manor. 1 bordar. 1 plough. 3 acres of meadow. 1 mill. 20 sheep. Then it was worth 8s., now 10s. In the same place 17 free men and half a [free man], commended to the same person, [held] 60 acres. Then 2 ploughs, now 1; 1 acre of meadow. Then it was worth 17s., now 15s. William Malet was seised [thereof] on the day on which he died. It is 1 league long and a half broad. In geld 22d. Odo holds this from Hervey.

In Dallinghoo 40 acres which 3 free men held, worth 6s. In the same place 2 free men, commended half to Swærting and half to Brunmann, [held] 20 acres. Then half a plough. It is worth 3s. It is 1 league long and 3 furlongs broad. In geld 7½d. In the same place 2 half [free] men commended to Eadric [held] 5 acres, worth 12d.

HUNDRED OF PLUMESGATE.

Azur, commended to Eadric of Laxfield, held Cransford with 80 acres of land as a manor. Then as now 1 bordar. Then 2 ploughs, now 1; 1 acre of meadow. Then 2 horses. Then 24 pigs, now 1; 16 sheep. Then 40 goats. Then it was worth 20s., now 13s. 4d.

LXVIII. Lands of Gilbert the Crossbowman.

HUNDRED OF BLYTHING.

In Easton [Bavents] Ælfric, son of Wulfgeat, commended to Earl Harold, held TRE 2 carucates of land; now Gilbert holds it from the king. Then 5 villans, now 3. Then as now 5 bordars and 1 slave. Then 1½ ploughs in demesne, now none. Then as now 3 ploughs belonging to the men. Woodland for 8 pigs. 3 acres of meadow. Then 1 salt-pan,

[Folio 444v: SUFFOLK]

now none. Then 1 horse, 3 head of cattle, 2 pigs and 80 sheep, now none. Then it was worth 40s., now 20s. The king and the earl have the soke. Also in Uggeshall 1 villan, Wulfric, with 20 acres and half a plough. The king and the earl have the soke In Chediston 1 villan, Eskil, with 20 acres and half a plough and it is in the same valuation of Easton [Bavents]. The same Gilbert holds in Chediston 1 free man, Godric, under the same commendation with 20 acres. 2 bordars and half a plough and half an acre of meadow. Woodland for 6 pigs. It is worth 4s. And in Easton [Bavents] there are 2 free men, Godric and Eskil, under the same commendation, with 20 acres of land.

Then as now 1 plough. It is worth 4s. The king and the earl have the soke. Easton [Bavents] is 1 league long and a half broad. In geld 6d. Others hold [land] there.

HUNDRED OF HARTISMERE.

Alsige, a free man, held Gislingham with 2 carucates of land as a manor and 2 bordars. Then and afterwards 2 ploughs in demesne, now 1; 2 acres of meadow. Woodland for 4 pigs. It is worth 40s. During the lifetime of King Edward this manor was in the demesne of Abbot Leofstan of St Edmund and Leofstan the abbot leased it to Alsige and his wife on the agreement that after their death the abbot should have his manor back, and one other manor of Alsige, Euston by name. The king and the earl have the soke. In the same place 8 free men commended to Alsige [held] 16 acres. Then 1 plough, now a half. They are in the above valuation. In the same place 3 free men commended to the predecessor of Aubrey de Vere [held] 6 acres, worth 12d. The king and the earl have the soke. It is 1 league long and 7 furlongs broad. 10d. in geld.

[Folio 445: SUFFOLK]

LXVIIII. Lands of Ralph the Crossbowman.

HALF-HUNDRED OF LOTHINGLAND.

Bishop Stigand held Burgh [Castle] together with the soke TRE, with 4 carucates of land as a manor. Then as now 10 villans and 5 bordars. Then 2 slaves, now none. Then in demesne 3 ploughs, now 2. Then 4 ploughs belonging to the men, now 3; 10 acres of meadow. 3 salt-pans. Then as now 3 horses, 6 head of cattle, 17 pigs and 160 sheep. 1 church with 10 acres. 1 acre of meadow. Then it was worth 100s., now 106s.

Bondi, commended to Gyrth, held Caldecott TRE with 1 carucate of land as a manor. Then 1 bordar, now 3. Then 1 plough, now a half. Then it was worth 10s., now 8s. In Corton 1 free man, Ketil, commended to Ulf, [held] TRE 40 acres. Then 1 bordar, now none. Then as now half a plough. Then as now worth 4s.

In Somerleyton 1 free man, Alweald, commended to Gyrth, [held] 30 acres. Then half a plough, now none. Woodland for 5 pigs. It is worth 2s.

LXX. Lands of Reginald the Bretonwhich he claims in alms of the king.

HUNDRED OF RISBRIDGE.

3 free men held Lidgate as 4 carucates of land. Then 9 villans, afterwards 7, now 3. Then 1 bordar, afterwards 4, now 6. Then 3 slaves, afterwards 1, now none. Then and afterwards 3 ploughs, now 1. Then and afterwards 7 ploughs belonging to the men, now 2. Woodland for 10 pigs. 10 acres of meadow. Then 2 pigs, now 30. Then as now 7 sheep. Then it was worth 80s., now 60s. This land W[illiam de] Vatteville's men claim for his fief.

LXXI. Land of Robert of Stafford.

HUNDRED OF SAMFORD.

Swein Swart held Boynton TRE with 1 carucate of land as a manor. Then 2 bordars, now 6. Then 2 ploughs in demesne. Then as now 1 plough belonging to the men. 5 acres of meadow. Then it was worth 40s.; now 30s. The soke is in [East] Bergholt. In the same place Beorhtsige, a free man, held 1 carucate of land as a manor TRE. Then 1 bordar, now 2. Then as now 1 plough in demesne. Now 1 horse and 6 sheep. It is worth 20s. It is 7 furlongs long and 6 broad. 14d. in geld. Others hold [land] there. The soke is in [East] Bergholt.

In Belstead Thorir held 80 acres as a manor. Then as now 3 villans and 2 bordars. Then 1 plough in demesne. Then as now 1 plough belonging to the men. 2 acres of meadow. The fourth part of a church. It is worth 23s. The soke is in [East] Bergholt.

LXXII. Land of Stanheard, son of Æthelwig.

HUNDRED OF RISBRIDGE.

In Ousden Wihtgar held 30 acres TRE. Then as now 1 bordar and 1 plough. 2 acres of meadow. It is worth 20s.

LXXIII. Land of Wulfmær.

HUNDRED OF RISBRIDGE.

In "Lafham" 24 acres and half a plough. It is worth 4s. St Edmund has the soke. In the same place the same Wulfmær holds 9 acres which he appropriated in the time of King William from Ralph Pinel's predecessor for 21s. It is worth 12d. Roger the sheriff had heriot from his father.

[Folio 446: SUFFOLK]

LXXIIII. Land of Vavassors.

HUNDRED OF BOSMERE.

In Hemingstone 1 free man with 20 acres in the king's soke. 5 bordars. Then as now 1 plough. It is worth 5s.

In "Facheduna" 3 free men in the king's soke with 30 acres. Then as now 1 plough. It is worth 5s. In the same Hundred. In Battisford 1 free man, Durand, held 30 acres TRE; now Siward [holds it] in the king's soke. Then half a plough, now 2 oxen. 2 acres.

In Olden [in Coddenham] 4 free men, Radbodo, Leofric, Eadric, Wulfric, [held] 8 acres, worth 16d. These men were added to the farm in the time of King William and Roger is warrant thereof to Wulfmær the reeve who added them. And they did not belong to any farm. In the same place 1 free man, Wulfmær, [had] the fourth part of an acre, worth 2d. Beorhtmær the beadle held this man and he gave a pledge. Wulfmær the reeve is the surety. In the same place 1 free man, Leofwine, with 2½ acres, worth 8d.

In Hemingstone 1 free man, Beorhtweald, with 4 acres, worth 8d.

In Creeting a free woman, Ealdgyth, with half an acre, worth 1d.

HUNDRED OF CLAYDON.

In Hemingstone 1 free man, Alwine, commended to Gyrth, [held] 30 acres. Then half a plough. It is worth 5s. Wulfmær the reeve added this free man to the king's farm at Bramford and Roger the sheriff is warrant thereof to him. He renders 5s. each year. The king and the earl have the soke.

In Thurlston Hrolf held TRE 12 acres; now Ælfric his son, a burgess of Ipswich, [holds it]. It is worth 2s. The king and the earl have the soke. Earl Ralph was seised of this when he forfeited. The same Ælfric holds the church

[Folio 446v: SUFFOLK]

of St Julian in the borough of Ipswich, with 20 acres of land, worth 40d. Earl Ralph was seised of this church.

In Claydon Ælfric, a free man, held 6½ acres TRE; now the same Ælfric holds it. It is worth 14d. The king and the earl have half the soke and St Æthelthryth the other half. That man Ælfric held this land in pledge and he did not have a guarantor for it. [...] These men are in the king's hand.

In Westerfield 6 free men Alwine, Flint, Alwine, Eadric, Wulfric, Æthelstan [hold] between them 15 acres and 1 plough, worth 30d. One of these, Flint by name, gave pledge for this, that he said that they gave farm in Ipswich and the sheriff proved that he lied. And the same sheriff is surety for this. The king and the earl have the soke.

In Thurlston 1 free man, Godwine, commended to Stigand, [held] 10 acres, worth 20d.

In this Hundred the king has 30 [sic] free men with 147½ acres. A church in Whitton with 10 acres. Then as now 3 ploughs. 1 acre of meadow. It is worth 40s. 4d. These are their names: Æthelstan, Godric, Godwine, Offa, Rictan, Goding, Ælfric, Eastræd, Ælfric, Tofa-Hildr, Leofwine, Ælfric, Gunnhvati, Wulfric, Thorkil, Godric, Edith, Deorsige, Beorhtmær, Leofgifu, Ælfric, Wulfric, Northmann, Leofric, Sahsleib, Alwine, Wulfwine, Eadric, Sigar. The sheriff holds these men in the king's hand. The king and the earl have the soke. In Westerfield Ælfric the priest holds then as now 12 acres. 2 acres of meadow. It is worth 3s. The king and the earl have the soke.

In Thurlston 2 free men, Wulfric and Ordmær, [held] 6 acres, worth 12d. The soke is the king's. The sheriff has custody in the king's hand.

[Folio 447: SUFFOLK]

In Coddenham 1 priest, Frideb[...], with half an acre in alms. It is worth 1d.

LXXV

These are the free men of Suffolk who remain in the hand of the king.

HUNDRED OF BRADMERE.

In [Ixworth] Thorpe 1 free man [held] 30 acres TRE. Then and afterwards half a plough, now 2 oxen. It is worth 2s. 6d. Robert Blund held this man thinking that he was of the abbot's holding and the same man confirmed that he belonged to Robert of the abbot's fief, but the abbot was not his guarantor for this. Now at last he has acknowledged that he is not of the abbot's fief. He has remitted him into the king's hand and he has given a pledge concerning this.

In Ixworth 1 free man [held] 12 acres, worth 2s. St Edmund [had] half the commendation TRE and the soke and sake and the predecessor of Peter de Valognes [had] half the commendation. Richard, Robert Blund's man, held this man and he gave a pledge. Robert is not a guarantor for him.

HUNDRED OF BISHOP.

In Horham 1 free man with 6 acres, worth 12d. Herbert Blacun held this man in the king's hand by order of Bishop Herfast but Judicael the priest claims him by the king's gift and he was seised thereof. His predecessor had the commendation TRE. The soke is in Hoxne.

In Instead 1 free man, over whom Bishop Æthelmær had the commendation, with 10½ acres and the fourth part of a mill. 1 bordar. Then half a plough, now 2 oxen. It is worth 2s. William Malet held this; afterwards Robert his son [held it], thinking it belonged to his father's fief.

[Folio 447v: SUFFOLK]

In Bedingfield 2 free men who remain in the king's hand through respite of the plea between the Bishop of Bayeux and Robert Malet's mother. One was commended to Stigand and the other half to Leofric, Robert Malet's predecessor, and half to Saxi. They have 40 acres and 3 bordars. Then as now 1 plough. Woodland for 20 pigs. It is worth 10s. The soke is in Hoxne.

LXXVI. Encroachments On the King.

HUNDRED OF RISBRIDGE.

Richard, son of Count Gilbert.

In [Great and Little] Bradley 4 free men: Wulfwine, Leofric [and] Wulfwine have 15 acres and the fourth, Bondi, has 1 carucate of land. Then as now 2 ploughs. 5 acres of meadow. It is worth 22s. 6d. His predecessor never had commendation over these men. Malvoisin holds the carucate. St Edmund has the whole soke.

TWO HUNDREDS OF BABERGH.

In Groton Richard fitzGilbert holds 1 free man of Robert fitzWymarc by commendation only with 60 acres of land. Then 4 bordars, now 1. Then and afterwards 1 plough, now none. 1 acre of meadow. Then and afterwards worth 10s., now 18s. Roger d'Orbec appropriated this and he holds it under Richard fitzGilbert. Richard's men claim it for the fief of Wihtgar, his predecessor. But according to the testimony of that Hundred it never belonged [to that fief], nor did the commendation nor the soke. In Cave Ælfric, brother of the aforesaid Eadric, and a man of Wihtgar, appropriated half of his brother's land, [namely] 60 acres. Now Roger de Saint-Germain holds it

[Folio 448: SUFFOLK]

as of Richard's fief but it never belonged to the fief by commendation or soke. Then as now there is there 1 villan and 1 bordar. 1 acre of meadow.

In [Great and Little] Cornard Ælfric Cempa held 2 free men by commendation only in the soke of St Edmund TRE but when King William came Wihtgar appropriated them before the agreement with Richard who now holds. They have 2 carucates of land and 40 acres. Then and afterwards 4 bordars, now 11. Then 5 slaves, now 4. Then 3 ploughs in demesne, now 3 between him and the men. Woodland for 30 pigs. 8 acres of meadow. Then 3 horses, now 4 head of cattle. Now 30 pigs. Now 110 sheep. A church with 15 acres of free land. Then and afterwards worth 20s.; now it renders £6. It is 8 furlongs long and 4 broad. In geld 24d., whoever holds there.

In "Saibamus" Richard holds 1 free man of Robert fitzWymarc by commendation and in the soke and sake of St Edmund. But Wihtgar held him when he forfeited. Now Richard his successor holds him. He has 1 carucate of land and 3 bordars and 2 slaves. Then as now 1 plough. 7 acres of meadow. Now 50 sheep and 7 pigs. It is worth 20s.

In Cavendish Alweald, 1 free man by commendation and soke and sake, had 1 carucate of land TRE and after King William came. Now Richard has appropriated him. Then as now 1½ ploughs. 2 acres of meadow. It is worth 20s.

In the same place Richard of Clare appropriated a free man of King Edward but his predecessor had no interest at all in him. He had 1 carucate of land. Then 4 villans, afterwards and now 2; 7 bordars. Then and afterwards 2 ploughs, now 1; 1 plough belonging to the men. 4 acres of meadow. Now 1 mill. Woodland for 10 pigs. It is worth 20s.

[Folio 448v: SUFFOLK]

HUNDRED OF BLACKBOURN.

In Stanton 1 free woman commended to St Edmund TRE [held] 30 acres. It is worth 5s.

In Knettishall St Edmund held 30 acres TRE and half a mill, worth 5s.

In Bardwell the dwellings of a certain free man of St Edmund. In the same place half a free man of St Edmund with 8 acres, worth 16d. In the same place 10 acres of a certain free [woman] of St Edmund, worth 20d. W[illiam] de Parthenay appropriated all this from the abbot and he holds the commendation of one free man.

HUNDRED OF BOSMERE.

In Somersham 1 free man, Wulfric by name, with 12 acres, worth 4s. Earl Ralph was seised of this when he forfeited and his predecessor had the commendation in Nettlestead. Wulfmær, the king's reeve, appropriated this and gave a pledge. Roger Bigod is surety. It is in the king's hand. The king and the earl have the soke.

In [Great and Little] Bricett there are 20 acres which belong in the manor of William d'Auberville which Eskil held TRE. Now Bothild, a certain woman, holds them and calls Hugh de Houdain as guarantor. But he himself is in the king's custody and he cannot respond. Now they are in the king's hand and Wulfmær the reeve has charge of them. It is worth 5s.

In Baylham Queen Edith held half a church with 12 acres TRE and as long as she lived. Afterwards William de Bournville held it. Now it is in the king's hand. It is worth 2s. He gave a pledge of this. Turstin fitzGuy is his surety.

HUNDRED OF STOW.

In [Great and Little] Finborough 1 free man over whom Roger [d'Auberville]'s predecessor had half the commendation and Eustace the other half of the commendation. Afterwards the Count of Mortain held him but Roger held him when he left the land and Robert the crossbowman

[Folio 449: SUFFOLK]

under him. Now Roger Bigod holds him in the king's hand until it be adjudged. He has 15 acres of land. Then half a plough, now none. It is worth 3s.

HUNDRED OF BLYTHING.

In Wissett, Count Alan's manor, belonged a free man with 4 acres which belong in Covehithe and are worth 8d. Robert de Courson appropriated this. Earl Ralph held this man when he forfeited. He has given a pledge of this. In the same place 1 free man with 8 acres, worth 16d. William de Warenne's predecessor had the commendation over him TRE and he had it as his land by exchange. Robert also appropriated these together with the 4 aforesaid acres.

In Uggeshall 2 free men, Northmann and Ketil, with 18 acres and half a plough, worth 3s. Berengar, a man of St Edmund appropriated this and he is in the king's mercy. This man was sick and he could not come to the plea. Now they are in the sheriff's charge.

In Cavendish Ralph de Limésy holds 1 free man of Harold's, whom Eadric the deacon, who died with him in the battle, held. It was delivered to Baynard as an estate. Edgar added it to Cavendish after Baynard lost it. Now Ralph de Limésy holds it in the demesne of the hall.

In Lavenham Aubrey de Vere holds 3 free [men] belonging to Wulfwine, Aubrey de Vere's predecessor, by commendation only in the soke of St Edmund. They have 50 acres. Then between them all 2 ploughs, now 1. Then as now worth 6s.

In Coddenham Walter de Saint-Valéry held 2 free men by commendation only.

[Folio 449v: SUFFOLK]

Now Roger de Rames holds them but the Hundred does not know how. Nor was there anyone on his behalf who could say how. They have 20 acres of land. Then and afterwards 10s., now nothing.

HUNDRED OF HARTISMERE.

In Eye Robert Malet held 1 free man, Svartrikr by name, commended to Harold and in his soke, with 120 acres as a manor. Then as now 4 bordars and 1 plough in demesne. 4 acres of meadow. Woodland for 13 pigs. It is worth 20s.

[Folio 450: SUFFOLK]

CONCERNING THE DISPUTES between the Bishop of Bayeux and the mother of Robert Malet.

HUNDRED OF HARTISMERE.

In Occold Beorhthere, a free man of Stigand, held 20 acres. Then as now 1 bordar. It is worth 40d. Stigand gave this land to Robert Malet's mother and she later held it from the queen. Now the bishop [holds it]. In the same vill Cyneric, a free man half commended to the predecessor of Robert Malet and half commended to Saxi, the predecessor of Ranulf Peverel, held 20 acres and 2 bordars and 1 plough, worth 40d.

HUNDRED OF BISHOP.

In Bedingfield the above-mentioned Beorhthere and Cyneric held 40 acres in the aforesaid manner. Then 1 plough, now a half. Woodland for 40 pigs. 1 free man commended to Beorhtræd with 5 acres. The whole is worth 11s.

HUNDRED OF HARTISMERE.

In Aspall 4 free men Deorwulf commended to the Abbot of Ely and Thorsten commended to Saxi and Markulf commended to Eadric, Robert Malet's predecessor, and Gunnulf commended to Robert Malet's predecessor [held] 86 acres and 7 bordars. Then as now 3 ploughs. 2 acres of meadow. Then as now worth 40s. William Malet was seised of this land before the Bishop of Bayeux, as the Hundred testifies. And afterwards Hubert de Port came and proved the land free and gave seisin of this land to the bishop because the free men used to hold it. On the day when Earl Ralph forfeited, Robert Malet's mother was seised thereof, as the Hundred testifies and until the plea at Odiham [Hants]. Now it is in the king's peace as the king ordered, between the bishop and Robert's mother.

THIS SURVEY WAS MADE IN THE YEAR ONE THOUSAND AND EIGHTY SIX FROM THE INCARNATION OF THE LORD AND THE TWENTIETH OF THE REIGN OF WILLIAM, NOT ONLY THROUGHOUT THESE THREE COUNTIES BUT ALSO THROUGHOUT THE OTHERS.

[Folio 450v: SUFFOLK]

Henry D'Oilli [1150-1160]
Sanson

[Folio 451: SUFFOLK]

There are 444 folios in this book
[Edward Fauconberg, 1659]

Index of Places

The Index of Places shows the modern name followed by the county in ( ) in which the place is to be found in Domesday. Annotation in square brackets helps identify more closely where the place mentioned is to be found geographically. So 'Aislaby [near Pickering], (Yorks)' This is followed by the name of the place (and its variants) as used in the actual text of *Domesday Book* and then the page reference. Places are listed in modern name order.

St Martins [in Canterbury], (Kent), Sanctus Martinus, 9
St Mary Cray [London], (Kent), Sudcrai, 16
St Marychurch, (Devon.), aecclesia Sanctae Mariae, Sanctae Mariae cerce, 283, 294
St Michael Church, (Som.), Michaeliscerce, 273
St Michaels Burton, (Sussex), Botechitone, 57
St Michael's on Wyre [Lancs.], (Yorks.), Michelescherche, 795
St Neot, (Corn.), Neotestou, Nietestou, 345, 354
St Osyth, (Essex), Cice, Cita, 976, 993, 1026
St Pancras, (Middx.), Sanctus Pancratius, 360
St Paul's Cray [London], (Kent), alia Craie, 16
St Paul's Walden, (Herts.), Waldene, 376
St Peters Chapel, (Essex), Effecestra, Effecestre, 984, 1009
St Stephens, (Corn.), Lanscauetone, 343
St Winnow, (Corn.), Sanwinuec, 343
Stackhouse, (Yorks.), Stacuse, 854
Stadbury, (Devon.), Stotberie, 309
Staddiscombe, (Devon.), Stotescome, 311
Staddon, (Devon.), Stotdone, 311
Stafford, (Devon.), Staford, 332
Stafford, (Staffs.), Stadford, Statford, 672, 676, 677, 678, 680
Stafford, West, (Dorset), Staford, Stanford, 210, 223
Stagenhoe, (Herts.), Stagnehou, 383
Stagsden, (Beds.), Stachedene, 563, 567, 571, 584
Stainborough, (Yorks.), Stainburg, Stanburg, 826, 868
Stainburn, (Yorks.), Stainburne, Stanburne, 795, 869
Stainby, (Lincs.), Stigandebi, 928
Staines [Surrey], (Middx.), Stanes, 361, 363, 366
Stainfield [in Haconby], (Lincs.), Steintone, Stentuith, 943, 953
Stainfield [near Lincoln], (Lincs.), Stainfelde, Steinfelde, 918, 960
Stainforth [in Hatfield], (Yorks.), Steinforde, Stenforde, 832, 833, 858
Stainforth [near Settle], (Yorks.), Stainforde, Stranforde, 854
Staining [Lancs.], (Yorks.), Staininghe, 795
Stainland, (Yorks.), Stanland, 868
Stainley, North, (Yorks.), Nordstanlai, Nordstanlaia, Staneleia, Stanlei, 800, 811, 869
Stainley, South, (Yorks.), Stanlai, Stanlei, Stanleie, 789, 800, 870
Stainsby, (Derby.), Steinesbi, 744
Stainsby, (Yorks.), Steinesbi, 803, 871
Stainton [in Bank Newton], (Yorks.), Stainton, Staintone, 795, 854, 870
'Stainton' [in Waddingham], (Lincs.), Staintone, Stantone, 887, 894, 915, 931, 953
Stainton [Lancs.], (Yorks.), Steintun, 796
Stainton [near Thornaby-on-Tees], (Yorks.), Steintun, 803, 831, 871
Stainton [near Tickhill], (Yorks.), Stainton, Staintone, Stantone, 829, 866
Stainton [Westm.], (Yorks.), Steintun, 796
Stainton by Langworth, (Lincs.), Staintune, 907
Stainton le Vale, (Lincs.), Stainton, Staintone, 919, 924, 934, 942
Staintondale, (Yorks.), Steintun, 787, 871
Stakesby, High, (Yorks.), Staxebi, 802, 870

Stalbridge, (Dorset), Staplebrige, 202
Stalbridge Weston, (Dorset), Westone, 202
Stalham, (Norfolk), Stalha, Stalham, Stanham, 1080, 1104, 1110, 1137, 1179
Stalisfield [Stalisfield and Stalisfield Green], (Kent), Stanefelle, 24
Stallenge Thorne, (Devon.), Stanlinz, 333
Stallingborough, (Lincs.), Stalinburg, Stalingeburg, 889, 890, 895, 924, 936, 961
Stalmine [Lancs.], (Yorks.), Stalmine, 796
Stambourne, (Essex), Stanburna, Stanburne, 1010, 1011, 1046
Stambridge, Great and Little, (Essex), Stanbruge, 974, 986, 1002, 1045
Stamford, (Lincs.), Stanford, 883, 884, 929
Stanage [Wales], (Shrops.), Stanege, 713
Stancil, (Yorks.), Steineshale, 857
Stancombe, (Devon.), Stancome, 309
Standen, (Sussex), Standene, 54
Standen [Berks.], (Wilts.), Standene, 186
Standen, Great East or Little East, I.o.W., (Hants.), Standone, 131
Standen, North [Berks.], (Wilts.), Standone, 178
Standerwick, (Som.), Stalrewiche, 258
Standish, (Glos.), Stanedis, 452
Standlynch, (Wilts.), Staninges, 185, 186, 193
Standon, (Herts.), Standone, 393
Standon, (Staffs.), Stantone, 681
Stanfield, (Norfolk), Stanfelda, Stanuelda, 1077, 1092
Stanford, (Beds.), Stanford, Stanforde, 570, 572, 574, 577, 586, 588
Stanford, (Norfolk), Estanforda, Stanforda, 1106, 1118, 1147, 1153, 1174
Stanford Bishop, (Herefs.), Stanford, 511
Stanford Dingley, (Berks.), Stanworde, 149
Stanford in the Vale, (Berks.), Stanford, 148
Stanford on Avon, (Northants.), Stanford, 614
Stanford on Avon [Northants.], (Leics.), Stanford, 642
Stanford on Soar, (Notts.), Stanford, 767, 779
Stanford on Teme, (Worcs.), Stanford, 487, 488
Stanford Regis, (Herefs.), Stanford, 497
Stanford Rivers, (Essex), Parva Stanfort, Stanfort, 992
Stanground [in Peterborough], (Hunts.), Stangrun, 555
Stanhoe, (Norfolk), Stanho, Stanhou, 1053, 1054, 1076, 1093
Stanion, (Northants.), Stanere, 591, 595
Stanley, (Derby.), Stanlei, 753
Stanley, (Wilts.), Stanlege, 186
Stanley, (Yorks.), Stanlei, Stanleie, 789, 867
Stanley Pontlarge, (Glos.), Stanlege, 449
Stanmer, (Essex), Stantmere, 1040
Stanmer, (Sussex), Stanmere, 38
Stanmore, (Middx.), Stanmere, 363
'Stanmore' [in Preshute], (Wilts.), Stamere, 184
Stanmore, Little, (Middx.), Stanmera, 366
Stanney [Stanney and Stanney, Little], (Ches.), Stanei, 720
Stanningfield, (Suffolk), Stanesfelda, Stanfella, 1194, 1242, 1279
Stanninghall, (Norfolk), Staningehalla, 1074
Stanpit, (Hants.), Stanpeta, 111

Glossary

This Glossary contains not only those terms found in *Domesday Book* but also a number of others commonly used in Medieval Studies and which may be unfamiliar to the general reader.

ACRE (Latin *acra*, from *ager*, field). (1) Unlike the modern acre the medieval acre could be used to estimate length as well as area. As a square measure 4 x 40 PERCHES, as a linear measure 66 ft (the length of a modern cricket pitch). (2) A unit of assessment to GELD: in some areas 120 geld-acres equalled one HIDE.

ALOD, allod (Old German *alod*, latinized). Land held by freehold. *Allodarii* are usually regarded as tenants in freehold..

AMBER (poss. from Latin *amphora*, a large jar; Old German *einpar*). (1) As a liquid measure, 48 SESTERS. (2) As a dry measure, used for salt: a pennyworth.

ANTECESSOR (Latin). In *Domesday Book*, the preceding landholder, usually the pre-Conquest landholder, from whom the 1086 holder might claim legal title.

ARPENT (Latin *arepennis*). A term originally meaning 100 square PERCHES imported from France in the eleventh century, and used in *Great Domesday Book* particularly for measuring vineyards.

ASSART, -ING (Latin *exsartun, -are*). As a noun, a clearing, not yet fully incorporated into the main arable land. As a verb, to make such a clearing.

ASSAY, -ING. The practice of testing the purity of coins, measured by silver content, by melting or 'burning' a sample. *See* FARM (1): BLANCH FARM.

AT FARM. *See* FARM (2).

ÆTHELING (Old English). A term applied to the royal princes of the Old English kingdom, the sons and brothers of the reigning king from whom the next ruler was chosen.

BAILEY (from Old French *baillier*, to enclose, to control). A defended enclosure. *See* MOTTE.

BEADLE (Latin *bedellus*; Old English *bydel*). A manorial official, subordinate to the REEVE.

BEREWICK (Old English *berewic*, literally 'barley wick'). An outlying estate, or an estate devoted to some specialized function.

BLANCH, BLANCH FARM. *See* FARM (1).

BLOOM (Latin *blomae, plumbei*). A measure used for iron, probably equivalent to the ingot (Latin *massa*).

BODYGUARD. In *Domesday Book*, *heuuard* (Old English *here-weard*, army guard). The duty of providing a bodyguard for a specified period, either for the king or for some other LORD.

BOOKLAND (Old English *bocland*). Land to which the title is a royal charter; the essential factor in bookland tenure is freedom to dispose of the land as the holder wishes.

BOOR (Latin *burcus*; Old English *gebur*). An inferior peasant: equated in *Domesday Book* with COLIBERT. Archaic in 1086, being replaced by VILLAN.

BORDAR (from Old French *borde*, a wooden hut). A cottager: a peasant of lower economic status than a VILLAN. Since *Domesday Book* distinguishes bordars from COTTARS and both from COTSETS, there must have been some distinction between them not now readily apparent. All three are also commonly associated with towns.

BOROUGH (Old English *burh*). An urban as opposed to a rural settlement, usually fortified.

BOVATE (from Latin *bos*, an ox). One-eighth of a CARUCATE; the Anglo-Scandinavian translation is OXGANG.

BURGESS (from Old English *burh*; Old French *burgeis*). A townsman usually from the upper stratum of town-dwellers, holding by a special form of tenure characterized by the payment of a money-rent.

BUTSECARL (Old Norse *batr*, boat + *karl*, man). A seaman; c.f. Anglo-Scandinavian *batswegen*, which gives Modern English boatswain, a term of more limited application now than in the eleventh century.

CAPUT (Latin, head). A principal manor. *See* MANOR.

CARTAGE. In *Domesday Book*, *avera* (Latin, property, cattle; Old French *ovre*, work). The duty of providing carts for the transport of the LORD's goods.

CARUCATE (from Latin *caruca*, a plough). A ploughland: notionally the area which could be ploughed with an eight-ox team, used in the north and east as a unit of assessment to tax instead of the HIDE.

CASTLE (Latin *castellum, castrum*; Old French *castel*). The fortified residence of a LORD.

CEORL (Old English). A peasant or non-noble FREE MAN, with a WERGELD of 200s.

CHURCHSCOT. In *Domesday Book*, usually *cirset* (Old English *ciric-sceat*, literally 'churchtax'). An annual render in kind paid to the church; c.f. TITHE.

CIRCUIT. The area for which one group of commissioners was responsible, consisting of several shires (usually five).

COLIBERT (Latin *colibertus, quolibertus*, from *libere*, to set free). A FREEDMAN: a former slave, emancipated and (usually) given a small piece of land.

COMMEND, COMMENDATION (from Latin *commendo, -are*, literally 'to put into the hands of'). A form of VASSALAGE.

COMMOTE (Old Welsh *cymwd*). An Old Welsh administrative division, roughly comparable to the English HUNDRED.

CONSTABLE (Latin *comes stabuli*; Old French *conestable*, officer of the stable). See STALLER.

COTSET (Old English *kotsetla*, a cottage-dweller). A cottager. See BORDAR.

COTTAR (from Old English *kot*, a cottage). A cottager. See BORDAR.

COUNT (Latin *comes*, companion). A continental title, denoting a man in authority over a specific area (county) with administrative and judicial powers: used to translate the English EARL.

COURT (Latin *curia*). Apart from its judicial use, the word also denotes the residence of the LORD (*see also* HALL and MANOR) to which dues were paid.

CROFT (Old English, enclosed field). The field or garden belonging to a peasant's house. See *also* TOFT.

CUSTOM, CUSTOMARY DUE (from Latin *consuetudo*). (1) Fixed RENDERS, financial, administrative or judicial. (2) Deriving from (1), traditional practices, whence the 'customs' of shires and boroughs in *Domesday Book*.

DANEGELD (Old English). Originally the tribute-money paid to the invading Danish armies at the time of Æthelræd II. Subsequently used for the HEREGELD.

DEMESNE (Latin *dominium*; Old French adj. *demeigne*, owned). Land 'in LORDSHIP' whose produce is devoted to the LORD rather than his tenants: (1) MANORS held in the LORD's personal possession as opposed to those granted to his men; (2) that part of an individual estate exploited directly for the LORD's 'home-farm'. Also expressed as INLAND (Old English), as opposed to WARLAND.

DENARIUS. See PENNY.

DICKER (Latin *decarius*). Literally 'a bundle of ten' used for leather and skins; also gloves, shoes and, in *Great Domesday Book*, horseshoes.

DOMESDAY MONACHORUM. A survey collected within an existing manuscript (now in Canterbury Cathedral library) compiled from *Domesday Book* or from the 'original returns' for the use of the Archbishop and monks of Christ Church, Canterbury.

DRENG (Old Norse *drengr*, fellow, warrior). In Lancashire and Yorkshire a man personally free, holding land in return for service, including military service.

DUEL (Latin *duellum*, from *duo*, two). The judicial battle in which accuser and accused fought either in person or through champions, introduced after 1066.

EARL (Old Norse *jarl*, nobleman, commander). In the Old English period, the chief administrative officers of the king, set over the main divisions of the kingdom (Wessex, Mercia, East Anglia and Northumbria): also the highest rank of the Old English aristocracy after the

ÆTHELINGS. It replaces the earlier title *ealdorman* (Old English *ealdor*, lord + *mann*, man) in the early eleventh century. The title survived the Conquest but the earls of the Norman period had more restricted areas of command (usually a single shire).

ENFEOFFMENT, TO ENFEOFF. See FIEF.

ESCHEAT (Latin *ex + cadere*, to fall out; Old French *cheoir*). To forfeit (land) for some misdemeanour or for lack of heirs.

ESCORT. In *Domesday Book*, *inweard* (Old English). The duty of riding escort to one's LORD, or of providing someone to do so. See RADKNIGHT.

EXON DOMESDAY (usually abbr. Exon). The manuscript containing the circuit-return for the five south-western shires, now kept in the Treasury of Exeter Cathedral.

FARM (Latin *firma*; Old English *feorm*, tribute). Never an agricultural unit, as in modern usage. (1) A RENDER, originally in kind, but by the eleventh century frequently commuted to money. NIGHT'S FARM: the amount of produce which would support the king and his retinue for one 24-hour period, paid by certain groups of royal estates. BLANCH FARM: (Latin *blanca*, white) royal dues paid in money ASSAYED for its purity ('white silver', 'white pennies') and usually reckoned as 21 shillings to the pound of silver instead of 20. (2) Land or office held AT FARM: in effect, leased at a specific rent in return for which the tenant, known as the 'farmer', received the profits of the estate or office.

FARTHING. See FERDING.

FEALTY (from Latin *fides*, oath, *fidelitas*, loyalty). (1) The oath sworn by a VASSAL to his LORD in the ceremony of VASSALAGE: usually sworn on holy relics or on the Gospels. (2) The duty owed by a VASSAL to his LORD including tributary service, aid and counsel.

FERDING, FERDINC, FERLING (Old English *feortha*, fourth). (1) A measurement of land, used for fiscal purposes and equalling one quarter VIRGATE. (2) The subdivision of a SHIRE, usually one of four.

FIEF. In *Domesday Book*, *feudum* (latinized from Old German *febu*, property). In general, a piece of land held in return for military service; in *Domesday Book*, often used as a synonym for HONOUR, which is the collective term for the fiefs of any one individual. From fief comes the verb 'TO ENFEOFF' (to give land in exchange for military service – 'IN FEE'); the adjectival 'IN FEE' (land or other property held in exchange for military service – 'as a fief'); and the nouns 'feudalism', 'SUBINFEUDATION'.

FOREST (Latin *foresta*, from *foris*, outside). Land set aside for the king's hunting. Not necessarily wooded.

FRANKPLEDGE (Old English *frith-borh*, peace-pledge). See TITHING.

FREEDMAN. See COLIBERT.

FREE MAN. In *Domesday Book*, *liber homo* (Latin). In eastern England a non-noble landholder, usually COMMENDED to a LORD (c.f. SOKEMAN) but sometimes used as an equivalent of THEGN.

FRENCHMAN. In *Domesday Book*, *francus homo*, *francigena* (Latin). A non-noble immigrant, usually found as a peasant settler of free status: hence *franklin* (Frenchman), a name sometimes given to freeholders in the later Middle Ages.

FURLONG. In *Domesday Book*, *quarentina* (Latin; Old English *furlong*, from *furh*, furrow + *lang*, long). The length of a furrow: 40 PERCHES.

FYRD (Old English). The Old English military levy or host.

GELD (Old English, money, tax). The English land-tax (DANEGELD, HEREGELD) assessed on the HIDE.

GLEBE (Latin *gleba*, clod, soil). The land belonging to a village church or priest.

HALL (Old English *heall*, hall). The characteristic feature of a MANOR; the lordly residence to which rents and dues were paid.

HEARTH-TAX. In *Domesday Book*, *fumagium* (Latin, smoke-tax; also *herdigelt*, Old English, hearth-tax). A levy on households counted by hearths.

HELVEWECHA (Old English *healf*, half + *wice*, week). Literally 'half-week', but the meaning of the word (which only occurs on p. 425) is obscure.

HEREGELD (Old English *here*, army + *geld*, tax). An annual tax raised to pay the standing fleet from 1012 to 1051, and reinstituted by William I. *See* GELD.

HERIOT. In *Domesday Book*, *relevium* (Latin, relief; Old English *heregeatu*, literally 'wargear'). In pre-Conquest England the RENDER in arms and/or money paid at death by a man to his LORD.

HIDE (Old English *hid*, *hida*). The standard unit of assessment to tax, especially GELD. Notionally the amount of land which would support a household: divided into four VIRGATES.

HOCCUS (derivation uncertain). Possibly a salt-mound, used for drying and purifying salt.

HOMAGE (Latin *homo*; French *homme*, man). The act of COMMENDATION in which someone became the man or VASSAL of a LORD by placing his clasped hands between those of his LORD and exchanging a kiss. *See* FEALTY.

HONOUR, HONOR (Latin *honor*, worth). The collection of FIEFS held by a TENANT-IN-CHIEF or a MESNE-TENANT.

HOUSECARL (Old Norse *huskarl*, a retainer, servant). A Scandinavian term introduced into England in the time of Cnut (1016–35), originally meaning a retainer; but by 1066 it could also be used instead of THEGN when applied to men of Scandinavian descent.

HUNDRED (Latin *hundredum*; Old English *hund*; Old French *hundret*, a hundred). An administrative subdivision of the SHIRE with fiscal, judicial and military functions. The men of the hundred are the members of the hundred-court (*see also* WAPENTAKE). The number and size of the hundreds varies greatly from shire to shire, but notionally, and sometimes actually, comprises 100 (or a 'long' hundred of 120) hides.

INCREMENT. In *Domesday Book*, *de cremento* (from Latin *increscare*, to increase). Increase: usually an additional sum of money added to existing dues.

IN FEE. *See* FIEF.

INLAND. *See* DEMESNE (2).

INQUISITIO COMITATUS CANTABRIGIENSIS (abbr. ICC). An existing document containing a copy of the returns for Cambridgeshire, arranged by HUNDREDS instead of the *Great Domesday Book* feudal arrangement and representing a stage in the collection of material for *Great Domesday Book*.

INQUISITIO ELIENSIS (abbr. IE). An existing document (now in Trinity College, Cambridge) containing a copy of the returns for the lands of Ely Abbey extracted from the *Great Domesday Book* and *Little Domesday Book* material at an early stage.

KNIGHT. In *Domesday Book*, *miles* (Latin; Old English *cniht*, a boy or servant). A military retainer. *See also* VASSAL.

LATHE (Old Norse poet., *lath*, land; Old English *læth*). A subdivision of the SHIRE, exclusive to Kent, similar to the RAPES of Sussex.

LAUND (Old French *launde*; Old Celtic *landa*, a stretch of woodland). A glade or open space among woods.

LEAGUE (Latin *leuga*). A Gaulish measure of $1\frac{1}{2}$ Roman miles of 1,000 paces. In medieval England one league = 12 FURLONGS, whereas the mile = 8 FURLONGS.

LIBRUM. In *Domesday Book*, *lib.*, *l.* (Latin, a pound). A money of account amounting to 240 silver pennies which were minted from a pound of silver.

LIVERY (from Latin *deliberare*, to deliver). The legal process of conveying title to land: the king's *liberator* was the agent who performed this function.

LOANLAND (Old English *lænland*). Land held on a lease, frequently for three lives, i.e. generations.

LORD. In *Domesday Book*, *dominus* (Latin; Old English *hlaford*, lord; literally 'loaf-giver'). The lord is the holder of the HOMAGE of his VASSALS, to whom he gives protection and land in return for support. The lady (Old English *hlafdige*, 'loaf-maker') is the lord's wife.

LORDSHIP. In *Domesday Book*, *dominium* (Latin). Territory or personnel under the direct authority of a LORD.

LOWY (Latin *leugata*, square LEAGUE). Probably a square LEAGUE, but also used simply to mean a large property (e.g. the lowy of Tonbridge).

MANOR (Latin *manerium*, from *manere*, to dwell; Old French *manoir*). An estate, varying in size; the estate-centre as opposed to the outlying BEREWICKS. The capital manor (CAPUT) was the administrative centre of the HONOUR where the LORD'S chief residence, often his CASTLE, was situated, and where his COURT was held.

MARK (Old Norse *mork*, mark). (1) A weight defining a unit of account equivalent to two-thirds of a pound (LIBRUM) i.e. in silver 13s 4d; (2) a gold mark which was equivalent to 6*l*. Neither was an actual coin.

MESNE-TENANT (Old French *mesnie*, retinue). A man holding land of a LORD other than the king.

MESSUAGE (from Latin *mansio*, dwelling). The unit of a land-tenure within a BOROUGH, comprising a house or houses with appurtenant property.

MILL (from Latin *molendinum*). A rotary engine driven by water, in most cases for grinding corn. The windmill does not appear in England for at least a century after *Domesday Book*. It is possible that mills in the northern regions were 'Norse mills', with the wheel pivoting horizontally, while mills in the south and west were driven by vertically positioned water-wheels.

MINSTER (Latin *monasterium*, monastery, church). The mother-church of an area, often in origin a small monastery. The territories assigned to minsters were usually larger than modern parishes.

MINT (from Latin *moneta*). The centres of coin production situated in towns of BOROUGH status. 78 mints are known to exist before 1066, and 64 at the time of the survey. The mint name as well as that of the issuing MONEYER appears on the reverse of every coin. Associated with the mint was the exchange (Latin *cambium*) where silver bullion and old coin were ASSAYED and bought in for new.

MITTA (Old English *mitte*, measure of capacity). A horse-load, specifically of salt; *see* SUMMA. In the tenth century the salt-tolls of Droitwich were reckoned at 1d on the horse-load and 1s on the cart-load.

MODIUS (Latin; Old French *muid*). (1) A liquid measure used for wine: the Roman *modius* = 8.75 litres, but the *Domesday Book* equivalent is unknown; (2) a dry measure, used (exceptionally) for grain.

MONEYER (Latin *monetarius*). An official responsible for the minting of coins, on which his name invariably appeared. Several moneyers operated at important MINTS such as London, Canterbury and Winchester.

MOTTE (Old French, mound, embankment). The mound of earth supporting a timber or stone TOWER. Invariably surrounded by, or attached to, a defended enclosure (BAILEY) to constitute the commonest form of CASTLE in the eleventh century.

MULTURE (from Latin *molere*, to grind). A toll paid to the miller for grinding corn.

NIGHT'S FARM. *See* FARM (1).

ORA (Old Norse *øre*, an ounce). One-eighth of a MARK: a unit of account, usually reckoned as equivalent to 20d, but sometimes as 16d.

ORDEAL (Old English *ordal*). The judicial trial, of which several kinds are recorded. The most common are: (1) the ordeal of cold water, in which the suspect was dropped into a specially dug pit filled with holy water; if innocent he sank, if guilty he floated; (2) the ordeal of hot iron, in which the suspect carried a red-hot iron for a specified number of paces. His wounds were bound up for a specific time; if when they were unwrapped they were healed, he was innocent, if they had turned septic, guilty. In both cases, the idea was to appeal to the judgement of God. *See also* DUEL.

OXGANG. *See* BOVATE.

PANNAGE (Latin *pannagium*). The autumn feed for pigs — acorns and beechnuts. Also, a payment for pasturing pigs: this may be the primary sense of the term in *Domesday Book*.

PARAGE, IN PARAGE (from Latin *par*, equal). Shared ownership of land by kinsmen: a French usage which is not found in pre-Conquest sources.

PENNY, PENCE. In *Domesday Book*, *d.*, *den.* = *denarius* (Latin; Old English *pending*, penny). The only actual coin in circulation in the eleventh century. 240 pence were struck from one pound (LIBRUM) of silver.

PERCH (Latin *pertica*). In the Middle Ages in England, the size of the perch varied from 14 to 18 ft and could sometimes be 25 to 28 ft.

PLOUGHLAND (Old English *plog*, plough). The number of ploughlands may: (1) estimate the arable capacity of an estate in terms of the number of eight-ox plough-teams needed to work it; or (2) record an assessment of the dues required from the estate.

PURPRESTURE (Latin *propestura*; Old French *pourpresure*). Encroachment, specifically encroachments on land used: (1) in the sense of ASSART; (2) in the sense of illegal encroachment on the land of another.

RADKNIGHT, RADMAN (Old English *radcniht*, riding servant, from Old English *rad*, road). A retainer who performed specific services, including that of riding ESCORT to his LORD.

RAPE (derivation uncertain). One of five (later six) subdivisions of Sussex, each with its LORD and CASTLE. Similar to the Kentish LATHE.

REEVE. In *Domesday Book*, *praepositus* (Latin; Old English *gerefa*). An administrative officer: used for (1) the king's officials in charge of royal estates; (2) manorial officials of other LORDS in charge of estates; (3) village representatives who oversaw the performance of manorial duties.

RELIEF (Latin *relevium*; Old French *relef*). The sum proffered by an heir for succession to his inheritance. In *Domesday Book* sometimes used to translate HERIOT.

RENDER (Latin *redditum*, from *reddere*, to give). A customary payment usually in kind rather than cash, but sometimes used for manorial values in money.

REVELAND (from Old English *gerefa*, REEVE). Meaning uncertain: perhaps land set aside for the use of a REEVE.

ROUNCEY (Latin *runcinus*). A cheap riding-horse; at this date probably a harrowing-horse also.

RUSCA (Old Irish *rusc*; Gaelic *rusq, rusg*). A vessel of straw or bark; thus a measure for butter in Cheshire, size unknown.

SAKE AND SOKE (Old English *sac* and *soc*). Literally 'cause' and 'suit'; the case heard in a COURT and the duty of attending it. Used to denote the judicial and dominical rights associated with the possession of land, especially BOOKLAND.

SEISIN (Old French). Lawful possession, usually of land. The phrase 'to be seised of' means 'to possess' or 'to be in possession of'.

SERGEANT, SERGEANTY (from Latin *serviens*, servant). A tenant who held his land by rendering a specific service, e.g. as a forester or cook; SERGEANTY was the name given to this form of tenure.

SESTER (Latin *sextarius*). (1) As a liquid measure, used for honey and wine; the size varied but sesters of 24 oz and 32 oz are recorded in eleventh-century England. (2) As a dry measure, used for grain: perhaps equivalent to 12 bushels.

SHERIFF (Old English *scir-gerefa*). The royal officer set over a SHIRE, whose duties included judicial and financial functions, as well as the overseeing of royal estates and, in the post-Conquest period, custody of royal CASTLES. The Normans translated the word as *vicecomes* (Latin), viscount.

SHIRE (Old English *scira*, an area of authority, a county). The main unit of English local administration. The word is used both for the county and for the county- or shire-COURT. The Normans translated the word as *comitatus* (Latin), county.

SOKE (Old English *soc*). Right of jurisdiction enjoyed by a LORD over specified places and personnel. *See* SAKE AND SOKE.

SOKELAND (Old English *soc*). Used to describe lands appurtenant to a MANOR.

SOKEMAN (Old English *socmann*). A FREE MAN (though often only a peasant) owing service, including suit of COURT, to the LORD of a SOKE (*see* SAKE AND SOKE).

SOLIDUS (Latin). A money of account amounting to 12 silver PENCE. The *Domesday Book* abbr. *sol., s.,* stand equally for Old English *scilling*, shilling, which was probably the term in common use.

SORE HAWK (Old French *sor*, saure). A hawk in its second year which has not moulted and still has red plumage: nowadays a 'red' hawk.

STALLER (Old Norse *stallari*, a marshal, from *stallr*, a stall or seat). In the Old English period, a high-ranking holder of a recognized office. Sometimes translated in *Domesday Book* as *comes stabuli*, CONSTABLE.

STEERMAN (Old English *stirmann*). In the Old English period, the commander of a ship, especially of the ships provided for the king's service.

STICK (Old English *sticca, sticha, estika*). A measure for eels: 25 held together by a stick or cord passed through the gills.

SUBINFEUDATE, SUBINFEUDATION (Latin *subinfeudatio*, from *feudum*, FIEF). The practice of LORDS in receipt of land from the king entrusting part of it to MESNE-TENANTS.

SULUNG (Old English *sulh*, plough). A Kentish unit of assessment usually regarded as equivalent to two HIDES.

SUMMA (Greek, latinized *sagma*, saddle). A horse-load, equivalent to MITTA: hence SUMPTER HORSE for pack-horse. No precise equivalent can be given as there was probably local variation.

SUMPTER HORSE (Greek, latinized *sagma*, saddle). A pack-horse.

TALE, BY TALE. In *Domesday Book*, *ad numerum* (Latin; Old English *getal*, reckoning, number). Payments made by counting out coins ('telling' them) as opposed to weighing them. *See also* TALLAGE.

TALLAGE (Old French *tail*). A tax or impost in cash or kind, usually in the sense of a levy by a LORD on unfree peasants.

TENANT-IN-CHIEF (Latin *tenens-in-capite*, holding-in-chief). A man who holds his land directly of the king.

THEGN. In *Domesday Book*, *tainus* (Old English, latinized, servant, nobleman). A man of noble status as opposed to a peasant (CEORL), having a WERGELD of 1,200s. A king's thegn was COMMENDED to the king; a median thegn to some other LORD. The nobility of pre-Conquest England was ranked according to the HERIOT they paid in the following descending order: EARL, king's thegn, median thegn.

THEGNLAND (Old English). Land belonging to a THEGN; sometimes apparently used as the equivalent of LOAN-LAND.

THIRD PENNY. The portion of the dues (particularly the judicial renders including penalties) from the SHIRE and HUNDRED apportioned to the EARL. The other two PENCE went to the king.

THRAVE (of Scandinavian origin, e.g. Danish *trave*). Two shocks of 12 sheaves each of reaped corn.

TIMBER (Old French *timbre*). A bundle of 40 pelts.

TITHE. In *Domesday Book*, *decima* (Latin; Old English *teotha*, a tenth). A render to the church amounting to one-tenth of the annual produce. In the eleventh century one-third of the tithe was paid to the church of the MANOR and two-thirds to the mother-church (MINSTER) on which the manorial church was dependent.

TITHING (Old English *teotha*, a tenth). The subdivision of a HUNDRED, notionally ten men, the main function of which was to organize sureties so as to ensure that its members appeared in court when summoned. Later the system was known as FRANKPLEDGE.

TOFT (Old English; Old Norse *topt*, homestead). A peasant's house or cottage, to which belonged his garden or field. *See* CROFT.

TOLL AND TEAM (Old English *toll*, tax + *team*, cattle). The right to receive tolls on merchandise and probably to hold a market.

TOWER (Latin *turris*). The tower of a CASTLE, especially the upstanding donjon (Latin *dominium*), or keep. The tower, or the MOTTE in a motte and bailey, is used symbolically for the whole building since it represents the LORD's authority (also Latin *dominium*).

TRE (abbr. for Latin *Tempore Regis Edwardi*). The formula commonly used in *Domesday Book* to indicate the position 'in the time of King Edward', i.e. before the Conquest in 1066. In EXON a more exact phrase is sometimes used: 'the day when King Edward was alive and dead', i.e. 5 January 1066.

TRW (abbr. for Latin *Tempore Regis Willelmi*). The formula used today (by analogy with TRE) to indicate the position after the Conquest, 'in the time of King William', more especially in 1086 when the survey was being compiled.

TURBARY (Old English *torvelande*). A place from which turves were taken; the right to cut turves of peat.

VASSAL, VASSALAGE (Latin *vassus*; Old Celtic *gwas*, a boy or servant). A man, usually of noble rank, who subordinates himself to a LORD. Vassalage is the status of a vassal, which was entered by COMMENDATION in the ceremony of HOMAGE, sealed by the oath of FEALTY. The relationship might be personal or, if the vassal received a FIEF, tenurial.

VAVASOUR (Old French). In eleventh-century Normandy, a retainer of lower status than a VASSAL.

VILL (Latin *villa*, village; Old English *tun*, township). (1) The unit of local administration at its lowest level: GELD for instance was levied on the SHIRE, HUNDRED and vill, in that descending order. Not necessarily a village in the modern sense: a vill represents an area of land rather than the site of a specific settlement, and may contain more than one settlement. (2) In *Domesday Book* occasionally used of urban sites which were not fully-fledged BOROUGHS

VILLAN (Latin *villanus*, a villager, which translates Old English *tunsman*). A peasant of higher economic status than a BORDAR and living in a village. Notionally unfree because subject to the manorial COURT.

VIRGATE (Latin *virgata*, from *virga*, a rod). One-quarter of a HIDE: the equivalent of the English YARDLAND.

WAPENTAKE (Old Norse *vapnan tak*, 'the taking up of weapons' laid aside during peaceful assemblies after agreement). In northern and eastern England, a division of the SHIRE with the same functions exercised by the HUNDRED in the south and west.

WARA (Old English). The obligations (especially for the payment of GELD) owed by an estate to the royal service; literally 'defence', hence the common formula in *Domesday Book*, *x se defendit pro y hidae* to indicate liability to GELD.

WARLAND (*see* WARA). Land which owes service (as opposed to the exempt DEMESNE or INLAND): thus

land held by peasants and tenants as opposed to their LORD.

WARNODE (Old Danish *værned*, assurance, pledge). The service (specifically GELD) owed by WARLAND; the land which owes this service.

WASTE. In *Domesday Book*, *wasta* (Latin; poss. Old English *wæste*, uninhabited, desolate; Old French *wast*). Land which does not RENDER dues either because it has been physically devastated, or because the dues have been attached to some other MANOR, or because they have been withheld. Some manors described as 'waste' are nevertheless credited with values and with population or other appurtenances in *Domesday Book*. Land on which GELD was not paid is also sometimes described as 'waste'.

WEIGHED AND BURNT. Coin which has been ASSAYED. *See* FARM (1): BLANCH FARM.

WERGELD (Old English *wer*, man + *geld*, money). Originally the recompense paid to the kin of a slain man by the kin of the slayer to avert the blood-feud: the amount varied according to the rank of the slain man, 1,200s for a THEGN, 200s for a CEORL. By the tenth century the wergeld was used to assess the amount of judicial fines.

WEY (Old English *wæge*). A measure for cheese (40d worth on p. 141): later weys varied between 175 and 196 pounds.

YARDLAND. *See* VIRGATE.

YOKE. In *Domesday Book*, *iugum* (Latin; Old English *ioclet*). One-quarter of a SULUNG in Kent. Oxen were yoked in pairs and a full plough-team would have consisted of four pairs of oxen.